WOMEN of DESTINY Bible

PRESENTED TO

GIVEN BY

DATE

OCCASION

WOMEN of DESTINY™ Bible

CONTENTS

BOOKS OF THE BIBLE

The Old Testament

The New Testament

Welcome to the *Women of Destiny Bible*. I'd like to welcome you to this wonderful book, which is full of God's words. As you may already know, this is a very special and unique book, unlike any other in the whole world.

Many believers today are crying out to God for a mighty move of the Holy Spirit in the form of a sweeping revival. History tells us that the great revivals of the past have each been marked by heroines of the faith. The coming wave of God's power that is about to crest in the nations of the earth will be no exception. Scripture tells us in Acts 2:17, 18 that in the last days He will pour out His Spirit on all flesh, and that includes the women of the earth. Surely it will come to pass in measure greater than those women of faith who went before us could ever imagine—your daughters shall prophesy.

The promise of God that a great outpouring will come upon His handmaidens rings in the hearts of the contributors to the *Women of Destiny Bible*. As we live in the twenty-first century, a whole new army of women who love God with all of their hearts is getting ready to rise up to proclaim the good news of Jesus Christ and His resurrection. They will encompass the earth with shouts of "He's alive!"

As I have talked to the women writers of this Bible, my life has been touched by their understanding that we must mentor the next generation. We greatly need discipleship to prepare the rising Deborahs, Esthers, and other new leaders. Moms need help in knowing how to discipline their children. Women ministers are searching for those who have gone before them to teach them how to walk in integrity.

I cannot write this section without thanking the woman who has really made this Bible possible. She has worked long hours, dreamed big dreams, and refused to give up when deadlines looked impossible. My special thanks to Beth Clark of Nelson Bibles, whom I have the honor of calling my friend. Marcus Yoars, Beth's assistant, has put up with more from us than any man should have to handle. Also, thanks to Nelson Bibles' publisher, John Eames, for believing in this product, and to the expert editorial and design team at Nelson. You are a blessing! Thanks to my wonderful husband, Mike, who is my best supporter. I must thank Polly Simchen, my secretary, for all her assistance. Last, but not least, my appreciation to all of the women who have written for the Bible for going the extra mile, often with near-to-impossible deadlines. I admire and love you all.

Women of God, this Bible is a special gift from God to you. It will teach you how to be an overcomer in your life and how to become a woman of destiny. Let nothing stand in your way as you reach the full potential for which the Father placed you on this earth.

With His love,

Cindy Jacobs

Notes

From the Executive Editor . . .

As Executive Editor of the *Spirit-Filled Life*® Bibles and other resources, I am delighted to welcome the *Women of Destiny Bible* as the newest member of this family of products.

I am excited about the work of the Holy Spirit among women today as He is empowering them in so many ways. I believe in this project and in the call of God on your life. I pray that you will be blessed by God's Word and by the godly mentoring you will receive in this book.

May God bless you as you take your place in His kingdom.

Jack W. Hayford

From the Publisher . . .

From time to time, a publisher is blessed to participate in a project that seems unusually touched by the grace and favor of God. At Nelson Bibles, we have had that kind of experience with the *Women of Destiny Bible*. We have walked this path along with some very special people, who deserve recognition for their efforts.

The Publisher expresses appreciation to Jack Hayford, Executive Editor of the *Spirit-Filled Life*® product line, for the excellent spirit and commitment with which he serves Nelson Bibles, for the wise counsel he continually provides, and for his enthusiastic support of the *Women of Destiny Bible*.

We wish to thank Cindy Jacobs for the extraordinary leadership she has given to this Bible and to the team of people who have worked to produce it. She has brought us the guidance of a true visionary and the heart of a true servant. She is a woman of destiny in every way, a great friend, and a consummate mentor. It has been our privilege and our pleasure to work with her.

We would also like to thank all of our contributors, who have so graciously shared their wisdom, their experiences, and their encouragement. We have been overwhelmed by their support for this Bible and by their love for the women of destiny who will read this book. They are an amazing group of God's leading ladies, and we are honored to publish the pieces of their hearts and lives that they have shared with us.

We remain deeply grateful to the host of intercessors in the United States and around the world, who have faithfully stood in the gap for us and for the *Women of Destiny Bible*. They are the invisible army that has made victory possible. Though we may not know their names or list them in this book, their prayers are precious and their contribution is without measure.

"Yet who knows whether [we] have come to the kingdom for such a time as this?"—Esther 4:14b

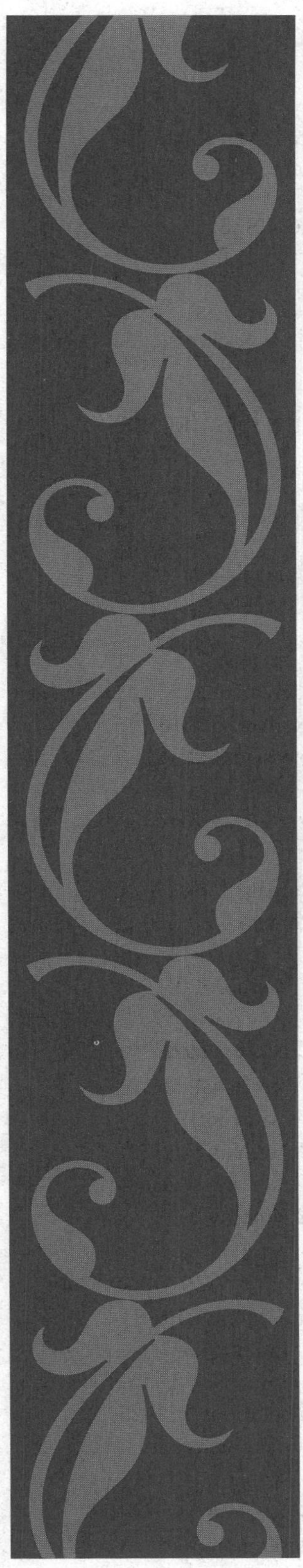

The Hope Chest

In the next several pages you will find a gift. It is a Hope Chest. It is *your* Hope Chest, filled with the great and precious promises that your Bridegroom, Jesus Christ, has given to you, His Bride.

Perhaps you have grown up with a hope chest of your own. If so, this section will hold a warm place in your heart, a place that represents promises fulfilled, promises of hope for the future, and promises of provision for the moment. May you receive all that your heavenly Bridegroom has to give you; His promises will exceed your greatest expectations.

You may be a woman who has never had a hope chest of your own. Maybe you always wanted one or looked longingly at someone else's. This Hope Chest is a gift to you. It has been lavishly poured out for you, and contains many of God's unfailing promises. As you read through it, may you bask in the immensity of His love and care for you.

Maybe you have experienced the disappointment of having a hope chest that was once full of dreams and expectant promises, but that came to represent broken promises, failure, hurt, or abuse. Dear one, this Hope Chest is for you; but it will *never fail you*. It is filled with promises from the One who is called Faithful and True. They are made by the One who gave His only Son to save you. As you sit and begin to go through this gift that is your Hope Chest, may your heart begin to be healed by the faithfulness, lovingkindness, compassion, mercy, and joy of the One who calls you His Bride.

The glorious thing about this Hope Chest is that what you find in these few pages is just the beginning! So rich and so vast are the promises of God toward you that you will find them flowing throughout the Bible. Search beyond the references you find here. A tremendous treasure awaits you. May this Hope Chest be a place to which you can come in times of joy and in times of sorrow, in times of plenty and in times of want, in times of sickness and in times of health. These are the promises of your Bridegroom to you, His precious Bride.

The Hope Chest

(Note: A ❦ attached to a reference in the list below indicates you will find a "Woman of Destiny" letter connected with that Bible verse or passage.)

The Basis for the Bridegroom's Promises:

Psalm 33:11
Psalm 18:30
Mark 13:31
Acts 20:32
Ephesians 1:13, 14

The Faithfulness of the Bridegroom to Fulfill His Promises:

1 Kings 8:56
Psalm 105:42
Isaiah 40:8
Isaiah 46:11
Hebrews 13:8

Promises of:

Salvation

❦John 3:16, 17
Romans 3:20–24
Romans 5:6–8
Ephesians 1:7
❦2 Peter 3:9

Grace

Psalm 84:11
Romans 5:15
Romans 6:14
❦2 Timothy 1:9
Hebrews 4:15, 16

Mercy

1 Chronicles 16:34
Psalm 103:8
Psalm 118
Isaiah 55:7
1 Peter 1:3–5

Love

Isaiah 43:4
Jeremiah 31:3
❦John 3:16, 17
Romans 5:5–8
Titus 3:4–7

Forgiveness

❦Isaiah 1:18
Isaiah 43:25
Jeremiah 33:8
Romans 5:9, 10
Colossians 1:21–23

Righteousness

Psalm 89:16
Romans 1:16, 17
Romans 10:9, 10
Titus 2:11–13
❦1 John 1:9

Deliverance

Psalm 34:4, 5
Psalm 34:19
1 Corinthians 10:13
Galatians 1:3, 4
2 Timothy 4:18

God's Faithfulness

Deuteronomy 31:6–8
Psalm 36:5
Psalm 89:1, 2
❦Lamentations 3:21–25
1 Corinthians 1:9

Hearing God's Voice

Deuteronomy 5:24

Deuteronomy 30:19, 20
1 Kings 19:11, 12
John 10:4, 5
John 10:16, 27

Guidance

Ezra 8:21
Psalm 37:23
Psalm 48:14
Proverbs 3:6
Proverbs 16:9

Acceptance

Ezekiel 20:41
John 6:37
2 Corinthians 5:18, 19
Ephesians 2:13–16
1 Peter 2:4, 5

God's Presence

Exodus 33:14
Deuteronomy 31:8
Psalm 23:4
Isaiah 60:19
John 14:23

Protection

Psalm 5:12
Psalm 46:1–3
Psalm 91
Isaiah 43:2
John 10:29

The Bridegroom's Return

John 14:3
1 Thessalonians 4:16, 17
Titus 2:13
Hebrews 9:28
Revelation 1:7

Freedom from Fear

Psalm 91:1, 4–7
Isaiah 35:3, 4
John 14:27
Romans 8:15
2 Timothy 1:7

Provision

Psalm 37:25, 26
Proverbs 10:3
Matthew 6:31–33
2 Corinthians 9:6–8
Philippians 4:19

Everlasting Glory

John 14:1–3
Romans 8:17, 18
Philippians 3:20, 21
Colossians 3:4
Revelation 21:3–5

Promises for Your Business

Deuteronomy 8:18
Deuteronomy 28:1–6
Deuteronomy 29:9
Psalm 1:1–3
Proverbs 3:3–10

Promises for Unsaved Loved Ones

Matthew 18:11–14
1 Corinthians 7:13–16
2 Corinthians 4:3–6
1 Peter 3:1, 2
2 Peter 3:9

Promises That God Will Hear Your Prayer

Psalm 37:4
Psalm 55:16, 17
Jeremiah 33:2, 3
Matthew 7:7, 8
John 15:7

Promises That God Will Keep You

Numbers 6:24–26
Isaiah 26:3, 4
Romans 8:38, 39
1 Peter 1:3–5
Jude 24

Promises When You Are:

Having Family Problems

❦Genesis 22:17
Deuteronomy 11:19–21
Proverbs 29:15, 17
❦Nahum 1:7
1 Peter 5:7

Feeling Lonely

Psalm 9:9, 10
Psalm 55:22
❦Psalm 68:6
Isaiah 41:10
❦John 14:16–18

Fearing Satan

Romans 16:20
❦Ephesians 6:10–12
2 Thessalonians 3:3
James 4:7
1 John 4:4

Anxious and Worried

Psalm 94:19
❦Matthew 6:31–34
Matthew 10:19, 20
Luke 12:22–28
❦Philippians 4:6

Facing Difficulties

Deuteronomy 31:6
Isaiah 43:1, 2
Isaiah 44:2, 3
2 Corinthians 4:8, 9
❦1 Peter 5:6–11

Considering Abortion

Genesis 1:26, 27
Deuteronomy 30:19
❦Psalm 139:13–16
Isaiah 49:1
Jeremiah 1:5

Unhappy

❦Psalm 43:5
Psalm 126:5
❦Psalm 147:3
Isaiah 30:19
John 16:22

Persecuted

Romans 8:35–37
2 Corinthians 1:8–11
2 Thessalonians 3:3
1 Peter 4:12–14
❦Revelation 12:11

Sick

Psalm 41:3
Isaiah 53:5
2 Corinthians 4:16–18
2 Corinthians 12:9
❦James 5:14–16

Feeling Impatient

❦Ecclesiastes 3
❦Psalm 31:14, 15
Hebrews 6:12
Hebrews 10:35–37
❦James 1:3, 4

Grieving

Psalm 116:15
Isaiah 51:3, 11
Isaiah 61:2
1 Thessalonians 4:13, 14
Revelation 21:4

Frustrated

Psalm 37:5–8
❦Isaiah 26:3
❦James 1:3
James 3:16–18
1 Peter 4:12, 13

Suffering

Psalm 55:22
Isaiah 40:29–31
Romans 8:17, 18
2 Corinthians 1:3–5
Philippians 3:10, 11

Discouraged

Psalm 27:13, 14
Psalm 138:7
Galatians 6:9
❦Philippians 1:6
Hebrews 10:35, 36

Depressed

Isaiah 41:10
Isaiah 49:15, 16
Isaiah 61:3
❦Romans 8:26, 27, 38, 39
❦Philippians 4:8

In Need

❦2 Chronicles 6:30
❦Psalm 23:3
Isaiah 41:17
❦Habakkuk 3:17–19
James 2:5

Having Problems in Your Marriage

Joshua 24:15
Malachi 2:14–16
1 Corinthians 7:2–4
❦1 Corinthians 13
Ephesians 4:31, 32

Dealing with Divorce

Proverbs 3:5–7
Isaiah 40:29
Matthew 19:3–9
1 Corinthians 7:10–16
Philippians 4:6, 7

Being Tempted

1 Corinthians 10:13
Galatians 5:16
Hebrews 2:18
James 1:12
❦1 Peter 5:8–10

Promises When You Need:

Finances

Psalm 23:1, 5
Psalm 34:9, 10
Proverbs 3:9, 10
❦Malachi 3:10–12
Luke 16:10

Wisdom

Proverbs 3:13–15
Proverbs 9:10
Proverbs 10:31
Proverbs 16:20
James 1:5

Perseverance

Isaiah 40:29–31
Colossians 1:22–25
Hebrews 10:35, 36
1 Peter 1:7–9
Revelation 3:5

Strength

Psalm 31:24
Psalm 68:35
Isaiah 35:3, 4
Isaiah 40:31
❦Habakkuk 3:17–19

To Know Truth

Psalm 25:12–15
Psalm 32:8
Psalm 119:160
❦John 8:31, 32
John 14:16, 17

A Miracle

Matthew 18:19
Mark 9:23, 24
John 14:12–14
Ephesians 3:20
❦James 5:14, 16

To Know You Are Loved

Isaiah 43:1
❦Jeremiah 29:11
❦Zephaniah 3:17
Romans 8:38, 39
1 John 4:16

To Be Filled with the Holy Spirit

Matthew 3:11
Luke 11:9–13
❦John 14:16, 17
❦Acts 1:8; 2:1–4
Acts 2:38, 39

To Forgive

Matthew 6:12
Mark 11:25
Luke 6:35, 37
Ephesians 4:31, 32
Colossians 3:13

To Know God's Will

Proverbs 2:4–7
Proverbs 3:5, 6
Proverbs 28:5
Isaiah 42:16
John 16:13

Peace of Mind

Numbers 6:24–26
Isaiah 26:3
Isaiah 32:17
Philippians 4:6, 7
2 Timothy 1:7

To Surrender to God

Isaiah 57:15
Jeremiah 42:6
Matthew 11:29
James 4:7, 10
1 Peter 5:5, 6

PROMISES WHEN YOU FEEL:

Insecure

Isaiah 32:18
John 10:29
Romans 8:37–39
2 Corinthians 12:9, 10
Philippians 1:6

Condemned

Romans 8:1, 2
Romans 8:38, 39
1 Corinthians 6:11
1 John 1:9
1 John 2:1, 2

Your Life Has No Value

Psalm 139
Jeremiah 29:11
Matthew 10:29–31
1 Corinthians 6:19, 20
1 John 3:16

Angry

Psalm 37:7, 8
Proverbs 14:29
Proverbs 29:22
Ephesians 4:26
James 1:19, 20

Bitter

Deuteronomy 29:18
Hebrews 12:15
2 Kings 14:26, 27
Isaiah 38:17
Ephesians 4:31

Guilty

Psalm 32:1, 2
Romans 5:6–11
Romans 5:18, 19
Romans 8:33, 34
2 Corinthians 7:10

Joyful

Psalm 16:11
Psalm 33:1–3
Psalm 100
Isaiah 51:11
Philippians 4:4

Weak

Psalm 18:1–3
Psalm 27:1
Psalm 29:11
Psalm 138:1–3
Isaiah 40:26–31

Hopeless

Psalm 33:18–22
Psalm 42:11
Psalm 71:1–6
Romans 5:1–5
Hebrews 6:18, 19

Promises When You Have:

Been Rebellious

Romans 6:12, 13
Hebrews 13:17
James 4:7–10
1 Peter 1:13–15
1 Peter 5:5, 6

Walked Away from the Lord

Isaiah 59:1, 2
James 1:12–14
James 4:7–10
2 Peter 1:9, 10
1 John 1:9

Children Who Have Walked Away from the Lord

Isaiah 54:13
Hosea 14:4
Luke 15:11–32
2 Corinthians 4:3–6
Hebrews 10:35, 36

Promises When You Want To:

Grow Spiritually

2 Corinthians 3:18
Ephesians 3:17, 19
Philippians 1:6, 9–11
1 Peter 2:1–3
2 Peter 1:5–8

Experience More Freedom

John 8:32, 36
Romans 6:21–23
Romans 8:1–5
2 Corinthians 3:17
Galatians 5:1

Live in Holiness

Ezekiel 11:19, 20
Luke 1:74, 75
2 Corinthians 7:1
2 Timothy 1:9
2 Timothy 2:21

Pray

Deuteronomy 32:30
Jeremiah 33:3
Mark 11:24
Romans 8:26
Philemon 4–7

Praise the Lord

Psalm 147:1
Psalm 150
Isaiah 25:1
Acts 16:25, 26
1 Peter 2:9

Be a Better Wife

Psalm 128:3
Proverbs 12:4
Proverbs 14:1
Proverbs 31:10–31
Ephesians 5:21–33

Be a Better Mother

Deuteronomy 6:6–9
1 Samuel 1:25–28
Psalm 128:1–4
Proverbs 22:6
Proverbs 29:15, 17

Be a Better Daughter

Deuteronomy 5:16
Proverbs 1:8, 9
Proverbs 23:22, 24, 25
2 Corinthians 6:17—7:1
Ephesians 6:1–3

Be Financially Responsible

Proverbs 3:9, 10
Matthew 6:20, 21, 33
Luke 6:38
2 Corinthians 9:6–8
1 Timothy 6:17–19

Repent

Acts 2:38, 39
Acts 3:19
Romans 2:4
2 Peter 3:9
1 John 1:8, 9

Witness to Others

1 Chronicles 16:23, 24
Proverbs 11:30
Matthew 28:18–20
Romans 1:16
2 Timothy 4:1–5

Promises When You Are Overcoming:

Lust

Galatians 5:16
1 Thessalonians 4:1–7
Titus 2:11–14
James 4:1–10
1 John 2:15–17

Being Deserted

Deuteronomy 31:6
Psalm 37:25
Psalm 68:5
Isaiah 49:15, 16
Isaiah 62:4

An Unfaithful Spouse

Psalm 32:7
Psalm 34:18
Psalm 147:3
Romans 12:17–20
Hebrews 13:5, 6

An Alcoholic Spouse

Psalm 27:5–8
Psalm 46
Psalm 91
John 14:27
Hebrews 12:1–3

A Heart Attack

Psalm 18:1–3, 6
Psalm 27:14
Psalm 31:24
Psalm 73:26
Psalm 145:18

Cancer

Psalm 23:1–4
Psalm 73:26
Psalm 91
Isaiah 40:29–31
Isaiah 53:5

A Negative Environment

Psalm 1:1–3
Psalm 46:1, 2
Psalm 91
Isaiah 54:17
Philippians 4:8, 9

Addiction

Proverbs 21:31
John 8:36
2 Timothy 4:18
Hebrews 4:15, 16
Hebrews 12:1–13

Criticism

Nehemiah 4:1–3
Psalm 27:11–14
Psalm 31:13–24
Psalm 35:11–24
Psalm 41:9–13

Abortion

Psalm 3:3–5
Psalm 51:14
Psalm 147:3
Isaiah 43:25
1 John 1:9

Mental Illness

Psalm 9:9, 10
Psalm 107:20
Proverbs 3:24–26
Philippians 4:6, 7
2 Timothy 1:7

A Mistake

Galatians 6:1, 2
Philippians 3:13, 14
James 4:10
1 Peter 5:6, 7
1 John 1:9

Women of Destiny Letters

Heroines of the Faith

Praying the Word

Words of Wisdom

Contributors to the Women of Destiny Bible

Sue Ahn
Lora Allison
Beth Alves
Julie Anderson
Maria Annacondia
Shirley Arnold
Jill Austin
Lori Graham Bakker
Kim Bangs
Vicki Bartholomew
Rebecca Bauer
Naomi Beard
Lisa Bevere
Connie Broome
Rachel Burchfield
Doris Bush
Cecilia Caballeros
Agatha Chan
Bonnie Chavda
Pat Chen
Beth Clark
Nancy Corbett Cole
Jamie Owens Collins
Germaine Copeland
Sue Curran
Sharon Damazio
Sharon Daugherty
Joy Dawson
Kathleen Dillard
Naomi Dowdy
Megan Doyle
Dee Eastman
Tommi Femrite
Mary Forsythe
Betty Freidzon
Ruthanne Garlock
Mary Glazier
Michal Ann Goll
Kathy Gray
Melody Green
Catherine Berg Greig
Doris Greig
Jill Griffith
Diana Hagee
Jane Hamon
Jane Hansen
Anna Hayford
Ruth Ward Heflin
Solveig Henderson
Marilyn Hickey
Jeri Hill
Nancy Hinkle
Suzanne Hinn
Sally Horton
Esther Ilnisky
Cindy Jacobs
Serita Jakes
Barbara James
Brenda Kilpatrick
Cathy Lechner
Freda Lindsay
Ginger Lindsay
Katie Luce
Colleen Marocco
Judith Christie-McAllister
Terry Meeuwsen
Bobbie Jean Merck
Linda Mintle
Margaret Moberly
Susan Moore
Leslyn Musch
Betsy Neuenschwander
Carol Noe
Agnes Numer
LaDonna Osborn
Lisa Otis
Carol Owens
Fawn Parish
Gina Pearson
Fuchsia Pickett
Mary Jean Pidgeon
Pam Pierce
Faeona Pratney
Judy Radachy
Gloria Richards
Evelyn Roberts
Lindsay Roberts
A.G. Rodriguez
Susan Ryan
Cheryl Sacks
Paula Sandford
Kathleen Scataglini
Gwen Shaw
Ceci Sheets
Dana Sherrard
Quin Sherrer
Ruth Silvoso
Polly Simchen
Alice Smith
Judy Smith
Kara Quinn-Smith
Rebecca Wagner Sytsema
Thetus Tenney
Lila Terhune
Betty Thiessen
Brenda Timberlake
Iverna Tompkins
LaNora Van Arsdall
Doris Wagner
Nola Warren
Joann Cole Webster
Barbara Wentroble
Miriam Witt
Barbara Yoder

How to Use This Bible

Having a new Bible is so exciting! Whether this is your first Bible or your twenty-first, it will be an important piece of your spiritual journey. Here is a "clean copy" of God's Word, just waiting for you to make notes in the margins as you read or to underline verses that are special to you. As you mark it, as you travel with it, as you share it with others, may it be life-giving and life-changing. Whether its pages end up with stains from your coffee or stains from your tears, may this edition of God's Word be a beloved companion to you in your adventures with God.

Following are the unique features of this Bible and explanations of how to use them.

Book Introductions: Opening pages from Marilyn Hickey and Cindy Jacobs will help you understand the general theme and intent of each book of the Bible, while explaining what that book offers you as a woman. They will also provide you with information on the author and date of each book, and list key words you might want to watch for as you read that book.

Women of Destiny Letters: These letters were written especially for you from more than 100 of the most respected women in ministry today. You will find more than 200 of these letters throughout the Scriptures, from Genesis to Revelation. Each letter corresponds to a specific Bible verse or passage. Those corresponding Scriptures will be printed in purple and will be set off with decorations that look like this: . Anytime you see a purple passage in the Bible, you will find a "Women of Destiny letter" appearing near it.

The Hope Chest: This section offers biblical hope and encouragement for a variety of issues you are facing now or may be facing at some future time. When you see a beside a Bible reference in The Hope Chest, you will know that you can gain particular insight to that scripture because a "Women of Destiny letter" corresponds to it.

Praying the Word: More than 300 prayers, based on specific Bible verses, will help you learn how to pray God's Word for a variety of situations in your life. Each prayer will contain one or more blank spaces into which you may insert the name or names of friends or family members for whom that prayer is appropriate. As you learn from these examples, begin to include God's Word more and more in your prayer life.

Heroines of the Faith: Biographies of heroines of the faith will challenge and inspire you as you learn about more than fifty women of destiny who have preceded you in God's kingdom. Each of these women was "called according to His purpose" (see Rom. 8:28). Let their stories give you hope and encouragement to answer His call for your life.

Words of Wisdom: A sample of great thoughts spoken or written by giants of the faith throughout history, these quotations will give you a sense of God's dealings with His servants in days gone by. They help link the present to the past and put you in touch with the rich heritage of faith available to all believers.

Hope Chest Journal: These blank pages are your opportunity to express yourself. You may want to use them to write down Bible verses that are meaningful to you, prayer requests, or praise reports. You may also want to write down what you believe God is revealing to you about His destiny for your life, or to ask one of your own mentors to write a personal "Women of Destiny letter" to you.

Enjoy the Word of God, a love letter to you.

Knowing God

JOY DAWSON

My life's motto is "To Know God and To Make Him Known." My opening prayer for everyone who reads this article is from Ephesians 1:17: "That the God of our Lord Jesus Christ, the Father of glory, may give to you the spirit of wisdom and revelation in the knowledge of Him."

To know God means to have an understanding of His character and ways—the principles by which He operates. Sadly, many spend a lifetime only knowing about Him.

We only know people to the degree we know their characters—not just their personalities. This entails observing their actions and reactions to God and men over a long period of time. Only then can we explain them to others. When we don't take time to study the character of God, we'll inevitably have, and give, a distorted view of Him.

Satan is trying to distort God's character to humanity all the time. Second Corinthians 5:20 says, "Now then, we are ambassadors for Christ, as though God were pleading [or making His appeal] through us." An ambassador is meant to be a true representative of the authority who has commissioned him for that purpose. As Christ's ambassadors in this world we need to frequently ask God to show us where, in any way, we have a distorted view of His character and ways.

All our spiritual problems come from our lack of the knowledge of God. Therefore, it's of paramount importance that we make our pursuit of Him our greatest passion. "In all your getting, get understanding" (Prov. 4:7). "The knowledge of the Holy One is understanding" (Prov. 9:10). From the overflow of that revelation we're strongly motivated to make God known through the power and Person of the Holy Spirit. In fact, the more God reveals Himself to us, the more we're ruined for the ordinary. Period!

I've discovered Him to be supreme in authority, timeless in His existence, ingenious in His creativity, total in His ownership, awesome in His holiness, blazing in His glory, dazzling in His beauty, unparalleled in His greatness, majestic in His splendor, unswerving in His faithfulness, unending in His mercy, absolute in His justice, unfathomable in His love, infinite in His understanding, terrible in His wrath, incomprehensible in His humility, fascinating in His personality, intriguing in His mystery, and unquestionable in His sovereignty. He's totally unique, the ruling reigning monarch of the universe, King God, the lover of my soul, who has totally captivated me and the only One who can totally fulfill me.

God's Word not only says that "my beloved is mine and I am his" (Song 2:16), but "I am my beloved's, and his desire is toward me" (Song 7:10). Now that really gets my attention. The Creator and Sustainer of the universe, who accomplishes it by His spoken words, wants to become my lover? The incredible becomes reality when we make the pursuit of God, for Himself, the passion of our life.

Well, how do we get there? By getting our priorities in the right order.

Our vision and goals determine our priorities, and our priorities determine our destinies. Jeremiah 9:23, 24 says, "Thus says the LORD: 'Let not the wise man glory in his wisdom, let not the mighty man glory in his might, nor let the rich man glory in his riches; but let him who glories glory in this, that he understands and knows Me, that I am the LORD, exercising lovingkindness, judgment, and righteousness in the earth. For in these I delight,' says the LORD."

The three things that impress the majority of the people the most about other people are the very things God says He's unimpressed with—gaining earthly knowledge, positions of authority, and wealth. Think about it.

The above verses also give us a powerful insight into three fundamental aspects of God's overall character: His love, His justice, and His holiness.

Let me ask you a penetrating question. Are you really more excited about what God does than about who God is? It's a sign of spiritual maturity when we're honestly more excited about having greater revelation of some aspect of God's character than in a display of His power, as wonderful as that is. The children of Israel saw awesome acts of God's power when He brought them out of Egypt, but apart from a few leaders, they didn't pass God's tests in the wilderness because they didn't understand God's character and His ways.

We need to heed the words of the prophets: "For My people are foolish, they have not known Me" (Jer. 4:22). "Hear the word of the LORD . . . for the LORD brings a charge against [His people]. There is no truth or mercy or knowledge of God in the land" (Hos. 4:1).

God wants to bring us to the place where we obey Him, instantly, joyfully, and wholly for *who* He *is* regardless of what He tells us to do. The latter aspect should be incidental.

King David wanted his son Solomon to have the maximum effectiveness in his role as the future spiritual leader. That's why the advice David gave Solomon in 1 Chronicles 28:9 is so significant. He said, "Know the God of your father [first requirement], and serve Him with a loyal heart and with a willing mind [second requirement]."

Too often that order is reversed. "For I desire mercy and not sacrifice, and the knowledge of God more than burnt offerings" (Hos. 6:6).

We'll only make God known effectively to the degree we've taken time to know Him, and that means studying both the many facets of His character and His ways.

How do we do that? We diligently search the Scriptures. David said, "I will meditate on Your precepts, and contemplate Your ways" (Ps. 119:15). In Proverbs 2:1–6, Solomon makes it starkly clear that the knowledge of God is only revealed to diligent seekers, not to casual inquirers. He says we're to search for this understanding like we would hunt for hidden treasure.

One time when I was teaching the Word of God in Chile, I stayed in an apartment where I had a partial view of the beautiful snow-capped Andes Mountains. Other people have traveled to the foot of the mountains to enjoy a far better view. But only those who have climbed the Andes Mountains know them and can speak about them with authority. Can we speak about God's character and ways with authority?

Moses had his priorities right when he prayed in Exodus 33:13, "Show me now Your way, that I may know You and that I may find grace in Your sight." And again in verse 18, "Please, show me Your glory." God's glory is the sum total of all God's attributes. Moses had to leave the securities and comfort zones of being with his other leaders, elders, and Joshua and climb rugged Mount Sinai to be alone with God for long periods of time.

His reward? God "made known His ways to Moses, His acts to the children of Israel" (Ps. 103:7). Moses was also rewarded with a revelation of eight aspects of God's character at one time as God placed Moses in a cleft of a rock and passed by him (see Ex. 34:6, 7). He was also called a friend of God. That friendship was so close that in one conversation with God, Moses' intercession released God to spare a nation doomed for judgment.

David prayed in Psalm 25:4, "Show me Your ways, O LORD; teach me Your paths." That's very good. But it's David's impassioned heart cries to know God that strongly inspire and motivate us to seek Him with greater intensity. There's always a desperation related to great thirst. Listen to it in Psalm 42:1, 2: "As the deer pants for water brooks, so pants my soul for You, O God. My soul thirsts for God, for the living God." His reward? David is described as "a man after His [God's] own heart" (1 Sam. 13:14). What a tribute! And God gave David great revelation of His character. In Psalm 145, David describes twenty-one attributes of God's character in twenty-one verses!

Paul prayed in Philippians 3:10, "that I may know Him and the power of His resurrection, and the fellowship of His sufferings, being conformed to His death." That prayer prayed in sincerity inevitably has enormous implications including multiple sufferings. Paul also said, "I also count all things loss for the excellence of the knowledge of Christ Jesus my Lord, for whom I have suffered the loss of all things, and count them as rubbish, that I may gain Christ" (Phil. 3:8).

His reward? Paul received so much revelation from God that he wasn't permitted to share it all. We obviously couldn't handle it. Think about that! We can choose to pray the prayers of these men and to seek God with intense desire. It's over to us.

Let's get real and tell God how little we know and understand Him. The more I've studied the many attributes of God, the more I see how little I know. His knowableness is so vast. But that excites me. If I could fully understand Him, I'd know as much as He does about Himself. Only God knows that, because He's God, infinite in knowledge and wisdom.

Only God can handle all that knowledge and not be bored. Learning is exciting, especially when it's about the most exciting, unpredictable being in the universe, God. Predictable in His character, but often unpredictable in the ways in which it is expressed. Fascinating. He's not moldy because He's not in a mold. I adore Him and praise and worship Him.

Let's tell God we want the supreme desire of our lives to be to know Him intimately so we can make Him known effectively. If you already have that desire, ask Him to increase it. He'd be delighted! "Then you will call upon Me and go and pray to Me, and I will listen to you. And you will seek Me and find Me, when you search for Me with all your heart" (Jer. 29:12, 13).

When Jesus was on the Emmaus road with two of His disciples after His resurrection, He indicated that He would have gone further, when the disciples came to their destination. Luke 24:29 says, "But they constrained Him, saying, 'Abide with us' . . . and He went in to stay with them." Verse 30 says Jesus fellowshiped with them and broke bread. And verse 31 says, "Then their eyes were opened and they knew Him."

When we desperately want to have greater revelation of the Lord Jesus, we'll spend more time getting to know Him, and He'll reveal more of the wonders of Himself to us.

In Exodus 3:2, 3, we find that the angel of the Lord appeared to Moses in flames of fire within a bush. But the bush didn't burn up, so Moses took the time to go over and look closely at this phenomenon. Then we read these important words in verse 4: "So when the LORD saw that he turned aside to look, God called to him from the midst of the bush and said, 'Moses, Moses!' And he said, 'Here I am.'" The rest is history.

Many times the bush burns (God manifests His presence and power), but we don't take the time to turn aside to seek *Him* for Himself, to understand His character and His ways. We don't wait in His presence until we hear His voice speaking to us. We don't wait upon Him to see if there's some new direction He may want us to take. Let's change that.

Each time before you read your Bible, you can ask God to reveal Himself and His ways to you, and thank Him that He will. The main purpose in having the Bible is not that we may study its historical backgrounds, the lives of the people recorded in it, or its Hebrew or Greek. Nor is it that we may memorize it or gain a lot of general knowledge about it. Rather, the main purpose in having the Bible is that we may seek to understand the Author of the Book and live in intimate friendship with Him.

It is important to meditate on God's Word by reading it slowly and by asking the Holy Spirit to give us revelation of the hidden truths, believing that He will. One ounce of meditation is worth a ton of memorization, as important as that is. Because meditation produces revelation. And revelation motivates us to worship Him and obey Him. And obedience to the truth is the only thing that releases God to conform us more to the image of His Son, which is what the Christian life is all about (see Rom. 8:29).

I have found several ways to effectively study the character and ways of God from His Word.

(1) Underline the verses in your Bible that refer to God's character and His ways as you read the Bible daily, and write or type them out under the appropriate headings. Then compile your personal concordance over the years. Meditate on what you've compiled, asking and believing for the Holy Spirit's revelation.

If you're writing, you'll need a big notebook (He's a big God), and you'll need a loose-leaf notebook so that you can put in additional pages. You'll also need alphabetical tabs, *A* through *Z*. For example: Say you're reading in Hebrews 12, and verse 10 says that the reason God brings chastening in our lives is for our good, "that we may be partakers of His holiness." Holiness is part of God's character, so you underline this verse and put a heading in your notebook under "H," "The Holiness of God," and write out the verse.

Then you see that one of the ways of God is also in this verse. So under the "C" section you write the heading "God's Chastening (or correcting) of His Children." Write out the verse again. When you come to verse 14, you see another reference to the holiness of God, so you underline it and write that one out in addition. "Pursue peace with all people, and holiness, without which no one will see the Lord." So you meditate on what you've written and understanding comes on how important living a holy life is in relation to receiving revelation of who God is, and that it has a lot to do with living peaceably with people . . . and so much more which you'll discover. Then ask God how what you've found can be applied to your life and put it into practice in an ongoing way. God will trust us with more revelation of truth to the degree we obey the truth we already know.

(2) Ask God to direct you concerning which facet of His character you're to study and/or which one of His ways you're to study, and follow through one by one. Add them to your personal concordance. Write down in other notebooks how the truths apply to everyday living.

(3) Make an in-depth study of the life of the Lord Jesus from the Gospels. This is very revealing and extremely rewarding. After all, He is our mentor.

(4) Turn frequently to portions of the Word of God that describe the Lord in His glory, and take a long look at Him and worship Him. See, for example, Isaiah 6:1–5, Ezekiel 1:26–28, Daniel 10:5, 6, Revelation 1:12–16, Revelation 4, and Revelation 19.

(5) As a way of life pray the Word of God into your personal spiritual experience, and use the Word of God in intercessory prayer for others and for situations. This greatly releases and enlarges the knowledge of God's character and ways into your spirit. We can easily be textually aware of the Bible, but spiritually unenlightened. The methods I'm suggesting will keep that from happening.

The results of knowing God will be as follows:

(1) We will become like Him. "But we all, with unveiled face, beholding as in a mirror the glory of the Lord, are being transformed into the same image from glory to glory, just as by the Spirit of the Lord" (2 Cor. 3:18).

(2) The greater the revelation we have of who God is, the less likely we'll want to touch His glory and to give it to ourselves or anyone else. The thought is obnoxious.

(3) The more we know God and understand His ways, the more ludicrous disobedience becomes. We do ourselves the greatest favor by obeying Him.

(4) The more we know Him and understand His ways, the more He'll create opportunities for us to make Him known. ". . . The people who know their God shall be strong, and carry out great exploits. And those of the people who understand shall instruct many" (Dan. 11:32, 33).

(5) Other lives are inevitably influenced and motivated to know God according to the time we've taken to know and understand Him. "Now thanks be to God who always leads us in triumph in Christ, and through us diffuses the fragrance of His knowledge in every place" (2 Cor. 2:14). That means we are to make God known in the circles of our influence, including world evangelism.

I join with the apostle Paul in praying for everyone who reads this article: "We also, since the day we heard it, do not cease to pray for you, and to ask that you may be filled with the knowledge of His will in all wisdom and spiritual understanding; that you may walk worthy of the Lord, fully pleasing Him, being fruitful in every good work and *increasing in the knowledge of God*" (Col. 1:9,10, emphasis added).

How to Receive Divine Revelation from the Bible

FUCHSIA PICKETT

There are many ways to interact with the Bible. Some people spend years studying it for its literary or historical qualities, while others read it in order to gain intellectual knowledge of Christianity. Sadly, some believers practice daily Bible reading out of a sense of fear or obligation and never realize that "the Word of God is living and powerful, . . . piercing even to the division of soul and spirit . . . and is a discerner of the thoughts and intents of the heart" (Heb. 4:12). There is only one way to discover the power and life of God's Word and to enter into the type of relationship with Him that He intends for His children to enjoy.

To experience the friendship, the fellowship, and the fatherhood of God, we must come to know Him by divine revelation of His Word. When we speak of divine revelation, we are talking about the unveiling of Jesus Christ to believers. Simply put, the wonder of divine revelation is that it unveils Christ's mind to your mind, His emotions to your emotions, and His will to your will. As you experience that unveiling, your character will be transformed into the likeness of Jesus Christ. It makes who you are more like who He is.

Jesus Christ is the beautiful, radiant, all-powerful Son of God. His character is so deep, so rich, so multifaceted that the human spirit cannot contain all that He is. God, our Father, in His grace and wisdom, allows the lovely nature of Christ to be unveiled, or made clear, to us by the process of divine revelation. Little by little, we get to know our Savior. As that happens, our affection and longing for Him will grow. We discover a passion for His presence and an ever-deepening desire to please Him. In the process, we are changed, little by little, "from glory to glory" (2 Cor. 3:18).

A careful search of the Scriptures shows that Christ comes to live in our spirits when we are born again—when we accept the sacrifice of His blood for the forgiveness of our sins. That is why you may hear the salvation experience referred to as "receiving Jesus." But once we are converted, the mysterious divine life of Christ in our spirits must be revealed, or unveiled, to our souls—our minds, wills, and emotions—in order for us to enjoy a vibrant, intimate relationship with the Father, the Son, and the Holy Spirit.

The revelation of Christ brings the rending of the "veil of flesh" that divides our souls and our spirits. This veil of flesh dropped between our souls and our spirits when sin entered the world through Adam and separated us from the presence of the Lord. Because God is Spirit (see John 4:24) and He speaks to us in our spirits, the veil of flesh keeps us from full communion with Him. The veil must be torn in order for us to know the glorious Person of Christ. Revelation allows us to see Him as He is—the Exalted One, the Brightness of God's Glory, the Express Image of His Person, the King of Glory, the Pearl of Great Price, the Rock in a weary land, the Cup that runs over, the Rod and Staff, the Father to the orphan, the Husband to the widow, the Bright and Morning Star, the Lily of the Valley, the Rose of Sharon, the Honey in the rock, the Passover Lamb, the Captain of our salvation, the Mighty to save, the Messenger of beautiful feet, the Avenger of God's elect, the Justifier, the Sanctifier. This Christ cannot be seen with the eye, touched with the hand, or heard with the ear of the natural man.

As mentioned earlier, the Scriptures declare that the Word of God is sharper than a two-edged sword, able to divide the soul and the spirit (see Heb. 4:12) The dividing doesn't happen out in the atmosphere somewhere. It happens inside us. It is a work of the Holy Spirit—the infinite, omnipotent, omniscient, omnipresent, blessed Third Person of the Godhead.

The Bible teaches that the Holy Spirit came to take the things of Jesus and show them to us (see John 16:15). He came to reveal Jesus in us and to fill our temples with God. In order to do that, He has a divine mandate to split the veil of flesh between our soul and spirit so that the life of Jesus can be manifest in our lives.

True revelation of God cannot take place apart from the Word of God. Jesus Christ is the living Word, and the Holy Spirit's job is to unveil Him by teaching us to apply the truth of the written Word to our lives. By the power of the Holy Spirit, the written Word works in us a divine process of revelation that changes us forever—from the inside out.

The revelation of God is a lifelong process, a continual unfolding of the endless wonders of the Godhead. We will never finish receiving revelation. It is not an easy endeavor, but there are seven steps that will be helpful in receiving divine revelation from the Word of God.

1. Information

The first step toward divine revelation is to receive *information*. We must first receive a basic truth in our minds and hearts before the Holy Spirit can bring it to our remembrance. This cannot happen without spending time daily reading and meditating on the Word of God. It makes sense, doesn't it? We cannot expect the Word to come to life inside of us if we do not know what it says.

As Christians, we need to spend time reading and memorizing the Word of God. In this way, we make it possible for the Holy Spirit to do His wonderful work of bringing us divine revelation.

Joshua received a mandate that would guarantee his success—to meditate day and night on the law of God (see Josh. 1:8). Our faithfulness in following this same mandate will determine our success or failure in walking toward true revelation. Without a knowledge of the information contained in the Scriptures, we cannot have a fuller revelation of Christ within us, even if we are born-again Christians.

2. Illumination

Have you ever enjoyed reading a familiar passage of Scripture and suddenly had a light come on in your mind? When this happens, you instantly see how a biblical principle applies to your life, or perhaps you see why God responded to a Bible character's situation the way He did. In that moment, information has taken on another dimension. The ancient words of the Bible become treasures to you as you begin to understand how powerfully they speak to your personal situations.

When information begins to be a light to our spirits, it becomes *illumination*. We understand, in a way we never understood before, the depth and power of biblical truths that once seemed like mere academic facts. At that point, it becomes our responsibility to walk in obedience to the truth we understand.

3. Inspiration

As the Holy Spirit continues His process of bringing revelation, we find ourselves responding to the truth with His joy. The Holy Spirit receives the Word, and as we receive it from Him, it becomes *inspiration* to us. We get excited about the Scriptures, and a new desire to obey the Word takes hold of us.

Inspiration makes us hungry for the Word of God. The divine work of the Holy Spirit causes a "hunger and thirst for righteousness" (Matt. 5:6). No human being can create hunger for the Word. If you find yourself hungering for truth, you are being invited by the Holy Spirit to receive greater revelation.

People who sit in church and are bored to death with the preached Word are not hungry. Hungry folks will devour anything. The Scriptures declare: "A satisfied soul loathes the honeycomb, but to a hungry soul every bitter thing is sweet" (Prov. 27:7).

When we are hungry for the Word, we are crying out for more of God. The blessed Holy Spirit then splits the veil of our darkened minds, emotions, and wills, and brings the light and life of Jesus to the deepest parts of us.

4. New Revelation

The written Word of God (*logos* in the Greek) can be viewed as a transcription of God's voice. It allows us to read and experience what God is actually saying to us on a deep and personal level. When the transcribed Word moves from our heads to our hearts and inspires us to its reality, it becomes a living Word (*rhema*). That living Word is revelation.

Jesus says, "I am the way, *the truth*, and the life" (John 14:6, emphasis mine). Revelation causes the truth to become a living Person to us. We realize that Jesus Christ does not just bring us information concerning the truth, but that He actually *becomes* truth to our hearts. As we respond to the revelation of Christ, we yield our minds, wills, and emotions to His divine character of truth, holiness, and righteousness, and His life is unveiled within us. When the Holy Spirit breathes a revealed truth into our spirits, it becomes life to us. We actually experience firsthand what we had previously heard only as information.

Our obedience to the revelation we receive is what enables the Holy Spirit to keep giving new revelation. *Once revelation begins to flow, it keeps flowing unless we resist it.* It is a serious matter indeed to disobey divine revelation that has come to our hearts. Darkness is dispelled only by the light that pierces it. If we give place to darkness rather than walking in the light we have received, we will suffer the consequences of our disobedience. God loves us enough to convict and correct us when we are not living in the full measure of understanding He desires for us.

5. Realization

After revelation begins to work in our hearts, the next step in the divine growth process is *realization*. Realization is the recognition that we are being changed through our obedience to the revelation we have received. We realize that the change that is taking place in us is real and that it affects the way we live.

We may not know exactly how it happened, but one day, for example, we may realize that we are not losing our temper as we used to. That we are walking in a grace we did not have before. That we are able to love those we once avoided. Other people, too, can observe this change. Our spirits are sensitive to the truth that has become a living reality in us, and we become increasingly careful not to disobey it.

6. Transformation

Transformation of character occurs as we allow death to come to the self-life through the rending of the veil of flesh. Those deep, inward tendencies of self-centeredness and lovelessness that reside in our natural selves are fundamentally changed—transformed—into holy desires and Christlike love. The rich and powerful life of Christ can then be lived through us in the world.

Consistently walking in greater depths of revelation brings a gradual *transformation* to our lives. We are changed from glory to glory into the image of the Son through our obedience to the revelation we receive.

7. Manifestation

The final step the Spirit of Truth works in us is the *manifestation* of Jesus' character in our lives. Maturity is the beauty of Jesus as it is seen in people who have allowed revelation to touch every area of their souls and spirits. In obedience to God, they have continually turned from sin and allowed the nature of Christ to be fully unveiled in them.

The beautiful part of the process of revelation is that different truth may be operating at different stages in us simultaneously. One truth may be at the fourth stage—*revelation*—becoming a reality and preparing us to move on to *realization* and *transformation*. Another truth we have just received as *information* may inspire us to seek God for *revelation*. In this way, as we consistently avail ourselves of the reading and hearing of the Word, the Holy Spirit takes the Book and writes it on our hearts.

Information is transferring someone else's notes to our minds. It has no eternal value unless it goes beyond that. But in our search for wisdom, we pray that God will make His Word real to us and open our minds to receive divine *revelation*. It was the Son of God Himself who declared in the face of the tempter: "Man shall not live by bread alone, but by every word that proceeds from the mouth of God" (Matt. 4:4). It is God's proceeding Word that contains the power to save our souls (see James 1:21).

How Revelation Deepens

We cannot overestimate the time and energy required to make us students of the Word—students who can receive an ever-greater revelation of God. We dare not expect to enter into intimate relationship with the Almighty God as easily as we would microwave a potato or flip a light switch. Even human relationships require time to cultivate and nurture to any level of intimacy.

We can be assured of deepening our relationship with God as we give priority to the Word and learn to yield to the Holy Spirit when He speaks something fresh to us. If we are willing to go through the process required to receive revelation, we will never be disappointed in our walk with Him. As we yield to the Holy Spirit's prompting and allow Him to tear away the veil of flesh that keeps us from knowing God intimately, we will behold "wondrous things" from His law (see Ps. 119:18). Then we will find our attitudes, actions, and priorities transformed by Jesus Christ, the Living Word, who is being unveiled *through* us as He is being revealed *to* us.

My prayer for you is that you may know how living, how powerful, and how sharp God's Word is. I pray for you according to Ephesians 1:17–19, "that the God of our Lord Jesus Christ, the Father of glory, may give you the spirit of wisdom and revelation in the knowledge of Him." I pray "that you may know what is the hope of His calling, what are the riches of the glory of His inheritance in the saints, and what is the exceeding greatness of His power toward us who believe."

May God bless you, my sisters, as you study His Word, as you receive divine revelation by His Holy Spirit, and as the beautiful character of Jesus Christ is unveiled in you.

How to Be Born Again

CINDY JACOBS

I assume that you are reading this Bible because you are interested in learning more about God. Maybe a friend has told you about Him and His Son, Jesus Christ. In order to fully understand the words you are about to read, it is important to have the key to this Book. This key is something the Bible calls being *born again* (see John 3:3–9).

You might wonder, *How can I be born again when I've been born once as a baby?* Someone else asked the same question long ago. His name was Nicodemus, and his story is found in the Book of John (you can find this account on page 1277).

Jesus told Nicodemus that in addition to his physical birth, he also needed to be born into the kingdom of God. He told him that God had sent Him into the world so that we would believe on Him and have eternal life. This is what we call "becoming a Christian."

You see, all of us on this earth commit sins and do wrong. Perhaps they are only things no one can see; but none of us is perfect (see Rom. 3:23). Only Jesus Christ was perfect, because He is God. He died for you on the cross to pay the price for your sins. In essence, He gave His life for yours so you would not have to die and go to a place called hell.

Hell was not prepared for you, but for Satan. However, all those who have ever sinned have been sentenced to go to that awful place. That is why Jesus had to die in your place—so that you could ask Him to forgive your sins, be cleansed of them, and go to heaven instead.

I don't believe it is by chance that you have picked up this Book today. God Himself has directed you to read it. If you pray to ask Jesus into your life and pray that your sins be forgiven, you will then become a child of God.

Why not take a moment and pray this prayer with me? It will change your life forever:

Dear God,
I realize that I am a sinner and I need to be forgiven. Please come into my heart and life and forgive me of my sin and all the wrong things that I have done in my life. I want to be born again and become Your child. In Jesus' name, Amen.

Dear friend, if you prayed that prayer, you are now my sister in the Lord. If you were to die now (and we are believing that you are not going to do that), you would go directly to heaven. You are forgiven and washed clean from your sins.

It is now important to find a good church that believes in being born again. I am praying that the Lord will lead you to the right church for you—one where you can grow as a Christian and learn more about how to be a child of God.

How to Be Filled With the Holy Spirit

MARILYN HICKEY

I know that God must have highly esteemed the baptism of the Holy Spirit, for He prophesied about it: "And it shall come to pass afterward that I will pour out My Spirit on all flesh . . . " (Joel 2:28).

The baptism of the Holy Spirit is a gift that God wants you to have. Believe that God wants to give you His best, just as He gave His best when He gave you His Son, Jesus Christ. If Jesus, the disciples, and the early church were all baptized in the Holy Spirit, then this baptism is for you, too. You are a member of the same body, and God will withhold no good thing from you: "If you then, being evil, know how to give good gifts to your children, how much more will your heavenly Father give the Holy Spirit to those who ask Him!" (Luke 11:13).

The Father gives good gifts, and He will not give you a counterfeit. Receive the baptism of the Holy Spirit by faith, just as you received salvation by faith. God imparts the baptism of the Holy Spirit in two ways:

(1) By sovereign outpouring (see Acts 2:1–4; 10:44–48). Many times Jesus simply baptizes people with the Holy Spirit anywhere they are, wherever they ask Him. Other times, they may not even ask, and they are baptized with the Holy Spirit because of someone's prayer for them. Jesus is a giver, and He loves to give people His most precious gift—the Spirit of God.

(2) By the ministry of laying on of hands. Sometimes Christians may have another member of the body of Christ lay hands on them to receive the baptism of the Holy Spirit (see Acts 8:14–19).

Speaking in tongues is one evidence of the Holy Spirit inside you. Speaking in tongues is one way that God builds you up spiritually: "But you, beloved, building yourselves up on your most holy faith, praying in the Holy Spirit . . . " (Jude 20).

When you pray in the Spirit, you pray directly to God and bypass your understanding. Praying in tongues eliminates selfishness from our prayers as they are guided directly by God. You pray according to His will, and even pray over matters that you may know nothing about! "Likewise the Spirit also helps in our weaknesses. For we do not know what we should pray for as we ought, but the Spirit Himself makes intercession for us with groanings which cannot be uttered. Now He who searches the hearts knows what the mind of the Spirit is, because He makes intercession for the saints according to the will of God. And we know that all things work together for good to those who love God, to those who are the called according to His purpose" (Rom. 8:26–28).

Your baptism with the Holy Spirit is a one-time event. But your "infilling" is continuous. Being filled with the Spirit begins at Holy Spirit baptism, but you should never stop receiving from the Spirit of the Lord. The filling of the Holy Spirit goes on and on (see Eph. 5:18). You have a fountain within you. Don't allow sin or self-life to stop this flow. You can be filled daily. Keep being filled, keep being filled, keep being filled. You are on your way to the richest life you have ever had, as you walk in the abundance of the Living Christ each day.

The Gifts of the Holy Spirit

Did you know that you are uniquely gifted and equipped for a specific purpose in God's kingdom? The Holy Spirit gives gifts to each member of the body of Christ in order to equip us to fulfill His purposes. As you move toward discovering God's destiny for your life, it will be important to know what your spiritual gifts are and how you can use them to serve the cause and kingdom of Jesus Christ.

There are several places in the New Testament that list the various gifts of the Holy Spirit. You will find them in Romans 12:3–8; 1 Corinthians 12:7–11; Ephesians 4:7–12. In Galatians 5:22, 23, you will also find the fruit of the Holy Spirit—the virtues that the Holy Spirit produces in a Spirit-filled life.

The gifts of the Holy Spirit are placed in the church as resources to be used to meet ministry needs in the body. This means that not every believer will have the same gifts as every other believer. Rather, the Holy Spirit is the giver of the gifts, dispensing them as He sees fit for the edification of the body, integrity in worship, and the building of the kingdom. Your gifts are to be developed, embraced, and enjoyed, just as the gifts in others are to be honored and not envied.

Following you will find, from Peter Wagner's book *Your Spiritual Gifts Can Help Your Church Grow*, a list of the spiritual gifts and some definitions that will help you begin to understand each gift. For further understanding, see the scriptures at the end of each definition.

Prophecy—the special ability that God gives to certain members of the body of Christ to receive and communicate an immediate message of God to His people through a divinely anointed utterance (see 1 Cor. 12:10, 28; Eph. 4:11–14; Rom. 12:6; Luke 7:26; Acts 15:32; 21:9–11).

Pastor—the special ability that God gives to certain members of the body of Christ to assume a long-term personal responsibility for the spiritual welfare of a group of believers (see Eph. 4:11–14; 1 Tim. 3:1–7; John 10:1–18; 1 Pet. 5:1–3).

Teaching—the special ability that God gives to certain members of the body of Christ to communicate information relevant to the health and ministry of the body and its members in such a way that others will learn (see 1 Cor. 12:28; Eph. 4:11–14; Rom. 12:7; Acts 8:24–28; 20:20, 21).

Wisdom—the special ability that God gives to certain members of the body of Christ to know the mind of the Holy Spirit in such a way as to receive insight into how given knowledge may best be applied to specific needs arising in the body of Christ (see 1 Cor. 2:1–13; 12:8; Acts 6:3, 10; James 1:5, 6; 2 Pet. 3:15, 16). [In addition, wisdom can be supernatural knowledge of events that are to come.—*Cindy Jacobs*]

Knowledge—the special ability that God gives to certain members of the body of Christ to discover, accumulate, analyze, and clarify information and ideas which are pertinent to the well-being of the body (see 1 Cor. 2:14; 12:8; Acts 5:1–11; Col. 2:2, 3; 2 Cor. 11:6). [In addition, knowledge can be supernatural insight into present needs, e.g., the need for healing.—*Cindy Jacobs*]

Exhortation—the special ability that God gives to certain members of the body of Christ to minister words of comfort, consolation, encouragement, and counsel to other members of the body in such a way that they feel helped and healed (see Rom. 12:8; 1 Tim. 4:13; Heb. 10:25; Act 14:22).

Discerning of Spirits—the special ability that God gives to certain members of the body of Christ to know with assurance whether certain behavior purported to be of God is in reality divine, human, or Satanic (see 1 Cor. 12:10; Acts 5:1–11; 16:16–18; 1 John 4:1–6; Matt. 16:21–23).

Giving—the special ability that God gives to certain members of the body of Christ to contribute their material resources to the work of the Lord with liberality and cheerfulness (see Rom. 12:8; 2 Cor. 8:1–7; 9:2–8; Mark 12:41–44).

Helps—the special ability that God gives to certain members of the body of Christ to invest the talents they have in the life and ministry of other members of the body, thus enabling those others to increase the effectiveness of their own spiritual gifts (see 1 Cor. 12:28; Rom. 16:1, 2; Acts 9:36; Luke 8:2, 3; Mark 15:40, 41).

Mercy—the special ability that God gives to certain members of the body of Christ to feel genuine empathy and compassion for individuals (both Christian and non-Christian) who suffer distressing physical, mental, or emotional problems, and to translate that compassion into cheerfully done deeds which reflect Christ's love and alleviate the suffering (see Rom. 12:8; Mark 9:41; Acts 16:33, 34; Luke 10:33–35; Matt. 20:29–34; 25:34–40; Acts 11:28–30).

Missionary—the special ability that God gives to certain members of the body of Christ to minister whatever other spiritual gifts they have in a second culture (see 1 Cor. 9:19–23; Acts 8:4; 13:2, 3; 22:21; Rom. 10:15).

Evangelist—the special ability that God gives to certain members of the body of Christ to share the gospel with unbelievers in such a way that men and women become Jesus' disciples and responsible members of the body of Christ (see Eph. 4:11–14; 2 Tim. 4:5; Acts 8:5, 6; 8:26–40; 14:21; 21:8).

Hospitality—the special ability that God gives to certain members of the body of Christ to provide an open house and a warm welcome to those in need of food and lodging (see 1 Pet. 4:9; Rom. 12:9–13; 16:23; Acts 16:14, 15; Heb. 13:1, 2).

Faith—the special ability that God gives to certain members of the body of Christ to discern with extraordinary confidence the will and purposes of God for His work (see 1 Cor. 12:9; Acts 11:22–24; 27:21–25; Heb. 11; Rom. 4:18–21).

Leadership—the special ability that God gives to certain members of the body of Christ to set goals in accordance with God's purpose for the future and to communicate these goals to others in such a way that they voluntarily and harmoniously work together to accomplish those goals for the glory of God (see 1 Tim. 5:17; Acts 7:10; 15:7–11; Rom. 12:8; Heb. 13:17; Luke 9:51).

Administration—the special ability that God gives to certain members of the body of Christ to understand clearly the immediate and long-range goals of a particular unit of the body of Christ and to devise and execute effective plans for the accomplishment of those goals (see 1 Cor. 12:28; Acts 6:1–7; 27:11; Luke 14:28–30; Titus 1:5).

Miracles—the special ability that God gives to certain members of the body of Christ to serve as human intermediaries through whom it pleases God to perform powerful acts that are perceived by observers to have altered the ordinary course of nature (see 1 Cor. 12:10, 28; Acts 9:36–42; 19:11–20; 20:7–12; Rom. 15:18, 19; 2 Cor. 12:12).

Healing—the special ability that God gives to certain members of the body of Christ to serve as human intermediaries through whom it pleases God to cure illness and restore health apart from the use of natural means (see 1 Cor. 12:9, 28; Acts 3:1–10; 5:12–16; 9:32–35; 28:7–10).

Tongues—the special ability that God gives to certain members of the body of Christ (a) to speak to God in a language they have never learned and/or (b) to receive and communicate an immediate message of God to His people through a divinely anointed utterance in a language they never learned (see Acts 2:1–13; 10:44–46; 19:1–7; Mark 16:17).

Interpretation—the special ability that God gives to certain members of the body of Christ to make known in the vernacular the message of one who speaks in tongues (see 1 Cor. 12:10, 30; 14:13; 14:26–28).

Voluntary Poverty—the special ability that God gives to certain members of the body of Christ to renounce material comfort and luxury and adopt a personal lifestyle equivalent to those living at the poverty level in a given society in order to serve God more effectively (see 1 Cor. 13:1–3; Acts 2:44, 45; 4:34–37; 2 Cor. 6:10; 8:9).

Celibacy—the special ability that God gives to certain members of the body of Christ to remain single and enjoy it; to be unmarried and not suffer undue sexual temptations (see 1 Cor. 7:7, 8; Matt. 19:10–12).

Intercession—the special ability that God gives to certain members of the body of Christ to pray for extended periods of time on a regular basis and see frequent and specific answers to their prayers, to a degree much greater than that which is expected of the average Christian (James 5:14–16; 1 Tim. 2:1, 2; Col. 1:9–12; 4:12, 13; Acts 12:12; Luke 22:41–44).

Exorcism—the special ability that God gives to certain members of the body of Christ to cast out demons and evil spirits (Matt. 12:22–32; Luke 10:12–20; Acts 8:5–8; 16:16–18).

Service—the special ability that God gives to certain members of the body of Christ to identify the unmet needs involved in a task related to God's work, and to make use of available resources to meet those needs and help accomplish the desired results (2 Tim. 1:16–18; Rom. 12:7; Acts 6:1–7; Titus 3:14; Gal. 6:2, 10).

May you be abundantly blessed as you discover and use your spiritual gifts to the glory of God!

The Old Testament

AUTHOR: *Traditionally Moses*
DATE: *Approximately 1440 B.C.*
THEME: *Beginnings*
KEY WORDS: *Create, Covenant, Genealogy*

GENESIS

Dear Woman of Destiny,

Genesis is an excellent book for women like us because we understand the power and potential of beginnings. Here we see the fullness of Creation and the seed-promise of redemption. Let these pictures of God's faithfulness bring renewed life to the potential all around you.

His love and mine,

Marilyn Hickey

The History of Creation

In the [a]beginning [b]God created the heavens and the earth. 2 The earth was [a]without form, and void; and darkness [1]*was* on the face of the deep. [b]And the Spirit of God was hovering over the face of the waters.

3 [a]Then God said, [b]"Let there be [c]light"; and there was light. 4 And God saw the light, that *it was* good; and God divided the light from the darkness. 5 God called the light Day, and the [a]darkness He called Night. [1]So the evening and the morning were the first day.

6 Then God said, [a]"Let there be a [1]firmament in the midst of the waters, and let it divide the waters from the waters." 7 Thus God made the firmament, [a]and divided the waters which *were* under the firmament from the waters which *were* [b]above the firmament; and it was so. 8 And God called the firmament Heaven. So the evening and the morning were the second day.

9 Then God said, [a]"Let the waters under the heavens be gathered together into one place, and [b]let the dry *land* appear"; and it was so. 10 And God called the dry *land* Earth, and the gathering together of the waters He called Seas. And God saw that *it was* good.

11 Then God said, "Let the earth [a]bring forth grass, the herb *that* yields seed, *and* the [b]fruit tree *that* yields fruit according to its kind, whose seed *is* in itself, on the earth"; and it was so. 12 And the earth brought forth grass, the herb *that* yields seed according to its kind, and the tree *that* yields fruit, whose seed *is* in itself according to its kind. And God saw that *it was* good. 13 So the evening and the morning were the third day.

14 Then God said, "Let there be [a]lights in the firmament of the heavens to divide the day from the night; and let them be for signs and [b]seasons, and for days and years; 15 and let them be for lights in the firmament of the heavens to give light on the earth"; and it was so. 16 Then God made two great [1]lights: the [a]greater light to rule the day, and the [b]lesser light to rule the night. *He made* [c]the stars also. 17 God set them in the firmament of the [a]heavens to give light on the earth, 18 and to [a]rule over the day and over the night, and to divide the light from the darkness. And God saw that *it was* good. 19 So the evening and the morning were the fourth day.

20 Then God said, "Let the waters abound with an abundance of living [1]creatures, and let birds fly above the earth across the face of the [2]firmament of the heavens." 21 So [a]God created great sea creatures and every living thing that moves, with which the waters abounded, according to their kind, and every winged bird according to its kind. And God saw that *it was* good. 22 And God blessed them, saying, [a]"Be fruitful and multiply, and fill the waters in the seas, and let birds multiply on the earth." 23 So the evening and the morning were the fifth day.

24 Then God said, "Let the earth bring forth the living creature according to its kind: cattle and creeping thing and beast of the earth, *each* according to its kind"; and it was so. 25 And God made the beast of the earth according to its kind, cattle according to its kind, and everything that creeps on the earth according to its kind. And God saw that *it was* good.

There is nothing created for mere show, no useless part of creation. The aim of God in all His modes and works is the highest good to all His creatures.

CATHERINE BOOTH

26 Then God said, [a]"Let Us make man in Our image, according to Our likeness; [b]let them have dominion over the fish of the sea, over the birds of the air, and over the cattle, over [1]all the earth and over every creeping thing that creeps on the earth." 27 So God created man [a]in His *own* image; in the image of God He created him; [b]male and female He created them. 28 Then God blessed them, and God said to them, [a]"Be fruitful and multiply; fill the earth and [b]subdue it; have dominion over the fish of the sea, over the birds of the air, and over every living thing that [1]moves on the earth."

29 And God said, "See, I have given you every herb *that* yields seed which *is* on the face of all the earth, and every tree whose fruit yields seed; [a]to you it shall be for

CHAPTER 1

1 a [John 1:1–3] b Acts 17:24

2 a Jer. 4:23 b Is. 40:13, 14 1 Words in italic type have been added for clarity. They are not found in the original Hebrew or Aramaic.

3 a Ps. 33:6, 9 b 2 Cor. 4:6 c [Heb. 11:3]

5 a Ps. 19:2; 33:6; 74:16; 104:20; 136:5 1 Lit. *And evening was, and morning was, a day, one.*

6 a Jer. 10:12 1 *expanse*

7 a Prov. 8:27–29 b Ps. 148:4

9 a Job 26:10 b Ps. 24:1, 2; 33:7; 95:5

11 a Heb. 6:7 b 2 Sam. 16:1

14 a Ps. 74:16; 136:5–9 b Ps. 104:19

16 a Ps. 136:8 b Ps. 8:3 c Job 38:7 1 *luminaries*

17 a Gen. 15:5

18 a Jer. 31:35

20 1 *souls* 2 *expanse*

21 a Ps. 104:25–28

22 a Gen. 8:17

26 a [Eph. 4:24] b Gen. 9:2 1 Syr. *all the wild animals of*

27 a Gen. 5:2 b Matt. 19:4

28 a Gen. 9:1, 7 b 1 Cor. 9:27 1 *moves about on*

29 a Gen. 9:3

GENESIS 1:27

Dear Woman of Destiny,

The church, which has not yet come into a proper relationship with the Holy Spirit, is living without a true understanding of God's divine order for mankind. A basic misunderstanding arises from our definition of "man." The word translated from the Hebrew as "man" actually has no gender; it is more accurately rendered "mankind." When God said, "It is not good that man should be alone; I will make him a helper comparable to him" (Gen. 2:18), He was announcing His plans to do "surgery" to separate mankind into two sexes. In mankind—in Adam—was both "male" and "female." His purpose was for them to walk together as one in fellowship with God.

When God was about to create Adam, He said, "Let Us make man in Our image, according to Our likeness. . . . God created man [mankind] in His own image; in the image of God He created him; male and female" (Gen. 1:26, 27). So Adam was created in God's image.

But after the fall of man, Adam "begot a son in his own likeness, after his image" (Gen. 5:3). This means that Adam's descendants—including us—were born not in the image of God, their heavenly Father, but rather in the image of Adam—and with his nature.

God's eternal plan for us was not thwarted, however, for He had anticipated Adam's failure before the foundation of the world and had prepared a Savior for mankind. When we accept this Savior, Jesus Christ, who is called the "last Adam," the Holy Spirit begins the process of restoring us to the image of God. Restoration is a wonderful reality that promises we will become all God ordained for us to become in His eternal purpose, experiencing a completeness and maturity that mankind would have known if the first pair had walked on with Him.

Because of Calvary, we are being changed into Christ's image so male and female can walk together in their own realms of authority. Husband and wife, male and female preachers, man and woman lay leaders will walk in the cool of the day with Jesus, who is talking to us, fellowshiping with us, giving us authority, and changing us into His image. Divine order is higher than the plight of fallen man. As God meets the innermost needs of both men and women, we will find that it is far more liberating than having to live under the curse of a fallen Adam and a fallen Eve.

As God delivers His church from the bondage of tradition and culture—and from fallen man's doctrine of divine order—we will see men and women function together to build godly homes and to fulfill God's purpose for the building of His kingdom. When redemption cleanses us from the desire to rule, man and woman will not be threatened by each other, but will welcome each other's godly counsel. This is the hour.

Fuchsia Pickett

food. 30Also, to [a]every beast of the earth,
to every [b]bird of the air, and to everything
that creeps on the earth, in which *there is*
[1]life, *I have given* every green herb for
food"; and it was so. 31Then [a]God saw everything that He had made, and indeed *it*
was very good. So the evening and the
morning were the sixth day.

Bless _____, O Lord, and may they be fruitful.

FROM GENESIS 1:28

2

2 Thus the heavens and the earth, and
[a]all the host of them, were finished.
2[a]And on the seventh day God ended His
work which He had done, and He rested
on the seventh day from all His work
which He had done. 3Then God [a]blessed
the seventh day and sanctified it, because
in it He rested from all His work which
God had created and made.

If man is not made for God, why is he only happy in God?

BLAISE PASCAL

4[a]This *is* the [1]history of the heavens
and the earth when they were created, in
the day that the LORD God made the earth
and the heavens, 5before any [a]plant of the
field was in the earth and before any herb
of the field had grown. For the LORD God
had not [b]caused it to rain on the earth,
and *there was* no man [c]to till the ground;
6but a mist went up from the earth and
watered the whole face of the ground.
7And the LORD God formed man *of* the
[a]dust of the ground, and [b]breathed into
his [c]nostrils the breath of life; and [d]man
became a living being.

The emptied vessel is filled with the constantly inflowing and outflowing water of life. His breath is our breath. The life that flows in the head of the body is the life that flows in the veins of the body, and this walk of communion is a conscious reality to us.

ZELMA ARGUE

Life in God's Garden

8The LORD God planted [a]a garden [b]east-
ward in [c]Eden, and there He put the man
whom He had formed. 9And out of the
ground the LORD God made [a]every tree
grow that is pleasant to the sight and good
for food. [b]The tree of life *was* also in the
midst of the garden, and the tree of the
knowledge of good and [c]evil.
10Now a river went out of Eden to water
the garden, and from there it parted and
became four riverheads. 11The name of
the first *is* Pishon; it *is* the one which
skirts [a]the whole land of Havilah, where
there is gold. 12And the gold of that land
is good. [a]Bdellium and the onyx stone *are*
there. 13The name of the second river *is*
Gihon; it *is* the one which goes around
the whole land of Cush. 14The name of the
third river *is* [a]Hiddekel;[1] it *is* the one
which goes toward the east of [2]Assyria.
The fourth river *is* the Euphrates.
15Then the LORD God took [1]the man
and put him in the garden of Eden to
[2]tend and keep it. 16And the LORD God
commanded the man, saying, "Of every
tree of the garden you may freely eat;
17but of the tree of the knowledge of good
and evil [a]you shall not eat, for in the day
that you eat of it [b]you[1] shall surely [c]die."
18And the LORD God said, "*It is* not good
that man should be alone; [a]I will make
him a helper comparable to him." 19[a]Out
of the ground the LORD God formed every
beast of the field and every bird of the air,

30 a Ps. 145:15 b Job 38:41 *1 a living soul*
31 a [Ps. 104:24]
CHAPTER 2
1 a Ps. 33:6
2 a Ex. 20:9–11; 31:17
3 a [Is. 58:13]
4 a Gen. 1:1 *1* Heb. *toledoth;* lit. *generations*
5 a Gen. 1:11, 12 b Gen. 7:4 c Gen. 3:23
7 a Gen. 3:19, 23 b Job 33:4 c Gen. 7:22 d 1 Cor. 15:45
8 a Is. 51:3 b Gen. 3:23, 24 c Gen. 4:16
9 a Ezek. 31:8 b [Gen. 3:22] c [Deut. 1:39]
11 a Gen. 25:18
12 a Num. 11:7
14 a Dan. 10:4 *1* Or *Tigris* *2* Heb. *Ashshur*
15 *1* Or *Adam* *2 cultivate*
17 a Gen. 3:1, 3, 11, 17 b Gen. 3:3, 19 c Rom. 5:12 *1* Lit. *dying you shall die*
18 a 1 Cor. 11:8, 9
19 a Gen. 1:20, 24

and [b]brought *them* to [1]Adam to see what
he would call them. And whatever Adam
called each living creature, that *was* its
name. 20So Adam gave names to all cattle,
to the birds of the air, and to every beast
of the field. But for Adam there was not
found a helper comparable to him.
21And the LORD God caused a [a]deep
sleep to fall on Adam, and he slept; and He
took one of his ribs, and closed up the
flesh in its place. 22Then the rib which the
LORD God had taken from man He [1]made
into a woman, [a]and He [b]brought her to
the man.
23And Adam said:

"This *is* now [a]bone of my bones
And flesh of my flesh;
She shall be called [1]Woman,
Because she was [b]taken out of
[2]Man."

24[a]Therefore a man shall leave his father
and mother and [b]be[1] joined to his wife,
and they shall become one flesh.
25[a]And they were both naked, the man
and his wife, and were not [b]ashamed.

The Temptation and Fall of Man

3 Now [a]the serpent was [b]more cunning
than any beast of the field which the
LORD God had made. And he said to the
woman, "Has God indeed said, 'You shall
not eat of every tree of the garden'?"
2And the woman said to the serpent,
"We may eat the [a]fruit of the trees of the
garden; 3but of the fruit of the tree which
is in the midst of the garden, God has said,
'You shall not eat it, nor shall you [a]touch
it, lest you die.' "
4[a]Then the serpent said to the woman,
"You will not surely die. 5For God knows
that in the day you eat of it your eyes will
be opened, and you will be like God,
knowing good and evil."
6So when the woman [a]saw that the tree
was good for food, that it *was* [1]pleasant to
the eyes, and a tree desirable to make *one*
wise, she took of its fruit [b]and ate. She
also gave to her husband with her, and he
ate. 7Then the eyes of both of them were
opened, [a]and they knew that they *were*
naked; and they sewed fig leaves together
and made themselves [1]coverings.
8And they heard [a]the [1]sound of the
LORD God walking in the garden in the
[2]cool of the day, and Adam and his wife
[b]hid themselves from the presence of the
LORD God among the trees of the garden.
9Then the LORD God called to Adam and
said to him, "Where *are* you?"
10So he said, "I heard Your voice in the
garden, [a]and I was afraid because I was
naked; and I hid myself."
11And He said, "Who told you that you
were naked? Have you eaten from the tree
of which I commanded you that you
should not eat?"
12Then the man said, [a]"The woman
whom You gave *to be* with me, she gave
me of the tree, and I ate."
13And the LORD God said to the woman,
"What *is* this you have done?"
The woman said, [a]"The serpent deceived me, and I ate."
14So the LORD God said to the serpent:

"Because you have done this,
You *are* cursed more than all cattle,
And more than every beast of the
field;
On your belly you shall go,
And [a]you shall eat dust
All the days of your life.
15 And I will put enmity
Between you and the woman,
And between [a]your seed and [b]her
Seed;
[c]He shall bruise your head,
And you shall bruise His heel."

16To the woman He said:

"I will greatly multiply your
sorrow and your conception;
[a]In pain you shall bring forth
children;
[b]Your desire *shall be* [1]for your
husband,
And he shall [c]rule over you."

17Then to Adam He said, [a]"Because you
have heeded the voice of your wife, and
have eaten from the tree [b]of which I commanded you, saying, 'You shall not eat
of it':

[c]"Cursed *is* the ground for your sake;
[d]In toil you shall eat *of* it
All the days of your life.
18 Both thorns and thistles it shall
[1]bring forth for you,
And [a]you shall eat the herb of the
field.
19 [a]In the sweat of your face you shall
eat bread
Till you return to the ground,
For out of it you were taken;

---

19 [b] Ps. 8:6 [1] Or *the man*
21 [a] 1 Sam. 26:12
22 [a] 1 Tim. 2:13 [b] Heb. 13:4 [1] Lit. *built*
23 [a] Gen. 29:14 [b] 1 Cor. 11:8, 9 [1] Heb. *Ishshah* [2] Heb. *Ish*
24 [a] Matt. 19:5 [b] Mark 10:6–8 [1] Lit. *cling*
25 [a] Gen. 3:7, 10 [b] Is. 47:3

CHAPTER 3
1 [a] 1 Chr. 21:1 [b] 2 Cor. 11:3
2 [a] Gen. 2:16, 17
3 [a] Ex. 19:12, 13
4 [a] [2 Cor. 11:3]
6 [a] 1 John 2:16 [b] 1 Tim. 2:14 [1] Lit. *a desirable thing*
7 [a] Gen. 2:25 [1] *girding coverings*
8 [a] Job 38:1 [b] Job 31:33 [1] Or *voice* [2] Or *wind, breeze*
10 [a] Gen. 2:25
12 [a] [Prov. 28:13]
13 [a] 2 Cor. 11:3
14 [a] Deut. 28:15–20
15 [a] John 8:44 [b] Is. 7:14 [c] Rom. 16:20
16 [a] John 16:21 [b] Gen. 4:7 [c] 1 Cor. 11:3 [1] Lit. *toward*
17 [a] 1 Sam. 15:23 [b] Gen. 2:17 [c] Rom. 8:20–22 [d] Eccl. 2:23
18 [a] Ps. 104:14 [1] *cause to grow*
19 [a] 2 Thess. 3:10

GENESIS 2:21–24

Dear Woman of Destiny,

When God created the heavens and the earth, He observed that it was not good for man to be alone, and so He said, "I will make him a helper comparable to him" (Gen. 2:18). From the deep sleep of Adam, from his very side, God created the woman as the perfect complement and crown of His creation. It is amazing to see how God has created man and woman with such distinct characteristics. But it is precisely our differences that can unite us and cause us to complement each other. For this reason God created woman to be man's helper—his companion walking next to him, sharing all her life with him, and carrying with him his yoke in an equal manner.

Many years ago God changed my vision of my role as a wife. He spoke to me, saying, "When your husband comes to you tired, you must offer him your heart as a place of rest. I will give you a ministry of consolation and of love so that he will rest in you." This changed my life. It's important that we women understand that while a man has the strength and authority God has given him as the head of the family, when he comes home he needs a place to lay his head, someone with listening ears, and someone to whom he can open his heart.

From that time I began to look at my husband with different eyes. I had to tell my index finger to stop pointing out errors, while saying, "The next time he needs to do it better!" The man that God has given to each of us needs to be listened to and sustained. There are women who ask their husbands, "Why don't you ever tell me anything? Why do you spend so much time away from home?" But the answer is obvious: What man would want to return home if only reproach and recrimination await him there?

God has called us to be suitable helpers of our husbands. We mustn't think, *Well, he's the servant of God and I will just live my life quietly at home*. No! The yoke needs to be equal. We need to share the burdens, interceding, praying. Personally, I feel my primary ministry is taking care of him, enjoying the privilege of having him as my husband. The Lord taught me the importance of being a true friend to my husband, of accompanying him in doing those things that he enjoys, and of sharing the same God-given vision.

I give thanks to God because He changed my way of thinking toward my husband. He gave me a new, deeper love for him. I had never before loved with such infinite love that covers all defects. And every day I am more in love with my husband! We continue to strengthen each other in unity and companionship.

Unity in marriage is the pleasing and perfect will of God for our lives. I encourage you to live this truth by faith. You will see wonderful changes in your life—changes you would never accomplish on your own. God, who is all-powerful, will surpass your expectations if you understand and accept His call.

Betty Freidzon

[b]For dust you *are,*
And [c]to dust you shall return."

20 And Adam called his wife's name
[a]Eve,[1] because she was the mother of all
living.
21 Also for Adam and his wife the LORD
God made tunics of skin, and clothed
them.
22 Then the LORD God said, "Behold, the
man has become like one of Us, to know
good and evil. And now, lest he put out his
hand and take also of the tree of life, and
eat, and live forever"— 23 therefore the
LORD God sent him out of the garden of
Eden [a]to till the ground from which he
was taken. 24 So [a]He drove out the man;
and He placed [b]cherubim [c]at the east of
the garden of Eden, and a flaming sword
which turned every way, to guard the way
to the tree of [d]life.

Cain Murders Abel

4 Now Adam knew Eve his wife, and she
conceived and bore [1]Cain, and said, "I
have acquired a man from the LORD."
2 Then she bore again, this time his
brother [1]Abel. Now [a]Abel was a keeper of
sheep, but Cain was a tiller of the ground.
3 And [1]in the process of time it came to
pass that Cain brought an offering of the
fruit [a]of the ground to the LORD. 4 Abel
also brought of [a]the firstborn of his flock
and of [b]their fat. And the LORD [c]respected
Abel and his offering, 5 but He did not respect Cain and his offering. And Cain was
very angry, and his countenance fell.
6 So the LORD said to Cain, "Why are you
angry? And why has your countenance
fallen? 7 If you do well, will you not be accepted? And if you do not do well, sin lies
at the door. And its desire *is* [1]for you, but
you should rule over it."
8 Now Cain [1]talked with Abel his
[2]brother; and it came to pass, when they
were in the field, that Cain rose up against
Abel his brother and [a]killed him.
9 Then the LORD said to Cain, "Where *is*
Abel your brother?"
He said, [a]"I do not know. *Am* I [b]my
brother's keeper?"
10 And He said, "What have you done?
The voice of your brother's blood [a]cries
out to Me from the ground. 11 So now [a]you
are cursed from the earth, which has
opened its mouth to receive your
brother's blood from your hand. 12 When
you till the ground, it shall no longer yield
its strength to you. A fugitive and a vagabond you shall be on the earth."
13 And Cain said to the LORD, "My [1]pun-
ishment *is* greater than I can bear!
14 Surely You have driven me out this day
from the face of the ground; [a]I shall be
[b]hidden from Your face; I shall be a fugitive and a vagabond on the earth, and it
will happen *that* [c]anyone who finds me
will kill me."
15 And the LORD said to him, [1]"Therefore, whoever kills Cain, vengeance shall
be taken on him [a]sevenfold." And the
LORD set a [b]mark on Cain, lest anyone
finding him should kill him.

The measure of the stature of fullness is seldom mentioned, much less demonstrated, while the stature of littleness, emptiness, and powerlessness of Christianity is often emphasized and demonstrated.

FINIS JENNINGS DAKE

The Family of Cain

16 Then Cain [a]went out from the [b]pres-
ence of the LORD and dwelt in the land
of [1]Nod on the east of Eden. 17 And Cain
knew his wife, and she conceived and bore
Enoch. And he built a city, [a]and called the
name of the city after the name of his
son—Enoch. 18 To Enoch was born Irad;
and Irad begot Mehujael, and Mehujael
begot Methushael, and Methushael begot
Lamech.
19 Then Lamech took for himself [a]two
wives: the name of one *was* Adah, and the
name of the second *was* Zillah. 20 And
Adah bore Jabal. He was the father of
those who dwell in tents and have livestock. 21 His brother's name *was* Jubal. He
was the father of all those who play the
harp and [1]flute. 22 And as for Zillah, she
also bore Tubal-Cain, an instructor of every craftsman in bronze and iron. And the
sister of Tubal-Cain *was* Naamah.
23 Then Lamech said to his wives:

---

19 [b] Gen. 2:7; 5:5 [c] Job 21:26
20 [a] 2 Cor. 11:3 [1] Lit. *Life* or *Living*
23 [a] Gen. 4:2; 9:20
24 [a] Ezek. 31:3, 11 [b] Ps. 104:4 [c] Gen. 2:8 [d] Gen. 2:9

CHAPTER 4
1 [1] Lit. *Acquire*
2 [a] Luke 11:50, 51 [1] Lit. *Breath* or *Nothing*
3 [a] Num. 18:12 [1] Lit. *at the end of days*
4 [a] Num. 18:17 [b] Lev. 3:16 [c] Heb. 11:4
7 [1] Lit. *toward*
8 [a] [1 John 3:12–15] [1] Lit. *said to* [2] Sam., LXX, Syr., Vg. add *"Let us go out to the field."*
9 [a] John 8:44 [b] 1 Cor. 8:11–13
10 [a] Heb. 12:24
11 [a] Gen. 3:14
13 [1] *iniquity*
14 [a] Ps. 51:11 [b] Is. 1:15 [c] Num. 35:19, 21, 27
15 [a] Gen. 4:24 [b] Ezek. 9:4, 6 [1] So with MT, Tg.; LXX, Syr., Vg. *Not so;*
16 [a] 2 Kin. 13:23; 24:20 [b] Jon. 1:3 [1] Lit. *Wandering*
17 [a] Ps. 49:11
19 [a] Gen. 2:24; 16:3
21 [1] *pipe*

Genesis 3:16b

Dear Woman of Destiny,

We are fashioned for intimacy. We long for love and a sense of true caring. Yet, because of the Fall, we are broken people living in a world of broken people. We move toward others, based not so much on what they need, but rather on what we need, endeavoring somehow to slake the hidden thirst deep within our souls.

Our need for relationship is legitimate; it is there by God's design. To have healthy, functional relationships, however, it is essential that we sort out what God, our "Source," intended to be to us.

One of the foundations being exposed today is the "desire of the woman"—the belief that her husband can be her source of life, that he can meet her need for unfailing love, worth, security, and purpose. Because she is looking to him for her life, he will "rule" her emotionally. She is "up" if things are going well. If not, she becomes hurt, discouraged, and depressed. Ruled by her husband—her heart, her "center," having been turned from God to man—she is not able to be the help for him she was created to be. She is drinking from a broken cistern (see Jer. 2:13). She has the right expectation, but the wrong source.

Whatever we think will satisfy our longing will become our god. Satisfaction found in a wrong source, a false god, is always temporary, doomed to failure and disappointment. False gods are addictive because we must come again and again for refilling; what they can give us is never enough. We become slaves to what we think will fill the empty wells inside of us.

God wants us to find our "being" needs in Him; no human can fulfill them. When we find our life in Him, we will discover we can let go of our demands on others. We can then begin to move in genuine relationship with them because they are no longer the source of our identity and security. Until this occurs, real intimacy cannot begin to take place.

When a woman's heart is turned—when she sets her desire back on God—a new freedom comes. The grasping in her voice and her attitude goes. She is able to move into relationship with her husband based on wholeness rather than inappropriate neediness, hurt, and woundedness. She is able to speak into his life with more effectiveness because her worth and identity no longer depend on his response. When the woman stops looking to her husband for the needs he cannot meet, she frees him to meet the ones he can: the need for intimacy and shared responsibility for the marriage and family.

This is a key factor in what God is doing today in the hearts of women around the world. He is turning the centers of women, teaching them to deny themselves, their own wisdom, their own strength, and to find their Source in Him. God is teaching them to live by the "tree of life," the life of God in them. He is freeing them from the broken cisterns of their own making and fashioning them anew, restoring the man's help to him.

Jane Hansen

"Adah and Zillah, hear my voice;
Wives of Lamech, listen to my
speech!
For I have [1]killed a man for
wounding me,
Even a young man [2]for hurting me.
24 [a]If Cain shall be avenged sevenfold,
Then Lamech seventy-sevenfold."

A New Son

[25]And Adam knew his wife again, and
she bore a son and [a]named him [1]Seth,
"For God has appointed another seed for
me instead of Abel, whom Cain killed."
[26]And as for Seth, [a]to him also a son was
born; and he named him [1]Enosh. Then
men began [b]to call on the name of the
LORD.

The Family of Adam

5 This is the book of the [a]genealogy of
Adam. In the day that God created
man, He made him in [b]the likeness of
God. [2]He created them [a]male and female,
and [b]blessed them and called them Mankind in the day they were created. [3]And
Adam lived one hundred and thirty years,
and begot *a son* [a]in his own likeness, after
his image, and [b]named him Seth. [4]After
he begot Seth, [a]the days of Adam were
eight hundred years; [b]and he had sons
and daughters. [5]So all the days that Adam
lived were nine hundred and thirty years;
[a]and he died.
[6]Seth lived one hundred and five years,
and begot [a]Enosh. [7]After he begot Enosh,
Seth lived eight hundred and seven years,
and had sons and daughters. [8]So all the
days of Seth were nine hundred and
twelve years; and he died.
[9]Enosh lived ninety years, and begot
[1]Cainan. [10]After he begot Cainan, Enosh
lived eight hundred and fifteen years, and
had sons and daughters. [11]So all the days
of Enosh were nine hundred and five
years; and he died.
[12]Cainan lived seventy years, and begot
Mahalalel. [13]After he begot Mahalalel, Cainan lived eight hundred and forty years,
and had sons and daughters. [14]So all the
days of Cainan were nine hundred and ten
years; and he died.

23 [1] *slain a man for my wound* [2] *for my hurt*
24 [a] Gen. 4:15
25 [a] Gen. 5:3 [1] Lit. *Appointed*
26 [a] Gen. 5:6 [b] Zeph. 3:9 [1] Gr. *Enos,* Luke 3:38

CHAPTER 5
1 [a] Gen. 2:4; 6:9 [b] Gen. 1:26; 9:6
2 [a] Mark 10:6 [b] Gen. 1:28; 9:1
3 [a] 1 Cor. 15:48, 49 [b] Gen. 4:25
4 [a] Luke 3:36–38 [b] Gen. 1:28; 4:25
5 [a] [Heb. 9:27]
6 [a] Gen. 4:26
9 [1] Heb. *Qenan*

EVE

Eve was the original first lady. She was not only a woman's first experience with God, but God's first experience with a woman. She was the first to delight the Father's heart as only a daughter can. She was the first to grace this Earth with the ways of a woman and the first to encounter the wiles of the devil. She was the first to love a man and the first to mislead one. She was the first to try to hide from God and the first to break His heart with her sin. She was the first to bear—and the first to bury—a child. She was the first to know the love of God and the first to suffer the curse of fallen humanity. She was the one after whom every woman who has ever lived has followed.

You, too, are a daughter of God. You were created and called according to His purpose. He may be calling you, like Eve, to pioneer. His destiny for your life may include some unexplored or unexpected territory. So go boldly after Him. Follow Him with all your heart. And if He asks you to do for Him what has not been done before, remember Eve. She had no mentor, no mother, no older female friend to help her on her way. She had only God; and if you ever find yourself as a first lady, He will be there to help you blaze every trail and break open every new day.

15Mahalalel lived sixty-five years, and
begot Jared. 16After he begot Jared, Mahalalel lived eight hundred and thirty years,
and had sons and daughters. 17So all the
days of Mahalalel were eight hundred and
ninety-five years; and he died.

18Jared lived one hundred and sixty-
two years, and begot [a]Enoch. 19After he
begot Enoch, Jared lived eight hundred
years, and had sons and daughters. 20So
all the days of Jared were nine hundred
and sixty-two years; and he died.

21Enoch lived sixty-five years, and begot Methuselah. 22After he begot Methuselah, Enoch [a]walked with God three
hundred years, and had sons and daughters. 23So all the days of Enoch were three
hundred and sixty-five years. 24And
[a]Enoch walked with God; and he *was* not,
for God [b]took him.

25Methuselah lived one hundred and
eighty-seven years, and begot Lamech.
26After he begot Lamech, Methuselah
lived seven hundred and eighty-two years,
and had sons and daughters. 27So all the
days of Methuselah were nine hundred
and sixty-nine years; and he died.

28Lamech lived one hundred and
eighty-two years, and had a son. 29And he
called his name [a]Noah,[1] saying, "This *one*
will comfort us concerning our work and
the toil of our hands, because of the
ground [b]which the LORD has cursed."
30After he begot Noah, Lamech lived five
hundred and ninety-five years, and had
sons and daughters. 31So all the days of
Lamech were seven hundred and seventy-
seven years; and he died.

32And Noah was five hundred years old,
and Noah begot [a]Shem, Ham, [b]and Japheth.

The Wickedness and Judgment of Man

6 Now it came to pass, [a]when men began to multiply on the face of the
earth, and daughters were born to them,
2that the sons of God saw the daughters of
men, that they *were* beautiful; and they
[a]took wives for themselves of all whom
they chose.

3And the LORD said, [a]"My Spirit shall
not [b]strive[1] with man forever, [c]for he *is*
indeed flesh; yet his days shall be one
hundred and twenty years." 4There were
[1]giants on the earth in those [a]days, and
also afterward, when the sons of God
came in to the daughters of men and they
bore *children* to them. Those *were* the
mighty men who *were* of old, men of renown.

5Then [1]the LORD saw that the wickedness of man *was* great in the earth, and
that every [a]intent[2] of the thoughts of his
heart *was* only evil [3]continually. 6And
[a]the LORD was sorry that He had made
man on the earth, and [b]He was grieved in
His [c]heart. 7So the LORD said, "I will [a]de-
stroy man whom I have created from the
face of the earth, both man and beast,
creeping thing and birds of the air, for I
am sorry that I have made them." 8But
Noah [a]found grace in the eyes of the
LORD.

Father, may ____ find grace in Your eyes.
FROM GENESIS 6:8

Noah Pleases God

9 This is the genealogy of Noah.
[a]Noah was a just man, [1]perfect in his generations. Noah [b]walked with God. 10And
Noah begot three sons: [a]Shem, Ham, and
Japheth.

11The earth also was corrupt [a]before
God, and the earth was [b]filled with violence. 12So God [a]looked upon the earth,
and indeed it was corrupt; for [b]all flesh
had corrupted their way on the earth.

The Ark Prepared

13And God said to Noah, [a]"The end of
all flesh has come before Me, for the earth
is filled with violence through them; [b]and
behold, [c]I will destroy them with the
earth. 14Make yourself an ark of
gopherwood; make [1]rooms in the ark, and
cover it inside and outside with pitch.
15And this is how you shall make it: The
length of the ark *shall be* three hundred
[1]cubits, its width fifty cubits, and its
height thirty cubits. 16You shall make a
window for the ark, and you shall finish it
to a cubit from above; and set the door of
the ark in its side. You shall make it *with*
lower, second, and third *decks*. 17[a]And behold, I Myself am bringing [b]floodwaters
on the earth, to destroy from under heav-
en all flesh in which *is* the breath of life;

---

18 a Jude 14, 15
22 a Gen. 6:9; 17:1; 24:40; 48:15
24 a 2 Kin. 2:11 b Heb. 11:5
29 a Luke 3:36 b Gen. 3:17–19; 4:11 *1* Lit. *Rest*
32 a Gen. 6:10; 7:13 b Gen. 10:21

CHAPTER 6
1 a Gen. 1:28
2 a Deut. 7:3, 4
3 a [Gal. 5:16, 17] b 2 Thess. 2:7 c Ps. 78:39 *1* LXX, Syr., Tg., Vg. *abide*
4 a Num. 13:32, 33 *1* Heb. *nephilim, fallen* or *mighty ones*
5 a Gen. 8:21 *1* So with MT, Tg.; Vg. *God;* LXX *LORD God* *2 thought* *3 all the day*
6 a 1 Sam. 15:11, 29 b Is. 63:10 c Mark 3:5
7 a Gen. 7:4, 23
8 a Gen. 19:19
9 a 2 Pet. 2:5 b Gen. 5:22, 24 *1 blameless* or *having integrity*
10 a Gen. 5:32; 7:13
11 a Rom. 2:13 b Ezek. 8:17
12 a Ps. 14:2; 53:2, 3 b Ps. 14:1–3
13 a 1 Pet. 4:7 b Gen. 6:17 c 2 Pet. 2:4–10
14 *1* Lit. *compartments* or *nests*
15 *1* A cubit is about 18 inches.
17 a 2 Pet. 2:5 b 2 Pet. 3:6

Genesis 6:9–13

Dear Woman of Destiny,

Noah lived in an ungodly era, a time when the earth was corrupt and filled with violence. The sin that was so rampant in those days brought chaos, disorder, anarchy, and confusion. Scripture might just as well have been describing our world today. Yet even in the midst of the evil of his day, Noah is described as "a just man, perfect in his generations," who "walked with God." So what lesson can we learn from Noah about pleasing God in an ungodly world? The answer is rest!

The very name *Noah* means "Rest." To rest is to recuperate, stand still, pause, stop, or cease. Noah's name was prophetic in that God's purpose for Noah was to bring rest to the earth from the chaos of sin. Because of our personal relationship with God, we, like Noah, have the unique opportunity to bring rest to a world filled with chaos. Every time we offer comfort or exhortation to a friend or compassion to someone who does not know the Lord, we have planted a seed toward bringing them to Christ, which is bringing the ultimate rest from the chaos of death, hell, and the grave.

Noah was a just man. Although he was not sinless (only Jesus has that distinction), Noah led a holy life before the Lord. I doubt it is possible to please God in our ungodly world without holiness. Holiness must be a priority in each of our lives. In fact, it is part of our destiny. Every time we choose to obey the Lord and resist temptation, we bring rest from sin and its effects into our lives and homes. We, like Noah, are destined to be the ministers of God's rest by the very lives we lead.

This passage also tells us that Noah walked with God. The two of them had a personal, direct relationship. When intimacy with God is missing, holiness in and of itself can lead to legalism and religiosity, which does not provide us with rest from sin, but rather with an impossible standard that we strive to live up to in our own strength. Striving to be holy leads to exhaustion, not rest. Noah, on the other hand, knew how to hear the voice of the Lord and obey His word—not through legalism, but through relationship. Our relationship with God should provide the basis for how we live our lives. It is through that relationship that we gain the strength to live holy lives. And as we learn to rest quietly in Him, we, like Noah, will know His voice. First Peter 3:4 tells us that "the incorruptible beauty of a gentle and quiet spirit . . . is very precious in the sight of God." What a picture of rest!

So, how do we please God in an ungodly world? Learn to rest in Him and to minister His rest in a world otherwise filled with chaos.

Rebecca Wagner Sytsema

everything that *is* on the earth shall [c]die.
[18]But I will establish My [a]covenant with
you; and [b]you shall go into the ark—you,
your sons, your wife, and your sons' wives
with you. [19]And of every living thing of all
flesh you shall bring [a]two of every *sort*
into the ark, to keep *them* alive with you;
they shall be male and female. [20]Of the
birds after their kind, of animals after
their kind, and of every creeping thing of
the earth after its kind, two of every *kind*
[a]will come to you to keep *them* alive.
[21]And you shall take for yourself of all food
that is eaten, and you shall gather *it* to
yourself; and it shall be food for you and
for them."

[22][a]Thus Noah did; [b]according to all that
[c]God commanded him, so he did.

Father, may ____ be righteous before You in this generation.
FROM GENESIS 7:1

The Great Flood

7 Then the [a]LORD said to Noah, [b]"Come
into the ark, you and all your household, because I have seen *that* [c]you *are*
righteous before Me in this generation.
[2]You shall take with you seven each of
every [a]clean animal, a male and his female; [b]two each of animals that *are* unclean, a male and his female; [3]also seven
each of birds of the air, male and female,
to keep [1]the species alive on the face of all
the earth. [4]For after [a]seven more days I
will cause it to rain on the earth [b]forty
days and forty nights, and I will [1]destroy
from the face of the earth all living things
that I have made." [5][a]And Noah did according to all that the LORD commanded him.
[6]Noah *was* [a]six hundred years old when
the floodwaters were on the earth.

[7][a]So Noah, with his sons, his wife, and
his sons' wives, went into the ark because
of the waters of the flood. [8]Of clean animals, of animals that *are* unclean, of
birds, and of everything that creeps on the
earth, [9]two by two they went into the ark
to Noah, male and female, as God had
commanded Noah. [10]And it came to pass
after seven days that the waters of the
flood were on the earth. [11]In the six hundredth year of Noah's life, in the second
month, the seventeenth day of the month,
on [a]that day all [b]the fountains of the great
deep were broken up, and the [c]windows of
heaven were opened. [12][a]And the rain was
on the earth forty days and forty nights.

[13]On the very same day Noah and
Noah's sons, Shem, Ham, and Japheth,
and Noah's wife and the three wives of his
sons with them, entered the ark— [14][a]they
and every beast after its kind, all cattle
after their kind, every creeping thing that
creeps on the earth after its kind, and every bird after its kind, every bird of every
[b]sort. [15]And they [a]went into the ark to
Noah, two by two, of all flesh in which *is*
the breath of life. [16]So those that entered,
male and female of all flesh, went in [a]as
God had commanded him; and the LORD
shut him in.

[17][a]Now the flood was on the earth forty
days. The waters increased and lifted up
the ark, and it rose high above the earth.
[18]The waters prevailed and greatly increased on the earth, [a]and the ark moved
about on the surface of the waters. [19]And
the waters prevailed exceedingly on the
earth, and all the high hills under the
whole heaven were covered. [20]The waters
prevailed fifteen cubits upward, and the
mountains were covered. [21][a]And all flesh
died that moved on [1]the earth: birds and
cattle and beasts and every creeping thing
that creeps on the earth, and every man.
[22]All in [a]whose nostrils *was* the breath [1]of
the spirit of life, all that *was* on the dry
land, died. [23]So He destroyed all living
things which were on the face of the
ground: both man and cattle, creeping
thing and bird of the air. They were destroyed from the earth. Only [a]Noah and
those who *were* with him in the ark remained *alive.* [24][a]And the waters prevailed
on the earth one hundred and fifty days.

Noah's Deliverance

8 Then God [a]remembered Noah, and
every living thing, and all the animals
that *were* with him in the ark. [b]And God
made a wind to pass over the earth, and
the waters subsided. [2][a]The fountains of
the deep and the windows of heaven were
also [b]stopped, and [c]the rain from heaven
was restrained. [3]And the waters receded
continually from the earth. At the end [a]of
the hundred and fifty days the waters decreased. [4]Then the ark rested in the sev-

17 c Luke 16:22
18 a Gen. 8:20—9:17; 17:7 b Gen. 7:1, 7, 13
19 a Gen. 7:2, 8, 9, 14–16
20 a Gen. 7:9, 15
22 a Gen. 7:5; 12:4, 5 b Gen. 7:5, 9, 16 c [1 John 5:3]

CHAPTER 7
1 a Matt. 11:28 b Matt. 24:38 c Gen. 6:9
2 a Lev. 11 b Lev. 10:10
3 *1* Lit. *seed*
4 a Gen. 7:10 b Gen. 7:12, 17 *1* Lit. *blot out*
5 a Gen. 6:22
6 a Gen. 5:4, 32
7 a Matt. 24:38
11 a Matt. 24:39 b Gen. 8:2 c Ps. 78:23
12 a Gen. 7:4, 17
14 a Gen. 6:19 b Gen. 1:21
15 a Gen. 6:19, 20; 7:9
16 a Gen. 7:2, 3
17 a Gen. 7:4, 12; 8:6
18 a Ps. 104:26
21 a Gen. 6:7, 13, 17; 7:4 *1 the land*
22 a Gen. 2:7 *1* LXX, Vg. omit *of the spirit*
23 a 2 Pet. 2:5
24 a Gen. 8:3, 4

CHAPTER 8
1 a Gen. 19:29 b Ex. 14:21; 15:10
2 a Gen. 7:11 b Deut. 11:17 c Job 38:37
3 a Gen. 7:24

enth month, the seventeenth day of the
month, on the mountains of Ararat. 5And
the waters decreased continually until the
tenth month. In the tenth *month,* on the
first *day* of the month, the tops of the
mountains were seen.
6So it came to pass, at the end of forty
days, that Noah opened [a]the window of
the ark which he had made. 7Then he sent
out a raven, which kept going to and fro
until the waters had dried up from the
earth. 8He also sent out from himself a
dove, to see if the waters had receded from
the face of the ground. 9But the dove
found no resting place for the sole of her
foot, and she returned into the ark to him,
for the waters *were* on the face of the
whole earth. So he put out his hand and
took her, and drew her into the ark to
himself. 10And he waited yet another sev-
en days, and again he sent the dove out
from the ark. 11Then the dove came to
him in the evening, and behold, a freshly
plucked olive leaf *was* in her mouth; and
Noah knew that the waters had receded
from the earth. 12So he waited yet another
seven days and sent out the dove, which
did not return again to him anymore.
13And it came to pass in the six hundred
and first year, in the first *month,* the first
day of the month, that the waters were
dried up from the earth; and Noah removed the covering of the ark and looked,
and indeed the surface of the ground was
dry. 14And in the second month, on the
twenty-seventh day of the month, the
earth was dried.
15Then God spoke to Noah, saying,
16"Go out of the ark, [a]you and your wife,
and your sons and your sons' wives with
you. 17Bring out with you every living
thing of all flesh that *is* with you: birds
and cattle and every creeping thing that
creeps on the earth, so that they may
abound on the earth, and [a]be fruitful and
multiply on the earth." 18So Noah went
out, and his sons and his wife and his
sons' wives with him. 19Every animal, every creeping thing, every bird, *and* whatever creeps on the earth, according to
their families, went out of the ark.

God's Covenant with Creation

20Then Noah built an [a]altar to the
LORD, and took of [b]every clean animal and
of every clean bird, and offered [c]burnt
offerings on the altar. 21And the LORD
smelled [a]a soothing aroma. Then the
LORD said in His heart, "I will never again
[b]curse the ground for man's sake, although the [c]imagination[1] of man's heart
is evil from his youth; [d]nor will I again
destroy every living thing as I have done.

22 "While the earth [a]remains,
Seedtime and harvest,
Cold and heat,
Winter and summer,
And [b]day and night
Shall not cease."

9 So God blessed Noah and his sons,
and said to them: [a]"Be fruitful and
multiply, and fill the earth. 2[a]And the fear
of you and the dread of you shall be on
every beast of the earth, on every bird of
the air, on all that move *on* the earth, and
on all the fish of the sea. They are given
into your hand. 3[a]Every moving thing
that lives shall be food for you. I have giv-
en you [b]all things, even as the [c]green
herbs. 4[a]But you shall not eat flesh with
its life, *that is,* its blood. 5Surely for your
lifeblood I will demand *a reckoning;*
[a]from the hand of every beast I will require it, and [b]from the hand of man. From
the hand of every [c]man's brother I will
require the life of man.

6 "Whoever [a]sheds man's blood,
By man his blood shall be shed;
[b]For in the image of God
He made man.
7 And as for you, [a]be fruitful and
multiply;
Bring forth abundantly in the earth
And multiply in it."

8Then God spoke to Noah and to his
sons with him, saying: 9"And as for Me,
[a]behold, I establish [b]My covenant with
you and with your [1]descendants after you,
10[a]and with every living creature that *is*
with you: the birds, the cattle, and every
beast of the earth with you, of all that go
out of the ark, every beast of the earth.
11Thus [a]I establish My covenant with you:
Never again shall all flesh be cut off by the
waters of the flood; never again shall there
be a flood to destroy the earth."
12And God said: [a]"This *is* the sign of the
covenant which I make between Me and
you, and every living creature that *is* with
you, for perpetual generations: 13I set [a]My
rainbow in the cloud, and it shall be for
the sign of the covenant between Me and
the earth. 14It shall be, when I bring a
cloud over the earth, that the rainbow

6 a Gen. 6:16
16 a Gen. 7:13
17 a Gen. 1:22, 28; 9:1, 7
20 a Gen. 12:7 b Lev. 11 c Ex. 10:25
21 a Ex. 29:18, 25 b Gen. 3:17; 6:7, 13, 17 c Gen. 6:5; 11:6 d Gen. 9:11, 15 *1 intent* or *thought*
22 a Is. 54:9 b Jer. 33:20, 25

CHAPTER 9
1 a Gen. 1:28, 29; 8:17; 9:7, 19; 10:32
2 a Ps. 8:6
3 a Deut. 12:15; 14:3, 9, 11 b Rom. 14:14, 20 c Gen. 1:29
4 a 1 Sam. 14:33, 34
5 a Ex. 21:28 b Gen. 4:9, 10 c Acts 17:26
6 a Lev. 24:17 b Gen. 1:26, 27
7 a Gen. 9:1, 19
9 a Gen. 6:18 b Is. 54:9 *1* Lit. *seed*
10 a Ps. 145:9
11 a Is. 54:9
12 a Gen. 9:13, 17; 17:11
13 a Ezek. 1:28

shall be seen in the cloud; 15and [a]I will
remember My covenant which *is* between
Me and you and every living creature of all
flesh; the waters shall never again become
a flood to destroy all flesh. 16The rainbow
shall be in the cloud, and I will look on it
to remember [a]the everlasting covenant
between God and every living creature of
all flesh that *is* on the earth." 17And God
said to Noah, "This *is* the sign of the covenant which I have established between
Me and all flesh that *is* on the earth."

Noah and His Sons

18Now the sons of Noah who went out
of the ark were Shem, Ham, and Japheth.
[a]And Ham *was* the father of Canaan.
19[a]These three *were* the sons of Noah,
[b]and from these the whole earth was pop-
ulated.

20And Noah began *to be* [a]a farmer, and
he planted a vineyard. 21Then he drank of
the wine [a]and was drunk, and became uncovered in his tent. 22And Ham, the father
of Canaan, saw the nakedness of his father, and told his two brothers outside.
23[a]But Shem and Japheth took a garment,
laid *it* on both their shoulders, and went
backward and covered the nakedness of
their father. Their faces *were* [1]turned
away, and they did not see their father's
nakedness.

24So Noah awoke from his wine, and
knew what his younger son had done to
him. 25Then he said:

[a]"Cursed *be* Canaan;
A [b]servant of servants
He shall be to his brethren."

26And he said:

[a]"Blessed *be* the LORD,
The God of Shem,
And may Canaan be his servant.
27 May God [a]enlarge Japheth,
[b]And may he dwell in the tents of
Shem;
And may Canaan be his servant."

28And Noah lived after the flood three
hundred and fifty years. 29So all the days
of Noah were nine hundred and fifty years;
and he died.

Nations Descended from Noah

10 Now this *is* the genealogy of the
sons of Noah: Shem, Ham, and Japheth. [a]And sons were born to them after
the flood.

2[a]The sons of Japheth *were* Gomer, Magog, Madai, Javan, Tubal, Meshech, and
Tiras. 3The sons of Gomer *were* Ashkenaz,
[1]Riphath, and Togarmah. 4The sons of Javan *were* Elishah, Tarshish, Kittim, and
[1]Dodanim. 5From these [a]the coastland
peoples of the Gentiles were separated
into their lands, everyone according to his
language, according to their families, into
their nations.

6[a]The sons of Ham *were* Cush, Mizraim, [1]Put, and Canaan. 7The sons of Cush
were Seba, Havilah, Sabtah, Raamah, and
Sabtechah; and the sons of Raamah *were*
Sheba and Dedan.

8Cush begot [a]Nimrod; he began to be
a mighty one on the earth. 9He was a
mighty [a]hunter [b]before the LORD; therefore it is said, "Like Nimrod the mighty
hunter before the LORD." 10[a]And the beginning of his kingdom was [b]Babel,
Erech, Accad, and Calneh, in the land of
Shinar. 11From that land he went [a]to Assyria and built Nineveh, Rehoboth Ir, Calah, 12and Resen between Nineveh and
Calah (that *is* the principal city).

13Mizraim begot Ludim, Anamim, Le-
habim, Naphtuhim, 14Pathrusim, and
Casluhim [a](from whom came the Philistines and Caphtorim).

15Canaan begot Sidon his firstborn, and
[a]Heth; 16[a]the Jebusite, the Amorite, and
the Girgashite; 17the Hivite, the Arkite,
and the Sinite; 18the Arvadite, the Zemarite, and the Hamathite. Afterward the
families of the Canaanites were dispersed.
19[a]And the border of the Canaanites was
from Sidon as you go toward Gerar, as far
as Gaza; then as you go toward Sodom,
Gomorrah, Admah, and Zeboiim, as far as
Lasha. 20These *were* the sons of Ham, according to their families, according to
their languages, in their lands *and* in
their nations.

21And *children* were born also to Shem,
the father of all the children of Eber, [1]the
brother of Japheth the elder. 22The [a]sons
of Shem *were* Elam, Asshur, [b]Arphaxad,
Lud, and Aram. 23The sons of Aram *were*
Uz, Hul, Gether, and [1]Mash. 24[1]Arphaxad
begot [a]Salah, and Salah begot Eber. 25[a]To
Eber were born two sons: the name of one
was [1]Peleg, for in his days the earth was
divided; and his brother's name *was* Joktan. 26Joktan begot Almodad, Sheleph,
Hazarmaveth, Jerah, 27Hadoram, Uzal,
Diklah, 28[1]Obal, Abimael, Sheba, 29Ophir,

15 a Lev. 26:42, 45
16 a Gen. 17:13, 19
18 a Gen. 9:25–27; 10:6
19 a Gen. 5:32 b 1 Chr. 1:4
20 a Gen. 3:19, 23; 4:2
21 a Prov. 20:1
23 a Ex. 20:12 *1* Lit. *backwards*
25 a Deut. 27:16 b Josh. 9:23
26 a Gen. 14:20; 24:27
27 a Gen. 10:2–5; 39:3 b Eph. 2:13, 14; 3:6

CHAPTER 10
1 a Gen. 9:1, 7, 19
2 a 1 Chr. 1:5–7
3 *1 Diphath,* 1 Chr. 1:6
4 *1* Sam. *Rodanim* and 1 Chr. 1:7
5 a Ps. 72:10
6 a 1 Chr. 1:8–16 *1* Or *Phut*
8 a Mic. 5:6
9 a Jer. 16:16 b Gen. 21:20
10 a Mic. 5:6 b Gen. 11:9
11 a Mic. 5:6
14 a 1 Chr. 1:12
15 a Gen. 23:3
16 a Gen. 14:7; 15:19–21
19 a Num. 34:2–12
21 *1* Or *the older brother of Japheth*
22 a 1 Chr. 1:17–28 b Luke 3:36
23 *1* LXX *Meshech* and 1 Chr. 1:17
24 a Gen. 11:12 *1* So with MT, Vg., Tg.; LXX *Arphaxad begot Cainan, and Cainan begot Salah* (cf. Luke 3:35, 36)
25 a 1 Chr. 1:19 *1* Lit. *Division*

28 *1 Ebal,* 1 Chr. 1:22

Havilah, and Jobab. All these *were* the sons of Joktan. 30 And their dwelling place was from Mesha as you go toward Sephar, the mountain of the east. 31 These *were* the sons of Shem, according to their families, according to their languages, in their lands, according to their nations.

32 [a]These *were* the families of the sons of Noah, according to their generations, in their nations; [b]and from these the nations were divided on the earth after the flood.

The Tower of Babel

11 Now the whole earth had one language and one [1]speech. 2 And it came to pass, as they journeyed from the east, that they found a plain in the land [a]of Shinar, and they dwelt there. 3 Then they said to one another, "Come, let us make bricks and [1]bake *them* thoroughly." They had brick for stone, and they had asphalt for mortar. 4 And they said, "Come, let us build ourselves a city, and a tower [a]whose top *is* in the heavens; let us make a [b]name for ourselves, lest we [c]be scattered abroad over the face of the whole earth."

5 [a]But the LORD came down to see the city and the tower which the sons of men had built. 6 And the LORD said, "Indeed [a]the people *are* one and they all have [b]one language, and this is what they begin to do; now nothing that they [c]propose to do will be withheld from them. 7 Come, [a]let Us go down and there [b]confuse their language, that they may not understand one another's speech." 8 So [a]the LORD scattered them abroad from there [b]over the face of all the earth, and they ceased building the city. 9 Therefore its name is called [1]Babel, [a]because there the LORD confused the language of all the earth; and from there the LORD scattered them abroad over the face of all the earth.

Shem's Descendants

10 [a]This *is* the genealogy of Shem: Shem *was* one hundred years old, and begot Arphaxad two years after the flood. 11 After he begot Arphaxad, Shem lived five hundred years, and begot sons and daughters.

12 Arphaxad lived thirty-five years, [a]and begot Salah. 13 After he begot Salah, Arphaxad lived four hundred and three years, and begot sons and daughters.

14 Salah lived thirty years, and begot Eber. 15 After he begot Eber, Salah lived four hundred and three years, and begot sons and daughters.

16 [a]Eber lived thirty-four years, and begot [b]Peleg. 17 After he begot Peleg, Eber lived four hundred and thirty years, and begot sons and daughters.

18 Peleg lived thirty years, and begot Reu. 19 After he begot Reu, Peleg lived two hundred and nine years, and begot sons and daughters.

20 Reu lived thirty-two years, and begot [a]Serug. 21 After he begot Serug, Reu lived two hundred and seven years, and begot sons and daughters.

22 Serug lived thirty years, and begot Nahor. 23 After he begot Nahor, Serug lived two hundred years, and begot sons and daughters.

24 Nahor lived twenty-nine years, and begot [a]Terah. 25 After he begot Terah, Nahor lived one hundred and nineteen years, and begot sons and daughters.

26 Now Terah lived seventy years, and [a]begot [1]Abram, Nahor, and Haran.

Terah's Descendants

27 This *is* the genealogy of Terah: Terah begot [a]Abram, Nahor, and Haran. Haran begot Lot. 28 And Haran died before his father Terah in his native land, in Ur of the Chaldeans. 29 Then Abram and Nahor took wives: the name of Abram's wife *was* [a]Sarai,[1] and the name of Nahor's wife, [b]Milcah, the daughter of Haran the father of Milcah and the father of Iscah. 30 But [a]Sarai was barren; she had no child.

31 And Terah [a]took his son Abram and his grandson Lot, the son of Haran, and his daughter-in-law Sarai, his son Abram's wife, and they went out with them from [b]Ur of the Chaldeans to go to [c]the land of Canaan; and they came to Haran and dwelt there. 32 So the days of Terah were two hundred and five years, and Terah died in Haran.

> *Man without God is in total ignorance and inevitable misery. For it is wretched to have the wish, but not the power.*
>
> BLAISE PASCAL

32 a Gen. 10:1 b Gen. 9:19; 11:8
CHAPTER 11
1 *1* Lit. *lip*
2 a Gen. 10:10; 14:1
3 *1* Lit. *burn*
4 a Deut. 1:28; 9:1 b Gen. 6:4 c Deut. 4:27
5 a Gen. 18:21
6 a Gen. 9:19 b Gen. 11:1 c Ps. 2:1
7 a Gen. 1:26 b Ex. 4:11
8 a [Luke 1:51] b Gen. 10:25, 32
9 a 1 Cor. 14:23 *1* Lit. *Confusion,* Babylon
10 a Gen. 10:22–25
12 a Luke 3:35
16 a 1 Chr. 1:19 b Luke 3:35
20 a Luke 3:35
24 a Josh. 24:2
26 a 1 Chr. 1:26 *1 Abraham,* Gen. 17:5
27 a Gen. 11:31; 17:5
29 a Gen. 17:15; 20:12 b Gen. 22:20, 23; 24:15 *1 Sarah,* Gen. 17:15
30 a Gen. 16:1, 2
31 a Gen. 12:1 b Acts 7:4 c Gen. 10:19

Promises to Abram

12 Now the [a]LORD had said to Abram:
"Get [b]out of your country,
From your family
And from your father's house,
To a land that I will show you.
2 [a]I will make you a great nation;
[b]I will bless you
And make your name great;
[c]And you shall be a blessing.
3 [a]I will bless those who bless you,
And I will curse him who curses
you;
And in [b]you all the families of the
earth shall be [c]blessed."

4 So Abram departed as the LORD had
spoken to him, and Lot went with him.
And Abram *was* seventy-five years old
when he departed from Haran. 5 Then
Abram took Sarai his wife and Lot his
brother's son, and all their possessions
that they had gathered, and [a]the [1]people
whom they had acquired [b]in Haran, and
they [c]departed to go to the land of Canaan. So they came to the land of Canaan.
6 Abram [a]passed through the land to the
place of Shechem, [b]as far as [1]the terebinth tree of Moreh. [c]And the Canaanites
were then in the land.
7 [a]Then the LORD appeared to Abram
and said, [b]"To your [1]descendants I will
give this land." And there he built an [c]al-
tar to the LORD, who had appeared to him.
8 And he moved from there to the mountain east of Bethel, and he pitched his tent
with Bethel on the west and Ai on the east;
there he built an altar to the LORD and
[a]called on the name of the LORD. 9 So
Abram journeyed, [a]going on still toward
the [1]South.

Abram in Egypt

10 Now there was [a]a famine in the land,
and Abram [b]went down to Egypt to dwell
there, for the famine *was* [c]severe in the
land. 11 And it came to pass, when he was
close to entering Egypt, that he said to
Sarai his wife, "Indeed I know that you
are [a]a woman of beautiful countenance.
12 Therefore it will happen, when the

CHAPTER 12
1 [a]Acts 7:2, 3 [b]Gen. 13:9
2 [a]Deut. 26:5 [b]Gen. 22:17; 24:35 [c]Gen. 28:4
3 [a]Num. 24:9 [b]Acts 3:25 [c]Is. 41:27
5 [a]Gen. 14:14 [b]Gen. 11:31 [c]Gen. 13:18 [1]Lit. *souls*
6 [a]Heb. 11:9 [b]Deut. 11:30 [c]Gen. 10:18, 19 [1]Heb. *Alon Moreh*
7 [a]Gen. 17:1; 18:1 [b]Gen. 13:15; 15:18; 17:8 [c]Gen. 13:4, 18; 22:9 [1]Lit. *seed*
8 [a]Gen. 4:26; 13:4; 21:33
9 [a]Gen. 13:1, 3; 20:1; 24:62 [1]Heb. *Negev*
10 [a]Gen. 26:1 [b]Ps. 105:13 [c]Gen. 43:1
11 [a]Gen. 12:14; 26:7; 29:17

SARAH

Being the wife of a wanderer could not have been easy, but Sarah was faithful to follow Abraham when God spoke to him saying, "Get out of your country, from your family and from your father's house, to a land that I will show you." She was a loyal wife, but she was not a perfect woman. She was a party to Abraham's deceit of King Abimelech (see Gen. 20:2–7), she ran ahead of God and tried to fulfill His covenant in her timing (see Gen. 16:1, 2), and she laughed at the possibility of a miracle (Gen. 18:1–12).

But God had mercy on Sarah. He visited her in her old age and gave her Isaac, the son of His promise. He took a woman who had been barren for years and made her the mother of a great nation.

Perhaps you are living in a Sarah season. Perhaps you are struggling with disappointment over a dream denied or a promise postponed. Maybe you feel like it's too late for God to perform His word to you. It is time to rest in Him. He never fails. And in Jesus Christ, all the promises of God are Yes and Amen (see 2 Cor. 1:20). Do not force an Ishmael into your life. God's timing is perfect. Always make room for a sovereign surprise from the Lord, and always allow for a miracle. You never know when you'll give birth to a promise.

Egyptians see you, that they will say, 'This *is* his wife'; and they [a]will kill me, but they will let you live. 13 [a]Please say you *are* my [b]sister, that it may be well with me for your sake, and that [1]I may live because of you."

14 So it was, when Abram came into Egypt, that the Egyptians saw the woman, that she *was* very beautiful. 15 The princes of Pharaoh also saw her and commended her to Pharaoh. And the woman was taken to Pharaoh's house. 16 He [a]treated Abram well for her sake. He [b]had sheep, oxen, male donkeys, male and female servants, female donkeys, and camels.

17 But the LORD [a]plagued Pharaoh and his house with great plagues because of Sarai, Abram's wife. 18 And Pharaoh called Abram and said, [a]"What *is* this you have done to me? Why did you not tell me that she *was* your wife? 19 Why did you say, 'She *is* my sister'? I might have taken her as my wife. Now therefore, here is your wife; take *her* and go your way." 20 [a]So Pharaoh commanded *his* men concerning him; and they sent him away, with his wife and all that he had.

Abram Inherits Canaan

13 Then Abram went up from Egypt, he and his wife and all that he had, and [a]Lot with him, [b]to the [1]South. 2 [a]Abram *was* very rich in livestock, in silver, and in gold. 3 And he went on his journey [a]from the South as far as Bethel, to the place where his tent had been at the beginning, between Bethel and Ai, 4 to the [a]place of the altar which he had made there at first. And there Abram [b]called on the name of the LORD.

5 Lot also, who went with Abram, had flocks and herds and tents. 6 Now [a]the land was not able to [1]support them, that they might dwell together, for their possessions were so great that they could not dwell together. 7 And there was [a]strife between the herdsmen of Abram's livestock and the herdsmen of Lot's livestock. [b]The Canaanites and the Perizzites then dwelt in the land.

8 So Abram said to Lot, [a]"Please let there be no strife between you and me, and between my herdsmen and your herdsmen; for we *are* brethren. 9 [a]*Is* not the whole land before you? Please [b]separate from me. [c]If *you take* the left, then I will go to the right; or, if *you go* to the right, then I will go to the left."

10 And Lot lifted his eyes and saw all [a]the plain of Jordan, that it *was* well watered everywhere (before the LORD [b]destroyed Sodom and Gomorrah) [c]like the garden of the LORD, like the land of Egypt as you go toward [d]Zoar. 11 Then Lot chose for himself all the plain of Jordan, and Lot journeyed east. And they separated from each other. 12 Abram dwelt in the land of Canaan, and Lot [a]dwelt in the cities of the plain and [b]pitched *his* tent even as far as Sodom. 13 But the men of Sodom [a]*were* exceedingly wicked and [b]sinful against the LORD.

14 And the LORD said to Abram, after Lot [a]had separated from him: "Lift your eyes now and look from the place where you are—[b]northward, southward, eastward, and westward; 15 for all the land which you see [a]I give to you and [b]your [1]descendants forever. 16 And [a]I will make your descendants as the dust of the earth; so that if a man could number the dust of the earth, *then* your descendants also could be numbered. 17 Arise, walk in the land through its length and its width, for I give it to you."

18 [a]Then Abram moved *his* tent, and went and [b]dwelt by [1]the terebinth trees of Mamre, [c]which *are* in Hebron, and built an [d]altar there to the LORD.

Lot's Captivity and Rescue

14 And it came to pass in the days of Amraphel king [a]of Shinar, Arioch king of Ellasar, Chedorlaomer king of [b]Elam, and Tidal king of [1]nations, 2 *that* they made war with Bera king of Sodom, Birsha king of Gomorrah, Shinab king of [a]Admah, Shemeber king of Zeboiim, and the king of Bela (that is, [b]Zoar). 3 All these joined together in the Valley of Siddim [a](that is, the Salt Sea). 4 Twelve years [a]they served Chedorlaomer, and in the thirteenth year they rebelled.

5 In the fourteenth year Chedorlaomer and the kings that *were* with him came and attacked [a]the Rephaim in Ashteroth Karnaim, [b]the Zuzim in Ham, [c]the Emim in Shaveh Kiriathaim, 6 [a]and the Horites in their mountain of Seir, as far as El Paran, which *is* by the wilderness. 7 Then they turned back and came to En Mishpat (that *is,* Kadesh), and attacked all the country of the Amalekites, and also the

12 a Gen. 20:11; 26:7
13 a Gen. 20:1–18; 26:6–11 b Gen. 20:12 *1* Lit. *my soul*
16 a Gen. 20:14 b Gen. 13:2
17 a 1 Chr. 16:21
18 a Gen. 20:9, 10; 26:10
20 a [Prov. 21:1]

CHAPTER 13
1 a Gen. 12:4; 14:12, 16 b Gen. 12:9 *1* Heb. *Negev*
2 a Gen. 24:35; 26:14
3 a Gen. 12:8, 9
4 a Gen. 12:7, 8; 21:33 b Ps. 116:17
6 a Gen. 36:7 *1* Lit. *bear*
7 a Gen. 26:20 b Gen. 12:6; 15:20, 21
8 a 1 Cor. 6:7
9 a Gen. 20:15; 34:10 b Gen. 13:11, 14 c [Rom. 12:18]
10 a Gen. 19:17–29 b Gen. 19:24 c Gen. 2:8, 10 d Deut. 34:3
12 a Gen. 19:24, 25, 29 b Gen. 14:12; 19:1
13 a Gen. 18:20, 21 b Gen. 6:11; 39:9
14 a Gen. 13:11 b Gen. 28:14
15 a Acts 7:5 b 2 Chr. 20:7 *1* Lit. *seed*
16 a Gen. 22:17
18 a Gen. 26:17 b Gen. 14:13 c Gen. 23:2; 35:27 d Gen. 8:20; 22:8, 9 *1* Heb. *Alon Mamre*

CHAPTER 14
1 a Gen. 10:10; 11:2 b Is. 11:11; 21:2 *1* Heb. *goyim*
2 a Deut. 29:23 b Gen. 13:10; 19:22 3 a Num. 34:12
4 a Gen. 9:26 5 a Gen. 15:20 b Deut. 2:20 c Deut. 2:10
6 a Deut. 2:12, 22

Amorites who dwelt [a]in Hazezon Tamar.
8And the king of Sodom, the king of
Gomorrah, the king of Admah, the king of
Zeboiim, and the king of Bela (that *is,*
Zoar) went out and joined together in battle in the Valley of Siddim 9against Chedorlaomer king of Elam, Tidal king of
[1]nations, Amraphel king of Shinar, and
Arioch king of Ellasar—four kings
against five. 10Now the Valley of Siddim
was full of [a]asphalt pits; and the kings
of Sodom and Gomorrah fled; *some* fell
there, and the remainder fled [b]to the
mountains. 11Then they took [a]all the
goods of Sodom and Gomorrah, and all
their provisions, and went their way.
12They also took Lot, Abram's [a]brother's
son [b]who dwelt in Sodom, and his goods,
and departed.
13Then one who had escaped came and
told Abram the [a]Hebrew, for [b]he dwelt by
[1]the terebinth trees of Mamre the Amorite, brother of Eshcol and brother of
Aner; [c]and they *were* allies with Abram.
14Now [a]when Abram heard that [b]his
brother was taken captive, he armed his
three hundred and eighteen trained *ser-*
vants who were [c]born in his own house,
and went in pursuit [d]as far as Dan. 15He
divided his forces against them by night,
and he and his servants [a]attacked them
and pursued them as far as Hobah, which
is [1]north of Damascus. 16So he [a]brought
back all the goods, and also brought back
his brother Lot and his goods, as well as
the women and the people.
17And the king of Sodom [a]went out to
meet him at the Valley of Shaveh (that *is,*
the [b]King's Valley), [c]after his return from
[1]the defeat of Chedorlaomer and the
kings who *were* with him.

Abram and Melchizedek

18Then [a]Melchizedek king of Salem
brought out [b]bread and wine; he *was* [c]the
priest of [d]God Most High. 19And he
blessed him and said:

[a]"Blessed be Abram of God Most
High,
[b]Possessor of heaven and earth;
20 And [a]blessed be God Most High,
Who has delivered your enemies
into your hand."

And he [b]gave him [1]a tithe of all.
21Now the king of Sodom said to
Abram, "Give me the [1]persons, and take
the goods for yourself."

22But Abram [a]said to the king of Sodom, "I [b]have raised my hand to the LORD,
God Most High, [c]the Possessor of heaven
and earth, 23that [a]I *will take* nothing,
from a thread to a sandal strap, and that
I will not take anything that *is* yours, lest
you should say, 'I have made Abram
rich'— 24except only what the young men
have eaten, and the portion of the men
who went with me: Aner, Eshcol, and
Mamre; let them take their portion."

Lord, I pray that _____ will not be afraid.

FROM GENESIS 15:1

God's Covenant with Abram

15 After these things the word of the
LORD came to Abram [a]in a vision,
saying, [b]"Do not be afraid, Abram. I *am*
your [c]shield, [1]your exceedingly [d]great reward."
2[a]But Abram said, "Lord GOD, what will
You give me, [b]seeing I [1]go childless, and
the heir of my house *is* Eliezer of Damascus?" 3Then Abram said, "Look, You have
given me no offspring; indeed [a]one[1] born
in my house is my heir!"
4And behold, the word of the LORD
came to him, saying, "This one shall not
be your heir, but one who [a]will come
from your own body shall be your heir."
5Then He brought him outside and said,
"Look now toward heaven, and [a]count the
[b]stars if you are able to number them."
And He said to him, [c]"So shall your [d]de-
scendants be."
6And he [a]believed in the LORD, and He
[b]accounted it to him for righteousness.
7Then He said to him, "I *am* the LORD,
who [a]brought you out of [b]Ur of the Chaldeans, [c]to give you this land to inherit it."
8And he said, "Lord GOD, [a]how shall I
know that I will inherit it?"
9So He said to him, "Bring Me a three-
year-old heifer, a three-year-old female
goat, a three-year-old ram, a turtledove,
and a young pigeon." 10Then he brought
all these to Him and [a]cut them in two,
down the middle, and placed each piece

7 a 2 Chr. 20:2
9 *1* Heb. *goyim*
10 a Gen. 11:3 b Gen. 19:17, 30
11 a Gen. 14:16, 21
12 a Gen. 11:27; 12:5 b Gen. 13:12
13 a Gen. 39:14; 40:15 b Gen. 13:18 c Gen. 14:24; 21:27, 32 *1* Heb. *Alon Mamre*
14 a Gen. 19:29 b Gen. 13:8; 14:12 c Gen. 12:5; 15:3; 17:27 d Deut. 34:1
15 a Is. 41:2, 3 *1* Lit. *on the left hand of*
16 a Gen. 31:18
17 a 1 Sam. 18:6 b 2 Sam. 18:18 c Heb. 7:1 *1* Lit. *striking*
18 a Heb. 7:1–10 b Gen. 18:5 c Ps. 110:4 d Acts 16:17
19 a Ruth 3:10 b Gen. 14:22
20 a Gen. 24:27 b Heb. 7:4 *1 one-tenth*
21 *1* Lit. *souls*
22 a Gen. 14:2, 8, 10 b Dan. 12:7 c Gen. 14:19
23 a 2 Kin. 5:16

CHAPTER 15
1 a Dan. 10:1 b Gen. 21:17; 26:24 c Deut. 33:29 d Prov. 11:18 *1 Or your reward shall be very great*
2 a Gen. 17:18 b Acts 7:5 *1 am childless*
3 a Gen. 14:14 *1 a servant*
4 a 2 Sam. 7:12
5 a Ps. 147:4 b Jer. 33:22 c Ex. 32:13 d Gen. 17:19
6 a Rom. 4:3, 9, 22 b Ps. 32:2; 106:31

7 a Gen. 12:1 b Gen. 11:28, 31 c Ps. 105:42, 44 **8** a Luke 1:18 **10** a Jer. 34:18

opposite the other; but he did not cut [b]the
birds in two. [11]And when the vultures
came down on the carcasses, Abram drove
them away.
[12]Now when the sun was going down,
[a]a deep sleep fell upon Abram; and behold,
horror *and* great darkness fell upon him.
[13]Then He said to Abram: "Know certainly
[a]that your descendants will be strangers
in a land *that is* not theirs, and will serve
them, and [b]they will afflict them four
hundred years. [14]And also the nation
whom they serve [a]I will judge; afterward
[b]they shall come out with great possessions. [15]Now as for you, [a]you shall [1]go [b]to
your fathers in peace; [c]you shall be buried
at a good old age. [16]But [a]in the fourth
generation they shall return here, for the
iniquity [b]of the Amorites [c]*is* not yet complete."
[17]And it came to pass, when the sun
went down and it was dark, that behold,
there appeared a smoking oven and a
burning torch that [a]passed between those
pieces. [18]On the same day the LORD [a]made
a covenant with Abram, saying:
[b]"To your descendants I have given this
land, from the river of Egypt to the great
river, the River Euphrates— [19]the Kenites, the Kenezzites, the Kadmonites,
[20]the Hittites, the Perizzites, the Rephaim, [21]the Amorites, the Canaanites, the
Girgashites, and the Jebusites."

Hagar and Ishmael

16 Now Sarai, Abram's wife, [a]had
borne him no *children.* And she
had [b]an Egyptian maidservant whose
name was [c]Hagar. [2][a]So Sarai said to
Abram, "See now, the LORD [b]has restrained me from bearing *children.*
Please, [c]go in to my maid; perhaps I shall
[1]obtain children by her." And Abram
[d]heeded the voice of Sarai. [3]Then Sarai,
Abram's wife, took Hagar her maid, the
Egyptian, and gave her to her husband
Abram to be his wife, after Abram [a]had
dwelt ten years in the land of Canaan. [4]So
he went in to Hagar, and she conceived.
And when she saw that she had conceived,
her mistress became [a]despised in her
[1]eyes.
[5]Then Sarai said to Abram, [1]"My wrong
be upon you! I gave my maid into your
embrace; and when she saw that she had
conceived, I became despised in her eyes.
[a]The LORD judge between you and me."

10 [b]Lev. 1:17
12 [a]Gen. 2:21; 28:11
13 [a]Ex. 1:11 [b]Ex. 12:40
14 [a]Ex. 6:6 [b]Ex. 12:36
15 [a]Job 5:26 [b]Gen. 25:8; 47:30 [c]Gen. 25:8 [1]*Die and join your ancestors*
16 [a]Ex. 12:41 [b]1 Kin. 21:26 [c]Matt. 23:32
17 [a]Jer. 34:18, 19
18 [a]Gen. 24:7 [b]Gen. 12:7; 17:8

CHAPTER 16
1 [a]Gen. 11:30; 15:2, 3 [b]Gen. 12:16; 21:9 [c]Gal. 4:24
2 [a]Gen. 30:3 [b]Gen. 20:18 [c]Gen. 30:3, 9 [d]Gen. 3:17 [1]Lit. *be built up from*
3 [a]Gen. 12:4, 5
4 [a][Prov. 30:21, 23] [1]*sight*
5 [a]Gen. 31:53 [1]*The wrong done to me be*
6 [a]1 Pet. 3:7 [b]Ex. 2:15
7 [a]Gen. 21:17, 18; 22:11, 15; 31:11 [b]Gen. 20:1; 25:18 [c]Ex. 15:22
9 [a][Titus 2:9]
10 [a]Gen. 17:20
11 [a]Luke 1:13, 31 [1]Lit. *God Hears*
12 [a]Gen. 21:20 [b]Gen. 25:18
13 [a]Gen. 31:42 [1]Heb. *El Roi* [2]*Seen the back of*
14 [a]Gen. 24:62 [b]Num. 13:26 [1]Lit. *Well of the One Who Lives and Sees Me*
15 [a]Gal. 4:22

[6][a]So Abram said to Sarai, "Indeed your
maid *is* in your hand; do to her as you
please." And when Sarai dealt harshly
with her, [b]she fled from her presence.
[7]Now the [a]Angel of the LORD found her
by a spring of water in the wilderness, [b]by
the spring on the way to [c]Shur. [8]And He
said, "Hagar, Sarai's maid, where have you
come from, and where are you going?"
She said, "I am fleeing from the presence of my mistress Sarai."
[9]The Angel of the LORD said to her, "Return to your mistress, and [a]submit yourself under her hand." [10]Then the Angel of
the LORD said to her, [a]"I will multiply
your descendants exceedingly, so that
they shall not be counted for multitude."
[11]And the Angel of the LORD said to her:

"Behold, you *are* with child,
[a]And you shall bear a son.
You shall call his name [1]Ishmael,
Because the LORD has heard your
affliction.
12 [a]He shall be a wild man;
His hand *shall be* against every
man,
And every man's hand against him.
[b]And he shall dwell in the presence
of all his brethren."

[13]Then she called the name of the LORD
who spoke to her, You-Are-[1]the-God-
Who-Sees; for she said, "Have I also here
[2]seen Him [a]who sees me?" [14]Therefore
the well was called [a]Beer Lahai Roi;[1] observe, *it is* [b]between Kadesh and Bered.
[15]So [a]Hagar bore Abram a son; and
Abram named his son, whom Hagar bore,
Ishmael. [16]Abram *was* eighty-six years old
when Hagar bore Ishmael to Abram.

The Sign of the Covenant

17 When Abram was ninety-nine
years old, the LORD [a]appeared to
Abram and said to him, [b]"I *am* [1]Almighty
God; [c]walk before Me and be [d]blameless.
[2]And I will make My [a]covenant between
Me and you, and [b]will multiply you exceedingly." [3]Then Abram fell on his face,
and God talked with him, saying: [4]"As for
Me, behold, My covenant is with you, and
you shall be [a]a father of [1]many nations.
[5]No longer shall [a]your name be called

CHAPTER 17 **1** [a]Gen. 12:7; 18:1 [b]Gen. 28:3; 35:11 [c]2 Kin. 20:3 [d]Deut. 18:13 [1]Heb. *El Shaddai* **2** [a]Gen. 15:18 [b]Gen. 12:2; 13:16; 15:5; 18:18 **4** [a][Rom. 4:11, 12, 16] [1]Lit. *multitude of nations* **5** [a]Neh. 9:7

[1]Abram, but your name shall be [2]Abraham; [b]for I have made you a father of [3]many nations. 6I will make you exceedingly fruitful; and I will make [a]nations of you, and [b]kings shall come from you. 7And I will [a]establish My covenant between Me and you and your descendants after you in their generations, for an everlasting covenant, [b]to be God to you and [c]your descendants after you. 8Also [a]I give to you and your descendants after you the land [b]in[1] which you are a stranger, all the land of Canaan, as an everlasting possession; and [c]I will be their God."

9And God said to Abraham: "As for you, [a]you shall keep My covenant, you and your descendants after you throughout their generations. 10This *is* My covenant which you shall keep, between Me and you and your descendants after you: [a]Every male child among you shall be circumcised; 11and you shall be circumcised in the flesh of your foreskins, and it shall be [a]a sign of the covenant between Me and you. 12He who is eight days old among you [a]shall be circumcised, every male child in your generations, he who is born in your house or bought with money from any foreigner who is not your descendant. 13He who is born in your house and he who is bought with your money must be circumcised, and My covenant shall be in your flesh for an everlasting covenant. 14And the uncircumcised male child, who is not circumcised in the flesh of his foreskin, that person [a]shall be cut off from his people; he has broken My covenant."

15Then God said to Abraham, "As for Sarai your wife, you shall not call her name Sarai, but [1]Sarah *shall be* her name. 16And I will bless her [a]and also give you a son by her; then I will bless her, and she shall be *a mother* [b]*of* nations; [c]kings of peoples shall be from her."

17Then Abraham fell on his face [a]and laughed, and said in his heart, "Shall *a child* be born to a man who is one hundred years old? And shall Sarah, who is ninety years old, bear *a child?*" 18And Abraham [a]said to God, "Oh, that Ishmael might live before You!"

19Then God said: "No, [a]Sarah your wife shall bear you a son, and you shall call his name Isaac; I will establish My [b]covenant with him for an everlasting covenant, *and* with his descendants after him. 20And as for Ishmael, I have heard you. Behold, I have blessed him, and will make him fruitful, and [a]will multiply him exceedingly. He shall beget [b]twelve princes, [c]and I will make him a great nation. 21But My [a]covenant I will establish with Isaac, [b]whom Sarah shall bear to you at this [c]set time next year." 22Then He finished talking with him, and God went up from Abraham.

23So Abraham took Ishmael his son, all who were born in his house and all who were bought with his money, every male among the men of Abraham's house, and circumcised the flesh of their foreskins that very same day, as God had said to him. 24Abraham *was* ninety-nine years old when he was circumcised in the flesh of his foreskin. 25And Ishmael his son *was* thirteen years old when he was circumcised in the flesh of his foreskin. 26That very same day Abraham was circumcised, and his son Ishmael; 27and [a]all the men of his house, born in the house or bought with money from a foreigner, were circumcised with him.

The Son of Promise

18 Then the LORD appeared to him by [1]the [a]terebinth trees of Mamre, as he was sitting in the tent door in the heat of the day. 2[a]So he lifted his eyes and looked, and behold, three men were standing by him; [b]and when he saw *them,* he ran from the tent door to meet them, and bowed himself to the ground, 3and said, "My Lord, if I have now found favor in Your sight, do not pass on by Your servant. 4Please let [a]a little water be brought, and wash your feet, and rest yourselves under the tree. 5And [a]I will bring a morsel of bread, that [b]you may refresh your hearts. After that you may pass by, [c]inasmuch as you have come to your servant."

They said, "Do as you have said."

6So Abraham hurried into the tent to Sarah and said, "Quickly, make ready three measures of fine meal; knead *it* and make cakes." 7And Abraham ran to the herd, took a tender and good calf, gave *it* to a young man, and he hastened to prepare it. 8So [a]he took butter and milk and the calf which he had prepared, and set *it* before them; and he stood by them under the tree as they ate.

9Then they said to him, "Where *is* Sarah your wife?"

So he said, "Here, [a]in the tent."

10And He said, "I will certainly return to you [a]according to the time of life, and be-

5 [b]Rom. 4:17 [1] Lit. *Exalted Father* [2] Lit. *Father of a Multitude* [3] *a multitude of*
6 [a]Gen. 17:16; 35:11 [b]Matt. 1:6
7 [a][Gal. 3:17] [b]Gen. 26:24; 28:13 [c]Rom. 9:8
8 [a]Acts 7:5 [b]Gen. 23:4; 28:4 [c]Lev. 26:12 [1] Lit. *of your sojournings*
9 [a]Ex. 19:5
10 [a]Acts 7:8
11 [a]Ex. 12:13, 48
12 [a]Lev. 12:3
14 [a]Ex. 4:24–26
15 [1] Lit. *Princess*
16 [a]Gen. 18:10 [b]Gen. 35:11 [c]Gen. 17:6; 36:31
17 [a]Gen. 17:3; 18:12; 21:6
18 [a]Gen. 18:23
19 [a]Gen. 18:10; 21:2 [b]Gen. 22:16
20 [a]Gen. 16:10 [b]Gen. 25:12–16 [c]Gen. 21:13, 18
21 [a]Gen. 26:2–5 [b]Gen. 21:2 [c]Gen. 18:14
27 [a]Gen. 18:19

CHAPTER 18
1 [a]Gen. 13:18; 14:13 [1] Heb. *Alon Mamre*
2 [a]Heb. 13:2 [b]Gen. 19:1
4 [a]Gen. 19:2; 24:32; 43:24
5 [a]Judg. 6:18, 19; 13:15, 16 [b]Judg. 19:5 [c]Gen. 19:8; 33:10
8 [a]Gen. 19:3
9 [a]Gen. 24:67
10 [a]2 Kin. 4:16

hold, [b]Sarah your wife shall have a son."
(Sarah was listening in the tent door
which *was* behind him.) 11Now [a]Abraham
and Sarah were old, well advanced in age;
and [1]Sarah [b]had passed the age of childbearing. 12Therefore Sarah [a]laughed
within herself, saying, [b]"After I have
grown old, shall I have pleasure, my [c]lord
being old also?"
13And the LORD said to Abraham, "Why
did Sarah laugh, saying, 'Shall I surely
bear *a child,* since I am old?' 14[a]Is anything too hard for the LORD? [b]At the appointed time I will return to you,
according to the time of life, and Sarah
shall have a son."
15But Sarah denied *it,* saying, "I did not
laugh," for she was afraid.
And He said, "No, but you did laugh!"

Abraham Intercedes for Sodom

16Then the men rose from there and
looked toward Sodom, and Abraham went
with them [a]to send them on the way.
17And the LORD said, [a]"Shall I hide from
Abraham what I am doing, 18since Abraham shall surely become a great and
mighty nation, and all the nations of the
earth shall be [a]blessed in him? 19For I
have known him, in order [a]that he may
command his children and his household
after him, that they keep the way of the
LORD, to do righteousness and justice,
that the LORD may bring to Abraham what
He has spoken to him." 20And the LORD
said, "Because [a]the outcry against Sodom
and Gomorrah is great, and because their
[b]sin is very grave, 21[a]I will go down now
and see whether they have done altogether according to the outcry against it that
has come to Me; and if not, [b]I will know."
22Then the men turned away from
there [a]and went toward Sodom, but Abraham still stood before the LORD. 23And
Abraham [a]came near and said, [b]"Would
You also [c]destroy the [d]righteous with the
wicked? 24Suppose there were fifty righteous within the city; would You also destroy the place and not spare *it* for the fifty
righteous that were in it? 25Far be it from
You to do such a thing as this, to slay the
righteous with the wicked, so [a]that the
righteous should be as the wicked; far be
it from You! [b]Shall not the Judge of all the
earth do right?"

10 [b] Rom. 9:9
11 [a] Gen. 17:17 [b] Gen. 31:35 [1] Lit. *the manner of women had ceased to be with Sarah*
12 [a] Gen. 17:17 [b] Luke 1:18 [c] 1 Pet. 3:6
14 [a] Jer. 32:17 [b] Gen. 17:21; 18:10
16 [a] Rom. 15:24
17 [a] Ps. 25:14
18 [a] [Acts 3:25, 26]
19 [a] [Deut. 4:9, 10; 6:6, 7]
20 [a] Gen. 4:10; 19:13 [b] Gen. 13:13
21 [a] Gen. 11:5 [b] Deut. 8:2; 13:3
22 [a] Gen. 18:16; 19:1
23 [a] [Heb. 10:22] [b] Num. 16:22 [c] Job 9:22 [d] Gen. 20:4
25 [a] Is. 3:10, 11 [b] Deut. 1:16, 17; 32:4
26 [a] Jer. 5:1
27 [a] [Gen. 3:19]
32 [a] Judg. 6:39 [b] James 5:16
CHAPTER 19
1 [a] Gen. 18:2, 16, 22 [b] Gen. 18:1–5
2 [a] [Heb. 13:2] [b] Gen. 18:4; 24:32 [c] Luke 24:28
3 [a] Gen. 18:6–8 [b] Ex. 12:8
5 [a] Is. 3:9 [b] Judg. 19:22

26So the LORD said, [a]"If I find in Sodom
fifty righteous within the city, then I will
spare all the place for their sakes."
27Then Abraham answered and said,
"Indeed now, I who *am* [a]*but* dust and ashes have taken it upon myself to speak to
the Lord: 28Suppose there were five less
than the fifty righteous; would You destroy all of the city for *lack of* five?"
So He said, "If I find there forty-five, I
will not destroy *it.*"
29And he spoke to Him yet again and
said, "Suppose there should be forty found
there?"
So He said, "I will not do *it* for the sake
of forty."
30Then he said, "Let not the Lord be
angry, and I will speak: Suppose thirty
should be found there?"
So He said, "I will not do *it* if I find
thirty there."
31And he said, "Indeed now, I have tak-
en it upon myself to speak to the Lord:
Suppose twenty should be found there?"
So He said, "I will not destroy *it* for the
sake of twenty."
32Then he said, [a]"Let not the Lord be
angry, and I will speak but once more:
Suppose ten should be found there?"
[b]And He said, "I will not destroy *it* for
the sake of ten." 33So the LORD went His
way as soon as He had finished speaking
with Abraham; and Abraham returned to
his place.

Sodom's Depravity

19 Now [a]the two angels came to Sodom in the evening, and [b]Lot was
sitting in the gate of Sodom. When Lot
saw *them,* he rose to meet them, and he
bowed himself with his face toward the
ground. 2And he said, "Here now, my
lords, please [a]turn in to your servant's
house and spend the night, and [b]wash
your feet; then you may rise early and go
on your way."
And they said, [c]"No, but we will spend
the night in the open square."
3But he insisted strongly; so they
turned in to him and entered his house.
[a]Then he made them a feast, and baked
[b]unleavened bread, and they ate.
4Now before they lay down, the men of
the city, the men of Sodom, both old and
young, all the people from every quarter,
surrounded the house. 5[a]And they called
to Lot and said to him, "Where are the
men who came to you tonight? [b]Bring

them out to us that we [c]may know them
carnally."
6So [a]Lot went out to them through the
doorway, shut the door behind him, 7and
said, "Please, my brethren, do not do so
wickedly! 8[a]See now, I have two daughters
who have not known a man; please, let me
bring them out to you, and you may do to
them as you wish; only do nothing to
these men, [b]since this is the reason they
have come under the shadow of my roof."
9And they said, "Stand back!" Then they
said, "This one [a]came in to [1]stay *here,*
[b]and he keeps acting as a judge; now we
will deal worse with you than with them."
So they pressed hard against the man Lot,
and came near to break down the door.
10But the men reached out their hands
and pulled Lot into the house with them,
and shut the door. 11And they [a]struck the
men who *were* at the doorway of the
house with blindness, both small and
great, so that they became weary *trying* to
find the door.

Sodom and Gomorrah Destroyed

12Then the men said to Lot, "Have you
anyone else here? Son-in-law, your sons,
your daughters, and whomever you have
in the city—[a]take *them* out of this place!
13For we will destroy this place, because
the [a]outcry against them has grown great
before the face of the LORD, and [b]the LORD
has sent us to destroy it."
14So Lot went out and spoke to his
sons-in-law, [a]who had married his
daughters, and said, [b]"Get up, get out of
this place; for the LORD will destroy this
city!" [c]But to his sons-in-law he seemed
to be joking.
15When the morning dawned, the angels urged Lot to hurry, saying, [a]"Arise,
take your wife and your two daughters
who are here, lest you be consumed in the
punishment of the city." 16And while he
lingered, the men [a]took hold of his hand,
his wife's hand, and the hands of his two
daughters, the [b]LORD being merciful to
him, [c]and they brought him out and set
him outside the city. 17So it came to pass,
when they had brought them outside, that
[1]he said, [a]"Escape for your life! [b]Do not
look behind you nor stay anywhere in the
plain. Escape [c]to the mountains, lest you
be [2]destroyed."
18Then Lot said to them, "Please, [a]no,
my lords! 19Indeed now, your servant has
found favor in your sight, and you have
increased your mercy which you have
shown me by saving my life; but I cannot
escape to the mountains, lest some evil
overtake me and I die. 20See now, this city
is near *enough* to flee to, and it *is* a little
one; please let me escape there (*is* it not
a little one?) and my soul shall live."
21And he said to him, "See, [a]I have favored you concerning this thing also, in
that I will not overthrow this city for
which you have spoken. 22Hurry, escape
there. For [a]I cannot do anything until you
arrive there."
Therefore [b]the name of the city was
called [1]Zoar.
23The sun had risen upon the earth
when Lot entered Zoar. 24Then the LORD
rained [a]brimstone and [b]fire on Sodom
and Gomorrah, from the LORD out of the
heavens. 25So He [1]overthrew those cities,
all the plain, all the inhabitants of the cities, and [a]what grew on the ground.
26But his wife looked back behind him,
and she became [a]a pillar of salt.
27And Abraham went early in the morning to the place where [a]he had stood before the LORD. 28Then he looked toward
Sodom and Gomorrah, and toward all the
land of the plain; and he saw, and behold,
[a]the smoke of the land which went up like
the smoke of a furnace. 29And it came to
pass, when God destroyed the cities of the
plain, that God [a]remembered Abraham,
and sent Lot out of the midst of the overthrow, when He overthrew the cities in
which Lot had dwelt.

The Descendants of Lot

30Then Lot went up out of Zoar and
[a]dwelt in the mountains, and his two
daughters were with him; for he was
afraid to dwell in Zoar. And he and his two
daughters dwelt in a cave. 31Now the firstborn said to the younger, "Our father *is*
old, and *there is* no man on the earth [a]to
come in to us as is the custom of all the
earth. 32Come, let us make our father
drink wine, and we will lie with him, that
we [a]may preserve the [1]lineage of our father." 33So they made their father drink
wine that night. And the firstborn went in
and lay with her father, and he did not
know when she lay down or when she
arose.
34It happened on the next day that the
firstborn said to the younger, "Indeed I lay
with my father last night; let us make him

5 [c]Gen. 4:1
6 [a]Judg. 19:23
8 [a]Judg. 19:24 [b]Gen. 18:5
9 [a]2 Pet. 2:7, 8 [b]Ex. 2:14 [1]As a resident alien
11 [a]Gen. 20:17, 18
12 [a]2 Pet. 2:7, 9
13 [a]Gen. 18:20 [b]1 Chr. 21:15
14 [a]Matt. 1:18 [b]Num. 16:21, 24, 26, 45 [c]Ex. 9:21
15 [a]Rev. 18:4
16 [a]2 Pet. 2:7 [b]Luke 18:13 [c]Ps. 34:22
17 [a]Jer. 48:6 [b]Matt. 24:16–18 [c]Gen. 14:10 [1]LXX, Syr., Vg. *they* [2]Lit. *swept away*
18 [a]Acts 10:14
21 [a]Job 42:8, 9
22 [a]Ex. 32:10 [b]Gen. 13:10; 14:2 [1]Lit. *Little* or *Insignificant*
24 [a]Deut. 29:23 [b]Lev. 10:2
25 [a]Ps. 107:34 [1]*devastated*
26 [a]Luke 17:32
27 [a]Gen. 18:22
28 [a]Rev. 9:2; 18:9
29 [a]Gen. 8:1; 18:23
30 [a]Gen. 19:17, 19
31 [a]Gen. 16:2, 4; 38:8, 9
32 [a][Mark 12:19] [1]Lit. *seed*

drink wine tonight also, and you go in *and* lie with him, that we may preserve the [1]lineage of our father." 35Then they made their father drink wine that night also. And the younger arose and lay with him, and he did not know when she lay down or when she arose.

36Thus both the daughters of Lot were with child by their father. 37The firstborn bore a son and called his name Moab; [a]he *is* the father of the Moabites to this day. 38And the younger, she also bore a son and called his name Ben-Ammi; [a]he *is* the father of the people of Ammon to this day.

Abraham and Abimelech

20 And Abraham journeyed from [a]there to the South, and dwelt between [b]Kadesh and Shur, and [c]stayed in Gerar. 2Now Abraham said of Sarah his wife, [a]"She *is* my sister." And Abimelech king of Gerar sent and [b]took Sarah.

3But [a]God came to Abimelech [b]in a dream by night, and said to him, [c]"Indeed you *are* a dead man because of the woman whom you have taken, for she *is* [1]a man's wife."

4But Abimelech had not come near her; and he said, "Lord, [a]will You slay a righteous nation also? 5Did he not say to me, 'She *is* my sister'? And she, even she herself said, 'He *is* my brother.' [a]In the [1]integrity of my heart and innocence of my hands I have done this."

6And God said to him in a dream, "Yes, I know that you did this in the integrity of your heart. For [a]I also withheld you from sinning [b]against Me; therefore I did not let you touch her. 7Now therefore, restore the man's wife; [a]for he *is* a prophet, and he will pray for you and you shall live. But if you do not restore *her,* [b]know that you shall surely die, you [c]and all who *are* yours."

8So Abimelech rose early in the morning, called all his servants, and told all these things in their hearing; and the men were very much afraid. 9And Abimelech called Abraham and said to him, "What have you done to us? How have I [1]offended you, [a]that you have brought on me and on my kingdom a great sin? You have done deeds to me [b]that ought not to be done." 10Then Abimelech said to Abraham, "What did you have in view, that you have done this thing?"

11And Abraham said, "Because I thought, surely [a]the fear of God *is* not in this place; and [b]they will kill me on account of my wife. 12But indeed [a]*she is* truly my sister. She *is* the daughter of my father, but not the daughter of my mother; and she became my wife. 13And it came to pass, when [a]God caused me to wander from my father's house, that I said to her, 'This *is* your kindness that you should do for me: in every place, wherever we go, [b]say of me, "He *is* my brother." ' "

14Then Abimelech [a]took sheep, oxen, and male and female servants, and gave *them* to Abraham; and he restored Sarah his wife to him. 15And Abimelech said, "See, [a]my land *is* before you; dwell where it pleases you." 16Then to Sarah he said, "Behold, I have given your brother a thousand *pieces* of silver; [a]indeed this [1]vindicates you [b]before all who *are* with you and before everybody." Thus she was [2]rebuked.

17So Abraham [a]prayed to God; and God [b]healed Abimelech, his wife, and his female servants. Then they bore *children;* 18for the LORD [a]had closed up all the wombs of the house of Abimelech because of Sarah, Abraham's wife.

Isaac Is Born

21 And the LORD [a]visited Sarah as He had said, and the LORD did for Sarah [b]as He had spoken. 2For Sarah [a]conceived and bore Abraham a son in his old age, [b]at the set time of which God had spoken to him. 3And Abraham called the name of his son who was born to him—whom Sarah bore to him—[a]Isaac.[1] 4Then Abraham [a]circumcised his son Isaac when he was eight days old, [b]as God had commanded him. 5Now [a]Abraham was one hundred years old when his son Isaac was born to him. 6And Sarah said, [a]"God has [1]made me laugh, *and* all who hear [b]will laugh with me." 7She also said, "Who would have said to Abraham that Sarah would nurse children? [a]For I have borne *him* a son in his old age."

Hagar and Ishmael Depart

8So the child grew and was weaned. And Abraham made a great feast on the same day that Isaac was weaned.

9And Sarah saw the son of Hagar [a]the Egyptian, whom she had borne to Abraham, [b]scoffing.[1] 10Therefore she said to

34 [1] Lit. *seed*
37 a Deut. 2:9
38 a Deut. 2:19

CHAPTER 20
1 a Gen. 18:1 b Gen. 12:9; 16:7, 14 c Gen. 26:1, 6
2 a Gen. 12:11–13; 26:7 b Gen. 12:15
3 a Ps. 105:14 b Job 33:15 c Gen. 20:7 [1] Lit. *married to a husband*
4 a Gen. 18:23–25
5 a 2 Kin. 20:3 [1] *innocence*
6 a 1 Sam. 25:26, 34 b Gen. 39:9
7 a 1 Sam. 7:5 b Gen. 2:17 c Num. 16:32, 33
9 a Gen. 26:10; 39:9 b Gen. 34:7 [1] *sinned against*
11 a Prov. 16:6 b Gen. 12:12; 26:7
12 a Gen. 11:29
13 a Gen. 12:1–9, 11 b Gen. 12:13; 20:5
14 a Gen. 12:16
15 a Gen. 13:9; 34:10; 47:6
16 a Gen. 26:11 b Mal. 2:9 [1] Lit. *is a covering of the eyes for you to all* [2] Or *justified*
17 a Job 42:9 b Gen. 21:2
18 a Gen. 12:17

CHAPTER 21
1 a 1 Sam. 2:21 b [Gal. 4:23, 28]
2 a Heb. 11:11, 12 b Gen. 17:21; 18:10, 14
3 a Gen. 17:19, 21 [1] Lit. *Laughter*
4 a Acts 7:8 b Gen. 17:10, 12
5 a Gen. 17:1, 17
6 a Is. 54:1 b Luke 1:58 [1] Lit. *made laughter for me*
7 a Gen. 18:11, 12
9 a Gen. 16:1, 4, 15 b [Gal. 4:29] [1] Lit. *laughing*

Abraham, [a]"Cast out this bondwoman and her son; for the son of this bondwoman shall not be heir with my son, *namely* with Isaac." 11And the matter was very [1]displeasing in Abraham's sight [a]because of his son.

12But God said to Abraham, "Do not let it be displeasing in your sight because of the lad or because of your bondwoman. Whatever Sarah has said to you, listen to her voice; for [a]in Isaac your seed shall be called. 13Yet I will also make [a]a nation of the son of the bondwoman, because he *is* your [1]seed."

14So Abraham rose early in the morning, and took bread and [1]a skin of water; and putting *it* on her shoulder, he gave *it* and the boy to Hagar, and [a]sent her away. Then she departed and wandered in the Wilderness of Beersheba. 15And the water in the skin was used up, and she placed the boy under one of the shrubs. 16Then she went and sat down across from *him* at a distance of about a bowshot; for she said to herself, "Let me not see the death of the boy." So she sat opposite *him,* and lifted her voice and wept.

17And [a]God heard the voice of the lad. Then the [b]angel of God called to Hagar out of heaven, and said to her, "What ails you, Hagar? Fear not, for God has heard the voice of the lad where he *is.* 18Arise, lift up the lad and hold him with your hand, for [a]I will make him a great nation."

19Then [a]God opened her eyes, and she saw a well of water. And she went and filled the skin with water, and gave the lad a drink. 20So God [a]was with the lad; and he grew and dwelt in the wilderness, [b]and became an archer. 21He dwelt in the Wilderness of Paran; and his mother [a]took a wife for him from the land of Egypt.

A Covenant with Abimelech

22And it came to pass at that time that [a]Abimelech and Phichol, the commander of his army, spoke to Abraham, saying, [b]"God *is* with you in all that you do. 23Now therefore, [a]swear[1] to me by God that you will not deal falsely with me, with my offspring, or with my posterity; but that according to the kindness that I have done to you, you will do to me and to the land in which you have dwelt."

24And Abraham said, "I will swear."

25Then Abraham rebuked Abimelech because of a well of water which Abimelech's servants [a]had seized. 26And Abimelech said, "I do not know who has done this thing; you did not tell me, nor had I heard *of it* until today." 27So Abraham took sheep and oxen and gave them to Abimelech, and the two of them [a]made a [1]covenant. 28And Abraham set seven ewe lambs of the flock by themselves.

29Then Abimelech asked Abraham, [a]"What *is the meaning of* these seven ewe lambs which you have set by themselves?"

30And he said, "You will take *these* seven ewe lambs from my hand, that [a]they may be my witness that I have dug this well." 31Therefore he [a]called that place [1]Beersheba, because the two of them swore an oath there.

32Thus they made a covenant at Beersheba. So Abimelech rose with Phichol, the commander of his army, and they returned to the land of the Philistines. 33Then *Abraham* planted a tamarisk tree in Beersheba, and [a]there called on the name of the LORD, [b]the Everlasting God. 34And Abraham stayed in the land of the Philistines many days.

Abraham's Faith Confirmed

22 Now it came to pass after these things that [a]God tested Abraham, and said to him, "Abraham!"

And he said, "Here I am."

2Then He said, "Take now your son, [a]your only *son* Isaac, whom you [b]love, and go [c]to the land of Moriah, and offer him there as a [d]burnt offering on one of the mountains of which I shall tell you."

3So Abraham rose early in the morning and saddled his donkey, and took two of his young men with him, and Isaac his son; and he split the wood for the burnt offering, and arose and went to the place of which God had told him. 4Then on the third day Abraham lifted his eyes and saw the place afar off. 5And Abraham said to his young men, "Stay here with the donkey; the [1]lad and I will go yonder and worship, and we will [a]come back to you."

6So Abraham took the wood of the burnt offering and [a]laid *it* on Isaac his son; and he took the fire in his hand, and a knife, and the two of them went together. 7But Isaac spoke to Abraham his father and said, "My father!"

And he said, "Here I am, my son."

Then he said, "Look, the fire and the wood, but where *is* the [1]lamb for a burnt offering?"

10 [a]Gal. 3:18; 4:30
11 [a]Gen. 17:18 [1]*distressing*
12 [a][Rom. 9:7, 8]
13 [a]Gen. 16:10; 17:20; 21:18; 25:12–18 [1]*descendant*
14 [a]John 8:35 [1]A water bottle made of skins
17 [a]Ex. 3:7 [b]Gen. 22:11
18 [a]Gen. 16:10; 21:13; 25:12–16
19 [a]Num. 22:31
20 [a]Gen. 28:15; 39:2, 3, 21 [b]Gen. 16:12
21 [a]Gen. 24:4
22 [a]Gen. 20:2, 14; 26:26 [b]Gen. 26:28
23 [a]Josh. 2:12 [1]*take an oath*
25 [a]Gen. 26:15, 18, 20–22
27 [a]Gen. 26:31; 31:44 [1]*treaty*
29 [a]Gen. 33:8
30 [a]Gen. 31:48, 52
31 [a]Gen. 21:14; 26:33 [1]Lit. *Well of the Oath* or *Well of the Seven*
33 [a]Gen. 4:26; 12:8; 13:4; 26:25 [b]Deut. 32:40; 33:27

CHAPTER 22
1 [a]Heb. 11:17
2 [a]Gen. 22:12, 16 [b]John 5:20 [c]2 Chr. 3:1 [d]Gen. 8:20; 31:54
5 [a][Heb. 11:19] [1]Or *young man*
6 [a]John 19:17
7 [1]Or *goat*

8And Abraham said, "My son, God will provide for Himself the [a]lamb for a [b]burnt offering." So the two of them went together.

9Then they came to the place of which God had told him. And Abraham built an altar there and placed the wood in order; and he bound Isaac his son and [a]laid him on the altar, upon the wood. 10And Abraham stretched out his hand and took the knife to slay his son.

11But the [a]Angel of the LORD called to him from heaven and said, "Abraham, Abraham!"

So he said, "Here I am."

12And He said, [a]"Do not lay your hand on the lad, or do anything to him; for [b]now I know that you fear God, since you have not [c]withheld your son, your only *son,* from Me."

To commit suggests not only bringing the matter to God, but also leaving it there.

GORDON LINDSAY

13Then Abraham lifted his eyes and looked, and there behind *him was* a ram caught in a thicket by its horns. So Abraham went and took the ram, and offered it up for a burnt offering instead of his son. 14And Abraham called the name of the place, [1]The-LORD-Will-Provide; as it is said *to* this day, "In the Mount of the LORD it shall be provided."

15Then the Angel of the LORD called to Abraham a second time out of heaven, 16and said: [a]"By Myself I have sworn, says the LORD, because you have done this thing, and have not withheld your son, your only *son*— 17blessing I will [a]bless you, and multiplying I will multiply your descendants [b]as the stars of the heaven [c]and as the sand which *is* on the seashore; and [d]your descendants shall possess the gate of their enemies. 18[a]In your seed all the nations of the earth shall be blessed, [b]because you have obeyed My voice." 19So Abraham returned to his young men, and they rose and went together to [a]Beersheba; and Abraham dwelt at Beersheba.

8 [a] John 1:29, 36 [b] Ex. 12:3–6
9 [a] [Heb. 11:17–19]
11 [a] Gen. 16:7–11; 21:17, 18; 31:11
12 [a] 1 Sam. 15:22 [b] James 2:21, 22 [c] Gen. 22:2, 16
14 [1] Heb. *YHWH Yireh*
16 [a] Ps. 105:9
17 [a] Gen. 17:16; 26:3, 24 [b] Gen. 15:5; 26:4 [c] Gen. 13:16; 32:12 [d] Gen. 24:60
18 [a] Gen. 12:3; 18:18; 26:4 [b] Gen. 18:19; 22:3, 10; 26:5
19 [a] Gen. 21:31
20 [a] Gen. 11:29; 24:15
21 [a] Job 1:1 [b] Job 32:2
23 [a] Gen. 24:15 [1] *Rebecca,* Rom. 9:10

CHAPTER 23
2 [a] Josh. 14:15; 15:13; 21:11 [b] Gen. 13:18; 23:19
3 [a] Gen. 10:15; 15:20
4 [a] [Gen. 17:8] [b] Acts 7:5, 16
6 [a] Gen. 13:2; 14:14; 24:35 [1] Lit. *prince of God*
8 [1] *entreat*
9 [a] Gen. 25:9
10 [a] Gen. 23:18; 34:20, 24
11 [a] 2 Sam. 24:21–24

The Family of Nahor

20Now it came to pass after these things that it was told Abraham, saying, "Indeed [a]Milcah also has borne children to your brother Nahor: 21[a]Huz his firstborn, Buz his brother, Kemuel the father [b]of Aram, 22Chesed, Hazo, Pildash, Jidlaph, and Bethuel." 23And [a]Bethuel begot [1]Rebekah. These eight Milcah bore to Nahor, Abraham's brother. 24His concubine, whose name was Reumah, also bore Tebah, Gaham, Thahash, and Maachah.

Sarah's Death and Burial

23 Sarah lived one hundred and twenty-seven years; *these were* the years of the life of Sarah. 2So Sarah died in [a]Kirjath Arba (that *is,* [b]Hebron) in the land of Canaan, and Abraham came to mourn for Sarah and to weep for her.

3Then Abraham stood up from before his dead, and spoke to the sons of [a]Heth, saying, 4[a]"I *am* a foreigner and a visitor among you. [b]Give me property for a burial place among you, that I may bury my dead out of my sight."

5And the sons of Heth answered Abraham, saying to him, 6"Hear us, my lord: You *are* [a]a [1]mighty prince among us; bury your dead in the choicest of our burial places. None of us will withhold from you his burial place, that you may bury your dead."

7Then Abraham stood up and bowed himself to the people of the land, the sons of Heth. 8And he spoke with them, saying, "If it is your wish that I bury my dead out of my sight, hear me, and [1]meet with Ephron the son of Zohar for me, 9that he may give me the cave of [a]Machpelah which he has, which *is* at the end of his field. Let him give it to me at the full price, as property for a burial place among you."

10Now Ephron dwelt among the sons of Heth; and Ephron the Hittite answered Abraham in the presence of the sons of Heth, all who [a]entered at the gate of his city, saying, 11[a]"No, my lord, hear me: I give you the field and the cave that *is* in it; I give it to you in the presence of the sons of my people. I give it to you. Bury your dead!"

12Then Abraham bowed himself down before the people of the land; 13and he spoke to Ephron in the hearing of the people of the land, saying, "If you *will give it,* please hear me. I will give you money for

Genesis 22:17, 18

Dear Woman of Destiny,

As I meditated on Genesis 22:17, 18, I was amazed at the breadth and scope of this promise God gave to Abraham for his family. In fact, the first time I remember reading the words of verse 17 after I had children, I boldly went to the Lord and said, "Lord, I'd like to make covenant with You, too, regarding my own children. I want them to possess the gate of the enemy."

This verse so burned in my heart that I titled my book on intercessory prayer *Possessing the Gates of the Enemy*. Why? I felt that God wanted the mothers and fathers He had raised up to spiritually impact whole nations through intercession. We can be blessed and multiply even if we aren't natural, physical parents. I don't think it is stretching this verse too far to believe that God will give us a harvest of those we have led to the Lord, even those who are gatekeepers for their nations. This also includes the influencers of society who stand in important gates into our cities—for example, our government officials, lawyers, and teachers.

The key to receiving this promise for yourself and your generation is obedience. When we walk in obedience to God, He will bless us. What kind of blessing do you want from God for your obedience? I personally want souls for the Kingdom as my reward. I want to lead people to the Lord, to see them saved, and to cheer them on as they go out and change the world for Jesus Christ.

To those of you who have children, either physical or spiritual, don't be afraid to ask great things for them. Make covenant with the Almighty God concerning those little ones. Mark them for God as your inheritance and declare that each succeeding generation will do greater things for God than the last. Pray that they will shake their known world and make a mighty impact in their place of destiny.

Beloved, I am believing for great things for you and your seed. Don't be afraid to ask God for big things for your children and for your children's children. I personally want my children to accomplish twice what I've been able to achieve in God during my life. They are my legacy and joy. I am asking God to give them the double portion.

As a woman of destiny, you can change not only your own world, but that of those who come after you.

Cindy Jacobs

the field; take *it* from me and I will bury
my dead there."
[14]And Ephron answered Abraham, saying to him, [15]"My lord, listen to me; the
land *is worth* four hundred [a]shekels of silver. What *is* that between you and me? So
bury your dead." [16]And Abraham listened
to Ephron; and Abraham [a]weighed out
the silver for Ephron which he had named
in the hearing of the sons of Heth, four
hundred shekels of silver, currency of the
merchants.
[17]So [a]the field of Ephron which *was* in
Machpelah, which *was* before Mamre, the
field and the cave which *was* in it, and all
the trees that *were* in the field, which
were within all the surrounding borders,
were deeded [18]to Abraham as a possession
in the presence of the sons of Heth, before
all who went in at the gate of his city.
[19]And after this, Abraham buried Sarah
his wife in the cave of the field of Machpelah, before Mamre (that *is,* Hebron) in the
land of Canaan. [20]So the field and the cave
that *is* in it [a]were deeded to Abraham by
the sons of Heth as property for a burial
place.

A Bride for Isaac

24 Now Abraham [a]was old, well advanced in age; and the LORD [b]had
blessed Abraham in all things. [2]So Abraham said [a]to the oldest servant of his
house, who [b]ruled over all that he had,
"Please, [c]put your hand under my thigh,
[3]and I will make you [a]swear[1] by the LORD,
the God of heaven and the God of the
earth, that [b]you will not take a wife for my
son from the daughters of the Canaanites,
among whom I dwell; [4][a]but you shall go
[b]to my country and to my family, and take
a wife for my son Isaac."
[5]And the servant said to him, "Perhaps
the woman will not be willing to follow
me to this land. Must I take your son back
to the land from which you came?"
[6]But Abraham said to him, "Beware
that you do not take my son back there.
[7]The LORD God of heaven, who [a]took me
from my father's house and from the land
of my family, and who spoke to me and
swore to me, saying, [b]'To your [1]descen-
dants I give this land,' [c]He will send His
angel before you, and you shall take a wife
for my son from there. [8]And if the woman
is not willing to follow you, then [a]you will
be released from this oath; only do not
take my son back there." [9]So the servant
put his hand under the thigh of Abraham
his master, and swore to him concerning
this matter.
[10]Then the servant took ten of his master's camels and departed, [a]for all his
master's goods *were in* his hand. And he
arose and went to Mesopotamia, to [b]the
city of Nahor. [11]And he made his camels
kneel down outside the city by a well of
water at evening time, the time [a]when
women go out to draw *water.* [12]Then he
[a]said, "O LORD God of my master Abraham, please [b]give me success this day, and
show kindness to my master Abraham.
[13]Behold, *here* [a]I stand by the well of water, and [b]the daughters of the men of the
city are coming out to draw water. [14]Now
let it be that the young woman to whom
I say, 'Please let down your pitcher that I
may drink,' and she says, 'Drink, and I will
also give your camels a drink'—*let* her *be
the one* You have appointed for Your servant Isaac. And [a]by this I will know that
You have shown kindness to my master."
[15]And it happened, [a]before he had finished speaking, that behold, [b]Rebekah,[1]
who was born to Bethuel, son of [c]Milcah,
the wife of Nahor, Abraham's brother,
came out with her pitcher on her shoulder. [16]Now the young woman [a]*was* very
beautiful to behold, a virgin; no man had
known her. And she went down to the
well, filled her pitcher, and came up.
[17]And the servant ran to meet her and
said, "Please let me drink a little water
from your pitcher."
[18][a]So she said, "Drink, my lord." Then
she quickly let her pitcher down to her
hand, and gave him a drink. [19]And when
she had finished giving him a drink, she
said, "I will draw *water* for your camels
also, until they have finished drinking."
[20]Then she quickly emptied her pitcher
into the trough, ran back to the well to
draw *water,* and drew for all his camels.
[21]And the man, wondering at her, remained silent so as to know whether [a]the
LORD had made his journey prosperous or
not.
[22]So it was, when the camels had finished drinking, that the man took a gold-
en [a]nose ring weighing half a shekel, and
two bracelets for her wrists weighing ten
shekels of gold, [23]and said, "Whose daughter *are* you? Tell me, please, is there room
in your father's house for us [1]to lodge?"
[24]So she said to him, [a]"I *am* the daughter of Bethuel, Milcah's son, whom she

15 a Ex. 30:13
16 a Jer. 32:9, 10
17 a Gen. 25:9; 49:29–32; 50:13
20 a Jer. 32:10, 11

CHAPTER 24
1 a Gen. 18:11; 21:5 b Gen. 12:2; 13:2; 24:35
2 a Gen. 15:2 b Gen. 24:10; 39:4–6 c Gen. 47:29
3 a Gen. 14:19, 22 b Deut. 7:3 *1 take an oath*
4 a Gen. 28:2 b Gen. 12:1
7 a Gen. 12:1; 24:3 b Gen. 12:7; 13:15; 15:18; 17:8 c Ex. 23:20, 23; 33:2 *1* Lit. *seed*
8 a Josh. 2:17–20
10 a Gen. 24:2, 22 b Gen. 11:31, 32; 22:20; 27:43; 29:5
11 a Ex. 2:16
12 a Ex. 3:6, 15 b Neh. 1:11
13 a Gen. 24:43 b Ex. 2:16
14 a Judg. 6:17, 37
15 a Is. 65:24 b Gen. 24:45; 25:20 c Gen. 22:20, 23 *1 Rebecca,* Rom. 9:10
16 a Gen. 12:11; 26:7; 29:17
18 a [1 Pet. 3:8, 9]
21 a Gen. 24:12–14, 27, 52
22 a Ex. 32:2, 3
23 *1 to spend the night*
24 a Gen. 22:23; 24:15

bore to Nahor." 25Moreover she said to
him, "We have both straw and feed
enough, and room to lodge."
26Then the man [a]bowed down his head
and worshiped the LORD. 27And he said,
[a]"Blessed *be* the LORD God of my master
Abraham, who has not forsaken [b]His mercy and His truth toward my master. As for
me, being on the way, the LORD [c]led me
to the house of my master's brethren."
28So the young woman ran and told her
mother's household these things.
29Now Rebekah had a brother whose
name *was* [a]Laban, and Laban ran out to
the man by the well. 30So it came to pass,
when he saw the nose ring, and the bracelets on his sister's wrists, and when he
heard the words of his sister Rebekah, saying, "Thus the man spoke to me," that he
went to the man. And there he stood by
the camels at the well. 31And he said,
"Come in, [a]O blessed of the LORD! Why do
you stand outside? For I have prepared the
house, and a place for the camels."
32Then the man came to the house. And
he unloaded the camels, and [a]provided
straw and feed for the camels, and water
to [b]wash his feet and the feet of the men
who *were* with him. 33*Food* was set before
him to eat, but he said, [a]"I will not eat
until I have told about my errand."
And he said, "Speak on."
34So he said, "I *am* Abraham's servant.
35The LORD [a]has blessed my master greatly, and he has become great; and He has
given him flocks and herds, silver and
gold, male and female servants, and camels and donkeys. 36And Sarah my master's
wife [a]bore a son to my master when she
was old; and [b]to him he has given all that
he has. 37Now my master [a]made me
swear, saying, 'You shall not take a wife
for my son from the daughters of the Canaanites, in whose land I dwell; 38[a]but you
shall go to my father's house and to my
family, and take a wife for my son.' 39[a]And
I said to my master, 'Perhaps the woman
will not follow me.' 40[a]But he said to me,
'The LORD, [b]before whom I walk, will send
His angel with you and [1]prosper your way;
and you shall take a wife for my son from
my family and from my father's house.
41[a]You will be clear from this oath when
you arrive among my family; for if they
will not give *her* to you, then you will be
released from my oath.'
42"And this day I came to the well and
said, [a]'O LORD God of my master Abraham, if You will now prosper the way in
which I go, 43[a]behold, I stand by the well
of water; and it shall come to pass that
when the virgin comes out to draw *water*,
and I say to her, "Please give me a little
water from your pitcher to drink," 44and
she says to me, "Drink, and I will draw for
your camels also,"—*let* her *be* the woman
whom the LORD has appointed for my
master's son.'
45[a]"But before I had finished [b]speaking
in my heart, there was Rebekah, coming
out with her pitcher on her shoulder; and
she went down to the well and drew *water*. And I said to her, 'Please let me drink.'
46And she made haste and let her pitcher
down from her *shoulder*, and said, 'Drink,
and I will give your camels a drink also.'
So I drank, and she gave the camels a
drink also. 47Then I asked her, and said,
'Whose daughter *are* you?' And she said,
'The daughter of Bethuel, Nahor's son,
whom Milcah bore to him.' So I put the
nose ring on her nose and the bracelets on
her wrists. 48[a]And I bowed my head and
worshiped the LORD, and blessed the LORD
God of my master Abraham, who had led
me in the way of truth to [b]take the daughter of my master's brother for his son.
49Now if you will [a]deal kindly and truly
with my master, tell me. And if not, tell
me, that I may turn to the right hand or
to the left."
50Then Laban and Bethuel answered
and said, [a]"The thing comes from the
LORD; we cannot [b]speak to you either bad
or good. 51[a]Here *is* Rebekah before you;
take *her* and go, and let her be your master's son's wife, as the LORD has spoken."
52And it came to pass, when Abraham's
servant heard their words, that [a]he worshiped the LORD, *bowing himself* to the
earth. 53Then the servant brought out
[a]jewelry of silver, jewelry of gold, and
clothing, and gave *them* to Rebekah. He
also gave [b]precious things to her brother
and to her mother.
54And he and the men who *were* with
him ate and drank and stayed all night.
Then they arose in the morning, and he
said, [a]"Send me away to my master."
55But her brother and her mother said,
"Let the young woman stay with us *a few*
days, at least ten; after that she may go."
56And he said to them, "Do not [1]hinder
me, since the LORD has prospered my way;
send me away so that I may go to my
master."

26 a Ex. 4:31
27 a Ex. 18:10 b Gen. 32:10 c Gen. 24:21, 48
29 a Gen. 29:5, 13
31 a Judg. 17:2
32 a Gen. 43:24 b Gen. 19:2
33 a John 4:34
35 a Gen. 13:2; 24:1
36 a Gen. 21:1–7 b Gen. 21:10; 25:5
37 a Gen. 24:2–4
38 a Gen. 24:4
39 a Gen. 24:5
40 a Gen. 24:7 b Gen. 5:22, 24; 17:1 *1 make your way successful*
41 a Gen. 24:8
42 a Gen. 24:12
43 a Gen. 24:13
45 a Gen. 24:15 b 1 Sam. 1:13
48 a Gen. 24:26, 52 b Gen. 22:23; 24:27
49 a Josh. 2:14
50 a Ps. 118:23 b Gen. 31:24, 29
51 a Gen. 20:15
52 a Gen. 24:26, 48
53 a Ex. 3:22; 11:2; 12:35 b 2 Chr. 21:3
54 a Gen. 24:56, 59; 30:25
56 *1 delay*

57So they said, "We will call the young
woman and ask her personally." 58Then
they called Rebekah and said to her, "Will
you go with this man?"
And she said, "I will go."
59So they sent away Rebekah their sister [a]and her nurse, and Abraham's servant
and his men. 60And they blessed Rebekah
and said to her:

"Our sister, *may* you *become*
[a]*The mother of* thousands of ten
thousands;
[b]And may your descendants possess
The gates of those who hate them."

61Then Rebekah and her maids arose,
and they rode on the camels and followed
the man. So the servant took Rebekah and
departed.
62Now Isaac came from the way of
[a]Beer Lahai Roi, for he dwelt in the
South. 63And Isaac went out [a]to meditate
in the field in the evening; and he lifted
his eyes and looked, and there, the camels
were coming. 64Then Rebekah lifted her
eyes, and when she saw Isaac [a]she dismounted from her camel; 65for she had
said to the servant, "Who *is* this man
walking in the field to meet us?"
The servant said, "It *is* my master." So
she took a veil and covered herself.
66And the servant told Isaac all the
things that he had done. 67Then Isaac
brought her into his mother Sarah's tent;
and he [a]took Rebekah and she became his
wife, and he loved her. So Isaac [b]was comforted after his mother's *death*.

Abraham and Keturah

25 Abraham again took a wife, and her
name *was* [a]Keturah. 2And [a]she
bore him Zimran, Jokshan, Medan, Midian, Ishbak, and Shuah. 3Jokshan begot
Sheba and Dedan. And the sons of Dedan
were Asshurim, Letushim, and Leum-
mim. 4And the sons of Midian *were*
Ephah, Epher, Hanoch, Abidah, and Eldaah. All these *were* the children of Keturah.
5And [a]Abraham gave all that he had to
Isaac. 6But Abraham gave gifts to the sons
of the concubines which Abraham had;
and while he was still living he [a]sent them
eastward, away from Isaac his son, to [b]the
country of the east.

Abraham's Death and Burial

7This *is* the sum of the years of Abraham's life which he lived: one hundred
and seventy-five years. 8Then Abraham
breathed his last and [a]died in a good old
age, an old man and full *of years,* and
[b]was gathered to his people. 9And [a]his
sons Isaac and Ishmael buried him in the
cave of [b]Machpelah, which *is* before Mamre, in the field of Ephron the son of Zohar
the Hittite, 10[a]the field which Abraham
purchased from the sons of Heth. [b]There
Abraham was buried, and Sarah his wife.
11And it came to pass, after the death of
Abraham, that God blessed his son Isaac.
And Isaac dwelt at [a]Beer Lahai Roi.

The Families of Ishmael and Isaac

12Now this *is* the [a]genealogy of Ishmael, Abraham's son, whom Hagar the Egyptian, Sarah's maidservant, bore to
Abraham. 13And [a]these *were* the names of
the sons of Ishmael, by their names, according to their generations: The firstborn of Ishmael, Nebajoth; then Kedar,
Adbeel, Mibsam, 14Mishma, Dumah, Massa, 15[1]Hadar, Tema, Jetur, Naphish, and
Kedemah. 16These *were* the sons of Ishmael and these *were* their names, by their
towns and their [1]settlements, [a]twelve
princes according to their nations.
17These *were* the years of the life of Ishmael: one hundred and thirty-seven
years; and [a]he breathed his last and died,
and was gathered to his people. 18[a](They
dwelt from Havilah as far as Shur, which
is east of Egypt as you go toward Assyria.)
He [1]died [b]in the presence of all his
brethren.
19This *is* the [a]genealogy of Isaac, Abraham's son. [b]Abraham begot Isaac. 20Isaac
was forty years old when he took Rebekah
as wife, [a]the daughter of Bethuel the Syrian of Padan Aram, [b]the sister of Laban the
Syrian. 21Now Isaac pleaded with the
LORD for his wife, because she *was* barren;
[a]and the LORD granted his plea, [b]and Rebekah his wife conceived. 22But the children struggled together within her; and
she said, "If *all is* well, why *am I like*
this?" [a]So she went to inquire of the
LORD.
23And the LORD said to her:

[a]"Two nations *are* in your womb,
Two peoples shall be separated from
your body;
One people shall be stronger than
[b]the other,

59 a Gen. 35:8
60 a Gen. 17:16 b Gen. 22:17; 28:14
62 a Gen. 16:14; 25:11
63 a Josh. 1:8
64 a Josh. 15:18
67 a Gen. 25:20; 29:20 b Gen. 23:1, 2; 38:12

CHAPTER 25

1 a 1 Chr. 1:32, 33
2 a 1 Chr. 1:32, 33
5 a Gen. 24:35, 36
6 a Gen. 21:14 b Judg. 6:3
8 a Gen. 15:15; 47:8, 9 b Gen. 25:17; 35:29; 49:29, 33
9 a Gen. 35:29; 50:13 b Gen. 23:9, 17; 49:30
10 a Gen. 23:3–16 b Gen. 49:31
11 a Gen. 16:14
12 a Gen. 11:10, 27; 16:15
13 a 1 Chr. 1:29–31
15 1 MT *Hadad*
16 a Gen. 17:20 1 *camps*
17 a Gen. 25:8; 49:33
18 a 1 Sam. 15:7 b Gen. 16:12 1 *fell*
19 a Gen. 36:1, 9 b Matt. 1:2
20 a Gen. 22:23; 24:15, 29, 67 b Gen. 24:29
21 a 1 Chr. 5:20 b Rom. 9:10–13
22 a 1 Sam. 1:15; 9:9; 10:22
23 a Gen. 17:4–6, 16; 24:60 b 2 Sam. 8:14

[c]And the older shall serve the
younger."

[24]So when her days were fulfilled *for
her* to give birth, indeed *there were* twins
in her womb. [25]And the first came out red.
He was [a]like a hairy garment all over; so
they called his name [1]Esau. [26]Afterward
his brother came out, and [a]his hand took
hold of Esau's heel; so [b]his name was
called [1]Jacob. Isaac *was* sixty years old
when she bore them.

[27]So the boys grew. And Esau was [a]a
skillful hunter, a man of the field; but Jacob was [b]a [1]mild man, [c]dwelling in tents.
[28]And Isaac loved Esau because he [a]ate *of
his* game, [b]but Rebekah loved Jacob.

Esau Sells His Birthright

[29]Now Jacob cooked a stew; and Esau
came in from the field, and he *was* weary.
[30]And Esau said to Jacob, "Please feed me
with that same red *stew,* for I *am* weary."
Therefore his name was called [1]Edom.

[31]But Jacob said, "Sell me your birthright as of this day."

[32]And Esau said, "Look, I *am* about to
die; so [a]what *is* this birthright to me?"

[33]Then Jacob said, [1]"Swear to me as of
this day."

So he swore to him, and [a]sold his birthright to Jacob. [34]And Jacob gave Esau
bread and stew of lentils; then [a]he ate and
drank, arose, and went his way. Thus Esau
[b]despised *his* birthright.

Isaac and Abimelech

26 There was a famine in the land, besides [a]the first famine that was in
the days of Abraham. And Isaac went to
[b]Abimelech king of the Philistines, in
Gerar.

[2]Then the LORD appeared to him and
said: [a]"Do not go down to Egypt; live in
[b]the land of which I shall tell you. [3][a]Dwell
in this land, and [b]I will be with you and
[c]bless you; for to you and your descendants [d]I give all these lands, and I will
perform [e]the oath which I swore to Abraham your father. [4]And [a]I will make your
descendants multiply as the stars of heav-
en; I will give to your descendants all
these lands; [b]and in your seed all the nations of the earth shall be blessed; [5][a]be-
cause Abraham obeyed My voice and kept
My charge, My commandments, My statutes, and My laws."

[6]So Isaac dwelt in Gerar. [7]And the men
of the place asked about his wife. And [a]he
said, "She *is* my sister"; for [b]he was afraid
to say, *"She is* my wife," *because he
thought,* "lest the men of the place kill me
for Rebekah, because she *is* [c]beautiful to
behold." [8]Now it came to pass, when he
had been there a long time, that Abimelech king of the Philistines looked
through a window, and saw, and there was
Isaac, [1]showing endearment to Rebekah
his wife. [9]Then Abimelech called Isaac and
said, "Quite obviously she *is* your wife; so
how could you say, 'She *is* my sister'?"

Isaac said to him, "Because I said, 'Lest
I die on account of her.' "

[10]And Abimelech said, "What *is* this you
have done to us? One of the people might
soon have lain with your wife, and [a]you
would have brought guilt on us." [11]So
Abimelech charged all *his* people, saying,
"He who [a]touches this man or his wife
shall surely be put to death."

[12]Then Isaac sowed in that land, and
reaped in the same year [a]a hundredfold;
and the LORD [b]blessed him. [13]The man
[a]began to prosper, and continued prospering until he became very prosperous;
[14]for he had possessions of flocks and possessions of herds and a great number of
servants. So the Philistines [a]envied him.
[15]Now the Philistines had stopped up all
the wells [a]which his father's servants had
dug in the days of Abraham his father, and
they had filled them with earth. [16]And
Abimelech said to Isaac, "Go away from
us, for [a]you are much mightier than we."

[17]Then Isaac departed from there and
[1]pitched his tent in the Valley of Gerar,
and dwelt there. [18]And Isaac dug again the
wells of water which they had dug in the
days of Abraham his father, for the Philistines had stopped them up after the death
of Abraham. [a]He called them by the
names which his father had called them.

[19]Also Isaac's servants dug in the valley,
and found a well of running water there.
[20]But the herdsmen of Gerar [a]quarreled
with Isaac's herdsmen, saying, "The water
is ours." So he called the name of the well
[1]Esek, because they quarreled with him.
[21]Then they dug another well, and they
quarreled over that *one* also. So he called
its name [1]Sitnah. [22]And he moved from
there and dug another well, and they did
not quarrel over it. So he called its name
[1]Rehoboth, because he said, "For now the

23 [c]Rom. 9:12
25 [a]Gen. 27:11, 16, 23 [1]Lit. *Hairy*
26 [a]Hos. 12:3 [b]Gen. 27:36 [1]*Supplanter* or *Deceitful,* lit. *One Who Takes the Heel*
27 [a]Gen. 27:3, 5 [b]Job 1:1, 8 [c]Heb. 11:9 [1]Lit. *complete*
28 [a]Gen. 27:4, 19, 25, 31 [b]Gen. 27:6–10
30 [1]Lit. *Red*
32 [a]Mark 8:36, 37
33 [a]Heb. 12:16 [1]*Take an oath*
34 [a]Eccl. 8:15 [b]Heb. 12:16, 17

CHAPTER 26
1 [a]Gen. 12:10 [b]Gen. 20:1, 2
2 [a]Gen. 12:7; 17:1; 18:1; 35:9 [b]Gen. 12:1
3 [a]Heb. 11:9 [b]Gen. 28:13, 15 [c]Gen. 12:2 [d]Gen. 12:7; 13:15; 15:18 [e]Gen. 22:16
4 [a]Gen. 15:5; 22:17 [b]Gen. 12:3; 22:18
5 [a]Gen. 22:16, 18
7 [a]Gen. 12:13; 20:2, 12, 13 [b]Prov. 29:25 [c]Gen. 12:11; 24:16; 29:17
8 [1]*caressing*
10 [a]Gen. 20:9
11 [a]Ps. 105:15
12 [a]Matt. 13:8, 23 [b]Gen. 24:1; 25:8, 11; 26:3
13 [a][Prov. 10:22]
14 [a]Gen. 37:11
15 [a]Gen. 21:25, 30
16 [a]Ex. 1:9
17 [1]*camped*
18 [a]Gen. 21:31
20 [a]Gen. 21:25 [1]Lit. *Quarrel*
21 [1]Lit. *Enmity*
22 [1]Lit. *Spaciousness*

LORD has made room for us, and we shall
[a]be fruitful in the land."
[23]Then he went up from there to Beersheba. [24]And the LORD [a]appeared to him
the same night and said, [b]"I *am* the God
of your father Abraham; [c]do not fear, for
[d]I *am* with you. I will bless you and multiply your descendants for My servant Abraham's sake." [25]So he [a]built an altar there
and [b]called on the name of the LORD, and
he pitched his tent there; and there Isaac's
servants dug a well.
[26]Then Abimelech came to him from
Gerar with Ahuzzath, one of his friends,
[a]and Phichol the commander of his army.
[27]And Isaac said to them, "Why have you
come to me, [a]since you hate me and have
[b]sent me away from you?"
[28]But they said, "We have certainly seen
that the LORD [a]is with you. So we said,
'Let there now be an oath between us, between you and us; and let us make a [1]cov-
enant with you, [29]that you will do us no
harm, since we have not touched you, and
since we have done nothing to you but
good and have sent you away in peace.
[a]You *are* now the blessed of the LORD.'"
[30][a]So he made them a feast, and they
ate and drank. [31]Then they arose early in
the morning and [a]swore an oath with one
another; and Isaac sent them away, and
they departed from him in peace.
[32]It came to pass the same day that
Isaac's servants came and told him about
the well which they had dug, and said
to him, "We have found water." [33]So he
called it [1]Shebah. [a]Therefore the name of
the city *is* [2]Beersheba to this day.
[34][a]When Esau was forty years old, he
took as wives Judith the daughter of Beeri
the Hittite, and Basemath the daughter of
Elon the Hittite. [35]And [a]they were a grief
of mind to Isaac and Rebekah.

Isaac Blesses Jacob

27 Now it came to pass, when Isaac
was [a]old and [b]his eyes were so dim
that he could not see, that he called Esau
his older son and said to him, "My son."
And he answered him, "Here I am."
[2]Then he said, "Behold now, I am old.
I [a]do not know the day of my death.
[3][a]Now therefore, please take your weapons, your quiver and your bow, and go out
to the field and hunt game for me. [4]And
make me [1]savory food, such as I love, and
bring *it* to me that I may eat, that my soul
[a]may bless you before I die."
[5]Now Rebekah was listening when Isaac
spoke to Esau his son. And Esau went to
the field to hunt game and to bring *it*. [6]So
Rebekah spoke to Jacob her son, saying,
"Indeed I heard your father speak to Esau
your brother, saying, [7]'Bring me game
and make [1]savory food for me, that I may
eat it and bless you in the presence of the
LORD before my death.' [8]Now therefore,
my son, [a]obey my voice according to what
I command you. [9]Go now to the flock and
bring me from there two choice kids of
the goats, and I will make [a]savory food
from them for your father, such as he
loves. [10]Then you shall take *it* to your father, that he may eat *it*, and that he [a]may
bless you before his death."
[11]And Jacob said to Rebekah his
mother, "Look, [a]Esau my brother *is* a
hairy man, and I *am* a smooth-*skinned*
man. [12]Perhaps my father will [a]feel me,
and I shall seem to be a deceiver to him;
and I shall bring [b]a curse on myself and
not a blessing."
[13]But his mother said to him, [a]"*Let*
your curse *be* on me, my son; only obey
my voice, and go, get *them* for me." [14]And
he went and got *them* and brought *them*
to his mother, and his mother [a]made [1]sa-
vory food, such as his father loved. [15]Then
Rebekah took [a]the choice clothes of her
elder son Esau, which *were* with her in
the house, and put them on Jacob her
younger son. [16]And she put the skins of
the kids of the goats on his hands and on
the smooth part of his neck. [17]Then she
gave the savory food and the bread, which
she had prepared, into the hand of her son
Jacob.
[18]So he went to his father and said, "My
father."
And he said, "Here I am. Who *are* you,
my son?"
[19]Jacob said to his father, "I *am* Esau
your firstborn; I have done just as you told
me; please arise, sit and eat of my game,
[a]that your soul may bless me."
[20]But Isaac said to his son, "How *is it*
that you have found *it* so quickly, my
son?"
And he said, "Because the LORD your
God brought *it* to me."
[21]Isaac said to Jacob, "Please come
near, that I [a]may feel you, my son, whether you *are* really my son Esau or not."
[22]So Jacob went near to Isaac his father,
and he felt him and said, "The voice *is*
Jacob's voice, but the hands *are* the hands

22 a Gen. 17:6; 28:3; 41:52
24 a Gen. 26:2 b Gen. 17:7, 8; 24:12 c Gen. 15:1 d Gen. 26:3, 4
25 a Gen. 12:7, 8; 13:4, 18; 22:9; 33:20 b Ps. 116:17
26 a Gen. 21:22
27 a Judg. 11:7 b Gen. 26:16
28 a Gen. 21:22, 23 *1 treaty*
29 a Gen. 24:31
30 a Gen. 19:3
31 a Gen. 21:31
33 a Gen. 21:31; 28:10 *1* Lit. *Oath* or *Seven* *2* Lit. *Well of the Oath* or *Well of the Seven*
34 a Gen. 28:8; 36:2
35 a Gen. 27:46; 28:1, 8

CHAPTER 27
1 a Gen. 35:28 b Gen. 48:10
2 a [Prov. 27:1]
3 a Gen. 25:27, 28
4 a Deut. 33:1 *1 tasty*
7 *1 tasty*
8 a Gen. 27:13, 43
9 a Gen. 27:4
10 a Gen. 27:4; 48:16
11 a Gen. 25:25
12 a Gen. 27:21, 22 b Deut. 27:18
13 a Gen. 43:9
14 a Prov. 23:3 *1 tasty*
15 a Gen. 27:27
19 a Gen. 27:4
21 a Gen. 27:12

of Esau." 23And he did not recognize him,
because [a]his hands were hairy like his
brother Esau's hands; so he blessed him.
24Then he said, "*Are* you really my son
Esau?"
He said, "I *am.*"
25He said, "Bring *it* near to me, and I
will eat of my son's game, so [a]that my soul
may bless you." So he brought *it* near
to him, and he ate; and he brought him
wine, and he drank. 26Then his father
Isaac said to him, "Come near now and
kiss me, my son." 27And he came near and
[a]kissed him; and he smelled the smell of
his clothing, and blessed him and said:

"Surely, [b]the smell of my son
Is like the smell of a field
Which the LORD has blessed.
28 Therefore may [a]God give you
Of [b]the dew of heaven,
Of [c]the fatness of the earth,
And [d]plenty of grain and wine.
29 [a]Let peoples serve you,
And nations bow down to you.
Be master over your brethren,
And [b]let your mother's sons bow
down to you.
[c]Cursed *be* everyone who curses you,
And blessed *be* those who bless
you!"

Esau's Lost Hope

30Now it happened, as soon as Isaac had
finished blessing Jacob, and Jacob had
scarcely gone out from the presence of
Isaac his father, that Esau his brother
came in from his hunting. 31He also had
made [1]savory food, and brought it to his
father, and said to his father, "Let my father arise and [a]eat of his son's game, that
your soul may bless me."
32And his father Isaac said to him, "Who
are you?"
So he said, "I *am* your son, your firstborn, Esau."
33Then Isaac trembled exceedingly, and
said, "Who? Where *is* the one who hunted
game and brought *it* to me? I ate all *of it*
before you came, and I have blessed
him—[a]*and* indeed he shall be blessed."
34When Esau heard the words of his father, [a]he cried with an exceedingly great
and bitter cry, and said to his father,
"Bless me—me also, O my father!"
35But he said, "Your brother came with
deceit and has taken away your blessing."

36And *Esau* said, [a]"Is he not rightly
named [1]Jacob? For he has supplanted me
these two times. He took away my birthright, and now look, he has taken away my
blessing!" And he said, "Have you not reserved a blessing for me?"
37Then Isaac answered and said to Esau,
[a]"Indeed I have made him your master,
and all his brethren I have given to him
as servants; with [b]grain and wine I have
[1]sustained him. What shall I do now for
you, my son?"
38And Esau said to his father, "Have you
only one blessing, my father? Bless me—
me also, O my father!" And Esau lifted up
his voice [a]and wept.
39Then Isaac his father answered and
said to him:

"Behold, [a]your dwelling shall be of
the [1]fatness of the earth,
And of the dew of heaven from
above.
40 By your sword you shall live,
And [a]you shall serve your brother;
And [b]it shall come to pass, when
you become restless,
That you shall break his yoke from
your neck."

Jacob Escapes from Esau

41So Esau [a]hated Jacob because of the
blessing with which his father blessed
him, and Esau said in his heart, [b]"The
days of mourning for my father [1]are at
hand; [c]then I will kill my brother Jacob."
42And the words of Esau her older son
were told to Rebekah. So she sent and
called Jacob her younger son, and said to
him, "Surely your brother Esau [a]comforts
himself concerning you *by intending* to
kill you. 43Now therefore, my son, obey
my voice: arise, flee to my brother Laban
[a]in Haran. 44And stay with him a [a]few
days, until your brother's fury turns away,
45until your brother's anger turns away
from you, and he forgets what you have
done to him; then I will send and bring
you from there. Why should I be bereaved
also of you both in one day?"
46And Rebekah said to Isaac, [a]"I am
weary of my life because of the daughters
of Heth; [b]if Jacob takes a wife of the
daughters of Heth, like these *who are* the
daughters of the land, what good will my
life be to me?"

23 [a]Gen. 27:16
25 [a]Gen. 27:4, 10, 19, 31
27 [a]Gen. 29:13 [b]Song 4:11
28 [a]Heb. 11:20 [b]Deut. 33:13, 28 [c]Gen. 45:18 [d]Deut. 7:13; 33:28
29 [a]Gen. 9:25; 25:23 [b]Gen. 37:7, 10; 49:8 [c]Gen. 12:2, 3
31 [a]Gen. 27:4 [1] *tasty*
33 [a]Gen. 25:23; 28:3, 4
34 [a][Heb. 12:17]
36 [a]Gen. 25:26, 32–34 [1] *Supplanter* or *Deceitful,* lit. *One Who Takes the Heel*
37 [a]2 Sam. 8:14 [b]Gen. 27:28, 29 [1] *provided support for*
38 [a]Heb. 12:17
39 [a]Heb. 11:20 [1] *fertility*
40 [a]Gen. 25:23; 27:29 [b]2 Kin. 8:20–22
41 [a]Gen. 26:27; 32:3–11; 37:4, 5, 8 [b]Gen. 50:2–4, 10 [c]Obad. 10 [1] *are soon here*
42 [a]Ps. 64:5
43 [a]Gen. 11:31; 25:20; 28:2, 5
44 [a]Gen. 31:41
46 [a]Gen. 26:34, 35; 28:8 [b]Gen. 24:3

28 Then Isaac called Jacob and
[a]blessed him, and [1]charged him,
and said to him: [b]"You shall not take a
wife from the daughters of Canaan.
2[a]Arise, go to [b]Padan Aram, to the house
of [c]Bethuel your mother's father; and take
yourself a wife from there of the daughters of [d]Laban your mother's brother.

God Almighty, I pray that You will bless ____, and that You will make them fruitful and multiply them.

FROM GENESIS 28:3

3 "May [a]God Almighty bless you,
And make you [b]fruitful and
multiply you,
That you may be an assembly of
peoples;
4 And give you [a]the blessing of
Abraham,
To you and your descendants with
you,
That you may inherit the land
[b]In[1] which you are a stranger,
Which God gave to Abraham."

5So Isaac sent Jacob away, and he went to
Padan Aram, to Laban the son of Bethuel
the Syrian, the brother of Rebekah, the
mother of Jacob and Esau.

Esau Marries Mahalath

6Esau saw that Isaac had blessed Jacob
and sent him away to Padan Aram to take
himself a wife from there, *and that* as he
blessed him he gave him a charge, saying,
"You shall not take a wife from the daughters of Canaan," 7and that Jacob had
obeyed his father and his mother and had
gone to Padan Aram. 8Also Esau saw [a]that
the daughters of Canaan did not please his
father Isaac. 9So Esau went to Ishmael
and [a]took [b]Mahalath the daughter of Ishmael, Abraham's son, [c]the sister of Nebajoth, to be his wife in addition to the wives
he had.

Jacob's Vow at Bethel

10Now Jacob [a]went out from Beersheba
and went toward [b]Haran. 11So he came to
a certain place and stayed there all night,
because the sun had set. And he took one
of the stones of that place and put it at his
head, and he lay down in that place to
sleep. 12Then he [a]dreamed, and behold, a
ladder *was* set up on the earth, and its top
reached to heaven; and there [b]the angels
of God were ascending and descending
on it.

13[a]And behold, the LORD stood above it
and said: [b]"I *am* the LORD God of Abraham
your father and the God of Isaac; [c]the land
on which you lie I will give to you and
your descendants. 14Also your [a]descen-
dants shall be as the dust of the earth; you
shall spread abroad [b]to the west and the
east, to the north and the south; and in
you and [c]in your seed all the families of
the earth shall be blessed. 15Behold, [a]I *am*
with you and will [b]keep[1] you wherever
you go, and will [c]bring you back to this
land; for [d]I will not leave you [e]until I have
done what I have spoken to you."

16Then Jacob awoke from his sleep and
said, "Surely the LORD is in [a]this place,
and I did not know *it.*" 17And he was afraid
and said, "How awesome *is* this place!
This *is* none other than the house of God,
and this *is* the gate of heaven!"

18Then Jacob rose early in the morning,
and took the stone that he had put at his
head, [a]set it up as a pillar, [b]and poured oil
on top of it. 19And he called the name of
[a]that place [1]Bethel; but the name of that
city had been Luz previously. 20[a]Then Jacob made a vow, saying, "If [b]God will be
with me, and keep me in this way that I
am going, and give me [c]bread to eat and
clothing to put on, 21so that [a]I come back
to my father's house in peace, [b]then the
LORD shall be my God. 22And this stone
which I have set as a pillar [a]shall be God's
house, [b]and of all that You give me I will
surely give a [1]tenth to You."

Jacob Meets Rachel

29 So Jacob went on his journey [a]and
came to the land of the people of
the East. 2And he looked, and saw a [a]well
in the field; and behold, there *were* three
flocks of sheep lying by it; for out of that
well they watered the flocks. A large stone
was on the well's mouth. 3Now all the
flocks would be gathered there; and they
would roll the stone from the well's
mouth, water the sheep, and put the stone
back in its place on the well's mouth.

CHAPTER 28
1 a Gen. 27:33 b Gen. 24:3 *1 commanded*
2 a Hos. 12:12 b Gen. 25:20 c Gen. 22:23 d Gen. 24:29; 27:43; 29:5
3 a Gen. 17:16; 35:11; 48:3 b Gen. 26:4, 24
4 a Gen. 12:2, 3; 22:17 b Gen. 17:8; 23:4; 36:7 *1 Lit. Of your sojournings*
8 a Gen. 24:3; 26:34, 35; 27:46
9 a Gen. 26:34, 35 b Gen. 36:2, 3 c Gen. 25:13
10 a Hos. 12:12 b Gen. 12:4, 5; 27:43; 29:4
12 a Gen. 31:10; 41:1 b John 1:51
13 a Gen. 35:1; 48:3 b Gen. 26:24 c Gen. 13:15, 17; 26:3; 35:12
14 a Gen. 13:16; 22:17 b Gen. 13:14, 15 c Gen. 12:3; 18:18; 22:18; 26:4
15 a Gen. 26:3, 24; 31:3 b Gen. 48:16 c Gen. 35:6; 48:21 d Deut. 7:9; 31:6, 8 e Num. 23:19 *1 protect*
16 a Ex. 3:5
18 a Gen. 31:13, 45 b Lev. 8:10–12
19 a Judg. 1:23, 26 *1 Lit. House of God*
20 a Judg. 11:30 b Gen. 28:15 c 1 Tim. 6:8
21 a Judg. 11:31 b Deut. 26:17
22 a Gen. 35:7, 14 b Gen. 14:20 *1 tithe*

CHAPTER 29
1 a Num. 23:7
2 a Gen. 24:10, 11

4 And Jacob said to them, "My brethren,
where *are* you from?"
And they said, "We *are* from [a]Haran."
5 Then he said to them, "Do you know
[a]Laban the son of Nahor?"
And they said, "We know him."
6 So he said to them, [a]"Is he well?"
And they said, "*He is* well. And look, his
daughter Rachel [b]is coming with the
sheep."
7 Then he said, "Look, *it is* still [1]high
day; *it is* not time for the cattle to be gathered together. Water the sheep, and go
and feed *them*."
8 But they said, "We cannot until all the
flocks are gathered together, and they
have rolled the stone from the well's
mouth; then we water the sheep."
9 Now while he was still speaking with
them, [a]Rachel came with her father's
sheep, for she was a shepherdess. 10 And it
came to pass, when Jacob saw Rachel the
daughter of Laban his mother's brother,
and the sheep of Laban his mother's
brother, that Jacob went near and [a]rolled
the stone from the well's mouth, and watered the flock of Laban his mother's
brother. 11 Then Jacob [a]kissed Rachel, and
lifted up his voice and wept. 12 And Jacob
told Rachel that he *was* [a]her father's relative and that he *was* Rebekah's son. [b]So
she ran and told her father.
13 Then it came to pass, when Laban
heard the report about Jacob his sister's
son, that [a]he ran to meet him, and embraced him and kissed him, and brought
him to his house. So he told Laban all
these things. 14 And Laban said to him,
[a]"Surely you *are* my bone and my flesh."
And he stayed with him for a month.

Jacob Marries Leah and Rachel

15 Then Laban said to Jacob, "Because
you *are* my relative, should you therefore
serve me for nothing? Tell me, [a]what

4 a Gen. 11:31; 28:10
5 a Gen. 24:24, 29; 28:2
6 a Gen. 43:27 b Ex. 2:16, 17
7 *1 early in the day*
9 a Ex. 2:16
10 a Ex. 2:17
11 a Gen. 33:4; 45:14, 15
12 a Gen. 13:8; 14:14, 16; 28:5 b Gen. 24:28
13 a Gen. 24:29–31
14 a Gen. 2:23; 37:27
15 a Gen. 30:28; 31:41

LEAH

She was the unwanted one, the unattractive one, the one her father used as a trick. She was Leah. By birth, she was Rachel's older sister. And, by deceit, she was Jacob's first wife. She must have seen the disappointment in his eyes when he discovered she wasn't the woman he'd spent seven years longing and working for. And she must have known, as well as any woman today, the deep and lasting sting of rejection.

But, for all his weakness and all his cunning, her father did provide for her. And for every woman who stands in the shadow of one who seems more beautiful or more brilliant, there is a Father who says, "This one is worthy." There is a Father who is looking out for you. There is a Father in whose eyes you are the loveliest of all. He is a Father who delights in you so much that He sings and rejoices over you (see Zeph. 3:17). It is time to see yourself as He sees you—the apple of His eye, the joy of His heart, the masterpiece of His hand.

Leah may have felt inferior to Rachel, and we know she felt unloved by Jacob (see Gen. 29:31); but her heavenly Father had a purpose for her life. She bore Jacob a daughter and six sons, among them Levi and Judah. From Levi, the priestly tribe arose and ministered to God for the entire nation of Israel. From Judah came King David and his royal lineage, which included Jesus Christ.

God has a destiny for you, too. Find a place to be alone with Him, not simply to seek His will, but to let Him show you who He created you to be, and to let Him tell you how beautiful He thinks you are.

should your wages *be?*" 16Now Laban had
two daughters: the name of the elder *was*
Leah, and the name of the younger *was*
Rachel. 17Leah's eyes *were* [1]delicate, but
Rachel was [a]beautiful of form and appear-
ance.

18Now Jacob loved Rachel; so he said,
[a]"I will serve you seven years for Rachel
your younger daughter."

19And Laban said, "*It is* better that I
give her to you than that I should give her
to another man. Stay with me." 20So Jacob [a]served seven years for Rachel, and
they seemed *only* a few days to him because of the love he had for her.

21Then Jacob said to Laban, "Give *me*
my wife, for my days are fulfilled, that I
may [a]go in to her." 22And Laban gathered
together all the men of the place and
[a]made a feast. 23Now it came to pass in the
evening, that he took Leah his daughter
and brought her to Jacob; and he went in
to her. 24And Laban gave his maid [a]Zilpah
to his daughter Leah *as* a maid. 25So it
came to pass in the morning, that behold,
it *was* Leah. And he said to Laban, "What
is this you have done to me? Was it not for
Rachel that I served you? Why then have
you [a]deceived me?"

26And Laban said, "It must not be done
so in our [1]country, to give the younger
before the firstborn. 27[a]Fulfill her week,
and we will give you this one also for the
service which you will serve with me still
another seven years."

28Then Jacob did so and fulfilled her
week. So he gave him his daughter Rachel
as wife also. 29And Laban gave his maid
[a]Bilhah to his daughter Rachel as a maid.
30Then *Jacob* also went in to Rachel, and
he also [a]loved Rachel more than Leah.
And he served with Laban [b]still another
seven years.

The Children of Jacob

31When the LORD [a]saw that Leah *was*
[1]unloved, He [b]opened her womb; but Rachel *was* barren. 32So Leah conceived and
bore a son, and she called his name [1]Reu-
ben; for she said, "The LORD has surely
[a]looked on my affliction. Now therefore,
my husband will love me." 33Then she
conceived again and bore a son, and said,
"Because the LORD has heard that I *am*
[1]unloved, He has therefore given me this
son also." And she called his name [2]Sime-
on. 34She conceived again and bore a son,
and said, "Now this time my husband will
become attached to me, because I have
borne him three sons." Therefore his
name was called [1]Levi. 35And she conceived again and bore a son, and said,
"Now I will praise the LORD." Therefore
she called his name [a]Judah.[1] Then she
stopped bearing.

30 Now when Rachel saw that [a]she
bore Jacob no children, Rachel
[b]envied her sister, and said to Jacob, "Give
me children, [c]or else I die!"

2And Jacob's anger was aroused against
Rachel, and he said, [a]"*Am* I in the place of
God, who has withheld from you the fruit
of the womb?"

3So she said, "Here is [a]my maid Bilhah;
go in to her, [b]and she will bear *a child* on
my knees, [c]that I also may [1]have children
by her." 4Then she gave him Bilhah her
maid [a]as wife, and Jacob went in to her.
5And Bilhah conceived and bore Jacob a
son. 6Then Rachel said, "God has [a]judged
my case; and He has also heard my voice
and given me a son." Therefore she called
his name [1]Dan. 7And Rachel's maid Bilhah conceived again and bore Jacob a second son. 8Then Rachel said, "With [1]great
wrestlings I have wrestled with my sister,
and indeed I have prevailed." So she called
his name [2]Naphtali.

9When Leah saw that she had stopped
bearing, she took Zilpah her maid and
[a]gave her to Jacob as wife. 10And Leah's
maid Zilpah bore Jacob a son. 11Then
Leah said, [1]"A troop comes!" So she called
his name [2]Gad. 12And Leah's maid Zilpah
bore Jacob a second son. 13Then Leah
said, "I am happy, for the daughters [a]will
call me blessed." So she called his name
[1]Asher.

14Now Reuben went in the days of
wheat harvest and found mandrakes in
the field, and brought them to his mother
Leah. Then Rachel said to Leah, [a]"Please
give me *some* of your son's mandrakes."

15But she said to her, [a]"*Is it* a small
matter that you have taken away my husband? Would you take away my son's
mandrakes also?"

And Rachel said, "Therefore he will lie
with you tonight for your son's mandrakes."

16When Jacob came out of the field in
the evening, Leah went out to meet him
and said, "You must come in to me, for I
have surely hired you with my son's mandrakes." And he lay with her that night.

17 [a]Gen. 12:11, 14; 26:7 [1]Or *weak*
18 [a]Gen. 31:41
20 [a]Gen. 30:26
21 [a]Judg. 15:1
22 [a]John 2:1, 2
24 [a]Gen. 30:9, 10
25 [a]1 Sam. 28:12
26 [1]Lit. *place*
27 [a]Judg. 14:2
29 [a]Gen. 30:3–5
30 [a]Deut. 21:15–17 [b]Gen. 30:26; 31:41
31 [a]Ps. 127:3 [b]Gen. 30:1 [1]Lit. *hated*
32 [a]Deut. 26:7 [1]Lit. *See, a Son*
33 [1]Lit. *hated* [2]Lit. *Heard*
34 [1]Lit. *Attached*
35 [a]Matt. 1:2 [1]Lit. *Praise*

CHAPTER 30

1 [a]Gen. 16:1, 2; 29:31 [b]Gen. 37:11 [c][Job 5:2]
2 [a]1 Sam. 1:5
3 [a]Gen. 16:2 [b]Gen. 50:23 [c]Gen. 16:2, 3 [1]Lit. *be built up by her*
4 [a]Gen. 16:3, 4
6 [a]Lam. 3:59 [1]Lit. *Judge*
8 [1]Lit. *wrestlings of God* [2]Lit. *My Wrestling*
9 [a]Gen. 30:4
11 [1]So with Qr., Syr., Tg.; Kt., LXX, Vg. *in fortune* [2]Lit. *Troop* or *Fortune*
13 [a]Luke 1:48 [1]Lit. *Happy*
14 [a]Gen. 25:30
15 [a][Num. 16:9, 13]

GENESIS 30:1

Dear Woman of Destiny,

After being married for several years, I came face-to-face with the same situation as Rachel in Genesis 30:1—unwanted barrenness. I had read this verse many times and continued through the story. But how could Rachel's life speak personally to me?

The one thing lovely Rachel could not force or create was the blessing of a child. She had a situation she could not change, a problem she could not solve, and a circumstance she did not deserve. Where was God? Only His sovereignty understood the plans that went beyond her natural comprehension.

Rachel's barrenness was a journey of faith that ultimately brought her a child of destiny, one who was key to the life and history of Israel. But what pain she suffered on this journey—so much that she felt her life was over because of her inability to bear children.

Like Rachel, I began to understand that a barren woman goes through very deep waters: Her worth as a woman is challenged to its very core, her God-given motherly instinct has no focus, embarrassing fertility tests are conducted to discover what is wrong, she endures the emotional trauma similar to dealing with death and loss, and she is a target for Satanic harassment and spiritual confusion. As any barren woman can testify, she asks herself many agonizing questions and endures insensitive questions from other people.

My own barrenness journey taught me many things about myself, about life, and about God. Today my home is busy and noisy, with four children coming and going (two adopted and two biological children after twelve years of barrenness). I have learned to trust God in a way I would never have understood before. He alone knows the reasons and the timing. I've learned to totally dedicate and commit myself to God, recognizing that my value and dignity come from Him alone, because I belong to Him and not because of what I can do or create. I've learned that God is more concerned about my character, who I am, my inner strength and ability to endure than about temporal accomplishments and personal gain. I've learned to be more compassionate and caring, realizing that every woman has a story to tell; and every life touches pain, sickness, sorrow, loss, and good-byes, as well as joy, growth, belonging, memories, change, celebration, and hope.

If you are in a season of barrenness, what do you do? First, realize that you are, in fact, a woman of destiny. God has not forgotten you, and He does have a plan. Let Him have total control of your life and future. Second, don't withdraw from children because of your own pain. There are so many that are "motherless" and "fatherless" in both the physical and the emotional sense. Reach out and love—you have so much to give. Third, don't isolate yourself and believe no one understands what you are going through. Many women have been on this journey before, and you will receive much encouragement and support by sharing your heart with them. Above all, don't give up hope. Hope in the One who created you and understands every detail of your life. Let Him weave together the tapestry of your life according to His beautiful design.

Sharon Damazio

17 And God listened to Leah, and she
conceived and bore Jacob a fifth son.
18 Leah said, "God has given me my wages,
because I have given my maid to my husband." So she called his name [1]Issachar.
19 Then Leah conceived again and bore Jacob a sixth son. 20 And Leah said, "God has
endowed me *with* a good endowment;
now my husband will dwell with me, because I have borne him six sons." So she
called his name [1]Zebulun. 21 Afterward
she bore a [a]daughter, and called her name
[1]Dinah.

22 Then God [a]remembered Rachel, and
God listened to her and [b]opened her
womb. 23 And she conceived and bore a
son, and said, "God has taken away [a]my
reproach." 24 So she called his name [1]Jo-
seph, and said, [a]"The LORD shall add to me
another son."

Jacob's Agreement with Laban

25 And it came to pass, when Rachel had
borne Joseph, that Jacob said to Laban,
[a]"Send me away, that I may go to [b]my
own place and to my country. 26 Give *me*
my wives and my children [a]for whom I
have served you, and let me go; for you
know my service which I have done for
you."

27 And Laban said to him, "Please *stay,*
if I have found favor in your eyes, *for* [a]I
have learned by experience that the LORD
has blessed me for your sake." 28 Then he
said, [a]"Name me your wages, and I will
give *it.*"

29 So *Jacob* said to him, [a]"You know
how I have served you and how your livestock has been with me. 30 For what you
had before I *came was* little, and it has
increased to a great amount; the LORD has
blessed you [1]since my coming. And now,
when shall I also [a]provide for my own
house?"

31 So he said, "What shall I give you?"

And Jacob said, "You shall not give me
anything. If you will do this thing for me,
I will again feed and keep your flocks:
32 Let me pass through all your flock today, removing from there all the speckled
and spotted sheep, and all the brown ones
among the lambs, and the spotted and
speckled among the goats; and [a]*these*
shall be my wages. 33 So my [a]righteous-
ness will answer for me in time to come,
when the subject of my wages comes before you: every one that *is* not speckled
and spotted among the goats, and brown
among the lambs, will be considered stolen, if *it is* with me."

34 And Laban said, "Oh, that it were according to your word!" 35 So he removed
that day the male goats that were [a]speck-
led and spotted, all the female goats that
were speckled and spotted, every one that
had *some* white in it, and all the brown
ones among the lambs, and gave *them*
into the hand of his sons. 36 Then he put
three days' journey between himself and
Jacob, and Jacob fed the rest of Laban's
flocks.

37 Now [a]Jacob took for himself rods of
green poplar and of the almond and chest-
nut trees, peeled white strips in them, and
exposed the white which *was* in the rods.
38 And the rods which he had peeled, he set
before the flocks in the gutters, in the watering troughs where the flocks came to
drink, so that they should conceive when
they came to drink. 39 So the flocks conceived before the rods, and the flocks
brought forth streaked, speckled, and
spotted. 40 Then Jacob separated the
lambs, and made the flocks face toward
the streaked and all the brown in the flock
of Laban; but he put his own flocks by
themselves and did not put them with Laban's flock.

41 And it came to pass, whenever the
stronger livestock conceived, that Jacob
placed the rods before the eyes of the livestock in the gutters, that they might conceive among the rods. 42 But when the
flocks were feeble, he did not put *them* in;
so the feebler were Laban's and the stronger Jacob's. 43 Thus the man [a]became exceedingly prosperous, and [b]had large
flocks, female and male servants, and
camels and donkeys.

Jacob Flees from Laban

31 Now *Jacob* heard the words of Laban's sons, saying, "Jacob has tak-
en away all that was our father's, and from
what was our father's he has acquired all
this [a]wealth." 2 And Jacob saw the [a]coun-
tenance of Laban, and indeed it *was* not
[b]*favorable* toward him as before. 3 Then
the LORD said to Jacob, [a]"Return to the
land of your fathers and to your family,
and I will [b]be with you."

4 So Jacob sent and called Rachel and
Leah to the field, to his flock, 5 and said to
them, [a]"I see your father's [1]countenance,
that it *is* not *favorable* toward me as before; but the God of my father [b]has been

18 1 Lit. *Wages*
20 1 Lit. *Dwelling*
21 a Gen. 34:1 1 Lit. *Judgment*
22 a 1 Sam. 1:19, 20 b Gen. 29:31
23 a Luke 1:25
24 a Gen. 35:16–18 1 Lit. *He Will Add*
25 a Gen. 24:54, 56 b Gen. 18:33
26 a Gen. 29:18–20, 27, 30
27 a Gen. 26:24; 39:3
28 a Gen. 29:15; 31:7, 41
29 a Gen. 31:6, 38–40
30 a [1 Tim. 5:8] 1 Lit. *at my foot*
32 a Gen. 31:8
33 a Ps. 37:6
35 a Gen. 31:9–12
37 a Gen. 31:9–12
43 a Gen. 12:16; 30:30 b Gen. 13:2; 24:35; 26:13, 14

CHAPTER 31
1 a Ps. 49:16
2 a Gen. 4:5 b Deut. 28:54
3 a Gen. 28:15, 20, 21; 32:9 b Gen. 46:4
5 a Gen. 31:2, 3 b Is. 41:10 1 Lit. *face*

with me. 6And [a]you know that with all my
might I have served your father. 7Yet your
father has deceived me and [a]changed my
wages [b]ten times, but God [c]did not allow
him to hurt me. 8If he said thus: [a]'The
speckled shall be your wages,' then all the
flocks bore speckled. And if he said thus:
'The streaked shall be your wages,' then
all the flocks bore streaked. 9So God has
[a]taken away the livestock of your father
and given *them* to me.
10"And it happened, at the time when
the flocks conceived, that I lifted my eyes
and saw in a dream, and behold, the rams
which leaped upon the flocks *were*
streaked, speckled, and gray-spotted.
11Then [a]the Angel of God spoke to me in
a dream, saying, 'Jacob.' And I said, 'Here
I am.' 12And He said, 'Lift your eyes now
and see, all the rams which leap on the
flocks *are* streaked, speckled, and gray-
spotted; for [a]I have seen all that Laban is
doing to you. 13I *am* the God of Bethel,
[a]where you anointed the pillar *and* where
you made a vow to Me. Now [b]arise, get out
of this land, and return to the land of your
family.' "
14Then Rachel and Leah answered and
said to him, [a]"Is there still any portion or
inheritance for us in our father's house?
15Are we not considered strangers by him?
For [a]he has sold us, and also completely
consumed our money. 16For all these
riches which God has taken from our father are *really* ours and our children's;
now then, whatever God has said to you,
do it."
17Then Jacob rose and set his sons and
his wives on camels. 18And he carried
away all his livestock and all his possessions which he had gained, his acquired
livestock which he had gained in Padan
Aram, to go to his father Isaac in the land
of [a]Canaan. 19Now Laban had gone to
shear his sheep, and Rachel had stolen the
[a]household[1] idols that were her father's.
20And Jacob stole away, unknown to Laban the Syrian, in that he did not tell him
that he intended to flee. 21So he fled with
all that he had. He arose and crossed the
river, and [a]headed[1] toward the mountains
of Gilead.

Laban Pursues Jacob

22And Laban was told on the third day
that Jacob had fled. 23Then he took [a]his
brethren with him and pursued him for
seven days' journey, and he overtook him
in the mountains of Gilead. 24But God
[a]had come to Laban the Syrian in a dream
by night, and said to him, "Be careful that
you [b]speak to Jacob neither good nor
bad."
25So Laban overtook Jacob. Now Jacob
had pitched his tent in the mountains,
and Laban with his brethren pitched in
the mountains of Gilead.
26And Laban said to Jacob: "What have
you done, that you have stolen away unknown to me, and [a]carried away my
daughters like captives *taken* with the
sword? 27Why did you flee away secretly,
and steal away from me, and not tell me;
for I might have sent you away with joy
and songs, with timbrel and harp? 28And
you did not allow me [a]to kiss my sons and
my daughters. Now [b]you have done foolishly in *so* doing. 29It is in my power to do
you harm, but the [a]God of your father
spoke to me [b]last night, saying, 'Be careful that you speak to Jacob neither good
nor bad.' 30And now you have surely gone
because you greatly long for your father's
house, *but* why did you [a]steal my gods?"
31Then Jacob answered and said to Laban, "Because I was [a]afraid, for I said,
'Perhaps you would take your daughters
from me by force.' 32With whomever you
find your gods, [a]do not let him live. In the
presence of our brethren, identify what I
have of yours and take *it* with you." For
Jacob did not know that Rachel had stolen
them.
33And Laban went into Jacob's tent,
into Leah's tent, and into the two maids'
tents, but he did not find *them.* Then he
went out of Leah's tent and entered Rachel's tent. 34Now Rachel had taken the
[1]household idols, put them in the camel's
saddle, and sat on them. And Laban
[2]searched all about the tent but did not
find *them.* 35And she said to her father,
"Let it not displease my lord that I cannot
[a]rise before you, for the manner of wom-
en *is* with me." And he searched but did
not find the [1]household idols.
36Then Jacob was angry and rebuked
Laban, and Jacob answered and said to Laban: "What *is* my [1]trespass? What *is* my
sin, that you have so hotly pursued me?
37Although you have searched all my
things, what part of your household
things have you found? Set *it* here before
my brethren and your brethren, that they
may judge between us both! 38These
twenty years I *have been* with you; your

6 a Gen. 30:29; 31:38–41
7 a Gen. 29:25; 31:41 b Num. 14:22 c Job 1:10
8 a Gen. 30:32
9 a Gen. 31:1, 16
11 a Gen. 16:7–11; 22:11, 15; 31:13; 48:16
12 a Ex. 3:7
13 a Gen. 28:16–22; 35:1, 6, 15 b Gen. 31:3; 32:9
14 a Gen. 2:24
15 a Gen. 29:15, 20, 23, 27
18 a Gen. 17:8; 33:18; 35:27
19 a Judg. 17:5 *1* Heb. *teraphim*
21 a 2 Kin. 12:17 *1* Lit. *set his face toward*
23 a Gen. 13:8
24 a Gen. 20:3; 31:29; 46:2–4 b Gen. 24:50; 31:7, 29
26 a 1 Sam. 30:2
28 a Gen. 31:55 b 1 Sam. 13:13
29 a Gen. 28:13; 31:5, 24, 42, 53 b Gen. 31:24
30 a Judg. 17:5; 18:24
31 a Gen. 26:7; 32:7, 11
32 a Gen. 44:9
34 *1* Heb. *teraphim* *2* Lit. *felt*
35 a Lev. 19:32 *1* Heb. *teraphim*
36 *1 transgression*

ewes and your female goats have not mis-
carried their young, and I have not eaten
the rams of your flock. 39[a]That which was
torn *by beasts* I did not bring to you; I
bore the loss of it. [b]You required it from
my hand, *whether* stolen by day or stolen
by night. 40*There* I was! In the day the
drought consumed me, and the frost by
night, and my sleep departed from my
eyes. 41Thus I have been in your house
twenty years; I [a]served you fourteen years
for your two daughters, and six years for
your flock, and [b]you have changed my
wages ten times. 42[a]Unless the God of my
father, the God of Abraham and [b]the Fear
of Isaac, had been with me, surely now
you would have sent me away empty-
handed. [c]God has seen my affliction and
the labor of my hands, and [d]rebuked *you*
last night."

Laban's Covenant with Jacob

43And Laban answered and said to Jacob, "*These* daughters *are* my daughters,
and *these* children *are* my children, and
this flock *is* my flock; all that you see *is*
mine. But what can I do this day to these
my daughters or to their children whom
they have borne? 44Now therefore, come,
[a]let us make a [1]covenant, [b]you and I, and
let it be a witness between you and me."

Lord, I pray that You will watch between ____ and ____ while they are absent one from another.

FROM GENESIS 31:49

45So Jacob [a]took a stone and set it up *as*
a pillar. 46Then Jacob said to his brethren,
"Gather stones." And they took stones and
made a heap, and they ate there on the
heap. 47Laban called it [1]Jegar Sahadutha,
but Jacob called it [2]Galeed. 48And Laban
said, [a]"This heap *is* a witness between you
and me this day." Therefore its name was
called Galeed, 49also [a]Mizpah,[1] because he
said, "May the LORD watch between you
and me when we are absent one from another. 50If you afflict my daughters, or if
you take *other* wives besides my daughters, *although* no man *is* with us—see,
God *is* witness between you and me!"
51Then Laban said to Jacob, "Here is
this heap and here is *this* pillar, which I
have placed between you and me. 52This
heap *is* a witness, and *this* pillar *is* a witness, that I will not pass beyond this heap
to you, and you will not pass beyond this
heap and this pillar to me, for harm. 53The
God of Abraham, the God of Nahor, and
the God of their father [a]judge between
us." And Jacob [b]swore by [c]the [1]Fear of his
father Isaac. 54Then Jacob offered a sacrifice on the mountain, and called his
brethren to eat bread. And they ate bread
and stayed all night on the mountain.
55And early in the morning Laban arose,
and [a]kissed his sons and daughters and
[b]blessed them. Then Laban departed and
[c]returned to his place.

Esau Comes to Meet Jacob

32 So Jacob went on his way, and [a]the
angels of God met him. 2When Jacob saw them, he said, "This *is* God's
[a]camp." And he called the name of that
place [1]Mahanaim.
3Then Jacob sent messengers before
him to Esau his brother [a]in the land of
Seir, [b]the [1]country of Edom. 4And he
commanded them, saying, [a]"Speak thus
to my lord Esau, 'Thus your servant Jacob
says: "I have dwelt with Laban and stayed
there until now. 5[a]I have oxen, donkeys,
flocks, and male and female servants; and
I have sent to tell my lord, that [b]I may find
favor in your sight." ' "
6Then the messengers returned to Jacob, saying, "We came to your brother
Esau, and [a]he also is coming to meet you,
and four hundred men *are* with him." 7So
Jacob was greatly afraid and [a]distressed;
and he divided the people that *were* with
him, and the flocks and herds and camels,
into two companies. 8And he said, "If Esau
comes to the one company and [1]attacks it,
then the other company which is left will
escape."
9[a]Then Jacob said, [b]"O God of my father Abraham and God of my father Isaac,
the LORD [c]who said to me, 'Return to your
country and to your family, and I will deal
well with you': 10I am not worthy of the
least of all the [a]mercies and of all the
truth which You have shown Your servant; for I crossed over this Jordan with
[b]my staff, and now I have become two
companies. 11[a]Deliver me, I pray, from
the hand of my brother, from the hand of

39 a Ex. 22:10 b Ex. 22:10–13
41 a Gen. 29:20, 27–30 b Gen. 31:7
42 a Ps. 124:1, 2 b Is. 8:13 c Ex. 3:7 d 1 Chr. 12:17
44 a Gen. 21:27, 32; 26:28 b Josh. 24:27 1 *treaty*
45 a Gen. 28:18; 35:14
47 1 Lit., in Aram., *Heap of Witness* 2 Lit., in Heb., *Heap of Witness*
48 a Josh. 24:27
49 a Judg. 10:17; 11:29 1 Lit. *Watch*
53 a Gen. 16:5 b Gen. 21:23 c Gen. 31:42 1 A reference to God
55 a Gen. 29:11, 13; 31:28, 43 b Gen. 28:1 c Num. 24:25

CHAPTER 32
1 a Num. 22:31
2 a Josh. 5:14 1 Lit. *Double Camp*
3 a Gen. 14:6; 33:14, 16 b Gen. 25:30; 36:6–9 1 Lit. *field*
4 a Prov. 15:1
5 a Gen. 30:43 b Gen. 33:8, 15
6 a Gen. 33:1
7 a Gen. 32:11; 35:3
8 1 Lit. *strikes*
9 a [Ps. 50:15] b Gen. 28:13; 31:42 c Gen. 31:3, 13
10 a Gen. 24:27 b Job 8:7
11 a Ps. 59:1, 2

Esau; for I fear him, lest he come and [1]at-
tack me *and* [b]the mother with the children. 12 For [a]You said, 'I will surely treat
you well, and make your descendants as
the [b]sand of the sea, which cannot be
numbered for multitude.' "
13 So he lodged there that same night,
and took what [1]came to his hand as [a]a
present for Esau his brother: 14 two hundred female goats and twenty male goats,
two hundred ewes and twenty rams,
15 thirty milk camels with their colts, forty
cows and ten bulls, twenty female donkeys
and ten foals. 16 Then he delivered *them* to
the hand of his servants, every drove by
itself, and said to his servants, "Pass over
before me, and put some distance between
successive droves." 17 And he commanded
the first one, saying, "When Esau my
brother meets you and asks you, saying,
'To whom do you belong, and where are
you going? Whose *are* these in front of
you?' 18 then you shall say, 'They *are* your
servant Jacob's. It *is* a present sent to my
lord Esau; and behold, he also *is* behind
us.' " 19 So he commanded the second, the
third, and all who followed the droves,
saying, "In this manner you shall speak to
Esau when you find him; 20 and also say,
'Behold, your servant Jacob *is* behind
us.' " For he said, "I will [a]appease him
with the present that goes before me, and
afterward I will see his face; perhaps he
will accept me." 21 So the present went on
over before him, but he himself lodged
that night in the camp.

Wrestling with God

22 And he arose that night and took his
two wives, his two female servants, and
his eleven sons, [a]and crossed over the ford
of Jabbok. 23 He took them, sent them
[1]over the brook, and sent over what he
had. 24 Then Jacob was left alone; and [a]a
Man wrestled with him until the [1]break-
ing of day. 25 Now when He saw that He
did not prevail against him, He [1]touched
the socket of his hip; and [a]the socket of
Jacob's hip was out of joint as He wrestled
with him. 26 And [a]He said, "Let Me go, for
the day breaks."
But he said, [b]"I will not let You go unless You bless me!"
27 So He said to him, "What *is* your
name?"
He said, "Jacob."
28 And He said, [a]"Your name shall no
longer be called Jacob, but [1]Israel; for you

11 [b]Hos. 10:14 [1]Lit. *strike*
12 [a]Gen. 28:13–15 [b]Gen. 22:17
13 [a]Gen. 43:11 [1]*he had received*
20 [a][Prov. 21:14]
22 [a]Deut. 3:16
23 [1]*across*
24 [a]Hos. 12:2–4 [1]*dawn*
25 [a]2 Cor. 12:7 [1]*struck*
26 [a]Luke 24:28 [b]Hos. 12:4
28 [a]Gen. 35:10 [b]Hos. 12:3, 4 [c]Gen. 25:31; 27:33 [1]Lit. *Prince with God*
29 [a]Judg. 13:17, 18 [b]Gen. 35:9
30 [a]Gen. 16:13 [1]Lit. *Face of God*
31 [1]Lit. *Face of God;* same as *Peniel,* v. 30
32 [1]*struck*
CHAPTER 33
1 [a]Gen. 32:6
3 [a]Gen. 18:2; 42:6
4 [a]Gen. 32:28 [b]Gen. 45:14, 15
5 [a]Gen. 48:9
8 [a]Gen. 32:13–16 [b]Gen. 32:5

*O Lord, may _____ hold
onto You and not give up
until You bless them.*
FROM GENESIS 32:26

have [b]struggled with God and [c]with men,
and have prevailed."
29 Then Jacob asked, saying, "Tell *me*
Your name, I pray."
And He said, [a]"Why *is* it *that* you ask
about My name?" And He [b]blessed him
there.
30 So Jacob called the name of the place
[1]Peniel: "For [a]I have seen God face to
face, and my life is preserved." 31 Just as he
crossed over [1]Penuel the sun rose on him,
and he limped on his hip. 32 Therefore to
this day the children of Israel do not eat
the muscle that shrank, which *is* on the
hip socket, because He [1]touched the socket of Jacob's hip in the muscle that
shrank.

Jacob and Esau Meet

33 Now Jacob lifted his eyes and
looked, and there, [a]Esau was coming, and with him were four hundred
men. So he divided the children among
Leah, Rachel, and the two maidservants.
2 And he put the maidservants and their
children in front, Leah and her children
behind, and Rachel and Joseph last. 3 Then
he crossed over before them and [a]bowed
himself to the ground seven times, until
he came near to his brother.
4 [a]But Esau ran to meet him, and embraced him, [b]and fell on his neck and
kissed him, and they wept. 5 And he lifted
his eyes and saw the women and children,
and said, "Who *are* these with you?"
So he said, "The children [a]whom God
has graciously given your servant." 6 Then
the maidservants came near, they and
their children, and bowed down. 7 And
Leah also came near with her children,
and they bowed down. Afterward Joseph
and Rachel came near, and they bowed
down.
8 Then Esau said, "What *do you mean
by* [a]all this company which I met?"
And he said, "*These are* [b]to find favor in
the sight of my lord."

9But Esau said, "I have enough, my
brother; keep what you have for yourself."
10And Jacob said, "No, please, if I have
now found favor in your sight, then receive my present from my hand, inasmuch as I [a]have seen your face as though
I had seen the face of God, and you were
pleased with me. 11Please, take [a]my blessing that is brought to you, because God
has dealt [b]graciously with me, and because I have [1]enough." [c]So he urged him,
and he took *it*.
12Then Esau said, "Let us take our journey; let us go, and I will go before you."
13But Jacob said to him, "My lord
knows that the children *are* weak, and the
flocks and herds which are nursing *are*
with me. And if the men should drive
them hard one day, all the flock will die.
14Please let my lord go on ahead before his
servant. I will lead on slowly at a pace
which the livestock that go before me, and
the children, [1]are able to endure, until I
come to my lord [a]in Seir."
15And Esau said, "Now let me leave with
you *some* of the people who *are* with me."
But he said, "What need is there? [a]Let
me find favor in the sight of my lord."
16So Esau returned that day on his way to
Seir. 17And Jacob journeyed to [a]Succoth,
built himself a house, and made [1]booths
for his livestock. Therefore the name of
the place is called [2]Succoth.

Jacob Comes to Canaan

18Then Jacob came [1]safely to [a]the city
of [b]Shechem, which *is* in the land of Canaan, when he came from Padan Aram;
and he pitched his tent before the city.
19And [a]he bought the parcel of [1]land,
where he had pitched his tent, from the
children of Hamor, Shechem's father, for
one hundred pieces of money. 20Then he
erected an altar there and called it [a]El[1]
Elohe Israel.

The Dinah Incident

34 Now [a]Dinah the daughter of Leah,
whom she had borne to Jacob,
went out to see the daughters of the land.
2And when Shechem the son of Hamor
the Hivite, prince of the country, saw her,
he [a]took her and lay with her, and violated her. 3His soul [1]was strongly attracted
to Dinah the daughter of Jacob, and he
loved the young woman and spoke [2]kindly
to the young woman. 4So Shechem
[a]spoke to his father Hamor, saying, "Get
me this young woman as a wife."
5And Jacob heard that he had defiled
Dinah his daughter. Now his sons were
with his livestock in the field; so Jacob
[a]held[1] his peace until they came. 6Then
Hamor the father of Shechem went out to
Jacob to speak with him. 7And the sons of
Jacob came in from the field when they
heard *it;* and the men were grieved and
very angry, because he [a]had done a disgraceful thing in Israel by lying with Jacob's daughter, [b]a thing which ought not
to be done. 8But Hamor spoke with them,
saying, "The soul of my son Shechem
longs for your daughter. Please give her to
him as a wife. 9And make marriages with
us; give your daughters to us, and take
our daughters to yourselves. 10So you
shall dwell with us, and the land shall be
before you. Dwell and trade in it, and acquire possessions for yourselves in it."
11Then Shechem said to her father and
her brothers, "Let me find favor in your
eyes, and whatever you say to me I will
give. 12Ask me ever so much [a]dowry[1] and
gift, and I will give according to what you
say to me; but give me the young woman
as a wife."
13But the sons of Jacob answered Shechem and Hamor his father, and spoke
[a]deceitfully, because he had defiled Dinah
their sister. 14And they said to them, "We
cannot do this thing, to give our sister
to one who is [a]uncircumcised, for [b]that
would be a reproach to us. 15But on this
condition we will consent to you: If you
will become as we *are,* if every male of you
is circumcised, 16then we will give our
daughters to you, and we will take your
daughters to us; and we will dwell with
you, and we will become one people. 17But
if you will not heed us and be circumcised, then we will take our daughter and
be gone."
18And their words pleased Hamor and
Shechem, Hamor's son. 19So the young
man did not delay to do the thing, because
he delighted in Jacob's daughter. He *was*
[a]more honorable than all the household
of his father.
20And Hamor and Shechem his son
came to the [a]gate of their city, and spoke
with the men of their city, saying:
21"These men *are* at peace with us. Therefore let them dwell in the land and trade
in it. For indeed the land *is* large enough
for them. Let us take their daughters to us

10 [a]Gen. 43:3
11 [a]1 Sam. 25:27; 30:26 [b]Ex. 33:19 [c]2 Kin. 5:23 [1]Lit. *all*
14 [a]Gen. 32:3; 36:8 [1]*can stand*
15 [a]Ruth 2:13
17 [a]Josh. 13:27 [1]*shelters* [2]Lit. *Booths*
18 [a]John 3:23 [b]Josh. 24:1 [1]Or *to Shalem, a city of*
19 [a]John 4:5 [1]Lit. *the field*
20 [a]Gen. 35:7 [1]Lit. *God, the God of Israel*

CHAPTER 34
1 [a]Gen. 30:21
2 [a]Gen. 20:2
3 [1]Lit. *clung to* [2]*tenderly*
4 [a]Judg. 14:2
5 [a]2 Sam. 13:22 [1]*kept silent*
7 [a]Judg. 20:6 [b]2 Sam. 13:12
12 [a]Ex. 22:16, 17 [1]*bride-price*
13 [a]Gen. 31:7
14 [a]Ex. 12:48 [b]Josh. 5:2–9
19 [a]1 Chr. 4:9
20 [a]Ruth 4:1, 11

as wives, and let us give them our daughters. 22 Only on this *condition* will the men
consent to dwell with us, to be one people:
if every male among us is circumcised
as they *are* circumcised. 23 *Will* not their
livestock, their property, and every animal
of theirs *be* ours? Only let us consent to
them, and they will dwell with us." 24 And
all who went out of the gate of his city
heeded Hamor and Shechem his son; every male was circumcised, all who [a]went
out of the gate of his city.
25 Now it came to pass on the third day,
when they were in pain, that two of the
sons of Jacob, [a]Simeon and Levi, Dinah's
brothers, each took his sword and came
boldly upon the city and killed all the
males. 26 And they [a]killed Hamor and Shechem his son with the edge of the sword,
and took Dinah from Shechem's house,
and went out. 27 The sons of Jacob came
upon the slain, and plundered the city,
because their sister had been defiled.
28 They took their sheep, their oxen, and
their donkeys, what *was* in the city and
what *was* in the field, 29 and all their
wealth. All their little ones and their wives
they took captive; and they plundered
even all that *was* in the houses.
30 Then Jacob said to Simeon and Levi,
[a]"You have [b]troubled me [c]by making me
obnoxious among the inhabitants of the
land, among the Canaanites and the Perizzites; [d]and since I *am* few in number,
they will gather themselves together
against me and kill me. I shall be destroyed, my household and I."
31 But they said, "Should he treat our
sister like a harlot?"

Jacob's Return to Bethel

35 Then God said to Jacob, "Arise, go
up to [a]Bethel and dwell there; and
make an altar there to God, [b]who appeared to you [c]when you fled from the
face of Esau your brother."
2 And Jacob said to his [a]household and
to all who *were* with him, "Put away [b]the
foreign gods that *are* among you, [c]purify
yourselves, and change your garments.
3 Then let us arise and go up to Bethel; and
I will make an altar there to God, [a]who
answered me in the day of my distress
[b]and has been with me in the way which
I have gone." 4 So they gave Jacob all the
foreign [1]gods which *were* in their hands,
and the [a]earrings which *were* in their
ears; and Jacob hid them under [b]the terebinth tree which *was* by Shechem.
5 And they journeyed, and [a]the terror
of God was upon the cities that *were* all
around them, and they did not pursue the
sons of Jacob. 6 So Jacob came to [a]Luz
(that *is,* Bethel), which *is* in the land of
Canaan, he and all the people who *were*
with him. 7 And he [a]built an altar there
and called the place [1]El Bethel, because
[b]there God appeared to him when he fled
from the face of his brother.
8 Now [a]Deborah, Rebekah's nurse, died,
and she was buried below Bethel under
the terebinth tree. So the name of it was
called [1]Allon Bachuth.
9 Then [a]God appeared to Jacob again,
when he came from Padan Aram, and
[b]blessed him. 10 And God said to him,
"Your name *is* Jacob; [a]your name shall
not be called Jacob anymore, [b]but Israel
shall be your name." So He called his
name Israel. 11 Also God said to him: [a]"I
am God Almighty. [b]Be fruitful and multiply; [c]a nation and a company of nations
shall proceed from you, and kings shall
come from your body. 12 The [a]land which
I gave Abraham and Isaac I give to you;
and to your descendants after you I give
this land." 13 Then God [a]went[1] up from
him in the place where He talked with
him. 14 So Jacob [a]set up a pillar in the
place where He talked with him, a pillar of
stone; and he poured a drink offering on
it, and he poured oil on it. 15 And Jacob
called the name of the place where God
spoke with him, [a]Bethel.

Death of Rachel

16 Then they journeyed from Bethel.
And when there was but a little distance to

> *Impurity is the biggest problem in the lives of God's servants. . . . The Lord's Name does not suffer because of your lack of life, but because of your flow of impurities.*
>
> WATCHMAN NEE

24 a Gen. 23:10, 18
25 a Gen. 29:33, 34; 42:24; 49:5–7
26 a Gen. 49:5, 6
30 a Gen. 49:6 b Josh. 7:25 c Ex. 5:21 d Deut. 4:27

CHAPTER 35
1 a Gen. 28:19; 31:13 b Gen. 28:13 c Gen. 27:43
2 a Josh. 24:15 b Josh. 24:2, 14, 23 c Ex. 19:10, 14
3 a Gen. 32:7, 24 b Gen. 28:15, 20; 31:3, 42
4 a Hos. 2:13 b Josh. 24:26 1 *idols*
5 a Ex. 15:16; 23:27
6 a Gen. 28:19, 22; 48:3
7 a Eccl. 5:4 b Gen. 28:13 1 Lit. *God of the House of God*
8 a Gen. 24:59 1 Lit. *Terebinth of Weeping*
9 a Josh. 5:13 b Gen. 32:29
10 a Gen. 17:5 b Gen. 32:28
11 a Ex. 6:3 b Gen. 9:1, 7 c Gen. 17:5, 6, 16; 28:3; 48:4
12 a Gen. 12:7; 13:15; 26:3, 4; 28:13; 48:4
13 a Gen. 17:22; 18:33 1 *departed*
14 a Gen. 28:18, 19; 31:45
15 a Gen. 28:19

go to Ephrath, Rachel labored *in child-*
birth, and she had hard labor. 17Now it
came to pass, when she was in hard labor,
that the midwife said to her, "Do not fear;
[a]you will have this son also." 18And so it
was, as her soul was departing (for she
died), that she called his name [1]Ben-Oni;
but his father called him [2]Benjamin. 19So
[a]Rachel died and was buried on the way to
[b]Ephrath (that *is,* Bethlehem). 20And Jacob set a pillar on her grave, which *is* the
pillar of Rachel's grave [a]to this day.
21Then Israel journeyed and pitched his
tent beyond [a]the tower of Eder. 22And it
happened, when Israel dwelt in that land,
that Reuben went and [a]lay with Bilhah
his father's concubine; and Israel heard
about it.

Jacob's Twelve Sons

Now the sons of Jacob were twelve:
23the sons of Leah *were* [a]Reuben, Jacob's
firstborn, and Simeon, Levi, Judah, Issachar, and Zebulun; 24the sons of Rachel
were Joseph and Benjamin; 25the sons of
Bilhah, Rachel's maidservant, *were* Dan
and Naphtali; 26and the sons of Zilpah,
Leah's maidservant, *were* Gad and Asher.
These *were* the sons of Jacob who were
born to him in Padan Aram.

Death of Isaac

27Then Jacob came to his father Isaac at
[a]Mamre, or [b]Kirjath Arba[1] (that *is,* Hebron), where Abraham and Isaac had
dwelt. 28Now the days of Isaac were one
hundred and eighty years. 29So Isaac
breathed his last and died, and [a]was
[1]gathered to his people, *being* old and full
of days. And [b]his sons Esau and Jacob buried him.

The Family of Esau

36 Now this *is* the genealogy of Esau,
[a]who is Edom. 2[a]Esau took his
wives from the daughters of Canaan: Adah
the daughter of Elon the [b]Hittite; [c]Aholi-
bamah[1] the daughter of Anah, the daughter of Zibeon the Hivite; 3and [a]Basemath,
Ishmael's daughter, sister of Nebajoth.
4Now [a]Adah bore Eliphaz to Esau, and
Basemath bore Reuel. 5And [1]Aholibamah
bore Jeush, Jaalam, and Korah. These
were the sons of Esau who were born to
him in the land of Canaan.
6Then Esau took his wives, his sons,
his daughters, and all the persons of his
household, his cattle and all his animals,
and all his goods which he had gained in
the land of Canaan, and went to a country
away from the presence of his brother Jacob. 7[a]For their possessions were too
great for them to dwell together, and [b]the
land where they were strangers could not
support them because of their livestock.
8So Esau dwelt in [a]Mount Seir. [b]Esau *is*
Edom.
9And this *is* the genealogy of Esau the
father of the Edomites in Mount Seir.
10These *were* the names of Esau's sons:
[a]Eliphaz the son of Adah the wife of Esau,
and Reuel the son of Basemath the wife of
Esau. 11And the sons of Eliphaz were Teman, Omar, [1]Zepho, Gatam, and Kenaz.
12Now Timna was the concubine of Eliphaz, Esau's son, and she bore [a]Amalek to
Eliphaz. These *were* the sons of Adah,
Esau's wife.
13These *were* the sons of Reuel: Nahath,
Zerah, Shammah, and Mizzah. These
were the sons of Basemath, Esau's wife.
14These were the sons of [1]Aholibamah,
Esau's wife, the daughter of Anah, the
daughter of Zibeon. And she bore to Esau:
Jeush, Jaalam, and Korah.

The Chiefs of Edom

15These *were* the chiefs of the sons of
Esau. The sons of Eliphaz, the firstborn
son of Esau, were Chief Teman, Chief
Omar, Chief Zepho, Chief Kenaz, 16[1]Chief
Korah, Chief Gatam, *and* Chief Amalek.
These *were* the chiefs of Eliphaz in the
land of Edom. They *were* the sons of Adah.
17These *were* the sons of Reuel, Esau's
son: Chief Nahath, Chief Zerah, Chief
Shammah, and Chief Mizzah. These *were*
the chiefs of Reuel in the land of Edom.
These *were* the sons of Basemath, Esau's
wife.
18And these *were* the sons of [1]Aholiba-
mah, Esau's wife: Chief Jeush, Chief Jaalam, and Chief Korah. These *were* the
chiefs *who descended* from Aholibamah,
Esau's wife, the daughter of Anah. 19These
were the sons of Esau, who is Edom, and
these *were* their chiefs.

The Sons of Seir

20[a]These *were* the sons of Seir [b]the Ho-
rite who inhabited the land: Lotan, Shobal, Zibeon, Anah, 21Dishon, Ezer, and
Dishan. These *were* the chiefs of the Horites, the sons of Seir, in the land of
Edom.

17 a Gen. 30:24
18 *1* Lit. *Son of My Sorrow* *2* Lit. *Son of the Right Hand*
19 a Gen. 48:7 b Mic. 5:2
20 a 1 Sam. 10:2
21 a Mic. 4:8
22 a Gen. 49:4
23 a Ex. 1:1–4
27 a Gen. 13:18; 18:1; 23:19 b Josh. 14:15 *1* Lit. *Town* or *City of Arba*
29 a Gen. 15:15; 25:8; 49:33 b Gen. 25:9; 49:31 *1* Joined his ancestors

CHAPTER 36
1 a Gen. 25:30
2 a Gen. 26:34; 28:9 b 2 Kin. 7:6 c Gen. 36:25 *1* Or *Oholibamah*
3 a Gen. 28:9
4 a 1 Chr. 1:35
5 *1* Or *Oholibamah*
7 a Gen. 13:6, 11 b Gen. 17:8; 28:4
8 a Gen. 32:3 b Gen. 36:1, 19
10 a 1 Chr. 1:35
11 *1 Zephi,* 1 Chr. 1:36
12 a Num. 24:20
14 *1* Or *Oholibamah*
16 *1* Sam. omits *Chief Korah*
18 *1* Or *Oholibamah*
20 a 1 Chr. 1:38–42 b Gen. 14:6

22And the sons of Lotan were Hori and
[1]Hemam. Lotan's sister *was* Timna.
23These *were* the sons of Shobal: [1]Al-
van, Manahath, Ebal, [2]Shepho, and
Onam.
24These *were* the sons of Zibeon: both
Ajah and Anah. This *was the* Anah who
found the [1]water in the wilderness as he
pastured [a]the donkeys of his father Zibeon. 25These *were* the children of Anah: Dishon and [1]Aholibamah the daughter of
Anah.
26These *were* the sons of [1]Dishon:
[2]Hemdan, Eshban, Ithran, and Cheran.
27These *were* the sons of Ezer: Bilhan, Za-
avan, and [1]Akan. 28These *were* the sons of
Dishan: [a]Uz and Aran.
29These *were* the chiefs of the Horites:
Chief Lotan, Chief Shobal, Chief Zibeon,
Chief Anah, 30Chief Dishon, Chief Ezer,
and Chief Dishan. These *were* the chiefs of
the Horites, according to their chiefs in
the land of Seir.

The Kings of Edom

31[a]Now these *were* the kings who
reigned in the land of Edom before any
king reigned over the children of Israel:
32Bela the son of Beor reigned in Edom,
and the name of his city *was* Dinhabah.
33And when Bela died, Jobab the son of
Zerah of Bozrah reigned in his place.
34When Jobab died, Husham of the land of
the Temanites reigned in his place. 35And
when Husham died, Hadad the son of Bedad, who attacked Midian in the field of
Moab, reigned in his place. And the name
of his city *was* Avith. 36When Hadad died,
Samlah of Masrekah reigned in his place.
37And when Samlah died, Saul of
[a]Rehoboth-*by*-the-River reigned in his
place. 38When Saul died, Baal-Hanan the
son of Achbor reigned in his place. 39And
when Baal-Hanan the son of Achbor died,
[1]Hadar reigned in his place; and the name
of his city *was* [2]Pau. His wife's name *was*
Mehetabel, the daughter of Matred, the
daughter of Mezahab.

The Chiefs of Esau

40And these *were* the names of the
chiefs of Esau, according to their families
and their places, by their names: Chief
Timnah, Chief [1]Alvah, Chief Jetheth,
41Chief [1]Aholibamah, Chief Elah, Chief
Pinon, 42Chief Kenaz, Chief Teman, Chief
Mibzar, 43Chief Magdiel, and Chief Iram.
These *were* the chiefs of Edom, according
to their dwelling places in the land of
their possession. Esau *was* the father of
[1]the Edomites.

Joseph Dreams of Greatness

37 Now Jacob dwelt in the land
[a]where his father was a [1]stranger,
in the land of Canaan. 2This *is* the history
of Jacob.
Joseph, *being* seventeen years old, was
feeding the flock with his brothers. And
the lad *was* with the sons of Bilhah and
the sons of Zilpah, his father's wives; and
Joseph brought [a]a bad report of them to
his father.
3Now Israel loved Joseph more than all
his children, because he *was* [a]the son of
his old age. Also he [b]made him a tunic of
many colors. 4But when his brothers saw
that their father loved him more than all
his brothers, they [a]hated him and could
not speak peaceably to him.
5Now Joseph had a dream, and he told
it to his brothers; and they hated him
even more. 6So he said to them, "Please
hear this dream which I have dreamed:
7[a]There we were, binding sheaves in the
field. Then behold, my sheaf arose and
also stood upright; and indeed your
sheaves stood all around and bowed down
to my sheaf."
8And his brothers said to him, "Shall
you indeed reign over us? Or shall you
indeed have dominion over us?" So they
hated him even more for his dreams and
for his words.
9Then he dreamed still another dream
and told it to his brothers, and said,
"Look, I have dreamed another dream.
And this time, [a]the sun, the moon, and
the eleven stars bowed down to me."
10So he told *it* to his father and his
brothers; and his father rebuked him and
said to him, "What *is* this dream that you
have dreamed? Shall your mother and I
and [a]your brothers indeed come to bow
down to the earth before you?" 11And [a]his
brothers envied him, but his father [b]kept
the matter *in mind.*

Joseph Sold by His Brothers

12Then his brothers went to feed their
father's flock in [a]Shechem. 13And Israel
said to Joseph, "Are not your brothers
feeding *the flock* in Shechem? Come, I
will send you to them."
So he said to him, "Here I am."

---

22 [1] *Homam,* 1 Chr. 1:39
23 [1] *Alian,* 1 Chr. 1:40 [2] *Shephi,* 1 Chr. 1:40
24 [a] Lev. 19:19 [1] So with MT, Vg. (*hot springs*); LXX *Jamin;* Tg. *mighty men;* Talmud *mules*
25 [1] Or *Oholibamah*
26 [1] Heb. *Dishan* [2] *Hamran,* 1 Chr. 1:41
27 [1] *Jaakan,* 1 Chr. 1:42
28 [a] Job 1:1
31 [a] 1 Chr. 1:43
37 [a] Gen. 10:11
39 [1] Sam., Syr. *Hadad* and 1 Chr. 1:50 [2] *Pai,* 1 Chr. 1:50
40 [1] *Aliah,* 1 Chr. 1:51
41 [1] Or *Oholibamah*
43 [1] Heb. *Edom*

CHAPTER 37
1 [a] Gen. 17:8; 23:4; 28:4; 36:7 [1] *sojourner,* temporary resident
2 [a] 1 Sam. 2:22–24
3 [a] Gen. 44:20 [b] Gen. 37:23, 32
4 [a] Gen. 27:41; 49:23
7 [a] Gen. 42:6, 9; 43:26; 44:14
9 [a] Gen. 46:29; 47:25
10 [a] Gen. 27:29
11 [a] Acts 7:9 [b] Dan. 7:28
12 [a] Gen. 33:18–20

14Then he said to him, "Please go and
see if it is well with your brothers and well
with the flocks, and bring back word to
me." So he sent him out of the Valley of
[a]Hebron, and he went to Shechem.
15Now a certain man found him, and
there he was, wandering in the field. And
the man asked him, saying, "What are you
seeking?"
16So he said, "I am seeking my
brothers. [a]Please tell me where they are
feeding *their flocks.*"
17And the man said, "They have departed from here, for I heard them say, 'Let us
go to Dothan.'" So Joseph went after his
brothers and found them in [a]Dothan.
18Now when they saw him afar off, even
before he came near them, [a]they conspired against him to kill him. 19Then
they said to one another, "Look, this
[1]dreamer is coming! 20[a]Come therefore,
let us now kill him and cast him into
some pit; and we shall say, 'Some wild
beast has devoured him.' We shall see
what will become of his dreams!"
21But [a]Reuben heard *it,* and he delivered him out of their hands, and said, "Let
us not kill him." 22And Reuben said to
them, "Shed no blood, *but* cast him into
this pit which *is* in the wilderness, and do
not lay a hand on him"—that he might
deliver him out of their hands, and bring
him back to his father.
23So it came to pass, when Joseph had
come to his brothers, that they [a]stripped
Joseph *of* his tunic, the tunic of *many* colors that *was* on him. 24Then they took
him and cast him into a pit. And the pit
was empty; *there was* no water in it.

The power of God is equal to every emergency and is great enough for the deliverance of every soul from every oppression.

JOHN G. LAKE

25[a]And they sat down to eat a meal.
Then they lifted their eyes and looked, and
there was a company of [b]Ishmaelites,
coming from Gilead with their camels,
bearing spices, [c]balm, and myrrh, on
their way to carry *them* down to Egypt.
26So Judah said to his brothers, "What
profit *is there* if we kill our brother and
[a]conceal his blood? 27Come and let us sell
him to the Ishmaelites, and [a]let not our
hand be upon him, for he *is* [b]our brother
and [c]our flesh." And his brothers listened.
28Then [a]Midianite traders passed by; so
the brothers pulled Joseph up and lifted
him out of the pit, [b]and sold him to the
Ishmaelites for [c]twenty *shekels* of silver.
And they took Joseph to Egypt.
29Then Reuben returned to the pit, and
indeed Joseph *was* not in the pit; and he
[a]tore his clothes. 30And he returned to his
brothers and said, "The lad [a]*is* no *more;*
and I, where shall I go?"
31So they took [a]Joseph's tunic, killed a
kid of the goats, and dipped the tunic in
the blood. 32Then they sent the tunic of
many colors, and they brought *it* to their
father and said, "We have found this. Do
you know whether it *is* your son's tunic or
not?"
33And he recognized it and said, "*It is*
my son's tunic. A [a]wild beast has devoured him. Without doubt Joseph is torn
to pieces." 34Then Jacob [a]tore his clothes,
put sackcloth on his waist, and [b]mourned
for his son many days. 35And all his sons
and all his daughters [a]arose to comfort
him; but he refused to be comforted, and
he said, "For [b]I shall go down into the
grave to my son in mourning." Thus his
father wept for him.
36Now [a]the [1]Midianites had sold him in
Egypt to Potiphar, an officer of Pharaoh
and captain of the guard.

Judah and Tamar

38 It came to pass at that time that
Judah departed from his brothers,
and [a]visited a certain Adullamite whose
name *was* Hirah. 2And Judah [a]saw there
a daughter of a certain Canaanite whose
name *was* [b]Shua, and he married her and
went in to her. 3So she conceived and
bore a son, and he called his name [a]Er.
4She conceived again and bore a son, and
she called his name [a]Onan. 5And she conceived yet again and bore a son, and called
his name [a]Shelah. He was at Chezib when
she bore him.
6Then Judah [a]took a wife for Er his
firstborn, and her name *was* [b]Tamar. 7But
[a]Er, Judah's firstborn, was wicked in the
sight of the LORD, [b]and the LORD killed

14 a Gen. 13:18; 23:2, 19; 35:27
16 a Song 1:7
17 a 2 Kin. 6:13
18 a Mark 14:1
19 1 Lit. *master of dreams*
20 a Prov. 1:11
21 a Gen. 42:22
23 a Matt. 27:28
25 a Prov. 30:20 b Gen. 16:11, 12; 37:28, 36; 39:1 c Jer. 8:22
26 a Gen. 37:20
27 a 1 Sam. 18:17 b Gen. 42:21 c Gen. 29:14
28 a Judg. 6:1–3; 8:22, 24 b Ps. 105:17 c Matt. 27:9
29 a Job 1:20
30 a Gen. 42:13, 36
31 a Gen. 37:3, 23
33 a Gen. 37:20
34 a 2 Sam. 3:31 b Gen. 50:10
35 a 2 Sam. 12:17 b Gen. 25:8; 35:29; 42:38; 44:29, 31
36 a Gen. 39:1 1 MT *Medanites*

CHAPTER 38
1 a 2 Kin. 4:8
2 a Gen. 34:2 b 1 Chr. 2:3
3 a Gen. 46:12
4 a Num. 26:19
5 a Num. 26:20
6 a Gen. 21:21 b Ruth 4:12
7 a Gen. 46:12 b 1 Chr. 2:3

him. 8And Judah said to Onan, "Go in to
[a]your brother's wife and marry her, and
raise up an heir to your brother." 9But
Onan knew that the heir would not be
[a]his; and it came to pass, when he went in
to his brother's wife, that he emitted on
the ground, lest he should give an heir to
his brother. 10And the thing which he did
[1]displeased the LORD; therefore He killed
[a]him also.

11Then Judah said to Tamar his
daughter-in-law, [a]"Remain a widow in
your father's house till my son Shelah is
grown." For he said, "Lest he also die like
his brothers." And Tamar went and dwelt
[b]in her father's house.

12Now in the process of time the daughter of Shua, Judah's wife, died; and Judah
[a]was comforted, and went up to his sheepshearers at Timnah, he and his friend Hirah the Adullamite. 13And it was told
Tamar, saying, "Look, your father-in-law
is going up [a]to Timnah to shear his
sheep." 14So she took off her widow's garments, covered *herself* with a veil and
wrapped herself, and [a]sat in an open place
which *was* on the way to Timnah; for she
saw [b]that Shelah was grown, and she was
not given to him as a wife. 15When Judah
saw her, he thought she *was* a harlot, because she had covered her face. 16Then he
turned to her by the way, and said, "Please
let me come in to you"; for he did not
know that she *was* his daughter-in-law.

So she said, "What will you give me,
that you may come in to me?"

17And he said, [a]"I will send a young
goat from the flock."

So she said, [b]"Will you give *me* a pledge
till you send *it?*"

18Then he said, "What pledge shall I
give you?"

So she said, [a]"Your signet and cord, and
your staff that *is* in your hand." Then he
gave *them* to her, and went in to her, and
she conceived by him. 19So she arose and
went away, and [a]laid aside her veil and put
on the garments of her widowhood.

20And Judah sent the young goat by the
hand of his friend the Adullamite, to receive *his* pledge from the woman's hand,
but he did not find her. 21Then he asked
the men of that place, saying, "Where is
the harlot who *was* [1]openly by the road-
side?"

And they said, "There was no harlot in
this *place*."

22So he returned to Judah and said, "I
cannot find her. Also, the men of the place
said there was no harlot in this *place*."

23Then Judah said, "Let her take *them*
for herself, lest we be shamed; for I sent
this young goat and you have not found
her."

24And it came to pass, about three
months after, that Judah was told, saying,
"Tamar your daughter-in-law has [a]played
the harlot; furthermore she *is* [1]with child
by harlotry."

So Judah said, "Bring her out [b]and let
her be burned!"

25When she *was* brought out, she sent
to her father-in-law, saying, "By the man
to whom these belong, I *am* with child."
And she said, [a]"Please determine whose
these *are*—the signet and cord, and staff."

26So Judah [a]acknowledged *them* and
said, [b]"She has been more righteous than
I, because [c]I did not give her to Shelah my
son." And he [d]never knew her again.

27Now it came to pass, at the time for
giving birth, that behold, twins *were* in
her womb. 28And so it was, when she was
giving birth, that *the one* put out *his*
hand; and the midwife took a scarlet
thread and bound it on his hand, saying,
"This one came out first." 29Then it happened, as he drew back his hand, that his
brother came out unexpectedly; and she
said, "How did you break through? *This*
breach *be* upon you!" Therefore his name
was called [a]Perez.[1] 30Afterward his
brother came out who had the scarlet
thread on his hand. And his name was
called [a]Zerah.

Joseph a Slave in Egypt

39 Now Joseph had been taken [a]down
to Egypt. And [b]Potiphar, an officer
of Pharaoh, captain of the guard, an Egyptian, [c]bought him from the Ishmaelites
who had taken him down there. 2[a]The
LORD was with Joseph, and he was a successful man; and he was in the house of
his master the Egyptian. 3And his master
saw that the LORD *was* with him and that
the LORD [a]made all he did [1]to prosper in
his hand. 4So Joseph [a]found favor in his
sight, and served him. Then he made him
[b]overseer of his house, and all *that* he had
he put [1]under his authority. 5So it was,
from the time *that* he had made him overseer of his house and all that he had, that
[a]the LORD blessed the Egyptian's house
for Joseph's sake; and the blessing of the

8 [a]Deut. 25:5, 6
9 [a]Deut. 25:6
10 [a]Gen. 46:12 [1]Lit. *was evil in the eyes of*
11 [a]Ruth 1:12, 13 [b]Lev. 22:13
12 [a]2 Sam. 13:39
13 [a]Josh. 15:10, 57
14 [a]Prov. 7:12 [b]Gen. 38:11, 26
17 [a]Ezek. 16:33 [b]Gen. 38:20
18 [a]Gen. 38:25; 41:42
19 [a]Gen. 38:14
21 [1]*in full view*
24 [a]Judg. 19:2 [b]Lev. 20:14; 21:9 [1]*pregnant*
25 [a]Gen. 37:32; 38:18
26 [a]Gen. 37:33 [b]1 Sam. 24:17 [c]Gen. 38:14 [d]Job 34:31, 32
29 [a]Gen. 46:12 [1]Lit. *Breach* or *Breakthrough*
30 [a]1 Chr. 2:4

CHAPTER 39
1 [a]Gen. 12:10; 43:15 [b]Gen. 37:36 [c]Gen. 37:28; 45:4
2 [a]Acts 7:9
3 [a]Ps. 1:3 [1]*to be a success*
4 [a]Gen. 18:3; 19:19; 39:21 [b]Gen. 24:2, 10; 39:8, 22; 41:40 [1]Lit. *in his hand*
5 [a]Gen. 18:26; 30:27

LORD was on all that he had in the house
and in the field. [6]Thus he left all that he
had in Joseph's [1]hand, and he did not
know what he had except for the [2]bread
which he ate.
Now Joseph [a]was handsome in form
and appearance.
[7]And it came to pass after these things
that his master's wife [1]cast longing eyes
on Joseph, and she said, [a]"Lie with me."
[8]But he refused and said to his master's
wife, "Look, my master does not know
what *is* with me in the house, and he has
committed all that he has to my hand.

6 a 1 Sam. 16:12
1 Care
2 Food

7 a 2 Sam. 13:11
1 Lit. *lifted up her eyes toward*

9 a Prov. 6:29, 32
b Ps. 51:4

10 a Prov. 1:10

12 a Prov. 7:13

[9]*There is* no one greater in this house
than I, nor has he kept back anything
from me but you, because you *are* his
wife. [a]How then can I do this great wickedness, and [b]sin against God?"
[10]So it was, as she spoke to Joseph day
by day, that he [a]did not heed her, to lie
with her *or* to be with her.
[11]But it happened about this time,
when Joseph went into the house to do his
work, and none of the men of the house
was inside, [12]that she [a]caught him by his
garment, saying, "Lie with me." But he
left his garment in her hand, and fled and

JEANNE GUYON

Described by John Wesley as "a pattern of true holiness," Jeanne Guyon (1648–1717) suffered much in her relentless pursuit of Jesus Christ.

Born in Montargis, France, Jeanne was drawn to God at an early age. She devoured the Word and even attached a paper with the name of Christ to herself, to be continually reminded of Him.

Her marriage to Jacques Guyon swept her into the wealthy Parisian society and gained her a mother-in-law who took great pains to humiliate her. Enduring ridicule and rejection, Jeanne believed that suffering was necessary to develop Christlikeness.

As she welcomed tribulation, it came often for Jeanne. She battled smallpox successfully herself, but lost both a son and a daughter to the same disease. Her grief only fueled her desire to help the poor and needy. She was often found nursing the wounds of commoners, feeding the hungry, or paying for the funerals of paupers.

At 28, Jeanne was widowed. After many unsuccessful attempts for peace with her mother-in-law, she eventually left home with her three surviving children. Five years later, she embraced the "apostolic life" and embarked on an eight-year spiritual pilgrimage through France and Switzerland. She taught on effective prayer and stressed the importance of holiness based solely on faith.

Her popularity among the masses rose, as did the religious attacks against her. Jealous church leaders labeled her a heretic, burned her books publicly, destroyed her house, and stole her servants. Eventually, Jeanne spent seven years in prison for her beliefs, four of them in the horrific conditions of the Bastille. For the last two years, she was forbidden to speak or write to anyone. As a result, she devoted herself more passionately to prayer and writing, developing an inner spiritual strength few Christians have known.

Jeanne Guyon suffered tremendously, yet her profound influence on others came through her determination to glorify God. "My life is consecrated to God," she said, "to suffer for Him, as well as to enjoy Him."

ran outside. 13 And so it was, when she saw
that he had left his garment in her hand
and fled outside, 14 that she called to the
men of her house and spoke to them, saying, "See, he has brought in to us a [a]He-
brew to [1]mock us. He came in to me to lie
with me, and I cried out with a loud voice.
15 And it happened, when he heard that I
lifted my voice and cried out, that he left
his garment with me, and fled and went
outside."
16 So she kept his garment with her until his master came home. 17 Then she
[a]spoke to him with words like these, saying, "The Hebrew servant whom you
brought to us came in to me to mock me;
18 so it happened, as I lifted my voice and
cried out, that he left his garment with
me and fled outside."

Father, because You are with ____, may they prosper in whatever they do according to Your will.

FROM GENESIS 39:23

19 So it was, when his master heard the
words which his wife spoke to him, saying, "Your servant did to me after this
manner," that his [a]anger was aroused.
20 Then Joseph's master took him and [a]put
him into the [b]prison, a place where the
king's prisoners *were* confined. And he
was there in the prison. 21 But the LORD
was with Joseph and showed him mercy,
and He [a]gave[1] him favor in the sight of
the keeper of the prison. 22 And the keeper
of the prison [a]committed to Joseph's
hand all the prisoners who *were* in the
prison; whatever they did there, it was his
doing. 23 The keeper of the prison did not
look into anything *that was* under [1]*Joseph's* authority, because [a]the LORD was
with him; and whatever he did, the LORD
made *it* prosper.

The Prisoners' Dreams

40 It came to pass after these things
that the [a]butler and the baker of
the king of Egypt offended their lord, the
king of Egypt. 2 And Pharaoh was [a]angry
with his two officers, the chief butler and
the chief baker. 3 [a]So he put them in custody in the house of the captain of the
guard, in the prison, the place where Joseph *was* confined. 4 And the captain of the
guard charged Joseph with them, and he
served them; so they were in custody for
a while.
5 Then the butler and the baker of the
king of Egypt, who *were* confined in the
prison, [a]had a dream, both of them, each
man's dream in one night *and* each man's
dream with its *own* interpretation. 6 And
Joseph came in to them in the morning
and looked at them, and saw that they
were [1]sad. 7 So he asked Pharaoh's officers
who *were* with him in the custody of his
lord's house, saying, [a]"Why do you look *so*
sad today?"
8 And they said to him, [a]"We each have
had a dream, and *there is* no interpreter
of it."
So Joseph said to them, [b]"Do not interpretations belong to God? Tell *them* to
me, please."
9 Then the chief butler told his dream to
Joseph, and said to him, "Behold, in my
dream a vine *was* before me, 10 and in the
vine *were* three branches; it *was* as
though it budded, its blossoms shot forth,
and its clusters brought forth ripe grapes.
11 Then Pharaoh's cup *was* in my hand;
and I took the grapes and pressed them
into Pharaoh's cup, and placed the cup in
Pharaoh's hand."
12 And Joseph said to him, [a]"This *is* the
interpretation of it: The three branches
[b]*are* three days. 13 Now within three days
Pharaoh will [a]lift up your head and restore you to your [1]place, and you will put
Pharaoh's cup in his hand according to
the former manner, when you were his
butler. 14 But [a]remember me when it is
well with you, and [b]please show kindness
to me; make mention of me to Pharaoh,
and get me out of this house. 15 For indeed
I was [a]stolen away from the land of the
Hebrews; [b]and also I have done nothing
here that they should put me into the
dungeon."
16 When the chief baker saw that the interpretation was good, he said to Joseph,
"I also *was* in my dream, and there *were*
three [1]white baskets on my head. 17 In the
uppermost basket *were* all kinds of baked
goods for Pharaoh, and the birds ate them
out of the basket on my head."
18 So Joseph answered and said, [a]"This
is the interpretation of it: The three bas-

14 a Gen. 14:13; 41:12
1 *laugh at*
17 a Ex. 23:1
19 a Prov. 6:34, 35
20 a Ps. 105:18 b Gen. 40:3, 15; 41:14
21 a Acts 7:9, 10
1 Caused him to be viewed with favor by
22 a Gen. 39:4; 40:3, 4
23 a Gen. 39:2, 3
1 Lit. *his hand*

CHAPTER 40
1 a Neh. 1:11
2 a Prov. 16:14
3 a Gen. 39:1, 20, 23; 41:10
5 a Gen. 37:5; 41:1
6 1 *dejected*
7 a Neh. 2:2
8 a Gen. 41:15 b [Dan. 2:11, 20–22, 27, 28, 47]
12 a Dan. 2:36; 4:18, 19 b Gen. 40:18; 42:17
13 a 2 Kin. 25:27
1 *position*
14 a Luke 23:42 b Josh. 2:12
15 a Gen. 37:26–28 b Gen. 39:20
16 1 Or *baskets of white bread*
18 a Gen. 40:12

kets *are* three days. 19[a]Within three days
Pharaoh will lift [1]off your head from you
and [b]hang you on a tree; and the birds will
eat your flesh from you."
20Now it came to pass on the third day,
which was Pharaoh's [a]birthday, that he
[b]made a feast for all his servants; and he
[c]lifted up the head of the chief butler and
of the chief baker among his servants.
21Then he [a]restored the chief butler to his
butlership again, and [b]he placed the cup
in Pharaoh's hand. 22But he [a]hanged the
chief baker, as Joseph had interpreted to
them. 23Yet the chief butler did not remember Joseph, but [a]forgot him.

Pharaoh's Dreams

41 Then it came to pass, at the end of
two full years, that [a]Pharaoh had a
dream; and behold, he stood by the river.
2Suddenly there came up out of the river
seven cows, fine looking and fat; and they
fed in the meadow. 3Then behold, seven
other cows came up after them out of the
river, ugly and gaunt, and stood by the
other cows on the bank of the river. 4And
the ugly and gaunt cows ate up the seven
fine looking and fat cows. So Pharaoh
awoke. 5He slept and dreamed a second
time; and suddenly seven heads of grain
came up on one stalk, plump and good.
6Then behold, seven thin heads, blighted
by the [a]east wind, sprang up after them.
7And the seven thin heads devoured the
seven plump and full heads. So Pharaoh
awoke, and indeed, *it was* a dream. 8Now
it came to pass in the morning [a]that his
spirit was troubled, and he sent and called
for all [b]the magicians of Egypt and all its
[c]wise men. And Pharaoh told them his
dreams, but *there was* no one who could
interpret them for Pharaoh.
9Then the [a]chief butler spoke to Pharaoh, saying: "I remember my faults this
day. 10When Pharaoh was [a]angry with his
servants, [b]and put me in custody in the
house of the captain of the guard, *both* me
and the chief baker, 11[a]we each had a
dream in one night, he and I. Each of us
dreamed according to the interpretation
of his *own* dream. 12Now there *was* a
young [a]Hebrew man with us there, a [b]ser-
vant of the captain of the guard. And we
told him, and he [c]interpreted our dreams
for us; to each man he interpreted according to his *own* dream. 13And it came to
pass, just [a]as he interpreted for us, so it
happened. He restored me to my office,
and he hanged him."
14[a]Then Pharaoh sent and called Joseph, and they [b]brought him quickly [c]out
of the dungeon; and he shaved, [d]changed
his clothing, and came to Pharaoh. 15And
Pharaoh said to Joseph, "I have had a
dream, and *there is* no one who can interpret it. [a]But I have heard it said of you
that you can understand a dream, to interpret it."

Lord, I pray that You will give ____ an answer of peace.

FROM GENESIS 41:16

16So Joseph answered Pharaoh, saying,
[a]"*It is* not in me; [b]God will give Pharaoh
an answer of peace."
17Then Pharaoh said to Joseph: "Behold, [a]in my dream I stood on the bank of
the river. 18Suddenly seven cows came up
out of the river, fine looking and fat; and
they fed in the meadow. 19Then behold,
seven other cows came up after them,
poor and very ugly and gaunt, such ugli-
ness as I have never seen in all the land of
Egypt. 20And the gaunt and ugly cows ate
up the first seven, the fat cows. 21When
they had eaten them up, no one would
have known that they had eaten them, for
they *were* just as ugly as at the beginning.
So I awoke. 22Also I saw in my dream, and
suddenly seven [1]heads came up on one
stalk, full and good. 23Then behold, seven
heads, withered, thin, *and* blighted by the
east wind, sprang up after them. 24And
the thin heads devoured the seven good
heads. So [a]I told *this* to the magicians,
but *there was* no one who could explain *it*
to me."
25Then Joseph said to Pharaoh, "The
dreams of Pharaoh *are* one; [a]God has
shown Pharaoh what He *is* about to do:
26The seven good cows *are* seven years,
and the seven good [1]heads *are* seven
years; the dreams *are* one. 27And the sev-
en thin and ugly cows which came up after them *are* seven years, and the seven
empty heads blighted by the east wind are
[a]seven years of famine. 28[a]This *is* the
thing which I have spoken to Pharaoh.

19 a Gen. 40:13 b Deut. 21:22 *1* Lit. *up*
20 a Matt. 14:6–10 b Mark 6:21 c Gen. 40:13, 19
21 a Gen. 40:13 b Neh. 2:1
22 a Gen. 40:19
23 a Eccl. 9:15, 16
CHAPTER 41
1 a Gen. 40:5
6 a Ex. 10:13
8 a Dan. 2:1, 3; 4:5, 19 b Ex. 7:11, 22 c Matt. 2:1
9 a Gen. 40:1, 14, 23
10 a Gen. 40:2, 3 b Gen. 39:20
11 a Gen. 40:5
12 a Gen. 39:14; 43:32 b Gen. 37:36 c Gen. 40:12
13 a Gen. 40:21, 22
14 a Ps. 105:20 b Dan. 2:25 c [1 Sam. 2:8] d 2 Kin. 25:27–29
15 a Dan. 5:16
16 a Dan. 2:30 b Dan. 2:22, 28, 47
17 a Gen. 41:1
22 *1* Heads of grain
24 a Is. 8:19
25 a Dan. 2:28, 29, 45
26 *1* Heads of grain
27 a 2 Kin. 8:1
28 a [Gen. 41:25, 32]

God has shown Pharaoh what He *is* about
to do. 29Indeed [a]seven years of great plenty will come throughout all the land of
Egypt; 30but after them seven years of
famine will [a]arise, and all the plenty will
be forgotten in the land of Egypt; and the
famine [b]will deplete the land. 31So the
plenty will not be known in the land because of the famine following, for it *will*
be very severe. 32And the dream was repeated to Pharaoh twice because the
[a]thing *is* established by God, and God will
shortly bring it to pass.
33"Now therefore, let Pharaoh select a
discerning and wise man, and set him
over the land of Egypt. 34Let Pharaoh do
this, and let him appoint [1]officers over the
land, [a]to collect one-fifth *of the produce*
of the land of Egypt in the seven plentiful
years. 35And [a]let them gather all the food
of those good years that are coming, and
store up grain under the [1]authority of
Pharaoh, and let them keep food in the
cities. 36Then that food shall be as a [1]re-
serve for the land for the seven years of
famine which shall be in the land of
Egypt, that the land [a]may not [2]perish
during the famine."

Joseph's Rise to Power

37So [a]the advice was good in the eyes of
Pharaoh and in the eyes of all his servants.
38And Pharaoh said to his servants, "Can
we find *such a one* as this, a man [a]in
whom *is* the Spirit of God?"
39Then Pharaoh said to Joseph, "Inasmuch as God has shown you all this, *there*
is no one as discerning and wise as you.
40[a]You shall be [1]over my house, and all
my people shall be ruled according to
your word; only in regard to the throne
will I be greater than you." 41And Pharaoh
said to Joseph, "See, I have [a]set you over
all the land of Egypt."
42Then Pharaoh [a]took his signet ring
off his hand and put it on Joseph's hand;
and he [b]clothed him in garments of fine
linen [c]and put a gold chain around his
neck. 43And he had him ride in the second
[a]chariot which he had; [b]and they cried
out before him, "Bow the knee!" So he set
him [c]over all the land of Egypt. 44Pharaoh
also said to Joseph, "I *am* Pharaoh, and
without your consent no man may lift his
hand or foot in all the land of Egypt."
45And Pharaoh called Joseph's name
[1]Zaphnath-Paaneah. And he gave him as
a wife [a]Asenath, the daughter of Poti-
Pherah priest of On. So Joseph went out
over *all* the land of Egypt.
46Joseph was thirty years old when he
[a]stood before Pharaoh king of Egypt. And
Joseph went out from the presence of
Pharaoh, and went throughout all the
land of Egypt. 47Now in the seven plentiful
years the ground brought forth [1]abun-
dantly. 48So he gathered up all the food of
the seven years which were in the land of
Egypt, and laid up the food in the cities;
he laid up in every city the food of the
fields which surrounded them. 49Joseph
gathered very much grain, [a]as the sand of
the sea, until he stopped counting, for *it*
was immeasurable.
50[a]And to Joseph were born two sons
before the years of famine came, whom
Asenath, the daughter of Poti-Pherah
priest of On, bore to him. 51Joseph called
the name of the firstborn [1]Manasseh: "For
God has made me forget all my toil and all
my [a]father's house." 52And the name of
the second he called [1]Ephraim: "For God
has caused me to be [a]fruitful in the land
of my affliction."
53Then the seven years of plenty which
were in the land of Egypt ended, 54[a]and
the seven years of famine began to come,
[b]as Joseph had said. The famine was in all
lands, but in all the land of Egypt there
was bread. 55So when all the land of Egypt
was famished, the people cried to Pharaoh
for bread. Then Pharaoh said to all the
Egyptians, "Go to Joseph; [a]whatever he
says to you, do." 56The famine was over all
the face of the earth, and Joseph opened
[1]all the storehouses and [a]sold to the
Egyptians. And the famine became severe
in the land of Egypt. 57[a]So all countries
came to Joseph in Egypt to [b]buy *grain,*
because the famine was severe in all lands.

Joseph's Brothers Go to Egypt

42 When [a]Jacob saw that there was
grain in Egypt, Jacob said to his
sons, "Why do you look at one another?"
2And he said, "Indeed I have heard that
there is grain in Egypt; go down to that
place and buy for us there, that we may
[a]live and not die."
3So Joseph's ten brothers went down to
buy grain in Egypt. 4But Jacob did not
send Joseph's brother Benjamin with his
brothers, for he said, [a]"Lest some calamity befall him." 5And the sons of Israel
went to buy *grain* among those who jour-

29 a Gen. 41:47
30 a Gen. 41:54, 56 b Gen. 47:13
32 a Num. 23:19
34 a [Prov. 6:6–8] *1 overseers*
35 a Gen. 41:48 *1* Lit. *hand*
36 a Gen. 47:15, 19 *1* Lit. *supply* *2 be cut off*
37 a Acts 7:10
38 a Num. 27:18
40 a Ps. 105:21 *1* In charge of
41 a Dan. 6:3
42 a Esth. 3:10 b Esth. 8:2, 15 c Dan. 5:7, 16, 29
43 a Gen. 46:29 b Esth. 6:9 c Gen. 42:6
45 a Gen. 46:20 *1* Probably Egyptian for *God Speaks and He Lives*
46 a 1 Sam. 16:21
47 *1* Lit. *by handfuls*
49 a Gen. 22:17
50 a Gen. 46:20; 48:5
51 a Ps. 45:10 *1* Lit. *Making Forgetful*
52 a Gen. 17:6; 28:3; 49:22 *1* Lit. *Fruitfulness*
54 a Acts 7:11 b Gen. 41:30
55 a John 2:5
56 a Gen. 42:6 *1* Lit. *all that was in them*
57 a Ezek. 29:12 b Gen. 27:28, 37; 42:3

CHAPTER 42
1 a Acts 7:12
2 a Gen. 43:8
4 a Gen. 42:38

neyed, for the famine was [a]in the land of
Canaan.
6Now Joseph *was* governor [a]over the
land; and it was he who sold to all the
people of the land. And Joseph's brothers
came and [b]bowed down before him with
their faces to the earth. 7Joseph saw his
brothers and recognized them, but he
acted as [a]a stranger to them and spoke
[1]roughly to them. Then he said to them,
"Where do you come from?"
And they said, "From the land of Canaan to buy food."
8So Joseph recognized his brothers, but
they did not recognize him. 9Then Joseph
[a]remembered the dreams which he had
dreamed about them, and said to them,
"You *are* spies! You have come to see the
[1]nakedness of the land!"
10And they said to him, "No, my lord,
but your servants have come to buy food.
11We *are* all one man's sons; we *are* honest *men;* your servants are not spies."
12But he said to them, "No, but you
have come to see the nakedness of the
land."
13And they said, "Your servants *are*
twelve brothers, the sons of one man in
the land of Canaan; and in fact, the youngest *is* with our father today, and one [a]*is*
no more."
14But Joseph said to them, "It *is* as I
spoke to you, saying, 'You *are* spies!' 15In
this *manner* you shall be tested: [a]By the
life of Pharaoh, you shall not leave this
place unless your youngest brother comes
here. 16Send one of you, and let him bring
your brother; and you shall be [1]kept in
prison, that your words may be tested to
see whether *there is* any truth in you; or
else, by the life of Pharaoh, surely you *are*
spies!" 17So he [1]put them all together in
prison [a]three days.
18Then Joseph said to them the third
day, "Do this and live, [a]*for* I fear God: 19If
you *are* honest *men,* let one of your
brothers be confined to your prison
house; but you, go and carry grain for the
famine of your houses. 20And [a]bring your
youngest brother to me; so your words
will be verified, and you shall not die."
And they did so. 21Then they said to one
another, [a]"We *are* truly guilty concerning
our brother, for we saw the anguish of his
soul when he pleaded with us, and we
would not hear; [b]therefore this distress
has come upon us."
22And Reuben answered them, saying,
[a]"Did I not speak to you, saying, 'Do not
sin against the boy'; and you would not
listen? Therefore behold, his blood is now
[b]required of us." 23But they did not know
that Joseph understood *them,* for he
spoke to them through an interpreter.
24And he turned himself away from them
and [a]wept. Then he returned to them
again, and talked with them. And he took
[b]Simeon from them and bound him before their eyes.

The Brothers Return to Canaan

25Then Joseph [a]gave a command to fill
their sacks with grain, to [b]restore every
man's money to his sack, and to give them
provisions for the journey. [c]Thus he did
for them. 26So they loaded their donkeys
with the grain and departed from there.
27But as [a]one *of them* opened his sack to
give his donkey feed at the encampment,
he saw his money; and there it was, in the
mouth of his sack. 28So he said to his
brothers, "My money has been restored,
and there it is, in my sack!" Then their
hearts [1]failed *them* and they were afraid,
saying to one another, "What *is* this *that*
God has done to us?"
29Then they went to Jacob their father
in the land of Canaan and told him all that
had happened to them, saying: 30"The
man *who is* lord of the land [a]spoke
[1]roughly to us, and took us for spies of the
country. 31But we said to him, 'We *are*
honest *men;* we are not spies. 32We *are*
twelve brothers, sons of our father; one *is*
no *more,* and the youngest *is* with our
father this day in the land of Canaan.'
33Then the man, the lord of the country,
said to us, [a]'By this I will know that you
are honest *men:* Leave one of your
brothers *here* with me, take *food for* the
famine of your households, and be gone.
34And bring your [a]youngest brother to
me; so I shall know that you *are* not spies,
but *that* you *are* honest *men.* I will grant
your brother to you, and you may [b]trade
in the land.' "
35Then it happened as they emptied
their sacks, that surprisingly [a]each man's
bundle of money *was* in his sack; and
when they and their father saw the bundles of money, they were afraid. 36And Jacob their father said to them, "You have
[a]bereaved me: Joseph is no *more,* Simeon

5 a Acts 7:11
6 a Gen. 41:41, 55 b Gen. 37:7–10; 41:43
7 a Gen. 45:1, 2 *1 harshly*
9 a Gen. 37:5–9 *1* Exposed parts
13 a Gen. 37:30; 42:32; 44:20
15 a 1 Sam. 1:26; 17:55
16 *1* Lit. *bound*
17 a Gen. 40:4, 7, 12 *1* Lit. *gathered*
18 a Lev. 25:43
20 a Gen. 42:34; 43:5; 44:23
21 a Hos. 5:15 b Prov. 21:13
22 a Gen. 37:21, 22, 29 b Gen. 9:5, 6
24 a Gen. 43:30; 45:14, 15 b Gen. 34:25, 30; 43:14, 23
25 a Gen. 44:1 b Gen. 43:12 c [Rom. 12:17, 20, 21]
27 a Gen. 43:21, 22
28 *1 sank*
30 a Gen. 42:7 *1 harshly*
33 a Gen. 42:15, 19, 20
34 a Gen. 42:20; 43:3, 5 b Gen. 34:10
35 a Gen. 43:12, 15, 21
36 a Gen. 43:14

is no *more,* and you want to take [b]Benja-
min. All these things are against me."
37 Then Reuben spoke to his father, saying, "Kill my two sons if I do not bring
him *back* to you; put him in my hands,
and I will bring him back to you."
38 But he said, "My son shall not go
down with you, for [a]his brother is dead,
and he is left alone. [b]If any calamity
should befall him along the way in which
you go, then you would [c]bring down my
gray hair with sorrow to the grave."

Joseph's Brothers Return with Benjamin

43 Now the famine *was* [a]severe in the
land. 2 And it came to pass, when
they had eaten up the grain which they
had brought from Egypt, that their father
said to them, "Go [a]back, buy us a little
food."
3 But Judah spoke to him, saying, "The
man solemnly warned us, saying, 'You
shall not see my face unless your [a]brother
is with you.' 4 If you send our brother with
us, we will go down and buy you food.
5 But if you will not send *him,* we will not
go down; for the man said to us, 'You shall
not see my face unless your brother *is*
with you.' "
6 And Israel said, "Why did you deal *so*
[1]wrongfully with me *as* to tell the man
whether you had still *another* brother?"
7 But they said, "The man asked us
pointedly about ourselves and our family,
saying, '*Is* your father still alive? Have you
another brother?' And we told him according to these words. Could we possibly
have known that he would say, 'Bring
your brother down'?"
8 Then Judah said to Israel his father,
"Send the lad with me, and we will arise
and go, that we may [a]live and not die,
both we and you *and* also our little ones.
9 I myself will be surety for him; from my
hand you shall require him. [a]If I do not
bring him *back* to you and set him before
you, then let me bear the blame forever.
10 For if we had not lingered, surely by
now we would have returned this second
time."
11 And their father Israel said to them,
"If *it must be* so, then do this: Take some
of the best fruits of the land in your vessels and [a]carry down a present for the
man—a little [b]balm and a little honey,
spices and myrrh, pistachio nuts and almonds. 12 Take double money in your
hand, and take back in your hand the
money [a]that was returned in the mouth of
your sacks; perhaps it was an oversight.
13 Take your brother also, and arise, go
back to the man. 14 And may God [a]Al-
mighty [b]give you mercy before the man,
that he may release your other brother
and Benjamin. [c]If I am bereaved, I am bereaved!"
15 So the men took that present and
Benjamin, and they took double money in
their hand, and arose and went [a]down
to Egypt; and they stood before Joseph.
16 When Joseph saw Benjamin with them,
he said to the [a]steward of his house, "Take
these men to my home, and slaughter [1]an
animal and make ready; for *these* men will
dine with me at noon." 17 Then the man
did as Joseph ordered, and the man
brought the men into Joseph's house.
18 Now the men were [a]afraid because
they were brought into Joseph's house;
and they said, "*It is* because of the money,
which was returned in our sacks the first
time, that we are brought in, so that he
may [1]make a case against us and seize us,
to take us as slaves with our donkeys."
19 When they drew near to the steward
of Joseph's house, they talked with him at
the door of the house, 20 and said, "O sir,
[a]we indeed came down the first time to
buy food; 21 but [a]it happened, when we
came to the encampment, that we opened
our sacks, and there, *each* man's money
was in the mouth of his sack, our money
in full weight; so we have brought it back
in our hand. 22 And we have brought down
other money in our hands to buy food. We
do not know who put our money in our
sacks."
23 But he said, "Peace *be* with you, do
not be afraid. Your God and the God of
your father has given you treasure in your
sacks; I had your money." Then he
brought [a]Simeon out to them.
24 So the man brought the men into Joseph's house and [a]gave *them* water, and
they washed their feet; and he gave their
donkeys feed. 25 Then they made the present ready for Joseph's coming at noon,
for they heard that they would eat bread
there.
26 And when Joseph came home, they
brought him the present which *was* in
their hand into the house, and [a]bowed
down before him to the earth. 27 Then he
asked them about *their* well-being, and

36 b [Rom. 8:28, 31]
38 a Gen. 37:22; 42:13; 44:20, 28 b Gen. 42:4; 44:29 c Gen. 37:35; 44:31

CHAPTER 43
1 a Gen. 41:54, 57; 42:5; 45:6, 11
2 a Gen. 42:2; 44:25
3 a Gen. 42:20; 43:5; 44:23
6 1 Lit. *wickedly*
8 a Gen. 42:2; 47:19
9 a Gen. 42:37; 44:32
11 a Gen. 32:20; 33:10; 43:25, 26 b Jer. 8:22
12 a Gen. 42:25, 35; 43:21, 22
14 a Gen. 17:1; 28:3; 35:11; 48:3 b Ps. 106:46 c Esth. 4:16
15 a Gen. 39:1; 46:3, 6
16 a Gen. 24:2; 39:4; 44:1 1 Lit. *a slaughter*
18 a Gen. 42:28 1 Lit. *roll himself upon us*
20 a Gen. 42:3, 10
21 a Gen. 42:27, 35
23 a Gen. 42:24
24 a Gen. 18:4; 19:2; 24:32
26 a Gen. 37:7, 10; 42:6; 44:14

said, "*Is* your father well, the old man [a]of whom you spoke? *Is* he still alive?"

28 And they answered, "Your servant our father *is* in good health; he *is* still alive." [a]And they bowed their heads down and prostrated themselves.

29 Then he lifted his eyes and saw his brother Benjamin, [a]his mother's son, and said, "*Is* this your younger brother [b]of whom you spoke to me?" And he said, "God be gracious to you, my son." 30 Now [a]his heart yearned for his brother; so Joseph made haste and sought *somewhere* to weep. And he went into *his* chamber and [b]wept there. 31 Then he washed his face and came out; and he restrained himself, and said, "Serve the [a]bread."

32 So they set him a place by himself, and them by themselves, and the Egyptians who ate with him by themselves; because the Egyptians could not eat food with the [a]Hebrews, for that *is* [b]an abomination to the Egyptians. 33 And they sat before him, the firstborn according to his [a]birthright and the youngest according to his youth; and the men looked in astonishment at one another. 34 Then he took servings to them from before him, but Benjamin's serving was [a]five times as much as any of theirs. So they drank and were merry with him.

Joseph's Cup

44 And he commanded [1]the [a]steward of his house, saying, [b]"Fill the men's sacks with food, as much as they can carry, and put each man's money in the mouth of his sack. 2 Also put my cup, the silver cup, in the mouth of the sack of the youngest, and his grain money." So he did according to the word that Joseph had spoken. 3 As soon as the morning dawned, the men were sent away, they and their donkeys. 4 When they had gone out of the city, *and* were not *yet* far off, Joseph said to his steward, "Get up, follow the men; and when you overtake them, say to them, 'Why have you [a]repaid evil for good? 5 *Is* not this *the one* from which my lord drinks, and with which he indeed practices divination? You have done evil in so doing.' "

6 So he overtook them, and he spoke to them these same words. 7 And they said to him, "Why does my lord say these words? Far be it from us that your servants should do such a thing. 8 Look, we brought back to you from the land of Canaan [a]the money which we found in the mouth of our sacks. How then could we steal silver or gold from your lord's house? 9 With whomever of your servants it is found, [a]let him die, and we also will be my lord's slaves."

10 And he said, "Now also *let* it *be* according to your words; he with whom it is found shall be my slave, and you shall be blameless." 11 Then each man speedily let down his sack to the ground, and each opened his sack. 12 So he searched. He began with the oldest and [1]left off with the youngest; and the cup was found in Benjamin's sack. 13 Then they [a]tore their clothes, and each man loaded his donkey and returned to the city.

14 So Judah and his brothers came to Joseph's house, and he *was* still there; and they [a]fell before him on the ground. 15 And Joseph said to them, "What deed *is* this you have done? Did you not know that such a man as I can certainly practice divination?"

16 Then Judah said, "What shall we say to my lord? What shall we speak? Or how shall we clear ourselves? God has [a]found out the iniquity of your servants; here [b]we are, my lord's slaves, both we and *he* also with whom the cup was found."

17 But he said, [a]"Far be it from me that I should do so; the man in whose hand the cup was found, he shall be my slave. And as for you, go up in peace to your father."

Judah Intercedes for Benjamin

18 Then Judah came near to him and said: "O my lord, please let your servant speak a word in my lord's hearing, and [a]do not let your anger burn against your servant; for you *are* even like Pharaoh. 19 My lord asked his servants, saying, 'Have you a father or a brother?' 20 And we said to my lord, 'We have a father, an old man, and [a]a child of *his* old age, *who is* young; his brother is [b]dead, and he [c]alone is left of his mother's children, and his [d]father loves him.' 21 Then you said to your servants, [a]'Bring him down to me, that I may set my eyes on him.' 22 And we said to my lord, 'The lad cannot leave his father, for *if* he should leave his father, *his father* would die.' 23 But you said to your servants, [a]'Unless your youngest brother comes down with you, you shall see my face no more.'

27 a Gen. 29:6; 42:11, 13; 43:7; 45:3
28 a Gen. 37:7, 10
29 a Gen. 35:17, 18 b Gen. 42:13
30 a 1 Kin. 3:26 b Gen. 42:24; 45:2, 14, 15; 46:29
31 a Gen. 43:25
32 a Gen. 41:12 b Gen. 46:34
33 a Gen. 27:36; 42:7
34 a Gen. 35:24; 45:22

CHAPTER 44
1 a Gen. 43:16 b Gen. 42:25 *1 Lit. the one over*
4 a 1 Sam. 25:21
8 a Gen. 43:21
9 a Gen. 31:32
12 *1 finished with*
13 a 2 Sam. 1:11
14 a Gen. 37:7, 10
16 a [Num. 32:23] b Gen. 44:9
17 a Prov. 17:15
18 a Ex. 32:22
20 a Gen. 37:3; 43:8; 44:30 b Gen. 42:38 c Gen. 46:19 d Gen. 42:4
21 a Gen. 42:15, 20
23 a Gen. 43:3, 5

24“So it was, when we went up to your
servant my father, that we told him the
words of my lord. 25And [a]our father said,
‘Go back *and* buy us a little food.’ 26But we
said, ‘We cannot go down; if our youngest
brother is with us, then we will go down;
for we may not see the man’s face unless
our youngest brother *is* with us.’ 27Then
your servant my father said to us, ‘You
know that [a]my wife bore me two sons;
28and the one went out from me, and I
said, [a]“Surely he is torn to pieces”; and
I have not seen him since. 29But if you
[a]take this one also from me, and calamity
befalls him, you shall bring down my gray
hair with sorrow to the grave.’
30“Now therefore, when I come to your
servant my father, and the lad *is* not with
us, since [a]his life is bound up in the lad’s
life, 31it will happen, when he sees that the
lad *is* not *with us,* that he will die. So your
servants will bring down the gray hair of
your servant our father with sorrow to the
grave. 32For your servant became surety
for the lad to my father, saying, [a]‘If I do
not bring him *back* to you, then I shall
bear the blame before my father forever.’
33Now therefore, please [a]let your servant
remain instead of the lad as a slave to
my lord, and let the lad go up with his
brothers. 34For how shall I go up to my
father if the lad *is* not with me, lest perhaps I see the evil that would [1]come upon
my father?”

Joseph Revealed to His Brothers

45 Then Joseph could not restrain
himself before all those who stood
by him, and he cried out, “Make everyone
go out from me!” So no one stood with
him [a]while Joseph made himself known
to his brothers. 2And he [a]wept aloud, and
the Egyptians and the house of Pharaoh
heard *it.*
3Then Joseph said to his brothers, [a]“I
am Joseph; does my father still live?” But
his brothers could not answer him, for
they were dismayed in his presence. 4And
Joseph said to his brothers, “Please come
near to me.” So they came near. Then he
said: “I *am* Joseph your brother, [a]whom
you sold into Egypt. 5But now, do not
therefore be grieved or angry with yourselves because you sold me here; [a]for God
sent me before you to preserve life. 6For
these two years the [a]famine *has been* in
the land, and *there are* still five years in
which *there will be* neither plowing nor
harvesting. 7And God [a]sent me before you
to preserve a [1]posterity for you in the
earth, and to save your lives by a great
deliverance. 8So now *it was* not you *who*
sent me here, but [a]God; and He has made
me [b]a father to Pharaoh, and lord of all his
house, and a [c]ruler throughout all the
land of Egypt.
9“Hurry and go up to my father, and say
to him, ‘Thus says your son Joseph: “God
has made me lord of all Egypt; come down
to me, do not [1]tarry. 10[a]You shall dwell in
the land of Goshen, and you shall be near
to me, you and your children, your children’s children, your flocks and your
herds, and all that you have. 11There I will
[a]provide for you, lest you and your household, and all that you have, come to poverty; for *there are* still five years of
famine.” ’
12“And behold, your eyes and the eyes of
my brother Benjamin see that *it is* [a]my
mouth that speaks to you. 13So you shall
tell my father of all my glory in Egypt, and
of all that you have seen; and you shall
hurry and [a]bring my father down here.”
14Then he fell on his brother Benjamin’s neck and wept, and Benjamin wept
on his neck. 15Moreover he [a]kissed all his
brothers and wept over them, and after
that his brothers talked with him.
16Now the report of it was heard in Pharaoh’s house, saying, “Joseph’s brothers
have come.” So it pleased Pharaoh and his
servants well. 17And Pharaoh said to Joseph, “Say to your brothers, ‘Do this: Load
your animals and depart; go to the land
of Canaan. 18Bring your father and your
households and come to me; I will give
you the best of the land of Egypt, and you
will eat [a]the [1]fat of the land. 19Now you
are commanded—do this: Take carts out
of the land of Egypt for your little ones
and your wives; bring your father and
come. 20Also do not be concerned about
your goods, for the best of all the land of
Egypt *is* yours.’ ”
21Then the sons of Israel did so; and
Joseph gave them [a]carts,[1] according to
the command of Pharaoh, and he gave
them provisions for the journey. 22He
gave to all of them, to each man, [a]changes
of garments; but to Benjamin he gave
three hundred *pieces* of silver and [b]five
changes of garments. 23And he sent to his
father these *things:* ten donkeys loaded
with the good things of Egypt, and ten

25 a Gen. 43:2
27 a Gen. 30:22–24; 35:16–18; 46:19
28 a Gen. 37:31–35
29 a Gen. 42:36, 38; 44:31
30 a [1 Sam. 18:1; 25:29]
32 a Gen. 43:9
33 a Ex. 32:32
34 *1* Lit. *find*

CHAPTER 45
1 a Acts 7:13
2 a Gen. 43:30; 46:29
3 a Acts 7:13
4 a Gen. 37:28; 39:1
5 a Gen. 45:7, 8; 50:20
6 a Gen. 43:1; 47:4, 13
7 a Gen. 45:5; 50:20 *1 remnant*
8 a [Rom. 8:28] b Is. 22:21 c Gen. 41:43; 42:6
9 *1 delay*
10 a Gen. 46:28, 34; 47:1, 6
11 a Gen. 47:12
12 a Gen. 42:23
13 a Acts 7:14
15 a Gen. 48:10
18 a Gen. 27:28; 47:6 *1* The choicest produce
21 a Gen. 45:19; 46:5 *1 wagons*
22 a 2 Kin. 5:5 b Gen. 43:34

female donkeys loaded with grain, bread, and food for his father for the journey. [24]So he sent his brothers away, and they departed; and he said to them, "See that you do not become troubled along the way."

[25]Then they went up out of Egypt, and came to the land of Canaan to Jacob their father. [26]And they told him, saying, "Joseph *is* still alive, and he *is* governor over all the land of Egypt." [a]And Jacob's heart stood still, because he did not believe them. [27]But when they told him all the words which Joseph had said to them, and when he saw the carts which Joseph had sent to carry him, the spirit [a]of Jacob their father revived. [28]Then Israel said, "*It is* enough. Joseph my son *is* still alive. I will go and see him before I die."

Jacob's Journey to Egypt

46 So Israel took his journey with all that he had, and came to [a]Beersheba, and offered sacrifices [b]to the God of his father Isaac. [2]Then God spoke to Israel [a]in the visions of the night, and said, "Jacob, Jacob!"

And he said, "Here I am."

[3]So He said, "I *am* God, [a]the God of your father; do not fear to go down to Egypt, for I will [b]make of you a great nation there. [4a]I will go down with you to Egypt, and I will also surely [b]bring you up *again;* and [c]Joseph [1]will put his hand on your eyes."

[5]Then [a]Jacob arose from Beersheba; and the sons of Israel carried their father Jacob, their little ones, and their wives, in the [1]carts [b]which Pharaoh had sent to carry him. [6]So they took their livestock and their goods, which they had acquired in the land of Canaan, and went to Egypt, [a]Jacob and all his descendants with him. [7]His sons and his sons' sons, his daughters and his sons' daughters, and all his descendants he brought with him to Egypt.

[8]Now [a]these *were* the names of the children of Israel, Jacob and his sons, who went to Egypt: [b]Reuben *was* Jacob's firstborn. [9]The [a]sons of Reuben *were* Hanoch, Pallu, Hezron, and Carmi. [10a]The sons of Simeon *were* [1]Jemuel, Jamin, Ohad, [2]Jachin, [3]Zohar, and Shaul, the son of a Canaanite woman. [11]The sons of [a]Levi *were* Gershon, Kohath, and Merari. [12]The sons of [a]Judah *were* [b]Er, Onan, Shelah, Perez, and Zerah (but Er and Onan died in the land of Canaan). [c]The sons of Perez were Hezron and Hamul. [13]The sons of Issachar *were* Tola, [1]Puvah, [2]Job, and Shimron. [14]The [a]sons of Zebulun *were* Sered, Elon, and Jahleel. [15]These *were* the [a]sons of Leah, whom she bore to Jacob in Padan Aram, with his daughter Dinah. All the persons, his sons and his daughters, *were* thirty-three.

[16]The sons of Gad *were* [1]Ziphion, Haggi, Shuni, [2]Ezbon, Eri, [3]Arodi, and Areli. [17a]The sons of Asher *were* Jimnah, Ishuah, Isui, Beriah, and Serah, their sister. And the sons of Beriah *were* Heber and Malchiel. [18a]These *were* the sons of Zilpah, [b]whom Laban gave to Leah his daughter; and these she bore to Jacob: sixteen persons.

[19]The [a]sons of Rachel, [b]Jacob's wife, *were* Joseph and Benjamin. [20a]And to Joseph in the land of Egypt were born Manasseh and Ephraim, whom Asenath, the daughter of Poti-Pherah priest of On, bore to him. [21a]The sons of Benjamin *were* Belah, Becher, Ashbel, Gera, Naaman, [b]Ehi, Rosh, [c]Muppim, [1]Huppim, and Ard. [22]These *were* the sons of Rachel, who were born to Jacob: fourteen persons in all.

[23]The son of Dan *was* [1]Hushim. [24a]The sons of Naphtali *were* [1]Jahzeel, Guni, Jezer, and [2]Shillem. [25a]These *were* the sons of Bilhah, [b]whom Laban gave to Rachel his daughter, and she bore these to Jacob: seven persons in all.

[26a]All the persons who went with Jacob to Egypt, who came from his body, [b]besides Jacob's sons' wives, *were* sixty-six persons in all. [27]And the sons of Joseph who were born to him in Egypt *were* two persons. [a]All the persons of the house of Jacob who went to Egypt were seventy.

Jacob Settles in Goshen

[28]Then he sent Judah before him to Joseph, [a]to point out before him *the way* to Goshen. And they came [b]to the land of Goshen. [29]So Joseph made ready his [a]chariot and went up to Goshen to meet his father Israel; and he presented himself to him, and [b]fell on his neck and wept on his neck a good while.

26 a Job 29:24
27 a Judg. 15:19

CHAPTER 46
1 a Gen. 21:31, 33; 26:32, 33; 28:10 b Gen. 26:24, 25; 28:13; 31:42; 32:9
2 a Gen. 15:1; 22:11; 31:11
3 a Gen. 17:1; 28:13 b Deut. 26:5
4 a Gen. 28:15; 31:3; 48:21 b Gen. 15:16; 50:12, 24, 25 c Gen. 50:1 *1* Will close your eyes when you die
5 a Acts 7:15 b Gen. 45:19–21 *1 wagons*
6 a Deut. 26:5
8 a Ex. 1:1–4 b Num. 26:4, 5
9 a Ex. 6:14
10 a Ex. 6:15 *1 Nemuel,* 1 Chr. 4:24 *2 Jarib,* 1 Chr. 4:24 *3 Zerah,* 1 Chr. 4:24
11 a 1 Chr. 6:1, 16
12 a 1 Chr. 2:3; 4:21 b Gen. 38:3, 7, 10 c Gen. 38:29
13 *1 Puah,* Num. 26:23; 1 Chr. 7:1 *2 Jashub,* Num. 26:24; 1 Chr. 7:1
14 a Num. 26:26
15 a Gen. 35:23; 49:31
16 *1* Sam., LXX *Zephon* and Num. 26:15 *2 Ozni,* Num. 26:16 *3 Arod,* Num. 26:17
17 a 1 Chr. 7:30
18 a Gen. 30:10; 37:2 b Gen. 29:24
19 a Gen. 35:24 b Gen. 44:27
20 a Gen. 41:45, 50–52; 48:1
21 a 1 Chr. 7:6; 8:1 b Num. 26:38 c Num. 26:39 *1 Hupham,* Num. 26:39
23 *1 Shuham,* Num. 26:42 **24** a Num. 26:48 *1 Jahziel,* 1 Chr. 7:13 *2 Shallum,* 1 Chr. 7:13 **25** a Gen. 30:5, 7 b Gen. 29:29 **26** a Ex. 1:5 b Gen. 35:11 **27** a Deut. 10:22
28 a Gen. 31:21 b Gen. 47:1 **29** a Gen. 41:43 b Gen. 45:14, 15

30And Israel said to Joseph, [a]"Now let
me die, since I have seen your face, because you *are* still alive."
31Then Joseph said to his brothers and
to his father's household, [a]"I will go up
and tell Pharaoh, and say to him, 'My
brothers and those of my father's house,
who *were* in the land of Canaan, have
come to me. 32And the men *are* [a]shep-
herds, for their occupation has been to
feed livestock; and they have brought
their flocks, their herds, and all that they
have.' 33So it shall be, when Pharaoh calls
you and says, [a]'What is your occupation?'
34that you shall say, 'Your servants' [a]oc-
cupation has been with livestock [b]from
our youth even till now, both we *and* also
our fathers,' that you may dwell in the
land of Goshen; for every shepherd *is* [c]an[1]
abomination to the Egyptians."

47 Then Joseph [a]went and told Pharaoh, and said, "My father and my
brothers, their flocks and their herds and
all that they possess, have come from the
land of Canaan; and indeed they *are* in
[b]the land of Goshen." 2And he took five
men from among his brothers and [a]pre-
sented them to Pharaoh. 3Then Pharaoh
said to his brothers, [a]"What *is* your occupation?"
And they said to Pharaoh, [b]"Your servants *are* shepherds, both we *and* also our
fathers." 4And they said to Pharaoh, [a]"We
have come to dwell in the land, because
your servants have no pasture for their
flocks, [b]for the famine *is* severe in the
land of Canaan. Now therefore, please let
your servants [c]dwell in the land of Goshen."
5Then Pharaoh spoke to Joseph, saying,
"Your father and your brothers have come
to you. 6[a]The land of Egypt *is* before you.
Have your father and brothers dwell in the
best of the land; let them dwell [b]in the
land of Goshen. And if you know *any* com-
petent men among them, then make
them chief herdsmen over my livestock."
7Then Joseph brought in his father Jacob and set him before Pharaoh; and Jacob [a]blessed Pharaoh. 8Pharaoh said to
Jacob, "How old *are* you?"
9And Jacob said to Pharaoh, [a]"The days
of the years of my [1]pilgrimage *are* [b]one
hundred and thirty years; [c]few and evil
have been the days of the years of my life,
and [d]they have not attained to the days of
the years of the life of my fathers in the
days of their pilgrimage." 10So Jacob
[a]blessed Pharaoh, and went out from before Pharaoh.
11And Joseph situated his father and his
brothers, and gave them a possession in
the land of Egypt, in the best of the land,
in the land of [a]Rameses, [b]as Pharaoh had
commanded. 12Then Joseph provided [a]his
father, his brothers, and all his father's
household with bread, according to the
number in *their* families.

Joseph Deals with the Famine

13Now *there was* no bread in all the
land; for the famine *was* very severe, [a]so
that the land of Egypt and the land of Canaan languished because of the famine.
14[a]And Joseph gathered up all the money
that was found in the land of Egypt and in
the land of Canaan, for the grain which
they bought; and Joseph brought the
money into Pharaoh's house.
15So when the money failed in the land
of Egypt and in the land of Canaan, all the
Egyptians came to Joseph and said, "Give
us bread, for [a]why should we die in your
presence? For the money has failed."
16Then Joseph said, "Give your livestock, and I will give you *bread* for your
livestock, if the money is gone." 17So they
brought their livestock to Joseph, and Joseph gave them bread *in exchange* for the
horses, the flocks, the cattle of the herds,
and for the donkeys. Thus he [1]fed them
with bread *in exchange* for all their livestock that year.
18When that year had ended, they came
to him the next year and said to him, "We
will not hide from my lord that our money
is gone; my lord also has our herds of livestock. There is nothing left in the sight of
my lord but our bodies and our lands.
19Why should we die before your eyes,
both we and our land? Buy us and our
land for bread, and we and our land will be
servants of Pharaoh; give *us* seed, that we
may [a]live and not die, that the land may
not be desolate."
20Then Joseph [a]bought all the land of
Egypt for Pharaoh; for every man of the
Egyptians sold his field, because the famine was severe upon them. So the land
became Pharaoh's. 21And as for the people, he [1]moved them into the cities, from
one end of the borders of Egypt to the
other end. 22[a]Only the land of the [b]priests
he did not buy; for the priests had rations
allotted to them by Pharaoh, and they ate

30 a Luke 2:29, 30
31 a Gen. 47:1
32 a Gen. 47:3
33 a Gen. 47:2, 3
34 a Gen. 47:3 b Gen. 30:35; 34:5; 37:17 c Gen. 43:32 *1 loathsome*

CHAPTER 47
1 a Gen. 46:31 b Gen. 45:10; 46:28; 50:8
2 a Acts 7:13
3 a Gen. 46:33 b Gen. 46:32, 34
4 a Deut. 26:5 b Gen. 43:1 c Gen. 46:34
6 a Gen. 20:15; 45:10, 18; 47:11 b Gen. 47:4
7 a Gen. 47:10; 48:15, 20
9 a [Heb. 11:9, 13] b Gen. 47:28 c [Job 14:1] d Gen. 5:5; 11:10, 11; 25:7, 8; 35:28 *1* Lit. *sojourning*
10 a Gen. 47:7
11 a Ex. 1:11; 12:37 b Gen. 47:6, 27
12 a Gen. 45:11; 50:21
13 a Gen. 41:30
14 a Gen. 41:56; 42:6
15 a Gen. 47:19
17 *1 supplied*
19 a Gen. 43:8
20 a Jer. 32:43
21 *1* So with MT, Tg.; Sam., LXX, Vg. *made the people virtual slaves*
22 a Ezra 7:24 b Gen. 41:45

their rations which Pharaoh gave them; therefore they did not sell their lands.

23Then Joseph said to the people, "Indeed I have bought you and your land this day for Pharaoh. Look, *here is* seed for you, and you shall sow the land. 24And it shall come to pass in the harvest that you shall give one-fifth to Pharaoh. Four-fifths shall be your own, as seed for the field and for your food, for those of your households and as food for your little ones."

25So they said, "You have saved [a]our lives; let us find favor in the sight of my lord, and we will be Pharaoh's servants." 26And Joseph made it a law over the land of Egypt to this day, *that* Pharaoh should have one-fifth, [a]except for the land of the priests only, *which* did not become Pharaoh's.

Joseph's Vow to Jacob

27So Israel [a]dwelt in the land of Egypt, in the country of Goshen; and they had possessions there and [b]grew and multiplied exceedingly. 28And Jacob lived in the land of Egypt seventeen years. So the length of Jacob's life was one hundred and forty-seven years. 29When the time [a]drew near that Israel must die, he called his son Joseph and said to him, "Now if I have found favor in your sight, please [b]put your hand under my thigh, and [c]deal kindly and truly with me. [d]Please do not bury me in Egypt, 30but [a]let me lie with my fathers; you shall carry me out of Egypt and [b]bury me in their burial place."

And he said, "I will do as you have said."

31Then he said, "Swear to me." And he swore to him. So [a]Israel bowed himself on the head of the bed.

Jacob Blesses Joseph's Sons

48 Now it came to pass after these things that Joseph was told, "Indeed your father *is* sick"; and he took with him his two sons, [a]Manasseh and Ephraim. 2And Jacob was told, "Look, your son Joseph is coming to you"; and Israel [1]strengthened himself and sat up on the bed. 3Then Jacob said to Joseph: "God [a]Almighty appeared to me at [b]Luz in the land of Canaan and blessed me, 4and said to me, 'Behold, I will [a]make you fruitful and multiply you, and I will make of you a multitude of people, and [b]give this land to your descendants after you [c]*as* an everlasting possession.' 5And now your [a]two sons, Ephraim and Manasseh, who were born to you in the land of Egypt before I came to you in Egypt, *are* mine; as Reuben and Simeon, they shall be mine. 6Your [1]offspring [2]whom you beget after them shall be yours; they will be called by the name of their brothers in their inheritance. 7But as for me, when I came from Padan, [a]Rachel died beside me in the land of Canaan on the way, when *there was* but a little distance to go to Ephrath; and I buried her there on the way to Ephrath (that is, Bethlehem)."

8Then Israel saw Joseph's sons, and said, "Who *are* these?"

9Joseph said to his father, "They *are* my sons, whom God has given me in this *place.*"

And he said, "Please bring them to me, and [a]I will bless them." 10Now [a]the eyes of Israel were dim with age, *so that* he could not see. Then Joseph brought them near him, and he [b]kissed them and embraced them. 11And Israel said to Joseph, [a]"I had not thought to see your face; but in fact, God has also shown me your offspring!"

12So Joseph brought them from beside his knees, and he bowed down with his face to the earth. 13And Joseph took them both, Ephraim with his right hand toward Israel's left hand, and Manasseh with his left hand toward Israel's right hand, and brought *them* near him. 14Then Israel stretched out his right hand and [a]laid *it* on Ephraim's head, who *was* the younger, and his left hand on Manasseh's head, [b]guiding his hands knowingly, for Manasseh *was* the [c]firstborn. 15And [a]he blessed Joseph, and said:

"God, [b]before whom my fathers
Abraham and Isaac walked,
The God who has fed me all my life
long to this day,
16 The Angel [a]who has redeemed me
from all evil,
Bless the lads;
Let [b]my name be named upon
them,
And the name of my fathers
Abraham and Isaac;
And let them [c]grow into a
multitude in the midst of the
earth."

17Now when Joseph saw that his father [a]laid his right hand on the head of Ephraim, it displeased him; so he took hold of his father's hand to remove it from

25 a Gen. 33:15
26 a Gen. 47:22
27 a Gen. 47:11 b Gen. 17:6; 26:4; 35:11; 46:3
29 a Deut. 31:14 b Gen. 24:2–4 c Gen. 24:49 d Gen. 50:25
30 a 2 Sam. 19:37 b Gen. 49:29; 50:5–13
31 a 1 Kin. 1:47
CHAPTER 48
1 a Gen. 41:51, 56; 46:20; 50:23
2 1 Collected his strength
3 a Gen. 43:14; 49:25 b Gen. 28:13, 19; 35:6, 9
4 a Gen. 46:3 b Ex. 6:8 c Gen. 17:8
5 a Josh. 13:7; 14:4
6 1 *children* 2 Who are born to you
7 a Gen. 35:9, 16, 19, 20
9 a Gen. 27:4; 47:15
10 a Gen. 27:1 b Gen. 27:27; 45:15; 50:1
11 a Gen. 45:26
14 a Matt. 19:15 b Gen. 48:19 c Josh. 17:1
15 a [Heb. 11:21] b Gen. 17:1; 24:40
16 a Gen. 22:11, 15–18; 28:13–15; 31:11 b Amos 9:12 c Num. 26:34, 37
17 a Gen. 48:14

Ephraim's head to Manasseh's head. [18]And
Joseph said to his father, "Not so, my
father, for this *one is* the firstborn; put
your right hand on his head."
[19]But his father refused and said, [a]"I
know, my son, I know. He also shall become a people, and he also shall be great;
but truly [b]his younger brother shall be
greater than he, and his descendants shall
become a multitude of nations."
[20]So he blessed them that day, saying,
[a]"By you Israel will bless, saying, 'May
God make you as Ephraim and as Manasseh!'" And thus he set Ephraim before
Manasseh.
[21]Then Israel said to Joseph, "Behold, I
am dying, but [a]God will be with you and
bring you back to the land of your fathers.
[22]Moreover [a]I have given to you one [1]por-
tion above your brothers, which I took
from the hand [b]of the Amorite with my
sword and my bow."

Jacob's Last Words to His Sons

49 And Jacob called his sons and said,
"Gather together, that I may [a]tell
you what shall befall you [b]in the last days:

2 "Gather together and hear, you sons of Jacob,
And listen to Israel your father.

3 "Reuben, you are [a]my firstborn,
My might and the beginning of my strength,
The excellency of dignity and the excellency of power.
4 Unstable as water, you shall not excel,
Because you [a]went up to your father's bed;
Then you defiled *it*—
He went up to my couch.

5 "Simeon and Levi *are* brothers;
Instruments of [1]cruelty *are in* their dwelling place.
6 [a]Let not my soul enter their council;
Let not my honor be united [b]to their assembly;
[c]For in their anger they slew a man,
And in their self-will they [1]hamstrung an ox.
7 Cursed *be* their anger, for *it is* fierce;
And their wrath, for it is cruel!
[a]I will divide them in Jacob
And scatter them in Israel.

8 "Judah,[a] you *are he* whom your brothers shall praise;
[b]Your hand *shall be* on the neck of your enemies;
[c]Your father's children shall bow down before you.
9 Judah *is* [a]a lion's whelp;
From the prey, my son, you have gone up.
[b]He [1]bows down, he lies down as a lion;
And as a lion, who shall rouse him?
10 [a]The [1]scepter shall not depart from Judah,
Nor [b]a lawgiver from between his feet,
[c]Until Shiloh comes;
[d]And to Him *shall be* the obedience of the people.
11 Binding his donkey to the vine,
And his donkey's colt to the choice vine,
He washed his garments in wine,
And his clothes in the blood of grapes.
12 His eyes *are* darker than wine,
And his teeth whiter than milk.

13 "Zebulun[a] shall dwell by the haven of the sea;
He *shall become* a haven for ships,
And his border shall [b]adjoin Sidon.

14 "Issachar[a] is a strong donkey,
Lying down between two burdens;
15 He saw that rest *was* good,
And that the land *was* pleasant;
He bowed [a]his shoulder to bear *a burden,*
And became a band of slaves.

16 "Dan[a] shall judge his people
As one of the tribes of Israel.
17 [a]Dan shall be a serpent by the way,
A viper by the path,
That bites the horse's heels
So that its rider shall fall backward.
18 [a]I have waited for your salvation, O LORD!

19 "Gad,[a1] a troop shall [2]tramp upon him,
But he shall [2]triumph at last.

20 "Bread from [a]Asher *shall be* rich,
And he shall yield royal dainties.

21 "Naphtali[a] *is* a deer let loose;
He uses beautiful words.

19 [a]Gen. 48:14 [b]Num. 1:33, 35
20 [a]Ruth 4:11, 12
21 [a]Gen. 28:15; 46:4; 50:24
22 [a]Josh. 24:32 [b]Gen. 34:28 [1]Lit. *shoulder*

CHAPTER 49
1 [a]Deut. 33:1, 6–25 [b]Is. 2:2; 39:6
3 [a]Gen. 29:32
4 [a]Gen. 35:22
5 [1]*violence*
6 [a]Prov. 1:15, 16 [b]Ps. 26:9 [c]Gen. 34:26 [1]*lamed*
7 [a]Josh. 19:1, 9; 21:1–42
8 [a]Deut. 33:7 [b]Ps. 18:40 [c]1 Chr. 5:2
9 [a][Rev. 5:5] [b]Num. 23:24; 24:9 [1]*couches*
10 [a]Num. 24:17 [b]Ps. 60:7 [c]Is. 11:1 [d]Ps. 2:6–9; 72:8–11 [1]A symbol of kingship
13 [a]Deut. 33:18, 19 [b]Gen. 10:19
14 [a]1 Chr. 12:32
15 [a]1 Sam. 10:9
16 [a]Deut. 33:22
17 [a]Judg. 18:27
18 [a]Is. 25:9
19 [a]Deut. 33:20 [1]Lit. *Troop* [2]Lit. *raid*
20 [a]Deut. 33:24
21 [a]Deut. 33:23

22 "Joseph *is* a fruitful bough,
A fruitful bough by a well;
His branches run over the wall.
23 The archers have [a]bitterly grieved him,
Shot *at him* and hated him.
24 But his [a]bow remained in strength,
And the arms of his hands were [1]made strong
By the hands of [b]the Mighty *God* of Jacob
[c](From there [d]*is* the Shepherd, [e]the Stone of Israel),
25 [a]By the God of your father who will help you,
[b]And by the Almighty [c]who will bless you
With blessings of heaven above,
Blessings of the deep that lies beneath,
Blessings of the breasts and of the womb.
26 The blessings of your father
Have excelled the blessings of my ancestors,
[a]Up to the utmost bound of the everlasting hills.
[b]They shall be on the head of Joseph,
And on the crown of the head of him who was separate from his brothers.

O God, help ____ and bless them with the blessings of heaven above.

FROM GENESIS 49:25

27 "Benjamin is a [a]ravenous wolf;
In the morning he shall devour the prey,
[b]And at night he shall divide the spoil."

28 All these *are* the twelve tribes of Israel, and this *is* what their father spoke to them. And he blessed them; he blessed each one according to his own blessing.

Jacob's Death and Burial

29 Then he charged them and said to them: "I [a]am to be gathered to my people; [b]bury me with my fathers [c]in the cave that *is* in the field of Ephron the Hittite,
30 in the cave that *is* in the field of Machpelah, which *is* before Mamre in the land of Canaan, [a]which Abraham bought with the field of Ephron the Hittite as a possession
for a burial place. 31 [a]There they buried
Abraham and Sarah his wife, [b]there they buried Isaac and Rebekah his wife, and
there I buried Leah. 32 The field and the
cave that *is* there *were* purchased from
the sons of Heth." 33 And when Jacob had
finished commanding his sons, he drew his feet up into the bed and breathed his last, and was gathered to his people.

50

1 Then Joseph [a]fell on his father's face and [b]wept over him, and
kissed him. 2 And Joseph commanded his
servants the physicians to [a]embalm his father. So the physicians embalmed Israel.
3 Forty days were required for him, for
such are the days required for those who are embalmed; and the Egyptians [a]mourned[1] for him seventy days.

4 Now when the days of his mourning
were past, Joseph spoke to [a]the household of Pharaoh, saying, "If now I have found favor in your eyes, please speak in the
hearing of Pharaoh, saying, 5 [a]'My father
made me swear, saying, "Behold, I am dying; in my grave [b]which I dug for myself in the land of Canaan, there you shall bury me." Now therefore, please let me go up and bury my father, and I will come back.' "

6 And Pharaoh said, "Go up and bury your father, as he made you swear."

7 So Joseph went up to bury his father;
and with him went up all the servants of Pharaoh, the elders of his house, and all
the elders of the land of Egypt, 8 as well as
all the house of Joseph, his brothers, and his father's house. Only their little ones, their flocks, and their herds they left in
the land of Goshen. 9 And there went up
with him both chariots and horsemen, and it was a very great gathering.

10 Then they came to the threshing floor of Atad, which *is* beyond the Jordan, and they [a]mourned there with a great and
very solemn lamentation. [b]He observed
seven days of mourning for his father.
11 And when the inhabitants of the land,
the Canaanites, saw the mourning at the threshing floor of Atad, they said, "This *is* a deep mourning of the Egyptians."
Therefore its name was called [1]Abel Mizraim, which *is* beyond the Jordan.

---

23 [a] Gen. 37:4, 24
24 [a] Job 29:20 [b] Ps. 132:2, 5 [c] Gen. 45:11; 47:12 [d] [Ps. 23:1; 80:1] [e] Is. 28:16 [1] Or *supple*
25 [a] Gen. 28:13; 32:9; 35:3; 43:23; 50:17 [b] Gen. 17:1; 35:11 [c] Deut. 33:13
26 [a] Deut. 33:15 [b] Deut. 33:16
27 [a] Judg. 20:21, 25 [b] Zech. 14:1
29 [a] Gen. 15:15; 25:8; 35:29 [b] Gen. 47:30 [c] Gen. 23:16–20; 50:13
30 [a] Gen. 23:3–20
31 [a] Gen. 23:19, 20; 25:9 [b] Gen. 35:29; 50:13

CHAPTER 50
1 [a] Gen. 46:4, 29 [b] 2 Kin. 13:14
2 [a] Gen. 50:26
3 [a] Deut. 34:8 [1] Lit. *wept*
4 [a] Esth. 4:2
5 [a] Gen. 47:29–31 [b] Is. 22:16
10 [a] Acts 8:2 [b] 1 Sam. 31:13
11 [1] Lit. *Mourning of Egypt*

12 So his sons did for him just as he had
commanded them. 13 For [a]his sons carried
him to the land of Canaan, and buried
him in the cave of the field of Machpelah,
before Mamre, which Abraham [b]bought
with the field from Ephron the Hittite as
property for a burial place. 14 And after he
had buried his father, Joseph returned to
Egypt, he and his brothers and all who
went up with him to bury his father.

O Lord, as for ____, they
meant evil against ____; but
You meant it for good,
in order to bring about
Your purposes.
FROM GENESIS 50:20

Joseph Reassures His Brothers

15 When Joseph's brothers saw that
their father was dead, [a]they said, "Perhaps
Joseph will hate us, and may [1]actually repay us for all the evil which we did to
him." 16 So they sent *messengers* to Joseph, saying, "Before your father died he
commanded, saying, 17 'Thus you shall say
to Joseph: "I beg you, please forgive the
trespass of your brothers and their sin;
[a]for they did evil to you."' Now, please,
forgive the trespass of the servants of [b]the
God of your father." And Joseph wept
when they spoke to him.
18 Then his brothers also went and [a]fell
down before his face, and they said, "Behold, we *are* your servants."
19 Joseph said to them, [a]"Do not be
afraid, [b]for *am* I in the place of God?
20 [a]But as for you, you meant evil against
me; *but* [b]God meant it for good, in order
to bring it about as *it is* this day, to save
many people alive. 21 Now therefore, do
not be afraid; [a]I will provide for you and
your little ones." And he comforted them
and spoke [1]kindly to them.

Death of Joseph

22 So Joseph dwelt in Egypt, he and his
father's household. And Joseph lived one
hundred and ten years. 23 Joseph saw
Ephraim's children [a]to the third *generation.* [b]The children of Machir, the son of
Manasseh, [c]were also brought up on Joseph's knees.
24 And Joseph said to his brethren, "I am
dying; but [a]God will surely visit you, and
bring you out of this land to the land [b]of
which He swore to Abraham, to Isaac, and
to Jacob." 25 Then [a]Joseph took an oath
from the children of Israel, saying, "God
will surely [1]visit you, and [b]you shall carry
up my [c]bones from here." 26 So Joseph
died, *being* one hundred and ten years
old; and they embalmed him, and he was
put in a coffin in Egypt.

13 a Acts 7:16 b Gen. 23:16–20
15 a [Job 15:21] *1 fully*
17 a [Prov. 28:13] b Gen. 49:25
18 a Gen. 37:7–10; 41:43; 44:14
19 a Gen. 45:5 b 2 Kin. 5:7
20 a Ps. 56:5 b [Acts 3:13–15]
21 a [Matt. 5:44] *1 Lit. to their hearts*
23 a Job 42:16 b Num. 26:29; 32:39 c Gen. 30:3
24 a Ex. 3:16, 17 b Gen. 26:3; 35:12; 46:4
25 a Ex. 13:19 b Deut. 1:8; 30:1–8 c Ex. 13:19 *1 give attention to*

AUTHOR: *Traditionally Moses*
DATE: *Approximately 1400 B.C.*
THEME: *Deliverance*
KEY WORDS: *Deliver, Sacrifice, Sign, Tabernacle, Sanctuary*

EXODUS

Dear Woman of Destiny,

How important and precious family is to us! In the Book of Exodus, we see God's hand on His family, delivering them from bondage and walking with them through the wilderness, ever faithful and merciful, providing for their every need. How good it is to know He will do the same for us and our families.

His love and mine,

Marilyn Hickey

Israel's Suffering in Egypt

NOW [a]these *are* the names of the
children of Israel who came to
Egypt; each man and his household came with Jacob: 2Reuben, Simeon,
Levi, and Judah; 3Issachar, Zebulun, and
Benjamin; 4Dan, Naphtali, Gad, and Asher. 5All those [1]who were descendants of
Jacob were [a]seventy[2] persons (for Joseph
was in Egypt *already*). 6And [a]Joseph died,
all his brothers, and all that generation.
7[a]But the children of Israel were fruitful
and increased abundantly, multiplied and
[1]grew exceedingly mighty; and the land
was filled with them.

8Now there arose a new king over
Egypt, [a]who did not know Joseph. 9And
he said to his people, "Look, the people
of the children of Israel *are* more and
[a]mightier than we; 10[a]come, let us [b]deal
shrewdly with them, lest they multiply,
and it happen, in the event of war, that
they also join our enemies and fight
against us, and *so* go up out of the land."
11Therefore they set taskmasters over
them [a]to afflict them with their [b]burdens.
And they built for Pharaoh [c]supply cities,
Pithom [d]and Raamses. 12But the more
they afflicted them, the more they multiplied and grew. And they were in dread of
the children of Israel. 13So the Egyptians
made the children of Israel [a]serve with
[1]rigor. 14And they [a]made their lives bitter
with hard bondage—[b]in mortar, in brick,
and in all manner of service in the field.
All their service in which they made them
serve *was* with rigor.

15Then the king of Egypt spoke to the
[a]Hebrew midwives, of whom the name of
one *was* Shiphrah and the name of the
other Puah; 16and he said, "When you do
the duties of a midwife for the Hebrew
women, and see *them* on the birthstools,
if it *is* a [a]son, then you shall kill him; but
if it *is* a daughter, then she shall live."
17But the midwives [a]feared God, and did
not do [b]as the king of Egypt commanded
them, but saved the male children alive.
18So the king of Egypt called for the midwives and said to them, "Why have you
done this thing, and saved the male children alive?"

19And [a]the midwives said to Pharaoh,
"Because the Hebrew women *are* not like
the Egyptian women; for they [1]*are* lively
and give birth before the midwives come
to them."

20[a]Therefore God dealt well with the
midwives, and the people multiplied and
[1]grew very mighty. 21And so it was, because the midwives feared God, [a]that He
[1]provided households for them.

22So Pharaoh commanded all his people, saying, [a]"Every son who is [1]born you
shall cast into the river, and every daughter you shall save alive."

Moses Is Born

2 And [a]a man of the house of Levi went
and took *as wife* a daughter of Levi.
2So the woman conceived and bore a son.
And [a]when she saw that he *was* a beautiful
child, she hid him three months. 3But
when she could no longer hide him, she
took an ark of [a]bulrushes for him, daubed
it with [b]asphalt and [c]pitch, put the child
in it, and laid *it* in the reeds [d]by the river's
bank. 4[a]And his sister stood afar off, to
know what would be done to him.

5Then the [a]daughter of Pharaoh came
down to bathe at the river. And her maidens walked along the riverside; and when
she saw the ark among the reeds, she sent
her maid to get it. 6And when she opened
it, she saw the child, and behold, the baby
wept. So she had compassion on him, and
said, "This is one of the Hebrews' children."

7Then his sister said to Pharaoh's
daughter, "Shall I go and call a nurse for
you from the Hebrew women, that she
may nurse the child for you?"

8And Pharaoh's daughter said to her,
"Go." So the maiden went and called the
child's mother. 9Then Pharaoh's daughter
said to her, "Take this child away and
nurse him for me, and I will give *you* your
wages." So the woman took the child and
nursed him. 10And the child grew, and she
brought him to Pharaoh's daughter, and
he became [a]her son. So she called his
name [1]Moses, saying, "Because I drew
him out of the water."

Moses Flees to Midian

11Now it came to pass in those days,
[a]when Moses was grown, that he went out
to his brethren and looked at their burdens. And he saw an Egyptian beating a
Hebrew, one of his brethren. 12So he
looked this way and that way, and when
he saw no one, he [a]killed the Egyptian
and hid him in the sand. 13And [a]when he
went out the second day, behold, two He-

CHAPTER 1
1 a Gen. 46:8–27
5 a Gen. 46:26, 27
1 Lit. *who came from the loins of*
2 DSS, LXX *seventy-five;* cf. Acts 7:14
6 a Gen. 50:26
7 a Acts 7:17
1 *became very numerous*
8 a Acts 7:18, 19
9 a Gen. 26:16
10 a Ps. 83:3, 4
b Acts 7:19
11 a Ex. 3:7; 5:6
b Ex. 1:14; 2:11; 5:4–9; 6:6
c 1 Kin. 9:19
d Gen. 47:11
13 a Gen. 15:13
1 *harshness*
14 a Num. 20:15
b Ps. 81:6
15 a Ex. 2:6
16 a Acts 7:19
17 a Prov. 16:6
b Dan. 3:16, 18
19 a Josh. 2:4
1 *have vigor of life,* bear quickly, easily
20 a [Prov. 11:18]
1 *became very numerous*
21 a 1 Sam. 2:35
1 *gave them families*
22 a Acts 7:19
1 Sam., LXX, Tg. add *to the Hebrews*

CHAPTER 2
1 a Ex. 6:16–20
2 a Acts 7:20
3 a Is. 18:2
b Gen. 14:10
c Gen. 6:14
d Is. 19:6
4 a Num. 26:59
5 a Acts 7:21
10 a Acts 7:21
1 Heb. *Mosheh,* lit. *Drawn Out*
11 a Heb. 11:24–26
12 a Acts 7:24, 25
13 a Acts 7:26–28

brew men [b]were fighting, and he said to
the one who did the wrong, "Why are you
striking your companion?"
14Then he said, [a]"Who made you a
prince and a judge over us? Do you intend
to kill me as you killed the Egyptian?"
So Moses [b]feared and said, "Surely this
thing is known!" 15When Pharaoh heard
of this matter, he sought to kill Moses.
But [a]Moses fled from [1]the face of Pharaoh
and dwelt in the land of [b]Midian; and he
sat down by [c]a well.
16[a]Now the priest of Midian had seven
daughters. [b]And they came and drew water, and they filled the [c]troughs to water
their father's flock. 17Then the [a]shepherds
came and [b]drove them away; but Moses
stood up and helped them, and [c]watered
their flock.
18When they came to [a]Reuel[1] their father, [b]he said, "How *is it that* you have
come so soon today?"
19And they said, "An Egyptian delivered
us from the hand of the shepherds, and he
also drew enough water for us and watered the flock."
20So he said to his daughters, "And
where *is* he? Why *is* it *that* you have left
the man? Call him, that he may [a]eat
bread."
21Then Moses was content to live with
the man, and he gave [a]Zipporah his
daughter to Moses. 22And she bore *him* a
son. He called his name [a]Gershom,[1] for

13 b Prov. 25:8
14 a Acts 7:27, 28 b Judg. 6:27
15 a Acts 7:29 b Ex. 3:1 c Gen. 24:11; 29:2 *1 the presence of Pharaoh*
16 a Ex. 3:1; 4:18; 18:12 b Gen. 24:11, 13, 19; 29:6–10 c Gen. 30:38
17 a Gen. 47:3 b Gen. 26:19–21 c Gen. 29:3, 10
18 a Num. 10:29 b Ex. 3:1; 4:18 *1 Jethro,* Ex. 3:1
20 a Gen. 31:54; 43:25
21 a Ex. 4:25; 18:2
22 a Ex. 4:20; 18:3, 4 *1* Lit. *Stranger There*

JOCHEBED

A mother's love can make her do things for her children—things that will cause her heart to break. After Jochebed gave birth to Moses, she struggled with the same wrenching dilemma that every Hebrew boy's mother faced in the days when the birth of a baby boy brought fear and the need for a quick decision. Knowing that the Egyptian king had decreed death for every male child born to the Israelites, she wondered what she could do to spare her son's life.

There was only one way to save Moses, and that was to let him go. It must have shattered her heart to realize she had no choice but to send him away. With an amazing faith in the God of Israel, this ingenious woman waterproofed a basket, laid baby Moses inside, and gently placed him on the water. Then she felt the cradle slip from her fingers and watched it float away, surely hoping that the river would rock him to sleep and carry him to safety.

With remarkable bravery, she emptied her arms of her three-month-old son; and with remarkable grace, God allowed her to hold him again. He allowed her to become Moses' nurse and to take care of him for a season. When he was old enough, she surrendered him once again, this time knowing he would safely enjoy the best that Egypt had to offer as the adopted grandson of the king who would have killed him.

Moses is often called "the deliverer" of God's people. But before he could lead the Israelites out of bondage and send them on their way to the Promised Land, he had to escape Pharaoh's fatal hand. Because Jochebed had the faith to let him go and the courage to embrace a devastating loss, she delivered the one who would later deliver a nation.

he said, "I have been [b]a [2]stranger in a
foreign land."
23Now it happened [a]in the process of
time that the king of Egypt died. Then the
children of Israel [b]groaned because of the
bondage, and they cried out; and [c]their
cry came up to God because of the bondage. 24So God [a]heard their groaning, and
God [b]remembered His [c]covenant with
Abraham, with Isaac, and with Jacob.
25And God [a]looked upon the children of
Israel, and God [b]acknowledged *them.*

May ____ know Your name Lord, "I AM WHO I AM." This is Your name forever.

FROM EXODUS 3:14, 15

Moses at the Burning Bush

3 Now Moses was tending the flock of
[a]Jethro his father-in-law, [b]the priest
of Midian. And he led the flock to the back
of the desert, and came to [c]Horeb, [d]the
mountain of God. 2And [a]the Angel of the
LORD appeared to him in a flame of fire
from the midst of a bush. So he looked,
and behold, the bush was burning with
fire, but the bush *was* not consumed.
3Then Moses said, "I will now turn aside
and see this [a]great sight, why the bush
does not burn."
4So when the LORD saw that he turned
aside to look, God called [a]to him from
the midst of the bush and said, "Moses,
Moses!"
And he said, "Here I am."
5Then He said, "Do not draw near this
place. [a]Take your sandals off your feet,
for the place where you stand *is* holy
ground." 6Moreover He said, [a]"I *am* the
God of your father—the God of Abraham,
the God of Isaac, and the God of Jacob."
And Moses hid his face, for [b]he was afraid
to look upon God.
7And the LORD said: [a]"I have surely seen
the oppression of My people who *are* in
Egypt, and have heard their cry [b]because
of their taskmasters, [c]for I know their
[1]sorrows. 8So [a]I have come down to [b]de-
liver them out of the hand of the Egyptians, and to bring them up from that land

22 [b]Acts 7:29 [2]*sojourner, temporary resident*
23 [a]Acts 7:34 [b]Deut. 26:7 [c]James 5:4
24 [a]Ex. 6:5 [b]Gen. 15:13; 22:16–18; 26:2–5; 28:13–15 [c]Gen. 12:1–3; 15:14; 17:1–14
25 [a]Ex. 4:31 [b]Ex. 3:7

CHAPTER 3
1 [a]Ex. 4:18 [b]Ex. 2:16 [c]Ex. 17:6 [d]Ex. 18:5
2 [a]Deut. 33:16
3 [a]Acts 7:31
4 [a]Deut. 33:16
5 [a]Josh. 5:15
6 [a][Matt. 22:32] [b]1 Kin. 19:13
7 [a]Ex. 2:23–25 [b]Ex. 1:11 [c]Ex. 2:25 [1]*pain*
8 [a]Gen. 15:13–16; 46:4; 50:24, 25 [b]Ex. 6:6–8; 12:51 [c]Deut. 1:25; 8:7–9 [d]Jer. 11:5 [e]Gen. 15:19–21
9 [a]Ex. 2:23 [b]Ex. 1:11, 13, 14
10 [a][Mic. 6:4]
11 [a]Ex. 4:10; 6:12
12 [a]Gen. 31:3 [b]Ex. 4:8; 19:3
14 [a][John 8:24, 28, 58]
15 [a]Ps. 30:4; 97:12; 102:12; 135:13
16 [a]Ex. 4:29 [b]Ex. 2:25; 4:31
17 [a]Gen. 15:13–21; 46:4; 50:24, 25

[c]to a good and large land, to a land [d]flow-
ing with milk and honey, to the place of
[e]the Canaanites and the Hittites and the
Amorites and the Perizzites and the Hivites and the Jebusites. 9Now therefore,
behold, [a]the cry of the children of Israel
has come to Me, and I have also seen the
[b]oppression with which the Egyptians oppress them. 10[a]Come now, therefore, and
I will send you to Pharaoh that you may
bring My people, the children of Israel,
out of Egypt."
11But Moses said to God, [a]"Who *am* I
that I should go to Pharaoh, and that I
should bring the children of Israel out of
Egypt?"
12So He said, [a]"I will certainly be with
you. And this *shall be* a [b]sign to you that
I have sent you: When you have brought
the people out of Egypt, you shall serve
God on this mountain."
13Then Moses said to God, "Indeed,
when I come to the children of Israel and
say to them, 'The God of your fathers has
sent me to you,' and they say to me, 'What
is His name?' what shall I say to them?"

God's name is, "I am that I am." He is the Almighty; He is omnipotent; He is omniscient. He brings the eternal past and the eternal future into the present.

HOWARD CARTER

14And God said to Moses, "I AM WHO I
AM." And He said, "Thus you shall say to
the children of Israel, [a]'I AM has sent me
to you.'" 15Moreover God said to Moses,
"Thus you shall say to the children of Israel: 'The LORD God of your fathers, the God
of Abraham, the God of Isaac, and the God
of Jacob, has sent me to you. This *is* [a]My
name forever, and this *is* My memorial to
all generations.' 16Go and [a]gather the elders of Israel together, and say to them,
'The LORD God of your fathers, the God of
Abraham, of Isaac, and of Jacob, appeared
to me, saying, [b]"I have surely visited you
and *seen* what is done to you in Egypt;
17and I have said [a]I will bring you up out

Exodus 3:1–6

Dear Woman of Destiny,

The Lord is revealing Himself in our day in intense, glorious ways, just as He did for Moses in the burning bush. When He comes blazing on the scene, things change. The ordinary becomes extraordinary; the unholy is made holy. He is raising up passionate and pure women who reflect His fiery character.

For me, bitterness and pride formed a stranglehold on my personality most of my life. This became the "taproot" of my personality, feeding every other attitude. After so many years of nurturing this root, I became the "professional" minister, pretending to have the fire of God. My passion for Jesus was being snuffed out.

I could teach other women the "Scriptural Formula for Freedom from Bitterness," but I was not free. Fasting and prayer only suppressed this taproot before it would spring up again. Whenever I would get close to true repentance and change, self-justification would rise up, quenching my freedom. This vicious cycle dulled me, making me ineffective as a believer.

I needed fire, not a formula! I needed a direct encounter with God's burning presence. I needed Him to do something *in* me that was beyond my self-effort.

In the midst of a mighty outpouring of the Holy Spirit in our church, I would watch while other women were supernaturally touched by God's fire. Yet, fear mixed with pride held me back from receiving. My husband finally told me with tears in his eyes, "You are going to miss your destiny if you don't yield to the glory of God."

By then, I was desperate to experience God intensely. My pride *and* my body ended up on the floor as I heard women praying, "Jesus, plunge your hand in Kathy's soul and free her from that taproot of bitterness and pride!" As I yielded to the fire of God, I felt the weightiness of His glory on me and a burning within me. Lasting freedom came!

At my burning bush, my destiny was restored. It was an intimate, intense time where the Lord consumed my lifelong stranglehold. Years later, I am still free while learning the height and depth of the real me. My passion is burning brighter each day.

This testimony has touched the lives of many women around the world, helping them to have an intense encounter with God. Now I understand the words of John Wesley. When asked once why thousands came to hear him preach, he replied, "I set myself on fire and they come to watch me burn." That's the way I want to be!

My prayer for you is that you will meet face-to-face with the power of God and allow Him to do what you cannot do on your own. May He consume all that is not of Him and replace it with His fire. May He set you ablaze!

Kathy Gray

of the affliction of Egypt to the land of the Canaanites and the Hittites and the Amorites and the Perizzites and the Hivites and the Jebusites, to a land flowing with milk and honey." ' 18Then [a]they will heed your voice; and [b]you shall come, you and the elders of Israel, to the king of Egypt; and you shall say to him, 'The LORD God of the Hebrews has [c]met with us; and now, please, let us go three days' journey into the wilderness, that we may sacrifice to the LORD our God.' 19But I am sure that the king of Egypt [a]will not let you go, no, not even by a mighty hand. 20So I will [a]stretch out My hand and strike Egypt with [b]all My wonders which I will do in its midst; and [c]after that he will let you go. 21And [a]I will give this people favor in the sight of the Egyptians; and it shall be, when you go, that you shall not go empty-handed. 22[a]But every woman shall ask of her neighbor, namely, of her who dwells near her house, [b]articles of silver, articles of gold, and clothing; and you shall put *them* on your sons and on your daughters. So [c]you shall plunder the Egyptians."

Miraculous Signs for Pharaoh

4 Then Moses answered and said, "But suppose they will not believe me or listen to my voice; suppose they say, 'The LORD has not appeared to you.' "

2So the LORD said to him, "What *is* that in your hand?"

He said, "A rod."

3And He said, "Cast it on the ground." So he cast it on the ground, and it became a serpent; and Moses fled from it. 4Then the LORD said to Moses, "Reach out your hand and take *it* by the tail" (and he reached out his hand and caught it, and it became a rod in his hand), 5"that they may [a]believe that the [b]LORD God of their fathers, the God of Abraham, the God of Isaac, and the God of Jacob, has appeared to you."

6Furthermore the LORD said to him, "Now put your hand in your bosom." And he put his hand in his bosom, and when he took it out, behold, his hand *was* leprous, [a]like snow. 7And He said, "Put your hand in your bosom again." So he put his hand in his bosom again, and drew it out of his bosom, and behold, [a]it was restored like his *other* flesh. 8"Then it will be, if they do not believe you, nor heed the message of the [a]first sign, that they may believe the message of the latter sign. 9And it shall be, if they do not believe even these two signs, or listen to your voice, that you shall take water from [1]the river and pour *it* on the dry *land.* [a]The water which you take from the river will become blood on the dry *land.*"

10Then Moses said to the LORD, "O my Lord, I *am* not eloquent, neither before nor since You have spoken to Your servant; but [a]I *am* slow of speech and [1]slow of tongue."

I praise You, O Lord, that You have made our mouths. Teach ____ how to speak and what they should say.

FROM EXODUS 4:11, 12

11So the LORD said to him, [a]"Who has made man's mouth? Or who makes the mute, the deaf, the seeing, or the blind? *Have* not I, the LORD? 12Now therefore, go, and I will be [a]with your mouth and teach you what you shall say."

13But he said, "O my Lord, [a]please send by the hand of whomever *else* You may send."

14So [a]the anger of the LORD was kindled against Moses, and He said: "Is not Aaron the Levite your [b]brother? I know that he can speak well. And look, [c]he is also coming out to meet you. When he sees you, he will be glad in his heart. 15Now [a]you shall speak to him and [b]put the words in his mouth. And I will be with your mouth and with his mouth, and [c]I will teach you what you shall do. 16So he shall be your spokesman to the people. And he himself shall be as a mouth for you, and [a]you shall be to him as God. 17And you shall take this rod in your hand, with which you shall do the signs."

Moses Goes to Egypt

18So Moses went and returned to [a]Jethro his father-in-law, and said to him, "Please let me go and return to my brethren who *are* in Egypt, and see whether they are still alive."

And Jethro said to Moses, [b]"Go in peace."

18 a Ex. 4:31 b Ex. 5:1, 3 c Num. 23:3, 4, 15, 16
19 a Ex. 5:2
20 a Ex. 6:6; 9:15 b Deut. 6:22 c Ex. 11:1; 12:31–37
21 a Ex. 11:3; 12:36
22 a Ex. 11:2 b Ex. 33:6 c Job 27:17

CHAPTER 4
5 a Ex. 4:31; 19:9 b Ex. 3:6, 15
6 a Num. 12:10
7 a Deut. 32:39
8 a Ex. 7:6–13
9 a Ex. 7:19, 20 *1 The Nile*
10 a Ex. 3:11; 4:1; 6:12 *1 heavy* or *dull of tongue;* cannot talk very well
11 a Ps. 94:9; 146:8
12 a Is. 50:4
13 a Jon. 1:3
14 a Num. 11:1, 33 b Num. 26:59 c Ex. 4:27
15 a Ex. 4:12, 30; 7:1, 2 b Num. 23:5, 12 c Deut. 5:31
16 a Ex. 7:1, 2
18 a Ex. 2:21; 3:1; 4:18 b Judg. 18:6

19Now the LORD said to Moses in [a]Midi-
an, "Go, return to [b]Egypt; for [c]all the men
who sought your life are dead." 20Then
Moses [a]took his wife and his sons and set
them on a donkey, and he returned to the
land of Egypt. And Moses took [b]the rod of
God in his hand.

21And the LORD said to Moses, "When
you go back to Egypt, see that you do all
those [a]wonders before Pharaoh which I
have put in your hand. But [b]I will harden
his heart, so that he will not let the people
go. 22Then you shall [a]say to Pharaoh,
'Thus says the LORD: [b]"Israel *is* My son,
[c]My firstborn. 23So I say to you, let My son
go that he may serve Me. But if you refuse
to let him go, indeed [a]I will kill your son,
your firstborn." ' "

24And it came to pass on the way, at the
[a]encampment, that the LORD [b]met him
and sought to [c]kill him. 25Then [a]Zipporah
took [b]a sharp stone and cut off the foreskin of her son and [1]cast *it* at [2]*Moses'* feet,
and said, "Surely you *are* a husband of
blood to me!" 26So He let him go. Then
she said, *"You are* a [1]husband of
blood!"—because of the circumcision.

27And the LORD said to Aaron, "Go into
the wilderness [a]to meet Moses." So he
went and met him on [b]the mountain of
God, and kissed him. 28So Moses [a]told
Aaron all the words of the LORD who had
sent him, and all the [b]signs which He
had commanded him. 29Then Moses and
Aaron [a]went and gathered together all the
elders of the children of Israel. 30[a]And
Aaron spoke all the words which the LORD
had spoken to Moses. Then he did the
signs in the sight of the people. 31So the
people [a]believed; and when they heard
that the LORD had [b]visited the children of
Israel and that He [c]had looked on their
affliction, then [d]they bowed their heads
and worshiped.

First Encounter with Pharaoh

5 Afterward Moses and Aaron went in
and told Pharaoh, "Thus says the
LORD God of Israel: 'Let My people go, that
they may [1]hold [a]a feast to Me in the wilderness.' "

2And Pharaoh said, [a]"Who *is* the LORD,
that I should obey His voice to let Israel
go? I do not know the LORD, [b]nor will I let
Israel go."

3So they said, [a]"The God of the Hebrews has [b]met with us. Please, let us go
three days' journey into the desert and
sacrifice to the LORD our God, lest He fall
upon us with [c]pestilence or with the
sword."

4Then the king of Egypt said to them,
"Moses and Aaron, why do you take the
people from their work? Get *back* to your
[a]labor." 5And Pharaoh said, "Look, the
people of the land *are* [a]many now, and
you make them rest from their labor!"

6So the same day Pharaoh commanded
the [a]taskmasters of the people and their
officers, saying, 7"You shall no longer give
the people straw to make [a]brick as before.
Let them go and gather straw for themselves. 8And you shall lay on them the
quota of bricks which they made before.
You shall not reduce it. For they are idle;
therefore they cry out, saying, 'Let us go
and sacrifice to our God.' 9Let more work
be laid on the men, that they may labor in
it, and let them not regard false words."

10And the taskmasters of the people and
their officers went out and spoke to the
people, saying, "Thus says Pharaoh: 'I will
not give you straw. 11Go, get yourselves
straw where you can find it; yet none of
your work will be reduced.' " 12So the people were scattered abroad throughout all
the land of Egypt to gather stubble instead
of straw. 13And the taskmasters forced
them to hurry, saying, "Fulfill your work,
your daily quota, as when there was
straw." 14Also the [a]officers of the children
of Israel, whom Pharaoh's taskmasters
had set over them, were [b]beaten *and* were
asked, "Why have you not fulfilled your
task in making brick both yesterday and
today, as before?"

15Then the officers of the children of
Israel came and cried out to Pharaoh, saying, "Why are you dealing thus with your
servants? 16There is no straw given to
your servants, and they say to us, 'Make
brick!' And indeed your servants *are* beat-
en, but the fault *is* in your *own* people."

17But he said, "You *are* idle! Idle!
Therefore you say, 'Let us go *and* sacrifice
to the LORD.' 18Therefore go now *and*
work; for no straw shall be given you, yet
you shall deliver the quota of bricks."
19And the officers of the children of Israel
saw *that* they *were* in trouble after it was
said, "You shall not reduce *any* bricks
from your daily quota."

20Then, as they came out from Pharaoh, they met Moses and Aaron who
stood there to meet them. 21[a]And they
said to them, "Let the LORD look on you

19 a Ex. 3:1; 18:1 b Gen. 46:3, 6 c Ex. 2:15, 23
20 a Ex. 18:2–5 b Num. 20:8, 9, 11
21 a Ex. 3:20; 11:9, 10 b John 12:40
22 a Ex. 5:1 b Hos. 11:1 c Jer. 31:9
23 a Ex. 11:5; 12:29
24 a Gen. 42:27 b Num. 22:22 c Gen. 17:14
25 a Ex. 2:21; 18:2 b Josh. 5:2, 3 *1 Lit. made it touch* *2* Lit. *his*
26 *1 bridegroom*
27 a Ex. 4:14 b Ex. 3:1; 18:5; 24:13
28 a Ex. 4:15, 16 b Ex. 4:8, 9
29 a Ex. 3:16; 12:21
30 a Ex. 4:15, 16
31 a Ex. 3:18; 4:8, 9; 19:9 b Gen. 50:24 c Ex. 2:25; 3:7 d Gen. 24:26

CHAPTER 5
1 a Ex. 3:18; 7:16; 10:9 *1 keep a pilgrim-feast*
2 a 2 Kin. 18:35 b Ex. 3:19; 7:14
3 a Ex. 3:18; 7:16 b Num. 23:3 c Ex. 9:15
4 a Ex. 1:11; 2:11; 6:6
5 a Ex. 1:7, 9
6 a Ex. 1:11; 3:7; 5:10, 13, 14
7 a Ex. 1:14
14 a Ex. 5:6 b Is. 10:24
21 a Ex. 6:9; 14:11; 15:24; 16:2

and judge, because you have made [1]us abhorrent in the sight of Pharaoh and in the sight of his servants, to put a sword in their hand to kill us."

Israel's Deliverance Assured

22So Moses returned to the LORD and said, "Lord, why have You brought trouble on this people? Why *is* it You have sent me? 23For since I came to Pharaoh to speak in Your name, he has done evil to this people; neither have You delivered Your people at all."

6 Then the LORD said to Moses, "Now you shall see what I will do to Pharaoh. For [a]with a strong hand he will let them go, and with a strong hand [b]he will drive them out of his land."

O Father, bring ______ out from under their burdens, rescue them from their bondage and redeem them.

FROM EXODUS 6:6

2And God spoke to Moses and said to him: "I *am* [1]the LORD. 3[a]I appeared to Abraham, to Isaac, and to Jacob, as [b]God Almighty, but *by* My name [c]LORD[1] I was not known to them. 4[a]I have also [1]established My covenant with them, [b]to give them the land of Canaan, the land of their [2]pilgrimage, [c]in which they were [3]strangers. 5And [a]I have also heard the groaning of the children of Israel whom the Egyptians keep in bondage, and I have remembered My covenant. 6Therefore say to the children of Israel: [a]'I *am* the LORD; [b]I will bring you out from under the burdens of the Egyptians, I will [c]rescue you from their bondage, and I will redeem you with [1]an outstretched arm and with great judgments. 7I will [a]take you as My people, and [b]I will be your God. Then you shall know that I *am* the LORD your God who brings you out [c]from under the burdens of the Egyptians. 8And I will bring you into the land which I [a]swore[1] to give to Abraham, Isaac, and Jacob; and I will give it to you *as* a heritage: I *am* the LORD.'" 9So Moses spoke thus to the children of Israel; [a]but they did not heed Moses, because of [b]anguish[1] of spirit and cruel bondage.

10And the LORD spoke to Moses, saying, 11"Go in, tell Pharaoh king of Egypt to let the children of Israel go out of his land."

12And Moses spoke before the LORD, saying, "The children of Israel have not heeded me. How then shall Pharaoh heed me, for [a]I *am* [1]of uncircumcised lips?"

13Then the LORD spoke to Moses and Aaron, and gave them a [a]command[1] for the children of Israel and for Pharaoh king of Egypt, to bring the children of Israel out of the land of Egypt.

The Family of Moses and Aaron

14These *are* the heads of their fathers' houses: [a]The sons of Reuben, the firstborn of Israel, *were* Hanoch, Pallu, Hezron, and Carmi. These are the families of Reuben. 15[a]And the sons of Simeon *were* [1]Jemuel, Jamin, Ohad, Jachin, Zohar, and Shaul the son of a Canaanite woman. These *are* the families of Simeon. 16These *are* the names of [a]the sons of Levi according to their generations: Gershon, Kohath, and Merari. And the years of the life of Levi *were* one hundred and thirty-seven. 17[a]The sons of Gershon *were* Libni and Shimi according to their families. 18And [a]the sons of Kohath *were* Amram, Izhar, Hebron, and Uzziel. And the years of the life of Kohath *were* one hundred and thirty-three. 19[a]The sons of Merari *were* Mahli and Mushi. These *are* the families of Levi according to their generations.

20Now [a]Amram took for himself [b]Jochebed, his father's sister, as wife; and she bore him [b]Aaron and Moses. And the years of the life of Amram *were* one hundred and thirty-seven. 21[a]The sons of Izhar *were* Korah, Nepheg, and Zichri. 22And [a]the sons of Uzziel *were* Mishael, Elzaphan, and Zithri. 23Aaron took to himself Elisheba, daughter of [a]Amminadab, sister of Nahshon, as wife; and she bore him [b]Nadab, Abihu, [c]Eleazar, and Ithamar. 24And [a]the sons of Korah *were* Assir, Elkanah, and Abiasaph. These are the families of the Korahites. 25Eleazar, Aaron's son, took for himself one of the daughters of Putiel as wife; and [a]she bore him Phinehas. These *are* the heads of the fathers'

21 [1] Lit. *our scent to stink before*

CHAPTER 6

1 a Ex. 3:19 b Ex. 12:31, 33, 39

2 [1] Heb. *YHWH*

3 a Gen. 17:1; 35:9; 48:3 b Gen. 28:3; 35:11 c Ps. 68:4; 83:18 [1] Heb. *YHWH*, traditionally *Jehovah*

4 a Gen. 12:7; 15:18; 17:4, 7, 8; 26:3; 28:4, 13 b Lev. 25:23 c Gen. 28:4 [1] *made* or *ratified* [2] *sojournings* [3] *sojourners*, temporary residents

5 a Ex. 2:24

6 a Deut. 6:12 b Deut. 26:8 c Deut. 7:8 [1] Mighty power

7 a 2 Sam. 7:24 b Ex. 29:45, 46 c Ex. 5:4, 5

8 a Gen. 15:18; 26:3 [1] *promised*, lit. *lifted up My hand*

9 a Ex. 5:21 b Ex. 2:23 [1] Lit. *shortness*

12 a Jer. 1:6 [1] One who does not speak well

13 a Deut. 31:14 [1] *charge*

14 a Gen. 46:9

15 a Gen. 46:10 [1] *Nemuel*, Num. 26:12

16 a Gen. 46:11

17 a 1 Chr. 6:17

18 a 1 Chr. 6:2, 18

19 a 1 Chr. 6:19; 23:21

20 a Ex. 2:1, 2 b Num. 26:59

21 a 1 Chr. 6:37, 38

22 a Lev. 10:4

23 a Ruth 4:19, 20 b Lev. 10:1 c Ex. 28:1

24 a Num. 26:11

25 a Num. 25:7, 11

houses of the Levites according to their
families.
26 These *are the same* Aaron and Moses
to whom the LORD said, "Bring out the
children of Israel from the land of Egypt
according to their [a]armies."[1] 27 These *are*
the ones who spoke to Pharaoh king of
Egypt, [a]to bring out the children of Israel
from Egypt. These *are the same* Moses
and Aaron.

Aaron Is Moses' Spokesman

28 And it came to pass, on the day the
LORD spoke to Moses in the land of Egypt,
29 that the LORD spoke to Moses, saying, "I
am the LORD. [a]Speak to Pharaoh king of
Egypt all that I say to you."
30 But Moses said before the LORD, "Behold, [a]I *am* [1]of uncircumcised lips, and
how shall Pharaoh heed me?"
7 So the LORD said to Moses: "See, I
have made you [a]*as* God to Pharaoh,
and Aaron your brother shall be [b]your
prophet. 2 You [a]shall speak all that I command you. And Aaron your brother shall
tell Pharaoh to send the children of Israel
out of his land. 3 And [a]I will harden Pharaoh's heart, and [b]multiply My [c]signs and
My wonders in the land of Egypt. 4 But
[a]Pharaoh will not heed you, so [b]that I may
lay My hand on Egypt and bring My [1]ar-
mies *and* My people, the children of Israel,
out of the land of Egypt [c]by great judgments. 5 And the Egyptians [a]shall know
that I *am* the LORD, when I [b]stretch out
My hand on Egypt and [c]bring out the children of Israel from among them."
6 Then Moses and Aaron [a]did *so;* just as
the LORD commanded them, so they did.
7 And Moses *was* [a]eighty years old and
[b]Aaron eighty-three years old when they
spoke to Pharaoh.

Aaron's Miraculous Rod

8 Then the LORD spoke to Moses and
Aaron, saying, 9 "When Pharaoh speaks to
you, saying, [a]'Show a miracle for yourselves,' then you shall say to Aaron, [b]'Take
your rod and cast *it* before Pharaoh, *and*
let it become a serpent.'" 10 So Moses and
Aaron went in to Pharaoh, and they did so,
just [a]as the LORD commanded. And Aaron
cast down his rod before Pharaoh and before his servants, and it [b]became a serpent.
11 But Pharaoh also [a]called the wise
men and [b]the [1]sorcerers; so the magicians of Egypt, they also [c]did in like man-

26 [a]Ex. 7:4; 12:17, 51 *[1] hosts*
27 [a]Ps. 77:20
29 [a]Ex. 6:11; 7:2
30 [a]Ex. 4:10; 6:12 [1] One who does not speak well

CHAPTER 7
1 [a]Ex. 4:16 [b]Ex. 4:15, 16
2 [a]Ex. 4:15
3 [a]Ex. 4:21; 9:12 [b]Ex. 11:9 [c]Deut. 4:34
4 [a]Ex. 3:19, 20; 10:1; 11:9 [b]Ex. 9:14 [c]Ex. 6:6; 12:12 *[1] hosts*
5 [a]Ps. 9:16 [b]Ex. 9:15 [c]Ex. 3:20; 6:6; 12:51
6 [a]Ex. 7:2
7 [a]Deut. 29:5; 31:2; 34:7 [b]Num. 33:39
9 [a]Is. 7:11 [b]Ex. 4:2, 3, 17
10 [a]Ex. 7:9 [b]Ex. 4:3
11 [a]Gen. 41:8 [b]2 Tim. 3:8 [c]Ex. 7:22; 8:7, 18 *[1] soothsayers* *[2] secret arts*
14 [a]Ex. 8:15; 10:1, 20, 27
15 [a]Ex. 2:5; 8:20 [b]Ex. 4:2, 3; 7:10
16 [a]Ex. 3:13, 18; 4:22 [b]Ex. 3:12, 18; 4:23; 5:1, 3; 8:1 *[1] worship*
17 [a]Ex. 5:2; 7:5; 10:2 [b]Ex. 4:9; 7:20 [c]Rev. 11:6; 16:4, 6
18 [a]Ex. 7:24 *[1] be weary of drinking*
19 [a]Ex. 8:5, 6, 16; 9:22; 10:12, 21; 14:21, 26

ner with their [2]enchantments. 12 For
every man threw down his rod, and they
became serpents. But Aaron's rod swallowed up their rods. 13 And Pharaoh's
heart grew hard, and he did not heed
them, as the LORD had said.

So I will trust that the greatest of all miracles will be wrought once more. The humanly impossible will become the divinely possible, to the greater praise of His glory. The exceeding greatness of His power to you who believe will be made manifest.

AMY CARMICHAEL

The First Plague: Waters Become Blood

14 So the LORD said to Moses: [a]"Pharaoh's heart *is* hard; he refuses to let the
people go. 15 Go to Pharaoh in the morning, when he goes out to the [a]water, and
you shall stand by the river's bank to meet
him; and [b]the rod which was turned to a
serpent you shall take in your hand. 16 And
you shall say to him, [a]'The LORD God of
the Hebrews has sent me to you, saying,
"Let My people go, [b]that they may [1]serve
Me in the wilderness"; but indeed, until
now you would not hear! 17 Thus says the
LORD: "By this [a]you shall know that I *am*
the LORD. Behold, I will strike the waters
which *are* in the river with the rod that *is*
in my hand, and [b]they shall be turned [c]to
blood. 18 And the fish that *are* in the river
shall die, the river shall stink, and the
Egyptians will [a]loathe[1] to drink the water
of the river."'"
19 Then the LORD spoke to Moses, "Say
to Aaron, 'Take your rod and [a]stretch out
your hand over the waters of Egypt, over
their streams, over their rivers, over their
ponds, and over all their pools of water,
that they may become blood. And there

shall be blood throughout all the land of
Egypt, both in *buckets of* wood and *pitchers of* stone.' " 20And Moses and Aaron did
so, just as the LORD commanded. So he
[a]lifted up the rod and struck the waters
that *were* in the river, in the sight of Pharaoh and in the sight of his servants. And
all the [b]waters that *were* in the river were
turned to blood. 21The fish that *were* in
the river died, the river stank, and the
Egyptians [a]could not drink the water of
the river. So there was blood throughout
all the land of Egypt.
22[a]Then the magicians of Egypt did [b]so
with their [1]enchantments; and Pharaoh's
heart grew hard, and he did not heed
them, [c]as the LORD had said. 23And Pharaoh turned and went into his house. Neither was his heart moved by this. 24So all
the Egyptians dug all around the river for
water to drink, because they could not
drink the water of the river. 25And seven
days passed after the LORD had struck the
river.

The Second Plague: Frogs

8 And the LORD spoke to Moses, "Go to
Pharaoh and say to him, 'Thus says
the LORD: "Let My people go, [a]that they
may serve Me. 2But if you [a]refuse to let
them go, behold, I will smite all your territory with [b]frogs. 3So the river shall
bring forth frogs abundantly, which shall
go up and come into your house, into
your [a]bedroom, on your bed, into the
houses of your servants, on your people,
into your ovens, and into your kneading
bowls. 4And the frogs shall come up on
you, on your people, and on all your servants." ' "
5Then the LORD spoke to Moses, "Say to
Aaron, [a]'Stretch out your hand with your
rod over the streams, over the rivers, and
over the ponds, and cause frogs to come
up on the land of Egypt.' " 6So Aaron
stretched out his hand over the waters of
Egypt, and [a]the frogs came up and covered the land of Egypt. 7[a]And the magicians did so with their [1]enchantments,
and brought up frogs on the land of
Egypt.
8Then Pharaoh called for Moses and
Aaron, and said, [a]"Entreat[1] the LORD that
He may take away the frogs from me and
from my people; and I will let the people
[b]go, that they may sacrifice to the LORD."
9And Moses said to Pharaoh, "Accept
the honor of saying when I shall intercede
for you, for your servants, and for your
people, to destroy the frogs from you and
your houses, *that* they may remain in the
river only."
10So he said, "Tomorrow." And he said,
"*Let it be* according to your word, that
you may know that [a]*there is* no one like
the LORD our God. 11And the frogs shall
depart from you, from your houses, from
your servants, and from your people. They
shall remain in the river only."

O Lord, may ______ know that there is no one like You.

FROM EXODUS 8:10

12Then Moses and Aaron went out from
Pharaoh. And Moses [a]cried out to the
LORD concerning the frogs which He had
brought against Pharaoh. 13So the LORD
did according to the word of Moses. And
the frogs died out of the houses, out of the
courtyards, and out of the fields. 14They
gathered them together in heaps, and the
land stank. 15But when Pharaoh saw that
there was [a]relief, [b]he hardened his heart
and did not heed them, as the LORD had
said.

The Third Plague: Lice

16So the LORD said to Moses, "Say to
Aaron, 'Stretch out your rod, and strike
the dust of the land, so that it may become
[1]lice throughout all the land of Egypt.' "
17And they did so. For Aaron stretched out
his hand with his rod and struck the dust
of the earth, and [a]it became lice on man
and beast. All the dust of the land became
lice throughout all the land of Egypt.
18Now [a]the magicians so worked with
their [1]enchantments to bring forth lice,
but they [b]could not. So there were lice on
man and beast. 19Then the magicians said
to Pharaoh, "This *is* [a]the[1] finger of God."
But Pharaoh's [b]heart grew hard, and he
did not heed them, just as the LORD had
said.

The Fourth Plague: Flies

20And the LORD said to Moses, [a]"Rise
early in the morning and stand before
Pharaoh as he comes out to the water.
Then say to him, 'Thus says the LORD:

20 a Ex. 17:5 b Ps. 78:44; 105:29, 30
21 a Ex. 7:18
22 a Ex. 7:11 b Ex. 8:7 c Ex. 3:19; 7:3 *1 secret arts*
CHAPTER 8
1 a Ex. 3:12, 18; 4:23; 5:1, 3
2 a Ex. 7:14; 9:2 b Rev. 16:13
3 a Ps. 105:30
5 a Ex. 7:19
6 a Ps. 78:45; 105:30
7 a Ex. 7:11, 22 *1 secret arts*
8 a Ex. 8:28; 9:28; 10:17 b Ex. 10:8, 24 *1 Pray to, Make supplication to*
10 a Ex. 9:14; 15:11
12 a Ex. 8:30; 9:33; 10:18; 32:11
15 a Eccl. 8:11 b Ex. 7:14, 22; 9:34
16 *1 gnats*
17 a Ps. 105:31
18 a Ex. 7:11, 12; 8:7 b Dan. 5:8 *1 secret arts*
19 a Ex. 7:5; 10:7 b Ex. 8:15 *1 An act of God*
20 a Ex. 7:15; 9:13

[b]"Let My people go, that they may serve Me. 21Or else, if you will not let My people go, behold, I will send swarms *of flies* on you and your servants, on your people and into your houses. The houses of the Egyptians shall be full of swarms *of flies,* and also the ground on which they *stand.* 22And in that day [a]I will set apart the land of [b]Goshen, in which My people dwell, that no swarms *of flies* shall be there, in order that you may [c]know that I *am* the LORD in the midst of the [d]land. 23I will [1]make a difference between My people and your people. Tomorrow this [a]sign shall be." ' " 24And the LORD did so. [a]Thick swarms *of flies* came into the house of Pharaoh, *into* his servants' houses, and into all the land of Egypt. The land was corrupted because of the swarms *of flies.*

25Then Pharaoh called for Moses and Aaron, and said, "Go, sacrifice to your God in the land."

26And Moses said, "It is not right to do so, for we would be sacrificing [a]the abomination of the Egyptians to the LORD our God. If we sacrifice the abomination of the Egyptians before their eyes, then will they not [1]stone us? 27We will go [a]three days' journey into the wilderness and sacrifice to the LORD our God as [b]He will command us."

28So Pharaoh said, "I will let you go, that you may sacrifice to the LORD your God in the wilderness; only you shall not go very far away. [a]Intercede for me."

29Then Moses said, "Indeed I am going out from you, and I will entreat the LORD, that the swarms *of flies* may depart tomorrow from Pharaoh, from his servants, and from his people. But let Pharaoh not [a]deal deceitfully anymore in not letting the people go to sacrifice to the LORD."

30So Moses went out from Pharaoh and [a]entreated the LORD. 31And the LORD did according to the word of Moses; He removed the swarms *of flies* from Pharaoh, from his servants, and from his people. Not one remained. 32But Pharaoh [a]hardened his heart at this time also; neither would he let the people go.

The Fifth Plague: Livestock Diseased

9 Then the LORD said to Moses, [a]"Go in to Pharaoh and tell him, 'Thus says the LORD God of the Hebrews: "Let My people go, that they may [b]serve Me. 2For if you [a]refuse to let *them* go, and still hold them, 3behold, the [a]hand of the LORD will be on your cattle in the field, on the horses, on the donkeys, on the camels, on the oxen, and on the sheep—a very severe pestilence. 4And [a]the LORD will make a difference between the livestock of Israel and the livestock of Egypt. So nothing shall die of all *that* belongs to the children of Israel." ' " 5Then the LORD appointed a set time, saying, "Tomorrow the LORD will do this thing in the land."

6So the LORD did this thing on the next day, and [a]all the livestock of Egypt died; but of the livestock of the children of Israel, not one died. 7Then Pharaoh sent, and indeed, not even one of the livestock of the Israelites was dead. But the [a]heart of Pharaoh became hard, and he did not let the people go.

The Sixth Plague: Boils

8So the LORD said to Moses and Aaron, "Take for yourselves handfuls of ashes from a furnace, and let Moses scatter it toward the heavens in the sight of Pharaoh. 9And it will become fine dust in all the land of Egypt, and it will cause [a]boils that break out in sores on man and beast throughout all the land of Egypt." 10Then they took ashes from the furnace and stood before Pharaoh, and Moses scattered *them* toward heaven. And *they* caused [a]boils that break out in sores on man and beast. 11And the [a]magicians could not stand before Moses because of the [b]boils, for the boils were on the magicians and on all the Egyptians. 12But the LORD hardened the heart of Pharaoh; and he [a]did not heed them, just [b]as the LORD had spoken to Moses.

The Seventh Plague: Hail

13Then the LORD said to Moses, [a]"Rise early in the morning and stand before Pharaoh, and say to him, 'Thus says the LORD God of the Hebrews: "Let My people go, that they may [b]serve Me, 14for at this time I will send all My plagues to your very heart, and on your servants and on your people, [a]that you may know that *there is* none like Me in all the earth. 15Now if I had [a]stretched out My hand and struck you and your people with [b]pestilence, then you would have been cut off from the earth. 16But indeed for [a]this *purpose* I have raised you up, that I may [b]show My power *in* you, and that My [c]name may be declared in all the earth.

20 b Ex. 3:18; 4:23; 5:1, 3; 8:1
22 a Ex. 9:4, 6, 26; 10:23; 11:6, 7; 12:13 b Gen. 50:8 c Ex. 7:5, 17; 10:2; 14:4 d Ex. 9:29
23 a Ex. 4:8 *1* Lit. *set a ransom,* Ex. 9:4; 11:7
24 a Ps. 78:45; 105:31
26 a Gen. 43:32; 46:34 *1* Put us to death by stoning
27 a Ex. 3:18; 5:3 b Ex. 3:12
28 a Ex. 8:8, 15, 29, 32; 9:28
29 a Ex. 8:8, 15
30 a Ex. 8:12
32 a Ex. 4:21; 8:8, 15

CHAPTER 9
1 a Ex. 4:23; 8:1 b Ex. 7:16
2 a Ex. 8:2
3 a Ex. 7:4
4 a Ex. 8:22
6 a Ps. 78:48, 50
7 a Ex. 7:14; 8:32
9 a Rev. 16:2
10 a Deut. 28:27
11 a [Ex. 8:18, 19] b Job 2:7
12 a Ex. 7:13 b Ex. 4:21
13 a Ex. 8:20 b Ex. 9:1
14 a Ex. 8:10
15 a Ex. 3:20; 7:5 b Ex. 5:3
16 a [Rom. 9:17, 18] b Ex. 7:4, 5; 10:1; 11:9; 14:17 c 1 Kin. 8:43

17As yet you exalt yourself against My people in that you will not let them go. 18Be-
hold, tomorrow about this time I will
cause very heavy hail to rain down, such
as has not been in Egypt since its found-
ing until now. 19Therefore send now *and*
gather your livestock and all that you have
in the field, for the hail shall come down
on every man and every animal which is
found in the field and is not brought
home; and they shall die." ' "
20He who [a]feared the word of the LORD
among the [b]servants of Pharaoh made his
servants and his livestock flee to the houses. 21But he who did not regard the word
of the LORD left his servants and his livestock in the field.
22Then the LORD said to Moses, "Stretch
out your hand toward heaven, that there
may be [a]hail in all the land of Egypt—on
man, on beast, and on every herb of the
field, throughout the land of Egypt."
23And Moses stretched out his rod toward
heaven; and [a]the LORD sent thunder and
hail, and fire darted to the ground. And
the LORD rained hail on the land of Egypt.
24So there was hail, and fire mingled with
the hail, so very heavy that there was none
like it in all the land of Egypt since it
became a nation. 25And the [a]hail struck
throughout the whole land of Egypt, all
that *was* in the field, both man and beast;
and the hail struck every herb of the field
and broke every tree of the field. 26[a]Only
in the land of Goshen, where the children
of Israel *were,* there was no hail.
27And Pharaoh sent and [a]called for Moses and Aaron, and said to them, [b]"I have
sinned this time. [c]The LORD *is* righteous,
and my people and I *are* wicked. 28[a]En-
treat[1] the LORD, that there may be no
more [2]mighty thundering and hail, for *it*
is enough. I will let you [b]go, and you shall
stay no longer."
29So Moses said to him, "As soon as I
have gone out of the city, I will [a]spread
out my hands to the LORD; the thunder
will cease, and there will be no more hail,
that you may know that the [b]earth *is* the
LORD's. 30But as for you and your servants, [a]I know that you will not yet fear
the LORD God."
31Now the flax and the barley were
struck, [a]for the barley *was* in the head and
the flax *was* in bud. 32But the wheat and
the spelt were not struck, for they *are*
[1]late crops.
33So Moses went out of the city from
Pharaoh and [a]spread out his hands to the
LORD; then the thunder and the hail
ceased, and the rain was not poured on
the earth. 34And when Pharaoh saw that
the rain, the hail, and the thunder had
ceased, he sinned yet more; and he hardened his heart, he and his servants. 35So
[a]the heart of Pharaoh was hard; neither
would he let the children of Israel go, as
the LORD had spoken by Moses.

The Eighth Plague: Locusts

10 Now the LORD said to Moses, "Go in
to Pharaoh; [a]for I have hardened
his heart and the hearts of his servants,
[b]that I may show these signs of Mine before him, 2and that [a]you may tell in the
hearing of your son and your son's son the
mighty things I have done in Egypt, and
My signs which I have done among them,
that you may [b]know that I *am* the LORD."
3So Moses and Aaron came in to Pharaoh and said to him, "Thus says the LORD
God of the Hebrews: 'How long will you
refuse to [a]humble yourself before Me? Let
My people go, that they may [b]serve Me.
4Or else, if you refuse to let My people go,
behold, tomorrow I will bring [a]locusts
into your territory. 5And they shall cover
the face of the earth, so that no one will
be able to see the earth; and [a]they shall
eat the residue of what is left, which remains to you from the hail, and they shall
eat every tree which grows up for you out
of the field. 6They shall [a]fill your houses,
the houses of all your servants, and the
houses of all the Egyptians—which neither your fathers nor your fathers' fathers
have seen, since the day that they were on
the earth to this day.' " And he turned and
went out from Pharaoh.
7Then Pharaoh's [a]servants said to him,
"How long shall this man be [b]a snare to
us? Let the men go, that they may serve
the LORD their God. Do you not yet know
that Egypt is destroyed?"
8So Moses and Aaron were brought
again to Pharaoh, and he said to them,
"Go, serve the LORD your God. Who *are*
the ones that are going?"
9And Moses said, "We will go with our
young and our old; with our sons and our
daughters, with our flocks and our herds
we will go, for [a]we must hold a feast to the
LORD."
10Then he said to them, "The LORD had
better be with you when I let you and your

20 a [Prov. 13:13] b Ex. 8:19; 10:7
22 a Rev. 16:21
23 a Josh. 10:11
25 a Ps. 78:47, 48; 105:32, 33
26 a Ex. 8:22, 23; 9:4, 6; 10:23; 11:7; 12:13
27 a Ex. 8:8 b Ex. 9:34; 10:16, 17 c 2 Chr. 12:6
28 a Ex. 8:8, 28; 10:17 b Ex. 8:25; 10:8, 24 *1 Pray to, Make supplication to* *2* Lit. *voices of God* or *sounds of God*
29 a Is. 1:15 b Ps. 24:1
30 a [Is. 26:10]
31 a Ruth 1:22; 2:23
32 *1* Lit. *darkened*
33 a Ex. 8:12; 9:29
35 a Ex. 4:21

CHAPTER 10
1 a John 12:40 b Ex. 7:4; 9:16
2 a Joel 1:3 b Ex. 7:5, 17; 8:22
3 a [1 Kin. 21:29] b Ex. 4:23; 8:1; 9:1
4 a Rev. 9:3
5 a Ex. 9:32
6 a Ex. 8:3, 21
7 a Ex. 7:5; 8:19; 9:20; 12:33 b Ex. 23:33
9 a Ex. 5:1; 7:16

little ones go! Beware, for evil is ahead of you. 11Not so! Go now, you *who are* men, and serve the LORD, for that is what you desired." And they were driven [a]out from Pharaoh's presence.

12Then the LORD said to Moses, [a]"Stretch out your hand over the land of Egypt for the locusts, that they may come upon the land of Egypt, and [b]eat every herb of the land—all that the hail has left." 13So Moses stretched out his rod over the land of Egypt, and the LORD brought an east wind on the land all that day and all *that* night. When it was morning, the east wind brought the locusts. 14And [a]the locusts went up over all the land of Egypt and rested on all the territory of Egypt. *They were* very severe; [b]previously there had been no such locusts as they, nor shall there be such after them. 15For they [a]covered the face of the whole earth, so that the land was darkened; and they [b]ate every herb of the land and all the fruit of the trees which the hail had left. So there remained nothing green on the trees or on the plants of the field throughout all the land of Egypt.

16Then Pharaoh called [a]for Moses and Aaron in haste, and said, [b]"I have sinned against the LORD your God and against you. 17Now therefore, please forgive my sin only this once, and [a]entreat[1] the LORD your God, that He may take away from me this death only." 18So he [a]went out from Pharaoh and entreated the LORD. 19And the LORD turned a very strong west wind, which took the locusts away and blew them [a]into the Red Sea. There remained not one locust in all the territory of Egypt. 20But the LORD [a]hardened Pharaoh's heart, and he did not let the children of Israel go.

The Ninth Plague: Darkness

21Then the LORD said to Moses, [a]"Stretch out your hand toward heaven, that there may be darkness over the land of Egypt, [1]darkness *which* may even be felt." 22So Moses stretched out his hand toward heaven, and there was [a]thick darkness in all the land of Egypt [b]three days. 23They did not see one another; nor did anyone rise from his place for three days. [a]But all the children of Israel had light in their dwellings.

24Then Pharaoh called to Moses and [a]said, "Go, serve the LORD; only let your flocks and your herds be kept back. Let your [b]little ones also go with you."

25But Moses said, "You must also give [1]us sacrifices and burnt offerings, that we may sacrifice to the LORD our God. 26Our [a]livestock also shall go with us; not a hoof shall be left behind. For we must take some of them to serve the LORD our God, and even we do not know with what we must serve the LORD until we arrive there."

27But the LORD [a]hardened Pharaoh's heart, and he would not let them go. 28Then Pharaoh said to him, [a]"Get away from me! Take heed to yourself and see my face no more! For in the day you see my face you shall die!"

29So Moses said, "You have spoken well. [a]I will never see your face again."

Death of the Firstborn Announced

11 And the LORD said to Moses, "I will bring one more plague on Pharaoh and on Egypt. [a]Afterward he will let you go from here. [b]When he lets *you* go, he will surely drive you out of here altogether. 2Speak now in the hearing of the people, and let every man ask from his neighbor and every woman from her neighbor, [a]articles of silver and articles of gold." 3[a]And the LORD gave the people favor in the sight of the Egyptians. Moreover the man [b]Moses *was* very great in the land of Egypt, in the sight of Pharaoh's servants and in the sight of the people.

4Then Moses said, "Thus says the LORD: [a]'About midnight I will go out into the midst of Egypt; 5and [a]all the firstborn in the land of Egypt shall die, from the firstborn of Pharaoh who sits on his throne, even to the firstborn of the female servant who *is* behind the handmill, and all the firstborn of the animals. 6[a]Then there shall be a great cry throughout all the land of Egypt, [b]such as was not like it *before,* nor shall be like it again. 7[a]But against none of the children of Israel [b]shall a dog [1]move its tongue, against man or beast, that you may know that the LORD does make a difference between the Egyptians and Israel.' 8And [a]all these your servants shall come down to me and bow down to me, saying, 'Get out, and all the people who follow you!' After that I will go out." [b]Then he went out from Pharaoh in great anger.

11 a Ex. 10:28
12 a Ex. 7:19 b Ex. 10:5, 15
14 a Ps. 78:46; 105:34 b Joel 1:4, 7; 2:1–11
15 a Ex. 10:5 b Ps. 105:35
16 a Ex. 8:8 b Ex. 9:27
17 a 1 Kin. 13:6 *1 make supplication to*
18 a Ex. 8:30
19 a Joel 2:20
20 a Ex. 4:21; 10:1; 11:10
21 a Ex. 9:22 *1 Lit. that one may feel the darkness*
22 a Ps. 105:28 b Ex. 3:18
23 a Ex. 8:22, 23
24 a Ex. 8:8, 25; 10:8 b Ex. 10:10
25 *1 Lit. into our hands*
26 a Ex. 10:9
27 a Ex. 4:21; 10:1, 20; 14:4, 8
28 a Ex. 10:11
29 a Heb. 11:27

CHAPTER 11
1 a Ex. 12:31, 33, 39 b Ex. 6:1; 12:39
2 a Ex. 3:22; 12:35, 36
3 a Ex. 3:21; 12:36 b Deut. 34:10–12
4 a Ex. 12:12, 23, 29
5 a Ex. 4:23; 12:12, 29
6 a Ex. 12:30 b Ex. 10:14
7 a Ex. 8:22 b Josh. 10:21 *1 sharpen*
8 a Ex. 12:31–33 b Heb. 11:27

9 But the LORD said to Moses, [a]"Pharaoh will not heed you, so that [b]My wonders may be multiplied in the land of Egypt." 10 So Moses and Aaron did all these wonders before Pharaoh; [a]and the LORD hardened Pharaoh's heart, and he did not let the children of Israel go out of his land.

The Passover Instituted

12 Now the LORD spoke to Moses and Aaron in the land of Egypt, saying, 2 [a]"This month *shall be* your beginning of months; it *shall be* the first month of the year to you. 3 Speak to all the congregation of Israel, saying: 'On the [a]tenth of this month every man shall take for himself a lamb, according to the house of *his* father, a lamb for a household. 4 And if the household is too small for the lamb, let him and his neighbor next to his house take *it* according to the number of the persons; according to each man's need you shall make your count for the lamb. 5 Your lamb shall be [a]without[1] blemish, a male [2]of the first year. You may take *it* from the sheep or from the goats. 6 Now you shall keep it until the [a]fourteenth day of the same month. Then the whole assembly of the congregation of Israel shall kill it at twilight. 7 And they shall take *some* of the blood and put *it* on the two doorposts and on the lintel of the houses where they eat it. 8 Then they shall eat the flesh on that [a]night; [b]roasted in fire, with [c]unleavened bread *and* with bitter *herbs* they shall eat it. 9 Do not eat it raw, nor boiled at all with water, but [a]roasted in fire—its head with its legs and its entrails. 10 [a]You shall let none of it remain until morning, and what remains of it until morning you shall burn with fire. 11 And thus you shall eat it: [1]*with* a belt on your waist, your sandals on your feet, and your staff in your hand. So you shall eat it in haste. [a]It *is* the LORD's Passover.

12 'For I [a]will pass through the land of Egypt on that night, and will strike all the firstborn in the land of Egypt, both man and beast; and [b]against all the gods of Egypt I will execute judgment: [c]I *am* the LORD. 13 Now the blood shall be a sign for you on the houses where you *are*. And when I see the blood, I will pass over you; and the plague shall not be on you to destroy *you* when I strike the land of Egypt.

14 'So this day shall be to you [a]a memorial; and you shall keep it as a [b]feast to the LORD throughout your generations. You shall keep it as a feast [c]by an everlasting ordinance. 15 [a]Seven days you shall eat unleavened bread. On the first day you shall remove leaven from your houses. For whoever eats leavened bread from the first day until the seventh day, [b]that [1]person shall be [2]cut off from Israel. 16 On the first day *there shall be* [a]a holy convocation, and on the seventh day there shall be a holy convocation for you. No manner of work shall be done on them; but *that* which everyone must eat—that only may be prepared by you. 17 So you shall observe *the Feast of* Unleavened Bread, for [a]on this same day I will have brought your [1]armies [b]out of the land of Egypt. Therefore you shall observe this day throughout your generations as an everlasting ordinance. 18 [a]In the first *month,* on the fourteenth day of the month at evening, you shall eat unleavened bread, until the twenty-first day of the month at evening. 19 For [a]seven days no leaven shall be found in your houses, since whoever eats what is leavened, that same person shall be cut off from the congregation of Israel, whether *he is* a stranger or a native of the land. 20 You shall eat nothing leavened; in all your dwellings you shall eat unleavened bread.' "

21 Then [a]Moses called for all the [b]elders of Israel and said to them, [c]"Pick out and take lambs for yourselves according to your families, and kill the Passover *lamb.* 22 [a]And you shall take a bunch of hyssop, dip *it* in the blood that *is* in the basin, and [b]strike the lintel and the two doorposts with the blood that *is* in the basin. And none of you shall go out of the door of his house until morning. 23 [a]For the LORD will pass through to strike the Egyptians; and when He sees the [b]blood on the [1]lintel and on the two doorposts, the LORD will pass over the door and [c]not allow [d]the destroyer to come into your houses to strike *you.* 24 And you shall [a]observe this thing as an ordinance for you and your sons forever. 25 It will come to pass when you come to the land which the LORD will give you, [a]just as He promised, that you shall keep this service. 26 [a]And it shall be, when your children say to you, 'What do you mean by this service?' 27 that you shall say, [a]'It *is* the Passover sacrifice of the LORD, who passed over the houses of the children of Israel in Egypt when He struck the Egyptians and delivered our households.' " So the people [b]bowed their

---

9 a Ex. 3:19; 7:4; 10:1 b Ex. 7:3; 9:16
10 a Rom. 2:5

CHAPTER 12
2 a Deut. 16:1
3 a Josh. 4:19
5 a [1 Pet. 1:19] *1 perfect* or *sound* *2 a year old*
6 a Lev. 23:5
8 a Num. 9:12 b Deut. 16:7 c 1 Cor. 5:8
9 a Deut. 16:7
10 a Ex. 16:19; 23:18; 34:25
11 a Ex. 12:13, 21, 27, 43 *1* Made ready to travel
12 a Ex. 11:4, 5 b Num. 33:4 c Ex. 6:2
14 a Ex. 13:9 b Lev. 23:4, 5 c Ex. 12:17, 24; 13:10
15 a Lev. 23:6 b Gen. 17:14 *1 soul* *2* Put to death
16 a Lev. 23:2, 7, 8
17 a Ex. 12:14; 13:3, 10 b Num. 33:1 *1 hosts*
18 a Lev. 23:5–8
19 a Ex. 12:15; 23:15; 34:18
21 a [Heb. 11:28] b Ex. 3:16 c Num. 9:4
22 a Heb. 11:28 b Ex. 12:7
23 a Ex. 11:4; 12:12, 13 b Ex. 24:8 c Rev. 7:3; 9:4 d Heb. 11:28 *1* Crosspiece at top of door
24 a Ex. 12:14, 17; 13:5, 10
25 a Ex. 3:8, 17
26 a Ex. 10:2; 13:8, 14, 15
27 a Ex. 12:11 b Ex. 4:31

heads and worshiped. 28Then the children of Israel went away and [a]did *so;* just as the LORD had commanded Moses and Aaron, so they did.

The Tenth Plague: Death of the Firstborn

29[a]And it came to pass at midnight that [b]the LORD struck all the firstborn in the land of Egypt, from the firstborn of Pharaoh who sat on his throne to the firstborn of the captive who *was* [1]in the dungeon, and all the firstborn of [c]livestock. 30So Pharaoh rose in the night, he, all his servants, and all the Egyptians; and there was a great cry in Egypt, for *there was* not a house where *there was* not one dead.

The Exodus

31Then he [a]called for Moses and Aaron by night, and said, "Rise, go out from among my people, [b]both you and the children of Israel. And go, serve the LORD as you have [c]said. 32[a]Also take your flocks and your herds, as you have said, and be gone; and bless me also."

33[a]And the Egyptians [b]urged the people, that they might send them out of the land in haste. For they said, "We *shall* all *be* dead." 34So the people took their dough before it was leavened, having their kneading bowls bound up in their clothes on their shoulders. 35Now the children of Israel had done according to the word of Moses, and they had asked from the Egyptians [a]articles of silver, articles of gold, and clothing. 36[a]And the LORD had given the people favor in the sight of the Egyptians, so that they granted them *what they requested.* Thus [b]they plundered the Egyptians.

37Then [a]the children of Israel journeyed from [b]Rameses to Succoth, about [c]six hundred thousand men on foot, besides children. 38A [a]mixed multitude went up with them also, and flocks and herds—a great deal of [b]livestock. 39And they baked unleavened cakes of the dough which they had brought out of Egypt; for it was not leavened, because [a]they were driven out of Egypt and could not wait, nor had they prepared provisions for themselves.

40Now the [1]sojourn of the children of Israel who lived in [2]Egypt *was* [a]four hundred and thirty years. 41And it came to pass at the end of the four hundred and thirty years—on that very same day—it came to pass that [a]all the armies of the LORD went out from the land of Egypt. 42It *is* [a]a [1]night of solemn observance to the LORD for bringing them out of the land of Egypt. This *is* that night of the LORD, a solemn observance for all the children of Israel throughout their generations.

Passover Regulations

43And the LORD said to Moses and Aaron, "This *is* [a]the ordinance of the Passover: No foreigner shall eat it. 44But every man's servant who is bought for money, when you have [a]circumcised him, then he may eat it. 45[a]A sojourner and a hired servant shall not eat it. 46In one house it shall be eaten; you shall not carry any of the flesh outside the house, [a]nor shall you break one of its bones. 47[a]All the congregation of Israel shall keep it. 48And [a]when a stranger [1]dwells with you *and wants* to keep the Passover to the LORD, let all his males be circumcised, and then let him come near and keep it; and he shall be as a native of the land. For no uncircumcised person shall eat it. 49[a]One law shall be for the native-born and for the stranger who dwells among you."

50Thus all the children of Israel did; as the LORD commanded Moses and Aaron, so they did. 51[a]And it came to pass, on that very same day, that the LORD brought the children of Israel out of the land of Egypt [b]according to their armies.

The Firstborn Consecrated

13 Then the LORD spoke to Moses, saying, 2[a]"Consecrate[1] to Me all the firstborn, whatever opens the womb among the children of Israel, *both* of man and beast; it is Mine."

The Feast of Unleavened Bread

3And Moses said to the people: [a]"Remember this day in which you went out of Egypt, out of the house of [1]bondage; for [b]by strength of hand the LORD brought you out of this *place.* [c]No leavened bread shall be eaten. 4[a]On this day you are going out, in the month Abib. 5And it shall be, when the LORD [a]brings you into the [b]land of the Canaanites and the Hittites and the Amorites and the Hivites and the Jebusites, which He [c]swore to your fathers to

---

28 a [Heb. 11:28]
29 a Ex. 11:4, 5 b Num. 8:17; 33:4 c Ex. 9:6 *1 in prison*
31 a Ex. 10:28, 29 b Ex. 8:25; 11:1 c Ex. 10:9
32 a Ex. 10:9, 26
33 a Ex. 10:7 b Ps. 105:38
35 a Ex. 3:21, 22; 11:2, 3
36 a Ex. 3:21 b Gen. 15:14
37 a Num. 33:3, 5 b Gen. 47:11 c Ex. 38:26
38 a Num. 11:4 b Deut. 3:19
39 a Ex. 6:1; 11:1; 12:31–33
40 a Acts 7:6 *1* Length of the stay *2* Sam., LXX *Egypt and Canaan*
41 a Ex. 3:8, 10; 6:6; 7:4
42 a Deut. 16:1, 6 *1 night of vigil*
43 a Num. 9:14
44 a Gen. 17:12, 13
45 a Lev. 22:10
46 a [John 19:33, 36]
47 a Ex. 12:6
48 a Num. 9:14 *1* As a resident alien
49 a Num. 15:15, 16
51 a Ex. 12:41; 20:2 b Ex. 6:26

CHAPTER 13
2 a Luke 2:23 *1 Set apart*
3 a Deut. 16:3 b Ex. 3:20; 6:1 c Ex. 12:8, 19 *1* Lit. *slaves*
4 a Ex. 12:2; 23:15; 34:18
5 a Ex. 3:8, 17 b Gen. 17:8 c Ex. 6:8

give you, a land flowing with milk and
honey, [d]that you shall keep this service in
this month. 6[a]Seven days you shall eat
unleavened bread, and on the seventh day
there shall be a feast to the LORD. 7Unleav-
ened bread shall be eaten seven days. And
[a]no leavened bread shall be seen among
you, nor shall leaven be seen among you
in all your quarters. 8And you shall [a]tell
your son in that day, saying, '*This is done*
because of what the LORD did for me when
I came up from Egypt.' 9It shall be as [a]a
sign to you on your hand and as a memorial between your eyes, that the LORD's
law may be in your mouth; for with a
strong hand the LORD has brought you
out of Egypt. 10[a]You shall therefore keep
this [1]ordinance in its season from year to
year.

The Law of the Firstborn

11"And it shall be, when the LORD
[a]brings you into the land of the [b]Canaan-
ites, as He swore to you and your fathers,
and gives it to you, 12[a]that you shall [1]set
apart to the LORD all that open the womb,
that is, every firstborn that comes from an
animal which you have; the males *shall be*
the LORD's. 13But [a]every firstborn of a
donkey you shall redeem with a lamb; and
if you will not redeem *it,* then you shall
break its neck. And all the firstborn of
man among your sons [b]you shall redeem.
14[a]So it shall be, when your son asks you
in time to come, saying, 'What *is* this?'
that you shall say to him, [b]'By strength of
hand the LORD brought us out of Egypt,
out of the house of bondage. 15And it
came to pass, when Pharaoh was stubborn
about letting us go, that [a]the LORD killed
all the firstborn in the land of Egypt, both
the firstborn of man and the firstborn of
beast. Therefore I sacrifice to the LORD all
males that open the womb, but all the
firstborn of my sons I redeem.' 16It shall
be as [a]a sign on your hand and as frontlets
between your eyes, for by strength of hand
the LORD brought us out of Egypt."

The Wilderness Way

17Then it came to pass, when Pharaoh
had let the people go, that God did not
lead them *by* way of the land of the Philistines, although that *was* near; for God
said, "Lest perhaps the people [a]change
their minds when they see war, and [b]re-
turn to Egypt." 18So God [a]led the people
around *by* way of the wilderness of the
Red Sea. And the children of Israel went
up in orderly ranks out of the land of
Egypt.

19And Moses took the [a]bones of [b]Joseph
with him, for he had placed the children
of Israel under solemn oath, saying,
[c]"God will surely [1]visit you, and you shall
carry up my bones from here with you."
20So [a]they took their journey from
[b]Succoth and camped in Etham at the
edge of the wilderness. 21And [a]the LORD
went before them by day in a pillar of
cloud to lead the way, and by night in a
pillar of fire to give them light, so as to go
by day and night. 22He did not take away
the pillar of cloud by day or the pillar of
fire by night *from* before the people.

The Red Sea Crossing

14 Now the LORD spoke to Moses, saying: 2"Speak to the children of Israel, [a]that they turn and camp before [b]Pi
Hahiroth, between [c]Migdol and the sea,
opposite Baal Zephon; you shall camp before it by the sea. 3For Pharaoh will say of
the children of Israel, [a]'They *are* bewildered by the land; the wilderness has
closed them in.' 4Then [a]I will harden Pharaoh's heart, so that he will pursue them;
and I [b]will gain honor over Pharaoh and
over all his army, [c]that the Egyptians may
know that I *am* the LORD." And they
did so.

Lord, may ____ not be afraid. Let them stand still and see the salvation of the Lord, which You will accomplish for them.

FROM EXODUS 14:13

5Now it was told the king of Egypt that
the people had fled, and [a]the heart of Pharaoh and his servants was turned against
the people; and they said, "Why have we
done this, that we have let Israel go from
serving us?" 6So he [1]made ready his chariot and took his people with him. 7Also, he
took [a]six hundred choice chariots, and all
the chariots of Egypt with captains over
every one of them. 8And the LORD [a]hard-
ened the heart of Pharaoh king of Egypt,

5 [d]Ex. 12:25, 26
6 [a]Ex. 12:15–20
7 [a]Ex. 12:19
8 [a]Ex. 10:2; 12:26; 13:14
9 [a]Deut. 6:8; 11:18
10 [a]Ex. 12:14, 24 [1]*regulation*
11 [a]Ex. 13:5 [b]Num. 21:3
12 [a]Lev. 27:26 [1]*Lit. cause to pass over*
13 [a]Ex. 34:20 [b]Num. 3:46, 47; 18:15, 16
14 [a]Deut. 6:20 [b]Ex. 13:3, 9
15 [a]Ex. 12:29
16 [a]Ex. 13:9
17 [a]Ex. 14:11 [b]Deut. 17:16
18 [a]Num. 33:6
19 [a]Gen. 50:24, 25 [b]Ex. 1:6; Deut. 33:13–17 [c]Ex. 4:31 [1]*give attention to*
20 [a]Num. 33:6–8 [b]Ex. 12:37
21 [a]Deut. 1:33
CHAPTER 14
2 [a]Ex. 13:18 [b]Num. 33:7 [c]Jer. 44:1
3 [a]Ps. 71:11
4 [a]Ex. 4:21; 7:3; 14:17 [b]Ex. 9:16; 14:17, 18, 23 [c]Ex. 7:5; 14:25
5 [a]Ps. 105:25
6 [1]*harnessed*
7 [a]Ex. 15:4
8 [a]Ex. 14:4

and he pursued the children of Israel; and
[b]the children of Israel went out with boldness. 9So the [a]Egyptians pursued them,
all the horses *and* chariots of Pharaoh, his
horsemen and his army, and overtook
them camping by the sea beside Pi Hahiroth, before Baal Zephon.

10And when Pharaoh drew near, the
children of Israel lifted their eyes, and behold, the Egyptians marched after them.
So they were very afraid, and the children
of Israel [a]cried out to the LORD. 11[a]Then
they said to Moses, "Because *there were*
no graves in Egypt, have you taken us
away to die in the wilderness? Why have
you so dealt with us, to bring us up out of
Egypt? 12[a]*Is* this not the word that we told
you in Egypt, saying, 'Let us alone that we
may serve the Egyptians'? For *it would*
have been better for us to serve the Egyptians than that we should die in the wilderness."

God is the God of the people who are at their wit's end, who are right up against it with their backs to the wall, and He delights to come to our help when we need Him most.

JAMES SALTER

13And Moses said to the people, [a]"Do
not be afraid. [b]Stand still, and see the
[c]salvation[1] of the LORD, which He will accomplish for you today. For the Egyptians
whom you see today, you shall [d]see again
no more forever. 14[a]The LORD will fight
for you, and you shall [b]hold[1] your peace."

15And the LORD said to Moses, "Why do
you cry to Me? Tell the children of Israel
to go forward. 16But [a]lift up your rod, and
stretch out your hand over the sea and
divide it. And the children of Israel shall
go on dry *ground* through the midst of
the sea. 17And I indeed will [a]harden the
hearts of the Egyptians, and they shall follow them. So I will [b]gain honor over Pharaoh and over all his army, his chariots,
and his horsemen. 18Then the Egyptians
shall know that I *am* the LORD, when I
have gained honor for Myself over Pharaoh, his chariots, and his horsemen."

19And the Angel of God, [a]who went before the camp of Israel, moved and went
behind them; and the pillar of cloud went
from before them and stood behind them.
20So it came between the camp of the
Egyptians and the camp of Israel. Thus it
was a cloud and darkness *to the one,* and
it gave light by night *to the other,* so that
the one did not come near the other all
that night.

21Then Moses stretched out his hand
over the sea; and the LORD caused the sea
to go *back* by a strong east wind all that
night, and [a]made the sea into dry *land,*
and the waters were [b]divided. 22So [a]the
children of Israel went into the midst of
the sea on the dry *ground,* and the waters
were [b]a wall to them on their right hand
and on their left. 23And the Egyptians pursued and went after them into the midst
of the sea, all Pharaoh's horses, his chariots, and his horsemen.

24Now it came to pass, in the morning
[a]watch, that [b]the LORD looked down upon
the army of the Egyptians through the pillar of fire and cloud, and He [1]troubled the
army of the Egyptians. 25And He [1]took off
their chariot wheels, so that they drove
them with difficulty; and the Egyptians
said, "Let us flee from the face of Israel,
for the LORD [a]fights for them against the
Egyptians."

26Then the LORD said to Moses, "Stretch
out your hand over the sea, that the waters may come back upon the Egyptians,
on their chariots, and on their horsemen." 27And Moses stretched out his hand
over the sea; and when the morning appeared, the sea [a]returned to its full depth,
while the Egyptians were fleeing into it.
So the LORD [b]overthrew[1] the Egyptians in
the midst of the sea. 28Then [a]the waters
returned and covered the chariots, the
horsemen, *and* all the army of Pharaoh
that came into the sea after them. Not so
much as one of them remained. 29But
[a]the children of Israel had walked on dry
land in the midst of the sea, and the waters *were* a wall to them on their right
hand and on their left.

30So the LORD [a]saved[1] Israel that day
out of the hand of the Egyptians, and Israel [b]saw the Egyptians dead on the seashore. 31Thus Israel saw the great [1]work
which the LORD had done in Egypt; so the

8 [b] Num. 33:3
9 [a] Josh. 24:6
10 [a] Neh. 9:9
11 [a] Ps. 106:7, 8
12 [a] Ex. 5:21; 6:9
13 [a] 2 Chr. 20:15, 17 [b] Ps. 46:10, 11 [c] Ex. 14:30; 15:2 [d] Deut. 28:68 [1] *deliverance*
14 [a] Deut. 1:30; 3:22 [b] [Is. 30:15] [1] Lit. *be quiet*
16 [a] Num. 20:8, 9, 11
17 [a] Ex. 14:8 [b] Ex. 14:4
19 [a] [Is. 63:9]
21 [a] Ps. 66:6; 106:9; 136:13, 14 [b] Is. 63:12, 13
22 [a] Ex. 15:19 [b] Ex. 14:29; 15:8
24 [a] Judg. 7:19 [b] Ex. 13:21 [1] *confused*
25 [a] Ex. 7:5; 14:4, 14, 18 [1] Sam., LXX, Syr. *bound*
27 [a] Josh. 4:18 [b] Ex. 15:1, 7 [1] Lit. *shook off*
28 [a] Ps. 78:53; 106:11
29 [a] Ps. 66:6; 78:52, 53
30 [a] Ps. 106:8, 10 [b] Ps. 58:10; 59:10 [1] *delivered*
31 [1] Lit. *hand with which the LORD worked*

people feared the LORD, and [a]believed the LORD and His servant Moses.

The Song of Moses

15 Then [a]Moses and the children of Israel sang this song to the LORD, and spoke, saying:

"I will [b]sing to the LORD,
For He has triumphed gloriously!
The horse and its rider
He has thrown into the sea!
2 The LORD *is* my strength and [a]song,
And He has become my salvation;
He *is* my God, and [b]I will praise Him;
My [c]father's God, and I [d]will exalt Him.
3 The LORD *is* a man of [a]war;
The LORD *is* His [b]name.
4 [a]Pharaoh's chariots and his army He has cast into the sea;
[b]His chosen captains also are drowned in the Red Sea.
5 The depths have covered them;
[a]They sank to the bottom like a stone.

6 "Your [a]right hand, O LORD, has become glorious in power;
Your right hand, O LORD, has dashed the enemy in pieces.
7 And in the greatness of Your [a]excellence
You have overthrown those who rose against You;
You sent forth [b]Your wrath;
It [c]consumed them [d]like stubble.
8 And [a]with the blast of Your nostrils
The waters were gathered together;
[b]The floods stood upright like a heap;
The depths [1]congealed in the heart of the sea.
9 [a]The enemy said, 'I will pursue,
I will overtake,
I will [b]divide the spoil;
My desire shall be satisfied on them.
I will draw my sword,
My hand shall destroy them.'
10 You blew with Your wind,
The sea covered them;
They sank like lead in the mighty waters.

11 "Who[a] *is* like You, O LORD, among the [1]gods?
Who *is* like You, [b]glorious in holiness,
Fearful in [c]praises, [d]doing wonders?
12 You stretched out Your right hand;
The earth swallowed them.
13 You in Your mercy have [a]led forth
The people whom You have redeemed;
You have guided *them* in Your strength
To [b]Your holy habitation.

Who is like You, O Lord, among the gods? Who is like You, glorious in holiness, fearful in praises, doing wonders? In Your mercy, guide ____ to Your holy habitation.

FROM EXODUS 15:11, 13

14 "The [a]people will hear *and* be afraid;
[b]Sorrow[1] will take hold of the inhabitants of Philistia.
15 [a]Then [b]the chiefs of Edom will be dismayed;
[c]The mighty men of Moab,
Trembling will take hold of them;
[d]All the inhabitants of Canaan will [e]melt away.
16 [a]Fear and dread will fall on them;
By the greatness of Your arm
They will be [b]*as* still as a stone,
Till Your people pass over, O LORD,
Till the people pass over
[c]Whom You have purchased.
17 You will bring them in and [a]plant them
In the [b]mountain of Your inheritance,
In the place, O LORD, *which* You have made
For Your own dwelling,
The [c]sanctuary, O LORD, *which* Your hands have established.
18 "The[a] LORD shall reign forever and ever."

31 a John 2:11; 11:45

CHAPTER 15
1 a Ps. 106:12 b Is. 12:1–6
2 a Is. 12:2 b Gen. 28:21, 22 c Ex. 3:6, 15, 16 d Is. 25:1
3 a Rev. 19:11 b Ps. 24:8; 83:18
4 a Ex. 14:28 b Ex. 14:7
5 a Neh. 9:11
6 a Ps. 17:7; 118:15
7 a Deut. 33:26 b Ps. 78:49, 50 c Ps. 59:13 d Is. 5:24
8 a Ex. 14:21, 22, 29 b Ps. 78:13 1 *became firm*
9 a Judg. 5:30 b Is. 53:12
11 a 1 Kin. 8:23 b Is. 6:3 c 1 Chr. 16:25 d Ps. 77:11, 14 1 *mighty ones*
13 a [Ps. 77:20] b Ps. 78:54
14 a Josh. 2:9 b Ps. 48:6 1 *Anguish*
15 a Gen. 36:15, 40 b Deut. 2:4 c Num. 22:3, 4 d Josh. 5:1 e Josh. 2:9–11, 24
16 a Josh. 2:9 b 1 Sam. 25:37 c Jer. 31:11
17 a Ps. 44:2; 80:8, 15 b Ps. 2:6; 78:54, 68 c Ps. 68:16; 76:2; 132:13, 14
18 a Is. 57:15

19 For the [a]horses of Pharaoh went with his chariots and his horsemen into the sea, and [b]the LORD brought back the waters of the sea upon them. But the children of Israel went on dry *land* in the midst of the sea.

The Song of Miriam

20 Then Miriam [a]the prophetess, [b]the sister of Aaron, [c]took the timbrel in her hand; and all the women went out after her [d]with timbrels and with dances. 21 And Miriam [a]answered them:

[b]"Sing to the LORD,
For He has triumphed gloriously!
The horse and its rider
He has thrown into the sea!"

Bitter Waters Made Sweet

22 So Moses brought Israel from the Red Sea; then they went out into the Wilderness of [a]Shur. And they went three days in the wilderness and found no [b]water. 23 Now when they came to [a]Marah, they could not drink the waters of Marah, for they *were* bitter. Therefore the name of it was called [1]Marah. 24 And the people [a]complained against Moses, saying, "What shall we drink?" 25 So he cried out to the LORD, and the LORD showed him a tree. [a]When he cast *it* into the waters, the waters were made sweet.

There He [b]made a statute and an [1]ordinance for them, and there [c]He tested them, 26 and said, [a]"If you diligently heed the voice of the LORD your God and do what is right in His sight, give ear to His commandments and keep all His statutes, I will put none of the [b]diseases on you which I have brought on the Egyptians. For I *am* the LORD [c]who heals you."

27 [a]Then they came to Elim, where there *were* twelve wells of water and seventy palm trees; so they camped there by the waters.

Bread from Heaven

16 And they [a]journeyed from Elim, and all the congregation of the children of Israel came to the Wilderness of Sin, which is between Elim and [b]Sinai, on the fifteenth day of the second month after they departed from the land of Egypt. 2 Then the whole congregation of the children of Israel [a]complained against Moses and Aaron in the wilderness. 3 And the children of Israel said to them, [a]"Oh, that we had died by the hand of the LORD in the land of Egypt, [b]when we sat by the pots of meat *and* when we ate bread to the full! For you have brought us out into this wilderness to kill this whole assembly with hunger."

4 Then the LORD said to Moses, "Behold, I will rain [a]bread from heaven for you. And the people shall go out and gather [1]a certain quota every day, that I may [b]test them, whether they will [c]walk in My law or not. 5 And it shall be on the sixth day that they shall prepare what they bring in, and [a]it shall be twice as much as they gather daily."

6 Then Moses and Aaron said to all the children of Israel, [a]"At evening you shall know that the LORD has brought you out of the land of Egypt. 7 And in the morning you shall see [a]the glory of the LORD; for He [b]hears your complaints against the LORD. But [c]what *are* we, that you complain against us?" 8 Also Moses said, "*This shall be seen* when the LORD gives you meat to eat in the evening, and in the morning bread to the full; for the LORD hears your complaints which you make against Him. And what *are* we? Your complaints *are* not against us but [a]against the LORD."

9 Then Moses spoke to Aaron, "Say to all the congregation of the children of Israel, [a]'Come near before the LORD, for He has heard your complaints.' " 10 Now it came to pass, as Aaron spoke to the whole congregation of the children of Israel, that they looked toward the wilderness, and behold, the glory of the LORD [a]appeared in the cloud.

11 And the LORD spoke to Moses, saying, 12 [a]"I have heard the complaints of the children of Israel. Speak to them, saying, [b]'At twilight you shall eat meat, and [c]in the morning you shall be filled with bread. And you shall know that I *am* the LORD your God.' "

13 So it was that [a]quails came up at evening and covered the camp, and in the morning [b]the dew lay all around the camp. 14 And when the layer of dew lifted, there, on the surface of the wilderness, was [a]a small round [b]substance, *as* fine as frost on the ground. 15 So when the children of Israel saw *it,* they said to one another, "What is it?" For they did not know what it *was.*

And Moses said to them, [a]"This *is* the bread which the LORD has given you to

19 a Ex. 14:23 b Ex. 14:28
20 a Judg. 4:4 b Num. 26:59 c 1 Sam. 18:6 d Judg. 11:34; 21:21
21 a 1 Sam. 18:7 b Ex. 15:1
22 a Gen. 16:7; 20:1; 25:18 b Num. 20:2
23 a Num. 33:8 *1 Lit. Bitter*
24 a Ex. 14:11; 16:2
25 a 2 Kin. 2:21 b Josh. 24:25 c Deut. 8:2, 16 *1 regulation*
26 a Deut. 7:12, 15 b Deut. 28:27, 58, 60 c Ex. 23:25
27 a Num. 33:9

CHAPTER 16
1 a Num. 33:10, 11 b Ex. 12:6, 51; 19:1
2 a 1 Cor. 10:10
3 a Lam. 4:9 b Num. 11:4, 5
4 a [John 6:31–35] b Deut. 8:2, 16 c Judg. 2:22 *1 Lit. the portion of a day in its day*
5 a Lev. 25:21
6 a Ex. 6:7
7 a John 11:4, 40 b Num. 14:27; 17:5 c Num. 16:11
8 a 1 Sam. 8:7
9 a Num. 16:16
10 a Num. 16:19
12 a Ex. 16:8 b Ex. 16:6 c Ex. 16:7
13 a Num. 11:31 b Num. 11:9
14 a Num. 11:7, 8 b Ps. 147:16
15 a 1 Cor. 10:3

Exodus 15:20

Dear Woman of Destiny,

Many times in biblical history, prophets emphasized the word God had given them to deliver by acting it out before the people. In some of the more unusual cases, like Hosea's, it was an actual lifestyle, graphically illustrating the word God was bringing to His people. At other times, the actions would simply accompany the words. In the Book of Acts, the prophet Agabus prophesied the captivity of Paul, taking Paul's belt and binding his own hands to illustrate what would happen in the future of this great apostle of faith (see Acts 21:11). Combining the words with physical action brought not only heightened understanding of the prophet's words, but special significance to the people the Lord intended to impact, much like the parables Jesus used to teach His disciples.

Today we see prophetic words acted out in this same manner, as well as in drama and in dance. Christian prophetic dance is merely the acting out of a timely word from God, and it can be accompanied by music. We know that Samuel's schools of prophets often used music to accompany their prophetic utterances (see 1 Sam. 10:5). The prophetess Miriam, another example, went out with dances and tambourines and songs. Her prophetic gifting was released in more than just the spoken word.

Dancing before the Lord is something I have been familiar with for a long time. Praising His name in the dance (see Ps. 149:3) is always a joy. But sometimes the Lord takes this expression a bit further. When anointed and inspired by the Holy Spirit, physical movements can communicate a visible expression of what God is saying.

Once in a small gathering to say good-bye to a friend, the Lord used me in this way. My friend was shy and very close to her friends. She and her family were moving to another city, and she was apprehensive. As the others sang "with the spirit" (1 Cor. 14:15), I found myself moving in weaving motions around her kneeling figure. Then the Lord used me to speak a prophetic word to her, assuring her that He was weaving a cocoon of His love around her and that she would be so insulated by His love that she would have no fear in her new environment. The comfort and love of the Holy Spirit had ministered to her in a deep way by the prophetic dance, and she left with fresh confidence and hope.

You and I have the ability when inspired by the Holy Spirit to bring the love, comfort, and message of the Lord to His people in all kinds of wonderful and creative ways. Allow your body to be a living sacrifice in your worship to Him. He may desire to speak through you to bring life and deeper understanding to someone else. And He may use more than just your vocal chords! You would not hesitate to use actions to communicate with children or with someone of another country and language. Break out of your comfort zone, and be obedient to communicate God's word in all of His eternal, life-giving ways!

May you have great freedom of expression in God's Spirit!

Lora Allison

eat. [16]This is the thing which the LORD
has commanded: 'Let every man gather it
[a]according to each one's need, one [b]omer
for each person, *according to the* number
of persons; let every man take for *those*
who *are* in his tent.' "
[17]Then the children of Israel did so and
gathered, some more, some less. [18]So
when they measured *it* by omers, [a]he who
gathered much had nothing left over, and
he who gathered little had no lack. Every
man had gathered according to each one's
need. [19]And Moses said, "Let no one [a]leave
any of it till morning." [20]Notwithstanding
they did not [1]heed Moses. But some of
them left part of it until morning, and it
bred worms and stank. And Moses was angry with them. [21]So they gathered it every
morning, every man according to his
need. And when the sun became hot, it
melted.
[22]And so it was, on the sixth day, *that*
they gathered twice as much bread, two
omers for each one. And all the rulers of
the congregation came and told Moses.
[23]Then he said to them, "This *is what* the

16 a Ex. 12:4 b Ex. 16:32, 36
18 a 2 Cor. 8:15
19 a Ex. 12:10; 16:23; 23:18
20 1 *listen to*

Kathryn Kuhlman

Was it the way she walked onto the stage and theatrically paraded across in her sweeping white dress that left such a mark on people? Or was it the "Hell-ooo there, and have you been waiting for me?" which began each of her radio broadcasts? Possibly it was her distinctive accent and enunciation of words, leaving such phrases as, "I beeeeliEEEEVE in meeeericles," ringing in the ears of her listeners. Wherever she went, whatever she did, Kathryn Kuhlman (1907–1976) left an impression on all.

Raised in Concordia, Missouri, the lanky, red-headed girl had her first taste of the trials of ministry in 1924 when she joined her older sister and brother-in-law, who was a traveling evangelist. The team struggled both financially and relationally, and Kathryn eventually left. After preaching throughout Idaho, Kuhlman arrived in Denver, Colorado, where for five months she ministered in a warehouse filled to capacity every night. Eventually, the Denver Revival Tabernacle was built; and as people came from across the country, Kuhlman witnessed thousands saved over the next few years.

With Kuhlman's rise came several setbacks. Her father, with whom she held a special bond, was killed in a car accident. Members of her own staff betrayed her, publicly attacked her character, and attempted to take a share of the ministry's earnings on their way down. But most heart-wrenching of all was her marriage to evangelist Burroughs Waltrip and their eventual divorce—an extremely atypical point in her life in which she ignored the warnings of the Holy Spirit. Kuhlman suffered the consequences of a relationship doomed from the start.

Through these and other trials, however, Kuhlman became more broken and dependent on the Holy Spirit. She approached every meeting with the same desperation—if the Holy Spirit did not use her, she would be made a fool. She was used powerfully, however, and throughout the 1960s and 70s millions of skeptics, outcasts, and unbelievers were drawn to Christ through the miraculous signs and healings seen during her meetings.

LORD has said: 'Tomorrow *is* [a]a Sabbath
rest, a holy Sabbath to the LORD. Bake
what you will bake *today,* and boil what
you will boil; and lay up for yourselves all
that remains, to be kept until morning.' "
24So they laid it up till morning, as Moses
commanded; and it did not [a]stink, nor
were there any worms in it. 25Then Moses
said, "Eat that today, for today *is* a Sabbath to the LORD; today you will not find
it in the field. 26[a]Six days you shall gather
it, but on the seventh day, the Sabbath,
there will be none."

27Now it happened *that some* of the
people went out on the seventh day to
gather, but they found none. 28And the
LORD said to Moses, "How long [a]do you
refuse to keep My commandments and My
laws? 29See! For the LORD has given you
the Sabbath; therefore He gives you on
the sixth day bread for two days. Let every
man remain in his place; let no man go
out of his place on the seventh day." 30So
the people rested on the seventh day.

31And the house of Israel called its
name [1]Manna. And [a]it *was* like white coriander seed, and the taste of it *was* like
wafers *made* with honey.

32Then Moses said, "This *is* the thing
which the LORD has commanded: 'Fill an
omer with it, to be kept for your generations, that they may see the bread with
which I fed you in the wilderness, when I
brought you out of the land of Egypt.' "
33And Moses said to Aaron, [a]"Take a pot
and put an omer of manna in it, and lay
it up before the LORD, to be kept for your
generations." 34As the LORD commanded
Moses, so Aaron laid it up [a]before the Testimony, to be kept. 35And the children of
Israel [a]ate manna [b]forty years, [c]until they
came to an inhabited land; they ate manna until they came to the border of the
land of Canaan. 36Now an omer *is* one-
tenth of an ephah.

Water from the Rock

17 Then [a]all the congregation of the
children of Israel set out on their
journey from the Wilderness of [b]Sin, according to the commandment of the
LORD, and camped in Rephidim; but *there*
was no water for the people to [c]drink.
2[a]Therefore the people contended with
Moses, and said, "Give us water, that we
may drink."
So Moses said to them, "Why do you
contend with me? Why do you [b]tempt the
LORD?"

3And the people thirsted there for water, and the people [a]complained against
Moses, and said, "Why *is* it you have
brought us up out of Egypt, to kill us and
our children and our [b]livestock with
thirst?"

> *A murmuring spirit is often the cause of lack of victory. When the children of Israel murmured, they grieved and angered God. We are commanded to "offer the sacrifice of praise to God continually"—not merely with our hearts but with our lips. And if we obey this command there will not be much room left for murmuring.*
>
> CARRIE JUDD MONTGOMERY

4So Moses [a]cried out to the LORD, saying, "What shall I do with this people?
They are almost ready to [b]stone[1] me!"

5And the LORD said to Moses, [a]"Go on
before the people, and take with you some
of the elders of Israel. Also take in your
hand your rod with which [b]you struck the
river, and go. 6[a]Behold, I will stand before
you there on the rock in Horeb; and you
shall strike the rock, and water will come
out of it, that the people may drink."

And Moses did so in the sight of the
elders of Israel. 7So he called the name of
the place [a]Massah[1] and [2]Meribah, because
of the contention of the children of Israel,
and because they [3]tempted the LORD, saying, "Is the LORD among us or not?"

Victory over the Amalekites

8[a]Now Amalek came and fought with
Israel in Rephidim. 9And Moses said to
Joshua, "Choose us some men and go out,

---

23 a Gen. 2:3
24 a Ex. 16:20
26 a Ex. 20:9, 10
28 a 2 Kin. 17:14
31 a Num. 11:7–9 1 Lit. *What?* Ex. 16:15
33 a Heb. 9:4
34 a Num. 17:10
35 a Deut. 8:3, 16 b Num. 33:38 c Josh. 5:12

CHAPTER 17
1 a Ex. 16:1 b Num. 33:11–15 c Ex. 15:22
2 a Num. 20:2, 3, 13 b [Deut. 6:16]
3 a Ex. 16:2, 3 b Ex. 12:38
4 a Ex. 14:15 b John 8:59; 10:31 1 Put me to death by stoning
5 a Ezek. 2:6 b Num. 20:8
6 a Num. 20:10, 11
7 a Num. 20:13, 24; 27:14 1 Lit. *Tempted* 2 Lit. *Contention* 3 *tested*
8 a Gen. 36:12

fight with Amalek. Tomorrow I will stand
on the top of the hill with [a]the rod of God
in my hand." 10So Joshua did as Moses
said to him, and fought with Amalek. And
Moses, Aaron, and Hur went up to the top
of the hill. 11And so it was, when Moses
[a]held up his hand, that Israel prevailed;
and when he let down his hand, Amalek
prevailed. 12But Moses' hands *became*
[1]heavy; so they took a stone and put *it*
under him, and he sat on it. And Aaron
and Hur supported his hands, one on one
side, and the other on the other side; and
his hands were steady until the going
down of the sun. 13So Joshua defeated
Amalek and his people with the edge of
the sword.
14Then the LORD said to Moses, [a]"Write
this *for* a memorial in the book and recount *it* in the hearing of Joshua, that [b]I
will utterly blot out the remembrance of
Amalek from under heaven." 15And Moses
built an altar and called its name, [1]The-
LORD-Is-My-Banner; 16for he said, "Because [1]the LORD has [a]sworn: the LORD *will
have* war with Amalek from generation to
generation."

Jethro's Advice

18 And [a]Jethro, the priest of Midian,
Moses' father-in-law, heard of all
that [b]God had done for Moses and for Israel His people—that the LORD had brought
Israel out of Egypt. 2Then Jethro, Moses'
father-in-law, took [a]Zipporah, Moses'
wife, after he had sent her back, 3with her
[a]two sons, of whom the name of one *was*
[1]Gershom (for he said, [b]"I have been a
[2]stranger in a foreign land") 4and the
name of the other *was* [1]Eliezer (for *he
said,* "The God of my father *was* my [a]help,
and delivered me from the sword of Pharaoh"); 5and Jethro, Moses' father-in-law,
came with his sons and his wife to Moses
in the wilderness, where he was encamped
at [a]the mountain of God. 6Now he had
said to Moses, "I, your father-in-law Jethro, am coming to you with your wife and
her two sons with her."
7So Moses [a]went out to meet his
father-in-law, bowed down, and [b]kissed
him. And they asked each other about
their well-being, and they went into the
tent. 8And Moses told his father-in-law all
that the LORD had done to Pharaoh and
to the Egyptians for Israel's sake, all the
hardship that had come upon them on the
way, and *how* the LORD had [a]delivered
them. 9Then Jethro rejoiced for all the
[a]good which the LORD had done for Israel,
whom He had delivered out of the hand
of the Egyptians. 10And Jethro said,
[a]"Blessed *be* the LORD, who has delivered
you out of the hand of the Egyptians and
out of the hand of Pharaoh, *and* who has
delivered the people from under the hand
of the Egyptians. 11Now I know that the
LORD *is* [a]greater than all the gods; [b]for in
the very thing in which they [1]behaved
[c]proudly, *He was* above them." 12Then
Jethro, Moses' father-in-law, [1]took a
burnt [a]offering and *other* sacrifices *to offer* to God. And Aaron came with all the
elders of Israel [b]to eat bread with Moses'
father-in-law before God.

O Father, I pray that ____ will know that You are greater than all other gods.

FROM EXODUS 18:11

13And so it was, on the next day, that
Moses [a]sat to judge the people; and the
people stood before Moses from morning
until evening. 14So when Moses' father-
in-law saw all that he did for the people,
he said, "What *is* this thing that you are
doing for the people? Why do you alone
[1]sit, and all the people stand before you
from morning until evening?"
15And Moses said to his father-in-law,
"Because [a]the people come to me to inquire of God. 16When they have [a]a [1]diffi-
culty, they come to me, and I judge
between one and another; and I make
known the statutes of God and His laws."
17So Moses' father-in-law said to him,
"The thing that you do *is* not good. 18Both
you and these people who *are* with you
will surely wear yourselves out. For this
thing *is* too much for you; [a]you are not
able to perform it by yourself. 19Listen
now to my voice; I will give you [1]counsel,
and God will be with you: Stand [a]before
God for the people, so that you may
[b]bring the difficulties to God. 20And you
shall [a]teach them the statutes and the
laws, and show them the way in which
they must walk and [b]the work they must
do. 21Moreover you shall select from all
the people [a]able men, such as [b]fear God,

9 a Ex. 4:20
11 a [James 5:16]
12 1 Weary of being held up
14 a Ex. 24:4; 34:27 b 1 Sam. 15:3
15 1 Heb. *YHWH Nissi*
16 a Gen. 22:14–16 1 Lit. *a hand is upon the throne of the LORD*

CHAPTER 18
1 a Ex. 2:16, 18; 3:1 b [Ps. 106:2, 8]
2 a Ex. 2:21; 4:20–26
3 a Acts 7:29 b Ex. 2:22 1 Lit. *Stranger There* 2 *sojourner,* temporary resident
4 a Gen. 49:25 1 Lit. *My God Is Help*
5 a Ex. 3:1, 12; 4:27; 24:13
7 a Gen. 18:2 b Ex. 4:27
8 a Ex. 15:6, 16
9 a [Is. 63:7–14]
10 a Gen. 14:20
11 a 2 Chr. 2:5 b Ex. 1:10, 16, 22; 5:2, 7 c Luke 1:51 1 *acted presumptuously*
12 a Ex. 24:5 b Deut. 12:7 1 So with MT, LXX; Syr., Tg., Vg. *offered*
13 a Matt. 23:2
14 1 Sit as judge
15 a Lev. 24:12
16 a Ex. 24:14 1 *dispute*
18 a Num. 11:14, 17
19 a Ex. 4:16; 20:19 b Num. 9:8; 27:5 1 *advice*
20 a Deut. 5:1 b Deut. 1:18
21 a Acts 6:3 b 2 Sam. 23:3

[c]men of truth, [d]hating covetousness; and
place *such* over them *to be* rulers of thousands, rulers of hundreds, rulers of fifties,
and rulers of tens. 22And let them judge
the people at all times. [a]Then it will be
that every great matter they shall bring to
you, but every small matter they themselves shall judge. So it will be easier for
you, for [b]they will bear *the burden* with
you. 23If you do this thing, and God *so*
commands you, then you will be able to
endure, and all this people will also go to
their [a]place in peace."
24So Moses heeded the voice of his
father-in-law and did all that he had said.
25And [a]Moses chose able men out of all
Israel, and made them heads over the people: rulers of thousands, rulers of hundreds, rulers of fifties, and rulers of tens.
26So they judged the people at all times;
the [a]hard[1] cases they brought to Moses,
but they judged every small case themselves.
27Then Moses let his father-in-law depart, and [a]he went his way to his own
land.

Israel at Mount Sinai

19 In the third month after the children of Israel had gone out of the
land of Egypt, on the same day, [a]they
came *to* the Wilderness of Sinai. 2For they
had departed from [a]Rephidim, had come
to the Wilderness of Sinai, and camped in
the wilderness. So Israel camped there before [b]the mountain.
3And [a]Moses went up to God, and the
LORD [b]called to him from the mountain,
saying, "Thus you shall say to the house
of Jacob, and tell the children of Israel:
4[a]'You have seen what I did to the Egyptians, and *how* [b]I [1]bore you on eagles'
wings and brought you to Myself. 5Now
[a]therefore, if you will indeed obey My
voice and [b]keep My covenant, then [c]you
shall be a special treasure to Me above all
people; for all the earth *is* [d]Mine. 6And you
shall be to Me a [a]kingdom of priests and
a [b]holy nation.' These *are* the words
which you shall speak to the children of
Israel."
7So Moses came and called for the [a]el-
ders of the people, and [1]laid before them
all these words which the LORD commanded him. 8Then [a]all the people answered together and said, "All that the
LORD has spoken we will do." So Moses
brought back the words of the people to
the LORD. 9And the LORD said to Moses,
"Behold, I come to you [a]in the thick
cloud, [b]that the people may hear when I
speak with you, and believe you forever."
So Moses told the words of the people
to the LORD.
10Then the LORD said to Moses, "Go to
the people and [a]consecrate them today
and tomorrow, and let them wash their
clothes. 11And let them be ready for the
third day. For on the third day the LORD
will come down upon Mount Sinai in the
sight of all the people. 12You shall set
bounds for the people all around, saying,
'Take heed to yourselves *that* you do *not*
go up to the mountain or touch its base.
[a]Whoever touches the mountain shall
surely be put to death. 13Not a hand shall
touch him, but he shall surely be stoned
or shot *with an arrow;* whether man or
beast, he shall not live.' When the trumpet sounds long, they shall come near the
mountain."
14So Moses went down from the mountain to the people and sanctified the people, and they washed their clothes. 15And
he said to the people, "Be ready for the
third day; [a]do not come near *your* wives."
16Then it came to pass on the third day,
in the morning, that there were [a]thunder-
ings and lightnings, and a thick cloud on
the mountain; and the sound of the trumpet was very loud, so that all the people
who *were* in the camp [b]trembled. 17And
[a]Moses brought the people out of the
camp to meet with God, and they stood at
the foot of the mountain. 18Now [a]Mount
Sinai *was* completely in smoke, because
the LORD descended upon [b]it in fire. [c]Its
smoke ascended like the smoke of a furnace, and [1]the [d]whole mountain quaked
greatly. 19And when the blast of the trumpet sounded long and became louder and
louder, [a]Moses spoke, and [b]God answered
him by voice. 20Then the LORD came down
upon Mount Sinai, on the top of the
mountain. And the LORD called Moses to
the top of the mountain, and Moses
went up.
21And the LORD said to Moses, "Go
down and warn the people, lest they break
through [a]to gaze at the LORD, and many
of them perish. 22Also let the [a]priests who
come near the LORD [b]consecrate themselves, lest the LORD [c]break out against
them."
23But Moses said to the LORD, "The people cannot come up to Mount Sinai; for

21 c Ezek. 18:8 d Deut. 16:19
22 a Deut. 1:17 b Num. 11:17
23 a Ex. 16:29
25 a Deut. 1:15
26 a Job 29:16 *1 difficult matters*
27 a Num. 10:29, 30

CHAPTER 19
1 a Num. 33:15
2 a Ex. 17:1 b Ex. 3:1, 12; 18:5
3 a Acts 7:38 b Ex. 3:4
4 a Deut. 29:2 b Is. 63:9 *1 sustained*
5 a Ex. 15:26; 23:22 b Deut. 5:2 c Ps. 135:4 d Ex. 9:29
6 a [1 Pet. 2:5, 9] b Deut. 7:6; 14:21; 26:19
7 a Ex. 4:29, 30 *1 set*
8 a Deut. 5:27; 26:17
9 a Ex. 19:16; 20:21; 24:15 b Deut. 4:12, 36
10 a Lev. 11:44, 45
12 a Heb. 12:20
15 a [1 Cor. 7:5]
16 a Heb. 12:18, 19 b Heb. 12:21
17 a Deut. 4:10
18 a Deut. 4:11 b Ex. 3:2; 24:17 c Gen. 15:17; 19:28 d Ps. 68:8 *1 LXX all the people*
19 a Heb. 12:21 b Ps. 81:7
21 a 1 Sam. 6:19
22 a Ex. 19:24; 24:5 b Lev. 10:3; 21:6–8 c 2 Sam. 6:7, 8

You warned us, saying, [a]'Set bounds
around the mountain and consecrate it.' "
24 Then the LORD said to him, "Away!
Get down and then come up, you and
Aaron with you. But do not let the priests
and the people break through to come up
to the LORD, lest He break out against
them." 25 So Moses went down to the people and spoke to them.

The Ten Commandments

20 And God spoke [a]all these words,
saying:
2 [a]"I *am* the LORD your God, who
brought you out of the land of
Egypt, [b]out of the house of
[1]bondage.
3 [a]"You shall have no other gods before Me.

Lord, may _____ not make for themselves any carved image nor bow down and serve any idol, for You are a jealous God.

FROM EXODUS 20:4, 5

4 [a]"You shall not make for yourself a
carved image—any likeness *of
anything* that *is* in heaven above,
or that *is* in the earth beneath, or
that *is* in the water under the
earth; 5 [a]you shall not bow down to
them nor [1]serve them. [b]For I, the
LORD your God, *am* a jealous God,
[c]visiting[2] the iniquity of the fathers upon the children to the
third and fourth *generations* of
those who hate Me, 6 but [a]showing
mercy to thousands, to those who
love Me and keep My commandments.
7 [a]"You shall not take the name of the
LORD your God in vain, for the
LORD [b]will not hold *him* guiltless
who takes His name in vain.
8 [a]"Remember the Sabbath day, to keep
it holy. 9 [a]Six days you shall labor
and do all your work, 10 but the
[a]seventh day *is* the Sabbath of the
LORD your God. *In it* you shall do
no work: you, nor your son, nor
your daughter, nor your male servant, nor your female servant, nor
your cattle, [b]nor your stranger
who *is* within your gates. 11 For [a]*in*
six days the LORD made the heavens and the earth, the sea, and all
that *is* in them, and rested the seventh day. Therefore the LORD
blessed the Sabbath day and hallowed it.
12 [a]"Honor your father and your mother,
that your days may be [b]long upon
the land which the LORD your God
is giving you.
13 [a]"You shall not murder.
14 [a]"You shall not commit [b]adultery.
15 [a]"You shall not steal.
16 [a]"You shall not bear false witness
against your neighbor.
17 [a]"You shall not covet your neighbor's
house; [b]you shall not covet your
neighbor's wife, nor his male servant, nor his female servant, nor
his ox, nor his donkey, nor anything that *is* your neighbor's."

Loving Lord, show _____ Your mercy as You do to all those who keep Your commandments.

FROM EXODUS 20:6

The People Afraid of God's Presence

18 Now [a]all the people [b]witnessed the
thunderings, the lightning flashes, the
sound of the trumpet, and the mountain
[c]smoking; and when the people saw *it,*
they trembled and stood afar off. 19 Then
they said to Moses, [a]"You speak with us,
and we will hear; but [b]let not God speak
with us, lest we die."
20 And Moses said to the people, [a]"Do
not fear; [b]for God has come to test you,
and [c]that His fear may be before you, so
that you may not sin." 21 So the people
stood afar off, but Moses drew near [a]the
thick darkness where God *was.*

23 a Ex. 19:12

CHAPTER 20
1 a Deut. 5:22
2 a Hos. 13:4 b Ex. 13:3 1 *slaves*
3 a Jer. 25:6; 35:15
4 a Deut. 4:15–19; 27:15
5 a Is. 44:15, 19 b Deut. 4:24 c Num. 14:18, 33 1 *worship* 2 *punishing*
6 a Deut. 7:9
7 a Lev. 19:12 b Mic. 6:11
8 a Lev. 26:2
9 a Luke 13:14
10 a Gen. 2:2, 3 b Neh. 13:16–19
11 a Ex. 31:17
12 a Lev. 19:3 b Deut. 5:16, 33; 6:2; 11:8, 9
13 a Rom. 13:9
14 a Matt. 5:27 b Deut. 5:18
15 a Lev. 19:11, 13
16 a Deut. 5:20
17 a [Eph. 5:3, 5] b [Matt. 5:28]
18 a Heb. 12:18, 19 b Rev. 1:10, 12 c Ex. 19:16, 18
19 a Heb. 12:19 b Deut. 5:5, 23–27
20 a [Is. 41:10, 13] b [Deut. 13:3] c Is. 8:13
21 a Ex. 19:16

Exodus 20:1–17

Dear Woman of Destiny,

It is difficult for us to read Exodus 20 without judging it to be a list of God's rules, which, if broken, carry great penalty. The words "thou shalt" and "thou shalt not" we may remember from the King James Version, were fearsome words from the mouth of the Almighty. That was exactly the reaction of the children of Israel.

Just three months earlier, they had experienced the deliverance from Egypt. In this they had experienced what God was trying to show them now—Himself. His desire to always be there for them was contingent only on their recognition of His Lordship and their obedience (see Ex. 19:5).

We must ask ourselves if a God of love would ask us to obey a set of impossible rules. If the answer is no, then what is the purpose of the Ten Commandments? God is not like many parents who demand of their children what they don't do themselves, instructing them to "do as I say and not as I do."

God's first role with us is that of a Father, and His ultimate desire is for us to know Him. It is in knowing Him that we can trust Him implicitly.

The very nature and character of God is revealed in this *Torah,* which is the word translated over two hundred times for "law." To observe the commandments, which are only a summary of the entire law, without knowing the God who gave them, would result only in a legalistic obedience, which was bound to fail. Jesus made this clear in His teachings in Matthew 5:21–28.

Let's just look at the first command to shed light on this. "You shall have no other gods before Me." Is this the controlling voice of an egomaniac or the loving awareness that any other than Himself could not deliver, provide for, lead, or bless them? We already know that God is perfect, almighty, and the supreme authority, so what is the lesson in this passage for us? Paul shares his understanding in Romans 8:3 and 13:8–10. The perfection and holiness God requires of His chosen people is to be experienced by every believer who has died to self and been resurrected in Christ. In other words, our loving, caring God wants us to reflect His likeness and live in His blessing; and He has made that possible by sending His Son to live in and through us.

The people's response to this demonstration of the Almighty who had just claimed them as His own and promised to care for them always was to remove themselves from the display of glory, which was evidenced in thunder, lightning, trumpet sounding, smoke, and fire (see Ex. 20:18).

May we not react similarly. God help us to rejoice in His Person, His callings, and His enablings and to enter boldly the place of grace and mercy so we may truly fulfill our destiny. In this place we join the psalmist in saying, "I delight to do Your will, O my God, and Your law is within my heart" (Ps. 40:8).

Iverna Tompkins

The Law of the Altar

[22]Then the LORD said to Moses, "Thus
you shall say to the children of Israel: 'You
have seen that I have talked with you
[a]from heaven. [23]You shall not make *anything to be* [a]with Me—gods of silver or
gods of gold you shall not make for yourselves. [24]An altar of [a]earth you shall make
for Me, and you shall sacrifice on it your
burnt offerings and your peace offerings,
[b]your sheep and your oxen. In every
[c]place where I [1]record My name I will
come to you, and I will [d]bless you. [25]And
[a]if you make Me an altar of stone, you
shall not build it of hewn stone; for if you
[b]use your tool on it, you have profaned it.
[26]Nor shall you go up by steps to My altar,
that your [a]nakedness may not be exposed
on it.'

The Law Concerning Servants

21 "Now these *are* the [1]judgments
which you shall [a]set before them:
[2][a]If you buy a Hebrew servant, he shall
serve six years; and in the seventh he shall
go out free and pay nothing. [3]If he comes
in by himself, he shall go out by himself;
if he *comes in* married, then his wife shall
go out with him. [4]If his master has given
him a wife, and she has borne him sons or
daughters, the wife and her children shall
be her master's, and he shall go out by
himself. [5][a]But if the servant plainly says,
'I love my master, my wife, and my children; I will not go out free,' [6]then his master shall bring him to the [a]judges. He
shall also bring him to the door, or to the
doorpost, and his master shall pierce his
ear with an awl; and he shall serve him
forever.

[7]"And if a man [a]sells his daughter to
be a female slave, she shall not go out
as the male slaves do. [8]If she [1]does not
please her master, who has betrothed
her to himself, then he shall let her be
redeemed. He shall have no right to sell
her to a foreign people, since he has
dealt deceitfully with her. [9]And if he
has betrothed her to his son, he shall
deal with her according to the custom of
daughters. [10]If he takes another *wife,* he
shall not diminish her food, her clothing, [a]and her marriage rights. [11]And if
he does not do these three for her, then
she shall go out free, without *paying*
money.

22 a Deut. 4:36; 5:24, 26
23 a Ex. 32:1, 2, 4
24 a Ex. 20:25; 27:1–8 b Ex. 24:5 c 2 Chr. 6:6 d Gen. 12:2 *1 cause My name to be remembered*
25 a Deut. 27:5 b Josh. 8:30, 31
26 a Ex. 28:42, 43

CHAPTER 21
1 a Deut. 4:14; 6:1 *1 ordinances*
2 a Jer. 34:14
5 a Deut. 15:16, 17
6 a Ex. 12:12; 22:8, 9
7 a Neh. 5:5
8 *1* Lit. *is evil in the eyes of*
10 a [1 Cor. 7:3, 5]
12 a [Matt. 26:52]
13 a Deut. 19:4, 5 b 1 Sam. 24:4, 10, 18 c Num. 35:11
14 a Deut. 19:11, 12 b 1 Kin. 2:28–34
16 a Deut. 24:7 b Gen. 37:28 c Ex. 22:4
17 a Mark 7:10
19 a 2 Sam. 3:29 *1 exempt from punishment*
21 a Lev. 25:44–46
22 a Ex. 18:21, 22; 21:30 *1 struggle* *2* Lit. *her children come out*
24 a Lev. 24:20
28 a Gen. 9:5 *1 exempt from punishment*
29 *1 was inclined*

The Law Concerning Violence

[12][a]"He who strikes a man so that he
dies shall surely be put to death. [13]Howev-
er, [a]if he did not lie in wait, but God [b]de-
livered *him* into his hand, then [c]I will
appoint for you a place where he may flee.
[14]"But if a man acts with [a]premedita-
tion against his neighbor, to kill him by
treachery, [b]you shall take him from My
altar, that he may die.

[15]"And he who strikes his father or his
mother shall surely be put to death.

[16][a]"He who kidnaps a man and [b]sells
him, or if he is [c]found in his hand, shall
surely be put to death.

[17]"And [a]he who curses his father or his
mother shall surely be put to death.

[18]"If men contend with each other, and
one strikes the other with a stone or with
his fist, and he does not die but is confined
to *his* bed, [19]if he rises again and walks
about outside [a]with his staff, then he who
struck *him* shall be [1]acquitted. He shall
only pay *for* the loss of his time, and shall
provide *for him* to be thoroughly healed.

[20]"And if a man beats his male or female
servant with a rod, so that he dies under
his hand, he shall surely be punished.
[21]Notwithstanding, if he remains alive a
day or two, he shall not be punished; for
he *is* his [a]property.

[22]"If men [1]fight, and hurt a woman
with child, so that [2]she gives birth prematurely, yet no harm follows, he shall surely be punished accordingly as the
woman's husband imposes on him; and he
shall [a]pay as the judges *determine.* [23]But
if *any* harm follows, then you shall give
life for life, [24][a]eye for eye, tooth for tooth,
hand for hand, foot for foot, [25]burn for
burn, wound for wound, stripe for stripe.

[26]"If a man strikes the eye of his male
or female servant, and destroys it, he shall
let him go free for the sake of his eye.
[27]And if he knocks out the tooth of his
male or female servant, he shall let him
go free for the sake of his tooth.

Animal Control Laws

[28]"If an ox gores a man or a woman to
death, then [a]the ox shall surely be stoned,
and its flesh shall not be eaten; but the
owner of the ox *shall be* [1]acquitted. [29]But
if the ox [1]tended to thrust with its horn in
times past, and it has been made known to
his owner, and he has not kept it confined,
so that it has killed a man or a woman, the
ox shall be stoned and its owner also shall

be put to death. 30If there is imposed on
him a sum of money, then he shall pay [a]to
redeem his life, whatever is imposed on
him. 31Whether it has gored a son or
gored a daughter, according to this judgment it shall be done to him. 32If the ox
gores a male or female servant, he shall
give to their master [a]thirty shekels of silver, and the [b]ox shall be stoned.

33"And if a man opens a pit, or if a man
digs a pit and does not cover it, and an ox
or a donkey falls in it, 34the owner of the
pit shall make *it* good; he shall give money to their owner, but the dead *animal*
shall be his.

35"If one man's ox hurts another's, so
that it dies, then they shall sell the live ox
and divide the money from it; and the
dead *ox* they shall also divide. 36Or if it
was known that the ox tended to thrust in
time past, and its owner has not kept it
confined, he shall surely pay ox for ox, and
the dead animal shall be his own.

Responsibility for Property

22 "If a man steals an ox or a sheep,
and slaughters it or sells it, he shall
[a]restore five oxen for an ox and four sheep
for a sheep. 2If the thief is found [a]break-
ing in, and he is struck so that he dies,
there shall be [b]no guilt for his bloodshed.
3If the sun has risen on him, *there shall
be* guilt for his bloodshed. He should
make full restitution; if he has nothing,
then he shall be [a]sold[1] for his theft. 4If the
theft is certainly [a]found alive in his hand,
whether it is an ox or donkey or sheep, he
shall [b]restore double.

5"If a man causes a field or vineyard to
be grazed, and lets loose his animal, and
it feeds in another man's field, he shall
make restitution from the best of his own
field and the best of his own vineyard.

6"If fire breaks out and catches in
thorns, so that stacked grain, standing
grain, or the field is consumed, he who
kindled the fire shall surely make restitution.

7"If a man [a]delivers to his neighbor
money or articles to keep, and it is stolen
out of the man's house, [b]if the thief is
found, he shall pay double. 8If the thief is
not found, then the master of the house
shall be brought to the [a]judges *to see*
whether he has put his hand into his
neighbor's goods.

9"For any kind of trespass, *whether it
concerns* an ox, a donkey, a sheep, or
clothing, *or* for any kind of lost thing
which *another* claims to be his, the
[a]cause of both parties shall come before
the judges; *and* whomever the judges condemn shall pay double to his neighbor.
10If a man delivers to his neighbor a donkey, an ox, a sheep, or any animal to keep,
and it dies, is hurt, or driven away, no one
seeing *it,* 11*then* an [a]oath of the LORD
shall be between them both, that he has
not put his hand into his neighbor's
goods; and the owner of it shall accept
that, and he shall not make *it* good. 12But
[a]if, in fact, it is stolen from him, he shall
make restitution to the owner of it. 13If it
is [a]torn to pieces *by a beast, then* he shall
bring it as evidence, *and* he shall not
make good what was torn.

14"And if a man borrows *anything* from
his neighbor, and it becomes injured or
dies, the owner of it not *being* with it, he
shall surely make *it* good. 15If its owner
was with it, he shall not make *it* good; if
it *was* hired, it came for its hire.

Moral and Ceremonial Principles

16[a]"If a man entices a virgin who is not
betrothed, and lies with her, he shall surely pay the bride-price for her *to be* his
wife. 17If her father utterly refuses to give
her to him, he shall pay money according
to the [a]bride-price of virgins.

18[a]"You shall not permit a sorceress to
live.

19[a]"Whoever lies with an animal shall
surely be put to death.

20[a]"He who sacrifices to *any* god, except to the LORD only, he shall be utterly
destroyed.

21[a]"You shall neither mistreat a
[1]stranger nor oppress him, for you were
strangers in the land of Egypt.

22[a]"You shall not afflict any widow or
fatherless child. 23If you afflict them in
any way, *and* they [a]cry at all to Me, I will
surely [b]hear their cry; 24and My [a]wrath
will become hot, and I will kill you with
the sword; [b]your wives shall be widows,
and your children fatherless.

25[a]"If you lend money to *any of* My people *who are* poor among you, you shall
not be like a moneylender to him; you
shall not charge him [b]interest. 26[a]If you
ever take your neighbor's garment as a
pledge, you shall return it to him before
the sun goes down. 27For that *is* his only
covering, it *is* his garment for his skin.

30 a Num. 35:31
32 a Zech. 11:12, 13 b Ex. 21:28
CHAPTER 22
1 a 2 Sam. 12:6
2 a Matt. 6:19; 24:43 b Num. 35:27
3 a Ex. 21:2 *1* Sold as a slave
4 a Ex. 21:16 b Prov. 6:31
7 a Lev. 6:1–7 b Ex. 22:4
8 a Ex. 21:6, 22; 22:28
9 a Deut. 25:1
11 a Heb. 6:16
12 a Gen. 31:39
13 a Gen. 31:39
16 a Deut. 22:28, 29
17 a Gen. 34:12
18 a 1 Sam. 28:3–10
19 a Lev. 18:23; 20:15, 16
20 a Ex. 32:8; 34:15
21 a Deut. 10:19 *1 sojourner*
22 a [James 1:27]
23 a [Luke 18:7] b Ps. 18:6
24 a Ps. 69:24 b Ps. 109:9
25 a Lev. 25:35–37 b Ps. 15:5
26 a Deut. 24:6, 10–13

What will he sleep in? And it will be that
when he cries to Me, I will hear, for I *am*
[a]gracious.
28[a]"You shall not revile God, nor curse
a [b]ruler of your people.
29"You shall not delay *to offer* [a]the first
of your ripe produce and your juices. [b]The
firstborn of your sons you shall give to
Me. 30[a]Likewise you shall do with your
oxen *and* your sheep. It shall be with its
mother [b]seven days; on the eighth day
you shall give it to Me.
31"And you shall be [a]holy men to Me:
[b]you shall not eat meat torn *by beasts* in
the field; you shall throw it to the dogs.

Justice for All

23 "You [a]shall not circulate a false report. Do not put your hand with
the wicked to be an [b]unrighteous witness.
2[a]You shall not follow a crowd to do evil;
[b]nor shall you testify in a dispute so as to
turn aside after many to pervert *justice.*
3You shall not show partiality to a [a]poor
man in his dispute.
4[a]"If you meet your enemy's ox or his
donkey going astray, you shall surely
bring it back to him again. 5[a]If you see the
donkey of one who hates you lying under
its burden, and you would refrain from
helping it, you shall surely help him
with it.
6[a]"You shall not pervert the judgment
of your poor in his dispute. 7[a]Keep yourself far from a false matter; [b]do not kill the
innocent and righteous. For [c]I will not
justify the wicked. 8And [a]you shall take no
bribe, for a bribe blinds the discerning
and perverts the words of the righteous.
9"Also [a]you shall not oppress a [1]strang-
er, for you know the heart of a stranger,
because you were strangers in the land of
Egypt.

The Law of Sabbaths

10[a]"Six years you shall sow your land
and gather in its produce, 11but the seventh *year* you shall let it rest and lie fallow, that the poor of your people may eat;
and what they leave, the beasts of the field
may eat. In like manner you shall do with
your vineyard *and* your [1]olive grove.
12[a]Six days you shall do your work, and on
the seventh day you shall rest, that your
ox and your donkey may rest, and the son
of your female servant and the stranger
may be refreshed.

13"And in all that I have said to you, [a]be
circumspect and [b]make no mention of the
name of other gods, nor let it be heard
from your mouth.

Three Annual Feasts

14[a]"Three times you shall keep a feast to
Me in the year: 15[a]You shall keep the Feast
of Unleavened Bread (you shall eat unleavened bread seven days, as I commanded you, at the time appointed in the
month of Abib, for in it you came out of
Egypt; [b]none shall appear before Me empty); 16[a]and the Feast of Harvest, the firstfruits of your labors which you have sown
in the field; and [b]the Feast of Ingathering
at the end of the year, when you have
gathered in *the fruit of* your labors from
the field.
17[a]"Three times in the year all your
males shall appear before the Lord [1]GOD.
18[a]"You shall not offer the blood of My
sacrifice with leavened [b]bread; nor shall
the fat of My [1]sacrifice remain until
morning. 19[a]The first of the firstfruits of
your land you shall bring into the house
of the LORD your God. [b]You shall not boil
a young goat in its mother's milk.

The Angel and the Promises

20[a]"Behold, I send an Angel before you
to keep you in the way and to bring you
into the place which I have prepared.
21Beware of Him and obey His voice; [a]do
not provoke Him, for He will [b]not pardon
your transgressions; for [c]My name *is* in
Him. 22But if you indeed obey His voice
and do all that I speak, then [a]I will be an
enemy to your enemies and an adversary
to your adversaries. 23[a]For My Angel will
go before you and [b]bring you in to the
Amorites and the Hittites and the Perizzites and the Canaanites and the Hivites
and the Jebusites; and I will [1]cut them off.
24You shall not [a]bow down to their gods,
nor serve them, [b]nor do according to
their works; [c]but you shall utterly overthrow them and completely break down
their *sacred* pillars.
25"So you shall [a]serve the LORD your
God, and [b]He will bless your bread and
your water. And [c]I will take sickness away
from the midst of you. 26[a]No one shall
suffer miscarriage or be barren in your

27 a Ex. 34:6, 7
28 a Eccl. 10:20 b Acts 23:5
29 a Ex. 23:16, 19 b Ex. 13:2, 12, 15
30 a Deut. 15:19 b Lev. 22:27
31 a Lev. 11:44; 19:2 b Ezek. 4:14

CHAPTER 23
1 a Ps. 101:5 b Deut. 19:16–21
2 a Gen. 7:1 b Lev. 19:15
3 a Deut. 1:17; 16:19
4 a [Rom. 12:20]
5 a Deut. 22:4
6 a Eccl. 5:8
7 a Eph. 4:25 b Matt. 27:4 c Rom. 1:18
8 a Prov. 15:27; 17:8, 23
9 a Ex. 22:21 *1 sojourner*
10 a Lev. 25:1–7
11 *1 olive yards*
12 a Luke 13:14
13 a 1 Tim. 4:16 b Josh. 23:7
14 a Ex. 23:17; 34:22–24
15 a Ex. 12:14–20 b Ex. 22:29; 34:20
16 a Ex. 34:22 b Deut. 16:13
17 a Deut. 16:16 *1* Heb. *YHWH,* usually translated *LORD*
18 a Ex. 34:25 b Deut. 16:4 *1 feast*
19 a Deut. 26:2, 10 b Deut. 14:21
20 a Ex. 3:2; 13:15; 14:19
21 a Ps. 78:40, 56 b Deut. 18:19 c Is. 9:6
22 a Deut. 30:7
23 a Ex. 23:20 b Josh. 24:8, 11 *1 annihilate them*
24 a Ex. 20:5; 23:13, 33 b Deut. 12:30, 31 c Num. 33:52
25 a Deut. 6:13 b Deut. 28:5 c Ex. 15:26
26 a Deut. 7:14; 28:4

land; I will [b]fulfill the number of your
days.
27“I will send [a]My fear before you, I will
[b]cause confusion among all the people to
whom you come, and will make all your
enemies turn *their* backs to you. 28And [a]I
will send hornets before you, which shall
drive out the Hivite, the Canaanite, and
the Hittite from before you. 29[a]I will not
drive them out from before you in one
year, lest the land become desolate and
the beasts of the field become too numerous for you. 30Little by little I will drive
them out from before you, until you have
increased, and you inherit the land. 31And
[a]I will set your [1]bounds from the Red Sea
to the sea, Philistia, and from the desert to
the [2]River. For I will [b]deliver the inhabitants of the land into your hand, and you
shall drive them out before you. 32[a]You
shall make no [1]covenant with them, nor
with their gods. 33They shall not dwell in
your land, lest they make you sin against
Me. For *if* you serve their gods, [a]it will
surely be a snare to you.”

Father, send an angel
before ____, as You did
before Israel, to keep them in
the way and to bring them
into the place which You
have prepared.

FROM EXODUS 23:20

Israel Affirms the Covenant

24 Now He said to Moses, “Come up to
the LORD, you and Aaron, [a]Nadab
and Abihu, [b]and seventy of the elders of
Israel, and worship from afar. 2And Moses
alone shall come near the LORD, but they
shall not come near; nor shall the people
go up with him.”
3So Moses came and told the people all
the words of the LORD and all the [1]judg-
ments. And all the people answered with
one voice and said, [a]“All the words which
the LORD has said we will do.” 4And Moses
[a]wrote all the words of the LORD. And he
rose early in the morning, and built an
altar at the foot of the mountain, and
twelve [b]pillars according to the twelve
tribes of Israel. 5Then he sent young men
of the children of Israel, who offered
[a]burnt offerings and sacrificed peace offerings of oxen to the LORD. 6And Moses
[a]took half the blood and put *it* in basins,
and half the blood he sprinkled on the altar. 7Then he [a]took the Book of the Covenant and read in the hearing of the
people. And they said, “All that the LORD
has said we will do, and be obedient.” 8And
Moses took the blood, sprinkled *it* on the
people, and said, “This is [a]the blood of the
covenant which the LORD has made with
you according to all these words.”

On the Mountain with God

9Then Moses went up, also Aaron, Nadab, and Abihu, and seventy of the elders
of Israel, 10and they [a]saw the God of Israel. And *there was* under His feet as it were
a paved work of [b]sapphire stone, and it
was like the [c]very[1] heavens in *its* clarity.
11But on the nobles of the children of Israel He [a]did not [1]lay His hand. So [b]they saw
God, and they [c]ate and drank.
12Then the LORD said to Moses, [a]“Come
up to Me on the mountain and be there;
and I will give you [b]tablets of stone, and
the law and commandments which I have
written, that you may teach them.”
13So Moses arose with [a]his assistant
Joshua, and Moses went up to the mountain of God. 14And he said to the elders,
“Wait here for us until we come back to
you. Indeed, Aaron and [a]Hur *are* with
you. If any man has a difficulty, let him go
to them.” 15Then Moses went up into the
mountain, and [a]a cloud covered the
mountain.
16Now [a]the glory of the LORD rested on
Mount Sinai, and the cloud covered it six
days. And on the seventh day He called to
Moses out of the midst of the cloud. 17The
sight of the glory of the LORD *was* like [a]a
consuming fire on the top of the mountain in the eyes of the children of Israel.
18So Moses went into the midst of the
cloud and went up into the mountain.
And [a]Moses was on the mountain forty
days and forty nights.

Offerings for the Sanctuary

25 Then the LORD spoke to Moses,
saying: 2“Speak to the children of
Israel, that they bring Me an [1]offering.
[a]From everyone who gives it willingly
with his heart you shall take My offering.
3And this *is* the offering which you shall

26 b 1 Chr. 23:1
27 a Ex. 15:16 b Deut. 7:23
28 a Josh. 24:12
29 a Deut. 7:22
31 a Gen. 15:18 b Josh. 21:44 *1 boundaries* *2* Heb. *Nahar,* the Euphrates
32 a Ex. 34:12, 15 *1 treaty*
33 a Ps. 106:36

CHAPTER 24
1 a Lev. 10:1, 2 b Num. 11:16
3 a Ex. 19:8; 24:7 *1 ordinances*
4 a Deut. 31:9 b Gen. 28:18
5 a Ex. 18:12; 20:24
6 a Heb. 9:18
7 a Heb. 9:19
8 a [Luke 22:20]
10 a [John 1:18; 6:46] b Ezek. 1:26 c Matt. 17:2 *1* Lit. *substance of heaven*
11 a Ex. 19:21 b Gen. 32:30 c 1 Cor. 10:18 *1 stretch out His*
12 a Ex. 24:2, 15 b Ex. 31:18; 32:15
13 a Ex. 32:17
14 a Ex. 17:10, 12
15 a Ex. 19:9
16 a Ex. 16:10; 33:18
17 a Deut. 4:26, 36; 9:3
18 a Ex. 34:28

CHAPTER 25
2 a Ex. 35:4–9, 21 *1 heave offering*

take from them: gold, silver, and bronze; 4blue, purple, and scarlet *thread,* fine linen, and goats' *hair;* 5ram skins dyed red, [1]badger skins, and acacia wood; 6[a]oil for the light, and [b]spices for the anointing oil and for the sweet incense; 7onyx stones, and stones to be set in the [a]ephod and in the breastplate. 8And let them make Me a [a]sanctuary,[1] that [b]I may dwell among them. 9According to all that I show you, *that is,* the pattern of the tabernacle and the pattern of all its furnishings, just so you shall make *it.*

The Ark of the Testimony

10[a]"And they shall make an ark of acacia wood; two and a half cubits *shall be* its length, a cubit and a half its width, and a cubit and a half its height. 11And you shall overlay it with pure gold, inside and out you shall overlay it, and shall make on it a molding of [a]gold all around. 12You shall cast four rings of gold for it, and put *them* in its four corners; two rings *shall be* on one side, and two rings on the other side. 13And you shall make poles *of* acacia wood, and overlay them with gold. 14You shall put the poles into the rings on the sides of the ark, that the ark may be carried by them. 15[a]The poles shall be in the rings of the ark; they shall not be taken from it. 16And you shall put into the ark [a]the Testimony which I will give you.

17[a]"You shall make a mercy seat of pure gold; two and a half cubits *shall be* its length and a cubit and a half its width. 18And you shall make two cherubim of gold; of hammered work you shall make them at the two ends of the mercy seat. 19Make one cherub at one end, and the other cherub at the other end; you shall make the cherubim at the two ends of it *of one piece* with the mercy seat. 20And [a]the cherubim shall stretch out *their* wings above, covering the mercy seat with their wings, and they shall face one another; the faces of the cherubim *shall be* toward the mercy seat. 21[a]You shall put the mercy seat on top of the ark, and [b]in the ark you shall put the Testimony that I will give you. 22And [a]there I will meet with you, and I will speak with you from above the mercy seat, from [b]between the two cherubim which *are* on the ark of the Testimony, about everything which I will give you in commandment to the children of Israel.

5 [1] Or *dolphin*
6 [a] Ex. 27:20 [b] Ex. 30:23
7 [a] Ex. 28:4, 6–14
8 [a] Heb. 9:1, 2 [b] [2 Cor. 6:16] [1] *sacred place*
10 [a] Ex. 37:1–9
11 [a] Ex. 37:2
15 [a] 1 Kin. 8:8
16 [a] Heb. 9:4
17 [a] Ex. 37:6
20 [a] 1 Kin. 8:7
21 [a] Ex. 26:34; 40:20 [b] Ex. 25:16
22 [a] Ex. 29:42, 43; 30:6, 36 [b] Num. 7:89
23 [a] Ex. 37:10–16
29 [a] Ex. 37:16
30 [a] Lev. 24:5–9
31 [a] Zech. 4:2
33 [a] Ex. 37:19
34 [a] Ex. 37:20–22
37 [a] Lev. 24:3, 4 [b] Num. 8:2
40 [a] [Heb. 8:5]

The Table for the Showbread

23[a]"You shall also make a table of acacia wood; two cubits *shall be* its length, a cubit its width, and a cubit and a half its height. 24And you shall overlay it with pure gold, and make a molding of gold all around. 25You shall make for it a frame of a handbreadth all around, and you shall make a gold molding for the frame all around. 26And you shall make for it four rings of gold, and put the rings on the four corners that *are* at its four legs. 27The rings shall be close to the frame, as holders for the poles to bear the table. 28And you shall make the poles of acacia wood, and overlay them with gold, that the table may be carried with them. 29You shall make [a]its dishes, its pans, its pitchers, and its bowls for pouring. You shall make them of pure gold. 30And you shall set the [a]showbread on the table before Me always.

The Gold Lampstand

31[a]"You shall also make a lampstand of pure gold; the lampstand shall be of hammered work. Its shaft, its branches, its bowls, its *ornamental* knobs, and flowers shall be *of one piece.* 32And six branches shall come out of its sides: three branches of the lampstand out of one side, and three branches of the lampstand out of the other side. 33[a]Three bowls *shall be* made like almond *blossoms* on one branch, *with* an *ornamental* knob and a flower, and three bowls made like almond *blossoms* on the other branch, *with* an *ornamental* knob and a flower—and so for the six branches that come out of the lampstand. 34[a]On the lampstand itself four bowls *shall be* made like almond *blossoms, each with* its *ornamental* knob and flower. 35And *there shall be* a knob under the *first* two branches of the same, a knob under the *second* two branches of the same, and a knob under the *third* two branches of the same, according to the six branches that extend from the lampstand. 36Their knobs and their branches *shall be of one piece;* all of it *shall be* one hammered piece of pure gold. 37You shall make seven lamps for it, and [a]they shall arrange its lamps so that they [b]give light in front of it. 38And its wick-trimmers and their trays *shall be* of pure gold. 39It shall be made of a talent of pure gold, with all these utensils. 40And [a]see to it that you make *them* according to the pattern which was shown you on the mountain.

The Tabernacle

26 "Moreover [a]you shall make the
tabernacle *with* ten curtains *of* fine
woven linen and blue, purple, and scarlet
thread; with artistic designs of cherubim
you shall weave them. 2 The length of each
curtain *shall be* twenty-eight cubits, and
the width of each curtain four cubits. And
every one of the curtains shall have [1]the
same measurements. 3 Five curtains shall
be coupled to one another, and *the other*
five curtains *shall be* coupled to one another. 4 And you shall make loops of blue
yarn on the edge of the curtain on the
selvedge of *one* set, and likewise you shall
do on the outer edge of *the other* curtain
of the second set. 5 Fifty loops you shall
make in the one curtain, and fifty loops
you shall make on the edge of the curtain
that *is* on the end of the second set, that
the loops may be clasped to one another.
6 And you shall make fifty clasps of gold,
and couple the curtains together with the
clasps, so that it may be one tabernacle.
7 [a]"You shall also make curtains of
goats' *hair,* to be a tent over the tabernacle. You shall make eleven curtains. 8 The
length of each curtain *shall be* thirty cubits, and the width of each curtain four
cubits; and the eleven curtains shall all
have the same measurements. 9 And you
shall couple five curtains by themselves
and six curtains by themselves, and you
shall double over the sixth curtain at the
forefront of the tent. 10 You shall make fifty loops on the edge of the curtain that is
outermost in *one* set, and fifty loops on
the edge of the curtain of the second set.
11 And you shall make fifty bronze clasps,
put the clasps into the loops, and couple
the tent together, that it may be one.
12 The remnant that remains of the curtains of the tent, the half curtain that remains, shall hang over the back of the
tabernacle. 13 And a cubit on one side and
a cubit on the other side, of what remains
of the length of the curtains of the tent,
shall hang over the sides of the tabernacle, on this side and on that side, to cover it.
14 [a]"You shall also make a covering of
ram skins dyed red for the tent, and a covering of badger skins above that.
15 "And for the tabernacle you shall
[a]make the boards of acacia wood, standing upright. 16 Ten cubits *shall be* the
length of a board, and a cubit and a half
shall be the width of each board. 17 Two
[1]tenons *shall be* in each board for binding
one to another. Thus you shall make for
all the boards of the tabernacle. 18 And you
shall make the boards for the tabernacle,
twenty boards for the south side. 19 You
shall make forty sockets of silver under
the twenty boards: two sockets under each
of the boards for its two tenons. 20 And for
the second side of the tabernacle, the
north side, *there shall be* twenty boards
21 and their forty sockets of silver: two
sockets under each of the boards. 22 For
the far side of the tabernacle, westward,
you shall make six boards. 23 And you shall
also make two boards for the two back
corners of the tabernacle. 24 They shall be
[1]coupled together at the bottom and they
shall be coupled together at the top by one
ring. Thus it shall be for both of them.
They shall be for the two corners. 25 So
there shall be eight boards with their
sockets of silver—sixteen sockets—two
sockets under each of the boards.
26 "And you shall make bars of acacia
wood: five for the boards on one side of
the tabernacle, 27 five bars for the boards
on the other side of the tabernacle, and
five bars for the boards of the side of the
tabernacle, for the far side westward.
28 The [a]middle bar shall pass through the
midst of the boards from end to end.
29 You shall overlay the boards with gold,
make their rings of gold *as* holders for the
bars, and overlay the bars with gold. 30 And
you shall raise up the tabernacle [a]accord-
ing to its pattern which you were shown
on the mountain.
31 [a]"You shall make a veil woven of blue,
purple, and scarlet *thread,* and fine woven
linen. It shall be woven with an artistic
design of cherubim. 32 You shall hang it
upon the four pillars of acacia *wood* overlaid with gold. Their hooks *shall be* gold,
upon four sockets of silver. 33 And you
shall hang the veil from the clasps. Then
you shall bring [a]the ark of the Testimony
in there, behind the veil. The veil shall be
a divider for you between [b]the holy *place*
and the Most Holy. 34 [a]You shall put the
mercy seat upon the ark of the Testimony
in the Most Holy. 35 [a]You shall set the table outside the veil, and [b]the lampstand
across from the table on the side of the
tabernacle toward the south; and you
shall put the table on the north side.
36 [a]"You shall make a screen for the
door of the tabernacle, *woven of* blue, purple, and scarlet *thread,* and fine woven

CHAPTER 26
1 [a]Ex. 36:8–19
2 [1]Lit. *one measure*
7 [a]Ex. 36:14
14 [a]Ex. 35:7, 23; 36:19
15 [a]Ex. 36:20–34
17 [1]Projections for joining, lit. *hands*
24 [1]Lit. *doubled*
28 [a]Ex. 36:33
30 [a]Acts 7:44
31 [a]Matt. 27:51
33 [a]Ex. 25:10–16; 40:21 [b]Heb. 9:2, 3
34 [a]Ex. 25:17–22; 40:20
35 [a]Ex. 40:22 [b]Ex. 40:24
36 [a]Ex. 36:37

linen, made by a weaver. 37And you shall
make for the screen [a]five pillars of acacia
wood, and overlay them with gold; their
hooks *shall be* gold, and you shall cast five
sockets of bronze for them.

The Altar of Burnt Offering

27 "You shall make [a]an altar of acacia
wood, five cubits long and five cubits wide—the altar shall be square—and
its height *shall be* three cubits. 2You shall
make its horns on its four corners; its
horns shall be of one piece with it. And
you shall overlay it with bronze. 3Also you
shall make its pans to receive its ashes,
and its shovels and its basins and its forks
and its firepans; you shall make all its
utensils of bronze. 4You shall make a
grate for it, a network of bronze; and on
the network you shall make four bronze
rings at its four corners. 5You shall put it
under the rim of the altar beneath, that
the network may be midway up the altar.
6And you shall make poles for the altar,
poles of acacia wood, and overlay them
with bronze. 7The poles shall be put in the
rings, and the poles shall be on the two
sides of the altar to bear it. 8You shall
make it hollow with boards; [a]as it was
shown you on the mountain, so shall they
make *it.*

The Court of the Tabernacle

9[a]"You shall also make the court of the
tabernacle. For the south side *there shall*
be hangings for the court *made of* fine
woven linen, one hundred cubits long for
one side. 10And its twenty pillars and their
twenty sockets *shall be* bronze. The hooks
of the pillars and their bands *shall be* silver. 11Likewise along the length of the
north side *there shall be* hangings one
hundred *cubits* long, with its twenty pillars and their twenty sockets of bronze,
and the hooks of the pillars and their
bands of silver.

12"And along the width of the court on
the west side *shall be* hangings of fifty cubits, with their ten pillars and their ten
sockets. 13The width of the court on the
east side *shall be* fifty cubits. 14The hangings on *one* side *of the gate shall be* fifteen cubits, *with* their three pillars and
their three sockets. 15And on the other
side *shall be* hangings of fifteen *cubits,*
with their three pillars and their three
sockets.

16"For the gate of the court *there shall*
be a screen twenty cubits long, *woven of*
blue, purple, and scarlet *thread,* and fine
woven linen, made by a weaver. It *shall*
have four pillars and four sockets. 17All
the pillars around the court shall have
bands of silver; their [a]hooks *shall be* of
silver and their sockets of bronze. 18The
length of the court *shall be* one hundred
cubits, the width fifty throughout, and the
height five cubits, *made of* fine woven lin-
en, and its sockets of bronze. 19All the
utensils of the tabernacle for all its service, all its pegs, and all the pegs of the
court, *shall be* of bronze.

The Care of the Lampstand

20"And [a]you shall command the children of Israel that they bring you pure oil
of pressed olives for the light, to cause the
lamp to [1]burn continually. 21In the tabernacle of meeting, [a]outside the veil which
is before the Testimony, [b]Aaron and his
sons shall tend it from evening until
morning before the LORD. [c]*It shall be* a
statute forever to their generations on behalf of the children of Israel.

Garments for the Priesthood

28 "Now take [a]Aaron your brother,
and his sons with him, from
among the children of Israel, that he may
minister to Me as [b]priest, Aaron *and*
Aaron's sons: [c]Nadab, Abihu, [d]Eleazar,
and Ithamar. 2And [a]you shall make [1]holy
garments for Aaron your brother, for glory and for beauty. 3So [a]you shall speak to
all *who are* gifted artisans, [b]whom I have
filled with the spirit of wisdom, that they
may make Aaron's garments, to consecrate him, that he may minister to Me as
priest. 4And these *are* the garments which
they shall make: [a]a breastplate, [b]an
[1]ephod, [c]a robe, [d]a skillfully woven tunic,
a turban, and [e]a sash. So they shall make
holy garments for Aaron your brother and
his sons, that he may minister to Me as
priest.

The Ephod

5"They shall take the gold, blue, purple,
and scarlet *thread,* and the fine linen,
6[a]and they shall make the ephod of gold,
blue, purple, *and* scarlet *thread,* and fine
woven linen, artistically worked. 7It shall
have two shoulder straps joined at its two
edges, and *so* it shall be joined together.
8And the [1]intricately woven band of the

37 a Ex. 36:38

CHAPTER 27
1 a Ex. 38:1
8 a Ex. 25:40; 26:30
9 a Ex. 38:9–20
17 a Ex. 38:19
20 a Lev. 24:1–4 *1* Lit. *ascend*
21 a Ex. 26:31, 33 b Ex. 30:8 c Lev. 3:17; 16:34

CHAPTER 28
1 a Num. 3:10; 18:7 b Heb. 5:4 c Lev. 10:1 d Ex. 6:23
2 a Ex. 29:5, 29; 31:10; 39:1–31 *1* *sacred*
3 a Ex. 31:6; 36:1 b Ex. 31:3; 35:30, 31
4 a Ex. 28:15 b Ex. 28:6 c Ex. 28:31 d Ex. 28:39 e Lev. 8:7 *1* Ornamented vest
6 a Ex. 39:2–7
8 *1* *ingenious work of*

ephod, which *is* on it, shall be of the same
workmanship, *made of* gold, blue, purple,
and scarlet *thread,* and fine woven linen.
9“Then you shall take two onyx [a]stones
and engrave on them the names of the
sons of Israel: 10six of their names on one
stone and six names on the other stone, in
order of their [a]birth. 11With the work of
an [a]engraver in stone, *like* the engravings
of a signet, you shall engrave the two
stones with the names of the sons of Israel. You shall set them in settings of gold.
12And you shall put the two stones on
the shoulders of the ephod *as* memorial
stones for the sons of Israel. So [a]Aaron
shall bear their names before the LORD on
his two shoulders [b]as a memorial. 13You
shall also make settings of gold, 14and you
shall make two chains of pure gold like
braided cords, and fasten the braided
chains to the settings.

The Breastplate

15[a]“You shall make the breastplate of
judgment. Artistically woven according to
the workmanship of the ephod you shall
make it: of gold, blue, purple, and scarlet
thread, and fine woven linen, you shall
make it. 16It shall be doubled into a
square: a span *shall be* its length, and a
span *shall be* its width. 17[a]And you shall
put settings of stones in it, four rows of
stones: *The first* row *shall be* a [1]sardius, a
topaz, and an emerald; *this shall be* the
first row; 18the second row *shall be* a turquoise, a sapphire, and a diamond; 19the
third row, a [1]jacinth, an agate, and an amethyst; 20and the fourth row, a [1]beryl, an
[2]onyx, and a jasper. They shall be set in
gold settings. 21And the stones shall have
the names of the sons of Israel, twelve according to their names, *like* the engravings of a signet, each one with its own
name; they shall be according to the
twelve tribes.
22“You shall make chains for the breastplate at the end, like braided cords of pure
gold. 23And you shall make two rings of
gold for the breastplate, and put the two
rings on the two ends of the breastplate.
24Then you shall put the two braided
chains of gold in the two rings which are
on the ends of the breastplate; 25and the
other two ends of the two braided *chains*
you shall fasten to the two settings, and
put them on the shoulder straps of the
ephod in the front.
26“You shall make two rings of gold,
and put them on the two ends of the
breastplate, on the edge of it, which is on
the inner side of the ephod. 27And two
other rings of gold you shall make, and
put them on the two shoulder straps, underneath the ephod toward its front, right
at the seam above the [1]intricately woven
band of the ephod. 28They shall bind the
breastplate by means of its rings to the
rings of the ephod, using a blue cord, so
that it is above the intricately woven band
of the ephod, and so that the breastplate
does not come loose from the ephod.
29“So Aaron shall [a]bear the names of
the sons of Israel on the breastplate of
judgment over his heart, when he goes
into the holy *place,* as a memorial before
the LORD continually. 30And [a]you shall
put in the breastplate of judgment the
[1]Urim and the Thummim, and they shall
be over Aaron's heart when he goes in before the LORD. So Aaron shall bear the
judgment of the children of Israel over his
heart before the LORD continually.

Other Priestly Garments

31[a]“You shall make the robe of the
ephod all of blue. 32There shall be an
opening for his head in the middle of it; it
shall have a woven binding all around its
opening, like the opening in a coat of
mail, so that it does not tear. 33And upon
its hem you shall make pomegranates of
blue, purple, and scarlet, all around its
hem, and bells of gold between them all
around: 34a golden bell and a pomegranate, a golden bell and a pomegranate,
upon the hem of the robe all around.
35And it shall be upon Aaron when he
ministers, and its sound will be heard
when he goes into the holy *place* before
the LORD and when he comes out, that he
may not die.
36[a]“You shall also make a plate of pure
gold and engrave on it, *like* the engraving
of a signet:

HOLINESS TO THE LORD.

37And you shall put it on a blue cord, that
it may be on the turban; it shall be on the
front of the turban. 38So it shall be on
Aaron's forehead, that Aaron may [a]bear
the iniquity of the holy things which the
children of Israel hallow in all their [1]holy
gifts; and it shall always be on his forehead, that they may be [b]accepted before
the LORD.

9 a Ex. 35:27
10 a Gen. 29:31—30:24; 35:16–18
11 a Ex. 35:35
12 a Ex. 28:29, 30; 39:6, 7 b Josh. 4:7
15 a Ex. 39:8–21
17 a Ex. 39:10 *1 Or ruby*
19 *1 Or amber*
20 *1 Or yellow jasper 2 Or carnelian*
27 *1 ingenious work of*
29 a Ex. 28:12
30 a Lev. 8:8 *1 Lit. Lights and the Perfections*
31 a Ex. 39:22–26
36 a Ex. 39:30, 31
38 a [1 Pet. 2:24] b Lev. 1:4; 22:27; 23:11 *1 sacred*

39"You shall [a]skillfully weave the tunic
of fine linen *thread,* you shall make the
turban of fine linen, and you shall make
the sash of woven work.
40[a]"For Aaron's sons you shall make tunics, and you shall make sashes for them.
And you shall make [1]hats for them, for
glory and [b]beauty. 41So you shall put
them on Aaron your brother and on his
sons with him. You shall [a]anoint them,
[b]consecrate them, and [1]sanctify them,
that they may minister to Me as priests.
42And you shall make [a]for them linen
trousers to cover their [1]nakedness; they
shall [2]reach from the waist to the thighs.
43They shall be on Aaron and on his sons
when they come into the tabernacle of
meeting, or when they come near [a]the altar to minister in the holy *place,* that they
[b]do not incur [1]iniquity and die. [c]*It shall
be* a statute forever to him and his descendants after him.

Aaron and His Sons Consecrated

29 "And this is what you shall do to
them to hallow them for minister-
ing to Me as priests: [a]Take one young bull
and two rams without blemish, 2and [a]un-
leavened bread, unleavened cakes mixed
with oil, and unleavened wafers anointed
with oil (you shall make them of wheat
flour). 3You shall put them in one basket
and bring them in the basket, with the
bull and the two rams.
4"And Aaron and his sons you shall
bring to the door of the tabernacle of
meeting, [a]and you shall wash them with
water. 5[a]Then you shall take the garments, put the tunic on Aaron, and the
robe of the ephod, the ephod, and the
breastplate, and gird him with [b]the intricately woven band of the ephod. 6[a]You
shall put the turban on his head, and put
the holy crown on the turban. 7And you
shall take the anointing [a]oil, pour *it* on
his head, and anoint him. 8Then [a]you
shall bring his sons and put tunics on
them. 9And you shall gird them with sashes, Aaron and his sons, and put the hats
on them. [a]The priesthood shall be theirs
for a perpetual statute. So you shall [b]con-
secrate Aaron and his sons.
10"You shall also have the bull brought
before the tabernacle of meeting, and
[a]Aaron and his sons shall put their hands
on the head of the bull. 11Then you shall
kill the bull before the LORD, *by* the door
of the tabernacle of meeting. 12You shall
take *some* of the blood of the bull and put
it on [a]the horns of the altar with your
finger, and [b]pour all the blood beside the
base of the altar. 13And [a]you shall take all
the fat that covers the entrails, the fatty
lobe *attached* to the liver, and the two
kidneys and the fat that *is* on them, and
burn *them* on the altar. 14But [a]the flesh of
the bull, with its skin and its offal, you
shall burn with fire outside the camp. It *is*
a sin offering.
15[a]"You shall also take one ram, and
Aaron and his sons shall [b]put their hands
on the head of the ram; 16and you shall
kill the ram, and you shall take its blood
and [a]sprinkle *it* all around on the altar.
17Then you shall cut the ram in pieces,
wash its entrails and its legs, and put
them with its pieces and with its head.
18And you shall burn the whole ram on
the altar. It *is* a [a]burnt offering to the
LORD; it *is* a sweet aroma, an offering
made by fire to the LORD.
19[a]"You shall also take the other ram,
and Aaron and his sons shall put their
hands on the head of the ram. 20Then you
shall kill the ram, and take some of its
blood and put *it* on the tip of the right ear
of Aaron and on the tip of the right ear of
his sons, on the thumb of their right hand
and on the big toe of their right foot, and
sprinkle the blood all around on the altar.
21And you shall take some of the blood
that is on the altar, and some of [a]the
anointing oil, and sprinkle *it* on Aaron
and on his garments, on his sons and on
the garments of his sons with him; and
[b]he and his garments shall be hallowed,
and his sons and his sons' garments with
him.
22"Also you shall take the fat of the ram,
the fat tail, the fat that covers the entrails,
the fatty lobe *attached to* the liver, the
two kidneys and the fat on them, the right
thigh (for it *is* a ram of consecration),
23[a]one loaf of bread, one cake *made with*
oil, and one wafer from the basket of the
unleavened bread that *is* before the LORD;
24and you shall put all these in the hands
of Aaron and in the hands of his sons, and
you shall [a]wave them *as* a wave offering
before the LORD. 25[a]You shall receive
them back from their hands and burn
them on the altar as a burnt offering, as
a sweet aroma before the LORD. It *is* an
offering made by fire to the LORD.

39 a Ex. 35:35; 39:27–29
40 a Ezek. 44:17, 18 b Ex. 28:2 *1 headpieces* or *turbans*
41 a Lev. 10:7 b Lev. 8 *1 set them apart*
42 a Ex. 39:28 *1 bare flesh* *2* Lit. *be*
43 a Ex. 20:26 b Num. 9:13; 18:22 c Ex. 27:21 *1 guilt*

CHAPTER 29
1 a [Heb. 7:26–28]
2 a Lev. 2:4; 6:19–23
4 a Ex. 40:12
5 a Ex. 28:2 b Ex. 28:8
6 a Lev. 8:9
7 a Ex. 25:6; 30:25–31
8 a Ex. 28:39, 40
9 a Num. 3:10; 18:7; 25:13 b Ex. 28:41
10 a Lev. 1:4; 8:14
12 a Lev. 8:15 b Ex. 27:2; 30:2
13 a Lev. 1:8; 3:3, 4
14 a Lev. 4:11, 12, 21
15 a Lev. 8:18 b Lev. 1:4–9
16 a Ex. 24:6
18 a Ex. 20:24
19 a Lev. 8:22
21 a Ex. 30:25, 31 b [Heb. 9:22]
23 a Lev. 8:26
24 a Lev. 7:30; 10:14
25 a Lev. 8:28

26 "Then you shall take [a]the breast of
the ram of Aaron's consecration and wave
it *as* a wave offering before the LORD; and
it shall be your portion. 27 And from the
ram of the consecration you shall consecrate [a]the breast of the wave offering
which is waved, and the thigh of the heave
offering which is raised, of *that* which *is*
for Aaron and of *that* which is for his sons.
28 It shall be from the children of Israel *for*
Aaron and his sons [a]by a statute forever.
For it is a heave offering; [b]it shall be a
heave offering from the children of Israel
from the sacrifices of their peace offerings, *that is,* their heave offering to the
LORD.

29 "And the [a]holy garments of Aaron
[b]shall be his sons' after him, [c]to be
anointed in them and to be consecrated in
them. 30 [a]That son who becomes priest in
his place shall put them on for [b]seven
days, when he enters the tabernacle of
meeting to minister in the [1]holy *place.*

31 "And you shall take the ram of the
consecration and [a]boil its flesh in the holy
place. 32 Then Aaron and his sons shall eat
the flesh of the ram, and the [a]bread that
is in the basket, *by* the door of the tabernacle of meeting. 33 [a]They shall eat those
things with which the atonement was
made, to consecrate *and* to sanctify them;
[b]but an outsider shall not eat *them,* because they *are* holy. 34 And if any of the
flesh of the consecration offerings, or of
the bread, remains until the morning,
then [a]you shall burn the remainder with
fire. It shall not be eaten, because it *is*
holy.

35 "Thus you shall do to Aaron and his
sons, according to all that I have commanded you. [a]Seven days you shall consecrate them. 36 And you [a]shall offer a bull
every day *as* a sin offering for atonement.
[b]You shall cleanse the altar when you
make atonement for it, and you shall
anoint it to sanctify it. 37 Seven days you
shall make atonement for the altar and
sanctify it. And the altar shall be most
holy. [a]Whatever touches the altar must be
holy.

The Daily Offerings

38 "Now this *is* what you shall offer on
the altar: [a]two lambs of the first year, [b]day
by day continually. 39 One lamb you shall
offer [a]in the morning, and the other lamb
you shall offer [1]at twilight. 40 With the one
lamb shall be one-tenth *of an ephah* of
flour mixed with one-fourth of a hin of
pressed oil, and one-fourth of a hin of
wine *as* a drink offering. 41 And the other
lamb you shall [a]offer [1]at twilight; and you
shall offer with it the grain offering and
the drink offering, as in the morning, for
a sweet aroma, an offering made by fire to
the LORD. 42 *This shall be* [a]a continual
burnt offering throughout your generations *at* the door of the tabernacle of
meeting before the LORD, [b]where I will
meet you to speak with you. 43 And there
I will meet with the children of Israel, and
the tabernacle [a]shall be sanctified by My
glory. 44 So I will consecrate the tabernacle of meeting and the altar. I will also
[a]consecrate both Aaron and his sons to
minister to Me as priests. 45 [a]I will dwell
among the children of Israel and will [b]be
their God. 46 And they shall know that [a]I
am the LORD their God, who [b]brought
them up out of the land of Egypt, that I
may dwell among them. I *am* the LORD
their God.

The Altar of Incense

30 "You shall make [a]an altar to burn
incense on; you shall make it of
acacia wood. 2 A cubit *shall be* its length
and a cubit its width—it shall be
square—and two cubits *shall be* its
height. Its horns *shall be* of one piece
with it. 3 And you shall overlay its top, its
sides all around, and its horns with pure
gold; and you shall make for it a [1]molding
of gold all around. 4 Two gold rings you
shall make for it, under the molding on
both its sides. You shall place *them* on its
two sides, and they will be holders for the
poles with which to bear it. 5 You shall
make the poles of acacia wood, and overlay them with gold. 6 And you shall put it
before the [a]veil that *is* before the ark of
the Testimony, before the [b]mercy seat
that *is* over the Testimony, where I will
meet with you.

7 "Aaron shall burn on it [a]sweet incense
every morning; when [b]he tends the
lamps, he shall burn incense on it. 8 And
when Aaron lights the lamps [1]at twilight,
he shall burn incense on it, a perpetual
incense before the LORD throughout your
generations. 9 You shall not offer [a]strange
incense on it, or a burnt offering, or a
grain offering; nor shall you pour a drink
offering on it. 10 And [a]Aaron shall make
atonement upon its horns once a year
with the blood of the sin offering of

---

26 a Lev. 7:31, 34; 8:29
27 a Num. 18:11, 18
28 a Lev. 10:15 b Lev. 3:1; 7:34
29 a Ex. 28:2 b Num. 20:26, 28 c Num. 18:8
30 a Num. 20:28 b Lev. 8:35 *1 sanctuary*
31 a Lev. 8:31
32 a Matt. 12:4
33 a Lev. 10:14, 15, 17 b Lev. 22:10
34 a Lev. 7:18; 8:32
35 a Lev. 8:33–35
36 a Heb. 10:11 b Ex. 30:26–29; 40:10, 11
37 a Num. 4:15; Hag. 2:11–13; Matt. 23:19
38 a Num. 28:3–31; 29:6–38 b Dan. 12:11
39 a Ezek. 46:13–15 *1 Lit. between the two evenings*
41 a 2 Kin. 16:15 *1 Lit. between the two evenings*
42 a Ex. 30:8 b Ex. 25:22; 33:7, 9
43 a 1 Kin. 8:11
44 a Lev. 21:15
45 a [Rev. 21:3] b Gen. 17:8
46 a Ex. 16:12; 20:2 b Lev. 11:45

CHAPTER 30
1 a Ex. 37:25–29
3 *1 border*
6 a Ex. 26:31–35 b Ex. 25:21, 22
7 a 1 Sam. 2:28 b Ex. 27:20, 21
8 *1 Lit. between the two evenings*
9 a Lev. 10:1
10 a Lev. 16:3–34

atonement; once a year he shall make atonement upon it throughout your generations. It *is* most holy to the LORD."

The Ransom Money

11 Then the LORD spoke to Moses, saying: 12 [a]"When you take the census of the children of Israel for their number, then every man shall give [b]a [1] ransom for himself to the LORD, when you number them, that there may be no [c]plague among them when *you* number them. 13 [a]This is what everyone among those who are numbered shall give: half a shekel according to the shekel of the sanctuary [b](a shekel *is* twenty gerahs). [c]The half-shekel *shall be* an offering to the LORD. 14 Everyone included among those who are numbered, from twenty years old and above, shall give an [1]offering to the LORD. 15 The [a]rich shall not give more and the poor shall not give less than half a shekel, when *you* give an offering to the LORD, to make atonement for yourselves. 16 And you shall take the atonement money of the children of Israel, and [a]shall [1]appoint it for the service of the tabernacle of meeting, that it may be [b]a memorial for the children of Israel before the LORD, to make atonement for yourselves."

The Bronze Laver

17 Then the LORD spoke to Moses, saying: 18 [a]"You shall also make a [1]laver of bronze, with its base also of bronze, for washing. You shall [b]put it between the tabernacle of meeting and the altar. And you shall put water in it, 19 for Aaron and his sons [a]shall wash their hands and their feet in water from it. 20 When they go into the tabernacle of meeting, or when they come near the altar to minister, to burn an offering made by fire to the LORD, they shall wash with water, lest they die. 21 So they shall wash their hands and their feet, lest they die. And [a]it shall be a [1]statute forever to them—to him and his descendants throughout their generations."

The Holy Anointing Oil

22 Moreover the LORD spoke to Moses, saying: 23 "Also take for yourself [a]quality spices—five hundred *shekels* of liquid [b]myrrh, half as much sweet-smelling cinnamon (two hundred and fifty *shekels*), two hundred and fifty *shekels* of sweet-smelling [c]cane, 24 five hundred *shekels* of [a]cassia, according to the shekel of the sanctuary, and a [b]hin of olive oil. 25 And you shall make from these a holy anointing oil, an ointment compounded according to the art of the perfumer. It shall be [a]a holy anointing oil. 26 [a]With it you shall anoint the tabernacle of meeting and the ark of the Testimony; 27 the table and all its utensils, the lampstand and its utensils, and the altar of incense; 28 the altar of burnt offering with all its utensils, and the laver and its base. 29 You shall consecrate them, that they may be most holy; [a]whatever touches them must be holy. 30 [a]And you shall anoint Aaron and his sons, and consecrate them, that *they* may minister to Me as priests.

31 "And you shall speak to the children of Israel, saying: 'This shall be a holy anointing oil to Me throughout your generations. 32 It shall not be poured on man's flesh; nor shall you make *any other* like it, according to its composition. [a]It *is* holy, *and* it shall be holy to you. 33 [a]Whoever [1]compounds *any* like it, or whoever puts *any* of it on an outsider, [b]shall be [2]cut off from his people.' "

The Incense

34 And the LORD said to Moses: [a]"Take sweet spices, stacte and onycha and galbanum, and pure frankincense with *these* sweet spices; there shall be equal amounts of each. 35 You shall make of these an incense, a compound [a]according to the art of the perfumer, salted, pure, *and* holy. 36 And you shall beat *some* of it very fine, and put some of it before the Testimony in the tabernacle of meeting [a]where I will meet with you. [b]It shall be most holy to you. 37 But *as for* the incense which you shall make, [a]you shall not make any for yourselves, according to its [1]composition. It shall be to you holy for the LORD. 38 [a]Whoever makes *any* like it, to smell it, he shall be cut off from his people."

Artisans for Building the Tabernacle

31 Then the LORD spoke to Moses, saying: 2 [a]"See, I have called by name Bezalel the [b]son of Uri, the son of Hur, of the tribe of Judah. 3 And I have [a]filled him with the Spirit of God, in wisdom, in understanding, in knowledge, and in all *manner of* workmanship, 4 to design artistic works, to work in gold, in silver, in bronze, 5 in cutting jewels for

12 a Num. 1:2; 26:2 b [1 Pet. 1:18, 19] c 2 Sam. 24:15 *1 the price of a life*
13 a Matt. 17:24 b Num. 3:47 c Ex. 38:26
14 *1 contribution*
15 a [Eph. 6:9]
16 a Ex. 38:25–31 b Num. 16:40 *1 give*
18 a Ex. 38:8 b Ex. 40:30 *1 basin*
19 a Ex. 40:31, 32
21 a Ex. 28:43 *1 requirement*
23 a Ezek. 27:22 b Prov. 7:17 c Song 4:14
24 a Ps. 45:8 b Ex. 29:40
25 a Ex. 37:29; 40:9
26 a Lev. 8:10
29 a Ex. 29:37; Num. 4:15; Hag. 2:11–13
30 a Lev. 8:12
32 a Ex. 30:25, 37
33 a Ex. 30:38 b Gen. 17:14 *1 mixes* 2 Put to death
34 a Ex. 25:6; 37:29
35 a Ex. 30:25
36 a Ex. 29:42 b Lev. 2:3
37 a Ex. 30:32 *1 Lit. proportion*
38 a Ex. 30:33

CHAPTER 31
2 a Ex. 35:30—36:1 b 1 Chr. 2:20
3 a 1 Kin. 7:14

Exodus 30:22–30

Dear Woman of Destiny,

You frequently ask me how to receive the anointing for your life. Your desire for the empowering of the Lord is to be commended. Every believer should strive for excellence.

Shortly after I was filled with the Spirit, I heard a speaker say, "Don't ever stand up and speak without the anointing." I was in a church that did not teach about the anointing. At that point in my life, I had no plans to ever stand up and speak anywhere. I really don't know why that statement grabbed me, but I felt an intense longing to understand this thing called "anointing."

In the Old Testament, the tabernacle had to be anointed before anything supernatural happened. After researching the word *anointing* through the Bible and a concordance, I discovered that the keys to the anointing oil were found in its ingredients. As I learned about each component, I began to understand some of the things that are important in our lives if we are to receive the anointing.

An anointing compound containing several ingredients was used in Old Testament times (see Ex. 30:22–30). The formula used gives us a picture of the anointing provided for us as New Testament priests.

The first ingredient was myrrh, used to prepare bodies for burial. Its beautiful sweetness could only be obtained by crushing. Let the Lord use the difficult places, the "crushing" experiences, in your life to release a sweet aroma.

Another component used was sweet cinnamon. Cinnamon is used for flavoring and gives off a pleasant odor. The fragrance counteracted the stench of the Old Testament sacrifices. Allow the cinnamon to keep you sweet as you present yourself as a living sacrifice to the Lord.

A third ingredient was sweet-smelling cane, also called sweet calamus. The calamus plant grows in miry soil. The more the bark was beaten, the sweeter the fragrance of the plant. In the midst of difficult places and persecution, let the calamus produce a fragrant anointing in your life.

Cassia was another element of the anointing oil. The spice grows only at elevations higher than 8,000 feet. It is bitter to the taste and was used to purge the body so that healing could take place. Climb above the painful circumstances of life; and let the Lord bring purging, healing, and restoration in your life.

Finally, all the ingredients were mixed with olive oil, and the mixture was called "holy." The Lord will combine all the good and difficult things in your life with the oil of His Spirit. A sweet anointing will form in you, and it will minister healing and life to those you are called to reach. Jesus spoke about being anointed when He quoted the prophet Isaiah, saying, "The Spirit of the LORD is upon Me, because He has anointed Me to preach the gospel to the poor; He has sent Me to heal the brokenhearted, to proclaim liberty to the captives and recovery of sight to the blind, to set at liberty those who are oppressed" (Luke 4:18).

Woman of Destiny, I encourage you to receive the anointing of the Lord in your life.

Barbara Wentroble

setting, in carving wood, and to work in
all *manner of* workmanship.
6 "And I, indeed I, have appointed with
him [a]Aholiab the son of Ahisamach, of the
tribe of Dan; and I have put wisdom in the
hearts of all the [b]gifted artisans, that they
may make all that I have commanded you:
7 [a]the tabernacle of meeting, [b]the ark of
the Testimony and [c]the mercy seat that *is*
on it, and all the furniture of the tabernacle— 8 [a]the table and its utensils, [b]the
pure *gold* lampstand with all its utensils,
the altar of incense, 9 [a]the altar of burnt
offering with all its utensils, and [b]the laver and its base— 10 [a]the [1]garments of
ministry, the holy garments for Aaron the
priest and the garments of his sons, to
minister as priests, 11 [a]and the anointing
oil and [b]sweet incense for the holy *place*.
According to all that I have commanded
you they shall do."

O Lord, fill _____ with the Spirit of God, in wisdom, in understanding, in knowledge, and use the gifts that You have given them for Your glory.

FROM EXODUS 31:3

The Sabbath Law

12 And the LORD spoke to Moses, saying,
13 "Speak also to the children of Israel, saying: [a]'Surely My Sabbaths you shall keep,
for it *is* a sign between Me and you
throughout your generations, that *you*
may know that I *am* the LORD who [b]sanc-
tifies[1] you. 14 [a]You shall keep the Sabbath,
therefore, for *it is* holy to you. Everyone
who [1]profanes it shall surely be put to
death; for [b]whoever does *any* work on it,
that person shall be cut off from among
his people. 15 Work shall be done for [a]six
days, but the [b]seventh *is* the Sabbath of
rest, holy to the LORD. Whoever does *any*
work on the Sabbath day, he shall surely
be put to death. 16 Therefore the children
of Israel shall keep the Sabbath, to observe the Sabbath throughout their generations *as* a perpetual covenant. 17 It *is* [a]a
sign between Me and the children of Israel
forever; for [b]*in* six days the LORD made the
heavens and the earth, and on the seventh
day He rested and was refreshed.' "
18 And when He had made an end of
speaking with him on Mount Sinai, He
gave Moses [a]two tablets of the Testimony,
tablets of stone, written with the finger of
God.

The Gold Calf

32 Now when the people saw that Moses [a]delayed coming down from
the mountain, the people [b]gathered together to Aaron, and said to him, [c]"Come,
make us [1]gods that shall [d]go before us; for
as for this Moses, the man who [e]brought
us up out of the land of Egypt, we do not
know what has become of him."
2 And Aaron said to them, "Break off the
[a]golden earrings which *are* in the ears of
your wives, your sons, and your daughters, and bring *them* to me." 3 So all the
people broke off the golden earrings
which *were* in their ears, and brought
them to Aaron. 4 [a]And he received *the gold*
from their hand, and he fashioned it with
an engraving tool, and made a molded
calf.
Then they said, "This *is* your god,
O Israel, that [b]brought you out of the
land of Egypt!"
5 So when Aaron saw *it,* he built an altar
before it. And Aaron made a [a]proclama-
tion and said, "Tomorrow *is* a feast to the
LORD." 6 Then they rose early on the next
day, offered burnt offerings, and brought
peace offerings; and the people [a]sat down
to eat and drink, and rose up to play.
7 And the LORD said to Moses, [a]"Go, get
down! For your people whom you brought
out of the land of Egypt [b]have corrupted
themselves. 8 They have turned aside
quickly out of the way which [a]I commanded them. They have made themselves a molded calf, and worshiped it and
sacrificed to it, and said, [b]'This *is* your
god, O Israel, that brought you out of the
land of Egypt!' " 9 And the LORD said to
Moses, [a]"I have seen this people, and indeed it *is* a [1]stiff-necked people! 10 Now
therefore, [a]let Me alone, that [b]My wrath
may burn hot against them and I may
[1]consume them. And [c]I will make of you
a great nation."
11 [a]Then Moses pleaded with [1]the LORD
his God, and said: "LORD, why does Your
wrath burn hot against Your people
whom You have brought out of the land of

6 a Ex. 35:34 b Ex. 28:3; 35:10, 35; 36:1
7 a Ex. 36:8 b Ex. 37:1–5 c Ex. 37:6–9
8 a Ex. 37:10–16 b Ex. 37:17–24
9 a Ex. 38:1–7 b Ex. 38:8
10 a Ex. 39:1, 41 1 Or *woven garments*
11 a Ex. 30:23–33 b Ex. 30:34–38
13 a Ezek. 20:12, 20 b Lev. 20:8 1 *consecrates*
14 a Ex. 20:8 b Num. 15:32–36 1 *defiles*
15 a Ex. 20:9–11 b Gen. 2:2
17 a Ex. 31:13 b Gen. 1:31; 2:2, 3
18 a [Ex. 24:12; 32:15, 16]

CHAPTER 32
1 a Ex. 24:18; Deut. 9:9–12 b Ex. 17:1–3 c Acts 7:40 d Ex. 13:21 e Ex. 32:8 1 Or *a god*
2 a Ex. 11:2; 35:22
4 a Ex. 20:3, 4, 23 b Ex. 29:45, 46
5 a 2 Kin. 10:20
6 a Num. 25:2
7 a Deut. 9:8–21 b Gen. 6:11, 12
8 a Ex. 20:3, 4, 23 b 1 Kin. 12:28
9 a [Acts 7:51] 1 *stubborn*
10 a Deut. 9:14, 19 b Ex. 22:24 c Num. 14:12 1 *destroy*
11 a Deut. 9:18, 26–29 1 Lit. *the face of the LORD*

Egypt with great power and with a mighty
hand? 12 [a]Why should the Egyptians
speak, and say, 'He brought them out to
harm them, to kill them in the mountains, and to consume them from the face
of the earth'? Turn from Your fierce
wrath, and [b]relent from this harm to Your
people. 13 Remember Abraham, Isaac, and
Israel, Your servants, to whom You
[a]swore by Your own self, and said to them,
[b]'I will multiply your descendants as the
stars of heaven; and all this land that I
have spoken of I give to your descendants,
and they shall inherit *it* forever.' " 14 So
the LORD [a]relented from the harm which
He said He would do to His people.
15 And [a]Moses turned and went down
from the mountain, and the two tablets of
the Testimony *were* in his hand. The tablets *were* written on both sides; on the one
side and on the other they were written.
16 Now the [a]tablets *were* the work of God,
and the writing *was* the writing of God
engraved on the tablets.
17 And when Joshua heard the noise of
the people as they shouted, he said to Moses, "*There is* a noise of war in the camp."
18 But he said:

"*It is* not the noise of the shout of
victory,
Nor the noise of the cry of defeat,
But the sound of singing I hear."

19 So it was, as soon as he came near the
camp, that [a]he saw the calf *and* the dancing. So Moses' anger became hot, and he
cast the tablets out of his hands and broke
them at the foot of the mountain. 20 [a]Then
he took the calf which they had made,
burned *it* in the fire, and ground *it* to powder; and he scattered *it* on the water and
made the children of Israel drink *it*. 21 And
Moses said to Aaron, [a]"What did this people do to you that you have brought *so*
great a sin upon them?"
22 So Aaron said, "Do not let the anger
of my lord become hot. [a]You know the
people, that they *are set* on evil. 23 For
they said to me, 'Make us gods that shall
go before us; *as for* this Moses, the man
who brought us out of the land of Egypt,
we do not know what has become of him.'
24 And I said to them, 'Whoever has any
gold, let them break *it* off.' So they gave
it to me, and I cast it into the fire, and this
calf came out."
25 Now when Moses saw that the people
were [a]unrestrained (for Aaron [b]had not
restrained them, to *their* shame among
their enemies), 26 then Moses stood in the
entrance of the camp, and said, "Whoever
is on the LORD's side—*come* to me!" And
all the sons of Levi gathered themselves
together to him. 27 And he said to them,
"Thus says the LORD God of Israel: 'Let
every man put his sword on his side, and
go in and out from entrance to entrance
throughout the camp, and [a]let every man
kill his brother, every man his companion, and every man his neighbor.' " 28 So
the sons of Levi did according to the word
of Moses. And about three thousand men
of the people fell that day. 29 [a]Then Moses
said, [1]"Consecrate yourselves today to the
LORD, that He may bestow on you a blessing this day, for every man has opposed
his son and his brother."

I pray that ____ will set themselves apart to follow You today, O Lord.

FROM EXODUS 32:29

30 Now it came to pass on the next day
that Moses said to the people, [a]"You have
committed a great sin. So now I will go up
to the LORD; [b]perhaps I can [c]make atonement for your sin." 31 Then Moses [a]re-
turned to the LORD and said, "Oh, these
people have committed a great sin, and
have [b]made for themselves a god of gold!
32 Yet now, if You will forgive their sin—
but if not, I pray, [a]blot me [b]out of Your
book which You have written."
33 And the LORD said to Moses, [a]"Whoever has sinned against Me, I will [b]blot him
out of My book. 34 Now therefore, go, lead
the people to *the place* of which I have
[a]spoken to you. [b]Behold, My Angel shall
go before you. Nevertheless, [c]in the day
when I [d]visit for punishment, I will visit
punishment upon them for their sin."
35 So the LORD plagued the people because of [a]what they did with the calf
which Aaron made.

The Command to Leave Sinai

33 Then the LORD said to Moses, "Depart *and* go up from here, you [a]and
the people whom you have brought out of
the land of Egypt, to the land of which I

12 [a]Num. 14:13–19 [b]Ex. 32:14
13 [a][Heb. 6:13] [b]Gen. 12:7; 13:15; 15:7, 18; 22:17; 26:4; 35:11, 12
14 [a]2 Sam. 24:16
15 [a]Deut. 9:15
16 [a]Ex. 31:18
19 [a]Deut. 9:16, 17
20 [a]Deut. 9:21
21 [a]Gen. 26:10
22 [a]Deut. 9:24
25 [a]Ex. 33:4, 5 [b]2 Chr. 28:19
27 [a]Num. 25:5–13
29 [a]Ex. 28:41 [1]Lit. *Fill your hand*
30 [a]1 Sam. 12:20, 23 [b]2 Sam. 16:12 [c]Num. 25:13
31 [a]Deut. 9:18 [b]Ex. 20:23
32 [a]Ps. 69:28 [b]Dan. 12:1
33 [a][Ezek. 18:4; 33:2, 14, 15] [b]Ex. 17:14
34 [a]Ex. 3:17 [b]Ex. 23:20 [c]Deut. 32:35 [d]Ps. 89:32
35 [a]Neh. 9:18
CHAPTER 33
1 [a]Ex. 32:1, 7, 13

swore to Abraham, Isaac, and Jacob, saying, [b]'To your descendants I will give it.'
2 [a]And I will send *My* Angel before you,
[b]and I will drive out the Canaanite and the
Amorite and the Hittite and the Perizzite
and the Hivite and the Jebusite. 3 *Go up*
[a]to a land flowing with milk and honey;
for I will not go up in your midst, lest [b]I
[1]consume you on the way, for you *are* a
[c]stiff-necked[2] people."
4 And when the people heard this bad
news, [a]they mourned, [b]and no one put on
his ornaments. 5 For the LORD had said to
Moses, "Say to the children of Israel, 'You
are a stiff-necked people. I could come up
into your midst in one moment and consume you. Now therefore, take off your
[1]ornaments, that I may [a]know what to
do to you.'" 6 So the children of Israel
stripped themselves of their ornaments by
Mount Horeb.

Moses Meets with the Lord

7 Moses took his tent and pitched it outside the camp, far from the camp, and
[a]called it the tabernacle of meeting. And
it came to pass *that* everyone who [b]sought
the LORD went out to the tabernacle of
meeting which *was* outside the camp. 8 So
it was, whenever Moses went out to the
tabernacle, *that* all the people rose, and
each man stood [a]*at* his tent door and
watched Moses until he had gone into the
tabernacle. 9 And it came to pass, when
Moses entered the tabernacle, that the pillar of cloud descended and stood *at* the
door of the tabernacle, and *the LORD*
[a]talked with Moses. 10 All the people saw
the pillar of cloud standing *at* the tabernacle door, and all the people rose and [a]wor-
shiped, each man *in* his tent door. 11 So
[a]the LORD spoke to Moses face to face, as
a man speaks to his friend. And he would
return to the camp, but [b]his servant Joshua the son of Nun, a young man, did not
depart from the tabernacle.

The Promise of God's Presence

12 Then Moses said to the LORD, "See,
[a]You say to me, 'Bring up this people.' But
You have not let me know whom You will
send with me. Yet You have said, [b]'I know
you by name, and you have also found
grace in My sight.' 13 Now therefore, I
pray, [a]if I have found grace in Your sight,
[b]show me now Your way, that I may know
You and that I may find grace in Your
sight. And consider that this nation *is*
[c]Your people."

> *Father, may ____ find grace in Your sight. Show them Your way and in Your Presence give them rest.*
>
> FROM EXODUS 33:13, 14

14 And He said, [a]"My Presence will go
with you, and I will give you [b]rest."
15 Then he said to Him, [a]"If Your Presence does not go *with us,* do not bring us
up from here. 16 For how then will it be
known that Your people and I have found
grace in Your sight, [a]except You go with
us? So we [b]shall be separate, Your people
and I, from all the people who *are* upon
the face of the earth."
17 So the LORD said to Moses, [a]"I will
also do this thing that you have spoken;
for you have found grace in My sight, and
I know you by name."

> *To maintain and enjoy the right kind of fellowship with the Lord, we must always be mindful of who we are and how much we are indebted to His grace.*
>
> ANDREW MURRAY

18 And he said, "Please, show me [a]Your
glory."
19 Then He said, "I will make all My
[a]goodness pass before you, and I will proclaim the name of the LORD before you. [b]I
will be gracious to whom I will be [c]gra-
cious, and I will have compassion on
whom I will have compassion." 20 But He
said, "You cannot see My face; for [a]no
man shall see Me, and live." 21 And the
LORD said, "Here is a place by Me, and you
shall stand on the rock. 22 So it shall be,

1 b Gen. 12:7
2 a Ex. 32:34 b Josh. 24:11
3 a Ex. 3:8 b Num. 16:21, 45 c Ex. 32:9; 33:5 *1 destroy* *2 stubborn*
4 a Num. 14:1, 39 b Ezra 9:3
5 a [Ps. 139:23] *1 jewelry*
7 a Ex. 29:42, 43 b Deut. 4:29
8 a Num. 16:27
9 a Ps. 99:7
10 a Ex. 4:31
11 a Num. 12:8 b Ex. 24:13
12 a Ex. 3:10; 32:34 b Ex. 33:17
13 a Ex. 34:9 b Ps. 25:4; 27:11; 86:11; 119:33 c Deut. 9:26, 29
14 a Is. 63:9 b Josh. 21:44; 22:4
15 a Ex. 33:3
16 a Num. 14:14 b Ex. 34:10
17 a [James 5:16]
18 a [1 Tim. 6:16]
19 a Ex. 34:6, 7 b [Rom. 9:15, 16, 18] c [Rom. 4:4, 16]
20 a [Gen. 32:30]

EXODUS 33:12–15

Dear Woman of Destiny,

God said to Moses, "Here is a place by Me. Come here" (see Ex. 33:21–23). That's the place I want to be. That place is reserved for me, so that I can stay near Him.

He says to us, "Come over here by Me." It's like pulling up your chair and sitting next to your grandfather, your best friend, or your brother. There is a drawing near to the Lord that, in itself, is holy. There is a drawing near to the Lord that, in itself, is righteous. Just getting near Him, you begin to feel His presence and the manifestation of His glory.

You can't be in His presence without its becoming visible in your life. The shine on Moses' face was the evidence of the presence of God. Each of us who stays close to Him will have the glory look, a holy look, the look of one who has been gazing into the face of Jesus. You can often see it in people's eyes after they have been with God.

Moses was in God's presence longer than most of us, but as we go there more and more—spending time with Him, communing with Him, worshiping Him—we will find that the glorious light of the gospel of Jesus Christ will not only shine into our hearts, but will shine forth from our lives and our faces as well.

Many of us are just now beginning to come into the experience that Moses had on the mount with God. It happens when we genuinely hunger for His presence, when we cry out to Him, "Show me Your glory." Just as Jesus was changed before the eyes of the disciples, we are being changed by the manifestation of His glory. He is changing us from glory to glory. These are revival days in which He is working those transforming graces into our lives by the power of His Spirit.

I want to declare, as did Moses: If God's presence goes not with me, I just don't want to go. I don't want to go where He has not gone before me in the fullness of His glory. He is causing the veil to be taken from our eyes, the blinders to fall away, the scales to drop. He is removing the hindrances and the limitations of our minds and our own thinking, and is causing even the hard crust that has formed upon our hearts through the cares of this life to melt so that we might experience His glory in a new and greater way.

Ruth Ward Heflin

while My glory passes by, that I will put
you [a]in the cleft of the rock, and will [b]cov-
er you with My hand while I pass by.
23 Then I will take away My hand, and you
shall see My back; but My face shall [a]not
be seen."

Moses Makes New Tablets

34 And the LORD said to Moses, [a]"Cut
two tablets of stone like the first
ones, and [b]I will write on *these* tablets the
words that were on the first tablets which
you broke. 2 So be ready in the morning,
and come up in the morning to Mount
Sinai, and present yourself to Me there
[a]on the top of the mountain. 3 And no man
shall [a]come up with you, and let no man
be seen throughout all the mountain; let
neither flocks nor herds feed before that
mountain."

4 So he cut two tablets of stone like the
first *ones.* Then Moses rose early in the
morning and went up Mount Sinai, as the
LORD had commanded him; and he took
in his hand the two tablets of stone.

5 Now the LORD descended in the [a]cloud
and stood with him there, and [b]pro-
claimed the name of the LORD. 6 And the
LORD passed before him and proclaimed,
"The LORD, the LORD [a]God, merciful and
gracious, longsuffering, and abounding in
[b]goodness and [c]truth, 7 [a]keeping mercy
for thousands, [b]forgiving iniquity and
transgression and sin, [c]by no means
clearing *the guilty,* visiting the iniquity
of the fathers upon the children and the
children's children to the third and the
fourth generation."

8 So Moses made haste and [a]bowed his
head toward the earth, and worshiped.
9 Then he said, "If now I have found grace
in Your sight, O Lord, [a]let my Lord, I
pray, go among us, even though we *are* a
[b]stiff-necked[1] people; and pardon our iniquity and our sin, and take us as [c]Your
inheritance."

The Covenant Renewed

10 And He said: "Behold, [a]I make a covenant. Before all your people I will [b]do
[1]marvels such as have not been done in all
the earth, nor in any nation; and all the
people among whom you *are* shall see the
work of the LORD. For it *is* [c]an awesome
thing that I will do with you. 11 [a]Observe
what I command you this day. Behold, [b]I
am driving out from before you the Amorite and the Canaanite and the Hittite and
the Perizzite and the Hivite and the Jebusite. 12 [a]Take heed to yourself, lest you
make a covenant with the inhabitants of
the land where you are going, lest it be a
snare in your midst. 13 But you shall [a]de-
stroy their altars, break their *sacred* pillars, and [b]cut down their wooden images
14 (for you shall worship [a]no other god, for
the LORD, whose [b]name *is* Jealous, *is* a
[c]jealous God), 15 lest you make a covenant
with the inhabitants of the land, and they
[a]play the harlot with their gods and make
sacrifice to their gods, and *one of them*
[b]invites you and you [c]eat of his sacrifice,
16 and you take of [a]his daughters for your
sons, and his daughters [b]play the harlot
with their gods and make your sons play
the harlot with their gods.

17 [a]"You shall make no molded gods for
yourselves.

18 "The Feast of [a]Unleavened Bread you
shall keep. Seven days you shall eat unleavened bread, as I commanded you, in
the appointed time of the month of Abib;
for in the [b]month of Abib you came out
from Egypt.

19 [a]"All [1]that open the womb *are* Mine,
and every male firstborn among your livestock, *whether* ox or sheep. 20 But [a]the
firstborn of a donkey you shall redeem
with a lamb. And if you will not redeem
him, then you shall break his neck. All the
firstborn of your sons you shall redeem.

"And none shall appear before Me
[b]empty-handed.

21 [a]"Six days you shall work, but on the
seventh day you shall rest; in plowing
time and in harvest you shall rest.

22 "And you shall observe the Feast of
Weeks, of the firstfruits of wheat harvest,
and the Feast of Ingathering at the year's
end.

23 [a]"Three times in the year all your
men shall appear before the Lord, the
LORD God of Israel. 24 For I will [a]cast out
the nations before you and enlarge your
borders; neither will any man covet your
land when you go up to appear before the
LORD your God three times in the year.

25 "You shall not offer the blood of My
sacrifice with leaven, [a]nor shall the sacrifice of the Feast of the Passover be left
until morning.

26 [a]"The first of the firstfruits of your
land you shall bring to the house of the
LORD your God. You shall not boil a young
goat in its mother's milk."

---

22 a Is. 2:21 b Ps. 91:1, 4
23 a [John 1:18]
CHAPTER 34
1 a [Ex. 24:12; 31:18; 32:15, 16, 19] b Deut. 10:2, 4
2 a Ex. 19:11, 18, 20
3 a Ex. 19:12, 13; 24:9–11
5 a Ex. 19:9 b Ex. 33:19
6 a Neh. 9:17 b Rom. 2:4 c Ps. 108:4
7 a Ex. 20:6 b Ps. 103:3, 4 c Job 10:14
8 a Ex. 4:31
9 a Ex. 33:12–16 b Ex. 33:3 c Ps. 33:12; 94:14 *1 stubborn*
10 a Deut. 5:2 b Ps. 77:14 c Ps. 145:6 *1 wonderful acts*
11 a Deut. 6:25 b Ex. 23:20–33; 33:2
12 a Ex. 23:32, 33
13 a Deut. 12:3 b 2 Kin. 18:4
14 a [Ex. 20:3–5] b [Is. 9:6; 57:15] c [Deut. 4:24]
15 a Judg. 2:17 b Num. 25:1, 2 c 1 Cor. 8:4, 7, 10
16 a Gen. 28:1 b Num. 25:1, 2
17 a Ex. 20:4, 23; 32:8
18 a Ex. 12:15, 16 b Ex. 12:2; 13:4
19 a Ex. 13:2; 22:29 *1 the firstborn*
20 a Ex. 13:13 b Ex. 22:29; 23:15
21 a Ex. 20:9; 23:12; 31:15; 35:2
23 a Ex. 23:14–17
24 a [Ex. 33:2]
25 a Ex. 12:10
26 a Ex. 23:19

27 Then the LORD said to Moses, "Write
[a]these words, for according to the tenor of
these words I have made a covenant with
you and with Israel." 28 [a]So he was there
with the LORD forty days and forty nights;
he neither ate bread nor drank water. And
[b]He wrote on the tablets the words of the
covenant, the [1]Ten Commandments.

The Shining Face of Moses

29 Now it was so, when Moses came
down from Mount Sinai (and the [a]two
tablets of the Testimony *were* in Moses'
hand when he came down from the
mountain), that Moses did not know that
[b]the skin of his face shone while he talked
with Him. 30 So when Aaron and all the
children of Israel saw Moses, behold, the
skin of his face shone, and they were
afraid to come near him. 31 Then Moses
called to them, and Aaron and all the rulers of the congregation returned to him;
and Moses talked with them. 32 Afterward
all the children of Israel came near, [a]and
he gave them as commandments all that
the LORD had spoken with him on Mount
Sinai. 33 And when Moses had finished
speaking with them, he put [a]a veil on his
face. 34 But [a]whenever Moses went in before the LORD to speak with Him, he
would take the veil off until he came out;
and he would come out and speak to the
children of Israel whatever he had been
commanded. 35 And whenever the children of Israel saw the face of Moses, that
the skin of Moses' face shone, then Moses
would put the veil on his face again, until
he went in to speak with Him.

Sabbath Regulations

35 Then Moses gathered all the congregation of the children of Israel
together, and said to them, [a]"These *are*
the words which the LORD has commanded *you* to do: 2 Work shall be done for [a]six
days, but the seventh day shall be a holy
day for you, a Sabbath of rest to the LORD.
Whoever does any work on it shall be put
to [b]death. 3 [a]You shall kindle no fire
throughout your dwellings on the Sabbath day."

Offerings for the Tabernacle

4 And Moses spoke to all the congregation of the children of Israel, saying,
[a]"This *is* the thing which the LORD commanded, saying: 5 'Take from among you
an offering to the LORD. [a]Whoever *is* of a
willing heart, let him bring it as an offering to the LORD: [b]gold, silver, and bronze;
6 [a]blue, purple, and scarlet *thread,* fine
linen, and [b]goats' *hair;* 7 ram skins dyed
red, badger skins, and acacia wood; 8 oil
for the light, [a]and spices for the anointing
oil and for the sweet incense; 9 onyx
stones, and stones to be set in the ephod
and in the breastplate.

Articles of the Tabernacle

10 [a]'All *who are* gifted artisans among
you shall come and make all that the LORD
has commanded: 11 [a]the tabernacle, its
tent, its covering, its clasps, its boards, its
bars, its pillars, and its sockets; 12 [a]the ark
and its poles, *with* the mercy seat, and the
veil of the covering; 13 the [a]table and its
poles, all its utensils, [b]and the showbread;
14 also [a]the lampstand for the light, its
utensils, its lamps, and the oil for the
light; 15 [a]the incense altar, its poles, [b]the
anointing oil, [c]the sweet incense, and the
screen for the door at the entrance of
the tabernacle; 16 [a]the altar of burnt offering
with its bronze grating, its poles, all its
utensils, *and* the laver and its base; 17 [a]the
hangings of the court, its pillars, their
sockets, and the screen for the gate of the
court; 18 the pegs of the tabernacle, the
pegs of the court, and their cords; 19 [a]the
[1]garments of ministry, for ministering in
the holy *place*—the holy garments for
Aaron the priest and the garments of his
sons, to minister as priests.' "

The Tabernacle Offerings Presented

20 And all the congregation of the children of Israel departed from the presence
of Moses. 21 Then everyone came [a]whose
heart [1]was stirred, and everyone whose
spirit was willing, *and* they [b]brought the
LORD's offering for the work of the tabernacle of meeting, for all its service, and for
the holy garments. 22 They came, both
men and women, as many as had a willing
heart, *and* brought [a]earrings and nose
rings, rings and necklaces, all [b]jewelry of
gold, that is, every man who *made* an offering of gold to the LORD. 23 And [a]every
man, with whom was found blue, purple,
and scarlet *thread,* fine linen, goats' *hair,*
red skins of rams, and [1]badger skins,
brought *them.* 24 Everyone who offered an
offering of silver or bronze brought the
LORD's offering. And everyone with whom

27 a Deut. 31:9
28 a Ex. 24:18 b Ex. 34:1, 4 *1* Lit. *Ten Words*
29 a Ex. 32:15 b 2 Cor. 3:7
32 a Ex. 24:3
33 a [2 Cor. 3:13, 14]
34 a [2 Cor. 3:13–16]
CHAPTER 35
1 a Ex. 34:32
2 a Lev. 23:3 b Num. 15:32–36
3 a Ex. 12:16; 16:23
4 a Ex. 25:1, 2
5 a Ex. 25:2 b Ex. 38:24
6 a Ex. 36:8 b Ex. 36:14
8 a Ex. 25:6; 30:23–25
10 a Ex. 31:2–6; 36:1, 2
11 a Ex. 26:1, 2; 36:14
12 a Ex. 25:10–22
13 a Ex. 25:23 b Ex. 25:30
14 a Ex. 25:31
15 a Ex. 30:1 b Ex. 30:25 c Ex. 30:34–38
16 a Ex. 27:1–8
17 a Ex. 27:9–18
19 a Ex. 31:10; 39:1, 41 *1* Or *woven garments*
21 a Ex. 25:2; 35:5, 22, 26, 29; 36:2 b Ex. 35:24 *1* Lit. *lifted him up*
22 a Ex. 32:2, 3 b Ex. 11:2
23 a 1 Chr. 29:8 *1* Or *dolphin*

was found acacia wood for any work of the
service, brought *it.* 25All the women *who*
were [a]gifted artisans spun yarn with their
hands, and brought what they had spun,
of blue, purple, *and* scarlet, and fine linen.
26And all the women whose hearts
[1]stirred with wisdom spun yarn of goats'
hair. 27[a]The rulers brought onyx stones,
and the stones to be set in the ephod and
in the breastplate, 28and [a]spices and oil
for the light, for the anointing oil, and for
the sweet incense. 29The children of Israel
brought a [a]freewill offering to the LORD,
all the men and women whose hearts were
willing to bring *material* for all kinds of
work which the LORD, by the hand of Moses, had commanded to be done.

The Artisans Called by God

30And Moses said to the children of Israel, "See, [a]the LORD has called by name
Bezalel the son of Uri, the son of Hur, of
the tribe of Judah; 31and He has filled him
with the Spirit of God, in wisdom and understanding, in knowledge and all manner
of workmanship, 32to design artistic
works, to work in gold and silver and
bronze, 33in cutting jewels for setting, in
carving wood, and to work in all manner
of artistic workmanship.

34"And He has put in his heart the ability to teach, *in* him and [a]Aholiab the son
of Ahisamach, of the tribe of Dan. 35He
has [a]filled them with skill to do all manner of work of the engraver and the designer and the tapestry maker, in blue,
purple, and scarlet *thread,* and fine linen,
and of the weaver—those who do every
work and those who design artistic works.

36 "And Bezalel and Aholiab, and every [a]gifted artisan in whom the
LORD has put wisdom and understanding,
to know how to do all manner of work for
the service of the [b]sanctuary,[1] shall do according to all that the LORD has commanded."

The People Give More than Enough

2Then Moses called Bezalel and Aholiab, and every gifted artisan in whose heart
the LORD had put wisdom, everyone
[a]whose heart [1]was stirred, to come and do
the work. 3And they received from Moses
all the [a]offering which the children of Israel [b]had brought for the work of the service of making the sanctuary. So they
continued bringing to him freewill offerings every morning. 4Then all the craftsmen who were doing all the work of the
sanctuary came, each from the work he
was doing, 5and they spoke to Moses, saying, [a]"The people bring much more than
enough for the service of the work which
the LORD commanded *us* to do."

6So Moses gave a commandment, and
they caused it to be proclaimed throughout the camp, saying, "Let neither man
nor woman do any more work for the offering of the sanctuary." And the people
were restrained from bringing, 7for the
material they had was sufficient for all the
work to be done—indeed too [a]much.

Building the Tabernacle

8[a]Then all the gifted artisans among
them who worked on the tabernacle made
ten curtains woven of fine linen, and of
blue, purple, and scarlet *thread; with* artistic designs of cherubim they made
them. 9The length of each curtain *was*
twenty-eight cubits, and the width of
each curtain four cubits; the curtains
were all the same size. 10And he coupled
five curtains to one another, and *the other*
five curtains he coupled to one another.
11He made loops of blue *yarn* on the edge
of the curtain on the selvedge of one set;
likewise he did on the outer edge of *the*
other curtain of the second set. 12[a]Fifty
loops he made on one curtain, and fifty
loops he made on the edge of the curtain
on the end of the second set; the loops
held one *curtain* to another. 13And he
made fifty clasps of gold, and coupled the
curtains to one another with the clasps,
that it might be one tabernacle.

14[a]He made curtains of goats' *hair* for
the tent over the tabernacle; he made
eleven curtains. 15The length of each curtain *was* thirty cubits, and the width of
each curtain four cubits; the eleven curtains *were* the same size. 16He coupled
five curtains by themselves and six curtains by themselves. 17And he made fifty
loops on the edge of the curtain that is
outermost in one set, and fifty loops he
made on the edge of the curtain of the
second set. 18He also made fifty bronze
clasps to couple the tent together, that it
might be one. 19[a]Then he made a covering
for the tent of ram skins dyed red, and a
covering of [1]badger skins above *that.*

20For the tabernacle [a]he made boards
of acacia wood, standing upright. 21The

---

25 [a]Ex. 28:3; 31:6; 36:1
26 [1]Lit. *lifted them up*
27 [a]Ezra 2:68
28 [a]Ex. 30:23
29 [a]1 Chr. 29:9
30 [a]Ex. 31:1–6
34 [a]Ex. 31:6
35 [a]1 Kin. 7:14

CHAPTER 36
1 [a]Ex. 28:3; 31:6; 35:10, 35 [b]Ex. 25:8 [1]*holy place*
2 [a]1 Chr. 29:5, 9, 17 [1]*lifted him up*
3 [a]Ex. 35:5 [b]Ex. 35:27
5 [a][2 Cor. 8:2, 3]
7 [a]1 Kin. 8:64
8 [a]Ex. 26:1–14
12 [a]Ex. 26:5
14 [a]Ex. 26:7
19 [a]Ex. 26:14 [1]Or *dolphin*
20 [a]Ex. 26:15–29

length of each board *was* ten cubits, and
the width of each board a cubit and a half.
22 Each board had two [1]tenons [a]for binding one to another. Thus he made for all
the boards of the tabernacle. 23 And he
made boards for the tabernacle, twenty
boards for the south side. 24 Forty sockets
of silver he made to go under the twenty
boards: two sockets under each of the
boards for its two tenons. 25 And for the
other side of the tabernacle, the north
side, he made twenty boards 26 and their
forty sockets of silver: two sockets under
each of the boards. 27 For the west side of
the tabernacle he made six boards. 28 He
also made two boards for the two back
corners of the tabernacle. 29 And they were
coupled at the bottom and [1]coupled together at the top by one ring. Thus he
made both of them for the two corners.
30 So there were eight boards and their
sockets—sixteen sockets of silver—two
sockets under each of the boards.
31 And he made [a]bars of acacia wood:
five for the boards on one side of the tabernacle, 32 five bars for the boards on the
other side of the tabernacle, and five bars
for the boards of the tabernacle on the far
side westward. 33 And he made the middle
bar to pass through the boards from one
end to the other. 34 He overlaid the boards
with gold, made their rings of gold *to be*
holders for the bars, and overlaid the bars
with gold.
35 And he made [a]a veil of blue, purple,
and scarlet *thread,* and fine woven linen;
it was worked *with* an artistic design of
cherubim. 36 He made for it four pillars of
acacia *wood,* and overlaid them with gold,
with their hooks of gold; and he cast four
sockets of silver for them.
37 He also made a [a]screen for the tabernacle door, of blue, purple, and scarlet
thread, and fine woven linen, made by a
[1]weaver, 38 and its five pillars with their
hooks. And he overlaid their capitals and
their rings with gold, but their five sockets *were* bronze.

Making the Ark of the Testimony

37 Then [a]Bezalel made [b]the ark of
acacia wood; two and a half cubits
was its length, a cubit and a half its width,
and a cubit and a half its height. 2 He overlaid it with pure gold inside and outside,
and made a molding of gold all around it.
3 And he cast for it four rings of gold *to be*

22 [a]Ex. 26:17 [1]Projections for joining, lit. *hands*

29 [1]Lit. *doubled*

31 [a]Ex. 26:26–29

35 [a]Ex. 26:31–37

37 [a]Ex. 26:36 [1]Lit. *variegator,* a weaver in colors

CHAPTER 37
1 [a]Ex. 35:30; 36:1 [b]Ex. 25:10–20

6 [a]Ex. 25:17

9 [a]Ex. 25:20

10 [a]Ex. 25:23–29

16 [a]Ex. 25:29

17 [a]Ex. 25:31–39

set in its four corners: two rings on one
side, and two rings on the other side of it.
4 He made poles of acacia wood, and overlaid them with gold. 5 And he put the poles
into the rings at the sides of the ark, to
bear the ark. 6 He also made the [a]mercy
seat of pure gold; two and a half cubits
was its length and a cubit and a half its
width. 7 He made two cherubim of beaten
gold; he made them of one piece at the
two ends of the mercy seat: 8 one cherub
at one end on this side, and the other
cherub at the *other* end on that side. He
made the cherubim at the two ends *of one
piece* with the mercy seat. 9 The cherubim
spread out *their* wings above, *and* covered
the [a]mercy seat with their wings. They
faced one another; the faces of the cherubim were toward the mercy seat.

Making the Table for the Showbread

10 He made [a]the table of acacia wood;
two cubits *was* its length, a cubit its
width, and a cubit and a half its height.
11 And he overlaid it with pure gold, and
made a molding of gold all around it.
12 Also he made a frame of a handbreadth
all around it, and made a molding of gold
for the frame all around it. 13 And he cast
for it four rings of gold, and put the rings
on the four corners that *were* at its four
legs. 14 The rings were close to the frame,
as holders for the poles to bear the table.
15 And he made the poles of acacia wood to
bear the table, and overlaid them with
gold. 16 He made of pure gold the utensils
which were on the table: its [a]dishes, its
cups, its bowls, and its pitchers for
pouring.

Making the Gold Lampstand

17 He also made the [a]lampstand of pure
gold; of hammered work he made the
lampstand. Its shaft, its branches, its
bowls, its *ornamental* knobs, and its flowers were of the same piece. 18 And six
branches came out of its sides: three
branches of the lampstand out of one side,
and three branches of the lampstand out
of the other side. 19 There were three
bowls made like almond *blossoms* on one
branch, with an *ornamental* knob and a
flower, and three bowls made like almond
blossoms on the other branch, with an *ornamental* knob and a flower—and so for
the six branches coming out of the lamp-

stand. [20]And on the lampstand itself *were* four bowls made like almond *blossoms, each with* its *ornamental* knob and flower. [21]*There was* a knob under the *first* two branches of the same, a knob under the *second* two branches of the same, and a knob under the *third* two branches of the same, according to the six branches extending from it. [22]Their knobs and their branches were of one piece; all of it *was* one hammered piece of pure gold. [23]And he made its seven lamps, its [a]wick-trimmers, and its trays of pure gold. [24]Of a talent of pure gold he made it, with all its utensils.

Making the Altar of Incense

[25][a]He made the incense altar of acacia wood. Its length *was* a cubit and its width a cubit—*it was* square—and two cubits *was* its height. Its horns were *of one piece* with it. [26]And he overlaid it with pure gold: its top, its sides all around, and its horns. He also made for it a molding of gold all around it. [27]He made two rings of gold for it under its molding, by its two corners on both sides, as holders for the poles with which to bear it. [28]And he [a]made the poles of acacia wood, and overlaid them with gold.

Making the Anointing Oil and the Incense

[29]He also made [a]the holy anointing oil and the pure incense of sweet spices, according to the work of the perfumer.

Making the Altar of Burnt Offering

38 He made [a]the altar of burnt offering of acacia wood; five cubits *was* its length and five cubits its width—*it was* square—and its height *was* three cubits. [2]He made its horns on its four corners; the horns were *of one piece* with it. And he overlaid it with bronze. [3]He made all the utensils for the altar: the pans, the shovels, the basins, the forks, and the firepans; all its utensils he made of bronze. [4]And he made a grate of bronze network for the altar, under its rim, midway from the bottom. [5]He cast four rings for the four corners of the bronze grating, *as* holders for the poles. [6]And he made the poles of acacia wood, and overlaid them with bronze. [7]Then he put the poles into the rings on the sides of the altar, with which to bear it. He made the altar hollow with boards.

Making the Bronze Laver

[8]He made [a]the laver of bronze and its base of bronze, from the bronze mirrors of the serving women who assembled at the door of the tabernacle of meeting.

Making the Court of the Tabernacle

[9]Then he made [a]the court on the south side; the hangings of the court *were of* fine woven linen, one hundred cubits long. [10]There *were* twenty pillars for them, with twenty bronze sockets. The hooks of the pillars and their bands *were* silver. [11]On the north side *the hangings were* one hundred cubits *long,* with twenty pillars and their twenty bronze sockets. The hooks of the pillars and their bands *were* silver. [12]And on the west side *there were* hangings of fifty cubits, with ten pillars and their ten sockets. The hooks of the pillars and their bands *were* silver. [13]For the east side *the hangings were* fifty cubits. [14]The hangings of one side *of the gate were* fifteen cubits *long, with* their three pillars and their three sockets, [15]and the same for the other side of the court gate; on this side and that *were* hangings of fifteen cubits, *with* their three pillars and their three sockets. [16]All the hangings of the court all around *were of* fine woven linen. [17]The sockets for the pillars *were* bronze, the hooks of the pillars and their bands *were* silver, and the overlay of their capitals *was* silver; and all the pillars of the court had bands of silver. [18]The screen for the gate of the court *was* woven of blue, purple, and scarlet *thread,* and of fine woven linen. The length *was* twenty cubits, and the height along its width *was* five cubits, corresponding to the hangings of the court. [19]And *there were* four pillars *with* their four sockets of bronze; their hooks *were* silver, and the overlay of their capitals and their bands *was* silver. [20]All the [a]pegs of the tabernacle, and of the court all around, *were* bronze.

Materials of the Tabernacle

[21][1]This is the inventory of the tabernacle, [a]the tabernacle of the Testimony, which was counted according to the commandment of Moses, for the service of the

---

23 [a]Num. 4:9
25 [a]Ex. 30:1–5
28 [a]Ex. 30:5
29 [a]Ex. 30:23–25
CHAPTER 38
1 [a]Ex. 27:1–8
8 [a]Ex. 30:18
9 [a]Ex. 27:9–19
20 [a]Ex. 27:19
21 [a]Acts 7:44
1 Lit. *These are the things appointed for*

Exodus 38:8

Dear Woman of Destiny,

There is an old saying, "The New Testament in the Old Testament is concealed; the Old Testament in the New Testament is revealed." In Exodus 38:8, we see one of those passages whose meaning is revealed in the New Testament.

We notice first that there were "serving women" at the door of the tabernacle. Even in the Old Testament, women were important in the spiritual life of their communities. As far back as Moses' day, we see women serving the Lord.

God told Moses to make the laver of bronze from the mirrors of the women. God didn't waste words with Moses, but directed him in spiritually significant steps to build the tabernacle. What was so significant about taking the mirrors from the women?

In the New Testament, we read in 1 Peter 3:1, 2 that a man can be won without a word by observing the godly life of a woman and noticing her chaste behavior. In that sense, the woman's purity becomes a mirror or gives vision to the man, not only to win him to Christ but also to aid him in his development in Christ. The woman has a powerful God-given influence on the man.

The laver was strategically placed and filled with water so the priests could do their ceremonial cleansing before they went into the presence of God. Symbolically, the Word of God is likened to water, as in Ephesians 5:26, which states that Jesus will sanctify and cleanse His church through the washing of the water of the Word.

As women, when we are filled with God's Word and obey and abide in His Word, we become just like that laver, filled with the living water and able to be an effective instrument of cleansing to those around us. We have the opportunity to bring purity and holiness to our environments. When people look into our lives and see that we are clean and pure, they begin to trust us.

The women who contributed the mirrors were the women who "assembled at the door of the tabernacle of meeting" (Ex. 38:8). "Assembled" infers that they gathered as to go to war. Isn't that interesting? These women who contributed the mirrors and the vision were the women who took their job of "womanhood" as seriously as any soldier in an army. These were women who were willing to give whatever it took to fulfill their call as a woman—to fulfill their destiny as a cleansing influence.

I pray that you feel that way about your call as a woman and that you will follow the example of the "serving women" in Exodus 38:8. May you serve Him with purity and holiness, walking in the sanctified place to which the Lord Jesus has called you. And may you take that job seriously as you minister to Him and to the people around you.

Mary Jean Pidgeon

Levites, [b]by the hand of [c]Ithamar, son of Aaron the priest.

22 [a]Bezalel the son of Uri, the son of Hur, of the tribe of Judah, made all that the LORD had commanded Moses. 23 And with him *was* [a]Aholiab the son of Ahisamach, of the tribe of Dan, an engraver and [1]designer, a weaver of blue, purple, and scarlet *thread,* and of fine linen.

24 All the gold that was used in all the work of the holy *place,* that is, the gold of the [a]offering, was twenty-nine talents and seven hundred and thirty shekels, according to [b]the shekel of the sanctuary. 25 And the silver from those who were [a]numbered of the congregation *was* one hundred talents and one thousand seven hundred and seventy-five shekels, according to the shekel of the sanctuary: 26 [a]a bekah for [1]each man (*that is,* half a shekel, according to the shekel of the sanctuary), for everyone included in the numbering from twenty years old and above, for [b]six hundred and three thousand, five hundred and fifty *men.* 27 And from the hundred talents of silver were cast [a]the sockets of the sanctuary and the bases of the veil: one hundred sockets from the hundred talents, one talent for each socket. 28 Then from the one thousand seven hundred and seventy-five *shekels* he made hooks for the pillars, overlaid their capitals, and [a]made bands for them.

29 The offering of bronze *was* seventy talents and two thousand four hundred shekels. 30 And with it he made the sockets for the door of the tabernacle of meeting, the bronze altar, the bronze grating for it, and all the utensils for the altar, 31 the sockets for the court all around, the bases for the court gate, all the pegs for the tabernacle, and all the pegs for the court all around.

Making the Garments of the Priesthood

39 Of the [a]blue, purple, and scarlet *thread* they made [b]garments[1] of ministry, for ministering in the [2]holy *place,* and made the holy garments for Aaron, [c]as the LORD had commanded Moses.

Making the Ephod

2 [a]He made the [b]ephod of gold, blue, purple, and scarlet *thread,* and of fine woven linen. 3 And they beat the gold into thin sheets and cut *it into* threads, to work *it* in *with* the blue, purple, and scarlet *thread,* and the fine linen, *into* artistic designs. 4 They made shoulder straps for it to couple *it* together; it was coupled together at its two edges. 5 And the intricately woven band of his ephod that *was* on it *was* of the same workmanship, *woven of* gold, blue, purple, and scarlet *thread,* and of fine woven linen, as the LORD had commanded Moses.

6 [a]And they set onyx stones, enclosed in [1]settings of gold; they were engraved, as signets are engraved, with the names of the sons of Israel. 7 He put them on the shoulders of the ephod *as* [a]memorial stones for the sons of Israel, as the LORD had commanded Moses.

Making the Breastplate

8 [a]And he made the breastplate, artistically woven like the workmanship of the ephod, of gold, blue, purple, and scarlet *thread,* and of fine woven linen. 9 They made the breastplate square by doubling it; a span *was* its length and a span its width when doubled. 10 [a]And they set in it four rows of stones: a row with a sardius, a topaz, and an emerald was the first row; 11 the second row, a turquoise, a sapphire, and a diamond; 12 the third row, a jacinth, an agate, and an amethyst; 13 the fourth row, a beryl, an onyx, and a jasper. *They were* enclosed in settings of gold in their mountings. 14 *There were* [a]twelve stones according to the names of the sons of Israel: according to their names, *engraved like* a signet, each one with its own name according to the twelve tribes. 15 And they made chains for the breastplate at the ends, like braided cords of pure gold. 16 They also made two settings of gold and two gold rings, and put the two rings on the two ends of the breastplate. 17 And they put the two braided *chains* of gold in the two rings on the ends of the breastplate. 18 The two ends of the two braided *chains* they fastened in the two settings, and put them on the shoulder straps of the ephod in the front. 19 And they made two rings of gold and put *them* on the two ends of the breastplate, on the edge of it, which *was* on the inward side of the ephod. 20 They made two *other* gold rings and put them on the two shoulder straps, underneath the ephod toward its front, right at the seam above the intricately woven band of

---

21 [b] Num. 4:28, 33 [c] Lev. 10:6, 16
22 [a] Ex. 31:2, 6
23 [a] Ex. 31:6; 36:1 [1] *skillful workman*
24 [a] Ex. 35:5, 22 [b] Ex. 30:13, 24
25 [a] Ex. 30:11–16
26 [a] Ex. 30:13, 15 [b] Num. 1:46; 26:51 [1] Lit. *a head*
27 [a] Ex. 26:19, 21, 25, 32
28 [a] Ex. 27:17

CHAPTER 39
1 [a] Ex. 25:4; 35:23 [b] Ex. 31:10; 35:19 [c] Ex. 28:4 [1] Or *woven garments* [2] *sanctuary*
2 [a] Ex. 28:6–14 [b] Lev. 8:7
6 [a] Ex. 28:9–11 [1] *plaited work*
7 [a] Ex. 28:12, 29
8 [a] Ex. 28:15–30
10 [a] Ex. 28:17
14 [a] Rev. 21:12

the ephod. 21And they bound the breastplate by means of its rings to the rings of
the ephod with a blue cord, so that it
would be above the intricately woven
band of the ephod, and that the breastplate would not come loose from the
ephod, as the LORD had commanded
Moses.

Making the Other Priestly Garments

22[a]He made the [b]robe of the ephod of
woven work, all of blue. 23And *there was*
an opening in the middle of the robe, like
the opening in a coat of mail, *with* a woven binding all around the opening, so
that it would not tear. 24They made on the
hem of the robe pomegranates of blue,
purple, and scarlet, and of fine woven *lin-
en.* 25And they made [a]bells of pure gold,
and put the bells between the pomegranates on the hem of the robe all around
between the pomegranates: 26a bell and a
pomegranate, a bell and a pomegranate,
all around the hem of the robe to [1]minis-
ter in, as the LORD had commanded
Moses.

27[a]They made tunics, artistically woven
of fine linen, for Aaron and his sons, 28[a]a
turban of fine linen, exquisite hats of fine
linen, [b]short trousers of fine woven linen,
29[a]and a sash of fine woven linen with
blue, purple, and scarlet *thread,* made by
a weaver, as the LORD had commanded
Moses.

30[a]Then they made the plate of the holy
crown of pure gold, and wrote on it an
inscription *like* the engraving of a signet:

[b]HOLINESS TO THE LORD.

31And they tied to it a blue cord, to fasten
it above on the turban, as the LORD had
commanded Moses.

The Work Completed

32Thus all the work of the tabernacle of
the tent of meeting was [a]finished. And the
children of Israel did [b]according to all
that the LORD had commanded Moses; so
they did. 33And they brought the tabernacle to Moses, the tent and all its furnishings: its clasps, its boards, its bars, its
pillars, and its sockets; 34the covering of
ram skins dyed red, the covering of badger
skins, and the veil of the covering; 35the
ark of the Testimony with its poles, and
the mercy seat; 36the table, all its utensils,
and the [a]showbread; 37the pure *gold*
lampstand with its lamps (the lamps set
in order), all its utensils, and the oil for
light; 38the gold altar, the anointing oil,
and the sweet incense; the screen for the
tabernacle door; 39the bronze altar, its
grate of bronze, its poles, and all its utensils; the laver with its base; 40the hangings
of the court, its pillars and its sockets, the
screen for the court gate, its cords, and its
pegs; all the utensils for the service of the
tabernacle, for the tent of meeting; 41and
the [1]garments of ministry, to [2]minister
in the holy *place:* the holy garments for
Aaron the priest, and his sons' garments,
to minister as priests.

42According to all that the LORD had
commanded Moses, so the children of Israel [a]did all the work. 43Then Moses
looked over all the work, and indeed they
had done it; as the LORD had commanded,
just so they had done it. And Moses
[a]blessed them.

The Tabernacle Erected and Arranged

40 Then the LORD [a]spoke to Moses,
saying: 2"On the first day of the
[a]first month you shall set up [b]the tabernacle of the tent of meeting. 3[a]You shall
put in it the ark of the Testimony, and
[1]partition off the ark with the veil. 4[a]You
shall bring in the table and [b]arrange the
things that are to be set in order on it;
[c]and you shall bring in the lampstand and
[1]light its lamps. 5[a]You shall also set the
altar of gold for the incense before the ark
of the Testimony, and put up the screen
for the door of the tabernacle. 6Then you
shall set the [a]altar of the burnt offering
before the door of the tabernacle of the
tent of meeting. 7And [a]you shall set the
laver between the tabernacle of meeting
and the altar, and put water in it. 8You
shall set up the court all around, and hang
up the screen at the court gate.

9"And you shall take the anointing oil,
and [a]anoint the tabernacle and all that *is*
in it; and you shall hallow it and all its
utensils, and it shall be holy. 10You shall
[a]anoint the altar of the burnt offering and
all its utensils, and consecrate the altar.
[b]The altar shall be most holy. 11And you
shall anoint the laver and its base, and
consecrate it.

12[a]"Then you shall bring Aaron and his
sons to the door of the tabernacle of meeting and wash them with water. 13You shall

22 a Ex. 28:31–35 b Ex. 29:5
25 a Ex. 28:33
26 *1 serve*
27 a Ex. 28:39, 40
28 a Ex. 28:4, 39 b Ex. 28:42
29 a Ex. 28:39
30 a Ex. 28:36, 37 b Zech. 14:20
32 a Ex. 40:17 b Ex. 25:40; 39:42, 43
36 a Ex.23–30
41 *1 Or woven garments 2 serve*
42 a Ex. 35:10
43 a Lev. 9:22, 23

CHAPTER 40
1 a Ex. 25:1—31:18
2 a Ex. 12:2; 13:4 b Ex. 26:1, 30; 40:17
3 a Num. 4:5 *1 screen*
4 a Ex. 26:35; 40:22 b Ex. 25:30; 40:23 c Ex. 40:24, 25 *1 set up*
5 a Ex. 40:26
6 a Ex. 39:39
7 a Ex. 30:18; 40:30
9 a Ex. 30:26
10 a Ex. 30:26–30 b Ex. 29:36, 37
12 a Lev. 8:1–13

put the holy [a]garments on Aaron, [b]and anoint him and consecrate him, that he may minister to Me as priest. [14]And you shall bring his sons and clothe them with tunics. [15]You shall anoint them, as you anointed their father, that they may minister to Me as priests; for their anointing shall surely be [a]an everlasting priesthood throughout their generations."

[16]Thus Moses did; according to all that the LORD had commanded him, so he did.

[17]And it came to pass in the first month of the second year, on the first *day* of the month, *that* the [a]tabernacle was [1]raised up. [18]So Moses raised up the tabernacle, fastened its sockets, set up its boards, put in its bars, and raised up its pillars. [19]And he spread out the tent over the tabernacle and put the covering of the tent on top of it, as the LORD had commanded Moses. [20]He took [a]the Testimony and put *it* into the ark, inserted the poles through the rings of the ark, and put the mercy seat on top of the ark. [21]And he brought the ark into the tabernacle, [a]hung up the veil of the covering, and partitioned off the ark of the Testimony, as the LORD had commanded Moses.

[22][a]He put the table in the tabernacle of meeting, on the north side of the tabernacle, outside the veil; [23][a]and he set the bread in order upon it before the LORD, as the LORD had commanded Moses. [24][a]He put the lampstand in the tabernacle of meeting, across from the table, on the south side of the tabernacle; [25]and [a]he lit the lamps before the LORD, as the LORD had commanded Moses. [26][a]He put the gold altar in the tabernacle of meeting in front of the veil; [27][a]and he burned sweet incense on it, as the LORD had commanded Moses. [28][a]He hung up the screen *at* the door of the tabernacle. [29][a]And he put the altar of burnt offering *before* the door of the tabernacle of the tent of meeting, and [b]offered upon it the burnt offering and the grain offering, as the LORD had commanded Moses. [30][a]He set the laver between the tabernacle of meeting and the altar, and put water there for washing; [31]and Moses, Aaron, and his sons would [a]wash their hands and their feet *with water* from it. [32]Whenever they went into the tabernacle of meeting, and when they came near the altar, they washed, [a]as the LORD had commanded Moses. [33][a]And he raised up the court all around the tabernacle and the altar, and hung up the screen of the court gate. So Moses [b]finished the work.

The Cloud and the Glory

[34][a]Then the [b]cloud covered the tabernacle of meeting, and the [c]glory of the LORD filled the tabernacle. [35]And Moses [a]was not able to enter the tabernacle of meeting, because the cloud rested above it, and the glory of the LORD filled the tabernacle. [36][a]Whenever the cloud was taken up from above the tabernacle, the children of Israel would [1]go onward in all their journeys. [37]But [a]if the cloud was not taken up, then they did not journey till the day that it was taken up. [38]For [a]the cloud of the LORD *was* above the tabernacle by day, and fire was over it by night, in the sight of all the house of Israel, throughout all their journeys.

13 a Ex. 29:5; 39:1, 41 b [Ex. 28:41]
15 a Num. 25:13
17 a Ex. 40:2 *1 erected*
20 a Ex. 25:16
21 a Ex. 26:33
22 a Ex. 26:35
23 a Ex. 40:4
24 a Ex. 26:35
25 a Ex. 25:37; 30:7, 8; 40:4
26 a Ex. 30:1, 6; 40:5
27 a Ex. 30:7
28 a Ex. 26:36; 40:5
29 a Ex. 40:6 b Ex. 29:38–42
30 a Ex. 30:18; 40:7
31 a Ex. 30:19, 20
32 a Ex. 30:19
33 a Ex. 27:9–18; 40:8 b [Heb. 3:2–5]
34 a Num. 9:15 b 1 Kin. 8:10, 11 c Lev. 9:6, 23
35 a 1 Kin. 8:11
36 a Num. 9:17 *1 journey*
37 a Num. 9:19–22
38 a Ex. 13:21

AUTHOR: *Traditionally Moses*
DATE: *Approximately 1445 B.C.*
THEME: *The Sanctity of God and Holiness in Everyday Life*
KEY WORDS: *Holiness, Offering, Sacrifice*

LEVITICUS

Dear Woman of Destiny,

The wedding is a symbol of pure and perfect union and, to Christians, is an illustration of the ultimate, most desirable relationship with God. Leviticus teaches us how to approach God, pointing to the sacrifice and high priesthood of Jesus Christ, so that we will be without spot or wrinkle for our Bridegroom's return.

His love and mine,

Marilyn Hickey

The Burnt Offering

Now the LORD [a]called to Moses, and
spoke to him [b]from the tabernacle
of meeting, saying, 2"Speak to the
children of Israel, and say to them:
[a]'When any one of you brings an offering
to the LORD, you shall bring your offering
of the livestock—of the herd and of the
flock.

3'If his offering *is* a burnt sacrifice of
the herd, let him offer a male [a]without
blemish; he shall offer it of his own free
will at the door of the tabernacle of meeting before the LORD. 4[a]Then he shall put
his hand on the head of the burnt offering, and it will be [b]accepted on his behalf
[c]to make atonement for him. 5He shall
kill the [a]bull before the LORD; [b]and the
priests, Aaron's sons, shall bring the blood
[c]and sprinkle the blood all around on the
altar that *is by* the door of the tabernacle
of meeting. 6And he shall [a]skin the burnt
offering and cut it into its pieces. 7The
sons of Aaron the priest shall put [a]fire on
the altar, and [b]lay the wood in order on
the fire. 8Then the priests, Aaron's sons,
shall lay the parts, the head, and the fat in
order on the wood that *is* on the fire upon
the altar; 9but he shall wash its entrails
and its legs with water. And the priest
shall burn all on the altar as a burnt sacrifice, an offering made by fire, a [a]sweet[1]
aroma to the LORD.

10'If his offering *is* of the flocks—of the
sheep or of the goats—as a burnt sacrifice, he shall bring a male [a]without blemish. 11[a]He shall kill it on the north side of
the altar before the LORD; and the priests,
Aaron's sons, shall sprinkle its blood all
around on the altar. 12And he shall cut it
into its pieces, with its head and its fat;
and the priest shall lay them in order on
the wood that *is* on the fire upon the altar;
13but he shall wash the entrails and the
legs with water. Then the priest shall
bring *it* all and burn *it* on the altar; it *is*
a burnt sacrifice, an [a]offering made by
fire, a sweet aroma to the LORD.

14'And if the burnt sacrifice of his offering to the LORD *is* of birds, then he shall
bring his offering of [a]turtledoves or
young pigeons. 15The priest shall bring it
to the altar, [1]wring off its head, and burn
it on the altar; its blood shall be drained
out at the side of the altar. 16And he shall
remove its crop with its feathers and cast
it [a]beside the altar on the east side, into
the place for ashes. 17Then he shall split it
at its wings, *but* [a]shall not divide *it* completely; and the priest shall burn it on the
altar, on the wood that *is* on the fire. [b]It
is a burnt sacrifice, an offering made by
fire, a [1]sweet aroma to the LORD.

The Grain Offering

2 'When anyone offers [a]a grain offering
to the LORD, his offering shall be *of*
fine flour. And he shall pour oil on it, and
put [b]frankincense on it. 2He shall bring it
to Aaron's sons, the priests, one of whom
shall take from it his handful of fine flour
and oil with all the frankincense. And the
priest shall burn [a]*it as* a memorial on the
altar, an offering made by fire, a sweet
aroma to the LORD. 3[a]The rest of the grain
offering *shall be* Aaron's and his [b]sons'.
[c]*It is* most holy of the offerings to the
LORD made by fire.

4'And if you bring as an offering a grain
offering baked in the oven, *it shall be* unleavened cakes of fine flour mixed with
oil, or unleavened wafers [a]anointed[1] with
oil. 5But if your offering *is* a grain offering
baked in a [1]pan, *it shall be of* fine flour,
unleavened, mixed with oil. 6You shall
break it in pieces and pour oil on it; it *is*
a grain offering.

7'If your offering *is* a grain offering
baked in a [a]covered pan, it shall be made
of fine flour with oil. 8You shall bring the
grain offering that is made of these things
to the LORD. And when it is presented to
the priest, he shall bring it to the altar.
9Then the priest shall take from the grain
offering [a]a memorial portion, and burn *it*
on the altar. *It is* an [b]offering made by
fire, a sweet aroma to the LORD. 10And
[a]what is left of the grain offering *shall be*
Aaron's and his sons'. *It is* most holy of
the offerings to the LORD made by fire.

11'No grain offering which you bring to
the LORD shall be made with [a]leaven, for
you shall burn no leaven nor any honey in
any offering to the LORD made by fire.
12[a]As for the offering of the firstfruits, you
shall offer them to the LORD, but they
shall not be burned on the altar for a
sweet aroma. 13And every offering of your
grain offering [a]you shall season with salt;
you shall not allow [b]the salt of the covenant of your God to be lacking from your
grain offering. [c]With all your offerings
you shall offer salt.

14'If you offer a grain offering of your
firstfruits to the LORD, [a]you shall offer for
the grain offering of your firstfruits green

CHAPTER 1
1 a Ex. 19:3; 25:22 b Ex. 40:34
2 a Lev. 22:18, 19
3 a Eph. 5:27
4 a Lev. 3:2, 8, 13; 4:15 b [Rom. 12:1] c 2 Chr. 29:23, 24
5 a Mic. 6:6 b 2 Chr. 35:11 c [Heb. 12:24]
6 a Lev. 7:8
7 a Mal. 1:10 b Gen. 22:9
9 a Gen. 8:21 *1 soothing* or *pleasing aroma*
10 a Lev. 1:3
11 a Lev. 1:5
13 a Num. 15:4–7; 28:12–14
14 a Lev. 5:7, 11; 12:8
15 *1* Lit. *nip* or *chop off*
16 a Lev. 6:10
17 a Gen. 15:10 b Lev. 1:9, 13 *1 soothing* or *pleasing aroma*

CHAPTER 2
1 a Num. 15:4 b Lev. 5:11
2 a Lev. 2:9; 5:12; 6:15; 24:7
3 a Lev. 7:9 b Lev. 6:6; 10:12, 13 c Num. 18:9
4 a Ex. 29:2 *1 spread*
5 *1 flat plate* or *griddle*
7 a Lev. 7:9
9 a Lev. 2:2, 16; 5:12; 6:15 b Ex. 29:18
10 a Lev. 2:3; 6:16
11 a Lev. 6:16, 17
12 a Lev. 23:10, 11, 17, 18
13 a [Col. 4:6] b Num. 18:19 c Ezek. 43:24
14 a Lev. 23:10, 14

heads of grain roasted on the fire, grain
beaten from [b]full heads. 15And [a]you shall
put oil on it, and lay frankincense on it. It
is a grain offering. 16Then the priest shall
burn [a]the memorial portion: *part* of its
beaten grain and *part* of its oil, with all
the frankincense, as an offering made by
fire to the LORD.

The Peace Offering

3 'When his offering *is* a [a]sacrifice of a
peace offering, if he offers *it* of the
herd, whether male or female, he shall offer it [b]without [1]blemish before the LORD.
2And [a]he shall lay his hand on the head of
his offering, and kill it *at* the door of the
tabernacle of meeting; and Aaron's sons,
the priests, shall [b]sprinkle the blood all
around on the altar. 3Then he shall offer
from the sacrifice of the peace offering an
offering made by fire to the LORD. [a]The fat
that covers the entrails and all the fat that
is on the entrails, 4the two kidneys and
the fat that *is* on them by the flanks, and
the fatty lobe *attached* to the liver above
the kidneys, he shall remove; 5and Aaron's
sons [a]shall burn it on the altar upon the
[b]burnt sacrifice, which *is* on the wood
that *is* on the fire, *as* an [c]offering made by
fire, a [d]sweet aroma to the LORD.

6'If his offering as a sacrifice of a peace
offering to the LORD *is* of the flock, *whether* male or female, [a]he shall offer it without blemish. 7If he offers a [a]lamb as his
offering, then he shall [b]offer it [c]before the
LORD. 8And he shall lay his hand on the
head of his offering, and kill it before the
tabernacle of meeting; and Aaron's sons
shall sprinkle its blood all around on the
altar.

9'Then he shall offer from the sacrifice
of the peace offering, as an offering made
by fire to the LORD, its fat *and* the whole
fat tail which he shall remove close to the
backbone. And the fat that covers the entrails and all the fat that *is* on the entrails,
10the two kidneys and the fat that *is* on
them by the flanks, and the fatty lobe *attached* to the liver above the kidneys, he
shall remove; 11and the priest shall burn
them on the altar *as* [a]food, an offering
made by fire to the LORD.

12'And if his [a]offering *is* a goat, then [b]he
shall offer it before the LORD. 13He shall
lay his hand on its head and kill it before
the tabernacle of meeting; and the sons of
Aaron shall sprinkle its blood all around
on the altar. 14Then he shall offer from it
his offering, as an offering made by fire to
the LORD. The fat that covers the entrails
and all the fat that *is* on the entrails, 15the
two kidneys and the fat that *is* on them by
the flanks, and the fatty lobe *attached* to
the liver above the kidneys, he shall remove; 16and the priest shall burn them on
the altar *as* food, an offering made by fire
for a sweet aroma; [a]all the fat *is* the
LORD's.

17'*This shall be* a [a]perpetual[1] statute
throughout your generations in all your
dwellings: you shall eat neither fat nor
[b]blood.' "

The Sin Offering

4 Now the LORD spoke to Moses, saying,
2"Speak to the children of Israel, saying: [a]'If a person sins [1]unintentionally
against any of the commandments of the
LORD *in anything* which ought not to be
done, and does any of them, 3[a]if the
anointed priest sins, bringing guilt on the
people, then let him offer to the LORD for
his sin which he has sinned [b]a young bull
without blemish as a [c]sin offering. 4He
shall bring the bull [a]to the door of the
tabernacle of meeting before the LORD, lay
his hand on the bull's head, and kill the
bull before the LORD. 5Then the anointed
priest [a]shall take some of the bull's blood
and bring it to the tabernacle of meeting.
6The priest shall dip his finger in the
blood and sprinkle some of the blood sev-
en times before the LORD, in front of the
[a]veil of the sanctuary. 7And the priest
shall [a]put some of the blood on the horns
of the altar of sweet incense before the
LORD, which is in the tabernacle of meeting; and he shall pour [b]the remaining
blood of the bull at the base of the altar of
the burnt offering, which is at the door of
the tabernacle of meeting. 8He shall take
from it all the fat of the bull as the sin
offering. The fat that covers the entrails
and all the fat which *is* on the entrails,
9the two kidneys and the fat that *is* on
them by the flanks, and the fatty lobe *attached* to the liver above the kidneys, he
shall remove, 10[a]as it was taken from the
bull of the sacrifice of the peace offering;
and the priest shall burn them on the altar of the burnt offering. 11[a]But the bull's
hide and all its flesh, with its head and
legs, its entrails and offal— 12the whole
bull he shall carry outside the camp to a
clean place, [a]where the ashes are poured
out, and [b]burn it on wood with fire; where

14 [b] 2 Kin. 4:42
15 [a] Lev. 2:1
16 [a] Lev. 2:2

CHAPTER 3
1 [a] Lev. 7:11, 29 [b] Lev. 1:3; 22:20–24 [1] *imperfection or defect*
2 [a] Lev. 1:4, 5; 16:21 [b] Lev. 1:5
3 [a] Lev. 1:8; 3:16; 4:8, 9
5 [a] Ex. 29:13 [b] 2 Chr. 35:14 [c] Num. 28:3–10 [d] Num. 15:8–10
6 [a] Lev. 3:1; 22:20–24
7 [a] Num. 15:4, 5 [b] 1 Kin. 8:62 [c] Lev. 17:8, 9
11 [a] Num. 28:2
12 [a] Num. 15:6–11 [b] Lev. 3:1, 7
16 [a] Lev. 7:23–25
17 [a] Lev. 6:18; 7:36; 17:7; 23:14 [b] Lev. 7:23, 26; 17:10, 14 [1] *everlasting or never-ending*

CHAPTER 4
2 [a] Lev. 5:15–18 [1] *through error*
3 [a] Lev. 8:12 [b] Lev. 3:1; 9:2 [c] Lev. 9:7
4 [a] Lev. 1:3, 4; 4:15
5 [a] Lev. 16:14
6 [a] Ex. 40:21, 26
7 [a] Lev. 4:18, 25, 30, 34; 8:15; 9:9; 16:18 [b] Ex. 40:5, 6; Lev. 5:9
10 [a] Lev. 3:3–5
11 [a] Ex. 29:14
12 [a] Lev. 4:21; 6:10, 11; 16:27 [b] [Heb. 13:11, 12]

the ashes are poured out it shall be burned.

13‘Now [a]if the whole congregation of Israel sins unintentionally, [b]and the thing is hidden from the eyes of the assembly, and they have done *something against* any of the commandments of the LORD *in anything* which should not be done, and are guilty; 14when the sin which they have committed becomes known, then the assembly shall offer a young bull for the sin, and bring it before the tabernacle of meeting. 15And the elders of the congregation [a]shall lay their hands on the head of the bull before the LORD. Then the bull shall be killed before the LORD. 16[a]The anointed priest shall bring some of the bull’s blood to the tabernacle of meeting. 17Then the priest shall dip his finger in the blood and sprinkle *it* seven times before the LORD, in front of the veil. 18And he shall put *some* of the blood on the horns of the altar which *is* before the LORD, which *is* in the tabernacle of meeting; and he shall pour the remaining blood at the base of the altar of burnt offering, which is at the door of the tabernacle of meeting. 19He shall take all the fat from it and burn *it* on the altar. 20And he shall do [a]with the bull as he did with the bull as a sin offering; thus he shall do with it. [b]So the priest shall make [1]atonement for them, and it shall be forgiven them. 21Then he shall carry the bull outside the camp, and burn it as he burned the first bull. It *is* a sin offering for the assembly.

22‘When a [1]ruler has sinned, and [a]done *something* unintentionally *against* any of the commandments of the LORD his God *in anything* which should not be done, and is guilty, 23or [a]if his sin which he has committed [1]comes to his knowledge, he shall bring as his offering a kid of the goats, a male without blemish. 24And [a]he shall lay his hand on the head of the goat, and kill it at the place where they kill the burnt offering before the LORD. It *is* a sin offering. 25[a]The priest shall take some of the blood of the sin offering with his finger, put *it* on the horns of the altar of burnt offering, and pour its blood at the base of the altar of burnt offering. 26And he shall burn all its fat on the altar, like [a]the fat of the sacrifice of the peace offering. [b]So the priest shall make [1]atonement for him concerning his sin, and it shall be forgiven him.

27[a]‘If [1]anyone of the [2]common people sins unintentionally by doing *something against* any of the commandments of the LORD *in anything* which ought not to be done, and is guilty, 28or [a]if his sin which he has committed comes to his knowledge, then he shall bring as his offering a kid of the goats, a female without blemish, for his sin which he has committed. 29[a]And he shall lay his hand on the head of the sin offering, and kill the sin offering at the place of the burnt offering. 30Then the priest shall take *some* of its blood with his finger, put *it* on the horns of the altar of burnt offering, and pour all *the remaining* blood at the base of the altar. 31[a]He shall remove all its fat, [b]as fat is removed from the sacrifice of the peace offering; and the priest shall burn it on the altar for a [c]sweet aroma to the LORD. [d]So the priest shall make atonement for him, and it shall be forgiven him.

32‘If he brings a lamb as his sin offering, [a]he shall bring a female without blemish. 33Then he shall [a]lay his hand on the head of the sin offering, and kill it as a sin offering at the place where they kill the burnt offering. 34The priest shall take *some* of the blood of the sin offering with his finger, put *it* on the horns of the altar of burnt offering, and pour all *the remaining* blood at the base of the altar. 35He shall remove all its fat, as the fat of the lamb is removed from the sacrifice of the peace offering. Then the priest shall burn it on the altar, [a]according to the offerings made by fire to the LORD. [b]So the priest shall make atonement for his sin that he has committed, and it shall be forgiven him.

The Trespass Offering

5 ‘If a person sins in [a]hearing the utterance of an oath, and *is* a witness, whether he has seen or known *of the matter*—if he does not tell *it*, he [b]bears [1]guilt.

2‘Or [a]if a person touches any unclean thing, whether *it is* the carcass of an unclean beast, or the carcass of unclean livestock, or the carcass of unclean creeping things, and he is unaware of it, he also shall be unclean and [b]guilty. 3Or if he touches [a]human uncleanness—whatever uncleanness with which a man may be defiled, and he is unaware of it—when he realizes *it*, then he shall be guilty.

4‘Or if a person [1]swears, speaking thoughtlessly with *his* lips [a]to do evil or

13 a Num. 15:24–26 b Lev. 5:2–4, 17
15 a Lev. 1:3, 4
16 a Lev. 4:5
20 a Lev. 4:3 b Num. 15:25 *1* Lit. *covering*
22 a Lev. 4:2, 13, 27 *1 leader*
23 a Lev. 4:14; 5:4 *1 is made known to him*
24 a [Is. 53:6]
25 a Lev. 4:7, 18, 30, 34
26 a Lev. 3:3–5 b Lev. 4:20 *1* Lit. *covering*
27 a Num. 15:27 *1* Lit. *any soul* *2* Lit. *people of the land*
28 a Lev. 4:23
29 a Lev. 1:4; 4:4, 24
31 a Lev. 3:14 b Lev. 3:3, 4 c Ex. 29:18 d Lev. 4:26
32 a Lev. 4:28
33 a Num. 8:12
35 a Lev. 3:5 b Lev. 4:26, 31

CHAPTER 5
1 a Prov. 29:24 b Num. 9:13 *1 his iniquity*
2 a Num. 19:11–16 b Lev. 5:17
3 a Lev. 5:12, 13, 15
4 a Acts 23:12 *1 vows*

[b]to do good, whatever *it is* that a man may
pronounce by an oath, and he is unaware
of it—when he realizes *it,* then he shall be
guilty in any of these *matters.*
5'And it shall be, when he is guilty in
any of these *matters,* that he shall [a]con-
fess that he has sinned in that *thing;* 6and
he shall bring his trespass offering to the
LORD for his sin which he has committed,
a female from the flock, a lamb or a kid of
the goats as a sin offering. So the priest
shall make atonement for him concerning
his sin.
7[a]'If he is not able to bring a lamb, then
he shall bring to the LORD, for his trespass
which he has committed, two [b]turtle-
doves or two young pigeons: one as a sin
offering and the other as a burnt offering.
8And he shall bring them to the priest,
who shall offer *that* which *is* for the sin
offering first, and [a]wring off its head from
its neck, but shall not divide *it* [1]complete-
ly. 9Then he shall sprinkle *some* of the
blood of the sin offering on the side of the
altar, and the [a]rest of the blood shall be
drained out at the base of the altar. It *is* a
sin offering. 10And he shall offer the second *as* a burnt offering according to the
[a]prescribed manner. So [b]the priest shall
make atonement on his behalf for his sin
which he has committed, and it shall be
forgiven him.
11'But if he is [a]not able to bring two
turtledoves or two young pigeons, then he
who sinned shall bring for his offering
one-tenth of an ephah of fine flour as a
sin offering. [b]He shall put no oil on it, nor
shall he put frankincense on it, for it *is* a
sin offering. 12Then he shall bring it to the
priest, and the priest shall take his handful of it [a]as a memorial portion, and burn
it on the altar [b]according to the offerings
made by fire to the LORD. It *is* a sin offering. 13[a]The priest shall make atonement
for him, [1]for his sin that he has committed in any of these matters; and it shall
be forgiven him. [b]*The rest* shall be the
priest's as a grain offering.' "

Offerings with Restitution

14Then the LORD spoke to Moses, saying: 15[a]"If a person commits a trespass,
and sins unintentionally in regard to the
holy things of the LORD, then [b]he shall
bring to the LORD as his trespass offering
a ram without blemish from the flocks,
with your valuation in shekels of silver
according to [c]the shekel of the sanctuary,
as a trespass offering. 16And he shall make
restitution for the harm that he has done
in regard to the holy thing, [a]and shall add
one-fifth to it and give it to the priest. [b]So
the priest shall make atonement for him
with the ram of the trespass offering, and
it shall be forgiven him.
17"If a person sins, and commits any of
these things which are forbidden to be
done by the commandments of the LORD,
[a]though he does not know *it,* yet he is
[b]guilty and shall bear his [1]iniquity.
18[a]And he shall bring to the priest a ram
without blemish from the flock, with your
valuation, as a trespass offering. So the
priest shall make atonement for him regarding his ignorance in which he erred
and did not know *it,* and it shall be forgiv-
en him. 19It is a trespass offering; [a]he has
certainly trespassed against the LORD."

Ignorance will rob us of what we could otherwise possess and use.
HOWARD CARTER

6

And the LORD spoke to Moses, saying:
2"If a person sins and [a]commits a
trespass against the LORD by [b]lying[1] to his
neighbor about [c]what was delivered to
him for safekeeping, or about [2]a pledge,
or about a robbery, or if he has [d]extorted
from his neighbor, 3or if he [a]has found
what was lost and lies concerning it, and
[b]swears falsely—in any one of these
things that a man may do in which he
sins: 4then it shall be, because he has
sinned and is guilty, that he shall [1]restore
[a]what he has stolen, or the thing which
he has extorted, or what was delivered
to him for safekeeping, or the lost thing
which he found, 5or all that about which
he has sworn falsely. He shall [a]restore its
full value, add one-fifth more to it, *and*
give it to whomever it belongs, on the day
of his trespass offering. 6And he shall
bring his trespass offering to the LORD, [a]a
ram without blemish from the flock, with
your [1]valuation, as a trespass offering, to
the priest. 7[a]So the priest shall make
atonement for him before the LORD, and

---

4 b [James 5:12]
5 a Prov. 28:13
7 a Lev. 12:6, 8; 14:21 b Lev. 1:14
8 a Lev. 1:15–17 *1 Lit. apart*
9 a Lev. 4:7, 18, 30, 34
10 a Lev. 1:14–17 b Lev. 4:20, 26; 5:13, 16
11 a Lev. 14:21–32 b Num. 5:15
12 a Lev. 2:2 b Lev. 4:35
13 a Lev. 4:26 b Lev. 2:3; 6:17, 26 *1 concerning his sin*
15 a Lev. 4:2; 22:14 b Ezra 10:19 c Ex. 30:13
16 a Num. 5:7 b Lev. 4:26
17 a Lev. 4:2, 13, 22, 27 b Lev. 5:1, 2 *1 punishment*
18 a Lev. 5:15
19 a Ezra 10:2

CHAPTER 6
2 a Num. 5:6 b Lev. 19:11 c Ex. 22:7, 10 d Prov. 24:28 *1 deceiving his associate 2 an entrusted security*
3 a Deut. 22:1–4 b Ex. 22:11
4 a Lev. 24:18, 21 *1 return*
5 a Lev. 5:16
6 a Lev. 1:3; 5:15 *1 appraisal*
7 a Lev. 4:26

he shall be forgiven for any one of these
things that he may have done in which he
trespasses."

The Law of the Burnt Offering

8 Then the LORD spoke to Moses, saying,
9 "Command Aaron and his sons, saying,
'This *is* the [a]law of the burnt offering: The
burnt offering *shall be* on the hearth
upon the altar all night until morning,
and the fire of the altar shall be kept burning on it. 10 [a]And the priest shall put on
his linen garment, and his linen trousers
he shall put on his body, and take up the
ashes of the burnt offering which the fire
has consumed on the altar, and he shall
put them [b]beside the altar. 11 Then [a]he
shall take off his garments, put on other
garments, and carry the ashes outside the
camp [b]to a clean place. 12 And the fire on
the altar shall be kept burning on it; it
shall not be put out. And the priest shall
burn wood on it every morning, and lay
the burnt offering in order on it; and he
shall burn on it [a]the fat of the peace offerings. 13 A fire shall always be burning on
the [a]altar; it shall never go out.

The Law of the Grain Offering

14 'This *is* the law of the grain offering:
The sons of Aaron shall offer it on the
altar before the LORD. 15 He shall take from
it his handful of the fine flour of the grain
offering, with its oil, and all the frankincense which *is* on the grain offering, and
shall burn *it* on the altar *for* a sweet aroma, as a memorial to the LORD. 16 And the
remainder of it Aaron and his sons shall
eat; with unleavened bread it shall be eat-
en in a holy place; in the court of the tabernacle of meeting they shall eat it. 17 It
shall not be baked with leaven. I have giv-
en it *as* their [1]portion of My offerings
made by fire; it *is* most holy, like the sin
offering and the [a]trespass offering. 18 [a]All
the males among the children of Aaron
may eat it. [b]*It shall be* a statute forever in
your generations concerning the offerings made by fire to the LORD. [c]Everyone
who touches them must be holy.' "

19 And the LORD spoke to Moses, saying,
20 [a]"This *is* the offering of Aaron and his
sons, which they shall offer to the LORD,
beginning on the day when he is anointed:
one-tenth of an [b]ephah of fine flour as a
daily grain offering, half of it in the morning and half of it at night. 21 It shall be
made in a [a]pan with oil. *When it is* mixed,
you shall bring it in. The baked pieces of
the grain offering you shall offer *for* a
[1]sweet aroma to the LORD. 22 The priest
from among his sons, [a]who is anointed in
his place, shall offer it. *It is* a statute forever to the LORD. [b]It shall be [1]wholly
burned. 23 For every grain offering for the
priest shall be wholly burned. It shall not
be eaten."

The Law of the Sin Offering

24 Also the LORD spoke to Moses, saying,
25 "Speak to Aaron and to his sons, saying,
'This *is* the law of the sin offering: [a]In the
place where the burnt offering is killed,
the sin offering shall be killed before the
LORD. It *is* most holy. 26 [a]The priest who
offers it for sin shall eat it. In a holy place
it shall be eaten, in the court of the tabernacle of meeting. 27 [a]Everyone who touches its flesh [1]must be holy. And when its
blood is sprinkled on any garment, you
shall wash that on which it was sprinkled,
in a holy place. 28 But the earthen vessel in
which it is boiled [a]shall be broken. And if
it is boiled in a bronze pot, it shall be both
scoured and rinsed in water. 29 All the
males among the priests may eat it. It *is*
most holy. 30 [a]But no sin offering from
which *any* of the blood is brought into the
tabernacle of meeting, to make atonement in [1]the holy [b]*place,* shall be [c]eaten.
It shall be [d]burned in the fire.

The Law of the Trespass Offering

7 'Likewise [a]this *is* the law of the trespass offering (it *is* most holy): 2 In the
place where they kill the burnt offering
they shall kill the trespass offering. And
its blood he shall sprinkle all around on
the altar. 3 And he shall offer from it all its
fat. The fat tail and the fat that covers the
entrails, 4 the two kidneys and the fat that
is on them by the flanks, and the fatty lobe
attached to the liver above the kidneys, he
shall remove; 5 and the priest shall burn
them on the altar *as* an offering made by
fire to the LORD. It *is* a trespass offering.
6 [a]Every male among the priests may eat
it. It shall be eaten in a holy place. [b]It *is*
most holy. 7 [a]The trespass offering *is* like
the sin offering; *there is* one law for them
both: the priest who makes atonement
with it shall have *it.* 8 And the priest who

9 a Ex. 29:38–42
10 a Ex. 28:39–43 b Lev. 1:16
11 a Ezek. 44:19 b Lev. 4:12
12 a Lev. 3:3, 5, 9, 14
13 a Lev. 1:7
17 a Lev. 7:7 *1 share*
18 a Lev. 6:29; 7:6 b Lev. 3:17 c Ex. 29:37; Num. 4:15; Hag. 2:11–13
20 a Ex. 29:2 b Ex. 16:36
21 a Lev. 2:5; 7:9 *1 pleasing*
22 a Lev. 4:3 b Ex. 29:25 *1 completely*
25 a Lev. 1:1, 3, 5, 11
26 a [Ezek. 44:28, 29]
27 a Ex. 29:37; Num. 4:15; Hag. 2:11–13 *1* Lit. *shall*
28 a Lev. 11:33; 15:12
30 a Lev. 4:7, 11, 12, 18, 21; 10:18; 16:27 b Ex. 26:33 c Lev. 6:16, 23, 26 d Lev. 16:27 *1* The Most Holy Place when capitalized

CHAPTER 7
1 a Lev. 5:14—6:7
6 a Lev. 6:16–18, 29 b Lev. 2:3
7 a Lev. 6:24–30; 14:13

offers anyone's burnt offering, that priest shall have for himself the skin of the burnt offering which he has offered. [9]Also [a]every grain offering that is baked in the oven and all that is prepared in the covered pan, or [1]in a pan, shall be the priest's who offers it. [10]Every grain offering, *whether* mixed with oil or dry, shall belong to all the sons of Aaron, to one *as much* as the other.

The Law of Peace Offerings

[11][a]'This *is* the law of the sacrifice of peace offerings which he shall offer to the LORD: [12]If he offers it for a thanksgiving, then he shall offer, with the sacrifice of thanksgiving, unleavened cakes mixed with oil, unleavened wafers [a]anointed with oil, or cakes of blended flour mixed with oil. [13]Besides the cakes, *as* his offering he shall offer [a]leavened bread with the sacrifice of thanksgiving of his peace offering. [14]And from it he shall offer one cake from each offering *as* a heave offering to the LORD. [a]It shall belong to the priest who sprinkles the blood of the peace offering.

[15][a]'The flesh of the sacrifice of his peace offering for thanksgiving shall be eaten the same day it is offered. He shall not leave any of it until morning. [16]But [a]if the sacrifice of his offering *is* a vow or a voluntary offering, it shall be eaten the same day that he offers his sacrifice; but on the next day the remainder of it also may be eaten; [17]the remainder of the flesh of the sacrifice on the third day must be burned with fire. [18]And if *any* of the flesh of the sacrifice of his peace offering is eaten at all on the third day, it shall not be accepted, nor shall it be [a]imputed to him; it shall be an [b]abomination *to* him who offers it, and the person who eats of it shall bear [1]guilt.

[19]'The flesh that touches any unclean thing shall not be eaten. It shall be burned with fire. And as for the *clean* flesh, all who are [1]clean may eat of it. [20]But the person who eats the flesh of the sacrifice of the peace offering that *belongs* to the [a]LORD, [b]while he is unclean, that person [c]shall be cut off from his people. [21]Moreover the person who touches any unclean thing, *such as* [a]human uncleanness, *an* [b]unclean animal, or any [c]abominable[1] unclean thing, and who eats the flesh of the sacrifice of the peace offering that *belongs* to the LORD, that person [d]shall be cut off from his people.' "

Fat and Blood May Not Be Eaten

[22]And the LORD spoke to Moses, saying, [23]"Speak to the children of Israel, saying: [a]'You shall not eat any fat, of ox or sheep or goat. [24]And the fat of an animal that dies *naturally,* and the fat of what is torn by wild beasts, may be used in any other way; but you shall by no means eat it. [25]For whoever eats the fat of the animal of which men offer an offering made by fire to the LORD, the person who eats *it* shall be cut off from his people. [26][a]Moreover you shall not eat any blood in any of your dwellings, *whether* of bird or beast. [27]Whoever eats any blood, that person shall be cut off from his people.' "

The Portion of Aaron and His Sons

[28]Then the LORD spoke to Moses, saying, [29]"Speak to the children of Israel, saying: [a]'He who offers the sacrifice of his peace offering to the LORD shall bring his offering to the LORD from the sacrifice of his peace offering. [30][a]His own hands shall bring the offerings made by fire to the LORD. The fat with the breast he shall bring, that the [b]breast may be waved *as* a wave offering before the LORD. [31][a]And the priest shall burn the fat on the altar, but the [b]breast shall be Aaron's and his sons'. [32][a]Also the right thigh you shall give to the priest *as* a heave offering from the sacrifices of your peace offerings. [33]He among the sons of Aaron, who offers the blood of the peace offering and the fat, shall have the right thigh for *his* part. [34]For [a]the breast of the wave offering and the thigh of the heave offering I have taken from the children of Israel, from the sacrifices of their peace offerings, and I have given them to Aaron the priest and to his sons from the children of Israel by a statute forever.' "

[35]This *is* the consecrated portion for Aaron and his sons, from the offerings made by fire to the LORD, on the day when *Moses* presented them to [1]minister to the LORD as priests. [36]The LORD commanded this to be given to them by the children of Israel, [a]on the day that He anointed them, *by* a statute forever throughout their generations.

9 a Lev. 2:3, 10 *1 on a griddle*
11 a Lev. 3:1; 22:18, 21
12 a Num. 6:15
13 a Amos 4:5
14 a Num. 18:8, 11, 19
15 a Lev. 22:29, 30
16 a Lev. 19:5–8
18 a Num. 18:27 b Lev. 11:10, 11, 41; 19:7 *1 his iniquity*
19 *1 pure*
20 a [Heb. 2:17] b Num. 19:13 c Gen. 17:14
21 a Lev. 5:2, 3, 5 b Lev. 11:24, 28 c Ezek. 4:14 d Lev. 7:20 *1* So with MT, LXX, Vg.; Sam., Syr., Tg. *swarming thing* (cf. 5:2)
23 a Lev. 3:17; 17:10–15
26 a Acts 15:20, 29
29 a Lev. 3:1; 22:21
30 a Lev. 3:3, 4, 9, 14 b Ex. 29:24, 27
31 a Lev. 3:5, 11, 16 b Deut. 18:3
32 a Num. 6:20
34 a Lev. 10:14, 15
35 *1 serve*
36 a Lev. 8:12, 30

37This *is* the law [a]of the burnt offering, [b]the grain offering, [c]the sin offering, [d]the trespass offering, [e]the consecrations, and [f]the sacrifice of the peace offering, 38which the LORD commanded Moses on Mount Sinai, on the day when He commanded the children of Israel [a]to offer their offerings to the LORD in the Wilderness of Sinai.

Aaron and His Sons Consecrated

8 And the LORD spoke to Moses, saying: 2[a]"Take Aaron and his sons with him, and [b]the garments, [c]the anointing oil, a [d]bull as the sin offering, two [e]rams, and a basket of unleavened bread; 3and gather all the congregation together at the door of the tabernacle of meeting."

4So Moses did as the LORD commanded him. And the congregation was gathered together at the door of the tabernacle of meeting. 5And Moses said to the congregation, "This *is* what the LORD commanded to be done."

6Then Moses brought Aaron and his sons and [a]washed them with water. 7And he [a]put the tunic on him, girded him with the sash, clothed him with the robe, and put the ephod on him; and he girded him with the intricately woven band of the ephod, and with it tied *the ephod* on him. 8Then he put the breastplate on him, and he [a]put the [1]Urim and the Thummim in the breastplate. 9[a]And he put the turban on his head. Also on the turban, on its front, he put the golden plate, the holy crown, as the LORD had commanded Moses.

10[a]Also Moses took the anointing oil, and anointed the tabernacle and all that *was* in it, and consecrated them. 11He sprinkled some of it on the altar seven times, anointed the altar and all its utensils, and the laver and its base, to [1]consecrate them. 12And he [a]poured some of the anointing oil on Aaron's head and anointed him, to consecrate him.

13[a]Then Moses brought Aaron's sons and put tunics on them, girded them with sashes, and put [1]hats on them, as the LORD had commanded Moses.

14[a]And he brought the bull for the sin offering. Then Aaron and his sons [b]laid their hands on the head of the bull for the sin offering, 15and Moses killed *it*. [a]Then he took the blood, and put *some* on the horns of the altar all around with his finger, and purified the altar. And he poured the blood at the base of the altar, and consecrated it, to make [1]atonement for it. 16[a]Then he took all the fat that *was* on the entrails, the fatty lobe *attached to* the liver, and the two kidneys with their fat, and Moses burned *them* on the altar. 17But the bull, its hide, its flesh, and its offal, he burned with fire outside the camp, as the LORD [a]had commanded Moses.

18[a]Then he brought the ram as the burnt offering. And Aaron and his sons laid their hands on the head of the ram, 19and Moses killed *it*. Then he sprinkled the blood all around on the altar. 20And he cut the ram into pieces; and Moses [a]burned the head, the pieces, and the fat. 21Then he washed the entrails and the legs in water. And Moses burned the whole ram on the altar. It *was* a burnt sacrifice for a [1]sweet aroma, an offering made by fire to the LORD, [a]as the LORD had commanded Moses.

22And [a]he brought the second ram, the ram of consecration. Then Aaron and his sons laid their hands on the head of the ram, 23and Moses killed *it*. Also he took *some* of [a]its blood and put it on the tip of Aaron's right ear, on the thumb of his right hand, and on the big toe of his right foot. 24Then he brought Aaron's sons. And Moses put *some* of the [a]blood on the tips of their right ears, on the thumbs of their right hands, and on the big toes of their right feet. And Moses sprinkled the blood all around on the altar. 25[a]Then he took the fat and the fat tail, all the fat that *was* on the entrails, the fatty lobe *attached to* the liver, the two kidneys and their fat, and the right thigh; 26[a]and from the basket of unleavened bread that was before the LORD he took one unleavened cake, a cake of bread *anointed with* oil, and one wafer, and put *them* on the fat and on the right thigh; 27and he put all *these* [a]in Aaron's hands and in his sons' hands, and waved them *as* a wave offering before the LORD. 28[a]Then Moses took them from their hands and burned *them* on the altar, on the burnt offering. They *were* consecration offerings for a sweet aroma. That *was* an offering made by fire to the LORD. 29And [a]Moses took the [b]breast and waved it *as* a wave offering before the LORD. It was Moses' [c]part of the ram of consecration, as the LORD had commanded Moses.

37 a Lev. 6:9 b Lev. 6:14 c Lev. 6:25 d Lev. 7:1 e Ex. 29:1 f Lev. 7:11
38 a Lev. 1:1, 2

CHAPTER 8
2 a Ex. 29:1–3 b Ex. 28:2, 4 c Ex. 30:24, 25 d Ex. 29:10 e Ex. 29:15, 19
6 a Heb. 10:22
7 a Ex. 39:1–31
8 a Ex. 28:30 *1* Lit. *Lights and the Perfections,* Ex. 28:30
9 a Ex. 28:36, 37; 29:6
10 a Ex. 30:26–29; 40:10, 11
11 *1 set them apart* for the LORD
12 a Ps. 133:2
13 a Ex. 29:8, 9 *1 headpieces*
14 a Ezek. 43:19 b Lev. 4:4
15 a Lev. 4:7 *1* Lit. *covering*
16 a Ex. 29:13
17 a Lev. 4:11, 12
18 a Ex. 29:15
20 a Lev. 1:8
21 a Ex. 29:18 *1 pleasing*
22 a Ex. 29:19, 31
23 a Lev. 14:14
24 a [Heb. 9:13, 14, 18–23]
25 a Ex. 29:22
26 a Ex. 29:23
27 a Ex. 29:24
28 a Ex. 29:25
29 a Ps. 99:6 b Ex. 29:27 c Ex. 29:26

30Then [a]Moses took some of the anointing oil and some of the blood which *was*
on the altar, and sprinkled *it* on Aaron,
on his garments, on his sons, and on the
garments of his sons with him; and he
consecrated Aaron, his garments, his
sons, and the garments of his sons with
him.
31And Moses said to Aaron and his sons,
[a]"Boil the flesh *at* the door of the tabernacle of meeting, and eat it there with the
bread that *is* in the basket of consecration
offerings, as I commanded, saying, 'Aaron
and his sons shall eat it.' 32[a]What remains
of the flesh and of the bread you shall
burn with fire. 33And you shall not go outside the door of the tabernacle of meeting
for seven days, until the days of your consecration are ended. For [a]seven days he
shall consecrate you. 34[a]As he has done
this day, *so* the LORD has commanded to
do, to make atonement for you. 35There-
fore you shall stay *at* the door of the tabernacle of meeting day and night for seven
days, and [a]keep the [1]charge of the LORD,
so that you may not die; for so I have been
commanded." 36So Aaron and his sons did
all the things that the LORD had commanded by the hand of Moses.

The Priestly Ministry Begins

9 It came to pass on the [a]eighth day
that Moses called Aaron and his sons
and the elders of Israel. 2And he said to
Aaron, "Take for yourself a young [a]bull as
a sin offering and a ram as a burnt offering, without blemish, and offer *them* before the LORD. 3And to the children of
Israel you shall speak, saying, [a]'Take a kid
of the goats as a sin offering, and a calf
and a lamb, *both* of the first year, without
blemish, as a burnt offering, 4also a bull
and a ram as peace offerings, to sacrifice
before the LORD, and [a]a grain offering
mixed with oil; for [b]today the LORD will
appear to you.' "
5So they brought what Moses commanded before the tabernacle of meeting.
And all the congregation drew near and
stood [1]before the LORD. 6Then Moses said,
"This *is* the thing which the LORD commanded you to do, and the glory of the
LORD will appear to you." 7And Moses said
to Aaron, "Go to the altar, [a]offer your sin
offering and your burnt offering, and
make atonement for yourself and for the
people. [b]Offer the offering of the people,
and make atonement for them, as the
LORD commanded."
8Aaron therefore went to the altar and
killed the calf of the sin offering, which
was for himself. 9Then the sons of Aaron
brought the blood to him. And he dipped
his finger in the blood, put *it* on the horns
of the altar, and poured the blood at the
base of the altar. 10[a]But the fat, the kidneys, and the fatty lobe from the liver of
the sin offering he burned on the altar, as
the LORD had commanded Moses. 11[a]The
flesh and the hide he burned with fire outside the camp.
12And he killed the burnt offering; and
Aaron's sons presented to him the blood,
[a]which he sprinkled all around on the altar. 13[a]Then they presented the burnt offering to him, with its pieces and head,
and he burned *them* on the altar. 14[a]And
he washed the entrails and the legs, and
burned *them* with the burnt offering on
the altar.
15[a]Then he brought the people's offering, and took the goat, which *was* the sin
offering for the people, and killed it and
offered it for sin, like the first one. 16And
he brought the burnt offering and offered
it [a]according to the [1]prescribed manner.
17Then he brought the grain offering,
took a handful of it, and burned *it* on the
altar, [a]besides the burnt sacrifice of the
morning.
18He also killed the bull and the ram *as*
[a]sacrifices of peace offerings, which *were*
for the people. And Aaron's sons presented
to him the blood, which he sprinkled all
around on the altar, 19and the fat from the
bull and the ram—the fatty tail, what covers *the entrails* and the kidneys, and the
fatty lobe *attached to* the liver; 20and they
put the fat on the breasts. [a]Then he
burned the fat on the altar; 21but the
breasts and the right thigh Aaron waved
[a]*as* a wave offering before the LORD, as
Moses had commanded.
22Then Aaron lifted his hand toward the
people, [a]blessed them, and came down
from offering the sin offering, the burnt
offering, and peace offerings. 23And Moses
and Aaron went into the tabernacle of
meeting, and came out and blessed the
people. Then the glory of the LORD appeared to all the people, 24and [a]fire came
out from before the LORD and consumed
the burnt offering and the fat on the altar.
When all the people saw *it,* they [b]shouted
and fell on their [c]faces.

30 a Ex. 29:21; 30:30
31 a Ex. 29:31, 32
32 a Ex. 29:34
33 a Ex. 29:30, 35
34 a [Heb. 7:16]
35 a Deut. 11:1 *1 office*

CHAPTER 9
1 a Ezek. 43:27
2 a Lev. 4:1–12
3 a Lev. 4:23, 28
4 a Lev. 2:4 b Ex. 29:43
5 *1 in the presence of*
7 a [Heb. 5:3–5; 7:27] b Lev. 4:16, 20
10 a Lev. 8:16
11 a Lev. 4:11, 12; 8:17
12 a Lev. 1:5; 8:19
13 a Lev. 8:20
14 a Lev. 8:21
15 a [Is. 53:10]
16 a Lev. 1:1–13 *1 ordinance*
17 a Ex. 29:38, 39
18 a Lev. 3:1–11
20 a Lev. 3:5, 16
21 a Lev. 7:30–34
22 a Luke 24:50
24 a Judg. 6:21 b Ezra 3:11 c 1 Kin. 18:38, 39

The Profane Fire of Nadab and Abihu

10 Then [a]Nadab and Abihu, the sons
of Aaron, [b]each took his censer and
put fire in it, put incense on it, and offered
[c]profane fire before the LORD, which He
had not commanded them. 2So [a]fire went
out from the LORD and devoured them,
and they died before the LORD. 3And Moses said to Aaron, "This is what the LORD
spoke, saying:

'By those [a]who come near Me
I must be regarded as holy;
And before all the people
I must be glorified.' "

So Aaron held his peace.

Father, by Your mercy we draw near to You. Teach ____ to regard You as holy and to glorify You before all people.

FROM LEVITICUS 10:3

4Then Moses called Mishael and Elzaphan, the sons of Uzziel the uncle of
Aaron, and said to them, "Come near,
[a]carry your brethren from [1]before the
sanctuary out of the camp." 5So they went
near and carried them by their tunics out
of the camp, as Moses had said.
6And Moses said to Aaron, and to Eleazar and Ithamar, his sons, "Do not [1]un-
cover your heads nor tear your clothes,
lest you die, and [a]wrath come upon all the
people. But let your brethren, the whole
house of Israel, [2]bewail the burning
which the LORD has kindled. 7[a]You shall
not go out from the door of the tabernacle
of meeting, lest you die, [b]for the anointing oil of the LORD *is* upon you." And they
did according to the word of Moses.

Conduct Prescribed for Priests

8Then the LORD spoke to Aaron, saying:
9[a]"Do not drink wine or intoxicating
drink, you, nor your sons with you, when
you go into the tabernacle of meeting,
lest you die. *It shall be* a statute forever
throughout your generations, 10that you
may [a]distinguish between holy and unholy, and between unclean and clean,
11[a]and that you may teach the children of
Israel all the statutes which the LORD has
spoken to them by the hand of Moses."
12And Moses spoke to Aaron, and to Eleazar and Ithamar, his sons who were left:
[a]"Take the grain offering that remains of
the offerings made by fire to the LORD,
and eat it without leaven beside the altar;
[b]for it *is* most holy. 13You shall eat it in a
[a]holy place, because it *is* your [1]due and
your sons' due, of the sacrifices made by
fire to the LORD; for [b]so I have been commanded. 14[a]The breast of the wave offering and the thigh of the heave offering
you shall eat in a clean place, you, your
sons, and your [b]daughters with you; for
they are your due and your sons' [c]due,
which are given from the sacrifices of
peace offerings of the children of Israel.
15[a]The thigh of the heave offering and the
breast of the wave offering they shall
bring with the offerings of fat made by
fire, to offer *as* a wave offering before the
LORD. And it shall be yours and your sons'
with you, by a statute forever, as the LORD
has commanded."
16Then Moses made careful inquiry
about [a]the goat of the sin offering, and
there it was—burned up. And he was angry with Eleazar and Ithamar, the sons of
Aaron *who were* left, saying, 17[a]"Why have
you not eaten the sin offering in a holy
place, since it *is* most holy, and *God* has
given it to you to bear [b]the guilt of the
congregation, to make atonement for
them before the LORD? 18See! [a]Its blood
was not brought inside [1]the holy *place;*
indeed you should have eaten it in a holy
place, [b]as I commanded."
19And Aaron said to Moses, "Look, [a]this
day they have offered their sin offering
and their burnt offering before the LORD,
and such things have befallen me! *If* I had
eaten the sin offering today, [b]would it
have been accepted in the sight of the
LORD?" 20So when Moses heard *that,* he
was content.

Foods Permitted and Forbidden

11 Now the LORD spoke to Moses and
Aaron, saying to them, 2"Speak to
the children of Israel, saying, [a]'These *are*
the animals which you may eat among all
the animals that *are* on the earth: 3Among
the animals, whatever divides the hoof,

CHAPTER 10
1 [a]Num. 3:2–4 [b]Lev. 16:12 [c]Ex. 30:9
2 [a]Num. 11:1; 16:35
3 [a]Ex. 19:22
4 [a]Acts 5:6, 10 [1]in front of
6 [a]2 Sam. 24:1 [1]An act of mourning [2]weep bitterly
7 [a]Lev. 8:33; 21:12 [b]Lev. 8:30
9 [a]Ezek. 44:21
10 [a]Ezek. 22:26; 44:23
11 [a]Deut. 24:8
12 [a]Num. 18:9 [b]Lev. 21:22
13 [a]Num. 18:10 [b]Lev. 2:3; 6:16 [1]portion
14 [a]Num. 18:11 [b]Lev. 22:13 [c]Num. 18:10
15 [a]Lev. 7:29, 30, 34
16 [a]Lev. 9:3, 15
17 [a]Lev. 6:24–30 [b]Ex. 28:38
18 [a]Lev. 6:30 [b]Lev. 6:26, 30 [1]The Most Holy Place when capitalized
19 [a]Lev. 9:8, 12 [b][Is. 1:11–15]

CHAPTER 11
2 [a]Deut. 14:4

having cloven hooves *and* chewing the cud—that you may eat. 4 Nevertheless these you shall [a]not eat among those that chew the cud or those that have cloven hooves: the camel, because it chews the cud but does not have cloven hooves, is [1]unclean to you; 5 the [1]rock hyrax, because it chews the cud but does not have cloven hooves, *is* [2]unclean to you; 6 the hare, because it chews the cud but does not have cloven hooves, *is* unclean to you; 7 and the swine, though it divides the hoof, having cloven hooves, yet does not chew the cud, [a]*is* unclean to you. 8 Their flesh you shall not eat, and their carcasses you shall not touch. [a]They *are* unclean to you.

9 [a]'These you may eat of all that *are* in the water: whatever in the water has fins and scales, whether in the seas or in the rivers—that you may eat. 10 But all in the seas or in the rivers that do not have fins and scales, all that move in the water or any living thing which *is* in the water, they *are* [1]an [a]abomination to you. 11 They shall be an abomination to you; you shall not eat their flesh, but you shall regard their carcasses as an abomination. 12 Whatever in the water does not have fins or scales—that *shall be* an abomination to you.

13 [a]'And these you shall regard as an abomination among the birds; they shall not be eaten, they *are* an abomination: the eagle, the vulture, the buzzard, 14 the kite, and the falcon after its kind; 15 every raven after its kind, 16 the ostrich, the short-eared owl, the sea gull, and the hawk after its kind; 17 the little owl, the fisher owl, and the screech owl; 18 the white owl, the jackdaw, and the carrion vulture; 19 the stork, the heron after its kind, the hoopoe, and the bat.

20 'All flying insects that creep on *all* fours *shall be* an abomination to you. 21 Yet these you may eat of every flying insect that creeps on *all* fours: those which have jointed legs above their feet with which to leap on the earth. 22 These you may eat: [a]the locust after its kind, the destroying locust after its kind, the cricket after its kind, and the grasshopper after its kind. 23 But all *other* flying insects which have four feet *shall be* an abomination to you.

Unclean Animals

24 'By these you shall become [1]unclean; whoever touches the carcass of any of them shall be unclean until evening; 25 whoever carries part of the carcass of any of them [a]shall wash his clothes and be unclean until evening: 26 *The carcass* of any animal which divides the foot, but is not cloven-hoofed or does not chew the cud, *is* unclean to you. Everyone who touches it shall be unclean. 27 And whatever goes on its paws, among all kinds of animals that go on *all* fours, those *are* unclean to you. Whoever touches any such carcass shall be unclean until evening. 28 Whoever carries *any such* carcass shall wash his clothes and be unclean until evening. It *is* unclean to you.

29 'These also *shall be* unclean to you among the creeping things that creep on the earth: the mole, [a]the mouse, and the large lizard after its kind; 30 the gecko, the monitor lizard, the sand reptile, the sand lizard, and the chameleon. 31 These *are* unclean to you among all that creep. Whoever [a]touches them when they are dead shall be unclean until evening. 32 Anything on which *any* of them falls, when they are dead shall be [1]unclean, whether *it is* any item of wood or clothing or skin or sack, whatever item *it is,* in which *any* work is done, [a]it must be put in water. And it shall be unclean until evening; then it shall be clean. 33 Any [a]earthen vessel into which *any* of them falls [b]you shall break; and whatever *is* in it shall be unclean: 34 in such a vessel, any edible food upon which water falls becomes unclean, and any drink that may be drunk from it becomes unclean. 35 And everything on which *a part* of *any such* carcass falls shall be unclean; *whether it is* an oven or cooking stove, it shall be broken down; *for* they *are* unclean, and shall be unclean to you. 36 Nevertheless a spring or a cistern, *in which there is* plenty of water, shall be clean, but whatever touches any such carcass becomes unclean. 37 And if a part of *any such* carcass falls on any planting seed which is to be sown, it *remains* clean. 38 But if water is put on the seed, and if *a part* of *any such* carcass falls on it, it *becomes* [1]unclean to you.

39 'And if any animal which you may eat dies, he who touches its carcass shall be [a]unclean until evening. 40 [a]He who eats of its carcass shall wash his clothes and be unclean until evening. He also who carries its carcass shall wash his clothes and be unclean until evening.

4 a Acts 10:14 *1 impure*
5 *1 rock badger* *2 impure*
7 a Is. 65:4; 66:3, 17
8 a Is. 52:11
9 a Deut. 14:9
10 a Lev. 7:18, 21 *1 detestable*
13 a Is. 66:17
22 a Matt. 3:4
24 *1 impure*
25 a Num. 19:10, 21, 22; 31:24
29 a Is. 66:17
31 a Hag. 2:13
32 a Lev. 15:12 *1 impure*
33 a Lev. 6:28 b Lev. 15:12
38 *1 impure*
39 a Hag. 2:11–13
40 a Lev. 17:15; 22:8

41 'And every creeping thing that creeps on the earth *shall be* [1]an abomination. It shall not be eaten. 42 Whatever crawls on its belly, whatever goes on *all* fours, or whatever has many feet among all creeping things that creep on the earth—these you shall not eat, for they *are* an abomination. 43 [a]You shall not make [1]yourselves [2]abominable with any creeping thing that creeps; nor shall you make yourselves unclean with them, lest you be defiled by them. 44 For I *am* the LORD your [a]God. You shall therefore consecrate yourselves, and [b]you shall be holy; for I *am* holy. Neither shall you defile yourselves with any creeping thing that creeps on the earth. 45 [a]For I *am* the LORD who brings you up out of the land of Egypt, to be your God. [b]You shall therefore be holy, for I *am* holy.

Lord, God of Deliverance, I pray that _____ will be holy, for You are holy.

FROM LEVITICUS 11:45

46 'This *is* the law [1]of the animals and the birds and every living creature that moves in the waters, and of every creature that creeps on the earth, 47 [a]to distinguish between the unclean and the clean, and between the animal that may be eaten and the animal that may not be eaten.' "

The Ritual After Childbirth

12 Then the LORD spoke to Moses, saying, 2 "Speak to the children of Israel, saying: 'If a [a]woman has conceived, and borne a male child, then [b]she shall be [1]unclean seven days; [c]as in the days of her customary impurity she shall be unclean. 3 And on the [a]eighth day the flesh of his foreskin shall be circumcised. 4 She shall then continue in the blood of *her* purification thirty-three days. She shall not touch any [1]hallowed thing, nor come into the sanctuary until the days of her purification are fulfilled.

5 'But if she bears a female child, then she shall be unclean two weeks, as in her customary impurity, and she shall continue in the blood of *her* purification sixty-six days.

6 [a]'When the days of her purification are fulfilled, whether for a son or a daughter, she shall bring to the priest a [b]lamb [1]of the first year as a burnt offering, and a young pigeon or a turtledove as a [c]sin offering, to the door of the tabernacle of meeting. 7 Then he shall offer it before the LORD, and make [1]atonement for her. And she shall be clean from the flow of her blood. This *is* the law for her who has borne a male or a female.

8 [a]'And if she is not able to bring a lamb, then she may bring two turtledoves or two young pigeons—one as a burnt offering and the other as a sin offering. [b]So the priest shall make atonement for her, and she will be [1]clean.' "

The Law Concerning Leprosy

13 And the LORD spoke to Moses and Aaron, saying: 2 "When a man has on the skin of his body a swelling, [a]a scab, or a bright spot, and it becomes on the skin of his body *like* a [1]leprous sore, [b]then he shall be brought to Aaron the priest or to one of his sons the priests. 3 The priest shall examine the sore on the skin of the body; and if the hair on the sore has turned white, and the sore appears *to be* deeper than the skin of his body, it *is* a leprous sore. Then the priest shall examine him, and pronounce him [1]unclean. 4 But if the bright spot *is* white on the skin of his body, and does not appear *to be* deeper than the skin, and its hair has not turned white, then the priest shall isolate *the one who has* the sore [a]seven days. 5 And the priest shall examine him on the seventh day; and indeed *if* the sore appears to be as it was, *and* the sore has not spread on the skin, then the priest shall isolate him another seven days. 6 Then the priest shall examine him again on the seventh day; and indeed *if* the sore has faded, *and* the sore has not spread on the skin, then the priest shall pronounce him clean; it *is only* a scab, and he [a]shall wash his clothes and be clean. 7 But if the scab should at all spread over the skin, after he has been seen by the priest for his cleansing, he shall be seen by the priest again. 8 And *if* the priest sees that the scab has indeed spread on the skin, then the priest shall pronounce him [1]unclean. It *is* leprosy.

9 "When the leprous sore is on a person, then he shall be brought to the priest. 10 [a]And the priest shall examine *him;* and

41 [1] *detestable*
43 [a] Lev. 20:25 [1] Lit. *your souls* [2] *impure*
44 [a] Ex. 6:7 [b] 1 Pet. 1:15, 16
45 [a] Ex. 6:7; 20:2 [b] Lev. 11:44
46 [1] *concerning*
47 [a] Ezek. 44:23

CHAPTER 12
2 [a] Lev. 15:19 [b] Luke 2:22 [c] Lev. 18:19 [1] *impure*
3 [a] Gen. 17:12
4 [1] *consecrated*
6 [a] Luke 2:22 [b] [John 1:29] [c] Lev. 5:7 [1] Lit. *a son of his year*
7 [1] Lit. *covering*
8 [a] Lev. 5:7 [b] Lev. 4:26 [1] *pure*

CHAPTER 13
2 [a] Is. 3:17 [b] Mal. 2:7 [1] Heb. *saraath,* disfiguring skin diseases, including leprosy, and so in vv. 2–46 and 14:2–32
3 [1] *defiled*
4 [a] Lev. 14:8
6 [a] Lev. 11:25; 14:8
8 [1] *defiled*
10 [a] Num. 12:10, 12

LEVITICUS 11:44

Dear Woman of Destiny,

Most of us would be moderately uncomfortable with the thought that we could be holy. Holiness seems to be an attribute reserved for God, but beyond that a lot of us would have a difficult time trying to verbalize exactly what it is. Yet in Leviticus 11:44, God clearly says to His people, "You shall therefore consecrate yourselves, and you shall be holy; for I am holy."

It is almost impossible for me to comprehend God's holiness. His holiness is the antithesis of what I am, and it evokes all kinds of feelings in me—from sheer terror to trembling reverence. I recently considered how cavalierly we treat God in the midst of such incredible blessings: family, friends, homes, lakes and trees, stores stocked with everything we could desire. Thinking about it all, I am overwhelmed with how much God has provided for us and how seldom we acknowledge Him for it.

This biblical warning came to mind: "Beware that you do not forget the LORD your God . . . lest—when you have eaten and are full, and have built beautiful houses and dwell in them; and when your herds and your flocks multiply, and your silver and your gold are multiplied, and all that you have is multiplied; when your heart is lifted up, and you forget the LORD your God" (Deut. 8:11–14). These are words we need to heed.

When we glimpse the greatness of our God, we often want to do something to honor Him. We are like Peter when he saw Jesus in His glory with Moses and Elijah. He said, "If You wish, let us make here three tabernacles" (Matt. 17:4).

But in the Book of Micah, God tells us what He requires of us: "With what shall I come before the LORD, and bow myself before the High God? . . . Will the LORD be pleased with thousands of rams, ten thousand rivers of oil? Shall I give my firstborn for my transgression, the fruit of my body for the sin of my soul? He has shown you, O man, what is good; and what does the LORD require of you but to do justly, to love mercy, and to walk humbly with your God?" (6:6–8).

God isn't looking for perfect men and women; God isn't asking us to build great monuments to Him. God is looking for people who will reverence Him in their hearts and in their lifestyles. God is looking for people in whom He can take up residence, with whom He can speak and walk, through whom He can work. He is looking for people who are willing to be set apart.

Lord, I know that You understand my shortcomings, for You created me. But I also know that You are holy and awesome and that Your purposes for Your people far exceed what I could dream or imagine. Forgive me for being distracted from You. I bow my heart and my knee to You. Perform a work in me that I might be pleasing in Your sight, O God. My heart cries out with Your angels as they call to one another, "Holy, holy, holy is the LORD of hosts; the whole earth is full of His glory!" (Is. 6:3).

Terry Meeuwsen

indeed *if* the swelling on the skin *is* white, and it has turned the hair white, and *there is* a spot of raw flesh in the swelling, [11]it *is* an old leprosy on the skin of his body. The priest shall pronounce him [1]unclean, and shall not isolate him, for he *is* unclean.

[12]"And if leprosy breaks out all over the skin, and the leprosy covers all the skin of *the one who has* the sore, from his head to his foot, wherever the priest looks, [13]then the priest shall consider; and indeed *if* the leprosy has covered all his body, he shall pronounce *him* clean *who has* the sore. It has all turned [a]white. He *is* clean. [14]But when raw flesh appears on him, he shall be unclean. [15]And the priest shall examine the raw flesh and pronounce him to be unclean; *for* the raw flesh *is* unclean. It *is* leprosy. [16]Or if the raw flesh changes and turns white again, he shall come to the priest. [17]And the priest shall examine him; and indeed *if* the sore has turned white, then the priest shall pronounce *him* clean *who has* the sore. He *is* clean.

[18]"If the body develops a [a]boil in the skin, and it is healed, [19]and in the place of the boil there comes a white swelling or a bright spot, reddish-white, then it shall be shown to the priest; [20]and *if*, when the priest sees it, it indeed *appears* deeper than the skin, and its hair has turned white, the priest shall pronounce him unclean. It *is* a leprous sore which has broken out of the boil. [21]But if the priest examines it, and indeed *there are* no white hairs in it, and it *is* not deeper than the skin, but has faded, then the priest shall isolate him seven days; [22]and if it should at all spread over the skin, then the priest shall pronounce him unclean. It *is* a [1]leprous sore. [23]But if the bright spot stays in one place, *and* has not spread, it *is* the scar of the boil; and the priest shall pronounce him clean.

[24]"Or if the body receives a [a]burn on its skin by fire, and the raw *flesh* of the burn becomes a bright spot, reddish-white or white, [25]then the priest shall examine it; and indeed *if* the hair of the bright spot has turned white, and it appears deeper than the skin, it *is* leprosy broken out in the burn. Therefore the priest shall pronounce him unclean. It *is* a leprous sore. [26]But if the priest examines it, and indeed *there are* no white hairs in the bright spot, and it *is* not deeper than the skin, but has faded, then the priest shall isolate him seven days. [27]And the priest shall examine him on the seventh day. If it has at all spread over the skin, then the priest shall pronounce him unclean. It *is* a leprous sore. [28]But if the bright spot stays in one place, *and* has not spread on the skin, but has faded, it *is* a swelling from the burn. The priest shall pronounce him clean, for it *is* the scar from the burn.

[29]"If a man or woman has a sore on the head or the beard, [30]then the priest shall examine the sore; and indeed if it appears deeper than the skin, *and there is* in it thin yellow hair, then the priest shall pronounce him unclean. It *is* a scaly leprosy of the head or beard. [31]But if the priest examines the scaly sore, and indeed it does not appear deeper than the skin, and *there is* no black hair in it, then the priest shall isolate *the one who has* the scale seven days. [32]And on the seventh day the priest shall examine the sore; and indeed *if* the scale has not spread, and there is no yellow hair in it, and the scale does not appear deeper than the skin, [33]he shall shave himself, but the scale he shall not shave. And the priest shall isolate *the one who has* the scale another seven days. [34]On the seventh day the priest shall examine the scale; and indeed *if* the scale has not spread over the skin, and does not appear deeper than the skin, then the priest shall pronounce him clean. He shall wash his clothes and be clean. [35]But if the scale should at all spread over the skin after his cleansing, [36]then the priest shall examine him; and indeed *if* the scale has spread over the skin, the priest need not seek for yellow hair. He *is* unclean. [37]But if the scale appears to be at a standstill, and there is black hair grown up in it, the scale has healed. He *is* clean, and the priest shall pronounce him clean.

[38]"If a man or a woman has bright spots on the skin of the body, *specifically* white bright spots, [39]then the priest shall look; and indeed *if* the bright spots on the skin of the body *are* dull white, it *is* a white spot *that* grows on the skin. He *is* clean.

[40]"As for the man whose hair has fallen from his head, he *is* bald, *but* he *is* clean. [41]He whose hair has fallen from his forehead, he *is* bald on the forehead, *but* he *is* clean. [42]And if there is on the bald head or bald [a]forehead a reddish-white sore, it *is* leprosy breaking out on his bald head or his bald forehead. [43]Then the priest shall

11 *1 defiled*
13 a Ex. 4:6
18 a Ex. 9:9; 15:26
22 *1 infection*
24 a Is. 3:24
42 a 2 Chr. 26:19

examine it; and indeed *if* the swelling of
the sore *is* reddish-white on his bald head
or on his bald forehead, as the appearance
of leprosy on the skin of the body, 44he is
a leprous man. He *is* unclean. The priest
shall surely pronounce him [1]unclean; his
sore *is* on his [a]head.
45"Now the leper on whom the sore *is,*
his clothes shall be torn and his head
[a]bare; and he shall [b]cover his mustache,
and cry, [c]'Unclean! Unclean!' 46He shall
be unclean. All the days he has the sore he
shall be unclean. He *is* unclean, and he
shall [1]dwell alone; his dwelling *shall be*
[a]outside the camp.

The Law Concerning Leprous Garments

47"Also, if a garment has a [1]leprous
plague in it, *whether it is* a woolen garment or a linen garment, 48whether *it is*
in the warp or woof of linen or wool,
whether in leather or in anything made of
leather, 49and if the plague is greenish or
reddish in the garment or in the leather,
whether in the warp or in the woof, or in
anything made of leather, it *is* a leprous
[1]plague and shall be shown to the priest.
50The priest shall examine the plague and
isolate *that which has* the plague seven
days. 51And he shall examine the plague
on the seventh day. If the plague has
spread in the garment, either in the warp
or in the woof, in the leather *or* in anything made of leather, the plague *is* [a]an
active leprosy. It *is* unclean. 52He shall
therefore burn that garment in which is
the plague, whether warp or woof, in wool
or in linen, or anything of leather, for it
is an active leprosy; *the garment* shall be
burned in the fire.
53"But if the priest examines *it,* and indeed the plague has not spread in the garment, either in the warp or in the woof, or
in anything made of leather, 54then the
priest shall command that they wash *the
thing* in which *is* the plague; and he shall
isolate it another seven days. 55Then the
priest shall examine the plague after it has
been washed; and indeed *if* the plague has
not changed its color, though the plague
has not spread, it *is* unclean, and you shall
burn it in the fire; it continues eating
away, *whether* the damage *is* outside or
inside. 56If the priest examines *it,* and indeed the plague has faded after washing it,
then he shall tear it out of the garment,
whether out of the warp or out of the
woof, or out of the leather. 57But if it appears again in the garment, either in the
warp or in the woof, or in anything made
of leather, it *is* a spreading *plague;* you
shall burn with fire that in which is the
plague. 58And if you wash the garment,
either warp or woof, or whatever is made
of leather, if the plague has disappeared
from it, then it shall be washed a second
time, and shall be clean.
59"This *is* the law of the leprous plague
in a garment of wool or linen, either in
the warp or woof, or in anything made of
leather, to pronounce it clean or to pronounce it unclean."

The Ritual for Cleansing Healed Lepers

14 Then the LORD spoke to Moses,
saying, 2"This shall be the law of
the [1]leper for the day of his cleansing: He
[a]shall be brought to the priest. 3And the
priest shall go out of the camp, and the
priest shall examine *him;* and indeed, *if*
the [1]leprosy is healed in the leper, 4then
the priest shall command to take for him
who is to be cleansed two living *and* clean
birds, [a]cedar wood, [b]scarlet, and [c]hyssop.
5And the priest shall command that one of
the birds be killed in an earthen vessel
over running water. 6As for the living
bird, he shall take it, the cedar wood and
the scarlet and the hyssop, and dip them
and the living bird in the blood of the bird
that was killed over the running water.
7And he shall [a]sprinkle it [b]seven times on
him who is to be cleansed from the leprosy, and shall pronounce him clean, and
shall let the living bird loose in the open
field. 8He who is to be cleansed [a]shall
wash his clothes, shave off all his hair, and
[b]wash himself in water, that he may be
clean. After that he shall come into the
camp, and [c]shall stay outside his tent sev-
en days. 9But on the [a]seventh day he shall
shave all the hair off his head and his
beard and his eyebrows—all his hair he
shall shave off. He shall wash his clothes
and wash his body in water, and he shall
be clean.
10"And on the eighth day [a]he shall take
two male lambs without blemish, one ewe
lamb of the first year without blemish,
three-tenths *of an ephah* of fine flour
mixed with oil as [b]a grain offering, and
one log of oil. 11Then the priest who
makes *him* clean shall present the man
who is to be made clean, and those things,

44 a Is. 1:5 *1 altogether defiled*
45 a Lev. 10:6; 21:10 b Ezek. 24:17, 22 c Lam. 4:15
46 a Num. 5:1–4; 12:14 *1 live alone*
47 *1* A mold, fungus, or similar infestation, and so in vv. 47–59
49 *1 mark*
51 a Lev. 14:44

CHAPTER 14
2 a Matt. 8:2, 4 *1* See note at 13:2
3 *1* Heb. *saraath,* disfiguring skin diseases, including leprosy, and so in vv. 2–32
4 a Num. 19:6 b Ex. 25:4 c Ps. 51:7
7 a Num. 19:18, 19 b Ps. 51:2
8 a Num. 8:7 b [Heb. 10:22] c Num. 5:2, 3; 12:14, 15
9 a Num. 19:19
10 a Matt. 8:4 b Lev. 2:1

before the LORD, *at* the door of the tabernacle of meeting. 12And the priest shall
take one male lamb and [a]offer it as a trespass offering, and the log of oil, and [b]wave
them *as* a wave offering before the LORD.
13Then he shall kill the lamb [a]in the place
where he kills the sin offering and the
burnt offering, in a holy place; for [b]as the
sin offering *is* the priest's, so *is* the trespass offering. [c]It *is* most holy. 14The priest
shall take *some* of the blood of the trespass offering, and the priest shall put *it*
[a]on the tip of the right ear of him who is
to be cleansed, on the thumb of his right
hand, and on the big toe of his right foot.
15And the priest shall take *some* of the log
of oil, and pour *it* into the palm of his own
left hand. 16Then the priest shall dip his
right finger in the oil that *is* in his left
hand, and shall [a]sprinkle some of the oil
with his finger seven times before the
LORD. 17And of the rest of the oil in his
hand, the priest shall put *some* on the
tip of the right ear of him who is to be
cleansed, on the thumb of his right hand,
and on the big toe of his right foot, on the
blood of the trespass offering. 18The rest
of the oil that *is* in the priest's hand he
shall put on the head of him who is to
be cleansed. [a]So the priest shall make
[1]atonement for him before the LORD.

19"Then the priest shall offer [a]the sin
offering, and make atonement for him
who is to be cleansed from his uncleanness. Afterward he shall kill the burnt offering. 20And the priest shall offer the
burnt offering and the grain offering on
the altar. So the priest shall make atonement for him, and he shall be [a]clean.

21"But [a]if he *is* poor and cannot afford
it, then he shall take one male lamb *as* a
trespass offering to be waved, to make
atonement for him, [1]one-tenth *of an
ephah* of fine flour mixed with oil as a
grain offering, a log of oil, 22[a]and two
turtledoves or two young pigeons, such as
he is able to afford: one shall be a sin offering and the other a burnt offering. 23[a]He
shall bring them to the priest on the
eighth day for his cleansing, to the door
of the tabernacle of meeting, before the
LORD. 24[a]And the priest shall take the
lamb of the trespass offering and the log
of oil, and the priest shall wave them *as* a
wave offering before the LORD. 25Then he
shall kill the lamb of the trespass offering,
[a]and the priest shall take *some* of the
blood of the trespass offering and put *it* on
the tip of the right ear of him who is to be
cleansed, on the thumb of his right hand,
and on the big toe of his right foot. 26And
the priest shall pour some of the oil into
the palm of his own left hand. 27Then the
priest shall sprinkle with his right finger
some of the oil that *is* in his left hand
seven times before the LORD. 28And the
priest shall put *some* of the oil that *is* in
his hand on the tip of the right ear of him
who is to be cleansed, on the thumb of the
right hand, and on the big toe of his right
foot, on the place of the blood of the trespass offering. 29The rest of the oil that *is*
in the priest's hand he shall put on the
head of him who is to be cleansed, to
make atonement for him before the LORD.
30And he shall offer one of [a]the turtledoves or young pigeons, such as he can
afford— 31such as he is able to afford, the
one *as* a sin offering and the other *as* a
burnt offering, with the grain offering. So
the priest shall make atonement for him
who is to be cleansed before the LORD.
32This *is* the law *for one* who had a leprous
sore, who cannot afford [a]the usual
cleansing."

The Law Concerning Leprous Houses

33And the LORD spoke to Moses and
Aaron, saying: 34[a]"When you have come
into the land of Canaan, which I give you
as a possession, and [b]I put the [1]leprous
plague in a house in the land of your possession, 35and he who owns the house
comes and tells the priest, saying, 'It
seems to me that *there is* [a]some plague in
the house,' 36then the priest shall command that they empty the house, before
the priest goes *into it* to examine the
plague, that all that *is* in the house may
not be made unclean; and afterward the
priest shall go in to examine the house.
37And he shall examine the plague; and
indeed *if* the plague *is* on the walls of the
house with ingrained streaks, greenish or
reddish, which appear to be [1]deep in the
wall, 38then the priest shall go out of the
house, to the door of the house, and [1]shut
up the house seven days. 39And the priest
shall come again on the seventh day and
look; and indeed *if* the plague has spread
on the walls of the house, 40then the
priest shall command that they take away
the stones in which *is* the plague, and
they shall cast them into an unclean place
outside the city. 41And he shall cause the

12 [a]Lev. 5:6, 18; 6:6; 14:19 [b]Ex. 29:22–24, 26
13 [a]Ex. 29:11 [b]Lev. 6:24–30; 7:7 [c]Lev. 2:3; 7:6; 21:22
14 [a]Lev. 8:23, 24
16 [a]Lev. 4:6
18 [a]Lev. 4:26; 5:6 [1]Lit. *covering*
19 [a]Lev. 5:1, 6; 12:7
20 [a]Lev. 14:8, 9
21 [a]Lev. 5:7, 11; 12:8; 27:8 [1]Approximately two dry quarts
22 [a]Lev. 12:8; 15:14, 15
23 [a]Lev. 14:10, 11
24 [a]Lev. 14:12
25 [a]Lev. 14:14, 17
30 [a]Lev. 14:22; 15:14, 15
32 [a]Lev. 14:10
34 [a]Deut. 7:1; 32:49 [b][Prov. 3:33] [1]Decomposition by mildew, mold, dry rot, etc., and so in vv. 34–53
35 [a][Ps. 91:9, 10]
37 [1]Lit. *lower than the wall*
38 [1]*quarantine*

house to be scraped inside, all around, and the dust that they scrape off they shall pour out in an unclean place outside the city. 42Then they shall take other stones and put *them* in the place of *those* stones, and he shall take other mortar and plaster the house.

43"Now if the plague comes back and breaks out in the house, after he has taken away the stones, after he has scraped the house, and after it is plastered, 44then the priest shall come and look; and indeed *if* the plague has spread in the house, it *is* [a]an active leprosy in the house. It *is* unclean. 45And he shall break down the house, its stones, its timber, and all the plaster of the house, and he shall carry *them* outside the city to an unclean place. 46Moreover he who goes into the house at all while it is shut up shall be [1]unclean [a]until evening. 47And he who lies down in the house shall [a]wash his clothes, and he who eats in the house shall wash his clothes.

48"But if the priest comes in and examines *it,* and indeed the plague has not spread in the house after the house was plastered, then the priest shall pronounce the house clean, because the plague is healed. 49And [a]he shall take, to cleanse the house, two birds, cedar wood, scarlet, and hyssop. 50Then he shall kill one of the birds in an earthen vessel over running water; 51and he shall take the cedar wood, the hyssop, the scarlet, and the living bird, and dip them in the blood of the slain bird and in the running water, and sprinkle the house seven times. 52And he shall [1]cleanse the house with the blood of the bird and the running water and the living bird, with the cedar wood, the hyssop, and the scarlet. 53Then he shall let the living bird loose outside the city in the open field, and [a]make atonement for the house, and it shall be clean.

54"This *is* the law for any [a]leprous sore and scale, 55for the [a]leprosy of a garment [b]and of a house, 56[a]for a swelling and a scab and a bright spot, 57to [a]teach when *it is* unclean and when *it is* clean. This *is* the law of leprosy."

The Law Concerning Bodily Discharges

15 And the LORD spoke to Moses and Aaron, saying, 2"Speak to the children of Israel, and say to them: [a]'When any man has a discharge from his body, his discharge *is* unclean. 3And this shall be his uncleanness in regard to his discharge—whether his body runs with his discharge, or his body is stopped up by his discharge, it *is* his uncleanness. 4Every bed is [1]unclean on which he who has the discharge lies, and everything on which he sits shall be unclean. 5And whoever [a]touches his bed shall [b]wash his clothes and [c]bathe in water, and be unclean until evening. 6He who sits on anything on which he who has the [a]discharge sat shall wash his clothes and bathe in water, and be unclean until evening. 7And he who touches the body of him who has the discharge shall wash his clothes and bathe in water, and be unclean until evening. 8If he who has the discharge [a]spits on him who is clean, then he shall wash his clothes and bathe in water, and be unclean until evening. 9Any saddle on which he who has the discharge rides shall be unclean. 10Whoever touches anything that was under him shall be unclean until evening. He who carries *any of* those things shall wash his clothes and bathe in water, and be unclean until evening. 11And whomever the one who has the discharge touches, and has not rinsed his hands in water, he shall wash his clothes and bathe in water, and be unclean until evening. 12The [a]vessel of earth that he who has the discharge touches shall be broken, and every vessel of wood shall be rinsed in water.

13'And when he who has a discharge is cleansed of his discharge, then [a]he shall count for himself seven days for his cleansing, wash his clothes, and bathe his body in running water; then he shall be clean. 14On the eighth day he shall take for himself [a]two turtledoves or two young pigeons, and come before the LORD, to the door of the tabernacle of meeting, and give them to the priest. 15Then the priest shall offer them, [a]the one *as* a sin offering and the other *as* a burnt offering. [b]So the priest shall make [1]atonement for him before the LORD because of his discharge.

16[a]'If any man has an emission of semen, then he shall wash all his body in water, and be unclean until evening. 17And any garment and any leather on which there is semen, it shall be washed with water, and be unclean until evening. 18Also, when a woman lies with a man, and *there is* an emission of semen, they

---

44 a Lev. 13:51
46 a Lev. 11:24; 15:5 1 *defiled*
47 a Lev. 14:8
49 a Lev. 14:4
52 1 *ceremonially cleanse*
53 a Lev. 14:20
54 a Lev. 13:30; 26:21
55 a Lev. 13:47–52 b Lev. 14:34
56 a Lev. 13:2
57 a Deut. 24:8

CHAPTER 15
2 a Num. 5:2
4 1 *defiled*
5 a Lev. 5:2; 14:46 b Lev. 14:8, 47 c Lev. 11:25; 17:15
6 a Deut. 23:10
8 a Num. 12:14
12 a Lev. 6:28; 11:32, 33
13 a Lev. 14:8; 15:28
14 a Lev. 14:22, 23, 30, 31
15 a Lev. 14:30, 31 b Lev. 14:19, 31 1 Lit. *covering*
16 a Lev. 22:4

shall bathe in water, and [a]be unclean until evening.

19[a]'If a woman has a discharge, *and* the
discharge from her body is blood, she
shall be [1]set apart seven days; and whoever touches her shall be unclean until evening. 20Everything that she lies on during
her impurity shall be unclean; also everything that she sits on shall be unclean.
21Whoever touches her bed shall wash his
clothes and bathe in water, and be unclean until evening. 22And whoever
touches anything that she sat on shall
wash his clothes and bathe in water, and
be unclean until evening. 23If *anything* is
on *her* bed or on anything on which she
sits, when he touches it, he shall be unclean until evening. 24And [a]if any man lies
with her at all, so that her impurity is on
him, he shall be [1]unclean seven days; and
every bed on which he lies shall be unclean.

25'If [a]a woman has a discharge of blood
for many days, other than at the time of
her *customary* impurity, or if it runs beyond her *usual time of* impurity, all the
days of her unclean discharge shall be as
the days of her *customary* impurity. She
shall be unclean. 26Every bed on which
she lies all the days of her discharge shall
be to her as the bed of her impurity; and
whatever she sits on shall be unclean, as
the uncleanness of her impurity. 27Who-
ever touches those things shall be unclean; he shall wash his clothes and bathe
in water, and be unclean until evening.

28'But [a]if she is cleansed of her discharge, then she shall count for herself
seven days, and after that she shall be
clean. 29And on the eighth day she shall
take for herself two turtledoves or two
young pigeons, and bring them to the
priest, to the door of the tabernacle of
meeting. 30Then the priest shall offer the
one *as* a sin offering and the other *as* a
[a]burnt offering, and the priest shall make
atonement for her before the LORD for the
discharge of her uncleanness.

31'Thus you shall [a]separate the children
of Israel from their uncleanness, lest they
die in their uncleanness when they [b]defile
My tabernacle that *is* among them.
32[a]This *is* the law for one who has a discharge, [b]and *for him* who emits semen
and is unclean thereby, 33[a]and for her
who is indisposed because of her *customary* impurity, and for one who has a discharge, either man [b]or woman, [c]and for
him who lies with her who is unclean.' "

The Day of Atonement

16 Now the LORD spoke to Moses after
[a]the death of the two sons of
Aaron, when they offered *profane fire* before the LORD, and died; 2 and the LORD
said to Moses: "Tell Aaron your brother
[a]not to come at *just* any time into the
Holy *Place* inside the veil, before the mercy seat which *is* on the ark, lest he die; for
[b]I will appear in the cloud above the mercy seat.

3[1]"Thus Aaron shall [a]come into the
Holy *Place*: [b]with *the blood of* a young
bull as a sin offering, and *of* a ram as a
burnt offering. 4He shall put the [a]holy lin-
en tunic and the linen trousers on his
body; he shall be girded with a linen sash,
and with the linen turban he shall be at-
tired. These *are* holy garments. Therefore
[b]he shall wash his body in water, and put
them on. 5And he shall take from [a]the
congregation of the children of Israel two
kids of the goats as a sin offering, and one
ram as a burnt offering.

6"Aaron shall offer the bull as a sin offering, which *is* for himself, and [a]make
atonement for himself and for his house.
7He shall take the two goats and present
them before the LORD *at* the door of the
tabernacle of meeting. 8Then Aaron shall
cast lots for the two goats: one lot for the
LORD and the other lot for the scapegoat.
9And Aaron shall bring the goat on which
the LORD's lot fell, and offer it *as* a sin
offering. 10But the goat on which the lot
fell to be the scapegoat shall be presented
alive before the LORD, to make [a]atone-
ment upon it, *and* to let it go as the scapegoat into the wilderness.

11"And Aaron shall bring the bull of the
sin offering, which is for [a]himself, and
make atonement for himself and for his
house, and shall kill the bull as the sin
offering which *is* for himself. 12Then he
shall take [a]a censer full of burning coals
of fire from the altar before the LORD, with
his hands full of [b]sweet incense beaten
fine, and bring *it* inside the veil. 13[a]And he
shall put the incense on the fire before the
LORD, that the cloud of incense may cover
the [b]mercy seat that *is* on the Testimony,
lest he [c]die. 14[a]He shall take some of the
blood of the bull and [b]sprinkle *it* with
his finger on the mercy seat on the east
side; and before the mercy seat he shall

18 a [1 Sam. 21:4]
19 a Lev. 12:2 *1* Lit. *in her impurity*
24 a Lev. 18:19; 20:18 *1 defiled*
25 a Matt. 9:20
28 a Lev. 15:13–15
30 a Lev. 5:7
31 a Deut. 24:8 b Num. 5:3; 19:13, 20
32 a Lev. 15:2 b Lev. 15:16
33 a Lev. 15:19 b Lev. 15:25 c Lev. 15:24

CHAPTER 16
1 a Lev. 10:1, 2
2 a Ex. 30:10 b Ex. 25:21, 22; 40:34
3 a [Heb. 9:7, 12, 24, 25] b Lev. 4:3 *1* Lit. *With this*
4 a Ex. 28:39, 42, 43 b Ex. 30:20
5 a Lev. 4:14
6 a [Heb. 5:3; 7:27, 28; 9:7]
10 a [1 John 2:2]
11 a [Heb. 7:27; 9:7]
12 a Lev. 10:1 b Ex. 30:34–38
13 a Ex. 30:7, 8 b Ex. 25:21 c Ex. 28:43
14 a [Heb. 9:25; 10:4] b Lev. 4:6, 17

Leviticus 16:2

Dear Woman of Destiny,

In Old Testament times it was forbidden for a woman to enter the temple area. The requirements were exclusively for the Levitical priesthood; and only Aaron, the high priest, was allowed to enter the holiest of places once a year. Aaron's sons died when they attempted to enter the Most Holy Place. Then the Lord said to Moses: "Tell Aaron your brother not to come at just any time into the Holy Place inside the veil, before the mercy seat which is on the ark, lest he die; for I will appear in the cloud above the mercy seat" (Lev. 16:2).

Today we have the joy of freely going inside the veil into the inner sanctum anytime we wish. Hebrews 10:19–22 tells us, "Therefore, brethren, having boldness to enter the Holiest by the blood of Jesus, by a new and living way which He consecrated for us, through the veil, that is, His flesh, and having a High Priest over the house of God, let us draw near with a true heart in full assurance of faith, having our hearts sprinkled from an evil conscience and our bodies washed with pure water."

There are conditions to our coming into the Holy Place:

We must come to Him with boldness and confidence.
We must approach the Lord with a sincere heart.
We are to come into His presence with a heart of faith, even if it is small.
We should have repented from known sin.

Woman of Destiny, the Lord invites you into His courts. There is no need to be shy or hesitant. Jesus has placed a welcome mat at the entrance of His throne room, "Come in."

There is a story told of Alexander the Great that illustrates how God delights in our coming to Him. A general in his army was held in such high favor that Alexander told him to draw from the treasury any amount he desired. He presented a request for such an enormous amount that the treasurer was astonished and would not honor it. The general reported to the emperor, who called the treasurer and said, "Did I not tell you to honor the draft of the general?"

"But," replied the treasurer, "do you understand its amount?"

"Never mind what it is," answered the emperor, "he honors me and my kingdom by making a great draft."

Woman of Destiny, you can make a draft from the coffer of heaven as you discover the treasures that are found beyond the veil.

Alice Smith

sprinkle some of the blood with his finger seven times.

15[a]“Then he shall kill the goat of the sin offering, which *is* for the people, bring its blood [b]inside the veil, do with that blood as he did with the blood of the bull, and sprinkle it on the mercy seat and before the mercy seat. 16So he shall [a]make atonement for the Holy *Place,* because of the uncleanness of the children of Israel, and because of their transgressions, for all their sins; and so he shall do for the tabernacle of meeting which remains among them in the midst of their uncleanness. 17There shall be [a]no man in the tabernacle of meeting when he goes in to make atonement in the Holy *Place,* until he comes out, that he may make atonement for himself, for his household, and for all the assembly of Israel. 18And he shall go out to the altar that *is* before the LORD, and make atonement for [a]it, and shall take some of the blood of the bull and some of the blood of the goat, and put it on the horns of the altar all around. 19Then he shall sprinkle some of the blood on it with his finger seven times, cleanse it, and [a]consecrate[1] it from the [2]uncleanness of the children of Israel.

> *By neglecting to take care of what we call our little actions, we are led into great transgressions.*
>
> CHARLES WESLEY

20“And when he has made an end of atoning for the Holy *Place,* the tabernacle of meeting, and the altar, he shall bring the live goat. 21Aaron shall lay both his hands on the head of the live goat, [a]confess over it all the iniquities of the children of Israel, and all their transgressions, concerning all their sins, [b]putting them on the head of the goat, and shall send *it* away into the wilderness by the hand of a suitable man. 22The goat [1]shall [a]bear on itself all their iniquities to an [2]uninhabited land; and he shall [b]release the goat in the wilderness.

23“Then Aaron shall come into the tabernacle of meeting, [a]shall take off the linen garments which he put on when he went into the Holy *Place,* and shall leave them there. 24And he shall wash his body with water in a holy place, put on his garments, come out and offer his burnt offering and the burnt offering of the people, and make [1]atonement for himself and for the people. 25[a]The fat of the sin offering he shall burn on the altar. 26And he who released the goat as the scapegoat shall wash his clothes [a]and bathe his body in water, and afterward he may come into the camp. 27[a]The bull *for* the sin offering and the goat *for* the sin offering, whose blood was brought in to make atonement in the Holy *Place,* shall be carried outside the camp. And they shall burn in the fire their skins, their flesh, and their offal. 28Then he who burns them shall wash his clothes and bathe his body in water, and afterward he may come into the camp.

29“*This* shall be a statute forever for you: [a]In the seventh month, on the tenth *day* of the month, you shall [1]afflict your souls, and do no work at all, *whether* a native of your own country or a stranger who [2]dwells among you. 30For on that day *the priest* shall make [1]atonement for you, to [a]cleanse you, *that* you may be clean from all your sins before the LORD. 31[a]It *is* a sabbath of solemn rest for you, and you shall afflict your souls. *It is* a statute forever. 32[a]And the priest, who is anointed and [b]consecrated to minister as priest in his father’s place, shall make atonement, and put on the linen clothes, the holy garments; 33then he shall make [1]atonement for [2]the Holy Sanctuary, and he shall make atonement for the tabernacle of meeting and for the altar, and he shall make atonement for the priests and for all the people of the assembly. 34[a]This shall be an everlasting statute for you, to make atonement for the children of Israel, for all their sins, [b]once a year.” And he did as the LORD commanded Moses.

The Sanctity of Blood

17 And the LORD spoke to Moses, saying, 2“Speak to Aaron, to his sons, and to all the children of Israel, and say to them, ‘This *is* the thing which the LORD has commanded, saying: 3“Whatever man of the house of Israel who [a]kills an ox or lamb or goat in the camp, or who kills *it* outside the camp, 4and does not bring it to the door of the tabernacle of meeting to offer an offering to the LORD before the

---

15 a [Heb. 2:17] b [Heb. 6:19; 7:27; 9:3, 7, 12]
16 a Ex. 29:36; 30:10
17 a Luke 1:10
18 a Ex. 29:36
19 a Ezek. 43:20 *1 set it apart* *2 impurity*
21 a Lev. 5:5; 26:40 b [Is. 53:6]
22 a [Is. 53:6, 11, 12] b Lev. 14:7 *1 shall carry* *2 solitary land*
23 a Ezek. 42:14; 44:19
24 1 Lit. *covering*
25 a Lev. 1:8; 4:10
26 a Lev. 15:5
27 a Heb. 13:11
29 a Lev. 23:27–32 *1 humble yourselves* 2 As a resident alien
30 a Jer. 33:8 1 Lit. *covering*
31 a Lev. 23:27, 32
32 a Lev. 4:3, 5, 16; 21:10 b Ex. 29:29, 30
33 1 Lit. *covering* 2 The Most Holy Place
34 a Lev. 23:31 b [Heb. 9:7, 25, 28]

CHAPTER 17
3 a Deut. 12:5, 15, 21

tabernacle of the LORD, the guilt of bloodshed shall be [a]imputed to that man. He has shed blood; and that man shall be [1]cut off from among his people, 5to the end that the children of Israel may bring their sacrifices [a]which they offer in the open field, that they may bring them to the LORD at the door of the tabernacle of meeting, to the priest, and offer them *as* peace offerings to the LORD. 6And the priest [a]shall sprinkle the blood on the altar of the LORD *at* the door of the tabernacle of meeting, and [b]burn the fat for a sweet aroma to the LORD. 7They shall no more offer their sacrifices [a]to [1]demons, after whom they [b]have played the harlot. This shall be a statute forever for them throughout their generations."'

8"Also you shall say to them: 'Whatever man of the house of Israel, or of the strangers who dwell among you, [a]who offers a burnt offering or sacrifice, 9and does not [a]bring it to the door of the tabernacle of meeting, to offer it to the LORD, that man shall be [1]cut off from among his people.

10[a]'And whatever man of the house of Israel, or of the strangers who dwell among you, who eats any blood, [b]I will set My face against that person who eats blood, and will cut him off from among his people. 11For the [a]life of the flesh *is* in the blood, and I have given it to you upon the altar [b]to make atonement for your souls; for [c]it *is* the blood *that* makes atonement for the soul.' 12Therefore I said to the children of Israel, 'No one among you shall eat blood, nor shall any stranger who dwells among you eat blood.'

13"Whatever man of the children of Israel, or of the strangers who dwell among you, who [a]hunts and catches any animal or bird that may be eaten, he shall [b]pour out its blood and [c]cover it with dust; 14[a]for *it is* the life of all flesh. Its blood sustains its life. Therefore I said to the children of Israel, 'You shall not eat the blood of any flesh, for the life of all flesh is its blood. Whoever eats it shall be cut off.'

15[a]"And every person who eats what died *naturally* or what was torn *by beasts, whether he is* a native of your own country or a stranger, [b]he shall both wash his clothes and [c]bathe in water, and be unclean until evening. Then he shall be clean. 16But if he does not wash *them* or bathe his body, then [a]he shall bear his [1]guilt."

Laws of Sexual Morality

18 Then the LORD spoke to Moses, saying, 2"Speak to the children of Israel, and say to them: [a]'I am the LORD your God. 3[a]According to [1]the doings of the land of Egypt, where you dwelt, you shall not do; and [b]according to the doings of the land of Canaan, where I am bringing you, you shall not do; nor shall you walk in their [2]ordinances. 4[a]You shall observe My judgments and keep My ordinances, to walk in them: I *am* the LORD your God. 5You shall therefore keep My statutes and My judgments, which if a man does, he shall live by them: I *am* the LORD.

Lord, I pray that ______ will live according to Your ways. For You, Lord, are God.

FROM LEVITICUS 18:4, 5

6'None of you shall approach anyone who is near of kin to him, to uncover his nakedness: I *am* the LORD. 7The nakedness of your father or the nakedness of your mother you shall not uncover. She *is* your mother; you shall not uncover her nakedness. 8The nakedness of your [a]father's wife you shall not uncover; it *is* your father's nakedness. 9[a]The nakedness of your sister, the daughter of your father, or the daughter of your mother, *whether* born at home or elsewhere, their nakedness you shall not uncover. 10The nakedness of your son's daughter or your daughter's daughter, their nakedness you shall not uncover; for theirs *is* your own nakedness. 11The nakedness of your father's wife's daughter, begotten by your father—she *is* your sister—you shall not uncover her nakedness. 12[a]You shall not uncover the nakedness of your father's sister; she *is* near of kin to your father. 13You shall not uncover the nakedness of your mother's sister, for she *is* near of kin to your mother. 14[a]You shall not uncover the nakedness of your father's brother. You shall not approach his wife; she *is* your aunt. 15You shall not uncover the

4 [a]Rom. 5:13 [1]Put to death
5 [a]Deut. 12:1–27
6 [a]Lev. 3:2 [b]Num. 18:17
7 [a]Deut. 32:17 [b]Ezek. 23:8 [1]Having the form of a goat or satyr
8 [a]Lev. 1:2, 3; 18:26
9 [a]Lev. 14:23 [1]Put to death
10 [a]Gen. 9:4 [b]Lev. 20:3, 5, 6
11 [a]Gen. 9:4 [b][Matt. 26:28] [c][Heb. 9:22]
13 [a]Lev. 7:26 [b]Deut. 12:16, 24 [c]Ezek. 24:7
14 [a]Gen. 9:4
15 [a]Ex. 22:31 [b]Lev. 11:25 [c]Lev. 15:5
16 [a]Lev. 5:1 [1]*iniquity*

CHAPTER 18
2 [a]Ex. 6:7
3 [a]Ezek. 20:7, 8 [b]Lev. 18:24–30; 20:23 [1]*what is done in* [2]*statutes*
4 [a]Ezek. 20:19
8 [a]Gen. 35:22
9 [a]Deut. 27:22
12 [a]Lev. 20:19
14 [a]Lev. 20:20

nakedness of your daughter-in-law—she
is your son's wife—you shall not uncover
her nakedness. 16You shall not uncover
the nakedness of your brother's wife; it *is*
your brother's nakedness. 17You shall not
uncover the nakedness of a woman and
her [a]daughter, nor shall you take her
son's daughter or her daughter's daughter, to uncover her nakedness. They *are*
near of kin to her. It *is* wickedness. 18Nor
shall you take a woman [a]as a rival to her
sister, to uncover her nakedness while the
other is alive.
19'Also you shall not approach a woman
to uncover her nakedness as [a]long as she
is in her [b]*customary* impurity. 20[a]More-
over you shall not lie carnally with your
[b]neighbor's wife, to defile yourself with
her. 21And you shall not let any of your
descendants [a]pass through [b]*the fire* to
[c]Molech, nor shall you profane the name
of your God: I *am* the LORD. 22You shall
not lie with [a]a male as with a woman. It
is an abomination. 23Nor shall you mate
with any [a]animal, to defile yourself with
it. Nor shall any woman stand before an
animal to mate with it. It *is* perversion.
24[a]'Do not defile yourselves with any of
these things; [b]for by all these the nations
are defiled, which I am casting out before
you. 25For [a]the land is defiled; therefore
I [b]visit[1] the punishment of its iniquity
upon it, and the land [c]vomits out its
inhabitants. 26[a]You shall therefore [1]keep
My statutes and My judgments, and shall
not commit *any* of these abominations,
either any of your own nation or any
stranger who dwells among you 27(for all
these abominations the men of the land
have done, who *were* before you, and thus
the land is defiled), 28lest [a]the land vomit
you out also when you defile it, as it vomited out the nations that *were* before you.
29For whoever commits any of these
abominations, the persons who commit
them shall be [1]cut off from among their
people.
30'Therefore you shall keep My [1]ordi-
nance, so [a]that *you* do not commit *any* of
these abominable customs which were
committed before you, and that you do
not defile yourselves by them: [b]I *am* the
LORD your God.' "

Moral and Ceremonial Laws

19 And the LORD spoke to Moses, saying, 2"Speak to all the congregation of the children of Israel, and say to
them: [a]'You shall be holy, for I the LORD
your God *am* holy.
3[a]'Every one of you shall revere his
mother and his father, and [b]keep My Sabbaths: I *am* the LORD your God.
4[a]'Do not turn to idols, [b]nor make for
yourselves [1]molded gods: I *am* the LORD
your God.
5'And [a]if you offer a sacrifice of a peace
offering to the LORD, you shall offer it of
your own free will. 6It shall be eaten the
same day you offer *it,* and on the next day.
And if any remains until the third day, it
shall be burned in the fire. 7And if it is
eaten at all on the third day, it *is* an abomination. It shall not be accepted. 8There-
fore *everyone* who eats it shall bear his
iniquity, because he has profaned the hallowed *offering* of the LORD; and that person shall be cut off from his people.

> *Go forward. Live holy lives. . . Love and seek the lost. Bring them to the Blood. Make the people good. Inspire them with the Spirit of Jesus Christ. Love one another. Help your comrades in dark hours.*
>
> CATHERINE BOOTH

9[a]'When you reap the harvest of your
land, you shall not wholly reap the corners of your field, nor shall you gather the
gleanings of your harvest. 10And you shall
not glean your vineyard, nor shall you
gather *every* grape of your vineyard; you
shall leave them for the poor and the
stranger: I *am* the LORD your God.
11[a]'You shall not steal, nor deal falsely,
[b]nor lie to one another. 12And you shall
not [a]swear by My name falsely, [b]nor shall
you profane the name of your God: I *am*
the LORD.
13[a]'You shall not cheat your neighbor,
nor rob *him.* [b]The wages of him who is
hired shall not remain with you all night
until morning. 14You shall not curse the
deaf, [a]nor put a stumbling block before

17 a Lev. 20:14
18 a 1 Sam. 1:6, 8
19 a Ezek. 18:6 b Lev. 15:24; 20:18
20 a [Prov. 6:25–33] b Lev. 20:10
21 a Lev. 20:2–5 b 2 Kin. 16:3 c 1 Kin. 11:7, 33
22 a Lev. 20:13
23 a Ex. 22:19
24 a Matt. 15:18–20 b Deut. 18:12
25 a Num. 35:33, 34 b Jer. 5:9 c Lev. 18:28; 20:22 1 *bring judgment for*
26 a Lev. 18:5, 30 1 *obey*
28 a Jer. 9:19
29 1 Put to death
30 a Lev. 18:3; 22:9 b Lev. 18:2 1 *charge*

CHAPTER 19
2 a Lev. 11:44; 20:7, 26
3 a Ex. 20:12 b Ex. 16:23; 20:8; 31:13
4 a Ex. 20:4 b Ex. 34:17 1 *molten*
5 a Lev. 7:16
9 a Deut. 24:19–22
11 a Ex. 20:15, 16 b Eph. 4:25
12 a Deut. 5:11 b Lev. 18:21
13 a Ex. 22:7–15, 21–27 b Deut. 24:15
14 a Deut. 27:18

the blind, but shall fear your God: I *am* the LORD.

15 'You shall do no injustice in [a]judgment. You shall not [b]be partial to the poor, nor honor the person of the mighty. In righteousness you shall judge your neighbor. 16 You shall not go about *as* a [a]talebearer among your people; nor shall you [b]take a stand against the life of your neighbor: I *am* the LORD.

17 [a]'You shall not hate your brother in your heart. [b]You shall surely [1]rebuke your neighbor, and not bear sin because of him. 18 [a]You shall not take vengeance, nor bear any grudge against the children of your people, [b]but you shall love your neighbor as yourself: I *am* the LORD.

19 'You shall keep My statutes. You shall not let your livestock breed with another kind. You shall not sow your field with mixed seed. Nor shall a garment of mixed linen and wool come upon you.

20 'Whoever lies carnally with a woman who *is* [a]betrothed to a man as a concubine, and who has not at all been redeemed nor given her freedom, for this there shall be [1]scourging; *but* they shall not be put to death, because she was not free. 21 And he shall bring his trespass offering to the LORD, to the door of the tabernacle of meeting, a ram as a trespass offering. 22 The priest shall make [1]atonement for him with the ram of the trespass offering before the LORD for his sin which he has committed. And the sin which he has committed shall be forgiven him.

23 'When you come into the land, and have planted all kinds of trees for food, then you shall count their fruit as [1]uncircumcised. Three years it shall be as uncircumcised to you. *It* shall not be eaten. 24 But in the fourth year all its fruit shall be holy, a praise to the LORD. 25 And in the fifth year you may eat its fruit, that it may yield to you its increase: I *am* the LORD your God.

26 'You shall not eat *anything* with the blood, nor shall you practice divination or soothsaying. 27 You shall not shave around the sides of your head, nor shall you disfigure the edges of your beard. 28 You shall not [a]make any cuttings in your flesh for the dead, nor tattoo any marks on you: I *am* the LORD.

29 [a]'Do not prostitute your daughter, to cause her to be a harlot, lest the land fall into harlotry, and the land become full of wickedness.

30 'You shall [1]keep My Sabbaths and [a]reverence My sanctuary: I *am* the LORD.

31 'Give no regard to mediums and familiar spirits; do not seek after [a]them, to be defiled by them: I *am* the LORD your God.

32 [a]'You shall [1]rise before the gray headed and honor the presence of an old man, and [b]fear your God: I *am* the LORD.

33 'And [a]if a stranger dwells with you in your land, you shall not mistreat him. 34 [a]The stranger who dwells among you shall be to you as [1]one born among you, and [b]you shall love him as yourself; for you were strangers in the land of Egypt: I *am* the LORD your God.

35 'You shall do no injustice in judgment, in measurement of length, weight, or volume. 36 You shall have [a]honest scales, honest weights, an honest ephah, and an honest hin: I *am* the LORD your God, who brought you out of the land of Egypt.

37 [a]'Therefore you shall observe all My statutes and all My judgments, and perform them: I *am* the LORD.' "

Penalties for Breaking the Law

20 Then the LORD spoke to Moses, saying, 2 [a]"Again, you shall say to the children of Israel: [b]'Whoever of the children of Israel, or of the strangers who [1]dwell in Israel, who gives *any* of his descendants to Molech, he shall surely be put to death. The people of the land shall [c]stone him with stones. 3 [a]I will set My face against that man, and will [1]cut him off from his people, because he has given *some* of his descendants to Molech, to defile My sanctuary and profane My holy name. 4 And if the people of the land should in any way [1]hide their eyes from the man, when he gives *some* of his descendants to Molech, and they do not kill him, 5 then I will set My face against that man and against his family; and I will cut him off from his people, and all who prostitute themselves with him to commit harlotry with Molech.

6 'And [a]the person who turns to mediums and familiar spirits, to prostitute himself with them, I will set My face against that person and cut him off from his people. 7 [a]Consecrate[1] yourselves therefore, and be holy, for I *am* the LORD your God. 8 And you shall keep [a]My

15 a Deut. 16:19 b Ex. 23:3, 6
16 a Prov. 11:13; 18:8; 20:19 b 1 Kin. 21:7–19
17 a [1 John 2:9, 11; 3:15] b Matt. 18:15 1 *reprove*
18 a [Deut. 32:35] b Mark 12:31
20 a Deut. 22:23–27 1 *punishment*
22 1 Lit. *covering*
23 1 *unclean*
28 a Jer. 16:6
29 a Deut. 22:21; 23:17, 18
30 a Lev. 26:2 1 *observe*
31 a Lev. 20:6, 27
32 a 1 Tim. 5:1 b Lev. 19:14 1 *rise to give honor*
33 a Ex. 22:21
34 a Ex. 12:48 b Deut. 10:19 1 *native among you*
36 a Deut. 25:13–15
37 a Lev. 18:4, 5

CHAPTER 20
2 a Lev. 18:2 b Lev. 18:21 c Deut. 17:2–5 1 As resident aliens
3 a Lev. 17:10 1 Put him to death
4 1 *disregard*
6 a Lev. 19:31
7 a Lev. 19:2 1 *Set yourselves apart for the* LORD
8 a Lev. 19:19, 37

Leviticus 19:16

Dear Woman of Destiny,

Many people don't realize that the Bible talks a lot about gossip. It is not just a "little sin" as we sometimes rationalize. The Lord clearly commands us to "not go about as a talebearer" (Lev. 19:16). However, at times all of us have not only listened to gossip, but we've spread it and become the victim of it, too. I believe it's all equally painful to the Lord.

When we share things we shouldn't, we usually try to justify it by saying, "We need to pray for so-and-so; they're really struggling with this problem." But too often we just "talk it through" and forget to pray. Then, of course, it is always interesting to listen to the latest tale about someone or some church. We justify this, too, by thinking, "Well, it's important to keep up with what's going on. Besides, I need to know how to pray," which again, usually doesn't happen.

A statement doesn't have to be a lie to make it gossip. Many of us think, *Well, it's true, so I can tell anyone I want to.* Not so! This is called slander. Telling the truth for the wrong motive can be even more destructive than telling a lie. Gossip and slander are Satan's tools. God warns us, "Whoever secretly slanders his neighbor, him I will destroy" (Ps. 101:5).

Gossip divides us, and that's why it is so serious to the Lord. The enemy knows that if he can get us to come against each other, we'll be far too busy to unify and stand against him! The Lord lists gossips together with those who are untrustworthy; unloving; unrighteous; full of envy, strife, and deceit; murderers and haters of God (see Rom. 1:29–31). He also says, "The perverse mouth I hate" (Prov. 8:13).

Here's a good definition of gossip: Gossip is sharing anything about someone when the act of sharing it is not part of the solution to that person's problem. If you've developed a habit of gossip, there are some simple things you can do to change. Ask the Lord to remind you to think before you speak. Make a conscious decision to never receive or repeat gossip again. Learn to gracefully stop someone from telling you something you shouldn't hear. Once you determine to make the right choices, God will give you the grace to follow through.

Take some time to pray. Do you need to humbly ask anyone for forgiveness for gossiping about them? Or maybe you've been wounded by gossip, and bitterness has set in that needs to be confessed and healed. Go to the Lord first. He will help you get your heart right and give you the power to do the rest. "Let us be glad and rejoice and give Him glory, for the marriage of the Lamb has come, and His wife has made herself ready" (Rev. 19:7). It may seem like a huge task; but God is calling a holy bride, and we need to do everything we possibly can to "make ourselves ready"!

Melody Green

I pray that ____ will consecrate themselves and be holy. For You, our God, have set them apart.

FROM LEVITICUS 20:7, 8

statutes, and perform them: [b]I *am* the
LORD who [1]sanctifies you.
9 'For [a]everyone who curses his father
or his mother shall surely be put to death.
He has cursed his father or his mother.
[b]His blood *shall be* upon him.
10 [a]'The man who commits adultery
with *another* man's wife, *he* who commits
adultery with his neighbor's wife, the
adulterer and the adulteress, shall surely
be put to death. 11 The man who lies with
his [a]father's wife has uncovered his father's nakedness; both of them shall surely be put to death. Their blood *shall be*
upon them. 12 If a man lies with his
[a]daughter-in-law, both of them shall
surely be put to death. They have committed perversion. Their blood *shall be* upon
them. 13 [a]If a man lies with a male as he
lies with a woman, both of them have
committed an abomination. They shall
surely be put to death. Their blood *shall*
be upon them. 14 If a man marries a woman and her [a]mother, it *is* wickedness.
They shall be burned with fire, both he
and they, that there may be no wickedness
among you. 15 If a man mates with an [a]an-
imal, he shall surely be put to death, and
you shall kill the animal. 16 If a woman
approaches any animal and mates with it,
you shall kill the woman and the animal.
They shall surely be put to death. Their
blood *is* upon them.
17 'If a man takes his [a]sister, his father's
daughter or his mother's daughter, and
sees her nakedness and she sees his nakedness, it *is* a wicked thing. And they
shall be [1]cut off in the sight of their people. He has uncovered his sister's nakedness. He shall bear his [2]guilt. 18 [a]If a man
lies with a woman during her [1]sickness
and uncovers her nakedness, he has [2]ex-
posed her flow, and she has uncovered the
flow of her blood. Both of them shall be
[3]cut off from their people.

8 b Ex. 31:13 1 *sets you apart*
9 a Ex. 21:17 b 2 Sam. 1:16
10 a Ex. 20:14
11 a Lev. 18:7, 8
12 a Lev. 18:15
13 a Lev. 18:22
14 a Lev. 18:17
15 a Lev. 18:23
17 a Lev. 18:9 1 Put to death 2 *iniquity*
18 a Lev. 15:24; 18:19 1 Or *customary impurity* 2 Lit. *made bare* 3 Put to death
19 a Lev. 18:13 b Lev. 18:12
20 a Lev. 18:14
21 a Lev. 18:16 1 *indecent, impure*
22 a Lev. 18:26; 19:37 b Lev. 18:25, 28
23 a Lev. 18:3, 24 b Deut. 9:5
24 a Ex. 3:17; 6:8; 13:5; 33:1–3 b Ex. 19:5; 33:16
25 a Lev. 10:10; 11:1–47 b Lev. 11:43 1 *detestable* or *loathsome* 2 *defiled*
26 a Lev. 19:2
27 a Lev. 19:31

19 'You shall not uncover the nakedness
of your [a]mother's sister nor of your [b]fa-
ther's sister, for that would uncover his
near of kin. They shall bear their guilt. 20 If
a man lies with his [a]uncle's wife, he has
uncovered his uncle's nakedness. They
shall bear their sin; they shall die childless. 21 If a man takes his [a]brother's wife,
it *is* an [1]unclean thing. He has uncovered
his brother's nakedness. They shall be
childless.
22 'You shall therefore keep all My [a]stat-
utes and all My judgments, and perform
them, that the land where I am bringing
you to dwell [b]may not vomit you out.
23 [a]And you shall not walk in the statutes
of the nation which I am casting out before you; for they commit all these things,
and [b]therefore I abhor them. 24 But [a]I
have said to you, "You shall inherit their
land, and I will give it to you to possess,
a land flowing with milk and honey." I *am*
the LORD your God, [b]who has separated
you from the peoples. 25 [a]You shall therefore distinguish between clean animals
and unclean, between unclean birds and
clean, [b]and you shall not make yourselves
[1]abominable by beast or by bird, or by any
kind of living thing that creeps on the
ground, which I have separated from you
as [2]unclean. 26 And you shall be holy to
Me, [a]for I the LORD *am* holy, and have
separated you from the peoples, that you
should be Mine.

We lay it down as an elemental principle of religion, that no large growth in holiness was ever gained by one who did not take time to be often and long alone with God.

AUSTIN PHELPS

27 [a]'A man or a woman who is a medium, or who has familiar spirits, shall
surely be put to death; they shall stone
them with stones. Their blood *shall be*
upon them.' "

Regulations for Conduct of Priests

21 And the LORD said to Moses, "Speak to the priests, the sons of Aaron, and say to them: [a]'None shall defile himself for the dead among his people, 2except for his relatives who are nearest to him: his mother, his father, his son, his daughter, and his brother; 3also his virgin sister who is near to him, who has had no husband, for her he may defile himself. 4*Otherwise* he shall not defile himself, *being* a [1]chief man among his people, to profane himself.

5[a]'They shall not make any bald *place* on their heads, nor shall they shave the edges of their beards nor make any cuttings in their flesh. 6They shall be [a]holy to their God and not profane the name of their God, for they offer the offerings of the LORD made by fire, *and* the [b]bread of their God; [c]therefore they shall be holy. 7[a]They shall not take a wife *who is* a harlot or a defiled woman, nor shall they take a woman [b]divorced from her husband; for [1]*the priest* is holy to his God. 8Therefore you shall [1]consecrate him, for he offers the bread of your God. He shall be holy to you, for [a]I the LORD, who [b]sanctify you, *am* holy. 9The daughter of any priest, if she profanes herself by playing the harlot, she profanes her father. She shall be [a]burned with fire.

10'*He who is* the high priest among his brethren, on whose head the anointing oil was [a]poured and who is consecrated to wear the garments, shall not [b]uncover[1] his head nor tear his clothes; 11nor shall he go [a]near any dead body, nor defile himself for his father or his mother; 12[a]nor shall he go out of the sanctuary, nor profane the sanctuary of his God; for the [b]consecration of the anointing oil of his God *is* upon him: I *am* the LORD. 13And he shall take a wife in her virginity. 14A widow or a divorced woman or a defiled woman *or* a harlot—these he shall not marry; but he shall take a virgin of his own people as wife. 15Nor shall he profane his posterity among his people, for I the LORD sanctify him.' "

16And the LORD spoke to Moses, saying, 17"Speak to Aaron, saying: 'No man of your descendants in *succeeding* generations, who has *any* defect, may approach to offer the bread of his God. 18For any man who has a [a]defect shall not approach: a man blind or lame, who has a marred *face* or any *limb* [b]too long, 19a man who has a broken foot or broken hand, 20or is a hunchback or a dwarf, or *a man* who has a defect in his eye, or eczema or scab, or is a eunuch. 21No man of the descendants of Aaron the priest, who has a defect, shall come near to offer the offerings made by fire to the LORD. He has a defect; he shall not come near to offer the bread of his God. 22He may eat the bread of his God, *both* the most holy and the holy; 23only he shall not go near the [a]veil or approach the altar, because he has a defect, lest [b]he profane My sanctuaries; for I the LORD sanctify them.' "

24And Moses told *it* to Aaron and his sons, and to all the children of Israel.

22 Then the LORD spoke to Moses, saying, 2"Speak to Aaron and his sons, that they [a]separate[1] themselves from the holy things of the children of Israel, and that they [b]do not profane My holy name *by* what they [c]dedicate to Me: I *am* the LORD. 3Say to them: 'Whoever of all your descendants throughout your generations, who goes near the holy things which the children of Israel dedicate to the LORD, [a]while he has [1]uncleanness upon him, that person shall be cut off from My presence: I *am* the LORD.

4'Whatever man of the descendants of Aaron, who *is* a [a]leper or has [b]a discharge, shall not eat the holy offerings [c]until he is clean. And [d]whoever touches anything made unclean *by* a corpse, or [e]a man who has had an emission of semen, 5or [a]whoever touches any creeping thing by which he would be made unclean, or [b]any person by whom he would become unclean, whatever his uncleanness may be— 6the person who has touched any such thing shall be unclean until evening, and shall not eat the holy *offerings* unless he [a]washes his body with water. 7And when the sun goes down he shall be clean; and afterward he may eat the holy *offerings,* because [a]it *is* his food. 8[a]Whatever dies *naturally* or is torn *by beasts* he shall not eat, to defile himself with it: I *am* the LORD.

9'They shall therefore keep [a]My [1]ordinance, [b]lest they bear sin for it and die thereby, if they profane it: I the LORD sanctify them.

10[a]'No outsider shall eat the holy *offering;* one who [1]dwells with the priest, or a hired servant, shall not eat the holy thing.

CHAPTER 21
1 a Ezek. 44:25
4 1 Lit. *master* or *husband*
5 a Deut. 14:1
6 a Ex. 22:31 b Lev. 3:11 c Is. 52:11
7 a Ezek. 44:22 b Deut. 24:1, 2 1 Lit. *he*
8 a Lev. 11:44, 45 b Lev. 8:12, 30 1 *set him apart*
9 a Deut. 22:21
10 a Lev. 8:12 b Lev. 10:6, 7 1 In mourning
11 a Num. 19:14
12 a Lev. 10:7 b Ex. 29:6, 7
18 a Lev. 22:19–25 b Lev. 22:23
23 a Lev. 16:2 b Lev. 21:12

CHAPTER 22
2 a Num. 6:3 b Lev. 18:21 c Ex. 28:38 1 *keep themselves apart from*
3 a Lev. 7:20, 21 1 *defilement*
4 a Num. 5:2 b Lev. 15:2 c Lev. 14:2; 15:13 d Num. 19:11 e Lev. 15:16, 17
5 a Lev. 11:23–28 b Lev. 15:7, 19
6 a Lev. 15:5
7 a Num. 18:11, 13
8 a Lev. 7:24; 11:39, 40; 17:15
9 a Lev. 18:30 b Ex. 28:43 1 *charge*
10 a Ex. 29:33 1 As a visitor

11 But if the priest [a]buys a person with his money, he may eat it; and one who is born in his house may eat his food. 12 If the priest's daughter is married to an outsider, she may not eat of the holy offerings. 13 But if the priest's daughter is a widow or divorced, and has no child, and has returned to her father's house as in her youth, she may eat her father's food; but no outsider shall eat it.

14 'And if a man eats the holy *offering* unintentionally, then he shall restore a holy *offering* to the priest, and add one-fifth to it. 15 They shall not profane the [a]holy *offerings* of the children of Israel, which they offer to the LORD, 16 or allow them to bear the guilt of trespass when they eat their holy *offerings;* for I the LORD sanctify them.' "

Offerings Accepted and Not Accepted

17 And the LORD spoke to Moses, saying, 18 "Speak to Aaron and his sons, and to all the children of Israel, and say to them: [a]'Whatever man of the house of Israel, or of the strangers in Israel, who [1]offers his sacrifice for any of his vows or for any of his freewill offerings, which they offer to the LORD as a burnt offering— 19 [a]*you shall offer* of your own free will a male without blemish from the cattle, from the sheep, or from the goats. 20 [a]Whatever has a defect, you shall not offer, for it shall not be acceptable on your behalf. 21 And [a]whoever offers a sacrifice of a peace offering to the LORD, [b]to fulfill *his* vow, or a freewill offering from the cattle or the sheep, it must be perfect to be accepted; there shall be no defect in it. 22 [a]Those *that are* blind or broken or maimed, or have an [1]ulcer or eczema or scabs, you shall not offer to the LORD, nor make [b]an offering by fire of them on the altar to the LORD. 23 Either a bull or a lamb that has any limb [a]too long or too short you may offer *as* a freewill offering, but for a vow it shall not be accepted.

24 'You shall not offer to the LORD what is bruised or crushed, or torn or cut; nor shall you make *any offering of them* in your land. 25 Nor [a]from a foreigner's hand shall you offer any of these as [b]the bread of your God, because their [c]corruption *is* in them, *and* defects *are* in them. They shall not be accepted on your behalf.' "

26 And the LORD spoke to Moses, saying: 27 [a]"When a bull or a sheep or a goat is born, it shall be seven days with its mother; and from the eighth day and thereafter it shall be accepted as an offering made by fire to the LORD. 28 *Whether it is* a cow or ewe, do not kill both her [a]and her young on the same day. 29 And when you [a]offer a sacrifice of thanksgiving to the LORD, offer *it* of your own free will. 30 On the same day it shall be eaten; you shall leave [a]none of it until morning: I *am* the LORD.

31 [a]"Therefore you shall keep My commandments, and perform them: I *am* the LORD. 32 [a]You shall not profane My holy name, but [b]I will be [1]hallowed among the children of Israel. I *am* the LORD who [c]sanctifies you, 33 [a]who brought you out of the land of Egypt, to be your God: I *am* the LORD."

Feasts of the Lord

23 And the LORD spoke to Moses, saying, 2 "Speak to the children of Israel, and say to them: 'The feasts of the LORD, which you shall proclaim *to be* [a]holy convocations, these *are* My feasts.

The Sabbath

3 [a]'Six days shall work be done, but the seventh day *is* a Sabbath of solemn rest, a holy convocation. You shall do no work *on it;* it *is* the Sabbath of the LORD in all your dwellings.

The Passover and Unleavened Bread

4 [a]'These *are* the feasts of the LORD, holy convocations which you shall proclaim at their appointed times. 5 [a]On the fourteenth *day* of the first month at twilight *is* the LORD's Passover. 6 And on the fifteenth day of the same month *is* the Feast of Unleavened Bread to the LORD; seven days you must eat unleavened bread. 7 [a]On the first day you shall have a holy convocation; you shall do no [1]customary work on it. 8 But you shall offer an offering made by fire to the LORD for seven days. The seventh day *shall be* a holy convocation; you shall do no customary work *on it.*' "

The Feast of Firstfruits

9 And the LORD spoke to Moses, saying, 10 "Speak to the children of Israel, and say to them: [a]'When you come into the land which I give to you, and reap its harvest,

---

11 [a]Ex. 12:44
15 [a]Num. 18:32
18 [a]Lev. 1:2, 3, 10 [1]*brings his offering*
19 [a]Lev. 1:3
20 [a]Deut. 15:21; 17:1
21 [a]Lev. 3:1, 6 [b]Num. 15:3, 8
22 [a]Mal. 1:8 [b]Lev. 1:9, 13; 3:3, 5 [1]*running sore*
23 [a]Lev. 21:18
25 [a]Num. 15:15, 16 [b]Lev. 21:6, 17 [c]Mal. 1:14
27 [a]Ex. 22:30
28 [a]Deut. 22:6, 7
29 [a]Lev. 7:12
30 [a]Lev. 7:15
31 [a]Deut. 4:40
32 [a]Lev. 18:21 [b]Lev. 10:3 [c]Lev. 20:8 [1]*treated as holy*
33 [a]Lev. 19:36, 37

CHAPTER 23
2 [a]Ex. 12:16
3 [a]Luke 13:14
4 [a]Ex. 23:14–16
5 [a]Ex. 12:1–28
7 [a]Ex. 12:16 [1]*occupational*
10 [a]Ex. 23:19; 34:26

then you shall bring a sheaf of [b]the firstfruits of your harvest to the priest. 11He
shall [a]wave the sheaf before the LORD, to
be accepted on your behalf; on the day
after the Sabbath the priest shall wave it.
12And you shall offer on that day, when
you wave the sheaf, a male lamb of the
first year, without blemish, as a burnt offering to the LORD. 13Its grain offering
shall be two-tenths *of an ephah* of fine
flour mixed with oil, an offering made by
fire to the LORD, for a [1]sweet aroma; and
its drink offering *shall be* of wine, one-
fourth of a hin. 14You shall eat neither
bread nor parched grain nor fresh grain
until the same day that you have brought
an offering to your God; *it shall be* a statute forever throughout your generations
in all your dwellings.

The Feast of Weeks

15'And you shall count for yourselves
from the day after the Sabbath, from the
day that you brought the sheaf of the wave
offering: seven Sabbaths shall be completed. 16Count [a]fifty days to the day after the
seventh Sabbath; then you shall offer [b]a
new grain offering to the LORD. 17You
shall bring from your dwellings two wave
loaves of two-tenths *of an ephah.* They
shall be of fine flour; they shall be baked
with leaven. *They are* [a]the firstfruits to
the LORD. 18And you shall offer with the
bread seven lambs of the first year, without blemish, one young bull, and two
rams. They shall be *as* a burnt offering to
the LORD, with their grain offering and
their drink offerings, an offering made by
fire for a sweet aroma to the LORD. 19Then
you shall sacrifice [a]one kid of the goats as
a sin offering, and two male lambs of the
first year as a sacrifice of a [b]peace offering.
20The priest shall wave them with the
bread of the firstfruits *as* a wave offering
before the LORD, with the two lambs.
[a]They shall be holy to the LORD for the
priest. 21And you shall proclaim on the
same day *that* it is a holy convocation to
you. You shall do no customary work *on
it. It shall be* a statute forever in all your
dwellings throughout your generations.

22[a]'When you reap the harvest of your
land, you shall not wholly reap the corners of your field when you reap, nor shall
you gather any gleaning from your harvest. You shall leave them for the poor
and for the stranger: I *am* the LORD your
God.' "

10 [b][Rom. 11:16]
11 [a]Ex. 29:24
13 *1 pleasing*
16 [a]Acts 2:1 [b]Num. 28:26
17 [a]Num. 15:17–21
19 [a]Num. 28:30 [b]Lev. 3:1
20 [a]Deut. 18:4
22 [a]Lev. 19:9, 10
24 [a]Num. 29:1 [b]Lev. 25:9
27 [a]Num. 29:7
28 [a]Lev. 16:34
29 [a]Jer. 31:9 [b]Num. 5:2
30 [a]Lev. 20:3–6
32 *1 humble yourselves 2 observe your sabbath*
34 [a]Num. 29:12
36 [a]Num. 29:12–34 [b]Num. 29:35–38 [c]Deut. 16:8 *1 solemn*
37 [a]Lev. 23:2, 4
38 [a]Num. 29:39

The Feast of Trumpets

23Then the LORD spoke to Moses, saying, 24"Speak to the children of Israel, saying: 'In the [a]seventh month, on the first
day of the month, you shall have a
sabbath-*rest,* [b]a memorial of blowing of
trumpets, a holy convocation. 25You shall
do no customary work *on it;* and you shall
offer an offering made by fire to the
LORD.' "

The Day of Atonement

26And the LORD spoke to Moses, saying:
27[a]"Also the tenth *day* of this seventh
month *shall be* the Day of Atonement. It
shall be a holy convocation for you; you
shall afflict your souls, and offer an offering made by fire to the LORD. 28And you
shall do no work on that same day, for it
is the Day of Atonement, [a]to make atonement for you before the LORD your God.
29For any person who is not [a]afflicted *in
soul* on that same day [b]shall be cut off
from his people. 30And any person who
does any work on that same day, [a]that
person I will destroy from among his people. 31You shall do no manner of work; *it
shall be* a statute forever throughout your
generations in all your dwellings. 32It
shall be to you a sabbath of *solemn* rest,
and you shall [1]afflict your souls; on the
ninth *day* of the month at evening, from
evening to evening, you shall [2]celebrate
your sabbath."

The Feast of Tabernacles

33Then the LORD spoke to Moses, saying, 34"Speak to the children of Israel, saying: [a]'The fifteenth day of this seventh
month *shall be* the Feast of Tabernacles
for seven days to the LORD. 35On the first
day *there shall be* a holy convocation. You
shall do no customary work *on it.* 36*For*
seven days you shall offer an [a]offering
made by fire to the LORD. [b]On the eighth
day you shall have a holy convocation, and
you shall offer an offering made by fire to
the LORD. It *is* a [c]sacred[1] assembly, *and*
you shall do no customary work *on it.*
37[a]'These *are* the feasts of the LORD
which you shall proclaim *to be* holy convocations, to offer an offering made by fire
to the LORD, a burnt offering and a grain
offering, a sacrifice and drink offerings,
everything on its day— 38[a]besides the
Sabbaths of the LORD, besides your gifts,
besides all your vows, and besides all your

freewill offerings which you give to the LORD.

39'Also on the fifteenth day of the seventh month, when you have [a]gathered in the fruit of the land, you shall keep the feast of the LORD *for* seven days; on the first day *there shall be* a sabbath-*rest,* and on the eighth day a sabbath-*rest.* 40And [a]you shall take for yourselves on the first day the [1]fruit of beautiful trees, branches of palm trees, the boughs of leafy trees, and willows of the brook; [b]and you shall rejoice before the LORD your God for seven days. 41[a]You shall keep it as a feast to the LORD for seven days in the year. *It shall be* a statute forever in your generations. You shall celebrate it in the seventh month. 42[a]You shall dwell in [1]booths for seven days. [b]All who are native Israelites shall dwell in booths, 43[a]that your generations may [b]know that I made the children of Israel dwell in booths when [c]I brought them out of the land of Egypt: I *am* the LORD your God.' "

44So Moses [a]declared to the children of Israel the feasts of the LORD.

Care of the Tabernacle Lamps

24 Then the LORD spoke to Moses, saying: 2[a]"Command the children of Israel that they bring to you pure oil of pressed olives for the light, to make the lamps burn continually. 3Outside the veil of the Testimony, in the tabernacle of meeting, Aaron shall be in charge of it from evening until morning before the LORD continually; *it shall be* a statute forever in your generations. 4He shall [1]be in charge of the lamps on [a]the pure *gold* lampstand before the LORD continually.

The Bread of the Tabernacle

5"And you shall take fine flour and bake twelve [a]cakes with it. Two-tenths *of an ephah* shall be in each cake. 6You shall set them in two rows, six in a row, [a]on the pure *gold* table before the LORD. 7And you shall put pure frankincense on *each* row, that it may be on the bread for a [a]memorial, an offering made by fire to the LORD. 8[a]Every Sabbath he shall set it in order before the LORD continually, *being taken* from the children of Israel by an everlasting covenant. 9And [a]it shall be for Aaron and his sons, [b]and they shall eat it in a holy place; for it *is* most holy to him from the offerings of the LORD made by fire, by a perpetual statute."

The Penalty for Blasphemy

10Now the son of an Israelite woman, whose father *was* an Egyptian, went out among the children of Israel; and this Israelite *woman's* son and a man of Israel fought each other in the camp. 11And the Israelite woman's son [a]blasphemed the name *of the LORD* and [b]cursed; and so they [c]brought him to Moses. (His mother's name *was* Shelomith the daughter of Dibri, of the tribe of Dan.) 12Then they [a]put him [1]in custody, [b]that [2]the mind of the LORD might be shown to them.

13And the LORD spoke to Moses, saying, 14"Take outside the camp him who has cursed; then let all who heard *him* [a]lay their hands on his head, and let all the congregation stone him.

15"Then you shall speak to the children of Israel, saying: 'Whoever curses his God [a]shall [1]bear his sin. 16And whoever [a]blasphemes the name of the LORD shall surely be put to death. All the congregation shall certainly stone him, the stranger as well as him who is born in the land. When he blasphemes the name *of the LORD,* he shall be put to death.

17[a]'Whoever kills any man shall surely be put to death. 18[a]Whoever kills an animal shall make it good, animal for animal.

19'If a man causes disfigurement of his neighbor, as [a]he has done, so shall it be done to him— 20fracture for [a]fracture, [b]eye for eye, tooth for tooth; as he has caused disfigurement of a man, so shall it be done to him. 21And whoever kills an animal shall restore it; but whoever kills a man shall be put to death. 22You shall have [a]the[1] same law for the stranger and for one from your own country; for I *am* the LORD your God.' "

23Then Moses spoke to the children of Israel; and they took outside the camp him who had cursed, and stoned him with stones. So the children of Israel did as the LORD commanded Moses.

The Sabbath of the Seventh Year

25 And the LORD spoke to Moses on Mount [a]Sinai, saying, 2"Speak to the children of Israel, and say to them: 'When you come into the land which I give you, then the land shall [a]keep a sab-

---

39 a Ex. 23:16
40 a Neh. 8:15 b Deut. 12:7; 16:14, 15 *1 foliage*
41 a Num. 29:12
42 a [Is. 4:6] b Neh. 8:14–16 *1 tabernacles; shelters made of boughs*
43 a Deut. 31:13 b Ex. 10:2 c Lev. 22:33
44 a Lev. 23:2

CHAPTER 24
2 a Ex. 27:20, 21
4 a Ex. 25:31; 31:8; 37:17 *1 arrange* or *set in order*
5 a Ex. 25:30; 39:36; 40:23
6 a 1 Kin. 7:48
7 a Lev. 2:2, 9, 16
8 a 1 Chr. 9:32
9 a Matt. 12:4 b Ex. 29:33
11 a Ex. 22:28 b Is. 8:21 c Ex. 18:22, 26
12 a Num. 15:34 b Num. 27:5 *1 under guard* *2 Lit. it might be declared to them from the mouth of the LORD*
14 a Deut. 13:9; 17:7
15 a Lev. 20:17 *1 be responsible for*
16 a [Mark 3:28, 29]
17 a Ex. 21:12
18 a Lev. 24:21
19 a Ex. 21:24
20 a Ex. 21:23 b [Matt. 5:38, 39]
22 a Ex. 12:49 *1 one standard of judgment*

CHAPTER 25
1 a Lev. 26:46
2 a Lev. 26:34, 35

bath to the LORD. 3Six years you shall sow your field, and six years you shall prune your vineyard, and gather its fruit; 4but in the [a]seventh year there shall be a sabbath of solemn [b]rest for the land, a sabbath to the LORD. You shall neither sow your field nor prune your vineyard. 5[a]What grows of its own accord of your harvest you shall not reap, nor gather the grapes of your untended vine, *for* it is a year of rest for the land. 6And the sabbath *produce* of the land shall be food for you: for you, your male and female servants, your hired man, and the stranger who dwells with you, 7for your livestock and the beasts that *are* in your land—all its produce shall be for food.

The Year of Jubilee

8'And you shall count seven sabbaths of years for yourself, seven times seven years; and the time of the seven sabbaths of years shall be to you forty-nine years. 9Then you shall cause the trumpet of the Jubilee to sound on the tenth *day* of the seventh month; [a]on the Day of Atonement you shall make the trumpet to sound throughout all your land. 10And you shall consecrate the fiftieth year, and [a]proclaim liberty throughout *all* the land to all its inhabitants. It shall be a Jubilee for you; [b]and each of you shall return to his possession, and each of you shall return to his family. 11That fiftieth year shall be a Jubilee to you; in it [a]you shall neither sow nor reap what grows of its own accord, nor gather *the grapes* of your untended vine. 12For it *is* the Jubilee; it shall be holy to you; [a]you shall eat its produce from the field.

13[a]'In this Year of Jubilee, each of you shall return to his possession. 14And if you sell anything to your neighbor or buy from your neighbor's hand, you shall not [a]oppress one another. 15[a]According to the number of years after the Jubilee you shall buy from your neighbor, and according to the number of years of crops he shall sell to you. 16According to the multitude of years you shall increase its price, and according to the fewer number of years you shall diminish its price; for he sells to you *according* to the number *of the years* of the crops. 17Therefore [a]you shall not [1]oppress one another, [b]but you shall fear your God; for I *am* the LORD your God.

Provisions for the Seventh Year

18[a]'So you shall observe My statutes and keep My judgments, and perform them; [b]and you will dwell in the land in safety. 19Then the land will yield its fruit, and [a]you will eat your fill, and dwell there in safety.

Merciful Father, teach
to walk in Your ways
so they will live safely and
peacefully in a fruitful land.
FROM LEVITICUS 25:18, 19

20'And if you say, [a]"What shall we eat in the seventh year, since [b]we shall not sow nor gather in our produce?" 21Then I will [a]command My blessing on you in the [b]sixth year, and it will bring forth produce enough for three years. 22[a]And you shall sow in the eighth year, and eat [b]old produce until the ninth year; until its produce comes in, you shall eat *of* the old *harvest*.

Redemption of Property

23'The land shall not be sold permanently, for [a]the land *is* Mine; for you *are* [b]strangers and sojourners with Me. 24And in all the land of your possession you shall grant redemption of the land.

25[a]'If one of your brethren becomes poor, and has sold *some* of his possession, and if [b]his redeeming relative comes to redeem it, then he may redeem what his brother sold. 26Or if the man has no one to redeem it, but he himself becomes able to redeem it, 27then [a]let him count the years since its sale, and restore the remainder to the man to whom he sold it, that he may return to his possession. 28But if he is not able to have *it* restored to himself, then what was sold shall remain in the hand of him who bought it until the Year of Jubilee; [a]and in the Jubilee it shall be released, and he shall return to his possession.

29'If a man sells a house in a walled city, then he may redeem it within a whole year after it is sold; *within* a full year he

4 a Deut. 15:1 b [Heb. 4:9]
5 a 2 Kin. 19:29
9 a Lev. 23:24, 27
10 a Jer. 34:8, 15, 17 b Num. 36:4
11 a Lev. 25:5
12 a Lev. 25:6, 7
13 a Lev. 25:10; 27:24
14 a Lev. 19:13
15 a Lev. 27:18, 23
17 a Lev. 25:14 b Lev. 19:14, 32; 25:43 *1 mistreat*
18 a Lev. 19:37 b Deut. 12:10
19 a Lev. 26:5
20 a Matt. 6:25, 31 b Lev. 25:4, 5
21 a Deut. 28:8 b Ex. 16:29
22 a 2 Kin. 19:29 b Josh. 5:11
23 a Ex. 19:5 b Ps. 39:12
25 a Ruth 2:20; 4:4, 6 b Ruth 3:2, 9, 12
27 a Lev. 25:50–52
28 a Lev. 25:10, 13

may redeem it. 30But if it is not redeemed within the space of a full year, then the house in the walled city shall belong permanently to him who bought it, throughout his generations. It shall not be released in the Jubilee. 31However the houses of villages which have no wall around them shall be counted as the fields of the country. They may be redeemed, and they shall be released in the Jubilee. 32Nevertheless [a]the cities of the Levites, *and* the houses in the cities of their possession, the Levites may redeem at any time. 33And if a man purchases a house from the Levites, then the house that was sold in the city of his possession shall be released in the Jubilee; for the houses in the cities of the Levites *are* their possession among the children of Israel. 34But [a]the field of the common-land of their cities may not be [b]sold, for it *is* their perpetual possession.

Lending to the Poor

35'If one of your brethren becomes poor, and [1]falls into poverty among you, then you shall [a]help him, like a stranger or a sojourner, that he may live with you. 36[a]Take no usury or interest from him; but [b]fear your God, that your brother may live with you. 37You shall not lend him your money for usury, nor lend him your food at a profit. 38[a]I *am* the LORD your God, who brought you out of the land of Egypt, to give you the land of Canaan *and* to be your God.

The Law Concerning Slavery

39'And if *one of* your brethren *who dwells* by you becomes poor, and sells himself to you, you shall not compel him to serve as a slave. 40As a hired servant *and* a sojourner he shall be with you, *and* shall serve you until the Year of Jubilee. 41And *then* he shall depart from you—he and his children [a]with him—and shall return to his own family. He shall return to the possession of his fathers. 42For they *are* [a]My servants, whom I brought out of the land of Egypt; they shall not be sold as slaves. 43[a]You shall not rule over him [b]with [1]rigor, but you [c]shall fear your God. 44And as for your male and female slaves whom you may have—from the nations that are around you, from them you may buy male and female slaves. 45Moreover you may buy [a]the children of the strangers who dwell among you, and their families who are with you, which they beget in your land; and they shall become your property. 46And [a]you may take them as an inheritance for your children after you, to inherit *them as* a possession; they shall be your permanent slaves. But regarding your brethren, the children of Israel, you shall not rule over one another with rigor.

47'Now if a sojourner or stranger close to you becomes rich, and *one of* your brethren *who dwells* by him becomes poor, and sells himself to the stranger *or* sojourner close to you, or to a member of the stranger's family, 48after he is sold he may be redeemed again. One of his brothers may redeem him; 49or his uncle or his uncle's son may redeem him; or *anyone* who is near of kin to him in his family may redeem him; or if he is able he may redeem himself. 50Thus he shall reckon with him who bought him: The price of his release shall be according to the number of years, from the year that he was sold to him until the Year of Jubilee; *it shall be* [a]according to the time of a hired servant for him. 51If *there are* still many years *remaining,* according to them he shall repay the price of his redemption from the money with which he was bought. 52And if there remain but a few years until the Year of Jubilee, then he shall reckon with him, *and* according to his years he shall repay him the price of his redemption. 53He shall be with him as a yearly hired servant, and he shall not rule with rigor over him in your sight. 54And if he is not redeemed in these *years,* then he shall be released in the Year of Jubilee—he and his children with him. 55For the children of Israel *are* servants to Me; they *are* My servants whom I brought out of the land of Egypt: I *am* the LORD your God.

Promise of Blessing and Retribution

26 'You shall [a]not make idols for
 yourselves;
neither a carved image nor a *sacred*
 pillar shall you rear up for yourselves;
nor shall you set up an engraved
 stone in your land, to bow down
 to it;
for I *am* the LORD your God.
2 [a]You shall [1]keep My Sabbaths and
 reverence My sanctuary:
 I *am* the LORD.

32 a Num. 35:1–8
34 a Num. 35:2–5 b Acts 4:36, 37
35 a Deut. 15:7–11; 24:14, 15 *1* Lit. *his hand fails*
36 a Ex. 22:25 b Neh. 5:9
38 a Lev. 11:45; 22:32, 33
41 a Ex. 21:3
42 a [Rom. 6:22]
43 a Eph. 6:9 b Ex. 1:13, 14 c Mal. 3:5 *1 severity*
45 a [Is. 56:3, 6, 7]
46 a Is. 14:2
50 a Job 7:1
CHAPTER 26
1 a Ex. 20:4, 5
2 a Lev. 19:30 *1 observe*

3 [a]'If you walk in My statutes and keep My commandments, and perform them,
4 [a]then I will give you rain in its season, [b]the land shall yield its produce, and the trees of the field shall yield their fruit.
5 [a]Your threshing shall last till the time of vintage, and the vintage shall last till the time of sowing;
you shall eat your bread to the full, and [b]dwell in your land safely.
6 [a]I will give peace in the land, and [b]you shall lie down, and none will make *you* afraid;
I will rid the land of [c]evil[1] beasts,
and [d]the sword will not go through your land.
7 You will chase your enemies, and they shall fall by the sword before you.
8 [a]Five of you shall chase a hundred, and a hundred of you shall put ten thousand to flight;
your enemies shall fall by the sword before you.

O Lord, I pray that you will look favorably on ____ as You did on Israel. Make them fruitful, and confirm Your covenant. Walk with them, for You are their God.

FROM LEVITICUS 26:9, 12

9 'For I will [a]look on you favorably and [b]make you fruitful, multiply you and confirm My [c]covenant with you.
10 You shall eat the [a]old harvest, and clear out the old because of the new.
11 [a]I will set My [1]tabernacle among you, and My soul shall not abhor you.
12 [a]I will walk among you and be your God, and you shall be My people.
13 I *am* the LORD your God, who brought you out of the land of Egypt, that *you* should not be their slaves;
I have broken the bands of your [a]yoke and made you walk [1]upright.

3 a Deut. 28:1–14
4 a Is. 30:23 b Ps. 67:6
5 a Amos 9:13 b Lev. 25:18, 19
6 a Is. 45:7 b Job 11:19 c 2 Kin. 17:25 d Ezek. 14:17 1 wild beasts
8 a Deut. 32:30
9 a Ex. 2:25 b Gen. 17:6, 7 c Gen. 17:1–7
10 a Lev. 25:22
11 a Ex. 25:8; 29:45, 46 1 dwelling place
12 a [2 Cor. 6:16]
13 a Gen. 27:40 1 erect
16 a Deut. 28:22 b 1 Sam. 2:33 c Ezek. 24:23; 33:10 d Judg. 6:3–6 1 without profit
17 a Ps. 34:16 b Deut. 28:25 c Ps. 106:41 d Prov. 28:1 1 oppose you
18 a 1 Sam. 2:5
19 a Is. 25:11 b Deut. 28:23
20 a Ps. 127:1 b Gen. 4:12
22 a Deut. 32:24 b Judg. 5:6
23 a Amos 4:6–12
24 a Lev. 26:28, 41
25 a Ezek. 5:17 b Deut. 28:21
26 a Ps. 105:16

14 'But if you do not obey Me, and do not observe all these commandments,
15 and if you despise My statutes, or if your soul abhors My judgments, so that you do not perform all My commandments, *but* break My covenant,
16 I also will do this to you:
I will even appoint terror over you, [a]wasting disease and fever which shall [b]consume the eyes and [c]cause sorrow of heart.
And [d]you shall sow your seed [1]in vain, for your enemies shall eat it.
17 I will [1]set [a]My face against you, and [b]you shall be defeated by your enemies.
[c]Those who hate you shall reign over you, and you shall [d]flee when no one pursues you.
18 'And after all this, if you do not obey Me, then I will punish you [a]seven times more for your sins.
19 I will [a]break the pride of your power;
I [b]will make your heavens like iron and your earth like bronze.
20 And your [a]strength shall be spent in vain;
for your [b]land shall not yield its produce, nor shall the trees of the land yield their fruit.
21 'Then, if you walk contrary to Me, and are not willing to obey Me, I will bring on you seven times more plagues, according to your sins.
22 [a]I will also send wild beasts among you, which shall rob you of your children, destroy your livestock, and make you few in number;
and [b]your highways shall be desolate.
23 'And if [a]by these things you are not reformed by Me, but walk contrary to Me,
24 [a]then I also will walk contrary to you, and I will punish you yet seven times for your sins.
25 And [a]I will bring a sword against you that will execute the vengeance of the covenant;
when you are gathered together within your cities [b]I will send pestilence among you;
and you shall be delivered into the hand of the enemy.
26 [a]When I have cut off your supply of

bread, ten women shall bake your bread in one oven, and they shall bring back your bread by weight,
[b]and you shall eat and not be satisfied.

27 'And after all this, if you do not obey
Me, but walk contrary to Me,
28 then I also will walk contrary to you
in fury;
and I, even I, will chastise you seven
times for your sins.
29 [a]You[1] shall eat the flesh of your sons,
and you shall eat the flesh of your
daughters.
30 [a]I will destroy your high places, cut
down your incense altars, and cast
your carcasses on the lifeless forms
of your idols;
and My soul shall abhor you.
31 I will lay your [a]cities waste and
[b]bring your sanctuaries to desolation, and I will not [c]smell the fragrance of your [1]sweet aromas.
32 [a]I will bring the land to desolation,
and your enemies who dwell in it
shall be astonished at it.
33 [a]I will scatter you among the nations
and draw out a sword after you;
your land shall be desolate and your
cities waste.
34 [a]Then the land shall enjoy its sabbaths as long as it lies desolate and
you *are* in your enemies' land;
then the land shall rest and enjoy its
sabbaths.
35 As long as *it* lies desolate it shall
rest—
for the time it did not rest on your
[a]sabbaths when you dwelt in it.

36 'And as for those of you who are left,
I will send [a]faintness[1] into their
hearts in the lands of their enemies;
the sound of a shaken leaf shall cause
them to flee;
they shall flee as though fleeing from
a sword, and they shall fall when
no one pursues.
37 [a]They shall stumble over one another, as it were before a sword, when
no one pursues;
and [b]you shall have no *power* to stand
before your enemies.
38 You shall [a]perish among the nations, and the land of your enemies
shall eat you up.
39 And those of you who are left [a]shall
[1]waste away in their iniquity in
your enemies' lands;
also in their [b]fathers' iniquities,
which are with them, they shall
waste away.

40 '*But* [a]if they confess their iniquity
and the iniquity of their fathers,
with their unfaithfulness in which
they were unfaithful to Me, and
that they also have walked contrary to Me,
41 and *that* I also have walked contrary
to them and have brought them
into the land of their enemies;
if their [a]uncircumcised hearts are
[b]humbled, and they [c]accept their
guilt—
42 then I will [a]remember My covenant
with Jacob, and My covenant with
Isaac and My covenant with Abraham I will remember;
I will [b]remember the land.
43 [a]The land also shall be left empty by
them, and will enjoy its sabbaths
while it lies desolate without them;
they will accept their guilt, because
they [b]despised My judgments and
because their soul abhorred My
statutes.
44 Yet for all that, when they are in the
land of their enemies, [a]I will not
cast them away, nor shall I abhor
them, to utterly destroy them and
break My covenant with them;
for I *am* the LORD their God.
45 But [a]for their sake I will remember
the covenant of their ancestors,
[b]whom I brought out of the land of
Egypt [c]in the sight of the nations,
that I might be their God:
I *am* the LORD.' "

46 [a]These *are* the statutes and judgments and laws which the LORD made between Himself and the children of Israel
[b]on Mount Sinai by the hand of Moses.

Redeeming Persons and Property Dedicated to God

27 Now the LORD spoke to Moses, saying, 2"Speak to the children of Israel, and say to them: [a]'When a man
[1]consecrates by a vow certain persons to
the LORD, according to your [2]valuation,
3if your valuation is of a male from twenty
years old up to sixty years old, then your

26 [b] Mic. 6:14
29 [a] 2 Kin. 6:28, 29 *[1] In time of famine*
30 [a] 2 Chr. 34:3
31 [a] 2 Kin. 25:4, 10 [b] Ps. 74:7 [c] Is. 1:11–15 *[1] pleasing*
32 [a] Jer. 9:11; 18:16
33 [a] Deut. 4:27
34 [a] 2 Chr. 36:21
35 [a] Lev. 25:2
36 [a] Ezek. 21:7, 12, 15 *[1] fear*
37 [a] 1 Sam. 14:15, 16 [b] Josh. 7:12, 13
38 [a] Deut. 4:26
39 [a] Ezek. 4:17; 33:10 [b] Ex. 34:7 *[1] rot away*
40 [a] Neh. 9:2
41 [a] Acts 7:51 [b] 2 Chr. 12:6, 7, 12 [c] Dan. 9:7
42 [a] Ex. 2:24; 6:5 [b] Ps. 136:23
43 [a] Lev. 26:34, 35 [b] Lev. 26:15
44 [a] Deut. 4:31
45 [a] [Rom. 11:28] [b] Lev. 22:33; 25:38 [c] Ps. 98:2
46 [a] [John 1:17] [b] Lev. 25:1

CHAPTER 27
2 [a] Num. 6:2 *[1] Or makes a difficult or extraordinary vow* *[2] appraisal*

valuation shall be fifty shekels of silver,
[a]according to the shekel of the sanctuary.
4If it *is* a female, then your valuation shall
be thirty shekels; 5and if from five years
old up to twenty years old, then your valuation for a male shall be twenty shekels,
and for a female ten shekels; 6and if from
a month old up to five years old, then your
valuation for a male shall be five shekels
of silver, and for a female your valuation
shall be three shekels of silver; 7and if
from sixty years old and above, if *it is* a
male, then your valuation shall be fifteen
shekels, and for a female ten shekels.

8'But if he is too poor to pay your valuation, then he shall present himself before
the priest, and the priest shall set a value
for [a]him; according to the ability of him
who vowed, the priest shall value him.

9'If *it is* an animal that men may bring
as an offering to the LORD, all that *anyone*
gives to the LORD shall be holy. 10He shall
not substitute it or exchange it, good for
bad or bad for good; and if he at all exchanges animal for animal, then both it
and the one exchanged for it shall be
[a]holy. 11If *it is* an unclean animal which
they do not offer as a sacrifice to the LORD,
then he shall present the animal before
the priest; 12and the priest shall set a value for it, whether it is good or bad; as you,
the priest, value it, so it shall be. 13[a]But if
he *wants* at all *to* redeem it, then he must
add one-fifth to your valuation.

14'And when a man [1]dedicates his
house *to be* holy to the LORD, then the
priest shall set a value for it, whether it is
good or bad; as the priest values it, so it
shall stand. 15If he who dedicated it *wants*
to [1]redeem his house, then he must add
one-fifth of the money of your valuation
to it, and it shall be his.

16'If a man [1]dedicates to the LORD *part*
of a field of his possession, then your valuation shall be according to the seed for it.
A homer of barley seed *shall be valued* at
fifty shekels of silver. 17If he dedicates his
field from the Year of Jubilee, according
to your valuation it shall stand. 18But if he
dedicates his field after the Jubilee, then
the priest shall [a]reckon to him the money
due according to the years that remain till
the Year of Jubilee, and it shall be deduct-
ed from your valuation. 19And if he who
dedicates the field ever wishes to redeem
it, then he must add one-fifth of the
money of your valuation to it, and it shall
belong to him. 20But if he does not want
to redeem the field, or if he has sold the
field to another man, it shall not be redeemed anymore; 21but the field, [a]when
it is released in the Jubilee, shall be holy
to the LORD, as a [b]devoted field; it shall
be [c]the possession of the priest.

22'And if a man dedicates to the LORD a
field which he has bought, which is not
the field of [a]his possession, 23then the
priest shall reckon to him the worth of
your valuation, up to the Year of Jubilee,
and he shall give your valuation on that
day *as* a holy *offering* to the LORD. 24[a]In
the Year of Jubilee the field shall return to
him from whom it was bought, to the one
who *owned* the land as a possession. 25And
all your valuations shall be according to
the shekel of the sanctuary: [a]twenty gerahs to the shekel.

26'But the [a]firstborn of the animals,
which should be the LORD's firstborn, no
man shall dedicate; whether *it is* an ox or
sheep, it *is* the LORD's. 27And if *it is* an
unclean animal, then he shall redeem *it*
according to your valuation, and [a]shall
add one-fifth to it; or if it is not redeemed,
then it shall be sold according to your valuation.

28[a]'Nevertheless no [1]devoted *offering*
that a man may devote to the LORD of all
that he has, *both* man and beast, or the
field of his possession, shall be sold or redeemed; every devoted *offering is* most
holy to the LORD. 29[a]No person under the
ban, who may become doomed to destruction among men, shall be redeemed, *but*
shall surely be put to death. 30And [a]all the
tithe of the land, *whether* of the seed of
the land *or* of the fruit of the tree, *is* the
LORD's. It *is* holy to the LORD. 31[a]If a man
wants at all to redeem *any* of his tithes, he
shall add one-fifth to it. 32And concerning
the tithe of the herd or the flock, of whatever [a]passes under the rod, the tenth one
shall be holy to the LORD. 33He shall not
inquire whether it is good or bad, [a]nor
shall he exchange it; and if he exchanges
it at all, then both it and the one exchanged for it shall be holy; it shall not be
redeemed.' "

34[a]These *are* the commandments
which the LORD commanded Moses for
the children of Israel on Mount [b]Sinai.

3 a Ex. 30:13
8 a Lev. 5:11; 14:21–24
10 a Lev. 27:33
13 a Lev. 6:5; 22:14; 27:15, 19
14 *1 sets apart*
15 *1 buy back*
16 *1 sets apart*
18 a Lev. 25:15, 16, 28
21 a Lev. 25:10, 28, 31 b Lev. 27:28 c Num. 18:14
22 a Lev. 25:10, 25
24 a Lev. 25:10–13, 28
25 a Ex. 30:13
26 a Ex. 13:2, 12; 22:30
27 a Lev. 27:11, 12
28 a Josh. 6:17–19 *1* Given exclusively and irrevocably
29 a Num. 21:2
30 a Gen. 28:22
31 a Lev. 27:13
32 a Jer. 33:13
33 a Lev. 27:10
34 a Lev. 26:46 b [Heb. 12:18–29]

AUTHOR: *Traditionally Moses*
DATE: *Approximately 1400 B.C.*
THEME: *Yahweh's Guiding Presence for the Journey from Sinai to Transjordan*
KEY WORDS: *Census, Murmuring, Purity, Tabernacle of Meeting*

NUMBERS

Dear Woman of Destiny,

The Book of Numbers is important to women, because we are concerned for our offspring and our generations. We want God's name on our children so that He will bless them. We desire to see them spared the pain of sin and rebellion. As you read and pray, meditate on the goodness of God's mercy and the sacrifice of His Son.

His love and mine,

Marilyn Hickey

The First Census of Israel

Now the LORD spoke to Moses [a]in
the Wilderness of Sinai, [b]in the
tabernacle of meeting, on the
[c]first *day* of the second month, in the second year after they had come out of the
land of Egypt, saying: 2[a]"Take a census of
all the congregation of the children of Israel, by their families, by their fathers'
houses, according to the number of
names, every male [b]individually, 3from
[a]twenty years old and above—all who *are*
able to go to war in Israel. You and Aaron
shall number them by their armies. 4And
with you there shall be a man from every
tribe, each one the head of his father's
house.
5"These are the names of the men who
shall stand with you: from Reuben, Elizur
the son of Shedeur; 6from Simeon, Shelumiel the son of Zurishaddai; 7from Judah,
Nahshon the son of Amminadab; 8from Issachar, Nethanel the son of Zuar; 9from
Zebulun, Eliab the son of Helon; 10from
the sons of Joseph: from Ephraim, Elishama the son of Ammihud; from Manasseh,
Gamaliel the son of Pedahzur; 11from
Benjamin, Abidan the son of Gideoni;
12from Dan, Ahiezer the son of Ammishaddai; 13from Asher, Pagiel the son of
Ocran; 14from Gad, Eliasaph the son of
[a]Deuel;[1] 15from Naphtali, Ahira the son of
Enan." 16[a]These *were* [b]chosen[1] from the
congregation, leaders of their fathers'
tribes, [c]heads of the divisions in Israel.
17Then Moses and Aaron took these
men who had been [1]mentioned [a]by name,
18and they assembled all the congregation
together on the first *day* of the second
month; and they recited their [a]ancestry
by families, by their fathers' houses, according to the number of names, from
twenty years old and above, each one individually. 19As the LORD commanded Moses, so he numbered them in the
Wilderness of Sinai.
20Now the [a]children of Reuben, Israel's
oldest son, their genealogies by their families, by their fathers' house, according to
the number of names, every male individually, from twenty years old and above,
all who *were able to* go to war: 21those
who were numbered of the tribe of Reuben *were* forty-six thousand five hundred.
22From the [a]children of Simeon, their
genealogies by their families, by their fathers' house, of those who were numbered, according to the number of names,
every male individually, from twenty
years old and above, all who *were able to*
go to war: 23those who were numbered of
the tribe of Simeon *were* fifty-nine thousand three hundred.
24From the [a]children of Gad, their genealogies by their families, by their fathers' house, according to the number of
names, from twenty years old and above,
all who *were able to* go to war: 25those
who were numbered of the tribe of Gad
were forty-five thousand six hundred and
fifty.
26From the [a]children of Judah, their
genealogies by their families, by their fathers' house, according to the number of
names, from twenty years old and above,
all who *were able to* go to war: 27those
who were numbered of the tribe of Judah
were [a]seventy-four thousand six hundred.
28From the [a]children of Issachar, their
genealogies by their families, by their fathers' house, according to the number of
names, from twenty years old and above,
all who *were able to* go to war: 29those
who were numbered of the tribe of Issachar *were* fifty-four thousand four hundred.
30From the [a]children of Zebulun, their
genealogies by their families, by their fathers' house, according to the number of
names, from twenty years old and above,
all who *were able to* go to war: 31those
who were numbered of the tribe of Zebulun *were* fifty-seven thousand four hundred.
32From the sons of Joseph, the [a]chil-
dren of Ephraim, their genealogies by
their families, by their fathers' house, according to the number of names, from
twenty years old and above, all who *were*
able to go to war: 33those who were numbered of the tribe of Ephraim *were* forty
thousand five hundred.
34From the [a]children of Manasseh,
their genealogies by their families, by
their fathers' house, according to the
number of names, from twenty years old
and above, all who *were able to* go to war:
35those who were numbered of the tribe of
Manasseh *were* thirty-two thousand two
hundred.
36From the [a]children of Benjamin,
their genealogies by their families, by
their fathers' house, according to the
number of names, from twenty years old
and above, all who *were able to* go to war:

CHAPTER 1
1 [a]Ex. 19:1 [b]Ex. 25:22 [c]Num. 9:1; 10:11
2 [a]Num. 26:2, 63, 64 [b]Ex. 30:12, 13; 38:26
3 [a]Ex. 30:14; 38:26
14 [a]Num. 7:42 [1] *Reuel,* Num. 2:14
16 [a]Num. 7:2 [b]Num. 16:2 [c]Ex. 18:21, 25 [1] *called*
17 [a]Is. 43:1 [1] *designated*
18 [a]Ezra 2:59
20 [a]Num. 2:10, 11; 26:5–11; 32:6, 15, 21, 29
22 [a]Num. 2:12, 13; 26:12–14
24 [a]Num. 26:15–18
26 [a]2 Sam. 24:9
27 [a]2 Chr. 17:14
28 [a]Num. 2:5, 6
30 [a]Num. 2:7, 8; 26:26, 27
32 [a]Num. 26:28–37
34 [a]Num. 2:20, 21; 26:28–34
36 [a]Num. 26:38–41

[37]those who were numbered of the tribe of Benjamin *were* thirty-five thousand four hundred.

[38]From the [a]children of Dan, their genealogies by their families, by their fathers' house, according to the number of names, from twenty years old and above, all who *were able to* go to war: [39]those who were numbered of the tribe of Dan *were* sixty-two thousand seven hundred.

[40]From the [a]children of Asher, their genealogies by their families, by their fathers' house, according to the number of names, from twenty years old and above, all who *were able to* go to war: [41]those who were numbered of the tribe of Asher *were* forty-one thousand five hundred.

[42]From the children of Naphtali, their genealogies by their families, by their fathers' house, according to the number of names, from twenty years old and above, all who *were able to* go to war: [43]those who were numbered of the tribe of Naphtali *were* fifty-three thousand four hundred.

[44][a]These are the ones who were numbered, whom Moses and Aaron numbered, with the leaders of Israel, twelve men, each one representing his father's house. [45]So all who were numbered of the children of Israel, by their fathers' houses, from twenty years old and above, all who *were able to* go to war in Israel— [46]all who were numbered were [a]six hundred and three thousand five hundred and fifty.

[47]But [a]the Levites were not numbered among them by their fathers' tribe; [48]for the LORD had spoken to Moses, saying: [49][a]"Only the tribe of Levi you shall not number, nor take a census of them among the children of Israel; [50][a]but you shall appoint the Levites over the tabernacle of the Testimony, over all its furnishings, and over all things that belong to it; they shall carry the tabernacle and all its furnishings; they shall attend to it [b]and camp around the tabernacle. [51][a]And when the tabernacle is to go forward, the Levites shall take it down; and when the tabernacle is to be set up, the Levites shall set it [b]up. [c]The outsider who comes near shall be put to death. [52]The children of Israel shall pitch their tents, [a]everyone by his own camp, everyone by his own standard, according to their armies; [53][a]but the Levites shall camp around the tabernacle of the Testimony, that there may be no [b]wrath on the congregation of the children of Israel; and the Levites shall [c]keep[1] charge of the tabernacle of the Testimony."

[54]Thus the children of Israel did; according to all that the LORD commanded Moses, so they did.

The Tribes and Leaders by Armies

2 And the LORD spoke to Moses and Aaron, saying: [2][a]"Everyone of the children of Israel shall camp by his own [1]standard, beside the emblems of his father's house; they shall camp [b]some distance from the tabernacle of meeting. [3]On the [a]east side, toward the rising of the sun, those of the standard of the forces with Judah shall camp according to their armies; and [b]Nahshon the son of Amminadab *shall be* the leader of the children of Judah." [4]And his army was numbered at seventy-four thousand six hundred.

[5]"Those who camp next to him *shall be* the tribe of Issachar, and Nethanel the son of Zuar *shall be* the leader of the children of Issachar." [6]And his army was numbered at fifty-four thousand four hundred.

[7]"Then *comes* the tribe of Zebulun, and Eliab the son of Helon *shall be* the leader of the children of Zebulun." [8]And his army was numbered at fifty-seven thousand four hundred. [9]"All who were numbered according to their armies of the forces with Judah, one hundred and eighty-six thousand four hundred— [a]these shall [1]break camp first.

[10]"On the [a]south side *shall be* the standard of the forces with Reuben according to their armies, and the leader of the children of Reuben *shall be* Elizur the son of Shedeur." [11]And his army was numbered at forty-six thousand five hundred.

[12]"Those who camp next to him *shall be* the tribe of Simeon, and the leader of the children of Simeon *shall be* Shelumiel the son of Zurishaddai." [13]And his army was numbered at fifty-nine thousand three hundred.

[14]"Then *comes* the tribe of Gad, and the leader of the children of Gad *shall be* Eliasaph the son of [1]Reuel." [15]And his army was numbered at forty-five thousand six hundred and fifty. [16]"All who were numbered according to their armies of the forces with Reuben, one hundred and fifty-one thousand four hundred and fifty— [a]they shall [1]be the second to break camp.

38 a Gen. 30:6; 46:23
40 a Num. 2:27, 28; 26:44–47
44 a Num. 26:64
46 a Ex. 12:37; 38:26
47 a Num. 2:33; 3:14–22; 26:57–62
49 a Num. 2:33; 26:62
50 a Ex. 38:21 b Num. 3:23, 29, 35, 38
51 a Num. 4:5–15; 10:17, 21 b Num. 10:21 c Num. 3:10, 38; 4:15, 19, 20; 18:22
52 a Num. 2:2, 34; 24:2
53 a Num. 1:50 b Lev. 10:6 c 1 Chr. 23:32 *1 have in their care*

CHAPTER 2
2 a Num. 1:52; 24:2 b Josh. 3:4 *1 banner*
3 a Num. 10:5 b 1 Chr. 2:10
9 a Num. 10:14 *1 Lit. set forth*
10 a Num. 10:6
14 *1 Deuel,* Num. 1:14; 7:42
16 a Num. 10:18 *1 Lit. set forth second*

17[a]"And the tabernacle of meeting shall
move out with the [1]camp of the Levites
[b]in the middle of the [2]camps; as they
camp, so they shall move out, everyone in
his place, by their [3]standards.
18"On the west side *shall be* the standard of the forces with Ephraim according
to their armies, and the leader of the children of Ephraim *shall be* Elishama the
son of Ammihud." 19And his army was
numbered at forty thousand five hundred.
20"Next to him *comes* the tribe of Manasseh, and the leader of the children of
Manasseh *shall be* Gamaliel the son of Pedahzur." 21And his army was numbered at
thirty-two thousand two hundred.
22"Then *comes* the tribe of Benjamin,
and the leader of the children of Benjamin
shall be Abidan the son of Gideoni." 23And
his army was numbered at thirty-five
thousand four hundred. 24"All who were
numbered according to their armies of
the forces with Ephraim, one hundred
and eight thousand one hundred—[a]they
shall [1]be the third to break camp.
25"The [1]standard of the forces with Dan
shall be on the north side according to
their armies, and the leader of the children of Dan *shall be* Ahiezer the son of
Ammishaddai." 26And his army was numbered at sixty-two thousand seven hundred.
27"Those who camp next to him *shall
be* the tribe of Asher, and the leader of the
children of Asher *shall be* Pagiel the son
of Ocran." 28And his army was numbered
at forty-one thousand five hundred.
29"Then *comes* the tribe of Naphtali,
and the leader of the children of Naphtali
shall be Ahira the son of Enan." 30And his
army was numbered at fifty-three thousand four hundred. 31"All who were numbered of the forces with Dan, one hundred
and fifty-seven thousand six hundred—
[a]they shall [1]break camp last, with their
[2]standards."
32These *are* the ones who were numbered of the children of Israel by their fathers' houses. [a]All who were numbered
according to their armies of the forces
were six hundred and three thousand five
hundred and fifty. 33But [a]the Levites were
not numbered among the children of Israel, just as the LORD commanded Moses.
34Thus the children of Israel [a]did according to all that the LORD commanded
Moses; [b]so they camped by their [1]stan-
dards and so they broke camp, each one
by his family, according to their fathers'
houses.

The Sons of Aaron

3 Now these *are* the [a]records[1] of Aaron
and Moses when the LORD spoke with
Moses on Mount Sinai. 2And these *are* the
names of the sons of Aaron: Nadab, the
[a]firstborn, and [b]Abihu, Eleazar, and Ithamar. 3These *are* the names of the sons of
Aaron, [a]the anointed priests, [1]whom he
consecrated to minister as priests. 4[a]Na-
dab and Abihu had died before the LORD
when they offered profane fire before the
LORD in the Wilderness of Sinai; and they
had no children. So Eleazar and Ithamar
ministered as priests in the presence of
Aaron their father.

The Levites Serve in the Tabernacle

5And the LORD spoke to Moses, saying:
6[a]"Bring the tribe of Levi near, and present them before Aaron the priest, that
they may serve him. 7And they shall attend to his needs and the needs of the
whole congregation before the tabernacle
of meeting, to do [a]the work of the tabernacle. 8Also they shall attend to all the
furnishings of the tabernacle of meeting,
and to the needs of the children of Israel,
to do the work of the tabernacle. 9And
[a]you shall give the Levites to Aaron and
his sons; they *are* given entirely to [1]him
from among the children of Israel. 10So
you shall appoint Aaron and his sons,
[a]and they shall attend to their priesthood;
[b]but the outsider who comes near shall be
put to death."
11Then the LORD spoke to Moses, saying: 12"Now behold, [a]I Myself have taken
the Levites from among the children of
Israel instead of every firstborn who opens
the womb among the children of Israel.
Therefore the Levites shall be [b]Mine, 13be-
cause [a]all the firstborn *are* Mine. [b]On the
day that I struck all the firstborn in the
land of Egypt, I sanctified to Myself all the
firstborn in Israel, both man and beast.
They shall be Mine: I *am* the LORD."

Census of the Levites Commanded

14Then the LORD spoke to Moses in the
Wilderness of Sinai, saying: 15"Number
the children of Levi by their fathers' houses, by their families; you shall number

17 [a] Num. 10:17, 21 [b] Num. 1:53 [1] *company* [2] *whole company* [3] *banners*
24 [a] Num. 10:22 [1] Lit. *set forth third*
25 [1] *banner*
31 [a] Num. 10:25 [1] Lit. *set forth last* [2] *banners*
32 [a] Ex. 38:26
33 [a] Num. 1:47; 26:57–62
34 [a] Num. 1:54 [b] Num. 24:2, 5, 6 [1] *banners*

CHAPTER 3
1 [a] Ex. 6:16–27 [1] Lit. *generations*
2 [a] Ex. 6:23 [b] Num. 26:60, 61
3 [a] Ex. 28:41 [1] Lit. *whose hands he filled*
4 [a] 1 Chr. 24:2
6 [a] Num. 8:6–22; 18:1–7
7 [a] Num. 1:50; 8:11, 15, 24, 26
9 [a] Num. 8:19; 18:6, 7 [1] Sam., LXX *Me*
10 [a] Ex. 29:9 [b] Num. 1:51; 3:38; 16:40
12 [a] Num. 3:41; 8:16; 18:6 [b] Num. 3:45; 8:14
13 [a] Ex. 13:2 [b] Num. 8:17

[a]every male from a month old and above."

16 So Moses numbered them according to the [1]word of the LORD, as he was commanded. 17 [a]These were the sons of Levi by their names: Gershon, Kohath, and Merari. 18 And these *are* the names of the sons of [a]Gershon by their families: [b]Libni and Shimei. 19 And the sons of [a]Kohath by their families: [b]Amram, Izehar, Hebron, and Uzziel. 20 [a]And the sons of Merari by their families: Mahli and Mushi. These *are* the families of the Levites by their fathers' houses.

21 From Gershon *came* the family of the Libnites and the family of the Shimites; these *were* the families of the Gershonites. 22 Those who were numbered, according to the number of all the males from a month old and above—of those who were numbered *there were* seven thousand five hundred. 23 [a]The families of the Gershonites were to camp behind the tabernacle westward. 24 And the leader of the father's house of the Gershonites *was* Eliasaph the son of Lael. 25 [a]The duties of the children of Gershon in the tabernacle of meeting *included* [b]the tabernacle, [c]the tent with [d]its covering, [e]the screen for the door of the tabernacle of meeting, 26 [a]the screen for the door of the court, [b]the hangings of the court which *are* around the tabernacle and the altar, and [c]their cords, according to all the work relating to them.

27 [a]From Kohath *came* the family of the Amramites, the family of the Izharites, the family of the Hebronites, and the family of the Uzzielites; these *were* the families of the Kohathites. 28 According to the number of all the males, from a month old and above, *there were* eight thousand [1]six hundred [2]keeping charge of the sanctuary. 29 [a]The families of the children of Kohath were to camp on the south side of the tabernacle. 30 And the leader of the fathers' house of the families of the Kohathites *was* Elizaphan the son of [a]Uzziel. 31 [a]Their duty *included* [b]the ark, [c]the table, [d]the lampstand, [e]the altars, the utensils of the sanctuary with which they ministered, [f]the screen, and all the work relating to them.

32 And Eleazar the son of Aaron the priest *was to be* chief over the leaders of the Levites, *with* oversight of those who kept charge of the sanctuary.

33 From Merari *came* the family of the Mahlites and the family of the Mushites; these *were* the families of Merari. 34 And those who were numbered, according to the number of all the males from a month old and above, *were* six thousand two hundred. 35 The leader of the fathers' house of the families of Merari *was* Zuriel the son of Abihail. [a]These *were* to camp on the north side of the tabernacle. 36 And [a]the appointed duty of the children of Merari *included* the boards of the tabernacle, its bars, its pillars, its sockets, its utensils, all the work relating to them, 37 and the pillars of the court all around, with their sockets, their pegs, and their cords.

38 [a]Moreover those who were to camp before the tabernacle on the east, before the tabernacle of meeting, *were* Moses, Aaron, and his sons, [b]keeping charge of the sanctuary, [c]to meet the needs of the children of Israel; but [d]the outsider who came near was to be put to death. 39 [a]All who were numbered of the Levites, whom Moses and Aaron numbered at the commandment of the LORD, by their families, all the males from a month old and above, *were* twenty-two thousand.

Levites Dedicated Instead of the Firstborn

40 Then the LORD said to Moses: [a]"Number[1] all the firstborn males of the children of Israel from a month old and above, and take the number of their names. 41 [a]And you shall take the Levites for Me—I *am* the LORD—instead of all the firstborn among the children of Israel, and the livestock of the Levites instead of all the firstborn among the livestock of the children of Israel." 42 So Moses numbered all the firstborn among the children of Israel, as the LORD commanded him. 43 And all the firstborn males, according to the number of names from a month old and above, of those who were numbered of them, were twenty-two thousand two hundred and seventy-three.

44 Then the LORD spoke to Moses, saying: 45 [a]"Take the Levites instead of all the firstborn among the children of Israel, and the livestock of the Levites instead of their livestock. The Levites shall be Mine: I *am* the LORD. 46 And for [a]the redemption of the two hundred and seventy-three of the firstborn of the children of Israel, [b]who are more than the number of the Levites, 47 you shall take [a]five shekels for each one [b]individually; you shall take *them* in the currency of the shekel of the sanctuary, [c]the shekel of twenty gerahs.

---

15 a Num. 3:39; 26:62
16 1 Lit. *mouth*
17 a Ex. 6:16–22
18 a Num. 4:38–41 b Ex. 6:17
19 a Num. 4:34–37 b Ex. 6:18
20 a Ex. 6:19
23 a Num. 1:53
25 a Num. 4:24–26 b Ex. 25:9 c Ex. 26:1 d Ex. 26:7, 14 e Ex. 26:36
26 a Ex. 27:9, 12, 14, 15 b Ex. 27:16 c Ex. 35:18
27 a 1 Chr. 26:23
28 1 Some LXX mss. *three* 2 *taking care of*
29 a Num. 1:53
30 a Lev. 10:4
31 a Num. 4:15 b Ex. 25:10 c Ex. 25:23 d Ex. 25:31 e Ex. 27:1; 30:1 f Ex. 26:31–33
35 a Num. 1:53; 2:25
36 a Num. 4:31, 32
38 a Num. 1:53 b Num. 18:5 c Num. 3:7, 8 d Num. 3:10
39 a Num. 3:43; 4:48; 26:62
40 a Num. 3:15 1 *Take a census of*
41 a Num. 3:12, 45
45 a Num. 3:12, 41
46 a Ex. 13:13, 15 b Num. 3:39, 43
47 a Lev. 27:6 b Num. 1:2, 18, 20 c Ex. 30:13

48 And you shall give the money, with
which the excess number of them is redeemed, to Aaron and his sons."
49 So Moses took the redemption money
from those who were over and above those
who were redeemed by the Levites.
50 From the firstborn of the children of Israel he took the money, [a]one thousand
three hundred and sixty-five *shekels,* according to the shekel of the sanctuary.
51 And Moses [a]gave their redemption money to Aaron and his sons, according to the
word of the LORD, as the LORD commanded Moses.

Duties of the Sons of Kohath

4 Then the LORD spoke to Moses and
Aaron, saying: 2 "Take a census of the
sons of [a]Kohath from among the children
of Levi, by their families, by their fathers'
house, 3 [a]from thirty years old and above,
even to fifty years old, all who enter the
service to do the work in the tabernacle of
meeting.
4 [a]"This *is* the service of the sons of Kohath in the tabernacle of meeting, *relating to* [b]the most holy things: 5 When the
camp prepares to journey, Aaron and his
sons shall come, and they shall take down
[a]the covering veil and cover the [b]ark of
the Testimony with it. 6 Then they shall
put on it a covering of badger skins, and
spread over *that* a cloth entirely of [a]blue;
and they shall insert [b]its poles.
7 "On the [a]table of showbread they shall
spread a blue cloth, and put on it the dishes, the pans, the bowls, and the [1]pitchers
for pouring; and the [b]showbread[2] shall be
on it. 8 They shall spread over them a scarlet cloth, and cover the same with a covering of badger skins; and they shall insert
its poles. 9 And they shall take a blue cloth
and cover the [a]lampstand of the light,
[b]with its lamps, its wick-trimmers, its
trays, and all its oil vessels, with which
they service it. 10 Then they shall put it
with all its utensils in a covering of badger
skins, and put *it* on a carrying beam.
11 "Over [a]the golden altar they shall
spread a blue cloth, and cover it with a
covering of badger skins; and they shall
insert its poles. 12 Then they shall take all
the [a]utensils of service with which they
minister in the sanctuary, put *them* in a
blue cloth, cover them with a covering of
badger skins, and put *them* on a carrying
beam. 13 Also they shall take away the ashes from the altar, and spread a purple
cloth over it. 14 They shall put on it all its
implements with which they minister
there—the firepans, the forks, the shovels, the [1]basins, and all the utensils of the
altar—and they shall spread on it a covering of badger skins, and insert its poles.
15 And when Aaron and his sons have finished covering the sanctuary and all the
furnishings of the sanctuary, when the
camp is set to go, then [a]the sons of Kohath shall come to carry *them;* [b]but they
shall not touch any holy thing, lest they
die.
[c]"These *are* the things in the tabernacle of meeting which the sons of Kohath
are to carry.
16 "The appointed duty of Eleazar the
son of Aaron the priest *is* [a]the oil for the
light, the [b]sweet incense, [c]the daily grain
offering, the [d]anointing oil, the oversight
of all the tabernacle, of all that *is* in it,
with the sanctuary and its furnishings."
17 Then the LORD spoke to Moses and
Aaron, saying: 18 "Do not cut off the tribe
of the families of the Kohathites from
among the Levites; 19 but do this in regard
to them, that they may live and not die
when they approach [a]the most holy
things: Aaron and his sons shall go in and
[1]appoint each of them to his service and
his task. 20 [a]But they shall not go in to
watch while the holy things are being covered, lest they die."

Duties of the Sons of Gershon

21 Then the LORD spoke to Moses, saying: 22 "Also take a census of the sons of
[a]Gershon, by their fathers' house, by their
families. 23 [a]From thirty years old and
above, even to fifty years old, you shall
number them, all who enter to perform
the service, to do the work in the tabernacle of meeting. 24 This *is* the [a]service of the
families of the Gershonites, in serving and
carrying: 25 [a]They shall carry the [b]curtains
of the tabernacle and the tabernacle of
meeting *with* its covering, the covering of
[c]badger skins that *is* on it, the screen for
the door of the tabernacle of meeting,
26 the screen for the door of the gate of the
court, the hangings of the court which
are around the tabernacle and altar, and
their cords, all the furnishings for their
service and all that is made for these
things: so shall they serve.
27 "Aaron and his sons shall [1]assign all
the service of the sons of the Gershonites,
all their tasks and all their service. And

---

50 a Num. 3:46, 47
51 a Num. 3:48

CHAPTER 4
2 a Num. 3:27–32
3 a Num. 4:23, 30, 35; 8:24
4 a Num. 4:15 b Num. 4:19
5 a Ex. 26:31 b Ex. 25:10, 16
6 a Ex. 39:1 b Ex. 25:13
7 a Ex. 25:23, 29, 30 b Lev. 24:5–9 *1 jars for the drink offering* *2 Lit. continual bread*
9 a Ex. 25:31 b Ex. 25:37, 38
11 a Ex. 30:1–5
12 a Ex. 25:9
14 *1 bowls*
15 a Deut. 31:9 b 2 Sam. 6:6, 7 c Num. 3:31
16 a Lev. 24:2 b Ex. 30:34 c Ex. 29:38 d Ex. 30:23–25
19 a Num. 4:4 *1 assign*
20 a Ex. 19:21
22 a Num. 3:22
23 a Num. 4:3
24 a Num. 7:7
25 a Num. 3:25, 26 b Ex. 36:8 c Ex. 26:14
27 *1 command*

you shall [2]appoint to them all their tasks as their duty. 28This *is* the service of the families of the sons of Gershon in the tabernacle of meeting. And their duties *shall be* [a]under the [1]authority of Ithamar the son of Aaron the priest.

Duties of the Sons of Merari

29"*As for* the sons of [a]Merari, you shall number them by their families and by their fathers' house. 30[a]From thirty years old and above, even to fifty years old, you shall number them, everyone who enters the service to do the work of the tabernacle of meeting. 31And [a]this *is* [b]what they must carry as all their service for the tabernacle of meeting: [c]the boards of the tabernacle, its bars, its pillars, its sockets, 32and the pillars around the court with their sockets, pegs, and cords, with all their furnishings and all their service; and you shall [a]assign *to each man* by name the items he must carry. 33This *is* the service of the families of the sons of Merari, as all their service for the tabernacle of meeting, under the [1]authority of Ithamar the son of Aaron the priest."

Census of the Levites

34[a]And Moses, Aaron, and the leaders of the congregation numbered the sons of the Kohathites by their families and by their fathers' house, 35from thirty [a]years old and above, even to fifty years old, everyone who entered the service for work in the tabernacle of meeting; 36and those who were numbered by their families were two thousand seven hundred and fifty. 37These *were* the ones who were numbered of the families of the Kohathites, all who might serve in the tabernacle of meeting, whom Moses and Aaron numbered according to the commandment of the LORD by the hand of Moses.

38And those who were numbered of the sons of Gershon, by their families and by their fathers' house, 39from thirty years old and above, even to fifty years old, everyone who entered the service for work in the tabernacle of meeting— 40those who were numbered by their families, by their fathers' house, were two thousand six hundred and thirty. 41[a]These *are* the ones who were numbered of the families of the sons of Gershon, of all who might serve in the tabernacle of meeting, whom Moses and Aaron numbered according to the commandment of the LORD.

42Those of the families of the sons of Merari who were numbered, by their families, by their fathers' [1]house, 43from thirty years old and above, even to fifty years old, everyone who entered the service for work in the tabernacle of meeting— 44those who were numbered by their families were three thousand two hundred. 45These *are* the ones who were numbered of the families of the sons of Merari, whom Moses and Aaron numbered [a]according to the word of the LORD by the hand of Moses.

46All who were [a]numbered of the Levites, whom Moses, Aaron, and the leaders of Israel numbered, by their families and by their fathers' houses, 47[a]from thirty years old and above, even to fifty years old, everyone who came to do the work of service and the work of bearing burdens in the tabernacle of meeting— 48those who were numbered were eight thousand five hundred and eighty.

49According to the commandment of the LORD they were numbered by the hand of Moses, [a]each according to his service and according to his task; thus were they numbered by him, [b]as the LORD commanded Moses.

Ceremonially Unclean Persons Isolated

5 And the LORD spoke to Moses, saying: 2"Command the children of Israel that they put out of the camp every [a]leper, everyone who has a [b]discharge, and whoever becomes [c]defiled [1]by a corpse. 3You shall put out both male and female; you shall put them outside the camp, that they may not defile their camps [a]in the midst of which I dwell." 4And the children of Israel did so, and put them outside the camp; as the LORD spoke to Moses, so the children of Israel did.

Confession and Restitution

5Then the LORD spoke to Moses, saying, 6"Speak to the children of Israel: [a]'When a man or woman commits any sin that men commit in unfaithfulness against the LORD, and that person is guilty, 7[a]then he shall confess the sin which he has committed. He shall make restitution for his trespass [b]in full, plus one-fifth of it, and give *it* to the one he has wronged. 8But if the man has no [1]relative to whom restitution may be made for the wrong, the resti-

---

27 [2] *assign*
28 [a] Num. 4:33 [1] Lit. *hand*
29 [a] Num. 3:33–37
30 [a] Num. 4:3; 8:24–26
31 [a] Num. 3:36, 37 [b] Num. 7:8 [c] Ex. 26:15
32 [a] Ex. 25:9; 38:21
33 [1] Lit. *hand*
34 [a] Num. 4:2
35 [a] Num. 4:47
41 [a] Num. 4:22
42 [1] *household*
45 [a] Num. 4:29
46 [a] 1 Chr. 23:3–23
47 [a] Num. 4:3, 23, 30
49 [a] Num. 4:15, 24, 31 [b] Num. 4:1, 21

CHAPTER 5
2 [a] Lev. 13:3, 8, 46 [b] Lev. 15:2 [c] Lev. 21:1 [1] *by contact with*
3 [a] Lev. 26:11, 12
6 [a] Lev. 5:14—6:7
7 [a] Lev. 5:5; 26:40, 41 [b] Lev. 6:4, 5
8 [1] *redeemer,* Heb. *goel*

tution for the wrong *must go* to the LORD
for the priest, in addition to [a]the ram of
the atonement with which atonement is
made for him. 9Every [a]offering[1] of all the
holy things of the children of Israel,
which they bring to the priest, shall be
[b]his. 10And every man's [1]holy things shall
be his; whatever any man gives the priest
shall be [a]his.' "

Concerning Unfaithful Wives

11And the LORD spoke to Moses, saying,
12"Speak to the children of Israel, and say
to them: 'If any man's wife goes astray and
behaves unfaithfully toward him, 13and a
man [a]lies with her carnally, and it is hidden from the eyes of her husband, and it
is concealed that she has defiled herself,
and *there was* no witness against her, nor
was she [b]caught— 14if the spirit of jealousy comes upon him and he becomes [a]jeal-
ous of his wife, who has defiled herself; or
if the spirit of jealousy comes upon him
and he becomes jealous of his wife, although she has not defiled herself—
15then the man shall bring his wife to the
priest. He shall [a]bring the offering required for her, one-tenth of an ephah of
barley meal; he shall pour no oil on it and
put no frankincense on it, because it *is* a
grain offering of jealousy, an offering for
remembering, for [b]bringing iniquity to
remembrance.

16'And the priest shall bring her near,
and set her before the LORD. 17The priest
shall take holy water in an earthen vessel,
and take some of the dust that is on the
floor of the tabernacle and put *it* into the
water. 18Then the priest shall stand the
woman before the [a]LORD, uncover
the woman's head, and put the offering
for remembering in her hands, which *is*
the grain offering of jealousy. And the
priest shall have in his hand the bitter water that brings a curse. 19And the priest
shall put her under oath, and say to the
woman, "If no man has lain with you, and
if you have not gone astray to uncleanness
while under your husband's *authority,* be
free from this bitter water that brings a
curse. 20But if you have gone astray *while*
under your husband's *authority,* and if
you have defiled yourself and some man
other than your husband has lain with
you"— 21then the priest shall [a]put the
woman under the oath of the curse, and
he shall say to the woman—[b]"the LORD
make you a curse and an oath among your
people, when the LORD makes your thigh
[1]rot and your belly swell; 22and may this
water that causes the curse [a]go into your
stomach, and make *your* belly swell and
your thigh rot."

[b]"Then the woman shall say, "Amen, so
be it."

23'Then the priest shall write these
curses in a book, and he shall scrape *them*
off into the bitter water. 24And he shall
make the woman drink the bitter water
that brings a curse, and the water that
brings the curse shall enter her *to become*
bitter. 25[a]Then the priest shall take the
grain offering of jealousy from the woman's hand, shall [b]wave the offering before
the LORD, and bring it to the altar; 26and
the priest shall take a handful of the offering, [a]as its memorial portion, burn *it* on
the altar, and afterward make the woman
drink the water. 27When he has made her
drink the water, then it shall be, if she has
defiled herself and behaved unfaithfully
toward her husband, that the water that
brings a [a]curse will enter her *and become*
bitter, and her belly will swell, her thigh
will rot, and the woman [b]will become a
curse among her people. 28But if the
woman has not defiled herself, and is
clean, then she shall be free and may conceive children.

29'This *is* the law of jealousy, when a
wife, *while* under her husband's *authority,* [a]goes astray and defiles herself, 30or
when the spirit of jealousy comes upon a
man, and he becomes jealous of his wife;
then he shall stand the woman before the
LORD, and the priest shall execute all this
law upon her. 31Then the man shall be
free from [1]iniquity, but that woman [a]shall
bear her [2]guilt.' "

The Law of the Nazirite

6 Then the LORD spoke to Moses, saying, 2"Speak to the children of Israel,
and say to them: 'When either a man or
woman [1]consecrates an offering to take
the vow of a Nazirite, [a]to separate himself
to the LORD, 3[a]he shall separate himself
from wine and *similar* drink; he shall
drink neither vinegar made from wine nor
vinegar made from *similar* drink; neither
shall he drink any grape juice, nor eat
fresh grapes or raisins. 4All the days of his
[1]separation he shall eat nothing that is
produced by the grapevine, from seed to
skin.

8 [a]Lev. 5:15; 6:6, 7; 7:7
9 [a]Ex. 29:28 [b]Lev. 7:32–34; 10:14, 15 [1]*heave offering*
10 [a]Lev. 10:13 [1]*consecrated*
13 [a]Lev. 18:20; 20:10 [b]John 8:4
14 [a]Prov. 6:34
15 [a]Lev. 5:11 [b]1 Kin. 17:18
18 [a]Heb. 13:4
21 [a]Josh. 6:26 [b]Jer. 29:22 [1]Lit. *fall away*
22 [a]Ps. 109:18 [b]Deut. 27:15–26
25 [a]Lev. 8:27 [b]Lev. 2:2, 9
26 [a]Lev. 2:2, 9
27 [a]Jer. 24:9; 29:18, 22; 42:18 [b]Num. 5:21
29 [a]Num. 5:19
31 [a]Lev. 20:17, 19, 20 [1]*guilt* [2]*iniquity*

CHAPTER 6
2 [a]Judg. 13:5 [1]Or *makes a difficult vow*
3 [a]Luke 1:15
4 [1]Separation as a Nazirite

5 'All the days of the vow of his separation no [a]razor shall come upon his head; until the days are fulfilled for which he separated himself to the LORD, he shall be holy. *Then* he shall let the locks of the hair of his head grow. 6 All the days that he separates himself to the LORD [a]he shall not go near a dead body. 7 [a]He shall not [1]make himself unclean even for his father or his mother, for his brother or his sister, when they die, because his separation to God *is* on his head. 8 [a]All the days of his separation he shall be holy to the LORD.

9 'And if anyone dies very suddenly beside him, and he defiles his consecrated head, then he shall [a]shave his head on the day of his cleansing; on the seventh day he shall shave it. 10 Then [a]on the eighth day he shall bring two turtledoves or two young pigeons to the priest, to the door of the tabernacle of meeting; 11 and the priest shall offer one as a sin offering and *the* other as a burnt offering, and make atonement for him, because he sinned in regard to the corpse; and he shall sanctify his head that same day. 12 He shall consecrate to the LORD the days of his separation, and bring a male lamb in its first year [a]as a trespass offering; but the former days shall be [1]lost, because his separation was defiled.

13 'Now this *is* the law of the Nazirite: [a]When the days of his separation are fulfilled, he shall be brought to the door of the tabernacle of meeting. 14 And he shall present his offering to the LORD: one male lamb in its first year without blemish as a burnt offering, one ewe lamb in its first year without blemish [a]as a sin offering, one ram without blemish [b]as a peace offering, 15 a basket of unleavened bread, [a]cakes of fine flour mixed with oil, unleavened wafers [b]anointed with oil, and their grain offering with their [c]drink offerings.

16 'Then the priest shall bring *them* before the LORD and offer his sin offering and his burnt offering; 17 and he shall offer the ram as a sacrifice of a peace offering to the LORD, with the basket of unleavened bread; the priest shall also offer its grain offering and its drink offering. 18 [a]Then the Nazirite shall shave his consecrated head *at* the door of the tabernacle of meeting, and shall take the hair from his consecrated head and put *it* on the fire which is under the sacrifice of the peace offering.

5 a 1 Sam. 1:11
6 a Num. 19:11–22
7 a Num. 9:6 *1* By touching a dead body
8 a [2 Cor. 6:17, 18]
9 a Lev. 14:8, 9
10 a Lev. 5:7; 14:22; 15:14, 29
12 a Lev. 5:6 *1 void*
13 a Acts 21:26
14 a Lev. 4:2, 27, 32 b Lev. 3:6
15 a Lev. 2:4 b Ex. 29:2 c Num. 15:5, 7, 10
18 a Acts 21:23, 24
19 a 1 Sam. 2:15 b Ex. 29:23, 24 c Lev. 7:30
20 a Ex. 29:27, 28
24 a Deut. 28:3–6 b John 7:11
25 a Dan. 9:17 b Mal. 1:9
26 a Ps. 4:6; 89:15 b Lev. 26:6 *1* Look upon you with favor
27 a Is. 43:7 b Num. 23:20 *1 invoke*
CHAPTER 7
1 a Ex. 40:17–33 b Lev. 8:10, 11

19 'And the priest shall take the [a]boiled shoulder of the ram, one [b]unleavened cake from the basket, and one unleavened wafer, and [c]put *them* upon the hands of the Nazirite after he has shaved his consecrated *hair,* 20 and the priest shall wave them as a wave offering before the LORD; [a]they *are* holy for the priest, together with the breast of the wave offering and the thigh of the heave offering. After that the Nazirite may drink wine.'

21 "This is the law of the Nazirite who vows to the LORD the offering for his separation, and besides that, whatever else his hand is able to provide; according to the vow which he takes, so he must do according to the law of his separation."

Father, I pray that You will bless ____ and keep them; that You will make Your face to shine upon them, and be gracious to them; that You will lift up Your countenance upon them, and give them peace.

FROM NUMBERS 6:24–26

The Priestly Blessing

22 And the LORD spoke to Moses, saying: 23 "Speak to Aaron and his sons, saying, 'This is the way you shall bless the children of Israel. Say to them:

24 "The LORD [a]bless you and [b]keep you;
25 The LORD [a]make His face shine upon you,
And [b]be gracious to you;
26 [a]The LORD [1]lift up His countenance upon you,
And [b]give you peace." '

27 [a]"So they shall [1]put My name on the children of Israel, and [b]I will bless them."

Offerings of the Leaders

7 Now it came to pass, when Moses had finished [a]setting up the tabernacle, that he [b]anointed it and consecrated it and all its furnishings, and the altar and all its utensils; so he anointed them and

consecrated them. 2 Then [a]the leaders of
Israel, the heads of their fathers' houses,
who *were* the leaders of the tribes [1]and
over those who were numbered, made an
offering. 3 And they brought their offering
before the LORD, six covered carts and
twelve oxen, a cart for *every* two of the
leaders, and for each one an ox; and they
presented them before the tabernacle.
4 Then the LORD spoke to Moses, saying,
5 "Accept *these* from them, that they may
be used in doing the work of the tabernacle of meeting; and you shall give them to
the Levites, *to* every man according to his
service." 6 So Moses took the carts and the
oxen, and gave them to the Levites. 7 Two
carts and four oxen [a]he gave to the sons
of Gershon, according to their service;
8 [a]and four carts and eight oxen he gave to
the sons of Merari, according to their service, under the [1]authority of Ithamar the
son of Aaron the priest. 9 But to the sons
of Kohath he gave none, because theirs
was [a]the service of the holy things,
[b]*which* they carried on their shoulders.
10 Now the leaders offered [a]the dedication *offering* for the altar when it was
anointed; so the leaders offered their offering before the altar. 11 For the LORD said
to Moses, "They shall offer their offering,
one leader each day, for the dedication of
the altar."
12 And the one who offered his offering
on the first day *was* [a]Nahshon the son
of Amminadab, from the tribe of Judah.
13 His offering *was* one silver platter, the
weight of which *was* one hundred and
thirty *shekels,* and one silver bowl of seventy shekels, according to [a]the shekel of
the sanctuary, both of them full of fine
flour mixed with oil as a [b]grain offering;
14 one gold pan of ten *shekels,* full of [a]in-
cense; 15 [a]one young bull, one ram, and
one male lamb [b]in its first year, as a burnt
offering; 16 one kid of the goats as a [a]sin
offering; 17 and for [a]the sacrifice of peace
offerings: two oxen, five rams, five male
goats, and five male lambs in their first
year. This *was* the offering of Nahshon the
son of Amminadab.
18 On the second day Nethanel the son
of Zuar, leader of Issachar, presented *an
offering.* 19 *For* his offering he offered one
silver platter, the weight of which *was* one
hundred and thirty *shekels,* and one silver
bowl of seventy shekels, according to the
shekel of the sanctuary, both of them full
of fine flour mixed with oil as a grain offering; 20 one gold pan of ten *shekels,* full
of incense; 21 one young bull, one ram, and
one male lamb in its first year, as a burnt
offering; 22 one kid of the goats as a sin
offering; 23 and as the sacrifice of peace
offerings: two oxen, five rams, five male
goats, and five male lambs in their first
year. This *was* the offering of Nethanel the
son of Zuar.
24 On the third day Eliab the son of Helon, leader of the children of Zebulun,
presented an offering. 25 His offering *was*
one silver platter, the weight of which *was*
one hundred and thirty *shekels,* and one
silver bowl of seventy shekels, according
to the shekel of the sanctuary, both of
them full of fine flour mixed with oil as a
grain offering; 26 one gold pan of ten *shekels,* full of incense; 27 one young bull, one
ram, and one male lamb in its first year,
as a burnt offering; 28 one kid of the goats
as a sin offering; 29 and for the sacrifice of
peace offerings: two oxen, five rams, five
male goats, and five male lambs in their
first year. This *was* the offering of Eliab
the son of Helon.
30 On the fourth day [a]Elizur the son of
Shedeur, leader of the children of Reuben,
presented an offering. 31 His offering *was*
one silver platter, the weight of which *was*
one hundred and thirty *shekels,* and one
silver bowl of seventy shekels, according
to the shekel of the sanctuary, both of
them full of fine flour mixed with oil as a
grain offering; 32 one gold pan of ten *shekels,* full of incense; 33 one young bull, one
ram, and one male lamb in its first year,
as a burnt offering; 34 one kid of the goats
as a sin offering; 35 and as the sacrifice of
peace offerings: two oxen, five rams, five
male goats, and five male lambs in their
first year. This *was* the offering of Elizur
the son of Shedeur.
36 On the fifth day [a]Shelumiel the son
of Zurishaddai, leader of the children of
Simeon, *presented an offering.* 37 His offering *was* one silver platter, the weight of
which *was* one hundred and thirty *shekels,* and one silver bowl of seventy shekels,
according to the shekel of the sanctuary,
both of them full of fine flour mixed with
oil as a grain offering; 38 one gold pan of
ten *shekels,* full of incense; 39 one young
bull, one ram, and one male lamb in its
first year, as a burnt offering; 40 one kid of
the goats as a sin offering; 41 and as the
sacrifice of peace offerings: two oxen, five
rams, five male goats, and five male lambs

2 [a]Num. 1:4 [1]Lit. *who stood over*
7 [a]Num. 4:24–28
8 [a]Num. 4:29–33 [1]Lit. *hand*
9 [a]Num. 4:15 [b]Num. 4:6–14
10 [a]2 Chr. 7:5, 9
12 [a]Num. 2:3
13 [a]Ex. 30:13 [b]Lev. 2:1
14 [a]Ex. 30:34, 35
15 [a]Lev. 1:2 [b]Ex. 12:5
16 [a]Lev. 4:23
17 [a]Lev. 3:1
30 [a]Num. 1:5; 2:10
36 [a]Num. 1:6; 2:12; 7:41

in their first year. This *was* the offering of Shelumiel the son of Zurishaddai.

[42]On the sixth day [a]Eliasaph the son of [1]Deuel, leader of the children of Gad, *presented an offering.* [43]His offering *was* one silver platter, the weight of which *was* one hundred and thirty *shekels,* and one silver bowl of seventy shekels, according to the shekel of the sanctuary, both of them full of fine flour mixed with oil as a grain offering; [44]one gold pan of ten *shekels,* full of incense; [45]one young bull, one ram, and one male lamb in its first year, as [a]a burnt offering; [46]one kid of the goats as a sin offering; [47]and as the sacrifice of peace offerings: two oxen, five rams, five male goats, and five male lambs in their first year. This *was* the offering of Eliasaph the son of Deuel.

[48]On the seventh day [a]Elishama the son of Ammihud, leader of the children of Ephraim, *presented an offering.* [49]His offering *was* one silver platter, the weight of which *was* one hundred and thirty *shekels,* and one silver bowl of seventy shekels, according to the shekel of the sanctuary, both of them full of fine flour mixed with oil as a grain offering; [50]one gold pan of ten *shekels,* full of incense; [51]one young bull, one ram, and one male lamb in its first year, as a burnt offering; [52]one kid of the goats as a sin offering; [53]and as the sacrifice of peace offerings: two oxen, five rams, five male goats, and five male lambs in their first year. This *was* the offering of Elishama the son of Ammihud.

[54]On the eighth day [a]Gamaliel the son of Pedahzur, leader of the children of Manasseh, *presented an offering.* [55]His offering *was* one silver platter, the weight of which *was* one hundred and thirty *shekels,* and one silver bowl of seventy shekels, according to the shekel of the sanctuary, both of them full of fine flour mixed with oil as a grain offering; [56]one gold pan of ten *shekels,* full of incense; [57]one young bull, one ram, and one male lamb in its first year, as a burnt offering; [58]one kid of the goats as a sin offering; [59]and as the sacrifice of peace offerings: two oxen, five rams, five male goats, and five male lambs in their first year. This *was* the offering of Gamaliel the son of Pedahzur.

[60]On the ninth day [a]Abidan the son of Gideoni, leader of the children of Benjamin, *presented an offering.* [61]His offering *was* one silver platter, the weight of which *was* one hundred and thirty *shekels,* and one silver bowl of seventy shekels, according to the shekel of the sanctuary, both of them full of fine flour mixed with oil as a grain offering; [62]one gold pan of ten *shekels,* full of incense; [63]one young bull, one ram, and one male lamb in its first year, as a burnt offering; [64]one kid of the goats as a sin offering; [65]and as the sacrifice of peace offerings: two oxen, five rams, five male goats, and five male lambs in their first year. This *was* the offering of Abidan the son of Gideoni.

[66]On the tenth day [a]Ahiezer the son of Ammishaddai, leader of the children of Dan, *presented an offering.* [67]His offering *was* one silver platter, the weight of which *was* one hundred and thirty *shekels,* and one silver bowl of seventy shekels, according to the shekel of the sanctuary, both of them full of fine flour mixed with oil as a grain offering; [68]one gold pan of ten *shekels,* full of incense; [69]one young bull, one ram, and one male lamb in its first year, as a burnt offering; [70]one kid of the goats as a sin offering; [71]and as the sacrifice of peace offerings: two oxen, five rams, five male goats, and five male lambs in their first year. This *was* the offering of Ahiezer the son of Ammishaddai.

[72]On the eleventh day [a]Pagiel the son of Ocran, leader of the children of Asher, *presented an offering.* [73]His offering *was* one silver platter, the weight of which *was* one hundred and thirty *shekels,* and one silver bowl of seventy shekels, according to the shekel of the sanctuary, both of them full of fine flour mixed with oil as a grain offering; [74]one gold pan of ten *shekels,* full of incense; [75]one young bull, one ram, and one male lamb in its first year, as a burnt offering; [76]one kid of the goats as a sin offering; [77]and as the sacrifice of peace offerings: two oxen, five rams, five male goats, and five male lambs in their first year. This *was* the offering of Pagiel the son of Ocran.

[78]On the twelfth day [a]Ahira the son of Enan, leader of the children of Naphtali, *presented an offering.* [79]His offering *was* one silver platter, the weight of which *was* one hundred and thirty *shekels,* and one silver bowl of seventy shekels, according to the shekel of the sanctuary, both of them full of fine flour mixed with oil as a grain offering; [80]one gold pan of ten *shekels,* full of incense; [81]one young bull, one ram, and one male lamb in its first year, as a burnt offering; [82]one kid of the goats

42 [a] Num. 1:14; 2:14; 10:20 [1] *Reuel,* Num. 2:14
45 [a] Ps. 40:6
48 [a] Num. 1:10; 2:18
54 [a] Num. 1:10; 2:20
60 [a] Num. 1:11; 2:22
66 [a] Num. 1:12; 2:25
72 [a] Num. 1:13; 2:27
78 [a] Num. 1:15; 2:29

as a sin offering; 83 and as the sacrifice of peace offerings: two oxen, five rams, five male goats, and five male lambs in their first year. This *was* the offering of Ahira the son of Enan.

84 This *was* [a]the dedication *offering* for the altar from the leaders of Israel, when it was anointed: twelve silver platters, twelve silver bowls, and twelve gold pans. 85 Each silver platter *weighed* one hundred and thirty *shekels* and each bowl seventy *shekels.* All the silver of the vessels *weighed* two thousand four hundred *shekels,* according to the shekel of the sanctuary. 86 The twelve gold pans full of incense *weighed* ten *shekels* apiece, according to the shekel of the sanctuary; all the gold of the pans *weighed* one hundred and twenty *shekels.* 87 All the oxen for the burnt offering *were* twelve young bulls, the rams twelve, the male lambs in their first year twelve, with their grain offering, and the kids of the goats as a sin offering twelve. 88 And all the oxen for the sacrifice of peace offerings were twenty-four bulls, the rams sixty, the male goats sixty, and the lambs in their first year sixty. This *was* the dedication *offering* for the altar after it was [a]anointed.

89 Now when Moses went into the tabernacle of meeting [a]to speak with Him, he heard [b]the voice of One speaking to him from above the mercy seat that *was* on the ark of the Testimony, from [c]between the two cherubim; thus He spoke to him.

Arrangement of the Lamps

8 And the LORD spoke to Moses, saying: 2 "Speak to Aaron, and say to him, 'When you [a]arrange the lamps, the seven [b]lamps shall give light in front of the lampstand.'" 3 And Aaron did so; he arranged the lamps to face toward the front of the lampstand, as the LORD commanded Moses. 4 [a]Now this workmanship of the lampstand *was* hammered gold; from its shaft to its flowers it *was* [b]hammered work. [c]According to the pattern which the LORD had shown Moses, so he made the lampstand.

Cleansing and Dedication of the Levites

5 Then the LORD spoke to Moses, saying: 6 "Take the Levites from among the children of Israel and cleanse them *ceremonially.* 7 Thus you shall do to them to cleanse them: Sprinkle [a]water of purification on them, and [b]let[1] them shave all their body, and let them wash their clothes, and *so* make themselves clean. 8 Then let them take a young bull with [a]its grain offering of fine flour mixed with oil, and you shall take another young bull as a sin offering. 9 [a]And you shall bring the Levites before the tabernacle of meeting, [b]and you shall gather together the whole congregation of the children of Israel. 10 So you shall bring the Levites before the LORD, and the children of Israel [a]shall lay their hands on the Levites; 11 and Aaron shall [1]offer the Levites before the LORD *like* a [a]wave offering from the children of Israel, that they may perform the work of the LORD. 12 [a]Then the Levites shall lay their hands on the heads of the young bulls, and you shall offer one as a sin offering and the other as a burnt offering to the LORD, to make atonement for the Levites.

> *We cannot measure the love He showers on our souls who give and abandon themselves to Him, and who have no higher aspiration than to do all that they believe to be pleasing to Him.*
>
> JEANNE DE CHANTAL

13 "And you shall stand the Levites before Aaron and his sons, and then offer them *like* a wave offering to the LORD. 14 Thus you shall [a]separate the Levites from among the children of Israel, and the Levites shall be [b]Mine. 15 After that the Levites shall go in to service the tabernacle of meeting. So you shall cleanse them and [a]offer them *like* a wave offering. 16 For they *are* [a]wholly given to Me from among the children of Israel; I have taken them for Myself [b]instead of all who open the womb, the firstborn of all the children of Israel. 17 [a]For all the firstborn among the children of Israel *are* Mine, *both* man and

84 a Num. 7:10
88 a Num. 7:1, 10
89 a [Ex. 33:9, 11] b Ex. 25:21, 22 c Ps. 80:1; 99:1

CHAPTER 8
2 a Lev. 24:2–4 b Ex. 25:37; 40:25
4 a Ex. 25:31 b Ex. 25:18 c Ex. 25:40
7 a Num. 19:9, 13, 17, 20 b Lev. 14:8, 9 *1* Heb. *let them cause a razor to pass over*
8 a Lev. 2:1
9 a Ex. 29:4; 40:12 b Lev. 8:3
10 a Lev. 1:4
11 a Num. 18:6 *1 present*
12 a Ex. 29:10
14 a Num. 16:9 b Num. 3:12, 45; 16:9
15 a Num. 8:11, 13
16 a Num. 3:9 b Num. 3:12, 45
17 a Ex. 12:2, 12, 13, 15

beast; on the day that I struck all the firstborn in the land of Egypt I [1]sanctified them to Myself. 18I have taken the Levites instead of all the firstborn of the children of Israel. 19And [a]I have given the Levites as a gift to Aaron and his sons from among the children of Israel, to do the work for the children of Israel in the tabernacle of meeting, and to make atonement for the children of Israel, [b]that there be no plague among the children of Israel when the children of Israel come near the sanctuary."

20Thus Moses and Aaron and all the congregation of the children of Israel did to the Levites; according to all that the LORD commanded Moses concerning the Levites, so the children of Israel did to them. 21[a]And the Levites purified themselves and washed their clothes; then Aaron presented them *like* a wave offering before the LORD, and Aaron made atonement for them to cleanse them. 22[a]After that the Levites went in to do their work in the tabernacle of meeting before Aaron and his sons; [b]as the LORD commanded Moses concerning the Levites, so they did to them.

23Then the LORD spoke to Moses, saying, 24"This *is* what *pertains* to the Levites: [a]From twenty-five years old and above one may enter to perform service in the work of the tabernacle of meeting; 25and at the age of fifty years they must cease performing this work, and shall work no more. 26They may minister with their brethren in the tabernacle of meeting, [a]to attend to needs, but they *themselves* shall do no work. Thus you shall do to the Levites regarding their duties."

The Second Passover

9 Now the LORD spoke to Moses in the Wilderness of Sinai, in the first month of the second year after they had come out of the land of Egypt, saying: 2"Let the children of Israel keep [a]the Passover at its appointed [b]time. 3On the fourteenth day of this month, [1]at twilight, you shall [2]keep it at its appointed time. According to all its [3]rites and ceremonies you shall keep it." 4So Moses told the children of Israel that they should keep the Passover. 5And [a]they kept the Passover on the fourteenth day of the first month, at twilight, in the Wilderness of Sinai; according to all that the LORD commanded Moses, so the children of Israel did.

6Now there were *certain* men who were [a]defiled by a human corpse, so that they could not keep the Passover on that day; [b]and they came before Moses and Aaron that day. 7And those men said to him, "We *became* defiled by a human corpse. Why are we kept from presenting the offering of the LORD at its appointed time among the children of Israel?"

8And Moses said to them, "Stand still, that [a]I may hear what the LORD will command concerning you."

9Then the LORD spoke to Moses, saying, 10"Speak to the children of Israel, saying: 'If anyone of you or your [1]posterity is unclean because of a corpse, or *is* far away on a journey, he may still keep the LORD's Passover. 11On [a]the fourteenth day of the second month, at twilight, they may keep it. They shall [b]eat it with unleavened bread and bitter herbs. 12[a]They shall leave none of it until morning, [b]nor break one of its bones. [c]According to all the [1]ordinances of the Passover they shall keep it. 13But the man who *is* clean and is not on a journey, and ceases to keep the Passover, that same person [a]shall be cut off from among his people, because he [b]did not bring the offering of the LORD at its appointed time; that man shall [c]bear his sin.

14'And if a stranger [1]dwells among you, and would keep the LORD's Passover, he must do so according to the rite of the Passover and according to its ceremony; [a]you shall have one [2]ordinance, both for the stranger and the native of the land.' "

The Cloud and the Fire

15Now [a]on the day that the tabernacle was raised up, the cloud [b]covered the tabernacle, the tent of the Testimony; [c]from evening until morning it was above the tabernacle like the appearance of fire. 16So it was always: the cloud covered it *by day,* and the appearance of fire by night. 17 Whenever the cloud [a]was [1]taken up from above the tabernacle, after that the children of Israel would journey; and in the place where the cloud settled, there the children of Israel would pitch their tents. 18At the [1]command of the LORD the children of Israel would journey, and at the command of the LORD they would camp; [a]as long as the cloud stayed above the tabernacle they remained encamped. 19Even when the cloud continued long, many days above the tabernacle, the

17 [1] *set them apart*
19 [a] Num. 3:9 [b] Num. 1:53; 16:46; 18:5
21 [a] Num. 8:7
22 [a] Num. 8:15 [b] Num. 8:5
24 [a] Num. 4:3
26 [a] Num. 1:53

CHAPTER 9
2 [a] Lev. 23:5 [b] 2 Chr. 30:1–15
3 [1] Lit. *between the evenings* [2] *observe* [3] *statutes*
5 [a] Josh. 5:10
6 [a] Num. 5:2; 19:11–22 [b] Num. 27:2
8 [a] Num. 27:5
10 [1] *descendants*
11 [a] 2 Chr. 30:2, 15 [b] Ex. 12:8
12 [a] Ex. 12:10 [b] Ex. 12:46 [c] Ex. 12:43 [1] *statutes*
13 [a] Ex. 12:15, 47 [b] Num. 9:7 [c] Num. 5:31
14 [a] Ex. 12:49 [1] *As a resident alien* [2] *statute*
15 [a] Ex. 40:33, 34 [b] Is. 4:5 [c] Ex. 13:21, 22; 40:38
17 [a] Ex. 40:36–38 [1] *lifted up*
18 [a] 1 Cor. 10:1 [1] Lit. *mouth*

Numbers 9:17–23

Dear Woman of Destiny,

You are God's temporary dwelling place on the earth—fashioned to be full of His manifest glorious presence. When Israel left Egypt and journeyed through the wilderness, God placed His tabernacle in their midst to house His ark and be His resting place. Upon that tabernacle God sent His cloud like "the appearance of fire" (Num. 9:16). God's manifest presence over the ark and the tabernacle gave Israel guidance and protection from their enemies. God charged Israel to abide continually with the cloud. When you were born again, God built you into a new creation to house Jesus, the true ark of God's covenant. You are His second temple destined for greater glory than His former house enjoyed. This glory appears as the cloud of God, the Holy Spirit, rests on you just as He dwelt over Israel's tabernacle. God's victory comes to you as you stay under the cloud of His presence, daily following the Holy Spirit.

At Pentecost, tongues of fire rested on each person. Pentecost is the fullness of the cloud that appeared like fire and rested on the tabernacle day and night. For as long as the cloud remained, the people encamped. When it moved, the people journeyed also. God says, "As many as are led by the Spirit of God, these are sons of God" (Rom. 8:14). The indication that you are God's offspring is the manifest presence of the Holy Spirit resting on you.

If you have never received the fullness of the Holy Spirit, do so today. This is your Pentecost appointment! Turn your face to heaven, open wide your mouth and say, "Come in, Holy Spirit! Fill me! Rest on me just as You rested on the Christians in the Upper Room—just as You rested on the tabernacle of old. Appear in me and through me to all!"

Whatever your present circumstance or previous experience, this is the hour of your visitation. God's words to Zerubbabel are for you, too, "Yet now be strong . . . and work; for I am with you,' says the LORD of hosts. 'According to the word that I covenanted with you when you came out of Egypt, so My Spirit remains among you; do not fear! . . . I will fill this temple with glory . . . the glory of this latter temple shall be greater than the former, . . . And in this place I will give peace'" (see Hag. 2:4–9). How shall God accomplish this work? He completes His building as you abide daily in His Spirit. It is: "'Not by might nor by power, but by My Spirit,' says the LORD of hosts" (Zech. 4:6).

Your key to victory is to welcome the Holy Spirit afresh today. Your divine strategy for success is to hear His voice and follow Him. If He rests today, rest. If He moves today, move with Him. Take courage. He has promised to "never leave you nor forsake you" (Heb. 13:5). He who began a good work in you will complete it! (see Phil. 1:6). It is not by your might, it is not by your power, but by the power of His Spirit dwelling in you.

Bonnie Chavda

children of Israel [a]kept the charge of the LORD and did not journey. [20]So it was, when the cloud was above the tabernacle a few days: according to the command of the LORD they would remain encamped, and according to the command of the LORD they would journey. [21]So it was, when the cloud remained only from evening until morning: when the cloud was taken up in the morning, then they would journey; whether by day or by night, whenever the cloud was taken up, they would journey. [22]*Whether it was* two days, a month, or a year that the cloud remained above the tabernacle, the children of Israel [a]would remain encamped and not journey; but when it was taken up, they would journey. [23]At the command of the LORD they remained encamped, and at the command of the LORD they journeyed; they [a]kept the charge of the LORD, at the command of the LORD by the hand of Moses.

Two Silver Trumpets

10 And the LORD spoke to Moses, saying: [2]"Make two silver trumpets for yourself; you shall make them of hammered work; you shall use them for [a]calling the congregation and for directing the movement of the camps. [3]When [a]they blow both of them, all the congregation shall gather before you at the door of the tabernacle of meeting. [4]But if they blow *only* one, then the leaders, the [a]heads of the divisions of Israel, shall gather to you. [5]When you sound the [a]advance, [b]the camps that lie on the east side shall then begin their journey. [6]When you sound the advance the second time, then the camps that lie [a]on the south side shall begin their journey; they shall sound the call for them to begin their journeys. [7]And when the assembly is to be gathered together, [a]you shall blow, but not [b]sound the advance. [8][a]The sons of Aaron, the priests, shall blow the trumpets; and these shall be to you as an [1]ordinance forever throughout your generations.

[9][a]"When you go to war in your land against the enemy who [b]oppresses you, then you shall sound an alarm with the trumpets, and you will be [c]remembered before the LORD your God, and you will be saved from your enemies. [10]Also [a]in the day of your gladness, in your appointed feasts, and at the beginning of your months, you shall blow the trumpets over your burnt offerings and over the sacrifices of your peace offerings; and they shall be [b]a memorial for you before your God: I *am* the LORD your God."

Departure from Sinai

[11]Now it came to pass on the twentieth *day* of the second month, in the second year, that the cloud [a]was taken up from above the tabernacle of the Testimony. [12]And the children of Israel set out from the [a]Wilderness of Sinai on [b]their journeys; then the cloud settled down in the [c]Wilderness of Paran. [13]So they started out for the first time [a]according to the command of the LORD by the hand of Moses.

[14]The [1]standard of the camp of the children of Judah [a]set out first according to their armies; over their army was [b]Nahshon the son of Amminadab. [15]Over the army of the tribe of the children of Issachar *was* Nethanel the son of Zuar. [16]And over the army of the tribe of the children of Zebulun *was* Eliab the son of Helon.

[17]Then [a]the tabernacle was taken down; and the sons of Gershon and the sons of Merari set out, [b]carrying the tabernacle.

[18]And [a]the standard of the camp of Reuben set out according to their armies; over their army *was* Elizur the son of Shedeur. [19]Over the army of the tribe of the children of Simeon *was* Shelumiel the son of Zurishaddai. [20]And over the army of the tribe of the children of Gad *was* Eliasaph the son of Deuel.

[21]Then the Kohathites set out, carrying the [a]holy things. (The tabernacle would be [1]prepared for their arrival.)

[22]And [a]the standard of the camp of the children of Ephraim set out according to their armies; over their army *was* Elishama the son of Ammihud. [23]Over the army of the tribe of the children of Manasseh *was* Gamaliel the son of Pedahzur. [24]And over the army of the tribe of the children of Benjamin *was* Abidan the son of Gideoni.

[25]Then [a]the standard of the camp of the children of Dan (the rear guard of all the camps) set out according to their armies; over their army *was* Ahiezer the son of Ammishaddai. [26]Over the army of the tribe of the children of Asher *was* Pagiel the son of Ocran. [27]And over the army of the tribe of the children of Naphtali *was* Ahira the son of Enan.

19 a Num. 1:53; 3:8
22 a Ex. 40:36, 37
23 a Num. 9:19

CHAPTER 10
2 a Is. 1:13
3 a Jer. 4:5
4 a Ex. 18:21
5 a Joel 2:1 b Num. 2:3
6 a Num. 2:10
7 a Num. 10:3 b Joel 2:1
8 a Num. 31:6 *1 statute*
9 a Josh. 6:5 b Judg. 2:18; 4:3; 6:9; 10:8, 12 c Gen. 8:1
10 a Lev. 23:24 b Num. 10:9
11 a Num. 9:17
12 a Ex. 19:1 b Ex. 40:36 c Gen. 21:21
13 a Num. 10:5, 6
14 a Num. 2:3–9 b Num. 1:7 *1 banner*
17 a Num. 1:51 b Num. 4:21–32; 7:7–9
18 a Num. 2:10–16
21 a Num. 4:4–20; 7:9 *1* Prepared by the Gershonites and the Merarites
22 a Num. 2:18–24
25 a Num. 2:25–31

28[a]Thus *was* the order of march of the
children of Israel, according to their armies, when they began their journey.
29Now Moses said to [a]Hobab the son of
[b]Reuel[1] the Midianite, Moses' father-in-
law, "We are setting out for the place of
which the LORD said, [c]'I will give it to
you.' Come with us, and [d]we will treat you
well; for [e]the LORD has promised good
things to Israel."
30And he said to him, "I will not go, but
I will depart to my *own* land and to my
relatives."
31So *Moses* said, "Please do not leave,
inasmuch as you know how we are to
camp in the wilderness, and you can [1]be
our [a]eyes. 32And it shall be, if you go with
us—indeed it shall be—that [a]whatever
good the LORD will do to us, the same we
will do to you."
33So they departed from [a]the mountain
of the LORD on a journey of three days;
and the ark of the covenant of the LORD
[b]went before them for the three days'
journey, to search out a resting place for
them. 34And [a]the cloud of the LORD *was*
above them by day when they went out
from the camp.

> *Through the eyes of faith we see enemies scattered, their force broken as missiles fall harmlessly at the feet of the faithful servant of God.*
>
> PHOEBE PALMER

35So it was, whenever the ark set out,
that Moses said:

[a]"Rise up, O LORD!
Let Your enemies be scattered,
And let those who hate You flee
before You."

36And when it rested, he said:

"Return, O LORD,
To the many thousands of Israel."

The People Complain

11 Now [a]*when* the people complained, it displeased the LORD;
[b]for the LORD heard *it,* and His anger was
aroused. So the [c]fire of the LORD burned
among them, and consumed *some* in the
outskirts of the camp. 2Then the people
[a]cried out to Moses, and when Moses
[b]prayed to the LORD, the fire was
[1]quenched. 3So he called the name of the
place [1]Taberah, because the fire of the
LORD had burned among them.
4Now the [a]mixed multitude who were
among them [1]yielded to [b]intense craving;
so the children of Israel also wept again
and said: [c]"Who will give us meat to eat?
5[a]We remember the fish which we ate
freely in Egypt, the cucumbers, the mel-
ons, the leeks, the onions, and the garlic;
6but now [a]our whole being *is* dried up;
there is nothing at all except this manna
before our eyes!"
7Now [a]the manna *was* like coriander
seed, and its color like the color of bdelli-
um. 8The people went about and gathered
it, ground *it* on millstones or beat *it* in the
mortar, cooked *it* in pans, and made cakes
of it; and [a]its taste was like the taste of
pastry prepared with oil. 9And [a]when the
dew fell on the camp in the night, the
manna fell on it.
10Then Moses heard the people weeping
throughout their families, everyone at the
door of his tent; and [a]the anger of the
LORD was greatly aroused; Moses also was
displeased. 11[a]So Moses said to the LORD,
"Why have You afflicted Your servant?
And why have I not found favor in Your
sight, that You have laid the [1]burden of all
these people on me? 12Did I conceive all
these people? Did I beget them, that You
should say to me, [a]'Carry them in your
bosom, as a [b]guardian carries a nursing
child,' to the land which You [c]swore[1] to
their fathers? 13[a]Where am I to get meat
to give to all these people? For they weep
all over me, saying, 'Give us meat, that we
may eat.' 14[a]I am not able to bear all these
people alone, because the burden *is* too
heavy for me. 15If You treat me like this,
please kill me here and now—if I have
found favor in Your sight—and [a]do not
let me see my wretchedness!"

The Seventy Elders

16So the LORD said to Moses: "Gather to
Me [a]seventy men of the elders of Israel,
whom you know to be the elders of the
people and [b]officers over them; bring
them to the tabernacle of meeting, that
they may stand there with you. 17Then I
will come down and talk with you there.

---

28 a Num. 2:34
29 a Judg. 4:11 b Ex. 2:18; 3:1; 18:12 c Gen. 12:7 d Judg. 1:16 e Ex. 3:8 *1 Jethro,* Ex. 3:1; LXX *Raguel*
31 a Job 29:15 *1* Act as our guide
32 a Judg. 1:16
33 a Ex. 3:1 b Deut. 1:33
34 a Ex. 13:21
35 a Ps. 68:1, 2; 132:8
CHAPTER 11
1 a Num. 14:2; 16:11; 17:5 b Ps. 78:21 c Lev. 10:2
2 a Num. 12:11, 13; 21:7 b [James 5:16] *1 extinguished*
3 *1* Lit. *Burning*
4 a Ex. 12:38 b 1 Cor. 10:6 c [Ps. 78:18] *1* Lit. *lusted intensely*
5 a Ex. 16:3
6 a Num. 21:5
7 a Ex. 16:14, 31
8 a Ex. 16:31
9 a Ex. 16:13, 14
10 a Ps. 78:21
11 a Deut. 1:12 *1 responsibility*
12 a Is. 40:11 b Is. 49:23 c Gen. 26:3 *1 solemnly promised*
13 a Mark 8:4
14 a Ex. 18:18
15 a Rev. 3:17
16 a Ex. 18:25; 24:1, 9 b Deut. 16:18

[a]I will take of the Spirit that *is* upon you and will put *the same* upon them; and they shall bear the burden of the people with you, that you may not bear *it* yourself alone. 18 Then you shall say to the people, [1]'Consecrate yourselves for tomorrow, and you shall eat meat; for you have wept [a]in the hearing of the LORD, saying, "Who will give us meat to eat? For *it was* well with us in Egypt." Therefore the LORD will give you meat, and you shall eat. 19 You shall eat, not one day, nor two days, nor five days, nor ten days, nor twenty days, 20 [a]but *for* a whole month, until it comes out of your nostrils and becomes loathsome to you, because you have [b]despised the LORD who is among you, and have wept before Him, saying, [c]"Why did we ever come up out of Egypt?" ' "

21 And Moses said, [a]"The people whom I *am* among *are* six hundred thousand men on foot; yet You have said, 'I will give them meat, that they may eat *for* a whole month.' 22 [a]Shall flocks and herds be slaughtered for them, to provide enough for them? Or shall all the fish of the sea be gathered together for them, to provide enough for them?"

23 And the LORD said to Moses, [a]"Has[1] the LORD's arm been shortened? Now you shall see whether [b]what I say will happen to you or not."

24 So Moses went out and told the people the words of the LORD, and he [a]gathered the seventy men of the elders of the people and placed them around the tabernacle. 25 Then the LORD came down in the cloud, and spoke to him, and took of the Spirit that *was* upon him, and placed *the same* upon the seventy elders; and it happened, [a]when the Spirit rested upon them, that [b]they prophesied, [1]although they never did *so* again.

26 But two men had remained in the camp: the name of one *was* Eldad, and the name of the other Medad. And the Spirit rested upon them. Now they *were* among those listed, but who [a]had not gone out to the tabernacle; yet they prophesied in the camp. 27 And a young man ran and told Moses, and said, "Eldad and Medad are prophesying in the camp."

28 So Joshua the son of Nun, Moses' assistant, *one* of his choice men, answered and said, "Moses my lord, [a]forbid them!"

29 Then Moses said to him, "Are you [1]zealous for my sake? [a]Oh, that all the LORD's people were prophets *and* that the LORD would put His Spirit upon them!" 30 And Moses returned to the camp, he and the elders of Israel.

The Lord Sends Quail

31 Now a [a]wind went out from the LORD, and it brought quail from the sea and left *them* fluttering near the camp, about a day's journey on this side and about a day's journey on the other side, all around the camp, and about two cubits above the surface of the ground. 32 And the people stayed up all that day, all night, and all the next day, and gathered the quail (he who gathered least gathered ten [a]homers); and they spread *them* out for themselves all around the camp. 33 But while the [a]meat *was* still between their teeth, before it was chewed, the wrath of the LORD was aroused against the people, and the LORD struck the people with a very great plague. 34 So he called the name of that place [1]Kibroth Hattaavah, because there they buried the people who had yielded to craving.

35 [a]From Kibroth Hattaavah the people moved to Hazeroth, and camped at Hazeroth.

Dissension of Aaron and Miriam

12 Then [a]Miriam and Aaron [1]spoke [b]against Moses because of the [2]Ethiopian woman whom he had married; for [c]he had married an Ethiopian woman. 2 So they said, "Has the LORD indeed spoken only through [a]Moses? [b]Has He not spoken through us also?" And the LORD [c]heard *it*. 3 (Now the man Moses *was* very humble, more than all men who *were* on the face of the earth.)

4 [a]Suddenly the LORD said to Moses, Aaron, and Miriam, "Come out, you three, to the tabernacle of meeting!" So the three came out. 5 [a]Then the LORD came down in the pillar of cloud and stood *in* the door of the tabernacle, and called Aaron and Miriam. And they both went forward. 6 Then He said,

"Hear now My words:
If there is a prophet among you,
I, the LORD, make Myself known to
him [a]in a vision;
I speak to him [b]in a dream.
7 Not so with [a]My servant Moses;
[b]He *is* faithful in all [c]My house.

17 a 1 Sam. 10:6
18 a Ex. 16:7 1 *Set yourselves apart*
20 a Ps. 78:29; 106:15 b 1 Sam. 10:19 c Num. 21:5
21 a Gen. 12:2
22 a 2 Kin. 7:2
23 a Is. 50:2; 59:1 b Num. 23:19 1 Is the LORD's power limited?
24 a Num. 11:16
25 a 2 Kin. 2:15 b Joel 2:28 1 Tg., Vg. *and they did not cease*
26 a Jer. 36:5
28 a [Mark 9:38–40]
29 a 1 Cor. 14:5 1 *jealous*
31 a Ex. 16:13
32 a Ezek. 45:11
33 a Ps. 78:29–31; 106:15
34 1 Lit. *Graves of Craving*
35 a Num. 33:17

CHAPTER 12
1 a Num. 20:1 b Num. 11:1 c Ex. 2:21 1 *criticized* 2 *Cushite*
2 a Num. 16:3 b Mic. 6:4 c Ezek. 35:12, 13
4 a [Ps. 76:9]
5 a Ex. 19:9; 34:5
6 a Gen. 46:2 b Gen. 31:10
7 a Josh. 1:1 b Heb. 3:2, 5 c 1 Tim. 1:12

8 I speak with him [a]face to face,
Even [b]plainly,[1] and not in [2]dark
sayings;
And he sees [c]the form of the LORD.
Why then [d]were you not afraid
To speak against My servant
Moses?"
9So the anger of the LORD was aroused
against them, and He departed. 10And
when the cloud departed from above the
tabernacle, [a]suddenly Miriam *became*
[b]leprous, as *white as* snow. Then Aaron
turned toward Miriam, and there she was,
a leper. 11So Aaron said to Moses, "Oh, my
lord! Please [a]do not lay [1]*this* sin on us,
in which we have done foolishly and in
which we have sinned. 12Please [a]do not let
her be as one dead, whose flesh is half
consumed when he comes out of his
mother's womb!"
13So Moses cried out to the LORD, saying, "Please [a]heal her, O God, I pray!"
14Then the LORD said to Moses, "If her
father had but [a]spit in her face, would she
not be shamed seven days? Let her be
[b]shut[1] out of the camp seven days, and
afterward she may be received *again.*"
15[a]So Miriam was shut out of the camp
seven days, and the people did not journey
till Miriam was brought in *again.* 16And
afterward the people moved from [a]Haze-
roth and camped in the Wilderness of
Paran.

8 a Deut. 34:10 b [1 Cor. 13:12] c Ex. 33:19–23 d 2 Pet. 2:10 *1 appearing* *2 riddles*
10 a Deut. 24:9 b 2 Kin. 5:27; 15:5
11 a 2 Sam. 19:19; 24:10 *1 the penalty for this*
12 a Ps. 88:4
13 a Ps. 103:3
14 a Deut. 25:9 b Lev. 13:46 *1 exiled*
15 a Deut. 24:9
16 a Num. 11:35; 33:17, 18

MIRIAM

Miriam teaches us what to do and what not to do. She may be the only woman in the Bible who experienced both God's miraculous grace in the life of her nation and His personal dispensation of judgment upon her as an individual. She watched Him work miracles of provision, six days a week for forty years. And for those same years of walking through the desert, He gave her shoes that never wore out. She saw Him in the cloud and in the fire, and she heard the waters rush as He rolled back the sea. As a prophetess, she spoke His holy words; and as a dancer and musician, she led the women of Israel in declaring His victory.

But Miriam also offended the Father. She passed judgment on Moses and, with Aaron, spoke against him for marrying a foreigner. This invoked God's anger, and they received a summons to His presence. There, God affirmed His faithful servant Moses and chastised them for their actions. When God's presence departed, Miriam was covered with leprosy—a visible sign of His displeasure. She might have suffered long, if not for the intercession of her brothers, after which God restored her.

Miriam was a watchwoman, a witness, a worshiper, and a warning. As a watchwoman, her early life teaches us to be vigilant and to speak up at our appointed time; and later, she established the precedent for female prophets among the people of God. As a witness, she experienced miracles the world has not seen since her day. As a worshiper, she is an example of passionate devotion and praise. But she is also a warning for those who may be tempted to speak against God's chosen leaders.

As women of destiny, may we be diligent to avoid Miriam's mistake, walking consistently in the fear of the Lord and in humility with His people. And when we fail, may we, too, receive His restoration and His mercy.

Spies Sent into Canaan

13 And the LORD spoke to Moses, saying, 2 [a]"Send men to spy out the land of Canaan, which I am giving to the children of Israel; from each tribe of their fathers you shall send a man, every one a leader among them."

3 So Moses sent them [a]from the Wilderness of Paran according to the command of the LORD, all of them men who *were* heads of the children of Israel. 4 Now these *were* their names: from the tribe of Reuben, Shammua the son of Zaccur; 5 from the tribe of Simeon, Shaphat the son of Hori; 6 [a]from the tribe of Judah, [b]Caleb the son of Jephunneh; 7 from the tribe of Issachar, Igal the son of Joseph; 8 from the tribe of Ephraim, [1]Hoshea the son of Nun; 9 from the tribe of Benjamin, Palti the son of Raphu; 10 from the tribe of Zebulun, Gaddiel the son of Sodi; 11 from the tribe of Joseph, *that is,* from the tribe of Manasseh, Gaddi the son of Susi; 12 from the tribe of Dan, Ammiel the son of Gemalli; 13 from the tribe of Asher, Sethur the son of Michael; 14 from the tribe of Naphtali, Nahbi the son of Vophsi; 15 from the tribe of Gad, Geuel the son of Machi.

16 These *are* the names of the men whom Moses sent to [1]spy out the land. And Moses called [a]Hoshea[2] the son of Nun, Joshua.

17 Then Moses sent them to spy out the land of Canaan, and said to them, "Go up this *way* into the South, and go up to [a]the mountains, 18 and see what the land is like: whether the people who dwell in it *are* strong or weak, few or many; 19 whether the land they dwell in *is* good or bad; whether the cities they inhabit *are* like camps or strongholds; 20 whether the land *is* [1]rich or poor; and whether there are forests there or not. [a]Be of good courage. And bring some of the fruit of the land." Now the time *was* the season of the first ripe grapes.

21 So they went up and spied out the land [a]from the Wilderness of Zin as far as [b]Rehob, near the entrance of [c]Hamath. 22 And they went up through the South and came to [a]Hebron; Ahiman, Sheshai, and Talmai, the descendants of [b]Anak, *were* there. (Now Hebron was built seven years before Zoan in Egypt.) 23 [a]Then they came to the [1]Valley of Eshcol, and there cut down a branch with one cluster of grapes; they carried it between two of them on a pole. *They* also *brought* some of the pomegranates and figs. 24 The place was called the Valley of [1]Eshcol, because of the cluster which the men of Israel cut down there. 25 And they returned from spying out the land after forty days.

26 Now they departed and came back to Moses and Aaron and all the congregation of the children of Israel in the Wilderness of Paran, at [a]Kadesh; they brought back word to them and to all the congregation, and showed them the fruit of the land. 27 Then they told him, and said: "We went to the land where you sent us. It truly [1]flows with [a]milk and honey, [b]and this *is* its fruit. 28 Nevertheless the [a]people who dwell in the land *are* strong; the cities *are* fortified *and* very large; moreover we saw the descendants of [b]Anak there. 29 [a]The Amalekites dwell in the land of the South; the Hittites, the Jebusites, and the Amorites dwell in the mountains; and the Canaanites dwell by the sea and along the banks of the Jordan."

30 Then [a]Caleb quieted the people before Moses, and said, "Let us go up at once and take possession, for we are well able to overcome it."

Lord God, give ____ the ability to see obstacles and challenges through eyes of faith like Caleb did. For by Your power, You have made them more than able to overcome.

FROM NUMBERS 13:30

31 [a]But the men who had gone up with him said, "We are not able to go up against the people, for they *are* stronger than we." 32 And they [a]gave the children of Israel a bad report of the land which they had spied out, saying, "The land through which we have gone as spies *is* a land that devours its inhabitants, and [b]all the people whom we saw in it *are* men of *great* stature. 33 There we saw the [1]giants ([a]the descendants of Anak came from the giants); and we were [b]like[2] grasshoppers in our own sight, and so we were [c]in their sight."

CHAPTER 13
2 a Deut. 1:22; 9:23
3 a Num. 12:16; 32:8
6 a Num. 34:19 b Josh. 14:6, 7
8 *1* LXX, Vg. *Oshea*
16 a Ex. 17:9 *1 secretly search* *2* LXX, Vg. *Oshea*
17 a Judg. 1:9
20 a Deut. 31:6, 7, 23 *1 fertile or barren*
21 a Num. 20:1; 27:14; 33:36 b Josh. 19:28 c Josh. 13:5
22 a Josh. 15:13, 14 b Josh. 11:21, 22
23 a Deut. 1:24, 25 *1 Wadi*
24 *1* Lit. *Cluster*
26 a Deut. 1:19
27 a Ex. 3:8, 17; 13:5; 33:3 b Deut. 1:25 *1* Has an abundance of food
28 a Deut. 1:28; 9:1, 2 b Josh. 11:21, 22
29 a Judg. 6:3
30 a Num. 14:6, 24
31 a Deut. 1:28; 9:1–3
32 a Num. 14:36, 37 b Amos 2:9
33 a Deut. 1:28; 9:2 b Is. 40:22 c 1 Sam. 17:42 *1* Heb. *nephilim* *2* As mere insects

NUMBERS 13:16

Dear Woman of Destiny,

Today I thought of the many changes you are experiencing. Once I heard a person say, "We might as well face it. Change is here to stay." How true that is. It seems that people hardly get out of one place of change until they are in another.

One of the most difficult changes to make is to come into a new identity. Remember when you went through identity changes as you changed from a little girl to a teenager and then to an adult? There were times when your emotions made you feel like a little girl; but at the same time, you wanted to be treated like a young lady and not a child. How confusing it was!

Changes that come while we are growing in the Lord are no different. Our emotions sometimes long for an earlier or more comfortable time in life, and yet we cry out to be a mature woman of God. The difficulties you are going through during this season remind me of similar times in my own life.

As I began to move into the ministry, the transition was sometimes difficult. Someone once explained it by telling me the people who had known me in the previous season of my life still identified me according to the roles I had played in the past. Many knew me as a mother, a wife, a friend, or good helper, but not as a minister of the gospel. They knew me as I was, but they did not know how to relate to who I was becoming.

The Lord had, through transition, put me in a new place. The new place required a new identity. Not receiving the new identity would cause me to function as I had in past seasons. Before others could recognize my new identity, I had to accept it myself. Since my Father in heaven had spoken, I could receive everything He had for me including a new "name" as a minister, in addition to the names I had in other areas of my life.

In the Bible, Joshua received a new name when he came into a new season (see Num. 13:16). In order for Joshua to fulfill his destiny, he had to receive a new identity. Many people are never able to function properly in the new season because of names that hold them in the past. Some of the names a person can have from the old season are: Failure, Rejected, Abandoned, and Unloved. A new name will bring a person out of captivity and set her on a road to success.

As you sit in the presence of the Father and pour out your heart to Him, listen for Him to speak your new name. Your new identity will free you from old names that hold you in captivity. A new confidence will arise. Let the Lord give you the name He calls you.

Barbara Wentroble

Israel Refuses to Enter Canaan

14 So all the congregation lifted up their voices and cried, and the people [a]wept that night. 2[a]And all the children of Israel complained against Moses and Aaron, and the whole congregation said to them, "If only we had died in the land of Egypt! Or if only we had died in this wilderness! 3Why has the LORD brought us to this land to [1]fall by the sword, that our wives and [a]children should become victims? Would it not be better for us to return to Egypt?" 4So they said to one another, [a]"Let us select a leader and [b]return to Egypt."

5Then Moses and Aaron [1]fell on their faces before all the assembly of the congregation of the children of Israel.

6But Joshua the son of Nun and Caleb the son of Jephunneh, *who were* among those who had spied out the land, tore their clothes; 7and they spoke to all the congregation of the children of Israel, saying: [a]"The land we passed through to spy out *is* an exceedingly good land. 8If the LORD [a]delights in us, then He will bring us into this land and give it to us, [b]'a land which flows with milk and honey.' 9Only [a]do not rebel against the LORD, [b]nor fear the people of the land, for [c]they[1] *are* our bread; their protection has departed from them, [d]and the LORD *is* with us. Do not fear them."

10[a]And all the congregation said to stone them with stones. Now [b]the glory of the LORD appeared in the tabernacle of meeting before all the children of Israel.

Moses Intercedes for the People

11Then the LORD said to Moses: "How long will these people [a]reject[1] Me? And how long will they not [b]believe Me, with all the [2]signs which I have performed among them? 12I will strike them with the pestilence and disinherit them, and I will [a]make of you a nation greater and mightier than they."

13And [a]Moses said to the LORD: [b]"Then the Egyptians will hear *it,* for by Your might You brought these people up from among them, 14and they will tell *it* to the inhabitants of this land. They have [a]heard that You, LORD, *are* among these people; that You, LORD, are seen face to face and Your cloud stands above them, and You go before them in a pillar of cloud by day and in a pillar of fire by night. 15Now *if* You kill these people as one man, then the nations which have heard of Your fame will speak, saying, 16'Because the LORD was not [a]able to bring this people to the land which He swore to give them, therefore He killed them in the wilderness.' 17And now, I pray, let the power of my Lord be great, just as You have spoken, saying, 18[a]'The LORD is longsuffering and abundant in mercy, forgiving iniquity and transgression; but He by no means clears *the guilty,* [b]visiting the iniquity of the fathers on the children to the third and fourth *generation.*' 19[a]Pardon the iniquity of this people, I pray, [b]according to the greatness of Your mercy, just [c]as You have forgiven this people, from Egypt even until now."

20Then the LORD said: "I have pardoned, [a]according to your word; 21 but truly, as I live, [a]all the earth shall be filled with the glory of the LORD— 22[a]because all these men who have seen My glory and the signs which I did in Egypt and in the wilderness, and have put Me to the test now [b]these ten times, and have not heeded My voice, 23they certainly shall not [a]see the land of which I [1]swore to their fathers, nor shall any of those who rejected Me see it. 24But My servant [a]Caleb, because he has a different spirit in him and [b]has followed Me fully, I will bring into the land where he went, and his descendants shall inherit it. 25Now the Amalekites and the Canaanites dwell in the valley; tomorrow turn and [a]move out into the wilderness by the Way of the Red Sea."

Death Sentence on the Rebels

26And the LORD spoke to Moses and Aaron, saying, 27[a]"How long *shall I bear with* this evil congregation who complain against Me? [b]I have heard the complaints which the children of Israel make against Me. 28Say to them, [a]'As I live,' says the LORD, 'just as you have spoken in My hearing, so I will do to you: 29The carcasses of you who have complained against Me shall fall in this wilderness, [a]all of you who were numbered, according to your entire number, from twenty years old and above. 30[a]Except for Caleb the son of Jephunneh and Joshua the son of Nun, you

CHAPTER 14
1 a Deut. 1:45
2 a Ex. 16:2; 17:3
3 a Deut. 1:39 *1 be killed in battle*
4 a Neh. 9:17 b Acts 7:39
5 *1 prostrated themselves*
7 a Num. 13:27
8 a Deut. 10:15 b Num. 13:27
9 a Deut. 1:26; 9:7, 23, 24 b Deut. 7:18 c Num. 24:8 d Deut. 20:1, 3, 4; 31:6–8 *1* They shall be as food for our consumption.
10 a Ex. 17:4 b Ex. 16:10
11 a Heb. 3:8 b Deut. 9:23 *1 despise 2 miraculous signs*
12 a Ex. 32:10
13 a Ps. 106:23 b Ex. 32:12
14 a Deut. 2:25
16 a Deut. 9:28
18 a Ex. 34:6, 7 b Ex. 20:5
19 a Ex. 32:32; 34:9 b Ps. 51:1; 106:45 c Ps. 78:38
20 a Mic. 7:18–20
21 a Ps. 72:19
22 a Deut. 1:35 b Gen. 31:7
23 a Num. 26:65; 32:11 *1 solemnly promised*
24 a Josh. 14:6, 8, 9 b Num. 32:12
25 a Deut. 1:40
27 a Ex. 16:28 b Ex. 16:12
28 a Heb. 3:16–19
29 a Num. 1:45, 46; 26:64
30 a Deut. 1:36–38

NUMBERS 14:21

Dear Woman of Destiny,

For many years, I had little understanding of the term "the glory of God." There seemed to be a vague, mysterious aura about it that defied definition. As I began to study the glory of God, however, I realized that, though there are several different meanings to be considered, the simplest definition we can give to the glory of the Lord is "the manifest presence of God."

In the Old Testament, the glory of God was resident in the cloud by day and the pillar of fire by night that guarded the children of Israel throughout their exodus. The glory was not the cloud or the pillar, but the manifest presence of God dwelling in them.

The glory of human achievement is an ascribed glory. It exists in the eye of the beholder. But the glory of God is objective. It is rooted in His very nature, not in the evaluation of others. When God's glory is unveiled and recognized, all those things in which human beings take pride fade to nothingness. When Moses begged God to show him His glory, He obliged (see Ex. 33:19), thus linking the glory of God with His loving character.

In Moses' tabernacle there was a veil between the Most Holy Place and the Holy Place that hid the manifest presence of God from the view of the people. The glory of God dwelt in the tabernacle of David and in the temples of Solomon and of Zerubbabel as well. But that was not God's original plan or desire; He desired to indwell His human creation, making mankind His temple and pouring His glory into Adam and Eve as He walked with them and talked with them in the cool of the evening. If man had not fallen, God would have poured His glory—the weight of His divine presence—into man as He walked with him and communed with him. We witness in the transfiguration of Jesus the glory of God's presence as He had intended to give it to Adam. Because of the Fall, however, God's original plan was interrupted.

What then is our response to be to the glory of God? We are to ascribe to the Lord glory (see 1 Chr. 16:28) and we are to "glory in His holy name" (v. 10). We are to worship Him by recognizing His presence and praising Him for those qualities that His actions on our behalf unveil. We glorify God by offering Him our praise and by being channels through which the Holy Spirit, who lives within us, can communicate God to those around us.

As you allow the precious Holy Spirit to fulfill His mandate in your life, rending the veil of flesh, you will be filled with His glory—the manifest presence of God. In that way, through the lives of believers, "the earth will be filled with the knowledge of the glory of the LORD, as the waters cover the sea" (Hab. 2:14).

Fuchsia Pickett

shall by no means enter the land which I
[1]swore I would make you dwell in. 31[a]But
your little ones, whom you said would be
victims, I will bring in, and they shall
[1]know the land which [b]you have despised.
32But *as for* you, [a]your[1] carcasses shall
fall in this wilderness. 33And your sons
shall [a]be [1]shepherds in the wilderness
[b]forty years, and [c]bear the brunt of your
infidelity, until your carcasses are consumed in the wilderness. 34[a]According to
the number of the days in which you spied
out the land, [b]forty days, for each day you
shall bear your [1]guilt one year, *namely*
forty years, [c]and you shall know My [2]re-
jection. 35[a]I the LORD have spoken this. I
will surely do so to all [b]this evil congregation who are gathered together against
Me. In this wilderness they shall be consumed, and there they shall die.' "
36Now the men whom Moses sent to spy
out the land, who returned and made all
the congregation complain against him
by bringing a bad report of the land,
37those very men who brought the evil report about the land, [a]died by the plague
before the LORD. 38[a]But Joshua the son of
Nun and Caleb the son of Jephunneh remained alive, of the men who went to spy
out the land.

A Futile Invasion Attempt

39Then Moses told these words to all
the children of Israel, [a]and the people
mourned greatly. 40And they rose early in
the morning and went up to the top of the
mountain, saying, [a]"Here we are, and we
will go up to the place which the LORD has
promised, for we have sinned!"
41And Moses said, "Now why do you
[1]transgress the command of the LORD?
For this will not succeed. 42[a]Do not go up,
lest you be defeated by your enemies,
for the LORD *is* not among you. 43For
the Amalekites and the Canaanites *are*
there before you, and you shall fall by
the sword; [a]because you have turned
away from the LORD, the LORD will not be
with you."
44[a]But they presumed to go up to the
mountaintop. Nevertheless, neither the
ark of the covenant of the LORD nor Moses
departed from the camp. 45Then the Amalekites and the Canaanites who dwelt in
that mountain came down and attacked
them, and drove them back as far as
[a]Hormah.

Laws of Grain and Drink Offerings

15 And the LORD spoke to Moses, saying, 2[a]"Speak to the children of Israel, and say to them: 'When you have
come into the land you are to inhabit,
which I am giving to you, 3and you [a]make
an offering by fire to the LORD, a burnt
offering or a sacrifice, [b]to fulfill a vow or
as a freewill offering or [c]in your appointed
feasts, to make a [d]sweet[1] aroma to the
LORD, from the herd or the flock, 4then
[a]he who presents his offering to the LORD
shall bring [b]a grain offering of one-tenth
of an ephah of fine flour mixed [c]with one-
fourth of a hin of oil; 5[a]and one-fourth of
a hin of wine as a drink offering you shall
prepare with the burnt offering or the sacrifice, for each [b]lamb. 6[a]Or for a ram you
shall prepare as a grain offering two-
tenths *of an ephah* of fine flour mixed
with one-third of a hin of oil; 7and as a
drink offering you shall offer one-third of
a hin of wine as a sweet aroma to the
LORD. 8And when you prepare a young
bull as a burnt offering, or as a sacrifice to
fulfill a vow, or as a [a]peace offering to the
LORD, 9then shall be offered [a]with the
young bull a grain offering of three-
tenths *of an ephah* of fine flour mixed
with half a hin of oil; 10and you shall bring
as the drink offering half a hin of wine as
an offering made by fire, a sweet aroma to
the LORD.
11[a]'Thus it shall be done for each young
bull, for each ram, or for each lamb or
young goat. 12According to the number
that you prepare, so you shall do with everyone according to their number. 13All
who are native-born shall do these things
in this manner, in presenting an offering
made by fire, a sweet aroma to the LORD.
14And if a stranger [1]dwells with you, or
whoever *is* among you throughout your
generations, and would present an offering made by fire, a sweet aroma to the
LORD, just as you do, so shall he do.
15[a]One [1]ordinance *shall be* for you of the
assembly and for the stranger who dwells
with you, an ordinance forever throughout your generations; as you are, so shall
the stranger be before the LORD. 16One
law and one custom shall be for you and
for the stranger who dwells with you.' "
17Again the LORD spoke to Moses, saying, 18[a]"Speak to the children of Israel,
and say to them: 'When you come into the

30 [1] *solemnly promised*
31 [a] Deut. 1:39 [b] Ps. 106:24 [1] *be acquainted with*
32 [a] Num. 26:64, 65; 32:13 [1] You shall die.
33 [a] Ps. 107:40 [b] Deut. 2:14 [c] Ezek. 23:35 [1] Vg. *wanderers*
34 [a] Num. 13:25 [b] Ezek. 4:6 [c] [Heb. 4:1] [1] *iniquity* [2] *opposition*
35 [a] Num. 23:19 [b] 1 Cor. 10:5
37 [a] [1 Cor. 10:10]
38 [a] Josh. 14:6, 10
39 [a] Ex. 33:4
40 [a] Deut. 1:41–44
41 [1] *overstep*
42 [a] Deut. 1:42; 31:17
43 [a] 2 Chr. 15:2
44 [a] Deut. 1:43
45 [a] Num. 21:3

CHAPTER 15
2 [a] Lev. 23:10
3 [a] Lev. 1:2, 3 [b] Lev. 7:16; 22:18, 21 [c] Lev. 23:2, 8, 12, 38 [d] Ex. 29:18 [1] *pleasing*
4 [a] Lev. 2:1; 6:14 [b] Ex. 29:40 [c] Num. 28:5
5 [a] Num. 28:7, 14 [b] Lev. 1:10; 3:6
6 [a] Num. 28:12, 14
8 [a] Lev. 7:11
9 [a] Num. 28:12, 14
11 [a] Num. 28
14 [1] *As a resident alien*
15 [a] Num. 9:14; 15:29 [1] *statute*
18 [a] Deut. 26:1

land to which I bring you, [19]then it will
be, when you eat of [a]the bread of the land,
that you shall offer up a heave offering to
the LORD. [20][a]You shall offer up a cake of
the first of your ground meal *as* a heave
offering; as [b]a heave offering of the
threshing floor, so shall you offer it up.
[21]Of the first of your ground meal you
shall give to the LORD a heave offering
throughout your generations.

Laws Concerning Unintentional Sin

[22][a]'If you sin unintentionally, and do
not observe all these commandments
which the LORD has spoken to Moses—
[23]all that the LORD has commanded you
by the hand of Moses, from the day the
LORD gave commandment and onward
throughout your generations— [24]then it
will be, [a]if it is unintentionally committed, [1]without the knowledge of the congregation, that the whole congregation
shall offer one young bull as a burnt offering, as a sweet aroma to the LORD, [b]with
its grain offering and its drink offering,
according to the ordinance, and [c]one kid
of the goats as a sin offering. [25][a]So the
priest shall make atonement for the whole
congregation of the children of Israel, and
it shall be forgiven them, for it was unin-
tentional; they shall bring their offering,
an offering made by fire to the LORD, and
their sin offering before the LORD, for
their unintended sin. [26]It shall be forgiven
the whole congregation of the children of
Israel and the stranger who dwells among
them, because all the people *did it* unintentionally.

[27]'And [a]if a person sins unintentionally,
then he shall bring a female goat in its
first year as a sin offering. [28][a]So the priest
shall make atonement for the person who
sins unintentionally, when he sins unintentionally before the LORD, to make
atonement for him; and it shall be forgiv-
en him. [29][a]You shall have one law for him
who sins unintentionally, *for* him who is
native-born among the children of Israel
and for the stranger who dwells among
them.

Law Concerning Presumptuous Sin

[30][a]'But the person who does *anything*
[1]presumptuously, *whether he is* native-
born or a stranger, that one [2]brings reproach on the LORD, and he shall be [3]cut
off from among his people. [31]Because he
has [a]despised the word of the LORD, and
has broken His commandment, that person shall be completely cut off; his [1]guilt
shall be upon him.' "

Penalty for Violating the Sabbath

[32]Now while the children of Israel were
in the wilderness, [a]they found a man
gathering sticks on the Sabbath day.
[33]And those who found him gathering
sticks brought him to Moses and Aaron,
and to all the congregation. [34]They put
him [a]under guard, because it had not
been explained what should be done to
him.

[35]Then the LORD said to Moses, [a]"The
man must surely be put to death; all the
congregation shall [b]stone him with
stones outside the camp." [36]So, as the
LORD commanded Moses, all the congregation brought him outside the camp and
stoned him with stones, and he died.

Tassels on Garments

[37]Again the LORD spoke to Moses, saying, [38]"Speak to the children of Israel: Tell
[a]them to make tassels on the corners of
their garments throughout their generations, and to put a blue thread in the tassels of the corners. [39]And you shall have
the tassel, that you may look upon it and

19 a Josh. 5:11, 12
20 a Lev. 23:10, 14, 17 b Lev. 2:14; 23:10, 16
22 a Lev. 4:2
24 a Lev. 4:13 b Num. 15:8–10 c Lev. 4:23 *1* Lit. *away from the eyes*
25 a [Heb. 2:17]
27 a Lev. 4:27–31
28 a Lev. 4:35
29 a Num. 15:15
30 a Deut. 1:43; 17:12 *1 defiantly,* lit. *with a high hand* *2 blasphemes* *3* Put to death
31 a Prov. 13:13 *1 iniquity*
32 a Ex. 31:14, 15; 35:2, 3
34 a Lev. 24:12
35 a Ex. 31:14, 15 b Lev. 24:14
38 a Matt. 23:5

There are three elements in the spiritual life that we must know if we are to live and die as believers. We must know: how great our sin is, how we can be delivered from our sins, and how we should live in thankfulness to God for this deliverance.

ANDREW MURRAY

[a]remember all the commandments of the
LORD and do them, and that you [b]*may* not
[c]follow the harlotry to which your own
heart and your own eyes are inclined,
40and that you may remember and do all
My commandments, and be [a]holy for your
God. 41I *am* the LORD your God, who
brought you out of the land of Egypt, to
be your God: I *am* the LORD your God."

Rebellion Against Moses and Aaron

16 Now [a]Korah the son of Izhar, the
son of Kohath, the son of Levi,
with [b]Dathan and Abiram the sons of Eliab, and On the son of Peleth, sons of Reuben, took *men;* 2and they rose up before
Moses with some of the children of Israel,
two hundred and fifty leaders of the congregation, [a]representatives of the congregation, men of renown. 3[a]They gathered
together against Moses and Aaron, and
said to them, "*You* [1]*take* too much upon
yourselves, for [b]all the congregation *is*
holy, every one of them, [c]and the LORD *is*
among them. Why then do you exalt yourselves above the assembly of the LORD?"
4So when Moses heard *it,* he [a]fell on his
face; 5and he spoke to Korah and all his
company, saying, "Tomorrow morning
the LORD will show who *is* [a]His and *who*
is [b]holy,[1] and will cause *him* to come near
to Him. That one whom He chooses He
will cause to [c]come near to Him. 6Do this:
Take censers, Korah and all your company; 7put fire in them and put incense in
them before the LORD tomorrow, and it
shall be *that* the man whom the LORD
chooses *is* the holy one. *You take* too
much upon yourselves, you sons of Levi!"
8Then Moses said to Korah, "Hear now,
you sons of Levi: 9*Is it* [a]a small thing to
you that the God of Israel has [b]separated
you from the congregation of Israel, to
bring you near to Himself, to do the work
of the tabernacle of the LORD, and to stand
before the congregation to serve them;
10and that He has brought you near *to*
Himself, you and all your brethren, the
sons of Levi, with you? And are you seeking the priesthood also? 11Therefore you
and all your company *are* gathered together against the LORD. [a]And what *is*
Aaron that you complain against him?"
12And Moses sent to call Dathan and
Abiram the sons of Eliab, but they said,
"We will not come up! 13*Is it* a small thing
that you have brought us up out of [a]a land
flowing with milk and honey, to kill us in
the wilderness, that you should [b]keep acting like a prince over us? 14Moreover [a]you
have not brought us into [b]a land flowing
with milk and honey, nor given us inheritance of fields and vineyards. Will you put
out the eyes of these men? We will not
come up!"
15Then Moses was very angry, and said
to the LORD, [a]"Do not [1]respect their offering. [b]I have not taken one donkey from
them, nor have I hurt one of them."
16And Moses said to Korah, "Tomorrow,
you and all your company be present [a]be-
fore the LORD—you and they, as well as
Aaron. 17Let each take his censer and put
incense in it, and each of you bring his
censer before the LORD, two hundred and
fifty censers; both you and Aaron, each
with his censer." 18So every man took his
censer, put fire in it, laid incense on it,
and stood at the door of the tabernacle of
meeting with Moses and Aaron. 19And Korah gathered all the congregation against
them at the door of the tabernacle of
meeting. Then [a]the glory of the LORD appeared to all the congregation.
20And the LORD spoke to Moses and
Aaron, saying, 21[a]"Separate yourselves
from among this congregation, that I may
[b]consume them in a moment."
22Then they [a]fell[1] on their faces, and
said, "O God, [b]the God of the spirits of all
flesh, shall one man sin, and You be angry
with all the [c]congregation?"
23So the LORD spoke to Moses, saying,
24"Speak to the congregation, saying, 'Get
away from the tents of Korah, Dathan, and
Abiram.' "
25Then Moses rose and went to Dathan
and Abiram, and the elders of Israel followed him. 26And he spoke to the congregation, saying, [a]"Depart now from the
tents of these wicked men! Touch nothing
of theirs, lest you be consumed in all their
sins." 27So they got away from around the
tents of Korah, Dathan, and Abiram; and
Dathan and Abiram came out and stood at
the door of their tents, with their wives,
their sons, and their little [a]children.
28And Moses said: [a]"By this you shall
know that the LORD has sent me to do all
these works, for *I have* not *done them* [b]of
my own will. 29If these men die naturally
like all men, or if they are [a]visited by the
common fate of all men, *then* the LORD
has not sent me. 30But if the LORD creates
[a]a new thing, and the earth opens its

39 a Ps. 103:18 b Deut. 29:19 c James 4:4
40 a [Lev. 11:44, 45]
CHAPTER 16
1 a Ex. 6:21 b Num. 26:9
2 a Num. 1:16; 26:9
3 a Ps. 106:16 b Ex. 19:6 c Ex. 29:45 *1 assume too much for*
4 a Num. 14:5; 20:6
5 a [2 Tim. 2:19] b Lev. 21:6–8, 12 c Ezek. 40:46; 44:15, 16 *1 set aside* for His use only
9 a Is. 7:13 b Deut. 10:8
11 a Ex. 16:7, 8
13 a Num. 11:4–6 b Ex. 2:14
14 a Num. 14:1–4 b Ex. 3:8
15 a Gen. 4:4, 5 b 1 Sam. 12:3 *1 graciously regard*
16 a 1 Sam. 12:3, 7
19 a Num. 14:10
21 a Gen. 19:17 b Ex. 32:10; 33:5
22 a Num. 14:5 b Num. 27:16 c Gen. 18:23–32; 20:4 *1 prostrated themselves*
26 a Gen. 19:12, 14, 15, 17
27 a Num. 26:11
28 a John 5:36 b John 5:30
29 a Ex. 20:5
30 a Job 31:3

mouth and swallows them up with all that belongs to them, and they [b]go down alive into the pit, then you will understand that these men have rejected the LORD."

31 [a]Now it came to pass, as he finished speaking all these words, that the ground split apart under them, 32 and the earth opened its mouth and swallowed them up, with their households and [a]all the men with Korah, with all *their* goods. 33 So they and all those with them went down alive into the pit; the earth closed over them, and they perished from among the assembly. 34 Then all Israel who *were* around them fled at their cry, for they said, "Lest the earth swallow us up *also!*"

35 And [a]a fire came out from the LORD and consumed the two hundred and fifty men who were offering incense.

36 Then the LORD spoke to Moses, saying: 37 "Tell Eleazar, the son of Aaron the priest, to pick up the censers out of the blaze, for [a]they are holy, and scatter the fire some distance away. 38 The censers of [a]these men who sinned [1]against their own souls, let them be made into hammered plates as a covering for the altar. Because they presented them before the LORD, therefore they are holy; [b]and they shall be a sign to the children of Israel." 39 So Eleazar the priest took the bronze censers, which those who were burned up had presented, and they were hammered out as a covering on the altar, 40 *to be* a [1]memorial to the children of Israel [a]that no outsider, who *is* not a descendant of Aaron, should come near to offer incense before the LORD, that he might not become like Korah and his companions, just as the LORD had said to him through Moses.

Complaints of the People

41 On the next day [a]all the congregation of the children of Israel complained against Moses and Aaron, saying, "You have killed the people of the LORD." 42 Now it happened, when the congregation had gathered against Moses and Aaron, that they turned toward the tabernacle of meeting; and suddenly [a]the cloud covered it, and the glory of the LORD appeared. 43 Then Moses and Aaron came before the tabernacle of meeting.

44 And the LORD spoke to Moses, saying, 45 "Get away from among this congregation, that I may consume them in a moment." And they fell on their faces.

46 So Moses said to Aaron, "Take a censer and put fire in it from the altar, put incense *on it,* and take it quickly to the congregation and make [1]atonement for them; [a]for wrath has gone out from the LORD. The plague has begun." 47 Then Aaron took *it* as Moses commanded, and ran into the midst of the assembly; and already the plague had begun among the people. So he put in the incense and made atonement for the people. 48 And he stood between the dead and the living; so [a]the plague was stopped. 49 Now those who died in the plague were fourteen thousand seven hundred, besides those who died in the Korah incident. 50 So Aaron returned to Moses at the door of the tabernacle of meeting, for the plague had stopped.

The Budding of Aaron's Rod

17 And the LORD spoke to Moses, saying: 2 "Speak to the children of Israel, and get from them a rod from each father's house, all their leaders according to their fathers' houses—twelve rods. Write each man's name on his rod. 3 And you shall write Aaron's name on the rod of Levi. For there shall be one rod for the head of *each* father's house. 4 Then you shall place them in the tabernacle of meeting before [a]the Testimony, [b]where I meet with you. 5 And it shall be *that* the rod of the man [a]whom I choose will blossom; thus I will rid Myself of the complaints of the children of Israel, [b]which they make against you."

6 So Moses spoke to the children of Israel, and each of their leaders gave him a rod apiece, for each leader according to their fathers' houses, twelve rods; and the rod of Aaron *was* among their rods. 7 And Moses placed the rods before the LORD in [a]the tabernacle of witness.

8 Now it came to pass on the next day that Moses went into the tabernacle of witness, and behold, the [a]rod of Aaron, of the house of Levi, had sprouted and put forth buds, had produced blossoms and yielded ripe almonds. 9 Then Moses brought out all the rods from before the LORD to all the children of Israel; and they looked, and each man took his rod.

10 And the LORD said to Moses, "Bring [a]Aaron's rod back before the Testimony, to be kept [b]as a sign against the rebels, [c]that you may put their complaints away from Me, lest they die." 11 Thus did Moses;

30 b [Ps. 55:15]
31 a Num. 26:10
32 a Num. 26:11
35 a Num. 11:1–3; 26:10
37 a Lev. 27:28
38 a Hab. 2:10 b Num. 17:10 *1* Or *at the cost of their own lives*
40 a Num. 3:10 *1 reminder*
41 a Num. 14:2
42 a Ex. 40:34
46 a Num. 18:5 *1* Lit. *covering*
48 a Num. 25:8

CHAPTER 17
4 a Ex. 25:16 b Ex. 25:22; 29:42, 43; 30:36
5 a Num. 16:5 b Num. 16:11
7 a Ex. 38:21
8 a [Ezek. 17:24]
10 a Heb. 9:4 b Deut. 9:7, 24 c Num. 17:5

just as the LORD had commanded him, so
he did.
12So the children of Israel spoke to Moses, saying, "Surely we die, we perish, we
all perish! 13[a]Whoever even comes near
the tabernacle of the LORD must die. Shall
we all utterly die?"

Duties of Priests and Levites

18 Then the LORD said to Aaron:
[a]"You and your sons and your father's house with you shall [b]bear the [1]in-
iquity *related to* the sanctuary, and you
and your sons with you shall bear the iniquity *associated with* your priesthood.
2Also bring with you your brethren of the
[a]tribe of Levi, the tribe of your father, that
they may be [b]joined with you and serve
you while you and your sons *are* with you
before the tabernacle of [1]witness. 3They
shall attend to your [1]needs and [a]all the
needs of the tabernacle; [b]but they shall
not come near the articles of the sanctuary and the altar, [c]lest they die—they and
you also. 4They shall be joined with you
and attend to the needs of the tabernacle
of meeting, for all the work of the tabernacle; [a]but an outsider shall not come
near you. 5And you shall attend to [a]the
duties of the sanctuary and the duties of
the altar, [b]that there *may* be no more
wrath on the children of Israel. 6Behold,
I Myself have [a]taken your brethren the
Levites from among the children of Israel;
[b]*they are* a gift to you, given by the LORD,
to do the work of the tabernacle of meeting. 7Therefore [a]you and your sons with
you shall attend to your priesthood for everything at the altar and [b]behind the veil;
and you shall serve. I give your priesthood
to you as a [c]gift for service, but the outsider who comes near shall be put to
death."

Offerings for Support of the Priests

8And the LORD spoke to Aaron: "Here, [a]I
Myself have also given you [1]charge of My
heave offerings, all the holy gifts of the
children of Israel; I have given them [b]as a
portion to you and your sons, as an ordinance forever. 9This shall be yours of the
most holy things *reserved* from the fire:
every offering of theirs, every [a]grain offering and every [b]sin offering and every
[c]trespass offering which they render to
Me, *shall be* most holy for you and your
sons. 10[a]In a most holy *place* you shall eat
it; every male shall eat it. It shall be holy
to you.
11"This also *is* yours: [a]the heave offering of their gift, with all the wave offerings of the children of Israel; I have given
them to you, and your sons and daughters
with you, as an ordinance forever. [b]Every-
one who is [1]clean in your house may
eat it.
12[a]"All the [1]best of the oil, all the best
of the new wine and the grain, [b]their firstfruits which they offer to the LORD, I have
given them to you. 13Whatever first ripe
fruit is in their land, [a]which they bring to
the LORD, shall be yours. Everyone who is
clean in your house may eat it.
14[a]"Every [1]devoted thing in Israel shall
be yours.
15"Everything that first opens [a]the
womb of all flesh, which they bring to the
LORD, whether man or beast, shall be
yours; nevertheless [b]the firstborn of man
you shall surely redeem, and the firstborn
of unclean animals you shall redeem.
16And those redeemed of the devoted
things you shall redeem when one month
old, [a]according to your valuation, for five
shekels of silver, according to the shekel
of the sanctuary, which *is* [b]twenty gerahs.
17[a]But the firstborn of a cow, the firstborn
of a sheep, or the firstborn of a goat you
shall not redeem; they *are* holy. [b]You
shall sprinkle their blood on the altar, and
burn their fat *as* an offering made by fire
for a sweet aroma to the LORD. 18And their
flesh shall be yours, just as the [a]wave[1]
breast and the right thigh are yours.
19"All the heave offerings of the holy
things, which the children of Israel offer
to the LORD, I have given to you and your
sons and daughters with you as an ordinance forever; [a]it *is* a covenant of salt forever before the LORD with you and your
descendants with you."
20Then the LORD said to Aaron: "You
shall have [a]no inheritance in their land,
nor shall you have any portion among
them; [b]I *am* your portion and your inheritance among the children of Israel.

Tithes for Support of the Levites

21"Behold, [a]I have given the children of
Levi all the tithes in Israel as [1]an inheritance in return for the work which they
perform, [b]the work of the tabernacle of
meeting. 22[a]Hereafter the children of Is-

13 a Num. 1:51, 53; 18:4, 7

CHAPTER 18
1 a Num. 17:13 b Ex. 28:38 *1 guilt*
2 a Num. 1:47 b Num. 3:5–10 *1 testimony*
3 a Num. 3:25, 31, 36 b Num. 16:40 c Num. 4:15 *1 service*
4 a Num. 3:10
5 a Lev. 24:3 b Num. 8:19; 16:46
6 a Num. 3:12, 45 b Num. 3:9
7 a Num. 3:10; 18:5 b Heb. 9:3, 6 c 1 Pet. 5:2, 3
8 a Lev. 6:16, 18; 7:28–34 b Ex. 29:29; 40:13, 15 *1 custody*
9 a Lev. 2:2, 3; 10:12, 13 b Lev. 6:25, 26 c Lev. 7:7
10 a Lev. 6:16, 26
11 a Deut. 18:3–5 b Lev. 22:1–16 *1 purified*
12 a Ex. 23:19 b Ex. 22:29 *1 Lit. fat*
13 a Ex. 22:29; 23:19; 34:26
14 a Lev. 27:1–33 *1 consecrated*
15 a Ex. 13:2 b Ex. 13:12–15
16 a Lev. 27:6 b Ex. 30:13
17 a Deut. 15:19 b Lev. 3:2, 5
18 a Ex. 29:26–28 *1 breast of the wave offering*
19 a 2 Chr. 13:5
20 a Josh. 13:14, 33 b Ezek. 44:28
21 a Lev. 27:30–33 b Num. 3:7, 8 *1 a possession*
22 a Num. 1:51

rael shall not come near the tabernacle of meeting, [b]lest they bear sin and die. 23 But the Levites shall perform the work of the tabernacle of meeting, and they shall bear their iniquity; *it shall be* a statute forever, throughout your generations, that among the children of Israel they shall have no inheritance. 24 For the tithes of the children of Israel, which they offer up *as* a heave offering to the LORD, I have given to the Levites [1]as an inheritance; therefore I have said to them, 'Among the children of Israel they shall have no inheritance.' "

The Tithe of the Levites

25 Then the LORD spoke to Moses, saying, 26 "Speak thus to the Levites, and say to them: 'When you take from the children of Israel the tithes which I have given you from them as your inheritance, then you shall offer up a heave offering of it to the LORD, [a]a tenth of the tithe. 27 And your heave offering shall be reckoned to you as though *it were* the grain of the [a]threshing floor and as the fullness of the winepress. 28 Thus you shall also offer a heave offering to the LORD from all your tithes which you receive from the children of Israel, and you shall give the LORD's heave offering from it to Aaron the priest. 29 Of all your gifts you shall offer up every heave offering due to the LORD, from all the [1]best of them, the consecrated part of them.' 30 Therefore you shall say to them: 'When you have lifted up the best of it, then *the rest* shall be accounted to the Levites as the produce of the threshing floor and as the produce of the winepress. 31 You may eat it in any place, you and your households, for it *is* [a]your [1]reward for your work in the tabernacle of meeting. 32 And you shall [a]bear no sin because of it, when you have lifted up the best of it. But you shall not [b]profane the holy gifts of the children of Israel, lest you die.' "

Laws of Purification

19 Now the LORD spoke to Moses and Aaron, saying, 2 "This *is* the [1]ordinance of the law which the LORD has commanded, saying: 'Speak to the children of Israel, that they bring you a red heifer without [2]blemish, in which there *is* no [a]defect [b]*and* on which a yoke has never come. 3 You shall give it to Eleazar the priest, that he may take it [a]outside the camp, and it shall be slaughtered before him; 4 and Eleazar the priest shall take some of its blood with his finger, and [a]sprinkle some of its blood seven times directly in front of the tabernacle of meeting. 5 Then the heifer shall be burned in his sight: [a]its hide, its flesh, its blood, and its offal shall be burned. 6 And the priest shall take [a]cedar wood and [b]hyssop and scarlet, and cast *them* into the midst of the fire burning the heifer. 7 [a]Then the priest shall wash his clothes, he shall bathe in water, and afterward he shall come into the camp; the priest shall be unclean until evening. 8 And the one who burns it shall wash his clothes in water, bathe in water, and shall be unclean until evening. 9 Then a man *who is* clean shall gather up [a]the ashes of the heifer, and store *them* outside the camp in a clean place; and they shall be kept for the congregation of the children of Israel [b]for the water of [1]purification; it *is* for purifying from sin. 10 And the one who gathers the ashes of the heifer shall wash his clothes, and be unclean until evening. It shall be a statute forever to the children of Israel and to the stranger who dwells among them.

11 [a]'He who touches the dead [1]body of anyone shall be unclean seven days. 12 [a]He shall purify himself with the water on the third day and on the seventh day; *then* he will be clean. But if he does not purify himself on the third day and on the seventh day, he will not be clean. 13 Whoever touches the body of anyone who has died, and [a]does not purify himself, [b]defiles the tabernacle of the LORD. That person shall be cut off from Israel. He shall be unclean, because [c]the water of purification was not sprinkled on him; [d]his uncleanness *is* still on him.

14 'This *is* the law when a man dies in a tent: All who come into the tent and all who *are* in the tent shall be unclean seven days; 15 and every [a]open vessel, which has no cover fastened on it, *is* unclean. 16 [a]Whoever in the open field touches one who is slain by a sword or who has died, or a bone of a man, or a grave, shall be unclean seven days.

17 'And for an unclean *person* they shall take some of the [a]ashes of the heifer burnt for purification from sin, and [1]running water shall be put on them in a vessel. 18 [a]A clean person shall take [a]hyssop and dip *it* in the water, sprinkle *it* on the tent, on all the vessels, on the persons who were

---

22 b Lev. 22:9
24 *1 for a possession*
26 a Neh. 10:38
27 a Num. 15:20
29 1 Lit. *fat*
31 a [Luke 10:7] *1 wages*
32 a Lev. 19:8; 22:16 b Lev. 22:2, 15

CHAPTER 19
2 a Lev. 22:20–25 b Deut. 21:3 *1 statute* *2 defect*
3 a Lev. 4:12, 21
4 a Lev. 4:6
5 a Ex. 29:14
6 a Lev. 14:4, 6, 49 b Ex. 12:22
7 a Lev. 11:25; 15:5; 16:26, 28
9 a [Heb. 9:13, 14] b Num. 19:13, 20, 21 1 Lit. *impurity*
11 a Lev. 21:1, 11 1 Lit. *soul of man*
12 a Num. 19:19; 31:19
13 a Lev. 22:3–7 b Lev. 15:31 c Num. 8:7; 19:9 d Lev. 7:20; 22:3
15 a Num. 31:20
16 a Num. 19:11; 31:19
17 a Num. 19:9 1 Lit. *living*
18 a Ps. 51:7

NUMBERS 19:2

Dear Woman of Destiny,

It has been said, "The moral state of a nation is an expression of the spiritual state of its women." Through types and shadows in Scripture, the female often symbolizes the purifying element for society, as is true in this verse from Numbers 19. In the Old Testament sacrificial system, the sprinkled blood of the sacrificed heifer, a female, cleansed the people from sin. Her ashes mixed with water purified those touched by death. Ashes can represent the sacrifice of prayer, and the water symbolizes the Word of God. In other words, great cleansing and deliverance can come through the Word and prayer. How we need cleansing and deliverance in our world today!

Throughout the Pentateuch, we read that "the life of the flesh is in the blood . . . for it is the blood that makes atonement for the soul" (Lev. 17:11). In the New Testament, we learn that only the blood of Jesus cleanses us from sin. We find spiritual life by applying the blood of Jesus to our lives. It makes us clean, pure, righteous, and acceptable to our holy God (see Matt. 26:28; Eph. 2:13; Heb. 9:14, 22). Jesus Christ fulfilled the types and shadows seen in the Old Testament. He *was* our sacrifice. He continues to make us pure.

Years ago, I complained to a wise friend about my stepsons' misbehaving. She replied, "They don't need a judge; they need an intercessor." That sentence snatched me off my path of self-pity and anger and onto a spiritual path of prayer, applying the Word, appropriating the Blood, and speaking life over a situation headed for death. The result is two terrific sons!

Death comes in various forms. Divorce is the death of a marriage. Bankruptcy is financial death. When a family or friends are in the throes of any death, the woman's role, with her spiritual acumen and sensitivity to the Holy Spirit, is to rise in that spiritual darkness and pray for life.

The red heifer sacrificed in Numbers 19:2 was a cow that had never mated or worked—in other words, an unencumbered animal. In the same way, as women lay down earthly concerns and focus on our mighty purpose in God, we can be used to purify the world around us. And as others see our holy lives, they see how they can walk in paths of righteousness (see 1 Pet. 3:1, 2).

Think how Satan loves to detour women to misuse their power and neglect their role. Instead of holy lives, the images of women in pornography and sexy ads lead people down a path of sin, which ultimately leads to death. The moral fiber of a nation deteriorates when its women regard themselves cheaply. But when we follow Christ, what a great honor it is to be a woman! Contrary to what some people believe, Jesus is the greatest liberator of women in history. How God cherishes us! How He longs for us to pray, use His Word, apply Christ's blood, and bring purity to the world around us. Rise up! And shine as woman!

Joann Cole Webster

there, or on the one who touched a bone,
the slain, the dead, or a grave. 19The clean
person shall sprinkle the unclean on the
third day and on the seventh day; [a]and on
the seventh day he shall purify himself,
wash his clothes, and bathe in water; and
at evening he shall be clean.
20'But the man who is unclean and does
not purify himself, that person shall be
cut off from among the assembly, because
he has [a]defiled the sanctuary of the LORD.
The water of purification has not been
sprinkled on him; he *is* unclean. 21It shall
be a perpetual statute for them. He who
sprinkles the water of purification shall
wash his clothes; and he who touches the
water of purification shall be unclean until evening. 22[a]Whatever the unclean *per-*
son touches shall be unclean; and [b]the
person who touches *it* shall be unclean
until evening.' "

Moses' Error at Kadesh

20 Then[a] the children of Israel, the
whole congregation, came into the
Wilderness of Zin in the first month, and
the people stayed in [b]Kadesh; and [c]Miri-
am died there and was buried there.
2[a]Now there was no water for the congregation; [b]so they gathered together
against Moses and Aaron. 3And the people
[a]contended with Moses and spoke, saying:
"If only we had died [b]when our brethren
died before the LORD! 4[a]Why have you
brought up the assembly of the LORD into
this wilderness, that we and our animals
should die here? 5And why have you made
us come up out of Egypt, to bring us to
this evil place? It *is* not a place of grain or
figs or vines or pomegranates; nor *is* there
any water to drink." 6So Moses and Aaron
went from the presence of the assembly to
the door of the tabernacle of meeting, and
[a]they [1]fell on their faces. And [b]the glory
of the LORD appeared to them.
7Then the LORD spoke to Moses, saying,
8[a]"Take the rod; you and your brother
Aaron gather the congregation together.
Speak to the rock before their eyes, and it
will yield its water; thus [b]you shall bring
water for them out of the rock, and give
drink to the congregation and their animals." 9So Moses took the rod [a]from before the LORD as He commanded him.
10And Moses and Aaron gathered the assembly together before the rock; and he
said to them, [a]"Hear now, you rebels!
Must we bring water for you out of this
rock?" 11Then Moses lifted his hand and
struck the rock twice with his rod; [a]and
water came out abundantly, and the congregation and their animals drank.
12Then the LORD spoke to Moses and
Aaron, "Because [a]you did not believe Me,
to [b]hallow Me in the eyes of the children
of Israel, therefore you shall not bring this
assembly into the land which I have given
them."

> *Strive to think what God thinks and will what God wills. In everything be of the same mind that God is. Grow by His Word and have it dwell in you. Then you will be established.*
>
> ANDREW MURRAY

13[a]This *was* the water of [1]Meribah, because the children of Israel contended
with the LORD, and He was hallowed
among them.

Passage Through Edom Refused

14[a]Now Moses sent messengers from
Kadesh to the king of [b]Edom. [c]"Thus says
your brother Israel: 'You know all the
hardship that has befallen us, 15[a]how our
fathers went down to Egypt, [b]and we
dwelt in Egypt a long time, [c]and the
Egyptians [1]afflicted us and our fathers.
16[a]When we cried out to the LORD, He
heard our voice and [b]sent the Angel and
brought us up out of Egypt; now here we
are in Kadesh, a city on the edge of your
border. 17Please [a]let us pass through your
country. We will not pass through fields
or vineyards, nor will we drink water from
wells; we will go along the King's Highway; we will not turn aside to the right
hand or to the left until we have passed
through your territory.' "
18Then [a]Edom said to him, "You shall
not pass through my *land,* lest I come out
against you with the sword."
19So the children of Israel said to him,
"We will go by the Highway, and if I or my

19 a Lev. 14:9
20 a Num. 19:13
22 a Hag. 2:11–13 b Lev. 15:5

CHAPTER 20
1 a Num. 13:21; 33:36 b Num. 13:26 c Ex. 15:20
2 a Ex. 17:1 b Num. 16:19, 42
3 a Ex. 17:2 b Num. 11:1, 33; 14:37; 16:31–35, 49
4 a Ex. 17:3
6 a Num. 14:5; 16:4, 22, 45 b Num. 14:10 *1 prostrated themselves*
8 a Ex. 4:17, 20; 17:5, 6 b Neh. 9:15
9 a Num. 17:10
10 a Ps. 106:33
11 a [1 Cor. 10:4]
12 a Deut. 1:37; 3:26, 27; 34:5 b Lev. 10:3
13 a Deut. 33:8 *1 Lit. Contention*
14 a Judg. 11:16, 17 b Gen. 36:31–39 c Deut. 2:4
15 a Gen. 46:6 b Ex. 12:40 c Deut. 26:6 *1 did evil to*
16 a Ex. 2:23; 3:7 b Ex. 3:2; 14:19
17 a Num. 21:22
18 a Num. 24:18

livestock drink any of your water, [a]then I will pay for it; let me only pass through on foot, nothing *more*."

20 Then he said, [a]"You shall not pass through." So Edom came out against them with many men and with a strong hand. 21 Thus Edom [a]refused to give Israel passage through his territory; so Israel [b]turned away from him.

Death of Aaron

22 Now the children of Israel, the whole congregation, journeyed from [a]Kadesh [b]and came to Mount Hor. 23 And the LORD spoke to Moses and Aaron in Mount Hor by the border of the land of Edom, saying: 24 "Aaron shall [1]be [a]gathered to his people, for he shall not enter the land which I have given to the children of Israel, because you rebelled against My word at the water of Meribah. 25 [a]Take Aaron and Eleazar his son, and bring them up to Mount Hor; 26 and strip Aaron of his garments and put them on Eleazar his son; for Aaron shall be gathered *to his people* and die there." 27 So Moses did just as the LORD commanded, and they went up to Mount Hor in the sight of all the congregation. 28 [a]Moses stripped Aaron of his garments and put them on Eleazar his son; and [b]Aaron died there on the top of the mountain. Then Moses and Eleazar came down from the mountain. 29 Now when all the congregation saw that Aaron was dead, all the house of Israel mourned for Aaron [a]thirty days.

Canaanites Defeated at Hormah

21 The [a]king of Arad, the Canaanite, who dwelt in the South, heard that Israel was coming on the road to Atharim. Then he fought against Israel and took *some* of them prisoners. 2 [a]So Israel made a vow to the LORD, and said, "If You will indeed deliver this people into my hand, then [b]I will utterly destroy their cities." 3 And the LORD listened to the voice of Israel and delivered up the Canaanites, and they utterly destroyed them and their cities. So the name of that place was called [1]Hormah.

The Bronze Serpent

4 Then they journeyed from Mount Hor by the Way of the Red Sea, to [a]go around the land of Edom; and the soul of the people became very [1]discouraged on the way. 5 And the people [a]spoke against God and against Moses: "Why have you brought us up out of Egypt to die in the wilderness? For *there is* no food and no water, and our soul [1]loathes this worthless bread." 6 So [a]the LORD sent [b]fiery serpents among the people, and they bit the people; and many of the people of Israel died.

7 [a]Therefore the people came to Moses, and said, "We have [b]sinned, for we have spoken against the LORD and against you; [c]pray to the LORD that He take away the serpents from us." So Moses prayed for the people.

8 Then the LORD said to Moses, [a]"Make a [b]fiery *serpent,* and set it on a pole; and it shall be that everyone who is bitten, when he looks at it, shall live." 9 So [a]Moses made a bronze serpent, and put it on a pole; and so it was, if a serpent had bitten anyone, when he looked at the bronze serpent, he lived.

Just believe what God says that Jesus has done for you, body, soul, and spirit—think about it, talk about it, sing about it, shout about it, and the praise cure has begun.

DR. LILIAN B. YEOMANS

From Mount Hor to Moab

10 Now the children of Israel moved on and [a]camped in Oboth. 11 And they journeyed from Oboth and camped at [1]Ije Abarim, in the wilderness which *is* east of Moab, toward the sunrise. 12 [a]From there they moved and camped in the Valley of Zered. 13 From there they moved and camped on the other side of the Arnon, which *is* in the wilderness that extends from the border of the Amorites; for [a]the Arnon *is* the border of Moab, between Moab and the Amorites. 14 Therefore it is said in the Book of the Wars of the LORD:

[1]"Waheb in Suphah,
The brooks of the Arnon,
15 And the slope of the brooks
That reaches to the dwelling of [a]Ar,

---

19 a Deut. 2:6, 28
20 a Judg. 11:17
21 a Deut. 2:27, 30 b Judg. 11:18
22 a Num. 33:37 b Num. 21:4
24 a Gen. 25:8 1 Die and join his ancestors
25 a Num. 33:38
28 a Ex. 29:29, 30 b Num. 33:38
29 a Deut. 34:8
CHAPTER 21
1 a Judg. 1:16
2 a Gen. 28:20 b Deut. 2:34
3 1 Lit. *Utter Destruction*
4 a Judg. 11:18 1 *impatient*
5 a Num. 20:4, 5 1 *detests*
6 a 1 Cor. 10:9 b Deut. 8:15
7 a Num. 11:2 b Lev. 26:40 c Ex. 8:8
8 a [John 3:14, 15] b Is. 14:29; 30:6
9 a John 3:14, 15
10 a Num. 33:43, 44
11 1 Lit. *The Heaps of Abarim*
12 a Deut. 2:13
13 a Num. 22:36
14 1 Ancient unknown places; Vg. *What He did in the Red Sea*
15 a Deut. 2:9, 18, 29

And lies on the border of Moab."

[16]From there *they went* [a]to Beer, which *is* the well where the LORD said to Moses, "Gather the people together, and I will give them water." [17a]Then Israel sang this song:

"Spring up, O well!
All of you sing to it—
18 The well the leaders sank,
Dug by the nation's nobles,
By the [a]lawgiver, with their staves."

And from the wilderness *they went* to Mattanah, [19]from Mattanah to Nahaliel, from Nahaliel to Bamoth, [20]and from Bamoth, *in* the valley that *is* in the [1]country of Moab, to the top of Pisgah which looks [a]down on the [2]wasteland.

King Sihon Defeated

[21]Then [a]Israel sent messengers to Sihon king of the Amorites, saying, [22a]"Let me pass through your land. We will not turn aside into fields or vineyards; we will not drink water from wells. We will go by the King's Highway until we have passed through your territory." [23a]But Sihon would not allow Israel to pass through his territory. So Sihon gathered all his people together and [1]went out against Israel in the wilderness, [b]and he came to Jahaz and fought against Israel. [24]Then [a]Israel defeated him with the edge of the sword, and took possession of his land from the Arnon to the Jabbok, as far as the people of Ammon; for the border of the people of Ammon *was* fortified. [25]So Israel took all these cities, and Israel [a]dwelt in all the cities of the Amorites, in Heshbon and in all its villages. [26]For Heshbon *was* the city of Sihon king of the Amorites, who had fought against the former king of Moab, and had taken all his land from his hand as far as the Arnon. [27]Therefore those who speak in [1]proverbs say:

"Come to Heshbon, let it be built;
Let the city of Sihon be repaired.
28 "For [a]fire went out from Heshbon,
A flame from the city of Sihon;
It consumed [b]Ar of Moab,
The lords of the [c]heights of the
Arnon.
29 Woe to you, [a]Moab!
You have perished, O people of
[b]Chemosh!
He has given his [c]sons as fugitives,

16 a Judg. 9:21
17 a Ex. 15:1
18 a Is. 33:22
20 a Num. 23:28 1 Lit. *field* 2 Heb. *Jeshimon*
21 a Deut. 2:26–37
22 a Num. 20:16, 17
23 a Deut. 29:7 b Judg. 11:20 1 *attacked*
24 a Amos 2:9
25 a Amos 2:10
27 1 *parables*
28 a Jer. 48:45, 46 b Is. 15:1 c Num. 22:41; 33:52
29 a Jer. 48:46 b Judg. 11:24 c Is. 15:2, 5 d Is. 16:2
30 a Num. 32:3, 34 b Is. 15:2
32 a Jer. 48:32 1 *secretly search*
33 a Deut. 29:7 b Deut. 3:1 c Josh. 13:12
34 a Deut. 3:2 b Num. 21:24 1 *given you victory over him*
35 a Deut. 3:3, 4; 29:7
CHAPTER 22
1 a Num. 33:48, 49
2 a Judg. 11:25
3 a Ex. 15:15
4 a Num. 25:15–18; 31:1–3 1 *consume*
5 a 2 Pet. 2:15 b Deut. 23:4 1 The Euphrates 2 Or *the people of Amau*
6 a Num. 22:17; 23:7, 8 b Num. 22:12; 24:9
7 a 1 Sam. 9:7, 8

And his [d]daughters into captivity,
To Sihon king of the Amorites.
30 "But we have shot at them;
Heshbon has perished [a]as far as
Dibon.
Then we laid waste as far as
Nophah,
Which *reaches* to [b]Medeba."

[31]Thus Israel dwelt in the land of the Amorites. [32]Then Moses sent to [1]spy out [a]Jazer; and they took its villages and drove out the Amorites who *were* there.

King Og Defeated

[33a]And they turned and went up by the way to [b]Bashan. So Og king of Bashan went out against them, he and all his people, to battle [c]at Edrei. [34]Then the LORD said to Moses, [a]"Do not fear him, for I have [1]delivered him into your hand, with all his people and his land; and [b]you shall do to him as you did to Sihon king of the Amorites, who dwelt at Heshbon." [35a]So they defeated him, his sons, and all his people, until there was no survivor left him; and they took possession of his land.

Balak Sends for Balaam

22 Then [a]the children of Israel moved, and camped in the plains of Moab on the side of the Jordan *across from* Jericho.

[2]Now [a]Balak the son of Zippor saw all that Israel had done to the Amorites. [3]And [a]Moab was exceedingly afraid of the people because they *were* many, and Moab was sick with dread because of the children of Israel. [4]So Moab said to [a]the elders of Midian, "Now this company will [1]lick up everything around us, as an ox licks up the grass of the field." And Balak the son of Zippor *was* king of the Moabites at that time. [5]Then [a]he sent messengers to Balaam the son of Beor at [b]Pethor, which *is* near [1]the River in the land of [2]the sons of his people, to call him, saying: "Look, a people has come from Egypt. See, they cover the face of the earth, and are settling next to me! [6a]Therefore please come at once, [b]curse this people for me, for they *are* too mighty for me. Perhaps I shall be able to defeat them and drive them out of the land, for I know that he whom you bless *is* blessed, and he whom you curse is cursed."

[7]So the elders of Moab and the elders of Midian departed with [a]the diviner's fee in

their hand, and they came to Balaam and
spoke to him the words of Balak. 8And he
said to them, [a]"Lodge here tonight, and I
will bring back word to you, as the LORD
speaks to me." So the princes of Moab
stayed with Balaam.
9[a]Then God came to Balaam and said,
"Who *are* these men with you?"
10So Balaam said to God, "Balak the son
of Zippor, king of Moab, has sent to me,
saying, 11'Look, a people has come out
of Egypt, and they cover the face of the
earth. Come now, curse them for me; perhaps I shall be able to overpower them
and drive them out.' "
12And God said to Balaam, "You shall
not go with them; you shall not curse the
people, for [a]they *are* blessed."
13So Balaam rose in the morning and
said to the princes of Balak, "Go back to
your land, for the LORD has refused to give
me permission to go with you."
14And the princes of Moab rose and
went to Balak, and said, "Balaam refuses
to come with us."
15Then Balak again sent princes, more
numerous and more [1]honorable than
they. 16And they came to Balaam and said
to him, "Thus says Balak the son of Zippor: 'Please let nothing hinder you from
coming to me; 17for I will certainly [a]hon-
or you greatly, and I will do whatever you
say to me. [b]Therefore please come, curse
this people for me.' "
18Then Balaam answered and said to
the servants of Balak, [a]"Though Balak
were to give me his house full of silver and
gold, [b]I could not go beyond the word of
the LORD my God, to do less or more.
19Now therefore, please, you also [a]stay
here tonight, that I may know what more
the LORD will say to me."
20[a]And God came to Balaam at night
and said to him, "If the men come to call
you, rise *and* go with them; but [b]only the
word which I speak to you—that you
shall do." 21So Balaam rose in the morning, saddled his donkey, and went with
the princes of Moab.

Balaam, the Donkey, and the Angel

22Then God's anger was aroused because he went, [a]and the Angel of the LORD
took His stand in the way as an adversary
against him. And he was riding on his
donkey, and his two servants *were* with
him. 23Now [a]the donkey saw the Angel of
the LORD standing in the way with His
drawn sword in His hand, and the donkey
turned aside out of the way and went into
the field. So Balaam struck the donkey to
turn her back onto the road. 24Then the
Angel of the LORD stood in a narrow path
between the vineyards, *with* a wall on this
side and a wall on that side. 25And when
the donkey saw the Angel of the LORD,
she pushed herself against the wall and
crushed Balaam's foot against the wall; so
he struck her again. 26Then the Angel of
the LORD went further, and stood in a narrow place where there *was* no way to turn
either to the right hand or to the left.
27And when the donkey saw the Angel of
the LORD, she lay down under Balaam;
so Balaam's anger was aroused, and he
struck the donkey with his staff.
28Then the LORD [a]opened the mouth of
the donkey, and she said to Balaam, "What
have I done to you, that you have struck
me these three times?"
29And Balaam said to the donkey, "Because you have [1]abused me. I wish there
were a sword in my hand, [a]for now I
would kill you!"
30[a]So the donkey said to Balaam, "*Am* I
not your donkey on which you have ridden, ever since *I became* yours, to this
day? Was I ever [1]disposed to do this to
you?"
And he said, "No."
31Then the LORD [a]opened Balaam's
eyes, and he saw the Angel of the LORD
standing in the way with His drawn sword
in His hand; and he bowed his head and
fell flat on his face. 32And the Angel of the
LORD said to him, "Why have you struck
your donkey these three times? Behold, I
have come out [1]to stand against you, because *your* way is [a]perverse[2] before Me.
33The donkey saw Me and turned aside
from Me these three times. If she had not
turned aside from Me, surely I would also
have killed you by now, and let her live."
34And Balaam said to the Angel of the
LORD, [a]"I have sinned, for I did not know
You stood in the way against me. Now
therefore, if it [1]displeases You, I will turn
back."
35Then the Angel of the LORD said to
Balaam, "Go with the men, [a]but only the
word that I speak to you, that you shall
speak." So Balaam went with the princes
of Balak.
36Now when Balak heard that Balaam
was coming, [a]he went out to meet him at

8 a Num. 22:19
9 a Gen. 20:3
12 a [Rom. 11:28]
15 *1 distinguished*
17 a Num. 24:11 b Num. 22:6
18 a Num. 22:38; 24:13 b 1 Kin. 22:14
19 a Num. 22:8
20 a Num. 22:9 b Num. 22:35; 23:5, 12, 16, 26; 24:13
22 a Ex. 4:24
23 a Josh. 5:13
28 a 2 Pet. 2:16
29 a [Prov. 12:10] *1 mocked*
30 a 2 Pet. 2:16 *1 accustomed*
31 a Gen. 21:19
32 a [2 Pet. 2:14, 15] *1 as an adversary 2 contrary*
34 a 2 Sam. 12:13 *1 Lit. is evil in your eyes*
35 a Num. 22:20
36 a Gen. 14:17

the city of Moab, [b]which *is* on the border
at the Arnon, the boundary of the territory. 37Then Balak said to Balaam, "Did I not
earnestly send to you, calling for you?
Why did you not come to me? Am I not
able [a]to honor you?"
38And Balaam said to Balak, "Look, I
have come to you! Now, have I any power
at all to say anything? [a]The word that God
puts in my mouth, that I must speak."
39So Balaam went with Balak, and they
came to Kirjath Huzoth. 40Then Balak offered oxen and sheep, and he sent *some* to
Balaam and to the princes who *were* with
him.

Faith is a product of your spirit, not of your intellect. Your intellect does not produce faith. Your knowledge may give you ground for faith, but faith is resident in your spirit.

JOHN G. LAKE

Balaam's First Prophecy

41So it was, the next day, that Balak
took Balaam and brought him up to the
[a]high places of Baal, that from there he
might observe [1]the extent of the people.
23 Then Balaam said to Balak, [a]"Build
seven altars for me here, and prepare for me here seven bulls and seven
rams."
2And Balak did just as Balaam had spoken, and Balak and Balaam [a]offered a bull
and a ram on *each* altar. 3Then Balaam
said to Balak, [a]"Stand by your burnt offering, and I will go; perhaps the LORD will
come [b]to meet me, and whatever He
shows me I will tell you." So he went to a
desolate height. 4[a]And God met Balaam,
and he said to Him, "I have prepared the
seven altars, and I have offered on *each*
altar a bull and a ram."
5Then the LORD [a]put a word in Balaam's mouth, and said, "Return to Balak,
and thus you shall speak." 6So he returned to him, and there he was, standing
by his burnt offering, he and all the princes of Moab.
7And he [a]took up his [1]oracle and said:

"Balak the king of Moab has brought
me from Aram,
From the mountains of the east.
[b]'Come, curse Jacob for me,
And come, [c]denounce Israel!'

8 "How[a] shall I curse whom God has
not cursed?
And how shall I denounce *whom*
the LORD has not denounced?
9 For from the top of the rocks I see
him,
And from the hills I behold him;
There! [a]A people dwelling alone,
[b]Not reckoning itself among the
nations.

10 "Who[a] can count the [1]dust of
Jacob,
Or number one-fourth of Israel?
Let me die [b]the death of the
righteous,
And let my end be like his!"

11Then Balak said to Balaam, "What
have you done to me? [a]I took you to curse
my enemies, and look, you have blessed
them bountifully!"
12So he answered and said, [a]"Must I not
take heed to speak what the LORD has put
in my mouth?"

Balaam's Second Prophecy

13Then Balak said to him, "Please come
with me to another place from which you
may see them; you shall see only the outer
part of them, and shall not see them all;
curse them for me from there." 14So he
brought him to the field of Zophim, to the
top of Pisgah, [a]and built seven altars, and
offered a bull and a ram on *each* altar.
15And he said to Balak, "Stand here by
your burnt offering while I [1]meet *the
LORD* over there."
16Then the LORD met Balaam, and [a]put
a word in his mouth, and said, "Go back
to Balak, and thus you shall speak." 17So
he came to him, and there he was, standing by his burnt offering, and the princes
of Moab were with him. And Balak said to
him, "What has the LORD spoken?"
18Then he took up his oracle and said:

[a]"Rise up, Balak, and hear!
Listen to me, son of Zippor!

36 [b] Num. 21:13
37 [a] Num. 22:17; 24:11
38 [a] 1 Kin. 22:14
41 [a] Num. 21:28
[1] *the farthest extent*
CHAPTER 23
1 [a] Num. 23:29
2 [a] Num. 23:14, 30
3 [a] Num. 23:15
[b] Num. 23:4, 16
4 [a] Num. 23:16
5 [a] Deut. 18:18
7 [a] Deut. 23:4
[b] Num. 22:6, 11, 17
[c] 1 Sam. 17:10
[1] *prophetic discourse*
8 [a] Num. 22:12
9 [a] Deut. 32:8; 33:28
[b] Ex. 33:16
10 [a] Gen. 13:16; 22:17; 28:14
[b] Ps. 116:15
[1] *Or dust cloud*
11 [a] Num. 22:11
12 [a] Num. 22:38
14 [a] Num. 23:1, 2
15 [1] So with MT, Tg., Vg.; Syr. *call;* LXX *go and ask God*
16 [a] Num. 22:35; 23:5
18 [a] Judg. 3:20

19 "God[a] *is* not a man, that He should
lie,
Nor a son of man, that He should
repent.
Has He [b]said, and will He not do?
Or has He spoken, and will He not
make it good?
20 Behold, I have received *a
command* to bless;
[a]He has blessed, and I cannot
reverse it.

21 "He[a] has not observed iniquity in
Jacob,
Nor has He seen [1]wickedness in
Israel.
The LORD his God *is* with him,
[b]And the shout of a King *is* among
them.
22 [a]God brings them out of Egypt;
He has [b]strength like a wild ox.

23 "For *there is* no [1]sorcery against
Jacob,
Nor any [2]divination against Israel.
It now must be said of Jacob
And of Israel, 'Oh, [a]what God has
done!'
24 Look, a people rises [a]like a
lioness,
And lifts itself up like a lion;
[b]It shall not lie down until it
devours the prey,
And drinks the blood of the slain."

[25]Then Balak said to Balaam, "Neither
curse them at all, nor bless them at all!"
[26]So Balaam answered and said to Balak, "Did I not tell you, saying, [a]'All that
the LORD speaks, that I must do'?"

Balaam's Third Prophecy

[27]Then Balak said to Balaam, "Please
come, I will take you to another place;
perhaps it will please God that you may
curse them for me from there." [28]So Balak
took Balaam to the top of Peor, that [a]over-
looks the [1]wasteland. [29]Then Balaam said
to Balak, "Build for me here seven altars,
and prepare for me here seven bulls and
seven rams." [30]And Balak did as Balaam
had said, and offered a bull and a ram on
every altar.

24 Now when Balaam saw that it
pleased the LORD to bless Israel, he
did not go as at [a]other times, to seek to
use [1]sorcery, but he set his face toward
the wilderness. [2]And Balaam raised his
eyes, and saw Israel [a]encamped according

19 a Mal. 3:6 b 1 Kin. 8:56
20 a Num. 22:12
21 a [Rom. 4:7, 8] b Ps. 89:15–18 *1 trouble*
22 a Num. 24:8 b Deut. 33:17
23 a Ps. 31:19; 44:1 *1 enchantment 2 fortune-telling*
24 a Gen. 49:9 b Gen. 49:27
26 a Num. 22:38
28 a Num. 21:20 *1 Heb. Jeshimon*

CHAPTER 24
1 a Num. 23:3, 15 *1 enchantments*
2 a Num. 2:2, 34 b Num. 11:25
3 a Num. 23:7, 18
4 a Ezek. 1:28
6 a Jer. 17:8 b Ps. 104:16
7 a Jer. 51:13 b 1 Sam. 15:8, 9 c 2 Sam. 5:12
8 a Num. 23:22 b Num. 14:9; 23:24 c Ps. 2:9 d Ps. 45:5
9 a Gen. 49:9 b Gen. 12:3; 27:29
10 a Ezek. 21:14, 17 b Num. 23:11

to their tribes; and [b]the Spirit of God
came upon him.
[3][a]Then he took up his oracle and said:
"The utterance of Balaam the son of
Beor,
The utterance of the man whose
eyes are opened,
4 The utterance of him who hears
the words of God,
Who sees the vision of the
Almighty,
Who [a]falls down, with eyes wide
open:

5 "How lovely are your tents, O Jacob!
Your dwellings, O Israel!
6 Like valleys that stretch out,
Like gardens by the riverside,
[a]Like aloes [b]planted by the LORD,
Like cedars beside the waters.
7 He shall pour water from his
buckets,
And his seed *shall be* [a]in many
waters.

"His king shall be higher than
[b]Agag,
And his [c]kingdom shall be exalted.

8 "God[a] brings him out of Egypt;
He has strength like a wild ox;
He shall [b]consume the nations, his
enemies;
He shall [c]break their bones
And [d]pierce *them* with his arrows.
9 'He[a] bows down, he lies down as a
lion;
And as a lion, who shall rouse
him?'
[b]"Blessed *is* he who blesses you,
And cursed *is* he who curses you."

Father, I pray that those who bless ______ would be blessed.

FROM NUMBERS 24:9

[10]Then Balak's anger was aroused
against Balaam, and he [a]struck his hands
together; and Balak said to Balaam, [b]"I
called you to curse my enemies, and look,
you have bountifully blessed *them* these

three times! 11Now therefore, flee to your
place. [a]I said I would greatly honor you,
but in fact, the LORD has kept you back
from honor."
12So Balaam said to Balak, "Did I not
also speak to your messengers whom you
sent to me, saying, 13'If Balak were to give
me his house full of silver and gold, I
could not go beyond the word of the LORD,
to do good or bad of my own will. What
the LORD says, that I must speak'? 14And
now, indeed, I am going to my people.
Come, [a]I will advise you what this people
will do to your people in the [b]latter days."

Balaam's Fourth Prophecy

15So he took up his oracle and said:

"The utterance of Balaam the son of
Beor,
And the utterance of the man
whose eyes are opened;
16 The utterance of him who hears
the words of God,
And has the knowledge of the Most
High,
Who sees the vision of the
Almighty,
Who falls down, with eyes wide
open:

17 "I[a] see Him, but not now;
I behold Him, but not near;
[b]A Star shall come out of Jacob;
[c]A Scepter shall rise out of Israel,
And [1]batter the brow of Moab,
And destroy all the sons of [2]tumult.

18 "And [a]Edom shall be a possession;
Seir also, his enemies, shall be a
possession,
While Israel does [1]valiantly.
19 [a]Out of Jacob One [1]shall have
dominion,
And destroy the remains of the city."

20Then he looked on Amalek, and he
took up his oracle and said:

"Amalek *was* first among the
nations,
But *shall be* last until he perishes."

21Then he looked on the Kenites, and
he took up his oracle and said:

"Firm is your dwelling place,
And your nest is set in the rock;
22 Nevertheless Kain shall be burned.
How long until Asshur carries you
away captive?"

23Then he took up his oracle and said:

"Alas! Who shall live when God does
this?
24 But ships *shall come* from the
coasts of [a]Cyprus,[1]
And they shall afflict Asshur and
afflict [b]Eber,
And so shall [2]*Amalek*, until he
perishes."

25So Balaam rose and departed and [a]re-
turned to his place; Balak also went his
way.

Israel's Harlotry in Moab

25 Now Israel remained in [a]Acacia
Grove,[1] and the [b]people began to
commit harlotry with the women of
Moab. 2[a]They invited the people to [b]the
sacrifices of their gods, and the people ate
and [c]bowed down to their gods. 3So Israel
was joined to Baal of Peor, and [a]the anger
of the LORD was aroused against Israel.
4Then the LORD said to Moses, [a]"Take
all the leaders of the people and hang the
offenders before the LORD, out in the sun,
[b]that the fierce anger of the LORD may
turn away from Israel."
5So Moses said to [a]the judges of Israel,
[b]"Every one of you kill his men who were
joined to Baal of Peor."
6And indeed, one of the children of Israel came and presented to his brethren a
Midianite woman in the sight of Moses
and in the sight of all the congregation of
the children of Israel, [a]who *were* weeping
at the door of the tabernacle of meeting.
7Now [a]when Phinehas [b]the son of Eleazar, the son of Aaron the priest, saw *it,* he
rose from among the congregation and
took a javelin in his hand; 8and he went
after the man of Israel into the tent and
thrust both of them through, the man of
Israel, and the woman through her body.
So [a]the plague was [b]stopped among the
children of Israel. 9And [a]those who died in
the plague were twenty-four thousand.
10Then the LORD spoke to Moses, saying: 11[a]"Phinehas the son of Eleazar, the
son of Aaron the priest, has turned back
My wrath from the children of Israel, because he was zealous with My zeal among
them, so that I did not consume the children of Israel in [b]My zeal. 12Therefore say,
[a]'Behold, I give to him My [b]covenant of
peace; 13and it shall be to him and [a]his
descendants after him a covenant of [b]an
everlasting priesthood, because he was

11 [a]Num. 22:17, 37
14 [a][Mic. 6:5] [b]Gen. 49:1
17 [a]Rev. 1:7 [b]Matt. 2:2 [c]Gen. 49:10 [1]*shatter the forehead* [2]Heb. *Sheth,* Jer. 48:45
18 [a]2 Sam. 8:14 [1]*mightily*
19 [a]Amos 9:11, 12 [1]*shall rule*
24 [a]Gen. 10:4 [b]Gen. 10:21, 25 [1]Heb. *Kittim* [2]Lit. *he* or *that one*
25 [a]Num. 22:5; 31:8

CHAPTER 25
1 [a]Josh. 2:1 [b]Rev. 2:14 [1]Heb. *Shittim*
2 [a]Hos. 9:10 [b]Ex. 34:15 [c]Ex. 20:5
3 [a]Ps. 106:28, 29
4 [a]Deut. 4:3 [b]Num. 25:11
5 [a]Ex. 18:21 [b]Deut. 13:6, 9
6 [a]Joel 2:17
7 [a]Ps. 106:30 [b]Ex. 6:25
8 [a]Ps. 106:30 [b]Num. 16:46–48
9 [a]Deut. 4:3
11 [a]Ps. 106:30 [b][Ex. 20:5]
12 [a][Mal. 2:4, 5; 3:1] [b]Is. 54:10
13 [a]1 Chr. 6:4–15 [b]Ex. 40:15

[c]zealous for his God, and [d]made [1]atone-
ment for the children of Israel.' "
14 Now the name of the Israelite who
was killed, who was killed with the Midianite woman, *was* Zimri the son of Salu,
a leader of a father's house among the
Simeonites. 15 And the name of the Midianite woman who was killed *was* Cozbi
the daughter of [a]Zur; he *was* head of the
people of a father's house in Midian.
16 Then the LORD spoke to Moses, saying: 17 [a]"Harass the Midianites, and [1]at-
tack them; 18 for they harassed you with
their [a]schemes[1] by which they seduced
you in the matter of Peor and in the matter of Cozbi, the daughter of a leader of
Midian, their sister, who was killed in the
day of the plague because of Peor."

The Second Census of Israel

26 And it came to pass, after the
[a]plague, that the LORD spoke to
Moses and Eleazar the son of Aaron the
priest, saying: 2 [a]"Take a census of all the
congregation of the children of Israel
[b]from twenty years old and above, by their
fathers' houses, all who are able to go to
war in Israel." 3 So Moses and Eleazar the
priest spoke with them [a]in the plains of
Moab by the Jordan, *across from* Jericho,
saying: 4 "*Take a census of the people* from
twenty years old and above, just as the
LORD [a]commanded Moses and the children of Israel who came out of the land of
Egypt."
5 [a]Reuben *was* the firstborn of Israel.
The children of Reuben *were: of* Hanoch,
the family of the Hanochites; *of* Pallu, the
family of the Palluites; 6 *of* Hezron, the
family of the Hezronites; *of* Carmi, the
family of the Carmites. 7 These *are*
the families of the Reubenites: those who
were numbered of them were forty-three
thousand seven hundred and thirty. 8 And
the son of Pallu *was* Eliab. 9 The sons of
Eliab *were* Nemuel, Dathan, and Abiram.
These *are* the Dathan and Abiram, [a]re-
presentatives of the congregation, who
contended against Moses and Aaron in the
company of Korah, when they contended
against the LORD; 10 [a]and the earth opened
its mouth and swallowed them up together with Korah when that company died,
when the fire devoured two hundred and
fifty men; [b]and they became a sign. 11 Nevertheless [a]the children of Korah did not
die.

12 The sons of Simeon according to
their families *were: of* [1]Nemuel, the family of the Nemuelites; *of* Jamin, the family
of the Jaminites; *of* [2]Jachin, the family of
the Jachinites; 13 *of* [1]Zerah, the family of
the Zarhites; *of* Shaul, the family of the
Shaulites. 14 These *are* the families of the
Simeonites: twenty-two thousand two
hundred.
15 The sons of Gad according to their
families *were: of* [1]Zephon, the family of
the Zephonites; *of* Haggi, the family of the
Haggites; *of* Shuni, the family of the Shu-
nites; 16 *of* [1]Ozni, the family of the Oz-
nites; *of* Eri, the family of the Erites; 17 *of*
[1]Arod, the family of the Arodites; *of* Areli,
the family of the Arelites. 18 These *are* the
families of the sons of Gad according to
those who were numbered of them: forty
thousand five hundred.
19 [a]The sons of Judah *were* Er and Onan;
and Er and Onan died in the land of Canaan. 20 And [a]the sons of Judah according
to their families were: *of* Shelah, the family of the Shelanites; *of* Perez, the family of
the Parzites; *of* Zerah, the family of the
Zarhites. 21 And the sons of Perez were: *of*
Hezron, the family of the Hezronites; *of*
Hamul, the family of the Hamulites.
22 These *are* the families of Judah according to those who were numbered of them:
seventy-six thousand five hundred.
23 The sons of Issachar according to
their families *were: of* Tola, the family of
the Tolaites; of [1]Puah, the family of the
[2]Punites; 24 of [1]Jashub, the family of the
Jashubites; of Shimron, the family of the
Shimronites. 25 These *are* the families of
Issachar according to those who were
numbered of them: sixty-four thousand
three hundred.
26 [a]The sons of Zebulun according to
their families *were:* of Sered, the family of
the Sardites; of Elon, the family of the
Elonites; of Jahleel, the family of the Jah-
leelites. 27 These *are* the families of the
Zebulunites according to those who were
numbered of them: sixty thousand five
hundred.
28 [a]The sons of Joseph according to
their families, by Manasseh and Ephraim,
were: 29 The sons of [a]Manasseh: of [b]Ma-
chir, the family of the Machirites; and Machir begot Gilead; of Gilead, the family of
the Gileadites. 30 These *are* the sons of Gilead: *of* [1]Jeezer, the family of the Jeezer-
ites; of Helek, the family of the Helekites;
31 *of* Asriel, the family of the Asrielites; *of*

13 c Acts 22:3 d [Heb. 2:17] *1* Lit. *covering*
15 a Num. 31:8
17 a Num. 31:1–3 *1 be hostile toward*
18 a Rev. 2:14 *1 tricks*
CHAPTER 26
1 a Num. 25:9
2 a Num. 1:2; 14:29 b Num. 1:3
3 a Num. 22:1; 31:12; 33:48; 35:1
4 a Num. 1:1
5 a Ex. 6:14
9 a Num. 1:16; 16:1, 2
10 a Num. 16:32–35 b Num. 16:38–40
11 a Ex. 6:24
12 *1 Jemuel,* Gen. 46:10; Ex. 6:15 *2 Jarib,* 1 Chr. 4:24
13 *1 Zohar,* Gen. 46:10
15 *1 Ziphion,* Gen. 46:16
16 *1 Ezbon,* Gen. 46:16
17 *1* Sam., Syr. *Arodi* and Gen. 46:16
19 a Gen. 38:2; 46:12
20 a 1 Chr. 2:3
23 *1* So with Sam., LXX, Syr., Vg.; Heb. *Puvah,* Gen. 46:13; 1 Chr. 7:1 *2* Sam., LXX, Syr., Vg. *Puaites*
24 *1 Job,* Gen. 46:13
26 a Gen. 46:14
28 a Gen. 46:20
29 a Josh. 17:1 b 1 Chr. 7:14, 15
30 *1 Abiezer,* Josh. 17:2

Shechem, the family of the Shechemites;
32*of* Shemida, the family of the Shemida-
ites; *of* Hepher, the family of the Hepher-
ites. 33Now [a]Zelophehad the son of
Hepher had no sons, but daughters; and
the names of the daughters of Zelophehad
were Mahlah, Noah, Hoglah, Milcah, and
Tirzah. 34These *are* the families of Manasseh; and those who were numbered of
them *were* fifty-two thousand seven hundred.

35These *are* the sons of Ephraim according to their families: of Shuthelah,
the family of the Shuthalhites; of [1]Becher,
the family of the Bachrites; of Tahan, the
family of the Tahanites. 36And these *are*
the sons of Shuthelah: of Eran, the family
of the Eranites. 37These *are* the families of
the sons of Ephraim according to those
who were numbered of them: thirty-two
thousand five hundred.

These *are* the sons of Joseph according
to their families.

38[a]The sons of Benjamin according to
their families were: of Bela, the family of
the Belaites; of Ashbel, the family of the
Ashbelites; of [b]Ahiram, the family of the
Ahiramites; 39of [a]Shupham,[1] the family of
the Shuphamites; of [2]Hupham, the family
of the Huphamites. 40And the sons of Bela
were [1]Ard and Naaman: [a]*of Ard,* the family of the Ardites; of Naaman, the family
of the Naamites. 41These *are* the sons of
Benjamin according to their families; and
those who were numbered of them *were*
forty-five thousand six hundred.

42These *are* the sons of Dan according
to their families: of [1]Shuham, the family
of the Shuhamites. These *are* the families
of Dan according to their families. 43All
the families of the Shuhamites, according
to those who were numbered of them,
were sixty-four thousand four hundred.

44[a]The sons of Asher according to their
families *were:* of Jimna, the family of the
Jimnites; of Jesui, the family of the Je-
suites; of Beriah, the family of the Beri-
ites. 45Of the sons of Beriah: of Heber, the
family of the Heberites; of Malchiel, the
family of the Malchielites. 46And the name
of the daughter of Asher *was* Serah.
47These *are* the families of the sons of
Asher according to those who were numbered of them: fifty-three thousand four
hundred.

48[a]The sons of Naphtali according to
their families *were:* of [1]Jahzeel, the family
of the Jahzeelites; of Guni, the family of
the Gunites; 49of Jezer, the family of the
Jezerites; of [a]Shillem, the family of the
Shillemites. 50These *are* the families of
Naphtali according to their families; and
those who were numbered of them *were*
forty-five thousand four hundred.

51[a]These *are* those who were numbered
of the children of Israel: six hundred and
one thousand seven hundred and thirty.

52Then the LORD spoke to Moses, saying: 53[a]"To these the land shall be [b]divid-
ed as an inheritance, according to the
number of names. 54[a]To a large *tribe* you
shall give a larger inheritance, and to a
small *tribe* you shall give a smaller inheritance. Each shall be given its inheritance
according to those who were numbered of
them. 55But the land shall be [a]divided by
lot; they shall inherit according to the
names of the tribes of their fathers. 56Ac-
cording to the lot their inheritance shall
be divided between the larger and the
smaller."

57[a]And these *are* those who were numbered of the Levites according to their
families: of Gershon, the family of the
Gershonites; of Kohath, the family of the
Kohathites; of Merari, the family of the
Merarites. 58These *are* the families of
the Levites: the family of the Libnites, the
family of the Hebronites, the family of the
Mahlites, the family of the Mushites, and
the family of the Korathites. And Kohath
begot Amram. 59The name of Amram's
wife *was* [a]Jochebed the daughter of Levi,
who was born to Levi in Egypt; and to
Amram she bore Aaron and Moses and
their sister Miriam. 60[a]To Aaron were
born Nadab and Abihu, Eleazar and Ithamar. 61And [a]Nadab and Abihu died when
they offered profane fire before the LORD.

62[a]Now those who were numbered of
them were twenty-three thousand, every
male from a month old and above; [b]for
they were not numbered among the other
children of Israel, because there was [c]no
inheritance given to them among the
children of Israel.

63These *are* those who were numbered
by Moses and Eleazar the priest, who
numbered the children of Israel [a]in the
plains of Moab by the Jordan, *across from*
Jericho. 64[a]But among these there was
not a man of those who were numbered by
Moses and Aaron the priest when they
numbered the children of Israel in the
[b]Wilderness of Sinai. 65For the LORD had
said of them, "They [a]shall surely die in the

33 [a]Num. 27:1; 36:11
35 [1] *Bered,* 1 Chr. 7:20
38 [a]Gen. 46:21 [b]1 Chr. 8:1, 2
39 [a]1 Chr. 7:12 [1] MT *Shephupham; Shephuphan,* 1 Chr. 8:5 [2] *Huppim,* Gen. 46:21
40 [a]1 Chr. 8:3 [1] *Addar,* 1 Chr. 8:3
42 [1] *Hushim,* Gen. 46:23
44 [a]Gen. 46:17
48 [a]1 Chr. 7:13 [1] *Jahziel,* 1 Chr. 7:13
49 [a]1 Chr. 7:13
51 [a]Num. 1:46; 11:21
53 [a]Josh. 11:23; 14:1 [b]Num. 33:54
54 [a]Num. 33:54
55 [a]Num. 33:54; 34:13
57 [a]Gen. 46:11
59 [a]Ex. 2:1, 2; 6:20
60 [a]Num. 3:2
61 [a]Lev. 10:1, 2
62 [a]Num. 3:39 [b]Num. 1:49 [c]Num. 18:20, 23, 24
63 [a]Num. 26:3
64 [a]Num. 14:29–35 [b]Num. 1:1–46
65 [a]Num. 14:26–35

wilderness." So there was not left a man of them, [b]except Caleb the son of Jephunneh and Joshua the son of Nun.

Inheritance Laws

27 Then came the daughters of [a]Zelophehad the son of Hepher, the son of Gilead, the son of Machir, the son of Manasseh, from the families of Manasseh the son of Joseph; and these *were* the names of his daughters: Mahlah, Noah, Hoglah, Milcah, and Tirzah. 2And they stood before Moses, before Eleazar the priest, and before the leaders and all the congregation, *by* the doorway of the tabernacle of meeting, saying: 3"Our father [a]died in the wilderness; but he was not in the company of those who gathered together against the LORD, [b]in company with Korah, but he died in his own sin; and he had no sons. 4Why should the name of our father be [a]removed[1] from among his family because he had no son? [b]Give us a [2]possession among our father's brothers."

5So Moses [a]brought their case before the LORD.

6And the LORD spoke to Moses, saying: 7"The daughters of Zelophehad speak *what is* right; [a]you shall surely give them a possession of inheritance among their father's brothers, and cause the inheritance of their father to pass to them. 8And you shall speak to the children of Israel, saying: 'If a man dies and has no son, then you shall cause his inheritance to pass to his daughter. 9If he has no daughter, then you shall give his inheritance to his brothers. 10If he has no brothers, then you shall give his inheritance to his father's brothers. 11And if his father has no brothers, then you shall give his inheritance to the relative closest to him in his family, and he shall possess it.'" And it shall be to the children of Israel [a]a statute of judgment, just as the LORD commanded Moses.

Joshua the Next Leader of Israel

12Now the LORD said to Moses: [a]"Go up into this Mount Abarim, and see the land which I have given to the children of Israel. 13And when you have seen it, you also [a]shall [1]be gathered to your people, as Aaron your brother was gathered. 14For in the Wilderness of Zin, during the strife of the congregation, you [a]rebelled against My command to hallow Me at the waters before their eyes." (These *are* the [b]waters of Meribah, at Kadesh in the Wilderness of Zin.)

Father, I pray that You will set faithful leaders over the congregation of ____, so that they will not be like sheep which have no shepherd.

FROM NUMBERS 27:16, 17

15Then Moses spoke to the LORD, saying: 16"Let the LORD, [a]the God of the spirits of all flesh, set a man over the congregation, 17[a]who may go out before them and go in before them, who may lead them out and bring them in, that the congregation of the LORD may not be [b]like sheep which have no shepherd."

18And the LORD said to Moses: "Take Joshua the son of Nun with you, a man [a]in whom *is* the Spirit, and [b]lay your hand on him; 19set him before Eleazar the priest and before all the congregation, and [a]inaugurate[1] him in their sight. 20And [a]you shall give *some* of your authority to him, that all the congregation of the children of Israel [b]may be obedient. 21[a]He shall stand before Eleazar the priest, who shall inquire before the LORD for him [b]by the judgment of the Urim. [c]At his word they shall go out, and at his word they shall come in, he and all the children of Israel with him—all the congregation."

22So Moses did as the LORD commanded him. He took Joshua and set him before Eleazar the priest and before all the congregation. 23And he laid his hands on him [a]and [1]inaugurated him, just as the LORD commanded by the hand of Moses.

Daily Offerings

28 Now the LORD spoke to Moses, saying, 2"Command the children of Israel, and say to them, 'My offering, [a]My food for My offerings made by fire as a sweet aroma to Me, you shall be careful to offer to Me at their appointed time.'

---

65 [b]Num. 14:30

CHAPTER 27

1 [a]Num. 26:33; 36:1, 11
3 [a]Num. 14:35; 26:64, 65 [b]Num. 16:1, 2
4 [a]Deut. 25:6 [b]Josh. 17:4 [1]*withdrawn* [2]*inheritance*
5 [a]Ex. 18:13–26
7 [a]Num. 36:2
11 [a]Num. 35:29
12 [a]Num. 33:47
13 [a]Deut. 10:6; 34:5, 6 [1]Die and join your ancestors
14 [a]Ps. 106:32, 33 [b]Ex. 17:7
16 [a]Num. 16:22
17 [a]Deut. 31:2 [b]Zech. 10:2
18 [a]Gen. 41:38 [b]Deut. 34:9
19 [a]Deut. 3:28; 31:3, 7, 8, 23 [1]*commission*
20 [a]Num. 11:17 [b]Josh. 1:16–18
21 [a]1 Sam. 23:9; 30:7 [b]Ex. 28:30 [c]1 Sam. 22:10
23 [a]Deut. 3:28; 31:7, 8 [1]*commissioned*

CHAPTER 28

2 [a]Lev. 3:11; 21:6, 8

3"And you shall say to them, [a]'This *is* the offering made by fire which you shall offer to the LORD: two male lambs in their first year without blemish, day by day, as a regular burnt offering. 4The one lamb you shall offer in the morning, the other lamb you shall offer in the evening, 5and [a]one-tenth of an ephah of fine flour as a [b]grain offering mixed with one-fourth of a hin of pressed oil. 6*It is* [a]a regular burnt offering which was ordained at Mount Sinai for a sweet aroma, an offering made by fire to the LORD. 7And its drink offering *shall be* one-fourth of a hin for each lamb; [a]in a holy *place* you shall pour out the drink to the LORD as an offering. 8The other lamb you shall offer in the evening; as the morning grain offering and its drink offering, you shall offer *it* as an offering made by fire, a [1]sweet aroma to the LORD.

Sabbath Offerings

9'And on the Sabbath day two lambs in their first year, without blemish, and two-tenths *of an ephah* of fine flour as a grain offering, mixed with oil, with its drink offering— 10*this is* [a]the burnt offering for every Sabbath, besides the regular burnt offering with its drink offering.

Monthly Offerings

11[a]'At the beginnings of your months you shall present a burnt offering to the LORD: two young bulls, one ram, and seven lambs in their first year, without blemish; 12[a]three-tenths *of an ephah* of fine flour as a grain offering, mixed with oil, for each bull; two-tenths *of an ephah* of fine flour as a grain offering, mixed with oil, for the one ram; 13and one-tenth *of an ephah* of fine flour, mixed with oil, as a grain offering for each lamb, as a burnt offering of sweet aroma, an offering made by fire to the LORD. 14Their drink offering shall be half a hin of wine for a bull, one-third of a hin for a ram, and one-fourth of a hin for a lamb; this *is* the burnt offering for each month throughout the months of the year. 15Also [a]one kid of the goats as a sin offering to the LORD shall be offered, besides the regular burnt offering and its drink offering.

Offerings at Passover

16[a]'On the fourteenth day of the first month *is* the Passover of the LORD. 17[a]And on the fifteenth day of this month *is* the feast; unleavened bread shall be eaten for seven days. 18On the [a]first day *you shall have* a holy [1]convocation. You shall do no [2]customary work. 19And you shall present an offering made by fire as a burnt offering to the LORD: two young bulls, one ram, and seven lambs in their first year. [a]Be sure they are without blemish. 20Their grain offering shall be of fine flour mixed with oil: three-tenths *of an ephah* you shall offer for a bull, and two-tenths for a ram; 21you shall offer one-tenth *of an ephah* for each of the seven lambs; 22also [a]one goat *as* a sin offering, to make [1]atonement for you. 23You shall offer these besides the burnt offering of the morning, which *is* for a regular burnt offering. 24In this manner you shall offer the food of the offering made by fire daily for seven days, as a sweet aroma to the LORD; it shall be offered besides the regular burnt offering and its drink offering. 25And [a]on the seventh day you shall have a holy convocation. You shall do no customary work.

Offerings at the Feast of Weeks

26'Also [a]on the day of the firstfruits, when you bring a new grain offering to the LORD at your *Feast of* Weeks, you shall have a holy convocation. You shall do no customary work. 27You shall present a burnt offering as a sweet aroma to the LORD: [a]two young bulls, one ram, and seven lambs in their first year, 28with their grain offering of fine flour mixed with oil: three-tenths *of an ephah* for each bull, two-tenths for the one ram, 29and one-tenth for each of the seven lambs; 30*also* one kid of the goats, to make [1]atonement for you. 31[a]Be sure they are without [1]blemish. You shall present *them* with their drink offerings, besides the regular burnt offering with its grain offering.

Offerings at the Feast of Trumpets

29 'And in the seventh month, on the first *day* of the month, you shall have a holy convocation. You shall do no customary work. For you [a]it is a day of blowing the trumpets. 2You shall offer a burnt offering as a sweet aroma to the LORD: one young bull, one ram, *and* seven lambs in their first year, without blemish. 3Their grain offering *shall be* fine flour mixed with oil: three-tenths *of an ephah*

3 [a]Ex. 29:38–42
5 [a]Ex. 16:36 [b]Lev. 2:1
6 [a]Ex. 29:42
7 [a]Ex. 29:42
8 [1]*pleasing*
10 [a]Ezek. 46:4
11 [a]Num. 10:10
12 [a]Num. 15:4–12
15 [a]Num. 15:24; 28:3, 22
16 [a]Lev. 23:5–8
17 [a]Lev. 23:6
18 [a]Lev. 23:7 [1]*assembly* or *gathering* [2]*occupational*
19 [a]Deut. 15:21
22 [a]Num. 28:15 [1]Lit. *covering*
25 [a]Lev. 23:8
26 [a]Deut. 16:9–12
27 [a]Lev. 23:18, 19
30 [1]Lit. *covering*
31 [a]Num. 28:3, 19 [1]*defect*
CHAPTER 29
1 [a]Lev. 23:23–25

for the bull, two-tenths for the ram, 4and
one-tenth for each of the seven lambs;
5also one kid of the goats *as* a sin offering,
to make atonement for you; 6besides [a]the
burnt offering with its grain offering for
the New Moon, [b]the regular burnt offering with its grain offering, and their drink
offerings, [c]according to their ordinance,
as a sweet aroma, an offering made by fire
to the LORD.

Offerings on the Day of Atonement

7[a]'On the tenth *day* of this seventh
month you shall have a holy convocation.
You shall [b]afflict your souls; you shall not
do any work. 8You shall present a burnt
offering to the LORD *as* a sweet aroma: one
young bull, one ram, *and* seven lambs in
their first year. [a]Be sure they are without
blemish. 9Their grain offering *shall be of*
fine flour mixed with oil: three-tenths *of
an ephah* for the bull, two-tenths for the
one ram, 10and one-tenth for each of the
seven lambs; 11also one kid of the goats *as*
a sin offering, besides [a]the sin offering for
atonement, the regular burnt offering
with its grain offering, and their drink offerings.

Offerings at the Feast of Tabernacles

12[a]'On the fifteenth day of the seventh
month you shall have a holy convocation.
You shall do no customary work, and you
shall keep a feast to the LORD seven days.
13[a]You shall present a burnt offering, an
offering made by fire as a sweet aroma to
the LORD: thirteen young bulls, two rams,
and fourteen lambs in their first year.
They shall be without blemish. 14Their
grain offering *shall be of* fine flour mixed
with oil: three-tenths *of an ephah* for
each of the thirteen bulls, two-tenths for
each of the two rams, 15and one-tenth for
each of the fourteen lambs; 16also one kid
of the goats *as* a sin offering, besides the
regular burnt offering, its grain offering,
and its drink offering.

17'On the [a]second day *present* twelve
young bulls, two rams, fourteen lambs in
their first year without blemish, 18and
their grain offering and their drink offerings for the bulls, for the rams, and for the
lambs, by their number, [a]according to the
ordinance; 19also one kid of the goats *as* a
sin offering, besides the regular burnt offering with its grain offering, and their
drink offerings.

20'On the third day *present* eleven bulls,
two rams, fourteen lambs in their first
year without blemish, 21and their grain
offering and their drink offerings for the
bulls, for the rams, and for the lambs, by
their number, [a]according to the ordinance; 22also one goat *as* a sin offering,
besides the regular burnt offering, its
grain offering, and its drink offering.

23'On the fourth day *present* ten bulls,
two rams, *and* fourteen lambs in their
first year, without blemish, 24and their
grain offering and their drink offerings for
the bulls, for the rams, and for the lambs,
by their number, according to the ordinance; 25also one kid of the goats *as* a sin
offering, besides the regular burnt offering, its grain offering, and its drink offering.

26'On the fifth day *present* nine bulls,
two rams, *and* fourteen lambs in their
first year without blemish, 27and their
grain offering and their drink offerings for
the bulls, for the rams, and for the lambs,
by their number, according to the ordinance; 28also one goat *as* a sin offering,
besides the regular burnt offering, its
grain offering, and its drink offering.

29'On the sixth day *present* eight bulls,
two rams, *and* fourteen lambs in their
first year without blemish, 30and their
grain offering and their drink offerings for
the bulls, for the rams, and for the lambs,
by their number, according to the ordinance; 31also one goat *as* a sin offering,
besides the regular burnt offering, its
grain offering, and its drink offering.

32'On the seventh day *present* seven
bulls, two rams, *and* fourteen lambs in
their first year without blemish, 33and
their grain offering and their drink offerings for the bulls, for the rams, and for the
lambs, by their number, according to the
ordinance; 34also one goat *as* a sin offering, besides the regular burnt offering, its
grain offering, and its drink offering.

35'On the eighth day you shall have a
[a]sacred[1] assembly. You shall do no customary work. 36You shall present a burnt
offering, an offering made by fire as a
sweet aroma to the LORD: one bull, one
ram, seven lambs in their first year without blemish, 37and their grain offering
and their drink offerings for the bull, for
the ram, and for the lambs, by their number, according to the ordinance; 38also

---

6 a Num. 28:11–15 b Num. 28:3 c Num. 15:11, 12
7 a Lev. 16:29–34; 23:26–32 b Is. 58:5
8 a Num. 28:19
11 a Lev. 16:3, 5
12 a Deut. 16:13–15
13 a Ezra 3:4
17 a Lev. 23:36
18 a Num. 15:12; 28:7, 14; 29:3, 4, 9, 10
21 a Num. 29:18
35 a Lev. 23:36 1 *solemn*

one goat *as* a sin offering, besides the regular burnt offering, its grain offering, and
its drink offering.
39'These you shall present to the LORD
at your [a]appointed feasts (besides your
[b]vowed offerings and your freewill offerings) as your burnt offerings and your
grain offerings, as your drink offerings
and your peace offerings.' "
40So Moses told the children of Israel
everything, just as the LORD commanded
Moses.

The Law Concerning Vows

30 Then Moses spoke to [a]the heads of
the tribes concerning the children
of Israel, saying, "This *is* the thing which
the LORD has commanded: 2[a]If a man
makes a vow to the LORD, or [b]swears an
oath to bind himself by some agreement,
he shall not break his word; he shall [c]do
according to all that proceeds out of his
mouth.
3"Or if a woman makes a vow to the
LORD, and binds *herself* by some agreement while in her father's house in her
youth, 4and her father hears her vow and
the agreement by which she has bound
herself, and her father [1]holds his peace,
then all her vows shall stand, and every
agreement with which she has bound herself shall stand. 5But if her father over-
rules her on the day that he hears, then
none of her vows nor her agreements by
which she has bound herself shall stand;
and the LORD will release her, because her
father overruled her.
6"If indeed she takes a husband, while
bound by her vows or by a rash utterance
from her lips by which she bound herself,
7and her husband hears *it,* and makes no
response to her on the day that he hears,
then her vows shall stand, and her agreements by which she bound herself shall
stand. 8But if her husband [a]overrules her
on the day that he hears *it,* he shall make
void her vow which she took and what she
uttered with her lips, by which she bound
herself, and the LORD will release her.
9"Also any vow of a widow or a divorced
woman, by which she has bound herself,
shall stand against her.
10"If she vowed in her husband's house,
or bound herself by an agreement with an
oath, 11and her husband heard *it,* and
made no response to her *and* did not over-
rule her, then all her vows shall stand, and
every agreement by which she bound herself shall stand. 12But if her husband truly
made them void on the day he heard
them, then whatever proceeded from her
lips concerning her vows or concerning
the agreement binding her, it shall not
stand; her husband has made them [1]void,
and the LORD will release her. 13Every vow
and every binding oath to afflict her soul,
her husband may confirm it, or her husband may make it void. 14Now if her husband makes no response whatever to her
from day to day, then he confirms all her
vows or all the agreements that bind her;
he confirms them, because he made no
response to her on the day that he heard
them. 15But if he does make them void
after he has heard *them,* then he shall
bear her guilt."
16These *are* the statutes which the
LORD commanded Moses, between a man
and his wife, and between a father and his
daughter in her youth in her father's
house.

Vengeance on the Midianites

31 And the LORD spoke to Moses, saying: 2[a]"Take vengeance on the
Midianites for the children of Israel. Afterward you shall [b]be gathered to your
people."
3So Moses spoke to the people, saying,
"Arm some of yourselves for war, and let
them go against the Midianites to take
vengeance for the LORD on [a]Midian. 4A
thousand from each tribe of all the tribes
of Israel you shall send to the war."
5So there were recruited from the divisions of Israel one thousand from *each*
tribe, twelve thousand armed for war.
6Then Moses sent them to the war, one
thousand from *each* tribe; he sent them to
the war with Phinehas the son of Eleazar
the priest, with the holy articles and [a]the
signal trumpets in his hand. 7And they
warred against the Midianites, just as the
LORD commanded Moses, and [a]they killed
all the [b]males. 8They killed the kings of
Midian with *the rest of* those who were
killed—[a]Evi, Rekem, [b]Zur, Hur, and
Reba, the five kings of Midian. [c]Balaam
the son of Beor they also killed with the
sword.
9And the children of Israel took the
women of Midian captive, with their little
ones, and took as spoil all their cattle, all
their flocks, and all their goods. 10They
also burned with fire all the cities where
they dwelt, and all their forts. 11And [a]they

---

39 a Lev. 23:1–44 b Lev. 7:16; 22:18, 21, 23; 23:38

CHAPTER 30
1 a Num. 1:4, 16; 7:2
2 a Lev. 27:2 b Matt. 14:9 c Job 22:27
4 *1 says nothing* to interfere
8 a [Gen. 3:16]
12 *1 annulled* or *invalidated*

CHAPTER 31
2 a Num. 25:17 b Num. 27:12, 13
3 a Josh. 13:21
6 a Num. 10:9
7 a Deut. 20:13 b Gen. 34:25
8 a Josh. 13:21 b Num. 25:15 c Josh. 13:22
11 a Deut. 20:14

took all the spoil and all the booty—of man and beast.

Return from the War

12Then they brought the captives, the booty, and the spoil to Moses, to Eleazar the priest, and to the congregation of the children of Israel, to the camp in the plains of Moab by the Jordan, *across from* Jericho. 13And Moses, Eleazar the priest, and all the leaders of the congregation, went to meet them outside the camp. 14But Moses was angry with the officers of the army, *with* the captains over thousands and captains over hundreds, who had come from the battle.

15And Moses said to them: "Have you kept [a]all the women alive? 16Look, [a]these *women* caused the children of Israel, through the [b]counsel of Balaam, to trespass against the LORD in the incident of Peor, and [c]there was a plague among the congregation of the LORD. 17Now therefore, [a]kill every male among the little ones, and kill every woman who has known a man intimately. 18But keep alive [a]for yourselves all the young girls who have not known a man intimately. 19And as for you, [a]remain outside the camp seven days; whoever has killed any person, and [b]whoever has touched any slain, purify yourselves and your captives on the third day and on the seventh day. 20Purify every garment, everything made of leather, everything woven of goats' *hair,* and everything made of wood."

21Then Eleazar the priest said to the men of war who had gone to the battle, "This *is* the [1]ordinance of the law which the LORD commanded Moses: 22"Only the gold, the silver, the bronze, the iron, the tin, and the lead, 23everything that can endure fire, you shall put through the fire, and it shall be clean; and it shall be purified [a]with the water of purification. But all that cannot endure fire you shall put through water. 24[a]And you shall wash your clothes on the seventh day and be clean, and afterward you may come into the camp."

Division of the Plunder

25Now the LORD spoke to Moses, saying: 26"Count up the plunder that was [1]taken—of man and beast—you and Eleazar the priest and the chief fathers of the congregation; 27and [a]divide the plunder into two parts, between those who took part in the war, who went out to battle, and all the congregation. 28And levy a [1]tribute for the LORD on the men of war who went out to battle: [a]one of every five hundred of the persons, the cattle, the donkeys, and the sheep; 29take *it* from their half, and [a]give *it* to Eleazar the priest as a heave offering to the LORD. 30And from the children of Israel's half you shall take [a]one of every fifty, drawn from the persons, the cattle, the donkeys, and the sheep, from all the livestock, and give them to the Levites [b]who [1]keep charge of the tabernacle of the LORD." 31So Moses and Eleazar the priest did as the LORD commanded Moses.

32The booty remaining from the plunder, which the men of war had taken, was six hundred and seventy-five thousand sheep, 33seventy-two thousand cattle, 34sixty-one thousand donkeys, 35and thirty-two thousand persons in all, of women who had not known a man intimately. 36And the half, the portion for those who had gone out to war, was in number three hundred and thirty-seven thousand five hundred sheep; 37and the LORD's [1]tribute of the sheep was six hundred and seventy-five. 38The cattle *were* thirty-six thousand, of which the LORD's tribute *was* seventy-two. 39The donkeys *were* thirty thousand five hundred, of which the LORD's tribute *was* sixty-one. 40The persons *were* sixteen thousand, of which the LORD's tribute *was* thirty-two persons. 41So Moses gave the tribute *which was* the LORD's heave offering to Eleazar the priest, [a]as the LORD commanded Moses.

42And from the children of Israel's half, which Moses separated from the men who fought— 43now the half belonging to the congregation was three hundred and thirty-seven thousand five hundred sheep, 44thirty-six thousand cattle, 45thirty thousand five hundred donkeys, 46and sixteen thousand persons— 47and [a]from the children of Israel's half Moses took one of every fifty, drawn from man and beast, and gave them to the Levites, who kept charge of the tabernacle of the LORD, as the LORD commanded Moses.

48Then the officers who *were* over thousands of the army, the captains of thousands and captains of hundreds, came near to Moses; 49and they said to Moses, "Your servants have taken a count of the men of war who *are* under our command, and not a man of us is missing. 50There-

15 [a]Deut. 20:14
16 [a]Num. 25:2 [b]Rev. 2:14 [c]Num. 25:9
17 [a]Deut. 7:2; 20:16–18
18 [a]Deut. 21:10–14
19 [a]Num. 5:2 [b]Num. 19:11–22
21 [1]*statute*
23 [a]Num. 19:9, 17
24 [a]Lev. 11:25
26 [1]*captured*
27 [a]Josh. 22:8
28 [a]Num. 31:30, 47 [1]*tax*
29 [a]Deut. 18:1–5
30 [a]Num. 31:42–47 [b]Num. 3:7, 8, 25, 31, 36; 18:3, 4 [1]*perform the service*
37 [1]*tax*
41 [a]Num. 5:9, 10; 18:8, 19
47 [a]Num. 31:30

fore we have brought an offering for the
LORD, what every man found of ornaments of gold: armlets and bracelets and
signet rings and earrings and necklaces,
[a]to make [1]atonement for ourselves before
the LORD." 51So Moses and Eleazar the
priest received the gold from them, all the
fashioned ornaments. 52And all the gold of
the offering that they offered to the LORD,
from the captains of thousands and captains of hundreds, was sixteen thousand
seven hundred and fifty shekels. 53[a](The
men of war had taken spoil, every man for
himself.) 54And Moses and Eleazar the
priest received the gold from the captains
of thousands and of hundreds, and
brought it into the tabernacle of meeting
[a]as a memorial for the children of Israel
before the LORD.

The Tribes Settling East of the Jordan

32 Now the children of Reuben and
the children of Gad had a very
great multitude of livestock; and when
they saw the land of [a]Jazer and the land
of [b]Gilead, that indeed the region *was* a
place for livestock, 2the children of Gad
and the children of Reuben came and
spoke to Moses, to Eleazar the priest, and
to the leaders of the congregation, saying,
3"Ataroth, Dibon, Jazer, [a]Nimrah, [b]Hesh-
bon, Elealeh, [c]Shebam, Nebo, and [c]Beon,
4the country [a]which the LORD defeated
before the congregation of Israel, *is* a land
for livestock, and your servants have livestock." 5Therefore they said, "If we have
found favor in your sight, let this land be
given to your servants as a possession. Do
not take us over the Jordan."

6And Moses said to the children of Gad
and to the children of Reuben: "Shall your
brethren go to war while you sit here?
7Now why will you [a]discourage the heart
of the children of Israel from going over
into the land which the LORD has given
them? 8Thus your fathers did [a]when I
sent them away from Kadesh Barnea [b]to
see the land. 9For [a]when they went up to
the Valley of Eshcol and saw the land, they
discouraged the heart of the children of
Israel, so that they did not go into the land
which the LORD had given them. 10[a]So the
LORD's anger was aroused on that day, and
He swore an oath, saying, 11'Surely none
of the men who came up from Egypt,
[a]from twenty years old and above, shall
see the land of which I swore to Abraham,
Isaac, and Jacob, because [b]they have not
wholly followed Me, 12except Caleb the
son of Jephunneh, the Kenizzite, and
Joshua the son of Nun, [a]for they have
wholly followed the LORD.' 13So the
LORD's anger was aroused against Israel,
and He made them [a]wander in the wilderness forty years, until [b]all the generation
that had done evil in the sight of the LORD
was gone. 14And look! You have risen in
your fathers' place, a brood of sinful men,
to increase still more the [a]fierce anger of
the LORD against Israel. 15For if you [a]turn
away from following Him, He will once
again leave them in the wilderness, and
you will destroy all these people."

16Then they came near to him and said:
"We will build sheepfolds here for our
livestock, and cities for our little ones,
17but [a]we ourselves will be armed, ready
to go before the children of Israel until we
have brought them to their place; and our
little ones will dwell in the fortified cities
because of the inhabitants of the land.
18[a]We will not return to our homes until
every one of the children of Israel has [1]re-
ceived his inheritance. 19For we will not
inherit with them on the other side of the
Jordan and beyond, [a]because our inheritance has fallen to us on this eastern side
of the Jordan."

20Then [a]Moses said to them: "If you do
this thing, if you arm yourselves before
the LORD for the war, 21and all your armed
men cross over the Jordan before the
LORD until He has driven out His enemies
from before Him, 22and [a]the land is subdued before the LORD, then afterward
[b]you may return and be blameless before
the LORD and before Israel; and [c]this land
shall be your possession before the LORD.
23But if you do not do so, then take note,
you have sinned against the LORD; and be
sure [a]your sin will find you out. 24[a]Build
cities for your little ones and folds for
your sheep, and do [1]what has proceeded
out of your mouth."

25And the children of Gad and the children of Reuben spoke to Moses, saying:
"Your servants will do as my lord commands. 26[a]Our little ones, our wives, our
flocks, and all our livestock will be there
in the cities of Gilead; 27[a]but your servants will cross over, every man armed for
war, before the LORD to battle, just as my
lord says."

28So Moses gave command [a]concerning
them to Eleazar the priest, to Joshua the

50 a Ex. 30:12–16 1 Lit. *covering*
53 a Deut. 20:14
54 a Ex. 30:16

CHAPTER 32
1 a Num. 21:32 b Deut. 3:13
3 a Num. 32:36 b Josh. 13:17, 26 c Num. 32:38
4 a Num. 21:24, 34, 35
7 a Num. 13:27—14:4
8 a Num. 13:3, 26 b Deut. 1:19–25
9 a Deut. 1:24, 28
10 a Deut. 1:34–36
11 a Num. 14:28, 29; 26:63–65 b Num. 14:24, 30
12 a Deut. 1:36
13 a Num. 14:33–35 b Num. 26:64, 65
14 a Deut. 1:34
15 a Deut. 30:17, 18
17 a Josh. 4:12, 13
18 a Josh. 22:1–4 1 *possessed*
19 a Josh. 12:1; 13:8
20 a Deut. 3:18
22 a Deut. 3:20 b Josh. 22:4 c Deut. 3:12, 15, 16, 18
23 a Is. 59:12
24 a Num. 32:16 1 *what you said you would do*
26 a Josh. 1:14
27 a Josh. 4:12
28 a Josh. 1:13

son of Nun, and to the chief fathers of the tribes of the children of Israel. 29And Moses said to them: "If the children of Gad and the children of Reuben cross over the Jordan with you, every man armed for battle before the LORD, and the land is subdued before you, then you shall give them the land of Gilead as a possession. 30But if they do not cross over armed with you, they shall have possessions among you in the land of Canaan."

31Then the children of Gad and the children of Reuben answered, saying: "As the LORD has said to your servants, so we will do. 32We will cross over armed before the LORD into the land of Canaan, but the possession of our inheritance *shall remain* with us on this side of the Jordan."

33So [a]Moses gave to the children of Gad, to the children of Reuben, and to half the tribe of Manasseh the son of Joseph, [b]the kingdom of Sihon king of the Amorites and the kingdom of Og king of Bashan, the land with its cities within the borders, the cities of the surrounding country. 34And the children of Gad built [a]Dibon and Ataroth and [b]Aroer, 35Atroth and Shophan and [a]Jazer and Jogbehah, 36[a]Beth Nimrah and Beth Haran, [b]fortified cities, and folds for sheep. 37And the children of Reuben built [a]Heshbon and Elealeh and Kirjathaim, 38[a]Nebo and [b]Baal Meon [c](*their* names being changed) and Shibmah; and they gave *other* names to the cities which they built.

39And the children of [a]Machir the son of Manasseh went to Gilead and took it, and [1]dispossessed the Amorites who *were* in it. 40So Moses [a]gave Gilead to Machir the son of Manasseh, and he dwelt in it. 41Also [a]Jair the son of Manasseh went and took its small towns, and called them [b]Havoth Jair.[1] 42Then Nobah went and took Kenath and its villages, and he called it Nobah, after his own name.

Israel's Journey from Egypt Reviewed

33 These *are* the journeys of the children of Israel, who went out of the land of Egypt by their armies under the [a]hand of Moses and Aaron. 2Now Moses wrote down the starting points of their journeys at the command of the LORD. And these *are* their journeys according to their starting points:

3They [a]departed from Rameses in [b]the first month, on the fifteenth day of the first month; on the day after the Passover the children of Israel went out [c]with boldness in the sight of all the Egyptians. 4For the Egyptians were burying all *their* firstborn, [a]whom the LORD had killed among them. Also [b]on their gods the LORD had executed judgments.

5[a]Then the children of Israel moved from Rameses and camped at Succoth. 6They departed from [a]Succoth and camped at Etham, which *is* on the edge of the wilderness. 7[a]They moved from Etham and turned back to Pi Hahiroth, which *is* east of Baal Zephon; and they camped near Migdol. 8They departed [1]from before Hahiroth and [a]passed through the midst of the sea into the wilderness, went three days' journey in the Wilderness of Etham, and camped at Marah. 9They moved from Marah and [a]came to Elim. At Elim *were* twelve springs of water and seventy palm trees; so they camped there.

10They moved from Elim and camped by the Red Sea. 11They moved from the Red Sea and camped in the [a]Wilderness of Sin. 12They journeyed from the Wilderness of Sin and camped at Dophkah. 13They departed from Dophkah and camped at Alush. 14They moved from Alush and camped at [a]Rephidim, where there was no water for the people to drink.

15They departed from Rephidim and camped in the [a]Wilderness of Sinai. 16They moved from the Wilderness of Sinai and camped [a]at [1]Kibroth Hattaavah. 17They departed from Kibroth Hattaavah and [a]camped at Hazeroth. 18They departed from Hazeroth and camped at [a]Rithmah. 19They departed from Rithmah and camped at Rimmon Perez. 20They departed from Rimmon Perez and camped at Libnah. 21They moved from Libnah and camped at Rissah. 22They journeyed from Rissah and camped at Kehelathah. 23They went from Kehelathah and camped at Mount Shepher. 24They moved from Mount Shepher and camped at Haradah. 25They moved from Haradah and camped at Makheloth. 26They moved from Makheloth and camped at Tahath. 27They departed from Tahath and camped at Terah. 28They moved from Terah and camped at Mithkah. 29They went from Mithkah and camped at Hashmonah. 30They departed from Hashmonah and [a]camped at Moseroth. 31They departed from Moseroth and camped at Bene Jaakan. 32They moved

33 a Deut. 3:8–17; 29:8 b Num. 21:24, 33, 35
34 a Num. 33:45, 46 b Deut. 2:36
35 a Num. 32:1, 3
36 a Num. 32:3 b Num. 32:24
37 a Num. 21:27
38 a Is. 46:1 b Ezek. 25:9 c Ex. 23:13
39 a Gen. 50:23 *1 drove out*
40 a Deut. 3:12, 13, 15
41 a Deut. 3:14 b Judg. 10:4 1 Lit. *Towns of Jair*

CHAPTER 33
1 a Ps. 77:20
3 a Ex. 12:37 b Ex. 12:2; 13:4 c Ex. 14:8
4 a Ex. 12:29 b Is. 19:1
5 a Ex. 12:37
6 a Ex. 13:20
7 a Ex. 14:1, 2, 9
8 a Ex. 14:22; 15:22, 23 1 Many Heb. mss., Sam., Syr., Tg., Vg. *from Pi Hahiroth;* cf. Num. 33:7
9 a Ex. 15:27
11 a Ex. 16:1
14 a Ex. 17:1; 19:2
15 a Ex. 16:1; 19:1, 2
16 a Num. 11:34 1 Lit. *Graves of Craving*
17 a Num. 11:35
18 a Num. 12:16
30 a Deut. 10:6

from [a]Bene Jaakan and [b]camped at Hor Hagidgad. 33They went from Hor Hagidgad and camped at Jotbathah. 34They moved from Jotbathah and camped at Abronah. 35They departed from Abronah [a]and camped at Ezion Geber. 36They moved from Ezion Geber and camped in the [a]Wilderness of Zin, which *is* Kadesh. 37They moved from [a]Kadesh and camped at Mount Hor, on the boundary of the land of Edom.

38Then [a]Aaron the priest went up to Mount Hor at the command of the LORD, and died there in the fortieth year after the children of Israel had come out of the land of Egypt, on the first *day* of the fifth month. 39Aaron *was* one hundred and twenty-three years old when he died on Mount Hor.

40Now [a]the king of Arad, the Canaanite, who dwelt in the South in the land of Canaan, heard of the coming of the children of Israel.

41So they departed from Mount Hor and camped at Zalmonah. 42They departed from Zalmonah and camped at Punon. 43They departed from Punon and [a]camped at Oboth. 44[a]They departed from Oboth and camped at Ije Abarim, at the border of Moab. 45They departed from [1]Ijim and camped [a]at Dibon Gad. 46They moved from Dibon Gad and camped at [a]Almon Diblathaim. 47They moved from Almon Diblathaim [a]and camped in the mountains of Abarim, before Nebo. 48They departed from the mountains of Abarim and [a]camped in the plains of Moab by the Jordan, *across from* Jericho. 49They camped by the Jordan, from Beth Jesimoth as far as the [a]Abel Acacia Grove[1] in the plains of Moab.

Instructions for the Conquest of Canaan

50Now the LORD spoke to Moses in the plains of Moab by the Jordan, *across from* Jericho, saying, 51"Speak to the children of Israel, and say to them: [a]'When you have crossed the Jordan into the land of Canaan, 52[a]then you shall drive out all the inhabitants of the land from before you, destroy all their engraved stones, destroy all their molded images, and demolish all their [1]high places; 53you shall dispossess *the inhabitants of* the land and dwell in it, for I have given you the land to [a]possess. 54And [a]you shall divide the land by lot as an inheritance among your families; to the larger you shall give a larger inheritance, and to the smaller you shall give a smaller inheritance; there everyone's *inheritance* shall be whatever falls to him by lot. You shall inherit according to the tribes of your fathers. 55But if you do not drive out the inhabitants of the land from before you, then it shall be that those whom you let remain *shall be* [a]irritants in your eyes and thorns in your sides, and they shall harass you in the land where you dwell. 56Moreover it shall be *that* I will do to you as I thought to do to them.' "

The Appointed Boundaries of Canaan

34 Then the LORD spoke to Moses, saying, 2"Command the children of Israel, and say to them: 'When you come into [a]the land of Canaan, this *is* the land that shall fall to you as an inheritance—the land of Canaan to its boundaries. 3[a]Your southern border shall be from the Wilderness of Zin along the border of Edom; then your southern border shall extend eastward to the end of [b]the Salt Sea; 4your border shall turn from the southern side of [a]the Ascent of Akrabbim, continue to Zin, and be on the south of [b]Kadesh Barnea; then it shall go on to [c]Hazar Addar, and continue to Azmon; 5the border shall turn from Azmon [a]to the Brook of Egypt, and it shall end at the Sea.

6'As for the [a]western border, you shall have the Great Sea for a border; this shall be your western border.

7'And this shall be your northern border: From the Great Sea you shall mark out your *border* line to [a]Mount Hor; 8from Mount Hor you shall mark out *your border* [a]to the entrance of Hamath; then the direction of the border shall be toward [b]Zedad; 9the border shall proceed to Ziphron, and it shall end at [a]Hazar Enan. This shall be your northern border.

10'You shall mark out your eastern border from Hazar Enan to Shepham; 11the border shall go down from Shepham [a]to Riblah on the east side of Ain; the border shall go down and reach to the eastern [1]side of the Sea [b]of Chinnereth; 12the border shall go down along the Jordan, and it shall end at [a]the Salt Sea. This shall be your land with its surrounding boundaries.' "

32 a Deut. 10:6 b Deut. 10:7
35 a Deut. 2:8
36 a Num. 20:1; 27:14
37 a Num. 20:22, 23; 21:4
38 a Num. 20:25, 28
40 a Num. 21:1
43 a Num. 21:10
44 a Num. 21:11
45 a Num. 32:34 *1* Same as *Ije Abarim*, v. 44
46 a Jer. 48:22
47 a Deut. 32:49
48 a Num. 22:1; 31:12; 35:1
49 a Num. 25:1 *1* Heb. *Abel Shittim*
51 a Josh. 3:17
52 a Deut. 7:2, 5; 12:3 *1* Places for pagan worship
53 a Deut. 11:31
54 a Num. 26:53–56
55 a Josh. 23:13

CHAPTER 34
2 a Gen. 17:8
3 a Josh. 15:1–3 b Gen. 14:3
4 a Josh. 15:3 b Num. 13:26; 32:8 c Josh. 15:3, 4
5 a Josh. 15:4, 47
6 a Ezek. 47:20
7 a Num. 33:37
8 a Num. 13:21 b Ezek. 47:15
9 a Ezek. 47:17
11 a 2 Kin. 23:33 b Deut. 3:17 *1* Lit. *shoulder*
12 a Num. 34:3

13 Then Moses commanded the children of Israel, saying: [a]"This *is* the land which you shall inherit by lot, which the LORD has commanded to give to the nine tribes and to the half-tribe. 14 [a]For the tribe of the children of Reuben according to the house of their fathers, and the tribe of the children of Gad according to the house of their fathers, have received *their inheritance*; and the half-tribe of Manasseh has received its inheritance. 15 The two tribes and the half-tribe have received their inheritance on this side of the Jordan, *across from* Jericho eastward, toward the sunrise."

The Leaders Appointed to Divide the Land

16 And the LORD spoke to Moses, saying, 17 "These *are* the names of the men who shall divide the land among you as an inheritance: [a]Eleazar the priest and Joshua the son of Nun. 18 And you shall take one [a]leader of every tribe to divide the land for the inheritance. 19 These *are* the names of the men: from the tribe of Judah, Caleb the son of Jephunneh; 20 from the tribe of the children of Simeon, Shemuel the son of Ammihud; 21 from the tribe of Benjamin, Elidad the son of Chislon; 22 a leader from the tribe of the children of Dan, Bukki the son of Jogli; 23 from the sons of Joseph: a leader from the tribe of the children of Manasseh, Hanniel the son of Ephod, 24 and a leader from the tribe of the children of Ephraim, Kemuel the son of Shiphtan; 25 a leader from the tribe of the children of Zebulun, Elizaphan the son of Parnach; 26 a leader from the tribe of the children of Issachar, Paltiel the son of Azzan; 27 a leader from the tribe of the children of Asher, Ahihud the son of Shelomi; 28 and a leader from the tribe of the children of Naphtali, Pedahel the son of Ammihud."

29 These *are* the ones the LORD commanded to [1]divide the inheritance among the children of Israel in the land of Canaan.

Cities for the Levites

35 And the LORD spoke to Moses in [a]the plains of Moab by the Jordan *across from* Jericho, saying: 2 [a]"Command the children of Israel that they give the Levites cities to dwell in from the inheritance of their possession, and you shall *also* give the Levites [b]common-land around the cities. 3 They shall have the cities to dwell in; and their common-land shall be for their cattle, for their herds, and for all their animals. 4 The common-land of the cities which you will give the Levites *shall extend* from the wall of the city outward a thousand cubits all around. 5 And you shall measure outside the city on the east side two thousand cubits, on the south side two thousand cubits, on the west side two thousand cubits, and on the north side two thousand cubits. The city *shall be* in the middle. This shall belong to them as common-land for the cities.

6 "Now among the cities which you will give to the Levites *you shall appoint* [a]six cities of refuge, to which a manslayer may flee. And to these you shall add forty-two cities. 7 So all the cities you will give to the Levites *shall be* [a]forty-eight; these *you shall give* with their common-land. 8 And the cities which you will give *shall be* [a]from the possession of the children of Israel; [b]from the larger *tribe* you shall give many, from the smaller you shall give few. Each shall give some of its cities to the Levites, in proportion to the inheritance that each receives."

Cities of Refuge

9 Then the LORD spoke to Moses, saying, 10 "Speak to the children of Israel, and say to them: [a]'When you cross the Jordan into the land of Canaan, 11 then [a]you shall appoint cities to be cities of refuge for you, that the manslayer who kills any person accidentally may flee there. 12 [a]They shall be cities of refuge for you from the avenger, that the manslayer may not die until he stands before the congregation in judgment. 13 And of the cities which you give, you shall have [a]six cities of refuge. 14 [a]You shall appoint three cities on this side of the Jordan, and three cities you shall appoint in the land of Canaan, *which* will be cities of refuge. 15 These six cities shall be for refuge for the children of Israel, [a]for the stranger, and for the sojourner among them, that anyone who kills a person accidentally may flee there.

16 [a]'But if he strikes him with an iron implement, so that he dies, he *is* a murderer; the murderer shall surely be put to death. 17 And if he strikes him with a stone in the hand, by which one could die, and he does die, he *is* a murderer; the murder-

34:13 [a] Josh. 14:1–5
14 [a] Num. 32:33
17 [a] Josh. 14:1, 2; 19:51
18 [a] Num. 1:4, 16
29 [1] *apportion*

CHAPTER 35
1 [a] Num. 33:50
2 [a] Josh. 14:3, 4; 21:2, 3 [b] Lev. 25:32–34
6 [a] Josh. 20:2, 7, 8; 21:3, 13
7 [a] Josh. 21:41
8 [a] Josh. 21:3 [b] Num. 26:54; 33:54
10 [a] Josh. 20:1–9
11 [a] Ex. 21:13
12 [a] Deut. 19:6
13 [a] Num. 35:6
14 [a] Deut. 4:41
15 [a] Num. 15:16
16 [a] Lev. 24:17

er shall surely be put to death. 18Or *if* he
strikes him with a wooden hand weapon,
by which one could die, and he does die,
he *is* a murderer; the murderer shall surely be put to death. 19[a]The[1] avenger of
blood himself shall put the murderer to
death; when he meets him, he shall put
him to death. 20[a]If he pushes him out
of hatred or, [b]while lying in wait, hurls
something at him so that he dies, 21or in
enmity he strikes him with his hand so
that he dies, the one who struck *him* shall
surely be put to death. He *is* a murderer.
The avenger of blood shall put the murderer to death when he meets him.
22'However, if he pushes him suddenly
[a]without enmity, or throws anything at
him without lying in wait, 23or uses a
stone, by which a man could die, throwing *it* at him without seeing *him,* so that
he dies, while he was not his enemy or
seeking his harm, 24then [a]the congregation shall judge between the manslayer
and the avenger of blood according to
these judgments. 25So the congregation
shall deliver the manslayer from the hand
of the avenger of blood, and the congregation shall return him to the city of refuge
where he had fled, and [a]he shall remain
there until the death of the high priest
[b]who was anointed with the holy oil.
26But if the manslayer at any time goes
outside the limits of the city of refuge
where he fled, 27and the avenger of blood
finds him outside the limits of his city of
refuge, and the avenger of blood kills the
manslayer, he shall not be guilty of
[1]blood, 28because he should have remained in his city of refuge until the
death of the high priest. But after the
death of the high priest the manslayer
may return to the land of his possession.
29'And these *things* shall be [a]a statute
of judgment to you throughout your generations in all your dwellings. 30Whoever
kills a person, the murderer shall be put
to death on the [a]testimony of witnesses;
but one witness is not *sufficient* testimony against a person for the death *penalty.*
31Moreover you shall take no ransom for
the life of a murderer who *is* guilty of
death, but he shall surely be put to death.
32And you shall take no ransom for him
who has fled to his city of refuge, that he
may return to dwell in the land before the
death of the priest. 33So you shall not pollute the land where you *are;* for blood [a]de-
files the land, and no [1]atonement can be
made for the land, for the blood that is
shed on it, except [b]by the blood of him
who shed it. 34Therefore [a]do not defile the
land which you inhabit, in the midst of
which I dwell; for [b]I the LORD dwell
among the children of Israel.' "

Marriage of Female Heirs

36 Now the chief fathers of the families of the [a]children of Gilead the
son of Machir, the son of Manasseh, of the
families of the sons of Joseph, came near
and [b]spoke before Moses and before the
leaders, the chief fathers of the children of
Israel. 2And they said: [a]"The LORD commanded my lord *Moses* to give the land as
an inheritance by lot to the children of
Israel, and [b]my lord was commanded by
the LORD to give the inheritance of our
brother Zelophehad to his daughters.
3Now if they are married to any of the
sons of the *other* tribes of the children of
Israel, then their inheritance will be [a]tak-
en from the inheritance of our fathers,
and it will be added to the inheritance of
the tribe into which they marry; so it will
be taken from the lot of our inheritance.
4And when [a]the Jubilee of the children of
Israel comes, then their inheritance will
be added to the inheritance of the tribe
into which they marry; so their inheritance will be taken away from the inheritance of the tribe of our fathers."
5Then Moses commanded the children
of Israel according to the word of the
LORD, saying: [a]"What the tribe of the sons
of Joseph speaks is right. 6This *is* what the
LORD commands concerning the daughters of Zelophehad, saying, 'Let them
[1]marry whom they think best, [a]but they
may marry only within the family of their
father's tribe.' 7So the inheritance of
the children of Israel shall not change
hands from tribe to tribe, for every one
of the children of Israel shall [a]keep the
inheritance of the tribe of his fathers.
8And [a]every daughter who possesses an
inheritance in any tribe of the children of
Israel shall be the wife of one of the family
of her father's tribe, so that the children
of Israel each may possess the inheritance
of his fathers. 9Thus no inheritance shall
change hands from *one* tribe to another,
but every tribe of the children of Israel
shall keep its own inheritance."
10Just as the LORD commanded Moses,

19 [a] Num. 35:21, 24, 27 [1] A family member who is to avenge the victim
20 [a] Gen. 4:8 [b] Ex. 21:14
22 [a] Ex. 21:13
24 [a] Josh. 20:6
25 [a] Josh. 20:6 [b] Ex. 29:7
27 [1] Murder
29 [a] Num. 27:11
30 [a] Deut. 17:6; 19:15
33 [a] Ps. 106:38 [b] Gen. 9:6 [1] Lit. *covering*
34 [a] Lev. 18:24, 25 [b] Ex. 29:45, 46

CHAPTER 36
1 [a] Num. 26:29 [b] Num. 27:1–11
2 [a] Josh. 17:4 [b] Num. 27:1, 5–7
3 [a] Num. 27:4
4 [a] Lev. 25:10
5 [a] Num. 27:7
6 [a] Num. 36:11, 12 [1] Lit. *be wives to*
7 [a] 1 Kin. 21:3
8 [a] 1 Chr. 23:22

so did the daughters of Zelophehad; 11[a]for
Mahlah, Tirzah, Hoglah, Milcah, and
Noah, the daughters of Zelophehad, were
married to the sons of their father's
brothers. 12They were married into the
families of the children of Manasseh the
son of Joseph, and their inheritance remained in the tribe of their father's
family.

13These *are* the commandments and
the judgments which the LORD commanded the children of Israel by the hand of
Moses [a]in the plains of Moab by the Jordan, *across from* Jericho.

11 a Num. 26:33; 27:1

13 a Num. 26:3; 33:50

AUTHOR: *Traditionally Moses*
DATE: *Approximately 1400 B.C.*
THEME: *Obedience Brings Blessing, Disobedience Cursing*
KEY WORDS: *Covenant, Obey, Remember, Blessed, Cursed*

DEUTERONOMY

Dear Woman of Destiny,

In Deuteronomy, Moses carefully summarizes the law and the wilderness experience. In three outstanding sermons, he looks back over victories and lessons of the past. He looks inward at the law, and he looks ahead with hope in God's promises. As women of excellence, we also value past experiences as we seek Him and press on to our own land of promise.

His love and mine,

Marilyn Hickey

The Previous Command to Enter Canaan

These *are* the words which Moses spoke to all Israel [a]on this side of the Jordan in the wilderness, in the [1]plain opposite [2]Suph, between Paran, Tophel, Laban, Hazeroth, and Dizahab. 2 *It is* eleven days' *journey* from Horeb by way of Mount Seir [a]to Kadesh Barnea. 3 Now it came to pass [a]in the fortieth year, in the eleventh month, on the first *day* of the month, *that* Moses spoke to the children of Israel according to all that the LORD had given him as commandments to them, 4 [a]after he had killed Sihon king of the Amorites, who dwelt in Heshbon, and Og king of Bashan, who dwelt at Ashtaroth [b]in[1] Edrei.

5 On this side of the Jordan in the land of Moab, Moses began to explain this law, saying, 6 "The LORD our God spoke to us [a]in Horeb, saying: 'You have dwelt long [b]enough at this mountain. 7 Turn and take your journey, and go to the mountains of the Amorites, to all the neighboring *places* in the [1]plain, in the mountains and in the lowland, in the South and on the seacoast, to the land of the Canaanites and to Lebanon, as far as the great river, the River Euphrates. 8 See, I have set the land before you; go in and possess the land which the LORD [1]swore to your fathers—to [a]Abraham, Isaac, and Jacob—to give to them and their descendants after them.'

Tribal Leaders Appointed

9 "And [a]I spoke to you at that time, saying: 'I [1]alone am not able to bear you. 10 The LORD your God has multiplied you, [a]and here you *are* today, as the stars of heaven in multitude. 11 [a]May the LORD God of your fathers make you a thousand times more numerous than you are, and bless you [b]as He has promised you! 12 [a]How can I alone bear your problems and your burdens and your complaints? 13 Choose wise, understanding, and knowledgeable men from among your tribes, and I will make them [1]heads over you.' 14 And you answered me and said, 'The thing which you have told *us* to do *is* good.' 15 So I took [a]the heads of your tribes, wise and knowledgeable men, and [1]made them heads over you, leaders of thousands, leaders of hundreds, leaders of fifties, leaders of tens, and officers for your tribes.

16 "Then I commanded your judges at that time, saying, 'Hear *the cases* between your brethren, and [a]judge righteously between a man and his [b]brother or the stranger who is with him. 17 [a]You shall not show partiality in judgment; you shall hear the small as well as the great; you shall not be afraid in any man's presence, for [b]the judgment *is* God's. The case that is too hard for you, [c]bring to me, and I will hear it.' 18 And I commanded you at that time all the things which you should do.

Israel's Refusal to Enter the Land

19 "So we departed from Horeb, [a]and went through all that great and terrible wilderness which you saw on the way to the mountains of the Amorites, as the LORD our God had commanded us. Then [b]we came to Kadesh Barnea. 20 And I said to you, 'You have come to the mountains of the Amorites, which the LORD our God is giving us. 21 Look, the LORD your God has set the land before you; go up *and* possess *it,* as the LORD God of your fathers has spoken to you; [a]do not fear or be discouraged.'

22 "And every one of you came near to me and said, 'Let us send men before us, and let them search out the land for us, and bring back word to us of the way by which we should go up, and of the cities into which we shall come.'

23 "The plan pleased me well; so [a]I took twelve of your men, one man from *each* tribe. 24 [a]And they departed and went up into the mountains, and came to the Valley of Eshcol, and spied it out. 25 They also took *some* of the fruit of the land in their hands and brought *it* down to us; and they brought back word to us, saying, '*It is* a [a]good land which the LORD our God is giving us.'

26 [a]"Nevertheless you would not go up, but rebelled against the command of the LORD your God; 27 and you [a]complained in your tents, and said, 'Because the LORD [b]hates us, He has brought us out of the land of Egypt to deliver us into the hand of the Amorites, to destroy us. 28 Where can we go up? Our brethren have [1]discouraged our hearts, saying, [a]"The people *are* greater and taller than we; the cities *are* great and fortified up to heaven; moreover we have seen the sons of the [b]Anakim there." '

CHAPTER 1
1 a Deut. 4:44–46 *1* Heb. *arabah* *2* One LXX ms., Tg., Vg. *Red Sea*
2 a Num. 13:26; 32:8
3 a Num. 33:38
4 a Num. 21:23, 24, 33–35 b Josh. 13:12 *1* LXX, Syr., Vg. *and;* cf. Josh. 12:4
6 a Ex. 3:1, 12 b Ex. 19:1, 2
7 *1* Heb. *arabah*
8 a Gen. 12:7; 15:5; 22:17; 26:3; 28:13 *1 promised*
9 a Ex. 18:18, 24 *1 am not able to bear you by myself*
10 a Gen. 15:5; 22:17
11 a 2 Sam. 24:3 b Gen. 15:5
12 a 1 Kin. 3:8, 9
13 *1 rulers*
15 a Ex. 18:25 *1 appointed*
16 a Deut. 16:18 b Lev. 24:22
17 a Prov. 24:23–26 b 2 Chr. 19:6 c Ex. 18:22, 26
19 a Deut. 2:7; 8:15; 32:10 b Num. 13:26
21 a Josh. 1:6, 9
23 a Num. 13:2, 3
24 a Num. 13:21–25
25 a Num. 13:27
26 a Num. 14:1–4
27 a Ps. 106:25 b Deut. 9:28
28 a Deut. 9:1, 2 b Num. 13:28 *1* Lit. *melted*

29"Then I said to you, 'Do not be terrified, [a]or afraid of them. 30[a]The LORD your God, who goes before you, He will fight for you, according to all He did for you in Egypt before your eyes, 31and in the wilderness where you saw how the LORD your God carried you, as a [a]man carries his son, in all the way that you went until you came to this place.' 32Yet, for all that, [a]you did not believe the LORD your God, 33[a]who went in the way before you [b]to search out a place for you to pitch your tents, to show you the way you should go, in the fire by night and in the cloud by day.

O Lord our God, I pray that _____ will not be terrified or afraid, because You go before them. You will fight for them and carry them everywhere they go.

FROM DEUTERONOMY 1:29–31

The Penalty for Israel's Rebellion

34"And the LORD heard the sound of your words, and was angry, [a]and took an oath, saying, 35[a]'Surely not one of these men of this evil generation shall see that good land of which I [1]swore to give to your fathers, 36[a]except Caleb the son of Jephunneh; he shall see it, and to him and his children I am giving the land on which he walked, because [b]he [1]wholly followed the LORD.' 37[a]The LORD was also angry with me for your sakes, saying, 'Even you shall not go in there. 38[a]Joshua the son of Nun, [b]who stands before you, he shall go in there. [c]Encourage him, for he shall cause Israel to inherit it.

39[a]'Moreover your little ones and your children, who [b]you say will be victims, who today [c]have no knowledge of good and evil, they shall go in there; to them I will give it, and they shall possess it. 40[a]But *as for* you, turn and take your journey into the wilderness by the Way of the Red Sea.'

41"Then you answered and said to me, [a]'We have sinned against the LORD; we will go up and fight, just as the LORD our God commanded us.' And when everyone of you had girded on his weapons of war, you were ready to go up into the mountain.

42"And the LORD said to me, 'Tell them, [a]"Do not go up nor fight, for I *am* not among you; lest you be defeated before your enemies." ' 43So I spoke to you; yet you would not listen, but [a]rebelled against the command of the LORD, and [b]presumptuously[1] went up into the mountain. 44And the Amorites who dwelt in that mountain came out against you and chased you [a]as bees do, and drove you back from Seir to Hormah. 45Then you returned and wept before the LORD, but the LORD would not listen to your voice nor give ear to you.

46[a]"So you remained in Kadesh many days, according to the days that you spent *there*.

The Desert Years

2 "Then we turned and [a]journeyed into the wilderness of the Way of the Red Sea, [b]as the LORD spoke to me, and we [1]skirted Mount Seir for many days.

2"And the LORD spoke to me, saying: 3'You have skirted this mountain [a]long enough; turn northward. 4And command the people, saying, [a]"You *are about to* pass through the territory of [b]your brethren, the descendants of Esau, who live in Seir; and they will be afraid of you. Therefore watch yourselves carefully. 5Do not meddle with them, for I will not give you *any* of their land, no, not so much as one footstep, [a]because I have given Mount Seir to Esau *as* a possession. 6You shall buy food from them with money, that you may eat; and you shall also buy water from them with money, that you may drink.

7"For the LORD your God has blessed you in all the work of your hand. He knows your [1]trudging through this great wilderness. [a]These forty years the LORD your God *has been* with you; you have lacked nothing." '

8"And when we passed beyond our brethren, the descendants of Esau who dwell in Seir, away from the road of the plain, away from [a]Elath and Ezion Geber, we [b]turned and passed by way of the Wilderness of Moab. 9Then the LORD said to me, 'Do not harass Moab, nor contend with them in battle, for I will not give you

---

29 a Num. 14:9
30 a Ex. 14:14
31 a Is. 46:3, 4; 63:9
32 a Jude 5
33 a Ex. 13:21 b Num. 10:33
34 a Deut. 2:14, 15
35 a Num. 14:22, 23 1 *promised*
36 a [Josh. 14:9] b Num. 32:11, 12 1 *fully*
37 a Deut. 3:26; 4:21; 34:4
38 a Num. 14:30 b 1 Sam. 16:22 c Deut. 31:7, 23
39 a Num. 14:31 b Num. 14:3 c Is. 7:15, 16
40 a Num. 14:25
41 a Num. 14:40
42 a Num. 14:41–43
43 a Num. 14:44 b Deut. 17:12, 13 1 *willfully*
44 a Ps. 118:12
46 a Deut. 2:7, 14

CHAPTER 2
1 a Deut. 1:40 b Num. 14:25 1 *circled around*
3 a Deut. 2:7, 14
4 a Num. 20:14–21 b Deut. 23:7
5 a Gen. 36:8
7 a Deut. 8:2–4 1 Lit. *goings*
8 a Judg. 11:18 b Num. 21:4

any of their land *as* a possession, because
I have given [a]Ar to [b]the descendants of
Lot *as* a possession.' "
10[a](The Emim had dwelt there in times
past, a people as great and numerous and
tall as [b]the Anakim. 11They were also regarded as [1]giants, like the Anakim, but
the Moabites call them Emim. 12[a]The Horites formerly dwelt in Seir, but the descendants of Esau dispossessed them and
destroyed them from before them, and
dwelt in their [1]place, just as Israel did to
the land of their possession which the
LORD gave them.)
13" 'Now rise and cross over [a]the [1]Val-
ley of the Zered.' So we crossed over the
Valley of the Zered. 14And the time we
took to come [a]from Kadesh Barnea until
we crossed over the Valley of the Zered
was thirty-eight years, [b]until all the generation of the men of war [1]was consumed
from the midst of the camp, [c]just as the
LORD had sworn to them. 15For indeed the
hand of the LORD was against them, to
destroy them from the midst of the camp
until they [1]were consumed.
16"So it was, when all the men of war
had finally perished from among the people, 17that the LORD spoke to me, saying:
18'This day you are to cross over at Ar, the
boundary of Moab. 19And *when* you come
near the people of Ammon, do not harass
them or meddle with them, for I will not
give you *any* of the land of the people of
Ammon *as* a possession, because I have
given it to [a]the descendants of Lot *as* a
possession.' "
20(That was also regarded as a land of
[1]giants; giants formerly dwelt there. But
the Ammonites call them [a]Zamzummim,
21[a]a people as great and numerous and
tall as the Anakim. But the LORD destroyed them before them, and they dispossessed them and dwelt in their place,
22just as He had done for the descendants
of Esau, [a]who dwelt in Seir, when He destroyed [b]the Horites from before them.
They dispossessed them and dwelt in their
place, even to this day. 23And [a]the Avim,
who dwelt in villages as far as Gaza—[b]the
Caphtorim, who came from Caphtor, destroyed them and dwelt in their place.)
24" 'Rise, take your journey, and [a]cross
over the River Arnon. Look, I have given
into your hand [b]Sihon the Amorite, king
of Heshbon, and his land. Begin [1]to possess *it,* and engage him in battle. 25[a]This
day I will begin to put the dread and fear
of you upon the nations [1]under the whole
heaven, who shall hear the report of you,
and shall [b]tremble and be in anguish because of you.'

King Sihon Defeated

26"And I [a]sent messengers from the
Wilderness of Kedemoth to Sihon king of
Heshbon, [b]with words of peace, saying,
27[a]'Let me pass through your land; I will
keep strictly to the road, and I will turn
neither to the right nor to the left. 28You
shall sell me food for money, that I may
eat, and give me water for money, that I
may drink; [a]only let me pass through on
foot, 29[a]just as the descendants of Esau
who dwell in Seir and the Moabites who
dwell in Ar did for me, until I cross the
Jordan to the land which the LORD our
God is giving us.'
30[a]"But Sihon king of Heshbon would
not let us pass through, for [b]the LORD
your God [c]hardened his spirit and made
his heart obstinate, that He might deliver
him into your hand, as *it is* this day.
31"And the LORD said to me, 'See, I have
begun to [a]give Sihon and his land over to
you. Begin to possess *it,* that you may inherit his land.' 32[a]Then Sihon and all his
people came out against us to fight at Jahaz. 33And [a]the LORD our God delivered
him [1]over to us; so [b]we defeated him, his
sons, and all his people. 34We took all his
cities at that time, and we [a]utterly destroyed the men, women, and little ones
of every city; we left none remaining.
35We took only the livestock as plunder
for ourselves, with the spoil of the cities
which we took. 36[a]From Aroer, which *is*
on the bank of the River Arnon, and *from*
[b]the city that *is* in the ravine, as far as
Gilead, there was not one city too strong
for us; [c]the LORD our God delivered all to
us. 37Only you did not go near the land of
the people of Ammon—anywhere along
the River [a]Jabbok, or to the cities of the
mountains, or [b]wherever the LORD our
God had forbidden us.

King Og Defeated

3 "Then we turned and went up the
road to Bashan; and [a]Og king of Bashan came out against us, he and all his
people, to battle [b]at Edrei. 2And the LORD
said to me, 'Do not fear him, for I have
delivered him and all his people and his

9 [a]Deut. 2:18, 29 [b]Gen. 19:36–38
10 [a]Gen. 14:5 [b]Deut. 9:2
11 [1]Heb. *rephaim*
12 [a]Deut. 2:22 [1]*stead*
13 [a]Num. 21:12 [1]*Wadi* or *Brook*
14 [a]Num. 13:26 [b]Deut. 1:34, 35 [c]Num. 14:35 [1]*perished*
15 [1]*perished*
19 [a]Gen. 19:38
20 [a]Gen. 14:5 [1]Heb. *rephaim*
21 [a]Deut. 2:10
22 [a]Gen. 36:8 [b]Gen. 14:6; 36:20–30
23 [a]Josh. 13:3 [b]Gen. 10:14
24 [a]Judg. 11:18 [b]Deut. 1:4 [1]*to take possession*
25 [a]Ex. 23:27 [b]Ex. 15:14–16 [1]*everywhere under the heavens*
26 [a]Num. 21:21–32 [b]Deut. 20:10
27 [a]Judg. 11:19
28 [a]Num. 20:19
29 [a]Deut. 23:3, 4
30 [a]Num. 21:23 [b]Josh. 11:20 [c]Ex. 4:21
31 [a]Deut. 1:3, 8
32 [a]Num. 21:23
33 [a]Deut. 7:2 [b]Num. 21:24 [1]Lit. *before us*
34 [a]Lev. 27:28
36 [a]Deut. 3:12; 4:48 [b]Josh. 13:9, 16 [c]Ps. 44:3
37 [a]Gen. 32:22 [b]Deut. 2:5, 9, 19

CHAPTER 3 **1** [a]Num. 21:33–35 [b]Deut. 1:4

land into your hand; you shall do to him
as you did to [a]Sihon king of the Amorites,
who dwelt at Heshbon.’
3“So the LORD our God also delivered
into our hands Og king of Bashan, with all
his people, and we [1]attacked him until he
had no survivors remaining. 4And we took
all his cities at that time; there was not a
city which we did not take from them:
sixty cities, [a]all the region of Argob, the
kingdom of Og in Bashan. 5All these cities
were fortified with high walls, gates, and
bars, besides a great many rural towns.
6And we utterly destroyed them, as we did
to Sihon king [a]of Heshbon, utterly destroying the men, women, and children of
every city. 7But all the livestock and the
spoil of the cities we took as booty for ourselves.
8“And at that time we took the [a]land
from the hand of the two kings of the Amorites who *were* on this side of the Jordan,
from the River Arnon to Mount [b]Hermon
9(the Sidonians call [a]Hermon Sirion, and
the Amorites call it Senir), 10[a]all the cities
of the plain, all Gilead, and [b]all Bashan, as
far as Salcah and Edrei, cities of the kingdom of Og in Bashan.
11[a]“For only Og king of Bashan remained of the remnant of [b]the [1]giants.
Indeed his bedstead *was* an iron bedstead.
(*Is* it not in [c]Rabbah of the people of Ammon?) Nine cubits *is* its length and four
cubits its width, according to the standard
cubit.

The Land East of the Jordan Divided

12“And this [a]land, *which* we possessed
at that time, [b]from Aroer, which *is* by the
River Arnon, and half the mountains of
Gilead and [c]its cities, I gave to the Reubenites and the Gadites. 13[a]The rest of Gilead, and all Bashan, the kingdom of Og, I
gave to half the tribe of Manasseh. (All the
region of Argob, with all Bashan, was
called the land of the [1]giants. 14[a]Jair the
son of Manasseh took all the region of Argob, [b]as far as the border of the Geshurites and the Maachathites, and [c]called
Bashan after his own name, [1]Havoth Jair,
to this day.)
15“Also I gave [a]Gilead to Machir. 16And
to the Reubenites [a]and the Gadites I gave
from Gilead as far as the River Arnon, the
middle of the river as *the* border, as far as
the River Jabbok, [b]the border of the people of Ammon; 17the plain also, with the
Jordan as *the* border, from Chinnereth [a]as
far as the east side of the Sea of the Arabah
[b](the Salt Sea), below the slopes of Pisgah.
18“Then I commanded you at that time,
saying: ‘The LORD your God has given you
this land to possess. [a]All you men of valor
shall cross over armed before your brethren, the children of Israel. 19But your
wives, your little ones, and your livestock
(I know that you have much livestock)
shall stay in your cities which I have given
you, 20until the LORD has given [a]rest to
your brethren as to you, and they also
possess the land which the LORD your God
is giving them beyond the Jordan. Then
each of you may [b]return to his possession
which I have given you.’
21“And [a]I commanded Joshua at that
time, saying, ‘Your eyes have seen all that
the LORD your God has done to these two
kings; so will the LORD do to all the kingdoms through which you pass. 22You
must not fear them, for [a]the LORD your
God Himself fights for you.’

Moses Forbidden to Enter the Land

23“Then [a]I pleaded with the LORD at
that time, saying: 24‘O Lord GOD, You
have begun to show Your servant [a]Your
greatness and Your [1]mighty hand, for
[b]what god *is there* in heaven or on earth
who can do *anything* like Your works and
Your mighty *deeds?* 25I pray, let me cross
over and see [a]the good land beyond the
Jordan, those pleasant mountains, and
Lebanon.’
26“But the LORD [a]was angry with me on
your account, and would not listen to me.
So the LORD said to me: ‘Enough of that!
Speak no more to Me of this matter. 27[a]Go
up to the top of Pisgah, and lift your eyes
toward the west, the north, the south, and
the east; behold *it* with your eyes, for you
shall not cross over this Jordan. 28But
[a]command[1] Joshua, and encourage him
and strengthen him; for he shall go over
before this people, and he shall cause
them to inherit the land which you will
see.’
29“So we stayed in [a]the valley opposite
Beth Peor.

Moses Commands Obedience

4 “Now, O Israel, listen to [a]the statutes
and the judgments which I teach you
to observe, that you may live, and go in

2 a Num. 21:34
3 *1 struck*
4 a Deut. 3:13, 14
6 a Deut. 2:24, 34, 35
8 a Josh. 12:6; 13:8–12 b 1 Chr. 5:23
9 a 1 Chr. 5:23
10 a Deut. 4:49 b Josh. 12:5; 13:11
11 a Amos 2:9 b Deut. 2:11, 20 c Jer. 49:2 *1 Heb. rephaim*
12 a Num. 32:33 b Deut. 2:36 c Num. 34:14
13 a Josh. 13:29–31; 17:1 *1 Heb. rephaim*
14 a 1 Chr. 2:22 b Josh. 13:13 c Num. 32:41 *1 Lit. Towns of Jair*
15 a Num. 32:39, 40
16 a 2 Sam. 24:5 b Num. 21:24
17 a Num. 34:11, 12 b Gen. 14:3
18 a Num. 32:20
20 a Deut. 12:9, 10 b Josh. 22:4
21 a [Num. 27:22, 23]
22 a Ex. 14:14
23 a [2 Cor. 12:8, 9]
24 a Deut. 5:24; 11:2 b 2 Sam. 7:22 *1 strong*
25 a Deut. 4:22
26 a Num. 20:12; 27:14
27 a Num. 23:14; 27:12
28 a Num. 27:18, 23 *1 charge*
29 a Deut. 4:46; 34:6
CHAPTER 4
1 a [Rom. 10:5]

and [1]possess the land which the LORD God
of your fathers is giving you. 2[a]You shall
not add to the word which I command
you, nor take from it, that you may keep
the commandments of the LORD your God
which I command you. 3Your eyes have
seen what the LORD did at [a]Baal Peor; for
the LORD your God has destroyed from
among you all the men who followed Baal
of Peor. 4But you who held fast to the
LORD your God *are* alive today, every one
of you.

5"Surely I have taught you statutes and
judgments, just as the LORD my God commanded me, that you should act according *to them* in the land which you go to
possess. 6Therefore be careful to observe
them; for this *is* [a]your wisdom and your
understanding in the sight of the peoples
who will hear all these statutes, and say,
'Surely this great nation *is* a wise and understanding people.'

7"For [a]what great nation *is there* that
has [b]God[1] *so* near to it, as the LORD our
God *is* to us, for whatever *reason* we may
call upon Him? 8And what great nation *is*
there that has *such* statutes and righteous
judgments as are in all this law which I set
before you this day? 9Only take heed to
yourself, and diligently [a]keep yourself,
lest you [b]forget the things your eyes have
seen, and lest they depart from your heart
all the days of your life. And [c]teach them
to your children and your grandchildren,
10*especially concerning* [a]the day you
stood before the LORD your God in Horeb,
when the LORD said to me, 'Gather the
people to Me, and I will let them hear My
words, that they may learn to fear Me all
the days they live on the earth, and *that*
they may teach their children.'

11"Then you came near and stood at the
foot of the mountain, and the mountain
burned with fire to the midst of heaven,
with darkness, cloud, and thick darkness.
12[a]And the LORD spoke to you out of the
midst of the fire. You heard the sound of
the words, but saw no [1]form; [b]*you* only
heard a voice. 13[a]So He declared to you
His covenant which He commanded you
to perform, [b]the Ten Commandments;
and [c]He wrote them on two tablets of
stone. 14And [a]the LORD commanded me
at that time to teach you statutes and
judgments, that you might [1]observe
them in the land which you cross over
to possess.

Beware of Idolatry

15[a]"Take careful heed to yourselves, for
you saw no [b]form when the LORD spoke to
you at Horeb out of the midst of the fire,
16lest you [a]act corruptly and [b]make for
yourselves a carved image in the [1]form of
any figure: [c]the likeness of male or female, 17the likeness of any animal that *is*
on the earth or the likeness of any winged
bird that flies in the air, 18the likeness of
anything that creeps on the ground or the
likeness of any fish that *is* in the water
beneath the earth. 19And *take heed,* lest
you [a]lift your eyes to heaven, and *when*
you see the sun, the moon, and the stars,
[b]all the host of heaven, you feel driven to
[c]worship them and serve them, which the
LORD your God has [1]given to all the peoples under the whole heaven as a heritage.
20But the LORD has taken you and
[a]brought you out of the iron furnace, out
of Egypt, to be [b]His people, an inheritance, as you are this day. 21Furthermore
[a]the LORD was angry with me for your
sakes, and swore that [b]I would not cross
over the Jordan, and that I would not enter the good land which the LORD your
God is giving you as an inheritance. 22But
[a]I must die in this land, [b]I must not cross
over the Jordan; but you shall cross over
and [1]possess [c]that good land. 23Take heed
to yourselves, lest you forget the covenant
of the LORD your God which He made with
you, [a]and make for yourselves a carved
image in the form of anything which the
LORD your God has forbidden you. 24For
[a]the LORD your God *is* a consuming fire,
[b]a jealous God.

25"When you beget children and grandchildren and have grown old in the land,
and act corruptly and make a carved image in the form of anything, and [a]do evil
in the sight of the LORD your God to provoke Him to anger, 26[a]I call heaven and
earth to witness against you this day, that
you will soon utterly perish from the land
which you cross over the Jordan to possess; you will not [1]prolong *your* days in it,
but will be utterly destroyed. 27And the
LORD [a]will scatter you among the peoples,
and you will be left few in number among
the nations where the LORD will drive you.
28And [a]there you will serve gods, the work
of men's hands, wood and stone, [b]which
neither see nor hear nor eat nor smell.
29[a]But from there you will seek the LORD
your God, and you will find *Him* if you
seek Him with all your heart and with all

1 *1 take possession of*
2 a Prov. 30:6
3 a Num. 25:1–9
6 a [2 Tim. 3:15]
7 a [2 Sam. 7:23] b [Is. 55:6] *1 Or a god*
9 a Prov. 4:23 b Deut. 29:2–8 c Gen. 18:19
10 a Ex. 19:9, 16, 17
12 a Deut. 5:4, 22 b 1 Kin. 19:11–18 *1 similitude*
13 a Deut. 9:9, 11 b Ex. 34:28 c Ex. 24:12
14 a Ex. 21:1 *1 do or perform*
15 a Josh. 23:11 b Is. 40:18
16 a Deut. 9:12; 31:29 b Ex. 20:4, 5 c Rom. 1:23 *1 similitude*
19 a Deut. 17:3 b 2 Kin. 21:3 c [Rom. 1:25] *1 divided*
20 a Jer. 11:4 b Deut. 7:6; 27:9
21 a Num. 20:12 b Num. 27:13, 14
22 a 2 Pet. 1:13–15 b Deut. 3:27 c Deut. 3:25 *1 take possession of*
23 a Deut. 4:16
24 a Deut. 9:3 b Ex. 20:5; 34:14
25 a 2 Kin. 17:17
26 a Deut. 30:18, 19 *1 live long on it*
27 a Deut. 28:62
28 a Jer. 16:13 b Ps. 115:4–7; 135:15–17
29 a [2 Chr. 15:4]

your soul. 30When you are in [1]distress, and all these things come upon you in the [a]latter days, when you [b]turn to the LORD your God and obey His voice 31(for the LORD your God *is* a merciful God), He will not forsake you nor [a]destroy you, nor forget the covenant of your fathers which He swore to them.

Lord, enable ____ to find You when they seek You with all of their heart and with all of their soul.
FROM DEUTERONOMY 4:29

32"For [a]ask now concerning the days that are past, which were before you, since the day that God created man on the earth, and *ask* [b]from one end of heaven to the other, whether *any* great *thing* like this has happened, or *anything* like it has been heard. 33[a]Did *any* people *ever* hear the voice of God speaking out of the midst of the fire, as you have heard, and live? 34Or did God *ever* try to go *and* take for Himself a nation from the midst of *another* nation, [a]by trials, [b]by signs, by wonders, by war, [c]by a mighty hand and [d]an outstretched arm, [e]and by great [1]terrors, according to all that the LORD your God did for you in Egypt before your eyes? 35To you it was shown, that you might know that the LORD Himself *is* God; [a]*there is* none other besides Him. 36[a]Out of heaven He let you hear His voice, that He might instruct you; on earth He showed you His great fire, and you heard His words out of the midst of the fire. 37And because [a]He loved your fathers, therefore He chose their [1]descendants after them; and [b]He brought you out of Egypt with His Presence, with His mighty power, 38[a]driving out from before you nations greater and mightier than you, to bring you in, to give you their land *as* an inheritance, as *it is* this day. 39Therefore know this day, and consider *it* in your heart, that [a]the LORD Himself *is* God in heaven above and on the earth beneath; *there is* no other. 40[a]You shall therefore keep His statutes and His commandments which I command you today, that [1]it may go well with you and with your children after you, and that you may [2]prolong *your* days in the land which the LORD your God is giving you for all time."

Cities of Refuge East of the Jordan

41Then Moses [a]set apart three cities on this side of the Jordan, toward the rising of the sun, 42[a]that the manslayer might flee there, who kills his neighbor unintentionally, without having hated him in time past, and that by fleeing to one of these cities he might live: 43[a]Bezer in the wilderness on the plateau for the Reubenites, Ramoth in Gilead for the Gadites, and Golan in Bashan for the Manassites.

Introduction to God's Law

44Now this *is* the law which Moses set before the children of Israel. 45These *are* the testimonies, the statutes, and the judgments which Moses spoke to the children of Israel after they came out of Egypt, 46on this side of the Jordan, [a]in the valley opposite Beth Peor, in the land of Sihon king of the Amorites, who dwelt at Heshbon, whom Moses and the children of Israel [b]defeated[1] after they came out of Egypt. 47And they took possession of his land and the land [a]of Og king of Bashan, two kings of the Amorites, who *were* on this side of the Jordan, toward the [1]rising of the sun, 48[a]from Aroer, which *is* on the bank of the River Arnon, even to Mount [1]Sion (that is, [b]Hermon), 49and all the plain on the east side of the Jordan as far as the Sea of the Arabah, below the [a]slopes of Pisgah.

The Ten Commandments Reviewed

5 And Moses called all Israel, and said to them: "Hear, O Israel, the statutes and judgments which I speak in your hearing today, that you may learn them and be careful to observe them. 2[a]The LORD our God made a covenant with us in Horeb. 3The LORD [a]did not make this covenant with our fathers, but with us, those who *are* here today, all of us who *are* alive. 4[a]The LORD talked with you face to face on the mountain from the midst of the fire. 5[a]I stood between the LORD and you at that time, to declare to you the word of the LORD; for [b]you were afraid because of

---

30 a Hos. 3:5 b Joel 2:12 1 *tribulation*
31 a Jer. 30:11
32 a Job 8:8 b Matt. 24:31
33 a Deut. 5:24–26
34 a Deut. 7:19 b Ex. 7:3 c Ex. 13:3 d Ex. 6:6 e Deut. 26:8 1 *calamities*
35 a Mark 12:32
36 a Heb. 12:19, 25
37 a Deut. 7:7, 8; 10:15; 33:3 b Ex. 13:3, 9, 14 1 Lit. *seed*
38 a Deut. 7:1
39 a Josh. 2:11
40 a Lev. 22:31 1 *you may prosper* 2 *live long*
41 a Num. 35:6
42 a Deut. 19:4
43 a Josh. 20:8
46 a Deut. 3:29 b Num. 21:24 1 *struck*
47 a Num. 21:33–35 1 *east*
48 a Deut. 2:36; 3:12 b Deut. 3:9 1 Syr. *Sirion*
49 a Deut. 3:17

CHAPTER 5
2 a Ex. 19:5
3 a Heb. 8:9
4 a Ex. 19:9
5 a Gal. 3:19 b Ex. 19:16

the fire, and you did not go up the mountain. *He* said:
6 [a]'I *am* the LORD your God who brought
you out of the land of Egypt, out of
the house of [1]bondage.
7 [a]'You shall have no other gods [1]be-
fore Me.
8 [a]'You shall not make for yourself a
carved image—any likeness *of*
anything that *is* in heaven above,
or that *is* in the earth beneath, or
that *is* in the water under the
earth; [9]you shall not [a]bow[1] down
to them nor serve them. For I, the
LORD your God, *am* a jealous God,
[2]visiting the iniquity of the fathers
upon the children to the third and
fourth *generations* of those who
hate Me, [10][a]but showing mercy to
thousands, to those who love Me
and [1]keep My commandments.
11 [a]'You shall not take the name of the
LORD your God in vain, for the
LORD will not hold *him* [1]guiltless
who takes His name in vain.
12 [a]'Observe the Sabbath day, to [1]keep it
holy, as the LORD your God commanded you. [13][a]Six days you shall
labor and do all your work, [14]but
the seventh day *is* the [a]Sabbath of
the LORD your God. *In it* you shall
do no work: you, nor your son, nor
your daughter, nor your male servant, nor your female servant, nor
your ox, nor your donkey, nor any
of your cattle, nor your stranger
who *is* within your gates, that your
male servant and your female servant may rest as well as you.
[15][a]And remember that you were a
slave in the land of Egypt, and the
LORD your God brought you out
from there [b]by a mighty hand and
by an outstretched arm; therefore
the LORD your God commanded
you to keep the Sabbath day.
16 [a]'Honor your father and your mother,
as the LORD your God has commanded you, [b]that your days may
be long, and that it may be well
with [c]you in the land which the
LORD your God is giving you.
17 [a]'You shall not murder.
18 [a]'You shall not commit adultery.
19 [a]'You shall not steal.
20 [a]'You shall not bear false witness
against your neighbor.
21 [a]'You shall not covet your neighbor's
wife; and you shall not desire your
neighbor's house, his field, his
male servant, his female servant,
his ox, his donkey, or anything that
is your neighbor's.'
[22]"These words the LORD spoke to all
your assembly, in the mountain from the
midst of the fire, the cloud, and the thick
darkness, with a loud voice; and He added
no more. And [a]He wrote them on two tablets of stone and gave them to me.

The People Afraid of God's Presence

[23][a]"So it was, when you heard the voice
from the midst of the darkness, while the
mountain was burning with fire, that you
came near to me, all the heads of your
tribes and your elders. [24]And you said:
'Surely the LORD our God has shown us
His glory and His greatness, and [a]we have
heard His voice from the midst of the fire.
We have seen this day that God speaks
with man; yet he [b]*still* lives. [25]Now therefore, why should we die? For this great
fire will consume us; [a]if we hear the voice
of the LORD our God anymore, then we
shall die. [26][a]For who *is there* of all flesh
who has heard the voice of the living God
speaking from the midst of the fire, as we
have, and lived? [27]You go near and hear
all that the LORD our God may say, and
[a]tell us all that the LORD our God says to
you, and we will hear and do *it.*'
[28]"Then the LORD heard the voice of
your words when you spoke to me, and
the LORD said to me: 'I have heard the
voice of the words of this people which
they have spoken to you. [a]They are right
in all that they have spoken. [29][a]Oh, that
they had such a heart in them that they
would fear Me and [b]always keep all My
commandments, [c]that it might be well
with them and with their children forever! [30]Go and say to them, "Return to
your tents." [31]But as for you, stand here
by Me, [a]and I will speak to you all the commandments, the statutes, and the judgments which you shall teach them, that
they may observe *them* in the land which
I am giving them to possess.'
[32]"Therefore you shall [1]be careful to do
as the LORD your God has commanded
you; [a]you shall not turn aside to the right
hand or to the left. [33]You shall walk in [a]all
the ways which the LORD your God has
commanded you, that you may live [b]and

6 a Ex. 20:2–17 *1 slavery*
7 a Hos. 13:4 *1 besides*
8 a Ex. 20:4
9 a Ex. 34:7, 14–16 *1 worship them* *2 punishing*
10 a Dan. 9:4 *1 observe*
11 a Ex. 20:7 *1 innocent*
12 a Ex. 20:8 *1 sanctify it*
13 a Ex. 23:12; 35:2
14 a [Heb. 4:4]
15 a Deut. 15:15 b Deut. 4:34, 37
16 a Lev. 19:3 b Deut. 6:2 c Deut. 4:40
17 a Matt. 5:21
18 a Ex. 20:14
19 a [Rom. 13:9]
20 a Ex. 20:16; 23:1
21 a Ex. 20:17
22 a Deut. 4:13
23 a Ex. 20:18, 19
24 a Ex. 19:19 b Deut. 4:33
25 a Deut. 18:16
26 a Deut. 4:33
27 a Ex. 20:19
28 a Deut. 18:17
29 a Ps. 81:13 b Deut. 11:1 c Deut. 4:40
31 a [Gal. 3:19]
32 a Deut. 17:20; 28:14 *1 observe*
33 a Deut. 10:12 b Deut. 4:40

Father, I pray that ____ will be careful to do as You have commanded them, turning neither to the right nor to the left. Let them walk in all of Your ways that it may be well with them.

FROM DEUTERONOMY 5:32, 33

that it may be well with you, and *that* you may prolong *your* days in the land which you shall possess.

The Greatest Commandment

6 "Now this *is* [a]the commandment, *and these are* the statutes and judgments which the LORD your God has commanded to teach you, that you may observe *them* in the land which you are crossing over to possess, [2a]that you may fear the LORD your God, to keep all His statutes and His commandments which I command you, you and your son and your grandson, all the days of your life, [b]and that your days may be prolonged. [3]Therefore hear, O Israel, and [1]be careful to observe *it,* that it may be well with you, and that you may [a]multiply greatly [b]as the LORD God of your fathers has promised you—[c]'a land flowing with milk and honey.'

Love to the King and concern for His interests must be the master passion of the soul.

CATHERINE BOOTH

[4a]"Hear, O Israel: [1]The LORD our God, the LORD *is* one! [5][a]You shall love the LORD your God with all your heart, [b]with all your soul, and with all your strength.

[6]"And [a]these words which I command you today shall be in your heart. [7a]You shall teach them diligently to your children, and shall talk of them when you sit in your house, when you walk by the way, when you lie down, and when you rise up. [8a]You shall bind them as a sign on your hand, and they shall be as frontlets between your eyes. [9a]You shall write them on the doorposts of your house and on your gates.

Caution Against Disobedience

[10]"So it shall be, when the LORD your God brings you into the land of which He [1]swore to your fathers, to Abraham, Isaac, and Jacob, to give you large and beautiful cities [a]which you did not build, [11]houses full of all good things, which you did not fill, hewn-out wells which you did not dig, vineyards and olive trees which you did not plant—[a]when you have eaten and are full— [12]*then* beware, lest you forget the [a]LORD who brought you out of the land of Egypt, from the house of bondage. [13]You shall [a]fear the LORD your God and serve Him, and [b]shall take oaths in His name. [14]You shall not go after other gods, [a]the gods of the peoples who *are* all around you [15](for [a]the LORD your God *is* a jealous God [b]among you), lest the anger of the LORD your God be aroused against you and destroy you from the face of the earth.

[16a]"You shall not [1]tempt the LORD your God [b]as you [2]tempted *Him* in Massah. [17]You shall [a]diligently keep the commandments of the LORD your God, His testimonies, and His statutes which He has commanded you. [18]And you [a]shall do *what is* right and good in the sight of the LORD, that it may be well with you, and that you may go in and possess the good land of which the LORD swore to your fathers, [19a]to cast out all your enemies from before you, as the LORD has spoken.

[20a]"When your son asks you in time to come, saying, 'What *is the meaning of* the testimonies, the statutes, and the judgments which the LORD our God has commanded you?' [21]then you shall say to your son: 'We were slaves of Pharaoh in Egypt, and the LORD brought us out of Egypt [a]with a mighty hand; [22]and the LORD showed signs and wonders before our eyes, great and severe, against Egypt, Pharaoh, and all his household. [23]Then He brought us out from there, that He might bring us in, to give us the land of which He [1]swore to our fathers. [24]And the LORD commanded us to [1]observe all these

CHAPTER 6
1 a Deut. 12:1
2 a [Eccl. 12:13] b Deut. 4:40
3 a Deut. 7:13 b Gen. 22:17 c Ex. 3:8, 17 *1* Lit. *observe to do*
4 a [1 Cor. 8:4, 6] *1* Or *The LORD is our God, the LORD alone,* i.e., the only one
5 a Matt. 22:37 b 2 Kin. 23:25
6 a Deut. 11:18–20
7 a Deut. 4:9; 11:19
8 a Prov. 3:3; 6:21; 7:3
9 a Deut. 11:20
10 a Josh. 24:13 *1 promised*
11 a Deut. 8:10; 11:15; 14:29
12 a Deut. 8:11–18
13 a Matt. 4:10 b Deut. 5:11
14 a Deut. 13:7
15 a Ex. 20:5 b Ex. 33:3
16 a Luke 4:12 b [1 Cor. 10:9] *1 test* *2 tested*
17 a Deut. 11:22
18 a Ex. 15:26
19 a Num. 33:52, 53
20 a Ex. 13:8, 14
21 a Ex. 13:3
23 *1 promised*
24 *1 do*

Deuteronomy 6:5

Dear Woman of Destiny,

You are very special in God's eyes and He requires only one thing from you—your very best—to love Him with all your heart, soul, and strength. That means to put Him first in all you do. Loving Him is the basis of everything else you do.

The issues of life come from the heart—from how you feel inside the deepest recesses of yourself that no one knows except you (see Prov. 4:23). The great love of your life comes from that part of you. I'm reminded of the times I held my babies in my arms and loved them so much I almost hurt. That's the kind of love God wants from us.

Your mind and emotions can go up and down like a yo-yo, and Satan is constantly trying to steal your thoughts. He will come to you with some wild thought that is exactly opposite to what God's Word says. You have to fight him with the sword of the Spirit—God's Word. That's why you need to fill yourself with His Word every day to keep your mind and emotions under subjection. The Word is spirit and life to you (see John 6:63).

Loving God with all your strength is like trying to get the lid of a jar open—you use all the strength you have, and it pops open. Then you are so elated. Having the joy of the Lord in your heart gives you strength. Then you can use it to tell others about God's love for them. That's part of loving God with all your strength.

When we lost our daughter in a plane crash, I was devastated. Always before I had hymns and Christian music playing in my home as I went about my duties. But then I didn't want to have it. I turned everything off and felt very depressed—so much that I went to the doctor because I thought I was sick. He told me it was just the trauma I had been through and that I would feel better as time went on.

That night, as I lay down to sleep, I opened my Bible to Nehemiah 8:10 and read, "The joy of the LORD is your strength." Quietly, I thought, *Well, I certainly don't have any strength. Where did it go?* Then I remembered that sacred music had always brought joy to me. I had cut off the source! So I said to the devil, "All right, Satan, you have harassed me enough, and you won't do it anymore."

The next day I turned the music back on in every room of the house. My joy came back, and my strength came back. God's Word is true. The joy of the Lord is your strength. I'm a long way from perfect, but I'm learning every day to love God more, to check the recesses of my heart to bring my mind under subjection, and to use my strength to love God and to worship and adore Him. I hope you are doing this, too.

Evelyn Roberts

[2]statutes, [a]to fear the LORD our God, [b]for our good always, that [c]He might preserve us alive, as *it is* [3]this day. 25Then [a]it will be righteousness for us, if we are careful to observe all these commandments before the LORD our God, as He has commanded us.'

A Chosen People

7 "When the LORD your God brings you into the land which you go to [a]possess, and has cast out many [b]nations before you, [c]the Hittites and the Girgashites and the Amorites and the Canaanites and the Perizzites and the Hivites and the Jebusites, seven nations greater and mightier than you, 2and when the LORD your God delivers [a]them over to you, you shall conquer them *and* utterly destroy them. [b]You shall make no covenant with them nor show mercy to them. 3[a]Nor shall you make marriages with them. You shall not give your daughter to their son, nor take their daughter for your son. 4For they will turn your sons away from following Me, to serve other gods; [a]so the anger of the LORD will be aroused against you and destroy you suddenly. 5But thus you shall deal with them: you shall [a]destroy their altars, and break down their *sacred* pillars, and cut down their [1]wooden images, and burn their carved images with fire.

6"For you *are* a [1]holy people to the LORD your God; [a]the LORD your God has chosen you to be a people for Himself, a special treasure above all the peoples on the face of the earth. 7The LORD did not set His [a]love on you nor choose you because you were more in number than any other people, for you were [b]the least of all peoples; 8but [a]because the LORD loves you, and because He would keep [b]the oath which He swore to your fathers, [c]the LORD has brought you out with a mighty hand, and redeemed you from the house of [1]bondage, from the hand of Pharaoh king of Egypt.

9"Therefore know that the LORD your God, He *is* God, [a]the faithful God [b]who keeps covenant and mercy for a thousand generations with those who love Him and keep His commandments; 10and He repays those who hate Him to their face, to destroy them. He will not [1]be [a]slack with him who hates Him; He will repay him to his face. 11Therefore you shall keep the commandment, the statutes, and the judgments which I command you today, to observe them.

Blessings of Obedience

12"Then it shall come to pass, because you listen to these judgments, and keep and do them, that the LORD your God will keep with you the covenant and the mercy which He swore to your fathers. 13And He will [a]love you and bless you and [1]multiply you; [b]He will also bless the fruit of your womb and the fruit of your land, your grain and your new wine and your oil, the increase of your cattle and the offspring of your flock, in the land of which He [2]swore to your fathers to give you. 14You shall be blessed above all peoples; there shall not be a male or female [a]barren among you or among your livestock. 15And the LORD will take away from you all sickness, and will afflict you with none of the [a]terrible diseases of Egypt which you have known, but will lay *them* on all those who hate you. 16Also you shall [1]destroy all the peoples whom the LORD your God delivers over to you; your eye shall have no pity on them; nor shall you serve their gods, for that *will* [a]*be* a snare to you.

O Lord, may ___ know that You are the faithful God who keeps covenant and mercy for a thousand generations with those who love You and keep Your commandments.

FROM DEUTERONOMY 7:9

17"If you should say in your heart, 'These nations are greater than I; how can I dispossess them?'— 18you shall not be afraid of them, *but* you shall [a]remember well what the LORD your God did to Pharaoh and to all Egypt: 19[a]the great trials which your eyes saw, the signs and the wonders, the mighty hand and the outstretched arm, by which the LORD your God brought you out. So shall the LORD your God do to all the peoples of whom you are afraid. 20[a]Moreover the LORD your God will send the hornet among them

---

24 a Deut. 6:2 b Jer. 32:39 c Deut. 4:1 *2 ordinances 3 today*
25 a [Rom. 10:3, 5]

CHAPTER 7
1 a Deut. 6:10 b Gen. 15:19–21 c Ex. 33:2
2 a Num. 31:17 b Josh. 2:14
3 a 1 Kin. 11:2
4 a Deut. 6:15
5 a Ex. 23:24; 34:13 *1 Heb. Asherim,* Canaanite deities
6 a Ex. 19:5, 6 *1 set-apart*
7 a Deut. 4:37 b Deut. 10:22
8 a Deut. 10:15 b Luke 1:55, 72, 73 c Ex. 13:3, 14 *1 slavery*
9 a 1 Cor. 1:9 b Neh. 1:5
10 a [2 Pet. 3:9, 10] *1 delay*
13 a John 14:21 b Deut. 28:4 *1 cause you to increase 2 promised*
14 a Ex. 23:26
15 a Ex. 9:14; 15:26
16 a Judg. 8:27 *1 consume*
18 a Ps. 105:5
19 a Deut. 4:34; 29:3
20 a Josh. 24:12

until those who are left, who hide themselves from you, are destroyed. 21You shall not be terrified of them; for the LORD your God, the great and awesome God, *is* among you. 22And the LORD your God will drive out those nations before you [a]little by little; you will be unable to [1]destroy them at once, lest the beasts of the field become *too* numerous for you. 23But the LORD your God will deliver them over to you, and will inflict defeat upon them until they are destroyed. 24And [a]He will deliver their kings into your hand, and you will destroy their name from under heaven; [b]no one shall be able to stand [1]against you until you have destroyed them. 25You shall burn the carved images of their gods with fire; you shall not [a]covet[1] the silver or gold *that is* on them, nor take *it* for yourselves, lest you be snared by it; for it *is* an abomination to the LORD your God. 26Nor shall you bring an abomination into your house, lest you be doomed to destruction like it. You shall utterly detest it and utterly abhor it, [a]for it *is* an [1]accursed thing.

Remember the Lord Your God

8 "Every commandment which I command you today [a]you must [1]be careful to observe, that you may live and [b]multiply,[2] and go in and possess the land of which the LORD [3]swore to your fathers. 2And you shall remember that the LORD your God [a]led you all the way these forty years in the wilderness, to humble you *and* [b]test you, [c]to know what *was* in your heart, whether you would keep His commandments or not. 3So He humbled you, [a]allowed you to hunger, and [b]fed you with manna which you did not know nor did your fathers know, that He might make you know that man shall [c]not live by bread alone; but man lives by every *word* that proceeds from the mouth of the LORD. 4[a]Your garments did not wear out on you, nor did your foot swell these forty years. 5[a]You should [1]know in your heart that as a man chastens his son, *so* the LORD your God chastens you.

6"Therefore you shall keep the commandments of the LORD your God, [a]to walk in His ways and to fear Him. 7For the LORD your God is bringing you into a good land, [a]a land of brooks of water, of fountains and springs, that flow out of valleys and hills; 8a land of wheat and barley, of vines and fig trees and pomegranates, a land of olive oil and honey; 9[a] land in which you will eat bread without scarcity, in which you will lack nothing; a land whose stones *are* iron and out of whose hills you can dig copper. 10[a]When you have eaten and are full, then you shall bless the LORD your God for the good land which He has given you.

11"Beware that you do not forget the LORD your God by not keeping His commandments, His judgments, and His statutes which I command you today, 12[a]lest—*when* you have eaten and are [1]full, and have built beautiful houses and dwell *in them;* 13and *when* your herds and your flocks multiply, and your silver and your gold are [1]multiplied, and all that you have is multiplied; 14[a]when your heart [1]is lifted up, and you [b]forget the LORD your God who brought you out of the land of Egypt, from the house of bondage; 15who [a]led you through that great and terrible wilderness, [b]*in which were* fiery serpents and scorpions and thirsty land where there was no water; [c]who brought water for you out of the flinty rock; 16who fed you in the wilderness with [a]manna, which your fathers did not know, that He might humble you and that He might test you, [b]to do you good in the end— 17then you say in your heart, 'My power and the might of my hand have gained me this wealth.'

Father, may ____ know that they cannot live by bread alone; but they will live by every word that proceeds from Your mouth.

FROM DEUTERONOMY 8:3

18"And you shall remember the LORD your God, [a]for *it is* He who gives you power to get wealth, [b]that He may [1]establish His covenant which He swore to your fathers, as *it is* this day. 19Then it shall be, if you by any means forget the LORD your God, and follow other gods, and serve them and worship them, [a]I testify against you this day that you shall surely perish. 20As the nations which the LORD destroys before you, [a]so you shall perish, because

22 a Ex. 23:29, 30 1 *consume*
24 a Josh. 10:24, 42; 12:1–24 b Josh. 23:9 1 *before*
25 a Prov. 23:6 1 *desire*
26 a Deut. 13:17 1 *devoted* or *banned*

CHAPTER 8
1 a Deut. 4:1; 6:24 b Deut. 30:16 1 *observe to do* 2 *increase in number* 3 *promised*
2 a Amos 2:10 b Ex. 16:4 c [John 2:25]
3 a Ex. 16:2, 3 b Ex. 16:12, 14, 35 c Matt. 4:4
4 a Neh. 9:21
5 a 2 Sam. 7:14 1 *consider*
6 a [Deut. 5:33]
7 a Deut. 11:9–12
10 a Deut. 6:11, 12
12 a Hos. 13:6 1 *satisfied*
13 1 *increased*
14 a 1 Cor. 4:7 b Ps. 106:21 1 *becomes proud*
15 a Is. 63:12–14 b Num. 21:6 c Num. 20:11
16 a Ex. 16:15 b [Heb. 12:11]
18 a Hos. 2:8 b Deut. 7:8, 12 1 *confirm*
19 a Deut. 4:26; 30:18
20 a [Dan. 9:11, 12]

you would not be obedient to the voice of the LORD your God.

Israel's Rebellions Reviewed

9 "Hear, O Israel: You *are* to cross over the Jordan today, and go in to dispossess nations greater and mightier than yourself, cities great and fortified up to heaven, 2 a people great and tall, the [a]descendants of the Anakim, whom you know, and *of whom* you heard *it said,* 'Who can stand before the descendants of Anak?' 3 Therefore understand today that the LORD your God *is* He who [a]goes over before you *as* a [b]consuming fire. [c]He will destroy them and bring them down before you; [d]so you shall drive them out and destroy them quickly, as the LORD has said to you.

4 [a]"Do not think in your heart, after the LORD your God has cast them out before you, saying, 'Because of my righteousness the LORD has brought me in to possess this land'; but *it is* [b]because of the wickedness of these nations *that* the LORD is driving them out from before you. 5 [a]*It is* not because of your righteousness or the uprightness of your heart *that* you go in to possess their land, but because of the wickedness of these nations *that* the LORD your God drives them out from before you, and that He may [1]fulfill the [b]word which the LORD swore to your fathers, to Abraham, Isaac, and Jacob. 6 Therefore understand that the LORD your God is not giving you this good land to possess because of your righteousness, for you *are* a [a]stiff-necked[1] people.

7 "Remember! Do not forget how you [a]provoked the LORD your God to wrath in the wilderness. [b]From the day that you departed from the land of Egypt until you came to this place, you have been rebellious against the LORD. 8 Also [a]in Horeb you provoked the LORD to wrath, so that the LORD was angry *enough* with you to have destroyed you. 9 [a]When I went up into the mountain to receive the tablets of stone, the tablets of the covenant which the LORD made with you, then I stayed on the mountain forty days and [b]forty nights. I neither ate bread nor drank water. 10 [a]Then the LORD delivered to me two tablets of stone written with the finger of God, and on them *were* all the words which the LORD had spoken to you on the mountain from the midst of the fire [b]in[1] the day of the assembly. 11 And it came to pass, at the end of forty days and forty nights, *that* the LORD gave me the two tablets of stone, the tablets of the covenant.

12 "Then the LORD said to me, [a]'Arise, go down quickly from here, for your people whom you brought out of Egypt have acted corruptly; they have [b]quickly turned aside from the way which I commanded them; they have made themselves a molded image.'

13 "Furthermore [a]the LORD spoke to me, saying, 'I have seen this people, and indeed [b]they are a [1]stiff-necked people. 14 [a]Let Me alone, that I may destroy them and [b]blot out their name from under heaven; [c]and I will make of you a nation mightier and greater than they.'

15 [a]"So I turned and came down from the mountain, and [b]the mountain burned with fire; and the two tablets of the covenant *were* in my two hands. 16 And [a]I looked, and behold, you had sinned against the LORD your God—had made for yourselves a molded calf! You had turned aside quickly from the way which the LORD had commanded you. 17 Then I took the two tablets and threw them out of my two hands and [a]broke them before your eyes. 18 And I [a]fell[1] down before the LORD, as at the first, forty days and forty nights; I neither ate bread nor drank water, because of all your sin which you committed in doing wickedly in the sight of the LORD, to provoke Him to anger. 19 [a]For I was afraid of the anger and hot displeasure with which the LORD was angry with you, to destroy you. [b]But the LORD listened to me at that time also. 20 And the LORD was very angry with Aaron *and* would have destroyed him; so I prayed for Aaron also at the same time. 21 Then I took your sin, the calf which you had made, and burned it with fire and crushed it *and* ground *it* very small, until it was as fine as dust; and I [a]threw its dust into the brook that descended from the mountain.

22 "Also at [a]Taberah and [b]Massah and [c]Kibroth Hattaavah you [1]provoked the LORD to wrath. 23 Likewise, [a]when the LORD sent you from Kadesh Barnea, saying, 'Go up and possess the land which I have given you,' then you rebelled against the commandment of the LORD your God, and [b]you did not believe Him nor obey His voice. 24 [a]You have been rebellious against the LORD from the day that I knew you.

CHAPTER 9
2 a Num. 13:22, 28, 33
3 a Josh. 3:11; 5:14 b Deut. 4:24 c Deut. 7:24 d Ex. 23:31
4 a Deut. 8:17 b Lev. 18:3, 24–30
5 a [Titus 3:5] b Gen. 50:24 *1 perform*
6 a Deut. 31:27 *1 stubborn* or *rebellious*
7 a Num. 14:22 b Ex. 14:11
8 a Ex. 32:1–8
9 a Deut. 5:2–22 b Ex. 24:18
10 a Deut. 4:13 b Ex. 19:17 *1 when you were all gathered together*
12 a Ex. 32:7, 8 b Deut. 31:29
13 a Ex. 32:9 b Deut. 9:6 *1 stubborn* or *rebellious*
14 a Ex. 32:10 b Deut. 29:20 c Num. 14:12
15 a Ex. 32:15–19 b Ex. 19:18
16 a Ex. 32:19
17 a Ex. 32:19
18 a Ex. 34:28 *1 prostrated myself*
19 a Ex. 32:10, 11 b Ex. 32:14
21 a Ex. 32:20
22 a Num. 11:1, 3 b Ex. 17:7 c Num. 11:4, 34 *1 caused the LORD to be angry*
23 a Num. 13:3 b Ps. 106:24, 25
24 a Deut. 9:7; 31:27

25 [a]“Thus I [1]prostrated myself before the LORD; forty days and forty nights I kept prostrating myself, because the LORD had said He would destroy you. 26 Therefore I prayed to the LORD, and said: ‘O Lord GOD, do not destroy Your people and [a]Your inheritance whom You have redeemed through Your greatness, whom You have brought out of Egypt with a mighty hand. 27 Remember Your servants, Abraham, Isaac, and Jacob; do not look on the stubbornness of this people, or on their wickedness or their sin, 28 lest the land from which You brought us should say, “Because the LORD was not able to bring them to the land which He promised them, and because He hated them, He has brought them out to kill them in the wilderness.” 29 Yet they *are* Your people and Your inheritance, whom You brought out by Your mighty power and by Your outstretched arm.’

The Second Pair of Tablets

10 “At that time the LORD said to me, [1]‘Hew for yourself two tablets of stone like the first, and come up to Me on the mountain and make yourself an [a]ark of wood. 2 And I will write on the tablets the words that were on the first tablets, which you broke; and [a]you shall put them in the ark.’

3 “So I made an ark of acacia wood, hewed two tablets of stone like the first, and went up the mountain, having the two tablets in my hand. 4 And He wrote on the tablets according to the first writing, the Ten [1]Commandments, [a]which the LORD had spoken to you in the mountain from the midst of the fire in the day of the assembly; and the LORD gave them to me. 5 Then I turned and [a]came down from the mountain, and [b]put the tablets in the ark which I had made; [c]and there they are, just as the LORD commanded me.”

6 (Now the children of Israel journeyed from the wells of Bene Jaakan to Moserah, where Aaron [a]died, and where he was buried; and Eleazar his son ministered as priest in his [1]stead. 7 [a]From there they journeyed to Gudgodah, and from Gudgodah to Jotbathah, a land of [1]rivers of water. 8 At that time [a]the LORD [1]separated the tribe of Levi [b]to bear the ark of the covenant of the LORD, [c]to stand before the LORD to minister to Him and [d]to bless in His name, to this day. 9 [a]Therefore Levi has no portion nor inheritance with his

25 a Deut. 9:18 1 fell down
26 a Deut. 32:9
CHAPTER 10
1 a Ex. 25:10 1 Cut out
2 a Ex. 25:16, 21
4 a Ex. 20:1; 34:28 1 Lit. Words
5 a Ex. 34:29 b Ex. 40:20 c 1 Kin. 8:9
6 a Num. 20:25–28; 33:38 1 place
7 a Num. 33:32–34 1 brooks
8 a Num. 3:6 b Num. 4:5, 15; 10:21 c Deut. 18:5 d Num. 6:23 1 set apart
9 a Deut. 18:1, 2
10 a Deut. 9:18 b Ex. 32:14
11 a Ex. 33:1
12 a Mic. 6:8 b Deut. 6:5
13 a Deut. 6:24 1 benefit or welfare
14 a [Neh. 9:6]
15 1 Lit. seed
16 a Jer. 4:4 b Deut. 9:6, 13 1 rebellious
17 a Dan. 2:47 b Rev. 19:16 c Deut. 7:21 d Acts 10:34
18 a Ps. 68:5; 146:9
20 a Matt. 4:10

brethren; the LORD *is* his inheritance, just as the LORD your God promised him.)

10 “As at the first time, [a]I stayed in the mountain forty days and forty nights; [b]the LORD also heard me at that time, *and* the LORD chose not to destroy you. 11 [a]Then the LORD said to me, ‘Arise, begin *your* journey before the people, that they may go in and possess the land which I swore to their fathers to give them.’

Lord, I pray that _____ would remember what You require of them: to fear You, to walk in all Your ways and to love You, serving You with all their heart and soul, and keeping Your commandments and statutes.

FROM DEUTERONOMY 10:12, 13

The Essence of the Law

12 “And now, Israel, [a]what does the LORD your God require of you, but to fear the LORD your God, to walk in all His ways and to [b]love Him, to serve the LORD your God with all your heart and with all your soul, 13 *and* to keep the commandments of the LORD and His statutes which I command you today [a]for your [1]good? 14 Indeed heaven and the highest heavens belong to the [a]LORD your God, *also* the earth with all that *is* in it. 15 The LORD delighted only in your fathers, to love them; and He chose their [1]descendants after them, you above all peoples, as *it is* this day. 16 Therefore circumcise the foreskin of your [a]heart, and be [b]stiff-necked[1] no longer. 17 For the LORD your God *is* [a]God of gods and [b]Lord of lords, the great God, [c]mighty and awesome, who [d]shows no partiality nor takes a bribe. 18 [a]He administers justice for the fatherless and the widow, and loves the stranger, giving him food and clothing. 19 Therefore love the stranger, for you were strangers in the land of Egypt. 20 [a]You shall fear the LORD your God; you shall serve Him, and to Him you shall hold fast, and take oaths in His name. 21 He *is* your praise, and He *is* your God, who has done for you these great and

awesome things which your eyes have
seen. 22Your fathers went down to Egypt
with seventy persons, and now the LORD
your God has made you as the stars of
heaven in multitude.

Love and Obedience Rewarded

11 "Therefore you shall love the LORD
your God, and keep His charge, His
statutes, His judgments, and His commandments always. 2Know today that *I do*
not *speak* with your children, who have
not known and who have not seen the
[1]chastening of the LORD your God, His
greatness and His mighty hand and His
outstretched arm— 3His signs and His
acts which He did in the midst of Egypt,
to Pharaoh king of Egypt, and to all his
land; 4what He did to the army of Egypt,
to their horses and their chariots: [a]how
He made the waters of the Red Sea overflow them as they pursued you, and *how*
the LORD has destroyed them to this day;
5what He did for you in the wilderness
until you came to this place; 6and [a]what
He did to Dathan and Abiram the sons of
Eliab, the son of Reuben: how the earth
opened its mouth and swallowed them up,
their households, their tents, and all the
substance that *was* [1]in their possession,
in the midst of all Israel— 7but your eyes
have [a]seen every great [1]act of the LORD
which He did.

8"Therefore you shall keep every commandment which I command you today,
that you may [a]be strong, and go in and
possess the land which you cross over to
possess, 9and [a]that you may prolong *your*
days in the land [b]which the LORD [1]swore
to give your fathers, to them and their
descendants, [c]'a land flowing with milk
and honey.' 10For the land which you go
to possess *is* not like the land of Egypt
from which you have come, where you
sowed your seed and watered *it* by foot, as
a vegetable garden; 11[a]but the land which
you cross over to possess *is* a land of hills
and valleys, which drinks water from the
rain of heaven, 12a land for which the
LORD your God cares; [a]the eyes of the
LORD your God *are* always on it, from
the beginning of the year to the very end
of the year.

13'And it shall be that if you earnestly
[1]obey My commandments which I command you today, to love the LORD your
God and serve Him with all your heart and
with all your soul, 14then [a]I[1] will give *you*

CHAPTER 11
2 [1] *discipline*
4 [a] Ps. 106:11
6 [a] Ps. 106:16–18 [1] *at their feet*
7 [a] Deut. 10:21; 29:2 [1] *work*
8 [a] Josh. 1:6, 7
9 [a] Deut. 4:40; 5:16, 33; 6:2 [b] Deut. 9:5 [c] Ex. 3:8 [1] *promised*
11 [a] Deut. 8:7
12 [a] 1 Kin. 9:3
13 [1] Lit. *listen to*
14 [a] Deut. 28:12 [b] Joel 2:23 [1] So with MT, Tg.; Sam., LXX, Vg. *He*
15 [a] Ps. 104:14 [b] Deut. 6:11 [1] *satisfied*
16 [a] Job 31:27 [b] Deut. 8:19
17 [a] Deut. 6:15; 9:19 [b] 2 Chr. 6:26; 7:13 [c] Deut. 4:26
18 [a] Deut. 6:6–9 [b] Ps. 119:2, 34 [c] Deut. 6:8 [1] Lit. *put*
19 [a] Deut. 4:9, 10; 6:7
20 [a] Deut. 6:9
21 [a] Deut. 4:40 [b] Ps. 72:5; 89:29

the rain for your land in its season, [b]the
early rain and the latter rain, that you
may gather in your grain, your new wine,
and your oil. 15[a]And I will send grass in
your fields for your livestock, that you
may [b]eat and be [1]filled.' 16Take heed to
yourselves, [a]lest your heart be deceived,
and you turn aside and [b]serve other gods
and worship them, 17lest [a]the LORD's anger be aroused against you, and He [b]shut
up the heavens so that there be no rain,
and the land yield no produce, and [c]you
perish quickly from the good land which
the LORD is giving you.

Father God, I pray that ____ will store these words of Yours in their heart and soul, binding them as a sign on their hands, and keeping them ever before their eyes.

FROM DEUTERONOMY 11:18

18"Therefore [a]you shall [1]lay up these
words of mine in your heart and in your
[b]soul, and [c]bind them as a sign on your
hand, and they shall be as frontlets between your eyes. 19[a]You shall teach them
to your children, speaking of them when
you sit in your house, when you walk by
the way, when you lie down, and when
you rise up. 20[a]And you shall write them
on the doorposts of your house and on
your gates, 21that [a]your days and the days
of your children may be multiplied in the
land of which the LORD swore to your fathers to give them, like [b]the days of the
heavens above the earth.

Enable ____ to teach Your words to their children, speaking of them at home, while traveling and throughout the day.

FROM DEUTERONOMY 11:19

22"For if [a]you carefully keep all these
commandments which I command you to
do—to love the LORD your God, to walk in
all His ways, and [b]to hold fast to Him—
23then the LORD will [a]drive out all these
nations from before you, and you will
[b]dispossess greater and mightier nations
than yourselves. 24[a]Every place on which
the sole of your foot treads shall be yours:
[b]from the wilderness and Lebanon, from
the river, the River Euphrates, even to the
[1]Western Sea, shall be your territory.
25No man shall be able to [a]stand [1]against
you; the LORD your God will put the
[b]dread of you and the fear of you upon all
the land where you tread, just as He has
said to you.

26[a]"Behold, I set before you today a
blessing and a curse: 27[a]the blessing, if
you obey the commandments of the LORD
your God which I command you today;
28and the [a]curse, if you do not obey the
commandments of the LORD your God,
but turn aside from the way which I command you today, to go after other gods
which you have not known. 29Now it shall
be, when the LORD your God has brought
you into the land which you go to possess,
that you shall put the [a]blessing on Mount
Gerizim and the [b]curse on Mount Ebal.
30*Are* they not on the other side of the
Jordan, toward the setting sun, in the
land of the Canaanites who dwell in the
plain opposite Gilgal, [a]beside the terebinth trees of Moreh? 31For you will cross
over the Jordan and go in to possess the
land which the LORD your God is giving
you, and you will possess it and dwell in
it. 32And you shall be careful to observe all
the statutes and judgments which I set
before you today.

A Prescribed Place of Worship

12 "These [a]*are* the statutes and judgments which you shall be careful
to observe in the land which the LORD God
of your fathers is giving you to possess,
[b]all[1] the days that you live on the earth.
2[a]You shall utterly destroy all the places
where the nations which you shall dispossess served their gods, [b]on the high
mountains and on the hills and under ev-

22 [a]Deut. 11:1 [b]Deut. 10:20
23 [a]Deut. 4:38 [b]Deut. 9:1
24 [a]Josh. 1:3; 14:9 [b]Gen. 15:18 [1]Mediterranean
25 [a]Deut. 7:24 [b]Deut. 2:25 [1]*before*
26 [a]Deut. 30:1, 15, 19
27 [a]Deut. 28:1–14
28 [a]Deut. 28:15–68
29 [a]Josh. 8:33 [b]Deut. 27:13–26
30 [a]Gen. 12:6

CHAPTER 12
1 [a]Deut. 6:1 [b]Deut. 4:9, 10 [1]As long as
2 [a]Ex. 34:13 [b]2 Kin. 16:4; 17:10, 11

ANTHUSA

"Heavens! What women these Christians have!" This was the astonished reply of Libanius, a noted pagan orator when he learned of the self-sacrifice and purity of Anthusa, mother of John Chrysostom. Even the non-Christian world has been influenced by godly mothers. Throughout history, God has used women to touch people—even devoted pagans, such as Libanius.

Anthusa lived from approximately A.D. 347 to 407 in the city of Antioch, where Paul began his missionary journeys. Her son John, because of his eloquence as a Christian preacher, became known as Chrysostom, which translates to English as "Golden-Mouthed."

Like many women today, Anthusa was a student of the Bible and was concerned about the corruption and lack of righteousness in her city. As Chrysostom's mother, Anthusa taught her son at an early age to love the Scriptures and often studied them together with him. The time they spent together reading God's Word instilled in Chrysostom a deep love for Scripture, which would later be evident in the homilies he wrote. As a result of his mother's godly influence, Chrysostom became one of the greatest expository preachers the world has ever known.

ery green tree. 3And [a]you shall destroy
their altars, break their *sacred* pillars, and
burn their [1]wooden images with fire; you
shall cut down the carved images of their
gods and destroy their names from that
place. 4You shall not [a]worship the LORD
your God *with* such *things*.
5"But you shall seek the [a]place where
the LORD your God chooses, out of all
your tribes, to put His name for His
[b]dwelling[1] place; and there you shall go.
6[a]There you shall take your burnt offerings, your sacrifices, your tithes, the
heave offerings of your hand, your vowed
offerings, your freewill offerings, and the
[b]firstborn of your herds and flocks. 7And
[a]there you shall eat before the LORD your
God, and [b]you shall rejoice in [1]all to
which you have put your hand, you and
your households, in which the LORD your
God has blessed you.
8"You shall not at all do as we are doing
here today—[a]every man doing whatever
is right in his own eyes— 9for as yet you
have not come to the [a]rest[1] and the inheritance which the LORD your God is giving
you. 10But *when* you cross over the Jordan
and dwell in the land which the LORD your
God is giving you to inherit, and He gives
you [a]rest from all your enemies round
about, so that you dwell in safety, 11then
there will be the place where the LORD
your God chooses to make His name
abide. There you shall bring all that I
command you: your burnt offerings, your
sacrifices, your tithes, the heave offerings
of your hand, and all your choice offerings
which you vow to the LORD. 12And [a]you
shall rejoice before the LORD your God,
you and your sons and your daughters,
your male and female servants, and the
[b]Levite who *is* within your gates, since he
has no portion nor inheritance with you.
13Take heed to yourself that you do not
offer your burnt offerings in every place
that you see; 14but in the place which the
LORD chooses, in one of your tribes, there
you shall offer your burnt offerings, and
there you shall do all that I command you.
15"However, [a]you may slaughter and
eat meat within all your gates, whatever
your heart desires, according to the blessing of the LORD your God which He has
given you; [b]the unclean and the clean
may eat of it, [c]of the gazelle and the deer
alike. 16[a]Only you shall not eat the blood;
you shall pour it on the earth like water.
17You may not eat within your gates the
tithe of your grain or your new wine or
your oil, of the firstborn of your herd or
your flock, of any of your offerings which
you vow, of your freewill offerings, or of
the [1]heave offering of your hand. 18But
you must eat them before the LORD your
God in the place which the LORD your God
chooses, you and your son and your
daughter, your male servant and your female servant, and the Levite who *is* within
your gates; and you shall rejoice before
the LORD your God in [1]all to which you
put your hands. 19[1]Take heed to yourself
that you do not forsake the Levite as long
as you live in your land.
20"When the LORD your God [a]enlarges
your border as He has promised you, and
you say, 'Let me eat meat,' because you
long to eat meat, you may eat as much
meat as your heart desires. 21If the place
where the LORD your God chooses to put
His name is too far from [a]you, then you
may slaughter from your herd and from
your flock which the LORD has given you,
just as I have commanded you, and you
may eat within your gates as much as
your heart desires. 22Just as the gazelle
and the deer are eaten, so you may eat
them; the unclean and the clean alike may
eat them. 23Only be sure that you do not
eat the blood, [a]for the blood *is* the life;
you may not eat the life with the meat.
24You shall not eat it; you shall pour it on
the earth like water. 25You shall not eat it,
[a]that it may go well with you and your
children after you, [b]when you do *what is*
right in the sight of the LORD. 26Only the
[a]holy things which you have, and your
vowed offerings, you shall take and go to
the place which the LORD chooses. 27And
[a]you shall offer your burnt offerings, the
meat and the blood, on the altar of the
LORD your God; and the blood of your sacrifices shall be poured out on the altar of
the LORD your God, and you shall eat the
meat. 28Observe and obey all these words
which I command you, [a]that it may go
well with you and your children after you
forever, when you do *what is* good and
right in the sight of the LORD your God.

Beware of False Gods

29"When [a]the LORD your God cuts off
from before you the nations which you go
to dispossess, and you displace them and
dwell in their land, 30take heed to yourself
that you are not ensnared to follow them,
after they are destroyed from before you,

3 [a]Num. 33:52 [1]Heb. *Asherim*
4 [a]Deut. 12:31
5 [a]Ex. 20:24 [b]Ex. 15:13 [1]*home*
6 [a]Lev. 17:3, 4 [b]Deut. 14:23
7 [a]Deut. 14:26 [b]Deut. 12:12, 18 [1]*all that you undertake*
8 [a]Judg. 17:6; 21:25
9 [a]Deut. 3:20; 25:19 [1]*Or place of rest*
10 [a]Josh. 11:23
12 [a]Deut. 12:18; 26:11 [b]Deut. 10:9; 14:29
15 [a]Deut. 12:21 [b]Deut. 12:22 [c]Deut. 14:5
16 [a]Gen. 9:4
17 [1]*contribution*
18 [1]*all your undertakings*
19 [1]*Be careful*
20 [a]Ex. 34:24
21 [a]Deut. 14:24
23 [a]Gen. 9:4
25 [a]Deut. 4:40; 6:18 [b]Ex. 15:26
26 [a]Num. 5:9, 10; 18:19
27 [a]Lev. 1:5, 9, 13, 17
28 [a]Deut. 12:25
29 [a]Ex. 23:23

and that you do not inquire after their
gods, saying, 'How did these nations serve
their gods? I also will do likewise.' 31 [a]You
shall not worship the LORD your God in
that way; for every [1]abomination to the
LORD which He hates they have done to
their gods; for [b]they burn even their sons
and daughters in the fire to their gods.
32 "Whatever I command you, be careful
to observe it; [a]you shall not add to it nor
take away from it.

Punishment of Apostates

13 "If there arises among you a prophet or a [a]dreamer of dreams, [b]and
he gives you a sign or a wonder, 2 and [a]the
sign or the wonder comes to pass, of
which he spoke to you, saying, 'Let us go
after other gods'—which you have not
known—'and let us serve them,' 3 you
shall not listen to the words of that prophet or that dreamer of dreams, for the LORD
your God [a]is testing you to know whether
you love the LORD your God with all your
heart and with all your soul. 4 You shall
[a]walk[1] after the LORD your God and fear
Him, and keep His commandments and
obey His voice; you shall serve Him and
[b]hold fast to Him. 5 But [a]that prophet or
that dreamer of dreams shall be put to
death, because he has spoken in order to
turn *you* away from the LORD your God,
who brought you out of the land of Egypt
and redeemed you from the house of
bondage, to entice you from the way in
which the LORD your God commanded
you to walk. [b]So you shall [1]put away the
evil from your midst.

The success of your life as a child of God will be in exact accordance with the consciousness of the Christ and the power of God that is in your heart.

JOHN G. LAKE

6 [a]"If your brother, the son of your
mother, your son or your daughter, [b]the
wife [1]of your bosom, or your friend [c]who
is as your own soul, secretly entices you,
saying, 'Let us go and serve other gods,'
which you have not known, neither you
nor your fathers, 7 of the gods of the people which *are* all around you, near to you
or far off from you, from *one* end of the
earth to the *other* end of the earth, 8 you
shall [a]not [1]consent to him or listen to
him, nor shall your eye pity him, nor shall
you spare him or conceal him; 9 but you
shall surely kill him; your hand shall be
first against him to put him to [a]death, and
afterward the hand of all the people. 10 And
you shall stone him with stones until he
dies, because he sought to entice you
away from the LORD your God, who
brought you out of the land of Egypt,
from the house of bondage. 11 So all Israel
shall hear and [a]fear, and not again do
such wickedness as this among you.
12 [a]"If you hear someone in one of your
cities, which the LORD your God gives you
to dwell in, saying, 13 [1]'Corrupt men have
gone out from among you and enticed the
inhabitants of their city, saying, "Let us
go and serve other gods" '—which you
have not known— 14 then you shall inquire, search out, and ask diligently. And
if it is indeed true *and* certain *that* such
an [1]abomination was committed among
you, 15 you shall surely strike the inhabitants of that city with the edge of the
sword, utterly destroying it, all that is in
it and its livestock—with the edge of the
sword. 16 And you shall gather all its plunder into the middle of the street, and
[1]completely [a]burn with fire the city and
all its plunder, for the LORD your God. It
shall be [b]a [2]heap forever; it shall not be
built again. 17 [a]So none of the accursed
things shall remain in your hand, that the
LORD may [b]turn from the fierceness of His
anger and show you mercy, have compassion on you and [1]multiply you, just as He
swore to your fathers, 18 because you have
listened to the voice of the LORD your
God, [a]to keep all His commandments
which I command you today, to do *what*
is right in the eyes of the LORD your God.

Improper Mourning

14 "You *are* [a]the children of the LORD
your God; [b]you shall not cut yourselves nor [1]shave the front of your head
for the dead. 2 [a]For you *are* a holy people
to the LORD your God, and the LORD has
chosen you to be a people for Himself, a
special treasure above all the peoples who
are on the face of the earth.

---

31 a Lev. 18:3, 26, 30; 20:1, 2 b Deut. 18:10 *1 detestable action*
32 a Rev. 22:18, 19

CHAPTER 13
1 a Zech. 10:2 b Matt. 24:24
2 a Deut. 18:22
3 a Deut. 8:2, 16
4 a 2 Kin. 23:3 b Deut. 30:20 *1 follow the LORD*
5 a Jer. 14:15 b Deut. 17:5, 7 *1 exterminate*
6 a Deut. 17:2 b Gen. 16:5 c 1 Sam. 18:1, 3 *1 Whom you cherish*
8 a Prov. 1:10 *1 yield*
9 a Deut. 17:7
11 a Deut. 17:13
12 a Judg. 20:1–48
13 *1* Lit. *Sons of Belial*
14 *1 detestable action*
16 a Josh. 6:24 b Josh. 8:28 *1 Or as a whole-offering* 2 Lit. *mound* or *ruin*
17 a Josh. 6:18 b Josh. 7:26 *1 increase*
18 a Deut. 12:25, 28, 32

CHAPTER 14
1 a [Rom. 8:16] b Lev. 19:28; 21:1–5 *1 make any baldness between your eyes*
2 a Lev. 20:26

Clean and Unclean Meat

3[a]“You shall not eat any [1]detestable
thing. 4[a]These *are* the animals which you
may eat: the ox, the sheep, the goat, 5the
deer, the gazelle, the roe deer, the wild
goat, the [1]mountain goat, the antelope,
and the mountain sheep. 6And you may
eat every animal with cloven hooves, having the hoof split into two parts, *and that*
chews the cud, among the animals. 7Nev-
ertheless, of those that chew the cud or
have cloven hooves, you shall not eat,
such as these: the camel, the hare, and
the rock hyrax; for they chew the cud but
do not have cloven hooves; they *are* unclean for you. 8Also the swine is unclean
for you, because it has cloven hooves, yet
does not *chew* the cud; you shall not eat
their flesh [a]or touch their dead carcasses.

9[a]“These you may eat of all that *are* in
the waters: you may eat all that have fins
and scales. 10And whatever does not have
fins and scales you shall not eat; it *is* unclean for you.

11“All clean birds you may eat. 12[a]But
these you shall not eat: the eagle, the vulture, the buzzard, 13the red kite, the falcon, and the kite after their kinds; 14every
raven after its kind; 15the ostrich, the
short-eared owl, the sea gull, and the
hawk after their kinds; 16the little owl, the
screech owl, the white owl, 17the jackdaw,
the carrion vulture, the fisher owl, 18the
stork, the heron after its kind, and the
hoopoe and the bat.

19“Also [a]every [1]creeping thing that flies
is unclean for you; [b]they shall not be
eaten.

20“You may eat all clean birds.

21[a]“You shall not eat anything that dies
of itself; you may give it to the alien who
is within your gates, that he may eat it, or
you may sell it to a foreigner; [b]for you *are*
a holy people to the LORD your God.

[c]“You shall not boil a young goat in its
mother’s milk.

Tithing Principles

22[a]“You shall truly tithe all the increase
of your grain that the field produces year
by year. 23[a]And you shall eat before the
LORD your God, in the place where He
chooses to make His name abide, the tithe
of your grain and your new wine and your
oil, of [b]the firstborn of your herds and
your flocks, that you may learn to fear the
LORD your God always. 24But if the journey is too long for you, so that you are not
able to carry *the tithe, or* [a]if the place
where the LORD your God chooses to put
His name is too far from you, when the
LORD your God has blessed you, 25then
you shall exchange *it* for money, take the
money in your hand, and go to the place
which the LORD your God chooses. 26And
you shall spend that money for whatever
your heart desires: for oxen or sheep, for
wine or similar drink, for whatever your
heart desires; you shall eat there before
the LORD your God, and you shall [a]rejoice,
you and your household. 27You shall not
[1]forsake the [a]Levite who *is* within your
gates, for he has no part nor inheritance
with you.

28[a]“At the end of *every* third year you
shall bring out the [b]tithe of your produce
of that year and store *it* up within your
gates. 29And the Levite, because he has no
portion nor inheritance with you, and the
stranger and the fatherless and the widow
who *are* within your gates, may come and
eat and be satisfied, that the LORD your
God may bless you in all the work of your
hand which you do.

Debts Canceled Every Seven Years

15 “At the end of [a]*every* seven years
you shall grant a [1]release *of debts.*
2And this *is* the form of the release: Every
creditor who has lent *anything* to his
neighbor shall [1]release *it;* he shall not
[2]require *it* of his neighbor or his brother,
because it is called the LORD’s release. 3Of
a foreigner you may require *it;* but you
shall give up your claim to what is owed
by your brother, 4except when there may
be no poor among you; for the LORD will
greatly [a]bless you in the land which the
LORD your God is giving you to possess *as*
an inheritance— 5only if you carefully
obey the voice of the LORD your God, to
observe with care all these commandments which I command you today. 6For
the LORD your God will bless you just as
He promised you; [a]you shall lend to many
nations, but you shall not borrow; you
shall reign over many nations, but they
shall not reign over you.

Generosity to the Poor

7“If there is among you a poor man of
your brethren, within any of the [1]gates in
your land which the LORD your God is giving you, [a]you shall not harden your heart

---

3 a Ezek. 4:14 1 *abominable*
4 a Lev. 11:2–45
5 1 Or *addax*
8 a Lev. 11:26, 27
9 a Lev. 11:9
12 a Lev. 11:13
19 a Lev. 11:20 b Lev. 11:23 1 *swarming*
21 a Lev. 17:15; 22:8 b Deut. 14:2 c Ex. 23:19; 34:26
22 a Lev. 27:30
23 a Deut. 12:5–7 b Deut. 15:19, 20
24 a Deut. 12:5, 21
26 a Deut. 12:7
27 a Deut. 12:12 1 *neglect*
28 a Deut. 26:12 b Num. 18:21–24

CHAPTER 15
1 a Ex. 21:2; 23:10, 11 1 *remission*
2 1 *cancel the debt* 2 *exact it*
4 a Deut. 7:13
6 a Deut. 28:12, 44
7 a Lev. 25:35–37 1 *towns*

nor shut your hand from your poor
brother, 8but [a]you shall *1*open your hand
wide to him and willingly lend him sufficient for his need, whatever he needs.
9Beware lest there be a wicked thought in
your heart, saying, 'The seventh year, the
year of release, is at hand,' and your [a]eye
be evil against your poor brother and you
give him nothing, and [b]he cry out to the
LORD against you, and [c]it become sin
among you. 10You shall surely give to
him, and [a]your heart should not be
grieved when you give to him, because
[b]for this thing the LORD your God will
bless you in all your works and in all to
which you put your hand. 11For [a]the poor
will never cease from the land; therefore
I command you, saying, 'You shall *1*open
your hand wide to your brother, to your
poor and your needy, in your land.'

Lord, help ____ to be aware of the poor around them so that they can give freely and willingly to meet their needs.

FROM DEUTERONOMY 15:7, 8

The Law Concerning Bondservants

12[a]"If your brother, a Hebrew man, or a
Hebrew woman, is [b]sold to you and serves
you six years, then in the seventh year you
shall let him go free from you. 13And
when you *1*send him away free from you,
you shall not let him go away empty-
handed; 14you shall supply him liberally
from your flock, from your threshing
floor, and from your winepress. *From
what* the LORD has [a]blessed you with, you
shall give to him. 15[a]You shall remember
that you were a slave in the land of Egypt,
and the LORD your God redeemed you;
therefore I command you this thing today. 16And [a]if it happens that he says to
you, 'I will not go away from you,' because
he loves you and your house, since he
prospers with you, 17then you shall take
an awl and thrust *it* through his ear to the
door, and he shall be your servant forever.
Also to your female servant you shall do
likewise. 18It shall not seem hard to you
when you send him away free from you;
for he has been worth [a]a double hired servant in serving you six years. Then the
LORD your God will bless you in all that
you do.

The Law Concerning Firstborn Animals

19[a]"All the firstborn males that come
from your herd and your flock you shall
*1*sanctify to the LORD your God; you shall
do no work with the firstborn of your
herd, nor shear the firstborn of your flock.
20[a]You and your household shall eat *it* before the LORD your God year by year in the
place which the LORD chooses. 21[a]But if
there is a defect in it, *if it is* lame or blind
or has any serious defect, you shall not
sacrifice it to the LORD your God. 22You
may eat it within your gates; [a]the unclean
and the clean *person* alike *may eat it,* as
if it were a gazelle or a deer. 23Only you
shall not eat its blood; you shall pour it on
the ground like water.

The Passover Reviewed

16 "Observe the [a]month of Abib, and
keep the Passover to the LORD your
God, for [b]in the month of Abib the LORD
your God brought you out of Egypt by
night. 2Therefore you shall sacrifice the
Passover to the LORD your God, from the
flock and [a]the herd, in the [b]place where
the LORD chooses to put His name. 3You
shall eat no leavened bread with it; [a]seven
days you shall eat unleavened bread with
it, *that is,* the bread of affliction (for you
came out of the land of Egypt in haste),
that you may [b]remember the day in which
you came out of the land of Egypt all the
days of your life. 4[a]And no leaven shall be
seen among you in all your territory for
seven days, nor shall *any* of the meat
which you sacrifice the first day at twilight remain overnight until [b]morning.
5"You may not sacrifice the Passover
within any of your gates which the LORD
your God gives you; 6but at the place
where the LORD your God chooses to
make His name abide, there you shall sacrifice the Passover [a]at twilight, at the going down of the sun, at the time you came
out of Egypt. 7And you shall roast and eat
it [a]in the place which the LORD your God
chooses, and in the morning you shall
turn and go to your tents. 8Six days you

8 a Matt. 5:42
1 freely open
9 a Deut. 28:54, 56
b Deut. 24:15
c [Matt. 25:41, 42]
10 a 2 Cor. 9:5, 7
b Deut. 14:29
11 a Matt. 26:11
1 freely open
12 a Ex. 21:2–6
b Lev. 25:39–46
13 *1 set him free*
14 a Prov. 10:22
15 a Deut. 5:15
16 a Ex. 21:5, 6
18 a Is. 16:14
19 a Ex. 13:2, 12
1 set apart or *consecrate*
20 a Deut. 12:5; 14:23
21 a Lev. 22:19–25
22 a Deut. 12:15, 16, 22
CHAPTER 16
1 a Ex. 12:2
b Ex. 13:4
2 a Num. 28:19
b Deut. 12:5, 26; 15:20
3 a Num. 29:12
b Ex. 13:3
4 a Ex. 13:7
b Num. 9:12
6 a Ex. 12:7–10
7 a 2 Kin. 23:23

shall eat unleavened bread, and [a]on the
seventh day there *shall be* a [1]sacred assembly to the LORD your God. You shall
do no work *on it*.

The Feast of Weeks Reviewed

9"You shall count seven weeks for yourself; begin to count the seven weeks from
the time you begin *to put* the sickle to the
grain. 10Then you shall keep the [a]Feast of
Weeks to the LORD your God with the tribute of a freewill offering from your hand,
which you shall give [b]as the LORD your
God blesses you. 11[a]You shall rejoice before the LORD your God, you and your son
and your daughter, your male servant and
your female servant, the Levite who *is*
within your gates, the stranger and the
fatherless and the widow who *are* among
you, at the place where the LORD your God
chooses to make His name abide. 12[a]And
you shall remember that you were a slave
in Egypt, and you shall be careful to observe these statutes.

The Feast of Tabernacles Reviewed

13[a]"You shall observe the Feast of Tabernacles seven days, when you have gathered from your threshing floor and from
your winepress. 14And [a]you shall rejoice
in your feast, you and your son and your
daughter, your male servant and your female servant and the Levite, the stranger
and the fatherless and the widow, who *are*
within your [1]gates. 15[a]Seven days you
shall keep a sacred feast to the LORD your
God in the place which the LORD chooses,
because the LORD your God will bless you
in all your produce and in all the work of
your hands, so that you surely rejoice.
16[a]"Three times a year all your males
shall appear before the LORD your God in
the place which He chooses: at the Feast
of Unleavened Bread, at the Feast of
Weeks, and at the Feast of Tabernacles;
and [b]they shall not appear before the
LORD empty-handed. 17Every man *shall
give* as he is able, [a]according to the blessing of the LORD your God which He has
given you.

Justice Must Be Administered

18"You shall appoint [a]judges and officers in all your [1]gates, which the LORD
your God gives you, according to your
tribes, and they shall judge the people

8 a Lev. 23:8, 36
1 Lit. *restraint*
10 a Ex. 34:22 b 1 Cor. 16:2
11 a Deut. 16:14
12 a Deut. 15:15
13 a Ex. 23:16
14 a Neh. 8:9
1 towns
15 a Lev. 23:39–41
16 a Ex. 23:14–17; 34:22–24 b Ex. 23:15
17 a Deut. 16:10
18 a Deut. 1:16, 17
1 towns
19 a Ex. 23:2, 6 b Deut. 1:17 c Ex. 23:8
1 Lit. *regard faces*
2 perverts
20 a Ezek. 18:5–9
21 a Ex. 34:13
1 Or *Asherah*
22 a Lev. 26:1
CHAPTER 17
1 a Deut. 15:21
1 Lit. *evil thing*
2 detestable thing
2 a Deut. 13:6 b Josh. 7:11
1 towns
3 a Deut. 4:19 b Jer. 7:22
4 a Deut. 13:12, 14
1 detestable thing
5 a Lev. 24:14–16 b Deut. 13:6–18
6 a Num. 35:30
7 a Deut. 13:5; 19:19
8 a Deut. 1:17 b Deut. 12:5; 16:2
9 a Jer. 18:18 b Deut. 19:17–19 c Ezek. 44:24

with just judgment. 19[a]You shall not pervert justice; [b]you shall not [1]show partiality, [c]nor take a bribe, for a bribe blinds the
eyes of the wise and [2]twists the words of
the righteous. 20You shall follow what is
altogether just, that you may [a]live and inherit the land which the LORD your God is
giving you.
21[a]"You shall not plant for yourself any
tree, as a [1]wooden image, near the altar
which you build for yourself to the LORD
your God. 22[a]You shall not set up a *sacred*
pillar, which the LORD your God hates.

17 "You [a]shall not sacrifice to the
LORD your God a bull or sheep
which has any [1]blemish *or* defect, for that
is an [2]abomination to the LORD your God.
2[a]"If there is found among you, within
any of your [1]gates which the LORD your
God gives you, a man or a woman who has
been wicked in the sight of the LORD your
God, [b]in transgressing His covenant,
3who has gone and served other gods and
worshiped them, either [a]the sun or moon
or any of the host of heaven, [b]which I have
not commanded, 4[a]and it is told you, and
you hear *of it,* then you shall inquire diligently. And if *it is* indeed true *and* certain
that such an [1]abomination has been committed in Israel, 5then you shall bring out
to your gates that man or woman who has
committed that wicked thing, and [a]shall
stone [b]to death that man or woman with
stones. 6Whoever is deserving of death
shall be put to death on the testimony of
two or three [a]witnesses; he shall not be
put to death on the testimony of one witness. 7The hands of the witnesses shall be
the first against him to put him to death,
and afterward the hands of all the people.
So you shall put away the evil from among
[a]you.
8[a]"If a matter arises which is too hard
for you to judge, between degrees of guilt
for bloodshed, between one judgment or
another, or between one punishment or
another, matters of controversy within
your gates, then you shall arise and go up
to the [b]place which the LORD your God
chooses. 9And [a]you shall come to the
priests, the Levites, and [b]to the judge
there in those days, and inquire *of them;*
[c]they shall pronounce upon you the sentence of judgment. 10You shall do according to the sentence which they pronounce
upon you in that place which the LORD
chooses. And you shall be careful to do
according to all that they order you.

11According to the sentence of the law in
which they instruct you, according to the
judgment which they tell you, you shall
do; you shall not turn aside *to* the right
hand or *to* the left from the sentence
which they pronounce upon you. 12Now
[a]the man who acts presumptuously and
will not heed the priest who stands to
minister there before the LORD your God,
or the judge, that man shall die. So you
shall put away the evil from Israel. 13[a]And
all the people shall hear and fear, and no
longer act presumptuously.

Principles Governing Kings

14"When you come to the land which
the LORD your God is giving you, and possess it and dwell in it, and say, [a]'I will set
a king over me like all the nations that *are*
around me,' 15you shall surely set a king
over you [a]whom the LORD your God
chooses; *one* [b]from among your brethren
you shall set as king over you; you may
not set a foreigner over you, who *is* not
your brother. 16But he shall not multiply
[a]horses for himself, nor cause the people
[b]to return to Egypt to multiply horses, for
[c]the LORD has said to you, [d]'You shall not
return that way again.' 17Neither shall he
multiply wives for himself, lest his heart
turn away; nor shall he greatly multiply
silver and [a]gold for himself.

18"Also it shall be, when he sits on the
throne of his kingdom, that he shall write
for himself a copy of this law in a book,
from *the one* [a]before the priests, the Levites. 19And [a]it shall be with him, and he
shall read it all the days of his life, that he
may learn to fear the LORD his God and be
careful to observe all the words of this law
and these statutes, 20that his heart may
not [1]be lifted above his brethren, that he
[a]may not turn aside from the commandment *to* the right hand or *to* the left, and
that he may [2]prolong *his* days in his kingdom, he and his children in the midst of
Israel.

The Portion of the Priests and Levites

18 "The priests, the Levites—all the
tribe of Levi—shall have [1]no part
nor [a]inheritance with Israel; they shall eat
the offerings of the LORD made by fire, and
His portion. 2Therefore they shall have no
inheritance among their brethren; the
LORD is their inheritance, as He said to
them.

3"And this shall be the priest's [a]due[1]
from the people, from those who offer a
sacrifice, whether *it is* bull or sheep: they
shall give to the priest the shoulder, the
cheeks, and the stomach. 4[a]The firstfruits
of your grain and your new wine and your
oil, and the first of the fleece of your
sheep, you shall give him. 5For [a]the LORD
your God has chosen him out of all your
tribes [b]to stand to minister in the name of
the LORD, him and his sons forever.

6"So if a Levite comes from any of your
[1]gates, from where he [a]dwells among all
Israel, and comes with all the desire of his
mind [b]to the place which the LORD chooses, 7then he may serve in the name of the
LORD his God [a]as all his brethren the Levites *do,* who stand there before the LORD.
8They shall have equal [a]portions to eat,
besides what comes from the sale of his
inheritance.

Avoid Wicked Customs

9"When you come into the land which
the LORD your God is giving you, [a]you
shall not learn to follow the [1]abomina-
tions of those nations. 10There shall not
be found among you *anyone* who makes
his son or his daughter [a]pass[1] through
the fire, [b]*or one* who practices witchcraft,
or a soothsayer, or one who interprets
omens, or a sorcerer, 11[a]or one who con-
jures spells, or a medium, or a spiritist, or
[b]one who calls up the dead. 12For all who
do these things *are* [1]an abomination to
the LORD, and [a]because of these abominations the LORD your God drives them out
from before you. 13You shall be [1]blame-
less before the LORD your God. 14For these
nations which you will dispossess listened
to soothsayers and diviners; but as for
you, the LORD your God has not [1]appoint-
ed such for you.

A New Prophet Like Moses

15[a]"The LORD your God will raise up for
you a Prophet like me from your midst,
from your brethren. Him you shall hear,
16according to all you desired of the LORD
your God in Horeb [a]in the day of the assembly, saying, [b]'Let me not hear again
the voice of the LORD my God, nor let me
see this great fire anymore, lest I die.'

17"And the LORD said to me: [a]'What
they have spoken is good. 18[a]I will raise up
for them a Prophet like you from among

12 a Num. 15:30
13 a Deut. 13:11
14 a 1 Sam. 8:5, 19, 20; 10:19
15 a 1 Sam. 9:15, 16; 10:24; 16:12, 13 b Jer. 30:21
16 a 1 Kin. 4:26; 10:26–29 b Ezek. 17:15 c Ex. 13:17, 18 d Deut. 28:68
17 a 1 Kin. 10:14
18 a Deut. 31:24–26
19 a Ps. 119:97, 98
20 a Deut. 5:32 *1 become proud* *2 continue long in his kingdom*

CHAPTER 18
1 a Deut. 10:9 *1 no portion*
3 a Lev. 7:32–34; 1 Sam. 2:13–16, 29 *1 right*
4 a Ex. 22:29
5 a Ex. 28:1 b Deut. 10:8
6 a Num. 35:2 b Deut. 12:5; 14:23 *1 towns*
7 a 2 Chr. 31:2
8 a 2 Chr. 31:4
9 a Deut. 12:29, 30; 20:16–18 *1 detestable acts*
10 a Deut. 12:31 b Is. 8:19 *1 Be burned as an offering to an idol*
11 a Lev. 20:27 b 1 Sam. 28:7
12 a Lev. 18:24 *1 detestable*
13 *1 Lit. perfect*
14 *1 allowed you to do so*
15 a Acts 3:22
16 a Deut. 5:23–27 b Ex. 20:18, 19
17 a Deut. 5:28
18 a John 1:45

their brethren, and [b]will put My words in
His mouth, [c]and He shall speak to them
all that I command Him. 19[a]And it shall be
that whoever will not hear My words,
which He speaks in My name, I will require *it* of him. 20But [a]the prophet who
presumes to speak a word in My name,
which I have not commanded him to
speak, or [b]who speaks in the name of other gods, that prophet shall die.’ 21And if
you say in your heart, ‘How shall we know
the word which the LORD has not spoken?’— 22[a]when a prophet speaks in the
name of the LORD, [b]if the thing does not
happen or come to pass, that *is* the thing
which the LORD has not spoken; the
prophet has spoken it [c]presumptuously;
you shall not be afraid of him.

The Word of God becomes the thing men live by, the thing men will die for, when the Word of God becomes a present, living reality.

JOHN G. LAKE

Three Cities of Refuge

19 “When the LORD your God [a]has cut
off the nations whose land the
LORD your God is giving you, and you dispossess them and dwell in their cities and
in their houses, 2[a]you shall separate three
cities for yourself in the midst of your
land which the LORD your God is giving
you to possess. 3You shall prepare roads
for yourself, and divide into three parts
the territory of your land which the LORD
your God is giving you to inherit, that any
manslayer may flee there.
4“And [a]this *is* the case of the manslayer
who flees there, that he may live: Whoever
kills his neighbor [1]unintentionally, not
having hated him in time past— 5as when
a man goes to the woods with his neighbor to cut timber, and his hand swings a
stroke with the ax to cut down the tree,
and the head slips from the handle and
strikes his neighbor so that he dies—he
shall flee to one of these cities and live;
6[a]lest the avenger of blood, while his anger is hot, pursue the manslayer and overtake him, because the way is long, and kill
him, though he *was* not deserving of
death, since he had not hated the victim
in time past. 7Therefore I command you,
saying, ‘You shall separate three cities for
yourself.’
8“Now if the LORD your God [a]enlarges
your territory, as He swore to [b]your fathers, and gives you the land which He
promised to give to your fathers, 9and if
you keep all these commandments and do
them, which I command you today, to
love the LORD your God and to walk always in His ways, [a]then you shall add
three more cities for yourself besides
these three, 10[a]lest innocent blood be
shed in the midst of your land which the
LORD your God is giving you *as* an inheritance, and *thus* guilt of bloodshed be
upon you.
11“But [a]if anyone hates his neighbor,
lies in wait for him, rises against him and
strikes him mortally, so that he dies, and
he flees to one of these cities, 12then the
elders of his city shall send and bring him
from there, and deliver him over to the
hand of the avenger of blood, that he may
die. 13[a]Your eye shall not pity him, [b]but
you shall [1]put away *the guilt of* innocent
blood from Israel, that it may go well with
you.

Property Boundaries

14[a]“You shall not remove your neighbor’s landmark, which the men of old
have set, in your inheritance which you
will inherit in the land that the LORD your
God is giving you to possess.

The Law Concerning Witnesses

15[a]“One witness shall not rise against a
man concerning any iniquity or any sin
that he commits; by the mouth of two or
three witnesses the matter shall be established. 16If a false witness [a]rises against
any man to testify against him of wrongdoing, 17then both men in the controversy shall stand before the LORD, [a]before the
priests and the judges who serve in those
days. 18And the judges shall make careful
inquiry, and indeed, *if* the witness *is* a
false witness, who has testified falsely
against his brother, 19[a]then you shall do
to him as he thought to have done to his
brother; so [b]you shall put away the evil
from among you. 20[a]And those who

---

18 [b] Is. 49:2; 51:16 [c] [John 4:25; 8:28]
19 [a] [Heb. 12:25]
20 [a] Jer. 14:14, 15 [b] Jer. 2:8
22 [a] Jer. 28:9 [b] Deut. 13:2 [c] Deut. 18:20

CHAPTER 19
1 [a] Deut. 12:29
2 [a] Num. 35:10–15
4 [a] Num. 35:9–34 [1] *ignorantly,* lit. *without knowledge*
6 [a] Num. 35:12
8 [a] Deut. 12:20 [b] Gen. 15:18–21
9 [a] Josh. 20:7–9
10 [a] Deut. 21:1–9
11 [a] Num. 35:16, 24
13 [a] Deut. 13:8 [b] 1 Kin. 2:31 [1] *purge the blood of the innocent*
14 [a] Prov. 22:28
15 [a] Num. 35:30
16 [a] Ex. 23:1
17 [a] Deut. 17:8–11; 21:5
19 [a] Prov. 19:5 [b] Deut. 13:5; 17:7; 21:21; 22:21
20 [a] Deut. 17:13; 21:21

remain shall hear and fear, and hereafter
they shall not again commit such evil
among you. 21[a]Your eye shall not pity:
[b]life *shall be* for life, eye for eye, tooth for
tooth, hand for hand, foot for foot.

Principles Governing Warfare

20 "When you go out to battle against
your enemies, and see [a]horses and
chariots *and* people more numerous than
you, do not be [b]afraid of them; for the
LORD your God *is* [c]with you, who brought
you up from the land of Egypt. 2So it shall
be, when you are on the verge of battle,
that the priest shall approach and speak to
the people. 3And he shall say to them,
'Hear, O Israel: Today you are on the
verge of battle with your enemies. Do not
let your heart faint, do not be afraid, and
do not tremble or be terrified because of
them; 4for the LORD your God *is* He who
goes with you, [a]to fight for you against
your enemies, to save you.'

> *The very essence of the spirit of evil is antagonistic to the spirit of good. Good and evil are as diametrically opposed to each other as ever; therefore they can never be brought into contact without conflict, without war, and sometimes of the most deadly kind, ending in the death and martyrdom of the saints.*
>
> CATHERINE BOOTH

5"Then the officers shall speak to the
people, saying: 'What man *is there* who
has built a new house and has not [a]dedi-
cated it? Let him go and return to his
house, lest he die in the battle and another man dedicate it. 6Also what man *is*
there who has planted a vineyard and has
not eaten of it? Let him go and return to
his house, lest he die in the battle and
another man eat of it. 7[a]And what man *is*
there who is betrothed to a woman and
has not married her? Let him go and return to his house, lest he die in the battle
and another man marry her.'
8"The officers shall speak further to the
people, and say, [a]'What man *is there who*
is fearful and fainthearted? Let him go
and return to his house, [1]lest the heart of
his brethren faint like his heart.' 9And so
it shall be, when the officers have finished
speaking to the people, that they shall
make captains of the armies to lead the
people.
10"When you go near a city to fight
against it, [a]then proclaim an offer of
peace to it. 11And it shall be that if they
accept your offer of peace, and open to
you, then all the people *who are* found in
it shall be placed under tribute to you, and
serve you. 12Now if *the city* will not make
peace with you, but war against you, then
you shall besiege it. 13And when the LORD
your God delivers it into your hands, [a]you
shall strike every male in it with the edge
of the sword. 14But the women, the little
ones, [a]the livestock, and all that is in the
city, all its spoil, you shall plunder for
yourself; and [b]you shall eat the enemies'
plunder which the LORD your God gives
you. 15Thus you shall do to all the cities
which are very far from you, which *are*
not of the cities of these nations.
16"But [a]of the cities of these peoples
which the LORD your God gives you *as* an
inheritance, you shall let nothing that
breathes remain alive, 17but you shall utterly destroy them: the Hittite and the
Amorite and the Canaanite and the Perizzite and the Hivite and the Jebusite, just
as the LORD your God has commanded
you, 18lest [a]they teach you to do according to all their [1]abominations which they
have done for their gods, and you [b]sin
against the LORD your God.
19"When you besiege a city for a long
time, while making war against it to take
it, you shall not destroy its trees by wield-
ing an ax against them; if you can eat of
them, do not cut them down to use in the
siege, for the tree of the field *is* man's
food. 20Only the trees which you know *are*
not trees for food you may destroy and cut
down, to build siegeworks against the city
that makes war with you, until it is subdued.

21 a Deut. 19:13 b Ex. 21:23, 24

CHAPTER 20
1 a Ps. 20:7 b Deut. 7:18 c 2 Chr. 13:12; 32:7, 8
4 a Josh. 23:10
5 a Neh. 12:27
7 a Deut. 24:5
8 a Judg. 7:3 *1* So with MT, Tg.; Sam., LXX, Syr., Vg. *lest he make his brother's heart faint*
10 a 2 Sam. 10:19
13 a Num. 31:7
14 a Josh. 8:2 b 1 Sam. 14:30
16 a Deut. 7:1–5
18 a Deut. 7:4; 12:30; 18:9 b Ex. 23:33 *1 detestable things*

The Law Concerning Unsolved Murder

21 "If *anyone* is found slain, lying in the field in the land which the LORD your God is giving you to possess, *and* it is not known who killed him, 2then your elders and your judges shall go out and measure *the distance* from the slain man to the surrounding cities. 3And it shall be *that* the elders of the city nearest to the slain man will take a heifer which has not been worked *and* which has not pulled with a [a]yoke. 4The elders of that city shall bring the heifer down to a valley with flowing water, which is neither plowed nor sown, and they shall break the heifer's neck there in the valley. 5Then the priests, the sons of Levi, shall come near, for [a]the LORD your God has chosen them to minister to Him and to bless in the name of the LORD; [b]by their word every controversy and every [1]assault shall be *settled.* 6And all the elders of that city nearest to the slain *man* [a]shall wash their hands over the heifer whose neck was broken in the valley. 7Then they shall answer and say, 'Our hands have not shed this blood, nor have our eyes seen *it.* 8Provide atonement, O LORD, for Your people Israel, whom You have redeemed, [a]and do not lay innocent blood to the charge of Your people Israel.' And atonement shall be provided on their behalf for the blood. 9So [a]you shall put away the *guilt of* innocent blood from among you when you do *what is* right in the sight of the LORD.

Female Captives

10"When you go out to war against your enemies, and the LORD your God delivers them into your hand, and you take them captive, 11and you see among the captives a beautiful woman, and desire her and would take her for your [a]wife, 12then you shall bring her home to your house, and she shall [a]shave her head and trim her nails. 13She shall put off the clothes of her captivity, remain in your house, and [a]mourn her father and her mother a full month; after that you may go in to her and be her husband, and she shall be your wife. 14And it shall be, if you have no delight in her, then you shall set her free, but you certainly shall not sell her for money; you shall not treat her brutally, because you have [a]humbled her.

Firstborn Inheritance Rights

15"If a man has two wives, one loved [a]and the other unloved, and they have borne him children, *both* the loved and the unloved, and *if* the firstborn son is of her who is unloved, 16then it shall be, [a]on the day he bequeaths his possessions to his sons, *that* he must not bestow firstborn status on the son of the loved wife in preference to the son of the unloved, the *true* firstborn. 17But he shall acknowledge the son of the unloved wife *as* the firstborn [a]by giving him a double portion of all that he has, for he [b]*is* the beginning of his strength; [c]the right of the firstborn *is* his.

The Rebellious Son

18"If a man has a stubborn and rebellious son who will not obey the voice of his father or the voice of his mother, and *who,* when they have chastened him, will not heed them, 19then his father and his mother shall take hold of him and bring him out to the elders of his city, to the gate of his city. 20And they shall say to the elders of his city, 'This son of ours is stubborn and rebellious; he will not obey our voice; he is a glutton and a drunkard.' 21Then all the men of his city shall stone him to death with stones; [a]so you shall put away the evil from among you, [b]and all Israel shall hear and fear.

Miscellaneous Laws

22"If a man has committed a sin [a]deserving of death, and he is put to death, and you hang him on a tree, 23[a]his body shall not remain overnight on the tree, but you shall surely bury him that day, so that [b]you do not defile the land which the LORD your God is giving you *as* an inheritance; for [c]he who is hanged *is* accursed of God.

22 "You [a]shall not see your brother's ox or his sheep going astray, and [1]hide yourself from them; you shall certainly bring them back to your brother. 2And if your brother *is* not near you, or if you do not know him, then you shall bring it to your own house, and it shall remain with you until your brother seeks it; then you shall restore it to him. 3You shall do the same with his donkey, and so shall you do with his garment; with any lost thing of your brother's, which he has

CHAPTER 21
3 a Num. 19:2
5 a 1 Chr. 23:13 b Deut. 17:8, 9 *1 Lit. stroke*
6 a Matt. 27:24
8 a Jon. 1:14
9 a Deut. 19:13
11 a Num. 31:18
12 a Lev. 14:8, 9
13 a Ps. 45:10
14 a Judg. 19:24
15 a Gen. 29:33
16 a 1 Chr. 5:2; 26:10
17 a 2 Kin. 2:9 b Gen. 49:3 c Gen. 25:31, 33
21 a Deut. 13:5; 19:19, 20; 22:21, 24 b Deut. 13:11
22 a Acts 23:29
23 a John 19:31 b Lev. 18:25 c Gal. 3:13

CHAPTER 22
1 a Ex. 23:4 *1 ignore them*

lost and you have found, you shall do likewise; you [1]must not hide yourself.

4a“You shall not see your brother’s donkey or his ox fall down along the road, and hide yourself from them; you shall surely help him lift *them* up again.

5“A woman shall not wear anything that pertains to a man, nor shall a man put on a woman’s garment, for all who do so *are* [1]an abomination to the LORD your God.

6“If a bird’s nest happens to be before you along the way, in any tree or on the ground, with young ones or eggs, with the mother sitting on the young or on the eggs, [a]you shall not take the mother with the young; 7you shall surely let the mother go, and take the young for yourself, [a]that it may be well with you and *that* you may prolong *your* days.

8“When you build a new house, then you shall make a parapet for your roof, that you may not bring guilt of bloodshed on your household if anyone falls from it.

9a“You shall not sow your vineyard with different kinds of seed, lest the yield of the seed which you have sown and the fruit of your vineyard be defiled.

10a“You shall not plow with an ox and a donkey together.

11a“You shall not wear a garment of different sorts, *such as* wool and linen mixed together.

12“You shall make [a]tassels on the four corners of the clothing with which you cover *yourself.*

Laws of Sexual Morality

13“If any man takes a wife, and goes in to her, and [a]detests her, 14and charges her with shameful conduct, and brings a bad name on her, and says, ‘I took this woman, and when I came to her I found she *was* not a virgin,’ 15then the father and mother of the young woman shall take and bring out *the evidence of* the young woman’s virginity to the elders of the city at the gate. 16And the young woman’s father shall say to the elders, ‘I gave my daughter to this man as wife, and he detests her. 17Now he has charged her with shameful conduct, saying, “I found your daughter *was* not a virgin,” and yet these *are the evidences of* my daughter’s virginity.’ And they shall spread the cloth before the elders of the city. 18Then the elders of that city shall take that man and punish him; 19and they shall fine him one hundred *shekels* of silver and give *them* to the father of the young woman, because he has brought a bad name on a virgin of Israel. And she shall be his wife; he cannot divorce her all his days.

20“But if the thing is true, *and evidences of* virginity are not found for the young woman, 21then they shall bring out the young woman to the door of her father’s house, and the men of her city shall stone her to death with [a]stones, because she has [b]done a disgraceful thing in Israel, to play the harlot in her father’s house. [c]So you shall [1]put away the evil from among you.

22a“If a man is found lying with a woman married to a husband, then both of them shall die—the man that lay with the woman, and the woman; so you shall put away the evil from Israel.

23“If a young woman *who is* a virgin is [a]betrothed to a husband, and a man finds her in the city and lies with her, 24then you shall bring them both out to the gate of that city, and you shall stone them to death with stones, the young woman because she did not cry out in the city, and the man because he [a]humbled his neighbor’s wife; [b]so you shall put away the evil from among you.

25“But if a man finds a betrothed young woman in the countryside, and the man forces her and lies with her, then only the man who lay with her shall die. 26But you shall do nothing to the young woman; *there is* in the young woman no sin *deserving* of death, for just as when a man rises against his neighbor and kills him, even so *is* this matter. 27For he found her in the countryside, *and* the betrothed young woman cried out, but *there was* no one to save her.

28a“If a man finds a young woman *who is* a virgin, who is not betrothed, and he seizes her and lies with her, and they are found out, 29then the man who lay with her shall give to the young woman’s father [a]fifty *shekels* of silver, and she shall be his wife [b]because he has humbled her; he shall not be permitted to divorce her all his days.

30a“A man shall not take his father’s wife, nor [b]uncover his father’s bed.

Those Excluded from the Congregation

23 “He who is emasculated by crushing or mutilation shall [a]not enter the assembly of the LORD.

---

3 [1] *may not avoid responsibility*
4 a Ex. 23:5
5 [1] *detestable*
6 a Lev. 22:28
7 a Deut. 4:40
9 a Lev. 19:19
10 a [2 Cor. 6:14–16]
11 a Lev. 19:19
12 a Num. 15:37–41
13 a Deut. 21:15; 24:3
21 a Deut. 21:21 b Gen. 34:7 c Deut. 13:5 [1] *purge the evil person*
22 a Lev. 20:10
23 a Matt. 1:18, 19
24 a Deut. 21:14 b Deut. 22:21, 22
28 a Ex. 22:16, 17
29 a Ex. 22:16, 17 b Deut. 22:24
30 a Deut. 27:20 b Ezek. 16:8
CHAPTER 23
1 a Lev. 21:20; 22:24

2"One of illegitimate birth shall not enter the assembly of the LORD; even to the tenth generation none of his *descendants* shall enter the assembly of the LORD.

3[a]"An Ammonite or Moabite shall not enter the assembly of the LORD; even to the tenth generation none of his *descendants* shall enter the assembly of the LORD forever, 4[a]because they did not meet you with bread and water on the road when you came out of Egypt, and [b]because they hired against you Balaam the son of Beor from Pethor of [1]Mesopotamia, to curse you. 5 Nevertheless the LORD your God would not listen to Balaam, but the LORD your God turned the curse into a blessing for you, because the LORD your God [a]loves you. 6[a]You shall not seek their peace nor their prosperity all your days forever.

Father, I pray that You will turn any curse into a blessing for _____ because You love them.

FROM DEUTERONOMY 23:5

7"You shall not abhor an Edomite, [a]for he *is* your brother. You shall not abhor an Egyptian, because [b]you were an alien in his land. 8The children of the third generation born to them may enter the assembly of the LORD.

Cleanliness of the Camp Site

9"When the army goes out against your enemies, then keep yourself from every wicked thing. 10[a]If there is any man among you who becomes unclean by some occurrence in the night, then he shall go outside the camp; he shall not come inside the camp. 11But it shall be, when evening comes, that [a]he shall wash with water; and when the sun sets, he may come into the camp.

12"Also you shall have a place outside the camp, where you may go out; 13and you shall have an implement among your equipment, and when you sit down outside, you shall dig with it and turn and cover your refuse. 14For the LORD your God [a]walks in the midst of your camp, to deliver you and give your enemies over to you; therefore your camp shall be holy, that He may see no unclean thing among you, and turn away from you.

Miscellaneous Laws

15[a]"You shall not give back to his master the slave who has escaped from his master to you. 16He may dwell with you in your midst, in the place which he chooses within one of your gates, where it [1]seems best to him; [a]you shall not oppress him.

17"There shall be no *ritual* [1]harlot [a]of the daughters of Israel, or a [b]perverted[2] one of the sons of Israel. 18You shall not bring the wages of a harlot or the price of a dog to the house of the LORD your God for any vowed offering, for both of these *are* [1]an abomination to the LORD your God.

19[a]"You shall not charge interest to your brother—interest on money *or* food *or* anything that is lent out at interest. 20[a]To a foreigner you may charge interest, but to your brother you shall not charge interest, [b]that the LORD your God may bless you in all to which you set your hand in the land which you are entering to possess.

21[a]"When you make a vow to the LORD your God, you shall not delay to pay it; for the LORD your God will surely require it of you, and it would be sin to you. 22But if you abstain from vowing, it shall not be sin to you. 23[a]That which has gone from your lips you shall keep and perform, for you voluntarily vowed to the LORD your God what you have promised with your mouth.

24"When you come into your neighbor's vineyard, you may eat your fill of grapes at your pleasure, but you shall not put *any* in your container. 25When you come into your neighbor's standing grain, [a]you may pluck the heads with your hand, but you shall not use a sickle on your neighbor's standing grain.

Law Concerning Divorce

24 "When a [a]man takes a wife and marries her, and it happens that she finds no favor in his eyes because he has found some [1]uncleanness in her, and he writes her a [b]certificate of divorce, puts *it* in her hand, and sends her out of his house, 2when she has departed from his house, and goes and becomes another man's *wife,* 3*if* the latter husband detests her and writes her a certificate of divorce,

3 [a] Neh. 13:1, 2
4 [a] Deut. 2:27–30 [b] Num. 22:5, 6; 23:7 [1] Heb. *Aram Naharaim*
5 [a] Deut. 4:37
6 [a] Ezra 9:12
7 [a] Obad. 10, 12 [b] Deut. 10:19
10 [a] Lev. 15:16
11 [a] Lev. 15:5
14 [a] Lev. 26:12
15 [a] 1 Sam. 30:15
16 [a] Ex. 22:21 [1] *pleases him best*
17 [a] Lev. 19:29 [b] 2 Kin. 23:7 [1] Heb. *qedeshah,* fem. of *qadesh* (note 2) [2] Heb. *qadesh,* one practicing sodomy and prostitution in religious rituals
18 [1] *detestable*
19 [a] Ex. 22:25
20 [a] Deut. 15:3 [b] Deut. 15:10
21 [a] Eccl. 5:4, 5
23 [a] Ps. 66:13, 14
25 [a] Luke 6:1

CHAPTER 24
1 [a] [Matt. 5:31; 19:7] [b] [Jer. 3:8] [1] *indecency,* lit. *nakedness of a thing*

Deuteronomy 23:5

Dear Woman of Destiny,

As a woman of destiny, you are in a time of preparation that is equipping you for the plans and purpose that God has carried in His heart for you since before you were formed in your mother's womb. As a woman called by God to fulfill His divine purposes, you must be trained and equipped with revelation, understanding, inner strength, and wisdom. The "school of the Spirit" that God orchestrates in your life can come in an unusual package. My classroom was five life-changing years in a federal prison. In this intense and difficult environment, I learned that I had a destiny and purpose in God that was being hindered by generational curses and bondage from wrong choices.

Within two months of being incarcerated, the Lord delivered me and filled me with His Holy Spirit. The Holy Spirit opened my eyes to the devastating choices and generational curses that had entangled my life in darkness and bondage. I was perishing for lack of knowledge of God's Word and His ways. God rescued me by teaching me how to plead the blood of Jesus over generational curses that had drawn me into sin and darkness. He gave me inner strength to stand against falling back into old thought patterns and wisdom about how to resist repeated demonic attacks. His lessons included teaching me how to pray and worship Him, despite the intense pressures of prison life. Step by step, God began to turn the curses in my life into blessings. He was leading me to the place of freedom that Jesus had paid for with His redemptive work on the cross (see Gal. 3:13).

You may find yourself in the school of the Spirit through a broken relationship, or financial struggle, or deep grief, or another form of personal devastation. Even if the pain of such circumstances has come into your life intended as a curse from others, the Lord specializes in turning the curse into a blessing. He is able to bring blessings out of the bleakest situations.

Allow the Holy Spirit to lead you through this season. He will show you how to experience joy in the midst of tribulation and peace in the midst of turmoil. He will take you on a path that ends with the blessings of God being made manifest in your life. Everything that the enemy intended for harm and destruction in my life, the Lord has turned into blessings. And He wants to do the same for you.

Whatever "cursed" circumstances you may be in, I pray that you will open your heart to the leading of the Holy Spirit. This time of preparation will not be in vain. The lessons and experiences that you are going through are vital for the days ahead. Obedience to His Word and His prompting is critical as He leads you on the path of redemption and blessing so that you will fulfill the purposes that God has ordained for you.

Mary Forsythe

puts *it* in her hand, and sends her out of
his house, or if the latter husband dies
who took her as his wife, 4[a]*then* her former husband who divorced her must not
take her back to be his wife after she has
been defiled; for that *is* [1]an abomination
before the LORD, and you shall not bring
sin on the land which the LORD your God
is giving you *as* an inheritance.

Miscellaneous Laws

5[a]"When a man has taken a new wife,
he shall not go out to war or be charged
with any business; he shall be free at
home one year, and [b]bring happiness to
his wife whom he has taken.
6"No man shall take the lower or the
upper millstone in pledge, for he takes
[1]*one's* living in pledge.
7"If a man is [a]found [1]kidnapping any of
his brethren of the children of Israel, and
mistreats him or sells him, then that kid-
napper shall die; [b]and you shall put away
the evil from among you.
8"Take heed in [a]an outbreak of leprosy,
that you carefully observe and do according to all that the priests, the Levites,
shall teach you; just as I commanded
them, *so* you shall be careful to do. 9[a]Re-
member what the LORD your God did [b]to
Miriam on the way when you came out of
Egypt!
10"When you [a]lend your brother anything, you shall not go into his house to
get his pledge. 11You shall stand outside,
and the man to whom you lend shall bring
the pledge out to you. 12And if the man *is*
poor, you shall not [1]keep his pledge overnight. 13[a]You shall in any case return the
pledge to him again when the sun goes
down, that he may sleep in his own garment and [b]bless you; and [c]it shall be righteousness to you before the LORD your
God.
14"You shall not [a]oppress a hired servant *who is* poor and needy, *whether* one
of your brethren or one of the aliens who
is in your land within your gates. 15Each
day [a]you shall give *him* his wages, and not
let the sun go down on it, for he *is* poor
and has set his heart on it; [b]lest he cry out
against you to the LORD, and it be sin to
you.
16[a]"Fathers shall not be put to death for
their children, nor shall children be put to
death for *their* fathers; a person shall be
put to death for his own sin.
17[a]"You shall not pervert justice due
the stranger or the fatherless, [b]nor take a
widow's garment as a pledge. 18But [a]you
shall remember that you were a slave in
Egypt, and the LORD your God redeemed
you from there; therefore I command you
to do this thing.
19[a]"When you reap your harvest in your
field, and forget a sheaf in the field, you
shall not go back to get it; it shall be for
the stranger, the fatherless, and the widow, that the LORD your God may [b]bless
you in all the work of your hands. 20When
you beat your olive trees, you shall not go
over the boughs again; it shall be for the
stranger, the fatherless, and the widow.
21When you gather the grapes of your
vineyard, you shall not glean *it* afterward;
it shall be for the stranger, the fatherless,
and the widow. 22And you shall remember
that you were a slave in the land of Egypt;
therefore I command you to do this thing.

25

"If there is a [a]dispute between
men, and they come to [1]court, that
the judges may judge them, and they [b]jus-
tify the righteous and condemn the wicked, 2then it shall be, if the wicked man
[a]deserves to be beaten, that the judge will
cause him to lie down [b]and be beaten in
his presence, according to his guilt, with
a certain number of blows. 3[a]Forty blows
he may give him *and* no more, lest he
should exceed this and beat him with
many blows above these, and your brother
[b]be humiliated in your sight.
4[a]"You shall not muzzle an ox while it
[1]treads out *the grain.*

Marriage Duty of the Surviving Brother

5[a]"If brothers dwell together, and one
of them dies and has no son, the widow of
the dead man shall not be *married* to a
stranger outside *the family;* her husband's brother shall go in to her, take her
as his wife, and perform the duty of a husband's brother to her. 6And it shall be *that*
the firstborn son which she bears [a]will
succeed to the name of his dead brother,
that [b]his name may not be blotted out of
Israel. 7But if the man does not want to
take his brother's wife, then let his
brother's wife go up to the [a]gate to the
elders, and say, 'My husband's brother refuses to raise up a name to his brother in
Israel; he will not perform the duty of my
husband's brother.' 8Then the elders of
his city shall call him and speak to him.

4 a [Jer. 3:1] *1 a detestable thing*
5 a Deut. 20:7 b Prov. 5:18
6 *1 life*
7 a Ex. 21:16 b Deut. 19:19 *1* Lit. *stealing*
8 a Lev. 13:2; 14:2
9 a [1 Cor. 10:6] b Num. 12:10
10 a Matt. 5:42
12 *1* Lit. *sleep with his pledge*
13 a Ex. 22:26 b 2 Tim. 1:18 c Deut. 6:25
14 a [Mal. 3:5]
15 a Lev. 19:13 b James 5:4
16 a Ezek. 18:20
17 a Ex. 23:6 b Ex. 22:26
18 a Deut. 24:22
19 a Lev. 19:9, 10 b Ps. 41:1

CHAPTER 25
1 a Deut. 17:8–13; 19:17 b Prov. 17:15 *1* Lit. *the judgment*
2 a Prov. 19:29 b Matt. 10:17
3 a 2 Cor. 11:24 b Job 18:3
4 a [Prov. 12:10] *1 threshes*
5 a Matt. 22:24
6 a Gen. 38:9 b Ruth 4:5, 10
7 a Ruth 4:1, 2

But *if* he stands firm and says, [a]'I do not
want to take her,' 9then his brother's wife
shall come to him in the presence of the
elders, [a]remove his sandal from his foot,
spit in his face, and answer and say, 'So
shall it be done to the man who will not
[b]build up his brother's house.' 10And his
name shall be called in Israel, 'The house
of him who had his sandal removed.'

Miscellaneous Laws

11"If *two* men fight together, and the
wife of one draws near to rescue her husband from the hand of the one attacking
him, and puts out her hand and seizes
him by the genitals, 12then you shall cut
off her hand; [a]your eye shall not pity *her.*
13[a]"You shall not have in your bag differing weights, a heavy and a light. 14You
shall not have in your house differing
measures, a large and a small. 15You shall
have a perfect and just weight, a perfect
and just measure, [a]that your days may be
lengthened in the land which the LORD
your God is giving you. 16For [a]all who do
such things, all who behave unrighteously, *are* [1]an abomination to the LORD your
God.

Destroy the Amalekites

17[a]"Remember what Amalek did to you
on the way as you were coming out of
Egypt, 18how he met you on the way and
attacked your rear ranks, all the stragglers
at your rear, when you *were* tired and
weary; and he [a]did not fear God. 19Therefore it shall be, [a]when the LORD your God
has given you rest from your enemies all
around, in the land which the LORD your
God is giving you to possess *as* an inheritance, *that* you will [b]blot out the remembrance of Amalek from under heaven. You
shall not forget.

Offerings of Firstfruits and Tithes

26 "And it shall be, when you come
into the land which the LORD your
God is giving you *as* an inheritance, and
you possess it and dwell in it, 2[a]that you
shall take some of the first of all the produce of the ground, which you shall bring
from your land that the LORD your God is
giving you, and put *it* in a basket and [b]go
to the place where the LORD your God
chooses to make His name abide. 3And
you shall go to the one who is priest in
those days, and say to him, 'I declare today
to the LORD [1]your God that I have come
to the country which the LORD swore to
our fathers to give us.'
4"Then the priest shall take the basket
out of your hand and set it down before
the altar of the LORD your God. 5And you
shall answer and say before the LORD your
God: 'My father *was* [a]a [1]Syrian, [b]about to
perish, and [c]he went down to Egypt and
[2]dwelt there, [d]few in number; and there
he became a nation, [e]great, mighty, and
populous. 6But the [a]Egyptians mistreated
us, afflicted us, and laid hard bondage on
us. 7[a]Then we cried out to the LORD God
of our fathers, and the LORD heard our
voice and looked on our affliction and our
labor and our oppression. 8So [a]the LORD
brought us out of Egypt with a mighty
hand and with an outstretched arm, [b]with
great terror and with signs and wonders.
9He has brought us to this place and has
given us this land, [a]"a land flowing with
milk and honey"; 10and now, behold, I
have brought the firstfruits of the land
which you, O LORD, have given me.'
"Then you shall set it before the LORD
your God, and worship before the LORD
your God. 11So [a]you shall rejoice in every
good *thing* which the LORD your God has
given to you and your house, you and the
Levite and the stranger who *is* among
you.
12"When you have finished laying aside
all the [a]tithe of your increase in the third
year—[b]the year of tithing—and have given *it* to the Levite, the stranger, the fatherless, and the widow, so that they may
eat within your gates and be filled, 13then
you shall say before the LORD your God: 'I
have removed the [1]holy *tithe* from *my*
house, and also have given them to the
Levite, the stranger, the fatherless, and
the widow, according to all Your commandments which You have commanded
me; I have not transgressed Your commandments, [a]nor have I forgotten *them.*
14[a]I have not eaten any of it [1]when in
mourning, nor have I removed *any* of it
[2]for an unclean *use,* nor given *any* of it for
the dead. I have obeyed the voice of the
LORD my God, and have done according
to all that You have commanded me.
15[a]Look down from Your holy [1]habitation, from heaven, and bless Your people
Israel and the land which You have given
us, just as You swore to our fathers, [b]"a
land flowing with milk and honey."'

8 a Ruth 4:6
9 a Ruth 4:7, 8 b Ruth 4:11
12 a Deut. 7:2; 19:13
13 a Mic. 6:11
15 a Ex. 20:12
16 a Prov. 11:1 *1 detestable*
17 a Ex. 17:8–16
18 a Rom. 3:18
19 a 1 Sam. 15:3 b Ex. 17:14

CHAPTER 26
2 a Ex. 22:29; 23:16, 19 b Deut. 12:5
3 *1* LXX *my*
5 a Hos. 12:12 b Gen. 43:1, 2; 45:7, 11 c Acts 7:15 d Deut. 10:22 e Deut. 1:10 *1* Or *Aramean* *2* As a resident alien
6 a Ex. 1:8–11, 14
7 a Ex. 2:23–25; 3:9; 4:31
8 a Deut. 5:15 b Deut. 4:34; 34:11, 12
9 a Ex. 3:8, 17
11 a Deut. 12:7; 16:11
12 a Lev. 27:30 b Deut. 14:28, 29
13 a Ps. 119:141, 153, 176 *1 hallowed things*
14 a Hos. 9:4 *1* Lit. *in my mourning* *2* Or *while I was unclean*
15 a Is. 63:15 b Ex. 3:8 *1 home*

A Special People of God

16“This day the LORD your God commands you to observe these statutes and
judgments; therefore you shall be careful
to observe them with all your heart and
with all your soul. 17Today you have [a]pro-
claimed the LORD to be your God, and that
you will walk in His ways and keep His
statutes, His commandments, and His
judgments, and that you will [b]obey His
voice. 18Also today [a]the LORD has proclaimed you to be His special people, just
as He promised you, that *you* should keep
all His commandments, 19and that He will
set you [a]high above all nations which He
has made, in praise, in name, and in hon-
or, and that you may be [b]a [1]holy people
to the LORD your God, just as He has
spoken.”

Look down from heaven,
Father, and bless ____.
FROM DEUTERONOMY 26:15

The Law Inscribed on Stones

27 Now Moses, with the elders of Israel, commanded the people, saying:
“Keep all the commandments which I
command you today. 2And it shall be, on
the day [a]when you cross over the Jordan
to the land which the LORD your God is
giving you, that [b]you shall set up for yourselves large stones, and whitewash them
with lime. 3You shall write on them all
the words of this law, when you have
crossed over, that you may enter the land
which the LORD your God is giving you,
[a]‘a land flowing with milk and honey,’ just
as the LORD God of your fathers promised
you. 4Therefore it shall be, when you have
crossed over the Jordan, *that* [a]on Mount
Ebal you shall set up these stones, which
I command you today, and you shall
whitewash them with lime. 5And there
you shall build an altar to the LORD your
God, an altar of stones; [a]you shall not use
an iron *tool* on them. 6You shall build
with [1]whole stones the altar of the LORD
your God, and offer burnt offerings on it
to the LORD your God. 7You shall offer
peace offerings, and shall eat there, and
[a]rejoice before the LORD your God. 8And
you shall [a]write very plainly on the stones
all the words of this law.”
9Then Moses and the priests, the Levites, spoke to all Israel, saying, “Take
heed and listen, O Israel: [a]This day you
have become the people of the LORD your
God. 10Therefore you shall obey the voice
of the LORD your God, and observe His
commandments and His statutes which I
command you today.”

Curses Pronounced from Mount Ebal

11And Moses commanded the people on
the same day, saying, 12“These shall stand
[a]on Mount Gerizim to bless the people,
when you have crossed over the Jordan:
Simeon, Levi, Judah, Issachar, Joseph,
and Benjamin; 13and [a]these shall stand on
Mount Ebal to curse: Reuben, Gad, Asher,
Zebulun, Dan, and Naphtali.
14“And [a]the Levites shall speak with a
loud voice and say to all the men of Israel:
15[a]‘Cursed *is* the one who makes a carved
or molded image, [1]an abomination to the
LORD, the work of the hands of the craftsman, and sets *it* up in secret.’
[b]“And all the people shall answer and
say, ‘Amen!’
16[a]‘Cursed *is* the one who treats his father or his mother with contempt.’
“And all the people shall say, ‘Amen!’
17[a]‘Cursed *is* the one who moves his
neighbor’s landmark.’
“And all the people shall say, ‘Amen!’
18[a]‘Cursed *is* the one who makes the
blind to wander off the road.’
“And all the people shall say, ‘Amen!’
19[a]‘Cursed *is* the one who perverts the
justice due the stranger, the fatherless,
and widow.’
“And all the people shall say, ‘Amen!’
20[a]‘Cursed *is* the one who lies with his
father’s wife, because he has uncovered
his father’s bed.’
“And all the people shall say, ‘Amen!’
21[a]‘Cursed *is* the one who lies with any
kind of animal.’
“And all the people shall say, ‘Amen!’
22[a]‘Cursed *is* the one who lies with his
sister, the daughter of his father or the
daughter of his mother.’
“And all the people shall say, ‘Amen!’
23[a]‘Cursed *is* the one who lies with his
mother-in-law.’
“And all the people shall say, ‘Amen!’
24[a]‘Cursed *is* the one who attacks his
neighbor secretly.’

---

17 a Ex. 20:19 b Deut. 15:5
18 a Ex. 6:7; 19:5
19 a Deut. 4:7, 8; 28:1 b [1 Pet. 2:9] *1 consecrated*

CHAPTER 27
2 a Josh. 4:1 b Josh. 8:32
3 a Ex. 3:8
4 a Deut. 11:29
5 a Ex. 20:25
6 *1 uncut*
7 a Deut. 26:11
8 a Josh. 8:32
9 a Deut. 26:18
12 a Josh. 8:33
13 a Deut. 11:29
14 a Deut. 33:10
15 a Ex. 20:4, 23; 34:17 b Num. 5:22 *1 a detestable thing*
16 a Ezek. 22:7
17 a Deut. 19:14
18 a Lev. 19:14
19 a Ex. 22:21, 22; 23:9
20 a Deut. 22:30
21 a Lev. 18:23; 20:15, 16
22 a Lev. 18:9
23 a Lev. 18:17; 20:14
24 a Ex. 20:13; 21:12

"And all the people shall say, 'Amen!'
25[a]'Cursed *is* the one who takes a bribe
to slay an innocent person.'
"And all the people shall say, 'Amen!'
26[a]'Cursed *is* the one who does not confirm *all* the words of this law by observing
them.'
"And all the people shall say, 'Amen!' "

O Lord, I pray that ____ will diligently obey Your voice and observe carefully all Your commandments, so that Your blessings will be on them and overtake them.

FROM DEUTERONOMY 28:1, 2

Blessings on Obedience

28 "Now it shall come to pass, [a]if you
diligently obey the voice of the
LORD your God, to observe carefully all
His commandments which I command
you today, that the LORD your God [b]will
set you high above all nations of the earth.
2And all these blessings shall come upon
you and [a]overtake you, because you obey
the voice of the LORD your God:
3[a]"Blessed *shall* you *be* in the city, and
blessed *shall* you *be* [b]in the country.
4"Blessed *shall be* [a]the [1]fruit of your
body, the produce of your ground and the
increase of your herds, the increase of
your cattle and the offspring of your
flocks.
5"Blessed *shall be* your basket and your
kneading bowl.
6[a]"Blessed *shall* you *be* when you come
in, and blessed *shall* you *be* when you go
out.
7"The LORD [a]will cause your enemies
who rise against you to be defeated before
your face; they shall come out against you
one way and flee before you seven ways.
8"The LORD will [a]command the blessing on you in your storehouses and in all
to which you [b]set your hand, and He will
bless you in the land which the LORD your
God is giving you.
9[a]"The LORD will establish you as a holy
people to Himself, just as He has sworn to
you, if you keep the commandments of
the LORD your God and walk in His ways.
10Then all peoples of the earth shall see
that you are [a]called by the name of the
LORD, and they shall be [b]afraid of you.
11And [a]the LORD will grant you plenty of
goods, in the fruit of your body, in the
increase of your livestock, and in the produce of your ground, in the land of which
the LORD [1]swore to your fathers to give
you. 12The LORD will open to you His good
[1]treasure, the heavens, [a]to give the rain to
your land in its season, and [b]to bless all
the work of your hand. [c]You shall lend to
many nations, but you shall not borrow.
13And the LORD will make [a]you the head
and not the tail; you shall be above only,
and not be beneath, if you [1]heed the commandments of the LORD your God, which
I command you today, and are careful to
observe *them.* 14[a]So you shall not turn
aside from any of the words which I command you this day, *to* the right or the left,
to go after other gods to serve them.

Curses on Disobedience

15"But it shall come to pass, [a]if you do
not obey the voice of the LORD your God,
to observe carefully all His commandments and His statutes which I command
you today, that all these curses will come
upon you and overtake you:
16"Cursed *shall* you *be* in the city, and
cursed *shall* you *be* in the country.
17"Cursed *shall be* your basket and your
kneading bowl.
18"Cursed *shall be* the [1]fruit of your
body and the produce of your land, the
increase of your cattle and the offspring of
your flocks.
19"Cursed *shall* you *be* when you come
in, and cursed *shall* you *be* when you go
out.
20"The LORD will send on you [a]cursing,
[b]confusion, and [c]rebuke in all that you set
your hand to do, until you are destroyed
and until you perish quickly, because of
the wickedness of your doings in which
you have forsaken Me. 21The LORD will
make the [1]plague cling to you until He
has consumed you from the land which
you are going to possess. 22[a]The LORD will
strike you with consumption, with fever,
with inflammation, with severe burning
fever, with the sword, with [b]scorching,[1]
and with mildew; they shall pursue you
until you perish. 23And [a]your heavens
which *are* over your head shall be bronze,
and the earth which is under you *shall be*
iron. 24The LORD will change the rain of

25 a Ex. 23:7
26 a Gal. 3:10
CHAPTER 28
1 a Ex. 15:26 b Deut. 26:19
2 a Deut. 28:15
3 a Ps. 128:1, 4 b Gen. 39:5
4 a Gen. 22:17 *1 offspring*
6 a Ps. 121:8
7 a Lev. 26:7, 8
8 a Lev. 25:21 b Deut. 15:10
9 a Ex. 19:5, 6
10 a Num. 6:27 b Deut. 11:25
11 a Deut. 30:9 *1 promised*
12 a Lev. 26:4 b Deut. 14:29 c Deut. 15:6 *1 storehouse*
13 a [Is. 9:14, 15] *1 listen to*
14 a Deut. 5:32
15 a Lev. 26:14–39
18 *1 offspring*
20 a Mal. 2:2 b Is. 65:14 c Is. 30:17
21 *1 pestilence*
22 a Lev. 26:16 b Amos 4:9 *1 blight*
23 a Lev. 26:19

your land to powder and dust; from the heaven it shall come down on you until you are destroyed.

25[a]“The LORD will cause you to be defeated before your enemies; you shall go out one way against them and flee seven ways before them; and you shall become [1]troublesome to all the kingdoms of the earth. 26[a]Your carcasses shall be food for all the birds of the air and the beasts of the earth, and no one shall frighten *them* away. 27The LORD will strike you with [a]the boils of Egypt, with [b]tumors, with the scab, and with the itch, from which you cannot be healed. 28The LORD will strike you with madness and blindness and [a]confusion of heart. 29And you shall [a]grope at noonday, as a blind man gropes in darkness; you shall not prosper in your ways; you shall be only oppressed and plundered continually, and no one shall save *you.*

30[a]“You shall betroth a wife, but another man shall lie with her; [b]you shall build a house, but you shall not dwell in it; [c]you shall plant a vineyard, but shall not gather its grapes. 31Your ox *shall be* slaughtered before your eyes, but you shall not eat of it; your donkey *shall be* violently taken away from before you, and shall not be restored to you; your sheep *shall be* given to your enemies, and you shall have no one to rescue *them.* 32Your sons and your daughters *shall be* given to [a]another people, and your eyes shall look and [b]fail *with longing* for them all day long; and *there shall be* [1]no strength in your [c]hand. 33A nation whom you have not known shall eat [a]the fruit of your land and the produce of your labor, and you shall be only oppressed and crushed continually. 34So you shall be driven mad because of the sight which your eyes see. 35The LORD will strike you in the knees and on the legs with severe boils which cannot be healed, and from the sole of your foot to the top of your head.

36“The LORD will [a]bring you and the king whom you set over you to a nation which neither you nor your fathers have known, and [b]there you shall serve other gods—wood and stone. 37And you shall become [a]an[1] astonishment, a proverb, [b]and a byword among all nations where the LORD will drive you.

38[a]“You shall carry much seed out to the field but gather little in, for [b]the locust shall [1]consume it. 39You shall plant vineyards and tend *them,* but you shall neither drink *of* the [a]wine nor gather the *grapes;* for the worms shall eat them. 40You shall have olive trees throughout all your territory, but you shall not anoint *yourself* with the oil; for your olives shall drop off. 41You shall beget sons and daughters, but they shall not be yours; for [a]they shall go into captivity. 42Locusts shall [1]consume all your trees and the produce of your land.

43“The alien who *is* among you shall rise higher and higher above you, and you shall come down lower and lower. 44He shall lend to you, but you shall not lend to him; he shall be the head, and you shall be the tail.

45“Moreover all these curses shall come upon you and pursue and overtake you, until you are destroyed, because you [1]did not obey the voice of the LORD your God, to keep His commandments and His statutes which He commanded you. 46And they shall be upon [a]you for a sign and a wonder, and on your descendants forever.

47[a]“Because you did not serve the LORD your God with joy and gladness of heart, [b]for the abundance of everything, 48therefore you shall serve your enemies, whom the LORD will send against you, in [a]hunger, in thirst, in nakedness, and in need of everything; and He [b]will put a yoke of iron on your neck until He has destroyed you. 49[a]The LORD will bring a nation against you from afar, from the end of the earth, [b]*as swift* as the eagle flies, a nation whose language you will not understand, 50a nation of fierce countenance, [a]which does not respect the elderly nor show favor to the young. 51And they shall eat the increase of your livestock and the produce of your land, until you are destroyed; they shall not leave you grain or new wine or oil, *or* the increase of your cattle or the offspring of your flocks, until they have destroyed you.

52“They shall [a]besiege you at all your gates until your high and fortified walls, in which you trust, come down throughout all your land; and they shall besiege you at all your gates throughout all your land which the LORD your God has given you. 53[a]You shall eat the [1]fruit of your own body, the flesh of your sons and your daughters whom the LORD your God has given you, in the siege and desperate straits in which your enemy shall distress you. 54The [1]sensitive and very refined

25 a Deut. 32:30 *1 a terror*
26 a 1 Sam. 17:44
27 a Ex. 15:26 b 1 Sam. 5:6
28 a Jer. 4:9
29 a Job 5:14
30 a Jer. 8:10 b Amos 5:11 c Deut. 20:6
32 a 2 Chr. 29:9 b Ps. 119:82 c Neh. 5:5 *1 nothing you can do*
33 a Jer. 5:15, 17
36 a Jer. 39:1–9 b Deut. 4:28
37 a 1 Kin. 9:7, 8 b Ps. 44:14 *1 a thing of horror*
38 a Mic. 6:15 b Joel 1:4 *1 devour*
39 a Zeph. 1:13
41 a Lam. 1:5
42 *1 possess*
45 *1 did not listen to*
46 a Is. 8:18
47 a Neh. 9:35–37 b Deut. 32:15
48 a Lam. 4:4–6 b Jer. 28:13, 14
49 a Jer. 5:15 b Jer. 48:40; 49:22
50 a 2 Chr. 36:17
52 a 2 Kin. 25:1, 2, 4
53 a Lev. 26:29 *1 offspring*
54 *1 Lit. tender*

man among you [a]will[2] be hostile toward
his brother, toward [b]the wife of his bosom, and toward the rest of his children
whom he leaves behind, 55 so that he will
not give any of them the flesh of his children whom he will eat, because he has
nothing left in the siege and desperate
straits in which your enemy shall distress
you at all your gates. 56 The [1]tender and
[2]delicate woman among you, who would
not venture to set the sole of her foot on
the ground because of her delicateness
and sensitivity, [3]will refuse to the husband of her bosom, and to her son and her
daughter, 57 her [1]placenta which comes
out [a]from between her feet and her children whom she bears; for she will eat
them secretly for lack of everything in the
siege and desperate straits in which your
enemy shall distress you at all your gates.
58 "If you do not carefully observe all the
words of this law that are written in this
book, that you may fear [a]this glorious and
awesome name, THE LORD YOUR GOD,
59 then the LORD will bring upon you
and your descendants [a]extraordinary
plagues—great and prolonged plagues—
and serious and prolonged sicknesses.
60 Moreover He will bring back on you all
[a]the diseases of Egypt, of which you were
afraid, and they shall cling to you. 61 Also
every sickness and every plague, which *is*
not written in this Book of the Law, will
the LORD bring upon you until you are
destroyed. 62 You [a]shall be left few in number, whereas you were [b]as the stars of
heaven in multitude, because you would
not obey the voice of the LORD your God.
63 And it shall be, *that* just as the LORD
[a]rejoiced over you to do you good and
multiply you, so the LORD [b]will rejoice
over you to destroy you and bring you to
nothing; and you shall be [c]plucked[1] from
off the land which you go to possess.
64 "Then the LORD [a]will scatter you
among all peoples, from one end of the
earth to the other, and [b]there you shall
serve other gods, which neither you nor
your fathers have known—wood and
stone. 65 And [a]among those nations you
shall find no rest, nor shall the sole of
your foot have a resting place; [b]but there
the LORD will give you a [1]trembling heart,
failing eyes, and [c]anguish of soul. 66 Your
life shall hang in doubt before you; you
shall fear day and night, and have no assurance of life. 67 [a]In the morning you
shall say, 'Oh, that it were evening!' And
at evening you shall say, 'Oh, that it were
morning!' because of the fear which terrifies your heart, and [b]because of the sight
which your eyes see.
68 "And the LORD [a]will take you back to
Egypt in ships, by the way of which I said
to you, [b]'You shall never see it again.' And
there you shall be offered for sale to your
enemies as male and female slaves, but no
one will buy *you*."

The Covenant Renewed in Moab

29 These *are* the words of the covenant which the LORD commanded
Moses to make with the children of Israel
in the land of Moab, besides the [a]covenant
which He made with them in Horeb.
2 Now Moses called all Israel and said to
them: [a]"You have seen all that the LORD
did before your eyes in the land of Egypt,
to Pharaoh and to all his servants and to
all his land— 3 [a]the great trials which
your eyes have seen, the signs, and those
great wonders. 4 Yet [a]the LORD has not
given you a heart to [1]perceive and eyes to
see and ears to hear, to this *very* day.
5 [a]And I have led you forty years in the
wilderness. [b]Your clothes have not worn
out on you, and your sandals have not
worn out on your feet. 6 [a]You have not
eaten bread, nor have you drunk wine or
similar drink, that you may know that I
am the LORD your God. 7 And when you
came to this place, [a]Sihon king of Heshbon and Og king of Bashan came out
against us to battle, and we conquered
them. 8 We took their land and [a]gave it as
an inheritance to the Reubenites, to the
Gadites, and to half the tribe of Manasseh.
9 Therefore [a]keep the words of this covenant, and do them, that you may [b]pros-
per in all that you do.
10 "All of you stand today before the
LORD your God: your leaders and your
tribes and your elders and your officers,
all the men of Israel, 11 your little ones and
your wives—also the stranger who *is* in
your camp, from [a]the one who cuts your
wood to the one who draws your water—
12 that you may enter into covenant with
the LORD your God, and [a]into His oath,
which the LORD your God makes with you
today, 13 that He may [a]establish you today
as a people for Himself, and *that* He may
be God to you, [b]just as He has spoken to
you, and [c]just as He has sworn to your
fathers, to Abraham, Isaac, and Jacob.

54 a Deut. 15:9 b Deut. 13:6 *2 Lit. his eye shall be evil toward*
56 *1 sensitive 2 refined 3 Lit. her eye shall be evil toward*
57 a Gen. 49:10 *1 afterbirth*
58 a Ex. 6:3
59 a Dan. 9:12
60 a Deut. 7:15
62 a Deut. 4:27 b Neh. 9:23
63 a Jer. 32:41 b Prov. 1:26 c Jer. 12:14; 45:4 *1 torn*
64 a Jer. 16:13 b Deut. 28:36
65 a Amos 9:4 b Lev. 26:36 c Lev. 26:16 *1 anxious*
67 a Job 7:4 b Deut. 28:34
68 a Hos. 8:13 b Deut. 17:16

CHAPTER 29
1 a Deut. 5:2, 3
2 a Ex. 19:4
3 a Deut. 4:34; 7:19
4 a [Acts 28:26, 27] *1 understand or know*
5 a Deut. 1:3; 8:2 b Deut. 8:4
6 a Deut. 8:3
7 a Num. 21:23, 24
8 a Deut. 3:12, 13
9 a Deut. 4:6 b Josh. 1:7
11 a Josh. 9:21, 23, 27
12 a Neh. 10:29
13 a Deut. 28:9 b Ex. 6:7 c Gen. 17:7, 8

14“I make this covenant and this oath,
[a]not with you alone, 15but with *him* who
stands here with us today before the LORD
our God, [a]as well as with *him* who *is* not
here with us today 16(for you know that
we dwelt in the land of Egypt and that we
came through the nations which you
passed by, 17and you saw their [1]abomina-
tions and their idols which *were* among
them—wood and stone and silver and
gold); 18so that there may not be among
you man or woman or family or tribe,
[a]whose heart turns away today from the
LORD our God, to go *and* serve the gods of
these nations, [b]and that there may not be
among you a root bearing [c]bitterness or
wormwood; 19and so it may not happen,
when he hears the words of this curse,
that he blesses himself in his heart, saying, ‘I shall have peace, even though I
[1]follow the [a]dictates of my heart’—[b]as
though the drunkard could be included
with the sober.
20[a]“The LORD would not spare him; for
then [b]the anger of the LORD and [c]His jealousy would burn against that man, and
every curse that is written in this book
would settle on him, and the LORD [d]would
blot out his name from under heaven.
21And the LORD [a]would separate him from
all the tribes of Israel for adversity, according to all the curses of the covenant
that are written in this Book of the [b]Law,
22so that the coming generation of your
children who rise up after you, and the
foreigner who comes from a far land,
would say, when they [a]see the plagues of
that land and the sicknesses which the
LORD has laid on it:
23‘The whole land *is* brimstone, [a]salt,
and burning; it is not sown, nor does it
bear, nor does any grass grow there, [b]like
the overthrow of Sodom and Gomorrah,
Admah, and Zeboiim, which the LORD
overthrew in His anger and His wrath.’
24All nations would say, [a]‘Why has the
LORD done so to this land? What does the
heat of this great anger mean?’ 25Then
people would say: ‘Because they have forsaken the covenant of the LORD God of
their fathers, which He made with them
when He brought them out of the land of
Egypt; 26for they went and served other
gods and worshiped them, gods that they
did not know and that He had not given to
them. 27Then the anger of the LORD was
aroused against this land, [a]to bring on it
every curse that is written in this book.
28And the LORD [a]uprooted them from
their land in anger, in wrath, and in great
indignation, and cast them into another
land, as *it is* this day.’
29“The secret *things belong* to the LORD
our God, but those *things which are* revealed *belong* to us and to our children
forever, that *we* may do all the words of
this law.

The Blessing of Returning to God

30 “Now [a]it shall come to pass, when
[b]all these things come upon you,
the blessing and the [c]curse which I have
set before you, and [d]you [1]call *them* to
mind among all the nations where the
LORD your God drives you, 2and you [a]re-
turn to the LORD your God and obey His
voice, according to all that I command
you today, you and your children, with all
your heart and with all your soul, 3[a]that
the LORD your God will bring you back
from captivity, and have compassion on
you, and [b]gather you again from all the
nations where the LORD your God has
scattered you. 4[a]If *any* of you are driven
out to the farthest *parts* under heaven,
from there the LORD your God will gather
you, and from there He will bring you.
5Then the LORD your God will bring you
to the land which your fathers possessed,
and you shall possess it. He will prosper
you and multiply you more than your fathers. 6And [a]the LORD your God will circumcise your heart and the heart of your
descendants, to love the LORD your God
with all your heart and with all your soul,
that you may live.
7“Also the LORD your God will put all
these [a]curses on your enemies and on
those who hate you, who persecuted you.
8And you will [a]again obey the voice of
the LORD and do all His commandments
which I command you today. 9[a]The LORD
your God will make you abound in all the
work of your hand, in the [1]fruit of your
body, in the increase of your livestock,
and in the produce of your land for good.
For the LORD will again [b]rejoice over you
for good as He rejoiced over your fathers,
10if you obey the voice of the LORD your
God, to keep His commandments and His
statutes which are written in this Book of
the Law, *and* if you turn to the LORD your
God with all your heart and with all your
soul.

14 a [Jer. 31:31]
15 a Acts 2:39
17 *1 detestable things*
18 a Deut. 11:16 b Heb. 12:15 c Deut. 32:32
19 a Jer. 3:17; 7:24 b Is. 30:1 *1 walk in the stubbornness* or *imagination*
20 a Ezek. 14:7 b Ps. 74:1 c Ps. 79:5 d Deut. 9:14
21 a [Matt. 24:51] b Deut. 30:10
22 a Jer. 19:8; 49:17; 50:13
23 a Zeph. 2:9 b Gen. 19:24, 25
24 a 1 Kin. 9:8
27 a Dan. 9:11
28 a 1 Kin. 14:15

CHAPTER 30
1 a Lev. 26:40 b Deut. 28:2 c Deut. 28:15–45 d Deut. 4:29, 30 *1 Lit. cause them to return to your heart*
2 a Neh. 1:9
3 a Jer. 29:14 b Ezek. 34:13
4 a Neh. 1:9
6 a Deut. 10:16
7 a Jer. 30:16, 20
8 a Zeph. 3:20
9 a Deut. 28:11 b Jer. 32:41 *1 offspring*

Deuteronomy 29:18

Dear Woman of Destiny,

You've probably figured out by now that being a Christian is not a bed of roses. There are definitely some thorns in life's garden. Some people naively think when we give our lives to Jesus that the Holy Spirit touches us with a magic wand and life will be perfect with no more pain and no more suffering. God does promise that to us, but not on this earth. That's in heaven, where He is preparing a beautiful mansion decorated just the way we like and everything is self-cleaning (at least I'm sure hoping for that).

But in the meantime, He said we would have tribulation or problems on this earth. God sees these seasons in our lives as character building times. (Wouldn't it be easier if He had spiritual microwaves that He could pop us into, push the timer for two minutes, and out we would come—"Godly Woman of Faith and Power.")

Our response to disappointments can become His appointments to truly shape us into being women of destiny. Just as a goldsmith allows the gold to stay in the refining fire until he can see a reflection of himself, our heavenly Father uses each problem, disappointment, and even each crisis to purify our lives and to paint a portrait of His image on our hearts. We have a choice. We can get better, or we can get bitter.

Deuteronomy 29:18 and Hebrews 12:15 both talk about a root of bitterness that can spring up and cause trouble. I know of a woman who chose years ago to not forgive someone who had hurt her, but instead, allowed a seed of resentment to be planted into her heart. One disappointment after another came into her life until the seed of resentment began to take root as bitterness. Now lines of bitterness are etched into her face and scathing words from her mouth reflect the root-bound callousness of her soul. She remained a victim instead of becoming a victor. Never underestimate the power locked within a tiny seed!

The first part of Hebrews 12:15 exhorts us to look carefully not to "fall short of the grace of God." We must carefully and frequently examine our hearts to make sure we are not allowing any seeds of resentment to even dwell in our minds. Those seeds can so quickly fall from our minds and take root in our hearts and souls. We must daily take a spiritual "shower" with the blood of Jesus that cleanses us, and clothe ourselves in His graciousness and kindness.

My first husband, who was a dynamic evangelist, died of cancer in 1982. I was a widow with two small children at 34 years old. I chose to not get bitter and blame God, but cried out for His grace and strength to walk through the toughest valley in my life. My husband's death became another one of God's refining fires in my life. I am now a much stronger woman and have a deeper level of compassion for hurting people.

Let's "make lemonade" with the lemons we have been given and distribute it to the world around us to let them "taste and see that the LORD is good" (see Ps. 34:8).

Judy Radachy

The Choice of Life or Death

11"For this commandment which I command you today [a]*is* [1]not *too* mysterious for you, nor *is* it far off. 12[a]It *is* not in heaven, that you should say, 'Who will ascend into heaven for us and bring it to us, that we may hear it and do it?' 13Nor *is* it beyond the sea, that you should say, 'Who will go over the sea for us and bring it to us, that we may hear it and do it?' 14But the word *is* very near you, [a]in your mouth and in your heart, that you may do it.

There comes a crisis, a moment when every human soul which enters the kingdom of God has to make its choice of that kingdom in preference to everything else that it holds and owns.

CATHERINE BOOTH

15"See, [a]I have set before you today life and good, death and evil, 16in that I command you today to love the LORD your God, to walk in His ways, and to keep His commandments, His statutes, and His judgments, that you may live and multiply; and the LORD your God will bless you in the land which you go to possess. 17But if your heart turns away so that you do not hear, and are drawn away, and worship other gods and serve them, 18[a]I announce to you today that you shall surely perish; you shall not prolong *your* days in the land which you cross over the Jordan to go in and possess. 19 [a]I call heaven and earth as witnesses today against you, *that* [b]I have set before you life and death, blessing and cursing; therefore choose life, that both you and your descendants may live; 20that you may love the LORD your God, that you may obey His voice, and that you may cling to Him, for He *is* your [a]life and the length of your days; and that you may dwell in the land which the LORD swore to your fathers, to Abraham, Isaac, and Jacob, to give them."

11 a Is. 45:19 *1 not hidden from*
12 a Rom. 10:6–8
14 a Rom. 10:8
15 a Deut. 30:1, 19
18 a Deut. 4:26; 8:19
19 a Deut. 4:26 b Deut. 30:15
20 a [John 11:25; 14:6]

CHAPTER 31
2 a Deut. 34:7 b 1 Kin. 3:7 c Num. 20:12
3 a Deut. 9:3 b Num. 27:18 c Num. 27:21
4 a Deut. 3:21 b Num. 21:24, 33
5 a Deut. 7:2; 20:10–20
6 a Josh. 10:25 b Deut. 1:29 c Deut. 20:4 d Heb. 13:5
7 a Deut. 31:23
8 a Ex. 13:21 b Josh. 1:5
9 a Deut. 17:18; 31:25, 26 b Josh. 3:3
10 a Deut. 15:1, 2 b Lev. 23:34
11 a Deut. 16:16 b Deut. 12:5 c Josh. 8:34
12 a Deut. 4:10
13 a Deut. 11:2 b Ps. 78:6, 7

Joshua the New Leader of Israel

31 Then Moses went and spoke these words to all Israel. 2And he said to them: "I [a]*am* one hundred and twenty years old today. I can no longer [b]go out and come in. Also the LORD has said to me, [c]'You shall not cross over this Jordan.' 3The LORD your God [a]Himself crosses over before you; He will destroy these nations from before you, and you shall dispossess them. [b]Joshua himself crosses over before you, just [c]as the LORD has said. 4[a]And the LORD will do to them [b]as He did to Sihon and Og, the kings of the Amorites and their land, when He destroyed them. 5[a]The LORD will give them over to you, that you may do to them according to every commandment which I have commanded you. 6[a]Be strong and of good courage, [b]do not fear nor be afraid of them; for the LORD your God, [c]He *is* the One who goes with you. [d]He will not leave you nor forsake you."

7Then Moses called Joshua and said to him in the sight of all Israel, [a]"Be strong and of good courage, for you must go with this people to the land which the LORD has sworn to their fathers to give them, and you shall cause them to inherit it. 8And the LORD, [a]He *is* the One who goes before you. [b]He will be with you, He will not leave you nor forsake you; do not fear nor be dismayed."

The Law to Be Read Every Seven Years

9So Moses wrote this law [a]and delivered it to the priests, the sons of Levi, [b]who bore the ark of the covenant of the LORD, and to all the elders of Israel. 10And Moses commanded them, saying: "At the end of *every* seven years, at the appointed time in the [a]year of release, [b]at the Feast of Tabernacles, 11when all Israel comes to [a]appear before the LORD your God in the [b]place which He chooses, [c]you shall read this law before all Israel in their hearing. 12[a]Gather the people together, men and women and little ones, and the stranger who *is* within your gates, that they may hear and that they may learn to fear the LORD your God and carefully observe all the words of this law, 13and *that* their children, [a]who have not known it, [b]may hear and learn to fear the LORD your God

Deuteronomy 30:19

Dear Woman of Destiny,

Notice that God has to tell us to choose life. You would think it's obvious that we'd choose life, right? I believe that somewhere inside of us we all have a panic button we could push in the toughest situations for easy escape when Satan comes and throws catastrophe in our faces. But God set before us life and death, blessing and cursing. His Word says we can make a choice, and that choice can be life.

It's easy to talk about choosing life, but do we actually follow through with it in tough times? Deuteronomy 8:3 says, "Man shall not live by bread alone; but man lives by every word that proceeds from the mouth of the LORD." If we live by His every word, we need to find out what He is saying. When we find out what God has said, we need to do something with it and make the conscious choice to put it into action.

It's not always so easy, however. The Bible says that Satan comes to steal, kill, and destroy (see John 10:10). The word *steal* used there translates "to cut off from the limb or the shoot, to be broken off from its branches." Satan comes to steal your life, and the way he does that is by cutting you off from your life source. He cuts you off from the very branches of God that send life into you.

Later in that verse, however, Jesus adds a "but" when He says, "I have come that they may have life, and that they may have it more abundantly." The life Jesus is talking about here is life in the same sense God has it, not just being biologically alive and breathing. He is saying, "I have come that you might have all the highest and best." God has given us the highest and best by sending Christ to earth.

But that isn't all. Jesus says, "Not only do I come so that you might have life—all of My Father's highest and best—I come so that you might have it more abundantly." The word *abundantly* means "enough to spare, beyond measure, superabundant in quantity and superior in quality." Jesus came to remove everything put on you by the world and to replace it with everything that He is. He said, "I have come that they may have life" (John 10:10). There's a choice in this matter. "May have life" doesn't mean that because Jesus came and did all those things to redeem us—which He did—we automatically get to appropriate them into our lives. "May" means there's a condition, and we have to meet that condition in order to see the fruits of that abundant life.

The Bible says we walk by faith and not by sight (see 2 Cor. 5:7). The sight of things today can shake us to our core. It can destroy us if we start to believe the enemy's reports. So what do you do when the lies of the devil manifest themselves in the flesh? You get back into the Word of God and decide to make a choice. I believe God is saying, "Woman of Destiny, I have set before you life and death, blessing and cursing." Now it's up to you to choose life. And that's so that you and your descendants may live exceedingly abundantly, above all you could ever ask or think (see Eph. 3:20).

Lindsay Roberts

as long as you live in the land which you
cross the Jordan to possess."

Prediction of Israel's Rebellion

14 Then the LORD said to Moses, [a]"Behold, the days approach when you must
die; call Joshua, and present yourselves in
the tabernacle of meeting, that [b]I may
[1]inaugurate him."
So Moses and Joshua went and presented themselves in the tabernacle of meeting. 15 Now [a]the LORD appeared at the
tabernacle in a pillar of cloud, and the pillar of cloud stood above the door of the
tabernacle.
16 And the LORD said to Moses: "Behold,
you will [1]rest with your fathers; and this
people will [a]rise and [b]play the harlot with
the gods of the foreigners of the land,
where they go *to be* among them, and
they will [c]forsake Me and [d]break My covenant which I have made with them.
17 Then My anger shall be [a]aroused against
them in that day, and [b]I will forsake them,
and I will [c]hide My face from them, and
they shall be [1]devoured. And many evils
and troubles shall befall them, so that
they will say in that day, [d]'Have not these
evils come upon us because our God *is*
[e]not among us?' 18 And [a]I will surely hide
My face in that day because of all the evil
which they have done, in that they have
turned to other gods.
19 "Now therefore, write down this song
for yourselves, and teach it to the children
of Israel; put it in their mouths, that this
song may be [a]a witness for Me against the
children of Israel. 20 When I have brought
them to the land flowing with milk and
honey, of which I swore to their fathers,
and they have eaten and filled themselves
[a]and grown fat, [b]then they will turn to
other gods and serve them; and they will
provoke Me and break My covenant.
21 Then it shall be, [a]when many evils and
troubles have come upon them, that this
song will testify against them as a witness;
for it will not be forgotten in the mouths
of their descendants, for [b]I know the inclination [c]of their behavior today, even before I have brought them to the land of
which I swore *to give them.*"
22 Therefore Moses wrote this song the
same day, and taught it to the children of
Israel. 23 [a]Then He inaugurated Joshua
the son of Nun, and said, [b]"Be strong and
of good courage; for you shall bring the
children of Israel into the land of which I
swore to them, and I will be with you."
24 So it was, when Moses had completed
writing the words of this law in a book,
when they were finished, 25 that Moses
commanded the Levites, who bore the ark
of the covenant of the LORD, saying:
26 "Take this Book of the Law, [a]and put it
beside the ark of the covenant of the LORD
your God, that it may be there [b]as a witness against you; 27 [a]for I know your rebellion and your [b]stiff neck. *If* today, while I
am yet alive with you, you have been rebellious against the LORD, then how much
more after my death? 28 Gather to me all
the elders of your tribes, and your officers,
that I may speak these words in their
hearing [a]and call heaven and earth to witness against them. 29 For I know that after
my death you will [a]become utterly corrupt, and turn aside from the way which
I have commanded you. And [b]evil will befall you [c]in the latter days, because you
will do evil in the sight of the LORD, to
provoke Him to anger through the work
of your hands."

The Song of Moses

30 Then Moses spoke in the hearing of
all the assembly of Israel the words of this
song until they were ended:

32 "Give [a]ear, O heavens, and I will
speak;
And hear, O [b]earth, the words of
my mouth.
2 Let [a]my [1]teaching drop as the rain,
My speech distill as the dew,
[b]As raindrops on the tender herb,
And as showers on the grass.
3 For I proclaim the [a]name of the
LORD:
[b]Ascribe greatness to our God.
4 *He is* [a]the Rock, [b]His work *is*
perfect;
For all His ways *are* justice,
[c]A God of truth and [d]without
injustice;
Righteous and upright *is* He.
5 "They[a] have corrupted themselves;
They are not His children,
Because of their blemish:
A [b]perverse and crooked generation.
6 Do you thus [a]deal[1] with the LORD,
O foolish and unwise people?
Is He not [b]your Father, *who*
[c]bought you?

14 a Num. 27:13 b Deut. 3:28 1 *commission*
15 a Ex. 33:9
16 a Deut. 29:22 b Ex. 34:15 c Deut. 32:15 d Judg. 2:20 1 *Die and join your ancestors*
17 a Judg. 2:14; 6:13 b 2 Chr. 15:2 c Deut. 32:20 d Judg. 6:13 e Num. 14:42 1 *consumed*
18 a Deut. 31:17
19 a Deut. 31:22, 26
20 a Deut. 32:15–17 b Deut. 31:16
21 a Deut. 31:17 b Hos. 5:3 c Amos 5:25, 26
23 a Num. 27:23 b Deut. 31:7
26 a 2 Kin. 22:8 b Deut. 31:19
27 a Deut. 9:7, 24 b Ex. 32:9
28 a Deut. 30:19
29 a Judg. 2:19 b Deut. 28:15 c Gen. 49:1
CHAPTER 32
1 a Deut. 4:26 b Jer. 6:19
2 a Is. 55:10, 11 b Ps. 72:6 1 *doctrine*
3 a Deut. 28:58 b 1 Chr. 29:11
4 a Ps. 18:2 b 2 Sam. 22:31 c Is. 65:16 d Job 34:10
5 a Deut. 4:25; 31:29 b Phil. 2:15
6 a Ps. 116:12 b Is. 63:16 c Ps. 74:2 1 *repay the*

Has He not [d]made you and
established you?

7 "Remember[a] the days of old,
Consider the years of many
generations.
[b]Ask your father, and he will show
you;
Your elders, and they will tell you:
8 When the Most High [a]divided their
inheritance to the nations,
When He [b]separated the sons of
Adam,
He set the boundaries of the
peoples
According to the number of the
[1]children of Israel.
9 For [a]the LORD's portion *is* His
people;
Jacob *is* the place of His
inheritance.

10 "He found him [a]in a desert land
And in the wasteland, a howling
wilderness;
He encircled him, He instructed
him,
He [b]kept him as the [1]apple of His
eye.
11 [a]As an eagle stirs up its nest,
Hovers over its young,
Spreading out its wings, taking
them up,
Carrying them on its wings,
12 *So* the LORD alone led him,
And *there was* no foreign god with
him.

13 "He[a] made him ride in the heights
of the earth,
That he might eat the produce of
the fields;
He made him draw honey from the
rock,
And oil from the flinty rock;
14 Curds from the cattle, and milk of
the flock,
[a]With fat of lambs;
And rams of the breed of Bashan,
and goats,
With the choicest wheat;
And you drank wine, the [b]blood of
the grapes.

15 "But Jeshurun grew fat and kicked;
[a]You grew fat, you grew thick,
You are obese!
Then he [b]forsook God *who* [c]made
him,
And scornfully esteemed the [d]Rock
of his salvation.
16 [a]They provoked Him to jealousy
with foreign *gods;*
With [1]abominations they provoked
Him to anger.
17 [a]They sacrificed to demons, not to
God,
To gods they did not know,
To new *gods,* new arrivals
That your fathers did not fear.
18 [a]Of the Rock *who* begot you, you
are unmindful,
And have [b]forgotten the God who
fathered you.

19 "And[a] when the LORD saw *it,* He
spurned *them,*
Because of the provocation of His
sons and His daughters.
20 And He said: 'I will hide My face
from them,
I will see what their end *will be,*
For they *are* a perverse generation,
[a]Children in whom *is* no faith.
21 [a]They have provoked Me to jealousy
by *what* is not God;
They have moved Me to anger [b]by
their [1]foolish idols.
But [c]I will provoke them to
jealousy by *those who are* not a
nation;
I will move them to anger by a
foolish nation.
22 For [a]a fire is kindled in My anger,
And shall burn to the [1]lowest [2]hell;
It shall consume the earth with her
increase,
And set on fire the foundations of
the mountains.

23 'I will [a]heap disasters on them;
[b]I will spend My arrows on them.
24 *They shall be* wasted with hunger,
Devoured by pestilence and bitter
destruction;
I will also send against them the
[a]teeth of beasts,
With the poison of serpents of the
dust.
25 The sword shall destroy outside;
There shall be terror within
For the young man and virgin,
The nursing child with the man of
gray hairs.
26 [a]I would have said, "I will dash
them in pieces,
I will make the memory of them to
cease from among men,"

6 [d]Deut. 32:15
7 [a]Ps. 44:1 [b]Ps. 78:5–8
8 [a]Acts 17:26 [b]Gen. 11:8 [1]LXX, DSS *angels of God;* Symmachus, Lat. *sons of God*
9 [a]Ex. 19:5
10 [a]Jer. 2:6 [b]Ps. 17:8 [1]*pupil*
11 [a]Is. 31:5
13 [a]Is. 58:14
14 [a]Ps. 81:16 [b]Gen. 49:11
15 [a]Deut. 31:20 [b]Is. 1:4 [c]Is. 51:13 [d]Ps. 95:1
16 [a]1 Cor. 10:22 [1]*detestable acts*
17 [a]Rev. 9:20
18 [a]Is. 17:10 [b]Jer. 2:32
19 [a]Judg. 2:14
20 [a]Matt. 17:17
21 [a]Ps. 78:58 [b]Ps. 31:6 [c]Rom. 10:19 [1]*foolishness,* lit. *vanities*
22 [a]Lam. 4:11 [1]*lowest part of* [2]Or *Sheol*
23 [a]Ex. 32:12 [b]Ps. 7:12, 13
24 [a]Lev. 26:22
26 [a]Ezek. 20:23

27 Had I not feared the wrath of the enemy,
Lest their adversaries should misunderstand,
Lest they should say, [a]"Our hand *is* high;
And it is not the LORD who has done all this." '

28 "For they *are* a nation void of counsel,
Nor *is there any* understanding in them.
29 [a]Oh, that they were wise, *that* they understood this,
That they would consider their [b]latter end!
30 How could one chase a thousand,
And two put ten thousand to flight,
Unless their Rock [a]had sold them,
And the LORD had surrendered them?
31 For their rock *is* not like our Rock,
[a]Even our enemies themselves *being* judges.
32 For [a]their vine *is* of the vine of Sodom
And of the fields of Gomorrah;
Their grapes *are* grapes of gall,
Their clusters *are* bitter.
33 Their wine *is* [a]the poison of serpents,
And the cruel [b]venom of cobras.

34 '*Is* this not [a]laid up in store with Me,
Sealed up among My treasures?
35 [a]Vengeance is Mine, and recompense;
Their foot shall slip in *due* time;
[b]For the day of their calamity *is* at hand,
And the things to come hasten upon them.'

36 "For[a] the LORD will judge His people
[b]And have compassion on His servants,
When He sees that *their* power is gone,
And [c]*there is* no one *remaining,* bond or free.
37 He will say: [a]'Where *are* their gods,
The rock in which they sought refuge?
38 Who ate the fat of their sacrifices,
And drank the wine of their drink offering?
Let them rise and help you,
And be your refuge.

39 'Now see that [a]I, *even* I, *am* He,
And [b]*there is* no God besides Me;
[c]I kill and I make alive;
I wound and I heal;
Nor *is there any* who can deliver from My hand.
40 For I raise My hand to heaven,
And say, "*As* I live forever,
41 [a]If I [1]whet My glittering sword,
And My hand takes hold on judgment,
I will render vengeance to My enemies,
And repay those who hate Me.
42 I will make My arrows drunk with blood,
And My sword shall devour flesh,
With the blood of the slain and the captives,
From the heads of the leaders of the enemy." '

43 "Rejoice,[a] O Gentiles, *with* His [1]people;
For He will [b]avenge the blood of His servants,
And render vengeance to His adversaries;
He [c]will provide atonement for His land *and* His people."

44So Moses came with [1]Joshua the son
of Nun and spoke all the words of this
song in the hearing of the people. 45Moses
finished speaking all these words to all Israel, 46and he said to them: [a]"Set your
hearts on all the words which I testify
among you today, which you shall command your [b]children to be careful to observe—all the words of this law. 47For it
is not a [1]futile thing for you, because it *is*
your [a]life, and by this word you shall prolong *your* days in the land which you
cross over the Jordan to possess."

Moses to Die on Mount Nebo

48Then the LORD spoke to Moses that
very same day, saying: 49[a]"Go up this
mountain of the Abarim, Mount Nebo,
which *is* in the land of Moab, across from
Jericho; view the land of Canaan, which I
give to the children of Israel as a possession; 50and die on the mountain which
you ascend, and be [1]gathered to your

27 a Is. 10:12–15
29 a [Luke 19:42] b Deut. 31:29
30 a Judg. 2:14
31 a [1 Sam. 4:7, 8]
32 a Is. 1:8–10
33 a Ps. 58:4 b Rom. 3:13
34 a [Jer. 2:22]
35 a Heb. 10:30 b 2 Pet. 2:3
36 a Ps. 135:14 b Jer. 31:20 c 2 Kin. 14:26
37 a Judg. 10:14
39 a Is. 41:4; 43:10 b Is. 45:5 c 1 Sam. 2:6
41 a Is. 1:24; 66:16 *1 sharpen*
43 a Rom. 15:10 b Rev. 6:10; 19:2 c Ps. 65:3; 79:9; 85:1 *1* DSS fragment adds *And let all the gods (angels) worship Him;* cf. LXX and Heb. 1:6
44 *1* Heb. *Hoshea,* Num. 13:8, 16
46 a Ezek. 40:4; 44:5 b Deut. 11:19
47 a Deut. 8:3; 30:15–20 *1 vain*
49 a Num. 27:12–14
50 *1* Join your ancestors

Deuteronomy 32:30

Dear Woman of Destiny,

What a joy to know that you are growing in your prayer life! Prayer will empower you to accomplish the will of the Lord for your life. It will give you victory in the many battles you face. Your faith will grow as you hear the Lord in times of prayer, and battle strategy to defeat the enemy will be revealed. I remember how the Lord once spoke strategy to me during a difficult time in the ministry.

The ministry had grown to a place where we needed extra help. After I'd prayed for someone to help, a close friend agreed to work for me. She had only worked for the ministry for two weeks when she was involved in an accident. While driving on the freeway to pick me up for a meeting, her van was hit by another car. The van spun around and then rolled off the road. The only thing she was able to do at the time was cry out a one-word prayer: "Jesus!" In an emergency, that one word is more than enough.

The hand surgeon spent fifty-two hours suturing my friend's tendons, ligaments, and skin. Afterward, she spent weeks in physical therapy, but how thankful we were that her life was spared!

However, we still needed help in the office. Another person came to work for us at that time. Two weeks later, her husband's car was stolen. After purchasing another car, the new one was stolen. The car had been parked at their home for only a few hours. What was wrong? There were about two hundred intercessors throughout the nation praying for the ministry at that time. Why was all this happening to us? I had to have an answer.

After several days of fasting and prayer, I felt that the Lord spoke an answer. "How could one chase a thousand, and two put ten thousand to flight?" (Deut. 32:30). I continued to sense His instruction that each increase in the ministry required a corresponding increase in the foundation of prayer to lift up the ministry. Although there were many individual intercessors praying for us, we did not have corporate prayer meetings where the intercessors came together. The Lord's strategy had been revealed! A corporate prayer leader was appointed. She gathered several local intercessors together for prayer. Immediately, the attacks stopped. Since that time we have continued to seek the Lord for strategy as the ministry has grown. He has been faithful to speak to us. Prayer has been the foundation to hold the ministry up through the years. The Lord will do the same thing for you.

Your growth is important to the Lord. However, resistance to that growth will be a genuine obstacle. God wants to give you strategy to overcome the resistance and hindrance. As you spend time in prayer, He will speak to you. Obey Him. A new strength will come as you experience each conquest.

Woman of Destiny, spend much time in prayer. While in the place of prayer, listen to the Lord's instructions. Then, whatever He says, do it.

Barbara Wentroble

people, just as [a]Aaron your brother died on
Mount Hor and was gathered to his people; 51 because [a]you trespassed against Me
among the children of Israel at the waters
of [1]Meribah Kadesh, in the Wilderness of
Zin, because you [b]did not hallow Me in
the midst of the children of Israel. 52 [a]Yet
you shall see the land before *you,* though
you shall not go there, into the land
which I am giving to the children of Israel."

Moses' Final Blessing on Israel

33 Now this *is* [a]the blessing with which Moses [b]the man of God blessed the children of Israel before his death. 2 And he said:

[a]"The LORD came from Sinai,
And dawned on them from [b]Seir;
He shone forth from [c]Mount Paran,
And He came with [d]ten thousands
of saints;
From His right hand
Came a fiery law for them.
3 Yes, [a]He loves the people;
[b]All His saints *are* in Your hand;
They [c]sit down at Your feet;
Everyone [d]receives Your words.
4 [a]Moses [1]commanded a law for us,
[b]A heritage of the congregation of
Jacob.
5 And He was [a]King in [b]Jeshurun,
When the leaders of the people
were gathered,
All the tribes of Israel together.
6 "Let [a]Reuben live, and not die,
Nor let his men be few."

7 And this he said of [a]Judah:

"Hear, LORD, the voice of Judah,
And bring him to his people;
[b]Let his hands be sufficient for him,
And may You be [c]a help against his
enemies."

8 And of [a]Levi he said:

[b]"*Let* Your [1]Thummim and Your
Urim *be* with Your holy one,
[c]Whom You tested at Massah,
And with whom You contended at
the waters of Meribah,
9 [a]Who says of his father and mother,
'I have not [b]seen them';
[c]Nor did he acknowledge his
brothers,
Or know his own children;
For [d]they have observed Your word
And kept Your covenant.
10 [a]They shall teach Jacob Your
judgments,
And Israel Your law.
They shall put incense before You,
[b]And a whole burnt sacrifice on
Your altar.
11 Bless his substance, LORD,
And [a]accept the work of his hands;
Strike the loins of those who rise
against him,
And of those who hate him, that
they rise not again."

Bless the substance and ability of _____, Lord, and accept the work of their hands.

FROM DEUTERONOMY 33:11

12 Of Benjamin he said:

"The beloved of the LORD shall dwell
in safety by Him,
Who shelters him all the day long;
And he shall dwell between His
shoulders."

13 And of Joseph he said:

[a]"Blessed of the LORD *is* his land,
With the precious things of heaven,
with the [b]dew,
And the deep lying beneath,
14 With the precious fruits of the
sun,
With the precious produce of the
months,
15 With the best things of [a]the
ancient mountains,
With the precious things [b]of the
everlasting hills,
16 With the precious things of the
earth and its fullness,
And the favor of [a]Him who dwelt in
the bush.
Let *the blessing* come [b]'on the head
of Joseph,
And on the crown of the head of
him *who was* separate from his
brothers.'
17 His glory *is like* a [a]firstborn bull,

50 [a]Num. 20:25, 28; 33:38
51 [a]Num. 20:11–13 [b]Lev. 10:3 [1]Lit. *Contention at Kadesh*
52 [a]Deut. 34:1–5
CHAPTER 33
1 [a]Gen. 49:28 [b]Ps. 90
2 [a]Ps. 68:8, 17 [b]Deut. 2:1, 4 [c]Num. 10:12 [d]Dan. 7:10
3 [a]Hos. 11:1 [b]1 Sam. 2:9 [c][Luke 10:39] [d]Prov. 2:1
4 [a]John 1:17; 7:19 [b]Ps. 119:111 [1]*charged us with*
5 [a]Ex. 15:18 [b]Deut. 32:15
6 [a]Gen. 49:3, 4
7 [a]Gen. 49:8–12 [b]Gen. 49:8 [c]Ps. 146:5
8 [a]Gen. 49:5 [b]Ex. 28:30 [c]Ps. 81:7 [1]Lit. *Perfections and Your Lights*
9 [a][Num. 25:5–8] [b][Gen. 29:32] [c]Ex. 32:26–28 [d]Mal. 2:5, 6
10 [a]Lev. 10:11 [b]Ps. 51:19
11 [a]2 Sam. 24:23
13 [a]Gen. 49:22–26 [b]Gen. 27:28
15 [a]Gen. 49:26 [b]Hab. 3:6
16 [a]Ex. 3:2–4 [b]Gen. 49:26
17 [a]1 Chr. 5:1

And his horns *like* the [b]horns of
the wild ox;
Together with them
[c]He shall push the peoples
To the ends of the earth;
[d]They *are* the ten thousands of
Ephraim,
And they *are* the thousands of
Manasseh."

18 And of Zebulun he said:

[a]"Rejoice, Zebulun, in your going
out,
And Issachar in your tents!
19 They shall [a]call the peoples *to* the
mountain;
There [b]they shall offer sacrifices of
righteousness;
For they shall partake *of* the
abundance of the seas
And *of* treasures hidden in the
sand."

20 And of Gad he said:

"Blessed *is* he who [a]enlarges Gad;
He dwells as a lion,
And tears the arm and the crown of
his head.
21 [a]He provided the first *part* for
himself,
Because a lawgiver's portion was
reserved there.
[b]He came *with* the heads of the
people;
He administered the justice of the
LORD,
And His judgments with Israel."

22 And of Dan he said:

"Dan *is* a lion's whelp;
[a]He shall leap from Bashan."

23 And of Naphtali he said:

"O Naphtali, [a]satisfied with favor,
And full of the blessing of the LORD,
[b]Possess the west and the south."

24 And of Asher he said:

[a]"Asher *is* most blessed of sons;
Let him be favored by his brothers,
And let him [b]dip his foot in oil.
25 Your sandals *shall be* [a]iron and
bronze;
As your days, *so shall* your strength
be.

26 "*There is* [a]no one like the God of
[b]Jeshurun,
[c]*Who* rides the heavens to help you,
And in His excellency on the
clouds.
27 The eternal God *is your* [a]refuge,
And underneath *are* the everlasting
arms;
[b]He will thrust out the enemy from
before you,
And will say, 'Destroy!'
28 Then [a]Israel shall dwell in safety,
[b]The fountain of Jacob [c]alone,
In a land of grain and new wine;
His [d]heavens shall also drop dew.
29 [a]Happy *are* you, O Israel!
[b]Who *is* like you, a people saved by
the LORD,
[c]The shield of your help
And the sword of your majesty!
Your enemies [d]shall submit to
you,
And [e]you shall tread down their
[1]high places."

Moses Dies on Mount Nebo

34 Then Moses went up from the
plains of Moab [a]to Mount Nebo, to
the top of Pisgah, which is across from
Jericho. And the LORD showed him all the
land of Gilead as far as Dan, 2 all Naphtali
and the land of Ephraim and Manasseh,
all the land of Judah as far as the [1]Western
Sea, 3 the South, and the plain of the Valley of Jericho, [a]the city of palm trees, as
far as Zoar. 4 Then the LORD said to him,
[a]"This *is* the land of which I swore to give
Abraham, Isaac, and Jacob, saying, 'I will
give it to your descendants.' [b]I have
caused you to see *it* with your eyes, but
you shall not cross over there."
5 [a]So Moses the servant of the LORD died
there in the land of Moab, according to
the word of the LORD. 6 And He buried him
in a valley in the land of Moab, opposite
Beth Peor; but [a]no one knows his grave to
this day. 7 [a]Moses *was* one hundred and
twenty years old when he died. [b]His [1]eyes
were not dim nor his natural vigor [2]di-
minished. 8 And the children of Israel wept
for Moses in the plains of Moab [a]thirty
days. So the days of weeping *and* mourning for Moses ended.
9 Now Joshua the son of Nun was full of
the [a]spirit of wisdom, for [b]Moses had laid
his hands on him; so the children of Israel
heeded him, and did as the LORD had commanded Moses.
10 But since then there [a]has not arisen

17 [b] Num. 23:22 [c] Ps. 44:5 [d] Gen. 48:19
18 [a] Gen. 49:13–15
19 [a] Is. 2:3 [b] Ps. 4:5; 51:19
20 [a] 1 Chr. 12:8
21 [a] Num. 32:16, 17 [b] Josh. 4:12
22 [a] Josh. 19:47
23 [a] Gen. 49:21 [b] Josh. 19:32
24 [a] Gen. 49:20 [b] Job 29:6
25 [a] Deut. 8:9
26 [a] Ex. 15:11 [b] Deut. 32:15 [c] Ps. 68:3, 33, 34; 104:3
27 [a] [Ps. 90:1; 91:2, 9] [b] Deut. 9:3–5
28 [a] Jer. 23:6; 33:16 [b] Deut. 8:7, 8 [c] Num. 23:9 [d] Gen. 27:28
29 [a] Ps. 144:15 [b] 2 Sam. 7:23 [c] Ps. 115:9 [d] Ps. 18:44; 66:3 [e] Num. 33:52 *[1] Places for pagan worship*

CHAPTER 34
1 [a] Deut. 32:49
2 *[1] Mediterranean*
3 [a] 2 Chr. 28:15
4 [a] Gen. 12:7 [b] Deut. 3:27
5 [a] Deut. 32:50; Josh. 1:1, 2
6 [a] Jude 9
7 [a] Deut. 31:2 [b] Gen. 27:1; 48:10 *[1] eyesight was not weakened [2] reduced*
8 [a] Gen. 50:3, 10
9 [a] Is. 11:2 [b] Num. 27:18, 23
10 [a] Deut. 18:15, 18

in Israel a prophet like Moses, [b]whom the
LORD knew face to face, 11in all [a]the signs
and wonders which the LORD sent him to
do in the land of Egypt, before Pharaoh,
before all his servants, and in all his land,
12and by all that mighty power and all the
great terror which Moses performed in
the sight of all Israel.

10 [b] Ex. 33:11
11 [a] Deut. 7:19

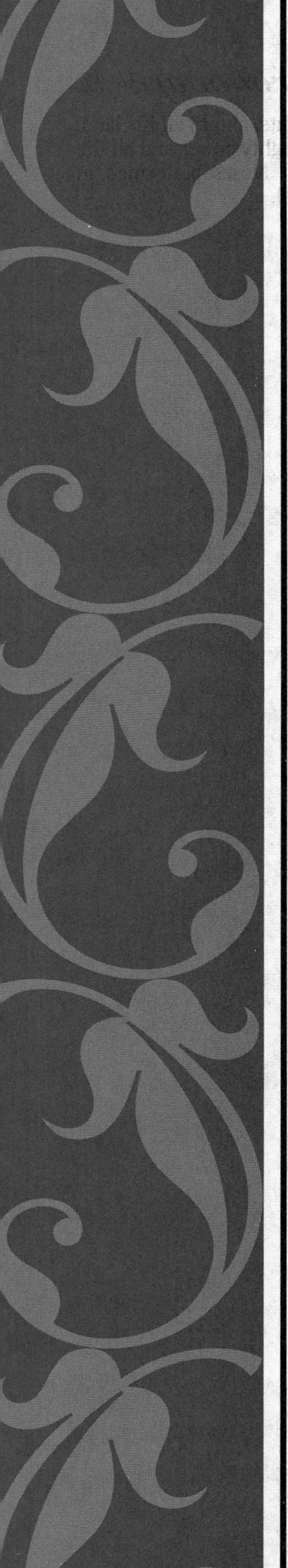

AUTHOR: *Uncertain*
DATE: *1400–1375 B.C.*
THEME: *Possessing the Inheritance*
KEY WORDS: *Obedience, Covenant, Courage*

JOSHUA

Dear Woman of Destiny,

The Book of Joshua is a book of encouragement. Often, women are called to stand in faith and lead by example. Like Joshua, we can be enabled by God's grace to banish the enemy and take charge of our circumstances. As we follow God's command to meditate in His Word day and night, we are empowered, not only to believe, but also to enter into the promise.

His love and mine,

Marilyn Hickey

God's Commission to Joshua

After the death of Moses the servant
of the LORD, it came to pass that
the LORD spoke to Joshua the son
of Nun, Moses' [a]assistant, saying: 2[a]"Moses My servant is dead. Now therefore,
arise, go over this Jordan, you and all this
people, to the land which I am giving to
them—the children of Israel. 3[a]Every
place that the sole of your foot will tread
upon I have given you, as I said to Moses.
4[a]From the wilderness and this Lebanon
as far as the great river, the River Euphrates, all the land of the Hittites, and to the
Great Sea toward the going down of the
sun, shall be your territory. 5[a]No man
shall *be able to* stand before you all the
days of your life; [b]as I was with Moses, *so*
[c]I will be with you. [d]I will not leave you
nor forsake you. 6[a]Be strong and of good
courage, for to this people you shall [1]di-
vide as an inheritance the land which I
swore to their fathers to give them.
7 Only be strong and very courageous,
that you may observe to do according
to all the law [a]which Moses My servant
commanded you; [b]do not turn from
it to the right hand or to the left, that
you may [1]prosper wherever you go.
8[a]This Book of the Law shall not depart
from your mouth, but [b]you[1] shall meditate in it day and night, that you may
observe to do according to all that is
written in it. For then you will make
your way prosperous, and then you will
have good success. 9[a]Have I not commanded you? Be strong and of good courage; [b]do not be afraid, nor be dismayed,
for the LORD your God *is* with you wherever you go."

I pray, Father, that _____ will meditate on this Book of the Law both day and night so that they may do all that is written in it. Then may their way be prosperous and successful.

FROM JOSHUA 1:8

The Order to Cross the Jordan

10Then Joshua commanded the officers
of the people, saying, 11"Pass through the
camp and command the people, saying,
'Prepare provisions for yourselves, for
[a]within three days you will cross over this
Jordan, to go in to possess the land which
the LORD your God is giving you to possess.' "
12And to the Reubenites, the Gadites,
and half the tribe of Manasseh Joshua
spoke, saying, 13"Remember [a]the word
which Moses the servant of the LORD commanded you, saying, 'The LORD your God
is giving you rest and is giving you this
land.' 14Your wives, your little ones, and
your livestock shall remain in the land
which Moses gave you on this side of the
Jordan. But you shall [1]pass before your
brethren armed, all your mighty men of
valor, and help them, 15until the LORD has
given your brethren rest, as He *gave* you,
and they also have taken possession of the
land which the LORD your God is giving
them. [a]Then you shall return to the land
of your possession and enjoy it, which Moses the LORD's servant gave you on this
side of the Jordan toward the sunrise."
16So they answered Joshua, saying, "All
that you command us we will do, and
wherever you send us we will go. 17Just as
we heeded Moses in all things, so we will
heed you. Only the LORD your God [a]be
with you, as He was with Moses. 18Who-
ever rebels against your command and
does not heed your words, in all that you
command him, shall be put to death. Only
be strong and of good courage."

Rahab Hides the Spies

2 Now Joshua the son of Nun sent out
two men [a]from [1]Acacia Grove to spy
secretly, saying, "Go, view the land, especially Jericho."
So they went, and [b]came to the house
of a harlot named [c]Rahab, and [2]lodged
there. 2And [a]it was told the king of Jericho, saying, "Behold, men have come here
tonight from the children of Israel to
search out the country."
3So the king of Jericho sent to Rahab,
saying, "Bring out the men who have
come to you, who have entered your
house, for they have come to search out
all the country."

CHAPTER 1
1 a Ex. 24:13
2 a Deut. 34:5
3 a Deut. 11:24
4 a Gen. 15:18
5 a Deut. 7:24 b Ex. 3:12 c Deut. 31:8, 23 d Deut. 31:6, 7
6 a Deut. 31:7, 23 *1 give as a possession*
7 a Deut. 31:7 b Deut. 5:32 *1 have success* or *act wisely*
8 a Josh. 8:34 b Ps. 1:1–3 *1 you shall be constantly in*
9 a Deut. 31:7 b Ps. 27:1
11 a Deut. 9:1
13 a Num. 32:20–28
14 *1 cross over ahead of*
15 a Josh. 22:1–4
17 a 1 Sam. 20:13

CHAPTER 2
1 a Num. 25:1 b James 2:25 c Matt. 1:5 1 Heb. *Shittim* 2 Lit. *lay down*
2 a Josh. 2:22

Joshua 1:7–9

Dear Woman of Destiny,

If you have met and conquered these enemies of the Spirit-led life—hatred, fear, unbelief, and despair—then no doubt you are living courageously and joyously. Courage and joy are built on faith and love and grow out of a healthy, well-nourished spirit.

Courage has nothing to do with natural reason. Courage says in the face of reason, "I will not quit." That is the posture of faith. Nor is courage merely natural stubbornness or human grit and determination. It is not a human quality; it is a spiritual outgrowth of faith in the integrity of God, as revealed in His Word. Things may look bleak, but courage will carry you above your circumstances.

Courage embraces failure and breathes victory into it. Courage redeems the defeats and failures of the past, and uses them as a foundation upon which to build future successes. Courage rallies a weak and tired body, driving out exhaustion. It will not let you quit or give up.

Is your courage rooted in the promises of God? The devil hates courage, and that is why he fights your faith. Courage will cause you to bounce right back. You may get knocked down, but you won't stay down (see 2 Cor. 4:8–10). When you live by faith and allow courage to flow out of your conviction, you are being led by the Spirit.

The Spirit-led life is also marked by joy. Joy is not the same as happiness. Happiness requires a happening, connected with physical circumstances around you. But joy does not depend upon what other people say or don't say, do or don't do. Happiness comes from the senses. Joy comes from the Spirit.

Joy bubbles up from within even when everything has gone wrong. It is a pulsing, creative, indestructible thing, a force that flows from your recreated spirit. And how that frustrates the enemy! No one can quench your joy but you. You are not crazy when you are joyful in the tough times; you are behaving like a normal Spirit-led person who has refused to be led about by circumstances.

Have you ever been in a situation when you were so physically weary you wondered if you could put one foot in front of the other? Do you remember how your mind turned to God's promises? You simply said, "Thank You, Jesus. You know right where I am and just what I have been through, and You care."

Draw on the One who is at work within you. Be led every day with His courage and joy. Study the revelation of His Word, especially the exemplary life of Jesus. Allow the Holy Spirit to reveal truth to you; then conform your own thinking to it. Put every newly discovered revelation into practice.

Then, as you walk in the redemptive truth, your lifestyle will be dynamic. You will truly be directed by the Spirit, and His limitless creativity will begin to be expressed in every area of your life.

LaDonna Osborn

4[a]Then the woman took the two men
and hid them. So she said, "Yes, the men
came to me, but I did not know where
they *were* from. 5And it happened as the
gate was being shut, when it was dark,
that the men went out. Where the men
went I do not know; pursue them quickly,
for you may overtake them." 6(But [a]she
had brought them up to the roof and hidden them with the stalks of flax, which
she had laid in order on the roof.) 7Then
the men pursued them by the road to the
Jordan, to the fords. And as soon as those
who pursued them had gone out, they
shut the gate.

8Now before they lay down, she came
up to them on the roof, 9and said to the
men: [a]"I know that the LORD has given
you the land, that [b]the terror of you has
fallen on us, and that all the inhabitants
of the land [c]are fainthearted because of
you. 10For we have heard how the LORD
[a]dried up the water of the Red Sea for you
when you came out of Egypt, and [b]what
you did to the two kings of the Amorites
who *were* on the other side of the Jordan,
Sihon and Og, whom you [c]utterly destroyed. 11And as soon as we [a]heard *these
things,* [b]our hearts melted; neither did
there remain any more courage in anyone
because of you, for [c]the LORD your God,
He *is* God in heaven above and on earth
beneath. 12Now therefore, I beg you,
[a]swear to me by the LORD, since I have
shown you kindness, that you also will
show kindness to [b]my father's house, and
[c]give me [1]a true token, 13and [a]spare my
father, my mother, my brothers, my sisters, and all that they have, and deliver
our lives from death."

14So the men answered her, "Our lives
for yours, if none of you tell this business
of ours. And it shall be, when the LORD has
given us the land, that [a]we will deal kindly
and truly with you."

15Then she [a]let them down by a rope
through the window, for her house *was*
on the city wall; she dwelt on the wall.
16And she said to them, "Get to the mountain, lest the pursuers meet you. Hide
there three days, until the pursuers have
returned. Afterward you may go your
way."

17So the men said to her: "We *will be*
[a]blameless[1] of this oath of yours which
you have made us swear, 18[a]unless, *when*
we come into the land, you bind this line
of scarlet cord in the window through
which you let us down, [b]and unless you
[1]bring your father, your mother, your
brothers, and all your father's household
to your own home. 19So it shall be *that*
whoever goes outside the doors of your
house into the street, his blood *shall be*
on his own head, and we *will be* [1]guiltless.
And whoever is with you in the house,
[a]his [2]blood *shall be* on our head if a hand
is laid on him. 20And if you tell this business of ours, then we will be [1]free from
your oath which you made us swear."

21Then she said, "According to your
words, so *be* it." And she sent them away,
and they departed. And she bound the
scarlet cord in the window.

22They departed and went to the mountain, and stayed there three days until the
pursuers returned. The pursuers sought
them all along the way, but did not find
them. 23So the two men returned, descended from the mountain, and crossed
over; and they came to Joshua the son of
Nun, and told him all that had befallen
them. 24And they said to Joshua, "Truly
[a]the LORD has delivered all the land into
our hands, for indeed all the inhabitants
of the country are fainthearted because
of us."

Israel Crosses the Jordan

3 Then Joshua rose early in the morning; and they set out [a]from [1]Acacia
Grove and came to the Jordan, he and all
the children of Israel, and lodged there
before they crossed over. 2So it was, [a]after
three days, that the officers went through
the camp; 3and they commanded the people, saying, [a]"When you see the ark of the
covenant of the LORD your God, [b]and the
priests, the Levites, [1]bearing it, then you
shall set out from your place and go after
it. 4[a]Yet there shall be a space between
you and it, about two thousand cubits by
measure. Do not come near it, that you
may know the way by which you must go,
for you have not passed *this* way before."

5And Joshua said to the people, [a]"Sanctify[1] yourselves, for tomorrow the LORD
will do wonders among you." 6Then Joshua spoke to the priests, saying, [a]"Take up
the ark of the covenant and cross over before the people."

So they took up the ark of the covenant
and went before the people.

7And the LORD said to Joshua, "This day
I will begin to [a]exalt[1] you in the sight of
all Israel, that they may know that, [b]as I

---

4 a 2 Sam. 17:19, 20
6 a Ex. 1:17
9 a Deut. 1:8 b Deut. 2:25; 11:25 c Josh. 5:1
10 a Ex. 14:21 b Num. 21:21–35 c Josh. 6:21
11 a Ex. 15:14, 15 b Josh. 5:1; 7:5 c Deut. 4:39
12 a 1 Sam. 20:14, 15, 17 b 1 Tim. 5:8 c Josh. 2:18 *1 a pledge of truth*
13 a Josh. 6:23–25
14 a Judg. 1:24
15 a Acts 9:25
17 a Ex. 20:7 *1 free from obligation to this oath*
18 a Josh. 2:12 b Josh. 6:23 *1 Lit. gather*
19 a 1 Kin. 2:32 *1 free from obligation* *2 guilt of bloodshed*
20 *1 free from obligation to*
24 a Ex. 23:31

CHAPTER 3
1 a Josh. 2:1 *1 Heb. Shittim*
2 a Josh. 1:10, 11
3 a Num. 10:33 b Deut. 31:9, 25 *1 carrying*
4 a Ex. 19:12
5 a Josh. 7:13 *1 Consecrate*
6 a Num. 4:15
7 a Josh. 4:14 b Josh. 1:5, 9 *1 make you great*

was with Moses, *so* I will be with you.
8You shall command [a]the priests who
bear the ark of the covenant, saying,
'When you have come to the edge of the
water of the Jordan, [b]you shall stand in
the Jordan.' "
9So Joshua said to the children of Israel, "Come here, and hear the words of the
LORD your God." 10And Joshua said, "By
this you shall know that [a]the living God *is*
among you, and *that* He will without fail
[b]drive out from before you the [c]Canaan-
ites and the Hittites and the Hivites and
the Perizzites and the Girgashites and the
Amorites and the Jebusites: 11Behold, the
ark of the covenant of [a]the Lord of all the
earth is crossing over before you into
the Jordan. 12Now therefore, [a]take for
yourselves twelve men from the tribes of
Israel, one man from every tribe. 13And it
shall come to pass, [a]as soon as the soles
of the feet of the priests who bear the ark
of the LORD, [b]the Lord of all the earth,
shall rest in the waters of the Jordan, *that*
the waters of the Jordan shall be cut off,
the waters that come down from upstream, and they [c]shall stand as a heap."
14So it was, when the people set out
from their camp to cross over the Jordan,
with the priests bearing the [a]ark of the
covenant before the people, 15and as those
who bore the ark came to the Jordan, and
[a]the feet of the priests who bore the ark
dipped in the edge of the water (for the
[b]Jordan overflows all its banks [c]during
the whole time of harvest), 16that the waters which came down from upstream
stood *still, and* rose in a heap very far
away [1]at Adam, the city that *is* beside
[a]Zaretan. So the waters that went down
[b]into the Sea of the Arabah, [c]the Salt Sea,
failed, *and* were cut off; and the people
crossed over opposite Jericho. 17Then the
priests who bore the ark of the covenant
of the LORD stood firm on dry ground in
the midst of the Jordan; [a]and all Israel
crossed over on dry ground, until all the
people had crossed completely over the
Jordan.

The Memorial Stones

4 And it came to pass, when all the people had completely crossed [a]over the
Jordan, that the LORD spoke to Joshua,
saying: 2[a]"Take for yourselves twelve men
from the people, one man from every
tribe, 3and command them, saying, 'Take
for yourselves twelve stones from here,
out of the midst of the Jordan, from the
place where [a]the priests' feet stood firm.
You shall carry them over with you and
leave them in [b]the lodging place where
you lodge tonight.' "
4Then Joshua called the twelve men
whom he had appointed from the children
of Israel, one man from every tribe; 5and
Joshua said to them: "Cross over before
the ark of the LORD your God into the
midst of the Jordan, and each one of you
take up a stone on his shoulder, according
to the number of the tribes of the children
of Israel, 6that this may be [a]a sign among
you [b]when your children ask in time to
come, saying, 'What do these stones *mean*
to you?' 7Then you shall answer them that
[a]the waters of the Jordan were cut off before the ark of the covenant of the LORD;
when it crossed over the Jordan, the waters of the Jordan were cut off. And these
stones shall be for [b]a memorial to the
children of Israel forever."
8And the children of Israel did so, just
as Joshua commanded, and took up
twelve stones from the midst of the Jordan, as the LORD had spoken to Joshua,
according to the number of the tribes of
the children of Israel, and carried them
over with them to the place where they
lodged, and laid them down there. 9Then
Joshua set up twelve stones in the midst
of the Jordan, in the place where the feet
of the priests who bore the ark of the covenant stood; and they are there to this
day.
10So the priests who bore the ark stood
in the midst of the Jordan until everything was finished that the LORD had
commanded Joshua to speak to the people, according to all that Moses had commanded Joshua; and the people hurried
and crossed over. 11Then it came to pass,
when all the people had completely
crossed over, that the [a]ark of the LORD
and the priests crossed over in the presence of the people. 12And [a]the men of
Reuben, the men of Gad, and half the tribe
of Manasseh crossed over armed before
the children of Israel, as Moses had spoken to them. 13About forty thousand [1]pre-
pared for war crossed over before the
LORD for battle, to the plains of Jericho.
14On that day the LORD [a]exalted[1] Joshua
in the sight of all Israel; and they feared
him, as they had feared Moses, all the days
of his life.

8 [a]Josh. 3:3 [b]Josh. 3:17
10 [a]1 Thess. 1:9 [b]Ex. 33:2 [c]Acts 13:19
11 [a]Zech. 4:14; 6:5
12 [a]Josh. 4:2, 4
13 [a]Josh. 3:15, 16 [b]Josh. 3:11 [c]Ps. 78:13; 114:3
14 [a]Acts 7:44, 45
15 [a]Josh. 3:13 [b]1 Chr. 12:15 [c]Josh. 4:18; 5:10, 12
16 [a]1 Kin. 4:12; 7:46 [b]Deut. 3:17 [c]Gen. 14:3 [1]Qr., many mss. and vss., *from Adam*
17 [a]Ex. 3:8; 6:1–8; 14:21, 22, 29; 33:1
CHAPTER 4
1 [a]Deut. 27:2
2 [a]Josh. 3:12
3 [a]Josh. 3:13 [b]Josh. 4:19, 20
6 [a]Deut. 27:2 [b]Deut. 6:20
7 [a]Josh. 3:13, 16 [b]Num. 16:40
11 [a]Josh. 3:11; 6:11
12 [a]Num. 32:17, 20, 27, 28
13 [1]*equipped*
14 [a]Josh. 3:7 [1]*made Joshua great*

15 Then the LORD spoke to Joshua, saying, 16 "Command the priests who bear
[a]the ark of the Testimony to come up
from the Jordan." 17 Joshua therefore
commanded the priests, saying, "Come up
from the Jordan." 18 And it came to pass,
when the priests who bore the ark of the
covenant of the LORD had come from the
midst of the Jordan, *and* the soles of the
priests' feet touched the dry land, that
the waters of the Jordan returned to their
place [a]and overflowed all its banks as before.
19 Now the people came up from the
Jordan on the tenth *day* of the first
month, and they camped [a]in Gilgal on
the east border of Jericho. 20 And [a]those
twelve stones which they took out of the
Jordan, Joshua set up in Gilgal. 21 Then he
spoke to the children of Israel, saying:
[a]"When your children ask their fathers in
time to come, saying, 'What *are* these
stones?' 22 then you shall let your children
know, saying, [a]'Israel crossed over this
Jordan on [b]dry land'; 23 for the LORD your
God dried up the waters of the Jordan before you until you had crossed over, as the
LORD your God did to the Red Sea, [a]which
He dried up before us until we had crossed
over, 24 [a]that all the peoples of the earth
may know the hand of the LORD, that it
is [b]mighty, that you may [c]fear the LORD
your God [1]forever."

Father, may ___ know
Your hand is mighty and
fear You forever.
FROM JOSHUA 4:24

The Second Generation Circumcised

5 So it was, when all the kings of the
Amorites who *were* on the west side of
the Jordan, and all the kings of the Canaanites [a]who *were* by the sea, [b]heard
that the LORD had dried up the waters of
the Jordan from before the children of
Israel until [1]we had crossed over, that
[2]their heart melted; [c]and there was no
spirit in them any longer because of the
children of Israel.

2 At that time the LORD said to Joshua,
"Make [a]flint knives for yourself, and circumcise the sons of Israel again the second time." 3 So Joshua made flint knives
for himself, and circumcised the sons of
Israel at [1]the hill of the foreskins. 4 And
this *is* the reason why Joshua circumcised
them: [a]All the people who came out of
Egypt *who were* males, all the men of war,
had died in the wilderness on the way,
after they had come out of Egypt. 5 For all
the people who came out had been circumcised, but all the people born in the
wilderness, on the way as they came out
of Egypt, had not been circumcised. 6 For
the children of Israel walked [a]forty years
in the wilderness, till all the people *who*
were men of war, who came out of Egypt,
were [1]consumed, because they did not
obey the voice of the LORD—to whom the
LORD swore that [b]He would not show
them the land which the LORD had sworn
to their fathers that He would give us, [c]"a
land flowing with milk and honey." 7 Then
Joshua circumcised [a]their sons *whom* He
raised up in their place; for they were uncircumcised, because they had not been
circumcised on the way.
8 So it was, when they had finished cir-
cumcising all the people, that they stayed
in their places in the camp [a]till they were
healed. 9 Then the LORD said to Joshua,
"This day I have rolled away [a]the reproach
of Egypt from you." Therefore the name of
the place is called [b]Gilgal[1] to this day.
10 Now the children of Israel camped in
Gilgal, and kept the Passover [a]on the
fourteenth day of the month at twilight
on the plains of Jericho. 11 And they ate of
the produce of the land on the day after
the Passover, unleavened bread and
[1]parched grain, on the very same day.
12 Then [a]the manna ceased on the day after they had eaten the produce of the land;
and the children of Israel no longer had
manna, but they ate the food of the land
of Canaan that year.

The Commander of the Army of the Lord

13 And it came to pass, when Joshua was
by Jericho, that he lifted his eyes and
looked, and behold, [a]a Man stood opposite
him [b]with His sword drawn in His hand.
And Joshua went to Him and said to Him,
"*Are* You for us or for our adversaries?"
14 So He said, "No, but *as* Commander
of the army of the LORD I have now come."

16 a Ex. 25:16, 22
18 a Josh. 3:15
19 a Josh. 5:9
20 a Josh. 4:3; 5:9, 10
21 a Josh. 4:6
22 a Deut. 26:5–9 b Josh. 3:17
23 a Ex. 14:21
24 a 1 Kin. 8:42 b 1 Chr. 29:12 c Jer. 10:7 *1* Lit. *all days*

CHAPTER 5
1 a Num. 13:29 b Ex. 15:14, 15 c Josh. 2:10, 11; 9:9 *1* So with Kt.; Qr., some Heb. mss. and editions, LXX, Syr., Tg., Vg. *they* *2 their courage failed*
2 a Ex. 4:25
3 *1* Heb. *Gibeath Haaraloth*
4 a Deut. 2:14–16
6 a Num. 14:33 b Heb. 3:11 c Ex. 3:8 *1 destroyed*
7 a Deut. 1:39
8 a Gen. 34:25
9 a Gen. 34:14 b Josh. 4:19 *1* Lit. *Rolling*
10 a Ex. 12:6
11 *1 roasted*
12 a Ex. 16:35
13 a Gen. 18:1, 2; 32:24, 30 b Num. 22:23

And Joshua [a]fell on his face to the earth and [b]worshiped, and said to Him, "What does my Lord say to His servant?"

15Then the Commander of the LORD's army said to Joshua, [a]"Take your sandal off your foot, for the place where you stand *is* holy." And Joshua did so.

The Destruction of Jericho

6 Now [a]Jericho was securely shut up because of the children of Israel; none went out, and none came in. 2And the LORD said to Joshua: "See! [a]I have given Jericho into your hand, its [b]king, *and* the mighty men of valor. 3You shall march around the city, all *you* men of war; you shall go all around the city once. This you shall do six days. 4And seven priests shall bear seven [a]trumpets of rams' horns before the ark. But the seventh day you shall march around the city [b]seven times, and [c]the priests shall blow the trumpets. 5It shall come to pass, when they make a long *blast* with the ram's horn, *and* when you hear the sound of the trumpet, that all the people shall shout with a great shout; then the wall of the city will fall down flat. And the people shall go up every man straight before him."

6Then Joshua the son of Nun called the priests and said to them, "Take up the ark of the covenant, and let seven priests bear seven trumpets of rams' horns before the ark of the LORD." 7And he said to the people, "Proceed, and march around the city, and let him who is armed advance before the ark of the LORD."

8So it was, when Joshua had spoken to the people, that the seven priests bearing the seven trumpets of rams' horns before the LORD advanced and blew the trumpets, and the ark of the covenant of the LORD followed them. 9The armed men went before the priests who blew the trumpets, [a]and the rear guard came after the ark, while *the priests* continued blowing the trumpets. 10Now Joshua had commanded the people, saying, "You shall not shout or make any noise with your voice, nor shall a word proceed out of your mouth, until the day I say to you, 'Shout!' Then you shall shout." 11So he had [a]the ark of the LORD circle the city, going around *it* once. Then they came into the camp and [1]lodged in the camp.

12And Joshua rose early in the morning, [a]and the priests took up the ark of the LORD. 13Then seven priests bearing seven trumpets of rams' horns before the ark of the LORD went on continually and blew with the trumpets. And the armed men went before them. But the rear guard came after the ark of the LORD, while *the priests* continued blowing the trumpets. 14And the second day they marched around the city once and returned to the camp. So they did six days.

15But it came to pass on the seventh day that they rose early, about the dawning of the day, and marched around the city seven times in the same manner. On that day only they marched around the city seven times. 16And the seventh time it happened, when the priests blew the trumpets, that Joshua said to the people: "Shout, for the LORD has given you the city! 17Now the city shall be [a]doomed by the LORD to destruction, it and all who *are* in it. Only [b]Rahab the harlot shall live, she and all who *are* with her in the house, because [c]she hid the messengers that we sent. 18And you, [a]by all means abstain from the accursed things, lest you become accursed when you take of the accursed things, and make the camp of Israel a curse, [b]and trouble it. 19But all the silver and gold, and vessels of bronze and iron, *are* [1]consecrated to the LORD; they [2]shall come into the treasury of the LORD."

20So the people shouted when *the priests* blew the trumpets. And it happened when the people heard the sound of the trumpet, and the people shouted with a great shout, that [a]the wall fell down flat. Then the people went up into the city, every man straight before him, and they took the city. 21And they [a]utterly destroyed all that *was* in the city, both man and woman, young and old, ox and sheep and donkey, with the edge of the sword.

22But Joshua had said to the two men who had spied out the country, "Go into the harlot's house, and from there bring out the woman and all that she has, [a]as you swore to her." 23And the young men who had been spies went in and brought out Rahab, [a]her father, her mother, her brothers, and all that she had. So they brought out all her relatives and left them outside the camp of Israel. 24But they burned the city and all that *was* in it with fire. Only the silver and gold, and the vessels of bronze and iron, they put into the treasury of the house of the LORD. 25And Joshua spared Rahab the harlot, her father's household, and all that she had. So

14 a Gen. 17:3 b Ex. 34:8
15 a Ex. 3:5

CHAPTER 6
1 a Josh. 2:1
2 a Josh. 2:9, 24; 8:1 b Deut. 7:24
4 a Lev. 25:9 b 1 Kin. 18:43 c Num. 10:8
9 a Num. 10:25
11 a Josh. 4:11 *1 spent the night*
12 a Deut. 31:25
17 a Deut. 13:17 b Matt. 1:5 c Josh. 2:4, 6
18 a Deut. 7:26 b Josh. 7:1, 12, 25
19 *1 set apart 2 shall go*
20 a Heb. 11:30
21 a Deut. 7:2; 20:16, 17
22 a Josh. 2:12–19
23 a Josh. 2:13

[a]she dwells in Israel to this day, because
she hid the messengers whom Joshua
sent to spy out Jericho.
26 Then Joshua [1]charged *them* at that
time, saying, [a]"Cursed *be* the man before
the LORD who rises up and builds this city
Jericho; he shall lay its foundation with
his firstborn, and with his youngest he
shall set up its gates."
27 So the LORD was with Joshua, and his
fame spread throughout all the country.

Defeat at Ai

7 But the children of Israel [1]committed
a [a]trespass regarding the [b]accursed[2]
things, for [c]Achan the son of Carmi, the
son of [3]Zabdi, the son of Zerah, of the
tribe of Judah, took of the accursed
things; so the anger of the LORD burned
against the children of Israel.
2 Now Joshua sent men from Jericho to
Ai, which *is* beside Beth Aven, on the east
side of Bethel, and spoke to them, saying,
"Go up and spy out the country." So the
men went up and spied out Ai. 3 And they
returned to Joshua and said to him, "Do
not let all the people go up, but let about
two or three thousand men go up and attack Ai. Do not weary all the people there,
for *the people of Ai are* few." 4 So about
three thousand men went up there from
the people, [a]but they fled before the men
of Ai. 5 And the men of Ai struck down
about thirty-six men, for they chased
them *from* before the gate as far as Sheba-
rim, and struck them down on the

25 a [Matt. 1:5]
26 a 1 Kin. 16:34
1 *warned*

CHAPTER 7
1 a Josh. 7:20, 21
b Josh. 6:17–19
c Josh. 22:20
1 *acted unfaithfully*
2 *devoted*
3 *Zimri,* 1 Chr. 2:6

4 a Lev. 26:17

RAHAB

When people in Jericho talked about Rahab, they probably whispered. She was a harlot; but she was a harlot with a destiny. She did not know the God of Israel, but He knew her. And He had a plan for her before her plans included Him.

She was brave enough to hide Joshua's two spies and cunning enough to keep from getting caught. She was crucial to the success of their mission and, therefore, to Israel's victorious arrival in the land that God had promised. But as important as Rahab's cooperation was to Joshua's military strategy, Rahab herself was even more important to God. He wanted to make the harlot holy. He wanted to clean her up and make her pure. He wanted to be her God and to give her a love unlike any she had ever known. So He arranged for the spies to show up on her doorstep, and sometime during that divine appointment, she rejected her pagan ways and declared, "The LORD your God, He is God" (Josh. 2:11).

God is not looking for women who appear to be perfect. He is looking for women who are willing. He is looking for women who have Rahab's kind of courage. He is looking for women who will risk everything to trust Him. He is eager to forgive sin and to use people in spite of their past. God redeemed Rahab to the point that she is listed along with other godly men and women in the Hebrews 11 "Hall of Faith."

Woman of Destiny, do you have a past you are not proud of? Never think that you have exhausted God's mercy. Never think that He cannot make you clean. Never think that you are not good enough to be used mightily in His service. Whatever you have done, whatever has been done to you, He wants you. And He calls you now to take your place in His eternal plan.

descent; therefore [a]the[1] hearts of the people melted and became like water.
6Then Joshua [a]tore his clothes, and fell
to the earth on his face before the ark of
the LORD until evening, he and the elders
of Israel; and they [b]put dust on their
heads. 7And Joshua said, "Alas, Lord
[1]GOD, [a]why have You brought this people
over the Jordan at all—to deliver us into
the hand of the Amorites, to destroy us?
Oh, that we had been content, and dwelt
on the other side of the Jordan! 8O Lord,
what shall I say when Israel turns its
[1]back before its enemies? 9For the Canaanites and all the inhabitants of the
land will hear *it,* and surround us, and
[a]cut off our name from the earth. Then
[b]what will You do for Your great name?"

The Sin of Achan

10So the LORD said to Joshua: "Get up!
Why do you lie thus on your face? 11Israel
has sinned, and they have also transgressed My covenant which I commanded
them. [a]For they have even taken some of
the [1]accursed things, and have both stolen and [b]deceived; and they have also put
it among their own stuff. 12[a]Therefore the
children of Israel could not stand before
their enemies, *but* turned *their* backs before their enemies, because [b]they have become doomed to destruction. Neither will
I be with you anymore, unless you destroy
the accursed from among you. 13Get up,
[a]sanctify[1] the people, and say, [b]'Sanctify
yourselves for tomorrow, because thus
says the LORD God of Israel: "*There is* an
accursed thing in your midst, O Israel;
you cannot stand before your enemies until you take away the accursed thing from
among you." 14In the morning therefore
you shall be brought according to your
tribes. And it shall be *that* the tribe which
[a]the LORD takes shall come according to
families; and the family which the LORD
takes shall come by households; and the
household which the LORD takes shall
come man by man. 15[a]Then it shall be
that he who is taken with the accursed
thing shall be burned with fire, he and
all that he has, because he has [b]trans-
gressed[1] the covenant of the LORD, and
because he [c]has done a disgraceful thing
in Israel.' "
16So Joshua rose early in the morning
and brought Israel by their tribes, and the
tribe of Judah was taken. 17He brought
the clan of Judah, and he took the family
of the Zarhites; and he brought the family
of the Zarhites man by man, and Zabdi
was taken. 18Then he brought his household man by man, and Achan the son of
Carmi, the son of Zabdi, the son of Zerah,
of the tribe of Judah, [a]was taken.
19Now Joshua said to Achan, "My son, I
beg you, [a]give glory to the LORD God of
Israel, [b]and make confession to Him, and
[c]tell me now what you have done; do not
hide *it* from me."
20And Achan answered Joshua and said,
"Indeed [a]I have sinned against the LORD
God of Israel, and this is what I have done:
21When I saw among the spoils a beautiful
Babylonian garment, two hundred shekels of silver, and a wedge of gold weighing
fifty shekels, I [1]coveted them and took
them. And there they are, hidden in the
earth in the midst of my tent, with the
silver under it."
22So Joshua sent messengers, and they
ran to the tent; and there it was, hidden in
his tent, with the silver under it. 23And
they took them from the midst of the tent,
brought them to Joshua and to all the
children of Israel, and laid them out before the LORD. 24Then Joshua, and all Israel with him, took Achan the son of Zerah,
the silver, the garment, the wedge of gold,
his sons, his daughters, his oxen, his donkeys, his sheep, his tent, and [a]all that he
had, and they brought them to [b]the Valley
of Achor. 25And Joshua said, [a]"Why have
you troubled us? The LORD will trouble
you this day." [b]So all Israel stoned him
with stones; and they burned them with
fire after they had stoned them with
stones.
26Then they [a]raised over him a great
heap of stones, still there to this day. So
[b]the LORD turned from the fierceness of
His anger. Therefore the name of that
place has been called [c]the Valley of [1]Achor
to this day.

The Fall of Ai

8 Now the LORD said to Joshua: [a]"Do
not be afraid, nor be dismayed; take
all the people of war with you, and arise,
go up to Ai. See, [b]I have given into your
hand the king of Ai, his people, his city,
and his land. 2And you shall do to Ai and
its king as you did to [a]Jericho and its king.
Only [b]its spoil and its cattle you shall take
as booty for yourselves. Lay an ambush for
the city behind it."

5 a Lev. 26:36
1 *the people's courage failed*
6 a Gen. 37:29, 34
b 1 Sam. 4:12
7 a Ex. 17:3
1 Heb. *YHWH,* LORD
8 1 Lit. *neck*
9 a Deut. 32:26
b Ex. 32:12
11 a Josh. 6:17–19
b Acts 5:1, 2
1 *devoted*
12 a Judg. 2:14
b [Hag. 2:13, 14]
13 a Ex. 19:10
b Josh. 3:5
1 *set apart*
14 a [Prov. 16:33]
15 a 1 Sam. 14:38, 39
b Josh. 7:11
c Gen. 34:7
1 *overstepped*
18 a 1 Sam. 14:42
19 a Jer. 13:16
b Num. 5:6, 7
c 1 Sam. 14:43
20 a Num. 22:34
21 1 *desired*
24 a Num. 16:32, 33
b Josh. 7:26; 15:7
25 a Josh. 6:18
b Deut. 17:5
26 a 2 Sam. 18:17
b Deut. 13:17
c Is. 65:10
1 Lit. *Trouble*
CHAPTER 8
1 a Josh. 1:9; 10:8
b Josh. 6:2
2 a Josh. 6:21
b Deut. 20:14

3So Joshua arose, and all the people of
war, to go up against Ai; and Joshua chose
thirty thousand mighty men of valor and
sent them away by night. 4And he commanded them, saying: "Behold, [a]you shall
lie in ambush against the city, behind the
city. Do not go very far from the city, but
all of you be ready. 5Then I and all the
people who *are* with me will approach the
city; and it will come about, when they
come out against us as at the first, that
[a]we shall flee before them. 6For they will
come out after us till we have drawn them
from the city, for they will say, '*They are*
fleeing before us as at the first.' Therefore
we will flee before them. 7Then you shall
rise from the ambush and seize the city,
for the LORD your God will deliver it into
your hand. 8And it will be, when you have
taken the city, *that* you shall set the city
on fire. According to the commandment
of the LORD you shall do. [a]See, I have
commanded you."

9Joshua therefore sent them out; and
they went to lie in ambush, and stayed
between Bethel and Ai, on the west side of
Ai; but Joshua lodged that night among
the people. 10Then Joshua rose up early in
the morning and mustered the people,
and went up, he and the elders of Israel,
before the people to Ai. 11[a]And all the people of war who *were* with him went up and
drew near; and they came before the city
and camped on the north side of Ai. Now
a valley *lay* between them and Ai. 12So he
took about five thousand men and set
them in ambush between Bethel and Ai,
on the west side of [1]the city. 13And when
they had set the people, all the army that
was on the north of the city, and its rear
guard on the west of the city, Joshua went
that night into the midst of the valley.

14Now it happened, when the king of Ai
saw *it,* that the men of the city hurried
and rose early and went out against Israel
to battle, he and all his people, at an appointed place before the plain. But he [a]did
not know that *there was* an ambush
against him behind the city. 15And Joshua
and all Israel [a]made as if they were beaten
before them, and fled by the way of the
wilderness. 16So all the people who *were*
in Ai were called together to pursue them.
And they pursued Joshua and were drawn
away from the city. 17There was not a man
left in Ai or Bethel who did not go out
after Israel. So they left the city open and
pursued Israel.

18Then the LORD said to Joshua,
"Stretch out the spear that *is* in your hand
toward Ai, for I will give it into your
hand." And Joshua stretched out the spear
that *was* in his hand toward the city. 19So
those in ambush arose quickly out of their
place; they ran as soon as he had stretched
out his hand, and they entered the city
and took it, and hurried to set the city on
fire. 20And when the men of Ai looked
behind them, they saw, and behold, the
smoke of the city ascended to heaven. So
they had no power to flee this way or that
way, and the people who had fled to the
wilderness turned back on the pursuers.

21Now when Joshua and all Israel saw
that the ambush had taken the city and
that the smoke of the city ascended, they
turned back and struck down the men of
Ai. 22Then the others came out of the city
against them; so they were *caught* in the
midst of Israel, some on this side and
some on that side. And they struck them
down, so that they [a]let none of them remain or escape. 23But the king of Ai they
took alive, and brought him to Joshua.

24And it came to pass when Israel had
made an end of slaying all the inhabitants
of Ai in the field, in the wilderness where
they pursued them, and when they all had
fallen by the edge of the sword until they
were consumed, that all the Israelites returned to Ai and struck it with the edge of
the sword. 25So it was *that* all who fell
that day, both men and women, *were*
twelve thousand—all the people of Ai.
26For Joshua did not draw back his hand,
with which he stretched out the spear,
until he had [a]utterly destroyed all the
inhabitants of Ai. 27[a]Only the livestock
and the spoil of that city Israel took as
booty for themselves, according to the
word of the LORD which He had [b]com-
manded Joshua. 28So Joshua burned Ai
and made it [a]a heap forever, a desolation
to this day. 29[a]And the king of Ai he
hanged on a tree until evening. [b]And as
soon as the sun was down, Joshua commanded that they should take his corpse
down from the tree, cast it at the entrance
of the gate of the city, and [c]raise over it a
great heap of stones *that remains* to this
day.

Joshua Renews the Covenant

30Now Joshua built an altar to the LORD
God of Israel [a]in Mount Ebal, 31as Moses
the servant of the LORD had commanded

4 [a] Judg. 20:29
5 [a] Judg. 20:32
8 [a] 2 Sam. 13:28
11 [a] Josh. 8:5
12 [1] Ai
14 [a] Judg. 20:34
15 [a] Judg. 20:36
22 [a] Deut. 7:2
26 [a] Josh. 6:21
27 [a] Num. 31:22, 26 [b] Josh. 8:2
28 [a] Deut. 13:16
29 [a] Josh. 10:26 [b] Deut. 21:22, 23 [c] Josh. 7:26; 10:27
30 [a] Deut. 27:4–8

the children of Israel, as it is written in the Book of the Law of Moses: [a]"an altar of whole stones over which no man has wielded an iron *tool.*" And [b]they offered on it burnt offerings to the LORD, and sacrificed peace offerings. 32 And there, in the presence of the children of Israel, [a]he wrote on the stones a copy of the law of Moses, which he had written. 33 Then all Israel, with their elders and officers and judges, stood on either side of the ark before the priests, the Levites, [a]who bore the ark of the covenant of the LORD, [b]the stranger as well as he who was born among them. Half of them *were* in front of Mount Gerizim and half of them in front of Mount Ebal, [c]as Moses the servant of the LORD had commanded before, that they should bless the people of Israel. 34 And afterward [a]he read all the words of the law, [b]the blessings and the cursings, according to all that is written in the [c]Book of the Law. 35 There was not a word of all that Moses had commanded which Joshua did not read before all the assembly of Israel, [a]with the women, the little ones, [b]and the strangers who were living among them.

The Treaty with the Gibeonites

9 And it came to pass when [a]all the kings who *were* on this side of the Jordan, in the hills and in the lowland and in all the coasts of [b]the Great Sea toward Lebanon—[c]the Hittite, the Amorite, the Canaanite, the Perizzite, the Hivite, and the Jebusite—heard *about it,* 2 that they [a]gathered together to fight with Joshua and Israel with one [1]accord.

3 But when the inhabitants of [a]Gibeon [b]heard what Joshua had done to Jericho and Ai, 4 they worked craftily, and went and [1]pretended to be ambassadors. And they took old sacks on their donkeys, old wineskins torn and [2]mended, 5 old and patched sandals on their feet, and old garments on themselves; and all the bread of their provision was dry *and* moldy. 6 And they went to Joshua, [a]to the camp at Gilgal, and said to him and to the men of Israel, "We have come from a far country; now therefore, make a [1]covenant with us."

7 Then the men of Israel said to the [a]Hivites, "Perhaps you dwell among us; so [b]how can we make a covenant with you?"

8 But they said to Joshua, [a]"We *are* your servants."

And Joshua said to them, "Who *are* you, and where do you come from?"

9 So they said to him: [a]"From a very far country your servants have come, because of the name of the LORD your God; for we have [b]heard of His fame, and all that He did in Egypt, 10 and [a]all that He did to the two kings of the Amorites who *were* beyond the Jordan—to Sihon king of Heshbon, and Og king of Bashan, who was at Ashtaroth. 11 Therefore our elders and all the inhabitants of our country spoke to us, saying, 'Take provisions with you for the journey, and go to meet them, and say to them, "We *are* your servants; now therefore, make a covenant with us."' 12 This bread of ours we took hot *for* our provision from our houses on the day we departed to come to you. But now look, it is dry and moldy. 13 And these wineskins which we filled *were* new, and see, they are torn; and these our garments and our sandals have become old because of the very long journey."

14 Then the men of Israel took some of their provisions; [a]but they [1]did not ask counsel of the LORD. 15 So Joshua [a]made peace with them, and made a covenant with them to let them live; and the rulers of the congregation swore to them.

16 And it happened at the end of three days, after they had made a covenant with them, that they heard that they *were* their neighbors who dwelt near them. 17 Then the children of Israel journeyed and came to their cities on the third day. Now their cities *were* [a]Gibeon, Chephirah, Beeroth, and Kirjath Jearim. 18 But the children of Israel did not [1]attack them, [a]because the rulers of the congregation had sworn to them by the LORD God of Israel. And all the congregation complained against the rulers.

19 Then all the rulers said to all the congregation, "We have sworn to them by the LORD God of Israel; now therefore, we may not touch them. 20 This we will do to them: We will let them live, lest [a]wrath be upon us because of the oath which we swore to them." 21 And the rulers said to them, "Let them live, but let them be [a]woodcutters and water carriers for all the congregation, as the rulers had [b]promised them."

22 Then Joshua called for them, and he spoke to them, saying, "Why have you deceived us, saying, [a]'We *are* very far from you,' when [b]you dwell near us? 23 Now

---

31 [a] Ex. 20:25 [b] Ex. 20:24
32 [a] Deut. 27:2, 3, 8
33 [a] Deut. 31:9, 25 [b] Deut. 31:12 [c] Deut. 11:29; 27:12
34 [a] Neh. 8:3 [b] Deut. 28:2, 15, 45; 29:20, 21; 30:19 [c] Josh. 1:8
35 [a] Deut. 31:12 [b] Josh. 8:33

CHAPTER 9
1 [a] Josh. 3:10 [b] Num. 34:6 [c] Ex. 3:17; 23:23
2 [a] Ps. 83:3, 5 [1] Lit. *mouth*
3 [a] Josh. 9:17, 22; 10:2; 21:17 [b] Josh. 6:27
4 [1] *acted as envoys* [2] Lit. *tied up*
6 [a] Josh. 5:10 [1] *treaty*
7 [a] Josh. 9:1; 11:19 [b] Ex. 23:32
8 [a] Deut. 20:11
9 [a] Deut. 20:15 [b] Josh. 2:9, 10; 5:1
10 [a] Num. 21:24, 33
14 [a] Num. 27:21 [1] Lit. *did not inquire at the mouth of*
15 [a] 2 Sam. 21:2
17 [a] Josh. 18:25
18 [a] Ps. 15:4 [1] *strike*
20 [a] 2 Sam. 21:1, 2, 6
21 [a] Deut. 29:11 [b] Josh. 9:15
22 [a] Josh. 9:6, 9 [b] Josh. 9:16

therefore, you *are* [a]cursed, and none of you shall be freed from being slaves—woodcutters and water carriers for the house of my God."

24 So they answered Joshua and said, "Because your servants were clearly told that the LORD your God [a]commanded His servant Moses to give you all the land, and to destroy all the inhabitants of the land from before you; therefore [b]we were very much afraid for our lives because of you, and have done this thing. 25 And now, here we are, [a]in your hands; do with us as it seems good and right to do to us." 26 So he did to them, and delivered them out of the hand of the children of Israel, so that they did not kill them. 27 And that day Joshua made them [a]woodcutters and water carriers for the congregation and for the altar of the LORD, [b]in the place which He would choose, even to this day.

The Sun Stands Still

10 Now it came to pass when Adoni-Zedek king of Jerusalem [a]heard how Joshua had taken [b]Ai and had utterly destroyed it—[c]as he had done to Jericho and its king, so he had done to [d]Ai and its king—and [e]how the inhabitants of Gibeon had made peace with Israel and were among them, 2 that they [a]feared greatly, because Gibeon *was* a great city, like one of the royal cities, and because it *was* greater than Ai, and all its men *were* mighty. 3 Therefore Adoni-Zedek king of Jerusalem sent to Hoham king of Hebron, Piram king of Jarmuth, Japhia king of Lachish, and Debir king of Eglon, saying, 4 "Come up to me and help me, that we may attack Gibeon, for [a]it has made peace with Joshua and with the children of Israel." 5 Therefore the five kings of the [a]Amorites, the king of Jerusalem, the king of Hebron, the king of Jarmuth, the king of Lachish, *and* the king of Eglon, [b]gathered together and went up, they and all their armies, and camped before Gibeon and made war against it.

6 And the men of Gibeon sent to Joshua at the camp [a]at Gilgal, saying, "Do not forsake your servants; come up to us quickly, save us and help us, for all the kings of the Amorites who dwell in the mountains have gathered together against us."

7 So Joshua ascended from Gilgal, he and [a]all the people of war with him, and all the mighty men of valor. 8 And the LORD said to Joshua, [a]"Do not fear them, for I have delivered them into your hand; [b]not a man of them shall [c]stand before you." 9 Joshua therefore came upon them suddenly, having marched all night from Gilgal. 10 So the LORD [a]routed them before Israel, killed them with a great slaughter at Gibeon, chased them along the road that goes [b]to Beth Horon, and struck them down as far as [c]Azekah and Makkedah. 11 And it happened, as they fled before Israel *and* were on the descent of Beth Horon, [a]that the LORD cast down large hailstones from heaven on them as far as Azekah, and they died. *There were* more who died from the hailstones than the children of Israel killed with the sword.

I know the power obedience has of making things easy which seem impossible.

TERESA OF ÁVILA

12 Then Joshua spoke to the LORD in the day when the LORD delivered up the Amorites before the children of Israel, and he said in the sight of Israel:

[a]"Sun, stand still over Gibeon;
And Moon, in the Valley of
[b]Aijalon."
13 So the sun stood still,
And the moon stopped,
Till the people had revenge
Upon their enemies.

[a]*Is* this not written in the Book of Jasher? So the sun stood still in the midst of heaven, and did not hasten to go *down* for about a whole day. 14 And there has been [a]no day like that, before it or after it, that the LORD heeded the voice of a man; for [b]the LORD fought for Israel.

15 [a]Then Joshua returned, and all Israel with him, to the camp at Gilgal.

The Amorite Kings Executed

16 But these five kings had fled and hidden themselves in a cave at Makkedah. 17 And it was told Joshua, saying, "The five

23 [a]Gen. 9:25
24 [a]Deut. 7:1, 2 [b]Ex. 15:14
25 [a]Gen. 16:6
27 [a]Josh. 9:21, 23 [b]Deut. 12:5

CHAPTER 10
1 [a]Josh. 9:1 [b]Josh. 8:1 [c]Josh. 6:21 [d]Josh. 8:22, 26, 28 [e]Josh. 9:15
2 [a]Ex. 15:14–16
4 [a]Josh. 9:15; 10:1
5 [a]Num. 13:29 [b]Josh. 9:2
6 [a]Josh. 5:10; 9:6
7 [a]Josh. 8:1
8 [a]Josh. 11:6 [b]Josh. 1:5, 9 [c]Josh. 21:44
10 [a]Is. 28:21 [b]Josh. 16:3, 5 [c]Josh. 15:35
11 [a]Is. 30:30
12 [a]Hab. 3:11 [b]Judg. 12:12
13 [a]2 Sam. 1:18
14 [a]Is. 38:7, 8 [b]Deut. 1:30; 20:4
15 [a]Josh. 10:43

kings have been found hidden in the cave
at Makkedah."
18So Joshua said, "Roll large stones
against the mouth of the cave, and set
men by it to guard them. 19And do not
stay *there* yourselves, *but* pursue your enemies, and attack their rear *guard*. Do not
allow them to enter their cities, for the
LORD your God has delivered them into
your hand." 20Then it happened, while
Joshua and the children of Israel made an
end of slaying them with a very great
slaughter, till they had finished, that
those who escaped entered fortified cities.
21And all the people returned to the camp,
to Joshua at Makkedah, in peace.
[a]No one [1]moved his tongue against any
of the children of Israel.
22Then Joshua said, "Open the mouth
of the cave, and bring out those five kings
to me from the cave." 23And they did so,
and brought out those five kings to him
from the cave: the king of Jerusalem, the
king of Hebron, the king of Jarmuth, the
king of Lachish, *and* the king of Eglon.
24So it was, when they brought out
those kings to Joshua, that Joshua called
for all the men of Israel, and said to the
captains of the men of war who went with
him, "Come near, put your feet on the
necks of these kings." And they drew near
and [a]put their feet on their necks. 25Then
Joshua said to [1]them, [a]"Do not be afraid,
nor be dismayed; be strong and of good
courage, for [b]thus the LORD will do to all
your enemies against whom you fight."
26And afterward Joshua struck [1]them and
killed them, and hanged them on five
trees; and they [a]were hanging on the trees
until evening. 27So it was at the time of
the going down of the sun *that* Joshua
commanded, and they [a]took them down
from the trees, cast them into the cave
where they had been hidden, and laid
large stones against the cave's mouth,
which remain until this very day.

Conquest of the Southland

28On that day Joshua took Makkedah,
and struck it and its king with the edge of
the sword. He utterly [a]destroyed [1]them—
all the people who *were* in it. He let none
remain. He also did to the king of Makkedah [b]as he had done to the king of Jericho.
29Then Joshua passed from Makkedah,
and all Israel with him, to [a]Libnah; and
they fought against Libnah. 30And the
LORD also delivered it and its king into the
hand of Israel; he struck it and all the people who *were* in it with the edge of the
sword. He let none remain in it, but did to
its king as he had done to the king of Jericho.
31Then Joshua passed from Libnah, and
all Israel with him, to Lachish; and they
encamped against it and fought against it.
32And the LORD delivered Lachish into the
hand of Israel, who took it on the second
day, and struck it and all the people who
were in it with the edge of the sword, according to all that he had done to Libnah.
33Then Horam king of Gezer came up to
help Lachish; and Joshua struck him and
his people, until he left him none remaining.
34From Lachish Joshua passed to Eglon, and all Israel with him; and they encamped against it and fought against it.
35They took it on that day and struck it
with the edge of the sword; all the people
who *were* in it he utterly destroyed that
day, according to all that he had done to
Lachish.
36So Joshua went up from Eglon, and
all Israel with him, to [a]Hebron; and they
fought against it. 37And they took it and
struck it with the edge of the sword—its
king, all its cities, and all the people who
were in it; he left none remaining, according to all that he had done to Eglon, but
utterly destroyed it and all the people who
were in it.
38Then Joshua returned, and all Israel
with him, to [a]Debir; and they fought
against it. 39And he took it and its king
and all its cities; they struck them with
the edge of the sword and utterly destroyed all the people who *were* in it. He
left none remaining; as he had done to
Hebron, so he did to Debir and its king, as
he had done also to Libnah and its king.
40So Joshua conquered all the land: the
[a]mountain country and the [1]South and
the lowland and the wilderness slopes,
and [b]all their kings; he left none remaining, but [c]utterly destroyed all that
breathed, as the LORD God of Israel had
commanded. 41And Joshua conquered
them from [a]Kadesh Barnea as far as
[b]Gaza, [c]and all the country of Goshen,
even as far as Gibeon. 42All these kings
and their land Joshua took at one time,
[a]because the LORD God of Israel fought for
Israel. 43Then Joshua returned, and all Israel with him, to the camp at Gilgal.

21 a Ex. 11:7
1 *criticized,* lit. *sharpened his tongue*
24 a Mal. 4:3
25 a Deut. 31:6–8
b Deut. 3:21; 7:19
1 The captains
26 a Josh. 8:29
1 The kings
27 a Deut. 21:22, 23
28 a Deut. 7:2, 16
b Josh. 6:21
1 So with MT and most authorities; many Heb. mss., some LXX mss., and some Tg. mss. *it*
29 a Josh. 15:42; 21:13
36 a Josh. 14:13–15; 15:13
38 a Josh. 15:15
40 a Deut. 1:7
b Deut. 7:24
c Deut. 20:16, 17
1 Heb. *Negev,* and so throughout the book
41 a Deut. 9:23
b Gen. 10:19
c Josh. 11:16; 15:51
42 a Josh. 10:14

The Northern Conquest

11 And it came to pass, when Jabin
king of Hazor heard *these things,*
that he [a]sent to Jobab king of Madon, to
the king [b]of Shimron, to the king of Achshaph, 2and to the kings who *were* from
the north, in the mountains, in the plain
south of [a]Chinneroth, in the lowland, and
in the heights [b]of Dor on the west, 3to the
Canaanites in the east and in the west, the
[a]Amorite, the Hittite, the Perizzite, the
Jebusite in the mountains, [b]and the Hivite below [c]Hermon [d]in the land of Mizpah. 4So they went out, they and all their
armies with them, *as* many people [a]*as* the
sand that *is* on the seashore in multitude,
with very many horses and chariots. 5And
when all these kings had [1]met together,
they came and camped together at the waters of Merom to fight against Israel.
6But the LORD said to Joshua, [a]"Do not
be afraid because of them, for tomorrow
about this time I will deliver all of them
slain before Israel. You shall [b]hamstring
their horses and burn their chariots with
fire." 7So Joshua and all the people of war
with him came against them suddenly by
the waters of Merom, and they attacked
them. 8And the LORD delivered them into
the hand of Israel, who defeated them and
chased them to [1]Greater [a]Sidon, to the
[2]Brook [b]Misrephoth, and to the Valley of
Mizpah eastward; they attacked them until they left none of them remaining. 9So
Joshua did to them as the LORD had told
him: he hamstrung their horses and
burned their chariots with fire.
10Joshua turned back at that time and
took Hazor, and struck its king with the
sword; for Hazor was formerly the head of
all those kingdoms. 11And they struck all
the people who *were* in it with the edge
of the sword, [a]utterly destroying *them.*
There was none left [b]breathing. Then he
burned Hazor with fire.
12So all the cities of those kings, and all
their kings, Joshua took and struck with
the edge of the sword. He utterly destroyed them, [a]as Moses the servant of the
LORD had commanded. 13But *as for* the
cities that stood on their [1]mounds, Israel
burned none of them, except Hazor only,
which Joshua burned. 14And all the [a]spoil
of these cities and the livestock, the children of Israel took as booty for themselves; but they struck every man with the
edge of the sword until they had destroyed
them, and they left none breathing. 15[a]As
the LORD had commanded Moses his servant, so [b]Moses commanded Joshua, and
[c]so Joshua did. [1]He left nothing undone
of all that the LORD had commanded
Moses.

It is not faith in God's power that secures His blessings but faith in His love and in His will.

F. F. Bosworth

Summary of Joshua's Conquests

16Thus Joshua took all this land: [a]the
mountain country, all the South, [b]all the
land of Goshen, the lowland, and the Jordan [1]plain—the mountains of Israel and
its lowlands, 17[a]from [1]Mount Halak and
the ascent to Seir, even as far as Baal Gad
in the Valley of Lebanon below Mount
Hermon. He captured [b]all their kings, and
struck them down and killed them.
18Joshua made war a long time with all
those kings. 19There was not a city that
made peace with the children of Israel,
except [a]the Hivites, the inhabitants of
Gibeon. All *the others* they took in battle.
20For [a]it was of the LORD [1]to harden their
hearts, that they should come against Israel in battle, that He might utterly destroy them, *and* that they might receive
no mercy, but that He might destroy
them, [b]as the LORD had commanded
Moses.
21And at that time Joshua came and cut
off [a]the Anakim from the mountains:
from Hebron, from Debir, from Anab,
from all the mountains of Judah, and
from all the mountains of Israel; Joshua
utterly destroyed them with their cities.
22None of the Anakim were left in the land
of the children of Israel; they remained
only [a]in Gaza, in Gath, [b]and in Ashdod.
23So Joshua took the whole land, [a]ac-
cording to all that the LORD had said to
Moses; and Joshua gave it as an inheritance to Israel [b]according to their divisions by their tribes. Then the land
[c]rested from war.

CHAPTER 11
1 a Josh. 10:3 b Josh. 19:15
2 a Num. 34:11 b Josh. 17:11
3 a Josh. 9:1 b Judg. 3:3, 5 c Josh. 11:17; 13:5, 11 d Gen. 31:49
4 a Judg. 7:12
5 *1* Lit. *assembled by appointment*
6 a Josh. 10:8 b 2 Sam. 8:4
8 a Gen. 49:13 b Josh. 13:6 *1* Heb. *Sidon Rabbah* *2* Heb. *Misrephoth Maim,* lit. *Burnings of Water*
11 a Deut. 20:16 b Josh. 10:40
12 a Num. 33:50–56
13 *1* Heb. *tel,* a heap of successive city ruins
14 a Deut. 20:14–18
15 a Ex. 34:10–17 b Deut. 31:7, 8 c Josh. 1:7 *1* Lit. *He turned aside from nothing*
16 a Josh. 12:8 b Josh. 10:40, 41 *1* Heb. *arabah*
17 a Josh. 12:7 b Deut. 7:24 *1* Lit. *The Smooth* or *Bald Mountain*
19 a Josh. 9:3–7
20 a Deut. 2:30 b Deut. 20:16, 17 *1* Lit. *to make strong*
21 a Num. 13:22, 33
22 a 1 Sam. 17:4 b Josh. 15:46
23 a Num. 34:2–15 b Num. 26:53 c Deut. 12:9, 10; 25:19

The Kings Conquered by Moses

12 These *are* the kings of the land
whom the children of Israel defeated, and whose land they possessed on the
other side of the Jordan toward the rising
of the sun, [a]from the River Arnon [b]to
Mount Hermon, and all the eastern Jordan plain: 2*One king was* [a]Sihon king of
the Amorites, who dwelt in Heshbon *and*
ruled half of Gilead, from Aroer, which is
on the bank of the River Arnon, from the
middle of that river, even as far as the
River Jabbok, *which is* the border of the
Ammonites, 3and [a]the eastern Jordan
plain from the [1]Sea of Chinneroth as far
as the [2]Sea of the Arabah (the Salt Sea),
[b]the road to Beth Jeshimoth, and [3]south-
ward below [c]the[4] slopes of Pisgah. 4[a]*The*
other king was Og king of Bashan and his
territory, *who was* of [b]the remnant of the
giants, [c]who dwelt at Ashtaroth and at Edrei, 5and reigned over [a]Mount Hermon,
[b]over Salcah, over all Bashan, [c]as far as
the border of the Geshurites and the Maachathites, and over half of Gilead *to* the
border of Sihon king of Heshbon.
6[a]These Moses the servant of the LORD
and the children of Israel had conquered;
and [b]Moses the servant of the LORD had
given it *as* a possession to the Reubenites,
the Gadites, and half the tribe of Manasseh.

The Kings Conquered by Joshua

7And these *are* the kings of the country
[a]which Joshua and the children of Israel
conquered on this side of the Jordan, on
the west, from Baal Gad in the Valley of
Lebanon as far as [1]Mount Halak and the
ascent to [b]Seir, which Joshua [c]gave to the
tribes of Israel *as* a possession according
to their divisions, 8[a]in the mountain
country, in the lowlands, in the *Jordan*
plain, in the slopes, in the wilderness, and
in the South—[b]the Hittites, the Amorites, the Canaanites, the Perizzites, the
Hivites, and the Jebusites: 9[a]the king of
Jericho, one; [b]the king of Ai, which *is* beside Bethel, one; 10[a]the king of Jerusalem,
one; the king of Hebron, one; 11the king
of Jarmuth, one; the king of Lachish, one;
12the king of Eglon, one; [a]the king of Gezer, one; 13[a]the king of Debir, one; the
king of Geder, one; 14the king of Hormah,
one; the king of Arad, one; 15[a]the king of
Libnah, one; the king of Adullam, one;
16[a]the king of Makkedah, one; [b]the king of
Bethel, one; 17the king of Tappuah, one;
[a]the king of Hepher, one; 18the king of
Aphek, one; the king of [1]Lasharon, one;
19the king of Madon, one; [a]the king of Hazor, one; 20the king of [a]Shimron Meron,
one; the king of Achshaph, one; 21the king
of Taanach, one; the king of Megiddo, one;
22[a]the king of Kedesh, one; the king of
Jokneam in Carmel, one; 23the king of
Dor in the [a]heights of Dor, one; the king
of [b]the people of Gilgal, one; 24the king of
Tirzah, one—[a]all the kings, thirty-one.

Remaining Land to Be Conquered

13 Now Joshua [a]was old, advanced in
years. And the LORD said to him:
"You are old, advanced in years, and there
remains very much land yet to be possessed. 2[a]This is the land that yet remains:
[b]all the territory of the Philistines and all
[c]*that of* the Geshurites, 3[a]from Sihor,
which *is* east of Egypt, as far as the border
of Ekron northward (*which* is counted as
Canaanite); the [b]five lords of the Philistines—the Gazites, the Ashdodites, the
Ashkelonites, the Gittites, and the Ekronites; also [c]the Avites; 4from the south, all
the land of the Canaanites, and Mearah
that belongs to the Sidonians [a]as far as
Aphek, to the border of [b]the Amorites;
5the land of [a]the [1]Gebalites, and all Lebanon, toward the sunrise, [b]from Baal Gad
below Mount Hermon as far as the entrance to Hamath; 6all the inhabitants of
the mountains from Lebanon as far as
[a]the [1]Brook Misrephoth, *and* all the Sidonians—them [b]I will drive out from before
the children of Israel; only [c]divide[2] it by
lot to Israel as an inheritance, as I have
commanded you. 7Now therefore, divide
this land as an inheritance to the nine
tribes and half the tribe of Manasseh."

The Land Divided East of the Jordan

8With the other half-tribe the Reubenites and the Gadites received their inheritance, [a]which Moses had given them,
[b]beyond the Jordan eastward, as Moses
the servant of the LORD had given them:

CHAPTER 12
1 a Num. 21:24 b Deut. 3:8
2 a Deut. 2:24–27
3 a Deut. 3:17 b Josh. 13:20 c Deut. 3:17; 4:49 *1* Sea of Galilee *2* Lit. *Sea of the Plain,* the Dead Sea *3* Or *Teman* *4* Or *Ashdoth Pisgah*
4 a Num. 21:33 b Deut. 3:11 c Deut. 1:4
5 a Deut. 3:8 b Deut. 3:10 c Deut. 3:14
6 a Num. 21:24, 35 b Num. 32:29–33
7 a Josh. 11:17 b Gen. 14:6; 32:3 c Josh. 11:23 *1* Lit. *The Bald Mountain*
8 a Josh. 10:40; 11:16 b Ex. 3:8; 23:23
9 a Josh. 6:2 b Josh. 8:29
10 a Josh. 10:23
12 a Josh. 10:33
13 a Josh. 10:38, 39
15 a Josh. 10:29, 30
16 a Josh. 10:28 b Judg. 1:22
17 a 1 Kin. 4:10
18 *1* Or *Sharon*
19 a Josh. 11:10
20 a Josh. 11:1; 19:15
22 a Josh. 19:37; 20:7; 21:32
23 a Josh. 11:2 b Is. 9:1
24 a Deut. 7:24

CHAPTER 13
1 a Josh. 14:10; 23:1, 2
2 a Judg. 3:1–3 b Joel 3:4 c 2 Sam. 3:3
3 a Jer. 2:18 b Judg. 3:3 c Deut. 2:23

4 a Josh. 12:18; 19:30 b Judg. 1:34 **5** a 1 Kin. 5:18; Ezek. 27:9 b Josh. 12:7 *1* Or *Giblites* **6** a Josh. 11:8 b Josh. 23:13 c Josh. 14:1, 2 *1* Heb. *Misrephoth Maim,* lit. *Burnings of Water* *2* apportion **8** a Num. 32:33 b Josh. 12:1–6

9 from Aroer which *is* on the bank of the River Arnon, and the town that *is* in the midst of the ravine, [a]and all the plain of Medeba as far as Dibon; 10 [a]all the cities of Sihon king of the Amorites, who reigned in Heshbon, as far as the border of the children of Ammon; 11 [a]Gilead, and the border of the Geshurites and Maachathites, all Mount Hermon, and all Bashan as far as Salcah; 12 all the kingdom of Og in Bashan, who reigned in Ashtaroth and Edrei, who remained of [a]the remnant of the giants; [b]for Moses had [1]defeated and [2]cast out these.

13 Nevertheless the children of Israel [a]did not drive out the Geshurites or the Maachathites, but the Geshurites and the Maachathites dwell among the Israelites until this day.

14 [a]Only to the tribe of Levi he had given [1]no inheritance; the sacrifices of the LORD God of Israel made by fire *are* their inheritance, [b]as He said to them.

The Land of Reuben

15 [a]And Moses had given to the tribe of the children of Reuben *an inheritance* according to their families. 16 Their territory was [a]from Aroer, which *is* on the bank of the River Arnon, [b]and the city that *is* in the midst of the ravine, [c]and all the plain by Medeba; 17 [a]Heshbon and all its cities that *are* in the plain: Dibon, Bamoth Baal, Beth Baal Meon, 18 [a]Jahaza, Kedemoth, Mephaath, 19 [a]Kirjathaim, [b]Sibmah, Zereth Shahar on the mountain of the valley, 20 Beth Peor, [a]the slopes of Pisgah, and Beth Jeshimoth— 21 [a]all the cities of the plain and all the kingdom of Sihon king of the Amorites, who reigned in Heshbon, [b]whom Moses had struck [c]with the princes of Midian: Evi, Rekem, Zur, Hur, and Reba, who *were* princes of Sihon dwelling in the country. 22 The children of Israel also killed with the sword [a]Balaam the son of Beor, the [1]soothsayer, among those who were killed by them. 23 And the border of the children of Reuben was the bank of the Jordan. This *was* the inheritance of the children of Reuben according to their families, the cities and their villages.

The Land of Gad

24 [a]Moses also had given *an inheritance* to the tribe of Gad, to the children of Gad according to their families. 25 [a]Their territory was Jazer, and all the cities of Gilead, [b]and half the land of the Ammonites as far as Aroer, which *is* before [c]Rabbah, 26 and from Heshbon to Ramath Mizpah and Betonim, and from Mahanaim to the border of Debir, 27 and in the valley [a]Beth Haram, Beth Nimrah, [b]Succoth, and Zaphon, the rest of the kingdom of Sihon king of Heshbon, with the Jordan as *its* border, as far as the edge [c]of the [1]Sea of Chinnereth, on the other side of the Jordan eastward. 28 This *is* the inheritance of the children of Gad according to their families, the cities and their villages.

Half the Tribe of Manasseh (East)

29 [a]Moses also had given *an inheritance* to half the tribe of Manasseh; it was for half the tribe of the children of Manasseh according to their families: 30 Their territory was from Mahanaim, all Bashan, all the kingdom of Og king of Bashan, and [a]all the towns of Jair which are in Bashan, sixty cities; 31 half of Gilead, and [a]Ashtaroth and Edrei, cities of the kingdom of Og in Bashan, *were* for the [b]children of Machir the son of Manasseh, for half of the children of Machir according to their families.

32 These *are the areas* which Moses had [1]distributed as an inheritance in the plains of Moab on the other side of the Jordan, by Jericho eastward. 33 [a]But to the tribe of Levi Moses had given no inheritance; the LORD God of Israel *was* their inheritance, [b]as He had said to them.

The Land Divided West of the Jordan

14 These *are the areas* which the children of Israel inherited in the land of Canaan, [a]which Eleazar the priest, Joshua the son of Nun, and the heads of the fathers of the tribes of the children of Israel distributed as an inheritance to them. 2 Their inheritance *was* [a]by lot, as the LORD had commanded by the hand of Moses, for the nine tribes and the half-tribe. 3 [a]For Moses had given the inheritance of the two tribes and the half-tribe on the other side of the Jordan; but to the Levites he had given no inheritance among them. 4 For [a]the children of Joseph were two tribes: Manasseh and Ephraim. And they gave no part to the Levites in the

9 a Num. 21:30
10 a Num. 21:24, 25
11 a Josh. 12:5
12 a Deut. 3:11 b Num. 21:24, 34, 35 *1 Lit. struck* *2 dispossessed*
13 a Josh. 13:11
14 a Josh. 14:3, 4 b Josh. 13:33 *1 no land as a possession*
15 a Num. 34:14
16 a Josh. 12:2 b Num. 21:28 c Num. 21:30
17 a Num. 21:28, 30
18 a Num. 21:23
19 a Num. 32:37 b Num. 32:38
20 a Deut. 3:17
21 a Deut. 3:10 b Num. 21:24 c Num. 31:8
22 a Num. 22:5; 31:8 *1 diviner*
24 a Num. 34:14
25 a Num. 32:1, 35 b Judg. 11:13, 15 c Deut. 3:11
27 a Num. 32:36 b Gen. 33:17 c Num. 34:11 *1* Sea of Galilee
29 a Num. 34:14
30 a Num. 32:41
31 a Josh. 9:10; 12:4; 13:12 b Num. 32:39, 40
32 *1 apportioned*
33 a Josh. 13:14; 18:7 b Num. 18:20

CHAPTER 14
1 a Num. 34:16–29
2 a Num. 26:55; 33:54; 34:13
3 a Josh. 13:8, 32, 33
4 a 2 Chr. 30:1

land, except [b]cities to dwell *in,* with their
common-lands for their livestock and
their property. 5[a]As the LORD had commanded Moses, so the children of Israel
did; and they divided the land.

Caleb Inherits Hebron

6Then the children of Judah came to
Joshua in Gilgal. And Caleb the son of Jephunneh the [a]Kenizzite said to him: "You
know [b]the word which the LORD said to
Moses the man of God concerning [c]you
and me in Kadesh Barnea. 7I *was* forty
years old when Moses the servant of the
LORD [a]sent me from Kadesh Barnea to spy
out the land, and I brought back word to
him as *it was* in my heart. 8Nevertheless
[a]my brethren who went up with me made
the [1]heart of the people melt, but I wholly
[b]followed the LORD my God. 9So Moses
swore on that day, saying, [a]'Surely the
land [b]where your foot has trodden shall be
your inheritance and your children's forever, because you have wholly followed
the LORD my God.' 10And now, behold, the
LORD has kept me [a]alive, [b]as He said,
these forty-five years, ever since the LORD
spoke this word to Moses while Israel
[1]wandered in the wilderness; and now,
here I am this day, eighty-five years old.
11[a]As yet I *am as* strong this day as on
the day that Moses sent me; just as my
strength *was* then, so now *is* my strength
for war, both [b]for going out and for coming in. 12Now therefore, give me this
mountain of which the LORD spoke in that
day; for you heard in that day how [a]the
Anakim *were* there, and *that* the cities
were great *and* fortified. [b]It may be that
the LORD *will be* with me, and [c]I shall be
able to drive them out as the LORD said."
13And Joshua [a]blessed him, [b]and gave
Hebron to Caleb the son of Jephunneh as
an inheritance. 14[a]Hebron therefore became the inheritance of Caleb the son of
Jephunneh the Kenizzite to this day, because he [b]wholly followed the LORD God
of Israel. 15And [a]the name of Hebron formerly was Kirjath Arba (*Arba was* the
greatest man among the Anakim).
[b]Then the land had rest from war.

The Land of Judah

15 So *this* was the [1]lot of the tribe of
the children of Judah according to
their families:
[a]The border of Edom at the [b]Wilder-
ness of Zin southward *was* the extreme
southern boundary. 2And their [a]southern
border began at the shore of the Salt Sea,
from the bay that faces southward. 3Then
it went out to the southern side of [a]the
Ascent of Akrabbim, passed along to Zin,
ascended on the south side of Kadesh Barnea, passed along to Hezron, went up to
Adar, and went around to Karkaa. 4*From
there* it passed [a]toward Azmon and went
out to the Brook of Egypt; and the border
ended at the sea. This shall be your southern border.
5The east border *was* the Salt Sea as far
as the mouth of the Jordan.
And the [a]border on the northern quarter *began* at the bay of the sea at the
mouth of the Jordan. 6The border went up
to [a]Beth Hoglah and passed north of Beth
Arabah; and the border went up [b]to the
stone of Bohan the son of Reuben. 7Then
the border went up toward [a]Debir from
[b]the Valley of Achor, and it turned northward toward Gilgal, which *is* before the
Ascent of Adummim, which *is* on the
south side of the valley. The border continued toward the waters of En Shemesh
and ended at [c]En Rogel. 8And the border
went up [a]by the Valley of the Son of Hinnom to the southern slope of the [b]Jebu-
site *city* (which *is* Jerusalem). The border
went up to the top of the mountain that
lies before the Valley of Hinnom westward, which *is* at the end of the Valley [c]of
[1]Rephaim northward. 9Then the border
went around from the top of the hill to
[a]the fountain of the water of Nephtoah,
and extended to the cities of Mount
Ephron. And the border went around [b]to
Baalah (which *is* [c]Kirjath Jearim). 10Then
the border [1]turned westward from Baalah
to Mount Seir, passed along to the side
of Mount Jearim on the north (which *is*
Chesalon), went down to Beth Shemesh,
and passed on to [a]Timnah. 11And the border went out to the side of [a]Ekron northward. Then the border went around to
Shicron, passed along to Mount Baalah,
and extended to Jabneel; and the border
ended at the sea.
12The west border *was* [a]the coastline of
the Great Sea. This *is* the boundary of the
children of Judah all around according to
their families.

Caleb Occupies Hebron and Debir

13[a]Now to Caleb the son of Jephunneh
he gave a share among the children of

4 b Num. 35:2–8
5 a Josh. 21:2
6 a Num. 32:11, 12 b Num. 14:24, 30 c Num. 13:26
7 a Num. 13:6, 17; 14:6
8 a Num. 13:31, 32 b Num. 14:24 *1 courage of the people fail*
9 a Num. 14:23, 24 b Deut. 1:36
10 a Num. 14:24, 30, 38 b Josh. 5:6 *1 Lit. walked*
11 a Deut. 34:7 b Deut. 31:2
12 a Num. 13:28, 33 b Rom. 8:31 c Josh. 15:14
13 a Josh. 22:6 b Josh. 10:37; 15:13
14 a Josh. 21:12 b Josh. 14:8, 9
15 a Gen. 23:2 b Josh. 11:23

CHAPTER 15
1 a Num. 34:3 b Num. 33:36 *1 allotment*
2 a Num. 34:3, 4
3 a Num. 34:4
4 a Num. 34:5
5 a Josh. 18:15–19
6 a Josh. 18:19, 21 b Josh. 18:17
7 a Josh. 13:26 b Josh. 7:26 c 2 Sam. 17:17
8 a Josh. 18:16 b Judg. 1:21; 19:10 c Josh. 18:16 *1 Lit. Giants*
9 a Josh. 18:15 b 1 Chr. 13:6 c Judg. 18:12
10 a Gen. 38:13 *1 turned around*
11 a Josh. 19:43
12 a Num. 34:6, 7
13 a Josh. 14:13

[b]Judah, according to the commandment
of the LORD to Joshua, *namely,* [c]Kirjath
Arba, which *is* Hebron (*Arba was* the father of Anak). 14Caleb drove out [a]the
three sons of Anak from there: [b]Sheshai,
Ahiman, and Talmai, the children of Anak.
15Then [a]he went up from there to the
inhabitants of Debir (formerly the name
of Debir *was* Kirjath Sepher).

16[a]And Caleb said, "He who [1]attacks
Kirjath Sepher and takes it, to him I will
give Achsah my daughter as wife." 17So
[a]Othniel the [b]son of Kenaz, the brother of
Caleb, took it; and he gave him [c]Achsah
his daughter as wife. 18[a]Now it was so,
when she came *to him,* that she persuaded him to ask her father for a field. So
[b]she dismounted from *her* donkey, and
Caleb said to her, "What do you wish?"
19She answered, "Give me a [a]blessing;
since you have given me land in the
South, give me also springs of water." So
he gave her the upper springs and the
lower springs.

The Cities of Judah

20This *was* the inheritance of the tribe
of the children of Judah according to their
families:

21The cities at the limits of the tribe of
the children of Judah, toward the border
of Edom in the South, were Kabzeel,
[a]Eder, Jagur, 22Kinah, Dimonah, Adadah,
23Kedesh, Hazor, Ithnan, 24[a]Ziph, Telem,
Bealoth, 25Hazor, Hadattah, Kerioth, Hezron (which *is* Hazor), 26Amam, Shema,
Moladah, 27Hazar Gaddah, Heshmon,
Beth Pelet, 28Hazar Shual, [a]Beersheba,
Bizjothjah, 29Baalah, Ijim, Ezem, 30Elto-
lad, Chesil, [a]Hormah, 31[a]Ziklag, Madmannah, Sansannah, 32Lebaoth, Shilhim, Ain,
and [a]Rimmon: all the cities *are* twenty-
nine, with their villages.

33In the lowland: [a]Eshtaol, Zorah, Ashnah, 34Zanoah, En Gannim, Tappuah,
Enam, 35Jarmuth, [a]Adullam, Socoh, Azekah, 36Sharaim, Adithaim, Gederah, and
Gederothaim: fourteen cities with their
villages; 37Zenan, Hadashah, Migdal Gad,
38Dilean, Mizpah, [a]Joktheel, 39[a]Lachish,
Bozkath, [b]Eglon, 40Cabbon, [1]Lahmas,
Kithlish, 41Gederoth, Beth Dagon, Naamah, and Makkedah: sixteen cities with
their villages; 42[a]Libnah, Ether, Ashan,
43Jiphtah, Ashnah, Nezib, 44Keilah, Achzib, and Mareshah: nine cities with their
villages; 45Ekron, with its towns and villages; 46from Ekron to the sea, all that *lay*
near [a]Ashdod, with their villages; 47Ash-
dod with its towns and villages, Gaza with
its towns and villages—as far as [a]the
Brook of Egypt and [b]the Great Sea with *its*
coastline.

48And in the mountain country: Shamir, Jattir, Sochoh, 49Dannah, Kirjath
Sannah (which *is* Debir), 50Anab, Eshte-
moh, Anim, 51[a]Goshen, Holon, and Giloh:
eleven cities with their villages; 52Arab,
Dumah, Eshean, 53Janum, Beth Tappuah,
Aphekah, 54Humtah, [a]Kirjath Arba
(which *is* Hebron), and Zior: nine cities
with their villages; 55[a]Maon, Carmel,
Ziph, Juttah, 56Jezreel, Jokdeam, Zanoah,
57Kain, Gibeah, and Timnah: ten cities
with their villages; 58Halhul, Beth Zur,
Gedor, 59Maarath, Beth Anoth, and Elte-
kon: six cities with their villages; 60[a]Kir-
jath Baal (which *is* Kirjath Jearim) and
Rabbah: two cities with their villages.

61In the wilderness: Beth Arabah, Mid-
din, Secacah, 62Nibshan, the City of Salt,
and [a]En Gedi: six cities with their villages.

63As for the Jebusites, the inhabitants of
Jerusalem, [a]the children of Judah could
not drive them out; [b]but the Jebusites
dwell with the children of Judah at Jerusalem to this day.

Ephraim and West Manasseh

16 The lot [1]fell to the children of Joseph from the Jordan, by Jericho,
to the waters of Jericho on the east, to the
[a]wilderness that goes up from Jericho
through the mountains to [2]Bethel, 2then
went out [1]from [a]Bethel to Luz, passed
along to the border of the Archites at Ataroth, 3and went down westward to the
boundary of the Japhletites, [a]as far as the
boundary of Lower Beth Horon to [b]Gezer;
and [1]it ended at the sea.

4[a]So the children of Joseph, Manasseh
and Ephraim, took their [1]inheritance.

The Land of Ephraim

5[a]The border of the children of Ephraim, according to their families, was *thus:*
The border of their inheritance on the
east side was [b]Ataroth Addar [c]as far as Upper Beth Horon.

6And the border went out toward the
sea on the north side of [a]Michmethath;
then the border went around eastward to
Taanath Shiloh, and passed by it on the

13 b Num. 13:6 c Josh. 14:15
14 a Judg. 1:10, 20 b Num. 13:22
15 a Judg. 1:11
16 a Judg. 1:12 1 Lit. *strikes*
17 a Judg. 1:13; 3:9 b Num. 32:12 c Judg. 1:12
18 a Judg. 1:14 b Gen. 24:64
19 a Gen. 33:11
21 a Gen. 35:21
24 a 1 Sam. 23:14
28 a Gen. 21:31
30 a Josh. 19:4
31 a 1 Sam. 27:6; 30:1
32 a Judg. 20:45, 47
33 a Judg. 13:25; 16:31
35 a 1 Sam. 22:1
38 a 2 Kin. 14:7
39 a 2 Kin. 14:19 b Josh. 10:3
40 1 Or *Lahmam*
42 a Josh. 21:13
46 a Josh. 11:22
47 a Josh. 15:4 b Num. 34:6
51 a Josh. 10:41; 11:16
54 a Josh. 14:15
55 a 1 Sam. 23:24, 25
60 a Josh. 18:14
62 a 1 Sam. 23:29
63 a 2 Sam. 5:6 b Judg. 1:21

CHAPTER 16
1 a Josh. 8:15; 18:12 1 Lit. *went out* 2 LXX *Bethel Luz*
2 a Josh. 18:13 1 LXX *to Bethel,*
3 a 2 Chr. 8:5 b 1 Kin. 9:15 1 Lit. *the goings out of it were at the sea*

4 a Josh. 17:14 1 *possession* **5** a Judg. 1:29 b Josh. 18:13 c 2 Chr. 8:5 **6** a Josh. 17:7

east of Janohah. [7]Then it went down from
Janohah to Ataroth and [1]Naarah, reached
to Jericho, and came out at the Jordan.
[8]The border went out from [a]Tappuah
westward to the [b]Brook Kanah, and [1]it
ended at the sea. This *was* the inheritance
of the tribe of the children of Ephraim
according to their families. [9a]The separate cities for the children of Ephraim
were among the inheritance of the children of Manasseh, all the cities with their
villages.
[10a]And they did not drive out the Canaanites who dwelt in Gezer; but the Canaanites dwell among the Ephraimites to
this day and have become forced laborers.

The Other Half-Tribe of Manasseh (West)

17 There was also a lot for the tribe of
Manasseh, for he *was* the [a]first-
born of Joseph: *namely* for [b]Machir the
firstborn of Manasseh, the father of Gilead, because he was a man of war; therefore he was given [c]Gilead and Bashan.
[2]And there was *a lot* for [a]the rest of the
children of Manasseh according to their
families: [b]for the children of [1]Abiezer, the
children of Helek, [c]the children of Asriel,
the children of Shechem, [d]the children
of Hepher, and the children of Shemida;
these *were* the male children of Manasseh
the son of Joseph according to their families.
[3]But [a]Zelophehad the son of Hepher,
the son of Gilead, the son of Machir, the
son of Manasseh, had no sons, but only
daughters. And these *are* the names of his
daughters: Mahlah, Noah, Hoglah, Milcah, and Tirzah. [4]And they came near before [a]Eleazar the priest, before Joshua the
son of Nun, and before the rulers, saying,
[b]"The LORD commanded Moses to give us
an [1]inheritance among our brothers."
Therefore, according to the commandment of the LORD, he gave them an inheri-

7 *1 Naaran,* 1 Chr. 7:28
8 a Josh. 17:8 b Josh. 17:9 *1 Lit. the goings out of it were at the sea*
9 a Josh. 17:9
10 a Judg. 1:29

CHAPTER 17
1 a Gen. 41:51; 46:20; 48:18 b Gen. 50:23 c Deut. 3:15
2 a Num. 26:29–33 b 1 Chr. 7:18 c Num. 26:31 d Num. 26:32 *1 Jeezer,* Num. 26:30
3 a Num. 26:33; 27:1; 36:2
4 a Josh. 14:1 b Num. 27:2–11 *1 possession*

THE DAUGHTERS OF ZELOPHEHAD

In biblical times, Hebrew law dictated that a man's possessions, particularly his land, were to be left to his sons upon his death. When Zelophehad died, leaving five daughters and no sons, the women were not content to be left out of his estate. Instead, they decided to ask for their inheritance. They were not arrogant; they were not pushy; but they were brave enough to claim what they believed to be rightfully theirs. Their request was so radical that even Moses did not know how to respond to it.

Moses asked the Lord what to do, and God told him that the women were right. Not only did the daughters of Zelophehad receive the inheritance of their father, their case set a precedent throughout Israel. The Lord went on to tell Moses that he should "speak to the children of Israel, saying: 'If a man dies and has no son, then you shall cause his inheritance to pass to his daughter'" (Num. 27:8).

There is an inheritance from the Lord for everyone, men and women alike. God has put your name on something. There is something He wants to give you and something He wants you to do with it, but you must discover what your inheritance is. So press into the heart of God until you find out what His legacy is for you. And when you do, stake your claim and refuse to let go. When God calls, He also equips. Your inheritance is part of the equipment you will need in order to answer His call and to walk in His purpose for your life. Receive your portion from the Father.

tance among their father's brothers. 5Ten
shares fell to [a]Manasseh, besides the land
of Gilead and Bashan, which *were* on the
other side of the Jordan, 6because the
daughters of Manasseh received an inheritance among his sons; and the rest of Manasseh's sons had the land of Gilead.

7And the territory of Manasseh was
from Asher to [a]Michmethath, that *lies*
east of Shechem; and the border went
along south to the inhabitants of En Tappuah. 8Manasseh had the land of Tappuah,
but [a]Tappuah on the border of Manasseh
belonged to the children of Ephraim.
9And the [1]border descended to the [2]Brook
Kanah, southward to the brook. [a]These
cities of Ephraim *are* among the cities of
Manasseh. The border of Manasseh *was* on
the north side of the brook; and it ended
at the sea.

10Southward *it was* Ephraim's, northward *it was* Manasseh's, and the sea was
its border. Manasseh's territory was adjoining Asher on the north and Issachar
on the east. 11And in Issachar and in Asher, [a]Manasseh had [b]Beth Shean and its
towns, Ibleam and its towns, the inhabitants of Dor and its towns, the inhabitants of En Dor and its towns, the
inhabitants of Taanach and its towns, and
the inhabitants of Megiddo and its
towns—three hilly regions. 12Yet [a]the
children of Manasseh could not drive out
the inhabitants of those cities, but the Canaanites were determined to dwell in that
land. 13And it happened, when the children of Israel grew strong, that they put
the Canaanites to [a]forced labor, but did
not utterly drive them out.

More Land for Ephraim and Manasseh

14[a]Then the children of Joseph spoke to
Joshua, saying, "Why have you given us
only [b]one [1]lot and one share to inherit,
since we *are* [c]a great people, inasmuch as
the LORD has blessed us until now?"

15So Joshua answered them, "If you *are*
a great people, *then* go up to the forest
country and clear a place for yourself
there in the land of the Perizzites and the
giants, since the mountains of Ephraim
are too confined for you."

16But the children of Joseph said, "The
mountain country is not enough for us;
and all the Canaanites who dwell in the
land of the valley have [a]chariots of iron,
both those who *are* of Beth Shean and its
towns and *those* who *are* [b]of the Valley of
Jezreel."

17And Joshua spoke to the house of Joseph—to Ephraim and Manasseh—saying, "You *are* a great people and have
great power; you shall not have *only* one
[1]lot, 18but the mountain country shall be
yours. Although it *is* wooded, you shall
cut it down, and its [1]farthest extent shall
be yours; for you shall drive out the Canaanites, [a]though they have iron chariots
and are strong."

The Remainder of the Land Divided

18 Now the whole congregation of the
children of Israel assembled together [a]at Shiloh, and [b]set up the tabernacle of meeting there. And the land was
subdued before them. 2But there remained among the children of Israel sev-
en tribes which had not yet received their
inheritance.

3Then Joshua said to the children of Israel: [a]"How long will you neglect to go
and possess the land which the LORD God
of your fathers has given you? 4Pick out
from among you three men for *each* tribe,
and I will send them; they shall rise and
go through the land, survey it according
to their inheritance, and come *back* to
me. 5And they shall divide it into seven
parts. [a]Judah shall remain in their territory on the south, and the [b]house of Joseph
shall remain in their territory on the
north. 6You shall therefore [1]survey the
land in seven parts and bring *the survey*
here to me, [a]that I may cast lots for you
here before the LORD our God. 7[a]But the
Levites have no part among you, for the
priesthood of the LORD *is* their inheritance. [b]And Gad, Reuben, and half the
tribe of Manasseh have received their inheritance beyond the Jordan on the east,
which Moses the servant of the LORD gave
them."

8Then the men arose to go away; and
Joshua charged those who went to [1]sur-
vey the land, saying, "Go, walk [a]through
the land, survey it, and come back to me,
that I may cast lots for you here before
the LORD in Shiloh." 9So the men went,
passed through the land, and [1]wrote the
survey in a book in seven parts by cities;
and they came to Joshua at the camp in
Shiloh. 10Then Joshua cast [a]lots for them
in Shiloh before the LORD, and there

5 a Josh. 22:7
7 a Josh. 16:6
8 a Josh. 16:8
9 a Josh. 16:9 *1 boundary* *2 Wadi*
11 a 1 Chr. 7:29 b 1 Kin. 4:12
12 a Judg. 1:19, 27, 28
13 a Josh. 16:10
14 a Josh. 16:4 b Gen. 48:22 c Gen. 48:19 *1 allotment*
16 a Judg. 1:19; 4:3 b 1 Kin. 4:12
17 *1 allotment*
18 a Deut. 20:1 *1 Lit. goings out*

CHAPTER 18
1 a Jer. 7:12 b Judg. 18:31
3 a Judg. 18:9
5 a Josh. 15:1 b Josh. 16:1—17:18
6 a Josh. 14:2; 18:10 *1 describe in writing*
7 a Josh. 13:33 b Josh. 13:8
8 a Gen. 13:17 *1 describe in writing*
9 *1 described it in writing*
10 a Acts 13:19

[b]Joshua divided the land to the children of
Israel according to their [1]divisions.

The Land of Benjamin

11[a]Now the lot of the tribe of the children of Benjamin came up according to
their families, and the territory of their lot
came out between the children of Judah
and the children of Joseph. 12[a]Their border on the north side began at the Jordan,
and the border went up to the side of Jericho on the north, and went up through
the mountains westward; it ended at the
Wilderness of Beth Aven. 13The border
went over from there toward Luz, to the
side of Luz [a](which *is* Bethel) southward;
and the border descended to Ataroth Addar, near the hill that *lies* on the south
side [b]of Lower Beth Horon.
14Then the border extended around the
west side to the south, from the hill that
lies before Beth Horon southward; and [1]it
ended at [a]Kirjath Baal (which *is* Kirjath
Jearim), a city of the children of Judah.
This *was* the west side.
15The south side *began* at the end of
Kirjath Jearim, and the border extended
on the west and went out to [a]the spring of
the waters of Nephtoah. 16Then the border came down to the end of the mountain that *lies* before [a]the Valley of the Son
of Hinnom, which *is* in the Valley of the
[1]Rephaim on the north, descended to the
Valley of Hinnom, to the side of the Jebusite *city* on the south, and descended to
[b]En Rogel. 17And it went around from the
north, went out to En Shemesh, and extended toward Geliloth, which is before
the Ascent of Adummim, and descended
to [a]the stone of Bohan the son of Reuben.
18Then it passed along toward the north
side of [1]Arabah, and went down to Arabah.
19And the border passed along to the
north side of Beth Hoglah; then [1]the border ended at the north bay at the [a]Salt
Sea, at the south end of the Jordan. This
was the southern boundary.
20The Jordan was its border on the east
side. This *was* the inheritance of the children of Benjamin, according to its boundaries all around, according to their
families.
21Now the cities of the tribe of the children of Benjamin, according to their families, were Jericho, Beth Hoglah, Emek
Keziz, 22Beth Arabah, Zemaraim, Bethel,
23Avim, Parah, Ophrah, 24Chephar Haam-
moni, Ophni, and Gaba: twelve cities with

10 [b]Num. 34:16–29 [1] *portions*
11 [a]Judg. 1:21
12 [a]Josh. 16:1
13 [a]Gen. 28:19 [b]Josh. 16:3
14 [a]Josh. 15:9 [1] Lit. *its goings out were*
15 [a]Josh. 15:9
16 [a]Josh. 15:8 [b]Josh. 15:7 [1] Lit. *Giants*
17 [a]Josh. 15:6
18 [1] *Beth Arabah,* Josh. 15:6; 18:22
19 [a]Josh. 15:2, 5 [1] Lit. *the goings out of the border were*
25 [a]1 Kin. 3:4, 5 [b]Jer. 31:15
28 [a]Josh. 15:8, 63
CHAPTER 19
1 [a]Judg. 1:3 [b]Josh. 19:9
2 [a]1 Chr. 4:28
8 [a]1 Sam. 30:27
9 [a]Josh. 19:1 [1] *too large* [2] Lit. *them*
11 [a]Gen. 49:13 [b]Josh. 12:22
12 [a]1 Chr. 6:72
13 [a]2 Kin. 14:25
14 [1] Lit. *the goings out of it were*

their villages; 25[a]Gibeon, [b]Ramah, Beeroth, 26Mizpah, Chephirah, Mozah, 27Re-
kem, Irpeel, Taralah, 28Zelah, Eleph,
[a]Jebus (which *is* Jerusalem), Gibeath, *and*
Kirjath: fourteen cities with their villages.
This was the inheritance of the children of
Benjamin according to their families.

Simeon's Inheritance with Judah

19 The [a]second lot came out for Simeon, for the tribe of the children of
Simeon according to their families. [b]And
their inheritance was within the inheritance of the children of Judah. 2[a]They had
in their inheritance Beersheba (Sheba),
Moladah, 3Hazar Shual, Balah, Ezem, 4El-
tolad, Bethul, Hormah, 5Ziklag, Beth Mar-
caboth, Hazar Susah, 6Beth Lebaoth, and
Sharuhen: thirteen cities and their villages; 7Ain, Rimmon, Ether, and Ashan: four
cities and their villages; 8and all the villages that *were* all around these cities as
far as Baalath Beer, [a]Ramah of the South.
This *was* the inheritance of the tribe of
the children of Simeon according to their
families.
9The inheritance of the children of
Simeon *was included* in the share of the
children of Judah, for the share of the
children of Judah was [1]too much for
them. [a]Therefore the children of Simeon
had *their* inheritance within the inheritance of [2]that people.

The Land of Zebulun

10The third lot came out for the children of Zebulun according to their families, and the border of their inheritance
was as far as Sarid. 11[a]Their border went
toward the west and to Maralah, went to
Dabbasheth, and extended along the
brook that is [b]east of Jokneam. 12Then
from Sarid it went eastward toward the
sunrise along the border of Chisloth Tabor, and went out toward [a]Daberath, bypassing Japhia. 13And from there it passed
along on the east of [a]Gath Hepher, toward
Eth Kazin, and extended to Rimmon,
which borders on Neah. 14Then the border went around it on the north side of
Hannathon, and [1]it ended in the Valley of
Jiphthah El. 15Included were Kattath, Na-
hallal, Shimron, Idalah, and Bethlehem:
twelve cities with their villages. 16This
was the inheritance of the children of

Zebulun according to their families, these
cities with their villages.

The Land of Issachar

17The fourth lot came out to Issachar,
for the children of Issachar according to
their families. 18And their territory went
to Jezreel, and *included* Chesulloth, Shunem, 19Haphraim, Shion, Anaharath,
20Rabbith, Kishion, Abez, 21Remeth, En
Gannim, En Haddah, and Beth Pazzez.
22And the border reached to Tabor, Sha-
hazimah, and [a]Beth Shemesh; their border ended at the Jordan: sixteen cities
with their villages. 23This *was* the inheritance of the tribe of the children of Issachar according to their families, the cities
and their villages.

The Land of Asher

24[a]The fifth lot came out for the tribe of
the children of Asher according to their
families. 25And their territory included
Helkath, Hali, Beten, Achshaph, 26Alam-
melech, Amad, and Mishal; it reached to
[a]Mount Carmel westward, along *the
Brook* Shihor Libnath. 27It turned toward
the sunrise to Beth Dagon; and it reached
to Zebulun and to the Valley of Jiphthah
El, then northward beyond Beth Emek
and Neiel, bypassing [a]Cabul *which was* on
the left, 28including [1]Ebron, Rehob, Hammon, and Kanah, [a]as far as Greater Sidon.
29And the border turned to Ramah and to
the fortified city of Tyre; then the border
turned to Hosah, and ended at the sea by
the region of [a]Achzib. 30Also Ummah,
Aphek, and Rehob *were included:* twenty-
two cities with their villages. 31This *was*
the inheritance of the tribe of the children
of Asher according to their families, these
cities with their villages.

The Land of Naphtali

32[a]The sixth lot came out to the children of Naphtali, for the children of Naphtali according to their families. 33And
their border began at Heleph, enclosing
the territory from the terebinth tree in
Zaanannim, Adami Nekeb, and Jabneel, as
far as Lakkum; [1]it ended at the Jordan.
34[a]From Heleph the border extended
westward to Aznoth Tabor, and went out
from there toward Hukkok; it adjoined
Zebulun on the south side and Asher on
the west side, and ended at Judah by the
Jordan toward the sunrise. 35And the fortified cities *are* Ziddim, Zer, Hammath,
Rakkath, Chinnereth, 36Adamah, Ramah,
Hazor, 37[a]Kedesh, Edrei, En Hazor,
38Iron, Migdal El, Horem, Beth Anath,
and Beth Shemesh: nineteen cities with
their villages. 39This *was* the inheritance
of the tribe of the children of Naphtali according to their families, the cities and
their villages.

The Land of Dan

40[a]The seventh lot came out for the
tribe of the children of Dan according to
their families. 41And the territory of their
inheritance was Zorah, [a]Eshtaol, Ir Shemesh, 42[a]Shaalabbin, [b]Aijalon, Jethlah,
43Elon, Timnah, [a]Ekron, 44Eltekeh, Gibbethon, Baalath, 45Jehud, Bene Berak,
Gath Rimmon, 46Me Jarkon, and Rakkon,
with the region [1]near [2]Joppa. 47And the
[a]border of the children of Dan went beyond these, because the children of Dan
went up to fight against Leshem and took
it; and they struck it with the edge of the
sword, took possession of it, and dwelt in
it. They called Leshem, [b]Dan, after the
name of Dan their father. 48This *is* the
inheritance of the tribe of the children of
Dan according to their families, these cities with their villages.

Joshua's Inheritance

49When they had [1]made an end of dividing the land as an inheritance according
to their borders, the children of Israel
gave an inheritance among them to Joshua the son of Nun. 50According to the
word of the LORD they gave him the city
which he asked for, [a]Timnath [b]Serah in
the mountains of Ephraim; and he built
the city and dwelt in it.
51[a]These *were* the inheritances which
Eleazar the priest, Joshua the son of Nun,
and the heads of the fathers of the tribes
of the children of Israel divided as an inheritance by lot [b]in Shiloh before the
LORD, at the door of the tabernacle of
meeting. So they made an end of dividing
the country.

The Cities of Refuge

20 The LORD also spoke to Joshua,
saying, 2"Speak to the children of
Israel, saying: [a]'Appoint[1] for yourselves
cities of refuge, of which I spoke to you
through Moses, 3that the slayer who kills
a person accidentally *or* unintentionally
may flee there; and they shall be your refuge from the avenger of blood. 4And when

---

22 a Josh. 15:10
24 a Judg. 1:31, 32
26 a Jer. 46:18
27 a 1 Kin. 9:13
28 a Judg. 1:31 *1* So with MT, Tg., Vg.; a few Heb. mss. *Abdon* (cf. 21:30 and 1 Chr. 6:74)
29 a Judg. 1:31
32 a Judg. 1:33
33 *1* Lit. *its goings out were*
34 a Deut. 33:23
37 a Josh. 20:7
40 a Judg. 1:34–36
41 a Josh. 15:33
42 a Judg. 1:35 b Josh. 10:12; 21:24
43 a Judg. 1:18
46 *1 over against* *2* Heb. *Japho*
47 a Judg. 18 b Judg. 18:29
49 *1 finished*
50 a Josh. 24:30 b 1 Chr. 7:24
51 a Num. 34:17 b Josh. 18:1, 10
CHAPTER 20
2 a Num. 35:6–34 *1 Designate*

he flees to one of those cities, and stands
at the entrance of the gate of the city, and
[1]declares his case in the hearing of the
elders of that city, they shall take him into
the city as one of them, and give him a
place, that he may dwell among them.
5[a]Then if the avenger of blood pursues
him, they shall not deliver the slayer into
his hand, because he struck his neighbor
unintentionally, but did not hate him beforehand. 6And he shall dwell in that city
[a]until he stands before the congregation
for judgment, *and* until the death of the
one who is high priest in those days. Then
the slayer may return and come to his
own city and his own house, to the city
from which he fled.' "
7So they appointed [a]Kedesh in Galilee,
in the mountains of Naphtali, [b]Shechem
in the mountains of Ephraim, and [c]Kir-
jath Arba (which *is* Hebron) in [d]the
mountains of Judah. 8And on the other
side of the Jordan, by Jericho eastward,
they assigned [a]Bezer in the wilderness on
the plain, from the tribe of Reuben, [b]Ra-
moth in Gilead, from the tribe of Gad, and
[c]Golan in Bashan, from the tribe of Manasseh. 9[a]These were the cities appointed
for all the children of Israel and for the
stranger who [1]dwelt among them, that
whoever killed a person accidentally
might flee there, and not die by the hand
of the avenger of blood [b]until he stood
before the congregation.

Cities of the Levites

21 Then the heads of the fathers'
houses of the [a]Levites came near
to [b]Eleazar the priest, to Joshua the son
of Nun, and to the heads of the fathers'
houses of the tribes of the children of Israel. 2And they spoke to them at [a]Shiloh in
the land of Canaan, saying, [b]"The LORD
commanded through Moses to give us cities to dwell in, with their common-lands
for our livestock." 3So the children of Israel gave to the Levites from their inheritance, at the commandment of the LORD,
these cities and their common-lands:
4Now the lot came out for the families
of the Kohathites. And [a]the children of
Aaron the priest, *who were* of the Levites,
[b]had thirteen cities by lot from the tribe
of Judah, from the tribe of Simeon, and
from the tribe of Benjamin. 5[a]The rest of
the children of Kohath had ten cities by
lot from the families of the tribe of Ephraim, from the tribe of Dan, and from the
half-tribe of Manasseh.
6And [a]the children of Gershon had thirteen cities by lot from the families of the
tribe of Issachar, from the tribe of Asher,
from the tribe of Naphtali, and from the
half-tribe of Manasseh in Bashan.
7[a]The children of Merari according to
their families had twelve cities from the
tribe of Reuben, from the tribe of Gad, and
from the tribe of Zebulun.
8[a]And the children of Israel gave these
cities with their common-lands by lot to
the Levites, [b]as the LORD had commanded
by the hand of Moses.
9So they gave from the tribe of the children of Judah and from the tribe of the
children of Simeon these cities which are
[1]designated by name, 10which were for
the children of Aaron, one of the families
of the Kohathites, *who were* of the children of Levi; for the lot was theirs first.
11[a]And they gave them [1]Kirjath Arba
(*Arba was* the father of [b]Anak), [c]which *is*
Hebron, in the mountains of Judah, with
the common-land surrounding it. 12But
[a]the fields of the city and its villages they
gave to Caleb the son of Jephunneh as his
possession.
13Thus [a]to the children of Aaron the
priest they gave [b]Hebron with its
common-land (a city of refuge for the
slayer), [c]Libnah with its common-land,
14[a]Jattir with its common-land, [b]Eshte-
moa with its common-land, 15[a]Holon
with its common-land, [b]Debir with its
common-land, 16[a]Ain with its common-
land, [b]Juttah with its common-land, and
[c]Beth Shemesh with its common-land:
nine cities from those two tribes; 17and
from the tribe of Benjamin, [a]Gibeon with
its common-land, [b]Geba with its
common-land, 18Anathoth with its
common-land, and [a]Almon with its
common-land: four cities. 19All the cities
of the children of Aaron, the priests, *were*
thirteen cities with their common-lands.
20[a]And the families of the children of
Kohath, the Levites, the rest of the children of Kohath, even they had the cities of
their [1]lot from the tribe of Ephraim. 21For
they gave them [a]Shechem with its
common-land in the mountains of
Ephraim (a city of refuge for the slayer),
[b]Gezer with its common-land, 22Kibzaim
with its common-land, and Beth Horon
with its common-land: four cities; 23and
from the tribe of Dan, Eltekeh with

---

4 [1] *states*
5 [a] Num. 35:12
6 [a] Num. 35:12, 24, 25
7 [a] 1 Chr. 6:76 [b] Josh. 21:21 [c] Josh. 14:15; 21:11, 13 [d] Luke 1:39
8 [a] Deut. 4:43 [b] Josh. 21:38 [c] Josh. 21:27
9 [a] Num. 35:15 [b] Josh. 20:6 [1] As a resident alien

CHAPTER 21
1 [a] Num. 35:1–8 [b] Josh. 14:1; 17:4
2 [a] Josh. 18:1 [b] Num. 35:2
4 [a] Josh. 21:8, 19 [b] Josh. 19:51
5 [a] Josh. 21:20
6 [a] Josh. 21:27
7 [a] Josh. 21:34
8 [a] Josh. 21:3 [b] Num. 35:2
9 [1] Lit. *called*
11 [a] 1 Chr. 6:55 [b] Josh. 14:15; 15:13, 14 [c] Josh. 20:7 [1] Lit. *City of Arba*
12 [a] Josh. 14:14
13 [a] 1 Chr. 6:57 [b] Josh. 15:54; 20:2, 7 [c] Josh. 15:42
14 [a] Josh. 15:48 [b] Josh. 15:50
15 [a] 1 Chr. 6:58 [b] Josh. 15:49
16 [a] 1 Chr. 6:59 [b] Josh. 15:55 [c] Josh. 15:10
17 [a] Josh. 18:25 [b] Josh. 18:24
18 [a] 1 Chr. 6:60
20 [a] 1 Chr. 6:66 [1] *allotment*
21 [a] Josh. 20:7 [b] Judg. 1:29

its common-land, Gibbethon with its
common-land, 24[a]Aijalon with its
common-land, *and* Gath Rimmon with
its common-land: four cities; 25and from
the half-tribe of Manasseh, Tanach with
its common-land and Gath Rimmon with
its common-land: two cities. 26All the ten
cities with their common-lands were for
the rest of the families of the children of
Kohath.

27[a]Also to the children of Gershon, of
the families of the Levites, from the *other*
half-tribe of Manasseh, *they gave* [b]Golan
in Bashan with its common-land (a city of
refuge for the slayer), and Be Eshterah
with its common-land: two cities; 28and
from the tribe of Issachar, Kishion with
its common-land, Daberath with its
common-land, 29Jarmuth with its
common-land, *and* En Gannim with its
common-land: four cities; 30and from the
tribe of Asher, Mishal with its common-
land, Abdon with its common-land,
31Helkath with its common-land, and Rehob with its common-land: four cities;
32and from the tribe of Naphtali, [a]Kedesh
in Galilee with its common-land (a city of
refuge for the slayer), Hammoth Dor with
its common-land, and Kartan with its
common-land: three cities. 33All the cities
of the Gershonites according to their families *were* thirteen cities with their
common-lands.

34[a]And to the families of the children of
Merari, the rest of the Levites, from the
tribe of Zebulun, Jokneam with its
common-land, Kartah with its common-
land, 35Dimnah with its common-land,
and Nahalal with its common-land: four
cities; 36[1]and from the tribe of Reuben,
[a]Bezer with its common-land, Jahaz with
its common-land, 37Kedemoth with its
common-land, and Mephaath with its
common-land: four cities; 38and from the
tribe of Gad, [a]Ramoth in Gilead with its
common-land (a city of refuge for the
slayer), Mahanaim with its common-land,
39Heshbon with its common-land, *and*
Jazer with its common-land: four cities in
all. 40So all the cities for the children of
Merari according to their families, the
rest of the families of the Levites, were *by*
their lot twelve cities.

41[a]All the cities of the Levites within
the possession of the children of Israel
were forty-eight cities with their
common-lands. 42Every one of these cities had its common-land surrounding it;
thus *were* all these cities.

The Promise Fulfilled

43So the LORD gave to Israel [a]all the
land of which He had sworn to give to
their fathers, and they [b]took possession of
it and dwelt in it. 44[a]The LORD gave them
[b]rest all around, according to all that He
had sworn to their fathers. And [c]not a
man of all their enemies stood against
them; the LORD delivered all their enemies into their hand. 45[a]Not a word failed
of any good thing which the LORD had
spoken to the house of Israel. All came to
pass.

Because _____ has served You faithfully, Lord, please give them rest. Do not let even one of their enemies stand against them.

FROM JOSHUA 21:44

Eastern Tribes Return to Their Lands

22 Then Joshua called the Reubenites,
the Gadites, and half the tribe of
Manasseh, 2and said to them: "You have
kept [a]all that Moses the servant of the
LORD commanded you, [b]and have obeyed
my voice in all that I commanded you.
3You have not [1]left your brethren these
many days, up to this day, but have kept
the charge of the commandment of the
LORD your God. 4And now the LORD your
God has given [a]rest to your brethren, as
He promised them; now therefore, return
and go to your tents *and* to the land of
your possession, [b]which Moses the servant of the LORD gave you on the other
side of the Jordan. 5But [a]take[1] careful
heed to do the commandment and the law
which Moses the servant of the LORD commanded you, [b]to love the LORD your God,
to walk in all His ways, to keep His commandments, to hold fast to Him, and to
serve Him with all your heart and with all
your soul." 6So Joshua [a]blessed them and
sent them away, and they went to their
tents.

---

24 a Josh. 10:12
27 a 1 Chr. 6:71 b Josh. 20:8
32 a Josh. 20:7
34 a 1 Chr. 6:77–81
36 a Josh. 20:8 *1 So with LXX, Vg. (cf. 1 Chr. 6:78, 79); MT, Bg., Tg. omit vv. 36, 37*
38 a Josh. 20:8
41 a Num. 35:7
43 a Gen. 12:7; 26:3, 4; 28:4, 13, 14 b Num. 33:53
44 a Deut. 7:23, 24 b Josh. 1:13, 15; 11:23 c Deut. 7:24
45 a Josh. 23:14

CHAPTER 22
2 a Num. 32:20–22 b Josh. 1:12–18
3 *1 forsaken*
4 a Josh. 21:44 b Num. 32:33
5 a Deut. 6:6, 17; 11:22 b Deut. 10:12; 11:13, 22 *1 be very careful to do*
6 a 2 Sam. 6:18

Lord, do Thou turn me all into love, and all my love into obedience. And let my obedience be without interruption.

St. Augustine

7Now to half the tribe of Manasseh Moses had given a possession in Bashan, [a]but
to the *other* half of it Joshua gave *a pos-*
session among their brethren on this side
of the Jordan, westward. And indeed,
when Joshua sent them away to their
tents, he blessed them, 8and spoke to
them, saying, "Return with much riches
to your tents, with very much livestock,
with silver, with gold, with bronze, with
iron, and with very much clothing. [a]Di-
vide the [1]spoil of your enemies with your
brethren."
9So the children of Reuben, the children of Gad, and half the tribe of Manasseh returned, and departed from the
children of Israel at Shiloh, which *is* in
the land of Canaan, to go to [a]the country
of Gilead, to the land of their possession,
which they had obtained according to the
word of the LORD by the hand of Moses.

An Altar by the Jordan

10And when they came to the region of
the Jordan which *is* in the land of Canaan,
the children of Reuben, the children of
Gad, and half the tribe of Manasseh built
an altar there by the Jordan—a great, im-
pressive altar. 11Now the children of Israel
[a]heard *someone* say, "Behold, the children of Reuben, the children of Gad, and
half the tribe of Manasseh have built an
altar on the [1]frontier of the land of Canaan, in the region of the Jordan—on the
children of Israel's side." 12And when the
children of Israel heard *of it,* [a]the whole
congregation of the children of Israel
gathered together at Shiloh to go to war
against them.
13Then the children of Israel [a]sent
[b]Phinehas the son of Eleazar the priest to
the children of Reuben, to the children of
Gad, and to half the tribe of Manasseh,
into the land of Gilead, 14and with him ten
rulers, one ruler each from the chief
house of every tribe of Israel; and [a]each
one *was* the head of the house of his father among the [1]divisions of Israel.
15Then they came to the children of Reuben, to the children of Gad, and to half the
tribe of Manasseh, to the land of Gilead,
and they spoke with them, saying, 16"Thus
says the whole congregation of the LORD:
'What [a]treachery[1] *is* this that you have
committed against the God of Israel, to
turn away this day from following the
LORD, in that you have built for yourselves
an altar, [b]that you might rebel this day
against the LORD? 17*Is* the iniquity [a]of
Peor not enough for us, from which we
are not cleansed till this day, although
there was a plague in the congregation of
the LORD, 18but that you must turn away
this day from following the LORD? And it
shall be, if you rebel today against the
LORD, that tomorrow [a]He will be angry
with the whole congregation of Israel.
19[1]Nevertheless, if the land of your possession *is* unclean, *then* cross over to the
land of the possession of the LORD, [a]where
the LORD's tabernacle stands, and take
possession among us; but do not rebel
against the LORD, nor rebel against us, by
building yourselves an altar besides the
altar of the LORD our God. 20[a]Did not
Achan the son of Zerah [1]commit a trespass in the [2]accursed thing, and wrath fell
on all the congregation of Israel? And that
man did not perish alone in his iniquity.' "
21Then the children of Reuben, the
children of Gad, and half the tribe of Manasseh answered and said to the heads of
the [1]divisions of Israel: 22"The LORD [a]God
of gods, the LORD God of gods, He [b]knows,
and let Israel itself know—if *it is* in rebellion, or if in treachery against the LORD,
do not save us this day. 23If we have built
ourselves an altar to turn from following
the LORD, or if to offer on it burnt offerings or grain offerings, or if to offer peace
offerings on it, let the LORD Himself [a]re-
quire *an account.* 24But in fact we have
done it [1]for fear, for a reason, saying, 'In
time to come your descendants may speak
to our descendants, saying, "What have
you to do with the LORD God of Israel?
25For the LORD has made the Jordan a border between you and us, *you* children of
Reuben and children of Gad. You have no
part in the LORD." So your descendants
would make our descendants cease fearing the LORD.' 26Therefore we said, 'Let us

7 a Josh. 17:1–13

8 a 1 Sam. 30:24 *1 plunder*

9 a Num. 32:1, 26, 29

11 a Judg. 20:12, 13 *1 Lit. front*

12 a Josh. 18:1

13 a Deut. 13:14 b Ex. 6:25

14 a Num. 1:4 *1 Lit. thousands*

16 a Deut. 12:5–14 b Lev. 17:8, 9 *1 unfaithful act*

17 a Num. 25:1–9

18 a Num. 16:22

19 a Josh. 18:1 *1 However*

20 a Josh. 7:1–26 *1 act unfaithfully 2 devoted thing*

21 *1 Lit. thousands*

22 a Deut. 4:35; 10:17 b [Jer. 12:3]

23 a 1 Sam. 20:16

24 *1 Lit. from fear*

now prepare to build ourselves an altar, not for burnt offering nor for sacrifice, [27]but *that* it *may be* [a]a [1]witness between you and us and our generations after us, that we may [b]perform the service of the LORD before Him with our burnt offerings, with our sacrifices, and with our peace offerings; that your descendants may not say to our descendants in time to come, "You have no part in the LORD." ' [28]Therefore we said that it will be, when they say *this* to us or to our generations in time to come, that we may say, 'Here is the replica of the altar of the LORD which our fathers made, though not for burnt offerings nor for sacrifices; but it *is* a witness between you and us.' [29]Far be it from us that we should rebel against the LORD, and turn from following the LORD this day, [a]to build an altar for burnt offerings, for grain offerings, or for sacrifices, besides the altar of the LORD our God which *is* before His tabernacle."

[30]Now when Phinehas the priest and the rulers of the congregation, the heads of the [1]divisions of Israel who *were* with him, heard the words that the children of Reuben, the children of Gad, and the children of Manasseh spoke, it pleased them. [31]Then Phinehas the son of Eleazar the priest said to the children of Reuben, the children of Gad, and the children of Manasseh, "This day we perceive that the LORD *is* [a]among us, because you have not committed this treachery against the LORD. Now you have delivered the children of Israel out of the hand of the LORD."

[32]And Phinehas the son of Eleazar the priest, and the rulers, returned from the children of Reuben and the children of Gad, from the land of Gilead to the land of Canaan, to the children of Israel, and brought back word to them. [33]So the thing pleased the children of Israel, and the children of Israel [a]blessed God; they spoke no more of going against them in battle, to destroy the land where the children of Reuben and Gad dwelt.

[34]The children of Reuben and the children of [1]Gad called the altar, *Witness,* "For *it is* a witness between us that the LORD *is* God."

Joshua's Farewell Address

23 Now it came to pass, a long time after the LORD [a]had given rest to Israel from all their enemies round about, that Joshua [b]was old, advanced in age. [2]And Joshua [a]called for all Israel, for their elders, for their heads, for their judges, and for their officers, and said to them:

"I am old, advanced in age. [3]You have seen all that the [a]LORD your God has done to all these nations because of you, for the [b]LORD your God *is* He who has fought for you. [4]See, [a]I have divided to you by lot these nations that remain, to be an inheritance for your tribes, from the Jordan, with all the nations that I have cut off, as far as the Great Sea westward. [5]And the LORD your God [a]will expel them from before you and drive them out of your sight. So you shall possess their land, [b]as the LORD your God promised you. [6][a]Therefore be very courageous to keep and to do all that is written in the Book of the Law of Moses, [b]lest you turn aside from it to the right hand or to the left, [7]*and* lest you [a]go[1] among these nations, these who remain among you. You shall not [b]make mention of the name of their gods, nor cause *anyone* to [c]swear *by them;* you shall not [d]serve them nor bow down to them, [8]but you shall [a]hold fast to the LORD your God, as you have done to this day. [9][a]For the LORD has [1]driven out from before you great and strong nations; but *as for* you, no one has been able to stand against you to this day. [10][a]One man of you shall chase a thousand, for the LORD your God *is* He who fights for you, [b]as He promised you. [11][a]Therefore take careful heed to yourselves, that you love the LORD your God. [12]Or else, if indeed you do [a]go back, and cling to the remnant of these nations—these that remain among you—and [b]make marriages with them, and go in to them and they to you, [13]know for certain that [a]the LORD your God will no longer drive out these nations from before you. [b]But they shall be snares and traps to you, and scourges on your sides and thorns in your eyes, until you perish from this good land which the LORD your God has given you.

[14]"Behold, this day [a]I[1] *am* going the way of all the earth. And you know in all your hearts and in all your souls that [b]not one thing has failed of all the good things which the LORD your God spoke concerning you. All have come to pass for you; not one word of them has failed. [15][a]Therefore it shall come to pass, that as all the good things have come upon you which the LORD your God promised you, so the LORD

27 a Gen. 31:48 b Deut. 12:5, 14 *1 testimony*
29 a Deut. 12:13, 14
30 *1* Lit. *thousands*
31 a Lev. 26:11, 12
33 a 1 Chr. 29:20
34 *1* LXX adds *and half the tribe of Manasseh*

CHAPTER 23
1 a Josh. 21:44; 22:4 b Josh. 13:1; 24:29
2 a Deut. 31:28
3 a Ps. 44:3 b Deut. 1:30
4 a Josh. 13:2, 6; 18:10
5 a Ex. 23:30; 33:2 b Num. 33:53
6 a Josh. 1:7 b Deut. 5:32
7 a Deut. 7:2, 3 b Ex. 23:13 c Deut. 6:13; 10:20 d Ex. 20:5 *1 associate with*
8 a Deut. 10:20
9 a Deut. 7:24; 11:23 *1 dispossessed*
10 a Lev. 26:8 b Ex. 14:14
11 a Josh. 22:5
12 a [2 Pet. 2:20, 21] b Deut. 7:3, 4
13 a Judg. 2:3 b Ex. 23:33; 34:12
14 a 1 Kin. 2:2 b Josh. 21:45 *1* I am going to die.
15 a Deut. 28:63

will bring upon you [b]all harmful things,
until He has destroyed you from this good
land which the LORD your God has given
you. 16 [1]When you have transgressed the
covenant of the LORD your God, which
He commanded you, and have gone and
served other gods, and bowed down to
them, then the [a]anger of the LORD will
burn against you, and you shall perish
quickly from the good land which He has
given you."

Lord, I pray that all of the
good things that You have
spoken concerning ____
would come to pass, that not
one of them would fail.

FROM JOSHUA 23:14

The Covenant at Shechem

24 Then Joshua gathered all the tribes
of Israel to [a]Shechem and [b]called
for the elders of Israel, for their heads, for
their judges, and for their officers; and
they [c]presented themselves before God.
2 And Joshua said to all the people, "Thus
says the LORD God of Israel: [a]'Your fathers, *including* Terah, the father of Abraham and the father of Nahor, dwelt on the
other side of [1]the River in old times; and
[b]they served other gods. 3 [a]Then I took
your father Abraham from the other side
of [1]the River, led him throughout all the
land of Canaan, and multiplied his [2]de-
scendants and [b]gave him Isaac. 4 To Isaac
I gave [a]Jacob and Esau. To [b]Esau I gave
the mountains of Seir to possess, [c]but Jacob and his children went down to Egypt.
5 [a]Also I sent Moses and Aaron, and [b]I
plagued Egypt, according to what I did
among them. Afterward I brought you
out.

6 'Then I [a]brought your fathers out of
Egypt, and you came to the sea; and the
Egyptians pursued your fathers with chariots and horsemen to the Red Sea. 7 So
they cried out to the LORD; and He put
[a]darkness between you and the Egyptians,
brought the sea upon them, and covered
them. And [b]your eyes saw what I did in
Egypt. Then you dwelt in the wilderness
[c]a long time. 8 And I brought you into the
land of the Amorites, who dwelt on the
other side of the Jordan, [a]and they fought
with you. But I gave them into your hand,
that you might possess their land, and I
destroyed them from before you. 9 Then
[a]Balak the son of Zippor, king of Moab,
arose to make war against Israel, and
[b]sent and called Balaam the son of Beor to
curse you. 10 [a]But I would not listen to
Balaam; [b]therefore he continued to bless
you. So I delivered you out of his hand.
11 Then [a]you went over the Jordan and
came to Jericho. And [b]the men of Jericho
fought against you—*also* the Amorites,
the Perizzites, the Canaanites, the Hittites, the Girgashites, the Hivites, and the
Jebusites. But I delivered them into your
hand. 12 [a]I sent the hornet before you
which drove them out from before you,
also the two kings of the Amorites, *but*
[b]not with your sword or with your bow.
13 I have given you a land for which you
did not labor, and [a]cities which you did
not build, and you dwell in them; you eat
of the vineyards and olive groves which
you did not plant.'

I pray, Father, that ____
will choose for themselves
today whom they will serve. I
pray that they will say, "As
for me and my house, we
will serve the Lord."

FROM JOSHUA 24:15

14 [a]"Now therefore, fear the LORD, serve
Him in [b]sincerity and in truth, and [c]put
away the gods which your fathers served
on the other side of [1]the River and [d]in
Egypt. Serve the LORD! 15 And if it seems
evil to you to serve the LORD, [a]choose for
yourselves this day whom you will serve,
whether [b]the gods which your fathers
served that *were* on the other side of [1]the
River, or [c]the gods of the Amorites, in
whose land you dwell. [d]But as for me and
my house, we will serve the LORD."

16 So the people answered and said: "Far
be it from us that we should forsake the
LORD to serve other gods; 17 for the LORD
our God *is* He who brought us and our
fathers up out of the land of Egypt, from

15 [b]Deut. 28:15–68
16 [a]Deut. 4:24–28 [1]Or *If ever*

CHAPTER 24
1 [a]Gen. 35:4 [b]Josh. 23:2 [c]1 Sam. 10:19
2 [a]Gen. 11:7–32 [b]Josh. 24:14 [1]The Euphrates
3 [a]Gen. 12:1; Acts 7:2, 3 [b][Ps. 127:3] [1]The Euphrates [2]Lit. *seed*
4 [a]Gen. 25:24–26 [b]Deut. 2:5 [c]Gen. 46:1, 3, 6
5 [a]Ex. 3:10 [b]Ex. 7—10
6 [a]Ex. 12:37, 51; 14:2–31
7 [a]Ex. 14:20 [b]Deut. 4:34 [c]Josh. 5:6
8 [a]Num. 21:21–35
9 [a]Judg. 11:25 [b]Num. 22:2–14
10 [a]Deut. 23:5 [b]Num. 23:11, 20; 24:10
11 [a]Josh. 3:14, 17 [b]Josh. 6:1; 10:1
12 [a]Ex. 23:28 [b]Ps. 44:3
13 [a]Deut. 6:10, 11
14 [a]1 Sam. 12:24 [b]2 Cor. 1:12 [c]Ezek. 20:18 [d]Ezek. 20:7, 8 [1]The Euphrates
15 [a]1 Kin. 18:21 [b]Josh. 24:2 [c]Ex. 23:24, 32 [d]Gen. 18:19 [1]The Euphrates

the house of bondage, who did those great
signs in our sight, and preserved us in all
the way that we went and among all the
people through whom we passed. 18And
the LORD drove out from before us all the
people, including the Amorites who dwelt
in the land. [a]We also will serve the LORD,
for He *is* our God."
19But Joshua said to the people, [a]"You
cannot serve the LORD, for He *is* a [b]holy
God. He *is* [c]a jealous God; [d]He will not
forgive your transgressions nor your sins.
20[a]If you forsake the LORD and serve foreign gods, [b]then He will turn and do you
harm and consume you, after He has done
you good."
21And the people said to Joshua, "No,
but we will serve the LORD!"
22So Joshua said to the people, "You *are*
witnesses against yourselves that [a]you
have chosen the LORD for yourselves, to
serve Him."
And they said, "*We are* witnesses!"
23"Now therefore," *he said,* [a]"put away
the foreign gods which *are* among you,
and [b]incline your heart to the LORD God
of Israel."
24And the people [a]said to Joshua, "The
LORD our God we will serve, and His voice
we will obey!"
25So Joshua [a]made[1] a covenant with
the people that day, and made for them a
statute and an ordinance [b]in Shechem.
26Then Joshua [a]wrote these words in
the Book of the Law of God. And he took
[b]a large stone, and [c]set it up there [d]under
the oak that *was* by the sanctuary of the
LORD. 27And Joshua said to all the people,
"Behold, this stone shall be [a]a witness to
us, for [b]it has heard all the words of the
LORD which He spoke to us. It shall therefore be a witness to you, lest you deny
your God." 28So [a]Joshua let the people depart, each to his own inheritance.

Death of Joshua and Eleazar

29[a]Now it came to pass after these
things that Joshua the son of Nun, the
servant of the LORD, died, *being* one hundred and ten years old. 30And they buried
him within the border of his inheritance
at [a]Timnath Serah, which *is* in the mountains of Ephraim, on the north side of
Mount Gaash.
31[a]Israel served the LORD all the days of
Joshua, and all the days of the elders who
outlived Joshua, who had [b]known all the
works of the LORD which He had done for
Israel.
32[a]The bones of Joseph, which the children of Israel had brought up out of
Egypt, they buried at Shechem, in the plot
of ground [b]which Jacob had bought from
the sons of Hamor the father of Shechem
for one hundred [1]pieces of silver, and
which had become an inheritance of the
children of Joseph.
33And [a]Eleazar the son of Aaron died.
They buried him in a hill *belonging to*
[b]Phinehas his son, which was given to
him in the mountains of Ephraim.

18 a Ps. 116:16
19 a Matt. 6:24 b 1 Sam. 6:20 c Ex. 20:5 d Ex. 23:21
20 a Ezra 8:22 b Deut. 4:24–26
22 a Ps. 119:173
23 a Gen. 35:2 b 1 Kin. 8:57, 58
24 a Deut. 5:24–27
25 a Ex. 15:25 b Josh. 24:1 1 Lit. *cut a covenant*
26 a Deut. 31:24 b Judg. 9:6 c Gen. 28:18 d Gen. 35:4
27 a Gen. 31:48 b Deut. 32:1
28 a Judg. 2:6, 7
29 a Judg. 2:8
30 a Josh. 19:50
31 a Judg. 2:7 b Deut. 11:2
32 a Gen. 50:25 b Gen. 33:19 1 Heb. *qesitah,* an unknown ancient measure of weight
33 a Ex. 28:1 b Ex. 6:25

AUTHOR: *Unknown*

DATE: *Approximately 1050–1000 B.C.*

THEME: *Apostasy, Oppression, Repentance, Deliverance*

KEY WORDS: *Did Evil, Cried Out, Delivered, Judged, Spirit of the Lord*

JUDGES

Dear Woman of Destiny,

In the Book of Judges, we see the impact a strong woman can make by being obedient to God's will. God worked through Deborah to lead His people to supernatural victory, and He can do the same through us. If He has called you to stand and fight for those you love, trust Him to bring deliverance through *you*.

His love and mine,

Marilyn Hickey

The Continuing Conquest of Canaan

Now after the [a]death of Joshua it came to pass that the children of Israel [b]asked the LORD, saying, "Who shall be first to go up for us against the [c]Canaanites to fight against them?"

2And the LORD said, [a]"Judah shall go up. Indeed I have delivered the land into his hand."

3So Judah said to [a]Simeon his brother, "Come up with me to my allotted territory, that we may fight against the Canaanites; and [b]I will likewise go with you to your allotted territory." And Simeon went with him. 4Then Judah went up, and the LORD delivered the Canaanites and the Perizzites into their hand; and they killed ten thousand men at [a]Bezek. 5And they found Adoni-Bezek in Bezek, and fought against him; and they defeated the Canaanites and the Perizzites. 6Then Adoni-Bezek fled, and they pursued him and caught him and cut off his thumbs and big toes. 7And Adoni-Bezek said, "Seventy kings with their thumbs and big toes cut off used to gather *scraps* under my table; [a]as I have done, so God has repaid me." Then they brought him to Jerusalem, and there he died.

8Now [a]the children of Judah fought against Jerusalem and took it; they struck it with the edge of the sword and set the city on fire. 9[a]And afterward the children of Judah went down to fight against the Canaanites who dwelt in the mountains, in the [1]South, and in the lowland. 10Then Judah [1]went against the Canaanites who dwelt in [a]Hebron. (Now the name of Hebron *was* formerly [b]Kirjath Arba.) And they killed Sheshai, Ahiman, and Talmai.

11[a]From there they went against the inhabitants of Debir. (The name of Debir *was* formerly Kirjath Sepher.)

12[a]Then Caleb said, "Whoever attacks Kirjath Sepher and takes it, to him I will give my daughter Achsah as wife." 13And Othniel the son of Kenaz, [a]Caleb's younger brother, took it; so he gave him his daughter Achsah as wife. 14[a]Now it happened, when she came *to him,* that [1]she urged him to ask her father for a field. And she dismounted from *her* donkey, and Caleb said to her, "What do you wish?" 15So she said to him, [a]"Give me a blessing; since you have given me land in the South, give me also springs of water." And Caleb gave her the upper springs and the lower springs.

16[a]Now the children of the Kenite, Moses' father-in-law, went up [b]from the City of Palms with the children of Judah into the Wilderness of Judah, which *lies* in the South *near* [c]Arad; [d]and they went and dwelt among the people. 17[a]And Judah went with his brother Simeon, and they attacked the Canaanites who inhabited Zephath, and utterly destroyed it. So the name of the city was called [b]Hormah. 18Also Judah took [a]Gaza with its territory, Ashkelon with its territory, and Ekron with its territory. 19So the LORD was with Judah. And they drove out the mountaineers, but they could not drive out the inhabitants of the lowland, because they had [a]chariots of iron. 20[a]And they gave Hebron to Caleb, as Moses had said. Then he [1]expelled from there the [b]three sons of Anak. 21[a]But the children of Benjamin did not drive out the Jebusites who inhabited Jerusalem; so the Jebusites dwell with the children of Benjamin in Jerusalem to this day.

22And the [1]house of Joseph also went up against Bethel, [a]and the LORD *was* with them. 23So the [1]house of Joseph [a]sent men to spy out Bethel. (The name of the city *was* formerly [b]Luz.) 24And when the spies saw a man coming out of the city, they said to him, "Please show us the entrance to the city, and [a]we will show you mercy." 25So he showed them the entrance to the city, and they struck the city with the edge of the sword; but they let the man and all his family go. 26And the man went to the land of the Hittites, built a city, and called its name Luz, which *is* its name to this day.

Incomplete Conquest of the Land

27[a]However, Manasseh did not drive out *the inhabitants of* Beth Shean and its villages, or [b]Taanach and its villages, or the inhabitants of [c]Dor and its villages, or the inhabitants of Ibleam and its villages, or the inhabitants of Megiddo and its villages; for the Canaanites were determined to dwell in that land. 28And it came to pass, when Israel was strong, that they put the Canaanites [1]under tribute, but did not completely drive them out.

29[a]Nor did Ephraim drive out the Canaanites who dwelt in Gezer; so the Canaanites dwelt in Gezer among them.

CHAPTER 1
1 a Josh. 24:29 b Num. 27:21 c Josh. 17:12, 13
2 a Gen. 49:8, 9
3 a Josh. 19:1 b Judg. 1:17
4 a 1 Sam. 11:8
7 a Lev. 24:19
8 a Josh. 15:63
9 a Josh. 10:36; 11:21; 15:13 *1 Heb. Negev, and so throughout the book*
10 a Josh. 15:13–19 b Josh. 14:15 *1 attacked*
11 a Josh. 15:15
12 a Josh. 15:16, 17
13 a Judg. 3:9
14 a Josh. 15:18, 19 *1 LXX, Vg. he urged her*
15 a Gen. 33:11
16 a Num. 10:29–32 b Deut. 34:3 c Josh. 12:14 d 1 Sam. 15:6
17 a Judg. 1:3 b Num. 21:3
18 a Josh. 11:22
19 a Josh. 17:16, 18
20 a Josh. 14:9, 14 b Josh. 15:14 *1 drove out from there*
21 a Josh. 15:63
22 a Judg. 1:19 *1 family*
23 a Josh. 2:1; 7:2 b Gen. 28:19 *1 family*
24 a Josh. 2:12, 14
27 a Josh. 17:11–13 b Josh. 21:25 c Josh. 17:11
28 *1 to forced labor*
29 a Josh. 16:10

30 Nor did [a]Zebulun drive out the inhabitants of Kitron or the inhabitants of Nahalol; so the Canaanites dwelt among them, and [1]were put under tribute.

31 [a]Nor did Asher drive out the inhabitants of Acco or the inhabitants of Sidon, or of Ahlab, Achzib, Helbah, Aphik, or Rehob. 32 So the Asherites [a]dwelt among the Canaanites, the inhabitants of the land; for they did not drive them out.

33 [a]Nor did Naphtali drive out the inhabitants of Beth Shemesh or the inhabitants of Beth Anath; but they dwelt among the Canaanites, the inhabitants of the land. Nevertheless the inhabitants of Beth Shemesh and Beth Anath were put under tribute to them.

34 And the Amorites forced the children of Dan into the mountains, for they would not allow them to come down to the valley; 35 and the Amorites were determined to dwell in Mount Heres, [a]in Aijalon, and in [1]Shaalbim; yet when the strength of the house of Joseph became greater, they [2]were put under tribute.

36 Now the boundary of the Amorites *was* [a]from the Ascent of Akrabbim, from Sela, and upward.

Israel's Disobedience

2 Then the Angel of the LORD came up from Gilgal to Bochim, and said: [a]"I led you up from Egypt and [b]brought you to the land of which I swore to your fathers; and [c]I said, 'I will never break My covenant with you. 2 And [a]you shall make no [1]covenant with the inhabitants of this land; [b]you shall tear down their altars.' [c]But you have not obeyed My voice. Why have you done this? 3 Therefore I also said, 'I will not drive them out before you; but they shall be [a]*thorns*[1] in your side, and [b]their gods shall [2]be a [c]snare to you.' " 4 So it was, when the Angel of the LORD spoke these words to all the children of Israel, that the people lifted up their voices and wept.

5 Then they called the name of that place [1]Bochim; and they sacrificed there to the LORD. 6 And when [a]Joshua had dismissed the people, the children of Israel went each to his own inheritance to possess the land.

Death of Joshua

7 [a]So the people served the LORD all the days of Joshua, and all the days of the elders who outlived Joshua, who had seen all the great works of the LORD which He had done for Israel. 8 Now [a]Joshua the son of Nun, the servant of the LORD, died *when he was* one hundred and ten years old. 9 [a]And they buried him within the border of his inheritance at [b]Timnath Heres, in the mountains of Ephraim, on the north side of Mount Gaash. 10 When all that generation had [1]been gathered to their fathers, another generation arose after them who [a]did not know the LORD nor the work which He had done for Israel.

> *How poor and malnourished are the saints who live without the diligent use of the Word of God.*
>
> CHARLES H. SPURGEON

Israel's Unfaithfulness

11 Then the children of Israel did [a]evil in the sight of the LORD, and served the Baals; 12 and they [a]forsook the LORD God of their fathers, who had brought them out of the land of Egypt; and they followed [b]other gods from *among* the gods of the people who *were* all around them, and they [c]bowed down to them; and they provoked the LORD to anger. 13 They forsook the LORD [a]and served [1]Baal and the [2]Ashtoreths. 14 [a]And the anger of the LORD was hot against Israel. So He [b]delivered them into the hands of plunderers who despoiled them; and [c]He sold them into the hands of their enemies all around, so that they [d]could no longer stand before their enemies. 15 Wherever they went out, the hand of the LORD was against them for calamity, as the LORD had said, and as the LORD had [a]sworn to them. And they were greatly distressed.

16 Nevertheless, [a]the LORD raised up judges who delivered them out of the hand of those who plundered them. 17 Yet they would not listen to their judges, but they [a]played the harlot with other gods, and bowed down to them. They turned quickly from the way in which their fathers walked, in obeying the commandments of the LORD; they did not do so. 18 And when the LORD raised up judges for

---

30 a Josh. 19:10–16 *1 became forced laborers*
31 a Josh. 19:24–31
32 a Ps. 106:34, 35
33 a Josh. 19:32–39
35 a Josh. 19:42 *1 Shaalabbin,* Josh. 19:42 *2 became forced laborers*
36 a Josh. 15:3

CHAPTER 2
1 a Ex. 20:2 b Deut. 1:8 c Gen. 17:7, 8
2 a Deut. 7:2 b Deut. 12:3 c Ps. 106:34 *1 treaty*
3 a Josh. 23:13 b Judg. 3:6 c Ps. 106:36 *1* LXX, Tg., Vg. *enemies to you 2 entrap you*
5 *1* Lit. *Weeping*
6 a Josh. 22:6; 24:28–31
7 a Josh. 24:31
8 a Josh. 24:29
9 a Josh. 24:30 b Josh. 19:49, 50
10 a 1 Sam. 2:12 *1* Died and joined their ancestors
11 a Judg. 3:7, 12; 4:1; 6:1
12 a Deut. 31:16 b Deut. 6:14 c Ex. 20:5
13 a Judg. 10:6 *1* A Canaanite god *2* Canaanite goddesses
14 a Deut. 31:17 b 2 Kin. 17:20 c Is. 50:1 d Lev. 26:37
15 a Lev. 26:14–26
16 a Ps. 106:43–45
17 a Ex. 34:15

them, [a]the LORD was with the judge and delivered them out of the hand of their enemies all the days of the judge; [b]for the LORD was moved to pity by their groaning because of those who oppressed them and harassed them. 19And it came to pass, [a]when the judge was dead, that they reverted and behaved more corruptly than their fathers, by following other gods, to serve them and bow down to them. They did not cease from their own doings nor from their stubborn way.

20Then the anger of the LORD was hot against Israel; and He said, "Because this nation has [a]transgressed My covenant which I commanded their fathers, and has not heeded My voice, 21I also will no longer drive out before them any of the nations which Joshua [a]left when he died, 22so [a]that through them I may [b]test Israel, whether they will keep the ways of the LORD, to walk in them as their fathers kept *them,* or not." 23Therefore the LORD left those nations, without driving them out immediately; nor did He deliver them into the hand of Joshua.

The Nations Remaining in the Land

3 Now these *are* [a]the nations which the LORD left, that He might test Israel by them, *that is,* all who had not [1]known any of the wars in Canaan 2(*this was* only so that the generations of the children of Israel might be taught to know war, at least those who had not formerly known it), 3*namely,* [a]five lords of the Philistines, all the Canaanites, the Sidonians, and the Hivites who dwelt in Mount Lebanon, from Mount Baal Hermon to the entrance of Hamath. 4And they were *left, that He might* test Israel by them, to [1]know whether they would obey the commandments of the LORD, which He had commanded their fathers by the hand of Moses.

5[a]Thus the children of Israel dwelt among the Canaanites, the Hittites, the Amorites, the Perizzites, the Hivites, and the Jebusites. 6And [a]they took their daughters to be their wives, and gave their daughters to their sons; and they served their gods.

Othniel

7So the children of Israel did [a]evil in the sight of the LORD. They [b]forgot the LORD their God, and served the Baals and [1]Asherahs. 8Therefore the anger of the LORD was hot against Israel, and He [a]sold them into the hand of [b]Cushan-Rishathaim king of Mesopotamia; and the children of Israel served Cushan-Rishathaim eight years. 9When the children of Israel [a]cried out to the LORD, the LORD [b]raised up a deliverer for the children of Israel, who delivered them: [c]Othniel the son of Kenaz, Caleb's younger brother. 10[a]The Spirit of the LORD came upon him, and he judged Israel. He went out to war, and the LORD delivered Cushan-Rishathaim king of Mesopotamia into his hand; and his hand prevailed over Cushan-Rishathaim. 11So the land had rest for forty years. Then Othniel the son of Kenaz died.

Ehud

12[a]And the children of Israel again did evil in the sight of the LORD. So the LORD strengthened [b]Eglon king of Moab against Israel, because they had done evil in the sight of the LORD. 13Then he gathered to himself the people of Ammon and [a]Amalek, went and [1]defeated Israel, and took possession of [b]the City of Palms. 14So the children of Israel [a]served Eglon king of Moab eighteen years.

15But when the children of Israel [a]cried out to the LORD, the LORD raised up a deliverer for them: Ehud the son of Gera, the Benjamite, a [b]left-handed man. By him the children of Israel sent tribute to Eglon king of Moab. 16Now Ehud made himself a dagger (it was double-edged and a cubit in length) and fastened it under his clothes on his right thigh. 17So he brought the tribute to Eglon king of Moab. (Now Eglon *was* a very fat man.) 18And when he had finished presenting the tribute, he sent away the people who had carried the tribute. 19But he himself turned back [a]from the [1]stone images that *were* at Gilgal, and said, "I have a secret message for you, O king."

He said, "Keep silence!" And all who attended him went out from him.

20So Ehud came to him (now he was sitting upstairs in his cool private chamber). Then Ehud said, "I have a message from God for you." So he arose from *his* seat. 21Then Ehud reached with his left hand, took the dagger from his right thigh, and thrust it into his belly. 22Even the [1]hilt went in after the blade, and the

18 a Josh. 1:5 b Gen. 6:6
19 a Judg. 3:12
20 a [Josh. 23:16]
21 a Josh. 23:4, 5, 13
22 a Judg. 3:1, 4 b Deut. 8:2, 16; 13:3

CHAPTER 3
1 a Judg. 1:1; 2:21, 22 *1 experienced*
3 a Josh. 13:3
4 *1 find out*
5 a Ps. 106:35
6 a Ex. 34:15, 16
7 a Judg. 2:11 b Deut. 32:18 *1* Name or symbol for Canaanite goddesses
8 a Judg. 2:14 b Hab. 3:7
9 a Judg. 3:15 b Judg. 2:16 c Judg. 1:13
10 a Num. 27:18
12 a Judg. 2:19 b 1 Sam. 12:9
13 a Judg. 5:14 b Judg. 1:16 *1 struck*
14 a Deut. 28:48
15 a Ps. 78:34 b Judg. 20:16
19 a Josh. 4:20 *1* Tg. *quarries*
22 *1 handle*

fat closed over the blade, for he did not
draw the dagger out of his belly; and his
entrails came out. 23Then Ehud went out
through the porch and shut the doors of
the upper room behind him and locked
them.
24When he had gone out, [1]*Eglon's* servants came to look, and *to their* surprise,
the doors of the upper room were locked.
So they said, "He is probably [a]attending[2]
to his needs in the cool chamber." 25So
they waited till they were [a]embarrassed,
and still he had not opened the doors of
the upper room. Therefore they took the
key and opened *them.* And there was their
master, fallen dead on the floor.
26But Ehud had escaped while they delayed, and passed beyond the [1]stone images and escaped to Seirah. 27And it
happened, when he arrived, that [a]he blew
the trumpet in the [b]mountains of Ephraim, and the children of Israel went down
with him from the mountains; and [1]he led
them. 28Then he said to them, "Follow
me, for [a]the LORD has delivered your enemies the Moabites into your hand." So
they went down after him, seized the
[b]fords of the Jordan leading to Moab, and
did not allow anyone to cross over. 29And
at that time they killed about ten thousand men of Moab, all stout men of valor;
not a man escaped. 30So Moab was subdued that day under the hand of Israel.
And [a]the land had rest for eighty years.

Shamgar

31After him was [a]Shamgar the son of
Anath, who killed six hundred men of the
Philistines [b]with an ox goad; [c]and he also
delivered [d]Israel.

Deborah

4 When Ehud was dead, [a]the children of
Israel again did [b]evil in the sight of
the LORD. 2So the LORD [a]sold them into
the hand of Jabin king of Canaan, who
reigned in [b]Hazor. The commander of his
army *was* [c]Sisera, who dwelt in [d]Haro-
sheth Hagoyim. 3And the children of Israel cried out to the LORD; for Jabin had
nine hundred [a]chariots of iron, and for
twenty years [b]he had harshly oppressed
the children of Israel.
4 Now Deborah, a prophetess, the wife
of Lapidoth, was judging Israel at that
time. 5[a]And she would sit under the
palm tree of Deborah between Ramah and
Bethel in the mountains of Ephraim. And

24 a 1 Sam. 24:3
1 Lit. *his*
2 Lit. *covering his feet*

25 a 2 Kin. 2:17; 8:11

26 1 Tg. *quarries*

27 a 1 Sam. 13:3
b Josh. 17:15
1 Lit. *he went before them*

28 a Judg. 7:9, 15
b Josh. 2:7

30 a Judg. 3:11

31 a Judg. 5:6
b 1 Sam. 17:47
c Judg. 2:16
d 1 Sam. 4:1

CHAPTER 4
1 a Judg. 2:19
b Judg. 2:11

2 a Judg. 2:14
b Josh. 11:1, 10
c 1 Sam. 12:9
d Judg. 4:13, 16

3 a Judg. 1:19
b Ps. 106:42

5 a Gen. 35:8

6 a Heb. 11:32
b Josh. 19:37; 21:32
c Judg. 8:18
1 *march*

7 a Ex. 14:4
b Ps. 83:9, 10
1 Lit. *draw*

9 a Judg. 2:14

10 a Judg. 5:18
b 1 Kin. 20:10
1 Lit. *at his feet*

11 a Judg. 1:16
b Num. 10:29
c Judg. 4:6

14 a Deut. 9:3; 31:3
1 *Arise!*

the children of Israel came up to her for
judgment. 6Then she sent and called for
[a]Barak the son of Abinoam from [b]Kedesh
in Naphtali, and said to him, "Has not the
LORD God of Israel commanded, 'Go and
[1]deploy *troops* at Mount [c]Tabor; take with
you ten thousand men of the sons of
Naphtali and of the sons of Zebulun; 7and
against you [a]I will deploy Sisera, the commander of Jabin's army, with his chariots
and his multitude at the [b]River Kishon;
and I will [1]deliver him into your hand'?"
8And Barak said to her, "If you will go
with me, then I will go; but if you will not
go with me, I will not go!"
9So she said, "I will surely go with you;
nevertheless there will be no glory for you
in the journey you are taking, for the
LORD will [a]sell Sisera into the hand of a
woman." Then Deborah arose and went
with Barak to Kedesh. 10And Barak called
[a]Zebulun and Naphtali to Kedesh; he
went up with ten thousand men [b]under[1]
his command, and Deborah went up with
him.
11Now Heber [a]the Kenite, of the children of [b]Hobab the father-in-law of Moses, had separated himself from the
Kenites and pitched his tent near the terebinth tree at Zaanaim, [c]which *is* beside
Kedesh.
12And they reported to Sisera that Barak the son of Abinoam had gone up to
Mount Tabor. 13So Sisera gathered together all his chariots, nine hundred
chariots of iron, and all the people who
were with him, from Harosheth Hagoyim
to the River Kishon.

O God, have mercy and keep from doing evil in Your sight.

FROM JUDGES 4:1

14Then Deborah said to Barak, [1]"Up!
For this *is* the day in which the LORD has
delivered Sisera into your hand. [a]Has not
the LORD gone out before you?" So Barak
went down from Mount Tabor with ten
thousand men following him. 15And the
LORD routed Sisera and all *his* chariots
and all *his* army with the edge of the

JUDGES 4:4

Dear Woman of Destiny,

Deborah is one of the Bible's great women of destiny. She was called by God to be a prophetess, as well as the only female judge in the land of Israel. She is an example to us of a woman of vision, evidenced by her ability to hear the voice of God for Israel during a time of tremendous bondage and oppression. The divine revelation she received enabled her to govern her nation effectively and to release to other leaders the battle plan that would secure Israel's liberty.

At the time of Deborah's rule as judge, Israel had fallen into idolatry and had, therefore, been delivered into the hand of the Canaanite king. This mighty, intimidating king, with nine hundred chariots of iron, had oppressed Israel for twenty years. Realizing that they would remain in bondage without God's intervention, Israel cried to the Lord for deliverance, just as many women today are crying out to God to free them from other forms of oppression.

When the word of the Lord came to her, Deborah was sitting under her palm tree. God gave her a revelation that dealt with the destiny of the nation and showed her the battle plan that would lead her people to freedom. Because she was a woman of vision, Deborah was able to look past the seemingly impossible situation her nation faced and lay hold of the hope of God's promise of deliverance. She is an example of women who desire to see beyond their natural situations, regardless of how hopeless or desperate they may seem, and look into the supernatural realm with the eyes of God's Spirit.

God is raising up a generation of women today who are willing to embrace His vision for their lives, their families, their circumstances, and even their nations, above and beyond that which the natural mind can see or comprehend. Women of vision have the courage that enables them to conquer and overcome in situations that would otherwise seem unconquerable. Someone once said, "People of vision see the invisible, hear the inaudible, believe the incredible, think the unthinkable, and do the impossible!" (Unknown)

Vision releases faith to do the impossible. It gives one the ability to grasp the mind and will of God for a given situation, or even for one's life, which will help to develop focus and establish priority. Vision penetrates the clouds of darkness, confusion, and fear, and releases the light of revelation that illuminates the path leading to one's destiny. Vision brings courage to overcome. Vision brings breakthrough!

Today, women everywhere can be partakers of the same spirit and anointing that Deborah possessed. God is calling you to know His voice and see His hand. In doing so, fear is destroyed, faith is established, and the impossible becomes possible!

Jane Hamon

sword before Barak; and Sisera alighted
from *his* chariot and fled away on foot.
[16]But Barak pursued the chariots and the
army as far as Harosheth Hagoyim, and all
the army of Sisera fell by the edge of the
sword; not a man was [a]left.
[17]However, Sisera had fled away on foot
to the tent of [a]Jael, the wife of Heber the
Kenite; for *there was* peace between Jabin
king of Hazor and the house of Heber the
Kenite. [18]And Jael went out to meet Sisera, and said to him, "Turn aside, my lord,
turn aside to me; do not fear." And when
he had turned aside with her into the tent,
she covered him with a [1]blanket.
[19]Then he said to her, "Please give me
a little water to drink, for I am thirsty." So
she opened [a]a jug of milk, gave him a
drink, and covered him. [20]And he said to
her, "Stand at the door of the tent, and if
any man comes and inquires of you, and
says, 'Is there any man here?' you shall
say, 'No.' "
[21]Then Jael, Heber's wife, [a]took a tent
peg and took a hammer in her hand, and
went softly to him and drove the peg into
his temple, and it went down into the
ground; for he was fast asleep and weary.
So he died. [22]And then, as Barak pursued
Sisera, Jael came out to meet him, and
said to him, "Come, I will show you the
man whom you seek." And when he went
into her *tent,* there lay Sisera, dead with
the peg in his temple.

16 [a]Ex. 14:28
17 [a]Judg. 5:6
18 [1]*rug*
19 [a]Judg. 5:24–27
21 [a]Judg. 5:24–27

Deborah

It doesn't matter whether a leader is male or female when that person rules with the authority of the Almighty. Deborah had more political authority than any woman in the Bible, and she governed God's people with a mother's heart and a soldier's strength (see Judg. 5:7; 4:6–9).

A trusted counselor for the children of Israel, Deborah's gift made room for her (see Prov. 18:16). She did not go looking for ways to exercise her leadership, but possessed the kind of godly wisdom that called the people to her. She sat patiently under a palm tree, fielding questions, mediating disputes, and bringing order and justice to the lives of a people miserably oppressed by the cruel Canaanite king, Jabin.

Deborah was also blessed with the gift that gives any leader an edge—she had the ability to hear, and the courage to act upon, the voice of God. When it was time for Israel to stand up to King Jabin, Deborah sent for Barak and reminded him of the word of the Lord, "Has not the LORD God of Israel commanded, 'Go and deploy troops . . . and against you I will deploy Sisera . . . and I will deliver him into your hand'?" (Judg. 4:6, 7). Even with such a promise from God, Barak refused to go to war without Deborah; and she marched into the battle with him, revealing to him God's strategy for victory .

Amid the fighting, the clamor of war thundered in her ears, while the voice of the Lord whispered to her spirit. And when the moment was right, she gave God's instructions to Barak: "Up! For this is the day in which the LORD has delivered Sisera into your hand. Has not the LORD gone out before you?" (Judg. 4:14). Thanks to her leadership, Israel won the war and escaped Jabin's tyranny.

May God raise up women today with the prophetic voice, the discerning mind and the courageous heart of Deborah.

[23]So on that day God subdued Jabin
king of Canaan in the presence of the children of Israel. [24]And the hand of the children of Israel grew stronger and stronger
against Jabin king of Canaan, until they
had destroyed Jabin king of Canaan.

The Song of Deborah

5 Then Deborah and Barak the son of Abinoam [a]sang on that day, saying:

2 "When[1] leaders [a]lead in Israel,
[b]When the people [2]willingly offer
themselves,
Bless the LORD!

3 "Hear,[a] O kings! Give ear,
O princes!
I, *even* [b]I, will sing to the LORD;
I will sing praise to the LORD God
of Israel.

4 "LORD, [a]when You went out from
Seir,
When You marched from [b]the field
of Edom,
The earth trembled and the heavens
poured,
The clouds also poured water;
5 [a]The mountains [1]gushed before the
LORD,
[b]This Sinai, before the LORD God of
Israel.

6 "In the days of [a]Shamgar, son of
Anath,
In the days of [b]Jael,
[c]The highways were deserted,
And the travelers walked along the
byways.
7 Village life ceased, it ceased in
Israel,
Until I, Deborah, arose,
Arose a mother in Israel.
8 They chose [a]new gods;
Then *there was* war in the gates;
Not a shield or spear was seen
among forty thousand in Israel.
9 My heart *is* with the rulers of
Israel
Who offered themselves willingly
with the people.
Bless the LORD!

10 "Speak, you who ride on white
[a]donkeys,
Who sit in judges' attire,
And who walk along the road.
11 Far from the noise of the archers,
among the watering places,
There they shall recount the
righteous acts of the LORD,
The righteous acts *for* His villagers
in Israel;
Then the people of the LORD shall
go down to the gates.

12 "Awake,[a] awake, Deborah!
Awake, awake, sing a song!
Arise, Barak, and lead your captives
away,
O son of Abinoam!

13 "Then the survivors came down,
the people against the nobles;
The LORD came down for me
against the mighty.
14 From Ephraim *were* those whose
roots were in [a]Amalek.
After you, Benjamin, with your
peoples,
From Machir rulers came down,
And from Zebulun those who bear
the recruiter's staff.
15 And [1]the princes of Issachar *were*
with Deborah;
As Issachar, so *was* Barak
Sent into the valley [2]under his
command;
Among the divisions of Reuben
There were great resolves of heart.
16 Why did you sit among the
sheepfolds,
To hear the pipings for the flocks?
The divisions of Reuben have great
searchings of heart.
17 [a]Gilead stayed beyond the Jordan,
And why did Dan remain [1]on ships?
[b]Asher continued at the seashore,
And stayed by his inlets.
18 [a]Zebulun *is* a people *who*
jeopardized their lives to the
point of death,
Naphtali also, on the heights of the
battlefield.

19 "The kings came *and* fought,
Then the kings of Canaan fought
In [a]Taanach, by the waters of
Megiddo;
They took no spoils of silver.
20 They fought from the heavens;
The stars from their courses fought
against Sisera.
21 [a]The torrent of Kishon swept them
away,
That ancient torrent, the torrent of
Kishon.
O my soul, march on in strength!
22 Then the horses' hooves pounded,

CHAPTER 5
1 [a]Judg. 4:4
2 [a]Ps. 18:47 [b]2 Chr. 17:16 *[1] Or When locks are loosed* *[2] volunteer*
3 [a]Deut. 32:1, 3 [b]Ps. 27:6
4 [a]Deut. 33:2 [b]Ps. 68:8
5 [a]Ps. 97:5 [b]Ex. 19:18 *[1] flowed*
6 [a]Judg. 3:31 [b]Judg. 4:17 [c]Is. 33:8
8 [a]Deut. 32:17
10 [a]Judg. 10:4; 12:14
12 [a]Ps. 57:8
14 [a]Judg. 3:13
15 [1] So with LXX, Syr., Tg., Vg.; MT *And my princes in Issachar* [2] Lit. *at his feet*
17 [a]Josh. 22:9 [b]Josh. 19:29, 31 [1] Or *at ease*
18 [a]Judg. 4:6, 10
19 [a]Judg. 1:27
21 [a]Judg. 4:7

The galloping, galloping of his
steeds.
23 'Curse Meroz,' said the [1]angel of
the LORD,
'Curse its inhabitants bitterly,
Because they did not come to the
help of the LORD,
To the help of the LORD against the
mighty.'

24 "Most blessed among women is
Jael,
The wife of Heber the Kenite;
[a]Blessed is she among women in
tents.
25 He asked for water, she gave milk;
She brought out cream in a lordly
bowl.
26 She stretched her hand to the tent
peg,
Her right hand to the workmen's
hammer;
She pounded Sisera, she pierced his
head,
She split and struck through his
temple.
27 At her feet he sank, he fell, he lay
still;
At her feet he sank, he fell;
Where he sank, there he fell [a]dead.

28 "The mother of Sisera looked
through the window,
And cried out through the lattice,
'Why is his chariot *so* long in
coming?
Why tarries the clatter of his
chariots?'
29 Her wisest [1]ladies answered her,
Yes, she [2]answered herself,
30 'Are they not finding and dividing
the spoil:
To every man a girl *or* two;
For Sisera, plunder of dyed
garments,
Plunder of garments embroidered
and dyed,
Two pieces of dyed embroidery for
the neck of the looter?'

31 "Thus let all Your enemies [a]perish,
O LORD!
But *let* those who love Him *be* [b]like
the [c]sun
When it comes out in full
[d]strength."
So the land had rest for forty years.

23 [1] Or *Angel*

24 [a] [Luke 1:28]

27 [a] Judg. 4:18–21

29 [1] *princesses* [2] Lit. *repeats her words to herself*

31 [a] Ps. 92:9 [b] 2 Sam. 23:4 [c] Ps. 37:6; 89:36, 37 [d] Ps. 19:5

CHAPTER 6

1 [a] Judg. 2:11 [b] Num. 22:4; 31:1–3

2 [a] 1 Sam. 13:6

3 [a] Judg. 7:12

4 [a] Lev. 26:16 [b] Deut. 28:31

5 [1] *innumerable*

6 [a] Hos. 5:15

8 [a] Josh. 24:17 [1] *slavery*

9 [a] Ps. 44:2, 3

10 [a] 2 Kin. 17:35, 37, 38 [b] Judg. 2:1, 2

11 [a] Josh. 17:2 [b] Heb. 11:32

12 [a] Judg. 13:3 [b] Josh. 1:5

13 [a] [Is. 59:1] [b] Ps. 44:1 [c] Ps. 44:9–16 [1] Heb. *adoni*, used of man

Midianites Oppress Israel

6 Then the children of Israel did [a]evil in
the sight of the LORD. So the LORD
delivered them into the hand of [b]Midian
for seven years, 2and the hand of Midian
prevailed against Israel. Because of the
Midianites, the children of Israel made for
themselves the dens, [a]the caves, and the
strongholds which *are* in the mountains.
3So it was, whenever Israel had sown,
Midianites would come up; also Amalekites and the [a]people of the East would
come up against them. 4Then they would
encamp against them and [a]destroy the
produce of the earth as far as Gaza, and
leave no sustenance for Israel, neither
sheep nor ox nor [b]donkey. 5For they
would come up with their livestock and
their tents, coming in as numerous as locusts; both they and their camels were
[1]without number; and they would enter
the land to destroy it. 6So Israel was greatly impoverished because of the Midianites, and the children of Israel [a]cried out
to the LORD.

7And it came to pass, when the children
of Israel cried out to the LORD because
of the Midianites, 8that the LORD sent a
prophet to the children of Israel, who said
to them, "Thus says the LORD God of Israel: 'I brought you up from Egypt and
brought you out of the [a]house of [1]bond-
age; 9and I delivered you out of the hand
of the Egyptians and out of the hand of all
who oppressed you, and [a]drove them out
before you and gave you their land. 10Also
I said to you, "I *am* the LORD your God;
[a]do not fear the gods of the Amorites, in
whose land you dwell." But you have not
obeyed My [b]voice.' "

Gideon

11Now the Angel of the LORD came and
sat under the terebinth tree which *was* in
Ophrah, which *belonged* to Joash [a]the
Abiezrite, while his son [b]Gideon threshed
wheat in the winepress, in order to hide *it*
from the Midianites. 12And the [a]Angel of
the LORD appeared to him, and said to
him, "The LORD *is* [b]with you, you mighty
man of valor!"

13Gideon said to Him, "O [1]my lord, if
the LORD is with us, why then has all this
happened to us? And [a]where *are* all His
miracles [b]which our fathers told us about,
saying, 'Did not the LORD bring us up
from Egypt?' But now the LORD has [c]for-

saken us and delivered us into the hands
of the Midianites."
14 Then the LORD turned to him and
said, [a]"Go in this might of yours, and you
shall save Israel from the hand of the Midianites. [b]Have I not sent you?"
15 So he said to Him, "O [1]my Lord, how
can I save Israel? Indeed [a]my clan *is* the
weakest in Manasseh, and I *am* the least
in my father's house."
16 And the LORD said to him, [a]"Surely I
will be with you, and you shall [1]defeat the
Midianites as one man."
17 Then he said to Him, "If now I have
found favor in Your sight, then [a]show me
a sign that it is You who talk with me.
18 [a]Do not depart from here, I pray, until
I come to You and bring out my offering
and set *it* before You."
And He said, "I will wait until you come
back."
19 [a]So Gideon went in and prepared a
young goat, and unleavened bread from
an ephah of flour. The meat he put in a
basket, and he put the broth in a pot; and
he brought *them* out to Him under the
terebinth tree and presented *them*. 20 The
Angel of God said to him, "Take the meat
and the unleavened bread and [a]lay *them*
on this rock, and [b]pour out the broth."
And he did so.
21 Then the Angel of the LORD put out
the end of the staff that *was* in His hand,
and touched the meat and the unleavened
bread; and [a]fire rose out of the rock and
consumed the meat and the unleavened
bread. And the Angel of the LORD departed
out of his sight.
22 Now Gideon [a]perceived that He *was*
the Angel of the LORD. So Gideon said,
"Alas, O Lord GOD! [b]For I have seen the
Angel of the LORD face to face."
23 Then the LORD said to him, [a]"Peace
be with you; do not fear, you shall not
die." 24 So Gideon built an altar there to
the LORD, and called it [1]The-LORD-*Is*-
Peace. To this day it *is* still [a]in Ophrah of
the Abiezrites.
25 Now it came to pass the same night
that the LORD said to him, "Take your father's young bull, the second bull of seven
years old, and [a]tear down the altar of
[b]Baal that your father has, and [c]cut down
the [1]wooden image that *is* beside it; 26 and
build an altar to the LORD your God on top
of this [1]rock in the proper arrangement,
and take the second bull and offer a burnt
sacrifice with the wood of the image
which you shall cut down." 27 So Gideon
took ten men from among his servants
and did as the LORD had said to him. But
because he feared his father's household
and the men of the city too much to do *it*
by day, he did *it* by night.

Gideon Destroys the Altar of Baal

28 And when the men of the city arose
early in the morning, there was the altar
of Baal, torn down; and the wooden image
that *was* beside it was cut down, and the
second bull was being offered on the altar
which had been built. 29 So they said to
one another, "Who has done this thing?"
And when they had inquired and asked,
they said, "Gideon the son of Joash has
done this thing." 30 Then the men of the
city said to Joash, "Bring out your son,
that he may die, because he has torn down
the altar of Baal, and because he has cut
down the wooden image that *was* beside it."
31 But Joash said to all who stood
against him, "Would you [1]plead for Baal?
Would you save him? Let the one who
would plead for him be put to death by
morning! If he *is* a god, let him plead for
himself, because his altar has been torn
down!" 32 Therefore on that day he called
him [a]Jerubbaal,[1] saying, "Let Baal plead
against him, because he has torn down his
altar."
33 Then all [a]the Midianites and Amalekites, the people of the East, gathered together; and they crossed over and
encamped in [b]the Valley of Jezreel. 34 But
[a]the Spirit of the LORD came upon Gideon; then he [b]blew the trumpet, and the
Abiezrites gathered behind him. 35 And he
sent messengers throughout all Manasseh, who also gathered behind him. He
also sent messengers to [a]Asher, [b]Zebulun,
and Naphtali; and they came up to meet
them.

The Sign of the Fleece

36 So Gideon said to God, "If You will
save Israel by my hand as You have said—
37 [a]look, I shall put a fleece of wool on the
threshing floor; if there is dew on the
fleece only, and *it is* dry on all the ground,
then I shall know that You will save Israel
by my hand, as You have said." 38 And it
was so. When he rose early the next morning and squeezed the fleece together, he

14 a 1 Sam. 12:11 b Josh. 1:9
15 a 1 Sam. 9:21 *1* Heb. *Adonai*, used of God
16 a Ex. 3:12 *1* Lit. *strike*
17 a Judg. 6:36, 37
18 a Gen. 18:3, 5
19 a Gen. 18:6–8
20 a Judg. 13:19 b 1 Kin. 18:33, 34
21 a Lev. 9:24
22 a Judg. 13:21, 22 b Gen. 16:13
23 a Dan. 10:19
24 a Judg. 8:32 *1* Heb. *YHWH Shalom*
25 a Judg. 2:2 b Judg. 3:7 c Ex. 34:13 *1* Heb. *Asherah*, a Canaanite goddess
26 *1 stronghold*
31 *1 contend*
32 a 1 Sam. 12:11 *1* Lit. *Let Baal Plead*
33 a Judg. 6:3 b Josh. 17:16
34 a Judg. 3:10 b Judg. 3:27
35 a Judg. 5:17; 7:23 b Judg. 4:6, 10; 5:18
37 a [Ex. 4:3–7]

wrung the dew out of the fleece, a bowlful
of water. 39Then Gideon said to God, [a]"Do
not be angry with me, but let me speak
just once more: Let me test, I pray, just
once more with the fleece; let it now be
dry only on the fleece, but on all the
ground let there be dew." 40And God did
so that night. It was dry on the fleece only,
but there was dew on all the ground.

Gideon's Valiant Three Hundred

7 Then [a]Jerubbaal (that *is,* Gideon) and
all the people who *were* with him rose
early and encamped beside the well of Ha-
rod, so that the camp of the Midianites
was on the north side of them by the hill
of Moreh in the valley.

Lord, I pray that _____ would be careful to give all glory to You, for You alone can save.

FROM JUDGES 7:2

2And the LORD said to Gideon, "The
people who *are* with you *are* too many for
Me to give the Midianites into their hands,
lest Israel [a]claim glory for itself against
Me, saying, 'My own hand has saved me.'
3Now therefore, proclaim in the hearing
of the people, saying, [a]'Whoever *is* fearful
and afraid, let him turn and depart at once
from Mount Gilead.'" And twenty-two
thousand of the people returned, and ten
thousand remained.
4But the LORD said to Gideon, "The people *are* still *too* many; bring them down to
the water, and I will test them for you
there. Then it will be, *that* of whom I say
to you, 'This one shall go with you,' the
same shall go with you; and of whomever
I say to you, 'This one shall not go with
you,' the same shall not go." 5So he
brought the people down to the water.
And the LORD said to Gideon, "Everyone
who laps from the water with his tongue,
as a dog laps, you shall set apart by himself; likewise everyone who gets down on
his knees to drink." 6And the number of
those who lapped, *putting* their hand to
their mouth, was three hundred men; but
all the rest of the people got down on their
knees to drink water. 7Then the LORD said
to Gideon, [a]"By the three hundred men
who lapped I will save you, and deliver the
Midianites into your hand. Let all the *other* people go, every man to his [1]place." 8So
the people took provisions and their
trumpets in their hands. And he sent away
all *the rest of* Israel, every man to his tent,
and retained those three hundred men.
Now the camp of Midian was below him in
the valley.
9It happened on the same [a]night that
the LORD said to him, "Arise, go down
against the camp, for I have delivered it
into your hand. 10But if you are afraid to
go down, go down to the camp with Purah
your servant, 11and you shall [a]hear what
they say; and afterward [1]your hands shall
be strengthened to go down against the
camp." Then he went down with Purah
his servant to the outpost of the armed
men who *were* in the camp. 12Now the
Midianites and Amalekites, [a]all the people
of the East, were lying in the valley [b]as
numerous as locusts; and their camels
were [1]without number, as the sand by the
seashore in multitude.
13And when Gideon had come, there
was a man telling a dream to his companion. He said, "I have had a dream: *To my*
surprise, a loaf of barley bread tumbled
into the camp of Midian; it came to a tent
and struck it so that it fell and overturned,
and the tent collapsed."
14Then his companion answered and
said, "This *is* nothing else but the sword
of Gideon the son of Joash, a man of Israel! Into his hand [a]God has delivered Midian and the whole camp."
15And so it was, when Gideon heard the
telling of the dream and its interpretation,
that he worshiped. He returned to the
camp of Israel, and said, "Arise, for the
LORD has delivered the camp of Midian
into your hand." 16Then he divided the
three hundred men *into* three companies,
and he put a trumpet into every man's
hand, with empty pitchers, and torches
inside the pitchers. 17And he said to them,
"Look at me and do likewise; watch, and
when I come to the edge of the camp you
shall do as I do: 18When I blow the trumpet, I and all who *are* with me, then you
also blow the trumpets on every side of
the whole camp, and say, '*The sword of*
the LORD and of Gideon!'"

39 a Gen. 18:32

CHAPTER 7
1 a Judg. 6:32
2 a Deut. 8:17
3 a Deut. 20:8
7 a 1 Sam. 14:6
1 home
9 a Judg. 6:25
11 a 1 Sam. 14:9, 10
1 you shall be encouraged
12 a Judg. 6:3, 33; 8:10
b Judg. 6:5
1 innumerable
14 a Judg. 6:14, 16

19So Gideon and the hundred men who
were with him came to the outpost of the
camp at the beginning of the middle
watch, just as they had posted the watch;
and they blew the trumpets and broke the
pitchers that *were* in their hands. 20Then
the three companies blew the trumpets
and broke the pitchers—they held the
torches in their left hands and the trumpets in their right hands for blowing—
and they cried, "The sword of the LORD
and of Gideon!" 21And [a]every man stood
in his place all around the camp; [b]and the
whole army ran and cried out and fled.
22When the three hundred [a]blew the
trumpets, [b]the LORD set [c]every man's
sword against his companion throughout
the whole camp; and the army fled to
[1]Beth Acacia, toward Zererah, as far as the
border of [d]Abel Meholah, by Tabbath.

The Bible itself is the greatest of miracles, and the Son of God more wonderful than any of the wonders that confirm His claims!

KATHRYN KUHLMAN

23And the men of Israel gathered together from [a]Naphtali, Asher, and all Manasseh, and pursued the Midianites.
24Then Gideon sent messengers
throughout all the [a]mountains of Ephraim, saying, "Come down against the Midianites, and seize from them the watering
places as far as Beth Barah and the Jordan." Then all the men of Ephraim gathered together and [b]seized the watering
places as far as [c]Beth Barah and the Jordan. 25And they captured [a]two princes of
the Midianites, [b]Oreb and Zeeb. They
killed Oreb at the rock of Oreb, and Zeeb
they killed at the winepress of Zeeb. They
pursued Midian and brought the heads of
Oreb and Zeeb to Gideon on the [c]other
side of the Jordan.

Gideon Subdues the Midianites

8 Now [a]the men of Ephraim said to
him, "Why have you done this to us by
not calling us when you went to fight with
the Midianites?" And they reprimanded
him sharply.
2So he said to them, "What have I done
now in comparison with you? *Is* not the
[1]gleaning *of the grapes* of Ephraim better
than [2]the vintage of [a]Abiezer? 3[a]God has
delivered into your hands the princes of
Midian, Oreb and Zeeb. And what was I
able to do in comparison with you?" Then
their [b]anger toward him subsided when
he said that.
4When Gideon came [a]to the Jordan, he
and [b]the three hundred men who *were*
with him crossed over, exhausted but still
in pursuit. 5Then he said to the men of
[a]Succoth, "Please give loaves of bread to
the people who follow me, for they are
exhausted, and I am pursuing Zebah and
Zalmunna, kings of Midian."
6And the leaders of Succoth said, [a]"*Are*[1]
the hands of Zebah and Zalmunna now in
your hand, that [b]we should give bread to
your army?"
7So Gideon said, "For this cause, when
the LORD has delivered Zebah and Zalmunna into my hand, [a]then I will tear
your flesh with the thorns of the wilderness and with briers!" 8Then he went up
from there [a]to Penuel and spoke to them
in the same way. And the men of Penuel
answered him as the men of Succoth had
answered. 9So he also spoke to the men of
Penuel, saying, "When I [a]come back in
peace, [b]I will tear down this tower!"
10Now Zebah and Zalmunna *were* at
Karkor, and their armies with them,
about fifteen thousand, all who were left
of [a]all the army of the people of the East;
for [b]one hundred and twenty thousand
men who drew the sword had fallen.
11Then Gideon went up by the road of
those who dwell in tents on the east of
[a]Nobah and Jogbehah; and he [1]attacked
the army while the camp felt [b]secure.
12When Zebah and Zalmunna fled, he pursued them; and he [a]took the two kings of
Midian, Zebah and Zalmunna, and routed
the whole army.
13Then Gideon the son of Joash returned from battle, from the Ascent of Heres. 14And he caught a young man of the
men of Succoth and interrogated him;
and he wrote down for him the leaders
of Succoth and its elders, seventy-seven
men. 15Then he came to the men of Succoth and said, "Here are Zebah and Zalmunna, about whom you [a]ridiculed me,
saying, '*Are* the hands of Zebah and

21 a 2 Chr. 20:17 b 2 Kin. 7:7
22 a Josh. 6:4, 16, 20 b Is. 9:4 c 1 Sam. 14:20 d 1 Kin. 4:12 *1* Heb. *Beth Shittah*
23 a Judg. 6:35
24 a Judg. 3:27 b Judg. 3:28 c John 1:28
25 a Judg. 8:3 b Ps. 83:11 c Judg. 8:4

CHAPTER 8
1 a Judg. 12:1
2 a Judg. 6:11 *1* Few grapes left after the harvest *2* The whole harvest
3 a Judg. 7:24, 25 b Prov. 15:1
4 a Judg. 7:25 b Judg. 7:6
5 a Gen. 33:17
6 a Judg. 8:15 b 1 Sam. 25:11 *1* Lit. *Is the palm*
7 a Judg. 8:16
8 a Gen. 32:30, 31
9 a 1 Kin. 22:27 b Judg. 8:17
10 a Judg. 7:12 b Judg. 6:5
11 a Num. 32:35, 42 b Judg. 18:27 *1* Lit. *struck*
12 a Ps. 83:11
15 a Judg. 8:6

Zalmunna now in your hand, that we should give bread to your weary men?' " 16[a]And he took the elders of the city, and thorns of the wilderness and briers, and with them he [1]taught the men of Succoth. 17[a]Then he tore down the tower of [b]Penuel and killed the men of the city.

18And he said to Zebah and Zalmunna, "What kind of men *were they* whom you killed at [a]Tabor?"

So they answered, "As you *are,* so *were* they; each one resembled the son of a king."

19Then he said, "They *were* my brothers, the sons of my mother. *As* the LORD lives, if you had let them live, I would not kill you." 20And he said to Jether his firstborn, "Rise, kill them!" But the youth would not draw his sword; for he was afraid, because he *was* still a youth.

21So Zebah and Zalmunna said, "Rise yourself, and kill us; for as a man *is, so is* his strength." So Gideon arose and [a]killed Zebah and Zalmunna, and took the crescent ornaments that *were* on their camels' necks.

> *I want to help you decide that, by the power of God, you will not be ordinary.*
>
> SMITH WIGGLESWORTH

Gideon's Ephod

22Then the men of Israel said to Gideon, [a]"Rule over us, both you and your son, and your grandson also; for you have [b]delivered us from the hand of Midian."

23But Gideon said to them, "I will not rule over you, nor shall my son rule over you; [a]the LORD shall rule over you." 24Then Gideon said to them, "I would like to [1]make a request of you, that each of you would give me the earrings from his plunder." For they had golden earrings, [a]because they *were* Ishmaelites.

25So they answered, "We will gladly give *them.*" And they spread out a garment, and each man threw into it the earrings from his plunder. 26Now the weight of the gold earrings that he requested was one thousand seven hundred *shekels* of gold, besides the crescent ornaments, pendants, and purple robes which *were* on the kings of Midian, and besides the chains that *were* around their camels' necks. 27Then Gideon [a]made it into an ephod and set it up in his city, [b]Ophrah. And all Israel [c]played the harlot with it there. It became [d]a snare to Gideon and to his house.

28Thus Midian was subdued before the children of Israel, so that they lifted their heads no more. [a]And the country was quiet for forty years in the days of Gideon.

Death of Gideon

29Then [a]Jerubbaal the son of Joash went and dwelt in his own house. 30Gideon had [a]seventy sons who were his own offspring, for he had many wives. 31[a]And his concubine who *was* in Shechem also bore him a son, whose name he called Abimelech. 32Now Gideon the son of Joash died [a]at a good old age, and was buried in the tomb of Joash his father, [b]in Ophrah of the Abiezrites.

33So it was, [a]as soon as Gideon was dead, that the children of Israel again [b]played the harlot with the Baals, [c]and made Baal-Berith their god. 34Thus the children of Israel [a]did not remember the LORD their God, who had delivered them from the hands of all their enemies on every side; 35[a]nor did they show kindness to the house of Jerubbaal (Gideon) in accordance with the good he had done for Israel.

Abimelech's Conspiracy

9 Then Abimelech the son of Jerubbaal went to Shechem, to [a]his mother's brothers, and spoke with them and with all the family of the house of his mother's father, saying, 2"Please speak in the hearing of all the men of Shechem: 'Which is better for you, that all [a]seventy of the sons of Jerubbaal reign over you, or that one reign over you?' Remember that I *am* your own flesh and [b]bone."

3And his mother's brothers spoke all these words concerning him in the hearing of all the men of Shechem; and their heart was inclined to follow Abimelech, for they said, "He is our [a]brother." 4So they gave him seventy *shekels* of silver from the temple of [a]Baal-Berith, with which Abimelech hired [b]worthless and reckless men; and they followed him.

---

16 a Judg. 8:7 *1 disciplined*
17 a Judg. 8:9 b 1 Kin. 12:25
18 a Judg. 4:6
21 a Ps. 83:11
22 a [Judg. 9:8] b Judg. 3:9; 9:17
23 a 1 Sam. 8:7; 10:19; 12:12
24 a Gen. 37:25, 28 *1 Lit. request a request*
27 a Judg. 17:5 b Judg. 6:11, 24 c [Ps. 106:39] d Deut. 7:16
28 a Judg. 5:31
29 a Judg. 6:32; 7:1
30 a Judg. 9:2, 5
31 a Judg. 9:1
32 a Gen. 25:8 b Judg. 6:24; 8:27
33 a Judg. 2:19 b Judg. 2:17 c Judg. 9:4, 46
34 a Deut. 4:9
35 a Judg. 9:16–18

CHAPTER 9
1 a Judg. 8:31, 35
2 a Judg. 8:30; 9:5, 18 b Gen. 29:14
3 a Gen. 29:15
4 a Judg. 8:33 b Judg. 11:3

5Then he went to his father's house [a]at Ophrah and [b]killed his brothers, the seventy sons of Jerubbaal, on one stone. But Jotham the youngest son of Jerubbaal was left, because he hid himself. 6And all the men of Shechem gathered together, all of Beth Millo, and they went and made Abimelech king beside the terebinth tree at the pillar that *was* in Shechem.

The Parable of the Trees

7Now when they told Jotham, he went and stood on top of [a]Mount Gerizim, and lifted his voice and cried out. And he said to them:

"Listen to me, you men of Shechem,
That God may listen to you!

8 "The[a] trees once went forth to
anoint a king over them.
And they said to the olive tree,
[b]'Reign over us!'
9 But the olive tree said to them,
'Should I cease giving my oil,
[a]With which they honor God and
men,
And go to sway over trees?'

10 "Then the trees said to the fig tree,
'You come *and* reign over us!'
11 But the fig tree said to them,
'Should I cease my sweetness and
my good fruit,
And go to sway over trees?'

12 "Then the trees said to the vine,
'You come *and* reign over us!'
13 But the vine said to them,
'Should I cease my new wine,
[a]Which cheers *both* God and men,
And go to sway over trees?'

14 "Then all the trees said to the
bramble,
'You come *and* reign over us!'
15 And the bramble said to the trees,
'If in truth you anoint me as king
over you,
Then come *and* take shelter in my
[a]shade;
But if not, [b]let fire come out of the
bramble
And devour the [c]cedars of
Lebanon!'

16"Now therefore, if you have acted in truth and sincerity in making Abimelech king, and if you have dealt well with Jerubbaal and his house, and have done to him [a]as[1] he deserves— 17for my [a]father fought for you, risked his life, and [b]delivered you out of the hand of Midian; 18[a]but you have risen up against my father's house this day, and killed his seventy sons on one stone, and made Abimelech, the son of his [b]female servant, king over the men of Shechem, because he is your brother— 19if then you have acted in truth and sincerity with Jerubbaal and with his house this day, *then* [a]rejoice in Abimelech, and let him also rejoice in you. 20But if not, [a]let fire come from Abimelech and devour the men of Shechem and Beth Millo; and let fire come from the men of Shechem and from Beth Millo and devour Abimelech!" 21And Jotham ran away and fled; and he went to [a]Beer and dwelt there, for fear of Abimelech his brother.

Downfall of Abimelech

22After Abimelech had reigned over Israel three years, 23[a]God sent a [b]spirit of ill will between Abimelech and the men of Shechem; and the men of Shechem [c]dealt treacherously with Abimelech, 24[a]that the crime *done* to the seventy sons of Jerubbaal might be settled and their [b]blood be laid on Abimelech their brother, who killed them, and on the men of Shechem, who aided him in the killing of his brothers. 25And the men of Shechem set [1]men in ambush against him on the tops of the mountains, and they robbed all who passed by them along that way; and it was told Abimelech.

26Now Gaal the son of Ebed came with his brothers and went over to Shechem; and the men of Shechem put their confidence in him. 27So they went out into the fields, and gathered *grapes* from their vineyards and trod *them,* and [1]made merry. And they went into [a]the house of their god, and ate and drank, and cursed Abimelech. 28Then Gaal the son of Ebed said, [a]"Who *is* Abimelech, and who *is* Shechem, that we should serve him? *Is he* not the son of Jerubbaal, and *is not* Zebul his officer? Serve the men of [b]Hamor the father of Shechem; but why should we serve him? 29[a]If only this people were under my [1]authority! Then I would remove Abimelech." So [2]he said to Abimelech, "Increase your army and come out!"

30When Zebul, the ruler of the city, heard the words of Gaal the son of Ebed, his anger was aroused. 31And he sent messengers to Abimelech secretly, saying,

5 a Judg. 6:24 b 2 Kin. 11:1, 2
7 a Deut. 11:29; 27:12
8 a 2 Kin. 14:9 b Judg. 8:22, 23
9 a [John 5:23]
13 a Ps. 104:15
15 a Is. 30:2 b Num. 21:28 c 2 Kin. 14:9
16 a Judg. 8:35 *1 Lit. according to the doing of his hands*
17 a Judg. 7 b Judg. 8:22
18 a Judg. 8:30, 35; 9:2, 5, 6 b Judg. 8:31
19 a Is. 8:6
20 a Judg. 9:15, 45, 56, 57
21 a Num. 21:16
23 a Is. 19:14 b 1 Sam. 16:14; 18:9, 10 c Is. 33:1
24 a 1 Kin. 2:32 b Num. 35:33
25 *1 Lit. liers-in-wait for*
27 a Judg. 9:4 *1 rejoiced*
28 a 1 Sam. 25:10 b Gen. 34:2, 6
29 a 2 Sam. 15:4 *1 Lit. hand* *2 So with MT, Tg.; DSS they; LXX I*

"Take note! Gaal the son of Ebed and his
brothers have come to Shechem; and here
they are, fortifying the city against you.
32Now therefore, get up by night, you and
the people who *are* with you, and [1]lie in
wait in the field. 33And it shall be, as soon
as the sun is up in the morning, *that* you
shall rise early and rush upon the city;
and *when* he and the people who are with
him come out against you, you may then
do to them [1]as you find opportunity."

34So Abimelech and all the people who
were with him rose by night, and [1]lay in
wait against Shechem in four companies.
35When Gaal the son of Ebed went out and
stood in the entrance to the city gate,
Abimelech and the people who *were* with
him rose from lying in wait. 36And when
Gaal saw the people, he said to Zebul,
"Look, people are coming down from the
tops of the mountains!"

But Zebul said to him, "You see the
shadows of the mountains as *if they were*
men."

37So Gaal spoke again and said, "See,
people are coming down from the center
of the land, and another company is coming from the [1]Diviners' Terebinth Tree."

38Then Zebul said to him, "Where indeed *is* your mouth now, with which you
[a]said, 'Who is Abimelech, that we should
serve him?' *Are* not these the people
whom you despised? Go out, if you will,
and fight with them now."

39So Gaal went out, leading the men of
Shechem, and fought with Abimelech.
40And Abimelech chased him, and he fled
from him; and many fell wounded, to the
very entrance of the gate. 41Then Abimelech dwelt at Arumah, and Zebul [1]drove
out Gaal and his brothers, so that they
would not dwell in Shechem.

42And it came about on the next day
that the people went out into the field,
and they told Abimelech. 43So he took his
people, divided them into three companies, and lay in wait in the field. And he
looked, and there were the people, coming out of the city; and he rose against
them and [1]attacked them. 44Then Abimelech and the company that *was* with him
rushed forward and stood at the entrance
of the gate of the city; and the *other* two
companies rushed upon all who *were* in
the fields and killed them. 45So Abimelech
fought against the city all that day; [a]he
took the city and killed the people who
were in it; and he [b]demolished the city
and sowed it with salt.

46Now when all the men of the tower of
Shechem had heard *that,* they entered the
[1]stronghold of the temple [a]of the god Be-
rith. 47And it was told Abimelech that all
the men of the tower of Shechem were
gathered together. 48Then Abimelech
went up to Mount [a]Zalmon, he and all the
people who *were* with him. And Abimelech took an ax in his hand and cut down
a bough from the trees, and took it and
laid *it* on his shoulder; then he said to the
people who were with him, "What you
have seen me do, make haste *and* do as I
have done." 49So each of the people likewise cut down his own bough and followed Abimelech, put *them* against the
[1]stronghold, and set the stronghold on
fire above them, so that all the people of
the tower of Shechem died, about a thousand men and women.

50 Then Abimelech went to Thebez,
and he [1]encamped against Thebez and
took it. 51But there was a strong tower in
the city, and all the men and women—all
the people of the city—fled there and shut
themselves in; then they went up to the
top of the tower. 52So Abimelech came as
far as the tower and fought against it; and
he drew near the door of the tower to
burn it with fire. 53But a certain woman
[a]dropped an upper millstone on Abimelech's head and crushed his skull. 54Then
[a]he called quickly to the young man, his
armorbearer, and said to him, "Draw your
sword and kill me, lest men say of me, 'A
woman killed him.' " So his young man
thrust him through, and he died. 55And
when the men of Israel saw that Abimelech was dead, they departed, every man
to his [1]place.

56[a]Thus God repaid the wickedness of
Abimelech, which he had done to his father by killing his seventy brothers.
57And all the evil of the men of Shechem
God returned on their own heads, and on
them came [a]the curse of Jotham the son
of Jerubbaal.

Tola

10 After Abimelech there [a]arose to
save Israel Tola the son of Puah,
the son of Dodo, a man of Issachar; and
he dwelt in Shamir in the mountains of
Ephraim. 2He judged Israel twenty-three
years; and he died and was buried in
Shamir.

32 [1] Set up an ambush
33 [1] Lit. *as your hand can find*
34 [1] Set up an ambush
37 [1] Heb. *Meonenim*
38 [a] Judg. 9:28, 29
41 [1] *exiled*
43 [1] Lit. *struck*
45 [a] Judg. 9:20 [b] 2 Kin. 3:25
46 [a] Judg. 8:33 [1] *fortified room*
48 [a] Ps. 68:14
49 [1] *fortified room*
50 [1] *besieged*
53 [a] 2 Sam. 11:21
54 [a] 1 Sam. 31:4
55 [1] *home*
56 [a] Job 31:3
57 [a] Judg. 9:20
CHAPTER 10
1 [a] Judg. 2:16

JUDGES 9:50–57

Dear Woman of Destiny,

Some of the unnamed women of the Bible are my heroines. Among my favorites is the no-name woman of Thebez who literally saved her city (see Judg. 9:50–57).

The wicked king Abimelech had ruled with terror for three years, killing seventy of his half brothers and destroying one village of a thousand. His next target was to burn Thebez.

When he came to Thebez, he and his men captured the city, but there was a strong tower in the center where the men and women had shut themselves up on the roof. Then comes the story of our heroine: "But a certain woman dropped an upper millstone on Abimelech's head and crushed his skull" (v. 53).

Then the wicked king told his armorbearer, "Draw your sword and kill me, lest men say of me, 'A woman killed him'" (v. 54). So the young man did.

I love this part. Abimelech knew only a woman would have used this upper revolving stone with a circular hole in the center because it was a domestic utensil used to grind corn—a woman's work. A man would have attacked with a weapon of war, such as a spear or a bow and arrow, no doubt.

This woman had nothing to lose. She knew she'd be dead if she didn't do something—and so would her people. She used what was available—an upper millstone. Her aim was on target, specific. The results: The wicked king was killed. She lived and her people were freed from terror.

We could say she hit the bull's-eye. The Hebrew root word for intercessor or intercession is *paga'* (paw-GAH) meaning, "to come between, to assail, to cause to entreat." When an Israeli soldier hits the mark in target practice, he shouts, "Paga'!"—the modern Hebrew equivalent of "Bull's-eye!" (Dutch Sheets on *Intercessory Prayer*). Effective intercessors learn to "hit the bull's-eye" with accuracy in their warfare.

We learn to see things from God's vantage point. The name of the Lord is our strong tower if we know Him. We hide in Him and are safe (see Ps. 61:3; Prov.18:10). This woman was in the right strategic place. Intercession keeps us by the Spirit in the right strategic spot. But unlike this woman, we wield our weapon using our mouth in intercession. For example:

The name of Jesus—our authority (Ps. 44:4–7; Luke 10:19)
The blood of Jesus—(1 John 1:7–9)
Praise to glorify God and terrify the enemy (2 Chr. 20)
Clap and shout (Ps. 47:1; Zeph. 3:14, 15)
Joy and laughter (Ps.126:1, 2)
Pray as led by the Holy Spirit (Rom. 8:26, 28; Eph. 6:18)
Travail (Ps. 126:5)
Fasting (Neh. 1:4–7; Is. 58:6; Dan. 9:3–5)

When interceding for others, we ask the Holy Spirit how to pray. Sometimes in prayer I find myself standing between a person and God, entreating God on her behalf; at other times I'm standing between that person and the devil, battling on her behalf. Let's align our prayers with what the Holy Spirit wants us to pray and hit the bull's-eye.

Quin Sherrer

Jair

[3]After him arose Jair, a Gileadite; and he judged Israel twenty-two years. [4]Now he had thirty sons who [a]rode on thirty donkeys; they also had thirty towns, [b]which are called [1]"Havoth Jair" to this day, which *are* in the land of Gilead. [5]And Jair died and was buried in Camon.

Merciful Lord, keep _____ from returning to evil so that they would never again forsake You.

FROM JUDGES 10:6

Israel Oppressed Again

[6]Then [a]the children of Israel again did evil in the sight of the LORD, and [b]served the Baals and the Ashtoreths, [c]the gods of Syria, the gods of [d]Sidon, the gods of Moab, the gods of the people of Ammon, and the gods of the Philistines; and they forsook the LORD and did not serve Him. [7]So the anger of the LORD was hot against Israel; and He [a]sold them into the hands of the [b]Philistines and into the hands of the people of [c]Ammon. [8]From that year they [1]harassed and oppressed the children of Israel for eighteen years—all the children of Israel who *were* on the other side of the Jordan in the [a]land of the Amorites, in Gilead. [9]Moreover the people of Ammon crossed over the Jordan to fight against Judah also, against Benjamin, and against the house of Ephraim, so that Israel was severely distressed.

[10][a]And the children of Israel cried out to the LORD, saying, "We have [b]sinned against You, because we have both forsaken our God and served the Baals!"

[11]So the LORD said to the children of Israel, *"Did I* not *deliver you* [a]from the Egyptians and [b]from the Amorites and [c]from the people of Ammon and [d]from the Philistines? [12]Also [a]the Sidonians [b]and Amalekites and [1]Maonites [c]oppressed you; and you cried out to Me, and I delivered you from their hand. [13][a]Yet you have forsaken Me and served other gods. Therefore I will deliver you no more. [14]Go and [a]cry out to the gods which you have chosen; let them deliver you in your time of distress."

[15]And the children of Israel said to the LORD, "We have sinned! [a]Do to us whatever seems best to You; only deliver us this day, we pray." [16][a]So they put away the foreign gods from among them and served the LORD. And [b]His soul could no longer endure the misery of Israel.

[17]Then the people of Ammon gathered together and encamped in Gilead. And the children of Israel assembled together and encamped in [a]Mizpah. [18]And the people, the leaders of Gilead, said to one another, "Who *is* the man who will begin the fight against the people of Ammon? He shall [a]be head over all the inhabitants of Gilead."

Jephthah

11 Now [a]Jephthah the Gileadite was [b]a mighty man of valor, but he *was* the son of a harlot; and Gilead begot Jephthah. [2]Gilead's wife bore sons; and when his wife's sons grew up, they drove Jephthah out, and said to him, "You shall have [a]no inheritance in our father's house, for you *are* the son of another woman." [3]Then Jephthah fled from his brothers and dwelt in the land of [a]Tob; and [b]worthless men banded together with Jephthah and went out *raiding* with him.

[4]It came to pass after a time that the [a]people of Ammon made war against Israel. [5]And so it was, when the people of Ammon made war against Israel, that the elders of Gilead went to get Jephthah from the land of Tob. [6]Then they said to Jephthah, "Come and be our commander, that we may fight against the people of Ammon."

[7]So Jephthah said to the elders of Gilead, [a]"Did you not hate me, and expel me from my father's house? Why have you come to me now when you are in [1]distress?"

[8][a]And the elders of Gilead said to Jephthah, "That is why we have [b]turned[1] again to you now, that you may go with us and fight against the people of Ammon, and be [c]our head over all the inhabitants of Gilead."

[9]So Jephthah said to the elders of Gilead, "If you take me back home to fight against the people of Ammon, and the LORD delivers them to me, shall I be your head?"

4 a Judg. 5:10; 12:14 b Deut. 3:14 *1* Lit. *Towns of Jair,* Num. 32:41; Deut. 3:14
6 a Judg. 2:11; 3:7; 6:1; 13:1 b Judg. 2:13 c Judg. 2:12 d 1 Kin. 11:33
7 a 1 Sam. 12:9 b Judg. 13:1 c Judg. 3:13
8 a Num. 32:33 *1* Lit. *shattered*
10 a 1 Sam. 12:10 b Deut. 1:41
11 a Ex. 14:30 b Num. 21:21, 24, 25 c Judg. 3:12, 13 d Judg. 3:31
12 a Judg. 1:31; 5:19 b Judg. 6:3; 7:12 c Ps. 106:42, 43 *1* LXX mss. *Midianites*
13 a [Jer. 2:13]
14 a Deut. 32:37, 38
15 a 1 Sam. 3:18
16 a Jer. 18:7, 8 b Is. 63:9
17 a Judg. 11:11, 29
18 a Judg. 11:8, 11

CHAPTER 11
1 a Heb. 11:32 b 2 Kin. 5:1
2 a Gen. 21:10
3 a 2 Sam. 10:6, 8 b 1 Sam. 22:2
4 a Judg. 10:9, 17
7 a Gen. 26:27 *1* *trouble*
8 a Judg. 10:18 b [Luke 17:4] c Judg. 10:18 *1* *returned*

10And the elders of Gilead said to Jephthah, [a]"The LORD will be a witness between us, if we do not do according to
your words." 11Then Jephthah went with
the elders of Gilead, and the people made
him [a]head and commander over them;
and Jephthah spoke all his words [b]before
the LORD in Mizpah.
12Now Jephthah sent messengers to the
king of the people of Ammon, saying,
[a]"What do you have against me, that you
have come to fight against me in my
land?"
13And the king of the people of Ammon
answered the messengers of Jephthah,
[a]"Because Israel took away my land when
they came up out of Egypt, from [b]the Arnon as far as [c]the Jabbok, and to the Jordan. Now therefore, restore those *lands*
peaceably."
14So Jephthah again sent messengers to
the king of the people of Ammon, 15and
said to him, "Thus says Jephthah: [a]'Israel
did not take away the land of Moab, nor
the land of the people of Ammon; 16for
when Israel came up from Egypt, they
walked through the wilderness as far as
the Red Sea and [a]came to Kadesh. 17Then
[a]Israel sent messengers to the king of
Edom, saying, "Please let me pass
through your land." [b]But the king of
Edom would not heed. And in like manner
they sent to the [c]king of Moab, but he
would not *consent*. So Israel [d]remained in
Kadesh. 18And they [a]went along through
the wilderness and [b]bypassed the land of
Edom and the land of Moab, came to the
east side of the land of Moab, and encamped on the other side of the Arnon.
But they did not enter the border of Moab,
for the Arnon *was* the border of Moab.
19Then [a]Israel sent messengers to Sihon
king of the Amorites, king of Heshbon;
and Israel said to him, "Please [b]let us pass
through your land into our place." 20[a]But
Sihon did not trust Israel to pass through
his territory. So Sihon gathered all his
people together, encamped in Jahaz, and
fought against Israel. 21And the LORD God
of Israel [a]delivered Sihon and all his people into the hand of Israel, and they [b]de-
feated[1] them. Thus Israel gained
possession of all the land of the Amorites,
who inhabited that country. 22They took
possession of [a]all the territory of the Amorites, from the Arnon to the Jabbok and
from the wilderness to the Jordan.
23'And now the LORD God of Israel has
[1]dispossessed the Amorites from before
His people Israel; should you then possess
it? 24Will you not possess whatever [a]Che-
mosh your god gives you to possess? So
whatever [b]the LORD our God takes possession of before us, we will possess. 25And
now, *are* you any better than [a]Balak the
son of Zippor, king of Moab? Did he ever
strive against Israel? Did he ever fight
against them? 26While Israel dwelt in
[a]Heshbon and its villages, in [b]Aroer and
its villages, and in all the cities along the
banks of the Arnon, for three hundred
years, why did you not recover *them* within that time? 27Therefore I have not
sinned against you, but you wronged me
by fighting against me. May the LORD,
[a]the Judge, [b]render judgment this day between the children of Israel and the people of Ammon.' " 28However, the king of
the people of Ammon did not heed the
words which Jephthah sent him.

Jephthah's Vow and Victory

29Then [a]the Spirit of the LORD came
upon Jephthah, and he passed through
Gilead and Manasseh, and passed through
Mizpah of Gilead; and from Mizpah of Gilead he advanced *toward* the people of Ammon. 30And Jephthah [a]made a vow to the
LORD, and said, "If You will indeed deliver
the people of Ammon into my hands,
31then it will be that whatever comes out
of the doors of my house to meet me,
when I return in peace from the people of
Ammon, [a]shall surely be the LORD's, [b]and
I will offer it up as a burnt offering."
32So Jephthah advanced toward the
people of Ammon to fight against them,
and the LORD delivered them into his
hands. 33And he [1]defeated them from Aroer as far as [a]Minnith—twenty cities—and
to [2]Abel Keramim, with a very great
slaughter. Thus the people of Ammon
were subdued before the children of Israel.

Jephthah's Daughter

34When Jephthah came to his house at
[a]Mizpah, there was [b]his daughter, coming
out to meet him with timbrels and dancing; and she *was his* only child. Besides
her he had neither son nor daughter.
35And it came to pass, when he saw her,
that he [a]tore his clothes, and said, "Alas,
my daughter! You have brought me very
low! You are among those who trouble

10 a Jer. 29:23; 42:5
11 a Judg. 11:8 b Judg. 10:17; 20:1
12 a 2 Sam. 16:10
13 a Num. 21:24–26 b Josh. 13:9 c Gen. 32:22
15 a Deut. 2:9, 19
16 a Num. 13:26; 20:1
17 a Num. 20:14 b Num. 20:14–21 c Josh. 24:9 d Num. 20:1
18 a Deut. 2:9, 18, 19 b Num. 21:4
19 a Num. 21:21 b Deut. 2:27
20 a Deut. 2:27
21 a Josh. 24:8 b Num. 21:24, 25 1 Lit. *struck*
22 a Deut. 2:36, 37
23 1 *driven out*
24 a Num. 21:29 b [Deut. 9:4, 5]
25 a Num. 22:2
26 a Num. 21:25, 26 b Deut. 2:36
27 a Gen. 18:25 b Gen. 16:5; 31:53
29 a Judg. 3:10
30 a Gen. 28:20
31 a Lev. 27:2, 3, 28 b Ps. 66:13
33 a Ezek. 27:17 1 Lit. *struck* 2 Lit. *Plain of Vineyards*
34 a Judg. 10:17; 11:11 b Ex. 15:20
35 a Gen. 37:29, 34

me! For I [b]have [1]given my word to the
LORD, and [c]I cannot [2]go back on it."
36 So she said to him, "My father, *if* you
have given your word to the LORD, [a]do to
me according to what has gone out of
your mouth, because [b]the LORD has
avenged you of your enemies, the people
of Ammon." 37 Then she said to her father,
"Let this thing be done for me: let me
alone for two months, that I may go and
wander on the mountains and [1]bewail my
virginity, my [2]friends and I."
38 So he said, "Go." And he sent her
away *for* two months; and she went with
her friends, and bewailed her virginity on
the mountains. 39 And it was so at the end
of two months that she returned to her
father, and he [a]carried out his vow with
her which he had vowed. She [1]knew no
man.
And it became a custom in Israel 40 *that*
the daughters of Israel went four days
each year to [1]lament the daughter of
Jephthah the Gileadite.

Jephthah's Conflict with Ephraim

12 Then [a]the men of Ephraim [1]gath-
ered together, crossed over toward
Zaphon, and said to Jephthah, "Why did
you cross over to fight against the people
of Ammon, and did not call us to go with
you? We will burn your house down on
you with fire!"
2 And Jephthah said to them, "My people
and I were in a great struggle with the
people of Ammon; and when I called you,
you did not deliver me out of their hands.
3 So when I saw that you would not deliver
me, I [a]took my life in my hands and
crossed over against the people of Ammon; and the LORD delivered them into
my hand. Why then have you come up to
me this day to fight against me?" 4 Now
Jephthah gathered together all the men of
Gilead and fought against Ephraim. And
the men of Gilead defeated Ephraim, because they said, "You Gileadites [a]*are* fugitives of Ephraim among the Ephraimites
and among the Manassites." 5 The Gileadites seized the [a]fords of the Jordan before
the Ephraimites *arrived.* And when *any*
Ephraimite who escaped said, "Let me
cross over," the men of Gilead would say
to him, "*Are* you an Ephraimite?" If he
said, "No," 6 then they would say to him,
"Then say, [a]'Shibboleth'!"[1] And he would
say, "Sibboleth," for he could not [2]pro-
nounce *it* right. Then they would take
him and kill him at the fords of the Jordan. There fell at that time forty-two
thousand Ephraimites.
7 And Jephthah judged Israel six years.
Then Jephthah the Gileadite died and was
buried among the cities of Gilead.

Ibzan, Elon, and Abdon

8 After him, Ibzan of Bethlehem judged
Israel. 9 He had thirty sons. And he gave
away thirty daughters in marriage, and
brought in thirty daughters from elsewhere for his sons. He judged Israel seven
years. 10 Then Ibzan died and was buried at
Bethlehem.
11 After him, Elon the Zebulunite
judged Israel. He judged Israel ten years.
12 And Elon the Zebulunite died and was
buried at Aijalon in the country of Zebulun.
13 After him, Abdon the son of Hillel the
Pirathonite judged Israel. 14 He had forty
sons and thirty grandsons, who [a]rode on
seventy young donkeys. He judged Israel
eight years. 15 Then Abdon the son of Hillel the Pirathonite died and was buried in
Pirathon in the land of Ephraim, [a]in the
mountains of the Amalekites.

The Birth of Samson

13 Again the children of Israel [a]did
evil in the sight of the LORD, and
the LORD delivered them [b]into the hand of
the Philistines for forty years.
2 Now there was a certain man from
[a]Zorah, of the family of the Danites,
whose name *was* Manoah; and his wife
was barren and had no children. 3 And
the [a]Angel of the LORD appeared to the
woman and said to her, "Indeed now, you
are barren and have borne no children,
but you shall conceive and bear a son.
4 Now therefore, please be careful [a]not to
drink wine or *similar* drink, and not to eat
anything unclean. 5 For behold, you shall
conceive and bear a son. And no [a]razor
shall come upon his head, for the child
shall be [b]a Nazirite to God from the
womb; and he shall [c]begin to deliver Israel out of the hand of the Philistines."
6 So the woman came and told her husband, saying, [a]"A Man of God came to me,
and His [b]countenance[1] *was* like the countenance of the Angel of God, very awesome; but I [c]did not ask Him where He
was from, and He did not tell me His
name. 7 And He said to me, 'Behold, you

35 b Eccl. 5:2, 4, 5 c Num. 30:2 *1* Lit. *opened my mouth* *2* Lit. *take it back*
36 a Num. 30:2 b 2 Sam. 18:19, 31
37 *1 lament* *2 companions*
39 a Judg. 11:31 *1* Remained a virgin
40 *1 commemorate*

CHAPTER 12
1 a Judg. 8:1 *1 were summoned*
3 a 1 Sam. 19:5; 28:21
4 a 1 Sam. 25:10
5 a Josh. 22:11
6 a Ps. 69:2, 15 *1* Lit. *a flowing stream;* used as a test of dialect *2* Lit. *speak so*
14 a Judg. 5:10; 10:4
15 a Judg. 3:13, 27; 5:14

CHAPTER 13
1 a Judg. 2:11 b 1 Sam. 12:9
2 a Josh. 19:41
3 a Judg. 6:12
4 a Num. 6:2, 3, 20
5 a Num. 6:5 b Num. 6:2 c 1 Sam. 7:13
6 a Gen. 32:24–30 b Matt. 28:3 c Judg. 13:17, 18 *1 appearance*

JUDGES 13:3

Dear Woman of Destiny,

This scripture holds great meaning for me, for my husband and I walked through years of physical barrenness. We were told by our infertility specialist years ago to give up our hopes and dreams, that we needed to face the fact that we would never have children. And yet, in that place of barrenness that reached to the very depths of our souls, the Lord saw our pain and hunger. He reached down with great love and compassion and gave my husband a dream. As a result of that dream, we knew beyond any doubt we would have a son.

To make a long story short, God miraculously healed us, and not only do we have a son named Justin, we also have a daughter named Grace Ann, a son named Tyler, and a daughter named Rachel. Each one of our children was announced to us before conception, and their names were given to us as well.

I've had dreams and other experiences concerning not only the births of our children, but also many other issues. Many of them came to me in just as clear and direct a fashion as we see in this passage of Scripture. You see, God has not changed! He is the same yesterday, today, and forever; and He still loves to talk with us! Among other things, He wants to talk with us concerning personal issues of barrenness. There are many ways a person can be barren besides the physical ability to have children. And there are also corporate issues of barrenness in the church that He wants to talk with us about.

Let's look at this issue for just a moment. We, as the church, have been barren. We've not been able to bring forth spiritual children. We've done a lot of swapping church memberships, but where are the new births? There have been a few, but not enough. If we will cry out to the Lord and acknowledge our barrenness, we can help open the door for angelic empowering to be released. God is waiting for us to cry out to Him with hearts filled with true repentance.

We can take courage and have hope that the Lord loves to give to us, His beloved. He is the Creator of life, and He loves to give us life! He is ready and waiting to release His angelic messengers to bring us news of His plans for our healing and deliverance. He has promised in His Word that the reproach of barrenness will be removed, and His church will be a fruitful vine.

I believe as God heals the womb of the church, these new lives birthed will carry a purity of devotion and will be powerful warriors for the kingdom of God. I believe God would love to see a whole generation of Samsons, who have learned the lesson of having nothing in common with the enemy, and in whom the Spirit of the Lord could move mightily once again.

So, let's press into God, and with expectant hearts await the angelic message, "You shall become pregnant, and bear a son."

Michal Ann Goll

shall conceive and bear a son. Now drink
no wine or *similar* drink, nor eat anything
unclean, for the child shall be a Nazirite
to God from the womb to the day of his
death.' "
8Then Manoah prayed to the LORD, and
said, "O my Lord, please let the Man of
God whom You sent come to us again and
teach us what we shall do for the child
who will be born."
9And God listened to the voice of Manoah, and the Angel of God came to the
woman again as she was sitting in the
field; but Manoah her husband *was* not
with her. 10Then the woman ran in haste
and told her husband, and said to him,
"Look, the Man who came to me the *other*
day has just now appeared to me!"
11So Manoah arose and followed his
wife. When he came to the Man, he said to
Him, "Are You the Man who spoke to this
woman?"
And He said, "I *am.*"
12Manoah said, "Now let Your words
come *to pass!* What will be the boy's rule
of life, and his work?"
13So the Angel of the LORD said to Manoah, "Of all that I said to the woman let
her be careful. 14She may not eat anything
that comes from the vine, [a]nor may she
drink wine or *similar* drink, nor eat anything unclean. All that I commanded her
let her observe."
15Then Manoah said to the Angel of the
LORD, "Please [a]let us detain You, and we
will prepare a young goat for You."
16And the Angel of the LORD said to Manoah, "Though you detain Me, I will not
eat your food. But if you offer a burnt offering, you must offer it to the LORD." (For
Manoah did not know He *was* the Angel of
the LORD.)
17Then Manoah said to the Angel of the
LORD, "What *is* Your name, that when
Your words come *to pass* we may honor
You?"
18And the Angel of the LORD said to
him, [a]"Why do you ask My name, seeing
it *is* wonderful?"
19So Manoah took the young goat with
the grain offering, [a]and offered it upon
the rock to the LORD. And He did a wondrous thing while Manoah and his wife
looked on— 20it happened as the flame
went up toward heaven from the altar—
the Angel of the LORD ascended in the
flame of the altar! When Manoah and his
wife saw *this,* they [a]fell on their faces to
the ground. 21When the Angel of the LORD
appeared no more to Manoah and his wife,
[a]then Manoah knew that He *was* the Angel of the LORD.
22And Manoah said to his wife, [a]"We
shall surely die, because we have seen
God!"
23But his wife said to him, "If the LORD
had desired to kill us, He would not have
accepted a burnt offering and a grain offering from our hands, nor would He have
shown us all these *things,* nor would He
have told us *such things* as these at this
time."
24So the woman bore a son and called
his name [a]Samson; and [b]the child grew,
and the LORD blessed him. 25[a]And the
Spirit of the LORD began to move upon
him at [1]Mahaneh Dan [b]between Zorah
and [c]Eshtaol.

Samson's Philistine Wife

14 Now Samson went down [a]to Timnah, and [b]saw a woman in Timnah
of the daughters of the Philistines. 2So he
went up and told his father and mother,
saying, "I have seen a woman in Timnah
of the daughters of the Philistines; now
therefore, [a]get her for me as a wife."
3Then his father and mother said to
him, "*Is there* no woman among the
daughters of [a]your brethren, or among all
my people, that you must go and get a
wife from the [b]uncircumcised Philistines?"
And Samson said to his father, "Get her
for me, for [1]she pleases me well."
4But his father and mother did not
know that it was [a]of the LORD—that He
was seeking an occasion to move against
the Philistines. For at that time [b]the Philistines had dominion over Israel.
5So Samson went down to Timnah with
his father and mother, and came to the
vineyards of Timnah.
Now *to his* surprise, a young lion *came*
roaring against him. 6And [a]the Spirit of
the LORD came mightily upon him, and he
tore the lion apart as one would have torn
apart a young goat, though *he had* nothing in his hand. But he did not tell his
father or his mother what he had done.
7Then he went down and talked with
the woman; and she pleased Samson well.
8After some time, when he returned to get
her, he turned aside to see the carcass of
the lion. And behold, a swarm of bees and
honey *were* in the carcass of the lion. 9He

14 a Num. 6:3, 4
15 a Gen. 18:5
18 a Gen. 32:29
19 a Judg. 6:19–21
20 a Ezek. 1:28
21 a Judg. 6:22
22 a Deut. 5:26
24 a Heb. 11:32 b 1 Sam. 3:19
25 a Judg. 3:10 b Judg. 18:11 c Judg. 16:31 1 Lit. *Camp of Dan,* Judg. 18:12

CHAPTER 14
1 a Josh. 15:10, 57 b Gen. 34:2
2 a Gen. 21:21
3 a Gen. 24:3, 4 b Gen. 34:14 1 Lit. *she is right in my eyes*
4 a Josh. 11:20 b Deut. 28:48
6 a Judg. 3:10

took some of it in his hands and went
along, eating. When he came to his father
and mother, he gave *some* to them, and
they also ate. But he did not tell them that
he had taken the honey out of the [a]carcass
of the lion.
10 So his father went down to the woman. And Samson gave a feast there, for
young men used to do so. 11 And it happened, when they saw him, that they
brought thirty companions to be with
him.
12 Then Samson said to them, "Let me
[a]pose a riddle to you. If you can correctly
solve and explain it to me [b]within the sev-
en days of the feast, then I will give you
thirty linen garments and thirty [c]changes
of clothing. 13 But if you cannot explain *it*
to me, then you shall give me thirty linen
garments and thirty changes of clothing."
And they said to him, [a]"Pose your riddle, that we may hear it."
14 So he said to them:

"Out of the eater came something to
eat,
And out of the strong came
something sweet."

Now for three days they could not explain
the riddle.
15 But it came to pass on the [1]seventh
day that they said to Samson's wife, [a]"Entice your husband, that he may explain
the riddle to us, [b]or else we will burn you
and your father's house with fire. Have
you invited us in order to take what is
ours? *Is that* not *so?*"
16 Then Samson's wife wept on him, and
said, [a]"You only hate me! You do not love
me! You have posed a riddle to the sons of
my people, but you have not explained *it*
to me."
And he said to her, "Look, I have not
explained *it* to my father or my mother; so
should I explain *it* to you?" 17 Now she had
wept on him the seven days while their
feast lasted. And it happened on the seventh day that he told her, because she
pressed him so much. Then she explained
the riddle to the sons of her people. 18 So
the men of the city said to him on the
seventh day before the sun went down:

"What *is* sweeter than honey?
And what *is* stronger than a lion?"

And he said to them:

"If you had not plowed with my
heifer,
You would not have solved my
riddle!"

19 Then [a]the Spirit of the LORD came
upon him mightily, and he went down to
Ashkelon and killed thirty of their men,
took their apparel, and gave the changes
of clothing to those who had explained
the riddle. So his anger was aroused, and
he went back up to his father's house.
20 And Samson's wife [a]was *given* to his
companion, who had been [b]his best man.

Samson Defeats the Philistines

15 After a while, in the time of wheat
harvest, it happened that Samson
visited his wife with a [a]young goat. And he
said, "Let me go in to my wife, into *her*
room." But her father would not permit
him to go in.
2 Her father said, "I really thought that
you thoroughly [a]hated her; therefore I
gave her to your companion. *Is* not her
younger sister better than she? Please,
take her instead."
3 And Samson said to them, "This time
I shall be blameless regarding the Philistines if I harm them!" 4 Then Samson
went and caught three hundred foxes; and
he took torches, turned *the foxes* tail to
tail, and put a torch between each pair of
tails. 5 When he had set the torches on fire,
he let *the foxes* go into the standing grain
of the Philistines, and burned up both the
shocks and the standing grain, as well as
the vineyards *and* olive groves.
6 Then the Philistines said, "Who has
done this?"
And they answered, "Samson, the son-
in-law of the Timnite, because he has tak-
en his wife and given her to his
companion." [a]So the Philistines came up
and burned her and her father with fire.
7 Samson said to them, "Since you
would do a thing like this, I will surely
take revenge on you, and after that I will
cease." 8 So he attacked them hip and
thigh with a great slaughter; then he went
down and dwelt in the cleft of the rock of
[a]Etam.
9 Now the Philistines went up, encamped in Judah, and deployed themselves [a]against Lehi. 10 And the men of
Judah said, "Why have you come up
against us?"
So they answered, "We have come up to
[1]arrest Samson, to do to him as he has
done to us."

9 [a]Lev. 11:27
12 [a]Ezek. 17:2 [b]Gen. 29:27 [c]2 Kin. 5:22
13 [a]Ezek. 17:2
15 [a]Judg. 16:5 [b]Judg. 15:6 [1]So with MT, Tg., Vg.; LXX, Syr. *fourth*
16 [a]Judg. 16:15
19 [a]Judg. 3:10; 13:25
20 [a]Judg. 15:2 [b]John 3:29
CHAPTER 15
1 [a]Gen. 38:17
2 [a]Judg. 14:20
6 [a]Judg. 14:15
8 [a]2 Chr. 11:6
9 [a]Judg. 15:19
10 [1]Lit. *bind*

11 Then three thousand men of Judah
went down to the cleft of the rock of
Etam, and said to Samson, "Do you not
know that the Philistines [a]rule over us?
What *is* this you have done to us?"
And he said to them, "As they did to me,
so I have done to them."
12 But they said to him, "We have come
down to arrest you, that we may deliver
you into the hand of the Philistines."
Then Samson said to them, "Swear to
me that you will not kill me yourselves."
13 So they spoke to him, saying, "No, but
we will tie you securely and deliver you
into their hand; but we will surely not kill
you." And they bound him with two [a]new
ropes and brought him up from the rock.
14 When he came to Lehi, the Philistines
came shouting against him. Then [a]the
Spirit of the LORD came mightily upon
him; and the ropes that *were* on his arms
became like flax that is burned with fire,
and his bonds [1]broke loose from his
hands. 15 He found a fresh jawbone of a
donkey, reached out his hand and took
it, and [a]killed a thousand men with it.
16 Then Samson said:

"With the jawbone of a donkey,
Heaps upon heaps,
With the jawbone of a donkey
I have slain a thousand men!"

17 And so it was, when he had finished
speaking, that he threw the jawbone from
his hand, and called that place [1]Ramath
Lehi.
18 Then he became very thirsty; so he
cried out to the LORD and said, [a]"You have
given this great deliverance by the hand of
Your servant; and now shall I die of thirst
and fall into the hand of the uncircumcised?" 19 So God split the hollow place
that *is* in [1]Lehi, and water came out, and
he drank; and [a]his spirit returned, and he
revived. Therefore he called its name [2]En
Hakkore, which is in Lehi to this day.
20 And [a]he judged Israel [b]twenty years [c]in
the days of the Philistines.

Samson and Delilah

16 Now Samson went to [a]Gaza and
saw a harlot there, and went in to
her. 2 *When* the Gazites *were told,* "Samson has come here!" they [a]surrounded *the
place* and lay in wait for him all night at
the gate of the city. They were quiet all
night, saying, "In the morning, when it is
daylight, we will kill him." 3 And Samson
lay *low* till midnight; then he arose at
midnight, took hold of the doors of the
gate of the city and the two gateposts,
pulled them up, bar and all, put *them* on
his shoulders, and carried them to the top
of the hill that faces Hebron.
4 Afterward it happened that he loved
a woman in the Valley of Sorek, whose
name *was* Delilah. 5 And the [a]lords of the
Philistines came up to her and said to her,
[b]"Entice him, and find out where his
great strength *lies,* and by what *means* we
may overpower him, that we may bind
him to afflict him; and every one of us will
give you eleven hundred *pieces* of silver."
6 So Delilah said to Samson, "Please tell
me where your great strength *lies,* and
with what you may be bound to afflict
you."
7 And Samson said to her, "If they bind
me with seven fresh bowstrings, not yet
dried, then I shall become weak, and be
like any *other* man."
8 So the lords of the Philistines brought
up to her seven fresh bowstrings, not yet
dried, and she bound him with them.
9 Now *men were* lying in wait, staying with
her in the room. And she said to him,
"The Philistines *are* upon you, Samson!"
But he broke the bowstrings as a strand of
yarn breaks when it touches fire. So the
secret of his strength was not known.
10 Then Delilah said to Samson, "Look,
you have mocked me and told me lies.
Now, please tell me what you may be
bound with."
11 So he said to her, "If they bind me
securely with [a]new ropes [1]that have never
been used, then I shall become weak, and
be like any *other* man."
12 Therefore Delilah took new ropes and
bound him with them, and said to him,
"The Philistines *are* upon you, Samson!"
And *men were* lying in wait, staying in the
room. But he broke them off his arms like
a thread.
13 Delilah said to Samson, "Until now
you have mocked me and told me lies. Tell
me what you may be bound with."
And he said to her, "If you weave the
seven locks of my head into the web of the
loom"—
14 So she wove *it* tightly with the batten
of the loom, and said to him, "The Philistines *are* upon you, Samson!" But he
awoke from his sleep, and pulled out the
batten and the web from the loom.

---

11 a Judg. 13:1; 14:4
13 a Judg. 16:11, 12
14 a Judg. 3:10; 14:6 *1* Lit. *were melted*
15 a Lev. 26:8
17 *1* Lit. *Jawbone Height*
18 a Ps. 3:7
19 a Is. 40:29 *1* Lit. *Jawbone,* Judg. 15:14 *2* Lit. *Spring of the Caller*
20 a Judg. 10:2; 12:7–14 b Judg. 16:31 c Judg. 13:1

CHAPTER 16
1 a Josh. 15:47
2 a 1 Sam. 23:26
5 a Josh. 13:3 b Judg. 14:15
11 a Judg. 15:13 *1* Lit. *with which work has never been done*

15 Then she said to him, [a]"How can you say, 'I love you,' when your heart *is* not with me? You have mocked me these three times, and have not told me where your great strength *lies.*" 16 And it came to pass, when she pestered him daily with her words and pressed him, *so* that his soul was [1]vexed to death, 17 that he [a]told her all his heart, and said to her, [b]"No razor has ever come upon my head, for I *have been* a Nazirite to God from my mother's womb. If I am shaven, then my strength will leave me, and I shall become weak, and be like any *other* man."

18 When Delilah saw that he had told her all his heart, she sent and called for the lords of the Philistines, saying, "Come up once more, for he has told me all his heart." So the lords of the Philistines came up to her and brought the money in their hand. 19 [a]Then she lulled him to sleep on her knees, and called for a man and had him shave off the seven locks of his head. Then [1]she began to torment him, and his strength left him. 20 And she said, "The Philistines *are* upon you, Samson!" So he awoke from his sleep, and said, "I will go out as before, at other times, and shake myself free!" But he did not know that the LORD [a]had departed from him.

21 Then the Philistines took him and [1]put out his [a]eyes, and brought him down to Gaza. They bound him with bronze fetters, and he became a grinder in the prison. 22 However, the hair of his head began to grow again after it had been shaven.

Samson Dies with the Philistines

23 Now the lords of the Philistines gathered together to offer a great sacrifice to [a]Dagon their god, and to rejoice. And they said:

"Our god has delivered into our
 hands
Samson our enemy!"

24 When the people saw him, they [a]praised their god; for they said:

"Our god has delivered into our
 hands our enemy,
The destroyer of our land,
And the one who multiplied our
 dead."

25 So it happened, when their hearts were [a]merry, that they said, "Call for Samson, that he may perform for us." So they called for Samson from the prison, and he performed for them. And they stationed him between the pillars. 26 Then Samson said to the lad who held him by the hand, "Let me feel the pillars which support the temple, so that I can lean on them." 27 Now the temple was full of men and women. All the lords of the Philistines *were* there—about three thousand men and women on the [a]roof watching while Samson performed.

28 Then Samson called to the LORD, saying, "O Lord GOD, [a]remember me, I pray! Strengthen me, I pray, just this once, O God, that I may with one *blow* take vengeance on the Philistines for my two eyes!" 29 And Samson took hold of the two middle pillars which supported the temple, and he braced himself against them, one on his right and the other on his left. 30 Then Samson said, "Let me die with the Philistines!" And he pushed with *all his* might, and the temple fell on the lords and all the people who *were* in it. So the dead that he killed at his death were more than he had killed in his life.

31 And his brothers and all his father's household came down and took him, and brought *him* up and [a]buried him between Zorah and Eshtaol in the tomb of his father Manoah. He had judged Israel [b]twenty years.

Micah's Idolatry

17 Now there was a man from the mountains of Ephraim, whose name *was* [a]Micah. 2 And he said to his mother, "The eleven hundred *shekels* of silver that were taken from you, and on which you [a]put a curse, even saying it in my ears—here *is* the silver with me; I took it."

And his mother said, [b]"*May you be* blessed by the LORD, my son!" 3 So when he had returned the eleven hundred *shekels* of silver to his mother, his mother said, "I had wholly dedicated the silver from my hand to the LORD for my son, to [a]make a carved image and a molded image; now therefore, I will return it to you." 4 Thus he returned the silver to his mother. Then his mother [a]took two hundred *shekels* of silver and gave them to the silversmith, and he made it into a carved image and a molded image; and they were in the house of Micah.

15 [a] Judg. 14:16
16 [1] Lit. *impatient to the point of*
17 [a] [Mic. 7:5] [b] Judg. 13:5
19 [a] Prov. 7:26, 27 [1] So with MT, Tg., Vg.; LXX *he began to be weak,*
20 [a] [Josh. 7:12]
21 [a] 2 Kin. 25:7 [1] Lit. *bored out*
23 [a] 1 Sam. 5:2
24 [a] Dan. 5:4
25 [a] Judg. 9:27
27 [a] Deut. 22:8
28 [a] Jer. 15:15
31 [a] Judg. 13:25 [b] Judg. 15:20

CHAPTER 17
1 [a] Judg. 18:2
2 [a] Lev. 5:1 [b] Gen. 14:19
3 [a] Ex. 20:4, 23; 34:17
4 [a] Is. 46:6

5The man Micah had a [a]shrine, and made an [b]ephod and [c]household[1] idols; and he consecrated one of his sons, who became his priest. 6[a]In those days *there was* no king in Israel; [b]everyone did *what was* right in his own eyes.

7Now there was a young man from [a]Bethlehem in Judah, of the family of Judah; he *was* a Levite, and [b]was staying there. 8The man departed from the city of Bethlehem in Judah to stay wherever he could find *a place.* Then he came to the mountains of Ephraim, to the house of Micah, as he journeyed. 9And Micah said to him, "Where do you come from?"

So he said to him, "I *am* a Levite from Bethlehem in Judah, and I am on my way to find *a place* to stay."

10Micah said to him, "Dwell with me, [a]and be a [b]father and a priest to me, and I will give you ten *shekels* of silver per year, a suit of clothes, and your sustenance." So the Levite went in. 11Then the Levite was content to dwell with the man; and the young man became like one of his sons to him. 12So Micah [a]consecrated[1] the Levite, and the young man [b]became his priest, and lived in the house of Micah. 13Then Micah said, "Now I know that the LORD will be good to me, since I have a Levite as [a]priest!"

The Danites Adopt Micah's Idolatry

18 In [a]those days *there was* no king in Israel. And in those days [b]the tribe of the Danites was seeking an inheritance for itself to dwell in; for until that day *their* inheritance among the tribes of Israel had not fallen to them. 2So the children of Dan sent five men of their family from their territory, men of valor from [a]Zorah and Eshtaol, [b]to spy out the land and search it. They said to them, "Go, search the land." So they went to the mountains of Ephraim, to the [c]house of Micah, and lodged there. 3While they *were* at the house of Micah, they recognized the voice of the young Levite. They turned aside and said to him, "Who brought you here? What are you doing in this *place?* What do you have here?"

4He said to them, "Thus and so Micah did for me. He has [a]hired me, and I have become his priest."

5So they said to him, "Please [a]inquire [b]of God, that we may know whether the journey on which we go will be prosperous."

6And the priest said to them, [a]"Go in peace. [1]The presence of the LORD *be* with you on your way."

7So the five men departed and went to [a]Laish. They saw the people who *were* there, [b]how they dwelt safely, in the manner of the Sidonians, quiet and secure. *There were* no rulers in the land who might put *them* to shame for anything. They *were* far from the [c]Sidonians, and they had no ties [1]with anyone.

8Then *the spies* came back to their brethren at [a]Zorah and Eshtaol, and their brethren said to them, "What *is* your *report?*"

9So they said, [a]"Arise, let us go up against them. For we have seen the land, and indeed it *is* very good. *Would* you [b]*do* nothing? Do not hesitate to go, *and* enter to possess the land. 10When you go, you will come to a [a]secure people and a large land. For God has given it into your hands, [b]a place where *there is* no lack of anything that *is* on the earth."

11And six hundred men of the family of the Danites went from there, from Zorah and Eshtaol, armed with weapons of war. 12Then they went up and encamped in [a]Kirjath Jearim in Judah. (Therefore they call that place [b]Mahaneh Dan[1] to this day. There *it is,* west of Kirjath Jearim.) 13And they passed from there to the mountains of Ephraim, and came to [a]the house of Micah.

14[a]Then the five men who had gone to spy out the country of Laish answered and said to their brethren, "Do you know that [b]there are in these houses an ephod, household idols, a carved image, and a molded image? Now therefore, consider what you should do." 15So they turned aside there, and came to the house of the young Levite man—to the house of Micah—and greeted him. 16The [a]six hundred men armed with their weapons of war, who *were* of the children of Dan, stood by the entrance of the gate. 17Then [a]the five men who had gone to spy out the land went up. Entering there, they took [b]the carved image, the ephod, the household idols, and the molded image. The priest stood at the entrance of the gate with the six hundred men *who were* armed with weapons of war.

18When these went into Micah's house and took the carved image, the ephod, the

---

5 a Judg. 18:24 b Judg. 8:27; 18:14 c Gen. 31:19, 30 *1* Heb. *teraphim*
6 a Judg. 18:1; 19:1 b Deut. 12:8
7 a Matt. 2:1, 5, 6 b Deut. 18:6
10 a Judg. 18:19 b Gen. 45:8
12 a Judg. 17:5 b Judg. 18:30 *1* Lit. *filled the hand of*
13 a Judg. 18:4

CHAPTER 18
1 a Judg. 17:6; 19:1; 21:25 b Josh. 19:40–48
2 a Judg. 13:25 b Num. 13:17 c Judg. 17:1
4 a Judg. 17:10, 12
5 a Hos. 4:12 b Judg. 1:1; 17:5; 18:14
6 a 1 Kin. 22:6 *1* Lit. *The LORD is before the way in which you go*
7 a Josh. 19:47 b Judg. 18:27–29 c Judg. 10:12 *1* So with MT, Tg., Vg.; LXX *with Syria*
8 a Judg. 18:2
9 a Num. 13:30 b 1 Kin. 22:3
10 a Judg. 18:7, 27 b Deut. 8:9
12 a Josh. 15:60 b Judg. 13:25 *1* Lit. *Camp of Dan*
13 a Judg. 18:2
14 a 1 Sam. 14:28 b Judg. 17:5
16 a Judg. 18:11
17 a Judg. 18:2, 14 b Judg. 17:4, 5

household idols, and the molded image, the priest said to them, "What are you doing?"

19 And they said to him, "Be quiet, [a]put your hand over your mouth, and come with us; [b]be a father and a priest to us. *Is it* better for you to be a priest to the household of one man, or that you be a priest to a tribe and a family in Israel?" 20 So the priest's heart was glad; and he took the ephod, the household idols, and the carved image, and took his place among the people.

21 Then they turned and departed, and put the little ones, the livestock, and the goods in front of them. 22 When they were a good way from the house of Micah, the men who *were* in the houses near Micah's house gathered together and overtook the children of Dan. 23 And they called out to the children of Dan. So they turned around and said to Micah, [a]"What ails you, that you have gathered such a company?"

24 So he said, "You have [a]taken away my [1]gods which I made, and the priest, and you have gone away. Now what more do I have? How can you say to me, 'What ails you?' "

25 And the children of Dan said to him, "Do not let your voice be heard among us, lest [1]angry men fall upon you, and you lose your life, with the lives of your household!" 26 Then the children of Dan went their way. And when Micah saw that they *were* too strong for him, he turned and went back to his house.

Danites Settle in Laish

27 So they took *the things* Micah had made, and the priest who had belonged to him, and went to Laish, to a people quiet and secure; [a]and they struck them with the edge of the sword and burned the city with fire. 28 *There was* no deliverer, because it *was* [a]far from Sidon, and they had no ties with anyone. It was in the valley that belongs [b]to Beth Rehob. So they rebuilt the city and dwelt there. 29 And [a]they called the name of the city [b]Dan, after the name of Dan their father, who was born to Israel. However, the name of the city formerly *was* Laish.

30 Then the children of Dan set up for themselves the carved image; and Jonathan the son of Gershom, the son of [1]Manasseh, and his sons were priests to the tribe of Dan [a]until the day of the captivity of the land. 31 So they set up for themselves Micah's carved image which he made, [a]all the time that the house of God was in Shiloh.

The Levite's Concubine

19 And it came to pass in those days, [a]when *there was* no king in Israel, that there was a certain Levite staying in the remote mountains of Ephraim. He took for himself a concubine from [b]Bethlehem in Judah. 2 But his concubine played the harlot against him, and went away from him to her father's house at Bethlehem in Judah, and was there four whole months. 3 Then her husband arose and went after her, to [a]speak [1]kindly to her *and* bring her back, having his servant and a couple of donkeys with him. So she brought him into her father's house; and when the father of the young woman saw him, he was glad to meet him. 4 Now his father-in-law, the young woman's father, detained him; and he stayed with him three days. So they ate and drank and lodged there.

5 Then it came to pass on the fourth day that they arose early in the morning, and he stood to depart; but the young woman's father said to his son-in-law, [a]"Refresh your heart with a morsel of bread, and afterward go your way."

6 So they sat down, and the two of them ate and drank together. Then the young woman's father said to the man, "Please be content to stay all night, and let your heart be merry." 7 And when the man stood to depart, his father-in-law urged him; so he lodged there again. 8 Then he arose early in the morning on the fifth day to depart, but the young woman's father said, "Please refresh your heart." So they delayed until afternoon; and both of them ate.

9 And when the man stood to depart—he and his concubine and his servant—his father-in-law, the young woman's father, said to him, "Look, the day is now drawing toward evening; please spend the night. See, the day is coming to an end; lodge here, that your heart may be merry. Tomorrow go your way early, so that you may get [1]home."

10 However, the man was not willing to spend that night; so he rose and departed, and came opposite [a]Jebus (that *is,* Jerusalem). With him were the two saddled donkeys; his concubine *was* also with him.

19 a Job 21:5; 29:9; 40:4 b Judg. 17:10
23 a 2 Kin. 6:28
24 a Gen. 31:30 *1 idols*
25 *1* Lit. *bitter of soul*
27 a Josh. 19:47
28 a Judg. 18:7 b 2 Sam. 10:6
29 a Josh. 19:47 b Judg. 20:1
30 a 2 Kin. 15:29 *1* LXX, Vg. *Moses*
31 a Josh. 18:1, 8

CHAPTER 19
1 a Judg. 17:6; 18:1; 21:25 b Judg. 17:7
3 a Gen. 34:3; 50:21 *1* Lit. *to her heart*
5 a Gen. 18:5
9 *1* Lit. *to your tent*
10 a 1 Chr. 11:4, 5

11They *were* near Jebus, and the day was far spent; and the servant said to his master, "Come, please, and let us turn aside into this city [a]of the Jebusites and lodge in it."

12But his master said to him, "We will not turn aside here into a city of foreigners, who *are* not of the children of Israel; we will go on [a]to Gibeah." 13So he said to his servant, "Come, let us draw near to one of these places, and spend the night in Gibeah or in [a]Ramah." 14And they passed by and went their way; and the sun went down on them near Gibeah, which belongs to Benjamin. 15They turned aside there to go in to lodge in Gibeah. And when he went in, he sat down in the open square of the city, for no one would [a]take them into *his* house to spend the night.

16Just then an old man came in from [a]his work in the field at evening, who also *was* from the mountains of Ephraim; he was staying in Gibeah, whereas the men of the place *were* Benjamites. 17And when he raised his eyes, he saw the traveler in the open square of the city; and the old man said, "Where are you going, and where do you come from?"

18So he said to him, "We *are* passing from Bethlehem in Judah toward the remote mountains of Ephraim; I *am* from there. I went to Bethlehem in Judah; *now* I am going to [a]the house of the LORD. But there *is* no one who will take me into his house, 19although we have both straw and fodder for our donkeys, and bread and wine for myself, for your female servant, and for the young man *who is* with your servant; *there is* no lack of anything."

20And the old man said, [a]"Peace *be* with you! However, *let* all your needs *be* my responsibility; [b]only do not spend the night in the open square." 21[a]So he brought him into his house, and gave fodder to the donkeys. [b]And they washed their feet, and ate and drank.

Gibeah's Crime

22As they were [a]enjoying themselves, suddenly [b]certain men of the city, [c]perverted[1] men, surrounded the house *and* beat on the door. They spoke to the master of the house, the old man, saying, [d]"Bring out the man who came to your house, that we may know him *carnally!*"

23But [a]the man, the master of the house, went out to them and said to them, "No, my brethren! I beg you, do not act *so* wickedly! Seeing this man has come into my house, [b]do not commit this outrage. 24[a]Look, *here is* my virgin daughter and [1]*the man's* concubine; let me bring them out now. [b]Humble them, and do with them as you please; but to this man do not do such a vile thing!" 25But the men would not heed him. So the man took his concubine and brought *her* out to them. And they [a]knew her and abused her all night until morning; and when the day began to break, they let her go.

26Then the woman came as the day was dawning, and fell down at the door of the man's house where her master *was,* till it was light.

27When her master arose in the morning, and opened the doors of the house and went out to go his way, there was his concubine, fallen *at* the door of the house with her hands on the threshold. 28And he said to her, "Get up and let us be going." But [a]there was no answer. So the man lifted her onto the donkey; and the man got up and went to his place.

29When he entered his house he took a knife, laid hold of his concubine, and [a]divided her into twelve pieces, [1]limb by limb, and sent her throughout all the territory of Israel. 30And so it was that all who saw it said, "No such deed has been done or seen from the day that the children of Israel came up from the land of Egypt until this day. Consider it, [a]confer, and speak up!"

Israel's War with the Benjamites

20 So [a]all the children of Israel came out, from [b]Dan to [c]Beersheba, as well as from the land of Gilead, and the congregation gathered together as one man before the LORD [d]at Mizpah. 2And the leaders of all the people, all the tribes of Israel, presented themselves in the assembly of the people of God, four hundred thousand foot soldiers [a]who drew the sword. 3(Now the children of Benjamin heard that the children of Israel had gone up to Mizpah.)

Then the children of Israel said, "Tell *us,* how did this wicked deed happen?"

4So the Levite, the husband of the woman who was murdered, answered and said, "My concubine and [a]I went into Gibeah, which belongs to Benjamin, to spend the night. 5[a]And the men of Gibeah rose against me, and surrounded the house at

11 a Josh. 15:8, 63
12 a Josh. 18:28
13 a Josh. 18:25
15 a Matt. 25:43
16 a Ps. 104:23
18 a Josh. 18:1
20 a Gen. 43:23 b Gen. 19:2
21 a Gen. 24:32; 43:24 b John 13:5
22 a Judg. 16:25; 19:6, 9 b Hos. 9:9; 10:9 c Deut. 13:13 d [Rom. 1:26, 27] 1 Lit. *sons of Belial*
23 a Gen. 19:6, 7 b 2 Sam. 13:12
24 a Gen. 19:8 b Gen. 34:2 1 Lit. *his*
25 a Gen. 4:1
28 a Judg. 20:5
29 a 1 Sam. 11:7 1 Lit. *with her bones*
30 a Judg. 20:7

CHAPTER 20
1 a Josh. 22:12 b 2 Sam. 3:10; 24:2 c Josh. 19:2 d 1 Sam. 7:5
2 a Judg. 8:10
4 a Judg. 19:15
5 a Judg. 19:22

night because of me. They intended to kill me, [b]but instead they ravished my concubine so that she died. 6So [a]I took hold of my concubine, cut her in pieces, and sent her throughout all the territory of the inheritance of Israel, because they [b]committed lewdness and outrage in Israel. 7Look! All of you *are* children of Israel; [a]give your advice and counsel here and now!"

8So all the people arose as one man, saying, "None *of us* will go to his tent, nor will any turn back to his house; 9but now this *is* the thing which we will do to Gibeah: *We will go up* [a]against it by lot. 10We will take ten men out of *every* hundred throughout all the tribes of Israel, a hundred out of *every* thousand, and a thousand out of *every* ten thousand, to make provisions for the people, that when they come to Gibeah in Benjamin, they may repay all the vileness that they have done in Israel." 11So all the men of Israel were gathered against the city, united together as one man.

12[a]Then the tribes of Israel sent men through all the tribe of Benjamin, saying, "What *is* this wickedness that has occurred among you? 13Now therefore, deliver up the men, [a]the [1]perverted men who *are* in Gibeah, that we may put them to death and [b]remove the evil from Israel!" But the children of Benjamin would not listen to the voice of their brethren, the children of Israel. 14Instead, the children of Benjamin gathered together from their cities to Gibeah, to go to battle against the children of Israel. 15And from their cities at that time [a]the children of Benjamin numbered twenty-six thousand men who drew the sword, besides the inhabitants of Gibeah, who numbered seven hundred select men. 16Among all this people *were* seven hundred select men *who were* [a]left-handed; every one could sling a stone at a hair's *breadth* and not miss. 17Now besides Benjamin, the men of Israel numbered four hundred thousand men who drew the sword; all of these *were* men of war.

18Then the children of Israel arose and [a]went up to [1]the house of God to [b]inquire of God. They said, "Which of us shall go up first to battle against the children of Benjamin?"

The LORD said, [c]"Judah first!"

19So the children of Israel rose in the morning and encamped against Gibeah. 20And the men of Israel went out to battle against Benjamin, and the men of Israel put themselves in battle array to fight against them at Gibeah. 21Then [a]the children of Benjamin came out of Gibeah, and on that day cut down to the ground twenty-two thousand men of the Israelites. 22And the people, that is, the men of Israel, encouraged themselves and again formed the battle line at the place where they had put themselves in array on the first day. 23[a]Then the children of Israel went up and wept before the LORD until evening, and asked counsel of the LORD, saying, "Shall I again draw near for battle against the children of my brother Benjamin?"

And the LORD said, "Go up against him."

24So the children of Israel approached the children of Benjamin on the second day. 25And [a]Benjamin went out against them from Gibeah on the second day, and cut down to the ground eighteen thousand more of the children of Israel; all these drew the sword.

26Then all the children of Israel, that is, all the people, [a]went up and came to [1]the house of God and wept. They sat there before the LORD and fasted that day until evening; and they offered burnt offerings and peace offerings before the LORD. 27So the children of Israel inquired of the LORD ([a]the ark of the covenant of God *was* there in those days, 28[a]and Phinehas the son of Eleazar, the son of Aaron, [b]stood before it in those days), saying, "Shall I yet again go out to battle against the children of my brother Benjamin, or shall I cease?"

And the LORD said, "Go up, for tomorrow I will deliver them into your hand."

29Then Israel [a]set men in ambush all around Gibeah. 30And the children of Israel went up against the children of Benjamin on the third day, and put themselves in battle array against Gibeah as at the other times. 31So the children of Benjamin went out against the people, *and* were drawn away from the city. They began to strike down *and* kill some of the people, as at the other times, in the highways [a](one of which goes up to Bethel and the other to Gibeah) and in the field, about thirty men of Israel. 32And the children of Benjamin said, "They *are* defeated before us, as at first."

But the children of Israel said, "Let us flee and draw them away from the city to

5 [b]Judg. 19:25, 26
6 [a]Judg. 19:29 [b]Josh. 7:15
7 [a]Judg. 19:30
9 [a]Judg. 1:3
12 [a]Deut. 13:14
13 [a]Deut. 13:13 [b]Deut. 17:12 [1]Lit. *sons of Belial*
15 [a]Num. 1:36, 37; 2:23; 26:41
16 [a]1 Chr. 12:2
18 [a]Judg. 20:23, 26 [b]Num. 27:21 [c]Judg. 1:1, 2 [1]Or *Bethel*
21 [a][Gen. 49:27]
23 [a]Judg. 20:26, 27
25 [a]Judg. 20:21
26 [a]Judg. 20:18, 23; 21:2 [1]Or *Bethel*
27 [a]Josh. 18:1
28 [a]Josh. 24:33 [b]Deut. 10:8; 18:5
29 [a]Josh. 8:4
31 [a]Judg. 21:19

the highways." 33So all the men of Israel
rose from their place and put themselves
in battle array at Baal Tamar. Then Israel's men in ambush burst forth from their
position in the plain of Geba. 34And ten
thousand select men from all Israel came
against Gibeah, and the battle was fierce.
[a]But [1]*the Benjamites* did not know that
disaster *was* upon them. 35The LORD [1]de-
feated Benjamin before Israel. And the
children of Israel destroyed that day
twenty-five thousand one hundred Benjamites; all these drew the sword.
36So the children of Benjamin saw that
they were defeated. [a]The men of Israel
had given ground to the Benjamites, because they relied on the men in ambush
whom they had set against Gibeah. 37[a]And
the men in ambush quickly rushed upon
Gibeah; the men in ambush spread out
and struck the whole city with the edge of
the sword. 38Now the appointed signal between the men of Israel and the men in
ambush was that they would make a great
cloud of [a]smoke rise up from the city,
39whereupon the men of Israel would turn
in battle. Now Benjamin had begun [1]to
strike *and* kill about thirty of the men of
Israel. For they said, "Surely they are defeated before us, as *in* the first battle."
40But when the cloud began to rise from
the city in a column of smoke, the Benjamites [a]looked behind them, and there was
the whole city going up *in smoke* to heav-
en. 41And when the men of Israel turned
back, the men of Benjamin panicked, for
they saw that disaster had come upon
them. 42Therefore they [1]turned *their*
backs before the men of Israel in the direction of the wilderness; but the battle
overtook them, and whoever *came* out of
the cities they destroyed in their midst.
43They surrounded the Benjamites,
chased them, *and* easily trampled them
down as far as the front of Gibeah toward
the east. 44And eighteen thousand men of
Benjamin fell; all these *were* men of valor.
45Then [1]they turned and fled toward the
wilderness to the rock of [a]Rimmon; and
they cut down five thousand of them on
the highways. Then they pursued them
relentlessly up to Gidom, and killed two
thousand of them. 46So all who fell of
Benjamin that day were twenty-five thousand men who drew the sword; all these
were [1]men of valor.
47[a]But six hundred men turned and fled
toward the wilderness to the rock of Rimmon, and they stayed at the rock of Rimmon for four months. 48And the men of
Israel turned back against the children of
Benjamin, and struck them down with the
edge of the sword—from *every* city, men
and beasts, all who were found. They also
set fire to all the cities they came to.

Wives Provided for the Benjamites

21 Now [a]the men of Israel had sworn
an oath at Mizpah, saying, "None of
us shall give his daughter to Benjamin as
a wife." 2Then the people came [a]to [1]the
house of God, and remained there before
God till evening. They lifted up their voices and wept bitterly, 3and said, "O LORD
God of Israel, why has this come to pass
in Israel, that today there should be one
tribe *missing* in Israel?"

Prayer and prayer alone, much prayer, persistent prayer, is the door of entrance into the heart of God.

JOHN G. LAKE

4So it was, on the next morning, that
the people rose early and [a]built an altar
there, and offered burnt offerings and
peace offerings. 5The children of Israel
said, "Who *is there* among all the tribes of
Israel who did not come up with the assembly to the LORD?" [a]For they had made
a great oath concerning anyone who had
not come up to the LORD at Mizpah, saying, "He shall surely be put to death."
6And the children of Israel grieved for
Benjamin their brother, and said, "One
tribe is cut off from Israel today. 7What
shall we do for wives for those who remain, seeing we have sworn by the LORD
that we will not give them our daughters
as wives?"
8And they said, "What one *is there* from
the tribes of Israel who did not come up
to Mizpah to the LORD?" And, in fact, no
one had come to the camp from [a]Jabesh
Gilead to the assembly. 9For when the
people were counted, indeed, not one of

34 [a]Josh. 8:14 [1]Lit. *they*
35 [1]Lit. *struck*
36 [a]Josh. 8:15
37 [a]Josh. 8:19
38 [a]Josh. 8:20
39 [1]Lit. *to strike the slain ones*
40 [a]Josh. 8:20
42 [1]*fled*
45 [a]Josh. 15:32 [1]LXX *the rest*
46 [1]*valiant warriors*
47 [a]Judg. 21:13

CHAPTER 21
1 [a]Judg. 20:1
2 [a]Judg. 20:18, 26 [1]Or *Bethel*
4 [a]2 Sam. 24:25
5 [a]Judg. 20:1–3
8 [a]1 Sam. 11:1; 31:11

the inhabitants of Jabesh Gilead *was*
there. 10 So the congregation sent out
there twelve thousand of their most valiant men, and commanded them, saying,
[a]"Go and strike the inhabitants of Jabesh
Gilead with the edge of the sword, including the women and children. 11 And this *is*
the thing that you shall do: [a]You shall
utterly destroy every male, and every
woman who has known a man intimately." 12 So they found among the inhabitants of Jabesh Gilead four hundred
young virgins who had not known a man
intimately; and they brought them to the
camp at [a]Shiloh, which is in the land of
Canaan.

13 Then the whole congregation sent
word to the children of Benjamin [a]who
were at the rock of Rimmon, and announced peace to them. 14 So Benjamin
came back at that time, and they gave
them the women whom they had saved
alive of the women of Jabesh Gilead; and
yet they had not found enough for them.

15 And the people [a]grieved for Benjamin, because the LORD had made a void in
the tribes of Israel.

16 Then the elders of the congregation
said, "What shall we do for wives for those
who remain, since the women of Benjamin have been destroyed?" 17 And they
said, "*There must be* an inheritance for
the survivors of Benjamin, that a tribe
may not be destroyed from Israel. 18 However, we cannot give them wives from our
daughters, [a]for the children of Israel have
sworn an oath, saying, 'Cursed *be* the one
who gives a wife to Benjamin.' " 19 Then
they said, "In fact, *there is* a yearly [a]feast
of the LORD in [b]Shiloh, which *is* north of
Bethel, on the east side of the [c]highway
that goes up from Bethel to Shechem, and
south of Lebonah."

10 [a]Num. 31:17
11 [a]Num. 31:17
12 [a]Josh. 18:1
13 [a]Judg. 20:47
15 [a]Judg. 21:6
18 [a]Judg. 11:35; 21:1
19 [a]Lev. 23:2 [b]1 Sam. 1:3 [c]Judg. 20:31
21 [a]Judg. 11:34
23 [a]Judg. 20:48
25 [a]Judg. 17:6; 18:1; 19:1 [b]Judg. 17:6

20 Therefore they instructed the children of Benjamin, saying, "Go, lie in wait
in the vineyards, 21 and watch; and just
when the daughters of Shiloh come out
[a]to perform their dances, then come out
from the vineyards, and every man catch
a wife for himself from the daughters of
Shiloh; then go to the land of Benjamin.
22 Then it shall be, when their fathers or
their brothers come to us to complain,
that we will say to them, 'Be kind to them
for our sakes, because we did not take a
wife for any of them in the war; for *it is*
not *as though* you have given the *women*
to them at this time, making yourselves
guilty of your oath.' "

23 And the children of Benjamin did so;
they took enough wives for their number
from those who danced, whom they
caught. Then they went and returned to
their inheritance, and they [a]rebuilt the
cities and dwelt in them. 24 So the children
of Israel departed from there at that time,
every man to his tribe and family; they
went out from there, every man to his inheritance.

O God, You alone are King! I pray that you would keep _____ from rejecting You and doing what is right in their own eyes.

FROM JUDGES 21:25

25 [a]In those days *there was* no king in
Israel; [b]everyone did *what was* right in his
own eyes.

AUTHOR: *Unknown. Jewish Tradition Ascribes It to Samuel.*
DATE: *1050–500 B.C.*
THEME: *God's Sovereign Intervention Brings Universal Redemption*
KEY WORDS: *Sovereignty, The Almighty, Redeemer*

RUTH

Dear Woman of Destiny,

Ruth is the story of one woman's love, friendship, and devotion. The effects of her faithfulness reached down through generations all the way to her most famous descendant, Jesus Christ. Why is her example so valuable to women today? From Ruth, we learn to remain in the place of blessing, and to exercise the patience that allows God to bring His wonderful redemptive plan to completion.

His love and mine,

Marilyn Hickey

Elimelech's Family Goes to Moab

Now it came to pass, in the days
when [a]the judges [1]ruled, that
there was [b]a famine in the land.
And a certain man of [c]Bethlehem, Judah,
went to [2]dwell in the country of [d]Moab, he
and his wife and his two sons. 2The name
of the man *was* Elimelech, the name of
his wife *was* Naomi, and the names of his
two sons *were* Mahlon and Chilion—
[a]Ephrathites of Bethlehem, Judah. And
they went [b]to the country of Moab and
remained there. 3Then Elimelech, Naomi's husband, died; and she was left, and
her two sons. 4Now they took wives of the
women of Moab: the name of the one *was*
Orpah, and the name of the other Ruth.
And they [1]dwelt there about ten years.
5Then both Mahlon and Chilion also died;
so the woman survived her two sons and
her husband.

Naomi Returns with Ruth

6Then she arose with her daughters-in-
law that she might return from the country of Moab, for she had heard in the
country of Moab that the LORD had [a]visit-
ed[1] His people by [b]giving them bread.
7Therefore she went out from the place
where she was, and her two daughters-in-
law with her; and they went on the way to
return to the land of Judah. 8And Naomi
said to her two daughters-in-law, [a]"Go,
return each to her mother's house. [b]The
LORD deal kindly with you, as you have

CHAPTER 1
1 [a]Judg. 2:16–18 [b]Gen. 12:10; 26:1 [c]Judg. 17:8 [d]Gen. 19:37 [1]Lit. *judged* [2]As a resident alien
2 [a]Gen. 35:19 [b]Judg. 3:30
4 [1]*lived*
6 [a]Ex. 3:16; 4:31 [b]Matt. 6:11 [1]*attended to*
8 [a]Josh. 24:15 [b]2 Tim. 1:16–18

Naomi's life is one of the Bible's beautiful tales of redemption. While in Moab, she endured one loss after another, and one of the first things we learn about her is that she was a survivor (see Ruth 1:5). As every survivor knows, the business of survival leaves little time or energy for joy, and Naomi certainly had lost hers. She took it upon herself to try and change her name from Naomi, which means "Pleasant, Delightful, or Lovely" to Mara, which means "Bitter." And, indeed, she had responded to her circumstances with bitterness, saying that "the hand of the LORD [had] gone out against" her (Ruth 1:13). Her bitterness had made her unable to feel the tender touch of God, but it had not made Him unable to touch her. In her sadness and hardness of heart, Naomi did not know that God had a merciful surprise in store for her.

Eventually, Naomi made the choice survivors always make. She chose to live on. She chose to make the best of her situation. She got busy thinking about what relatives she might have in Bethlehem and was instrumental in arranging Ruth's marriage to Boaz. In helping to redeem Ruth's situation, she also helped herself. God used Ruth and Boaz to provide for Naomi and to bring happiness to her later years as she enjoyed her grandson Obed, who would later be the grandfather of King David.

Naomi learned that survival is worth everything it costs. She learned that it is never too late for God to redeem. There was a time when Naomi could not see the hand of God moving on her behalf. She could not see her destiny unfolding until she had already lived much of her life. But, through her heartbreak and beyond her bitterness, God wanted to bless her and to use her to bless others. And He wants to do the same for you.

dealt [c]with the dead and with me. 9The
LORD grant that you may find [a]rest, each
in the house of her husband."
So she kissed them, and they lifted up
their voices and wept. 10And they said to
her, "Surely we will return with you to
your people."
11But Naomi said, "Turn back, my
daughters; why will you go with me? *Are*
there still sons in my womb, [a]that they
may be your husbands? 12Turn back, my
daughters, go—for I am too old to have a
husband. If I should say I have hope, *if*
I should have a husband tonight and
should also bear sons, 13would you wait
for them till they were grown? Would you
restrain yourselves from having husbands? No, my daughters; for it grieves
me very much for your sakes that [a]the
hand of the LORD has gone out
against me!"

Thou hast made us for Thyself, and our hearts are restless until they find their rest in Thee.

ST. AUGUSTINE

14Then they lifted up their voices and
wept again; and Orpah kissed her mother-
in-law, but Ruth [a]clung to her.
15And she said, "Look, your sister-in-
law has gone back to [a]her people and to
her gods; [b]return after your sister-in-
law."
16But Ruth said:

[a]"Entreat[1] me not to leave you,
Or to turn back from following
after you;
For wherever you go, I will go;
And wherever you lodge, I will
lodge;
[b]Your people *shall be* my people,
And your God, my God.
17 Where you die, I will die,
And there will I be buried.
[a]The LORD do so to me, and more
also,
If *anything but* death parts you and
me."

18[a]When she saw that she [1]was determined to go with her, she stopped speaking to her.
19Now the two of them went until they
came to Bethlehem. And it happened,
when they had come to Bethlehem, that
[a]all the city was excited because of them;
and the women said, [b]"*Is* this Naomi?"
20But she said to them, "Do not call me
[1]Naomi; call me [2]Mara, for the Almighty
has dealt very bitterly with me. 21I went
out full, [a]and the LORD has brought me
home again empty. Why do you call me
Naomi, since the LORD has testified
against me, and [1]the Almighty has afflicted me?"
22So Naomi returned, and Ruth the Moabitess her daughter-in-law with her,
who returned from the country of Moab.
Now they came to Bethlehem [a]at the beginning of barley harvest.

Ruth Meets Boaz

2 There was a [a]relative of Naomi's husband, a man of great wealth, of the
family of [b]Elimelech. His name *was*
[c]Boaz. 2So Ruth the Moabitess said to Naomi, "Please let me go to the [a]field, and
glean heads of grain after *him* in whose
sight I may find favor."
And she said to her, "Go, my daughter."
3Then she left, and went and gleaned in
the field after the reapers. And she happened to come to the part of the field *belonging* to Boaz, who *was* of the family of
Elimelech.
4Now behold, Boaz came from [a]Bethle-
hem, and said to the reapers, [b]"The LORD
be with you!"
And they answered him, "The LORD
bless you!"
5Then Boaz said to his servant who was

Hope for nothing from your own labors, from your own understanding: trust solely in God, and in the influence of His Spirit.

MARTIN LUTHER

8 [c] Ruth 2:20
9 [a] Ruth 3:1
11 [a] Deut. 25:5
13 [a] Judg. 2:15
14 [a] [Prov. 17:17]
15 [a] Judg. 11:24 [b] Josh. 1:15
16 [a] 2 Kin. 2:2, 4, 6 [b] Ruth 2:11, 12 [1] *Urge me not*
17 [a] 1 Sam. 3:17
18 [a] Acts 21:14 [1] Lit. *made herself strong to go*
19 [a] Matt. 21:10 [b] Lam. 2:15
20 [1] Lit. *Pleasant* [2] Lit. *Bitter*
21 [a] Job 1:21 [1] Heb. *Shaddai*
22 [a] 2 Sam. 21:9

CHAPTER 2
1 [a] Ruth 3:2, 12 [b] Ruth 1:2 [c] Ruth 4:21
2 [a] Lev. 19:9, 10; 23:22
4 [a] Ruth 1:1 [b] Ps. 129:7, 8

in charge of the reapers, "Whose young
woman *is* this?"
[6]So the servant who was in charge of
the reapers answered and said, "It *is* the
young Moabite woman [a]who came back
with Naomi from the country of Moab.
[7]And she said, 'Please let me glean and
gather after the reapers among the
sheaves.' So she came and has continued
from morning until now, though she rested a little in the house."
[8]Then Boaz said to Ruth, "You will listen, my daughter, will you not? Do not go
to glean in another field, nor go from
here, but stay close by my young women.
[9]*Let* your eyes *be* on the field which they
reap, and go after them. Have I not commanded the young men not to touch you?
And when you are thirsty, go to the vessels and drink from what the young men
have drawn."
[10]So she [a]fell on her face, bowed down
to the ground, and said to him, "Why have
I found [b]favor in your eyes, that you
should take notice of me, since I *am* a
foreigner?"
[11]And Boaz answered and said to her,
"It has been fully reported to me, [a]all that
you have done for your mother-in-law
since the death of your husband, and *how*
you have left your father and your mother
and the land of your birth, and have come
to a people whom you did not know before. [12][a]The LORD repay your work, and a

6 a Ruth 1:22
10 a 1 Sam. 25:23 b 1 Sam. 1:18
11 a Ruth 1:14–18
12 a 1 Sam. 24:19

RUTH

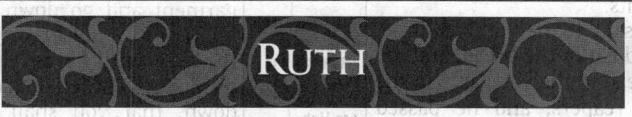

Who knows why women through the centuries have called Ruth one of their favorite Bible characters? Perhaps it is because there is something in us that longs to be as faithful, as courageous, as obedient, as loyal, and as blessed as this woman of destiny.

As a young widow, Ruth undoubtedly had many choices to make. One of her first decisions was whether to stay in Moab, a familiar place with familiar people, or to let go of what was comfortable to her and return to Bethlehem with Naomi. She went with Naomi wholeheartedly—not just physically, but spiritually. She let go of the security of her homeland and embraced all the uncertainties of a new home, a new culture, and a new religion. She demonstrated her commitment to a covenant relationship with Naomi by saying these familiar words, "Your people shall be my people, and your God, my God" (Ruth 1:16). In a beautiful act of commitment, she gave herself completely to Naomi, to Naomi's land, and to Naomi's God.

In Bethlehem, Ruth was a stranger. She had nothing but her mother-in-law, her newfound faith, and a determination to stick with both. Naomi directed her to Boaz's field, where she could glean behind the reapers and hopefully gather enough wheat to provide food for herself and Naomi. Being a gleaner was a lowly occupation, but Ruth went about her duties with a spirit of humility and service. Eventually, Boaz took notice of Ruth, they married, and God used him to redeem her life.

Ruth understood something that is crucial to any woman of destiny. She knew when it was time to move on. She knew when it was time to give up everything in order to walk with God and to live among His people. She took the risk, gained the Lord's favor, and became a paragon of faith and virtue who remains a role model for women today.

O God of Israel,
may ______ take refuge
under Your wings.
FROM RUTH 2:12

full reward be given you by the LORD God
of Israel, [b]under whose wings you have
come for refuge."
13Then she said, [a]"Let me find favor in
your sight, my lord; for you have comforted me, and have spoken [1]kindly to your
maidservant, [b]though I am not like one of
your maidservants."
14Now Boaz said to her at mealtime,
"Come here, and eat of the bread, and dip
your piece of bread in the vinegar." So she
sat beside the reapers, and he passed
parched *grain* to her; and she ate and
[a]was satisfied, and kept some back. 15And
when she rose up to [1]glean, Boaz commanded his young men, saying, "Let her
glean even among the sheaves, and do not
[2]reproach her. 16Also let *grain* from the
bundles fall purposely for her; leave *it* that
she may glean, and do not rebuke her."
17So she gleaned in the field until evening, and beat out what she had gleaned,
and it was about an ephah of [a]barley.
18Then she took *it* up and went into the
city, and her mother-in-law saw what she
had gleaned. So she brought out and gave
to her [a]what she had kept back after she
had been satisfied.
19And her mother-in-law said to her,
"Where have you gleaned today? And
where did you work? Blessed be the one
who [a]took notice of you."
So she told her mother-in-law with
whom she had worked, and said, "The
man's name with whom I worked today *is*
Boaz."
20Then Naomi said to her daughter-in-
law, [a]"Blessed *be* he of the LORD, who [b]has
not forsaken His kindness to the living
and the dead!" And Naomi said to her,
"This man *is* a relation of ours, [c]one of
[1]our close relatives."
21Ruth the Moabitess said, "He also said
to me, 'You shall stay close by my young
men until they have finished all my harvest.' "
22And Naomi said to Ruth her
daughter-in-law, "*It is* good, my daughter, that you go out with his young wom-
en, and that people do not [1]meet you in
any other field." 23So she stayed close by
the young women of Boaz, to glean until
the end of barley harvest and wheat harvest; and she dwelt with her mother-in-
law.

Ruth's Redemption Assured

3 Then Naomi her mother-in-law said
to her, "My daughter, [a]shall I not seek
[b]security[1] for you, that it may be well with
you? 2Now Boaz, [a]whose young women
you were with, *is he* not our relative? In
fact, he is winnowing barley tonight at the
threshing floor. 3 Therefore wash yourself and [a]anoint yourself, put on your *best*
garment and go down to the threshing
floor; *but* do not make yourself known to
the man until he has finished eating and
drinking. 4Then it shall be, when he lies
down, that you shall notice the place
where he lies; and you shall go in, uncover
his feet, and lie down; and he will tell you
what you should do."
5And she said to her, "All that you say
to me I will do."
6So she went down to the threshing
floor and did according to all that her
mother-in-law instructed her. 7And after
Boaz had eaten and drunk, and [a]his heart
was cheerful, he went to lie down at the
end of the heap of grain; and she came
softly, uncovered his feet, and lay down.
8Now it happened at midnight that the
man was startled, and turned himself; and
there, a woman was lying at his feet. 9And
he said, "Who *are* you?"
So she answered, "I *am* Ruth, your
maidservant. [a]Take[1] your maidservant
under your wing, for you are [b]a [2]close relative."
10Then he said, [a]"Blessed *are* you of the
LORD, my daughter! For you have shown
more kindness at the end than [b]at the
beginning, in that you did not go after
young men, whether poor or rich. 11And
now, my daughter, do not fear. I will do
for you all that you request, for all the
people of my town know that you *are* [a]a
virtuous woman. 12Now it is true that I
am a [a]close relative; however, [b]there is a
relative closer than I. 13Stay this night,
and in the morning it shall be *that* if he
will [a]perform the duty of a close relative
for you—good; let him do it. But if he
does not want to perform the duty for you,

12 [b]Ruth 1:16
13 [a]Gen. 33:15 [b]1 Sam. 25:41 [1]Lit. *to the heart of*
14 [a]Ruth 2:18
15 [1]Gather after the reapers [2]*rebuke*
17 [a]Ruth 1:22
18 [a]Ruth 2:14
19 [a][Ps. 41:1]
20 [a]2 Sam. 2:5 [b]Prov. 17:17 [c]Ruth 3:9; 4:4, 6 [1]*our redeemers,* Heb. *goalenu*
22 [1]*encounter*
CHAPTER 3
1 [a]1 Tim. 5:8 [b]Ruth 1:9 [1]Lit. *rest*
2 [a]Ruth 2:3, 8
3 [a]2 Sam. 14:2
7 [a]Judg. 19:6, 9, 22
9 [a]Ezek. 16:8 [b]Ruth 2:20; 3:12 [1]Or *Spread the corner of your garment over your maidservant* [2]*redeemer,* Heb. *goel*
10 [a]Ruth 2:20 [b]Ruth 1:8
11 [a]Prov. 12:4; 31:10–31
12 [a]Ruth 3:9 [b]Ruth 4:1
13 [a]Deut. 25:5–10

Ruth 3:3

Dear Woman of Destiny,

God is all about love—redeeming love. That is why I so appreciate the beautiful love story of Ruth and Boaz. The name *Ruth* means "Friend." God's heart is to have a deep, abiding friendship with you; He loves you dearly and always. Ruth's kinsman-redeemer was Boaz, whose name means "In Him Is Strength." Boaz is a type of Christ, and it is in Christ alone that we will find our strength from day to day.

The three primary responsibilities of the kinsman-redeemer were to protect the widow of a deceased kinsman; to purchase her freedom, if necessary; and to marry her in order to carry on the family name. In this story Ruth finds herself newly bereaved, in a strange culture, far from her own home. She is dependent upon her mother-in-law, Naomi, to guide her through the unfamiliar rituals. Since Ruth respects and loves Naomi, she clings to her, listens to her wisdom and counsel, and obeys. It is because of Ruth's submission to Naomi's Spirit-led instruction that she is later prepared for her destiny and consequently becomes the bride of Boaz.

We can be assured that Christ, like Boaz, will also fulfill His obligations to His bride, the church. We are living in the day of accelerated preparation that will help bring about the fulfillment of destiny in Him. Though this time has been speeded up, Jesus, our Beloved Kinsman-Redeemer, will not quickly brush over one detail of our character and personality development in order to fulfill His eternal purposes. He is preparing His bride. Ultimately, we will be made ready to live with Him in His heavenly home forever. Presently, we are experiencing a dress rehearsal for our wedding and coming together.

God, our Father, is meticulous and detailed in His expectations of us—His bride. He is after the hidden things in our lives that do not please Him, desiring that we present ourselves to Him in a garment that is wrinkle-free, without spot or blemish. He also wants to bring forth the hidden treasures (gifts, talents, and callings) within us to bless the body of Christ and the world. Do you know about the deep dealings of God? Have you been dealt with in the depths of your heart by God in this preparation process?

The lessons to be learned from this passage will help you fulfill your destiny:

- Wash yourself—with the water of the Word and a lifestyle of repentance and forgiveness.
- Anoint yourself—by spending time in His Presence, in prayer, praise, and worship.
- Put on your best clothes—of righteousness, holiness, humility, right motives, and attitudes.
- Go down to the threshing floor—because you are made of dust. Let God do His sifting work in you.
- Do not make yourself known until He has finished with you—God has His own timing. Don't run ahead of it; stay in step with Him.

There is more to share, and I pray that the Holy Spirit will give you further revelation as only He can.

Pat Chen

then I will perform the duty for you, [b]*as* the LORD lives! Lie down until morning."

14 So she lay at his feet until morning, and she arose before one could recognize another. Then he said, [a]"Do not let it be known that the woman came to the threshing floor." 15 Also he said, "Bring the [1]shawl that *is* on you and hold it." And when she held it, he measured six *ephahs* of barley, and laid *it* on her. Then [2]she went into the city.

16 When she came to her mother-in-law, she said, [1]"*Is* that you, my daughter?"

Then she told her all that the man had done for her. 17 And she said, "These six *ephahs* of barley he gave me; for he said to me, 'Do not go empty-handed to your mother-in-law.' "

18 Then she said, [a]"Sit still, my daughter, until you know how the matter will turn out; for the man will not rest until he has concluded the matter this day."

Boaz Redeems Ruth

4 Now Boaz went up to the gate and sat down there; and behold, [a]the close relative of whom Boaz had spoken came by. So Boaz said, "Come aside, [1]friend, sit down here." So he came aside and sat down. 2 And he took ten men of [a]the elders of the city, and said, "Sit down here." So they sat down. 3 Then he said to the close relative, "Naomi, who has come back from the country of Moab, sold the piece of land [a]which *belonged* to our brother Elimelech. 4 And I thought to [1]inform you, saying, [a]'Buy *it* back [b]in the presence of the inhabitants and the elders of my people. If you will redeem *it,* redeem *it;* but if [2]you will not redeem *it, then* tell me, that I may know; [c]for *there is* no one but you to redeem *it,* and I *am* next after you.' "

And he said, "I will redeem *it.*"

5 Then Boaz said, "On the day you buy the field from the hand of Naomi, you must also buy *it* from Ruth the Moabitess, the wife of the dead, [a]to [1]perpetuate the name of the dead through his inheritance."

6 [a]And the close relative said, "I cannot redeem *it* for myself, lest I ruin my own inheritance. You redeem my right of redemption for yourself, for I cannot redeem *it.*"

7 [a]Now this *was the custom* in former times in Israel concerning redeeming and exchanging, to confirm anything: one man took off his sandal and gave *it* to the other, and this *was* a confirmation in Israel.

8 Therefore the close relative said to Boaz, "Buy *it* for yourself." So he took off his sandal. 9 And Boaz said to the elders and all the people, "You *are* witnesses this day that I have bought all that was Elimelech's, and all that *was* Chilion's and Mahlon's, from the hand of Naomi. 10 Moreover, Ruth the Moabitess, the widow of Mahlon, I have acquired as my wife, to perpetuate the name of the dead through his inheritance, [a]that the name of the dead may not be cut off from among his brethren and from [1]his position at the gate. You *are* witnesses this day."

11 And all the people who *were* at the gate, and the elders, said, "*We are* witnesses. [a]The LORD make the woman who is coming to your house like Rachel and Leah, the two who [b]built the house of Israel; and may you prosper in [c]Ephrathah and be famous in [d]Bethlehem. 12 May your house be like the house of [a]Perez, [b]whom Tamar bore to Judah, because of [c]the offspring which the LORD will give you from this young woman."

Lord, I pray that You would redeem and restore the life of ____, even as You did for Naomi.

FROM RUTH 4:15

Descendants of Boaz and Ruth

13 So Boaz [a]took Ruth and she became his wife; and when he went in to her, [b]the LORD gave her conception, and she bore a son. 14 Then [a]the women said to Naomi, "Blessed *be* the LORD, who has not left you this day without a [1]close relative; and may his name be famous in Israel! 15 And may he be to you a restorer of life and a [1]nourisher of your old age; for your daughter-in-law, who loves you, who is [a]better to you than seven sons, has borne him." 16 Then Naomi took the child and laid him on her bosom, and became a nurse to him. 17 [a]Also the neighbor women gave him a name, saying, "There is a son born

---

13 b Jer. 4:2; 12:16
14 a [1 Cor. 10:32]
15 *1 cloak* 2 Many Heb. mss., Syr., Vg. *she;* MT, LXX, Tg. *he*
16 *1* Or *How are you,*
18 a [Ps. 37:3, 5]

CHAPTER 4
1 a Ruth 3:12 *1* Heb. *peloni almoni,* lit. *so and so*
2 a 1 Kin. 21:8
3 a Lev. 25:25
4 a Jer. 32:7, 8 b Gen. 23:18 c Lev. 25:25 *1* Lit. *uncover your ear* *2* So with many Heb. mss., LXX, Syr., Tg., Vg.; MT *he*
5 a Matt. 22:24 *1* Lit. *raise up*
6 a Ruth 3:12, 13
7 a Deut. 25:7–10
10 a Deut. 25:6 *1* Probably his civic office
11 a Ps. 127:3; 128:3 b Gen. 29:25–30 c Gen. 35:16–18 d Mic. 5:2
12 a Matt. 1:3 b Gen. 38:6–29 c 1 Sam. 2:20
13 a Ruth 3:11 b Gen. 29:31; 33:5
14 a Luke 1:58 *1 redeemer,* Heb. *goel*
15 a 1 Sam. 1:8 *1 sustainer*
17 a Luke 1:58

to Naomi." And they called his name
Obed. He *is* the father of Jesse, the father
of David.
18 [a]Now this *is* the genealogy of Perez:
[b]Perez begot Hezron; 19 Hezron begot
Ram, and Ram begot Amminadab; 20 Amminadab begot [a]Nahshon, and Nahshon
begot [b]Salmon;[1] 21 Salmon begot Boaz,
and Boaz begot Obed; 22 Obed begot Jesse,
and Jesse begot [a]David.

18 a 1 Chr. 2:4, 5 b Num. 26:20, 21
20 a Num. 1:7 b Matt. 1:4 *1* Heb. *Salmah*
22 a Matt. 1:6

AUTHOR: *Uncertain*
DATE: *931–722 B.C.*
THEME: *God Is Working in History*
KEY PEOPLE: *Samuel, Saul, David*

1 SAMUEL

Dear Woman of Destiny,

First Samuel illustrates that any one of us can become a true woman of destiny through prayer and righteousness. Consider Hannah, a barren woman praying fervently for a son. God granted her heart's desire with the birth of Samuel, and then used the boy to accomplish His will for Israel. As you pray today, consider the power of your words to release destiny in the mighty name of Jesus!

His love and mine,

Marilyn Hickey

The Family of Elkanah

Now there was a certain man of Ra-
mathaim Zophim, of the [a]moun-
tains of Ephraim, and his name
was [b]Elkanah the son of Jeroham, the son
of [1]Elihu, the son of [2]Tohu, the son of
Zuph, [c]an Ephraimite. [2]And he had [a]two
wives: the name of one *was* Hannah, and
the name of the other Peninnah. Peninnah had children, but Hannah had no
children. [3]This man went up from his city
[a]yearly [b]to worship and sacrifice to the
LORD of hosts in [c]Shiloh. Also the two
sons of Eli, Hophni and Phinehas, the
priests of the LORD, *were* there. [4]And
whenever the time came for Elkanah to
make an [a]offering, he would give portions
to Peninnah his wife and to all her sons
and daughters. [5]But to Hannah he would
give a double portion, for he loved Hannah, [a]although the LORD had closed her
womb. [6]And her rival also [a]provoked her
severely, to make her miserable, because
the LORD had closed her womb. [7]So it was,
year by year, when she went up to the
house of the LORD, that she provoked her;
therefore she wept and did not eat.

Hannah's Vow

[8]Then Elkanah her husband said to her,
"Hannah, why do you weep? Why do you
not eat? And why is your heart grieved?
Am I not [a]better to you than ten sons?"
[9]So Hannah arose after they had finished eating and drinking in Shiloh. Now
Eli the priest was sitting on the seat by the
doorpost of [a]the [1]tabernacle of the LORD.

CHAPTER 1
1 a Josh. 17:17, 18; 24:33 b 1 Chr. 6:27, 33–38 c Ruth 1:2 *1 Eliel,* 1 Chr. 6:34 *2 Toah,* 1 Chr. 6:34
2 a Deut. 21:15–17
3 a Luke 2:41 b Deut. 12:5–7; 16:16 c Josh. 18:1
4 a Deut. 12:17, 18
5 a Gen. 16:1; 30:1, 2
6 a Job 24:21
8 a Ruth 4:15
9 a 1 Sam. 3:3 *1 palace* or *temple,* Heb. *heykal*

HANNAH

Hannah was desperate. Maybe more than any other woman in the Bible, she was absolutely driven by desperation. And it drove her to a place of reckless prayer and weeping before the Lord. She abandoned her dignity, forgot formality, and begged God with all her might to give her a son.

She had to fight for her destiny. No doubt she had to fight the consuming ache of inadequacy within herself. She also had to fight against the cruelty of her husband's other wife, who "provoked her severely, to make her miserable, because the LORD had closed her womb" (1 Sam. 1:6). And she had to fight a long and recurring battle with disappointment and, in her Old Testament culture, social disgrace.

But Hannah had a fervent desire in her heart. She refused to let it go until, as the Bible says, she had "poured out [her] soul before the LORD" (1 Sam. 1:15). She was willing to go to war in order to fulfill the destiny to which she believed God had called her. She fought with some of the same weapons that are available to women today—tears, prayer, faith, passion. She also made and kept a vow to the Lord, promising to dedicate her son to His service if He would simply allow her to have a son. God saw her tears. He heard her prayers. He rewarded her faith. And He responded to the passion of her broken heart.

Woman of God, develop a zeal to fulfill God's destiny for you. Bring passion to your prayers. Get to the point where you, too, can say, "I have poured out my soul before the Lord." And when you have, like Hannah, may you leave your place of prayer in peace. May you find the favor of the Lord. And may God grant you the desires of your heart (see 1 Sam. 1:17, 18).

10[a]And she *was* in bitterness of soul, and prayed to the LORD and [1]wept in anguish. 11Then she [a]made a vow and said, "O LORD of hosts, if You will indeed [b]look on the affliction of Your maidservant and [c]remember me, and not forget Your maidservant, but will give Your maidservant a male child, then I will give him to the LORD all the days of his life, and [d]no razor shall come upon his head."

12And it happened, as she continued praying before the LORD, that Eli watched her mouth. 13Now Hannah spoke in her heart; only her lips moved, but her voice was not heard. Therefore Eli thought she was drunk. 14So Eli said to her, "How long will you be drunk? Put your wine away from you!"

15But Hannah answered and said, "No, my lord, I *am* a woman of sorrowful spirit. I have drunk neither wine nor intoxicating drink, but have [a]poured out my soul before the LORD. 16Do not consider your maidservant a [a]wicked[1] woman, for out of the abundance of my complaint and grief I have spoken until now."

17Then Eli answered and said, [a]"Go in peace, and [b]the God of Israel grant your petition which you have asked of Him."

18And she said, [a]"Let your maidservant find favor in your sight." So the woman [b]went her way and ate, and her face was no longer *sad.*

Dear mothers, live the Christ life before your children. Teach them how to pray from their infancy. When they grow up, they will very seldom depart from it.

SISTER MARY CANFIELD

Samuel Is Born and Dedicated

19Then they rose early in the morning and worshiped before the LORD, and returned and came to their house at Ramah. And Elkanah [a]knew Hannah his wife, and the LORD [b]remembered her. 20So it came to pass in the process of time that Hannah conceived and bore a son, and called his name [1]Samuel, *saying,* "Because I have asked for him from the LORD."

21Now the man Elkanah and all his house [a]went up to offer to the LORD the yearly sacrifice and his vow. 22But Hannah did not go up, for she said to her husband, "*Not* until the child is weaned; then I will [a]take him, that he may appear before the LORD and [b]remain there [c]forever."

23So [a]Elkanah her husband said to her, "Do what seems best to you; wait until you have weaned him. Only let the LORD [1]establish [2]His word." Then the woman stayed and nursed her son until she had weaned him.

24Now when she had weaned him, she [a]took him up with her, with [1]three bulls, one ephah of flour, and a skin of wine, and brought him to [b]the house of the LORD in Shiloh. And the child *was* young. 25Then they slaughtered a bull, and [a]brought the child to Eli. 26And she said, "O my lord! [a]As your soul lives, my lord, I *am* the woman who stood by you here, praying to the LORD. 27[a]For this child I prayed, and the LORD has granted me my petition which I asked of Him. 28Therefore I also have lent him to the LORD; as long as he lives he shall be [1]lent to the LORD." So they [a]worshiped the LORD there.

May ____ smile at their enemies, O God, because they rejoice in Your salvation.

FROM 1 SAMUEL 2:1

Hannah's Prayer

2 And Hannah [a]prayed and said:

[b]"My heart rejoices in the LORD;
[c]My [1]horn is exalted in the LORD.
[2]I smile at my enemies,
Because I [d]rejoice in Your salvation.

2 "No[a] one is holy like the LORD,
For *there is* [b]none besides You,
Nor *is there* any [c]rock like our God.

---

10 [a]Job 7:11 [1]Lit. *wept greatly*
11 [a]Num. 30:6–11 [b]Ps. 25:18 [c]Gen. 8:1 [d]Num. 6:5
15 [a]Ps. 42:4; 62:8
16 [a]Deut. 13:13 [1]Lit. *daughter of Belial*
17 [a]Mark 5:34 [b]Ps. 20:3–5
18 [a]Ruth 2:13 [b]Rom. 15:13
19 [a]Gen. 4:1 [b]Gen. 21:1; 30:22
20 [1]Lit. *Heard by God*
21 [a]1 Sam. 1:3
22 [a]Luke 2:22 [b]1 Sam. 1:11, 28 [c]Ex. 21:6
23 [a]Num. 30:7, 10, 11 [1]*confirm* [2]So with MT, Tg., Vg.; DSS, LXX, Syr. *your*
24 [a]Num. 15:9, 10 [b]Josh. 18:1 [1]DSS, LXX, Syr. *a three-year-old bull*
25 [a]Luke 2:22
26 [a]2 Kin. 2:2, 4, 6; 4:30
27 [a][Matt. 7:7]
28 [a]Gen. 24:26, 52 [1]*granted*

CHAPTER 2
1 [a]Phil. 4:6 [b]Luke 1:46–55 [c]Ps. 75:10; 89:17, 24; 92:10; 112:9 [d]Ps. 9:14; 13:5; 35:9 [1]Strength [2]Lit. *My mouth is enlarged*
2 [a]Ex. 15:11 [b]Deut. 4:35 [c]Deut. 32:4, 30, 31

1 Samuel 1:25–28

Dear Woman of Destiny,

As mothers, we must realize children are God's gift to us—our heritage—and we are merely their caretakers. What gifts He's entrusted to us for the short time we'll have to impact and influence their lives!

The barren Hannah came to the Lord, weeping in anguish for a child. "O LORD of Hosts, if You will indeed look on the affliction of Your maidservant and . . . give [me] a male child, then I will give him to the LORD all the days of his life" (1 Sam. 1:11). Hers is the first recorded prayer of a woman in the Old Testament.

In the course of time, Hannah conceived and gave birth to a son whom she named Samuel, saying, "Because I have asked for him from the LORD" (v. 20). Every time she called her son's name, Hannah was reminded of God's faithfulness. When she took little Samuel to live in the tabernacle with Eli, she said, "For this child I prayed, and the LORD has granted me my petition" (v. 27). Then she worshiped the Lord there.

Later, we see that Hannah's prayer life has matured. She begins with an outpouring of praise to God for His power and righteousness. Finally, she prophesies that God will give strength to His king—in a land that had never before been ruled by a king! (see 1 Sam. 2:1–10). Eventually, her firstborn son, Samuel, would anoint Israel's first king.

As a godly mother, Hannah no doubt prayed earnestly for each of her children—three sons and two daughters—all of their lives. Mary's prayer before the birth of Jesus resembles Hannah's magnificent praise prayer. Because the prayers of these two women are recorded, they can serve as patterns for us to pray aloud, and may also encourage us to write down our own prayers as a legacy for our children.

You may want to pray as I did some years ago: "Lord, as You did for Hannah, take this child of mine, ______ (name). I give her to You. For her whole life, she will be dedicated to You" (see 1 Sam. 1:28).

Dedicating our children to God, whether in a church or home service, means we will not only depend on the Lord to help us bring them up, but that we will accept our children just as God made them. We must learn how to pray more effectively—fervently, frequently, and confidently—for God's destiny to be fulfilled in each of them. We learn to pray for our children by (1) giving them back to God, (2) forgiving them, and (3) loving them unconditionally.

Some mothers harbor deep resentments toward their children. Believe me, most of us will experience some disappointment in our youngsters—it goes with the territory of parenting. But if we want our prayers answered, Jesus tells us we must continually forgive them (see Mark 11:25).

If you have a hard time some days loving your kids, let alone liking them, you might try paraphrasing Romans 5:5 like this: "God, pour out Your love in my heart by the Holy Spirit so I can love with Your love."

Quin Sherrer

3 "Talk no more so very proudly;
[a]Let no arrogance come from your
mouth,
For the LORD *is* the God of
[b]knowledge;
And by Him actions are weighed.

4 "The[a] bows of the mighty men *are*
broken,
And those who stumbled are girded
with strength.
5 *Those who were* full have hired
themselves out for bread,
And the hungry have ceased *to
hunger.*
Even [a]the barren has borne seven,
And [b]she who has many children
has become feeble.

6 "The[a] LORD kills and makes alive;
He brings down to the grave and
brings up.
7 The LORD [a]makes poor and makes
rich;
[b]He brings low and lifts up.
8 [a]He raises the poor from the dust
And lifts the beggar from the ash
heap,
[b]To set *them* among princes
And make them inherit the throne
of glory.

[c]"For the pillars of the earth *are* the
LORD's,
And He has set the world upon
them.
9 [a]He will guard the feet of His saints,
But the [b]wicked shall be silent in
darkness.

"For by strength no man shall
prevail.
10 The adversaries of the LORD shall
be [a]broken in pieces;
[b]From heaven He will thunder
against them.
[c]The LORD will judge the ends of the
earth.

[d]"He will give [e]strength to His king,
And [f]exalt the [1]horn of His
anointed."

11 Then Elkanah went to his house at Ramah. But the child [1]ministered to the LORD before Eli the priest.

The Wicked Sons of Eli

12 Now the sons of Eli *were* [a]corrupt;[1] [b]they did not know the LORD. 13 And the priests' custom with the people *was that* when any man offered a sacrifice, the priest's servant would come with a three-pronged fleshhook in his hand while the meat was boiling. 14 Then he would thrust *it* into the pan, or kettle, or caldron, or pot; and the priest would take for himself all that the fleshhook brought up. So they did in [a]Shiloh to all the Israelites who came there. 15 Also, before they [a]burned the fat, the priest's servant would come and say to the man who sacrificed, "Give meat for roasting to the priest, for he will not take boiled meat from you, but raw."

16 And *if* the man said to him, "They should really burn the fat first; *then* you may take *as much* as your heart desires," he would then answer him, "*No,* but you must give *it* now; and if not, I will take *it* by force."

17 Therefore the sin of the young men was very great [a]before the LORD, for men [b]abhorred[1] the offering of the LORD.

Samuel's Childhood Ministry

18 [a]But Samuel ministered before the LORD, *even as* a child, [b]wearing a linen ephod. 19 Moreover his mother used to make him a little robe, and bring *it* to him year by year when she [a]came up with her husband to offer the yearly sacrifice. 20 And Eli [a]would bless Elkanah and his wife, and say, "The LORD give you descendants from this woman for the [1]loan that was [b]given to the LORD." Then they would go to their own home.

21 And the LORD [a]visited[1] Hannah, so that she conceived and bore three sons and two daughters. Meanwhile the child Samuel [b]grew before the LORD.

Prophecy Against Eli's Household

22 Now Eli was very old; and he heard everything his sons did to all Israel, [1]and how they lay with [a]the women who assembled at the door of the tabernacle of meeting. 23 So he said to them, "Why do you do such things? For I hear of your evil dealings from all the people. 24 No, my sons! For *it is* not a good report that I hear. You make the LORD's people transgress. 25 If one man sins against another, [a]God[1] will judge him. But if a man [b]sins against the LORD, who will intercede for him?" Nevertheless they did not heed the voice of their father, [c]because the LORD desired to kill them.

---

3 a Ps. 94:4 b 1 Sam. 16:7
4 a Ps. 37:15; 46:9
5 a Ps. 113:9 b Is. 54:1
6 a Deut. 32:39
7 a Deut. 8:17, 18 b Ps. 75:7
8 a Luke 1:52 b Job 36:7 c Job 38:4–6
9 a [1 Pet. 1:5] b [Rom. 3:19]
10 a Ps. 2:9 b Ps. 18:13, 14 c Ps. 96:13; 98:9 d [Matt. 28:18] e Ps. 21:1, 7 f Ps. 89:24 *1* Strength
11 *1 served*
12 a Deut. 13:13 b Judg. 2:10 *1* Lit. *sons of Belial*
14 a 1 Sam. 1:3
15 a Lev. 3:3–5, 16
17 a Gen. 6:11 b [Mal. 2:7–9] *1 despised*
18 a 1 Sam. 2:11; 3:1 b Ex. 28:4
19 a 1 Sam. 1:3, 21
20 a Gen. 14:19 b 1 Sam. 1:11, 27, 28 *1 gift*
21 a Gen. 21:1 b 1 Sam. 2:26; 3:19–21 *1 attended to*
22 a Ex. 38:8 *1* So with MT, Tg., Vg.; DSS, LXX omit rest of verse
25 a Deut. 1:17; 25:1, 2 b Num. 15:30 c Josh. 11:20 *1* Tg. *the Judge*

26 And the child Samuel [a]grew in stature, and [b]in favor both with the LORD and
men.
27 Then a [a]man of God came to Eli and
said to him, "Thus says the LORD: [b]'Did I
not clearly reveal Myself to the house of
your father when they were in Egypt in
Pharaoh's house? 28 Did I not [a]choose him
out of all the tribes of Israel *to be* My
priest, to offer upon My altar, to burn incense, and to wear an ephod before Me?
And [b]did I not give to the house of your
father all the offerings of the children of
Israel made by fire? 29 Why do you [a]kick at
My sacrifice and My offering which I have
commanded *in My* [b]dwelling place, and
honor your sons more than [c]Me, to make
yourselves fat with the best of all the offerings of Israel My people?' 30 Therefore the
LORD God of Israel says: [a]'I said indeed
that your house and the house of your
father would walk before Me forever.' But
now the LORD says: [b]'Far be it from Me;
for those who honor Me I will honor, and
[c]those who despise Me shall be lightly esteemed. 31 Behold, [a]the days are coming
that I will cut off your [1]arm and the arm
of your father's house, so that there will
not be an old man in your house. 32 And
you will see an enemy *in My* dwelling
place, *despite* all the good which God does
for Israel. And there shall not be [a]an old
man in your house forever. 33 But any of
your men *whom* I do not cut off from My
altar shall consume your eyes and grieve
your heart. And all the descendants of
your house shall die in the flower of their
age. 34 Now this *shall be* [a]a sign to you that
will come upon your two sons, on Hophni
and Phinehas: [b]in one day they shall die,
both of them. 35 Then [a]I will raise up for
Myself a faithful priest *who* shall do according to what *is* in My heart and in My
mind. [b]I will build him a sure house, and
he shall walk before [c]My anointed forever.
36 [a]And it shall come to pass that everyone
who is left in your house will come *and*
bow down to him for a piece of silver and
a morsel of bread, and say, "Please, [1]put
me in one of the priestly positions, that I
may eat a piece of bread." ' "

Samuel's First Prophecy

3 Now [a]the boy Samuel ministered to
the LORD before Eli. And [b]the word of
the LORD was rare in those days; *there was*
no widespread revelation. 2 And it came
to pass at that time, while Eli *was* lying
down in his place, and when his eyes had
begun to grow [a]so dim that he could not
see, 3 and before [a]the lamp of God went
out in the [1]tabernacle of the LORD where
the ark of God *was,* and while Samuel was
lying down, 4 that the LORD called Samuel.
And he answered, "Here I am!" 5 So he
ran to Eli and said, "Here I am, for you
called me."
And he said, "I did not call; lie down
again." And he went and lay down.
6 Then the LORD called yet again,
"Samuel!"
So Samuel arose and went to Eli, and
said, "Here I am, for you called me." He
answered, "I did not call, my son; lie down
again." 7 (Now Samuel [a]did not yet know
the LORD, nor was the word of the LORD
yet revealed to him.)
8 And the LORD called Samuel again the
third time. So he arose and went to Eli,
and said, "Here I am, for you did call me."
Then Eli perceived that the LORD had
called the boy. 9 Therefore Eli said to Samuel, "Go, lie down; and it shall be, if He
calls you, that you must say, [a]'Speak,
LORD, for Your servant hears.' " So Samuel went and lay down in his place.

When You call ____, Lord, may they respond like Samuel, saying, "Speak, for Your servant hears."

FROM 1 SAMUEL 3:10

10 Now the LORD came and stood and
called as at other times, "Samuel!
Samuel!"
And Samuel answered, "Speak, for Your
servant hears."
11 Then the LORD said to Samuel: "Behold, I will do something in Israel [a]at
which both ears of everyone who hears it
will tingle. 12 In that day I will perform
against Eli [a]all that I have spoken concerning his house, from beginning to end.
13 [a]For I have told him that I will [b]judge
his house forever for the iniquity which
he knows, because [c]his sons made themselves vile, and he [d]did not [1]restrain
them. 14 And therefore I have sworn to the
house of Eli that the iniquity of Eli's

26 a 1 Sam. 2:21 b Prov. 3:4
27 a 1 Kin. 13:1 b Ex. 4:14–16; 12:1
28 a Ex. 28:1, 4 b Num. 5:9
29 a Deut. 32:15 b Deut. 12:5 c Matt. 10:37
30 a Ex. 29:9 b Jer. 18:9, 10 c Mal. 2:9–12
31 a 1 Kin. 2:27, 35 *1 strength*
32 a Zech. 8:4
34 a 1 Kin. 13:3 b 1 Sam. 4:11, 17
35 a 1 Kin. 2:35 b 1 Kin. 11:38 c Ps. 18:50
36 a 1 Kin. 2:27 *1 assign*

CHAPTER 3
1 a 1 Sam. 2:11, 18 b Ps. 74:9
2 a 1 Sam. 4:15
3 a Ex. 27:20, 21 *1 palace* or *temple*
7 a 1 Sam. 2:12
9 a 1 Kin. 2:17
11 a 2 Kin. 21:12
12 a 1 Sam. 2:27–36
13 a 1 Sam. 2:29–31 b 1 Sam. 2:22 c 1 Sam. 2:12, 17, 22 d 1 Sam. 2:23, 25 *1 Lit. rebuke*

house [a]shall not be atoned for by sacrifice or offering forever."

15So Samuel lay down until [1]morning, and opened the doors of the house of the LORD. And Samuel was afraid to tell Eli the vision. 16Then Eli called Samuel and said, "Samuel, my son!"

He answered, "Here I am."

17And he said, "What *is* the word that *the LORD* spoke to you? Please do not hide *it* from me. [a]God do so to you, and more also, if you hide anything from me of all the things that He said to you." 18Then Samuel told him everything, and hid nothing from him. And he said, [a]"It *is* the LORD. Let Him do what seems good to Him."

19So Samuel [a]grew, and [b]the LORD was with him [c]and let none of his words [1]fall to the ground. 20And all Israel [a]from Dan to Beersheba knew that Samuel *had been* [1]established as a prophet of the LORD. 21Then the LORD appeared again in Shiloh. For the LORD revealed Himself to Samuel in Shiloh by [a]the word of the LORD.

4 And the word of Samuel came to all [1]Israel.

The Ark of God Captured

Now Israel went out to battle against the Philistines, and encamped beside [a]Ebenezer; and the Philistines encamped in Aphek. 2Then the [a]Philistines put themselves in battle array against Israel. And when they joined battle, Israel was [1]defeated by the Philistines, who killed about four thousand men of the army in the field. 3And when the people had come into the camp, the elders of Israel said, "Why has the LORD defeated us today before the Philistines? [a]Let us bring the ark of the covenant of the LORD from Shiloh to us, that when it comes among us it may save us from the hand of our enemies." 4So the people sent to Shiloh, that they might bring from there the ark of the covenant of the LORD of hosts, [a]who dwells *between* [b]the cherubim. And the [c]two sons of Eli, Hophni and Phinehas, *were* there with the ark of the covenant of God.

5And when the ark of the covenant of the LORD came into the camp, all Israel shouted so loudly that the earth shook. 6Now when the Philistines heard the noise of the shout, they said, "What *does* the sound of this great shout in the camp of the Hebrews *mean?*" Then they understood that the ark of the LORD had come into the camp. 7So the Philistines were afraid, for they said, "God has come into the camp!" And they said, [a]"Woe to us! For such a thing has never happened before. 8Woe to us! Who will deliver us from the hand of these mighty gods? These *are* the gods who struck the Egyptians with all the plagues in the wilderness. 9[a]Be strong and conduct yourselves like men, you Philistines, that you do not become servants of the Hebrews, [b]as they have been to you. [1]Conduct yourselves like men, and fight!"

10So the Philistines fought, and [a]Israel was [1]defeated, and every man fled to his tent. There was a very great slaughter, and there fell of Israel thirty thousand foot soldiers. 11Also [a]the ark of God was captured; and [b]the two sons of Eli, Hophni and Phinehas, died.

Death of Eli

12Then a man of Benjamin ran from the battle line the same day, and [a]came to Shiloh with his clothes torn and [b]dirt on his head. 13Now when he came, there was Eli, sitting on [a]a seat [1]by the wayside watching, for his heart [2]trembled for the ark of God. And when the man came into the city and told *it,* all the city cried out. 14When Eli heard the noise of the outcry, he said, "What *does* the sound of this tumult *mean?*" And the man came quickly and told Eli. 15Eli was ninety-eight years old, and [a]his eyes were so [1]dim that he could not see.

16Then the man said to Eli, "I *am* he who came from the battle. And I fled today from the battle line."

And he said, [a]"What happened, my son?"

17So the messenger answered and said, "Israel has fled before the Philistines, and there has been a great slaughter among the people. Also your two sons, Hophni and Phinehas, are dead; and the ark of God has been captured."

18Then it happened, when he made mention of the ark of God, that Eli fell off the seat backward by the side of the gate; and his neck was broken and he died, for the man was old and heavy. And he had judged Israel forty years.

Ichabod

19Now his daughter-in-law, Phinehas' wife, was with child, *due* to be delivered;

---

14 a Num. 15:30, 31
15 *1* So with MT, Tg., Vg.; LXX adds *and he arose in the morning*
17 a Ruth 1:17
18 a Is. 39:8
19 a 1 Sam. 2:21 b Gen. 21:22; 28:15; 39:2, 21, 23 c 1 Sam. 9:6 *1 fail*
20 a Judg. 20:1 *1 confirmed*
21 a 1 Sam. 3:1, 4

CHAPTER 4
1 a 1 Sam. 7:12 *1* So with MT, Tg.; LXX, Vg. add *And it came to pass in those days that the Philistines gathered themselves together to fight;* LXX adds further *against Israel*
2 a 1 Sam. 12:9 *1* Lit. *struck*
3 a Josh. 6:6–21
4 a 1 Sam. 6:2 b Num. 7:89 c 1 Sam. 2:12
7 a Ex. 15:14
9 a 1 Cor. 16:13 b Judg. 13:1 *1* Lit. *Be men*
10 a Deut. 28:15, 25 *1* Lit. *struck down*
11 a Ps. 78:60, 61 b 1 Sam. 2:34
12 a 2 Sam. 1:2 b Josh. 7:6
13 a 1 Sam. 1:9; 4:18 *1* So with MT, Vg.; LXX *beside the gate watching the road* *2 trembled with anxiety*
15 a 1 Sam. 3:2 *1 fixed*
16 a 2 Sam. 1:4

and when she heard the news that the ark of God was captured, and that her father-in-law and her husband were dead, she bowed herself and gave birth, for her labor pains came upon her. 20And about the time of her death [a]the women who stood by her said to her, "Do not fear, for you have borne a son." But she did not answer, nor did she [1]regard *it.* 21Then she named the child [a]Ichabod,[1] saying, [b]"The glory has departed from Israel!" because the ark of God had been captured and because of her father-in-law and her husband. 22And she said, "The glory has departed from Israel, for the ark of God has been captured."

The Philistines and the Ark

5 Then the Philistines took the ark of God and brought it [a]from Ebenezer to Ashdod. 2When the Philistines took the ark of God, they brought it into the house of [a]Dagon[1] and set it by Dagon. 3And when the people of Ashdod arose early in the morning, there was Dagon, [a]fallen on its face to the earth before the ark of the LORD. So they took Dagon and [b]set it in its place again. 4And when they arose early the next morning, there was Dagon, fallen on its face to the ground before the ark of the LORD. [a]The head of Dagon and both the palms of its hands *were* broken off on the threshold; only [1]Dagon's torso was left of it. 5Therefore neither the priests of Dagon nor any who come into Dagon's house [a]tread on the threshold of Dagon in Ashdod to this day.

6But the [a]hand of the LORD was heavy on the people of Ashdod, and He [b]ravaged them and struck them with [c]tumors,[1] *both* Ashdod and its [d]territory. 7And when the men of Ashdod saw how *it was,* they said, "The ark of the [a]God of Israel must not remain with us, for His hand is harsh toward us and Dagon our god." 8Therefore they sent and gathered to themselves all the [a]lords of the Philistines, and said, "What shall we do with the ark of the God of Israel?"

And they answered, "Let the ark of the God of Israel be carried away to [b]Gath." So they carried the ark of the God of Israel away. 9So it was, after they had carried it away, that [a]the hand of the LORD was against the city with a very great destruction; and He struck the men of the city, both small and great, [1]and tumors broke out on them.

10Therefore they sent the ark of God to Ekron. So it was, as the ark of God came to Ekron, that the Ekronites cried out, saying, "They have brought the ark of the God of Israel to us, to kill us and our people!" 11So they sent and gathered together all the lords of the Philistines, and said, "Send away the ark of the God of Israel, and let it go back to its own place, so that it does not kill us and our people." For there was a deadly destruction throughout all the city; the hand of God was very heavy there. 12And the men who did not die were stricken with the tumors, and the [a]cry of the city went up to heaven.

The Ark Returned to Israel

6 Now the ark of the LORD was in the country of the Philistines seven months. 2And the Philistines [a]called for the priests and the diviners, saying, "What shall we do with the ark of the LORD? Tell us how we should send it to its place."

3So they said, "If you send away the ark of the God of Israel, do not send it [a]empty; but by all means return *it* to Him *with* [b]a trespass offering. Then you will be healed, and it will be known to you why His hand is not removed from you."

4Then they said, "What *is* the trespass offering which we shall return to Him?"

They answered, [a]"Five golden tumors and five golden rats, *according to* the number of the lords of the Philistines. For the same plague *was* on all of [1]you and on your lords. 5Therefore you shall make images of your tumors and images of your rats that [a]ravage the land, and you shall [b]give glory to the God of Israel; perhaps He will [c]lighten[1] His hand from you, from [d]your gods, and from your land. 6Why then do you harden your hearts [a]as the Egyptians and Pharaoh hardened their hearts? When He did mighty things among them, [b]did they not let the people go, that they might depart? 7Now therefore, make [a]a new cart, take two milk cows [b]which have never been yoked, and hitch the cows to the cart; and take their calves home, away from them. 8Then take the ark of the LORD and set it on the cart; and put [a]the articles of gold which you are returning to Him *as* a trespass offering in a chest by its side. Then send it away, and let it go. 9And watch: if it goes up the road to its own territory, to [a]Beth Shemesh,

20 [a]Gen. 35:16–19 [1] *pay any attention to*
21 [a]1 Sam. 14:3 [b]Ps. 26:8; 78:61 [1] Lit. *Inglorious*

CHAPTER 5
1 [a]1 Sam. 4:1; 7:12
2 [a]1 Chr. 10:8–10 [1] A Philistine idol
3 [a]Is. 19:1; 46:1, 2 [b]Is. 46:7
4 [a]Mic. 1:7 [1] So with LXX, Syr., Tg., Vg.; MT *Dagon*
5 [a]Zeph. 1:9
6 [a]Ex. 9:3 [b]1 Sam. 6:5 [c]Deut. 28:27; Ps. 78:66 [d]Josh. 15:46, 47 [1] Probably bubonic plague. LXX, Vg. add *And in the midst of their land rats sprang up, and there was a great death panic in the city.*
7 [a]1 Sam. 6:5
8 [a]1 Sam. 6:4 [b]Josh. 11:22
9 [a]Deut. 2:15 [1] Vg. *and they had tumors in their secret parts*
12 [a]Jer. 14:2

CHAPTER 6
2 [a]Gen. 41:8
3 [a]Deut. 16:16 [b]Lev. 5:15, 16
4 [a]1 Sam. 5:6, 9, 12; 6:17 [1] Lit. *them*
5 [a]1 Sam. 5:6 [b]Josh. 7:19 [c]1 Sam. 5:6, 11 [d]1 Sam. 5:3, 4, 7 [1] *ease*
6 [a]Ex. 7:13; 8:15; 9:34; 14:17 [b]Ex. 12:31
7 [a]2 Sam. 6:3 [b]Num. 19:2
8 [a]1 Sam. 6:4, 5 **9** [a]Josh. 15:10; 21:16

then He has done [1]us this great evil. But
if not, then [b]we shall know that *it is* not
His hand *that* struck us—it happened to
us by chance."
[10]Then the men did so; they took two
milk cows and hitched them to the cart,
and shut up their calves at home. [11]And
they set the ark of the LORD on the cart,
and the chest with the gold rats and the
images of their tumors. [12]Then the cows
headed straight for the road to Beth Shemesh, *and* went along the [a]highway, lowing as they went, and did not turn aside to
the right hand or the left. And the lords of
the Philistines went after them to the border of Beth Shemesh.
[13]Now *the people of* Beth Shemesh
were reaping their [a]wheat harvest in the
valley; and they lifted their eyes and saw
the ark, and rejoiced to see *it.* [14]Then the
cart came into the field of Joshua of Beth
Shemesh, and stood there; a large stone
was there. So they split the wood of the
cart and offered the cows as a burnt offering to the LORD. [15]The Levites took down
the ark of the LORD and the chest that *was*
with it, in which *were* the articles of gold,
and put *them* on the large stone. Then the
men of Beth Shemesh offered burnt offerings and made sacrifices the same day to
the LORD. [16]So when [a]the five lords of the
Philistines had seen *it,* they returned to
Ekron the same day.
[17][a]These *are* the golden tumors which
the Philistines returned *as* a trespass offering to the LORD: one for Ashdod, one
for Gaza, one for Ashkelon, one for [b]Gath,
one for Ekron; [18]and the golden rats, *according to* the number of all the cities of
the Philistines *belonging* to the five lords,
both fortified cities and country villages,
even as far as the large *stone of* Abel on
which they set the ark of the LORD, *which
stone remains* to this day in the field of
Joshua of Beth Shemesh.
[19]Then [a]He struck the men of Beth
Shemesh, because they had looked into
the ark of the LORD. [1]He [b]struck fifty
thousand and seventy men of the people,
and the people lamented because the
LORD had struck the people with a great
slaughter.

The Ark at Kirjath Jearim

[20]And the men of Beth Shemesh said,
[a]"Who is able to stand before this holy
LORD God? And to whom shall it go up
from us?" [21]So they sent messengers to
the inhabitants of [a]Kirjath Jearim, saying,
"The Philistines have brought back the
ark of the LORD; come down *and* take it up
with you."

7 Then the men of [a]Kirjath Jearim
came and took the ark of the LORD,
and brought it into the house of [b]Abina-
dab on the hill, and [c]consecrated Eleazar
his son to keep the ark of the LORD.

Samuel Judges Israel

[2]So it was that the ark remained in Kirjath Jearim a long time; it was there twenty years. And all the house of Israel
lamented after the LORD.

Father, I pray that ____ will return to You with all their heart. May they prepare their heart for You and serve You, for You alone will deliver them.

FROM 1 SAMUEL 7:3

[3]Then Samuel spoke to all the house of
Israel, saying, "If you [a]return to the LORD
with all your hearts, *then* [b]put away the
foreign gods and the [c]Ashtoreths[1] from
among you, and [d]prepare your hearts for
the LORD, and [e]serve Him only; and He
will deliver you from the hand of the Philistines." [4]So the children of Israel put
away the [a]Baals and the [1]Ashtoreths, and
served the LORD only.
[5]And Samuel said, [a]"Gather all Israel to
Mizpah, and [b]I will pray to the LORD for
you." [6]So they gathered together at Mizpah, [a]drew water, and poured *it* out before
the LORD. And they [b]fasted that day, and
said there, [c]"We have sinned against the
LORD." And Samuel judged the children of
Israel at Mizpah.
[7]Now when the Philistines heard that
the children of Israel had gathered together at Mizpah, the lords of the Philistines went up against Israel. And when the
children of Israel heard *of it,* they were
afraid of the Philistines. [8]So the children
of Israel said to Samuel, [a]"Do not cease to
cry out to the LORD our God for us, that
He may save us from the hand of the Philistines."

9 [b] 1 Sam. 6:3 [1] *this calamity to us*
12 [a] Num. 20:19
13 [a] 1 Sam. 12:17
16 [a] Josh. 13:3
17 [a] 1 Sam. 6:4 [b] 1 Sam. 5:8
19 [a] Ex. 19:21 [b] 2 Sam. 6:7 [1] Or *He struck seventy men of the people and fifty oxen of a man*
20 [a] Mal. 3:2
21 [a] 1 Chr. 13:5, 6

CHAPTER 7
1 [a] 1 Sam. 6:21 [b] 2 Sam. 6:3, 4 [c] Lev. 21:8
3 [a] Deut. 30:2–10 [b] Gen. 35:2 [c] Judg. 2:13 [d] Job 11:13 [e] Luke 4:8 [1] Images of Canaanite goddesses
4 [a] Judg. 2:11; 10:16 [1] Images of Canaanite goddesses
5 [a] Judg. 10:17; 20:1 [b] 1 Sam. 12:17–19
6 [a] 2 Sam. 14:14 [b] Neh. 9:1, 2 [c] 1 Sam. 12:10
8 [a] Is. 37:4

9And Samuel took a [a]suckling lamb and
offered *it as* a whole burnt offering to the
LORD. Then [b]Samuel cried out to the
LORD for Israel, and the LORD answered
him. 10Now as Samuel was offering up the
burnt offering, the Philistines drew near
to battle against Israel. [a]But the LORD
thundered with a loud thunder upon the
Philistines that day, and so confused them
that they were overcome before Israel.
11And the men of Israel went out of Mizpah and pursued the Philistines, and
[1]drove them back as far as below Beth
Car. 12Then Samuel [a]took a stone and
set *it* up between Mizpah and Shen, and
called its name [1]Ebenezer, saying, "Thus
far the LORD has helped us."
13[a]So the Philistines were subdued, and
they [b]did not come anymore into the territory of Israel. And the hand of the LORD
was against the Philistines all the days of
Samuel. 14Then the cities which the Philistines had taken from Israel were restored to Israel, from Ekron to Gath; and
Israel recovered its territory from the
hands of the Philistines. Also there was
peace between Israel and the Amorites.
15And Samuel [a]judged Israel all the
days of his life. 16He went from year to
year on a circuit to Bethel, Gilgal, and
Mizpah, and judged Israel in all those
places. 17But [a]he always returned to Ramah, for his home *was* there. There he
judged Israel, and there he [b]built an altar
to the LORD.

Israel Demands a King

8 Now it came to pass when Samuel was
[a]old that he [b]made his [c]sons judges
over Israel. 2The name of his firstborn was
Joel, and the name of his second, Abijah;
they were judges in Beersheba. 3But his
sons [a]did not walk in his ways; they
turned aside [b]after dishonest gain, [c]took
bribes, and perverted justice.
4Then all the elders of Israel gathered
together and came to Samuel at Ramah,
5and said to him, "Look, you are old, and
your sons do not walk in your ways. Now
[a]make us a king to judge us like all the
nations."
6But the thing [a]displeased Samuel
when they said, "Give us a king to judge
us." So Samuel [b]prayed to the LORD. 7And
the LORD said to Samuel, "Heed the voice
of the people in all that they say to you; for
[a]they have not rejected you, but [b]they
have rejected Me, that I should not reign
over them. 8According to all the works
which they have done since the day that I
brought them up out of Egypt, even to
this day—with which they have forsaken
Me and served other gods—so they are
doing to you also. 9Now therefore, heed
their voice. However, you shall solemnly
forewarn them, and [a]show them the behavior of the king who will reign over
them."
10So Samuel told all the words of the
LORD to the people who asked him for a
king. 11And he said, [a]"This will be the behavior of the king who will reign over you:
He will take your [b]sons and appoint *them*
for his own [c]chariots and *to be* his horsemen, and *some* will run before his chariots. 12He will [a]appoint captains over his
thousands and captains over his fifties,
will set some to plow his ground and reap
his harvest, and *some* to make his weapons of war and equipment for his chariots.
13He will take your daughters *to be* perfumers, cooks, and bakers. 14And [a]he will
take the best of your fields, your vineyards, and your olive groves, and give
them to his servants. 15He will take a
tenth of your grain and your vintage, and
give it to his officers and servants. 16And
he will take your male servants, your female servants, your finest [1]young men,
and your donkeys, and put *them* to his
work. 17He will take a tenth of your sheep.
And you will be his servants. 18And you
will cry out in that day because of your
king whom you have chosen for yourselves, and the LORD [a]will not hear you in
that day."
19Nevertheless the people [a]refused to
obey the voice of Samuel; and they said,
"No, but we will have a king over us,
20that we also may be [a]like all the nations,
and that our king may judge us and go out
before us and fight our battles."
21And Samuel heard all the words of the
people, and he repeated them in the hearing of the LORD. 22So the LORD said to
Samuel, [a]"Heed their voice, and make
them a king."
And Samuel said to the men of Israel,
"Every man go to his city."

Saul Chosen to Be King

9 There was a man of Benjamin whose
name *was* [a]Kish the son of Abiel, the
son of Zeror, the son of Bechorath, the
son of Aphiah, a Benjamite, a mighty man
of [1]power. 2And he had a choice and

9 [a]Lev. 22:27 [b]1 Sam. 12:18
10 [a]2 Sam. 22:14, 15
11 [1]*struck them down*
12 [a]Josh. 4:9; 24:26 [1]Lit. *Stone of Help*
13 [a]Judg. 13:1 [b]1 Sam. 13:5
15 [a]1 Sam. 12:11
17 [a]1 Sam. 8:4 [b]Judg. 21:4

CHAPTER 8
1 [a]1 Sam. 12:2 [b]Deut. 16:18, 19 [c]Judg. 10:4
3 [a]Jer. 22:15–17 [b]Ex. 18:21 [c]Ex. 23:6–8
5 [a]Deut. 17:14, 15
6 [a]1 Sam. 12:17 [b]1 Sam. 7:9
7 [a]Ex. 16:8 [b]1 Sam. 10:19
9 [a]1 Sam. 8:11–18
11 [a]Deut. 17:14–20 [b]1 Sam. 14:52 [c]2 Sam. 15:1
12 [a]1 Sam. 22:7
14 [a]1 Kin. 21:7
16 [1]LXX *cattle*
18 [a]Is. 1:15
19 [a]Jer. 44:16
20 [a]1 Sam. 8:5
22 [a]Hos. 13:11

CHAPTER 9
1 [a]1 Chr. 8:33; 9:36–39 [1]*wealth*

handsome son whose name *was* Saul. *There was* not a more handsome person than he among the children of Israel. [a]From his shoulders upward *he was* taller than any of the people.

3Now the donkeys of Kish, Saul's father, were lost. And Kish said to his son Saul, "Please take one of the servants with you, and arise, go and look for the donkeys." 4So he passed through the mountains of Ephraim and through the land of [a]Shalisha, but they did not find *them.* Then they passed through the land of Shaalim, and *they were* not *there.* Then he passed through the land of the Benjamites, but they did not find *them.*

5When they had come to the land of [a]Zuph, Saul said to his servant who *was* with him, "Come, let [b]us return, lest my father cease *caring* about the donkeys and become worried about us."

6And he said to him, "Look now, *there is* in this city [a]a man of God, and *he is* an honorable man; [b]all that he says surely comes to pass. So let us go there; perhaps he can show us the way that we should go."

7Then Saul said to his servant, "But look, *if* we go, [a]what shall we bring the man? For the bread in our vessels is all gone, and *there is* no present to bring to the man of God. What do we have?"

8And the servant answered Saul again and said, "Look, I have here at hand one-fourth of a shekel of silver. I will give *that* to the man of God, to tell us our way." 9(Formerly in Israel, when a man [a]went [1]to inquire of God, he spoke thus: "Come, let us go to the seer"; for *he who is* now *called* a prophet was formerly called [b]a seer.)

10Then Saul said to his servant, [1]"Well said; come, let us go." So they went to the city where the man of God *was.*

11As they went up the hill to the city, [a]they met some young women going out to draw water, and said to them, "Is the seer here?"

12And they answered them and said, "Yes, there he is, just ahead of you. Hurry now; for today he came to this city, because [a]there is a sacrifice of the people today [b]on the high place. 13As soon as you come into the city, you will surely find him before he goes up to the high place to eat. For the people will not eat until he comes, because he must bless the sacrifice; afterward those who are invited will eat. Now therefore, go up, for about this time you will find him." 14So they went up to the city. As they were coming into the city, there was Samuel, coming out toward them on his way up to the high place.

15[a]Now the LORD had told Samuel in his ear the day before Saul came, saying, 16"Tomorrow about this time [a]I will send you a man from the land of Benjamin, [b]and you shall anoint him [1]commander over My people Israel, that he may save My people from the hand of the Philistines; for I have [c]looked upon My people, because their cry has come to Me."

17So when Samuel saw Saul, the LORD said to him, [a]"There he is, the man of whom I spoke to you. This one shall reign over My people." 18Then Saul drew near to Samuel in the gate, and said, "Please tell me, where *is* the seer's house?"

19Samuel answered Saul and said, "I *am* the seer. Go up before me to the high place, for you shall eat with me today; and tomorrow I will let you go and will tell you all that *is* in your heart. 20But as for [a]your donkeys that were lost three days ago, do not be anxious about them, for they have been found. And [1]on whom [b]*is* all the desire of Israel? *Is it* not on you and on all your father's house?"

21And Saul answered and said, [a]"*Am* I not a Benjamite, of the [b]smallest of the tribes of Israel, and [c]my family the least of all the families of the [1]tribe of Benjamin? Why then do you speak like this to me?"

22Now Samuel took Saul and his servant and brought them into the hall, and had them sit in the place of honor among those who were invited; there *were* about thirty persons. 23And Samuel said to the cook, "Bring the portion which I gave you, of which I said to you, 'Set it apart.'" 24So the cook took up [a]the thigh with its upper part and set *it* before Saul. And *Samuel* said, "Here it is, what was kept back. *It* was set apart for you. Eat; for until this time it has been kept for you, since I said I invited the people." So Saul ate with Samuel that day.

25When they had come down from the high place into the city, [1]*Samuel* spoke with Saul on [a]the top of the house. 26They arose early; and it was about the dawning of the day that Samuel called to Saul on the top of the house, saying, "Get up, that I may send you on your way." And Saul

2 a 1 Sam. 10:23
4 a 2 Kin. 4:42
5 a 1 Sam. 1:1 b 1 Sam. 10:2
6 a Deut. 33:1 b 1 Sam. 3:19
7 a Judg. 6:18; 13:17
9 a Gen. 25:22 b 2 Kin. 17:13 1 Lit. *to seek God*
10 1 Lit. *Your word is good*
11 a Ex. 2:16
12 a Gen. 31:54 b 1 Kin. 3:2
15 a 1 Sam. 15:1
16 a Deut. 17:15 b 1 Sam. 10:1 c Ex. 2:23–25; 3:7, 9 1 *prince* or *ruler*
17 a 1 Sam. 16:12
20 a 1 Sam. 9:3 b 1 Sam. 8:5, 19; 12:13 1 *for whom*
21 a 1 Sam. 15:17 b Judg. 20:46–48 c Judg. 6:15 1 Lit. *tribes*
24 a Lev. 7:32, 33
25 a Deut. 22:8 1 So with MT, Tg.; LXX omits *He spoke with Saul on the top of the house;* LXX, Vg. afterward add *And he prepared a bed for Saul on the top of the house, and he slept.*

arose, and both of them went outside, he and Samuel.

Saul Anointed King

27As they were going down to the outskirts of the city, Samuel said to Saul, "Tell the servant to go on ahead of us." And he went on. "But you stand here [1]awhile, that I may announce to you the word of God."

10

Then [a]Samuel took a flask of oil and poured *it* on his head, [b]and kissed him and said: "*Is it* not because [c]the LORD has anointed you commander over [d]His [1]inheritance? 2When you have departed from me today, you will find two men by [a]Rachel's tomb in the territory of Benjamin [b]at Zelzah; and they will say to you, 'The donkeys which you went to look for have been found. And now your father has ceased caring about the donkeys and is worrying about [c]you, saying, "What shall I do about my son?"' 3Then you shall go on forward from there and come to the terebinth tree of Tabor. There three men going up [a]to God at Bethel will meet you, one carrying three young goats, another carrying three loaves of bread, and another carrying a skin of wine. 4And they will [1]greet you and give you two *loaves* of bread, which you shall receive from their hands. 5After that you shall come to the hill of God [a]where the Philistine garrison *is*. And it will happen, when you have come there to the city, that you will meet a group of prophets coming down [b]from the high place with a stringed instrument, a tambourine, a flute, and a harp before them; [c]and they will be prophesying. 6Then [a]the Spirit of the LORD will come upon you, and [b]you will prophesy with them and be turned into another man. 7And let it be, when these [a]signs come to you, *that* you do as the occasion demands; for [b]God *is* with you. 8You shall go down before me [a]to Gilgal; and surely I will come down to you to offer burnt offerings *and* make sacrifices of peace offerings. [b]Seven days you shall wait, till I come to you and show you what you should do."

9So it was, when he had turned his back to go from Samuel, that God [1]gave him another heart; and all those signs came to pass that day. 10[a]When they came there to the hill, there was [b]a group of prophets to meet him; then the Spirit of God came upon him, and he prophesied among them. 11And it happened, when all who knew him formerly saw that he indeed prophesied among the prophets, that the people said to one another, "What *is* this *that* has come upon the son of Kish? [a]*Is* Saul also among the prophets?" 12Then a man from there answered and said, "But [a]who *is* their father?" Therefore it became a proverb: "*Is* Saul also among the prophets?" 13And when he had finished prophesying, he went to the high place.

14Then Saul's [a]uncle said to him and his servant, "Where did you go?"

So he said, "To look for the donkeys. When we saw that *they were* nowhere *to be found,* we went to Samuel."

15And Saul's uncle said, "Tell me, please, what Samuel said to you."

16So Saul said to his uncle, "He told us plainly that the donkeys had been [a]found." But about the matter of the kingdom, he did not tell him what Samuel had said.

Saul Proclaimed King

17Then Samuel called the people together [a]to the LORD [b]at Mizpah, 18and said to the children of Israel, [a]"Thus says the LORD God of Israel: 'I brought up Israel out of Egypt, and delivered you from the hand of the Egyptians *and* from the hand of all kingdoms and from those who oppressed you.' 19[a]But you have today rejected your God, who Himself saved you from all your adversities and your tribulations; and you have said to Him, 'No, set a king over us!' Now therefore, present yourselves before the LORD by your tribes and by your [1]clans."

20And when Samuel had [a]caused all the tribes of Israel to come near, the tribe of Benjamin was chosen. 21When he had caused the tribe of Benjamin to come near by their families, the family of Matri was chosen. And Saul the son of Kish was chosen. But when they sought him, he could not be found. 22Therefore they [a]inquired of the LORD further, "Has the man come here yet?"

And the LORD answered, "There he is, hidden among the equipment."

23So they ran and brought him from there; and when he stood among the people, [a]he was taller than any of the people from his shoulders upward. 24And Samuel said to all the people, "Do you see him [a]whom the LORD has chosen, that *there is*

---

27 *1 now*

CHAPTER 10

1 a 2 Kin. 9:3, 6 b Ps. 2:12 c Acts 13:21 d Deut. 32:9 *1* So with MT, Tg., Vg.; LXX *people Israel; and you shall rule the people of the Lord;* LXX, Vg. add *And you shall deliver His people from the hands of their enemies all around them. And this shall be a sign to you, that God has anointed you to be a prince.*

2 a Gen. 35:16–20; 48:7 b Josh. 18:28 c 1 Sam. 9:3–5

3 a Gen. 28:22; 35:1, 3, 7

4 *1 ask you about your welfare*

5 a 1 Sam. 13:2, 3 b 1 Sam. 19:12, 20 c 2 Kin. 3:15

6 a Num. 11:25, 29 b 1 Sam. 10:10; 19:23, 24

7 a Ex. 4:8 b Judg. 6:12

8 a 1 Sam. 11:14, 15; 13:8 b 1 Sam. 13:8–10

9 *1 changed his heart*

10 a 1 Sam. 10:5 b 1 Sam. 19:20

11 a Matt. 13:54–57

12 a John 5:30, 36

14 a 1 Sam. 14:50

16 a 1 Sam. 9:20

17 a Judg. 20:1 b 1 Sam. 7:5, 6

18 a Judg. 6:8, 9

19 a 1 Sam. 8:7, 19; 12:12 *1* Lit. *thousands*

20 a Acts 1:24, 26

22 a 1 Sam. 23:2, 4, 10, 11 **23** a 1 Sam. 9:2 **24** a 2 Sam. 21:6

no one like him among all the people?"

So all the people shouted and said, [b]"Long[1] live the king!"

25 Then Samuel explained to the people [a]the behavior of royalty, and wrote *it* in a book and laid *it* up before the LORD. And Samuel sent all the people away, every man to his house. 26 And Saul also went home [a]to Gibeah; and valiant *men* went with him, whose hearts God had touched. 27 [a]But some [b]rebels said, "How can this man save us?" So they despised him, [c]and brought him no presents. But he [1]held his peace.

Saul Saves Jabesh Gilead

11 Then [a]Nahash the Ammonite came up and [1]encamped against [b]Jabesh Gilead; and all the men of Jabesh said to Nahash, [c]"Make a covenant with us, and we will serve you."

2 And Nahash the Ammonite answered them, "On this *condition* I will make *a covenant* with you, that I may put out all your right eyes, and bring [a]reproach on all Israel."

3 Then the elders of Jabesh said to him, "Hold off for seven days, that we may send messengers to all the territory of Israel. And then, if *there is* no one to [1]save us, we will come out to you."

4 So the messengers came [a]to Gibeah of Saul and told the news in the hearing of the people. And [b]all the people lifted up their voices and wept. 5 Now there was Saul, coming behind the herd from the field; and Saul said, "What *troubles* the people, that they weep?" And they told him the words of the men of Jabesh. 6 [a]Then the Spirit of God came upon Saul when he heard this news, and his anger was greatly aroused. 7 So he took a yoke of oxen and [a]cut them in pieces, and sent *them* throughout all the territory of Israel by the hands of messengers, saying, [b]"Whoever does not go out with Saul and Samuel to battle, so it shall be done to his oxen."

And the fear of the LORD fell on the people, and they came out [1]with one consent. 8 When he numbered them in [a]Bezek, the children [b]of Israel were three hundred thousand, and the men of Judah thirty thousand. 9 And they said to the messengers who came, "Thus you shall say to the men of Jabesh Gilead: 'Tomorrow, by *the time* the sun is hot, you shall have help.'" Then the messengers came and reported *it* to the men of Jabesh, and they were glad. 10 Therefore the men of Jabesh said, "Tomorrow we will come out to you, and you may do with us whatever seems good to you."

11 So it was, on the next day, that [a]Saul put the people [b]in three companies; and they came into the midst of the camp in the morning watch, and killed Ammonites until the heat of the day. And it happened that those who survived were scattered, so that no two of them were left together.

12 Then the people said to Samuel, [a]"Who *is* he who said, 'Shall Saul reign over us?' [b]Bring the men, that we may put them to death."

13 But Saul said, [a]"Not a man shall be put to death this day, for today [b]the LORD has accomplished salvation in Israel."

14 Then Samuel said to the people, "Come, let us go [a]to Gilgal and renew the kingdom there." 15 So all the people went to Gilgal, and there they made Saul king [a]before the LORD in Gilgal. [b]There they made sacrifices of peace offerings before the LORD, and there Saul and all the men of Israel rejoiced greatly.

Samuel's Address at Saul's Coronation

12 Now Samuel said to all Israel: "Indeed I have [1]heeded [a]your voice in all that you said to me, and [b]have made a king over you. 2 And now here is the king, [a]walking before you; [b]and I am old and grayheaded, and look, my sons *are* with you. I have walked before you from my childhood to this day. 3 Here I am. Witness against me before the LORD and before [a]His anointed: [b]Whose ox have I taken, or whose donkey have I taken, or whom have I cheated? Whom have I oppressed, or from whose hand have I received *any* [c]bribe with which to [d]blind my eyes? I will restore *it* to you."

4 And they said, [a]"You have not cheated us or oppressed us, nor have you taken anything from any man's hand."

5 Then he said to them, "The LORD *is* witness against you, and His anointed *is* witness this day, [a]that you have not found anything [b]in my hand."

And they answered, "*He is* witness."

6 Then Samuel said to the people, [a]"*It is* the LORD who raised up Moses and Aaron, and who brought your fathers up from the land of Egypt. 7 Now therefore, stand still,

---

24 b 1 Kin. 1:25, 39
1 Lit. *May the king live*
25 a 1 Sam. 8:11–18
26 a Judg. 20:14
27 a 1 Sam. 11:12
b Deut. 13:13
c 1 Kin. 4:21; 10:25
1 *kept silent*

CHAPTER 11
1 a 1 Sam. 12:12
b Judg. 21:8
c Gen. 26:28
1 *besieged*
2 a Gen. 34:14
3 1 *deliver*
4 a 1 Sam. 10:26; 15:34
b Judg. 2:4; 20:23, 26; 21:2
6 a Judg. 3:10; 6:34; 11:29; 13:25; 14:6
7 a Judg. 19:29
b Judg. 21:5, 8, 10
1 Lit. *as one man*
8 a Judg. 1:5
b 2 Sam. 24:9
11 a 1 Sam. 31:11
b Judg. 7:16, 20
12 a 1 Sam. 10:27
b Luke 19:27
13 a 2 Sam. 19:22
b Ex. 14:13, 30
14 a 1 Sam. 7:16; 10:8
15 a 1 Sam. 10:17
b 1 Sam. 10:8

CHAPTER 12
1 a 1 Sam. 8:5, 7, 9, 20, 22
b 1 Sam. 10:24; 11:14, 15
1 *listened to*
2 a Num. 27:17
b 1 Sam. 8:1, 5
3 a 1 Sam. 10:1; 24:6
b Num. 16:15
c Ex. 23:8
d Deut. 16:19
4 a Lev. 19:13
5 a Acts 23:9; 24:20
b Ex. 22:4
6 a Mic. 6:4

that I may [a]reason with you before the
LORD concerning all the [b]righteous acts of
the LORD which He did to you and your
fathers: 8[a]When Jacob had gone into
[1]Egypt, and your fathers [b]cried out to the
LORD, then the LORD [c]sent Moses and
Aaron, who brought your fathers out of
Egypt and made them dwell in this place.
9And when they [a]forgot the LORD their
God, He sold them into the hand of [b]Sis-
era, commander of the army of Hazor,
into the hand of the [c]Philistines, and into
the hand of the king of [d]Moab; and they
fought against them. 10Then they cried
out to the LORD, and said, [a]'We have
sinned, because we have forsaken the
LORD [b]and served the Baals and [1]Ashto-
reths; but now deliver us from the hand
of our enemies, and we will serve You.'
11And the LORD sent [1]Jerubbaal, [2]Bedan,
[a]Jephthah, and [b]Samuel,[3] and delivered
you out of the hand of your enemies on
every side; and you dwelt in safety. 12And
when you saw that [a]Nahash king of the
Ammonites came against you, [b]you said
to me, 'No, but a king shall reign over us,'
when [c]the LORD your God *was* your king.

I pray, Father, that _____ will fear You, serve You, and obey Your voice, so they will not rebel against Your commandments.

FROM 1 SAMUEL 12:14

13"Now therefore, [a]here is the king
[b]whom you have chosen *and* whom you
have desired. And take note, [c]the LORD
has set a king over you. 14If you [a]fear the
LORD and serve Him and obey His voice,
and do not rebel against the commandment of the LORD, then both you and the
king who reigns over you will continue
following the LORD your God. 15However,
if you do [a]not obey the voice of the LORD,
but [b]rebel against the commandment of
the LORD, then the hand of the LORD will
be against you, as *it was* against your fathers.
16"Now therefore, [a]stand and see this
great thing which the LORD will do before
your eyes: 17*Is* today not the [a]wheat harvest? [b]I will call to the LORD, and He will
send thunder and [c]rain, that you may perceive and see that [d]your wickedness *is*
great, which you have done in the sight of
the LORD, in asking a king for yourselves."
18So Samuel called to the LORD, and the
LORD sent thunder and rain that day; and
[a]all the people greatly feared the LORD and
Samuel.
19And all the people said to Samuel,
[a]"Pray for your servants to the LORD your
God, that we may not die; for we have added to all our sins the evil of asking a king
for ourselves."
20Then Samuel said to the people, "Do
not fear. You have done all this wickedness; [a]yet do not turn aside from following the LORD, but serve the LORD with all
your heart. 21And [a]do not turn aside; [b]for
then you would go after empty things
which cannot profit or deliver, for they
are nothing. 22For [a]the LORD will not forsake [b]His people, [c]for His great name's
sake, because [d]it has pleased the LORD to
make you His people. 23Moreover, as for
me, far be it from me that I should sin
against the LORD [a]in ceasing to pray for
you; but [b]I will teach you the [c]good and
the right way. 24[a]Only fear the LORD, and
serve Him in truth with all your heart; for
[b]consider what [c]great things He has done
for you. 25But if you still do wickedly, [a]you
shall be swept away, [b]both you and your
king."

Saul's Unlawful Sacrifice

13 Saul [1]reigned one year; and when
he had reigned two years over Israel, 2Saul chose for himself three thousand
men of Israel. Two thousand were with
Saul in [a]Michmash and in the mountains
of Bethel, and a thousand were with [b]Jon-
athan in [c]Gibeah of Benjamin. The rest of
the people he sent away, every man to his
tent.
3And Jonathan attacked [a]the garrison
of the Philistines that *was* in [b]Geba, and
the Philistines heard *of it*. Then Saul blew
the trumpet throughout all the land, saying, "Let the Hebrews hear!" 4Now all Israel heard it said *that* Saul had attacked a
garrison of the Philistines, and *that* Israel
had also become [1]an abomination to the

7 a Is. 1:18 b Judg. 5:11 **8** a Gen. 46:5, 6 b Ex. 2:23–25 c Ex. 3:10; 4:14–16 *1* So with MT, Tg., Vg.; LXX adds *and the Egyptians afflicted them* **9** a Judg. 3:7 b Judg. 4:2 c Judg. 3:31; 10:7; 13:1 d Judg. 3:12–30 **10** a Judg. 10:10 b Judg. 2:13; 3:7 *1* Images of Canaanite goddesses **11** a Judg. 11:1 b 1 Sam. 7:13 *1* Gideon, cf. Judg. 6:25–32; Syr. *Deborah;* Tg. *Gideon* *2* LXX, Syr. *Barak;* Tg. *Simson* *3* Syr. *Simson* **12** a 1 Sam. 11:1, 2 b 1 Sam. 8:5, 19, 20 c Judg. 8:23 **13** a 1 Sam. 10:24 b 1 Sam. 8:5; 12:17, 19 c Hos. 13:11 **14** a Josh. 24:14 **15** a Deut. 28:15 b Is. 1:20 **16** a Ex. 14:13, 31 **17** a Gen. 30:14 b [James 5:16–18] c Ezra 10:9 d 1 Sam. 8:7 **18** a Ex. 14:31 **19** a Ex. 9:28 **20** a Deut. 11:16 **21** a 2 Chr. 25:15 b Is. 41:29 **22** a Deut. 31:6 b Is. 43:21 c Jer. 14:21 d Deut. 7:6–11 **23** a Rom. 1:9 b Ps. 34:11 c 1 Kin. 8:36 **24** a Eccl. 12:13 b Is. 5:12 c Deut. 10:21

25 a Josh. 24:20 b Deut. 28:36 **CHAPTER 13** **1** *1* Heb. is difficult; cf. 2 Sam. 5:4; 2 Kin. 14:2; see also 2 Sam. 2:10; Acts 13:21 **2** a 1 Sam. 14:5, 31 b 1 Sam. 14:1 c 1 Sam. 10:26 **3** a 1 Sam. 10:5 b 2 Sam. 5:25 **4** *1* *odious*

Philistines. And the people were called together to Saul at Gilgal.
5 Then the Philistines gathered together
to fight with Israel, [1]thirty thousand chariots and six thousand horsemen, and people [a]as the sand which *is* on the seashore
in multitude. And they came up and encamped in Michmash, to the east of [b]Beth
Aven. 6 When the men of Israel saw that
they were in danger (for the people were
distressed), then the people [a]hid in caves,
in thickets, in rocks, in holes, and in pits.
7 And *some of* the Hebrews crossed over
the Jordan to the [a]land of Gad and Gilead.
As for Saul, he *was* still in Gilgal, and
all the people followed him trembling.
8 [a]Then he waited seven days, according to
the time set by Samuel. But Samuel did
not come to Gilgal; and the people were
scattered from him. 9 So Saul said, "Bring
a burnt offering and peace offerings here
to me." And he offered the burnt offering.
10 Now it happened, as soon as he had finished presenting the burnt offering, that
Samuel came; and Saul went out to meet
him, that he might [1]greet him.
11 And Samuel said, "What have you
done?"
Saul said, "When I saw that the people
were scattered from me, and *that* you did
not come within the days appointed, and
that the Philistines gathered together at
Michmash, 12 then I said, 'The Philistines
will now come down on me at Gilgal, and
I have not made supplication to the LORD.'
Therefore I felt compelled, and offered a
burnt offering."
13 And Samuel said to Saul, [a]"You have
done foolishly. [b]You have not kept the
commandment of the LORD your God,
which He commanded you. For now the
LORD would have established your kingdom over Israel forever. 14 [a]But now your
kingdom shall not continue. [b]The LORD
has sought for Himself a man [c]after His
own heart, and the LORD has commanded
him *to be* commander over His people,
because you have [d]not kept what the LORD
commanded you."
15 Then Samuel arose and went up from
Gilgal to Gibeah of [1]Benjamin. And Saul
numbered the people present with him,
[a]about six hundred men.

No Weapons for the Army

16 Saul, Jonathan his son, and the people present with them remained in [1]Gibe-
ah of Benjamin. But the Philistines
encamped in Michmash. 17 Then raiders
came out of the camp of the Philistines in
three companies. One company turned
onto the road to [a]Ophrah, to the land of
Shual, 18 another company turned to the
road *to* [a]Beth Horon, and another company turned *to* the road of the border that
overlooks the Valley of [b]Zeboim toward
the wilderness.
19 Now [a]there was no blacksmith to be
found throughout all the land of Israel,
for the Philistines said, "Lest the Hebrews
make swords or spears." 20 But all the Israelites would go down to the Philistines to
sharpen each man's plowshare, his mat-
tock, his ax, and his sickle; 21 and the
charge for a sharpening was a [1]pim for the
plowshares, the mattocks, the forks, and
the axes, and to set the points of the
goads. 22 So it came about, on the day of
battle, that [a]there was neither sword nor
spear found in the hand of any of the people who *were* with Saul and Jonathan. But
they were found with Saul and Jonathan
his son.
23 [a]And the garrison of the Philistines
went out to the pass of Michmash.

Jonathan Defeats the Philistines

14 Now it happened one day that Jonathan the son of Saul said to the
young man who [1]bore his armor, "Come,
let us go over to the Philistines' garrison
that *is* on the other side." But he did not
tell his father. 2 And Saul was sitting in the
outskirts of [a]Gibeah under a pomegranate
tree which *is* in Migron. The people who
were with him *were* about six hundred
men. 3 [a]Ahijah the son of Ahitub, [b]Icha-
bod's brother, the son of Phinehas, the
son of Eli, the LORD's priest in Shiloh, was
[c]wearing an ephod. But the people did not
know that Jonathan had gone.
4 Between the passes, by which Jonathan sought to go over [a]to the Philistines'
garrison, *there was* a sharp rock on one
side and a sharp rock on the other side.
And the name of one *was* Bozez, and the
name of the other Seneh. 5 The front of
one faced northward opposite Michmash,
and the other southward opposite Gibeah.
6 Then Jonathan said to the young man
who bore his armor, "Come, let us go over
to the garrison of these [a]uncircumcised;
it may be that the LORD will work for us.
For nothing restrains the LORD [b]from saving by many or by few."

---

5 a Judg. 7:12 b Josh. 7:2 *1* So with MT, LXX, Tg., Vg.; Syr. and some mss. of LXX *three thousand*
6 a Judg. 6:2
7 a Num. 32:1–42
8 a 1 Sam. 10:8
10 *1* Lit. *bless him*
13 a 2 Chr. 16:9 b 1 Sam. 15:11, 22, 28
14 a 1 Sam. 15:28; 31:6 b 1 Sam. 16:1 c Acts 7:46; 13:22 d 1 Sam. 15:11, 19
15 a 1 Sam. 13:2, 6, 7; 14:2 *1* So with MT, Tg.; LXX, Vg. add *And the rest of the people went up after Saul to meet the people who fought against them, going from Gilgal to Gibeah in the hill of Benjamin.*
16 *1* Heb. *Geba*
17 a Josh. 18:23
18 a Josh. 16:3; 18:13, 14 b Neh. 11:34
19 a Judg. 5:8
21 *1* About two-thirds shekel weight
22 a Judg. 5:8
23 a 1 Sam. 14:1, 4

CHAPTER 14
1 *1 carried*
2 a 1 Sam. 13:15, 16
3 a 1 Sam. 22:9, 11, 20 b 1 Sam. 4:21 c 1 Sam. 2:28
4 a 1 Sam. 13:23
6 a 1 Sam. 17:26, 36 b Judg. 7:4, 7

7So his armorbearer said to him, "Do
all that is in your heart. Go then; here I
am with you, according to your heart."
8Then Jonathan said, "Very well, let us
cross over to *these* men, and we will show
ourselves to them. 9If they say thus to us,
'Wait until we come to you,' then we will
stand still in our place and not go up to
them. 10But if they say thus, 'Come up to
us,' then we will go up. For the LORD has
delivered them into our hand, and [a]this
will be a sign to us."
11So both of them showed themselves
to the garrison of the Philistines. And the
Philistines said, "Look, the Hebrews are
coming out of the holes where they have
[a]hidden." 12Then the men of the garrison
called to Jonathan and his armorbearer,
and said, "Come up to us, and we will
[1]show you something."

Jonathan said to his armorbearer,
"Come up after me, for the LORD has delivered them into the hand of Israel."
13And Jonathan climbed up on his hands
and knees with his armorbearer after him;
and they [a]fell before Jonathan. And as he
came after him, his armorbearer killed
them. 14That first slaughter which Jonathan and his armorbearer made was about
twenty men within about [1]half an acre of
land.
15And [a]there was [1]trembling in the
camp, in the field, and among all the people. The garrison and [b]the raiders also
trembled; and the earth quaked, so that it
was [c]a very great trembling. 16Now the
watchmen of Saul in Gibeah of Benjamin
looked, and *there* was the multitude,
melting away; and they [a]went here and
there. 17Then Saul said to the people who
were with him, "Now call the roll and see
who has gone from us." And when they
had called the roll, surprisingly, Jonathan
and his armorbearer *were* not *there.*
18And Saul said to Ahijah, "Bring the [1]ark
of God here" (for at that time the ark of
God was with the children of Israel).
19Now it happened, while Saul [a]talked to
the priest, that the noise which *was* in the
camp of the Philistines continued to increase; so Saul said to the priest, "Withdraw your hand." 20Then Saul and all the
people who *were* with him assembled, and
they went to the battle; and indeed [a]every
man's sword was against his neighbor,
and there was very great confusion.
21Moreover the Hebrews *who* were with
the Philistines before that time, who went
up with them into the camp *from the* surrounding *country,* they also joined the Israelites who *were* with Saul and Jonathan.
22Likewise all the men of Israel who [a]had
hidden in the mountains of Ephraim,
when they heard that the Philistines fled,
they also followed hard after them in the
battle. 23[a]So the LORD saved Israel that
day, and the battle shifted [b]to Beth Aven.

Saul's Rash Oath

24And the men of Israel were distressed
that day, for Saul had [a]placed the people
under oath, saying, "Cursed *is* the man
who eats *any* food until evening, before I
have taken vengeance on my enemies." So
none of the people tasted food. 25[a]Now all
the people of the land came to a forest;
and there was [b]honey on the ground.
26And when the people had come into the
woods, there was the honey, dripping; but
no one put his hand to his mouth, for the
people feared the oath. 27But Jonathan
had not heard his father charge the people
with the oath; therefore he stretched out
the end of the rod that *was* in his hand
and dipped it in a honeycomb, and put his
hand to his mouth; and his [1]countenance
brightened. 28Then one of the people said,
"Your father strictly charged the people
with an oath, saying, 'Cursed *is* the man
who eats food this day.'" And the people
were faint.
29But Jonathan said, "My father has
troubled the land. Look now, how my
countenance has brightened because I
tasted a little of this honey. 30How much
better if the people had eaten freely today
of the spoil of their enemies which they
found! For now would there not have
been a much greater slaughter among the
Philistines?"
31Now they had [1]driven back the Philistines that day from Michmash to Aijalon.
So the people were very faint. 32And the
people rushed on the [1]spoil, and took
sheep, oxen, and calves, and slaughtered
them on the ground; and the people ate
them [a]with the blood. 33Then they told
Saul, saying, "Look, the people are sinning against the LORD by eating with the
blood!"

So he said, "You have dealt treacherously; roll a large stone to me this day."
34Then Saul said, "Disperse yourselves
among the people, and say to them, 'Bring
me here every man's ox and every man's
sheep, slaughter *them* here, and eat; and

10 a Gen. 24:14
11 a 1 Sam. 13:6; 14:22
12 1 *teach*
13 a Lev. 26:8
14 1 Lit. *half the area plowed by a yoke* of oxen in a day
15 a Job 18:11 b 1 Sam. 13:17 c Gen. 35:5 1 *terror*
16 a 1 Sam. 14:20
18 1 So with MT, Tg., Vg.; LXX *ephod*
19 a Num. 27:21
20 a Judg. 7:22
22 a 1 Sam. 13:6
23 a Ex. 14:30 b 1 Sam. 13:5
24 a Josh. 6:26
25 a Deut. 9:28 b Ex. 3:8
27 1 Lit. *eyes*
31 1 Lit. *struck*
32 a Deut. 12:16, 23, 24 1 *plunder*

do not sin against the LORD by eating with the blood.' " So every one of the people brought his ox with him that night, and slaughtered *it* there. 35Then Saul [a]built an altar to the LORD. This was the first altar that he built to the LORD.

36Now Saul said, "Let us go down after the Philistines by night, and plunder them until the morning light; and let us not leave a man of them."

And they said, "Do whatever seems good to you."

Then the priest said, "Let us draw near to God here."

37So Saul [a]asked counsel of God, "Shall I go down after the Philistines? Will You deliver them into the hand of Israel?" But [b]He did not answer him that day. 38And Saul said, [a]"Come over here, all you chiefs of the people, and know and see what this sin was today. 39For [a]*as* the LORD lives, who saves Israel, though it be in Jonathan my son, he shall surely die." But not a man among all the people answered him. 40Then he said to all Israel, "You be on one side, and my son Jonathan and I will be on the other side."

And the people said to Saul, "Do what seems good to you."

41Therefore Saul said to the LORD God of Israel, [a]"Give[1] a perfect *lot.*" [b]So Saul and Jonathan were taken, but the people escaped. 42And Saul said, "Cast *lots* between my son Jonathan and me." So Jonathan was taken. 43Then Saul said to Jonathan, [a]"Tell me what you have done."

And Jonathan told him, and said, [b]"I only tasted a little honey with the end of the rod that *was* in my hand. So now I must die!"

44Saul answered, [a]"God do so and more also; [b]for you shall surely die, Jonathan."

45But the people said to Saul, "Shall Jonathan die, who has accomplished this great deliverance in Israel? Certainly not! [a]*As* the LORD lives, not one hair of his head shall fall to the ground, for he has worked [b]with God this day." So the people rescued Jonathan, and he did not die.

46Then Saul returned from pursuing the Philistines, and the Philistines went to their own place.

Saul's Continuing Wars

47So Saul established his sovereignty over Israel, and fought against all his enemies on every side, against Moab, against the people of [a]Ammon, against Edom, against the kings of [b]Zobah, and against the Philistines. Wherever he turned, he [1]harassed *them.* 48And he gathered an army and [a]attacked[1] the Amalekites, and delivered Israel from the hands of those who plundered them.

49[a]The sons of Saul were Jonathan, [1]Jishui, and Malchishua. And the names of his two daughters *were these:* the name of the firstborn Merab, and the name of the younger [b]Michal. 50The name of Saul's wife *was* Ahinoam the daughter of Ahimaaz. And the name of the commander of his army *was* Abner the son of Ner, Saul's [a]uncle. 51[a]Kish *was* the father of Saul, and Ner the father of Abner *was* the son of Abiel.

52Now there was fierce war with the Philistines all the days of Saul. And when Saul saw any strong man or any valiant man, [a]he took him for himself.

Saul Spares King Agag

15 Samuel also said to Saul, [a]"The LORD sent me to anoint you king over His people, over Israel. Now therefore, heed the voice of the words of the LORD. 2Thus says the LORD of hosts: 'I will punish Amalek *for* what he did to Israel, [a]how he ambushed him on the way when he came up from Egypt. 3Now go and [a]attack[1] Amalek, and [b]utterly destroy all that they have, and do not spare them. But kill both man and woman, infant and nursing child, ox and sheep, camel and donkey.' "

4So Saul gathered the people together and numbered them in Telaim, two hundred thousand foot soldiers and ten thousand men of Judah. 5And Saul came to a city of Amalek, and lay in wait in the valley.

6Then Saul said to [a]the Kenites, [b]"Go, depart, get down from among the Amalekites, lest I destroy you with them. For [c]you showed kindness to all the children of Israel when they came up out of Egypt." So the Kenites departed from among the Amalekites. 7[a]And Saul attacked the Amalekites, from [b]Havilah all the way to [c]Shur, which is east of Egypt. 8[a]He also took Agag king of the Amalekites alive, and [b]utterly destroyed all the people with the edge of the sword. 9But Saul and the people [a]spared Agag and the best of the sheep, the oxen, the fatlings, the lambs, and all *that was* good, and were unwilling

35 a 1 Sam. 7:12, 17
37 a Judg. 20:18 b 1 Sam. 28:6
38 a Josh. 7:14
39 a 2 Sam. 12:5
41 a Acts 1:24–26 b 1 Sam. 10:20, 21 *1* So with MT, Tg.; LXX, Vg. *Why do You not answer Your servant today? If the injustice is with me or Jonathan my son, O LORD God of Israel, give proof; and if You say it is with Your people Israel, give holiness.*
43 a Josh. 7:19 b 1 Sam. 14:27
44 a Ruth 1:17 b 1 Sam. 14:39
45 a 1 Kin. 1:52 b [2 Cor. 6:1]
47 a 1 Sam. 11:1–13 b 2 Sam. 10:6 *1* LXX, Vg. *prospered*
48 a 1 Sam. 15:3–7 *1* Lit. *struck*
49 a 1 Sam. 31:2 b 1 Sam. 18:17–20, 27; 19:12 *1 Abinadab,* 1 Chr. 8:33; 9:39
50 a 1 Sam. 10:14
51 a 1 Sam. 9:1, 21
52 a 1 Sam. 8:11

CHAPTER 15
1 a 1 Sam. 9:16; 10:1
2 a Deut. 25:17–19
3 a Deut. 25:19 b Num. 24:20 *1* Lit. *strike*
6 a Num. 24:21 b Gen. 18:25; 19:12, 14 c Ex. 18:10, 19
7 a 1 Sam. 14:48 b Gen. 2:11; 25:17, 18 c Gen. 16:7

8 a 1 Sam. 15:32, 33 b 1 Sam. 27:8, 9 **9** a 1 Sam. 15:3, 15, 19

to utterly destroy them. But everything
despised and worthless, that they utterly
destroyed.

Saul Rejected as King

10Now the word of the LORD came to
Samuel, saying, 11[a]"I greatly regret that
I have set up Saul *as* king, for he has
[b]turned back from following Me, [c]and has
not performed My commandments." And
it [d]grieved Samuel, and he cried out to
the LORD all night. 12So when Samuel
rose early in the morning to meet Saul, it
was told Samuel, saying, "Saul went to
[a]Carmel, and indeed, he set up a monument for himself; and he has gone on
around, passed by, and gone down to Gilgal." 13Then Samuel went to Saul, and
Saul said to him, [a]"Blessed *are* you of the
LORD! I have performed the commandment of the LORD."
14But Samuel said, "What then *is* this
bleating of the sheep in my ears, and the
lowing of the oxen which I hear?"
15And Saul said, "They have brought
them from the Amalekites; [a]for the people
spared the best of the sheep and the oxen,
to sacrifice to the LORD your God; and the
rest we have utterly destroyed."
16Then Samuel said to Saul, "Be quiet!
And I will tell you what the LORD said to
me last night."
And he said to him, "Speak on."
17So Samuel said, [a]"When you *were* little in your own eyes, *were* you not head of
the tribes of Israel? And did not the LORD
anoint you king over Israel? 18Now the
LORD sent you on a mission, and said, 'Go,
and utterly destroy the sinners, the Amalekites, and fight against them until they
are [1]consumed.' 19Why then did you not
obey the voice of the LORD? Why did you
swoop down on the [1]spoil, and do evil in
the sight of the LORD?"
20And Saul said to Samuel, [a]"But I have
obeyed the voice of the LORD, and gone on
the mission on which the LORD sent me,
and brought back Agag king of Amalek;
I have utterly destroyed the Amalekites.
21[a]But the people took of the plunder,
sheep and oxen, the best of the things
which should have been utterly destroyed,
to sacrifice to the LORD your God in
Gilgal."
22So Samuel said:

[a]"Has the LORD *as great* delight in
burnt offerings and sacrifices,
As in obeying the voice of the
LORD?
Behold, [b]to obey is better than
sacrifice,
And to heed than the fat of rams.
23 For rebellion *is as* the sin of
[1]witchcraft,
And stubbornness *is as* iniquity and
idolatry.
Because you have rejected the word
of the LORD,
[a]He also has rejected you from *being*
king."

*Lord, teach _____ to hear
Your voice and to obey You,
for obedience is better
than sacrifice.*

FROM 1 SAMUEL 15:22

24[a]Then Saul said to Samuel, "I have
sinned, for I have transgressed the commandment of the LORD and your words,
because I [b]feared the people and obeyed
their voice. 25Now therefore, please pardon my sin, and return with me, that I
may worship the LORD."
26But Samuel said to Saul, "I will not
return with you, [a]for you have rejected
the word of the LORD, and the LORD has
rejected you from being king over Israel."
27And as Samuel turned around to go
away, [a]*Saul* seized the edge of his robe,
and it tore. 28So Samuel said to him,
[a]"The LORD has torn the kingdom of Israel from you today, and has given it to a
neighbor of yours, *who is* better than you.
29And also the Strength of Israel [a]will not
lie nor relent. For He *is* not a man, that
He should relent."
30Then he said, "I have sinned; *yet*
[a]honor me now, please, before the elders
of my people and before Israel, and return
with me, that I may worship the LORD
your God." 31So Samuel turned back after
Saul, and Saul worshiped the LORD.
32Then Samuel said, "Bring Agag king
of the Amalekites here to me." So Agag
came to him cautiously.
And Agag said, "Surely the bitterness of
death is past."

11 [a]Gen. 6:6, 7 [b]1 Kin. 9:6 [c]1 Sam. 13:13; 15:3, 9 [d]1 Sam. 15:35; 16:1
12 [a]Josh. 15:55
13 [a]Judg. 17:2
15 [a][Gen. 3:12, 13]; 1 Sam. 15:9, 21
17 [a]1 Sam. 9:21; 10:22
18 [1]*exterminated*
19 [1]*plunder*
20 [a]1 Sam. 15:13
21 [a]1 Sam. 15:15
22 [a][Is. 1:11–17] [b][Hos. 6:6]
23 [a]1 Sam. 13:14; 16:1 [1]*divination*
24 [a]Josh. 7:20 [b][Is. 51:12, 13]
26 [a]1 Sam. 2:30
27 [a]1 Kin. 11:30, 31
28 [a]1 Kin. 11:31
29 [a]Num. 23:19
30 [a][John 5:44; 12:43]

33 But Samuel said, [a]"As your sword has made women childless, so shall your mother be childless among women." And Samuel hacked Agag in pieces before the LORD in Gilgal.

34 Then Samuel went to [a]Ramah, and Saul went up to his house at [b]Gibeah of Saul. 35 And [a]Samuel went no more to see Saul until the day of his death. Nevertheless Samuel mourned for Saul, and the LORD regretted that He had made Saul king over Israel.

David Anointed King

16 Now the LORD said to Samuel, [a]"How long will you mourn for Saul, seeing I have rejected him from reigning over Israel? [b]Fill your horn with oil, and go; I am sending you to [c]Jesse the Bethlehemite. For [d]I have [1]provided Myself a king among his sons."

2 And Samuel said, "How can I go? If Saul hears *it,* he will kill me."

But the LORD said, "Take a heifer with you, and say, [a]'I have come to sacrifice to the LORD.' 3 Then invite Jesse to the sacrifice, and I will show you what you shall do; you shall anoint for Me the one I name to you."

The Spirit ought to be poured out like oil on our heads, to give us knowledge of the deep things of God. The Lord says we shall prophesy.

MARIA WOODWORTH-ETTER

4 So Samuel did what the LORD said, and went to Bethlehem. And the elders of the town [a]trembled at his coming, and said, [b]"Do you come peaceably?"

5 And he said, "Peaceably; I have come to sacrifice to the LORD. [a]Sanctify[1] yourselves, and come with me to the sacrifice." Then he consecrated Jesse and his sons, and invited them to the sacrifice.

6 So it was, when they came, that he looked at [a]Eliab and [b]said, "Surely the LORD's anointed *is* before Him!"

7 But the LORD said to Samuel, [a]"Do not look at his appearance or at his physical stature, because I have [1]refused him. [b]For[2] *the LORD does* not *see* as man sees; for man [c]looks at the outward appearance, but the LORD looks at the [d]heart."

8 So Jesse called Abinadab, and made him pass before Samuel. And he said, "Neither has the LORD chosen this one." 9 Then Jesse made Shammah pass by. And he said, "Neither has the LORD chosen this one." 10 Thus Jesse made seven of his sons pass before Samuel. And Samuel said to Jesse, "The LORD has not chosen these." 11 And Samuel said to Jesse, "Are all the young men here?" Then he said, "There remains yet the youngest, and there he is, keeping the [a]sheep."

And Samuel said to Jesse, "Send and bring him. For we will not [1]sit down till he comes here." 12 So he sent and brought him in. Now he *was* [a]ruddy, [b]with [1]bright eyes, and good-looking. [c]And the LORD said, "Arise, anoint him; for this *is* the one!" 13 Then Samuel took the horn of oil and anointed him in the midst of his brothers; and [a]the Spirit of the LORD came upon David from that day forward. So Samuel arose and went to Ramah.

A Distressing Spirit Troubles Saul

14 [a]But the Spirit of the LORD departed from Saul, and [b]a distressing spirit from the LORD troubled him. 15 And Saul's servants said to him, "Surely, a distressing spirit from God is troubling you. 16 Let our master now command your servants, *who are* before you, to seek out a man *who is* a skillful player on the harp. And it shall be that he will [a]play it with his hand when the [1]distressing spirit from God is upon you, and you shall be well."

17 So Saul said to his servants, [1]"Provide me now a man who can play well, and bring *him* to me."

18 Then one of the servants answered and said, "Look, I have seen a son of Jesse the Bethlehemite, *who is* skillful in playing, a mighty man of valor, a man of war, prudent in speech, and a handsome person; and [a]the LORD *is* with him."

19 Therefore Saul sent messengers to Jesse, and said, "Send me your son David, who *is* with the sheep." 20 And Jesse [a]took a donkey *loaded with* bread, a skin of wine, and a young goat, and sent *them* by his son David to Saul. 21 So David came to Saul and [a]stood before him. And he loved him greatly, and he became his armorbearer. 22 Then Saul sent to Jesse, saying,

33 a [Gen. 9:6]
34 a 1 Sam. 7:17 b 1 Sam. 11:4
35 a 1 Sam. 19:24

CHAPTER 16
1 a 1 Sam. 15:23, 35 b 1 Sam. 9:16; 10:1 c Ruth 4:18–22 d Acts 13:22 *1* Lit. *seen*
2 a 1 Sam. 9:12
4 a 1 Sam. 21:1 b 1 Kin. 2:13
5 a Ex. 19:10 *1 Consecrate*
6 a 1 Sam. 17:13, 28 b 1 Kin. 12:26
7 a Ps. 147:10 b Is. 55:8, 9 c 2 Cor. 10:7 d 1 Kin. 8:39 *1 rejected* *2* LXX *For God does not see as man sees;* Tg. *It is not by the appearance of a man;* Vg. *Nor do I judge according to the looks of a man*
11 a 2 Sam. 7:8 *1* So with LXX, Vg.; MT *turn around;* Tg., Syr. *turn away*
12 a 1 Sam. 17:42 b Gen. 39:6 c 1 Sam. 9:17 *1* Lit. *beautiful*
13 a Num. 27:18
14 a Judg. 16:20 b Judg. 9:23
16 a 1 Sam. 18:10; 19:9 *1* Lit. *evil*
17 *1* Lit. *Look now for a man for me*
18 a 1 Sam. 3:19; 18:12, 14
20 a 1 Sam. 10:4, 27
21 a Gen. 41:46

1 Samuel 16:1

Dear Woman of Destiny,

Pain and grief are part of life. We all suffer loss, whether through death, broken relationships, financial ruin, unrealized dreams, or a myriad of other causes. Changes in our circumstances often result in losing something—or someone—precious to us. It is important for us not to deny our pain, and to take time to mourn our losses. Without giving ourselves time to grieve, our wounds may never heal.

Samuel was grieving over the loss of Saul as king. But Samuel's grief was extended beyond the season God had appointed. In this passage, God confronts Samuel and admonishes him to move on with his life. Why? Because Samuel's grief could have caused him to miss the next move of God through David.

Ecclesiastes 3:4 reminds us there is "a time to weep, and a time to laugh; a time to mourn, and a time to dance." God does not expect us to ignore loss and deny ourselves time to mourn and to work through our pain. But there is a time to cast off mourning. Satan knows that if he can prolong our seasons of grief, he can keep us from moving into the new things God has for us. Just as Samuel was in danger of missing the transition that took Israel from Saul's reign to David's reign, we, too, may be in danger of missing the transition into God's new order for our lives.

Grieving robs us of strength—often the very strength we need to launch ourselves into God's new purpose and plan. During an appropriate season of grief, God's grace covers our lack of natural strength. But when the Lord is ready to move us on, that grace lifts and we can be left in a vulnerable and weak place, unable to make the necessary leap from mourning to morning! We may miss King David while grieving for King Saul!

How do we make the transition? By trusting God in the changing seasons, and by not resisting when the Holy Spirit nudges us forward. God provides the oil of joy for mourning. He gives beauty for ashes. He brings resurrection life where we have experienced death—if we will let Him. As we lean on God, trusting the Holy Spirit to see us through, He will take us beyond mourning, ashes, and death into joy, beauty, and new life!

The losses you have suffered will always be a part of your history, a part of what has made you who you are today. It's all right to feel pain from time to time as you revisit those places. But don't allow the enemy of your soul to steal the beautiful future God has ordained for you because you are still grieving the losses of your past!

Rebecca Wagner Sytsema

"Please let David stand before me, for he
has found favor in my sight." 23 And so it
was, whenever the spirit from God was
upon Saul, that David would take a harp
and play *it* with his hand. Then Saul
would become refreshed and well, and the
distressing spirit would depart from him.

David and Goliath

17 Now the Philistines gathered their
armies together to battle, and were
gathered at [a]Sochoh, which *belongs* to
Judah; they encamped between Sochoh
and Azekah, in Ephes Dammim. 2 And
Saul and the men of Israel were gathered
together, and they encamped in the Valley
of Elah, and drew up in battle array
against the Philistines. 3 The Philistines
stood on a mountain on one side, and Israel stood on a mountain on the other
side, with a valley between them.

4 And a champion went out from the
camp of the Philistines, named [a]Goliath,
from [b]Gath, whose height *was* six cubits
and a span. 5 *He had* a bronze helmet on
his head, and he *was* [1]armed with a coat
of mail, and the weight of the coat *was* five
thousand shekels of bronze. 6 And *he had*
bronze armor on his legs and a bronze
javelin between his shoulders. 7 Now the
staff of his spear *was* like a weaver's beam,
and his iron spearhead *weighed* six hundred shekels; and a shield-bearer went before him. 8 Then he stood and cried out to
the armies of Israel, and said to them,
"Why have you come out to line up for
battle? *Am* I not a Philistine, and you the
[a]servants of Saul? Choose a man for yourselves, and let him come down to me. 9 If
he is able to fight with me and kill me,
then we will be your servants. But if I prevail against him and kill him, then you
shall be our servants and [a]serve us." 10 And
the Philistine said, "I [a]defy the armies of
Israel this day; give me a man, that we
may fight together." 11 When Saul and all
Israel heard these words of the Philistine,
they were dismayed and greatly afraid.

12 Now David *was* [a]the son of that [b]Eph-
rathite of Bethlehem Judah, whose name
was Jesse, and who had [c]eight sons. And
the man was old, advanced *in years,* in the
days of Saul. 13 The three oldest sons of
Jesse had gone to follow Saul to the battle.
The [a]names of his three sons who went to
the battle *were* Eliab the firstborn, next to
him Abinadab, and the third Shammah.
14 David *was* the youngest. And the three
oldest followed Saul. 15 But David occasionally went and returned from Saul [a]to
feed his father's sheep at Bethlehem.

16 And the Philistine drew near and presented himself forty days, morning and
evening.

17 Then Jesse said to his son David,
"Take now for your brothers an ephah of
this dried *grain* and these ten loaves, and
run to your brothers at the camp. 18 And
carry these ten cheeses to the captain of
their thousand, and [a]see how your
brothers fare, and bring back news of
them." 19 Now Saul and they and all the
men of Israel *were* in the Valley of Elah,
fighting with the Philistines.

20 So David rose early in the morning,
left the sheep with a keeper, and took *the
things* and went as Jesse had commanded
him. And he came to the camp as the
army was going out to the fight and
shouting for the battle. 21 For Israel and
the Philistines had drawn up in battle array, army against army. 22 And David left
his supplies in the hand of the supply
keeper, ran to the army, and came and
greeted his brothers. 23 Then as he talked
with them, there was the champion, the
Philistine of Gath, Goliath by name, coming up from the armies of the Philistines;
and he spoke [a]according to the same
words. So David heard *them.* 24 And all the
men of Israel, when they saw the man,
fled from him and were dreadfully afraid.
25 So the men of Israel said, "Have you
seen this man who has come up? Surely
he has come up to defy Israel; and it shall
be *that* the man who kills him the king
will enrich with great riches, [a]will give
him his daughter, and give his father's
house exemption *from taxes* in Israel."

26 Then David spoke to the men who
stood by him, saying, "What shall be done
for the man who kills this Philistine and
takes away [a]the reproach from Israel? For
who *is* this [b]uncircumcised Philistine,
that he should [c]defy the armies of [d]the
living God?"

27 And the people answered him in this
manner, saying, [a]"So shall it be done for
the man who kills him."

28 Now Eliab his oldest brother heard
when he spoke to the men; and Eliab's
[a]anger was aroused against David, and he
said, "Why did you come down here? And
with whom have you left those few sheep
in the wilderness? I know your pride and

CHAPTER 17
1 a Josh. 15:35
4 a 2 Sam. 21:19 b Josh. 11:21, 22
5 *1 clothed with scaled body armor*
8 a 1 Sam. 8:17
9 a 1 Sam. 11:1
10 a 1 Sam. 17:26, 36, 45
12 a Ruth 4:22 b Gen. 35:19 c 1 Sam. 16:10, 11
13 a 1 Sam. 16:6, 8, 9
15 a 1 Sam. 16:11, 19
18 a Gen. 37:13, 14
23 a 1 Sam. 17:8–10
25 a Josh. 15:16
26 a 1 Sam. 11:2 b 1 Sam. 14:6; 17:36 c 1 Sam. 17:10 d Deut. 5:26
27 a 1 Sam. 17:25
28 a [Matt. 10:36]

the insolence of your heart, for you have
come down to see the battle."
29And David said, "What have I done
now? [a]*Is*[1] *there* not a cause?" 30Then he
turned from him toward another and
[a]said the same thing; and these people answered him as the first ones *did.*
31Now when the words which David
spoke were heard, they reported *them* to
Saul; and he sent for him. 32Then David
said to Saul, [a]"Let no man's heart fail because of him; [b]your servant will go and
fight with this Philistine."
33And Saul said to David, [a]"You are not
able to go against this Philistine to fight
with him; for you *are* a youth, and he a
man of war from his youth."
34But David said to Saul, "Your servant
used to keep his father's sheep, and when
a [a]lion or a bear came and took a lamb out
of the flock, 35I went out after it and
struck it, and delivered *the lamb* from its
mouth; and when it arose against me, I
caught *it* by its beard, and struck and
killed it. 36Your servant has killed both
lion and bear; and this uncircumcised
Philistine will be like one of them, seeing
he has defied the armies of the living
God." 37Moreover David said, [a]"The LORD,
who delivered me from the paw of the lion
and from the paw of the bear, He will deliver me from the hand of this Philistine."
And Saul said to David, [b]"Go, and the
LORD be with you!"
38So Saul clothed David with his [1]ar-
mor, and he put a bronze helmet on his
head; he also clothed him with a coat of
mail. 39David fastened his sword to his armor and tried to walk, for he had not tested *them.* And David said to Saul, "I cannot
walk with these, for I have not tested
them." So David took them off.
40Then he took his staff in his hand; and
he chose for himself five smooth stones
from the brook, and put them in a shepherd's bag, in a pouch which he had, and
his sling was in his hand. And he drew
near to the Philistine. 41So the Philistine
came, and began drawing near to David,
and the man who bore the shield *went*
before him. 42And when the Philistine
looked about and saw David, he [a]dis-
dained[1] him; for he was *only* a youth,
[b]ruddy and good-looking. 43So the Philistine [a]said to David, "*Am* I a dog, that you
come to me with sticks?" And the Philistine cursed David by his gods. 44And the
Philistine [a]said to David, "Come to me,

29 [a] 1 Sam. 17:17
[1] Lit. *Is it not a word?* or *matter?*

30 [a] 1 Sam. 17:26, 27

32 [a] Deut. 20:1–4
[b] 1 Sam. 16:18

33 [a] Num. 13:31

34 [a] Judg. 14:5

37 [a] [2 Cor. 1:10]
[b] 1 Chr. 22:11, 16

38 [1] Lit. *clothes*

42 [a] [Ps. 123:4]
[b] 1 Sam. 16:12
[1] *belittled*

43 [a] 2 Kin. 8:13

44 [a] 1 Kin. 20:10, 11

45 [a] Heb. 11:33, 34
[b] 1 Sam. 17:10

46 [a] Deut. 28:26
[b] Josh. 4:24

47 [a] Hos. 1:7
[b] 2 Chr. 20:15

48 [a] Ps. 27:3

50 [a] Judg. 3:31; 15:15; 20:16

51 [a] 1 Sam. 21:9
[b] Heb. 11:34

52 [a] Josh. 15:36
[1] So with MT, Syr., Tg., Vg.; LXX *Gath*

and I will give your flesh to the birds of
the air and the beasts of the field!"
45Then David said to the Philistine,
"You come to me with a sword, with a
spear, and with a javelin. [a]But I come to
you in the name of the LORD of hosts, the
God of the armies of Israel, whom you
have [b]defied. 46This day the LORD will deliver you into my hand, and I will strike
you and take your head from you. And this
day I will give [a]the carcasses of the camp
of the Philistines to the birds of the air
and the wild beasts of the earth, [b]that all
the earth may know that there is a God in
Israel. 47Then all this assembly shall know
that the LORD [a]does not save with sword
and spear; for [b]the battle *is* the LORD's,
and He will give you into our hands."

Father God, may ____ know that the Lord does not save through human strength, for the battle is the Lord's.

FROM 1 SAMUEL 17:47

48So it was, when the Philistine arose
and came and drew near to meet David,
that David hurried and [a]ran toward the
army to meet the Philistine. 49Then David
put his hand in his bag and took out a
stone; and he slung *it* and struck the Philistine in his forehead, so that the stone
sank into his forehead, and he fell on his
face to the earth. 50So David prevailed
over the Philistine with a [a]sling and a
stone, and struck the Philistine and killed
him. But *there was* no sword in the hand
of David. 51Therefore David ran and stood
over the Philistine, took his [a]sword and
drew it out of its sheath and killed him,
and cut off his head with it.
And when the Philistines saw that their
champion was dead, [b]they fled. 52Now the
men of Israel and Judah arose and shouted, and pursued the Philistines as far as
the entrance of [1]the valley and to the
gates of Ekron. And the wounded of the
Philistines fell along the road to [a]Shaara-
im, even as far as Gath and Ekron. 53Then
the children of Israel returned from chas-
ing the Philistines, and they plundered

their tents. 54 And David took the head of
the Philistine and brought it to Jerusalem, but he put his armor in his tent.
55 When Saul saw David going out
against the Philistine, he said to [a]Abner,
the commander of the army, "Abner,
[b]whose son *is* this youth?"
And Abner said, "As your soul lives,
O king, I do not know."
56 So the king said, "Inquire whose son
this young man *is*."
57 Then, as David returned from the
slaughter of the Philistine, Abner took
him and brought him before Saul [a]with
the head of the Philistine in his hand.
58 And Saul said to him, "Whose son *are*
you, young man?"
So David answered, [a]"*I am* the son of
your servant Jesse the Bethlehemite."

Saul Resents David

18 Now when he had finished speaking to Saul, [a]the [1]soul of Jonathan
was knit to the soul of David, [b]and Jonathan loved him as his own soul. 2 Saul
took him that day, [a]and would not let him
go home to his father's house anymore.
3 Then Jonathan and David made a [a]cov-
enant, because he loved him as his own
soul. 4 And Jonathan took off the robe that
was on him and gave it to David, with his
armor, even to his sword and his bow and
his belt.
5 So David went out wherever Saul sent
him, *and* [1]behaved wisely. And Saul set
him over the men of war, and he was accepted in the sight of all the people and
also in the sight of Saul's servants. 6 Now
it had happened as they were coming
home, when David was returning from
the slaughter of the [1]Philistine, that [a]the
women had come out of all the cities of
Israel, singing and dancing, to meet King
Saul, with tambourines, with joy, and
with musical instruments. 7 So the wom-
en [a]sang as they danced, and said:

[b]"Saul has slain his thousands,
And David his ten thousands."

8 Then Saul was very angry, and the saying
[a]displeased him; and he said, "They have
ascribed to David ten thousands, and to
me they have ascribed *only* thousands.
Now *what* more can he have but [b]the
kingdom?" 9 So Saul [1]eyed David from
that day forward.
10 And it happened on the next day that
[a]the distressing spirit from God came
upon Saul, [b]and he prophesied inside the
house. So David [c]played *music* with his
hand, as at other times; [d]but *there was* a
spear in Saul's hand. 11 And Saul [a]cast the
spear, for he said, "I will pin David to the
wall!" But David escaped his presence
twice.
12 Now Saul was [a]afraid of David, because [b]the LORD was with him, but had
[c]departed from Saul. 13 Therefore Saul removed him from [1]his presence, and made
him his captain over a thousand; and [a]he
went out and came in before the people.
14 And David behaved wisely in all his
ways, and [a]the LORD *was* with him.
15 Therefore, when Saul saw that he behaved very wisely, he was afraid of him.
16 But [a]all Israel and Judah loved David,
because he went out and came in before
them.

David Marries Michal

17 Then Saul said to David, "Here is my
older daughter Merab; [a]I will give her to
you as a wife. Only be valiant for me,
and fight [b]the LORD's battles." For Saul
thought, [c]"Let my hand not be against
him, but let the hand of the Philistines be
against him."
18 So David said to Saul, [a]"Who *am* I,
and what *is* my life *or* my father's family
in Israel, that I should be son-in-law to
the king?" 19 But it happened at the time
when Merab, Saul's daughter, should have
been given to David, that she was given to
[a]Adriel the [b]Meholathite as a wife.
20 [a]Now Michal, Saul's daughter, loved
David. And they told Saul, and the thing
pleased him. 21 So Saul said, "I will give
her to him, that she may [1]be a snare to
him, and that [a]the hand of the Philistines
may be against him." Therefore Saul said
to David a second time, [b]"You shall be my
son-in-law today."
22 And Saul commanded his servants,
"Communicate with David secretly, and
say, 'Look, the king has delight in you,
and all his servants love you. Now therefore, become the king's son-in-law.' "
23 So Saul's servants spoke those words
in the hearing of David. And David said,
"Does it seem to you *a* light *thing* to be a
king's son-in-law, seeing I *am* a poor and
lightly esteemed man?" 24 And the servants of Saul told him, saying, [1]"In this
manner David spoke."
25 Then Saul said, "Thus you shall say
to David: 'The king does not desire any

55 [a] 1 Sam. 14:50 [b] 1 Sam. 16:21, 22
57 [a] 1 Sam. 17:54
58 [a] 1 Sam. 17:12

CHAPTER 18
1 [a] Gen. 44:30 [b] 1 Sam. 20:17 [1] *life of Jonathan was bound up with the life of*
2 [a] 1 Sam. 17:15
3 [a] 1 Sam. 20:8–17
5 [1] *Or prospered*
6 [a] Ex. 15:20, 21 [1] *Philistines*
7 [a] Ex. 15:21 [b] 1 Sam. 21:11; 29:5
8 [a] Eccl. 4:4 [b] 1 Sam. 15:28
9 [1] *Viewed with suspicion*
10 [a] 1 Sam. 16:14 [b] 1 Sam. 19:24 [c] 1 Sam. 16:23 [d] 1 Sam. 19:9, 10
11 [a] 1 Sam. 19:10; 20:33
12 [a] 1 Sam. 18:15, 29 [b] 1 Sam. 16:13, 18 [c] 1 Sam. 16:14; 28:15
13 [a] Num. 27:17 [1] Lit. *himself*
14 [a] Josh. 6:27
16 [a] 1 Sam. 18:5
17 [a] 1 Sam. 14:49; 17:25 [b] Num. 32:20, 27, 29 [c] 1 Sam. 18:21, 25
18 [a] 2 Sam. 7:18
19 [a] 2 Sam. 21:8 [b] Judg. 7:22
20 [a] 1 Sam. 18:28
21 [a] 1 Sam. 18:17 [b] 1 Sam. 18:26 [1] *be bait for*
24 [1] Lit. *According to these words*

[a]dowry but one hundred foreskins of the Philistines, to take [b]vengeance on the king's enemies.' " But Saul [c]thought to make David fall by the hand of the Philistines. 26So when his servants told David these words, it pleased David well to become the king's son-in-law. Now [a]the days had not expired; 27therefore David arose and went, he and [a]his men, and killed two hundred men of the Philistines. And [b]David brought their foreskins, and they gave them in full count to the king, that he might become the king's son-in-law. Then Saul gave him Michal his daughter as a wife.

28Thus Saul saw and knew that the LORD *was* with David, and *that* Michal, Saul's daughter, loved him; 29and Saul was still more afraid of David. So Saul became David's enemy [1]continually. 30Then the princes of the Philistines [a]went out *to war.* And so it was, whenever they went out, *that* David [b]behaved more wisely than all the servants of Saul, so that his name became highly esteemed.

Saul Persecutes David

19 Now Saul spoke to Jonathan his son and to all his servants, that they should kill [a]David; but Jonathan, Saul's son, [b]delighted greatly in David. 2So Jonathan told David, saying, "My father Saul seeks to kill you. Therefore please be on your guard until morning, and stay in a secret *place* and hide. 3And I will go out and stand beside my father in the field where you *are,* and I will speak with my father about you. Then what I observe, I will tell [a]you."

4Thus Jonathan [a]spoke well of David to Saul his father, and said to him, "Let not the king [b]sin against his servant, against David, because he has not sinned against you, and because his works *have been* very good toward you. 5For he took his [a]life in his hands and [b]killed the Philistine, and [c]the LORD brought about a great deliverance for all Israel. You saw *it* and rejoiced. [d]Why then will you [e]sin against innocent blood, to kill David without a cause?"

6So Saul heeded the voice of Jonathan, and Saul swore, "*As* the LORD lives, he shall not be killed." 7Then Jonathan called David, and Jonathan told him all these things. So Jonathan brought David to Saul, and he was in his presence [a]as in times past.

8And there was war again; and David went out and fought with the Philistines, [a]and struck them with a mighty blow, and they fled from him.

9Now [a]the distressing spirit from the LORD came upon Saul as he sat in his house with his spear in his hand. And David was playing *music* with *his* hand. 10Then Saul sought to pin David to the wall with the spear, but he slipped away from Saul's presence; and he drove the spear into the wall. So David fled and escaped that night.

11[a]Saul also sent messengers to David's house to watch him and to kill him in the morning. And Michal, David's wife, told him, saying, "If you do not save your life tonight, tomorrow you will be killed." 12So Michal [a]let David down through a window. And he went and fled and escaped. 13And Michal took [1]an image and laid *it* in the bed, put a cover of goats' *hair* for his head, and covered *it* with clothes. 14So when Saul sent messengers to take David, she said, "He *is* sick."

15Then Saul sent the messengers *back* to see David, saying, "Bring him up to me in the bed, that I may kill him." 16And when the messengers had come in, there was the image in the bed, with a cover of goats' *hair* for his head. 17Then Saul said to Michal, "Why have you deceived me like this, and sent my enemy away, so that he has escaped?"

And Michal answered Saul, "He said to me, 'Let me go! [a]Why should I kill you?' "

18So David fled and escaped, and went to [a]Samuel at [b]Ramah, and told him all that Saul had done to him. And he and Samuel went and stayed in Naioth. 19Now it was told Saul, saying, "Take note, David *is* at Naioth in Ramah!" 20Then [a]Saul sent messengers to take David. [b]And when they saw the group of prophets prophesying, and Samuel standing *as* leader over them, the Spirit of God came upon the messengers of Saul, and they also [c]prophesied. 21And when Saul was told, he sent other messengers, and they prophesied likewise. Then Saul sent messengers again the third time, and they prophesied also. 22Then he also went to Ramah, and came to the great well that *is* at Sechu. So he asked, and said, "Where *are* Samuel and David?"

And *someone* said, "Indeed *they are* at Naioth in Ramah." 23So he went there to Naioth in Ramah. Then [a]the Spirit of God

25 a Ex. 22:17 b 1 Sam. 14:24 c 1 Sam. 18:17
26 a 1 Sam. 18:21
27 a 1 Sam. 18:13 b 2 Sam. 3:14
29 *1 all the days*
30 a 2 Sam. 11:1 b 1 Sam. 18:5

CHAPTER 19
1 a 1 Sam. 8:8, 9 b 1 Sam. 18:1
3 a 1 Sam. 20:8–13
4 a [Prov. 31:8, 9] b [Prov. 17:13]
5 a Judg. 9:17; 12:3 b 1 Sam. 17:49, 50 c 1 Sam. 11:13 d 1 Sam. 20:32 e [Deut. 19:10–13]
7 a 1 Sam. 16:21; 18:2, 10, 13
8 a 1 Sam. 18:27; 23:5
9 a 1 Sam. 16:14; 18:10, 11
11 a Ps. 59:title
12 a Josh. 2:15
13 *1 household idols,* Heb. *teraphim*
17 a 2 Sam. 2:22
18 a 1 Sam. 16:13 b 1 Sam. 7:17
20 a John 7:32 b 1 Sam. 10:5, 6, 10 c Joel 2:28
23 a 1 Sam. 10:10

was upon him also, and he went on and
prophesied until he came to Naioth in
Ramah. 24 [a]And he also stripped off his
clothes and prophesied before Samuel in
like manner, and lay down [b]naked all that
day and all that night. Therefore they say,
[c]"*Is* Saul also among the prophets?"

Jonathan's Loyalty to David

20 Then David fled from Naioth in Ramah, and went and said to Jonathan, "What have I done? What *is* my
iniquity, and what *is* my sin before your
father, that he seeks my life?"
2 So Jonathan said to him, "By no
means! You shall not die! Indeed, my father will do nothing either great or small
without first telling me. And why should
my father hide this thing from me? It *is*
not *so!*"
3 Then David took an oath again, and
said, "Your father certainly knows that I
have found favor in your eyes, and he has
said, 'Do not let Jonathan know this, lest
he be grieved.' But [a]truly, *as* the LORD
lives and *as* your soul lives, *there is* but a
step between me and death."
4 So Jonathan said to David, "Whatever
you yourself desire, I will do *it* for you."
5 And David said to Jonathan, "Indeed
tomorrow *is* the [a]New Moon, and I should
not fail to sit with the king to eat. But let
me go, that I may [b]hide in the field until
the third *day* at evening. 6 If your father
misses me at all, then say, 'David earnestly asked *permission* of me that he might
run over [a]to Bethlehem, his city, for *there*
is a yearly sacrifice there for all the family.' 7 [a]If he says thus: '*It is* well,' your servant will be safe. But if he is very angry,
be sure that [b]evil is determined by him.
8 Therefore you shall [a]deal kindly with
your servant, for [b]you have brought your
servant into a covenant of the LORD with
you. Nevertheless, [c]if there is iniquity in
me, kill me yourself, for why should you
bring me to your father?"
9 But Jonathan said, "Far be it from you!
For if I knew certainly that evil was determined by my father to come upon you,
then would I not tell you?"
10 Then David said to Jonathan, "Who
will tell me, or what *if* your father answers
you roughly?"
11 And Jonathan said to David, "Come,
let us go out into the field." So both of
them went out into the field. 12 Then Jonathan said to David: "The LORD God of
Israel *is witness!* When I have [1]sounded
out my father sometime tomorrow, *or* the
third *day,* and indeed *there is* good toward
David, and I do not send to you and tell
you, 13 may [a]the LORD do so and much
more to Jonathan. But if it pleases my father *to do* you evil, then I will report it to
you and send you away, that you may go
in safety. And [b]the LORD be with you as He
has [c]been with my father. 14 And you shall
not only show me the kindness of the
LORD while I still live, that I may not die;
15 but [a]you shall not [1]cut off your kindness from my [2]house forever, no, not
when the LORD has cut off every one of the
enemies of David from the face of the
earth." 16 So Jonathan made *a covenant*
with the [1]house of David, *saying,* [a]"Let
the LORD require *it* at the hand of David's
enemies."
17 Now Jonathan again caused David to
vow, because he loved him; [a]for he loved
him as he loved his own soul. 18 Then Jonathan said to David, [a]"Tomorrow *is* the
New Moon; and you will be missed, because your seat will be empty. 19 And *when*
you have stayed three days, go down
quickly and come to [a]the place where you
hid on the day of the deed; and remain by
the stone Ezel. 20 Then I will shoot three
arrows to the side, as though I shot at a
target; 21 and there I will send a lad, *say-*
ing, 'Go, find the arrows.' If I expressly say
to the lad, 'Look, the arrows *are* on this
side of you; get them and come'—then,
[a]as the LORD lives, *there is* safety for you
and no harm. 22 But if I say thus to the
young man, 'Look, the arrows *are* beyond
you'—go your way, for the LORD has sent
you away. 23 And as for [a]the matter which
you and I have spoken of, indeed the LORD
be between you and me forever."
24 Then David hid in the field. And when
the New Moon had come, the king sat
down to eat the feast. 25 Now the king sat
on his seat, as at other times, on a seat by
the wall. And [1]Jonathan arose, and Abner
sat by Saul's side, but David's place was
empty. 26 Nevertheless Saul did not say
anything that day, for he thought, "Something has happened to him; he *is* unclean,
surely he *is* [a]unclean." 27 And it happened
the next day, the second *day* of the
month, that David's place was empty. And
Saul said to Jonathan his son, "Why has
the son of Jesse not come to eat, either
yesterday or today?"

24 a Is. 20:2 b Mic. 1:8 c 1 Sam. 10:10–12

CHAPTER 20
3 a 1 Sam. 27:1
5 a Num. 10:10; 28:11–15 b 1 Sam. 19:2, 3
6 a 1 Sam. 16:4; 17:12
7 a 2 Sam. 17:4 b 1 Sam. 25:17
8 a Josh. 2:14 b 1 Sam. 18:3; 20:16; 23:18 c 2 Sam. 14:32
12 *1 searched out*
13 a Ruth 1:17 b Josh. 1:5 c 1 Sam. 10:7
15 a 2 Sam. 9:1, 3, 7; 21:7 *1 stop being kind* *2 family*
16 a 1 Sam. 25:22; 31:2 *1 family*
17 a 1 Sam. 18:1
18 a 1 Sam. 20:5, 24
19 a 1 Sam. 19:2
21 a Jer. 4:2
23 a 1 Sam. 20:14, 15
25 *1* So with MT, Syr., Tg., Vg.; LXX *he sat across from Jonathan*
26 a Lev. 7:20, 21; 15:5

28So Jonathan [a]answered Saul, "David
earnestly asked *permission* of me *to go* to
Bethlehem. 29And he said, 'Please let me
go, for our family has a sacrifice in the
city, and my brother has commanded me
to be there. And now, if I have found favor
in your eyes, please let me get away and
see my brothers.' Therefore he has not
come to the king's table."
30Then Saul's anger was aroused
against Jonathan, and he said to him,
"You son of a perverse, rebellious *woman!*
Do I not know that you have chosen the
son of Jesse to your own shame and to the
shame of your mother's nakedness? 31For
as long as the son of Jesse lives on the
earth, you shall not be established, nor
your kingdom. Now therefore, send and
bring him to me, for he [1]shall surely die."
32And Jonathan answered Saul his father, and said to him, [a]"Why should he be
killed? What has he done?" 33Then Saul
[a]cast a spear at him to [1]kill him, [b]by
which Jonathan knew that it was determined by his father to kill David.
34So Jonathan arose from the table in
fierce anger, and ate no food the second
day of the month, for he was grieved for
David, because his father had treated him
shamefully.
35And so it was, in the morning, that
Jonathan went out into the field at the
time appointed with David, and a little lad
was with him. 36Then he said to his lad,
"Now run, find the arrows which I shoot."
As the lad ran, he shot an arrow beyond
him. 37When the lad had come to the
place where the arrow was which Jonathan had shot, Jonathan cried out after
the lad and said, "*Is* not the arrow beyond
you?" 38And Jonathan cried out after the
lad, "Make haste, hurry, do not delay!" So
Jonathan's lad gathered up the arrows and
came back to his master. 39But the lad did
not know anything. Only Jonathan and
David knew of the matter. 40Then Jonathan gave his [1]weapons to his lad, and
said to him, "Go, carry *them* to the city."
41As soon as the lad had gone, David
arose from *a place* toward the south, fell
on his face to the ground, and bowed
down three times. And they kissed one another; and they wept together, but David
more so. 42Then Jonathan said to David,
[a]"Go in peace, since we have both sworn
in the name of the LORD, saying, 'May
the LORD be between you and me, and
between your descendants and my
descendants, forever.' " So he arose and
departed, and Jonathan went into the city.

David and the Holy Bread

21 Now David came to Nob, to Ahimelech the priest. And [a]Ahimelech
was [b]afraid when he met David, and said
to him, "Why *are* you alone, and no one is
with you?"
2So David said to Ahimelech the priest,
"The king has ordered me on some business, and said to me, 'Do not let anyone
know anything about the business on
which I send you, or what I have commanded you.' And I have directed *my*
young men to such and such a place.
3Now therefore, what have you on hand?
Give *me* five *loaves of* bread in my hand,
or whatever can be found."
4And the priest answered David and
said, "*There is* no [1]common bread on
hand; but there is [a]holy[2] bread, [b]if the
young men have at least kept themselves
from women."
5Then David answered the priest, and
said to him, "Truly, women *have been*
kept from us about three days since I
came out. And [1]the [a]vessels of the young
men are holy, and *the bread is* in effect
common, even though it was consecrated
[b]in the vessel this day."
6So the priest [a]gave him holy *bread;* for
there was no bread there but the showbread [b]which had been taken from before
the LORD, in order to put hot bread *in its
place* on the day when it was taken away.
7Now a certain man of the servants of
Saul *was* there that day, detained before
the LORD. And his name *was* [a]Doeg, an
Edomite, the chief of the herdsmen who
belonged to Saul.
8And David said to Ahimelech, "Is there
not here on hand a spear or a sword? For
I have brought neither my sword nor my
weapons with me, because the king's business required haste."
9So the priest said, "The sword of Goliath the Philistine, whom you killed in
[a]the Valley of Elah, [b]there it is, wrapped
in a cloth behind the ephod. If you will
take that, take *it.* For *there is* no other
except that one here."
And David said, "*There is* none like it;
give it to me."

David Flees to Gath

10Then David arose and fled that day
from before Saul, and went to Achish the

---

28 a 1 Sam. 20:6
31 1 Lit. *is a son of death*
32 a Gen. 31:36
33 a 1 Sam. 18:11; 19:10 b 1 Sam. 20:7 1 *strike him down*
40 1 *equipment*
42 a 1 Sam. 1:17

CHAPTER 21
1 a 1 Sam. 14:3 b 1 Sam. 16:4
4 a Lev. 24:5–9 b Ex. 19:15 1 *ordinary* 2 *consecrated*
5 a 1 Thess. 4:4 b Lev. 8:26 1 *The young men are ceremonially undefiled*
6 a Luke 6:3, 4 b Lev. 24:8, 9
7 a 1 Sam. 14:47; 22:9
9 a 1 Sam. 17:2, 50 b 1 Sam. 31:10

king of Gath. 11And [a]the servants of
Achish said to him, "*Is* this not David the
king of the land? Did they not sing of him
to one another in dances, saying:

[b]'Saul has slain his thousands,
And David his ten thousands'?"

12Now David [a]took these words [1]to
heart, and was very much afraid of Achish
the king of Gath. 13So [a]he changed his
behavior before them, pretended [1]mad-
ness in their hands, [2]scratched on the
doors of the gate, and let his saliva fall
down on his beard. 14Then Achish said to
his servants, "Look, you see the man is
insane. Why have you brought him to me?
15Have I need of madmen, that you have
brought this *fellow* to play the madman in
my presence? Shall this *fellow* come into
my house?"

David's Four Hundred Men

22 David therefore departed from
there and [a]escaped [b]to the cave of
Adullam. So when his brothers and all his
father's house heard *it,* they went down
there to him. 2[a]And everyone *who was* in
distress, everyone who *was* in debt, and
everyone *who was* [1]discontented gathered
to him. So he became captain over them.
And there were about [b]four hundred men
with him.

3Then David went from there to Mizpah
of [a]Moab; and he said to the king of Moab,
"Please let my father and mother come
here with you, till I know what God will do
for me." 4So he brought them before the
king of Moab, and they dwelt with him all
the time that David was in the stronghold.

5Now the prophet [a]Gad said to David,
"Do not stay in the stronghold; depart,
and go to the land of Judah." So David
departed and went into the forest of He-
reth.

Saul Murders the Priests

6When Saul heard that David and the
men who *were* with him had been discovered—now Saul was staying in [a]Gibeah
under a tamarisk tree in Ramah, with his
spear in his hand, and all his servants
standing about him— 7then Saul said to
his servants who stood about him, "Hear
now, you Benjamites! Will the son of Jesse
[a]give every one of you fields and vineyards, *and* make you all captains of thousands and captains of hundreds? 8All of
you have conspired against me, and *there*
is no one who reveals to me that [a]my son
has made a covenant with the son of Jesse;
and *there is* not one of you who is sorry
for me or reveals to me that my son has
stirred up my servant against me, to lie in
wait, as *it is* this day."

9Then answered [a]Doeg the Edomite,
who was set over the servants of Saul, and
said, "I saw the son of Jesse going to Nob,
to [b]Ahimelech the son of [c]Ahitub. 10[a]And
he inquired of the LORD for him, [b]gave
him provisions, and gave him the sword of
Goliath the Philistine."

11So the king sent to call Ahimelech the
priest, the son of Ahitub, and all his father's house, the priests who *were* in Nob.
And they all came to the king. 12And Saul
said, "Hear now, son of Ahitub!"

He answered, "Here I am, my lord."

13Then Saul said to him, "Why have you
conspired against me, you and the son of
Jesse, in that you have given him bread
and a sword, and have inquired of God for
him, that he should rise against me, to lie
in wait, as it is this day?"

14So Ahimelech answered the king and
said, "And who among all your servants *is*
as [a]faithful as David, who is the king's
son-in-law, who goes at your bidding,
and is honorable in your house? 15Did I
then begin to inquire of God for him? Far
be it from me! Let not the king impute
anything to his servant, *or* to any in the
house of my father. For your servant knew
nothing of all this, little or much."

16And the king said, "You shall surely
die, Ahimelech, you and all [a]your father's
house!" 17Then the king said to the guards
who stood about him, "Turn and kill the
priests of the LORD, because their hand
also *is* with David, and because they knew
when he fled and did not tell it to me." But
the servants of the king [a]would not lift
their hands to strike the priests of the
LORD. 18And the king said to Doeg, "You
turn and kill the priests!" So Doeg the
Edomite turned and [1]struck the priests,
and [a]killed on that day eighty-five men
who wore a linen ephod. 19[a]Also Nob, the
city of the priests, he struck with the edge
of the sword, both men and women, children and nursing infants, oxen and donkeys and sheep—with the edge of the
sword.

20[a]Now one of the sons of Ahimelech
the son of Ahitub, named Abiathar, [b]es-
caped and fled after David. 21And Abiathar
told David that Saul had killed the LORD's

11 a Ps. 56:title b 1 Sam. 18:6–8; 29:5
12 a Luke 2:19 *1 Lit. in his heart*
13 a Ps. 34:title *1 insanity* *2 scribbled*

CHAPTER 22
1 a Ps. 57:title; 142:title b 2 Sam. 23:13
2 a Judg. 11:3 b 1 Sam. 25:13 *1 Lit. bitter of soul*
3 a 2 Sam. 8:2
5 a 2 Sam. 24:11
6 a 1 Sam. 15:34
7 a 1 Sam. 8:14
8 a 1 Sam. 18:3; 20:16, 30
9 a 1 Sam. 21:7; 22:22 b 1 Sam. 21:1 c 1 Sam. 14:3
10 a Num. 27:21 b 1 Sam. 21:6, 9
14 a 1 Sam. 19:4, 5; 20:32; 24:11
16 a Deut. 24:16
17 a Ex. 1:17
18 a 1 Sam. 2:31 *1 attacked*
19 a 1 Sam. 22:9, 11
20 a 1 Sam. 23:6, 9; 30:7 b 1 Sam. 2:33

priests. 22So David said to Abiathar, "I knew that day, when Doeg the Edomite *was* there, that he would surely tell Saul. I have caused *the death* of all the persons of your father's [1]house. 23Stay with me; do not fear. [a]For he who seeks my life seeks your life, but with me you *shall be* safe."

David Saves the City of Keilah

23 Then they told David, saying, "Look, the Philistines are fighting against [a]Keilah, and they are robbing the threshing floors."

2Therefore David [a]inquired of the LORD, saying, "Shall I go and [1]attack these Philistines?"

And the LORD said to David, "Go and attack the Philistines, and save Keilah."

3But David's men said to him, "Look, we are afraid here in Judah. How much more then if we go to Keilah against the armies of the Philistines?" 4Then David inquired of the LORD once again.

And the LORD answered him and said, "Arise, go down to Keilah. For I will deliver the Philistines into your hand." 5And David and his men went to Keilah and [a]fought with the Philistines, struck them with a mighty blow, and took away their livestock. So David saved the inhabitants of Keilah.

6Now it happened, when Abiathar the son of Ahimelech [a]fled to David at Keilah, *that* he went down *with* an ephod in his hand.

7And Saul was told that David had gone to Keilah. So Saul said, "God has delivered him into my hand, for he has shut himself in by entering a town that has gates and bars." 8Then Saul called all the people together for war, to go down to Keilah to besiege David and his men.

9When David knew that Saul plotted evil against him, [a]he said to Abiathar the priest, "Bring the ephod here." 10Then David said, "O LORD God of Israel, Your servant has certainly heard that Saul seeks to come to Keilah [a]to destroy the city for my sake. 11Will the men of Keilah deliver me into his hand? Will Saul come down, as Your servant has heard? O LORD God of Israel, I pray, tell Your servant."

And the LORD said, "He will come down."

12Then David said, "Will the men of Keilah [1]deliver me and my men into the hand of Saul?"

And the LORD said, "They will deliver *you*."

13So David and his men, [a]about six hundred, arose and departed from Keilah and went wherever they could go. Then it was told Saul that David had escaped from Keilah; so he halted the expedition.

David in Wilderness Strongholds

14And David stayed in strongholds in the wilderness, and remained in [a]the mountains in the Wilderness of [b]Ziph. Saul [c]sought him every day, but God did not deliver him into his hand. 15So David saw that Saul had come out to seek his life. And David *was* in the Wilderness of Ziph [1]in a forest. 16Then Jonathan, Saul's son, arose and went to David in the woods and [1]strengthened his hand in God. 17And he said to him, [a]"Do not fear, for the hand of Saul my father shall not find you. You shall be king over Israel, and I shall be next to you. [b]Even my father Saul knows that." 18So the two of them [a]made a covenant before the LORD. And David stayed in the woods, and Jonathan went to his own house.

19Then the Ziphites [a]came up to Saul at Gibeah, saying, "Is David not hiding with us in strongholds in the woods, in the hill of Hachilah, which *is* on the south of Jeshimon? 20Now therefore, O king, come down according to all the desire of your soul to come down; and [a]our part *shall be* to deliver him into the king's hand."

21And Saul said, "Blessed *are* you of the LORD, for you have compassion on me. 22Please go and find out for sure, and see the place where his hideout is, *and* who has seen him there. For I am told he is very crafty. 23See therefore, and take knowledge of all the lurking places where he hides; and come back to me with certainty, and I will go with you. And it shall be, if he is in the land, that I will search for him throughout all the [1]clans of Judah."

24So they arose and went to Ziph before Saul. But David and his men *were* in the Wilderness [a]of Maon, in the plain on the south of Jeshimon. 25When Saul and his men went to seek *him*, they told David. Therefore he went down [1]to the rock, and stayed in the Wilderness of Maon. And

22 [1] *family*
23 [a] 1 Kin. 2:26

CHAPTER 23
1 [a] Josh. 15:44
2 [a] 2 Sam. 5:19, 23 [1] Lit. *strike*
5 [a] 1 Sam. 19:8
6 [a] 1 Sam. 22:20
9 [a] 1 Sam. 23:6; 30:7
10 [a] 1 Sam. 22:19
12 [1] Lit. *shut up*
13 [a] 1 Sam. 22:2; 25:13
14 [a] Ps. 11:1 [b] Josh. 15:55 [c] Ps. 32:7; 54:3, 4
15 [1] Or *in Horesh*
16 [1] *encouraged him*
17 [a] [Heb. 13:6] [b] 1 Sam. 20:31; 24:20
18 [a] 2 Sam. 9:1; 21:7
19 [a] 1 Sam. 26:1
20 [a] Ps. 54:3
23 [1] Lit. *thousands*
24 [a] 1 Sam. 25:2
25 [1] Or *from the rock*

when Saul heard *that,* he pursued David in the Wilderness of Maon. [26]Then Saul went on one side of the mountain, and David and his men on the other side of the mountain. [a]So David made haste to get away from Saul, for Saul and his men [b]were encircling David and his men to take them.

[27][a]But a messenger came to Saul, saying, "Hurry and come, for the Philistines have invaded the land!" [28]Therefore Saul returned from pursuing David, and went against the Philistines; so they called that place [1]the Rock of Escape. [29]Then David went up from there and dwelt in strongholds at [a]En Gedi.

David Spares Saul

24 Now it happened, [a]when Saul had returned from following the Philistines, that it was told him, saying, "Take note! David *is* in the Wilderness of En Gedi." [2]Then Saul took three thousand chosen men from all Israel, and [a]went to seek David and his men on the Rocks of the Wild Goats. [3]So he came to the sheepfolds by the road, where there *was* a cave; and [a]Saul went in to [b]attend to his needs. ([c]David and his men were staying in the recesses of the cave.) [4][a]Then the men of David said to him, "This is the day of which the LORD said to you, 'Behold, I will deliver your enemy into your hand, that you may do to him as it seems good to you.' " And David arose and secretly cut off a corner of Saul's robe. [5]Now it happened afterward that [a]David's heart troubled him because he had cut Saul's *robe.* [6]And he said to his men, [a]"The LORD forbid that I should do this thing to my master, the LORD's anointed, to stretch out my hand against him, seeing he *is* the anointed of the LORD." [7]So David [a]restrained his servants with *these* words, and did not allow them to rise against Saul. And Saul got up from the cave and went on *his* way.

[8]David also arose afterward, went out of the cave, and called out to Saul, saying, "My lord the king!" And when Saul looked behind him, David stooped with his face to the earth, and bowed down. [9]And David said to Saul: [a]"Why do you listen to the words of men who say, 'Indeed David seeks your harm'? [10]Look, this day your eyes have seen that the LORD delivered you today into my hand in the cave, and *someone* urged *me* to kill you. But *my eye* spared you, and I said, 'I will not stretch out my hand against my lord, for he *is* the LORD's anointed.' [11]Moreover, my father, see! Yes, see the corner of your robe in my hand! For in that I cut off the corner of your robe, and did not kill you, know and see that *there is* [a]neither evil nor rebellion in my hand, and I have not sinned against you. Yet you [b]hunt my life to take it. [12][a]Let the LORD judge between you and me, and let the LORD avenge me on you. But my hand shall not be against you. [13]As the proverb of the ancients says, [a]'Wickedness proceeds from the wicked.' But my hand shall not be against you. [14]After whom has the king of Israel come out? Whom do you pursue? [a]A dead dog? [b]A flea? [15][a]Therefore let the LORD be judge, and judge between you and me, and [b]see and [c]plead my case, and deliver me out of your hand."

Peace be to ____, Father, peace to their house, and peace to all that they have!

FROM 1 SAMUEL 25:6

[16]So it was, when David had finished speaking these words to Saul, that Saul said, [a]"*Is* this your voice, my son David?" And Saul lifted up his voice and wept. [17][a]Then he said to David: "You *are* [b]more righteous than I; for [c]you have rewarded me with good, whereas I have rewarded you with evil. [18]And you have shown this day how you have dealt well with me; for when [a]the LORD delivered me into your hand, you did not kill me. [19]For if a man finds his enemy, will he let him get away safely? Therefore may the LORD reward you with good for what you have done to me this day. [20]And now [a]I know indeed that you shall surely be king, and that the kingdom of Israel shall be established in your hand. [21][a]Therefore swear now to me by the LORD [b]that you will not cut off my descendants after me, and that you will not destroy my name from my father's house."

[22]So David swore to Saul. And Saul went home, but David and his men went up to [a]the stronghold.

26 a Ps. 31:22 b Ps. 17:9
27 a 2 Kin. 19:9
28 *1* Heb. *Sela Hammahlekoth*
29 a 2 Chr. 20:2

CHAPTER 24
1 a 1 Sam. 23:19, 28, 29
2 a 1 Sam. 26:2
3 a 1 Sam. 24:10 b Judg. 3:24 c Ps. 57:title; 142:title
4 a 1 Sam. 26:8–11
5 a 2 Sam. 24:10
6 a 1 Sam. 26:11
7 a [Matt. 5:44]
9 a Ps. 141:6
11 a Ps. 7:3; 35:7 b 1 Sam. 26:20
12 a 1 Sam. 26:10–23
13 a [Matt. 7:16–20]
14 a 2 Sam. 9:8 b 1 Sam. 26:20
15 a 1 Sam. 24:12 b 2 Chr. 24:22 c Ps. 35:1; 43:1; 119:154
16 a 1 Sam. 26:17
17 a 1 Sam. 26:21 b Gen. 38:26 c [Matt. 5:44]
18 a 1 Sam. 26:23
20 a 1 Sam. 23:17
21 a Gen. 21:23 b 2 Sam. 21:6–8
22 a 1 Sam. 23:29

Death of Samuel

25 Then [a]Samuel died; and the Israelites gathered together and [b]la-
mented for him, and buried him at his
home in Ramah. And David arose and
went down [c]to the Wilderness of [1]Paran.

David and the Wife of Nabal

2 Now *there was* a man [a]in Maon whose
business *was* in [b]Carmel, and the man
was very rich. He had three thousand
sheep and a thousand goats. And he was
shearing his sheep in Carmel. 3 The name
of the man *was* Nabal, and the name of his
wife Abigail. And *she was* a woman of
good understanding and beautiful appearance; but the man *was* harsh and evil in
his doings. He *was of the house of* [a]Caleb.
4 When David heard in the wilderness
that Nabal was [a]shearing his sheep, 5 David sent ten young men; and David said to
the young men, "Go up to Carmel, go to
Nabal, and greet him in my name. 6 And
thus you shall say to him who lives *in
prosperity:* [a]'Peace *be* to you, peace to
your house, and peace to all that you
have! 7 Now I have heard that you have
shearers. Your shepherds were with us,
and we did not hurt them, [a]nor was there
anything missing from them all the while
they were in Carmel. 8 Ask your young
men, and they will tell you. Therefore [1]let

CHAPTER 25
1 [a]1 Sam. 28:3 [b]Deut. 34:8 [c]Gen. 21:21 [1]So with MT, Syr., Tg., Vg.; LXX *Maon*
2 [a]1 Sam. 23:24 [b]Josh. 15:55
3 [a]Josh. 15:13
4 [a]Gen. 38:13
6 [a]1 Chr. 12:18
7 [a]1 Sam. 25:15, 21
8 [1]*be gracious to the young men*

Abigail

Married to a "harsh and evil" rascal named Nabal (1 Sam. 25:3), Abigail was probably accustomed to trying to calm the chaos he created and redeem the harm he inflicted. But the incident with King David's men took the cake. He had offended them by refusing to give them food and water. Never before had she had to find the king to apologize for something Nabal had done; but as soon as she heard of his rudeness, off she went.

She greeted David with the ultimate act of humility—falling on her face before him. She started with a passionate plea for him to regard Nabal's iniquity as her own, and ended by praising David, acknowledging his greatness, and reminding him of "all the good" that God had spoken concerning him (1 Sam. 25:30).

Knowing that King David had determined to kill Nabal, Abigail found herself trying to persuade him to spare Nabal's life more for his own benefit than for Nabal's. She encouraged him to let God take His own revenge, and to keep his royal hands free from bloodshed. In her disarming way, she diffused the king's anger, saved Nabal's life, and kept David from doing something he would have later regretted.

Abigail pursued David in order to do for him what Nabal had refused. She was determined to bless him and to right the wrong her husband had committed. Her generous act of hospitality and her humble, zealous appeal to David earned her the favor, the respect, and the gratitude of the king (see 1 Sam. 25:35). He blessed her. He blessed God for her. And in the end, he made her his wife.

As women of destiny, let us be like Abigail and care deeply when people offend our King, Jesus Christ. Let us follow her model of intercession, loving Him enough to drop everything and run after Him on someone else's behalf.

my young men find favor in your eyes, for
we come on [a]a feast day. Please give whatever comes to your hand to your servants
and to your son David.' "
9So when David's young men came,
they spoke to Nabal according to all these
words in the name of David, and waited.
10Then Nabal answered David's servants, and said, [a]"Who *is* David, and who
is the son of Jesse? There are many servants nowadays who break away each one
from his master. 11[a]Shall I then take my
bread and my water and my [1]meat that I
have killed for my shearers, and give *it* to
men when I do not know where they *are*
from?"
12So David's young men turned on
their heels and went back; and they came
and told him all these words. 13Then David said to his men, "Every man gird on
his sword." So every man girded on his
sword, and David also girded on his
sword. And about four hundred men went
with David, and two hundred [a]stayed with
the supplies.
14Now one of the young men told Abigail, Nabal's wife, saying, "Look, David
sent messengers from the wilderness to
greet our master; and he [1]reviled them.
15But the men *were* very good to us, and
[a]we were not hurt, nor did we miss anything as long as we accompanied them,
when we were in the fields. 16They were [a]a
wall to us both by night and day, all the
time we were with them keeping the
sheep. 17Now therefore, know and consider what you will do, for [a]harm is determined against our master and against all
his household. For he *is such* a [b]scoun-
drel[1] that *one* cannot speak to him."
18Then Abigail made haste and [a]took
two hundred *loaves* of bread, two skins of
wine, five sheep already dressed, five seahs
of roasted *grain,* one hundred clusters of
raisins, and two hundred cakes of figs, and
loaded *them* on donkeys. 19And she said to
her servants, [a]"Go on before me; see, I am
coming after you." But she did not tell her
husband Nabal.
20So it was, *as* she rode on the donkey,
that she went down under cover of the
hill; and there were David and his men,
coming down toward her, and she met
them. 21Now David had said, "Surely in
vain I have protected all that this *fellow*
has in the wilderness, so that nothing was
missed of all that *belongs* to him. And he
has [a]repaid me evil for good. 22[a]May God
do so, and more also, to the enemies of
David, if I [b]leave [c]one male of all who *be-*
long to him by morning light."
23Now when Abigail saw David, she
[a]dismounted quickly from the donkey,
fell on her face before David, and bowed
down to the ground. 24So she fell at his
feet and said: "On me, my lord, *on* me *let*
this iniquity *be!* And please let your maidservant [1]speak in your ears, and hear the
words of your maidservant. 25Please, let
not my lord [1]regard this scoundrel Nabal.
For as his name *is,* so *is* he: [2]Nabal *is* his
name, and folly *is* with him! But I, your
maidservant, did not see the young men
of my lord whom you sent. 26Now therefore, my lord, [a]*as* the LORD lives and *as*
your soul lives, since the LORD has [b]held
you back from coming to bloodshed and
from [c]avenging[1] yourself with your own
hand, now then, [d]let your enemies and
those who seek harm for my lord be as
Nabal. 27And now [a]this present which
your maidservant has brought to my lord,
let it be given to the young men who follow my lord. 28Please forgive the trespass
of your maidservant. For [a]the LORD will
certainly make for my lord an enduring
house, because my lord [b]fights the battles
of the LORD, [c]and evil is not found in you
throughout your days. 29Yet a man has
risen to pursue you and seek your life, but
the life of my lord shall be [a]bound in the
bundle of the living with the LORD your
God; and the lives of your enemies He
shall [b]sling out, *as from* the pocket of a
sling. 30And it shall come to pass, when
the LORD has done for my lord according
to all the good that He has spoken concerning you, and has appointed you [a]ruler
over Israel, 31that this will be no grief to
you, nor offense of heart to my lord, either
that you have shed blood without cause,
or that my lord has avenged himself. But
when the LORD has dealt well with my
lord, then remember your maidservant."
32Then David said to Abigail: [a]"Blessed
is the LORD God of Israel, who sent you
this day to meet me! 33And blessed *is* your
advice and blessed *are* you, because you
have [a]kept me this day from coming to
bloodshed and from avenging myself with
my own hand. 34For indeed, *as* the LORD
God of Israel lives, who has [a]kept me back
from hurting you, unless you had hurried
and come to meet me, surely [b]by morning
light no males would have been left to Nabal!" 35So David received from her hand

8 a Esth. 8:17; 9:19, 22
10 a Judg. 9:28
11 a Judg. 8:6, 15 · *1* Lit. *slaughter*
13 a 1 Sam. 30:24
14 *1 scolded or scorned at*
15 a 1 Sam. 25:7, 21
16 a Ex. 14:22
17 a 1 Sam. 20:7 · b Deut. 13:13 · *1* Lit. *son of Belial*
18 a Gen. 32:13
19 a Gen. 32:16, 20
21 a Ps. 109:5
22 a 1 Sam. 3:17; 20:13, 16 · b 1 Sam. 25:34 · c 1 Kin. 14:10; 21:21
23 a Judg. 1:14
24 *1 speak to you*
25 *1 pay attention to* · *2* Lit. *Fool*
26 a 2 Kin. 2:2 · b Gen. 20:6 · c [Rom. 12:19] · d 2 Sam. 18:32 · *1* Lit. *saving yourself*
27 a Gen. 33:11
28 a 2 Sam. 7:11–16, 27 · b 1 Sam. 18:17 · c 1 Sam. 24:11
29 a [Col. 3:3] · b Jer. 10:18
30 a 1 Sam. 13:14; 15:28
32 a Luke 1:68
33 a 1 Sam. 25:26
34 a 1 Sam. 25:26 · b 1 Sam. 25:22

what she had brought him, and said to her, [a]"Go up in peace to your house. See, I have heeded your voice and [b]respected your person."

36 Now Abigail went to Nabal, and there he was, [a]holding a feast in his house, like the feast of a king. And Nabal's heart *was* merry within him, for he *was* very drunk; therefore she told him nothing, little or much, until morning light. 37 So it was, in the morning, when the wine had gone from Nabal, and his wife had told him these things, that his heart died within him, and he became *like* a stone. 38 Then it happened, *after* about ten days, that the LORD [a]struck Nabal, and he died.

39 So when David heard that Nabal was dead, he said, [a]"Blessed *be* the LORD, who has [b]pleaded the cause of my reproach from the hand of Nabal, and has [c]kept His servant from evil! For the LORD has [d]returned the wickedness of Nabal on his own head."

And David sent and proposed to Abigail, to take her as his wife. 40 When the servants of David had come to Abigail at Carmel, they spoke to her saying, "David sent us to you, to ask you to become his wife."

41 Then she arose, bowed her face to the earth, and said, "Here is your maidservant, a servant to [a]wash the feet of the servants of my lord." 42 So Abigail rose in haste and rode on a donkey, [1]attended by five of her maidens; and she followed the messengers of David, and became his wife. 43 David also took Ahinoam [a]of Jezreel, [b]and so both of them were his wives.

44 But Saul had given [a]Michal his daughter, David's wife, to [1]Palti the son of Laish, who *was* from [b]Gallim.

David Spares Saul a Second Time

26 Now the Ziphites came to Saul at Gibeah, saying, [a]"Is David not hiding in the hill of Hachilah, opposite Jeshimon?" 2 Then Saul arose and went down to the Wilderness of Ziph, having [a]three thousand chosen men of Israel with him, to seek David in the Wilderness of Ziph. 3 And Saul encamped in the hill of Hachilah, which *is* opposite Jeshimon, by the road. But David stayed in the wilderness, and he saw that Saul came after him into the wilderness. 4 David therefore sent out spies, and understood that Saul had indeed come.

5 So David arose and came to the place where Saul had encamped. And David saw the place where Saul lay, and [a]Abner the son of Ner, the commander of his army. Now Saul lay within the camp, with the people encamped all around him. 6 Then David answered, and said to Ahimelech the Hittite and to Abishai [a]the son of Zeruiah, brother of [b]Joab, saying, "Who will [c]go down with me to Saul in the camp?"

And [d]Abishai said, "I will go down with you."

7 So David and Abishai came to the people by night; and there Saul lay sleeping within the camp, with his spear stuck in the ground by his head. And Abner and the people lay all around him. 8 Then Abishai said to David, [a]"God has delivered your enemy into your hand this day. Now therefore, please, let me strike him [1]at once with the spear, right to the earth; and I will not *have to strike* him a second time!"

9 But David said to Abishai, "Do not destroy him; [a]for who can stretch out his hand against the LORD's anointed, and be guiltless?" 10 David said furthermore, "*As* the LORD lives, [a]the LORD shall strike him, or [b]his day shall come to die, or he shall [c]go out to battle and perish. 11 [a]The LORD forbid that I should stretch out my hand against the LORD's anointed. But please, take now the spear and the jug of water that *are* by his head, and let us go." 12 So David took the spear and the jug of water *by* Saul's head, and they got away; and no man saw or knew *it* or awoke. For they *were* all asleep, because [a]a deep sleep from the LORD had fallen on them.

13 Now David went over to the other side, and stood on the top of a hill afar off, a great distance *being* between them. 14 And David called out to the people and to Abner the son of Ner, saying, "Do you not answer, Abner?"

Then Abner answered and said, "Who *are* you, calling out to the king?"

15 So David said to Abner, "*Are* you not a man? And who *is* like you in Israel? Why then have you not guarded your lord the king? For one of the people came in to destroy your lord the king. 16 This thing that you have done *is* not good. *As* the LORD lives, you deserve to die, because you have not guarded your master, the LORD's anointed. And now see where the king's spear *is,* and the jug of water that *was* by his head."

---

35 [a]2 Kin. 5:19 [b]Gen. 19:21
36 [a]2 Sam. 13:28
38 [a]1 Sam. 26:10
39 [a]1 Sam. 25:32 [b]Prov. 22:23 [c]1 Sam. 25:26, 34 [d]1 Kin. 2:44
41 [a]Luke 7:38, 44
42 [1]Lit. *with five of her maidens at her feet*
43 [a]Josh. 15:56 [b]1 Sam. 27:3; 30:5
44 [a]2 Sam. 3:14 [b]Is. 10:30 [1]*Paltiel,* 2 Sam. 3:15

CHAPTER 26
1 [a]1 Sam. 23:19
2 [a]1 Sam. 13:2; 24:2
5 [a]1 Sam. 14:50, 51; 17:55
6 [a]1 Chr. 2:16 [b]2 Sam. 2:13 [c]Judg. 7:10, 11 [d]2 Sam. 2:18, 24
8 [a]1 Sam. 24:4 [1]Or *one time*
9 [a]1 Sam. 24:6, 7
10 [a]1 Sam. 25:26, 38 [b][Job 7:1; 14:5] [c]1 Sam. 31:6
11 [a]1 Sam. 24:6–12
12 [a]Gen. 2:21; 15:12

17 Then Saul knew David's voice, and
said, [a]"*Is* that your voice, my son David?"
David said, "*It is* my voice, my lord,
O king." 18 And he said, [a]"Why does my
lord thus pursue his servant? For what
have I done, or what evil *is* in my hand?
19 Now therefore, please, let my lord the
king hear the words of his servant: If the
LORD has [a]stirred you up against me, let
Him accept an offering. But if *it is* the
children of men, *may* they *be* cursed before the LORD, [b]for they have driven me
out this day from sharing in the [c]inheri-
tance of the LORD, saying, 'Go, serve other
gods.' 20 So now, do not let my blood fall
to the earth before the face of the LORD.
For the king of Israel has come out to seek
[a]a flea, as when one hunts a partridge in
the mountains."
21 Then Saul said, [a]"I have sinned. Return, my son David. For I will harm you
no more, because my life was precious in
your eyes this day. Indeed I have played
the fool and erred exceedingly."
22 And David answered and said, "Here is
the king's spear. Let one of the young
men come over and get it. 23 [a]May the
LORD [b]repay every man *for* his righteousness and his faithfulness; for the LORD
delivered you into *my* hand today, but I
would not stretch out my hand against
the LORD's anointed. 24 And indeed, as
your life was valued much this day in my
eyes, so let my life be valued much in the
eyes of the LORD, and let Him deliver me
out of all tribulation."
25 Then Saul said to David, "*May* you *be*
blessed, my son David! You shall both do
great things and also still [a]prevail."
So David went on his way, and Saul returned to his place.

David Allied with the Philistines

27 And David said in his heart, "Now
I shall perish someday by the hand
of Saul. *There is* nothing better for me
than that I should speedily escape to the
land of the Philistines; and Saul will [1]de-
spair of me, to seek me anymore in any
part of Israel. So I shall escape out of his
hand." 2 Then David arose [a]and went over
with the six hundred men who *were* with
him [b]to Achish the son of Maoch, king
of Gath. 3 So David dwelt with Achish at
Gath, he and his men, each man with his
household, *and* David [a]with his two wives,
Ahinoam the Jezreelitess, and Abigail the
Carmelitess, Nabal's widow. 4 And it was
told Saul that David had fled to Gath; so
he sought him no more.
5 Then David said to Achish, "If I have
now found favor in your eyes, let them
give me a place in some town in the country, that I may dwell there. For why
should your servant dwell in the royal city
with you?" 6 So Achish gave him Ziklag
that day. Therefore [a]Ziklag has belonged
to the kings of Judah to this day. 7 Now
[1]the time that David [a]dwelt in the country
of the Philistines was one full year and
four months.
8 And David and his men went up and
raided [a]the Geshurites, [b]the [1]Girzites,
and the [c]Amalekites. For those nations
were the inhabitants of the land from [2]of
old, [d]as you go to Shur, even as far as the
land of Egypt. 9 Whenever David [1]attacked
the land, he left neither man nor woman
alive, but took away the sheep, the oxen,
the donkeys, the camels, and the apparel,
and returned and came to Achish. 10 Then
Achish would say, "Where have you made
a raid today?" And David would say,
"Against the southern *area* of Judah, or
against the southern *area* of [a]the Jerahmeelites, or against the southern *area* of
[b]the Kenites." 11 David would save neither
man nor woman alive, to bring *news* to
Gath, saying, "Lest they should inform on
us, saying, 'Thus David did.'" And thus
was his behavior all the time he dwelt in
the country of the Philistines. 12 So Achish
believed David, saying, "He has made his
people Israel utterly abhor him; therefore
he will be my servant forever."

28 Now [a]it happened in those days
that the Philistines gathered their
armies together for war, to fight with Israel. And Achish said to David, "You assuredly know that you will go out with me
to battle, you and your men."
2 So David said to Achish, "Surely you
know what your servant can do."
And Achish said to David, "Therefore I
will make you one of my chief guardians
forever."

Saul Consults a Medium

3 Now [a]Samuel had died, and all Israel
had lamented for him and buried him in
[b]Ramah, in his own city. And Saul had put
[c]the mediums and the spiritists out of the
land.
4 Then the Philistines gathered together, and came and encamped at [a]Shunem.

---

17 a 1 Sam. 24:16
18 a 1 Sam. 24:9, 11–14
19 a 2 Sam. 16:11; 24:1 b Deut. 4:27, 28 c 2 Sam. 14:16; 20:19
20 a 1 Sam. 24:14
21 a 1 Sam. 15:24, 30; 24:17
23 a Ps. 7:8; 18:20; 62:12 b 2 Sam. 22:21
25 a Gen. 32:28

CHAPTER 27
1 *1 despair of searching for*
2 a 1 Sam. 25:13 b 1 Sam. 21:10
3 a 1 Sam. 25:42, 43
6 a Josh. 15:31; 19:5
7 a 1 Sam. 29:3 1 Lit. *the number of days*
8 a Josh. 13:2, 13 b Judg. 1:29 c Ex. 17:8, 16 d Gen. 25:18 1 Or *Gezrites* 2 *ancient times*
9 1 Lit. *struck*
10 a 1 Chr. 2:9, 25 b Judg. 1:16

CHAPTER 28
1 a 1 Sam. 29:1, 2
3 a 1 Sam. 25:1 b 1 Sam. 1:19 c Deut. 18:10, 11
4 a Josh. 19:18

So Saul gathered all Israel together, and they encamped at [b]Gilboa. [5]When Saul saw the army of the Philistines, he was [a]afraid, and his heart trembled greatly. [6]And when Saul inquired of the LORD, [a]the LORD did not answer him, either by [b]dreams or [c]by Urim or by the prophets.

[7]Then Saul said to his servants, "Find me a woman who is a medium, [a]that I may go to her and inquire of her."

And his servants said to him, "In fact, *there is* a woman who is a medium at En Dor."

[8]So Saul disguised himself and put on other clothes, and he went, and two men with him; and they came to the woman by night. And [a]he said, "Please conduct a séance for me, and bring up for me the one I shall name to you."

[9]Then the woman said to him, "Look, you know what Saul has done, how he has [a]cut off the mediums and the spiritists from the land. Why then do you lay a snare for my life, to cause me to die?"

[10]And Saul swore to her by the LORD, saying, "*As* the LORD lives, no punishment shall come upon you for this thing."

[11]Then the woman said, "Whom shall I bring up for you?"

And he said, "Bring up Samuel for me."

[12]When the woman saw Samuel, she cried out with a loud voice. And the woman spoke to Saul, saying, "Why have you deceived me? For you *are* Saul!"

[13]And the king said to her, "Do not be afraid. What did you see?"

And the woman said to Saul, "I saw [a]a[1] spirit ascending out of the earth."

[14]So he said to her, "What *is* his form?"

And she said, "An old man is coming up, and he *is* covered with [a]a mantle." And Saul perceived that it *was* Samuel, and he stooped with *his* face to the ground and bowed down.

[15]Now Samuel said to Saul, "Why have you [a]disturbed me by bringing me up?"

And Saul answered, "I am deeply distressed; for the Philistines make war against me, and [b]God has departed from me and [c]does not answer me anymore, neither by prophets nor by dreams. Therefore I have called you, that you may reveal to me what I should do."

[16]Then Samuel said: "So why do you ask me, seeing the LORD has departed from you and has become your enemy? [17]And the LORD has done for [1]Himself [a]as He spoke by me. For the LORD has torn the kingdom out of your hand and given it to your neighbor, David. [18][a]Because you did not obey the voice of the LORD nor execute His fierce wrath upon [b]Amalek, therefore the LORD has done this thing to you this day. [19]Moreover the LORD will also deliver Israel with you into the hand of the Philistines. And tomorrow you and your sons *will be* with [a]me. The LORD will also deliver the army of Israel into the hand of the Philistines."

[20]Immediately Saul fell full length on the ground, and was dreadfully afraid because of the words of Samuel. And there was no strength in him, for he had eaten no food all day or all night.

[21]And the woman came to Saul and saw that he was severely troubled, and said to him, "Look, your maidservant has obeyed your voice, and I have [a]put my life in my hands and heeded the words which you spoke to me. [22]Now therefore, please, heed also the voice of your maidservant, and let me set a piece of bread before you; and eat, that you may have strength when you go on *your* way."

[23]But he refused and said, "I will not eat."

So his servants, together with the woman, urged him; and he heeded their voice. Then he arose from the ground and sat on the bed. [24]Now the woman had a fatted calf in the house, and she hastened to kill it. And she took flour and kneaded *it,* and baked unleavened bread from it. [25]So she brought *it* before Saul and his servants, and they ate. Then they rose and went away that night.

The Philistines Reject David

29 Then [a]the Philistines gathered together all their armies [b]at Aphek, and the Israelites encamped by a fountain which *is* in Jezreel. [2]And the [a]lords of the Philistines [1]passed in review by hundreds and by thousands, but [b]David and his men passed in review at the rear with Achish. [3]Then the princes of the Philistines said, "What *are* these Hebrews *doing here?*"

And Achish said to the princes of the Philistines, "*Is* this not David, the servant of Saul king of Israel, who has been with me [a]these days, or these years? And to this day I have [b]found no fault in him since he defected *to me.*"

[4]But the princes of the Philistines were angry with him; so the princes of the Philistines said to him, [a]"Make this fellow

4 [b] 1 Sam. 31:1
5 [a] Job 18:11
6 [a] 1 Sam. 14:37 [b] Num. 12:6 [c] Ex. 28:30
7 [a] 1 Chr. 10:13
8 [a] Deut. 18:10, 11
9 [a] 1 Sam. 28:3
13 [a] Ex. 22:28 [1] Heb. *elohim*
14 [a] 1 Sam. 15:27
15 [a] Is. 14:9 [b] 1 Sam. 16:14; 18:12 [c] 1 Sam. 28:6
17 [a] 1 Sam. 15:28 [1] Or *him,* i.e., David
18 [a] 1 Chr. 10:13 [b] 1 Sam. 15:3–9
19 [a] Job 3:17–19
21 [a] Job 13:14

CHAPTER 29
1 [a] 1 Sam. 28:1 [b] 1 Sam. 4:1
2 [a] 1 Sam. 6:4; 7:7 [b] 1 Sam. 28:1, 2 [1] *passed on in the rear*
3 [a] 1 Sam. 27:7 [b] Dan. 6:5
4 [a] 1 Sam. 27:6

return, that he may go back to the place
which you have appointed for him, and do
not let him go down with us to [b]battle,
lest [c]in the battle he become our adversary. For with what could he reconcile
himself to his master, if not with the
heads of these [d]men? 5*Is* this not David,
[a]of whom they sang to one another in
dances, saying:

> [b]'Saul has slain his thousands,
> And David his ten thousands'?"

6Then Achish called David and said to
him, "Surely, *as* the LORD lives, you have
been upright, and [a]your going out and
your coming in with me in the army *is*
good in my sight. For to this day [b]I have
not found evil in you since the day of your
coming to me. Nevertheless the lords do
not favor you. 7Therefore return now, and
go in peace, that you may not displease
the lords of the Philistines."

8So David said to Achish, "But what
have I done? And to this day what have
you found in your servant as long as I
have been with you, that I may not go and
fight against the enemies of my lord the
king?"

9Then Achish answered and said to David, "I know that you *are* as good in my
sight [a]as an angel of God; nevertheless
[b]the princes of the Philistines have said,
'He shall not go up with us to the battle.'
10Now therefore, rise early in the morning
with your master's servants [a]who have
come with [1]you. And as soon as you are up
early in the morning and have light, depart."

11So David and his men rose early to
depart in the morning, to return to the
land of the Philistines. [a]And the Philistines went up to Jezreel.

David's Conflict with the Amalekites

30 Now it happened, when David and
his men came to [a]Ziklag, on the
third day, that the [b]Amalekites had invaded the South and Ziklag, attacked Ziklag
and burned it with fire, 2and had taken
captive the [a]women and those who *were*
there, from small to great; they did not
kill anyone, but carried *them* away and
went their way. 3So David and his men
came to the city, and there it was, burned
with fire; and their wives, their sons, and
their daughters had been taken captive.

4 [b]1 Sam. 14:21 [c]1 Sam. 29:9 [d]1 Chr. 12:19, 20
5 [a]1 Sam. 21:11 [b]1 Sam. 18:7
6 [a]2 Sam. 3:25 [b]1 Sam. 29:3
9 [a]2 Sam. 14:17, 20; 19:27 [b]1 Sam. 29:4
10 [a]1 Chr. 12:19, 22 [1]So with MT, Tg., Vg.; LXX adds *and go to the place which I have selected for you there; and set no bothersome word in your heart, for you are good before me. And rise on your way*
11 [a]2 Sam. 4:4

CHAPTER 30
1 [a]1 Sam. 27:6 [b]1 Sam. 15:7; 27:8
2 [a]1 Sam. 27:2, 3
5 [a]1 Sam. 25:42, 43
6 [a]Ex. 17:4 [b]Hab. 3:17–19 [1]Lit. *bitter*
7 [a]1 Sam. 23:2–9 [b]1 Sam. 23:6
8 [a]1 Sam. 23:2, 4
10 [a]1 Sam. 30:9, 21
12 [a]1 Sam. 25:18 [b]Judg. 15:19
14 [a]2 Sam. 8:18 [b]Josh. 14:13; 15:13
15 [a]Deut. 23:15
16 [a]1 Thess. 5:3

4Then David and the people who *were*
with him lifted up their voices and wept,
until they had no more power to weep.
5And David's two [a]wives, Ahinoam the
Jezreelitess, and Abigail the widow of Nabal the Carmelite, had been taken captive.
6Now David was greatly distressed, for
[a]the people spoke of stoning him, because
the soul of all the people was [1]grieved,
every man for his sons and his daughters.
[b]But David strengthened himself in the
LORD his God.

7[a]Then David said to Abiathar the
priest, Ahimelech's son, "Please bring the
ephod here to me." And [b]Abiathar
brought the ephod to David. 8[a]So David
inquired of the LORD, saying, "Shall I pursue this troop? Shall I overtake them?"

And He answered him, "Pursue, for you
shall surely overtake *them* and without
fail recover *all.*"

9So David went, he and the six hundred
men who *were* with him, and came to the
Brook Besor, where those stayed who
were left behind. 10But David pursued, he
and four hundred men; [a]for two hundred
stayed *behind,* who were so weary that
they could not cross the Brook Besor.

11Then they found an Egyptian in the
field, and brought him to David; and they
gave him bread and he ate, and they let
him drink water. 12And they gave him a
piece of [a]a cake of figs and two clusters
of raisins. So [b]when he had eaten, his
strength came back to him; for he had
eaten no bread nor drunk water for three
days and three nights. 13Then David said
to him, "To whom do you *belong,* and
where *are* you from?"

And he said, "I *am* a young man from
Egypt, servant of an Amalekite; and my
master left me behind, because three days
ago I fell sick. 14We made an invasion of
the southern *area* of [a]the Cherethites, in
the *territory* which *belongs* to Judah, and
of the southern *area* [b]of Caleb; and we
burned Ziklag with fire."

15And David said to him, "Can you take
me down to this troop?"

So he said, "Swear to me by God that
you will neither kill me nor deliver me
into the hands of my [a]master, and I will
take you down to this troop."

16And when he had brought him down,
there they were, spread out over all the
land, [a]eating and drinking and dancing,
because of all the great spoil which they

1 Samuel 30:6

Dear Woman of Destiny,

When my husband, Bishop Mack Timberlake, was diagnosed with cancer of the throat, we were brought to a point of crisis that threatened the stability of everything in our lives. In June 1996, I noticed an enlarged growth on the side of Mack's neck. When we went to see a doctor, we were told that he was suffering from a sinus condition.

But in March 1997, while he was eating, his jaw suddenly locked. After being assured by a doctor that nothing was wrong, we were prompted by the Holy Spirit to set up another appointment. When this doctor began examining my husband, he looked down his throat, stepped back, and said, "You know you're in serious trouble, don't you?" We could sense through the Holy Spirit that something was gravely wrong. Like David, we were "greatly distressed," but determined to strengthen ourselves in the Lord. I thank God that, in the middle of this crisis, I prayed, "God, You said that the steps of a righteous man and woman are ordered of the Lord. I ask You to order our steps." Even when the devil attacks, God intervenes.

The results from a second tissue biopsy were positive for cancer. The first plan of attack was to begin treating my husband with radiation and chemotherapy. If that did not work, the doctor would do surgery to remove his tongue. When we heard this, we became determined to believe God for a miracle. At the time, we knew Mack's condition was bad, but we didn't know that the cancer was already in the fourth stage.

In just two weeks, I saw my husband go from a vibrant, healthy-looking, 230-pound man to a bedridden, 185-pound invalid. Mack was usually the one in control of everything—the one who was there to fight the devil for *me*. But now, *he* was the one being attacked, so I had to move into his position.

God knew all the while that we would come through this test stronger than before; He knew that many would be watching and taking note and that He would be glorified in a great way. I was believing for my husband's total healing. I saw him whole, healed, and back in the pulpit. We're not supposed to walk by sight or by feelings. It's out of the abundance of the heart that the mouth speaks (see Luke 6:45). Our hearts must be filled with faith. The Word of God tells us God calls those things that are not as though they already exist (see Rom. 4:17). It doesn't matter how crazy people say you are. There is no mountain too big for God! (see Mark 11:23).

My husband's recovery has been amazing. The survival rate for this particular cancer, especially when it is first detected at such a late stage, is extremely low. But Mack is more determined now than ever to minister the compassion of Christ to those who are suffering and to fulfill the calling of God on his life as a man of God and a preacher of the gospel.

Brenda Timberlake

had taken from the land of the Philistines and from the land of Judah. 17 Then David attacked them from twilight until the evening of the next day. Not a man of them escaped, except four hundred young men who rode on camels and fled. 18 So David recovered all that the Amalekites had carried away, and David rescued his two wives. 19 And nothing of theirs was lacking, either small or great, sons or daughters, spoil or anything which they had taken from them; [a]David recovered all. 20 Then David took all the flocks and herds they had driven before those *other* livestock, and said, "This *is* David's spoil."

21 Now David came to the [a]two hundred men who had been so weary that they could not follow David, whom they also had made to stay at the Brook Besor. So they went out to meet David and to meet the people who *were* with him. And when David came near the people, he [1]greeted them. 22 Then all the wicked and [a]worthless[1] men of those who went with David answered and said, "Because they did not go with us, we will not give them *any* of the spoil that we have recovered, except for every man's wife and children, that they may lead *them* away and depart."

23 But David said, "My brethren, you shall not do so with what the LORD has given us, who has preserved us and delivered into our hand the troop that came against us. 24 For who will heed you in this matter? But [a]as his part *is* who goes down to the battle, so *shall* his part *be* who stays by the supplies; they shall share alike." 25 So it was, from that day forward; he made it a statute and an ordinance for Israel to this day.

26 Now when David came to Ziklag, he sent *some* of the [1]spoil to the elders of Judah, to his friends, saying, "Here is a present for you from the spoil of the enemies of the LORD"— 27 to *those* who *were* in Bethel, *those* who *were* in [a]Ramoth of the South, *those* who *were* in [b]Jattir, 28 *those* who *were* in [a]Aroer, *those* who *were* in [b]Siphmoth, *those* who *were* in [c]Eshtemoa, 29 *those* who *were* in Rachal, *those* who *were* in the cities of [a]the Jerahmeelites, *those* who *were* in the cities of the [b]Kenites, 30 *those* who *were* in [a]Hormah, *those* who *were* in [1]Chorashan, *those* who *were* in Athach, 31 *those* who *were* in [a]Hebron, and to all the places where David himself and his men were accustomed to [b]rove.

The Tragic End of Saul and His Sons

31 Now [a]the Philistines fought against Israel; and the men of Israel fled from before the Philistines, and fell slain on Mount [b]Gilboa. 2 Then the Philistines followed hard after Saul and his sons. And the Philistines killed [a]Jonathan, Abinadab, and Malchishua, Saul's sons. 3 [a]The battle became fierce against Saul. The archers [1]hit him, and he was severely wounded by the archers.

4 [a]Then Saul said to his armorbearer, "Draw your sword, and thrust me through with it, lest [b]these uncircumcised men come and thrust me through and [1]abuse me."

But his armorbearer would not, [c]for he was greatly afraid. Therefore Saul took a sword and [d]fell on it. 5 And when his armorbearer saw that Saul was dead, he also fell on his sword, and died with him. 6 So Saul, his three sons, his armorbearer, and all his men died together that same day.

7 And when the men of Israel who *were* on the other side of the valley, and *those* who *were* on the other side of the Jordan, saw that the men of Israel had fled and that Saul and his sons were dead, they forsook the cities and fled; and the Philistines came and dwelt in them. 8 So it happened the next day, when the Philistines came to strip the slain, that they found Saul and his three sons fallen on Mount Gilboa. 9 And they cut off his head and stripped off his armor, and sent *word* throughout the land of the Philistines, to [a]proclaim *it in* the temple of their idols and among the people. 10 [a]Then they put his armor in the temple of the [b]Ashtoreths, and [c]they fastened his body to the wall of [d]Beth[1] Shan.

11 [a]Now when the inhabitants of Jabesh Gilead heard what the Philistines had done to Saul, 12 [a]all the valiant men arose and traveled all night, and took the body of Saul and the bodies of his sons from the wall of Beth Shan; and they came to Jabesh and [b]burned them there. 13 Then they took their bones and [a]buried *them* under the tamarisk tree at Jabesh, [b]and fasted seven days.

---

19 a 1 Sam. 30:8
21 a 1 Sam. 30:10 *1 asked them concerning their welfare*
22 a Deut. 13:13 *1* Lit. *men of Belial*
24 a Josh. 22:8
26 *1 booty*
27 a Josh. 19:8 b Josh. 15:48; 21:14
28 a Josh. 13:16 b 1 Chr. 27:27 c Josh. 15:50
29 a 1 Sam. 27:10 b Judg. 1:16
30 a Judg. 1:17 *1* Or *Borashan*
31 a 2 Sam. 2:1 b 1 Sam. 23:22

CHAPTER 31
1 a 1 Chr. 10:1–12 b 1 Sam. 28:4
2 a 1 Sam. 14:49
3 a 2 Sam. 1:6 *1* Lit. *found him*
4 a Judg. 9:54 b 1 Sam. 14:6; 17:26, 36 c 2 Sam. 1:14 d 2 Sam. 1:6, 10 *1 torture*
9 a 2 Sam. 1:20
10 a 1 Sam. 21:9 b Judg. 2:13 c 2 Sam. 21:12 d Judg. 1:27 *1 Beth Shean,* Josh. 17:11
11 a 1 Sam. 11:1–13
12 a 2 Sam. 2:4–7 b 2 Chr. 16:14
13 a 2 Sam. 2:4, 5; 21:12–14 b Gen. 50:10

AUTHOR: *Possibly Abiathar the Priest*
DATE: *931–722 B.C.*
THEME: *King David, Forerunner of the Messiah*
KEY PEOPLE: *David, Nathan, Absalom, Joab, Bathsheba*

2 SAMUEL

Dear Woman of Destiny,

In 2 Samuel, personal and political challenges threatened David's very life. Through both David's strengths and weaknesses, God reigned; and He built Israel into a powerful nation. Be assured that, with God on the throne of your life, His outstanding ways will shine through all you do. As you read, prayerfully consider the overriding power of God's faithful love.

His love and mine,

Marilyn Hickey

The Report of Saul's Death

Now it came to pass after the [a]death of Saul, when David had returned from [b]the slaughter of the Amalekites, and David had stayed two days in Ziklag, 2 on the third day, behold, it happened that [a]a man came from Saul's camp [b]with his clothes [1]torn and dust on his head. So it was, when he came to David, that he [c]fell to the ground and prostrated himself.

3 And David said to him, "Where have you come from?"

So he said to him, "I have escaped from the camp of Israel."

4 Then David said to him, [a]"How did the matter go? Please tell me."

And he answered, "The people have fled from the battle, many of the people are fallen and dead, and Saul and [b]Jonathan his son are dead also."

5 So David said to the young man who told him, "How do you know that Saul and Jonathan his son are dead?"

6 Then the young man who told him said, "As I happened by chance *to be* on [a]Mount Gilboa, there was [b]Saul, leaning on his spear; and indeed the chariots and horsemen followed hard after him. 7 Now when he looked behind him, he saw me and called to me. And I answered, 'Here I am.' 8 And he said to me, 'Who *are* you?' So I answered him, 'I *am* an Amalekite.' 9 He said to me again, 'Please stand over me and kill me, for [1]anguish has come upon me, but my life still *remains* in me.' 10 So I stood over him and [a]killed him, because I was sure that he could not live after he had fallen. And I took the crown that *was* on his head and the bracelet that *was* on his arm, and have brought them here to my lord."

11 Therefore David took hold of his own clothes and [a]tore them, and *so did* all the men who *were* with him. 12 And they [a]mourned and wept and [b]fasted until evening for Saul and for Jonathan his son, for the [c]people of the LORD and for the house of Israel, because they had fallen by the sword.

13 Then David said to the young man who told him, "Where *are* you from?"

And he answered, "I *am* the son of an alien, an Amalekite."

14 So David said to him, "How [a]was it you were not [b]afraid to [c]put forth your hand to destroy the LORD's anointed?" 15 Then [a]David called one of the young men and said, "Go near, *and* execute him!" And he struck him so that he died. 16 So David said to him, [a]"Your blood *is* on your own head, for [b]your own mouth has testified against you, saying, 'I have killed the LORD's anointed.' "

The Song of the Bow

17 Then David lamented with this lamentation over Saul and over Jonathan his son, 18 [a]and he told *them* to teach the children of Judah *the Song of* the Bow; indeed *it is* written [b]in the Book [1]of Jasher:

19 "The beauty of Israel is slain on
your high places!
[a]How the mighty have fallen!
20 [a]Tell *it* not in Gath,
Proclaim *it* not in the streets of
[b]Ashkelon—
Lest [c]the daughters of the
Philistines rejoice,
Lest the daughters of [d]the
uncircumcised triumph.

21 "O [a]mountains of Gilboa,
[b]*Let there be* no dew nor rain upon
you,
Nor fields of offerings.
For the shield of the mighty is
[1]cast away there!
The shield of Saul, not [c]anointed
with oil.
22 From the blood of the slain,
From the fat of the mighty,
[a]The bow of Jonathan did not turn
back,
And the sword of Saul did not
return empty.

23 "Saul and Jonathan *were* beloved
and pleasant in their lives,
And in their [a]death they were not
divided;
They were swifter than eagles,
They were [b]stronger than lions.

24 "O daughters of Israel, weep over
Saul,
Who clothed you in scarlet, with
luxury;
Who put ornaments of gold on your
apparel.

25 "How the mighty have fallen in the
midst of the battle!
Jonathan *was* slain in your high
places.
26 I am distressed for you, my
brother Jonathan;

CHAPTER 1
1 a 1 Sam. 31:6 b 1 Sam. 30:1, 17, 26
2 a 2 Sam. 4:10 b 1 Sam. 4:12 c 1 Sam. 25:23 *1 To show grief*
4 a 1 Sam. 4:16; 31:3 b 1 Sam. 31:2
6 a 1 Sam. 31:1 b 1 Sam. 31:2–4
9 *1 agony*
10 a Judg. 9:54
11 a 2 Sam. 3:31; 13:31
12 a 2 Sam. 3:31 b 1 Sam. 31:13 c 2 Sam. 6:21
14 a Num. 12:8 b 1 Sam. 31:4 c 1 Sam. 24:6; 26:9
15 a 2 Sam. 4:10, 12
16 a 1 Kin. 2:32–37 b Luke 19:22
18 a 1 Sam. 31:3 b Josh. 10:13 *1 Lit. of the Upright*
19 a 2 Sam. 1:27
20 a Mic. 1:10 b Jer. 25:20 c Ex. 15:20 d 1 Sam. 31:4
21 a 1 Sam. 31:1 b Ezek. 31:15 c 1 Sam. 10:1 *1 Lit. defiled*
22 a 1 Sam. 18:4
23 a 1 Sam. 31:2–4 b Judg. 14:18

You have been very pleasant to me;
[a]Your love to me was wonderful,
Surpassing the love of women.

27 "How[a] the mighty have fallen,
And the weapons of war perished!"

David Anointed King of Judah

2 It happened after this that David [a]in-
quired of the LORD, saying, "Shall I go
up to any of the cities of Judah?"
And the LORD said to him, "Go up."
David said, "Where shall I go up?"
And He said, "To [b]Hebron."
2So David went up there, and his [a]two
wives also, Ahinoam the Jezreelitess, and
Abigail the widow of Nabal the Carmelite.
3And David brought up [a]the men who
were with him, every man with his household. So they dwelt in the cities of Hebron.
4[a]Then the men of Judah came, and
there they [b]anointed David king over the
house of Judah. And they told David, saying, [c]"The men of Jabesh Gilead *were the*
ones who buried Saul." 5So David sent
messengers to the men of Jabesh Gilead,
and said to them, [a]"You *are* blessed of the
LORD, for you have shown this kindness to
your lord, to Saul, and have buried him.
6And now may [a]the LORD show kindness
and truth to you. I also will repay you this
kindness, because you have done this
thing. 7Now therefore, let your hands be
strengthened, and be valiant; for your
master Saul is dead, and also the house of
Judah has anointed me king over them."

Lord, I pray that You will show kindness and truth to ______. May their hands be strengthened, and may they be valiant.

FROM 2 SAMUEL 2:6, 7

Ishbosheth Made King of Israel

8But [a]Abner the son of Ner, commander of Saul's army, took [1]Ishbosheth the
son of Saul and brought him over to [b]Ma-
hanaim; 9and he made him king over
[a]Gilead, over the [b]Ashurites, over [c]Jezre-
el, over Ephraim, over Benjamin, and over
all Israel. 10Ishbosheth, Saul's son, *was*
forty years old when he began to reign
over Israel, and he reigned two years. Only
the house of Judah followed David. 11And
[a]the [1]time that David was king in Hebron
over the house of Judah was seven years
and six months.

Israel and Judah at War

12Now Abner the son of Ner, and the
servants of Ishbosheth the son of Saul,
went out from Mahanaim to [a]Gibeon.
13And [a]Joab the son of Zeruiah, and the
servants of David, went out and met them
by [b]the pool of Gibeon. So they sat down,
one on one side of the pool and the other
on the other side of the pool. 14Then Abner said to Joab, "Let the young men now
arise and compete before us."
And Joab said, "Let them arise."
15So they arose and went over by number, twelve from Benjamin, *followers* of
Ishbosheth the son of Saul, and twelve
from the servants of David. 16And each
one grasped his opponent by the head and
thrust his sword in his opponent's side; so
they fell down together. Therefore that
place was called [1]the Field of Sharp
Swords, which *is* in Gibeon. 17So there
was a very fierce battle that day, and Abner and the men of Israel were beaten before the servants of David.
18Now the [a]three sons of Zeruiah were
there: Joab and Abishai and Asahel. And
Asahel *was* [b]*as* fleet of foot [c]as a wild gazelle. 19So Asahel pursued Abner, and in
going he did not turn to the right hand or
to the left from following Abner.
20Then Abner looked behind him and
said, "*Are* you Asahel?"
He answered, "I *am*."
21And Abner said to him, "Turn aside to
your right hand or to your left, and lay
hold on one of the young men and take
his armor for yourself." But Asahel would
not turn aside from following him. 22So
Abner said again to Asahel, "Turn aside
from following me. Why should I strike
you to the ground? How then could I face
your brother Joab?" 23However, he refused to turn aside. Therefore Abner
struck him [a]in the stomach with the
blunt end of the spear, so that the spear
came out of his back; and he fell down
there and died on the spot. So it was *that*

26 a 1 Sam. 18:1–4; 19:2; 20:17
27 a 2 Sam. 1:19, 25

CHAPTER 2
1 a Judg. 1:1 b 1 Sam. 30:31
2 a 1 Sam. 25:42, 43; 30:5
3 a 1 Chr. 12:1
4 a 1 Sam. 30:26 b 1 Sam. 16:13 c 1 Sam. 31:11–13
5 a Ruth 2:20; 3:10
6 a 2 Tim. 1:16, 18
8 a 1 Sam. 14:50 b 2 Sam. 17:24 *1 Esh-Baal,* 1 Chr. 8:33; 9:39
9 a Josh. 22:9 b Judg. 1:32 c 1 Sam. 29:1
11 a 2 Sam. 5:5 *1* Lit. *number of days*
12 a Josh. 10:2–12; 18:25
13 a 1 Chr. 2:16; 11:6 b Jer. 41:12
16 *1* Heb. *Helkath Hazzurim*
18 a 1 Chr. 2:16 b 1 Chr. 12:8 c Ps. 18:33
23 a 2 Sam. 3:27; 4:6; 20:10

as many as came to the place where Asahel fell down and died, stood [b]still.
24Joab and Abishai also pursued Abner.
And the sun was going down when they
came to the hill of Ammah, which *is* before Giah by the road to the Wilderness of
Gibeon. 25Now the children of Benjamin
gathered together behind Abner and became [1]a unit, and took their stand on top
of a hill. 26Then Abner called to Joab and
said, "Shall the sword devour forever? Do
you not know that it will be bitter in the
latter end? How long will it be then until
you tell the people to return from pursuing their brethren?"
27And Joab said, "*As* God lives, [1]unless
[a]you had spoken, surely then by morning
all the people would have given up pursuing their brethren." 28So Joab blew a
trumpet; and all the people stood still and
did not pursue Israel anymore, nor did
they fight anymore. 29Then Abner and his
men went on all that night through the
plain, crossed over the Jordan, and went
through all Bithron; and they came to Mahanaim.
30So Joab returned from pursuing Abner. And when he had gathered all the
people together, there were missing of
David's servants nineteen men and Asahel. 31But the servants of David had struck
down, of Benjamin and Abner's men,
three hundred and sixty men who died.
32Then they took up Asahel and buried
him in his father's tomb, which *was in*
[a]Bethlehem. And Joab and his men went
all night, and they came to Hebron at daybreak.

3 Now there was a long [a]war between
the house of Saul and the house of
David. But David grew stronger and stronger, and the house of Saul grew weaker
and weaker.

Sons of David

2Sons were born [a]to David in Hebron:
His firstborn was Amnon [b]by Ahinoam
the Jezreelitess; 3his second, [1]Chileab, by
Abigail the widow of Nabal the Carmelite;
the third, [a]Absalom the son of Maacah,
the daughter of Talmai, king [b]of Geshur;
4the fourth, [a]Adonijah the son of Haggith;
the fifth, Shephatiah the son of Abital;
5and the sixth, Ithream, by David's wife
Eglah. These were born to David in Hebron.

Abner Joins Forces with David

6Now it was so, while there was war between the house of Saul and the house of
David, that Abner was strengthening *his*
hold on the house of Saul.
7And Saul had a concubine, whose
name *was* [a]Rizpah, the daughter of Aiah.
So *Ishbosheth* said to Abner, "Why have
you [b]gone in to my father's concubine?"
8Then Abner became very angry at the
words of Ishbosheth, and said, "*Am* I [a]a
dog's head that belongs to Judah? Today I
show loyalty to the house of Saul your
father, to his brothers, and to his friends,
and have not delivered you into the hand
of David; and you charge me today with a
fault concerning this woman? 9[a]May God
do so to Abner, and more also, if I do not
do for David [b]as the LORD has sworn to
him— 10to transfer the kingdom from the
[1]house of Saul, and set up the throne of
David over Israel and over Judah, [a]from
Dan to Beersheba." 11And he could not
answer Abner another word, because he
feared him.
12Then Abner sent messengers on his
behalf to David, saying, "Whose *is* the
land?" saying *also,* "Make your covenant
with me, and indeed my hand *shall be*
with you to bring all Israel to you."
13And *David* said, "Good, I will make a
covenant with you. But one thing I require of you: [a]you shall not see my face
unless you first bring [b]Michal, Saul's
daughter, when you come to see my face."
14So David sent messengers to [a]Ish-
bosheth, Saul's son, saying, "Give *me* my
wife Michal, whom I betrothed to myself
[b]for a hundred foreskins of the Philistines." 15And Ishbosheth sent and took
her from *her* husband, from [1]Paltiel the
son of Laish. 16Then her husband went
along with her to [a]Bahurim, [1]weeping behind her. So Abner said to him, "Go, return!" And he returned.
17Now Abner had communicated with
the elders of Israel, saying, "In time past
you were seeking for David *to be* king over
you. 18Now then, do *it!* [a]For the LORD has
spoken of David, saying, 'By the hand of
My servant David, [1]I will save My people
Israel from the hand of the Philistines and
the hand of all their enemies.' " 19And Abner also spoke in the hearing of [a]Benja-
min. Then Abner also went to speak in
the hearing of David in Hebron all that

23 [b] 2 Sam. 20:12
25 [1] *one band*
27 [a] 2 Sam. 2:14 [1] *if you had not spoken*
32 [a] 1 Sam. 20:6

CHAPTER 3
1 [a] 1 Kin. 14:30
2 [a] 1 Chr. 3:1–4 [b] 1 Sam. 25:42, 43
3 [a] 2 Sam. 15:1–10 [b] Josh. 13:13 [1] *Daniel,* 1 Chr. 3:1
4 [a] 1 Kin. 1:5
7 [a] 2 Sam. 21:8–11 [b] 2 Sam. 16:21
8 [a] 1 Sam. 24:14
9 [a] 1 Kin. 19:2 [b] 1 Chr. 12:23
10 [a] 1 Sam. 3:20 [1] *family*
13 [a] Gen. 43:3 [b] 1 Sam. 18:20; 19:11; 25:44
14 [a] 2 Sam. 2:10 [b] 1 Sam. 18:25–27
15 [1] *Palti,* 1 Sam. 25:44
16 [a] 2 Sam. 16:5; 19:16 [1] Lit. *going and weeping*
18 [a] 2 Sam. 3:9 [1] So with many Heb. mss., LXX, Syr., Tg.; MT *he*
19 [a] 1 Chr. 12:29

seemed good to Israel and the whole
house of Benjamin.
20 So Abner and twenty men with him
came to David at Hebron. And David made
a feast for Abner and the men who *were*
with him. 21 Then Abner said to David, "I
will arise and go, and [a]gather all Israel to
my lord the king, that they may make a
covenant with you, and that you may
[b]reign over all that your heart desires." So
David sent Abner away, and he went in
peace.

Joab Murders Abner

22 At that moment the servants of David
and Joab came from a raid and brought
much [1]spoil with them. But Abner *was*
not with David in Hebron, for he had sent
him away, and he had gone in peace.
23 When Joab and all the troops that *were*
with him had come, they told Joab, saying,
"Abner the son of Ner came to the
king, and he sent him away, and he has
gone in peace." 24 Then Joab came to the
king and said, "What have you done?
Look, Abner came to you; why *is* it *that*
you sent him away, and he has already
gone? 25 Surely you realize that Abner the
son of Ner came to deceive you, to know
[a]your going out and your coming in, and
to know all that you are doing."
26 And when Joab had gone from David's
presence, he sent messengers after Abner,
who brought him back from the well of
Sirah. But David did not know *it.* 27 Now
when Abner had returned to Hebron, Joab
[a]took him aside in the gate to speak with
him privately, and there [1]stabbed him [b]in
the stomach, so that he died for the blood
of [c]Asahel his brother.
28 Afterward, when David heard *it,* he
said, "My kingdom and I *are* [1]guiltless before
the LORD forever of the blood of Abner
the son of Ner. 29 [a]Let it rest on the
head of Joab and on all his father's house;
and let there never fail to be in the [1]house
of Joab one [b]who has a discharge or is a
leper, who leans on a staff or falls by the
sword, or who lacks bread." 30 So Joab and
Abishai his brother killed Abner, because
he had killed their brother [a]Asahel at Gibeon
in the battle.

David's Mourning for Abner

31 Then David said to Joab and to all the
people who were with him, [a]"Tear your
clothes, [b]gird yourselves with sackcloth,
and mourn for Abner." And King David
followed the coffin. 32 So they buried Abner
in Hebron; and the king lifted up his
voice and wept at the grave of Abner, and
all the people wept. 33 And the king sang *a*
lament over Abner and said:

"Should Abner die as a [a]fool dies?
34 Your hands were not bound
Nor your feet put into fetters;
As a man falls before wicked men,
so you fell."

Then all the people wept over him again.
35 And when all the people came [a]to persuade
David to eat food while it was still
day, David took an oath, saying, [b]"God do
so to me, and more also, if I taste bread or
anything else [c]till the sun goes down!"
36 Now all the people took note *of it,* and
it pleased them, since whatever the king
did pleased all the people. 37 For all the
people and all Israel understood that day
that it had not been the king's *intent* to
kill Abner the son of Ner. 38 Then the king
said to his servants, "Do you not know
that a prince and a great man has fallen
this day in Israel? 39 And I *am* weak today,
though anointed king; and these men, the
sons of Zeruiah, [a]*are* too harsh for me.
[b]The LORD shall repay the evildoer according
to his wickedness."

Ishbosheth Is Murdered

4 When Saul's [1]son heard that Abner
had died in Hebron, [a]he[2] lost heart,
and all Israel was [b]troubled. 2 Now Saul's
son *had* two men *who were* captains of
troops. The name of one *was* Baanah and
the name of the other Rechab, the sons of
Rimmon the Beerothite, of the children of
Benjamin. (For [a]Beeroth also was [1]*part* of
Benjamin, 3 because the Beerothites fled
to [a]Gittaim and have been sojourners
there until this day.)
4 [a]Jonathan, Saul's son, had a son *who*
was lame in *his* feet. He was five years old
when the news about Saul and Jonathan
came [b]from Jezreel; and his nurse took
him up and fled. And it happened, as she
made haste to flee, that he fell and became
lame. His name *was* [c]Mephibosheth.[1]
5 Then the sons of Rimmon the Beerothite,
Rechab and Baanah, set out and
came at about the heat of the day to the
[a]house of Ishbosheth, who was lying on
his bed at noon. 6 And they came there, all
the way into the house, *as though* to get
wheat, and they [1]stabbed him [a]in the
stomach. Then Rechab and Baanah his

21 a 2 Sam. 3:10, 12 b 1 Kin. 11:37
22 1 *booty*
25 a 1 Sam. 29:6
27 a 1 Kin. 2:5 b 2 Sam. 4:6 c 2 Sam. 2:23 1 Lit. *struck*
28 1 *innocent*
29 a 1 Kin. 2:32, 33 b Lev. 15:2 1 *family*
30 a 2 Sam. 2:23
31 a Josh. 7:6 b Gen. 37:34
33 a 2 Sam. 13:12, 13
35 a 2 Sam. 12:17 b Ruth 1:17 c 2 Sam. 1:12
39 a 2 Sam. 19:5–7 b 1 Kin. 2:5, 6, 32–34

CHAPTER 4
1 a Ezra 4:4 b Matt. 2:3 1 Ishbosheth 2 Lit. *his hands dropped*
2 a Josh. 18:25 1 *considered part of*
3 a Neh. 11:33
4 a 2 Sam. 9:3 b 1 Sam. 29:1, 11 c 2 Sam. 9:6 1 *Merib-Baal,* 1 Chr. 8:34; 9:40
5 a 2 Sam. 2:8, 9
6 a 2 Sam. 2:23; 20:10 1 Lit. *struck*

brother escaped. 7For when they came into the house, he was lying on his bed in his bedroom; then they struck him and killed him, beheaded him and took his head, and were all night escaping through the plain. 8And they brought the head of Ishbosheth to David at Hebron, and said to the king, "Here is the head of Ishbosheth, the son of Saul your enemy, [a]who sought your life; and the LORD has avenged my lord the king this day of Saul and his descendants."

9But David answered Rechab and Baanah his brother, the sons of Rimmon the Beerothite, and said to them, "*As* the LORD lives, [a]who has redeemed my life from all adversity, 10when [a]someone told me, saying, 'Look, Saul is dead,' thinking to have brought good news, I arrested him and had him executed in Ziklag—the one who *thought* I would give him a reward for *his* news. 11How much more, when wicked men have killed a righteous person in his own house on his bed? Therefore, shall I not now [a]require his [1]blood at your hand and [2]remove you from the earth?" 12So David [a]commanded his young men, and they executed them, cut off their hands and feet, and hanged *them* by the pool in Hebron. But they took the head of Ishbosheth and buried *it* in the [b]tomb of Abner in Hebron.

David Reigns over All Israel

5 Then all the tribes of Israel [a]came to David at Hebron and spoke, saying, "Indeed [b]we *are* your bone and your flesh. 2Also, in time past, when Saul was king over us, [a]you were the one who led Israel out and brought them in; and the LORD said to you, [b]'You shall shepherd My people Israel, and be ruler over Israel.'" 3[a]Therefore all the elders of Israel came to the king at Hebron, [b]and King David made a covenant with them at Hebron [c]before the LORD. And they anointed David king over Israel. 4David *was* [a]thirty years old when he began to reign, *and* [b]he reigned forty years. 5In Hebron he reigned over Judah [a]seven years and six months, and in Jerusalem he reigned thirty-three years over all Israel and Judah.

The Conquest of Jerusalem

6[a]And the king and his men went to Jerusalem against [b]the Jebusites, the inhabitants of the land, who spoke to David, saying, "You shall not come in here; but the blind and the lame will repel you," thinking, "David cannot come in here." 7Nevertheless David took the stronghold of Zion [a](that *is,* the City of David).

8Now David said on that day, "Whoever climbs up by way of the water shaft and defeats the Jebusites (the lame and the blind, *who are* hated by David's soul), [a]*he shall be chief and captain*." Therefore they say, "The blind and the lame shall not come into the house."

9Then David dwelt in the stronghold, and called it [a]the City of David. And David built all around from [1]the Millo and inward. 10So David went on and became great, and [a]the LORD God of hosts *was* with [b]him.

11Then [a]Hiram [b]king of Tyre sent messengers to David, and cedar trees, and carpenters and masons. And they built David a house. 12So David knew that the LORD had established him as king over Israel, and that He had [a]exalted His kingdom [b]for the sake of His people Israel.

13And [a]David took more concubines and wives from Jerusalem, after he had come from Hebron. Also more sons and daughters were born to David. 14Now [a]these *are* the names of those who were born to him in Jerusalem: [1]Shammua, Shobab, Nathan, [b]Solomon, 15Ibhar, [1]Elishua, Nepheg, Japhia, 16Elishama, Eliada, and Eliphelet.

The Philistines Defeated

17[a]Now when the Philistines heard that they had anointed David king over Israel, all the Philistines went up to search for David. And David heard *of it* [b]and went down to the stronghold. 18The Philistines also went and deployed themselves in [a]the Valley of Rephaim. 19So David [a]inquired of the LORD, saying, "Shall I go up against the Philistines? Will You deliver them into my hand?"

And the LORD said to David, "Go up, for I will doubtless deliver the Philistines into your hand."

20So David went to [a]Baal Perazim, and David defeated them there; and he said, "The LORD has broken through my enemies before me, like a breakthrough of water." Therefore he called the name of that place [1]Baal Perazim. 21And they left their [1]images there, and David and his men [a]carried them away.

---

8 a 1 Sam. 19:2, 10, 11; 23:15; 25:29
9 a Gen. 48:16
10 a 2 Sam. 1:2–16
11 a [Gen. 9:5, 6] *1 Or bloodshed* *2 Lit. consume you*
12 a 2 Sam. 1:15 b 2 Sam. 3:32

CHAPTER 5
1 a 1 Chr. 11:1–3 b 2 Sam. 19:12, 13
2 a 1 Sam. 18:5, 13, 16 b 1 Sam. 16:1
3 a 2 Sam. 3:17 b 2 Kin. 11:17 c 1 Sam. 23:18
4 a Gen. 41:46 b 1 Chr. 26:31; 29:27
5 a 2 Sam. 2:11
6 a Judg. 1:21 b Josh. 15:63
7 a 1 Kin. 2:10; 8:1; 9:24
8 a 1 Chr. 11:6–9
9 a 2 Sam. 5:7 *1 Lit. The Landfill*
10 a 1 Sam. 17:45 b 1 Sam. 18:12, 28
11 a 1 Kin. 5:1–18 b 1 Chr. 14:1
12 a Num. 24:7 b Is. 45:4
13 a [Deut. 17:17]
14 a 1 Chr. 3:5–8 b 2 Sam. 12:24 *1 Shimea,* 1 Chr. 3:5
15 *1 Elishama,* 1 Chr. 3:6
17 a 1 Chr. 11:16 b 2 Sam. 23:14
18 a 1 Chr. 11:15
19 a 1 Sam. 23:2
20 a Is. 28:21 *1 Lit. Master of Breakthroughs*
21 a Deut. 7:5, 25 *1 idols*

[22][a]Then the Philistines went up once
again and deployed themselves in the Valley of Rephaim. [23]Therefore [a]David inquired of the LORD, and He said, "You
shall not go up; circle around behind
them, and come upon them in front of the
mulberry trees. [24]And it shall be, when
you [a]hear the sound of marching in the
tops of the mulberry trees, then you shall
advance quickly. For then [b]the LORD will
go out before you to strike the camp of the
Philistines." [25]And David did so, as the
LORD commanded him; and he drove back
the Philistines from [a]Geba[1] as far as
[b]Gezer.

The Ark Brought to Jerusalem

6 Again David gathered all *the* choice
men of Israel, thirty thousand. [2]And
[a]David arose and went with all the people
who *were* with him from [1]Baale Judah to
bring up from there the ark of God, whose
name is called [2]by the Name, the LORD of
Hosts, [b]who dwells *between* the cherubim. [3]So they set the ark of God on a new
cart, and brought it out of the house of
Abinadab, which *was* on [a]the hill; and Uzzah and Ahio, the sons of Abinadab, drove
the new [1]cart. [4]And they brought it out of
[a]the house of Abinadab, which *was* on the
hill, accompanying the ark of God; and
Ahio went before the ark. [5]Then David and
all the house of Israel [a]played *music* before the LORD on all kinds of *instruments*
of fir wood, on harps, on stringed instruments, on tambourines, on sistrums, and
on cymbals.

[6]And when they came to [a]Nachon's
threshing floor, Uzzah put out *his* [b]*hand*
to the ark of God and [1]took hold of it, for
the oxen stumbled. [7]Then the anger of the
LORD was aroused against Uzzah, and God
struck him there for *his* [1]error; and he
died there by the ark of God. [8]And David
became angry because of the LORD's outbreak against Uzzah; and he called the
name of the place [1]Perez Uzzah to this
day.

[9][a]David was afraid of the LORD that day;
and he said, "How can the ark of the LORD
come to me?" [10]So David would not move
the ark of the LORD with him into the
[a]City of David; but David took it aside into
the house of Obed-Edom the [b]Gittite.
[11][a]The ark of the LORD remained in the
house of Obed-Edom the Gittite three
months. And the LORD [b]blessed Obed-
Edom and all his household.

[12]Now it was told King David, saying,
"The LORD has blessed the house of Obed-
Edom and all that *belongs* to him, because of the ark of God." [a]So David went
and brought up the ark of God from the
house of Obed-Edom to the City of David
with gladness. [13]And so it was, when
[a]those bearing the ark of the LORD had
gone six paces, that he sacrificed [b]oxen
and fatted sheep. [14]Then David [a]danced[1]
before the LORD with all *his* might; and
David *was* wearing [b]a linen ephod. [15][a]So
David and all the house of Israel brought
up the ark of the LORD with shouting and
with the sound of the trumpet.

[16]Now as the ark of the LORD came
into the City of David, [a]Michal, Saul's
daughter, looked through a window and
saw King David leaping and whirling before the LORD; and she despised him in
her heart. [17]So [a]they brought the ark of
the LORD, and set it in [b]its place in the
midst of the tabernacle that David had
erected for it. Then David [c]offered burnt
offerings and peace offerings before the
LORD. [18]And when David had finished offering burnt offerings and peace offerings,
[a]he blessed the people in the name of the
LORD of hosts. [19][a]Then he distributed
among all the people, among the whole
multitude of Israel, both the women and
the men, to everyone a loaf of bread, a
piece *of meat,* and a cake of raisins. So
all the people departed, everyone to his
house.

[20][a]Then David returned to bless his
household. And Michal the daughter of
Saul came out to meet David, and said,
"How glorious was the king of Israel today, [b]uncovering himself today in the eyes
of the maids of his servants, as one of the
[c]base fellows [1]shamelessly uncovers himself!"

[21]So David said to Michal, "*It was* before the LORD, [a]who chose me instead of
your father and all his house, to appoint
me ruler over the [b]people of the LORD,
over Israel. Therefore I will play *music* before the LORD. [22]And I will be even more
undignified than this, and will be humble
in my own sight. But as for the maidservants of whom you have spoken, by
them I will be held in honor."

22 a 1 Chr. 14:13
23 a 2 Sam. 5:19
24 a 1 Chr. 14:15 b Judg. 4:14
25 a 1 Chr. 14:16 b Josh. 16:10 *1* So with MT, Tg., Vg.; LXX *Gibeon*

CHAPTER 6
2 a 1 Chr. 13:5, 6 b Ps. 80:1 *1 Baalah, Kirjath Jearim,* Josh. 15:9; 1 Chr. 13:6 *2* LXX, Tg., Vg. omit *by the Name;* many Heb. mss., Syr. *there*
3 a 1 Sam. 26:1 *1* LXX adds *with the ark*
4 a 1 Sam. 7:1
5 a 1 Sam. 18:6, 7
6 a 1 Chr. 13:9 b Num. 4:15, 19, 20 *1 held it*
7 *1* Or *irreverence*
8 *1* Lit. *Outburst Against Uzzah*
9 a Ps. 119:120
10 a 2 Sam. 5:7 b 1 Chr. 13:13; 26:4–8
11 a 1 Chr. 13:14 b Gen. 30:27; 39:5
12 a 1 Chr. 15:25—16:3
13 a Josh. 3:3 b 1 Kin. 8:5
14 a Ps. 30:11; 149:3 b 1 Sam. 2:18, 28 *1 whirled about*
15 a 1 Chr. 15:28
16 a 2 Sam. 3:14
17 a 1 Chr. 16:1 b 1 Chr. 15:1 c 1 Kin. 8:5, 62, 63
18 a 1 Kin. 8:14, 15, 55
19 a 1 Chr. 16:3
20 a Ps. 30:title b 2 Sam. 6:14, 16 c Judg. 9:4 *1 openly*
21 a 1 Sam. 13:14; 15:28 b 2 Kin. 11:17

2 Samuel 6:16

Dear Woman of Destiny,

The psalmist exhorts us: "Let them praise His name with the dance; let them sing praises to Him with the timbrel and harp" (Ps. 149:3). Music and dance are important in the praises of His people. When we excuse ourselves from dancing by being overly self-conscious or inhibited, we miss out on one of the most powerful expressions of worship to God.

It is interesting that we have no problem releasing the excitement and tensions of football or other sports with physical demonstrations: shouting, clapping, or leaping up and down. The benefit from releasing all of our heart, mind, and strength in worship and praise of the One who created us is infinitely more important and exciting. And it has eternal significance.

Music and dance were created by God. Dancing before the Lord is simply an outward or physical expression of the inner relationship or experience with the Lord. It is interesting that in the hundreds of references in Scripture commanding us to rejoice, most of the original Hebrew or Greek words refer to physical movements: to leap, jump, or spin. We leap, dance, and spin for joy in His presence, not because of circumstantial or emotional stimulus, but because of who He is. As we choose to break forth in this expression of praise, we will find ourselves breaking out of our "natural" resistance to physical expression, as well as fear, anger, and other unpleasant deterrents to our joy.

King David had a heart of worship. He spent many of his days on the hillsides with only his sheep and his harp, singing praises to his God. He chose to praise and worship even in times of great distress or fear. He brought the ark of the Lord into a new dwelling place where he instituted Levites to praise and worship the Lord twenty-four hours a day. He was not afraid to dance out this exuberant and joyous praise publicly, which was not exactly kingly behavior in those days.

"Be glad in the LORD and rejoice, you righteous; and shout for joy, all you upright in heart!" (Ps. 32:11). The Hebrew word *gul* is translated here as "rejoice." It literally means, "to spin around under the influence of violent emotion." *Gul* is the same word translated "rejoice" when we read about the Lord's expressive demonstration over us: "The LORD your God in your midst, the Mighty One, will save; He will rejoice over you with gladness, He will quiet you with His love, He will *rejoice* over you with singing" (Zeph. 3:17, italics mine).

God Himself, the King of All Kings, spins around us in exultant love. He loved us first. How much more then should we exult before Him in extravagant and unmeasured love for His boundless mercy, love, and grace! Woman of Destiny, get alone in your time with your Maker, and express your love and adoration of Him with dances, with shouts of joy, and with singing. That very outpouring will bring Him closer to you than your own heartbeat, as He inhabits the praises of His people (see Ps. 22:3).

Dance before Him as David did!

Lora Allison

23 Therefore Michal the daughter of
Saul had no children [a]to the day of her
death.

God's Covenant with David

7 Now it came to pass [a]when the king
was dwelling in his house, and the
LORD had given him rest from all his enemies all around, 2 that the king said to Nathan the prophet, "See now, I dwell in [a]a
house of cedar, [b]but the ark of God dwells
inside tent [c]curtains."
3 Then Nathan said to the king, "Go, do
all that *is* in your [a]heart, for the LORD *is*
with you."
4 But it happened that night that the
word of the LORD came to Nathan, saying,
5 "Go and tell My servant David, 'Thus says
the LORD: [a]"Would you build a house for
Me to dwell in? 6 For I have not dwelt in a
house [a]since the time that I brought the
children of Israel up from Egypt, even to
this day, but have moved about in [b]a tent
and in a tabernacle. 7 Wherever I have
[a]moved about with all the children of Israel, have I ever spoken a word to anyone
from the tribes of Israel, whom I commanded [b]to shepherd My people Israel,
saying, 'Why have you not built Me a
house of cedar?' " ' 8 Now therefore, thus
shall you say to My servant David, 'Thus
says the LORD of hosts: [a]"I took you from
the sheepfold, from following the sheep,
to be ruler over My people, over Israel.
9 And [a]I have been with you wherever you
have gone, [b]and have [1]cut off all your enemies from before you, and have made you
a great name, like the name of the great
men who *are* on the earth. 10 Moreover I
will appoint a place for My people Israel,
and will [a]plant them, that they may dwell
in a place of their own and move no more;
[b]nor shall the sons of wickedness oppress
them anymore, as previously, 11 [a]since the
time that I commanded judges *to be* over
My people Israel, and have caused you to
rest from all your enemies. Also the LORD
[1]tells you [b]that He will make you a
[2]house.
12 [a]"When your days are fulfilled and
you [b]rest with your fathers, [c]I will set up
your seed after you, who will come from
your body, and I will establish his kingdom. 13 [a]He shall build a house for My
name, and I will [b]establish the throne of
his kingdom forever. 14 [a]I will be his Father, and he shall be [b]My son. If he commits iniquity, I will chasten him with the
rod of men and with the [1]blows of the
sons of men. 15 But My mercy shall not
depart from him, [a]as I took *it* from Saul,
whom I removed from before you. 16 And
[a]your house and your kingdom shall be
established forever before [1]you. Your
throne shall be established forever." ' "
17 According to all these words and according to all this vision, so Nathan spoke
to David.

David's Thanksgiving to God

18 Then King David went in and sat before the LORD; and he said: [a]"Who *am* I,
O Lord GOD? And what is my house, that
You have brought me this far? 19 And yet
this was a small thing in Your sight,
O Lord GOD; and You have also spoken of
Your servant's house for a great while to
come. [a]*Is* this the manner of man, O Lord
GOD? 20 Now what more can David say to
You? For You, Lord GOD, [a]know Your servant. 21 For Your word's sake, and according to Your own heart, You have done all
these great things, to make Your servant
know *them.* 22 Therefore [a]You are great,
[1]O Lord GOD. For [b]*there is* none like You,
nor *is there any* God besides You, according to all that we have heard with our
[c]ears. 23 And who *is* like Your people, like
Israel, [a]the one nation on the earth whom
God went to redeem for Himself as a people, to make for Himself a name—and to
do for Yourself great and awesome deeds
for Your land—before [b]Your people
whom You redeemed for Yourself from
Egypt, the nations, and their gods? 24 For
[a]You have made Your people Israel Your
very own people forever; [b]and You, LORD,
have become their God.

Lord God, show ____ that You are great. For there is none like You, nor is there any God besides You.

FROM 2 SAMUEL 7:22

25 "Now, O LORD God, the word which
You have spoken concerning Your servant
and concerning his house, establish *it* forever and do as You have said. 26 So let Your
name be magnified forever, saying, 'The

23 a Is. 22:14

CHAPTER 7

1 a 1 Chr. 17:1–27
2 a 2 Sam. 5:11 b Acts 7:46 c Ex. 26:1
3 a 1 Kin. 8:17, 18
5 a 1 Kin. 5:3, 4; 8:19
6 a 1 Kin. 8:16 b Ex. 40:18, 34
7 a Lev. 26:11, 12 b 2 Sam. 5:2
8 a 1 Sam. 16:11, 12
9 a 2 Sam. 5:10 b 1 Sam. 31:6 *1 destroyed*
10 a Ps. 44:2; 80:8 b Ps. 89:22, 23
11 a Judg. 2:14–16 b 2 Sam. 7:27 *1 declares to you* 2 Royal dynasty
12 a 1 Kin. 2:1 b Deut. 31:16 c Ps. 132:11
13 a 1 Kin. 5:5; 8:19 b [Is. 9:7; 49:8]
14 a [Heb. 1:5] b [Ps. 2:7; 89:26, 27, 30] *1 strokes*
15 a 1 Sam. 15:23, 28; 16:14
16 a 2 Sam. 7:13 1 LXX *Me*
18 a Ex. 3:11
19 a [Is. 55:8, 9]
20 a John 21:17
22 a Deut. 10:17 b Ex. 15:11 c Ex. 10:2 1 Tg., Syr. *O LORD God*
23 a Ps. 147:20 b Deut. 9:26; 33:29
24 a [Deut. 26:18] b Ps. 48:14

LORD of hosts *is* the God over Israel.' And
let the house of Your servant David be established before You. 27For You, O LORD
of hosts, God of Israel, have revealed
this to Your servant, saying, 'I will build
you a house.' Therefore Your servant has
found it in his heart to pray this prayer
to You.

> *Prayer unites with God's purposes and lays itself out to secure those purposes.*
>
> E. M. BOUNDS

28"And now, O Lord GOD, You are God,
and [a]Your words are true, and You have
promised this goodness to Your servant.
29Now therefore, let it please You to bless
the house of Your servant, that it may
continue before You forever; for You,
O Lord GOD, have spoken *it,* and with
Your blessing let the house of Your servant be blessed [a]forever."

David's Further Conquests

8 After this it came to pass that David
[1]attacked the Philistines and subdued
them. And David took [2]Metheg Ammah
from the hand of the Philistines.
2Then [a]he defeated Moab. Forcing
them down to the ground, he measured
them off with a line. With two lines he
measured off those to be put to death, and
with one full line those to be kept alive. So
the Moabites became David's [b]servants,
and [c]brought tribute.
3David also defeated Hadadezer the son
of Rehob, king of [a]Zobah, as he went to
recover [b]his territory at the River Euphrates. 4David took from him one thousand
chariots, [1]seven hundred horsemen, and
twenty thousand foot soldiers. Also David
[a]hamstrung all the chariot horses, except
that he spared *enough* of them for one
hundred chariots.
5[a]When the Syrians of Damascus came
to help Hadadezer king of Zobah, David
killed twenty-two thousand of the Syrians. 6Then David put garrisons in Syria of
Damascus; and the Syrians became David's servants, *and* brought tribute. So
[a]the LORD preserved David wherever he
went. 7And David took [a]the shields of gold
that had belonged to the servants of Hadadezer, and brought them to Jerusalem.
8Also from [1]Betah and from [a]Berothai,[2]
cities of Hadadezer, King David took a
large amount of bronze.
9When [1]Toi king of [a]Hamath heard
that David had defeated all the army of
Hadadezer, 10then Toi sent [1]Joram his son
to King David, to [2]greet him and bless
him, because he had fought against Hadadezer and defeated him (for Hadadezer
had been at war with Toi); and *Joram*
brought with him articles of silver, articles of gold, and articles of bronze. 11King
David also [a]dedicated these to the LORD,
along with the silver and gold that he had
dedicated from all the nations which he
had subdued— 12from [1]Syria, from Moab,
from the people of Ammon, from the
[a]Philistines, from Amalek, and from the
spoil of Hadadezer the son of Rehob, king
of Zobah.
13And David made *himself* a [a]name
when he returned from killing [b]eighteen
thousand [1]Syrians in [c]the Valley of Salt.
14He also put garrisons in Edom;
throughout all Edom he put garrisons,
and [a]all the Edomites became David's servants. And the LORD preserved David
wherever he went.

David's Administration

15So David reigned over all Israel; and
David administered judgment and justice
to all his people. 16[a]Joab the son of Zeruiah *was* over the army; [b]Jehoshaphat the
son of Ahilud *was* recorder; 17[a]Zadok the
son of Ahitub and Ahimelech the son of
Abiathar *were* the priests; [1]Seraiah *was*
the [2]scribe; 18[a]Benaiah the son of Jehoiada *was over* both the [b]Cherethites and the
Pelethites; and David's sons were [1]chief
ministers.

David's Kindness to Mephibosheth

9 Now David said, "Is there still anyone
who is left of the house of Saul, that
I may [a]show him [1]kindness for Jonathan's
sake?"
2And *there was* a servant of the house

---

28 [a]John 17:17
29 [a]2 Sam. 22:51

CHAPTER 8
1 [1]Lit. *struck* [2]Lit. *The Bridle of the Mother City*
2 [a]Num. 24:17 [b]2 Sam. 12:31 [c]1 Kin. 4:21
3 [a]1 Sam. 14:47 [b]2 Sam. 10:15–19
4 [a]Josh. 11:6, 9 [1]*seven thousand,* 1 Chr. 18:4
5 [a]1 Kin. 11:23–25
6 [a]2 Sam. 7:9; 8:14
7 [a]1 Kin. 10:16
8 [a]Ezek. 47:16 [1]*Tibhath,* 1 Chr. 18:8 [2]*Chun,* 1 Chr. 18:8
9 [a]1 Kin. 8:65 [1]*Tou,* 1 Chr. 18:9
10 [1]*Hadoram,* 1 Chr. 18:10 [2]Lit. *ask him of his welfare*
11 [a]1 Kin. 7:51
12 [a]2 Sam. 5:17–25 [1]LXX, Syr., Heb. mss. *Edom*
13 [a]2 Sam. 7:9 [b]2 Kin. 14:7 [c]1 Chr. 18:12 [1]LXX, Syr., Heb. mss. *Edomites* and 1 Chr. 18:12
14 [a]Gen. 27:29, 37–40
16 [a]2 Sam. 19:13; 20:23 [b]1 Kin. 4:3
17 [a]1 Chr. 6:4–8; 24:3 [1]*Shavsha,* 1 Chr. 18:16 [2]*secretary*
18 [a]1 Chr. 18:17 [b]1 Sam. 30:14 [1]Lit. *priests*

CHAPTER 9
1 [a]1 Sam. 18:3; 20:14–16 [1]*covenant faithfulness*

of Saul whose name *was* [a]Ziba. So when
they had called him to David, the king
said to him, "*Are* you Ziba?"
He said, "At your service!"
3Then the king said, "*Is* there not still
someone of the house of Saul, to whom I
may show [a]the kindness of God?"
And Ziba said to the king, "There is still
a son of Jonathan *who is* [b]lame in *his*
feet."
4So the king said to him, "Where
is he?"
And Ziba said to the king, "Indeed he *is*
in the house of [a]Machir the son of Ammiel, in Lo Debar."
5Then King David sent and brought
him out of the house of Machir the son of
Ammiel, from Lo Debar.
6Now when [a]Mephibosheth[1] the son of
Jonathan, the son of Saul, had come to
David, he fell on his face and prostrated
himself. Then David said, "Mephibosheth?"
And he answered, "Here is your servant!"
7So David said to him, "Do not fear, for
I will surely show you kindness for Jonathan your father's sake, and will restore to
you all the land of Saul your grandfather;
and you shall eat bread at my table continually."
8Then he bowed himself, and said,
"What *is* your servant, that you should
look upon such [a]a dead dog as I?"
9And the king called to Ziba, Saul's servant, and said to him, [a]"I have given to
your master's son all that belonged to
Saul and to all his house. 10You therefore,
and your sons and your servants, shall
work the land for him, and you shall bring
in *the harvest,* that your master's son may
have food to eat. But Mephibosheth your
master's son [a]shall eat bread at my table
always." Now Ziba had [b]fifteen sons and
twenty servants.
11Then Ziba said to the king, "According to all that my lord the king has commanded his servant, so will your
servant do."
"As for Mephibosheth," *said the king,*
"he shall eat at [1]my table like one of the
king's sons." 12Mephibosheth had a young
son [a]whose name *was* Micha. And all who
dwelt in the house of Ziba *were* servants
of Mephibosheth. 13So Mephibosheth
dwelt in Jerusalem, [a]for he ate continually at the king's table. And he [b]was lame in
both his feet.

The Ammonites and Syrians Defeated

10 It happened after this that the
[a]king of the people of Ammon died,
and Hanun his son reigned in his place.
2Then David said, "I will show [a]kindness
to Hanun the son of [b]Nahash, as his father
showed kindness to me."
So David sent by the hand of his servants to comfort him concerning his father. And David's servants came into the
land of the people of Ammon. 3And the
princes of the people of Ammon said to
Hanun their lord, "Do you think that David really honors your father because he
has sent comforters to you? Has David not
rather sent his servants to you to search
the city, to spy it out, and to overthrow it?"
4Therefore Hanun took David's servants, shaved off half of their beards, cut
off their garments in the middle, [a]at their
buttocks, and sent them away. 5When
they told David, he sent to meet them,
because the men were greatly [1]ashamed.
And the king said, "Wait at Jericho until
your beards have grown, and *then* return."
6When the people of Ammon saw that
they [a]had made themselves repulsive to
David, the people of Ammon sent and
hired [b]the Syrians of [c]Beth Rehob and the
Syrians of Zoba, twenty thousand foot soldiers; and from the king of [d]Maacah one
thousand men, and from [e]Ish-Tob twelve
thousand men. 7Now when David heard *of
it,* he sent Joab and all the army of [a]the
mighty men. 8Then the people of Ammon
came out and put themselves in battle array at the entrance of the gate. And [a]the
Syrians of Zoba, Beth Rehob, Ish-Tob,
and Maacah *were* by themselves in the
field.
9When Joab saw that the battle line was
against him before and behind, he chose
some of Israel's best and put *them* in battle array against the Syrians. 10And the
rest of the people he put under the command of [a]Abishai his brother, that he
might set *them* in battle array against the
people of Ammon. 11Then he said, "If the
Syrians are too strong for me, then you
shall help me; but if the people of Ammon
are too strong for you, then I will come
and help you. 12[a]Be of good courage, and
let us [b]be strong for our people and for

---

2 [a] 2 Sam. 16:1–4; 19:17, 29
3 [a] 1 Sam. 20:14 [b] 2 Sam. 4:4
4 [a] 2 Sam. 17:27–29
6 [a] 2 Sam. 16:4; 19:24–30 [1] Or *Merib-Baal*
8 [a] 2 Sam. 16:9
9 [a] 2 Sam. 16:4; 19:29
10 [a] 2 Sam. 9:7, 11, 13; 19:28 [b] 2 Sam. 19:17
11 [1] LXX *David's table*
12 [a] 1 Chr. 8:34
13 [a] 2 Sam. 9:7, 10, 11 [b] 2 Sam. 9:3

CHAPTER 10
1 [a] 1 Chr. 19:1
2 [a] 2 Sam. 9:1 [b] 1 Sam. 11:1
4 [a] Is. 20:4; 47:2
5 [1] *humiliated*
6 [a] Gen. 34:30 [b] 2 Sam. 8:3, 5 [c] Judg. 18:28 [d] Deut. 3:14 [e] Judg. 11:3, 5
7 [a] 2 Sam. 23:8
8 [a] 2 Sam. 10:6
10 [a] 2 Sam. 3:30
12 [a] Deut. 31:6 [b] 1 Cor. 16:13

the cities of our God. And may [c]the LORD
do *what is* good in His sight."
13So Joab and the people who *were* with
him drew near for the battle against the
Syrians, and they fled before him. 14When
the people of Ammon saw that the Syrians
were fleeing, they also fled before Abishai,
and entered the city. So Joab returned
from the people of Ammon and went to
[a]Jerusalem.
15When the Syrians saw that they had
been defeated by Israel, they gathered together. 16Then [1]Hadadezer sent and
brought out the Syrians who *were* beyond
[2]the River, and they came to Helam. And
[3]Shobach the commander of Hadadezer's
army *went* before them. 17When it was
told David, he gathered all Israel, crossed
over the Jordan, and came to Helam. And
the Syrians set themselves in battle array
against David and fought with him.
18Then the Syrians fled before Israel; and
David killed seven hundred charioteers
and forty thousand [a]horsemen of the Syrians, and struck Shobach the commander
of their army, who died there. 19And when
all the kings *who were* servants to [1]Had-
adezer saw that they were defeated by Israel, they made peace with Israel and
[a]served them. So the Syrians were afraid
to help the people of Ammon anymore.

David, Bathsheba, and Uriah

11 It happened in the spring of the
year, at the [a]time when kings go
out *to battle,* that [b]David sent Joab and
his servants with him, and all Israel; and
they destroyed the people of Ammon and
besieged [c]Rabbah. But David remained at
Jerusalem.
2Then it happened one evening that David arose from his bed [a]and walked on the
roof of the king's house. And from the
roof he [b]saw a woman bathing, and the
woman *was* very beautiful to behold. 3So
David sent and inquired about the woman. And *someone* said, "*Is* this not [1]Bath-
sheba, the daughter of [2]Eliam, the wife
[a]of Uriah the [b]Hittite?" 4Then David sent
messengers, and took her; and she came
to him, and [a]he lay with her, for she was
[b]cleansed from her impurity; and she returned to her house. 5And the woman
conceived; so she sent and told David, and
said, "I *am* with child."
6Then David sent to Joab, *saying,* "Send
me Uriah the Hittite." And Joab sent Uriah
to David. 7When Uriah had come to him,
David asked how Joab was doing, and how
the people were doing, and how the war
prospered. 8And David said to Uriah, "Go
down to your house and [a]wash your feet."
So Uriah departed from the king's house,
and a gift *of food* from the king followed
him. 9But Uriah slept at the [a]door of the
king's house with all the servants of his
lord, and did not go down to his house.
10So when they told David, saying, "Uriah
did not go down to his house," David said
to Uriah, "Did you not come from a journey? Why did you not go down to your
house?"
11And Uriah said to David, [a]"The ark
and Israel and Judah are dwelling in tents,
and [b]my lord Joab and the servants of my
lord are encamped in the open fields.
Shall I then go to my house to eat and
drink, and to lie with my wife? *As* you live,
and *as* your soul lives, I will not do this
thing."
12Then David said to Uriah, "Wait here
today also, and tomorrow I will let you
depart." So Uriah remained in Jerusalem
that day and the next. 13Now when David
called him, he ate and drank before him;
and he made him [a]drunk. And at evening
he went out to lie on his bed [b]with the
servants of his lord, but he did not go
down to his house.
14In the morning it happened that David [a]wrote a letter to Joab and sent *it* by
the hand of Uriah. 15And he wrote in the
letter, saying, "Set Uriah in the forefront
of the [1]hottest battle, and retreat from
him, that he may [a]be struck down and
die." 16So it was, while Joab besieged the
city, that he assigned Uriah to a place
where he knew there *were* valiant men.
17Then the men of the city came out and
fought with Joab. And *some* of the people
of the servants of David fell; and Uriah the
Hittite died also.
18Then Joab sent and told David all the
things concerning the war, 19and charged
the messenger, saying, "When you have
finished telling the matters of the war to
the king, 20if it happens that the king's
wrath rises, and he says to you: 'Why did
you approach so near to the city when you
fought? Did you not know that they would
shoot from the wall? 21Who struck [a]Abim-
elech the son of [1]Jerubbesheth? Was it not
a woman who cast a piece of a millstone
on him from the wall, so that he died in
Thebez? Why did you go near the wall?'—

12 [c]1 Sam. 3:18
14 [a]2 Sam. 11:1
16 [1] Heb. *Hadarezer* [2] The Euphrates [3] *Shophach,* 1 Chr. 19:16
18 [a]1 Chr. 19:18
19 [a]2 Sam. 8:6 [1] Heb. *Hadarezer*

CHAPTER 11
1 [a]1 Kin. 20:22–26 [b]1 Chr. 20:1 [c]2 Sam. 12:26
2 [a]Deut. 22:8 [b]Gen. 34:2
3 [a]2 Sam. 23:39 [b]1 Sam. 26:6 [1] *Bathshua,* 1 Chr. 3:5 [2] *Ammiel,* 1 Chr. 3:5
4 [a][James 1:14, 15] [b]Lev. 15:19, 28
8 [a]Gen. 18:4; 19:2
9 [a]1 Kin. 14:27, 28
11 [a]2 Sam. 7:2, 6 [b]2 Sam. 20:6–22
13 [a]Gen. 19:33, 35 [b]2 Sam. 11:9
14 [a]1 Kin. 21:8, 9
15 [a]2 Sam. 12:9 [1] *fiercest*
21 [a]Judg. 9:50–54 [1] *Jerubbaal* (Gideon), Judg. 6:32ff.

then you shall say, 'Your servant Uriah the
Hittite is dead also.' "
22So the messenger went, and came and
told David all that Joab had sent by him.
23And the messenger said to David, "Surely the men prevailed against us and came
out to us in the field; then we drove them
back as far as the entrance of the gate.
24The archers shot from the wall at your
servants; and *some* of the king's servants
are dead, and your servant Uriah the Hittite is dead also."
25Then David said to the messenger,
"Thus you shall say to Joab: 'Do not let
this thing [1]displease you, for the sword
devours one as well as another. Strength-
en your attack against the city, and overthrow it.' So encourage him."
26When the wife of Uriah heard that
Uriah her husband was dead, she
mourned for her husband. 27And when
her mourning was over, David sent and
brought her to his house, and she [a]be-
came his wife and bore him a son. But the
thing that David had done [b]displeased[1]
the LORD.

Nathan's Parable and David's Confession

12 Then the LORD sent Nathan to David. And [a]he came to him, and
[b]said to him: "There were two men in one
city, one rich and the other poor. 2The
rich *man* had exceedingly many flocks
and herds. 3But the poor *man* had nothing, except one little ewe lamb which he
had bought and nourished; and it grew up
together with him and with his children.
It ate of his own food and drank from his
own cup and lay in his bosom; and it was
like a daughter to him. 4And a traveler
came to the rich man, who refused to take
from his own flock and from his own herd
to prepare one for the wayfaring man who
had come to him; but he took the poor
man's lamb and prepared it for the man
who had come to him."
5So David's anger was greatly aroused
against the man, and he said to Nathan,
"*As* the LORD lives, the man who has done
this [1]shall surely die! 6And he shall restore [a]fourfold for the lamb, because he
did this thing and because he had no
pity."
7Then Nathan said to David, "You *are*
the man! Thus says the LORD God of Israel: 'I [a]anointed you king over Israel, and
I delivered you from the hand of Saul. 8I
gave you your master's house and your
master's wives into your keeping, and
gave you the house of Israel and Judah.
And if *that had been* too little, I also
would have given you much more! 9[a]Why
have you [b]despised the commandment of
the LORD, to do evil in His sight? [c]You
have killed Uriah the Hittite with the
sword; you have taken his wife *to be* your
wife, and have killed him with the sword
of the people of Ammon. 10Now therefore,
[a]the sword shall never depart from your
house, because you have despised Me, and
have taken the wife of Uriah the Hittite to
be your wife.' 11Thus says the LORD: 'Behold, I will raise up adversity against you
from your own house; and I will [a]take
your wives before your eyes and give *them*
to your neighbor, and he shall lie with
your wives in the sight of this sun. 12For
you did *it* secretly, [a]but I will do this thing
before all Israel, before the sun.' "
13[a]So David said to Nathan, [b]"I have
sinned against the LORD."
And Nathan said to David, "The LORD
also has [c]put away your sin; you shall not
die. 14However, because by this deed you
have given great occasion to the enemies
of the LORD [a]to blaspheme, the child also
who is born to you shall surely die."
15Then Nathan departed to his house.

The Death of David's Son

And the [a]LORD struck the child that
Uriah's wife bore to David, and it became
ill. 16David therefore pleaded with God for
the child, and David fasted and went in
and [a]lay all night on the ground. 17So the
elders of his house arose *and went* to him,
to raise him up from the ground. But he
would not, nor did he eat food with them.
18Then on the seventh day it came to pass
that the child died. And the servants of
David were afraid to tell him that the child
was dead. For they said, "Indeed, while the
child was alive, we spoke to him, and he
would not heed our voice. How can we tell
him that the child is dead? He may do
some harm!"
19When David saw that his servants
were whispering, David perceived that the
child was dead. Therefore David said to his
servants, "Is the child dead?"
And they said, "He is dead."
20So David arose from the ground,
washed and [a]anointed himself, and
changed his clothes; and he went into the
house of the LORD and [b]worshiped. Then

25 [1] Lit. *be evil in your sight*
27 [a] 2 Sam. 12:9 [b] 1 Chr. 21:7 [1] Lit. *was evil in the eyes of*
CHAPTER 12
1 [a] Ps. 51:title [b] 1 Kin. 20:35–41
5 [1] *deserves to die*, lit. *is a son of death*
6 [a] [Ex. 22:1]
7 [a] 1 Sam. 16:13
9 [a] 1 Sam. 15:19 [b] Num. 15:31 [c] 2 Sam. 11:14–17, 27
10 [a] [Amos 7:9]
11 [a] 2 Sam. 16:21, 22
12 [a] 2 Sam. 16:22
13 [a] 1 Sam. 15:24 [b] 2 Sam. 24:10 [c] [Mic. 7:18]
14 [a] Is. 52:5
15 [a] 1 Sam. 25:38
16 [a] 2 Sam. 13:31
20 [a] Ruth 3:3 [b] Job 1:20

he went to his own house; and when he
requested, they set food before him, and
he ate. 21 Then his servants said to him,
"What *is* this that you have done? You
fasted and wept for the child *while he was*
alive, but when the child died, you arose
and ate food."
22 And he said, "While the child was
alive, I fasted and wept; [a]for I said, 'Who
can tell *whether* [1]the LORD will be gracious to me, that the child may live?'
23 But now he is dead; why should I fast?
Can I bring him back again? I shall go [a]to
him, but [b]he shall not return to me."

Solomon Is Born

24 Then David comforted Bathsheba his
wife, and went in to her and lay with her.
So [a]she bore a son, and [b]he[1] called his
name Solomon. Now the LORD loved him,
25 and He sent *word* by the hand of Nathan
the prophet: So [1]he called his name [2]Jedi-
diah, because of the LORD.

Rabbah Is Captured

26 Now [a]Joab fought against [b]Rabbah of
the people of Ammon, and took the royal
city. 27 And Joab sent messengers to David,
and said, "I have fought against Rabbah,
and I have taken the city's water *supply*.
28 Now therefore, gather the rest of the
people together and encamp against the
city and take it, lest I take the city and it
be called after my name." 29 So David gathered all the people together and went to
Rabbah, fought against it, and took it.
30 [a]Then he took their king's crown from
his head. Its weight *was* a talent of gold,
with precious stones. And it was *set* on
David's head. Also he brought out the
[1]spoil of the city in great abundance.
31 And he brought out the people who
were in it, and put *them to work* with saws
and iron picks and iron axes, and made
them cross over to the brick works. So he
did to all the cities of the people of Ammon. Then David and all the people returned to Jerusalem.

Amnon and Tamar

13 After this [a]Absalom the son of
David had a lovely sister, whose
name *was* [b]Tamar; and [c]Amnon the son
of David loved her. 2 Amnon was so distressed over his sister Tamar that he became sick; for she *was* a virgin. And it was
improper for Amnon to do anything to
her. 3 But Amnon had a friend whose
name *was* Jonadab [a]the son of Shimeah,
David's brother. Now Jonadab *was* a very
crafty man. 4 And he said to him, "Why
are you, the king's son, becoming thinner
day after day? Will you not tell me?"
Amnon said to him, "I love Tamar, my
brother Absalom's sister."
5 So Jonadab said to him, "Lie down on
your bed and pretend to be ill. And when
your father comes to see you, say to him,
'Please let my sister Tamar come and give
me food, and prepare the food in my sight,
that I may see *it* and eat it from her
hand.' " 6 Then Amnon lay down and pretended to be ill; and when the king came
to see him, Amnon said to the king,
"Please let Tamar my sister come and
[a]make a couple of cakes for me in my
sight, that I may eat from her hand."
7 And David sent home to Tamar, saying, "Now go to your brother Amnon's
house, and prepare food for him." 8 So Tamar went to her brother Amnon's house;
and he was lying down. Then she took
flour and kneaded *it*, made cakes in his
sight, and baked the cakes. 9 And she took
the pan and placed *them* out before him,
but he refused to eat. Then Amnon said,
[a]"Have everyone go out from me." And
they all went out from him. 10 Then Amnon said to Tamar, "Bring the food into
the bedroom, that I may eat from your
hand." And Tamar took the cakes which
she had made, and brought *them* to Amnon her brother in the bedroom. 11 Now
when she had brought *them* to him to eat,
[a]he took hold of her and said to her,
"Come, lie with me, my sister."
12 But she answered him, "No, my
brother, do not [1]force me, for [a]no such
thing should be done in Israel. Do not do
this [b]disgraceful thing! 13 And I, where
could I take my shame? And as for you,
you would be like one of the fools in Israel. Now therefore, please speak to the
king; [a]for he will not withhold me from
you." 14 However, he would not heed her
voice; and being stronger than she, he
[a]forced her and lay with her.
15 Then Amnon hated her [1]exceedingly,
so that the hatred with which he hated
her *was* greater than the love with which
he had loved her. And Amnon said to her,
"Arise, be gone!"
16 So she said to him, "No, indeed! This
evil of sending me away *is* worse than the
other that you did to me."

22 a Jon. 3:9 *1* Heb. mss., Syr. *God*
23 a Gen. 37:35 b Job 7:8–10
24 a Matt. 1:6 b 1 Chr. 22:9 *1* So with Kt., LXX, Vg.; Qr., a few Heb. mss., Syr., Tg. *she*
25 *1* Qr., some Heb. mss., Syr., Tg. *she* *2* Lit. *Beloved of the LORD*
26 a 1 Chr. 20:1 b Deut. 3:11
30 a 1 Chr. 20:2 *1 plunder*
CHAPTER 13
1 a 2 Sam. 3:2, 3 b 1 Chr. 3:9 c 2 Sam. 3:2
3 a 1 Sam. 16:9
6 a Gen. 18:6
9 a Gen. 45:1
11 a Gen. 39:12
12 a [Lev. 18:9–11; 20:17] b Judg. 19:23; 20:6 *1* Lit. *humble me*
13 a Gen. 20:12
14 a 2 Sam. 12:11
15 *1 with a very great hatred*

2 Samuel 13:4–14

Dear Woman of Destiny,

Sexual abuse within family circles is one of the worst kinds of crimes. If a thief broke into your home and stole some of your possessions, you would immediately report it to the police. But what if someone was able to break into your life and steal your feelings of self-worth, cripple your ability to trust others, and beat you down until you were bruised with fear? What if you were a child, and that "someone" was your father or brother or grandfather or uncle?

If you have suffered through sexual abuse, your life has been drastically affected. But however much your experiences may affect your life, they don't have to ruin it! I am living proof of that. For me, I first needed to get rid of my wrong ideas about what happened. Jesus said, "And you shall know the truth, and the truth shall make you free" (John 8:32). So let's start with the truth: You are not responsible for the wrong choices of others.

At this very moment, God wants to reach down tenderly into that little child's heart of yours—a heart that's been crushed under such a heavy load—and lift your burden. Open your wound of pain, and pour out everything you feel to God. Be totally honest and share every hurt with Him. Tell God what happened. Tell Him how it made you feel. He wants to heal you and comfort your soul. He is waiting with open arms, longing to hold you and love you. Let Him cleanse you and heal you. One of the most wonderful promises we have from God is that "the blood of Jesus Christ His Son cleanses us from all sin" (1 John 1:7). Not only will He forgive and cleanse you from your own sin, but Jesus will cleanse you and heal you from the hurtful effects of other people's sin as well. He's there for you right now . . . just call out to Him.

All it takes is the turn of a key to set a prisoner free. But once they're out, there's an awkward period of readjustment. Forgiveness was the key releasing me from the prison of my past, but I needed to learn some things before I was really adjusted. Because I spent so many years walking in bitterness and resentment, my whole outlook toward men, sex, and relationships needed a total overhaul. I needed to start looking to God to discover my true value—believing in His unwavering love and acceptance.

Piece by piece, His love transformed me from victim to joyful overcomer. A happy marriage, children, and a productive life for God are the proof that He gives "beauty for ashes" (Is. 61:3). If there's any hope for me, then there's hope for you.

The Bible says, "If anyone is in Christ, he is a new creation; old things have passed away; behold, all things have become new" (2 Cor. 5:17). Jesus has made me a new person and given me a new life. I pray that you will find the same peace in God and forgiveness in your heart that I have found. "'For I will restore health to you and heal you of your wounds,' says the LORD" (Jer. 30:17).

A Victorious Overcomer

Woman of Destiny, I have chosen to remain anonymous because I have young children who are not aware of this aspect of my life. God has freed me from shame, as I pray He will do for you if you have ever been sexually abused.

But he would not listen to her. 17Then
he called his servant who attended him,
and said, "Here! Put this *woman* out,
away from me, and bolt the door behind
her." 18Now she had on [a]a robe of many
colors, for the king's virgin daughters
wore such apparel. And his servant put
her out and bolted the door behind her.
19Then Tamar put [a]ashes on her head,
and tore her robe of many colors that *was*
on her, and [b]laid her hand on her head
and went away crying bitterly. 20And Absalom her brother said to her, "Has Amnon your brother been with you? But now
hold your peace, my sister. He *is* your
brother; do not take this thing to heart."
So Tamar remained desolate in her
brother Absalom's house.
21But when King David heard of all
these things, he was very angry. 22And Absalom spoke to his brother Amnon [a]nei-
ther good nor bad. For Absalom [b]hated
Amnon, because he had forced his sister
Tamar.

Absalom Murders Amnon

23And it came to pass, after two full
years, that Absalom [a]had sheepshearers in
Baal Hazor, which *is* near Ephraim; so Absalom invited all the king's sons. 24Then
Absalom came to the king and said,
"Kindly note, your servant has sheepshearers; please, let the king and his servants go with your servant."
25But the king said to Absalom, "No, my
son, let us not all go now, lest we be a
burden to you." Then he urged him, but
he would not go; and he blessed him.
26Then Absalom said, "If not, please let
my brother Amnon go with us."
And the king said to him, "Why should
he go with you?" 27But Absalom urged
him; so he let Amnon and all the king's
sons go with him.
28Now Absalom had commanded his
servants, saying, "Watch now, when Amnon's [a]heart is merry with wine, and
when I say to you, 'Strike Amnon!' then
kill him. Do not be afraid. Have I not commanded you? Be courageous and [1]val-
iant." 29So the servants of Absalom [a]did
to Amnon as Absalom had commanded.
Then all the king's sons arose, and each
one got on [b]his mule and fled.
30And it came to pass, while they were
on the way, that news came to David, saying, "Absalom has killed all the king's
sons, and not one of them is left!" 31So the
king arose and [a]tore his garments and
[b]lay on the ground, and all his servants
stood by with their clothes torn. 32Then
[a]Jonadab the son of Shimeah, David's
brother, answered and said, "Let not my
lord suppose they have killed all the
young men, the king's sons, for only Amnon is dead. For by the command of Absalom this has been determined from the
day that he forced his sister Tamar. 33Now
therefore, [a]let not my lord the king take
the thing to his heart, to think that all the
king's sons are dead. For only Amnon is
dead."

Absalom Flees to Geshur

34[a]Then Absalom fled. And the young
man who was keeping watch lifted his
eyes and looked, and there, many people
were coming from the road on the hillside
behind [1]him. 35And Jonadab said to the
king, "Look, the king's sons are coming;
as your servant said, so it is." 36So it was,
as soon as he had finished speaking, that
the king's sons indeed came, and they lifted up their voice and wept. Also the king
and all his servants wept very bitterly.
37But Absalom fled and went to [a]Talmai
the son of Ammihud, king of Geshur. And
David mourned for his son every day. 38So
Absalom fled and went to [a]Geshur, and
was there three years. 39And [1]King David
[2]longed to go to Absalom. For he had
been [a]comforted concerning Amnon, because he was dead.

Absalom Returns to Jerusalem

14 So Joab the son of Zeruiah perceived that the king's heart *was*
concerned [a]about Absalom. 2And Joab
sent to [a]Tekoa and brought from there a
wise woman, and said to her, "Please pretend to be a mourner, [b]and put on
mourning apparel; do not anoint yourself
with oil, but act like a woman who has
been mourning a long time for the dead.
3Go to the king and speak to him in this
manner." So Joab [a]put the words in her
mouth.
4And when the woman of Tekoa [1]spoke
to the king, she [a]fell on her face to the
ground and prostrated herself, and said,
[b]"Help, O king!"
5Then the king said to her, "What troubles you?"
And she answered, [a]"Indeed I *am* a widow, my husband is dead. 6Now your maidservant had two sons; and the two fought

18 a Gen. 37:3
19 a Josh. 7:6 b Jer. 2:37
22 a Gen. 24:50; 31:24 b [Lev. 19:17, 18]
23 a 1 Sam. 25:4
28 a 1 Sam. 25:36 *1* Lit. *sons of valor*
29 a 2 Sam. 12:10 b 2 Sam. 18:9
31 a 2 Sam. 1:11 b 2 Sam. 12:16
32 a 2 Sam. 13:3–5
33 a 2 Sam. 19:19
34 a 2 Sam. 13:37, 38 *1* LXX adds *And the watchman went and told the king, and said, "I see men from the way of Horonaim, from the regions of the mountains."*
37 a 2 Sam. 3:3
38 a 2 Sam. 14:23, 32; 15:8
39 a 2 Sam. 12:19, 23 *1* So with MT, Syr., Vg.; LXX *the spirit of the king;* Tg. *the soul of King David* *2* So with MT, Tg.; LXX, Vg. *ceased to pursue after*

CHAPTER 14
1 a 2 Sam. 13:39
2 a 2 Chr. 11:6 b Ruth 3:3
3 a 2 Sam. 14:19
4 a 1 Sam. 20:41; 25:23 b 2 Kin. 6:26, 28 *1* Many Heb. mss., LXX, Syr., Vg. *came*
5 a [Zech. 7:10]

with each other in the field, and *there was*
no one to part them, but the one struck
the other and killed him. 7And now the
whole family has risen up against your
maidservant, and they said, 'Deliver him
who struck his brother, that we may execute him [a]for the life of his brother whom
he killed; and we will destroy the heir
also.' So they would extinguish my ember
that is left, and leave to my husband *neither* name nor remnant on the earth."
8Then the king said to the woman, "Go
to your house, and I will give orders concerning you."
9And the woman of Tekoa said to the
king, "My lord, O king, *let* [a]the [1]iniquity
be on me and on my father's house, [b]and
the king and his throne *be* guiltless."
10So the king said, "Whoever says *anything* to you, bring him to me, and he
shall not touch you anymore."
11Then she said, "Please let the king remember the LORD your God, and do not
permit [a]the avenger of blood to destroy
anymore, lest they destroy my son."
And he said, [b]"*As* the LORD lives, not
one hair of your son shall fall to the
ground."
12Therefore the woman said, "Please,
let your maidservant speak *another* word
to my lord the king."
And he said, "Say on."

7 [a]Deut. 19:12, 13

9 [a]1 Sam. 25:24 [b]1 Kin. 2:33 [1]*guilt*

11 [a]Num. 35:19, 21 [b]1 Sam. 14:45

The Wise Woman of Tekoa

Why would David's trusted servant, Joab, send all the way to Tekoa for a woman to approach David during a time of personal distress? Surely the palace contained a variety of counselors, scholars, and others who could advise David. Apparently, Joab did not think those advisors would be successful in this situation.

David's son Absalom had fled Jerusalem, banished from the kingdom after murdering his brother Amnon. Perceiving that David was upset about Absalom and hoping to convince him to allow Absalom to come home, Joab wanted someone who could speak to King David in such a way that he would permit Absalom's return. He needed someone poised enough to conduct herself properly in the presence of royalty, teachable enough to follow his instructions, and smart enough to handle any unexpected question or statement from the king. He needed someone with one of the most valuable virtues a person can possess—wisdom. The only character description we have for the woman he called is that she was indeed "a wise woman" (2 Sam. 14:2), a woman whose wise reputation preceded beyond the city limits of Tekoa, all the way to the palace.

Wisdom remains a precious virtue in women today. It is so important to God that He gave Solomon "both riches and honor" because he requested wisdom when God said to him, "Ask! What shall I give you?" (1 Kin. 3:5, 13). The woman of Tekoa did not have access to all the Scriptures, as we do today, nor was she familiar with the wisdom of Solomon because it was not yet recorded. Her wisdom came from God, who still imparts His wisdom today through His Word and through His Spirit.

Let us pray, as Paul did, "that the God of our Lord Jesus Christ, the Father of glory, may give to [us] the spirit of wisdom and revelation in the knowledge of Him" (Eph. 1:17) and that, like the woman of Tekoa, we, too, may be known for our godly wisdom.

13 So the woman said: "Why then have
you schemed such a thing against [a]the
people of God? For the king speaks this
thing as one who is guilty, *in that* the king
does not bring [b]his banished one home
again. 14 For we [a]will surely die and *be-*
come like water spilled on the ground,
which cannot be gathered up again. Yet
God does not [b]take away a life; but He
[c]devises means, so that His banished ones
are not [1]expelled from Him. 15 Now therefore, I have come to speak of this thing to
my lord the king because the people have
made me afraid. And your maidservant
said, 'I will now speak to the king; it may
be that the king will perform the request
of his maidservant. 16 For the king will
hear and deliver his maidservant from the
hand of the man *who would* destroy me
and my son together from the [a]inheri-
tance of God.' 17 Your maidservant said,
'The word of my lord the king will now be
comforting; for [a]as the angel of God, so *is*
my lord the king in [b]discerning good and
evil. And may the LORD your God be with
you.' "

18 Then the king answered and said to
the woman, "Please do not hide from me
anything that I ask you."

And the woman said, "Please, let my
lord the king speak."

19 So the king said, "*Is* the hand of Joab
with you in all this?" And the woman answered and said, "*As* you live, my lord the
king, no one can turn to the right hand or
to the left from anything that my lord the
king has spoken. For your servant Joab
commanded me, and [a]he put all these
words in the mouth of your maidservant.
20 To bring about this change of affairs
your servant Joab has done this thing; but
my lord *is* wise, [a]according to the wisdom
of the angel of God, to know everything
that *is* in the earth."

21 And the king said to Joab, "All right,
I have granted this thing. Go therefore,
bring back the young man Absalom."

22 Then Joab fell to the ground on his
face and bowed himself, and [1]thanked the
king. And Joab said, "Today your servant
knows that I have found favor in your
sight, my lord, O king, in that the king
has fulfilled the request of his servant."
23 So Joab arose [a]and went to Geshur, and
brought Absalom to Jerusalem. 24 And the
king said, "Let him return to his own
house, but [a]do not let him see my face."
So Absalom returned to his own house,
but did not see the king's face.

David Forgives Absalom

25 Now in all Israel there was no one
who was praised as much as Absalom for
his good looks. [a]From the sole of his foot
to the crown of his head there was no
blemish in him. 26 And when he cut the
hair of his head—at the end of every year
he cut *it* because it was heavy on him—
when he cut it, he weighed the hair of his
head at two hundred shekels according to
the king's standard. 27 [a]To Absalom were
born three sons, and one daughter whose
name *was* Tamar. She was a woman of
beautiful appearance.

28 And Absalom dwelt two full years in
Jerusalem, [a]but did not see the king's
face. 29 Therefore Absalom sent for Joab, to
send him to the king, but he would not
come to him. And when he sent again the
second time, he would not come. 30 So he
said to his servants, "See, Joab's field is
near mine, and he has barley there; go and
set it on fire." And Absalom's servants set
the field on fire.

31 Then Joab arose and came to Absalom's house, and said to him, "Why have
your servants set my field on fire?"

32 And Absalom answered Joab, "Look, I
sent to you, saying, 'Come here, so that I
may send you to the king, to say, "Why
have I come from Geshur? *It would be*
better for me *to be* there still." ' Now
therefore, let me see the king's face; but
[a]if there is iniquity in me, let him execute me."

33 So Joab went to the king and told
him. And when he had called for Absalom,
he came to the king and bowed himself on
his face to the ground before the king.
Then the king [a]kissed Absalom.

Absalom's Treason

15 After this [a]it happened that Absalom [b]provided himself with chariots and horses, and fifty men to run before
him. 2 Now Absalom would rise early and
stand beside the way to the gate. *So* it was,
whenever anyone who had a [a]lawsuit[1]
came to the king for a decision, that Absalom would call to him and say, "What city
are you from?" And he would say, "Your
servant *is* from such and such a tribe of
Israel." 3 Then Absalom would say to him,
"Look, your [1]case *is* good and right; but
there is no [2]deputy of the king to hear

---

13 a Judg. 20:2 b 2 Sam. 13:37, 38
14 a [Heb. 9:27] b Job 34:19 c Num. 35:15 1 *cast out*
16 a Deut. 32:9
17 a 2 Sam. 19:27 b 1 Kin. 3:9
19 a 2 Sam. 14:3
20 a 2 Sam. 14:17; 19:27
22 1 Lit. *blessed*
23 a 2 Sam. 13:37, 38
24 a 2 Sam. 3:13
25 a Is. 1:6
27 a 2 Sam. 13:1; 18:18
28 a 2 Sam. 14:24
32 a 1 Sam. 20:8
33 a Luke 15:20

CHAPTER 15
1 a 2 Sam. 12:11 b 1 Kin. 1:5
2 a Deut. 19:17 1 Lit. *controversy*
3 1 Lit. *words* 2 Lit. *listener*

you." 4 Moreover Absalom would say, [a]"Oh, that I were made judge in the land, and everyone who has any suit or cause would come to me; then I would give him justice." 5 And *so* it was, whenever anyone came near to bow down to him, that he would put out his hand and take him and [a]kiss him. 6 In this manner Absalom acted toward all Israel who came to the king for judgment. [a]So Absalom stole the hearts of the men of Israel.

7 Now it came to pass [a]after [1]forty years that Absalom said to the king, "Please, let me go to [b]Hebron and pay the vow which I made to the LORD. 8 [a]For your servant [b]took a vow [c]while I dwelt at Geshur in Syria, saying, 'If the LORD indeed brings me back to Jerusalem, then I will serve the LORD.' "

9 And the king said to him, "Go in peace." So he arose and went to Hebron.

10 Then Absalom sent spies throughout all the tribes of Israel, saying, "As soon as you hear the sound of the trumpet, then you shall say, 'Absalom [a]reigns in Hebron!' " 11 And with Absalom went two hundred men [a]invited from Jerusalem, and they [b]went along innocently and did not know anything. 12 Then Absalom sent for Ahithophel the Gilonite, [a]David's counselor, from his city—from [b]Giloh—while he offered sacrifices. And the conspiracy grew strong, for the people with Absalom [c]continually increased in number.

David Escapes from Jerusalem

13 Now a messenger came to David, saying, [a]"The hearts of the men of Israel are [1]with Absalom."

14 So David said to all his servants who *were* with him at Jerusalem, "Arise, and let us [a]flee, or we shall not escape from Absalom. Make haste to depart, lest he overtake us suddenly and bring disaster upon us, and strike the city with the edge of the sword."

15 And the king's servants said to the king, "We *are* your servants, *ready to do* whatever my lord the king commands." 16 Then [a]the king went out with all his household after him. But the king left [b]ten women, concubines, to keep the house. 17 And the king went out with all the people after him, and stopped at the outskirts. 18 Then all his servants passed [1]before him; [a]and all the Cherethites, all the Pelethites, and all the Gittites, [b]six hundred men who had followed him from Gath, passed before the king.

> *Jesus Christ did not call us to fight each other, but He called us to present one bold front to the enemy. He bade us go and take captive the hearts and souls of men, and not merely to change their opinions. Get a man's heart right, and his opinions will soon follow.*
>
> CATHERINE BOOTH

19 Then the king said to [a]Ittai the Gittite, "Why are you also going with us? Return and remain with the king. For you *are* a foreigner and also an exile from your own place. 20 In fact, you came *only* yesterday. Should I make you wander up and down with us today, since I go [a]I know not where? Return, and take your brethren back. Mercy and truth *be* with you."

21 But Ittai answered the king and said, [a]"*As* the LORD lives, and *as* my lord the king lives, surely in whatever place my lord the king shall be, whether in death or life, even there also your servant will be."

22 So David said to Ittai, "Go, and cross over." Then Ittai the Gittite and all his men and all the little ones who *were* with him crossed over. 23 And all the country wept with a loud voice, and all the people crossed over. The king himself also crossed over the Brook Kidron, and all the people crossed over toward the way of the [a]wilderness.

24 There was [a]Zadok also, and all the Levites with him, bearing the [b]ark of the covenant of God. And they set down the ark of God, and [c]Abiathar went up until all the people had finished crossing over

4 a Judg. 9:29
5 a 2 Sam. 14:33; 20:9
6 a [Rom. 16:18]
7 a [Deut. 23:21] b 2 Sam. 3:2, 3 1 LXX mss., Syr., Josephus *four*
8 a 1 Sam. 16:2 b Gen. 28:20, 21 c 2 Sam. 13:38
10 a 1 Kin. 1:34
11 a 1 Sam. 16:3, 5 b Gen. 20:5
12 a 1 Chr. 27:33 b Josh. 15:51 c Ps. 3:1
13 a Judg. 9:3 1 Lit. *after*
14 a Ps. 3:title
16 a Ps. 3:title b 2 Sam. 12:11; 16:21, 22
18 a 2 Sam. 8:18 b 1 Sam. 23:13; 25:13; 30:1, 9 1 Lit. *by his hand*
19 a 2 Sam. 18:2
20 a 1 Sam. 23:13
21 a Ruth 1:16, 17
23 a 2 Sam. 15:28; 16:2
24 a 2 Sam. 8:17 b Num. 4:15 c 1 Sam. 22:20

from the city. 25Then the king said to Zadok, "Carry the ark of God back into the
city. If I find favor in the eyes of the LORD,
He [a]will bring me back and show me *both*
it and [b]His dwelling place. 26But if He says
thus: 'I have no [a]delight in you,' here I
am, [b]let Him do to me as seems good to
Him." 27The king also said to Zadok the
priest, "*Are* you *not* a [a]seer?[1] Return to
the city in peace, and [b]your two sons with
you, Ahimaaz your son, and Jonathan the
son of Abiathar. 28See, [a]I will wait in the
plains of the wilderness until word comes
from you to inform me." 29Therefore Zadok and Abiathar carried the ark of God
back to Jerusalem. And they remained
there.

30So David went up by the Ascent of the
Mount of Olives, and wept as he went up;
and he [a]had his head covered and went
[b]barefoot. And all the people who *were*
with him [c]covered their heads and went
up, [d]weeping as they went up. 31Then
someone told David, saying, [a]"Ahithophel
is among the conspirators with Absalom."
And David said, "O LORD, I pray, [b]turn the
counsel of Ahithophel into foolishness!"

32Now it happened when David had
come to the top *of the mountain,* where
he worshiped God—there was Hushai the
[a]Archite coming to meet him [b]with his
robe torn and dust on his head. 33David
said to him, "If you go on with me, then
you will become [a]a burden to me. 34But if
you return to the city, and say to Absalom,
[a]'I will be your servant, O king; *as* I *was*
your father's servant previously, so I *will*
now also *be* your servant,' then you may
defeat the counsel of Ahithophel for me.
35And *do* you not *have* Zadok and Abiathar
the priests with you there? Therefore it
will be *that* whatever you hear from the
king's house, you shall tell to [a]Zadok and
Abiathar the priests. 36Indeed *they have*
there [a]with them their two sons, Ahimaaz, Zadok's *son,* and Jonathan, Abiathar's
son; and by them you shall send me everything you hear."

37So Hushai, [a]David's friend, went into
the city. [b]And Absalom came into Jerusalem.

Mephibosheth's Servant

16 When[a] David was a little past the
top *of the mountain,* there was
[b]Ziba the servant of Mephibosheth, who
met him with a couple of saddled donkeys,
and on them two hundred *loaves* of bread,
one hundred clusters of raisins, one hundred summer fruits, and a skin of wine.
2And the king said to Ziba, "What do you
mean to do with these?"

So Ziba said, "The donkeys *are* for the
king's household to ride on, the bread and
summer fruit for the young men to eat,
and the wine for [a]those who are faint in
the wilderness to drink."

3Then the king said, "And where *is* your
[a]master's son?"

[b]And Ziba said to the king, "Indeed he
is staying in Jerusalem, for he said, 'Today
the house of Israel will restore the kingdom of my father to me.' "

4So the king said to Ziba, "Here, all that
belongs to Mephibosheth *is* yours."

And Ziba said, "I humbly bow before
you, *that* I may find favor in your sight,
my lord, O king!"

Shimei Curses David

5Now when King David came to [a]Bahu-
rim, there was a man from the family
of the house of Saul, whose name *was*
[b]Shimei the son of Gera, coming from
there. He came out, cursing continuously
as he came. 6And he threw stones at David
and at all the servants of King David. And
all the people and all the mighty men
were on his right hand and on his left.
7Also Shimei said thus when he cursed:
"Come out! Come out! You [1]bloodthirsty
man, [a]you [2]rogue! 8The LORD has
[a]brought upon you all [b]the blood of the
house of Saul, in whose place you have
reigned; and the LORD has delivered the
kingdom into the hand of Absalom your
son. So now you *are caught* in your own
evil, because you are a [1]bloodthirsty
man!"

9Then Abishai the son of Zeruiah said
to the king, "Why should this [a]dead dog
[b]curse my lord the king? Please, let me go
over and take off his head!"

10But the king said, [a]"What have I to do
with you, you sons of Zeruiah? So let him
curse, because [b]the LORD has said to him,
'Curse David.' [c]Who then shall say, 'Why
have you done so?' "

11And David said to Abishai and all his
servants, "See how [a]my son who [b]came
from my own body seeks my life. How
much more now *may this* Benjamite? Let
him alone, and let him curse; for so the

25 a [Ps. 43:3] b Ex. 15:13
26 a Num. 14:8 b 1 Sam. 3:18
27 a 1 Sam. 9:6–9 b 2 Sam. 17:17–20 *1 prophet*
28 a 2 Sam. 17:16
30 a Esth. 6:12 b Is. 20:2–4 c Jer. 14:3, 4 d [Ps. 126:6]
31 a Ps. 3:1, 2; 55:12 b 2 Sam. 16:23; 17:14, 23
32 a Josh. 16:2 b 2 Sam. 1:2
33 a 2 Sam. 19:35
34 a 2 Sam. 16:19
35 a 2 Sam. 17:15, 16
36 a 2 Sam. 15:27
37 a 1 Chr. 27:33 b 2 Sam. 16:15

CHAPTER 16
1 a 2 Sam. 15:30, 32 b 2 Sam. 9:2; 19:17, 29
2 a 2 Sam. 15:23; 17:29
3 a 2 Sam. 9:9, 10 b 2 Sam. 19:27
5 a 2 Sam. 3:16 b 2 Sam. 19:21
7 a Deut. 13:13 *1 Lit. man of bloodshed* *2 worthless man*
8 a Judg. 9:24, 56, 57 b 2 Sam. 1:16; 3:28, 29; 4:11, 12 *1 Lit. man of bloodshed*
9 a 2 Sam. 9:8 b Ex. 22:28
10 a 2 Sam. 3:39; 19:22 b [Lam. 3:38] c [Rom. 9:20]
11 a 2 Sam. 12:11 b Gen. 15:4

LORD has ordered him. 12 It may be that the LORD will look on [1]my affliction, and that the LORD will [a]repay me with [b]good for his cursing this day." 13 And as David and his men went along the road, Shimei went along the hillside opposite him and cursed as he went, threw stones at him and [1]kicked up dust. 14 Now the king and all the people who *were* with him became weary; so they refreshed themselves there.

The Advice of Ahithophel

15 Meanwhile [a]Absalom and all the people, the men of Israel, came to Jerusalem; and Ahithophel *was* with him. 16 And so it was, when Hushai the Archite, [a]David's friend, came to Absalom, that [b]Hushai said to Absalom, "*Long* live the king! *Long* live the king!"

17 So Absalom said to Hushai, "*Is* this your loyalty to your friend? [a]Why did you not go with your friend?"

18 And Hushai said to Absalom, "No, but whom the LORD and this people and all the men of Israel choose, his I will be, and with him I will remain. 19 "Furthermore, [a]whom should I serve? *Should I* not *serve* in the presence of his son? As I have served in your father's presence, so will I be in your presence."

20 Then Absalom said to [a]Ahithophel, "Give advice as to what we should do."

21 And Ahithophel said to Absalom, "Go in to your father's [a]concubines, whom he has left to keep the house; and all Israel will hear that you [b]are abhorred by your father. Then [c]the hands of all who are with you will be strong." 22 So they pitched a tent for Absalom on the top of the house, and Absalom went in to his father's concubines [a]in the sight of all Israel.

23 Now the advice of Ahithophel, which he gave in those days, *was* as if one had inquired at the oracle of God. So *was* all the advice of Ahithophel [a]both with David and with Absalom.

17 Moreover Ahithophel said to Absalom, "Now let me choose twelve thousand men, and I will arise and pursue David tonight. 2 I will come upon him while he *is* [a]weary and weak, and make him [1]afraid. And all the people who *are* with him will flee, and I will [b]strike only the king. 3 Then I will bring back all the people to you. When all return except the man whom you seek, all the people will be at peace." 4 And the saying pleased Absalom and all the [a]elders of Israel.

12 [a]Prov. 20:22 [b][Rom. 8:28] [1]So with Kt., LXX, Syr., Vg.; Qr. *my eyes;* Tg. *tears of my eyes*

13 [1]Lit. *dusted him with dust*

15 [a]2 Sam. 15:12, 37

16 [a]2 Sam. 15:37 [b]2 Sam. 15:34

17 [a]2 Sam. 19:25

19 [a]2 Sam. 15:34

20 [a]2 Sam. 15:12

21 [a]2 Sam. 15:16; 20:3 [b]Gen. 34:30 [c]2 Sam. 2:7

22 [a]2 Sam. 12:11, 12

23 [a]2 Sam. 15:12

CHAPTER 17

2 [a]2 Sam. 16:14 [b]Zech. 13:7 [1]*tremble with fear*

4 [a]2 Sam. 5:3; 19:11

5 [a]2 Sam. 15:32–34

8 [a]Hos. 13:8

10 [a]Josh. 2:11

11 [a]2 Sam. 3:10 [b]Gen. 22:17

13 [a]Mic. 1:6

14 [a]2 Sam. 15:31, 34

15 [a]2 Sam. 15:35, 36

16 [a]2 Sam. 15:28

The Advice of Hushai

5 Then Absalom said, "Now call Hushai the Archite also, and let us hear what he [a]says too." 6 And when Hushai came to Absalom, Absalom spoke to him, saying, "Ahithophel has spoken in this manner. Shall we do as he says? If not, speak up."

7 So Hushai said to Absalom: "The advice that Ahithophel has given *is* not good at this time. 8 For," said Hushai, "you know your father and his men, that they *are* mighty men, and they *are* enraged in their minds, like [a]a bear robbed of her cubs in the field; and your father *is* a man of war, and will not camp with the people. 9 Surely by now he is hidden in some pit, or in some *other* place. And it will be, when some of them are overthrown at the first, that whoever hears *it* will say, 'There is a slaughter among the people who follow Absalom.' 10 And even he *who is* valiant, whose heart *is* like the heart of a lion, will [a]melt completely. For all Israel knows that your father *is* a mighty man, and *those* who *are* with him *are* valiant men. 11 Therefore I advise that all Israel be fully gathered to you, [a]from Dan to Beersheba, [b]like the sand that *is* by the sea for multitude, and that you go to battle in person. 12 So we will come upon him in some place where he may be found, and we will fall on him as the dew falls on the ground. And of him and all the men who *are* with him there shall not be left so much as one. 13 Moreover, if he has withdrawn into a city, then all Israel shall bring ropes to that city; and we will [a]pull it into the river, until there is not one small stone found there."

14 So Absalom and all the men of Israel said, "The advice of Hushai the Archite *is* better than the advice of Ahithophel." For [a]the LORD had purposed to defeat the good advice of Ahithophel, to the intent that the LORD might bring disaster on Absalom.

Hushai Warns David to Escape

15 [a]Then Hushai said to Zadok and Abiathar the priests, "Thus and so Ahithophel advised Absalom and the elders of Israel, and thus and so I have advised. 16 Now therefore, send quickly and tell David, saying, 'Do not spend this night [a]in the plains of the wilderness, but speedily cross over, lest the king and all the people who

are with him be swallowed up.' " [17][a]Now Jonathan and Ahimaaz [b]stayed at [c]En Rogel, for they dared not be seen coming into the city; so a female servant would come and tell them, and they would go and tell King David. [18]Nevertheless a lad saw them, and told Absalom. But both of them went away quickly and came to a man's house [a]in Bahurim, who had a well in his court; and they went down into it. [19][a]Then the woman took and spread a covering over the well's mouth, and spread ground grain on it; and the thing was not known. [20]And when Absalom's servants came to the woman at the house, they said, "Where *are* Ahimaaz and Jonathan?"

So [a]the woman said to them, "They have gone over the water brook."

And when they had searched and could not find *them,* they returned to Jerusalem. [21]Now it came to pass, after they had departed, that they came up out of the well and went and told King David, and said to David, [a]"Arise and cross over the water quickly. For thus has Ahithophel advised against you." [22]So David and all the people who *were* with him arose and crossed over the Jordan. By morning light not one of them was left who had not gone over the Jordan.

[23]Now when Ahithophel saw that his advice was not followed, he saddled a donkey, and arose and went home to [a]his house, to his city. Then he [1]put his [b]household in order, and [c]hanged himself, and died; and he was buried in his father's tomb.

[24]Then David went to [a]Mahanaim. And Absalom crossed over the Jordan, he and all the men of Israel with him. [25]And Absalom made [a]Amasa captain of the army instead of Joab. This Amasa *was* the son of a man whose name *was* [1]Jithra, an [2]Israelite, who had gone in to [b]Abigail the daughter of Nahash, sister of Zeruiah, Joab's mother. [26]So Israel and Absalom encamped in the land of Gilead.

[27]Now it happened, when David had come to Mahanaim, that [a]Shobi the son of Nahash from Rabbah of the people of Ammon, [b]Machir the son of Ammiel from Lo Debar, and [c]Barzillai the Gileadite from Rogelim, [28]brought beds and basins, earthen vessels and wheat, barley and flour, parched *grain* and beans, lentils and parched *seeds,* [29]honey and curds, sheep and cheese of the herd, for David and the people who *were* with him to eat. For they said, "The people are hungry and weary and thirsty [a]in the wilderness."

Absalom's Defeat and Death

18 And David [1]numbered the people who *were* with him, and [a]set captains of thousands and captains of hundreds over them. [2]Then David sent out one third of the people under the hand of Joab, [a]one third under the hand of Abishai the son of Zeruiah, Joab's brother, and one third under the hand of [b]Ittai the Gittite. And the king said to the people, "I also will surely go out with you myself."

[3][a]But the people answered, "You shall not go out! For if we flee away, they will not care about us; nor if half of us die, will they care about us. But *you are* worth ten thousand of us now. For you are now more help to us in the city."

[4]Then the king said to them, "Whatever seems best to you I will do." So the king stood beside the gate, and all the people went out by hundreds and by thousands. [5]Now the king had commanded Joab, Abishai, and Ittai, saying, "*Deal* gently for my sake with the young man Absalom." [a]And all the people heard when the king gave all the captains orders concerning Absalom.

[6]So the people went out into the field of battle against Israel. And the battle was in the [a]woods of Ephraim. [7]The people of Israel were overthrown there before the servants of David, and a great slaughter of twenty thousand took place there that day. [8]For the battle there was scattered over the face of the whole countryside, and the woods devoured more people that day than the sword devoured.

[9]Then Absalom met the servants of David. Absalom rode on a mule. The mule went under the thick boughs of a great terebinth tree, and [a]his head caught in the terebinth; so he was left hanging between heaven and earth. And the mule which *was* under him went on. [10]Now a certain man saw *it* and told Joab, and said, "I just saw Absalom hanging in a terebinth tree!"

[11]So Joab said to the man who told him, "You just saw *him!* And why did you not strike him there to the ground? I would have given you ten *shekels* of silver and a belt."

[12]But the man said to Joab, "Though I were to receive a thousand *shekels* of sil-

---

17 a 2 Sam. 15:27, 36 b Josh. 2:4–6 c Josh. 15:7; 18:16
18 a 2 Sam. 3:16; 16:5
19 a Josh. 2:4–6
20 a Josh. 2:3–5
21 a 2 Sam. 17:15, 16
23 a 2 Sam. 15:12 b 2 Kin. 20:1 c Matt. 27:5 *1* Lit. *gave charge concerning his house*
24 a 2 Sam. 2:8; 19:32
25 a 1 Kin. 2:5, 32 b 1 Chr. 2:16 *1 Jether,* 1 Chr. 2:17 *2* So with MT, some LXX mss., Tg.; some LXX mss. *Ishmaelite* (cf. 1 Chr. 2:17); Vg. *of Jezrael*
27 a 2 Sam. 10:1; 12:29 b 2 Sam. 9:4 c 2 Sam. 19:31, 32
29 a 2 Sam. 16:2, 14

CHAPTER 18
1 a Ex. 18:25 *1* Lit. *attended to*
2 a Judg. 7:16 b 2 Sam. 15:19–22
3 a 2 Sam. 21:17
5 a 2 Sam. 18:12
6 a Josh. 17:15, 18
9 a 2 Sam. 14:26

ver in my hand, I would not raise my hand against the king's son. [a]For in our hearing the king commanded you and Abishai and Ittai, saying, [1]'Beware lest anyone *touch* the young man Absalom!' 13Otherwise I would have dealt falsely against my own life. For there is nothing hidden from the king, and you yourself would have set yourself against *me*."

14Then Joab said, "I cannot linger with you." And he took three spears in his hand and thrust them through Absalom's heart, while he was *still* alive in the midst of the terebinth tree. 15And ten young men who bore Joab's armor surrounded Absalom, and struck and killed him.

16So Joab blew the trumpet, and the people returned from pursuing Israel. For Joab held back the people. 17And they took Absalom and cast him into a large pit in the woods, and [a]laid a very large heap of stones over him. Then all Israel [b]fled, everyone to his tent.

18Now Absalom in his lifetime had taken and set up a [1]pillar for himself, which *is* in [a]the King's Valley. For he said, [b]"I have no son to keep my name in remembrance." He called the pillar after his own name. And to this day it is called Absalom's Monument.

David Hears of Absalom's Death

19Then [a]Ahimaaz the son of Zadok said, "Let me run now and take the news to the king, how the LORD has [1]avenged him of his enemies."

20And Joab said to him, "You shall not take the news this day, for you shall take the news another day. But today you shall take no news, because the king's son is dead." 21Then Joab said to the Cushite, "Go, tell the king what you have seen." So the Cushite bowed himself to Joab and ran.

22And Ahimaaz the son of Zadok said again to Joab, "But [1]whatever happens, please let me also run after the Cushite."

So Joab said, "Why will you run, my son, since you have no news ready?"

23"But whatever happens," *he said,* "let me run."

So he said to him, "Run." Then Ahimaaz ran by way of the plain, and outran the Cushite.

24Now David was sitting between the [a]two gates. And the watchman went up to the roof over the gate, to the wall, lifted his eyes and looked, and there was a man, running alone. 25Then the watchman cried out and told the king. And the king said, "If he *is* alone, *there is* news in his mouth." And he came rapidly and drew near.

26Then the watchman saw *another* man running, and the watchman called to the gatekeeper and said, "There is *another* man, running alone!"

And the king said, "He also brings news."

27So the watchman said, [1]"I think the running of the first is like the running of Ahimaaz the son of Zadok."

And the king said, "He *is* a good man, and comes with [a]good news."

28So Ahimaaz called out and said to the king, [1]"All is well!" Then he bowed down with his face to the earth before the king, and said, [a]"Blessed *be* the LORD your God, who has delivered up the men who raised their hand against my lord the king!"

29The king said, "Is the young man Absalom safe?"

Ahimaaz answered, "When Joab sent the king's servant and *me* your servant, I saw a great tumult, but I did not know what *it was about*."

30And the king said, "Turn aside *and* stand here." So he turned aside and stood still.

31Just then the Cushite came, and the Cushite said, "There is good news, my lord the king! For the LORD has avenged you this day of all those who rose against you."

32And the king said to the Cushite, "Is the young man Absalom safe?"

So the Cushite answered, "May the enemies of my lord the king, and all who rise against you to do harm, be like *that* young man!"

David's Mourning for Absalom

33Then the king was deeply moved, and went up to the chamber over the gate, and wept. And as he went, he said thus: [a]"O my son Absalom—my son, my son Absalom—if only I had died in your place! O Absalom my son, [b]my son!"

19 And Joab was told, "Behold, the king is weeping and [a]mourning for Absalom." 2So the victory that day was *turned* into [a]mourning for all the people. For the people heard it said that day, "The king is grieved for his son." 3And the

12 [a]2 Sam. 18:5 [1]Vss. *'Protect the young man Absalom for me!'*
17 [a]Josh. 7:26; 8:29 [b]2 Sam. 19:8; 20:1, 22
18 [a]Gen. 14:17 [b]2 Sam. 14:27 [1]*monument*
19 [a]2 Sam. 15:36; 17:17 [1]*vindicated*
22 [1]Lit. *be what may*
24 [a]2 Kin. 9:17
27 [a]1 Kin. 1:42 [1]Lit. *I see the running*
28 [a]2 Sam. 16:12 [1]*Peace be to you*
33 [a]2 Sam. 12:10 [b]2 Sam. 19:4
CHAPTER 19
1 [a]Jer. 14:2
2 [a]Esth. 4:3

people [1]stole back [a]into the city that day,
as people who are ashamed steal away
when they flee in battle. 4But the king
[a]covered his face, and the king cried out
with a loud voice, [b]"O my son Absalom!
O Absalom, my son, my son!"
5Then [a]Joab came into the house to the
king, and said, "Today you have disgraced
all your servants who today have saved
your life, the lives of your sons and daughters, the lives of your wives and the lives
of your concubines, 6in that you love your
enemies and hate your friends. For you
have declared today that you [1]regard neither princes nor servants; for today I perceive that if Absalom had lived and all
of us had died today, then it would have
pleased you well. 7Now therefore, arise, go
out and speak [1]comfort to your servants.
For I swear by the LORD, if you do not go
out, not one will stay with you this night.
And that will be worse for you than all the
evil that has befallen you from your youth
until now." 8Then the king arose and sat
in the [a]gate. And they told all the people,
saying, "There is the king, sitting in the
gate." So all the people came before the
king.
For everyone of Israel had [b]fled to his
tent.

David Returns to Jerusalem

9Now all the people were in a dispute
throughout all the tribes of Israel, saying,
"The king saved us from the hand of our
[a]enemies, he delivered us from the hand
of the [b]Philistines, and now he has [c]fled
from the land because of Absalom. 10But
Absalom, whom we anointed over us, has
died in battle. Now therefore, why do you
say nothing about bringing back the
king?"
11So King David sent to [a]Zadok and
Abiathar the priests, saying, "Speak to the
elders of Judah, saying, 'Why are you the
last to bring the king back to his house,
since the words of all Israel have come to
the king, to his *very* house? 12You *are* my
brethren, you *are* [a]my bone and my flesh.
Why then are you the last to bring back
the king?' 13[a]And say to Amasa, '*Are* you
not my bone and my flesh? [b]God do so to
me, and more also, if you are not commander of the army before me [1]continu-
ally in place of Joab.' " 14So he swayed the
hearts of all the men of Judah, [a]just as *the*
heart of one man, so that they sent *this*
word to the king: "Return, you and all
your servants!"
15Then the king returned and came to
the Jordan. And Judah came to [a]Gilgal, to
go to meet the king, to escort the king
[b]across the Jordan. 16And [a]Shimei the son
of Gera, a Benjamite, who *was* from Bahurim, hurried and came down with the
men of Judah to meet King David. 17*There*
were a thousand men of [a]Benjamin with
him, and [b]Ziba the servant of the house of
Saul, and his fifteen sons and his twenty
servants with him; and they went over the
Jordan before the king. 18Then a ferryboat
went across to carry over the king's
household, and to do what he thought
good.

David's Mercy to Shimei

Now Shimei the son of Gera fell down
before the king when he had crossed the
Jordan. 19Then he said to the king, [a]"Do
not let my lord [1]impute iniquity to me, or
remember what [b]wrong your servant did
on the day that my lord the king left Jerusalem, that the king should [c]take *it* to
heart. 20For I, your servant, know that I
have sinned. Therefore here I am, the first
to come today of all [a]the house of Joseph
to go down to meet my lord the king."
21But Abishai the son of Zeruiah answered and said, "Shall not Shimei be put
to death for this, [a]because he [b]cursed the
LORD's anointed?"
22And David said, [a]"What have I to do
with you, you sons of Zeruiah, that you
should be adversaries to me today? [b]Shall
any man be put to death today in Israel?
For do I not know that today I *am* king
over Israel?" 23Therefore [a]the king said to
Shimei, "You shall not die." And the king
swore to him.

David and Mephibosheth Meet

24Now [a]Mephibosheth the son of Saul
came down to meet the king. And he had
not cared for his feet, nor trimmed his
mustache, nor washed his clothes, from
the day the king departed until the day he
returned in peace. 25So it was, when he
had come to Jerusalem to meet the king,
that the king said to him, [a]"Why did you
not go with me, Mephibosheth?"
26And he answered, "My lord, O king,
my servant deceived me. For your servant
said, 'I will saddle a donkey for myself,

3 [a]2 Sam. 17:24, 27; 19:32 [1]*went by stealth*
4 [a]2 Sam. 15:30 [b]2 Sam. 18:33
5 [a]2 Sam. 18:14
6 [1]*have no respect for*
7 [1]Lit. *to the heart of*
8 [a]2 Sam. 15:2; 18:24 [b]2 Sam. 18:17
9 [a]2 Sam. 8:1–14 [b]2 Sam. 3:18 [c]2 Sam. 15:14
11 [a]2 Sam. 15:24
12 [a]2 Sam. 5:1
13 [a]2 Sam. 17:25 [b]Ruth 1:17 [1]*permanently*
14 [a]Judg. 20:1
15 [a]Josh. 5:9 [b]2 Sam. 17:22
16 [a]2 Sam. 16:5
17 [a]1 Kin. 12:21 [b]2 Sam. 9:2, 10; 16:1, 2
19 [a]1 Sam. 22:15 [b]2 Sam. 16:5, 6 [c]2 Sam. 13:33 [1]*charge me with iniquity*
20 [a]Judg. 1:22
21 [a][Ex. 22:28] [b][1 Sam. 26:9]
22 [a]2 Sam. 3:39; 16:10 [b]1 Sam. 11:13
23 [a]1 Kin. 2:8, 9, 37, 46
24 [a]2 Sam. 9:6; 21:7
25 [a]2 Sam. 16:17

that I may ride on it and go to the king,' because your servant *is* lame. 27And [a]he has slandered your servant to my lord the king, [b]but my lord the king *is* like the angel of God. Therefore do *what is* good in your eyes. 28For all my father's house were but dead men before my lord the king. [a]Yet you set your servant among those who eat at your own table. Therefore what right have I still to [1]cry out anymore to the king?"

29So the king said to him, "Why do you speak anymore of your matters? I have said, 'You and Ziba divide the land.' "

30Then Mephibosheth said to the king, "Rather, let him take it all, inasmuch as my lord the king has come back in peace to his own house."

David's Kindness to Barzillai

31And [a]Barzillai the Gileadite came down from Rogelim and went across the Jordan with the king, to escort him across the Jordan. 32Now Barzillai was a very aged man, eighty years old. And [a]he had provided the king with supplies while he stayed at Mahanaim, for he *was* a very rich man. 33And the king said to Barzillai, "Come across with me, and I will provide for you while you are with me in Jerusalem."

34But Barzillai said to the king, "How long have I to live, that I should go up with the king to Jerusalem? 35I *am* today [a]eighty years old. Can I discern between the good and bad? Can your servant taste what I eat or what I drink? Can I hear any longer the voice of singing men and singing women? Why then should your servant be a further burden to my lord the king? 36Your servant will go a little way across the Jordan with the king. And why should the king repay me *with* such a reward? 37Please let your servant turn back again, that I may die in my own city, near the grave of my father and mother. But here is your servant [a]Chimham; let him cross over with my lord the king, and do for him what seems good to you."

38And the king answered, "Chimham shall cross over with me, and I will do for him what seems good to you. Now whatever you request of me, I will do for you." 39Then all the people went over the Jordan. And when the king had crossed over, the king [a]kissed Barzillai and blessed him, and he returned to his own place.

The Quarrel About the King

40Now the king went on to Gilgal, and [1]Chimham went on with him. And all the people of Judah escorted the king, and also half the people of Israel. 41Just then all the men of Israel came to the king, and said to the king, "Why have our brethren, the men of Judah, stolen you away and [a]brought the king, his household, and all David's men with him across the Jordan?"

42So all the men of Judah answered the men of Israel, "Because the king *is* [a]a close relative of ours. Why then are you angry over this matter? Have we ever eaten at the king's *expense?* Or has he given us any gift?"

43And the men of Israel answered the men of Judah, and said, "We have [a]ten shares in the king; therefore we also have more *right* to David than you. Why then do you despise us—were we not the first to advise bringing back our king?"

Yet [b]the words of the men of Judah were [1]fiercer than the words of the men of Israel.

The Rebellion of Sheba

20 And there happened to be there a [1]rebel, whose name *was* Sheba the son of Bichri, a Benjamite. And he blew a trumpet, and said:

[a]"We have no share in David,
Nor do we have inheritance in the
son of Jesse;
[b]Every man to his tents, O Israel!"

2So every man of Israel deserted David, *and* followed Sheba the son of Bichri. But the [a]men of Judah, from the Jordan as

Our souls may lose their peace and even disturb other people's, if we are always criticizing trivial actions—which often are not real defects at all, but we construe them wrongly through our ignorance of their motives.

TERESA OF ÁVILA

27 [a] 2 Sam. 16:3, 4 [b] 2 Sam. 14:17, 20
28 [a] 2 Sam. 9:7–13 [1] *complain*
31 [a] 1 Kin. 2:7
32 [a] 2 Sam. 17:27–29
35 [a] Ps. 90:10
37 [a] Jer. 41:17
39 [a] Gen. 31:55
40 [1] MT *Chimhan*
41 [a] 2 Sam. 19:15
42 [a] 2 Sam. 19:12
43 [a] 1 Kin. 11:30, 31 [b] Judg. 8:1; 12:1 [1] *harsher*

CHAPTER 20
1 [a] 1 Kin. 12:16 [b] 2 Sam. 18:17 [1] Lit. *man of Belial*
2 [a] 2 Sam. 19:14

far as Jerusalem, remained loyal to their king.

[3]Now David came to his house at Jerusalem. And the king took the ten women, [a]his concubines whom he had left to keep the house, and put them in seclusion and supported them, but did not go in to them. So they were shut up to the day of their death, living in widowhood.

[4]And the king said to Amasa, [a]"Assemble the men of Judah for me within three days, and be present here yourself." [5]So Amasa went to assemble *the men of* Judah. But he delayed longer than the set time which David had appointed him. [6]And David said to [a]Abishai, "Now Sheba the son of Bichri will do us more harm than Absalom. Take [b]your lord's servants and pursue him, lest he find for himself fortified cities, and escape us." [7]So Joab's men, with the [a]Cherethites, the Pelethites, and [b]all the mighty men, went out after him. And they went out of Jerusalem to pursue Sheba the son of Bichri. [8]When they *were* at the large stone which *is* in Gibeon, Amasa came before them. Now Joab was dressed in battle armor; on it was a belt *with* a sword fastened in its sheath at his hips; and as he was going forward, it fell out. [9]Then Joab said to Amasa, "*Are* you in health, my brother?" [a]And Joab took Amasa by the beard with his right hand to kiss him. [10]But Amasa did not notice the sword that *was* in Joab's hand. And [a]he struck him with it [b]in the stomach, and his entrails poured out on the ground; and he did not *strike* him again. Thus he died.

Then Joab and Abishai his brother pursued Sheba the son of Bichri. [11]Meanwhile one of Joab's men stood near Amasa, and said, "Whoever favors Joab and whoever *is* for David—follow Joab!" [12]But Amasa wallowed in *his* blood in the middle of the highway. And when the man saw that all the people stood still, he moved Amasa from the highway to the field and threw a garment over him, when he saw that everyone who came upon him halted. [13]When he was removed from the highway, all the people went on after Joab to pursue Sheba the son of Bichri.

[14]And he went through all the tribes of Israel to [a]Abel and Beth Maachah and all the Berites. So they were gathered together and also went after [1]*Sheba.* [15]Then they came and besieged him in Abel of Beth Maachah; and they [a]cast up a siege mound against the city, and it stood by the rampart. And all the people who *were* with Joab battered the wall to throw it down.

[16]Then a wise woman cried out from the city, "Hear, hear! Please say to Joab, 'Come nearby, that I may speak with you.' " [17]When he had come near to her, the woman said, "*Are* you Joab?"

He answered, "I *am.*"

Then she said to him, "Hear the words of your maidservant."

And he answered, "I am listening."

[18]So she spoke, saying, "They used to talk in former times, saying, 'They shall surely seek *guidance* at Abel,' and so they would end *disputes.* [19]I *am among the* peaceable *and* faithful in Israel. You seek to destroy a city and a mother in Israel. Why would you swallow up [a]the inheritance of the LORD?"

[20]And Joab answered and said, "Far be it, far be it from me, that I should swallow up or destroy! [21]That *is* not so. But a man from the mountains of Ephraim, Sheba the son of Bichri by name, has raised his hand against the king, against David. Deliver him only, and I will depart from the city."

So the woman said to Joab, "Watch, his head will be thrown to you over the wall." [22]Then the woman [a]in her wisdom went to all the people. And they cut off the head of Sheba the son of Bichri, and threw *it* out to Joab. Then he blew a trumpet, and they withdrew from the city, every man to his tent. So Joab returned to the king at Jerusalem.

David's Government Officers

[23]And [a]Joab *was* over all the army of Israel; Benaiah the son of Jehoiada *was* over the Cherethites and the Pelethites; [24]Adoram *was* [a]in charge of revenue; [b]Jehoshaphat the son of Ahilud *was* recorder; [25]Sheva *was* scribe; [a]Zadok and Abiathar *were* the priests; [26][a]and Ira the Jairite was [1]a chief minister under David.

David Avenges the Gibeonites

21 Now there was a famine in the days of David for three years, year after year; and David [a]inquired of the LORD. And the LORD answered, "*It is* because of Saul and *his* [1]bloodthirsty house, because he killed the Gibeonites." [2]So the king called the Gibeonites and spoke to them.

3 [a]2 Sam. 15:16; 16:21, 22
4 [a]2 Sam. 17:25; 19:13
6 [a]2 Sam. 21:17 [b]2 Sam. 11:11
7 [a]1 Kin. 1:38, 44 [b]2 Sam. 15:18
9 [a]Matt. 26:49
10 [a]1 Kin. 2:5 [b]2 Sam. 2:23
14 [a]2 Kin. 15:29 [1]Lit. *him*
15 [a]2 Kin. 19:32
19 [a]1 Sam. 26:19
22 [a][Eccl. 9:13–16]
23 [a]2 Sam. 8:16–18
24 [a]1 Kin. 4:6 [b]2 Sam. 8:16
25 [a]1 Kin. 4:4
26 [a]2 Sam. 8:18 [1]Or *David's priest*

CHAPTER 21
1 [a]Num. 27:21 [1]Lit. *house of bloodshed*

Now the Gibeonites *were* not of the children of Israel, but [a]of the remnant of the
Amorites; the children of Israel had sworn
protection to them, but Saul had sought
to kill them [b]in his zeal for the children
of Israel and Judah.
3 Therefore David said to the Gibeonites, "What shall I do for you? And with
what shall I make atonement, that you
may bless [a]the inheritance of the LORD?"
4 And the Gibeonites said to him, "We
will have no silver or gold from Saul or
from his house, nor shall you kill any man
in Israel for us."
So he said, "Whatever you say, I will do
for you."
5 Then they answered the king, "As for
the man who consumed us and plotted
against us, *that* we should be destroyed
from remaining in any of the territories of
Israel, 6 let seven men of his descendants
be delivered [a]to us, and we will hang them
before the LORD [b]in Gibeah of Saul,
[c]*whom* the LORD chose."
And the king said, "I will give *them*."
7 But the king spared [a]Mephibosheth
the son of Jonathan, the son of Saul, because of [b]the LORD's oath that *was* between them, between David and Jonathan
the son of Saul. 8 So the king took Armoni
and Mephibosheth, the two sons of [a]Riz-
pah the daughter of Aiah, whom she bore
to Saul, and the five sons of [1]Michal the
daughter of Saul, whom she [2]brought up
for Adriel the son of Barzillai the Mehola-
thite; 9 and he delivered them into the
hands of the Gibeonites, and they hanged
them on the hill [a]before the LORD. So they
fell, *all* seven together, and were put to
death in the days of harvest, in the first
days, in the beginning of barley harvest.
10 Now [a]Rizpah the daughter of Aiah
took sackcloth and spread it for herself on
the rock, [b]from the beginning of harvest
until the late rains poured on them from
heaven. And she did not allow the birds of
the air to rest on them by day nor the
beasts of the field by night.
11 And David was told what Rizpah the
daughter of Aiah, the concubine of Saul,
had done. 12 Then David went and took the
bones of Saul, and the bones of Jonathan
his son, from the men of [a]Jabesh Gilead
who had stolen them from the street of
[1]Beth Shan, where the [b]Philistines had
hung them up, after the Philistines had
struck down Saul in Gilboa. 13 So he
brought up the bones of Saul and the
bones of Jonathan his son from there; and
they gathered the bones of those who had
been hanged. 14 They buried the bones of
Saul and Jonathan his son in the country
of Benjamin in [a]Zelah, in the tomb of
Kish his father. So they performed all that
the king commanded. And after that [b]God
heeded the prayer for the land.

Philistine Giants Destroyed

15 When the Philistines were at war
again with Israel, David and his servants
with him went down and fought against
the Philistines; and David grew faint.
16 Then Ishbi-Benob, who *was* one of the
sons of [1]the [a]giant, the weight of whose
bronze spear *was* three hundred *shekels,*
who was bearing a new *sword,* thought he
could kill David. 17 But [a]Abishai the son of
Zeruiah came to his aid, and struck the
Philistine and killed him. Then the men of
David swore to him, saying, [b]"You shall go
out no more with us to battle, lest you
quench the [c]lamp of Israel."
18 [a]Now it happened afterward that
there was again a battle with the Philistines at Gob. Then [b]Sibbechai the Hushathite killed [1]Saph, who *was* one of the
sons of [2]the giant. 19 Again there was war
at Gob with the Philistines, where [a]Elha-
nan the son of [1]Jaare-Oregim the Bethlehemite killed [b]*the brother of* Goliath the
Gittite, the shaft of whose spear *was* like
a weaver's beam.
20 Yet again [a]there was war at Gath,
where there was a man of *great* stature,
who had six fingers on each hand and six
toes on each foot, twenty-four in number;
and he also was born to [1]the giant. 21 So
when he [a]defied Israel, Jonathan the son
of [1]Shimea, David's brother, killed him.
22 [a]These four were born to [1]the giant in
Gath, and fell by the hand of David and by
the hand of his servants.

Praise for God's Deliverance

22 Then David [a]spoke to the LORD the
words of this song, on the day
when the LORD had [b]delivered him from
the hand of all his enemies, and from the
hand of Saul. 2 And he [a]said:

[b]"The LORD *is* my rock and my
[c]fortress and my deliverer;
3 The God of my strength, [a]in whom
I will trust;
My [b]shield and the [c]horn[1] of my
salvation,

---

2 a Josh. 9:3, 15–20 b [Ex. 34:11–16]
3 a 2 Sam. 20:19
6 a Num. 25:4 b 1 Sam. 10:26 c 1 Sam. 10:24
7 a 2 Sam. 4:4; 9:10 b 2 Sam. 9:1–7
8 a 2 Sam. 3:7 *1 Merab,* 1 Sam. 18:19; 25:44; 2 Sam. 3:14; 6:23 *2* Lit. *bore to Adriel*
9 a 2 Sam. 6:17
10 a 2 Sam. 3:7; 21:8 b Deut. 21:23
12 a 1 Sam. 31:11–13 b 1 Sam. 31:8 *1 Beth Shean,* Josh. 17:11
14 a Josh. 18:28 b 2 Sam. 24:25
16 a 2 Sam. 21:18–22 *1* Or *Rapha*
17 a 2 Sam. 20:6–10 b 2 Sam. 18:3 c 1 Kin. 11:36
18 a 1 Chr. 20:4–8 b 1 Chr. 11:29; 27:11 *1 Sippai,* 1 Chr. 20:4 *2* Or *Rapha*
19 a 2 Sam. 23:24 b 1 Chr. 20:5 *1 Jair,* 1 Chr. 20:5
20 a 1 Chr. 20:6 *1* Or *Rapha*
21 a 1 Sam. 17:10 *1 Shammah,* 1 Sam. 16:9 and elsewhere
22 a 1 Chr. 20:8 *1* Or *Rapha*

CHAPTER 22
1 a Ex. 15:1 b Ps. 18:title; 34:19
2 a Ps. 18 b Deut. 32:4 c Ps. 91:2
3 a Heb. 2:13 b Gen. 15:1 c Luke 1:69 *1* Strength

My [d]stronghold and my [e]refuge;
My Savior, You save me from
violence.
4 I will call upon the LORD, *who is worthy* to be praised;
So shall I be saved from my
enemies.

Lord, You are our strength and shield, our stronghold and refuge. May ____ call upon You and be saved from their enemies.

FROM 2 SAMUEL 22:3, 4

5 "When the waves of death
surrounded me,
The floods of ungodliness [1]made
me afraid.
6 The [a]sorrows of Sheol surrounded
me;
The snares of death confronted me.
7 In my distress [a]I called upon the
LORD,
And cried out to my God;
He [b]heard my voice from His
temple,
And my cry *entered* His ears.
8 "Then [a]the earth shook and
trembled;
[b]The foundations of [1]heaven quaked
and were shaken,
Because He was angry.
9 Smoke went up from His nostrils,
And devouring [a]fire from His
mouth;
Coals were kindled by it.
10 He [a]bowed the heavens also, and
came down
With [b]darkness under His feet.
11 He rode upon a cherub, and flew;
And He [1]was seen [a]upon the wings
of the wind.
12 He made [a]darkness canopies
around Him,
Dark waters *and* thick clouds of the
skies.
13 From the brightness before Him
Coals of fire were kindled.
14 "The LORD [a]thundered from
heaven,
And the Most High uttered His
voice.
15 He sent out [a]arrows and scattered
them;
Lightning bolts, and He vanquished
them.
16 Then the channels of the sea
[a]were seen,
The foundations of the world were
uncovered,
At the [b]rebuke of the LORD,
At the blast of the breath of His
nostrils.

Oh, what a cause of thankfulness it is that we have a gracious God to whom to go on all occasions. Use and enjoy this privilege and you can never be miserable.

LADY MAXWELL OF EDINBURGH

17 "He[a] sent from above, He took me,
He drew me out of many waters.
18 He delivered me from my strong
enemy,
From those who hated me;
For they were too strong for me.
19 They confronted me in the day of
my calamity,
But the LORD was my [a]support.
20 [a]He also brought me out into a
broad place;
He delivered me because He
[b]delighted in me.
21 "The[a] LORD rewarded me according
to my righteousness;
According to the [b]cleanness of my
hands
He has recompensed me.
22 For I have [a]kept the ways of the
LORD,
And have not wickedly departed
from my God.
23 For all His [a]judgments *were*
before me;
And *as for* His statutes, I did not
depart from them.
24 I was also [a]blameless before Him,
And I kept myself from my iniquity.

3 [d] Prov. 18:10 [e] Ps. 9:9; 46:1, 7, 11
5 [1] Or *overwhelmed*
6 [a] Ps. 116:3
7 [a] Ps. 116:4; 120:1 [b] Ex. 3:7
8 [a] Judg. 5:4 [b] Job 26:11 [1] So with MT, LXX, Tg.; Syr., Vg. *hills* (cf. Ps. 18:7)
9 [a] Heb. 12:29
10 [a] Is. 64:1 [b] Ex. 20:21
11 [a] Ps. 104:3 [1] So with MT, LXX; many Heb. mss., Syr., Vg. *flew* (cf. Ps. 18:10); Tg. *spoke with power*
12 [a] Job 36:29
14 [a] Job 37:2–5
15 [a] Deut. 32:23
16 [a] Nah. 1:4 [b] Ex. 15:8
17 [a] Ps. 144:7
19 [a] Is. 10:20
20 [a] Ps. 31:8; 118:5 [b] 2 Sam. 15:26
21 [a] 1 Sam. 26:23 [b] Ps. 24:4
22 [a] Ps. 119:3
23 [a] [Deut. 6:6–9; 7:12]
24 [a] [Eph. 1:4]

25 Therefore [a]the LORD has
[1]recompensed me according to
my righteousness,
According to [2]my cleanness in His
eyes.

26 "With [a]the merciful You will show
Yourself merciful;
With a blameless man You will
show Yourself blameless;
27 With the pure You will show
Yourself pure;
And [a]with the devious You will
show Yourself shrewd.
28 You will save the [a]humble[1]
people;
But Your eyes *are* on [b]the haughty,
that You may bring *them* down.

29 "For You *are* my [a]lamp, O LORD;
The LORD shall enlighten my
darkness.
30 For by You I can run against a
troop;
By my God I can leap over a [a]wall.
31 *As for* God, [a]His way *is* perfect;
[b]The word of the LORD *is* proven;
He *is* a shield to all who trust in
Him.

32 "For [a]who *is* God, except the LORD?
And who *is* a rock, except our God?
33 [1]God *is* my [a]strength *and* power,
And He [b]makes [2]my way [c]perfect.
34 He makes [1]my feet [a]like the *feet*
of deer,
And [b]sets me on my high places.
35 He teaches my hands [1]to make
war,
So that my arms can bend a bow of
bronze.

36 "You have also given me the shield
of Your salvation;
Your gentleness has made me great.
37 You [a]enlarged my path under me;
So my feet did not slip.

38 "I have pursued my enemies and
destroyed them;
Neither did I turn back again till
they were destroyed.
39 And I have destroyed them and
wounded them,
So that they could not rise;
They have fallen [a]under my feet.
40 For You have [a]armed me with
strength for the battle;
You have [1]subdued under me
[b]those who rose against me.

41 You have also [1]given me the
[a]necks of my enemies,
So that I destroyed those who hated
me.
42 They looked, but *there was* none
to save;
Even [a]to the LORD, but He did not
answer them.
43 Then I beat them as fine [a]as the
dust of the earth;
I trod them [b]like dirt in the streets,
And I [1]spread them out.

44 "You[a] have also delivered me from
the [1]strivings of my people;
You have kept me as the [b]head of
the nations.
[c]A people I have not known shall
serve me.
45 The foreigners submit to me;
As soon as they hear, they obey me.
46 The foreigners fade away,
And [1]come frightened [a]from their
hideouts.

47 "The LORD lives!
Blessed *be* my Rock!
Let God be exalted,
The [a]Rock of my salvation!
48 *It is* God who avenges me,
And [a]subdues the peoples under
me;
49 He delivers me from my enemies.
You also lift me up above those
who rise against me;
You have delivered me from the
[a]violent man.
50 Therefore I will give thanks to
You, O LORD, among [a]the
Gentiles,
And sing praises to Your [b]name.

51 *He*[a] *is* the tower of salvation to
His king,
And shows mercy to His [b]anointed,
To David and [c]his descendants
forevermore."

David's Last Words

23 Now these *are* the last words of
David.

Thus says David the son of Jesse;
Thus says [a]the man raised up on
high,
[b]The anointed of the God of Jacob,

25 [a] 2 Sam. 22:21 [1] *rewarded* [2] LXX, Syr., Vg. *the cleanness of my hands in His sight* (cf. Ps. 18:24); Tg. *my cleanness before His word*
26 [a] [Matt. 5:7]
27 [a] [Lev. 26:23, 24]
28 [a] Ps. 72:12 [b] Job 40:11 [1] *afflicted*
29 [a] Ps. 119:105; 132:17
30 [a] 2 Sam. 5:6–8
31 [a] [Matt. 5:48] [b] Ps. 12:6
32 [a] Is. 45:5, 6
33 [a] Ps. 27:1 [b] [Heb. 13:21] [c] Ps. 101:2, 6 [1] DSS, LXX, Syr., Vg. *It is God who arms me with strength* (cf. Ps. 18:32); Tg. *It is God who sustains me with strength* [2] So with Qr., LXX, Syr., Tg., Vg. (cf. Ps. 18:32); Kt. *His*
34 [a] 2 Sam. 2:18 [b] Is. 33:16 [1] So with Qr., LXX, Syr., Tg., Vg. (cf. Ps. 18:33); Kt. *His*
35 [1] Lit. *for the war*
37 [a] Prov. 4:12
39 [a] Mal. 4:3
40 [a] [Ps. 18:32] [b] [Ps. 44:5] [1] Lit. *caused to bow down*
41 [a] Gen. 49:8 [1] *given me victory over*
42 [a] 1 Sam. 28:6
43 [a] Ps. 18:42 [b] Is. 10:6 [1] *scattered*
44 [a] 2 Sam. 3:1 [b] Deut. 28:13 [c] [Is. 55:5] [1] *contentions*
46 [a] [Mic. 7:17] [1] So with LXX, Tg., Vg. (cf. Ps. 18:45); MT *gird themselves*
47 [a] Ps. 89:26 **48** [a] Ps. 144:2 **49** [a] Ps. 140:1, 4, 11 **50** [a] 2 Sam. 8:1–14 [b] Rom. 15:9 **51** [a] Ps. 144:10 [b] Ps. 89:20 [c] 2 Sam. 7:12–16 **CHAPTER 23 1** [a] 2 Sam. 7:8, 9 [b] 1 Sam. 16:12, 13

And the sweet psalmist of Israel:
2 "The[a] Spirit of the LORD spoke by me,
And His word *was* on my tongue.
3 The God of Israel said,
[a]The Rock of Israel spoke to me:
'He who rules over men *must be* just,
Ruling [b]in the fear of God.
4 And [a]*he shall be* like the light of the morning *when* the sun rises,
A morning without clouds,
Like the tender grass *springing* out of the earth,
By clear shining after rain.'

I seek the will of the Spirit of God through the Word of God. The Spirit and the Word must be combined.

GEORGE MUELLER

5 "Although my house *is* not so with God,
[a]Yet He has made with me an everlasting covenant,
Ordered in all *things* and secure.
For *this is* all my salvation and all *my* desire;
Will He not make *it* increase?
6 But *the sons* of rebellion *shall* all *be* as thorns thrust away,
Because they cannot be taken with hands.
7 But the man *who* touches them
Must be [1]armed with iron and the shaft of a spear,
And they shall be utterly burned with fire in *their* place."

David's Mighty Men

[8]These *are* the names of the mighty
men whom David had: [1]Josheb-
Basshebeth the Tachmonite, chief among
[2]the captains. He was called Adino the Ez-
nite, because he had killed eight hundred
men at one time. [9]And after him *was* [a]Ele-
azar the son of [1]Dodo, the Ahohite, *one* of
the three mighty men with David when
they defied the Philistines *who* were gathered there for battle, and the men of Israel
had retreated. [10]He arose and attacked the
Philistines until his hand was [a]weary, and
his hand stuck to the sword. The LORD
brought about a great victory that day;
and the people returned after him only to
[b]plunder. [11]And after him *was* [a]Shammah
the son of Agee the Hararite. [b]The Philistines had gathered together into a troop
where there was a piece of ground full of
lentils. So the people fled from the Philistines. [12]But he stationed himself in the
middle of the field, defended it, and killed
the Philistines. So the LORD brought
about a great victory.

[13]Then [a]three of the thirty chief men
went down at harvest time and came to
David at [b]the cave of Adullam. And the
troop of Philistines encamped in [c]the Valley of Rephaim. [14]David *was* then in [a]the
stronghold, and the garrison of the Philistines *was* then *in* Bethlehem. [15]And David
said with longing, "Oh, that someone
would give me a drink of the water from
the well of Bethlehem, which *is* by the
gate!" [16]So the three mighty men broke
through the camp of the Philistines, drew
water from the well of Bethlehem that
was by the gate, and took it and brought
it to David. Nevertheless he would not
drink it, but poured it out to the LORD.
[17]And he said, "Far be it from me, O LORD,
that I should do this! Is *this not* [a]the
blood of the men who went in *jeopardy of*
their lives?" Therefore he would not
drink it.

These things were done by the three
mighty men.

[18]Now [a]Abishai the brother of Joab, the
son of Zeruiah, was chief of [1]*another*
three. He lifted his spear against three
hundred *men,* killed *them,* and won a
name among *these* three. [19]Was he not
the most honored of three? Therefore he
became their captain. However, he did not
attain to the *first* three.

[20]Benaiah *was* the son of Jehoiada, the
son of a valiant man from [a]Kabzeel, [1]who
had done many deeds. [b]He had killed two
lion-like heroes of Moab. He also had
gone down and killed a lion in the midst
of a pit on a snowy day. [21]And he killed an
Egyptian, [1]a spectacular man. The Egyptian *had* a spear in his hand; so he went
down to him with a staff, wrested the
spear out of the Egyptian's hand, and
killed him with his own spear. [22]These
things Benaiah the son of Jehoiada did,
and won a name among three mighty

2 a [2 Pet. 1:21]
3 a [Deut. 32:4] b Ex. 18:21
4 a Ps. 89:36
5 a Ps. 89:29
7 *1* Lit. *filled*
8 *1* Lit. *One Who Sits in the Seat* (1 Chr. 11:11) *2* So with MT, Tg.; LXX, Vg. *the three*
9 a 1 Chr. 11:12; 27:4 *1 Dodai,* 1 Chr. 27:4
10 a Judg. 8:4 b 1 Sam. 30:24, 25
11 a 1 Chr. 11:27 b 1 Chr. 11:13, 14
13 a 1 Chr. 11:15 b 1 Sam. 22:1 c 2 Sam. 5:18
14 a 1 Sam. 22:4, 5
17 a [Lev. 17:10]
18 a 1 Chr. 11:20 *1* So with MT, LXX, Vg.; some Heb. mss., Syr. *thirty;* Tg. *the mighty men*
20 a Josh. 15:21 b Ex. 15:15 *1* Lit. *great of acts*
21 *1* Lit. *a man of appearance*

men. 23He was more honored than the thirty, but he did not attain to the *first* three. And David appointed him [a]over his guard.

24[a]Asahel the brother of Joab *was* one of the thirty; Elhanan the son of Dodo of Bethlehem, 25[a]Shammah the Harodite, Elika the Harodite, 26Helez the Paltite, Ira the son of Ikkesh the Tekoite, 27Abiezer the Anathothite, Mebunnai the Hushathite, 28Zalmon the Ahohite, Maharai the Netophathite, 29Heleb the son of Baanah (the Netophathite), Ittai the son of Ribai from Gibeah of the children of Benjamin, 30Benaiah a Pirathonite, Hiddai from the brooks of [a]Gaash, 31Abi-Albon the Arbathite, Azmaveth the Barhumite, 32Eliahba the Shaalbonite (of the sons of Jashen), Jonathan, 33[a]Shammah the [1]Hararite, Ahiam the son of Sharar the Hararite, 34Eliphelet the son of Ahasbai, the son of the Maachathite, Eliam the son of [a]Ahithophel the Gilonite, 35[1]Hezrai the Carmelite, Paarai the Arbite, 36Igal the son of Nathan of [a]Zobah, Bani the Gadite, 37Zelek the Ammonite, Naharai the Beerothite (armorbearer of Joab the son of Zeruiah), 38[a]Ira the Ithrite, Gareb the Ithrite, 39*and* [a]Uriah the Hittite: thirty-seven in all.

David's Census of Israel and Judah

24 Again [a]the anger of the LORD was aroused against Israel, and He moved David against them to say, [b]"Go, [1]number Israel and Judah."

2So the king said to Joab the commander of the army who *was* with him, "Now go throughout all the tribes of Israel, [a]from Dan to Beersheba, and count the people, that [b]I may know the number of the people."

3And Joab said to the king, "Now may the LORD your God [a]add to the people a hundred times more than there are, and may the eyes of my lord the king see *it*. But why does my lord the king desire this thing?" 4Nevertheless the king's word [1]prevailed against Joab and against the captains of the army. Therefore Joab and the captains of the army went out from the presence of the king to count the people of Israel.

5And they crossed over the Jordan and camped in [a]Aroer, on the right side of the town which *is* in the midst of the ravine of Gad, and toward [b]Jazer. 6Then they came to Gilead and to the land of Tahtim Hodshi; they came to [a]Dan Jaan and around to [b]Sidon; 7and they came to the stronghold of [a]Tyre and to all the cities of the [b]Hivites and the Canaanites. Then they went out to South Judah *as far as* Beersheba. 8So when they had gone through all the land, they came to Jerusalem at the end of nine months and twenty days. 9Then Joab gave the sum of the number of the people to the king. [a]And there were in Israel eight hundred thousand valiant men who drew the sword, and the men of Judah were five hundred thousand men.

The Judgment on David's Sin

10And [a]David's heart condemned him after he had numbered the people. So [b]David said to the LORD, [c]"I have sinned greatly in what I have done; but now, I pray, O LORD, take away the iniquity of Your servant, for I have [d]done very foolishly."

11Now when David arose in the morning, the word of the LORD came to the prophet [a]Gad, David's [b]seer, saying, 12"Go and tell David, 'Thus says the LORD: "I offer you three *things;* choose one of them for yourself, that I may do *it* to you." ' " 13So Gad came to David and told him; and he said to him, "Shall [a]seven[1] years of famine come to you in your land? Or shall you flee three months before your enemies, while they pursue you? Or shall there be three days' plague in your land? Now consider and see what answer I should take back to Him who sent me."

14And David said to Gad, "I am in great distress. Please let us fall into the hand of the LORD, [a]for His mercies *are* great; but [b]do not let me fall into the hand of man."

15So [a]the LORD sent a plague upon Israel from the morning till the appointed time. From Dan to Beersheba seventy thousand men of the people died. 16[a]And when the [1]angel stretched out His hand over Jerusalem to destroy it, [b]the LORD relented from the destruction, and said to the angel who was destroying the people, "It is enough; now restrain your hand." And the angel of the LORD was by the threshing floor of [2]Araunah the Jebusite.

17Then David spoke to the LORD when he saw the angel who was striking the people, and said, "Surely [a]I have sinned, and I have done wickedly; but these sheep, what have they done? Let Your hand, I

23 a 2 Sam. 8:18; 20:23
24 a 2 Sam. 2:18
25 a 1 Chr. 11:27
30 a Judg. 2:9
33 a 2 Sam. 23:11 *1* Or *Ararite*
34 a 2 Sam. 15:12
35 *1 Hezro,* 1 Chr. 11:37
36 a 2 Sam. 8:3
38 a 1 Chr. 2:53
39 a 2 Sam. 11:3, 6

CHAPTER 24
1 a 2 Sam. 21:1, 2 b 1 Chr. 27:23, 24 *1 take a census of*
2 a Judg. 20:1 b [Jer. 17:5]
3 a Deut. 1:11
4 *1 overruled*
5 a Deut. 2:36 b Num. 32:1, 3
6 a Judg. 18:29 b Josh. 19:28
7 a Josh. 19:29 b Josh. 11:3
9 a 1 Chr. 21:5
10 a 1 Sam. 24:5 b 2 Sam. 23:1 c 2 Sam. 12:13 d 1 Sam. 13:13
11 a 1 Sam. 22:5 b 1 Sam. 9:9
13 a Ezek. 14:21 *1* So with MT, Syr., Tg., Vg.; LXX *three* (cf. 1 Chr. 21:12)
14 a [Ps. 51:1; 103:8, 13, 14; 119:156; 130:4, 7] b [Is. 47:6]
15 a 1 Chr. 21:14
16 a Ex. 12:23 b Gen. 6:6 *1* Or *Angel* *2 Ornan,* 1 Chr. 21:15
17 a Ps. 74:1

pray, be against me and against my father's house."

The Altar on the Threshing Floor

18And Gad came that day to David and
said to him, [a]"Go up, erect an altar to the
LORD on the threshing floor of Araunah
the Jebusite." 19So David, according to the
word of Gad, went up as the LORD commanded.
20Now Araunah looked, and saw
the king and his servants coming toward him. So Araunah went out and bowed before the king with his face to the ground.
21Then Araunah said, "Why has my lord
the king come to his servant?"
[a]And David said, "To buy the threshing floor from you, to build an altar to the LORD, that [b]the plague may be withdrawn from the people."
22Now Araunah said to David, "Let my
lord the king take and offer up whatever *seems* good to him. [a]Look, *here are* oxen for burnt sacrifice, and threshing implements and the yokes of the oxen for wood.
23All these, O king, Araunah has given to
the king."
And Araunah said to the king, "May the LORD your God [a]accept you."
24Then the king said to Araunah, "No,
but I will surely buy *it* from you for a price; nor will I offer burnt offerings to the LORD my God with that which costs me nothing." So [a]David bought the threshing floor and the oxen for fifty shekels of silver.
25And David built there
an altar to the LORD, and offered burnt offerings and peace offerings. [a]So the LORD heeded the prayers for the land, and [b]the plague was withdrawn from Israel.

> *Everything depends on prayer, and yet we neglect it—not only to our own spiritual hurt, but also to the delay and injury of our Lord's cause upon earth.*
>
> E. M. BOUNDS

18 [a] 1 Chr. 21:18
21 [a] Gen. 23:8–16 [b] Num. 16:48, 50
22 [a] 1 Kin. 19:21
23 [a] [Ezek. 20:40, 41]
24 [a] 1 Chr. 21:24, 25
25 [a] 2 Sam. 21:14 [b] 2 Sam. 24:21

AUTHOR: *Unknown; Attributed to Jeremiah*
DATE: *Probably 560–538 B.C.*
THEME: *Lessons from the Dividing of the United Kingdom*
KEY WORDS: *King, House, Prophet*

1 KINGS

Dear Woman of Destiny,

First Kings shows us that, for a nation to thrive, faithfulness must be its foundation. What is the secret of faithfulness? It is the realization that observance of God's laws produces blessings, while obedience brings His judgment. The obedience of the widow at Zarephath illustrates the simple road to victory—a road that we, too, can follow.

His love and mine,

Marilyn Hickey

Adonijah Presumes to Be King

Now King David was [a]old, [1]ad-
vanced in years; and they put covers on him, but he could not get
warm. 2Therefore his servants said to
him, "Let a young woman, a virgin, be
sought for our lord the king, and let her
[1]stand before the king, and let her care for
him; and let her lie in your bosom, that
our lord the king may be warm." 3So they
sought for a lovely young woman
throughout all the territory of Israel, and
found [a]Abishag the [b]Shunammite, and
brought her to the king. 4The young
woman *was* very lovely; and she cared for
the king, and served him; but the king did
not know her.

5Then [a]Adonijah the [1]son of Haggith
exalted himself, saying, "I will [2]be king";
and [b]he prepared for himself chariots and
horsemen, and fifty men to run before
him. 6(And his father had not [1]rebuked
him at any time by saying, "Why have you
done so?" He *was* also very good-looking.
[a]*His mother* had borne him after Absalom.) 7Then he conferred with [a]Joab the
son of Zeruiah and with [b]Abiathar the
priest, and [c]they followed and helped Adonijah. 8But [a]Zadok the priest, [b]Benaiah
the son of Jehoiada, [c]Nathan the prophet,
[d]Shimei, Rei, and [e]the mighty men who
belonged to David were not with Adonijah.

9And Adonijah sacrificed sheep and
oxen and fattened cattle by the stone of
[1]Zoheleth, which *is* by [a]En Rogel;[2] he also
invited all his brothers, the king's sons,
and all the men of Judah, the king's servants. 10But he did not invite Nathan the
prophet, Benaiah, the mighty men, or
[a]Solomon his brother.

11So Nathan spoke to Bathsheba the
mother of Solomon, saying, "Have you
not heard that Adonijah the son of [a]Hag-
gith has become king, and David our lord
does not know *it?* 12Come, please, let me
now give you advice, that you may save
your own life and the life of your son Solomon. 13Go immediately to King David
and say to him, 'Did you not, my lord,
O king, swear to your maidservant, saying, [a]"Assuredly your son Solomon shall
reign after me, and he shall sit on my
throne"? Why then has Adonijah become
king?' 14Then, while you are still talking
there with the king, I also will come in
after you and confirm your words."

15So Bathsheba went into the chamber
to the king. (Now the king was very old,
and Abishag the Shunammite was serving
the king.) 16And Bathsheba bowed and did
homage to the king. Then the king said,
"What is your wish?"

17Then she said to him, "My lord, [a]you
swore by the LORD your God to your maidservant, *saying,* 'Assuredly Solomon your
son shall reign after me, and he shall sit
on my throne.' 18So now, look! Adonijah
has become king; and now, my lord the
king, you do not know about *it.* 19[a]He has
sacrificed oxen and fattened cattle and
sheep in abundance, and has invited all
the sons of the king, Abiathar the priest,
and Joab the commander of the army; but
Solomon your servant he has not invited.
20And as for you, my lord, O king, the eyes
of all Israel *are* on you, that you should
tell them who will sit on the throne of my
lord the king after him. 21Otherwise it will
happen, when my lord the king [a]rests
with his fathers, that I and my son Solomon will be counted as offenders."

22And just then, while she was still talking with the king, Nathan the prophet
also came in. 23So they told the king, saying, "Here is Nathan the prophet." And
when he came in before the king, he
bowed down before the king with his face
to the ground. 24And Nathan said, "My
lord, O king, have you said, 'Adonijah
shall reign after me, and he shall sit on my
throne'? 25[a]For he has gone down today,
and has sacrificed oxen and fattened cattle
and sheep in abundance, and has invited
all the king's sons, and the commanders
of the army, and Abiathar the priest; and
look! They are eating and drinking before
him; and they say, [b]'*Long*[1] live King Adonijah!' 26But he has not invited me—me
your servant—nor Zadok the priest, nor
Benaiah the son of Jehoiada, nor your servant Solomon. 27Has this thing been done
by my lord the king, and you have not told
your servant who should sit on the throne
of my lord the king after him?"

David Proclaims Solomon King

28Then King David answered and said,
"Call Bathsheba to me." So she came into
the king's presence and stood before the
king. 29And the king took an oath and
said, [a]"*As* the LORD lives, who has re-

CHAPTER 1
1 [a] 1 Chr. 23:1 [1] Seventy years
2 [1] Or *serve*
3 [a] 1 Kin. 2:17 [b] Josh. 19:18
5 [a] 2 Sam. 3:4 [b] 2 Sam. 15:1 [1] The fourth son [2] Lit. *reign*
6 [a] 2 Sam. 3:3, 4 [1] Lit. *pained*
7 [a] 1 Chr. 11:6 [b] 2 Sam. 20:25 [c] 1 Kin. 2:22, 28
8 [a] 1 Kin. 2:35 [b] 1 Kin. 2:25 [c] 2 Sam. 12:1 [d] 1 Kin. 4:18 [e] 2 Sam. 23:8
9 [a] Josh. 15:7; 18:16 [1] Lit. *Serpent* [2] A spring south of Jerusalem in the Kidron Valley
10 [a] 2 Sam. 12:24
11 [a] 2 Sam. 3:4
13 [a] 1 Chr. 22:9–13
17 [a] 1 Kin. 1:13, 30
19 [a] 1 Kin. 1:7–9, 25
21 [a] Deut. 31:16
25 [a] 1 Kin. 1:9, 19 [b] 1 Sam. 10:24 [1] Lit. *Let King Adonijah live*
29 [a] 2 Sam. 4:9; 12:5

deemed my life from every distress,
30[a]just as I swore to you by the LORD God
of Israel, saying, 'Assuredly Solomon your
son shall be king after me, and he shall sit
on my throne in my place,' so I certainly
will do this day."
31Then Bathsheba bowed with *her* face
to the earth, and paid homage to the king,
and said, [a]"Let my lord King David live
forever!"
32And King David said, "Call to me Zadok the priest, Nathan the prophet, and
Benaiah the son of Jehoiada." So they
came before the king. 33The king also said
to them, [a]"Take with you the servants of
your lord, and have Solomon my son ride
on my own [b]mule, and take him down to
[c]Gihon.[1] 34There let Zadok the priest and
Nathan the prophet [a]anoint him king
over Israel; and [b]blow the horn, and say,
[1]'*Long* live King Solomon!' 35Then you
shall come up after him, and he shall
come and sit on my throne, and he shall
be king in my place. For I have appointed
him to be ruler over Israel and Judah."
36Benaiah the son of Jehoiada answered
the king and said, [a]"Amen! May the LORD
God of my lord the king say so *too*. 37[a]As
the LORD has been with my lord the king,
even so may He be with Solomon, and
[b]make his throne greater than the throne
of my lord King David."
38So Zadok the priest, Nathan the
prophet, [a]Benaiah the son of Jehoiada,
the [b]Cherethites, and the Pelethites went
down and had Solomon ride on King David's mule, and took him to Gihon. 39Then
Zadok the priest took a horn of [a]oil from
the tabernacle and [b]anointed Solomon.
And they blew the horn, [c]and all the people said, [1]"*Long* live King Solomon!"
40And all the people went up after him;
and the people played the flutes and rejoiced with great joy, so that the earth
seemed to split with their sound.
41Now Adonijah and all the guests who
were with him heard *it* as they finished
eating. And when Joab heard the sound of
the horn, he said, "Why *is* the city in such
a noisy uproar?" 42While he was still
speaking, there came [a]Jonathan, the son
of Abiathar the priest. And Adonijah said
to him, "Come in, for [b]you *are* a prominent man, and bring good news."
43Then Jonathan answered and said to
Adonijah, "No! Our lord King David has
made Solomon king. 44The king has sent

30 a 1 Kin. 1:13, 17
31 a Dan. 2:4; 3:9
33 a 2 Sam. 20:6 b Esth. 6:8 c 2 Chr. 32:30; 33:14 *1* A spring east of Jerusalem in the Kidron Valley
34 a 1 Sam. 10:1; 16:3, 12 b 2 Sam. 15:10 *1* Lit. *Let King Solomon live*
36 a Jer. 28:6
37 a 1 Sam. 20:13 b 1 Kin. 1:47
38 a 2 Sam. 8:18; 23:20–23 b 2 Sam. 20:7
39 a Ps. 89:20 b 1 Chr. 29:22 c 1 Sam. 10:24 *1* Lit. *Let King Solomon live*
42 a 2 Sam. 17:17, 20 b 2 Sam. 18:27
46 a 1 Chr. 29:23
47 a 1 Kin. 1:37 b Gen. 47:31
48 a 1 Kin. 3:6 b 2 Sam. 7:12
50 a 1 Kin. 2:28
52 a 1 Sam. 14:45
CHAPTER 2
1 a Gen. 47:29 *1 commanded*
2 a Josh. 23:14 b Deut. 31:7, 23
3 a [Deut. 29:9]
4 a 2 Sam. 7:25 b [Ps. 132:12] c 2 Kin. 20:3

with him Zadok the priest, Nathan the
prophet, Benaiah the son of Jehoiada, the
Cherethites, and the Pelethites; and they
have made him ride on the king's mule.
45So Zadok the priest and Nathan the
prophet have anointed him king at Gihon;
and they have gone up from there rejoicing, so that the city is in an uproar. This
is the noise that you have heard. 46Also
Solomon [a]sits on the throne of the kingdom. 47And moreover the king's servants
have gone to bless our lord King David,
saying, [a]'May God make the name of Solomon better than your name, and may
He make his throne greater than your
throne.' [b]Then the king bowed himself on
the bed. 48Also the king said thus, 'Blessed
be the LORD God of Israel, who has [a]given
one to sit on my throne this day, while my
eyes see [b]*it!*' "
49So all the guests who were with Adonijah were afraid, and arose, and each one
went his way.
50Now Adonijah was afraid of Solomon;
so he arose, and went and [a]took hold of
the horns of the altar. 51And it was told
Solomon, saying, "Indeed Adonijah is
afraid of King Solomon; for look, he has
taken hold of the horns of the altar, saying, 'Let King Solomon swear to me today
that he will not put his servant to death
with the sword.' "
52Then Solomon said, "If he proves
himself a worthy man, [a]not one hair of
him shall fall to the earth; but if wickedness is found in him, he shall die." 53So
King Solomon sent them to bring him
down from the altar. And he came and fell
down before King Solomon; and Solomon
said to him, "Go to your house."

David's Instructions to Solomon

2 Now [a]the days of David drew near that
he should die, and he [1]charged Solomon his son, saying: 2[a]"I go the way of
all the earth; [b]be strong, therefore, and
prove yourself a man. 3And keep the
charge of the LORD your God: to walk in
His ways, to keep His statutes, His commandments, His judgments, and His testimonies, as it is written in the Law of
Moses, that you may [a]prosper in all that
you do and wherever you turn; 4that the
LORD may [a]fulfill His word which He
spoke concerning me, saying, [b]'If your
sons take heed to their way, to [c]walk

before Me in truth with all their heart and with all their soul,’ He said, [d]‘you shall not lack a man on the throne of Israel.’

I pray that _____ will keep Your charge: to walk in Your ways that they may prosper in all they do and in every place they go.

FROM I KINGS 2:3

5“Moreover you know also what Joab the son of Zeruiah [a]did to me, *and* what he did to the two commanders of the armies of Israel, to [b]Abner the son of Ner and [c]Amasa the son of Jether, whom he killed. And he shed the blood of war in peacetime, and put the blood of war on his belt that *was* around his waist, and on his sandals that *were* on his feet. 6Therefore do [a]according to your wisdom, and do not let his gray hair go down to the grave in peace.

7“But show kindness to the sons of [a]Barzillai the Gileadite, and let them be among those who [b]eat at your table, for so [c]they came to me when I fled from Absalom your brother.

8“And see, *you have* with you [a]Shimei the son of Gera, a Benjamite from Bahurim, who cursed me with a malicious curse in the day when I went to Mahanaim. But [b]he came down to meet me at the Jordan, and [c]I swore to him by the LORD, saying, ‘I will not put you to death with the sword.’ 9Now therefore, [a]do not hold him guiltless, for you *are* a wise man and know what you ought to do to him; but [b]bring his gray hair down to the grave with blood.”

Death of David

10So [a]David [1]rested with his fathers, and was buried in [b]the City of David. 11The period that David [a]reigned over Israel *was* forty years; seven years he reigned in Hebron, and in Jerusalem he reigned thirty-three years. 12[a]Then Solomon sat on the throne of his father David; and his kingdom was [b]firmly established.

Solomon Executes Adonijah

13Now Adonijah the son of Haggith came to Bathsheba the mother of Solomon. So she said, [a]“Do you come peaceably?”

And he said, “Peaceably.” 14Moreover he said, “I have something *to say* to you.”

And she said, “Say it.”

15Then he said, “You know that the kingdom was [a]mine, and all Israel had set their expectations on me, that I should reign. However, the kingdom has been turned over, and has become my brother’s; for [b]it was his from the LORD. 16Now I ask one petition of you; do not [1]deny me.”

And she said to him, “Say it.”

17Then he said, “Please speak to King Solomon, for he will not refuse you, that he may give me [a]Abishag the Shunammite as wife.”

18So Bathsheba said, “Very well, I will speak for you to the king.”

19Bathsheba therefore went to King Solomon, to speak to him for Adonijah. And the king rose up to meet her and [a]bowed down to her, and sat down on his throne and had a throne set for the king’s mother; [b]so she sat at his right hand. 20Then she said, “I desire one small petition of you; do not [1]refuse me.”

And the king said to her, “Ask it, my mother, for I will not refuse you.”

21So she said, “Let Abishag the Shunammite be given to Adonijah your brother as wife.”

22And King Solomon answered and said to his mother, “Now why do you ask Abishag the Shunammite for Adonijah? Ask for him the kingdom also—for he *is* my [a]older brother—for him, and for [b]Abiathar the priest, and for Joab the son of Zeruiah.” 23Then King Solomon swore by the LORD, saying, [a]“May God do so to me, and more also, if Adonijah has not spoken this word against his own life! 24Now therefore, *as* the LORD lives, who has confirmed me and set me on the throne of David my father, and who has established a [1]house for me, as He [a]promised, Adonijah shall be put to death today!”

25So King Solomon sent by the hand of [a]Benaiah the son of Jehoiada; and he struck him down, and he died.

4 d 2 Sam. 7:12, 13
5 a 2 Sam. 3:39; 18:5, 12, 14 b 2 Sam. 3:27 c 2 Sam. 20:10
6 a 1 Kin. 2:9
7 a 2 Sam. 19:31–39 b 2 Sam. 9:7, 10; 19:28 c 2 Sam. 17:17–29
8 a 2 Sam. 16:5–13 b 2 Sam. 19:18 c 2 Sam. 19:23
9 a Ex. 20:7 b Gen. 42:38; 44:31
10 a Acts 2:29; 13:36 b 2 Sam. 5:7 1 Died and joined his ancestors
11 a 2 Sam. 5:4, 5
12 a 1 Chr. 29:23 b 2 Chr. 1:1
13 a 1 Sam. 16:4, 5
15 a 1 Kin. 1:11, 18 b [Dan. 2:21]
16 1 Lit. *turn away the face*
17 a 1 Kin. 1:3, 4
19 a [Ex. 20:12] b Ps. 45:9
20 1 Lit. *turn away the face*
22 a 1 Chr. 3:2, 5 b 1 Kin. 1:7
23 a Ruth 1:17
24 a 2 Sam. 7:11, 13 1 Royal dynasty
25 a 2 Sam. 8:18

Abiathar Exiled, Joab Executed

26And to Abiathar the priest the king said, "Go to [a]Anathoth, to your own fields, for [1]you *are* deserving of death; but I will not put you to death at this time, [b]because you carried the ark of the Lord GOD before my father David, and because you were afflicted every time my father was afflicted." 27So Solomon removed Abiathar from being priest to the LORD, that he might [a]fulfill the word of the LORD which He spoke concerning the house of Eli at Shiloh.

28Then news came to Joab, for Joab [a]had defected to Adonijah, though he had not defected to Absalom. So Joab fled to the tabernacle of the LORD, and [b]took hold of the horns of the altar. 29And King Solomon was told, "Joab has fled to the tabernacle of the LORD; there *he is,* by the altar." Then Solomon sent Benaiah the son of Jehoiada, saying, "Go, [a]strike him down." 30So Benaiah went to the tabernacle of the LORD, and said to him, "Thus says the king, [a]'Come out!' "

And he said, "No, but I will die here." And Benaiah brought back word to the king, saying, "Thus said Joab, and thus he answered me."

31Then the king said to him, [a]"Do as he has said, and strike him down and bury him, [b]that you may take away from me and from the house of my father the innocent blood which Joab shed. 32So the LORD [a]will return his [1]blood on his head, because he struck down two men more righteous [b]and better than he, and killed them with the sword—[c]Abner the son of Ner, the commander of the army of Israel, and [d]Amasa the son of Jether, the commander of the army of Judah—though my father David did not know *it.* 33Their blood shall therefore return upon the head of Joab and [a]upon the head of his descendants forever. [b]But upon David and his descendants, upon his house and his throne, there shall be peace forever from the LORD."

34So Benaiah the son of Jehoiada went up and struck and killed him; and he was buried in his own house in the wilderness. 35The king put Benaiah the son of Jehoiada in his place over the army, and the king put [a]Zadok the priest in the place of [b]Abiathar.

26 a Josh. 21:18 b 2 Sam. 15:14, 29 *1 Lit. you are a man of death*
27 a 1 Sam. 2:31–35
28 a 1 Kin. 1:7 b 1 Kin. 1:50
29 a 1 Kin. 2:5, 6
30 a [Ex. 21:14]
31 a [Ex. 21:14] b [Num. 35:33]
32 a Judg. 9:24, 57 b 2 Chr. 21:13, 14 c 2 Sam. 3:27 d 2 Sam. 20:9, 10 *1 Or bloodshed*
33 a 2 Sam. 3:29 b [Prov. 25:5]
35 a 1 Sam. 2:35 b 1 Kin. 2:27
36 a 1 Kin. 2:8
37 a 2 Sam. 15:23 b Josh. 2:19 *1 Or bloodshed*
39 a 1 Sam. 27:2
44 a 2 Sam. 16:5–13 b 1 Sam. 25:39
45 a [Prov. 25:5]
46 a 2 Chr. 1:1

CHAPTER 3
1 a 1 Kin. 7:8; 9:24 b 2 Sam. 5:7 c 1 Kin. 7:1 d 1 Kin. 6 e 1 Kin. 9:15, 19 *1 an alliance*
2 a [Deut. 12:2–5, 13, 14]
3 a [Rom. 8:28] b [1 Kin. 3:6, 14]

Shimei Executed

36Then the king sent and called for [a]Shimei, and said to him, "Build yourself a house in Jerusalem and dwell there, and do not go out from there anywhere. 37For it shall be, on the day you go out and cross [a]the Brook Kidron, know for certain you shall surely die; [b]your [1]blood shall be on your own head."

38And Shimei said to the king, "The saying *is* good. As my lord the king has said, so your servant will do." So Shimei dwelt in Jerusalem many days.

39Now it happened at the end of three years, that two slaves of Shimei ran away to [a]Achish the son of Maachah, king of Gath. And they told Shimei, saying, "Look, your slaves *are* in Gath!" 40So Shimei arose, saddled his donkey, and went to Achish at Gath to seek his slaves. And Shimei went and brought his slaves from Gath. 41And Solomon was told that Shimei had gone from Jerusalem to Gath and had come back. 42Then the king sent and called for Shimei, and said to him, "Did I not make you swear by the LORD, and warn you, saying, 'Know for certain that on the day you go out and travel anywhere, you shall surely die'? And you said to me, 'The word I have heard *is* good.' 43Why then have you not kept the oath of the LORD and the commandment that I gave you?" 44The king said moreover to Shimei, "You know, as your heart acknowledges, [a]all the wickedness that you did to my father David; therefore the LORD will [b]return your wickedness on your own head. 45But King Solomon *shall be* blessed, and [a]the throne of David shall be established before the LORD forever."

46So the king commanded Benaiah the son of Jehoiada; and he went out and struck him down, and he died. Thus the [a]kingdom was established in the hand of Solomon.

Solomon Requests Wisdom

3 Now [a]Solomon made [1]a treaty with Pharaoh king of Egypt, and married Pharaoh's daughter; then he brought her [b]to the City of David until he had finished building his [c]own house, and [d]the house of the LORD, and [e]the wall all around Jerusalem. 2[a]Meanwhile the people sacrificed at the high places, because there was no house built for the name of the LORD until those days. 3And Solomon [a]loved the LORD, [b]walking in the statutes of his

father David, except that he sacrificed and
burned incense at the high places.
4Now [a]the king went to Gibeon to sacrifice there, [b]for that *was* the great high
place: Solomon offered a thousand burnt
offerings on that altar. 5[a]At Gibeon the
LORD appeared to Solomon [b]in a dream by
night; and God said, "Ask! What shall I
give you?"
6[a]And Solomon said: "You have shown
great mercy to Your servant David my father, because he [b]walked before You in
truth, in righteousness, and in uprightness of heart with You; You have continued this great kindness for him, and You
[c]have given him a son to sit on his throne,
as *it is* this day. 7Now, O LORD my God,
You have made Your servant king instead
of my father David, but I *am* a [a]little child;
I do not know *how* [b]to go out or come in.
8And Your servant *is* in the midst of Your
people whom You [a]have chosen, a great
people, [b]too numerous to be numbered or
counted. 9[a]Therefore give to Your servant an [1]understanding heart [b]to judge
Your people, that I may [c]discern between
good and evil. For who is able to judge
this great people of Yours?"

Give to _____ an understanding heart like Solomon's to discern between good and evil.

FROM 1 KINGS 3:9

10The speech pleased the LORD, that
Solomon had asked this thing. 11Then
God said to him: "Because you have asked
this thing, and have [a]not asked long life
for yourself, nor have asked riches for
yourself, nor have asked the life of your
enemies, but have asked for yourself understanding to discern justice, 12[a]behold,
I have done according to your words; [b]see,
I have given you a wise and understanding
heart, so that there has not been anyone
like you before you, nor shall any like you
arise after you. 13And I have also [a]given
you what you have not asked: both [b]riches
and honor, so that there shall not be anyone like you among the kings all your
days. 14So [a]if you walk in My ways, to keep
My statutes and My commandments, [b]as
your father David walked, then I will
[c]lengthen[1] your days."
15Then Solomon [a]awoke; and indeed it
had been a dream. And he came to Jerusalem and stood before the ark of the covenant of the LORD, offered up burnt
offerings, offered peace offerings, and
[b]made a feast for all his servants.

Solomon's Wise Judgment

16Now two women *who were* harlots
came to the king, and [a]stood before him.
17And one woman said, "O my lord, this
woman and I dwell in the same house; and
I gave birth while she *was* in the house.
18Then it happened, the third day after I
had given birth, that this woman also gave
birth. And we *were* together; [1]no one *was*
with us in the house, except the two of us
in the house. 19And this woman's son died
in the night, because she lay on him. 20So
she arose in the middle of the night and
took my son from my side, while your
maidservant slept, and laid him in her bosom, and laid her dead child in my bosom.
21And when I rose in the morning to
nurse my son, there he was, dead. But
when I had examined him in the morning,
indeed, he was not my son whom I had
borne."
22Then the other woman said, "No! But
the living one *is* my son, and the dead one
is your son."
And the first woman said, "No! But the
dead one *is* your son, and the living one *is*
my son."
Thus they spoke before the king.
23And the king said, "The one says,
'This *is* my son, who lives, and your son *is*
the dead one'; and the other says, 'No! But
your son *is* the dead one, and my son *is*
the living one.' " 24Then the king said,
"Bring me a sword." So they brought a
sword before the king. 25And the king
said, "Divide the living child in two, and
give half to one, and half to the other."
26Then the woman whose son *was* living spoke to the king, for [a]she yearned
with compassion for her son; and she said,
"O my lord, give her the living child, and
by no means kill him!"
But the other said, "Let him be neither
mine nor yours, *but* divide *him*."
27So the king answered and said, "Give
the first woman the living child, and by no
means kill him; she *is* his mother."

4 a 2 Chr. 1:3 b 1 Chr. 16:39; 21:29
5 a 1 Kin. 9:2; 11:9 b Num. 12:6
6 a 2 Chr. 1:8 b 1 Kin. 2:4; 9:4 c 1 Kin. 1:48
7 a Jer. 1:6, 7 b Num. 27:17
8 a [Deut. 7:6] b Gen. 13:6; 15:5; 22:17
9 a 2 Chr. 1:10 b Ps. 72:1, 2 c [Heb. 5:14] *1 Lit. hearing*
11 a [James 4:3]
12 a [1 John 5:14, 15] b Eccl. 1:16
13 a [Matt. 6:33] b 1 Kin. 4:21, 24; 10:23
14 a [1 Kin. 6:12] b 1 Kin. 15:5 c Ps. 91:16 *1 prolong*
15 a Gen. 41:7 b 1 Kin. 8:65
16 a Num. 27:2
18 *1 Lit. no stranger*
26 a Jer. 31:20

1 Kings 3:9

Dear Woman of Destiny,

"You can have anything in the universe your heart desires! Ask of Me, and I will give it to you!" How do you think you would answer if God came to you with this incredible proposition? God *did* appear to King Solomon in a dream, as recorded in 1 Kings 3:5–9, and Solomon was faced with the choice of a lifetime.

The question posed to Solomon was based on a two-way trust—God had to trust Solomon to give him a choice, and Solomon had to trust God enough to believe he would receive what he asked for.

Solomon knew that God's blessing was on his life because of the mercy He had shown to King David, his father. Solomon's rich heritage guaranteed him many privileges. Many of you may not be able to claim this kind of heritage, but the instant you accept Jesus Christ as your Savior, you begin a brand-new heritage. You are living in the King's house and are given all it has to offer! No matter where you come from, this new heritage in Jesus begins.

Solomon didn't ask for more land, riches, or influence. If he had been self-serving and greedy, he could have asked for the world—and received it! Instead, he humbly admitted to God his inexperience, telling Him that he was just a child (1 Kin. 3:7). So Solomon asked God to give him an understanding, or a hearing, heart (1 Kin. 3:9). He knew that, in order to fulfill God's destiny in his life, he needed a heart to hear God's voice and an understanding of His ways. My friend, as you grow in the Lord, you, too, must ask God for an understanding heart, that you may know Him and fulfill His purposes in your life. Only then can you help others to do the same. Solomon didn't just ask for himself; he had others in mind. Likewise, God always anoints you with others in mind. You must know God and then make Him known.

Solomon asked for this hearing heart so that he might know the difference between good and evil, right and wrong (1 Kin. 3:9). Even though Solomon seemingly had everything, he still recognized his need for total dependency on God.

Solomon's response pleased God, and God gave him the wisdom he requested. God was, and is, ever true to His word. But Solomon did not continue to make wise choices. He was not a good steward of what God had given him.

In a time when the lines between good and evil, right and wrong, have clearly been erased, you, too, must have total dependency on God to show you the difference. If not, you will not make wise choices when it comes to your individual life, your family, or those you lead.

My friend, it's not how we start the race that counts, but how we finish! Let's humbly admit our daily need for God to help us make wise choices in determining the difference between right and wrong, thus fulfilling His divine destiny in our lives. Only then can we effectively reach out and help others do the same.

Nancy Hinkle

28And all Israel heard of the judgment
which the king had rendered; and they
feared the king, for they saw that the [a]wis-
dom of God *was* in him to administer justice.

The deepest and most profitable lesson is this: the true knowledge and contempt of ourselves. It is great wisdom and high perfection to esteem nothing of ourselves, and to think always well and highly of others.

THOMAS À KEMPIS

Solomon's Administration

4 So King Solomon was king over all
Israel. 2And these *were* his officials:
Azariah the son of Zadok, the priest; 3Eli-
horeph and Ahijah, the sons of Shisha,
[1]scribes; [a]Jehoshaphat the son of Ahilud,
the recorder; 4[a]Benaiah the son of Jehoiada, over the army; Zadok and [b]Abiathar,
the priests; 5Azariah the son of Nathan,
over [a]the officers; Zabud the son of Nathan, [b]a priest *and* [c]the king's friend;
6Ahishar, over the household; and [a]Adoni-
ram the son of Abda, over the labor force.
7And Solomon had twelve governors
over all Israel, who provided food for the
king and his household; each one made
provision for one month of the year.
8These *are* their names: [1]Ben-Hur, in the
mountains of Ephraim; 9[1]Ben-Deker, in
Makaz, Shaalbim, Beth Shemesh, and
Elon Beth Hanan; 10[1]Ben-Hesed, in Arub-
both; to him *belonged* Sochoh and all the
land of Hepher; 11[1]Ben-Abinadab, *in* all
the regions of Dor; he had Taphath the
daughter of Solomon as wife; 12Baana the
son of Ahilud, *in* Taanach, Megiddo, and
all Beth Shean, which *is* beside Zaretan
below Jezreel, from Beth Shean to Abel
Meholah, as far as the other side of Jokneam; 13[1]Ben-Geber, in Ramoth Gilead; to
him *belonged* [a]the towns of Jair the son of
Manasseh, in Gilead; to him *also belonged*
[b]the region of Argob in Bashan—sixty
large cities with walls and bronze gate-
bars; 14Ahinadab the son of Iddo, *in* Mahanaim; 15[a]Ahimaaz, in Naphtali; he also
took Basemath the daughter of Solomon
as wife; 16Baanah the son of [a]Hushai, in
Asher and Aloth; 17Jehoshaphat the son of
Paruah, in Issachar; 18[a]Shimei the son of
Elah, in Benjamin; 19Geber the son of Uri,
in the land of Gilead, *in* [a]the country of
Sihon king of the Amorites, and of Og
king of Bashan. *He was* the only governor
who *was* in the land.

Prosperity and Wisdom of Solomon's Reign

20Judah and Israel *were* as numerous
[a]as the sand by the sea in multitude, [b]eat-
ing and drinking and rejoicing. 21So [a]Sol-
omon reigned over all kingdoms from
[b]the[1] River *to* the land of the Philistines,
as far as the border of Egypt. [c]*They*
brought tribute and served Solomon all
the days of his life.
22[a]Now Solomon's [1]provision for one
day was thirty [2]kors of fine flour, sixty
kors of meal, 23ten fatted oxen, twenty
oxen from the pastures, and one hundred
sheep, besides deer, gazelles, roebucks,
and fatted fowl.
24For he had dominion over all *the region* on this side of [1]the River from Tiph-
sah even to Gaza, namely over [a]all the
kings on this side of the River; and [b]he
had peace on every side all around him.
25And Judah and Israel [a]dwelt[1] safely,
[b]each man under his vine and his fig tree,
[c]from Dan as far as Beersheba, all the days
of Solomon.
26[a]Solomon had [1]forty thousand stalls
of [b]horses for his chariots, and twelve
thousand horsemen. 27And [a]these governors, each man in his month, provided
food for King Solomon and for all who
came to King Solomon's table. There was
no lack in their supply. 28They also
brought barley and straw to the proper
place, for the horses and steeds, each man
according to his charge.
29And [a]God gave Solomon wisdom and
exceedingly great understanding, and
largeness of heart like the sand on the seashore. 30Thus Solomon's wisdom excelled
the wisdom of all the men [a]of the East and
all [b]the wisdom of Egypt. 31For he was
[a]wiser than all men—[b]than Ethan the
Ezrahite, [c]and Heman, Chalcol, and Darda,

28 a 1 Kin. 3:9, 11, 12

CHAPTER 4

3 a 2 Sam. 8:16; 20:24 *1 secretaries*

4 a 1 Kin. 2:35 b 1 Kin. 2:27

5 a 1 Kin. 4:7 b 2 Sam. 8:18; 20:26 c 2 Sam. 15:37; 16:16

6 a 1 Kin. 5:14

8 *1* Lit. *Son of Hur*

9 *1* Lit. *Son of Deker*

10 *1* Lit. *Son of Hesed*

11 *1* Lit. *Son of Abinadab*

13 a Num. 32:41 b Deut. 3:4 *1* Lit. *Son of Geber*

15 a 2 Sam. 15:27

16 a 1 Chr. 27:33

18 a 1 Kin. 1:8

19 a Deut. 3:8–10

20 a Gen. 22:17; 32:12 b Mic. 4:4

21 a Ps. 72:8 b Gen. 15:18 c Ps. 68:29 *1* The Euphrates

22 a Neh. 5:18 *1* Lit. *bread* *2* Each about 5 bushels

24 a Ps. 72:11 b 1 Chr. 22:9 *1* The Euphrates

25 a [Jer. 23:6] b [Mic. 4:4] c Judg. 20:1 *1 lived in safety*

26 a 1 Kin. 10:26 b [Deut. 17:16] *1* So with MT, most other authorities; some LXX mss. *four thousand;* cf. 2 Chr. 9:25

27 a 1 Kin. 4:7

29 a 1 Kin. 3:12

30 a Gen. 25:6 b Is. 19:11, 12

31 a 1 Kin. 3:12 b 1 Chr. 15:19 c 1 Chr. 2:6

the sons of Mahol; and his fame was in
all the surrounding nations. 32[a]He spoke
three thousand proverbs, and his [b]songs
were one thousand and five. 33Also he
spoke of trees, from the cedar tree of Lebanon even to the hyssop that springs out
of the wall; he spoke also of animals, of
birds, of creeping things, and of fish.
34And men of all nations, from all the
kings of the earth who had heard of his
wisdom, [a]came to hear the wisdom of Solomon.

Solomon Prepares to Build the Temple

5 Now [a]Hiram king of Tyre sent his servants to Solomon, because he heard
that they had anointed him king in place
of his father, [b]for Hiram had always loved
David. 2Then [a]Solomon sent to Hiram,
saying:

3 [a]You know how my father David
could not build a house for the
name of the LORD his God [b]because
of the wars which were fought
against him on every side, until the
LORD put [1]*his foes* under the soles
of his feet.
4 But now the LORD my God has giv-
en me [a]rest[1] on every side; *there is*
neither adversary nor [2]evil occurrence.

Father, I pray that You will give rest and peace to ____ in all areas of their lives and keep evil far from them.

FROM 1 KINGS 5:4

5 [a]And behold, [1]I propose to build a
house for the name of the LORD my
God, [b]as the LORD spoke to my father David, saying, "Your son,
whom I will set on your throne in
your place, he shall build the house
for My name."
6 Now therefore, command that they
cut down [a]cedars for me from Lebanon; and my servants will be with
your servants, and I will pay you
wages for your servants according
to whatever you say. For you know
there is none among us who has
skill to cut timber like the Sidonians.

7So it was, when Hiram heard the
words of Solomon, that he rejoiced greatly and said,

Blessed *be* the LORD this day, for
He has given David a wise son over
this great people!

8Then Hiram sent to Solomon, saying:

I have considered *the message*
which you sent me, *and* I will do
all you desire concerning the cedar
and cypress logs.
9 My servants shall bring *them* down
[a]from Lebanon to the sea; I will
float them in rafts by sea to the
place you indicate to me, and will
have them broken apart there; then
you can take *them* away. And you
shall fulfill my desire [b]by giving
food for my household.

10Then Hiram gave Solomon cedar and
cypress logs *according to* all his desire.
11[a]And Solomon gave Hiram twenty thousand [1]kors of wheat *as* food for his household, and [2]twenty kors of pressed oil.
Thus Solomon gave to Hiram year by
year.
12So the LORD gave Solomon wisdom,
[a]as He had promised him; and there was
peace between Hiram and Solomon, and
the two of them made a treaty together.
13Then King Solomon raised up a labor
force out of all Israel; and the labor force
was thirty thousand men. 14And he sent
them to Lebanon, ten thousand a month
in shifts: they were one month in Lebanon
and two months at home; [a]Adoniram *was*
in charge of the labor force. 15[a]Solomon
had seventy thousand who carried burdens, and eighty thousand who quarried
stone in the mountains, 16besides three
thousand [1]three hundred from the [a]chiefs
of Solomon's deputies, who supervised
the people who labored in the work. 17And
the king commanded them to quarry
large stones, costly stones, *and* [a]hewn
stones, to lay the foundation of the [1]tem-
ple. 18So Solomon's builders, Hiram's
builders, and the Gebalites quarried *them;*
and they prepared timber and stones to
build the [1]temple.

---

32 [a]Eccl. 12:9 [b]Song 1:1
34 [a]1 Kin. 10:1

CHAPTER 5
1 [a]2 Chr. 2:3 [b]2 Sam. 5:11
2 [a]2 Chr. 2:3
3 [a]1 Chr. 28:2, 3 [b]1 Chr. 22:8; 28:3 [1]Lit. *them*
4 [a]1 Kin. 4:24 [1]*peace* [2]*misfortune*
5 [a]2 Chr. 2:4 [b]2 Sam. 7:12, 13 [1]Lit. *I am saying*
6 [a]2 Chr. 2:8, 10
9 [a]Ezra 3:7 [b]Ezek. 27:17
11 [a]2 Chr. 2:10 [1]Each about 5 bushels [2]So with MT, Tg., Vg.; LXX, Syr. *twenty thousand kors*
12 [a]1 Kin. 3:12
14 [a]1 Kin. 12:18
15 [a]2 Chr. 2:17, 18
16 [a]1 Kin. 9:23 [1]So with MT, Tg., Vg.; LXX *six hundred*
17 [a]1 Kin. 6:7 [1]Lit. *house*
18 [1]Lit. *house*

Solomon Builds the Temple

6 And [a]it came to pass in the four hundred and [1]eightieth year after the children of Israel had come out of the land of Egypt, in the fourth year of Solomon's reign over Israel, in the month of [2]Ziv, which *is* the second month, [b]that he began to build the house of the LORD. 2Now [a]the house which King Solomon built for the LORD, its length *was* sixty cubits, its width twenty, and its height thirty cubits. 3The vestibule in front of the [1]sanctuary of the house *was* [2]twenty cubits long across the width of the house, *and* the width of [3]*the vestibule extended* [4]ten cubits from the front of the house. 4And he made for the house [a]windows with beveled frames.

5Against the wall of the [1]temple he built [a]chambers all around, *against* the walls of the temple, all around the sanctuary [b]and the [2]inner sanctuary. Thus he made side chambers all around it. 6The lowest chamber *was* five cubits wide, the middle *was* six cubits wide, and the third *was* seven cubits wide; for he made narrow ledges around the outside of the temple, so that *the support beams* would not be fastened into the walls of the [1]temple. 7And [a]the temple, when it was being built, was built with stone finished at the quarry, so that no hammer or chisel *or* any iron tool was heard in the temple while it was being built. 8The doorway for the [1]middle story *was* on the right side of the temple. They went up by stairs to the middle *story,* and from the middle to the third.

9[a]So he built the [1]temple and finished it, and he paneled the temple with beams and boards of cedar. 10And he built side chambers against the entire temple, each five cubits high; they were attached to the temple with cedar beams.

11Then the word of the LORD came to Solomon, saying: 12"*Concerning* this [1]temple which you are building, [a]if you walk in My statutes, execute My judgments, keep all My commandments, and walk in them, then I will perform My [2]word with you, [b]which I spoke to your father David. 13And [a]I will dwell among the children of Israel, and will not [b]forsake My people Israel."

14So Solomon built the temple and finished it. 15And he built the inside walls of the temple with cedar boards; from the floor of the temple to the ceiling he paneled the inside with wood; and he covered the floor of the temple with planks of cypress. 16Then he built the twenty-cubit room at the rear of the temple, from floor to ceiling, with cedar boards; he built *it* inside as the inner sanctuary, as the [a]Most Holy *Place.* 17And in front of it the temple sanctuary was forty cubits *long.* 18The inside of the temple was cedar, carved with ornamental buds and open flowers. All *was* cedar; there was no stone *to be* seen.

> *I feel it is far better to begin with God, to see His face first, to get my soul near Him before it is near another.*
>
> ROBERT MURRAY MCCHEYNE

19And he prepared the [1]inner sanctuary inside the temple, to set the ark of the covenant of the LORD there. 20The inner sanctuary *was* twenty cubits long, twenty cubits wide, and twenty cubits high. He overlaid it with pure gold, and overlaid the altar of cedar. 21So Solomon overlaid the inside of the temple with pure gold. He stretched gold chains across the front of the inner sanctuary, and overlaid it with gold. 22The whole temple he overlaid with gold, until he had finished all the temple; also he overlaid with gold [a]the entire altar that *was* by the inner sanctuary.

23Inside the inner sanctuary [a]he made two cherubim *of* olive wood, *each* ten cubits high. 24One wing of the cherub *was* five cubits, and the other wing of the cherub five cubits: ten cubits from the tip of one wing to the tip of the other. 25And the other cherub *was* ten cubits; both cherubim *were* of the same size and shape. 26The height of one cherub *was* ten cubits, and so *was* the other cherub. 27Then he set the cherubim inside the inner [1]room; and [a]they stretched out the wings of the cherubim so that the wing of the one touched *one* wall, and the wing of the other cherub touched the other wall. And their wings touched each other in the middle of the room. 28Also he overlaid the cherubim with gold.

29Then he carved all the walls of the temple all around, both the inner and

CHAPTER 6
1 [a]2 Chr. 3:1, 2 [b]Acts 7:47 [1]So with MT, Tg., Vg.; LXX *fortieth* [2]Or *Ayyar,* April or May
2 [a]Ezek. 41:1
3 [1]Heb. *heykal;* here the main room of the temple; elsewhere called the holy place, Ex. 26:33; Ezek. 41:1 [2]About 30 feet [3]Lit. *it* [4]About 15 feet
4 [a]Ezek. 40:16; 41:16
5 [a]Ezek. 41:6 [b]1 Kin. 6:16, 19–21, 31 [1]Lit. *house* [2]Heb. *debir;* here the inner room of the temple; elsewhere called the Most Holy Place, v. 16
6 [1]Lit. *house*
7 [a]Deut. 27:5, 6
8 [1]So with MT, Vg.; LXX *upper story;* Tg. *ground story*
9 [a]1 Kin. 6:14, 38 [1]Lit. *house*
12 [a]1 Kin. 2:4; 9:4 [b][2 Sam. 7:13] [1]Lit. *house* [2]*promise*
13 [a]Ex. 25:8 [b][Deut. 31:6]
16 [a]Ex. 26:33
19 [1]The Most Holy Place
22 [a]Ex. 30:1, 3, 6
23 [a]2 Chr. 3:10–12
27 [a]2 Chr. 5:8 [1]Lit. *house*

outer *sanctuaries,* with carved [a]figures of
cherubim, palm trees, and open flowers.
30 And the floor of the temple he overlaid
with gold, both the inner and outer *sanctuaries.*
31 For the entrance of the inner sanctuary he made doors *of* olive wood; the lintel
and doorposts *were* [1]one-fifth *of the wall.*
32 The two doors *were of* olive wood; and
he carved on them figures of cherubim,
palm trees, and open flowers, and overlaid
them with gold; and he spread gold on the
cherubim and on the palm trees. 33 So for
the door of the [1]sanctuary he also made
doorposts *of* olive wood, [2]one-fourth *of
the wall.* 34 And the two doors *were of* cypress wood; [a]two panels *comprised* one
folding door, and two panels *comprised*
the other folding door. 35 Then he carved
cherubim, palm trees, and open flowers
on them, and overlaid *them* with gold applied evenly on the carved work.
36 And he built the [a]inner court with
three rows of hewn stone and a row of
cedar beams.
37 [a]In the fourth year the foundation of
the house of the LORD was laid, in the
month of [1]Ziv. 38 And in the eleventh year,
in the month of [1]Bul, which is the eighth
month, the house was finished in all its
details and according to all its plans. So
he was [a]seven years in building it.

Solomon's Other Buildings

7 But Solomon took [a]thirteen years to
build his own house; so he finished all
his house.
2 He also built the [a]House of the Forest
of Lebanon; its length *was* [1]one hundred
cubits, its width [2]fifty cubits, and its
height thirty cubits, with four rows of cedar pillars, and cedar beams on the pillars.
3 And *it was* paneled with cedar above the
beams that *were* on forty-five pillars, fifteen *to* a row. 4 *There were* windows *with
beveled frames in* three rows, and window
was opposite window *in* three tiers. 5 And
all the doorways and doorposts *had* rect-
angular frames; and window *was* opposite
window *in* three tiers.
6 He also made the Hall of Pillars: its
length *was* fifty cubits, and its width thirty cubits; and in front of them *was* a porti-
co with pillars, and a canopy *was* in front
of them.
7 Then he made a hall for the throne,
the Hall of Judgment, where he might
judge; and *it was* paneled with cedar from
floor to [1]ceiling.
8 And the house where he dwelt *had* another court inside the hall, of like workmanship. Solomon also made a house like
this hall for Pharaoh's daughter, [a]whom
he had taken *as wife.*
9 All these *were of* costly stones cut to
size, trimmed with saws, inside and out,
from the foundation to the eaves, and also
on the outside to the great court. 10 The
foundation *was of* costly stones, large
stones, some ten cubits and some eight
cubits. 11 And above *were* costly stones,
hewn to size, and cedar wood. 12 The great
court *was* enclosed with three rows of
hewn stones and a row of cedar beams. So
were the [a]inner court of the house of the
LORD [b]and the vestibule of the temple.

Hiram the Craftsman

13 Now King Solomon sent and brought
[1]Huram from Tyre. 14 [a]He *was* the son of
a widow from the tribe of Naphtali, and
[b]his father *was* a man of Tyre, a bronze
worker; [c]he was filled with wisdom and
understanding and skill in working with
all kinds of bronze work. So he came to
King Solomon and did all his work.

The Bronze Pillars for the Temple

15 And he [1]cast [a]two pillars of bronze,
each one eighteen cubits high, and a line
of twelve cubits measured the circumference of each. 16 Then he made two capitals
of cast bronze, to set on the tops of the
pillars. The height of one capital *was* five
cubits, and the height of the other capital
was five cubits. 17 *He made* a lattice network, with wreaths of chainwork, for the
capitals which *were* on top of the pillars:
seven chains for one capital and seven for
the other capital. 18 So he made the pillars,
and two rows of pomegranates above the
network all around to cover the capitals
that *were* on top; and thus he did for the
other capital.
19 The capitals which *were* on top of the
pillars in the hall *were* in the shape of
lilies, four cubits. 20 The capitals on the
two pillars also *had pomegranates* above,
by the convex surface which *was* next to
the network; and there *were* [a]two hundred such pomegranates in rows on each
of the capitals all around.

29 [a] Ex. 36:8, 35
31 [1] Or *five-sided*
33 [1] *temple* [2] Or *four-sided*
34 [a] Ezek. 41:23–25
36 [a] 1 Kin. 7:12
37 [a] 1 Kin. 6:1 [1] Or *Ayyar,* April or May
38 [a] 1 Kin. 5:5; 6:1; 8:19 [1] Or *Heshvan,* October or November

CHAPTER 7
1 [a] 2 Chr. 8:1
2 [a] 2 Chr. 9:16 [1] About 150 feet [2] About 75 feet
7 [1] Lit. *floor* of the upper level
8 [a] 2 Chr. 8:11
12 [a] 1 Kin. 6:36 [b] John 10:23
13 [1] Heb. *Hiram;* cf. 2 Chr. 2:13, 14
14 [a] 2 Chr. 2:14 [b] 2 Chr. 4:16 [c] Ex. 31:3; 36:1
15 [a] Jer. 52:21 [1] *fashioned*
20 [a] Jer. 52:23

21[a]Then he set up the pillars by the vestibule of the temple; he set up the pillar
on the right and called its name [1]Jachin,
and he set up the pillar on the left and
called its name [2]Boaz. 22The tops of the
pillars were in the shape of lilies. So the
work of the pillars was finished.

The Sea and the Oxen

23And he made [a]the Sea of cast bronze,
ten cubits from one brim to the other; *it*
was completely round. Its height *was* five
cubits, and a line of thirty cubits measured its circumference.
24Below its brim *were* ornamental buds
encircling it all around, ten to a cubit, [a]all
the way around the Sea. The ornamental
buds *were* cast in two rows when it was
cast. 25It stood on [a]twelve oxen: three
looking toward the north, three looking
toward the west, three looking toward the
south, and three looking toward the east;
the Sea *was set* upon them, and all their
back parts *pointed* inward. 26It *was* a
handbreadth thick; and its brim was
shaped like the brim of a cup, *like* a lily
blossom. It contained [1]two thousand
baths.

The Carts and the Lavers

27He also made ten [1]carts of bronze;
four cubits *was* the length of each cart,
four cubits its width, and three cubits its
height. 28And this *was* the design of the
carts: They had panels, and the panels
were between frames; 29on the panels that
were between the frames *were* lions, oxen,
and cherubim. And on the frames *was* a
pedestal on top. Below the lions and oxen
were wreaths of plaited work. 30Every cart
had four bronze wheels and axles of
bronze, and its four feet had supports. Under the laver *were* supports of cast *bronze*
beside each wreath. 31Its opening inside
the crown at the top *was* one cubit in
diameter; and the opening *was* round,
shaped *like* a pedestal, one and a half cubits in outside diameter; and also on the
opening *were* engravings, but the panels
were square, not round. 32Under the panels *were* the four wheels, and the axles of
the wheels *were joined* to the cart. The
height of a wheel *was* one and a half cubits. 33The workmanship of the wheels
was like the workmanship of a chariot
wheel; their axle pins, their rims, their
spokes, and their hubs *were* all of cast
bronze. 34And *there were* four supports at
the four corners of each cart; its supports
were part of the cart itself. 35On the top of
the cart, at the height of half a cubit, *it*
was perfectly round. And on the top of the
cart, its flanges and its panels *were* of the
same casting. 36On the plates of its flanges
and on its panels he engraved cherubim,
lions, and palm trees, wherever there was
a clear space on each, with wreaths all
around. 37Thus he made the ten carts. All
of them were of [1]the same mold, one measure, *and* one shape.
38Then [a]he made ten lavers of bronze;
each laver contained [1]forty baths, *and*
each laver *was* four cubits. On each of the
ten carts *was* a laver. 39And he put five
carts on the right side of the house, and
five on the left side of the house. He set
the Sea on the right side of the house,
toward the southeast.

Furnishings of the Temple

40[a]Huram[1] made the lavers and the
shovels and the bowls. So Huram finished
doing all the work that he was to do for
King Solomon *for* the house of the LORD:
41the two pillars, the *two* bowl-shaped
capitals that *were* on top of the two pillars; the two [a]networks covering the two
bowl-shaped capitals which *were* on top
of the pillars; 42[a]four hundred pomegranates for the two networks (two rows of
pomegranates for each network, to cover
the two bowl-shaped capitals that *were* on
top of the pillars); 43the ten carts, and ten
lavers on the carts; 44one Sea, and twelve
oxen under the Sea; 45[a]the pots, the shovels, and the bowls.
All these articles which [1]Huram made
for King Solomon *for* the house of the
LORD *were of* burnished bronze. 46[a]In the
plain of Jordan the king had them cast in
clay molds, between [b]Succoth and [c]Zare-
tan. 47And Solomon did not weigh all the
articles, because *there were* so many; the
weight of the bronze was not [a]deter-
mined.
48Thus Solomon had all the furnishings
made for the house of the LORD: [a]the altar
of gold, and [b]the table of gold on which
was [c]the showbread; 49the lampstands of
pure gold, five on the right *side* and five
on the left in front of the inner sanctuary,
with the flowers and the lamps and the
wick-trimmers of gold; 50the basins, the
trimmers, the bowls, the ladles, and the
[1]censers of pure gold; and the hinges of
gold, *both* for the doors of the inner room

---

21 [a] 2 Chr. 3:17 [1] Lit. *He Shall Establish* [2] Lit. *In It Is Strength*
23 [a] 2 Chr. 4:2
24 [a] 2 Chr. 4:3
25 [a] Jer. 52:20
26 [1] About 12,000 gallons; *three thousand,* 2 Chr. 4:5
27 [1] Or *stands*
37 [1] *one*
38 [a] 2 Chr. 4:6 [1] About 240 gallons
40 [a] 2 Chr. 4:11—5:1 [1] Heb. *Hiram;* cf. 2 Chr. 2:13, 14
41 [a] 1 Kin. 7:17, 18
42 [a] 1 Kin. 7:20
45 [a] Ex. 27:3 [1] Heb. *Hiram;* cf. 2 Chr. 2:13, 14
46 [a] 2 Chr. 4:17 [b] Gen. 33:17 [c] Josh. 3:16
47 [a] 1 Chr. 22:3, 14
48 [a] Ex. 37:25, 26; 2 Chr. 4:8 [b] Ex. 37:10, 11 [c] Lev. 24:5–8
50 [1] *firepans*

(the Most Holy *Place*) *and* for the doors of
the main hall of the temple.
51 So all the work that King Solomon
had done for the house of the LORD was
finished; and Solomon brought in the
things [a]which his father David had dedicated: the silver and the gold and the furnishings. He put them in the treasuries of
the house of the LORD.

The Ark Brought into the Temple

8 Now [a]Solomon assembled the elders
of Israel and all the heads of the
tribes, the chief fathers of the children of
Israel, to King Solomon in Jerusalem,
[b]that they might bring [c]up the ark of the
covenant of the LORD from the City of David, which *is* Zion. 2 Therefore all the men
of Israel assembled with King Solomon
at the [a]feast in the month of [1]Ethanim,
which *is* the seventh month. 3 So all the
elders of Israel came, [a]and the priests
took up the ark. 4 Then they brought up
the ark of the LORD, [a]the [1]tabernacle of
meeting, and all the holy furnishings that
were in the tabernacle. The priests and
the Levites brought them up. 5 Also King
Solomon, and all the congregation of Israel who were assembled with him, *were*
with him before the ark, [a]sacrificing
sheep and oxen that could not be counted
or numbered for multitude. 6 Then the
priests [a]brought in the ark of the covenant of the LORD to [b]its place, into the
inner sanctuary of the temple, to the Most
Holy *Place,* [c]under the wings of the cherubim. 7 For the cherubim spread *their* two
wings over the place of the ark, and the
cherubim overshadowed the ark and its
poles. 8 The poles [a]extended so that the
[1]ends of the poles could be seen from the
holy *place,* in front of the inner sanctuary;
but they could not be seen from outside.
And they are there to this day. 9 [a]Nothing
was in the ark [b]except the two tablets of
stone which Moses [c]put there at Horeb,
[d]when the LORD made *a covenant* with
the children of Israel, when they came out
of the land of Egypt.
10 And it came to pass, when the priests
came out of the holy *place,* that the cloud
[a]filled the house of the LORD, 11 so that the
priests could not continue ministering
because of the cloud; for the [a]glory of the
LORD filled the house of the LORD.

12 [a]Then Solomon spoke:

"The LORD said He would dwell [b]in
the dark cloud.
13 [a]I have surely built You an exalted
house,
[b]And a place for You to dwell in
forever."

Solomon's Speech at Completion of the Work

14 Then the king turned around and
[a]blessed the whole assembly of Israel,
while all the assembly of Israel was standing. 15 And he said: [a]"Blessed *be* the LORD
God of Israel, who [b]spoke with His mouth
to my father David, and with His hand has
fulfilled *it,* saying, 16 'Since the day that I
brought My people Israel out of Egypt, I
have chosen no city from any tribe of Israel *in which* to build a house, that [a]My
name might be there; but I chose [b]David
to be over My people Israel.' 17 Now [a]it was
in the heart of my father David to build a
[1]temple for the name of the LORD God of
Israel. 18 [a]But the LORD said to my father
David, 'Whereas it was in your heart to
build a temple for My name, you did well
that it was in your heart. 19 Nevertheless
[a]you shall not build the temple, but your
son who will come from your body, he
shall build the temple for My name.' 20 So
the LORD has fulfilled His word which He
spoke; and I have [1]filled the position of
my father David, and sit on the throne of
Israel, [a]as the LORD promised; and I have
built a temple for the name of the LORD
God of Israel. 21 And there I have made a
place for the ark, in which *is* [a]the covenant of the LORD which He made with
our fathers, when He brought them out of
the land of Egypt."

Solomon's Prayer of Dedication

22 Then Solomon stood before [a]the altar
of the LORD in the presence of all the
assembly of Israel, and [b]spread out his
hands toward heaven; 23 and he said:
"LORD God of Israel, [a]*there is* no God in
heaven above or on earth below like You,
[b]who keep *Your* covenant and mercy with
Your servants who [c]walk before You with
all their hearts. 24 You have kept what You
promised Your servant David my father;
You have both spoken with Your mouth
and fulfilled *it* with Your hand, as *it is* this

51 [a]2 Sam. 8:11

CHAPTER 8
1 [a]2 Chr. 5:2–14 [b]2 Sam. 6:12–17 [c]2 Sam. 5:7; 6:12, 16
2 [a]Lev. 23:34 [1]Or *Tishri,* September or October
3 [a]Num. 4:15; 7:9
4 [a]2 Chr. 1:3 [1]*tent*
5 [a]2 Sam. 6:13
6 [a]2 Sam. 6:17 [b]1 Kin. 6:19 [c]1 Kin. 6:27
8 [a]Ex. 25:13–15; 37:4, 5 [1]*heads*
9 [a]Ex. 25:21 [b]Deut. 10:5 [c]Ex. 24:7, 8; 40:20 [d]Ex. 34:27, 28
10 [a]Ex. 40:34, 35
11 [a]2 Chr. 7:1, 2
12 [a]2 Chr. 6:1 [b]Ps. 18:11; 97:2
13 [a]2 Sam. 7:13 [b]Ps. 132:14
14 [a]2 Sam. 6:18
15 [a]Luke 1:68 [b]2 Sam. 7:2, 12, 13, 25
16 [a]1 Kin. 8:29 [b]2 Sam. 7:8
17 [a]2 Sam. 7:2, 3 [1]Lit. *house,* and so in vv. 18–20
18 [a]2 Chr. 6:8, 9
19 [a]2 Sam. 7:5, 12, 13
20 [a]1 Chr. 28:5, 6 [1]*risen in the place of*
21 [a]Deut. 31:26
22 [a]2 Chr. 6:12 [b]Ezra 9:5
23 [a]Ex. 15:11 [b][Neh. 1:5] [c][Gen. 17:1]

day. 25Therefore, LORD God of Israel, now
keep what You promised Your servant David my father, saying, [a]'You shall not fail
to have a man sit before Me on the throne
of Israel, only if your sons take heed to
their way, that they walk before Me as you
have walked before Me.' 26[a]And now I
pray, O God of Israel, let Your word come
true, which You have spoken to Your servant David my father.

27"But [a]will God indeed dwell on the
earth? Behold, heaven and the [b]heaven of
heavens cannot contain You. How much
less this temple which I have built! 28Yet
regard the prayer of Your servant and his
supplication, O LORD my God, and listen
to the cry and the prayer which Your servant is praying before You today: 29that
Your eyes may be open toward this [1]tem-
ple night and day, toward the place of
which You said, [a]'My name shall be
[b]there,' that You may hear the prayer
which Your servant makes [c]toward this
place. 30[a]And may You hear the supplication of Your servant and of Your people
Israel, when they pray toward this place.
Hear in heaven Your dwelling place; and
when You hear, forgive.

31"When anyone sins against his neighbor, and is forced to take [a]an oath, and
comes *and* takes an oath before Your altar
in this temple, 32then hear in heaven, and
act, and judge Your servants, [a]condemn-
ing the wicked, bringing his way on his
head, and justifying the righteous by giving him according to his righteousness.

33[a]"When Your people Israel are defeated before an enemy because they have
sinned against You, and [b]when they turn
back to You and confess Your name, and
pray and make supplication to You in this
temple, 34then hear in heaven, and forgive
the sin of Your people Israel, and bring
them back to the land which You gave to
their [a]fathers.

35[a]"When the heavens are shut up and
there is no rain because they have sinned
against You, when they pray toward this
place and confess Your name, and turn
from their sin because You afflict them,
36then hear in heaven, and forgive the sin
of Your servants, Your people Israel, that
You may [a]teach them [b]the good way in
which they should walk; and send rain on
Your land which You have given to Your
people as an inheritance.

37[a]"When there is famine in the land,
pestilence *or* blight *or* mildew, locusts *or*
grasshoppers; when their enemy besieges
them in the land of their [1]cities; whatever
plague or whatever sickness *there is;*
38whatever prayer, whatever supplication
is made by anyone, *or* by all Your people
Israel, when each one knows the plague of
his own heart, and spreads out his hands
toward this temple: 39then hear in heaven
Your dwelling place, and forgive, and act,
and give to everyone according to all his
ways, whose heart You know (for You
alone [a]know the hearts of all the sons of
men), 40[a]that they may fear You all the
days that they live in the land which You
gave to our fathers.

41"Moreover, concerning a foreigner,
who *is* not of Your people Israel, but has
come from a far country for Your name's
sake 42(for they will hear of Your great
name and Your [a]strong hand and Your
outstretched arm), when he comes and
prays toward this temple, 43hear in heav-
en Your dwelling place, and do according
to all for which the foreigner calls to You,
[a]that all peoples of the earth may know
Your name and [b]fear You, as *do* Your people Israel, and that they may know that
this temple which I have built is called by
Your name.

44"When Your people go out to battle
against their enemy, wherever You send
them, and when they pray to the LORD
toward the city which You have chosen
and the temple which I have built for Your
name, 45then hear in heaven their prayer
and their supplication, and maintain their
[1]cause.

46"When they sin against You [a](for
there is no one who does not sin), and You
become angry with them and deliver
them to the enemy, and they take them
captive [b]to the land of the enemy, far or
near; 47[a]*yet* when they [1]come to themselves in the land where they were carried
captive, and repent, and make supplication to You in the land of those who took
them captive, [b]saying, 'We have sinned
and done wrong, we have committed
wickedness'; 48and *when* they [a]return to
You with all their heart and with all their
soul in the land of their enemies who led
them away captive, and [b]pray to You toward their land which You gave to their
fathers, the city which You have chosen
and the temple which I have built for Your
name: 49then hear in heaven Your dwelling place their prayer and their supplication, and maintain their [1]cause, 50and

25 a 1 Kin. 2:4; 9:5
26 a 2 Sam. 7:25
27 a [Acts 7:49; 17:24] b 2 Cor. 12:2
29 a Deut. 12:11 b 1 Kin. 9:3 c Dan. 6:10 1 Lit. *house*
30 a Neh. 1:6
31 a Ex. 22:8–11
32 a Deut. 25:1
33 a Deut. 28:25 b Lev. 26:39, 40
34 a [Lev. 26:40–42]
35 a Deut. 28:23
36 a Ps. 25:4; 27:11; 94:12 b 1 Sam. 12:23
37 a Lev. 26:16, 25, 26 1 Lit. *gates*
39 a [1 Sam. 16:7]
40 a [Ps. 130:4]
42 a Deut. 3:24
43 a [1 Sam. 17:46] b Ps. 102:15
45 1 *justice*
46 a Ps. 130:3 b Lev. 26:34, 44
47 a [Lev. 26:40–42] b Dan. 9:5 1 Lit. *bring back to their heart*
48 a Jer. 29:12–14 b Dan. 6:10
49 1 *justice*

forgive Your people who have sinned
against You, and all their transgressions
which they have transgressed against
You; and [a]grant them compassion before
those who took them captive, that they
may have compassion on them 51(for
[a]they *are* Your people and Your inheritance, whom You brought out of Egypt,
[b]out of the iron furnace), 52[a]that Your
eyes may be open to the supplication of
Your servant and the supplication of Your
people Israel, to listen to them whenever
they call to You. 53For You separated
them from among all the peoples of the
earth *to be* Your inheritance, [a]as You
spoke by Your servant Moses, when You
brought our fathers out of Egypt, O Lord
GOD."

Solomon Blesses the Assembly

54[a]And so it was, when Solomon had
finished praying all this prayer and supplication to the LORD, that he arose from
before the altar of the LORD, from kneeling on his knees with his hands spread up
to heaven. 55Then he stood [a]and blessed
all the assembly of Israel with a loud
voice, saying: 56"Blessed *be* the LORD, who
has given [a]rest[1] to His people Israel, according to all that He promised. [b]There
has not failed one word of all His good
promise, which He promised through His
servant Moses. 57May the LORD our God be
with us, as He was with our fathers. [a]May
He not leave us nor forsake us, 58that He
may [a]incline our hearts to Himself, to
walk in all His ways, and to keep His commandments and His statutes and His
judgments, which He commanded our fathers. 59And may these words of mine,
with which I have made supplication before the LORD, be near the LORD our God
day and night, that He may maintain the
cause of His servant and the cause of His
people Israel, as each day may require,
60[a]that all the peoples of the earth may
know that [b]the LORD *is* God; *there is* no
other. 61Let your [a]heart therefore be [1]loy-
al to the LORD our God, to walk in His
statutes and keep His commandments, as
at this day."

Solomon Dedicates the Temple

62Then [a]the king and all Israel with him
offered sacrifices before the LORD. 63And
Solomon offered a sacrifice of peace offer-

50 a Ps. 106:46
51 a Deut. 9:26–29 b Jer. 11:4
52 a 1 Kin. 8:29
53 a Ex. 19:5, 6
54 a 2 Chr. 7:1
55 a 2 Sam. 6:18
56 a 1 Chr. 22:18 b Deut. 12:10 *1 peace*
57 a Deut. 31:6
58 a Ps. 119:36
60 a 1 Sam. 17:46 b Deut. 4:35, 39
61 a Deut. 18:13 *1 Lit. at peace with*
62 a 2 Chr. 7:4–10
64 a 2 Chr. 7:7 b 2 Chr. 4:1
65 a Lev. 23:34 b Num. 34:8 c Gen. 15:18 d 2 Chr. 7:8
66 a 2 Chr. 7:9 *1 thanked*
CHAPTER 9
1 a 2 Chr. 7:11 b 1 Kin. 7:1 c 2 Chr. 8:6

ings, which he offered to the LORD,
twenty-two thousand bulls and one hundred and twenty thousand sheep. So the
king and all the children of Israel dedicated the house of the LORD. 64On [a]the same
day the king consecrated the middle of the
court that *was* in front of the house of the
LORD; for there he offered burnt offerings,
grain offerings, and the fat of the peace
offerings, because the [b]bronze altar that
was before the LORD *was* too small to receive the burnt offerings, the grain offerings, and the fat of the peace offerings.

> *My heart is fixed. I'll be loyal to Him at any cost, at any price. Loyalty is much more than a casual interest in someone or something. It's a personal commitment. In the final analysis, it means, "Here I am. You can count on me. I won't fail you."*
>
> KATHRYN KUHLMAN

65At that time Solomon held [a]a feast,
and all Israel with him, a great assembly
from [b]the entrance of Hamath to [c]the
Brook of Egypt, before the LORD our God,
[d]seven days and seven *more* days—fourteen days. 66[a]On the eighth day he sent
the people away; and they [1]blessed the
king, and went to their tents joyful and
glad of heart for all the good that the LORD
had done for His servant David, and for
Israel His people.

God's Second Appearance to Solomon

9 And [a]it came to pass, when Solomon
had finished building the house of the
LORD [b]and the king's house, and [c]all Solomon's desire which he wanted to do,
2that the LORD appeared to Solomon the

second time, [a]as He had appeared to him at Gibeon. 3And the LORD said to him: [a]"I have heard your prayer and your supplication that you have made before Me; I have consecrated this house which you have built [b]to put My name there forever, [c]and My eyes and My heart will be there perpetually. 4Now if you [a]walk before Me [b]as your father David walked, in integrity of heart and in uprightness, to do according to all that I have commanded you, *and* if you [c]keep My statutes and My judgments, 5then I will establish the throne of your kingdom over Israel forever, [a]as I promised David your father, saying, 'You shall not fail to have a man on the throne of Israel.' 6[a]*But* if you or your sons at all [1]turn from following Me, and do not keep My commandments *and* My statutes which I have set before you, but go and serve other gods and worship them, 7[a]then I will [1]cut off Israel from the land which I have given them; and this house which I have consecrated [b]for My name I will cast out of My sight. [c]Israel will be a proverb and a byword among all peoples. 8And *as for* [a]this house, *which* is exalted, everyone who passes by it will be astonished and will hiss, and say, [b]'Why has the LORD done thus to this land and to this house?' 9Then they will answer, 'Because they forsook the LORD their God, who brought their fathers out of the land of Egypt, and have embraced other gods, and worshiped them and served them; therefore the LORD has brought all this [a]calamity on them.' "

Solomon and Hiram Exchange Gifts

10Now [a]it happened at the end of twenty years, when Solomon had built the two houses, the house of the LORD and the king's house 11[a](Hiram the king of Tyre had supplied Solomon with cedar and cypress and gold, as much as he desired), *that* King Solomon then gave Hiram twenty cities in the land of Galilee. 12Then Hiram went from Tyre to see the cities which Solomon had given him, but they did not please him. 13So he said, "What *kind of* cities *are* these which you have given me, my brother?" [a]And he called them the land of [1]Cabul, as they are to this day. 14Then Hiram sent the king one hundred and twenty talents of gold.

Solomon's Additional Achievements

15And this *is* the reason for [a]the labor force which King Solomon raised: to build the house of the LORD, his own house, [1]the [b]Millo, the wall of Jerusalem, [c]Hazor, [d]Megiddo, and [e]Gezer. 16(Pharaoh king of Egypt had gone up and taken Gezer and burned it with fire, [a]had killed the Canaanites who dwelt in the city, and had given it *as* a dowry to his daughter, Solomon's wife.) 17And Solomon built Gezer, Lower [a]Beth Horon, 18[a]Baalath, and Tadmor in the wilderness, in the land *of Judah,* 19all the storage cities that Solomon had, cities for [a]his chariots and cities for his [b]cavalry, and whatever Solomon [c]desired to build in Jerusalem, in Lebanon, and in all the land of his dominion.

20[a]All the people *who were* left of the Amorites, Hittites, Perizzites, Hivites, and Jebusites, who *were* not of the children of Israel— 21that is, their descendants [a]who were left in the land after them, [b]whom the children of Israel had not been able to destroy completely—[c]from these Solomon raised [d]forced labor, as it is to this day. 22But of the children of Israel Solomon [a]made no forced laborers, because they *were* men of war and his servants: his officers, his captains, commanders of his chariots, and his cavalry.

23Others *were* chiefs of the officials who *were* over Solomon's work: [a]five hundred and fifty, who ruled over the people who did the work.

24But [a]Pharaoh's daughter came up from the City of David to [b]her house which [1]*Solomon* had built for her. [c]Then he built the Millo.

25[a]Now three times a year Solomon offered burnt offerings and peace offerings on the altar which he had built for the LORD, and he burned incense with them *on the altar* that *was* before the LORD. So he finished the temple.

26[a]King Solomon also built a fleet of ships at [b]Ezion Geber, which *is* near [1]Elath on the shore of the Red Sea, in the land of Edom. 27[a]Then Hiram sent his servants with the fleet, seamen who knew the sea, to work with the servants of Solomon. 28And they went to [a]Ophir, and acquired four hundred and twenty talents of gold from there, and brought *it* to King Solomon.

2 a 1 Kin. 3:5; 11:9
3 a Ps. 10:17 b 1 Kin. 8:29 c Deut. 11:12
4 a Gen. 17:1 b 1 Kin. 11:4, 6; 15:5 c 1 Kin. 8:61
5 a 2 Sam. 7:12, 16
6 a 2 Sam. 7:14–16 *1 turn back*
7 a [Lev. 18:24–29] b [Jer. 7:4–14] c Ps. 44:14 *1 destroy*
8 a 2 Chr. 7:21 b [Deut. 29:24–26]
9 a [Deut. 29:25–28]
10 a 2 Chr. 8:1
11 a 1 Kin. 5:1
13 a Josh. 19:27 *1* Lit. *Good for Nothing*
15 a 1 Kin. 5:13 b 2 Sam. 5:9 c Josh. 11:1; 19:36 d Josh. 17:11 e Josh. 16:10 *1* Lit. *The Landfill*
16 a Josh. 16:10
17 a 2 Chr. 8:5
18 a Josh. 19:44
19 a 1 Kin. 10:26 b 1 Kin. 4:26 c 1 Kin. 9:1
20 a 2 Chr. 8:7
21 a Judg. 1:21–36; 3:1 b Josh. 15:63; 17:12, 13 c Judg. 1:28, 35 d Ezra 2:55, 58
22 a [Lev. 25:39]
23 a 2 Chr. 8:10
24 a 1 Kin. 3:1 b 1 Kin. 7:8 c 2 Sam. 5:9 *1* Lit. *he;* cf. 2 Chr. 8:11
25 a Ex. 23:14–17
26 a 2 Chr. 8:17, 18 b Num. 33:35 *1* Heb. *Eloth*
27 a 1 Kin. 5:6, 9; 10:11
28 a Job 22:24

The Queen of Sheba's Praise of Solomon

10 Now when the [a]queen of Sheba
heard of the fame of Solomon concerning the name of the LORD, she came
[b]to test him with hard questions. 2She
came to Jerusalem with a very great [1]reti-
nue, with camels that bore spices, very
much gold, and precious stones; and
when she came to Solomon, she spoke
with him about all that was in her heart.
3So Solomon answered all her questions;
there was nothing [1]so difficult for the
king that he could not explain *it* to her.
4And when the queen of Sheba had seen
all the wisdom of Solomon, the house that
he had built, 5the food on his table, the
seating of his servants, the service of his
waiters and their apparel, his cupbearers,
[a]and his entryway by which he went up to
the house of the LORD, there was no more
spirit in her. 6Then she said to the king:
"It was a true report which I heard in my
own land about your words and your wisdom. 7However I did not believe the words
until I came and saw with my own eyes;
and indeed the half was not told me. Your
wisdom and prosperity exceed the fame of
which I heard. 8[a]Happy *are* your men and
happy *are* these your servants, who stand
continually before you *and* hear your wisdom! 9[a]Blessed be the LORD your God,
who [b]delighted in you, setting you on the
throne of Israel! Because the LORD has
loved Israel forever, therefore He made
you king, [c]to do justice and righteousness."

10Then she [a]gave the king one hundred
and twenty talents of gold, spices in great
quantity, and precious stones. There never again came such abundance of spices
as the queen of Sheba gave to King Solomon. 11[a]Also, the ships of Hiram, which
brought gold from Ophir, brought great
quantities of [1]almug wood and precious
stones from Ophir. 12[a]And the king made
[1]steps of the almug wood for the house of
the LORD and for the king's house, also
harps and stringed instruments for singers. There never again came such [b]almug
wood, nor has the like been seen to this
day.

13Now King Solomon gave the queen of
Sheba all she desired, whatever she asked,
besides what Solomon had given her according to the royal generosity. So she
turned and went to her own country, she
and her servants.

Solomon's Great Wealth

14The weight of gold that came to Solomon yearly was six hundred and sixty-
six talents of gold, 15besides *that* from the
[a]traveling merchants, from the income of
traders, [b]from all the kings of Arabia, and
from the governors of the country.

16And King Solomon made two hundred large shields *of* hammered gold; six
hundred *shekels* of gold went into each
shield. 17He also *made* [a]three hundred
shields *of* hammered gold; three minas of
gold went into each shield. The king put
them in the [b]House of the Forest of Lebanon.

18[a]Moreover the king made a great
throne of ivory, and overlaid it with pure
gold. 19The throne had six steps, and the
top of the throne *was* round at the back;
there were armrests on either side of the
place of the seat, and two lions stood beside the armrests. 20Twelve lions stood
there, one on each side of the six steps;
nothing like *this* had been made for any
other kingdom.

21[a]All King Solomon's drinking vessels
were gold, and all the vessels of the House
of the Forest of Lebanon *were* pure gold.
Not *one was* silver, for this was accounted
as nothing in the days of Solomon. 22For
the king had [a]merchant[1] ships at sea with
the fleet of Hiram. Once every three years
the merchant [b]ships came bringing gold,
silver, ivory, apes, and [2]monkeys. 23So
[a]King Solomon surpassed all the kings of
the earth in riches and wisdom.

Glory not in wealth if you have it, nor in friends because they are powerful, but in God who gives all things, and above all desires to give you Himself.

THOMAS À KEMPIS

24Now all the earth sought the presence
of Solomon to hear his wisdom, which
God had put in his heart. 25Each man

CHAPTER 10
1 a Matt. 12:42
b Judg. 14:12
2 *1 company*
3 *1 too*
5 a 1 Chr. 26:16
8 a Prov. 8:34
9 a 1 Kin. 5:7
b 2 Sam. 22:20
c Ps. 72:2
10 a Ps. 72:10, 15
11 a 1 Kin. 9:27, 28
1 algum, 2 Chr. 9:10, 11
12 a 2 Chr. 9:11
b 2 Chr. 9:10
1 Or *supports*
15 a 2 Chr. 1:16
b Ps. 72:10
17 a 1 Kin. 14:26
b 1 Kin. 7:2
18 a 2 Chr. 9:17
21 a 2 Chr. 9:20
22 a Gen. 10:4
b 1 Kin. 9:26–28; 22:48
1 Lit. *ships of Tarshish,* deep-sea vessels
2 Or *peacocks*
23 a 1 Kin. 3:12, 13; 4:30

brought his present: articles of silver and
gold, garments, armor, spices, horses, and
mules, at a set rate year by year.
26[a]And Solomon [b]gathered chariots
and horsemen; he had one thousand four
hundred chariots and twelve thousand
horsemen, whom he [1]stationed in the
chariot cities and with the king at Jerusalem. 27[a]The king made silver *as common*
in Jerusalem as stones, and he made cedar
trees as abundant as the sycamores which
are in the lowland.
28[a]Also Solomon had horses imported
from Egypt and Keveh; the king's merchants bought them in Keveh at the *cur-*
rent price. 29Now a chariot that was
imported from Egypt cost six hundred
shekels of silver, and a horse one hundred
and fifty; [a]and [1]thus, through their
agents, they exported *them* to all the
kings of the Hittites and the kings of
Syria.

Solomon's Heart Turns from the Lord

11 But [a]King Solomon loved [b]many
foreign women, as well as the
daughter of Pharaoh: women of the Moabites, Ammonites, Edomites, Sidonians,
and Hittites— 2from the nations of whom
the LORD had said to the children of Israel,
[a]"You shall not intermarry with them,
nor they with you. Surely they will turn
away your hearts after their gods." Solomon clung to these in love. 3And he had
seven hundred wives, princesses, and
three hundred concubines; and his wives
turned away his heart. 4For it was so,
when Solomon was old, [a]that his wives
turned his heart after other gods; and his
[b]heart was not [1]loyal to the LORD his God,
[c]as *was* the heart of his father David. 5For
Solomon went after [a]Ashtoreth the goddess of the Sidonians, and after [b]Milcom[1]
the abomination of the [c]Ammonites.
6Solomon did evil in the sight of the
LORD, and did not fully follow the LORD,
as *did* his father David. 7[a]Then Solomon
built a [1]high place for [b]Chemosh the
abomination of Moab, on [c]the hill that
is east of Jerusalem, and for Molech the
abomination of the people of Ammon.
8And he did likewise for all his foreign
wives, who burned incense and sacrificed
to their gods.
9So the LORD became angry with Solomon, because his heart had turned from
the LORD God of Israel, [a]who had appeared to him twice, 10and [a]had commanded him concerning this thing, that
he should not go after other gods; but he
did not keep what the LORD had commanded. 11Therefore the LORD said to Solomon, "Because you have done this, and
have not kept My covenant and My statutes, which I have commanded you, [a]I
will surely tear the kingdom away from
you and give it to your [b]servant. 12Never-
theless I will not do it in your days, for the
sake of your father David; I will tear it out
of the hand of your son. 13[a]However I will
not tear away the whole kingdom; I will
give [b]one tribe to your son [c]for the sake
of My servant David, and for the sake of
Jerusalem [d]which I have chosen."

Adversaries of Solomon

14Now the LORD [a]raised up an adversary
against Solomon, Hadad the Edomite; he
was a descendant of the king in Edom.
15[a]For it happened, when David was in
Edom, and Joab the commander of the
army had gone up to bury the slain, [b]after
he had killed every male in Edom 16(because for six months Joab remained there
with all Israel, until he had cut down every male in Edom), 17that Hadad fled to go
to Egypt, he and certain Edomites of his
father's servants with him. Hadad *was* still
a little child. 18Then they arose from Midian and came to Paran; and they took men
with them from Paran and came to Egypt,
to Pharaoh king of Egypt, who gave him
a house, apportioned food for him, and
gave him land. 19And Hadad found great
favor in the sight of Pharaoh, so that he
gave him as wife the sister of his own wife,
that is, the sister of Queen Tahpenes.
20Then the sister of Tahpenes bore him
Genubath his son, whom Tahpenes
weaned in Pharaoh's house. And Genubath was in Pharaoh's household among
the sons of Pharaoh.
21[a]So when Hadad heard in Egypt that
David [1]rested with his fathers, and that
Joab the commander of the army was
dead, Hadad said to Pharaoh, [2]"Let me depart, that I may go to my own country."
22Then Pharaoh said to him, "But what
have you lacked with me, that suddenly
you seek to go to your own country?"
So he answered, "Nothing, but do let
me go anyway."
23And God raised up *another* adversary
against him, Rezon the son of Eliadah,
who had fled from his lord, [a]Hadadezer

---

26 a 1 Kin. 4:26 b 1 Kin. 9:19 *1* So with LXX, Syr., Tg., Vg. (cf. 2 Chr. 9:25); MT *led*

27 a 2 Chr. 1:15–17

28 a [Deut. 17:16]

29 a 2 Kin. 7:6, 7 *1* Lit. *by their hands*

CHAPTER 11

1 a [Neh. 13:26] b [Deut. 17:17]

2 a [Deut. 7:3, 4]

4 a [Deut. 17:17] b 1 Kin. 8:61 c 1 Kin. 9:4 *1* Lit. *at peace with*

5 a Judg. 2:13 b [Lev. 20:2–5] c 2 Kin. 23:13 *1* Or *Molech*

7 a Num. 33:52 b Judg. 11:24 c 2 Kin. 23:13 *1* A place for pagan worship

9 a 1 Kin. 3:5; 9:2

10 a 1 Kin. 6:12; 9:6, 7

11 a 1 Kin. 11:31; 12:15, 16 b 1 Kin. 11:31, 37

13 a 2 Sam. 7:15 b 1 Kin. 12:20 c 2 Sam. 7:15, 16 d Deut. 12:11

14 a 1 Chr. 5:26

15 a 2 Sam. 8:14 b Num. 24:18, 19

21 a 1 Kin. 2:10, 34 *1* Died and joined his ancestors *2* Lit. *Send me away*

23 a 2 Sam. 8:3; 10:16

king of Zobah. 24So he gathered men to
him and became captain over a band *of*
raiders, [a]when David killed those *of Zo-*
bah. And they went to Damascus and
dwelt there, and reigned in Damascus.
25He was an adversary of Israel all the days
of Solomon (besides the trouble that Hadad *caused*); and he abhorred Israel, and
reigned over Syria.

Jeroboam's Rebellion

26Then Solomon's servant, [a]Jeroboam
the son of Nebat, an Ephraimite from Zer-
eda, whose mother's name *was* Zeruah, a
widow, [b]also [c]rebelled against the king.
27And this *is* what caused him to rebel
against the king: [a]Solomon had built the
Millo *and* [1]repaired the damages to the
City of David his father. 28The man Jeroboam *was* a mighty man of valor; and Solomon, seeing that the young man was
[a]industrious, made him the officer over
all the labor force of the house of Joseph.
29Now it happened at that time, when
Jeroboam went out of Jerusalem, that the
prophet [a]Ahijah the Shilonite met him on
the way; and he had clothed himself with
a new garment, and the two *were* alone in
the field. 30Then Ahijah took hold of the
new garment that *was* on him, and [a]tore
it *into* twelve pieces. 31And he said to Jeroboam, "Take for yourself ten pieces, for
[a]thus says the LORD, the God of Israel:
'Behold, I will tear the kingdom out of the
hand of Solomon and will give ten tribes
to you 32(but he shall have one tribe for
the sake of My servant David, and for the
sake of Jerusalem, the city which I have
chosen out of all the tribes of Israel),
33[a]because [1]they have forsaken Me, and
worshiped Ashtoreth the goddess of the
Sidonians, Chemosh the god of the Moabites, and Milcom the god of the people of
Ammon, and have not walked in My ways
to do *what is* right in My eyes and *keep* My
statutes and My judgments, as *did* his father David. 34However I will not take the
whole kingdom out of his hand, because I
have made him ruler all the days of his life
for the sake of My servant David, whom
I chose because he kept My commandments and My statutes. 35But [a]I will take
the kingdom out of his son's hand and
give it to you—ten tribes. 36And to his son
I will give one tribe, that [a]My servant David may always have a lamp before Me in
Jerusalem, the city which I have chosen
for Myself, to put My name there. 37So I
will take you, and you shall reign over all
your heart desires, and you shall be king
over Israel. 38Then it shall be, if you heed
all that I command you, walk in My ways,
and do *what is* right in My sight, to keep
My statutes and My commandments, as
My servant David did, then [a]I will be with
you and [b]build for you an enduring house,
as I built for David, and will give Israel to
you. 39And I will afflict the descendants of
David because of this, but not forever.' "
40Solomon therefore sought to kill Jeroboam. But Jeroboam arose and fled to
Egypt, to [a]Shishak king of Egypt, and was
in Egypt until the death of Solomon.

Death of Solomon

41Now [a]the rest of the acts of Solomon,
all that he did, and his wisdom, *are* they
not written in the book of the acts of Solomon? 42[a]And the period that Solomon
reigned in Jerusalem over all Israel *was*
forty years. 43[a]Then Solomon [1]rested with
his fathers, and was buried in the City of
David his father. And Rehoboam his son
reigned in his [b]place.

The Revolt Against Rehoboam

12 And [a]Rehoboam went to [b]She-
chem, for all Israel had gone to
Shechem to make him king. 2So it happened, when [a]Jeroboam the son of Nebat
heard *it* (he was still in [b]Egypt, for he had
fled from the presence of King Solomon
and had been dwelling in Egypt), 3that
they sent and called him. Then Jeroboam
and the whole assembly of Israel came and
spoke to Rehoboam, saying, 4"Your father
made our [a]yoke [1]heavy; now therefore,
lighten the burdensome service of your
father, and his heavy yoke which he put
on us, and we will serve you."
5So he said to them, "Depart *for* three
days, then come back to me." And the people departed.
6Then King Rehoboam consulted the
elders who stood before his father Solomon while he still lived, and he said,
"How do you advise *me* to answer these
people?"
7And they spoke to him, saying, [a]"If you
will be a servant to these people today,
and serve them, and answer them, and
speak good words to them, then they will
be your servants forever."

24 a 2 Sam. 8:3; 10:8, 18
26 a 1 Kin. 12:2 b 2 Chr. 13:6 c 2 Sam. 20:21
27 a 1 Kin. 9:15, 24 *1* Lit. *closed up the breaches*
28 a [Prov. 22:29]
29 a 2 Chr. 9:29
30 a 1 Sam. 15:27, 28; 24:5
31 a 1 Kin. 11:11, 13
33 a 1 Kin. 11:5–8 *1* So with MT, Tg.; LXX, Syr., Vg. *he has*
35 a 1 Kin. 12:16, 17
36 a [1 Kin. 15:4]
38 a Josh. 1:5 b 2 Sam. 7:11, 27
40 a 2 Chr. 12:2–9
41 a 2 Chr. 9:29
42 a 2 Chr. 9:30
43 a 2 Chr. 9:31 b 2 Chr. 10:1 *1* Died and joined his ancestors

CHAPTER 12
1 a 2 Chr. 10:1 b Judg. 9:6
2 a 1 Kin. 11:26 b 1 Kin. 11:40
4 a 1 Sam. 8:11–18 *1 hard*
7 a 2 Chr. 10:7

8But he rejected the advice which the
elders had given him, and consulted the
young men who had grown up with him,
who stood before him. 9And he said to
them, "What advice do you give? How
should we answer this people who have
spoken to me, saying, 'Lighten the yoke
which your father put on us'?"
10Then the young men who had grown
up with him spoke to him, saying, "Thus
you should speak to this people who have
spoken to you, saying, 'Your father made
our yoke heavy, but you make *it* lighter on
us'—thus you shall say to them: 'My little
finger shall be thicker than my father's
waist! 11And now, whereas my father put
a heavy yoke on you, I will add to your
yoke; my father chastised you with whips,
but I will chastise you with [1]scourges!' "
12So Jeroboam and all the people came
to Rehoboam the third day, as the king
had directed, saying, "Come back to me
the third day." 13Then the king answered
the people [1]roughly, and rejected the advice which the elders had given him;
14and he spoke to them according to the
advice of the young men, saying, "My father made your yoke heavy, but I will add
to your yoke; my father chastised you with
whips, but I will chastise you with
[1]scourges!" 15So the king did not listen to
the people; for [a]the turn *of events* was
from the LORD, that He might fulfill His
word, which the LORD had [b]spoken by
Ahijah the Shilonite to Jeroboam the son
of Nebat.
16Now when all Israel saw that the king
did not listen to them, the people answered the king, saying:

[a]"What share have we in David?
We have no inheritance in the son
of Jesse.
To your tents, O Israel!
Now, see to your own house,
O David!"

So Israel departed to their tents. 17But
Rehoboam reigned over [a]the children of
Israel who dwelt in the cities of Judah.
18Then King Rehoboam [a]sent Adoram,
who *was* in charge of the revenue; but all
Israel stoned him with stones, and he
died. Therefore King Rehoboam mounted
his chariot in haste to flee to Jerusalem.
19So [a]Israel has been in rebellion against
the house of David to this day.
20Now it came to pass when all Israel
heard that Jeroboam had come back, they
sent for him and called him to the congregation, and made him king over all [a]Isra-
el. There was none who followed the
house of David, but the tribe of Judah
[b]only.
21And when [a]Rehoboam came to Jerusalem, he assembled all the house of Judah with the tribe of [b]Benjamin, one
hundred and eighty thousand chosen *men*
who were warriors, to fight against the
house of Israel, that he might restore the
kingdom to Rehoboam the son of Solomon. 22But [a]the word of God came to
Shemaiah the man of God, saying,
23"Speak to Rehoboam the son of Solomon, king of Judah, to all the house of
Judah and Benjamin, and to the rest of
the people, saying, 24'Thus says the LORD:
"You shall not go up nor fight against
your brethren the children of Israel. Let
every man return to his house, [a]for this
thing is from Me." ' " Therefore they
obeyed the word of the LORD, and turned
back, according to the word of the LORD.

Jeroboam's Gold Calves

25Then Jeroboam [a]built[1] Shechem in
the mountains of Ephraim, and dwelt
there. Also he went out from there and
built [b]Penuel. 26And Jeroboam said in his
heart, "Now the kingdom may return to
the house of David: 27If these people [a]go
up to offer sacrifices in the house of the
LORD at Jerusalem, then the heart of this
people will turn back to their lord, Rehoboam king of Judah, and they will kill me
and go back to Rehoboam king of Judah."
28Therefore the king asked advice,
[a]made two calves of gold, and said to the
people, "It is too much for you to go up to
Jerusalem. [b]Here are your gods, O Israel,
which brought you up from the land of
Egypt!" 29And he set up one in [a]Bethel,
and the other he put in [b]Dan. 30Now this
thing became [a]a sin, for the people went
to worship before the one as far as Dan.
31He made [1]shrines on the high places,
[a]and made priests from every class of people, who were not of the sons of Levi.
32Jeroboam [1]ordained a feast on the fifteenth day of the eighth month, like [a]the
feast that *was* in Judah, and offered sacrifices on the altar. So he did at Bethel, sacrificing to the calves that he had made.
[b]And at Bethel he installed the priests of

11 [1]Scourges with points or barbs, lit. *scorpions*

13 [1]*harshly*

14 [1]Lit. *scorpions*

15 [a]Judg. 14:4 [b]1 Kin. 11:11, 29, 31

16 [a]2 Sam. 20:1

17 [a]1 Kin. 11:13, 36

18 [a]1 Kin. 4:6; 5:14

19 [a]2 Kin. 17:21

20 [a]2 Kin. 17:21 [b]1 Kin. 11:13, 32, 36

21 [a]2 Chr. 11:1–4 [b]2 Sam. 19:17

22 [a]2 Chr. 11:2; 12:5–7

24 [a]1 Kin. 12:15

25 [a]Judg. 9:45–49 [b]Judg. 8:8, 17 [1]*fortified*

27 [a][Deut. 12:5–7, 14]

28 [a]2 Kin. 10:29; 17:16 [b]Ex. 32:4, 8

29 [a]Gen. 28:19 [b]Judg. 18:26–31

30 [a]1 Kin. 13:34

31 [a]2 Kin. 17:32 [1]Lit. *a house;* cf. 1 Kin. 13:32, lit. *houses*

32 [a]Lev. 23:33, 34 [b]Amos 7:10–13 [1]*instituted*

the high places which he had made. 33So
he made offerings on the altar which he
had made at Bethel on the fifteenth day of
the eighth month, in the month which he
had [a]devised in his own heart. And he [1]or-
dained a feast for the children of Israel,
and offered sacrifices on the altar and
[b]burned incense.

The Message of the Man of God

13 And behold, [a]a man of God went
from Judah to Bethel [1]by the word
of the LORD, [b]and Jeroboam stood by the
altar to burn incense. 2Then he cried out
against the altar [1]by the word of the LORD,
and said, "O altar, altar! Thus says the
LORD: 'Behold, a child, [a]Josiah by name,
shall be born to the house of David; and
on you he shall sacrifice the priests of the
high places who burn incense on you, and
men's bones shall be [b]burned on you.'"
3And he gave [a]a sign the same day, saying,
"This *is* the sign which the LORD has spoken: Surely the altar shall split apart, and
the ashes on it shall be poured out."

4So it came to pass when King Jeroboam heard the saying of the man of God,
who cried out against the altar in Bethel,
that he stretched out his hand from the
altar, saying, "Arrest him!" Then his hand,
which he stretched out toward him, withered, so that he could not pull it back to
himself. 5The altar also was split apart,
and the ashes poured out from the altar,
according to the sign which the man of
God had given by the word of the LORD.
6Then the king answered and said to the
man of God, "Please [a]entreat the favor of
the LORD your God, and pray for me, that
my hand may be restored to me."

So the man of God entreated the LORD,
and the king's hand was restored to him,
and became as before. 7Then the king said
to the man of God, "Come home with me
and refresh yourself, and [a]I will give you
a reward."

8But the man of God said to the king,
[a]"If you were to give me half your house,
I would not go in with you; nor would I
eat bread nor drink water in this place.
9For so it was commanded me by the word
of the LORD, saying, [a]'You shall not eat
bread, nor drink water, nor return by the
same way you came.'" 10So he went another way and did not return by the way
he came to Bethel.

Death of the Man of God

11Now an [a]old prophet dwelt in Bethel,
and his [1]sons came and told him all the
works that the man of God had done that
day in Bethel; they also told their father
the words which he had spoken to the
king. 12And their father said to them,
"Which way did he go?" For his sons [1]had
seen which way the man of God went who
came from Judah. 13Then he said to his
sons, "Saddle the donkey for me." So they
saddled the donkey for him; and he rode
on it, 14and went after the man of God,
and found him sitting under an oak. Then
he said to him, "*Are* you the man of God
who came from Judah?"

And he said, "I *am*."

15Then he said to him, "Come home
with me and eat bread."

16And he said, [a]"I cannot return with
you nor go in with you; neither can I eat
bread nor drink water with you in this
place. 17For [1]I have been told [a]by the
word of the LORD, 'You shall not eat bread
nor drink water there, nor return by going the way you came.'"

18He said to him, "I too *am* a prophet as
you *are*, and an angel spoke to me by the
word of the LORD, saying, 'Bring him back
with you to your house, that he may eat
bread and drink water.'" (He was lying to
him.)

19So he went back with him, and ate
bread in his house, and drank water.

20Now it happened, as they sat at the
table, that the word of the LORD came to
the prophet who had brought him back;
21and he cried out to the man of God who
came from Judah, saying, "Thus says the
LORD: 'Because you have disobeyed the
word of the LORD, and have not kept the
commandment which the LORD your God
commanded you, 22but you came back,
ate bread, and drank water in the [a]place of
which *the LORD* said to you, "Eat no bread
and drink no water," your corpse shall not
come to the tomb of your fathers.'"

23So it was, after he had eaten bread
and after he had drunk, that he saddled
the donkey for him, the prophet whom he
had brought back. 24When he was gone,
[a]a lion met him on the road and killed
him. And his corpse was thrown on the
road, and the donkey stood by it. The lion
also stood by the corpse. 25And there, men
passed by and saw the corpse thrown on
the road, and the lion standing by the

---

33 a Num. 15:39 b 1 Kin. 13:1 *1 instituted*

CHAPTER 13

1 a 2 Kin. 23:17 b 1 Kin. 12:32, 33 *1 at the LORD's command*

2 a 2 Kin. 23:15, 16 b [Lev. 26:30] *1 at the LORD's command*

3 a Is. 7:14; 38:7

6 a [James 5:16]

7 a 1 Sam. 9:7

8 a Num. 22:18; 24:13

9 a [1 Cor. 5:11]

11 a 1 Kin. 13:25 *1* Lit. *son*

12 *1* LXX, Syr., Tg., Vg. *showed him*

16 a 1 Kin. 13:8, 9

17 a 1 Kin. 20:35 *1* Lit. *a command came to me by*

22 a 1 Kin. 13:9

24 a 1 Kin. 20:36

corpse. Then they went and told *it* in the city where the old prophet dwelt.

26 Now when the prophet who had brought him back from the way heard *it,* he said, "It *is* the man of God who was disobedient to the word of the LORD. Therefore the LORD has delivered him to the lion, which has torn him and killed him, according to the word of the LORD which He spoke to him." 27 And he spoke to his sons, saying, "Saddle the donkey for me." So they saddled *it.* 28 Then he went and found his corpse thrown on the road, and the donkey and the lion standing by the corpse. The lion had not eaten the corpse nor torn the donkey. 29 And the prophet took up the corpse of the man of God, laid it on the donkey, and brought it back. So the old prophet came to the city to mourn, and to bury him. 30 Then he laid the corpse in his own tomb; and they mourned over him, *saying,* [a]"Alas, my brother!" 31 So it was, after he had buried him, that he spoke to his sons, saying, "When I am dead, then bury me in the tomb where the man of God *is* buried; [a]lay my bones beside his bones. 32 [a]For the [1]saying which he cried out by the word of the LORD against the altar in Bethel, and against all the [2]shrines on the high places which *are* in the cities of [b]Samaria, will surely come to pass."

33 [a]After this event Jeroboam did not turn from his evil way, but again he made priests from every class of people for the high places; whoever wished, he consecrated him, and he became *one* of the priests of the high places. 34 [a]And this thing was the sin of the house of Jeroboam, so as [b]to exterminate and destroy *it* from the face of the earth.

Judgment on the House of Jeroboam

14 At that time Abijah the son of Jeroboam became sick. 2 And Jeroboam said to his wife, "Please arise, and disguise yourself, that they may not recognize you as the wife of Jeroboam, and go to Shiloh. Indeed, Ahijah the prophet *is* there, who told me that [a]*I would be* king over this people. 3 [a]Also take [1]with you ten loaves, *some* cakes, and a jar of honey, and go to him; he will tell you what will become of the child." 4 And Jeroboam's wife did so; she arose [a]and went to Shiloh, and came to the house of Ahijah. But Ahijah could not see, for his eyes were [1]glazed by reason of his age.

5 Now the LORD had said to Ahijah, "Here is the wife of Jeroboam, coming to ask you something about her son, for he *is* sick. Thus and thus you shall say to her; for it will be, when she comes in, that she will pretend *to be* another *woman.*"

6 And so it was, when Ahijah heard the sound of her footsteps as she came through the door, he said, "Come in, wife of Jeroboam. Why do you pretend *to be* another *person?* For I *have been* sent to you *with* bad *news.* 7 Go, tell Jeroboam, 'Thus says the LORD God of Israel: [a]"Because I exalted you from among the people, and made you ruler over My people Israel, 8 and [a]tore the kingdom away from the house of David, and gave it to you; and *yet* you have not been as My servant David, [b]who kept My commandments and who followed Me with all his heart, to do only *what was* right in My eyes; 9 but you have done more evil than all who were before you, [a]for you have gone and made for yourself other gods and molded images to provoke Me to anger, and [b]have cast Me behind your back— 10 therefore behold! [a]I will bring disaster on the house of Jeroboam, and [b]will cut off from Jeroboam every male in Israel, [c]bond and free; I will take away the remnant of the house of Jeroboam, as one takes away refuse until it is all gone. 11 The dogs shall eat [a]whoever belongs to Jeroboam and dies in the city, and the birds of the air shall eat whoever dies in the field; for the LORD has spoken!"' 12 Arise therefore, go to your own house. [a]When your feet enter the city, the child shall die. 13 And all Israel shall mourn for him and bury him, for he is the only one of Jeroboam who shall [1]come to the grave, because in him [a]there is found something good toward the LORD God of Israel in the house of Jeroboam.

14 [a]"Moreover the LORD will raise up for Himself a king over Israel who shall cut off the house of Jeroboam; [1]this is the day. What? Even now! 15 For the LORD will strike Israel, as a reed is shaken in the water. He will [a]uproot Israel from this [b]good land which He gave to their fathers, and will scatter them [c]beyond [1]the River, [d]because they have made their [2]wooden images, provoking the LORD to anger. 16 And He will give Israel up because of the sins of Jeroboam, [a]who sinned and who made Israel sin."

30 a Jer. 22:18
31 a 2 Kin. 23:17, 18
32 a 2 Kin. 23:16, 19 b 1 Kin. 16:24 1 Lit. *word* 2 Lit. *houses*
33 a 1 Kin. 12:31, 32
34 a 1 Kin. 12:30 b [1 Kin. 14:10; 15:29, 30]

CHAPTER 14
2 a 1 Kin. 11:29–31
3 a 1 Sam. 9:7, 8 1 Lit. *in your hand*
4 a 1 Kin. 11:29 1 Lit. *set*
7 a 1 Kin. 16:2
8 a 1 Kin. 11:31 b 1 Kin. 11:33, 38; 15:5
9 a 1 Kin. 12:28 b Ps. 50:17
10 a 1 Kin. 15:29 b 1 Kin. 21:21 c Deut. 32:36
11 a 1 Kin. 16:4; 21:24
12 a 1 Kin. 14:17
13 a 2 Chr. 12:12; 19:3 1 Be buried
14 a 1 Kin. 15:27–29 1 Or *this day and from now on*
15 a 2 Kin. 17:6 b [Josh. 23:15, 16] c 2 Kin. 15:29 d [Ex. 34:13, 14] 1 The Euphrates 2 Heb. *Asherim,* Canaanite deities
16 a 1 Kin. 12:30; 13:34; 15:30, 34; 16:2

17Then Jeroboam's wife arose and departed, and came to [a]Tirzah. [b]When she
came to the threshold of the house, the
child died. 18And they buried him; and all
Israel mourned for him, [a]according to the
word of the LORD which He spoke through
His servant Ahijah the prophet.

Death of Jeroboam

19Now the rest of the acts of Jeroboam,
how he [a]made war and how he reigned,
indeed they *are* written in the book of the
chronicles of the kings of Israel. 20The period that Jeroboam reigned *was* twenty-
two years. So he rested with his fathers.
Then [a]Nadab his son reigned in his place.

Rehoboam Reigns in Judah

21And Rehoboam the son of Solomon
reigned in Judah. [a]Rehoboam *was* forty-
one years old when he became king. He
reigned seventeen years in Jerusalem, the
city [b]which the LORD had chosen out of all
the tribes of Israel, to put His name there.
[c]His mother's name *was* Naamah, an Ammonitess. 22[a]Now Judah did evil in the
sight of the LORD, and they [b]provoked
Him to jealousy with their sins which
they committed, more than all that their
fathers had done. 23For they also built for
themselves [a]high places,[1] [b]*sacred* pillars,
and [c]wooden images on every high hill
and [d]under every green tree. 24[a]And there
were also [1]perverted persons in the land.
They did according to all the [b]abomina-
tions of the nations which the LORD had
cast out before the children of [c]Israel.
25[a]It happened in the fifth year of King
Rehoboam *that* Shishak king of Egypt
came up against Jerusalem. 26[a]And he
took away the treasures of the house of
the LORD and the treasures of the king's
house; he took away everything. He also
took away all the gold shields [b]which Solomon had made. 27Then King Rehoboam
made bronze shields in their place, and
[1]committed *them* to the hands of the captains of the [2]guard, who guarded the
doorway of the king's house. 28And whenever the king entered the house of the
LORD, the guards carried them, then
brought them back into the guardroom.
29[a]Now the rest of the acts of Rehoboam, and all that he did, *are* they not written in the book of the chronicles of the
kings of Judah? 30And there was [a]war between Rehoboam and Jeroboam all *their*
days. 31[a]So Rehoboam [1]rested with his fathers, and was buried with his fathers in
the City of David. [b]His mother's name *was*
Naamah, an Ammonitess. Then [c]Abijam[2]
his son reigned in his place.

Abijam Reigns in Judah

15 [a]In the eighteenth year of King
Jeroboam the son of Nebat, Abijam
became king over Judah. 2He reigned
three years in Jerusalem. [a]His mother's
name *was* [b]Maachah the granddaughter
of [c]Abishalom. 3And he walked in all the
sins of his father, which he had done before him; [a]his heart was not [1]loyal to the
LORD his God, as was the heart of his
father David. 4Nevertheless [a]for David's
sake the LORD his God gave him a lamp in
Jerusalem, by setting up his son after him
and by establishing Jerusalem; 5because
David [a]did *what was* right in the eyes of
the LORD, and had not turned aside from
anything that He commanded him all the
days of his life, [b]except in the matter of
Uriah the Hittite. 6[a]And there was war between [1]Rehoboam and Jeroboam all the
days of his life. 7[a]Now the rest of the acts
of Abijam, and all that he did, *are* they not
written in the book of the chronicles of
the kings of Judah? And there was war
between Abijam and Jeroboam.
8[a]So Abijam [1]rested with his fathers,
and they buried him in the City of David.
Then Asa his son reigned in his place.

Asa Reigns in Judah

9In the twentieth year of Jeroboam king
of Israel, Asa became king over Judah.
10And he reigned forty-one years in Jerusalem. His grandmother's name *was* Maachah the granddaughter of Abishalom.
11[a]Asa did *what was* right in the eyes of
the LORD, as *did* his father David. 12[a]And
he banished the [1]perverted persons from
the land, and removed all the idols that
his fathers had made. 13Also he removed
[a]Maachah his grandmother from *being*
queen mother, because she had made an
obscene image of [1]Asherah. And Asa cut
down her obscene image and [b]burned *it*
by the Brook Kidron. 14[a]But the [1]high
places were not removed. Nevertheless
Asa's [b]heart was loyal to the LORD all his

17 a Song 6:4 b 1 Kin. 14:12
18 a 1 Kin. 14:13
19 a 2 Chr. 13:2–20
20 a 1 Kin. 15:25
21 a 2 Chr. 12:13 b 1 Kin. 11:32, 36 c 1 Kin. 14:31
22 a 2 Chr. 12:1, 14 b Deut. 32:21
23 a Deut. 12:2 b [Deut. 16:22] c [2 Kin. 17:9, 10] d Is. 57:5 *1* Places for pagan worship
24 a Deut. 23:17 b Deut. 20:18 c [Deut. 9:4, 5] *1* Heb. *qadesh,* one practicing sodomy and prostitution in religious rituals
25 a 1 Kin. 11:40
26 a 2 Chr. 12:9–11 b 1 Kin. 10:17
27 *1 entrusted* *2* Lit. *runners*
29 a 2 Chr. 12:15, 16
30 a 1 Kin. 12:21–24; 15:6
31 a 2 Chr. 12:16 b 1 Kin. 14:21 c 2 Chr. 12:16 *1* Died and joined his ancestors *2 Abijah,* 2 Chr. 12:16

CHAPTER 15
1 a 2 Chr. 13:1
2 a 2 Chr. 11:20–22 b 2 Chr. 13:2 c 2 Chr. 11:21
3 a Ps. 119:80 *1* Lit. *at peace with*
4 a 2 Sam. 21:17
5 a 1 Kin. 9:4; 14:8 b 2 Sam. 11:3, 15–17; 12:9, 10
6 a 1 Kin. 14:30 *1* So with MT, LXX, Tg., Vg.; some Heb. mss., Syr. *Abijam*

7 a 2 Chr. 13:2–22 8 a 2 Chr. 14:1 *1* Died and joined his ancestors 11 a 2 Chr. 14:2 12 a 1 Kin. 14:24; 22:46 *1* Heb. *qedeshim,* those practicing sodomy and prostitution in religious rituals 13 a 2 Chr. 15:16–18 b Ex. 32:20 *1* A Canaanite goddess 14 a 1 Kin. 3:2; 22:43 b 1 Kin. 8:61; 15:3 *1* Places for pagan worship

days. 15He also brought into the house of the LORD the things which his father [a]had dedicated, and the things which he himself had dedicated: silver and gold and utensils.

16Now there was war between Asa and Baasha king of Israel all their days. 17And [a]Baasha king of Israel came up against Judah, and built [b]Ramah, [c]that he might let none go out or come in to Asa king of Judah. 18Then Asa took all the silver and gold *that was* left in the treasuries of the house of the LORD and the treasuries of the king's house, and delivered them into the hand of his servants. And King Asa sent them to [a]Ben-Hadad the son of Tabrimmon, the son of Hezion, king of Syria, who dwelt in [b]Damascus, saying, 19"*Let there be* a treaty between you and me, as there was between my father and your father. See, I have sent you a present of silver and gold. Come and break your treaty with Baasha king of Israel, so that he will withdraw from me."

20So Ben-Hadad heeded King Asa, and [a]sent the captains of his armies against the cities of Israel. He attacked [b]Ijon, [c]Dan, [d]Abel Beth Maachah, and all Chinneroth, with all the land of Naphtali. 21Now it happened, when Baasha heard *it,* that he stopped building Ramah, and remained in [a]Tirzah.

22[a]Then King Asa made a proclamation throughout all Judah; none *was* exempted. And they took away the stones and timber of Ramah, which Baasha had used for building; and with them King Asa built [b]Geba of Benjamin, and [c]Mizpah.

23The rest of all the acts of Asa, all his might, all that he did, and the cities which he built, *are* they not written in the book of the chronicles of the kings of Judah? But [a]in the time of his old age he was diseased in his feet. 24So Asa [1]rested with his fathers, and was buried with his fathers in the City of David his father. [a]Then [b]Jehoshaphat his son reigned in his place.

Nadab Reigns in Israel

25Now [a]Nadab the son of Jeroboam became king over Israel in the second year of Asa king of Judah, and he reigned over Israel two years. 26And he did evil in the sight of the LORD, and walked in the way of his father, and in [a]his sin by which he had made Israel sin.

27[a]Then Baasha the son of Ahijah, of the house of Issachar, conspired against him. And Baasha killed him at [b]Gibbethon, which *belonged* to the Philistines, while Nadab and all Israel laid siege to Gibbethon. 28Baasha killed him in the third year of Asa king of Judah, and reigned in his place. 29And it was so, when he became king, *that* he killed all the house of Jeroboam. He did not leave to Jeroboam anyone that breathed, until he had destroyed him, according to [a]the word of the LORD which He had spoken by His servant Ahijah the Shilonite, 30[a]because of the sins of Jeroboam, which he had sinned and by which he had made Israel sin, because of his provocation with which he had provoked the LORD God of Israel to anger.

31Now the rest of the acts of Nadab, and all that he did, *are* they not written in the book of the chronicles of the kings of Israel? 32[a]And there was war between Asa and Baasha king of Israel all their days.

Baasha Reigns in Israel

33In the third year of Asa king of Judah, Baasha the son of Ahijah became king over all Israel in Tirzah, and *reigned* twenty-four years. 34He did evil in the sight of the LORD, and walked in [a]the way of Jeroboam, and in his sin by which he had made Israel sin.

16 Then the word of the LORD came to [a]Jehu the son of [b]Hanani, against [c]Baasha, saying: 2[a]"Inasmuch as I lifted you out of the dust and made you ruler over My people Israel, and [b]you have walked in the way of Jeroboam, and have made My people Israel sin, to provoke Me to anger with their sins, 3surely I will [a]take[1] away the posterity of Baasha and the posterity of his house, and I will make your house like [b]the house of Jeroboam the son of Nebat. 4The dogs shall eat [a]whoever belongs to Baasha and dies in the city, and the birds of the air shall eat whoever dies in the fields."

5Now the rest of the acts of Baasha, what he did, and his might, [a]*are* they not written in the book of the chronicles of the kings of Israel? 6So Baasha [1]rested with his fathers and was buried in [a]Tirzah. Then Elah his son reigned in his place.

7And also the word of the LORD came by the prophet [a]Jehu the son of Hanani against Baasha and his house, because of

15 a 1 Kin. 7:51
17 a 2 Chr. 16:1–6 b Josh. 18:25 c 1 Kin. 12:26–29
18 a 2 Chr. 16:2 b 1 Kin. 11:23, 24
20 a 1 Kin. 20:1 b 2 Kin. 15:29 c Judg. 18:29 d 2 Sam. 20:14, 15
21 a 1 Kin. 14:17; 16:15–18
22 a 2 Chr. 16:6 b Josh. 21:17 c Josh. 18:26
23 a 2 Chr. 16:11–14
24 a 2 Chr. 17:1 b Matt. 1:8 *1 Died and joined his ancestors*
25 a 1 Kin. 14:20
26 a 1 Kin. 12:28–33; 14:16
27 a 1 Kin. 14:14 b Josh. 19:44; 21:23
29 a 1 Kin. 14:10–14
30 a 1 Kin. 14:9, 16
32 a 1 Kin. 15:16
34 a 1 Kin. 13:33; 14:16

CHAPTER 16
1 a 2 Chr. 19:2; 20:34 b 2 Chr. 16:7–10 c 1 Kin. 15:27
2 a 1 Kin. 14:7 b 1 Kin. 12:25–33; 15:34
3 a 1 Kin. 16:11; 21:21 b 1 Kin. 14:10; 15:29 *1 consume*
4 a 1 Kin. 14:11; 21:24
5 a 2 Chr. 16:11
6 a 1 Kin. 14:17; 15:21 *1 Died and joined his ancestors*
7 a 1 Kin. 16:1

all the evil that he did in the sight of the
LORD in provoking Him to anger with the
work of his hands, in being like the house
of Jeroboam, and because [b]he killed them.

Elah Reigns in Israel

8In the twenty-sixth year of Asa king of
Judah, Elah the son of Baasha became
king over Israel, *and reigned* two years in
Tirzah. 9[a]Now his servant Zimri, commander of half *his* chariots, conspired
against him as he was in Tirzah drinking
himself drunk in the house of Arza, [b]stew-
ard[1] of *his* house in Tirzah. 10And Zimri
went in and struck him and killed him in
the twenty-seventh year of Asa king of Judah, and reigned in his place.

11Then it came to pass, when he began
to reign, as soon as he was seated on his
throne, *that* he killed all the household of
Baasha; he [a]did not leave him one male,
neither of his relatives nor of his friends.
12Thus Zimri destroyed all the household
of Baasha, [a]according to the word of the
LORD, which He spoke against Baasha by
Jehu the prophet, 13for all the sins of Baasha and the sins of Elah his son, by which
they had sinned and by which they had
made Israel sin, in provoking the LORD
God of Israel to anger [a]with their [1]idols.
14Now the rest of the acts of Elah, and
all that he did, *are* they not written in the
book of the chronicles of the kings of Israel?

Zimri Reigns in Israel

15In the twenty-seventh year of Asa
king of Judah, Zimri had reigned in Tirzah seven days. And the people *were* encamped [a]against Gibbethon, which
belonged to the Philistines. 16Now the
people *who were* encamped heard it said,
"Zimri has conspired and also has killed
the king." So all Israel made Omri, the
commander of the army, king over Israel
that day in the camp. 17Then Omri and all
Israel with him went up from Gibbethon,
and they besieged Tirzah. 18And it happened, when Zimri saw that the city was
[1]taken, that he went into the citadel of the
king's house and burned the king's house
[2]down upon himself with fire, and died,
19because of the sins which he had committed in doing evil in the sight of the
LORD, [a]in walking in the [b]way of Jeroboam, and in his sin which he had committed to make Israel sin.

20Now the rest of the acts of Zimri, and
the treason he committed, *are* they not
written in the book of the chronicles of
the kings of Israel?

Omri Reigns in Israel

21Then the people of Israel were divided
into two parts: half of the people followed
Tibni the son of Ginath, to make him
king, and half followed Omri. 22But the
people who followed Omri prevailed over
the people who followed Tibni the son of
Ginath. So Tibni died and Omri reigned.
23In the thirty-first year of Asa king of
Judah, Omri became king over Israel, *and
reigned* twelve years. Six years he reigned
in [a]Tirzah. 24And he bought the hill of
Samaria from Shemer for two talents of
silver; then he built on the hill, and called
the name of the city which he built, [a]Sa-
maria,[1] after the name of Shemer, owner
of the hill. 25[a]Omri did evil in the eyes of
the LORD, and did worse than all who *were*
before him. 26For he [a]walked in all the
ways of Jeroboam the son of Nebat, and in
his sin by which he had made Israel sin,
provoking the LORD God of Israel to anger
with their [b]idols.[1]

27Now the rest of the acts of Omri
which he did, and the might that he
showed, *are* they not written in the book
of the chronicles of the kings of Israel?
28So Omri rested with his fathers and
was buried in Samaria. Then Ahab his son
reigned in his place.

Ahab Reigns in Israel

29In the thirty-eighth year of Asa king
of Judah, Ahab the son of Omri became
king over Israel; and Ahab the son of Omri
reigned over Israel in Samaria twenty-
two years. 30Now Ahab the son of Omri did
evil in the sight of the LORD, more than all
who *were* before him. 31And it came to
pass, as though it had been a trivial thing
for him to walk in the sins of Jeroboam
the son of Nebat, [a]that he took as wife
Jezebel the daughter of Ethbaal, king of
the [b]Sidonians; [c]and he went and served
Baal and worshiped him. 32Then he set up
an altar for Baal in [a]the temple of Baal,
which he had built in Samaria. 33[a]And
Ahab made a [1]wooden image. Ahab [b]did
more to provoke the LORD God of Israel
to anger than all the kings of Israel who
were before him. 34In his days Hiel of
Bethel built Jericho. He laid its foundation [1]with Abiram his firstborn, and with

7 b 1 Kin. 15:27, 29
9 a 2 Kin. 9:30–33 b 1 Kin. 18:3 1 Lit. *who was over the house*
11 a 1 Sam. 25:22
12 a 1 Kin. 16:3
13 a Deut. 32:21 1 Lit. *vanities*
15 a 1 Kin. 15:27
18 1 *captured* 2 Lit. *over him*
19 a 1 Kin. 15:26, 34 b 1 Kin. 12:25–33
23 a 1 Kin. 15:21
24 a 1 Kin. 13:32 1 Heb. *Shomeron*
25 a Mic. 6:16
26 a 1 Kin. 16:19 b 1 Kin. 16:13 1 Lit. *vanities*
31 a Deut. 7:3 b Judg. 18:7 c 1 Kin. 21:25, 26
32 a 2 Kin. 10:21, 26, 27
33 a 2 Kin. 13:6 b 1 Kin. 14:9; 16:29, 30; 21:25 1 Heb. *Asherah*, a Canaanite goddess
34 1 At the cost of the life of

his youngest *son* Segub he set up its
gates, [a]according to the word of the LORD,
which He had spoken through Joshua the
son of Nun.

Elijah Proclaims a Drought

17 And Elijah the Tishbite, of the
[a]inhabitants of Gilead, said to
Ahab, [b]"*As* the LORD God of Israel lives,
[c]before whom I stand, [d]there shall not be
dew nor rain [e]these years, except at my
word."
2Then the word of the LORD came to
him, saying, 3"Get away from here and
turn eastward, and hide by the Brook Cherith, which flows into the Jordan. 4And
it will be *that* you shall drink from the
brook, and I have commanded the [a]ravens
to feed you there."
5So he went and did according to the
word of the LORD, for he went and stayed
by the Brook Cherith, which flows into
the Jordan. 6The ravens brought him
bread and meat in the morning, and bread
and meat in the evening; and he drank
from the brook. 7And it happened after a
while that the brook dried up, because
there had been no rain in the land.

Elijah and the Widow

8Then the word of the LORD came to
him, saying, 9"Arise, go to [a]Zarephath,

34 [a]Josh. 6:26

CHAPTER 17
1 [a]Judg. 12:4
[b]2 Kin. 3:14; 5:20
[c]Deut. 10:8
[d]James 5:17
[e]Luke 4:25

4 [a]Job 38:41

9 [a]Obad. 20

THE WIDOW OF ZAREPHATH

All women of destiny must learn to be obedient to the Lord. In fulfilling God's purpose for our lives, obedience is not simply an admirable trait, but an absolute requirement. One of the Old Testament's shining examples of obedience is the widow of Zarephath.

Just before meeting the widow, Elijah the prophet found himself depending on God for every meal. During a time of drought, God had directed him to get his water from the Brook Cherith and had commanded the ravens to feed him (see 1 Kin. 17:3, 4). But one day the brook dried up and the situation required Elijah to be obedient to the word of the Lord to "Arise, go to Zarephath. . . . I have commanded a widow there to provide for you" (1 Kin. 17:9).

Elijah arrived in the city to find the widow gathering sticks for what she thought would be the last meal she would ever eat or prepare for her son. When Elijah asked her for bread, she told him that she only had enough ingredients to make bread for herself and her son, and when that bread was gone, they would die.

But Elijah spoke the word of the Lord to her, saying, "For thus says the LORD God of Israel: 'The bin of flour shall not be used up, nor shall the jar of oil run dry, until the day the LORD sends rain on the earth'" (1 Kin. 17:14). And we see that she obeyed the word—not being able to provide for herself and her son by doing as the prophet directed. Perhaps it seemed strange to her that a so-called "man of God" would ask for her last meal, but God had prepared her to receive and respond to His command given through Elijah.

The widow did exactly as Elijah had instructed and ended up surviving the famine. The requests and instructions of the Lord do not always make sense to the natural mind. Woman of Destiny, cultivate and develop a life of obedience to God, and watch Him work miracles for you and through you.

which *belongs* to [b]Sidon, and dwell there.
See, I have commanded a widow there to
provide for you." [10]So he arose and went
to Zarephath. And when he came to the
gate of the city, indeed a widow *was* there
gathering sticks. And he called to her and
said, "Please bring me a little water in a
cup, that I may drink." [11]And as she was
going to get *it,* he called to her and said,
"Please bring me a morsel of bread in your
hand."

Heavenly Father, give ____ faith to know that when they follow You faithfully, You will provide for them as You did for Elijah.

FROM 1 KINGS 17:9

[12]So she said, "As the LORD your God
lives, I do not have bread, only a handful
of flour in a bin, and a little oil in a [1]jar;
and see, I *am* gathering a couple of sticks
that I may go in and prepare it for myself
and my son, that we may eat it, and [a]die."
[13]And Elijah said to her, "Do not fear;
go *and* do as you have said, but make me
a small cake from it first, and bring *it* to
me; and afterward make *some* for yourself
and your son. [14]For thus says the LORD
God of Israel: 'The bin of flour shall not be
used up, nor shall the jar of oil run dry,
until the day the LORD sends rain on the
earth.' "
[15]So she went away and did according
to the word of Elijah; and she and he and
her household ate for *many* days. [16]The
bin of flour was not used up, nor did the
jar of oil run dry, according to the word of
the LORD which He spoke by Elijah.

Elijah Revives the Widow's Son

[17]Now it happened after these things
that the son of the woman who owned the
house became sick. And his sickness was
so [1]serious that [2]there was no breath left
in him. [18]So she said to Elijah, [a]"What
have I to do with you, O man of God?
Have you come to me to bring my sin to
remembrance, and to kill my son?"
[19]And he said to her, "Give me your
son." So he took him out of her arms and
carried him to the upper room where he
was staying, and laid him on his own bed.
[20]Then he cried out to the LORD and said,
"O LORD my God, have You also brought
tragedy on the widow with whom I lodge,
by killing her son?" [21][a]And he stretched
himself out on the child three times, and
cried out to the LORD and said, "O LORD
my God, I pray, let this child's soul come
back to him." [22]Then the LORD heard the
voice of Elijah; and the soul of the child
came back to him, and he [a]revived.
[23]And Elijah took the child and brought
him down from the upper room into the
house, and gave him to his mother. And
Elijah said, "See, your son lives!"
[24]Then the woman said to Elijah, "Now
by this [a]I know that you *are* a man of God,
and that the word of the LORD in your
mouth *is* the truth."

When God calls you out for His work, He will take care of you, give you something to eat and clothe you; there are so many who run before they are sent; better not go at all.

MARIA WOODWORTH-ETTER

Elijah's Message to Ahab

18 And it came to pass *after* [a]many
days that the word of the LORD
came to Elijah, in the third year, saying,
"Go, present yourself to Ahab, and [b]I will
send rain on the earth."
[2]So Elijah went to present himself to
Ahab; and *there was* a severe famine in
Samaria. [3]And Ahab had called Obadiah,
who *was* [1]in charge of *his* house. (Now
Obadiah feared the LORD greatly. [4]For so
it was, while Jezebel [1]massacred the
prophets of the LORD, that Obadiah had
taken one hundred prophets and hidden
them, fifty to a cave, and had fed them
with bread and water.) [5]And Ahab had said
to Obadiah, "Go into the land to all the
springs of water and to all the brooks;

9 b 2 Sam. 24:6
12 a Deut. 28:23, 24
1 Lit. *pitcher or water jar*
17 1 *severe*
2 He died.
18 a Luke 5:8
21 a 2 Kin. 4:34, 35
22 a Heb. 11:35
24 a John 2:11; 3:2; 16:30
CHAPTER 18
1 a Luke 4:25
b Deut. 28:12
3 1 Lit. *over the house*
4 1 Lit. *cut off*

perhaps we may find grass to keep the horses and mules alive, so that we will not have to kill any livestock." 6So they divided the land between them to explore it; Ahab went one way by himself, and Obadiah went another way by himself.

7Now as Obadiah was on his way, suddenly Elijah met him; and he [a]recognized him, and fell on his face, and said, "*Is* that you, my lord Elijah?"

8And he answered him, "*It is* I. Go, tell your master, 'Elijah *is here.*' "

9So he said, "How have I sinned, that you are delivering your servant into the hand of Ahab, to kill me? 10*As* the LORD your God lives, there is no nation or kingdom where my master has not sent someone to hunt for you; and when they said, '*He is* not *here,*' he took an oath from the kingdom or nation that they could not find you. 11And now you say, 'Go, tell your master, "Elijah *is here*" '! 12And it shall come to pass, *as soon as* I am gone from you, that [a]the Spirit of the LORD will carry you to a place I do not know; so when I go and tell Ahab, and he cannot find you, he will kill me. But I your servant have feared the LORD from my youth. 13Was it not reported to my lord what I did when Jezebel killed the prophets of the LORD, how I hid one hundred men of the LORD's prophets, fifty to a cave, and fed them with bread and water? 14And now you say, 'Go, tell your master, "Elijah *is here.*" ' He will kill me!"

15Then Elijah said, "*As* the LORD of hosts lives, before whom I stand, I will surely present myself to him today."

16So Obadiah went to meet Ahab, and told him; and Ahab went to meet Elijah.

17Then it happened, when Ahab saw Elijah, that Ahab said to him, [a]"*Is that* you, O [b]troubler of Israel?"

18And he answered, "I have not troubled Israel, but you and your father's house *have,* [a]in that you have forsaken the commandments of the LORD and have followed the Baals. 19Now therefore, send *and* gather all Israel to me on [a]Mount Carmel, the four hundred and fifty prophets of Baal, [b]and the four hundred prophets of [1]Asherah, who [2]eat at Jezebel's table."

Elijah's Mount Carmel Victory

20So Ahab sent for all the children of Israel, and [a]gathered the prophets together on Mount Carmel. 21And Elijah came to all the people, and said, [a]"How long will you falter between two opinions? If the LORD *is* God, follow Him; but if Baal, [b]follow him." But the people answered him not a word. 22Then Elijah said to the people, [a]"I alone am left a prophet of the LORD; [b]but Baal's prophets *are* four hundred and fifty men. 23Therefore let them give us two bulls; and let them choose one bull for themselves, cut it in pieces, and lay *it* on the wood, but put no fire *under it;* and I will prepare the other bull, and lay *it* on the wood, but put no fire *under it.* 24Then you call on the name of your gods, and I will call on the name of the LORD; and the God who [a]answers by fire, He is God."

So all the people answered and said, [1]"It is well spoken."

25Now Elijah said to the prophets of Baal, "Choose one bull for yourselves and prepare *it* first, for you *are* many; and call on the name of your god, but put no fire *under it.*"

26So they took the bull which was given them, and they prepared *it,* and called on the name of Baal from morning even till noon, saying, "O Baal, [1]hear us!" But *there was* [a]no voice; no one answered. Then they [2]leaped about the altar which they had made.

27And so it was, at noon, that Elijah mocked them and said, "Cry [1]aloud, for he *is* a god; either he is meditating, or he is busy, or he is on a journey, *or* perhaps he is sleeping and must be awakened." 28So they cried aloud, and [a]cut themselves, as was their custom, with [1]knives and lances, until the blood gushed out on them. 29And when midday was past, [a]they prophesied until the *time* of the offering of the *evening* sacrifice. But *there was* [b]no voice; no one answered, no one paid attention.

30Then Elijah said to all the people, "Come near to me." So all the people came near to him. [a]And he repaired the altar of the LORD *that was* broken down. 31And Elijah took twelve stones, according to the number of the tribes of the sons of Jacob, to whom the word of the LORD had come, saying, [a]"Israel shall be your name." 32Then with the stones he built an altar [a]in the name of the LORD; and he made a trench around the altar large enough to hold two seahs of seed. 33And he [a]put the wood in order, cut the bull in pieces, and laid *it* on the wood, and said,

7 a 2 Kin. 1:6–8
12 a Acts 8:39
17 a 1 Kin. 21:20 b Josh. 7:25
18 a [2 Chr. 15:2]
19 a Josh. 19:26 b 1 Kin. 16:33 *1* A Canaanite goddess *2* Are provided for by Jezebel
20 a 1 Kin. 22:6
21 a [Matt. 6:24] b Josh. 24:15
22 a 1 Kin. 19:10, 14 b 1 Kin. 18:19
24 a 1 Chr. 21:26 *1* Lit. *The word is good*
26 a Jer. 10:5 *1 answer* *2* Lit. *limped about, leaped in dancing around*
27 *1 with a loud voice*
28 a [Deut. 14:1] *1 swords*
29 a Ex. 29:39, 41 b 1 Kin. 18:26
30 a 2 Chr. 33:16
31 a Gen. 32:28; 35:10
32 a [Col. 3:17]
33 a Lev. 1:6–8

"Fill four waterpots with water, and [b]pour
it on the burnt sacrifice and on the wood."
34Then he said, "Do *it* a second time," and
they did *it* a second time; and he said, "Do
it a third time," and they did *it* a third
time. 35So the water ran all around the
altar; and he also filled [a]the trench with
water.

36And it came to pass, at *the time of* the
offering of the *evening* sacrifice, that Elijah the prophet came near and said, "LORD
[a]God of Abraham, Isaac, and Israel, [b]let it
be known this day that You *are* God in
Israel and I *am* Your servant, and *that* [c]I
have done all these things at Your word.
37Hear me, O LORD, hear me, that this
people may know that You *are* the LORD
God, and *that* You have turned their
hearts back *to You* again."

38Then [a]the fire of the LORD fell and
consumed the burnt sacrifice, and the
wood and the stones and the dust, and it
licked up the water that *was* in the trench.
39Now when all the people saw *it,* they fell
on their faces; and they said, [a]"The LORD,
He *is* God! The LORD, He *is* God!"

Lord, show Your mighty deeds to ____ so that they will know that You, Lord, are God!

FROM 1 KINGS 18:39

40And Elijah said to them, [a]"Seize the
prophets of Baal! Do not let one of them
escape!" So they seized them; and Elijah
brought them down to the Brook [b]Kishon
and [c]executed them there.

The Drought Ends

41Then Elijah said to Ahab, "Go up, eat
and drink; for *there is* the sound of abundance of rain." 42So Ahab went up to eat
and drink. And Elijah went up to the top
of Carmel; [a]then he bowed down on the
ground, and put his face between his
knees, 43and said to his servant, "Go up
now, look toward the sea."

So he went up and looked, and said,
"*There is* nothing." And seven times he
said, "Go again."

44Then it came to pass the seventh
time, that he said, "There is a cloud, as
small as a man's hand, rising out of the
sea!" So he said, "Go up, say to Ahab,
[1]'Prepare *your chariot,* and go down before the rain stops you.' "

45Now it happened in the meantime
that the sky became black with clouds and
wind, and there was a heavy rain. So Ahab
rode away and went to Jezreel. 46Then the
[a]hand of the LORD came upon Elijah; and
he [b]girded[1] up his loins and ran ahead of
Ahab to the entrance of Jezreel.

Elijah Escapes from Jezebel

19 And Ahab told Jezebel all that Elijah had done, also how he had [a]ex-
ecuted all the prophets with the sword.
2Then Jezebel sent a messenger to Elijah,
saying, [a]"So let the gods do *to me,* and
more also, if I do not make your life as the
life of one of them by tomorrow about this
time." 3And when he saw *that,* he arose
and ran for his life, and went to Beersheba, which *belongs* to Judah, and left his
servant there.

4But he himself went a day's journey
into the wilderness, and came and sat
down under a [1]broom tree. And he
[a]prayed that he might die, and said, "It is
enough! Now, LORD, take my life, for I *am*
no better than my fathers!"

5Then as he lay and slept under a
broom tree, suddenly an [1]angel touched
him, and said to him, "Arise *and* eat."
6Then he looked, and there by his head
was a cake baked on [1]coals, and a jar of
water. So he ate and drank, and lay down
again. 7And the [1]angel of the LORD came
back the second time, and touched him,
and said, "Arise *and* eat, because the journey *is* too great for you." 8So he arose,
and ate and drank; and he went in the
strength of that food forty days and [a]forty
nights as far as [b]Horeb, the mountain of
God.

9And there he went into a cave, and
spent the night in that place; and behold,
the word of the LORD *came* to him, and He
said to him, "What are you doing here,
Elijah?"

10So he said, [a]"I have been very [b]zeal-
ous for the LORD God of hosts; for the
children of Israel have forsaken Your
covenant, torn down Your altars, and
[c]killed Your prophets with the sword. [d]I
alone am left; and they seek to take my
life."

33 [b] Judg. 6:20
35 [a] 1 Kin. 18:32, 38
36 [a] Ex. 3:6; 4:5 [b] 1 Kin. 8:43 [c] Num. 16:28
38 [a] 1 Chr. 21:26
39 [a] 1 Kin. 18:21, 24
40 [a] 2 Kin. 10:25 [b] Judg. 4:7; 5:21 [c] [Deut. 13:5; 18:20]
42 [a] James 5:17, 18
44 [1] Lit. *Bind* or *Harness*
46 [a] 2 Kin. 3:15 [b] 2 Kin. 4:29; 9:1 [1] Tucked the skirts of his robe in his belt in preparation for quick travel

CHAPTER 19
1 [a] 1 Kin. 18:40
2 [a] Ruth 1:17
4 [a] Num. 11:15 [1] *juniper*
5 [1] Or *Angel*
6 [1] *hot stones*
7 [1] Or *Angel*
8 [a] Matt. 4:2 [b] Ex. 3:1; 4:27
10 [a] Rom. 11:3 [b] Ps. 69:9 [c] 1 Kin. 18:4 [d] 1 Kin. 18:22

God's Revelation to Elijah

11Then He said, "Go out, and stand [a]on
the mountain before the LORD." And behold, the LORD [b]passed by, and [c]a great
and strong wind tore into the mountains
and broke the rocks in pieces before the
LORD, *but* the LORD *was* not in the wind;
and after the wind an earthquake, *but* the
LORD *was* not in the earthquake; 12and after the earthquake a fire, *but* the LORD
was not in the fire; and after the fire [1]a
still small voice.
13So it was, when Elijah heard *it,* that
[a]he wrapped his face in his mantle and
went out and stood in the entrance of the
cave. [b]Suddenly a voice *came* to him, and
said, "What are you doing here, Elijah?"
14[a]And he said, "I have been very zealous for the LORD God of hosts; because the
children of Israel have forsaken Your covenant, torn down Your altars, and killed
Your prophets with the sword. I alone am
left; and they seek to take my life."
15Then the LORD said to him: "Go, return on your way to the Wilderness of
Damascus; [a]and when you arrive, anoint
Hazael *as* king over Syria. 16Also you shall
anoint [a]Jehu the son of Nimshi *as* king
over Israel. And [b]Elisha the son of Shaphat of Abel Meholah you shall anoint *as*
prophet in your place. 17[a]It shall be *that*
whoever escapes the sword of Hazael,
Jehu will [b]kill; and whoever escapes the
sword of Jehu, [c]Elisha will kill. 18[a]Yet I
have reserved seven thousand in Israel, all
whose knees have not bowed to Baal, [b]and
every mouth that has not kissed him."

Elisha Follows Elijah

19So he departed from there, and found
Elisha the son of Shaphat, who *was* plowing *with* twelve yoke *of oxen* before him,
and he was with the twelfth. Then Elijah
passed by him and threw his [a]mantle on
him. 20And he left the oxen and ran after
Elijah, and said, [a]"Please let me kiss my
father and my mother, and *then* I will follow you."
And he said to him, "Go back again, for
what have I done to you?"
21So *Elisha* turned back from him, and
took a yoke of oxen and slaughtered them
and [a]boiled their flesh, using the oxen's
equipment, and gave it to the people, and
they ate. Then he arose and followed Elijah, and became his servant.

Ahab Defeats the Syrians

20 Now [a]Ben-Hadad the king of Syria
gathered all his forces together;
thirty-two kings *were* with him, with
horses and chariots. And he went up and
besieged [b]Samaria, and made war against
it. 2Then he sent messengers into the city
to Ahab king of Israel, and said to him,
"Thus says Ben-Hadad: 3'Your silver and
your gold *are* mine; your loveliest wives
and children are mine.' "
4And the king of Israel answered and
said, "My lord, O king, just as you say, I
and all that I have *are* yours."
5Then the messengers came back and
said, "Thus speaks Ben-Hadad, saying,
'Indeed I have sent to you, saying, "You
shall deliver to me your silver and your
gold, your wives and your children"; 6but
I will send my servants to you tomorrow
about this time, and they shall search
your house and the houses of your servants. And it shall be, *that* whatever is
[1]pleasant in your eyes, they will put *it* in
their hands and take *it.*' "
7So the king of Israel called all the elders of the land, and said, "Notice, please,
and see how this *man* seeks trouble, for
he sent to me for my wives, my children,
my silver, and my gold; and I did not deny
him."
8And all the elders and all the people
said to him, "Do not listen or consent."
9Therefore he said to the messengers of
Ben-Hadad, "Tell my lord the king, 'All
that you sent for to your servant the first
time I will do, but this thing I cannot do.' "
And the messengers departed and
brought back word to him.
10Then Ben-Hadad sent to him and
said, [a]"The gods do so to me, and more
also, if enough dust is left of Samaria for
a handful for each of the people [1]who follow me."
11So the king of Israel answered and
said, "Tell *him,* 'Let not the one who puts
on *his armor* [a]boast like the one who
takes *it off.*' "
12And it happened when *Ben-Hadad*
heard this message, as he and the kings
were [a]drinking at the [1]command post,
that he said to his servants, "Get ready."
And they got ready to attack the city.
13Suddenly a prophet approached Ahab
king of Israel, saying, "Thus says the
LORD: 'Have you seen all this great multitude? Behold, [a]I will deliver it into your

11 a Ex. 19:20; 24:12, 18 b Ex. 33:21, 22 c Ezek. 1:4; 37:7
12 *1 a delicate whispering voice*
13 a Ex. 3:6 b 1 Kin. 19:9
14 a 1 Kin. 19:10
15 a 2 Kin. 8:8–15
16 a 2 Kin. 9:1–10 b 2 Kin. 2:9–15
17 a 2 Kin. 8:12; 13:3, 22 b 2 Kin. 9:14—10:28 c [Hos. 6:5]
18 a Rom. 11:4 b Hos. 13:2
19 a 2 Kin. 2:8, 13, 14
20 a [Matt. 8:21, 22]
21 a 2 Sam. 24:22

CHAPTER 20
1 a 2 Kin. 6:24 b 1 Kin. 16:24
6 *1 pleasing*
10 a 1 Kin. 19:2 *1 Lit. at my feet*
11 a Prov. 27:1
12 a 1 Kin. 20:16 *1 Lit. booths* or *shelters*
13 a 1 Kin. 20:28

hand today, and you shall know that I *am* the LORD.' "

14 So Ahab said, "By whom?"

And he said, "Thus says the LORD: 'By the young leaders of the provinces.' "

Then he said, "Who will set the battle in order?"

And he answered, "You."

15 Then he mustered the young leaders of the provinces, and there were two hundred and thirty-two; and after them he mustered all the people, all the children of Israel—seven thousand.

16 So they went out at noon. Meanwhile Ben-Hadad and the thirty-two kings helping him were [a]getting drunk at the command post. 17 The young leaders of the provinces went out first. And Ben-Hadad sent out *a patrol,* and they told him, saying, "Men are coming out of Samaria!" 18 So he said, "If they have come out for peace, take them alive; and if they have come out for war, take them alive."

19 Then these young leaders of the provinces went out of the city with the army which followed them. 20 And each one killed his man; so the Syrians fled, and Israel pursued them; and Ben-Hadad the king of Syria escaped on a horse with the cavalry. 21 Then the king of Israel went out and attacked the horses and chariots, and killed the Syrians with a great slaughter.

22 And the prophet came to the king of Israel and said to him, "Go, strengthen yourself; take note, and see what you should do, [a]for [1]in the spring of the year the king of Syria will come up against you."

The Syrians Again Defeated

23 Then the servants of the king of Syria said to him, "Their gods *are* gods of the hills. Therefore they were stronger than we; but if we fight against them in the plain, surely we will be stronger than they. 24 So do this thing: Dismiss the kings, each from his position, and put captains in their [1]places; 25 and you shall muster an army like the army [1]that you have lost, horse for horse and chariot for chariot. Then we will fight against them in the plain; surely we will be stronger than they."

And he listened to their voice and did so.

26 So it was, in the spring of the year, that Ben-Hadad mustered the Syrians and went up to [a]Aphek to fight against Israel. 27 And the children of Israel were mustered and given provisions, and they went against them. Now the children of Israel encamped before them like two little flocks of goats, while the Syrians filled the [a]countryside.

28 Then a [a]man of God came and spoke to the king of Israel, and said, "Thus says the LORD: 'Because the Syrians have said, "The LORD *is* God of the hills, but He *is* not God of the valleys," therefore [b]I will deliver all this great multitude into your hand, and you shall know that I *am* the LORD.' " 29 And they encamped opposite each other for seven days. So it was that on the seventh day the battle was joined; and the children of Israel killed one hundred thousand foot soldiers *of* the Syrians in one day. 30 But the rest fled to Aphek, into the city; then a wall fell on twenty-seven thousand of the men *who were* left.

And Ben-Hadad fled and went into the city, into an inner chamber.

Ahab's Treaty with Ben-Hadad

31 Then his servants said to him, "Look now, we have heard that the kings of the house of Israel *are* merciful kings. Please, let us [a]put sackcloth around our waists and ropes around our heads, and go out to the king of Israel; perhaps he will spare your life." 32 So they wore sackcloth around their waists and *put* ropes around their heads, and came to the king of Israel and said, "Your servant Ben-Hadad says, 'Please let me live.' "

And he said, "*Is* he still alive? He *is* my brother."

33 Now the men were watching closely to see whether *any sign of mercy would come* from him; and they quickly grasped *at this word* and said, "Your brother Ben-Hadad."

So he said, "Go, bring him." Then Ben-Hadad came out to him; and he had him come up into the chariot.

34 So *Ben-Hadad* said to him, [a]"The cities which my father took from your father I will restore; and you may set up marketplaces for yourself in Damascus, as my father did in Samaria."

Then *Ahab said,* "I will send you away with this treaty." So he made a treaty with him and sent him away.

16 [a]1 Kin. 16:9; 20:12
22 [a]2 Sam. 11:1 [1]Lit. *at the return*
24 [1]*positions*
25 [1]Lit. *that fell from you*
26 [a]Josh. 13:4
27 [a]Judg. 6:3–5
28 [a]1 Kin. 17:18 [b]1 Kin. 20:13
31 [a]Gen. 37:34
34 [a]1 Kin. 15:20

Ahab Condemned

35 Now a certain man of [a]the sons of the prophets said to his neighbor [b]by the word of the LORD, "Strike me, please." And the man refused to strike him. 36 Then he said to him, "Because you have not obeyed the voice of the LORD, surely, as soon as you depart from me, a lion shall kill you." And as soon as he left him, [a]a lion found him and killed him.

37 And he found another man, and said, "Strike me, please." So the man struck him, inflicting a wound. 38 Then the prophet departed and waited for the king by the road, and disguised himself with a bandage over his eyes. 39 Now [a]as the king passed by, he cried out to the king and said, "Your servant went out into the midst of the battle; and there, a man came over and brought a man to me, and said, 'Guard this man; if by any means he is missing, [b]your life shall be for his life, or else you shall [1]pay a talent of silver.' 40 While your servant was busy here and there, he was gone."

Then the king of Israel said to him, "So *shall* your judgment *be;* you yourself have decided *it.*"

41 And he hastened to take the bandage away from his eyes; and the king of Israel recognized him as one of the prophets. 42 Then he said to him, "Thus says the LORD: [a]'Because you have let slip out of *your* hand a man whom I appointed to utter destruction, therefore your life shall go for his life, and your people for his people.' "

43 So the king of Israel [a]went to his house sullen and displeased, and came to Samaria.

Naboth Is Murdered for His Vineyard

21 And it came to pass after these things *that* Naboth the Jezreelite had a vineyard which *was* in [a]Jezreel, next to the palace of Ahab king of Samaria. 2 So Ahab spoke to Naboth, saying, "Give me your [a]vineyard, that I may have it for a vegetable garden, because it *is* near, next to my house; and for it I will give you a vineyard better than it. *Or,* if it seems good to you, I will give you its worth in money."

3 But Naboth said to Ahab, "The LORD forbid [a]that I should give the inheritance of my fathers to you!"

4 So Ahab went into his house sullen and displeased because of the word which Naboth the Jezreelite had spoken to him; for he had said, "I will not give you the inheritance of my fathers." And he lay down on his bed, and turned away his face, and would eat no food. 5 But [a]Jezebel his wife came to him, and said to him, "Why is your spirit so sullen that you eat no food?"

6 He said to her, "Because I spoke to Naboth the Jezreelite, and said to him, 'Give me your vineyard for money; or else, if it pleases you, I will give you *another* vineyard for it.' And he answered, 'I will not give you my vineyard.' "

7 Then Jezebel his wife said to him, "You now exercise authority over Israel! Arise, eat food, and let your heart be cheerful; I will give you the vineyard of Naboth the Jezreelite."

8 And she wrote letters in Ahab's name, sealed *them* with his seal, and sent the letters to the elders and the nobles who *were* dwelling in the city with Naboth. 9 She wrote in the letters, saying,

> Proclaim a fast, and seat Naboth [1]with high honor among the people; 10 and seat two men, scoundrels, before him to bear witness against him, saying, You have [a]blasphemed God and the king. *Then* take him out, and [b]stone him, that he may die.

11 So the men of his city, the elders and nobles who were inhabitants of his city, did as Jezebel had sent to them, as it *was* written in the letters which she had sent to them. 12 [a]They proclaimed a fast, and seated Naboth with high honor among the people. 13 And two men, scoundrels, came in and sat before him; and the scoundrels [a]witnessed against him, against Naboth, in the presence of the people, saying, "Naboth has blasphemed God and the king!" [b]Then they took him outside the city and stoned him with stones, so that he died. 14 Then they sent to Jezebel, saying, "Naboth has been stoned and is dead."

15 And it came to pass, when Jezebel heard that Naboth had been stoned and was dead, that Jezebel said to Ahab, "Arise, take possession of the vineyard of Naboth the Jezreelite, which he refused to give you for money; for Naboth is not alive, but

35 [a]2 Kin. 2:3, 5, 7, 15 [b]1 Kin. 13:17, 18
36 [a]1 Kin. 13:24
39 [a]2 Sam. 12:1 [b]2 Kin. 10:24 [1]Lit. *weigh*
42 [a]1 Kin. 22:31–37
43 [a]1 Kin. 21:4

CHAPTER 21
1 [a]1 Kin. 18:45, 46
2 [a]1 Sam. 8:14
3 [a][Num. 36:7]
5 [a]1 Kin. 19:1, 2
9 [1]Lit. *at the head*
10 [a][Ex. 22:28] [b][Lev. 24:14]
12 [a]Is. 58:4
13 [a][Ex. 20:16; 23:1, 7] [b]2 Kin. 9:26

1 KINGS 21:7–14

Dear Woman of Destiny,

Have you ever been around a controlling person? A person who typifies Jezebel in the Bible? While we need to be careful about labeling any strong woman as a Jezebel, it is important to be able to recognize the tendencies of one.

I wonder if Jezebel was always an evil, manipulative, and controlling woman, or if events in her life caused her to end up that way. I once was praying for a woman who struggled with issues that made her controlling. As we prayed together, I asked her, "Why do you have to control those around you?" She paused a moment and then answered with a sigh, "I suppose to keep the pain level down. I think that I do it out of fear."

Each of us must examine our lives to be able to recognize areas where we are wounded, or we can easily become the typical "bossy" woman that men hate.

However, the Jezebel from this passage went far beyond being bossy. She was a wicked woman who was intentionally evil. Her tactics included lying, stealing, and murder. She stopped at nothing to obtain what her husband wanted. She used the power of her position as queen to control the whole city, while destroying a righteous man in the process.

It is possible for such people to infiltrate the church today. Sometimes they are witches who slip in and other times they carry a spirit of Jezebel, which causes chaos and havoc. They often draw people to their side to take away power from those in authority. Others willfully seduce both mentally and sexually innocent people. Those affected by this spirit—and it can be men or women—set their agenda over that of leadership. Often accompanying the Jezebel spirit is an occult spirit, which disguises the true purpose of why they are attending church.

While we must be careful not to let these spirits function in the church, please make sure the person has a true spirit of Jezebel and is not just wounded. Some are unknowingly affected by the spirit. For these, it is possible to simply bind its power. However, some carry the spirit and knowingly try to rob vision and take control. These must be confronted in love and not allowed to operate in the church.

Each of us must ask the Lord if we are affected on some level by this kind of spirit. If we are controlling and manipulating, we must seek the Lord for help to be healed of this problem.

Lastly, if you know someone who seemingly is a true Jezebel, do not participate in their agenda. Be careful that you are not seduced and drawn into something that will hurt the church and pastor. Pray for wisdom and discernment, and God will be faithful to guide you and protect you from the Jezebel spirit.

Cindy Jacobs

dead." 16So it was, when Ahab heard that
Naboth was dead, that Ahab got up and
went down to take possession of the vineyard of Naboth the Jezreelite.

The Lord Condemns Ahab

17[a]Then the word of the LORD came to
[b]Elijah the Tishbite, saying, 18"Arise, go
down to meet Ahab king of Israel, [a]who
lives in Samaria. There *he is,* in the vineyard of Naboth, where he has gone down
to take possession of it. 19You shall speak
to him, saying, 'Thus says the LORD: "Have
you murdered and also taken possession?" ' And you shall speak to him, saying, 'Thus says the LORD: [a]"In the place
where dogs licked the blood of Naboth,
dogs shall lick your blood, even yours." ' "
20So Ahab said to Elijah, [a]"Have you
found me, O my enemy?"
And he answered, "I have found *you,*
because [b]you have sold yourself to do evil
in the sight of the LORD: 21'Behold, [a]I will
bring calamity on you. I will take away
your [b]posterity, and will cut off from Ahab
[c]every male in Israel, both [d]bond and free.
22I will make your house like the house of
[a]Jeroboam the son of Nebat, and like the
house of [b]Baasha the son of Ahijah, because of the provocation with which you
have provoked *Me* to anger, and made Israel sin.' 23And [a]concerning Jezebel the
LORD also spoke, saying, 'The dogs shall
eat Jezebel by the [1]wall of Jezreel.'
24The dogs shall eat [a]whoever belongs to
Ahab and dies in the city, and the birds
of the air shall eat whoever dies in the
field."
25But [a]there was no one like Ahab who
sold himself to do wickedness in the sight
of the LORD, [b]because Jezebel his wife
[1]stirred him up. 26And he behaved very
abominably in following idols, according
to all [a]*that* the Amorites had done, whom
the LORD had cast out before the children
of Israel.
27So it was, when Ahab heard those
words, that he tore his clothes and [a]put
sackcloth on his body, and fasted and
lay in sackcloth, and went about mourning.
28And the word of the LORD came to
Elijah the Tishbite, saying, 29"See how
Ahab has humbled himself before Me? Because he [a]has humbled himself before Me,
I will not bring the calamity in his days.
[b]In the days of his son I will bring the
calamity on his house."

17 a [Ps. 9:12] b 1 Kin. 19:1
18 a 2 Chr. 22:9
19 a 1 Kin. 22:38
20 a 1 Kin. 18:17 b [Rom. 7:14]
21 a 1 Kin. 14:10 b 2 Kin. 10:10 c 1 Sam. 25:22 d 1 Kin. 14:10
22 a 1 Kin. 15:29 b 1 Kin. 16:3, 11
23 a 2 Kin. 9:10, 30–37 *1* So with MT, LXX; some Heb. mss., Syr., Tg., Vg. *plot of ground* instead of *wall* (cf. 2 Kin. 9:36)
24 a 1 Kin. 14:11; 16:4
25 a 1 Kin. 16:30–33; 21:20 b 1 Kin. 16:31 *1 incited him*
26 a 2 Kin. 21:11
27 a Gen. 37:34
29 a [2 Kin. 22:19] b 2 Kin. 9:25; 10:11, 17

CHAPTER 22
2 a 2 Chr. 18:2
3 a Deut. 4:43
4 a 2 Kin. 3:7
5 a 2 Kin. 3:11
6 a 1 Kin. 18:19 *1* The false prophets
7 a 2 Kin. 3:11 *1* Or *him*
11 a Zech. 1:18–21 b Deut. 33:17

Micaiah Warns Ahab

22 Now three years passed without
war between Syria and Israel.
2Then it came to pass, in the third year,
that [a]Jehoshaphat the king of Judah went
down to *visit* the king of Israel.
3And the king of Israel said to his servants, "Do you know that [a]Ramoth in Gilead *is* ours, but we hesitate to take it out
of the hand of the king of Syria?" 4So he
said to Jehoshaphat, "Will you go with me
to fight at Ramoth Gilead?"
Jehoshaphat said to the king of Israel,
[a]"I *am* as you *are,* my people as your people, my horses as your horses." 5Also Jehoshaphat said to the king of Israel,
[a]"Please inquire for the word of the LORD
today."
6Then the king of Israel [a]gathered [1]the
prophets together, about four hundred
men, and said to them, "Shall I go against
Ramoth Gilead to fight, or shall I refrain?"
So they said, "Go up, for the Lord will
deliver *it* into the hand of the king."
7And [a]Jehoshaphat said, "*Is there* not
still a prophet of the LORD here, that we
may inquire of [1]Him?"
8So the king of Israel said to Jehoshaphat, "*There is* still one man, Micaiah the
son of Imlah, by whom we may inquire of
the LORD; but I hate him, because he does
not prophesy good concerning me, but
evil."
And Jehoshaphat said, "Let not the king
say such things!"
9Then the king of Israel called an officer
and said, "Bring Micaiah the son of Imlah
quickly!"
10The king of Israel and Jehoshaphat
the king of Judah, having put on *their*
robes, sat each on his throne, at a threshing floor at the entrance of the gate of
Samaria; and all the prophets prophesied
before them. 11Now Zedekiah the son of
Chenaanah had made [a]horns of iron for
himself; and he said, "Thus says the LORD:
'With these you shall [b]gore the Syrians
until they are destroyed.' " 12And all the
prophets prophesied so, saying, "Go up to
Ramoth Gilead and prosper, for the LORD
will deliver *it* into the king's hand."
13Then the messenger who had gone to
call Micaiah spoke to him, saying, "Now
listen, the words of the prophets with one
accord encourage the king. Please, let
your word be like the word of one of them,
and speak encouragement."

14 And Micaiah said, "*As* the LORD lives,
[a]whatever the LORD says to me, that I will
speak."

My prayer for _____ is that whatever they hear You say to them, O Lord, they will speak.

FROM 1 KINGS 22:14

15 Then he came to the king; and the
king said to him, "Micaiah, shall we go to
war against Ramoth Gilead, or shall we
refrain?"
And he answered him, "Go and prosper,
for the LORD will deliver *it* into the hand
of the king!"
16 So the king said to him, "How many
times shall I make you swear that you tell
me nothing but the truth in the name of
the LORD?"
17 Then he said, "I saw all Israel [a]scat-
tered on the mountains, as sheep that
have no shepherd. And the LORD said,
'These have no master. Let each return to
his house in peace.' "
18 And the king of Israel said to Jehoshaphat, "Did I not tell you he would not
prophesy good concerning me, but evil?"
19 Then *Micaiah* said, "Therefore hear
the word of the LORD: [a]I saw the LORD
sitting on His throne, [b]and all the host of
heaven standing by, on His right hand and
on His left. 20 And the LORD said, 'Who will
persuade Ahab to go up, that he may fall
at Ramoth Gilead?' So one spoke in this
manner, and another spoke in that manner. 21 Then a spirit came forward and
stood before the LORD, and said, 'I will
persuade him.' 22 The LORD said to him, 'In
what way?' So he said, 'I will go out and
be a lying spirit in the mouth of all his
prophets.' And the LORD said, [a]'You shall
persuade *him,* and also prevail. Go out
and do so.' 23 [a]Therefore look! The LORD
has put a lying spirit in the mouth of all
these prophets of yours, and the LORD has
declared disaster against you."
24 Now Zedekiah the son of Chenaanah
went near and [a]struck Micaiah on the
cheek, and said, [b]"Which way did the
spirit from the LORD go from me to speak
to you?"
25 And Micaiah said, "Indeed, you shall
see on that day when you go into an [a]in-
ner chamber to hide!"
26 So the king of Israel said, "Take Micaiah, and return him to Amon the governor
of the city and to Joash the king's son;
27 and say, 'Thus says the king: "Put this
fellow in [a]prison, and feed him with bread
of affliction and water of affliction, until I
come in peace." ' "
28 But Micaiah said, "If you ever return
in peace, [a]the LORD has not spoken by
me." And he said, "Take heed, all you
people!"

Ahab Dies in Battle

29 So the king of Israel and Jehoshaphat
the king of Judah went up to Ramoth Gilead. 30 And the king of Israel said to Jehoshaphat, "I will disguise myself and go
into battle; but you put on your robes." So
the king of Israel [a]disguised himself and
went into battle.
31 Now the [a]king of Syria had commanded the thirty-two [b]captains of his
chariots, saying, "Fight with no one small
or great, but only with the king of Israel."
32 So it was, when the captains of the chariots saw Jehoshaphat, that they said,
"Surely it *is* the king of Israel!" Therefore
they turned aside to fight against him,
and Jehoshaphat [a]cried out. 33 And it happened, when the captains of the chariots
saw that it *was* not the king of Israel, that
they turned back from pursuing him.
34 Now a *certain* man drew a bow at ran-
dom, and struck the king of Israel between the joints of his armor. So he said
to the driver of his chariot, "Turn around
and take me out of the battle, for I am
wounded."
35 The battle increased that day; and the
king was propped up in his chariot, facing
the Syrians, and died at evening. The
blood ran out from the wound onto the
floor of the chariot. 36 Then, as the sun was
going down, a shout went throughout the
army, saying, "Every man to his city, and
every man to his own country!"
37 So the king died, and was brought to
Samaria. And they buried the king in Samaria. 38 Then *someone* washed the chariot at a pool in Samaria, and the dogs
licked up his blood while [1]the harlots
bathed, according [a]to the word of the
LORD which He had spoken.

14 [a]Num. 22:38; 24:13
17 [a]Matt. 9:36
19 [a]Is. 6:1 [b]Dan. 7:10
22 [a]Judg. 9:23
23 [a][Ezek. 14:9]
24 [a]Jer. 20:2 [b]2 Chr. 18:23
25 [a]1 Kin. 20:30
27 [a]2 Chr. 16:10; 18:25–27
28 [a]Num. 16:29
30 [a]2 Chr. 35:22
31 [a]1 Kin. 20:1 [b]1 Kin. 20:24
32 [a]2 Chr. 18:31
38 [a]1 Kin. 21:19 [1]Tg., Syr. *they washed his armor*

39 Now the rest of the acts of Ahab, and
all that he did, [a]the ivory house which he
built and all the cities that he built, *are*
they not written in the book of the chronicles of the kings of Israel? 40 So Ahab [1]rest-
ed with his fathers. Then [a]Ahaziah his son
reigned in his place.

Jehoshaphat Reigns in Judah

41 [a]Jehoshaphat the son of Asa had become king over Judah in the fourth year
of Ahab king of Israel. 42 Jehoshaphat *was*
thirty-five years old when he became
king, and he reigned twenty-five years in
Jerusalem. His mother's name *was* Azubah the daughter of Shilhi. 43 And [a]he
walked in all the ways of his father Asa. He
did not turn aside from them, doing *what*
was right in the eyes of the LORD. Nevertheless [b]the high places were not taken
away, *for* the people offered sacrifices and
burned incense on the high places. 44 Also
[a]Jehoshaphat made [b]peace with the king
of Israel.

45 Now the rest of the acts of Jehoshaphat, the might that he showed, and how
he made war, *are* they not written [a]in the
book of the chronicles of the kings of Judah? 46 [a]And the rest of the [1]perverted persons, who remained in the days of his
father Asa, he banished from the land.
47 [a]*There was* then no king in Edom, only
a deputy of the king.

48 [a]Jehoshaphat [b]made [1]merchant ships
to go to [c]Ophir for gold; [d]but they never
sailed, for the ships were wrecked at [e]Ezi-
on Geber. 49 Then Ahaziah the son of Ahab
said to Jehoshaphat, "Let my servants go
with your servants in the ships." But Jehoshaphat would not.

50 And [a]Jehoshaphat [1]rested with his fathers, and was buried with his fathers in
the City of David his father. Then Jehoram
his son reigned in his place.

Ahaziah Reigns in Israel

51 [a]Ahaziah the son of Ahab became
king over Israel in Samaria in the seventeenth year of Jehoshaphat king of Judah,
and reigned two years over Israel. 52 He did
evil in the sight of the LORD, and [a]walked
in the way of his father and in the way of
his mother and in the way of Jeroboam
the son of Nebat, who had made Israel sin;
53 for [a]he served Baal and worshiped him,
and provoked the LORD God of Israel to
anger, [b]according[1] to all that his father
had done.

52 a 1 Kin. 15:26; 21:25 **53** a Judg. 2:11 b 1 Kin. 16:30–32
1 In the same way that

39 a Amos 3:15
40 a 2 Kin. 1:2, 18
1 Died and joined his ancestors
41 a 2 Chr. 20:31
43 a 2 Chr. 17:3; 20:32, 33
b 2 Kin. 12:3
44 a 2 Chr. 19:2
b 2 Chr. 18:1
45 a 2 Chr. 20:34
46 a 1 Kin. 14:24; 15:12
1 Heb. *qadesh,* one practicing sodomy and prostitution in religious rituals
47 a 2 Sam. 8:14
48 a 2 Chr. 20:35–37
b 1 Kin. 10:22
c 1 Kin. 9:28
d 2 Chr. 20:37
e 1 Kin. 9:26
1 Or *ships of Tarshish*
50 a 2 Chr. 21:1
1 Died and joined his ancestors
51 a 1 Kin. 22:40

AUTHOR: *Unknown; Attributed to Jeremiah*
DATE: *Uncertain; Probably 560–538 B.C.*
THEME: *Lessons from the Ruin of Israel and Judah*
KEY WORDS: *King, House, Prophet*

2 KINGS

Dear Woman of Destiny,

In the midst of rebellion, there has always been a remnant who are determined to stick to God's path. In 2 Kings, against a backdrop of evil rulers, we see the widow whose sons were saved from slavery by the miracle of the overflowing oil. Though we may be surrounded by evil in this world and beset by the difficulties of life, we can look to God daily and He *will* direct our paths.

His love and mine,

Marilyn Hickey

God Judges Ahaziah

Moab [a]rebelled against Israel [b]after the death of Ahab.

2 Now [a]Ahaziah fell through the lattice of his upper room in Samaria, and was injured; so he sent messengers and said to them, "Go, inquire of [b]Baal-Zebub,[1] the god of [c]Ekron, whether I shall recover from this injury." 3 But the [1]angel of the LORD said to Elijah the Tishbite, "Arise, go up to meet the messengers of the king of Samaria, and say to them, '*Is it* because *there is* no God in Israel *that* you are going to inquire of Baal-Zebub, the god of Ekron?' 4 Now therefore, thus says the LORD: 'You shall not come down from the bed to which you have gone up, but you shall surely die.' " So Elijah departed.

5 And when the messengers returned to [1]him, he said to them, "Why have you come back?"

6 So they said to him, "A man came up to meet us, and said to us, 'Go, return to the king who sent you, and say to him, "Thus says the LORD: '*Is it* because *there is* no God in Israel *that* you are sending to inquire of Baal-Zebub, the god of Ekron? Therefore you shall not come down from the bed to which you have gone up, but you shall surely die.' " ' "

7 Then he said to them, "What kind of man *was it* who came up to meet you and told you these words?"

8 So they answered him, [a]"A hairy man wearing a leather belt around his waist."

And he said, [b]"It *is* Elijah the Tishbite."

9 Then the king sent to him a captain of fifty with his fifty men. So he went up to him; and there he was, sitting on the top of a hill. And he spoke to him: "Man of God, the king has said, 'Come down!' "

10 So Elijah answered and said to the captain of fifty, "If I *am* a man of God, then [a]let fire come down from heaven and consume you and your fifty men." And fire came down from heaven and consumed him and his fifty. 11 Then he sent to him another captain of fifty with his fifty men.

And he answered and said to him: "Man of God, thus has the king said, 'Come down quickly!' "

12 So Elijah answered and said to them, "If I *am* a man of God, let fire come down from heaven and consume you and your fifty men." And the fire of God came down from heaven and consumed him and his fifty.

13 Again, he sent a third captain of fifty with his fifty men. And the third captain of fifty went up, and came and [1]fell on his knees before Elijah, and pleaded with him, and said to him: "Man of God, please let my life and the life of these fifty servants of yours [a]be precious in your sight. 14 Look, fire has come down from heaven and burned up the first two captains of fifties with their fifties. But let my life now be precious in your sight."

15 And the [1]angel of the LORD said to Elijah, "Go down with him; do not be afraid of him." So he arose and went down with him to the king. 16 Then he said to him, "Thus says the LORD: 'Because you have sent messengers to inquire of Baal-Zebub, the god of Ekron, *is it* because *there is* no God in Israel to inquire of His word? Therefore you shall not come down from the bed to which you have gone up, but you shall surely die.' "

17 So *Ahaziah* died according to the word of the LORD which Elijah had spoken. Because he had no son, [a]Jehoram[1] became king in his place, in the second year of Jehoram the son of Jehoshaphat, king of Judah.

18 Now the rest of the acts of Ahaziah which he did, *are* they not written in the book of the chronicles of the kings of Israel?

Elijah Ascends to Heaven

2 And it came to pass, when the LORD was about to [a]take up Elijah into heaven by a whirlwind, that Elijah went with [b]Elisha from Gilgal. 2 Then Elijah said to Elisha, [a]"Stay here, please, for the LORD has sent me on to Bethel."

But Elisha said, "*As* the LORD lives, and [b]*as* your soul lives, I will not leave you!" So they went down to Bethel.

3 Now [a]the sons of the prophets who *were* at Bethel came out to Elisha, and said to him, "Do you know that the LORD will take away your master [1]from over you today?"

And he said, "Yes, I know; keep silent!"

4 Then Elijah said to him, "Elisha, stay here, please, for the LORD has sent me on to Jericho."

But he said, "*As* the LORD lives, and *as* your soul lives, I will not leave you!" So they came to Jericho.

5 Now the sons of the prophets who *were* at Jericho came to Elisha and said to him, "Do you know that the LORD will

CHAPTER 1
1 [a]2 Sam. 8:2 [b]2 Kin. 3:5
2 [a]1 Kin. 22:40 [b]Matt. 10:25 [c]1 Sam. 5:10 [1]Lit. *Lord of Flies*
3 [1]Or *Angel*
5 [1]Ahaziah
8 [a]Zech. 13:4 [b]1 Kin. 18:7
10 [a]Luke 9:54
13 [a]1 Sam. 26:21 [1]Lit. *bowed down*
15 [1]Or *Angel*
17 [a]1 Kin. 22:50 [1]The son of Ahab king of Israel, 2 Kin. 3:1

CHAPTER 2
1 [a]Gen. 5:24 [b]1 Kin. 19:16–21
2 [a]Ruth 1:15, 16 [b]1 Sam. 1:26
3 [a]1 Kin. 20:35 [1]Lit. *from your head*

take away your master from over you today?"

So he answered, "Yes, I know; keep silent!"

[6]Then Elijah said to him, "Stay here, please, for the LORD has sent me on to the Jordan."

But he said, "*As* the LORD lives, and *as* your soul lives, I will not leave you!" So the two of them went on. [7]And fifty men of the sons of the prophets went and stood facing *them* at a distance, while the two of them stood by the Jordan. [8]Now Elijah took his mantle, rolled *it* up, and struck the water; and [a]it was divided this way and that, so that the two of them crossed over on dry [b]ground.

[9]And so it was, when they had crossed over, that Elijah said to Elisha, "Ask! What may I do for you, before I am taken away from you?"

Elisha said, "Please let a double portion of your spirit be upon me."

[10]So he said, "You have asked a hard thing. *Nevertheless,* if you see me *when I am* taken from you, it shall be so for you; but if not, it shall not be *so.*" [11]Then it happened, as they continued on and talked, that suddenly [a]a chariot of fire *appeared* with horses of fire, and separated the two of them; and Elijah [b]went up by a whirlwind into heaven.

[12]And Elisha saw *it,* and he cried out, [a]"My father, my father, the chariot of Israel and its horsemen!" So he saw him no more. And he took hold of his own clothes and tore them into two pieces. [13]He also took up the mantle of Elijah that had fallen from him, and went back and stood by the bank of the Jordan. [14]Then he took the mantle of Elijah that had fallen from him, and struck the water, and said, "Where *is* the LORD God of Elijah?" And when he also had struck the water, [a]it was divided this way and that; and Elisha crossed over.

[15]Now when the sons of the prophets who *were* [a]from[1] Jericho saw him, they said, "The spirit of Elijah rests on Elisha." And they came to meet him, and bowed to the ground before him. [16]Then they said to him, "Look now, there are fifty strong men with your servants. Please let them go and search for your master, [a]lest perhaps the Spirit of the LORD has taken him up and cast him upon some mountain or into some valley."

And he said, "You shall not send anyone."

[17]But when they urged him till he was [a]ashamed, he said, "Send *them!*" Therefore they sent fifty men, and they searched for three days but did not find him. [18]And when they came back to him, for he had stayed in Jericho, he said to them, "Did I not say to you, 'Do not go'?"

> *Oh, that God would give me more practical faith in Him! Where is now the Lord God of Elijah? He is waiting for Elijah to call on Him.*
>
> JAMES GILMOUR

Elisha Performs Miracles

[19]Then the men of the city said to Elisha, "Please notice, the situation of this city *is* pleasant, as my lord sees; but the water *is* bad, and the ground barren."

[20]And he said, "Bring me a new bowl, and put salt in it." So they brought *it* to him. [21]Then he went out to the source of the water, and [a]cast in the salt there, and said, "Thus says the LORD: 'I have [1]healed this water; from it there shall be no more death or barrenness.'" [22]So the water remains [a]healed to this day, according to the word of Elisha which he spoke.

[23]Then he went up from there to Bethel; and as he was going up the road, some youths came from the city and mocked him, and said to him, "Go up, you baldhead! Go up, you baldhead!"

[24]So he turned around and looked at them, and [a]pronounced a curse on them in the name of the LORD. And two female bears came out of the woods and mauled forty-two of the youths.

[25]Then he went from there to [a]Mount Carmel, and from there he returned to Samaria.

Moab Rebels Against Israel

3 Now [a]Jehoram the son of Ahab became king over Israel at Samaria in the eighteenth year of Jehoshaphat king of Judah, and reigned twelve years. [2]And he did evil in the sight of the LORD, but not like his father and mother; for he put

8 a Ex. 14:21, 22 b Josh. 3:17
11 a 2 Kin. 6:17 b Heb. 11:5
12 a 2 Kin. 13:14
14 a 2 Kin. 2:8
15 a 2 Kin. 2:7 *1 Or at Jericho opposite him saw*
16 a 1 Kin. 18:12
17 a 2 Kin. 8:11
21 a Ex. 15:25, 26 *1 purified*
22 a Ezek. 47:8, 9
24 a Deut. 27:13–26
25 a 2 Kin. 4:25
CHAPTER 3
1 a 2 Kin. 1:17

away the *sacred* pillar of Baal [a]that his father had made. 3Nevertheless he persisted in [a]the sins of Jeroboam the son of Nebat, who had made Israel sin; he did not depart from them.

4Now Mesha king of Moab was a sheepbreeder, and he [a]regularly paid the king of Israel one hundred thousand [b]lambs and the wool of one hundred thousand rams. 5But it happened, when [a]Ahab died, that the king of Moab rebelled against the king of Israel.

6So King Jehoram went out of Samaria at that time and mustered all Israel. 7Then he went and sent to Jehoshaphat king of Judah, saying, "The king of Moab has rebelled against me. Will you go with me to fight against Moab?"

And he said, "I will go up; [a]I *am* as you *are,* my people as your people, my horses as your horses." 8Then he said, "Which way shall we go up?"

And he answered, "By way of the Wilderness of Edom."

9So the king of Israel went with the king of Judah and the king of Edom, and they marched on that roundabout route seven days; and there was no water for the army, nor for the animals that followed them. 10And the king of Israel said, "Alas! For the LORD has called these three kings together to deliver them into the hand of Moab."

11But [a]Jehoshaphat said, "*Is there* no prophet of the LORD here, that we may inquire of the LORD by him?"

So one of the servants of the king of Israel answered and said, "Elisha the son of Shaphat *is* here, who [b]poured[1] water on the hands of Elijah."

12And Jehoshaphat said, "The word of the LORD is with him." So the king of Israel and Jehoshaphat and the king of Edom [a]went down to him.

13Then Elisha said to the king of Israel, [a]"What have I to do with you? [b]Go to [c]the prophets of your father and the [d]prophets of your mother."

But the king of Israel said to him, "No, for the LORD has called these three kings *together* to deliver them into the hand of Moab."

14And Elisha said, [a]"*As* the LORD of hosts lives, before whom I stand, surely were it not that I regard the presence of Jehoshaphat king of Judah, I would not look at you, nor see you. 15But now bring me [a]a musician."

Then it happened, when the musician [b]played, that [c]the hand of the LORD came upon him. 16And he said, "Thus says the LORD: [a]'Make this valley full of [1]ditches.' 17For thus says the LORD: 'You shall not see wind, nor shall you see rain; yet that valley shall be filled with water, so that you, your cattle, and your animals may drink.' 18And this is a simple matter in the sight of the LORD; He will also deliver the Moabites into your hand. 19Also you shall attack every fortified city and every choice city, and shall cut down every good tree, and stop up every spring of water, and ruin every good piece of land with stones."

20Now it happened in the morning, when [a]the grain offering was offered, that suddenly water came by way of Edom, and the land was filled with water.

21And when all the Moabites heard that the kings had come up to fight against them, all who were able to bear arms and older were [1]gathered; and they stood at the border. 22Then they rose up early in the morning, and the sun was shining on the water; and the Moabites saw the water on the other side *as* red as blood. 23And they said, "This is blood; the kings have surely struck swords and have killed one another; now therefore, Moab, to the spoil!"

24So when they came to the camp of Israel, Israel rose up and attacked the Moabites, so that they fled before them; and they entered *their* land, killing the Moabites. 25Then they destroyed the cities, and each man threw a stone on every good piece of land and filled it; and they stopped up all the springs of water and cut down all the good trees. But they left the stones of [a]Kir Haraseth *intact.* However the slingers surrounded and attacked it.

26And when the king of Moab saw that the battle was too fierce for him, he took with him seven hundred men who drew swords, to break through to the king of Edom, but they could not. 27Then [a]he took his eldest son who would have reigned in his place, and offered him *as* a burnt offering upon the wall; and there was great [1]indignation against Israel. [b]So they departed from him and returned to *their own* land.

Elisha and the Widow's Oil

4 A certain woman of the wives of [a]the sons of the prophets cried out to Elisha, saying, "Your servant my husband

2 [a] 1 Kin. 16:31, 32
3 [a] 1 Kin. 12:28–32
4 [a] 2 Sam. 8:2 [b] Is. 16:1, 2
5 [a] 2 Kin. 1:1
7 [a] 1 Kin. 22:4
11 [a] 1 Kin. 22:7 [b] 1 Kin. 19:21 [1] *Was the personal servant of*
12 [a] 2 Kin. 2:25
13 [a] [Ezek. 14:3] [b] Judg. 10:14 [c] 1 Kin. 22:6–11 [d] 1 Kin. 18:19
14 [a] 1 Kin. 17:1
15 [a] 1 Sam. 10:5 [b] 1 Sam. 16:16, 23 [c] Ezek. 1:3; 3:14, 22; 8:1
16 [a] Jer. 14:3 [1] *water canals*
20 [a] Ex. 29:39, 40
21 [1] *summoned*
25 [a] Is. 16:7, 11
27 [a] [Amos 2:1] [b] 2 Kin. 8:20 [1] *wrath*
CHAPTER 4
1 [a] 1 Kin. 20:35

2 Kings 3:15

Dear Woman of Destiny,

Let me share some wonderful words with you: "Music is a fair and glorious gift of God. I am strongly persuaded that after theology, there is no art which can be placed on the level with music. The devil flees before the sound of music almost as much as before the word of God." The exciting revelational truth from Martin Luther is just as true today as it was in his day and in the days of the biblical kings.

Through the Scriptures and through long personal experience, I have learned that anointed music is a mysterious but potent spiritual tool. It is a marvelous means of worship, a biblical aid to prophecy and a dynamic weapon of spiritual warfare.

Before writing this letter, I read again how God used the music of David to calm the demon-tormented soul of Saul (see 1 Sam. 16:23). I read of the young prophets coming down the mountain, prophesying to the world, heralded by consecrated musicians (see 1 Sam. 10:5). I read about the courageous choir, chosen by King Jehoshapat under the guidance of the Holy Spirit, leading the outnumbered army of Israel into battle with their song. In the face of their blazing praise, their enemies self-destructed (see 2 Chr. 20:21–23).

Yes, anointed music provides songs of deliverance and mighty armaments of war . . . *if* we understand its power and purpose and use it in faith.

Surely few would deny that music is also our most biblical and expressive means of corporate worship. As we sing in expectant trust, the results can be dynamic: God, invoked by our united praise, faithfully manifests His presence (see Ps. 22:3). But what I want to share with you is this: Exactly the same thing can happen in your personal worship.

I believe that as we invoke God's presence in our private times, the Holy Spirit will inhabit our praise there, too. As He does, He brings His person and His gifts. Here dreams and visions, words of wisdom, heavenly language, and prophetic knowledge are born. Music can lead us there. For instance, a friend of mine can use her spiritual language only when she worships by playing her piano and singing: God is very creative in the way He releases His gifts!

Sing to the glory of God when the enemy harasses you. Yes, all by yourself; just let it flow. Fill your mouth and your house with songs of praise and the declaration of Jesus' victory and authority. Even in a public place, you can hum "A Mighty Fortress"! Believe me, the devil knows the lyrics.

With all my heart I encourage you to learn about music's amazing influence and experience the blessing and victory it can bring. Use contemporary Christian music for your teenagers and simple praise songs for your little ones. Just let it all ring! As you do, the joy and glory of God will permeate your home, your family, and your own soul.

Carol Owens

is dead, and you know that your servant
feared the LORD. And the creditor is coming [b]to take my two sons to be his slaves."
2So Elisha said to her, "What shall I do
for you? Tell me, what do you have in the
house?" And she said, "Your maidservant
has nothing in the house but a jar of oil."
3Then he said, "Go, borrow vessels from
everywhere, from all your neighbors—
empty vessels; [a]do not gather just a few.
4And when you have come in, you shall
shut the door behind you and your sons;
then pour it into all those vessels, and set
aside the full ones."
5So she went from him and shut the
door behind her and her sons, who
brought *the vessels* to her; and she poured
it out. 6Now it came to pass, when the
vessels were full, that she said to her son,
"Bring me another vessel."

And he said to her, "*There is* not another vessel." So the oil ceased. 7Then she
came and told the man of God. And he
said, "Go, sell the oil and pay your debt;
and you *and* your sons live on the rest."

Elisha Raises the Shunammite's Son

8Now it happened one day that Elisha
went to [a]Shunem, where there *was* a
[1]notable woman, and she [2]persuaded him
to eat some food. So it was, as often as he
passed by, he would turn in there to eat

1 b [Lev. 25:39–41, 48]

3 a 2 Kin. 3:16

8 a Josh. 19:18 *1* Lit. *great* *2* Lit. *laid hold on him*

The Shunammite Woman

It is amazing to see how God provides for His people, especially when the people have sacrificed their whole lives to serve Him. Throughout the Bible, we find story after story of God's miraculous and creative provision for those who love Him. The prophet Elisha was no exception.

Second Kings 4:8 tells us that Elisha visited Shunem often enough to regularly stop and eat at the home of a certain family. The lady of the house said to her husband, "Look now, I know that this is a holy man of God" (2 Kin. 4:9), and she wanted to serve the prophet by providing a place for him to stay when he was in Shunem. She not only said to Elisha, "Keep stopping by when you're in the neighborhood," but even prepared a room in her home especially for him.

Elisha was so touched by her ministry to him that he, in turn, ministered to her, prophetically speaking the words she longed to hear: "About this time next year you shall embrace a son" (2 Kin. 4:16). She did have a son; and later, when the child died, Elisha prayed for him and God restored his life.

But what were the keys to her miracle? First of all, she recognized Elisha as a *true* man of God. Second, she wanted nothing from him. When he asked, "What can I do for you?" she responded, "I dwell among my own people" (1 Kin. 4:13). In other words, "I don't need anything." In effect, she turned down his open-ended request to do something for her, even though she knew he was a man of miracles.

Woman of Destiny, let us follow the Shunammite woman's example and honor the servants of God. Let us discern, with the help of God's Word and His Spirit, who His true servants are; and when we encounter a man of God or a woman of God who can benefit from our support, let us give generously to the work of the ministry.

some food. 9And she said to her husband,
"Look now, I know that this *is* a holy
man of God, who passes by us regularly.
10Please, let us make [1]a small upper room
on the wall; and let us put a bed for him
there, and a table and a chair and a lampstand; so it will be, whenever he comes to
us, he can turn in there."

11And it happened one day that he came
there, and he turned in to the upper room
and lay down there. 12Then he said to [a]Ge-
hazi his servant, "Call this Shunammite
woman." When he had called her, she
stood before him. 13And he said to him,
"Say now to her, 'Look, you have been
concerned for us with all this care. What
can I do for you? Do you want me to speak
on your behalf to the king or to the commander of the army?' "

She answered, "I dwell among my own
people."

14So he said, "What then *is* to be done
for her?"

And Gehazi answered, "Actually, she
has no son, and her husband is old."

15So he said, "Call her." When he had
called her, she stood in the doorway.
16Then he said, [1]"About this time next
year you shall embrace a son."

And she said, "No, my lord. Man of God,
[a]do not lie to your maidservant!"

17But the woman conceived, and bore a
son when the appointed time had come, of
which Elisha had told her.

18And the child grew. Now it happened
one day that he went out to his father, to
the reapers. 19And he said to his father,
"My head, my head!"

So he said to a servant, "Carry him to
his mother." 20When he had taken him
and brought him to his mother, he sat on
her knees till noon, and *then* died. 21And
she went up and laid him on the bed of the
man of God, shut *the door* upon him, and
went out. 22Then she called to her husband, and said, "Please send me one of the
young men and one of the donkeys, that
I may run to the man of God and come
back."

23So he said, "Why are you going to him
today? *It is* neither the [a]New Moon nor
the Sabbath."

And she said, [1]"*It is* well." 24Then she
saddled a donkey, and said to her servant,
"Drive, and go forward; do not slacken the
pace for me unless I tell you." 25And so
she departed, and went to the man of God
[a]at Mount Carmel.

So it was, when the man of God saw her
afar off, that he said to his servant Gehazi,
"Look, the Shunammite woman! 26Please
run now to meet her, and say to her, '*Is it*
well with you? *Is it* well with your husband? *Is it* well with the child?' "

And she answered, "*It is* well." 27Now
when she came to the man of God at the
hill, she caught him by the feet, but Gehazi came near to push her away. But the
man of God said, "Let her alone; for her
soul *is* in deep distress, and the LORD has
hidden *it* from me, and has not told me."

28So she said, "Did I ask a son of my
lord? [a]Did I not say, 'Do not deceive me'?"

29Then he said to Gehazi, [a]"Get[1] yourself ready, and take my staff in your hand,
and be on your way. If you meet anyone,
[b]do not greet him; and if anyone greets
you, do not answer him; but [c]lay my staff
on the face of the child."

30And the mother of the child said, [a]"*As*
the LORD lives, and *as* your soul lives, I
will not [b]leave you." So he arose and followed her. 31Now Gehazi went on ahead of
them, and laid the staff on the face of the
child; but *there was* neither voice nor
hearing. Therefore he went back to meet
him, and told him, saying, "The child has
[a]not awakened."

32When Elisha came into the house,
there was the child, lying dead on his bed.
33He [a]went in therefore, shut the door behind the two of them, [b]and prayed to the
LORD. 34And he went up and lay on the
child, and put his mouth on his mouth,
his eyes on his eyes, and his hands on his
hands; and [a]he stretched himself out on
the child, and the flesh of the child became warm. 35He returned and walked
back and forth in the house, and again
went up [a]and stretched himself out on
him; then [b]the child sneezed seven times,
and the child opened his eyes. 36And he
called Gehazi and said, "Call this Shunammite woman." So he called her. And
when she came in to him, he said, "Pick
up your son." 37So she went in, fell at his
feet, and bowed to the ground; then she
[a]picked up her son and went out.

Elisha Purifies the Pot of Stew

38And Elisha returned to [a]Gilgal, and
there was a [b]famine in the land. Now the
sons of the prophets *were* [c]sitting before
him; and he said to his servant, "Put on
the large pot, and boil stew for the sons of

10 [1] Or *a small walled upper chamber*
12 [a] 2 Kin. 4:29–31; 5:20–27; 8:4, 5
16 [a] 2 Kin. 4:28 [1] Lit. *About this season, as the time of life*
23 [a] 1 Chr. 23:31 [1] Or *It will be well*
25 [a] 2 Kin. 2:25
28 [a] 2 Kin. 4:16
29 [a] 1 Kin. 18:46 [b] Luke 10:4 [c] Ex. 7:19; 14:16 [1] Lit. *Gird up your loins.* The skirt of the robe was wrapped around the legs and tucked in the belt to gain freedom of movement.
30 [a] 2 Kin. 2:2 [b] 2 Kin. 2:4
31 [a] John 11:11
33 [a] [Matt. 6:6] [b] 1 Kin. 17:20
34 [a] 1 Kin. 17:21–23
35 [a] 1 Kin. 17:21 [b] 2 Kin. 8:1, 5
37 [a] [Heb. 11:35]
38 [a] 2 Kin. 2:1 [b] 2 Kin. 8:1 [c] Acts 22:3

the prophets." 39 So one went out into the field to gather herbs, and found a wild vine, and gathered from it a lapful of wild gourds, and came and sliced *them* into the pot of stew, though they did not know *what they were.* 40 Then they served it to the men to eat. Now it happened, as they were eating the stew, that they cried out and said, "Man of God, *there is* [a]death in the pot!" And they could not eat *it.*

41 So he said, "Then bring some flour." And [a]he put *it* into the pot, and said, "Serve *it* to the people, that they may eat." And there was nothing harmful in the pot.

Elisha Feeds One Hundred Men

42 Then a man came from [a]Baal Shalisha, [b]and brought the man of God bread of the firstfruits, twenty loaves of barley bread, and newly ripened grain in his knapsack. And he said, "Give *it* to the people, that they may eat."

43 But his servant said, [a]"What? Shall I set this before one hundred men?"

He said again, "Give it to the people, that they may eat; for thus says the LORD: [b]'They shall eat and have *some* left over.' " 44 So he set *it* before them; and they ate [a]and had *some* left over, according to the word of the LORD.

Naaman's Leprosy Healed

5 Now [a]Naaman, commander of the army of the king of Syria, was [b]a great and honorable man in the eyes of his master, because by him the LORD had given victory to Syria. He was also a mighty man of valor, *but* a leper. 2 And the Syrians had gone out [a]on[1] raids, and had brought back captive a young girl from the land of Israel. She [2]waited on Naaman's wife. 3 Then she said to her mistress, "If only my master *were* with the prophet who *is* in Samaria! For he would heal him of his leprosy." 4 And *Naaman* went in and told his master, saying, "Thus and thus said the girl who *is* from the land of Israel."

5 Then the king of Syria said, "Go now, and I will send a letter to the king of Israel."

So he departed and [a]took with him ten talents of silver, six thousand *shekels* of gold, and ten changes of clothing. 6 Then he brought the letter to the king of Israel, which said,

> Now be advised, when this letter comes to you, that I have sent Naaman my servant to you, that you may heal him of his leprosy.

7 And it happened, when the king of Israel read the letter, that he tore his clothes and said, "*Am* I [a]God, to kill and make alive, that this man sends a man to me to heal him of his leprosy? Therefore please consider, and see how he seeks a quarrel with me."

8 So it was, when Elisha the man of God heard that the king of Israel had torn his clothes, that he sent to the king, saying, "Why have you torn your clothes? Please let him come to me, and he shall know that there is a prophet in Israel."

9 Then Naaman went with his horses and chariot, and he stood at the door of Elisha's house. 10 And Elisha sent a messenger to him, saying, "Go and [a]wash in the Jordan seven times, and your flesh shall be restored to you, and *you shall* be clean." 11 But Naaman became furious, and went away and said, "Indeed, I said to myself, 'He will surely come out *to me,* and stand and call on the name of the LORD his God, and wave his hand over the place, and heal the leprosy.' 12 *Are* not the [1]Abanah and the Pharpar, the rivers of Damascus, better than all the waters of Israel? Could I not wash in them and be clean?" So he turned and went away in a rage. 13 And his [a]servants came near and spoke to him, and said, "My father, *if* the prophet had told you *to do* something great, would you not have done *it?* How much more then, when he says to you, 'Wash, and be clean'?" 14 So he went down and dipped seven times in the Jordan, according to the saying of the man of God; and his [a]flesh was restored like the flesh of a little child, and [b]he was clean.

15 And he returned to the man of God, he and all his aides, and came and stood before him; and he said, "Indeed, now I know that *there is* [a]no God in all the earth, except in Israel; now therefore, please take [b]a gift from your servant."

16 But he said, [a]"*As* the LORD lives, before whom I stand, [b]I will receive nothing." And he urged him to take *it,* but he refused.

17 So Naaman said, "Then, if not, please let your servant be given two mule-loads of earth; for your servant will no longer offer either burnt offering or sacrifice to other gods, but to the LORD. 18 Yet in this thing may the LORD pardon your servant:

---

40 [a]Ex. 10:17
41 [a]Ex. 15:25
42 [a]1 Sam. 9:4 [b][1 Cor. 9:11]
43 [a]John 6:9 [b]Luke 9:17
44 [a]John 6:13

CHAPTER 5
1 [a]Luke 4:27 [b]Ex. 11:3
2 [a]2 Kin. 6:23; 13:20 [1] Or *in bands* [2] Served, lit. *was before*
5 [a]1 Sam. 9:8
7 [a][Gen. 30:2]
10 [a]John 9:7
12 [1] So with Kt., LXX, Vg.; Qr., Syr., Tg. *Amanah*
13 [a]1 Sam. 28:23
14 [a]Job 33:25 [b]Luke 4:27; 5:13
15 [a]Dan. 2:47; 3:29; 6:26, 27 [b]Gen. 33:11
16 [a]2 Kin. 3:14 [b]Gen. 14:22, 23

when my master goes into the temple of
Rimmon to worship there, and [a]he leans
on my hand, and I bow down in the temple of Rimmon—when I bow down in the
temple of Rimmon, may the LORD please
pardon your servant in this thing."
19Then he said to him, "Go in peace."
So he departed from him a short distance.

Gehazi's Greed

20But [a]Gehazi, the servant of Elisha the
man of God, said, "Look, my master has
spared Naaman this Syrian, while not receiving from his hands what he brought;
but *as* the LORD lives, I will run after him
and take something from him." 21So Gehazi pursued Naaman. When Naaman saw
him running after him, he got down from
the chariot to meet him, and said, "*Is* all
well?"
22And he said, "All *is* [a]well. My master
has sent me, saying, 'Indeed, just now two
young men of the sons of the prophets
have come to me from the mountains of
Ephraim. Please give them a talent of silver and two changes of garments.' "

18 a 2 Kin. 7:2, 17
20 a 2 Kin. 4:12; 8:4, 5
22 a 2 Kin. 4:26

Naaman's Maid

The young woman kidnapped and forced into servitude in Naaman's house offers us valuable lessons about how to deal with one of life's most inevitable situations—captivity.

Most women of destiny, at some time in their lives, find themselves held captive to something: disappointment, fear, low self-esteem, anxiety, frustration, unwise decisions. One of the things we all go through on our way to destiny is the process of getting free. Often, we find ourselves free from one form of bondage only to recognize another. But women of destiny walk in freedom, having been released from every captivity of the enemy.

What can we learn from the nameless girl whisked away from home and family by the Syrian army and given a job as a maidservant to Naaman's wife? In her captivity, if anything outweighs her confidence and her courage, it is her astounding compassion for her master, Naaman, who suffered from leprosy. Her first and only words recorded in Scripture are, "If only my master were with the prophet who is in Samaria! For he would heal him of his leprosy" (2 Kin. 5:3).

We see her guileless heart, eager for her master's restoration, though she had been drafted into his service against her will. Her love gave her the courage to speak up and tell Naaman's wife where to get help for this fatal disease. She speaks words of absolute faith, declaring that the prophet "would heal him of his leprosy." She did not say to her mistress, "Maybe the prophet can help," but spoke with complete confidence that Naaman would certainly be healed if he could just get to Elisha.

Given her circumstances, the young woman could have succumbed to fear instead of faith. She could have felt vindicated by Naaman's suffering. She could have walked in self-pity or bitterness instead of pointing her master toward a miracle. But she teaches us that any captivity requires courage and compassion, among a host of other virtues.

May we women of destiny today possess the amazing love and boldness of this little girl.

23 So Naaman said, "Please, take two talents." And he urged him, and bound two talents of silver in two bags, with two changes of garments, and handed *them* to two of his servants; and they carried *them* on ahead of him. 24 When he came to [1]the citadel, he took *them* from their hand, and stored *them* away in the house; then he let the men go, and they departed. 25 Now he went in and stood before his master. Elisha said to him, "Where *did you go,* Gehazi?"

And he said, "Your servant did not go anywhere."

26 Then he said to him, "Did not my heart go *with you* when the man turned back from his chariot to meet you? *Is it* [a]time to receive money and to receive clothing, olive groves and vineyards, sheep and oxen, male and female servants? 27 Therefore the leprosy of Naaman [a]shall cling to you and your descendants forever." And he went out from his presence [b]leprous, *as white* as snow.

The Floating Ax Head

6 And [a]the sons of the prophets said to Elisha, "See now, the place where we dwell with you is too small for us. 2 Please, let us go to the Jordan, and let every man take a beam from there, and let us make there a place where we may dwell."

So he answered, "Go."

3 Then one said, [a]"Please consent to go with your servants."

And he answered, "I will go." 4 So he went with them. And when they came to the Jordan, they cut down trees. 5 But as one was cutting down a tree, the iron *ax head* fell into the water; and he cried out and said, "Alas, master! For it was [a]borrowed."

6 So the man of God said, "Where did it fall?" And he showed him the place. So [a]he cut off a stick, and threw *it* in there; and he made the iron float. 7 Therefore he said, "Pick *it* up for yourself." So he reached out his hand and took it.

The Blinded Syrians Captured

8 Now the [a]king of Syria was making war against Israel; and he consulted with his servants, saying, "My camp *will be* in such and such a place." 9 And the man of God sent to the king of Israel, saying, "Beware that you do not pass this place, for the Syrians are coming down there." 10 Then the king of Israel sent *someone* to the place of which the man of God had told him. Thus he warned him, and he was watchful there, not just once or twice.

11 Therefore the heart of the king of Syria was greatly troubled by this thing; and he called his servants and said to them, "Will you not show me which of us *is* for the king of Israel?"

12 And one of his servants said, "None, my lord, O king; but Elisha, the prophet who *is* in Israel, tells the king of Israel the words that you speak in your bedroom." 13 So he said, "Go and see where he *is,* that I may send and get him."

And it was told him, saying, "Surely *he is* in [a]Dothan."

14 Therefore he sent horses and chariots and a great army there, and they came by night and surrounded the city. 15 And when the servant of the man of God arose early and went out, there was an army, surrounding the city with horses and chariots. And his servant said to him, "Alas, my master! What shall we do?"

I pray, Lord, that _____ will not fear, for those who are with them are more than those who are against them. Open their eyes that they may see.

FROM 2 KINGS 6:16, 17

16 So he answered, [a]"Do not fear, for [b]those who *are* with us *are* more than those who *are* with them." 17 And Elisha prayed, and said, "LORD, I pray, open his eyes that he may see." Then the LORD [a]opened the eyes of the young man, and he saw. And behold, the mountain *was* full of [b]horses and chariots of fire all around Elisha. 18 So when *the Syrians* came down to him, Elisha prayed to the LORD, and said, "Strike this people, I pray, with blindness." And [a]He struck them with blindness according to the word of Elisha.

19 Now Elisha said to them, "This *is* not the way, nor *is* this the city. Follow me, and I will bring you to the man whom you seek." But he led them to Samaria.

24 [1] Lit. *the hill*
26 [a] [Eccl. 3:1, 6]
27 [a] [1 Tim. 6:10] [b] Ex. 4:6
CHAPTER 6
1 [a] 2 Kin. 4:38
3 [a] 2 Kin. 5:23
5 [a] [Ex. 22:14]
6 [a] 2 Kin. 2:21; 4:41
8 [a] 2 Kin. 8:28, 29
13 [a] Gen. 37:17
16 [a] Ex. 14:13 [b] [Rom. 8:31]
17 [a] Num. 22:31 [b] 2 Kin. 2:11
18 [a] Gen. 19:11

20 So it was, when they had come to Samaria, that Elisha said, "LORD, open the eyes of these *men,* that they may see." And the LORD opened their eyes, and they saw; and there *they were,* inside Samaria!

21 Now when the king of Israel saw them, he said to Elisha, "My [a]father, shall I kill *them?* Shall I kill *them?*"

22 But he answered, "You shall not kill *them.* Would you kill those whom you have taken captive with your sword and your bow? [a]Set food and water before them, that they may eat and drink and go to their master." 23 Then he prepared a great feast for them; and after they ate and drank, he sent them away and they went to their master. So [a]the bands of Syrian *raiders* came no more into the land of Israel.

Syria Besieges Samaria in Famine

24 And it happened after this that [a]Ben-Hadad king of Syria gathered all his army, and went up and besieged Samaria. 25 And there was a great [a]famine in Samaria; and indeed they besieged it until a donkey's head was *sold* for eighty *shekels* of silver, and one-fourth of a [1]kab of dove droppings for five *shekels* of silver.

26 Then, as the king of Israel was passing by on the wall, a woman cried out to him, saying, "Help, my lord, O king!"

27 And he said, "If the LORD does not help you, where can I find help for you? From the threshing floor or from the winepress?" 28 Then the king said to her, "What is troubling you?"

And she answered, "This woman said to me, 'Give your son, that we may eat him today, and we will eat my son tomorrow.' 29 So [a]we boiled my son, and ate him. And I said to her on the next day, 'Give your son, that we may eat him'; but she has hidden her son."

30 Now it happened, when the king heard the words of the woman, that he [a]tore his clothes; and as he passed by on the wall, the people looked, and there underneath *he had* sackcloth on his body. 31 Then he said, [a]"God do so to me and more also, if the head of Elisha the son of Shaphat remains on him today!"

32 But Elisha was sitting in his house, and [a]the elders were sitting with him. And *the king* sent a man ahead of him, but before the messenger came to him, he said to the elders, [b]"Do you see how this son of [c]a murderer has sent someone to take away my head? Look, when the messenger comes, shut the door, and hold him fast at the door. *Is* not the sound of his master's feet behind him?" 33 And while he was still talking with them, there was the messenger, coming down to him; and then *the king* said, "Surely this calamity *is* from the LORD; [a]why should I wait for the LORD any longer?"

7 Then Elisha said, "Hear the word of the LORD. Thus says the LORD: [a]'Tomorrow about this time a [1]seah of fine flour *shall be sold* for a shekel, and two seahs of barley for a shekel, at the gate of Samaria.' "

2 [a]So an officer on whose hand the king leaned answered the man of God and said, "Look, [b]*if* the LORD would make windows in heaven, could this thing be?"

And he said, "In fact, you shall see *it* with your eyes, but you shall not eat of it."

The Syrians Flee

3 Now there were four leprous men [a]at the entrance of the gate; and they said to one another, "Why are we sitting here until we die? 4 If we say, 'We will enter the city,' the famine *is* in the city, and we shall die there. And if we sit here, we die also. Now therefore, come, let us surrender to the [a]army of the Syrians. If they keep us alive, we shall live; and if they kill us, we shall only die." 5 And they rose at twilight to go to the camp of the Syrians; and when they had come to the outskirts of the Syrian camp, to their surprise no one *was* there. 6 For the LORD had caused the army of the Syrians [a]to hear the noise of chariots and the noise of horses—the noise of a great army; so they said to one another, "Look, the king of Israel has hired against us [b]the kings of the Hittites and the kings of the Egyptians to attack us!" 7 Therefore they [a]arose and fled at twilight, and left the camp intact—their tents, their horses, and their donkeys—and they fled for their lives. 8 And when these lepers came to the outskirts of the camp, they went into one tent and ate and drank, and carried from it silver and gold and clothing, and went and hid *them;* then they came back and entered another tent, and carried *some* from there *also,* and went and hid *it.*

9 Then they said to one another, "We are not doing right. This day *is* a day of good news, and we remain silent. If we wait

21 a 2 Kin. 2:12; 5:13; 8:9
22 a [Rom. 12:20]
23 a 2 Kin. 5:2; 6:8, 9
24 a 1 Kin. 20:1
25 a 2 Kin. 4:38; 8:1
1 Approximately 1 pint
29 a Lev. 26:27–29
30 a 1 Kin. 21:27
31 a Ruth 1:17
32 a Ezek. 8:1; 14:1; 20:1
b Luke 13:32
c 1 Kin. 18:4, 13, 14; 21:10, 13
33 a Job 2:9

CHAPTER 7
1 a 2 Kin. 7:18, 19
1 A third of an ephah, or about 8 gallons
2 a 2 Kin. 5:18; 7:17, 19, 20
b Mal. 3:10
3 a [Num. 5:2–4; 12:10–14]
4 a 2 Kin. 6:24
6 a 2 Sam. 5:24
b 1 Kin. 10:29
7 a Ps. 48:4–6

until morning light, some [1]punishment will come upon us. Now therefore, come, let us go and tell the king's household." 10So they went and called to the gatekeepers of the city, and told them, saying, "We went to the Syrian camp, and surprisingly no one *was* there, not a human sound—only horses and donkeys tied, and the tents intact." 11And the gatekeepers called out, and they told *it* to the king's household inside.

12So the king arose in the night and said to his servants, "Let me now tell you what the Syrians have done to us. They know that we *are* [a]hungry; therefore they have gone out of the camp to [1]hide themselves in the field, saying, 'When they come out of the city, we shall catch them alive, and get into the city.' "

13And one of his servants answered and said, "Please, let several *men* take five of the remaining horses which are left in the city. Look, they *may either become* like all the multitude of Israel that are left in it; or indeed, *I say,* they *may become* like all the multitude of Israel left from those who are consumed; so let us send them and see." 14Therefore they took two chariots with horses; and the king sent them in the direction of the Syrian army, saying, "Go and see." 15And they went after them to the Jordan; and indeed all the road *was* full of garments and weapons which the Syrians had thrown away in their haste. So the messengers returned and told the king. 16Then the people went out and plundered the tents of the Syrians. So a seah of fine flour was *sold* for a shekel, and two seahs of barley for a shekel, [a]according to the word of the LORD.

17Now the king had appointed the officer on whose hand he leaned to have charge of the gate. But the people trampled him in the gate, and he died, just [a]as the man of God had said, who spoke when the king came down to him. 18So it happened just as the man of God had spoken to the king, saying, [a]"Two seahs of barley for a shekel, and a seah of fine flour for a shekel, shall be *sold* tomorrow about this time in the gate of Samaria."

19Then that officer had answered the man of God, and said, "Now look, *if* the LORD would make windows in heaven, could such a thing be?"

And he had said, "In fact, you shall see *it* with your eyes, but you shall not eat of it." 20And so it happened to him, for the people trampled him in the gate, and he died.

The King Restores the Shunammite's Land

8 Then Elisha spoke to the woman [a]whose son he had restored to life, saying, "Arise and go, you and your household, and stay wherever you can; for the LORD [b]has called for a [c]famine, and furthermore, it will come upon the land for seven years." 2So the woman arose and did according to the saying of the man of God, and she went with her household and dwelt in the land of the Philistines seven years.

3It came to pass, at the end of seven years, that the woman returned from the land of the Philistines; and she went to make an appeal to the king for her house and for her land. 4Then the king talked with [a]Gehazi, the servant of the man of God, saying, "Tell me, please, all the great things Elisha has done." 5Now it happened, as he was telling the king how he had restored the dead to life, that there was the woman whose son he had [a]restored to life, appealing to the king for her house and for her land. And Gehazi said, "My lord, O king, this *is* the woman, and this *is* her son whom Elisha restored to life." 6And when the king asked the woman, she told him.

So the king appointed a certain officer for her, saying, "Restore all that *was* hers, and all the proceeds of the field from the day that she left the land until now."

Death of Ben-Hadad

7Then Elisha went to Damascus, and [a]Ben-Hadad king of Syria was sick; and it was told him, saying, "The man of God has come here." 8And the king said to [a]Hazael, [b]"Take a present in your hand, and go to meet the man of God, and [c]inquire of the LORD by him, saying, 'Shall I recover from this disease?' " 9So [a]Hazael went to meet him and took a present with him, of every good thing of Damascus, forty camel-loads; and he came and stood before him, and said, "Your son Ben-Hadad king of Syria has sent me to you, saying, 'Shall I recover from this disease?' "

10And Elisha said to him, "Go, say to him, 'You shall certainly recover.' However the LORD has shown me that [a]he will really die." 11Then he [1]set his counte-

9 [1] Calamity
12 [a] 2 Kin. 6:24–29 [1] Hide themselves in ambush
16 [a] 2 Kin. 7:1
17 [a] 2 Kin. 6:32; 7:2
18 [a] 2 Kin. 7:1

CHAPTER 8
1 [a] 2 Kin. 4:18, 31–35 [b] Hag. 1:11 [c] 2 Sam. 21:1
4 [a] 2 Kin. 4:12; 5:20–27
5 [a] 2 Kin. 4:35
7 [a] 2 Kin. 6:24
8 [a] 1 Kin. 19:15 [b] 1 Sam. 9:7 [c] 2 Kin. 1:2
9 [a] 1 Kin. 19:15
10 [a] 2 Kin. 8:15
11 [1] *fixed his gaze*

nance in a stare until he was ashamed; and the man of God [a]wept. 12And Hazael said, "Why is my lord weeping?"

He answered, "Because I know [a]the evil that you will do to the children of Israel: Their strongholds you will set on fire, and their young men you will kill with the sword; and you [b]will dash their children, and rip open their women with child."

13So Hazael said, "But what [a]*is* your servant—a dog, that he should do this gross thing?"

And Elisha answered, [b]"The LORD has shown me that you *will become* king over Syria."

14Then he departed from Elisha, and came to his master, who said to him, "What did Elisha say to you?" And he answered, "He told me you would surely recover." 15But it happened on the next day that he took a thick cloth and dipped *it* in water, and spread *it* over his face so that he died; and Hazael reigned in his place.

Jehoram Reigns in Judah

16Now [a]in the fifth year of Joram the son of Ahab, king of Israel, Jehoshaphat *having been* king of Judah, [b]Jehoram the son of Jehoshaphat began to reign as [1]king of Judah. 17He was [a]thirty-two years old when he became king, and he reigned eight years in Jerusalem. 18And he walked in the way of the kings of Israel, just as the house of Ahab had done, for [a]the daughter of Ahab was his wife; and he did evil in the sight of the LORD. 19Yet the LORD would not destroy Judah, for the sake of His servant David, [a]as He promised him to give a lamp to him *and* his sons forever.

20In his days [a]Edom revolted against Judah's authority, [b]and made a king over themselves. 21So [1]Joram went to Zair, and all his chariots with him. Then he rose by night and attacked the Edomites who had surrounded him and the captains of the chariots; and the troops fled to their tents. 22Thus Edom has been in revolt against Judah's authority to this day. [a]And Libnah revolted at that time.

23Now the rest of the acts of Joram, and all that he did, *are* they not written in the book of the chronicles of the kings of Judah? 24So Joram [1]rested with his fathers, and was buried with his fathers in the City of David. Then [a]Ahaziah[2] his son reigned in his place.

Ahaziah Reigns in Judah

25In the twelfth year of Joram the son of Ahab, king of Israel, Ahaziah the son of Jehoram, king of Judah, began to reign. 26Ahaziah *was* [a]twenty-two years old when he became king, and he reigned one year in Jerusalem. His mother's name *was* Athaliah the granddaughter of Omri, king of Israel. 27[a]And he walked in the way of the house of Ahab, and did evil in the sight of the LORD, like the house of Ahab, for he *was* the son-in-law of the house of Ahab.

28Now he went [a]with Joram the son of Ahab to war against Hazael king of Syria at [b]Ramoth Gilead; and the Syrians wounded Joram. 29Then [a]King Joram went back to Jezreel to recover from the wounds which the Syrians had inflicted on him at [1]Ramah, when he fought against Hazael king of Syria. [b]And Ahaziah the son of Jehoram, king of Judah, went down to see Joram the son of Ahab in Jezreel, because he was sick.

Jehu Anointed King of Israel

9 And Elisha the prophet called one of [a]the sons of the prophets, and said to him, [b]"Get[1] yourself ready, take this flask of oil in your hand, [c]and go to Ramoth Gilead. 2Now when you arrive at that place, look there for Jehu the son of Jehoshaphat, the son of Nimshi, and go in and make him rise up from among [a]his associates, and take him to an inner room. 3Then [a]take the flask of oil, and pour *it* on his head, and say, 'Thus says the LORD: "I have anointed you king over Israel." ' Then open the door and flee, and do not delay."

4So the young man, the servant of the prophet, went to Ramoth Gilead. 5And when he arrived, there *were* the captains of the army sitting; and he said, "I have a message for you, Commander."

Jehu said, "For which *one* of us?"

And he said, "For you, Commander."

6Then he arose and went into the house. And he poured the oil on his head, and said to him, [a]"Thus says the LORD God of Israel: 'I have anointed you king over the people of the LORD, over Israel. 7You shall strike down the house of Ahab your master, that I may [a]avenge the blood of My servants the prophets, and the blood of all the servants of the LORD, [b]at the hand of Jezebel. 8For the whole house of Ahab shall perish; and [a]I will cut off from Ahab all [b]the males in Israel, both [c]bond and

---

11 a Luke 19:41
12 a Amos 1:3, 4 b Hos. 13:16
13 a 1 Sam. 17:43 b 1 Kin. 19:15
16 a 2 Kin. 1:17; 3:1 b 2 Chr. 21:3 *1* Co-regent with his father
17 a 2 Chr. 21:5–10
18 a 2 Kin. 8:26, 27
19 a 2 Sam. 7:13
20 a Gen. 27:40 b 1 Kin. 22:47
21 *1 Jehoram,* v. 16
22 a Josh. 21:13
24 a 2 Chr. 22:1, 7 *1* Died and joined his ancestors *2* Or *Azariah* or *Jehoahaz*
26 a 2 Chr. 22:2
27 a 2 Chr. 22:3, 4
28 a 2 Chr. 22:5 b 1 Kin. 22:3, 29
29 a 2 Kin. 9:15 b 2 Chr. 22:6, 7 *1 Ramoth,* v. 28

CHAPTER 9
1 a 1 Kin. 20:35 b 2 Kin. 4:29 c 2 Kin. 8:28, 29 *1* Lit. *Gird up your loins*
2 a 2 Kin. 9:5, 11
3 a 1 Kin. 19:16
6 a 2 Chr. 22:7
7 a [Deut. 32:35, 41] b 1 Kin. 18:4; 21:15
8 a 2 Kin. 10:17 b 1 Sam. 25:22 c Deut. 32:36

free. 9So I will make the house of Ahab
like the house of [a]Jeroboam the son of
Nebat, and like the house of [b]Baasha the
son of Ahijah. 10[a]The dogs shall eat Jezebel on the plot *of ground* at Jezreel, and
there shall be none to bury *her*.' " And he
opened the door and fled.

11Then Jehu came out to the servants of
his master, and *one* said to him, "*Is* all
well? Why did [a]this madman come to
you?"

And he said to them, "You know the
man and his babble."

12And they said, "A lie! Tell us now."

So he said, "Thus and thus he spoke to
me, saying, 'Thus says the LORD: "I have
anointed you king over Israel." ' "

13Then each man hastened [a]to take his
garment and put *it* [1]under him on the top
of the steps; and they blew trumpets, saying, "Jehu is king!"

Joram of Israel Killed

14So Jehu the son of Jehoshaphat, the
son of Nimshi, conspired against [a]Joram.
(Now Joram had been defending Ramoth
Gilead, he and all Israel, against Hazael
king of Syria. 15But [a]King [1]Joram had
returned to Jezreel to recover from the
wounds which the Syrians had inflicted
on him when he fought with Hazael king
of Syria.) And Jehu said, "If you are so
minded, let no one leave *or* escape from
the city to go and tell *it* in Jezreel." 16So
Jehu rode in a chariot and went to Jezreel,
for Joram was laid up there; [a]and Ahaziah
king of Judah had come down to see
Joram.

17Now a watchman stood on the tower
in Jezreel, and he saw the company of
Jehu as he came, and said, "I see a company of men."

And Joram said, "Get a horseman and
send him to meet them, and let him say,
[1]'*Is it* peace?' "

18So the horseman went to meet him,
and said, "Thus says the king: '*Is it*
peace?' "

And Jehu said, "What have you to do
with peace? [1]Turn around and follow me."

So the watchman reported, saying,
"The messenger went to them, but is not
coming back."

19Then he sent out a second horseman
who came to them, and said, "Thus says
the king: '*Is it* peace?' "

And Jehu answered, "What have you to
do with peace? Turn around and follow me."

20So the watchman reported, saying,
"He went up to them and is not coming
back; and the driving *is* like the driving of
Jehu the son of Nimshi, for he drives furiously!"

21Then Joram said, [1]"Make ready." And
his chariot was made ready. Then [a]Joram
king of Israel and Ahaziah king of Judah
went out, each in his chariot; and they
went out to meet Jehu, and [2]met him [b]on
the property of Naboth the Jezreelite.
22Now it happened, when Joram saw Jehu,
that he said, "*Is it* peace, Jehu?"

So he answered, "What peace, as long as
the harlotries of your mother Jezebel and
her witchcraft *are so* many?"

23Then Joram turned around and fled,
and said to Ahaziah, "Treachery, Ahaziah!" 24Now Jehu [1]drew his bow with full
strength and shot Jehoram between his
arms; and the arrow came out at his heart,
and he sank down in his chariot. 25Then
Jehu said to Bidkar his captain, "Pick *him*
up, *and* throw him into the tract of the
field of Naboth the Jezreelite; for remember, when you and I were riding together
behind Ahab his father, that [a]the LORD
laid this [b]burden upon him: 26'Surely I
saw yesterday the blood of Naboth and the
blood of his sons,' says the LORD, [a]'and I
will repay you [1]in this plot,' says the LORD.
Now therefore, take *and* throw him on the
plot *of ground,* according to the word of
the LORD."

Ahaziah of Judah Killed

27But when Ahaziah king of Judah saw
this, he fled by the road to [1]Beth Haggan.
So Jehu pursued him, and said, [2]"Shoot
him also in the chariot." *And they shot
him* at the Ascent of Gur, which is by Ibleam. Then he fled to [a]Megiddo, and died
there. 28And his servants carried him in
the chariot to Jerusalem, and buried him
in his tomb with his fathers in the City of
David. 29In the eleventh year of Joram the
son of Ahab, Ahaziah had become king
over Judah.

Jezebel's Violent Death

30Now when Jehu had come to Jezreel,
Jezebel heard *of it;* [a]and she put paint
on her eyes and adorned her head, and
looked through a window. 31Then, as Jehu

9 a 1 Kin. 14:10; 15:29; 21:22 b 1 Kin. 16:3, 11
10 a 1 Kin. 21:23
11 a Jer. 29:26
13 a Matt. 21:7, 8 1 Lit. *under his feet*
14 a 2 Kin. 8:28
15 a 2 Kin. 8:29 1 *Jehoram,* v. 24
16 a 2 Kin. 8:29
17 1 Are you peaceful?
18 1 Lit. *Turn behind me*
21 a 1 Kin. 19:17 b 1 Kin. 21:1–14 1 *Harness up* 2 Lit. *found*
24 1 Lit. *filled his hand*
25 a 1 Kin. 21:19, 24–29 b Is. 13:1
26 a 1 Kin. 21:13, 19 1 *on this property*
27 a 2 Chr. 22:7, 9 1 Lit. *The Garden House* 2 Lit. *Strike*
30 a Ezek. 23:40

entered at the gate, she said, [a]"*Is it* peace,
Zimri, murderer of your master?"
32And he looked up at the window, and
said, "Who *is* on my side? Who?" So two
or three eunuchs looked out at him.
33Then he said, "Throw her down." So
they threw her down, and *some* of her
blood spattered on the wall and on the
horses; and he trampled her underfoot.
34And when he had gone in, he ate and
drank. Then he said, "Go now, see to this
accursed *woman,* and bury her, for [a]she
was a king's daughter." 35So they went to
bury her, but they found no more of her
than the skull and the feet and the palms
of *her* hands. 36Therefore they came back
and told him. And he said, "This *is* the
word of the LORD, which He spoke by His
servant Elijah the Tishbite, saying, [a]'On
the plot *of ground* at Jezreel dogs shall eat
the flesh of Jezebel; 37and the corpse of
Jezebel shall be [a]as refuse on the surface
of the field, in the plot at Jezreel, so that
they shall not say, "Here *lies* Jezebel." ' "

Ahab's Seventy Sons Killed

10 Now Ahab had seventy sons in Samaria.
And Jehu wrote and sent
letters to Samaria, to the rulers of [1]Jezre-
el, to the elders, and to [2]those who reared
Ahab's *sons,* saying:

2 Now as soon as this letter comes
to you, since your master's sons *are*
with you, and you have chariots
and horses, a fortified city also, and
weapons, 3choose the [1]best qualified
of your master's sons, set *him* on
his father's throne, and fight for
your master's house.

4But they were exceedingly afraid, and
said, "Look, [a]two kings could not [1]stand
up to him; how then can we stand?" 5And
he who *was* in charge of the house, and he
who *was* in charge of the city, the elders
also, and those who reared *the sons,* sent
to Jehu, saying, "We *are* your servants, we
will do all you tell us; but we will not
make anyone king. Do *what is* good in
your sight." 6Then he wrote a second letter to them, saying:

If you *are* for me and will obey my
voice, take the heads of the men,
your master's sons, and come to me
at Jezreel by this time tomorrow.

Now the king's sons, seventy persons,
were with the great men of the city, *who*
were rearing them. 7So it was, when the
letter came to them, that they took the
king's sons and [a]slaughtered seventy persons, put their heads in baskets and sent
them to him at Jezreel.
8Then a messenger came and told him,
saying, "They have brought the heads of
the king's sons."
And he said, "Lay them in two heaps at
the entrance of the gate until morning."
9So it was, in the morning, that he went
out and stood, and said to all the people,
"You *are* righteous. Indeed [a]I conspired
against my master and killed him; but
who killed all these? 10Know now that
nothing shall [a]fall to the earth of the word
of the LORD which the LORD spoke concerning the house of Ahab; for the LORD
has done what He spoke [b]by His servant
Elijah." 11So Jehu killed all who remained
of the house of Ahab in Jezreel, and all his
great men and his close acquaintances
and his priests, until he left him none remaining.

Ahaziah's Forty-two Brothers Killed

12And he arose and departed and went
to Samaria. On the way, at [1]Beth Eked
of the Shepherds, 13[a]Jehu met with the
brothers of Ahaziah king of Judah, and
said, "Who *are* you?"
So they answered, "We *are* the brothers
of Ahaziah; we have come down to greet
the sons of the king and the sons of the
queen mother."
14And he said, "Take them alive!" So
they took them alive, and [a]killed them at
the well of [1]Beth Eked, forty-two men;
and he left none of them.

The Rest of Ahab's Family Killed

15Now when he departed from there, he
[1]met [a]Jehonadab the son of [b]Rechab,
coming to meet him; and he greeted him
and said to him, "Is your heart right, as
my heart *is* toward your heart?"
And Jehonadab answered, "It is."
Jehu said, "If it is, [c]give *me* your hand."
So he gave *him* his hand, and he took him
up to him into the chariot. 16Then he said,
"Come with me, and see my [a]zeal for the
LORD." So they had him ride in his chariot. 17And when he came to Samaria, [a]he
killed all who remained to Ahab in Samaria, till he had destroyed them, according

31 [a] 1 Kin. 16:9–20
34 [a] 1 Kin. 16:31
36 [a] 1 Kin. 21:23
37 [a] Ps. 83:10

CHAPTER 10
1 [1] So with MT, Syr., Tg.; LXX *Samaria;* Vg. *city* [2] *the guardians of*
3 [1] *most upright*
4 [a] 2 Kin. 9:24, 27 [1] Lit. *stand before*
7 [a] 1 Kin. 21:21
9 [a] 2 Kin. 9:14–24
10 [a] 1 Sam. 3:19 [b] 1 Kin. 21:17–24, 29
12 [1] Or *The Shearing House*
13 [a] 2 Chr. 22:8
14 [a] 2 Chr. 22:8 [1] Or *The Shearing House*
15 [a] Jer. 35:6 [b] 1 Chr. 2:55 [c] Ezra 10:19 [1] Lit. *found*
16 [a] 1 Kin. 19:10
17 [a] 2 Kin. 9:8

to the word of the LORD [b]which He spoke
to Elijah.

Worshipers of Baal Killed

18Then Jehu gathered all the people together, and said to them, [a]"Ahab served
Baal a little, Jehu will serve him much.
19Now therefore, call to me all the [a]proph-
ets of Baal, all his servants, and all his
priests. Let no one be missing, for I have
a great sacrifice for Baal. Whoever is missing shall not live." But Jehu acted decep-
tively, with the intent of destroying the
worshipers of Baal. 20And Jehu said,
[1]"Proclaim a solemn assembly for Baal."
So they proclaimed *it*. 21Then Jehu sent
throughout all Israel; and all the worshipers of Baal came, so that there was not a
man left who did not come. So they came
into the [1]temple of Baal, and the [a]temple
of Baal was full from one end to the other.
22And he said to the one in charge of the
wardrobe, "Bring out vestments for all the
worshipers of Baal." So he brought out
vestments for them. 23Then Jehu and Jehonadab the son of Rechab went into the
temple of Baal, and said to the worshipers
of Baal, "Search and see that no servants
of the LORD are here with you, but only
the worshipers of Baal." 24So they went
in to offer sacrifices and burnt offerings.
Now Jehu had appointed for himself
eighty men on the outside, and had said,
"*If* any of the men whom I have brought
into your hands escapes, *whoever lets him
escape, it shall be* [a]his life for the life of
the other."
25Now it happened, as soon as he had
made an end of offering the burnt offering, that Jehu said to the guard and to the
captains, "Go in *and* kill them; let no one
come out!" And they killed them with the
edge of the sword; then the guards and
the officers threw *them* out, and went into
the [1]inner room of the temple of Baal.
26And they brought the [a]*sacred* pillars out
of the temple of Baal and burned them.
27Then they broke down the *sacred* pillar
of Baal, and tore down the [1]temple of Baal
and [a]made it a refuse dump to this day.
28Thus Jehu destroyed Baal from Israel.
29However Jehu did not turn away from
the sins of Jeroboam the son of Nebat,
who had made Israel sin, *that is,* from
[a]the golden calves that *were* at Bethel and
Dan. 30And the LORD [a]said to Jehu, "Because you have done well in doing *what is*
right in My sight, *and* have done to the
house of Ahab all that *was* in My heart,
[b]your sons shall sit on the throne of Israel
to the fourth *generation*." 31But Jehu
[1]took no heed to walk in the law of the
LORD God of Israel with all his heart; for
he did not depart from [a]the sins of Jeroboam, who had made Israel sin.

Death of Jehu

32In those days the LORD began to cut
off *parts* of Israel; and [a]Hazael conquered
them in all the territory of Israel 33from
the Jordan eastward: all the land of Gilead—Gad, Reuben, and Manasseh—from
[a]Aroer, which *is* by the River Arnon, including [b]Gilead and Bashan.
34Now the rest of the acts of Jehu, all
that he did, and all his might, *are* they not
written in the book of the chronicles of
the kings of Israel? 35So Jehu [1]rested with
his fathers, and they buried him in Samaria. Then [a]Jehoahaz his son reigned
in his place. 36And the period that Jehu
reigned over Israel in Samaria *was*
twenty-eight years.

Athaliah Reigns in Judah

11 When [a]Athaliah [b]the mother of
Ahaziah saw that her son was
[c]dead, she arose and destroyed all the royal heirs. 2But [1]Jehosheba, the daughter of
King Joram, sister of [a]Ahaziah, took [2]Jo-
ash the son of Ahaziah, and stole him
away from among the king's sons *who
were* being murdered; and they hid him
and his nurse in the bedroom, from Athaliah, so that he was not killed. 3So he was
hidden with her in the house of the LORD
for six years, while Athaliah reigned over
the land.

Joash Crowned King of Judah

4In [a]the seventh year Jehoiada sent and
brought the captains of hundreds—of the
bodyguards and the [1]escorts—and
brought them into the house of the LORD
to him. And he made a covenant with
them and took an oath from them in the
house of the LORD, and showed them the
king's son. 5Then he commanded them,
saying, "This *is* what you shall do: One-
third of you who [1]come on duty [a]on the
Sabbath shall be keeping watch over the
king's house, 6one-third *shall be* at the
gate of Sur, and one-third at the gate behind the escorts. You shall keep the watch

17 [b]1 Kin. 21:21, 29
18 [a]1 Kin. 16:31, 32
19 [a]1 Kin. 18:19; 22:6
20 [1]*Consecrate*
21 [a]1 Kin. 16:32 [1]Lit. *house*
24 [a]1 Kin. 20:39
25 [1]Lit. *city*
26 [a][Deut. 7:5, 25]
27 [a]Ezra 6:11 [1]Lit. *house*
29 [a]1 Kin. 12:28–30; 13:33, 34
30 [a]2 Kin. 9:6, 7 [b]2 Kin. 13:1, 10; 14:23; 15:8, 12
31 [a]1 Kin. 14:16 [1]*was not careful*
32 [a]2 Kin. 8:12; 13:22
33 [a]Deut. 2:36 [b]Amos 1:3–5
35 [a]2 Kin. 13:1 [1]Died and joined his ancestors

CHAPTER 11
1 [a]2 Chr. 22:10 [b]2 Kin. 8:26 [c]2 Kin. 9:27
2 [a]2 Kin. 8:25 [1]*Jehoshabeath*, 2 Chr. 22:11 [2]Or *Jehoash*
4 [a]2 Chr. 23:1 [1]*guards*
5 [a]1 Chr. 9:25 [1]Lit. *enter in*

of the house, lest it be broken down. 7The two [1]contingents of you who go off duty on the Sabbath shall keep the watch of the house of the LORD for the king. 8But you shall surround the king on all sides, every man with his weapons in his hand; and whoever comes within range, let him be put to death. You are to be with the king as he goes out and as he comes in."

9[a]So the captains of the hundreds did according to all that Jehoiada the priest commanded. Each of them took his men who were to be on duty on the Sabbath, with those who were going off duty on the Sabbath, and came to Jehoiada the priest. 10And the priest gave the captains of hundreds the spears and shields which *had belonged* to King David, [a]that were in the temple of the LORD. 11Then the escorts stood, every man with his weapons in his hand, all around the king, from the right [1]side of the temple to the left side of the temple, by the altar and the house. 12And he brought out the king's son, put the crown on him, and *gave him* the [a]Testimony;[1] they made him king and anointed him, and they clapped their hands and said, [b]"Long live the king!"

Death of Athaliah

13[a]Now when Athaliah heard the noise of the escorts *and* the people, she came to the people *in* the temple of the LORD. 14When she looked, there was the king standing by [a]a pillar according to custom; and the leaders and the trumpeters were by the king. All the people of the land were rejoicing and blowing trumpets. So Athaliah tore her clothes and cried out, "Treason! Treason!"

15And Jehoiada the priest commanded the captains of the hundreds, the officers of the army, and said to them, "Take her outside [1]under guard, and slay with the sword whoever follows her." For the priest had said, "Do not let her be killed in the house of the LORD." 16So they seized her; and she went by way of the horses' entrance *into* the king's house, and there she was killed.

17[a]Then Jehoiada [b]made a covenant between the LORD, the king, and the people, that they should be the LORD's people, and *also* [c]between the king and the people. 18And all the people of the land went to the [a]temple of Baal, and tore it down. They thoroughly [b]broke in pieces its altars and [1]images, and [c]killed Mattan the priest of Baal before the altars. And [d]the priest appointed [2]officers over the house of the LORD. 19Then he took the captains of hundreds, the bodyguards, the escorts, and all the people of the land; and they brought the king down from the house of the LORD, and went by way of the gate of the escorts to the king's house. Then he sat on the throne of the kings. 20So all the people of the land rejoiced; and the city was quiet, for they had slain Athaliah with the sword *in* the king's house. 21Jehoash *was* [a]seven years old when he became king.

Jehoash Repairs the Temple

12 In the seventh year of Jehu, [a]Jehoash[1] became king, and he reigned forty years in Jerusalem. His mother's name *was* Zibiah of Beersheba. 2Jehoash did *what was* right in the sight of the LORD all the days in which [a]Jehoiada the priest instructed him. 3But [a]the [1]high places were not taken away; the people still sacrificed and burned incense on the high places.

4And Jehoash said to the priests, [a]"All the money of the dedicated gifts that are brought into the house of the LORD—each man's [b]census[1] money, each man's [c]assessment money—*and* all the money that [2]a man [d]purposes in his heart to bring into the house of the LORD, 5let the priests take *it* themselves, each from his constituency; and let them repair the [1]damages of the temple, wherever any dilapidation is found."

6Now it was so, by the twenty-third year of King Jehoash, [a]*that* the priests had not repaired the damages of the temple. 7[a]So King Jehoash called Jehoiada the priest and the *other* priests, and said to them, "Why have you not repaired the damages of the temple? Now therefore, do not take *more* money from your constituency, but deliver it for repairing the damages of the temple." 8And the priests agreed that they would neither receive *more* money from the people, nor repair the damages of the temple.

9Then Jehoiada the priest took [a]a chest, bored a hole in its lid, and set it beside the altar, on the right side as one comes into the house of the LORD; and the priests who [1]kept the door put [b]there all the money brought into the house of the LORD. 10So it was, whenever they saw that *there was* much money in the chest, that

7 [1] *companies*
9 [a] 2 Chr. 23:8
10 [a] 2 Sam. 8:7
11 [1] Lit. *shoulder*
12 [a] Ex. 25:16; 31:18 [b] 1 Sam. 10:24 [1] Law, Ex. 25:16, 21; Deut. 31:9
13 [a] 2 Chr. 23:12
14 [a] 2 Chr. 34:31
15 [1] Lit. *between ranks*
17 [a] 2 Chr. 23:16 [b] Josh. 24:24, 25 [c] 2 Sam. 5:3
18 [a] 2 Kin. 10:26, 27 [b] [Deut. 12:3] [c] 1 Kin. 18:40 [d] 2 Chr. 23:18 [1] Idols [2] Lit. *offices*
21 [a] 2 Chr. 24:1–14

CHAPTER 12
1 [a] 2 Chr. 24:1 [1] *Joash*, 2 Kin. 11:2ff.
2 [a] 2 Kin. 11:4
3 [a] 2 Kin. 14:4; 15:35 [1] Places for pagan worship
4 [a] 2 Kin. 22:4 [b] Ex. 30:13–16 [c] Lev. 27:2–28 [d] Ex. 35:5 [1] Lit. *the money coming over* [2] *any man's heart prompts him to bring*
5 [1] Lit. *breaches*
6 [a] 2 Chr. 24:5
7 [a] 2 Chr. 24:6
9 [a] 2 Chr. 23:1; 24:8 [b] Mark 12:41 [1] *guarded at the door*

the king's [a]scribe[1] and the high priest
came up and [2]put it in bags, and counted
the money that was found in the house of
the LORD. 11Then they gave the money,
which had been apportioned, into the
hands of those who did the work, who had
the oversight of the house of the LORD;
and they [1]paid it out to the carpenters and
builders who worked on the house of the
LORD, 12and to masons and stonecutters,
and for buying timber and hewn stone, to
[a]repair the damage of the house of the
LORD, and for all that was paid out to repair the temple. 13However [a]there were
not made for the house of the LORD basins
of silver, trimmers, sprinkling-bowls,
trumpets, any articles of gold or articles of
silver, from the money brought into the
house of the LORD. 14But they gave that to
the workmen, and they repaired the house
of the LORD with it. 15Moreover [a]they did
not require an account from the men into
whose hand they delivered the money to
be paid to workmen, for they dealt faithfully. 16[a]The money from the trespass offerings and the money from the sin
offerings was not brought into the house
of the LORD. [b]It belonged to the priests.

Hazael Threatens Jerusalem

17[a]Hazael king of Syria went up and
fought against Gath, and took it; then
[b]Hazael set his face to [1]go up to Jerusalem. 18And Jehoash king of Judah [a]took
all the sacred things that his fathers, Jehoshaphat and Jehoram and Ahaziah,
kings of Judah, had dedicated, and his
own sacred things, and all the gold found
in the treasuries of the house of the LORD
and in the king's house, and sent *them* to
Hazael king of Syria. Then he went away
from Jerusalem.

Death of Joash

19Now the rest of the acts of [1]Joash, and
all that he did, *are* they not written in the
book of the chronicles of the kings of
Judah?

20And [a]his servants arose and formed a
conspiracy, and killed Joash in the house
of [1]the Millo, which goes down to Silla.
21For [1]Jozachar the son of Shimeath and
Jehozabad the son of [2]Shomer, his servants, struck him. So he died, and they
buried him with his fathers in the City of
David. Then [a]Amaziah his son reigned in
his place.

Jehoahaz Reigns in Israel

13 In the twenty-third year of [a]Joash[1]
the son of Ahaziah, king of Judah,
[b]Jehoahaz the son of Jehu became king
over Israel in Samaria, *and reigned* seventeen years. 2And he did evil in the sight of
the LORD, and followed the [a]sins of Jeroboam the son of Nebat, who had made
Israel sin. He did not [1]depart from them.
3Then [a]the anger of the LORD was
aroused against Israel, and He delivered
them into the hand of [b]Hazael king of
Syria, and into the hand of [c]Ben-Hadad
the son of Hazael, all *their* days. 4So Jehoahaz [a]pleaded with the LORD, and the
LORD listened to him; for [b]He saw the oppression of Israel, because the king of Syria oppressed them. 5[a]Then the LORD gave
Israel a deliverer, so that they escaped
from under the hand of the Syrians; and
the children of Israel dwelt in their tents
as before. 6Nevertheless they did not depart from the sins of the house of Jeroboam, who had made Israel sin, *but* walked
in them; [a]and the [1]wooden image also remained in Samaria. 7For He left of the
army of Jehoahaz only fifty horsemen, ten
chariots, and ten thousand foot soldiers;
for the king of Syria had destroyed them
[a]and made them [b]like the dust at
threshing.
8Now the rest of the acts of Jehoahaz,
all that he did, and his might, *are* they not
written in the book of the chronicles of
the kings of Israel? 9So Jehoahaz [1]rested
with his fathers, and they buried him in
Samaria. Then [2]Joash his son reigned in
his place.

Jehoash Reigns in Israel

10In the thirty-seventh year of Joash
king of Judah, [1]Jehoash the son of Jehoahaz became king over Israel in Samaria,
and reigned sixteen years. 11And he did
evil in the sight of the LORD. He did not
depart from all the sins of Jeroboam the
son of Nebat, who made Israel sin, *but*
walked in them.
12[a]Now the rest of the acts of Joash, [b]all
that he did, and [c]his might with which he
fought against Amaziah king of Judah, *are*
they not written in the book of the chronicles of the kings of Israel? 13So Joash
[a]rested[1] with his fathers. Then Jeroboam
sat on his throne. And Joash was buried in
Samaria with the kings of Israel.

---

10 a 2 Sam. 8:17 *1 secretary* *2 tied it up*
11 *1* Lit. *weighed*
12 a 2 Kin. 22:5, 6
13 a 2 Chr. 24:14
15 a 2 Kin. 22:7
16 a [Lev. 5:15, 18] b [Num. 18:9]
17 a 2 Kin. 8:12 b 2 Chr. 24:23 *1* Advance upon
18 a 1 Kin. 15:18
19 *1 Jehoash,* vv. 1–18
20 a 2 Kin. 14:5 *1* Lit. *The Landfill*
21 a 2 Chr. 24:27 *1 Zabad,* 2 Chr. 24:26 *2 Shimrith,* 2 Chr. 24:26

CHAPTER 13
1 a 2 Kin. 12:1 b 2 Kin. 10:35 *1 Jehoash,* 2 Kin. 12:1–18
2 a 1 Kin. 12:26–33 *1* Lit. *turn*
3 a Judg. 2:14 b 2 Kin. 8:12 c Amos 1:4
4 a [Ps. 78:34] b [Ex. 3:7, 9]
5 a 2 Kin. 13:25; 14:25, 27
6 a 1 Kin. 16:33 *1* Heb. *Asherah,* a Canaanite goddess
7 a 2 Kin. 10:32 b [Amos 1:3]
9 *1* Died and joined his ancestors *2* Or *Jehoash*
10 *1 Joash,* v. 9
12 a 2 Kin. 14:8–15 b 2 Kin. 13:14–19, 25 c 2 Kin. 14:9
13 a 2 Kin. 14:16 *1* Died and joined his ancestors

Death of Elisha

14Elisha had become sick with the illness of which he would die. Then Joash
the king of Israel came down to him, and
wept over his face, and said, "O my father,
my father, [a]the chariots of Israel and their
horsemen!"
15And Elisha said to him, "Take a bow
and some arrows." So he took himself a
bow and some arrows. 16Then he said to
the king of Israel, "Put your hand on the
bow." So he put his hand *on it,* and Elisha
put his hands on the king's hands. 17And
he said, "Open the east window"; and he
opened *it.* Then Elisha said, "Shoot"; and
he shot. And he said, "The arrow of the
LORD's deliverance and the arrow of deliverance from Syria; for you must strike the
Syrians at [a]Aphek till you have destroyed
them." 18Then he said, "Take the arrows";
so he took *them.* And he said to the king
of Israel, "Strike the ground"; so he struck
three times, and stopped. 19And the man
of God was angry with him, and said, "You
should have struck five or six times; then
you would have struck Syria till you had
destroyed *it!* [a]But now you will strike Syria *only* three times."
20Then Elisha [1]died, and they buried
him. And the [a]*raiding* bands from Moab
invaded the land in the spring of the year.
21So it was, as they were burying a man,
that suddenly they spied a band *of raiders;*
and they put the man in the tomb of Elisha; and when the man was let down and
touched the bones of Elisha, he revived
and stood on his feet.

Israel Recaptures Cities from Syria

22And [a]Hazael king of Syria oppressed
Israel all the days of Jehoahaz. 23But the
LORD was [a]gracious to them, had compassion on them, and [b]regarded them, [c]be-
cause of His covenant with Abraham,
Isaac, and Jacob, and would not yet destroy them or cast them from His presence.
24Now Hazael king of Syria died. Then
Ben-Hadad his son reigned in his place.
25And [1]Jehoash the son of Jehoahaz recaptured from the hand of Ben-Hadad,
the son of Hazael, the cities which he had
taken out of the hand of Jehoahaz his father by war. [a]Three times Joash defeated
him and recaptured the cities of Israel.

Amaziah Reigns in Judah

14 In [a]the second year of Joash the
son of Jehoahaz, king of Israel,
[b]Amaziah the son of Joash, king of Judah,
became king. 2He was twenty-five years
old when he became king, and he reigned
twenty-nine years in Jerusalem. His
mother's name was Jehoaddan of Jerusalem. 3And he did *what was* right in the
sight of the LORD, yet not like his father
David; he did everything [a]as his father Joash had done. 4[a]However the [1]high places
were not taken away, and the people still
sacrificed and burned incense on the high
places.
5Now it happened, as soon as the kingdom was established in his hand, that he
executed his servants [a]who had murdered
his father the king. 6But the children of
the murderers he did not execute, according to what is written in the Book of the
Law of Moses, in which the LORD commanded, saying, [a]"Fathers shall not be
put to death for their children, nor shall
children be put to death for their fathers;
but a person shall be put to death for his
own sin."
7[a]He killed ten thousand Edomites in
[b]the Valley of Salt, and took [1]Sela by war,
[c]and called its name Joktheel to this day.
8[a]Then Amaziah sent messengers to
[1]Jehoash the son of Jehoahaz, the son of
Jehu, king of Israel, saying, "Come, let us
face one another *in battle.*" 9And Jehoash
king of Israel sent to Amaziah king of Judah, saying, [a]"The thistle that *was* in Lebanon sent to the [b]cedar that *was* in
Lebanon, saying, 'Give your daughter to
my son as wife'; and a wild beast that *was*
in Lebanon passed by and trampled the
thistle. 10You have indeed defeated Edom,
and [a]your heart has [1]lifted you up. Glory
in that, and stay at home; for why should
you meddle with trouble so that you fall—
you and Judah with you?"
11But Amaziah would not heed. Therefore Jehoash king of Israel went out; so he
and Amaziah king of Judah faced one another at [a]Beth Shemesh, which *belongs* to
Judah. 12And Judah was defeated by Israel,
and every man fled to his tent. 13Then
Jehoash king of Israel captured Amaziah
king of Judah, the son of Jehoash, the son
of Ahaziah, at Beth Shemesh; and he went
to Jerusalem, and broke down the wall of
Jerusalem from [a]the Gate of Ephraim to
[b]the Corner Gate—[1]four hundred cubits.
14And he took all [a]the gold and silver, all

---

14 a 2 Kin. 2:12
17 a 1 Kin. 20:26
19 a 2 Kin. 13:25
20 a 2 Kin. 3:5; 24:2 *1* Having prophesied at least 55 years
22 a 2 Kin. 8:12, 13
23 a 2 Kin. 14:27 b [Ex. 2:24, 25] c Ex. 32:13
25 a 2 Kin. 13:18, 19 *1 Joash,* vv. 12–14, 25

CHAPTER 14
1 a 2 Kin. 13:10 b 2 Chr. 25:1, 2
3 a 2 Kin. 12:2
4 a 2 Kin. 12:3 *1* Places for pagan worship
5 a 2 Kin. 12:20
6 a [Ezek. 18:4, 20]
7 a 2 Chr. 25:5–16 b 2 Sam. 8:13 c Josh. 15:38 *1* Lit. *The Rock;* the city of Petra
8 a 2 Chr. 25:17, 18 *1 Joash,* 2 Kin. 13:9, 12–14, 25; 2 Chr. 25:17ff.
9 a Judg. 9:8–15 b 1 Kin. 4:33
10 a Deut. 8:14 *1* Made you proud
11 a Josh. 19:38; 21:16
13 a Neh. 8:16; 12:39 b Jer. 31:38 *1* About 600 feet
14 a 1 Kin. 7:51

the articles that were found in the house of the LORD and in the treasuries of the king's house, and hostages, and returned to Samaria.

15 [a]Now the rest of the acts of Jehoash which he did—his might, and how he fought with Amaziah king of Judah—*are* they not written in the book of the chronicles of the kings of Israel? 16 So Jehoash [1]rested with his fathers, and was buried in Samaria with the kings of Israel. Then Jeroboam his son reigned in his place.

17 [a]Amaziah the son of Joash, king of Judah, lived fifteen years after the death of Jehoash the son of Jehoahaz, king of Israel. 18 Now the rest of the acts of Amaziah, *are* they not written in the book of the chronicles of the kings of Judah? 19 And [a]they formed a conspiracy against him in Jerusalem, and he fled to [b]Lachish; but they sent after him to Lachish and killed him there. 20 Then they brought him on horses, and he was buried at Jerusalem with his fathers in the City of David.

21 And all the people of Judah took [a]Azariah,[1] who *was* sixteen years old, and made him king instead of his father Amaziah. 22 He built [a]Elath[1] and restored it to Judah, after [2]the king rested with his fathers.

Jeroboam II Reigns in Israel

23 In the fifteenth year of Amaziah the son of Joash, king of Judah, Jeroboam the son of Joash, king of Israel, became king in Samaria, *and reigned* forty-one years. 24 And he did evil in the sight of the LORD; he did not depart from all the [a]sins of Jeroboam the son of Nebat, who had made Israel sin. 25 He [a]restored the [1]territory of Israel [b]from the entrance of Hamath to [c]the[2] Sea of the Arabah, according to the word of the LORD God of Israel, which He had spoken through His servant [d]Jonah the son of Amittai, the prophet who *was* from [e]Gath Hepher. 26 For the LORD [a]saw *that* the affliction of Israel *was* very bitter; and whether bond or free, [b]there was no helper for Israel. 27 [a]And the LORD did not say that He would blot out the name of Israel from under heaven; but He saved them by the hand of Jeroboam the son of Joash.

28 Now the rest of the acts of Jeroboam, and all that he did—his might, how he made war, and how he recaptured for Israel, from [a]Damascus and Hamath, [b]*what had belonged* to Judah—*are* they not written in the book of the chronicles of the kings of Israel? 29 So Jeroboam [1]rested with his fathers, the kings of Israel. Then [a]Zechariah his son reigned in his place.

Azariah Reigns in Judah

15 In the twenty-seventh year of Jeroboam king of Israel, [a]Azariah the son of Amaziah, king of Judah, [b]became king. 2 He was sixteen years old when he became king, and he reigned fifty-two years in Jerusalem. His mother's name *was* Jecholiah of Jerusalem. 3 And he did *what was* right in the sight of the LORD, according to all that his father Amaziah had done, 4 [a]except that the [1]high places were not removed; the people still sacrificed and burned incense on the high places. 5 Then the LORD [a]struck the king, so that he was a leper until the day of his [b]death; so he [c]dwelt in an isolated house. And Jotham the king's son *was* over the *royal* house, judging the people of the land.

6 Now the rest of the acts of Azariah, and all that he did, *are* they not written in the book of the chronicles of the kings of Judah? 7 So Azariah [1]rested with his fathers, and [a]they buried him with his fathers in the City of David. Then Jotham his son reigned in his place.

Zechariah Reigns in Israel

8 In the thirty-eighth year of Azariah king of Judah, [a]Zechariah the son of Jeroboam reigned over Israel in Samaria six months. 9 And he did evil in the sight of the LORD, [a]as his fathers had done; he did not depart from the sins of Jeroboam the son of Nebat, who had made Israel sin. 10 Then Shallum the son of Jabesh conspired against him, and [a]struck and killed him in front of the people; and he reigned in his place.

11 Now the rest of the acts of Zechariah, indeed they *are* written in the book of the chronicles of the kings of Israel.

12 This *was* the word of the LORD which He spoke to Jehu, saying, [a]"Your sons shall sit on the throne of Israel to the fourth *generation.*" And so it was.

Shallum Reigns in Israel

13 Shallum the son of Jabesh became king in the thirty-ninth year of [1]Uzziah king of Judah; and he reigned a full month in Samaria. 14 For Menahem the son of Gadi went up from [a]Tirzah, came

---

15 a 2 Kin. 13:12, 13
16 *1* Died and joined his ancestors
17 a 2 Chr. 25:25–28
19 a 2 Chr. 25:27 b Josh. 10:31
21 a 2 Kin. 15:13 *1 Uzziah,* 2 Chr. 26:1ff.; Is. 6:1; etc.
22 a 2 Kin. 16:6 *1* Heb. *Eloth* *2* Amaziah died and joined his ancestors.
24 a 1 Kin. 12:26–33
25 a 2 Kin. 10:32; 13:5, 25 b 1 Kin. 8:65 c Deut. 3:17 d Jon. 1:1 e Josh. 19:13 *1 border* *2* The Dead Sea
26 a 2 Kin. 13:4 b Deut. 32:36
27 a [2 Kin. 13:5, 23]
28 a 1 Kin. 11:24 b 2 Chr. 8:3
29 a 2 Kin. 15:8 *1* Died and joined his ancestors

CHAPTER 15
1 a 2 Kin. 15:13, 30 b 2 Kin. 14:21
4 a 2 Kin. 12:3; 14:4; 15:35 *1* Places for pagan worship
5 a 2 Chr. 26:19–23 b Is. 6:1 c [Lev. 13:46]
7 a 2 Chr. 26:23 *1* Died and joined his ancestors
8 a 2 Kin. 14:29
9 a 2 Kin. 14:24
10 a Amos 7:9
12 a 2 Kin. 10:30
13 *1 Azariah,* 2 Kin. 14:21ff.; 15:1ff.
14 a 1 Kin. 14:17

to Samaria, and struck Shallum the son of
Jabesh in Samaria and killed him; and he
reigned in his place.
15Now the rest of the acts of Shallum,
and the conspiracy which he [1]led, indeed
they *are* written in the book of the chronicles of the kings of Israel. 16Then from
Tirzah, Menahem attacked [a]Tiphsah, all
who *were* there, and its territory. Because
they did not surrender, therefore he attacked *it*. All [b]the women there who were
with child he ripped open.

Menahem Reigns in Israel

17In the thirty-ninth year of Azariah
king of Judah, Menahem the son of Gadi
became king over Israel, *and reigned* ten
years in Samaria. 18And he did evil in the
sight of the LORD; he did not depart all his
days from the sins of Jeroboam the son of
Nebat, who had made Israel sin. 19[a]Pul[1]
king of Assyria came against the land; and
Menahem gave Pul a thousand talents of
silver, that his [2]hand might be with him
to [b]strengthen the kingdom under his
control. 20And Menahem [a]exacted[1] the
money from Israel, from all the very
wealthy, from each man fifty shekels of
silver, to give to the king of Assyria. So the
king of Assyria turned back, and did not
stay there in the land.
21Now the rest of the acts of Menahem,
and all that he did, *are* they not written in
the book of the chronicles of the kings of
Israel? 22So Menahem [1]rested with his fathers. Then Pekahiah his son reigned in
his place.

Pekahiah Reigns in Israel

23In the fiftieth year of Azariah king of
Judah, Pekahiah the son of Menahem became king over Israel in Samaria, *and
reigned* two years. 24And he did evil in the
sight of the LORD; he did not depart from
the sins of Jeroboam the son of Nebat,
who had made Israel sin. 25Then Pekah
the son of Remaliah, an officer of his, conspired against him and [1]killed him in Samaria, in the [a]citadel of the king's house,
along with Argob and Arieh; and with him
were fifty men of Gilead. He killed him
and reigned in his place.
26Now the rest of the acts of Pekahiah,
and all that he did, indeed they *are* written in the book of the chronicles of the
kings of Israel.

Pekah Reigns in Israel

27In the fifty-second year of Azariah
king of Judah, [a]Pekah the son of Remaliah
became king over Israel in Samaria, *and
reigned* twenty years. 28And he did evil in
the sight of the LORD; he did not depart
from the sins of Jeroboam the son of Nebat, who had made Israel sin. 29In the days
of Pekah king of Israel, [1]Tiglath-Pileser
king of Assyria [a]came and took [b]Ijon, Abel
Beth Maachah, Janoah, Kedesh, Hazor,
Gilead, and Galilee, all the land of Naphtali; and he [c]carried them captive to Assyria.
30Then Hoshea the son of Elah led a conspiracy against Pekah the son of Remaliah, and struck and killed him; so he
[a]reigned in his place in the twentieth year
of Jotham the son of Uzziah.
31Now the rest of the acts of Pekah, and
all that he did, indeed they *are* written in
the book of the chronicles of the kings of
Israel.

Jotham Reigns in Judah

32In the second year of Pekah the son of
Remaliah, king of Israel, [a]Jotham the son
of Uzziah, king of Judah, began to reign.
33He was twenty-five years old when he
became king, and he reigned sixteen years
in Jerusalem. His mother's name *was* [1]Je-
rusha the daughter of Zadok. 34And he did
what was right in the sight of the LORD;
he did [a]according to all that his father
Uzziah had done. 35[a]However the [1]high
places were not removed; the people still
sacrificed and burned incense on the high
places. [b]He built the Upper Gate of the
house of the LORD.
36Now the rest of the acts of Jotham,
and all that he did, *are* they not written in
the book of the chronicles of the kings of
Judah? 37In those days the LORD began to
send [a]Rezin king of Syria and [b]Pekah the
son of Remaliah against Judah. 38So Jotham [1]rested with his fathers, and was
buried with his fathers in the City of David
his father. Then Ahaz his son reigned in
his place.

Ahaz Reigns in Judah

16 In the seventeenth year of Pekah
the son of Remaliah, Ahaz the son
of Jotham, king of Judah, began to reign.
2Ahaz *was* twenty years old when he became king, and he reigned sixteen years in
Jerusalem; and he did not do *what was*
right in the sight of the LORD his God, as

15 [1] Lit. *conspired*
16 [a] 1 Kin. 4:24 [b] 2 Kin. 8:12
19 [a] Hos. 8:9 [b] 2 Kin. 14:5 [1] Tiglath-Pileser III, v. 29 [2] Support
20 [a] 2 Kin. 23:35 [1] *took*
22 [1] Died and joined his ancestors
25 [a] 1 Kin. 16:18 [1] Lit. *struck*
27 [a] Is. 7:1
29 [a] 1 Chr. 5:26 [b] 1 Kin. 15:20 [c] 2 Kin. 17:6 [1] A later name of *Pul*, v. 19
30 [a] [Hos. 10:3, 7, 15]
32 [a] 2 Chr. 27:1
33 [1] *Jerushah*, 2 Chr. 27:1
34 [a] 2 Kin. 15:3, 4
35 [a] 2 Kin. 15:4 [b] 2 Chr. 23:20; 27:3 [1] Places for pagan worship
37 [a] 2 Kin. 16:5–9 [b] 2 Kin. 15:26, 27
38 [1] Died and joined his ancestors

his father David *had done.* 3But he walked
in the way of the kings of Israel; indeed
[a]he made his son pass through the fire,
according to the [b]abominations of the nations whom the LORD had cast out from
before the children of Israel. 4And he sacrificed and burned incense on the [a]high
places, [b]on the hills, and under every
green tree.
5[a]Then Rezin king of Syria and Pekah
the son of Remaliah, king of Israel, came
up to Jerusalem to *make* war; and they
besieged Ahaz but could not overcome
him. 6At that time Rezin king of Syria
[a]captured [1]Elath for Syria, and drove the
men of Judah from Elath. Then the
[2]Edomites went to Elath, and dwell there
to this day.
7So Ahaz sent messengers to [a]Tiglath-
Pileser[1] king of Assyria, saying, "I *am*
your servant and your son. Come up and
save me from the hand of the king of Syria
and from the hand of the king of Israel,
who rise up against me." 8And Ahaz [a]took
the silver and gold that was found in the
house of the LORD, and in the treasuries of
the king's house, and sent *it as* a present
to the king of Assyria. 9So the king of Assyria heeded him; for the king of Assyria
went up against [a]Damascus and [b]took it,
carried *its people* captive to [c]Kir, and
killed Rezin.
10Now King Ahaz went to Damascus to
meet Tiglath-Pileser king of Assyria, and
saw an altar that *was* at Damascus; and
King Ahaz sent to Urijah the priest the
design of the altar and its pattern, according to all its workmanship. 11Then [a]Urijah
the priest built an altar according to all
that King Ahaz had sent from Damascus.
So Urijah the priest made *it* before King
Ahaz came back from Damascus. 12And
when the king came back from Damascus,
the king saw the altar; and [a]the king approached the altar and made offerings on
it. 13So he burned his burnt offering and
his grain offering; and he poured his drink
offering and sprinkled the blood of his
peace offerings on the altar. 14He also
brought [a]the bronze altar which *was* before the LORD, from the front of the [1]tem-
ple—from between the *new* altar and the
house of the LORD—and put it on the
north side of the *new* altar. 15Then King
Ahaz commanded Urijah the priest, saying, "On the great *new* altar burn [a]the
morning burnt offering, the evening
grain offering, the king's burnt sacrifice,
and his grain offering, with the burnt offering of all the people of the land, their
grain offering, and their drink offerings;
and sprinkle on it all the blood of the
burnt offering and all the blood of the sacrifice. And the bronze altar shall be for me
to inquire *by.*" 16Thus did Urijah the
priest, according to all that King Ahaz
commanded.
17[a]And King Ahaz cut off [b]the panels of
the carts, and removed the lavers from
them; and he took down [c]the Sea from
the bronze oxen that *were* under it, and
put it on a pavement of stones. 18Also he
removed the Sabbath pavilion which they
had built in the temple, and he removed
the king's outer entrance from the house
of the LORD, on account of the king of
Assyria.
19Now the rest of the acts of Ahaz which
he did, *are* they not written in the book of
the chronicles of the kings of Judah? 20So
Ahaz rested with his fathers, and [a]was
buried with his fathers in the City of David. Then Hezekiah his son reigned in his
place.

Hoshea Reigns in Israel

17 In the twelfth year of Ahaz king of
Judah, [a]Hoshea the son of Elah became king of Israel in Samaria, *and he
reigned* nine years. 2And he did evil in the
sight of the LORD, but not as the kings of
Israel who were before him. 3[a]Shalmane-
ser king of Assyria came up against him;
and Hoshea [b]became his vassal, and paid
him tribute money. 4And the king of Assyria uncovered a conspiracy by Hoshea;
for he had sent messengers to So, king of
Egypt, and brought no tribute to the king
of Assyria, as *he had done* year by year.
Therefore the king of Assyria shut him up,
and bound him in prison.

Israel Carried Captive to Assyria

5Now [a]the king of Assyria went
throughout all the land, and went up to
Samaria and besieged it for three years.
6[a]In the ninth year of Hoshea, the king of
Assyria took Samaria and [b]carried Israel
away to Assyria, [c]and placed them in Halah and by the Habor, the River of Gozan,
and in the cities of the Medes.
7For [a]so it was that the children of Israel had sinned against the LORD their God,
who had brought them up out of the land

CHAPTER 16
3 a [Lev. 18:21] b [Deut. 12:31]
4 a 2 Kin. 15:34, 35 b [Deut. 12:2]
5 a Is. 7:1, 4
6 a 2 Kin. 14:22 *1* Lit. *Large Tree;* sing. of *Eloth* *2* A few ancient mss. *Syrians*
7 a 1 Chr. 5:26 *1* A later name of *Pul,* 2 Kin. 15:19
8 a 2 Kin. 12:17, 18
9 a 2 Kin. 14:28 b Amos 1:5 c Amos 9:7
11 a Is. 8:2
12 a 2 Chr. 26:16, 19
14 a 2 Chr. 4:1 *1* Lit. *house*
15 a Ex. 29:39–41
17 a 2 Chr. 28:24 b 1 Kin. 7:27–29 c 1 Kin. 7:23–25
20 a 2 Chr. 28:27

CHAPTER 17
1 a 2 Kin. 15:30
3 a 2 Kin. 18:9–12 b 2 Kin. 24:1
5 a Hos. 13:16
6 a Hos. 1:4; 13:16 b [Deut. 28:36, 64; 29:27, 28] c 1 Chr. 5:26
7 a [Josh. 23:16]

of Egypt, from under the hand of Pharaoh king of Egypt; and they had [b]feared other gods, 8and [a]had walked in the statutes of the nations whom the LORD had cast out from before the children of Israel, and of the kings of Israel, which they had made. 9Also the children of Israel secretly did against the LORD their God things that *were* not right, and they built for themselves [1]high places in all their cities, [a]from watchtower to fortified city. 10[a]They set up for themselves *sacred* pillars and [b]wooden images[1] [c]on every high hill and under every green tree. 11There they burned incense on all the high places, like the nations whom the LORD had carried away before them; and they did wicked things to provoke the LORD to anger, 12for they served idols, [a]of which the LORD had said to them, [b]"You shall not do this thing."

13Yet the LORD testified against Israel and against Judah, by all of His [a]prophets, [b]every seer, saying, [c]"Turn from your evil ways, and keep My commandments *and* My statutes, according to all the law which I commanded your fathers, and which I sent to you by My servants the prophets." 14Nevertheless they would not hear, but [a]stiffened their necks, like the necks of their fathers, who [b]did not believe in the LORD their God. 15And they [a]rejected His statutes [b]and His covenant that He had made with their fathers, and His testimonies which He had testified against them; they followed [c]idols, [d]became idolaters, and *went* after the nations who *were* all around them, *concerning* whom the LORD had charged them that they should [e]not do like them. 16So they left all the commandments of the LORD their God, [a]made for themselves a molded image *and* two calves, [b]made a wooden image and worshiped all the [c]host of heaven, [d]and served Baal. 17[a]And they caused their sons and daughters to pass through the fire, [b]practiced witchcraft and soothsaying, and [c]sold themselves to do evil in the sight of the LORD, to provoke Him to anger. 18Therefore the LORD was very angry with Israel, and removed them from His sight; there was none left [a]but the tribe of Judah alone.

19Also [a]Judah did not keep the commandments of the LORD their God, but walked in the statutes of Israel which they made. 20And the LORD rejected all the descendants of Israel, afflicted them, and [a]delivered them into the hand of plunderers, until He had cast them from His [b]sight. 21For [a]He tore Israel from the house of David, and [b]they made Jeroboam the son of Nebat king. Then Jeroboam drove Israel from following the LORD, and made them commit a great sin. 22For the children of Israel walked in all the sins of Jeroboam which he did; they did not depart from them, 23until the LORD removed Israel out of His sight, [a]as He had said by all His servants the prophets. [b]So Israel was carried away from their own land to Assyria, *as it is* to this day.

Assyria Resettles Samaria

24[a]Then the king of Assyria brought *people* from Babylon, Cuthah, [b]Ava, Hamath, and from Sepharvaim, and placed *them* in the cities of Samaria instead of the children of Israel; and they took possession of Samaria and dwelt in its cities. 25And it was so, at the beginning of their dwelling there, *that* they did not fear the LORD; therefore the LORD sent lions among them, which killed *some* of them. 26So they spoke to the king of Assyria, saying, "The nations whom you have removed and placed in the cities of Samaria do not know the rituals of the God of the land; therefore He has sent lions among them, and indeed, they are killing them because they do not know the rituals of the God of the land." 27Then the king of Assyria commanded, saying, "Send there one of the priests whom you brought from there; let him go and dwell there, and let him teach them the rituals of the God of the land." 28Then one of the priests whom they had carried away from Samaria came and dwelt in Bethel, and taught them how they should fear the LORD.

29However every nation continued to make gods of its own, and put *them* [a]in the shrines on the high places which the Samaritans had made, *every* nation in the cities where they dwelt. 30The men of [a]Babylon made Succoth Benoth, the men of Cuth made Nergal, the men of Hamath made Ashima, 31[a]and the Avites made Nibhaz and Tartak; and the Sepharvites [b]burned their children in fire to Adrammelech and Anammelech, the gods of Sepharvaim. 32So they feared the LORD, [a]and from every class they appointed for themselves priests of the [1]high places, who sacrificed for them in the shrines of the high places. 33[a]They feared the LORD,

7 [b] Judg. 6:10
8 [a] [Lev. 18:3]
9 [a] 2 Kin. 18:8 [1] Places for pagan worship
10 [a] Is. 57:5 [b] [Ex. 34:12–14] [c] [Deut. 12:2] [1] Heb. *Asherim,* Canaanite deities
12 [a] [Ex. 20:3–5] [b] [Deut. 4:19]
13 [a] Neh. 9:29, 30 [b] 1 Sam. 9:9 [c] [Jer. 18:11; 25:5; 35:15]
14 [a] [Acts 7:51] [b] Deut. 9:23
15 [a] Jer. 44:3 [b] Deut. 29:25 [c] Deut. 32:21 [d] [Rom. 1:21–23] [e] [Deut. 12:30, 31]
16 [a] 1 Kin. 12:28 [b] [1 Kin. 14:15] [c] [Deut. 4:19] [d] 1 Kin. 16:31; 22:53
17 [a] 2 Kin. 16:3 [b] [Deut. 18:10–12] [c] 1 Kin. 21:20
18 [a] 1 Kin. 11:13, 32
19 [a] Jer. 3:8
20 [a] 2 Kin. 13:3; 15:29 [b] 2 Kin. 24:20
21 [a] 1 Kin. 11:11, 31 [b] 1 Kin. 12:20, 28
23 [a] 1 Kin. 14:16 [b] 2 Kin. 17:6
24 [a] Ezra 4:2, 10 [b] 2 Kin. 18:34
29 [a] 1 Kin. 12:31; 13:32
30 [a] 2 Kin. 17:24
31 [a] Ezra 4:9 [b] [Deut. 12:31]
32 [a] 1 Kin. 12:31; 13:33 [1] Places for pagan worship
33 [a] Zeph. 1:5

yet served their own gods—according to
the rituals of the nations from among
whom they were carried away.

34To this day they continue practicing
the former rituals; they do not fear the
LORD, nor do they follow their statutes or
their ordinances, or the law and commandment which the LORD had commanded the children of Jacob, [a]whom He
named Israel, 35with whom the LORD had
made a covenant and charged them, saying: [a]"You shall not fear other gods, nor
[b]bow down to them nor serve them nor
sacrifice to them; 36but the LORD, who
[a]brought you up from the land of Egypt
with great power and [b]an outstretched
arm, [c]Him you shall fear, Him you shall
worship, and to Him you shall offer sacrifice. 37And the statutes, the ordinances,
the law, and the commandment which He
wrote for you, [a]you shall be careful to
observe forever; you shall not fear other
gods. 38And the covenant that I have made
with you, [a]you shall not forget, nor shall
you fear other gods. 39But the LORD your
God you shall fear; and He will deliver
you from the hand of all your enemies."
40However they did not obey, but they followed their former rituals. 41[a]So these nations feared the LORD, yet served their
carved images; also their children and
their children's children have continued
doing as their fathers did, even to this day.

Hezekiah Reigns in Judah

18 Now it came to pass in the third
year of [a]Hoshea the son of Elah,
king of Israel, *that* [b]Hezekiah the son of
Ahaz, king of Judah, began to reign. 2He
was twenty-five years old when he became king, and he reigned twenty-nine
years in Jerusalem. His mother's name
was [a]Abi[1] the daughter of Zechariah.
3And he did *what was* right in the sight of
the LORD, according to all that his father
David had done.

4[a]He removed the [1]high places and
broke the *sacred* pillars, cut down the
[2]wooden image and broke in pieces the
[b]bronze serpent that Moses had made; for
until those days the children of Israel
burned incense to it, and called it [3]Ne-
hushtan. 5He [a]trusted in the LORD God of
Israel, [b]so that after him was none like
him among all the kings of Judah, nor
who were before him. 6For he [a]held fast to
the LORD; he did not depart from following Him, but kept His commandments,
which the LORD had commanded Moses.
7The LORD [a]was with him; he [b]prospered
wherever he went. And he [c]rebelled
against the king of Assyria and did not
serve him. 8[a]He [1]subdued the Philistines,
as far as Gaza and its territory, [b]from
watchtower to fortified city.

9Now [a]it came to pass in the fourth year
of King Hezekiah, which *was* the seventh
year of Hoshea the son of Elah, king of
Israel, *that* Shalmaneser king of Assyria
came up against Samaria and besieged it.
10And at the end of three years they took
it. In the sixth year of Hezekiah, that *is,*
[a]the ninth year of Hoshea king of Israel,
Samaria was taken. 11[a]Then the king of
Assyria carried Israel away captive to Assyria, and put them [b]in Halah and by the
Habor, the River of Gozan, and in the cities of the Medes, 12because they [a]did not
obey the voice of the LORD their God, but
transgressed His covenant *and* all that
Moses the servant of the LORD had commanded; and they would neither hear nor
do *them.*

13And [a]in the fourteenth year of King
Hezekiah, Sennacherib king of Assyria
came up against all the fortified cities of
Judah and took them. 14Then Hezekiah
king of Judah sent to the king of Assyria
at Lachish, saying, "I have done wrong;
turn away from me; whatever you impose
on me I will pay." And the king of Assyria
assessed Hezekiah king of Judah three
hundred talents of silver and thirty talents
of gold. 15So Hezekiah [a]gave *him* all the
silver that was found in the house of the
LORD and in the treasuries of the king's
house. 16At that time Hezekiah stripped
the gold from the doors of the temple of
the LORD, and *from* the pillars which Hezekiah king of Judah had overlaid, and gave
[1]it to the king of Assyria.

Sennacherib Boasts Against the Lord

17Then the king of Assyria sent *the*
[1]Tartan, *the* [2]Rabsaris, *and the* [3]Rabsha-
keh from Lachish, with a great army
against Jerusalem, to King Hezekiah. And
they went up and came to Jerusalem.
When they had come up, they went and
stood by the [a]aqueduct from the upper
pool, [b]which *was* on the highway to the
Fuller's Field. 18And when they had called
to the king, [a]Eliakim the son of Hilkiah,
who *was* over the household, Shebna the
[1]scribe, and Joah the son of Asaph, the

34 a Gen. 32:28; 35:10
35 a Judg. 6:10 b [Ex. 20:5]
36 a Ex. 14:15–30 b Ex. 6:6; 9:15 c [Deut. 10:20]
37 a Deut. 5:32
38 a Deut. 4:23; 6:12
41 a 2 Kin. 17:32, 33

CHAPTER 18
1 a 2 Kin. 17:1 b 2 Chr. 28:27; 29:1
2 a Is. 38:5 *1 Abijah,* 2 Chr. 29:1ff.
4 a 2 Chr. 31:1 b Num. 21:5–9 *1* Places for pagan worship *2* Heb. *Asherah,* a Canaanite goddess *3* Lit. *Bronze Thing,* also similar to Heb. *nahash, serpent*
5 a 2 Kin. 19:10 b 2 Kin. 23:25
6 a Deut. 10:20
7 a [2 Chr. 15:2] b 1 Sam. 18:5, 14 c 2 Kin. 16:7
8 a Is. 14:29 b 2 Kin. 17:9 *1* Lit. *struck*
9 a 2 Kin. 17:3
10 a 2 Kin. 17:6
11 a 2 Kin. 17:6 b 1 Chr. 5:26
12 a 2 Kin. 17:7–18
13 a 2 Chr. 32:1
15 a 2 Kin. 12:18; 16:8
16 *1* Lit. *them*
17 a 2 Kin. 20:20 b Is. 7:3 *1* A title, probably *Commander in Chief* *2* A title, probably *Chief Officer* *3* A title, probably *Chief of Staff* or *Governor*
18 a Is. 22:20 *1 secretary*

recorder, came out to them. 19 Then *the* Rabshakeh said to them, "Say now to Hezekiah, 'Thus says the great king, the king of Assyria: [a]"What confidence *is* this in which you trust? 20 You speak of *having* plans and power for war; but *they are* [1]mere words. And in whom do you trust, that you rebel against me? 21 [a]Now look! You are trusting in the staff of this broken reed, Egypt, on which if a man leans, it will go into his hand and pierce it. So *is* Pharaoh king of Egypt to all who trust in him. 22 But if you say to me, 'We trust in the LORD our God,' *is* it not He [a]whose [1]high places and whose altars Hezekiah has taken away, and said to Judah and Jerusalem, 'You shall worship before this altar in Jerusalem'?" ' 23 Now therefore, I urge you, give a pledge to my master the king of Assyria, and I will give you two thousand horses—if you are able on your part to put riders on them! 24 How then will you repel one captain of the least of my master's servants, and put your trust in Egypt for chariots and horsemen? 25 Have I now come up without the LORD against this place to destroy it? The LORD said to me, 'Go up against this land, and destroy it.' "

26 [a]Then Eliakim the son of Hilkiah, Shebna, and Joah said to *the* Rabshakeh, "Please speak to your servants in [b]Aramaic, for we understand *it;* and do not speak to us in [1]Hebrew in the hearing of the people who *are* on the wall."

27 But *the* Rabshakeh said to them, "Has my master sent me to your master and to you to speak these words, and not to the men who sit on the wall, who will eat and drink their own waste with you?"

28 Then *the* Rabshakeh stood and called out with a loud voice in [1]Hebrew, and spoke, saying, "Hear the word of the great king, the king of Assyria! 29 Thus says the king: [a]'Do not let Hezekiah deceive you, for he shall not be able to deliver you from his hand; 30 nor let Hezekiah make you trust in the LORD, saying, "The LORD will surely deliver us; this city shall not be given into the hand of the king of Assyria." ' 31 Do not listen to Hezekiah; for thus says the king of Assyria: 'Make *peace* with me [1]by a present and come out to me; and every one of you eat from his own [a]vine and every one from his own fig tree, and every one of you drink the waters of his own cistern; 32 until I come and take you away to a land like your own land, [a]a land of grain and new wine, a land of bread and vineyards, a land of olive groves and honey, that you may live and not die. But do not listen to Hezekiah, lest he persuade you, saying, "The LORD will deliver us." 33 [a]Has any of the gods of the nations at all delivered its land from the hand of the king of Assyria? 34 Where *are* the gods of [a]Hamath and Arpad? Where *are* the gods of Sepharvaim and Hena and [b]Ivah? Indeed, have they delivered Samaria from my hand? 35 Who among all the gods of the lands have delivered their countries from my hand, [a]that the LORD should deliver Jerusalem from my hand?' "

36 But the people held their peace and answered him not a word; for the king's commandment was, "Do not answer him." 37 Then Eliakim the son of Hilkiah, who *was* over the household, Shebna the scribe, and Joah the son of Asaph, the recorder, came to Hezekiah [a]with *their* clothes torn, and told him the words of *the* Rabshakeh.

Isaiah Assures Deliverance

19 And [a]so it was, when King Hezekiah heard *it,* that he tore his clothes, covered himself with [b]sackcloth, and went into the house of the LORD. 2 Then he sent Eliakim, who *was* over the household, Shebna the scribe, and the elders of the priests, covered with sackcloth, to Isaiah the prophet, the son of Amoz. 3 And they said to him, "Thus says Hezekiah: 'This day *is* a day of trouble, and rebuke, and blasphemy; for the children have come to birth, but *there is* no strength to [1]bring them forth. 4 [a]It may be that the LORD your God will hear all the words of *the* Rabshakeh, whom his master the king of Assyria has sent to [b]reproach the living God, and will [c]rebuke the words which the LORD your God has heard. Therefore lift up *your* prayer for the remnant that is left.' "

5 So the servants of King Hezekiah came to Isaiah. 6 [a]And Isaiah said to them, "Thus you shall say to your master, 'Thus says the LORD: "Do not be [b]afraid of the words which you have heard, with which the [c]servants of the king of Assyria have blasphemed Me. 7 Surely I will send [a]a spirit upon him, and he shall hear a rumor and return to his own land; and I will cause him to fall by the sword in his own land." ' "

---

19 [a]2 Chr. 32:10
20 [1]Lit. *a word of the lips*
21 [a]Ezek. 29:6, 7
22 [a]2 Kin. 18:4 [1]Places for pagan worship
26 [a]Is. 36:11—39:8 [b]Ezra 4:7 [1]Lit. *Judean*
28 [1]Lit. *Judean*
29 [a]2 Chr. 32:15
31 [a]1 Kin. 4:20, 25 [1]By paying tribute
32 [a]Deut. 8:7–9; 11:12
33 [a]2 Kin. 19:12
34 [a]2 Kin. 19:13 [b]2 Kin. 17:24
35 [a]Dan. 3:15
37 [a]Is. 33:7

CHAPTER 19
1 [a]Is. 37:1 [b]Ps. 69:11
3 [1]*give birth*
4 [a]2 Sam. 16:12 [b]2 Kin. 18:35 [c]Ps. 50:21
6 [a]Is. 37:6 [b][Ps. 112:7] [c]2 Kin. 18:17
7 [a]2 Kin. 19:35–37

Sennacherib's Threat and Hezekiah's Prayer

8 Then *the* Rabshakeh returned and
found the king of Assyria warring against
Libnah, for he heard that he had departed
[a]from Lachish. 9 And [a]the king heard concerning Tirhakah king of Ethiopia, "Look,
he has come out to make war with you."
So he again sent messengers to Hezekiah,
saying, 10 "Thus you shall speak to Hezekiah king of Judah, saying: 'Do not let your
God [a]in whom you trust deceive you, saying, "Jerusalem shall not be given into the
hand of the king of Assyria." 11 Look! You
have heard what the kings of Assyria have
done to all lands by utterly destroying
them; and shall you be delivered? 12 [a]Have
the gods of the nations delivered those
whom my fathers have destroyed, Gozan
and Haran and Rezeph, and the people of
[b]Eden who *were* in Telassar? 13 [a]Where *is*
the king of Hamath, the king of Arpad,
and the king of the city of Sepharvaim,
Hena, and Ivah?' "

> *He who proves God will find that the very windows of heaven will open and a blessing will come down greater than he is able to receive.*
>
> GORDON LINDSAY

14 [a]And Hezekiah received the letter
from the hand of the messengers, and
read it; and Hezekiah went up to the
house of the LORD, and spread it before
the LORD. 15 Then Hezekiah prayed before
the LORD, and said: "O LORD God of Israel,
the One [a]who dwells *between* the cherubim, [b]You are God, You alone, of all the
kingdoms of the earth. You have made
heaven and earth. 16 [a]Incline Your ear,
O LORD, and hear; [b]open Your eyes,
O LORD, and see; and hear the words of
Sennacherib, [c]which he has sent to reproach the living God. 17 Truly, LORD, the
kings of Assyria have laid waste the nations and their lands, 18 and have cast their
gods into the fire; for they *were* [a]not gods,
but [b]the work of men's hands—wood and
stone. Therefore they destroyed them.
19 Now therefore, O LORD our God, I pray,
save us from his hand, [a]that all the kingdoms of the earth may [b]know that You *are*
the LORD God, You alone."

> *Mighty God, I pray that You will save ____ from the hand of their enemies, that all the kingdoms of the earth may know that You alone are God.*
>
> FROM 2 KINGS 19:19

The Word of the Lord Concerning Sennacherib

20 Then Isaiah the son of Amoz sent to
Hezekiah, saying, "Thus says the LORD
God of Israel: [a]'Because you have prayed
to Me against Sennacherib king of Assyria,
[b]I have heard.' 21 This *is* the word which
the LORD has spoken concerning him:

'The virgin, [a]the daughter of Zion,
Has despised you, laughed you to
scorn;
The daughter of Jerusalem
[b]Has shaken *her* head behind your
back!

22 'Whom have you reproached and
blasphemed?
Against whom have you raised *your*
voice,
And lifted up your eyes on high?
Against [a]the Holy *One* of Israel.
23 [a]By your messengers you have
reproached the Lord,
And said: [b]"By the multitude of my
chariots
I have come up to the height of the
mountains,
To the limits of Lebanon;
I will cut down its tall cedars
And its choice cypress trees;
I will enter the extremity of its
borders,
To its fruitful forest.
24 I have dug and drunk strange
water,

8 a 2 Kin. 18:14, 17
9 a 1 Sam. 23:27
10 a 2 Kin. 18:5
12 a 2 Kin. 18:33, 34 b Ezek. 27:23
13 a 2 Kin. 18:34
14 a Is. 37:14
15 a Ex. 25:22 b [Is. 44:6]
16 a Ps. 31:2 b 2 Chr. 6:40 c 2 Kin. 19:4
18 a [Jer. 10:3–5] b [Acts 17:29]
19 a Ps. 83:18 b 1 Kin. 8:42, 43
20 a Is. 37:21 b 2 Kin. 20:5
21 a Lam. 2:13 b Ps. 22:7, 8
22 a Jer. 51:5
23 a 2 Kin. 18:17 b Ps. 20:7

And with the soles of my feet I have
[a]dried up
All the brooks of defense.”

25 ‘Did you not hear long ago
How [a]I made it,
From ancient times that I formed
it?
Now I have brought it to pass,
That [b]you should be
For crushing fortified cities *into*
heaps of ruins.
26 Therefore their inhabitants had
little power;
They were dismayed and
confounded;
They were *as* the grass of the field
And the green herb,
As [a]the grass on the housetops
And *grain* blighted before it is
grown.
27 ‘But [a]I know your dwelling place,
Your going out and your coming
in,
And your rage against Me.
28 Because your rage against Me and
your tumult
Have come up to My ears,
Therefore [a]I will put My hook in
your nose
And My bridle in your lips,
And I will turn you back
[b]By the way which you came.

29‘This *shall be* a [a]sign to you:

You shall eat this year such as
grows [1]of itself,
And in the second year what
springs from the same;
Also in the third year sow and reap,
Plant vineyards and eat the fruit of
them.
30 [a]And the remnant who have
escaped of the house of Judah
Shall again take root downward,
And bear fruit upward.
31 For out of Jerusalem shall go a
remnant,
And those who escape from Mount
Zion.
[a]The zeal of the LORD [1]of hosts will
do this.’

32“Therefore thus says the LORD concerning the king of Assyria:

‘He shall [a]not come into this city,
Nor shoot an arrow there,
Nor come before it with shield,

24 a Is. 19:6
25 a [Is. 45:7] b Is. 10:5, 6
26 a Ps. 129:6
27 a Ps. 139:1–3
28 a Ezek. 29:4; 38:4 b 2 Kin. 19:33, 36
29 a 2 Kin. 20:8, 9 *1* Without cultivation
30 a 2 Chr. 32:22, 23
31 a Is. 9:7 *1* So with many Heb. mss. and ancient vss. (cf. Is. 37:32); MT omits *of hosts*
32 a Is. 8:7–10
34 a 2 Kin. 20:6 b Is. 31:5 c 1 Kin. 11:12, 13
35 a Is. 10:12–19; 37:36 *1* Or *Angel*
36 a Gen. 10:11
37 a 2 Kin. 17:31 b 2 Kin. 19:7 c Ezra 4:2
CHAPTER 20
1 a Is. 38:1–22
3 a Neh. 13:22
5 a 1 Sam. 9:16; 10:1 b Ps. 65:2 c Ps. 39:12; 56:8
6 a 2 Kin. 19:34

Nor build a siege mound against it.
33 By the way that he came,
By the same shall he return;
And he shall not come into this
city,’
Says the LORD.
34 ‘For [a]I will [b]defend this city, to
save it
For My own sake and [c]for My
servant David’s sake.’ ”

Sennacherib’s Defeat and Death

35And [a]it came to pass on a certain
night that the [1]angel of the LORD went
out, and killed in the camp of the Assyrians one hundred and eighty-five thousand; and when *people* arose early in the
morning, there were the corpses—all
dead. 36So Sennacherib king of Assyria departed and went away, returned *home,*
and remained at [a]Nineveh. 37Now it came
to pass, as he was worshiping in the temple of Nisroch his god, that his sons
[a]Adrammelech and Sharezer [b]struck him
down with the sword; and they escaped
into the land of Ararat. Then [c]Esarhaddon
his son reigned in his place.

Hezekiah’s Life Extended

20 In [a]those days Hezekiah was sick
and near death. And Isaiah the
prophet, the son of Amoz, went to him
and said to him, “Thus says the LORD: ‘Set
your house in order, for you shall die, and
not live.’ ”

2Then he turned his face toward the
wall, and prayed to the LORD, saying,
3[a]“Remember now, O LORD, I pray, how I
have walked before You in truth and with
a loyal heart, and have done *what was*
good in Your sight.” And Hezekiah wept
bitterly.

4And it happened, before Isaiah had
gone out into the middle court, that the
word of the LORD came to him, saying,
5“Return and tell Hezekiah [a]the leader of
My people, ‘Thus says the LORD, the God
of David your father: [b]“I have heard your
prayer, I have seen [c]your tears; surely I
will heal you. On the third day you shall
go up to the house of the LORD. 6And I will
add to your days fifteen years. I will deliver you and this city from the hand of the
king of Assyria; and [a]I will defend this city
for My own sake, and for the sake of My
servant David.” ’ ”

7 Then [a]Isaiah said, "Take a lump of
figs." So they took and laid *it* on the boil,
and he recovered.
8 And Hezekiah said to Isaiah, [a]"What *is*
the sign that the LORD will heal me, and
that I shall go up to the house of the LORD
the third day?"

Father, thank You that You have heard the prayers of ____ and have seen their tears; heal them, Lord, as You did Hezekiah.

FROM 2 KINGS 20:5

9 Then Isaiah said, [a]"This is the sign to
you from the LORD, that the LORD will do
the thing which He has spoken: *shall* the
shadow go forward ten degrees or go
backward ten degrees?"
10 And Hezekiah answered, "It is an easy
thing for the shadow to go down ten [1]de-
grees; no, but let the shadow go backward
ten degrees."
11 So Isaiah the prophet cried out to the
LORD, and [a]He brought the shadow ten
[1]degrees backward, by which it had gone
down on the sundial of Ahaz.

The Babylonian Envoys

12 [a]At that time [1]Berodach-Baladan the
son of Baladan, king of Babylon, sent letters and a present to Hezekiah, for he
heard that Hezekiah had been sick. 13 And
[a]Hezekiah was attentive to them, and
showed them all the house of his treasures—the silver and gold, the spices and
precious ointment, and [1]all [2]his armory—all that was found among his treasures. There was nothing in his house or
in all his dominion that Hezekiah did not
show them.
14 Then Isaiah the prophet went to King
Hezekiah, and said to him, "What did
these men say, and from where did they
come to you?"
So Hezekiah said, "They came from a
far country, from Babylon."
15 And he said, "What have they seen in
your house?"
So Hezekiah answered, [a]"They have
seen all that *is* in my house; there is noth-

7 a Is. 38:21
8 a Judg. 6:17, 37, 39
9 a Is. 38:7, 8
10 *1* Lit. *steps*
11 a Is. 38:8 *1* Lit. *steps*
12 a Is. 39:1–8 *1 Merodach-Baladan,* Is. 39:1
13 a 2 Chr. 32:27, 31 *1* So with many Heb. mss., Syr., Tg.; MT omits *all* *2* Lit. *the house of his armor*
15 a 2 Kin. 20:13
17 a Jer. 27:21, 22; 52:17
18 a 2 Kin. 24:12 b Dan. 1:3–7 c Dan. 1:11, 18 *1 be born from*
19 a 1 Sam. 3:18
20 a 2 Chr. 32:32 b Neh. 3:16 c Is. 7:3 d 2 Chr. 32:3, 30 *1 aqueduct*
21 a 2 Chr. 32:33 *1* Died and joined his ancestors

CHAPTER 21
1 a 2 Chr. 33:1–9
2 a 2 Kin. 16:3
3 a 2 Kin. 18:4, 22 b 1 Kin. 16:31–33 c [Deut. 4:19; 17:2–5] *1* Places for pagan worship *2* Heb. *Asherah,* a Canaanite goddess *3* The gods of the Assyrians
4 a Jer. 7:30; 32:34 b 1 Kin. 11:13
5 a 1 Kin. 6:36; 7:12
6 a [Lev. 18:21; 20:2] b [Deut. 18:10–14]
7 a 1 Kin. 8:29; 9:3

ing among my treasures that I have not
shown them."
16 Then Isaiah said to Hezekiah, "Hear
the word of the LORD: 17 'Behold, the days
are coming when all that *is* in your house,
and what your fathers have accumulated
until this day, [a]shall be carried to Babylon; nothing shall be left,' says the LORD.
18 'And [a]they shall take away some of your
sons who will [1]descend from you, whom
you will beget; [b]and they shall be [c]eu-
nuchs in the palace of the king of Babylon.' "
19 So Hezekiah said to Isaiah, [a]"The
word of the LORD which you have spoken
is good!" For he said, "Will there not be
peace and truth at least in my days?"

Death of Hezekiah

20 [a]Now the rest of the acts of Hezekiah—all his might, and how he [b]made a
[c]pool and a [1]tunnel and [d]brought water
into the city—*are* they not written in the
book of the chronicles of the kings of Judah? 21 So [a]Hezekiah [1]rested with his fathers. Then Manasseh his son reigned in
his place.

Manasseh Reigns in Judah

21 Manasseh [a]*was* twelve years old
when he became king, and he
reigned fifty-five years in Jerusalem. His
mother's name *was* Hephzibah. 2 And he
did evil in the sight of the LORD, [a]accord-
ing to the abominations of the nations
whom the LORD had cast out before the
children of Israel. 3 For he rebuilt the
[1]high places [a]which Hezekiah his father
had destroyed; he raised up altars for Baal,
and made a [2]wooden image, [b]as Ahab king
of Israel had done; and he [c]worshiped all
[3]the host of heaven and served them.
4 [a]He also built altars in the house of the
LORD, of which the LORD had said, [b]"In
Jerusalem I will put My name." 5 And he
built altars for all the host of heaven in
the [a]two courts of the house of the LORD.
6 [a]Also he made his son pass through the
fire, practiced [b]soothsaying, used witchcraft, and consulted spiritists and mediums. He did much evil in the sight of the
LORD, to provoke *Him* to anger. 7 He even
set a carved image of [1]Asherah that he had
made, in the [2]house of which the LORD
had said to David and to Solomon his son,
[a]"In this house and in Jerusalem, which I

1 A Canaanite goddess *2* Temple

have chosen out of all the tribes of Israel,
I will put My name forever; [8][a]and I will
not make the feet of Israel wander anymore from the land which I gave their
fathers—only if they are careful to do according to all that I have commanded
them, and according to all the law that My
servant Moses commanded them." [9]But
they paid no attention, and Manasseh [a]se-
duced them to do more evil than the nations whom the LORD had destroyed
before the children of Israel.
[10]And the LORD spoke [a]by His servants
the prophets, saying, [11][a]"Because Manasseh king of Judah has done these abominations ([b]he has acted more wickedly
than all the [c]Amorites who *were* before
him, and [d]has also made Judah sin with
his idols), [12]therefore thus says the LORD
God of Israel: 'Behold, *I* am bringing *such*
calamity upon Jerusalem and Judah, that
whoever hears of it, both [a]his ears will
tingle. [13]And I will stretch over Jerusalem
[a]the measuring line of Samaria and the
plummet of the house of Ahab; [b]I will
wipe Jerusalem as *one* wipes a dish, wip-
ing *it* and turning *it* upside down. [14]So I
will forsake the [a]remnant of My inheritance and deliver them into the hand of
their enemies; and they shall become victims of plunder to all their enemies, [15]be-
cause they have done evil in My sight, and
have provoked Me to anger since the day
their fathers came out of Egypt, even to
this day.' "
[16][a]Moreover Manasseh shed very much
innocent blood, till he had filled Jerusalem from one end to another, besides his
sin by which he made Judah sin, in doing
evil in the sight of the LORD.
[17]Now [a]the rest of the acts of [b]Manas-
seh—all that he did, and the sin that he
committed—*are* they not written in the
book of the chronicles of the kings of Judah? [18]So [a]Manasseh [1]rested with his fathers, and was buried in the garden of his
own house, in the garden of Uzza. Then
his son Amon reigned in his place.

Amon's Reign and Death

[19][a]Amon *was* twenty-two years old
when he became king, and he reigned two
years in Jerusalem. His mother's name
was Meshullemeth the daughter of Haruz
of Jotbah. [20]And he did evil in the sight of
the LORD, [a]as his father Manasseh had
done. [21]So he walked in all the ways that
his father had walked; and he served the
idols that his father had served, and worshiped them. [22]He [a]forsook the LORD God
of his fathers, and did not walk in the way
of the LORD.
[23][a]Then the servants of Amon [b]con-
spired against him, and killed the king in
his own house. [24]But the people of the
land [a]executed all those who had conspired against King Amon. Then the people of the land made his son Josiah king
in his place.
[25]Now the rest of the acts of Amon
which he did, *are* they not written in the
book of the chronicles of the kings of Judah? [26]And he was buried in his tomb in
the garden of Uzza. Then Josiah his son
reigned in his place.

Josiah Reigns in Judah

22 Josiah [a]*was* eight years old when
he became king, and he reigned
thirty-one years in Jerusalem. His
mother's name *was* Jedidah the daughter
of Adaiah of [b]Bozkath. [2]And he did
what was right in the sight of the LORD,
and walked in all the ways of his father
David; he [a]did not turn aside to the right
hand or to the left.

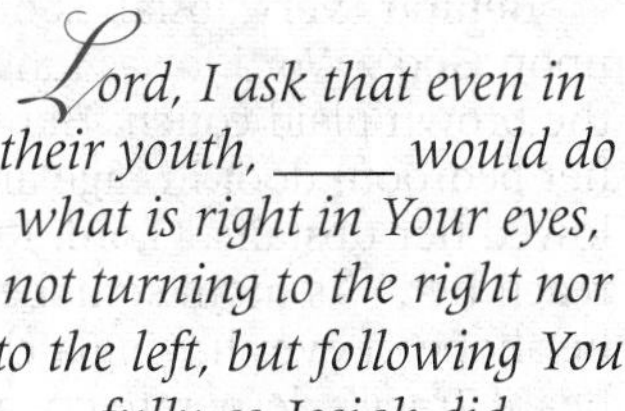

*Lord, I ask that even in
their youth, ____ would do
what is right in Your eyes,
not turning to the right nor
to the left, but following You
fully as Josiah did.*

FROM 2 KINGS 22:1, 2

Hilkiah Finds the Book of the Law

[3][a]Now it came to pass, in the eighteenth year of King Josiah, *that* the king
sent Shaphan the scribe, the son of Azali-
ah, the son of Meshullam, to the house of
the LORD, saying: [4]"Go up to Hilkiah the
high priest, that he may count the money
which has been [a]brought into the house
of the LORD, which [b]the doorkeepers have
gathered from the people. [5]And let them
[a]deliver it into the hand of those doing
the work, who are the overseers in the
house of the LORD; let them give it to

8 a 2 Sam. 7:10
9 a [Prov. 29:12]
10 a 2 Kin. 17:13
11 a 2 Kin. 23:26, 27; 24:3, 4 b 1 Kin. 21:26 c Gen. 15:16 d 2 Kin. 21:9
12 a Jer. 19:3
13 a Amos 7:7, 8 b 2 Kin. 22:16–19; 25:4–11
14 a Jer. 6:9
16 a 2 Kin. 24:4
17 a 2 Chr. 33:11–19 b 2 Kin. 20:21
18 a 2 Chr. 33:20 *1* Died and joined his ancestors
19 a 2 Chr. 33:21–23
20 a 2 Kin. 21:2–6, 11, 16
22 a 1 Kin. 11:33
23 a 2 Chr. 33:24, 25 b 2 Kin. 12:20; 14:19
24 a 2 Kin. 14:5
CHAPTER 22
1 a 2 Chr. 34:1 b Josh. 15:39
2 a Deut. 5:32
3 a 2 Chr. 34:8
4 a 2 Kin. 12:4 b 2 Kin. 12:9, 10
5 a 2 Kin. 12:11–14

2 Kings 22:2

Dear Woman of Destiny,

Josiah became king at eight years of age and led Judah into national revival at 20. At 26, he repaired the temple and declared a national Passover when the lost Law of Moses was found.

What was the secret to his courage? It has been said that "behind every move of God is a praying woman." I believe Josiah's mother, Jedidah, was the key to his godly thirty-one-year reign. Her husband, King Amon, was murdered and left a legacy of bloody idolatry. She had reason to be discouraged, yet her name meant "God's Darling," and that changed everything. When you are "God's Darling," heaven and hell will move on your behalf.

Let me tell you about two of "God's Darlings" and the Josiahs in their life. Jason looked like your typical eight-year-old summer camper. His fashion statement consisted of a three-day dirty T-shirt spattered with ketchup and go-cart mud, and swim trunks faded from chlorine abuse. The suitcase packed by his grandmother contained neatly folded and numbered camp clothes. It was never opened.

Jason wasn't a bad kid; but as eight-year-olds often do, he cut in the water-slide line, picked fights for fun, and tried to sneak out of the Discovery Camp's rally. Jason was caught and dragged to the front row of the miracle rally packed with a thousand kids. Within minutes, God's love melted this wiggly redhead, who found himself sobbing at the altar. He was even called to preach the gospel!

Was it the sermon that gripped him? The loving camp staff? Probably not. I discovered later that "God's Darling" for Jason was his praying grandmother.

Behind every Josiah is one of "God's Darlings" committed to pray and stand upon God's Word for as long as it takes. Tracy collapsed in discouragement on the brown plaid couch. Her teenage daughter, Ashley, had once again slammed her bedroom door in rage and rebellion. A trail of mud from her sneakers followed her upstairs. "Lord, I'm scared," Tracy whispered. "Show me how to reach her." As mom scrubbed the mud on her new carpet, it seemed to mock her hope of ever having a clean house or a pure daughter again. But God heard Tracy's desperate cry and turned her attention to the Bible on the couch. Her choice was divinely clear. Quit scrubbing the "mud" off Ashley and cling to the Word of God. The soiled cloths dropped to the floor as "God's Darling" claimed the precious promises of God's Word. Hope filled her heart and faith filled her words.

One thing was certain. God "watches over His Word to perform it," so a great performance was surely ahead. At midnight, a noise downstairs jolted Tracy out of bed. There grinned a repentant Ashley, rags in hand, pointing to the carpet. "All clean!" Big miracles sometimes start with small beginnings . . . perhaps a midnight smile. As they hugged, Tracy sensed the Father wink. His performance had begun.

Two stories. Two "Josiahs." Two breakthroughs. In both, "God's Darlings" made the difference.

Rachel Burchfield

those who *are* in the house of the LORD
doing the work, to repair the damages of
the house— 6 to carpenters and builders
and masons—and to buy timber and
hewn stone to repair the house. 7 However
[a]there need be no accounting made with
them of the money delivered into their
hand, because they deal faithfully."

8 Then Hilkiah the high priest said to
Shaphan the scribe, [a]"I have found the
Book of the Law in the house of the
LORD." And Hilkiah gave the book to Shaphan, and he read it. 9 So Shaphan the
scribe went to the king, bringing the king
word, saying, "Your servants have [1]gath-
ered the money that was found in the
house, and have delivered it into the hand
of those who do the work, who oversee the
house of the LORD." 10 Then Shaphan the
scribe showed the king, saying, "Hilkiah
the priest has given me a book." And Shaphan read it before the king.

11 Now it happened, when the king
heard the words of the Book of the Law,
that he tore his clothes. 12 Then the king
commanded Hilkiah the priest, [a]Ahikam
the son of Shaphan, [1]Achbor the son of
Michaiah, Shaphan the scribe, and Asaiah
a servant of the king, saying, 13 "Go, inquire of the LORD for me, for the people
and for all Judah, concerning the words of
this book that has been found; for great *is*
[a]the wrath of the LORD that is aroused
against us, because our fathers have not
obeyed the words of this book, to do according to all that is written concerning us."

14 So Hilkiah the priest, Ahikam, Achbor, Shaphan, and Asaiah went to Huldah
the prophetess, the wife of Shallum the
son of [a]Tikvah, the son of Harhas, keeper
of the wardrobe. (She dwelt in Jerusalem
in the Second Quarter.) And they spoke
with her. 15 Then she said to them, "Thus
says the LORD God of Israel, 'Tell the man
who sent you to Me, 16 "Thus says the
LORD: 'Behold, [a]I will bring calamity on
this place and on its inhabitants—all the
words of the book which the king of Judah
has read— 17 [a]because they have forsaken
Me and burned incense to other gods, that
they might provoke Me to anger with all
the works of their hands. Therefore My
wrath shall be aroused against this place
and shall not be quenched.' " ' 18 But as for
[a]the king of Judah, who sent you to inquire of the LORD, in this manner you
shall speak to him, 'Thus says the LORD
God of Israel: "*Concerning* the words
which you have heard— 19 because your
[a]heart was tender, and you [b]humbled
yourself before the LORD when you heard
what I spoke against this place and against
its inhabitants, that they would become [c]a
desolation and [d]a curse, and you tore your
clothes and wept before Me, I also have
heard *you*," says the LORD. 20 "Surely,
therefore, I will [1]gather you to your fathers, and you [a]shall [2]be gathered to your
grave in peace; and your eyes shall not see
all the calamity which I will bring on this
place." ' " So they brought back word to
the king.

> *The humbler a man is in himself, and the more resigned to God, the more prudent will he be in all things, and the more at peace.*
>
> THOMAS À KEMPIS

Josiah Restores True Worship

23 Now [a]the king sent them to
gather all the elders of Judah and
Jerusalem to him. 2 The king went up to
the house of the LORD with all the men of
Judah, and with him all the inhabitants of
Jerusalem—the priests and the prophets
and all the people, both small and great.
And he [a]read in their hearing all the
words of the Book of the Covenant [b]which
had been found in the house of the LORD.

3 Then the king [a]stood by a pillar and
made a [b]covenant before the LORD, to follow the LORD and to keep His commandments and His testimonies and His
statutes, with all *his* heart and all *his* soul,
to perform the words of this covenant that
were written in this book. And all the people took a stand for the covenant. 4 And
the king commanded Hilkiah the high
priest, the [a]priests of the second order,
and the doorkeepers, to bring [b]out of the
temple of the LORD all the articles that
were made for Baal, for [1]Asherah, and for
all [2]the host of heaven; and he burned
them outside Jerusalem in the fields of
Kidron, and carried their ashes to Bethel.

---

7 a 2 Kin. 12:15
8 a Deut. 31:24–26
9 *1* Lit. *poured out*
12 a Jer. 26:24 *1 Abdon the son of Micah,* 2 Chr. 34:20
13 a [Deut. 29:23–28; 31:17, 18]
14 a 2 Chr. 34:22
16 a Deut. 29:27
17 a Deut. 29:25–27
18 a 2 Chr. 34:26
19 a [Ps. 51:17] b 1 Kin. 21:29 c Lev. 26:31, 32 d Jer. 26:6; 44:22
20 a [Is. 57:1, 2] *1* Cause you to join your ancestors in death *2* Die a natural death

CHAPTER 23
1 a 2 Chr. 34:29, 30
2 a Deut. 31:10–13 b 2 Kin. 22:8
3 a 2 Kin. 11:14 b 2 Kin. 11:17
4 a 2 Kin. 25:18 b 2 Kin. 21:3–7 *1* A Canaanite goddess *2* The gods of the Assyrians

2 Kings 23:3–7

Dear Woman of Destiny,

Second Kings 23:25 says there was no king before or after who turned to the Lord like King Josiah did. What did he do to earn such words of honor and respect? Josiah, the last godly king of Judah, not only pledged to his people to keep the Lord's commandments, he was also determined to uproot the pervasive practice of idolatry through a sweeping destruction of all idols in the land, starting with all those in the temple.

An idol is an image that represents a false god, or a false god that is worshiped in an image. The second commandment reads, "You shall not make for yourself a carved image—any likeness of anything that is in heaven above, or that is in the earth beneath, or that is in the water under the earth; you shall not bow down to them nor serve them. For I, the LORD your God, am a jealous God . . . ." (Ex. 20:4, 5).

In the temple, Josiah removed horses, burned chariots bearing images of a sun-god, smashed the altars for Baal and the starry hosts, destroyed the sacred stones, and cut down the Asherah poles. He demolished all detestable things pertaining to idol worship, including portable household idols, throughout the Israelites' territories (see 2 Kin. 23).

Before Josiah, the other reforms under King Asa, King Jehoshaphat, the priest Jehoiada, King Joash, and King Hezekiah all involved physical removal of altars and images prior to the beginning of the blessings that came to their land.

On the other extreme, Josiah's grandfather, Manasseh, committed idolatry in every form. He went so far as to place idols in the temple itself. God's fierce anger toward him could not be turned away (see 2 Kin. 23:26). As a result, his abominations were the climactic cause of the Babylonian captivity, a severe judgment on Judah.

Today objects and items that are representative of and associated with idols, the occult, and powers opposed to God are to be avoided and removed from us and our own homes in the same way that Moses commanded the Israelites (see Deut. 7:25, 26). This is not to be taken as a ritual prescription, as idols are still abominations to Him. Because we are now the temple (as opposed to the temple in Jerusalem) of the living God, "let us cleanse ourselves from all filthiness of the flesh and spirit, perfecting holiness in the fear of God" (2 Cor. 7:1).

Because deception is a major weapon of the enemy, idolatrous things can come into our possessions knowingly and unknowingly, in different forms, and through different means. They can be arts or crafts, paintings or sculptures, memorable souvenirs, valuable jewelry, cultural artifacts, even toys and games for both children and adults.

In his final exhortation in his first letter to Thessalonica, Paul encouraged the new converts to "abstain from every form of evil" (1 Thess. 5:22). This was emphasized by another apostle, John, when writing to believers. Showing the importance he placed on the riddance of idols, John's final words in his letter are "Little children, keep yourselves from idols" (1 John 5:21).

Woman of Destiny, may you walk in holiness and purity, keeping yourself from any kind of idolatry, and completely devoting yourself to the Lord in every area of your life.

Agatha Chan

5 Then he removed the idolatrous priests
whom the kings of Judah had ordained to
burn incense on the high places in the
cities of Judah and in the places all around
Jerusalem, and those who burned incense
to Baal, to the sun, to the moon, to the
[1]constellations, and to [a]all the host of
heaven. 6 And he brought out the [a]wood-
en image[1] from the house of the LORD,
to the Brook Kidron outside Jerusalem,
burned it at the Brook Kidron and ground
it to [b]ashes, and threw its ashes on [c]the
graves of the common people. 7 Then he
tore down the *ritual* [1]booths [a]of the [2]per-
verted persons that *were* in the house of
the LORD, [b]where the [c]women wove hangings for the wooden image. 8 And he
brought all the priests from the cities of
Judah, and defiled the high places where
the priests had burned incense, from
[a]Geba to Beersheba; also he broke down
the high places at the gates which *were* at
the entrance of the Gate of Joshua the
governor of the city, which *were* to the
left of the city gate. 9 [a]Nevertheless the
priests of the high places did not come up
to the altar of the LORD in Jerusalem, [b]but
they ate unleavened bread among their
brethren.

10 And he defiled [a]Topheth, which *is* in
[b]the Valley of the [1]Son of Hinnom, [c]that
no man might make his son or his daughter [d]pass through the fire to Molech.
11 Then he removed the horses that the
kings of Judah had [1]dedicated to the sun,
at the entrance to the house of the LORD,
by the chamber of Nathan-Melech, the officer who *was* in the court; and he burned
the chariots of the sun with fire. 12 The
altars that *were* [a]on the roof, the upper
chamber of Ahaz, which the kings of Judah had made, and the altars which [b]Ma-
nasseh had made in the two courts of the
house of the LORD, the king broke down
and pulverized there, and threw their dust
into the Brook Kidron. 13 Then the king
defiled the [1]high places that *were* east of
Jerusalem, which *were* on the [2]south of
[3]the Mount of Corruption, which [a]Sol-
omon king of Israel had built for Ashtoreth the abomination of the Sidonians, for
Chemosh the abomination of the Moabites, and for Milcom the abomination of
the people of Ammon. 14 And he [a]broke in
pieces the *sacred* pillars and cut down the
wooden images, and filled their places
with the bones of men.

15 Moreover the altar that *was* at Bethel,
and the [1]high place [a]which Jeroboam the
son of Nebat, who made Israel sin, had
made, both that altar and the high place
he broke down; and he burned the high
place *and* crushed *it* to powder, and
burned the wooden image. 16 As Josiah
turned, he saw the tombs that *were* there
on the mountain. And he sent and took
the bones out of the tombs and burned
them on the altar, and defiled it according
to the [a]word of the LORD which the man
of God proclaimed, who proclaimed these
words. 17 Then he said, "What gravestone
is this that I see?"

So the men of the city told him, "*It is*
[a]the tomb of the man of God who came
from Judah and proclaimed these things
which you have done against the altar of
Bethel."

18 And he said, "Let him alone; let no
one move his bones." So they let his bones
alone, with the bones of [a]the prophet who
came from Samaria.

19 Now Josiah also took away all the
[1]shrines of the [2]high places that *were* [a]in
the cities of Samaria, which the kings of
Israel had made to provoke [3]the LORD to
anger; and he did to them according to all
the deeds he had done in Bethel. 20 [a]He
[b]executed all the priests of the [1]high places who *were* there, on the altars, and
[c]burned men's bones on them; and he returned to Jerusalem.

21 Then the king commanded all the
people, saying, [a]"Keep the Passover to the
LORD your God, [b]as *it is* written in this
Book of the Covenant." 22 [a]Such a Passover surely had never been held since the
days of the judges who judged Israel, nor
in all the days of the kings of Israel and
the kings of Judah. 23 But in the eighteenth year of King Josiah this Passover
was held before the LORD in Jerusalem.
24 Moreover Josiah put away those who
consulted mediums and spiritists, the
household gods and idols, all the abominations that were seen in the land of Judah and in Jerusalem, that he might
perform the words of [a]the law which were
written in the book [b]that Hilkiah the
priest found in the house of the LORD.
25 [a]Now before him there was no king like
him, who turned to the LORD with all his
heart, with all his soul, and with all his
might, according to all the Law of Moses;
nor after him did *any* arise like him.

5 a 2 Kin. 21:3 *1* Of the Zodiac
6 a 2 Kin. 21:7 b Ex. 32:20 c 2 Chr. 34:4 *1* Heb. *Asherah,* a Canaanite goddess
7 a 1 Kin. 14:24; 15:12 b Ezek. 16:16 c Ex. 38:8 *1* Lit. *houses* *2* Heb. *qedeshim,* those practicing sodomy and prostitution in religious rituals
8 a Josh. 21:17
9 a [Ezek. 44:10–14] b 1 Sam. 2:36
10 a Is. 30:33 b Josh. 15:8 c [Lev. 18:21] d 2 Kin. 21:6 *1* Kt. *Sons*
11 *1 given*
12 a Jer. 19:13 b 2 Kin. 21:5
13 a 1 Kin. 11:5–7 *1* Places for pagan worship *2* Lit. *right of* *3* The Mount of Olives
14 a [Ex. 23:24]
15 a 1 Kin. 12:28–33 *1* A place for pagan worship
16 a 1 Kin. 13:2
17 a 1 Kin. 13:1, 30, 31
18 a 1 Kin. 13:11, 31
19 a 2 Chr. 34:6, 7 *1* Lit. *houses* *2* Places for pagan worship *3* So with LXX, Syr., Vg.; MT, Tg. omit *the LORD*
20 a 1 Kin. 13:2 b 2 Kin. 10:25; 11:18 c 2 Chr. 34:5 *1* Places for pagan worship
21 a 2 Chr. 35:1 b Deut. 16:2–8
22 a 2 Chr. 35:18, 19
24 a [Lev. 19:31; 20:27] b 2 Kin. 22:8
25 a 2 Kin. 18:5

Impending Judgment on Judah

26 Nevertheless the LORD did not turn
from the fierceness of His great wrath,
with which His anger was aroused against
Judah, [a]because of all the provocations
with which Manasseh had provoked Him.
27 And the LORD said, "I will also remove
Judah from My sight, as [a]I have removed
Israel, and will cast off this city Jerusalem
which I have chosen, and the house of
which I said, [b]'My name shall be there.' "

Josiah Dies in Battle

28 Now the rest of the acts of Josiah, and
all that he did, *are* they not written in the
book of the chronicles of the kings of Judah? 29 [a]In his days Pharaoh Necho king of
Egypt went [1]to the aid of the king of Assyria, to the River Euphrates; and King
Josiah went against him. And *Pharaoh
Necho* killed him at [b]Megiddo when he
[c]confronted him. 30 [a]Then his servants
moved his body in a chariot from Megiddo, brought him to Jerusalem, and buried
him in his own tomb. And [b]the people of
the land took Jehoahaz the son of Josiah,
anointed him, and made him king in his
father's place.

The Reign and Captivity of Jehoahaz

31 [a]Jehoahaz *was* twenty-three years old
when he became king, and he reigned
three months in Jerusalem. His mother's
name *was* [b]Hamutal the daughter of Jeremiah of Libnah. 32 And he did evil in the
sight of the LORD, according to all that his
fathers had done. 33 Now Pharaoh Necho
put him in prison [a]at Riblah in the land of
Hamath, that he might not reign in Jerusalem; and he imposed on the land a tribute of one hundred talents of silver and
a talent of gold. 34 Then [a]Pharaoh Necho
made Eliakim the son of Josiah king in
place of his father Josiah, and [b]changed
his name to [c]Jehoiakim. And *Pharaoh*
took Jehoahaz [d]and went to Egypt, and
[1]he died there.

Jehoiakim Reigns in Judah

35 So Jehoiakim gave [a]the silver and
gold to Pharaoh; but he taxed the land to
give money according to the command of
Pharaoh; he exacted the silver and gold
from the people of the land, from every
one according to his assessment, to give
it to Pharaoh Necho. 36 [a]Jehoiakim *was*
twenty-five years old when he became
king, and he reigned eleven years in Jerusalem. His mother's name *was* Zebudah
the daughter of Pedaiah of Rumah. 37 And
he did evil in the sight of the LORD, according to all that his fathers had done.

Judah Overrun by Enemies

24 In [a]his days Nebuchadnezzar king
of [b]Babylon came up, and Jehoiakim became his vassal *for* three years.
Then he turned and rebelled against him.
2 [a]And the LORD sent against him *raiding*
[1]bands of Chaldeans, bands of Syrians,
bands of Moabites, and bands of the people of Ammon; He sent them against Judah to destroy it, [b]according to the word
of the LORD which He had spoken by His
servants the prophets. 3 Surely at the commandment of the LORD *this* came upon
Judah, to remove *them* from His sight
[a]because of the sins of Manasseh, according to all that he had done, 4 [a]and also
because of the innocent blood that he had
shed; for he had filled Jerusalem with innocent blood, which the LORD would not
pardon.
5 Now the rest of the acts of Jehoiakim,
and all that he did, *are* they not written in
the book of the chronicles of the kings of
Judah? 6 [a]So Jehoiakim rested with his fathers. Then Jehoiachin his son reigned in
his place.
7 And [a]the king of Egypt did not come
out of his land anymore, for [b]the king of
Babylon had taken all that belonged to the
king of Egypt from the Brook of Egypt to
the River Euphrates.

The Reign and Captivity of Jehoiachin

8 [a]Jehoiachin[1] *was* eighteen years old
when he became king, and he reigned in
Jerusalem three months. His mother's
name *was* Nehushta the daughter of Elnathan of Jerusalem. 9 And he did evil in the
sight of the LORD, according to all that his
father had done.
10 [a]At that time the servants of Nebuchadnezzar king of Babylon came up
against Jerusalem, and the city [1]was besieged. 11 And Nebuchadnezzar king of
Babylon came against the city, as his servants were besieging it. 12 [a]Then Jehoiachin king of Judah, his mother, his

---

26 a Jer. 15:4
27 a 2 Kin. 17:18, 20; 18:11; 21:13 b 1 Kin. 8:29; 9:3
29 a Jer. 2:16; 46:2 b Zech. 12:11 c 2 Kin. 14:8 *1 Or to attack,* Heb. *al* can mean *together with* or *against*
30 a 2 Chr. 35:24 b 2 Chr. 36:1–4
31 a Jer. 22:11 b 2 Kin. 24:18
33 a 2 Kin. 25:6
34 a 2 Chr. 36:4 b Dan. 1:7 c Matt. 1:11 d Ezek. 19:3, 4 *1* Jehoahaz
35 a 2 Kin. 23:33
36 a 2 Chr. 36:5

CHAPTER 24
1 a Dan. 1:1 b 2 Kin. 20:14
2 a Jer. 25:9; 32:28; 35:11 b 2 Kin. 20:17; 21:12–14; 23:27 *1 troops*
3 a 2 Kin. 21:2, 11; 23:26
4 a 2 Kin. 21:16
6 a Jer. 22:18, 19
7 a Jer. 37:5–7 b Jer. 46:2
8 a 2 Chr. 36:9 *1 Jeconiah,* 1 Chr. 3:16; Jer. 24:1; or *Coniah,* Jer. 22:24, 28
10 a Dan. 1:1 *1* Lit. *came into siege*
12 a Jer. 22:24–30; 24:1; 29:1, 2

servants, his princes, and his officers went out to the king of Babylon; and the king of Babylon, [b]in the eighth year of his reign, took him prisoner.

The Captivity of Jerusalem

13 [a]And he carried out from there all the treasures of the house of the LORD and the treasures of the king's house, and he [b]cut in pieces all the articles of gold which Solomon king of Israel had made in the temple of the LORD, [c]as the LORD had said. 14 Also [a]he carried into captivity all Jerusalem: all the captains and all the mighty men of valor, [b]ten thousand captives, and [c]all the craftsmen and smiths. None remained except [d]the poorest people of the land. 15 And [a]he carried Jehoiachin captive to Babylon. The king's mother, the king's wives, his officers, and the mighty of the land he carried into captivity from Jerusalem to Babylon. 16 [a]All the valiant men, seven thousand, and craftsmen and smiths, one thousand, all *who were* strong *and* fit for war, these the king of Babylon brought captive to Babylon.

Zedekiah Reigns in Judah

17 Then [a]the king of Babylon made Mattaniah, [b]*Jehoiachin's*[1] uncle, king in his place, and [c]changed his name to Zedekiah.

18 [a]Zedekiah *was* twenty-one years old when he became king, and he reigned eleven years in Jerusalem. His mother's name *was* [b]Hamutal the daughter of Jeremiah of Libnah. 19 [a]He also did evil in the sight of the LORD, according to all that Jehoiakim had done. 20 For because of the anger of the LORD *this* happened in Jerusalem and Judah, that He finally cast them out from His presence. [a]Then Zedekiah rebelled against the king of Babylon.

The Fall and Captivity of Judah

25 Now it came to pass [a]in the ninth year of his reign, in the tenth month, on the tenth *day* of the month, *that* Nebuchadnezzar king of Babylon and all his army came against Jerusalem and encamped against it; and they built a siege wall against it all around. 2 So the city was besieged until the eleventh year of King Zedekiah. 3 By the ninth *day* of the [a]*fourth* month the famine had become so severe in the city that there was no food for the people of the land.

4 Then [a]the city wall was broken through, and all the men of war *fled* at night by way of the gate between two walls, which was by the king's garden, even though the Chaldeans *were* still encamped all around against the city. And [b]*the king*[1] went by way of the [2]plain. 5 But the army of the Chaldeans pursued the king, and they overtook him in the plains of Jericho. All his army was scattered from him. 6 So they took the king and brought him up to the king of Babylon [a]at Riblah, and they pronounced judgment on him. 7 Then they killed the sons of Zedekiah before his eyes, [a]put[1] out the eyes of Zedekiah, bound him with bronze fetters, and took him to Babylon.

8 And in the fifth month, [a]on the seventh *day* of the month (which *was* [b]the nineteenth year of King Nebuchadnezzar king of Babylon), [c]Nebuzaradan the captain of the guard, a servant of the king of Babylon, came to Jerusalem. 9 [a]He burned the house of the LORD [b]and the king's house; all the houses of Jerusalem, that is, all the houses of the great, [c]he burned with fire. 10 And all the army of the Chaldeans who *were with* the captain of the guard [a]broke down the walls of Jerusalem all around.

11 Then Nebuzaradan the captain of the guard carried away captive [a]the rest of the people *who* remained in the city and the defectors who had deserted to the king of Babylon, with the rest of the multitude. 12 But the captain of the guard [a]left *some* of the poor of the land as vinedressers and farmers. 13 [a]The bronze [b]pillars that *were* in the house of the LORD, and [c]the carts and [d]the bronze Sea that *were* in the house of the LORD, the Chaldeans broke in pieces, and [e]carried their bronze to Babylon. 14 They also took away [a]the pots, the shovels, the trimmers, the spoons, and all the bronze utensils with which the priests ministered. 15 The firepans and the basins, the things of solid gold and solid silver, the captain of the guard took away. 16 The two pillars, one Sea, and the carts, which Solomon had made for the house of the LORD, [a]the bronze of all these articles was beyond measure. 17 [a]The height of one pillar *was* [1]eighteen cubits, and the capital on it *was* of bronze. The height of the capital was three cubits, and the network and pomegranates all around the capital were

---

12 b 2 Chr. 36:10
13 a Is. 39:6 b Dan. 5:2, 3 c Jer. 20:5
14 a Jer. 24:1 b 2 Kin. 24:16 c 1 Sam. 13:19 d 2 Kin. 25:12
15 a Jer. 22:24–28
16 a Jer. 52:28
17 a Jer. 37:1 b 2 Chr. 36:10 c 2 Chr. 36:4 1 Lit. *his*
18 a Jer. 52:1 b 2 Kin. 23:31
19 a 2 Chr. 36:12
20 a Ezek. 17:15

CHAPTER 25
1 a Jer. 6:6; 34:2
3 a Lam. 4:9, 10
4 a Jer. 39:2 b Ezek. 12:12 1 Lit. *he* 2 Or *Arabah,* the Jordan Valley
6 a Jer. 52:9
7 a Jer. 39:7 1 *blinded*
8 a Jer. 52:12 b 2 Kin. 24:12 c Jer. 39:9
9 a 2 Chr. 36:19 b Jer. 39:8 c Jer. 17:27
10 a Neh. 1:3
11 a Jer. 5:19; 39:9
12 a Jer. 39:10; 40:7; 52:16
13 a Jer. 52:17 b 1 Kin. 7:15 c 1 Kin. 7:27 d 1 Kin. 7:23 e Jer. 27:19–22
14 a Ex. 27:3
16 a 1 Kin. 7:47
17 a 1 Kin. 7:15–22 1 About 27 feet

all of bronze. The second pillar was the
same, with a network.
18[a]And the captain of the guard took
[b]Seraiah the chief priest, [c]Zephaniah the
second priest, and the three doorkeepers.
19He also took out of the city an officer
who had charge of the men of war, [a]five
men of [1]the king's close associates who
were found in the city, the chief recruiting officer of the army, who mustered the
people of the land, and sixty men of the
people of the land *who were* found in the
city. 20So Nebuzaradan, captain of
the guard, took these and brought them
to the king of Babylon at Riblah. 21Then
the king of Babylon struck them and put
them to death at Riblah in the land of Hamath. [a]Thus Judah was carried away captive from its own land.

Gedaliah Made Governor of Judah

22Then he made Gedaliah the son of
[a]Ahikam, the son of Shaphan, governor
over [b]the people who remained in the
land of Judah, whom Nebuchadnezzar
king of Babylon had left. 23Now when all
the [a]captains of the armies, they and *their*
men, heard that the king of Babylon had
made Gedaliah governor, they came to
Gedaliah at Mizpah—Ishmael the son of
Nethaniah, Johanan the son of Careah,
Seraiah the son of Tanhumeth the Netophathite, and [1]Jaazaniah the son of a
Maachathite, they and their men. 24And
Gedaliah took an oath before them and
their men, and said to them, "Do not be
afraid of the servants of the Chaldeans.
Dwell in the land and serve the king of
Babylon, and it shall be well with you."
25But [a]it happened in the seventh
month that Ishmael the son of Nethaniah,
the son of Elishama, of the royal family,
came with ten men and struck and killed
Gedaliah, the Jews, as well as the Chaldeans who were with him at Mizpah. 26And
all the people, small and great, and the
captains of the armies, arose [a]and went to
Egypt; for they were afraid of the Chaldeans.

Jehoiachin Released from Prison

27[a]Now it came to pass in the thirty-
seventh year of the captivity of Jehoiachin
king of Judah, in the twelfth month, on
the twenty-seventh *day* of the month,
that [1]Evil-Merodach king of Babylon, in
the year that he began to reign, [b]released
Jehoiachin king of Judah from prison.
28He spoke kindly to him, and gave him a
more prominent seat than those of the
kings who *were* with him in Babylon. 29So
Jehoiachin changed from his prison garments, and he [a]ate [1]bread regularly before the king all the days of his life. 30And
as for his [1]provisions, *there was* a [1]regu-
lar ration given him by the king, a portion
for each day, all the days of his life.

18 a Jer. 39:9–13; 52:12–16, 24 b Ezra 7:1 c Jer. 21:1; 29:25, 29
19 a Jer. 52:25 *1* Lit. *those seeing the king's face*
21 a Deut. 28:36, 64
22 a 2 Kin. 22:12 b Is. 1:9; Jer. 40:5
23 a Jer. 40:7–9 *1 Jezaniah,* Jer. 40:8
25 a Jer. 41:1–3
26 a Jer. 43:4–7
27 a Jer. 52:31–34 b Gen. 40:13, 20 *1* Lit. *Man of Marduk*
29 a 2 Sam. 9:7 *1* Food
30 *1* Lit. *allowance*

AUTHOR: *Attributed to Ezra*
DATE: *Probably 425–400 B.C.*
THEME: *Encouragement and Exhortation from Judah's Spiritual Heritage*
KEY WORDS: *King, House, David, Jerusalem, Priest*

1 CHRONICLES

Dear Woman of Destiny,

The emphasis on genealogies in 1 Chronicles reminds us that God is concerned with His offspring and remembers those who are faithful. We see, too, that His promises can be trusted. He promised David that the Savior would come from his line, and that promise stood. Take heart—God's promises to you are real and true!

His love and mine,

Marilyn Hickey

The Family of Adam—Seth to Abraham

Adam,[a] [b]Seth, Enosh, 2Cainan, Mahalalel, Jared, 3Enoch, Methuselah,
Lamech, 4[a]Noah,[1] Shem, Ham, and
Japheth.
5[a]The sons of Japheth *were* Gomer, Magog, Madai, Javan, Tubal, Meshech, and
Tiras. 6The sons of Gomer *were* Ashkenaz,
[1]Diphath, and Togarmah. 7The sons of Javan *were* Elishah, [1]Tarshishah, Kittim,
and [2]Rodanim.
8[a]The sons of Ham *were* Cush, Mizraim, Put, and Canaan. 9The sons of Cush
were Seba, Havilah, [1]Sabta, [2]Raama, and
Sabtecha. The sons of Raama *were* Sheba
and Dedan. 10Cush [a]begot Nimrod; he began to be a mighty one on the earth.
11Mizraim begot Ludim, Anamim, Leha-
bim, Naphtuhim, 12Pathrusim, Casluhim
(from whom came the Philistines and the
[a]Caphtorim). 13[a]Canaan begot Sidon, his
firstborn, and Heth; 14the Jebusite, the
Amorite, and the Girgashite; 15the Hivite,
the Arkite, and the Sinite; 16the Arvadite,
the Zemarite, and the Hamathite.
17The sons of [a]Shem *were* Elam, Asshur, [b]Arphaxad, Lud, Aram, Uz, Hul, Gether, and [1]Meshech. 18Arphaxad begot
Shelah, and Shelah begot Eber. 19To Eber
were born two sons: the name of one *was*
[1]Peleg, for in his days the [2]earth was divided; and his brother's name *was* Joktan.
20[a]Joktan begot Almodad, Sheleph, Hazarmaveth, Jerah, 21Hadoram, Uzal, Diklah, 22[1]Ebal, Abimael, Sheba, 23Ophir,
Havilah, and Jobab. All these *were* the
sons of Joktan.
24[a]Shem, Arphaxad, Shelah, 25[a]Eber,
Peleg, Reu, 26Serug, Nahor, Terah, 27and
[a]Abram, who *is* Abraham. 28[a]The sons of
Abraham *were* [b]Isaac and [c]Ishmael.

The Family of Ishmael

29These *are* their genealogies: The
[a]firstborn of Ishmael *was* Nebajoth; then
Kedar, Adbeel, Mibsam, 30Mishma, Dumah, Massa, [1]Hadad, Tema, 31Jetur, Naphish, and Kedemah. These *were* the sons
of Ishmael.

The Family of Keturah

32Now [a]the sons born to Keturah, Abraham's concubine, *were* Zimran, Jokshan,
Medan, Midian, Ishbak, and Shuah. The
sons of Jokshan *were* Sheba and Dedan.
33The sons of Midian *were* Ephah, Epher,
Hanoch, Abida, and Eldaah. All these were
the children of Keturah.

The Family of Isaac

34And [a]Abraham begot Isaac. [b]The sons
of Isaac *were* Esau and Israel. 35The sons
of [a]Esau *were* Eliphaz, Reuel, Jeush, Jaalam, and Korah. 36And the sons of Eliphaz
were Teman, Omar, [1]Zephi, Gatam, *and*
Kenaz; and *by* [a]Timna, Amalek. 37The
sons of Reuel *were* Nahath, Zerah, Shammah, and Mizzah.

The Family of Seir

38[a]The sons of Seir *were* Lotan, Shobal,
Zibeon, Anah, Dishon, Ezer, and Dishan.
39And the sons of Lotan *were* Hori and
[1]Homam; Lotan's sister *was* Timna. 40The
sons of Shobal *were* [1]Alian, Manahath,
Ebal, [2]Shephi, and Onam. The sons of
Zibeon *were* Ajah and Anah. 41The son of
Anah *was* [a]Dishon. The sons of Dishon
were [1]Hamran, Eshban, Ithran, and Cheran. 42The sons of Ezer *were* Bilhan, Zaa-
van, *and* [1]Jaakan. The sons of Dishan *were*
Uz and Aran.

The Kings of Edom

43Now these *were* the [a]kings who
reigned in the land of Edom before a king
reigned over the children of Israel: Bela
the son of Beor, and the name of his city
was Dinhabah. 44And when Bela died, Jobab the son of Zerah of Bozrah reigned in
his place. 45When Jobab died, Husham of
the land of the Temanites reigned in his
place. 46And when Husham died, Hadad
the son of Bedad, who [1]attacked Midian in
the field of Moab, reigned in his place. The
name of his city *was* Avith. 47When Hadad
died, Samlah of Masrekah reigned in his
place. 48[a]And when Samlah died, Saul of
Rehoboth-by-the-River reigned in his
place. 49When Saul died, Baal-Hanan the
son of Achbor reigned in his place. 50And
when Baal-Hanan died, [1]Hadad reigned
in his place; and the name of his city was
[2]Pai. His wife's name was Mehetabel the
daughter of Matred, the daughter of Mezahab. 51Hadad died also. And the chiefs of
Edom were Chief Timnah, Chief [1]Aliah,
Chief Jetheth, 52Chief Aholibamah, Chief
Elah, Chief Pinon, 53Chief Kenaz, Chief
Teman, Chief Mibzar, 54Chief Magdiel,

CHAPTER 1
1 a Gen. 1:27; 2:7; 5:1, 2, 5 b Gen. 4:25, 26; 5:3–9
4 a Gen. 5:28—10:1 *1* So with MT, Vg.; LXX adds *the sons of Noah*
5 a Gen. 10:2–4
6 *1 Riphath,* Gen. 10:3
7 *1 Tarshish,* Gen. 10:4 *2 Dodanim,* Gen. 10:4
8 a Gen. 10:6
9 *1 Sabtah,* Gen. 10:7 *2 Raamah,* Gen. 10:7
10 a Gen. 10:8–10, 13
12 a Deut. 2:23
13 a Gen. 9:18, 25–27; 10:15
17 a Gen. 10:22–29; 11:10 b Luke 3:36 *1 Mash,* Gen. 10:23
19 *1* Lit. *Division,* Gen. 10:25 *2* Or *land*
20 a Gen. 10:26
22 *1 Obal,* Gen. 10:28
24 a Luke 3:34–36
25 a Gen. 11:15
27 a Gen. 17:5
28 a Gen. 21:2, 3 b Gen. 21:2 c Gen. 16:11, 15
29 a Gen. 25:13–16
30 *1 Hadar,* Gen. 25:15
32 a Gen. 25:1–4
34 a Gen. 21:2 b Gen. 25:9, 25, 26, 29; 32:28
35 a Gen. 36:10–19
36 a Gen. 36:12 *1 Zepho,* Gen. 36:11
38 a Gen. 36:20–28
39 *1 Hemam* or *Heman,* Gen. 36:22
40 *1 Alvan,* Gen. 36:23 *2 Shepho,* Gen. 36:23 **41** a Gen. 36:25 *1 Hemdan,* Gen. 36:26 **42** *1 Akan,* Gen. 36:27 **43** a Gen. 36:31–43
46 *1* Lit. *struck* **48** a Gen. 36:37 **50** *1 Hadar,* Gen. 36:39 *2 Pau,* Gen. 36:39 **51** *1 Alvah,* Gen. 36:40

and Chief Iram. These *were* the chiefs of
Edom.

The Family of Israel

2 These *were* the [a]sons of [1]Israel: [b]Reu-
ben, Simeon, Levi, Judah, Issachar,
Zebulun, 2Dan, Joseph, Benjamin, Naphtali, Gad, and Asher.

From Judah to David

3The sons of [a]Judah *were* Er, Onan, and
Shelah. *These* three were born to him by
the daughter of [b]Shua, the Canaanitess.
[c]Er, the firstborn of Judah, was wicked in
the sight of the LORD; so He killed him.
4And [a]Tamar, his daughter-in-law, [b]bore
him Perez and Zerah. All the sons of Judah *were* five.
5The sons of [a]Perez *were* Hezron and
Hamul. 6The sons of Zerah *were* [1]Zimri,
[a]Ethan, Heman, Calcol, and [2]Dara—five
of them in all.
7The son of [a]Carmi *was* [1]Achar, the
troubler of Israel, who transgressed in the
[b]accursed[2] thing.
8The son of Ethan *was* Azariah.
9Also the sons of Hezron who were born
to him *were* Jerahmeel, [1]Ram, and [2]Che-
lubai. 10Ram [a]begot Amminadab, and Amminadab begot Nahshon, [b]leader of the
children of Judah; 11Nahshon begot [1]Sal-
ma, and Salma begot Boaz; 12Boaz begot
Obed, and Obed begot Jesse; 13[a]Jesse begot Eliab his firstborn, Abinadab the second, [1]Shimea the third, 14Nethanel the
fourth, Raddai the fifth, 15Ozem the sixth,
and David the [a]seventh.
16Now their sisters *were* Zeruiah and
Abigail. [a]And the sons of Zeruiah *were*
Abishai, Joab, and Asahel—three. 17Abi-
gail bore Amasa; and the father of Amasa
was [1]Jether the Ishmaelite.

The Family of Hezron

18Caleb the son of Hezron had children
by Azubah, *his* wife, and by Jerioth. Now
these were her sons: Jesher, Shobab, and
Ardon. 19When Azubah died, Caleb [1]took
[a]Ephrath[2] as his wife, who bore him Hur.
20And Hur begot Uri, and Uri begot [a]Bez-
alel.
21Now afterward Hezron went in to the
daughter of [a]Machir the father of Gilead,
whom he married when he *was* sixty years
old; and she bore him Segub. 22Segub begot [a]Jair,[1] who had twenty-three cities in
the land of Gilead. 23[a](Geshur and Syria
took from them the towns of Jair, with
Kenath and its towns—sixty towns.) All
these *belonged to* the sons of Machir the
father of Gilead. 24After Hezron died in
Caleb Ephrathah, Hezron's wife Abijah
bore him [a]Ashhur the father of Tekoa.

The Family of Jerahmeel

25The sons of Jerahmeel, the firstborn
of Hezron, *were* Ram, the firstborn, and
Bunah, Oren, Ozem, *and* Ahijah. 26Jerah-
meel had another wife, whose name was
Atarah; she was the mother of Onam.
27The sons of Ram, the firstborn of Jerah-
meel, were Maaz, Jamin, and Eker. 28The
sons of Onam were Shammai and Jada.
The sons of Shammai *were* Nadab and
Abishur.
29And the name of the wife of Abishur
was Abihail, and she bore him Ahban and
Molid. 30The sons of Nadab *were* Seled and
Appaim; Seled died without children.
31The son of Appaim *was* Ishi, the son of
Ishi *was* Sheshan, and [a]Sheshan's son *was*
Ahlai. 32The sons of Jada, the brother of
Shammai, *were* Jether and Jonathan; Jether died without children. 33The sons of
Jonathan *were* Peleth and Zaza. These
were the sons of Jerahmeel.
34Now Sheshan had no sons, only
daughters. And Sheshan had an Egyptian
servant whose name *was* Jarha. 35Sheshan
gave his daughter to Jarha his servant as
wife, and she bore him Attai. 36Attai begot
Nathan, and Nathan begot [a]Zabad; 37Za-
bad begot Ephlal, and Ephlal begot [a]Obed;
38Obed begot Jehu, and Jehu begot Azariah; 39Azariah begot Helez, and Helez begot Eleasah; 40Eleasah begot Sismai, and
Sismai begot Shallum; 41Shallum begot
Jekamiah, and Jekamiah begot Elishama.

The Family of Caleb

42The descendants of Caleb the brother
of Jerahmeel *were* Mesha, his firstborn,
who was the father of Ziph, and the sons
of Mareshah the father of Hebron. 43The
sons of Hebron *were* Korah, Tappuah, Rekem, and Shema. 44Shema begot Raham
the father of Jorkoam, and Rekem begot
Shammai. 45And the son of Shammai *was*
Maon, and Maon *was* the father of Beth
Zur.
46Ephah, Caleb's concubine, bore Haran, Moza, and Gazez; and Haran begot
Gazez. 47And the sons of Jahdai *were* Re-
gem, Jotham, Geshan, Pelet, Ephah, and
Shaaph.

CHAPTER 2
1 [a] Gen. 29:32–35; 35:23, 26; 46:8–27 [b] Gen. 29:32; 35:22 [1] *Jacob,* Gen. 32:28
3 [a] Num. 26:19 [b] Gen. 38:2 [c] Gen. 38:7
4 [a] Gen. 38:6 [b] Matt. 1:3
5 [a] Ruth 4:18
6 [a] 1 Kin. 4:31 [1] *Zabdi,* Josh. 7:1 [2] *Darda,* 1 Kin. 4:31
7 [a] 1 Chr. 4:1 [b] Josh. 6:18 [1] *Achan,* Josh. 7:1 [2] *banned* or *devoted*
9 [1] *Aram,* Matt. 1:3, 4 [2] *Caleb,* vv. 18, 42
10 [a] Matt. 1:4 [b] Num. 1:7; 2:3
11 [1] *Salmon,* Ruth 4:21; Luke 3:32
13 [a] 1 Sam. 16:6 [1] *Shammah,* 1 Sam. 16:9
15 [a] 1 Sam. 16:10, 11; 17:12
16 [a] 2 Sam. 2:18
17 [1] *Jithra the Israelite,* 2 Sam. 17:25
19 [a] 1 Chr. 2:50 [1] Lit. *took to himself* [2] Or *Ephrathah*
20 [a] Ex. 31:2; 38:22
21 [a] Num. 27:1
22 [a] Judg. 10:3 [1] Reckoned to Manasseh through the daughter of Machir, Num. 32:41; Deut. 3:14; 25:5, 6; 1 Kin. 4:13; 1 Chr. 7:14
23 [a] Deut. 3:14
24 [a] 1 Chr. 4:5
31 [a] 1 Chr. 2:34, 35
36 [a] 1 Chr. 11:41
37 [a] 2 Chr. 23:1

48 Maachah, Caleb's concubine, bore
Sheber and Tirhanah. 49 She also bore
Shaaph the father of Madmannah, Sheva
the father of Machbenah and the father
of Gibea. And the daughter of Caleb *was*
[a]Achsah.[1]

50 These were the descendants of Caleb:
The sons of [a]Hur, the firstborn of [1]Ephra-
thah, *were* Shobal the father of [b]Kirjath
Jearim, 51 Salma the father of Bethlehem,
and Hareph the father of Beth Gader.

52 And Shobal the father of Kirjath Jearim had descendants: [1]Haroeh, *and* half of
the [2]*families of* Manuhoth. 53 The families
of Kirjath Jearim *were* the Ithrites, the
Puthites, the Shumathites, and the Mish-
raites. From these came the Zorathites
and the Eshtaolites.

54 The sons of Salma *were* Bethlehem,
the Netophathites, [1]Atroth Beth Joab, half
of the Manahethites, and the Zorites.

55 And the families of the scribes who
dwelt at Jabez *were* the Tirathites, the
Shimeathites, *and* the Suchathites. These
were the [a]Kenites who came from Hammath, the father of the house of [b]Rechab.

The Family of David

3 Now these were the sons of David who
were born to him in Hebron: The
firstborn *was* [a]Amnon, by [b]Ahinoam the
[c]Jezreelitess; the second, [1]Daniel, by [d]Ab-
igail the Carmelitess; 2 the third, [a]Absa-
lom the son of Maacah, the daughter of
Talmai, king of Geshur; the fourth, [b]Ado-
nijah the son of Haggith; 3 the fifth,
Shephatiah, by Abital; the sixth, Ithream,
by his wife [a]Eglah.

4 *These* six were born to him in Hebron.
[a]There he reigned seven years and six
months, and [b]in Jerusalem he reigned
thirty-three years. 5 [a]And these were born
to him in Jerusalem: [1]Shimea, Shobab,
Nathan, and [b]Solomon—four by [2]Bath-
shua the daughter of [3]Ammiel. 6 Also
there were Ibhar, [1]Elishama, [2]Eliphelet,
7 Nogah, Nepheg, Japhia, 8 Elishama, [1]Eli-
ada, and Eliphelet—[a]nine *in all.* 9 *These*
were all the sons of David, besides the
sons of the concubines, and [a]Tamar their
sister.

The Family of Solomon

10 Solomon's son *was* [a]Rehoboam; [1]Abi-
jah *was* his son, Asa his son, Jehoshaphat
his son, 11 [1]Joram his son, [2]Ahaziah his
son, [3]Joash his son, 12 Amaziah his son,
[1]Azariah his son, Jotham his son, 13 Ahaz
his son, Hezekiah his son, Manasseh his
son, 14 Amon his son, *and* Josiah his son.
15 The sons of Josiah *were* Johanan the
firstborn, the second [1]Jehoiakim, the
third Zedekiah, and the fourth [2]Shallum.
16 The sons of [a]Jehoiakim *were* [1]Jeconiah
his son *and* [2]Zedekiah his son.

The Family of Jeconiah

17 And the sons of [1]Jeconiah [2]*were* As-
sir, Shealtiel [a]his son, 18 *and* Malchiram,
Pedaiah, Shenazzar, Jecamiah, Hoshama,
and Nedabiah. 19 The sons of Pedaiah *were*
Zerubbabel and Shimei. The sons of Ze-
rubbabel *were* Meshullam, Hananiah,
Shelomith their sister, 20 and Hashubah,
Ohel, Berechiah, Hasadiah, and Jushab-
Hesed—five *in all.*

21 The sons of Hananiah *were* Pelatiah
and Jeshaiah, the sons of Rephaiah, the
sons of Arnan, the sons of Obadiah, and
the sons of Shechaniah. 22 The son of
Shechaniah was Shemaiah. The sons of
Shemaiah *were* [a]Hattush, Igal, Bariah,
Neariah, and Shaphat—six *in all.* 23 The
sons of Neariah *were* Elioenai, Hezekiah,
and Azrikam—three *in all.* 24 The sons of
Elioenai *were* Hodaviah, Eliashib, Pelaiah,
Akkub, Johanan, Delaiah, and Anani—
seven *in all.*

The Family of Judah

4 The sons of Judah *were* [a]Perez, Hezron, [1]Carmi, Hur, and Shobal. 2 And
[1]Reaiah the son of Shobal begot Jahath,
and Jahath begot Ahumai and Lahad.
These *were* the families of the Zorathites.
3 These *were* the sons *of the father* of
Etam: Jezreel, Ishma, and Idbash; and the
name of their sister *was* Hazelelponi; 4 and
Penuel *was* the father of Gedor, and Ezer
was the father of Hushah.

These *were* the sons of [a]Hur, the firstborn of Ephrathah the father of Bethlehem.

5 And [a]Ashhur the father of Tekoa had
two wives, Helah and Naarah. 6 Naarah
bore him Ahuzzam, Hepher, Temeni, and
Haahashtari. These *were* the sons of Naarah. 7 The sons of Helah *were* Zereth, Zohar, and Ethnan; 8 and Koz begot Anub,

49 a Josh. 15:17 *1 Or Achsa*
50 a 1 Chr. 4:4 b Josh. 9:17; 18:14 *1 Ephrath,* v. 19
52 *1 Reaiah,* 1 Chr. 4:2 *2* Or *Manuhothites,* same as *Manahethites,* v. 54
54 *1* Or *Ataroth of the house of Joab*
55 a Judg. 1:16 b Jer. 35:2
CHAPTER 3
1 a 2 Sam. 3:2–5 b 1 Sam. 25:43 c Josh. 15:56 d 1 Sam. 25:39–42 *1 Chileab,* 2 Sam. 3:3
2 a 2 Sam. 13:37; 15:1 b 1 Kin. 1:5
3 a 2 Sam. 3:5
4 a 2 Sam. 2:11 b 2 Sam. 5:5
5 a 1 Chr. 14:4–7 b 2 Sam. 12:24, 25 *1 Shammua,* 1 Chr. 14:4; 2 Sam. 5:14 *2 Bathsheba,* 2 Sam. 11:3 *3 Eliam,* 2 Sam. 11:3
6 *1 Elishua,* 1 Chr. 14:5; 2 Sam. 5:15 *2 Elpelet,* 1 Chr. 14:5
8 a 2 Sam. 5:14–16 *1 Beeliada,* 1 Chr. 14:7
9 a 2 Sam. 13:1
10 a 1 Kin. 11:43 *1 Abijam,* 1 Kin. 15:1
11 *1 Jehoram,* 2 Kin. 1:17; 8:16 *2* Or *Azariah* or *Jehoahaz* *3 Jehoash,* 2 Kin. 12:1
12 *1 Uzziah,* Is. 6:1
15 *1 Eliakim,* 2 Kin. 23:34 *2 Jehoahaz,* 2 Kin. 23:31
16 a Matt. 1:11 *1 Jehoiachin,* 2 Kin. 24:8, or *Coniah,* Jer. 22:24 *2 Mattaniah,* 2 Kin. 24:17
17 a Matt. 1:12 *1 Jehoiachin,* 2 Kin. 24:8, or *Coniah,* Jer. 22:24 *2* Or *the captive were Shealtiel* 22 a Ezra 8:2
CHAPTER 4 1 a Gen. 38:29; 46:12 *1 Chelubai,* 1 Chr. 2:9 or *Caleb,* 1 Chr. 2:18 2 *1 Haroeh,* 1 Chr. 2:52 4 a 1 Chr. 2:50 5 a 1 Chr. 2:24

Zobebah, and the families of Aharhel the
son of Harum.
9 Now Jabez was [a]more honorable than
his brothers, and his mother called his
name [1]Jabez, saying, "Because I bore *him*
in pain." 10 And Jabez called on the God of
Israel saying, "Oh, that You would bless
me indeed, and enlarge my [1]territory,
that Your hand would be with me, and
that You would keep *me* from evil, that I
may not cause pain!" So God granted him
what he requested.
11 Chelub the brother of [a]Shuhah begot
Mehir, who *was* the father of Eshton.
12 And Eshton begot Beth-Rapha, Paseah,
and Tehinnah the father of [1]Ir-Nahash.
These *were* the men of Rechah.
13 The sons of Kenaz *were* [a]Othniel and
Seraiah. The sons of Othniel *were* [1]Ha-
thath, 14 and Meonothai *who* begot Ophrah. Seraiah begot Joab the father of [a]Ge
Harashim,[1] for they were craftsmen.
15 The sons of [a]Caleb the son of Jephunneh *were* Iru, Elah, and Naam. The son of
Elah *was* [1]Kenaz. 16 The sons of Jehallelel
were Ziph, Ziphah, Tiria, and Asarel.
17 The sons of Ezrah *were* Jether, Mered,
Epher, and Jalon. And [1]*Mered's wife bore*
Miriam, Shammai, and Ishbah the father
of Eshtemoa. 18 ([1]His wife Jehudijah bore
Jered the father of Gedor, Heber the father of Sochoh, and Jekuthiel the father of
Zanoah.) And these were the sons of Bithi-
ah the daughter of Pharaoh, whom Mered
took.
19 The sons of Hodiah's wife, the sister
of Naham, *were* the fathers of Keilah the
Garmite and of Eshtemoa the [a]Maacha-
thite. 20 And the sons of Shimon *were* Amnon, Rinnah, Ben-Hanan, and Tilon. And
the sons of Ishi *were* Zoheth and Ben-
Zoheth.
21 The sons of [a]Shelah [b]the son of Judah
were Er the father of Lecah, Laadah the
father of Mareshah, and the families of the
house of the linen workers of the house of
Ashbea; 22 also Jokim, the men of Choze-
ba, and Joash; Saraph, who ruled in Moab,
and Jashubi-Lehem. Now the [1]records are
ancient. 23 These *were* the potters and
those who dwell at [1]Netaim and [2]Gede-
rah; there they dwelt with the king for his
work.

The Family of Simeon

24 The [a]sons of Simeon *were* [1]Nemuel,
Jamin, [2]Jarib, [3]Zerah, *and* Shaul, 25 Shallum his son, Mibsam his son, and Mishma
his son. 26 And the sons of Mishma *were*
Hamuel his son, Zacchur his son, and
Shimei his son. 27 Shimei had sixteen sons
and six daughters; but his brothers did
not have many children, [a]nor did any of
their families multiply as much as the
children of Judah.
28 They dwelt at Beersheba, Moladah,
Hazar Shual, 29 [1]Bilhah, Ezem, [2]Tolad,
30 Bethuel, Hormah, Ziklag, 31 Beth Marca-
both, [1]Hazar Susim, Beth Biri, and at
Shaaraim. These *were* their cities until
the reign of David. 32 And their villages
were [1]Etam, Ain, Rimmon, Tochen, and
Ashan—five cities— 33 and all the villages
that *were* around these cities as far as
[1]Baal. These *were* their dwelling places,
and they maintained their genealogy:
34 Meshobab, Jamlech, and Joshah the son
of Amaziah; 35 Joel, and Jehu the son of
Joshibiah, the son of Seraiah, the son of
Asiel; 36 Elioenai, Jaakobah, Jeshohaiah,
Asaiah, Adiel, Jesimiel, and Benaiah;
37 Ziza the son of Shiphi, the son of Allon,
the son of Jedaiah, the son of Shimri, the
son of Shemaiah— 38 these mentioned by
name *were* leaders in their families, and
their father's house increased greatly.
39 So they went to the entrance of Gedor, as far as the east side of the valley, to
seek pasture for their flocks. 40 And they
found rich, good pasture, and the land
was broad, quiet, and peaceful; for some
Hamites formerly lived there.
41 These recorded by name came in the
days of Hezekiah king of Judah; and they
[a]attacked[1] their tents and the Meunites
who were found there, and [b]utterly destroyed them, as it is to this day. So they
dwelt in their place, because *there was*
pasture for their flocks there. 42 Now *some*
of them, five hundred men of the sons of
Simeon, went to Mount Seir, having as
their captains Pelatiah, Neariah, Rephaiah, and Uzziel, the sons of Ishi. 43 And
they [1]defeated [a]the rest of the Amalekites
who had escaped. They have dwelt there
to this day.

The Family of Reuben

5 Now the sons of Reuben the firstborn
of Israel—[a]he *was* indeed the firstborn, but because he [b]defiled his father's
bed, [c]his birthright was given to the sons
of Joseph, the son of Israel, so that the
genealogy is not listed according to the
birthright; 2 yet [a]Judah prevailed over his
brothers, and from him *came* a [b]ruler,

9 a Gen. 34:19 1 Lit. *He Will Cause Pain*
10 1 *border*
11 a Job 8:1
12 1 Lit. *City of Nahash*
13 a Josh. 15:17 1 LXX, Vg. add *and Meonothai*
14 a Neh. 11:35 1 Lit. *Valley of Craftsmen*
15 a 1 Chr. 6:56 1 Or *Uknaz*
17 1 Lit. *she*
18 1 Or *His Judean wife*
19 a 2 Kin. 25:23
21 a Gen. 38:11, 14 b Gen. 38:1–5; 46:12
22 1 Lit. *words*
23 1 Lit. *Plants* 2 Lit. *Hedges*
24 a Num. 26:12–14 1 *Jemuel,* Gen. 46:10; Ex. 6:15; Num. 26:12 2 *Jachin,* Gen. 46:10; Num. 26:12 3 *Zohar,* Gen. 46:10; Ex. 6:15
27 a Num. 2:9
29 1 *Balah,* Josh. 19:3 2 *Eltolad,* Josh. 19:4
31 1 *Hazar Susah,* Josh. 19:5
32 1 *Ether,* Josh. 19:7
33 1 *Baalath Beer,* Josh. 19:8
41 a 2 Kin. 18:8 b 2 Kin. 19:11 1 Lit. *struck*
43 a 1 Sam. 15:8; 30:17 1 Lit. *struck*

CHAPTER 5
1 a Gen. 29:32; 49:3 b Gen. 35:22; 49:4 c Gen. 48:15, 22
2 a Gen. 49:8, 10 b Mic. 5:2

although [1]the birthright was Joseph's— 3the sons of [a]Reuben the firstborn of Israel were Hanoch, Pallu, Hezron, and Carmi.

4The sons of Joel *were* Shemaiah his son, Gog his son, Shimei his son, 5Micah his son, Reaiah his son, Baal his son, 6and Beerah his son, whom [1]Tiglath-Pileser king of Assyria [a]carried into captivity. He *was* leader of the Reubenites. 7And his brethren by their families, [a]when the genealogy of their generations was registered: the chief, Jeiel, and Zechariah, 8and Bela the son of Azaz, the son of Shema, the son of Joel, who dwelt in [a]Aroer, as far as Nebo and Baal Meon. 9Eastward they settled as far as the [1]entrance of the wilderness this side of the River Euphrates, because their cattle had [2]multiplied [a]in the land of Gilead.

10Now in the days of Saul they made war [a]with the Hagrites, who fell by their hand; and they dwelt in their tents throughout the entire *area* east of Gilead.

The Family of Gad

11And the [a]children of Gad dwelt next to them in the land of [b]Bashan as far as [c]Salcah: 12Joel *was* the chief, Shapham the next, then Jaanai and Shaphat in Bashan, 13and their brethren of their father's house: Michael, Meshullam, Sheba, Jorai, Jachan, Zia, and Eber—seven *in all.* 14These *were* the children of Abihail the son of Huri, the son of Jaroah, the son of Gilead, the son of Michael, the son of Jeshishai, the son of Jahdo, the son of Buz; 15Ahi the son of Abdiel, the son of Guni, *was* chief of their father's house. 16And *the Gadites* dwelt in Gilead, in Bashan and in its villages, and in all the [1]common-lands of [a]Sharon within their borders. 17All these were registered by genealogies in the days of [a]Jotham king of Judah, and in the days of [b]Jeroboam king of Israel.

18The sons of Reuben, the Gadites, and half the tribe of Manasseh *had* forty-four thousand seven hundred and sixty valiant men, men able to bear shield and sword, to shoot with the bow, and skillful in war, who went to war. 19They made war with the Hagrites, [a]Jetur, Naphish, and Nodab. 20And [a]they were helped against them, and the Hagrites were delivered into their hand, and all who *were* with them, for they [b]cried out to God in the battle. He [1]heeded their prayer, because they [c]put their trust in Him. 21Then they took away their livestock—fifty thousand of their camels, two hundred and fifty thousand of their sheep, and two thousand of their donkeys—also one hundred thousand of their men; 22for many fell dead, because the war [a]*was* God's. And they dwelt in their place until [b]the captivity.

The Family of Manasseh (East)

23So the children of the half-tribe of Manasseh dwelt in the land. Their *numbers* increased from Bashan to Baal Hermon, that is, to [a]Senir, or Mount Hermon. 24These *were* the heads of their fathers' houses: Epher, Ishi, Eliel, Azriel, Jeremiah, Hodaviah, and Jahdiel. They were mighty men of valor, famous men, *and* heads of their fathers' houses.

25And they were unfaithful to the God of their fathers, and [a]played the harlot after the gods of the peoples of the land, whom God had destroyed before them. 26So the God of Israel stirred up the spirit of [a]Pul king of Assyria, that is, [b]Tiglath-Pileser[1] king of Assyria. He carried the Reubenites, the Gadites, and the half-tribe of Manasseh into captivity. He took them to [c]Halah, Habor, Hara, and the river of Gozan to this day.

The Family of Levi

6 The sons of Levi *were* [a]Gershon,[1] Kohath, and Merari. 2The sons of Kohath *were* Amram, [a]Izhar, Hebron, and Uzziel. 3The children of Amram *were* Aaron, Moses, and Miriam. And the sons of Aaron *were* [a]Nadab, Abihu, Eleazar, and Ithamar. 4Eleazar begot Phinehas, *and* Phinehas begot Abishua; 5Abishua begot Bukki, and Bukki begot Uzzi; 6Uzzi begot Zerahiah, and Zerahiah begot Meraioth; 7Meraioth begot Amariah, and Amariah begot Ahitub; 8[a]Ahitub begot [b]Zadok, and Zadok begot Ahimaaz; 9Ahimaaz begot Azariah, and Azariah begot Johanan; 10Johanan begot Azariah (it was he [a]who ministered as priest in the [b]temple[1] that Solomon built in Jerusalem); 11[a]Azariah begot [b]Amariah, and Amariah begot Ahitub; 12Ahitub begot Zadok, and Zadok begot [1]Shallum; 13Shallum begot Hilkiah, and Hilkiah begot Azariah; 14Azariah begot [a]Seraiah, and Seraiah begot Jehozadak. 15Jehozadak went *into captivity* [a]when the LORD carried Judah and Jerusalem into captivity by the hand of Nebuchadnezzar.

2 [1] *the right of the firstborn*
3 [a] Ex. 6:14
6 [a] 2 Kin. 18:11 [1] Heb. *Tilgath-Pilneser*
7 [a] 1 Chr. 5:17
8 [a] Josh. 12:2; 13:15, 16
9 [a] Josh. 22:8, 9 [1] *beginning* [2] *increased*
10 [a] Gen. 25:12
11 [a] Num. 26:15–18 [b] Josh. 13:11, 24–28 [c] Deut. 3:10
16 [a] 1 Chr. 27:29 [1] *open lands*
17 [a] 2 Kin. 15:5, 32 [b] 2 Kin. 14:16, 28
19 [a] Gen. 25:15
20 [a] [1 Chr. 5:22] [b] 2 Chr. 14:11–13 [c] Ps. 9:10; 20:7, 8; 22:4, 5 [1] Lit. *was entreated for them*
22 [a] [Josh. 23:10] [b] 2 Kin. 15:29; 17:6
23 [a] Deut. 3:9
25 [a] 2 Kin. 17:7
26 [a] 2 Kin. 15:19 [b] 2 Kin. 15:29 [c] 2 Kin. 17:6; 18:11 [1] Heb. *Tilgath-Pilneser*

CHAPTER 6
1 [a] Ex. 6:16 [1] Or *Gershom,* v. 16
2 [a] 1 Chr. 6:18, 22
3 [a] Lev. 10:1, 2
8 [a] 2 Sam. 8:17 [b] 2 Sam. 15:27
10 [a] 2 Chr. 26:17, 18 [b] 1 Kin. 6:1 [1] Lit. *house*
11 [a] Ezra 7:3 [b] 2 Chr. 19:11
12 [1] *Meshullam,* 1 Chr. 9:11
14 [a] Neh. 11:11
15 [a] 2 Kin. 25:21

16The sons of Levi *were* [a]Gershon,[1] Kohath, and Merari. 17These are the names
of the sons of Gershon: Libni and Shimei.
18The sons of Kohath *were* Amram, Izhar,
Hebron, and Uzziel. 19The sons of Merari
were Mahli and Mushi. Now these *are* the
families of the Levites according to their
fathers: 20Of Gershon *were* Libni his son,
Jahath his son, [a]Zimmah his son, 21[1]Joah
his son, [2]Iddo his son, Zerah his son, *and*
[3]Jeatherai his son. 22The sons of Kohath
were [1]Amminadab his son, [a]Korah his
son, Assir his son, 23Elkanah his son, Ebiasaph his son, Assir his son, 24Tahath his
son, Uriel his son, Uzziah his son, and
Shaul his son. 25The sons of Elkanah *were*
[a]Amasai and Ahimoth. 26*As for* Elkanah,
the sons of Elkanah *were* [1]Zophai his son,
[2]Nahath his son, 27[1]Eliab his son, Jeroham his son, *and* Elkanah his son. 28The
sons of Samuel *were* [1]*Joel* the firstborn,
and Abijah [2]the second. 29The sons of Merari *were* Mahli, Libni his son, Shimei his
son, Uzzah his son, 30Shimea his son,
Haggiah his son, *and* Asaiah his son.

Musicians in the House of the Lord

31Now these are [a]the men whom David
appointed over the service of song in the
house of the LORD, after the [b]ark came to
rest. 32They were ministering with music
before the dwelling place of the tabernacle
of meeting, until Solomon had built the
house of the LORD in Jerusalem, and they
served in their office according to their
order.
33And these *are* the ones who [1]minis-
tered with their sons: Of the sons of the
[a]Kohathites *were* Heman the singer, the
son of Joel, the son of Samuel, 34the son
of Elkanah, the son of Jeroham, the son
of [1]Eliel, the son of [2]Toah, 35the son of
Zuph, the son of Elkanah, the son of Mahath, the son of Amasai, 36the son of Elkanah, the son of Joel, the son of Azariah,
the son of Zephaniah, 37the son of Tahath,
the son of Assir, the son of [a]Ebiasaph, the
son of Korah, 38the son of Izhar, the son
of Kohath, the son of Levi, the son of Israel. 39And his brother [a]Asaph, who stood at
his right hand, *was* Asaph the son of Bera-
chiah, the son of Shimea, 40the son of
Michael, the son of Baaseiah, the son of
Malchijah, 41the son of [a]Ethni, the son
of Zerah, the son of Adaiah, 42the son of
Ethan, the son of Zimmah, the son
of Shimei, 43the son of Jahath, the son of
Gershon, the son of Levi.
44Their brethren, the sons of Merari, on
the left hand, *were* [1]Ethan the son of
[2]Kishi, the son of Abdi, the son of Malluch, 45the son of Hashabiah, the son of
Amaziah, the son of Hilkiah, 46the son of
Amzi, the son of Bani, the son of Shamer,
47the son of Mahli, the son of Mushi, the
son of Merari, the son of Levi.
48And their brethren, the Levites, *were*
appointed to every [a]kind of service of the
tabernacle of the house of God.

The Family of Aaron

49[a]But Aaron and his sons offered sacrifices [b]on the altar of burnt offering and
[c]on the altar of incense, for all the work
of the Most Holy *Place,* and to make
atonement for Israel, according to all that
Moses the servant of God had commanded. 50Now these *are* the [a]sons of Aaron:
Eleazar his son, Phinehas his son, Abishua his son, 51Bukki his son, Uzzi his son,
Zerahiah his son, 52Meraioth his son, Amariah his son, Ahitub his son, 53Zadok his
son, *and* Ahimaaz his son.

Dwelling Places of the Levites

54[a]Now these *are* their dwelling places
throughout their settlements in their territory, for they were *given* by lot to the
sons of Aaron, of the family of the Kohathites: 55[a]They gave them Hebron in the
land of Judah, with its surrounding
[1]common-lands. 56[a]But the fields of the
city and its villages they gave to Caleb the
son of Jephunneh. 57And [a]to the sons of
Aaron they gave *one of* the cities of refuge,
Hebron; also Libnah with its common-
lands, Jattir, Eshtemoa with its common-
lands, 58[1]Hilen with its common-lands,
Debir with its common-lands, 59[1]Ashan
with its common-lands, and Beth Shemesh with its common-lands. 60And
from the tribe of Benjamin: Geba with
its common-lands, [1]Alemeth with its
common-lands, and Anathoth with its
common-lands. All their cities among
their families *were* thirteen.
61[a]To the rest of the family of the tribe
of the Kohathites *they gave* [b]by lot ten
cities from half the tribe of Manasseh.
62And to the sons of Gershon, throughout
their families, *they gave* thirteen cities
from the tribe of Issachar, from the tribe

---

16 a Ex. 6:16 1 Heb. *Gershom,* an alternate spelling for *Gershon,* vv. 1, 17, 20, 43, 62, 71
20 a 1 Chr. 6:42
21 1 *Ethan,* v. 42 2 *Adaiah,* v. 41 3 *Ethni,* v. 41
22 a Num. 16:1 1 *Izhar,* vv. 2, 18
25 a 1 Chr. 6:35, 36
26 1 *Zuph,* v. 35; 1 Sam. 1:1 2 *Toah,* v. 34
27 1 *Eliel,* v. 34
28 1 So with LXX, Syr., Arab.; cf. v. 33 and 1 Sam. 8:2 2 Heb. *Vasheni*
31 a 1 Chr. 15:16–22, 27; 16:4–6 b 1 Chr. 15:25—16:1
33 a Num. 26:57 1 Lit. *stood with*
34 1 *Elihu,* 1 Sam. 1:1 2 *Tohu,* 1 Sam. 1:1
37 a Ex. 6:24
39 a 2 Chr. 5:12
41 a 1 Chr. 6:21
44 1 *Jeduthun,* 1 Chr. 9:16; 25:1, 3, 6; 2 Chr. 35:15; Ps. 62:title 2 Or *Kushaiah*
48 a 1 Chr. 9:14–34
49 a [Num. 18:1–8] b Lev. 1:8, 9 c Ex. 30:7
50 a 1 Chr. 6:4–8
54 a Josh. 21
55 a Josh. 14:13; 21:11, 12 1 *open lands*
56 a Josh. 14:13; 15:13
57 a Josh. 21:13, 19
58 1 *Holon,* Josh. 21:15
59 1 *Ain,* Josh. 21:16
60 1 *Almon,* Josh. 21:18
61 a 1 Chr. 6:66–70 b Josh. 21:5

of Asher, from the tribe of Naphtali, and from the tribe of Manasseh in Bashan. 63To the sons of Merari, throughout their families, *they gave* [a]twelve cities from the tribe of Reuben, from the tribe of Gad, and from the tribe of Zebulun. 64So the children of Israel gave *these* cities with their [1]common-lands to the Levites. 65And they gave by lot from the tribe of the children of Judah, from the tribe of the children of Simeon, and from the tribe of the children of Benjamin these cities which are called by *their* names.

66Now [a]some of the families of the sons of Kohath *were given* cities as their territory from the tribe of Ephraim. 67[a]And they gave them *one of* the cities of refuge, Shechem with its common-lands, in the mountains of Ephraim, also Gezer with its common-lands, 68[a]Jokmeam with its common-lands, Beth Horon with its common-lands, 69Aijalon with its common-lands, and Gath Rimmon with its common-lands. 70And from the half-tribe of Manasseh: Aner with its common-lands and Bileam with its common-lands, for the rest of the family of the sons of Kohath.

71From the family of the half-tribe of Manasseh the sons of Gershon *were given* Golan in Bashan with its common-lands and [1]Ashtaroth with its common-lands. 72And from the tribe of Issachar: [1]Kedesh with its common-lands, Daberath with its common-lands, 73Ramoth with its common-lands, and Anem with its common-lands. 74And from the tribe of Asher: Mashal with its common-lands, Abdon with its common-lands, 75Hukok with its common-lands, and Rehob with its common-lands. 76And from the tribe of Naphtali: Kedesh in Galilee with its common-lands, Hammon with its common-lands, and Kirjathaim with its common-lands.

77From the tribe of Zebulun the rest of the children of Merari *were given* [1]Rimmon with its common-lands and Tabor with its common-lands. 78And on the other side of the Jordan, across from Jericho, on the east side of the Jordan, *they were given* from the tribe of Reuben: Bezer in the wilderness with its common-lands, Jahzah with its common-lands, 79Kedemoth with its common-lands, and Mephaath with its common-lands. 80And from the tribe of Gad: Ramoth in Gilead with its common-lands, Mahanaim with its common-lands, 81Heshbon with its common-lands, and Jazer with its common-lands.

The Family of Issachar

7 The sons of Issachar *were* [a]Tola, [1]Puah, [2]Jashub, and Shimron—four *in all.* 2The sons of Tola *were* Uzzi, Rephaiah, Jeriel, Jahmai, Jibsam, and Shemuel, heads of their father's house. *The sons* of Tola *were* mighty men of valor in their generations; [a]their number in the days of David *was* twenty-two thousand six hundred. 3The son of Uzzi *was* Izrahiah, and the sons of Izrahiah *were* Michael, Obadiah, Joel, and Ishiah. All five of them *were* chief men. 4And with them, by their generations, according to their fathers' houses, *were* thirty-six thousand troops ready for war; for they had many wives and sons.

5Now their brethren among all the families of Issachar *were* mighty men of valor, listed by their genealogies, eighty-seven thousand in all.

The Family of Benjamin

6*The sons* of [a]Benjamin *were* Bela, Becher, and Jediael—three *in all.* 7The sons of Bela were Ezbon, Uzzi, Uzziel, Jerimoth, and Iri—five *in all.* They *were* heads of *their* fathers' houses, and they were listed by their genealogies, twenty-two thousand and thirty-four mighty men of valor.

8The sons of Becher *were* Zemirah, Joash, Eliezer, Elioenai, Omri, Jerimoth, Abijah, Anathoth, and Alemeth. All these *are* the sons of Becher. 9And they were recorded by genealogy according to their generations, heads of their fathers' houses, twenty thousand two hundred mighty men of valor. 10The son of Jediael *was* Bilhan, and the sons of Bilhan *were* Jeush, Benjamin, Ehud, Chenaanah, Zethan, Tharshish, and Ahishahar.

11All these sons of Jediael *were* heads of their fathers' houses; *there were* seventeen thousand two hundred mighty men of valor fit to go out for war *and* battle. 12[1]Shuppim and [2]Huppim *were* the sons of [3]Ir, *and* Hushim *was* the son of [4]Aher.

The Family of Naphtali

13The [a]sons of Naphtali *were* [1]Jahziel, Guni, Jezer, and [2]Shallum, the sons of Bilhah.

63 a Josh. 21:7, 34–40
64 *1 open lands*
66 a 1 Chr. 6:61
67 a Josh. 21:21
68 a Josh. 21:22
71 *1 Beeshterah,* Josh. 21:27
72 *1 Kishon,* Josh. 21:28
77 *1* Heb. *Rimmono,* an alternate spelling of *Rimmon,* 1 Chr. 4:32

CHAPTER 7
1 a Num. 26:23–25
1 Puvah, Gen. 46:13
2 Job, Gen. 46:13
2 a 2 Sam. 24:1–9
6 a Gen. 46:21
12 *1 Shupham,* Num. 26:39
2 Hupham, Num. 26:39
3 Iri, v. 7
4 Ahiram, Num. 26:38
13 a Num. 26:48–50
1 Jahzeel, Gen. 46:24
2 Shillem, Gen. 46:24

The Family of Manasseh (West)

14The [a]descendants of Manasseh: his
Syrian concubine bore him [b]Machir the
father of Gilead, the father of Asriel. 15Ma-
chir took as his wife *the sister* of [1]Huppim
and [2]Shuppim, whose name *was* Maachah. The name of *Gilead's* [3]grandson
was [a]Zelophehad, but Zelophehad begot
only daughters. 16(Maachah the wife of
Machir bore a son, and she called his
name Peresh. The name of his brother
was Sheresh, and his sons *were* Ulam and
Rakem. 17The son of Ulam *was* [a]Bedan.)
These *were* the descendants of Gilead the
son of Machir, the son of Manasseh.
18His sister Hammoleketh bore Ishhod,
[1]Abiezer, and Mahlah.
19And the sons of Shemida were Ahian,
Shechem, Likhi, and Aniam.

The Family of Ephraim

20[a]The sons of Ephraim *were* Shuthelah, Bered his son, Tahath his son, Eladah
his son, Tahath his son, 21Zabad his son,
Shuthelah his son, and Ezer and Elead.
The men of Gath who were born in *that*
land killed *them* because they came down
to take away their cattle. 22Then Ephraim
their father mourned many days, and his
brethren came to comfort him.
23And when he went in to his wife, she
conceived and bore a son; and he called
his name [1]Beriah, because tragedy had
come upon his house. 24Now his daughter
was Sheerah, who built Lower and Upper
[a]Beth Horon and Uzzen Sheerah; 25and
Rephah *was* his son, *as well* as Resheph,
and Telah his son, Tahan his son, 26Laa-
dan his son, Ammihud his son, [a]Elishama
his son, 27[1]Nun his son, and [a]Joshua his
son.
28Now their [a]possessions and dwelling
places *were* Bethel and its towns: to the
east [1]Naaran, to the west Gezer and its
towns, and Shechem and its towns, as far
as [2]Ayyah and its towns; 29and by the borders of the children of [a]Manasseh *were*
Beth Shean and its towns, Taanach and its
towns, [b]Megiddo and its towns, Dor and
its towns. In these dwelt the children of
Joseph, the son of Israel.

The Family of Asher

30[a]The sons of Asher *were* Imnah, Ish-
vah, Ishvi, Beriah, and their sister Serah.
31The sons of Beriah *were* Heber and Malchiel, who was the father of [1]Birzaith.
32And Heber begot Japhlet, [1]Shomer,
[2]Hotham, and their sister Shua. 33The
sons of Japhlet *were* Pasach, Bimhal, and
Ashvath. These *were* the children of Japhlet. 34The sons of [a]Shemer *were* Ahi, Roh-
gah, Jehubbah, and Aram. 35And the sons
of his brother Helem *were* Zophah, Imna,
Shelesh, and Amal. 36The sons of Zophah
were Suah, Harnepher, Shual, Beri, Im-
rah, 37Bezer, Hod, Shamma, Shilshah,
[1]Jithran, and Beera. 38The sons of Jether
were Jephunneh, Pispah, and Ara. 39The
sons of Ulla *were* Arah, Haniel, and Rizia.
40All these *were* the children of Asher,
heads of *their* fathers' houses, choice
men, mighty men of valor, chief leaders.
And they were recorded by genealogies
among the army fit for battle; their number *was* twenty-six thousand.

The Family Tree of King Saul of Benjamin

8 Now Benjamin begot [a]Bela his firstborn, Ashbel the second, [1]Aharah the
third, 2Nohah the fourth, and Rapha the
fifth. 3The sons of Bela *were* [1]Addar, Gera,
Abihud, 4Abishua, Naaman, Ahoah, 5Gera,
[1]Shephuphan, and Huram.
6These *are* the sons of Ehud, who were
the heads of the fathers' *houses* of the
inhabitants of [a]Geba, and who forced
them to move to [b]Manahath: 7Naaman,
Ahijah, and Gera who forced them to
move. He begot Uzza and Ahihud.
8Also Shaharaim had children in the
country of Moab, after he had sent away
Hushim and Baara his wives. 9By Hodesh
his wife he begot Jobab, Zibia, Mesha,
Malcam, 10Jeuz, Sachiah, and Mirmah.
These *were* his sons, heads of their fathers' *houses*.
11And by Hushim he begot Abitub and
Elpaal. 12The sons of Elpaal *were* Eber,
Misham, and Shemed, who built Ono and
Lod with its towns; 13and Beriah and
[a]Shema, who *were* heads of their fathers'
houses of the inhabitants of Aijalon, who
drove out the inhabitants of Gath. 14Ahio,
Shashak, Jeremoth, 15Zebadiah, Arad,
Eder, 16Michael, Ispah, and Joha *were* the
sons of Beriah. 17Zebadiah, Meshullam,
Hizki, Heber, 18Ishmerai, Jizliah, and Jobab *were* the sons of Elpaal. 19Jakim,
Zichri, Zabdi, 20Elienai, Zillethai, Eliel,
21Adaiah, Beraiah, and Shimrath *were* the
sons of [1]Shimei. 22Ishpan, Eber, Eliel,
23Abdon, Zichri, Hanan, 24Hananiah,

---

14 a Num. 26:29–34 b 1 Chr. 2:21

15 a Num. 26:30–33; 27:1 *1 Hupham,* v. 12; Num. 26:39 *2 Shupham,* v. 12; Num. 26:39 *3* Lit. *the second*

17 a 1 Sam. 12:11

18 *1 Jeezer,* Num. 26:30

20 a Num. 26:35–37

23 *1* Lit. *In Tragedy*

24 a Josh. 16:3, 5

26 a Num. 10:22

27 a Ex. 17:9, 14; 24:13; 33:11 *1* Heb. *Non*

28 a Josh. 16:1–10 *1 Naarath,* Josh. 16:7 *2* Many Heb. mss., Bg., LXX, Tg., Vg. *Gazza*

29 a Josh. 17:7 b Josh. 17:11

30 a Num. 26:44–47

31 *1* Or *Birzavith* or *Birzoth*

32 *1 Shemer,* 1 Chr. 7:34 *2 Helem,* 1 Chr. 7:35

34 a 1 Chr. 7:32

37 *1 Jether,* v. 38

CHAPTER 8

1 a Gen. 46:21 *1 Ahiram,* Num. 26:38

3 *1 Ard,* Num. 26:40

5 *1 Shupham,* Num. 26:39, or *Shuppim,* 1 Chr. 7:12

6 a 1 Chr. 6:60 b 1 Chr. 2:52

13 a 1 Chr. 8:21

21 *1 Shema,* 1 Chr. 7:13

Elam, Antothijah, 25Iphdeiah, and Penuel
were the sons of Shashak. 26Shamsherai,
Shehariah, Athaliah, 27Jaareshiah, Elijah,
and Zichri *were* the sons of Jeroham.
28These *were* heads of the fathers' *houses* by their generations, chief men. These
dwelt in Jerusalem.
29Now [1]the father of Gibeon, whose
[a]wife's name *was* Maacah, dwelt at Gibeon. 30And his firstborn son *was* Abdon,
then Zur, Kish, Baal, Nadab, 31Gedor,
Ahio, [1]Zecher, 32and Mikloth, *who* begot
[1]Shimeah. They also dwelt [2]alongside
their [3]relatives in Jerusalem, with their
brethren. 33[a]Ner[1] begot Kish, Kish begot
Saul, and Saul begot Jonathan, Malchishua, [2]Abinadab, and [3]Esh-Baal. 34The
son of Jonathan *was* [1]Merib-Baal, and
Merib-Baal begot [a]Micah. 35The sons of
Micah *were* Pithon, Melech, [1]Tarea, and
Ahaz. 36And Ahaz begot [1]Jehoaddah; Jehoaddah begot Alemeth, Azmaveth, and
Zimri; and Zimri begot Moza. 37Moza begot Binea, [1]Raphah his son, Eleasah his
son, *and* Azel his son.
38Azel had six sons whose names *were*
these: Azrikam, Bocheru, Ishmael, Sheariah, Obadiah, and Hanan. All these *were*
the sons of Azel. 39And the sons of Eshek
his brother *were* Ulam his firstborn, Jeush
the second, and Eliphelet the third.
40The sons of Ulam were mighty men of
valor—archers. *They* had many sons and
grandsons, one hundred and fifty *in all.*
These *were* all sons of Benjamin.

9 So [a]all Israel was [1]recorded by genealogies, and indeed, they *were* inscribed
in the book of the kings of Israel. But Judah was carried away captive to Babylon
because of their unfaithfulness. 2[a]And the
first inhabitants who *dwelt* in their possessions in their cities *were* Israelites,
priests, Levites, and [b]the Nethinim.

Dwellers in Jerusalem

3Now in [a]Jerusalem the children of Judah dwelt, and some of the children of
Benjamin, and of the children of Ephraim
and Manasseh: 4Uthai the son of Ammihud, the son of Omri, the son of Imri, the
son of Bani, of the descendants of Perez,
the son of Judah. 5Of the Shilonites: Asaiah the firstborn and his sons. 6Of the
sons of Zerah: Jeuel, and their brethren—
six hundred and ninety. 7Of the sons of
Benjamin: Sallu the son of Meshullam,
the son of Hodaviah, the son of Hassenuah; 8Ibneiah the son of Jeroham; Elah the
son of Uzzi, the son of Michri; Meshullam
the son of Shephatiah, the son of Reuel,
the son of Ibnijah; 9and their brethren,
according to their generations—nine
hundred and fifty-six. All these men *were*
heads of a father's *house* in their fathers'
houses.

The Priests at Jerusalem

10[a]Of the priests: Jedaiah, Jehoiarib,
and Jachin; 11[1]Azariah the son of Hilkiah,
the son of Meshullam, the son of Zadok,
the son of Meraioth, the son of Ahitub, the
[a]officer over the house of God; 12Adaiah
the son of Jeroham, the son of Pashur, the
son of Malchijah; Maasai the son of Adiel,
the son of Jahzerah, the son of Meshullam, the son of Meshillemith, the son of
Immer; 13and their brethren, heads of
their fathers' *houses*—one thousand sev-
en hundred and sixty. *They were* [1]very
able men for the work of the service of the
house of God.

The Levites at Jerusalem

14Of the Levites: Shemaiah the son of
Hasshub, the son of Azrikam, the son of
Hashabiah, of the sons of Merari; 15Bak-
bakkar, Heresh, Galal, and Mattaniah the
son of Micah, the son of [a]Zichri, the son
of Asaph; 16[a]Obadiah the son of [b]Shema-
iah, the son of Galal, the son of Jeduthun;
and Berechiah the son of Asa, the son of
Elkanah, who lived in the villages of the
Netophathites.

The Levite Gatekeepers

17And the gatekeepers *were* Shallum,
Akkub, Talmon, Ahiman, and their brethren. Shallum *was* the chief. 18Until then
they had been gatekeepers for the camps
of the children of Levi at the King's Gate
on the east.
19Shallum the son of Kore, the son of
Ebiasaph, the son of Korah, and his brethren, from his father's house, the Korahites, *were* in charge of the work of the
service, [1]gatekeepers of the tabernacle.
Their fathers had been keepers of the entrance to the camp of the LORD. 20And
[a]Phinehas the son of Eleazar had been the
officer over them in time past; the LORD
was with him. 21[a]Zechariah the son of Meshelemiah *was* [1]keeper of the door of the
tabernacle of meeting.
22All those chosen as gatekeepers *were*
two hundred and twelve. [a]They were recorded by their genealogy, in their villages.

29 [a] 1 Chr. 9:35–38 [1] Jeiel, 1 Chr. 9:35

31 [1] *Zechariah,* 1 Chr. 9:37

32 [1] *Shimeam,* 1 Chr.9:38 [2] Lit. *opposite* [3] *brethren*

33 [a] 1 Sam. 14:51 [1] Also the son of Gibeon, 1 Chr. 9:36, 39 [2] *Jishui,* 1 Sam. 14:49 [3] *Ishbosheth,* 2 Sam. 2:8

34 [a] 2 Sam. 9:12 [1] *Mephibosheth,* 2 Sam. 4:4

35 [1] *Tahrea,* 1 Chr. 9:41

36 [1] *Jarah,* 1 Chr. 9:42

37 [1] *Raphaiah,* 1 Chr. 9:43

CHAPTER 9

1 [a] Ezra 2:59 [1] *enrolled*

2 [a] Neh. 7:73 [b] Ezra 2:43; 8:20

3 [a] Neh. 11:1, 2

10 [a] Neh. 11:10–14

11 [a] Jer. 20:1 [1] *Seraiah,* Neh. 11:11

13 [1] Lit. *mighty men of strength*

15 [a] Neh. 11:17

16 [a] Neh. 11:17 [b] Neh. 11:17

19 [1] Lit. *thresholds*

20 [a] Num. 25:6–13; 31:6

21 [a] 1 Chr. 26:2, 14 [1] *gatekeeper*

22 [a] 1 Chr. 26:1, 2

David and Samuel [b]the seer had appointed them to their trusted office.
[23]So they and their children *were* in
charge of the gates of the house of the
LORD, the house of the tabernacle, by assignment. [24]The gatekeepers were assigned to the four directions: the east,
west, north, and south. [25]And their brethren in their villages *had* to come with
them from time to time [a]for seven days.
[26]For in this trusted office *were* four chief
gatekeepers; they were Levites. And they
had charge over the chambers and treasuries of the house of God. [27]And they
lodged *all* around the house of God because [1]they *had* the [a]responsibility, and
they *were* in charge of opening *it* every
morning.

Other Levite Responsibilities

[28]Now *some* of them were in charge of
the serving vessels, for they brought them
in and took them out by count. [29]*Some* of
them *were* appointed over the furnishings
and over all the implements of the sanctuary, and over the [a]fine flour and the wine
and the oil and the incense and the spices.
[30]And *some* of the sons of the priests made
[a]the ointment of the spices.

[31]Mattithiah of the Levites, the firstborn of Shallum the Korahite, had the
trusted office [a]over the things that were
baked in the pans. [32]And some of their
brethren of the sons of the Kohathites
[a]*were* in charge of preparing the showbread for every Sabbath.

[33]These are [a]the singers, heads of the
fathers' *houses* of the Levites, *who lodged*
in the chambers, *and were* free *from other
duties;* for they were employed in *that*
work day and night. [34]These heads of the
fathers' *houses* of the Levites *were* heads
throughout their generations. They dwelt
at Jerusalem.

The Family of King Saul

[35]Jeiel the father of Gibeon, whose
wife's name *was* [a]Maacah, dwelt at Gibeon. [36]His firstborn son *was* Abdon, then
Zur, Kish, Baal, Ner, Nadab, [37]Gedor,
Ahio, [1]Zechariah, and Mikloth. [38]And
Mikloth begot [1]Shimeam. They also dwelt
alongside their relatives in Jerusalem,
with their brethren. [39][a]Ner begot Kish,
Kish begot Saul, and Saul begot Jonathan,
Malchishua, Abinadab, and Esh-Baal.
[40]The son of Jonathan *was* Merib-Baal,
and Merib-Baal begot Micah. [41]The sons
of Micah *were* Pithon, Melech, [1]Tahrea,
[a]*and*[2] *Ahaz.* [42]And Ahaz begot [1]Jarah; Jarah begot Alemeth, Azmaveth, and Zimri;
and Zimri begot Moza; [43]Moza begot Binea, [1]Rephaiah his son, Eleasah his son,
and Azel his son.

[44]And Azel had six sons whose names
were these: Azrikam, Bocheru, Ishmael,
Sheariah, Obadiah, and Hanan; these
were the sons of Azel.

Tragic End of Saul and His Sons

10 Now [a]the Philistines fought
against Israel; and the men of Israel fled from before the Philistines, and fell
slain on Mount Gilboa. [2]Then the Philistines followed hard after Saul and his
sons. And the Philistines killed Jonathan,
[1]Abinadab, and Malchishua, Saul's sons.
[3]The battle became fierce against Saul.
The archers hit him, and he was wounded
by the archers. [4]Then Saul said to his
armorbearer, "Draw your sword, and
thrust me through with it, lest these uncircumcised men come and abuse me."
But his armorbearer would not, for he
was greatly afraid. Therefore Saul took a
sword and fell on it. [5]And when his armorbearer saw that Saul was dead, he also fell
on his sword and died. [6]So Saul and his
three sons died, and all his house died together. [7]And when all the men of Israel
who *were* in the valley saw that they had
fled and that Saul and his sons were dead,
they forsook their cities and fled; then the
Philistines came and dwelt in them.

[8]So it happened the next day, when the
Philistines came to [1]strip the slain, that
they found Saul and his sons fallen on
Mount Gilboa. [9]And they stripped him and
took his head and his armor, and sent
word *throughout* the land of the Philistines to proclaim the news *in the temple*
of their idols and among the people.
[10][a]Then they put his armor in the [1]temple
of their gods, and fastened his head in the
temple of Dagon.

[11]And when all Jabesh Gilead heard all
that the Philistines had done to Saul, [12]all
the [a]valiant men arose and took the body
of Saul and the bodies of his sons; and
they brought them to [b]Jabesh, and buried
their bones under the tamarisk tree at Jabesh, and fasted seven days.

[13]So Saul died for his unfaithfulness
which he had [1]committed against the
LORD, [a]because he did not keep the word

22 b 1 Sam. 9:9
25 a 2 Kin. 11:4–7
27 a 1 Chr. 23:30–32 *1 the watch was committed to them*
29 a 1 Chr. 23:29
30 a Ex. 30:22–25
31 a Lev. 2:5; 6:21
32 a Lev. 24:5–8
33 a 1 Chr. 6:31; 25:1
35 a 1 Chr. 8:29–32
37 *1 Zecher,* 1 Chr. 8:31
38 *1 Shimeah,* 1 Chr. 8:32
39 a 1 Chr. 8:33–38
41 a 1 Chr. 8:35 *1 Tarea,* 1 Chr. 8:35 *2* So with Arab., Syr., Tg., Vg. (cf. 8:35); MT, LXX omit *and Ahaz*
42 *1 Jehoaddah,* 1 Chr. 8:36
43 *1 Raphah,* 1 Chr. 8:37

CHAPTER 10
1 a 1 Sam. 31:1, 2
2 *1 Jishui,* 1 Sam. 14:49
8 *1 plunder*
10 a 1 Sam. 31:10 *1* Lit. *house*
12 a 1 Sam. 14:52 b 2 Sam. 21:12
13 a 1 Sam. 13:13, 14; 15:22–26 *1* Lit. *transgressed*

of the LORD, and also because [b]he consulted a medium for guidance. 14But *he* did not inquire of the LORD; therefore He killed him, and [a]turned the kingdom over to David the son of Jesse.

David Made King over All Israel

11 Then [a]all Israel came together to David at Hebron, saying, "Indeed we *are* your bone and your flesh. 2Also, in time past, even when Saul was king, you *were* the one who led Israel out and brought them in; and the LORD your [a]God said to you, 'You shall [b]shepherd My people Israel, and be ruler over My people Israel.' " 3Therefore all the elders of Israel came to the king at Hebron, and David made a covenant with them at Hebron before the LORD. And [a]they anointed David king over Israel, according to the word of the LORD [1]by [b]Samuel.

The City of David

4And David and all Israel [a]went to Jerusalem, which is Jebus, [b]where the Jebusites *were,* the inhabitants of the land. 5But the inhabitants of Jebus said to David, "You shall not come in here!" Nevertheless David took the stronghold of Zion (that is, the City of David). 6Now David said, "Whoever attacks the Jebusites first shall be [1]chief and captain." And Joab the son of Zeruiah went up first, and became chief. 7Then David dwelt in the stronghold; therefore they called it [1]the City of David. 8And he built the city around it, from [1]the Millo to the surrounding area. Joab [2]repaired the rest of the city. 9So David [a]went on and became great, and the LORD of hosts *was* with [b]him.

The Mighty Men of David

10Now [a]these *were* the heads of the mighty men whom David had, who strengthened themselves with him in his kingdom, with all Israel, to make him king, according to [b]the word of the LORD concerning Israel.

11And this *is* the number of the mighty men whom David had: [a]Jashobeam the son of a Hachmonite, [b]chief of [1]the captains; he had lifted up his spear against three hundred, killed *by him* at one time. 12After him *was* Eleazar the son of [a]Dodo, the Ahohite, who *was one* of the three mighty men. 13He was with David at [1]Pasdammim. Now there the Philistines were gathered for battle, and there was a piece of ground full of barley. So the people fled from the Philistines. 14But they [1]stationed themselves in the middle of *that* field, defended it, and killed the Philistines. So the LORD brought about a great victory.

15Now three of the thirty chief men [a]went down to the rock to David, into the cave of Adullam; and the army of the Philistines encamped [b]in the Valley of [1]Rephaim. 16David *was* then in the stronghold, and the garrison of the Philistines *was* then in Bethlehem. 17And David said with longing, "Oh, that someone would give me a drink of water from the well of Bethlehem, which is by the gate!" 18So the three broke through the camp of the Philistines, drew water from the well of Bethlehem that *was* by the gate, and took *it* and brought *it* to David. Nevertheless David would not drink it, but poured it out to the LORD. 19And he said, "Far be it from me, O my God, that I should do this! Shall I drink the blood of these men *who have put* their lives *in jeopardy?* For at the risk of their lives they brought it." Therefore he would not drink it. These things were done by the three mighty men.

20[a]Abishai the brother of Joab was chief of *another* [1]three. He had lifted up his spear against three hundred *men,* killed *them,* and won a name among *these* three. 21[a]Of the three he was more honored than the other two men. Therefore he became their captain. However he did not attain to the *first* three.

22Benaiah was the son of Jehoiada, the son of a valiant man from Kabzeel, who [1]had done many deeds. [a]He had killed two lion-like heroes of Moab. He also had gone down and killed a lion in the midst of a pit on a snowy day. 23And he killed an Egyptian, a man of *great* height, [1]five cubits tall. In the Egyptian's hand *there was* a spear like a weaver's beam; and he went down to him with a staff, wrested the spear out of the Egyptian's hand, and killed him with his own spear. 24These *things* Benaiah the son of Jehoiada did, and won a name among three mighty men. 25Indeed he was more honored than the thirty, but he did not attain to the *first* three. And David appointed him over his guard.

26Also the mighty warriors *were* [a]Asahel the brother of Joab, Elhanan the son

13 [b]1 Sam. 28:7
14 [a]1 Sam. 15:28

CHAPTER 11
1 [a]2 Sam. 5:1
2 [a]Ps. 78:70–72 [b]2 Sam. 7:7
3 [a]2 Sam. 5:3 [b]1 Sam. 16:1, 4, 12, 13 [1]Lit. *by the hand of Samuel*
4 [a]2 Sam. 5:6 [b]Judg. 1:21; 19:10, 11
6 [1]Lit. *head*
7 [1]*Zion,* 2 Sam. 5:7
8 [1]Lit. *The Landfill* [2]Lit. *revived*
9 [a]2 Sam. 3:1 [b]1 Sam. 16:18
10 [a]2 Sam. 23:8 [b]1 Sam. 16:1, 12
11 [a]1 Chr. 27:2 [b]1 Chr. 12:18 [1]So with Qr.; Kt., LXX, Vg. *the thirty* (cf. 2 Sam. 23:8)
12 [a]1 Chr. 27:4
13 [1]*Ephes Dammim,* 1 Sam. 17:1
14 [1]Lit. *took their stand*
15 [a]2 Sam. 23:13 [b]2 Sam. 5:18 [1]Lit. *Giants*
20 [a]2 Sam. 23:18 [1]So with MT, LXX, Vg.; Syr. *thirty*
21 [a]2 Sam. 23:19
22 [a]2 Sam. 23:20 [1]*was great in deeds*
23 [1]About 7 1/2 feet
26 [a]2 Sam. 23:24

of Dodo of Bethlehem, 27[1]Shammoth the
Harorite, [a]Helez the [2]Pelonite, 28[a]Ira the
son of Ikkesh the Tekoite, [b]Abiezer the
Anathothite, 29[1]Sibbechai the Hushathite,
[2]Ilai the Ahohite, 30[a]Maharai the Netophathite, [1]Heled the son of Baanah the Netophathite, 31[1]Ithai the son of Ribai of
Gibeah, of the sons of Benjamin, [a]Benaiah
the Pirathonite, 32[1]Hurai of the brooks of
Gaash, [2]Abiel the Arbathite, 33Azmaveth
the [1]Baharumite, Eliahba the Shaalbonite, 34the sons of [1]Hashem the Gizonite,
Jonathan the son of Shageh the Hararite,
35Ahiam the son of [1]Sacar the Hararite,
[2]Eliphal the son of [3]Ur, 36Hepher the Me-
cherathite, Ahijah the Pelonite, 37[1]Hezro
the Carmelite, [2]Naarai the son of Ezbai,
38Joel the brother of Nathan, Mibhar the
son of Hagri, 39Zelek the Ammonite, Naharai the [1]Berothite (the armorbearer of
Joab the son of Zeruiah), 40Ira the Ithrite,
Gareb the Ithrite, 41[a]Uriah the Hittite,
[1]Zabad the son of Ahlai, 42Adina the son of
Shiza the Reubenite (a chief of the Reubenites) and thirty with him, 43Hanan the
son of Maachah, Joshaphat the Mithnite,
44Uzzia the Ashterathite, Shama and Jeiel
the sons of Hotham the Aroerite, 45Jediael
the son of Shimri, and Joha his brother,
the Tizite, 46Eliel the Mahavite, Jeribai
and Joshaviah the sons of Elnaam, Ithmah
the Moabite, 47Eliel, Obed, and Jaasiel the
Mezobaite.

The Growth of David's Army

12 Now [a]these *were* the men who
came to David at [b]Ziklag while he
was still a fugitive from Saul the son of
Kish; and they *were* among the mighty
men, helpers in the war, 2armed with
bows, using both the right hand and [a]the
left in *hurling* stones and *shooting* arrows
with the bow. *They were* of Benjamin,
Saul's brethren.

3The chief *was* Ahiezer, then Joash, the
sons of [1]Shemaah the Gibeathite; Jeziel
and Pelet the sons of Azmaveth; Berachah, and Jehu the Anathothite; 4Ishma-
iah the Gibeonite, a mighty man among
the thirty, and over the thirty; Jeremiah,
Jahaziel, Johanan, and Jozabad the Gede-
rathite; 5Eluzai, Jerimoth, Bealiah, Shemariah, and Shephatiah the Haruphite;
6Elkanah, Jisshiah, Azarel, Joezer, and Ja-
shobeam, the Korahites; 7and Joelah and
Zebadiah the sons of Jeroham of Gedor.
8*Some* Gadites [1]joined David at the
stronghold in the wilderness, mighty men
of valor, men trained for battle, who could
handle shield and spear, whose faces *were
like* the faces of lions, and *were* [a]as swift
as gazelles on the mountains: 9Ezer the
first, Obadiah the second, Eliab the third,
10Mishmannah the fourth, Jeremiah the
fifth, 11Attai the sixth, Eliel the seventh,
12Johanan the eighth, Elzabad the ninth,
13Jeremiah the tenth, and Machbanai the
eleventh. 14These *were* from the sons of
Gad, captains of the army; the least was
over a hundred, and the greatest was over
a [a]thousand. 15These *are* the ones who
crossed the Jordan in the first month,
when it had overflowed all its [a]banks; and
they put to flight all *those* in the valleys,
to the east and to the west.

16Then some of the sons of Benjamin
and Judah came to David at the stronghold. 17And David went out [1]to meet
them, and answered and said to them, "If
you have come peaceably to me to help
me, my heart will be united with you; but
if to betray me to my enemies, since *there
is* no [2]wrong in my hands, may the God of
our fathers look and bring judgment."
18Then the Spirit [1]came upon [a]Amasai,
chief of the captains, *and he said:*

"*We are* yours, O David;
We *are* on your side, O son of
Jesse!
Peace, peace to you,
And peace to your helpers!
For your God helps you."

So David received them, and made them
captains of the troop.

19And *some* from Manasseh defected to
David [a]when he was going with the Philistines to battle against Saul; but they did
not help them, for the lords of the Philistines sent him away by agreement, saying,
[b]"He may defect to his master Saul *and
endanger* our heads." 20When he went to
Ziklag, those of Manasseh who defected to
him were Adnah, Jozabad, Jediael, Michael, Jozabad, Elihu, and Zillethai, captains
of the thousands who *were* from Manasseh. 21And they helped David against [a]the
bands *of raiders,* for they *were* all mighty
men of valor, and they were captains in
the army. 22For at *that* time they came to

27 [a] 1 Chr. 27:10 [1] *Shammah the Harodite,* 2 Sam. 23:25 [2] *Paltite,* 2 Sam. 23:26
28 [a] 1 Chr. 27:9 [b] 1 Chr. 27:12
29 [1] *Mebunnai,* 2 Sam. 23:27 [2] *Zalmon,* 2 Sam. 23:28
30 [a] 1 Chr. 27:13 [1] *Heleb,* 2 Sam. 23:29, or *Heldai,* 1 Chr. 27:15
31 [a] 1 Chr. 27:14 [1] *Ittai,* 2 Sam. 23:29
32 [1] *Hiddai,* 2 Sam. 23:30 [2] *Abi-Albon,* 2 Sam. 23:31
33 [1] *Barhumite,* 2 Sam. 23:31
34 [1] *Jashen,* 2 Sam. 23:32
35 [1] *Sharar,* 2 Sam. 23:33 [2] *Eliphelet,* 2 Sam. 23:34 [3] *Ahasbai,* 2 Sam. 23:34
37 [1] *Hezrai,* 2 Sam. 23:38 [2] *Paarai the Arbite,* 2 Sam. 23:35
39 [1] *Berothite,* 2 Sam. 23:37
41 [a] 2 Sam. 11 [1] The last sixteen are not added in 2 Sam. 23.

CHAPTER 12
1 [a] 1 Sam. 27:2 [b] 1 Sam. 27:6
2 [a] Judg. 3:15; 20:16
3 [1] Or *Hasmaah*
8 [a] 2 Sam. 2:18 [1] Lit. *separated themselves to*
14 [a] 1 Sam. 18:13
15 [a] Josh. 3:15; 4:18, 19
17 [1] Lit. *before them* [2] Lit. *violence*
18 [a] 2 Sam. 17:25 [1] Lit. *clothed*

19 [a] 1 Sam. 29:2 [b] 1 Sam. 29:4 **21** [a] 1 Sam. 30:1, 9, 10

David day by day to help him, until *it was*
a great army, [a]like the army of God.

David's Army at Hebron

[23]Now these *were* the numbers of the
[1]divisions *that were* equipped for war, *and*
[a]came to David at [b]Hebron to [c]turn *over*
the kingdom of Saul to him, [d]according to
the word of the LORD: [24]of the sons of Judah bearing shield and spear, six thousand
eight hundred [1]armed for war; [25]of the
sons of Simeon, mighty men of valor fit
for war, seven thousand one hundred; [26]of
the sons of Levi four thousand six hundred; [27]Jehoiada, the leader of the Aaronites, and with him three thousand seven
hundred; [28][a]Zadok, a young man, a valiant warrior, and from his father's house
twenty-two captains; [29]of the sons of Benjamin, relatives of Saul, three thousand
(until then [a]the greatest part of them had
remained loyal to the house of Saul); [30]of
the sons of Ephraim twenty thousand
eight hundred, mighty men of valor, [1]fa-
mous men throughout their father's
house; [31]of the half-tribe of Manasseh
eighteen thousand, who were designated
by name to come and make David king;
[32]❦ of the sons of Issachar [a]who had understanding of the times, to know what
Israel ought to do, their chiefs were two
hundred; and all their brethren were at
their command; ❦ [33]of Zebulun there
were fifty thousand who went out to battle, expert in war with all weapons of war,
[a]stouthearted men who could keep ranks;
[34]of Naphtali one thousand captains, and
with them thirty-seven thousand with
shield and spear; [35]of the Danites who
could keep battle formation, twenty-eight
thousand six hundred; [36]of Asher, those
who could go out to war, able to keep battle formation, forty thousand; [37]of the
Reubenites and the Gadites and the half-
tribe of Manasseh, from the other side of
the Jordan, one hundred and twenty thousand armed for battle with every *kind* of
weapon of war.

Father, may ____ be as
the sons of Issachar and have
understanding of the times.

FROM 1 CHRONICLES 12:32

[38]All these men of war, who could keep
ranks, came to Hebron with a loyal heart,
to make David king over all Israel; and all
the rest of Israel *were* of [a]one mind to
make David king. [39]And they were there
with David three days, eating and drinking, for their brethren had prepared for
them. [40]Moreover those who were near to
them, from as far away as Issachar and
Zebulun and Naphtali, were bringing food
on donkeys and camels, on mules and
oxen—provisions of flour and cakes of
figs and cakes of raisins, wine and oil and
oxen and sheep abundantly, for *there was*
joy in Israel.

The Ark Brought from Kirjath Jearim

13 Then David consulted with the
[a]captains of thousands and hundreds, *and* with every leader. [2]And David
said to all the assembly of Israel, "If *it*
seems good to you, and if it is of the LORD
our God, let us send out to our brethren
everywhere *who are* [a]left in all the land of
Israel, and with them to the priests and
Levites *who are* in their cities *and* their
common-lands, that they may gather together to us; [3]and let us bring the ark of
our God back to us, [a]for we have not inquired at it since the days of Saul." [4]Then
all the assembly said that they would do
so, for the thing was right in the eyes of
all the people.

[5]So [a]David gathered all Israel together,
from [b]Shihor in Egypt to as far as the entrance of Hamath, to bring the ark of God
[c]from Kirjath Jearim. [6]And David and all
Israel went up to [a]Baalah,[1] to Kirjath Jearim, which belonged to Judah, to bring up
from there the ark of God the LORD, [b]who
dwells *between* the cherubim, where *His*
name is proclaimed. [7]So they [1]carried the
ark of God [a]on a new cart [b]from the house
of Abinadab, and Uzza and Ahio drove the
cart. [8]Then [a]David and all Israel played
music before God with all *their* might,
with [1]singing, on harps, on stringed instruments, on tambourines, on cymbals,
and with trumpets.

[9]And when they came to [1]Chidon's
threshing floor, Uzza put out his hand
to hold the ark, for the oxen [2]stumbled.
[10]Then the anger of the LORD was aroused
against Uzza, and He struck him [a]because
he put his hand to the ark; and he [b]died
there before God. [11]And David became angry because of the LORD's outbreak

---

22 a Josh. 5:13–15
23 a 2 Sam. 2:1–4 b 1 Chr. 11:1 c 1 Chr. 10:14 d 1 Sam. 16:1–4 *1* Lit. *heads of those*
24 *1 equipped*
28 a 2 Sam. 8:17
29 a 2 Sam. 2:8, 9
30 *1* Lit. *men of names*
32 a Esth. 1:13
33 a Ps. 12:2
38 a 2 Chr. 30:12

CHAPTER 13
1 a 1 Chr. 11:15; 12:34
2 a Is. 37:4
3 a 1 Sam. 7:1, 2
5 a 1 Sam. 7:5 b Josh. 13:3 c 1 Sam. 6:21; 7:1, 2
6 a Josh. 15:9, 60 b Ex. 25:22 *1 Baale Judah,* 2 Sam. 6:2
7 a 1 Sam. 6:7 b 1 Sam. 7:1 *1* Lit. *caused the ark of God to ride*
8 a 2 Sam. 6:5 *1 songs*
9 *1 Nachon,* 2 Sam. 6:6 *2* Or *let it go off*
10 a [Num. 4:15] b Lev. 10:2

1 Chronicles 12:32

Dear Woman of Destiny,

The children of Issachar, who were able to discern the times in which they lived, had the right perspective on those times and could see where they fit into God's plan. Because of this, they knew what Israel ought to do.

What was true back then is true today. In order to know what to do, we must be discerners of the times in which we are living. God's plan for humankind, from beginning to end, has been carefully laid out for us in Scripture. He describes in great detail what will take place in the earth from now until Jesus' return—and even on into eternity. If we study the Scriptures, we can find descriptions of future events involving Israel, the church, and the rest of the world. From these descriptions, we can figure out approximately where we are in God's timetable. This knowledge gives us a tremendous advantage, because it enables us to get prepared for what's coming and gives us directions as to what to do. In other words, we can know what to do and when to do it.

We want to be discerners of the times, not only of God's plan for the world, but in our own lives as well. Sometimes we understand the plan, but are "off" on the timing, which can be tragic.

Abraham is a prime example of someone who understood the plan, but who tried to hurry the plan along, ahead of God's timing. He took matters into his own hands and the result was Ishmael, who was not the son of God's promise. God had promised him a son through Sarah, but he was not willing to wait.

Jesus was acutely aware that God had appointed specific times for events to occur in His life. And Jesus purposed to stay on God's timetable, as is evidenced by His saying in John 7:6, "My time has not yet come . . ." and again in verse 8, "You go up to this feast. I am not yet going up to this feast, for My time has not yet fully come."

As women of destiny, isn't it exciting to know that we all have a race to run, a course to finish, and a manifest destiny ahead for us in Christ? God has a plan and a purpose for each of us, and He has uniquely equipped each of us for the race we're to run. But we must stay on course and understand God's timing. To do this we must know His Word and hear His voice. This takes study, prayer, and meditation. I urge you to set aside time every single day to hear from God. Nothing is more important.

And as the end of your time on earth draws near, whenever that may be, won't it be exciting to be able to say as Paul did, "I have fought the good fight, I have finished the race, I have kept the faith"? (2 Tim. 4:7).

God bless you as you embark on this most exciting and important journey. May you, like the children of Issachar, be discerners of the times, knowing what you are to do and when you are to do it!

Dana Sherrard

against Uzza; therefore that place is called [1]Perez Uzza to this day. [12]David was afraid of God that day, saying, "How can I bring the ark of God to me?"

[13]So David would not move the ark with him into the City of David, but took it aside into the house of Obed-Edom the Gittite. [14][a]The ark of God remained with the family of Obed-Edom in his house three months. And the LORD blessed [b]the house of Obed-Edom and all that he had.

David Established at Jerusalem

14 Now [a]Hiram king of Tyre sent messengers to David, and cedar trees, with masons and carpenters, to build him a house. [2]So David knew that the LORD had established him as king over Israel, for his kingdom was [a]highly exalted for the sake of His people Israel.

[3]Then David took more wives in Jerusalem, and David begot more sons and daughters. [4]And [a]these are the names of his children whom he had in Jerusalem: [1]Shammua, Shobab, Nathan, Solomon, [5]Ibhar, [1]Elishua, [2]Elpelet, [6]Nogah, Nepheg, Japhia, [7]Elishama, [1]Beeliada, and Eliphelet.

The Philistines Defeated

[8]Now when the Philistines heard that [a]David had been anointed king over all Israel, all the Philistines went up to search for David. And David heard *of it* and went out against them. [9]Then the Philistines went and made a raid [a]on the Valley of [1]Rephaim. [10]And David [a]inquired of God, saying, "Shall I go up against the Philistines? Will You deliver them into my hand?"

The LORD said to him, "Go up, for I will deliver them into your hand."

[11]So they went up to Baal Perazim, and David defeated them there. Then David said, "God has broken through my enemies by my hand like a breakthrough of water." Therefore they called the name of that place [1]Baal Perazim. [12]And when they left their gods there, David gave a commandment, and they were burned with fire.

[13][a]Then the Philistines once again made a raid on the valley. [14]Therefore David inquired again of God, and God said to him, "You shall not go up after them; circle around them, [a]and come upon them in front of the mulberry trees. [15]And it shall be, when you hear a sound of marching in the tops of the mulberry trees, then you shall go out to battle, for God has gone out before you to strike the camp of the Philistines." [16]So David did as God commanded him, and they drove back the army of the Philistines from [1]Gibeon as far as Gezer. [17]Then [a]the fame of David went out into all lands, and the LORD [b]brought the fear of him upon all nations.

The Ark Brought to Jerusalem

15 *David* built houses for himself in the City of David; and he prepared a place for the ark of God, [a]and pitched a tent for it. [2]Then David said, "No one may carry the [a]ark of God but the Levites, for [b]the LORD has chosen them to carry the ark of God and to minister before Him forever." [3]And David [a]gathered all Israel together at Jerusalem, to bring up the ark of the LORD to its place, which he had prepared for it. [4]Then David assembled the children of Aaron and the Levites: [5]of the sons of Kohath, Uriel the chief, and one hundred and twenty of his [1]brethren; [6]of the sons of Merari, Asaiah the chief, and two hundred and twenty of his brethren; [7]of the sons of Gershom, Joel the chief, and one hundred and thirty of his brethren; [8]of the sons of [a]Elizaphan, Shemaiah the chief, and two hundred of his brethren; [9]of the sons of [a]Hebron, Eliel the chief, and eighty of his brethren; [10]of the sons of Uzziel, Amminadab the chief, and one hundred and twelve of his brethren.

[11]And David called for [a]Zadok and [b]Abiathar the priests, and for the Levites: for Uriel, Asaiah, Joel, Shemaiah, Eliel, and Amminadab. [12]He said to them, "You *are* the heads of the fathers' *houses* of the Levites; [1]sanctify yourselves, you and your brethren, that you may bring up the ark of the LORD God of Israel to *the place* I have prepared for it. [13]For [a]because you *did* not *do it* the first *time,* [b]the LORD our God broke out against us, because we did not consult Him [1]about the proper order."

[14]So the priests and the Levites [1]sanctified themselves to bring up the ark of the LORD God of Israel. [15]And the children of

---

11 [1] Lit. *Outburst Against Uzza*
14 [a] 2 Sam. 6:11 [b] 1 Chr. 26:4–8

CHAPTER 14
1 [a] 2 Sam. 5:11
2 [a] Num. 24:7
4 [a] 1 Chr. 3:5–8 [1] *Shimea,* 1 Chr. 3:5
5 [1] *Elishama,* 1 Chr. 3:6 [2] *Eliphelet,* 1 Chr. 3:6
7 [1] *Eliada,* 2 Sam. 5:6; 1 Chr. 3:8
8 [a] 2 Sam. 5:17–21
9 [a] 1 Chr. 11:15; 14:13 [1] Lit. *Giants*
10 [a] 1 Sam. 23:2, 4; 30:8
11 [1] Lit. *Master of Breakthroughs*
13 [a] 2 Sam. 5:22–25
14 [a] 2 Sam. 5:23
16 [1] *Geba,* 2 Sam. 5:25
17 [a] Josh. 6:27 [b] [Deut. 2:25; 11:25]

CHAPTER 15
1 [a] 1 Chr. 16:1
2 [a] [Num. 4:15] [b] Deut. 10:8; 31:9
3 [a] 1 Kin. 8:1
5 [1] *kinsmen*
8 [a] Ex. 6:22
9 [a] Ex. 6:18
11 [a] 1 Chr. 12:28 [b] 1 Kin. 2:22, 26, 27
12 [1] *consecrate*
13 [a] 2 Sam. 6:3 [b] 1 Chr. 13:7–11 [1] *regarding the ordinance*
14 [1] *consecrated*

the Levites bore the ark of God on their
shoulders, by its poles, as [a]Moses had
commanded according to the word of the
LORD.
16Then David spoke to the leaders of the
Levites to appoint their brethren *to be* the
singers accompanied by instruments of
music, stringed instruments, harps, and
cymbals, by raising the voice with resounding joy. 17So the Levites appointed
[a]Heman the son of Joel; and of his brethren, [b]Asaph the son of Berechiah; and of
their brethren, the sons of Merari, [c]Ethan
the son of Kushaiah; 18and with them
their brethren of the second *rank:* Zechariah, [1]Ben, Jaaziel, Shemiramoth, Jehiel,
Unni, Eliab, Benaiah, Maaseiah, Mattithiah, Elipheleh, Mikneiah, Obed-Edom, and
Jeiel, the gatekeepers; 19the singers, Heman, Asaph, and Ethan, *were* to sound the
cymbals of bronze; 20Zechariah, [1]Aziel,
Shemiramoth, Jehiel, Unni, Eliab, Maaseiah, and Benaiah, with strings according
to [a]Alamoth; 21Mattithiah, Elipheleh,
Mikneiah, Obed-Edom, Jeiel, and Azaziah, to direct with harps on the [a]Shemi-
nith; 22Chenaniah, leader of the Levites,
was instructor *in charge of* the music, because he *was* skillful; 23Berechiah and Elkanah *were* doorkeepers for the ark;
24Shebaniah, Joshaphat, Nethanel, Amasai, Zechariah, Benaiah, and Eliezer, the
priests, [a]were to blow the trumpets before
the ark of God; and [b]Obed-Edom and Je-
hiah, doorkeepers for the ark.
25So [a]David, the elders of Israel, and the
captains over thousands went to bring up
the ark of the covenant of the LORD from
the house of Obed-Edom with joy. 26And
so it was, when God helped the Levites
who bore the ark of the covenant of the
LORD, that they offered seven bulls and
seven rams. 27David was clothed with a
robe of fine [a]linen, as were all the Levites
who bore the ark, the singers, and Chenaniah the music master *with* the singers.
David also wore a linen ephod. 28[a]Thus all
Israel brought up the ark of the covenant
of the LORD with shouting and with the
sound of the horn, with trumpets and
with cymbals, making music with
stringed instruments and harps.
29And it happened, [a]*as* the ark of the
covenant of the LORD came to the City
of David, that Michal, Saul's daughter,
looked through a window and saw King
David whirling and playing music; and
she despised him in her heart.

The Ark Placed in the Tabernacle

16 So [a]they brought the ark of God,
and set it in the midst of the tabernacle that David had erected for it. Then
they offered burnt offerings and peace offerings before God. 2And when David had
finished offering the burnt offerings and
the peace offerings, [a]he blessed the people
in the name of the LORD. 3Then he distributed to everyone of Israel, both man and
woman, to everyone a loaf of bread, a
piece *of meat,* and a cake of raisins.
4And he appointed some of the Levites
to minister before the ark of the LORD, to
[a]commemorate, to thank, and to praise
the LORD God of Israel: 5Asaph the chief,
and next to him Zechariah, *then* [a]Jeiel,
Shemiramoth, Jehiel, Mattithiah, Eliab,
Benaiah, and Obed-Edom: Jeiel with
stringed instruments and harps, but
Asaph made music with cymbals; 6Bena-
iah and Jahaziel the priests regularly *blew*
the trumpets before the ark of the covenant of God.

Lord, may ____ seek You and Your strength. May they seek Your face forever.

FROM 1 CHRONICLES 16:11

David's Song of Thanksgiving

7On that day [a]David [b]first delivered *this*
psalm into the hand of Asaph and his
brethren, to thank the LORD:

8 [a]Oh, give thanks to the LORD!
Call upon His name;
Make known His deeds among the
peoples!
9 Sing to Him, sing psalms to Him;
Talk of all His wondrous works!
10 Glory in His holy name;
Let the hearts of those rejoice who
seek the LORD!
11 Seek the LORD and His strength;
Seek His face evermore!
12 Remember His marvelous works
which He has done,
His wonders, and the judgments of
His mouth,
13 O seed of Israel His servant,

15 [a]Ex. 25:14
17 [a]1 Chr. 6:33; 25:1 [b]1 Chr. 6:39 [c]1 Chr. 6:44
18 [1]So with MT, Vg.; LXX omits *Ben*
20 [a]Ps. 46:title [1]*Jaaziel,* v. 18
21 [a]Ps. 6:title
24 [a][Num. 10:8] [b]1 Chr. 13:13, 14
25 [a]1 Kin. 8:1
27 [a]1 Sam. 2:18, 28
28 [a]1 Chr. 13:8
29 [a]2 Sam. 3:13, 14; 6:16, 20–23
CHAPTER 16
1 [a]2 Sam. 6:17
2 [a]1 Kin. 8:14
4 [a]Ps. 38:title; 70:title
5 [a]1 Chr. 15:18
7 [a]2 Sam. 22:1; 23:1 [b]Ps. 105:1–15
8 [a]Ps. 105:1–15

You children of Jacob, His chosen
ones!

14 He *is* the LORD our God;
His [a]judgments *are* in all the earth.
15 Remember His covenant forever,
The word which He commanded,
for a thousand generations,
16 *The* [a]*covenant which* He made
with Abraham,
And His oath to Isaac,
17 And [a]confirmed it to [b]Jacob for a
statute,
To Israel *for* an everlasting
covenant,
18 Saying, "To you I will give the
land of Canaan
As the allotment of your
inheritance,"
19 When you were [a]few in number,
Indeed very few, and strangers in it.
20 When they went from one nation
to another,
And from *one* kingdom to another
people,
21 He permitted no man to do them
wrong;
Yes, He [a]rebuked kings for their
sakes,
22 *Saying,* [a]"Do not touch My
anointed ones,
And do My prophets no harm."
23 [a] Sing to the LORD, all the earth;
Proclaim the good news of His
salvation from day to day.
24 Declare His glory among the
nations,
His wonders among all peoples.
25 For the LORD *is* great and greatly
to be praised;
He *is* also to be feared above all
gods.
26 For all the gods [a]of the peoples
are [1]idols,
But the LORD made the heavens.
27 Honor and majesty *are* before
Him;
Strength and gladness are in His
place.
28 Give to the LORD, O families of
the peoples,
Give to the LORD glory and
strength.
29 Give to the LORD the glory *due*
His name;
Bring an offering, and come before
Him.
Oh, worship the LORD in the beauty
of holiness!
30 Tremble before Him, all the earth.
The world also is firmly established,
It shall not be moved.

31 Let the heavens rejoice, and let
the earth be glad;
And let them say among the
nations, "The LORD reigns."
32 Let the sea roar, and all its
fullness;
Let the field rejoice, and all that *is*
in it.
33 Then the [a]trees of the woods shall
rejoice before the LORD,
For He is [b]coming to judge the
earth.

34 [a]Oh, give thanks to the LORD, for
He is good!
For His mercy *endures* forever.
35 [a]And say, "Save us, O God of our
salvation;
Gather us together, and deliver us
from the Gentiles,
To give thanks to Your holy name,
To triumph in Your praise."
36 [a]Blessed *be* the LORD God of Israel
From everlasting to everlasting!

And all [b]the people said, "Amen!" and
praised the LORD.

Regular Worship Maintained

37So he left [a]Asaph and his brothers
there before the ark of the covenant of the
LORD to minister before the ark regularly,
as every day's work [b]required; 38and
[a]Obed-Edom with his sixty-eight brethren, including Obed-Edom the son of Jeduthun, and Hosah, *to be* gatekeepers;
39and Zadok the priest and his brethren
the priests, [a]before the tabernacle of the
LORD [b]at the [1]high place that *was* at Gibeon, 40to offer burnt offerings to the LORD
on the altar of burnt offering regularly
[a]morning and evening, and *to do* according to all that is written in the Law of the
LORD which He commanded Israel; 41and
with them Heman and Jeduthun and the
rest who were chosen, who were designated by name, to give thanks to the LORD,
[a]because His mercy *endures* forever;
42and with them Heman and Jeduthun, to
sound aloud with trumpets and cymbals
and the musical instruments of God. Now
the sons of Jeduthun *were* gatekeepers.

14 a [Is. 26:9]
16 a Gen. 17:2; 26:3; 28:13; 35:11
17 a Gen. 35:11, 12 b Gen. 28:10–15
19 a Gen. 34:30
21 a Gen. 12:17; 20:3
22 a Gen. 20:7
23 a Ps. 96:1–13
26 a Lev. 19:4 *1 worthless things*
33 a Is. 55:12, 13 b [Matt. 25:31–46]
34 a Ps. 106:1; 107:1; 118:1; 136:1
35 a Ps. 106:47, 48
36 a 1 Kin. 8:15, 56 b Deut. 27:15
37 a 1 Chr. 16:4, 5 b Ezra 3:4
38 a 1 Chr. 13:14
39 a 2 Chr. 1:3 b 1 Kin. 3:4 *1 Place for pagan worship*
40 a [Ex. 29:38–42]
41 a 2 Chr. 5:13; 7:3

1 Chronicles 16:23, 24

Dear Woman of Destiny,

As much as I enjoy Linda Strom's teaching, I love her gift for evangelism even more. For Linda, sharing Jesus is as natural as breathing. She never forgets, she never gets sidetracked, she never gets tired of sharing the love of God.

That's the way I want to be; but often busyness, weariness, or fear of rejection gets in the way. About a year ago, a friend was experiencing some difficulties in her marriage. I commiserated with her, offered sympathetic advice, and walked away. I felt her frustration and hopelessness. Later that day I began to pray for her when the Lord gently chided me. *Why didn't you tell her about Me?*

We often listen to people's pain, frustration, and anger, yet we never give them an understanding of who God is and what He wants to do in our lives. As I reflected on my conversation with my friend, I realized that I had not shared anything with her that would meet her need. I knew the One who was the answer to her problem and had failed to share Him.

As cohost of *The 700 Club*, I have the incredible privilege of sharing the love of God and His plan for our salvation with millions of people every single day. That privilege is awesome, and I do not take it for granted. But I lost the burden and urgency for the souls of people around me—the burden that kept me praying and waiting for God to open an opportunity. I've asked the Lord to rekindle that burden in me for my neighbors, my children's friends, the clerks, the service people, and others God brings my way.

The hardest situation we encounter in sharing our faith occurs when we desperately want to see someone in our family come to a saving knowledge of Jesus. It requires wisdom and perseverance.

I've learned from experience that people are more often won by the consistency of our lifestyles than by our theological expounding. Sometimes God opens opportunities immediately. Usually, however, we earn the right to speak candidly only after investing ourselves in relationships with genuine caring and sincere interest.

If you've been sharing and getting nowhere, be still—pray! The Spirit of God woos the heart, preparing it to hear and receive the great good news. Therefore, pray without ceasing; and beseech the Holy Spirit to touch the hearts of your family, your neighbors, your friends. "Now may the God of peace who brought up our Lord Jesus from the dead, that great Shepherd of the sheep, through the blood of the everlasting covenant, make you complete in every good work to do His will, working in you what is well pleasing in His sight, through Jesus Christ, to whom be glory forever and ever. Amen" (Heb. 13:20, 21).

Lord, my heart is burdened for my family and friends. I pray that my life will reflect Your goodness and love. And when I am able to speak of You, let my voice be gentle and my attitude winsome. Give me Your heart for the lost.

Terry Meeuwsen

43aThen all the people departed, every
man to his house; and David returned to
bless his house.

God's Covenant with David

17 Now ait came to pass, when David
was dwelling in his house, that David said to Nathan the prophet, "See now,
I dwell in a house of cedar, but the ark of
the covenant of the LORD *is* under tent
curtains."
2Then Nathan said to David, "Do all
that *is* in your heart, for God *is* with you."
3But it happened that night that the
word of God came to Nathan, saying, 4"Go
and tell My servant David, 'Thus says the
LORD: "You shall anot build Me a house to
dwell in. 5For I have not dwelt in a house
since the time that I brought up Israel,
even to this day, but have gone from tent
to tent, and from *one* tabernacle *to another.* 6Wherever I have moved about with all
Israel, have I ever spoken a word to any of
the judges of Israel, whom I commanded
to shepherd My people, saying, 'Why have
you not built Me a house of cedar?' " '
7Now therefore, thus shall you say to My
servant David, 'Thus says the LORD of
hosts: "I took you afrom the sheepfold,
from following the sheep, to be *1*ruler
over My people Israel. 8And I have been
with you wherever you have gone, and
have cut off all your enemies from before
you, and have *1*made you a name like the
name of the great men who *are* on the
earth. 9Moreover I will appoint a place for
My people Israel, and will aplant them,
that they may dwell in a place of their own
and move no more; nor shall the sons
of wickedness oppress them anymore, as
previously, 10since the time that I commanded judges *to be* over My people Israel. Also I will subdue all your enemies.
Furthermore I tell you that the LORD will
build you a *1*house. 11And it shall be, when
your days are afulfilled, when you must
1go to be with your fathers, that I will set
up your bseed after you, who will be of
your sons; and I will establish his kingdom. 12aHe shall build Me a house, and I
will establish his throne forever. 13aI will
be his Father, and he shall be My son; and
I will not take My mercy away from him,
bas I took *it* from *him* who was before you.
14And aI will establish him in My house
and in My kingdom forever; and his
throne shall be established forever." ' "

15According to all these words and according to all this vision, so Nathan spoke
to David.

For God reigns in the hearts of His servants; there is His kingdom. The power of grace hath subdued all His enemies; there is His power. They serve Him night and day, and give Him thanks and praise; that is His glory.

JEREMY TAYLOR

16aThen King David went in and sat before the LORD; and he said: "Who *am* I,
O LORD God? And what is my house, that
You have brought me this far? 17And *yet*
this was a small thing in Your sight,
O God; and You have *also* spoken of Your
servant's house for a great while to come,
and have regarded me according to the
rank of a man of high degree, O LORD
God. 18What more can David *say* to You
for the honor of Your servant? For You
know Your servant. 19O LORD, for Your
servant's sake, and according to Your own
heart, You have done all this greatness,
in making known all these great things.
20O LORD, *there is* none like You, nor *is
there any* God besides You, according to
all that we have heard with our ears.
21aAnd who *is* like Your people Israel, the
one nation on the earth whom God went
to redeem for Himself *as* a people—to
make for Yourself a name by great and
awesome deeds, by driving out nations
from before Your people whom You redeemed from Egypt? 22For You have made
Your people Israel Your very own people
forever; and You, LORD, have become their
God.
23"And now, O LORD, the word which
You have spoken concerning Your servant
and concerning his house, *let it* be established forever, and do as You have said.
24So let it be established, that Your name
may be magnified forever, saying, 'The
LORD of hosts, the God of Israel, *is* Israel's
God.' And let the house of Your servant

43 a 2 Sam. 6:18–20

CHAPTER 17
1 a 2 Sam. 7:1
4 a [1 Chr. 28:2, 3]
7 a 1 Sam. 16:11–13 *1 leader*
8 *1 given you prestige*
9 a Amos 9:14
10 *1 Royal dynasty*
11 a 1 Kin. 2:10 b [1 Chr. 22:9–13; 28:20] *1 Die and join your ancestors*
12 a [Ps. 89:20–37]
13 a Heb. 1:5 b [1 Sam. 15:23–28]
14 a [Luke 1:31–33]
16 a 2 Sam. 7:18
21 a Ps. 147:20

David be established before You. 25For You, O my God, [1]have revealed to Your servant that You will build him a house. Therefore Your servant has found it *in his heart* to pray before You. 26And now, LORD, [1]You are God, and have promised this goodness to Your servant. 27Now You have been pleased to bless the house of Your servant, that it may continue before You forever; for You have blessed it, O LORD, and *it shall be* blessed forever."

David's Further Conquests

18 After this [a]it came to pass that David [1]attacked the Philistines, subdued them, and took Gath and its towns from the hand of the Philistines. 2Then he [1]defeated [a]Moab, and the Moabites became David's [b]servants, *and* brought tribute.

3And [a]David [1]defeated [2]Hadadezer king of Zobah *as far as* Hamath, as he went to establish his power by the River Euphrates. 4David took from him one thousand chariots, [1]seven thousand horsemen, and twenty thousand foot soldiers. Also David [2]hamstrung all the chariot *horses,* except that he spared enough of them for one hundred chariots.

5When the [a]Syrians of Damascus came to help Hadadezer king of Zobah, David killed twenty-two thousand of the Syrians. 6Then David put *garrisons* in Syria of Damascus; and the Syrians became David's servants, *and* brought tribute. So the LORD preserved David wherever he went. 7And David took the shields of gold that were on the servants of Hadadezer, and brought them to Jerusalem. 8Also from [1]Tibhath and from [2]Chun, cities of [3]Hadadezer, David brought a large amount of [a]bronze, with which [b]Solomon made the bronze [4]Sea, the pillars, and the articles of bronze.

9Now when [1]Tou king of Hamath heard that David had [2]defeated all the army of Hadadezer king of Zobah, 10he sent [1]Hadoram his son to King David, to greet him and bless him, because he had fought against Hadadezer and [2]defeated him (for Hadadezer had been at war with Tou); and *Hadoram brought with him* all kinds of [a]articles of gold, silver, and bronze. 11King David also dedicated these to the LORD, along with the silver and gold that he had brought from all *these* nations—from Edom, from Moab, from the [a]people of Ammon, from the [b]Philistines, and from [c]Amalek.

12Moreover [a]Abishai the son of Zeruiah killed [b]eighteen thousand [1]Edomites in the Valley of Salt. 13[a]He also put garrisons in Edom, and all the Edomites became David's servants. And the LORD preserved David wherever he went.

David's Administration

14So David reigned over all Israel, and administered judgment and justice to all his people. 15Joab the son of Zeruiah *was* over the army; Jehoshaphat the son of Ahilud *was* recorder; 16Zadok the son of Ahitub and [1]Abimelech the son of Abiathar *were* the priests; [2]Shavsha *was* the scribe; 17[a]Benaiah the son of Jehoiada *was* over the Cherethites and the Pelethites; and David's sons *were* [1]chief ministers at the king's side.

The Ammonites and Syrians Defeated

19 It[a] happened after this that Nahash the king of the people of Ammon died, and his son reigned in his place. 2Then David said, "I will show kindness to Hanun the son of Nahash, because his father showed kindness to me." So David sent messengers to comfort him concerning his father. And David's servants came to Hanun in the land of the people of Ammon to comfort him.

3And the princes of the people of Ammon said to Hanun, [1]"Do you think that David really honors your father because he has sent comforters to you? Did his servants not come to you to search and to overthrow and to spy out the land?"

4Therefore Hanun took David's servants, shaved them, and cut off their garments [1]in the middle, at their [a]buttocks, and sent them away. 5Then *some* went and told David about the men; and he sent to meet them, because the men were greatly ashamed. And the king said, "Wait at Jericho until your beards have grown, and *then* return."

6When the people of Ammon saw that they had made themselves repulsive to David, Hanun and the people of Ammon sent a thousand talents of silver to hire for

25 [1] Lit. *have uncovered the ear of*
26 [1] Or *You alone are*

CHAPTER 18
1 [a] 2 Sam. 8:1–18 [1] Lit. *struck*
2 [a] 2 Sam. 8:2 [b] Ps. 60:8 [1] Lit. *struck*
3 [a] 2 Sam. 8:3 [1] Lit. *struck* [2] Heb. *Hadarezer*
4 [1] *seven hundred,* 2 Sam. 8:4 [2] *crippled*
5 [a] 2 Sam. 8:5, 6
8 [a] 2 Sam. 8:8 [b] 1 Kin. 7:15, 23 [1] *Betah,* 2 Sam. 8:8 [2] *Berothai,* 2 Sam. 8:8 [3] Heb. *Hadarezer* [4] Great laver or basin
9 [1] *Toi,* 2 Sam. 8:9, 10 [2] Lit. *struck*
10 [a] 2 Sam. 8:10–12 [1] *Joram,* 2 Sam. 8:10 [2] Lit. *struck*
11 [a] 2 Sam. 10:14 [b] 2 Sam. 5:17–25 [c] 2 Sam. 1:1
12 [a] 2 Sam. 23:18 [b] 2 Sam. 8:13 [1] *Syrians,* 2 Sam. 8:13
13 [a] 2 Sam. 8:14
16 [1] *Ahimelech,* 2 Sam. 8:17 [2] *Seraiah,* 2 Sam. 8:17, or *Shisha,* 1 Kin. 4:3
17 [a] 2 Sam. 8:18 [1] Lit. *at the hand of the king*

CHAPTER 19
1 [a] 2 Sam. 10:1–19
3 [1] Lit. *In your eyes is David honoring your father because*

4 [a] Is. 20:4 [1] *in half*

themselves chariots and horsemen from [1]Mesopotamia, from Syrian Maacah, [a]and from [2]Zobah. 7So they hired for themselves thirty-two thousand chariots, with the king of Maacah and his people, who came and encamped before Medeba. Also the people of Ammon gathered together from their cities, and came to battle.

8Now when David heard *of it,* he sent Joab and all the army of the mighty men. 9Then the people of Ammon came out and put themselves in battle array before the gate of the city, and the kings who had come *were* by themselves in the field.

10When Joab saw that the battle line was against him before and behind, he chose some of Israel's best, and put *them* in battle array against the Syrians. 11And the rest of the people he put under the command of Abishai his brother, and they set *themselves* in battle array against the people of Ammon. 12Then he said, "If the Syrians are too strong for me, then you shall help me; but if the people of Ammon are too strong for you, then I will help you. 13Be of good courage, and let us be strong for our people and for the cities of our God. And may the LORD do *what is* good in His sight."

14So Joab and the people who *were* with him drew near for the battle against the Syrians, and they fled before him. 15When the people of Ammon saw that the Syrians were fleeing, they also fled before Abishai his brother, and entered the city. So Joab went to Jerusalem.

16Now when the Syrians saw that they had been defeated by Israel, they sent messengers and brought the Syrians who were beyond [1]the River, and [2]Shophach the commander of Hadadezer's army *went* before them. 17When it was told David, he gathered all Israel, crossed over the Jordan and came upon them, and set up in battle array against them. So when David had set up in *battle* array against the Syrians, they fought with him. 18Then the Syrians fled before Israel; and David killed [1]seven thousand charioteers and forty thousand [2]foot soldiers of the Syrians, and killed Shophach the commander of the army. 19And when the servants of Hadadezer saw that they were defeated by Israel, they made peace with David and became his servants. So the Syrians were not willing to help the people of Ammon anymore.

Rabbah Is Conquered

20 It[a] happened [1]in the spring of the year, at the time kings go out *to battle,* that Joab led out the armed forces and ravaged the country of the people of Ammon, and came and besieged Rabbah. But [b]David stayed at Jerusalem. And [c]Joab defeated Rabbah and overthrew it. 2Then David [a]took their king's crown from his head, and found it to weigh a talent of gold, and *there were* precious stones in it. And it was set on David's head. Also he brought out the [1]spoil of the city in great abundance. 3And he brought out the people who *were* in it, and [1]put *them* to work with saws, with iron picks, and with axes. So David did to all the cities of the people of Ammon. Then David and all the people returned *to* Jerusalem.

Philistine Giants Destroyed

4Now it happened afterward [a]that war broke out at [1]Gezer with the Philistines, at which time [b]Sibbechai the Hushathite killed [2]Sippai, *who was one* of the sons of [3]the giant. And they were subdued.

5Again there was war with the Philistines, and Elhanan the son of [1]Jair killed Lahmi the brother of Goliath the Gittite, the shaft of whose spear *was* like a weaver's [a]beam.

6Yet again [a]there was war at Gath, where there was a man of *great* stature, with twenty-four fingers and toes, six *on each hand* and six *on each foot;* and he also was born to [1]the giant. 7So when he defied Israel, Jonathan the son of [1]Shimea, David's brother, killed him.

8These were born to the giant in Gath, and they fell by the hand of David and by the hand of his servants.

The Census of Israel and Judah

21 Now [a]Satan stood up against Israel, and moved David to [1]number Israel. 2So David said to Joab and to the leaders of the people, "Go, number Israel from Beersheba to Dan, [a]and bring the number of them to me that I may know *it.*"

3And Joab answered, "May the LORD make His people a hundred times more than they are. But, my lord the king, *are* they not all my lord's servants? Why then does my lord require this thing? Why should he be a cause of guilt in Israel?"

---

6 a 1 Chr. 18:5, 9 *1* Heb. *Aram Naharaim* *2 Zoba,* 2 Sam. 10:6

16 *1* The Euphrates *2 Zoba,* 2 Sam. 10:6, or *Shobach,* 2 Sam. 10:16

18 *1 seven hundred,* 2 Sam. 10:18 *2 horsemen,* 2 Sam. 10:18

CHAPTER 20

1 a 2 Sam. 11:1 b 2 Sam. 11:2—12:25 c 2 Sam. 12:26 *1* Lit. *at the return of the year*

2 a 2 Sam. 12:30, 31 *1 plunder*

3 *1* LXX *cut them with*

4 a 2 Sam. 21:18 b 1 Chr. 11:29 *1 Gob,* 2 Sam. 21:18 *2 Saph,* 2 Sam. 21:18 *3* Or *Raphah*

5 a 1 Sam. 17:7 *1 Jaare-Oregim,* 2 Sam. 21:19

6 a 2 Sam. 21:20 *1* Or *Raphah*

7 *1 Shammah,* 1 Sam. 16:9 or *Shimeah,* 2 Sam. 21:21

CHAPTER 21

1 a 2 Sam. 24:1–25 *1 take a census of*

2 a 1 Chr. 27:23, 24

4Nevertheless the king's word prevailed
against Joab. Therefore Joab departed and
went throughout all Israel and came to
Jerusalem. 5Then Joab gave the sum of
the number of the people to David. All
Israel *had* one million one hundred thousand men who drew the sword, and Judah
had four hundred and seventy thousand
men who drew the sword. 6[a]But he did
not count Levi and Benjamin among
them, for the king's [1]word was abominable to Joab.

7And [1]God was displeased with this
thing; therefore He struck Israel. 8So David said to God, [a]"I have sinned greatly,
because I have done this thing; [b]but now,
I pray, take away the iniquity of Your servant, for I have done very foolishly."

9Then the LORD spoke to Gad, David's
[a]seer, saying, 10"Go and tell David, [a]say-
ing, 'Thus says the LORD: "I offer you three
things; choose one of them for yourself,
that I may do *it* to you." ' "

11So Gad came to David and said to
him, "Thus says the LORD: 'Choose for
yourself, 12[a]either [1]three years of famine,
or three months to be defeated by your
foes with the sword of your enemies over-
taking *you,* or else for three days the
sword of the LORD—the plague in the
land, with the [2]angel of the LORD destroying throughout all the territory of Israel.'
Now consider what answer I should take
back to Him who sent me."

13And David said to Gad, "I am in great
distress. Please let me fall into the hand of
the LORD, for His [a]mercies *are* very great;
but do not let me fall into the hand of
man."

Sometimes God teaches us more in ten minutes when we are lost to this world, than we would otherwise learn in months.

MARIA WOODWORTH-ETTER

14So the LORD sent a [a]plague upon Israel, and seventy thousand men of Israel
fell. 15And God sent [1]an [a]angel to Jerusalem to destroy it. As [2]he was destroying,
the LORD looked and [b]relented of the disaster, and said to the angel who was destroying, "It is enough; now restrain
[3]your hand." And the angel of the LORD
stood by the [c]threshing floor of [4]Ornan
the Jebusite.

16Then David lifted his eyes and [a]saw
the angel of the LORD standing between
earth and heaven, having in his hand a
drawn sword stretched out over Jerusalem. So David and the elders, clothed in
sackcloth, fell on their faces. 17And David
said to God, "Was it not I who commanded the people to be numbered? I am the
one who has sinned and done evil indeed;
but these [a]sheep, what have they done?
Let Your hand, I pray, O LORD my God, be
against me and my father's house, but not
against Your people that they should be
plagued."

18Therefore, the [a]angel of the LORD
commanded Gad to say to David that David should go and erect an altar to the
LORD on the threshing floor of Ornan the
Jebusite. 19So David went up at the word
of Gad, which he had spoken in the name
of the LORD. 20Now Ornan turned and saw
the angel; and his four sons *who were*
with him hid themselves, but Ornan continued threshing wheat. 21So David came
to Ornan, and Ornan looked and saw David. And he went out from the threshing
floor, and bowed before David with *his*
face to the ground. 22Then David said to
Ornan, [1]"Grant me the place of *this*
threshing floor, that I may build an altar
on it to the LORD. You shall grant it to me
at the full price, that the plague may be
withdrawn from the people."

23But Ornan said to David, "Take *it* to
yourself, and let my lord the king do *what*
is good in his eyes. Look, I *also* give *you*
the oxen for burnt offerings, the threshing implements for wood, and the wheat
for the grain offering; I give *it* all."

24Then King David said to Ornan, "No,
but I will surely buy *it* for the full price,
for I will not take what is yours for the
LORD, nor offer burnt offerings with *that*
which costs *me* nothing." 25So [a]David
gave Ornan six hundred shekels of gold by
weight for the place. 26And David built
there an altar to the LORD, and offered
burnt offerings and peace offerings, and
called on the LORD; and [a]He answered
him from heaven by fire on the altar of
burnt offering.

27So the LORD commanded the angel,
and he returned his sword to its sheath.

6 a 1 Chr. 27:24 *1 command*
7 *1 Lit. it was evil in the eyes of God*
8 a 2 Sam. 24:10 b 2 Sam. 12:13
9 a 1 Sam. 9:9
10 a 2 Sam. 24:12–14
12 a 2 Sam. 24:13 *1 seven,* 2 Sam. 24:13 *2 Or Angel,* and so throughout the chapter
13 a Ps. 51:1; 130:4, 7
14 a 1 Chr. 27:24
15 a 2 Sam. 24:16 b Gen. 6:6 c 2 Chr. 3:1 *1 Or the Angel* *2 Or He* *3 Or Your* *4 Araunah,* 2 Sam. 24:16, 18–24
16 a 2 Chr. 3:1
17 a 2 Sam. 7:8
18 a 2 Chr. 3:1
22 *1 Lit. Give*
25 a 2 Sam. 24:24
26 a Lev. 9:24

28At that time, when David saw that the
LORD had answered him on the threshing
floor of Ornan the Jebusite, he sacrificed
there. 29[a]For the tabernacle of the LORD
and the altar of the burnt offering, which
Moses had made in the wilderness, *were* at
that time at the high place in [b]Gibeon.
30But David could not go before it to inquire of God, for he was afraid of the
sword of the angel of the LORD.

David Prepares to Build the Temple

22 Then David said, [a]"This *is* the
house of the LORD God, and this *is*
the altar of burnt offering for Israel." 2So
David commanded to gather the [a]aliens
who *were* in the land of Israel; and he appointed masons to [b]cut hewn stones to
build the house of God. 3And David prepared iron in abundance for the nails of
the doors of the gates and for the joints,
and bronze in abundance [a]beyond measure, 4and cedar trees in abundance; for
the [a]Sidonians and those from Tyre
brought much cedar wood to David.
5Now David said, [a]"Solomon my son *is*
young and inexperienced, and the house
to be built for the LORD *must be* exceedingly magnificent, famous and glorious
throughout all countries. I will now make
preparation for it." So David made abundant preparations before his death.
6Then he called for his son Solomon,
and [1]charged him to build a house for the
LORD God of Israel. 7And David said to
Solomon: "My son, as for me, [a]it was in
my mind to build a house [b]to the name of
the LORD my God; 8but the word of the
LORD came to me, saying, [a]'You have shed
much blood and have made great wars;
you shall not build a house for My name,
because you have shed much blood on the
earth in My sight. 9[a]Behold, a son shall be
born to you, who shall be a man of rest;
and I will give him [b]rest from all his enemies all around. His name shall be [1]Sol-
omon, for I will give peace and quietness
to Israel in his days. 10[a]He shall build a
house for My name, and [b]he shall be My
son, and I *will be* his Father; and I will
establish the throne of his kingdom over
Israel forever.' 11Now, my son, may [a]the
LORD be with you; and may you prosper,
and build the house of the LORD your God,
as He has said to you. 12Only may the
LORD [a]give you wisdom and understanding, and give you charge concerning Israel, that you may keep the law of the LORD
your God. 13[a]Then you will prosper, if you
take care to fulfill the statutes and judgments with which the LORD [1]charged Moses concerning Israel. [b]Be strong and of
good courage; do not fear nor be dismayed. 14Indeed I have taken much trouble to prepare for the house of the LORD
one hundred thousand talents of gold and
one million talents of silver, and bronze
and iron [a]beyond measure, for it is so
abundant. I have prepared timber and
stone also, and you may add to them.
15Moreover *there are* workmen with you
in abundance: woodsmen and stonecutters, and all types of skillful men for
every kind of work. 16Of gold and silver
and bronze and iron *there is* no limit.
Arise and begin working, and [a]the LORD
be with you."
17David also commanded all the [a]lead-
ers of Israel to help Solomon his son, *saying,* 18"*Is* not the LORD your God with
you? [a]And has He *not* given you rest on
every side? For He has given the inhabitants of the land into my hand, and the
land is subdued before the LORD and before His people. 19Now set your heart and
your soul to seek the LORD your God.
Therefore arise and build the sanctuary of
the LORD God, to [a]bring the ark of the
covenant of the LORD and the holy articles
of God into the house that is to be built
[b]for the name of the LORD."

Lord, I pray that ____ would set their heart and soul to seek You.

FROM 1 CHRONICLES 22:19

The Divisions of the Levites

23 So when David was old and full of
days, he made his son [a]Solomon
king over Israel.
2And he gathered together all the leaders of Israel, with the priests and the Levites. 3Now the Levites were numbered
from the age of [a]thirty years and above;
and the number of individual males was
thirty-eight thousand. 4Of these, twenty-
four thousand *were* to [a]look after the
work of the house of the LORD, six thou-

21:29 [a] 1 Kin. 3:4 [b] 1 Chr. 16:39

CHAPTER 22
1 [a] Deut. 12:5
2 [a] 1 Kin. 9:20, 21 [b] 1 Kin. 5:17, 18
3 [a] 1 Kin. 7:47
4 [a] 1 Kin. 5:6–10
5 [a] 1 Chr. 29:1, 2
6 [1] *commanded*
7 [a] 2 Sam. 7:1, 2 [b] Deut. 12:5, 11
8 [a] 1 Chr. 28:3
9 [a] 1 Chr. 28:5 [b] 1 Kin. 4:20, 25; 5:4 [1] Lit. *Peaceful*
10 [a] 1 Chr. 17:12, 13; 28:6 [b] Heb. 1:5
11 [a] 1 Chr. 22:16
12 [a] 1 Kin. 3:9–12
13 [a] 1 Chr. 28:7 [b] [Josh. 1:6, 7, 9] [1] *commanded*
14 [a] 1 Chr. 22:3
16 [a] 1 Chr. 22:11
17 [a] 1 Chr. 28:1–6
18 [a] Josh. 22:4
19 [a] 2 Chr. 5:2–14 [b] 1 Kin. 5:3

CHAPTER 23
1 [a] 1 Kin. 1:33–40
3 [a] Num. 4:1–3
4 [a] Ezra 3:8, 9

sand *were* [b]officers and judges, 5four thousand *were* gatekeepers, and four thousand [a]praised the LORD with *musical* instruments, [b]"which I made," *said David,* "for giving praise."

6Also [a]David separated them into [1]divisions among the sons of Levi: Gershon, Kohath, and Merari.

7Of the [a]Gershonites: [1]Laadan and Shimei. 8The sons of Laadan: the first Jehiel, then Zetham and Joel—three *in all.* 9The sons of Shimei: Shelomith, Haziel, and Haran—three *in all.* These were the heads of the fathers' *houses* of Laadan. 10And the sons of Shimei: Jahath, [1]Zina, Jeush, and Beriah. These *were* the four sons of Shimei. 11Jahath was the first and Zizah the second. But Jeush and Beriah did not have many sons; therefore they were assigned as one father's house.

12[a]The sons of Kohath: Amram, Izhar, Hebron, and Uzziel—four *in all.* 13The sons of [a]Amram: Aaron and Moses; and [b]Aaron was set apart, he and his sons forever, that he should [1]sanctify the most holy things, [c]to burn incense before the LORD, [d]to minister to Him, and [e]to give the blessing in His name forever. 14Now [a]the sons of Moses the man of God were reckoned to the tribe of Levi. 15[a]The sons of Moses *were* [1]Gershon and Eliezer. 16Of the sons of Gershon, [a]Shebuel[1] *was* the first. 17Of the descendants of Eliezer, [a]Rehabiah was the first. And Eliezer had no other sons, but the sons of Rehabiah were very many. 18Of the sons of Izhar, [a]Shelomith *was* the first. 19[a]Of the sons of Hebron, Jeriah *was* the first, Amariah the second, Jahaziel the third, and Jekameam the fourth. 20Of the sons of Uzziel, Michah *was* the first and Jesshiah the second.

21[a]The sons of Merari *were* Mahli and Mushi. The sons of Mahli *were* Eleazar and [b]Kish. 22And Eleazar died, and [a]had no sons, but only daughters; and their [1]brethren, the sons of Kish, [b]took them *as wives.* 23[a]The sons of Mushi *were* Mahli, Eder, and Jeremoth—three *in all.*

24These *were* the sons of [a]Levi by their fathers' houses—the heads of the fathers' *houses* as they were counted individually by the number of their names, who did the work for the service of the house of the LORD, from the age of [b]twenty years and above.

25For David said, "The LORD God of Israel [a]has given rest to His people, that they may dwell in Jerusalem forever"; 26and also to the Levites, "They shall no longer [a]carry the tabernacle, or any of the articles for its service." 27For by the [a]last words of David the Levites *were* numbered from twenty years old and above; 28because their duty *was* to help the sons of Aaron in the service of the house of the LORD, in the courts and in the chambers, in the purifying of all holy things and the work of the service of the house of God, 29both with [a]the showbread and [b]the fine flour for the grain offering, with [c]the unleavened cakes and [d]*what is baked in* the pan, with what is mixed and with all kinds of [e]measures and sizes; 30to stand every morning to thank and praise the LORD, and likewise at evening; 31and at every presentation of a burnt offering to the LORD [a]on the Sabbaths and on the New Moons and on the [b]set[1] feasts, by number according to the ordinance governing them, regularly before the LORD; 32and that they should [a]attend to the [b]needs of the tabernacle of meeting, the needs of the holy *place,* and the [c]needs of the sons of Aaron their brethren in the work of the house of the LORD.

Lord God, may ____ stand every morning and every evening to give You thanks and praise.

FROM 1 CHRONICLES 23:30

The Divisions of the Priests

24 Now *these are* the divisions of the sons of Aaron. [a]The sons of Aaron *were* Nadab, Abihu, Eleazar, and Ithamar. 2And [a]Nadab and Abihu died before their father, and had no children; therefore Eleazar and Ithamar ministered as priests. 3Then David with Zadok of the sons of Eleazar, and [a]Ahimelech of the sons of Ithamar, divided them according to the schedule of their service.

4There were more leaders found of the sons of Eleazar than of the sons of Ithamar, and *thus* they were divided. Among the sons of Eleazar *were* sixteen heads of *their* fathers' houses, and eight heads of their fathers' houses among the sons of

4 b Deut. 16:18–20
5 a 1 Chr. 15:16 b 2 Chr. 29:25–27
6 a Ex. 6:16 *1 groups*
7 a 1 Chr. 26:21 *1 Libni,* Ex. 6:17
10 *1* LXX, Vg. *Zizah* and v. 11
12 a Ex. 6:18
13 a Ex. 6:20 b Heb. 5:4 c 1 Sam. 2:28 d [Deut. 21:5] e Num. 6:23 *1 consecrate*
14 a 1 Chr. 26:20–24
15 a Ex. 18:3, 4 *1* Heb. *Gershom,* 1 Chr. 6:16
16 a 1 Chr. 26:24 *1 Shubael,* 1 Chr. 24:20
17 a 1 Chr. 26:25
18 a 1 Chr. 24:22
19 a 1 Chr. 24:23
21 a 1 Chr. 24:26 b 1 Chr. 24:29
22 a 1 Chr. 24:28 b Num. 36:6 *1 kinsmen*
23 a 1 Chr. 24:30
24 a Num. 10:17, 21 b Ezra 3:8
25 a 1 Chr. 22:18
26 a Num. 4:5, 15; 7:9
27 a 2 Sam. 23:1
29 a Ex. 25:30 b Lev. 6:20 c Lev. 2:1, 4 d Lev. 2:5, 7 e Lev. 19:35
31 a Num. 10:10 b Lev. 23:2–4 *1 appointed feasts*
32 a 2 Chr. 13:10, 11 b [Num. 1:53] c Num. 3:6–9, 38

CHAPTER 24
1 a Lev. 10:1–6
2 a Num. 3:1–4; 26:61
3 a 1 Chr. 18:16

Ithamar. 5Thus they were divided by lot,
one group as another, for there were officials of the sanctuary and officials *of the*
house of God, from the sons of Eleazar
and from the sons of Ithamar. 6And the
scribe, Shemaiah the son of Nethanel, *one*
of the Levites, wrote them down before
the king, the leaders, Zadok the priest,
Ahimelech the son of Abiathar, and the
heads of the fathers' *houses* of the priests
and Levites, one father's house taken for
Eleazar and *one* for Ithamar.
7Now the first lot fell to Jehoiarib, the
second to Jedaiah, 8the third to Harim,
the fourth to Seorim, 9the fifth to Malchijah, the sixth to Mijamin, 10the seventh to
Hakkoz, the eighth to [a]Abijah, 11the ninth
to Jeshua, the tenth to Shecaniah, 12the
eleventh to Eliashib, the twelfth to Jakim,
13the thirteenth to Huppah, the fourteenth to Jeshebeab, 14the fifteenth to Bilgah, the sixteenth to Immer, 15the
seventeenth to Hezir, the eighteenth to
[1]Happizzez, 16the nineteenth to Pethahiah, the twentieth to [1]Jehezekel, 17the
twenty-first to Jachin, the twenty-second
to Gamul, 18the twenty-third to Delaiah,
the twenty-fourth to Maaziah.
19This *was* the schedule of their service
[a]for coming into the house of the LORD
according to their ordinance by the hand
of Aaron their father, as the LORD God of
Israel had commanded him.

Other Levites

20And the rest of the sons of Levi: of the
sons of Amram, [1]Shubael; of the sons of
Shubael, Jehdeiah. 21Concerning [a]Reha-
biah, of the sons of Rehabiah, the first *was*
Isshiah. 22Of the Izharites, [1]Shelomoth; of
the sons of Shelomoth, Jahath. 23Of the
sons [1]*of* [a]*Hebron,* Jeriah [1]*was the first,*
Amariah the second, Jahaziel the third,
and Jekameam the fourth. 24*Of* the sons of
Uzziel, Michah; of the sons of Michah,
Shamir. 25The brother of Michah, Isshiah;
of the sons of Isshiah, Zechariah. 26[a]The
sons of Merari *were* Mahli and Mushi; the
son of Jaaziah, Beno. 27The sons of Merari
by Jaaziah *were* Beno, Shoham, Zaccur,
and Ibri. 28Of Mahli: Eleazar, [a]who had no
sons. 29Of Kish: the son of Kish, Jerahmeel.
30Also [a]the sons of Mushi *were* Mahli,
Eder, and Jerimoth. These *were* the sons
of the Levites according to their fathers'
houses.
31These also cast lots just as their
brothers the sons of Aaron did, in the
presence of King David, Zadok, Ahimelech, and the heads of the fathers' *houses*
of the priests and Levites. The chief fathers *did* just as their younger brethren.

The Musicians

25 Moreover David and the captains of
the army separated for the service
some of the sons of [a]Asaph, of Heman,
and of Jeduthun, who *should* prophesy
with harps, stringed instruments, and
cymbals. And the number of the skilled
men performing their service was: 2Of the
sons of Asaph: Zaccur, Joseph, Nethaniah,
and [1]Asharelah; the sons of Asaph *were*
[2]under the direction of Asaph, who prophesied according to the order of the king.
3Of [a]Jeduthun, the sons of Jeduthun:
Gedaliah, [1]Zeri, Jeshaiah, [2]Shimei, Hashabiah, and Mattithiah, [3]six, under the direction of their father Jeduthun, who
prophesied with a harp to give thanks and
to praise the LORD. 4Of Heman, the sons
of Heman: Bukkiah, Mattaniah, [1]Uzziel,
[2]Shebuel, [3]Jerimoth, Hananiah, Hanani,
Eliathah, Giddalti, Romamti-Ezer,
Joshbekashah, Mallothi, Hothir, *and*
Mahazioth. 5All these *were* the sons of Heman the king's seer in the words of God,
to [1]exalt his [a]horn. For God gave Heman
fourteen sons and three daughters.
6All these *were* under the direction of
their father for the music *in* the house of
the LORD, with cymbals, stringed instruments, and [a]harps, for the service of the
house of God. Asaph, Jeduthun, and Heman *were* [b]under the authority of the
king. 7So the [a]number of them, with their
brethren who were instructed in the
songs of the LORD, all who were skillful,
was two hundred and eighty-eight.
8And they cast lots for their duty, the
small as well as the great, [a]the teacher
with the student.
9Now the first lot for Asaph came out
for Joseph; the second for Gedaliah, him
with his brethren and sons, twelve; 10the
third for Zaccur, his sons and his brethren, twelve; 11the fourth for [1]Jizri, his
sons and his brethren, twelve; 12the fifth
for Nethaniah, his sons and his brethren,
twelve; 13the sixth for Bukkiah, his sons
and his brethren, twelve; 14the seventh for
[1]Jesharelah, his sons and his brethren,
twelve; 15the eighth for Jeshaiah, his sons
and his brethren, twelve; 16the ninth for

10 [a] Luke 1:5
15 [1] LXX, Vg. *Aphses*
16 [1] MT *Jehezkel*
19 [a] 1 Chr. 9:25
20 [1] *Shebuel,* 1 Chr. 23:16
21 [a] 1 Chr. 23:17
22 [1] *Shelomith,* 1 Chr. 23:18
23 [a] 1 Chr. 23:19; 26:31 [1] Supplied from 23:19 (following some Heb. mss. and LXX mss.)
26 [a] Ex. 6:19
28 [a] 1 Chr. 23:22
30 [a] 1 Chr. 23:23

CHAPTER 25
1 [a] 1 Chr. 6:30, 33, 39, 44
2 [1] *Jesharelah,* v. 14 [2] Lit. *at the hands of*
3 [a] 1 Chr. 16:41, 42 [1] *Jizri,* v. 11 [2] So with one Heb. ms., LXX mss. [3] Shimei is the sixth, v. 17
4 [1] *Azarel,* v. 18 [2] *Shubael,* v. 20 [3] *Jeremoth,* v. 22
5 [a] 1 Chr. 16:42 [1] Increase his power or influence
6 [a] 1 Chr. 15:16 [b] 1 Chr. 15:19; 25:2
7 [a] 1 Chr. 23:5
8 [a] 2 Chr. 23:13
11 [1] *Zeri,* v. 3
14 [1] *Asharelah,* v. 2

Mattaniah, his sons and his brethren, twelve; 17 the tenth for Shimei, his sons and his brethren, twelve; 18 the eleventh for [1]Azarel, his sons and his brethren, twelve; 19 the twelfth for Hashabiah, his sons and his brethren, twelve; 20 the thirteenth for [1]Shubael, his sons and his brethren, twelve; 21 the fourteenth for Mattithiah, his sons and his brethren, twelve; 22 the fifteenth for [1]Jeremoth, his sons and his brethren, twelve; 23 the sixteenth for Hananiah, his sons and his brethren, twelve; 24 the seventeenth for Joshbekashah, his sons and his brethren, twelve; 25 the eighteenth for Hanani, his sons and his brethren, twelve; 26 the nineteenth for Mallothi, his sons and his brethren, twelve; 27 the twentieth for Eliathah, his sons and his brethren, twelve; 28 the twenty-first for Hothir, his sons and his brethren, twelve; 29 the twenty-second for Giddalti, his sons and his brethren, twelve; 30 the twenty-third for Mahazioth, his sons and his brethren, twelve; 31 the twenty-fourth for Romamti-Ezer, his sons and his brethren, twelve.

The Gatekeepers

26 Concerning the divisions of the gatekeepers: of the Korahites, [1]Meshelemiah the son of [a]Kore, of the sons of [2]Asaph. 2 And the sons of Meshelemiah *were* [a]Zechariah the firstborn, Jediael the second, Zebadiah the third, Jathniel the fourth, 3 Elam the fifth, Jehohanan the sixth, Eliehoenai the seventh.

4 Moreover the sons of [a]Obed-Edom *were* Shemaiah the firstborn, Jehozabad the second, Joah the third, Sacar the fourth, Nethanel the fifth, 5 Ammiel the sixth, Issachar the seventh, Peulthai the eighth; for God blessed him.

6 Also to Shemaiah his son were sons born who governed their fathers' houses, because they *were* men of great ability. 7 The sons of Shemaiah *were* Othni, Rephael, Obed, and Elzabad, whose brothers Elihu and Semachiah *were* able men.

8 All these *were* of the sons of Obed-Edom, they and their sons and their brethren, [a]able men with strength for the work: sixty-two of Obed-Edom.

9 And Meshelemiah had sons and brethren, eighteen able men.

10 Also [a]Hosah, of the children of Merari, had sons: Shimri the first (for *though* he was not the firstborn, his father made him the first), 11 Hilkiah the second, Tebaliah the third, Zechariah the fourth; all the sons and brethren of Hosah *were* thirteen.

12 Among these *were* the divisions of the gatekeepers, among the chief men, *having* duties just like their brethren, to serve in the house of the LORD. 13 And they [a]cast lots for each gate, the small as well as the great, according to their father's house. 14 The lot for the East *Gate* fell to [1]Shelemiah. Then they cast lots *for* his son Zechariah, a wise counselor, and his lot came out for the North Gate; 15 to Obed-Edom the South Gate, and to his sons the [1]storehouse. 16 To Shuppim and Hosah *the lot came out* for the West Gate, with the Shallecheth Gate on the [a]ascending highway—watchman opposite watchman. 17 On the east were *six* Levites, on the north four each day, on the south four each day, and for the [1]storehouse two by two. 18 As for the [1]Parbar on the west, *there were* four on the highway *and* two at the Parbar. 19 These were the divisions of the gatekeepers among the sons of Korah and among the sons of Merari.

The Treasuries and Other Duties

20 Of the Levites, Ahijah *was* [a]over the treasuries of the house of God and over the treasuries of the [b]dedicated[1] things. 21 The sons of [1]Laadan, the descendants of the Gershonites of Laadan, heads of their fathers' *houses,* of Laadan the Gershonite: [2]Jehieli. 22 The sons of Jehieli, Zetham and Joel his brother, *were* over the treasuries of the house of the LORD. 23 Of the [a]Amramites, the Izharites, the Hebronites, and the Uzzielites: 24 [a]Shebuel the son of Gershom, the son of Moses, *was* overseer of the treasuries. 25 And his brethren by Eliezer *were* Rehabiah his son, Jeshaiah his son, Joram his son, Zichri his son, and [a]Shelomith his son.

26 This Shelomith and his brethren *were* over all the treasuries of the dedicated things [a]which King David and the heads of fathers' *houses,* the captains over thousands and hundreds, and the captains of the army, had dedicated. 27 Some of the [1]spoils won in battles they dedicated to maintain the house of the LORD. 28 And all that Samuel [a]the seer, Saul the son of Kish, Abner the son of Ner, and Joab the son of Zeruiah had dedicated, every dedicated *thing,* was under the hand of Shelomith and his brethren.

---

18 [1] *Uzziel,* v. 4
20 [1] *Shebuel,* v. 4
22 [1] *Jerimoth,* v. 4

CHAPTER 26
1 [a] Ps. 42:title [1] *Shelemiah,* v. 14 [2] *Ebiasaph,* 1 Chr. 6:37; 9:19
2 [a] 1 Chr. 9:21
4 [a] 1 Chr. 15:18, 21
8 [a] 1 Chr. 9:13
10 [a] 1 Chr. 16:38
13 [a] 1 Chr. 24:5, 31; 25:8
14 [1] *Meshelemiah,* v. 1
15 [1] Heb. *asuppim*
16 [a] 1 Kin. 10:5
17 [1] Heb. *asuppim*
18 [1] Probably a court or colonnade extending west of the temple
20 [a] 1 Chr. 9:26 [b] 1 Chr. 26:22, 24, 26; 28:12 [1] *holy things*
21 [1] *Libni,* 1 Chr. 6:17 [2] *Jehiel,* 1 Chr. 23:8; 29:8
23 [a] Ex. 6:18
24 [a] 1 Chr. 23:16
25 [a] 1 Chr. 23:18
26 [a] 2 Sam. 8:11
27 [1] *plunder*
28 [a] 1 Sam. 9:9

[29]Of the Izharites, Chenaniah and his sons [a]*performed* duties as [b]officials and judges over Israel outside Jerusalem.

[30]Of the Hebronites, [a]Hashabiah and his brethren, one thousand seven hundred able men, had the oversight of Israel on the west side of the Jordan for all the business of the LORD, and in the service of the king. [31]Among the Hebronites, [a]Jerijah *was* head of the Hebronites according to his genealogy of the fathers. In the fortieth year of the reign of David they were sought, and there were found among them capable men [b]at Jazer of Gilead. [32]And his brethren *were* two thousand seven hundred able men, heads of fathers' *houses,* whom King David made officials over the Reubenites, the Gadites, and the half-tribe of Manasseh, for every matter pertaining to God and the [a]affairs of the king.

The Military Divisions

27 And the children of Israel, according to their number, the heads of fathers' *houses,* the captains of thousands and hundreds and their officers, served the king in every matter of the *military* divisions. *These divisions* came in and went out month by month throughout all the months of the year, each division *having* twenty-four thousand.

[2]Over the first division for the first month *was* [a]Jashobeam the son of Zabdiel, and in his division *were* twenty-four thousand; [3]*he was* of the children of Perez, and the chief of all the captains of the army for the first month. [4]Over the division of the second month *was* [1]Dodai an Ahohite, and of his division Mikloth also *was* the leader; in his division *were* twenty-four thousand. [5]The third captain of the army for the third month *was* [a]Benaiah, the son of Jehoiada the priest, who was chief; in his division *were* twenty-four thousand. [6]This was the Benaiah *who was* [a]mighty *among* the thirty, and was over the thirty; in his division *was* Ammizabad his son. [7]The fourth *captain* for the fourth month *was* [a]Asahel the brother of Joab, and Zebadiah his son after him; in his division *were* twenty-four thousand. [8]The fifth *captain* for the fifth month *was* [1]Shamhuth the Izrahite; in his division were twenty-four thousand. [9]The sixth *captain* for the sixth month *was* [a]Ira the son of Ikkesh the Tekoite; in his division *were* twenty-four thousand. [10]The seventh *captain* for the seventh month *was* [a]Helez the Pelonite, of the children of Ephraim; in his division *were* twenty-four thousand. [11]The eighth *captain* for the eighth month *was* [a]Sibbechai the Hushathite, of the Zarhites; in his division *were* twenty-four thousand. [12]The ninth *captain* for the ninth month *was* [a]Abiezer the Anathothite, of the Benjamites; in his division *were* twenty-four thousand. [13]The tenth *captain* for the tenth month *was* [a]Maharai the Netophathite, of the Zarhites; in his division *were* twenty-four thousand. [14]The eleventh *captain* for the eleventh month *was* [a]Benaiah the Pirathonite, of the children of Ephraim; in his division *were* twenty-four thousand. [15]The twelfth *captain* for the twelfth month *was* [1]Heldai the Netophathite, of Othniel; in his division *were* twenty-four thousand.

Leaders of Tribes

[16]Furthermore, over the tribes of Israel: the officer over the Reubenites *was* Eliezer the son of Zichri; over the Simeonites, Shephatiah the son of Maachah; [17]*over* the Levites, [a]Hashabiah the son of Kemuel; over the Aaronites, Zadok; [18]*over* Judah, [a]Elihu, *one* of David's brothers; *over* Issachar, Omri the son of Michael; [19]*over* Zebulun, Ishmaiah the son of Obadiah; *over* Naphtali, Jerimoth the son of Azriel; [20]*over* the children of Ephraim, Hoshea the son of Azaziah; *over* the half-tribe of Manasseh, Joel the son of Pedaiah; [21]*over* the half-*tribe* of Manasseh in Gilead, Iddo the son of Zechariah; *over* Benjamin, Jaasiel the son of Abner; [22]*over* Dan, Azarel the son of Jeroham. These *were* the leaders of the tribes of Israel.

[23]But David did not take the number of those twenty years old and under, because [a]the LORD had said He would multiply Israel like the [b]stars of the heavens. [24]Joab the son of Zeruiah began a census, but he did not finish, for [a]wrath came upon Israel because of this census; nor was the number recorded in the account of the chronicles of King David.

Other State Officials

[25]And Azmaveth the son of Adiel *was* over the king's treasuries; and Jehonathan the son of Uzziah was over the storehouses in the field, in the cities, in the villages, and in the fortresses. [26]Ezri the son of Chelub was over those who did the

29 a Neh. 11:16 b 1 Chr. 23:4
30 a 1 Chr. 27:17
31 a 1 Chr. 23:19 b Josh. 21:39
32 a 2 Chr. 19:11
CHAPTER 27
2 a 1 Chr. 11:11
4 1 Heb. *Dodai,* usually spelled *Dodo,* 2 Sam. 23:9
5 a 1 Chr. 18:17
6 a 2 Sam. 23:20–23
7 a 1 Chr. 11:26
8 1 *Shammah,* 2 Sam. 23:11, or *Shammoth,* 1 Chr. 11:27
9 a 1 Chr. 11:28
10 a 1 Chr. 11:27
11 a 2 Sam. 21:18
12 a 1 Chr. 11:28
13 a 1 Chr. 11:30
14 a 1 Chr. 11:31
15 1 *Heleb,* 2 Sam. 23:29, or *Heled,* 1 Chr. 11:30
17 a 1 Chr. 26:30
18 a 1 Sam. 16:6
23 a [Deut. 6:3] b Gen. 15:5; 22:17; 26:4
24 a 1 Chr. 21:1–7

work of the field for tilling the ground.
27And Shimei the Ramathite *was* over
the vineyards, and Zabdi the Shiphmite
was over the produce of the vineyards
for the supply of wine. 28Baal-Hanan the
Gederite was over the olive trees and the
sycamore trees that *were* in the lowlands,
and Joash *was* over the store of oil. 29And
Shitrai the Sharonite *was* over the herds
that fed in Sharon, and Shaphat the son
of Adlai was over the herds *that were* in
the valleys. 30Obil the Ishmaelite *was* over
the camels, Jehdeiah the Meronothite *was*
over the donkeys, 31and Jaziz the [a]Hagrite
was over the flocks. All these *were* the officials over King David's property.
32Also Jehonathan, David's uncle, *was* a
counselor, a wise man, and a [1]scribe; and
Jehiel the [2]son of Hachmoni *was* with the
king's sons. 33[a]Ahithophel *was* the king's
counselor, and [b]Hushai the Archite *was*
the king's companion. 34After Ahithophel
was Jehoiada the son of Benaiah, then
[a]Abiathar. And the general of the king's
army *was* [b]Joab.

Solomon Instructed to Build the Temple

28 Now David assembled at Jerusalem
all [a]the leaders of Israel: the officers of the tribes and [b]the captains of the
divisions who served the king, the captains over thousands and captains over
hundreds, and [c]the stewards over all the
substance and [1]possessions of the king
and of his sons, with the officials, the valiant men, and all [d]the mighty men of
valor.
2Then King David rose to his feet and
said, "Hear me, my brethren and my people: [a]I *had* it in my heart to build a house
of rest for the ark of the covenant of the
LORD, and for [b]the footstool of our God,
and had made preparations to build it.
3But God said to me, [a]'You shall not build
a house for My name, because you *have
been* a man of war and have shed [b]blood.'
4However the LORD God of Israel [a]chose
me above all the house of my father to be
king over Israel forever, for He has chosen
[b]Judah *to be* the ruler. And of the house
of Judah, [c]the house of my father, and
[d]among the sons of my father, He was
pleased with me to make *me* king over all
Israel. 5[a]And of all my sons (for the LORD
has given me many sons) [b]He has chosen
my son Solomon to sit on the throne of
the kingdom of the LORD over Israel.
6Now He said to me, 'It is [a]your son Solomon *who* shall build My house and My
courts; for I have chosen him *to be* My
son, and I will be his Father. 7Moreover I
will establish his kingdom forever, [a]if he
is steadfast to observe My commandments
and My judgments, as it is this day.' 8Now
therefore, in the sight of all Israel, the assembly of the LORD, and in the hearing of
our God, be careful to seek out all the
commandments of the LORD your God,
that you may possess this good land, and
leave *it* as an inheritance for your children
after you forever.

> *We shall be judged according to our privileges, according to the light we have received, and the obedience we have rendered to it, not only outwardly, but inwardly, according to our rebellion or submission to God; according to our loyalty and obedience to Him, in our hearts as well as in our lives.*
>
> CATHERINE BOOTH

9"As for you, my son Solomon, [a]know
the God of your father, and serve Him
[b]with a loyal heart and with a willing
mind; for [c]the LORD searches all hearts
and understands all the intent of the
thoughts. [d]If you seek Him, He will be
found by you; but if you forsake Him, He
will [e]cast you off forever. 10Consider now,
[a]for the LORD has chosen you to build a
house for the sanctuary; be strong, and
do it."
11Then David gave his son Solomon
[a]the plans for the vestibule, its houses, its
treasuries, its upper chambers, its inner
chambers, and the place of the mercy seat;
12and the [a]plans for all that he had by the
Spirit, of the courts of the house of the

31 a 1 Chr. 5:10
32 1 secretary 2 Or Hachmonite
33 a 2 Sam. 15:12 b 2 Sam. 15:32–37
34 a 1 Kin. 1:7 b 1 Chr. 11:6
CHAPTER 28
1 a 1 Chr. 27:16 b 1 Chr. 27:1, 2 c 1 Chr. 27:25 d 1 Chr. 11:10–47 1 Or livestock
2 a 2 Sam. 7:2 b Ps. 99:5; 132:7
3 a 2 Sam. 7:5, 13 b [1 Chr. 17:4; 22:8]
4 a 1 Sam. 16:6–13 b Gen. 49:8–10 c 1 Sam. 16:1 d 1 Sam. 13:14; 16:12, 13
5 a 1 Chr. 3:1–9; 14:3–7; 23:1 b 1 Chr. 22:9; 29:1
6 a 2 Sam. 7:13, 14
7 a 1 Chr. 22:13
9 a [John 17:3] b 2 Kin. 20:3 c [1 Sam. 16:7] d 2 Chr. 15:2 e Deut. 31:17
10 a 1 Chr. 22:13; 28:6
11 a 1 Chr. 28:19
12 a Heb. 8:5

LORD, of all the chambers all around, [b]of
the treasuries of the house of God, and of
the treasuries for the dedicated things;
13also for the division of the priests and
the [a]Levites, for all the work of the service
of the house of the LORD, and for all the
articles of service in the house of the
LORD. 14*He gave* gold by weight for *things*
of gold, for all articles used in every kind
of service; also *silver* for all articles of silver by weight, for all articles used in every
kind of service; 15the weight for the
[a]lampstands of gold, and their lamps of
gold, by weight for each lampstand and its
lamps; for the lampstands of silver by
weight, for the lampstand and its lamps,
according to the use of each lampstand.
16And by weight *he gave* gold for the tables of the showbread, for each [a]table, and
silver for the tables of silver; 17also pure
gold for the forks, the basins, the pitchers
of pure gold, and the golden bowls—*he
gave gold* by weight for every bowl; and
for the silver bowls, *silver* by weight for
every bowl; 18and refined gold by weight
for the [a]altar of incense, and for the construction of the chariot, that is, the gold
[b]cherubim that spread *their wings* and
overshadowed the ark of the covenant of
the LORD. 19"All *this,*" *said David,* [a]"the
LORD made me understand in writing, by
His hand upon me, all the [1]works of these
plans."
20And David said to his son Solomon,
[a]"Be strong and of good courage, and do
it; do not fear nor be dismayed, for the
LORD God—my God—*will be* with you.
[b]He will not leave you nor forsake you,
until you have finished all the work for
the service of the house of the LORD.
21*Here are* [a]the divisions of the priests
and the Levites for all the service of the
house of God; and [b]every willing craftsman *will be* with you for all manner of
workmanship, for every kind of service;
also the leaders and all the people *will be*
completely at your command."

Offerings for Building the Temple

29 Furthermore King David said to all
the assembly: "My son Solomon,
whom alone God has [a]chosen, *is* [b]young
and inexperienced; and the work *is* great,
because the [1]temple *is* not for man but for
the LORD God. 2Now for the house of my
God I have prepared with all my might:
gold for *things to be made of* gold, silver
for *things of* silver, bronze for *things of*
bronze, iron for *things of* iron, wood for
things of wood, [a]onyx stones, *stones* to be
set, glistening stones of various colors, all
kinds of precious stones, and marble slabs
in abundance. 3Moreover, because I have
set my affection on the house of my God,
I have given to the house of my God, over
and above all that I have prepared for the
holy house, my own special treasure of
gold and silver: 4three thousand talents
of gold, of the gold of [a]Ophir, and seven
thousand talents of refined silver, to overlay the walls of the houses; 5the gold for
things of gold and the silver for *things of*
silver, and for all kinds of work *to be done*
by the hands of craftsmen. Who *then* is
[a]willing to [1]consecrate himself this day to
the LORD?"

Consecrate everything to God, day by day.

MARIA WOODWORTH-ETTER

6Then [a]the leaders of the fathers' *houses,* leaders of the tribes of Israel, the captains of thousands and of hundreds, with
[b]the officers over the king's work, [c]offered
willingly. 7They gave for the work of the
house of God five thousand talents and
ten thousand darics of gold, ten thousand
talents of silver, eighteen thousand talents of bronze, and one hundred thousand
talents of iron. 8And whoever had *precious* stones gave *them* to the treasury of
the house of the LORD, into the hand of
[a]Jehiel[1] the Gershonite. 9Then the people
rejoiced, for they had offered willingly, because with a loyal heart they had [a]offered
willingly to the LORD; and King David also
rejoiced greatly.

David's Praise to God

10Therefore David blessed the LORD before all the assembly; and David said:

"Blessed are You, LORD God of
Israel, our Father, forever and
ever.
11 [a]Yours, O LORD, *is* the greatness,

---

12 b 1 Chr. 26:20, 28
13 a 1 Chr. 23:6
15 a Ex. 25:31–39
16 a 1 Kin. 7:48
18 a Ex. 30:1–10 b Ex. 25:18–22
19 a Ex. 25:40 *1 details*
20 a 1 Chr. 22:13 b Josh. 1:5
21 a 1 Chr. 24—26 b Ex. 35:25–35; 36:1, 2

CHAPTER 29
1 a 1 Chr. 28:5 b 1 Kin. 3:7 *1 Lit. palace*
2 a Is. 54:11, 12
4 a 1 Kin. 9:28
5 a [2 Cor. 8:5, 12] *1 Lit. fill his hand*
6 a 1 Chr. 27:1; 28:1 b 1 Chr. 27:25–31 c Ex. 35:21–35
8 a 1 Chr. 23:8 *1 Possibly the same as Jehieli, 1 Chr. 26:21, 22*
9 a 2 Cor. 9:7
11 a 1 Tim. 1:17

1 Chronicles 29:18

Dear Woman of Destiny,

I watched a falling star streak across the northern skies recently. Living in Alaska, I often have the opportunity to gaze into the clear night sky and behold the brilliance of the stars twinkling against their deep, black background.

As I lifted my eyes to the diamond-clustered heaven, the haunting words of the wise shepherd boy David echoed once again in my mind. I knew he had also viewed the same starry expanse. "I will lift up my eyes to the hills—from whence comes my help? My help comes from the LORD, who made heaven and earth. He will not allow your foot to be moved; He who keeps you will not slumber. Behold, He who keeps Israel shall neither slumber nor sleep. The LORD is your keeper; the LORD is your shade at your right hand" (Ps 121:1–5).

As you know, this shepherd boy grew up to be king of Israel. He was the one whose royal lineage God promised to never cut off. He was the warrior and the worshiper who led God's people well, and he is the one called "a man after [God's] own heart" (see 1 Sam. 13:14; Acts 13:22).

Just as he would later pray for his son, Solomon, in 1 Chronicles 29:18, the sweet psalmist knew where to fix his eyes and his heart. As David watched his father's sheep, he sang praises to the God of Israel and lifted his eyes to higher ground. He became so full of the presence of God that the strength he needed to overcome the lion and the bear was there when he needed it.

In like fashion, your eyes were created to behold wondrous things. Your heart was created to sing. Don't allow your song to die from lack of use. Don't allow your eyes to become heavy-lidded with the affairs of this life. There is a distant horizon, full of promise and full of hope, beckoning you.

Every woman's life includes heartache and heartbreak, tests and trials. For every challenge you face, there is but one answer—to "fix your heart" on the Lord. By doing so you can avoid being swayed by your emotions or by the opinions of other people.

A heart that is fixed cannot be moved. In a way, it is "stuck." In your life, all sorts of things will try to win your heart, but you must determine that the passion and devotion will be firmly and continually set upon the Lord. He is the one refuge, the one safe place, for your tender heart.

Lift up your eyes, dear one. The One who created you will never fail.

Mary Glazier

The power and the glory,
The victory and the majesty;
For all *that is* in heaven and in
earth *is Yours;*
Yours *is* the kingdom, O LORD,
And You are exalted as head over
all.
12 [a]Both riches and honor *come* from
You,
And You reign over all.
In Your hand *is* power and might;
In Your hand *it is* to make great
And to give strength to all.

I thank You, O God, and praise Your glorious name. Lord, enable ____ to give to You abundantly and with a willing heart. For all things come from You.

FROM 1 CHRONICLES 29:13, 14

13 "Now therefore, our God,
We thank You
And praise Your glorious name.
14 But who *am* I, and who *are* my
people,
That we should be able to offer so
willingly as this?
For all things *come* from You,
And [1]of Your own we have given
You.
15 For [a]we *are* [1]aliens and [2]pilgrims
before You,
As *were* all our fathers;
[b]Our days on earth *are* as a shadow,
And without hope.

16"O LORD our God, all this abundance
that we have prepared to build You a
house for Your holy name is from Your
hand, and *is* all Your own. 17I know also,
my God, that You [a]test the heart and
[b]have pleasure in uprightness. As for me,
in the uprightness of my heart I have willingly offered all these *things;* and now
with joy I have seen Your people, who are
present here to offer willingly to You.
18 O LORD God of Abraham, Isaac, and
Israel, our fathers, keep this forever in the
intent of the thoughts of the heart of Your
people, and fix their heart toward You.
19And [a]give my son Solomon a loyal heart
to keep Your commandments and Your
testimonies and Your statutes, to do all
these things, and to build the [1]temple for
which [b]I have made provision."

20Then David said to all the assembly,
"Now bless the LORD your God." So all the
assembly blessed the LORD God of their
fathers, and bowed their heads and prostrated themselves before the LORD and the
king.

Solomon Anointed King

21And they made sacrifices to the LORD
and offered burnt offerings to the LORD on
the next day: a thousand bulls, a thousand
rams, a thousand lambs, with their drink
offerings, and [a]sacrifices in abundance for
all Israel. 22So they ate and drank before
the LORD with great gladness on that day.
And they made Solomon the son of David
king the second time, and [a]anointed *him*
before the LORD *to be* the leader, and Zadok *to be* priest. 23Then Solomon sat on
the throne of the LORD as king instead of
David his father, and prospered; and all
Israel obeyed him. 24All the leaders and
the mighty men, and also all the sons of
King David, [a]submitted[1] themselves to
King Solomon. 25So the LORD exalted Solomon exceedingly in the sight of all Israel,
and [a]bestowed on him *such* royal majesty
as had not been on any king before him in
Israel.

The Close of David's Reign

26Thus David the son of Jesse reigned
over all Israel. 27[a]And the period that he
reigned over Israel *was* forty years; [b]seven
years he reigned in Hebron, and thirty-
three *years* he reigned in Jerusalem. 28So
he [a]died in a good old age, [b]full of days
and riches and honor; and Solomon his
son reigned in his place. 29Now the acts of
King David, first and last, indeed they *are*
written in the [1]book of Samuel the seer,
in the book of Nathan the prophet, and in
the book of Gad the seer, 30with all his
reign and his might, [a]and the events that
happened to him, to Israel, and to all the
kingdoms of the lands.

12 [a]Rom. 11:36
14 [1]Lit. *of Your hand*
15 [a]Heb. 11:13, 14 [b]Job 14:2 [1]*sojourners,* temporary residents [2]*transients,* temporary residents in an even more temporary sense
17 [a][1 Chr. 28:9] [b]Prov. 11:20
19 [a][1 Chr. 28:9] [b]1 Chr. 29:1, 2 [1]Lit. *palace*
21 [a]1 Kin. 8:62, 63
22 [a]1 Kin. 1:32–35, 39
24 [a]Eccl. 8:2 [1]Lit. *gave the hand*
25 [a]1 Kin. 3:13
27 [a]1 Kin. 2:11 [b]2 Sam. 5:5
28 [a]Gen. 25:8 [b]1 Chr. 23:1
29 [1]Lit. *words*
30 [a]Dan. 2:21; 4:23, 25

AUTHOR: *Attributed to Ezra*
DATE: *Probably 425–400 B.C.*
THEME: *Encouragement and Exhortation from Judah's Spiritual Heritage*
KEY WORDS: *King, House, David, Jerusalem, Priest*

2 CHRONICLES

Dear Woman of Destiny,

Second Chronicles was written to remind God's people of their true calling and God's faithfulness. David's throne would be destroyed, but God's ultimate plan of salvation could not be stopped. Be encouraged as you read. Combine a sense of godly purpose with complete faith in Him, and God's ultimate plan for your life will be unstoppable, too!

His love and mine,

Marilyn Hickey

Solomon Requests Wisdom

Now [a]Solomon the son of David was
strengthened in his kingdom, and
[b]the LORD his God *was* with him
and [c]exalted him exceedingly.
2 And Solomon spoke to all Israel, to
[a]the captains of thousands and of hundreds, to the judges, and to every leader in
all Israel, the heads of the fathers' *houses.*
3 Then Solomon, and all the assembly with
him, went to [1]the high place that *was* at
[a]Gibeon; for the tabernacle of meeting
with God was there, which Moses the servant of the LORD had [b]made in the wilderness. 4 [a]But David had brought up the ark
of God from Kirjath Jearim to *the place*
David had prepared for it, for he had
pitched a tent for it at Jerusalem. 5 Now
[a]the bronze altar that [b]Bezalel the son of
Uri, the son of Hur, had made, [1]he put
before the tabernacle of the LORD; Solomon and the assembly sought Him
there. 6 And Solomon went up there to the
bronze altar before the LORD, which *was*
at the tabernacle of meeting, and [a]offered
a thousand burnt offerings on it.
7 [a]On that night God appeared to Solomon, and said to him, "Ask! What shall
I give you?"
8 And Solomon said to God: "You have
shown great [a]mercy to David my father,
and have made me [b]king in his place.
9 Now, O LORD God, let Your promise to
David my father be established, [a]for You
have made me king over a people like the
[b]dust of the earth in multitude. 10 [a]Now
give me wisdom and knowledge, that I
may [b]go out and come in before this people; for who can judge this great people of
Yours?"
11 [a]Then God said to Solomon: "Because
this was in your heart, and you have not
asked riches or wealth or honor or the life
of your enemies, nor have you asked long
life—but have asked wisdom and knowledge for yourself, that you may judge My
people over whom I have made you
king— 12 wisdom and knowledge *are*
granted to you; and I will give you riches
and wealth and honor, such as [a]none of
the kings have had who *were* before you,
nor shall any after you have the like."

Solomon's Military and Economic Power

13 So Solomon came to Jerusalem from
[1]the high place that *was* at Gibeon, from
before the tabernacle of meeting, and
reigned over Israel. 14 [a]And Solomon gathered chariots and horsemen; he had one
thousand four hundred chariots and
twelve thousand horsemen, whom he stationed in the chariot cities and with the
king in Jerusalem. 15 [a]Also the king made
silver and gold as common in Jerusalem
as stones, and he made cedars as abundant as the sycamores which *are* in the
lowland. 16 [a]And Solomon had horses imported from Egypt and Keveh; the king's
merchants bought them in Keveh at the
current price. 17 They also acquired and
imported from Egypt a chariot for six
hundred *shekels* of silver, and a horse for
one hundred and fifty; thus, [1]through
their agents, they exported them to all the
kings of the Hittites and the kings of
Syria.

Solomon Prepares to Build the Temple

2 Then Solomon [a]determined to build a
temple for the name of the LORD, and
a royal house for himself. 2 [a]Solomon selected seventy thousand men to bear burdens, eighty thousand to quarry *stone* in
the mountains, and three thousand six
hundred to oversee them.
3 Then Solomon sent to [1]Hiram king of
Tyre, saying:

> [a]As you have dealt with David my
> father, and sent him cedars to build
> himself a house to dwell in, *so deal*
> *with me.* 4 Behold, [a]I am building a
> temple for the name of the LORD
> my God, to dedicate *it* to Him, [b]to
> burn before Him [1]sweet incense,
> for [c]the continual showbread, for
> [d]the burnt offerings morning and
> evening, on the [e]Sabbaths, on the
> New Moons, and on the [2]set feasts
> of the LORD our God. This *is an or-*
> *dinance* forever to Israel.
>
> 5 And the temple which I build *will*
> *be* great, for [a]our God is greater
> than all gods. 6 [a]But who is able to
> build Him a temple, since heaven
> and the heaven of heavens cannot
> contain Him? Who *am* I then, that
> I should build Him a temple, except
> to burn sacrifice before Him?
>
> 7 Therefore send me at once a man
> skillful to work in gold and silver,
> in bronze and iron, in purple and

CHAPTER 1
1 [a]1 Kin. 2:46 [b]Gen. 39:2 [c]1 Chr. 29:25
2 [a]1 Chr. 27:1–34
3 [a]1 Kin. 3:4 [b]Ex. 25—27; 35:4—36:38 [1]Place for worship
4 [a]2 Sam. 6:2–17
5 [a]Ex. 27:1, 2; 38:1, 2 [b]Ex. 31:2 [1]Some authorities *it was there*
6 [a]1 Kin. 3:4
7 [a]1 Kin. 3:5–14; 9:2
8 [a]Ps. 18:50 [b]1 Chr. 28:5
9 [a]2 Sam. 7:8–16 [b]Gen. 13:16
10 [a]1 Kin. 3:9 [b]Deut. 31:2
11 [a]1 Kin. 3:11–13
12 [a]2 Chr. 9:22
13 [1]Place for worship
14 [a]1 Kin. 10:26
15 [a]2 Chr. 9:27
16 [a]1 Kin. 10:28; 22:36
17 [1]Lit. *by their hands*

CHAPTER 2
1 [a]1 Kin. 5:5
2 [a]2 Chr. 2:18
3 [a]1 Chr. 14:1 [1]Heb. *Huram;* cf. 1 Kin. 5:1
4 [a]2 Chr. 2:1 [b]Ex. 30:7 [c]Ex. 25:30 [d]Ex. 29:38–42 [e]Num. 28:3, 9–11 [1]Lit. *incense of spices* [2]*appointed*
5 [a]Ps. 135:5
6 [a]1 Kin. 8:27

crimson and blue, who has skill to
engrave with the skillful men who
are with me in Judah and Jerusalem, [a]whom David my father provided. 8 [a]Also send me cedar and
cypress and algum logs from Lebanon, for I know that your servants
have skill to cut timber in Lebanon;
and indeed my servants *will be* with
your servants, 9 to prepare timber
for me in abundance, for the [1]tem-
ple which I am about to build *shall*
be great and wonderful.

10 [a]And indeed I will give to your
servants, the woodsmen who cut
timber, twenty thousand kors of
ground wheat, twenty thousand
kors of barley, twenty thousand
baths of wine, and twenty thousand
baths of oil.

11 Then Hiram king of Tyre answered in
writing, which he sent to Solomon:

[a]Because the LORD loves His people,
He has made you king over them.

12 [1]Hiram also said:

[a]Blessed *be* the LORD God of Israel,
[b]who made heaven and earth, for
He has given King David a wise
son, endowed with prudence and
understanding, who will build a
temple for the LORD and a royal
house for himself!

13 And now I have sent a skillful
man, endowed with understanding,
[1]Huram my [2]master *craftsman*
14 [a](the son of a woman of the
daughters of Dan, and his father
was a man of Tyre), skilled to work
in gold and silver, bronze and iron,
stone and wood, purple and blue,
fine linen and crimson, and to
make any engraving and to accomplish any plan which may be given
to him, with your skillful men and
with the skillful men of my lord
David your father.

15 Now therefore, the wheat, the barley, the oil, and the wine which
[a]my lord has spoken of, let him
send to his servants. 16 [a]And we will
cut wood from Lebanon, as much
as you need; we will bring it to you
in rafts by sea to [1]Joppa, and you
will carry it up to Jerusalem.

17 [a]Then Solomon numbered all the
aliens who *were* in the land of Israel, after
the census in which [b]David his father had
numbered them; and there were found to
be one hundred and fifty-three thousand
six hundred. 18 And he made [a]seventy
thousand of them bearers of burdens,
eighty thousand stonecutters in the
mountain, and three thousand six hundred overseers to make the people work.

Solomon Builds the Temple

3 Now [a]Solomon began to build the
house of the LORD at [b]Jerusalem on
Mount Moriah, where [1]*the LORD* had appeared to his father David, at the place
that David had prepared on the threshing
floor of [c]Ornan[2] the Jebusite. 2 And he began to build on the second *day* of the second month in the fourth year of his reign.
3 This is the foundation [a]which Solomon laid for building the house of God:
The length *was* sixty cubits (by cubits according to the former measure) and the
width twenty cubits. 4 And the [a]vestibule
that *was* in front *of* [1]*the sanctuary* was
twenty cubits long across the width of the
house, and the height *was* [2]one hundred
and twenty. He overlaid the inside with
pure gold. 5 [a]The larger [1]room he [b]pan-
eled with cypress which he overlaid with
fine gold, and he carved palm trees and
chainwork on it. 6 And he decorated the
house with precious stones for beauty,
and the gold *was* gold from Parvaim. 7 He
also overlaid the house—the beams and
doorposts, its walls and doors—with gold;
and he carved cherubim on the walls.
8 And he made the [a]Most Holy Place. Its
length was according to the width of the
house, twenty cubits, and its width twenty
cubits. He overlaid it with six hundred talents of fine gold. 9 The weight of the nails
was fifty shekels of gold; and he overlaid
the upper [a]area with gold. 10 [a]In the Most
Holy Place he made two cherubim, fashioned by carving, and overlaid them with
gold. 11 The wings of the cherubim *were*
twenty cubits in *overall* length: one wing
of the one cherub was five cubits, touching the wall of the room, and the other
wing *was* five cubits, touching the wing of
the other cherub; 12 *one* wing of the other
cherub *was* five cubits, touching the wall
of the room, and the other wing *also was*
five cubits, touching the wing of the other
cherub. 13 The wings of these cherubim
spanned twenty cubits overall. They stood

7 a 1 Chr. 22:15
8 a 1 Kin. 5:6
9 *1* Lit. *house*
10 a 1 Kin. 5:11
11 a 2 Chr. 9:8
12 a 1 Kin. 5:7 b Rev. 10:6 *1* Heb. *Huram;* cf. 1 Kin. 5:1
13 *1 Hiram,* 1 Kin. 7:13 *2* Lit. *father,* 1 Kin. 7:13, 14
14 a 1 Kin. 7:13, 14
15 a 2 Chr. 2:10
16 a 1 Kin. 5:8, 9 *1* Heb. *Japho*
17 a 1 Kin. 5:13; 2 Chr. 8:7, 8 b 1 Chr. 22:2
18 a 2 Chr. 2:2

CHAPTER 3
1 a 1 Kin. 6:1 b Gen. 22:2–14 c 1 Chr. 21:18; 22:1 *1* Lit. *He,* following MT, Vg.; LXX *the LORD;* Tg. *the Angel of the LORD* *2 Araunah,* 2 Sam. 24:16
3 a 1 Kin. 6:2
4 a 1 Kin. 6:3 *1* The holy place, the main room of the temple, 1 Kin. 6:3 *2* So with MT, LXX, Vg.; Arab., some LXX mss., Syr. *twenty*
5 a 1 Kin. 6:17 b 1 Kin. 6:15 *1* Lit. *house*
8 a Ex. 26:33
9 a 1 Chr. 28:11
10 a 1 Kin. 6:23–28

on their feet, and they faced inward. 14And
he made the [a]veil of blue, purple, crimson, and fine linen, and wove cherubim
into it.
15Also he made in front of the [1]temple
[a]two pillars [2]thirty-five cubits [3]high, and
the capital that *was* on the top of each of
them was five cubits. 16He made wreaths
of chainwork, as in the inner sanctuary,
and put *them* on top of the pillars; and he
made [a]one hundred pomegranates, and
put *them* on the wreaths of chainwork.
17Then he [a]set up the pillars before the
temple, one on the right hand and the
other on the left; he called the name of the
one on the right hand [1]Jachin, and
the name of the one on the left [2]Boaz.

Furnishings of the Temple

4 Moreover he made [a]a bronze altar:
twenty cubits was its length, twenty
cubits its width, and ten cubits its height.
2[a]Then he made the [1]Sea of cast
bronze, ten cubits from one brim to the
other; *it was* completely round. Its height
was five cubits, and a line of thirty cubits
measured its circumference. 3[a]And under
it *was* the likeness of oxen encircling it all
around, ten to a cubit, all the way around
the Sea. The oxen *were* cast in two rows,
when it was cast. 4It stood on twelve
[a]oxen: three looking toward the north,
three looking toward the west, three looking toward the south, and three looking
toward the east; the Sea *was set* upon
them, and all their back parts *pointed* inward. 5It *was* a handbreadth thick; and its
brim was shaped like the brim of a cup,
like a lily blossom. It contained [1]three
thousand baths.
6He also made [a]ten lavers, and put five
on the right side and five on the left, to
wash in them; such things as they offered
for the burnt offering they would wash in
them, but the [1]Sea *was* for the [b]priests to
wash in. 7[a]And he made ten lampstands of
gold [b]according to their design, and set
them in the temple, five on the right side
and five on the left. 8[a]He also made ten
tables, and placed *them* in the temple, five
on the right side and five on the left. And
he made one hundred [b]bowls of gold.
9Furthermore [a]he made the court of
the priests, and the [b]great court and doors
for the court; and he overlaid these doors
with bronze. 10[a]He set the Sea on the
right side, toward the southeast.
11Then [a]Huram made the pots and the
shovels and the bowls. So Huram finished
doing the work that he was to do for King
Solomon for the house of God: 12the two
pillars and [a]the bowl-shaped capitals *that
were* on top of the two pillars; the two
networks covering the two bowl-shaped
capitals which *were* on top of the pillars;
13[a]four hundred pomegranates for the
two networks (two rows of pomegranates
for each network, to cover the two bowl-
shaped capitals that *were* on the pillars);
14he also made [a]carts and the lavers on
the carts; 15one Sea and twelve oxen under it; 16also the pots, the shovels, the
forks—and all their articles [a]Huram his
[1]master *craftsman* made of burnished
bronze for King Solomon for the house of
the LORD.
17In the plain of Jordan the king had
them cast in clay molds, between Succoth
and [1]Zeredah. 18[a]And Solomon had all
these articles made in such great abundance that the weight of the bronze was
not determined.
19Thus [a]Solomon had all the furnishings made for the house of God: the altar
of gold and the tables on which *was* [b]the
showbread; 20the lampstands with their
lamps of pure gold, to burn [a]in the prescribed manner in front of the inner sanctuary, 21with [a]the flowers and the lamps
and the wick-trimmers of gold, of purest
gold; 22the trimmers, the bowls, the ladles, and the censers of pure gold. As for
the entry of the [1]sanctuary, its inner
doors to the Most Holy *Place,* and the
doors of the main hall of the temple, *were*
gold.
5 So [a]all the work that Solomon had
done for the house of the LORD was
finished; and Solomon brought in the
things which his father David had dedicated: the silver and the gold and all the
furnishings. And he put *them* in the
treasuries of the house of God.

The Ark Brought into the Temple

2[a]Now Solomon assembled the elders
of Israel and all the heads of the tribes, the
chief fathers of the children of Israel, in
Jerusalem, that they might bring the ark
of the covenant of the LORD up [b]from the
City of David, which *is* Zion. 3[a]Therefore
all the men of Israel assembled with the
king [b]at the feast, which *was* in the seventh month. 4So all the elders of Israel

14 a Ex. 26:31
15 a 1 Kin. 7:15–20 *1* Lit. *house* *2 eighteen,* 1 Kin. 7:15; 2 Kin. 25:17; Jer. 52:21 *3* Lit. *long*
16 a 1 Kin. 7:20
17 a 1 Kin. 7:21 *1* Lit. *He Shall Establish* *2* Lit. *In It Is Strength*

CHAPTER 4
1 a Ex. 27:1, 2
2 a 1 Kin. 7:23–26 *1* Great laver or basin
3 a 1 Kin. 7:24–26
4 a 1 Kin. 7:25
5 *1* About 8,000 gallons; *two thousand,* 1 Kin. 7:26
6 a 1 Kin. 7:38, 40 b Ex. 30:19–21 *1* Great basin
7 a 1 Kin. 7:49 b Ex. 25:31
8 a 1 Kin. 7:48 b 1 Chr. 28:17
9 a 1 Kin. 6:36 b 2 Kin. 21:5
10 a 1 Kin. 7:39
11 a 1 Kin. 7:40–51
12 a 1 Kin. 7:41
13 a 1 Kin. 7:20
14 a 1 Kin. 7:27, 43
16 a 1 Kin. 7:45 *1* Lit. *father*
17 *1 Zaretan,* 1 Kin. 7:46
18 a 1 Kin. 7:47
19 a 1 Kin. 7:48–50 b Ex. 25:30
20 a Ex. 27:20, 21
21 a Ex. 25:31
22 *1* Lit. *house*

CHAPTER 5
1 a 1 Kin. 7:51
2 a 1 Kin. 8:1–9 b 2 Sam. 6:12
3 a 1 Kin. 8:2 b 2 Chr. 7:8–10

came, and the [a]Levites took up the ark.
5Then they brought up the ark, the tabernacle of meeting, and all the holy furnishings that *were* in the tabernacle. The
priests and the Levites brought them up.
6Also King Solomon, and all the congregation of Israel who were assembled with
him before the ark, were sacrificing sheep
and oxen that could not be counted or
numbered for multitude. 7Then the
priests brought in the ark of the covenant
of the LORD to its place, into the [a]inner
sanctuary of the [1]temple, to the Most
Holy *Place,* under the wings of the cherubim. 8For the cherubim spread *their*
wings over the place of the ark, and the
cherubim overshadowed the ark and its
poles. 9The poles extended so that the
ends of the [a]poles of the ark could be seen
from *the holy place,* in front of the inner
sanctuary; but they could not be seen
from outside. And [1]they are there to this
day. 10Nothing was in the ark except the
two tablets which Moses [a]put *there* at Horeb, [1]when the LORD made *a covenant*
with the children of Israel, when they had
come out of Egypt.
11 And it came to pass when the
priests came out of the *Most* Holy *Place*
(for all the priests who *were* present had
[1]sanctified themselves, without keeping
to their [a]divisions), 12[a]and the Levites
who were the singers, all those of Asaph
and Heman and Jeduthun, with their sons
and their brethren, stood at the east end
of the altar, clothed in white linen, having
cymbals, stringed instruments and harps,
[b]and with them one hundred and twenty
priests sounding with trumpets— 13in-
deed it came to pass, when the trumpeters
and singers *were* as one, to make one
sound to be heard in praising and thanking the LORD, and when they lifted up
their voice with the trumpets and cymbals
and instruments of music, and praised the
LORD, *saying:*

> [a]"*For He is* good,
> For His mercy *endures* forever,"

that the house, the house of the LORD, was
filled with a cloud, 14so that the priests
could not [1]continue ministering because
of the cloud; [a]for the glory of the LORD
filled the house of God.

6 Then [a]Solomon spoke:

> "The LORD said He would dwell in
> the [b]dark cloud.
> 2 I have surely built You an exalted
> house,
> And [a]a place for You to dwell in
> forever."

Solomon's Speech upon Completion of the Work

3Then the king turned around and
[a]blessed the whole assembly of Israel,
while all the assembly of Israel was standing. 4And he said: "Blessed *be* the LORD
God of Israel, who has fulfilled with His
hands *what* He spoke with His mouth to
my father David, [a]saying, 5'Since the day
that I brought My people out of the land
of Egypt, I have chosen no city from any
tribe of Israel *in which* to build a house,
that My name might be there, nor did I
choose any man to be a ruler over My people Israel. 6[a]Yet I have chosen Jerusalem,
that My name may be there, and I [b]have
chosen David to be over My people Israel.'
7Now [a]it was in the heart of my father
David to build a [1]temple for the name of
the LORD God of Israel. 8But the LORD said
to my father David, 'Whereas it was in
your heart to build a temple for My name,
you did well in that it was in your heart.
9Nevertheless you shall not build the temple, but your son who will come from
your body, he shall build the temple for
My [a]name.' 10So the LORD has fulfilled His
word which He spoke, and I have filled the
position of my father David, and [a]sit on
the throne of Israel, as the LORD promised; and I have built the temple for the
name of the LORD God of Israel. 11And
there I have put the ark, [a]in which *is* the
covenant of the LORD which He made with
the children of Israel."

Solomon's Prayer of Dedication

12[a]Then [1]*Solomon* stood before the altar of the LORD in the presence of all the
assembly of Israel, and spread out his
hands 13(for Solomon had made a bronze
platform five cubits long, five cubits wide,
and three cubits high, and had set it in the
midst of the court; and he stood on it,
knelt down on his knees before all the assembly of Israel, and spread out his hands
toward heaven); 14and he said: "LORD God
of Israel, [a]*there is* no God in heaven or on
earth like You, who keep *Your* [b]covenant
and mercy with Your servants who walk
before You with all their hearts. 15[a]You

---

4 a 1 Chr. 15:2, 15
7 a 2 Chr. 4:20 1 Lit. *house*
9 a Ex. 25:13–15 1 Lit. *it is*
10 a Deut. 10:2, 5 1 Or *where*
11 a 1 Chr. 24:1–5 1 *consecrated*
12 a 1 Chr. 25:1–7 b 1 Chr. 13:8; 15:16, 24
13 a 1 Chr. 16:34, 41; Ps. 100:5; 106:1; 136
14 a Ex. 40:35 1 Lit. *stand to minister*

CHAPTER 6
1 a 1 Kin. 8:12–21 b [Lev. 16:2]
2 a 2 Chr. 7:12
3 a 2 Sam. 6:18
4 a 1 Chr. 17:5
6 a Deut. 12:5–7 b 1 Chr. 28:4
7 a 2 Sam. 7:2 1 Lit. *house,* and so in vv. 8–10
9 a 1 Chr. 28:3–6
10 a 1 Kin. 2:12; 10:9
11 a 2 Chr. 5:7–10
12 a 1 Kin. 8:22 1 Lit. *he*
14 a [Ex. 15:11] b [Deut. 7:9]
15 a 1 Chr. 22:9, 10

2 Chronicles 5:11–14

Dear Woman of Destiny,

You are a treasure to the Lord, a temple to house the very glory of God. Whether He designed you with a gift in music or not, you are still called to be a worshiper, a vessel for Him to pour His glory through to the world around you.

As a young girl growing up on a small island on the West Coast of Norway, I was blessed with beautiful surroundings of deep blue fjords wrapping around the island and majestic mountains crowning the mainland across the water. The goodness of God portrayed in nature brings deep joy to the awakened heart. It's as if all of heaven and nature is beckoning us to unite in worship. Appreciating Him—who He is, what He does and creates—makes for quick pathways to worship.

But as it is with nature, so it is with music. Throughout history, humankind has been the target of a quest by Satan, who once was the worship leader in heaven, to switch our attention from worshiping the Creator to the created (see Rom. 1:25). We seem to think churches with great architectural grandeur must be more attractive to the Lord than the humble home of a heart. His original plan was never to dwell in a man-made temple; but we, His children, were to house Him inside of us. For all we know, maybe God was the first one to say, "Fancy hotels are nice for awhile, but nothing beats being home with your family!"

It is fascinating to see how nothing was spared in the construction of the temple. The finest metals, woods, and fabrics that were joyfully given as freewill offerings, were artfully composed, as revealed by the Spirit, into a symphony of praise performed by excellent craftsmen. King David, a skilled musician, taught his son Solomon to give worship high priority, seeing the musicians and singers as leaders who prophesied through song. In order to have 120 trumpet players, singers, and other musicians sound as one, there must have been a lot of practice! Also in preparation to minister, they all had first been in the Most Holy, laying aside their divisions and sanctifying themselves. Humility and purity go hand in hand with unity.

My husband, Ken, and I experienced a glimpse of the glory of God in what was considered to be the harshest prison in North Carolina. We watched as broken, hardened men, in an attempt to worship, sang about how they loved Jesus, to the accompaniment of just a single guitar. He answered by coming in His glory, causing us all, including the guards, to instantly tremble and sob, crumbling to the floor! This was a life-changing experience for all of us! It was then the Lord impressed upon Ken, "What you can do in twenty years of working for Me, I can do in two minutes!"

When we allow Him to fill us, His glory will come out, fulfilling the promise of "Christ in you, the hope of glory" (Col 1:27). It's all about making Him feel welcome!

Solveig Henderson

have kept what You promised Your servant David my father; You have both spoken with Your mouth and fulfilled *it* with
Your hand, as *it is* this day. 16Therefore,
LORD God of Israel, now keep what You
promised Your servant David my father,
saying, [a]'You shall not fail to have a man
sit before Me on the throne of Israel, [b]only
if your sons take heed to their way, that
they walk in My law as you have walked
before Me.' 17And now, O LORD God of Israel, let Your word come true, which You
have spoken to Your servant David.

Lord God of Israel, there is no God in heaven or on earth like You, who keep Your covenant and mercy with ____ who walks before You with all their heart.

FROM 2 CHRONICLES 6:14

18"But will God indeed dwell with men
on the earth? [a]Behold, heaven and the
heaven of heavens cannot contain You.
How much less this [1]temple which I have
built! 19Yet regard the prayer of Your servant and his supplication, O LORD my
God, and listen to the cry and the prayer
which Your servant is praying before You:
20that Your eyes may be [a]open toward this
temple day and night, toward the place
where *You* said *You would* put Your
name, that You may hear the prayer
which Your servant makes [b]toward this
place. 21And may You hear the supplications of Your servant and of Your people
Israel, when they pray toward this place.
Hear from heaven Your dwelling place,
and when You hear, [a]forgive.

22"If anyone sins against his neighbor,
and is forced to take an [a]oath, and comes
and takes an oath before Your altar in this
temple, 23then hear from heaven, and act,
and judge Your servants, bringing retribution on the wicked by bringing his way
on his own head, and justifying the righteous by giving him according to his
[a]righteousness.

24"Or if Your people Israel are defeated
before an [a]enemy because they have
sinned against You, and return and confess Your name, and pray and make supplication before You in this temple, 25then
hear from heaven and forgive the sin of
Your people Israel, and bring them back
to the land which You gave to them and
their fathers.

26"When the [a]heavens are shut up and
there is no rain because they have sinned
against You, when they pray toward this
place and confess Your name, and turn
from their sin because You afflict them,
27then hear *in* heaven, and forgive the sin
of Your servants, Your people Israel, that
You may teach them the good way in
which they should walk; and send rain on
Your land which You have given to Your
people as an inheritance.

28"When there [a]is famine in the land,
pestilence or blight or mildew, locusts or
grasshoppers; when their enemies besiege
them in the land of their cities; whatever
plague or whatever [b]sickness *there is;*
29whatever prayer, whatever supplication
is *made* by anyone, or by all Your people
Israel, when each one knows his own
burden and his own grief, and spreads
out his hands to this temple: 30 then
hear from heaven Your dwelling place,
and forgive, and give to everyone according to all his ways, whose heart You know
(for You alone [a]know the [b]hearts of the
sons of men), 31that they may fear
You, to walk in Your ways as long as
they live in the land which You gave to
our fathers.

32"Moreover, concerning a foreigner,
[a]who is not of Your people Israel, but has
come from a far country for the sake of
Your great name and Your mighty hand
and Your outstretched arm, when they
come and pray in this temple; 33then hear
from heaven Your dwelling place, and do
according to all for which the foreigner
calls to You, that all peoples of the earth
may know Your name and fear You, as *do*
Your people Israel, and that they may
know that [1]this temple which I have built
is called by Your name.

34"When Your people go out to battle
against their enemies, wherever You send
them, and when they pray to You toward
this city which You have chosen and the
temple which I have built for Your name,
35then hear from heaven their prayer and
their supplication, and maintain their
cause.

16 [a]2 Chr. 7:18 [b]Ps. 132:12
18 [a][2 Chr. 2:6] [1]Lit. *house*
20 [a]2 Chr. 7:15 [b]Dan. 6:10
21 [a][Mic. 7:18]
22 [a]Ex. 22:8–11
23 [a][Job 34:11]
24 [a]2 Kin. 21:14, 15
26 [a]1 Kin. 17:1
28 [a]2 Chr. 20:9 [b][Mic. 6:13]
30 [a][1 Chr. 28:9] [b][1 Sam. 16:7]
32 [a]John 12:20
33 [1]Lit. *Your name is called upon this house*

2 Chronicles 6:30

Dear Woman of Destiny,

I want to share with you what I've discovered to be one of the most liberating truths in God's Word—the release of the Holy Spirit through brokenness.

Brokenness is walking in the bright light of the truth about myself as I am before God, and immediately He reveals to me a sin, which inevitably causes darkness. Through confession, repentance, and restitution, I walk on in full light again. In Isaiah 2:5, God invites us to live like this: "Come and let us walk in the light of the LORD."

The purpose of brokenness is not to crush us and hurt us, but to release us. Read John 8:32: "You shall know the truth, and the truth shall make you free." However, Jeremiah 17:9 says, "The heart is deceitful above all things, and desperately wicked; who can know it?" The answer is found in 2 Chronicles 6:30—only God. That's why we desperately need to keep asking God to show us our hearts as He sees them. Only the Holy Spirit can reveal that truth.

We cannot see the root sins of pride and unbelief underlying all other sins, and we are often blind to our impure motives. We need to pray, "Make me know my transgression and my sin" (Job 13:23).

Some of God's methods of answering these prayers are:

1) Spiritual surgery with an instant answer, where the veil is lifted from our spiritual vision and we experience divine revelation and deep conviction of our pride and/or unbelief. "You have set our iniquities before You, our secret sins in the light of Your countenance" (Ps. 90:8).
2) Spiritual surgery again, but where we have to wrestle with God with intense desire and persistent faith until He answers us, as He did Jacob (see Hos. 12:4).
3) The drip-feed method—a gradual process whereby God allows circumstances in our lives that show, by our wrong reactions to them, what is in our hearts. Perhaps we responded ungraciously in a difficult situation, and the Holy Spirit reminds us that "God resists the proud, but gives grace to the humble" (James 4:6).

Making brokenness a way of life releases fresh revelation. "In Your light we see light" (Ps. 36:9). It means: (a) We'll be given fresh revelation of truth from God's Word; (b) We will have light on the pathway of life when we need directions from God; (c) Understanding will be given to us by God in relation to perplexing situations—the causes and purposes of them.

When the woman broke the alabaster flask of very costly oil in Simon the leper's home, and poured it over Jesus' head as an act of devotion to Him, she broke through the barrier of the fear of men. Jesus then broke through with His unique acclamation of approval of her spiritual insight and devotion—even saying that she would be remembered wherever the gospel would be proclaimed. The fragrance of that oil would linger on Jesus and be sensed by everyone who came in contact with Him (see Mark 14:3–9).

When we live with a broken and contrite spirit, being known for what we are as God sees us, we experience 2 Corinthians 2:14: "Now thanks be to God who always leads us in triumph in Christ, and through us diffuses the fragrance of His knowledge in every place."

Joy Dawson

36"When they sin against You (for *there*
is [a]no one who does not sin), and You
become angry with them and deliver
them to the enemy, and they take them
[b]captive to a land far or near; 37*yet* when
they [1]come to themselves in the land
where they were carried captive, and repent, and make supplication to You in the
land of their captivity, saying, 'We have
sinned, we have done wrong, and have
committed wickedness'; 38and *when* they
return to You with all their heart and with
all their soul in the land of their captivity,
where they have been carried captive, and
pray toward their land which You gave to
their fathers, the [a]city which You have
chosen, and toward the temple which I
have built for Your name: 39then hear
from heaven Your dwelling place their
prayer and their supplications, and maintain their cause, and forgive Your people
who have sinned against You. 40Now, my
God, I pray, let Your eyes be [a]open and *let*
Your ears *be* attentive to the prayer *made*
in this place.

41 "Now[a] therefore,
Arise, O LORD God, to Your [b]resting
place,
You and the ark of Your strength.
Let Your priests, O LORD God, be
clothed with salvation,
And let Your saints [c]rejoice in
goodness.

42 "O LORD God, do not turn away the
face of Your Anointed;
[a]Remember the mercies of Your
servant David."

Solomon Dedicates the Temple

7 When [a]Solomon had finished praying, [b]fire came down from heaven and
consumed the burnt offering and the sacrifices; and [c]the glory of the LORD filled
the [1]temple. 2[a]And the priests could not
enter the house of the LORD, because the
glory of the LORD had filled the LORD's
house. 3When all the children of Israel
saw how the fire came down, and the glory of the LORD on the temple, they bowed
their faces to the ground on the pavement, and worshiped and praised the
LORD, *saying:*

[a]"For *He is* good,
[b]For His mercy *endures* forever."

4[a]Then the king and all the people offered sacrifices before the LORD. 5King
Solomon offered a sacrifice of twenty-two
thousand bulls and one hundred and
twenty thousand sheep. So the king and
all the people dedicated the house of God.
6[a]And the priests attended to their services; the Levites also with instruments of
the music of the LORD, which King David
had made to praise the LORD, saying, "For
His mercy *endures* forever," whenever
David offered praise by their [1]ministry.
[b]The priests sounded trumpets opposite
them, while all Israel stood.

Fire is the motivating power in prayer. Religious principles that do not come out of fire have neither force nor effect. Fire is the wing on which faith ascends. Passion is the soul of prayer.

E. M. BOUNDS

7Furthermore [a]Solomon consecrated
the middle of the court that *was* in front
of the house of the LORD; for there he offered burnt offerings and the fat of the
peace offerings, because the bronze altar
which Solomon had made was not able to
receive the burnt offerings, the grain offerings, and the fat.
8[a]At that time Solomon kept the feast
seven days, and all Israel with him, a very
great assembly [b]from the entrance of Hamath to [c]the[1] Brook of Egypt. 9And on
the eighth day they held a [a]sacred assembly, for they observed the dedication of
the altar seven days, and the feast seven
days. 10[a]On the twenty-third day of the
seventh month he sent the people away to
their tents, joyful and glad of heart for the
good that the LORD had done for David,
for Solomon, and for His people Israel.
11Thus [a]Solomon finished the house of
the LORD and the king's house; and Solomon successfully accomplished all that
came into his heart to make in the house
of the LORD and in his own house.

36 [a][Rom. 3:9, 19; 5:12] [b]Deut. 28:63–68
37 [1]Lit. *bring back to their hearts*
38 [a]Dan. 6:10
40 [a]2 Chr. 6:20
41 [a]Ps. 132:8–10, 16 [b]1 Chr. 28:2 [c]Neh. 9:25
42 [a]Ps. 89:49; 132:1, 8–10
CHAPTER 7
1 [a]1 Kin. 8:54 [b]Lev. 9:24 [c]1 Kin. 8:10, 11 [1]Lit. *house*
2 [a]2 Chr. 5:14
3 [a]Ps. 106:1; 136:1 [b]2 Chr. 20:21
4 [a]1 Kin. 8:62, 63
6 [a]1 Chr. 15:16 [b]2 Chr. 5:12 [1]Lit. *hand*
7 [a]1 Kin. 8:64–66; 9:3
8 [a]1 Kin. 8:65 [b]1 Kin. 4:21, 24 [c]Josh. 13:3 [1]The Shihor, 1 Chr. 13:5
9 [a]Lev. 23:36
10 [a]1 Kin. 8:66
11 [a]1 Kin. 9:1

God's Second Appearance to Solomon

12Then the LORD [a]appeared to Solomon by night, and said to him: "I have heard your prayer, [b]and have chosen this [c]place for Myself as a house of sacrifice. 13[a]When I shut up heaven and there is no rain, or command the locusts to devour the land, or send pestilence among My people, 14 if My people who are [a]called by My name will [b]humble themselves, and pray and seek My face, and turn from their wicked ways, [c]then I will hear from heaven, and will forgive their sin and heal their land. 15Now [a]My eyes will be open and My ears attentive to prayer *made* in this place. 16For now [a]I have chosen and [1]sanctified this house, that My name may be there forever; and [2]My eyes and [3]My heart will be there perpetually. 17[a]As for you, if you walk before Me as your father David walked, and do according to all that I have commanded you, and if you keep My statutes and My judgments, 18then I will establish the throne of your kingdom, as I covenanted with David your father, saying, [a]'You shall not fail *to have* a man as ruler in Israel.'

Lord, if ____ who is called by Your name will humble themselves, and pray and seek Your face, and turn from their wicked ways, then You will hear from heaven, and forgive their sin and heal their land.

FROM 2 CHRONICLES 7:14

19[a]"But if you turn away and forsake My statutes and My commandments which I have set before you, and go and serve other gods, and worship them, 20[a]then I will uproot them from My land which I have given them; and this house which I have [1]sanctified for My name I will cast out of My sight, and will make it a proverb and a [b]byword among all peoples.

21"And *as for* [a]this [1]house, which [2]is exalted, everyone who passes by it will be [b]astonished and say, [c]'Why has the LORD done thus to this land and this house?' 22Then they will answer, 'Because they forsook the LORD God of their fathers, who brought them out of the land of Egypt, and embraced other gods, and worshiped them and served them; therefore He has brought all this calamity on them.' "

Solomon's Additional Achievements

8 It [a]came to pass at the end of [b]twenty years, when Solomon had built the house of the LORD and his own house, 2that the cities which [1]Hiram had given to Solomon, Solomon built them; and he settled the children of Israel there. 3And Solomon went to Hamath Zobah and seized it. 4[a]He also built Tadmor in the wilderness, and all the storage cities which he built in [b]Hamath. 5He built Upper Beth Horon and [a]Lower Beth Horon, fortified cities *with* walls, gates, and bars, 6also Baalath and all the storage cities that Solomon had, and all the chariot cities and the cities of the cavalry, and all that Solomon [a]desired to build in Jerusalem, in Lebanon, and in all the land of his dominion.

7[a]All the people *who were* left of the Hittites, Amorites, Perizzites, Hivites, and Jebusites, who *were* not of Israel— 8that is, their descendants who were left in the land after them, whom the children of Israel did not destroy—from these Solomon raised forced labor, as it is to this day. 9But Solomon did not make the children of Israel [1]servants for his work. Some *were* men of war, captains of his officers, captains of his chariots, and his cavalry. 10And others *were* chiefs of the officials of King Solomon: [a]two hundred and fifty, who ruled over the people.

11Now Solomon [a]brought the daughter of Pharaoh up from the City of David to the house he had built for her, for he said, "My wife shall not dwell in the house of David king of Israel, because *the places* to which the ark of the LORD has come are holy."

12Then Solomon offered burnt offerings to the LORD on the altar of the LORD which he had built before the vestibule, 13according to the [a]daily rate, offering according to the commandment of Moses, for the Sabbaths, the New Moons, and the [b]three appointed yearly [c]feasts—the

12 [a]1 Kin. 3:5; 11:9 [b]Deut. 12:5, 11 [c]2 Chr. 6:20
13 [a]2 Chr. 6:26–28
14 [a][Is. 43:7] [b][James 4:10] [c]2 Chr. 6:27, 30
15 [a]2 Chr. 6:20, 40
16 [a]2 Chr. 6:6 *1 set apart* *2* My attention *3* My concern
17 [a]1 Kin. 9:4
18 [a]2 Chr. 6:16
19 [a]Lev. 26:14, 33
20 [a]Deut. 28:63–68 [b]Ps. 44:14 *1 set apart*
21 [a]2 Kin. 25:9 [b]2 Chr. 29:8 [c][Deut. 29:24, 25] *1* Temple *2* Or *was*

CHAPTER 8
1 [a]1 Kin. 9:10–14 [b]1 Kin.6:38—7:1
2 *1* Heb. *Huram,* 2 Chr. 2:3
4 [a]1 Kin. 9:17, 18 [b]1 Chr. 18:3, 9
5 [a]1 Chr. 7:24
6 [a]2 Chr. 7:11
7 [a]1 Kin. 9:20
9 *1 slaves*
10 [a]1 Kin. 9:23
11 [a]1 Kin. 3:1; 7:8; 9:24; 11:1
13 [a]Num. 28:3, 9, 11, 26; 29:1 [b]Ex. 23:14–17; 34:22, 23 [c]Lev. 23:1–44

2 Chronicles 7:14

Dear Woman of Destiny,

This powerful scripture was given to Solomon during a visitation from God at night. It set forth God's conditions that determined whether or not a nation would receive His blessing. There is probably not another scripture that encapsulates how to obtain the favor of God and see the land on which they lived healed.

The first part of this verse is certainly a *kairon,* or living word, for us as women today. It deals with the issue of humility. We must come to God in a way that shows we realize He is the almighty, omnipotent Creator and we are willingly subjecting ourselves to Him.

The next admonition is to not only pray, but also seek His face as we pray. What does this mean? Seeking requires time and effort. It isn't something that happens when we talk to God for a few seconds while we are brushing our teeth. He must have a preeminent place in our lives and thoughts.

Another major portion of this scripture tells us we must turn from our wicked ways. God is bringing a sweeping move of holiness and purity upon the body of Christ that emphasizes this point. We cannot please God and engage ourselves with sexual sin, pornography, or movies full of things that grieve the heart of God. This includes movies that corrupt communication or those with foul language. The next time you watch a movie, why don't you actively invite Jesus to sit and watch it with you? See through His eyes what you are letting into your heart and mind.

Nations need to have times of repentance wherein we realize how far we have fallen away from biblical standards. Sin pollutes a nation. In fact, God's Word tells us that it even pollutes the physical land on which we live! (see Lev. 18:25). The good news is that if God's people follow the pattern of 2 Chronicles 7:14, God will heal the land.

Dream with me a moment. . . . What would your nation look like if it was healed? Crime rates would drop. The sound of violence would not ring from our inner cities. We wouldn't be prisoners in our own homes at night, fearing the dangers of the outside world. Sound impossible? Without God's intervention into the affairs of our nations, it certainly is impossible. We are on a downward spiral where children are killing children and hate abounds.

What must we do? We must pray. Woman of God, this is our call and this is our commission. Pray for our nation. Pray alone, and pray with others. We must stand up and fight against the darkness in our neighborhoods and cities. We must not give up until the tide turns, until revival comes to our land and it is healed.

Cindy Jacobs

Feast of Unleavened Bread, the Feast of
Weeks, and the Feast of Tabernacles.
[14]And, according to the [1]order of David
his father, he appointed the [a]divisions of
the priests for their service, [b]the Levites
for their duties (to praise and serve before
the priests) as the duty of each day required, and the [c]gatekeepers by their divisions at each gate; for so David the man of
God had commanded. [15]They did not depart from the command of the king to the
priests and Levites concerning any matter
or concerning the [a]treasuries.
[16]Now all the work of Solomon was
well-ordered [1]from the day of the foundation of the house of the LORD until it was
finished. So the house of the LORD was
completed.
[17]Then Solomon went to [a]Ezion Geber
and [1]Elath on the seacoast, in the land of
Edom. [18][a]And Hiram sent him ships by
the hand of his servants, and servants who
knew the sea. They went with the servants
of Solomon to [b]Ophir, and acquired four
hundred and fifty talents of gold from
there, and brought it to King Solomon.

The Queen of Sheba's Praise of Solomon

9 Now [a]when the queen of Sheba heard
of the fame of Solomon, she came to
Jerusalem to test Solomon with hard
questions, *having* a very great retinue,
camels that bore spices, gold in abundance, and precious stones; and when she
came to Solomon, she spoke with him
about all that was in her heart. [2]So Solomon answered all her questions; there
was nothing so difficult for Solomon that
he could not explain it to her. [3]And when
the queen of Sheba had seen the wisdom
of Solomon, the house that he had built,
[4]the food on his table, the seating of his
servants, the service of his waiters and
their apparel, his [a]cupbearers and their
apparel, and his entryway by which he
went up to the house of the LORD, there
was no more spirit in her.
[5]Then she said to the king: "*It was* a
true report which I heard in my own land
about your words and your wisdom.
[6]However I did not believe their words
until I came and saw with my own eyes;
and indeed the half of the greatness of
your wisdom was not told me. You exceed
the fame of which I heard. [7]Happy *are*
your men and happy *are* these your servants, who stand continually before you
and hear your wisdom! [8]Blessed be the
LORD your God, who delighted in you, setting you on His throne *to be* king for the
LORD your God! Because your God has
[a]loved Israel, to establish them forever,
therefore He made you king over them, to
do justice and righteousness."
[9]And she gave the king one hundred
and twenty talents of gold, spices in great
abundance, and precious stones; there
never were any spices such as those the
queen of Sheba gave to King Solomon.
[10]Also, the servants of Hiram and the
servants of Solomon, [a]who brought gold
from Ophir, brought [1]algum wood and
precious stones. [11]And the king made
walkways *of* the [1]algum wood for the
house of the LORD and for the king's
house, also harps and stringed instruments for singers; and there were none
such *as these* seen before in the land of
Judah.
[12]Now King Solomon gave to the queen
of Sheba all she desired, whatever she
asked, *much more* than she had brought
to the king. So she turned and went to her
own country, she and her servants.

Solomon's Great Wealth

[13][a]The weight of gold that came to Solomon yearly was six hundred and sixty-
six talents of gold, [14]besides *what* the
traveling merchants and traders brought.
And all the kings of Arabia and governors
of the country brought gold and silver to
Solomon. [15]And King Solomon made two
hundred large shields of hammered gold;
six hundred *shekels* of hammered gold
went into each shield. [16]*He* also *made*
three hundred shields of hammered gold;
[1]three hundred *shekels* of gold went into
each shield. The king put them in the
[a]House of the Forest of Lebanon.
[17]Moreover the king made a great
throne of ivory, and overlaid it with pure
gold. [18]The throne *had* six steps, with a
footstool of gold, *which were* fastened to
the throne; there were [1]armrests on either side of the place of the seat, and two
lions stood beside the armrests. [19]Twelve
lions stood there, one on each side of the
six steps; nothing like *this* had been made
for any *other* kingdom.
[20]All King Solomon's drinking vessels
were gold, and all the vessels of the House
of the Forest of Lebanon *were* pure gold.
Not *one was* silver, for this was accounted
as nothing in the days of Solomon. [21]For

14 a 1 Chr. 24:3 b 1 Chr. 25:1 c 1 Chr. 9:17; 26:1 *1 ordinance*
15 a 1 Chr. 26:20–28
16 *1* So with LXX, Syr., Vg.; MT *as far as*
17 a 1 Kin. 9:26 *1* Heb. *Eloth,* 2 Kin. 14:22
18 a 2 Chr. 9:10, 13 b 1 Chr. 29:4

CHAPTER 9
1 a [Matt. 12:42]
4 a Neh. 1:11
8 a Deut. 7:8
10 a 2 Chr. 8:18 *1 almug,* 1 Kin. 10:11, 12
11 *1 almug,* 1 Kin. 10:11, 12
13 a 1 Kin. 10:14–29
16 a 1 Kin. 7:2 *1 three minas,* 1 Kin. 10:17
18 *1* Lit. *hands*

the king's ships went to [a]Tarshish with
the servants of [1]Hiram. Once every three
years the [2]merchant ships came, bringing
gold, silver, ivory, apes, and [3]monkeys.
22So King Solomon surpassed all the
kings of the earth in riches and wisdom.
23And all the kings of the earth sought the
presence of Solomon to hear his wisdom,
which God had put in his heart. 24Each
man brought his present: articles of silver
and gold, garments, [a]armor, spices,
horses, and mules, at a set rate year by
year.
25Solomon [a]had four thousand stalls
for horses and chariots, and twelve thousand horsemen whom he stationed in the
chariot cities and with the king at Jerusalem.
26[a]So he reigned over all the kings
[b]from [1]the River to the land of the Philistines, as far as the border of Egypt. 27[a]The
king made silver *as common* in Jerusalem
as stones, and he made cedar trees [b]as
abundant as the sycamores which *are* in
the lowland. 28[a]And they brought horses
to Solomon from Egypt and from all
lands.

Death of Solomon

29[a]Now the rest of the acts of Solomon,
first and last, *are* they not written in the
book of Nathan the prophet, in the prophecy of [b]Ahijah the Shilonite, and in the
visions of [c]Iddo the seer concerning Jeroboam the son of Nebat? 30[a]Solomon
reigned in Jerusalem over all Israel forty
years. 31Then Solomon [1]rested with his
fathers, and was buried in the City of David his father. And Rehoboam his son
reigned in his place.

The Revolt Against Rehoboam

10 And [a]Rehoboam went to Shechem,
for all Israel had gone to Shechem
to make him king. 2So it happened, when
Jeroboam the son of Nebat heard *it* (he
was in Egypt, [a]where he had fled from the
presence of King Solomon), that Jeroboam returned from Egypt. 3Then they sent
for him and called him. And Jeroboam
and all Israel came and spoke to Rehoboam, saying, 4"Your father made our yoke
heavy; now therefore, lighten the burdensome service of your father and his heavy
yoke which he put on us, and we will serve
you."
5So he said to them, "Come back to me
after three days." And the people departed.
6Then King Rehoboam consulted the
elders who stood before his father Solomon while he still lived, saying, "How do
you advise *me* to answer these people?"
7And they spoke to him, saying, "If you
are kind to these people, and please them,
and speak good words to them, they will
be your servants forever."
8[a]But he rejected the advice which the
elders had given him, and consulted the
young men who had grown up with him,
who stood before him. 9And he said to
them, "What advice do you give? How
should we answer this people who have
spoken to me, saying, 'Lighten the yoke
which your father put on us'?"
10Then the young men who had grown
up with him spoke to him, saying, "Thus
you should speak to the people who have
spoken to you, saying, 'Your father made
our yoke heavy, but you make *it* lighter on
us'—thus you shall say to them: 'My little
finger shall be thicker than my father's
waist! 11And now, whereas my father put
a heavy yoke on you, I will add to your
yoke; my father chastised you with whips,
but I *will chastise you* with [1]scourges!' "
12So [a]Jeroboam and all the people came
to Rehoboam on the third day, as the king
had directed, saying, "Come back to me
the third day." 13Then the king answered
them roughly. King Rehoboam rejected
the advice of the elders, 14and he spoke to
them according to the advice of the young
men, saying, [1]"My father made your yoke
heavy, but I will add to it; my father chastised you with whips, but I *will chastise
you* with [2]scourges!" 15So the king did
not listen to the people; [a]for the turn *of
events* was from God, that the LORD might
fulfill His [b]word, which He had spoken by
the hand of Ahijah the Shilonite to Jeroboam the son of Nebat.
16Now when all Israel *saw* that the king
did not listen to them, the people answered the king, saying:

"What share have we in David?
We have no inheritance in the son
of Jesse.
Every man to your tents, O Israel!
Now see to your own house,
O David!"

So all Israel departed to their tents.
17But Rehoboam reigned over the

21 [a] 2 Chr. 20:36, 37 [1] Heb. *Huram;* cf. 1 Kin. 10:22 [2] Lit. *ships of Tarshish,* deep-sea vessels [3] Or *peacocks*
24 [a] 1 Kin. 20:11
25 [a] 1 Kin. 4:26; 10:26
26 [a] 1 Kin. 4:21 [b] Gen. 15:18 [1] The Euphrates
27 [a] 1 Kin. 10:27 [b] 2 Chr. 1:15–17
28 [a] 2 Chr. 1:16
29 [a] 1 Kin. 11:41 [b] 1 Kin. 11:29 [c] 2 Chr. 12:15; 13:22
30 [a] 1 Kin. 4:21; 11:42, 43
31 [1] Died and joined his ancestors

CHAPTER 10
1 [a] 1 Kin. 12:1–20
2 [a] 1 Kin. 11:40
8 [a] 1 Kin. 12:8–11
11 [1] Scourges with points or barbs, lit. *scorpions*
12 [a] 1 Kin. 12:12–14
14 [1] So with many Heb. mss., LXX, Syr., Vg. (cf. v. 10; 1 Kin. 12:14); MT / [2] Lit. *scorpions*
15 [a] 1 Chr. 5:22 [b] 1 Kin. 11:29–39

children of Israel who dwelt in the cities of Judah.

18Then King Rehoboam sent Hadoram, who *was* in charge of revenue; but the children of Israel stoned him with stones, and he died. Therefore King Rehoboam mounted *his* chariot in haste to flee to Jerusalem. 19[a]So Israel has been in rebellion against the house of David to this day.

11 Now [a]when Rehoboam came to Jerusalem, he assembled from the house of Judah and Benjamin one hundred and eighty thousand chosen *men* who were warriors, to fight against Israel, that he might restore the kingdom to Rehoboam.

2But the word of the LORD came [a]to Shemaiah the man of God, saying, 3"Speak to Rehoboam the son of Solomon, king of Judah, and to all Israel in Judah and Benjamin, saying, 4'Thus says the LORD: "You shall not go up or fight against your brethren! Let every man return to his house, for this thing is from Me." ' " Therefore they obeyed the words of the LORD, and turned back from attacking Jeroboam.

Rehoboam Fortifies the Cities

5So Rehoboam dwelt in Jerusalem, and built cities for defense in Judah. 6And he built Bethlehem, Etam, Tekoa, 7Beth Zur, Sochoh, Adullam, 8Gath, Mareshah, Ziph, 9Adoraim, Lachish, Azekah, 10Zorah, Aijalon, and Hebron, which are in Judah and Benjamin, fortified cities. 11And he fortified the strongholds, and put captains in them, and stores of food, oil, and wine. 12Also in every city *he put* shields and spears, and made them very strong, having Judah and Benjamin on his side.

Priests and Levites Move to Judah

13And from all their territories the priests and the Levites who *were* in all Israel took their stand with him. 14For the Levites left [a]their common-lands and their possessions and came to Judah and Jerusalem, for [b]Jeroboam and his sons had rejected them from serving as priests to the LORD. 15[a]Then he appointed for himself priests for the [1]high places, for [b]the demons, and [c]the calf idols which he had made. 16[a]And [1]after *the Levites left,* those from all the tribes of Israel, such as set their heart to seek the LORD God of Israel, [b]came to Jerusalem to sacrifice to the LORD God of their fathers. 17So they [a]strengthened the kingdom of Judah, and made Rehoboam the son of Solomon strong for three years, because they walked in the way of David and Solomon for three years.

> *Don't hurry into other forms of prayer when you are quiet before God. Simply allow yourself time to enjoy His presence and be filled full in your spirit.*
>
> MADAME JEANNE GUYON

The Family of Rehoboam

18Then Rehoboam took for himself as wife Mahalath the daughter of Jerimoth the son of David, *and of* Abihail the daughter of [a]Eliah the son of Jesse. 19And she bore him children: Jeush, Shamariah, and Zaham. 20After her he took [a]Maachah the [1]granddaughter of [b]Absalom; and she bore him [c]Abijah, Attai, Ziza, and Shelomith. 21Now Rehoboam loved Maachah the granddaughter of Absalom more than all his [a]wives and his concubines; for he took eighteen wives and sixty concubines, and begot twenty-eight sons and sixty daughters. 22And Rehoboam [a]appointed [b]Abijah the son of Maachah as chief, *to be* leader among his brothers; for he *intended* to make him king. 23He dealt wisely, and [1]dispersed some of his sons throughout all the territories of Judah and Benjamin, to every [a]fortified city; and he gave them provisions in abundance. He also sought many wives *for them.*

Egypt Attacks Judah

12 Now [a]it came to pass, when Rehoboam had established the kingdom and had strengthened himself, that [b]he forsook the law of the LORD, and all Israel along with him. 2[a]And it happened in the fifth year of King Rehoboam *that* Shishak king of Egypt came up against Jerusalem, because they had transgressed against the LORD, 3with twelve hundred chariots, sixty thousand horsemen, and people with-

---

19 a 1 Kin. 12:19

CHAPTER 11
1 a 1 Kin. 12:21–24
2 a 1 Chr. 12:5
14 a Num. 35:2–5 b 2 Chr. 13:9
15 a 1 Kin. 12:31; 13:33; 14:9 b [Lev. 17:7] c 1 Kin. 12:28 *1* Places for pagan worship
16 a 2 Chr. 14:7 b 2 Chr. 15:9, 10; 30:11, 18 *1* Lit. *after them*
17 a 2 Chr. 12:1, 13
18 a 1 Sam. 16:6
20 a 2 Chr. 13:2 b 1 Kin. 15:2 c 1 Kin. 14:31 *1* Lit. *daughter,* but in the broader sense of granddaughter
21 a Deut. 17:17
22 a Deut. 21:15–17 b 2 Chr. 13:1
23 a 2 Chr. 11:5 *1 distributed*

CHAPTER 12
1 a 2 Chr. 11:17 b 1 Kin. 14:22–24
2 a 1 Kin. 11:40; 14:25

out number who came with him out of
Egypt—[a]the Lubim and the Sukkiim and
the Ethiopians. 4And he took the fortified
cities of Judah and came to Jerusalem.

The reason people do not have rich, beautiful faith is because their spirit is denied the privilege of communion and fellowship with the Father.

JOHN G. LAKE

5Then [a]Shemaiah the prophet came to
Rehoboam and the leaders of Judah, who
were gathered together in Jerusalem because of Shishak, and said to them, "Thus
says the LORD: 'You have forsaken Me, and
therefore I also have left you in the hand
of Shishak.' "
6So the leaders of Israel and the king
[a]humbled themselves; and they said,
[b]"The LORD *is* righteous."
7Now when the LORD saw that they
humbled themselves, [a]the word of the
LORD came to Shemaiah, saying, "They
have humbled themselves; *therefore* I will
not destroy them, but I will grant them
some deliverance. My wrath shall not be
poured out on Jerusalem by the hand of
Shishak. 8Nevertheless [a]they will be his
servants, that they may distinguish [b]My
service from the service of the kingdoms
of the nations."
9[a]So Shishak king of Egypt came up
against Jerusalem, and took away the
treasures of the house of the LORD and the
treasures of the king's house; he took everything. He also carried away the gold
shields which Solomon had [b]made.
10Then King Rehoboam made bronze
shields in their place, and committed
them [a]to the hands of the captains of the
guard, who guarded the doorway of the
king's house. 11And whenever the king
entered the house of the LORD, the guard
would go and bring them out; then they
would take them back into the guardroom. 12When he humbled himself, the
wrath of the LORD turned from him, so as
not to destroy *him* completely; and things
also went well in Judah.

The End of Rehoboam's Reign

13Thus King Rehoboam strengthened
himself in Jerusalem and reigned. Now
[a]Rehoboam *was* forty-one years old when
he became king; and he reigned seventeen
years in Jerusalem, [b]the city which the
LORD had chosen out of all the tribes of
Israel, to put His name there. His
mother's name *was* Naamah, an [c]Am-
monitess. 14And he did evil, because he
did not prepare his heart to seek the LORD.
15The acts of Rehoboam, first and last,
are they not written in the book of Shemaiah the prophet, [a]and of Iddo the seer
concerning genealogies? [b]And *there were*
wars between Rehoboam and Jeroboam
all their days. 16So Rehoboam [1]rested
with his fathers, and was buried in the
City of David. Then [a]Abijah[2] his son
reigned in his place.

Abijah Reigns in Judah

13 In [a]the eighteenth year of King
Jeroboam, Abijah became king
over [b]Judah. 2He reigned three years in
Jerusalem. His mother's name *was* [1]Mi-
chaiah the daughter of Uriel of Gibeah.
And there was war between Abijah and
Jeroboam. 3Abijah set the battle in order
with an army of valiant warriors, four
hundred thousand choice men. Jeroboam
also drew up in battle formation against
him with eight hundred thousand choice
men, mighty men of valor.
4Then Abijah stood on Mount [a]Zemara-
im, which *is* in the mountains of Ephraim, and said, "Hear me, Jeroboam and all
Israel: 5Should you not know that the
LORD God of Israel [a]gave the dominion
over Israel to David forever, to him and
his sons, [b]by a covenant of salt? 6Yet Jeroboam the son of Nebat, the servant of
Solomon the son of David, rose up and
[a]rebelled against his lord. 7Then [a]worth-
less rogues gathered to him, and
strengthened themselves against Rehoboam the son of Solomon, when Rehoboam
was [b]young and inexperienced and could
not withstand them. 8And now you think
to withstand the kingdom of the LORD,
which is in the hand of the sons of David;
and you *are* a great multitude, and with
you are the gold calves which Jeroboam
[a]made for you as gods. 9[a]Have you not
cast out the priests of the LORD, the sons
of Aaron, and the Levites, and made for

3 a 2 Chr. 16:8
5 a 2 Chr. 11:2
6 a [James 4:10] b Ex. 9:27
7 a 1 Kin. 21:28, 29
8 a Is. 26:13 b [Deut. 28:47, 48]
9 a 1 Kin. 14:25, 26 b 2 Chr. 9:15, 16
10 a 1 Kin. 14:27
13 a 1 Kin. 14:21 b 2 Chr. 6:6 c 1 Kin. 11:1, 5
15 a 2 Chr. 9:29; 13:22 b 1 Kin. 14:30
16 a 2 Chr. 11:20–22 *1 Died and joined his ancestors* *2 Abijam,* 1 Kin. 14:31

CHAPTER 13
1 a 1 Kin. 15:1 b 1 Kin. 12:17
2 *1 Maachah,* 1 Kin. 15:2; 2 Chr. 11:20, 21
4 a Josh. 18:22
5 a 2 Sam. 7:8–16 b Num. 18:19
6 a 1 Kin. 11:28; 12:20
7 a Judg. 9:4 b 2 Chr. 12:13
8 a 1 Kin. 12:28; 14:9
9 a 2 Chr. 11:13–15

yourselves priests, like the peoples of *other* lands, [b]so that whoever comes to consecrate himself with a young bull and
seven rams may be a priest of [c]*things that
are* not gods? 10But as for us, the LORD *is*
our [a]God, and we have not forsaken Him;
and the priests who minister to the LORD
are the sons of Aaron, and the Levites *attend* to *their* duties. 11[a]And they burn to
the LORD every morning and every evening burnt sacrifices and sweet incense;
they also *set* the [b]showbread *in order on*
the pure *gold* table, and the lampstand of
gold with its lamps [c]to burn every evening; for we keep the command of the
LORD our God, but you have forsaken
Him. 12Now look, God Himself is with us
as *our* [a]head, [b]and His priests with sounding trumpets to sound the alarm against
you. O children of Israel, do not fight
against the LORD God of your fathers, for
you shall not prosper!"

13But Jeroboam caused an ambush to
go around behind them; so they were in
front of Judah, and the ambush *was* behind them. 14And when Judah looked
around, to their surprise the battle line
was at both front and rear; and they [a]cried
out to the LORD, and the priests sounded
the trumpets. 15Then the men of Judah
gave a shout; and as the men of Judah
shouted, it happened that God [a]struck
Jeroboam and all Israel before Abijah and
Judah. 16And the children of Israel fled
before Judah, and God delivered them
into their hand. 17Then Abijah and his
people struck them with a great slaughter; so five hundred thousand choice men
of Israel fell slain. 18Thus the children of
Israel were subdued at that time; and the
children of Judah prevailed, [a]because they
relied on the LORD God of their fathers.

19And Abijah pursued Jeroboam and
took cities from him: Bethel with its villages, Jeshanah with its villages, and
[a]Ephrain[1] with its villages. 20So Jeroboam did not recover strength again in the
days of Abijah; and the LORD [a]struck him,
and [b]he died.

21But Abijah grew mighty, married
fourteen wives, and begot twenty-two
sons and sixteen daughters. 22Now the
rest of the acts of Abijah, his ways, and his
sayings *are* written in [a]the [1]annals of the
prophet Iddo.

14 So Abijah rested with his fathers,
and they buried him in the City of
David. Then [a]Asa his son reigned in his
place. In his days the land was quiet for
ten years.

Asa Reigns in Judah

2Asa did *what was* good and right in the
eyes of the LORD his God, 3for he removed
the altars of the foreign *gods* and [a]the
[1]high places, and [b]broke down the *sacred*
pillars [c]and cut down the wooden images.
4He commanded Judah to [a]seek the LORD
God of their fathers, and to observe the
law and the commandment. 5He also removed the [1]high places and the incense
altars from all the cities of Judah, and the
kingdom was quiet under him. 6And he
built fortified cities in Judah, for the land
had rest; he had no war in those years,
because the LORD had given him [a]rest.
7Therefore he said to Judah, "Let us build
these cities and make walls around *them,*
and towers, gates, and bars, *while* the land
is yet before us, because we have sought
the LORD our God; we have sought *Him,*
and He has given us rest on every side." So
they built and prospered. 8And Asa had an
army of three hundred thousand from Judah who carried [1]shields and spears, and
from Benjamin two hundred and eighty
thousand men who carried shields and
drew [a]bows; all these *were* mighty men of
[b]valor.

9[a]Then Zerah the Ethiopian came out
against them with an army of a million
men and three hundred chariots, and he
came to [b]Mareshah. 10So Asa went out
against him, and they set the troops in
battle array in the Valley of Zephathah at
Mareshah. 11And Asa [a]cried out to the
LORD his God, and said, "LORD, *it is* [b]noth-
ing for You to help, whether with many or
with those who have no power; help us,
O LORD our God, for we rest on You, and
[c]in Your name we go against this multitude. O LORD, You *are* our God; do not let
man prevail against You!"

12So the LORD [a]struck the Ethiopians
before Asa and Judah, and the Ethiopians
fled. 13And Asa and the people who *were*
with him pursued them to [a]Gerar. So the
Ethiopians were overthrown, and they
could not recover, for they were broken
before the LORD and His army. And they
carried away very much [1]spoil. 14Then
they defeated all the cities around Gerar,
for [a]the fear of the LORD came upon them;
and they plundered all the cities, for there
was exceedingly much [1]spoil in them.

9 b Ex. 29:29–33 c Jer. 2:11; 5:7
10 a Josh. 24:15
11 a 2 Chr. 2:4 b Lev. 24:5–9 c Ex. 27:20, 21
12 a [Heb. 2:10] b [Num. 10:8–10]
14 a 2 Chr. 6:34, 35; 14:11
15 a 2 Chr. 14:12
18 a 2 Chr. 14:11
19 a Josh. 15:9 *1* Or *Ephron*
20 a 1 Sam. 2:6; 25:38 b 1 Kin. 14:20
22 a 2 Chr. 9:29 *1* Or *commentary,* Heb. *midrash*

CHAPTER 14
1 a 1 Kin. 15:8
3 a 1 Kin. 15:14 b [Ex. 34:13] c 1 Kin. 11:7 *1* Places for pagan worship
4 a [2 Chr. 7:14]
5 *1* Places for pagan worship
6 a 2 Chr. 15:15
8 a 1 Chr. 12:2 b 2 Chr. 13:3 *1 large shields*
9 a 2 Chr. 12:2, 3; 16:8 b Josh. 15:44
11 a Ex. 14:10 b [1 Sam. 14:6] c 1 Sam. 17:45
12 a 2 Chr. 13:15
13 a Gen. 10:19; 20:1 *1 plunder*
14 a 2 Chr. 17:10 *1 plunder*

15They also [1]attacked the livestock enclosures, and carried off sheep and camels in abundance, and returned to Jerusalem.

The Reforms of Asa

15 Now [a]the Spirit of God came upon Azariah the son of Oded. 2And he went out [1]to meet Asa, and said to him: "Hear me, Asa, and all Judah and Benjamin. [a]The LORD *is* with you while you are with Him. [b]If you seek Him, He will be found by you; but [c]if you forsake Him, He will forsake you. 3[a]For a long time Israel *has been* without the true God, without a [b]teaching priest, and without [c]law; 4but [a]when in their trouble they turned to the LORD God of Israel, and sought Him, He was found by them. 5And in those times *there was* no peace to the one who went out, nor to the one who came in, but great turmoil *was* on all the inhabitants of the lands. 6[a]So nation was [1]destroyed by nation, and city by city, for God troubled them with every adversity. 7But you, be strong and do not let your hands be weak, for your work shall be rewarded!"

Father, may ____ be strong and not let their hands be weak, for their work shall be rewarded!
FROM 2 CHRONICLES 15:7

8And when Asa heard these words and the prophecy of [1]Oded the prophet, he took courage, and removed the abominable idols from all the land of Judah and Benjamin and from the cities [a]which he had taken in the mountains of Ephraim; and he restored the altar of the LORD that *was* before the vestibule of the LORD. 9Then he gathered all Judah and Benjamin, and [a]those who dwelt with them from Ephraim, Manasseh, and Simeon, for they came over to him in great numbers from Israel when they saw that the LORD his God was with him.

10So they gathered together at Jerusalem in the third month, in the fifteenth year of the reign of Asa. 11[a]And they offered to the LORD [1]at that time seven hundred bulls and seven thousand sheep from the [2]spoil they had brought. 12Then they [a]entered into a covenant to seek the LORD God of their fathers with all their heart and with all their soul; 13[a]and whoever would not seek the LORD God of Israel [b]was to be put to death, whether small or great, whether man or woman. 14Then they took an oath before the LORD with a loud voice, with shouting and trumpets and rams' horns. 15And all Judah rejoiced at the oath, for they had sworn with all their heart and [a]sought Him with all their soul; and He was found by them, and the LORD gave them [b]rest all around.

16Also he removed [a]Maachah, the [1]mother of Asa the king, from *being* queen mother, because she had made an obscene image of [2]Asherah; and Asa cut down her obscene image, then crushed and burned *it* by the Brook Kidron. 17But [a]the [1]high places were not removed from Israel. Nevertheless the heart of Asa was loyal all his days.

18He also brought into the house of God the things that his father had dedicated and that he himself had dedicated: silver and gold and utensils. 19And there was no war until the thirty-fifth year of the reign of Asa.

Asa's Treaty with Syria

16 In the thirty-sixth year of the reign of Asa, [a]Baasha king of Israel came up against Judah and built Ramah, [b]that he might let none go out or come in to Asa king of Judah. 2Then Asa brought silver and gold from the treasuries of the house of the LORD and of the king's house, and sent to Ben-Hadad king of Syria, who dwelt in Damascus, saying, 3"*Let there be* a treaty between you and me, as there was between my father and your father. See, I have sent you silver and gold; come, break your treaty with Baasha king of Israel, so that he will withdraw from me."

4So Ben-Hadad heeded King Asa, and sent the captains of his armies against the cities of Israel. They attacked Ijon, Dan, Abel Maim, and all the storage cities of Naphtali. 5Now it happened, when Baasha heard *it,* that he stopped building Ramah and ceased his work. 6Then King Asa took all Judah, and they carried away the stones and timber of Ramah, which Baasha had used for building; and with them he built Geba and Mizpah.

---

15 [1] Lit. *struck*

CHAPTER 15
1 [a] 2 Chr. 20:14; 24:20
2 [a] [James 4:8] [b] [1 Chr. 28:9] [c] 2 Chr. 24:20 [1] Lit. *before*
3 [a] Hos. 3:4 [b] 2 Kin. 12:2 [c] Lev. 10:11
4 [a] [Deut. 4:29]
6 [a] Matt. 24:7 [1] Lit. *beaten in pieces*
8 [a] 2 Chr. 13:19 [1] So with MT, LXX; Syr., Vg. *Azariah the son of Oded* (cf. v. 1)
9 [a] 2 Chr. 11:16
11 [a] 2 Chr. 14:13–15 [1] Lit. *in that day* [2] *plunder*
12 [a] 2 Kin. 23:3
13 [a] Ex. 22:20 [b] Deut. 13:5–15
15 [a] 2 Chr. 15:2 [b] 2 Chr. 14:7
16 [a] 1 Kin. 15:2, 10, 13 [1] Or *grandmother* [2] A Canaanite deity
17 [a] 1 Kin. 15:14 [1] Places for pagan worship

CHAPTER 16
1 [a] 1 Kin. 15:17–22 [b] 2 Chr. 15:9

Hanani's Message to Asa

[7]And at that time [a]Hanani the seer came to Asa king of Judah, and said to him: [b]"Because you have relied on the king of Syria, and have not relied on the LORD your God, therefore the army of the king of Syria has escaped from your hand. [8]Were [a]the Ethiopians and [b]the Lubim not a huge army with very many chariots and horsemen? Yet, because you relied on the LORD, He delivered them into your [c]hand. [9][a]For the eyes of the LORD run to and fro throughout the whole earth, to show Himself strong on behalf of *those* whose heart *is* loyal to Him. In this [b]you have done foolishly; therefore from now on [c]you shall have wars." [10]Then Asa was angry with the seer, and [a]put him in prison, for *he was* enraged at him because of this. And Asa oppressed *some* of the people at that time.

Illness and Death of Asa

[11][a]Note that the acts of Asa, first and last, are indeed written in the book of the kings of Judah and Israel. [12]And in the thirty-ninth year of his reign, Asa became diseased in his feet, and his malady was severe; yet in his disease he [a]did not seek the LORD, but the physicians.

[13][a]So Asa [1]rested with his fathers; he died in the forty-first year of his reign. [14]They buried him in his own tomb, which he had [1]made for himself in the City of David; and they laid him in the bed which was filled [a]with spices and various ingredients prepared in a mixture of ointments. They made [b]a very great burning for him.

Jehoshaphat Reigns in Judah

17 Then [a]Jehoshaphat his son reigned in his place, and strengthened himself against Israel. [2]And he placed troops in all the fortified cities of Judah, and set garrisons in the land of [a]Judah and in the cities of Ephraim [b]which Asa his father had taken. [3]Now the LORD was with Jehoshaphat, because he walked in the former ways of his father David; he did not seek the Baals, [4]but sought [1]the God of his father, and walked in His commandments and not according to [a]the acts of Israel. [5]Therefore the LORD established the kingdom in his hand; and all Judah [a]gave presents to Jehoshaphat, [b]and he had riches and honor in abundance. [6]And his heart took delight in the ways of the LORD; moreover [a]he removed the [1]high places and wooden images from Judah.

[7]Also in the third year of his reign he sent his leaders, Ben-Hail, Obadiah, Zechariah, Nethanel, and Michaiah, [a]to teach in the cities of Judah. [8]And with them *he sent* Levites: Shemaiah, Nethaniah, Zebadiah, Asahel, Shemiramoth, Jehonathan, Adonijah, Tobijah, and Tobadonijah—the Levites; and with them Elishama and Jehoram, the priests. [9][a]So they taught in Judah, and *had* the Book of the Law of the LORD with them; they went throughout all the cities of Judah and taught the people.

[10]And [a]the fear of the LORD fell on all the kingdoms of the lands that *were* around Judah, so that they did not make war against Jehoshaphat. [11]Also *some* of the Philistines [a]brought Jehoshaphat presents and silver as tribute; and the Arabians brought him flocks, seven thousand seven hundred rams and seven thousand seven hundred male goats.

[12]So Jehoshaphat became increasingly powerful, and he built fortresses and storage cities in Judah. [13]He had much property in the cities of Judah; and the men of war, mighty men of valor, *were* in Jerusalem.

[14]These *are* their numbers, according to their fathers' houses. Of Judah, the captains of thousands: Adnah the captain, and with him three hundred thousand mighty men of valor; [15]and next to him *was* Jehohanan the captain, and with him two hundred and eighty thousand; [16]and next to him *was* Amasiah the son of Zichri, [a]who willingly offered himself to the LORD, and with him two hundred thousand mighty men of valor. [17]Of Benjamin: Eliada a mighty man of valor, and with him two hundred thousand men armed with bow and shield; [18]and next to him *was* Jehozabad, and with him one hundred and eighty thousand prepared for war. [19]These served the king, besides [a]those the king put in the fortified cities throughout all Judah.

Micaiah Warns Ahab

18 Jehoshaphat [a]had riches and honor in abundance; and by marriage he [b]allied himself with [c]Ahab. [2][a]After some years he went down to *visit* Ahab in Samaria; and Ahab killed sheep and oxen in abundance for him and the people who were with him, and persuaded him to go

---

7 a 2 Chr. 19:2 b [Jer. 17:5]
8 a 2 Chr. 14:9 b 2 Chr. 12:3 c 2 Chr. 13:16, 18
9 a Zech. 4:10 b 1 Sam. 13:13 c 1 Kin. 15:32
10 a Jer. 20:2
11 a 1 Kin. 15:23, 24
12 a [Jer. 17:5]
13 a 1 Kin. 15:24 *1 Died and joined his ancestors*
14 a John 19:39, 40 b 2 Chr. 21:19 *1 Lit. dug*

CHAPTER 17
1 a 1 Kin. 15:24
2 a 2 Chr. 11:5 b 2 Chr. 15:8
4 a 1 Kin. 12:28 *1 LXX the LORD God*
5 a 1 Kin. 10:25 b 2 Chr. 18:1
6 a 1 Kin. 22:43 *1 Places for pagan worship*
7 a 2 Chr. 15:3; 35:3
9 a Neh. 8:3, 7
10 a 2 Chr. 14:14
11 a 2 Chr. 9:14; 26:8
16 a Judg. 5:2, 9
19 a 2 Chr. 17:2

CHAPTER 18
1 a 2 Chr. 17:5 b 2 Kin. 8:18 c 1 Kin. 22:40
2 a 1 Kin. 22:2

up *with him* to Ramoth Gilead. 3So Ahab
king of Israel said to Jehoshaphat king of
Judah, "Will you go with me *against* Ramoth Gilead?"
And he answered him, "I *am* as you *are,*
and my people as your people; *we will be*
with you in the war."
4Also Jehoshaphat said to the king of
Israel, [a]"Please inquire for the word of the
LORD today."
5Then the king of Israel gathered the
prophets together, four hundred men,
and said to them, "Shall we go to war
against Ramoth Gilead, or shall I refrain?"
So they said, "Go up, for God will deliver it into the king's hand."
6But Jehoshaphat said, "*Is there* not
still a prophet of the LORD here, that we
may inquire of [a]Him?"[1]
7So the king of Israel said to Jehoshaphat, "*There is* still one man by whom we
may inquire of the LORD; but I hate him,
because he never prophesies good concerning me, but always evil. He *is* Micaiah
the son of Imla."
And Jehoshaphat said, "Let not the king
say such things!"
8Then the king of Israel called one *of
his* officers and said, "Bring Micaiah the
son of Imla quickly!"
9The king of Israel and Jehoshaphat
king of Judah, clothed in *their* robes, sat
each on his throne; and they sat at a
threshing floor at the entrance of the gate
of Samaria; and all the prophets prophesied before them. 10Now Zedekiah the son
of Chenaanah had made [a]horns of iron for
himself; and he said, "Thus says the LORD:
'With these you shall gore the Syrians until they are destroyed.' "
11And all the prophets prophesied so,
saying, "Go up to Ramoth Gilead and
prosper, for the LORD will deliver *it* into
the king's hand."
12Then the messenger who had gone to
call Micaiah spoke to him, saying, "Now
listen, the words of the prophets with one
accord encourage the king. Therefore
please let your word be like *the word of*
one of them, and speak encouragement."
13And Micaiah said, "*As* the LORD lives,
[a]whatever my God says, that I will speak."
14Then he came to the king; and the
king said to him, "Micaiah, shall we go to
war against Ramoth Gilead, or shall I refrain?"
And he said, "Go and prosper, and they
shall be delivered into your hand!"

4 a 2 Sam. 2:1
6 a 2 Kin. 3:11
1 Or *him*
10 a Zech. 1:18–21
13 a Num. 22:18–20, 35; 23:12, 26
16 a [Jer. 23:1–8; 31:10] b Matt. 9:36
18 a Is. 6:1–5
20 a Job 1:6
22 a Ezek. 14:9
23 a Jer. 20:2
26 a 2 Chr. 16:10

15So the king said to him, "How many
times shall I make you swear that you tell
me nothing but the truth in the name of
the LORD?"

He to whom the eternal Word speaks is set free from many opinions.

THOMAS À KEMPIS

16Then he said, "I saw all Israel [a]scat-
tered on the mountains, as sheep that
have no [b]shepherd. And the LORD said,
'These have no master. Let each return to
his house in peace.' "
17And the king of Israel said to Jehoshaphat, "Did I not tell you he would not
prophesy good concerning me, but evil?"
18Then *Micaiah* said, "Therefore hear
the word of the LORD: I saw the LORD sitting on His [a]throne, and all the host of
heaven standing on His right hand and
His left. 19And the LORD said, 'Who will
persuade Ahab king of Israel to go up, that
he may fall at Ramoth Gilead?' So one
spoke in this manner, and another spoke
in that manner. 20Then a [a]spirit came forward and stood before the LORD, and said,
'I will persuade him.' The LORD said to
him, 'In what way?' 21So he said, 'I will go
out and be a lying spirit in the mouth of
all his prophets.' And *the LORD* said, 'You
shall persuade *him* and also prevail; go
out and do so.' 22Therefore look! [a]The
LORD has put a lying spirit in the mouth
of these prophets of yours, and the LORD
has declared disaster against you."
23Then Zedekiah the son of Chenaanah
went near and [a]struck Micaiah on the
cheek, and said, "Which way did the spirit
from the LORD go from me to speak to
you?"
24And Micaiah said, "Indeed you shall
see on that day when you go into an inner
chamber to hide!"
25Then the king of Israel said, "Take Micaiah, and return him to Amon the governor of the city and to Joash the king's son;
26and say, 'Thus says the king: [a]"Put this
fellow in prison, and feed him with bread

of affliction and water of affliction, until I
return in peace.""'
27But Micaiah said, "If you ever return
in peace, the LORD has not spoken by
[a]me." And he said, "Take heed, all you
people!"

Ahab Dies in Battle

28So the king of Israel and Jehoshaphat
the king of Judah went up to Ramoth Gilead. 29And the king of Israel said to Jehoshaphat, "I will [a]disguise myself and go
into battle; but you put on your robes." So
the king of Israel disguised himself, and
they went into battle.
30Now the king of Syria had commanded the captains of the chariots who *were*
with him, saying, "Fight with no one
small or great, but only with the king of
Israel."
31So it was, when the captains of the
chariots saw Jehoshaphat, that they said,
"It *is* the king of Israel!" Therefore they
surrounded him to attack; but Jehoshaphat [a]cried out, and the LORD helped him,
and God diverted them from him. 32For so
it was, when the captains of the chariots
saw that it was not the king of Israel, that
they turned back from pursuing him.
33Now a certain man drew a bow at ran-
dom, and struck the king of Israel between the [1]joints of his armor. So he said
to the driver of his chariot, "Turn around
and take me out of the battle, for I am
wounded." 34The battle increased that
day, and the king of Israel propped *himself* up in *his* chariot facing the Syrians
until evening; and about the time of sun-
set he died.

19 Then Jehoshaphat the king of Judah returned safely to his house in
Jerusalem. 2And Jehu the son of Hanani
[a]the seer went out to meet him, and said
to King Jehoshaphat, "Should you help
the wicked and [b]love those who hate the
LORD? Therefore the [c]wrath of the LORD *is*
upon you. 3Nevertheless [a]good things are
found in you, in that you have removed
the [1]wooden images from the land, and
have [b]prepared your heart to seek God."

The Reforms of Jehoshaphat

4So Jehoshaphat dwelt at Jerusalem;
and he went out again among the people
from Beersheba to the mountains of
Ephraim, and brought them back to the
LORD God of their [a]fathers. 5Then he set
[a]judges in the land throughout all the fortified cities of Judah, city by city, 6and said
to the judges, "Take heed to what you are
doing, for [a]you do not judge for man but
for the LORD, [b]who *is* with you [1]in the
judgment. 7Now therefore, let the fear of
the LORD be upon you; take care and do *it*,
for [a]*there is* no iniquity with the LORD our
God, no [b]partiality, nor taking of bribes."
8Moreover in Jerusalem, for the judgment of the LORD and for controversies,
Jehoshaphat [a]appointed some of the Levites and priests, and some of the chief
fathers of Israel, [1]when they returned to
Jerusalem. 9And he commanded them,
saying, "Thus you shall act [a]in the fear of
the LORD, faithfully and with a loyal heart:
10[a]Whatever case comes to you from your
brethren who dwell in their cities, whether of bloodshed or offenses against law or
commandment, against statutes or ordinances, you shall warn them, lest they
trespass against the LORD and [b]wrath
come upon [c]you and your brethren. Do
this, and you will not be guilty. 11And take
notice: [a]Amariah the chief priest *is* over
you [b]in all matters of the LORD; and Zebadiah the son of Ishmael, the ruler of the
house of Judah, for all the king's matters;
also the Levites *will be* officials before
you. Behave courageously, and the LORD
will be [c]with the good."

Ammon, Moab, and Mount Seir Defeated

20 It happened after this *that* the people of [a]Moab with the people of
[b]Ammon, and *others* with them besides
the [c]Ammonites,[1] came to battle against
Jehoshaphat. 2Then some came and told
Jehoshaphat, saying, "A great multitude is
coming against you from beyond the sea,
from [1]Syria; and they are [a]in Hazazon Tamar" (which *is* [b]En Gedi). 3And Jehoshaphat feared, and set [1]himself to [a]seek the
LORD, and [b]proclaimed a fast throughout
all Judah. 4So Judah gathered together to
ask [a]*help* from the LORD; and from all the
cities of Judah they came to seek the
LORD.
5Then Jehoshaphat stood in the assembly of Judah and Jerusalem, in the house
of the LORD, before the new court, 6and
said: "O LORD God of our fathers, *are* You
not [a]God in heaven, and [b]do You *not* rule
over all the kingdoms of the nations, and
[c]in Your hand *is there not* power and
might, so that no one is able to withstand
You? 7*Are* You not [a]our God, *who* [b]drove

---

27 a Deut. 18:22
29 a 2 Chr. 35:22
31 a 2 Chr. 13:14, 15
33 *1* Or *scale armor and the breastplate*

CHAPTER 19
2 a 1 Kin. 16:1 b Ps. 139:21 c 2 Chr. 32:25
3 a 2 Chr. 17:4, 6 b 2 Chr. 30:19 *1* Or *Asherim*, Heb. *Asheroth*
4 a 2 Chr. 15:8–13
5 a [Deut. 16:18–20]
6 a [Deut. 1:17] b Ps. 82:1 *1* Lit. *in the matter of the judgment*
7 a [Deut. 32:4] b [Deut. 10:17, 18]
8 a 2 Chr. 17:8 *1* LXX, Vg. *for the inhabitants of Jerusalem*
9 a [2 Sam. 23:3]
10 a Deut. 17:8 b Num. 16:46 c [Ezek. 3:18]
11 a Ezra 7:3 b 1 Chr. 26:30 c [2 Chr. 15:2; 20:17]

CHAPTER 20
1 a 1 Chr. 18:2 b 1 Chr. 19:15 c 2 Chr. 26:7 *1* So with MT, Vg.; LXX *Meunites* (cf. 2 Chr. 26:7)
2 a Gen. 14:7 b Josh. 15:62 *1* So with MT, LXX, Vg.; Heb. mss., Old Lat. *Edom*
3 a 2 Chr. 19:3 b Ezra 8:21 *1* Lit. *his face*
4 a 2 Chr. 14:11
6 a Deut. 4:39 b Dan. 4:17, 25, 32 c 1 Chr. 29:12
7 a Ex. 6:7 b Ps. 44:2

out the inhabitants of this land before
Your people Israel, and gave it to the descendants of Abraham [c]Your friend forever? [8]And they dwell in it, and have built
You a sanctuary in it for Your name, saying, [9][a]'If disaster comes upon us—sword,
judgment, pestilence, or famine—we will
stand before this temple and in Your presence (for Your [b]name *is* in this temple),
and cry out to You in our affliction, and
You will hear and save.' [10]And now, here
are the people of Ammon, Moab, and
Mount Seir—whom You [a]would not let
Israel invade when they came out of the
land of Egypt, but [b]they turned from
them and did not destroy them— [11]here
they are, rewarding us [a]by coming to
throw us out of Your possession which
You have given us to inherit. [12]O our God,
will You not [a]judge them? For we have no
power against this great multitude that is
coming against us; nor do we know what
to do, but [b]our eyes *are* upon You."
[13]Now all Judah, with their little ones,
their wives, and their children, stood before the LORD.

7 c Is. 41:8
9 a 2 Chr. 6:28–30 b 2 Chr. 6:20
10 a Deut. 2:4, 9, 19 b Num. 20:21
11 a Ps. 83:1–18
12 a Judg. 11:27 b Ps. 25:15; 121:1, 2; 123:1, 2; 141:8

JOAN OF ARC

Joan of Arc (1412–1431) enjoyed an intimate relationship with God and called Him *Messire* ("my Master"). What she heard from Him was sweet and direct.

At age 16, she started receiving supernatural instruction regarding the political distress of her homeland, France. After some discouragement, Joan eventually appeared before France's disputed heir to the throne and said, "I am God's messenger, sent to tell you that you are . . . the true heir to France. And France is to be a Holy Kingdom."

Before she went, Joan cut her hair short and exchanged her dress for a soldier's uniform. Unfazed by much criticism for this, she believed God had instructed her to dress so that she could easily ride a horse and mingle with the soldiers.

After weeks of questioning, she was allowed to proceed. God gave her specific instructions to lead a battle at Orleans: "In God's Name go down against them, for they shall fall and not stay and shall be utterly discomforted; and you shall lose scarce any men. Arise and pursue them."

The troops took Orleans, and Joan led four more battles. She then instructed the heir to the throne to enter the city where the kings of France were traditionally crowned and saw that he was anointed with oil.

The day after his coronation, Joan was captured and tried by theologians and jurists as a witch and a heretic. She stood steadfast and answered clearly all the charges against her.

On May 31, 1431, nineteen-year-old Joan was tied to a stake and burned alive. Not once did she beg to be released, for she was not afraid of martyrdom. Her last words were simply the sweetest ones human lips can utter . . . *Jesus, Jesus.*

Joan did not consider her youth to be an obstacle in the path of her destiny in God. She died having fulfilled the purposes of God for her life in her generation (see Acts 13:36). The verdict against her was later reversed, and she was canonized in 1920 by Pope Benedict XV. Joan of Arc is a patroness of France.

14Then [a]the Spirit of the LORD came
upon Jahaziel the son of Zechariah, the
son of Benaiah, the son of Jeiel, the son of
Mattaniah, a Levite of the sons of Asaph,
in the midst of the assembly. 15And he
said, "Listen, all you of Judah and you
inhabitants of Jerusalem, and you, King
Jehoshaphat! Thus says the LORD to you:
[a]'Do not be afraid nor dismayed because
of this great multitude, [b]for the battle
is not yours, but God's. 16Tomorrow go
down against them. They will surely come
up by the Ascent of Ziz, and you will find
them at the end of the [1]brook before the
Wilderness of Jeruel. 17[a]You will not *need*
to fight in this *battle.* Position yourselves,
stand still and see the salvation of the
LORD, who is with you, O Judah and Jerusalem!' Do not fear or be dismayed; tomorrow go out against them, [b]for the
LORD *is* with you."

Lord God, if disaster comes upon ____, may they stand in Your presence and cry out to You in their affliction, for You will hear and save.

FROM 2 CHRONICLES 20:9

18And Jehoshaphat [a]bowed his head
with *his* face to the ground, and all Judah
and the inhabitants of Jerusalem bowed
before the LORD, worshiping the LORD.
19Then the Levites of the children of the
Kohathites and of the children of the Korahites stood up to praise the LORD God of
Israel with voices loud and high.
20 So they rose early in the morning
and went out into the Wilderness of Tekoa; and as they went out, Jehoshaphat
stood and said, "Hear me, O Judah and
you inhabitants of Jerusalem: [a]Believe in
the LORD your God, and you shall be established; believe His prophets, and you
shall prosper." 21And when he had consulted with the people, he appointed those
who should sing to the LORD, [a]and who
should praise the beauty of holiness, as
they went out before the army and were
saying:

[b]"Praise the LORD,
[c]For His mercy *endures* forever."

22Now when they began to sing and to
praise, [a]the LORD set ambushes against
the people of Ammon, Moab, and Mount
Seir, who had come against Judah; and
they were defeated. 23For the people of
Ammon and Moab stood up against the
inhabitants of Mount Seir to utterly kill
and destroy *them.* And when they [1]had
made an end of the inhabitants of Seir,
[a]they helped to destroy one another.
24So when Judah came to a place overlooking the wilderness, they looked toward the multitude; and there *were* their
dead bodies, fallen on the earth. No one
had escaped.
25When Jehoshaphat and his people
came to take away their spoil, they found
among them an abundance of valuables
on the [1]dead bodies, and precious jewelry,
which they stripped off for themselves,
more than they could carry away; and
they were three days gathering the spoil
because there was so much. 26And on the
fourth day they assembled in the Valley
of [1]Berachah, for there they blessed the
LORD; therefore the name of that place
was called The Valley of Berachah until
this day. 27Then they returned, every man
of Judah and Jerusalem, with Jehoshaphat
in front of them, to go back to Jerusalem
with joy, for the LORD had [a]made them
rejoice over their enemies. 28So they
came to Jerusalem, with stringed instruments and harps and trumpets, to the
house of the LORD. 29And [a]the fear of God
was on all the kingdoms of *those* countries when they heard that the LORD had
fought against the enemies of Israel.
30Then the realm of Jehoshaphat was quiet, for his [a]God gave him rest all around.

The End of Jehoshaphat's Reign

31[a]So Jehoshaphat was king over Judah. *He was* thirty-five years old when he
became king, and he reigned twenty-five
years in Jerusalem. His mother's name
was Azubah the daughter of Shilhi. 32And
he walked in the way of his father [a]Asa,
and did not turn aside from it, doing *what*
was right in the sight of the LORD. 33Nev-
ertheless [a]the [1]high places were not taken
away, for as yet the people had not [b]direct-
ed their hearts to the God of their fathers.
34Now the rest of the acts of Jehoshaphat, first and last, indeed they *are* written in the book of Jehu the son of Hanani,

14 a 2 Chr. 15:1; 24:20
15 a [Deut. 1:29, 30; 31:6, 8] b 1 Sam. 17:47
16 *1 stream-bed* or *wadi*
17 a Ex. 14:13, 14 b Num. 14:9
18 a Ex. 4:31
20 a Is. 7:9
21 a 1 Chr. 16:29 b Ps. 106:1; 136:1 c 2 Chr. 5:13
22 a Judg. 7:22
23 a 1 Sam. 14:20 *1 had finished*
25 *1* A few Heb. mss., Old Lat., Vg. *garments;* LXX *armor*
26 *1* Lit. *Blessing*
27 a Neh. 12:43
29 a 2 Chr. 14:14; 17:10
30 a Job 34:29
31 a [1 Kin. 22:41–43]
32 a 2 Chr. 14:2
33 a 2 Chr. 15:17; 17:6 b 2 Chr. 12:14; 19:3 *1* Places for pagan worship

2 Chronicles 20:20

Dear Woman of Destiny,

Second Chronicles 20:20, which tells us we will prosper if we believe God's prophets, is very important for us to understand. The context of this passage is that the children of Israel were being threatened by a great multitude of Ammonites. Things looked extremely bleak and discouraging for God's people! Without hearing the right battle strategy from God, they quite possibly could have died.

God spoke to them through the prophet Jahaziel and told them not to be afraid, that He would fight the battle for them. This, of course, was very comforting to the children of Israel. The Israelites' leader, Jehoshaphat, believed the prophetic word, interpreted it into battle strategy, and sent singers to do the battle.

Does God still speak to His people today? Yes, He does. Through prophetic people God will give us messages when we are in the midst of personal or national battles. God has often given me warning for cities and nations because He doesn't want judgments to fall upon them. Years ago, I was in Miami, Florida, one week before Hurricane Andrew caused massive destruction, and prophesied, "If this city does not repent for its witchcraft, God will judge it with the elements." One week later, Andrew roared through the city, leaving behind massive devastation.

We need to learn how to discern whether or not a prophecy is from God so that we will know whether or not to believe it. The Bible is clear that prophecy (not end-time prophecy, but that given from the gift of prophecy mentioned in 1 Corinthians 12:10) should edify, exhort, and/or comfort us.

If a prophetic word is from God, then we need to heed it. Many times God will speak specific directions for us to follow, often showing us certain conditions He wants us to meet. For example, the word about the sin of witchcraft in Miami asked for a response of repentance.

At times, we need to fight for the prophetic word to come to pass. Jehoshaphat and the children of Israel didn't just sit down and do nothing when they received the prophetic word; they went to war with worship. We may need to fight the good fight of faith to believe that what God has told us will come true (see 1 Tim. 1:18).

If God has given you a promise through a prophetic word and it has been judged to be accurate not only by you, but also by those you trust in spiritual authority, stand firm! You may be on the brink of financial disaster, and God has promised you a breakthrough. Hang on! Your marriage may be falling apart, and you have a word that God will heal your relationship. Don't give up! God is not a man who can lie (see Num. 23:19). Stand still, and see the deliverance of the Lord.

Cindy Jacobs

[a]which *is* mentioned in the book of the
kings of Israel.
[35]After this [a]Jehoshaphat king of Judah
allied himself with Ahaziah king of Israel,
[b]who acted very [c]wickedly. [36]And he allied
himself with him [a]to make ships to go to
Tarshish, and they made the ships in Ezion Geber. [37]But Eliezer the son of Doda-
vah of Mareshah prophesied against
Jehoshaphat, saying, "Because you have
allied yourself with Ahaziah, the LORD has
destroyed your works." [a]Then the ships
were wrecked, so that they were not able
to go [b]to Tarshish.

Jehoram Reigns in Judah

21 And [a]Jehoshaphat [1]rested with his
fathers, and was buried with his fathers in the City of David. Then Jehoram
his son reigned in his place. [2]He had
brothers, the sons of Jehoshaphat: Azariah, Jehiel, Zechariah, Azaryahu, Michael,
and Shephatiah; all these *were* the sons of
Jehoshaphat king of Israel. [3]Their father
gave them great gifts of silver and gold
and precious things, with fortified cities
in Judah; but he gave the kingdom to Jehoram, because he *was* the firstborn.
[4]Now when Jehoram [1]was established
over the kingdom of his father, he
strengthened himself and killed all his
brothers with the sword, and also *others*
of the princes of Israel.
[5][a]Jehoram *was* thirty-two years old
when he became king, and he reigned
eight years in Jerusalem. [6]And he walked
in the way of the kings of Israel, just as the
house of Ahab had done, for he had the
daughter of [a]Ahab as a wife; and he did
evil in the sight of the LORD. [7]Yet the
LORD would not destroy the house of David, because of the [a]covenant that He had
made with David, and since He had promised to give a lamp to him and to his [b]sons
forever.
[8][a]In his days Edom revolted against Judah's authority, and made a king over
themselves. [9]So Jehoram went out with
his officers, and all his chariots with him.
And he rose by night and attacked the
Edomites who had surrounded him and
the captains of the chariots. [10]Thus Edom
has been in revolt against Judah's authority to this day. At that time Libnah revolted against his rule, because he had
forsaken the LORD God of his fathers.
[11]Moreover he made [1]high places in the
mountains of Judah, and caused the
inhabitants of Jerusalem to [a]commit harlotry, and led Judah astray.
[12]And a letter came to him from Elijah
the prophet, saying,

> Thus says the LORD God of your father David:
> Because you have not walked in the ways of Jehoshaphat your father, or in the ways of Asa king of Judah,
> [13]but have walked in the way of the kings of Israel, and have [a]made Judah and the inhabitants of Jerusalem to [b]play the harlot like the [c]harlotry of the house of Ahab, and also have [d]killed your brothers, those of your father's household, *who were* better than yourself,
> [14]behold, the LORD will strike your people with a serious affliction—your children, your wives, and all your possessions;
> [15]and you *will become* very sick with a [a]disease of your intestines, until your intestines come out by reason of the sickness, day by day.

[16]Moreover the [a]LORD [b]stirred up
against Jehoram the spirit of the Philistines and the [c]Arabians who *were* near the
Ethiopians. [17]And they came up into Judah and invaded it, and carried away all
the possessions that were found in the
king's house, and also [a]his sons and his
wives, so that there was not a son left to
him except [1]Jehoahaz, the youngest of his
sons.
[18]After all this the LORD struck him [a]in
his intestines with an incurable disease.
[19]Then it happened in the course of time,
after the end of two years, that his intestines came out because of his sickness; so
he died in severe pain. And his people
made no [1]burning for him, like [a]the
burning for his fathers.
[20]He was thirty-two years old when he
became king. He reigned in Jerusalem
eight years and, to no one's sorrow, departed. However they buried him in the
City of David, but not in the tombs of the
kings.

Ahaziah Reigns in Judah

22 Then the inhabitants of Jerusalem
made [a]Ahaziah his youngest son
king in his place, for the raiders who came
with the [b]Arabians into the camp had
killed all the [c]older *sons*. So Ahaziah the
son of Jehoram, king of Judah, reigned.

---

34 [a] 1 Kin. 16:1, 7
35 [a] 2 Chr. 18:1 [b] 1 Kin. 22:48–53 [c] [2 Chr. 19:2]
36 [a] 1 Kin. 9:26; 10:22
37 [a] 1 Kin. 22:48 [b] 2 Chr. 9:21

CHAPTER 21
1 [a] 1 Kin. 22:50 [1] Died and joined his ancestors
4 [1] Lit. *arose*
5 [a] 2 Kin. 8:17–22
6 [a] 2 Chr. 18:1
7 [a] 2 Sam. 7:8–17 [b] 1 Kin. 11:36
8 [a] 2 Kin. 8:20; 14:7, 10
11 [a] [Lev. 20:5] [1] Places for pagan worship
13 [a] 2 Chr. 21:11 [b] Deut. 31:16 [c] 2 Kin. 9:22 [d] 2 Chr. 21:4
15 [a] 2 Chr. 21:18, 19
16 [a] 2 Chr. 33:11 [b] 1 Kin. 11:14, 23 [c] 2 Chr. 17:11
17 [a] 2 Chr. 24:7 [1] *Ahaziah* or *Azariah*, 2 Chr. 22:1
18 [a] 2 Chr. 13:20; 21:15
19 [a] 2 Chr. 16:14 [1] Burning of spices

CHAPTER 22
1 [a] 2 Chr. 21:17; 22:6 [b] 2 Chr. 21:16 [c] 2 Chr. 21:17

2 Ahaziah *was* [1]forty-two years old when
he became king, and he reigned one year
in Jerusalem. His mother's name *was*
[a]Athaliah the [2]granddaughter of Omri.
3 He also walked in the ways of the house
of Ahab, for his mother advised him to do
wickedly. 4 Therefore he did evil in the
sight of the LORD, like the house of Ahab;
for they were his counselors after the
death of his father, to his destruction. 5 He
also followed their advice, and went with
[1]Jehoram the son of Ahab king of Israel to
war against Hazael king of Syria at Ramoth Gilead; and the Syrians wounded
Joram. 6 [a]Then he returned to Jezreel to
recover from the wounds which he had
received at Ramah, when he fought
against Hazael king of Syria. And [1]Azariah
the son of Jehoram, king of Judah, went
down to see Jehoram the son of Ahab in
Jezreel, because he was sick.

7 His going to Joram [a]was God's occasion for Ahaziah's [1]downfall; for when he
arrived, [b]he went out with [2]Jehoram
against Jehu the son of Nimshi, [c]whom
the LORD had anointed to [3]cut off the
house of Ahab. 8 And it happened, when
Jehu was [a]executing judgment on the
house of Ahab, and [b]found the princes of
Judah and the sons of Ahaziah's brothers
who served Ahaziah, that he killed them.
9 [a]Then he searched for Ahaziah; and they
caught him (he was hiding in Samaria),
and brought him to Jehu. When they had
killed him, they buried him, "because,"
they said, "he is the son of [b]Jehoshaphat,
who [c]sought the LORD with all his heart."

So the house of Ahaziah had no one to
assume power over the kingdom.

Athaliah Reigns in Judah

10 [a]Now when Athaliah the mother of
Ahaziah saw that her son was dead, she
arose and destroyed all the royal heirs of
the house of Judah. 11 But [1]Jehoshabeath,
the daughter of the king, took [a]Joash the
son of Ahaziah, and stole him away from
among the king's sons who were being
murdered, and put him and his nurse in
a bedroom. So Jehoshabeath, the daughter of King Jehoram, the wife of Jehoiada
the priest (for she was the sister of Ahaziah), hid him from Athaliah so that she did
not kill him. 12 And he was hidden with
them in the house of God for six years,
while Athaliah reigned over the land.

Joash Crowned King of Judah

23 In [a]the seventh year [b]Jehoiada
strengthened himself, *and made a*
covenant with the captains of hundreds:
Azariah the son of Jeroham, Ishmael the
son of Jehohanan, Azariah the son of
[c]Obed, Maaseiah the son of Adaiah, and
Elishaphat the son of Zichri. 2 And they
went throughout Judah and gathered the
Levites from all the cities of Judah, and
the [a]chief fathers of Israel, and they came
to Jerusalem.

3 Then all the assembly made a covenant with the king in the house of God.
And he said to them, "Behold, the king's
son shall reign, as the LORD has [a]said of
the sons of David. 4 This *is* what you shall
do: One-third of you [a]entering on the
Sabbath, of the priests and the Levites,
shall be keeping watch over the doors;
5 one-third *shall be* at the king's house;
and one-third at the Gate of the Foundation. All the people *shall be* in the courts
of the house of the LORD. 6 But let no one
come into the house of the LORD except
the priests and [a]those of the Levites who
serve. They may go in, for they *are* holy;
but all the people shall keep the watch of
the LORD. 7 And the Levites shall surround
the king on all sides, every man with his
weapons in his hand; and whoever comes
into the house, let him be put to death.
You are to be with the king when he
comes in and when he goes out."

8 So the Levites and all Judah did according to all that Jehoiada the priest
commanded. And each man took his men
who were to be on duty on the Sabbath,
with those who were going *off duty* on the
Sabbath; for Jehoiada the priest had not
dismissed [a]the divisions. 9 And Jehoiada
the priest gave to the captains of hundreds
the spears and the large and small
[a]shields which *had belonged* to King David, that *were* in the temple of God.
10 Then he set all the people, every man
with his weapon in his hand, from the
right side of the temple to the left side of
the temple, along by the altar and by the
temple, all around the king. 11 And they
brought out the king's son, put the crown
on him, [a]*gave him* the [1]Testimony, and
made him king. Then Jehoiada and his
sons anointed him, and said, "*Long* live
the king!"

2 a 2 Chr. 21:6 *1 twenty-two,* 2 Kin. 8:26 *2* Lit. *daughter*
5 *1 Joram,* v. 7; 2 Kin. 8:28
6 a 2 Kin. 9:15 *1* Heb. mss., LXX, Syr., Vg. *Ahaziah* and 2 Kin. 8:29
7 a 2 Chr. 10:15 b 2 Kin. 9:21–24 c 2 Kin. 9:6, 7 *1* Lit. *crushing* *2 Joram,* vv. 5, 7; 2 Kin. 8:28 *3 destroy*
8 a 2 Kin. 9:22–24 b 2 Kin. 10:10–14
9 a [2 Kin. 9:27] b 1 Kin. 15:24 c 2 Chr. 17:4; 20:3, 4
10 a 2 Kin. 11:1–3
11 a 2 Kin. 12:18 *1 Jehosheba,* 2 Kin. 11:2

CHAPTER 23
1 a 2 Kin. 11:4 b 2 Kin. 12:2 c 1 Chr. 2:37, 38
2 a Ezra 1:5
3 a 2 Sam. 7:12
4 a 1 Chr. 9:25
6 a 1 Chr. 23:28–32
8 a 1 Chr. 24:1–31
9 a 2 Sam. 8:7
11 a Deut. 17:18 *1* Law, Ex. 25:16, 21; 31:18

Death of Athaliah

12Now when [a]Athaliah heard the noise of the people running and praising the king, she came to the people *in* the temple of the LORD. 13*When* she looked, there was the king standing by his pillar at the entrance; and the leaders and the trumpeters *were* by the king. All the people of the land were rejoicing and blowing trumpets, also the singers with musical instruments, and [a]those who led in praise. So Athaliah tore her clothes and said, [b]"Treason! Treason!"

14And Jehoiada the priest brought out the captains of hundreds who were set over the army, and said to them, "Take her outside under guard, and slay with the sword whoever follows her." For the priest had said, "Do not kill her in the house of the LORD."

15So they seized her; and she went by way of the entrance [a]of the Horse Gate *into* the king's house, and they killed her there.

16Then Jehoiada made a [a]covenant between himself, the people, and the king, that they should be the LORD's people. 17And all the people went to the [1]temple of Baal, and tore it down. They broke in pieces its altars and images, and [a]killed Mattan the priest of Baal before the altars. 18Also Jehoiada appointed the oversight of the house of the LORD to the hand of the priests, the Levites, whom David had [a]assigned in the house of the LORD, to offer the burnt offerings of the LORD, as *it is* written in the [b]Law of Moses, with rejoicing and with singing, *as it was established* by David. 19And he set the [a]gatekeepers at the gates of the house of the LORD, so that no one *who was* in any way unclean should enter.

20[a]Then he took the captains of hundreds, the nobles, the governors of the people, and all the people of the land, and brought the king down from the house of the LORD; and they went through the Upper Gate to the king's house, and set the king on the throne of the kingdom. 21So all the people of the land rejoiced; and the city was quiet, for they had slain Athaliah with the sword.

Joash Repairs the Temple

24 Joash [a]*was* seven years old when he became king, and he reigned forty years in Jerusalem. His mother's name *was* Zibiah of Beersheba. 2Joash [a]did *what was* right in the sight of the LORD all the days of Jehoiada the priest. 3And Jehoiada took two wives for him, and he had sons and daughters.

4Now it happened after this *that* Joash set his heart on repairing the house of the LORD. 5Then he gathered the priests and the Levites, and said to them, "Go out to the cities of Judah, and [a]gather from all Israel money to repair the house of your God from year to year, and see that you do it quickly."

However the Levites did not do it quickly. 6[a]So the king called Jehoiada the chief *priest,* and said to him, "Why have you not required the Levites to bring in from Judah and from Jerusalem the collection, *according to the commandment* of [b]Moses the servant of the LORD and of the assembly of Israel, for the [c]tabernacle of witness?" 7For [a]the sons of Athaliah, that wicked woman, had broken into the house of God, and had also presented all the [b]dedicated things of the house of the LORD to the Baals.

8Then at the king's command [a]they made a chest, and set it outside at the gate of the house of the LORD. 9And they made a proclamation throughout Judah and Jerusalem to bring to the LORD [a]the collection *that* Moses the servant of God *had imposed* on Israel in the wilderness. 10Then all the leaders and all the people rejoiced, brought their contributions, and put *them* into the chest until all had given. 11So it was, at that time, when the chest was brought to the king's official by the hand of the Levites, and [a]when they saw that *there was* much money, that the king's scribe and the high priest's officer came and emptied the chest, and took it and returned it to its place. Thus they did day by day, and gathered money in abundance.

12The king and Jehoiada gave it to those who did the work of the service of the house of the LORD; and they hired masons and carpenters to [a]repair the house of the LORD, and also those who worked in iron and bronze to restore the house of the LORD. 13So the workmen labored, and the work was completed by them; they restored the house of God to its original condition and reinforced it. 14When they had finished, they brought the rest of the money before the king and Jehoiada; [a]they made from it articles for the house of the LORD, articles for serving and offer-

12 [a]2 Chr. 22:10
13 [a]1 Chr. 25:6–8 [b]2 Kin. 9:23
15 [a]Neh. 3:28
16 [a]Josh. 24:24, 25
17 [a]Deut. 13:6–9 [1]Lit. *house*
18 [a]1 Chr. 23:6, 30, 31; 24:1 [b]Num. 28:2
19 [a]1 Chr. 26:1–19
20 [a]2 Kin. 11:19

CHAPTER 24
1 [a]2 Kin. 11:21; 12:1–15
2 [a]2 Chr. 26:4, 5
5 [a]2 Kin. 12:4
6 [a]2 Kin. 12:7 [b]Ex. 30:12–16 [c]Num. 1:50
7 [a]2 Chr. 21:17 [b]2 Kin. 12:4
8 [a]2 Kin. 12:9
9 [a]2 Chr. 24:6
11 [a]2 Kin. 12:10
12 [a]2 Chr. 30:12
14 [a]2 Kin. 12:13

ing, spoons and vessels of gold and silver. And they offered burnt offerings in the house of the LORD continually all the days of Jehoiada.

Apostasy of Joash

15But Jehoiada grew old and was full of days, and he died; *he was* one hundred and thirty years old when he died. 16And they buried him in the City of David among the kings, because he had done good in Israel, both toward God and His house.

17Now after the death of Jehoiada the leaders of Judah came and bowed down to the king. And the king listened to them. 18Therefore they left the house of the LORD God of their fathers, and served [a]wooden images and idols; and [b]wrath came upon Judah and Jerusalem because of their trespass. 19Yet He [a]sent prophets to them, to bring them back to the LORD; and they testified against them, but they would not listen.

20Then the Spirit of God [1]came upon [a]Zechariah the son of Jehoiada the priest, who stood above the people, and said to them, "Thus says God: [b]'Why do you transgress the commandments of the LORD, so that you cannot prosper? [c]Because you have forsaken the LORD, He also has forsaken you.' " 21So they conspired against him, and at the command of the king they [a]stoned him with stones in the court of the house of the LORD. 22Thus Joash the king did not remember the kindness which Jehoiada his [1]father had done to him, but killed his son; and as he died, he said, "The LORD look on *it,* and [a]repay!"

Death of Joash

23So it happened in the spring of the year *that* [a]the army of Syria came up against him; and they came to Judah and Jerusalem, and destroyed all the leaders of the people from among the people, and sent all their [1]spoil to the king of Damascus. 24For the army of the Syrians [a]came with a small company of men; but the LORD [b]delivered a very great army into their hand, because they had forsaken the LORD God of their fathers. So they [c]executed judgment against Joash. 25And when they had withdrawn from him (for they left him severely wounded), [a]his own servants conspired against him because of the blood of the [1]sons of Jehoiada the priest, and killed him on his bed. So he died. And they buried him in the City of David, but they did not bury him in the tombs of the kings.

26These are the ones who conspired against him: [1]Zabad the son of Shimeath the Ammonitess, and Jehozabad the son of [2]Shimrith the Moabitess. 27Now *concerning* his sons, and [a]the many oracles about him, and the repairing of the house of God, indeed they *are* written in the [1]annals of the book of the kings. [b]Then Amaziah his son reigned in his place.

Amaziah Reigns in Judah

25 Amaziah [a]*was* twenty-five years old *when* he became king, and he reigned twenty-nine years in Jerusalem. His mother's name *was* Jehoaddan of Jerusalem. 2And he did *what was* right in the sight of the LORD, [a]but not with a loyal heart.

3[a]Now it happened, as soon as the kingdom was established for him, that he executed his servants who had murdered his father the king. 4However he did not execute their children, but *did* as *it is* written in the Law in the Book of Moses, where the LORD commanded, saying, [a]"The fathers shall not be put to death for their children, nor shall the children be put to death for their fathers; but a person shall die for his own sin."

The War Against Edom

5Moreover Amaziah gathered Judah together and set over them captains of thousands and captains of hundreds, according to *their* fathers' houses, throughout all Judah and Benjamin; and he numbered them [a]from twenty years old and above, and found them to be three hundred thousand choice *men, able* to go to war, who could handle spear and shield. 6He also hired one hundred thousand mighty men of valor from Israel for one hundred talents of silver. 7But a [a]man of God came to him, saying, "O king, do not let the army of Israel go with you, for the LORD *is* not with Israel—*not with* any of the children of Ephraim. 8But if you go, be gone! Be strong in battle! *Even so,* God shall make you fall before the enemy; for God has [a]power to help and to overthrow."

9Then Amaziah said to the man of God, "But what *shall we* do about the hundred

18 a 1 Kin. 14:23 b [Ex. 34:12–14]
19 a 2 Chr. 36:15, 16
20 a Matt. 23:35 b Num. 14:41 c [2 Chr. 15:2] *1* Lit. *clothed*
21 a [Neh. 9:26]
22 a [Gen. 9:5] *1* Foster father
23 a 2 Kin. 12:17 *1 plunder*
24 a Lev. 26:8; Is. 30:17 b Lev. 26:25 c 2 Chr. 22:8
25 a 2 Kin. 12:20, 21 *1* LXX, Vg. *son* and vv. 20–22
26 *1 Jozachar,* 2 Kin. 12:21 *2 Shomer,* 2 Kin. 12:21
27 a 2 Kin. 12:18 b 2 Kin. 12:21 *1* Or *commentary,* Heb. *midrash*

CHAPTER 25
1 a 2 Kin. 14:1–6
2 a 2 Chr. 25:14
3 a 2 Kin. 14:5
4 a Deut. 24:16
5 a Num. 1:3
7 a 2 Chr. 11:2
8 a 2 Chr. 14:11; 20:6

talents which I have given to the troops of
Israel?"
And the man of God answered, [a]"The
LORD is able to give you much more than
this." 10So Amaziah discharged the troops
that had come to him from Ephraim, to
go back home. Therefore their anger was
greatly aroused against Judah, and they
returned home in great anger.
11Then Amaziah strengthened himself,
and leading his people, he went to [a]the
Valley of Salt and killed ten thousand of
the people of Seir. 12Also the children of
Judah took captive ten thousand alive,
brought them to the top of the rock, and
cast them down from the top of the rock,
so that they all were dashed in pieces.
13But as for the soldiers of the army
which Amaziah had discharged, so that
they would not go with him to battle, they
raided the cities of Judah from Samaria
to Beth Horon, killed three thousand in
them, and took much [1]spoil.
14Now it was so, after Amaziah came
from the slaughter of the Edomites, that
[a]he brought the gods of the people of Seir,
set them up *to be* [b]his gods, and bowed
down before them and burned incense to
them. 15Therefore the anger of the LORD
was aroused against Amaziah, and He sent
him a prophet who said to him, "Why
have you sought [a]the gods of the people,
which [b]could not rescue their own people
from your hand?"
16So it was, as he talked with him, that
the king said to him, "Have we made you
the king's counselor? Cease! Why should
you be killed?"
Then the prophet ceased, and said, "I
know that God has [a]determined to destroy you, because you have done this and
have not heeded my advice."

Israel Defeats Judah

17Now [a]Amaziah king of Judah asked
advice and sent to [1]Joash the son of Jehoahaz, the son of Jehu, king of Israel, saying, "Come, let us face one another *in
battle.*"
18And Joash king of Israel sent to Amaziah king of Judah, saying, "The thistle
that *was* in Lebanon sent to the cedar that
was in Lebanon, saying, 'Give your daughter to my son as wife'; and a wild beast
that *was* in Lebanon passed by and trampled the thistle. 19Indeed you say that you
have defeated the Edomites, and your
heart is lifted up to [a]boast. Stay at home
now; why should you meddle with trouble, that you should fall—you and Judah
with you?"
20But Amaziah would not heed, for [a]it
came from God, that He might give them
into the hand *of their enemies,* because
they [b]sought the gods of Edom. 21So Joash king of Israel went out; and he and
Amaziah king of Judah faced one another
at [a]Beth Shemesh, which *belongs* to Judah. 22And Judah was defeated by Israel,
and every man fled to his tent. 23Then Joash the king of Israel captured Amaziah
king of Judah, the son of Joash, the son
of [a]Jehoahaz, at Beth Shemesh; and he
brought him to Jerusalem, and broke
down the wall of Jerusalem from the Gate
of Ephraim to the Corner Gate—four
hundred cubits. 24And *he took* all the gold
and silver, all the articles that were found
in the house of God with [a]Obed-Edom,
the treasures of the king's house, and hostages, and returned to Samaria.

Death of Amaziah

25[a]Amaziah the son of Joash, king of
Judah, lived fifteen years after the death of
Joash the son of Jehoahaz, king of Israel.
26Now the rest of the acts of Amaziah,
from first to last, indeed *are* they not written in the book of the kings of Judah and
Israel? 27After the time that Amaziah
turned away from following the LORD,
they made a conspiracy against him in Jerusalem, and he fled to Lachish; but they
sent after him to Lachish and killed him
there. 28Then they brought him on horses
and buried him with his fathers in [1]the
City of Judah.

Uzziah Reigns in Judah

26 Now all the people of Judah took
[1]Uzziah, who *was* sixteen years old,
and made him king instead of his father
Amaziah. 2He built [1]Elath and restored it
to Judah, after the king rested with his
fathers.
3Uzziah *was* sixteen years old when he
became king, and he reigned fifty-two
years in Jerusalem. His mother's name
was Jecholiah of Jerusalem. 4And he did
what was [a]right in the sight of the LORD,
according to all that his father Amaziah
had done. 5[a]He sought God in the days of
Zechariah, who [b]had understanding in
the [1]visions of God; and as long as he
sought the LORD, God made him [c]prosper.

9 a [Deut. 8:18]
11 a 2 Kin. 14:7
13 *1 plunder*
14 a 2 Chr. 28:23 b [Ex. 20:3, 5]
15 a [Ps. 96:5] b 2 Chr. 25:11
16 a [1 Sam. 2:25]
17 a 2 Kin. 14:8–14 *1 Jehoash,* 2 Kin. 14:8ff.
19 a 2 Chr. 26:16; 32:25
20 a 1 Kin. 12:15 b 2 Chr. 25:14
21 a Josh. 19:38
23 a 2 Chr. 21:17; 22:1, 6
24 a 1 Chr. 26:15
25 a 2 Kin. 14:17–22
28 *1* The City of David

CHAPTER 26
1 *1 Azariah,* 2 Kin. 14:21ff.
2 *1* Heb. *Eloth*
4 a 2 Chr. 24:2
5 a 2 Chr. 24:2 b Dan. 1:17; 10:1 c [2 Chr. 15:2; 20:20; 31:21] *1* Heb. mss., LXX, Syr., Tg., Arab. *fear*

6Now he went out and [a]made war
against the Philistines, and broke down
the wall of Gath, the wall of Jabneh, and
the wall of Ashdod; and he built cities
around Ashdod and among the Philistines. 7God helped him against [a]the Philistines, against the Arabians who lived in
Gur Baal, and against the Meunites. 8Also
the Ammonites [a]brought tribute to Uzziah. His fame spread as far as the entrance
of Egypt, for he became exceedingly
strong.
9And Uzziah built towers in Jerusalem
at the [a]Corner Gate, at the Valley Gate,
and at the corner buttress of the wall;
then he fortified them. 10Also he built
towers in the desert. He dug many wells,
for he had much livestock, both in the
lowlands and in the plains; *he also had*
farmers and vinedressers in the mountains and in [1]Carmel, for he loved the soil.
11Moreover Uzziah had an army of
fighting men who went out to war by
companies, according to the number on
their roll as prepared by Jeiel the scribe
and Maaseiah the officer, under the hand
of Hananiah, *one* of the king's captains.
12The total number of [1]chief officers of
the mighty men of valor *was* two thousand six hundred. 13And under their authority *was* an army of three hundred and
seven thousand five hundred, that made
war with mighty power, to help the king
against the enemy. 14Then Uzziah prepared for them, for the entire army,
shields, spears, helmets, body armor,
bows, and slings *to cast* stones. 15And he
made devices in Jerusalem, invented by
[a]skillful men, to be on the towers and the
corners, to shoot arrows and large stones.
So his fame spread far and wide, for he
was marvelously helped till he became
strong.

The Penalty for Uzziah's Pride

16But [a]when he was strong his heart
was [b]lifted up, to *his* destruction, for he
transgressed against the LORD his God [c]by
entering the temple of the LORD to burn
incense on the altar of incense. 17So [a]Aza-
riah the priest went in after him, and with
him were eighty priests of the LORD—valiant men. 18And they withstood King Uzziah, and said to him, "*It* [a]*is* not for you,
Uzziah, to burn incense to the LORD, but
for the [b]priests, the sons of Aaron, who
are consecrated to burn incense. Get out
of the sanctuary, for you have trespassed!
You *shall have* no honor from the LORD
God."
19Then Uzziah became furious; and he
had a censer in his hand to burn incense.
And while he was angry with the priests,
[a]leprosy broke out on his forehead, before
the priests in the house of the LORD, beside the incense altar. 20And Azariah the
chief priest and all the priests looked at
him, and there, on his forehead, he *was*
leprous; so they thrust him out of that
place. Indeed he also [a]hurried to get out,
because the LORD had struck him.
21[a]King Uzziah was a leper until the day
of his death. He dwelt in an [b]isolated
house, because he was a leper; for he was
cut off from the house of the LORD. Then
Jotham his son *was* over the king's house,
judging the people of the land.
22Now the rest of the acts of Uzziah,
from first to last, the prophet [a]Isaiah the
son of Amoz wrote. 23[a]So Uzziah [1]rested
with his fathers, and they buried him with
his fathers in the field of burial which *belonged* to the kings, for they said, "He is
a leper." Then Jotham his son reigned in
his place.

Jotham Reigns in Judah

27 Jotham [a]*was* twenty-five years old
when he became king, and he
reigned sixteen years in Jerusalem. His
mother's name *was* [1]Jerushah the daughter of Zadok. 2And he did *what was* right
in the sight of the LORD, according to all
that his father Uzziah had done (although
he did not enter the temple of the LORD).
But still [a]the people acted corruptly.
3He built the Upper Gate of the house
of the LORD, and he built extensively on
the wall of [a]Ophel. 4Moreover he built cities in the mountains of Judah, and in the
forests he built fortresses and towers. 5He
also fought with the king of the [a]Ammon-
ites and defeated them. And the people of
Ammon gave him in that year one hundred talents of silver, ten thousand kors of
wheat, and ten thousand of barley. The
people of Ammon paid this to him in the
second and third years also. 6So Jotham
became mighty, [a]because he prepared his
ways before the LORD his God.
7Now the rest of the acts of Jotham, and
all his wars and his ways, indeed they *are*
written in the book of the kings of Israel
and Judah. 8He was twenty-five years old
when he became king, and he reigned

6 a Is. 14:29
7 a 2 Chr. 21:16
8 a 2 Chr. 17:11
9 a Neh. 3:13, 19, 32
10 *1 Or the fertile fields*
12 *1 Lit. chief fathers*
15 a Ex. 39:3, 8
16 a [Deut. 32:15] b 2 Chr. 25:19 c 2 Kin. 16:12, 13
17 a 1 Chr. 6:10
18 a [Num. 3:10; 16:39, 40; 18:7] b Ex. 30:7, 8
19 a 2 Kin. 5:25–27
20 a Esth. 6:12
21 a 2 Kin. 15:5 b [Lev. 13:46]
22 a Is. 1:1
23 a Is. 6:1 *1* Died and joined his ancestors

CHAPTER 27
1 a 2 Kin. 15:32–35 *1 Jerusha,* 2 Kin. 15:33
2 a 2 Kin. 15:35
3 a 2 Chr. 33:14
5 a 2 Chr. 26:8
6 a 2 Chr. 26:5

sixteen years in Jerusalem. [9][a]So Jotham [1]rested with his fathers, and they buried him in the City of David. Then [b]Ahaz his son reigned in his place.

Ahaz Reigns in Judah

28 Ahaz [a]*was* twenty years old when he became king, and he reigned sixteen years in Jerusalem; and he did not do *what was* right in the sight of the LORD, as his father David *had done.* [2]For he walked in the ways of the kings of Israel, and made [a]molded images for [b]the Baals. [3]He burned incense in [a]the Valley of the Son of Hinnom, and burned [b]his children in the [c]fire, according to the abominations of the nations whom the LORD had [d]cast out before the children of Israel. [4]And he sacrificed and burned incense on the [1]high places, on the hills, and under every green tree.

Syria and Israel Defeat Judah

[5]Therefore [a]the LORD his God delivered him into the hand of the king of Syria. They [b]defeated him, and carried away a great multitude of them as captives, and brought *them* to Damascus. Then he was also delivered into the hand of the king of Israel, who defeated him with a great slaughter. [6]For [a]Pekah the son of Remaliah killed one hundred and twenty thousand in Judah in one day, all valiant men, [b]because they had forsaken the LORD God of their fathers. [7]Zichri, a mighty man of Ephraim, killed Maaseiah the king's son, Azrikam the officer over the house, and Elkanah *who was* second to the king. [8]And the children of Israel carried away captive of their [a]brethren two hundred thousand women, sons, and daughters; and they also took away much [1]spoil from them, and brought the spoil to Samaria.

Israel Returns the Captives

[9]But a [a]prophet of the LORD was there, whose name *was* Oded; and he went out before the army that came to Samaria, and said to them: "Look, [b]because the LORD God of your fathers was angry with Judah, He has delivered them into your hand; but you have killed them in a rage *that* [c]reaches up to heaven. [10]And now you propose to force the children of Judah and Jerusalem to be your [a]male and female slaves; *but are* you not also guilty before the LORD your God? [11]Now hear me, therefore, and return the captives, whom you have taken captive from your brethren, [a]for the fierce wrath of the LORD *is* upon you."

[12]Then some of the heads of the children of Ephraim, Azariah the son of Johanan, Berechiah the son of Meshillemoth, Jehizkiah the son of Shallum, and Amasa the son of Hadlai, stood up against those who came from the war, [13]and said to them, "You shall not bring the captives here, for we *already* have offended the LORD. You intend to add to our sins and to our guilt; for our guilt is great, and *there is* fierce wrath against Israel." [14]So the armed men left the captives and the [1]spoil before the leaders and all the assembly. [15]Then the men [a]who were designated by name rose up and took the captives, and from the [1]spoil they clothed all who were naked among them, dressed them and gave them sandals, [b]gave them food and drink, and anointed them; and they let all the feeble ones ride on donkeys. So they brought them to their brethren at Jericho, [c]the city of palm trees. Then they returned to Samaria.

Assyria Refuses to Help Judah

[16][a]At the same time King Ahaz sent to the [1]kings of Assyria to help him. [17]For again the [a]Edomites had come, attacked Judah, and carried away captives. [18][a]The Philistines also had invaded the cities of the lowland and of the South of Judah, and had taken Beth Shemesh, Aijalon, Gederoth, Sochoh with its villages, Timnah with its villages, and Gimzo with its villages; and they dwelt there. [19]For the LORD [1]brought Judah low because of Ahaz king of [a]Israel, for he had [b]encouraged moral decline in Judah and had been continually unfaithful to the LORD. [20]Also [a]Tiglath-Pileser[1] king of Assyria came to him and distressed him, and did not assist him. [21]For Ahaz took part *of the treasures* from the house of the LORD, from the house of the king, and from the leaders, and he gave *it* to the king of Assyria; but he did not help him.

Apostasy and Death of Ahaz

[22]Now in the time of his distress King Ahaz became increasingly unfaithful to the LORD. This *is that* King Ahaz. [23]For

---

9 a 2 Kin. 15:38 b Is. 1:1 *1* Died and joined his ancestors

CHAPTER 28

1 a 2 Kin. 16:2–4

2 a Ex. 34:17 b Judg. 2:11

3 a Josh. 15:8 b 2 Kin. 23:10 c [Lev. 18:21] d [Lev. 18:24–30]

4 *1* Places for pagan worship

5 a [Is. 10:5] b Is. 7:1, 17

6 a 2 Kin. 15:27 b [2 Chr. 29:8]

8 a Deut. 28:25, 41 *1 plunder*

9 a 2 Chr. 25:15 b [Is. 10:5; 47:6] c Rev. 18:5

10 a [Lev. 25:39, 42, 43, 46]

11 a James 2:13

14 *1 plunder*

15 a 2 Chr. 28:12 b [Prov. 25:21, 22] c Deut. 34:3 *1 plunder*

16 a 2 Kin. 16:7 *1* LXX, Syr., Vg. *king* (cf. v. 20)

17 a Obad. 10–14

18 a Ezek. 16:27, 57

19 a 2 Chr. 21:2 b Ex. 32:25 *1 humbled Judah*

20 a 1 Chr. 5:26 *1* Heb. *Tilgath-Pilneser*

[a]he sacrificed to the gods of Damascus
which had defeated him, saying, "Because
the gods of the kings of Syria help them,
I will sacrifice to them [b]that they may
help me." But they were the ruin of him
and of all Israel. 24So Ahaz gathered the
articles of the house of God, cut in pieces
the articles of the house of God, [a]shut up
the doors of the house of the LORD, and
made for himself altars in every corner of
Jerusalem. 25And in every single city of
Judah he made [1]high places to burn incense to other gods, and provoked to anger the LORD God of his fathers.
26[a]Now the rest of his acts and all his
ways, from first to last, indeed they *are*
written in the book of the kings of Judah
and Israel. 27So Ahaz [1]rested with his fathers, and they buried him in the city, in
Jerusalem; but they [a]did not bring him
into the tombs of the kings of Israel. Then
Hezekiah his son reigned in his place.

Hezekiah Reigns in Judah

29 Hezekiah [a]became king *when he*
was twenty-five years old, and he
reigned twenty-nine years in Jerusalem.
His mother's name *was* [1]Abijah the
daughter of Zechariah. 2And he did *what*
was right in the sight of the LORD, according to all that his father David had done.

Hezekiah Cleanses the Temple

3In the first year of his reign, in the first
month, he [a]opened the doors of the house
of the LORD and repaired them. 4Then he
brought in the priests and the Levites, and
gathered them in the East Square, 5and
said to them: "Hear me, Levites! Now
[1]sanctify yourselves, [a]sanctify the house
of the LORD God of your fathers, and carry
out the rubbish from the holy *place.* 6For
our fathers have trespassed and done evil
in the eyes of the LORD our God; they have
forsaken Him, have [a]turned their faces
away from the [1]dwelling place of the
LORD, and turned *their* backs *on Him.*
7[a]They have also shut up the doors of the
vestibule, put out the lamps, and have not
burned incense or offered burnt offerings
in the holy *place* to the God of Israel.
8Therefore the [a]wrath of the LORD fell
upon Judah and Jerusalem, and He has
[b]given them up to trouble, to desolation,
and to [c]jeering, as you see with your
[d]eyes. 9For indeed, because of this [a]our
fathers have fallen by the sword; and our
sons, our daughters, and our wives *are* in
captivity.
10"Now *it is* in my heart to make [a]a covenant with the LORD God of Israel, that
His fierce wrath may turn away from us.
11My sons, do not be negligent now, for
the LORD has [a]chosen you to stand before
Him, to serve Him, and that you should
minister to Him and burn incense."
12Then these Levites arose: [a]Mahath
the son of Amasai and Joel the son of Azariah, of the sons of the [b]Kohathites; of the
sons of Merari, Kish the son of Abdi and
Azariah the son of Jehallelel; of the Gershonites, Joah the son of Zimmah and
Eden the son of Joah; 13of the sons of Elizaphan, Shimri and Jeiel; of the sons of
Asaph, Zechariah and Mattaniah; 14of the
sons of Heman, Jehiel and Shimei; and of
the sons of Jeduthun, Shemaiah and Uzziel.
15And they gathered their brethren,
[a]sanctified[1] themselves, and went according to the commandment of the king, at
the words of the LORD, [b]to cleanse the
house of the LORD. 16Then the priests
went into the inner part of the house of
the LORD to cleanse *it,* and brought out all
the debris that they found in the temple of
the LORD to the court of the house of the
LORD. And the Levites took *it* out and carried *it* to the Brook [a]Kidron.
17Now they began to [1]sanctify on the
first *day* of the first month, and on the
eighth day of the month they came to the
vestibule of the LORD. So they sanctified
the house of the LORD in eight days, and
on the sixteenth day of the first month
they finished.
18Then they went in to King Hezekiah
and said, "We have cleansed all the house
of the LORD, the altar of burnt offerings
with all its articles, and the table of the
showbread with all its articles. 19Moreover
all the articles which King Ahaz in his
reign had [a]cast aside in his transgression
we have prepared and [1]sanctified; and
there they *are,* before the altar of the
LORD."

Hezekiah Restores Temple Worship

20Then King Hezekiah rose early, gathered the rulers of the city, and went up to
the house of the LORD. 21And they brought
seven bulls, seven rams, seven lambs, and
seven male goats for a [a]sin offering for
the kingdom, for the sanctuary, and for

23 a 2 Chr. 25:14 b Jer. 44:17, 18
24 a 2 Chr. 29:3, 7
25 *1* Places for pagan worship
26 a 2 Kin. 16:19, 20
27 a 2 Chr. 21:20; 24:25 *1* Died and joined his ancestors

CHAPTER 29
1 a 2 Kin. 18:1 *1 Abi,* 2 Kin. 18:2
3 a 2 Chr. 28:24; 29:7
5 a 2 Chr. 29:15, 34; 35:6 *1 consecrate*
6 a Ezek. 8:16 *1* Temple
7 a 2 Chr. 28:24
8 a 2 Chr. 24:18 b 2 Chr. 28:5 c 1 Kin. 9:8 d Deut. 28:32
9 a 2 Chr. 28:5–8, 17
10 a 2 Chr. 15:12; 23:16
11 a Num. 3:6; 8:14; 18:2, 6
12 a 2 Chr. 31:13 b Num. 3:19, 20
15 a 2 Chr. 29:5 b 1 Chr. 23:28 *1 consecrated*
16 a 2 Chr. 15:16; 30:14
17 *1 consecrate*
19 a 2 Chr. 28:24 *1 consecrated*
21 a Lev. 4:3–14

Judah. Then he commanded the priests,
the sons of Aaron, to offer *them* on the altar of the LORD. 22 So they killed the bulls,
and the priests received the blood and
[a]sprinkled *it* on the altar. Likewise they
killed the rams and sprinkled the blood
on the altar. They also killed the lambs
and sprinkled the blood on the altar. 23 Then
they brought out the male goats *for* the
sin offering before the king and the assembly, and they laid their [a]hands on them.
24 And the priests killed them; and they
presented their blood on the altar as a sin
offering [a]to make an atonement for all
Israel, for the king commanded *that* the
burnt offering and the sin offering *be
made* for all Israel.
25 [a]And he stationed the Levites in the
house of the LORD with cymbals, with
stringed instruments, and with harps,
[b]according to the commandment of David, of [c]Gad the king's seer, and of Nathan
the prophet; [d]for thus *was* the commandment of the LORD by His prophets. 26 The
Levites stood with the instruments [a]of
David, and the priests with [b]the trumpets.
27 Then Hezekiah commanded *them* to offer the burnt offering on the altar. And
when the burnt offering began, [a]the song
of the LORD *also* began, with the trumpets
and with the instruments of David king of
Israel. 28 So all the assembly worshiped,
the singers sang, and the trumpeters
sounded; all *this continued* until the
burnt offering was finished. 29 And when
they had finished offering, [a]the king and
all who were present with him bowed and
worshiped. 30 Moreover King Hezekiah
and the leaders commanded the Levites to
sing praise to the LORD with the words of
David and of Asaph the seer. So they sang
praises with gladness, and they bowed
their heads and worshiped.
31 Then Hezekiah answered and said,
"Now *that* you have consecrated yourselves to the LORD, come near, and bring
sacrifices and [a]thank offerings into the
house of the LORD." So the assembly
brought in sacrifices and thank offerings,
and as many as were of a [b]willing heart
brought burnt offerings. 32 And the number of the burnt offerings which the assembly brought was seventy bulls, one
hundred rams, *and* two hundred lambs;
all these *were* for a burnt offering to the
LORD. 33 The consecrated things *were* six
hundred bulls and three thousand sheep.
34 But the priests were too few, so that
they could not skin all the burnt offerings;
therefore [a]their brethren the Levites
helped them until the work was ended
and until the *other* priests had [1]sanctified
themselves, [b]for the Levites were [c]more
diligent in [d]sanctifying themselves than
the priests. 35 Also the burnt offerings
were in abundance, with [a]the fat of the
peace offerings and *with* [b]the drink offerings for *every* burnt offering.
So the service of the house of the LORD
was set in order. 36 Then Hezekiah and all
the people rejoiced that God had prepared
the people, since the events took place so
suddenly.

> *We can stand on God's Word for salvation and healing after we have met God's conditions and have grounded every weapon of rebellion, and can praise our way through to perfect manifested victory.*
>
> DR. LILIAN B. YEOMANS

Hezekiah Keeps the Passover

30 And Hezekiah sent to all Israel and
Judah, and also wrote letters to
Ephraim and Manasseh, that they should
come to the house of the LORD at Jerusalem, to keep the Passover to the LORD God
of Israel. 2 For the king and his leaders and
all the assembly in Jerusalem had agreed
to keep the Passover in the second
[a]month. 3 For they could not keep it [a]at
[1]the regular time, [b]because a sufficient
number of priests had not consecrated
themselves, nor had the people gathered
together at Jerusalem. 4 And the matter
pleased the king and all the assembly. 5 So
they [1]resolved to make a proclamation
throughout all Israel, from Beersheba to
Dan, that they should come to keep the
Passover to the LORD God of Israel at Jerusalem, since they had not done *it* for a
long *time* in the *prescribed* manner.
6 Then the [a]runners went throughout
all Israel and Judah with the letters from
the king and his leaders, and spoke according to the command of the king:

22 [a]Lev. 8:14, 15, 19, 24
23 [a]Lev. 4:15, 24; 8:14
24 [a]Lev. 14:20
25 [a]1 Chr. 16:4; 25:6 [b]2 Chr. 8:14 [c]2 Sam. 24:11 [d]2 Chr. 30:12
26 [a]1 Chr. 23:5 [b]2 Chr. 5:12
27 [a]2 Chr. 23:18
29 [a]2 Chr. 20:18
31 [a]Lev. 7:12 [b]Ex. 35:5, 22
34 [a]2 Chr. 35:11 [b]2 Chr. 30:3 [c]Ps. 7:10 [d]2 Chr. 29:5 [1]*consecrated*
35 [a]Lev. 3:15, 16 [b]Num. 15:5–10

CHAPTER 30
2 [a]Num. 9:10, 11
3 [a]Ex. 12:6, 18 [b]2 Chr. 29:17, 34 [1]The first month, Lev. 23:5; lit. *that time*
5 [1]*established a decree to*
6 [a]Esth. 8:14

"Children of Israel, [b]return to the LORD God of Abraham, Isaac, and Israel; then He will return to the remnant of you who have escaped from the hand of [c]the kings of [d]Assyria. 7And do not be [a]like your fathers and your brethren, who trespassed against the LORD God of their fathers, so that He [b]gave them up to [c]desolation, as you see. 8Now do not be [a]stiff-necked,[1] as your fathers *were, but* yield yourselves to the LORD; and enter His sanctuary, which He has sanctified forever, and serve the LORD your God, [b]that the fierceness of His wrath may turn away from you. 9For if you return to the LORD, your brethren and your children *will be treated* with [a]compassion by those who lead them captive, so that they may come back to this land; for the LORD your God *is* [b]gracious and merciful, and will not turn *His* face from you if you [c]return to Him."

10So the runners passed from city to city through the country of Ephraim and Manasseh, as far as Zebulun; but [a]they laughed at them and mocked them. 11Nevertheless [a]some from Asher, Manasseh, and Zebulun humbled themselves and came to Jerusalem. 12Also [a]the hand of God was on Judah to give them singleness of heart to obey the command of the king and the leaders, [b]at the word of the LORD.

13Now many people, a very great assembly, gathered at Jerusalem to keep the Feast of [a]Unleavened Bread in the second month. 14They arose and took away the [a]altars that *were* in Jerusalem, and they took away all the incense altars and cast *them* into the Brook [b]Kidron. 15Then they slaughtered the Passover *lambs* on the fourteenth *day* of the second month. The priests and the Levites [1]were [a]ashamed, and [2]sanctified themselves, and brought the burnt offerings to the house of the LORD. 16They stood in their [a]place [1]according to their custom, according to the Law of Moses the man of God; the priests sprinkled the blood *received* from the hand of the Levites. 17For *there were* many in the assembly who had not [1]sanctified themselves; [a]therefore the Levites had charge of the slaughter of the Passover *lambs* for everyone *who was* not clean, to sanctify *them* to the LORD. 18For a multitude of the people, [a]many from Ephraim, Manasseh, Issachar, and Zebulun, had not cleansed themselves, [b]yet they ate the Passover contrary to what was written. But Hezekiah prayed for them, saying, "May the good LORD provide atonement for everyone 19*who* [a]prepares his heart to seek God, the LORD God of his fathers, though *he is* not *cleansed* according to the purification of the sanctuary." 20And the LORD listened to Hezekiah and healed the people.

21So the children of Israel who were present at Jerusalem kept [a]the Feast of Unleavened Bread seven days with great gladness; and the Levites and the priests praised the LORD day by day, *singing* to the LORD, accompanied by loud instruments. 22And Hezekiah gave encouragement to all the Levites [a]who taught the good knowledge of the LORD; and they ate throughout the feast seven days, offering peace offerings and [b]making confession to the LORD God of their fathers.

23Then the whole assembly agreed to keep *the feast* [a]another seven days, and they kept it *another* seven days with gladness. 24For Hezekiah king of Judah [a]gave to the assembly a thousand bulls and seven thousand sheep, and the leaders gave to the assembly a thousand bulls and ten thousand sheep; and a great number of priests [b]sanctified[1] themselves. 25The whole assembly of Judah rejoiced, also the priests and Levites, all the assembly that came from Israel, the sojourners [a]who came from the land of Israel, and those who dwelt in Judah. 26So there was great joy in Jerusalem, for since the time of [a]Solomon the son of David, king of Israel, *there had* been nothing like this in Jerusalem. 27Then the priests, the Levites, arose and [a]blessed the people, and their voice was heard; and their prayer came *up* to [b]His holy dwelling place, to heaven.

The Reforms of Hezekiah

31 Now when all this was finished, all Israel who were present went out to the cities of Judah and [a]broke the sacred pillars in pieces, cut down the wooden images, and threw down the [1]high places and the altars—from all Judah, Benjamin, Ephraim, and Manasseh—until they had utterly destroyed them all. Then all the children of Israel returned to their own cities, every man to his possession.

2And Hezekiah appointed [a]the divisions of the priests and the Levites according to their divisions, each man according to his service, the priests and Levites [b]for burnt

---

6 b [Jer. 4:1] c 2 Kin. 15:19, 29 d 2 Chr. 28:20
7 a Ezek. 20:18 b Is. 1:9 c 2 Chr. 29:8
8 a Ex. 32:9 b 2 Chr. 29:10 *1 Rebellious*
9 a Ps. 106:46 b [Ex. 34:6] c [Is. 55:7]
10 a 2 Chr. 36:16
11 a 2 Chr. 11:16; 30:18, 21
12 a [Phil. 2:13] b 2 Chr. 29:25
13 a Lev. 23:6
14 a 2 Chr. 28:24 b 2 Chr. 29:16
15 a 2 Chr. 29:34 *1 humbled themselves* *2 set themselves apart*
16 a 2 Chr. 35:10, 15 *1 Or in their proper order*
17 a 2 Chr. 29:34 *1 consecrated*
18 a 2 Chr. 30:1, 11, 25 b [Num. 9:10]
19 a 2 Chr. 19:3
21 a Ex. 12:15; 13:6
22 a 2 Chr. 17:9; 35:3 b Ezra 10:11
23 a 1 Kin. 8:65
24 a 2 Chr. 35:7, 8 b 2 Chr. 29:34 *1 consecrated*
25 a 2 Chr. 30:11, 18
26 a 2 Chr. 7:8–10
27 a Num. 6:23 b Deut. 26:15

CHAPTER 31
1 a 2 Kin. 18:4 *1 Places for pagan worship*
2 a 1 Chr. 23:6; 24:1 b 1 Chr. 23:30, 31

offerings and peace offerings, to serve, to give thanks, and to praise in the gates of the [1]camp of the LORD. 3 The king also *appointed* a [1]portion of his [a]possessions[2] for the burnt offerings: for the morning and evening burnt offerings, the burnt offerings for the Sabbaths and the New Moons and the set feasts, as *it is* written in the [b]Law of the LORD.

4 Moreover he commanded the people who dwelt in Jerusalem to contribute [a]support[1] for the priests and the Levites, that they might devote themselves to [b]the Law of the LORD.

5 As soon as the commandment was circulated, the children of Israel brought in abundance [a]the firstfruits of grain and wine, oil and honey, and of all the produce of the field; and they brought in abundantly the [b]tithe of everything. 6 And the children of Israel and Judah, who dwelt in the cities of Judah, brought the tithe of oxen and sheep; also the [a]tithe of holy things which were consecrated to the LORD their God they laid in heaps.

7 In the third month they began laying them in heaps, and they finished in the seventh month. 8 And when Hezekiah and the leaders came and saw the heaps, they blessed the LORD and His people Israel. 9 Then Hezekiah questioned the priests and the Levites concerning the heaps. 10 And Azariah the chief priest, from the [a]house of Zadok, answered him and said, [b]"Since *the people* began to bring the offerings into the house of the LORD, we have had enough to eat and have plenty left, for the LORD has blessed His people; and what is left *is* this great [c]abundance."

11 Now Hezekiah commanded *them* to prepare [a]rooms[1] in the house of the LORD, and they prepared them. 12 Then they faithfully brought in the offerings, the tithes, and the dedicated things; [a]Cononiah the Levite had charge of them, and Shimei his brother *was* the next. 13 Jehiel, Azaziah, Nahath, Asahel, Jerimoth, Jozabad, Eliel, Ismachiah, Mahath, and Benaiah *were* overseers under the hand of Cononiah and Shimei his brother, at the commandment of Hezekiah the king and Azariah the [a]ruler of the house of God. 14 Kore the son of Imnah the Levite, the keeper of the East Gate, *was* over the [a]freewill offerings to God, to distribute the offerings of the LORD and the most holy things. 15 And under him *were* [a]Eden, Miniamin, Jeshua, Shemaiah, Amariah, and Shecaniah, *his* faithful assistants in [b]the cities of the priests, to distribute [c]allotments to their brethren by divisions, to the great as well as the small.

16 Besides those males from three years old and up who were written in the genealogy, they distributed to everyone who entered the house of the LORD his daily portion for the work of his service, by his division, 17 and to the priests who were written in the genealogy according to their father's house, and to the Levites [a]from twenty years old and up according to their work, by their divisions, 18 and to all who were written in the genealogy—their little ones and their wives, their sons and daughters, the whole company of them—for in their faithfulness they [1]sanctified themselves in holiness.

> *A true love to God must begin with a delight in His holiness, and not with a delight in any other attribute; for no other attribute is truly lovely without this.*
>
> JONATHAN EDWARDS

19 Also for the sons of Aaron the priests, *who were* in [a]the fields of the common-lands of their cities, in every single city, *there were* men who were [b]designated by name to distribute portions to all the males among the priests and to all who were listed by genealogies among the Levites.

20 Thus Hezekiah did throughout all Judah, and he [a]did what *was* good and right and true before the LORD his God. 21 And in every work that he began in the service of the house of God, in the law and in the commandment, to seek his God, he did *it* with all his heart. So he [a]prospered.

Sennacherib Boasts Against the Lord

32 After [a]these deeds of faithfulness, Sennacherib king of Assyria came and entered Judah; he encamped against the fortified cities, thinking to win them over to himself. 2 And when Hezekiah saw

---

2 [1] Temple
3 [a] 2 Chr. 35:7 [b] Num. 28:1—29:40 [1] *share* [2] *property*
4 [a] Num. 18:8 [b] Mal. 2:7 [1] *the portion due*
5 [a] Ex. 22:29 [b] [Lev. 27:30]
6 [a] Deut. 14:28
10 [a] 1 Chr. 6:8, 9 [b] [Mal. 3:10] [c] Ex. 36:5
11 [a] 1 Kin. 6:5–8 [1] *storerooms*
12 [a] 2 Chr. 35:9
13 [a] Jer. 20:1
14 [a] Deut. 23:23
15 [a] 2 Chr. 29:12 [b] Josh. 21:1–3, 9 [c] 1 Chr. 9:26
17 [a] 1 Chr. 23:24, 27
18 [1] *consecrated*
19 [a] Lev. 25:34 [b] 2 Chr. 31:12–15
20 [a] 2 Kin. 20:3; 22:2
21 [a] Ps. 1:3
CHAPTER 32
1 [a] 2 Kin. 18:13—19:37

that Sennacherib had come, and that his
purpose was to make war against Jerusalem, 3he consulted with his leaders and
[1]commanders to stop the water from the
springs which *were* outside the city; and
they helped him. 4Thus many people
gathered together who stopped all the
[a]springs and the brook that ran through
the land, saying, "Why should the [1]kings
of Assyria come and find much water?"
5And [a]he strengthened himself, [b]built up
all the wall that was broken, raised *it* up
to the towers, and *built* another wall outside; also he repaired [1]the [c]Millo *in* the
City of David, and made [2]weapons and
shields in abundance. 6Then he set military captains over the people, gathered
them together to him in the open square
of the city gate, and [a]gave them encouragement, saying, 7[a]"Be strong and courageous; [b]do not be afraid nor dismayed
before the king of Assyria, nor before all
the multitude that *is* with him; for [c]*there*
are more with us than with him. 8With
him *is* an [a]arm of flesh; but [b]with us *is* the
LORD our God, to help us and to fight our
battles." And the people were strengthened by the words of Hezekiah king of
Judah.

9[a]After this Sennacherib king of Assyria
sent his servants to Jerusalem (but he and
all the forces with him *laid siege* against
Lachish), to Hezekiah king of Judah, and
to all Judah who *were* in Jerusalem, saying, 10[a]"Thus says Sennacherib king of
Assyria: 'In what do you trust, that you
remain under siege in Jerusalem? 11Does
not Hezekiah persuade you to give yourselves over to die by famine and by thirst,
saying, [a]"The LORD our God will deliver us
from the hand of the king of Assyria"?
12[a]Has not the same Hezekiah taken away
His high places and His altars, and commanded Judah and Jerusalem, saying,
"You shall worship before one altar and
burn incense on [b]it"? 13Do you not know
what I and my fathers have done to all the
peoples of *other* lands? [a]Were the gods of
the nations of those lands in any way able
to deliver their lands out of my hand?
14Who *was there* among all the gods of
those nations that my fathers utterly destroyed that could deliver his people from
my hand, that your God should be able to
deliver you from my [a]hand? 15Now therefore, [a]do not let Hezekiah deceive you or
persuade you like this, and do not believe
him; for no god of any nation or kingdom
was able to deliver his people from my
hand or the hand of my fathers. How
much less will your God deliver you from
my hand?' "

16Furthermore, his servants spoke
against the LORD God and against His servant Hezekiah.

17He also wrote letters to revile the
LORD God of Israel, and to speak against
Him, saying, [a]"As the gods of the nations
of *other* lands have not delivered their
people from my hand, so the God of Hezekiah will not deliver His people from my
[b]hand." 18[a]Then they called out with a
loud voice in [1]Hebrew to the people of
Jerusalem who *were* on the wall, to fright-
en them and trouble them, that they
might take the city. 19And they spoke
against the God of Jerusalem, as against
the gods of the people of the earth—[a]the
work of men's hands.

Sennacherib's Defeat and Death

20[a]Now because of this King Hezekiah
and [b]the prophet Isaiah, the son of Amoz,
prayed and cried out to heaven. 21[a]Then
the LORD sent an angel who cut down every mighty man of valor, leader, and captain in the camp of the king of Assyria. So
he returned [b]shamefaced to his own land.
And when he had gone into the temple of
his god, some of his own offspring struck
him down with the sword there.

22Thus the LORD saved Hezekiah and
the inhabitants of Jerusalem from the
hand of Sennacherib the king of Assyria,
and from the hand of all *others,* and
[1]guided them on every side. 23And many
brought gifts to the LORD at Jerusalem,
and [a]presents[1] to Hezekiah king of Judah,
so that he was [b]exalted in the sight of all
nations thereafter.

Hezekiah Humbles Himself

24[a]In those days Hezekiah was sick and
near death, and he prayed to the LORD;
and He spoke to him and gave him a sign.
25But Hezekiah [a]did not repay according
to the favor *shown* him, for [b]his heart was
lifted up; [c]therefore wrath was looming
over him and over Judah and Jerusalem.
26[a]Then Hezekiah humbled himself for
the pride of his heart, he and the inhabitants of Jerusalem, so that the wrath of

---

3 [1] Lit. *mighty men*
4 [a] 2 Kin. 20:20 [1] So with MT, Vg.; Arab., LXX, Syr. *king*
5 [a] Is. 22:9, 10 [b] 2 Chr. 25:23 [c] 2 Sam. 5:9 [1] Lit. *The Landfill* [2] *javelins*
6 [a] 2 Chr. 30:22
7 [a] [Deut. 31:6] [b] 2 Chr. 20:15 [c] 2 Kin. 6:16
8 [a] [Jer. 17:5] [b] [Rom. 8:31]
9 [a] 2 Kin. 18:17
10 [a] 2 Kin. 18:19
11 [a] 2 Kin. 18:30
12 [a] 2 Kin. 18:22 [b] 2 Chr. 31:1, 2
13 [a] 2 Kin. 18:33–35
14 [a] [Is. 10:5–12]
15 [a] 2 Kin. 18:29
17 [a] 2 Kin. 19:9 [b] 2 Kin. 19:12
18 [a] 2 Kin. 18:28 [1] Lit. *Judean*
19 [a] [Ps. 96:5; 115:4–8]
20 [a] 2 Kin. 19:15 [b] 2 Kin. 19:2
21 [a] Zech. 14:3 [b] Ps. 44:7
22 [1] LXX *gave them rest;* Vg. *gave them treasures*
23 [a] 2 Sam. 8:10 [b] 2 Chr. 1:1 [1] Lit. *precious things*
24 [a] Is. 38:1–8
25 [a] Ps. 116:12 [b] [Hab. 2:4] [c] 2 Chr. 24:18
26 [a] Jer. 26:18, 19

the LORD did not come upon them [b]in the
days of Hezekiah.

Hezekiah's Wealth and Honor

27Hezekiah had very great riches and
honor. And he made himself treasuries for
silver, for gold, for precious stones, for
spices, for shields, and for all kinds of desirable items; 28storehouses for the harvest of grain, wine, and oil; and stalls for
all kinds of livestock, and [1]folds for flocks.
29Moreover he provided cities for himself,
and possessions of flocks and herds in
abundance; for [a]God had given him very
much property. 30[a]This same Hezekiah
also stopped the water outlet of Upper Gihon, and [1]brought the water by tunnel to
the west side of the City of David. Hezekiah [b]prospered in all his works.
31However, *regarding* the ambassadors
of the princes of Babylon, whom they
[a]sent to him to inquire about the wonder
that was *done* in the land, God withdrew
from him, in order to [b]test him, that He
might know all *that was* in his heart.

Death of Hezekiah

32Now the rest of the acts of Hezekiah,
and his goodness, indeed they *are* written
in [a]the vision of Isaiah the prophet, the
son of Amoz, *and* in the [b]book of the kings
of Judah and Israel. 33[a]So Hezekiah [1]rest-
ed with his fathers, and they buried him
in the upper tombs of the sons of David;
and all Judah and the inhabitants of Jerusalem [b]honored him at his death. Then
Manasseh his son reigned in his place.

Manasseh Reigns in Judah

33 Manasseh [a]*was* twelve years old
when he became king, and he
reigned fifty-five years in Jerusalem. 2But
he did evil in the sight of the LORD, according to the [a]abominations of the nations whom the LORD had cast out before
the children of Israel. 3For he rebuilt the
[1]high places which Hezekiah his father
had [a]broken down; he raised up altars for
the Baals, and [b]made wooden images; and
he worshiped [c]all [2]the host of heaven and
served them. 4He also built altars in the
house of the LORD, of which the LORD had
said, [a]"In Jerusalem shall My name be forever." 5And he built altars for all the host
of heaven [a]in the two courts of the house
of the LORD. 6[a]Also he caused his sons to
pass through the fire in the Valley of the
Son of Hinnom; he practiced [b]sooth-
saying, used witchcraft and sorcery, and
[c]consulted mediums and spiritists. He did
much evil in the sight of the LORD, to provoke Him to anger. 7[a]He even set a carved
image, the idol which he had made, in the
[1]house of God, of which God had said to
David and to Solomon his son, [b]"In this
house and in Jerusalem, which I have
chosen out of all the tribes of Israel, I will
put My name forever; 8[a]and I will not
again remove the foot of Israel from the
land which I have appointed for your fathers—only if they are careful to do all
that I have commanded them, according
to the whole law and the statutes and the
ordinances by the hand of Moses." 9So
Manasseh seduced Judah and the inhabitants of Jerusalem to do more evil than
the nations whom the LORD had destroyed
before the children of Israel.

Manasseh Restored After Repentance

10And the LORD spoke to Manasseh and
his people, but they would not [1]listen.
11[a]Therefore the LORD brought upon
them the captains of the army of the king
of Assyria, who took Manasseh with
[1]hooks, [b]bound him with [2]bronze *fetters,*
and carried him off to Babylon. 12Now
when he was in affliction, he implored the
LORD his God, and [a]humbled himself
greatly before the God of his fathers, 13and
prayed to Him; and He [a]received his entreaty, heard his supplication, and
brought him back to Jerusalem into his
kingdom. Then Manasseh [b]knew that the
LORD *was* God.
14After this he built a wall outside the
City of David on the west side of [a]Gihon,
in the valley, as far as the entrance of the
Fish Gate; and *it* [b]enclosed Ophel, and he
raised it to a very great height. Then he
put military captains in all the fortified
cities of Judah. 15He took away [a]the foreign gods and the idol from the house of
the LORD, and all the altars that he had
built in the mount of the house of the
LORD and in Jerusalem; and he cast *them*
out of the city. 16He also repaired the altar
of the LORD, sacrificed peace offerings and
[a]thank offerings on it, and commanded
Judah to serve the LORD God of Israel.
17[a]Nevertheless the people still sacrificed
on the [1]high places, *but* only to the LORD
their God.

26 b 2 Kin. 20:19
28 *1* So with LXX, Vg.; Arab., Syr. omit *folds for flocks;* MT *flocks for sheepfolds*
29 a 1 Chr. 29:12
30 a Is. 22:9–11 b 2 Chr. 31:21 *1* Lit. *brought it straight to* (cf. 2 Kin. 20:20)
31 a Is. 39:1 b [Deut. 8:2, 16]
32 a Is. 36—39 b 2 Kin. 18—20
33 a 2 Kin. 20:21 b Prov. 10:7 *1* Died and joined his ancestors

CHAPTER 33
1 a 2 Kin. 21:1–9
2 a 2 Chr. 28:3
3 a 2 Kin. 18:4 b Deut. 16:21 c Deut. 17:3 *1* Places for pagan worship *2* The gods of the Assyrians
4 a 2 Chr. 6:6; 7:16
5 a 2 Chr. 4:9
6 a [Lev. 18:21] b Deut. 18:11 c 2 Kin. 21:6
7 a 2 Chr. 25:14 b Ps. 132:14 *1* Temple
8 a 2 Sam. 7:10
10 *1 obey*
11 a Deut. 28:36 b 2 Chr. 36:6 *1* Nose hooks, 2 Kin. 19:28 *2 chains*
12 a 2 Chr. 7:14; 32:26
13 a Ezra 8:23 b Dan. 4:25
14 a 1 Kin. 1:33 b 2 Chr. 27:3
15 a 2 Chr. 33:3, 5, 7
16 a Lev. 7:12
17 a 2 Chr. 32:12 *1* Places for pagan worship

Death of Manasseh

18 Now the rest of the acts of Manasseh,
his prayer to his God, and the words of
[a]the seers who spoke to him in the name
of the LORD God of Israel, indeed they *are*
written in the [1]book of the kings of Israel.
19 Also his prayer and *how God* received
his entreaty, and all his sin and trespass,
and the sites where he built [1]high places
and set up wooden images and carved images, before he was humbled, indeed they
are written among the sayings of [2]Hozai.
20 [a]So Manasseh rested with his fathers,
and they buried him in his own house.
Then his son Amon reigned in his place.

Amon's Reign and Death

21 [a]Amon *was* twenty-two years old
when he became king, and he reigned two
years in Jerusalem. 22 But he did evil in the
sight of the LORD, as his father Manasseh
had done; for Amon sacrificed to all the
carved images which his father Manasseh
had made, and served them. 23 And he did
not humble himself before the LORD, [a]as
his father Manasseh had humbled himself; but Amon trespassed more and more.
24 [a]Then his servants conspired against
him, and [b]killed him in his own house.
25 But the people of the land executed all
those who had conspired against King
Amon. Then the people of the land made
his son Josiah king in his place.

Josiah Reigns in Judah

34 Josiah [a]*was* eight years old when
he became king, and he reigned
thirty-one years in Jerusalem. 2 And he
did *what was* right in the sight of the
LORD, and walked in the ways of his father
David; *he* did *not* turn aside to the right
hand or to the left.
3 For in the eighth year of his reign,
while he was still [a]young, he began to
[b]seek the God of his father David; and in
the twelfth year he began [c]to purge Judah
and Jerusalem [d]of the [1]high places, the
wooden images, the carved images, and
the molded images. 4 [a]They broke down
the altars of the Baals in his presence, and
the incense altars which *were* above them
he cut down; and the wooden images, the
carved images, and the molded images he
broke in pieces, and made dust of them
[b]and scattered *it* on the graves of those
who had sacrificed to them. 5 He also
[a]burned the bones of the priests on their
[b]altars, and cleansed Judah and Jerusalem. 6 And *so he did* in the cities of Manasseh, Ephraim, and Simeon, as far as
Naphtali and all around, with [1]axes.
7 When he had broken down the altars and
the wooden images, had [a]beaten the
carved images into powder, and cut down
all the incense altars throughout all the
land of Israel, he returned to Jerusalem.

Hilkiah Finds the Book of the Law

8 [a]In the eighteenth year of his reign,
when he had purged the land and the
[1]temple, he sent [b]Shaphan the son of Aza-
liah, Maaseiah the [c]governor of the city,
and Joah the son of Joahaz the recorder,
to repair the house of the LORD his God.
9 When they came to Hilkiah the high
priest, they delivered [a]the money that was
brought into the house of God, which the
Levites who kept the doors had gathered
from the hand of Manasseh and Ephraim,
from all the [b]remnant of Israel, from all
Judah and Benjamin, and *which* they had
brought back to Jerusalem. 10 Then they
put *it* in the hand of the foremen who had
the oversight of the house of the LORD;
and they gave it to the workmen who
worked in the house of the LORD, to repair
and restore the house. 11 They gave *it* to
the craftsmen and builders to buy hewn
stone and timber for beams, and to floor
the houses which the kings of Judah had
destroyed. 12 And the men did the work
faithfully. Their overseers *were* Jahath
and Obadiah the Levites, of the sons of
Merari, and Zechariah and Meshullam, of
the sons of the Kohathites, to supervise.
Others of the Levites, all of whom were
skillful with instruments of music, 13 *were*
[a]over the burden bearers and *were* overseers of all who did work in any kind of
service. [b]And *some* of the Levites *were*
scribes, officers, and gatekeepers.
14 Now when they brought out the money that was brought into the house of the
LORD, Hilkiah the priest [a]found the Book
of the Law of the LORD *given* by Moses.
15 Then Hilkiah answered and said to Shaphan the scribe, "I have found the Book of
the Law in the house of the LORD." And
Hilkiah gave the [a]book to Shaphan. 16 So
Shaphan carried the book to the king,
bringing the king word, saying, "All that
was committed to your servants they are
doing. 17 And they have [1]gathered the
money that was found in the house of the

---

18 a 1 Sam. 9:9 1 Lit. *words*
19 1 Places for pagan worship 2 LXX *the seers*
20 a 2 Kin. 21:18
21 a 2 Kin. 21:19–24
23 a 2 Chr. 33:12, 19
24 a 2 Chr. 24:25 b 2 Chr. 25:27

CHAPTER 34
1 a 2 Kin. 22:1, 2
3 a Eccl. 12:1 b 2 Chr. 15:2 c 1 Kin. 13:2 d 2 Chr. 33:17–19, 22 1 Places for pagan worship
4 a Lev. 26:30 b 2 Kin. 23:6
5 a 1 Kin. 13:2 b 2 Kin. 23:20
6 1 Lit. *swords*
7 a Deut. 9:21
8 a 2 Kin. 22:3–20 b 2 Kin. 25:22 c 2 Chr. 18:25 1 Lit. *house*
9 a 2 Kin. 12:4 b 2 Chr. 30:6
13 a 2 Chr. 8:10 b 1 Chr. 23:4, 5
14 a 2 Kin. 22:8
15 a Deut. 31:24, 26
17 1 Lit. *poured out*

LORD, and have delivered it into the hand of the overseers and the workmen." 18Then Shaphan the scribe told the king, saying, "Hilkiah the priest has given me a book." And Shaphan read it before the king.

19Thus it happened, when the king heard the words of the Law, that he tore his clothes. 20Then the king commanded Hilkiah, [a]Ahikam the son of Shaphan, [1]Abdon the son of Micah, Shaphan the scribe, and Asaiah a servant of the king, saying, 21"Go, inquire of the LORD for me, and for those who are left in Israel and Judah, concerning the words of the book that is found; for great *is* the wrath of the LORD that is poured out on us, because our fathers have not [a]kept the word of the LORD, to do according to all that is written in this book."

> *The word of God is living. His word is sure to be living when we see it. For if we do not find it living, we simply have failed to see God's word.*
>
> WATCHMAN NEE

22So Hilkiah and those the king *had appointed* went to Huldah the prophetess, the wife of Shallum the son of [1]Tokhath, the son of [2]Hasrah, keeper of the wardrobe. (She dwelt in Jerusalem in the Second Quarter.) And they spoke to her to that *effect.*

23Then she answered them, "Thus says the LORD God of Israel, 'Tell the man who sent you to Me, 24"Thus says the LORD: 'Behold, I will [a]bring calamity on this place and on its inhabitants, all the curses that are written in the [b]book which they have read before the king of Judah, 25because they have forsaken Me and burned incense to other gods, that they might provoke Me to anger with all the works of their hands. Therefore My wrath will be poured out on this place, and not be quenched.' " ' 26But as for the king of Judah, who sent you to inquire of the LORD, in this manner you shall speak to him, 'Thus says the LORD God of Israel: "*Concerning* the words which you have heard— 27because your heart was tender, and you humbled yourself before God when you heard His words against this place and against its inhabitants, and you humbled yourself before Me, and you tore your clothes and wept before Me, I also have heard *you,*" says the [a]LORD. 28"Surely I will gather you to your fathers, and you shall be gathered to your grave in peace; and your eyes shall not see all the calamity which I will bring on this place and its inhabitants." ' " So they brought back word to the king.

Josiah Restores True Worship

29[a]Then the king sent and gathered all the elders of Judah and Jerusalem. 30The king went up to the house of the LORD, with all the men of Judah and the inhabitants of Jerusalem—the priests and the Levites, and all the people, great and small. And he [a]read in their hearing all the words of the Book of the Covenant which had been found in the house of the LORD. 31Then the king [a]stood in [b]his place and made a [c]covenant before the LORD, to follow the LORD, and to keep His commandments and His testimonies and His statutes with all his heart and all his soul, to perform the words of the covenant that were written in this book. 32And he made all who were present in Jerusalem and Benjamin take a stand. So the inhabitants of Jerusalem did according to the covenant of God, the God of their fathers. 33Thus Josiah removed all the [a]abominations from all the country that *belonged* to the children of Israel, and made all who were present in Israel [1]diligently serve the LORD their God. [b]All his days they did not depart from following the LORD God of their fathers.

Josiah Keeps the Passover

35 Now [a]Josiah kept a Passover to the LORD in Jerusalem, and they slaughtered the Passover *lambs* on the [b]fourteenth *day* of the first month. 2And he set the priests in their [a]duties and [b]encouraged them for the service of the house of the LORD. 3Then he said to the Levites [a]who taught all Israel, who were holy to the LORD: [b]"Put the holy ark [c]in the house which Solomon the son of David, king of Israel, built. [d]*It shall* no longer *be* a burden on *your* shoulders. Now serve the LORD your God and His people

---

20 [a]Jer. 26:24 [1]*Achbor the son of Micahiah,* 2 Kin. 22:12
21 [a]2 Kin. 17:15–19
22 [1]*Tikvah,* 2 Kin. 22:14 [2]*Harhas,* 2 Kin. 22:14
24 [a]2 Chr. 36:14–20 [b]Deut. 28:15–68
27 [a]2 Chr. 12:7; 30:6; 33:12, 13
29 [a]2 Kin. 23:1–3
30 [a]Neh. 8:1–3
31 [a]2 Chr. 6:13 [b]2 Kin. 11:14; 23:3 [c]2 Chr. 23:16; 29:10
33 [a]1 Kin. 11:5 [b]Jer. 3:10 [1]Lit. *serve to serve*

CHAPTER 35
1 [a]2 Kin. 23:21, 22 [b]Ex. 12:6
2 [a]2 Chr. 23:18 [b]2 Chr. 29:5–15
3 [a]Deut. 33:10 [b]2 Chr. 34:14 [c]2 Chr. 5:7 [d]1 Chr. 23:26

Israel. 4Prepare *yourselves* [a]according to
your fathers' [1]houses, according to your
divisions, following the [b]written instruction of David king of Israel and the [c]writ-
ten instruction of Solomon his son. 5And
[a]stand in the holy *place* according to the
divisions of the fathers' houses of your
brethren the *lay* people, and *according to*
the division of the father's house of the
Levites. 6So slaughter the Passover *offerings,* [a]consecrate yourselves, and prepare
them for your brethren, that *they* may do
according to the word of the LORD by the
hand of Moses."

7Then Josiah [a]gave the *lay* people
lambs and young goats from the flock, all
for Passover *offerings* for all who were
present, to the number of thirty thousand, as well as three thousand cattle;
these *were* from the king's [b]possessions.
8And his [a]leaders gave willingly to the
people, to the priests, and to the Levites.
Hilkiah, Zechariah, and Jehiel, rulers of
the house of God, gave to the priests for
the Passover *offerings* two thousand six
hundred *from the flock,* and three hundred cattle. 9Also [a]Conaniah, his brothers
Shemaiah and Nethanel, and Hashabiah
and Jeiel and Jozabad, chief of the Levites,
gave to the Levites for Passover *offerings*
five thousand *from the flock* and five hundred cattle.

10So the service was prepared, and the
priests [a]stood in their places, and the [b]Le-
vites in their divisions, according to the
king's command. 11And they slaughtered
the Passover *offerings;* and the priests
[a]sprinkled *the blood* with their hands,
while the Levites [b]skinned *the animals.*
12Then they removed the burnt offerings
that *they* might give them to the divisions
of the fathers' houses of the *lay* people, to
offer to the LORD, as *it is* written [a]in the
Book of Moses. And so *they did* with the
cattle. 13Also they [a]roasted the Passover
offerings with fire according to the ordinance; but the *other* holy *offerings* they
[b]boiled in pots, in caldrons, and in pans,
and divided *them* quickly among all the
lay people. 14Then afterward they prepared portions for themselves and for the
priests, because the priests, the sons of
Aaron, *were busy* in offering burnt offerings and fat until night; therefore the Levites prepared portions for themselves
and for the priests, the sons of Aaron.
15And the singers, the sons of Asaph, *were*
in their places, according to the [a]com-
mand of David, Asaph, Heman, and Jeduthun the king's seer. Also the gatekeepers
[b]were at each gate; they did not have to
leave their position, because their brethren the Levites prepared portions for
them.

16So all the service of the LORD was prepared the same day, to keep the Passover
and to offer burnt offerings on the altar of
the LORD, according to the command of
King Josiah. 17And the children of Israel
who were present kept the Passover at
that time, and the Feast of [a]Unleavened
Bread for seven days. 18[a]There had been
no Passover kept in Israel like that since
the days of Samuel the prophet; and none
of the kings of Israel had kept such a Passover as Josiah kept, with the priests and
the Levites, all Judah and Israel who were
present, and the inhabitants of Jerusalem.
19In the eighteenth year of the reign of
Josiah this Passover was kept.

Josiah Dies in Battle

20[a]After all this, when Josiah had prepared the temple, Necho king of Egypt
came up to fight against [b]Carchemish by
the Euphrates; and Josiah went out
against him. 21But he sent messengers to
him, saying, "What have I to do with you,
king of Judah? *I have* not *come* against
you this day, but against the house with
which I have war; for God commanded me
to make haste. Refrain *from meddling
with* God, who *is* with me, lest He destroy
you." 22Nevertheless Josiah would not
turn his face from him, but [a]disguised
himself so that he might fight with him,
and did not heed the words of Necho from
the mouth of God. So he came to fight in
the Valley of Megiddo.

23And the archers shot King Josiah; and
the king said to his servants, "Take me
away, for I am severely wounded." 24[a]His
servants therefore took him out of that
chariot and put him in the second chariot
that he had, and they brought him to Jerusalem. So he died, and was buried in
one of the tombs of his fathers. And [b]all
Judah and Jerusalem mourned for Josiah.

25Jeremiah also [a]lamented for [b]Josiah.
And to this day [c]all the singing men and
the singing women speak of Josiah in
their lamentations. [d]They made it a custom in Israel; and indeed they *are* written
in the Laments.

26Now the rest of the acts of Josiah
and his goodness, according to *what was*

4 [a] 1 Chr. 9:10–13 [b] 1 Chr. 23—26 [c] 2 Chr. 8:14 [1] *households*
5 [a] Ps. 134:1
6 [a] 2 Chr. 29:5, 15
7 [a] 2 Chr. 30:24 [b] 2 Chr. 31:3
8 [a] Num. 7:2
9 [a] 2 Chr. 31:12
10 [a] Ezra 6:18 [b] 2 Chr. 5:12; 7:6; 8:14, 15; 13:10; 29:25–34
11 [a] 2 Chr. 29:22 [b] 2 Chr. 29:34
12 [a] Ezra 6:18
13 [a] Ex. 12:8, 9 [b] 1 Sam. 2:13–15
15 [a] 1 Chr. 25:1–6 [b] 1 Chr. 9:17, 18
17 [a] Ex. 12:15; 13:6
18 [a] 2 Kin. 23:22, 23
20 [a] 2 Kin. 23:29 [b] Jer. 46:2
22 [a] 2 Chr. 18:29
24 [a] 2 Kin. 23:30 [b] Zech. 12:11
25 [a] Lam. 4:20 [b] Jer. 22:10, 11 [c] Matt. 9:23 [d] Jer. 22:20

written in the Law of the LORD, [27]and his deeds from first to last, indeed they *are* written in the book of the kings of Israel and Judah.

The Reign and Captivity of Jehoahaz

36 Then [a]the people of the land took Jehoahaz the son of Josiah, and made him king in his father's place in Jerusalem. [2][1]Jehoahaz *was* twenty-three years old when he became king, and he reigned three months in Jerusalem. [3]Now the king of Egypt deposed him at Jerusalem; and he imposed on the land a tribute of one hundred talents of silver and a talent of gold. [4]Then the king of Egypt made [1]*Jehoahaz's* brother Eliakim king over Judah and Jerusalem, and changed his name to Jehoiakim. And Necho took [2]Jehoahaz his brother and carried him off to Egypt.

The Reign and Captivity of Jehoiakim

[5][a]Jehoiakim *was* twenty-five years old when he became king, and he reigned eleven years in Jerusalem. And he did [b]evil in the sight of the LORD his God. [6][a]Nebuchadnezzar king of Babylon came up against him, and bound him in [1]bronze *fetters* to [b]carry him off to Babylon. [7][a]Nebuchadnezzar also carried off *some* of the articles from the house of the LORD to Babylon, and put them in his temple at Babylon. [8]Now the rest of the acts of Jehoiakim, the abominations which he did, and what was found against him, indeed they *are* written in the book of the kings of Israel and Judah. Then [1]Jehoiachin his son reigned in his place.

The Reign and Captivity of Jehoiachin

[9][a]Jehoiachin *was* [1]eight years old when he became king, and he reigned in Jerusalem three months and ten days. And he did evil in the sight of the LORD. [10]At the turn of the year [a]King Nebuchadnezzar summoned *him* and took him to Babylon, [b]with the costly articles from the house of the LORD, and made [c]Zedekiah,[1] [2]*Jehoiakim's* brother, king over Judah and Jerusalem.

Zedekiah Reigns in Judah

[11][a]Zedekiah *was* twenty-one years old when he became king, and he reigned eleven years in Jerusalem. [12]He did evil in the sight of the LORD his God, *and* [a]did not humble himself before Jeremiah the prophet, *who spoke* from the mouth of the LORD. [13]And he also [a]rebelled against King Nebuchadnezzar, who had made him swear *an oath* by God; but he [b]stiffened his neck and hardened his heart against turning to the LORD God of Israel. [14]Moreover all the leaders of the priests and the people transgressed more and more, *according* to all the abominations of the nations, and defiled the house of the LORD which He had consecrated in Jerusalem.

The Fall of Jerusalem

[15][a]And the LORD God of their fathers sent *warnings* to them by His messengers, rising up early and sending *them,* because He had compassion on His people and on His dwelling place. [16]But [a]they mocked the messengers of God, [b]despised His words, and [c]scoffed at His prophets, until the [d]wrath of the LORD arose against His people, till *there was* no remedy.

[17][a]Therefore He brought against them the king of the Chaldeans, who [b]killed their young men with the sword in the house of their sanctuary, and had no compassion on young man or virgin, on the aged or the weak; He gave *them* all into his hand. [18][a]And all the articles from the house of God, great and small, the treasures of the house of the LORD, and the treasures of the king and of his leaders, all *these* he took to Babylon. [19][a]Then they burned the house of God, broke down the wall of Jerusalem, burned all its palaces with fire, and destroyed all its precious possessions. [20]And [a]those who escaped from the sword he carried away to Babylon, [b]where they became servants to him and his sons until the rule of the kingdom of Persia, [21]to fulfill the word of the LORD by the mouth of [a]Jeremiah, until the land [b]had enjoyed her Sabbaths. As long as she lay desolate [c]she kept Sabbath, to fulfill seventy years.

The Proclamation of Cyrus

[22][a]Now in the first year of Cyrus king of Persia, that the word of the LORD by the mouth of [b]Jeremiah might be fulfilled,

CHAPTER 36
1 a 2 Kin. 23:30–34
2 *1* MT *Joahaz*
4 *1* Lit. *his* *2* MT *Joahaz*
5 a 2 Kin. 23:36, 37 b [Jer. 22:13–19]
6 a 2 Kin. 24:1 b Jer. 36:30 *1 chains*
7 a Dan. 1:1, 2
8 *1* Or *Jeconiah*
9 a 2 Kin. 24:8–17 *1* Heb. mss., LXX, Syr. *eighteen* and 2 Kin. 24:8
10 a 2 Kin. 24:10–17 b Dan. 1:1, 2 c Jer. 37:1 *1* Or *Mattaniah* *2* Lit. *his brother,* 2 Kin. 24:17
11 a Jer. 52:1
12 a Jer. 21:3–7; 44:10
13 a Ezek. 17:15 b 2 Kin. 17:14
15 a Jer. 7:13; 25:3, 4
16 a Jer. 5:12, 13 b [Prov. 1:24–32] c Jer. 38:6 d Ps. 79:5
17 a 2 Kin. 25:1 b Ps. 74:20
18 a 2 Kin. 25:13–15
19 a 2 Kin. 25:9
20 a 2 Kin. 25:11 b Jer. 17:4; 27:7
21 a Jer. 25:9–12; 27:6–8; 29:10 b Lev. 26:34–43 c Lev. 25:4, 5
22 a Ezra 1:1–3 b Jer. 29:10

the LORD stirred up the spirit of [c]Cyrus
king of Persia, so that he made a proclamation throughout all his kingdom, and
also *put it* in writing, saying,

23 [a]Thus says Cyrus king of Persia:
All the kingdoms of the earth the
LORD God of heaven has given me.
And He has commanded me to
build Him a [1]house at Jerusalem
which is in Judah. Who *is* among
you of all His people? May the LORD
his God *be* with him, and let him
go up!

22 [c] Is. 44:28; 45:1
23 [a] Ezra 1:2, 3 [1] Temple

AUTHOR: *Probably Ezra*
DATE: *538–457 B.C.*
THEME: *Exiles' Return to Jerusalem and Temple Reconstruction*
KEY WORDS: *Build, the Hand of the Lord, the House of God*

EZRA

Dear Woman of Destiny,

The Book of Ezra reemphasizes God's promise that observance of His laws will secure His blessings. As the people of Judah restored the temple, naysayers sought to discourage and frustrate them—but God sent two powerful prophets, Haggai and Zechariah, to revive their vision. They persevered, and the project was completed. Don't quit! As you read this powerful word, allow the Restorer of all things to inject new life into your situations.

His love and mine,

Marilyn Hickey

End of the Babylonian Captivity

Now in the first year of Cyrus king
of Persia, that the word of the
LORD [a]by the mouth of Jeremiah
might be fulfilled, the LORD stirred up the
spirit of Cyrus king of Persia, [b]so that he
made a proclamation throughout all his
kingdom, and also *put it* in writing,
saying,

2 Thus says Cyrus king of Persia:
All the kingdoms of the earth the
LORD God of heaven has given me.
And He has [a]commanded me to
build Him a [1]house at Jerusalem
which *is* in Judah. 3Who *is* among
you of all His people? May his God
be with him, and let him go up to
Jerusalem which *is* in Judah, and
build the house of the LORD God of
Israel [a](He *is* God), which *is* in Jerusalem. 4And whoever is left in
any place where he dwells, let the
men of his place help him with silver and gold, with goods and livestock, besides the freewill offerings
for the house of God which *is* in Jerusalem.

5Then the heads of the fathers' *houses*
of Judah and Benjamin, and the priests
and the Levites, with all whose spirits
[a]God [1]had moved, arose to go up and
build the house of the LORD which *is* in
Jerusalem. 6And all those who *were*
around them [1]encouraged them with articles of silver and gold, with goods and
livestock, and with precious things, besides all *that* was [a]willingly offered.
7[a]King Cyrus also brought out the articles of the house of the LORD, [b]which Nebuchadnezzar had taken from Jerusalem
and put in the [1]temple of his gods; 8and
Cyrus king of Persia brought them out by
the hand of Mithredath the treasurer, and
counted them out to [a]Sheshbazzar the
prince of Judah. 9This *is* the number of
them: thirty gold platters, one thousand
silver platters, twenty-nine knives, 10thir-
ty gold basins, four hundred and ten silver
basins of a similar *kind, and* one thousand
other articles. 11All the articles of gold and
silver *were* five thousand four hundred.
All *these* Sheshbazzar took with the captives who were brought from Babylon to
Jerusalem.

CHAPTER 1
1 a 2 Chr. 36:22, 23 b Ezra 5:13, 14
2 a Is. 44:28; 45:1, 13 1 Temple
3 a Dan. 6:26
5 a [Phil. 2:13] 1 *stirred up*
6 a Ezra 2:68 1 Lit. *strengthened their hands*
7 a Ezra 5:14; 6:5 b 2 Kin. 24:13 1 Lit. *house*
8 a Ezra 5:14, 16

CHAPTER 2
1 a Neh. 7:6–73 b 2 Kin. 24:14–16; 25:11
2 1 *Azariah,* Neh. 7:7 2 *Raamiah,* Neh. 7:7 3 *Mispereth,* Neh. 7:7 4 *Nehum,* Neh. 7:7
5 a Neh. 7:10
6 a Neh. 7:11
10 1 *Binnui,* Neh. 7:15
18 1 *Hariph,* Neh. 7:24
20 1 *Gibeon,* Neh. 7:25
24 1 *Beth Azmaveth,* Neh. 7:28
25 1 *Kirjath Jearim,* Neh. 7:29
31 a Ezra 2:7

The Captives Who Returned to Jerusalem

2 Now [a]these *are* the people of the province who came back from the captivity, of those who had been carried away,
[b]whom Nebuchadnezzar the king of Babylon had carried away to Babylon, and
who returned to Jerusalem and Judah, everyone to his *own* city.
2*Those* who came with Zerubbabel *were*
Jeshua, Nehemiah, [1]Seraiah, [2]Reelaiah,
Mordecai, Bilshan, [3]Mispar, Bigvai, [4]Re-
hum, *and* Baanah. The number of the
men of the people of Israel: 3the people of
Parosh, two thousand one hundred and
seventy-two; 4the people of Shephatiah,
three hundred and seventy-two; 5the people of Arah, [a]seven hundred and seventy-
five; 6the people of [a]Pahath-Moab, of the
people of Jeshua *and* Joab, two thousand
eight hundred and twelve; 7the people of
Elam, one thousand two hundred and
fifty-four; 8the people of Zattu, nine hundred and forty-five; 9the people of Zaccai,
seven hundred and sixty; 10the people of
[1]Bani, six hundred and forty-two; 11the
people of Bebai, six hundred and twenty-
three; 12the people of Azgad, one thousand two hundred and twenty-two; 13the
people of Adonikam, six hundred and
sixty-six; 14the people of Bigvai, two thousand and fifty-six; 15the people of Adin,
four hundred and fifty-four; 16the people
of Ater of Hezekiah, ninety-eight; 17the
people of Bezai, three hundred and
twenty-three; 18the people of [1]Jorah, one
hundred and twelve; 19the people of Hashum, two hundred and twenty-three;
20the people of [1]Gibbar, ninety-five; 21the
people of Bethlehem, one hundred and
twenty-three; 22the men of Netophah,
fifty-six; 23the men of Anathoth, one hundred and twenty-eight; 24the people of
[1]Azmaveth, forty-two; 25the people of
[1]Kirjath Arim, Chephirah, and Beeroth,
seven hundred and forty-three; 26the people of Ramah and Geba, six hundred and
twenty-one; 27the men of Michmas, one
hundred and twenty-two; 28the men of
Bethel and Ai, two hundred and twenty-
three; 29the people of Nebo, fifty-two;
30the people of Magbish, one hundred and
fifty-six; 31the people of the other [a]Elam,
one thousand two hundred and fifty-four;
32the people of Harim, three hundred and
twenty; 33the people of Lod, Hadid, and
Ono, seven hundred and twenty-five;

34 the people of Jericho, three hundred and forty-five; 35 the people of Senaah, three thousand six hundred and thirty.

36 The priests: the sons of [a]Jedaiah, of the house of Jeshua, nine hundred and seventy-three; 37 the sons of [a]Immer, one thousand and fifty-two; 38 the sons of [a]Pashhur, one thousand two hundred and forty-seven; 39 the sons of [a]Harim, one thousand and seventeen.

40 The Levites: the sons of Jeshua and Kadmiel, of the sons of [1]Hodaviah, seventy-four.

41 The singers: the sons of Asaph, one hundred and twenty-eight.

42 The sons of the gatekeepers: the sons of Shallum, the sons of Ater, the sons of Talmon, the sons of Akkub, the sons of Hatita, and the sons of Shobai, one hundred and thirty-nine *in* all.

43 [a]The Nethinim: the sons of Ziha, the sons of Hasupha, the sons of Tabbaoth, 44 the sons of Keros, the sons of [1]Siaha, the sons of Padon, 45 the sons of Lebanah, the sons of Hagabah, the sons of Akkub, 46 the sons of Hagab, the sons of Shalmai, the sons of Hanan, 47 the sons of Giddel, the sons of Gahar, the sons of Reaiah, 48 the sons of Rezin, the sons of Nekoda, the sons of Gazzam, 49 the sons of Uzza, the sons of Paseah, the sons of Besai, 50 the sons of Asnah, the sons of Meunim, the sons of [1]Nephusim, 51 the sons of Bakbuk, the sons of Hakupha, the sons of Harhur, 52 the sons of [1]Bazluth, the sons of Mehida, the sons of Harsha, 53 the sons of Barkos, the sons of Sisera, the sons of Tamah, 54 the sons of Neziah, and the sons of Hatipha.

55 The sons of [a]Solomon's servants: the sons of Sotai, the sons of [b]Sophereth, the sons of [1]Peruda, 56 the sons of Jaala, the sons of Darkon, the sons of Giddel, 57 the sons of Shephatiah, the sons of Hattil, the sons of Pochereth of Zebaim, and the sons of [1]Ami. 58 All the [a]Nethinim and the children of [b]Solomon's servants were three hundred and ninety-two.

59 And these *were* the ones who came up from Tel Melah, Tel Harsha, Cherub, [1]Addan, and Immer; but they could not [2]identify their father's house or their [3]genealogy, whether they *were* of Israel: 60 the sons of Delaiah, the sons of Tobiah, and the sons of Nekoda, six hundred and fifty-two; 61 and of the sons of the priests: the sons of [a]Habaiah, the sons of [1]Koz, and the sons of [b]Barzillai, who took a wife of the daughters of Barzillai the Gileadite, and was called by their name. 62 These sought their listing *among* those who were registered by genealogy, but they were not found; [a]therefore they *were excluded* from the priesthood as defiled. 63 And the [1]governor said to them that they [a]should not eat of the most holy things till a priest could consult with the [b]Urim and Thummim.

64 [a]The whole assembly together *was* forty-two thousand three hundred *and* sixty, 65 besides their male and female servants, of whom *there were* seven thousand three hundred and thirty-seven; and they had two hundred men and women singers. 66 Their horses *were* seven hundred and thirty-six, their mules two hundred and forty-five, 67 their camels four hundred and thirty-five, and *their* donkeys six thousand seven hundred and twenty.

68 [a]*Some* of the heads of the fathers' *houses,* when they came to the house of the LORD which *is* in Jerusalem, offered freely for the house of God, to erect it in its place: 69 According to their ability, they gave to the [a]treasury for the work sixty-one thousand gold drachmas, five thousand minas of silver, and one hundred priestly garments.

70 [a]So the priests and the Levites, *some* of the people, the singers, the gatekeepers, and the Nethinim, dwelt in their cities, and all Israel in their cities.

Worship Restored at Jerusalem

3 And when the [a]seventh month had come, and the children of Israel *were* in the cities, the people gathered together as one man to Jerusalem. 2 Then [1]Jeshua the son of [a]Jozadak[2] and his brethren the priests, [b]and Zerubbabel the son of [c]Shealtiel and his brethren, arose and built the altar of the God of Israel, to offer burnt offerings on it, as *it is* [d]written in the Law of Moses the man of God. 3 Though fear *had come* upon them because of the people of those countries, they set the altar on its [1]bases; and they offered [a]burnt offerings on it to the LORD, *both* the morning and evening burnt offerings. 4 [a]They also kept the Feast of Tabernacles, [b]as *it is* written, and [c]*offered* the daily burnt offerings in the number required by ordinance for each day. 5 Afterwards *they offered* the [a]regular burnt offering, and

---

36 a 1 Chr. 24:7–18
37 a 1 Chr. 24:14
38 a 1 Chr. 9:12
39 a 1 Chr. 24:8
40 *1 Judah,* Ezra 3:9, or *Hodevah,* Neh. 7:43
43 a 1 Chr. 9:2
44 *1 Sia,* Neh. 7:47
50 *1 Nephishesim,* Neh. 7:52
52 *1 Bazlith,* Neh. 7:54
55 a 1 Kin. 9:21 b Neh. 7:57–60 *1 Perida,* Neh. 7:57
57 *1 Amon,* Neh. 7:59
58 a 1 Chr. 9:2 b 1 Kin. 9:21
59 *1* Or *Addon,* Neh. 7:61 *2* Lit. *tell* *3* Lit. *seed*
61 a Neh. 7:63 b 2 Sam. 17:27 *1* Or *Hakkoz*
62 a Num. 3:10
63 a Lev. 22:2, 10, 15, 16 b Ex. 28:30 *1* Heb. *Tirshatha*
64 a Neh. 7:66
68 a Neh. 7:70
69 a Ezra 8:25–35
70 a Neh. 7:73

CHAPTER 3
1 a Neh. 7:73; 8:1, 2
2 a Neh. 12:1, 8 b Ezra 2:2; 4:2, 3; 5:2 c 1 Chr. 3:17 d Deut. 12:5, 6 *1* Or *Joshua* *2 Jehozadak,* 1 Chr. 6:14
3 a Num. 28:3 *1 foundations*
4 a Neh. 8:14–18 b Ex. 23:16 c Num. 29:12, 13
5 a Ex. 29:38

Ezra 3:3

Dear Woman of Destiny,

Fear. It's that emotion that comes upon all of us at one time or another. It makes our hearts pound, our blood pressure rise, our hands clammy and shaky, and our mouths dry. It's a feeling of agitation caused by what we perceive to be danger or trouble, and our first reaction is to run! To escape or to run away from a threatening situation is sometimes the best thing to do and is a natural reaction to what we feel is a danger to us.

However, there are times when running in fear from a situation is not necessarily the right thing to do. In this story in Ezra, the people of Israel were surrounded by idolatrous people who wanted nothing more than to destroy them and run them out of Jerusalem again. The people who had occupied Israel while the people of God were in captivity were not people who served God and weren't interested in seeing them return to Jerusalem to rebuild the city. Rather, they wanted them gone, and to reach that end they attacked them in war and tried to run them off. This caused those who had returned to Jerusalem to rebuild the city to be afraid. However, instead of following their natural instincts and running from that dangerous, threatening situation, they built an altar and offered sacrifices to God. Rather than give in to their fear, they remained faithful to God and were bold in their worship. As they did this, their fear turned into courage.

When I was 25, my husband was killed in a plane crash in the mountains of Mexico. The tragedy was a result of a prolonged period of religious persecution. As a result, fear came into my heart that not only had the persecutors taken his life, but that they would now turn their attention to me and to my three small children. My first instinct was to flee in fear. But God spoke to my heart and promised that He would be with me. Strengthened with His promise, I stayed in the same situation and continued the same work, while God turned my fear into faith and courage and did a great work in the country of Mexico.

Many times as we walk through our daily lives with the Lord, we feel that we are surrounded by hostile forces—that we are in danger from the anger and hatred we feel directed toward us from the outside world. Our first instinct is to flee. But as we hold steady in our worship of the Lord in the face of hostilities and in spite of our fear, we will find that God will give us special grace, and our fear will turn into courage.

Nola Warren

those for New Moons and for all the appointed feasts of the LORD that were consecrated, and *those* of everyone who
willingly offered a freewill offering to the
LORD. 6From the first day of the seventh
month they began to offer burnt offerings
to the LORD, although the foundation of
the temple of the LORD had not been laid.
7They also gave money to the masons and
the carpenters, and [a]food, drink, and oil
to the people of Sidon and Tyre to bring
cedar logs from Lebanon to the sea, to
[b]Joppa, [c]according to the permission
which they had from Cyrus king of Persia.

Restoration of the Temple Begins

8Now in the second month of the second year of their coming to the house of
God at Jerusalem, [a]Zerubbabel the son of
Shealtiel, Jeshua the son of [1]Jozadak, and
the rest of their brethren the priests and
the Levites, and all those who had come
out of the captivity to Jerusalem, began
work [b]and appointed the Levites from
twenty years old and above to oversee the
work of the house of the LORD. 9Then
Jeshua *with* his sons and brothers, Kadmiel *with* his sons, and the sons of [1]Ju-
dah, arose as one to oversee those
working on the house of God: the sons of
Henadad *with* their sons and their brethren the Levites.

Father, I pray that ____ will praise You and give thanks to You, for You are good, and Your mercy endures forever.

FROM EZRA 3:11

10When the builders laid the foundation
of the temple of the LORD, [a]the[1] priests
stood in their apparel with trumpets, and
the Levites, the sons of Asaph, with cymbals, to praise the LORD, according to the
[b]ordinance[2] of David king of Israel.
11[a]And they sang responsively, praising
and giving thanks to the LORD:

[b]"For *He is* good,
[c]For His mercy *endures* forever
toward Israel."

Then all the people shouted with a great
shout, when they praised the LORD, because the foundation of the house of the
LORD was laid.

12But many of the priests and Levites
and [a]heads of the fathers' *houses,* old men
who had seen the first temple, wept with
a loud voice when the foundation of this
temple was laid before their eyes. Yet
many shouted aloud for joy, 13so that the
people could not discern the noise of the
shout of joy from the noise of the weeping
of the people, for the people shouted with
a loud shout, and the sound was heard
afar off.

Resistance to Rebuilding the Temple

4 Now when [a]the [1]adversaries of Judah
and Benjamin heard that the descendants of the captivity were building the
temple of the LORD God of Israel, 2they
came to Zerubbabel and the heads of the
fathers' *houses,* and said to them, "Let us
build with you, for we seek your God as
you *do;* and we have sacrificed to Him
[a]since the days of Esarhaddon king of Assyria, who brought us here." 3But Zerubbabel and Jeshua and the rest of the heads
of the fathers' *houses* of Israel said to
them, [a]"You may do nothing with us to
build a [1]house for our God; but we alone
will build to the LORD God of Israel, as
[b]King Cyrus the king of Persia has commanded us." 4Then [a]the people of the land
tried to discourage the people of Judah.
They troubled them in building, 5and
hired counselors against them to frustrate
their purpose all the days of Cyrus king of
Persia, even until the reign of [a]Darius
king of Persia.

Rebuilding of Jerusalem Opposed

6In the reign of Ahasuerus, in the beginning of his reign, they wrote an accusation against the inhabitants of Judah
and Jerusalem.

7In the days of [a]Artaxerxes also, [1]Bish-
lam, Mithredath, Tabel, and the rest of
their companions wrote to Artaxerxes
king of Persia; and the letter *was* written
in [b]Aramaic script, and translated into the

7 [a]Acts 12:20 [b]2 Chr. 2:16 [c]Ezra 1:2; 6:3
8 [a]Ezra 3:2; 4:3 [b]1 Chr. 23:4, 24 [1]*Jehozadak,* 1 Chr. 6:14
9 [1]*Hodaviah,* Ezra 2:40
10 [a]1 Chr. 16:5, 6 [b]1 Chr. 6:31; 16:4; 25:1 [1]So with LXX, Syr., Vg.; MT *they stationed the priests* [2]Lit. *hands*
11 [a]Neh. 12:24 [b]Ps. 136:1 [c]Jer. 33:11
12 [a]Ezra 2:68
CHAPTER 4
1 [a]Ezra 4:7–9 [1]*enemies*
2 [a]2 Kin. 17:24; 19:37
3 [a]Neh. 2:20 [b]Ezra 1:1–4 [1]Temple
4 [a]Ezra 3:3
5 [a]Ezra 5:5; 6:1
7 [a]Ezra 7:1, 7, 21 [b]2 Kin. 18:26 [1]Or *in peace*

Aramaic language. 8[1]Rehum the commander and Shimshai the scribe wrote a
letter against Jerusalem to King Artaxerxes in this fashion:

9 [1]From Rehum the commander,
Shimshai the scribe, and the rest of
their companions—*representatives*
of [a]the Dinaites, the Apharsath-
chites, the Tarpelites, the people of
Persia and Erech and Babylon and
[2]Shushan, the Dehavites, the Elamites, 10[a]and the rest of the nations
whom the great and noble Osnap-
per took captive and settled in the
cities of Samaria and the remainder
beyond [1]the River—[b]and[2] so forth.

11(This *is* a copy of the letter that they
sent him)

To King Artaxerxes from your servants, the men *of the region* beyond the River, [1]and so forth:

12 Let it be known to the king that
the Jews who came up from you
have come to us at Jerusalem, and
are building the [a]rebellious and evil
city, and are finishing *its* [b]walls and
repairing the foundations. 13Let it
now be known to the king that, if
this city is built and the walls completed, they will not pay [a]tax, tribute, or custom, and the king's
treasury will be diminished. 14Now
because we receive support from
the palace, it was not proper for us
to see the king's dishonor; therefore
we have sent and informed the
king, 15that search may be made in
the book of the records of your fathers. And you will find in the book
of the records and know that this
city *is* a rebellious city, harmful to
kings and provinces, and that they
have incited sedition within the city
in former times, for which cause
this city was destroyed.

16 We inform the king that if this
city is rebuilt and its walls are completed, the result will be that you
will have no dominion beyond the
River.

17The king sent an answer:

To Rehum the commander, *to*
Shimshai the scribe, *to* the rest of
their companions who dwell in Samaria, and *to* the remainder beyond
the River:

Peace, [1]and so forth.

18 The letter which you sent to us
has been clearly read before me.
19And [1]I gave the command, and a
search has been made, and it was
found that this city in former times
has revolted against kings, and rebellion and sedition have been fos-
tered in it. 20There have also been
mighty kings over Jerusalem, who
have [a]ruled over all *the region* [b]be-
yond the River; and tax, tribute,
and custom were paid to them.
21Now [1]give the command to make
these men cease, that this city may
not be built until the command is
given by me.

22 Take heed now that you do not
fail to do this. Why should damage
increase to the hurt of the kings?

23Now when the copy of King Artaxerxes' letter *was* read before Rehum, Shimshai the scribe, and their companions,
they went up in haste to Jerusalem
against the Jews, and by force of arms
made them cease. 24Thus the work of the
house of God which *is* at Jerusalem
ceased, and it was discontinued until the
second year of the reign of Darius king of
Persia.

Restoration of the Temple Resumed

5 Then the prophet [a]Haggai and [b]Zech-
ariah the son of Iddo, prophets,
prophesied to the Jews who *were* in Judah
and Jerusalem, in the name of the God of
Israel, *who was* over them. 2So [a]Zerubba-
bel the son of Shealtiel and Jeshua the son
of [1]Jozadak rose up and began to build the
house of God which *is* in Jerusalem; and
[b]the prophets of God *were* with them,
helping them.

3At the same time [a]Tattenai the governor of *the region* beyond [1]the River and
Shethar-Boznai and their companions
came to them and spoke thus to them:
[b]"Who has commanded you to build this
[2]temple and finish this wall?" 4[a]Then, accordingly, we told them the names of the
men who were constructing this building.
5But [a]the eye of their God was upon the
elders of the Jews, so that they could not
make them cease till a report could go to

8 [1] The original language of Ezra 4:8 through 6:18 is Aramaic.

9 [a] 2 Kin. 17:30, 31 [1] Lit. *Then* [2] Or *Susa*

10 [a] 2 Kin. 17:24 [b] Ezra 4:11, 17; 7:12 [1] The Euphrates [2] Lit. *and now*

11 [1] Lit. *and now*

12 [a] 2 Chr. 36:13 [b] Ezra 5:3, 9

13 [a] Ezra 4:20; 7:24

17 [1] Lit. *and now*

19 [1] Lit. *by me a decree has been put forth*

20 [a] Ps. 72:8 [b] Gen. 15:18

21 [1] *put forth a decree*

CHAPTER 5

1 [a] Hag. 1:1 [b] Zech. 1:1

2 [a] Ezra 3:2 [b] Hag. 2:4 [1] *Jehozadak,* 1 Chr. 6:14

3 [a] Ezra 5:6; 6:6 [b] Ezra 1:3; 5:9 [1] The Euphrates [2] Lit. *house*

4 [a] Ezra 5:10

5 [a] Ps. 33:18

Darius. Then a [b]written answer was returned concerning this *matter.* 6This is a
copy of the letter that Tattenai sent:

The governor of *the region* beyond
the River, and Shethar-Boznai,
[a]and his companions, the Persians
who *were in the region* beyond the
River, to Darius the king.

7(They sent a letter to him, in which was
written thus)

To Darius the king:

All peace.

8 Let it be known to the king that
we went into the province of Judea,
to the [1]temple of the great God,
which is being built with [2]heavy
stones, and timber is being laid in
the walls; and this work goes on
diligently and prospers in their
hands.

9 Then we asked those elders, *and*
spoke thus to them: [a]"Who commanded you to build this temple
and to finish these walls?" 10We
also asked them their names to inform you, that we might write the
names of the men who *were* chief
among them.

11 And thus they returned us an answer, saying: "We are the servants
of the God of heaven and earth, and
we are rebuilding the [1]temple that
was built many years ago, which a
great king of Israel built [a]and completed. 12But [a]because our fathers
provoked the God of heaven to
wrath, He gave them into the hand
of [b]Nebuchadnezzar king of Babylon, the Chaldean, *who* destroyed
this temple and [c]carried the people
away to Babylon. 13However, in the
first year of [a]Cyrus king of Babylon,
King Cyrus issued a decree to build
this [1]house of God. 14Also, [a]the
gold and silver articles of the house
of God, which Nebuchadnezzar had
taken from the temple that *was* in
Jerusalem and carried into the temple of Babylon—those King Cyrus
took from the temple of Babylon,
and they were given to [b]one named
Sheshbazzar, whom he had made
governor. 15And he said to him,
'Take these articles; go, carry them
to the temple *site* that *is* in Jerusalem, and let the house of God be
rebuilt on its former site.' 16Then
the same Sheshbazzar came *and*
[a]laid the foundation of the house of
God which *is* in Jerusalem; but
from that time even until now it
has been under construction, and
[b]it is not finished."

17 Now therefore, if *it seems* good to
the king, [a]let a search be made in
the king's treasure house, which *is*
there in Babylon, whether it is *so*
that a decree was issued by King
Cyrus to build this house of God at
Jerusalem, and let the king send us
his pleasure concerning this *matter.*

The Decree of Darius

6 Then King Darius issued a decree,
[a]and a search was made in the [1]ar-
chives, where the treasures were stored in
Babylon. 2And at [1]Achmetha, in the palace that *is* in the province of [a]Media, a
scroll was found, and in it a record *was*
written thus:

3 In the first year of King Cyrus,
King Cyrus issued a [a]decree *concerning* the house of God at Jerusalem: "Let the house be rebuilt, the
place where they offered sacrifices;
and let the foundations of it be
firmly laid, its height sixty cubits
and its width sixty cubits, 4[a]*with*
three rows of heavy stones and one
row of new timber. Let the [b]expens-
es be paid from the king's treasury.
5Also let [a]the gold and silver articles of the house of God, which
Nebuchadnezzar took from the temple which *is* in Jerusalem and
brought to Babylon, be restored and
taken back to the temple which *is*
in Jerusalem, *each* to its place; and
deposit *them* in the house of
God"—

6 [a]Now *therefore,* Tattenai, governor
of *the region* beyond the River, and
Shethar-Boznai, and your companions the Persians who *are* beyond
the River, keep yourselves far from
there. 7Let the work of this house
of God alone; let the governor of
the Jews and the elders of the Jews
build this house of God on its site.

8 Moreover I issue a decree *as to*

---

5 b Ezra 6:6
6 a Ezra 4:7–10
8 *1* Lit. *house* *2* Lit. *stones of rolling,* stones too heavy to be carried
9 a Ezra 5:3, 4
11 a 1 Kin. 6:1, 38 *1* Lit. *house*
12 a 2 Chr. 34:25; 36:16, 17 b 2 Kin. 24:2; 25:8–11 c Jer. 13:19
13 a Ezra 1:1 *1* Temple
14 a Ezra 1:7, 8; 6:5 b Hag. 1:14; 2:2, 21
16 a Ezra 3:8–10 b Ezra 6:15
17 a Ezra 6:1, 2

CHAPTER 6
1 a Ezra 5:17 *1* Lit. *house of the scrolls*
2 a 2 Kin. 17:6 *1* Probably *Ecbatana,* the ancient capital of Media
3 a Ezra 1:1; 5:13
4 a 1 Kin. 6:36 b Ezra 3:7
5 a Ezra 1:7, 8; 5:14
6 a Ezra 5:3, 6

what you shall do for the elders of
these Jews, for the building of this
[1]house of God: Let the cost be paid
at the king's expense from taxes *on*
the region beyond the River; this is
to be given immediately to these
men, so that they are not hindered.
9 And whatever they need—young
bulls, rams, and lambs for the
burnt offerings of the God of heav-
en, wheat, salt, wine, and oil, according to the request of the priests
who *are* in Jerusalem—let it be
given them day by day without fail,
10 [a]that they may offer sacrifices of
sweet aroma to the God of heaven,
and pray for the life of the king and
his sons.

11 Also I issue a decree that whoever
alters this edict, let a timber be
pulled from his house and erected,
and let him be hanged on it; [a]and
let his house be made a refuse heap
because of this. 12 And may the God
who causes His [a]name to dwell
there destroy any king or people
who put their hand to alter it, or to
destroy this [1]house of God which is
in Jerusalem. I Darius issue a decree; let it be done diligently.

The Temple Completed and Dedicated

13 Then Tattenai, governor of *the region*
beyond the River, Shethar-Boznai, and
their companions diligently did according
to what King Darius had sent. 14 [a]So the
elders of the Jews built, and they prospered through the prophesying of Haggai
the prophet and Zechariah the son of
Iddo. And they built and finished *it,* according to the commandment of the God
of Israel, and according to the [1]command
of [b]Cyrus, [c]Darius, and [d]Artaxerxes king
of Persia. 15 Now the temple was finished
on the third day of the month of Adar,
which was in the sixth year of the reign of
King Darius. 16 Then the children of Israel,
the priests and the Levites and the rest of
the descendants of the captivity, celebrated [a]the dedication of this [1]house of God
with joy. 17 And they [a]offered sacrifices at
the dedication of this house of God, one
hundred bulls, two hundred rams, four
hundred lambs, and as a sin offering for
all Israel twelve male goats, according to
the number of the tribes of Israel. 18 They
assigned the priests to their [a]divisions
and the Levites to their [b]divisions, over
the service of God in Jerusalem, [c]as it is
written in the Book of Moses.

The renewal of our natures is a work of great importance. It is not to be done in a day. We have not only a new house to build up, but an old one to pull down.

GEORGE WHITEFIELD

The Passover Celebrated

19 [1]And the descendants of the captivity
kept the Passover [a]on the fourteenth *day*
of the first month. 20 For the priests and
the Levites had [a]purified themselves; all
of them *were ritually* clean. And they
[b]slaughtered the Passover *lambs* for all
the descendants of the captivity, for their
brethren the priests, and for themselves.
21 Then the children of Israel who had returned from the captivity ate together
with all who had separated themselves
from the [a]filth[1] of the nations of the land
in order to seek the LORD God of Israel.
22 And they kept the [a]Feast of Unleavened
Bread seven days with joy; for the LORD
made them joyful, and [b]turned the heart
[c]of the king of Assyria toward them, to
strengthen their hands in the work of the
house of God, the God of Israel.

The Arrival of Ezra

7 Now after these things, in the reign of
[a]Artaxerxes king of Persia, Ezra the
[b]son of Seraiah, [c]the son of Azariah, the
son of [d]Hilkiah, 2 the son of Shallum, the
son of Zadok, the son of Ahitub, 3 the son
of Amariah, the son of Azariah, the son of
Meraioth, 4 the son of Zerahiah, the son of
Uzzi, the son of Bukki, 5 the son of Abishua, the son of Phinehas, the son of Eleazar, the son of Aaron the chief priest—
6 this Ezra came up from Babylon; and he
was [a]a skilled scribe in the Law of Moses,
which the LORD God of Israel had given.
The king granted him all his request, [b]ac-
cording to the hand of the LORD his God
upon him. 7 [a]*Some* of the children of

8 [1]Temple

10 [a]Ezra 7:23

11 [a]Dan. 2:5; 3:29

12 [a]1 Kin. 9:3 [1]Temple

14 [a]Ezra 5:1, 2 [b]Ezra 1:1; 5:13; 6:3 [c]Ezra 4:24; 6:12 [d]Ezra 7:1, 11 [1]*decree*

16 [a]1 Kin. 8:63 [1]Temple

17 [a]Ezra 8:35

18 [a]1 Chr. 24:1 [b]1 Chr. 23:6 [c]Num. 3:6; 8:9

19 [a]Ex. 12:6 [1]The Hebrew language resumes in Ezra 6:19 and continues through 7:11.

20 [a]2 Chr. 29:34; 30:15 [b]2 Chr. 35:11

21 [a]Ezra 9:11 [1]*uncleanness*

22 [a]Ex. 12:15; 13:6, 7 [b][Prov. 21:1] [c]Ezra 1:1; 6:1

CHAPTER 7
1 [a]Neh. 2:1 [b]1 Chr. 6:14 [c]Jer. 52:24 [d]2 Chr. 35:8

6 [a]Ezra 7:11, 12, 21 [b]Ezra 7:9, 28; 8:22

7 [a]Ezra 8:1–14

Israel, the priests, [b]the Levites, the singers, the gatekeepers, and [c]the Nethinim
came up to Jerusalem in the seventh year
of King Artaxerxes. 8 And Ezra came to Jerusalem in the fifth month, which *was* in
the seventh year of the king. 9 On the first
day of the first month he began *his* journey from Babylon, and on the first *day* of
the fifth month he came to Jerusalem,
[a]according to the good hand of his God
upon him. 10 For Ezra had prepared his
heart to [a]seek[1] the Law of the LORD, and
to do *it,* and to [b]teach statutes and ordinances in Israel.

The Letter of Artaxerxes to Ezra

11 This *is* a copy of the letter that King
Artaxerxes gave Ezra the priest, the
scribe, expert in the words of the commandments of the LORD, and of His statutes to Israel:

12 [1]Artaxerxes, [a]king of kings,

To Ezra the priest, a scribe of the
Law of the God of heaven:

Perfect *peace,* [b]and[2] so forth.

13 I issue a decree that all those of
the people of Israel and the priests
and Levites in my realm, who volunteer to go up to Jerusalem, may
go with you. 14 And whereas you are
being sent [1]by the king and his
[a]seven counselors to inquire concerning Judah and Jerusalem, with
regard to the Law of your God
which *is* in your hand; 15 and *where-*
as you are to carry the silver and
gold which the king and his counselors have freely offered to the God
of Israel, [a]whose dwelling *is* in Jerusalem; 16 [a]and *whereas* all the silver and gold that you may find in
all the province of Babylon, along
with the freewill offering of the
people and the priests, *are to be*
[b]freely offered for the [1]house of
their God in Jerusalem— 17 now
therefore, be careful to buy with
this money bulls, rams, and lambs,
with their [a]grain offerings and their
drink offerings, and [b]offer them on
the altar of the house of your God
in Jerusalem.

18 And whatever seems good to you
and your brethren to do with the
rest of the silver and the gold, do it
according to the will of your God.
19 Also the articles that are given to
you for the service of the house of
your God, deliver in full before the
God of Jerusalem. 20 And whatever
more may be needed for the house
of your God, which you may have
occasion to provide, pay *for it* from
the king's treasury.

21 And I, *even* I, Artaxerxes the king,
issue a decree to all the treasurers
who *are in the region* beyond the
River, that whatever Ezra the priest,
the scribe of the Law of the God of
heaven, may require of you, let it
be done diligently, 22 up to one hundred talents of silver, one hundred
kors of wheat, one hundred baths of
wine, one hundred baths of oil, and
salt without prescribed limit.
23 Whatever [1]is commanded by the
God of heaven, let it diligently be
done for the [2]house of the God of
heaven. For why should there be
wrath against the realm of the king
and his sons?

24 Also we inform you that it shall
not be lawful to impose tax, tribute,
or custom *on* any of the priests, Levites, singers, gatekeepers, Nethinim, or servants of this house of
God. 25 And you, Ezra, according to
your God-given wisdom, [a]set magistrates and judges who may judge
all the people who *are in the region*
beyond the River, all such as know
the laws of your God; and [b]teach
those who do not know *them.*
26 Whoever will not observe the law
of your God and the law of the
king, let judgment be executed
speedily on him, whether *it be*
death, or [1]banishment, or confisca-
tion of goods, or imprisonment.

27 [a]Blessed[1] *be* the LORD God of our fathers, [b]who has put *such a thing* as this
in the king's heart, to beautify the house
of the LORD which *is* in Jerusalem, 28 and
[a]has extended mercy to me before the
king and his counselors, and before all the
king's mighty princes.

So I was encouraged, as [b]the hand of
the LORD my God *was* upon me; and I
gathered leading men of Israel to go up
with me.

7 [b] Ezra 8:15 [c] Ezra 2:43; 8:20
9 [a] Neh. 2:8, 18
10 [a] Ps. 119:45 [b] Deut. 33:10 [1] Study
12 [a] Dan. 2:37 [b] Ezra 4:10 [1] The original language of Ezra 7:12–26 is Aramaic. [2] Lit. *and now*
14 [a] Esth. 1:14 [1] *from before*
15 [a] Ezra 6:12
16 [a] Ezra 8:25 [b] 1 Chr. 29:6, 9 [1] Temple
17 [a] Num. 15:4–13 [b] Deut. 12:5–11
23 [1] Lit. *is from the decree* [2] Temple
25 [a] Ex. 18:21, 22 [b] [Mal. 2:7]
26 [1] Lit. *rooting out*
27 [a] 1 Chr. 29:10 [b] Ezra 6:22 [1] The Hebrew language resumes in Ezra 7:27.
28 [a] Ezra 9:9 [b] Ezra 5:5; 7:6, 9; 8:18

Exercise the spirit of faith as much as you do the act of prayer. Be humble and watchfully obedient, that faith be not clouded.

RAYMOND T. RICHEY

Heads of Families Who Returned with Ezra

8 These *are* the heads of their fathers'
houses, and *this is* the genealogy of
those who went up with me from Babylon,
in the reign of King Artaxerxes: 2of the
sons of Phinehas, Gershom; of the sons
of Ithamar, Daniel; of the sons of David,
[a]Hattush; 3of the sons of Shecaniah, of
the sons of [a]Parosh, Zechariah; and registered with him *were* one hundred and fifty
males; 4of the sons of [a]Pahath-Moab, Eliehoenai the son of Zerahiah, and with him
two hundred males; 5of [1]the sons of
Shechaniah, Ben-Jahaziel, and with him
three hundred males; 6of the sons of Adin,
Ebed the son of Jonathan, and with him
fifty males; 7of the sons of Elam, Jeshaiah
the son of Athaliah, and with him seventy
males; 8of the sons of Shephatiah, Zebadiah the son of Michael, and with him
eighty males; 9of the sons of Joab, Obadiah the son of Jehiel, and with him two
hundred and eighteen males; 10of [1]the
sons of Shelomith, Ben-Josiphiah, and
with him one hundred and sixty males;
11of the sons of [a]Bebai, Zechariah the son
of Bebai, and with him twenty-eight
males; 12of the sons of Azgad, Johanan
[1]the son of Hakkatan, and with him one
hundred and ten males; 13of the last sons
of Adonikam, whose names *are* these—
Eliphelet, Jeiel, and Shemaiah—and with
them sixty males; 14also of the sons of Bigvai, Uthai and [1]Zabbud, and with them
seventy males.

Servants for the Temple

15Now I gathered them by the river that
flows to Ahava, and we camped there
three days. And I looked among the people
and the priests, and found none of the
[a]sons of Levi there. 16Then I sent for Eliezer, Ariel, Shemaiah, Elnathan, Jarib, Elnathan, Nathan, Zechariah, and
[a]Meshullam, leaders; also for Joiarib and
Elnathan, men of understanding. 17And I
gave them a command for Iddo the chief
man at the place Casiphia, and [1]I told
them what they should say [2]to Iddo *and*
his brethren the Nethinim at the place Casiphia—that they should bring us servants for the house of our God. 18Then, by
the good hand of our God upon us, they
[a]brought us a man of understanding, of
the sons of Mahli the son of Levi, the son
of Israel, namely Sherebiah, with his sons
and brothers, eighteen men; 19and [a]Hash-
abiah, and with him Jeshaiah of the sons
of Merari, his brothers and their sons,
twenty men; 20[a]also of the Nethinim,
whom David and the leaders had appointed for the service of the Levites, two hundred and twenty Nethinim. All of them
were designated by name.

Humility is perfect quietness of heart. It is to be at rest when nobody praises me and when I am blamed or despised.

ANDREW MURRAY

Fasting and Prayer for Protection

21 Then I [a]proclaimed a fast there at
the river of Ahava, that we might [b]humble
ourselves before our God, to seek from
Him the [c]right way for us and our little
ones and all our possessions. 22For [a]I
was ashamed to request of the king an
escort of soldiers and horsemen to help us
against the enemy on the road, because
we had spoken to the king, saying, [b]"The
hand of our God *is* upon all those for
[c]good who seek Him, but His power and
His wrath *are* [d]against all those who [e]for-
sake Him." 23So we fasted and entreated
our God for this, and He [a]answered our
prayer.

Gifts for the Temple

24And I separated twelve of the leaders
of the priests—Sherebiah, Hashabiah,

CHAPTER 8
2 [a]1 Chr. 3:22
3 [a]Ezra 2:3
4 [a]Ezra 10:30
5 [1]So with MT, Vg.; LXX *the sons of Zatho, Shechaniah*
10 [1]So with MT, Vg.; LXX *the sons of Banni, Shelomith*
11 [a]Ezra 10:28
12 [1]Or *the youngest son,*
14 [1]Or *Zakkur*
15 [a]Ezra 7:7; 8:2
16 [a]Ezra 10:15
17 [1]Lit. *I put words in their mouths to say* [2]So with Vg.; MT *to Iddo his brother;* LXX *to their brethren*
18 [a]Neh. 8:7
19 [a]Neh. 12:24
20 [a]Ezra 2:43; 7:7
21 [a]1 Sam. 7:6 [b]Is. 58:3, 5 [c]Ps. 5:8
22 [a]1 Cor. 9:15 [b]Ezra 7:6, 9, 28 [c][Rom. 8:28] [d][Ps. 34:16] [e][2 Chr. 15:2]
23 [a]2 Chr. 33:13

Ezra 8:21

Dear Woman of Destiny,

God is a wonderful, loving God who delights in leading us through life. Read how David extolled God's leading: "O God, when You went out before Your people, when You marched through the wilderness . . . Selah" (Ps. 68:7). *Selah*—ponder that one. The Amplified Bible defines *selah* as "pause, and calmly think of that."

Yes, pause and think of it! The mighty Creator God marched right through the barren desert wilderness with His people, leading them by day with a cooling cloud and by night with a pillar of flame—not just a matchstick, but a big, red flaming pillar!

When my husband Edwin and I were just starting to pastor, we lived in a tiny parsonage next to a construction site and under the flight path for a major airport. The noise, dirt, and cramped living conditions were unnerving, especially with three small children underfoot and only one bedroom. But with hardly any income, where else could we live except where the church had provided?

When I cried to God for a way out, through His Word He spoke to me: "I called on the LORD in distress; the LORD answered me and set me in a broad place" (Ps. 118:5).

I knew He was right there, leading me through my wilderness. Even though I couldn't see it with my natural eyes, God was like a pillar of flame for me in the spiritual darkness of the moment. As He'd done for the Israelites in the wilderness, and for Ezra, God was more than willing to lead me safely to a place I could call "home."

But the Bible says even more about our path of life! "You comprehend my path and my lying down, and are acquainted with all my ways" (Ps. 139:3).

Figured into our path is not just the onward, surging, pressing missions and assignments of life, but also the cool, shady resting places where we lay down our burdens and sit peacefully beneath God's cloud of grace.

God's assurance that He was moving on my behalf gave me the ability to rest in the place where I was, regardless of the circumstances. A short time later, Edwin was called to pastor a church in a beautiful community where the parsonage was among a grove of trees. Best of all, it had three bedrooms for our growing family.

Certainly Edwin and I have walked through far bleaker wildernesses than merely having too small a house. But regardless of outward circumstances, God has not only desired to lead us, He has led us both day and night.

Our part is to dig into the Word of God and dedicate ourselves to prayer. Then, when we do the next thing God tells us to do, whether great or small, the flicker of His light becomes a flaming pillar that we can see in the blackest night.

Nancy Corbett Cole

and ten of their brethren with them—
25and weighed out to them [a]the silver, the
gold, and the articles, the offering for the
house of our God which the king and his
counselors and his princes, and all Israel
who were present, had offered. 26I
weighed into their hand six hundred and
fifty talents of silver, silver articles *weigh-*
ing one hundred talents, one hundred talents of gold, 27twenty gold basins *worth* a
thousand drachmas, and two vessels of
fine polished bronze, precious as gold.
28And I said to them, "You *are* [a]holy[1] to
the LORD; the articles *are* [b]holy also; and
the silver and the gold *are* a freewill offering to the LORD God of your fathers.
29Watch and keep *them* until you weigh
them before the leaders of the priests and
the Levites and [a]heads of the fathers'
houses of Israel in Jerusalem, *in* the
chambers of the house of the LORD." 30So
the priests and the Levites received the
silver and the gold and the articles by
weight, to bring *them* to Jerusalem to the
house of our God.

Lord, may ____ remember that Your hand is upon all those for good who seek You, but Your power and Your wrath are against all those who forsake You.

FROM EZRA 8:22

The Return to Jerusalem

31Then we departed from the river of
Ahava on the twelfth *day* of the first
month, to go to Jerusalem. And [a]the hand
of our God was upon us, and He delivered
us from the hand of the enemy and from
ambush along the road. 32So we [a]came
to Jerusalem, and stayed there three
days.
33Now on the fourth day the silver and
the gold and the articles were [a]weighed in
the house of our God by the hand of Meremoth the son of Uriah the priest, and
with him *was* Eleazar the son of Phinehas;
with them *were* the Levites, [b]Jozabad the
son of Jeshua and Noadiah the son of Binnui, 34with the number *and* weight of everything. All the weight was written down
at that time.
35The children of those who had been
[a]carried away captive, who had come from
the captivity, [b]offered burnt offerings to
the God of Israel: twelve bulls for all
Israel, ninety-six rams, seventy-seven
lambs, and twelve male goats *as* a sin offering. All *this was* a burnt offering to the
LORD.
36And they delivered the king's [a]orders
to the king's satraps and the governors *in*
the region beyond [1]the River. So they
gave support to the people and the [2]house
of God.

Intermarriage with Pagans

9 When these things were done, the
leaders came to me, saying, "The people of Israel and the priests and the Levites have not [a]separated themselves from
the peoples of the lands, [b]with respect to
the abominations of the Canaanites, the
Hittites, the Perizzites, the Jebusites, the
Ammonites, the Moabites, the Egyptians,
and the Amorites. 2For they have [a]taken
some of their daughters *as wives* for
themselves and their sons, so that the
[b]holy seed is [c]mixed with the peoples of
those lands. Indeed, the hand of the leaders and rulers has been foremost in this
[1]trespass." 3So when I heard this thing, [a]I
tore my garment and my robe, and
plucked out some of the hair of my head
and beard, and sat down [b]astonished.
4Then everyone who [a]trembled at the
words of the God of Israel assembled to
me, because of the transgression of those
who had been carried away captive, and I
sat astonished until the [b]evening sacrifice.
5At the evening sacrifice I arose from
my fasting; and having torn my garment
and my robe, I fell on my knees and
[a]spread out my hands to the LORD my
God. 6And I said: "O my God, I am too
[a]ashamed and humiliated to lift up my
face to You, my God; for [b]our iniquities
have risen higher than *our* heads, and
our guilt has [c]grown up to the heavens.
7Since the days of our fathers to this day
[a]we *have been* very guilty, and for our
iniquities [b]we, our kings, *and* our priests
have been delivered into the hand of the

25 a Ezra 7:15, 16
28 a Lev. 21:6–9 b Lev. 22:2, 3 *1 consecrated*
29 a Ezra 4:3
31 a Ezra 7:6, 9, 28
32 a Neh. 2:11
33 a Ezra 8:26, 30 b Neh. 11:16
35 a Ezra 2:1 b Ezra 6:17
36 a Ezra 7:21–24 *1* The Euphrates *2* Temple

CHAPTER 9
1 a Neh. 9:2 b Deut. 12:30, 31
2 a [Deut. 7:3] b Ex. 22:31 c [2 Cor. 6:14] *1 unfaithfulness*
3 a Job 1:20 b Ps. 143:4
4 a Ezra 10:3 b Ex. 29:39
5 a Ex. 9:29
6 a Dan. 9:7, 8 b Ps. 38:4 c Rev. 18:5
7 a Dan. 9:5, 6 b Deut. 28:36

kings of the lands, to the [c]sword, to captivity, to plunder, and to [d]humiliation,[1] as
it is this day. [8]And now for a little while
grace has been *shown* from the LORD our
God, to leave us a remnant to escape, and
to give us a peg in His holy place, that our
God may [a]enlighten our eyes and give us
a measure of revival in our bondage. [9][a]For
we *were* slaves. [b]Yet our God did not forsake us in our bondage; but [c]He extended
mercy to us in the sight of the kings of
Persia, to revive us, to repair the house of
our God, to rebuild its ruins, and to give
us [d]a wall in Judah and Jerusalem. [10]And
now, O our God, what shall we say after
this? For we have forsaken Your commandments, [11]which You commanded by
Your servants the prophets, saying, 'The
land which you are entering to possess is
an unclean land, with the [a]uncleanness of
the peoples of the lands, with their abominations which have filled it from one end
to another with their impurity. [12]Now
therefore, [a]do not give your daughters as
wives for their sons, nor take their daughters to your sons; and [b]never seek their
peace or prosperity, that you may be
strong and eat the good of the land, and
[c]leave *it* as an inheritance to your children forever.' [13]And after all that has
come upon us for our evil deeds and for
our great guilt, since You our God [a]have
punished us less than our iniquities *de-*
serve, and have given us *such* deliverance
as this, [14]should we [a]again break Your
commandments, and [b]join in marriage
with the people *committing* these abominations? Would You not be [c]angry with us
until You had [1]consumed *us,* so that *there*
would be no remnant or survivor?
[15]O LORD God of Israel, [a]You *are* righteous, for we are left as a remnant, as *it is*
this day. [b]Here we *are* before You, [c]in our
guilt, though no one can stand before You
because of this!"

Father, thank You that
You have punished ____ less
than their iniquities deserve,
and have given them such
deliverance.
FROM EZRA 9:13

Confession of Improper Marriages

10 Now [a]while Ezra was praying, and
while he was confessing, weeping,
and bowing down [b]before the house of
God, a very large assembly of men, wom-
en, and children gathered to him from Israel; for the people wept very [c]bitterly.
[2]And Shechaniah the son of Jehiel, *one* of
the sons of Elam, spoke up and said to
Ezra, "We have [a]trespassed[1] against our
God, and have taken pagan wives from the
peoples of the land; yet now there is hope
in Israel in spite of this. [3]Now therefore,
let us make [a]a covenant with our God to
put away all these wives and those who
have been born to them, according to the
advice of my master and of those who
[b]tremble at [c]the commandment of our
God; and let it be done according to the
[d]law. [4]Arise, for *this* matter *is* your *re-*
sponsibility. We also *are* with you. [a]Be of
good courage, and do *it.*"
[5]Then Ezra arose, and made the leaders
of the priests, the Levites, and all Israel
[a]swear an oath that they would do according to this word. So they swore an oath.
[6]Then Ezra rose up from before the house
of God, and went into the chamber of Jehohanan the son of Eliashib; and *when* he
came there, he [a]ate no bread and drank
no water, for he mourned because of the
guilt of those from the captivity.
[7]And they issued a proclamation
throughout Judah and Jerusalem to all
the descendants of the captivity, that they
must gather at Jerusalem, [8]and that whoever would not come within three days,
according to the instructions of the leaders and elders, all his property would be
confiscated, and he himself would be separated from the assembly of those from
the captivity.
[9]So all the men of Judah and Benjamin
gathered at Jerusalem within three days.
It *was* the ninth month, on the twentieth
of the month; and [a]all the people sat in
the open square of the house of God,
trembling because of *this* matter and because of heavy rain. [10]Then Ezra the priest
stood up and said to them, "You have
[1]transgressed and [2]have taken pagan
wives, adding to the guilt of Israel. [11]Now
therefore, [a]make confession to the LORD
God of your fathers, and do His will; [b]sep-
arate yourselves from the peoples of the
land, and from the pagan wives."

7 c Deut. 32:25 d Dan. 9:7, 8 1 Lit. *shame of faces*
8 a Ps. 34:5
9 a Neh. 9:36 b Ps. 136:23 c Ezra 7:28 d Is. 5:2
11 a Ezra 6:21
12 a [Deut. 7:3, 4] b Deut. 23:6 c [Prov. 13:22; 20:7]
13 a [Ps. 103:10]
14 a [John 5:14] b Neh. 13:23 c Deut. 9:8 1 *destroyed*
15 a Dan. 9:14 b [Rom. 3:19] c 1 Cor. 15:17

CHAPTER 10
1 a Dan. 9:4, 20 b 2 Chr. 20:9 c Neh. 8:1–9
2 a Neh. 13:23–27 1 *been unfaithful to*
3 a 2 Chr. 34:31 b Ezra 9:4 c Deut. 7:2, 3 d Deut. 24:1, 2
4 a 1 Chr. 28:10
5 a Neh. 5:12; 13:25
6 a Deut. 9:18
9 a 1 Sam. 12:18
10 1 *acted unfaithfully* 2 Heb. *have caused to dwell* or *have brought back*
11 a [Prov. 28:13] b Ezra 10:3

12 Then all the assembly answered and
said with a loud voice, "Yes! As you have
said, so we must do. 13 But *there are* many
people; *it is* the season for heavy rain, and
we are not able to stand outside. Nor *is*
this the work of one or two days, for *there*
are many of us who have transgressed in
this matter. 14 Please, let the leaders of our
entire assembly stand; and let all those in
our cities who have taken pagan wives
come at appointed times, together with
the elders and judges of their cities, until
[a]the fierce wrath of our God is turned
away from us in this matter." 15 Only Jonathan the son of Asahel and Jahaziah the
son of Tikvah opposed this, and [a]Meshul-
lam and Shabbethai the Levite gave them
support.

16 Then the descendants of the captivity
did so. And Ezra the priest, *with* certain
[a]heads of the fathers' *households,* were
set apart by the fathers' *households,* each
of them by name; and they sat down on
the first day of the tenth month to examine the matter. 17 By the first day of the
first month they finished *questioning* all
the men who had taken pagan wives.

Pagan Wives Put Away

18 And among the sons of the priests
who had taken pagan wives *the following*
were found of the sons of [a]Jeshua the son
of [1]Jozadak, and his brothers: Maaseiah,
Eliezer, Jarib, and Gedaliah. 19 And they
[a]gave their promise that they would put
away their wives; and *being* [b]guilty, *they*
presented a ram of the flock as their [c]tres-
pass offering.

20 Also of the sons of Immer: Hanani
and Zebadiah; 21 of the sons of Harim: Maaseiah, Elijah, Shemaiah, Jehiel, and Uzziah; 22 of the sons of Pashhur: Elioenai,
Maaseiah, Ishmael, Nethanel, Jozabad,
and Elasah.

23 Also of the Levites: Jozabad, Shimei,
Kelaiah (the same *is* Kelita), Pethahiah,
Judah, and Eliezer.

24 Also of the singers: Eliashib; and of
the gatekeepers: Shallum, Telem, and Uri.

25 And others of Israel: of the [a]sons of
Parosh: Ramiah, Jeziah, Malchiah, Mija-
min, Eleazar, Malchijah, and Benaiah; 26 of
the sons of Elam: Mattaniah, Zechariah,
Jehiel, Abdi, Jeremoth, and Eliah; 27 of the
sons of Zattu: Elioenai, Eliashib, Mattaniah, Jeremoth, Zabad, and Aziza; 28 of the
[a]sons of Bebai: Jehohanan, Hananiah,
Zabbai, *and* Athlai; 29 of the sons of Bani:
Meshullam, Malluch, Adaiah, Jashub,
Sheal, *and* [1]Ramoth; 30 of the [a]sons of
Pahath-Moab: Adna, Chelal, Benaiah, Maaseiah, Mattaniah, Bezalel, Binnui, and
Manasseh; 31 *of* the sons of Harim: Eliezer,
Ishijah, Malchijah, Shemaiah, Shimeon,
32 Benjamin, Malluch, *and* Shemariah;
33 of the sons of Hashum: Mattenai, Mat-
tattah, Zabad, Eliphelet, Jeremai, Manasseh, *and* Shimei; 34 of the sons of Bani:
Maadai, Amram, Uel, 35 Benaiah, Bedeiah,
[1]Cheluh, 36 Vaniah, Meremoth, Eliashib,
37 Mattaniah, Mattenai, [1]Jaasai, 38 Bani,
Binnui, Shimei, 39 Shelemiah, Nathan,
Adaiah, 40 Machnadebai, Shashai, Sharai,
41 Azarel, Shelemiah, Shemariah, 42 Shallum, Amariah, *and* Joseph; 43 of the sons of
Nebo: Jeiel, Mattithiah, Zabad, Zebina,
[1]Jaddai, Joel, *and* Benaiah.

44 All these had taken pagan wives, and
some of them had wives *by whom* they
had children.

14 [a] 2 Chr. 28:11–13; 29:10; 30:8
15 [a] Neh. 3:4
16 [a] Ezra 4:3
18 [a] Ezra 5:2 [1] *Jehozadak,* 1 Chr. 6:14
19 [a] 2 Kin. 10:15 [b] Lev. 6:4, 6 [c] Lev. 5:6, 15
25 [a] Ezra 2:3; 8:3
28 [a] Ezra 8:11
29 [1] Or *Jeremoth*
30 [a] Ezra 8:4
35 [1] Or *Cheluhi* or *Cheluhu*
37 [1] Or *Jaasu*
43 [1] Or *Jaddu*

AUTHOR: *Nehemiah*
DATE: *Approximately 423 B.C.*
THEME: *Godly Leadership, Cooperation, Opposition to Success*
KEY WORDS: *Distress, Praying, Work, the Book, Weeping, Joy, Service*

NEHEMIAH

Dear Woman of Destiny,

A man of prayer, Nehemiah wept when he heard about the broken walls of Jerusalem. When the king agreed to let him repair the walls, Nehemiah encountered fierce opposition. Undaunted, he proclaimed, "I am doing a great work. How can I come down?" As women of destiny, how can *we* quit? Strengthened with the joy of the Lord, we, too, can see great works completed in our lives.

His love and mine,

Marilyn Hickey

Nehemiah Prays for His People

The words of [a]Nehemiah the son of Hachaliah.

It came to pass in the month of Chislev, *in* the [b]twentieth year, as I was in [c]Shushan[1] the [2]citadel, 2that [a]Hanani one of my brethren came with men from Judah; and I asked them concerning the Jews who had escaped, who had survived the captivity, and concerning Jerusalem. 3And they said to me, "The survivors who are left from the captivity in the [a]province *are* there in great distress and [b]reproach. [c]The wall of Jerusalem [d]*is* also broken down, and its gates *are* burned with fire."

4So it was, when I heard these words, that I sat down and wept, and mourned *for many* days; I was fasting and praying before the God of heaven.

Lord God of heaven,
O great and awesome God,
You who keep Your covenant
and mercy with those who
love You and observe Your
commandments, may ____
know that You hear their
prayer as they confess their
sins to You.

FROM NEHEMIAH 1:5, 6

5And I said: "I pray, [a]LORD God of heaven, O great and [b]awesome God, [c]*You* who keep *Your* covenant and mercy with those who love [1]You and observe [2]Your commandments, 6please let Your ear be attentive and [a]Your eyes open, that You may hear the prayer of Your servant which I pray before You now, day and night, for the children of Israel Your servants, and [b]confess the sins of the children of Israel which we have sinned against You. Both my father's house and I have sinned. 7[a]We have acted very corruptly against You, and have [b]not kept the commandments, the statutes, nor the ordinances which You commanded Your servant Moses. 8Remember, I pray, the word that You commanded Your servant Moses, saying, [a]'*If* you [1]are unfaithful, I will scatter you among the nations; 9[a]but *if* you return to Me, and keep My commandments and do them, [b]though some of you were cast out to the farthest part of the heavens, *yet* I will gather them from there, and bring them to the place which I have chosen as a dwelling for My name.' 10[a]Now these *are* Your servants and Your people, whom You have redeemed by Your great power, and by Your strong hand. 11O Lord, I pray, please [a]let Your ear be attentive to the prayer of Your servant, and to the prayer of Your servants who [b]desire to fear Your name; and let Your servant prosper this day, I pray, and grant him mercy in the sight of this man."

For I was the king's [c]cupbearer.

Ardent desire is the basis of unceasing prayer. It is not a shallow, fickle tendency, but a strong yearning that permeates, glows, burns, and fixes the heart.

E. M. BOUNDS

Nehemiah Sent to Judah

2 And it came to pass in the month of Nisan, in the twentieth year of [a]King [1]Artaxerxes, *when* wine *was* before him, that [b]I took the wine and gave it to the king. Now I had never been sad in his presence before. 2Therefore the king said to me, "Why *is* your face sad, since you *are* not sick? This *is* nothing but [a]sorrow of heart."

So I became [1]dreadfully afraid, 3and said to the king, [a]"May the king live forever! Why should my face not be sad, when [b]the city, the place of my fathers' tombs, *lies* waste, and its gates are burned with [c]fire?"

4Then the king said to me, "What do you request?"

So I [a]prayed to the God of heaven. 5And I said to the king, "If it pleases the king, and if your servant has found favor in your sight, I ask that you send me to Judah, to the city of my fathers' tombs, that I may rebuild it."

CHAPTER 1
1 a Neh. 10:1 b Neh. 2:1 c Esth. 1:1, 2, 5 *1* Or *Susa* *2* Or *fortified palace,* and so elsewhere in the book
2 a Neh. 7:2
3 a Neh. 7:6 b Neh. 2:17 c Neh. 2:17 d 2 Kin. 25:10
5 a Dan. 9:4 b Neh. 4:14 c [Ex. 20:6; 34:6, 7] *1* Lit. *Him* *2* Lit. *His*
6 a 2 Chr. 6:40 b Dan. 9:20
7 a Dan. 9:5 b Deut. 28:15
8 a Lev. 26:33 *1 act treacherously*
9 a [Deut. 4:29–31; 30:2–5] b Deut. 30:4
10 a Deut. 9:29
11 a Neh. 1:6 b Is. 26:8 c Neh. 2:1

CHAPTER 2
1 a Ezra 7:1 b Neh. 1:11 *1* Artaxerxes Longimanus
2 a Prov. 15:13 *1* Lit. *very much*
3 a Dan. 2:4; 5:10; 6:6, 21 b 2 Chr. 36:19 c Neh. 1:3
4 a Neh. 1:4

6 Then the king said to me (the queen
also sitting beside him), "How long will
your journey be? And when will you return?" So it pleased the king to send me;
and I set him [a]a time.
7 Furthermore I said to the king, "If it
pleases the king, let letters be given to me
for the [a]governors *of the region* beyond
[1]the River, that they must permit me to
pass through till I come to Judah, 8 and a
letter to Asaph the keeper of the king's
forest, that he must give me timber to
make beams for the gates of the [1]citadel
which *pertains* [a]to the [2]temple, for the
city wall, and for the house that I will oc-
cupy." And the king granted *them* to me
[b]according to the good hand of my God
upon me.
9 Then I went to the governors *in the
region* beyond the River, and gave them
the king's letters. Now the king had sent
captains of the army and horsemen with
me. 10 When [a]Sanballat the Horonite and
Tobiah the Ammonite [1]official heard *of it,*
they were deeply disturbed that a man had
come to seek the well-being of the children of Israel.

Nehemiah Views the Wall of Jerusalem

11 So I [a]came to Jerusalem and was
there three days. 12 Then I arose in the
night, I and a few men with me; I told no
one what my God had put in my heart to
do at Jerusalem; nor was there any animal
with me, except the one on which I rode.
13 And I went out by night [a]through the
Valley Gate to the Serpent Well and the
[1]Refuse Gate, and [2]viewed the walls of Jerusalem which were [b]broken down and its
gates which were burned with fire. 14 Then
I went on to the [a]Fountain Gate and to
the [b]King's Pool, but *there was* no room
for the animal under me to pass. 15 So I
went up in the night by the [a]valley,[1] and
[2]viewed the wall; then I turned back and
entered by the Valley Gate, and so returned. 16 And the officials did not know
where I had gone or what I had done; I
had not yet told the Jews, the priests, the
nobles, the officials, or the others who did
the work.
17 Then I said to them, "You see the distress that we *are* in, how Jerusalem *lies*
[1]waste, and its gates are burned with fire.
Come and let us build the wall of Jerusalem, that we may no longer be [a]a reproach." 18 And I told them of [a]the hand of
my God which had been good upon me,
and also of the king's words that he had
spoken to me.
So they said, "Let us rise up and build."
Then they [b]set[1] their hands to *this* good
work.

The very same works that, before faith, are worthy to be rejected, are, after faith, an acceptable service to God.

ANDREW MURRAY

19 But when Sanballat the Horonite, Tobiah the Ammonite official, and Geshem
the Arab heard *of it,* they laughed at us
and despised us, and said, "What *is* this
thing that you are doing? [a]Will you rebel
against the king?"
20 So I answered them, and said to
them, "The God of heaven Himself will
prosper us; therefore we His servants will
arise and build, [a]but you have no heritage
or right or memorial in Jerusalem."

Rebuilding the Wall

3 Then [a]Eliashib the high priest rose up
with his brethren the priests [b]and
built the Sheep Gate; they consecrated it
and hung its doors. They built [c]as far as
the Tower of [1]the Hundred, *and* consecrated it, then as far as the Tower of [d]Han-
anel. 2 [1]Next to *Eliashib* [a]the men of
Jericho built. And next to them Zaccur
the son of Imri built.
3 Also the sons of Hassenaah built [a]the
Fish Gate; they laid its beams and [b]hung
its doors with its bolts and bars. 4 And next
to them [a]Meremoth the son of Urijah, the
son of [1]Koz, made repairs. Next to them
[b]Meshullam the son of Berechiah, the son
of Meshezabel, made repairs. Next to
them Zadok the son of Baana made repairs. 5 Next to them the Tekoites made
repairs; but their nobles did not put their
[1]shoulders to [a]the work of their Lord.
6 Moreover Jehoiada the son of Paseah
and Meshullam the son of Besodeiah repaired [a]the Old Gate; they laid its beams
and hung its doors, with its bolts and bars.
7 And next to them Melatiah the Gibeonite,

---

6 a Neh. 5:14; 13:6
7 a Ezra 7:21; 8:36 · 1 The Euphrates
8 a Neh. 3:7 · b Ezra 5:5; 7:6, 9, 28 · 1 *palace* · 2 Lit. *house*
10 a Neh. 2:19; 4:1 · 1 Lit. *servant*
11 a Ezra 8:32
13 a Neh. 3:13 · b Neh. 1:3; 2:17 · 1 *Dung* · 2 *examined*
14 a Neh. 3:15 · b 2 Kin. 20:20
15 a 2 Sam. 15:23 · 1 *torrent valley, wadi* · 2 *examined*
17 a Neh. 1:3 · 1 *desolate*
18 a Neh. 2:8 · b 2 Sam. 2:7 · 1 Lit. *strengthened*
19 a Neh. 6:6
20 a Ezra 4:3

CHAPTER 3
1 a Neh. 3:20; 12:10; 13:4, 7, 28 · b John 5:2 · c Neh. 12:39 · d Jer. 31:38 · 1 Heb. *Hammeah*
2 a Neh. 7:36 · 1 Lit. *On his hand*
3 a Zeph. 1:10 · b Neh. 6:1; 7:1
4 a Ezra 8:33 · b Ezra 10:15 · 1 Or *Hakkoz*
5 a [Judg. 5:23] · 1 Lit. *necks*
6 a Neh. 12:39

Jadon the Meronothite, the [a]men of Gibeon and Mizpah, repaired the [b]residence[1] of the governor *of the region* [2]beyond the River. 8Next to him Uzziel the son of Harhaiah, one of the goldsmiths, made repairs. Also next to him Hananiah, [1]one of the perfumers, made repairs; and they [2]fortified Jerusalem as far as the [a]Broad Wall. 9And next to them Rephaiah the son of Hur, leader of half the district of Jerusalem, made repairs. 10Next to them Jedaiah the son of Harumaph made repairs in front of his house. And next to him Hattush the son of Hashabniah made repairs.

11Malchijah the son of Harim and Hashub the son of Pahath-Moab repaired another section, [a]as well as the Tower of the Ovens. 12And next to him was Shallum the son of Hallohesh, leader of half the district of Jerusalem; he and his daughters made repairs.

13Hanun and the inhabitants of Zanoah repaired [a]the Valley Gate. They built it, hung its doors with its bolts and bars, and *repaired* a thousand cubits of the wall as far as [b]the Refuse Gate.

14Malchijah the son of Rechab, leader of the district of [a]Beth Haccerem, repaired the Refuse Gate; he built it and hung its doors with its bolts and bars.

15Shallun the son of Col-Hozeh, leader of the district of Mizpah, repaired [a]the Fountain Gate; he built it, covered it, hung its doors with its bolts and bars, and repaired the wall of the Pool of [b]Shelah[1] by the [c]King's Garden, as far as the stairs that go down from the City of David. 16After him Nehemiah the son of Azbuk, leader of half the district of Beth Zur, made repairs as far as *the place* in front of the [1]tombs of David, to the [a]man-made pool, and as far as the House of the Mighty.

17After him the Levites, *under* Rehum the son of Bani, made repairs. Next to him Hashabiah, leader of half the district of Keilah, made repairs for his district. 18After him their brethren, *under* [1]Bavai the son of Henadad, leader of the *other* half of the district of Keilah, made repairs. 19And next to him Ezer the son of Jeshua, the leader of Mizpah, repaired another section in front of the Ascent to the Armory at the [a]buttress.[1] 20After him Baruch the son of [1]Zabbai carefully repaired the other section, from the [2]buttress to the door of the house of Eliashib the high priest. 21After him Meremoth the son of Urijah, the son of [1]Koz, repaired another section, from the door of the house of Eliashib to the end of the house of Eliashib.

22And after him the priests, the men of the plain, made repairs. 23After him Benjamin and Hasshub made repairs opposite their house. After them Azariah the son of Maaseiah, the son of Ananiah, made repairs by his house. 24After him [a]Binnui the son of Henadad repaired another section, from the house of Azariah to [b]the [1]buttress, even as far as the corner. 25Palal the son of Uzai *made repairs* opposite the [1]buttress, and on the tower which projects from the king's upper house that *was* by the [a]court of the prison. After him Pedaiah the son of Parosh *made repairs.*

26Moreover [a]the Nethinim who dwelt in [b]Ophel *made repairs* as far as *the place* in front of [c]the Water Gate toward the east, and on the projecting tower. 27After them the Tekoites repaired another section, next to the great projecting tower, and as far as the wall of Ophel.

28Beyond the [a]Horse Gate the priests made repairs, each in front of his *own* house. 29After them Zadok the son of Immer made repairs in front of his *own* house. After him Shemaiah the son of Shechaniah, the keeper of the East Gate, made repairs. 30After him Hananiah the son of Shelemiah, and Hanun, the sixth son of Zalaph, repaired another section. After him Meshullam the son of Berechiah made repairs in front of his [1]dwelling. 31After him Malchijah, [1]one of the goldsmiths, made repairs as far as the house of the Nethinim and of the merchants, in front of the [2]Miphkad Gate, and as far as the upper room at the corner. 32And between the upper room at the corner, as far as the [a]Sheep Gate, the goldsmiths and the merchants made repairs.

The Wall Defended Against Enemies

4 But it so happened, [a]when Sanballat heard that we were rebuilding the wall, that he was furious and very indignant, and mocked the Jews. 2And he spoke before his brethren and the army of Samaria, and said, "What are these feeble Jews doing? Will they fortify themselves? Will they offer sacrifices? Will they complete it in a day? Will they revive the stones from the heaps of rubbish—*stones* that are burned?"

3Now [a]Tobiah the Ammonite *was* beside him, and he said, "Whatever they

---

7 [a]Neh. 7:25 [b]Neh. 2:7–9 [1]Lit. *throne* [2]West of the Euphrates

8 [a]Neh. 12:38 [1]Lit. *the son* [2]*restored*

11 [a]Neh. 12:38

13 [a]Neh. 2:13, 15 [b]Neh. 2:13

14 [a]Jer. 6:1

15 [a]Neh. 2:14 [b]Is. 8:6 [c]2 Kin. 25:4 [1]Or *Shiloah*

16 [a]2 Kin. 20:20 [1]LXX, Syr., Vg. *tomb*

18 [1]So with MT, Vg.; some Heb. mss., LXX, Syr. *Binnui* (cf. v. 24)

19 [a]2 Chr. 26:9 [1]Lit. *turning*

20 [1]A few Heb. mss., Syr., Vg. *Zaccai* [2]Lit. *turning*

21 [1]Or *Hakkoz*

24 [a]Ezra 8:33 [b]Neh. 3:19 [1]Lit. *turning*

25 [a]Jer. 32:2; 33:1; 37:21 [1]Lit. *turning*

26 [a]Neh. 11:21 [b]2 Chr. 27:3 [c]Neh. 8:1, 3; 12:37

28 [a]2 Chr. 23:15

30 [1]Lit. *room*

31 [1]Lit. *a son of the goldsmiths* [2]Lit. *Inspection* or *Recruiting*

32 [a]Neh. 3:1; 12:39

CHAPTER 4

1 [a]Neh. 2:10, 19

3 [a]Neh. 2:10, 19

Nehemiah 4:1–3

Dear Woman of Destiny,

The Lord is calling women today to attempt great things and take an active role in His kingdom building program. However, have you ever stepped out to do something great for the Lord, only to find yourself facing insurmountable challenges, fears, and discouragement?

Under Nehemiah, a small band of Israelites attempted the overwhelming task of rebuilding the burned walls of Jerusalem, with the daughters of Shallum helping (see Neh. 3:12). The builders faced many obstacles within their own ranks, including ridicule and weariness, as well as the opposition of outsiders Sanballat and Tobiah. Their weapon? Mocking words.

Ridicule definitely has a voice. It can speak through others, or it can bombard you as your own thoughts. It says, "You're weak, little, and unimportant." It asks, "Who do you think you are, trying to build something for God? Do you think *you* can help revive anything?"

I fought that voice for twelve years. My husband and I started our church in a tiny, Midwestern town in 1984. We knew the Lord had told us a mighty outpouring of His Spirit was coming to America. As we preached this message in that tiny, unimportant spot, we often heard the voices of ridicule taunting us.

Ridicule comes to rob you of fulfilling your destiny in God. When facing ridicule, I was sometimes tempted to give in to those voices and lay down my tools. Other times I wanted to become angry and defensive. Either way, I would have eliminated myself from God's building program.

I've learned to respond to ridicule the same way these Israelites did. Nehemiah 4:14 reveals that they made three godly choices that changes their destiny forever. They chose: not to fear; to remember the Lord, great and awesome; and to fight for what was right. So they stayed in God's building program, and the walls were completed.

Fear paralyzes faith and stifles the ability to rebuild. You must choose to meditate on the great power and salvation of the Lord, rather than on the discouraging voices of ridicule. When ridicule comes, I have learned to practice the Romans 12:21 principle: *Do not be overcome by evil, but overcome evil with good.* Since 1984, my husband and I have practiced this principle when faced with ridicule. Instead of giving up or letting down, we fight! We push harder for the good; preach with great conviction; praise louder and stronger; and do what is right with even more vigor.

God has graciously allowed us to help rebuild the walls. In our insignificant little town, we have experienced a wonderful outpouring of His Holy Spirit since March 24, 1996. It has literally touched the world, and many lives are being rebuilt. I'm so glad I didn't lay down my tools when the ridicule came.

Woman of God, you have a destiny as a rebuilder of the walls. Reject the voice of ridicule. Don't be afraid; remember the Lord, great and awesome; and fight!

Kathy Gray

build, if even a fox goes up *on it,* he will break down their stone wall." ℒ

4 [a]Hear, O our God, for we are despised; [b]turn their reproach on their own heads, and give them as plunder to a land of captivity! 5 [a]Do not cover their iniquity, and do not let their sin be blotted out from before You; for they have provoked *You* to anger before the builders.

6 So we built the wall, and the entire wall was joined together up to half its *height,* for the people had a mind to work.

7 Now it happened, [a]when Sanballat, Tobiah, [b]the Arabs, the Ammonites, and the Ashdodites heard that the walls of Jerusalem were being restored and the [1]gaps were beginning to be closed, that they became very angry, 8 and all of them [a]conspired together to come *and* attack Jerusalem and create confusion. 9 Nevertheless [a]we made our prayer to our God, and because of them we set a watch against them day and night.

10 Then Judah said, "The strength of the laborers is failing, and *there is* so much rubbish that we are not able to build the wall."

11 And our adversaries said, "They will neither know nor see anything, till we come into their midst and kill them and cause the work to cease."

12 So it was, when the Jews who dwelt near them came, that they told us ten times, "From whatever place you turn, *they will be* upon us."

13 Therefore I positioned *men* behind the lower parts of the wall, at the openings; and I set the people according to their families, with their swords, their spears, and their bows. 14 And I looked, and arose and said to the nobles, to the leaders, and to the rest of the people, [a]"Do not be afraid of them. Remember the Lord, [b]great and awesome, and [c]fight for your brethren, your sons, your daughters, your wives, and your houses."

15 And it happened, when our enemies heard that it was known to us, and [a]*that* God had brought their plot to nothing, that all of us returned to the wall, everyone to his work. 16 So it was, from that time on, *that* half of my servants worked at construction, while the other half held the spears, the shields, the bows, and *wore* armor; and the leaders [1]*were* behind all the house of Judah. 17 Those who built on the wall, and those who carried burdens, loaded themselves so that with one hand they worked at construction, and with the other held a weapon. 18 Every one of the builders had his sword girded at his side as he built. And the one who sounded the trumpet *was* beside me.

19 Then I said to the nobles, the rulers, and the rest of the people, "The work *is* great and extensive, and we are separated far from one another on the wall. 20 Wherever you hear the sound of the trumpet, rally to us there. [a]Our God will fight for us."

21 So we labored in the work, and half of [1]*the men* held the spears from daybreak until the stars appeared. 22 At the same time I also said to the people, "Let each man and his servant stay at night in Jerusalem, that they may be our guard by night and a working party by day." 23 So neither I, my brethren, my servants, nor the men of the guard who followed me took off our clothes, *except* that everyone took them off for washing.

Nehemiah Deals with Oppression

5 And there was a great [a]outcry of the people and their wives against their [b]Jewish brethren. 2 For there were those who said, "We, our sons, and our daughters *are* many; therefore let us get grain, that we may eat and live."

3 There were also *some* who said, "We have mortgaged our lands and vineyards and houses, that we might buy grain because of the famine."

4 There were also those who said, "We have borrowed money for the king's tax *on* our lands and vineyards. 5 Yet now [a]our flesh *is* as the flesh of our brethren, our children as their children; and indeed we [b]are forcing our sons and our daughters to be slaves, and *some* of our daughters have been brought into slavery. *It is* not in our power *to redeem them,* for other men have our lands and vineyards."

6 And I became very angry when I heard their outcry and these words. 7 After serious thought, I rebuked the nobles and rulers, and said to them, [a]"Each of you is [1]exacting usury from his brother." So I [2]called a great assembly against them. 8 And I said to them, "According to our ability we have [a]redeemed our Jewish brethren who were sold to the nations. Now indeed, will you even sell your brethren? Or should they be sold to us?"

4 a Ps. 123:3, 4 b Ps. 79:12
5 a Jer. 18:23
7 a Neh. 4:1 b Neh. 2:19 *1* Lit. *breaks*
8 a Ps. 83:3–5
9 a [Ps. 50:15]
14 a Deut. 1:29 b [Deut. 10:17] c 2 Sam. 10:12
15 a Job 5:12
16 *1* Supported
20 a Ex. 14:14, 25
21 *1* Lit. *them*

CHAPTER 5
1 a Neh. 5:7, 8 b Deut. 15:7
5 a Is. 58:7 b Ex. 21:7
7 a [Ex. 22:25] *1* *charging interest* *2* Lit. *held*
8 a Lev. 25:48

Then they were silenced and found
nothing *to say.* 9 Then I said, "What you
are doing *is* not good. Should you not
walk [a]in the fear of our God [b]because of
the reproach of the nations, our enemies?
10 I also, *with* my brethren and my servants, am lending them money and grain.
Please, let us stop this [1]usury! 11 Restore
now to them, even this day, their lands,
their vineyards, their olive groves, and
their houses, also a hundredth of the
money and the grain, the new wine and
the oil, that you have charged them."
12 So they said, "We will restore *it,* and
will require nothing from them; we will
do as you say."
Then I called the priests, [a]and required
an oath from them that they would do
according to this promise. 13 Then [a]I
shook out [1]the fold of my garment and
said, "So may God shake out each man
from his house, and from his property,
who does not perform this promise. Even
thus may he be shaken out and emptied."
And all the assembly said, "Amen!" and
praised the LORD. [b]Then the people did
according to this promise.

The Generosity of Nehemiah

14 Moreover, from the time that I was
appointed to be their governor in the land
of Judah, from the twentieth year [a]until
the thirty-second year of King Artaxerxes,
twelve years, neither I nor my brothers
[b]ate the governor's provisions. 15 But the
former governors who *were* before me
laid burdens on the people, and took from
them bread and wine, besides forty shekels of silver. Yes, even their servants bore
rule over the people, but [a]I did not do so,
because of the [b]fear of God. 16 Indeed, I
also continued the [a]work on this wall, and
[1]we did not buy any land. All my servants
were gathered there for the work.
17 And [a]at my table *were* one hundred
and fifty Jews and rulers, besides those
who came to us from the nations around
us. 18 Now *that* [a]which was prepared daily
was one ox *and* six choice sheep. Also fowl
were prepared for me, and once every ten
days an abundance of all kinds of wine.
Yet in spite of this [b]I did not demand the
governor's provisions, because the bondage was heavy on this people.
19 [a]Remember me, my God, for good,
according to all that I have done for this
people.

Conspiracy Against Nehemiah

6 Now it happened [a]when Sanballat,
Tobiah, [1]Geshem the Arab, and the
rest of our enemies heard that I had rebuilt the wall, and *that* there were no
breaks left in it [b](though at that time I
had not hung the doors in the gates),
2 that Sanballat and [1]Geshem [a]sent to me,
saying, "Come, let us meet together
[2]among the villages in the plain of [b]Ono."
But they [c]thought to do me harm.
3 So I sent messengers to them, saying,
"I *am* doing a great work, so that I cannot
come down. Why should the work cease
while I leave it and go down to you?"
4 But they sent me this message four
times, and I answered them in the same
manner.
5 Then Sanballat sent his servant to me
as before, the fifth time, with an open letter in his hand. 6 In it *was* written:

> It is reported among the nations,
> and [1]Geshem says, *that* you and the
> Jews plan to rebel; therefore, ac-
> cording to these rumors, you are
> rebuilding the wall, [a]that you may
> be their king. 7 And you have also
> appointed prophets to proclaim
> concerning you at Jerusalem, say-
> ing, "*There is* a king in Judah!"
> Now these matters will be reported
> to the king. So come, therefore,
> and let us consult together.

8 Then I sent to him, saying, "No such
things as you say are being done, but you
invent them in your own heart."
9 For they all *were trying to* make us
afraid, saying, "Their hands will be weakened in the work, and it will not be done."
Now therefore, *O God,* strengthen my
hands.
10 Afterward I came to the house of Shemaiah the son of Delaiah, the son of Mehetabel, who *was* a secret informer; and
he said, "Let us meet together in the
house of God, within the [1]temple, and let
us close the doors of the temple, for they
are coming to kill you; indeed, at night
they will come to kill you."
11 And I said, "Should such a man as
I flee? And who *is there* such as I who
would go into the temple to save his life?
I will not go in!" 12 Then I perceived that
God had not sent him at all, but that [a]he
pronounced *this* prophecy against me because Tobiah and Sanballat had hired
him. 13 For this reason he *was* hired, that

---

9 [a]Lev. 25:36 [b]2 Sam. 12:14
10 [1] *interest*
12 [a]Ezra 10:5
13 [a]Acts 13:51; 18:6 [b]2 Kin. 23:3 [1] Lit. *my lap*
14 [a]Neh. 2:1; 13:6 [b][1 Cor. 9:4–15]
15 [a]2 Cor. 11:9; 12:13 [b]Neh. 5:9
16 [a]Neh. 4:1; 6:1 [1] So with MT; LXX, Syr., Vg. *I*
17 [a]1 Kin. 18:19
18 [a]1 Kin. 4:22 [b]Neh. 5:14, 15
19 [a]Neh. 13:14, 22, 31

CHAPTER 6
1 [a]Neh. 2:10, 19; 4:1, 7; 13:28 [b]Neh. 3:1, 3 [1] Or *Gashmu*
2 [a]Prov. 26:24, 25 [b]1 Chr. 8:12 [c]Ps. 37:12, 32 [1] Or *Gashmu* [2] Or *in Kephirim,* exact location unknown
6 [a]Neh. 2:19 [1] Heb. *Gashmu*
10 [1] Lit. *house*
12 [a]Ezek. 13:22

NEHEMIAH 6:11

Dear Woman of Destiny,

I believe your response to this verse is the same as mine. That's the kind of leader I want to follow. That's the kind of person, leader, wife, mother, friend I want to be!

Nehemiah is so convinced of his direction and destiny that no threat of the enemy can deter his efforts, even the word of a pretended prophet. His present position is that of helping God's people rebuild broken walls. The mending of breaches is a true threat to the enemy, who wants God's people to hold onto their schisms, unforgiveness, prejudice, and anything else that will give him entrance into the "city."

The attempts used to stop the healing process include relentless warnings of disaster, impugning the motives of Nehemiah's leadership and even hiring false prophets. These "prophets" insist that they have Nehemiah's best interests at heart as they encourage him to quit his job and spend the remainder of his life in a religious setting.

Rather than becoming discouraged, Nehemiah is incensed at the thought of retreating to the temple to hide out before he has accomplished what he considers a high calling, a great work.

Once I experienced the temptation to quit what I was doing for God because of similar threats and so-called prophetic utterances. I was told that God never intended women to pastor and that, even though I appeared to be successful, it was only due to God's mercy for the people. I was instructed that if I would leave the ministry to men, I would find a happiness and completeness I'd never known. I was further instructed that if I continued ministering, I would know great disaster. Thankfully I learned early in my ministry that the enemy would use any tactic possible to divert me from fulfilling my destiny in God—even offering a religious motive.

Often these words are given to us when we are weary. Nehemiah had to be weary of prodding the people, encouraging others (though no one encouraged him), and working on a task that seemed greater than his ability. Yet his consistent responses reveal he had no intention of quitting.

Only when we understand that our place in Christ is high and holy can we stand strong in the face of opposition without becoming independent or unteachable.

Whether you are experiencing success or failure, strength or weakness, joy or sorrow, be encouraged today. We know that God who called us is faithful and will complete the work in us and through us (see Phil. 1:6). Remember that we are no surprise to God. He knew our frailties and strengths even before He revealed to us our destiny.

Let us say with the psalmist, "My heart is steadfast, O God, my heart is steadfast; I will sing and give praise" (Ps. 57:7). Lord, I have no intention of quitting the job You have given me. I intend to complete the task, and I thank You for allowing me to be part of Your great work. Amen.

Iverna Tompkins

I should be afraid and act that way and sin,
so *that* they might have *cause* for an evil
report, that they might reproach me.
14 [a]My God, remember Tobiah and Sanballat, according to these their works, and
the [b]prophetess Noadiah and the rest of
the prophets who would have made me
afraid.

The Wall Completed

15 So the wall was finished on the
twenty-fifth *day* of Elul, in fifty-two days.
16 And it happened, [a]when all our enemies
heard *of it,* and all the nations around us
saw *these things,* that they were very dis-
heartened in their own eyes; for [b]they perceived that this work was done by our
God.

> *Your spirit life is fortified and built up and enriched by communion with the Father and by reading His Word.*
>
> JOHN G. LAKE

17 Also in those days the nobles of Judah
sent many letters to Tobiah, and *the letters of* Tobiah came to them. 18 For many
in Judah were pledged to him, because he
was the [a]son-in-law of Shechaniah the
son of Arah, and his son Jehohanan had
married the daughter of [b]Meshullam the
son of Berechiah. 19 Also they reported his
good deeds before me, and reported my
[1]words to him. Tobiah sent letters to
frighten me.

7 Then it was, when the wall was built
and I had [a]hung the doors, when the
gatekeepers, the singers, and the Levites
had been appointed, 2 that I gave the
charge of Jerusalem to my brother [a]Hana-
ni, and Hananiah the leader [b]of the [1]cita-
del, for he *was* a faithful man and [c]feared
God more than many.
3 And I said to them, "Do not let the
gates of Jerusalem be opened until the
sun is hot; and while they stand *guard,* let
them shut and bar the doors; and appoint
guards from among the inhabitants of Jerusalem, one at his watch station and another in front of his own house."

The Captives Who Returned to Jerusalem

4 Now the city *was* large and spacious,
but the people in it *were* [a]few, and the
houses *were* not rebuilt. 5 Then my God
put it into my heart to gather the nobles,
the rulers, and the people, that they might
be registered by genealogy. And I found a
register of the genealogy of those who had
come up in the first *return,* and found
written in it:

6 [a]These *are* the people of the province who came back from the captivity, of those who had been carried away, whom Nebuchadnezzar the king of Babylon had carried away, and who returned to Jerusalem and Judah, everyone to his city.

7 Those who came with [a]Zerubbabel *were* Jeshua, Nehemiah, [1]Azariah, Raamiah, Nahamani, Mordecai, Bilshan, [2]Mispereth, Bigvai, Nehum, and Baanah.

The number of the men of the people of Israel: 8 the sons of Parosh,
two thousand one hundred and
seventy-two;
9 the sons of Shephatiah, three hundred and seventy-two;
10 the sons of Arah, six hundred and fifty-two;
11 the sons of Pahath-Moab, of the sons of Jeshua and Joab, two thousand eight hundred and eighteen;
12 the sons of Elam, one thousand two hundred and fifty-four;
13 the sons of Zattu, eight hundred and forty-five;
14 the sons of Zaccai, seven hundred and sixty;
15 the sons of [1]Binnui, six hundred and forty-eight;
16 the sons of Bebai, six hundred and twenty-eight;
17 the sons of Azgad, two thousand three hundred and twenty-two;
18 the sons of Adonikam, six hundred and sixty-seven;
19 the sons of Bigvai, two thousand and sixty-seven;
20 the sons of Adin, six hundred and fifty-five;
21 the sons of Ater of Hezekiah, ninety-eight;
22 the sons of Hashum, three hundred and twenty-eight;

---

14 [a]Neh. 13:29 [b]Ezek. 13:17
16 [a]Neh. 2:10, 20; 4:1, 7; 6:1 [b]Ps. 126:2
18 [a]Neh. 13:4, 28 [b]Ezra 10:15
19 [1]Or *affairs*

CHAPTER 7
1 [a]Neh. 6:1, 15
2 [a]Neh. 1:2 [b]Neh. 2:8; 10:23 [c]Ex. 18:21 [1]*palace*
4 [a]Deut. 4:27
6 [a]Ezra 2:1–70
7 [a]Ezra 5:2 [1]*Seraiah,* Ezra 2:2 [2]*Mispar,* Ezra 2:2
15 [1]*Bani,* Ezra 2:10

23 the sons of Bezai, three hundred
and twenty-four;
24 the sons of [1]Hariph, one hundred
and twelve;
25 the sons of [1]Gibeon, ninety-five;
26 the men of Bethlehem and Netophah, one hundred and eighty-
eight;
27 the men of Anathoth, one hundred and twenty-eight;
28 the men of [1]Beth Azmaveth,
forty-two;
29 the men of [1]Kirjath Jearim, Chephirah, and Beeroth, seven hundred
and forty-three;
30 the men of Ramah and Geba, six
hundred and twenty-one;
31 the men of Michmas, one hundred and twenty-two;
32 the men of Bethel and Ai, one
hundred and twenty-three;
33 the men of the other Nebo, fifty-
two;
34 the sons of the other [a]Elam, one
thousand two hundred and fifty-
four;
35 the sons of Harim, three hundred
and twenty;
36 the sons of Jericho, three hundred
and forty-five;
37 the sons of Lod, Hadid, and Ono,
seven hundred and twenty-one;
38 the sons of Senaah, three thousand nine hundred and thirty.

39 The priests: the sons of [a]Jedaiah,
of the house of Jeshua, nine hundred and seventy-three;
40 the sons of [a]Immer, one thousand
and fifty-two;
41 the sons of [a]Pashhur, one thousand two hundred and forty-seven;
42 the sons of [a]Harim, one thousand
and seventeen.

43 The Levites: the sons of Jeshua, of
Kadmiel, *and* of the sons of
[1]Hodevah, seventy-four.

44 The singers: the sons of Asaph,
one hundred and forty-eight.

45 The gatekeepers: the sons of
Shallum,
the sons of Ater,
the sons of Talmon,
the sons of Akkub,
the sons of Hatita,
the sons of Shobai, one hundred
and thirty-eight.

46 The Nethinim: the sons of Ziha,
the sons of Hasupha,
the sons of Tabbaoth,
47 the sons of Keros,
the sons of [1]Sia,
the sons of Padon,
48 the sons of [1]Lebana,
the sons of [2]Hagaba,
the sons of [3]Salmai,
49 the sons of Hanan,
the sons of Giddel,
the sons of Gahar,
50 the sons of Reaiah,
the sons of Rezin,
the sons of Nekoda,
51 the sons of Gazzam,
the sons of Uzza,
the sons of Paseah,
52 the sons of Besai,
the sons of Meunim,
the sons of [1]Nephishesim,
53 the sons of Bakbuk,
the sons of Hakupha,
the sons of Harhur,
54 the sons of [1]Bazlith,
the sons of Mehida,
the sons of Harsha,
55 the sons of Barkos,
the sons of Sisera,
the sons of Tamah,
56 the sons of Neziah,
and the sons of Hatipha.

57 The sons of Solomon's servants:
the sons of Sotai,
the sons of Sophereth,
the sons of [1]Perida,
58 the sons of Jaala,
the sons of Darkon,
the sons of Giddel,
59 the sons of Shephatiah,
the sons of Hattil,
the sons of Pochereth of Zebaim,
and the sons of [1]Amon.
60 All the Nethinim, and the sons of
Solomon's servants, *were* three
hundred and ninety-two.

61 And these *were* the ones who
came up from Tel Melah, Tel Harsha, Cherub, [1]Addon, and Immer,
but they could not identify their father's house nor their lineage,
whether they *were* of Israel: 62 the
sons of Delaiah,
the sons of Tobiah,

24 [1] *Jorah,* Ezra 2:18
25 [1] *Gibbar,* Ezra 2:20
28 [1] *Azmaveth,* Ezra 2:24
29 [1] *Kirjath Arim,* Ezra 2:25
34 [a] Neh. 7:12
39 [a] 1 Chr. 24:7
40 [a] 1 Chr. 9:12
41 [a] Ezra 2:38; 10:22
42 [a] 1 Chr. 24:8
43 [1] *Hodaviah,* Ezra 2:40; or *Judah,* Ezra 3:9
47 [1] *Siaha,* Ezra 2:44
48 [1] MT *Lebanah* [2] MT *Hogabah* [3] *Shalmai,* Ezra 2:46; or *Shamlai*
52 [1] *Nephusim,* Ezra 2:50
54 [1] *Bazluth,* Ezra 2:52
57 [1] *Peruda,* Ezra 2:55
59 [1] *Ami,* Ezra 2:57
61 [1] *Addan,* Ezra 2:59

the sons of Nekoda, six hundred
and forty-two;
63and of the priests: the sons of Ha-
baiah,
the sons of [1]Koz,
the sons of Barzillai, who took a
wife of the daughters of Barzillai
the Gileadite, and was called by
their name.
64These sought their listing *among*
those who were registered by genealogy, but it was not found;
therefore they were excluded from
the priesthood as defiled. 65And the
[1]governor said to them that they
should not eat of the most holy
things till a priest could consult
with the Urim and Thummim.

66 Altogether the whole assembly
was forty-two thousand three hundred and sixty, 67besides their male
and female servants, of whom *there*
were seven thousand three hundred
and thirty-seven; and they had two
hundred and forty-five men and
women singers. 68Their horses were
seven hundred and thirty-six, their
mules two hundred and forty-five,
69*their* camels four hundred and
thirty-five, *and* donkeys six thousand seven hundred and twenty.

70 And some of the heads of the fathers' houses gave to the work.
[a]The [1]governor gave to the treasury
one thousand gold drachmas, fifty
basins, and five hundred and thirty
priestly garments. 71Some of the
heads of the fathers' *houses* gave to
the treasury of the work [a]twenty
thousand gold drachmas, and two
thousand two hundred silver minas.
72And that which the rest of the
people gave *was* twenty thousand
gold drachmas, two thousand silver
minas, and sixty-seven priestly garments.

73So the priests, the Levites, the gatekeepers, the singers, *some* of the people,
the Nethinim, and all Israel dwelt in their
cities.

Ezra Reads the Law

[a]When the seventh month came, the
children of Israel *were* in their cities.

8 Now all [a]the people gathered together
as one man in the open square that
was [b]in front of the Water Gate; and they
told Ezra the [c]scribe to bring the Book of
the Law of Moses, which the LORD had
commanded Israel. 2So Ezra the priest
brought [a]the Law before the assembly of
men and women and all who *could* hear
with understanding [b]on the first day of
the seventh month. 3Then he [a]read from
it in the open square that *was* in front of
the Water Gate [1]from morning until midday, before the men and women and those
who could understand; and the ears of all
the people *were attentive* to the Book of
the Law.
4So Ezra the scribe stood on a platform
of wood which they had made for the purpose; and beside him, at his right hand,
stood Mattithiah, Shema, Anaiah, Urijah,
Hilkiah, and Maaseiah; and at his left
hand Pedaiah, Mishael, Malchijah, Hashum, Hashbadana, Zechariah, *and* Meshullam. 5And Ezra opened the book in
the sight of all the people, for he was
standing above all the people; and when
he opened it, all the people [a]stood up.
6And Ezra blessed the LORD, the great
God.
Then all the people [a]answered, "Amen,
Amen!" while [b]lifting up their hands.
And they [c]bowed their heads and worshiped the LORD with *their* faces to the
ground.

Father, as ____ reads to
Your people from the book,
in the Law of God, may they
give insight and help them to
understand the reading.
FROM NEHEMIAH 8:8

7Also Jeshua, Bani, Sherebiah, Jamin,
Akkub, Shabbethai, Hodijah, Maaseiah,
Kelita, Azariah, Jozabad, Hanan, Pelaiah,
and the Levites, [a]helped the people to understand the Law; and the people [b]*stood*
in their place. 8So they read distinctly
from the book, in the Law of God; and
they gave the sense, and helped *them* to
understand the reading.

63 [1] Or *Hakkoz*
65 [1] Heb. *Tirshatha*
70 [a] Neh. 8:9 [1] Heb. *Tirshatha*
71 [a] Ezra 2:69
73 [a] Ezra 3:1
CHAPTER 8
1 [a] Ezra 3:1 [b] Neh. 3:26 [c] Ezra 7:6
2 [a] [Deut. 31:11, 12] [b] Lev. 23:24
3 [a] 2 Kin. 23:2 [1] Lit. *from the light*
5 [a] Judg. 3:20
6 [a] Neh. 5:13 [b] Ps. 28:2 [c] 2 Chr. 20:18
7 [a] [Mal. 2:7] [b] Neh. 9:3

9[a]And Nehemiah, who *was* the [1]gover-
nor, Ezra the priest *and* scribe, and the
Levites who taught the people said to all
the people, [b]"This day *is* holy to the LORD
your God; [c]do not mourn nor weep." For
all the people wept, when they heard the
words of the Law.
10 Then he said to them, "Go your
way, eat the fat, drink the sweet, [a]and
send portions to those for whom nothing
is prepared; for *this* day *is* holy to our
Lord. Do not sorrow, for the joy of the
LORD is your strength."
11 So the Levites quieted all the people,
saying, "Be still, for the day *is* holy; do not
be grieved." 12And all the people went
their way to eat and drink, to [a]send portions and rejoice greatly, because they
[b]understood the words that were declared
to them.

The Feast of Tabernacles

13Now on the second day the heads of
the fathers' *houses* of all the people, with
the priests and Levites, were gathered to
Ezra the scribe, in order to understand
the words of the Law. 14And they found
written in the Law, which the LORD had
commanded by Moses, that the children
of Israel should dwell in [a]booths[1] during
the feast of the seventh month, 15and
[a]that they should announce and proclaim
in all their cities and [b]in Jerusalem, saying, "Go out to the mountain, and [c]bring
olive branches, branches of oil trees, myrtle branches, palm branches, and branches of leafy trees, to make booths, as *it is*
written."
16Then the people went out and
brought *them* and made themselves
booths, each one on the [a]roof of his
house, or in their courtyards or the courts
of the house of God, and in the open
square of the [b]Water Gate [c]and in the
open square of the Gate of Ephraim. 17So
the whole assembly of those who had returned from the captivity made [1]booths
and sat under the booths; for since the
days of Joshua the son of Nun until that
day the children of Israel had not done so.
And there was very [a]great gladness. 18Also
[a]day by day, from the first day until the
last day, he read from the Book of the Law
of God. And they kept the feast [b]seven
days; and on the [c]eighth day *there was*
a sacred assembly, according to the *prescribed* manner.

The People Confess Their Sins

9 Now on the twenty-fourth day of [a]this
month the children of Israel were assembled with fasting, in sackcloth, [b]and
with [1]dust on their heads. 2Then [a]those
of Israelite lineage separated themselves
from all foreigners; and they stood and
[b]confessed their sins and the iniquities of
their fathers. 3And they stood up in their
place and [a]read from the Book of the Law
of the LORD their God *for one*-fourth of
the day; and *for another* fourth they confessed and worshiped the LORD their God.
4Then Jeshua, Bani, Kadmiel, Shebaniah, Bunni, Sherebiah, Bani, *and* Chenani
stood on the [1]stairs of the Levites and
cried out with a loud voice to the LORD
their God. 5And the Levites, Jeshua, Kadmiel, Bani, Hashabniah, Sherebiah, Hodijah, Shebaniah, *and* Pethahiah, said:

"Stand up *and* bless the LORD your
God
Forever and ever!

"Blessed be [a]Your glorious name,
Which is exalted above all blessing
and praise!
6 [a]You alone *are* the LORD;
[b]You have made heaven,
[c]The heaven of heavens, with [d]all
their host,
The earth and everything on it,
The seas and all that is in them,
And You [e]preserve them all.
The host of heaven worships You.

7 "You *are* the LORD God,
Who chose [a]Abram,
And brought him out of Ur of the
Chaldeans,
And gave him the name [b]Abraham;
8 You found his heart [a]faithful before
You,
And made a [b]covenant with him
To give the land of the Canaanites,
The Hittites, the Amorites,
The Perizzites, the Jebusites,
And the Girgashites—
To give *it* to his descendants.
You [c]have performed Your words,
For You *are* righteous.

9 "You[a] saw the affliction of our
fathers in Egypt,
And [b]heard their cry by the Red
Sea.
10 You [a]showed signs and wonders
against Pharaoh,
Against all his servants,

9 a Neh. 7:65, 70; 10:1 b Num. 29:1 c Deut. 16:14 *1* Heb. *Tirshatha*
10 a Rev. 11:10
12 a Neh. 8:10 b Neh. 8:7, 8
14 a Lev. 23:34, 40, 42 *1* Temporary shelters
15 a Lev. 23:4 b Deut. 16:16 c Lev. 23:40
16 a Deut. 22:8 b Neh. 12:37 c 2 Kin. 14:13
17 a 2 Chr. 30:21 *1* Temporary shelters
18 a Deut. 31:11 b Lev. 23:36 c Num. 29:35

CHAPTER 9
1 a Neh. 8:2 b 1 Sam. 4:12 *1* Lit. *earth on them*
2 a Neh. 13:3, 30 b Neh. 1:6
3 a Neh. 8:7, 8
4 *1* Lit. *ascent*
5 a 1 Chr. 29:13
6 a 2 Kin. 19:15, 19 b Rev. 14:7 c [Deut. 10:14] d Gen. 2:1 e [Ps. 36:6]
7 a Gen. 11:31 b Gen. 17:5
8 a Gen. 15:6; 22:1–3 b Gen. 15:18 c Josh. 23:14
9 a Ex. 2:25; 3:7 b Ex. 14:10
10 a Ex. 7—14

NEHEMIAH 8:10

Dear Woman of Destiny,

Some time ago I saw an ad in the Christmas catalog for three wooden, gold-sprayed letters—JOY. The catalog showed them prominently displayed on a mantlepiece. I have a mantlepiece, so I just had to have them. When they arrived, I decided that, instead of setting the letters on the mantlepiece, I wanted to hang them on the wall above. The only catch was that the wooden letters weren't made to be hung on a wall. We tried sticky tape, super glue, and a hot-glue gun. The letters would stay up for a while, but eventually we would hear a crash and find that one of the letters had fallen off the wall.

Most of the problem was with the "J." I decided I would have JOY on my wall—not JO, not OY, not even JY—even if I had to weld the letters into place. The good news is I now have two-foot-high, gold letters spelling JOY over my fireplace. The bad news is that even if an earthquake occurs, I will have JOY on my wall for all of eternity—or until we knock out the wall.

Can I tell you that this is a spiritual lesson? It takes *perseverance* to keep your joy. I have worked long and hard to maintain my walk with God, but from time to time I have inevitably lost my JOY. The "J" would just be sucked right out of the JOY, and I would be left with OY. And we both know what that means. When my Jewish husband says, "OY VEY," it usually means, "Lady, you are giving me a migraine!"

What a difference the "J" makes! Every time I walk into my family room I start laughing when I think of all the people and all the different devices the Lord has used to keep that JOY level up—even in the midst of tremendous trials. His joy is my strength.

It is work to keep joy alive. Nehemiah declared this verse in the worst of circumstances, and yet the words he used sound like things you'd find at a party. Eating and drinking the sweet (see Neh. 8:10) sounds like a party to me, with cake and ice cream. Have a party in the midst of your trials. Let your joy know no bounds. Go through trials with dignity. God is not out to get you. He's out to get you through.

In the midst of your trials, there is only one place you will find true strength. In my life, getting at my Lord's feet is where the strength comes from. It comes from pouring out my heart in love, telling Him how much I trust Him even when I don't understand everything I am called to walk through. In return, He gives me joy, strength, and victory to face the test.

The pressures, distractions, and cares of this life will try to push out the very thing that is our source of life. Being in His presence is not an option—it is a necessity!

Cathy Lechner

And against all the people of his
land.
For You knew that they [b]acted
[1]proudly against them.
So You [c]made a name for Yourself,
as *it is* this day.
11 [a]And You divided the sea before
them,
So that they went through the
midst of the sea on the dry land;
And their persecutors You threw
into the deep,
[b]As a stone into the mighty waters.
12 Moreover You [a]led them by day
with a cloudy pillar,
And by night with a pillar of fire,
To give them light on the road
Which they should travel.

13 "You[a] came down also on Mount
Sinai,
And spoke with them from heaven,
And gave them [b]just ordinances and
true laws,
Good statutes and commandments.
14 You made known to them Your
[a]holy Sabbath,
And commanded them precepts,
statutes and laws,
By the hand of Moses Your servant.
15 You [a]gave them bread from
heaven for their hunger,
And [b]brought them water out of
the rock for their thirst,
And told them to [c]go in to possess
the land
Which You had [1]sworn to give
them.

16 "But[a] they and our fathers acted
[1]proudly,
[b]Hardened[2] their necks,
And did not heed Your
commandments.
17 They refused to obey,
And [a]they were not mindful of Your
wonders
That You did among them.
But they hardened their necks,
And [1]in their rebellion
They appointed [b]a leader
To return to their bondage.
But You *are* God,
Ready to pardon,
[c]Gracious and merciful,
Slow to anger,
Abundant in kindness,
And did not forsake them.

10 [b]Ex. 18:11 [c]Jer. 32:20 [1]*presumptuously* or *insolently*
11 [a]Ex. 14:20–28 [b]Ex. 15:1, 5
12 [a]Ex. 13:21, 22
13 [a]Ex. 20:1–18 [b][Rom. 7:12]
14 [a]Gen. 2:3
15 [a]Ex. 16:14–17 [b]Ex. 17:6 [c]Deut. 1:8 [1]Lit. *raised Your hand to*
16 [a]Ps. 106:6 [b]Deut. 1:26–33; 31:27 [1]*presumptuously* [2]*Stiffened their necks,* became stubborn
17 [a]Ps. 78:11, 42–45 [b]Num. 14:4 [c]Joel 2:13 [1]So with MT, Vg.; LXX *in Egypt*
18 [a]Ex. 32:4–8, 31
19 [a]Ps. 106:45 [b]1 Cor. 10:1
20 [a]Num. 11:17 [b]Ex. 16:14–16 [c]Ex. 17:6
21 [a]Deut. 2:7 [b]Deut. 8:4; 29:5
22 [a]Num. 21:21–35 [1]Lit. *corners* [2]So with MT, Vg.; LXX omits *The land of*
23 [a]Gen. 15:5; 22:17
24 [a]Josh. 1:2–4 [b][Ps. 44:2, 3] [1]Lit. *sons*

Is there anything too kind for Him to do? No, there is nothing too kind for Him to do.

AMY CARMICHAEL

18 "Even [a]when they made a molded
calf for themselves,
And said, 'This *is* your god
That brought you up out of Egypt,'
And worked great provocations,
19 Yet in Your [a]manifold mercies
You did not forsake them in the
wilderness.
The [b]pillar of the cloud did not
depart from them by day,
To lead them on the road;
Nor the pillar of fire by night,
To show them light,
And the way they should go.
20 You also gave Your [a]good Spirit to
instruct them,
And did not withhold Your [b]manna
from their mouth,
And gave them [c]water for their
thirst.
21 [a]Forty years You sustained them in
the wilderness;
They lacked nothing;
Their [b]clothes did not wear out
And their feet did not swell.

22 "Moreover You gave them
kingdoms and nations,
And divided them into [1]districts.
So they took possession of the land
of [a]Sihon,
[2]The land of the king of Heshbon,
And the land of Og king of Bashan.
23 You also multiplied [a]their children
as the stars of heaven,
And brought them into the land
Which You had told their fathers
To go in and possess.
24 So [a]the [1]people went in
And possessed the land;
[b]You subdued before them the
inhabitants of the land,
The Canaanites,
And gave them into their hands,
With their kings
And the people of the land,

That they might do with them as
they wished.
25 And they took strong cities and a
[a]rich land,
And possessed [b]houses full of all
goods,
Cisterns *already* dug, vineyards,
olive groves,
And [1]fruit trees in abundance.
So they ate and were filled and
[c]grew fat,
And delighted themselves in Your
great [d]goodness.

All the blessings which God hath bestowed upon man are of His mere grace, bounty or favor; His free, undeserved favor; favor altogether undeserved; man having no claim to the least of His mercies.

JOHN WESLEY

26 "Nevertheless they [a]were
disobedient
And rebelled against You,
[b]Cast Your law behind their backs
And killed Your [c]prophets, who
[1]testified against them
To turn them to Yourself;
And they worked great
provocations.
27 [a]Therefore You delivered them into
the hand of their enemies,
Who oppressed them;
And in the time of their trouble,
When they cried to You,
You [b]heard from heaven;
And according to Your abundant
mercies
[c]You gave them deliverers who saved
them
From the hand of their enemies.
28 "But after they had rest,
[a]They again did evil before You.

25 [a]Num. 13:27 [b]Deut. 6:11 [c][Deut. 32:15] [d]Hos. 3:5 [1]Lit. *trees for eating*

26 [a]Judg. 2:11 [b]1 Kin. 14:9 [c]1 Kin. 18:4; 19:10 [1]*admonished* or *warned them*

27 [a]Judg. 2:14 [b]Ps. 106:44 [c]Judg. 2:18

28 [a]Judg. 3:12 [b]Ps. 106:43

29 [a]Lev. 18:5 [1]*admonished them* [2]*presumptuously* [3]Became stubborn

30 [a]Jer. 7:25 [b][Acts 7:51] [c]Is. 5:5 [1]*admonished* or *warned them*

31 [a]Jer. 4:27

32 [a][Ex. 34:6, 7] [1]*hardship*

Therefore You left them in the
hand of their enemies,
So that they had dominion over
them;
Yet when they returned and cried
out to You,
You heard from heaven;
And [b]many times You delivered
them according to Your mercies,
29 And [1]testified against them,
That You might bring them back to
Your law.
Yet they acted [2]proudly,
And did not heed Your
commandments,
But sinned against Your judgments,
[a]'Which if a man does, he shall live
by them.'
And they shrugged their shoulders,
[3]Stiffened their necks,
And would not hear.
30 Yet for many years You had
patience with them,
And [1]testified [a]against them by
Your Spirit [b]in Your prophets.
Yet they would not listen;
[c]Therefore You gave them into the
hand of the peoples of the lands.
31 Nevertheless in Your great mercy
[a]You did not utterly consume them
nor forsake them;
For You *are* God, gracious and
merciful.

Many times ____ has sinned against You. Nevertheless in Your great mercy You did not utterly consume them nor forsake them; for You are God, gracious and merciful.

FROM NEHEMIAH 9:29, 31

32 "Now therefore, our God,
The great, the [a]mighty, and
awesome God,
Who keeps covenant and mercy:
Do not let all the [1]trouble seem
small before You
That has come upon us,
Our kings and our princes,
Our priests and our prophets,

Our fathers and on all Your people,
[b]From the days of the kings of
Assyria until this day.
33 However [a]You *are* just in all that
has befallen us;
For You have dealt faithfully,
But [b]we have done wickedly.
34 Neither our kings nor our princes,
Our priests nor our fathers,
Have kept Your law,
Nor heeded Your commandments
and Your testimonies,
With which You testified against
them.
35 For they have [a]not served You in
their kingdom,
Or in the many good *things* that
You gave them,
Or in the large and rich land which
You set before them;
Nor did they turn from their wicked
works.

36 "Here [a]we *are,* servants today!
And the land that You gave to our
fathers,
To eat its fruit and its bounty,
Here we *are,* servants in it!
37 And [a]it yields much increase to
the kings
You have set over us,
Because of our sins;
Also they have [b]dominion over our
bodies and our cattle
At their pleasure;
And we *are* in great distress.
38 "And because of all this,
We [a]make a sure *covenant* and
write *it;*
Our leaders, our Levites, *and* our
priests [b]seal *it.*"

The People Who Sealed the Covenant

10 Now those who placed *their* seal on
the document were:

1 Nehemiah the [1]governor, [a]the son of
Hacaliah, and Zedekiah, 2 [a]Seraiah, Azariah, Jeremiah, 3 Pashhur, Amariah, Malchijah, 4 Hattush, Shebaniah, Malluch,
5 Harim, Meremoth, Obadiah, 6 Daniel,
Ginnethon, Baruch, 7 Meshullam, Abijah,
Mijamin, 8 Maaziah, Bilgai, *and* Shemaiah.
These *were* the priests.
9 The Levites: Jeshua the son of Azaniah, Binnui of the sons of Henadad, *and*
Kadmiel.
10 Their brethren: Shebaniah, Hodijah,
Kelita, Pelaiah, Hanan, 11 Micha, Rehob,
Hashabiah, 12 Zaccur, Sherebiah, Shebaniah, 13 Hodijah, Bani, *and* Beninu.
14 The leaders of the people: [a]Parosh,
Pahath-Moab, Elam, Zattu, Bani, 15 Bunni, Azgad, Bebai, 16 Adonijah, Bigvai, Adin,
17 Ater, Hezekiah, Azzur, 18 Hodijah, Hashum, Bezai, 19 Hariph, Anathoth, Nebai,
20 Magpiash, Meshullam, Hezir, 21 Meshezabel, Zadok, Jaddua, 22 Pelatiah, Hanan,
Anaiah, 23 Hoshea, Hananiah, Hasshub,
24 Hallohesh, Pilha, Shobek, 25 Rehum, Ha-
shabnah, Maaseiah, 26 Ahijah, Hanan,
Anan, 27 Malluch, Harim, *and* Baanah.

The Covenant That Was Sealed

28 [a]Now the rest of the people—the
priests, the Levites, the gatekeepers, the
singers, the Nethinim, [b]and all those who
had separated themselves from the peoples of the lands to the Law of God, their
wives, their sons, and their daughters, everyone who had knowledge and understanding— 29 these joined with their
brethren, their nobles, [a]and entered into
a curse and an oath [b]to walk in God's Law,
which was given by Moses the servant of
God, and to observe and do all the commandments of the LORD our Lord, and His
ordinances and His statutes: 30 We would
not give [a]our daughters as wives to the
peoples of the land, nor take their daughters for our sons; 31 [a]*if* the peoples of the
land brought [1]wares or any grain to sell
on the Sabbath day, we would not buy it
from them on the Sabbath, or on a holy
day; and we would forego the [b]seventh
year's *produce* and the [c]exacting[2] of every
debt.
32 Also we made ordinances for ourselves, to exact from ourselves yearly
[a]one-third of a shekel for the service of
the house of our God: 33 for [a]the showbread, for the regular grain offering, for
the [b]regular burnt offering of the Sabbaths, the New Moons, and the set feasts;
for the holy things, for the sin offerings to
make atonement for Israel, and all the
work of the house of our God. 34 We cast
lots among the priests, the Levites, and
the people, [a]for *bringing* the wood offering into the house of our God, according
to our fathers' houses, at the appointed
times year by year, to burn on the altar of
the LORD our God [b]as *it is* written in the
Law.

32 [b]2 Kin. 15:19; 17:3–6
33 [a][Dan. 9:14] [b][Dan. 9:5, 6, 8]
35 [a]Deut. 28:47
36 [a]Deut. 28:48
37 [a]Deut. 28:33, 51 [b]Deut. 28:48
38 [a]2 Kin. 23:3 [b]Neh. 10:1

CHAPTER 10
1 [a]Neh. 1:1 [1]Heb. *Tirshatha*
2 [a]Neh. 12:1–21
14 [a]Ezra 2:3
28 [a]Ezra 2:36–43 [b]Neh. 13:3
29 [a]Deut. 29:12 [b]2 Kin. 23:3
30 [a]Ex. 34:16
31 [a]Ex. 20:10 [b]Lev. 25:4 [c][Deut. 15:1, 2] [1]*merchandise* [2]*collection*
32 [a]Matt. 17:24
33 [a]Lev. 24:5 [b]Num. 28; 29
34 [a]Neh. 13:31 [b]Lev. 6:12

[35]And *we made ordinances* [a]to bring the firstfruits of our ground and the firstfruits of all fruit of all trees, year by year, to the house of the LORD; [36]to bring the [a]firstborn of our sons and our cattle, as *it is* written in the Law, and the firstborn of our herds and our flocks, to the house of our God, to the priests who minister in the house of our God; [37][a]to bring the firstfruits of our dough, our offerings, the fruit from all kinds of trees, *the* new wine and oil, to the priests, to the storerooms of the [1]house of our God; and to bring [b]the tithes of our land to the Levites, for the Levites should receive the tithes in all our farming communities. [38]And the priest, the descendant of Aaron, shall be with the Levites [a]when the Levites receive tithes; and the Levites shall bring up a tenth of the tithes to the house of our God, to [b]the rooms of the storehouse.

[39]For the children of Israel and the children of Levi [a]shall bring the offering of the grain, of the new wine and the oil, to the storerooms where the articles of the sanctuary *are, where* the priests who minister and the gatekeepers [b]and the singers *are;* and we will not [c]neglect the house of our God.

The People Dwelling in Jerusalem

11 Now the leaders of the people dwelt at Jerusalem; the rest of the people cast lots to bring one out of ten to dwell in Jerusalem, [a]the holy city, and nine-tenths *were to dwell* in *other* cities. [2]And the people blessed all the men who [a]willingly offered themselves to dwell at Jerusalem.

[3][a]These *are* the heads of the province who dwelt in Jerusalem. (But in the cities of Judah everyone dwelt in his own possession in their cities—Israelites, priests, Levites, [b]Nethinim, and [c]descendants of Solomon's servants.) [4]Also [a]in Jerusalem dwelt *some* of the children of Judah and of the children of Benjamin.

The children of Judah: Athaiah the son of Uzziah, the son of Zechariah, the son of Amariah, the son of Shephatiah, the son of Mahalalel, of the children of [b]Perez; [5]and Maaseiah the son of Baruch, the son of Col-Hozeh, the son of Hazaiah, the son of Adaiah, the son of Joiarib, the son of Zechariah, the son of Shiloni. [6]All the sons of Perez who dwelt at Jerusalem *were* four hundred and sixty-eight valiant men.

[7]And these are the sons of Benjamin: Sallu the son of Meshullam, the son of Joed, the son of Pedaiah, the son of Kolaiah, the son of Maaseiah, the son of Ithiel, the son of Jeshaiah; [8]and after him Gabbai *and* Sallai, nine hundred and twenty-eight. [9]Joel the son of Zichri *was* their overseer, and Judah the son of [1]Senuah *was* second over the city.

[10][a]Of the priests: Jedaiah the son of Joiarib, and Jachin; [11]Seraiah the son of Hilkiah, the son of Meshullam, the son of Zadok, the son of Meraioth, the son of Ahitub, *was* the leader of the house of God. [12]Their brethren who did the work of the house *were* eight hundred and twenty-two; and Adaiah the son of Jeroham, the son of Pelaliah, the son of Amzi, the son of Zechariah, the son of Pashhur, the son of Malchijah, [13]and his brethren, heads of the fathers' *houses, were* two hundred and forty-two; and Amashai the son of Azarel, the son of Ahzai, the son of Meshillemoth, the son of Immer, [14]and their brethren, mighty men of valor, *were* one hundred and twenty-eight. Their overseer *was* Zabdiel [1]the son of *one of* the great men.

[15]Also of the Levites: Shemaiah the son of Hasshub, the son of Azrikam, the son of Hashabiah, the son of Bunni; [16][a]Shabbethai and [b]Jozabad, of the heads of the Levites, *had* the oversight of [c]the business outside of the [1]house of God; [17]Mattaniah the son of [1]Micha, the son of Zabdi, the son of Asaph, the leader *who* began the thanksgiving with prayer; Bakbukiah, the second among his brethren; and Abda the son of Shammua, the son of Galal, the son of Jeduthun. [18]All the Levites in [a]the holy city *were* two hundred and eighty-four.

[19]Moreover the gatekeepers, Akkub, Talmon, and their brethren who kept the gates, *were* one hundred and seventy-two.

[20]And the rest of Israel, of the priests *and* Levites, *were* in all the cities of Judah, everyone in his inheritance. [21][a]But the Nethinim dwelt in Ophel. And Ziha and Gishpa *were* over the Nethinim.

[22]Also the overseer of the Levites at Jerusalem *was* Uzzi the son of Bani, the son of Hashabiah, the son of Mattaniah, the son of Micha, of the sons of Asaph, the singers in charge of the [1]service of the [2]house of God. [23]For [a]*it was* the king's command concerning them that a [1]certain portion should be for the singers, a

---

35 a Ex. 23:19; 34:26
36 a Ex. 13:2, 12, 13
37 a Lev. 23:17 b Lev. 27:30 *1 Temple*
38 a Num. 18:26 b 1 Chr. 9:26
39 a Deut. 12:6, 11 b Neh. 13:10, 11 c [Heb. 10:25]

CHAPTER 11
1 a Matt. 4:5; 5:35; 27:53
2 a Judg. 5:9
3 a 1 Chr. 9:2, 3 b Ezra 2:43 c Ezra 2:55
4 a 1 Chr. 9:3 b Gen. 38:29
9 *1 Or Hassenuah*
10 a 1 Chr. 9:10
14 *1 Or the son of Haggedolim*
16 a Ezra 10:15 b Ezra 8:33 c 1 Chr. 26:29 *1 Temple*
17 *1 Or Michah*
18 a Neh. 11:1
21 a Neh. 3:26
22 *1 work 2 Temple*
23 a Ezra 6:8, 9; 7:20 *1 fixed share*

quota day by day. 24Pethahiah the son of
Meshezabel, of the children of [a]Zerah the
son of Judah, *was* [b]the[1] king's deputy in
all matters concerning the people.

The People Dwelling Outside Jerusalem

25And as for the villages with their
fields, *some* of the children of Judah dwelt
in [a]Kirjath Arba and its villages, Dibon
and its villages, Jekabzeel and its villages;
26in Jeshua, Moladah, Beth Pelet, 27Hazar
Shual, and Beersheba and its villages; 28in
Ziklag and Meconah and its villages; 29in
En Rimmon, Zorah, Jarmuth, 30Zanoah,
Adullam, and their villages; in Lachish
and its fields; in Azekah and its villages.
They dwelt from Beersheba to the Valley
of Hinnom.
31Also the children of Benjamin from
Geba *dwelt* in Michmash, Aija, and Bethel,
and their villages; 32in Anathoth, Nob, Ananiah; 33in Hazor, Ramah, Gittaim; 34in
Hadid, Zeboim, Neballat; 35in Lod, Ono,
and [a]the Valley of Craftsmen. 36Some of
the Judean divisions of Levites *were* in
Benjamin.

The Priests and Levites

12 Now these *are* the [a]priests and the
Levites who came up with [b]Zerub-
babel the son of Shealtiel, and Jeshua:
[c]Seraiah, Jeremiah, Ezra, 2Amariah,
[1]Malluch, Hattush, 3[1]Shechaniah, [2]Re-
hum, [3]Meremoth, 4Iddo, [1]Ginnethoi,
[a]Abijah, 5[1]Mijamin, [2]Maadiah, Bilgah,
6Shemaiah, Joiarib, Jedaiah, 7[1]Sallu,
Amok, Hilkiah, *and* Jedaiah.
These *were* the heads of the priests and
their brethren in the days of [a]Jeshua.
8Moreover the Levites *were* Jeshua,
Binnui, Kadmiel, Sherebiah, Judah, *and*
Mattaniah [a]*who led* the thanksgiving
psalms, he and his brethren. 9Also Bakbukiah and Unni, their brethren, *stood*
across from them in *their* duties.
10Jeshua begot Joiakim, Joiakim begot
Eliashib, Eliashib begot Joiada, 11Joiada
begot Jonathan, and Jonathan begot
Jaddua.
12Now in the days of Joiakim, the
priests, the [a]heads of the fathers' *houses*
were: of Seraiah, Meraiah; of Jeremiah,
Hananiah; 13of Ezra, Meshullam; of Amariah, Jehohanan; 14of [1]Melichu, Jonathan;
of [2]Shebaniah, Joseph; 15of [1]Harim, Adna;
of [2]Meraioth, Helkai; 16of Iddo, Zechariah;

24 a Gen. 38:30 b 1 Chr. 18:17 *1* Lit. *at the king's hand*
25 a Josh. 14:15
35 a 1 Chr. 4:14

CHAPTER 12
1 a Ezra 2:1, 2; 7:7 b Neh. 7:7 c Neh. 10:2–8
2 *1 Melichu,* v. 14
3 *1 Shebaniah,* v. 14 *2 Harim,* v. 15 *3 Meraioth,* v. 15
4 a Luke 1:5 *1 Ginnethon,* v. 16
5 *1 Minjamin,* v. 17 *2 Moadiah,* v. 17
7 a Zech. 3:1 *1 Sallai,* v. 20
8 a Neh. 11:17
12 a Neh. 7:70, 71; 8:13; 11:13
14 *1 Malluch,* v. 2 *2 Shechaniah,* v. 3
15 *1 Rehum,* v. 3 *2 Meremoth,* v. 3
17 *1 Mijamin,* v. 5 *2 Maadiah,* v. 5
20 *1 Sallu,* v. 7
22 a 1 Chr. 24:6
23 a 1 Chr. 9:14–22
24 a Neh. 11:17 b Ezra 3:11 c 1 Chr. 23—26 *1* Lit. *watch by watch*
26 a Neh. 8:9 b Ezra 7:6, 11 *1 Jehozadak,* 1 Chr. 6:14
27 a Deut. 20:5 b 1 Chr. 25:6
28 a 1 Chr. 9:16
30 a Neh. 13:22, 30
31 a Neh. 12:38 b Neh. 2:13; 3:13
35 a Num. 10:2, 8

of Ginnethon, Meshullam; 17of Abijah,
Zichri; *the son* of [1]Minjamin; of [2]Moadi-
ah, Piltai; 18of Bilgah, Shammua; of Shemaiah, Jehonathan; 19of Joiarib, Mattenai;
of Jedaiah, Uzzi; 20of [1]Sallai, Kallai; of
Amok, Eber; 21of Hilkiah, Hashabiah; *and*
of Jedaiah, Nethanel.
22During the reign of Darius the Persian, a record *was also kept* of the Levites
and priests *who had been* [a]heads of their
fathers' *houses* in the days of Eliashib, Joiada, Johanan, and Jaddua. 23The sons of
Levi, the heads of the fathers' *houses* until
the days of Johanan the son of Eliashib,
were written in the book of the [a]chroni-
cles.
24And the heads of the Levites *were*
Hashabiah, Sherebiah, and Jeshua the son
of Kadmiel, with their brothers across
from them, to [a]praise *and* give thanks,
[b]group[1] alternating with group, [c]accord-
ing to the command of David the man of
God. 25Mattaniah, Bakbukiah, Obadiah,
Meshullam, Talmon, and Akkub *were*
gatekeepers keeping the watch at the
storerooms of the gates. 26These *lived* in
the days of Joiakim the son of Jeshua, the
son of [1]Jozadak, and in the days of Nehemiah [a]the governor, and of Ezra the
priest, [b]the scribe.

Nehemiah Dedicates the Wall

27Now at [a]the dedication of the wall of
Jerusalem they sought out the Levites in
all their places, to bring them to Jerusalem to celebrate the dedication with gladness, [b]both with thanksgivings and
singing, *with* cymbals and stringed instruments and harps. 28And the sons of
the singers gathered together from the
countryside around Jerusalem, from the
[a]villages of the Netophathites, 29from the
house of Gilgal, and from the fields of
Geba and Azmaveth; for the singers had
built themselves villages all around Jerusalem. 30Then the priests and Levites [a]pu-
rified themselves, and purified the people,
the gates, and the wall.
31So I brought the leaders of Judah up
on the wall, and appointed two large
thanksgiving choirs. [a]*One* went to the
right hand on the wall [b]toward the Refuse
Gate. 32After them went Hoshaiah and
half of the leaders of Judah, 33and Azariah,
Ezra, Meshullam, 34Judah, Benjamin,
Shemaiah, Jeremiah, 35and some of the
priests' sons [a]with trumpets—Zechariah
the son of Jonathan, the son of Shemaiah,

the son of Mattaniah, the son of Michaiah, the son of Zaccur, the son of Asaph, 36and his brethren, Shemaiah, Azarel, Milalai, Gilalai, Maai, Nethanel, Judah, *and* Hanani, with [a]the musical [b]instruments of David the man of God. And Ezra the scribe *went* before them. 37[a]By the Fountain Gate, in front of them, they went up [b]the stairs of the [c]City of David, on the stairway of the wall, beyond the house of David, as far as [d]the Water Gate eastward.

38[a]The other thanksgiving choir went the opposite *way,* and I *was* behind them with half of the people on the wall, going past the [b]Tower of the Ovens as far as [c]the Broad Wall, 39[a]and above the Gate of Ephraim, above [b]the Old Gate, above [c]the Fish Gate, [d]the Tower of Hananel, the Tower of [1]the Hundred, as far as [e]the Sheep Gate; and they stopped by [f]the Gate of the Prison.

40So the two thanksgiving choirs stood in the house of God, likewise I and the half of the rulers with me; 41and the priests, Eliakim, Maaseiah, [1]Minjamin, Michaiah, Elioenai, Zechariah, *and* Hananiah, with trumpets; 42also Maaseiah, Shemaiah, Eleazar, Uzzi, Jehohanan, Malchijah, Elam, and Ezer. The singers [1]sang loudly with Jezrahiah the director.

43Also that day they offered great sacrifices, and rejoiced, for God had made them rejoice with great joy; the women and the children also rejoiced, so that the joy of Jerusalem was heard [a]afar off.

Temple Responsibilities

44[a]And at the same time some were appointed over the rooms of the storehouse for the offerings, the firstfruits, and the [b]tithes, to gather into them from the fields of the cities the portions specified by the Law for the priests and Levites; for Judah rejoiced over the priests and Levites who [1]ministered. 45Both the singers and the gatekeepers kept the charge of their God and the charge of the purification, [a]according to the command of David *and* Solomon his son. 46For in the days of David [a]and Asaph of old *there were* chiefs of the singers, and songs of praise and thanksgiving to God. 47In the days of Zerubbabel and in the days of Nehemiah all Israel gave the portions for the singers and the gatekeepers, a portion for [a]each day. [b]They also [1]consecrated *holy things* for the Levites, [c]and the Levites consecrated *them* for the children of Aaron.

Principles of Separation

13 On that day [a]they read from the Book of Moses in the hearing of the people, and in it was found written [b]that no Ammonite or Moabite should ever come into the assembly of God, 2because they had not met the children of Israel with bread and water, but [a]hired Balaam against them to curse them. [b]However, our God turned the curse into a blessing. 3So it was, when they had heard the Law, [a]that they separated all the mixed multitude from Israel.

The Reforms of Nehemiah

4Now before this, [a]Eliashib the priest, having authority over the storerooms of the house of our God, *was* allied with [b]Tobiah. 5And he had prepared for him a large room, [a]where previously they had stored the grain offerings, the frankincense, the articles, the tithes of grain, the new wine and oil, [b]which were commanded *to be given* to the Levites and singers and gatekeepers, and the offerings for the priests. 6But during all this I was not in Jerusalem, [a]for in the thirty-second year of Artaxerxes king of Babylon I had returned to the king. Then after certain days I obtained leave from the king, 7and I came to Jerusalem and discovered the evil that Eliashib had done for Tobiah, in [a]preparing a room for him in the courts of the [1]house of God. 8And it grieved me bitterly; therefore I threw all the household goods of Tobiah out of the room. 9Then I commanded them to [a]cleanse the rooms; and I brought back into them the articles of the house of God, with the grain offering and the frankincense.

10I also realized that the portions for the Levites had [a]not been given *them;* for each of the Levites and the singers who did the work had gone back to [b]his field. 11So [a]I contended with the rulers, and said, [b]"Why is the house of God forsaken?" And I gathered them together and set them in their place. 12[a]Then all Judah brought the tithe of the grain and the new wine and the oil to the storehouse. 13[a]And I appointed as treasurers over the storehouse Shelemiah the priest and Zadok the scribe, and of the Levites, Pedaiah; and next to them *was* Hanan the son of Zaccur, the son of Mattaniah; for they were

36 a 1 Chr. 23:5 b 2 Chr. 29:26, 27
37 a Neh. 2:14; 3:15 b Neh. 3:15 c 2 Sam. 5:7–9 d Neh. 3:26; 8:1, 3, 16
38 a Neh. 12:31 b Neh. 3:11 c Neh. 3:8
39 a 2 Kin. 14:13 b Neh. 3:6 c Neh. 3:3 d Neh. 3:1 e Neh. 3:32 f Jer. 32:2 *1* Heb. *Hammeah*
41 *1* Or *Mijamin,* v. 5
42 *1* Lit. *made their voice to be heard*
43 a Ezra 3:13
44 a Neh. 13:5, 12, 13 b Neh. 10:37–39 *1* Lit. *stood*
45 a 1 Chr. 25, 26
46 a 2 Chr. 29:30
47 a Neh. 11:23 b Num. 18:21, 24 c Num. 18:26 *1 set apart*

CHAPTER 13
1 a Neh. 8:3, 8; 9:3 b Deut. 23:3, 4
2 a Num. 22:5 b Num. 23:1; 24:10
3 a Neh. 9:2; 10:28
4 a Neh. 12:10 b Neh. 2:10; 4:3; 6:1
5 a Neh. 12:44 b Num. 18:21, 24
6 a Neh. 5:14–16
7 a Neh. 13:1, 5 *1* Temple
9 a 2 Chr. 29:5, 15, 16
10 a Neh. 10:37 b Num. 35:2
11 a Neh. 13:17, 25 b Neh. 10:39
12 a Neh. 10:38; 12:44
13 a 2 Chr. 31:12

considered [b]faithful, and their task *was* to
distribute to their brethren.
14 [a]Remember me, O my God, concerning this, and do not wipe out my good
deeds that I have done for the house of my
God, and for its services!
15 In those days I saw *people* in Judah
treading wine presses [a]on the Sabbath,
and bringing in sheaves, and loading donkeys with wine, grapes, figs, and all *kinds
of* burdens, [b]which they brought into Jerusalem on the Sabbath day. And I warned
them about the day on which they were
selling provisions. 16 Men of Tyre dwelt
there also, who brought in fish and all
kinds of goods, and sold *them* on the Sabbath to the children of Judah, and in Jerusalem.
17 Then I contended with the nobles of
Judah, and said to them, "What evil thing
is this that you do, by which you profane
the Sabbath day? 18 [a]Did not your fathers
do thus, and did not our God bring all this
disaster on us and on this city? Yet you
bring added wrath on Israel by profaning
the Sabbath."
19 So it was, at the gates of Jerusalem, as
it [a]began to be dark before the Sabbath,
that I commanded the gates to be shut,
and charged that they must not be opened
till after the Sabbath. [b]Then I posted *some*
of my servants at the gates, *so that* no
burdens would be brought in on the Sabbath day. 20 Now the merchants and sellers
of all kinds of [1]wares [2]lodged outside Jerusalem once or twice.
21 Then I warned them, and said to
them, "Why do you spend the night
[1]around the wall? If you do *so* again, I will
lay hands on you!" From that time on they
came no *more* on the Sabbath. 22 And I
commanded the Levites that [a]they should
cleanse themselves, and that they should
go and guard the gates, to sanctify the
Sabbath day.
Remember me, O my God, *concerning*
this also, and spare me according to the
greatness of Your mercy!
23 In those days I also saw Jews *who*
[a]had married women of [b]Ashdod, Ammon, *and* Moab. 24 And half of their children spoke the language of Ashdod, and
could not speak the language of Judah,
but spoke according to the language of
one or the other people.
25 So I [a]contended with them and
[1]cursed them, struck some of them and
pulled out their hair, and made them
[b]swear by God, *saying,* "You shall not give
your daughters as wives to their sons, nor
take their daughters for your sons or
yourselves. 26 [a]Did not Solomon king of
Israel sin by these things? Yet among
many nations there was no king like him,
[b]who was beloved of his God; and God
made him king over all Israel. [c]Neverthe-
less pagan women caused even him to sin.
27 Should we then hear of your doing all
this great evil, [a]transgressing against our
God by marrying pagan women?"
28 And *one* of the sons [a]of Joiada, the
son of Eliashib the high priest, *was* a son-
in-law of [b]Sanballat the Horonite; therefore I drove him from me.
29 [a]Remember them, O my God, because they have defiled the priesthood and
[b]the covenant of the priesthood and the
Levites.
30 [a]Thus I cleansed them of everything
pagan. I also [b]assigned duties to the
priests and the Levites, each to his service,
31 and *to bringing* [a]the wood offering and
the firstfruits at appointed times.
[b]Remember me, O my God, for good!

13 [b]1 Cor. 4:2
14 [a]Neh. 5:19; 13:22, 31
15 [a][Ex. 20:10] [b][Jer. 17:21]
18 [a][Jer. 17:21]
19 [a]Lev. 23:32 [b]Jer. 17:21, 22
20 *[1]merchandise [2]spent the night*
21 [1]Lit. *before*
22 [a]Neh. 12:30
23 [a]Ezra 9:2 [b]Neh. 4:7
25 [a]Prov. 28:4 [b]Neh. 10:29, 30 *[1]pronounced them cursed*
26 [a]1 Kin. 11:1, 2 [b]2 Sam. 12:24, 25 [c]1 Kin. 11:4–8
27 [a][Ezra 10:2]
28 [a]Neh. 12:10, 12 [b]Neh. 4:1, 7; 6:1, 2
29 [a]Neh. 6:14 [b]Mal. 2:4, 11, 12
30 [a]Neh. 10:30 [b]Neh. 12:1
31 [a]Neh. 10:34 [b]Neh. 13:14, 22

AUTHOR: *Unknown*
DATE: *Shortly After 465 B.C.*
THEME: *Teamwork That Shaped a Nation*
KEY WORDS: *Humility, Interdependence, the Fear of God*

ESTHER

Dear Woman of Destiny,

A true woman of destiny, Esther was willing to risk her own life for the welfare of her people and the furthering of God's plan. God strategically placed her to influence individuals and situations for His glory. As you read, ask God to reveal the divine opportunities that He has placed before you. Like Esther, you have been created for such a time as this!

His love and mine,

Marilyn Hickey

The King Dethrones Queen Vashti

Now it came to pass in the days of
[a]Ahasuerus[1] (this *was* the Ahasuerus who reigned [b]over one hundred and twenty-seven provinces, [c]from
India to Ethiopia), 2in those days when
King Ahasuerus [a]sat on the throne of his
kingdom, which *was* in [b]Shushan[1] the
[2]citadel, 3*that* in the third year of his
reign he [a]made a feast for all his officials
and servants—the powers of Persia and
Media, the nobles, and the princes of the
provinces *being* before him— 4when he
showed the riches of his glorious kingdom and the splendor of his excellent
majesty for many days, one hundred and
eighty days *in all.*

5And when these days were completed,
the king made a feast lasting seven days
for all the people who were present in
[1]Shushan the [2]citadel, from great to
small, in the court of the garden of the
king's palace. 6*There were* white and blue
linen *curtains* fastened with cords of fine
linen and purple on silver rods and marble pillars; *and the* [a]couches *were* of gold
and silver on a *mosaic* pavement of alabaster, turquoise, and white and black
marble. 7And they served drinks in golden
vessels, each vessel being different from
the other, with royal wine in abundance,
[a]according to the [1]generosity of the king.
8In accordance with the law, the drinking
was not compulsory; for so the king had
ordered all the officers of his household,
that they should do according to each
man's pleasure.

9Queen Vashti also made a feast for the
women *in* the royal palace which *belonged* to King Ahasuerus.

10On the seventh day, when the heart of
the king was merry with wine, he commanded Mehuman, Biztha, [a]Harbona,
Bigtha, Abagtha, Zethar, and Carcas, sev-
en eunuchs who served in the presence of
King Ahasuerus, 11to bring Queen Vashti
before the king, *wearing* her royal crown,
in order to show her beauty to the people
and the officials, for she *was* beautiful to
behold. 12But Queen Vashti refused to
come at the king's command *brought* by
his eunuchs; therefore the king was furious, and his anger burned within him.

13Then the king said to the [a]wise men
[b]who understood the times (for this *was*
the king's manner toward all who knew
law and justice, 14those closest to him
being Carshena, Shethar, Admatha, Tarshish, Meres, Marsena, and Memucan, the
[a]seven princes of Persia and Media, [b]who
had access to the king's presence, *and*
who [1]ranked highest in the kingdom):
15"What *shall we* do to Queen Vashti, according to law, because she did not obey
the command of King Ahasuerus *brought
to her* by the eunuchs?"

16And Memucan answered before the
king and the princes: "Queen Vashti has
not only wronged the king, but also all the
princes, and all the people who *are* in all
the provinces of King Ahasuerus. 17For
the queen's behavior will become known
to all women, so that they will [a]despise
their husbands in their eyes, when they
report, 'King Ahasuerus commanded
Queen Vashti to be brought in before him,
but she did not come.' 18This very day the
noble ladies of Persia and Media will say to
all the king's officials that they have heard
of the behavior of the queen. Thus *there
will be* excessive contempt and wrath. 19If
it pleases the king, let a royal [1]decree go
out from him, and let it be recorded in the
laws of the Persians and the Medes, so
that it will [a]not [2]be altered, that Vashti
shall come no more before King Ahasuerus; and let the king give her royal position to another who is better than she.
20When the king's decree which he will
make is proclaimed throughout all his
empire (for it is great), all wives will [a]hon-
or their husbands, both great and small."

21And the reply pleased the king and
the princes, and the king did according to
the word of Memucan. 22Then he sent letters to all the king's provinces, [a]to each
province in its own script, and to every
people in their own language, that each
man should [b]be master in his own house,
and speak in the language of his own
people.

Esther Becomes Queen

2 After these things, when the wrath
of King Ahasuerus subsided, he remembered Vashti, [a]what she had done,
and what had been decreed against her.
2Then the king's servants who attended
him said: "Let beautiful young virgins be
sought for the king; 3and let the king appoint officers in all the provinces of his
kingdom, that they may gather all the
beautiful young virgins to [1]Shushan the
[2]citadel, into the women's quarters,

CHAPTER 1
1 a Ezra 4:6 b Esth. 8:9 c Dan. 6:1 *1* Generally identified with Xerxes I (485–464 B.C.)
2 a 1 Kin. 1:46 b Neh. 1:1 *1* Or *Susa* *2* Or *fortified palace,* and so elsewhere in the book
3 a Gen. 40:20
5 *1* Or *Susa* *2 palace*
6 a Amos 2:8; 6:4
7 a Esth. 2:18 *1* Lit. *hand*
10 a Esth. 7:9
13 a Dan. 2:12 b 1 Chr. 12:32
14 a Ezra 7:14 b 2 Kin. 25:19 *1* Lit. *sat in first place*
17 a [Eph. 5:33]
19 a Esth. 8:8 *1* Lit. *word* *2 pass away*
20 a [Col. 3:18]
22 a Esth. 3:12; 8:9 b [Eph. 5:22–24]

CHAPTER 2
1 a Esth. 1:19, 20
3 *1* Or *Susa* *2 palace*

ESTHER 2:1–8

Dear Woman of Destiny,

What will you do when Jesus, your King, calls? The lives of Vashti and Esther—two women in Old Testament times who were a lot like us—illustrate the two choices we can make: We can refuse to respond when He invites us to come to Him, or we can answer, "I will."

King Ahasuerus and Queen Vashti were the crème de la crème of the land, and they were throwing a party—a royal banquet, to be exact. The king was upon his throne while Queen Vashti and her court were being entertained in another part of the palace. In the middle of the celebration, the king sent his servants scurrying with the command, "Tell Vashti that I, her king, require her immediate presence."

Imagine the servants' surprise when Queen Vashti, in front of everyone, said no to the king's command! The queen telling the king no? A wife telling her husband no? It was unheard of!

We could question the king's motives and the "political correctness" of his method. But what he wanted and why didn't matter. What mattered was that he called Vashti and she refused to come.

How many of us have refused the Lord when He has summoned us into His presence? He's called us over and over again, and we've told Him no just as many times in just as many ways.

What does He want? *What does it matter?* He has called!

Queen Vashti lost her crown and was banished because she refused her king. Fortunately for us, our King is the God of second chance. The Scriptures say that God is "married" to the backslider (see Jer. 3:14); and even though we may refuse to appear before Him, His mind is still set on us.

Esther was an unknown orphan when she chose to answer a call she did not yet fully understand. She became queen to King Ahasuerus, just as if she were the heroine in a fairy tale.

No doubt Esther did not come into the king's presence offering a list of excuses. Don't make the mistake of responding to the call of God by telling Him who you're *not* and what you *can't* do. He *knows* you—and He calls you anyway.

When the king called Esther, she responded, "I will." Later, when she asked to see him, he extended his royal scepter to her and declared, "Whatever you request is yours, Queen Esther." Rising to the occasion, she asked that her people, the nation of Israel living in captivity, be saved from annihilation. Her wish was granted, and she became known throughout history as a great deliverer.

Today, God is calling you "queen." You may not feel like a queen; you may not look like a queen; you may not deserve to be a queen. But the scepter is still extended to you. God is saying, "If you but answer My call, you can ask whatever you want, and it shall be done for you."

Serita Jakes

under the custody of [3]Hegai the king's eunuch, custodian of the women. And let beauty preparations be given *them.* 4 Then let the young woman who pleases the king be queen instead of Vashti."

This thing pleased the king, and he did so.

5 In [1]Shushan the [2]citadel there was a certain Jew whose name *was* Mordecai the son of Jair, the son of Shimei, the son of [a]Kish, a Benjamite. 6 [a]*Kish*[1] had been carried away from Jerusalem with the captives who had been captured with [2]Jeconiah king of Judah, whom Nebuchadnezzar the king of Babylon had carried away. 7 And *Mordecai* had brought up Hadassah, that *is,* Esther, [a]his uncle's daughter, for she had neither father nor mother. The young woman *was* lovely and beautiful. When her father and mother died, Mordecai took her as his own daughter.

8 So it was, when the king's command and decree were heard, and when many young women were [a]gathered at [1]Shushan the [2]citadel, *under* the custody of Hegai, that Esther also was taken to the king's palace, into the care of Hegai the custodian of the women. 9 Now the young woman pleased him, and she obtained his favor; so he readily gave [a]beauty preparations to her, besides [1]her allowance. Then seven choice maidservants were provided for her from the king's palace, and he moved her and her maidservants to the best *place* in the house of the women.

10 [a]Esther had not [1]revealed her people or family, for Mordecai had charged her not to reveal *it.* 11 And every day Mordecai paced in front of the court of the women's quarters, to learn of Esther's welfare and what was happening to her.

12 Each young woman's turn came to go in to King Ahasuerus after she had completed twelve months' preparation, according to the regulations for the women, for thus were the days of their preparation apportioned: six months with oil of myrrh, and six months with perfumes and preparations for beautifying women. 13 Thus *prepared, each* young woman went to the king, and she was given whatever she desired to take with her from the women's quarters to the king's palace. 14 In the evening she went, and in the morning she returned to the second house of the women, to the custody of Shaashgaz, the king's eunuch who kept the concubines. She would not go in to the king again unless the king delighted in her and called for her by name.

15 Now when the turn came for Esther [a]the daughter of Abihail the uncle of Mordecai, who had taken her as his daughter, to go in to the king, she requested nothing but what Hegai the king's eunuch, the custodian of the women, advised. And Esther [b]obtained favor in the sight of all who saw her. 16 So Esther was taken to King Ahasuerus, into his royal palace, in the tenth month, which *is* the month of Tebeth, in the seventh year of his reign. 17 The king loved Esther more than all the *other* women, and she obtained grace and favor in his sight more than all the virgins; so he set the royal [a]crown upon her head and made her queen instead of Vashti. 18 Then the king [a]made a great feast, the Feast of Esther, for all his officials and servants; and he proclaimed a holiday in the provinces and gave gifts according to the [1]generosity of a king.

May _____ obtain grace and favor in Your sight, O Lord.

FROM ESTHER 2:17

Mordecai Discovers a Plot

19 When virgins were gathered together a second time, Mordecai sat within the king's gate. 20 [a]*Now* Esther had not revealed her family and her people, just as Mordecai had charged her, for Esther obeyed the command of Mordecai as when she was brought up by him.

21 In those days, while Mordecai sat within the king's gate, two of the king's eunuchs, [1]Bigthan and Teresh, doorkeepers, became furious and sought to lay hands on King Ahasuerus. 22 So the matter became known to Mordecai, [a]who told Queen Esther, and Esther informed the king in Mordecai's name. 23 And when an inquiry was made into the matter, it was confirmed, and both were hanged on a gallows; and it was written in [a]the book of the chronicles in the presence of the king.

3 [3]Heb. *Hege*
5 [a]1 Sam. 9:1 [1]Or *Susa* [2]*palace*
6 [a]2 Kin. 24:14, 15 [1]Lit. *Who* [2]*Jehoiachin,* 2 Kin. 24:6
7 [a]Esth. 2:15
8 [a]Esth. 2:3 [1]Or *Susa* [2]*palace*
9 [a]Esth. 2:3, 12 [1]Lit. *her portions*
10 [a]Esth. 2:20 [1]Revealed the identity of
15 [a]Esth. 2:7; 9:29 [b]Esth. 5:2, 8
17 [a]Esth. 1:11
18 [a]Esth. 1:3 [1]Lit. *hand*
20 [a]Esth. 2:10
21 [1]*Bigthana,* Esth. 6:2
22 [a]Esth. 6:1, 2
23 [a]Esth. 6:1

Esther 4:4–8

Dear Woman of Destiny,

Your prayers can affect your nation!

Esther was an orphaned child of the captivity of her people, brought up by a guardian, her cousin Mordecai. She was an alert and beautiful daughter of God who overcame many struggles and replaced the Queen of Persia. In a dramatic encounter with her husband, the king, Esther was granted a release for the Jews in all the provinces of her nation, and saved her people from certain death.

Woman of Destiny, if you hope to impact a nation, you must *be prepared*. Before she approached the king, Esther allowed time for purification—a year-long ritual of beauty treatments, special diet, and hot baths. When the preparation was complete, she was brought forth at a strategic time for God's purposes and plans to be fully accomplished.

Woman of Destiny, in whatever way God is at work in you, submit to the process, and allow God to bring His purification. Obedience to God advances your life.

Make no demands. Esther could have asked for anything she wanted, but she asked for nothing for herself when her turn came. Instead, she waited to be appointed and showed an unassuming manner of humility and submission by seeking counsel from Hegai, the king's eunuch. She requested nothing but what he advised. Esther did not resort to beauty aids, yet she won the prize.

Woman of Destiny, be willing to be mentored—even to the point of accepting advice on how to dress for the King's business.

Pray to grow in grace each day. Esther honored Mordecai, pleased Hegai (the court custodian), and won the king's heart. He loved her more than all the other women in the palace and made her his queen.

Woman of Destiny, when promotion comes and you are elevated to rule, remember to be gracious to your benefactors and those who helped you to advance.

Don't value your own life too highly. Esther presented herself unbidden to the king to plead the case of her people and nation. She could have been killed! Esther was aware of the plans of the enemy, but she remained faithful and in step with God's purpose, and did not falter.

Woman of Destiny, don't be afraid when the stakes are high. Your life is in God's hands. Trust Him. Be strong and courageous.

Recognize and answer God's call. Become an expert in hearing God's voice. The Holy Spirit will help you every day, so be strengthened in your faith. As you respond and submit to God's timing, you will overcome.

Woman of Destiny, you can have a lasting impact on the history of your nation. Who knows if you have come to the kingdom for such a time as this?

Julie Anderson

Haman's Conspiracy Against the Jews

3 After these things King Ahasuerus promoted Haman, the son of Hammedatha the [a]Agagite, and [b]advanced him and set his seat above all the princes who *were* with him. [2]And all the king's servants who *were* [a]within the king's gate bowed and paid homage to Haman, for so the king had commanded concerning him. But Mordecai [b]would not bow or pay homage. [3]Then the king's servants who *were* within the king's gate said to Mordecai, "Why do you transgress the [a]king's command?" [4]Now it happened, when they spoke to him daily and he would not listen to them, that they told *it* to Haman, to see whether Mordecai's words would stand; for *Mordecai* had told them that he *was* a Jew. [5]When Haman saw that Mordecai [a]did not bow or pay him homage, Haman was [b]filled with wrath. [6]But he disdained to lay hands on Mordecai alone, for they had told him of the people of Mordecai. Instead, Haman [a]sought to destroy all the Jews who *were* throughout the whole kingdom of Ahasuerus—the people of Mordecai.

[7]In the first month, which is the month of Nisan, in the twelfth year of King Ahasuerus, [a]they cast Pur (that *is,* the lot), before Haman [1]to determine the day and the [2]month, [3]until *it fell on the* twelfth *month,* which *is* the month of Adar.

[8]Then Haman said to King Ahasuerus, "There is a certain people scattered and dispersed among the people in all the provinces of your kingdom; [a]their laws *are* different from all *other* people's, and they do not keep the king's laws. Therefore it *is* not fitting for the king to let them remain. [9]If it pleases the king, let *a decree* be written that they be destroyed, and I will pay ten thousand talents of silver into the hands of those who do the work, to bring *it* into the king's treasuries."

[10]So the king [a]took [b]his signet ring from his hand and gave it to Haman, the son of Hammedatha the Agagite, the [c]enemy of the Jews. [11]And the king said to Haman, "The money and the people *are* given to you, to do with them as seems good to you."

[12][a]Then the king's scribes were called on the thirteenth day of the first month, and *a decree* was written according to all that Haman commanded—to the king's satraps, to the governors who *were* over each province, to the officials of all people, to every province [b]according to its script, and to every people in their language. [c]In the name of King Ahasuerus it was written, and sealed with the king's signet ring. [13]And the letters were [a]sent by couriers into all the king's provinces, to destroy, to kill, and to annihilate all the Jews, both young and old, little children and women, [b]in one day, on the thirteenth *day* of the twelfth *month,* which *is* the month of Adar, and [c]to plunder their [1]possessions. [14][a]A copy of the document was to be issued as law in every province, being published for all people, that they should be ready for that day. [15]The couriers went out, hastened by the king's command; and the decree was proclaimed in [1]Shushan the [2]citadel. So the king and Haman sat down to drink, but [a]the city of Shushan was [3]perplexed.

Esther Agrees to Help the Jews

4 When Mordecai learned all that had happened, [1]he [a]tore his clothes and put on sackcloth [b]and ashes, and went out into the midst of the city. He [c]cried out with a loud and bitter cry. [2]He went as far as the front of the king's gate, for no one *might* enter the king's gate clothed with sackcloth. [3]And in every province where the king's command and decree arrived, *there was* great mourning among the Jews, with fasting, weeping, and wailing; and many lay in sackcloth and ashes.

[4]So Esther's maids and eunuchs came and told her, and the queen was deeply distressed. Then she sent garments to clothe Mordecai and take his sackcloth away from him, but he would not accept *them.* [5]Then Esther called Hathach, *one* of the king's eunuchs whom he had appointed to attend her, and she gave him a command concerning Mordecai, to learn what and why this *was.* [6]So Hathach went out to Mordecai in the city square that *was* in front of the king's gate. [7]And Mordecai told him all that had happened to him, and [a]the sum of money that Haman had promised to pay into the king's treasuries to destroy the Jews. [8]He also gave him [a]a copy of the written decree for their destruction, which was given at [1]Shushan, that he might show it to Esther and

CHAPTER 3
1 a Num. 24:7 b Esth. 5:11
2 a Esth. 2:19, 21; 5:9 b Ps. 15:4
3 a Esth. 3:2
5 a Esth. 3:2; 5:9 b Dan. 3:19
6 a Ps. 83:4
7 a Esth. 9:24–26 *1* Lit. *from day to day and month to month* *2* LXX adds *to destroy the people of Mordecai in one day;* Vg. adds *the nation of the Jews should be destroyed* *3* So with MT, Vg.; LXX *and the lot fell on the fourteenth of the month*
8 a Acts 16:20, 21
10 a Gen. 41:42 b Esth. 8:2, 8 c Esth. 7:6
12 a Esth. 8:9 b Esth. 1:22 c Esth. 8:8–10
13 a Esth. 8:10, 14 b Esth. 8:12 c Esth. 8:11; 9:10 *1* LXX adds the text of the letter here
14 a Esth. 8:13, 14
15 a Esth. 8:15 *1* Or *Susa* *2 palace* *3 in confusion*

CHAPTER 4
1 a 2 Sam. 1:11 b Josh. 7:6 c Gen. 27:34 *1* Lit. *Mordecai*
7 a Esth. 3:9
8 a Esth. 3:14, 15 *1* Or *Susa*

explain it to her, and that he might command her to go in to the king to make
supplication to him and plead before him
for her people. 9 So Hathach returned
and told Esther the words of Mordecai.
10 Then Esther spoke to Hathach, and
gave him a command for Mordecai: 11 "All
the king's servants and the people of the
king's provinces know that any man or
woman who goes into [a]the inner court to
the king, who has not been called, [b]*he has*
but one law: put *all* to death, except the
one [c]to whom the king holds out the
golden scepter, that he may live. Yet I myself have not been [d]called to go in to the
king these thirty days." 12 So they told
Mordecai Esther's words.
13 And Mordecai told *them* to answer
Esther: "Do not think in your heart that
you will escape in the king's palace any
more than all the other Jews. 14 For if
you remain completely silent at this time,
relief and deliverance will arise for the
Jews from another place, but you and
your father's house will perish. Yet who
knows whether you have come to the
kingdom for *such* a time as this?"

Lord, may ___ rise to the challenge before them, for You may have placed them, like Esther, in this situation for such a time as this.

FROM ESTHER 4:14

15 Then Esther told *them* to reply to
Mordecai: 16 "Go, gather all the Jews who
are present in [1]Shushan, and fast for me;
neither eat nor drink for [a]three days,
night or day. My maids and I will fast likewise. And so I will go to the king, which
is against the law; [b]and if I perish, I
perish!"
17 So Mordecai went his way and did
according to all that Esther commanded
[1]him.

Esther's Banquet

5 Now it happened [a]on the third day
that Esther put on *her* royal *robes* and
stood in [b]the inner court of the king's palace, across from the king's house, while
the king sat on his royal throne in the
royal house, facing the entrance of the
[1]house. 2 So it was, when the king saw
Queen Esther standing in the court, *that*
[a]she found favor in his sight, and [b]the
king held out to Esther the golden scepter
that *was* in his hand. Then Esther went
near and touched the top of the scepter.

It is high time for women to let their lights shine; to bring out their talents that have been hidden away rusting, and use them for the glory of God, and do with their might what their hands find to do, trusting God for strength, who has said, "I will never leave you."

MARIA WOODWORTH-ETTER

3 And the king said to her, "What do you
wish, Queen Esther? What *is* your request? [a]It shall be given to you—up to
half the kingdom!"
4 So Esther answered, "If it pleases the
king, let the king and Haman come today
to the banquet that I have prepared for
him."
5 Then the king said, "Bring Haman
quickly, that he may do as Esther has
said." So the king and Haman went to the
banquet that Esther had prepared.
6 At the banquet of wine [a]the king
said to Esther, [b]"What *is* your petition?
It shall be granted you. What *is* your request, up to half the kingdom? It shall be
done!"
7 Then Esther answered and said, "My
petition and request *is this:* 8 If I have
found favor in the sight of the king, and
if it pleases the king to grant my petition
and [1]fulfill my request, then let the king
and Haman come to the [a]banquet which
I will prepare for them, and tomorrow I
will do as the king has said."

11 a Esth. 5:1; 6:4 b Dan. 2:9 c Esth. 5:2; 8:4 d Esth. 2:14
16 a Esth. 5:1 b Gen. 43:14 *1* Or *Susa*
17 *1* LXX adds a prayer of Mordecai here

CHAPTER 5
1 a Esth. 4:16 b Esth. 4:11; 6:4 *1* LXX adds many extra details in vv. 1, 2
2 a [Prov. 21:1] b Esth. 4:11; 8:4
3 a Mark 6:23
6 a Esth. 7:2 b Esth. 9:12
8 a Esth. 6:14 *1* Lit. *to do*

Esther 4:14

Dear Woman of Destiny,

In July of 1968, I married the man of my dreams, John; and we have been in the ministry for thirty years. Through the years of our pastorates, I saw a lot of "living in the flesh," was hurt, and put up walls around myself. I had my own fears and insecurities; and I faced them with no friend to trust, no colleagues to share with. I would cry out to God for help and read His Word, but I knew I was not experiencing His peace and joy. I would pray, "Lord, something is wrong with me. If You will show me, I will repent." In prior years, when He spoke, I knew His voice; but now He seemed so far away and silent. I tried to live the best I knew how, but it seemed I had failed.

Four months before revival came to our Brownsville Assembly of God Church, I had a sudden encounter with the Lord. I went to Toronto and was prayed for. This intense heat came on my head and stopped at my neck. I was touched by His glory and was set free. He truly delivered me from all my fears (see Ps. 34:4–6).

I began to experience intimacy I never knew possible. Instead of offering prayer, I was being drawn in with an anticipation that was there as never before. I would get up early and sit in His presence for hours. Waves of His glory would flow over my body. Tears of gratitude would run down my face as I worshiped the Lord. It was like I was born again all over. I found a new language of love—silence. There was a love so deep between us, no words were spoken. He had quieted me in His love (see Zeph. 3:17). I was changed forever! Now I would be His radiant bride and fulfill my destiny.

The Book of Esther tells the story of a king throwing a celebration for the leaders of his nation. He calls for his bride, Vashti, to come and show her beauty. She refuses to come; she's too busy throwing a party for women.

Today our King is calling His bride to come forth and show her beauty, but many of us are like Vashti and don't understand our purpose in life. Vashti was beautiful, but aimless. Not so with Esther. Mordecai—a depiction of the Holy Spirit—had been grooming her for the day when she would show forth her beauty and save her people. She had a divine calling and destiny. Esther was willing to die for what she believed in, and she had been brought to the kingdom "for such a time as this."

This is the greatest time for women. It's a time the King of all kings is calling us out of apathy, self-centeredness, and feelings of inadequacies. The Deborahs are awakening, and the Baraks are rising up—the two working together in oneness. This is to be an army of the Lord arising with signs and wonders as our signature. His purity will be our garments, the beauty of His holiness our mirror, and His touch our anointing to a desperate and hungry world.

Brenda Kilpatrick

Haman's Plot Against Mordecai

[9]So Haman went out that day [a]joyful
and with a glad heart; but when Haman
saw Mordecai in the king's gate, and [b]that
he did not stand or tremble before him, he
was filled with indignation against Mordecai. [10]Nevertheless Haman [a]restrained
himself and went home, and he sent and
called for his friends and his wife Zeresh.
[11]Then Haman told them of his great
riches, [a]the multitude of his children, everything in which the king had promoted
him, and how he had [b]advanced him
above the officials and servants of the
king.
[12]Moreover Haman said, "Besides,
Queen Esther invited no one but me to
come in with the king to the banquet that
she prepared; and tomorrow I am again
invited by her, along with the king. [13]Yet
all this avails me nothing, so long as I see
Mordecai the Jew sitting at the king's
gate."
[14]Then his wife Zeresh and all his
friends said to him, "Let a [a]gallows[1] be
made, [2]fifty cubits high, and in the morning [b]suggest to the king that Mordecai be

9 a [Job 20:5] b Esth. 3:5
10 a 2 Sam. 13:22
11 a Esth. 9:7–10 b Esth. 3:1
14 a Esth. 7:9 b Esth. 6:4 *1* Lit. *tree* or *wood* *2* About 75 feet

Mary Slessor

Before there were officially women's rights, there was Mary Slessor (1848–1915). As a missionary, Slessor changed the lives of thousands of women across West Africa, literally freeing many of whom were slaves under ancient tribal laws.

Slessor grew up in a suburb of Aberdeen, Scotland, the daughter of an alcoholic father and a domineering mother. Although her mother discouraged her, saying missionary work was for men only, Mary set out to prepare herself for the mission field after the death of her second brother. Much like her hero David Livingstone, she worked twelve- to fourteen-hour days as a weaver, while also studying, attending church meetings at night and leading Sunday school classes. When Livingstone died, she took that as a sign that her time had come, and, in 1875, was assigned to Calabar by the Foreign Mission Board.

Slessor's years in Nigeria coincided with one of the most turbulent periods of the country's history. The conflict between new order and ancient traditions was seen everywhere. Slessor's greatest concerns were in overcoming the human sacrifice that routinely followed the death of a village leader, the ritual murder of twins, and the abhorrent treatment of women as property less valuable than cattle. Unlike many missionaries at the time, Slessor lived in native style and spoke the local Efik language. She was quick to serve, and thus received the respect she needed to gradually liberate the natives from their superstitions.

As soon as missionaries came to support her, Mary urged the Mission Board to send her further inland. Knowing she was risking her life, she felt driven by her call and was gifted with the ability to quickly establish relationship with tribes who had never seen a white person. By integrating herself into the tribal culture, Slessor became a mother among the tribes, earning her nickname of "Ma." As women of destiny, may we, too, possess the courage, determination, and belief in God's faithfulness that will allow us to impact the world around us.

hanged on it; then go merrily with the
king to the banquet."
And the thing pleased Haman; so he
had [c]the gallows made.

The King Honors Mordecai

6 That night [1]the king could not sleep.
So one was commanded to bring [a]the
book of the records of the chronicles; and
they were read before the king. 2And it
was found written that Mordecai had told
of [1]Bigthana and Teresh, two of the king's
eunuchs, the doorkeepers who had
sought to lay hands on King Ahasuerus.
3Then the king said, "What honor or dignity has been bestowed on Mordecai for
this?"
And the king's servants who attended
him said, "Nothing has been done for
him."
4So the king said, "Who *is* in the
court?" Now Haman had *just* entered [a]the
outer court of the king's palace [b]to suggest that the king hang Mordecai on the
gallows that he had prepared for him.
5The king's servants said to him, "Haman is there, standing in the court."
And the king said, "Let him come in."
6So Haman came in, and the king asked
him, "What shall be done for the man
whom the king delights to honor?"
Now Haman thought in his heart,
"Whom would the king delight to honor
more than [a]me?" 7And Haman answered
the king, "*For* the man whom the king
delights to honor, 8let a royal robe be
brought which the king has worn, and [a]a
horse on which the king has ridden,
which has a royal [1]crest placed on its
head. 9Then let this robe and horse be delivered to the hand of one of the king's
most noble princes, that he may array the
man whom the king delights to honor.
Then [1]parade him on horseback through
the city square, [a]and proclaim before him:
'Thus shall it be done to the man whom
the king delights to honor!' "
10Then the king said to Haman, "Hurry,
take the robe and the horse, as you have
suggested, and do so for Mordecai the Jew
who sits within the king's gate! Leave
nothing undone of all that you have
spoken."
11So Haman took the robe and the
horse, arrayed Mordecai and led him on
horseback through the city square, and
proclaimed before him, "Thus shall it be

14 [c]Esth. 7:10

CHAPTER 6
1 [a]Esth. 2:23; 10:2
[1] Lit. *the king's sleep fled away*
2 [1] *Bigthan,* Esth. 2:21
4 [a]Esth. 5:1
[b]Esth. 5:14
6 [a][Prov. 16:18; 18:12]
8 [a]1 Kin. 1:33
[1] *crown*
9 [a]Gen. 41:43
[1] Lit. *cause him to ride*
12 [a]2 Chr. 26:20
[b]2 Sam. 15:30
13 [a]Zech. 2:8
14 [a]Esth. 5:8

CHAPTER 7
2 [a]Esth. 5:6
4 [a]Esth. 3:9; 4:7
[b]Deut. 28:68

done to the man whom the king delights
to honor!"
12Afterward Mordecai went back to the
king's gate. But Haman [a]hurried to his
house, mourning [b]and with his head covered. 13When Haman told his wife Zeresh
and all his friends everything that had
happened to him, his wise men and his
wife Zeresh said to him, "If Mordecai, before whom you have begun to fall, is of
Jewish descent, you will not prevail
against [a]him but will surely fall before
him."
14While they *were* still talking with
him, the king's eunuchs came, and hastened to bring Haman to [a]the banquet
which Esther had prepared.

Haman Hanged Instead of Mordecai

7 So the king and Haman went to dine
with Queen Esther. 2And on the second day, [a]at the banquet of wine, the king
again said to Esther, "What *is* your petition, Queen Esther? It shall be granted
you. And what *is* your request, up to half
the kingdom? It shall be done!"
3Then Queen Esther answered and said,
"If I have found favor in your sight,
O king, and if it pleases the king, let my
life be given me at my petition, and my
people at my request. 4For we have been
[a]sold, my people and I, to be destroyed, to
be killed, and to be annihilated. Had we
been sold as [b]male and female slaves, I
would have held my tongue, although the
enemy could never compensate for the
king's loss."

Many pray about their needs and keep on praying as though they did not believe, and in consequence pray themselves out of faith.

GORDON LINDSAY

5So King Ahasuerus answered and said
to Queen Esther, "Who is he, and where is
he, who would dare presume in his heart
to do such a thing?"

6 And Esther said, "The adversary and
[a]enemy *is* this wicked Haman!"
So Haman was terrified before the king
and queen.
7 Then the king arose in his wrath from
the banquet of wine *and went* into the
palace garden; but Haman stood before
Queen Esther, pleading for his life, for he
saw that evil was determined against him
by the king. 8 When the king returned
from the palace garden to the place of the
banquet of wine, Haman had fallen across
[a]the couch where Esther *was*. Then the
king said, "Will he also assault the queen
while I *am* in the house?"
As the word left the king's mouth, they
[b]covered Haman's face. 9 Now [a]Harbonah,
one of the eunuchs, said to the king,
"Look! [b]The [1]gallows, fifty cubits high,
which Haman made for Mordecai, who
spoke [c]good on the king's behalf, is standing at the house of Haman."
Then the king said, "Hang him on it!"
10 So [a]they [b]hanged Haman on the gallows that he had prepared for Mordecai.
Then the king's wrath subsided.

Esther Saves the Jews

8 On that day King Ahasuerus gave
Queen Esther the house of Haman,
the [a]enemy of the Jews. And Mordecai
came before the king, for Esther had told

6 [a] Esth. 3:10
8 [a] Esth. 1:6 [b] Job 9:24
9 [a] Esth. 1:10 [b] Esth. 5:14 [c] Esth. 6:2 [1] Lit. *tree* or *wood*
10 [a] [Ps. 7:16; 94:23] [b] Dan. 6:24
CHAPTER 8
1 [a] Esth. 7:6

ESTHER

Esther exhibits several qualities that make a woman great: humility, wisdom, compassion, and courage. She had also learned how and when to exert her influence, and had the favor of her king.

Most likely, God's ultimate destiny for Esther was to use her to rescue an entire nation from certain destruction. Just as Esther had been prepared physically to become queen, God had prepared her spiritually to the point that He could trust her to ensure the deliverance of His beloved people.

Having lived so much of her life with her cousin Mordecai as her guardian, Esther had learned to submit to the wisdom of this man who clearly wanted nothing but the best for her. Throughout her story their long-established mentoring relationship continued. In fact, it was Mordecai who challenged her to embrace her destiny, saying, "Yet who knows whether you have come to the kingdom for such a time as this?" (Esth. 4:14b). With Mordecai, Esther displayed humility and wisdom as she sought and heeded his good counsel.

When Esther learned of Haman's plot to destroy her people, she continued her contact with Mordecai and was immediately moved to such deep compassion for her people that she called the Jews in Shushan to a three-day fast and joined them, seeking God and preparing herself for a strategic spiritual battle.

One key to accomplishing the purposes of God is knowing how and when to exert influence. Esther repeatedly demonstrated humility and honor as she addressed the king, saying, "If it pleases the king . . . ." She also approached him with passion and conviction when she fell before him weeping for her nation, begging him to let them live. And it worked. Not only were the Jews delivered, but Haman was killed.

God is calling Esthers to His kingdom today. Let us pray that He will give us the humility, wisdom, compassion, and courage of Queen Esther. And may we continually find favor in the eyes of our King.

[b]how he *was related* to her. 2So the king
took off [a]his signet ring, which he had
taken from Haman, and gave it to Mordecai; and Esther appointed Mordecai over
the house of Haman.
3Now Esther spoke again to the king,
fell down at his feet, and implored him
with tears to counteract the evil of Haman
the Agagite, and the scheme which he had
devised against the Jews. 4And [a]the king
held out the golden scepter toward Esther. So Esther arose and stood before the
king, 5and said, "If it pleases the king, and
if I have found favor in his sight and the
thing *seems* right to the king and I am
pleasing in his eyes, let it be written to
revoke the [a]letters devised by Haman, the
son of Hammedatha the Agagite, which he
wrote to annihilate the Jews who *are* in all
the king's provinces. 6For how can I endure to see [a]the evil that will come to my
people? Or how can I endure to see the
destruction of my countrymen?"
7Then King Ahasuerus said to Queen
Esther and Mordecai the Jew, "Indeed, [a]I
have given Esther the house of Haman,
and they have hanged him on the gallows
because he *tried to* lay his hand on the
Jews. 8You yourselves write *a decree* concerning the Jews, [1]as you please, in the
king's name, and seal *it* with the king's
signet ring; for whatever is written in the
king's name and sealed with the king's
signet ring [a]no one can revoke."
9[a]So the king's scribes were called at
that time, in the third month, which *is*
the month of Sivan, on the twenty-third
day; and it was written, according to all
that Mordecai commanded, to the Jews,
the satraps, the governors, and the princes of the provinces [b]from India to Ethiopia, one hundred and twenty-seven
provinces *in all,* to every province [c]in its
own script, to every people in their own
language, and to the Jews in their own
script and language. 10[a]And he wrote in
the name of King Ahasuerus, sealed *it*
with the king's signet ring, and sent letters by couriers on horseback, riding on
royal horses [1]bred from swift steeds.
11By these letters the king permitted
the Jews who *were* in every city to [a]gather
together and protect their lives—to [b]de-
stroy, kill, and annihilate all the forces of
any people or province that would assault
them, *both* little children and women,
and to plunder their possessions, 12[a]on
one day in all the provinces of King Ahasuerus, on the thirteenth *day* of the twelfth
month, which *is* the month of [1]Adar. 13[a]A
copy of the document was to be issued as
a decree in every province and published
for all people, so that the Jews would be
ready on that day to avenge themselves on
their enemies. 14The couriers who rode
on royal horses went out, hastened and
pressed on by the king's command. And
the decree was issued in [1]Shushan the
[2]citadel.
15So Mordecai went out from the presence of the king in royal apparel of [1]blue
and white, with a great crown of gold and
a garment of fine linen and purple; and
[a]the city of [2]Shushan rejoiced and was
glad. 16The Jews had [a]light and gladness,
joy and honor. 17And in every province
and city, wherever the king's command
and decree came, the Jews had joy and
gladness, a feast [a]and a holiday. Then
many of the people of the land [b]became
Jews, because [c]fear of the Jews fell upon
them.

The Jews Destroy Their Tormentors

9 Now [a]in the twelfth month, that *is,*
the month of Adar, on the thirteenth
day, [b]*the time* came for the king's command and his decree to be executed. On
the day that the enemies of the Jews had
hoped to overpower them, the opposite
occurred, in that the Jews themselves
[c]overpowered those who hated them.
2The Jews [a]gathered together in their cities throughout all the provinces of King
Ahasuerus to lay hands on those who
[b]sought their harm. And no one could
withstand them, [c]because fear of them fell
upon all people. 3And all the officials of
the provinces, the satraps, the governors,
and all those doing the king's work,
helped the Jews, because the fear of Mordecai fell upon them. 4For Mordecai *was*
great in the king's palace, and his fame
spread throughout all the provinces; for
this man Mordecai [a]became increasingly
prominent. 5Thus the Jews defeated all
their enemies with the stroke of the
sword, with slaughter and destruction,
and did what they pleased with those who
hated them.
6And in [a]Shushan[1] the [2]citadel the
Jews killed and destroyed five hundred
men. 7Also Parshandatha, Dalphon, Aspa-
tha, 8Poratha, Adalia, Aridatha, 9Parmash-
ta, Arisai, Aridai, and Vajezatha— 10[a]the

1 [b]Esth. 2:7, 15
2 [a]Esth. 3:10
4 [a]Esth. 4:11; 5:2
5 [a]Esth. 3:13
6 [a]Neh. 2:3
7 [a]Prov. 13:22
8 [a]Dan. 6:8, 12, 15 [1]Lit. *as is good in your eyes*
9 [a]Esth. 3:12 [b]Esth. 1:1 [c]Esth. 1:22; 3:12
10 [a]1 Kin. 21:8 [1]Lit. *sons of the swift horses*
11 [a]Esth. 9:2 [b]Esth. 9:10, 15, 16
12 [a]Esth. 3:13; 9:1 [1]LXX adds the text of the letter here
13 [a]Esth. 3:14, 15
14 [1]Or *Susa* [2]*palace*
15 [a]Prov. 29:2 [1]*violet* [2]Or *Susa*
16 [a]Ps. 97:11; 112:4
17 [a]Esth. 9:19 [b]Ps. 18:43 [c]Gen. 35:5

CHAPTER 9
1 [a]Esth. 8:12 [b]Esth. 3:13 [c]2 Sam. 22:41
2 [a]Esth. 8:11; 9:15–18 [b]Ps. 71:13, 14 [c]Esth. 8:17
4 [a]2 Sam. 3:1
6 [a]Esth. 1:2; 3:15; 4:16 [1]Or *Susa* [2]*palace*
10 [a]Esth. 5:11; 9:7–10

ten sons of Haman the son of Hammedatha, the enemy of the Jews—they killed;
[b]but they did not lay a hand on the
[1]plunder.
11On that day the number of those who
were killed in [1]Shushan the [2]citadel [3]was
brought to the king. 12And the king said
to Queen Esther, "The Jews have killed
and destroyed five hundred men in Shushan the citadel, and the ten sons of Haman. What have they done in the rest of
the king's provinces? Now [a]what *is* your
petition? It shall be granted to you. Or
what *is* your further request? It shall be
done."
13Then Esther said, "If it pleases the
king, let it be granted to the Jews who *are*
in Shushan to do again tomorrow [a]ac-
cording to today's decree, and let Haman's
ten sons [b]be hanged on the gallows."
14So the king commanded this to be
done; the decree was issued in Shushan,
and they hanged Haman's ten sons.
15And the Jews who *were* in [1]Shushan
[a]gathered together again on the fourteenth day of the month of Adar and killed
three hundred men at Shushan; [b]but they
did not lay a hand on the plunder.
16The remainder of the Jews in the
king's provinces [a]gathered together and
protected their lives, had rest from their
enemies, and killed seventy-five thousand
of their enemies; [b]but they did not lay a
hand on the plunder. 17*This was* on the
thirteenth day of the month of Adar. And
on the fourteenth of [1]*the month* they
rested and made it a day of feasting and
gladness.

The Feast of Purim

18But the Jews who *were* at [1]Shushan
assembled together [a]on the thirteenth
day, as well as on the fourteenth; and on
the fifteenth of [2]*the month* they rested,
and made it a day of feasting and gladness.
19Therefore the Jews of the villages who
dwelt in the unwalled towns celebrated
the fourteenth day of the month of Adar
[a]*with* gladness and feasting, [b]as a holiday,
and for [c]sending presents to one another.
20And Mordecai wrote these things and
sent letters to all the Jews, near and far,
who *were* in all the provinces of King
Ahasuerus, 21to establish among them
that they should celebrate yearly the fourteenth and fifteenth days of the month of
Adar, 22as the days on which the Jews had
rest from their enemies, as the month
which was turned from sorrow to joy for
them, and from mourning to a holiday;
that they should make them days of feasting and joy, of [a]sending presents to one
another and gifts to the [b]poor. 23So the
Jews accepted the custom which they had
begun, as Mordecai had written to them,
24because Haman, the son of Hammedatha the Agagite, the enemy of all the Jews,
[a]had plotted against the Jews to annihilate them, and had cast Pur (that *is,* the
lot), to consume them and destroy them;
25but [a]when [1]*Esther* came before the
king, he commanded by letter that [2]this
wicked plot which *Haman* had devised
against the Jews should [b]return on his
own head, and that he and his sons should
be hanged on the gallows.
26So they called these days Purim, after
the name [1]Pur. Therefore, because of all
the words of [a]this letter, what they had
seen concerning this matter, and what
had happened to them, 27the Jews established and imposed it upon themselves
and their descendants and all who would
[a]join them, that without fail they should
celebrate these two days every year, according to the written *instructions* and
according to the *prescribed* time, 28*that*
these days *should be* remembered and
kept throughout every generation, every
family, every province, and every city, that
these days of Purim should not fail *to be
observed* among the Jews, and *that* the
memory of them should not perish
among their descendants.
29Then Queen Esther, [a]the daughter
of Abihail, with Mordecai the Jew, wrote
with full authority to confirm this [b]sec-
ond letter about Purim. 30And *Mordecai*
sent letters to all the Jews, to [a]the one
hundred and twenty-seven provinces of
the kingdom of Ahasuerus, *with* words of
peace and truth, 31to confirm these days
of Purim at their *appointed* time, as Mordecai the Jew and Queen Esther had prescribed for them, and as they had decreed
for themselves and their descendants concerning matters of their [a]fasting and la-
menting. 32So the decree of Esther
confirmed these matters of Purim, and it
was written in the book.

Mordecai's Advancement

10 And King Ahasuerus imposed tribute on the land and *on* [a]the islands
of the sea. 2Now all the acts of his power
and his might, and the account of the

10 [b]Esth. 8:11 [1]*spoil*
11 [1]Or *Susa* [2]*palace* [3]Lit. *came*
12 [a]Esth. 5:6; 7:2
13 [a]Esth. 8:11; 9:15 [b]2 Sam. 21:6, 9
15 [a]Esth. 8:11; 9:2 [b]Esth. 9:10 [1]Or *Susa*
16 [a]Esth. 9:2 [b]Esth. 8:11
17 [1]Lit. *it*
18 [a]Esth. 9:11, 15 [1]Or *Susa* [2]Lit. *it*
19 [a]Deut. 16:11, 14 [b]Esth. 8:16, 17 [c]Neh. 8:10, 12
22 [a]Neh. 8:10 [b][Deut. 15:7–11]
24 [a]Esth. 3:6, 7; 9:26
25 [a]Esth. 7:4–10; 8:3; 9:13, 14 [b]Esth. 7:10 [1]Lit. *she* or *it* [2]Lit. *his*
26 [a]Esth. 9:20 [1]Lit. *Lot*
27 [a]Esth. 8:17
29 [a]Esth. 2:15 [b]Esth. 8:10; 9:20, 21
30 [a]Esth. 1:1
31 [a]Esth. 4:3, 16
CHAPTER 10
1 [a]Is. 11:11; 24:15

greatness of Mordecai, [a]to which the king
[1]advanced him, *are* they not written in
the book of the [b]chronicles of the kings of
Media and Persia? 3For Mordecai the Jew
was [a]second to King Ahasuerus, and was
great among the Jews and well received by
the multitude of his brethren, [b]seeking
the good of his people and speaking peace
to all his [1]countrymen.

2 **a** Esth. 8:15; 9:4
b Esth. 6:1
1 Lit. *made him great*

3 **a** Gen. 41:40, 43, 44
b Neh. 2:10

1 Lit. *seed.* LXX, Vg. add a dream of Mordecai here; Vg. adds six more chapters

AUTHOR:	*Uncertain; Perhaps Moses or Solomon*
DATE:	*Unspecified (Fifteenth–Second Century B.C.)*
THEME:	*The Suffering of the Godly and the Sovereignty of God*
KEY WORDS:	*Sin, Righteousness*

JOB

Dear Woman of Destiny,

The poetic Book of Job explores the mystery of human suffering and contrasts the invisible workings of the spirit realm against the reasonings of ordinary men. Godly women appreciate the value and rewards of patience—but this book teaches us far more than that. It proves that Satan is the author of all misery and that God is more than enough to support us through any trial.

His love and mine,

Marilyn Hickey

Job and His Family in Uz

There was a man [a]in the land of Uz,
whose name *was* [b]Job; and that
man was [c]blameless and upright,
and one who [d]feared God and [1]shunned
evil. 2And seven sons and three daughters
were born to him. 3Also, his possessions
were seven thousand sheep, three thousand camels, five hundred yoke of oxen,
five hundred female donkeys, and a very
large household, so that this man was the
greatest of all the [1]people of the East.

Father, may ____ live a blameless and upright life, fearing You and shunning evil.

FROM JOB 1:1

4And his sons would go and feast *in
their* houses, each on his *appointed* day,
and would send and invite their three sisters to eat and drink with them. 5So it
was, when the days of feasting had run
their course, that Job would send and
[1]sanctify them, and he would rise early in
the morning [a]and offer burnt offerings
according to the number of them all. For
Job said, "It may be that my sons have
sinned and [b]cursed[2] God in their hearts."
Thus Job did regularly.

Satan Attacks Job's Character

6Now [a]there was a day when the sons of
God came to present themselves before
the LORD, and [1]Satan also came among
them. 7And the LORD said to [1]Satan,
"From where do you come?"
So Satan answered the LORD and said,
"From [a]going to and fro on the earth, and
from walking back and forth on it."
8Then the LORD said to Satan, "Have
you [1]considered My servant Job, that
there is none like him on the earth, a
blameless and upright man, one who fears
God and [2]shuns evil?"
9So Satan answered the LORD and said,
"Does Job fear God for nothing? 10[a]Have
You not [1]made a hedge around him,
around his household, and around all that
he has on every side? [b]You have blessed
the work of his hands, and his possessions
have increased in the land. 11[a]But now,
stretch out Your hand and touch all that
he has, and he will surely [b]curse[1] You to
Your face!"
12And the LORD said to Satan, "Behold,
all that he has *is* in your [1]power; only do
not lay a hand on his *person.*"
So Satan went out from the presence of
the LORD.

Job Loses His Property and Children

13Now there was a day [a]when his sons
and daughters *were* eating and drinking
wine in their oldest brother's house; 14and
a messenger came to Job and said, "The
oxen were plowing and the donkeys feeding beside them, 15when the [1]Sabeans
[2]raided *them* and took them away—indeed they have killed the servants with the
edge of the sword; and I alone have escaped to tell you!"

Sometimes things are allowed to happen so that the quiet power of our Lord to arrange and rearrange events according to His purpose may be shown.

AMY CARMICHAEL

16While he *was* still speaking, another
also came and said, "The fire of God fell
from heaven and burned up the sheep and
the servants, and [1]consumed them; and I
alone have escaped to tell you!"
17While he *was* still speaking, another
also came and said, "The Chaldeans
formed three bands, raided the camels
and took them away, yes, and killed the
servants with the edge of the sword; and
I alone have escaped to tell you!"
18While he *was* still speaking, another
also came and said, [a]"Your sons and
daughters *were* eating and drinking wine
in their oldest brother's house, 19and suddenly a great wind came from [1]across the
wilderness and struck the four corners of
the house, and it fell on the young people,

CHAPTER 1
1 [a] 1 Chr. 1:17 [b] Ezek. 14:14, 20 [c] Gen. 6:9; 17:1 [d] [Prov. 16:6] [1] Lit. *turned away from*
3 [1] Lit. *sons*
5 [a] [Job 42:8] [b] 1 Kin. 21:10, 13 [1] *consecrate* [2] Lit. *blessed,* but in an evil sense; cf. Job 1:11; 2:5, 9
6 [a] Job 2:1 [1] Lit. *the Adversary*
7 [a] [1 Pet. 5:8] [1] Lit. *the Adversary*
8 [1] Lit. *set your heart on* [2] Lit. *turns away from*
10 [a] Ps. 34:7 [b] [Prov. 10:22] [1] Protected him
11 [a] Job 2:5; 19:21 [b] Is. 8:21 [1] Lit. *bless,* but in an evil sense; cf. Job 1:5
12 [1] Lit. *hand*
13 [a] [Eccl. 9:12]
15 [1] Lit. *Sheba;* cf. Job 6:19 [2] Lit. *fell upon*
16 [1] *destroyed*
18 [a] Job 1:4, 13
19 [1] LXX omits *across*

and they are dead; and I alone have escaped to tell you!"
20 Then Job arose, [a]tore his robe, and
shaved his head; and he [b]fell to the
ground and worshiped. 21 And he said:

[a]"Naked I came from my mother's
womb,
And naked shall I return there.
The LORD [b]gave, and the LORD has
[c]taken away;
[d]Blessed be the name of the LORD."

22 [a]In all this Job did not sin nor charge
God with wrong.

Merciful Lord, I pray as
_____ goes through this time
of suffering that You would
enable them, like Job,
not to sin nor to charge You
with wrong.

FROM JOB 1:22

Satan Attacks Job's Health

2 Again [a]there was a day when the sons
of God came to present themselves
before the LORD, and Satan came also
among them to present himself before the
LORD. 2 And the LORD said to Satan, "From
where do you come?"
3 [a]Satan answered the LORD and said,
"From going to and fro on the earth, and
from walking back and forth on it."
3 Then the LORD said to Satan, "Have
you considered My servant Job, that *there*
is none like him on the earth, [a]a blameless and upright man, one who fears God
and shuns evil? And still he [b]holds fast to
his integrity, although you incited Me
against him, [c]to [1]destroy him without
cause."
4 So Satan answered the LORD and said,
"Skin for skin! Yes, all that a man has he
will give for his life. 5 [a]But stretch out
Your hand now, and touch his [b]bone and
his flesh, and he will surely [1]curse You to
Your face!"
6 [a]And the LORD said to Satan, "Behold,
he *is* in your hand, but spare his life."
7 So Satan went out from the presence
of the LORD, and struck Job with painful
boils [a]from the sole of his foot to the
crown of his head. 8 And he took for himself a potsherd with which to scrape himself [a]while he sat in the midst of the ashes.
9 Then his wife said to him, "Do you still
hold fast to your integrity? [1]Curse God
and die!"
10 But he said to her, "You speak as one
of the foolish women speaks. [a]Shall we
indeed accept good from God, and shall
we not accept adversity?" [b]In all this Job
did not [c]sin with his lips.

Job's Three Friends

11 Now when Job's three friends heard of
all this adversity that had come upon him,
each one came from his own place—Eliphaz the [a]Temanite, Bildad the [b]Shuhite,
and Zophar the Naamathite. For they had
made an appointment together to come
[c]and mourn with him, and to comfort
him. 12 And when they raised their eyes
from afar, and did not recognize him, they
lifted their voices and wept; and each one
tore his robe and [a]sprinkled dust on his
head toward heaven. 13 So they sat down
with him on the ground [a]seven days and
seven nights, and no one spoke a word to
him, for they saw that *his* grief was very
great.

Job Deplores His Birth

3 After this Job opened his mouth and
cursed the day of his *birth*. 2 And Job
[1]spoke, and said:

3 "May[a] the day perish on which I
was born,
And the night *in which* it was said,
'A male child is conceived.'
4 May that day be darkness;
May God above not seek it,
Nor the light shine upon it.
5 May darkness and [a]the shadow of
death claim it;
May a cloud settle on it;
May the blackness of the day terrify
it.
6 *As for* that night, may darkness
seize it;
May it not [1]rejoice among the days
of the year,
May it not come into the number
of the months.
7 Oh, may that night be barren!
May no joyful shout come into it!

---

20 [a]Gen. 37:29, 34 [b][1 Pet. 5:6]
21 [a][Eccl. 5:15] [b][James 1:17] [c]Gen. 31:16 [d]Eph. 5:20
22 [a]Job 2:10

CHAPTER 2
1 [a]Job 1:6–8
2 [a]Job 1:7
3 [a]Job 1:1, 8 [b]Job 27:5, 6 [c]Job 9:17 [1]Lit. *consume*
5 [a]Job 1:11 [b]Job 19:20 [1]Lit. *bless,* but in an evil sense; cf. Job 1:5
6 [a]Job 1:12
7 [a]Is. 1:6
8 [a]Ezek. 27:30
9 [1]Lit. *Bless,* but in an evil sense; cf. Job 1:5
10 [a]Job 1:21, 22 [b]Job 1:22 [c]Ps. 39:1
11 [a]Gen. 36:11 [b]Gen. 25:2 [c]Rom. 12:15
12 [a]Neh. 9:1
13 [a]Gen. 50:10

CHAPTER 3
2 [1]Lit. *answered*
3 [a]Jer. 20:14–18
5 [a]Jer. 13:16
6 [1]LXX, Syr., Tg., Vg. *be joined*

8 May those curse it who curse the day,
Those [a]who are ready to arouse
Leviathan.
9 May the stars of its morning be
dark;
May it look for light, but *have*
none,
And not see the [1]dawning of the
day;
10 Because it did not shut up the
doors of my *mother's* womb,
Nor hide sorrow from my eyes.

11 "Why[a] did I not die at birth?
Why did I *not* [1]perish when I came
from the womb?
12 [a]Why did the knees receive me?
Or why the breasts, that I should
nurse?
13 For now I would have lain still
and been quiet,
I would have been asleep;
Then I would have been at rest
14 With kings and counselors of the
earth,

8 [a] Jer. 9:17
9 [1] *eyelids of the dawn*
11 [a] Job 10:18, 19
[1] *expire*
12 [a] Gen. 30:3

Mary Livingstone

Mary Livingstone (1822–1862) was known as the "Queen of the Wagon" because of her ability to travel with ease under the harsh conditions of Africa. But the rugged travel may have been the least of Mary's worries, as most of Mary's life was full of intense challenge and hardship.

Within the first five years of her marriage to the legendary David Livingstone, Mary gave birth to three children, suffered the loss of a baby girl, was paralyzed on the right side of her face and head, battled multiple illnesses, and moved five times across the rugged plains of Africa. In 1851, while traveling to establish a new mission settlement 870 miles north of their previous home, Mary watched as her children nearly died of dehydration. With children screaming and parents lifting parched prayers to God, the family could not find water for five days. Finally, they discovered a small muddy hole containing enough dirty water to save their lives.

However, perhaps Mary's most difficult hardship was being separated from her husband. David called Mary the "main spoke in my wheel," whose "shining example of simple goodness and purity is worth much more than all my exhortations." Mary's commitment to David stood the test of two lengthy separations while he traveled to establish new mission stations across Africa. During those years of not knowing whether David was alive or dead, Mary's strength was severely tested as local rumors swirled. These rumors accused the Livingstones of having an unhappy marriage and alleged that David left because Mary was difficult to live with.

But Mary, Queen of the Wagon, endured. The secret of her strength—and the strength of the man responsible for changing the face of Africa for Christ—is in a response she gave when David questioned whether their efforts were for any good: "But you and I are not fighting alone, dear." Through their many trials and sufferings, they stayed absolutely faithful to the God who had called them, equipped them, empowered them against impossible odds, and never once forsaken them.

Who [a]built ruins for themselves,
15 Or with princes who had gold,
Who filled their houses *with* silver;
16 Or *why* was I not hidden [a]like a stillborn child,
Like infants who never saw light?
17 There the wicked cease *from* troubling,
And there the [1]weary are at [a]rest.
18 *There* the prisoners [1]rest together;
[a]They do not hear the voice of the oppressor.
19 The small and great are there,
And the servant *is* free from his master.

20 "Why[a] is light given to him who is in misery,
And life to the [b]bitter of soul,
21 Who [a]long[1] for death, but it does not *come,*
And search for it more than [b]hidden treasures;
22 Who rejoice exceedingly,
And are glad when they can find the [a]grave?
23 *Why is light given* to a man whose way is hidden,
[a]And whom God has hedged in?
24 For my sighing comes before [1]I eat,
And my groanings pour out like water.
25 For the thing I greatly [a]feared has come upon me,
And what I dreaded has happened to me.
26 I am not at ease, nor am I quiet;
I have no rest, for trouble comes."

Eliphaz: Job Has Sinned

4 Then Eliphaz the Temanite answered and said:

2 "*If* one attempts a word with you, will you become weary?
But who can withhold himself from speaking?
3 Surely you have instructed many,
And you [a]have strengthened weak hands.
4 Your words have upheld him who was stumbling,
And you [a]have strengthened the [1]feeble knees;
5 But now it comes upon you, and you are weary;
It touches you, and you are troubled.
6 *Is* not [a]your reverence [b]your confidence?
And the integrity of your ways your hope?

7 "Remember now, [a]who *ever* perished being innocent?
Or where were the upright *ever* cut off?
8 Even as I have seen,
[a]Those who plow iniquity
And sow trouble reap the same.
9 By the blast of God they perish,
And by the breath of His anger they are consumed.
10 The roaring of the lion,
The voice of the fierce lion,
And [a]the teeth of the young lions are broken.
11 [a]The old lion perishes for lack of prey,
And the cubs of the lioness are scattered.

12 "Now a word was secretly brought to me,
And my ear received a whisper of it.
13 [a]In disquieting thoughts from the visions of the night,
When deep sleep falls on men,
14 Fear came upon me, and [a]trembling,
Which made all my bones shake.
15 Then a spirit passed before my face;
The hair on my body stood up.
16 It stood still,
But I could not discern its appearance.
A form *was* before my eyes;
There was silence;
Then I heard a voice *saying:*
17 'Can a mortal be more righteous than God?
Can a man be more pure than his Maker?
18 If He [a]puts no trust in His servants,
If He charges His angels with error,
19 How much more those who dwell in houses of clay,
Whose foundation is in the dust,
Who are crushed before a moth?
20 [a]They are broken in pieces from morning till evening;
They perish forever, with no one regarding.

---

14 a Job 15:28
16 a Ps. 58:8
17 a Job 17:16 *1* Lit. *weary of strength*
18 a Job 39:7 *1 are at ease*
20 a Jer. 20:18 b 2 Kin. 4:27
21 a Rev. 9:6 b Prov. 2:4 *1* Lit. *wait*
22 a Job 7:15, 16
23 a Job 19:8
24 *1* Lit. *my bread*
25 a [Job 9:28; 30:15]

CHAPTER 4
3 a Is. 35:3
4 a Is. 35:3 *1* Lit. *bending*
6 a Job 1:1 b Prov. 3:26
7 a [Ps. 37:25]
8 a [Prov. 22:8]
10 a Ps. 58:6
11 a Ps. 34:10
13 a Job 33:15
14 a Hab. 3:16
18 a Job 15:15
20 a Ps. 90:5, 6

21 Does not their own excellence go
away?
They die, even without wisdom.'

Eliphaz: Job Is Chastened by God

5 "Call out now;
Is there anyone who will answer
you?
And to which of the holy ones will
you turn?
2 For wrath kills a foolish man,
And envy slays a simple one.
3 [a]I have seen the foolish taking root,
But suddenly I cursed his dwelling
place.
4 His sons are [a]far from safety,
They are crushed in the gate,
And [b]*there is* no deliverer.
5 Because the hungry eat up his
harvest,
[1]Taking it even from the thorns,
[2]And a snare snatches their
[3]substance.
6 For affliction does not come from
the dust,
Nor does trouble spring from the
ground;
7 Yet man is [a]born to [1]trouble,
As the sparks fly upward.
8 "But as for me, I would seek God,
And to God I would commit my
cause—
9 Who does great things, and
unsearchable,
Marvelous things without number.
10 [a]He gives rain on the earth,
And sends waters on the fields.
11 [a]He sets on high those who are
lowly,
And those who mourn are lifted to
safety.
12 [a]He frustrates the devices of the
crafty,
So that their hands cannot carry
out their plans.
13 He catches the [a]wise in their own
craftiness,
And the counsel of the cunning
comes quickly upon them.
14 They meet with darkness in the
daytime,
And grope at noontime as in the
night.
15 But [a]He saves the needy from the
sword,
From the mouth of the mighty,
And from their hand.
16 [a]So the poor have hope,
And injustice shuts her mouth.
17 "Behold,[a] happy *is* the man whom
God corrects;
Therefore do not despise the
chastening of the Almighty.
18 [a]For He bruises, but He binds up;
He wounds, but His hands make
whole.
19 [a]He shall deliver you in six
troubles,
Yes, in seven [b]no evil shall touch
you.
20 [a]In famine He shall redeem you
from death,
And in war from the [1]power of the
sword.
21 [a]You shall be hidden from the
scourge of the tongue,
And you shall not be afraid of
destruction when it comes.
22 You shall laugh at destruction and
famine,
And [a]you shall not be afraid of the
[b]beasts of the earth.
23 [a]For you shall have a covenant
with the stones of the field,
And the beasts of the field shall be
at peace with you.
24 You shall know that your tent *is*
in peace;
You shall visit your dwelling and
find nothing amiss.
25 You shall also know that [a]your
descendants *shall be* many,
And your offspring [b]like the grass
of the earth.
26 [a]You shall come to the grave at a
full age,
As a sheaf of grain ripens in its
season.
27 Behold, this we have [a]searched
out;
It *is* true.
Hear it, and know for yourself."

Job: My Complaint Is Just

6 Then Job answered and said:
2 "Oh, that my grief were fully
weighed,
And my calamity laid with it on the
scales!
3 For then it would be heavier than
the sand of the sea—
Therefore my words have been rash.

CHAPTER 5
3 [a] Jer. 12:1–3
4 [a] Ps. 119:155 [b] Ps. 109:12
5 [1] LXX *They shall not be taken from evil men;* Vg. *And the armed man shall take him by violence* [2] LXX *The might shall draw them off;* Vg. *And the thirsty shall drink up their riches* [3] *wealth*
7 [a] Job 14:1 [1] *labor*
10 [a] [Job 36:27–29; 37:6–11; 38:26]
11 [a] Ps. 113:7
12 [a] Neh. 4:15
13 [a] [1 Cor. 3:19]
15 [a] Ps. 35:10
16 [a] 1 Sam. 2:8
17 [a] Ps. 94:12
18 [a] [1 Sam. 2:6, 7]
19 [a] Ps. 34:19; 91:3 [b] Ps. 91:10
20 [a] Ps. 33:19, 20; 37:19 [1] Lit. *hand*
21 [a] Ps. 31:20
22 [a] Ezek. 34:25 [b] Hos. 2:18
23 [a] Ps. 91:12
25 [a] Ps. 112:2 [b] Ps. 72:16
26 [a] [Prov. 9:11; 10:27]
27 [a] Ps. 111:2

4 [a]For the arrows of the Almighty *are* within me;
My spirit drinks in their poison;
[b]The terrors of God are arrayed [c]against me.
5 Does the [a]wild donkey bray when it has grass,
Or does the ox low over its fodder?
6 Can flavorless food be eaten without salt?
Or is there *any* taste in the white of an egg?
7 My soul refuses to touch them;
They *are* as loathsome food to me.

8 "Oh, that I might have my request,
That God would grant *me* the thing that I long for!
9 That it would please God to crush me,
That He would loose His hand and [a]cut me off!
10 Then I would still have comfort;
Though in anguish I would exult,
He will not spare;
For [a]I have not concealed the words of [b]the Holy One.

11 "What strength do I have, that I should hope?
And what *is* my end, that I should prolong my life?
12 *Is* my strength the strength of stones?
Or is my flesh bronze?
13 *Is* my help not within me?
And is success driven from me?

14 "To[a] him who is [1]afflicted, kindness *should be shown* by his friend,
Even though he forsakes the fear of the Almighty.
15 [a]My brothers have dealt deceitfully like a brook,
[b]Like the streams of the brooks that pass away,
16 Which are dark because of the ice,
And into which the snow vanishes.
17 When it is warm, they cease to flow;
When it is hot, they vanish from their place.
18 The paths of their way turn aside,
They go nowhere and perish.
19 The caravans of [a]Tema look,
The travelers of [b]Sheba hope for them.
20 They are [a]disappointed[1] because they were confident;
They come there and are confused.
21 For now [a]you are nothing,
You see terror and [b]are afraid.
22 Did I ever say, 'Bring *something* to me'?
Or, 'Offer a bribe for me from your wealth'?
23 Or, 'Deliver me from the enemy's hand'?
Or, 'Redeem me from the hand of oppressors'?

24 "Teach me, and I will hold my tongue;
Cause me to understand wherein I have erred.
25 How forceful are right words!
But what does your arguing prove?
26 Do you intend to rebuke *my* words,
And the speeches of a desperate one, *which are* as wind?
27 Yes, you overwhelm the fatherless,
And you [a]undermine your friend.
28 Now therefore, be pleased to look at me;
For I would never lie to your face.
29 [a]Yield now, let there be no injustice!
Yes, concede, my [b]righteousness [1]still stands!
30 Is there injustice on my tongue?
Cannot my [1]taste discern the unsavory?

Job: My Suffering Is Comfortless

7 "*Is there* not [a]a time of hard service for man on earth?
Are not his days also like the days of a hired man?
2 Like a servant who [1]earnestly desires the shade,
And like a hired man who eagerly looks for his wages,
3 So I have been allotted [a]months of futility,
And wearisome nights have been appointed to me.
4 [a]When I lie down, I say, 'When shall I arise,
And the night be ended?'
For I have had my fill of tossing till dawn.
5 My flesh is [a]caked with worms and dust,
My skin is cracked and breaks out afresh.

CHAPTER 6
4 [a]Ps. 38:2 [b]Ps. 88:15, 16 [c]Job 30:15
5 [a]Job 39:5–8
9 [a]Job 7:16; 9:21; 10:1
10 [a]Acts 20:20 [b][Is. 57:15]
14 [a][Prov. 17:17] [1]Or *despairing*
15 [a]Ps. 38:11 [b]Jer. 15:18
19 [a]Gen. 25:15 [b]1 Kin. 10:1
20 [a]Jer. 14:3 [1]Lit. *ashamed*
21 [a]Job 13:4 [b]Ps. 38:11
27 [a]Ps. 57:6
29 [a]Job 17:10 [b]Job 27:5, 6; 34:5 [1]Lit. *is in it*
30 [1]*palate*

CHAPTER 7
1 [a][Job 14:5, 13, 14]
2 [1]Lit. *pants for*
3 [a][Job 15:31]
4 [a]Deut. 28:67
5 [a]Is. 14:11

Father, like Job, ______ cannot even sleep because their sorrow is so deep. I ask that You would comfort them and pour out Your mercy upon them.

FROM JOB 7:4

6 "My[a] days are swifter than a
weaver's shuttle,
And are spent without hope.
7 Oh, remember that [a]my life *is* a
breath!
My eye will never again see good.
8 [a]The eye of him who sees me will
see me no *more;*
While your *eyes* are upon me, I
shall no longer *be.*
9 *As* the cloud disappears and
vanishes away,
So [a]he who goes down to the grave
does not come up.
10 He shall never return to his
house,
[a]Nor shall his place know him
anymore.

11 "Therefore I will [a]not restrain my
mouth;
I will speak in the anguish of my
spirit;
I will [b]complain in the bitterness of
my soul.
12 *Am* I a sea, or a sea serpent,
That You set a guard over me?
13 [a]When I say, 'My bed will comfort
me,
My couch will ease my complaint,'
14 Then You scare me with dreams
And terrify me with visions,
15 So that my soul chooses
strangling
And death rather than [1]my body.
16 [a]I loathe *my life;*
I would not live forever.
[b]Let me alone,
For [c]my days *are but* [1]a breath.

17 "What[a] *is* man, that You should
exalt him,
That You should set Your heart on
him,
18 That You should [1]visit him every
morning,
And test him every moment?
19 How long?
Will You not look away from me,
And let me alone till I swallow my
saliva?
20 Have I sinned?
What have I done to You,
[a]O watcher of men?
Why [b]have You set me as Your
target,
So that I am a burden [1]to myself?
21 Why then do You not pardon my
transgression,
And take away my iniquity?
For now I will lie down in the dust,
And You will seek me diligently,
But I *will* no longer *be.*"

Bildad: Job Should Repent

8 Then Bildad the Shuhite answered
and said:

2 "How long will you speak these
things,
And the words of your mouth *be*
like a strong wind?
3 [a]Does God subvert judgment?
Or does the Almighty pervert
justice?
4 If [a]your sons have sinned against
Him,
He has cast them away [1]for their
transgression.
5 [a]If you would earnestly seek God
And make your supplication to the
Almighty,
6 If you *were* pure and upright,
Surely now He would [1]awake for
you,
And prosper your rightful dwelling
place.
7 Though your beginning was small,
Yet your latter end would [a]increase
abundantly.

8 "For[a] inquire, please, of the former
age,
And consider the things discovered
by their fathers;
9 For [a]we *were born* yesterday, and
know [1]nothing,
Because our days on earth *are* a
shadow.
10 Will they not teach you and tell
you,
And utter words from their heart?

6 [a]Job 9:25; 16:22; 17:11
7 [a]Ps. 78:39; 89:47
8 [a]Job 8:18; 20:9
9 [a]2 Sam. 12:23
10 [a]Ps. 103:16
11 [a]Ps. 39:1, 9 [b]1 Sam. 1:10
13 [a]Job 9:27
15 [1]Lit. *my bones*
16 [a]Job 10:1 [b]Job 14:6 [c]Ps. 62:9 [1]Without substance, futile
17 [a]Ps. 8:4; 144:3
18 [1]*attend to*
20 [a]Ps. 36:6 [b]Ps. 21:12 [1]So with MT, Tg., Vg.; LXX, Jewish tradition *to You*

CHAPTER 8
3 [a][Deut. 32:4]
4 [a]Job 1:5, 18, 19 [1]Lit. *into the hand of their transgression*
5 [a][Job 5:17–27; 11:13]
6 [1]*arise*
7 [a]Job 42:12
8 [a]Deut. 4:32; 32:7
9 [a]Gen. 47:9 [1]Lit. *not*

11 "Can the papyrus grow up without
a marsh?
Can the reeds flourish without
water?
12 [a]While it *is* yet green *and* not cut
down,
It withers before any *other* plant.
13 So *are* the paths of all who [a]forget
God;
And the hope of the [b]hypocrite
shall perish,
14 Whose confidence shall be cut off,
And whose trust *is* [1]a spider's web.
15 [a]He leans on his house, but it does
not stand.
He holds it fast, but it does not
endure.
16 He grows green in the sun,
And his branches spread out in his
garden.
17 His roots wrap around the rock
heap,
And look for a place in the stones.
18 [a]If he is destroyed from his place,
Then *it* will deny him, *saying,* 'I
have not seen you.'

19 "Behold, this is the joy of His way,
And [a]out of the earth others will
grow.
20 Behold, [a]God will not [1]cast away
the blameless,
Nor will He uphold the evildoers.
21 He will yet fill your mouth with
laughing,
And your lips with [1]rejoicing.
22 Those who hate you will be
[a]clothed with shame,
And the dwelling place of the
wicked [1]will come to nothing."

Job: There Is No Mediator

9 Then Job answered and said:

2 "Truly I know *it is* so,
But how can a [a]man be [b]righteous
before God?
3 If one wished to [1]contend with
Him,
He could not answer Him one time
out of a thousand.
4 [a]*God is* wise in heart and mighty in
strength.
Who has hardened *himself* against
Him and prospered?
5 He removes the mountains, and
they do not know
When He overturns them in His
anger;
6 He [a]shakes the earth out of its
place,
And its [b]pillars tremble;
7 He commands the sun, and it does
not rise;
He seals off the stars;
8 [a]He alone spreads out the heavens,
And [1]treads on the [2]waves of the
sea;
9 [a]He made [1]the Bear, Orion, and the
Pleiades,
And the chambers of the south;
10 [a]He does great things past finding
out,
Yes, wonders without number.
11 [a]If He goes by me, I do not see
Him;
If He moves past, I do not perceive
Him;
12 [a]If He takes away, [1]who can hinder
Him?
Who can say to Him, 'What are You
doing?'
13 God will not withdraw His anger,
[a]The allies of [1]the proud lie
prostrate beneath Him.

14 "How then can I answer Him,
And choose my words *to reason*
with Him?
15 [a]For though I were righteous, I
could not answer Him;
I would beg mercy of my Judge.
16 If I called and He answered me,
I would not believe that He was
listening to my voice.
17 For He crushes me with a
tempest,
And multiplies my wounds [a]without
cause.
18 He will not allow me to catch my
breath,
But fills me with bitterness.
19 If *it is a matter* of strength,
indeed *He is* strong;
And if of justice, who will appoint
my day *in court?*
20 Though I were righteous, my own
mouth would condemn me;
Though I *were* blameless, it would
prove me perverse.

21 "I am blameless, yet I do not know
myself;
I despise my life.
22 It *is* all one *thing;*

---

12 [a]Ps. 129:6
13 [a]Ps. 9:17 [b]Job 11:20; 18:14; 27:8
14 [1]Lit. *a spider's house*
15 [a]Job 8:22; 27:18
18 [a]Job 7:10
19 [a]Ps. 113:7
20 [a]Job 4:7 [1]*reject*
21 [1]Lit. *shouts of joy*
22 [a]Ps. 35:26; 109:29 [1]Lit. *will not be*

CHAPTER 9
2 [a][Job 4:17; 15:14–16] [b][Hab. 2:4]
3 [1]*argue*
4 [a]Job 36:5
6 [a]Heb. 12:26 [b]Job 26:11
8 [a]Ps. 104:2, 3 [1]*walks* [2]Lit. *heights*
9 [a]Amos 5:8 [1]Heb. *Ash, Kesil,* and *Kimah*
10 [a]Job 5:9
11 [a][Job 23:8, 9; 35:14]
12 [a][Is. 45:9] [1]Lit. *who can turn Him back?*
13 [a]Job 26:12 [1]Heb. *rahab*
15 [a]Job 10:15; 23:1–7
17 [a]Job 2:3

Therefore I say, [a]'He destroys the
blameless and the wicked.'
23 If the scourge slays suddenly,
He laughs at the plight of the
innocent.
24 The earth is given into the hand
of the wicked.
He covers the faces of its judges.
If it is not *He,* who else could it be?

25 "Now [a]my days are swifter than a
runner;
They flee away, they see no good.
26 They pass by like [1]swift ships,
[a]Like an eagle swooping on its prey.
27 [a]If I say, 'I will forget my
complaint,
I will put off my sad face and wear
a smile,'
28 [a]I am afraid of all my sufferings;
I know that You [b]will not hold me
innocent.
29 *If* I am condemned,
Why then do I labor in vain?
30 [a]If I wash myself with snow water,
And cleanse my hands with [1]soap,
31 Yet You will plunge me into the
pit,
And my own clothes will [1]abhor
me.

32 "For [a]*He is* not a man, as I *am,*
That I may answer Him,
And that we should go to court
together.
33 [a]Nor is there any mediator between
us,
Who may lay his hand on us both.
34 [a]Let Him take His rod away from
me,
And do not let dread of Him terrify
me.
35 *Then* I would speak and not fear
Him,
But it is not so with me.

Job: I Would Plead with God

10 "My [a]soul loathes my life;
I will [1]give free course to my
complaint,
[b]I will speak in the bitterness of my
soul.
2 I will say to God, 'Do not condemn
me;
Show me why You contend with
me.
3 *Does it* seem good to You that You
should oppress,
That You should despise the work
of Your hands,
And smile on the counsel of the
wicked?
4 Do You have eyes of flesh?
Or [a]do You see as man sees?
5 *Are* Your days like the days of a
mortal man?
Are Your years like the days of a
mighty man,
6 That You should seek for my
iniquity
And search out my sin,
7 Although You know that I am not
wicked,
And *there is* no one who can
deliver from Your hand?

8 'Your[a] hands have made me and
fashioned me,
An intricate unity;
Yet You would [b]destroy me.
9 Remember, I pray, [a]that You have
made me like clay.
And will You turn me into dust
again?
10 [a]Did You not pour me out like
milk,
And curdle me like cheese,
11 Clothe me with skin and flesh,
And knit me together with bones
and sinews?
12 You have granted me life and
favor,
And Your care has preserved my
spirit.

Lord, even in the midst of trial, may _____ know that You are the One who has granted them life and favor and that Your care has preserved their spirit.

FROM JOB 10:12

13 'And these *things* You have hidden
in Your heart;
I know that this *was* with You:
14 If I sin, then [a]You mark me,
And will not acquit me of my
iniquity.
15 If I am wicked, [a]woe to me;

22 [a] Ezek. 21:3
25 [a] Job 7:6, 7
26 [a] Hab. 1:8 [1] Lit. *ships of reeds*
27 [a] Job 7:13
28 [a] Ps. 119:120 [b] Ex. 20:7
30 [a] [Jer. 2:22] [1] *lye*
31 [1] *loathe*
32 [a] [Is. 45:9]
33 [a] [1 Sam. 2:25]
34 [a] Job 13:20, 21

CHAPTER 10
1 [a] Job 7:16 [b] Job 7:11 [1] Lit. *leave on myself*
4 [a] [1 Sam. 16:7]
8 [a] Ps. 119:73 [b] [Job 9:22]
9 [a] Gen. 2:7
10 [a] [Ps. 139:14–16]
14 [a] Ps. 139:1
15 [a] Is. 3:11

[b]Even *if* I am righteous, I [1]cannot
lift up my head.
I am full of disgrace;
[c]See my misery!
16 If *my head* is exalted,
[a]You hunt me like a fierce lion,
And again You show Yourself
awesome against me.
17 You renew Your witnesses against
me,
And increase Your indignation
toward me;
Changes and war are *ever* with me.

18 'Why[a] then have You brought me
out of the womb?
Oh, that I had perished and no eye
had seen me!
19 I would have been as though I had
not been.
I would have been carried from the
womb to the grave.
20 [a]Are not my days few?
Cease! [b]Leave me alone, that I may
take a little comfort,
21 Before I go *to the place from
which* I shall not return,
[a]To the land of darkness [b]and the
shadow of death,
22 A land as dark as darkness *itself,*
As the shadow of death, without
any order,
Where even the light *is* like
darkness.' "

Zophar Urges Job to Repent

11 Then Zophar the Naamathite answered and said:

2 "Should not the multitude of words
be answered?
And should [1]a man full of talk be
vindicated?
3 Should your empty talk make men
[1]hold their peace?
And when you mock, should no one
rebuke you?
4 For you have said,
[a]'My doctrine *is* pure,
And I am clean in your eyes.'
5 But oh, that God would speak,
And open His lips against you,
6 That He would show you the
secrets of wisdom!
For *they would* double *your*
prudence.
Know therefore that [a]God [1]exacts
from you
Less than your iniquity *deserves.*

7 "Can[a] you search out the deep
things of God?
Can you find out the limits of the
Almighty?
8 *They are* higher than heaven—
what can you do?
Deeper than [1]Sheol—what can you
know?
9 Their measure *is* longer than the
earth
And broader than the sea.

10 "If[a] He passes by, imprisons, and
gathers *to judgment,*
Then who can [1]hinder Him?
11 For [a]He knows deceitful men;
He sees wickedness also.
Will He not then consider *it?*
12 For an [a]empty-headed man will
be wise,
When a wild donkey's colt is born a
man.

13 "If you would [a]prepare your heart,
And [b]stretch out your hands toward
Him;
14 If iniquity *were* in your hand, *and
you* put it far away,
And [a]would not let wickedness
dwell in your tents;
15 [a]Then surely you could lift up your
face without spot;
Yes, you could be steadfast, and not
fear;
16 Because you would [a]forget *your*
misery,
And remember *it* as waters *that
have* passed away,
17 And *your* life [a]would be brighter
than noonday.
Though you were dark, you would
be like the morning.
18 And you would be secure, because
there is hope;
Yes, you would dig *around you,
and* [a]take your rest in safety.
19 You would also lie down, and no
one would make *you* afraid;
Yes, many would court your favor.
20 But [a]the eyes of the wicked will
fail,
And they shall not escape,
And [b]their hope—[1]loss of life!"

Job Answers His Critics

12 Then Job answered and said:

2 "No doubt you *are* the people,
And wisdom will die with you!

---

15 b [Job 9:12, 15] c Ps. 25:18 *1* Lit. *will not*
16 a Is. 38:13
18 a Job 3:11–13
20 a Ps. 39:5 b Job 7:16, 19
21 a Ps. 88:12 b Ps. 23:4

CHAPTER 11
2 *1* Lit. *a man of lips*
3 *1 be silent*
4 a Job 6:30
6 a [Ezra 9:13] *1* Lit. *forgets some of your iniquity for you*
7 a [Eccl. 3:11]
8 *1* The abode of the dead
10 a [Rev. 3:7] *1 restrain*
11 a [Ps. 10:14]
12 a Rom. 1:22
13 a [1 Sam. 7:3] b Ps. 88:9
14 a Ps. 101:3
15 a Ps. 119:6
16 a Is. 65:16
17 a Is. 58:8, 10
18 a Lev. 26:5, 6
20 a Deut. 28:65 b [Prov. 11:7] *1* Lit. *the breathing out of life*

3 But I have [1]understanding as well
as you;
I *am* not [a]inferior to you.
Indeed, who does not *know* such
things as these?

4 "I[a] am one mocked by his friends,
Who [b]called on God, and He
answered him,
The just and blameless *who is*
ridiculed.
5 A [1]lamp is despised in the thought
of one who is at ease;
It is made ready for [a]those whose
feet slip.
6 [a]The tents of robbers prosper,
And those who provoke God are
secure—
In what God provides by His hand.
7 "But now ask the beasts, and they
will teach you;
And the birds of the air, and they
will tell you;
8 Or speak to the earth, and it will
teach you;
And the fish of the sea will explain
to you.
9 Who among all these does not
know
That the hand of the LORD has done
this,
10 [a]In whose hand *is* the [1]life of every
living thing,
And the [b]breath of [2]all mankind?
11 Does not the ear test words
And the [1]mouth taste its food?
12 Wisdom *is* with aged men,
And with [1]length of days,
understanding.

13 "With Him *are* [a]wisdom and
strength,
He has counsel and understanding.
14 If [a]He breaks *a thing* down, it
cannot be rebuilt;
If He imprisons a man, there can
be no release.
15 If He [a]withholds the waters, they
dry up;
If He [b]sends them out, they
overwhelm the earth.
16 With Him *are* strength and
prudence.
The deceived and the deceiver *are*
His.
17 He leads counselors away
plundered,
And makes fools of the judges.
18 He loosens the bonds of kings,
And binds their waist with a belt.
19 He leads [1]princes away plundered,
And overthrows the mighty.
20 [a]He deprives the trusted ones of
speech,
And takes away the discernment of
the elders.
21 [a]He pours contempt on princes,
And [1]disarms the mighty.
22 He [a]uncovers deep things out of
darkness,
And brings the shadow of death to
light.
23 [a]He makes nations great, and
destroys them;
He [1]enlarges nations, and guides
them.
24 He takes away the [1]understanding
of the chiefs of the people of the
earth,
And [a]makes them wander in a
pathless wilderness.
25 [a]They grope in the dark without
light,
And He makes them [b]stagger like a
drunken *man*.

13 "Behold, my eye has seen all *this*,
My ear has heard and understood
it.
2 [a]What you know, I also know;
I *am* not inferior to you.
3 [a]But I would speak to the Almighty,
And I desire to reason with God.
4 But you forgers of lies,
[a]You *are* all worthless physicians.
5 Oh, that you would be silent,
And [a]it would be your wisdom!
6 Now hear my reasoning,
And heed the pleadings of my lips.
7 [a]Will you speak [1]wickedly for God,
And talk deceitfully for Him?
8 Will you show partiality for Him?
Will you contend for God?
9 Will it be well when He searches
you out?
Or can you mock Him as one
mocks a man?
10 He will surely rebuke you
If you secretly show partiality.
11 Will not His [1]excellence make you
afraid,
And the dread of Him fall upon
you?
12 Your platitudes *are* proverbs of
ashes,
Your defenses are defenses of clay.

CHAPTER 12
3 [a]Job 13:2 [1]Lit. *a heart*
4 [a]Job 21:3 [b]Ps. 91:15
5 [a]Prov. 14:2 [1]Or *disaster*
6 [a][Job 9:24; 21:6–16]
10 [a][Acts 17:28] [b]Job 27:3; 33:4 [1]Or *soul* [2]Lit. *all flesh of men*
11 [1]*palate*
12 [1]Long life
13 [a]Job 9:4; 36:5
14 [a]Job 11:10
15 [a][1 Kin. 8:35, 36] [b]Gen. 7:11–24
19 [1]Lit. *priests*, but not in a technical sense
20 [a]Job 32:9
21 [a]Ps. 107:40 [1]*loosens the belt of*
22 [a][1 Cor. 4:5]
23 [a]Is. 9:3; 26:15 [1]Lit. *spreads out*
24 [a]Ps. 107:4 [1]Lit. *heart*
25 [a]Job 5:14; 15:30; 18:18 [b]Ps. 107:27

CHAPTER 13
2 [a]Job 12:3
3 [a]Job 23:3; 31:35
4 [a]Job 6:21
5 [a]Prov. 17:28
7 [a]Job 27:4; 36:4 [1]*unrighteously*
11 [1]Lit. *exaltation*

Faith must rest on the will of God alone, not on our desires or wishes. Appropriating faith is not believing that God can but that God will.

F. F. BOSWORTH

13 "Hold[1] your peace with me, and let me speak,
Then let come on me what *may!*
14 Why [a]do I take my flesh in my teeth,
And put my life in my hands?
15 [a]Though He slay me, yet will I trust Him.
[b]Even so, I will defend my own ways before Him.
16 He also *shall* be my salvation,
For a [a]hypocrite could not come before Him.
17 Listen carefully to my speech,
And to my declaration with your ears.
18 See now, I have prepared *my* case,
I know that I shall be [a]vindicated.
19 [a]Who *is* he *who* will contend with me?
If now I hold my tongue, I perish.

Job's Despondent Prayer

20 "Only[a] two *things* do not do to me,
Then I will not hide myself from You:
21 [a]Withdraw Your hand far from me,
And let not the dread of You make me afraid.
22 Then call, and I will [a]answer;
Or let me speak, then You respond to me.
23 How many *are* my iniquities and sins?
Make me know my transgression and my sin.
24 [a]Why do You hide Your face,
And [b]regard me as Your enemy?
25 [a]Will You frighten a leaf driven to and fro?
And will You pursue dry stubble?
26 For You write bitter things against me,
And [a]make me inherit the iniquities of my youth.
27 [a]You put my feet in the stocks,
And watch closely all my paths.
You [1]set a limit for the [2]soles of my feet.
28 "*Man*[1] decays like a rotten thing,
Like a garment that is moth-eaten.

14 "Man *who is* born of woman
Is of few days and [a]full of [1]trouble.
2 [a]He comes forth like a flower and fades away;
He flees like a shadow and does not continue.
3 And [a]do You open Your eyes on such a one,
And [b]bring [1]me to judgment with Yourself?
4 Who [a]can bring a clean *thing* out of an unclean?
No one!
5 [a]Since his days *are* determined,
The number of his months *is* with You;
You have appointed his limits, so that he cannot pass.
6 [a]Look away from him that he may [1]rest,
Till [b]like a hired man he finishes his day.
7 "For there is hope for a tree,
If it is cut down, that it will sprout again,
And that its tender shoots will not cease.
8 Though its root may grow old in the earth,
And its stump may die in the ground,
9 *Yet* at the scent of water it will bud
And bring forth branches like a plant.
10 But man dies and [1]is laid away;
Indeed he [2]breathes his last
And where *is* [a]he?
11 *As* water disappears from the sea,
And a river becomes parched and dries up,
12 So man lies down and does not rise.
[a]Till the heavens *are* no more,
They will not awake
Nor be roused from their sleep.
13 "Oh, that You would hide me in the grave,

---

13 [1] *Be silent*
14 [a] Job 18:4
15 [a] Ps. 23:4 [b] Job 27:5
16 [a] Job 8:13
18 [a] [Rom. 8:34]
19 [a] Is. 50:8
20 [a] Job 9:34
21 [a] Ps. 39:10
22 [a] Job 9:16; 14:15
24 [a] [Deut. 32:20] [b] Lam. 2:5
25 [a] Is. 42:3
26 [a] Job 20:11
27 [a] Job 33:11 [1] Lit. *inscribe a print* [2] Lit. *roots*
28 [1] Lit. *He*

CHAPTER 14
1 [a] Eccl. 2:23 [1] *turmoil*
2 [a] Job 8:9
3 [a] Ps. 8:4; 144:3 [b] [Ps. 143:2] [1] LXX, Syr., Vg. *him*
4 [a] [Ps. 51:2, 5, 10]
5 [a] Job 7:1; 21:21
6 [a] Ps. 39:13 [b] Job 7:1 [1] Lit. *cease*
10 [a] Job 10:21, 22 [1] *lies prostrate* [2] *expires*
12 [a] [Is. 51:6; 65:17; 66:22]

That You would conceal me until
Your wrath is past,
That You would appoint me a set
time, and remember me!
14 If a man dies, shall he live *again?*
All the days of my hard service [a]I
will wait,
Till my change comes.
15 [a]You shall call, and I will answer
You;
You shall desire the work of Your
hands.
16 For now [a]You number my steps,
But do not watch over my sin.
17 [a]My transgression *is* sealed up in a
bag,
And You [1]cover my iniquity.
18 "But *as* a mountain falls *and*
crumbles away,
And *as* a rock is moved from its
place;
19 *As* water wears away stones,
And as torrents wash away the soil
of the earth;
So You destroy the hope of man.
20 You prevail forever against him,
and he passes on;
You change his countenance and
send him away.
21 His sons come to honor, and [a]he
does not know *it;*
They are brought low, and he does
not perceive *it.*
22 But his flesh will be in pain over
it,
And his soul will mourn over it."

Eliphaz Accuses Job of Folly

15 Then [a]Eliphaz the Temanite answered and said:
2 "Should a wise man answer with
empty knowledge,
And fill [1]himself with the east
wind?
3 Should he reason with unprofitable
talk,
Or by speeches with which he can
do no good?
4 Yes, you cast off fear,
And restrain [1]prayer before God.
5 For your iniquity teaches your
mouth,
And you choose the tongue of the
crafty.
6 [a]Your own mouth condemns you,
and not I;

14 a Job 13:15
15 a Job 13:22
16 a Prov. 5:21
17 a Deut. 32:32–34
1 Lit. *plaster over*
21 a Eccl. 9:5
CHAPTER 15
1 a Job 4:1
2 1 Lit. *his belly*
4 1 *meditation* or *complaint*
6 a [Luke 19:22]
7 a Prov. 8:25
8 a Rom. 11:34
9 a Job 12:3; 13:2
10 a Job 8:8–10; 12:12; 32:6, 7
11 1 Or *a secret thing*
12 1 Or *why do your eyes flash*
14 a Prov. 20:9
15 a Job 4:18; 25:5
16 a Ps. 14:3; 53:3
b Prov. 19:28
18 a Job 8:8; 20:4
19 a Joel 3:17
1 Or *earth*
20 a Ps. 90:12
21 a 1 Thess. 5:3
1 *Terrifying*
22 a Job 14:10–12
23 a Ps. 59:15; 109:10

Yes, your own lips testify against
you.
7 "*Are* you the first man *who* was
born?
[a]Or were you made before the hills?
8 [a]Have you heard the counsel of
God?
Do you limit wisdom to yourself?
9 [a]What do you know that we do not
know?
What do you understand that *is* not
in us?
10 [a]Both the gray-haired and the aged
are among us,
Much older than your father.
11 *Are* the consolations of God too
small for you,
And the word *spoken* [1]gently with
you?
12 Why does your heart carry you
away,
And [1]what do your eyes wink at,
13 That you turn your spirit against
God,
And let *such* words go out of your
mouth?
14 "What[a] *is* man, that he could be
pure?
And *he who is* born of a woman,
that he could be righteous?
15 [a]If *God* puts no trust in His saints,
And the heavens are not pure in
His sight,
16 [a]How much less man, *who is*
abominable and filthy,
[b]Who drinks iniquity like water!
17 "I will tell you, hear me;
What I have seen I will declare,
18 What wise men have told,
Not hiding *anything received* [a]from
their fathers,
19 To whom alone the [1]land was
given,
And [a]no alien passed among them:
20 The wicked man writhes with pain
all *his* days,
[a]And the number of years is hidden
from the oppressor.
21 [1]Dreadful sounds *are* in his ears;
[a]In prosperity the destroyer comes
upon him.
22 He does not believe that he will
[a]return from darkness,
For a sword is waiting for him.
23 He [a]wanders about for bread,
saying, 'Where *is it?*'

He knows [b]that a day of darkness is
ready at his hand.
24 Trouble and anguish make him
afraid;
They overpower him, like a king
ready for [1]battle.
25 For he stretches out his hand
against God,
And acts defiantly against the
Almighty,
26 Running stubbornly against Him
With his strong, embossed shield.

27 "Though[a] he has covered his face
with his fatness,
And made *his* waist heavy with fat,
28 He dwells in desolate cities,
In houses which no one inhabits,
Which are destined to become
ruins.
29 He will not be rich,
Nor will his wealth [a]continue,
Nor will his possessions overspread
the earth.
30 He will not depart from darkness;
The flame will dry out his branches,
And [a]by the breath of His mouth
he will go away.
31 Let him not [a]trust in futile *things,*
deceiving himself,
For futility will be his reward.
32 It will be accomplished [a]before his
time,
And his branch will not be green.
33 He will shake off his unripe grape
like a vine,
And cast off his blossom like an
olive tree.
34 For the company of hypocrites *will
be* barren,
And fire will consume the tents of
bribery.
35 [a]They conceive trouble and bring
forth futility;
Their womb prepares deceit."

Job Reproaches His Pitiless Friends

16 Then Job answered and said:

2 "I have heard many such things;
[a]Miserable[1] comforters *are* you all!
3 Shall [1]words of wind have an end?
Or what provokes you that you
answer?
4 I also could speak as you *do,*
If your soul were in my soul's
place.

23 [b] Job 18:12
24 [1] *attack*
27 [a] Ps. 17:10; 73:7; 119:70
29 [a] Job 20:28; 27:16, 17
30 [a] Job 4:9
31 [a] Is. 59:4
32 [a] Job 22:16
35 [a] Is. 59:4

CHAPTER 16
2 [a] Job 13:4; 21:34 [1] *Troublesome*
3 [1] Empty words
4 [a] Ps. 22:7; 109:25
7 [a] Job 7:3 [b] Job 16:20; 19:13–15
8 [a] Job 10:17
9 [a] Hos. 6:1 [b] Job 13:24; 33:10
10 [a] Ps. 22:13; 35:21 [b] Lam. 3:30
11 [a] Job 1:15, 17
12 [a] Job 9:17 [b] Job 7:20
13 [1] Lit. *kidneys*
14 [1] Vg. *giant*
15 [a] Ps. 7:5 [1] Lit. *horn*
16 [1] Lit. *red*
18 [a] [Ps. 66:18]

I could heap up words against you,
And [a]shake my head at you;
5 *But* I would strengthen you with
my mouth,
And the comfort of my lips would
relieve *your grief.*

6 "Though I speak, my grief is not
relieved;
And *if* I remain silent, how am I
eased?
7 But now He has [a]worn me out;
You [b]have made desolate all my
company.
8 You have shriveled me up,
And it is a [a]witness *against me;*
My leanness rises up against me
And bears witness to my face.
9 [a]He tears *me* in His wrath, and
hates me;
He gnashes at me with His teeth;
[b]My adversary sharpens His gaze on
me.
10 They [a]gape at me with their
mouth,
They [b]strike me reproachfully on
the cheek,
They gather together against me.
11 God [a]has delivered me to the
ungodly,
And turned me over to the hands of
the wicked.
12 I was at ease, but He has
[a]shattered me;
He also has taken *me* by my neck,
and shaken me to pieces;
He has [b]set me up for His target,
13 His archers surround me.
He pierces my [1]heart and does not
pity;
He pours out my gall on the
ground.
14 He breaks me with wound upon
wound;
He runs at me like a [1]warrior.

15 "I have sewn sackcloth over my
skin,
And [a]laid my [1]head in the dust.
16 My face is [1]flushed from weeping,
And on my eyelids *is* the shadow of
death;
17 Although no violence *is* in my
hands,
And my prayer *is* pure.

18 "O earth, do not cover my blood,
And [a]let my cry have no *resting*
place!

19 Surely even now [a]my witness *is* in heaven,
And my evidence *is* on high.
20 My friends scorn me;
My eyes pour out *tears* to God.
21 [a]Oh, that one might plead for a man with God,
As a man *pleads* for his [1]neighbor!
22 For when a few years are finished,
I shall [a]go the way of no return.

Job Prays for Relief

17 "My spirit is broken,
My days are extinguished,
[a]The grave *is ready* for me.
2 *Are* not mockers with me?
And does not my eye [1]dwell on their [a]provocation?

3 "Now put down a pledge for me with Yourself.
Who *is* he *who* [a]will shake hands with me?
4 For You have hidden their heart from [a]understanding;
Therefore You will not exalt *them*.
5 He who speaks flattery to *his* friends,
Even the eyes of his children will [a]fail.

6 "But He has made me [a]a byword of the people,
And I have become one in whose face men spit.
7 [a]My eye has also grown dim because of sorrow,
And all my members *are* like shadows.
8 Upright *men* are astonished at this,
And the innocent stirs himself up against the hypocrite.
9 Yet the righteous will hold to his [a]way,
And he who has [b]clean hands will be stronger and stronger.

10 "But please, [a]come back again, [1]all of you,
For I shall not find *one* wise *man* among you.
11 [a]My days are past,
My purposes are broken off,
Even the [1]thoughts of my heart.
12 They change the night into day;
'The light *is* near,' *they say,* in the face of darkness.
13 If I wait *for* the grave *as* my house,
If I make my bed in the darkness,
14 If I say to corruption, 'You *are* my father,'
And to the worm, 'You *are* my mother and my sister,'
15 Where then *is* my [a]hope?
As for my hope, who can see it?
16 *Will* they go down [a]to the gates of [1]Sheol?
Shall *we have* [b]rest together in the dust?"

Bildad: The Wicked Are Punished

18 Then [a]Bildad the Shuhite answered and said:
2 "How long *till* you put an end to words?
Gain understanding, and afterward we will speak.
3 Why are we counted [a]as beasts,
And regarded as stupid in your sight?
4 [a]You[1] who tear yourself in anger,
Shall the earth be forsaken for you?
Or shall the rock be removed from its place?

5 "The[a] light of the wicked indeed goes out,
And the flame of his fire does not shine.
6 The light is dark in his tent,
[a]And his lamp beside him is put out.
7 The steps of his strength are shortened,
And [a]his own counsel casts him down.
8 For [a]he is cast into a net by his own feet,
And he walks into a snare.
9 The net takes *him* by the heel,
And [a]a snare lays hold of him.
10 A noose *is* hidden for him on the ground,
And a trap for him in the road.
11 [a]Terrors frighten him on every side,
And drive him to his feet.
12 His strength is starved,
And [a]destruction *is* ready at his side.
13 It devours patches of his skin;
The firstborn of death devours his [1]limbs.
14 He is uprooted from [a]the shelter of his tent,

---

19 a Rom. 1:9
21 a Job 31:35 1 *friend*
22 a Eccl. 12:5

CHAPTER 17
1 a Ps. 88:3, 4
2 a Job 12:4; 17:6; 30:1, 9; 34:7 1 Lit. *lodge*
3 a Prov. 6:1; 17:18; 22:26
4 a Job 12:20; 32:9
5 a Job 11:20
6 a Job 30:9
7 a Ps. 6:7; 31:9
9 a Prov. 4:18 b Ps. 24:4
10 a Job 6:29 1 So with some Heb. mss., LXX, Syr., Vg.; MT, Tg. *all of them*
11 a Job 7:6 1 *desires*
15 a Job 7:6; 13:15; 14:19; 19:10
16 a Jon. 2:6 b Job 3:17–19; 21:33 1 The abode of the dead

CHAPTER 18
1 a Job 8:1
3 a Ps. 73:22
4 a Job 13:14 1 Lit. *One who tears his soul*
5 a Prov. 13:9; 20:20; 24:20
6 a Job 21:17
7 a Job 5:12, 13; 15:6
8 a Job 22:10
9 a Job 5:5
11 a Jer. 6:25
12 a Job 15:23
13 1 *parts*
14 a Job 11:20

And they parade him before the
king of terrors.
15 They dwell in his tent *who are*
none of his;
Brimstone is scattered on his
dwelling.
16 [a]His roots are dried out below,
And his branch withers above.
17 [a]The memory of him perishes from
the earth,
And he has no name [1]among the
renowned.
18 [1]He is driven from light into
darkness,
And chased out of the world.
19 [a]He has neither son nor posterity
among his people,
Nor any remaining in his dwellings.
20 Those [1]in the west are astonished
[a]at his day,
As those [2]in the east are frightened.
21 Surely such *are* the dwellings of
the wicked,
And this *is* the place *of him who*
[a]does not know God."

Job Trusts in His Redeemer

19 Then Job answered and said:
2 "How long will you torment my
soul,
And break me in pieces with words?
3 These ten times you have
[1]reproached me;
You are not ashamed *that* you
[2]have wronged me.
4 And if indeed I have erred,
My error remains with me.
5 If indeed you [a]exalt *yourselves*
against me,
And plead my disgrace against me,
6 Know then that [a]God has wronged
me,
And has surrounded me with His
net.

7 "If I cry out concerning [1]wrong, I
am not heard.
If I cry aloud, *there is* no justice.
8 [a]He has [1]fenced up my way, so that
I cannot pass;
And He has set darkness in my
paths.
9 [a]He has stripped me of my glory,
And taken the crown *from* my head.
10 He breaks me down on every side,
And I am gone;
My [a]hope He has uprooted like a
tree.
11 He has also kindled His wrath
against me,
And [a]He counts me as *one of* His
enemies.
12 His troops come together
And build up their road against me;
They encamp all around my tent.

13 "He[a] has removed my brothers far
from me,
And my acquaintances are
completely estranged from me.
14 My relatives have failed,
And my close friends have forgotten
me.
15 Those who dwell in my house, and
my maidservants,
Count me as a stranger;
I am an alien in their sight.
16 I call my servant, but he gives no
answer;
I beg him with my mouth.
17 My breath is offensive to my wife,
And I am [1]repulsive to the children
of my own body.
18 Even [a]young children despise me;
I arise, and they speak against me.
19 [a]All my close friends abhor me,
And those whom I love have turned
against me.
20 [a]My bone clings to my skin and to
my flesh,
And I have escaped by the skin of
my teeth.

21 "Have pity on me, have pity on me,
O you my friends,
For the hand of God has struck me!
22 Why do you [a]persecute me as God
does,
And are not satisfied with my flesh?

23 "Oh, that my words were written!
Oh, that they were inscribed in a
book!
24 That they were engraved on a rock
With an iron pen and lead, forever!
25 For I know *that* my Redeemer
lives,
And He shall stand at last on the
earth;
26 And after my skin is [1]destroyed,
this *I know,*
That [a]in my flesh I shall see God,
27 Whom I shall see for myself,
And my eyes shall behold, and not
another.
How my [1]heart yearns within me!

16 a Job 29:19
17 a [Ps. 34:16] *1* Lit. *before the outside,* i.e., the distinguished or famous
18 *1* Or *They drive him*
19 a Is. 14:22
20 a Ps. 37:13 *1* Lit. *who came after* *2* Lit. *who have gone before*
21 a Jer. 9:3

CHAPTER 19
3 *1 shamed* or *disgraced* *2* A Jewish tradition *make yourselves strange to me*
5 a Ps. 35:26; 38:16; 55:12, 13
6 a Job 16:11
7 *1 violence*
8 a Job 3:23 *1 walled off my way*
9 a Ps. 89:44
10 a Job 17:14–16
11 a Job 13:24; 33:10
13 a Ps. 31:11; 38:11; 69:8; 88:8, 18
17 *1* Lit. *strange*
18 a 2 Kin. 2:23
19 a Ps. 38:11; 55:12, 13
20 a Ps. 102:5
22 a Ps. 69:26
26 a [Ps. 17:15] *1* Lit. *struck off*
27 *1* Lit. *kidneys*

28 If you should say, 'How shall we
persecute him?'—
Since the root of the matter is
found in me,
29 Be afraid of the sword for
yourselves;
For wrath *brings* the punishment of
the sword,
That you may know *there is* a
judgment."

Thank You, Lord, that ___ know that their Redeemer lives, and that You will stand at last on the earth; and that they know they will see You, O God.

FROM JOB 19:25, 26

Zophar's Sermon on the Wicked Man

20 Then [a]Zophar the Naamathite answered and said:
2 "Therefore my anxious thoughts
make me answer,
Because of the turmoil within me.
3 I have heard the rebuke [1]that
reproaches me,
And the spirit of my understanding
causes me to answer.

4 "Do you *not* know this of [a]old,
Since man was placed on earth,
5 [a]That the triumphing of the wicked
is short,
And the joy of the hypocrite is *but*
for a [b]moment?
6 [a]Though his haughtiness mounts up
to the heavens,
And his head reaches to the clouds,
7 *Yet* he will perish forever like his
own refuse;
Those who have seen him will say,
'Where is he?'
8 He will fly away [a]like a dream, and
not be found;
Yes, he [b]will be chased away like a
vision of the night.
9 The eye *that* saw him will *see him*
no more,
Nor will his place behold him
anymore.
10 His children will seek the favor of
the poor,
And his hands will restore his
wealth.
11 His bones are full of [a]his youthful
vigor,
[b]But it will lie down with him in the
dust.

12 "Though evil is sweet in his mouth,
And he hides it under his tongue,
13 *Though* he spares it and does not
forsake it,
But still keeps it in his [1]mouth,
14 *Yet* his food in his stomach turns
sour;
It becomes cobra venom within
him.
15 He swallows down riches
And vomits them up again;
God casts them out of his belly.
16 He will suck the poison of cobras;
The viper's tongue will slay him.
17 He will not see [a]the streams,
The rivers flowing with honey and
cream.
18 He will restore that for which he
labored,
And will not swallow *it* down;
From the proceeds of business
He will get no enjoyment.
19 For he has [1]oppressed *and*
forsaken the poor,
He has violently seized a house
which he did not build.

20 "Because[a] he knows no quietness
in his [1]heart,
He will not save anything he
desires.
21 Nothing is left for him to eat;
Therefore his well-being will not
last.
22 In his self-sufficiency he will be in
distress;
Every hand of [1]misery will come
against him.
23 *When* he is about to fill his
stomach,
God will cast on him the fury of
His wrath,
And will rain *it* on him while he is
eating.
24 [a]He will flee from the iron weapon;
A bronze bow will pierce him
through.

CHAPTER 20
1 a Job 11:1
3 1 Lit. *of my insulting correction*
4 a Job 8:8; 15:10
5 a Ps. 37:35, 36 b [Job 8:13; 13:16; 15:34; 27:8]
6 a Is. 14:13, 14
8 a Ps. 73:20; 90:5 b Job 18:18; 27:21–23
11 a Job 13:26 b Job 21:26
13 1 Lit. *palate*
17 a Jer. 17:8
19 1 *crushed*
20 a Eccl. 5:13–15 1 Lit. *belly*
22 1 Or *the wretched* or *sufferer*
24 a Amos 5:19

25 It is drawn, and comes out of the body;
Yes, [a]the glittering *point comes* out of his [1]gall.
[b]Terrors *come* upon him;
26 Total darkness *is* reserved for his treasures.
[a]An unfanned fire will consume him;
It shall go ill with him who is left in his tent.
27 The heavens will reveal his iniquity,
And the earth will rise up against him.
28 The increase of his house will depart,
And his goods will flow away in the day of His [a]wrath.
29 [a]This *is* the portion from God for a wicked man,
The heritage appointed to him by God."

Job's Discourse on the Wicked

21 Then Job answered and said:
2 "Listen carefully to my speech,
And let this be your [1]consolation.
3 Bear with me that I may speak,
And after I have spoken, keep [a]mocking.
4 "As for me, *is* my complaint against man?
And if *it were,* why should I not be impatient?
5 Look at me and be astonished;
[a]Put *your* hand over *your* mouth.
6 Even when I remember I am terrified,
And trembling takes hold of my flesh.
7 [a]Why do the wicked live *and* become old,
Yes, become mighty in power?
8 Their descendants are established with them in their sight,
And their offspring before their eyes.
9 Their houses *are* safe from fear,
[a]Neither *is* [1]the rod of God upon them.
10 Their bull breeds without failure;
Their cow calves [a]without miscarriage.
11 They send forth their little ones like a flock,
And their children dance.
12 They sing to the tambourine and harp,
And rejoice to the sound of the flute.
13 They [a]spend their days in wealth,
And [1]in a moment go down to the [2]grave.
14 [a]Yet they say to God, 'Depart from us,
For we do not desire the knowledge of Your ways.
15 [a]Who *is* the Almighty, that we should serve Him?
And [b]what profit do we have if we pray to Him?'
16 Indeed [1]their prosperity *is* not in their hand;
[a]The counsel of the wicked is far from me.
17 "How often is the lamp of the wicked put out?
How often does their destruction come upon them,
The sorrows *God* [a]distributes in His anger?
18 [a]They are like straw before the wind,
And like chaff that a storm [1]carries away.
19 *They say,* 'God [1]lays up [2]one's iniquity [a]for his children';
Let Him recompense him, that he may know *it.*
20 Let his eyes see his destruction,
And [a]let him drink of the wrath of the Almighty.
21 For what does he care about his household after him,
When the number of his months is cut in half?
22 "Can[a] *anyone* teach God knowledge,
Since He judges those on high?
23 One dies in his full strength,
Being wholly at ease and secure;
24 His [1]pails are full of milk,
And the marrow of his bones is moist.
25 Another man dies in the bitterness of his soul,
Never having eaten with pleasure.
26 They [a]lie down alike in the dust,
And worms cover them.
27 "Look, I know your thoughts,
And the schemes *with which* you would wrong me.
28 For you say,

20:25 a Job 16:13 b Job 18:11, 14 1 Gallbladder
26 a Ps. 21:9
28 a Job 20:15; 21:30
29 a Job 27:13; 31:2, 3

CHAPTER 21
2 1 *comfort*
3 a Job 16:10
5 a Judg. 18:19
7 a [Jer. 12:1]
9 a Ps. 73:5 1 The rod of God's chastisement
10 a Ex. 23:26
13 a Job 21:23; 36:11 1 Without lingering 2 Or *Sheol*
14 a Job 22:17
15 a Ex. 5:2 b Mal. 3:14
16 a Prov. 1:10 1 Lit. *their goal*
17 a [Luke 12:46]
18 a Ps. 1:4; 35:5 1 *steals away*
19 a [Ex. 20:5] 1 *stores up* 2 Lit. *his*
20 a Is. 51:17
22 a [Is. 40:13; 45:9]
24 1 LXX, Vg. *bowels;* Syr. *sides;* Tg. *breasts*
26 a Eccl. 9:2

'Where *is* the house of the prince?
And where *is* [1]the tent,
The dwelling place of the wicked?'
29 Have you not asked those who travel the road?
And do you not know their signs?
30 [a]For the wicked are reserved for the day of doom;
They shall be brought out on the day of wrath.
31 Who condemns his way to his face?
And who repays him *for what* he has done?
32 Yet he shall be brought to the grave,
And a vigil kept over the tomb.
33 The clods of the valley shall be sweet to him;
[a]Everyone shall follow him,
As countless *have gone* before him.
34 How then can you comfort me with empty words,
Since [1]falsehood remains in your answers?"

Eliphaz Accuses Job of Wickedness

22 Then [a]Eliphaz the Temanite answered and said:

2 "Can[a] a man be profitable to God,
Though he who is wise may be profitable to himself?
3 *Is it* any pleasure to the Almighty that you are righteous?
Or *is it* gain *to Him* that you make your ways blameless?

4 "Is it because of your fear of Him that He corrects you,
And enters into judgment with you?
5 *Is* not your wickedness great,
And your iniquity without end?
6 For you have [a]taken pledges from your brother for no reason,
And stripped the naked of their clothing.
7 You have not given the weary water to drink,
And you [a]have withheld bread from the hungry.
8 But the [1]mighty man possessed the land,
And the honorable man dwelt in it.
9 You have sent widows away empty,
And the [1]strength of the fatherless was crushed.
10 Therefore snares *are* all around you,
And sudden fear troubles you,
11 Or darkness *so that* you cannot see;
And an abundance of [a]water covers you.

12 "Is not God in the height of heaven?
And see the highest stars, how lofty they are!
13 And you say, [a]'What does God know?
Can He judge through the deep darkness?
14 [a]Thick clouds cover Him, so that He cannot see,
And He walks above the circle of heaven.'
15 Will you keep to the old way
Which wicked men have trod,
16 Who [a]were cut down before their time,
Whose foundations were swept away by a flood?
17 [a]They said to God, 'Depart from us!
What can the Almighty do to [1]them?'
18 Yet He filled their houses with good *things;*
But the counsel of the wicked is far from me.

19 "The[a] righteous see *it* and are glad,
And the innocent laugh at them:
20 'Surely our [1]adversaries are cut down,
And the fire consumes their remnant.'

21 "Now acquaint yourself with Him, and [a]be at peace;
Thereby good will come to you.
22 Receive, please, [a]instruction from His mouth,
And [b]lay up His words in your heart.
23 If you return to the Almighty, you will be built up;
You will remove iniquity far from your tents.
24 Then you will [a]lay your gold in the dust,
And the *gold* of Ophir among the stones of the brooks.
25 Yes, the Almighty will be your [1]gold
And your precious silver;

28 [1] Vg. omits *the tent*
30 [a] [Prov. 16:4]
33 [a] Heb. 9:27
34 [1] *faithlessness*

CHAPTER 22
1 [a] Job 4:1; 15:1; 42:9
2 [a] [Luke 17:10]
6 [a] [Ex. 22:26, 27]
7 [a] Deut. 15:7
8 [1] Lit. *man of arm*
9 [1] Lit. *arms*
11 [a] Ps. 69:1, 2; 124:5
13 [a] Ps. 73:11
14 [a] Ps. 139:11, 12
16 [a] Job 14:19; 15:32
17 [a] Job 21:14, 15
[1] LXX, Syr. *us*
19 [a] Ps. 52:6; 58:10; 107:42
20 [1] LXX *substance is*
21 [a] Is. 27:5
22 [a] Prov. 2:6
[b] [Ps. 119:11]
24 [a] 2 Chr. 1:15
25 [1] Ancient vss. suggest *defense;* MT *gold,* as in v. 24

Job 22:21

Dear Woman of Destiny,

The best relationship you can commit to is a relationship with the Lord. We know so many people; we know our friends' likes and dislikes, their patterns and desires—but do we know God? We know many things about God; we know His marvelous deeds of the past, and we may have memorized His words in the Bible—but do we really know Him?

In Job 22:21, you will notice the word *now*. It doesn't matter what experiences you have had with God in the past, or what you might do together in the future. The issue is "now." What is God saying to you at this moment? Have you experienced His nearness today? Is He dearer to you today than yesterday?

Always keep your relationship with God in the present tense. This verse calls us to intimate communion with Him. Where there is intimacy, there is conception and consequent birthing. We will continuously bear everlasting fruit of His glory. A lifestyle of acquaintance with Him will prevent lukewarmness, discouragement, and backsliding. This is how to survive every assault from the enemy and every disappointment that comes your way—by knowing Him as *El Shaddai*, the All-Sufficient One.

The second phrase of Job 22:21 speaks of peace. Jesus is our peace, and He came to guide our feet into the way of peace (see Luke 1:79; Eph. 2:14). The peace of the Lord will keep you in a state of rest, quietness, and calmness. It will cushion you from stress and strife. It can keep you prosperous, healthy, and happy. Trouble may be all around you, but you can be insulated from it. The more you acquaint yourself with Him, the more you will be at peace.

What does the Bible say will happen when you acquaint yourself with Him and enter into peace? "Thereby good will come to you." When you acquaint yourself with Him, "you will have your delight in the Almighty" (v. 26). He has promised that when you delight yourself in Him, He will give you the desires of your heart (see Ps. 37:4). I have experienced this over and over. In fact, I have experienced all the promises of this teaching over and over again. The Lord and His Word have never failed me.

God wants to reveal Himself to you, too. He wants to be known by His children. He wants you to know that He's your provider, your fortress, your haven of rest, your strong tower, your defender, your father, your friend, your confidant, your true love, your prince. He desires to be everything to you. So I encourage you, my sister, to acquaint yourself with Him—right *now!*

Bobbie Jean Merck

26 For then you will have your
[a]delight in the Almighty,
And lift up your face to God.
27 [a]You will make your prayer to
Him,
He will hear you,
And you will pay your vows.
28 You will also declare a thing,
And it will be established for you;
So light will shine on your ways.
29 When they cast *you* down, and
you say, 'Exaltation *will come!*'
Then [a]He will save the humble
person.
30 He will *even* deliver one who is
not innocent;
Yes, he will be delivered by the
purity of your hands."

Job Proclaims God's Righteous Judgments

23 Then Job answered and said:

2 "Even today my [a]complaint is bitter;
[1]My hand is listless because of my
groaning.
3 [a]Oh, that I knew where I might find
Him,
That I might come to His seat!
4 I would present *my* case before
Him,
And fill my mouth with arguments.
5 I would know the words *which* He
would answer me,
And understand what He would say
to me.
6 [a]Would He contend with me in His
great power?
No! But He would take *note* of me.
7 There the upright could reason
with Him,
And I would be delivered forever
from my Judge.
8 "Look,[a] I go forward, but He is not
there,
And backward, but I cannot
perceive Him;
9 When He works on the left hand, I
cannot behold *Him;*
When He turns to the right hand, I
cannot see *Him.*
10 But [a]He knows the way that I
take;
When [b]He has tested me, I shall
come forth as gold.
11 [a]My foot has held fast to His steps;
I have kept His way and not turned
aside.
12 I have not departed from the
[a]commandment of His lips;
[b]I have treasured the words of His
mouth
More than my [1]necessary *food.*

Faith is the hand with which we take from God. When we have met all the conditions and taken what God is offering us, we must believe that we have that thing.

MRS. C. NUZUM

13 "But He *is* unique, and who can
make Him change?
And *whatever* [a]His soul desires,
that He does.
14 For He performs *what is*
[a]appointed for me,
And many such *things are* with
Him.
15 Therefore I am terrified at His
presence;
When I consider *this,* I am afraid of
Him.
16 For God [a]made my heart weak,
And the Almighty terrifies me;
17 Because I was not [a]cut off [1]from
the presence of darkness,
And He did *not* hide deep darkness
from my face.

Job Complains of Violence on the Earth

24 "*Since* [a]times are not hidden
from the Almighty,
Why do those who know Him see
not His [b]days?
2 "*Some* remove [a]landmarks;
They seize flocks violently and feed
on them;
3 They drive away the donkey of the
fatherless;
They [a]take the widow's ox as a
pledge.
4 They push the needy off the road;

---

26 a Job 27:10; Ps. 37:4; Is. 58:14
27 a [Is. 58:9–11]
29 a [1 Pet. 5:5]
CHAPTER 23
2 a Job 7:11 *1* So with MT, Tg., Vg.; LXX, Syr. *His*
3 a Job 13:3, 18; 16:21; 31:35
6 a Is. 57:16
8 a Job 9:11; 35:14
10 a [Ps. 1:6; 139:1–3] b [James 1:12]
11 a Ps. 17:5
12 a Job 6:10; 22:22 b Ps. 44:18 *1* Lit. *appointed portion*
13 a [Ps. 115:3]
14 a [1 Thess. 3:2–4]
16 a Ps. 22:14
17 a Job 10:18, 19 *1* Or *by* or *before*
CHAPTER 24
1 a [Acts 1:7] b [Is. 2:12]
2 a [Deut. 19:14; 27:17]
3 a [Deut. 24:6, 10, 12, 17]

All the [a]poor of the land are forced
to hide.
5 Indeed, *like* wild donkeys in the
desert,
They go out to their work,
searching for food.
The wilderness *yields* food for them
and for *their* children.
6 They gather their fodder in the
field
And glean in the vineyard of the
wicked.
7 They [a]spend the night naked,
without clothing,
And have no covering in the cold.
8 They are wet with the showers of
the mountains,
And [a]huddle around the rock for
want of shelter.

9 "*Some* snatch the fatherless from
the breast,
And take a pledge from the poor.
10 They cause *the poor* to go naked,
without [a]clothing;
And they take away the sheaves
from the hungry.
11 They press out oil within their
walls,
And tread winepresses, yet suffer
thirst.
12 The dying groan in the city,
And the souls of the wounded cry
out;
Yet God does not charge *them* with
wrong.

13 "There are those who rebel against
the light;
They do not know its ways
Nor abide in its paths.
14 [a]The murderer rises with the light;
He kills the poor and needy;
And in the night he is like a thief.
15 [a]The eye of the adulterer waits for
the twilight,
[b]Saying, 'No eye will see me';
And he [1]disguises *his* face.
16 In the dark they break into houses
Which they marked for themselves
in the daytime;
[a]They do not know the light.
17 For the morning is the same to
them as the shadow of death;
If *someone* recognizes *them,*
They are in the terrors of the
shadow of death.

18 "They *should be* swift on the face
of the waters,
Their portion *should be* cursed in
the earth,
So that no *one would* turn into the
way of their vineyards.
19 As drought and heat [1]consume the
snow waters,
So [2]the grave *consumes those who*
have sinned.
20 The womb *should* forget him,
The worm *should* feed sweetly on
him;
[a]He *should* be remembered no more,
And wickedness *should* be broken
like a tree.
21 For he [1]preys on the barren *who*
do not bear,
And does no good for the widow.

22 "But *God* draws the mighty away
with His power;
He rises up, but no *man* is sure of
life.
23 He gives them security, and they
rely *on it;*
Yet [a]His eyes *are* on their ways.
24 They are exalted for a little while,
Then they are gone.
They are brought low;
They are [1]taken out of the way like
all *others;*
They dry out like the heads of
grain.

25 "Now if *it is* not *so,* who will prove
me a liar,
And make my speech worth
nothing?"

Bildad: How Can Man Be Righteous?

25 Then [a]Bildad the Shuhite answered and said:

2 "Dominion and fear *belong* to Him;
He makes peace in His high places.
3 [1]Is there any number to His armies?
Upon whom does [a]His light not
rise?
4 [a]How then can man be righteous
before God?
Or how can he be [b]pure *who is*
born of a woman?
5 If even the moon does not shine,
And the stars are not pure in His
[a]sight,
6 How much less man, *who is* [a]a
maggot,
And a son of man, *who is* a worm?"

---

4 a Prov. 28:28
7 a Ex. 22:26, 27
8 a Lam. 4:5
10 a Job 31:19
14 a Ps. 10:8
15 a Prov. 7:7–10 b Ps. 10:11 *1* Lit. *puts a covering on his face*
16 a [John 3:20]
19 *1* Lit. *seize* *2* Or *Sheol*
20 a Prov. 10:7
21 *1* Lit. *feeds on*
23 a [Prov. 15:3]
24 *1* Lit. *gathered up*

CHAPTER 25
1 a Job 8:1; 18:1
3 a James 1:17 *1* Can His armies be counted?
4 a Job 4:17; 15:14 b [Job 14:4]
5 a Job 15:15
6 a Ps. 22:6

Job: Man's Frailty and God's Majesty

26 But Job answered and said:

2 "How have you helped *him who is*
without power?
How have you saved the arm *that*
has no strength?
3 How have you counseled *one who*
has no wisdom?
And *how* have you declared sound
advice to many?
4 To whom have you uttered words?
And whose spirit came from you?

5 "The dead tremble,
Those under the waters and those
inhabiting them.
6 [a]Sheol *is* naked before Him,
And Destruction has no covering.
7 [a]He stretches out the north over
empty space;
He hangs the earth on nothing.
8 [a]He binds up the water in His thick
clouds,
Yet the clouds [1]are not broken
under it.
9 He covers the face of *His* throne,
And spreads His cloud over it.
10 [a]He drew a circular horizon on the
face of the waters,
At the boundary of light and
darkness.
11 The pillars of heaven tremble,
And are [1]astonished at His rebuke.
12 [a]He stirs up the sea with His
power,
And by His understanding He
breaks up [1]the storm.
13 [a]By His Spirit He adorned the
heavens;
His hand pierced [b]the fleeing
serpent.
14 Indeed these *are* the mere edges
of His ways,
And how small a whisper we hear
of Him!
But the thunder of His power who
can understand?"

Job Maintains His Integrity

27 Moreover Job continued his discourse, and said:

2 "*As* God lives, [a]*who* has taken away
my justice,
And the Almighty, *who* has made
my soul bitter,
3 As long as my breath *is* in me,
And the breath of God in my
nostrils,
4 My lips will not speak wickedness,
Nor my tongue utter deceit.
5 Far be it from me
That I should say you are right;
Till I die [a]I will not put away my
integrity from me.
6 My righteousness I [a]hold fast, and
will not let it go;
[b]My heart shall not [1]reproach *me* as
long as I live.

7 "May my enemy be like the wicked,
And he who rises up against me
like the unrighteous.
8 [a]For what is the hope of the
hypocrite,
Though he may gain *much,*
If God takes away his life?
9 [a]Will God hear his cry
When trouble comes upon him?
10 [a]Will he delight himself in the
Almighty?
Will he always call on God?

11 "I will teach you [1]about the hand
of God;
What *is* with the Almighty I will
not conceal.
12 Surely all of you have seen *it;*
Why then do you behave with
complete nonsense?

13 "This[a] is the portion of a wicked
man with God,
And the heritage of oppressors,
received from the Almighty:
14 [a]If his children are multiplied, *it is*
for the sword;
And his offspring shall not be
satisfied with bread.
15 Those who survive him shall be
buried in death,
And [a]their[1] widows shall not weep,
16 Though he heaps up silver like
dust,
And piles up clothing like clay—
17 He may pile *it* up, but [a]the just
will wear *it,*
And the innocent will divide the
silver.
18 He builds his house like a [1]moth,
[a]Like a [2]booth *which* a watchman
makes.

CHAPTER 26
6 [a]Prov. 15:11
7 [a]Job 9:8
8 [a]Prov. 30:4 [1]*do not break*
10 [a]Prov. 8:29
11 [1]*amazed*
12 [a]Is. 51:15 [1]Heb. *rahab*
13 [a]Ps. 33:6 [b]Is. 27:1

CHAPTER 27
2 [a]Job 34:5
5 [a]Job 2:9; 13:15
6 [a]Job 2:3; 33:9 [b]Acts 24:16 [1]*reprove*
8 [a]Matt. 16:26
9 [a]Jer. 14:12
10 [a]Job 22:26, 27
11 [1]Or *by*
13 [a]Job 20:29
14 [a]Deut. 28:41
15 [a]Ps. 78:64 [1]Lit. *his*
17 [a]Prov. 28:8
18 [a]Is. 1:8 [1]So with MT, Vg.; LXX, Syr. *spider* (cf. 8:14); Tg. *decay* [2]Temporary shelter

19 The rich man will lie down,
[1]But not be gathered *up;*
He opens his eyes,
And he *is* [a]no more.
20 [a]Terrors overtake him like a flood;
A tempest steals him away in the
night.
21 The east wind carries him away,
and he is gone;
It sweeps him out of his place.
22 It hurls against him and does not
[a]spare;
He flees desperately from its
[1]power.
23 *Men* shall clap their hands at
him,
And shall hiss him out of his place.

Job's Discourse on Wisdom

28 "Surely there is a mine for silver,
And a place *where* gold is
refined.
2 Iron is taken from the [1]earth,
And copper *is* smelted *from* ore.
3 *Man* puts an end to darkness,
And searches every recess
For ore in the darkness and the
shadow of death.
4 He breaks open a shaft away from
people;
In places forgotten by feet
They hang far away from men;
They swing to and fro.
5 *As for* the earth, from it comes
bread,
But underneath it is turned up as
by fire;
6 Its stones *are* the source of
sapphires,
And it contains gold dust.
7 *That* path no bird knows,
Nor has the falcon's eye seen it.
8 The [1]proud lions have not trodden
it,
Nor has the fierce lion passed over
it.
9 He puts his hand on the flint;
He overturns the mountains [1]at the
roots.
10 He cuts out channels in the rocks,
And his eye sees every precious
thing.
11 He dams up the streams from
trickling;
What is hidden he brings forth to
light.

12 "But[a] where can wisdom be found?
And where *is* the place of
understanding?
13 Man does not know its [a]value,
Nor is it found in the land of the
living.
14 [a]The deep says, *'It is* not in me';
And the sea says, *'It is* not with
me.'
15 It [a]cannot be purchased for gold,
Nor can silver be weighed *for* its
price.
16 It cannot be valued in the gold of
Ophir,
In precious onyx or sapphire.
17 Neither [a]gold nor crystal can
equal it,
Nor can it be exchanged for
[1]jewelry of fine gold.
18 No mention shall be made of
[1]coral or quartz,
For the price of wisdom *is* above
[a]rubies.
19 The topaz of Ethiopia cannot
equal it,
Nor can it be valued in pure [a]gold.

20 "From[a] where then does wisdom
come?
And where *is* the place of
understanding?
21 It is hidden from the eyes of all
living,
And concealed from the birds of the
[1]air.
22 [a]Destruction[1] and Death say,
'We have heard a report about it
with our ears.
23 God understands its way,
And He knows its place.
24 For He looks to the ends of the
earth,
And [a]sees under the whole heavens,
25 [a]To establish a weight for the wind,
And apportion the waters by
measure.
26 When He [a]made a law for the
rain,
And a path for the thunderbolt,
27 Then He saw [1]*wisdom* and
declared it;
He prepared it, indeed, He searched
it out.
28 And to man He said,
'Behold, [a]the fear of the Lord, that
is wisdom,
And to depart from evil *is*
understanding.' "

19 [a] Job 7:8, 21; 20:7 [1] So with MT, Tg.; LXX, Syr. *But shall not add* (i.e., do it again); Vg. *But take away nothing*
20 [a] Job 18:11
22 [a] Jer. 13:14 [1] Lit. *hand*

CHAPTER 28
2 [1] Lit. *dust*
8 [1] Lit. *sons of pride,* figurative of the great lions
9 [1] At the base
12 [a] Eccl. 7:24
13 [a] Prov. 3:15
14 [a] Job 28:22
15 [a] Prov. 3:13–15; 8:10, 11, 19
17 [a] Prov. 8:10; 16:16 [1] *vessels*
18 [a] Prov. 3:15; 8:11 [1] Heb. *ramoth*
19 [a] Prov. 8:19
20 [a] Job 28:12
21 [1] *heaven*
22 [a] Job 28:14 [1] Heb. *Abaddon*
24 [a] [Prov. 15:3]
25 [a] Ps. 135:7
26 [a] Job 37:3; 38:25
27 [1] Lit. *it*
28 [a] [Prov. 1:7; 9:10]

O God, may _____ understand that the fear of the Lord is wisdom. May they know that to depart from evil is understanding.

FROM JOB 28:28

Job's Summary Defense

29 Job further continued his discourse, and said:

2 "Oh, that I were as *in* months [a]past,
As *in* the days *when* God [b]watched over me;
3 [a]When His lamp shone upon my head,
And when by His light I walked *through* darkness;
4 Just as I was in the days of my prime,
When [a]the friendly counsel of God *was* over my tent;
5 When the Almighty *was* yet with me,
When my children *were* around me;
6 When [a]my steps were bathed with [1]cream,
And [b]the rock poured out rivers of oil for me!

7 "When I went out to the gate by the city,
When I took my seat in the open square,
8 The young men saw me and hid,
And the aged arose *and* stood;
9 The princes refrained from talking,
And [a]put *their* hand on their mouth;
10 The voice of nobles was hushed,
And their [a]tongue stuck to the roof of their mouth.
11 When the ear heard, then it blessed me,
And when the eye saw, then it approved me;
12 Because [a]I delivered the poor who cried out,
The fatherless and *the one who* had no helper.
13 The blessing of a perishing *man* came upon me,
And I caused the widow's heart to sing for joy.
14 [a]I put on righteousness, and it clothed me;
My justice *was* like a robe and a turban.
15 I *was* [a]eyes to the blind,
And I *was* feet to the lame.
16 I *was* a father to the poor,
And [a]I searched out the case *that* I did not know.
17 I broke [a]the fangs of the wicked,
And plucked the victim from his teeth.

18 "Then I said, [a]'I shall die in my nest,
And multiply *my* days as the sand.
19 [a]My root *is* spread out [b]to the waters,
And the dew lies all night on my branch.
20 My glory *is* fresh within me,
And my [a]bow is renewed in my hand.'

21 "*Men* listened to me and waited,
And kept silence for my counsel.
22 After my words they did not speak again,
And my speech settled on them *as dew*.
23 They waited for me *as* for the rain,
And they opened their mouth wide *as* for [a]the spring rain.
24 *If* I mocked at them, they did not believe *it*,
And the light of my countenance they did not cast down.
25 I chose the way for them, and sat as chief;
So I dwelt as a king in the army,
As one *who* comforts mourners.

30 "But now they mock at me, *men* [1]younger than I,
Whose fathers I disdained to put with the dogs of my flock.
2 Indeed, what *profit* is the strength of their hands to me?
Their vigor has perished.
3 *They are* gaunt from want and famine,
Fleeing late to the wilderness, desolate and waste,
4 Who pluck [1]mallow by the bushes,
And broom tree roots *for* their food.
5 They were driven out from among *men*,

CHAPTER 29
2 a Job 1:1–5 b Job 1:10
3 a Job 18:6
4 a [Ps. 25:14]
6 a Deut. 32:14; Job 20:17 b Ps. 81:16 *1* So with ancient vss. and a few Heb. mss. (cf. Job 20:17); MT *wrath*
9 a Job 21:5
10 a Ps. 137:6
12 a [Ps. 72:12]
14 a [Is. 59:17; 61:10]
15 a Num. 10:31
16 a Prov. 29:7
17 a Prov. 30:14
18 a Ps. 30:6
19 a Job 18:16 b Ps. 1:3
20 a Gen. 49:24
23 a [Zech. 10:1]

CHAPTER 30
1 *1* Lit. *of fewer days*
4 *1* A plant of the salty marshes

They shouted at them as *at* a thief.
6 *They had* to live in the clefts of the [1]valleys,
In [2]caves of the earth and the rocks.
7 Among the bushes they brayed,
Under the nettles they nestled.
8 *They were* sons of fools,
Yes, sons of vile men;
They were scourged from the land.

9 "And[a] now I am their taunting song;
Yes, I am their byword.
10 They abhor me, they keep far from me;
They do not hesitate [a]to spit in my face.
11 Because [a]He has loosed [1]my bowstring and afflicted me,
They have cast off restraint before me.
12 At *my* right *hand* the rabble arises;
They push away my feet,
And [a]they raise against me their ways of destruction.
13 They break up my path,
They promote my calamity;
They have no helper.
14 They come as broad breakers;
Under the ruinous storm they roll along.
15 Terrors are turned upon me;
They pursue my honor as the wind,
And my prosperity has passed like a cloud.

16 "And[a] now my soul is [b]poured out because of my *plight;*
The days of affliction take hold of me.
17 My bones are pierced in me at night,
And my gnawing pains take no rest.
18 By great force my garment is disfigured;
It binds me about as the collar of my coat.
19 He has cast me into the mire,
And I have become like dust and ashes.

20 "I [a]cry out to You, but You do not answer me;
I stand up, and You regard me.
21 *But* You have become cruel to me;
With the strength of Your hand You [a]oppose me.

6 [1] *wadis* [2] Lit. *holes*
9 [a] Job 17:6
10 [a] Is. 50:6
11 [a] Job 12:18 [1] So with MT, Syr., Tg.; LXX, Vg. *His*
12 [a] Job 19:12
16 [a] Ps. 42:4 [b] Ps. 22:14
20 [a] Job 19:7
21 [a] Job 10:3; 16:9, 14; 19:6, 22
23 [a] [Heb. 9:27]
25 [a] Ps. 35:13, 14
26 [a] Jer. 8:15
27 [1] *I seethe inside*
28 [a] Ps. 38:6; 42:9; 43:2
29 [a] Mic. 1:8
30 [a] Ps. 119:83 [b] Ps. 102:3

When contending with sickness, trouble, misunderstanding, discouragement, or depression, begin to see Jesus. Praise Him with all your heart, and the upward flight of His praises will lift you as with the wings of a great eagle above the woes of this earth.

AIMEE SEMPLE MCPHERSON

22 You lift me up to the wind and cause me to ride *on it;*
You spoil my success.
23 For I know *that* You will bring me *to* death,
And *to* the house [a]appointed for all living.

24 "Surely He would not stretch out *His* hand against a heap of ruins,
If they cry out when He destroys *it.*
25 [a]Have I not wept for him who was in trouble?
Has *not* my soul grieved for the poor?
26 [a]But when I looked for good, evil came *to me;*
And when I waited for light, then came darkness.
27 [1]My heart is in turmoil and cannot rest;
Days of affliction confront me.
28 [a]I go about mourning, but not in the sun;
I stand up in the assembly *and* cry out for help.
29 [a]I am a brother of jackals,
And a companion of ostriches.
30 [a]My skin grows black and falls from me;
[b]My bones burn with fever.
31 My harp is *turned* to mourning,
And my flute to the voice of those who weep.

31 "I have made a covenant with my eyes;
Why then should I [1]look upon a [a]young woman?
2 For what *is* the [a]allotment of God from above,
And the inheritance of the Almighty from on high?
3 *Is* it not destruction for the wicked,
And disaster for the workers of iniquity?
4 [a]Does He not see my ways,
And count all my steps?

5 "If I have walked with falsehood,
Or if my foot has hastened to deceit,
6 [1]Let me be weighed on honest scales,
That God may know my [a]integrity.
7 If my step has turned from the way,
Or [a]my heart walked after my eyes,
Or if any spot adheres to my hands,
8 *Then* [a]let me sow, and another eat;
Yes, let my harvest be [1]rooted out.

9 "If my heart has been enticed by a woman,
Or *if* I have lurked at my neighbor's door,
10 *Then* let my wife grind for [a]another,
And let others bow down over her.
11 For that *would be* wickedness;
Yes, [a]it *would be* iniquity *deserving of* judgment.
12 For that *would be* a fire *that* consumes to destruction,
And would root out all my increase.

13 "If I have [a]despised the cause of my male or female servant
When they complained against me,
14 What then shall I do when [a]God rises up?
When He punishes, how shall I answer Him?
15 [a]Did not He who made me in the womb make them?
Did not the same One fashion us in the womb?

16 "If I have kept the poor from *their* desire,
Or caused the eyes of the widow to [a]fail,
17 Or eaten my morsel by myself,
So that the fatherless could not eat of it
18 (But from my youth I reared him as a father,
And from my mother's womb I guided [1]*the widow*);
19 If I have seen anyone perish for lack of clothing,
Or any poor *man* without covering;
20 If his [1]heart has not [a]blessed me,
And *if* he was *not* warmed with the fleece of my sheep;
21 If I have raised my hand [a]against the fatherless,
When I saw I had help in the gate;
22 *Then* let my arm fall from my shoulder,
Let my arm be torn from the socket.
23 For [a]destruction *from* God *is* a terror to me,
And because of His magnificence I cannot endure.

24 "If[a] I have made gold my hope,
Or said to fine gold, '*You are* my confidence';
25 [a]If I have rejoiced because my wealth *was* great,
And because my hand had gained much;
26 [a]If I have observed the [1]sun when it shines,
Or the moon moving *in* brightness,
27 So that my heart has been secretly enticed,
And my mouth has kissed my hand;
28 This also *would be* an iniquity *deserving of* judgment,
For I would have denied God *who is* above.

29 "If[a] I have rejoiced at the destruction of him who hated me,
Or lifted myself up when evil found him
30 [a](Indeed I have not allowed my mouth to sin
By asking for a curse on his [1]soul);
31 If the men of my tent have not said,
'Who is there that has not been satisfied with his meat?'
32 [a](*But* no sojourner had to lodge in the street,
For I have opened my doors to the [1]traveler);
33 If I have covered my transgressions [a]as[1] Adam,

CHAPTER 31
1 a [Matt. 5:28] *1 look intently* or *gaze*
2 a Job 20:29
4 a [2 Chr. 16:9]
6 a Job 23:10; 27:5, 6 *1* Lit. *Let Him weigh me*
7 a Ezek. 6:9
8 a Lev. 26:16 *1 uprooted*
10 a Jer. 8:10
11 a Gen. 38:24
13 a [Deut. 24:14, 15]
14 a [Ps. 44:21]
15 a Job 34:19
16 a Job 29:12
18 *1* Lit. *her*
20 a [Deut. 24:13] *1* Lit. *loins*
21 a Job 22:9
23 a Is. 13:6
24 a [Mark 10:23–25]
25 a Ps. 62:10
26 a Ezek. 8:16 *1* Lit. *light*
29 a [Prov. 17:5; 24:17]
30 a [Matt. 5:44] *1* Or *life*
32 a Gen. 19:2, 3 *1* So with LXX, Syr., Tg., Vg.; MT *road*
33 a [Prov. 28:13] *1* Or *as men do*

By hiding my iniquity in my
bosom,
34 Because I feared the great
[a]multitude,
And dreaded the contempt of
families,
So that I kept silence
And did not go out of the door—
35 [a]Oh, that I had one to hear me!
Here is my mark.
Oh, [b]*that* the Almighty would
answer me,
That my [1]Prosecutor had written a
book!
36 Surely I would carry it on my
shoulder,
And bind it on me *like* a crown;
37 I would declare to Him the
number of my steps;
Like a prince I would approach
Him.

38 "If my land cries out against me,
And its furrows weep together;
39 If [a]I have eaten its [1]fruit without
money,
Or [b]caused its owners to lose their
lives;
40 *Then* let [a]thistles grow instead of
wheat,
And weeds instead of barley."

The words of Job are ended.

Elihu Contradicts Job's Friends

32 So these three men ceased answering Job, because he *was* [a]righteous
in his own eyes. 2Then the wrath of Elihu,
the son of Barachel the [a]Buzite, of the
family of Ram, was aroused against Job;
his wrath was aroused because he [b]justi-
fied himself rather than God. 3Also
against his three friends his wrath was
aroused, because they had found no answer, and *yet* had condemned Job.
4Now because they *were* years older
than he, Elihu had waited [1]to speak to
Job. 5When Elihu saw that *there was* no
answer in the mouth of these three men,
his wrath was aroused.
6So Elihu, the son of Barachel the Bu-
zite, answered and said:

"I *am* [a]young in years, and you *are*
very old;
Therefore I was afraid,
And dared not declare my opinion
to you.
7 I said, [1]'Age should speak,
And multitude of years should teach
wisdom.'
8 But *there is* a spirit in man,
And [a]the breath of the Almighty
gives him understanding.
9 [a]Great[1] men are not *always* wise,
Nor do the aged *always* understand
justice.

10 "Therefore I say, 'Listen to me,
I also will declare my opinion.'
11 Indeed I waited for your words,
I listened to your reasonings, while
you searched out what to say.
12 I paid close attention to you;
And surely not one of you
convinced Job,
Or answered his words—
13 [a]Lest you say,
'We have found wisdom';
God will vanquish him, not man.
14 Now he has not [1]directed *his*
words against me;
So I will not answer him with your
words.

15 "They are dismayed and answer no
more;
Words escape them.
16 And I have waited, because they
did not speak,
Because they stood still *and*
answered no more.
17 I also will answer my part,
I too will declare my opinion.
18 For I am full of words;
The spirit within me compels me.
19 Indeed my [1]belly *is* like wine *that*
has no [2]vent;
It is ready to burst like new
wineskins.
20 I will speak, that I may find relief;
I must open my lips and answer.
21 Let me not, I pray, show partiality
to anyone;
Nor let me flatter any man.
22 For I do not know how to flatter,
Else my Maker would soon take me
[a]away.

Elihu Contradicts Job

33 "But please, Job, hear my speech,
And listen to all my words.
2 Now, I open my mouth;
My tongue speaks in my mouth.
3 My words *come* from my upright
heart;
My lips utter pure knowledge.

34 a Ex. 23:2
35 a Job 19:7; 30:20, 24, 28 b Job 13:22, 24; 33:10 *1 Lit. Accuser*
39 a Job 24:6, 10–12 b 1 Kin. 21:19 *1 Lit. strength*
40 a Gen. 3:18
CHAPTER 32
1 a Job 6:29; 31:6; 33:9
2 a Gen. 22:21 b Job 27:5, 6
4 *1 Vg. till Job had spoken*
6 a Lev. 19:32
7 *1 Lit. Days,* i.e., years
8 a [Prov. 2:6]
9 a [1 Cor. 1:26] *1 Or Men of many years*
13 a [Jer. 9:23]
14 *1 ordered*
19 *1 bosom 2 opening*
22 a Job 27:8

4 [a]The Spirit of God has made me,
And the breath of the Almighty
gives me life.
5 If you can answer me,
Set *your words* in order before me;
Take your stand.
6 [a]Truly I *am* [1]as your spokesman
before God;
I also have been formed out of clay.
7 [a]Surely no fear of me will terrify
you,
Nor will my hand be heavy on you.

8 "Surely you have spoken [1]in my
hearing,
And I have heard the sound of *your*
words, *saying,*
9 'I[a] *am* pure, without transgression;
I *am* innocent, and *there is* no
iniquity in me.
10 Yet He finds occasions against me,
[a]He counts me as His enemy;
11 [a]He puts my feet in the stocks,
He watches all my paths.'

12 "Look, *in* this you are not
righteous.
I will answer you,
For God is greater than man.
13 Why do you [a]contend with Him?
For He does not give an accounting
of any of His words.
14 [a]For God may speak in one way, or
in another,
Yet man does not perceive it.
15 [a]In a dream, in a vision of the
night,
When deep sleep falls upon men,
While slumbering on their beds,
16 [a]Then He opens the ears of men,
And seals their instruction.
17 In order to turn man *from his*
deed,
And conceal pride from man,
18 He keeps back his soul from the
Pit,
And his life from [1]perishing by the
sword.

19 "*Man* is also chastened with pain
on his [a]bed,
And with strong *pain* in many of
his bones,
20 [a]So that his life abhors [b]bread,
And his soul [1]succulent food.
21 His flesh wastes away from sight,
And his bones stick out *which once*
were not seen.
22 Yes, his soul draws near the Pit,
And his life to the executioners.

CHAPTER 33
4 a [Gen. 2:7]
6 a Job 4:19
1 Lit. *as your mouth*
7 a Job 9:34
8 *1* Lit. *in my ears*
9 a Job 10:7
10 a Job 13:24; 16:9
11 a Job 13:27; 19:8
13 a [Is. 45:9]
14 a Ps. 62:11
15 a [Num. 12:6]
16 a [Job 36:10, 15]
18 *1* Lit. *passing*
19 a Job 30:17
20 a Ps. 107:18
b Job 3:24; 6:7
1 desirable
24 *1 an atonement*
27 a [Luke 15:21]
b [Rom. 6:21]
28 a Is. 38:17
1 Kt. *my*
30 a Ps. 56:13
33 a Ps. 34:11
1 Keep silent

23 "If there is a messenger for him,
A mediator, one among a thousand,
To show man His uprightness,
24 Then He is gracious to him, and
says,
'Deliver him from going down to
the Pit;
I have found [1]a ransom';
25 His flesh shall be young like a
child's,
He shall return to the days of his
youth.
26 He shall pray to God, and He will
delight in him,
He shall see His face with joy,
For He restores to man His
righteousness.
27 Then he looks at men and [a]says,
'I have sinned, and perverted *what*
was right,
And it [b]did not profit me.'
28 He will [a]redeem [1]his soul from
going down to the Pit,
And [1]his life shall see the light.

The salvation of God embraces deliverance, restoration, preservation and glorification.

CATHERINE BOOTH

29 "Behold, God works all these
things,
Twice, *in fact,* three *times* with a
man,
30 [a]To bring back his soul from the
Pit,
That he may be enlightened with
the light of life.

31 "Give ear, Job, listen to me;
Hold your peace, and I will speak.
32 If you have anything to say,
answer me;
Speak, for I desire to justify you.
33 If not, [a]listen to me;
[1]Hold your peace, and I will teach
you wisdom."

Elihu Proclaims God's Justice

34

Elihu further answered and said:

2 "Hear my words, you wise *men;*
Give ear to me, you who have knowledge.
3 [a]For the ear tests words
As the palate tastes food.
4 Let us choose justice for ourselves;
Let us know among ourselves what *is* good.

5 "For Job has said, [a]'I am righteous,
But [b]God has taken away my justice;
6 [a]Should I lie concerning my right?
My [1]wound *is* incurable, *though I am* without transgression.'
7 What man *is* like Job,
[a]*Who* drinks [1]scorn like water,
8 Who goes in company with the workers of iniquity,
And walks with wicked men?
9 For [a]he has said, 'It profits a man nothing
That he should delight in God.'

10 "Therefore listen to me, you [1]men of understanding:
[a]Far be it from God *to do* wickedness,
And *from* the Almighty to *commit* iniquity.
11 [a]For He repays man *according to* his work,
And makes man to find a reward according to *his* way.
12 Surely God will never do wickedly,
Nor will the Almighty [a]pervert justice.
13 Who gave Him charge over the earth?
Or who appointed *Him over* the whole world?
14 If He should set His heart on it,
If He should [a]gather to Himself His Spirit and His breath,
15 [a]All flesh would perish together,
And man would return to dust.

16 "If *you have* understanding, hear this;
Listen to the sound of my words:
17 [a]Should one who hates justice govern?
Will you [b]condemn *Him who is* most just?
18 [a]*Is it fitting* to say to a king, '*You are* worthless,'
And to nobles, '*You are* wicked'?
19 Yet He [a]is not partial to princes,
Nor does He regard the rich more than the poor;
For [b]they *are* all the work of His hands.
20 In a moment they die, [a]in the middle of the night;
The people are shaken and pass away;
The mighty are taken away without a hand.

21 "For[a] His eyes *are* on the ways of man,
And He sees all his steps.
22 [a]There is no darkness nor shadow of death
Where the workers of iniquity may hide themselves.
23 For He need not further consider a man,
That he should go before God in judgment.
24 [a]He breaks in pieces mighty men without inquiry,
And sets others in their place.
25 Therefore He knows their works;
He overthrows *them* in the night,
And they are crushed.
26 He strikes them as wicked *men*
In the open sight of others,
27 Because they [a]turned back from Him,
And [b]would not consider any of His ways,
28 So that they [a]caused the cry of the poor to come to Him;
For He [b]hears the cry of the afflicted.
29 When He gives quietness, who then can make trouble?
And when He hides *His* face, who then can see Him,
Whether *it is* against a nation or a man alone?—
30 That the hypocrite should not reign,
Lest the people be ensnared.

31 "For has *anyone* said to God,
'I have borne *chastening;*
I will offend no more;
32 Teach me *what* I do not see;
If I have done iniquity, I will do no more'?
33 Should He repay *it* according to your *terms,*
Just because you disavow it?

CHAPTER 34
3 a Job 6:30; 12:11
5 a Job 13:18; 33:9 b Job 27:2
6 a Job 6:4; 9:17 *1 Lit. arrow*
7 a Job 15:16 *1 derision*
9 a Mal. 3:14
10 a Job 8:3; 36:23 *1 men of heart*
11 a Ps. 62:12
12 a Job 8:3
14 a Ps. 104:29
15 a [Gen. 3:19]
17 a 2 Sam. 23:3 b Job 40:8
18 a Ex. 22:28
19 a [Deut. 10:17] b Job 31:15
20 a Ex. 12:29
21 a Job 31:4
22 a [Amos 9:2, 3]
24 a [Dan. 2:21]
27 a 1 Sam. 15:11 b Is. 5:12
28 a Job 35:9 b [Ex. 22:23]

You must choose, and not I;
Therefore speak what you know.

34 "Men of understanding say to me,
Wise men who listen to me:
35 'Job[a] speaks without knowledge,
His words *are* without wisdom.'
36 Oh, that Job were tried to the utmost,
Because *his* answers *are like* those of wicked men!
37 For he adds [a]rebellion to his sin;
He claps *his hands* among us,
And multiplies his words against God."

Elihu Condemns Self-Righteousness

35 Moreover Elihu answered and said:

2 "Do you think this is right?
Do you say,
'My righteousness is more than God's'?
3 For [a]you say,
'What advantage will it be to You?
What profit shall I have, more than *if* I had sinned?'

4 "I will answer you,
And [a]your companions with you.
5 [a]Look to the heavens and see;
And behold the clouds—
They are higher than you.
6 If you sin, what do you accomplish [a]against Him?
Or, *if* your transgressions are multiplied, what do you do to Him?
7 [a]If you are righteous, what do you give Him?
Or what does He receive from your hand?
8 Your wickedness affects a man such as you,
And your righteousness a son of man.

9 "Because[a] of the multitude of oppressions they cry out;
They cry out for help because of the arm of the mighty.
10 But no one says, [a]'Where *is* God my Maker,
[b]Who gives songs in the night,
11 Who [a]teaches us more than the beasts of the earth,
And makes us wiser than the birds of heaven?'
12 [a]There they cry out, but He does not answer,
Because of the pride of evil men.
13 [a]Surely God will not listen to empty *talk*,
Nor will the Almighty regard it.
14 [a]Although you say you do not see Him,
Yet justice *is* before Him, and [b]you must wait for Him.
15 And now, because He has not [a]punished in His anger,
Nor taken much notice of folly,
16 [a]Therefore Job opens his mouth in vain;
He multiplies words without knowledge."

Elihu Proclaims God's Goodness

36 Elihu also proceeded and said:

2 "Bear with me a little, and I will show you
That *there are* yet words to speak on God's behalf.
3 I will fetch my knowledge from afar;
I will ascribe righteousness to my Maker.
4 For truly my words *are* not false;
One who is perfect in knowledge *is* with you.

5 "Behold, God *is* mighty, but despises *no one;*
[a]*He is* mighty in strength [1]of understanding.
6 He does not preserve the life of the wicked,
But gives justice to the [a]oppressed.
7 [a]He does not withdraw His eyes from the righteous;
But [b]*they are* on the throne with kings,
For He has seated them forever,
And they are exalted.
8 And [a]if *they are* bound in [1]fetters,
Held in the cords of affliction,
9 Then He tells them their work and their transgressions—
That they have acted [1]defiantly.
10 [a]He also opens their ear to [1]instruction,
And commands that they turn from iniquity.
11 If they obey and serve *Him,*

34:35 a Job 35:16; 38:2
34:37 a Job 7:11; 10:1

CHAPTER 35
3 a Job 21:15; 34:9
4 a Job 34:8
5 a [Job 22:12]
6 a [Jer. 7:19]
7 a Prov. 9:12
9 a Job 34:28
10 a Is. 51:13 b Acts 16:25
11 a Ps. 94:12
12 a Prov. 1:28
13 a [Is. 1:15]
14 a Job 9:11 b [Ps. 37:5, 6]
15 a Ps. 89:32
16 a Job 34:35; 38:2

CHAPTER 36
5 a Job 12:13, 16; 37:23 *1 of heart*
6 a Job 5:15
7 a [Ps. 33:18; 34:15] b Ps. 113:8
8 a Ps. 107:10 *1 chains*
9 *1 proudly*
10 a Job 33:16; 36:15 *1 discipline*

Job 35:10

Dear Woman of Destiny,

Music is a powerful weapon that even scientists today recognize as influential in healing. But how much more effective music can be when it is God's music, played and sung by His people for His purposes! God's Word tells us that He inhabits the praises of His people (see 2 Chr. 5:13, 14). We are commanded often in His Word to sing, to praise, to clap and to rejoice with dancing and singing. Closer study of His Word reveals that throughout the ages, music was also used to prophesy to God's people (see 1 Chr. 25:1). That prophetic spirit, which is the testimony of Jesus (see Rev. 19:10), can bring insight not only into daily living, but into what is happening in the heavenlies, around God's throne! We can even sing, with the inspiration of the Holy Spirit, the actual music being sung by heavenly choirs!

Many times the psalmist cries, "Oh, sing to the LORD a new song!" (Ps. 96:1). What is a "new song"? It is one that has never been sung! To do that, we must sing "with the spirit," allowing the Holy Spirit to give us melodies and harmonies our minds have not yet embraced (see 1 Cor. 14:15). These songs will be whatever the Holy Spirit desires to minister that day. They might be songs the angels sing, or songs that Jesus is singing to His bride, the church. Song of Solomon, the Song of Songs, contains many songs from the bridegroom to the bride. Just as prophets spoke messages from God and acted out His word, so words from the Lord can come through song and music by voice or instrument (see 1 Sam. 10:5).

Hearing an articulated word from the Lord, whether audible or not, can bring us great comfort in times of darkness and distress in our lives. Hearing His word in music reaches places inside the heart of man that nothing else could penetrate. Often when we seek the Lord and He seems hidden from our view, we cry, "Where is God my Maker?" But when we have experienced the joy that songs in the darkness bring, we will add the rest of the sentence, "who gives songs in the night." As His music penetrates the darkness around us, we will experience the joy of the Lord that is our strength. Light will come to our path, and suddenly we will realize that the darkness is light to Him. He never sleeps, and at the deepest point of our need, He will come with songs of deliverance (see Ps. 32:7).

The key is that we must seek Him and His songs. As we pray and worship, we sing with the Spirit and give Him freedom to sing through us. Then, like Deborah in Judges 5, Moses in Exodus 15, or Miriam in Exodus 15:21, we can sing the "song of the LORD" (see 2 Chr. 29:25–27). God-breathed music will change our lives. Revelation will be released. Light will shine. God's glory will be revealed. Our hearts will be encouraged, comforted, and strengthened. But most of all, we will learn to know another wonderful facet of God, our Maker, who gives songs in the night!

Lora Allison

They shall [a]spend their days in prosperity,
And their years in pleasures.
12 But if they do not obey,
They shall perish by the sword,
And they shall die [1]without [a]knowledge.

13 "But the hypocrites in heart [a]store up wrath;
They do not cry for help when He binds them.
14 [a]They[1] die in youth,
And their life *ends* among the [2]perverted persons.
15 He delivers the poor in their affliction,
And opens their ears in oppression.

16 "Indeed He would have brought you out of dire distress,
[a]*Into* a broad place where *there is* no restraint;
And [b]what is set on your table *would be* full of [c]richness.
17 But you are filled with the judgment due the [a]wicked;
Judgment and justice take hold *of you.*
18 Because *there is* wrath, *beware* lest He take you away with *one* blow;
For [a]a large ransom would not help you avoid *it.*
19 [a]Will your riches,
Or all the mighty forces,
Keep you from distress?
20 Do not desire the night,
When people are cut off in their place.
21 Take heed, [a]do not turn to iniquity,
For [b]you have chosen this rather than affliction.

22 "Behold, God is exalted by His power;
Who teaches like Him?
23 [a]Who has assigned Him His way,
Or who has said, 'You have done [b]wrong'?

Elihu Proclaims God's Majesty

24 "Remember to [a]magnify His work,
Of which men have sung.
25 Everyone has seen it;
Man looks on *it* from afar.
26 "Behold, God *is* great, and we [a]do not know *Him;*
[b]Nor can the number of His years *be* discovered.
27 For He [a]draws up drops of water,
Which distill as rain from the mist,
28 [a]Which the clouds drop down
And pour abundantly on man.
29 Indeed, can *anyone* understand the spreading of clouds,
The thunder from His canopy?
30 Look, He [a]scatters His light upon it,
And covers the depths of the sea.
31 For [a]by these He judges the peoples;
He [b]gives food in abundance.
32 [a]He covers *His* hands with lightning,
And commands it to [1]strike.
33 [a]His thunder declares it,
The cattle also, concerning [1]the rising *storm.*

37 "At this also my heart trembles,
And leaps from its place.
2 Hear attentively the thunder of His voice,
And the rumbling *that* comes from His mouth.
3 He sends it forth under the whole heaven,
His [1]lightning to the ends of the earth.
4 After it [a]a voice roars;
He thunders with His majestic voice,
And He does not restrain them when His voice is heard.
5 God thunders marvelously with His voice;
[a]He does great things which we cannot comprehend.
6 For [a]He says to the snow, 'Fall *on* the earth';
Likewise to the [1]gentle rain and the heavy rain of His strength.
7 He seals the hand of every man,
[a]That [b]all men may know His work.
8 The beasts [a]go into dens,
And remain in their lairs.
9 From the chamber *of the south* comes the whirlwind,
And cold from the scattering winds *of the north.*

---

11 a [Is. 1:19, 20]
12 a Job 4:21 *1* MT *as one without knowledge*
13 a [Rom. 2:5]
14 a Ps. 55:23 *1* Lit. *Their soul dies* *2* Heb. *qedeshim,* those practicing sodomy or prostitution in religious rituals
16 a Ps. 18:19; 31:8; 118:5 b Ps. 23:5 c Ps. 36:8
17 a Job 22:5, 10, 11
18 a Ps. 49:7
19 a [Prov. 11:4]
21 a [Ps. 31:6; 66:18] b [Heb. 11:25]
23 a Job 34:13; [Is. 40:13, 14] b Job 8:3
24 a [Rev. 15:3]
26 a [1 Cor. 13:12] b Heb. 1:12
27 a Ps. 147:8
28 a [Prov. 3:20]
30 a Job 37:3
31 a [Acts 14:17] b Ps. 104:14, 15
32 a Ps. 147:8 *1 strike the mark*
33 a 1 Kin. 18:41 *1* Lit. *what is rising*

CHAPTER 37
3 *1* Or *light*
4 a Ps. 29:3
5 a Job 5:9; 9:10; 36:26
6 a Ps. 147:16, 17 *1* Lit. *shower of rain*
7 a Ps. 109:27 b Ps. 19:3, 4
8 a Ps. 104:21, 22

10 [a]By the breath of God ice is given,
And the broad waters are frozen.
11 Also with moisture He saturates
the thick clouds;
He scatters His [1]bright clouds.
12 And they swirl about, being turned
by His guidance,
That they may [a]do whatever He
commands them
On the face of [1]the whole earth.
13 [a]He causes it to come,
Whether for [1]correction,
Or [b]for His land,
Or [c]for mercy.

14 "Listen to this, O Job;
Stand still and [a]consider the
wondrous works of God.
15 Do you know when God
[1]dispatches them,
And causes the light of His cloud to
shine?
16 [a]Do you know how the clouds are
balanced,
Those wondrous works of [b]Him
who is perfect in knowledge?
17 Why *are* your garments hot,
When He quiets the earth by the
south *wind?*
18 With Him, have you [a]spread out
the [b]skies,
Strong as a cast metal mirror?

19 "Teach us what we should say to
Him,
For we can prepare nothing because
of the darkness.
20 Should He be told that I *wish to*
speak?
If a man were to speak, surely he
would be swallowed up.
21 Even now *men* cannot look at the
light *when it is* bright in the
skies,
When the wind has passed and
cleared them.
22 He comes from the north *as*
golden *splendor;*
With God *is* awesome majesty.
23 *As for* the Almighty, [a]we cannot
find Him;
[b]*He is* excellent in power,
In judgment and abundant justice;
He does not oppress.
24 Therefore men [a]fear Him;
He shows no partiality to any *who
are* [b]wise of heart."

10 a Ps. 147:17, 18
11 1 *clouds of light*
12 a Job 36:32 1 Lit. *the world of the earth*
13 a Ex. 9:18, 23 b Job 38:26, 27 c 1 Kin. 18:41–46 1 Lit. *a rod*
14 a Ps. 111:2
15 1 *places them*
16 a Job 36:29 b Job 36:4
18 a [Is. 44:24] b Ps. 104:2
23 a [1 Tim. 6:16] b [Job 9:4; 36:5]
24 a [Matt. 10:28] b [Matt. 11:25]

CHAPTER 38
1 a Ex. 19:16
2 a Job 34:35; 42:3 b 1 Tim. 1:7
3 a Job 40:7 1 Lit. *gird up your loins like*
4 a Ps. 104:5
5 1 *measuring line*
7 a Job 1:6
8 a Gen. 1:9
10 a Job 26:10
11 a [Ps. 89:9; 93:4]
12 a [Ps. 74:16; 148:5]
13 a Ps. 104:35
15 a Job 18:5 b Ps. 10:15; 37:17 1 Lit. *high*
16 a [Ps. 77:19]

The Lord Reveals His Omnipotence to Job

38 Then the LORD answered Job [a]out of the whirlwind, and said:

2 "Who[a] *is* this who darkens counsel
By [b]words without knowledge?
3 [a]Now [1]prepare yourself like a man;
I will question you, and you shall
answer Me.

4 "Where[a] were you when I laid the
foundations of the earth?
Tell *Me,* if you have understanding.
5 Who determined its measurements?
Surely you know!
Or who stretched the [1]line upon it?
6 To what were its foundations
fastened?
Or who laid its cornerstone,
7 When the morning stars sang
together,
And all [a]the sons of God shouted
for joy?

8 "Or[a] *who* shut in the sea with
doors,
When it burst forth *and* issued
from the womb;
9 When I made the clouds its
garment,
And thick darkness its swaddling
band;
10 When [a]I fixed My limit for it,
And set bars and doors;
11 When I said,
'This far you may come, but no
farther,
And here your proud waves [a]must
stop!'

12 "Have you [a]commanded the
morning since your days *began,*
And caused the dawn to know its
place,
13 That it might take hold of the
ends of the earth,
And [a]the wicked be shaken out of
it?
14 It takes on form like clay *under* a
seal,
And stands out like a garment.
15 From the wicked their [a]light is
withheld,
And [b]the [1]upraised arm is broken.

16 "Have you [a]entered the springs of
the sea?
Or have you walked in search of the
depths?

17 Have [a]the gates of death been
[1]revealed to you?
Or have you seen the doors of the
shadow of death?
18 Have you comprehended the
breadth of the earth?
Tell *Me,* if you know all this.

19 "Where *is* the way *to* the dwelling
of light?
And darkness, where *is* its place,
20 That you may take it to its
territory,
That you may know the paths *to* its
home?
21 Do you know *it,* because you were
born then,
Or *because* the number of your
days *is* great?

22 "Have you entered [a]the treasury of
snow,
Or have you seen the treasury of
hail,
23 [a]Which I have reserved for the
time of trouble,
For the day of battle and war?
24 By what way is light [1]diffused,
Or the east wind scattered over the
earth?

25 "Who [a]has divided a channel for
the overflowing *water,*
Or a path for the thunderbolt,
26 To cause it to rain on a land
where there is no one,
A wilderness in which *there is* no
man;
27 [a]To satisfy the desolate waste,
And cause to spring forth the
growth of tender grass?
28 [a]Has the rain a father?
Or who has begotten the drops of
dew?
29 From whose womb comes the ice?
And the [a]frost of heaven, who gives
it birth?
30 The waters harden like stone,
And the surface of the deep is
[a]frozen.[1]

31 "Can you bind the cluster of the
[a]Pleiades,[1]
Or loose the belt of Orion?
32 Can you bring out [1]Mazzaroth in
its season?
Or can you guide [2]the Great Bear
with its cubs?
33 Do you know [a]the ordinances of
the heavens?
Can you set their dominion over
the earth?

34 "Can you lift up your voice to the
clouds,
That an abundance of water may
cover you?
35 Can you send out lightnings, that
they may go,
And say to you, 'Here we *are!*'?
36 [a]Who has put wisdom in [1]the
mind?
Or who has given understanding to
the heart?
37 Who can number the clouds by
wisdom?
Or who can pour out the bottles of
heaven,
38 When the dust hardens in clumps,
And the clods cling together?

39 "Can[a] you hunt the prey for the
lion,
Or satisfy the appetite of the young
lions,
40 When they crouch in *their* dens,
Or lurk in their lairs to lie in wait?
41 [a]Who provides food for the raven,
When its young ones cry to God,
And wander about for lack of food?

39

"Do you know the time when the
wild [a]mountain goats bear
young?
Or can you mark when [b]the deer
gives birth?
2 Can you number the months *that*
they fulfill?
Or do you know the time when
they bear young?
3 They bow down,
They bring forth their young,
They deliver their [1]offspring.
4 Their young ones are healthy,
They grow strong with grain;
They depart and do not return to
them.

5 "Who set the wild donkey free?
Who loosed the bonds of the
[1]onager,
6 [a]Whose home I have made the
wilderness,
And the [1]barren land his dwelling?
7 He scorns the tumult of the city;
He does not heed the shouts of the
driver.
8 The range of the mountains *is* his
pasture,

17 a Ps. 9:13 1 Lit. *opened*
22 a Ps. 135:7
23 a Is. 30:30
24 1 Lit. *divided*
25 a Job 28:26
27 a Ps. 104:13, 14; 107:35
28 a Job 36:27, 28
29 a Ps. 147:16, 17
30 a [Job 37:10] 1 Lit. *imprisoned*
31 a Amos 5:8 1 Or *the Seven Stars*
32 1 Lit. *Constellations* 2 Or *Arcturus*
33 a Jer. 31:35, 36
36 a [Ps. 51:6] 1 Lit. *the inward parts*
39 a Ps. 104:21
41 a [Matt. 6:26]

CHAPTER 39
1 a Ps. 104:18 b Ps. 29:9
3 1 Lit. *pangs*
5 1 A species of wild donkey
6 a Jer. 2:24 1 Lit. *salt land*

And he searches after [a]every green thing.

9 "Will the [a]wild ox be willing to serve you?
Will he bed by your manger?
10 Can you bind the wild ox in the furrow with ropes?
Or will he plow the valleys behind you?
11 Will you trust him because his strength *is* great?
Or will you leave your labor to him?
12 Will you trust him to bring home your [1]grain,
And gather it to your threshing floor?

13 "The wings of the ostrich wave proudly,
But are her wings and pinions *like the* kindly stork's?
14 For she leaves her eggs on the ground,
And warms them in the dust;
15 She forgets that a foot may crush them,
Or that a wild beast may break them.
16 She [a]treats her young harshly, as though *they were* not hers;
Her labor is in vain, without [1]concern,
17 Because God deprived her of wisdom,
And did not [a]endow her with understanding.
18 When she lifts herself on high,
She scorns the horse and its rider.

19 "Have you given the horse strength?
Have you clothed his neck with [1]thunder?
20 Can you [1]frighten him like a locust?
His majestic snorting strikes terror.
21 He paws in the valley, and rejoices in *his* strength;
[a]He gallops into the clash of arms.
22 He mocks at fear, and is not frightened;
Nor does he turn back from the sword.
23 The quiver rattles against him,
The glittering spear and javelin.
24 He devours the distance with fierceness and rage;
Nor does he come to a halt because the trumpet *has* sounded.
25 At *the blast of* the trumpet he says, 'Aha!'
He smells the battle from afar,
The thunder of captains and shouting.

26 "Does the hawk fly by your wisdom,
And spread its wings toward the south?
27 Does the [a]eagle mount up at your command,
And [b]make its nest on high?
28 On the rock it dwells and resides,
On the crag of the rock and the stronghold.
29 From there it spies out the prey;
Its eyes observe from afar.
30 Its young ones suck up blood;
And [a]where the slain *are,* there it *is.*"

40 Moreover the LORD [a]answered Job, and said:

2 "Shall [a]the one who contends with the Almighty correct *Him?*
He who [b]rebukes God, let him answer it."

Job's Response to God

3 Then Job answered the LORD and said:

4 "Behold,[a] I am vile;
What shall I answer You?
[b]I lay my hand over my mouth.
5 Once I have spoken, but I will not answer;
Yes, twice, but I will proceed no further."

God's Challenge to Job

6 [a]Then the LORD answered Job out of
the whirlwind, and said:

7 "Now[a] [1]prepare yourself like a man;
[b]I will question you, and you shall answer Me:

8 "Would[a] you indeed [1]annul My judgment?
Would you condemn Me that you may be justified?
9 Have you an arm like God?
Or can you thunder with [a]a voice like His?
10 [a]Then adorn yourself *with* majesty and splendor,

---

8 a Gen. 1:29
9 a Num. 23:22
12 1 Lit. *seed*
16 a Lam. 4:3 1 Lit. *fear*
17 a Job 35:11
19 1 Or a *mane*
20 1 *make him spring*
21 a Jer. 8:6
27 a Prov. 30:18, 19 b Jer. 49:16
30 a Matt. 24:28
CHAPTER 40
1 a Job 38:1
2 a Job 9:3; 10:2; 33:13 b Job 13:3; 23:4
4 a Ezra 9:6 b Job 29:9
6 a Job 38:1
7 a Job 38:3 b Job 42:4 1 Lit. *gird up your loins*
8 a [Rom. 3:4] 1 *nullify*
9 a [Ps. 29:3, 4]
10 a Ps. 93:1; 104:1

And array yourself with glory and
beauty.
11 Disperse the rage of your wrath;
Look on everyone *who is* proud, and humble him.
12 Look on everyone *who is* [a]proud,
and bring him low;
Tread down the wicked in their place.
13 Hide them in the dust together,
Bind their faces in hidden *darkness.*
14 Then I will also confess to you
That your own right hand can save you.

I have learned that the nearer we get to Jesus, the smaller and more imperfect our own self life appears in our eyes.

AIMEE SEMPLE MCPHERSON

15 "Look now at the [1]behemoth,
which I made *along* with you;
He eats grass like an ox.
16 See now, his strength *is* in his hips,
And his power *is* in his stomach muscles.
17 He moves his tail like a cedar;
The sinews of his thighs are tightly knit.
18 His bones *are like* beams of bronze,
His ribs like bars of iron.
19 He *is* the first of the [a]ways of God;
Only He who made him can bring near His sword.
20 Surely the mountains [a]yield food for him,
And all the beasts of the field play there.
21 He lies under the lotus trees,
In a covert of reeds and marsh.
22 The lotus trees cover him *with* their shade;
The willows by the brook surround him.
23 Indeed the river may rage,
Yet he is not disturbed;
He is confident, though the Jordan gushes into his mouth,
24 *Though* he takes it in his eyes,
Or one pierces *his* nose with a snare.

41

"Can you draw out [a]Leviathan[1] with a hook,
Or *snare* his tongue with a line *which* you lower?
2 Can you [a]put a reed through his nose,
Or pierce his jaw with a [1]hook?
3 Will he make many supplications to you?
Will he speak softly to you?
4 Will he make a covenant with you?
Will you take him as a servant forever?
5 Will you play with him as *with* a bird,
Or will you leash him for your maidens?
6 Will *your* companions [1]make a banquet of him?
Will they apportion him among the merchants?
7 Can you fill his skin with harpoons,
Or his head with fishing spears?
8 Lay your hand on him;
Remember the battle—
Never do it again!
9 Indeed, *any* hope of *overcoming* him is false;
Shall *one not* be overwhelmed at the sight of him?
10 No one *is so* fierce that he would dare stir him up.
Who then is able to stand against Me?
11 [a]Who has preceded Me, that I should pay *him?*
[b]Everything under heaven is Mine.

12 "I will not [1]conceal his limbs,
His mighty power, or his graceful proportions.
13 Who can [1]remove his outer coat?
Who can approach *him* with a double bridle?
14 Who can open the doors of his face,
With his terrible teeth all around?
15 *His* rows of [1]scales are *his* pride,
Shut up tightly *as with* a seal;

---

12 [a]Dan. 4:37
15 [1]A large animal, exact identity unknown
19 [a]Job 26:14
20 [a]Ps. 104:14

CHAPTER 41
1 [a]Is. 27:1
[1]A large sea creature, exact identity unknown
2 [a]Is. 37:29
[1]*thorn*
6 [1]Or *bargain over him*
11 [a][Rom. 11:35]
[b]Ps. 24:1; 50:12
12 [1]Lit. *keep silent about*
13 [1]Lit. *take off the face of his garment*
15 [1]Lit. *shields*

16 One is so near another
That no air can come between
them;
17 They are joined one to another,
They stick together and cannot be
parted.
18 His sneezings flash forth light,
And his eyes *are* like the eyelids of
the morning.
19 Out of his mouth go burning
lights;
Sparks of fire shoot out.
20 Smoke goes out of his nostrils,
As *from* a boiling pot and burning
rushes.
21 His breath kindles coals,
And a flame goes out of his mouth.
22 Strength dwells in his neck,
And [1]sorrow dances before him.
23 The folds of his flesh are joined
together;
They are firm on him and cannot
be moved.
24 His heart is as hard as stone,
Even as hard as the lower
millstone.
25 When he raises himself up, the
mighty are afraid;
Because of his crashings they [1]are
beside themselves.
26 *Though* the sword reaches him, it
cannot avail;
Nor does spear, dart, or javelin.
27 He regards iron as straw,
And bronze as rotten wood.
28 The arrow cannot make him flee;
Slingstones become like stubble to
him.
29 Darts are regarded as straw;
He laughs at the threat of javelins.
30 His undersides *are* like sharp
potsherds;
He spreads pointed *marks* in the
mire.
31 He makes the deep boil like a pot;
He makes the sea like a pot of
ointment.
32 He leaves a shining wake behind
him;
One would think the deep had
white hair.
33 On earth there is nothing like
him,
Which is made without fear.
34 He beholds every high *thing;*
He *is* king over all the children of
pride."

22 [1] *despair*
25 [1] Or *purify themselves*

Job's Repentance and Restoration

42 Then Job answered the LORD and said:

2 "I know that You [a]can do
everything,
And that no purpose *of Yours* can
be withheld from You.
3 *You asked,* [a]'Who *is* this who hides
counsel without knowledge?'
Therefore I have uttered what I did
not understand,
[b]Things too wonderful for me, which
I did not know.
4 Listen, please, and let me speak;
You said, [a]'I will question you, and
you shall answer Me.'

5 "I have [a]heard of You by the
hearing of the ear,
But now my eye sees You.
6 Therefore I [a]abhor[1] *myself,*
And repent in dust and ashes."

7And so it was, after the LORD had spoken these words to Job, that the LORD said
to Eliphaz the Temanite, "My wrath is
aroused against you and your two friends,
for you have not spoken of Me *what is*
right, as My servant Job *has.* 8Now therefore, take for yourselves [a]seven bulls and
seven rams, [b]go to My servant Job, and
offer up for yourselves a burnt offering;
and My servant Job shall [c]pray for you.
For I will accept [1]him, lest I deal with you
according to your folly; because you have
not spoken of Me *what is* right, as My servant Job *has.*"
9So Eliphaz the Temanite and Bildad
the Shuhite *and* Zophar the Naamathite
went and did as the LORD commanded
them; for the LORD had [1]accepted Job.
10[a]And the LORD [1]restored Job's losses
when he prayed for his friends. Indeed the
LORD gave Job [b]twice as much as he had
before. 11Then [a]all his brothers, all his sisters, and all those who had been his acquaintances before, came to him and ate
food with him in his house; and they con-
soled him and comforted him for all the
adversity that the LORD had brought upon
him. Each one gave him a piece of silver
and each a ring of gold.
12Now the LORD blessed [a]the latter *days*
of Job more than his beginning; for he
had [b]fourteen thousand sheep, six thou-

CHAPTER 42
2 [a] [Matt. 19:26]
3 [a] Job 38:2 [b] Ps. 40:5; 131:1; 139:6
4 [a] Job 38:3; 40:7
5 [a] Job 26:14
6 [a] Ezra 9:6 [1] *despise*
8 [a] Num. 23:1 [b] [Matt. 5:24] [c] Gen. 20:17 [1] Lit. *his face*
9 [1] Lit. *lifted up the face of Job*
10 [a] Deut. 30:3 [b] Is. 40:2 [1] Lit. *turned the captivity of Job,* what was captured from Job
11 [a] Job 19:13
12 [a] James 5:11 [b] Job 1:3

sand camels, one thousand yoke of oxen,
and one thousand female donkeys. 13 [a]He
also had seven sons and three daughters.
14 And he called the name of the first [1]Je-
mimah, the name of the second [2]Keziah,
and the name of the third [3]Keren-
Happuch. 15 In all the land were found no
women *so* beautiful as the daughters of
Job; and their father gave them an inheritance among their brothers.
16 After this Job [a]lived one hundred and
forty years, and saw his children and
grandchildren *for* four generations. 17 So
Job died, old and [a]full of days.

13 a Job 1:2
14 1 Lit. *Handsome as the Day* 2 *Cassia,* a fragrance 3 Lit. *The Horn of Color* or *The Colorful Ray*
16 a Job 5:26; Prov. 3:16
17 a Gen. 15:15; 25:8

AUTHORS: *David, Asaph, Sons of Korah, and Others*
DATE: *1000–300 B.C.*
THEME: *Communion with God in Prayer and Praise*
KEY WORDS: *Rejoice, Mercy (Lovingkindness), Praise, Enemies, Lord, Righteousness*

PSALMS

Dear Woman of Destiny,

Psalms is less a book of doctrine than it is a description of the varieties of spiritual experience, providing guidance for our emotions. How often we need that guidance! David, the greatest psalmist, sang joyfully to God during the high points in his life and cried out to Him in times of desperate need. You cannot help but be deeply affected by the emotions, strengths, and petitions contained in the psalms. Enjoy God's presence as you read.

His love and mine,

Marilyn Hickey

BOOK ONE
Psalms 1—41

PSALM 1

The Way of the Righteous and the End of the Ungodly

Blessed [a]*is* the man
Who walks not in the counsel of
the [1]ungodly,
Nor stands in the path of
sinners,
[b]Nor sits in the seat of the
scornful;
2 But [a]his delight *is* in the law of
the LORD,
[b]And in His law he [1]meditates day
and night.
3 He shall be like a tree
[a]Planted by the [1]rivers of water,
That brings forth its fruit in its
season,
Whose leaf also shall not wither;
And whatever he does shall
[b]prosper.

4 The ungodly *are* not so,
But *are* [a]like the chaff which the
wind drives away.
5 Therefore the ungodly shall not
stand in the judgment,
Nor sinners in the congregation of
the righteous.

6 For [a]the LORD knows the way of
the righteous,
But the way of the ungodly shall
perish.

PSALM 2

The Messiah's Triumph and Kingdom

Why [a]do the [1]nations [2]rage,
And the people plot a [3]vain thing?
2 The kings of the earth set
themselves,
And the [a]rulers take counsel
together,
Against the LORD and against His
[b]Anointed,[1] *saying,*
3 "Let [a]us break Their bonds in pieces
And cast away Their cords from us."

4 He who sits in the heavens [a]shall
laugh;
The LORD shall hold them in
derision.
5 Then He shall speak to them in
His wrath,
And distress them in His deep
displeasure:
6 "Yet I have [1]set My King
[2]On My holy hill of Zion."

Lord, I pray that ____ would delight in Your law and that they would meditate on it, pondering it day and night.

FROM PSALM 1:2

7 "I will declare the [1]decree:
The LORD has said to Me,
[a]'You *are* My Son,
Today I have begotten You.
8 Ask of Me, and I will give *You*
The nations *for* Your inheritance,
And the ends of the earth *for* Your
possession.
9 [a]You shall [1]break them with a rod
of iron;
You shall dash them to pieces like a
potter's vessel.' "

10 Now therefore, be wise, O kings;
Be instructed, you judges of the
earth.
11 Serve the LORD with fear,
And rejoice with trembling.
12 [1]Kiss the Son, lest [2]He be angry,
And you perish *in* the way,
When [a]His wrath is kindled but a
little.
[b]Blessed *are* all those who put their
trust in Him.

PSALM 3

The Lord Helps His Troubled People

A Psalm of David [a]when he fled from
Absalom his son.

LORD, how they have increased who
trouble me!
Many *are* they who rise up against
me.
2 Many *are* they who say of me,
"*There is* no help for him in God."
Selah

PSALM 1
1 [a]Prov. 4:14 [b]Jer. 15:17 [1]*wicked*
2 [a]Ps. 119:14, 16, 35 [b][Josh. 1:8] [1]*ponders* by talking to himself
3 [a]Jer. 17:8 [b]Gen. 39:2, 3, 23 [1]*channels*
4 [a]Job 21:18
6 [a]Ps. 37:18

PSALM 2
1 [a]Acts 4:25–28 [1]*Gentiles* [2]*throng tumultuously* [3]*worthless* or *empty*
2 [a][Mark 3:6; 11:18] [b][John 1:41] [1]Christ, Commissioned One, Heb. *Messiah*
3 [a]Luke 19:14
4 [a]Ps. 37:13
6 [1]Lit. *installed* [2]Lit. *Upon Zion, the hill of My holiness*
7 [a][Heb. 1:5; 5:5] [1]Or *decree of the LORD: He said to Me*
9 [a]Ps. 89:23; 110:5, 6 [1]So with MT, Tg.; LXX, Syr., Vg. *rule* (cf. Rev. 2:27)
12 [a][Rev. 6:16, 17] [b][Ps. 5:11; 34:22] [1]LXX, Vg. *Embrace discipline;* Tg. *Receive instruction* [2]LXX *the LORD*

PSALM 3
title [a]2 Sam. 15:13–17

Psalm 2:8

Dear Woman of Destiny,

What a profound messianic scripture for world evangelism. Psalm 2 not only reveals the royal position of the Son as King, but also as Priest. In the declaration of "Ask of Me" is the nuance of intercession revealing the twofold title of King/Priest. This privilege has now been given to the "kingdom of priests," the church, through "our Great High Priest" Jesus. In the Gospels our Lord reveals the authority He is conferring upon the disciples of Christ. John 15:16 says, "You did not choose Me, but I chose you and appointed you that you should go and bear fruit, and that your fruit should remain, that whatever you ask the Father in My name He may give you."

The great commission for world evangelism is the last statement made by our Lord before His ascension: "But you shall receive power when the Holy Spirit has come upon you; and you shall be witnesses to Me in Jerusalem, and in all Judea and Samaria, and to the end of the earth" (Acts 1:8). When we translate that into our personal intercession in addition to evangelism, we see the great high calling of the church, to "make disciples of all the nations" (Matt. 28:19).

As I was leading a corporate intercession meeting one evening, a scripture was illuminated to one of our intercessors—Psalm 2:8. Attempting to be obedient to the leading of the Lord, we began to pray, asking "for the nations as an inheritance." While in the process of praying, this prophetic word was given: "I have given you the nations. Now take them." This presented quite a challenge to me as the leader, and as I waited on the Lord for additional direction, suddenly I remembered a large world map. I unfolded it, laid it on the floor and promptly jumped in the middle of the map and began to dance unrestrainedly over the nations. Declaring everywhere our feet stepped was to come under His authority, the other intercessors began to follow suit, calling out nations one by one at the direction of the Holy Spirit. It was very intense and inspirational.

This may seem a little radical to some and positively fanatical to others, but I can attest from that moment on we began to see an increase of Christian leaders from various nations coming to the services and receiving a fresh touch from God to serve their appointed nation. In addition, a Bible school has been established, with a strong emphasis on foreign missions, while many members of our congregation have had an opportunity to minister in various nations, reaping souls.

Am I advocating that if you purchase a map and dance upon it then your church will be released into higher purposes? No, that would be foolish. I am, however, encouraging you to hear what the Holy Spirit is saying and act upon that instruction. The plans of God must first be birthed in prayer, then the precious fruit of the earth will be harvested. It is our desire along with the apostle Paul "that the men pray everywhere, lifting up holy hands, without wrath and doubting" (1 Tim. 2:8).

Lila Terhune

3 But You, O LORD, *are* [a]a shield [1]for
me,
My glory and [b]the One who lifts up
my head.
4 I cried to the LORD with my voice,
And [a]He heard me from His [b]holy
hill. Selah
5 [a]I lay down and slept;
I awoke, for the LORD sustained me.
6 [a]I will not be afraid of ten
thousands of people
Who have set *themselves* against
me all around.
7 Arise, O LORD;
Save me, O my God!
[a]For You have struck all my enemies
on the cheekbone;
You have broken the teeth of the
ungodly.
8 [a]Salvation *belongs* to the LORD.
Your blessing *is* upon Your people.
Selah

PSALM 4

The Safety of the Faithful

To the [1]Chief Musician. With stringed instruments. A Psalm of David.

Hear me when I call, O God of my
righteousness!
You have relieved me in *my*
distress;
[1]Have mercy on me, and hear my
prayer.
2 How long, O you sons of men,
Will you turn my glory to shame?
How long will you love
worthlessness
And seek falsehood? Selah
3 But know that [a]the LORD has [1]set
apart for Himself him who is
godly;
The LORD will hear when I call to
Him.
4 [a]Be[1] angry, and do not sin.
[b]Meditate within your heart on your
bed, and be still. Selah
5 Offer [a]the sacrifices of
righteousness,
And [b]put your trust in the LORD.
6 *There are* many who say,
"Who will show us *any* good?"
[a]LORD, lift up the light of Your
countenance upon us.

3 [a]Ps. 5:12; 28:7 [b]Ps. 9:13; 27:6 [1]Lit. *around*
4 [a]Ps. 4:3; 34:4 [b]Ps. 2:6; 15:1; 43:3
5 [a]Lev. 26:6
6 [a]Ps. 23:4; 27:3
7 [a]Job 16:10
8 [a][Is. 43:11]

PSALM 4
title [1]*Choir Director*
1 [1]*Be gracious to me*
3 [a][2 Tim. 2:19] [1]Many Heb. mss., LXX, Tg., Vg. *made wonderful*
4 [a][Eph. 4:26] [b]Ps. 77:6 [1]Lit. *Tremble* or *Be agitated*
5 [a]Deut. 33:19 [b]Ps. 37:3, 5; 62:8
6 [a]Num. 6:26
7 [a]Is. 9:3
8 [a]Ps. 3:5 [b][Lev. 25:18]

PSALM 5
title [1]Heb. *nehiloth*
1 [a]Ps. 4:1 [1]Lit. *groaning*
3 [a]Ps. 55:17; 88:13
4 [1]Lit. *sojourn*
5 [a][Hab. 1:13] [b]Ps. 1:5
6 [a]Ps. 55:23
7 [1]Lit. *the temple of Your holiness*
8 [a]Ps. 25:4, 5; 27:11; 31:3
9 [a]Rom. 3:13 [1]*uprightness*

7 You have put [a]gladness in my
heart,
More than in the season that their
grain and wine increased.
8 [a]I will both lie down in peace, and
sleep;
[b]For You alone, O LORD, make me
dwell in safety.

PSALM 5

A Prayer for Guidance

To the Chief Musician. With [1]flutes. A Psalm of David.

Give [a]ear to my words, O LORD,
Consider my [1]meditation.
2 Give heed to the voice of my cry,
My King and my God,
For to You I will pray.
3 My voice You shall hear in the
morning, O LORD;
[a]In the morning I will direct *it* to
You,
And I will look up.
4 For You *are* not a God who takes
pleasure in wickedness,
Nor shall evil [1]dwell with You.
5 The [a]boastful shall not [b]stand in
Your sight;
You hate all workers of iniquity.
6 You shall destroy those who speak
falsehood;
The LORD abhors the [a]bloodthirsty
and deceitful man.
7 But as for me, I will come into
Your house in the multitude of
Your mercy;
In fear of You I will worship toward
[1]Your holy temple.
8 [a]Lead me, O LORD, in Your
righteousness because of my
enemies;
Make Your way straight before my
face.
9 For *there is* no [1]faithfulness in
their mouth;
Their inward part *is* destruction;
[a]Their throat *is* an open tomb;
They flatter with their tongue.
10 Pronounce them guilty, O God!
Let them fall by their own counsels;
Cast them out in the multitude of
their transgressions,
For they have rebelled against You.
11 But let all those rejoice who put
their trust in You;

Let them ever shout for joy,
because You [1]defend them;
Let those also who love Your name
Be joyful in You.
12 For You, O LORD, will bless the
righteous;
With favor You will surround him
as *with* a shield.

There is a joy which is not given to the ungodly, but to those who love Thee for Thine own sake, whose joy Thou Thyself art. And this is the happy life, to rejoice to Thee, of Thee, for Thee; this is it, and there is no other.

ST. AUGUSTINE

PSALM 6

A Prayer of Faith in Time of Distress

To the Chief Musician. With stringed instruments. [a]On [1]an eight-stringed harp. A Psalm of David.

O LORD, [a]do not rebuke me in Your
anger,
Nor chasten me in Your hot
displeasure.
2 Have mercy on me, O LORD, for I
am weak;
O LORD, [a]heal me, for my bones are
troubled.
3 My soul also is greatly [a]troubled;
But You, O LORD—how long?
4 Return, O LORD, deliver me!
Oh, save me for Your mercies' sake!
5 [a]For in death *there is* no
remembrance of You;
In the grave who will give You
thanks?
6 I am weary with my groaning;
[1]All night I make my bed swim;
I drench my couch with my tears.
7 [a]My eye wastes away because of
grief;
It grows old because of all my
enemies.
8 [a]Depart from me, all you workers of
iniquity;
For the LORD has [b]heard the voice
of my weeping.
9 The LORD has heard my
supplication;
The LORD will receive my prayer.
10 Let all my enemies be ashamed
and greatly troubled;
Let them turn back *and* be
ashamed suddenly.

PSALM 7

Prayer and Praise for Deliverance from Enemies

A [a]Meditation[1] of David, which he sang to the LORD [b]concerning the words of Cush, a Benjamite.

O LORD my God, in You I put my trust;
[a]Save me from all those who
persecute me;
And deliver me,
2 [a]Lest they tear me like a lion,
[b]Rending *me* in pieces, while *there*
is none to deliver.
3 O LORD my God, [a]if I have done
this:
If there is [b]iniquity in my hands,
4 If I have repaid evil to him who
was at peace with me,
Or [a]have plundered my enemy
without cause,
5 Let the enemy pursue me and
overtake *me;*
Yes, let him trample my life to the
earth,
And lay my honor in the dust.
Selah
6 Arise, O LORD, in Your anger;
[a]Lift Yourself up because of the rage
of my enemies;
[b]Rise up [1]for me *to* the judgment
You have commanded!
7 So the congregation of the peoples
shall surround You;
For their sakes, therefore, return on
high.
8 The LORD shall judge the peoples;
[a]Judge me, O LORD, [b]according to
my righteousness,

---

11 [1] *protect,* lit. *cover*

PSALM 6 title [a]Ps. 12:title [1]Heb. *sheminith*

1 [a]Ps. 38:1; 118:18

2 [a][Hos. 6:1]

3 [a]Ps. 88:3

5 [a][Eccl. 9:10]

6 [1]Or *Every night*

7 [a]Job 17:7

8 [a][Matt. 25:41] [b]Ps. 3:4; 28:6

PSALM 7 title [a]Hab. 3:1 [b]2 Sam. 16 [1]Heb. *Shiggaion*

1 [a]Ps. 31:15

2 [a]Is. 38:13 [b]Ps. 50:22

3 [a]2 Sam. 16:7 [b]1 Sam. 24:11

4 [a]1 Sam. 24:7; 26:9

6 [a]Ps. 94:2 [b]Ps. 35:23; 44:23 [1]So with MT, Tg., Vg.; LXX *O LORD my God*

8 [a]Ps. 26:1; 35:24; 43:1 [b]Ps. 18:20; 35:24

And according to my integrity
within me.

9 Oh, let the wickedness of the
wicked come to an end,
But establish the just;
[a]For the righteous God tests the
hearts and [1]minds.

10 [1]My defense *is* of God,
Who saves the [a]upright in heart.

11 God *is* a just judge,
And God is angry *with the wicked*
every day.

12 If he does not turn back,
He will [a]sharpen His sword;
He bends His bow and makes it
ready.

13 He also prepares for Himself
instruments of death;
He makes His arrows into fiery
shafts.

14 [a]Behold, *the wicked* brings forth
iniquity;
Yes, he conceives trouble and
brings forth falsehood.

15 He made a pit and dug it out,
[a]And has fallen into the ditch *which*
he made.

16 [a]His trouble shall return upon his
own head,
And his violent dealing shall come
down on [1]his own crown.

17 I will praise the LORD according to
His righteousness,
And will sing praise to the name of
the LORD Most High.

PSALM 8

The Glory of the Lord in Creation

To the Chief Musician. [1]On the instrument
of Gath. A Psalm of David.

O LORD, our Lord,
How [a]excellent *is* Your name in all
the earth,
Who have [b]set Your glory above the
heavens!

2 [a]Out of the mouth of babes and
nursing infants
You have [1]ordained strength,
Because of Your enemies,
That You may silence [b]the enemy
and the avenger.

3 When I [a]consider Your heavens,
the work of Your fingers,

The moon and the stars, which You
have ordained,

4 [a]What is man that You are mindful
of him,
And the son of man that You [b]visit[1]
him?

5 For You have made him a little
lower than [1]the angels,
And You have crowned him with
glory and honor.

We realize, and re-realize, our tininess, our nothingness, and the greatness and steadfastness of God.

EVELYN UNDERHILL

6 [a]You have made him to have
dominion over the works of Your
hands;
[b]You have put all *things* under his
feet,

7 All sheep and oxen—
Even the beasts of the field,

8 The birds of the air,
And the fish of the sea
That pass through the paths of the
seas.

9 [a]O LORD, our Lord,
How excellent *is* Your name in all
the earth!

PSALM 9

Prayer and Thanksgiving for the Lord's Righteous Judgments

To the Chief Musician. To *the tune of*
[1]"Death of the Son." A Psalm of David.

I will praise *You,* O LORD, with my
whole heart;
I will tell of all Your marvelous
works.

2 I will be glad and [a]rejoice in You;
I will sing praise to Your name,
[b]O Most High.

3 When my enemies turn back,
They shall fall and perish at Your
presence.

---

9 a[1 Sam. 16:7] *1* Lit. *kidneys, the most secret part of man*
10 a Ps. 97:10, 11; 125:4 *1* Lit. *My shield is upon God*
12 a Deut. 32:41
14 a Is. 59:4
15 a [Job 4:8]
16 a Esth. 9:25 *1* The crown of his own head

PSALM 8
title *1* Heb. *Al Gittith*
1 a Ps. 148:13 b Ps. 113:4
2 a [1 Cor. 1:27] b Ps. 44:16 *1 established*
3 a Ps. 111:2
4 a Job 7:17, 18 b [Job 10:12] *1 give attention to* or *care for*
5 *1* Heb. *Elohim, God;* LXX, Syr., Tg., Jewish tradition *angels*
6 a [Gen. 1:26, 28] b [Heb. 2:8]
9 a Ps. 8:1

PSALM 9
title *1* Heb. *Muth Labben*
2 a Ps. 5:11; 104:34 b [Ps. 83:18; 92:1]

4 For You have maintained my right
and my cause;
You sat on the throne judging in
righteousness.
5 You have rebuked the [1]nations,
You have destroyed the wicked;
You have [a]blotted out their name
forever and ever.
6 O enemy, destructions are finished
forever!
And you have destroyed cities;
Even their memory has [a]perished.
7 [a]But the LORD shall endure forever;
He has prepared His throne for
judgment.
8 [a]He shall judge the world in
righteousness,
And He shall administer judgment
for the peoples in uprightness.

Be a refuge for ____,
O Lord, a refuge in times
of trouble.

FROM PSALM 9:9

9 The LORD also will be a [a]refuge[1]
for the oppressed,
A refuge in times of trouble.
10 And those who [a]know Your name
will put their trust in You;
For You, LORD, have not forsaken
those who seek You.
11 Sing praises to the LORD, who
dwells in Zion!
[a]Declare His deeds among the
people.
12 [a]When He avenges blood, He
remembers them;
He does not forget the cry of the
[1]humble.
13 Have mercy on me, O LORD!
Consider my trouble from those
who hate me,
You who lift me up from the gates
of death,
14 That I may tell of all Your praise
In the gates of [1]the daughter of
Zion.
I will [a]rejoice in Your salvation.
15 [a]The [1]nations have sunk down in
the pit *which* they made;
In the net which they hid, their
own foot is caught.
16 The LORD is [a]known *by* the
judgment He executes;
The wicked is snared in the work of
his own hands.
[b]Meditation.[1] Selah
17 The wicked shall be turned into
hell,
And all the [1]nations [a]that forget
God.
18 [a]For the needy shall not always be
forgotten;
[b]The expectation of the poor shall
not perish forever.
19 Arise, O LORD,
Do not let man prevail;
Let the [1]nations be judged in Your
sight.
20 Put them in fear, O LORD,
That the [1]nations may know
themselves *to be but* men. Selah

PSALM 10

A Song of Confidence in God's Triumph over Evil

Why do You stand afar off, O LORD?
Why do You hide in times of
trouble?
2 The wicked in *his* pride [1]persecutes
the poor;
[a]Let them be caught in the plots
which they have devised.
3 For the wicked [a]boasts of his
heart's desire;
[1]He [b]blesses the greedy *and*
renounces the LORD.
4 The wicked in his proud
countenance does not seek *God;*
[1]God *is* in none of his [a]thoughts.
5 His ways [1]are always prospering;
Your judgments *are* far above, out
of his sight;
As for all his enemies, he sneers at
them.
6 [a]He has said in his heart, "I shall
not be moved;
[b]I shall never be in adversity."
7 [a]His mouth is full of cursing and
[b]deceit and oppression;
Under his tongue *is* trouble and
iniquity.
8 He sits in the lurking places of the
villages;

5 [a]Prov. 10:7 [1]*Gentiles*
6 [a][Ps. 34:16]
7 [a]Heb. 1:11
8 [a][Ps. 96:13; 98:9]
9 [a]Ps. 32:7; 46:1; 91:2 [1]Lit. *secure height*
10 [a]Ps. 91:14
11 [a]Ps. 66:16; 107:22
12 [a][Ps. 72:14] [1]*afflicted*
14 [a]Ps. 13:5; 20:5; 35:9 [1]Jerusalem
15 [a]Ps. 7:15, 16 [1]*Gentiles*
16 [a]Ex. 7:5 [b]Ps. 92:3 [1]Heb. *Higgaion*
17 [a]Job 8:13 [1]*Gentiles*
18 [a]Ps. 9:12; 12:5 [b]Prov. 23:18
19 [1]*Gentiles*
20 [1]*Gentiles*

PSALM 10
2 [a]Ps. 7:16; 9:16 [1]*hotly pursues*
3 [a]Ps. 49:6; 94:3, 4 [b]Prov. 28:4 [1]Or *The greedy man curses and spurns the* LORD
4 [a]Ps. 14:1; 36:1 [1]Or *All his thoughts are, "There is no God"*
5 [1]Lit. *are strong*
6 [a][Eccl. 8:11] [b]Rev. 18:7
7 [a][Rom. 3:14] [b]Ps. 55:10, 11

In the secret places he murders the innocent;
His eyes are secretly fixed on the helpless.
9 He lies in wait secretly, as a lion in his den;
He lies in wait to catch the poor;
He catches the poor when he draws him into his net.
10 So [1]he crouches, he lies low,
That the helpless may fall by his [2]strength.
11 He has said in his heart,
"God has forgotten;
He hides His face;
He will never see."

12 Arise, O LORD!
O God, [a]lift up Your hand!
Do not forget the [b]humble.
13 Why do the wicked renounce God?
He has said in his heart,
"You will not require *an account.*"

14 But You have [a]seen, for You observe trouble and grief,
To repay *it* by Your hand.
The helpless [b]commits[1] himself to You;
[c]You are the helper of the fatherless.
15 Break the arm of the wicked and the evil *man;*
Seek out his wickedness *until* You find none.

16 [a]The LORD *is* King forever and ever;
The nations have perished out of His land.
17 LORD, You have heard the desire of the humble;
You will prepare their heart;
You will cause Your ear to hear,
18 To [1]do justice to the fatherless and the oppressed,
That the man of the earth may [2]oppress no more.

PSALM 11

Faith in the Lord's Righteousness

To the Chief Musician. A Psalm of David.

In [a]the LORD I put my trust;
How can you say to my soul,
"Flee *as* a bird to your mountain"?
2 For look! [a]The wicked bend *their* bow,
They make ready their arrow on the string,
That they may shoot [1]secretly at the upright in heart.
3 [a]If the foundations are destroyed,
What can the righteous do?

4 The LORD *is* in His holy temple,
The LORD's [a]throne *is* in heaven;
[b]His eyes behold,
His eyelids test the sons of men.
5 The LORD [a]tests the righteous,
But the wicked and the one who loves violence His soul hates.
6 Upon the wicked He will rain coals;
Fire and brimstone and a burning wind
[a]*Shall be* [1]the portion of their cup.

7 For the LORD *is* righteous,
He [a]loves righteousness;
[1]His countenance beholds the upright.

PSALM 12

Man's Treachery and God's Constancy

To the Chief Musician. [a]On [1]an eight-stringed harp. A Psalm of David.

Help,[1] LORD, for the godly man [a]ceases!
For the faithful disappear from among the sons of men.
2 [a]They speak idly everyone with his neighbor;
With flattering lips *and* [1]a double heart they speak.

3 May the LORD [1]cut off all flattering lips,
And the tongue that speaks [2]proud things,
4 Who have said,
"With our tongue we will prevail;
Our lips *are* our own;
Who *is* lord over us?"

5 "For the oppression of the poor, for the sighing of the needy,
Now I will arise," says the LORD;
"I will set *him* in the safety for which he yearns."

6 The words of the LORD *are* [a]pure words,
Like silver tried in a furnace of earth,
Purified seven times.
7 You shall keep them, O LORD,
You shall preserve them from this generation forever.

---

10 [1] Or *he is crushed, is bowed* [2] Or *mighty ones*
12 a Mic. 5:9 b Ps. 9:12
14 a [Ps. 11:4] b [2 Tim. 1:12] c Ps. 68:5 [1] Lit. *leaves,* entrusts
16 a Ps. 29:10
18 [1] *vindicate* [2] *terrify*

PSALM 11
1 a Ps. 56:11
2 a Ps. 64:3, 4 [1] Lit. *in darkness*
3 a Ps. 82:5; 87:1; 119:152
4 a [Is. 66:1] b [Ps. 33:18; 34:15, 16]
5 a Gen. 22:1
6 a Ps. 75:8 [1] Their allotted portion or serving
7 a Ps. 33:5; 45:7 [1] Or *The upright beholds His countenance*

PSALM 12
title a Ps. 6:title [1] Heb. *sheminith*
1 a [Is. 57:1] [1] *Save*
2 a Ps. 10:7; 41:6 [1] An inconsistent mind
3 [1] *destroy* [2] *great*
6 a 2 Sam. 22:31; Ps. 18:30; 119:140

8 The wicked prowl on every side,
When vileness is exalted among the sons of men.

PSALM 13

Trust in the Salvation of the Lord

To the Chief Musician. A Psalm of David.

How long, O LORD? Will You forget me forever?
[a]How long will You hide Your face from me?
2 How long shall I take counsel in my soul,
Having sorrow in my heart daily?
How long will my enemy be exalted over me?
3 Consider *and* hear me, O LORD my God;
[a]Enlighten my eyes,
[b]Lest I sleep the *sleep of* death;
4 Lest my enemy say,
"I have prevailed against him";
Lest those who trouble me rejoice when I am moved.
5 But I have trusted in Your mercy;
My heart shall rejoice in Your salvation.
6 I will sing to the LORD,
Because He has dealt bountifully with me.

PSALM 14

Folly of the Godless, and God's Final Triumph

To the Chief Musician. A Psalm of David.

The [a]fool has said in his heart,
"*There is* no God."
They are corrupt,
They have done abominable works,
There is none who does good.
2 [a]The LORD looks down from heaven upon the children of men,
To see if there are any who understand, who seek God.
3 [a]They have all turned aside,
They have together become corrupt;
There is none who does good,
No, not one.
4 Have all the workers of iniquity no knowledge,
Who eat up my people *as* they eat bread,
And [a]do not call on the LORD?

PSALM 13
1 [a]Job 13:24
3 [a]Ezra 9:8 [b]Jer. 51:39

PSALM 14
1 [a]Ps. 10:4; 53:1
2 [a]Ps. 33:13, 14; 102:19
3 [a]Rom. 3:12
4 [a]Is. 64:7
6 [a]Ps. 9:9; 40:17; 46:1; 142:5
7 [a]Ps. 53:6 [b]Job 42:10 [1] Lit. *Who will give out of Zion the salvation of Israel?* [2] Or *His captive people*

PSALM 15
1 [a]Ps. 24:3–5 [1] *sojourn*
2 [a][Eph. 4:25]
3 [a][Lev. 19:16–18] [b]Ex. 23:1 [1] *receive*
4 [a]Esth. 3:2 [b]Lev. 5:4
5 [a]2 Pet. 1:10

PSALM 16
title [a]Ps. 56—60
1 [1] *Watch over*
2 [a]Job 35:7

5 There they are in great fear,
For God *is* with the generation of the righteous.
6 You shame the counsel of the poor,
But the LORD *is* his [a]refuge.
7 [a]Oh,[1] that the salvation of Israel *would come* out of Zion!
[b]When the LORD brings back [2]the captivity of His people,
Let Jacob rejoice *and* Israel be glad.

PSALM 15

The Character of Those Who May Dwell with the Lord

A Psalm of David.

LORD, [a]who may [1]abide in Your tabernacle?
Who may dwell in Your holy hill?
2 He who walks uprightly,
And works righteousness,
And speaks the [a]truth in his heart;
3 He *who* [a]does not backbite with his tongue,
Nor does evil to his neighbor,
[b]Nor does he [1]take up a reproach against his friend;
4 [a]In whose eyes a vile person is despised,
But he honors those who fear the LORD;
He *who* [b]swears to his own hurt and does not change;
5 He *who* does not put out his money at usury,
Nor does he take a bribe against the innocent.
He who does these *things* [a]shall never be moved.

PSALM 16

The Hope of the Faithful, and the Messiah's Victory

A [a]Michtam of David.

Preserve[1] me, O God, for in You I put my trust.
2 *O my soul,* you have said to the LORD,
"You *are* my Lord,
[a]My goodness is nothing apart from You."

3 As for the saints who *are* on the earth,
"They are the excellent ones, in [a]whom is all my delight."
4 Their sorrows shall be multiplied who hasten *after* another *god;*
Their drink offerings of [a]blood I will not offer,
[b]Nor take up their names on my lips.
5 O LORD, *You are* the portion of my inheritance and my cup;
You [1]maintain my lot.
6 The lines have fallen to me in pleasant *places;*
Yes, I have a good inheritance.
7 I will bless the LORD who has given me counsel;
My [1]heart also instructs me in the night seasons.
8 [a]I have set the LORD always before me;
Because *He is* at my right hand I shall not be moved.
9 Therefore my heart is glad, and my glory rejoices;
My flesh also will [1]rest in hope.
10 [a]For You will not leave my soul in [1]Sheol,
Nor will You allow Your Holy One to [2]see corruption.
11 You will show me the [a]path of life;
In Your presence *is* fullness of joy;
At Your right hand *are* pleasures forevermore.

PSALM 17

Prayer with Confidence in Final Salvation

A Prayer of David.

Hear a just cause, O LORD,
Attend to my cry;
Give ear to my prayer *which is* not from deceitful lips.
2 Let my vindication come from Your presence;
Let Your eyes look on the things that are upright.
3 You have tested my heart;
You have visited *me* in the night;
[a]You have [1]tried me and have found [2]nothing;
I have purposed that my mouth shall not [b]transgress.
4 Concerning the works of men,
By the word of Your lips,
I have kept away from the paths of the destroyer.
5 [a]Uphold my steps in Your paths,
That my footsteps may not slip.

Faith is the life of the soul.

CHARLES WESLEY

6 [a]I have called upon You, for You will hear me, O God;
Incline Your ear to me, *and* hear my speech.
7 Show Your marvelous lovingkindness by Your right hand,
O You who [1]save those who trust *in You*
From those who rise up *against them.*
8 Keep me as the [1]apple of Your eye;
Hide me under the shadow of Your wings,
9 From the wicked who oppress me,
From my deadly enemies who surround me.
10 They have closed up their [a]fat *hearts;*
With their mouths they [b]speak proudly.
11 They have now surrounded us in our steps;
They have set their eyes, crouching down to the earth,
12 As a lion is eager to tear his prey,
And like a young lion lurking in secret places.
13 Arise, O LORD,
Confront him, cast him down;
Deliver my life from the wicked with Your sword,
14 With Your hand from men, O LORD,
From men of the world *who have* their portion in *this* life,

---

3 a Ps. 119:63
4 a Ps. 106:37, 38 b [Ex. 23:13]
5 1 Lit. *uphold*
7 1 Mind, lit. *kidneys*
8 a [Acts 2:25–28]
9 1 Or *dwell securely*
10 a Ps. 49:15; 86:13 1 The abode of the dead 2 *undergo*
11 a [Matt. 7:14]

PSALM 17
3 a Job 23:10 b Ps. 39:1 1 *examined* 2 Nothing evil
5 a Ps. 44:18; 119:133
6 a Ps. 86:7; 116:2
7 1 *deliver*
8 1 *pupil*
10 a Ezek. 16:49 b [1 Sam. 2:3]

And whose belly You fill with Your
hidden treasure.
They are satisfied with children,
And leave the rest of their
possession for their babes.

15 As for me, [a]I will see Your face in
righteousness;
[b]I shall be satisfied when I [c]awake in
Your likeness.

O Father, keep _____ as the apple of Your eye; hide them under the shadow of Your wings, from the wicked who oppress them and from their deadly enemies who surround them.

FROM PSALM 17:8, 9

PSALM 18

God the Sovereign Savior

To the Chief Musician. A Psalm of David [a]the servant of the LORD, who spoke to the LORD the words of [b]this song on the day that the LORD delivered him from the hand of all his enemies and from the hand of Saul. And he said:

I [a]will love You, O LORD, my strength.
2 The LORD is my rock and my
fortress and my deliverer;
My God, my [1]strength, [a]in whom I
will trust;
My shield and the [2]horn of my
salvation, my stronghold.
3 I will call upon the LORD, [a]*who is worthy* to be praised;
So shall I be saved from my
enemies.

4 [a]The pangs of death surrounded me,
And the floods of [1]ungodliness
made me afraid.
5 The sorrows of Sheol surrounded
me;
The snares of death confronted me.
6 In my distress I called upon the
LORD,
And cried out to my God;
He heard my voice from His
temple,
And my cry came before Him, *even*
to His ears.

7 [a]Then the earth shook and
trembled;
The foundations of the hills also
quaked and were shaken,
Because He was angry.
8 Smoke went up from His nostrils,
And devouring fire from His mouth;
Coals were kindled by it.
9 [a]He bowed the heavens also, and
came down
With darkness under His feet.
10 [a]And He rode upon a cherub, and
flew;
[b]He flew upon the wings of the
wind.
11 He made darkness His secret
place;
[a]His canopy around Him *was* dark
waters
And thick clouds of the skies.
12 [a]From the brightness before Him,
His thick clouds passed with
hailstones and coals of fire.

13 The LORD thundered from heaven,
And the Most High uttered [a]His
voice,
[1]Hailstones and coals of fire.
14 [a]He sent out His arrows and
scattered [1]the foe,
Lightnings in abundance, and He
vanquished them.
15 Then the channels of the sea were
seen,
The foundations of the world were
uncovered
At Your rebuke, O LORD,
At the blast of the breath of Your
nostrils.

16 [a]He sent from above, He took me;
He drew me out of many waters.
17 He delivered me from my strong
enemy,
From those who hated me,
For they were too strong for me.
18 They confronted me in the day of
my calamity,
But the LORD was my support.
19 [a]He also brought me out into a
broad place;
He delivered me because He
delighted in me.

20 [a]The LORD rewarded me according
to my righteousness;

15 a [1 John 3:2] b Ps. 4:6, 7; 16:11 c [Is. 26:19]
PSALM 18
title a Ps. 36:title b 2 Sam. 22
1 a Ps. 144:1
2 a Heb. 2:13 *1* Lit. *rock* *2* Strength
3 a Rev. 5:12
4 a Ps. 116:3 *1* Lit. *Belial*
7 a Acts 4:31
9 a Ps. 144:5
10 a Ps. 80:1; 99:1 b [Ps. 104:3]
11 a Ps. 97:2
12 a Ps. 97:3; 140:10
13 a [Ps. 29:3–9; 104:7] *1* So with MT, Tg., Vg.; a few Heb. mss., LXX omit *Hailstones and coals of fire*
14 a Ps. 144:6 *1* Lit. *them*
16 a Ps. 144:7
19 a Ps. 4:1; 31:8; 118:5
20 a 1 Sam. 24:19

According to the cleanness of my hands
He has recompensed me.
21 For I have kept the ways of the LORD,
And have not wickedly departed from my God.
22 For all His judgments *were* before me,
And I did not put away His statutes from me.
23 I was also blameless [1]before Him,
And I kept myself from my iniquity.
24 [a]Therefore the LORD has recompensed me according to my righteousness,
According to the cleanness of my hands in His sight.

25 [a]With the merciful You will show Yourself merciful;
With a blameless man You will show Yourself blameless;
26 With the pure You will show Yourself pure;
And [a]with the devious You will show Yourself shrewd.
27 For You will save the humble people,
But will bring down [a]haughty looks.

28 [a]For You will light my lamp;
The LORD my God will enlighten my darkness.
29 For by You I can [1]run against a troop,
By my God I can leap over a wall.
30 *As for* God, [a]His way *is* perfect;
[b]The word of the LORD is [1]proven;
He *is* a shield [c]to all who trust in Him.

31 [a]For who *is* God, except the LORD?
And who *is* a rock, except our God?
32 *It is* God who [a]arms me with strength,
And makes my way perfect.
33 [a]He makes my feet like the *feet of* deer,
And [b]sets me on my high places.
34 [a]He teaches my hands to make war,
So that my arms can bend a bow of bronze.

35 You have also given me the shield of Your salvation;
Your right hand has held me up,
Your gentleness has made me great.

23 [1] *with*
24 a 1 Sam. 26:23
25 a [1 Kin. 8:32]
26 a [Lev. 26:23–28]
27 a [Ps. 101:5]
28 a Job 18:6
29 [1] Or *run through*
30 a Rev. 15:3 b Ps. 12:6; 119:140 c [Ps. 17:7] [1] Lit. *refined*
31 a [1 Sam. 2:2]
32 a [Ps. 91:2]
33 a Hab. 3:19 b Deut. 32:13; 33:29
34 a Ps. 144:1
36 a Prov. 4:12
39 [1] Lit. *caused to bow*
41 a Job 27:9
42 a Zech. 10:5
43 a 2 Sam. 8 b Is. 52:15 [1] *Gentiles*
44 [1] *feign submission*
45 a Mic. 7:17
47 a Ps. 47:3
48 a Ps. 27:6; 59:1
49 a Rom. 15:9 [1] *nations*
50 a Ps. 21:1; 144:10

36 You enlarged my path under me,
[a]So my feet did not slip.

37 I have pursued my enemies and overtaken them;
Neither did I turn back again till they were destroyed.
38 I have wounded them,
So that they could not rise;
They have fallen under my feet.
39 For You have armed me with strength for the battle;
You have [1]subdued under me those who rose up against me.
40 You have also given me the necks of my enemies,
So that I destroyed those who hated me.
41 They cried out, but *there was* none to save;
[a]*Even* to the LORD, but He did not answer them.
42 Then I beat them as fine as the dust before the wind;
I [a]cast them out like dirt in the streets.

43 You have delivered me from the strivings of the people;
[a]You have made me the head of the [1]nations;
[b]A people I have not known shall serve me.
44 As soon as they hear of me they obey me;
The foreigners [1]submit to me.
45 [a]The foreigners fade away,
And come frightened from their hideouts.

46 The LORD lives!
Blessed *be* my Rock!
Let the God of my salvation be exalted.
47 *It is* God who avenges me,
[a]And subdues the peoples under me;
48 He delivers me from my enemies.
[a]You also lift me up above those who rise against me;
You have delivered me from the violent man.
49 [a]Therefore I will give thanks to You, O LORD, among the [1]Gentiles,
And sing praises to Your name.
50 [a]Great deliverance He gives to His king,
And shows mercy to His anointed,

To David and his [1]descendants
forevermore.

50 [1] Lit. *seed*

PSALM 19

The Perfect Revelation of the Lord

To the Chief Musician. A Psalm of David.

The [a]heavens declare the glory of God;
And the [b]firmament[1] shows [2]His
handiwork.
2 Day unto day utters speech,
And night unto night reveals
knowledge.
3 *There is* no speech nor language
Where their voice is not heard.
4 [a]Their [1]line has gone out through
all the earth,
And their words to the end of the
world.

In them He has set a [2]tabernacle
for the sun,
5 Which *is* like a bridegroom coming
out of his chamber,
[a]*And* rejoices like a strong man to
run its race.
6 Its rising *is* from one end of
heaven,
And its circuit to the other end;
And there is nothing hidden from
its heat.

7 [a]The law of the LORD *is* perfect,
[1]converting the soul;
The testimony of the LORD *is* sure,
making [b]wise the simple;
8 The statutes of the LORD *are* right,
rejoicing the heart;
The commandment of the LORD *is*
pure, enlightening the eyes;
9 The fear of the LORD *is* clean,
enduring forever;
The judgments of the LORD *are* true
and righteous altogether.
10 More to be desired *are they* than
[a]gold,
Yea, than much fine gold;
Sweeter also than honey and the
[1]honeycomb.
11 Moreover by them Your servant is
warned,
And in keeping them *there is* great
reward.

12 Who can understand *his* errors?
[a]Cleanse me from secret *faults.*
13 Keep back Your servant also from
[a]presumptuous *sins;*
Let them not have [b]dominion over
me.
Then I shall be blameless,
And I shall be innocent of [1]great
transgression.

14 [a]Let the words of my mouth and
the meditation of my heart
Be acceptable in Your sight,
O LORD, my [1]strength and my
[b]Redeemer.

PSALM 19
1 [a]Is. 40:22 [b]Gen. 1:6, 7 [1] *expanse* of heaven [2] *the work of His hands*
4 [a]Rom. 10:18 [1] LXX, Syr., Vg. *sound;* Tg. *business* [2] *tent*
5 [a]Eccl. 1:5
7 [a]Ps. 111:7 [b]Ps. 119:130 [1] *restoring*
10 [a]Ps. 119:72, 127 [1] *honey in the combs*
12 [a][Ps. 51:1, 2]
13 [a]Num. 15:30 [b]Ps. 119:133 [1] Or *much*
14 [a]Ps. 51:15 [b]Is. 47:4 [1] Lit. *rock*

PSALM 20

The Assurance of God's Saving Work

To the Chief Musician. A Psalm of David.

May the LORD answer you in the day of
trouble;
May the name of the God of Jacob
[1]defend you;
2 May He send you help from the
sanctuary,
And strengthen you out of Zion;
3 May He remember all your
offerings,
And accept your burnt sacrifice.
Selah

4 May He grant you according to
your heart's *desire,*
And [a]fulfill all your [1]purpose.
5 We will rejoice in your salvation,
And in the name of our God we will
set up *our* banners!
May the LORD fulfill all your
petitions.

6 Now I know that the LORD saves
His [1]anointed;
He will answer him from His holy
heaven
With the saving strength of His
right hand.

7 Some *trust* in chariots, and some
in [a]horses;
But we will remember the name of
the LORD our God.
8 They have bowed down and fallen;
But we have risen and stand
upright.

9 Save, LORD!
May the King answer us when we
call.

PSALM 20
1 [1] Lit. *set you on high*
4 [a]Ps. 21:2 [1] *counsel*
6 [1] Commissioned one, Heb. *messiah*
7 [a]Ps. 33:16, 17

PSALM 21

Joy in the Salvation of the Lord

To the Chief Musician. A Psalm of David.

The king shall have joy in Your
strength, O LORD;
And in Your salvation how greatly
shall he rejoice!
2 You have given him his heart's
desire,
And have not withheld the [a]request
of his lips. Selah

Give me not life if I ought to be taken from it. Living or dying, I no longer desire anything but to be Thine.

FENELON

3 For You meet him with the
blessings of goodness;
You set a crown of pure gold upon
his head.
4 [a]He asked life from You, *and* You
gave *it* to him—
Length of days forever and ever.
5 His glory *is* great in Your salvation;
Honor and majesty You have placed
upon him.
6 For You have made him most
blessed forever;
[a]You have made him [1]exceedingly
glad with Your presence.
7 For the king trusts in the LORD,
And through the mercy of the Most
High he shall not be [1]moved.

8 Your hand will find all Your
enemies;
Your right hand will find those who
hate You.
9 You shall make them as a fiery
oven in the time of Your anger;
The LORD shall swallow them up in
His wrath,
And the fire shall devour them.
10 Their offspring You shall destroy
from the earth,
And their [1]descendants from among
the sons of men.
11 For they intended evil against
You;
They devised a plot *which* they are
not able *to* [a]*perform.*
12 Therefore You will make them
turn their back;
You will make ready *Your arrows*
on Your string toward their
faces.

13 Be exalted, O LORD, in Your own
strength!
We will sing and praise Your power.

PSALM 22

The Suffering, Praise, and Posterity of the Messiah

To the Chief Musician. Set to [1]"The Deer of the Dawn." A Psalm of David.

My [a]God, My God, why have You
forsaken Me?
Why are You so far from helping
Me,
And from the words of My
groaning?
2 O My God, I cry in the daytime,
but You do not hear;
And in the night season, and am
not silent.

Instead of complaining that God has hidden Himself, you will give Him thanks for having revealed so much of Himself.

BLAISE PASCAL

3 But You *are* holy,
Enthroned in the [a]praises of Israel.
4 Our fathers trusted in You;
They trusted, and You delivered
them.
5 They cried to You, and were
delivered;
[a]They trusted in You, and were not
ashamed.

6 But I *am* [a]a worm, and no man;
[b]A reproach of men, and despised by
the people.
7 [a]All those who see Me ridicule Me;
They [1]shoot out the lip, they shake
the head, *saying,*

PSALM 21
2 [a]2 Sam. 7:26–29
4 [a]Ps. 61:5, 6; 133:3
6 [a]Ps. 16:11; 45:7 [1]Lit. *joyful with gladness*
7 [1]*shaken*
10 [1]Lit. *seed*
11 [a]Ps. 2:1–4

PSALM 22
title [1]Heb. *Aijeleth Hashahar*
1 [a][Mark 15:34]
3 [a]Deut. 10:21
5 [a]Is. 49:23
6 [a]Is. 41:14 [b][Is. 53:3]
7 [a]Matt. 27:39 [1]*Show contempt with their mouth*

8 "He[a] [1]trusted in the LORD, let Him rescue Him;
[b]Let Him deliver Him, since He delights in Him!"

9 [a]But You *are* He who took Me out of the womb;
You made Me trust *while* on My mother's breasts.
10 I was cast upon You from birth.
From My mother's womb
[a]You *have been* My God.
11 Be not far from Me,
For trouble *is* near;
For *there is* none to help.

12 [a]Many bulls have surrounded Me;
Strong *bulls* of [b]Bashan have encircled Me.
13 [a]They [1]gape at Me *with* their mouths,
Like a raging and roaring lion.

14 I am poured out like water,
[a]And all My bones are out of joint;
My heart is like wax;
It has melted [1]within Me.
15 [a]My strength is dried up like a potsherd,
And [b]My tongue clings to My jaws;
You have brought Me to the dust of death.

16 For dogs have surrounded Me;
The congregation of the wicked has enclosed Me.
[a]They[1] pierced My hands and My feet;
17 I can count all My bones.
[a]They look *and* stare at Me.
18 [a]They divide My garments among them,
And for My clothing they cast lots.

19 But You, O LORD, do not be far from Me;
O My Strength, hasten to help Me!
20 Deliver Me from the sword,
[a]My[1] precious *life* from the power of the dog.
21 [a]Save Me from the lion's mouth
And from the horns of the wild oxen!

[b]You have answered Me.

22 [a]I will declare Your name to [b]My brethren;
In the midst of the assembly I will praise You.
23 [a]You who fear the LORD, praise Him!
All you [1]descendants of Jacob, glorify Him,
And fear Him, all you offspring of Israel!
24 For He has not despised nor abhorred the affliction of the afflicted;
Nor has He hidden His face from Him;
But [a]when He cried to Him, He heard.

25 [a]My praise *shall be* of You in the great assembly;
[b]I will pay My vows before those who fear Him.
26 The poor shall eat and be satisfied;
Those who seek Him will praise the LORD.
Let your heart live forever!

27 All the ends of the world
Shall remember and turn to the LORD,
And all the families of the [1]nations
Shall worship before [2]You.
28 [a]For the kingdom *is* the LORD's,
And He rules over the nations.

29 [a]All the prosperous of the earth
Shall eat and worship;
[b]All those who go down to [1]the dust
Shall bow before Him,
Even he who cannot keep himself alive.

30 A posterity shall serve Him.
It will be recounted of the Lord to the *next* generation,
31 They will come and declare His righteousness to a people who will be born,
That He has done *this*.

PSALM 23

The Lord the Shepherd of His People

A Psalm of David.

The LORD *is* [a]my shepherd;
[b]I shall not [1]want.
2 [a]He makes me to lie down in [1]green pastures;
[b]He leads me beside the [2]still waters.
3 He restores my soul;
[a]He leads me in the paths of righteousness
For His name's sake.

8 a Matt. 27:43 b Ps. 91:14 1 LXX, Syr., Vg. *hoped;* Tg. *praised*
9 a [Ps. 71:5, 6]
10 a [Is. 46:3; 49:1]
12 a Ps. 22:21; 68:30 b Deut. 32:14
13 a Job 16:10 1 Lit. *have opened their mouths at Me*
14 a Dan. 5:6 1 Lit. *in the midst of My bowels*
15 a Prov. 17:22 b John 19:28
16 a Matt. 27:35 1 So with some Heb. mss., LXX, Syr., Vg.; MT *Like a lion* instead of *They pierced*
17 a Luke 23:27, 35
18 a Matt. 27:35
20 a Ps. 35:17 1 Lit. *My only one*
21 a 2 Tim. 4:17 b Is. 34:7
22 a Heb. 2:12 b [Rom. 8:29]
23 a Ps. 135:19, 20 1 Lit. *seed*
24 a Heb. 5:7
25 a Ps. 35:18; 40:9, 10 b Eccl. 5:4
27 1 *Gentiles* 2 So with MT, LXX, Tg.; Arab., Syr., Vg. *Him*
28 a Matt. 6:13
29 a Ps. 17:10; 45:12 b [Is. 26:19] 1 Death

PSALM 23
1 a [Is. 40:11] b [Phil. 4:19] 1 *lack*
2 a Ezek. 34:14 b [Rev. 7:17] 1 Lit. *pastures of tender grass* 2 Lit. *waters of rest*
3 a Ps. 5:8; 31:3

Psalm 23:3

Dear Woman of Destiny,

Have you ever wondered what it means to have your soul restored, and just what is your soul? Let me share what I believe God's Word would have us understand about our spirit and soul.

"God formed man of the dust of the ground, and *breathed* into his nostrils the *breath of life* [Hebrew *ruach*]; and man *became* a living *being* [soul]" (Gen. 2:7). God formed woman from the rib of man (see Gen. 2:22), but she must have received her own individual gift of the breath of God, or she would not have had life in her body. "The body without the spirit is dead" (James 2:26). Your spirit was breathed into you at conception and is eternal. "The spirit will return to God who gave it" (Eccl. 12:7).

Even before our mind is fully formed, our spirit experiences life through our body, and reacts, and our *soul is formed*. "Soul" describes the structures of our heart, mind, character, and personality through which our spirit continues to encounter life and through which our spirit responds according to the way it has previously interpreted experience. As we develop structures of character, our entire soul becomes a temple through which our spirit worships God and meets, shares with, and blesses others. In other areas it becomes a prison of defensive walls to hide behind or an armored tank in which we rush out to attack.

When our spirit is wounded, it may lose ability to seek, empathize with, and embrace God and others. It may lose vitality to shape the soul with wholesome attitudes and expectations. Mind and heart are part of our soul. They are storehouses of memory, thought, and emotion. We act and speak not only from that which fills our mind, but also from that which fills and motivates us from the hidden areas of our heart (see Luke 6:45; 1 Cor. 4:5). Even a person who is truly striving to learn and perform well can be driven, scattered, or emotionally paralyzed because of deep wounds and resultant hidden agendas that often lie beneath the level of consciousness. She may be locked into senses of futility, unworthiness, rejection, and shame when she is unable to make significant changes in her feelings, thoughts, or behavior. A wound or unrepented sin (see Prov. 6:32; Matt. 10:28; 16:26), which continues to sicken or weaken our spirit, seriously impairs the healthy functioning of our soul's heart and mind. It disturbs and may eventually prevent stable integration and coordinated expression of every part of our body.

Our Lord Jesus Christ died for our sins, but Hebrews 12:15 warns us that we can fall short of His grace if we hold on to roots of bitterness that spring up and cause trouble. Even so, He invites us to pray as the psalmist did: "Search me, O God, and know my heart; try me, and know my anxieties; and see if there is any wicked way in me, and lead me in the way everlasting" (Ps. 139:23, 24). He heals our deep wounds, forgives, and enables us to forgive. He brings our soul out of prison that we may praise Him (see Ps. 142:7a). He finds green pastures for us, leads us beside *still* waters, and *restores* our soul so we *can* follow Him in paths of righteousness.

Paula Sandford

4 Yea, though I walk through the
valley of [a]the shadow of death,
[b]I will fear no evil;
[c]For You *are* with me;
Your rod and Your staff, they
comfort me.

5 You [a]prepare a table before me in
the presence of my enemies;
You [b]anoint my head with oil;
My cup runs over.

6 Surely goodness and mercy shall
follow me
All the days of my life;
And I will [1]dwell in the house of
the LORD
[2]Forever.

PSALM 24

The King of Glory and His Kingdom

A Psalm of David.

The [a]earth *is* the LORD's, and all its
fullness,
The world and those who dwell
therein.

2 For He has [a]founded it upon the
seas,
And established it upon the [1]waters.

God regards the personal purity of the man more than He regards any sacrifice or any ceremony.

E. M. BOUNDS

3 [a]Who may ascend into the hill of
the LORD?
Or who may stand in His holy
place?

4 He who has [a]clean hands and [b]a
pure heart,
Who has not lifted up his soul to
an idol,
Nor [c]sworn deceitfully.

5 He shall receive blessing from the
LORD,
And righteousness from the God of
his salvation.

6 This *is* Jacob, the generation of
those who [a]seek Him,
Who seek Your face. Selah

7 [a]Lift up your heads, O you gates!
And be lifted up, you everlasting
doors!
[b]And the King of glory shall come
in.

8 Who *is* this King of glory?
The LORD strong and mighty,
The LORD mighty in [a]battle.

9 Lift up your heads, O you gates!
Lift up, you everlasting doors!
And the King of glory shall come
in.

10 Who is this King of glory?
The LORD of hosts,
He *is* the King of glory. Selah

PSALM 25

A Plea for Deliverance and Forgiveness

A Psalm of David.

To [a]You, O LORD, I lift up my soul.
2 O my God, I [a]trust in You;
Let me not be ashamed;
[b]Let not my enemies triumph over
me.

3 Indeed, let no one who [1]waits on
You be ashamed;
Let those be ashamed who deal
treacherously without cause.

Show ____ Your ways, O Lord; teach them Your paths. Lead them in Your truth and teach them, for You are the God of their salvation.

FROM PSALM 25:4, 5

4 [a]Show me Your ways, O LORD;
Teach me Your paths.

5 Lead me in Your truth and teach
me,

---

4 a Job 3:5; 10:21, 22; 24:17 b [Ps. 3:6; 27:1] c [Is. 43:2]
5 a Ps. 104:15 b Ps. 92:10
6 *1* So with LXX, Syr., Tg., Vg.; MT *return* *2* Or *To the end of my days*, lit. *For length of days*

PSALM 24
1 a 1 Cor. 10:26, 28
2 a Ps. 89:11 *1* Lit. *rivers*
3 a Ps. 15:1–5
4 a [Job 17:9] b [Matt. 5:8] c Ps. 15:4
6 a Ps. 27:4, 8
7 a Is. 26:2 b Ps. 29:2, 9; 97:6
8 a Rev. 19:13–16

PSALM 25
1 a Ps. 86:4; 143:8
2 a Ps. 34:8 b Ps. 13:4; 41:11
3 *1* Waits for You in faith
4 a Ex. 33:13

Dear Woman of Destiny,

Many times in the past, you have hung your head in shame. There were times you found yourself in situations where you were haunted by the fear of being ashamed of something you might say or do. Hopefully, any temptation that has resulted in, or could result in, your being ashamed will be overcome as you remember the revelation of God's word of promise to you.

Keep David's prayer constantly before you, praying, "O my God, I trust in You; let me not be ashamed" (Ps. 25:2). This is the very prayer you can utter while putting your trust in Almighty God.

You need never be ashamed. When you cry out to God, you are turning away from self and from those around you. You are looking *only* to Him.

God commanded the prophet Jeremiah neither to consider nor to be afraid of the faces of men (see Jer. 1:8). Why? Because God was Jeremiah's Helper, his Strengthener, the One who was fighting for him—and the One who had called and chosen him.

When you consider God, and you do not consider the faces of men, you enter into a place of safety, confidence, and strength in Him. The Hebrew word for *trust* also means "shelter." What a picture of protection as you see yourself taking shelter with God!

Living a life without shame begins when you put your total trust and hope in Almighty God.

In Hebrew, the word for *ashamed* means "to be disappointed, disgraced, abashed, fearful, timid, confounded, struck dumb, confused, troubled, and dried up." Most of us can certainly look back and confess that we have experienced such negative feelings in our lives. We have even disappointed ourselves when we did not live up to our own expectations for ourselves.

Now we are looking for the fruit of God's Word in our lives—that we do not have to be ashamed. What peace and joy this prospect brings us! It can be our anchor, our rock of safety, in the midst of all circumstances!

When you look to God, you call to Him. You turn *to* Him and *away from* people and circumstances. You seek Him. You wait upon and for Him. You meditate (think) upon Him and His Word.

Psalm 34:5 tells us that "they looked to Him and were radiant, and their faces were not ashamed." Look to Him, Daughter of God. Let go of your shame in the presence of His radiance and His glory. Let us behold Him!

Bobbie Jean Merck

For You *are* the God of my
salvation;
On You I wait all the day.

6 Remember, O LORD, [a]Your tender
mercies and Your
lovingkindnesses,
For they *are* from of old.
7 Do not remember [a]the sins of my
youth, nor my transgressions;
[b]According to Your mercy remember
me,
For Your goodness' sake, O LORD.

8 Good and upright *is* the LORD;
Therefore He teaches sinners in the
way.
9 The humble He guides in justice,
And the humble He teaches His
way.
10 All the paths of the LORD *are*
mercy and truth,
To such as keep His covenant and
His testimonies.
11 [a]For Your name's sake, O LORD,
Pardon my iniquity, for it *is* great.

12 Who *is* the man that fears the
LORD?
[a]Him shall [1]He teach in the way [1]He
chooses.
13 [a]He himself shall dwell in
[1]prosperity,
And [b]his descendants shall inherit
the earth.
14 [a]The secret of the LORD *is* with
those who fear Him,
And He will show them His
covenant.
15 [a]My eyes *are* ever toward the LORD,
For He shall [1]pluck my feet out of
the net.

16 [a]Turn Yourself to me, and have
mercy on me,
For I *am* [1]desolate and afflicted.
17 The troubles of my heart have
enlarged;
Bring me out of my distresses!
18 [a]Look on my affliction and my
pain,
And forgive all my sins.
19 Consider my enemies, for they are
many;
And they hate me with [1]cruel
hatred.
20 Keep my soul, and deliver me;
Let me not be ashamed, for I put
my trust in You.
21 Let integrity and uprightness
preserve me,
For I wait for You.
22 [a]Redeem Israel, O God,
Out of all their troubles!

PSALM 26

A Prayer for Divine Scrutiny and Redemption

A Psalm of David.

Vindicate [a]me, O LORD,
For I have [b]walked in my integrity.
[c]I have also trusted in the LORD;
I shall not slip.
2 [a]Examine me, O LORD, and [1]prove
me;
Try my mind and my heart.
3 For Your lovingkindness *is* before
my eyes,
And [a]I have walked in Your truth.
4 I have not [a]sat with idolatrous
mortals,
Nor will I go in with hypocrites.
5 I have [a]hated the assembly of
evildoers,
And will not sit with the wicked.
6 I will wash my hands in innocence;
So I will go about Your altar,
O LORD,
7 That I may proclaim with the voice
of thanksgiving,
And tell of all Your wondrous
works.
8 LORD, [a]I have loved the habitation
of Your house,
And the place [1]where Your glory
dwells.

9 [a]Do[1] not gather my soul with
sinners,
Nor my life with bloodthirsty men,
10 In whose hands *is* a sinister
scheme,
And whose right hand is full of
[a]bribes.

11 But as for me, I will walk in my
integrity;
Redeem me and be merciful to me.
12 [a]My foot stands in an even place;
In the congregations I will bless the
LORD.

---

6 a Ps. 103:17; 106:1
7 a [Jer. 3:25] b Ps. 51:1
11 a Ps. 31:3; 79:9; 109:21; 143:11
12 a [Ps. 25:8; 37:23] *1 Or he*
13 a [Prov. 19:23] b Matt. 5:5 *1 Lit. goodness*
14 a [John 7:17]
15 a [Ps. 123:2; 141:8] *1 Lit. bring out*
16 a Ps. 69:16 *1 lonely*
18 a 2 Sam. 16:12
19 *1 violent hatred*
22 a [Ps. 130:8]

PSALM 26
1 a Ps. 7:8 b 2 Kin. 20:3 c [Ps. 13:5; 28:7]
2 a Ps. 17:3; 139:23 *1 test me*
3 a 2 Kin. 20:3
4 a Ps. 1:1
5 a Ps. 31:6; 139:21
8 a Ps. 27:4; 84:1–4, 10 *1 Lit. of the tabernacle of Your glory*
9 a Ps. 28:3 *1 Do not take away*
10 a 1 Sam. 8:3
12 a Ps. 40:2

PSALM 27

An Exuberant Declaration of Faith

A Psalm of David.

The LORD *is* my [a]light and my salvation;
Whom shall I fear?
The [b]LORD *is* the strength of my life;
Of whom shall I be afraid?
2 When the wicked came against me
To [a]eat[1] up my flesh,
My enemies and foes,
They stumbled and fell.
3 [a]Though an army may encamp against me,
My heart shall not fear;
Though war may rise against me,
In this I *will be* confident.

4 [a]One *thing* I have desired of the LORD,
That will I seek:
That I may [b]dwell in the house of the LORD
All the days of my life,
To behold the [1]beauty of the LORD,
And to inquire in His temple.
5 For [a]in the time of trouble
He shall hide me in His pavilion;
In the secret place of His tabernacle
He shall hide me;
He shall [b]set me high upon a rock.

6 And now [a]my head shall be [1]lifted up above my enemies all around me;
Therefore I will offer sacrifices of [2]joy in His tabernacle;
I will sing, yes, I will sing praises to the LORD.

7 Hear, O LORD, *when* I cry with my voice!
Have mercy also upon me, and answer me.
8 *When You said,* "Seek My face,"
My heart said to You, "Your face, LORD, I will seek."
9 [a]Do not hide Your face from me;
Do not turn Your servant away in anger;
You have been my help;
Do not leave me nor forsake me,
O God of my salvation.
10 [a]When my father and my mother forsake me,
Then the LORD will take care of me.

PSALM 27
1 a [Mic. 7:8] b Ps. 62:7; 118:14
2 a Ps. 14:4 *1 devour*
3 a Ps. 3:6
4 a Ps. 26:8; 65:4 b Luke 2:37 *1 delightfulness*
5 a Ps. 31:20; 91:1 b Ps. 40:2
6 a Ps. 3:3 *1* Lifted up in honor *2 joyous shouts*
9 a Ps. 69:17; 143:7
10 a Is. 49:15
11 a Ps. 25:4; 86:11; 119:33
12 a Ps. 35:11
13 a Ezek. 26:20
14 a Is. 25:9 *1* Wait in faith

PSALM 28
1 a Ps. 35:22; 39:12; 83:1 b Ps. 88:4; 143:7
2 a Ps. 5:7 b Ps. 138:2
3 a Ps. 12:2; 55:21; 62:4 *1 drag*
4 a [Rev. 18:6; 22:12]
5 a Is. 5:12
7 a Ps. 18:2; 59:17 b Ps. 13:5; 112:7

11 [a]Teach me Your way, O LORD,
And lead me in a smooth path, because of my enemies.
12 Do not deliver me to the will of my adversaries;
For [a]false witnesses have risen against me,
And such as breathe out violence.
13 *I would have lost heart,* unless I had believed
That I would see the goodness of the LORD
[a]In the land of the living.

14 [a]Wait[1] on the LORD;
Be of good courage,
And He shall strengthen your heart;
Wait, I say, on the LORD!

PSALM 28

Rejoicing in Answered Prayer

A Psalm of David.

To You I will cry, O LORD my Rock:
[a]Do not be silent to me,
[b]Lest, if You *are* silent to me,
I become like those who go down to the pit.
2 Hear the voice of my supplications
When I cry to You,
[a]When I lift up my hands [b]toward Your holy sanctuary.

3 Do not [1]take me away with the wicked
And with the workers of iniquity,
[a]Who speak peace to their neighbors,
But evil *is* in their hearts.
4 [a]Give them according to their deeds,
And according to the wickedness of their endeavors;
Give them according to the work of their hands;
Render to them what they deserve.
5 Because [a]they do not regard the works of the LORD,
Nor the operation of His hands,
He shall destroy them
And not build them up.

6 Blessed *be* the LORD,
Because He has heard the voice of my supplications!
7 The LORD *is* [a]my strength and my shield;
My heart [b]trusted in Him, and I am helped;

Therefore my heart greatly rejoices,
And with my song I will praise Him.
8 The LORD *is* [1]their strength,
And He *is* the [a]saving refuge of His [2]anointed.
9 Save Your people,
And bless [a]Your inheritance;
Shepherd them also,
[b]And bear them up forever.

PSALM 29

Praise to God in His Holiness and Majesty

A Psalm of David.

Give[1] [a]unto the LORD, O you mighty ones,
Give unto the LORD glory and strength.
2 [1]Give unto the LORD the glory [2]due to His name;
Worship the LORD in [a]the [3]beauty of holiness.
3 The voice of the LORD *is* over the waters;
[a]The God of glory thunders;
The LORD *is* over many waters.
4 The voice of the LORD *is* powerful;
The voice of the LORD *is* full of majesty.
5 The voice of the LORD breaks [a]the cedars,
Yes, the LORD splinters the cedars of Lebanon.
6 [a]He makes them also skip like a calf,
Lebanon and [b]Sirion like a young wild ox.
7 The voice of the LORD [1]divides the flames of fire.
8 The voice of the LORD shakes the wilderness;
The LORD shakes the Wilderness of [a]Kadesh.
9 The voice of the LORD makes the [a]deer give birth,
And strips the forests bare;
And in His temple everyone says, "Glory!"
10 The [a]LORD sat *enthroned* at the Flood,
And [b]the LORD sits as King forever.
11 [a]The LORD will give strength to His people;
The LORD will bless His people with peace.

PSALM 30

The Blessedness of Answered Prayer

A Psalm. A Song [a]at the dedication of the house of David.

I will extol You, O LORD, for You have [a]lifted me up,
And have not let my foes [b]rejoice over me.
2 O LORD my God, I cried out to You,
And You [a]healed me.
3 O LORD, [a]You brought my soul up from the grave;
You have kept me alive, [1]that I should not go down to the pit.
4 [a]Sing praise to the LORD, you saints of His,
And give thanks at the remembrance of [1]His holy name.
5 For [a]His anger *is but for* a moment,
[b]His favor *is for* life;
Weeping may endure for a night,
But [1]joy *comes* in the morning.
6 Now in my prosperity I said,
"I shall never be [1]moved."
7 LORD, by Your favor You have made my mountain stand strong;
[a]You hid Your face, *and* I was troubled.

Joys are always on their way to us. They are always traveling to us through the darkness of the night. There is never a night when they are not coming.

AMY CARMICHAEL

8 I cried out to You, O LORD;
And to the LORD I made supplication:
9 "What profit *is there* in my blood,
When I go down to the pit?

28:8 a Ps. 20:6 1 So with MT, Tg.; LXX, Syr., Vg. *the strength of His people* 2 Commissioned one, Heb. *messiah*
9 a [Deut. 9:29; 32:9] b Deut. 1:31

PSALM 29
1 a 1 Chr. 16:28, 29 1 *Ascribe*
2 a 2 Chr. 20:21 1 *Ascribe* 2 Lit. *of His name* 3 *majesty*
3 a [Job 37:4, 5]
5 a Is. 2:13; 14:8
6 a Ps. 114:4 b Deut. 3:9
7 1 *stirs up*, lit. *hews out*
8 a Num. 13:26
9 a Job 39:1
10 a Gen. 6:17 b Ps. 10:16
11 a Ps. 28:8; 68:35

PSALM 30
title a Deut. 20:5
1 a Ps. 28:9 b Ps. 25:2
2 a Ps. 6:2; 103:3
3 a Ps. 86:13 1 So with Qr., Tg.; Kt., LXX, Syr., Vg. *from those who descend to the pit*
4 a Ps. 97:12 1 Or *His holiness*
5 a Ps. 103:9 b Ps. 63:3 1 *a shout of joy*
6 1 *shaken*
7 a [Ps. 104:29; 143:7]

[a]Will the dust praise You?
Will it declare Your truth?
10 Hear, O LORD, and have mercy on me;
LORD, be my helper!"

11 [a]You have turned for me my mourning into dancing;
You have put off [1]my sackcloth and clothed me with gladness,
12 To the end that *my* [1]glory may sing praise to You and not be silent.
O LORD my God, I will give thanks to You forever.

PSALM 31

The Lord a Fortress in Adversity

To the Chief Musician. A Psalm of David.

In [a]You, O LORD, I [1]put my trust;
Let me never be ashamed;
Deliver me in Your righteousness.
2 [a]Bow down Your ear to me,
Deliver me speedily;
Be my rock of [1]refuge,
A [2]fortress of defense to save me.

3 [a]For You *are* my rock and my fortress;
Therefore, [b]for Your name's sake,
Lead me and guide me.
4 Pull me out of the net which they have secretly laid for me,
For You *are* my strength.
5 [a]Into Your hand I commit my spirit;
You have redeemed me, O LORD God of [b]truth.

6 I have hated those [a]who regard useless idols;
But I trust in the LORD.
7 I will be glad and rejoice in Your mercy,
For You have considered my trouble;
You have [a]known my soul in [1]adversities,
8 And have not [a]shut[1] me up into the hand of the enemy;
[b]You have set my feet in a wide place.

9 Have mercy on me, O LORD, for I am in trouble;
[a]My eye wastes away with grief,
Yes, my soul and my [1]body!
10 For my life is spent with grief,
And my years with sighing;
My strength fails because of my iniquity,
And my bones waste away.
11 [a]I am a [1]reproach among all my enemies,
But [b]especially among my neighbors,
And *am* repulsive to my acquaintances;
[c]Those who see me outside flee from me.
12 [a]I am forgotten like a dead man, out of mind;
I am like a [1]broken vessel.
13 [a]For I hear the slander of many;
[b]Fear *is* on every side;
While they [c]take counsel together against me,
They scheme to take away my life.

14 But as for me, I trust in You, O LORD;
I say, "You *are* my God."
15 My times *are* in Your [a]hand;
Deliver me from the hand of my enemies,
And from those who persecute me.
16 [a]Make Your face shine upon Your servant;
Save me for Your mercies' sake.
17 [a]Do not let me be ashamed, O LORD, for I have called upon You;
Let the wicked be ashamed;
[b]Let them be silent in the grave.
18 [a]Let the lying lips be put to silence,
Which [b]speak insolent things proudly and contemptuously against the righteous.

19 [a]Oh, how great *is* Your goodness,
Which You have laid up for those who fear You,
Which You have prepared for those who trust in You
In the presence of the sons of men!
20 [a]You shall hide them in the secret place of Your presence
From the plots of man;
[b]You shall keep them secretly in a [1]pavilion
From the strife of tongues.

21 Blessed *be* the LORD,
For [a]He has shown me His marvelous kindness in a [1]strong city!
22 For I said in my haste,

---

9 a [Ps. 6:5]
11 a Jer. 31:4 *1* The sackcloth of my mourning
12 *1 soul*

PSALM 31
1 a Ps. 22:5 *1 have taken refuge*
2 a Ps. 17:6; 71:2; 86:1; 102:2 *1 strength 2* Lit. *house of fortresses*
3 a [Ps. 18:2] b Ps. 23:3; 25:11
5 a Luke 23:46 b [Deut. 32:4]
6 a Jon. 2:8
7 a [John 10:27] *1 troubles*
8 a [Deut. 32:30] b [Ps. 4:1; 18:19] *1 given me over*
9 a Ps. 6:7 *1* Lit. *belly*
11 a [Is. 53:4] b Job 19:13 c Ps. 64:8 *1 despised thing*
12 a Ps. 88:4, 5 *1* Lit. *perishing*
13 a Jer. 20:10 b Lam. 2:22 c Matt. 27:1
15 a [Job 14:5; 24:1]
16 a Ps. 4:6; 80:3
17 a Ps. 25:2, 20 b Ps. 94:17; 115:17
18 a Ps. 109:2; 120:2 b Ps. 94:4
19 a [Rom. 2:4; 11:22]
20 a [Ps. 27:5; 32:7] b Job 5:21 *1 shelter*
21 a [Ps. 17:7] *1 fortified*

PSALM 31:14, 15

Dear Woman of Destiny,

Are you waiting for God to do something because of a vision, a dream, a prophecy, a heart's desire, or a prayer? Be encouraged by King David's words in Psalm 31:14, 15: "But as for me, I trust in You, O LORD; I say 'You are my God.' My times *are* in Your hand." Even though circumstances may seem to tell you that the enemy has succeeded in pushing you into a corner, or in holding you down in a small place with little hope of escape, be strengthened by God's word in Psalm 31:7, 8: "I will be glad and rejoice in Your mercy, for You have considered my trouble; You have known my soul in adversities, and have not shut me up into the hand of the enemy; You have set my feet in a wide place."

Take comfort in the knowledge that as you walk in obedience to God's will for your life, He will bring you out into the large places of victory! Your times *are* in His hand!

Before the foundations of the world were laid, God chose you in the Beloved, Jesus Christ (see Eph. 1:4). Therefore, as He chose you, He also chose a plan and purpose for your life (see John 15:16). God did the choosing, because He knows you best and He wants the best for you. And as you pursue God's plan, He will make everything beautiful in its time (see Eccl. 3:11).

You are *not* an accident! When your parents had you, it was by the direction of God. (Whether they realized it or not, God had you in His plans.) As you were being "fearfully and wonderfully made" in your mother's womb (see Ps. 139:14), the plan, the purpose, and the will of Almighty God were also being fashioned into you.

God longs for you and me to come into that place where His will, plan, and purpose are fulfilled in our lives.

Remember, "To everything there is a season, a time for every purpose under heaven" (Eccl. 3:1). Therefore, despise not "the day of small things" (Zech. 4:10). A small thing can grow into an enormous work for God, so continue to be a faithful steward in all things.

Your times are in His hands, and your time is coming!

Bobbie Jean Merck

"I am cut off from before Your eyes";
Nevertheless You heard the voice of my supplications
When I cried out to You.

23 Oh, love the LORD, all you His saints!
For the LORD preserves the faithful,
And fully repays the proud person.
24 [a]Be of good courage,
And He shall strengthen your heart,
All you who hope in the LORD.

PSALM 32

The Joy of Forgiveness

A Psalm of David. A [1]Contemplation.

Blessed *is he whose* [a]transgression *is* forgiven,
Whose sin *is* covered.
2 Blessed *is* the man to whom the LORD [a]does not [1]impute iniquity,
And [b]in whose spirit *there is* no deceit.

3 When I kept silent, my bones grew old
Through my groaning all the day long.
4 For day and night Your [a]hand was heavy upon me;
My vitality was turned into the drought of summer. Selah
5 I acknowledged my sin to You,
And my iniquity I have not hidden.
[a]I said, "I will confess my transgressions to the LORD,"
And You forgave the iniquity of my sin. Selah

6 [a]For this cause everyone who is godly shall [b]pray to You
In a time when You may be found;
Surely in a flood of great waters
They shall not come near him.
7 [a]You *are* my hiding place;
You shall preserve me from trouble;
You shall surround me with [b]songs of deliverance. Selah

8 I will instruct you and teach you in the way you should go;
I will guide you with My eye.
9 Do not be like the [a]horse *or* like the mule,
Which have no understanding,

24 a [Ps. 27:14]

PSALM 32
title 1 Heb. *Maschil*
1 a [Ps. 85:2; 103:3]
2 a [2 Cor. 5:19] b John 1:47 1 *charge his account with*
4 a 1 Sam. 5:6
5 a [Prov. 28:13]
6 a [1 Tim. 1:16] b Is. 55:6
7 a Ps. 9:9 b Ex. 15:1
9 a Prov. 26:3
10 a [Rom. 2:9] b Prov. 16:20
11 a Ps. 64:10; 68:3; 97:12

PSALM 33
1 a Ps. 32:11; 97:12
2 1 Lit. *Sing to Him*
6 a [Heb. 11:3] b Gen. 2:1 c [Job 26:13]
7 a Job 26:10; 38:8 1 LXX, Tg., Vg. *in a vessel*

Lord God, give ______ understanding to know that You are their hiding place. You will preserve them from trouble and surround them with songs of deliverance.

FROM PSALM 32:7

Which must be harnessed with bit and bridle,
Else they will not come near you.

10 [a]Many sorrows *shall be* to the wicked;
But [b]he who trusts in the LORD, mercy shall surround him.
11 [a]Be glad in the LORD and rejoice, you righteous;
And shout for joy, all *you* upright in heart!

PSALM 33

The Sovereignty of the Lord in Creation and History

Rejoice [a]in the LORD, O you righteous!
For praise from the upright is beautiful.
2 Praise the LORD with the harp;
[1]Make melody to Him with an instrument of ten strings.
3 Sing to Him a new song;
Play skillfully with a shout of joy.

4 For the word of the LORD *is* right,
And all His work *is done* in truth.
5 He loves righteousness and justice;
The earth is full of the goodness of the LORD.

6 [a]By the word of the LORD the heavens were made,
And all the [b]host of them [c]by the breath of His mouth.
7 [a]He gathers the waters of the sea together [1]as a heap;
He lays up the deep in storehouses.

8 Let all the earth fear the LORD;
Let all the inhabitants of the world stand in awe of Him.

9 For [a]He spoke, and it was *done;*
He commanded, and it stood fast.

10 [a]The LORD brings the counsel of the nations to nothing;
He makes the plans of the peoples of no effect.
11 [a]The counsel of the LORD stands forever,
The plans of His heart to all generations.
12 Blessed *is* the nation whose God *is* the LORD,
The people He has [a]chosen as His own inheritance.

13 [a]The LORD looks from heaven;
He sees all the sons of men.
14 From the place of His dwelling He looks
On all the inhabitants of the earth;
15 He fashions their hearts individually;
[a]He [1]considers all their works.

16 [a]No king *is* saved by the multitude of an army;
A mighty man is not delivered by great strength.
17 [a]A horse *is* a [1]vain hope for safety;
Neither shall it deliver *any* by its great strength.

18 [a]Behold, the eye of the LORD *is* on those who fear Him,
On those who hope in His mercy,
19 To deliver their soul from death,
And [a]to keep them alive in famine.

O Lord, let Your mercy be upon _____, just as they hope in You.

FROM PSALM 33:22

20 Our soul waits for the LORD;
He *is* our help and our shield.
21 For our heart shall rejoice in Him,
Because we have trusted in His holy name.
22 Let Your mercy, O LORD, be upon us,
Just as we hope in You.

9 a Gen. 1:3
10 a Is. 8:10; 19:3
11 a [Job 23:13]
12 a [Ex. 19:5]
13 a Job 28:24
15 a [Jer. 32:19] *1 understands*
16 a Ps. 44:6; 60:11
17 a [Prov. 21:31] *1 false*
18 a [Job 36:7]
19 a Job 5:20
PSALM 34 title a 1 Sam. 21:10–15
1 a [Eph. 5:20]
4 a [Matt. 7:7]
7 a Dan. 6:22 b 2 Kin. 6:17 *1 Or Angel*
8 a 1 Pet. 2:3 b Ps. 2:12
9 *1 lack*
10 a [Ps. 84:11]
11 a Ps. 32:8

PSALM 34

The Happiness of Those Who Trust in God

A Psalm of David [a]when he pretended madness before Abimelech, who drove him away, and he departed.

I will [a]bless the LORD at all times;
His praise *shall* continually *be* in my mouth.
2 My soul shall make its boast in the LORD;
The humble shall hear *of it* and be glad.
3 Oh, magnify the LORD with me,
And let us exalt His name together.

4 I [a]sought the LORD, and He heard me,
And delivered me from all my fears.
5 They looked to Him and were radiant,
And their faces were not ashamed.
6 This poor man cried out, and the LORD heard *him,*
And saved him out of all his troubles.
7 [a]The [1]angel of the LORD [b]encamps all around those who fear Him,
And delivers them.

I would prefer one mouthful of Christ's love and one sip of His fellowship than a whole world of carnal delights.

CHARLES H. SPURGEON

8 Oh, [a]taste and see that the LORD *is* good;
[b]Blessed *is* the man *who* trusts in Him!
9 Oh, fear the LORD, you His saints!
There is no [1]want to those who fear Him.
10 The young lions lack and suffer hunger;
[a]But those who seek the LORD shall not lack any good *thing.*

11 Come, you children, listen to me;
[a]I will teach you the fear of the LORD.

Psalm 34:1

Dear Woman of Destiny,

It is God's desire that we worship Him at all times, in spite of what may be going on in our lives. When David penned the words, "I will bless the LORD at all times; His praise [*Halal*] shall continually be in my mouth," he was running for his life. All "hell" seemed to be breaking loose around him. How could he find the strength in the midst of his adversity to bless God? How could he stare death in the face and yet praise, or more precisely *Halal* the Lord?

Halal is one of the many original Hebrew root words for "praise" in the Scriptures. The word literally means "to be clamorously foolish about the adoration of God"—to praise Him with passion and fervency, to lose all hang-ups about who we are or are not. This is the type of praise that David offered to the Lord when he led the ark of the covenant back into the city of Jerusalem. He took off his royal robe and gave praise, unashamedly, to the Almighty God. David was saying by this action: "I will not let my royal title hinder me from lavishly praising the One with whom I have intimate relationship. I will worship Him in spite of who I am or what I have attained!"

You see, my sister, worship is more than lifting our hands or singing a song in the house of the Lord; it is a lifestyle that must be lived out every single day. It is actually walking out the God-given purposes for our lives, which He has ordained before the foundation of this world. However, the understanding of that purpose comes through our times of intimacy and fellowship with Him.

David was able to "bless the LORD at all times" because he understood his purpose. He understood the power of praise. Whenever our praise (the vocalizing of the attributes of God) links up with our worship (the walking out of the purposes of God for our lives), we will walk in victory.

My dear sister, as you go about your busy day, make time for the Lord. Make time to become intimate with Him so that you might gain a complete understanding of the unique purpose He has placed you on this earth to fulfill.

Determine in your heart this day that you will live out your God-given assignment as you continue to offer to Him the fruit of your lips, giving thanks in the midst of all things, no matter how busy you are. This is God's will for all of us. Be encouraged my sister; the best is yet to come!

Judith Christie-McAllister

12 [a]Who *is* the man *who* desires life,
And loves *many* days, that he may
see good?
13 Keep your tongue from evil,
And your lips from speaking
[a]deceit.
14 [a]Depart from evil and do good;
[b]Seek peace and pursue it.
15 [a]The eyes of the LORD *are* on the
righteous,
And His ears *are open* to their cry.
16 [a]The face of the LORD *is* against
those who do evil,
[b]To [1]cut off the remembrance of
them from the earth.

17 *The righteous* cry out, and [a]the
LORD hears,
And delivers them out of all their
troubles.
18 [a]The LORD *is* near [b]to those who
have a broken heart,
And saves such as [1]have a contrite
spirit.
19 [a]Many *are* the afflictions of the
righteous,
[b]But the LORD delivers him out of
them all.
20 He guards all his bones;
[a]Not one of them is broken.
21 [a]Evil shall slay the wicked,
And those who hate the righteous
shall be [1]condemned.
22 The LORD [a]redeems the soul of
His servants,
And none of those who trust in
Him shall be condemned.

PSALM 35

The Lord the Avenger of His People

A Psalm of David.

Plead[1] *my cause,* O LORD, with those
who strive with me;
Fight against those who fight
against me.
2 Take hold of shield and [1]buckler,
And stand up for my help.
3 Also draw out the spear,
And stop those who pursue me.
Say to my soul,
"I *am* your salvation."

4 [a]Let those be put to shame and
brought to dishonor
Who seek after my life;
Let those be [b]turned back and
brought to confusion
Who plot my hurt.
5 [a]Let them be like chaff before the
wind,
And let the [1]angel of the LORD
chase *them.*
6 Let their way be [a]dark and
slippery,
And let the angel of the LORD
pursue them.
7 For without cause they have
[a]hidden their net for me *in* a pit,
Which they have dug without cause
for my life.
8 [1]Let [a]destruction come upon him
unexpectedly,
And let his net that he has hidden
catch himself;
Into that very destruction let him
fall.

9 And my soul shall be joyful in the
LORD;
It shall rejoice in His salvation.
10 [a]All my bones shall say,
"LORD, [b]who *is* like You,
Delivering the poor from him who
is too strong for him,
Yes, the poor and the needy from
him who plunders him?"

11 Fierce witnesses rise up;
They ask me *things* that I do not
know.
12 [a]They reward me evil for good,
To the sorrow of my soul.
13 But as for me, [a]when they were
sick,
My clothing *was* sackcloth;
I humbled myself with fasting;
And my prayer would return to my
own [1]heart.
14 I paced about as though *he were*
my friend *or* brother;
I bowed down [1]heavily, as one who
mourns *for his* mother.

15 But in my [1]adversity they rejoiced
And gathered together;
Attackers gathered against me,
And I did not know *it;*
They tore *at me* and did not cease;
16 With ungodly mockers at feasts
They gnashed at me with their
teeth.

17 Lord, how long will You [a]look on?
Rescue me from their destructions,
My precious *life* from the lions.

---

12 a [1 Pet. 3:10–12]
13 a [Eph. 4:25]
14 a Ps. 37:27 b [Rom. 14:19]
15 a Job 36:7
16 a Lev. 17:10 b [Prov. 10:7] *1 destroy*
17 a Ps. 34:6; 145:19
18 a [Ps. 145:18] b [Is. 57:15] *1 are crushed in spirit*
19 a Prov. 24:16 b Ps. 34:4, 6, 17
20 a John 19:33, 36
21 a Ps. 94:23; 140:11 *1 held guilty*
22 a 1 Kin. 1:29

PSALM 35
1 *1 Contend for me*
2 *1* A small shield
4 a Ps. 40:14, 15; 70:2, 3 b Ps. 129:5
5 a Job 21:18 *1* Or *Angel*
6 a Ps. 73:18
7 a Ps. 9:15
8 a [1 Thess. 5:3] *1* Lit. *Let destruction he does not know come upon him,*
10 a Ps. 51:8 b [Ex. 15:11]
12 a John 10:32
13 a Job 30:25 *1* Lit. *bosom*
14 *1 in mourning*
15 *1 limping, stumbling*
17 a [Hab. 1:13]

18 I will give You thanks in the great
assembly;
I will praise You among [1]many
people.
19 [a]Let them not rejoice over me who
are wrongfully my enemies;
Nor let them wink with the eye
who hate me without a cause.
20 For they do not speak peace,
But they devise deceitful matters
Against *the* quiet ones in the land.
21 They also opened their mouth
wide against me,
And said, "Aha, aha!
Our eyes have seen *it*."

22 *This* You have seen, O LORD;
Do not keep silence.
O Lord, do not be far from me.
23 Stir up Yourself, and awake to my
vindication,
To my cause, my God and my Lord.
24 Vindicate me, O LORD my God,
according to Your righteousness;
And let them not rejoice over me.
25 Let them not say in their hearts,
"Ah, so we would have it!"
Let them not say, "We have
swallowed him up."

26 Let them be ashamed and brought
to mutual confusion
Who rejoice at my hurt;
Let them be [a]clothed with shame
and dishonor
Who exalt themselves against me.

27 [a]Let them shout for joy and be
glad,
Who favor my righteous cause;
And let them say continually,
"Let the LORD be magnified,
Who has pleasure in the prosperity
of His servant."
28 And my tongue shall speak of
Your righteousness
And of Your praise all the day long.

PSALM 36

Man's Wickedness and God's Perfections

To the Chief Musician. A Psalm of David the servant of the LORD.

An oracle within my heart concerning
the transgression of the wicked:
[a]*There is* no fear of God before his
eyes.
2 For he flatters himself in his own
eyes,
When he finds out his iniquity *and*
when he hates.
3 The words of his mouth *are*
wickedness and deceit;
[a]He has ceased to be wise *and* to do
good.
4 [a]He devises wickedness on his bed;
He sets himself [b]in a way *that is*
not good;
He does not [1]abhor [c]evil.

5 Your mercy, O LORD, *is* in the
heavens;
Your faithfulness *reaches* to the
clouds.
6 Your righteousness *is* like the
[1]great mountains;
[a]Your judgments *are* a great deep;
O LORD, You preserve man and
beast.

7 How precious *is* Your
lovingkindness, O God!
Therefore the children of men [a]put
their trust under the shadow of
Your wings.
8 [a]They are abundantly satisfied with
the fullness of Your house,
And You give them drink from [b]the
river of Your pleasures.
9 [a]For with You *is* the fountain of
life;
[b]In Your light we see light.

10 Oh, continue Your lovingkindness
to those who know You,
And Your righteousness to the
upright in heart.
11 Let not the foot of pride come
against me,
And let not the hand of the wicked
drive me away.
12 There the workers of iniquity have
fallen;
They have been cast down and are
not able to rise.

PSALM 37

The Heritage of the Righteous and the Calamity of the Wicked

A Psalm of David.

Do[a] not fret because of evildoers,
Nor be envious of the workers of
iniquity.

---

18 [1] *a mighty*
19 a Ps. 69:4; 109:3
26 a Ps. 109:29
27 a Rom. 12:15

PSALM 36
1 a Rom. 3:18
3 a Jer. 4:22
4 a Prov. 4:16 b Is. 65:2 c [Rom. 12:9] [1] *reject, loathe*
6 a [Rom. 11:33] [1] Lit. *mountains of God*
7 a Ps. 17:8; 57:1; 91:4
8 a Ps. 63:5; 65:4 b Rev. 22:1
9 a [Jer. 2:13] b [1 Pet. 2:9]

PSALM 37
1 a Ps. 73:3

2 For they shall soon be cut down
[a]like the grass,
And wither as the green herb.

3 Trust in the LORD, and do good;
Dwell in the land, and feed on His
faithfulness.
4 [a]Delight yourself also in the LORD,
And He shall give you the desires of
your [b]heart.

I pray, Father, that ____ will delight themselves in You and that You would give them the desires of their heart.

FROM PSALM 37:4

5 [a]Commit[1] your way to the LORD,
Trust also in Him,
And He shall bring *it* to pass.
6 [a]He shall bring forth your
righteousness as the light,
And your justice as the noonday.

7 Rest in the LORD, [a]and wait
patiently for Him;
Do not fret because of him who
[b]prospers in his way,
Because of the man who brings
wicked schemes to pass.
8 [a]Cease from anger, and forsake
wrath;
[b]Do not fret—*it* only *causes* harm.

9 For evildoers shall be [1]cut off;
But those who wait on the LORD,
They shall [a]inherit the earth.
10 For [a]yet a little while and the
wicked *shall be* no *more;*
Indeed, [b]you will look carefully for
his place,
But it *shall be* no *more.*
11 [a]But the meek shall inherit the
earth,
And shall delight themselves in the
abundance of peace.

12 The wicked plots against the just,
[a]And gnashes at him with his teeth.
13 [a]The Lord laughs at him,
For He sees that [b]his day is
coming.
14 The wicked have drawn the sword
And have bent their bow,
To cast down the poor and needy,
To slay those who are of upright
conduct.
15 Their sword shall enter their own
heart,
And their bows shall be broken.

16 [a]A little that a righteous man has
Is better than the riches of many
wicked.
17 For the arms of the wicked shall
be broken,
But the LORD upholds the
righteous.

It is only when our hearts are . . . actually at rest in God, in peaceful and self-oblivious adoration, that we can hope to show His attractiveness to others.

EVELYN UNDERHILL

18 The LORD knows the days of the
upright,
And their inheritance shall be
forever.
19 They shall not be ashamed in the
evil time,
And in the days of famine they shall
be satisfied.
20 But the wicked shall perish;
And the enemies of the LORD,
Like the splendor of the meadows,
shall vanish.
Into smoke they shall vanish away.

21 The wicked borrows and does not
repay,
But [a]the righteous shows mercy
and gives.
22 [a]For *those* blessed by Him shall
inherit the earth,
But *those* cursed by Him shall be
[1]cut off.

23 [a]The steps of a *good* man are
[1]ordered by the LORD,
And He delights in his way.
24 [a]Though he fall, he shall not be
utterly cast down;

2 a Ps. 90:5, 6; 92:7
4 a Is. 58:14 b Ps. 21:2; 145:19
5 a [Ps. 55:22] *1 Lit. Roll off onto*
6 a Job 11:17
7 a [Lam. 3:26] b [Ps. 73:3–12]
8 a [Eph. 4:26] b Ps. 73:3
9 a [Is. 57:13; 60:21] *1 destroyed*
10 a [Heb. 10:37] b Job 7:10
11 a [Matt. 5:5]
12 a Ps. 35:16
13 a Ps. 2:4; 59:8 b 1 Sam. 26:10
16 a Prov. 15:16; 16:8
21 a Ps. 112:5, 9
22 a [Prov. 3:33] *1 destroyed*
23 a [1 Sam. 2:9] *1 established*
24 a Prov. 24:16

For the LORD upholds *him with* His hand.
25 I have been young, and *now* am old;
Yet I have not seen the righteous forsaken,
Nor his descendants begging bread.
26 [a]*He is* [1]ever merciful, and lends;
And his descendants *are* blessed.

27 Depart from evil, and do good;
And dwell forevermore.
28 For the LORD loves justice,
And does not forsake His saints;
They are preserved forever,
But the descendants of the wicked shall be cut off.
29 [a]The righteous shall inherit the land,
And dwell in it forever.

30 [a]The mouth of the righteous speaks wisdom,
And his tongue talks of justice.
31 The law of his God *is* in his heart;
None of his steps shall [1]slide.

32 The wicked [a]watches the righteous,
And seeks to slay him.
33 The LORD [a]will not leave him in his hand,
Nor condemn him when he is judged.

34 [a]Wait on the LORD,
And keep His way,
And He shall exalt you to inherit the land;
When the wicked are cut off, you shall see *it*.

35 I have seen the wicked in great power,
And spreading himself like a native green tree.
36 Yet [1]he passed away, and behold, he *was* no *more;*
Indeed I sought him, but he could not be found.

37 Mark the blameless *man,* and observe the upright;
For the future of *that* man *is* peace.
38 [a]But the transgressors shall be destroyed together;
The future of the wicked shall be cut off.

39 But the salvation of the righteous *is* from the LORD;
He is their strength [a]in the time of trouble.
40 And [a]the LORD shall help them and deliver them;
He shall deliver them from the wicked,
And save them,
[b]Because they trust in Him.

PSALM 38

Prayer in Time of Chastening

A Psalm of David. [a]To bring to remembrance.

O LORD, do not [a]rebuke me in Your wrath,
Nor chasten me in Your hot displeasure!
2 For Your arrows pierce me deeply,
And Your hand presses me down.

3 *There is* no soundness in my flesh
Because of Your anger,
Nor *any* health in my bones
Because of my sin.
4 For my iniquities have gone over my head;
Like a heavy burden they are too heavy for me.
5 My wounds are foul *and* festering
Because of my foolishness.
6 I am [1]troubled, I am bowed down greatly;
I go mourning all the day long.
7 For my loins are full of inflammation,
And *there is* no soundness in my flesh.
8 I am feeble and severely broken;
I groan because of the turmoil of my heart.

9 Lord, all my desire *is* before You;
And my sighing is not hidden from You.
10 My heart pants, my strength fails me;
As for the light of my eyes, it also has gone from me.
11 My loved ones and my friends [a]stand aloof from my plague,
And my relatives stand afar off.
12 Those also who seek my life lay snares *for me;*
Those who seek my hurt speak of destruction,
And plan deception all the day long.

---

26 a [Deut. 15:8] *1* Lit. *all the day*
29 a Prov. 2:21
30 a [Matt. 12:35]
31 *1 slip*
32 a Ps. 10:8; 17:11
33 a [2 Pet. 2:9]
34 a Ps. 27:14; 37:9
36 *1* So with MT, LXX, Tg.; Syr., Vg. *I passed by*
38 a [Ps. 1:4–6; 37:20, 28]
39 a Ps. 9:9; 37:19
40 a Is. 31:5 b 1 Chr. 5:20
PSALM 38 title a Ps. 70:title
1 a Ps. 6:1
6 *1* Lit. *bent down*
11 a Ps. 31:11; 88:18

13 But I, like a deaf *man,* do not hear;
And *I am* like a mute *who* does not open his mouth.
14 Thus I am like a man who does not hear,
And in whose mouth *is* no response.

15 For [1]in You, O LORD, [a]I hope;
You will [2]hear, O Lord my God.
16 For I said, *"Hear me,* lest they rejoice over me,
Lest, when my foot slips, they exalt *themselves* against me."

17 [a]For I *am* ready to fall,
And my sorrow *is* continually before me.
18 For I will [a]declare my iniquity;
I will be [b]in [1]anguish over my sin.
19 But my enemies *are* vigorous, *and* they are strong;
And those who hate me wrongfully have multiplied.
20 Those also [a]who render evil for good,
They are my adversaries, because I follow *what is* good.

21 Do not forsake me, O LORD;
O my God, [a]be not far from me!
22 Make haste to help me,
O Lord, my salvation!

PSALM 39

Prayer for Wisdom and Forgiveness

To the Chief Musician. To Jeduthun. A Psalm of David.

I said, "I will guard my ways,
Lest I sin with my [a]tongue;
I will restrain my mouth with a muzzle,
While the wicked are before me."
2 [a]I was mute with silence,
I held my peace *even* from good;
And my sorrow was stirred up.
3 My heart was hot within me;
While I was [1]musing, the fire burned.
Then I spoke with my tongue:

4 "LORD, [a]make me to know my end,
And what *is* the measure of my days,
That I may know how frail I *am.*
5 Indeed, You have made my days *as* handbreadths,
And my age *is* as nothing before You;
Certainly every man at his best state *is* but [a]vapor. Selah
6 Surely every man walks about like a shadow;
Surely they [1]busy themselves in vain;
He heaps up *riches,*
And does not know who will gather them.

7 "And now, Lord, what do I wait for?
My [a]hope *is* in You.
8 Deliver me from all my transgressions;
Do not make me [a]the reproach of the foolish.
9 [a]I was mute, I did not open my mouth,
Because it was [b]You who did *it.*
10 [a]Remove Your plague from me;
I am consumed by the blow of Your hand.
11 When with rebukes You correct man for iniquity,
You make his beauty [a]melt away like a moth;
Surely every man *is* vapor. Selah

12 "Hear my prayer, O LORD,
And give ear to my cry;
Do not be silent at my tears;
For I *am* a stranger with You,
A sojourner, [a]as all my fathers *were.*
13 [a]Remove Your gaze from me, that I may regain strength,
Before I go away and [b]am no more."

PSALM 40

Faith Persevering in Trial

To the Chief Musician. A Psalm of David.

I [a]waited patiently for the LORD;
And He inclined to me,
And heard my cry.
2 He also brought me up out of a horrible pit,
Out of [a]the miry clay,
And [b]set my feet upon a rock,
And established my steps.
3 [a]He has put a new song in my mouth—
Praise to our God;
Many will see *it* and fear,

15 [a][Ps. 39:7] [1] *I wait for You, O LORD* [2] *answer*
17 [a]Ps. 51:3
18 [a]Ps. 32:5 [b][2 Cor. 7:9, 10] [1] *anxiety*
20 [a]Ps. 35:12
21 [a]Ps. 22:19; 35:22

PSALM 39
1 [a][James 3:5–12]
2 [a]Ps. 38:13
3 [1] *meditating*
4 [a]Ps. 90:12; 119:84
5 [a]Ps. 62:9
6 [1] *make an uproar for nothing*
7 [a]Ps. 38:15
8 [a]Ps. 44:13; 79:4; 119:22
9 [a]Ps. 39:2 [b]Job 2:10
10 [a]Job 9:34; 13:21
11 [a]Job 13:28
12 [a]Gen. 47:9
13 [a]Job 7:19; 10:20, 21; 14:6 [b][Job 14:10]

PSALM 40
1 [a]Ps. 25:5; 27:14; 37:7
2 [a]Ps. 69:2, 14 [b]Ps. 27:5
3 [a]Ps. 32:7; 33:3

And will trust in the LORD.

4 [a]Blessed *is* that man who makes the
LORD his trust,
And does not respect the proud, nor
such as turn aside to lies.

5 [a]Many, O LORD my God, *are* Your
wonderful works
Which You have done;
[b]And Your thoughts toward us
Cannot be recounted to You in
order;
If I would declare and speak *of*
them,
They are more than can be
numbered.

6 [a]Sacrifice and offering You did not
desire;
My ears You have opened.
Burnt offering and sin offering You
did not require.

7 Then I said, "Behold, I come;
In the scroll of the book *it is*
written of me.

8 [a]I delight to do Your will, O my
God,
And Your law *is* [b]within my heart."

May ____ wait patiently for You, O Lord; turn to them and hear their cry. Bring ____ up out of a horrible pit, out of the miry clay. Lord, set their feet upon a rock, and establish their steps. Put a new song of praise in their mouth.

FROM PSALM 40:1–3

9 [a]I have proclaimed the good news of
righteousness
In the great assembly;
Indeed, [b]I do not restrain my lips,
O LORD, You Yourself know.

10 [a]I have not hidden Your
righteousness within my heart;
I have declared Your faithfulness
and Your salvation;
I have not concealed Your
lovingkindness and Your truth
From the great assembly.

4 a Ps. 34:8; 84:12
5 a Job 9:10 b [Is. 55:8]
6 a [Heb. 10:5–9]
8 a [John 4:34; 6:38] b [Jer. 31:33]
9 a Ps. 22:22, 25 b Ps. 119:13
10 a Acts 20:20, 27
11 a Ps. 61:7
12 a Ps. 38:4; 65:3
13 a Ps. 70:1
14 a Ps. 35:4, 26; 70:2; 71:13 *1* Lit. *soul*
15 a Ps. 73:19
16 a Ps. 70:4 b Ps. 35:27
17 a Ps. 70:5; 86:1; 109:22 b 1 Pet. 5:7

PSALM 41
1 *1 helpless* or *powerless*
2 a Ps. 27:12
3 *1 restore*
4 a Ps. 6:2; 103:3; 147:3

11 Do not withhold Your tender
mercies from me, O LORD;
[a]Let Your lovingkindness and Your
truth continually preserve me.

12 For innumerable evils have
surrounded me;
[a]My iniquities have overtaken me, so
that I am not able to look up;
They are more than the hairs of my
head;
Therefore my heart fails me.

13 [a]Be pleased, O LORD, to deliver me;
O LORD, make haste to help me!

14 [a]Let them be ashamed and brought
to mutual confusion
Who seek to destroy my [1]life;
Let them be driven backward and
brought to dishonor
Who wish me evil.

15 Let them be [a]confounded because
of their shame,
Who say to me, "Aha, aha!"

16 [a]Let all those who seek You rejoice
and be glad in You;
Let such as love Your salvation [b]say
continually,
"The LORD be magnified!"

17 [a]But I *am* poor and needy;
[b]*Yet* the LORD thinks upon me.
You *are* my help and my deliverer;
Do not delay, O my God.

PSALM 41

The Blessing and Suffering of the Godly

To the Chief Musician. A Psalm of David.

Blessed *is* he who considers the [1]poor;
The LORD will deliver him in time
of trouble.

2 The LORD will preserve him and
keep him alive,
And he will be blessed on the earth;
[a]You will not deliver him to the will
of his enemies.

3 The LORD will strengthen him on
his bed of illness;
You will [1]sustain him on his
sickbed.

4 I said, "LORD, be merciful to me;
[a]Heal my soul, for I have sinned
against You."

5 My enemies speak evil of me:
"When will he die, and his name
perish?"

6 And if he comes to see *me,* he
speaks [1]lies;
His heart gathers iniquity to itself;
When he goes out, he tells *it.*
7 All who hate me whisper together
against me;
Against me they [1]devise my hurt.
8 "An[1] evil disease," *they say,* "clings
to him.
And *now* that he lies down, he will
rise up no more."
9 [a]Even my own familiar friend in
whom I trusted,
[b]Who ate my bread,
Has [1]lifted up *his* heel against me.
10 But You, O LORD, be merciful to
me, and raise me up,
That I may repay them.
11 By this I know that You are well
pleased with me,
Because my enemy does not
triumph over me.
12 As for me, You uphold me in my
integrity,
And [a]set me before Your face
forever.
13 [a]Blessed *be* the LORD God of Israel
From everlasting to everlasting!
Amen and Amen.

BOOK TWO
Psalms 42—72

PSALM 42

Yearning for God in the Midst of Distresses

To the Chief Musician. A [1]Contemplation of the sons of Korah.

As the deer [1]pants for the water brooks,
So pants my soul for You, O God.
2 [a]My soul thirsts for God, for the
[b]living God.
When shall I come and [1]appear
before God?
3 [a]My tears have been my food day
and night,
While they continually say to me,
[b]"Where *is* your God?"
4 When I remember these *things,*
[a]I pour out my soul within me.
For I used to go with the
multitude;
[b]I went with them to the house of
God,
With the voice of joy and praise,
With a multitude that kept a
pilgrim feast.
5 [a]Why are you [1]cast down, O my
soul?
And *why* are you disquieted within
me?
[b]Hope in God, for I shall yet praise
Him
[2]*For* the help of His countenance.
6 [1]O my God, my soul is cast down
within me;
Therefore I will remember You
from the land of the Jordan,
And from the heights of Hermon,
From [2]the Hill Mizar.
7 Deep calls unto deep at the noise
of Your waterfalls;
[a]All Your waves and billows have
gone over me.
8 The LORD will [a]command His
lovingkindness in the daytime,
And [b]in the night His song *shall be*
with me—
A prayer to the God of my life.
9 I will say to God my Rock,
[a]"Why have You forgotten me?
Why do I go mourning because of
the oppression of the enemy?"
10 *As* with a [1]breaking of my bones,
My enemies [2]reproach me,
[a]While they say to me all day long,
"Where *is* your God?"
11 [a]Why are you cast down, O my
soul?
And why are you disquieted within
me?
Hope in God;
For I shall yet praise Him,
The [1]help of my countenance and
my God.

PSALM 43

Prayer to God in Time of Trouble

Vindicate [a]me, O God,
And [b]plead my cause against an
ungodly nation;
Oh, deliver me from the deceitful
and unjust man!
2 For You *are* the God of my
strength;
Why do You cast me off?
[a]Why do I go mourning because of
the oppression of the enemy?

---

6 [1] *empty words*
7 [1] *plot*
8 [1] Lit. *A thing of Belial*
9 [a] 2 Sam. 15:12 [b] John 13:18, 21–30 [1] Acted as a traitor
12 [a] [Job 36:7]
13 [a] Ps. 72:18, 19; 89:52; 106:48; 150:6

PSALM 42
title [1] Heb. *Maschil*
1 [1] Lit. *longs for*
2 [a] Ps. 63:1; 84:2; 143:6 [b] 1 Thess. 1:9 [1] So with MT, Vg.; some Heb. mss., LXX, Syr., Tg. *I see the face of God*
3 [a] Ps. 80:5; 102:9 [b] Ps. 79:10; 115:2
4 [a] Job 30:16 [b] Is. 30:29
5 [a] Ps. 42:11; 43:5 [b] Lam. 3:24 [1] Lit. *bowed down* [2] So with MT, Tg.; a few Heb. mss., LXX, Syr., Vg. *The help of my countenance, my God*
6 [1] So with MT, Tg.; a few Heb. mss., LXX, Syr., Vg. put *my God* at the end of v. 5 [2] Or *Mount*
7 [a] Ps. 69:1, 2; 88:7
8 [a] Deut. 28:8 [b] Job 35:10
9 [a] Ps. 38:6
10 [a] Joel 2:17 [1] Lit. *shattering* [2] *revile*
11 [a] Ps. 43:5 [1] Lit. *salvation*

PSALM 43
1 [a] [Ps. 26:1; 35:24] [b] Ps. 35:1
2 [a] Ps. 42:9

Psalm 42:5

Dear Woman of Destiny,

Our daughter was only four months old when we realized that there was something wrong with her health. We embarked on a six-year ordeal of tests and doctors that left us with more questions than answers and a little girl who was wasting away before our very eyes. Through the Lord's miraculous intervention, we found a doctor who was researching an extremely rare disease, the disease that had almost taken our daughter's life. Though the problem was identified, caring for her continued to call for round-the-clock vigilance. Daily we gave her life over to the Lord in prayer because of the constant potential for life-threatening complications. Into the midst of our exhaustion, when we felt like the psalmist, downcast and disquieted (weakened, bowed down, mourning, and crying out), the Lord spoke to us to put our hope in Him for He was with us. By His grace, He gave us hope beyond hope, the ability to trust Him even in the darkest of circumstances, the ability to believe that He had a future for our child.

I am writing this letter to you, dear sister, as you care for the chronically ill child in your life. I am praying that the Spirit of God would speak hope beyond hope to your heart as you, too, may be feeling disquieted and downcast. Jesus not only sees and understands what you are going through, but also is with you during the many hours of the night when you are trying to comfort your ill child. The long days of unending, vigilant care that go unseen by those around you do not go unseen by the Lord. He is beside you every moment and has promised never to leave you or forsake you. His heart is one of unfathomable compassion for your precious child. He longs to comfort you and to provide refuge under His wings (see Ps. 91:4, 5).

Our daughter received much prayer for healing throughout the years of her illness. We continued to hope that one day the Lord would heal her. Several months ago, my daughter came to me and said the Lord had told her that He wanted to heal her. During a conference shortly thereafter, Hannah received prayer for healing. The people at the conference prayed as though Hannah was their own child, and God powerfully touched her. Since then, she has grown significantly in both height and weight and is improving daily. We continue to put our hope in Him.

Though you may be in the deepest valley of darkness, disquieted and cast down, with great empathy I encourage you to hope in God, for you will yet praise Him. Remember He is with you. He is your help, your salvation, and your deliverance. May His lovingkindness be with you in the daytime and His song be with you in the night, as you put your hope in Him. May His everlasting arms surround you.

Leslyn Musch

3 [a]Oh, send out Your light and Your
truth!
Let them lead me;
Let them bring me to [b]Your holy
hill
And to Your [1]tabernacle.
4 Then I will go to the altar of God,
To God my exceeding joy;
And on the harp I will praise You,
O God, my God.

5 [a]Why are you cast down, O my
soul?
And why are you disquieted within
me?
Hope in God;
For I shall yet praise Him,
The [1]help of my countenance and
my God.

PSALM 44

Redemption Remembered in Present Dishonor

To the Chief Musician. A [a]Contemplation[1] of the sons of Korah.

We have heard with our ears, O God,
[a]Our fathers have told us,
The deeds You did in their days,
In days of old:
2 [a]You drove out the [1]nations with
Your hand,
But them You planted;
You afflicted the peoples, and cast
them out.
3 For [a]they did not gain possession
of the land by their own sword,
Nor did their own arm save them;
But it was Your right hand, Your
arm, and the light of Your
countenance,
[b]Because You favored them.

4 [a]You are my King, [1]O God;
[2]Command victories for Jacob.
5 Through You [a]we will push down
our enemies;
Through Your name we will
trample those who rise up
against us.
6 For [a]I will not trust in my bow,
Nor shall my sword save me.
7 But You have saved us from our
enemies,
And have put to shame those who
hated us.
8 [a]In God we boast all day long,
And praise Your name forever.
Selah

9 But [a]You have cast *us* off and put
us to shame,
And You do not go out with our
armies.
10 You make us [a]turn back from the
enemy,
And those who hate us have taken
[1]spoil for themselves.
11 [a]You have given us up like sheep
intended for food,
And have [b]scattered us among the
nations.
12 [a]You sell Your people for *next to*
nothing,
And are not enriched by selling
them.

13 [a]You make us a reproach to our
neighbors,
A scorn and a derision to those all
around us.
14 [a]You make us a byword among the
nations,
[b]A shaking of the head among the
peoples.
15 My dishonor *is* continually before
me,
And the shame of my face has
covered me,
16 Because of the voice of him who
reproaches and reviles,
[a]Because of the enemy and the
avenger.

17 [a]All this has come upon us;
But we have not forgotten You,
Nor have we dealt falsely with Your
covenant.
18 Our heart has not turned back,
[a]Nor have our steps departed from
Your way;
19 But You have severely broken us
in [a]the place of jackals,
And covered us [b]with the shadow of
death.

20 If we had forgotten the name of
our God,
Or [a]stretched[1] out our hands to a
foreign god,
21 [a]Would not God search this out?
For He knows the secrets of the
heart.
22 [a]Yet for Your sake we are killed all
day long;
We are accounted as sheep for the
slaughter.

---

3 a [Ps. 40:11] b Ps. 3:4 *1 dwelling places*
5 a Ps. 42:5, 11 *1* Lit. *salvation*

PSALM 44
title a Ps. 42:title *1* Heb. *Maschil*
1 a [Ex. 12:26, 27]
2 a Ex. 15:17 *1 Gentiles, heathen*
3 a [Deut. 8:17, 18] b [Deut. 4:37; 7:7, 8]
4 a [Ps. 74:12] *1* So with MT, Tg.; LXX, Vg. *and my God* *2* So with MT, Tg.; LXX, Syr., Vg. *Who commands*
5 a [Dan. 8:4]
6 a Ps. 33:16
8 a Ps. 34:2
9 a Ps. 60:1
10 a Lev. 26:17 *1 plunder*
11 a Rom. 8:36 b Deut. 4:27; 28:64
12 a Is. 52:3, 4
13 a Jer. 24:9
14 a Deut. 28:37 b Job 16:4
16 a Ps. 8:2
17 a Dan. 9:13
18 a Job 23:11
19 a Is. 34:13 b [Ps. 23:4]
20 a [Deut. 6:14] *1* Worshiped
21 a [Ps. 139:1, 2]
22 a Rom. 8:36

Psalm 43:5

Dear Woman of Destiny,

Depression is one of the most common and debilitating problems we face. Depression is more than feeling down or having a sad day. It involves a persistent sadness that affects most aspects of our lives. Symptoms last for more than two weeks and can include: a sad or down mood, loss of interest in normal activities, weight loss or gain, sleep problems, agitation, fatigue, feelings of worthlessness, inappropriate guilt, difficulty concentrating, hopelessness, and thoughts of suicide.

Some forms of depression are caused by genetic/biological factors, such as a lack of sleep, lack of exercise, PMS, delivery of a baby, menopause, side effects of drugs, poor diet, or disease. Other depressions are rooted in psychological, cognitive, and spiritual causes like troubled family experiences, stress over the multiple roles women face each day, social inequities like poverty and abuse, loss, negative thinking, sin, unresolved hurt and anger, and poor coping responses.

The voice of depression is hopeless, anxious, and negative—all counter to the Word of God. When you listen to the voice of depression, you give the enemy a stronghold, an area of your life in which to defeat you. You must fight negative thoughts, behave positively, and renew your mind through the promises of God. How do we do this?

1) Acknowledge the depression (see Prov. 12:25).
2) Trust in God to help you (see Ps. 46:1).
3) Praise Him despite the circumstances (see Ps. 34:1).
4) Speak hope into the situation (see Ps. 39:7).
5) Renew your negative thoughts through the positive Word of God (see Phil. 4:8).
6) Take steps to correct your behavior. Take care of your body and get active. Make yourself *do* it. Don't want to *feel* it.
7) Address the causes of the depression. For example, deal with anger, settle family conflicts, resolve inappropriate guilt, and forgive those who hurt you.

Nothing is hopeless or impossible with God. Be encouraged. God's Word gives us several examples of people struggling in the depths of despair—Moses, Job, Peter, the Israelites, Naomi, Jeremiah, David, and even Elijah.

The most powerful example God gave was Jesus. The night He grieved in the garden over His impending death, "He began to be sorrowful and deeply distressed" (Matt. 26:37). Jesus, confronted with despair and all alone, responded by praying even more earnestly. He submitted to the will of the Father. As He was nailed to the cross, He thought of others. Facing death, He was concerned that we be forgiven, that His mother be cared for, that the thief next to Him enter glory. What a model for us: Confront our darkest time, submit to the will of the Father, turn our attention to the needs of others, and praise God for the victory of the Cross.

Linda Mintle

23 [a]Awake! Why do You sleep, O Lord?
Arise! Do not cast *us* off forever.
24 [a]Why do You hide Your face,
And forget our affliction and our oppression?
25 For [a]our soul is bowed down to the [1]dust;
Our body clings to the ground.
26 Arise for our help,
And redeem us for Your mercies' sake.

PSALM 45

The Glories of the Messiah and His Bride

To the Chief Musician. [a]Set to [1]"The Lilies." A [2]Contemplation of the sons of Korah. A Song of Love.

My heart is overflowing with a good theme;
I recite my composition concerning the King;
My tongue *is* the pen of a [1]ready writer.

2 You are fairer than the sons of men;
[a]Grace is poured upon Your lips;
Therefore God has blessed You forever.
3 [1]Gird Your [a]sword upon *Your* thigh,
[b]O Mighty One,
With Your [c]glory and Your majesty.
4 [a]And in Your majesty ride prosperously because of truth, humility, *and* righteousness;
And Your right hand shall teach You awesome things.
5 Your arrows *are* sharp in the heart of the King's enemies;
The peoples fall under You.

6 [a]Your throne, O God, *is* forever and ever;
A [b]scepter of righteousness *is* the scepter of Your kingdom.
7 You love righteousness and hate wickedness;
Therefore God, Your God, has [a]anointed You
With the oil of [b]gladness more than Your companions.
8 All Your garments are [a]scented with myrrh and aloes *and* cassia,
Out of the ivory palaces, by which they have made You glad.
9 [a]Kings' daughters *are* among Your honorable women;
[b]At Your right hand stands the queen in gold from Ophir.

10 Listen, O daughter,
Consider and incline your ear;
[a]Forget your own people also, and your father's house;
11 So the King will greatly desire your beauty;
[a]Because He *is* your Lord, worship Him.
12 And the daughter of Tyre *will come* with a gift;
[a]The rich among the people will seek your favor.

13 The royal daughter *is* all glorious within *the palace;*
Her clothing *is* woven with gold.
14 [a]She shall be brought to the King in robes of many colors;
The virgins, her companions who follow her, shall be brought to You.
15 With gladness and rejoicing they shall be brought;
They shall enter the King's palace.

16 Instead of Your fathers shall be Your sons,
[a]Whom You shall make princes in all the earth.
17 [a]I will make Your name to be remembered in all generations;
Therefore the people shall praise You forever and ever.

PSALM 46

God the Refuge of His People and Conqueror of the Nations

To the Chief Musician. A Psalm of the sons of Korah. A Song [a]for Alamoth.

God *is* our [a]refuge and strength,
[b]A [1] very present help in trouble.
2 Therefore we will not fear,
Even though the earth be removed,
And though the mountains be carried into the [1]midst of the sea;
3 [a]*Though* its waters roar *and* be troubled,
Though the mountains shake with its swelling. Selah

4 *There is* a [a]river whose streams shall make glad the [b]city of God,

---

23 a Ps. 7:6
24 a Job 13:24
25 a Ps. 119:25 1 Ground, in humiliation

PSALM 45
title a Ps. 69:title 1 Heb. *Shoshannim* 2 Heb. *Maschil*
1 1 *skillful*
2 a Luke 4:22
3 a [Heb. 4:12] b [Is. 9:6] c Jude 25 1 *Belt on*
4 a Rev. 6:2
6 a [Ps. 93:2] b [Num. 24:17]
7 a Ps. 2:2 b Ps. 21:6
8 a Song 1:12, 13
9 a Song 6:8 b 1 Kin. 2:19
10 a Deut. 21:13
11 a [Is. 54:5]
12 a Is. 49:23
14 a Song 1:4
16 a [1 Pet. 2:9]
17 a Mal. 1:11

PSALM 46
title a 1 Chr. 15:20
1 a Ps. 62:7, 8 b [Deut. 4:7] 1 *An abundantly available help*
2 1 Lit. *heart*
3 a [Ps. 93:3, 4]
4 a [Ezek. 47:1–12] b Is. 60:14

The holy *place* of the [1]tabernacle of
the Most High.
5 God *is* [a]in the midst of her, she
shall not be [1]moved;
God shall help her, just [2]at the
break of dawn.
6 [a]The nations raged, the kingdoms
were moved;
He uttered His voice, the earth
melted.
7 The [a]LORD of hosts *is* with us;
The God of Jacob *is* our refuge.
Selah
8 Come, behold the works of the
LORD,
Who has made desolations in the
earth.
9 [a]He makes wars cease to the end of
the earth;
[b]He breaks the bow and cuts the
spear in two;
[c]He burns the chariot in the fire.
10 Be still, and know that I *am* God;
[a]I will be exalted among the nations,
I will be exalted in the earth!
11 The LORD of hosts *is* with us;
The God of Jacob *is* our refuge.
Selah

O God, You are our refuge and strength, a very present help in trouble. Therefore, may ____ not fear, even though the earth be removed and the mountains be carried into the midst of the sea.

FROM PSALM 46:1, 2

PSALM 47

Praise to God, the Ruler of the Earth

To the Chief Musician. A Psalm of the sons of Korah.

Oh, clap your hands, all you peoples!
Shout to God with the voice of
triumph!
2 For the LORD Most High *is*
awesome;
He is a great [a]King over all the
earth.
3 [a]He will subdue the peoples under
us,
And the nations under our feet.
4 He will choose our [a]inheritance for
us,
The excellence of Jacob whom He
loves. Selah
5 [a]God has gone up with a shout,
The LORD with the sound of a
trumpet.
6 Sing praises to God, sing praises!
Sing praises to our King, sing
praises!
7 [a]For God *is* the King of all the
earth;
[b]Sing praises with understanding.
8 [a]God reigns over the nations;
God [b]sits on His [c]holy throne.
9 The princes of the people have
gathered together,
[a]The people of the God of Abraham.
[b]For the shields of the earth *belong*
to God;
He is greatly exalted.

PSALM 48

The Glory of God in Zion

A Song. A Psalm of the sons of Korah.

Great *is* the LORD, and greatly to be
praised
In the [a]city of our God,
In His holy mountain.
2 [a]Beautiful in [1]elevation,
The joy of the whole earth,
Is Mount Zion *on* the sides of the
north,
The city of the great King.
3 God *is* in her palaces;
He is known as her refuge.
4 For behold, [a]the kings assembled,
They passed by together.
5 They saw *it, and* so they marveled;
They were troubled, they hastened
away.
6 Fear [a]took hold of them there,
And pain, as of a woman in birth
pangs,
7 *As when* You break the [a]ships of
Tarshish
With an east wind.
8 As we have heard,
So we have seen
In the city of the LORD of hosts,

---

4 [1] *dwelling places*
5 [a] [Zeph. 3:15] [1] *shaken* [2] Lit. *at the turning of the morning*
6 [a] Ps. 2:1, 2
7 [a] Num. 14:9
9 [a] Is. 2:4 [b] Ps. 76:3 [c] Ezek. 39:9
10 [a] [Is. 2:11, 17]

PSALM 47
2 [a] Neh. 1:5
3 [a] Ps. 18:47
4 [a] [1 Pet. 1:4]
5 [a] Ps. 68:24, 25
7 [a] Zech. 14:9 [b] 1 Cor. 14:15
8 [a] 1 Chr. 16:31 [b] Ps. 97:2 [c] Ps. 48:1
9 [a] [Rom. 4:11, 12] [b] [Ps. 89:18]

PSALM 48
1 [a] Ps. 46:4; 87:3
2 [a] Ps. 50:2 [1] *height*
4 [a] 2 Sam. 10:6, 14
6 [a] Ex. 15:15
7 [a] Ezek. 27:25

In the city of our God:
God will [a]establish it forever. Selah
9 We have thought, O God, on [a]Your
lovingkindness,
In the midst of Your temple.
10 According to [a]Your name, O God,
So *is* Your praise to the ends of the
earth;
Your right hand is full of
righteousness.
11 Let Mount Zion rejoice,
Let the daughters of Judah be glad,
Because of Your judgments.
12 Walk about Zion,
And go all around her.
Count her towers;
13 Mark well her bulwarks;
Consider her palaces;
That you may [a]tell *it* to the
generation following.
14 For this *is* God,
Our God forever and ever;
[a]He will be our guide
[1]*Even* to death.

PSALM 49

The Confidence of the Foolish

To the Chief Musician. A Psalm of the sons of Korah.

Hear this, all peoples;
Give ear, all inhabitants of the
world,
2 Both low and high,
Rich and poor together.
3 My mouth shall speak wisdom,
And the meditation of my heart
shall give understanding.
4 I will incline my ear to a proverb;
I will disclose my [1]dark saying on
the harp.

5 Why should I fear in the days of
evil,
When the iniquity at my heels
surrounds me?
6 Those who [a]trust in their wealth
And boast in the multitude of their
riches,
7 None *of them* can by any means
redeem *his* brother,
Nor [a]give to God a ransom for
him—
8 For [a]the redemption of their souls
is costly,
And it shall cease forever—
9 That he should continue to live
eternally,
And [a]not [1]see the Pit.
10 For he sees wise men die;
Likewise the fool and the senseless
person perish,
And leave their wealth to others.
11 [1]Their inner thought *is that* their
houses *will last* forever,
Their dwelling places to all
generations;
They [a]call *their* lands after their
own names.
12 Nevertheless man, *though* in
honor, does not [1]remain;
He is like the beasts *that* perish.
13 This is the way of those who *are*
[a]foolish,
And of their posterity who approve
their sayings. Selah
14 Like sheep they are laid in the
grave;
Death shall feed on them;
[a]The upright shall have dominion
over them in the morning;
[b]And their beauty shall be consumed
in [1]the grave, far from their
dwelling.
15 But God [a]will redeem my soul
from the power of [1]the grave,
For He shall [b]receive me. Selah
16 Do not be afraid when one
becomes rich,
When the glory of his house is
increased;
17 For when he dies he shall carry
nothing away;
His glory shall not descend after
him.
18 Though while he lives [a]he blesses
himself
(For *men* will praise you when you
do well for yourself),
19 He shall go to the generation of
his fathers;
They shall never see [a]light.[1]
20 A man *who is* in honor, yet does
not understand,
[a]Is like the beasts *that* perish.

PSALM 50

God the Righteous Judge

A Psalm of Asaph.

The [a]Mighty One, God the LORD,
Has spoken and called the earth

8 a [Ps. 87:5]
9 a Ps. 26:3
10 a Mal. 1:11
13 a [Ps. 78:5–7]
14 a Is. 58:11 *1* So with MT, Syr.; LXX, Vg. *Forever*

PSALM 49
4 *1 riddle*
6 a [Mark 10:23, 24]
7 a Job 36:18, 19
8 a [Matt. 16:26]
9 a Ps. 89:48 *1 experience corruption*
11 a Gen. 4:17 *1* LXX, Syr., Tg., Vg. *Their graves shall be their houses forever*
12 *1* So with MT, Tg.; LXX, Syr., Vg. *understand* (cf. v. 20)
13 a [Luke 12:20]
14 a [Dan. 7:18] b Job 4:21 *1* Or *Sheol*
15 a [Hos. 13:4] b Ps. 73:24 *1* Or *Sheol*
18 a Deut. 29:19
19 a Job 33:30 *1* The light of life
20 a Eccl. 3:19

PSALM 50
1 a Is. 9:6

From the rising of the sun to its
going down.
2 Out of Zion, the perfection of
beauty,
[a]God will shine forth.
3 Our God shall come, and shall not
keep silent;
[a]A fire shall devour before Him,
And it shall be very tempestuous all
around Him.

4 [a]He shall call to the heavens from
above,
And to the earth, that He may
judge His people:
5 "Gather [a]My saints together to Me,
[b]Those who have [1]made a covenant
with Me by sacrifice."
6 Let the [a]heavens declare His
righteousness,
For [b]God Himself *is* Judge. Selah

7 "Hear, O My people, and I will
speak,
O Israel, and I will testify against
you;
[a]I *am* God, your God!
8 [a]I will not [1]rebuke you [b]for your
sacrifices
Or your burnt offerings,
Which are continually before Me.
9 [a]I will not take a bull from your
house,
Nor goats out of your folds.
10 For every beast of the forest *is*
Mine,
And the cattle on a thousand hills.
11 I know all the birds of the
mountains,
And the wild beasts of the field *are*
Mine.

12 "If I were hungry, I would not tell
you;
[a]For the world *is* Mine, and all its
fullness.
13 [a]Will I eat the flesh of bulls,
Or drink the blood of goats?
14 [a]Offer to God thanksgiving,
And [b]pay your vows to the Most
High.
15 [a]Call upon Me in the day of
trouble;
I will deliver you, and you shall
glorify Me."

16 But to the wicked God says:
"What *right* have you to declare My
statutes,

2 **a** Ps. 80:1
3 **a** [Ps. 97:3]
4 **a** Is. 1:2
5 **a** Deut. 33:3
b Ex. 24:7
1 Lit. *cut*
6 **a** [Ps. 97:6]
b Ps. 75:7
7 **a** Ex. 20:2
8 **a** Jer. 7:22
b [Hos. 6:6]
1 reprove
9 **a** Ps. 69:31
12 **a** Ex. 19:5
13 **a** [Ps. 51:15–17]
14 **a** Heb. 13:15
b Deut. 23:21
15 **a** [Zech. 13:9]
17 **a** Rom. 2:21
18 **a** [Rom. 1:32]
b 1 Tim. 5:22
1 LXX, Syr., Tg., Vg. *ran*
19 **a** Ps. 52:2
21 **a** [Rom. 2:4]
b [Ps. 90:8]
22 **a** [Job 8:13]
23 **a** Gal. 6:16
PSALM 51
title **a** 2 Sam. 12:1
1 **a** [Is. 43:25; 44:22]
2 **a** [Heb. 9:14]

Or take My covenant in your
mouth,
17 [a]Seeing you hate instruction
And cast My words behind you?
18 When you saw a thief, you
[a]consented[1] with him,
And have been a [b]partaker with
adulterers.
19 You give your mouth to evil,
And [a]your tongue frames deceit.
20 You sit *and* speak against your
brother;
You slander your own mother's son.
21 These *things* you have done, and I
kept silent;
[a]You thought that I was altogether
like you;
But I will rebuke you,
And [b]set *them* in order before your
eyes.

22 "Now consider this, you who
[a]forget God,
Lest I tear *you* in pieces,
And *there be* none to deliver:
23 Whoever offers praise glorifies Me;
And [a]to him who orders *his*
conduct *aright*
I will show the salvation of God."

The best way to fight against sin is to fight it on our knees.

PHILIP HENRY

PSALM 51

A Prayer of Repentance

To the Chief Musician. A Psalm of David
[a]when Nathan the prophet went to him,
after he had gone in to Bathsheba.

Have mercy upon me, O God,
According to Your lovingkindness;
According to the multitude of Your
tender mercies,
[a]Blot out my transgressions.
2 [a]Wash me thoroughly from my
iniquity,
And cleanse me from my sin.

3 For I acknowledge my
transgressions,
And my sin *is* always before me.
4 [a]Against You, You only, have I
sinned,
And done *this* evil [b]in Your sight—
[c]That You may be found just [1]when
You speak,
And blameless when You judge.
5 [a]Behold, I was brought forth in
iniquity,
And in sin my mother conceived
me.
6 Behold, You desire truth in the
inward parts,
And in the hidden *part* You will
make me to know wisdom.
7 [a]Purge me with hyssop, and I shall
be clean;
Wash me, and I shall be [b]whiter
than snow.
8 Make me hear joy and gladness,

4 a 2 Sam. 12:13 b [Luke 5:21] c Rom. 3:4 *1* LXX, Tg., Vg. *in Your words*
5 a [Job 14:4]
7 a Heb. 9:19 b [Is. 1:18]

Ann Judson

Ann Judson's short life (1789–1826) was packed with the kind of adventure, heartache, danger, and opposition that can only be conquered by the power of God. In 1812, Ann and her husband, Adoniram, answered God's call to the mission field. They moved to the Burmese port of Rangoon (modern-day Myanmar), where a confession of Christianity could get a person killed. Not only did Ann stake her entire life on Jesus Christ, she called others to do the same.

For five years, Ann and Adoniram labored without seeing a single person converted. One thing in their favor was that they adapted well to Burmese society and were accepted into the culture. Men secretly visited Adoniram to ask him questions, while Ann met regularly with dozens of women fascinated with a God who loved women as much as He loved men. As a result of the Judsons' faithful efforts, ten Burmese committed themselves to Christ.

But when war erupted between Britain and Burma, the Judsons' lives became a battle for survival. Claiming Adoniram was a British spy, Burmese officials threw him in jail, where they kept him in near-torturous conditions. Ann immediately devoted herself to getting food and clothing to her husband and the other foreign prisoners, who would have starved without her efforts. She even smuggled in the manuscript of the New Testament translation Adoniram had been working on for years by sewing it into a pillow. Her risk proved invaluable as Adoniram's translation of the Bible became the cornerstone of the Burmese Christian Church.

When Adoniram was unexpectedly transferred, Ann gathered her things and her children, who were suffering from smallpox, to search for him. When she found him, he hardly recognized her, as he had been forced to march miles under the burning tropical sun without head covering or shoes. He was eventually released from prison only to find Ann desperately ill with spotted fever. Close to death, she revealed the source of her incredible strength and endurance, saying that her only hope was to "plead with that great and powerful Being who has said, 'Call upon Me in the day of trouble and I will hear.'"

That the bones You have broken
[a]may rejoice.
9 Hide Your face from my sins,
And blot out all my iniquities.

10 [a]Create in me a clean heart,
O God,
And renew a steadfast spirit within
me.
11 Do not cast me away from Your
presence,
And do not take Your [a]Holy Spirit
from me.

12 Restore to me the joy of Your
salvation,
And uphold me *by Your* [a]generous
Spirit.
13 *Then* I will teach transgressors
Your ways,
And sinners shall be converted to
You.

Create in ____ a clean heart, O God, and renew a steadfast spirit within them.
FROM PSALM 51:10

14 Deliver me from the guilt of
bloodshed, O God,
The God of my salvation,
And my tongue shall sing aloud of
Your righteousness.
15 O Lord, open my lips,
And my mouth shall show forth
Your praise.
16 For [a]You do not desire sacrifice,
or else I would give *it;*
You do not delight in burnt
offering.
17 [a]The sacrifices of God *are* a broken
spirit,
A broken and a contrite heart—
These, O God, You will not despise.

18 Do good in Your good pleasure to
Zion;
Build the walls of Jerusalem.
19 Then You shall be pleased with
[a]the sacrifices of righteousness,
With burnt offering and whole
burnt offering;
Then they shall offer bulls on Your
altar.

8 a [Matt. 5:4]
10 a [Ezek. 18:31]
11 a [Luke 11:13]
12 a [2 Cor. 3:17]
16 a [1 Sam. 15:22]
17 a Ps. 34:18
19 a Ps. 4:5
PSALM 52
title a 1 Sam. 22:9 b Ezek. 22:9 1 Heb. *Maschil*
7 1 Lit. *desire, in evil sense*
8 a Jer. 11:16
9 1 Or *has a good reputation*
PSALM 53
title 1 Heb. *Maschil*
1 a Ps. 10:4

PSALM 52

The End of the Wicked and the Peace of the Godly

To the Chief Musician. A [1]Contemplation of David [a]when Doeg the Edomite went and [b]told Saul, and said to him, "David has gone to the house of Ahimelech."

Why do you boast in evil, O mighty
man?
The goodness of God *endures*
continually.
2 Your tongue devises destruction,
Like a sharp razor, working
deceitfully.
3 You love evil more than good,
Lying rather than speaking
righteousness. Selah
4 You love all devouring words,
You deceitful tongue.

5 God shall likewise destroy you
forever;
He shall take you away, and pluck
you out of *your* dwelling place,
And uproot you from the land of
the living. Selah
6 The righteous also shall see and
fear,
And shall laugh at him, *saying,*
7 "Here is the man *who* did not make
God his strength,
But trusted in the abundance of his
riches,
And strengthened himself in his
[1]wickedness."

8 But I *am* [a]like a green olive tree in
the house of God;
I trust in the mercy of God forever
and ever.
9 I will praise You forever,
Because You have done *it;*
And in the presence of Your saints
I will wait on Your name, for *it* [1]*is*
good.

PSALM 53

Folly of the Godless, and the Restoration of Israel

To the Chief Musician. Set to "Mahalath." A [1]Contemplation of David.

The [a]fool has said in his heart,
"*There is* no God."

Psalm 51:14

Dear Woman of Destiny,

Psalm 51 has been a very powerful scripture for me to read and meditate on as I have journeyed (and still journey) through my healing from abortion. God's mercy is so awesome! No matter what we've done, He washes us thoroughly from our iniquity and cleanses us from our sins! (v. 2). There was a time, however, when I wasn't aware of this. . . .

For about five years I carried a heavy burden of guilt and shame after having two abortions. The first time I got pregnant, I was a senior in college preparing for graduation, less than two months away. I had an abortion because I thought I could not provide financially or emotionally for a child, and that I was too young. I was also ashamed that it happened in the first place. I had my whole life in front of me—an excellent job in an exciting new career. It just wasn't the right time. I honestly thought it was the best thing for the baby. But all of this was a lie I bought into, and I went ahead and took the "easy" way out.

When the procedure was over, I was supposed to feel relieved—but I didn't. In fact, I knew something was terribly wrong and that I had just made the biggest mistake of my life. Why didn't anyone warn me—or stop me? They didn't tell me anything at the clinic, and my college friends—even my boyfriend—all agreed this was the best option. But deep down I knew this decision would affect me far more than anyone would know.

I began to feel depressed, anxious, empty, ashamed, and totally out of control. Eventually, my state of mind led to many more wrong decisions, including another abortion. After that, I truly hit rock bottom. I was overwhelmed with anxiety, shame, depression, and thoughts of suicide.

At this low point in my life, God sent someone into my life to witness His loving-kindness in a way I had never heard. I gave my life to Jesus; and slowly God's truth dawned on me, and my healing process began.

It took a few years after I was saved to realize there was still something wrong. I was depressed and was suffering from panic attacks, but never connected them with the abortions. There was still too much shame. As I cried out to God for His healing and truth, I was divinely led to a crisis pregnancy center where I joined a postabortion Bible study. It was here that I began to learn about God's mercy and grace. It was also here that I related to David's cry of repentance in Psalm 51. David finally realized that his sin was ultimately against God, which led him to repent. And that's all God wants from us—to be honest and acknowledge our sin before Him.

If you are suffering from the pain and guilt that abortion leaves, please know you are not alone. God will forgive you, He loves you, and He will restore your heart. Let God purge you, and you shall be clean; let Him cleanse you, and you shall be whiter than snow. I know He can—He's done it for me!

Kara Quinn-Smith

They are corrupt, and have done abominable iniquity;
[b]*There is* none who does good.

2 God looks down from heaven upon the children of men,
To see if there are *any* who understand, who [a]seek God.
3 Every one of them has turned aside;
They have together become corrupt;
There is none who does good,
No, not one.

4 Have the workers of iniquity [a]no knowledge,
Who eat up my people *as* they eat bread,
And do not call upon God?
5 [a]There they are in great fear
Where no fear was,
For God has scattered the bones of him who encamps against you;
You have put *them* to shame,
Because God has despised them.

6 [a]Oh, that the salvation of Israel would come out of Zion!
When God brings back [1]the captivity of His people,
Let Jacob rejoice *and* Israel be glad.

PSALM 54

Answered Prayer for Deliverance from Adversaries

To the Chief Musician. With [1]stringed instruments. A [2]Contemplation of David [a]when the Ziphites went and said to Saul, "Is David not hiding with us?"

Save me, O God, by Your name,
And vindicate me by Your strength.
2 Hear my prayer, O God;
Give ear to the words of my mouth.
3 For strangers have risen up against me,
And oppressors have sought after my life;
They have not set God before them. Selah

4 Behold, God *is* my helper;
The Lord *is* with those who [1]uphold my life.
5 He will repay my enemies for their evil.
[1]Cut them off in Your [2]truth.

6 I will freely sacrifice to You;
I will praise Your name, O LORD, for *it is* good.
7 For He has delivered me out of all trouble;
[a]And my eye has seen *its desire* upon my enemies.

PSALM 55

Trust in God Concerning the Treachery of Friends

To the Chief Musician. With [1]stringed instruments. A [2]Contemplation of David.

Give ear to my prayer, O God,
And do not hide Yourself from my supplication.
2 Attend to me, and hear me;
I [a]am[1] restless in my complaint, and moan noisily,
3 Because of the voice of the enemy,
Because of the oppression of the wicked;
[a]For they bring down trouble upon me,
And in wrath they hate me.

4 [a]My heart is severely pained within me,
And the terrors of death have fallen upon me.
5 Fearfulness and trembling have come upon me,
And horror has overwhelmed me.
6 So I said, "Oh, that I had wings like a dove!
I would fly away and be at rest.
7 Indeed, I would wander far off,
And remain in the wilderness. Selah
8 I would hasten my escape
From the windy storm *and* tempest."

9 Destroy, O Lord, *and* divide their [1]tongues,
For I have seen [a]violence and strife in the city.
10 Day and night they go around it on its walls;
[a]Iniquity and trouble *are* also in the midst of it.
11 Destruction *is* in its midst;
[a]Oppression and deceit do not depart from its streets.
12 [a]For *it is* not an enemy *who* reproaches me;
Then I could bear *it*.

---

1 [b]Rom. 3:10–12
2 [a][2 Chr. 15:2]
4 [a]Jer. 4:22
5 [a]Prov. 28:1
6 [a]Ps. 14:7 [1]Or *His captive people*

PSALM 54
title [a]1 Sam. 23:19 [1]Heb. *neginoth* [2]Heb. *Maschil*
4 [1]*sustain my soul*
5 [1]*Destroy them* [2]Or *faithfulness*
7 [a]Ps. 59:10

PSALM 55
title [1]Heb. *neginoth* [2]Heb. *Maschil*
2 [a]Is. 38:14; 59:11 [1]*wander*
3 [a]2 Sam. 16:7, 8
4 [a]Ps. 116:3
9 [a]Jer. 6:7 [1]*speech,* their counsel
10 [a]Ps. 10:7
11 [a]Ps. 10:7
12 [a]Ps. 41:9

Nor *is it* one *who* hates me who
has [b]exalted *himself* against me;
Then I could hide from him.
13 But *it was* you, a man my equal,
[a]My companion and my
acquaintance.
14 We took sweet counsel together,
And [a]walked to the house of God in
the throng.

15 Let death seize them;
Let them [a]go down alive into [1]hell,
For wickedness *is* in their dwellings
and among them.

If you are in desperate need of deliverance, do not hesitate to cry to the Lord. He hears those who call upon Him with all their heart.

GORDON LINDSAY

16 As for me, I will call upon God,
And the LORD shall save me.
17 [a]Evening and morning and at noon
I will pray, and cry aloud,
And He shall hear my voice.
18 He has redeemed my soul in peace
from the battle *that was* against
me,
For [a]there were many against me.
19 God will hear, and afflict them,
[a]Even He who abides from of old.
Selah
Because they do not change,
Therefore they do not fear God.

20 He has [a]put forth his hands
against those who [b]were at peace
with him;
He has broken his [1]covenant.
21 [a]*The words* of his mouth were
smoother than butter,
But war *was* in his heart;
His words were softer than oil,
Yet they *were* drawn swords.

22 [a]Cast your burden on the LORD,
And [b]He shall sustain you;
He shall never permit the righteous
to be [1]moved.

23 But You, O God, shall bring them
down to the pit of destruction;
[a]Bloodthirsty and deceitful men
[b]shall not live out half their
days;
But I will trust in You.

PSALM 56

Prayer for Relief from Tormentors

To the Chief Musician. Set to [1]"The Silent Dove in Distant Lands." A Michtam of David when the [a]Philistines captured him in Gath.

Be [a]merciful to me, O God, for man
would swallow me up;
Fighting all day he oppresses me.
2 My enemies would [a]hound *me* all
day,
For *there are* many who fight
against me, O Most High.

3 Whenever I am afraid,
I will trust in You.
4 In God (I will praise His word),
In God I have put my trust;
[a]I will not fear.
What can flesh do to me?

5 All day they twist my words;
All their thoughts *are* against me
for evil.
6 They gather together,
They hide, they mark my steps,
When they lie in wait for my life.
7 Shall they escape by iniquity?
In anger cast down the peoples,
O God!

8 You number my wanderings;
Put my tears into Your bottle;
[a]*Are they* not in Your book?
9 When I cry out *to You,*
Then my enemies will turn back;
This I know, because [a]God *is* for
me.
10 In God (I will praise *His* word),
In the LORD (I will praise *His*
word),
11 In God I have put my trust;
I will not be afraid.
What can man do to me?

12 Vows *made* to You *are binding*
upon me, O God;
I will render praises to You,
13 [a]For You have delivered my soul
from death.
Have You not *kept* my feet from
falling,

---

12 [b]Ps. 35:26; 38:16
13 [a]2 Sam. 15:12
14 [a]Ps. 42:4
15 [a]Num. 16:30, 33 [1]Or *Sheol*
17 [a]Dan. 6:10
18 [a]2 Chr. 32:7, 8
19 [a][Deut. 33:27]
20 [a]Acts 12:1 [b]Ps. 7:4 [1]*treaty*
21 [a]Ps. 28:3; 57:4
22 [a][Ps. 37:5] [b]Ps. 37:24 [1]*shaken*
23 [a]Ps. 5:6 [b]Prov. 10:27

PSALM 56
title [a]1 Sam. 21:11 [1]Heb. *Jonath Elem Rechokim*
1 [a]Ps. 57:1
2 [a]Ps. 57:3
4 [a]Ps. 118:6
8 [a][Mal. 3:16]
9 [a][Rom. 8:31]
13 [a]Ps. 116:8, 9

That I may walk before God
In the [b]light of the living?

PSALM 57

Prayer for Safety from Enemies

To the Chief Musician. Set to [1]"Do Not Destroy." A Michtam of David [a]when he fled from Saul into the cave.

Be merciful to me, O God, be merciful
to me!
For my soul trusts in You;
[a]And in the shadow of Your wings I
will make my refuge,
[b]Until *these* calamities have passed
by.

2 I will cry out to God Most High,
To God [a]who performs *all things*
for me.
3 [a]He shall send from heaven and
save me;
He reproaches the one who [1]would
swallow me up. Selah
God [b]shall send forth His mercy
and His truth.

4 My soul *is* among lions;
I lie *among* the sons of men
Who are set on fire,
[a]Whose teeth *are* spears and arrows,
And their tongue a sharp sword.
5 [a]Be exalted, O God, above the
heavens;
Let Your glory *be* above all the
earth.

6 [a]They have prepared a net for my
steps;
My soul is bowed down;
They have dug a pit before me;
Into the midst of it they *themselves*
have fallen. Selah

7 [a]My heart is steadfast, O God, my
heart is steadfast;
I will sing and give praise.
8 Awake, [a]my glory!
Awake, lute and harp!
I will awaken the dawn.

9 [a]I will praise You, O Lord, among
the peoples;
I will sing to You among the
[1]nations.
10 [a]For Your mercy reaches unto the
heavens,
And Your truth unto the clouds.

11 [a]Be exalted, O God, above the
heavens;

13 [b]Job 33:30

PSALM 57
title [a]1 Sam. 22:1
[1]Heb. Al Tashcheth
1 [a]Ps. 17:8; 63:7 [b]Is. 26:20
2 [a][Ps. 138:8]
3 [a]Ps. 144:5, 7 [b]Ps. 43:3 *[1]snaps at* or *hounds me,* or *crushes me*
4 [a]Prov. 30:14
5 [a]Ps. 108:5
6 [a]Ps. 9:15
7 [a]Ps. 108:1–5
8 [a]Ps. 16:9
9 [a]Ps. 108:3 *[1]Gentiles*
10 [a]Ps. 103:11
11 [a]Ps. 57:5

PSALM 58
title *[1]Heb. Al Tashcheth*
3 [a][Is. 48:8]
4 [a]Eccl. 10:11
5 [a]Jer. 8:17
6 [a]Job 4:10 *[1]Break away*
7 [a]Josh. 2:11; 7:5
8 [a]Job 3:16
9 [a]Eccl. 7:6 [b]Prov. 10:25

In the prayer for grace, in the life of grace, the steadfast spirit must have a place.

ANDREW MURRAY

Let Your glory *be* above all the
earth.

PSALM 58

The Just Judgment of the Wicked

To the Chief Musician. Set to [1]"Do Not Destroy." A Michtam of David.

Do you indeed speak righteousness, you
silent ones?
Do you judge uprightly, you sons of
men?
2 No, in heart you work wickedness;
You weigh out the violence of your
hands in the earth.

3 [a]The wicked are estranged from the
womb;
They go astray as soon as they are
born, speaking lies.
4 [a]Their poison *is* like the poison of a
serpent;
They are like the deaf cobra *that*
stops its ear,
5 Which will not [a]heed the voice of
charmers,
Charming ever so skillfully.

6 [a]Break[1] their teeth in their mouth,
O God!
Break out the fangs of the young
lions, O LORD!
7 [a]Let them flow away as waters
which run continually;
When he bends *his bow,*
Let his arrows be as if cut in pieces.
8 *Let them be* like a snail which
melts away as it goes,
[a]*Like* a stillborn child of a woman,
that they may not see the sun.

9 Before your [a]pots can feel *the*
burning thorns,
He shall take them away [b]as with a
whirlwind,
As in His living and burning wrath.

10 The righteous shall rejoice when
he sees the [a]vengeance;
[b]He shall wash his feet in the blood
of the wicked,
11 [a]So that men will say,
"Surely *there is* a reward for the
righteous;
Surely He is God who [b]judges in
the earth."

PSALM 59

The Assured Judgment of the Wicked

To the Chief Musician. Set to [1]"Do Not Destroy." A Michtam of David [a]when Saul sent men, and they watched the house in order to kill him.

Deliver me from my enemies, O my
God;
[1]Defend me from those who rise up
against me.
2 Deliver me from the workers of
iniquity,
And save me from bloodthirsty
men.
3 For look, they lie in wait for my
life;
[a]The mighty gather against me,
Not *for* my transgression nor *for*
my sin, O LORD.
4 They run and prepare themselves
through no fault *of mine.*

[a]Awake to help me, and behold!
5 You therefore, O LORD God of
hosts, the God of Israel,
Awake to punish all the [1]nations;
Do not be merciful to any wicked
transgressors. Selah
6 [a]At evening they return,
They growl like a dog,
And go all around the city.
7 Indeed, they belch with their
mouth;
[a]Swords *are* in their lips;
For *they say,* [b]"Who hears?"
8 But [a]You, O LORD, shall laugh at
them;
You shall have all the [1]nations in
derision.
9 I will wait for You, O You [1]his
Strength;
[a]For God *is* my [2]defense.
10 [1]My God of mercy shall [a]come to
meet me;
God shall let [b]me see *my desire* on
my enemies.
11 Do not slay them, lest my people
forget;
Scatter them by Your power,
And bring them down,
O Lord our shield.
12 [a]*For* the sin of their mouth *and*
the words of their lips,
Let them even be taken in their
pride,
And for the cursing and lying
which they speak.
13 [a]Consume *them* in wrath, consume
them,
That they *may* not *be;*
And [b]let them know that God rules
in Jacob
To the ends of the earth. Selah
14 And [a]at evening they return,
They growl like a dog,
And go all around the city.
15 They [a]wander up and down for
food,
And [1]howl if they are not satisfied.

16 But I will sing of Your power;
Yes, I will sing aloud of Your mercy
in the morning;
For You have been my defense
And refuge in the day of my
trouble.
17 To You, [a]O my Strength, I will
sing praises;
For God *is* my defense,
My God of mercy.

PSALM 60

Urgent Prayer for the Restored Favor of God

To the Chief Musician. [a]Set to [1]"Lily of the Testimony." A Michtam of David. For teaching. [b]When he fought against Mesopotamia and Syria of Zobah, and Joab returned and killed twelve thousand Edomites in the Valley of Salt.

O God, [a]You have cast us off;
You have broken us down;
You have been displeased;
Oh, restore us again!
2 You have made the earth tremble;
You have broken it;
[a]Heal its breaches, for it is shaking.
3 [a]You have shown Your people hard
things;

---

10 a Jer. 11:20 b Ps. 68:23
11 a Ps. 92:15 b Ps. 50:6; 75:7
PSALM 59
title a 1 Sam. 19:11 *1* Heb. *Al Tashcheth*
1 *1* Lit. *Set me on high*
3 a Ps. 56:6
4 a Ps. 35:23
5 *1 Gentiles*
6 a Ps. 59:14
7 a Prov. 12:18 b Ps. 10:11
8 a Prov. 1:26 *1 Gentiles*
9 a [Ps. 62:2] *1* So with MT, Syr.; some Heb. mss., LXX, Tg., Vg. *my Strength* *2* Lit. *fortress*
10 a Ps. 21:3 b Ps. 54:7 *1* So with Qr.; some Heb. mss., LXX, Vg. *My God, His mercy;* Kt., some Heb. mss., Tg. *O God, my mercy;* Syr. *O God, Your mercy*
12 a Prov. 12:13
13 a Ps. 104:35 b Ps. 83:18
14 a Ps. 59:6
15 a Job 15:23 *1* So with LXX, Vg.; MT, Syr., Tg. *spend the night*
17 a Ps. 18:1
PSALM 60
title a Ps. 80 b 2 Sam. 8:3, 13 *1* Heb. *Shushan Eduth*
1 a Ps. 44:9
2 a [2 Chr. 7:14]
3 a Ps. 71:20

[b]You have made us drink the wine of [1]confusion.

4 [a]You have given a banner to those who fear You,
That it may be displayed because of the truth. Selah
5 [a]That Your beloved may be delivered,
Save *with* Your right hand, and hear me.

You have been a shelter for ____, O Lord, and a strong tower from the enemy. May they abide in Your tabernacle forever and trust in the shelter of Your wings.

FROM PSALM 61:3, 4

6 God has [a]spoken in His holiness:
"I will rejoice;
I will [b]divide [c]Shechem
And measure out [d]the Valley of Succoth.
7 Gilead *is* Mine, and Manasseh *is* Mine;
[a]Ephraim also *is* the [1]helmet for My head;
[b]Judah *is* My lawgiver.
8 [a]Moab *is* My washpot;
[b]Over Edom I will cast My shoe;
[c]Philistia, shout in triumph because of Me."

9 Who will bring me *to* the strong city?
Who will lead me to Edom?
10 *Is it* not You, O God, [a]*who* cast us off?
And You, O God, *who* did [b]not go out with our armies?
11 Give us help from trouble,
[a]For the help of man *is* useless.
12 Through God [a]we will do valiantly,
For *it is* He *who* shall tread down our enemies.

3 [b] Jer. 25:15 [1] *staggering*
4 [a] Ps. 20:5
5 [a] Ps. 108:6–13
6 [a] Ps. 89:35 [b] Josh. 1:6 [c] Gen. 12:6 [d] Josh. 13:27
7 [a] Deut. 33:17 [b] [Gen. 49:10] [1] Lit. *protection*
8 [a] 2 Sam. 8:2 [b] 2 Sam. 8:14 [c] 2 Sam. 8:1
10 [a] Ps. 108:11 [b] Josh. 7:12
11 [a] Ps. 118:8; 146:3
12 [a] Num. 24:18

PSALM 61
title [1] Heb. *neginah*
3 [a] Prov. 18:10
4 [a] Ps. 91:4 [1] *tent*
7 [a] Ps. 40:11 [1] Lit. *guard* or *keep*

PSALM 62
title [a] 1 Chr. 25:1
1 [a] Ps. 33:20
2 [a] Ps. 55:22 [1] *strong tower* [2] *shaken*
3 [a] Is. 30:13
4 [a] Ps. 28:3

PSALM 61

Assurance of God's Eternal Protection

To the Chief Musician. On [1]a stringed instrument. A Psalm of David.

Hear my cry, O God;
Attend to my prayer.
2 From the end of the earth I will cry to You,
When my heart is overwhelmed;
Lead me to the rock that is higher than I.
3 For You have been a shelter for me,
[a]A strong tower from the enemy.
4 I will abide in Your [1]tabernacle forever;
[a]I will trust in the shelter of Your wings. Selah

5 For You, O God, have heard my vows;
You have given *me* the heritage of those who fear Your name.
6 You will prolong the king's life,
His years as many generations.
7 He shall abide before God forever.
Oh, prepare mercy [a]and truth, *which* may [1]preserve him!
8 So I will sing praise to Your name forever,
That I may daily perform my vows.

PSALM 62

A Calm Resolve to Wait for the Salvation of God

To the Chief Musician. To [a]Jeduthun. A Psalm of David.

Truly [a]my soul silently *waits* for God;
From Him *comes* my salvation.
2 He only *is* my rock and my salvation;
He is my [1]defense;
I shall not be greatly [a]moved.[2]

3 How long will you attack a man?
You shall be slain, all of you,
[a]Like a leaning wall and a tottering fence.
4 They only consult to cast *him* down from his high position;
They [a]delight in lies;
They bless with their mouth,
But they curse inwardly. Selah

5 My soul, wait silently for God
alone,
For my [1]expectation *is* from Him.
6 He only *is* my rock and my
salvation;
He is my defense;
I shall not be [1]moved.
7 [a]In God *is* my salvation and my
glory;
The rock of my strength,
And my refuge, *is* in God.

8 Trust in Him at all times, you
people;
[a]Pour out your heart before Him;
God *is* a refuge for us. Selah

9 [a]Surely men of low degree *are* [1]a
vapor,
Men of high degree *are* a lie;
If they are weighed on the scales,
They *are* altogether *lighter* than
vapor.
10 Do not trust in oppression,
Nor vainly hope in robbery;
[a]If riches increase,
Do not set *your* heart *on them.*

11 God has spoken once,
Twice I have heard this:
That power *belongs* to God.
12 Also to You, O Lord, *belongs*
mercy;
For [a]You [1]render to each one
according to his work.

PSALM 63

Joy in the Fellowship of God

A Psalm of David [a]when he was in the
wilderness of Judah.

O God, You *are* my God;
Early will I seek You;
[a]My soul thirsts for You;
My flesh longs for You
In a dry and thirsty land
Where there is no water.
2 So I have looked for You in the
sanctuary,
To see [a]Your power and Your glory.

3 [a]Because Your lovingkindness *is*
better than life,
My lips shall praise You.
4 Thus I will bless You while I live;
I will [a]lift up my hands in Your
name.
5 My soul shall be satisfied as with
[1]marrow and [2]fatness,
And my mouth shall praise You
with joyful lips.

6 When [a]I remember You on my
bed,
I meditate on You in the *night*
watches.
7 Because You have been my help,
Therefore in the shadow of Your
wings I will rejoice.
8 My soul follows close behind You;
Your right hand upholds me.

9 But those *who* seek my life, to
destroy *it,*
Shall go into the lower parts of the
earth.
10 They shall [1]fall by the sword;
They shall be [2]a portion for jackals.

11 But the king shall rejoice in God;
[a]Everyone who swears by Him shall
glory;
But the mouth of those who speak
lies shall be stopped.

PSALM 64

Oppressed by the Wicked but Rejoicing in the Lord

To the Chief Musician. A Psalm of David.

Hear my voice, O God, in my
[1]meditation;
Preserve my life from fear of the
enemy.
2 Hide me from the secret plots of
the wicked,
From the rebellion of the workers
of iniquity,
3 Who sharpen their tongue like a
sword,
[a]And bend *their bows to shoot* their
arrows—bitter words,
4 That they may shoot in secret at
the blameless;
Suddenly they shoot at him and do
not fear.

5 They encourage themselves *in* an
evil matter;
They talk of laying snares secretly;
[a]They say, "Who will see them?"
6 They devise iniquities:
"We have perfected a shrewd
scheme."
Both the inward thought and the
heart of man are deep.

7 But God shall shoot at them *with*
an arrow;

---

5 [1]*hope*
6 [1]*shaken*
7 [a][Jer. 3:23]
8 [a]1 Sam. 1:15
9 [a]Is. 40:17 [1]*vanity*
10 [a][Luke 12:15]
12 [a][Matt. 16:27] [1]*reward*

PSALM 63
title [a]1 Sam. 22:5
1 [a]Ps. 42:2
2 [a]Ps. 27:4
3 [a]Ps. 138:2
4 [a]Ps. 28:2; 143:6
5 [1]Lit. *fat* [2]Abundance
6 [a]Ps. 42:8
10 [1]Lit. *pour him out by the hand of the sword* [2]Prey
11 [a]Deut. 6:13

PSALM 64
1 [1]*complaint*
3 [a]Ps. 58:7
5 [a]Ps. 10:11; 59:7

Psalm 62:12

Dear Woman of Destiny,

Need a raise? Looking for job satisfaction? Feeling used or useless? Perhaps the reason for your discontent in the home or workplace is that you are looking to the wrong source to receive reward for your labor. Your employer, spouse, kids, friends, peers—none of these relationships are primarily responsible for your financial reimbursement, emotional satisfaction, or psychological affirmation for a job well done.

According to the Scriptures, it is the Lord who recompenses "to each one according to his work" (Ps. 62:12). This promise is repeated almost word for word in both the Old and New Testaments. Saints of all time have been taught that they were ultimately accountable to God.

How would our lives change if we received this truth and began to look to God as our "Employer"? We cannot enjoy the quality of life He came to give us as long as we substitute human reward for divine recompense. This very practical reality teaches us that, even though our employer may sign our paycheck, we receive all that we receive from the hand of God.

As I have grasped in faith God's promise to recompense me according to my work, I have experienced miraculous changes in job satisfaction as well as in my financial status. Through a process of learning to acknowledge the Lord in all my ways, I have discovered true satisfaction in the workplace (see Prov. 3:6). I simply began to look to the Lord as my employer. I asked Him for wisdom with each task and for financial remuneration that would reflect the quality of my work, rather than the regional pay scale where I lived. And I became accountable to Him with my attitudes toward my work, my employer, and my fellow employees.

Jesus used parables about work to teach us how to grow spiritually. These parables deal with money, completing tasks, faithful stewardship, and honest emotional dealings with others. They teach a work ethic based on love under God. Work is a spiritual activity. In our work, we are made in the image of God, who is Himself a worker, a manager, a creator, a developer, a steward, and a healer. To be a Christian is to be a colaborer with God in the community of humanity.

Have you considered your work to be a spiritual activity? What liberating truth—to think that every ounce of energy you expend can work toward divine recompense. If you simply get up one more day to get to work reasonably on time, do only what you must to avoid reprimand, while anxiously watching the clock for the next moment of "escape," you will have failed to realize the high calling of God. But an eternal perspective makes earthly things of lesser priority. If you make yourself accountable to your eternal Father and do your best to please Him, His approval will provide true fulfillment—now and throughout eternity.

Carol Noe

Suddenly they shall be wounded.
8 So He will make them stumble
over their own tongue;
[a]All who see them shall flee away.
9 All men shall fear,
And shall [a]declare the work of God;
For they shall wisely consider His
doing.

10 [a]The righteous shall be glad in the
LORD, and trust in Him.
And all the upright in heart shall
glory.

PSALM 65

Praise to God for His Salvation and Providence

To the Chief Musician. A Psalm of David. A Song.

Praise is awaiting You, O God, in Zion;
And to You the [1]vow shall be
performed.
2 O You who hear prayer,
[a]To You all flesh will come.
3 Iniquities prevail against me;
As for our transgressions,
You will [a]provide atonement for
them.

4 [a]Blessed *is the man* You [b]choose,
And cause to approach *You,*
That he may dwell in Your courts.
[c]We shall be satisfied with the
goodness of Your house,
Of Your holy temple.

5 *By* awesome deeds in righteousness
You will answer us,
O God of our salvation,
You who are the confidence of all
the ends of the earth,
And of the far-off seas;
6 Who established the mountains by
His strength,
[a]*Being* clothed with power;
7 [a]You who still the noise of the seas,
The noise of their waves,
[b]And the tumult of the peoples.
8 They also who dwell in the farthest
parts are afraid of Your signs;
You make the outgoings of the
morning and evening [1]rejoice.

9 You [1]visit the earth and [a]water it,
You greatly enrich it;
[b]The river of God is full of water;
You provide their grain,
For so You have prepared it.

8 a Ps. 31:11
9 a Jer. 50:28; 51:10
10 a Ps. 32:11

PSALM 65
1 *1* A promised deed
2 a [Is. 66:23]
3 a [Heb. 9:14]
4 a Ps. 33:12
b Ps. 4:3
c Ps. 36:8
6 a Ps. 93:1
7 a Matt. 8:26
b Is. 17:12, 13
8 *1 shout for joy*
9 a Jer. 5:24
b Ps. 46:4; 104:13; 147:8
1 give attention to
13 a Is. 44:23; 55:12

PSALM 66
1 a Ps. 100:1
3 a Ps. 65:5
b Ps. 18:44
4 a Ps. 117:1
6 a Ex. 14:21

10 You water its ridges abundantly,
You settle its furrows;
You make it soft with showers,
You bless its growth.

We need never, never fear that the stream of love will run dry. The heavenly river, the river of God which is full of water never will.

AMY CARMICHAEL

11 You crown the year with Your
goodness,
And Your paths drip *with*
abundance.
12 They drop *on* the pastures of the
wilderness,
And the little hills rejoice on every
side.
13 The pastures are clothed with
flocks;
[a]The valleys also are covered with
grain;
They shout for joy, they also sing.

PSALM 66

Praise to God for His Awesome Works

To the Chief Musician. A Song. A Psalm.

Make [a]a joyful shout to God, all the
earth!
2 Sing out the honor of His name;
Make His praise glorious.
3 Say to God,
"How [a]awesome are Your works!
[b]Through the greatness of Your
power
Your enemies shall submit
themselves to You.
4 [a]All the earth shall worship You
And sing praises to You;
They shall sing praises *to* Your
name." Selah

5 Come and see the works of God;
He is awesome *in His* doing toward
the sons of men.
6 [a]He turned the sea into dry *land;*

[b]They went through the river on foot.
There we will rejoice in Him.
7 He rules by His power forever;
His eyes observe the nations;
Do not let the rebellious exalt themselves. Selah

8 Oh, bless our God, you peoples!
And make the voice of His praise to be heard,
9 Who keeps our soul among the living,
And does not allow our feet to [1]be moved.
10 For [a]You, O God, have tested us;
[b]You have refined us as silver is refined.
11 [a]You brought us into the net;
You laid affliction on our backs.
12 [a]You have caused men to ride over our heads;
[b]We went through fire and through water;
But You brought us out to [1]rich *fulfillment.*

13 [a]I will go into Your house with burnt offerings;
[b]I will pay You my [1]vows,
14 Which my lips have uttered
And my mouth has spoken when I was in trouble.
15 I will offer You burnt sacrifices of fat animals,
With the sweet aroma of rams;
I will offer bulls with goats. Selah

16 Come *and* hear, all you who fear God,
And I will declare what He has done for my soul.
17 I cried to Him with my mouth,
And He was [1]extolled with my tongue.
18 [a]If I regard iniquity in my heart,
The Lord will not hear.
19 *But* certainly God [a]has heard *me;*
He has attended to the voice of my prayer.

20 Blessed *be* God,
Who has not turned away my prayer,
Nor His mercy from me!

6 b Josh. 3:14–16
9 1 *slip*
10 a Ps. 17:3 b [1 Pet. 1:7]
11 a Lam. 1:13
12 a Is. 51:23 b Is. 43:2 1 *abundance*
13 a Ps. 100:4; 116:14, 17–19 b [Eccl. 5:4] 1 Promised deeds
17 1 *praised*
18 a Is. 1:15
19 a Ps. 116:1, 2
PSALM 67 title 1 Heb. *neginoth*
1 a Num. 6:25
2 a Acts 18:25 b Titus 2:11
4 a [Ps. 96:10, 13; 98:9]
6 a Lev. 26:4 1 *give her produce*
PSALM 68
1 a Num. 10:35
2 a [Is. 9:18] b Mic. 1:4
3 a Ps. 32:11
4 a Deut. 33:26 b [Ex. 6:3] 1 *Praise* 2 MT *deserts;* Tg. *heavens* (cf. v. 34 and Is. 19:1) 3 Lit. LORD, a shortened Heb. form
5 a [Ps. 10:14, 18; 146:9]

PSALM 67

An Invocation and a Doxology

To the Chief Musician. On [1]stringed instruments. A Psalm. A Song.

God be merciful to us and bless us,
And [a]cause His face to shine upon us, Selah
2 That [a]Your way may be known on earth,
[b]Your salvation among all nations.
3 Let the peoples praise You, O God;
Let all the peoples praise You.
4 Oh, let the nations be glad and sing for joy!
For [a]You shall judge the people righteously,
And govern the nations on earth. Selah
5 Let the peoples praise You, O God;
Let all the peoples praise You.
6 [a]*Then* the earth shall [1]yield her increase;
God, our own God, shall bless us.
7 God shall bless us,
And all the ends of the earth shall fear Him.

PSALM 68

The Glory of God in His Goodness to Israel

To the Chief Musician. A Psalm of David. A Song.

Let [a]God arise,
Let His enemies be scattered;
Let those also who hate Him flee before Him.
2 [a]As smoke is driven away,
So drive *them* away;
[b]As wax melts before the fire,
So let the wicked perish at the presence of God.
3 But [a]let the righteous be glad;
Let them rejoice before God;
Yes, let them rejoice exceedingly.
4 Sing to God, sing praises to His name;
[a]Extol[1] Him who rides on the [2]clouds,
[b]By His name [3]YAH,
And rejoice before Him.
5 [a]A father of the fatherless, a defender of widows,
Is God in His holy habitation.

6 [a]God sets the solitary in families;
[b]He brings out those who are bound into prosperity;
But [c]the rebellious dwell in a dry *land.*

I have found it easy to obtain the presence of God. He desires to be more present to us than we are to seek Him. He desires to give Himself to us more readily than we are to receive Him.

MADAME JEANNE GUYON

7 O God, [a]when You went out before Your people,
When You marched through the wilderness, Selah
8 The earth shook;
The heavens also dropped *rain* at the presence of God;
Sinai itself *was moved* at the presence of God, the God of Israel.
9 [a]You, O God, sent a plentiful rain,
Whereby You confirmed Your inheritance,
When it was weary.
10 Your congregation dwelt in it;
[a]You, O God, provided from Your goodness for the poor.

11 The Lord gave the word;
Great *was* the [1]company of those who proclaimed *it:*
12 "Kings[a] of armies flee, they flee,
And she who remains at home divides the [1]spoil.
13 [a]Though you lie down among the [1]sheepfolds,
[b]*You will be* like the wings of a dove covered with silver,
And her feathers with yellow gold."
14 [a]When the Almighty scattered kings in it,
It was *white* as snow in Zalmon.

15 A mountain of God *is* the mountain of Bashan;
A mountain *of many* peaks *is* the mountain of Bashan.
16 Why do you [1]fume with envy, you mountains of *many* peaks?
[a]*This is* the mountain *which* God desires to dwell in;
Yes, the LORD will dwell *in it* forever.

17 [a]The chariots of God *are* twenty thousand,
Even thousands of thousands;
The Lord is among them *as in* Sinai, in the Holy *Place.*
18 [a]You have ascended on high,
[b]You have led captivity captive;
[c]You have received gifts among men,
Even *from* [d]the rebellious,
[e]That the LORD God might dwell *there.*

19 Blessed *be* the Lord,
Who daily loads us *with benefits,*
The God of our salvation! Selah
20 Our God *is* the God of salvation;
And [a]to GOD the Lord *belong* escapes from death.

21 But [a]God will wound the head of His enemies,
[b]The hairy scalp of the one who still goes on in his trespasses.
22 The Lord said, "I will bring [a]back from Bashan,
I will bring *them* back [b]from the depths of the sea,
23 [a]That [1]your foot may crush *them* in blood,
[b]And the tongues of your dogs *may have* their portion from *your* enemies."

24 They have seen Your [1]procession, O God,
The procession of my God, my King, into the sanctuary.
25 [a]The singers went before, the players on instruments *followed* after;
Among *them were* the maidens playing timbrels.
26 Bless God in the congregations,
The Lord, from [a]the fountain of Israel.
27 [a]There *is* little Benjamin, their leader,
The princes of Judah *and* their [1]company,
The princes of Zebulun *and* the princes of Naphtali.

6 [a]Ps. 107:4–7 [b]Acts 12:6–11 [c]Ps. 107:34
7 [a]Ex. 13:21
9 [a]Deut. 11:11
10 [a]Deut. 26:5
11 [1]*host*
12 [a]Josh. 10:16 [1]*plunder*
13 [a]Ps. 81:6 [b]Ps. 105:37 [1]Or *saddlebags*
14 [a]Josh. 10:10
16 [a][Deut. 12:5] [1]Lit. *stare*
17 [a]Deut. 33:2
18 [a]Eph. 4:8 [b]Judg. 5:12 [c]Acts 2:4, 33; 10:44–46 [d][1 Tim. 1:13] [e]Ps. 78:60
20 [a][Deut. 32:39]
21 [a]Hab. 3:13 [b]Ps. 55:23
22 [a]Num. 21:33 [b]Ex. 14:22
23 [a]Ps. 58:10 [b]1 Kin. 21:19 [1]LXX, Syr., Tg., Vg. *you may dip your foot*
24 [1]Lit. *goings*
25 [a]1 Chr. 13:8
26 [a]Deut. 33:28
27 [a]1 Sam. 9:21 [1]*throng*

Psalm 68:6

Dear Woman of Destiny,

The words of each psalm greet our hearts with the same powerful revelation as when first written. Psalm 68:6 reveals the caring, consistent, just nature of our Father—He sets the solitary in families, releases those bound into prosperity, and exiles the rebellious to dryness.

Each word of the first line of this verse is a dramatic stroke of a master artist's brush. For the single woman, I pray that you will see the beauty of the painting. For those who are married, I pray you will see a painting you can enhance.

The verse begins where all life begins: *GOD*. The Hebrew word is *Elohim*. This base meaning is "strong creator, source of everything." Also, and perhaps most importantly for our discussion, it means "The Strong One who swears with an oath."

The Hebrew word for *sets* is *yashub*. The word isn't casual in meaning. It speaks of permanent dwelling, remaining, and abiding. It means to move in and abide, as to be at home.

The word *solitary* ranges from the nondesirable ("lonely, desolate") to the most desirable ("united, beloved, life, and darling")—what beautiful hues these last four words can add to the picture!

As a single woman, how do you picture yourself? Do you see yourself as a life united to the Father? Do you know you are beloved, God's darling, if you will? Or do you look at your life through a glass darkly with a sense of desolation . . . a loneliness that pierces your very heart?

Dear sister, *you* are God's beloved, *His* darling. This verse is your promise of fulfillment, placement, and connection. If you are "solitary," take the words of this verse *very, very* personally. This is not passive empathy, but active promise—God will set the solitary—YOU—in families.

When we hear the word *family*, we think of several different possibilities: the family we are raised in, a church family, a family of our own, or a family of friends. Specifically, this verse speaks of a family as a group in unity because of shared convictions. This "family" is where we are free to be who we really are—the beautiful and the not-so-beautiful parts of us. This is where true, honest, and pure relationship happens.

The promise: God will see to it that you are not lonely or desolate! He is committed to "setting" you into a family.

Woman of Destiny, here is the invitation:

For single women: Ask God to set you in a family; and, when He does, don't turn away. Have faith that your Father does know what is best for you.

For married women: When you hear God invite you to partner with Him in being "family," open your heart and have faith that your Father has chosen you because He knows what is best.

Throughout biblical history and through the ages that have followed, God has issued invitations of destiny to His women. What will you do with yours?

Kim Bangs

28 [1]Your God has [a]commanded your
strength;
Strengthen, O God, what You have
done for us.
29 Because of Your temple at
Jerusalem,
[a]Kings will bring presents to You.
30 Rebuke the beasts of the reeds,
[a]The herd of bulls with the calves of
the peoples,
Till everyone [b]submits himself with
pieces of silver.
Scatter the peoples *who* delight in
war.
31 [a]Envoys will come out of Egypt;
[b]Ethiopia will quickly [c]stretch out
her hands to God.

32 Sing to God, you [a]kingdoms of
the earth;
Oh, sing praises to the Lord, Selah
33 To Him [a]who rides on the heaven
of heavens, *which were* of old!
Indeed, He sends out His voice, a
[b]mighty voice.
34 [a]Ascribe strength to God;
His excellence *is* over Israel,
And His strength *is* in the clouds.
35 O God, [a]*You are* more awesome
than Your holy places.
The God of Israel *is* He who gives
strength and power to *His*
people.

Blessed *be* God!

PSALM 69

An Urgent Plea for Help in Trouble

To the Chief Musician. Set to [1]"The Lilies."
A Psalm of David.

Save me, O God!
For [a]the waters have come up to
my [1]neck.
2 [a]I sink in deep mire,
Where *there is* no standing;
I have come into deep waters,
Where the floods overflow me.
3 [a]I am weary with my crying;
My throat is dry;
[b]My eyes fail while I wait for my
God.

4 Those who [a]hate me without a
cause
Are more than the hairs of my
head;
They are mighty who would destroy
me,
Being my enemies wrongfully;
Though I have stolen nothing,
I *still* must restore *it*.

5 O God, You know my foolishness;
And my sins are not hidden from
You.
6 Let not those who [1]wait for You,
O Lord GOD of hosts, be ashamed
because of me;
Let not those who seek You be
[2]confounded because of me,
O God of Israel.
7 Because for Your sake I have borne
reproach;
Shame has covered my face.
8 [a]I have become a stranger to my
brothers,
And an alien to my mother's
children;
9 [a]Because zeal for Your house has
eaten me up,
[b]And the reproaches of those who
reproach You have fallen on me.
10 When I wept *and chastened* my
soul with fasting,
That became my reproach.
11 I also [1]made sackcloth my
garment;
I became a byword to them.
12 Those who [1]sit in the gate speak
against me,
And I *am* the song of the
[a]drunkards.

13 But as for me, my prayer *is* to
You,
O LORD, *in* the acceptable time;
O God, in the multitude of Your
mercy,
Hear me in the truth of Your
salvation.
14 Deliver me out of the mire,
And let me not sink;
Let me be delivered from those who
hate me,
And out of the deep waters.
15 Let not the floodwater overflow
me,
Nor let the deep swallow me up;
And let not the pit shut its mouth
on me.

16 Hear me, O LORD, for Your
lovingkindness *is* good;
Turn to me according to the
multitude of Your tender
mercies.

28 [a]Is. 26:12 [1]LXX, Syr., Tg., Vg. *Command, O God*
29 [a]Ps. 45:12; 72:10
30 [a]Ps. 22:12 [b]2 Sam. 8:2
31 [a]Is. 19:19–23 [b]Is. 45:14 [c]Ps. 44:20
32 [a][Ps. 67:3, 4]
33 [a]Ps. 18:10 [b]Ps. 46:6
34 [a]Ps. 29:1
35 [a]Ps. 76:12
PSALM 69
title [1]Heb. *Shoshannim*
1 [a]Jon. 2:5 [1]Lit. *soul*
2 [a]Ps. 40:2
3 [a]Ps. 6:6 [b]Ps. 119:82, 123
4 [a]John 15:25
6 [1]Wait in faith [2]*dishonored*
8 [a]Is. 53:3
9 [a]John 2:17 [b]Rom. 15:3
11 [1]Symbolic of sorrow
12 [a]Job 30:9 [1]Sit as judges

17 And do not hide Your face from
Your servant,
For I am in trouble;
Hear me speedily.
18 Draw near to my soul, *and* redeem
it;
Deliver me because of my enemies.

God draws very close to the praying soul. To see God, know God, and live for God—these form the objective of all true praying.

E. M. Bounds

19 You know [a]my reproach, my
shame, and my dishonor;
My adversaries *are* all before You.
20 Reproach has broken my heart,
And I am full of [1]heaviness;
[a]I looked *for someone* to take pity,
but *there was* none;
And for [b]comforters, but I found
none.
21 They also gave me gall for my
food,
[a]And for my thirst they gave me
vinegar to drink.
22 [a]Let their table become a snare
before them,
And their well-being a trap.
23 [a]Let their eyes be darkened, so that
they do not see;
And make their loins shake
continually.
24 [a]Pour out Your indignation upon
them,
And let Your wrathful anger take
hold of them.
25 [a]Let their dwelling place be
desolate;
Let no one live in their tents.
26 For they persecute the *ones* [a]You
have struck,
And talk of the grief of those You
have wounded.
27 [a]Add iniquity to their iniquity,
[b]And let them not come into Your
righteousness.
28 Let them [a]be blotted out of the
book of the living,
[b]And not be written with the
righteous.
29 But I *am* poor and sorrowful;
Let Your salvation, O God, set me
up on high.
30 [a]I will praise the name of God with
a song,
And will magnify Him with
thanksgiving.
31 [a]*This* also shall please the LORD
better than an ox *or* bull,
Which has horns and hooves.
32 [a]The humble shall see *this and* be
glad;
And you who seek God, [b]your
hearts shall live.
33 For the LORD hears the poor,
And does not despise [a]His
prisoners.
34 [a]Let heaven and earth praise Him,
The seas [b]and everything that
moves in them.
35 [a]For God will save Zion
And build the cities of Judah,
That they may dwell there and
possess it.
36 Also, [a]the [1]descendants of His
servants shall inherit it,
And those who love His name shall
dwell in it.

PSALM 70

Prayer for Relief from Adversaries

To the Chief Musician. *A Psalm* of David.
[a]To bring to remembrance.

Make haste, [a]O God, to deliver me!
Make haste to help me, O LORD!
2 [a]Let them be ashamed and
confounded
Who seek my life;
Let them be [1]turned back and
confused
Who desire my hurt.
3 [a]Let them be turned back because
of their shame,
Who say, [1]"Aha, aha!"
4 Let all those who seek You rejoice
and be glad in You;
And let those who love Your
salvation say continually,
"Let God be magnified!"
5 [a]But I *am* poor and needy;
[b]Make haste to me, O God!

19 a Ps. 22:6, 7
20 a Is. 63:5 b Job 16:2 *1* Lit. *sickness*
21 a Matt. 27:34, 48
22 a Rom. 11:9, 10
23 a Is. 6:9, 10
24 a [1 Thess. 2:16]
25 a Matt. 23:38
26 a [Is. 53:4]
27 a [Rom. 1:28] b [Is. 26:10]
28 a [Ex. 32:32] b Ezek. 13:9
30 a [Ps. 28:7]
31 a Ps. 50:13, 14, 23; 51:16
32 a Ps. 34:2 b Ps. 22:26
33 a Eph. 3:1
34 a Ps. 96:11 b Is. 55:12
35 a Is. 44:26
36 a Ps. 102:28 *1* Lit. *seed*
PSALM 70
title a Ps. 38:title
1 a Ps. 40:13–17
2 a Ps. 35:4, 26 *1* So with MT, LXX, Tg., Vg.; some Heb. mss., Syr. *appalled* (cf. 40:15)
3 a Ps. 40:15 *1* An expression of scorn
5 a Ps. 72:12, 13 b Ps. 141:1

You *are* my help and my deliverer;
O LORD, do not delay.

PSALM 71

God the Rock of Salvation

In [a]You, O LORD, I put my trust;
Let me never be put to shame.
2 [a]Deliver me in Your righteousness, and cause me to escape;
[b]Incline Your ear to me, and save me.
3 [a]Be my [1]strong refuge,
To which I may resort continually;
You have given the [b]commandment to save me,
For You *are* my rock and my fortress.
4 [a]Deliver me, O my God, out of the hand of the wicked,
Out of the hand of the unrighteous and cruel man.
5 For You are [a]my hope, O Lord GOD;
You are my trust from my youth.
6 [a]By You I have been [1]upheld from birth;
You are He who took me out of my mother's womb.
My praise *shall be* continually of You.
7 [a]I have become as a wonder to many,
But You *are* my strong refuge.
8 Let [a]my mouth be filled *with* Your praise
And with Your glory all the day.
9 Do not cast me off in the time of old age;
Do not forsake me when my strength fails.
10 For my enemies speak against me;
And those who lie in wait for my life [a]take counsel together,
11 Saying, "God has forsaken him;
Pursue and take him, for *there is* none to deliver *him*."
12 [a]O God, do not be far from me;
O my God, [b]make haste to help me!
13 Let them be [1]confounded *and* consumed
Who are adversaries of my life;
Let them be covered *with* reproach and dishonor
Who seek my hurt.

PSALM 71
1 a Ps. 25:2, 3
2 a Ps. 31:1
b Ps. 17:6
3 a Ps. 31:2, 3
b Ps. 44:4
1 Lit. *rock of refuge* or *rock of habitation*
4 a Ps. 140:1, 3
5 a Jer. 14:8; 17:7, 13, 17; 50:7
6 a Ps. 22:9, 10
1 *sustained from the womb*
7 a Is. 8:18
8 a Ps. 35:28
10 a 2 Sam. 17:1
12 a Ps. 35:22
b Ps. 70:1
13 1 *ashamed*
17 a Deut. 4:5; 6:7
18 a [Is. 46:4]
19 a Ps. 57:10
b Ps. 35:10
1 *great,* lit. *to the height of heaven*
20 a Ps. 60:3
b Hos. 6:1, 2
22 a Ps. 92:1–3
b 2 Kin. 19:22

14 But I will hope continually,
And will praise You yet more and more.
15 My mouth shall tell of Your righteousness
And Your salvation all the day,
For I do not know *their* limits.
16 I will go in the strength of the Lord GOD;
I will make mention of Your righteousness, of Yours only.

Father God, You have taught ____ from their youth; and to this day they declare Your wondrous works. Now also in their old age, let them declare Your strength to this generation, Your power to everyone who is to come.

FROM PSALM 71:17, 18

17 O God, You have taught me from my [a]youth;
And to this *day* I declare Your wondrous works.
18 Now also [a]when *I am* old and grayheaded,
O God, do not forsake me,
Until I declare Your strength to *this* generation,
Your power to everyone *who* is to come.
19 Also [a]Your righteousness, O God, *is* [1]very high,
You who have done great things;
[b]O God, who *is* like You?
20 [a]*You,* who have shown me great and severe troubles,
[b]Shall revive me again,
And bring me up again from the depths of the earth.
21 You shall increase my greatness,
And comfort me on every side.
22 Also [a]with the lute I will praise You—
And Your faithfulness, O my God!
To You I will sing with the harp,
O [b]Holy One of Israel.

23 My lips shall greatly rejoice when
I sing to You,
And [a]my soul, which You have
redeemed.
24 My tongue also shall talk of Your
righteousness all the day long;
For they are confounded,
For they are brought to shame
Who seek my hurt.

PSALM 72

Glory and Universality of the Messiah's Reign

A Psalm [a]of Solomon.

Give the king Your judgments, O God,
And Your righteousness to the
king's Son.
2 [a]He will judge Your people with
righteousness,
And Your poor with justice.
3 [a]The mountains will bring peace to
the people,
And the little hills, by
righteousness.
4 [a]He will bring justice to the poor of
the people;
He will save the children of the
needy,
And will [1]break in pieces the
oppressor.

5 [1]They shall fear You
[a]As long as the sun and moon
endure,
Throughout all generations.
6 [a]He shall come down like rain upon
the grass before mowing,
Like showers *that* water the earth.
7 In His days the righteous shall
flourish,
[a]And abundance of peace,
Until the moon is no more.

8 [a]He shall have dominion also from
sea to sea,
And from the River to the ends of
the earth.
9 [a]Those who dwell in the wilderness
will bow before Him,
[b]And His enemies will lick the dust.
10 [a]The kings of Tarshish and of the
isles
Will bring presents;
The kings of Sheba and Seba
Will offer gifts.
11 [a]Yes, all kings shall fall down
before Him;
All nations shall serve Him.

12 For He [a]will deliver the needy
when he cries,
The poor also, and *him* who has no
helper.
13 He will spare the poor and needy,
And will save the souls of the
needy.
14 He will redeem their life from
oppression and violence;
And [a]precious shall be their blood
in His sight.

15 And He shall live;
And the gold of [a]Sheba will be
given to Him;
Prayer also will be made for Him
continually,
And daily He shall be praised.
16 There will be an abundance of
grain in the earth,
On the top of the mountains;
Its fruit shall wave like Lebanon;
[a]And *those* of the city shall flourish
like grass of the earth.

17 [a]His name shall endure forever;
His name shall continue as long as
the sun.
And [b]*men* shall be blessed in Him;
[c]All nations shall call Him blessed.
18 [a]Blessed *be* the LORD God, the God
of Israel,
[b]Who only does wondrous things!
19 And [a]blessed *be* His glorious name
forever!
[b]And let the whole earth be filled
with His glory.
Amen and Amen.

20 The prayers of David the son of
Jesse are ended.

BOOK THREE

Psalms 73—89

PSALM 73

The Tragedy of the Wicked, and the Blessedness of Trust in God

A Psalm of [a]Asaph.

Truly God *is* good to Israel,
To such as are pure in heart.
2 But as for me, my feet had almost
stumbled;
My steps had nearly [a]slipped.

---

23 a Ps. 103:4
PSALM 72 title a Ps. 127:title
2 a [Is. 9:7; 11:2–5; 32:1]
3 a Ps. 85:10
4 a Is. 11:4 1 *crush*
5 a Ps. 72:7, 17; 89:36 1 So with MT, Tg.; LXX, Vg. *They shall continue*
6 a Hos. 6:3
7 a Is. 2:4
8 a Ex. 23:31
9 a Is. 23:13 b Is. 49:23
10 a 2 Chr. 9:21
11 a Is. 49:23
12 a Job 29:12
14 a [Ps. 116:15]
15 a Is. 60:6
16 a 1 Kin. 4:20
17 a [Ps. 89:36] b [Gen. 12:3] c Luke 1:48
18 a 1 Chr. 29:10 b Ex. 15:11
19 a [Neh. 9:5] b Num. 14:21
PSALM 73 title a Ps. 50:title
2 a Job 12:5

3 [a]For I *was* envious of the boastful,
When I saw the prosperity of the [b]wicked.
4 For *there are* no [1]pangs in their death,
But their strength *is* firm.
5 [a]They *are* not in trouble *as other* men,
Nor are they plagued like *other* men.
6 Therefore pride serves as their necklace;
Violence covers them [a]*like* a garment.
7 [a]Their [1]eyes bulge with abundance;
They have more than heart could wish.
8 [a]They scoff and speak wickedly *concerning* oppression;
They [b]speak [1]loftily.
9 They set their mouth [a]against the heavens,
And their tongue walks through the earth.
10 Therefore his people return here,
[a]And waters of a full *cup* are drained by them.
11 And they say, [a]"How does God know?
And is there knowledge in the Most High?"
12 Behold, these *are* the ungodly,
Who are always at ease;
They increase *in* riches.
13 Surely I have [1]cleansed my heart *in* [a]vain,
And washed my hands in innocence.
14 For all day long I have been plagued,
And chastened every morning.
15 If I had said, "I will speak thus,"
Behold, I would have been untrue to the generation of Your children.
16 When I thought *how* to understand this,
It *was* [1]too painful for me—
17 Until I went into the sanctuary of God;
Then I understood their [a]end.
18 Surely [a]You set them in slippery places;
You cast them down to destruction.
19 Oh, how they are *brought* to desolation, as in a moment!
They are utterly consumed with terrors.
20 As a dream when *one* awakes,
So, Lord, when You awake,
You shall despise their image.
21 Thus my heart was grieved,
And I was [1]vexed in my mind.
22 [a]I *was* so foolish and ignorant;
I was *like* a beast before You.
23 Nevertheless I *am* continually with You;
You hold *me* by my right hand.
24 [a]You will guide me with Your counsel,
And afterward receive me *to* glory.
25 [a]Whom have I in heaven *but You?*
And *there is* none upon earth *that* I desire besides You.
26 [a]My flesh and my heart fail;
But God *is* the [1]strength of my heart and my [b]portion forever.
27 For indeed, [a]those who are far from You shall perish;
You have destroyed all those who [1]desert You for harlotry.
28 But *it is* good for me to [a]draw near to God;
I have put my trust in the Lord GOD,
That I may [b]declare all Your works.

PSALM 74

A Plea for Relief from Oppressors

A [1]Contemplation of Asaph.

O God, why have You cast *us* off forever?
Why does Your anger smoke against the sheep of Your pasture?
2 Remember Your congregation, *which* You have purchased of old,
The tribe of Your inheritance, *which* You have redeemed—
This Mount Zion where You have dwelt.
3 Lift up Your feet to the perpetual desolations.
The enemy has damaged everything in the sanctuary.
4 [a]Your enemies roar in the midst of Your meeting place;
[b]They set up their banners *for* signs.
5 They seem like men who lift up
Axes among the thick trees.
6 And now they break down its carved work, all at once,

---

3 a Ps. 37:1, 7 b Job 21:5–16
4 *1 pains*
5 a Job 21:9
6 a Ps. 109:18
7 a Jer. 5:28 *1* Tg. *face bulges;* LXX, Syr., Vg. *iniquity bulges*
8 a Ps. 53:1 b 2 Pet. 2:18 *1* Proudly
9 a Rev. 13:6
10 a [Ps. 75:8]
11 a Job 22:13
13 a Job 21:15; 35:3 *1 kept my heart pure in vain*
16 *1 troublesome in my eyes*
17 a [Ps. 37:38; 55:23]
18 a Ps. 35:6
21 *1* Lit. *pierced in my kidneys*
22 a Ps. 92:6
24 a Ps. 32:8; 48:14
25 a [Phil. 3:8]
26 a Ps. 84:2 b Ps. 16:5 *1* Lit. *rock*
27 a [Ps. 119:155] *1* Are unfaithful to You
28 a [Heb. 10:22] b 2 Cor. 4:13
PSALM 74 title *1* Heb. *Maschil*
4 a Lam. 2:7 b Num. 2:2

With axes and hammers.
7 They have set fire to Your sanctuary;
They have defiled the dwelling place of Your name to the ground.
8 [a]They said in their hearts,
"Let us [1]destroy them altogether."
They have burned up all the meeting places of God in the land.

9 We do not see our signs;
[a]*There is* no longer any prophet;
Nor *is there* any among us who knows how long.
10 O God, how long will the adversary [1]reproach?
Will the enemy blaspheme Your name forever?
11 [a]Why do You withdraw Your hand, even Your right hand?
Take it out of Your bosom and destroy *them*.
12 For [a]God *is* my King from of old,
Working salvation in the midst of the earth.
13 [a]You divided the sea by Your strength;
You broke the heads of the [1]sea serpents in the waters.
14 You broke the heads of [1]Leviathan in pieces,
And gave him *as* food to the people inhabiting the wilderness.
15 [a]You broke open the fountain and the flood;
[b]You dried up mighty rivers.
16 The day *is* Yours, the night also *is* [a]Yours;
[b]You have prepared the light and the sun.
17 You have [a]set all the borders of the earth;
[b]You have made summer and winter.

18 Remember this, *that* the enemy has reproached, O LORD,
And *that* a foolish people has blasphemed Your name.
19 Oh, do not deliver the life of Your turtledove to the wild beast!
Do not forget the life of Your poor forever.
20 [a]Have respect to the covenant;
For the [1]dark places of the earth are full of the [2]haunts of [3]cruelty.
21 Oh, do not let the oppressed return ashamed!
Let the poor and needy praise Your name.

22 Arise, O God, plead Your own cause;
Remember how the foolish man [1]reproaches You daily.
23 Do not forget the voice of Your enemies;
The tumult of those who rise up against You increases continually.

PSALM 75

Thanksgiving for God's Righteous Judgment

To the Chief Musician. Set to [a]"Do[1] Not Destroy." A Psalm of Asaph. A Song.

We give thanks to You, O God, we give thanks!
For Your wondrous works declare *that* Your name is near.

2 "When I choose the [1]proper time,
I will judge uprightly.
3 The earth and all its inhabitants are dissolved;
I set up its pillars firmly. Selah

4 "I said to the boastful, 'Do not deal boastfully,'
And to the wicked, [a]'Do not [1]lift up the horn.
5 Do not lift up your horn on high;
Do *not* speak with [1]a stiff neck.'"
6 For exaltation *comes* neither from the east
Nor from the west nor from the south.
7 But [a]God *is* the Judge:
[b]He puts down one,
And exalts another.
8 For [a]in the hand of the LORD *there is* a cup,
And the wine is red;
It is fully mixed, and He pours it out;
Surely its dregs shall all the wicked of the earth
Drain *and* drink down.

9 But I will declare forever,
I will sing praises to the God of Jacob.

10 "All[a] the [1]horns of the wicked I will also cut off,

8 a Ps. 83:4 1 *oppress*
9 a Amos 8:11
10 1 *revile*
11 a Lam. 2:3
12 a Ps. 44:4
13 a Ex. 14:21 1 *sea monsters*
14 1 A large sea creature of unknown identity
15 a Ex. 17:5, 6 b Josh. 2:10; 3:13
16 a Job 38:12 b Gen. 1:14–18
17 a Acts 17:26 b Gen. 8:22
20 a Lev. 26:44, 45 1 *hiding places* 2 *homes* 3 *violence*
22 1 *reviles* or *taunts*
PSALM 75 title a Ps. 57:title 1 Heb. *Al Tashcheth*
2 1 *appointed*
4 a [1 Sam. 2:3] 1 Raise the head proudly like a horned animal
5 1 Insolent pride
7 a Ps. 50:6 b 1 Sam. 2:7
8 a Jer. 25:15
10 a Jer. 48:25 1 Strength

But [b]the horns of the righteous
shall be [c]exalted."

PSALM 76

The Majesty of God in Judgment

To the Chief Musician. On [1]stringed instruments. A Psalm of Asaph. A Song.

In [a]Judah God *is* known;
His name *is* great in Israel.
2 In [1]Salem also is His tabernacle,
And His dwelling place in Zion.
3 There He broke the arrows of the bow,
The shield and sword of battle. Selah

4 You *are* more glorious and excellent
[a]*Than* the mountains of prey.
5 [a]The stouthearted were plundered;
[b]They [1]have sunk into their sleep;
And none of the mighty men have found the use of their hands.
6 [a]At Your rebuke, O God of Jacob,
Both the chariot and horse were cast into a dead sleep.

7 You, Yourself, *are* to be feared;
And [a]who may stand in Your presence
When once You are angry?
8 [a]You caused judgment to be heard from heaven;
[b]The earth feared and was still,
9 When God [a]arose to judgment,
To deliver all the oppressed of the earth. Selah

10 [a]Surely the wrath of man shall praise You;
With the remainder of wrath You shall gird Yourself.

11 [a]Make vows to the LORD your God, and pay *them;*
[b]Let all who are around Him bring presents to Him who ought to be feared.
12 He shall cut off the spirit of princes;
[a]*He is* awesome to the kings of the earth.

10 [b]Ps. 89:17; 148:14 [c]1 Sam. 2:1

PSALM 76
title [1]Heb. *neginoth*
1 [a]Ps. 48:1, 3
2 [1]Jerusalem
4 [a]Ezek. 38:12
5 [a]Is. 10:12; 46:12 [b]Ps. 13:3 [1]Lit. *have slumbered their sleep*
6 [a]Ex. 15:1–21
7 [a][Nah. 1:6]
8 [a]Ex. 19:9 [b]2 Chr. 20:29
9 [a][Ps. 9:7–9]
10 [a]Rom. 9:17
11 [a][Eccl. 5:4–6] [b]2 Chr. 32:22, 23
12 [a]Ps. 68:35

PSALM 77
title [a]Ps. 39:title
6 [1]*ponders diligently*
8 [a][2 Pet. 3:8, 9] [1]Lit. *unto generation and generation*
10 [1]Lit. *infirmity*
13 [a]Ps. 73:17 [1]Or *holiness*

PSALM 77

The Consoling Memory of God's Redemptive Works

To the Chief Musician. [a]To Jeduthun. A Psalm of Asaph.

I cried out to God with my voice—
To God with my voice;
And He gave ear to me.
2 In the day of my trouble I sought the Lord;
My hand was stretched out in the night without ceasing;
My soul refused to be comforted.
3 I remembered God, and was troubled;
I complained, and my spirit was overwhelmed. Selah

4 You hold my eyelids *open;*
I am so troubled that I cannot speak.
5 I have considered the days of old,
The years of ancient times.
6 I call to remembrance my song in the night;
I meditate within my heart,
And my spirit [1]makes diligent search.

7 Will the Lord cast off forever?
And will He be favorable no more?
8 Has His mercy ceased forever?
Has *His* [a]promise failed
[1]forevermore?
9 Has God forgotten to be gracious?
Has He in anger shut up His tender mercies? Selah

10 And I said, "This *is* my [1]anguish;
But I will remember the years of the right hand of the Most High."
11 I will remember the works of the LORD;
Surely I will remember Your wonders of old.
12 I will also meditate on all Your work,
And talk of Your deeds.
13 Your way, O God, *is* in [1]the [a]sanctuary;
Who *is* so great a God as *our* God?
14 You *are* the God who does wonders;
You have declared Your strength among the peoples.

15 You have with *Your* arm redeemed
Your people,
The sons of Jacob and Joseph. Selah
16 The waters saw You, O God;
The waters saw You, they were
[a]afraid;
The depths also trembled.
17 The clouds poured out water;
The skies sent out a sound;
Your arrows also flashed about.
18 The voice of Your thunder *was* in
the whirlwind;
The lightnings lit up the world;
The earth trembled and shook.
19 Your way *was* in the sea,
Your path in the great waters,
And Your footsteps were not
known.
20 You led Your people like a flock
By the hand of Moses and Aaron.

PSALM 78

God's Kindness to Rebellious Israel

A [a]Contemplation[1] of Asaph.

Give ear, O my people, *to* my law;
Incline your ears to the words of
my mouth.
2 I will open my mouth in a
[a]parable;
I will utter [1]dark sayings of old,
3 Which we have heard and known,
And our fathers have told us.
4 [a]We will not hide *them* from their
children,
[b]Telling to the generation to come
the praises of the LORD,
And His strength and His wonderful
works that He has done.
5 For [a]He established a testimony in
Jacob,
And appointed a law in Israel,
Which He commanded our fathers,
That [b]they should make them
known to their children;
6 [a]That the generation to come might
know *them,*
The children *who* would be born,
That they may arise and declare
them to their children,
7 That they may set their hope in
God,
And not forget the works of God,
But keep His commandments;
8 And [a]may not be like their fathers,
[b]A stubborn and rebellious
generation,
A generation [c]*that* did not [1]set its
heart aright,
And whose spirit was not faithful to
God.

9 The children of Ephraim, *being*
armed *and* [1]carrying bows,
Turned back in the day of battle.
10 [a]They did not keep the covenant of
God;
They refused to walk in His law,
11 And [a]forgot His works
And His wonders that He had
shown them.

12 [a]Marvelous things He did in the
sight of their fathers,
In the land of Egypt, [b]*in* the field
of Zoan.
13 [a]He divided the sea and caused
them to pass through;
And [b]He made the waters stand up
like a heap.
14 [a]In the daytime also He led them
with the cloud,
And all the night with a light of
fire.
15 [a]He split the rocks in the
wilderness,
And gave *them* drink in abundance
like the depths.
16 He also brought [a]streams out of
the rock,
And caused waters to run down like
rivers.

17 But they sinned even more against
Him
By [a]rebelling against the Most High
in the wilderness.
18 And [a]they tested God in their
heart
By asking for the food of their
fancy.
19 [a]Yes, they spoke against God:
They said, "Can God prepare a table
in the wilderness?
20 [a]Behold, He struck the rock,
So that the waters gushed out,
And the streams overflowed.
Can He give bread also?
Can He provide meat for His
people?"
21 Therefore the LORD heard *this* and
[a]was furious;
So a fire was kindled against Jacob,

---

16 [a]Ex. 14:21
PSALM 78
title [a]Ps. 74:title [1]Heb. *Maschil*
2 [a]Matt. 13:34, 35 [1]*obscure sayings* or *riddles*
4 [a]Deut. 4:9; 6:7 [b]Ex. 13:8, 14
5 [a]Ps. 147:19 [b]Deut. 4:9; 11:19
6 [a]Ps. 102:18
8 [a]2 Kin. 17:14 [b]Ex. 32:9 [c]Ps. 78:37 [1]Lit. *prepare its heart*
9 [1]Lit. *bow shooters*
10 [a]2 Kin. 17:15
11 [a]Ps. 106:13
12 [a]Ex. 7—12 [b]Num. 13:22
13 [a]Ex. 14:21 [b]Ex. 15:8
14 [a]Ex. 13:21
15 [a]Num. 20:11
16 [a]Num. 20:8, 10, 11
17 [a]Heb. 3:16
18 [a]Ex. 16:2
19 [a]Num. 11:4; 20:3; 21:5
20 [a]Num. 20:11
21 [a]Num. 11:1

And anger also came up against
Israel,
22 Because they [a]did not believe in
God,
And did not trust in His salvation.
23 Yet He had commanded the clouds
above,
[a]And opened the doors of heaven,
24 [a]Had rained down manna on them
to eat,
And given them of the [1]bread of
[b]heaven.
25 Men ate angels' food;
He sent them food to [1]the full.
26 [a]He caused an east wind to blow in
the heavens;
And by His power He brought in
the south wind.
27 He also rained meat on them like
the dust,
Feathered fowl like the sand of the
seas;
28 And He let *them* fall in the midst
of their camp,
All around their dwellings.
29 [a]So they ate and were well filled,
For He gave them their own desire.
30 They were not [1]deprived of their
craving;
But [a]while their food *was* still in
their mouths,
31 The wrath of God came against
them,
And slew the stoutest of them,
And struck down the choice *men* of
Israel.

32 In spite of this [a]they still sinned,
And [b]did not believe in His
wondrous works.
33 [a]Therefore their days He consumed
in futility,
And their years in fear.
34 [a]When He slew them, then they
sought Him;
And they returned and sought
earnestly for God.
35 Then they remembered that [a]God
was their rock,
And the Most High God [b]their
Redeemer.
36 Nevertheless they [a]flattered Him
with their mouth,
And they lied to Him with their
tongue;
37 For their heart was not steadfast
with Him,
Nor were they faithful in His
covenant.
38 [a]But He, *being* full of [b]compassion,
forgave *their* iniquity,
And did not destroy *them*.
Yes, many a time [c]He turned His
anger away,
And [d]did not stir up all His wrath;
39 For [a]He remembered [b]that they
were but flesh,
[c]A breath that passes away and does
not come again.

40 How often they [a]provoked[1] Him
in the wilderness,
And grieved Him in the desert!
41 Yes, [a]again and again they
tempted God,
And limited the Holy One of Israel.
42 They did not remember His
[1]power:
The day when He redeemed them
from the enemy,
43 When He worked His signs in
Egypt,
And His wonders in the field of
Zoan;
44 [a]Turned their rivers into blood,
And their streams, that they could
not drink.
45 [a]He sent swarms of flies among
them, which devoured them,
And [b]frogs, which destroyed them.
46 He also gave their crops to the
caterpillar,
And their labor to the [a]locust.
47 [a]He destroyed their vines with hail,
And their sycamore trees with frost.
48 He also gave up their [a]cattle to
the hail,
And their flocks to fiery [1]lightning.
49 He cast on them the fierceness of
His anger,
Wrath, indignation, and trouble,
By sending angels of destruction
among them.
50 He made a path for His anger;
He did not spare their soul from
death,
But gave [1]their life over to the
plague,
51 And destroyed all the [a]firstborn in
Egypt,
The first of *their* strength in the
tents of Ham.
52 But He [a]made His own people go
forth like sheep,

22 a [Heb. 3:18]
23 a [Mal. 3:10]
24 a Ex. 16:4 b John 6:31 *1* Lit. *grain*
25 *1 satiation*
26 a Num. 11:31
29 a Num. 11:19, 20
30 a Num. 11:33 *1* Lit. *separated*
32 a Num. 14:16, 17 b Num. 14:11
33 a Num. 14:29, 35
34 a [Hos. 5:15]
35 a [Deut. 32:4, 15] b Is. 41:14; 44:6; 63:9
36 a Ezek. 33:31
38 a [Num. 14:18–20] b Ex. 34:6 c [Is. 48:9] d 1 Kin. 21:29
39 a Job 10:9 b John 3:6 c [Job 7:7, 16]
40 a Heb. 3:16 *1 rebelled against Him*
41 a Num. 14:22
42 *1* Lit. *hand*
44 a Ex. 7:20
45 a Ex. 8:24 b Ex. 8:6
46 a Ex. 10:14
47 a Ex. 9:23–25
48 a Ex. 9:19 *1 lightning bolts*
50 *1* Or *their beasts*
51 a Ex. 12:29, 30
52 a Ps. 77:20

And guided them in the wilderness like a flock;
53 And He [a]led them on safely, so that they did not fear;
But the sea [b]overwhelmed their enemies.
54 And He brought them to His [a]holy border,
This mountain [b]*which* His right hand had acquired.
55 [a]He also drove out the nations before them,
[b]Allotted them an inheritance by [1]survey,
And made the tribes of Israel dwell in their tents.

56 [a]Yet they tested and provoked the Most High God,
And did not keep His testimonies,
57 But [a]turned back and acted unfaithfully like their fathers;
They were turned aside [b]like a deceitful bow.
58 [a]For they provoked Him to anger with their [b]high places,
And moved Him to jealousy with their carved images.
59 When God heard *this,* He was furious,
And greatly abhorred Israel,
60 [a]So that He forsook the tabernacle of Shiloh,
The tent He had placed among men,
61 [a]And delivered His strength into captivity,
And His glory into the enemy's hand.
62 [a]He also gave His people over to the sword,
And was furious with His inheritance.
63 The fire consumed their young men,
And [a]their maidens were not given in marriage.
64 [a]Their priests fell by the sword,
And [b]their widows made no lamentation.

65 Then the Lord awoke as *from* sleep,
[a]Like a mighty man who shouts because of wine.
66 And [a]He beat back His enemies;
He put them to a perpetual reproach.

67 Moreover He rejected the tent of Joseph,
And did not choose the tribe of Ephraim,
68 But chose the tribe of Judah,
Mount Zion [a]which He loved.
69 And He built His [a]sanctuary like the heights,
Like the earth which He has established forever.
70 [a]He also chose David His servant,
And took him from the sheepfolds;
71 From following [a]the ewes that had young He brought him,
[b]To shepherd Jacob His people,
And Israel His inheritance.
72 So he shepherded them according to the [a]integrity of his heart,
And guided them by the skillfulness of his hands.

PSALM 79

A Dirge and a Prayer for Israel, Destroyed by Enemies

A Psalm of Asaph.

O God, the [1]nations have come into [a]Your inheritance;
Your holy temple they have defiled;
[b]They have laid Jerusalem [2]in heaps.
2 [a]The dead bodies of Your servants
They have given *as* food for the birds of the heavens,
The flesh of Your saints to the beasts of the earth.
3 Their blood they have shed like water all around Jerusalem,
And *there was* no one to bury *them.*
4 We have become a reproach to our [a]neighbors,
A scorn and derision to those who are around us.

5 [a]How long, LORD?
Will You be angry forever?
Will Your [b]jealousy burn like fire?
6 [a]Pour out Your wrath on the [1]nations that [b]do not know You,
And on the kingdoms that [c]do not call on Your name.
7 For they have devoured Jacob,
And laid waste his dwelling place.

---

53 [a] Ex. 14:19, 20 [b] Ex. 14:27, 28
54 [a] Ex. 15:17 [b] Ps. 44:3
55 [a] Ps. 44:2 [b] Josh. 13:7; 19:51; 23:4 [1] *surveyed measurement,* lit. *measuring cord*
56 [a] Judg. 2:11–13
57 [a] Ezek. 20:27, 28 [b] Hos. 7:16
58 [a] Judg. 2:12 [b] Deut. 12:2
60 [a] 1 Sam. 4:11
61 [a] Judg. 18:30
62 [a] 1 Sam. 4:10
63 [a] Jer. 7:34; 16:9; 25:10
64 [a] 1 Sam. 4:17; 22:18 [b] Job 27:15; Ezek. 24:23
65 [a] Is. 42:13
66 [a] 1 Sam. 5:6
68 [a] [Ps. 87:2]
69 [a] 1 Kin. 6:1–38
70 [a] 1 Sam. 16:11, 12
71 [a] [Is. 40:11] [b] 2 Sam. 5:2
72 [a] 1 Kin. 9:4

PSALM 79
1 [a] Ps. 74:2 [b] Mic. 3:12 [1] *Gentiles* [2] *in ruins*
2 [a] Jer. 7:33; 19:7; 34:20
4 [a] Ps. 44:13
5 [a] Ps. 74:1, 9 [b] [Zeph. 3:8]
6 [a] Jer. 10:25 [b] Is. 45:4, 5 [c] Ps. 53:4 [1] *Gentiles*

8 [a]Oh, do not remember [1]former
iniquities against us!
Let Your tender mercies come
speedily to meet us,
For we have been brought very low.
9 Help us, O God of our salvation,
For the glory of Your name;
And deliver us, and provide
atonement for our sins,
[a]For Your name's sake!
10 [a]Why should the [1]nations say,
"Where *is* their God?"
Let there be known among the
nations in our sight
The avenging of the blood of Your
servants *which has been* shed.
11 Let [a]the groaning of the prisoner
come before You;
According to the greatness of Your
[1]power
Preserve those who are appointed to
die;
12 And return to our neighbors
[a]sevenfold into their bosom
[b]Their reproach with which they
have reproached You, O Lord.

13 So [a]we, Your people and sheep of
Your pasture,
Will give You thanks forever;
[b]We will show forth Your praise to
all generations.

PSALM 80

Prayer for Israel's Restoration

To the Chief Musician. [a]Set to [1]"The Lilies." A [2]Testimony of Asaph. A Psalm.

Give ear, O Shepherd of Israel,
[a]You who lead Joseph [b]like a flock;
You who dwell *between* the
cherubim, [c]shine forth!
2 Before [a]Ephraim, Benjamin, and
Manasseh,
Stir up Your strength,
And come *and* save us!

3 [a]Restore us, O God;
[b]Cause Your face to shine,
And we shall be saved!

4 O LORD God of hosts,
[a]How long will You be angry
Against the prayer of Your people?
5 [a]You have fed them with the bread
of tears,
And given them tears to drink in
great measure.
6 You have made us a strife to our
neighbors,
And our enemies laugh among
themselves.

7 Restore us, O God of hosts;
Cause Your face to shine,
And we shall be saved!

8 You have brought [a]a vine out of
Egypt;
[b]You have cast out the [1]nations, and
planted it.
9 You prepared *room* for it,
And caused it to take deep root,
And it filled the land.
10 The hills were covered with its
shadow,
And the [1]mighty cedars with its
[a]boughs.
11 She sent out her boughs to [1]the
Sea,
And her branches to [2]the River.
12 Why have You [a]broken down her
[1]hedges,
So that all who pass by the way
pluck her *fruit?*
13 The boar out of the woods uproots
it,
And the wild beast of the field
devours it.

14 Return, we beseech You, O God of
hosts;
[a]Look down from heaven and see,
And visit this vine
15 And the vineyard which Your right
hand has planted,
And the branch *that* You made
strong [a]for Yourself.
16 *It is* burned with fire, *it is* cut
down;
[a]They perish at the rebuke of Your
countenance.
17 [a]Let Your hand be upon the man
of Your right hand,
Upon the son of man *whom* You
made strong for Yourself.
18 Then we will not turn back from
You;
Revive us, and we will call upon
Your name.

19 Restore us, O LORD God of hosts;
Cause Your face to shine,
And we shall be saved!

---

8 a Is. 64:9 *1 Or against us the iniquities of those who were before us*
9 a Jer. 14:7, 21
10 a Ps. 42:10 *1 Gentiles*
11 a Ps. 102:20 1 Lit. *arm*
12 a Gen. 4:15 b Ps. 74:10, 18, 22
13 a Ps. 74:1; 95:7 b Is. 43:21

PSALM 80
title a Ps. 45:title 1 Heb. *Shoshannim* 2 Heb. *Eduth*
1 a [Ex. 25:20–22] b Ps. 77:20 c Deut. 33:2
2 a Ps. 78:9, 67
3 a Lam. 5:21 b Num. 6:25
4 a Ps. 79:5
5 a Is. 30:20
8 a [Is. 5:1, 7] b Ps. 44:2 *1 Gentiles*
10 a Lev. 23:40 1 Lit. *cedars of God*
11 1 The Mediterranean 2 The Euphrates
12 a Is. 5:5 *1 walls* or *fences*
14 a Is. 63:15
15 a [Is. 49:5]
16 a [Ps. 39:11]
17 a Ps. 89:21

PSALM 81

An Appeal for Israel's Repentance

To the Chief Musician. [a]On [1] an instrument of Gath. A Psalm of Asaph.

Sing aloud to God our strength;
Make a joyful shout to the God of Jacob.
2 Raise a song and strike the timbrel,
The pleasant harp with the lute.

3 Blow the trumpet at the time of the New Moon,
At the full moon, on our solemn feast day.
4 For [a]this *is* a statute for Israel,
A law of the God of Jacob.
5 This He established in Joseph *as* a testimony,
When He went throughout the land of Egypt,
[a]*Where* I heard a language I did not understand.

6 "I removed his shoulder from the burden;
His hands were freed from the baskets.
7 [a]You called in trouble, and I delivered you;
[b]I answered you in the secret place of thunder;
I [c]tested you at the waters of [1]Meribah. Selah
8 "Hear,[a] O My people, and I will admonish you!
O Israel, if you will listen to Me!
9 There shall be no [a]foreign god among you;
Nor shall you worship any foreign god.
10 [a]I *am* the LORD your God,
Who brought you out of the land of Egypt;
[b]Open your mouth wide, and I will fill it.

11 "But My people would not heed My voice,
And Israel would *have* [a]none of Me.
12 [a]So I gave them over to [1]their own stubborn heart,
To walk in their own counsels.

13 "Oh,[a] that My people would listen to Me,
That Israel would walk in My ways!
14 I would soon subdue their enemies,
And turn My hand against their adversaries.
15 [a]The haters of the LORD would pretend submission to Him,
But their [1]fate would endure forever.
16 He would [a]have fed them also with [1]the finest of wheat;
And with honey [b]from the rock I would have satisfied you."

PSALM 82

A Plea for Justice

A Psalm of Asaph.

God [a]stands in the congregation of [1]the mighty;
He judges among [b]the [2]gods.
2 How long will you judge unjustly,
And [a]show partiality to the wicked? Selah
3 [1]Defend the poor and fatherless;
Do justice to the afflicted and [a]needy.
4 Deliver the poor and needy;
Free *them* from the hand of the wicked.

5 They do not know, nor do they understand;
They walk about in darkness;
All the [a]foundations of the earth are [1]unstable.

6 I said, [a]"You *are* [1]gods,
And all of you *are* children of the Most High.
7 But you shall die like men,
And fall like one of the princes."

8 Arise, O God, judge the earth;
[a]For You shall inherit all nations.

PSALM 83

Prayer to Frustrate Conspiracy Against Israel

A Song. A Psalm of Asaph.

Do[a] not keep silent, O God!
Do not hold Your peace,
And do not be still, O God!
2 For behold, [a]Your enemies make a [1]tumult;
And those who hate You have [2]lifted up their head.

PSALM 81
title a Ps. 8:title 1 Heb. *Al Gittith*
4 a Num. 10:10
5 a Ps. 114:1
7 a Ex. 2:23; 14:10 b Ex. 19:19; 20:18 c Ex. 17:6, 7 1 Lit. *Strife* or *Contention*
8 a [Ps. 50:7]
9 a [Is. 43:12]
10 a Ex. 20:2 b Ps. 103:5
11 a Deut. 32:15
12 a [Acts 7:42] 1 *the dictates of their heart*
13 a [Is. 48:18]
15 a Rom. 1:30 1 Lit. *time*
16 a Deut. 32:14 b Job 29:6 1 Lit. *fat of wheat*

PSALM 82
1 a [2 Chr. 19:6] b Ps. 82:6 1 Heb. *El*, lit. *God* 2 Judges; Heb. *elohim*, lit. *mighty ones* or *gods*
2 a [Deut. 1:17]
3 a [Deut. 24:17] 1 *Vindicate*
5 a Ps. 11:3 1 *moved*
6 a John 10:34 1 Judges; Heb. *elohim*, lit. *mighty ones* or *gods*
8 a [Rev. 11:15]

PSALM 83
1 a Ps. 28:1
2 a Ps. 81:15 1 *uproar* 2 Exalted themselves

3 They have taken crafty counsel
against Your people,
And consulted together [a]against
Your sheltered ones.
4 They have said, "Come, and [a]let us
cut them off from *being* a
nation,
That the name of Israel may be
remembered no more."

5 For they have consulted together
with one [1]consent;
They [2]form a confederacy against
You:
6 [a]The tents of Edom and the
Ishmaelites;
Moab and the Hagrites;
7 Gebal, Ammon, and Amalek;
Philistia with the inhabitants of
Tyre;
8 Assyria also has joined with them;
They have helped the children of
Lot. Selah

9 Deal with them as *with* [a]Midian,
As *with* [b]Sisera,
As *with* Jabin at the Brook Kishon,
10 Who perished at En Dor,
[a]*Who* became *as* refuse on the earth.
11 Make their nobles like [a]Oreb and
like Zeeb,
Yes, all their princes like [b]Zebah
and Zalmunna,
12 Who said, "Let us take for
ourselves
The pastures of God for a
possession."

13 [a]O my God, make them like the
whirling dust,
[b]Like the chaff before the wind!
14 As the fire burns the woods,
And as the flame [a]sets the
mountains on fire,
15 So pursue them with Your
tempest,
And frighten them with Your
storm.
16 Fill their faces with shame,
That they may seek Your name,
O LORD.
17 Let them be [1]confounded and
dismayed forever;
Yes, let them be put to shame and
perish,
18 [a]That they may know that You,
whose [b]name alone *is* the LORD,
Are [c]the Most High over all the
earth.

3 a [Ps. 27:5]
4 a Jer. 11:19; 31:36
5 1 Lit. *heart* 2 Lit. *cut a covenant*
6 a 2 Chr. 20:1, 10, 11
9 a Judg. 7:22 b Judg. 4:15–24; 5:20, 21
10 a Zeph. 1:17
11 a Judg. 7:25 b Judg. 8:12–21
13 a Is. 17:13 b Ps. 35:5
14 a Deut. 32:22
17 1 *ashamed*
18 a Ps. 59:13 b Ex. 6:3 c [Ps. 92:8]

PSALM 84
a title Ps. 8:title 1 Heb. *Al Gittith*
1 a Ps. 27:4; 46:4, 5 1 *are Your dwellings*
2 a Ps. 42:1, 2
4 a [Ps. 65:4]
6 a 2 Sam. 5:22–25 1 Lit. *Weeping* 2 Or *blessings*
7 a Prov. 4:18 b Deut. 16:16 1 LXX, Syr., Vg. *The God of gods shall be seen*
9 a Gen. 15:1

PSALM 84

The Blessedness of Dwelling in the House of God

To the Chief Musician. [a]On[1] an instrument of Gath. A Psalm of the sons of Korah.

How [a]lovely [1]*is* Your tabernacle,
O LORD of hosts!
2 [a]My soul longs, yes, even faints
For the courts of the LORD;
My heart and my flesh cry out for
the living God.

You, Lord God, are a sun and shield. You will give grace and glory; no good thing will You withhold from because they walk uprightly. O Lord of hosts, they are blessed because they trust in You!

FROM PSALM 84:11, 12

3 Even the sparrow has found a
home,
And the swallow a nest for herself,
Where she may lay her young—
Even Your altars, O LORD of hosts,
My King and my God.
4 Blessed *are* those who dwell in
Your [a]house;
They will still be praising You.
Selah

5 Blessed *is* the man whose strength
is in You,
Whose heart *is* set on pilgrimage.
6 *As they* pass through the Valley [a]of
[1]Baca,
They make it a spring;
The rain also covers it with [2]pools.
7 They go [a]from strength to
strength;
[1]*Each one* [b]appears before God in
Zion.

8 O LORD God of hosts, hear my
prayer;
Give ear, O God of Jacob! Selah
9 [a]O God, behold our shield,

And look upon the face of Your
[1]anointed.

10 For a day in Your courts *is* better
than a thousand.
I would rather [1]be a doorkeeper in
the house of my God
Than dwell in the tents of
wickedness.
11 For the LORD God *is* [a]a sun and
[b]shield;
The LORD will give grace and glory;
[c]No good *thing* will He withhold
From those who walk uprightly.

12 O LORD of hosts,
[a]Blessed *is* the man who trusts in
You!

PSALM 85

Prayer that the Lord Will Restore Favor to the Land

To the Chief Musician. A Psalm [a]of the sons of Korah.

LORD, You have been favorable to Your
land;
You have [a]brought back the
captivity of Jacob.
2 You have forgiven the iniquity of
Your people;
You have covered all their sin.
Selah
3 You have taken away all Your
wrath;
You have turned from the
fierceness of Your anger.
4 [a]Restore us, O God of our salvation,
And cause Your anger toward us to
cease.
5 [a]Will You be angry with us forever?
Will You prolong Your anger to all
generations?
6 Will You not [a]revive us again,
That Your people may rejoice in
You?
7 Show us Your mercy, LORD,
And grant us Your salvation.

8 I will hear what God the LORD will
speak,
For He will speak peace
To His people and to His saints;
But let them not turn back to
[1]folly.
9 Surely [a]His salvation *is* near to
those who fear Him,
[b]That glory may dwell in our land.

9 [1] Commissioned one, Heb. *messiah*
10 [1] *stand at the threshold*
11 [a] Is. 60:19, 20 [b] Gen. 15:1 [c] Ps. 34:9, 10
12 [a] [Ps. 2:12; 40:4]
PSALM 85
title [a] Ps. 42:title
1 [a] Joel 3:1
4 [a] Ps. 80:3, 7
5 [a] Ps. 79:5
6 [a] Hab. 3:2
8 [1] *foolishness*
9 [a] Is. 46:13 [b] Zech. 2:5
10 [a] Ps. 72:3
12 [a] [Ps. 84:11]
PSALM 86
2 [1] Lit. *soul*
4 [a] Ps. 25:1; 143:8 [1] *Make glad*
5 [a] [Joel 2:13]
8 [a] [Ex. 15:11]
10 [a] [Ex. 15:11] [b] Deut. 6:4
11 [a] Ps. 27:11; 143:8

10 Mercy and truth have met
together;
[a]Righteousness and peace have
kissed.
11 Truth shall spring out of the
earth,
And righteousness shall look down
from heaven.
12 [a]Yes, the LORD will give *what is*
good;
And our land will yield its increase.
13 Righteousness will go before Him,
And shall make His footsteps *our*
pathway.

PSALM 86

Prayer for Mercy, with Meditation on the Excellencies of the Lord

A Prayer of David.

Bow down Your ear, O LORD, hear me;
For I *am* poor and needy.
2 Preserve my [1]life, for I *am* holy;
You are my God;
Save Your servant who trusts in
You!
3 Be merciful to me, O Lord,
For I cry to You all day long.
4 [1]Rejoice the soul of Your servant,
[a]For to You, O Lord, I lift up my
soul.
5 For [a]You, Lord, *are* good, and
ready to forgive,
And abundant in mercy to all those
who call upon You.

6 Give ear, O LORD, to my prayer;
And attend to the voice of my
supplications.
7 In the day of my trouble I will call
upon You,
For You will answer me.

8 [a]Among the gods *there is* none like
You, O Lord;
Nor *are there any works* like Your
works.
9 All nations whom You have made
Shall come and worship before You,
O Lord,
And shall glorify Your name.
10 For You *are* great, and [a]do
wondrous things;
[b]You alone *are* God.

11 [a]Teach me Your way, O LORD;
I will walk in Your truth;

[1]Unite my heart to fear Your name.
12 I will praise You, O Lord my God, with all my heart,
And I will glorify Your name forevermore.
13 For great *is* Your mercy toward me,
And You have delivered my soul from the depths of [1]Sheol.

14 O God, the proud have risen against me,
And a mob of violent *men* have sought my life,
And have not set You before them.
15 But [a]You, O Lord, *are* a God full of compassion, and gracious,
Longsuffering and abundant in mercy and truth.

16 Oh, turn to me, and have mercy on me!
Give Your strength to Your servant,
And save the son of Your maidservant.
17 Show me a sign for good,
That those who hate me may see *it* and be ashamed,
Because You, LORD, have helped me and comforted me.

PSALM 87

The Glories of the City of God

A Psalm of the sons of Korah. A Song.

His foundation *is* in the holy mountains.
2 [a]The LORD loves the gates of Zion
More than all the dwellings of Jacob.
3 [a]Glorious things are spoken of you,
O city of God! Selah

4 "I will make mention of [1]Rahab and Babylon to those who know Me;
Behold, O Philistia and Tyre, with Ethiopia:
'This *one* was born there.' "

5 And of Zion it will be said,
"This *one* and that *one* were born in her;
And the Most High Himself shall establish her."
6 The LORD will record,
When He [a]registers the peoples:
"This *one* was born there." Selah

7 Both the singers and the players on instruments *say,*
"All my springs *are* in you."

11 [1]Give me singleness of heart

13 [1]The abode of the dead

15 [a]Ex. 34:6

PSALM 87
2 [a]Ps. 78:67, 68

3 [a]Is. 60:1

4 [1]Egypt

6 [a]Is. 4:3

PSALM 88
title [a]1 Kin. 4:31
[1]Heb. *Maschil*

1 [a]Ps. 27:9

2 [1]Listen to

3 [a]Ps. 107:18

4 [a][Ps. 28:1]
[b]Ps. 31:12
[1]Die

5 [1]Lit. *Free*

7 [a]Ps. 42:7

8 [a]Job 19:13, 19
[b]Lam. 3:7
[1]*taken away my friends*

9 [a]Ps. 86:3

PSALM 88

A Prayer for Help in Despondency

A Song. A Psalm of the sons of Korah. To the Chief Musician. Set to "Mahalath Leannoth." A [1]Contemplation of [a]Heman the Ezrahite.

O LORD, [a]God of my salvation,
I have cried out day and night before You.
2 Let my prayer come before You;
[1]Incline Your ear to my cry.

Prayer is the issue of the quiet mind, of untroubled thoughts, it is the daughter of charity and the sister of mercy.

JEREMY TAYLOR

3 For my soul is full of troubles,
And my life [a]draws near to the grave.
4 I am counted with those who [a]go[1] down to the pit;
[b]I am like a man *who has* no strength,
5 [1]Adrift among the dead,
Like the slain who lie in the grave,
Whom You remember no more,
And who are cut off from Your hand.

6 You have laid me in the lowest pit,
In darkness, in the depths.
7 Your wrath lies heavy upon me,
And You have afflicted *me* with all [a]Your waves. Selah
8 [a]You have [1]put away my acquaintances far from me;
You have made me an abomination to them;
[b]*I am* shut up, and I cannot get out;
9 My eye wastes away because of affliction.

[a]LORD, I have called daily upon You;
I have stretched out my hands to You.
10 Will You work wonders for the dead?

Shall [1]the dead arise *and* praise
You? Selah
11 Shall Your lovingkindness be
declared in the grave?
Or Your faithfulness in the place of
destruction?
12 Shall Your wonders be known in
the dark?
And Your righteousness in the land
of forgetfulness?

13 But to You I have cried out,
O LORD,
And in the morning my prayer
comes before You.
14 LORD, why do You cast off my
soul?
Why do You hide Your face from
me?
15 I *have been* afflicted and ready to
die from *my* youth;
I suffer Your terrors;
I am distraught.
16 Your fierce wrath has gone over
me;
Your terrors have [1]cut me off.
17 They came around me all day long
like water;
They engulfed me altogether.
18 [a]Loved one and friend You have
put far from me,
And my acquaintances into
darkness.

PSALM 89

Remembering the Covenant with David, and Sorrow for Lost Blessings

A [1]Contemplation of [a]Ethan the Ezrahite.

I will sing of the mercies of the LORD
forever;
With my mouth will I make known
Your faithfulness to all
generations.
2 For I have said, "Mercy shall be
built up forever;
[a]Your faithfulness You shall establish
in the very heavens."

3 "I[a] have made a covenant with My
chosen,
I have [b]sworn to My servant David:
4 'Your seed I will establish forever,
And build up your throne [a]to all
generations.' " Selah

10 [1] shades, ghosts

16 [1] destroyed me

18 [a] Ps. 31:11; 38:11

PSALM 89
title [a] 1 Kin. 4:31
[1] Heb. *Maschil*

2 [a] [Ps. 119:89, 90]

3 [a] 1 Kin. 8:16
[b] 2 Sam. 7:11

4 [a] [Luke 1:33]

5 [a] [Ps. 19:1]

6 [a] Ps. 86:8; 113:5

7 [a] Ps. 76:7, 11

9 [a] Ps. 65:7; 93:3, 4; 107:29

10 [a] Ps. 87:4
[1] Egypt

11 [a] [Gen. 1:1]

12 [a] Josh. 19:22
[b] Josh. 11:17; 12:1

15 [a] Ps. 98:6

17 [a] Ps. 75:10; 92:10; 132:17
[1] Strength

19 [1] So with many Heb. mss.; MT, LXX, Tg., Vg. *holy ones*

5 And [a]the heavens will praise Your
wonders, O LORD;
Your faithfulness also in the
assembly of the saints.
6 [a]For who in the heavens can be
compared to the LORD?
Who among the sons of the mighty
can be likened to the LORD?
7 [a]God is greatly to be feared in the
assembly of the saints,
And to be held in reverence by all
those around Him.
8 O LORD God of hosts,
Who *is* mighty like You, O LORD?
Your faithfulness also surrounds
You.
9 [a]You rule the raging of the sea;
When its waves rise, You still them.
10 [a]You have broken [1]Rahab in pieces,
as one who is slain;
You have scattered Your enemies
with Your mighty arm.
11 [a]The heavens *are* Yours, the earth
also *is* Yours;
The world and all its fullness, You
have founded them.
12 The north and the south, You
have created them;
[a]Tabor and [b]Hermon rejoice in Your
name.
13 You have a mighty arm;
Strong is Your hand, *and* high is
Your right hand.
14 Righteousness and justice *are* the
foundation of Your throne;
Mercy and truth go before Your
face.
15 Blessed *are* the people who know
the [a]joyful sound!
They walk, O LORD, in the light of
Your countenance.
16 In Your name they rejoice all day
long,
And in Your righteousness they are
exalted.
17 For You *are* the glory of their
strength,
And in Your favor our [1]horn is
[a]exalted.
18 For our shield *belongs* to the
LORD,
And our king to the Holy One of
Israel.

19 Then You spoke in a vision to
Your [1]holy one,
And said: "I have given help to *one
who is* mighty;

I have exalted one [a]chosen from the
people.
20 [a]I have found My servant David;
With My holy oil I have anointed
him,
21 [a]With whom My hand shall be
established;
Also My arm shall strengthen him.
22 The enemy shall not [1]outwit him,
Nor the son of wickedness afflict
him.
23 I will beat down his foes before
his face,
And plague those who hate him.

24 "But My faithfulness and My mercy
shall be with him,
And in My name his horn shall be
exalted.
25 Also I will [a]set his hand over the
sea,
And his right hand over the rivers.
26 He shall cry to Me, 'You *are* [a]my
Father,
My God, and [b]the rock of my
salvation.'
27 Also I will make him [a]*My*
firstborn,
[b]The highest of the kings of the
earth.
28 [a]My mercy I will keep for him
forever,
And My covenant shall stand firm
with him.
29 His seed also I will make *to
endure* forever,
[a]And his throne [b]as the days of
heaven.

30 "If[a] his sons [b]forsake My law
And do not walk in My judgments,
31 If they [1]break My statutes
And do not keep My
commandments,
32 Then I will punish their
transgression with the rod,
And their iniquity with stripes.
33 [a]Nevertheless My lovingkindness I
will not [1]utterly take from him,
Nor [2]allow My faithfulness to fail.
34 My covenant I will not break,
Nor [a]alter the word that has gone
out of My lips.
35 Once I have sworn [a]by My
holiness;
I will not lie to David:
36 [a]His seed shall endure forever,
And his throne [b]as the sun before
Me;

19 a 1 Kin. 11:34
20 a 1 Sam. 13:14; 16:1–12
21 a Ps. 80:17
22 *1 Or exact usury from him*
25 a Ps. 72:8
26 a [1 Chr. 22:10] b 2 Sam. 22:47
27 a [Col. 1:15, 18] b Rev. 19:16
28 a Is. 55:3
29 a Jer. 33:17 b Deut. 11:21
30 a [2 Sam. 7:14] b Ps. 119:53
31 *1 profane*
33 a 2 Sam. 7:14, 15 *1* Lit. *break off* *2* Lit. *deal falsely with My faithfulness*
34 a Jer. 33:20–22
35 a Amos 4:2
36 a [Luke 1:33] b Ps. 72:17
38 a [1 Chr. 28:9] b Deut. 32:19 *1 rejected* *2* Commissioned one, Heb. *messiah*
39 a Lam. 5:16 *1 defiled*
40 *1 fortresses*
41 a Ps. 80:12
44 *1 splendor* or *brightness*
47 a Ps. 90:9 b Ps. 62:9
48 a [Eccl. 3:19] *1 experience death* *2* Or *Sheol*
49 a [2 Sam. 7:15] b Ps. 54:5
50 a Ps. 69:9, 19
51 a Ps. 74:10, 18, 22 *1* Commissioned one, Heb. *messiah*

37 It shall be established forever like
the moon,
Even *like* the faithful witness in the
sky." Selah

38 But You have [a]cast off and
[b]abhorred,[1]
You have been furious with Your
[2]anointed.
39 You have renounced the covenant
of Your servant;
[a]You have [1]profaned his crown *by
casting it* to the ground.
40 You have broken down all his
hedges;
You have brought his [1]strongholds
to ruin.
41 All who pass by the way [a]plunder
him;
He is a reproach to his neighbors.
42 You have exalted the right hand of
his adversaries;
You have made all his enemies
rejoice.
43 You have also turned back the
edge of his sword,
And have not sustained him in the
battle.
44 You have made his [1]glory cease,
And cast his throne down to the
ground.
45 The days of his youth You have
shortened;
You have covered him with shame.
Selah

46 How long, LORD?
Will You hide Yourself forever?
Will Your wrath burn like fire?
47 Remember how short my time [a]is;
For what [b]futility have You created
all the children of men?
48 What man can live and not [1]see
[a]death?
Can he deliver his life from the
power of [2]the grave? Selah

49 Lord, where *are* Your former
lovingkindnesses,
Which You [a]swore to David [b]in
Your truth?
50 Remember, Lord, the reproach of
Your servants—
[a]*How* I bear in my bosom *the
reproach of* all the many peoples,
51 [a]With which Your enemies have
reproached, O LORD,
With which they have reproached
the footsteps of Your [1]anointed.

52 [a]Blessed *be* the LORD forevermore!
Amen and Amen.

BOOK FOUR
Psalms 90—106

PSALM 90

The Eternity of God, and Man's Frailty

A Prayer [a]of Moses the man of God.

Lord, [a]You have been our [1]dwelling place in all generations.
2 [a]Before the mountains were brought forth,
Or ever You [1]had formed the earth and the world,
Even from everlasting to everlasting, You *are* God.

3 You turn man to destruction,
And say, [a]"Return, O children of men."
4 [a]For a thousand years in Your sight
Are like yesterday when it is past,
And *like* a watch in the night.
5 You carry them away *like* a flood;
[a]*They are* like a sleep.
In the morning [b]they are like grass *which* grows up:
6 In the morning it flourishes and grows up;
In the evening it is cut down and withers.

7 For we have been consumed by Your anger,
And by Your wrath we are terrified.
8 [a]You have set our iniquities before You,
Our [b]secret *sins* in the light of Your countenance.
9 For all our days have passed away in Your wrath;
We finish our years like a sigh.
10 The days of our lives *are* seventy years;
And if by reason of strength *they are* eighty years,
Yet their boast *is* only labor and sorrow;
For it is soon cut off, and we fly away.
11 Who knows the power of Your anger?
For as the fear of You, *so is* Your wrath.
12 [a]So teach *us* to number our days,
That we may gain a heart of wisdom.

13 Return, O LORD!
How long?
And [a]have compassion on Your servants.
14 Oh, satisfy us early with Your mercy,
[a]That we may rejoice and be glad all our days!
15 Make us glad according to the days *in which* You have afflicted us,
The years *in which* we have seen evil.
16 Let [a]Your work appear to Your servants,
And Your glory to their children.
17 [a]And let the beauty of the LORD our God be upon us,
And [b]establish the work of our hands for us;
Yes, establish the work of our hands.

PSALM 91

Safety of Abiding in the Presence of God

He [a]who dwells in the secret place of the Most High
Shall abide [b]under the shadow of the Almighty.
2 [a]I will say of the LORD, "*He is* my refuge and my fortress;
My God, in Him I will trust."

3 Surely [a]He shall deliver you from the snare of the [1]fowler
And from the perilous pestilence.
4 [a]He shall cover you with His feathers,
And under His wings you shall take refuge;
His truth *shall be your* shield and [1]buckler.
5 [a]You shall not be afraid of the terror by night,
Nor of the arrow *that* flies by day,
6 *Nor* of the pestilence *that* walks in darkness,
Nor of the destruction *that* lays waste at noonday.

7 A thousand may fall at your side,
And ten thousand at your right hand;
But it shall not come near you.

---

52 a Ps. 41:13

PSALM 90
title a Deut. 33:1
1 a [Ezek. 11:16] *1* LXX, Tg., Vg. *refuge*
2 a [Prov. 8:25, 26] *1* Lit. *gave birth to*
3 a Gen. 3:19
4 a 2 Pet. 3:8
5 a Ps. 73:20 b Is. 40:6
8 a Ps. 50:21 b Ps. 19:12
12 a Ps. 39:4
13 a Deut. 32:36
14 a Ps. 85:6
16 a Hab. 3:2
17 a Ps. 27:4 b Is. 26:12

PSALM 91
1 a Ps. 27:5; 31:20; 32:7 b Ps. 17:8
2 a Ps. 142:5
3 a Ps. 124:7 *1* One who catches birds in a trap or snare
4 a Ps. 17:8 *1* A small shield
5 a [Job 5:19]

Psalm 91

Dear Woman of Destiny,

I live in a nation where Christians are often persecuted for their faith. We daily depend upon the Lord for His protection. He is the only One who can help. The psalmist David depicted God's response to his cry for help: "He shall call upon Me, and I will answer him; I will be with him in trouble; I will deliver him and honor him" (Ps. 91:15).

Psalm 91 has long been a source of comfort for believers. It includes some instructions for us: to dwell in "the secret place of the Most High" (v. 1), to set our love upon Him and to know His name (v. 14), and to call upon Him (v. 15). Then we can always count on God to be with us. We can always hide in Him.

I'll never forget the face of Dr. Assim [name changed]. The moment I stood before the crowd I noticed his face. It had a glow that set him apart. His peace was contagious, and his eyes were deep pools of love. Later I learned that his family had dealt him such a vicious beating after he confessed Jesus that he was hospitalized for six months. As I looked on his face, I couldn't help but think of Stephen, the first New Testament martyr, whose face must have shone like an angel when he "gazed into heaven and saw the glory of God" (Acts 7:55).

How could this be? Stephen must have been dwelling "in the secret place of the Most High" to offer forgiveness to a stone-throwing mob (Ps. 91:1). He was secure under the refuge of the Lord's wings (see v. 4). John Dawson says, "You can go through anything if you know your Father loves you." And David's words in Psalm 91 seem to highlight this truth as he proclaims, "He shall deliver you . . . He shall cover you with His feathers, and under His wings you shall take refuge; His truth shall be your shield and buckler . . . for He shall give His angels charge over you, to keep you in all your ways. . . . You shall tread upon the lion and the cobra" (vv. 3, 4, 11, 13).

Psalm 91 is an excellent antidote for fear. If you struggle with fear, the sixteen verses of this psalm would be good for you to memorize. The first step to overcoming fear is to "dwell in the secret place of the Most High," or to make sure that you live in close relationship with the Lord. James 4:8 tells us that if we draw near to God, He will draw near to us. He is as eager for us to live close to Him as we are to do so. Colossians 3:3 reminds us that, as believers, our lives are "hidden with Christ in God." Spiritual victory is assured as we "abide under the shadow of the Almighty" (Ps. 91:1).

Amy Carmichael knew about finding her refuge in Jesus. Her years of service as a pioneer worker in India yielded suffering and a life so fruitful it is beyond measure. She wrote a short poem that became her life's prayer. May your heart receive strength by these words as recorded in Frank Houghton's *Amy Carmichael of Dohnavur:* "Give me the love that leads the way, the faith that nothing can dismay, the hope no disappointments tire, the passion that will burn like fire, let me not sink to be a clod: Make me Thy fuel, Flame of God."

Kathleen Dillard

8 Only [a]with your eyes shall you
look,
And see the reward of the wicked.
9 Because you have made the LORD,
who is [a]my refuge,
Even the Most High, [b]your dwelling
place,
10 [a]No evil shall befall you,
Nor shall any plague come near
your dwelling;
11 [a]For He shall give His angels
charge over you,
To keep you in all your ways.
12 In *their* hands they shall [1]bear
you up,
[a]Lest you [2]dash your foot against a
stone.
13 You shall tread upon the lion and
the cobra,
The young lion and the serpent you
shall trample underfoot.
14 "Because he has set his love upon
Me, therefore I will deliver him;
I will [1]set him on high, because he
has [a]known My name.
15 He shall [a]call upon Me, and I will
answer him;
I *will be* [b]with him in trouble;
I will deliver him and honor him.
16 With [1]long life I will satisfy him,
And show him My salvation."

PSALM 92

Praise to the Lord for His Love and Faithfulness

A Psalm. A Song for the Sabbath day.

It is [a]good to give thanks to the LORD,
And to sing praises to Your name,
O Most High;
2 To [a]declare Your lovingkindness in
the morning,
And Your faithfulness every night,
3 [a]On an instrument of ten strings,
On the lute,
And on the harp,
With harmonious sound.
4 For You, LORD, have made me glad
through Your work;
I will triumph in the works of Your
hands.
5 [a]O LORD, how great are Your works!
[b]Your thoughts are very deep.
6 [a]A senseless man does not know,
Nor does a fool understand this.
7 When [a]the wicked [1]spring up like
grass,
And when all the workers of
iniquity flourish,
It is that they may be destroyed
forever.
8 [a]But You, LORD, *are* on high
forevermore.
9 For behold, Your enemies, O LORD,
For behold, Your enemies shall
perish;
All the workers of iniquity shall [a]be
scattered.
10 But [a]my [1]horn You have exalted
like a wild ox;
I have been [b]anointed with fresh
oil.
11 [a]My eye also has seen *my desire* on
my enemies;
My ears hear *my desire* on the
wicked
Who rise up against me.
12 [a]The righteous shall flourish like a
palm tree,
He shall grow like a cedar in
Lebanon.
13 Those who are planted in the
house of the LORD
Shall flourish in the courts of our
God.
14 They shall still bear fruit in old
age;
They shall be [1]fresh and
[2]flourishing,
15 To declare that the LORD is
upright;
[a]*He is* my rock, and [b]*there is* no
unrighteousness in Him.

PSALM 93

The Eternal Reign of the Lord

The [a]LORD reigns, He is clothed with
majesty;
The LORD is clothed,
[b]He has girded Himself with
strength.
Surely the world is established, so
that it cannot be [1]moved.
2 [a]Your throne *is* established from of
old;
You *are* from everlasting.
3 The floods have [1]lifted up, O LORD,
The floods have lifted up their
voice;
The floods lift up their waves.

---

8 a Mal. 1:5
9 a Ps. 91:2 b Ps. 90:1
10 a [Prov. 12:21]
11 a [Heb. 1:14]
12 a Matt. 4:6 *1 lift* *2 strike*
14 a [Ps. 9:10] *1 exalt him*
15 a Ps. 50:15 b Is. 43:2
16 1 Lit. *length of days*

PSALM 92
1 a Ps. 147:1
2 a Ps. 89:1
3 a 1 Chr. 23:5
5 a Ps. 40:5 b [Is. 28:29]
6 a Ps. 73:22
7 a Job 12:6 *1 sprout*
8 a [Ps. 83:18]
9 a Ps. 68:1
10 a Ps. 89:17 b Ps. 23:5 1 Strength
11 a Ps. 54:7
12 a Ps. 52:8
14 1 Full of oil or sap, lit. *fat* *2 green*
15 a [Deut. 32:4] b [Rom. 9:14]

PSALM 93
1 a Ps. 96:10 b Ps. 65:6 *1 shaken*
2 a Ps. 45:6
3 *1 raised up*

4 [a]The LORD on high *is* mightier
Than the noise of many waters,
Than the mighty waves of the sea.

5 Your testimonies are very sure;
Holiness adorns Your house,
O LORD, [1]forever.

PSALM 94

God the Refuge of the Righteous

O LORD God, [a]to whom vengeance belongs—
O God, to whom vengeance belongs, shine forth!
2 Rise up, O [a]Judge of the earth;
[1]Render punishment to the proud.
3 LORD, [a]how long will the wicked,
How long will the wicked triumph?

4 They [a]utter speech, *and* speak insolent things;
All the workers of iniquity boast in themselves.
5 They break in pieces Your people, O LORD,
And afflict Your heritage.
6 They slay the widow and the stranger,
And murder the fatherless.
7 [a]Yet they say, "The LORD does not see,
Nor does the God of Jacob [1]understand."

8 Understand, you senseless among the people;
And *you* fools, when will you be wise?
9 [a]He who planted the ear, shall He not hear?
He who formed the eye, shall He not see?
10 He who [1]instructs the [2]nations, shall He not correct,
He who teaches man knowledge?
11 The LORD [a]knows the thoughts of man,
That they *are* futile.

12 Blessed *is* the man whom You [a]instruct, O LORD,
And teach out of Your law,
13 That You may give him [1]rest from the days of adversity,
Until the pit is dug for the wicked.
14 For the LORD will not [1]cast off His people,
Nor will He forsake His inheritance.
15 But judgment will return to righteousness,
And all the upright in heart will follow it.

16 Who will rise up for me against the evildoers?
Who will stand up for me against the workers of iniquity?
17 Unless the LORD *had been* my help,
My soul would soon have settled in silence.
18 If I say, "My foot slips,"
Your mercy, O LORD, will hold me up.
19 In the multitude of my anxieties within me,
Your comforts delight my soul.

20 Shall [a]the throne of iniquity, which devises evil by law,
Have fellowship with You?
21 They gather together against the life of the righteous,
And condemn [a]innocent blood.
22 But the LORD has been my defense,
And my God the rock of my refuge.
23 He has brought on them their own iniquity,
And shall [1]cut them off in their own wickedness;
The LORD our God shall cut them off.

Blessed is ____, O Lord, whom You instruct and teach out of Your law. Lord, give them rest from the days of adversity.
FROM PSALM 94:12, 13

PSALM 95

A Call to Worship and Obedience

Oh come, let us sing to the LORD!
Let us shout joyfully to the Rock of our salvation.
2 Let us come before His presence with thanksgiving;
Let us shout joyfully to Him with [a]psalms.

---

4 a Ps. 65:7
5 1 Lit. *for length of days*
PSALM 94
1 a [Nah. 1:2]
2 a [Gen. 18:25]
1 *Repay with*
3 a [Job 20:5]
4 a Ps. 31:18
7 a Ps. 10:11
1 *pay attention*
9 a [Ex. 4:11]
10 1 *disciplines*
2 *Gentiles*
11 a 1 Cor. 3:20
12 a [Heb. 12:5, 6]
13 1 *relief*
14 1 *abandon*
20 a Amos 6:3
21 a [Ex. 23:7]
23 1 *destroy them*
PSALM 95
2 a James 5:13

3 For [a]the LORD *is* the great God,
And the great King above all gods.
4 [1]In His hand *are* the deep places of
the earth;
The heights of the hills *are* His
also.
5 [a]The sea *is* His, for He made it;
And His hands formed the dry *land.*

6 Oh come, let us worship and bow
down;
Let [a]us kneel before the LORD our
Maker.
7 For He *is* our God,
And [a]we *are* the people of His
pasture,
And the sheep [1]of His hand.

[b]Today, if you will hear His voice:
8 "Do not harden your hearts, as in
the [1]rebellion,
[a]As *in* the day of [2]trial in the
wilderness,
9 When [a]your fathers tested Me;
They tried Me, though they [b]saw
My work.
10 For [a]forty years I was [1]grieved
with *that* generation,
And said, 'It *is* a people who go
astray in their hearts,
And they do not know My ways.'
11 So [a]I swore in My wrath,
'They shall not enter My rest.' "

PSALM 96

A Song of Praise to God Coming in Judgment

Oh, [a]sing to the LORD a new song!
Sing to the LORD, all the earth.
2 Sing to the LORD, bless His name;
Proclaim the good news of His
salvation from day to day.
3 Declare His glory among the
[1]nations,
His wonders among all peoples.

4 For [a]the LORD *is* great and [b]greatly
to be praised;
[c]He *is* to be feared above all gods.
5 For [a]all the gods of the peoples *are*
idols,
[b]But the LORD made the heavens.
6 Honor and majesty *are* before Him;
Strength and [a]beauty *are* in His
sanctuary.

7 [a]Give[1] to the LORD, O families of
the peoples,
Give to the LORD glory and
strength.
8 [1]Give to the LORD the glory *due* His
name;
Bring an offering, and come into
His courts.
9 Oh, worship the LORD [a]in the
beauty of holiness!
Tremble before Him, all the earth.

10 Say among the [1]nations, [a]"The
LORD reigns;
The world also is firmly established,
It shall not be [2]moved;
[b]He shall judge the peoples
righteously."

11 [a]Let the heavens rejoice, and let
the earth be glad;
[b]Let the sea roar, and [1]all its
fullness;
12 Let the field be joyful, and all that
is in it.
Then all the trees of the woods will
rejoice before the LORD.
13 For He is coming, for He is
coming to judge the earth.
[a]He shall judge the world with
righteousness,
And the peoples with His truth.

PSALM 97

A Song of Praise to the Sovereign Lord

The LORD [a]reigns;
Let the earth rejoice;
Let the multitude of [1]isles be glad!
2 [a]Clouds and darkness surround
Him;
[b]Righteousness and justice *are* the
foundation of His throne.
3 [a]A fire goes before Him,
And burns up His enemies round
about.
4 [a]His lightnings light the world;
The earth sees and trembles.
5 [a]The mountains melt like wax at
the presence of the LORD,
At the presence of the Lord of the
whole earth.
6 [a]The heavens declare His
righteousness,
And all the peoples see His glory.

7 [a]Let all be put to shame who serve
carved images,
Who boast of idols.
[b]Worship Him, all *you* gods.

3 **a** [Ps. 96:4]
4 *1* In His possession
5 **a** Gen. 1:9, 10
6 **a** [Phil. 2:10]
7 **a** Ps. 79:13 **b** Heb. 3:7–11, 15; 4:7 *1* Under His care
8 **a** Ex. 17:2–7 *1* Or *Meribah,* lit. *Strife, Contention* *2* Or *Massah,* lit. *Trial, Testing*
9 **a** Ps. 78:18 **b** Num. 14:22
10 **a** Heb. 3:10, 17 *1 disgusted*
11 **a** Heb. 4:3, 5

PSALM 96
1 **a** 1 Chr. 16:23–33
3 *1 Gentiles*
4 **a** Ps. 145:3 **b** Ps. 18:3 **c** Ps. 95:3
5 **a** [Jer. 10:11] **b** Is. 42:5
6 **a** Ps. 29:2
7 **a** Ps. 29:1, 2 *1 Ascribe*
8 *1 Ascribe*
9 **a** Ps. 29:2
10 **a** Ps. 93:1; 97:1 **b** Ps. 67:4 *1 Gentiles* *2 shaken*
11 **a** Ps. 69:34 **b** Ps. 98:7 *1 all that is in it*
13 **a** [Rev. 19:11]

PSALM 97
1 **a** [Ps. 96:10] *1* Or *coastlands*
2 **a** Ps. 18:11 **b** [Ps. 89:14]
3 **a** Ps. 18:8
4 **a** Ex. 19:18
5 **a** Mic. 1:4
6 **a** Ps. 19:1
7 **a** [Ex. 20:4] **b** [Heb. 1:6]

8 Zion hears and is glad,
And the daughters of Judah rejoice
Because of Your judgments,
O LORD.
9 For You, LORD, *are* [a]most high
above all the earth;
[b]You are exalted far above all gods.

10 You who love the LORD, [a]hate evil!
[b]He preserves the souls of His saints;
[c]He delivers them out of the hand of
the wicked.
11 [a]Light is sown for the righteous,
And gladness for the upright in
heart.
12 [a]Rejoice in the LORD, you
righteous,
[b]And give thanks [1]at the
remembrance of [2]His holy name.

PSALM 98

A Song of Praise to the Lord for His Salvation and Judgment

A Psalm.

Oh, [a]sing to the LORD a new song!
For He has [b]done marvelous things;
His right hand and His holy arm
have gained Him the victory.
2 [a]The LORD has made known His
salvation;
[b]His righteousness He has revealed
in the sight of the [1]nations.
3 He has remembered His mercy and
His faithfulness to the house of
Israel;
[a]All the ends of the earth have seen
the salvation of our God.

4 Shout joyfully to the LORD, all the
earth;
Break forth in song, rejoice, and
sing praises.
5 Sing to the LORD with the harp,
With the harp and the sound of a
psalm,
6 With trumpets and the sound of a
horn;
Shout joyfully before the LORD, the
King.

7 Let the sea roar, and all its
fullness,
The world and those who dwell in
it;
8 Let the rivers clap *their* hands;
Let the hills be joyful together
before the LORD,
9 [a]For He is coming to judge the
earth.
With righteousness He shall judge
the world,
And the peoples with [1]equity.

PSALM 99

Praise to the Lord for His Holiness

The LORD reigns;
Let the peoples tremble!
[a]He dwells *between* the cherubim;
Let the earth be [1]moved!
2 The LORD *is* great in Zion,
And He *is* high above all the
peoples.
3 Let them praise Your great and
awesome name—
[1]He *is* holy.

4 The King's strength also loves
justice;
You have established equity;
You have executed justice and
righteousness in Jacob.
5 Exalt the LORD our God,
And worship at His footstool—
He *is* holy.

6 Moses and Aaron were among His
priests,
And Samuel was among those who
[a]called upon His name;
They called upon the LORD, and He
answered them.
7 He spoke to them in the cloudy
pillar;
They kept His testimonies and the
[1]ordinance He gave them.

8 You answered them, O LORD our
God;
You were to them
God-Who-Forgives,
Though You took vengeance on
their deeds.
9 Exalt the LORD our God,
And worship at His holy hill;
For the LORD our God *is* holy.

PSALM 100

A Song of Praise for the Lord's Faithfulness to His People

[a]A Psalm of Thanksgiving.

Make [a]a joyful shout to the LORD, [1]all
you lands!

97:9 a Ps. 83:18 b Ex. 18:11
10 a [Ps. 34:14] b Prov. 2:8 c Ps. 37:40
11 a Job 22:28
12 a Ps. 33:1 b Ps. 30:4 1 Or *for the memory* 2 Or *His holiness*

PSALM 98
1 a Is. 42:10 b Ex. 15:11
2 a Is. 52:10 b Is. 62:2 1 *Gentiles*
3 a Luke 3:6
9 a [Ps. 96:10, 13] 1 *uprightness*

PSALM 99
1 a Ex. 25:22 1 *shaken*
3 1 Or *It*
6 a 1 Sam. 7:9; 12:18
7 1 *statute*

PSALM 100
title a Ps. 145:title
1 a Ps. 95:1 1 Lit. *all the earth*

2 Serve the LORD with gladness;
Come before His presence with singing.
3 Know that the LORD, He *is* God;
[a]*It is* He *who* has made us, and [1]not we ourselves;
[b]*We are* His people and the sheep of His pasture.

3 a[Eph. 2:10] bEzek. 34:30, 31 *1* So with Kt., LXX, Vg.; Qr., many Heb. mss., Tg. *we are His*
4 aPs. 66:13; 116:17–19
5 aPs. 136:1

4 [a]Enter into His gates with thanksgiving,
And into His courts with praise.
Be thankful to Him, *and* bless His name.
5 For the LORD *is* good;
[a]His mercy *is* everlasting,
And His truth *endures* to all generations.

SUSANNA WESLEY

You know you've done something right in raising your children when your two youngest boys change the face of Christianity. And for all her strength and perseverance in raising her children, Susanna Wesley (1669–1742) can take some credit for the results: John founded Methodism, while Charles penned almost 1,900 poems and hymns, dozens of which are sung today.

Susanna was one of twenty-five children born to Dr. Samuel Annesley, a devout Puritan. While still a youth, her strong will and independence showed as she left her Dissent upbringing to join the Church of England. She soon met Samuel Wesley, who six years later became her husband. After they settled in Epworth, Samuel's imprudent handling of money left Susanna struggling to raise her children while he made frequent trips to London serving as an area representative in the Church of England's convocation.

In his absence, Susanna was determined to keep the worship of God forefront in her home, and since there were no Sunday evening services at church, she began reading and discussing sermons with her children. These "discussions" evolved into meetings where more than two hundred people packed her house to hear her speak—this in an era during which women were kept silent in church, were not allowed to vote, and were often treated no better than high servants.

Besides dealing with an oft-estranged husband, Wesley became familiar with trials and tragedies. She bore nineteen children in her first nineteen years of marriage. Of these nineteen, nine died before the age of two. The family's home twice burned to the ground.

Yet as sorrow continued to dwell in her household, she made sure her children received the best education and upbringing possible, instructing them in Hebrew and Greek, while teaching all the children to read and memorize Scripture as soon as they could dress themselves!

Susanna wasn't just a mother destined to raise two pioneers of faith, although that was certainly worthy of note! She served to give the world a peek at the godly strength a woman can possess and the powerful, lasting influence she can effect for the kingdom of God.

PSALM 101

Promised Faithfulness to the Lord

A Psalm of David.

I will sing of mercy and justice;
To You, O LORD, I will sing praises.

2 I will behave wisely in a [1]perfect way.
Oh, when will You come to me?
I will [a]walk within my house with a perfect heart.

3 I will set nothing [1]wicked before my eyes;
[a]I hate the work of those [b]who fall away;
It shall not cling to me.
4 A perverse heart shall depart from me;
I will not [a]know wickedness.

5 Whoever secretly slanders his neighbor,
Him I will destroy;
[a]The one who has a haughty look and a proud heart,
Him I will not endure.

6 My eyes *shall be* on the faithful of the land,
That they may dwell with me;
He who walks in a [1]perfect way,
He shall serve me.
7 He who works deceit shall not dwell within my house;
He who tells lies shall not [1]continue in my presence.
8 [a]Early I will destroy all the wicked of the land,
That I may cut off all the evildoers [b]from the city of the LORD.

PSALM 102

The Lord's Eternal Love

A Prayer of the afflicted, [a]when he is overwhelmed and pours out his complaint before the LORD.

Hear my prayer, O LORD,
And let my cry come to You.
2 [a]Do not hide Your face from me in the day of my trouble;
Incline Your ear to me;
In the day that I call, answer me speedily.

3 For my days [1]are [a]consumed like smoke,
And my bones are burned like a hearth.
4 My heart is stricken and withered like grass,
So that I forget to eat my bread.
5 Because of the sound of my groaning
My bones cling to my [1]skin.
6 I am like a pelican of the wilderness;
I am like an owl of the desert.
7 I lie awake,
And am like a sparrow alone on the housetop.

8 My enemies reproach me all day long;
Those who deride me swear an oath against me.
9 For I have eaten ashes like bread,
And mingled my drink with weeping,
10 Because of Your indignation and Your wrath;
For You have lifted me up and cast me away.
11 My days *are* like a shadow that lengthens,
And I wither away like grass.

12 But You, O LORD, shall endure forever,
And the remembrance of Your name to all generations.
13 You will arise *and* have mercy on Zion;
For the time to favor her,
Yes, the set time, has come.
14 For Your servants take pleasure in her stones,
And show favor to her dust.
15 So the [1]nations shall [a]fear the name of the LORD,
And all the kings of the earth Your glory.
16 For the LORD shall build up Zion;
[a]He shall appear in His glory.
17 [a]He shall regard the prayer of the destitute,
And shall not despise their prayer.

18 This will be [a]written for the generation to come,
That [b]a people yet to be created may praise the LORD.
19 For He [a]looked down from the height of His sanctuary;
From heaven the LORD viewed the earth,

PSALM 101
2 a 1 Kin. 11:4 *1 blameless*
3 a Ps. 97:10 b Josh. 23:6 *1 worthless*
4 a [Ps. 119:115]
5 a Prov. 6:17
6 *1 blameless*
7 *1 Lit. be established*
8 a Jer. 21:12 b Ps. 48:2, 8

PSALM 102
title a Ps. 61:2
2 a Ps. 27:9; 69:17
3 a James 4:14 *1 Lit. end in*
5 *1 flesh*
15 a 1 Kin. 8:43 *1 Gentiles*
16 a [Is. 60:1, 2]
17 a Neh. 1:6
18 a [Rom. 15:4] b Ps. 22:31
19 a Deut. 26:15

20 [a]To hear the groaning of the prisoner,
To release those appointed to death,
21 To [a]declare the name of the LORD in Zion,
And His praise in Jerusalem,
22 [a]When the peoples are gathered together,
And the kingdoms, to serve the LORD.

23 He weakened my strength in the way;
He [a]shortened my days.
24 [a]I said, "O my God,
Do not take me away in the midst of my days;
[b]Your years *are* throughout all generations.
25 [a]Of old You laid the foundation of the earth,
And the heavens *are* the work of Your hands.
26 [a]They will perish, but You will [1]endure;
Yes, they will all grow old like a garment;
Like a cloak You will change them,
And they will be changed.
27 But [a]You *are* the same,
And Your years will have no end.
28 [a]The children of Your servants will continue,
And their descendants will be established before You."

PSALM 103

Praise for the Lord's Mercies

A Psalm of David.

Bless [a]the LORD, O my soul;
And all that is within me, *bless* His holy name!
2 Bless the LORD, O my soul,
And forget not all His benefits:
3 [a]Who forgives all your iniquities,
Who [b]heals all your diseases,
4 Who redeems your life from destruction,
[a]Who crowns you with lovingkindness and tender mercies,
5 Who satisfies your mouth with good *things,*
So that [a]your youth is renewed like the eagle's.

20 a Ps. 79:11
21 a Ps. 22:22
22 a [Is. 2:2, 3; 49:22, 23; 60:3]
23 a Job 21:21
24 a Is. 38:10 b [Ps. 90:2]
25 a [Heb. 1:10–12]
26 a Is. 34:4; 51:6 *1 continue*
27 a [Mal. 3:6]
28 a Ps. 69:36
PSALM 103
1 a Ps. 104:1, 35
3 a Ps. 130:8 b [Ex. 15:26]
4 a [Ps. 5:12]
5 a [Is. 40:31]
7 a Ps. 147:19
8 a [Ex. 34:6, 7]
9 a [Ps. 30:5]
10 a [Ezra 9:13]
12 a [Is. 38:17; 43:25]
13 a Mal. 3:17
14 *1 Understands our constitution*
15 a 1 Pet. 1:24
16 a [Is. 40:7] b Job 7:10 *1 not*

6 The LORD executes righteousness
And justice for all who are oppressed.
7 [a]He made known His ways to Moses,
His acts to the children of Israel.
8 [a]The LORD *is* merciful and gracious,
Slow to anger, and abounding in mercy.
9 [a]He will not always strive *with us,*
Nor will He keep *His anger* forever.
10 [a]He has not dealt with us according to our sins,
Nor punished us according to our iniquities.

Eternal Father, I pray that ____ will bless You, not forgetting any of Your benefits: for You forgive all their iniquities, You heal all their diseases, You redeem their lives from destruction, You crown them with lovingkindness and tender mercies, You satisfy their mouths with good things, so that their youth is renewed like the eagle's.

FROM PSALM 103:2–5

11 For as the heavens are high above the earth,
So great is His mercy toward those who fear Him;
12 As far as the east is from the west,
So far has He [a]removed our transgressions from us.
13 [a]As a father pities *his* children,
So the LORD pities those who fear Him.
14 For He [1]knows our frame;
He remembers that we *are* dust.
15 *As for* man, [a]his days *are* like grass;
As a flower of the field, so he flourishes.
16 [a]For the wind passes over it, and it is [1]gone,
And [b]its place remembers it no more.

17 But the mercy of the LORD *is* from
everlasting to everlasting
On those who fear Him,
And His righteousness to children's
children,
18 [a]To such as keep His covenant,
And to those who remember His
commandments to do them.

19 The LORD has established His
throne in heaven,
And [a]His kingdom rules over all.

20 [a]Bless the LORD, you His angels,
Who excel in strength, who [b]do His
word,
Heeding the voice of His word.
21 Bless the LORD, all *you* His hosts,
[a]*You* [1]ministers of His, who do His
pleasure.
22 Bless the LORD, all His works,
In all places of His dominion.

Bless the LORD, O my soul!

PSALM 104

Praise to the Sovereign Lord for His Creation and Providence

Bless [a]the LORD, O my soul!

O LORD my God, You are very
great:
You are clothed with honor and
majesty,
2 Who cover *Yourself* with light as
with a garment,
Who stretch out the heavens like a
curtain.
3 [a]He lays the beams of His upper
chambers in the waters,
Who makes the clouds His chariot,
Who walks on the wings of the
wind,
4 Who makes His angels spirits,
His [1]ministers a flame of fire.
5 *You who* [1]laid the foundations of
the earth,
So *that* it should not be moved
forever,
6 You [a]covered it with the deep as
with a garment;
The waters stood above the
mountains.
7 At Your rebuke they fled;
At the voice of Your thunder they
hastened away.
8 [1]They went up over the mountains;
They went down into the valleys,
To the place which You founded for
them.
9 You have [a]set a boundary that they
may not pass over,
[b]That they may not return to cover
the earth.

10 He sends the springs into the
valleys;
They flow among the hills.
11 They give drink to every beast of
the field;
The wild donkeys quench their
thirst.
12 By them the birds of the heavens
have their home;
They sing among the branches.
13 [a]He waters the hills from His
upper chambers;
The earth is satisfied with [b]the fruit
of Your works.

14 [a]He causes the grass to grow for
the cattle,
And vegetation for the service of
man,
That he may bring forth [b]food from
the earth,
15 And [a]wine *that* makes glad the
heart of man,
Oil to make *his* face shine,
And bread *which* strengthens man's
heart.
16 The trees of the LORD are full *of
sap,*
The cedars of Lebanon which He
planted,
17 Where the birds make their nests;
The stork has her home in the fir
trees.
18 The high hills *are* for the wild
goats;
The cliffs are a refuge for the
[a]rock[1] badgers.

19 [a]He appointed the moon for
seasons;
The [b]sun knows its going down.
20 [a]You make darkness, and it is
night,
In which all the beasts of the forest
creep about.
21 [a]The young lions roar after their
prey,
And seek their food from God.
22 *When* the sun rises, they gather
together
And lie down in their dens.
23 Man goes out to [a]his work

---

18 a [Deut. 7:9]
19 a [Dan. 4:17, 25]
20 a Ps. 148:2 b [Matt. 6:10]
21 a [Heb. 1:14] *1 servants*

PSALM 104
1 a Ps. 103:1
3 a [Amos 9:6]
4 *1 servants*
5 *1* Lit. *founded the earth upon her bases*
6 a Gen. 1:6
8 *1* Or *The mountains rose up; The valleys sank down*
9 a [Jer. 5:22] b Gen. 9:11–15
13 a Ps. 147:8 b Jer. 10:13
14 a Gen. 1:29 b Job 28:5
15 a Judg. 9:13
18 a Lev. 11:5 *1 rock hyraxes*
19 a Gen. 1:14 b Ps. 19:6
20 a [Is. 45:7]
21 a Job 38:39
23 a Gen. 3:19

And to his labor until the evening.

24 [a]O LORD, how manifold are Your works!
In wisdom You have made them all.
The earth is full of Your [b]possessions—
25 This great and wide sea,
In which *are* innumerable teeming things,
Living things both small and great.
26 There the ships sail about;
There is that [a]Leviathan[1]
Which You have [2]made to play there.

27 [a]These all wait for You,
That You may give *them* their food in due season.
28 *What* You give them they gather in;
You open Your hand, they are filled with good.
29 You hide Your face, they are troubled;
[a]You take away their breath, they die and return to their dust.
30 [a]You send forth Your Spirit, they are created;
And You renew the face of the earth.

31 May the glory of the LORD endure forever;
May the LORD [a]rejoice in His works.
32 He looks on the earth, and it [a]trembles;
[b]He touches the hills, and they smoke.

33 [a]I will sing to the LORD as long as I live;
I will sing praise to my God while I have my being.
34 May my [a]meditation be sweet to Him;
I will be glad in the LORD.
35 May [a]sinners be consumed from the earth,
And the wicked be no more.

Bless the LORD, O my soul!
[1]Praise the LORD!

PSALM 105

The Eternal Faithfulness of the Lord

Oh, [a]give thanks to the LORD!
Call upon His name;
[b]Make known His deeds among the peoples!
2 Sing to Him, sing psalms to Him;
[a]Talk of all His wondrous works!
3 Glory in His holy name;
Let the hearts of those rejoice who seek the LORD!
4 Seek the LORD and His strength;
[a]Seek His face evermore!
5 [a]Remember His marvelous works which He has done,
His wonders, and the judgments of His mouth,
6 O seed of Abraham His servant,
You children of Jacob, His chosen ones!

7 He *is* the LORD our God;
[a]His judgments *are* in all the earth.
8 He [a]remembers His covenant forever,
The word *which* He commanded, for a thousand generations,
9 [a]*The covenant* which He made with Abraham,
And His oath to Isaac,
10 And confirmed it to Jacob for a statute,
To Israel *as* an everlasting covenant,
11 Saying, [a]"To you I will give the land of Canaan
As the allotment of your inheritance,"
12 [a]When they were few in number,
Indeed very few, [b]and strangers in it.
13 When they went from one nation to another,
From *one* kingdom to another people,
14 [a]He permitted no one to do them wrong;
Yes, [b]He rebuked kings for their sakes,
15 *Saying,* "Do not touch My anointed ones,
And do My prophets no harm."

16 Moreover [a]He called for a famine in the land;
He destroyed all the [b]provision of bread.
17 [a]He sent a man before them—
Joseph—*who* [b]was sold as a slave.
18 [a]They hurt his feet with fetters,
[1]He was laid in irons.
19 Until the time that his word came to pass,

---

24 a Prov. 3:19 b Ps. 65:9
26 a Job 41:1 *1* A large sea creature of unknown identity *2* Lit. *formed*
27 a Ps. 136:25
29 a Job 34:15
30 a Is. 32:15
31 a Gen. 1:31
32 a Hab. 3:10 b Ps. 144:5
33 a Ps. 63:4
34 a Ps. 19:14
35 a Ps. 37:38 *1* Heb. *Hallelujah*

PSALM 105
1 a Is. 12:4 b Ps. 145:12
2 a Ps. 119:27
4 a Ps. 27:8
5 a Ps. 77:11
7 a [Is. 26:9]
8 a Luke 1:72
9 a Gen. 17:2
11 a Gen. 13:15; 15:18
12 a [Deut. 7:7] b Heb. 11:9
14 a Gen. 35:5 b Gen. 12:17
16 a Gen. 41:54 b Lev. 26:26
17 a [Gen. 45:5] b Gen. 37:28, 36
18 a Gen. 40:15 *1* His soul came into iron

[a]The word of the LORD tested him.
20 [a]The king sent and released him,
The ruler of the people let him go
free.
21 [a]He made him lord of his house,
And ruler of all his possessions,
22 To [1]bind his princes at his
pleasure,
And teach his elders wisdom.

23 [a]Israel also came into Egypt,
And Jacob dwelt [b]in the land of
Ham.
24 [a]He increased His people greatly,
And made them stronger than their
enemies.
25 [a]He turned their heart to hate His
people,
To deal craftily with His servants.

26 [a]He sent Moses His servant,
And Aaron whom He had chosen.
27 They [a]performed His signs among
them,
And wonders in the land of Ham.
28 He sent darkness, and made *it*
dark;
And they did not rebel against His
word.
29 [a]He turned their waters into blood,
And killed their fish.
30 [a]Their land abounded with frogs,
Even in the chambers of their
kings.
31 [a]He spoke, and there came swarms
of flies,
And lice in all their territory.
32 [a]He gave them hail for rain,
And flaming fire in their land.
33 [a]He struck their vines also, and
their fig trees,
And splintered the trees of their
territory.
34 [a]He spoke, and locusts came,
Young locusts without number,
35 And ate up all the vegetation in
their land,
And devoured the fruit of their
ground.
36 [a]He also [1]destroyed all the
firstborn in their land,
[b]The first of all their strength.

37 [a]He also brought them out with
silver and gold,
And *there was* none feeble among
His tribes.
38 [a]Egypt was glad when they
departed,

19 a Gen. 39:11–21; 41:25, 42, 43
20 a Gen. 41:14
21 a Gen. 41:40–44
22 1 Bind as prisoners
23 a Gen. 46:6 b Ps. 78:51
24 a Ex. 1:7, 9
25 a Ex. 1:8–10; 4:21
26 a Ex. 3:10; 4:12–15
27 a Ps. 78:43
29 a Ex. 7:20, 21
30 a Ex. 8:6
31 a Ex. 8:16, 17
32 a Ex. 9:23–25
33 a Ps. 78:47
34 a Ex. 10:4
36 a Ex. 12:29; 13:15 b Gen. 49:3 1 Lit. *struck down*
37 a Ex. 12:35, 36
38 a Ex. 12:33
39 a Ex. 13:21
40 a Ex. 16:12 b Ps. 78:24
41 a Ex. 17:6
42 a Gen. 15:13, 14
43 1 *a joyful shout*
44 a Josh. 11:16–23; 13:7 1 *nations*
45 a [Deut. 4:1, 40] 1 Heb. *Hallelujah*
PSALM 106
1 a 1 Chr. 16:34, 41 1 Heb. *Hallelujah*
2 1 *express*
3 a Ps. 15:2 b [Gal. 6:9] 1 LXX, Syr., Tg., Vg. *those who do*
4 a Ps. 119:132
5 1 The people of Your inheritance
6 a [Dan. 9:5]

For the fear of them had fallen
upon them.
39 [a]He spread a cloud for a covering,
And fire to give light in the night.
40 [a]*The people* asked, and He brought
quail,
And [b]satisfied them with the bread
of heaven.
41 [a]He opened the rock, and water
gushed out;
It ran in the dry places *like* a river.

42 For He remembered [a]His holy
promise,
And Abraham His servant.
43 He brought out His people with
joy,
His chosen ones with [1]gladness.
44 [a]He gave them the lands of the
[1]Gentiles,
And they inherited the labor of the
nations,
45 [a]That they might observe His
statutes
And keep His laws.

[1]Praise the LORD!

PSALM 106

Joy in Forgiveness of Israel's Sins

Praise[1] the LORD!

[a]Oh, give thanks to the LORD, for *He*
is good!
For His mercy *endures* forever.

2 Who can [1]utter the mighty acts of
the LORD?
Who can declare all His praise?
3 Blessed *are* those who keep justice,
And [1]he who [a]does righteousness at
[b]all times!

4 [a]Remember me, O LORD, with the
favor *You have toward* Your
people.
Oh, visit me with Your salvation,
5 That I may see the benefit of Your
chosen ones,
That I may rejoice in the gladness
of Your nation,
That I may glory with [1]Your
inheritance.

6 [a]We have sinned with our fathers,
We have committed iniquity,
We have done wickedly.

7 Our fathers in Egypt did not
understand Your wonders;
They did not remember the
multitude of Your mercies,
[a]But rebelled by the sea—the Red
Sea.

8 Nevertheless He saved them for His
name's sake,
[a]That He might make His mighty
power known.
9 [a]He rebuked the Red Sea also, and
it dried up;
So [b]He led them through the
depths,
As through the wilderness.
10 He [a]saved them from the hand of
him who hated *them,*
And redeemed them from the hand
of the enemy.
11 [a]The waters covered their enemies;
There was not one of them left.
12 [a]Then they believed His words;
They sang His praise.

God rejoices when we manifest a faith that holds Him to His Word.

SMITH WIGGLESWORTH

13 [a]They soon forgot His works;
They did not wait for His counsel,
14 [a]But lusted exceedingly in the
wilderness,
And tested God in the desert.
15 [a]And He gave them their request,
But [b]sent leanness into their soul.
16 When [a]they envied Moses in the
camp,
And Aaron the saint of the LORD,
17 [a]The earth opened up and
swallowed Dathan,
And covered the faction of Abiram.
18 [a]A fire was kindled in their
company;
The flame burned up the wicked.
19 [a]They made a calf in Horeb,
And worshiped the molded image.

20 Thus [a]they changed their glory
Into the image of an ox that eats
grass.
21 They forgot God their Savior,
Who had done great things in
Egypt,
22 Wondrous works in the land of
Ham,
Awesome things by the Red Sea.
23 [a]Therefore He said that He would
destroy them,
Had not Moses His chosen one
[b]stood before Him in the breach,
To turn away His wrath, lest He
destroy *them.*

24 Then they despised [a]the pleasant
land;
They [b]did not believe His word,
25 [a]But complained in their tents,
And did not heed the voice of the
LORD.
26 [a]Therefore He raised His hand *in
an oath* against them,
[b]To [1]overthrow them in the
wilderness,
27 [a]To [1]overthrow their descendants
among the [2]nations,
And to scatter them in the lands.
28 [a]They joined themselves also to
Baal of Peor,
And ate sacrifices [1]made to the
dead.
29 Thus they provoked *Him* to anger
with their deeds,
And the plague broke out among
them.
30 [a]Then Phinehas stood up and
intervened,
And the plague was stopped.
31 And that was accounted to him
[a]for righteousness
To all generations forevermore.

32 [a]They angered *Him* also at the
waters of [1]strife,
[b]So that it went ill with Moses on
account of them;
33 [a]Because they rebelled against His
Spirit,
So that he spoke rashly with his
lips.

34 [a]They did not destroy the peoples,
[b]Concerning whom the LORD had
commanded them,

7 [a] Ex. 14:11, 12
8 [a] Ex. 9:16
9 [a] Ex. 14:21 [b] Is. 63:11–13
10 [a] Ex. 14:30
11 [a] Ex. 14:27, 28; 15:5
12 [a] Ex. 15:1–21
13 [a] Ex. 15:24; 16:2; 17:2
14 [a] 1 Cor. 10:6
15 [a] Num. 11:31 [b] Is. 10:16
16 [a] Num. 16:1–3
17 [a] Deut. 11:6
18 [a] Num. 16:35, 46
19 [a] Ex. 32:1–4
20 [a] Rom. 1:23
23 [a] Ex. 32:10 [b] Ezek. 22:30
24 [a] Deut. 8:7 [b] [Heb. 3:18, 19]
25 [a] Num. 14:2, 27
26 [a] Ezek. 20:15, 16 [b] Num. 14:28–30 [1] *make them fall*
27 [a] Lev. 26:33 [1] *make their descendants fall also* [2] *Gentiles*
28 [a] Hos. 9:10 [1] *offered*
30 [a] Num. 25:7, 8
31 [a] Num. 25:11–13
32 [a] Num. 20:3–13 [b] Deut. 1:37; 3:26 [1] Or *Meribah*
33 [a] Num. 20:3, 10
34 [a] Judg. 1:21 [b] [Deut. 7:2, 16]

35 [a]But they mingled with the
Gentiles
And learned their works;
36 [a]They served their idols,
[b]Which became a snare to them.
37 [a]They even sacrificed their sons
And their daughters to [b]demons,
38 And shed innocent blood,
The blood of their sons and
daughters,
Whom they sacrificed to the idols of
Canaan;
And [a]the land was polluted with
blood.
39 Thus they [1]were [a]defiled by their
own works,
And [b]played[2] the harlot by their
own deeds.

40 Therefore [a]the wrath of the LORD
was kindled against His people,
So that He abhorred [b]His own
inheritance.
41 And [a]He gave them into the hand
of the Gentiles,
And those who hated them ruled
over them.
42 Their enemies also oppressed
them,
And they were brought into
subjection under their hand.
43 [a]Many times He delivered them;
But they rebelled in their counsel,
And were brought low for their
iniquity.

44 Nevertheless He regarded their
affliction,
When [a]He heard their cry;
45 [a]And for their sake He remembered
His covenant,
And [b]relented [c]according to the
multitude of His mercies.
46 [a]He also made them to be pitied
By all those who carried them away
captive.

47 [a]Save us, O LORD our God,
And gather us from among the
Gentiles,
To give thanks to Your holy name,
To triumph in Your praise.

48 [a]Blessed *be* the LORD God of Israel
From everlasting to everlasting!
And let all the people say, "Amen!"
[1]Praise the LORD!

35 a Judg. 3:5, 6
36 a Judg. 2:12 b Deut. 7:16
37 a 2 Kin. 16:3; 17:17 b [Lev. 17:7]
38 a [Num. 35:33]
39 a Ezek. 20:18 b [Lev. 17:7] *1 became unclean* *2 Were unfaithful*
40 a Judg. 2:14 b [Deut. 9:29; 32:9]
41 a Judg. 2:14
43 a Judg. 2:16
44 a Judg. 3:9; 6:7; 10:10
45 a [Lev. 26:41, 42] b Judg. 2:18 c Ps. 69:16
46 a Ezra 9:9
47 a 1 Chr. 16:35, 36
48 a Ps. 41:13 *1 Heb. Hallelujah*

PSALM 107
1 a Ps. 106:1 *1 Heb. same as goodness, vv. 8, 15, 21, 31, and lovingkindness, v. 43*
3 a Is. 43:5, 6
4 a [Deut. 2:7; 32:10]
6 a Ps. 50:15
7 a Ezra 8:21
8 a Ps. 107:15, 21
9 a [Ps. 34:10]
10 a [Luke 1:79] b Job 36:8 *1 Prisoners*
11 a Lam. 3:42 b [Ps. 73:24] *1 scorned*
12 a Ps. 22:11
14 a Ps. 68:6

BOOK FIVE
Psalms 107—150

PSALM 107

Thanksgiving to the Lord for His Great Works of Deliverance

Oh, [a]give thanks to the LORD, for *He is*
good!
For His [1]mercy *endures* forever.
2 Let the redeemed of the LORD say
so,
Whom He has redeemed from the
hand of the enemy,
3 And [a]gathered out of the lands,
From the east and from the west,
From the north and from the
south.

4 They wandered in [a]the wilderness
in a desolate way;
They found no city to dwell in.
5 Hungry and thirsty,
Their soul fainted in them.
6 [a]Then they cried out to the LORD in
their trouble,
And He delivered them out of their
distresses.
7 And He led them forth by the
[a]right way,
That they might go to a city for a
dwelling place.
8 [a]Oh, that *men* would give thanks to
the LORD *for* His goodness,
And *for* His wonderful works to the
children of men!
9 For [a]He satisfies the longing soul,
And fills the hungry soul with
goodness.

10 Those who [a]sat in darkness and in
the shadow of death,
[b]Bound[1] in affliction and irons—
11 Because they [a]rebelled against the
words of God,
And [1]despised [b]the counsel of the
Most High,
12 Therefore He brought down their
heart with labor;
They fell down, and *there was*
[a]none to help.
13 Then they cried out to the LORD
in their trouble,
And He saved them out of their
distresses.
14 [a]He brought them out of darkness
and the shadow of death,
And broke their chains in pieces.

15 Oh, that *men* would give thanks
to the LORD *for* His goodness,
And *for* His wonderful works to the
children of men!
16 For He has [a]broken the gates of
bronze,
And cut the bars of iron in two.
17 Fools, [a]because of their
transgression,
And because of their iniquities,
were afflicted.
18 [a]Their soul abhorred all manner of
food,
And they [b]drew near to the gates of
death.
19 Then they cried out to the LORD
in their trouble,
And He saved them out of their
distresses.
20 [a]He sent His word and [b]healed
them,
And [c]delivered *them* from their
destructions.
21 Oh, that *men* would give thanks
to the LORD *for* His goodness,
And *for* His wonderful works to the
children of men!
22 [a]Let them sacrifice the sacrifices of
thanksgiving,
And [b]declare His works with
[1]rejoicing.
23 Those who go down to the sea in
ships,
Who do business on great waters,
24 They see the works of the LORD,
And His wonders in the deep.
25 For He commands and [a]raises the
stormy wind,
Which lifts up the waves of the sea.
26 They mount up to the heavens,
They go down again to the depths;
[a]Their soul melts because of trouble.
27 They reel to and fro, and stagger
like a drunken man,
And [1]are at their wits' end.
28 Then they cry out to the LORD in
their trouble,
And He brings them out of their
distresses.
29 [a]He calms the storm,
So that its waves are still.
30 Then they are glad because they
are quiet;
So He guides them to their desired
haven.
31 [a]Oh, that *men* would give thanks
to the LORD *for* His goodness,
And *for* His wonderful works to the
children of men!
32 Let them exalt Him also [a]in the
assembly of the people,
And praise Him in the company of
the elders.
33 He [a]turns rivers into a wilderness,
And the watersprings into dry
ground;
34 A [a]fruitful land into [1]barrenness,
For the wickedness of those who
dwell in it.
35 [a]He turns a wilderness into pools
of water,
And dry land into watersprings.
36 There He makes the hungry dwell,
That they may establish a city for a
dwelling place,
37 And sow fields and plant
vineyards,
That they may yield a fruitful
harvest.
38 [a]He also blesses them, and they
multiply greatly;
And He does not let their cattle
[b]decrease.
39 When they are [a]diminished and
brought low
Through oppression, affliction and
sorrow,
40 [a]He pours contempt on princes,
And causes them to wander in the
wilderness *where there is* no way;
41 [a]Yet He sets the poor on high, far
from affliction,
And [b]makes *their* families like a
flock.
42 [a]The righteous see *it* and rejoice,
And all [b]iniquity stops its mouth.
43 [a]Whoever *is* wise will observe these
things,
And they will understand the
lovingkindness of the LORD.

PSALM 108

Assurance of God's Victory over Enemies

A Song. A Psalm of David.

O [a]God, my heart is steadfast;
I will sing and give praise, even
with my glory.
2 [a]Awake, lute and harp!
I will awaken the dawn.
3 I will praise You, O LORD, among
the peoples,

16 a Is. 45:1, 2
17 a Lam. 3:39
18 a Job 33:20 b Job 33:22
20 a Matt. 8:8 b Ps. 30:2 c Job 33:28, 30
22 a Lev. 7:12 b Ps. 9:11 *1 joyful singing*
25 a Jon. 1:4
26 a Ps. 22:14
27 1 Lit. *all their wisdom is swallowed up*
29 a Ps. 89:9
31 a Ps. 107:8, 15, 21
32 a Ps. 22:22, 25
33 a 1 Kin. 17:1, 7
34 a Gen. 13:10 *1* Lit. *a salty waste*
35 a Ps. 114:8
38 a Gen. 12:2; 17:16, 20 b [Deut. 7:14]
39 a 2 Kin. 10:32
40 a Job 12:21, 24
41 a 1 Sam. 2:8 b Ps. 78:52
42 a Job 5:15, 16 b [Rom. 3:19]
43 a Jer. 9:12
PSALM 108
1 a Ps. 57:7–11
2 a Ps. 57:8–11

And I will sing praises to You
among the nations.
4 For Your mercy *is* great above the
[1]heavens,
And Your truth *reaches* to the
clouds.

5 [a]Be exalted, O God, above the
heavens,
And Your glory above all the earth;
6 [a]That Your beloved may be
delivered,
Save *with* Your right hand, and
[1]hear me.

7 God has spoken in His holiness:
"I will rejoice;
I will divide Shechem
And measure out the Valley of
Succoth.
8 Gilead *is* Mine; Manasseh *is* Mine;
Ephraim also *is* the [1]helmet for My
head;
[a]Judah *is* My lawgiver.
9 Moab *is* My washpot;
Over Edom I will cast My shoe;
Over Philistia I will triumph."

10 [a]Who will bring me *into* the strong
city?
Who will lead me to Edom?
11 *Is it* not *You,* O God, *who* cast us
off?
And *You,* O God, *who* did not go
out with our armies?
12 Give us help from trouble,
For the help of man is useless.
13 [a]Through God we will do valiantly,
For *it is* He *who* shall tread down
our enemies.

PSALM 109

Plea for Judgment of False Accusers

To the Chief Musician. A Psalm of David.

Do[a] not keep silent,
O God of my praise!
2 For the mouth of the wicked and
the mouth of the deceitful
Have opened against me;
They have spoken against me with a
[a]lying tongue.
3 They have also surrounded me with
words of hatred,
And fought against me [a]without a
cause.
4 In return for my love they are my
accusers,
But I *give myself to* prayer.
5 Thus [a]they have rewarded me evil
for good,
And hatred for my love.

6 Set a wicked man over him,
And let [a]an [1]accuser stand at his
right hand.
7 When he is judged, let him be
found guilty,
And [a]let his prayer become sin.
8 Let his days be [a]few,
And [b]let another take his office.
9 [a]Let his children be fatherless,
And his wife a widow.
10 Let his children [1]continually be
vagabonds, and beg;
Let them [2]seek *their bread* also
from their desolate places.
11 [a]Let the creditor seize all that he
has,
And let strangers plunder his labor.
12 Let there be none to extend mercy
to him,
Nor let there be any to favor his
fatherless children.
13 [a]Let his [1]posterity be cut off,
And in the generation following let
their [b]name be blotted out.

14 [a]Let the iniquity of his fathers be
remembered before the LORD,
And let not the sin of his mother
[b]be blotted out.
15 Let them be continually before the
LORD,
That He may [a]cut off the memory
of them from the earth;
16 Because he did not remember to
show mercy,
But persecuted the poor and needy
man,
That he might even slay the
[a]broken in heart.
17 [a]As he loved cursing, so let it come
to him;
As he did not delight in blessing, so
let it be far from him.
18 As he clothed himself with cursing
as with his garment,
So let it [a]enter his body like water,
And like oil into his bones.
19 Let it be to him like the garment
which covers him,
And for a belt with which he girds
himself continually.
20 *Let* this *be* the LORD's reward to
my accusers,

4 [1] *skies*
5 [a] Ps. 57:5, 11
6 [a] Ps. 60:5–12 [1] Lit. *answer*
8 [a] [Gen. 49:10] [1] Lit. *protection*
10 [a] Ps. 60:9
13 [a] Ps. 60:12

PSALM 109
1 [a] Ps. 83:1
2 [a] Ps. 27:12
3 [a] John 15:23–25
5 [a] Ps. 35:7, 12; 38:20
6 [a] Zech. 3:1 [1] Heb. *satan*
7 [a] [Prov. 28:9]
8 [a] [Ps. 55:23] [b] Acts 1:20
9 [a] Ex. 22:24
10 [1] *wander continuously* [2] So with MT, Tg.; LXX, Vg. *be cast out*
11 [a] Job 5:5; 18:9
13 [a] Job 18:19 [b] Prov. 10:7 [1] *descendants be destroyed*
14 [a] [Ex. 20:5] [b] Neh. 4:5
15 [a] Job 18:17
16 [a] [Ps. 34:18]
17 [a] Prov. 14:14
18 [a] Num. 5:22

And to those who speak evil against
my person.
21 But You, O GOD the Lord,
Deal with me for Your name's sake;
Because Your mercy *is* good, deliver
me.
22 For I *am* poor and needy,
And my heart is wounded within
me.
23 I am gone [a]like a shadow when it
lengthens;
I am shaken off like a locust.
24 My [a]knees are weak through
fasting,
And my flesh is feeble from lack of
fatness.
25 I also have become [a]a reproach to
them;
When they look at me, [b]they shake
their heads.

26 Help me, O LORD my God!
Oh, save me according to Your
mercy,
27 [a]That they may know that this *is*
Your hand—
That You, LORD, have done it!
28 [a]Let them curse, but You bless;
When they arise, let them be
ashamed,
But let [b]Your servant rejoice.
29 [a]Let my accusers be clothed with
shame,
And let them cover themselves with
their own disgrace as with a
mantle.
30 I will greatly praise the LORD with
my mouth;
Yes, [a]I will praise Him among the
multitude.
31 For [a]He shall stand at the right
hand of the poor,
To save *him* from those [1]who
condemn him.

PSALM 110

Announcement of the Messiah's Reign

A Psalm of David.

The [a]LORD said to my Lord,
"Sit at My right hand,
Till I make Your enemies Your
[b]footstool."
2 The LORD shall send the rod of
Your strength [a]out of Zion.
[b]Rule in the midst of Your enemies!
3 [a]Your people *shall be* volunteers
In the day of Your power;
[b]In the beauties of holiness, from
the womb of the morning,
You have the dew of Your youth.
4 The LORD has sworn
And [a]will not relent,
"You *are* a [b]priest forever
According to the order of
[c]Melchizedek."

5 The Lord *is* [a]at Your right hand;
He shall [1]execute kings [b]in the day
of His wrath.
6 He shall judge among the nations,
He shall fill *the places* with dead
bodies,
[a]He shall [1]execute the heads of
many countries.
7 He shall drink of the brook by the
wayside;
[a]Therefore He shall lift up the head.

PSALM 111

Praise to God for His Faithfulness and Justice

Praise[1] the LORD!
[a]I will praise the LORD with *my*
whole heart,
In the assembly of the upright and
in the congregation.
2 [a]The works of the LORD *are* great,
[b]Studied by all who have pleasure in
them.
3 His work *is* [a]honorable and
glorious,
And His righteousness endures
forever.
4 He has made His wonderful works
to be remembered;
[a]The LORD *is* gracious and full of
compassion.
5 He has given food to those who
fear Him;
He will ever be mindful of His
covenant.
6 He has declared to His people the
power of His works,
In giving them the [1]heritage of the
nations.
7 The works of His hands *are*
[a]verity[1] and justice;
All His precepts *are* sure.
8 [a]They stand fast forever and ever,

---

23 a Ps. 102:11
24 a Heb. 12:12
25 a Ps. 22:7 b Matt. 27:39
27 a Job 37:7
28 a 2 Sam. 6:11, 12 b Is. 65:14
29 a Ps. 35:26
30 a Ps. 35:18; 111:1
31 a [Ps. 16:8] *1* Lit. *judging his soul*

PSALM 110
1 a Matt. 22:44 b [1 Cor. 15:25]
2 a [Rom. 11:26, 27] b [Dan. 7:13, 14]
3 a Judg. 5:2 b Ps. 96:9
4 a [Num. 23:19] b [Zech. 6:13] c [Heb. 5:6, 10; 6:20]
5 a [Ps. 16:8] b Ps. 2:5, 12 *1* Lit. *break kings in pieces*
6 a Ps. 68:21 *1* Lit. *break in pieces*
7 a [Is. 53:12]

PSALM 111
1 a Ps. 35:18 *1* Heb. *Hallelujah*
2 a Ps. 92:5 b Ps. 143:5
3 a Ps. 145:4, 5
4 a [Ps. 86:5]
6 *1* *inheritance*
7 a [Rev. 15:3] *1* *truth*
8 a Is. 40:8

And are [b]done in truth and
uprightness.
9 [a]He has sent redemption to His
people;
He has commanded His covenant
forever:
[b]Holy and awesome *is* His name.

10 [a]The fear of the LORD *is* the
beginning of wisdom;
A good understanding have all
those who do *His
commandments.*
His praise endures forever.

PSALM 112

The Blessed State of the Righteous

Praise[1] the LORD!
Blessed *is* the man *who* fears the
LORD,
Who [a]delights greatly in His
commandments.

2 [a]His descendants will be mighty on
earth;
The generation of the upright will
be blessed.
3 [a]Wealth and riches *will be* in his
house,
And his righteousness [1]endures
forever.
4 [a]Unto the upright there arises light
in the darkness;
He is gracious, and full of
compassion, and righteous.
5 [a]A good man deals graciously and
lends;
He will guide his affairs [b]with
discretion.
6 Surely he will never be shaken;
[a]The righteous will be in everlasting
remembrance.
7 [a]He will not be afraid of evil tidings;
His heart is steadfast, trusting in
the LORD.
8 His [a]heart *is* established;
[b]He will not be afraid,
Until he [c]sees *his desire* upon his
enemies.

9 He has dispersed abroad,
He has given to the poor;
His righteousness endures forever;
His [1]horn will be exalted with
honor.

8 b [Rev. 15:3]

9 a Luke 1:68
b Luke 1:49

10 a Eccl. 12:13

PSALM 112
1 a Ps. 128:1
1 Heb. *Hallelujah*

2 a [Ps. 102:28]

3 a [Matt. 6:33]
1 stands

4 a Job 11:17

5 a [Luke 6:35]
b [Eph. 5:15]

6 a Prov. 10:7

7 a [Prov. 1:33]

8 a Heb. 13:9
b Prov. 1:33; 3:24
c Ps. 59:10

9 *1* Strength

PSALM 113
1 a Ps. 135:1
1 Heb. *Hallelujah*

2 a [Dan. 2:20]

3 a Is. 59:19

4 a Ps. 97:9; 99:2
b [Ps. 8:1]

5 a [Is. 57:15]

6 a [Ps. 11:4]

7 a 1 Sam. 2:8
b Ps. 72:12

8 a [Job 36:7]

9 a 1 Sam. 2:5
1 childless

PSALM 114
1 a Ex. 12:51; 13:3
b Ps. 81:5
1 who spoke unintelligibly

2 a Ex. 6:7; 19:6; 25:8; 29:45, 46

3 a Ex. 14:21
b Josh. 3:13–16

4 a Ps. 29:6

5 a Hab. 3:8

10 The wicked will see *it* and be
grieved;
He will gnash his teeth and melt
away;
The desire of the wicked shall
perish.

PSALM 113

The Majesty and Condescension of God

Praise[1] the LORD!

[a]Praise, O servants of the LORD,
Praise the name of the LORD!
2 [a]Blessed be the name of the LORD
From this time forth and
forevermore!
3 [a]From the rising of the sun to its
going down
The LORD's name *is* to be praised.

4 The LORD *is* [a]high above all
nations,
[b]His glory above the heavens.
5 [a]Who *is* like the LORD our God,
Who dwells on high,
6 [a]Who humbles Himself to behold
The things that are in the heavens
and in the earth?
7 [a]He raises the poor out of the dust,
And lifts the [b]needy out of the ash
heap,
8 That He may [a]seat *him* with
princes—
With the princes of His people.
9 [a]He grants the [1]barren woman a
home,
Like a joyful mother of children.

Praise the LORD!

PSALM 114

The Power of God in His Deliverance of Israel

When [a]Israel went out of Egypt,
The house of Jacob [b]from a people
[1]of strange language,
2 [a]Judah became His sanctuary,
And Israel His dominion.

3 [a]The sea saw *it* and fled;
[b]Jordan turned back.
4 [a]The mountains skipped like rams,
The little hills like lambs.
5 [a]What ails you, O sea, that you fled?
O Jordan, *that* you turned back?

6 O mountains, *that* you skipped like
rams?
O little hills, like lambs?

7 Tremble, O earth, at the presence
of the Lord,
At the presence of the God of Jacob,
8 [a]Who turned the rock *into* a pool of
water,
The flint into a fountain of waters.

PSALM 115

The Futility of Idols and the Trustworthiness of God

Not [a]unto us, O LORD, not unto us,
But to Your name give glory,
Because of Your mercy,
Because of Your truth.
2 Why should the [1]Gentiles say,
[a]"So where *is* their God?"

3 [a]But our God *is* in heaven;
He does whatever He pleases.
4 [a]Their idols *are* silver and gold,
The work of men's hands.
5 They have mouths, but they do not
speak;
Eyes they have, but they do not see;
6 They have ears, but they do not
hear;
Noses they have, but they do not
smell;
7 They have hands, but they do not
handle;
Feet they have, but they do not
walk;
Nor do they mutter through their
throat.
8 [a]Those who make them are like
them;
So is everyone who trusts in them.

9 [a]O Israel, trust in the LORD;
[b]He *is* their help and their shield.
10 O house of Aaron, trust in the
LORD;
He *is* their help and their shield.
11 You who fear the LORD, trust in
the LORD;
He *is* their help and their shield.

12 The LORD [1]has been mindful of *us;*
He will bless us;
He will bless the house of Israel;
He will bless the house of Aaron.
13 [a]He will bless those who fear the
LORD,
Both small and great.

14 May the LORD give you increase
more and more,
You and your children.
15 *May* you *be* [a]blessed by the LORD,
[b]Who made heaven and earth.

16 The heaven, *even* the heavens, *are*
the LORD's;
But the earth He has given to the
children of men.
17 [a]The dead do not praise the LORD,
Nor any who go down into silence.
18 [a]But we will bless the LORD
From this time forth and
forevermore.

Praise the LORD!

PSALM 116

Thanksgiving for Deliverance from Death

I [a]love the LORD, because He has heard
My voice *and* my supplications.
2 Because He has inclined His ear to
me,
Therefore I will call *upon Him* as
long as I live.

3 [a]The [1]pains of death surrounded
me,
And the [2]pangs of Sheol [3]laid hold
of me;
I found trouble and sorrow.
4 Then I called upon the name of the
LORD:
"O LORD, I implore You, deliver my
soul!"

5 [a]Gracious *is* the LORD, and
[b]righteous;
Yes, our God *is* merciful.
6 The LORD preserves the simple;
I was brought low, and He saved
me.
7 Return to your [a]rest, O my soul,
For [b]the LORD has dealt bountifully
with you.

8 [a]For You have delivered my soul
from death,
My eyes from tears,
And my feet from falling.
9 I will walk before the LORD
[a]In the land of the living.
10 [a]I believed, therefore I spoke,
"I am greatly afflicted."
11 [a]I said in my haste,
[b]"All men *are* liars."

114:8 [a]Ex. 17:6

PSALM 115
1 [a][Is. 48:11]
2 [a]Ps. 42:3, 10 · [1] *nations*
3 [a][1 Chr. 16:26]
4 [a]Jer. 10:3
8 [a]Is. 44:9–11
9 [a]Ps. 118:2, 3 · [b]Ps. 33:20
12 [1] *has remembered us*
13 [a]Ps. 128:1, 4
15 [a][Gen. 14:19] · [b]Gen. 1:1
17 [a][Is. 38:18]
18 [a]Dan. 2:20

PSALM 116
1 [a]Ps. 18:1
3 [a]Ps. 18:4–6 · [1] Lit. *cords* · [2] *distresses* · [3] Lit. *found me*
5 [a][Ps. 103:8] · [b][Ezra 9:15]
7 [a][Jer. 6:16] · [b]Ps. 13:6
8 [a]Ps. 56:13
9 [a]Ps. 27:13
10 [a]2 Cor. 4:13
11 [a]Ps. 31:22 · [b]Rom. 3:4

12 What shall I render to the LORD
For all His benefits toward me?
13 I will take up the cup of salvation,
And call upon the name of the LORD.
14 [a]I will pay my vows to the LORD
Now in the presence of all His people.

Rest. Rest. Rest in God's love. The only work you are required now to do is to give your most intense attention to His still, small voice within.

MADAME JEANNE GUYON

15 [a]Precious in the sight of the LORD
Is the death of His saints.

16 O LORD, truly [a]I *am* Your servant;
I *am* Your servant, [b]the son of Your maidservant;
You have loosed my bonds.
17 I will offer to You [a]the sacrifice of thanksgiving,
And will call upon the name of the LORD.

18 I will pay my vows to the LORD
Now in the presence of all His people,
19 In the [a]courts of the LORD's house,
In the midst of you, O Jerusalem.

[1]Praise the LORD!

PSALM 117

Let All Peoples Praise the Lord

Praise[a] the LORD, all you Gentiles!
[1]Laud Him, all you peoples!
2 For His merciful kindness is great toward us,
And [a]the truth of the LORD *endures* forever.

Praise the LORD!

14 a Ps. 116:18
15 a Ps. 72:14
16 a Ps. 119:125; 143:12 b Ps. 86:16
17 a Lev. 7:12
19 a Ps. 96:8 *1* Heb. *Hallelujah*

PSALM 117
1 a Rom. 15:11 *1 Praise*
2 a [Ps. 100:5]

PSALM 118
1 a 1 Chr. 16:8, 34 b [Ps. 136:1–26]
2 a [Ps. 115:9]
5 a Ps. 120:1 b Ps. 18:19
6 a Ps. 27:1; 56:9
7 a Ps. 54:4 b Ps. 59:10
8 a Ps. 40:4
9 a Ps. 146:3
11 a Ps. 88:17
12 a Deut. 1:44 b Nah. 1:10 *1 cut them off*
14 a Is. 12:2
16 a Ex. 15:6
17 a Hab. 1:12

PSALM 118

Praise to God for His Everlasting Mercy

Oh, [a]give thanks to the LORD, for *He is* good!
[b]For His mercy *endures* forever.

2 [a]Let Israel now say,
"His mercy *endures* forever."
3 Let the house of Aaron now say,
"His mercy *endures* forever."
4 Let those who fear the LORD now say,
"His mercy *endures* forever."

5 [a]I called on the LORD in distress;
The LORD answered me *and* [b]*set me* in a broad place.
6 [a]The LORD *is* on my side;
I will not fear.
What can man do to me?
7 [a]The LORD is for me among those who help me;
Therefore [b]I shall see *my desire* on those who hate me.
8 [a]*It is* better to trust in the LORD
Than to put confidence in man.
9 [a]*It is* better to trust in the LORD
Than to put confidence in princes.

10 All nations surrounded me,
But in the name of the LORD I will destroy them.
11 They [a]surrounded me,
Yes, they surrounded me;
But in the name of the LORD I will destroy them.
12 They surrounded me [a]like bees;
They were quenched [b]like a fire of thorns;
For in the name of the LORD I will [1]destroy them.
13 You pushed me violently, that I might fall,
But the LORD helped me.
14 [a]The LORD *is* my strength and song,
And He has become my salvation.

15 The voice of rejoicing and salvation
Is in the tents of the righteous;
The right hand of the LORD does valiantly.
16 [a]The right hand of the LORD is exalted;
The right hand of the LORD does valiantly.
17 [a]I shall not die, but live,

And [b]declare the works of the LORD.
18 The LORD has [a]chastened[1] me
severely,
But He has not given me over to
death.

19 [a]Open to me the gates of
righteousness;
I will go through them,
And I will praise the LORD.
20 [a]This is the gate of the LORD,
[b]Through which the righteous shall
enter.

21 I will praise You,
For You have [a]answered me,
And have become my salvation.

22 [a]The stone *which* the builders
rejected
Has become the chief cornerstone.
23 [1]This was the LORD's doing;
It *is* marvelous in our eyes.
24 This *is* the day the LORD has
made;
We will rejoice and be glad in it.

25 Save now, I pray, O LORD;
O LORD, I pray, send now
prosperity.
26 [a]Blessed *is* he who comes in the
name of the LORD!
We have blessed you from the
house of the LORD.
27 God *is* the LORD,
And He has given us [a]light;
Bind the sacrifice with cords to the
horns of the altar.
28 You *are* my God, and I will praise
You;
[a]*You are* my God, I will exalt You.

29 Oh, give thanks to the LORD, for
He is good!
For His mercy *endures* forever.

PSALM 119

Meditations on the Excellencies of the Word of God

א ALEPH

Blessed *are* the [1]undefiled in the way,
[a]Who walk in the law of the LORD!
2 Blessed *are* those who keep His
testimonies,
Who seek Him with the [a]whole
heart!
3 [a]They also do no iniquity;
They walk in His ways.

17 [b] Ps. 73:28
18 [a] 2 Cor. 6:9 [1] *disciplined*
19 [a] Is. 26:2
20 [a] Ps. 24:7 [b] Is. 35:8
21 [a] Ps. 116:1
22 [a] Matt. 21:42
23 [1] Lit. *This is from the LORD*
26 [a] Mark 11:9
27 [a] [1 Pet. 2:9]
28 [a] Is. 25:1

PSALM 119
1 [a] Ps. 128:1 [1] *blameless*
2 [a] Deut. 6:5; 10:12; 11:13; 13:3
3 [a] [1 John 3:9; 5:18]
6 [a] Job 22:26
10 [a] 2 Chr. 15:15
11 [a] Luke 2:19
13 [a] Ps. 34:11
15 [1] *look into*
16 [a] Ps. 1:2
17 [a] Ps. 116:7

4 You have commanded *us*
To keep Your precepts diligently.
5 Oh, that my ways were directed
To keep Your statutes!
6 [a]Then I would not be ashamed,
When I look into all Your
commandments.
7 I will praise You with uprightness
of heart,
When I learn Your righteous
judgments.
8 I will keep Your statutes;
Oh, do not forsake me utterly!

The Holy Scriptures were not given to us that we should enclose them in books, but that we should engrave them upon our hearts.

ST. JOHN CHRYSOSTOM

ב BETH

9 How can a young man cleanse
his way?
By taking heed according to Your
word.
10 With my whole heart I have
[a]sought You;
Oh, let me not wander from Your
commandments!
11 [a]Your word I have hidden in my
heart,
That I might not sin against You.
12 Blessed *are* You, O LORD!
Teach me Your statutes.
13 With my lips I have [a]declared
All the judgments of Your mouth.
14 I have rejoiced in the way of Your
testimonies,
As *much as* in all riches.
15 I will meditate on Your precepts,
And [1]contemplate Your ways.
16 I will [a]delight myself in Your
statutes;
I will not forget Your word.

ג GIMEL

17 [a]Deal bountifully with Your
servant,
That I may live and keep Your
word.

Psalm 119:9

Dear Woman of Destiny,

The child of God turns to the Bible as a babe turns to their mother's breast, seeking nourishment and strength. It is their heavenly Father's Word and is as necessary to the spiritual body as physical food is necessary for the natural body. Realizing that man cannot live by bread alone, they yearn for "every word that proceeds from the mouth of God" (Matt. 4:4). Therefore, my sister, constantly and faithfully study the Bible to apply its teaching to your own spiritual life and allow our Teacher, the Holy Spirit, to "life" the written Word. In turn, the written Word will "life" your inner man with the living Word, who is Christ—unveiling the life of our Lord to you and in you.

Many books of the Bible remain dead letters in the lives of Christians, however, mainly because readers have never caught the large vision of truth contained in them. There are several different approaches to understanding the Bible. One of the best is the study of the Book as a whole, also known as *synthetic study*. This type of Bible study can be likened to an explorer climbing a high mountain to get a bird's-eye view of the whole area before exploring it in detail.

Topical study is one of the most popular approaches to Bible study and, with the use of a good concordance, one of the easiest. The more you study, the more amazed you will be with the range of revealed truth.

Study by types involves using Old Testament persons, objects, and events that, by God's providence, were planned to foreshadow something higher in the Christian era, to enrich your understanding of the New Testament.

Biographical study will enable you to receive courage, instruction, example, and warning from the 2,930 very human beings mentioned in the Bible. With this method, it is helpful to consider the meaning of the person's name, ancestry, friends, and associates, the place where his or her story unfolds, traits of character, failures, great crises, contributions, and finally, lessons for us.

Study by chapters, verses, and words can be a rewarding experience. God reveals Himself through the words of His Word. For example, in Psalm 119, every verse speaks of the Word of God. In it, we find three rules for study: First, approach the Word with prayer (v. 18). Next, meditate upon the Word (v. 15). Finally, obey the Word (v. 9). Wherever possible, the Scripture should be interpreted literally. The Bible is filled with figures of speech, and one problem for interpreters is often the confusion over what is literal and what is figurative. However, the safest rule in understanding Scripture is to take it literally unless there is a clear indication that it is to be understood figuratively.

Above all, never forget for one moment that the Holy Spirit is the Author of the Book. Only He can reveal it to your spiritual man and make it eternal life in you, lived out through you.

Fuchsia Pickett

18 Open my eyes, that I may see
Wondrous things from Your law.
19 [a]I *am* a stranger in the earth;
Do not hide Your commandments
from me.
20 [a]My soul [1]breaks with longing
For Your judgments at all times.
21 You rebuke the proud—the
cursed,
Who stray from Your
commandments.
22 [a]Remove from me reproach and
contempt,
For I have kept Your testimonies.
23 Princes also sit *and* speak against
me,
But Your servant meditates on Your
statutes.
24 Your testimonies also *are* my
delight
And my counselors.

ד DALETH

25 [a]My soul clings to the dust;
[b]Revive me according to Your word.
26 I have declared my ways, and You
answered me;
[a]Teach me Your statutes.
27 Make me understand the way of
Your precepts;
So [a]shall I meditate on Your
wonderful works.
28 [a]My soul [1]melts from [2]heaviness;
Strengthen me according to Your
word.
29 Remove from me the way of lying,
And grant me Your law graciously.
30 I have chosen the way of truth;
Your judgments I have laid *before
me.*
31 I cling to Your testimonies;
O LORD, do not put me to shame!
32 I will run the course of Your
commandments,
For You shall [a]enlarge my heart.

ה HE

33 [a]Teach me, O LORD, the way of
Your statutes,
And I shall keep it *to* the end.
34 [a]Give me understanding, and I
shall keep Your law;
Indeed, I shall observe it with *my*
whole heart.
35 Make me walk in the path of Your
commandments,
For I delight in it.

19 a Heb. 11:13
20 a Ps. 42:1, 2; 63:1; 84:2 *1 is crushed*
22 a Ps. 39:8
25 a Ps. 44:25 b Ps. 143:11
26 a Ps. 25:4; 27:11; 86:11
27 a Ps. 145:5, 6
28 a Ps. 107:26 *1* Lit. *drops* *2 grief*
32 a Is. 60:5
33 a [Rev. 2:26]
34 a [Prov. 2:6]
36 a Ezek. 33:31 *1* Cause me to long for
37 a Is. 33:15 b Prov. 23:5 *1* Lit. *Cause my eyes to pass away from* *2* So with MT, LXX, Vg.; Tg. *Your words*
38 a 2 Sam. 7:25
42 *1 taunts*
45 a Prov. 4:12 *1* Lit. *in a wide place*
46 a Matt. 10:18
50 a [Rom. 15:4]

36 [1]Incline my heart to Your
testimonies,
And not to [a]covetousness.
37 [a]Turn[1] away my eyes from [b]looking
at worthless things,
And revive me in [2]Your way.
38 [a]Establish Your word to Your
servant,
Who *is devoted* to fearing You.
39 Turn away my reproach which I
dread,
For Your judgments *are* good.
40 Behold, I long for Your precepts;
Revive me in Your righteousness.

ו WAW

41 Let Your mercies come also to
me, O LORD—
Your salvation according to Your
word.
42 So shall I have an answer for him
who [1]reproaches me,
For I trust in Your word.
43 And take not the word of truth
utterly out of my mouth,
For I have hoped in Your
ordinances.
44 So shall I keep Your law
continually,
Forever and ever.
45 And I will walk [1]at [a]liberty,
For I seek Your precepts.
46 [a]I will speak of Your testimonies
also before kings,
And will not be ashamed.
47 And I will delight myself in Your
commandments,
Which I love.
48 My hands also I will lift up to
Your commandments,
Which I love,
And I will meditate on Your
statutes.

ז ZAYIN

49 Remember the word to Your
servant,
Upon which You have caused me to
hope.
50 This *is* my [a]comfort in my
affliction,
For Your word has given me life.
51 The proud have me in great
derision,
Yet I do not turn aside from Your
law.
52 I remembered Your judgments of
old, O LORD,

And have comforted myself.
53 [a]Indignation has taken hold of me
Because of the wicked, who forsake
Your law.
54 Your statutes have been my songs
In the house of my pilgrimage.
55 [a]I remember Your name in the
night, O LORD,
And I keep Your law.
56 This has become mine,
Because I kept Your precepts.

ח HETH

57 [a]*You are* my portion, O LORD;
I have said that I would keep Your
words.
58 I entreated Your favor with *my*
whole heart;
Be merciful to me according to
Your word.
59 I [a]thought about my ways,
And turned my feet to Your
testimonies.
60 I made haste, and did not delay
To keep Your commandments.
61 The cords of the wicked have
bound me,
But I have not forgotten Your law.
62 [a]At midnight I will rise to give
thanks to You,
Because of Your righteous
judgments.
63 I *am* a companion of all who fear
You,
And of those who keep Your
precepts.
64 [a]The earth, O LORD, is full of Your
mercy;
Teach me Your statutes.

ט TETH

65 You have dealt well with Your
servant,
O LORD, according to Your word.
66 Teach me good judgment and
[a]knowledge,
For I believe Your commandments.
67 Before I was [a]afflicted I went
astray,
But now I keep Your word.
68 You *are* [a]good, and do good;
Teach me Your statutes.
69 The proud have [a]forged[1] a lie
against me,
But I will keep Your precepts with
my whole heart.
70 [a]Their heart is [1]as fat as grease,
But I delight in Your law.

53 [a]Ezra 9:3
55 [a]Ps. 63:6
57 [a]Jer. 10:16
59 [a]Luke 15:17
62 [a]Acts 16:25
64 [a]Ps. 33:5
66 [a]Phil. 1:9
67 [a][Heb. 12:5–11]
68 [a][Matt. 19:17]
69 [a]Job 13:4 [1]Lit. *smeared me with a lie*
70 [a]Acts 28:27 [1]Insensible
72 [a]Ps. 19:10
73 [a]Job 10:8; 31:15
74 [a]Ps. 34:2
75 [a][Heb. 12:10] [1]Lit. *righteous*
78 [a]Ps. 25:3
81 [a]Ps. 73:26; 84:2
83 [a]Job 30:30
84 [a]Ps. 39:4 [b]Rev. 6:10
85 [a]Ps. 35:7
86 [a]Ps. 35:19

71 *It is* good for me that I have been
afflicted,
That I may learn Your statutes.
72 [a]The law of Your mouth *is* better
to me
Than thousands of *coins of* gold
and silver.

י YOD

73 [a]Your hands have made me and
fashioned me;
Give me understanding, that I may
learn Your commandments.
74 [a]Those who fear You will be glad
when they see me,
Because I have hoped in Your word.
75 I know, O LORD, [a]that Your
judgments *are* [1]right,
And *that* in faithfulness You have
afflicted me.
76 Let, I pray, Your merciful kindness
be for my comfort,
According to Your word to Your
servant.
77 Let Your tender mercies come to
me, that I may live;
For Your law *is* my delight.
78 Let the proud [a]be ashamed,
For they treated me wrongfully
with falsehood;
But I will meditate on Your
precepts.
79 Let those who fear You turn to
me,
Those who know Your testimonies.
80 Let my heart be blameless
regarding Your statutes,
That I may not be ashamed.

כ KAPH

81 [a]My soul faints for Your salvation,
But I hope in Your word.
82 My eyes fail *from searching* Your
word,
Saying, "When will You comfort
me?"
83 For [a]I have become like a
wineskin in smoke,
Yet I do not forget Your statutes.
84 [a]How many *are* the days of Your
servant?
[b]When will You execute judgment
on those who persecute me?
85 [a]The proud have dug pits for me,
Which *is* not according to Your law.
86 All Your commandments *are*
faithful;
They persecute me [a]wrongfully;

Help me!
87 They almost made an end of me
on earth,
But I did not forsake Your precepts.
88 Revive me according to Your
lovingkindness,
So that I may keep the testimony of
Your mouth.

ל LAMED

89 [a]Forever, O LORD,
Your word [1]is settled in heaven.
90 Your faithfulness *endures* to all
generations;
You established the earth, and it
[1]abides.
91 They continue this day according
to [a]Your ordinances,
For all *are* Your servants.
92 Unless Your law *had been* my
delight,
I would then have perished in my
affliction.
93 I will never forget Your precepts,
For by them You have given me
life.
94 I *am* Yours, save me;
For I have sought Your precepts.
95 The wicked wait for me to destroy
me,
But I will [1]consider Your
testimonies.
96 [a]I have seen the consummation of
all perfection,
But Your commandment *is*
exceedingly broad.

מ MEM

97 Oh, how I love Your law!
[a]It *is* my meditation all the day.
98 You, through Your
commandments, make me [a]wiser
than my enemies;
For they *are* ever with me.
99 I have more understanding than
all my teachers,
[a]For Your testimonies *are* my
meditation.
100 [a]I understand more than the
[1]ancients,
Because I keep Your precepts.
101 I have restrained my feet from
every evil way,
That I may keep Your word.
102 I have not departed from Your
judgments,
For You Yourself have taught me.

89 a Matt. 24:35
1 Lit. *stands firm*

90 *1* Lit. *stands*

91 a Jer. 33:25

95 *1 give attention to*

96 a Matt. 5:18

97 a Ps. 1:2

98 a Deut. 4:6

99 a [2 Tim. 3:15]

100 a [Job 32:7–9]
1 aged

103 a Prov. 8:11

105 a Prov. 6:23

106 a Neh. 10:29

108 a Hos. 14:2

109 a Job 13:14
1 In danger

110 a Ps. 140:5

111 a Deut. 33:4
1 inheritance

113 *1* Lit. *divided* in heart or mind

114 a [Ps. 32:7]

115 a Matt. 7:23

116 a [Rom. 5:5; 9:33; 10:11]

117 *1 Uphold me*

119 a Ezek. 22:18, 19
1 destroy, lit. *cause to cease*
2 slag or *refuse*

120 a Hab. 3:16

103 [a]How sweet are Your words to my
taste,
Sweeter than honey to my mouth!
104 Through Your precepts I get
understanding;
Therefore I hate every false way.

נ NUN

105 [a]Your word *is* a lamp to my feet
And a light to my path.
106 [a]I have sworn and confirmed
That I will keep Your righteous
judgments.
107 I am afflicted very much;
Revive me, O LORD, according to
Your word.
108 Accept, I pray, [a]the freewill
offerings of my mouth, O LORD,
And teach me Your judgments.
109 [a]My life *is* continually [1]in my
hand,
Yet I do not forget Your law.
110 [a]The wicked have laid a snare
for me,
Yet I have not strayed from Your
precepts.
111 [a]Your testimonies I have taken as
a [1]heritage forever,
For they *are* the rejoicing of my
heart.
112 I have inclined my heart to
perform Your statutes
Forever, to the very end.

ס SAMEK

113 I hate the [1]double-minded,
But I love Your law.
114 [a]You *are* my hiding place and my
shield;
I hope in Your word.
115 [a]Depart from me, you evildoers,
For I will keep the commandments
of my God!
116 Uphold me according to Your
word, that I may live;
And do not let me [a]be ashamed of
my hope.
117 [1]Hold me up, and I shall be safe,
And I shall observe Your statutes
continually.
118 You reject all those who stray
from Your statutes,
For their deceit *is* falsehood.
119 You [1]put away all the wicked of
the earth [a]*like* [2]dross;
Therefore I love Your testimonies.
120 [a]My flesh trembles for fear of You,
And I am afraid of Your judgments.

ע AYIN

121 I have done justice and
righteousness;
Do not leave me to my oppressors.
122 Be [a]surety[1] for Your servant for
good;
Do not let the proud oppress me.
123 My eyes fail *from seeking* Your
salvation
And Your righteous word.
124 Deal with Your servant according
to Your mercy,
And teach me Your statutes.
125 [a]I *am* Your servant;
Give me understanding,
That I may know Your testimonies.
126 *It is* time for *You* to act, O LORD,
For they have [1]regarded Your law
as void.
127 [a]Therefore I love Your
commandments
More than gold, yes, than fine gold!
128 Therefore all *Your* precepts
concerning all *things*
I consider *to be* right;
I hate every false way.

O Lord, my God, make Your face shine upon Your servant ____ and teach them Your statutes.

FROM PSALM 119:135

פ PE

129 Your testimonies are wonderful;
Therefore my soul keeps them.
130 The entrance of Your words gives
light;
[a]It gives understanding to the
[b]simple.
131 I opened my mouth and [a]panted,
For I longed for Your
commandments.
132 [a]Look upon me and be merciful
to me,
[b]As Your custom *is* toward those
who love Your name.
133 [a]Direct my steps by Your word,
And [b]let no iniquity have dominion
over me.
134 [a]Redeem me from the oppression
of man,
That I may keep Your precepts.
135 [a]Make Your face shine upon Your
servant,
And teach me Your statutes.
136 [a]Rivers of water run down from
my eyes,
Because *men* do not keep Your law.

צ TSADDE

137 [a]Righteous *are* You, O LORD,
And upright *are* Your judgments.
138 [a]Your testimonies, *which* You have
commanded,
Are righteous and very faithful.
139 [a]My zeal has [1]consumed me,
Because my enemies have forgotten
Your words.
140 [a]Your word *is* very [1]pure;
Therefore Your servant loves it.
141 I *am* small and despised,
Yet I do not forget Your precepts.
142 Your righteousness *is* an
everlasting righteousness,
And Your law *is* [a]truth.
143 Trouble and anguish have
[1]overtaken me,
Yet Your commandments *are* my
delights.
144 The righteousness of Your
testimonies *is* everlasting;
Give me understanding, and I shall
live.

ק QOPH

145 I cry out with *my* whole heart;
Hear me, O LORD!
I will keep Your statutes.
146 I cry out to You;
Save me, and I will keep Your
testimonies.
147 [a]I rise before the dawning of the
morning,
And cry for help;
I hope in Your word.
148 [a]My eyes are awake through the
night watches,
That I may meditate on Your word.
149 Hear my voice according to Your
lovingkindness;
O LORD, revive me according to
Your justice.
150 They draw near who follow after
wickedness;
They are far from Your law.
151 You *are* [a]near, O LORD,

122 a Heb. 7:22 *1 guaranty*
125 a Ps. 116:16
126 *1 broken Your law*
127 a Ps. 19:10
130 a Prov. 6:23 b [Ps. 19:7]
131 a Ps. 42:1
132 a Ps. 106:4 b [2 Thess. 1:6]
133 a Ps. 17:5 b [Rom. 6:12]
134 a Luke 1:74
135 a Ps. 4:6
136 a Jer. 9:1, 18; 14:17
137 a Neh. 9:33
138 a [Ps. 19:7–9]
139 a John 2:17 *1 put an end to*
140 a Ps. 12:6 *1* Lit. *refined* or *tried*
142 a [John 17:17]
143 *1* Lit. *found*
147 a Ps. 5:3
148 a Ps. 63:1, 6
151 a [Ps. 145:18]

And all Your commandments *are*
truth.
152 Concerning Your testimonies,
I have known of old that You have
founded them [a]forever.

ר RESH

153 [a]Consider my affliction and
deliver me,
For I do not forget Your law.
154 [a]Plead my cause and redeem me;
Revive me according to Your word.
155 Salvation *is* far from the wicked,
For they do not seek Your statutes.
156 [1]Great *are* Your tender mercies,
O LORD;
Revive me according to Your
judgments.
157 Many *are* my persecutors and my
enemies,
Yet I do not [a]turn from Your
testimonies.
158 I see the treacherous, and [a]am
disgusted,
Because they do not keep Your
word.
159 Consider how I love Your
precepts;
Revive me, O LORD, according to
Your lovingkindness.
160 The entirety of Your word *is*
truth,
And every one of Your righteous
judgments *endures* forever.

ש SHIN

161 [a]Princes persecute me without a
cause,
But my heart stands in awe of Your
word.
162 I rejoice at Your word
As one who finds great treasure.
163 I hate and abhor lying,
But I love Your law.
164 Seven times a day I praise You,
Because of Your righteous
judgments.
165 [a]Great peace have those who love
Your law,
And [1]nothing causes them to
stumble.
166 [a]LORD, I hope for Your salvation,
And I do Your commandments.
167 My soul keeps Your testimonies,
And I love them exceedingly.

152 a Luke 21:33
153 a Lam. 5:1
154 a 1 Sam. 24:15
156 1 Or *Many*
157 a Ps. 44:18
158 a Ezek. 9:4
161 a 1 Sam. 24:11; 26:18
165 a Prov. 3:2 1 Lit. *they have no stumbling block*
166 a Gen. 49:18
168 a Prov. 5:21
169 a Ps. 119:27, 144
170 1 Prayer of supplication
171 a Ps. 119:7
173 a Josh. 24:22
174 a Ps. 119:166 b Ps. 119:16, 24
176 a [Is. 53:6]
PSALM 120
1 a Jon. 2:2
4 1 *mighty one*
5 a Gen. 10:2 b Gen. 25:13

168 I keep Your precepts and Your
testimonies,
[a]For all my ways *are* before You.

ת TAU

169 Let my cry come before You,
O LORD;
[a]Give me understanding according
to Your word.
170 Let my [1]supplication come before
You;
Deliver me according to Your word.
171 [a]My lips shall utter praise,
For You teach me Your statutes.
172 My tongue shall speak of Your
word,
For all Your commandments *are*
righteousness.
173 Let Your hand become my help,
For [a]I have chosen Your precepts.
174 [a]I long for Your salvation, O LORD,
And [b]Your law *is* my delight.
175 Let my soul live, and it shall
praise You;
And let Your judgments help me.
176 [a]I have gone astray like a lost
sheep;
Seek Your servant,
For I do not forget Your
commandments.

PSALM 120

Plea for Relief from Bitter Foes

A Song of Ascents.

In [a]my distress I cried to the LORD,
And He heard me.
2 Deliver my soul, O LORD, from
lying lips
And from a deceitful tongue.
3 What shall be given to you,
Or what shall be done to you,
You false tongue?
4 Sharp arrows of the [1]warrior,
With coals of the broom tree!
5 Woe is me, that I dwell in
[a]Meshech,
[b]*That* I dwell among the tents of
Kedar!
6 My soul has dwelt too long
With one who hates peace.
7 I *am for* peace;
But when I speak, they *are* for war.

PSALM 121

God the Help of Those Who Seek Him

A Song of Ascents.

I [a]will lift up my eyes to the hills—
From whence comes my help?
2 [a]My help *comes* from the LORD,
Who made heaven and earth.

3 [a]He will not allow your foot to [1]be moved;
[b]He who keeps you will not slumber.
4 Behold, He who keeps Israel
Shall neither slumber nor sleep.

5 The LORD *is* your [1]keeper;
The LORD *is* [a]your shade [b]at your right hand.
6 [a]The sun shall not strike you by day,
Nor the moon by night.

7 The LORD shall [1]preserve you from all evil;
He shall [a]preserve your soul.
8 The LORD shall [a]preserve[1] your going out and your coming in
From this time forth, and even forevermore.

PSALM 122

The Joy of Going to the House of the Lord

A Song of Ascents. Of David.

I was glad when they said to me,
[a]"Let us go into the house of the LORD."
2 Our feet have been standing
Within your gates, O Jerusalem!

3 Jerusalem is built
As a city that is [a]compact together,
4 [a]Where the tribes go up,
The tribes of the LORD,
[1]To [b]the Testimony of Israel,
To give thanks to the name of the LORD.
5 [a]For thrones are set there for judgment,
The thrones of the house of David.

6 [a]Pray for the peace of Jerusalem:
"May they prosper who love you.
7 Peace be within your walls,
Prosperity within your palaces."
8 For the sake of my brethren and companions,
I will now say, "Peace *be* within you."
9 Because of the house of the LORD our God
I will [a]seek your good.

PSALM 123

Prayer for Relief from Contempt

A Song of Ascents.

Unto You [a]I lift up my eyes,
O You [b]who dwell in the heavens.
2 Behold, as the eyes of servants *look* to the hand of their masters,
As the eyes of a maid to the hand of her mistress,
[a]So our eyes *look* to the LORD our God,
Until He has mercy on us.

3 Have mercy on us, O LORD, have mercy on us!
For we are exceedingly filled with contempt.
4 Our soul is exceedingly filled
With the scorn of those who are at ease,
With the contempt of the proud.

PSALM 124

The Lord the Defense of His People

A Song of Ascents. Of David.

"If it had not been the LORD who was on our [a]side,"
[b]Let Israel now say—
2 "If it had not been the LORD who was on our side,
When men rose up against us,
3 Then they would have [a]swallowed us alive,
When their wrath was kindled against us;
4 Then the waters would have overwhelmed us,
The stream would have [1]gone over our soul;
5 Then the swollen waters
Would have [1]gone over our soul."

6 Blessed *be* the LORD,
Who has not given us *as* prey to their teeth.
7 [a]Our soul has escaped [b]as a bird from the snare of the [1]fowlers;
The snare is broken, and we have escaped.

PSALM 121
1 a [Jer. 3:23]
2 a [Ps. 124:8]
3 a 1 Sam. 2:9 b Is. 27:3 *1 slip*
5 a Is. 25:4 b Ps. 16:8 *1 protector*
6 a Is. 49:10
7 a Ps. 41:2 *1 keep*
8 a Deut. 28:6 *1 keep*

PSALM 122
1 a [Is. 2:3]
3 a 2 Sam. 5:9
4 a Deut. 16:16 b Ex. 16:34 1 Or *As a testimony to*
5 a Deut. 17:8
6 a Ps. 51:18
9 a Neh. 2:10

PSALM 123
1 a Ps. 121:1; 141:8 b Ps. 2:4; 11:4; 115:3
2 a Ps. 25:15

PSALM 124
1 a [Rom. 8:31] b Ps. 129:1
3 a Prov. 1:12
4 *1 swept over*
5 *1 swept over*
7 a Ps. 91:3 b Prov. 6:5 1 Persons who catch birds in a trap or snare

8 [a]Our help *is* in the name of the LORD,
[b]Who made heaven and earth.

PSALM 125

The Lord the Strength of His People

A Song of Ascents.

Those who trust in the LORD
Are like Mount Zion,
Which cannot be moved, *but* abides forever.
2 As the mountains surround Jerusalem,
So the LORD surrounds His people
From this time forth and forever.

3 For [a]the scepter of wickedness shall not rest
On the land allotted to the righteous,
Lest the righteous reach out their hands to iniquity.

4 Do good, O LORD, to *those who are* good,
And to *those who are* upright in their hearts.

5 As for such as turn aside to their [a]crooked ways,
The LORD shall lead them away
With the workers of iniquity.
[b]Peace *be* upon Israel!

PSALM 126

A Joyful Return to Zion

A Song of Ascents.

When [a]the LORD brought back [1]the captivity of Zion,
[b]We were like those who dream.
2 Then [a]our mouth was filled with laughter,
And our tongue with singing.
Then they said among the [1]nations,
"The LORD has done great things for them."
3 The LORD has done great things for us,
And we are glad.

4 Bring back our captivity, O LORD,
As the streams in the South.

5 [a]Those who sow in tears
Shall reap in joy.

8 a [Ps. 121:2]
b Gen. 1:1

PSALM 125
3 a Prov. 22:8

5 a Prov. 2:15
b [Gal. 6:16]

PSALM 126
1 a Hos. 6:11
b Acts 12:9
1 Those of the captivity

2 a Job 8:21
1 Gentiles

5 a Jer. 31:9

6 a Is. 61:3
1 to and fro
2 Lit. *a bag of seed for sowing*
3 with shouts of joy

PSALM 127
1 a [Ps. 121:3–5]

2 a [Gen. 3:17, 19]

3 a [Josh. 24:3, 4]
b Deut. 7:13; 28:4
c [Ps. 113:9]

5 a Ps. 128:2, 3
b Prov. 27:11

PSALM 128
1 a Ps. 119:1

2 a Is. 3:10
1 Fruit of the labor

6 He who continually goes [1]forth weeping,
Bearing [2]seed for sowing,
Shall doubtless come again [3]with [a]rejoicing,
Bringing his sheaves *with him.*

PSALM 127

Laboring and Prospering with the Lord

A Song of Ascents. Of Solomon.

Unless the LORD builds the house,
They labor in vain who build it;
Unless [a]the LORD guards the city,
The watchman stays awake in vain.
2 *It is* vain for you to rise up early,
To sit up late,
To [a]eat the bread of sorrows;
For so He gives His beloved sleep.

Father, bless the children of _____ who are a heritage from You; the fruit of their womb is a reward.

FROM PSALM 127:3

3 Behold, [a]children *are* a heritage from the LORD,
[b]The fruit of the womb *is* a [c]reward.
4 Like arrows in the hand of a warrior,
So *are* the children of one's youth.
5 [a]Happy *is* the man who has his quiver full of them;
[b]They shall not be ashamed,
But shall speak with their enemies in the gate.

PSALM 128

Blessings of Those Who Fear the Lord

A Song of Ascents.

Blessed [a]*is* every one who fears the LORD,
Who walks in His ways.
2 [a]When you eat the [1]labor of your hands,

You *shall be* happy, and *it shall be* [b]well with you.
3 Your wife *shall be* [a]like a fruitful vine
In the very heart of your house,
Your [b]children [c]like olive plants
All around your table.
4 Behold, thus shall the man be blessed
Who fears the LORD.

5 [a]The LORD bless you out of Zion,
And may you see the good of Jerusalem
All the days of your life.
6 Yes, may you [a]see your children's children.
[b]Peace *be* upon Israel!

PSALM 129

Song of Victory over Zion's Enemies

A Song of Ascents.

"Many a time they have [a]afflicted[1] me from [b]my youth,"
[c]Let Israel now say—
2 "Many a time they have afflicted me from my youth;
Yet they have not prevailed against me.
3 The plowers plowed on my back;
They made their furrows long."
4 The LORD *is* righteous;
He has cut in pieces the cords of the wicked.

5 Let all those who hate Zion
Be put to shame and turned back.
6 Let them be as the [a]grass *on* the housetops,
Which withers before it grows up,
7 With which the reaper does not fill his hand,
Nor he who binds sheaves, his [1]arms.
8 Neither let those who pass by them say,
[a]"The blessing of the LORD *be* upon you;
We bless you in the name of the LORD!"

2 b Deut. 4:40
3 a Ezek. 19:10 b Ps. 127:3–5 c Ps. 52:8; 144:12
5 a Ps. 134:3
6 a Job 42:16 b Ps. 125:5

PSALM 129
1 a [Jer. 1:19; 15:20] b Ezek. 23:3 c Ps. 124:1 *1 persecuted*
6 a Ps. 37:2
7 *1 armsful*, lit. *bosom*
8 a Ruth 2:4

PSALM 130
1 a Lam. 3:55
3 a [Ps. 143:2] b [Nah. 1:6] *1 take note of*
4 a [Ex. 34:7] b [1 Kin. 8:39, 40]
5 a [Ps. 27:14] b Ps. 119:81
6 a Ps. 119:147
7 a Ps. 131:3 b [Is. 55:7]
8 a [Ps. 103:3, 4]

PSALM 131
1 a [Rom. 12:16] *1* Proud *2* Arrogant *3* Lit. *walk in* *4 difficult*

PSALM 130

Waiting for the Redemption of the Lord

A Song of Ascents.

Out [a]of the depths I have cried to You, O LORD;
2 Lord, hear my voice!
Let Your ears be attentive
To the voice of my supplications.

3 [a]If You, LORD, should [1]mark iniquities,
O Lord, who could [b]stand?
4 But *there is* [a]forgiveness with You,
That [b]You may be feared.

Never be shaken in hope. Never be cooled in love. Never get tired of loving and hoping—yes, and believing.
AMY CARMICHAEL

5 [a]I wait for the LORD, my soul waits,
And [b]in His word I do hope.
6 [a]My soul *waits* for the Lord
More than those who watch for the morning—
Yes, more than those who watch for the morning.

7 [a]O Israel, hope in the LORD;
For [b]with the LORD *there is* mercy,
And with Him *is* abundant redemption.
8 And [a]He shall redeem Israel
From all his iniquities.

PSALM 131

Simple Trust in the Lord

A Song of Ascents. Of David.

LORD, my heart is not [1]haughty,
Nor my eyes [2]lofty.
[a]Neither do I [3]concern myself with great matters,
Nor with things too [4]profound for me.
2 Surely I have calmed and quieted my soul,

[a]Like a weaned child with his mother;
Like a weaned child *is* my soul within me.

3 [a]O Israel, hope in the LORD
From this time forth and forever.

PSALM 132

The Eternal Dwelling of God in Zion

A Song of Ascents.

LORD, remember David
And all his afflictions;
2 How he swore to the LORD,
[a]*And* vowed to [b]the Mighty One of Jacob:
3 "Surely I will not go into the chamber of my house,
Or go up to the comfort of my bed;
4 I will [a]not give sleep to my eyes
Or slumber to my eyelids,
5 Until I [a]find a place for the LORD,
A dwelling place for the Mighty One of Jacob."

6 Behold, we heard of it [a]in Ephrathah;
[b]We found it [c]in the fields of [1]the woods.
7 Let us go into His tabernacle;
[a]Let us worship at His footstool.
8 [a]Arise, O LORD, to Your resting place,
You and [b]the ark of Your strength.
9 Let Your priests [a]be clothed with righteousness,
And let Your saints shout for joy.

10 For Your servant David's sake,
Do not turn away the face of Your [1]Anointed.

11 [a]The LORD has sworn *in* truth to David;
He will not turn from it:
"I will set upon your throne [b]the [1]fruit of your body.
12 If your sons will keep My covenant
And My testimony which I shall teach them,
Their sons also shall sit upon your throne forevermore."

13 [a]For the LORD has chosen Zion;
He has desired *it* for His [1]dwelling place:
14 "This[a] *is* My resting place forever;
Here I will dwell, for I have desired it.
15 [a]I will abundantly bless her [1]provision;
I will satisfy her poor with bread.
16 [a]I will also clothe her priests with salvation,
[b]And her saints shall shout aloud for joy.
17 [a]There I will make the [1]horn of David grow;
[b]I will prepare a lamp for My [2]Anointed.
18 His enemies I will [a]clothe with shame,
But upon Himself His crown shall flourish."

PSALM 133

Blessed Unity of the People of God

A Song of Ascents. Of David.

Behold, how good and how pleasant *it is*
For [a]brethren to dwell together in unity!

2 *It is* like the precious oil upon the head,
Running down on the beard,
The beard of Aaron,
Running down on the edge of his garments.
3 *It is* like the dew of [a]Hermon,
Descending upon the mountains of Zion;
For [b]there the LORD commanded the blessing—
Life forevermore.

PSALM 134

Praising the Lord in His House at Night

A Song of Ascents.

Behold, bless the LORD,
All *you* servants of the LORD,
Who by night stand in the house of the LORD!
2 [a]Lift up your hands *in* the sanctuary,
And bless the LORD.

3 The LORD who made heaven and earth
Bless you from Zion!

PSALM 131
2 a[Matt. 18:3]
3 a[Ps. 130:7]

PSALM 132
2 a Ps. 65:1 b Gen. 49:24
4 a Prov. 6:4
5 a Acts 7:46
6 a 1 Sam. 17:12 b 1 Sam. 7:1 c 1 Chr. 13:5 *1* Heb. *Jaar,* lit. *Woods*
7 a Ps. 5:7; 99:5
8 a Num. 10:35 b Ps. 78:61
9 a Job 29:14
10 *1* Commissioned One, Heb. *Messiah*
11 a[Ps. 89:3, 4, 33; 110:4] b 2 Sam. 7:12 *1 offspring*
13 a[Ps. 48:1, 2] *1 home*
14 a Ps. 68:16
15 a Ps. 147:14 *1 supply of food*
16 a 2 Chr. 6:41 b 1 Sam. 4:5
17 a Ezek. 29:21 b 1 Kin. 11:36; 15:4 *1* Government *2* Heb. *Messiah*
18 a Ps. 35:26

PSALM 133
1 a Gen. 13:8
3 a Deut. 4:48 b Lev. 25:21

PSALM 134
2 a[1 Tim. 2:8]

PSALM 135

Praise to God in Creation and Redemption

Praise the LORD!

Praise the name of the LORD;
[a]Praise *Him,* O you servants of the LORD!
2 [a]You who stand in the house of the LORD,
In [b]the courts of the house of our God,
3 Praise the LORD, for [a]the LORD *is* good;
Sing praises to His name, [b]for *it is* pleasant.
4 For [a]the LORD has chosen Jacob for Himself,
Israel for His [1]special treasure.

5 For I know that [a]the LORD *is* great,
And our Lord *is* above all gods.
6 [a]Whatever the LORD pleases He does,
In heaven and in earth,
In the seas and in all deep places.
7 [a]He causes the [1]vapors to ascend from the ends of the earth;
[b]He makes lightning for the rain;
He brings the wind out of His [c]treasuries.
8 [a]He [1]destroyed the firstborn of Egypt,
[2]Both of man and beast.
9 [a]He sent signs and wonders into the midst of you, O Egypt,
[b]Upon Pharaoh and all his servants.
10 [a]He defeated many nations
And slew mighty kings—
11 Sihon king of the Amorites,
Og king of Bashan,
And [a]all the kingdoms of Canaan—
12 [a]And gave their land *as* a [1]heritage,
A heritage to Israel His people.

13 [a]Your name, O LORD, *endures* forever,
Your fame, O LORD, throughout all generations.
14 [a]For the LORD will judge His people,
And He will have compassion on His servants.

15 [a]The idols of the nations *are* silver and gold,
The work of men's hands.
16 They have mouths, but they do not speak;
Eyes they have, but they do not see;
17 They have ears, but they do not hear;
Nor is there *any* breath in their mouths.
18 Those who make them are like them;
So is everyone who trusts in them.

19 [a]Bless the LORD, O house of Israel!
Bless the LORD, O house of Aaron!
20 Bless the LORD, O house of Levi!
You who fear the LORD, bless the LORD!
21 Blessed be the LORD [a]out of Zion,
Who dwells in Jerusalem!

Praise the LORD!

PSALM 136

Thanksgiving to God for His Enduring Mercy

Oh, [a]give thanks to the LORD, for *He is* good!
[b]For His mercy *endures* forever.
2 Oh, give thanks to [a]the God of gods!
For His mercy *endures* forever.
3 Oh, give thanks to the Lord of lords!
For His mercy *endures* forever:

4 To Him [a]who alone does great wonders,
For His mercy *endures* forever;
5 [a]To Him who by wisdom made the heavens,
For His mercy *endures* forever;
6 [a]To Him who laid out the earth above the waters,
For His mercy *endures* forever;
7 [a]To Him who made great lights,
For His mercy *endures* forever—
8 [a]The sun to rule by day,
For His mercy *endures* forever;
9 The moon and stars to rule by night,
For His mercy *endures* forever.

10 [a]To Him who struck Egypt in their firstborn,
For His mercy *endures* forever;
11 [a]And brought out Israel from among them,
For His mercy *endures* forever;
12 [a]With a strong hand, and with [1]an outstretched arm,

PSALM 135
1 a Ps. 113:1
2 a Luke 2:37 b Ps. 116:19
3 a [Ps. 119:68] b Ps. 147:1
4 a [Ex. 19:5] *1 precious possession*
5 a Ps. 95:3; 97:9
6 a Ps. 115:3
7 a Jer. 10:13 b Job 28:25, 26; 38:24–28 c Jer. 51:16 *1* Water vapor
8 a Ex. 12:12 *1* Lit. *struck down* *2* Lit. *From man to beast*
9 a Ex. 7:10 b Ps. 136:15
10 a Num. 21:24
11 a Josh. 12:7–24
12 a Ps. 78:55; 136:21, 22 *1 inheritance*
13 a [Ex. 3:15]
14 a Deut. 32:36
15 a [Ps. 115:4–8]
19 a [Ps. 115:9]
21 a Ps. 134:3

PSALM 136
1 a Ps. 106:1 b 1 Chr. 16:34
2 a [Deut. 10:17]
4 a Ps. 72:18
5 a Jer. 51:15
6 a Jer. 10:12
7 a Gen. 1:14–18
8 a Gen. 1:16
10 a Ex. 12:29
11 a Ex. 12:51; 13:3, 16
12 a Ex. 6:6 *1* Mighty power

For His mercy *endures* forever;
13 [a]To Him who divided the Red Sea
in two,
For His mercy *endures* forever;
14 And made Israel pass through the
midst of it,
For His mercy *endures* forever;
15 [a]But overthrew Pharaoh and his
army in the Red Sea,
For His mercy *endures* forever;
16 [a]To Him who led His people
through the wilderness,
For His mercy *endures* forever;
17 [a]To Him who struck down great
kings,
For His mercy *endures* forever;
18 [a]And slew famous kings,
For His mercy *endures* forever—
19 [a]Sihon king of the Amorites,
For His mercy *endures* forever;
20 [a]And Og king of Bashan,
For His mercy *endures* forever—
21 [a]And gave their land as a [1]heritage,
For His mercy *endures* forever;
22 A heritage to Israel His servant,
For His mercy *endures* forever.

23 Who [a]remembered us in our lowly
state,
For His mercy *endures* forever;
24 And [a]rescued us from our
enemies,
For His mercy *endures* forever;
25 [a]Who gives food to all flesh,
For His mercy *endures* forever.

26 Oh, give thanks to the God of
heaven!
For His mercy *endures* forever.

PSALM 137

Longing for Zion in a Foreign Land

By the rivers of Babylon,
There we sat down, yea, we wept
When we remembered Zion.
2 We hung our harps
Upon the willows in the midst of it.
3 For there those who carried us
away captive asked of us a song,
And those who [a]plundered us
requested mirth,
Saying, "Sing us *one* of the songs
of Zion!"

4 How shall we sing the LORD's song
In a foreign land?
5 If I forget you, O Jerusalem,

13 [a]Ex. 14:21
15 [a]Ex. 14:27
16 [a]Ex. 13:18; 15:22
17 [a]Ps. 135:10–12
18 [a]Deut. 29:7
19 [a]Num. 21:21
20 [a]Num. 21:33
21 [a]Josh. 12:1 [1]*inheritance*
23 [a]Gen. 8:1
24 [a]Ps. 44:7
25 [a]Ps. 104:27; 145:15

PSALM 137
3 [a]Ps. 79:1
6 [a]Ezek. 3:26
7 [a]Jer. 49:7–22 [1]Lit. *Make bare*
8 [a]Is. 13:1–6; 47:1 [b]Jer. 50:15
9 [a]Is. 13:16

PSALM 138
1 [a]Ps. 119:46
2 [a]Ps. 28:2 [b]1 Kin. 8:29 [c]Is. 42:21
4 [a]Ps. 102:15
6 [a][Ps. 113:4–7] [b][James 4:6]
7 [a][Ps. 23:3, 4]
8 [a]Ps. 57:2 [1]*complete*

Let my right hand forget *its skill!*
6 If I do not remember you,
Let my [a]tongue cling to the roof of
my mouth—
If I do not exalt Jerusalem
Above my chief joy.

7 Remember, O LORD, against [a]the
sons of Edom
The day of Jerusalem,
Who said, [1]"Raze *it,* raze *it,*
To its very foundation!"

8 O daughter of Babylon, [a]who are to
be destroyed,
Happy the one [b]who repays you as
you have served us!
9 Happy the one who takes and
[a]dashes
Your little ones against the rock!

PSALM 138

The Lord's Goodness to the Faithful

A Psalm of David.

I will praise You with my whole heart;
[a]Before the gods I will sing praises
to You.
2 [a]I will worship [b]toward Your holy
temple,
And praise Your name
For Your lovingkindness and Your
truth;
For You have [c]magnified Your word
above all Your name.
3 In the day when I cried out, You
answered me,
And made me bold *with* strength in
my soul.

4 [a]All the kings of the earth shall
praise You, O LORD,
When they hear the words of Your
mouth.
5 Yes, they shall sing of the ways of
the LORD,
For great *is* the glory of the LORD.
6 [a]Though the LORD *is* on high,
Yet [b]He regards the lowly;
But the proud He knows from afar.

7 [a]Though I walk in the midst of
trouble, You will revive me;
You will stretch out Your hand
Against the wrath of my enemies,
And Your right hand will save me.
8 [a]The LORD will [1]perfect *that which*
concerns me;

Your mercy, O LORD, *endures*
forever;
[b]Do not forsake the works of Your
hands.

PSALM 139

God's Perfect Knowledge of Man

For the Chief Musician. A Psalm of David.

O LORD, [a]You have searched me and
known *me*.
2 [a]You know my sitting down and my
rising up;
You [b]understand my thought afar
off.
3 [a]You [1]comprehend my path and my
lying down,
And are acquainted with all my
ways.
4 For *there is* not a word on my
tongue,
But behold, O LORD, [a]You know it
altogether.
5 You have [1]hedged me behind and
before,
And laid Your hand upon me.
6 [a]*Such* knowledge *is* too wonderful
for me;
It is high, I cannot *attain* it.

Lord, I pray that ____ would understand how intimately You know them. You know when they sit down and rise up, You understand their thoughts, comprehend their path and their lying down. You are acquainted with all of their ways.

FROM PSALM 139:1–3

7 [a]Where can I go from Your Spirit?
Or where can I flee from Your
presence?
8 [a]If I ascend into heaven, You *are*
there;
[b]If I make my bed in [1]hell, behold,
You *are there*.
9 *If* I take the wings of the morning,
And dwell in the uttermost parts of
the sea,
10 Even there Your hand shall lead
me,
And Your right hand shall hold me.
11 If I say, "Surely the darkness shall
[1]fall on me,"
Even the night shall be light about
me;
12 Indeed, [a]the darkness [1]shall not
hide from You,
But the night shines as the day;
The darkness and the light *are* both
alike *to You*.
13 For You formed my inward parts;
You [1]covered me in my mother's
womb.
14 I will praise You, for [1]I am
fearfully *and* wonderfully made;
Marvelous are Your works,
And *that* my soul knows very well.
15 [a]My [1]frame was not hidden from
You,
When I was made in secret,
And skillfully wrought in the lowest
parts of the earth.
16 Your eyes saw my substance,
being yet unformed.
And in Your book they all were
written,
The days fashioned for me,
When *as yet there were* none of
them.
17 [a]How precious also are Your
thoughts to me, O God!
How great is the sum of them!
18 *If* I should count them, they
would be more in number than
the sand;
When I awake, I am still with You.
19 Oh, that You would [a]slay the
wicked, O God!
[b]Depart from me, therefore, you
[1]bloodthirsty men.
20 For they [a]speak against You
wickedly;
[1]Your enemies take *Your name* in
vain.
21 [a]Do I not hate them, O LORD, who
hate You?
And do I not loathe those who rise
up against You?
22 I hate them with [1]perfect hatred;
I count them my enemies.
23 [a]Search me, O God, and know my
heart;

8 [b]Job 10:3, 8

PSALM 139
1 [a]Ps. 17:3
2 [a]2 Kin. 19:27 [b]Matt. 9:4
3 [a]Job 14:16; 31:4 [1]Lit. *winnow*
4 [a][Heb. 4:13]
5 [1]*enclosed*
6 [a]Job 42:3
7 [a][Jer. 23:24]
8 [a][Amos 9:2–4] [b][Job 26:6] [1]Or *Sheol*
11 [1]Vg., Symmachus *cover*
12 [a]Job 26:6; 34:22 [1]Lit. *is not dark*
13 [1]*wove*
14 [1]So with MT, Tg.; LXX, Syr., Vg. *You are fearfully wonderful*
15 [a]Job 10:8, 9 [1]Lit. *bones were*
17 [a][Ps. 40:5]
19 [a][Is. 11:4] [b]Ps. 119:115 [1]Lit. *men of bloodshed*
20 [a]Jude 15 [1]LXX, Vg. *They take your cities in vain*
21 [a]2 Chr. 19:2
22 [1]*complete*
23 [a]Job 31:6

Psalm 139:15, 16

Dear Woman of Destiny,

It is so wonderful to know that God knew us and watched as we were being formed in the womb! Our days are already fashioned by Him; they are already written in His book. What a blessing to know that God has a plan for your life—a plan that He has known even before you were born.

Knowing this was important to me when I became pregnant with our first child. When I conceived our son, it wasn't quite our timing, as we were newly married. But through this Scripture and many others, God relieved the uncertainty with His faithful assurance that it was *His* time and *His* plan.

He began to gently instruct me to pray daily over the life that was forming inside of me. One of my first prayers was that our child would shine a light into the life of every person he met—and we are truly seeing that come to pass today! God specifically led me to pray that our child would know who he was in Christ, that God had a purpose for him, and that he would walk in his calling. The Lord continually led me to Scriptures to pray over our child concerning his temperament, health, peace, integrity, spirituality, protection, and many other areas of his life. I prayed and read aloud from Proverbs often to instill wisdom and knowledge. I prayed out of Galatians that our child would bear the fruits of the Spirit. I also prayed for his physical development, for each part of his body as it was being formed.

It is such a blessed experience to be a part of God's plan in bringing forth a new life. To pray for your child throughout your pregnancy is one of the best gifts you can give him. It starts the wonderful bonding process and sows seeds that will be harvested throughout his lifetime.

I have also realized through this Scripture that God knows about our children before we do! He has a plan for them, and it is important that we surrender them to God's plan—not our own. Pray that your child (and that you as parents) will know God's will for his life and that he will live with direction, that he will not be distracted or confused, but will walk boldly in his purpose.

If you are not expecting as you read this, pray for those who are facing an unplanned pregnancy. Pray for the unborn children in these circumstances and always remember—God has a plan!

Kara Quinn-Smith

Try me, and know my anxieties;
24 And see if *there is any* wicked way
in me,
And [a]lead me in the way
everlasting.

PSALM 140

Prayer for Deliverance from Evil Men

To the Chief Musician. A Psalm of David.

Deliver me, O LORD, from evil men;
Preserve me from violent men,
2 Who plan evil things in *their*
hearts;
[a]They continually gather together
for war.
3 They sharpen their tongues like a
serpent;
The [a]poison of asps *is* under their
lips. Selah

4 [a]Keep me, O LORD, from the hands
of the wicked;
Preserve me from violent men,
Who have purposed to make my
steps stumble.
5 The proud have hidden a [a]snare for
me, and cords;
They have spread a net by the
wayside;
They have set traps for me. Selah

6 I said to the LORD: "You *are* my
God;
Hear the voice of my supplications,
O LORD.
7 O GOD the Lord, the strength of
my salvation,
You have [1]covered my head in the
day of battle.
8 Do not grant, O LORD, the desires
of the wicked;
Do not further his *wicked* scheme,
[a]*Lest* they be exalted. Selah

9 "*As for* the head of those who
surround me,
Let the evil of their lips cover
them;
10 [a]Let burning coals fall upon them;
Let them be cast into the fire,
Into deep pits, that they rise not up
again.
11 Let not a slanderer be established
in the earth;
Let evil hunt the violent man to
overthrow *him*."

24 a Ps. 5:8; 143:10

PSALM 140
2 a Ps. 56:6
3 a Ps. 58:4
4 a Ps. 71:4
5 a Jer. 18:22
7 *1 sheltered*
8 a Deut. 32:27
10 a Ps. 11:6
12 a 1 Kin. 8:45

PSALM 141
2 a [Rev. 5:8; 8:3, 4]
b [1 Tim. 2:8]
c Ex. 29:39, 41
3 a [Prov. 13:3; 21:23]
4 a Prov. 23:6
5 a [Prov. 9:8]
6 *1 rock*

12 I know that the LORD will
[a]maintain
The cause of the afflicted,
And justice for the poor.
13 Surely the righteous shall give
thanks to Your name;
The upright shall dwell in Your
presence.

PSALM 141

Prayer for Safekeeping from Wickedness

A Psalm of David.

LORD, I cry out to You;
Make haste to me!
Give ear to my voice when I cry out
to You.
2 Let my prayer be set before You
[a]*as* incense,
[b]The lifting up of my hands *as* [c]the
evening sacrifice.

The life of prayer is just love to God, and the custom of being ever with Him.

TERESA OF ÁVILA

3 Set a guard, O LORD, over my
[a]mouth;
Keep watch over the door of my
lips.
4 Do not incline my heart to any evil
thing,
To practice wicked works
With men who work iniquity;
[a]And do not let me eat of their
delicacies.

5 [a]Let the righteous strike me;
It shall be a kindness.
And let him rebuke me;
It shall be as excellent oil;
Let my head not refuse it.

For still my prayer *is* against the
deeds of the wicked.
6 Their judges are overthrown by the
sides of the [1]cliff,
And they hear my words, for they
are sweet.

7 Our bones are scattered at the mouth of the grave,
As when one plows and breaks up the earth.

8 But [a]my eyes *are* upon You, O GOD the Lord;
In You I take refuge;
[1]Do not leave my soul destitute.

9 Keep me from [a]the snares they have laid for me,
And from the traps of the workers of iniquity.

10 [a]Let the wicked fall into their own nets,
While I escape safely.

PSALM 142

A Plea for Relief from Persecutors

A [a]Contemplation[1] of David. A Prayer [b]when he was in the cave.

I cry out to the LORD with my voice;
With my voice to the LORD I make my supplication.

2 I pour out my complaint before Him;
I declare before Him my trouble.

3 When my spirit [1]was [a]overwhelmed within me,
Then You knew my path.
In the way in which I walk
They have secretly [b]set a snare for me.

4 Look on *my* right hand and see,
For *there is* no one who acknowledges me;
Refuge has failed me;
No one cares for my soul.

5 I cried out to You, O LORD:
I said, "You *are* my refuge,
My portion in the land of the living.

6 [1]Attend to my cry,
For I am brought very low;
Deliver me from my persecutors,
For they are stronger than I.

7 Bring my soul out of prison,
That I may [a]praise Your name;
The righteous shall surround me,
For You shall deal bountifully with me."

8 a Ps. 25:15 *1* Lit. *Do not make my soul bare*
9 a Ps. 119:110
10 a Ps. 35:8
PSALM 142
title a Ps. 32:title b 1 Sam. 22:1 *1* Heb. *Maschil*
3 a Ps. 77:3 b Ps. 141:9 *1* Lit. *fainted*
6 *1 Give heed*
7 a Ps. 34:1, 2
PSALM 143
2 a [Gal. 2:16]
3 *1 dark places*
4 a Ps. 77:3
5 a Ps. 77:5, 10, 11 *1 ponder*
6 a Ps. 63:1
7 a Ps. 28:1 *1 become* *2* Die
8 a Ps. 46:5 b Ps. 5:8 c Ps. 25:1
9 *1* LXX, Vg. *To You I flee*
10 a Ps. 25:4, 5 b Neh. 9:20 c Is. 26:10
11 a Ps. 119:25
12 a Ps. 54:5 *1 put an end to*

PSALM 143

An Earnest Appeal for Guidance and Deliverance

A Psalm of David.

Hear my prayer, O LORD,
Give ear to my supplications!
In Your faithfulness answer me,
And in Your righteousness.

2 Do not enter into judgment with Your servant,
[a]For in Your sight no one living is righteous.

3 For the enemy has persecuted my soul;
He has crushed my life to the ground;
He has made me dwell in [1]darkness,
Like those who have long been dead.

4 [a]Therefore my spirit is overwhelmed within me;
My heart within me is distressed.

5 [a]I remember the days of old;
I meditate on all Your works;
I [1]muse on the work of Your hands.

6 I spread out my hands to You;
[a]My soul *longs* for You like a thirsty land. Selah

7 Answer me speedily, O LORD;
My spirit fails!
Do not hide Your face from me,
[a]Lest I [1]be like those who [2]go down into the pit.

8 Cause me to hear Your lovingkindness [a]in the morning,
For in You do I trust;
[b]Cause me to know the way in which I should walk,
For [c]I lift up my soul to You.

9 Deliver me, O LORD, from my enemies;
[1]In You I take shelter.

10 [a]Teach me to do Your will,
For You *are* my God;
[b]Your Spirit *is* good.
Lead me in [c]the land of uprightness.

11 [a]Revive me, O LORD, for Your name's sake!
For Your righteousness' sake bring my soul out of trouble.

12 In Your mercy [a]cut[1] off my enemies,

And destroy all those who afflict my
soul;
For I *am* Your servant.

PSALM 144

A Song to the Lord Who Preserves and Prospers His People

A Psalm of David.

Blessed *be* the LORD my Rock,
[a]Who trains my hands for war,
And my fingers for battle—
2 My lovingkindness and my fortress,
My high tower and my deliverer,
My shield and *the One* in whom I
take refuge,
Who subdues [1]my people under me.

3 [a]LORD, what *is* man, that You take
knowledge of him?
Or the son of man, that You are
mindful of him?
4 [a]Man is like a breath;
[b]His days *are* like a passing shadow.

5 [a]Bow down Your heavens, O LORD,
and come down;
[b]Touch the mountains, and they
shall smoke.
6 [a]Flash forth lightning and scatter
them;
Shoot out Your arrows and destroy
them.
7 Stretch out Your hand from above;
Rescue me and deliver me out of
great waters,
From the hand of foreigners,
8 Whose mouth [a]speaks [1]lying
words,
And whose right hand *is* a right
hand of falsehood.

9 I will [a]sing a new song to You,
O God;
On a harp of ten strings I will sing
praises to You,
10 *The One* who gives [1]salvation to
kings,
[a]Who delivers David His servant
From the deadly sword.

11 Rescue me and deliver me from
the hand of foreigners,
Whose mouth speaks lying words,
And whose right hand *is* a right
hand of falsehood—
12 That our sons *may be* [a]as plants
grown up in their youth;
That our daughters *may be* as
[1]pillars,
Sculptured in palace style;
13 *That* our barns *may be* full,
Supplying all kinds of produce;
That our sheep may bring forth
thousands
And ten thousands in our fields;
14 *That* our oxen *may be* well laden;
That there be no [1]breaking in or
going out;
That there be no outcry in our
streets.
15 [a]Happy *are* the people who are in
such a state;
Happy *are* the people whose God *is*
the LORD!

PSALM 145

A Song of God's Majesty and Love

[a]A Praise of David.

I will [1]extol You, my God, O King;
And I will bless Your name forever
and ever.
2 Every day I will bless You,
And I will praise Your name forever
and ever.
3 [a]Great *is* the LORD, and greatly to
be praised;
And [b]His greatness *is*
[1]unsearchable.

4 [a]One generation shall praise Your
works to another,
And shall declare Your mighty acts.
5 [1]I will meditate on the glorious
splendor of Your majesty,
And [2]on Your wondrous works.
6 *Men* shall speak of the might of
Your awesome acts,
And I will declare Your greatness.
7 They shall [1]utter the memory of
Your great goodness,
And shall sing of Your
righteousness.

8 [a]The LORD *is* gracious and full of
compassion,
Slow to anger and great in mercy.
9 [a]The LORD *is* good to all,
And His tender mercies *are* over all
His works.

10 [a]All Your works shall praise You,
O LORD,
And Your saints shall bless You.

PSALM 144
1 a 2 Sam. 22:35
2 1 So with MT, LXX, Vg.; Syr., Tg. *the peoples* (cf. 18:47)
3 a Heb. 2:6
4 a Ps. 39:11 b Job 8:9; 14:2
5 a Ps. 18:9 b Ps. 104:32
6 a Ps. 18:13, 14
8 a Ps. 12:2 1 *empty* or *worthless*
9 a Ps. 33:2, 3; 40:3
10 a Ps. 18:50 1 *deliverance*
12 a Ps. 128:3 1 *corner pillars*
14 1 Lit. *breach*
15 a [Ps. 33:12]

PSALM 145
title a Ps. 100:title
1 1 *praise*
3 a [Ps. 147:5] b [Rom. 11:33] 1 Beyond our understanding
4 a Is. 38:19
5 1 So with MT, Tg.; DSS, LXX, Syr., Vg. *They* 2 Lit. *on the words of Your wondrous works*
7 1 *eagerly utter,* lit. *bubble forth*
8 a [Num. 14:18]
9 a Nah. 1:7
10 a Ps. 19:1

11 They shall speak of the glory of
Your kingdom,
And talk of Your power,
12 To make known to the sons of
men His mighty acts,
And the glorious majesty of His
kingdom.
13 [a]Your kingdom *is* an everlasting
kingdom,
And Your dominion *endures*
throughout all [1]generations.

14 The LORD upholds all who fall,
And [a]raises up all *who are* bowed
down.
15 [a]The eyes of all look expectantly to
You,
And [b]You give them their food in
due season.
16 You open Your hand
[a]And satisfy the desire of every living
thing.

17 The LORD *is* righteous in all His
ways,
Gracious in all His works.
18 [a]The LORD *is* near to all who call
upon Him,
To all who call upon Him [b]in truth.
19 He will fulfill the desire of those
who fear Him;
He also will hear their cry and save
them.
20 [a]The LORD preserves all who love
Him,
But all the wicked He will destroy.
21 My mouth shall speak the praise
of the LORD,
And all flesh shall bless His holy
name
Forever and ever.

PSALM 146

The Happiness of Those Whose Help Is the Lord

Praise[1] the LORD!

[a]Praise the LORD, O my soul!
2 [a]While I live I will praise the LORD;
I will sing praises to my God while
I have my being.

3 [a]Do not put your trust in princes,
Nor in [1]a son of man, in whom
there is no [2]help.
4 [a]His spirit departs, he returns to his
earth;
In that very day [b]his plans perish.

13 **a** [1 Tim. 1:17] *1* So with MT, Tg.; DSS, LXX, Syr., Vg. add *The LORD is faithful in all His words, And holy in all His works*
14 **a** Ps. 146:8
15 **a** Ps. 104:27 **b** Ps. 136:25
16 **a** Ps. 104:21, 28
18 **a** [Deut. 4:7] **b** [John 4:24]
20 **a** [Ps. 31:23]

PSALM 146
1 **a** Ps. 103:1 *1* Heb. *Hallelujah*
2 **a** Ps. 104:33
3 **a** [Is. 2:22] *1* A human being *2 salvation*
4 **a** [Eccl. 12:7] **b** [1 Cor. 2:6]
5 **a** Jer. 17:7
6 **a** Rev. 14:7
7 **a** Ps. 103:6 **b** Ps. 107:9 **c** Ps. 107:10
8 **a** Matt. 9:30 **b** Luke 13:13
9 **a** Deut. 10:18 **b** Ps. 147:6 *1* Lit. *makes crooked*
10 **a** Ex. 15:18

PSALM 147
1 **a** Ps. 92:1 **b** Ps. 135:3 **c** Ps. 33:1 *1* Heb. *Hallelujah*
2 **a** Ps. 102:16 **b** Deut. 30:3
3 **a** [Ps. 51:17] *1* Lit. *sorrows*
4 **a** Is. 40:26

5 [a]Happy *is he* who *has* the God of
Jacob for his help,
Whose hope *is* in the LORD his God,
6 [a]Who made heaven and earth,
The sea, and all that *is* in them;
Who keeps truth forever,
7 [a]Who executes justice for the
oppressed,
[b]Who gives food to the hungry.
[c]The LORD gives freedom to the
prisoners.

Happy is ____ who has the God of Jacob for their help; may they put their hope in You, Lord, for You are their God.

FROM PSALM 146:5

8 [a]The LORD opens *the eyes of* the
blind;
[b]The LORD raises those who are
bowed down;
The LORD loves the righteous.
9 [a]The LORD watches over the
strangers;
He relieves the fatherless and
widow;
[b]But the way of the wicked He
[1]turns upside down.
10 [a]The LORD shall reign forever—
Your God, O Zion, to all
generations.

Praise the LORD!

PSALM 147

Praise to God for His Word and Providence

Praise[1] the LORD!
For [a]*it is* good to sing praises to
our God;
[b]For *it is* pleasant, *and* [c]praise is
beautiful.

2 The LORD [a]builds up Jerusalem;
[b]He gathers together the outcasts of
Israel.
3 [a]He heals the brokenhearted
And binds up their [1]wounds.
4 [a]He counts the number of the stars;

Psalm 147:3

Dear Woman of Destiny,

Losing a loved one is always difficult; but sudden, tragic loss has its own unique circumstances. When my husband, Keith Green, and two of our children died in a small plane crash, how could I be prepared? Keith was only twenty-eight years old, Josiah was three, and Bethany was two. My faith in Jesus was strong, but still I was devastated. Life, as I knew it, would never be the same.

There was much to do at first. The media sent helicopters and wanted interviews. I had to find x-rays so the coroner could identify bodies. I bought a casket, selected burial clothing, found a cemetery, and planned a memorial service and a funeral. Not my original plans for the week, but keeping busy was a helpful diversion from my mounting nightmare.

Once things quieted down and friends flew back home, I was left to live out a very different life. I was now a single mom. Rebekah was one year old, and I was pregnant with Rachel. I didn't understand why God had allowed something so terrible to happen, but I immediately decided to trust that He was good and would take care of us. If I turned my back on Him, I'd be cutting off my only source of comfort and healing. Healing? Would it ever come?

As the shock wore off, the worst of the grieving began. How do you live without those you've built your life around? How do you cope with mornings when for a moment before you open your eyes you feel good . . . then you remember? What do you do about the pain? The anger?

I had more questions than answers. But I knew one thing: I could trust God to be faithful. I threw myself on His mercy and asked Him to help me. It was during those long months of deep grief that I felt His profound, sweet presence in the most powerful way. For months I could only read the psalms—and I couldn't worship without crying. Sure, I got tired of always being the "needy" one in the room, but I was. Keith and the children were with Jesus. They were fine, but I was miserable. I was missing the years of relationship I'd counted on. Some thought my tears were selfish—but the Lord assured me that He cried when His Son died. He also told me He cried when Keith and the children died. I knew it was true. I saw His tears fall from heaven.

As time passed, I noticed that God was digging a deep well of compassion in my heart for others who were suffering. After awhile, He even told me to focus outwardly and to comfort others with the comfort He'd given me. And He told me to stay in fellowship and not to isolate myself from other believers. I needed to let people love me.

Even with God, grieving is a difficult process. But there is light at the end of the tunnel when we hold onto Jesus. I don't walk in the ever-present pain anymore, although I do still cry sometimes. My faith is much stronger now, too. I know for a fact that He "heals the brokenhearted and binds up their wounds" (Ps 147:3).

Melody Green

He calls them all by name.
5 [a]Great *is* our Lord, and [b]mighty in power;
[c]His understanding *is* infinite.
6 [a]The LORD lifts up the humble;
He casts the wicked down to the ground.

7 Sing to the LORD with thanksgiving;
Sing praises on the harp to our God,
8 [a]Who covers the heavens with clouds,
Who prepares rain for the earth,
Who makes grass to grow on the mountains.
9 [a]He gives to the beast its food,
And [b]to the young ravens that cry.

There is no one more beautiful than one who is broken!

WATCHMAN NEE

10 [a]He does not delight in the strength of the horse;
He takes no pleasure in the legs of a man.
11 The LORD takes pleasure in those who fear Him,
In those who hope in His mercy.

12 Praise the LORD, O Jerusalem!
Praise your God, O Zion!
13 For He has strengthened the bars of your gates;
He has blessed your children within you.
14 [a]He makes peace *in* your borders,
And [b]fills you with [1]the finest wheat.

15 [a]He sends out His command *to the* earth;
His word runs very swiftly.
16 [a]He gives snow like wool;
He scatters the frost like ashes;
17 He casts out His hail like [1]morsels;
Who can stand before His cold?
18 [a]He sends out His word and melts them;
He causes His wind to blow, *and* the waters flow.

19 [a]He declares His word to Jacob,
[b]His statutes and His judgments to Israel.
20 [a]He has not dealt thus with any nation;
And *as for His* judgments, they have not known them.

[1]Praise the LORD!

PSALM 148

Praise to the Lord from Creation

Praise[1] the LORD!

Praise the LORD from the heavens;
Praise Him in the heights!
2 Praise Him, all His angels;
Praise Him, all His hosts!
3 Praise Him, sun and moon;
Praise Him, all you stars of light!
4 Praise Him, [a]you heavens of heavens,
And [b]you waters above the heavens!

5 Let them praise the name of the LORD,
For [a]He commanded and they were created.
6 [a]He also established them forever and ever;
He made a decree which shall not pass away.

7 Praise the LORD from the earth,
[a]You great sea creatures and all the depths;
8 Fire and hail, snow and clouds;
Stormy wind, fulfilling His word;
9 [a]Mountains and all hills;
Fruitful trees and all cedars;
10 Beasts and all cattle;
Creeping things and flying fowl;
11 Kings of the earth and all peoples;
Princes and all judges of the earth;
12 Both young men and maidens;
Old men and children.

13 Let them praise the name of the LORD,
For His [a]name alone is exalted;
His glory *is* above the earth and heaven.
14 And He [a]has exalted the [1]horn of His people,

---

5 a Ps. 48:1 b Nah. 1:3 c Is. 40:28
6 a Ps. 146:8, 9
8 a Job 38:26
9 a Job 38:41 b [Matt. 6:26]
10 a Ps. 33:16, 17
14 a Is. 54:13; 60:17, 18 b Ps. 132:15 1 Lit. *fat of wheat*
15 a [Ps. 107:20]
16 a Job 37:6
17 1 *fragments* of food
18 a Job 37:10
19 a Deut. 33:4 b Mal. 4:4
20 a [Rom. 3:1, 2] 1 Heb. *Hallelujah*

PSALM 148
1 1 Heb. *Hallelujah*
4 a 1 Kin. 8:27 b Gen. 1:7
5 a Gen. 1:1, 6
6 a Ps. 89:37
7 a Is. 43:20
9 a Is. 44:23; 49:13
13 a Ps. 8:1
14 a Ps. 75:10 1 Strength or dominion

The praise of [b]all His saints—
Of the children of Israel,
[c]A people near to Him.

[2]Praise the LORD!

The trees, the fields, and the little snow birds flitting to and fro were praising the Lord and smiling upon me. So conscious was I of the pardoning blood of Jesus that I seemed to feel it flowing over me.

AIMEE SEMPLE MCPHERSON

PSALM 149

Praise to God for His Salvation and Judgment

Praise[1] the LORD!

[a]Sing to the LORD a new song,
And His praise in the assembly of saints.

2 Let Israel rejoice in their Maker;
Let the children of Zion be joyful in their [a]King.

3 [a]Let them praise His name with the dance;
Let them sing praises to Him with the timbrel and harp.

4 For [a]the LORD takes pleasure in His people;
[b]He will beautify the [1]humble with salvation.

5 Let the saints be joyful in glory;
Let them [a]sing aloud on their beds.

6 *Let* the high praises of God *be* in their mouth,
And [a]a two-edged sword in their hand,

7 To execute vengeance on the nations,
And punishments on the peoples;

8 To bind their kings with chains,
And their nobles with fetters of iron;

9 [a]To execute on them the written judgment—
[b]This honor have all His saints.

[1]Praise the LORD!

Praise the Lord! May _____ sing a new song to You, Lord. And may they praise You in the assembly of the saints.

FROM PSALM 149:1

PSALM 150

Let All Things Praise the Lord

Praise[a1] the LORD!

Praise God in His sanctuary;
Praise Him in His mighty [2]firmament!

2 Praise Him for His mighty acts;
Praise Him according to His excellent [a]greatness!

3 Praise Him with the sound of the [1]trumpet;
Praise Him with the lute and harp!

4 Praise Him with the timbrel and dance;
Praise Him with stringed instruments and flutes!

5 Praise Him with loud cymbals;
Praise Him with clashing cymbals!

6 Let everything that has breath praise the LORD.

[1]Praise the LORD!

---

14 [b]Ps. 149:9 [c]Eph. 2:17 [2]Heb. *Hallelujah*

PSALM 149
1 [a]Ps. 33:3 [1]Heb. *Hallelujah*
2 [a]Zech. 9:9
3 [a]Ps. 81:2
4 [a]Ps. 35:27 [b]Ps. 132:16 [1]*meek*
5 [a]Job 35:10
6 [a]Heb. 4:12
9 [a]Deut. 7:1, 2 [b]1 Cor. 6:2 [1]Heb. *Hallelujah*

PSALM 150
1 [a]Ps. 145:5, 6 [1]Heb. *Hallelujah* [2]*expanse* of heaven
2 [a]Deut. 3:24
3 [1]*cornet*
6 [1]Heb. *Hallelujah*

AUTHOR: *Solomon, with Portions by Agur and King Lemuel*
DATE: *Approximately 950 B.C., with Portions Approximately 720 B.C.*
THEME: *Universal Principles for Living*
KEY WORDS: *Wisdom, Knowledge, Understanding, Instruction, the Fear of the Lord*

PROVERBS

Dear Woman of Destiny,

If you've ever wondered why wisdom is stressed so much in the Book of Proverbs, the answer is found in Proverbs 1:7, *"The fear of the LORD is the beginning of knowledge, but fools despise wisdom and instruction."* Here is a book of simple truths upon which you can base your life. Read it again and again. It will fill your heart with understanding in every matter—and bring peace to you and those you love.

His love and mine,

Marilyn Hickey

The Beginning of Knowledge

The [a]proverbs of Solomon the son of David, king of Israel:

2 To know wisdom and instruction,
To [1]perceive the words of understanding,
3 To receive the instruction of wisdom,
Justice, judgment, and equity;
4 To give prudence to the [a]simple,
To the young man knowledge and discretion—
5 [a]A wise *man* will hear and increase learning,
And a man of understanding will [1]attain wise counsel,
6 To understand a proverb and an enigma,
The words of the wise and their [a]riddles.

7 [a]The fear of the LORD *is* the beginning of knowledge,
But fools despise wisdom and instruction.

CHAPTER 1
1 [a]1 Kin. 4:32
2 [1] *understand* or *discern*
4 [a]Prov. 9:4
5 [a]Prov. 9:9 [1] *acquire*
6 [a]Ps. 78:2
7 [a]Job 28:28

Teresa of Ávila

In a palace filled with the softest of beds, Teresa of Ávila (1515–1582) would have chosen to sleep in the dungeon on a layer of straw. Such was her commitment to a life of simplicity and humility.

Born in Ávila, a walled city in central Spain, Teresa early became fascinated with Bible stories and the lives of saints. At age 20, she joined the Carmelites and committed her life to serving the church. But the strict practices of a nun did not seem to fit Teresa. She was repeatedly sick and often fought bouts of depression.

Through these early years of struggle, she developed a method of prayer in which she "entered into herself." From this, her life as a mystic began. Though most of her supernatural experiences happened privately, those that were observed became the talk of the town. Such instances mattered little to Teresa. Rather, she chose to focus solely on becoming fully submitted to God in every area of her life.

In her 40s, Teresa's life was changed when she was gripped by a picture of Jesus covered with wounds. Instantly, she felt her worldly desires leave her, only to be replaced by a personal sense of the sufferings of Christ. Out of her new-found understanding of His love and sacrifice, she sought to serve the afflicted, the poor, and the needy. In 1561, though facing constant opposition, she devoted herself to a fifteen-year mission of opening convents and monasteries across Spain.

Teresa taught others how to blend the spiritual with practical advice and action. Though her prayers continued throughout the day, she could usually be found sweeping up refuse or digging wells to provide water for her nuns. She knew how to accomplish the necessary duties of life physically while her mind and spirit remained in constant prayer. A natural organizer, Teresa was a gifted leader who earned the respect of both men and women; and she became the first of three women who have been honored by the Catholic Church as Doctor of the Church.

Shun Evil Counsel

8 [a]My son, hear the instruction of your father,
And do not forsake the law of your mother;
9 For they *will be* a [a]graceful ornament on your head,
And chains about your neck.

10 My son, if sinners entice you,
[a]Do not consent.
11 If they say, "Come with us,
Let us [a]lie in wait to *shed* blood;
Let us lurk secretly for the innocent without cause;
12 Let us swallow them alive like [1]Sheol,
And whole, [a]like those who go down to the Pit;
13 We shall find all *kinds* of precious [1]possessions,
We shall fill our houses with [2]spoil;
14 Cast in your lot among us,
Let us all have one purse"—
15 My son, [a]do not walk in the way with them,
[b]Keep your foot from their path;
16 [a]For their feet run to evil,
And they make haste to shed blood.
17 Surely, in [1]vain the net is spread
In the sight of any [2]bird;
18 But they lie in wait for their *own* blood,
They lurk secretly for their *own* lives.
19 [a]So *are* the ways of everyone who is greedy for gain;
It takes away the life of its owners.

The Call of Wisdom

20 [a]Wisdom calls aloud [1]outside;
She raises her voice in the open squares.
21 She cries out in the [1]chief concourses,
At the openings of the gates in the city
She speaks her words:
22 "How long, you [1]simple ones, will you love [2]simplicity?
For scorners delight in their scorning,
And fools hate knowledge.
23 Turn at my rebuke;
Surely [a]I will pour out my spirit on you;
I will make my words known to you.
24 [a]Because I have called and you refused,
I have stretched out my hand and no one regarded,
25 Because you [a]disdained all my counsel,
And would have none of my rebuke,
26 [a]I also will laugh at your calamity;
I will mock when your terror comes,
27 When [a]your terror comes like a storm,
And your destruction comes like a whirlwind,
When distress and anguish come upon you.

28 "Then[a] they will call on me, but I will not answer;
They will seek me diligently, but they will not find me.
29 Because they [a]hated knowledge
And did not [b]choose the fear of the LORD,
30 [a]They would have none of my counsel
And despised my every rebuke.
31 Therefore [a]they shall eat the fruit of their own way,
And be filled to the full with their own fancies.
32 For the [1]turning away of the simple will slay them,
And the complacency of fools will destroy them;
33 But whoever listens to me will dwell [a]safely,
And [b]will be [1]secure, without fear of evil."

Father, because _____ listens to You, may they live safely, and be secure, without fear of evil.

FROM PROVERBS 1:33

The Value of Wisdom

2 My son, if you receive my words,
And [a]treasure my commands within you,
2 So that you incline your ear to wisdom,

---

8 a Prov. 4:1
9 a Prov. 3:22
10 a Gen. 39:7–10
11 a Jer. 5:26
12 a Ps. 28:1 1 *Or the grave*
13 1 Lit. *wealth* 2 *plunder*
15 a Ps. 1:1 b Ps. 119:101
16 a [Is. 59:7]
17 1 *futility* 2 Lit. *lord of the wing*
19 a [1 Tim. 6:10]
20 a [John 7:37] 1 *in the street*
21 1 LXX, Syr., Tg. *top of the walls;* Vg. *the head of multitudes*
22 1 *naive* 2 *naivete*
23 a Joel 2:28
24 a Jer. 7:13
25 a Luke 7:30
26 a Ps. 2:4
27 a [Prov. 10:24, 25]
28 a Is. 1:15
29 a Job 21:14 b Ps. 119:173
30 a Ps. 81:11
31 a Job 4:8
32 1 *waywardness*
33 a Prov. 3:24–26 b Ps. 112:7 1 *at ease*

CHAPTER 2
1 a [Prov. 4:21]

And apply your heart to understanding;
3 Yes, if you cry out for discernment,
And lift up your voice for understanding,
4 [a]If you seek her as silver,
And search for her as *for* hidden treasures;
5 [a]Then you will understand the fear of the LORD,
And find the knowledge of God.
6 [a]For the LORD gives wisdom;
From His mouth *come* knowledge and understanding;
7 He stores up sound wisdom for the upright;
[a]*He is* a shield to those who walk uprightly;
8 He guards the paths of justice,
And [a]preserves the way of His saints.
9 Then you will understand righteousness and justice,
Equity *and* every good path.

There are times when spiritual discernment is the chief gift of the Spirit. The praised and made-much-of seldom have it. But those who have suffered the loss of all things, even their reputations—these, if they live with their Lord, have this gift.

AMY CARMICHAEL

10 When wisdom enters your heart,
And knowledge is pleasant to your soul,
11 Discretion will preserve you;
[a]Understanding will keep you,
12 To deliver you from the way of evil,
From the man who speaks perverse things,
13 From those who leave the paths of uprightness
To [a]walk in the ways of darkness;
14 [a]Who rejoice in doing evil,
And delight in the perversity of the wicked;
15 [a]Whose ways *are* crooked,
And *who are* devious in their paths;
16 To deliver you from [a]the immoral woman,
[b]From the seductress *who* flatters with her words,
17 Who forsakes the companion of her youth,
And forgets the covenant of her God.
18 For [a]her house [1]leads down to death,
And her paths to the dead;
19 None who go to her return,
Nor do they [1]regain the paths of life—
20 So you may walk in the way of goodness,
And keep *to* the paths of righteousness.
21 For the upright will dwell in the [a]land,
And the blameless will remain in it;
22 But the wicked will be [1]cut off from the [2]earth,
And the unfaithful will be uprooted from it.

Guidance for the Young

3 My son, do not forget my law,
[a]But let your heart keep my commands;
2 For length of days and long life
And [a]peace they will add to you.

3 Let not mercy and truth forsake you;
[a]Bind them around your neck,
[b]Write them on the tablet of your heart,
4 [a]*And* so find favor and [1]high esteem
In the sight of God and man.

5 [a]Trust in the LORD with all your heart,
[b]And lean not on your own understanding;
6 [a]In all your ways acknowledge Him,
And He shall [1]direct your paths.

7 Do not be wise in your own [a]eyes;
Fear the LORD and depart from evil.
8 It will be health to your [1]flesh,
And [a]strength[2] to your bones.

9 [a]Honor the LORD with your possessions,

---

4 a [Prov. 3:14]
5 a [James 1:5, 6]
6 a 1 Kin. 3:9, 12
7 a [Ps. 84:11]
8 a [1 Sam. 2:9]
11 a Prov. 4:6; 6:22
13 a [John 3:19, 20]
14 a [Rom. 1:32]
15 a Ps. 125:5
16 a Prov. 5:20; 6:24; 7:5 b Prov. 5:3
18 a Prov. 7:27 1 *sinks*
19 1 Lit. *reach*
21 a Ps. 37:3
22 1 *destroyed* 2 *land*

CHAPTER 3
1 a Deut. 8:1
2 a Ps. 119:165
3 a Prov. 6:21 b [2 Cor. 3:3]
4 a Rom. 14:18 1 Lit. *good understanding*
5 a [Ps. 37:3, 5] b [Jer. 9:23, 24]
6 a [1 Chr. 28:9] 1 Or *make smooth* or *straight*
7 a Rom. 12:16
8 a Job 21:24 1 Body, lit. *navel* 2 Lit. *drink*
9 a Ex. 22:29

And with the firstfruits of all your
increase;
10 [a]So your barns will be filled with
plenty,
And your vats will overflow with
new wine.

11 [a]My son, do not despise the
chastening of the LORD,
Nor detest His correction;
12 For whom the LORD loves He
corrects,
[a]Just as a father the son *in whom* he
delights.

13 [a]Happy *is* the man *who* finds
wisdom,
And the man *who* gains
understanding;
14 [a]For her proceeds *are* better than
the profits of silver,
And her gain than fine gold.
15 She *is* more precious than rubies,
And [a]all the things you may desire
cannot compare with her.
16 [a]Length of days *is* in her right
hand,
In her left hand riches and honor.
17 [a]Her ways *are* ways of pleasantness,
And all her paths *are* peace.
18 She *is* [a]a tree of life to those who
take hold of her,
And happy *are all* who [1]retain her.

May ——— trust in You with all their heart, and lean not on their own understanding. I pray that they will acknowledge You in all their ways and that You would direct their paths.
FROM PROVERBS 3:5, 6

19 [a]The LORD by wisdom founded the
earth;
By understanding He established
the heavens;
20 By His knowledge the depths were
[a]broken up,
And clouds drop down the dew.

21 My son, let them not depart from
your eyes—
Keep sound wisdom and discretion;
22 So they will be life to your soul
And grace to your neck.
23 [a]Then you will walk safely in your
way,
And your foot will not stumble.
24 When you lie down, you will not
be afraid;
Yes, you will lie down and your
sleep will be sweet.
25 [a]Do not be afraid of sudden terror,
Nor of trouble from the wicked
when it comes;
26 For the LORD will be your
confidence,
And will keep your foot from being
caught.

27 [a]Do not withhold good from [1]those
to whom it is due,
When it is in the power of your
hand to do *so.*
28 [a]Do not say to your neighbor,
"Go, and come back,
And tomorrow I will give *it,*"
When *you have* it with you.
29 Do not devise evil against your
neighbor,
For he dwells by you for safety's
sake.
30 [a]Do not strive with a man without
cause,
If he has done you no harm.

31 [a]Do not envy the oppressor,
And choose none of his ways;
32 For the perverse *person is* an
abomination to the LORD,
[a]But His secret counsel *is* with the
upright.
33 [a]The curse of the LORD *is* on the
house of the wicked,
But [b]He blesses the home of the
just.
34 [a]Surely He scorns the scornful,
But gives grace to the humble.
35 The wise shall inherit glory,
But shame shall be the legacy of
fools.

Security in Wisdom

4
Hear, [a]*my* children, the instruction of
a father,
And give attention to know
understanding;
2 For I give you good doctrine:
Do not forsake my law.
3 When I was my father's son,

---

10 a Deut. 28:8
11 a Job 5:17
12 a Deut. 8:5
13 a Prov. 8:32, 34, 35
14 a Job 28:13
15 a Matt. 13:44
16 a [1 Tim. 4:8]
17 a [Matt. 11:29]
18 a Gen. 2:9
1 hold her fast
19 a Ps. 104:24
20 a Gen. 7:11
23 a Prov. 10:9
25 a Ps. 91:5
27 a Rom. 13:7
1 Lit. *its owners*
28 a Lev. 19:13
30 a [Rom. 12:18]
31 a Ps. 37:1
32 a Ps. 25:14
33 a Zech. 5:3, 4
b Ps. 1:3
34 a James 4:6
CHAPTER 4
1 a Ps. 34:11

[a]Tender and the only one in the sight of my mother,
4 [a]He also taught me, and said to me:
"Let your heart retain my words;
[b]Keep my commands, and live.
5 [a]Get wisdom! Get understanding!
Do not forget, nor turn away from the words of my mouth.
6 Do not forsake her, and she will preserve you;
[a]Love her, and she will keep you.
7 [a]Wisdom *is* the principal thing;
Therefore get wisdom.
And in all your getting, get understanding.
8 [a]Exalt her, and she will promote you;
She will bring you honor, when you embrace her.
9 She will place on your head [a]an ornament of grace;
A crown of glory she will deliver to you."

Lord, I pray that ____ would be taught in the way of wisdom and led in right paths.

FROM PROVERBS 4:11

10 Hear, my son, and receive my sayings,
[a]And the years of your life will be many.
11 I have [a]taught you in the way of wisdom;
I have led you in right paths.
12 When you walk, [a]your steps will not be hindered,
[b]And when you run, you will not stumble.
13 Take firm hold of instruction, do not let go;
Keep her, for she *is* your life.

14 [a]Do not enter the path of the wicked,
And do not walk in the way of evil.
15 Avoid it, do not travel on it;
Turn away from it and pass on.
16 [a]For they do not sleep unless they have done evil;
And their sleep is [1]taken away unless they make *someone* fall.
17 For they eat the bread of wickedness,
And drink the wine of violence.

18 [a]But the path of the just [b]*is* like the shining [1]sun,
That shines ever brighter unto the perfect day.
19 [a]The way of the wicked *is* like darkness;
They do not know what makes them stumble.

20 My son, give attention to my words;
Incline your ear to my sayings.
21 Do not let them depart from your eyes;
Keep them in the midst of your heart;
22 For they *are* life to those who find them,
And health to all their flesh.
23 Keep your heart with all diligence,
For out of it *spring* the issues of [a]life.
24 Put away from you a [1]deceitful mouth,
And put perverse lips far from you.
25 Let your eyes look straight ahead,
And your eyelids look right before you.
26 Ponder the path of your [a]feet,
And let all your ways be established.
27 Do not turn to the right or the left;
Remove your foot from evil.

The Peril of Adultery

5 My son, pay attention to my wisdom;
[1]Lend your ear to my understanding,
2 That you may [1]preserve discretion,
And your lips [a]may keep knowledge.
3 [a]For the lips of [1]an immoral woman drip honey,
And her mouth *is* [b]smoother than oil;
4 But in the end she is bitter as wormwood,
Sharp as a two-edged sword.
5 Her feet go down to death,
[a]Her steps lay hold of [1]hell.

3 a 1 Chr. 29:1
4 a 1 Chr. 28:9 b Prov. 7:2
5 a Prov. 2:2, 3
6 a 2 Thess. 2:10
7 a Matt. 13:44
8 a 1 Sam. 2:30
9 a Prov. 3:22
10 a Prov. 3:2
11 a 1 Sam. 12:23
12 a Ps. 18:36 b [Ps. 91:11]
14 a Ps. 1:1
16 a Ps. 36:4 *1* Lit. *robbed*
18 a Matt. 5:14, 45 b 2 Sam. 23:4 *1* Lit. *light*
19 a [Is. 59:9, 10]
23 a [Matt. 12:34; 15:18, 19]
24 *1 devious*
26 a Heb. 12:13

CHAPTER 5
1 *1* Lit. *Bow*
2 a Mal. 2:7 *1 appreciate good judgment*
3 a Prov. 2:16 b Ps. 55:21 *1* Lit. *a strange*
5 a Prov. 7:27 *1* Or *Sheol*

6 Lest you ponder *her* path of
life—
Her ways are unstable;
You do not know *them.*
7 Therefore hear me now, *my*
children,
And do not depart from the words
of my mouth.
8 Remove your way far from her,
And do not go near the door of her
house,
9 Lest you give your [1]honor to
others,
And your years to the cruel *one;*
10 Lest aliens be filled with your [1]wealth,
And your labors *go* to the house of
a foreigner;
11 And you mourn at last,
When your flesh and your body are
consumed,
12 And say:
"How I have hated instruction,
And my heart despised correction!
13 I have not obeyed the voice of my
teachers,
Nor inclined my ear to those who
instructed me!
14 I was on the verge of total ruin,

9 [1] *vigor*

10 [1] Lit. *strength*

Monica of Hippo

St. Augustine of Hippo spoke of his mother, Monica (331–387), as "God's handmaid who poured into my ears much about God, none of which sank into me until I was much older." For much of his early life, Augustine engaged in all sorts of unabashed depravity, including fathering a son outside of marriage when he was only 16 years old. He was a prodigal in every sense of the word, but he had a mother who prayed fervently for him. His autobiography, *The Confessions of St. Augustine,* says that God "drew his soul out of the profound darkness, because of his mother who wept on his behalf more than most mothers weep when their children die."

Monica's war for the soul of her son was not won overnight. In fact, for nine years she continued to pray as he sank deeper and deeper into sin. When Augustine moved from his hometown of Carthage to the city of Milan, Monica followed him. It was terribly dangerous for a woman to travel alone in those days, but Monica was determined to see Augustine redeemed. She persevered in prayer and faith, continually encouraging him to give up his decadent behavior. She had one ray of false hope when he sent his mistress of fifteen years home to Africa, only to take another one in her place.

But one day, alone in a garden, Augustine came to the end of himself and collided with God's destiny for his life—a destiny that had been secured by his mother on her knees. He cried out to God and felt God leading him to Romans 13:13, 14, which denounces "revelry and drunkenness" and encourages "[putting] on the Lord Jesus Christ." At that moment, Augustine was changed.

Monica was thrilled! She had spent so many years crying out to God for the prodigal to come home and had been there to welcome him with open arms. She lived only nine days after his return to Christ and did not see him save Christianity when the Roman Empire disintegrated. Monica died with her deepest prayers answered, knowing that Augustine had wholeheartedly surrendered his life to God and His holy purposes.

In the midst of the assembly and
congregation."

15 Drink water from your own
cistern,
And running water from your own
well.
16 Should your fountains be
dispersed abroad,
[1]Streams of water in the streets?
17 Let them be only your own,
And not for strangers with you.
18 Let your fountain be blessed,
And rejoice with [a]the wife of your
youth.
19 [a]*As a* loving deer and a graceful doe,
Let her breasts satisfy you at all times;
And always be [1]enraptured with her
love.
20 For why should you, my son, be
enraptured by [a]an immoral woman,
And be embraced in the arms of a
seductress?
21 [a]For the ways of man *are* before
the eyes of the LORD,
And He [1]ponders all his paths.
22 [a]His own iniquities entrap the
wicked *man,*
And he is caught in the cords of his
sin.
23 [a]He shall die for lack of
instruction,
And in the greatness of his folly he
shall go astray.

Dangerous Promises

6 My son, [a]if you become [1]surety for
your friend,
If you have [2]shaken hands in pledge
for a stranger,
2 You are snared by the words of
your mouth;
You are taken by the words of your
mouth.
3 So do this, my son, and deliver
yourself;
For you have come into the hand of
your friend:
Go and humble yourself;
Plead with your friend.
4 [a]Give no sleep to your eyes,
Nor slumber to your eyelids.
5 Deliver yourself like a gazelle from
the hand *of the hunter,*
And like a bird from the hand of
the [1]fowler.

16 [1] *Channels*
18 [a] Mal. 2:14
19 [a] Song 2:9 [1] Lit. *intoxicated*
20 [a] Prov. 2:16
21 [a] Hos. 7:2 [1] *observes,* lit. *weighs*
22 [a] Num. 32:23
23 [a] Job 4:21

CHAPTER 6
1 [a] Prov. 11:15 [1] *guaranty* or *collateral* [2] Lit. *struck*
4 [a] Ps. 132:4
5 [1] One who catches birds in a trap or snare
6 [a] Job 12:7
7 [1] Lit. *leader*
8 [1] Lit. *bread*
9 [a] Prov. 24:33, 34 [1] Lit. *lie down*
11 [a] Prov. 10:4
13 [a] Job 15:12 [1] *gives signals,* lit. *scrapes*
14 [a] Mic. 2:1 [b] Prov. 6:19
15 [a] Is. 30:13 [b] Jer. 19:11 [c] 2 Chr. 36:16
16 [1] Lit. *His soul*
17 [a] Ps. 101:5 [b] Ps. 120:2 [c] Is. 1:15 [1] Lit. *Haughty eyes*
18 [a] Gen. 6:5 [b] Is. 59:7
19 [a] Ps. 27:12 [b] Prov. 6:14
20 [a] Eph. 6:1
21 [a] Prov. 3:3
22 [a] [Prov. 3:23] [b] Prov. 2:11 [1] Lit. *it*

The Folly of Indolence

6 [a]Go to the ant, you sluggard!
Consider her ways and be wise,
7 Which, having no [1]captain,
Overseer or ruler,
8 Provides her [1]supplies in the
summer,
And gathers her food in the harvest.
9 [a]How long will you [1]slumber,
O sluggard?
When will you rise from your sleep?
10 A little sleep, a little slumber,
A little folding of the hands to
sleep—
11 [a]So shall your poverty come on
you like a prowler,
And your need like an armed man.

The Wicked Man

12 A worthless person, a wicked man,
Walks with a perverse mouth;
13 [a]He winks with his eyes,
He [1]shuffles his feet,
He points with his fingers;
14 Perversity *is* in his heart,
[a]He devises evil continually,
[b]He sows discord.
15 Therefore his calamity shall come
[a]suddenly;
Suddenly he shall [b]be broken
[c]without remedy.

16 These six *things* the LORD hates,
Yes, seven *are* an abomination to
[1]Him:
17 [a]A[1] proud look,
[b]A lying tongue,
[c]Hands that shed innocent blood,
18 [a]A heart that devises wicked plans,
[b]Feet that are swift in running to
evil,
19 [a]A false witness *who* speaks lies,
And one who [b]sows discord among
brethren.

Beware of Adultery

20 [a]My son, keep your father's
command,
And do not forsake the law of your
mother.
21 [a]Bind them continually upon your
heart;
Tie them around your neck.
22 [a]When you roam, [1]they will lead
you;
When you sleep, [b]they will keep
you;

And *when* you awake, they will
speak with you.
23 [a]For the commandment *is* a lamp,
And the law a light;
Reproofs of instruction *are* the way
of life,
24 [a]To keep you from the evil woman,
From the flattering tongue of a
seductress.
25 [a]Do not lust after her beauty in
your heart,
Nor let her allure you with her
eyelids.
26 For [a]by means of a harlot
A man is reduced to a crust of
bread;
[b]And [1]an adulteress will [c]prey upon
his precious life.
27 Can a man take fire to his bosom,
And his clothes not be burned?
28 Can one walk on hot coals,
And his feet not be seared?
29 So *is* he who goes in to his
neighbor's wife;
Whoever touches her shall not be
innocent.

30 *People* do not despise a thief
If he steals to satisfy himself when
he is starving.
31 Yet *when* he is found, [a]he must
restore sevenfold;
He may have to give up all the
substance of his house.
32 Whoever commits adultery with a
woman [a]lacks understanding;
He *who* does so destroys his own
soul.
33 Wounds and dishonor he will get,
And his reproach will not be wiped
away.
34 For [a]jealousy *is* a husband's fury;
Therefore he will not spare in the
day of vengeance.
35 He will [1]accept no recompense,
Nor will he be appeased though you
give many gifts.

7 My son, keep my words,
And [a]treasure my commands within
you.
2 [a]Keep my commands and live,
[b]And my law as the apple of your
eye.
3 [a]Bind them on your fingers;
Write them on the tablet of your
heart.
4 Say to wisdom, "You *are* my
sister,"
And call understanding *your*
nearest kin,
5 [a]That they may keep you from the
immoral woman,
From the seductress *who* flatters
with her words.

The Crafty Harlot

6 For at the window of my house
I looked through my lattice,
7 And saw among the simple,
I perceived among the [1]youths,
A young man [a]devoid[2] of
understanding,
8 Passing along the street near her
corner;
And he took the path to her house
9 [a]In the twilight, in the evening,
In the black and dark night.
10 And there a woman met him,
With the attire of a harlot, and a
crafty heart.
11 [a]She *was* loud and rebellious,
[b]Her feet would not stay at home.
12 At times *she was* outside, at times
in the open square,
Lurking at every corner.
13 So she caught him and kissed
him;
With an [1]impudent face she said to
him:
14 "*I have* peace offerings with me;
Today I have paid my vows.
15 So I came out to meet you,
Diligently to seek your face,
And I have found you.
16 I have spread my bed with
tapestry,
Colored coverings of [a]Egyptian
linen.
17 I have perfumed my bed
With myrrh, aloes, and cinnamon.
18 Come, let us take our fill of love
until morning;
Let us delight ourselves with love.
19 For [1]my husband *is* not at home;
He has gone on a long journey;
20 He has taken a bag of money
[1]with him,
And will come home [2]on the
appointed day."
21 [1]With [a]her enticing speech she
caused him to yield,
[b]With her flattering lips she
[2]seduced him.
22 Immediately he went after her, as
an ox goes to the slaughter,

---

23 a Ps. 19:8
24 a Prov. 2:16
25 a Matt. 5:28
26 a Prov. 29:3 b Gen. 39:14 c Ezek. 13:18 *1* Wife of another, lit. *a man's wife*
31 a Ex. 22:1–4
32 a Prov. 7:7
34 a Song 8:6
35 *1* Lit. *lift up the face of any*

CHAPTER 7
1 a Prov. 2:1
2 a Lev. 18:5 b Deut. 32:10
3 a Deut. 6:8
5 a Prov. 2:16; 5:3
7 a [Prov. 6:32; 9:4, 16] *1* Lit. *sons* *2 lacking*
9 a Job 24:15
11 a Prov. 9:13 b Titus 2:5
13 *1 shameless*
16 a Is. 19:9
19 *1* Lit. *the man*
20 *1* Lit. *in his hand* *2 at the full moon*
21 a Prov. 5:3 b Ps. 12:2 *1 By the greatness of her words* *2 compelled*

Or [1]as a fool to the correction of
the [2]stocks,
23 Till an arrow struck his liver.
[a]As a bird hastens to the snare,
He did not know it [1]*would cost* his
life.

24 Now therefore, listen to me, *my*
children;
Pay attention to the words of my
mouth:
25 Do not let your heart turn aside
to her ways,
Do not stray into her paths;
26 For she has cast down many
wounded,
And [a]all who were slain by her
were strong *men.*
27 [a]Her house *is* the way to [1]hell,
Descending to the chambers of
death.

The Excellence of Wisdom

8 Does not [a]wisdom cry out,
And understanding lift up her
voice?
2 She takes her stand on the top of
the [1]high hill,
Beside the way, where the paths
meet.
3 She cries out by the gates, at the
entry of the city,
At the entrance of the doors:
4 "To you, O men, I call,
And my voice *is* to the sons of men.
5 O you [1]simple ones, understand
prudence,
And you fools, be of an
understanding heart.
6 Listen, for I will speak of [a]excellent
things,
And from the opening of my lips
will come right things;
7 For my mouth will speak truth;
Wickedness *is* an abomination to
my lips.
8 All the words of my mouth *are*
with righteousness;
Nothing crooked or perverse *is* in
them.
9 They *are* all plain to him who
understands,
And right to those who find
knowledge.
10 Receive my instruction, and not
silver,
And knowledge rather than choice
gold;

22 [1]LXX, Syr., Tg. *as a dog to bonds;* Vg. *as a lamb . . . to bonds* [2]*shackles*

23 [a]Eccl. 9:12 [1]Lit. *is for*

26 [a]Neh. 13:26

27 [a]Prov. 2:18; 5:5; 9:18 [1]Or *Sheol*

CHAPTER 8

1 [a]Prov. 1:20, 21; 9:3

2 [1]Lit. *heights*

5 [1]*naive*

6 [a]Prov. 22:20

11 [a]Job 28:15

13 [a]Prov. 3:7; 16:6 [b][Prov. 16:17, 18] [c]Prov. 4:24

14 [a]Eccl. 7:19; 9:16

15 [a]Rom. 13:1

16 [1]MT, Syr., Tg., Vg. *righteousness;* LXX, Bg., some mss. and editions *earth*

17 [a][John 14:21] [b]James 1:5

18 [a]Prov. 3:16

20 [1]*walk about on*

22 [a]Prov. 3:19

23 [a][Ps. 2:6]

25 [a]Job 15:7, 8

26 [1]*outer places* [2]Lit. *beginning of the dust*

11 [a]For wisdom *is* better than rubies,
And all the things one may desire
cannot be compared with her.
12 "I, wisdom, dwell with prudence,
And find out knowledge *and*
discretion.
13 [a]The fear of the LORD *is* to hate
evil;
[b]Pride and arrogance and the evil
way
And [c]the perverse mouth I hate.
14 Counsel *is* mine, and sound
wisdom;
I *am* understanding, [a]I have
strength.
15 [a]By me kings reign,
And rulers decree justice.
16 By me princes rule, and nobles,
All the judges of [1]the earth.
17 [a]I love those who love me,
And [b]those who seek me diligently
will find me.
18 [a]Riches and honor *are* with me,
Enduring riches and righteousness.
19 My fruit *is* better than gold, yes,
than fine gold,
And my revenue than choice silver.
20 I [1]traverse the way of
righteousness,
In the midst of the paths of justice,
21 That I may cause those who love
me to inherit wealth,
That I may fill their treasuries.

22 "The[a] LORD possessed me at the
beginning of His way,
Before His works of old.
23 [a]I have been established from
everlasting,
From the beginning, before there
was ever an earth.
24 When *there were* no depths I was
brought forth,
When *there were* no fountains
abounding with water.
25 [a]Before the mountains were settled,
Before the hills, I was brought
forth;
26 While as yet He had not made the
earth or the [1]fields,
Or the [2]primal dust of the world.
27 When He prepared the heavens, I
was there,
When He drew a circle on the face
of the deep,
28 When He established the clouds
above,

When He strengthened the fountains of the deep,
29 [a]When He assigned to the sea its limit,
So that the waters would not transgress His command,
When [b]He marked out the foundations of the earth,
30 [a]Then I was beside Him *as* [1]a master craftsman;
[b]And I was daily *His* delight,
Rejoicing always before Him,
31 Rejoicing in His inhabited world,
And [a]my delight *was* with the sons of men.

I pray that ____ would hear instruction and be wise, that they would not disdain it.

FROM PROVERBS 8:33

32 "Now therefore, listen to me, *my* children,
For [a]blessed *are those who* keep my ways.
33 Hear instruction and be wise,
And do not disdain *it*.
34 [a]Blessed is the man who listens to me,
Watching daily at my gates,
Waiting at the posts of my doors.
35 For whoever finds me finds life,
And [a]obtains favor from the LORD;
36 But he who sins against me
[a]wrongs his own soul;
All those who hate me love death."

The Way of Wisdom

9 Wisdom has [a]built her house,
She has hewn out her seven pillars;
2 [a]She has slaughtered her meat,
[b]She has mixed her wine,
She has also [1]furnished her table.
3 She has sent out her maidens,
She cries out from the highest places of the city,
4 "Whoever[a] *is* simple, let him turn in here!"
As for him who lacks understanding, she says to him,
5 "Come,[a] eat of my bread
And drink of the wine I have mixed.
6 Forsake foolishness and live,
And go in the way of understanding.
7 "He who corrects a scoffer gets shame for himself,
And he who rebukes a wicked *man* *only* harms himself.
8 [a]Do not correct a scoffer, lest he hate you;
[b]Rebuke a wise *man*, and he will love you.
9 Give *instruction* to a wise *man*, and he will be still wiser;
Teach a just *man*, [a]and he will increase in learning.
10 "The[a] fear of the LORD *is* the beginning of wisdom,
And the knowledge of the Holy One *is* understanding.
11 [a]For by me your days will be multiplied,
And years of life will be added to you.
12 [a]If you are wise, you are wise for yourself,
And *if* you scoff, you will bear *it* alone."

The Way of Folly

13 [a]A foolish woman is [1]clamorous;
She is simple, and knows nothing.
14 For she sits at the door of her house,
On a seat [a]*by* the highest places of the city,
15 To call to those who pass by,
Who go straight on their way:
16 "Whoever[a] *is* [1]simple, let him turn in here";
And *as for* him who lacks understanding, she says to him,
17 "Stolen[a] water is sweet,
And bread *eaten* in secret is pleasant."
18 But he does not know that [a]the dead *are* there,
That her guests *are* in the depths of [1]hell.

Wise Sayings of Solomon

10 The proverbs of [a]Solomon:
[b]A wise son makes a glad father,
But a foolish son *is* the grief of his mother.

---

29 a Gen. 1:9, 10 b Job 28:4, 6
30 a [John 1:1–3, 18] b [Matt. 3:17] *1* A Jewish tradition *one brought up*
31 a Ps. 16:3
32 a Luke 11:28
34 a Prov. 3:13, 18
35 a [John 17:3]
36 a Prov. 20:2

CHAPTER 9
1 a [Matt. 16:18]
2 a Matt. 22:4 b Prov. 23:30 *1 arranged*
4 a Ps. 19:7
5 a Is. 55:1
8 a Matt. 7:6 b Ps. 141:5
9 a [Matt. 13:12]
10 a Job 28:28
11 a Prov. 3:2, 16
12 a Job 35:6, 7
13 a Prov. 7:11 *1 boisterous*
14 a Prov. 9:3
16 a Prov. 7:7, 8 *1 naive*
17 a Prov. 20:17
18 a Prov. 2:18; 7:27 *1* Or *Sheol*

CHAPTER 10
1 a Prov. 1:1; 25:1 b Prov. 15:20; 17:21, 25; 19:13; 29:3, 15

2 [a]Treasures of wickedness profit
nothing,
[b]But righteousness delivers from
death.
3 [a]The LORD will not allow the
righteous soul to famish,
But He casts away the desire of the
wicked.
4 [a]He who has a slack hand becomes
poor,
But [b]the hand of the diligent makes
rich.
5 He who gathers in [a]summer *is* a
wise son;
He who sleeps in harvest *is* [b]a son
who causes shame.
6 Blessings *are* on the head of the
righteous,
But violence covers the mouth of
the wicked.
7 [a]The memory of the righteous *is*
blessed,
But the name of the wicked will
rot.
8 The wise in heart will receive
commands,
[a]But [1]a prating fool will [2]fall.
9 [a]He who walks with integrity walks
securely,
But he who perverts his ways will
become known.
10 He who winks with the eye causes
trouble,
But a prating fool will fall.
11 The mouth of the righteous *is* a
well of life,
But violence covers the mouth of
the wicked.
12 Hatred stirs up strife,
But [a]love covers all sins.
13 Wisdom is found on the lips of
him who has understanding,
But [a]a rod *is* for the back of him
who [1]is devoid of understanding.
14 Wise *people* store up knowledge,
But [a]the mouth of the foolish *is*
near destruction.
15 The [a]rich man's wealth *is* his
strong city;
The destruction of the poor *is* their
poverty.

2 a [Luke 12:19, 20] b Dan. 4:27
3 a Ps. 34:9, 10; 37:25
4 a Prov. 19:15 b Prov. 12:24; 13:4; 21:5
5 a Prov. 6:8 b Prov. 19:26
7 a Eccl. 8:10
8 a Prov. 10:10 *1* Lit. *the foolish of lips* *2 be thrust down* or *ruined*
9 a [Ps. 23:4]
12 a [1 Cor. 13:4–7]
13 a Prov. 26:3 *1* Lit. *lacks heart*
14 a Prov. 18:7
15 a Job 31:24
16 a Prov. 6:23
17 *1 leads*
18 a Prov. 26:24 b Ps. 15:3; 101:5
19 a Eccl. 5:3 b [James 1:19; 3:2]
21 *1* Lit. *heart*
22 a Gen. 24:35; 26:12
23 a Prov. 2:14; 15:21
24 a Job 15:21 b Ps. 145:19
25 a Ps. 37:9, 10 b Ps. 15:5
27 a Prov. 9:11

16 The labor of the righteous *leads* to
[a]life,
The wages of the wicked to sin.
17 He who keeps instruction *is in* the
way of life,
But he who refuses correction
[1]goes astray.
18 Whoever [a]hides hatred *has* lying
lips,
And [b]whoever spreads slander *is* a
fool.
19 [a]In the multitude of words sin is
not lacking,
But [b]he who restrains his lips *is*
wise.
20 The tongue of the righteous *is*
choice silver;
The heart of the wicked *is worth*
little.
21 The lips of the righteous feed
many,
But fools die for lack of [1]wisdom.
22 [a]The blessing of the LORD makes
one rich,
And He adds no sorrow with it.
23 [a]To do evil *is* like sport to a fool,
But a man of understanding has
wisdom.
24 [a]The fear of the wicked will come
upon him,
And [b]the desire of the righteous
will be granted.
25 When the whirlwind passes by,
[a]the wicked *is* no *more,*
But [b]the righteous *has* an
everlasting foundation.

Faith is a sure foundation. He who stands on it will not be moved.

ANDREW MURRAY

26 As vinegar to the teeth and smoke
to the eyes,
So *is* the lazy *man* to those who
send him.
27 [a]The fear of the LORD prolongs
days,

But [b]the years of the wicked will be
shortened.
28 The hope of the righteous *will be*
gladness,
But the [a]expectation of the wicked
will perish.
29 The way of the LORD *is* strength
for the upright,
But [a]destruction *will come* to the
workers of iniquity.

30 [a]The righteous will never be
removed,
But the wicked will not inhabit the
[1]earth.
31 [a]The mouth of the righteous brings
forth wisdom,
But the perverse tongue will be cut
out.
32 The lips of the righteous know
what is acceptable,
But the mouth of the wicked *what*
is perverse.

11 Dishonest[a1] scales *are* an
abomination to the LORD,
But a [2]just weight *is* His delight.
2 When pride comes, then comes
[a]shame;
But with the humble *is* wisdom.

Nothing sets a person so much out of the devil's reach as humility.
JONATHAN EDWARDS

3 The integrity of the upright will
guide [a]them,
But the perversity of the unfaithful
will destroy them.
4 [a]Riches do not profit in the day of
wrath,
But [b]righteousness delivers from
death.
5 The righteousness of the blameless
will [1]direct his way aright,
But the wicked will fall by his own
[a]wickedness.
6 The righteousness of the upright
will deliver them,

27 b Job 15:32
28 a Job 8:13
29 a Ps. 1:6
30 a Ps. 37:22 *1 land*
31 a Ps. 37:30
CHAPTER 11
1 a Lev. 19:35, 36 *1 deceptive* *2* Lit. *perfect stone*
2 a Prov. 16:18; 18:12; 29:23
3 a Prov. 13:6
4 a Ezek. 7:19 b Gen. 7:1
5 a Prov. 5:22 *1* Or *make smooth* or *straight*
7 a Prov. 10:28
8 a Prov. 21:18
10 a Prov. 28:12
11 a Prov. 14:34
12 *1* Lit. *lacks heart*
13 a Lev. 19:16 b Prov. 19:11
14 a 1 Kin. 12:1
15 a Prov. 6:1, 2 *1 guaranty* *2 those pledging guaranty,* lit. *those who strike hands*
17 a [Matt. 5:7; 25:34–36]
18 a Hos. 10:12
19 a Prov. 10:16; 12:28 b [Rom. 6:23]
21 a Prov. 16:5 *1* Lit. *hand to hand*

But the unfaithful will be caught by
their lust.

7 When a wicked man dies, *his*
expectation will [a]perish,
And the hope of the unjust
perishes.
8 [a]The righteous is delivered from
trouble,
And it comes to the wicked instead.
9 The hypocrite with *his* mouth
destroys his neighbor,
But through knowledge the
righteous will be delivered.
10 [a]When it goes well with the
righteous, the city rejoices;
And when the wicked perish, *there*
is jubilation.
11 By the blessing of the upright the
city is [a]exalted,
But it is overthrown by the mouth
of the wicked.

12 He who [1]is devoid of wisdom
despises his neighbor,
But a man of understanding holds
his peace.
13 [a]A talebearer reveals secrets,
But he who is of a faithful spirit
[b]conceals a matter.

14 [a]Where *there is* no counsel, the
people fall;
But in the multitude of counselors
there is safety.

15 He who is [a]surety[1] for a stranger
will suffer,
But one who hates [2]being surety is
secure.

16 A gracious woman retains honor,
But ruthless *men* retain riches.
17 [a]The merciful man does good for
his own soul,
But *he who is* cruel troubles his
own flesh.
18 The wicked *man* does deceptive
work,
But [a]he who sows righteousness
will have a sure reward.
19 As righteousness *leads* to [a]life,
So he who pursues evil *pursues it*
to his own [b]death.
20 Those who are of a perverse heart
are an abomination to the LORD,
But *the* blameless in their ways *are*
His delight.
21 [a]*Though they join* [1]*forces*, the
wicked will not go unpunished;

But [b]the posterity of the righteous
will be delivered.

22 *As* a ring of gold in a swine's
snout,
So is a lovely woman who lacks
[1]discretion.

23 The desire of the righteous *is* only
good,
But the expectation of the wicked
[a]*is* wrath.

24 There is *one* who [a]scatters, yet
increases more;
And there is *one* who withholds
more than is right,
But it *leads* to poverty.

25 [a]The generous soul will be made
rich,
[b]And he who waters will also be
watered himself.

26 The people will curse [a]him who
withholds grain,
But [b]blessing *will be* on the head of
him who sells *it*.

27 He who earnestly seeks good
[1]finds favor,
[a]But trouble will come to him who
seeks *evil*.

28 [a]He who trusts in his riches will
fall,
But [b]the righteous will flourish like
foliage.

29 He who troubles his own house
[a]will inherit the wind,
And the fool *will be* [b]servant to the
wise of heart.

30 The fruit of the righteous *is a* tree
of life,
And [a]he who [1]wins souls *is* wise.

31 [a]If the righteous will be
[1]recompensed on the earth,
How much more the ungodly and
the sinner.

12 Whoever loves instruction loves
knowledge,
But he who hates correction *is*
stupid.

2 A good *man* obtains favor from the
LORD,
But a man of wicked intentions He
will condemn.

3 A man is not established by
wickedness,
But the [a]root of the righteous
cannot be moved.

4 [a]An[1] excellent wife *is* the crown of
her husband,
But she who causes shame *is* [b]like
rottenness in his bones.

5 The thoughts of the righteous *are*
right,
But the counsels of the wicked *are*
deceitful.

6 [a]The words of the wicked *are,* "Lie
in wait for blood,"
[b]But the mouth of the upright will
deliver them.

7 [a]The wicked are overthrown and *are*
no more,
But the house of the righteous will
stand.

8 A man will be commended
according to his wisdom,
[a]But he who is of a perverse heart
will be despised.

9 [a]Better *is the one* who is [1]slighted
but has a servant,
Than he who honors himself but
lacks bread.

10 [a]A righteous *man* regards the life
of his animal,
But the tender mercies of the
wicked *are* cruel.

11 [a]He who [1]tills his land will be
satisfied with [b]bread,
But he who follows [2]frivolity [c]*is*
devoid of [3]understanding.

12 The wicked covet the catch of evil
men,
But the root of the righteous yields
fruit.

13 [a]The wicked is ensnared by the
transgression of *his* lips,
[b]But the righteous will come
through trouble.

14 [a]A man will be satisfied with good
by the fruit of *his* mouth,
[b]And the recompense of a man's
hands will be rendered to him.

15 [a]The way of a fool *is* right in his
own eyes,
But he who heeds counsel *is* wise.

16 [a]A fool's wrath is known at once,
But a prudent *man* covers shame.

17 [a]He *who* speaks truth declares
righteousness,

---

21 [b] Ps. 112:2
22 [1] *taste*
23 [a] Rom. 2:8, 9
24 [a] Ps. 112:9
25 [a] [2 Cor. 9:6, 7] [b] [Matt. 5:7]
26 [a] Amos 8:5, 6 [b] Job 29:13
27 [a] Esth. 7:10 [1] Lit. *seeks*
28 [a] Job 31:24 [b] Ps. 1:3
29 [a] Eccl. 5:16 [b] Prov. 14:19
30 [a] [Dan. 12:3] [1] Lit. *takes,* in the sense of *brings,* cf. 1 Sam. 16:11
31 [a] Jer. 25:29 [1] *rewarded*

CHAPTER 12
3 [a] [Prov. 10:25]
4 [a] 1 Cor. 11:7 [b] Prov. 14:30 [1] Lit. *A wife of valor*
6 [a] Prov. 1:11, 18 [b] Prov. 14:3
7 [a] Matt. 7:24–27
8 [a] 1 Sam. 25:17
9 [a] Prov. 13:7 [1] *lightly esteemed*
10 [a] Deut. 25:4
11 [a] Gen. 3:19 [b] Prov. 28:19 [c] Prov. 6:32 [1] *works* or *cultivates* [2] Lit. *vain things* [3] Lit. *heart*
13 [a] Prov. 18:7 [b] [2 Pet. 2:9]
14 [a] Prov. 13:2; 15:23; 18:20 [b] [Is. 3:10, 11]
15 [a] Luke 18:11
16 [a] Prov. 11:13; 29:11
17 [a] Prov. 14:5

But a false witness, deceit.
18 [a]There is one who speaks like the piercings of a sword,
But the tongue of the wise *promotes* health.
19 The truthful lip shall be established forever,
[a]But a lying tongue *is* but for a moment.
20 Deceit is in the heart of those who devise evil,
But counselors of peace have joy.
21 [a]No grave [1]trouble will overtake the righteous,
But the wicked shall be filled with evil.
22 [a]Lying lips *are* an abomination to the LORD,
But those who deal truthfully *are* His delight.

23 [a]A prudent man conceals knowledge,
But the heart of fools proclaims foolishness.

24 [a]The hand of the diligent will rule,
But the lazy *man* will be put to forced labor.

25 [a]Anxiety in the heart of man causes depression,
But [b]a good word makes it glad.

26 The righteous should choose his friends carefully,
For the way of the wicked leads them astray.

27 The lazy *man* does not roast what he took in hunting,
But diligence *is* man's precious possession.

28 In the way of righteousness *is* life,
And in *its* pathway *there is* no death.

13 A wise son *heeds* his father's instruction,
[a]But a scoffer does not listen to rebuke.

2 [a]A man shall eat well by the fruit of *his* mouth,
But the soul of the unfaithful feeds on violence.
3 [a]He who guards his mouth preserves his life,
But he who opens wide his lips shall have destruction.

18 [a]Ps. 57:4
19 [a]Prov. 19:9
21 [a]1 Pet. 3:13 [1]*harm*
22 [a]Rev. 22:15
23 [a]Prov. 13:16
24 [a]Prov. 10:4
25 [a]Prov. 15:13 [b]Is. 50:4

CHAPTER 13
1 [a]Is. 28:14, 15
2 [a]Prov. 12:14
3 [a]Prov. 21:23
4 [a]Prov. 10:4
6 [a]Prov. 11:3, 5, 6
7 [a][Prov. 11:24; 12:9]
9 [a]Prov. 24:20
10 [a]Prov. 10:12
11 [a]Prov. 10:2; 20:21
12 [a]Prov. 13:19
13 [a]Num. 15:31
14 [a]Prov. 6:22; 10:11; 14:27 [b]2 Sam. 22:6
15 [a]Prov. 3:4 [1]*gives*
16 [a]Prov. 12:23
17 [a]Prov. 25:13
18 [1]Lit. *ignores*

4 [a]The soul of a lazy *man* desires, and *has* nothing;
But the soul of the diligent shall be made rich.

5 A righteous *man* hates lying,
But a wicked *man* is loathsome and comes to shame.
6 [a]Righteousness guards *him whose* way is blameless,
But wickedness overthrows the sinner.

7 [a]There is one who makes himself rich, yet *has* nothing;
And one who makes himself poor, yet *has* great riches.

8 The ransom of a man's life *is* his riches,
But the poor does not hear rebuke.
9 The light of the righteous rejoices,
[a]But the lamp of the wicked will be put out.
10 By pride comes nothing but [a]strife,
But with the well-advised *is* wisdom.
11 [a]Wealth *gained by* dishonesty will be diminished,
But he who gathers by labor will increase.

12 Hope deferred makes the heart sick,
But [a]*when* the desire comes, *it is* a tree of life.

13 He who [a]despises the word will be destroyed,
But he who fears the commandment will be rewarded.
14 [a]The law of the wise *is* a fountain of life,
To turn *one* away from [b]the snares of death.
15 Good understanding [1]gains [a]favor,
But the way of the unfaithful *is* hard.
16 [a]Every prudent *man* acts with knowledge,
But a fool lays open *his* folly.
17 A wicked messenger falls into trouble,
But [a]a faithful ambassador *brings* health.

18 Poverty and shame *will come* to him who [1]disdains correction,

Proverbs 13:24

Dear Woman of Destiny,

As a child, it seemed I was always getting into trouble for one thing or another. I have vivid memories of standing in the bathroom holding on to the towel rack while my mother administered my just punishment with a swift swat to my posterior. That system of sure punishment was a structure I was both familiar with and comforted by. It was a constant affirmation of safe limits in my life. I didn't realize this consciously until much later in my life, however.

I always knew that my parents loved me. I also knew they were proud of my accomplishments and talents. This knowledge combined with appropriately applied discipline prepared me for all the schools, instructors, and tests to come. I came to understand you can't grow correctly without finding out what you're doing wrong and changing it. Since my major in college was music, that truth was honed in with a vengeance. Mistakes were watched for with cruel diligence. My childhood punishment seemed a treat by comparison. Unfortunately, correction here *was* rejection to a degree. Mistakes were humiliating, because they were nearly always public.

Our Father's correction is *never* rejection! In fact, it is proof of His love. His love for us so far exceeds any earthly love we know that we cannot begin to measure it. We are His inheritance (see Ps. 94:14) and His joy (see Is. 65:19). The training and disciplining of our loving heavenly Father not only prepares us for life here and now, but trains us for our eternity with Him. As we come to know and trust Him, we learn and seek eagerly His ways and laws. Our minds and wills learn to gracefully submit to His loving instructions and corrections. We must become like the lambs He gently leads, guides, and teaches, rather than the rebellious old ewes who constantly stray into their own paths and balk at the Master's touch!

His plans and purposes are to change us from glory to glory (see 2 Cor. 3:18). Each correction saves us more painful ones later. Keeping ourselves soft and pliable before Him—humble and ready to be corrected—will help us see the glorious picture of our ultimate destiny. My parents did not "spare the rod," and I didn't appreciate it until much later. Sometimes with the Lord we will not see through the painful times until we have crossed to the other side. But relying on Him in faith as a little child prepares us for the greater glory to come.

With every distressing occasion, I try to ask my Father what I can learn from it. I ask for His perspective, because I have learned well that my perspective is limited. I desire to walk out my destiny according to *His* will: that which is good, acceptable, and perfect (see Rom. 12:2). I know I cannot do that unless I change, and most of the time I won't change unless I am corrected. Learn to glory in your weaknesses, Woman of Destiny, because when you are weak, and humble, and teachable, you will be strong in the power of *His* might! Joy in the discipline of the Lord as it takes you from glory to glory!

Lora Allison

But [a]he who regards a rebuke will
be honored.

19 A desire accomplished is sweet to
the soul,
But *it is* an abomination to fools to
depart from evil.

20 He who walks with wise *men* will
be wise,
But the companion of fools will be
destroyed.

21 [a]Evil pursues sinners,
But to the righteous, good shall be
repaid.

22 A good *man* leaves an inheritance
to his children's children,
But [a]the wealth of the sinner is
stored up for the righteous.

23 [a]Much food *is in* the [1]fallow
ground of the poor,
And for lack of justice there is
[2]waste.

24 [a]He who spares his rod hates his
son,
But he who loves him disciplines
him [1]promptly.

25 [a]The righteous eats to the
satisfying of his soul,
But the stomach of the wicked shall
be in want.

14

The wise woman builds her
house,
But the foolish pulls it down with
her hands.

2 He who walks in his uprightness
fears the LORD,
[a]But *he who is* perverse in his ways
despises Him.

3 In the mouth of a fool *is* a rod of
pride,
[a]But the lips of the wise will
preserve them.

4 Where no oxen *are,* the [1]trough *is*
clean;
But much increase *comes* by the
strength of an ox.

5 A [a]faithful witness does not lie,
But a false witness will utter [b]lies.

6 A scoffer seeks wisdom and does
not *find it,*
But [a]knowledge *is* easy to him who
understands.

7 Go from the presence of a foolish
man,
When you do not perceive *in him*
the lips of [a]knowledge.

8 The wisdom of the prudent *is* to
understand his way,
But the folly of fools *is* deceit.

9 [a]Fools mock at [1]sin,
But among the upright *there is*
favor.

10 The heart knows its own
bitterness,
And a stranger does not share its
joy.

11 [a]The house of the wicked will be
overthrown,
But the tent of the upright will
flourish.

12 [a]There is a way *that seems* right to
a man,
But [b]its end *is* the way of [c]death.

13 Even in laughter the heart may
sorrow,
And [a]the end of mirth *may be*
grief.

14 The backslider in heart will be
[a]filled with his own ways,
But a good man *will be satisfied*
[1]from [b]above.

15 The simple believes every word,
But the prudent considers well his
steps.

16 [a]A wise *man* fears and departs from
evil,
But a fool rages and is
self-confident.

17 A quick-tempered *man* acts
foolishly,
And a man of wicked intentions is
hated.

18 The simple inherit folly,
But the prudent are crowned with
knowledge.

19 The evil will bow before the good,
And the wicked at the gates of the
righteous.

20 [a]The poor *man* is hated even by his
own neighbor,
But [1]the rich *has* many [b]friends.

21 He who despises his neighbor sins;
[a]But he who has mercy on the poor,
happy *is* he.

22 Do they not go astray who devise
evil?

---

18 a Prov. 15:5, 31, 32
21 a Ps. 32:10
22 a [Eccl. 2:26]
23 a Prov. 12:11 *1 uncultivated* *2* Lit. *what is swept away*
24 a Prov. 19:18 *1 early*
25 a Ps. 34:10

CHAPTER 14
2 a [Rom. 2:4]
3 a Prov. 12:6
4 *1 manger* or *feed trough*
5 a Rev. 1:5; 3:14 b Prov. 6:19; 12:17
6 a Prov. 8:9; 17:24
7 a Prov. 23:9
9 a Prov. 10:23 *1* Lit. *guilt*
11 a Job 8:15
12 a Prov. 16:25 b Rom. 6:21 c Prov. 12:15
13 a Eccl. 2:1, 2
14 a Prov. 1:31; 12:15 b Prov. 13:2; 18:20 *1* Lit. *from above himself*
16 a Prov. 22:3
20 a Prov. 19:7 b Prov. 19:4 *1* Lit. *many are the lovers of the rich*
21 a Ps. 112:9

PROVERBS 14:1

Dear Woman of Destiny,

Houses and homes are very important to women. A woman's home reflects the warmth and atmosphere of the woman's heart. These attributes are independent of the size and expense of a home. It matters little if it is an apartment or a mansion. Without a woman's heart it is merely wood and stone.

Proverbs 14:1 tells us, "The wise woman builds her house, but the foolish pulls it down with her hands." I find this verse intriguing because women are rarely responsible for construction. Therefore this verse illustrates a deeper spiritual meaning. In this verse, I believe *house* represents our lives and *builds* represents control. A wise woman allows God to build her life while the foolish woman tries to build her life in her own strength.

All my life I found it difficult to relinquish control. I was afraid if I was not in charge I'd be left vulnerable. I feared the desires, dreams, and things I viewed as important would be neglected. So I sought to control my husband and other circumstances as much as I could. Though I am married, control is as much an issue for the single woman as it is for the married one. Control becomes an issue when we fail to trust.

I remember finding it hard to trust anyone in my life. But I don't believe God wants us to trust in man; He wants us to trust in Him. When we trust Him, then, no matter what surrounds us, He is in ultimate control.

Often when we are frustrated with the progress of God's process in our lives or in the lives of those around us, we decide to help out. But instead of building, we end up tearing down the walls of protection God provided for our relationships. This demolition occurs by the wrecking ball of criticism, belittling, nagging, and, worst of all, complaining.

In a desperate attempt to hold it all together, we watch it slip from our hands. I grasped and clutched, only to open my arms and find them empty. I was so thankful that God had exposed my folly before it was too late.

Too often we are afraid to trust God to build our homes or lives. We take matters into our hands, take out our blueprints, and start construction. Only when we run up against immovable walls, faulty foundations, and depleted resources, do we cry out for help!

Perhaps you're at just such a place. You have tried to build your life or house in your own strength only to find a pile of rubble at your feet. Every brick *you* placed for your protection and provision has failed you. God is waiting. He will step in from the shadows where He has patiently watched your frantic project. We have His gracious assurance that His plan for us is good. His blueprint contains not only our needs, but even our deepest unspoken desires. Woman of Destiny, let go of control and trust Him with the construction.

Lisa Bevere

But mercy and truth *belong* to
those who devise good.

23 In all labor there is profit,
But [1]idle chatter *leads* only to
poverty.

24 The crown of the wise is their
riches,
But the foolishness of fools *is* folly.

25 A true witness [1]delivers [a]souls,
But a deceitful *witness* speaks lies.

26 In the fear of the LORD *there is*
strong confidence,
And His children will have a place
of refuge.

27 [a]The fear of the LORD *is* a fountain
of life,
To turn *one* away from the snares
of death.

28 In a multitude of people *is* a
king's honor,
But in the lack of people *is* the
downfall of a prince.

29 [a]*He who is* slow to wrath has great
understanding,
But *he who is* [1]impulsive exalts
folly.

30 A sound heart *is* life to the body,
But [a]envy *is* [b]rottenness to the
bones.

31 [a]He who oppresses the poor
reproaches [b]his Maker,
But he who honors Him has mercy
on the needy.

32 The wicked is banished in his
wickedness,
But [a]the righteous has a refuge in
his death.

33 Wisdom rests in the heart of him
who has understanding,
But [a]*what is* in the heart of fools is
made known.

34 Righteousness exalts a [a]nation,
But sin *is* a [1]reproach to *any*
people.

35 [a]The king's favor *is* toward a wise
servant,
But his wrath *is against* him who
causes shame.

15 A [a]soft answer turns away wrath,
But [b]a harsh word stirs up anger.

2 The tongue of the wise uses
knowledge rightly,

I pray, Father, that _____
will give a soft answer to
turn away wrath, because
harsh words stir up anger.

FROM PROVERBS 15:1

[a]But the mouth of fools pours forth
foolishness.

3 [a]The eyes of the LORD *are* in every
place,
Keeping watch on the evil and the
good.

4 A [1]wholesome tongue *is* a tree of
life,
But perverseness in it breaks the
spirit.

5 [a]A fool despises his father's
instruction,
[b]But he who [1]receives correction is
prudent.

6 *In* the house of the righteous *there*
is much treasure,
But in the revenue of the wicked is
trouble.

7 The lips of the wise [1]disperse
knowledge,
But the heart of the fool *does* not
do so.

8 [a]The sacrifice of the wicked *is* an
abomination to the LORD,
But the prayer of the upright *is* His
delight.

9 The way of the wicked *is* an
abomination to the LORD,
But He loves him who [a]follows
righteousness.

10 [a]Harsh discipline *is* for him who
forsakes the way,
And [b]he who hates correction will
die.

11 [a]Hell[1] and [2]Destruction *are* before
the LORD;
So how much more [b]the hearts of
the sons of men.

12 [a]A scoffer does not love one who
corrects him,
Nor will he go to the wise.

23 [1] Lit. *talk of the lips*

25 [a] [Ezek. 3:18–21] [1] *saves lives*

27 [a] Prov. 13:14

29 [a] James 1:19 [1] Lit. *short of spirit*

30 [a] Ps. 112:10 [b] Prov. 12:4

31 [a] Matt. 25:40 [b] [Prov. 22:2]

32 [a] Job 13:15

33 [a] Prov. 12:16

34 [a] Prov. 11:11 [1] *shame* or *disgrace*

35 [a] Matt. 24:45–47

CHAPTER 15

1 [a] Prov. 25:15 [b] 1 Sam. 25:10

2 [a] Prov. 12:23

3 [a] Job 34:21

4 [1] Lit. *healing*

5 [a] Prov. 10:1 [b] Prov. 13:18 [1] Lit. *keeps*

7 [1] *spread*

8 [a] Is. 1:11

9 [a] Prov. 21:21

10 [a] 1 Kin. 22:8 [b] Prov. 5:12

11 [a] Job 26:6 [b] 2 Chr. 6:30 [1] Or *Sheol* [2] Heb. *Abaddon*

12 [a] Amos 5:10

13 [a]A merry heart makes a cheerful
[1]countenance,
But [b]by sorrow of the heart the
spirit is broken.

14 The heart of him who has
understanding seeks knowledge,
But the mouth of fools feeds on
foolishness.

15 All the days of the afflicted *are*
evil,
[a]But he who is of a merry heart *has*
a continual feast.

16 [a]Better *is* a little with the fear of
the LORD,
Than great treasure with trouble.

17 [a]Better *is* a dinner of [1]herbs where
love is,
Than a fatted calf with hatred.

18 [a]A wrathful man stirs up strife,
But *he who is* slow to anger allays
contention.

19 [a]The way of the lazy *man is* like a
hedge of thorns,
But the way of the upright *is* a
highway.

20 [a]A wise son makes a father glad,
But a foolish man despises his
mother.

21 [a]Folly *is* joy *to him who is*
destitute of [1]discernment,
[b]But a man of understanding walks
uprightly.

22 [a]Without counsel, plans go awry,
But in the multitude of counselors
they are established.

23 A man has joy by the answer of
his mouth,
And [a]a word *spoken* [1]in due season,
how good *it is!*

24 [a]The way of life *winds* upward for
the wise,
That he may [b]turn away from [1]hell
below.

25 [a]The LORD will destroy the house
of the proud,
But [b]He will establish the boundary
of the widow.

26 [a]The thoughts of the wicked *are* an
abomination to the LORD,
[b]But *the words* of the pure *are*
pleasant.

13 a Prov. 12:25 b Prov. 17:22 *1 face*
15 a Prov. 17:22
16 a Ps. 37:16
17 a Prov. 17:1 *1* Or *vegetables*
18 a Prov. 26:21
19 a Prov. 22:5
20 a Prov. 10:1
21 a Prov. 10:23 b Eph. 5:15 *1* Lit. *heart*
22 a Prov. 11:14
23 a Prov. 25:11 *1* Lit. *in its time*
24 a Phil. 3:20 b Prov. 14:16 *1* Or *Sheol*
25 a Prov. 12:7 b Ps. 68:5, 6
26 a Prov. 6:16, 18 b Ps. 37:30
27 a Is. 5:8
28 a 1 Pet. 3:15
29 a Ps. 10:1; 34:16 b Ps. 145:18
30 *1* Lit. *fat*
33 a Prov. 1:7 b Prov. 18:12
CHAPTER 16
1 a Jer. 10:23 b Matt. 10:19 *1 plans*
2 a Prov. 21:2
3 a Ps. 37:5 *1* Lit. *Roll*
4 a Is. 43:7 b [Rom. 9:22] *1* Lit. *evil*
5 a Prov. 6:17; 8:13

27 [a]He who is greedy for gain troubles
his own house,
But he who hates bribes will live.

28 The heart of the righteous
[a]studies how to answer,
But the mouth of the wicked pours
forth evil.

29 [a]The LORD *is* far from the wicked,
But [b]He hears the prayer of the
righteous.

30 The light of the eyes rejoices the
heart,
And a good report makes the bones
[1]healthy.

31 The ear that hears the rebukes of
life
Will abide among the wise.

32 He who disdains instruction
despises his own soul,
But he who heeds rebuke gets
understanding.

33 [a]The fear of the LORD *is* the
instruction of wisdom,
And [b]before honor *is* humility.

Humility must be in the praying character as light is in the sun.

E. M. BOUNDS

16

1 The [a]preparations[1] of the heart
belong to man,
[b]But the answer of the tongue *is*
from the LORD.

2 All the ways of a man *are* pure in
his own [a]eyes,
But the LORD weighs the spirits.

3 [a]Commit[1] your works to the LORD,
And your thoughts will be
established.

4 The [a]LORD has made all for
Himself,
[b]Yes, even the wicked for the day of
[1]doom.

5 [a]Everyone proud in heart *is* an
abomination to the LORD;

Though they join [1]forces, none will
go unpunished.

6 [a]In mercy and truth
Atonement is provided for iniquity;
And [b]by the fear of the LORD *one*
departs from evil.

7 When a man's ways please the
LORD,
He makes even his enemies to be at
peace with him.

8 [a]Better *is* a little with
righteousness,
Than vast revenues without justice.

9 [a]A man's heart plans his way,
[b]But the LORD directs his steps.

10 Divination *is* on the lips of the
king;
His mouth must not transgress in
judgment.

11 [a]Honest weights and scales *are* the
LORD's;
All the weights in the bag *are* His
[1]work.

12 *It is* an abomination for kings to
commit wickedness,
For [a]a throne is established by
righteousness.

13 [a]Righteous lips *are* the delight of
kings,
And they love him who speaks *what*
is right.

14 As messengers of death *is* the
king's wrath,
But a wise man will [a]appease it.

15 In the light of the king's face *is*
life,
And his favor *is* like a [a]cloud of the
latter rain.

16 [a]How much better to get wisdom
than gold!
And to get understanding is to be
chosen rather than silver.

17 The highway of the upright *is* to
depart from evil;
He who keeps his way preserves his
soul.

18 Pride *goes* before destruction,
And a haughty spirit before [1]a fall.

19 Better *to be* of a humble spirit
with the lowly,
Than to divide the [1]spoil with the
proud.

20 He who heeds the word wisely will
find good,
And whoever [a]trusts in the LORD,
happy *is* he.

21 The wise in heart will be called
prudent,
And sweetness of the lips increases
learning.

22 Understanding *is* a wellspring of
life to him who has it.
But the correction of fools *is* folly.

23 The heart of the wise teaches his
mouth,
And adds learning to his lips.

24 Pleasant words *are like* a
honeycomb,
Sweetness to the soul and health to
the bones.

25 There is a way *that seems* right to
a man,
But its end *is* the way of [a]death.

26 The person who labors, labors for
himself,
For his *hungry* mouth drives [a]him
on.

27 [1]An ungodly man digs up evil,
And *it is* on his lips like a burning
[a]fire.

28 A perverse man sows strife,
And [a]a whisperer separates the best
of friends.

29 A violent man entices his
neighbor,
And leads him in a way *that is* not
good.

30 He winks his eye to devise
perverse things;
He [1]purses his lips *and* brings
about evil.

31 [a]The silver-haired head *is* a crown
of glory,
If it is found in the way of
righteousness.

32 [a]*He who is* slow to anger *is* better
than the mighty,
And he who rules his spirit than he
who takes a city.

33 The lot is cast into the lap,
But its every decision *is* from the
LORD.

17 Better *is* [a]a dry morsel with
quietness,
Than a house full of [1]feasting *with*
strife.

---

5 *1* Lit. *hand to hand*
6 **a** Dan. 4:27 **b** Prov. 8:13; 14:16
8 **a** Ps. 37:16
9 **a** Prov. 19:21 **b** Jer. 10:23
11 **a** Lev. 19:36 *1 concern*
12 **a** Prov. 25:5
13 **a** Prov. 14:35
14 **a** Prov. 25:15
15 **a** Zech. 10:1
16 **a** Prov. 8:10, 11, 19
18 *1 stumbling*
19 *1 plunder*
20 **a** Ps. 34:8
25 **a** Prov. 14:12
26 **a** [Eccl. 6:7]
27 **a** [James 3:6] *1* Lit. *A man of Belial*
28 **a** Prov. 17:9
30 *1* Lit. *compresses*
31 **a** Prov. 20:29
32 **a** Prov. 14:29; 19:11

CHAPTER 17
1 **a** Prov. 15:17 *1* Or *sacrificial meals*

2 A wise servant will rule over [a]a son
who causes shame,
And will share an inheritance
among the brothers.

3 The refining pot *is* for silver and
the furnace for gold,
[a]But the LORD tests the hearts.

4 An evildoer gives heed to false lips;
A liar listens eagerly to a [1]spiteful
tongue.

5 [a]He who mocks the poor reproaches
his Maker;
[b]He who is glad at calamity will not
go unpunished.

6 [a]Children's children *are* the crown
of old men,
And the glory of children *is* their
father.

7 Excellent speech is not becoming
to a fool,
Much less lying lips to a prince.

8 A present *is* a precious stone in the
eyes of its possessor;
Wherever he turns, he prospers.

9 [a]He who covers a transgression
seeks love,
But [b]he who repeats a matter
separates friends.

10 [a]Rebuke is more effective for a wise
man
Than a hundred blows on a fool.

11 An evil *man* seeks only rebellion;
Therefore a cruel messenger will be
sent against him.

12 Let a man meet [a]a bear robbed of
her cubs,
Rather than a fool in his folly.

13 Whoever [a]rewards evil for good,
Evil will not depart from his house.

14 The beginning of strife *is like*
releasing water;
Therefore [a]stop contention before a
quarrel starts.

15 [a]He who justifies the wicked, and
he who condemns the just,
Both of them alike *are* an
abomination to the LORD.

16 Why *is there* in the hand of a fool
the purchase price of wisdom,
Since *he has* no heart *for it?*

17 [a]A friend loves at all times,
And a brother is born for adversity.

18 [a]A man devoid of [1]understanding
[2]shakes hands in a pledge,
And becomes [3]surety for his friend.

19 He who loves transgression loves
strife,
And [a]he who exalts his gate seeks
destruction.

20 He who has a [1]deceitful heart
finds no good,
And he who has [a]a perverse tongue
falls into evil.

21 He who begets a scoffer *does so* to
his sorrow,
And the father of a fool has no joy.

22 A [a]merry heart [1]does good, *like*
medicine,
But a broken spirit dries the
bones.

23 A wicked *man* accepts a bribe
[1]behind the back
To pervert the ways of justice.

24 [a]Wisdom *is* in the sight of him
who has understanding,
But the eyes of a fool *are* on the
ends of the earth.

25 A [a]foolish son *is* a grief to his
father,
And bitterness to her who bore
him.

26 Also, to punish the righteous *is*
not good,
Nor to strike princes for *their*
uprightness.

27 [a]He who has knowledge spares his
words,
And a man of understanding is of a
calm spirit.

28 [a]Even a fool is counted wise when
he holds his peace;
When he shuts his lips, *he is*
considered perceptive.

18 A man who isolates himself seeks
his own desire;
He rages against all [1]wise
judgment.

2 A fool has no delight in
understanding,
But in expressing his [a]own heart.

3 When the wicked comes, contempt
comes also;

2 a Prov. 10:5
3 a Jer. 17:10
4 1 Lit. *destructive*
5 a Prov. 14:31 b Job 31:29
6 a [Ps. 127:3; 128:3]
9 a [Prov. 10:12] b Prov. 16:28
10 a [Mic. 7:9]
12 a Hos. 13:8
13 a Ps. 109:4, 5
14 a [Prov. 20:3]
15 a Ex. 23:7
17 a Ruth 1:16
18 a Prov. 6:1 1 Lit. *heart* 2 Lit. *strikes the hands* 3 *guaranty* or *collateral*
19 a Prov. 16:18
20 a James 3:8 1 *crooked*
22 a Prov. 12:25; 15:13, 15 1 Or *makes medicine even better*
23 1 Under cover, lit. *from the bosom*
24 a Eccl. 2:14
25 a Prov. 10:1; 15:20; 19:13
27 a James 1:19
28 a Job 13:5

CHAPTER 18
1 1 *sound wisdom*
2 a Eccl. 10:3

Proverbs 17:22

Dear Woman of Destiny,

I don't know about you, but my life is very intense. The pressure rarely lets up unless I grab what fleeting moments there are to look on the lighter side.

Sadly, too many of us have lost our sense of humor. This is dangerous. If we lose our sense of humor, our mind might be the next thing to go! We might not think we can laugh in the midst of all the pressures of life, but we won't make it unless we do!

The gift of laughter may be one of our greatest blessings from God. Maybe that's why the enemy has corrupted humor the same way he's corrupted music. Today's humor is often crude, derogatory, or sexually exploitative. It makes fun of the weak, the needy and the different. I call this the easy "non-thinking" person's type of humor. It's just not creative.

The most godly people I know—those who've had the greatest spiritual impact on my life—always seem to have the greatest sense of humor! They're at home with laughter as long as it's not at someone's expense. And they can laugh at themselves, too. People who are "too spiritual" to enjoy a good belly laugh are missing the point.

Few people were more serious about God than my dear friend, the late Leonard Ravenhill. But his writings are laced with wit and the clever turning of a phrase. When I think of him, I always think of his warm laughter and ready smile.

George MacDonald, the famous Christian author from Scotland, said, "It is the heart that is not yet sure of its God that is afraid to laugh in His presence." Charles Spurgeon, who carried a pressing burden for England and survived poverty and the great plague of London, was often criticized for "frivolity" in the pulpit. He replied, "This preacher thinks it less a crime to cause momentary laughter than one hour of profound slumber!"

And God has a sense of humor, too. Look at the giraffe, the hippopotamus, and, well, look at us. People are funny! Volumes could be filled on the "humor of life" and all its little inconsistencies by just observing one day of silly human habits. Real life can be funnier than fiction.

Nobody can see the underside of life's "tapestry" as clearly as God, but He doesn't get uptight and stressed out. Maybe that's because He can see the final victorious outcome! Jesus said, "In the world you will have tribulation; but be of good cheer, I have overcome the world" (John 16:33).

As Christians, we want to be taken seriously because we are serious about God. We want to be seen as credible, stable, single-minded people. But let's not get "hyper-spiritual" to try to prove our integrity. And let's not let the enemy rob us of the ability to see the funny side of life and laugh at the downright silliness of some situations!

Can you keep a sense of humor in the midst of life's difficult situations? Do you laugh enough? If joyful laughter is an element that's missing from your life, then begin to smile more today than you did yesterday—and let the Lord fill your mouth with laughter!

Melody Green

Proverbs 18:16

Dear Woman of Destiny,

I feel privileged to be able to share with you one of my favorite Bible scriptures—Proverbs 18:16. I was 13 years old when I was first impacted by this verse as it spoke to me of a better life beyond my orphanage experiences—God's design for a future and a hope—for *me*.

Some time ago, I was again drawn to this text in preparation for a speaking engagement. Let me relate how it was unfolded to me. In looking at the first portion, "A [woman's] gift," I was given a picture of an immense exquisitely decorated gift box that God was elevating and showcasing for all to see. I understood that the gift represented each of us. So I chose as a topic: "I am a gift!" As women, this speaks of our value, uniqueness, beauty, dignity, creativity, stateliness, acceptance, resident resources, and contributions we make. So a woman's gift has to do with: 1) personal significance, 2) what's been given/poured into you, 3) what's been invested in you in the way of talents and abilities, and 4) who you are. "You are a *gift!*" This intimates that inside the package are "giftings" that are to be given away.

The verse continues, "makes room for [her]," meaning the gift/giftings create or prepare an appropriate or distinct place for you. This has to do with:

- *Opening a package against resistance*; you can't be held back though it seems you're being squeezed out!
- A fit or chosen opportunity; it's a properly selected moment or time for you to seize. You're there—possess it!
- Being successful in the designated position you're entering; where God places you, you *will not* fail!

The last portion of the text says "brings," meaning you will be ushered, escorted, conveyed, or showcased; and "before great men," meaning being brought to or into the presence of greatness or destinies you never imagined.

Therefore, you have been made a resource for every:

- appropriate place
- chosen opportunity
- designated position

in which God would place you.

The question is: Will God be given the privilege to *place you* "as a gift" *anywhere* He chooses?

It is sometimes difficult for women to not take control of the placements. But remember—"*You are a gift!*" A gift has no requirements, makes no requirements—it is offered!

And you, Woman of Destiny, are among the multiplicity of gifts that Jesus desires to place in various settings to bless others. For instance, your gift might be speaking a word of hope to one grappling with feelings of hopelessness and despair; showing acts of love and kindness to someone needing your genuine concern; tenderly taking someone by the hand, giving them your time, helping them find their way; rescuing teenagers/children, assisting the next generation in knowing the joys of serving Jesus; or reaching out and investing in young women as a Titus 2 woman.

May you always be reminded of your priceless value to God. You are not a "mere existence"—you *are* a gift!

Naomi Beard

And with dishonor *comes* reproach.

4 [a]The words of a man's mouth *are*
deep waters;
[b]The wellspring of wisdom *is* a
flowing brook.

5 *It is* not good to show partiality to
the wicked,
Or to overthrow the righteous in
[a]judgment.

6 A fool's lips enter into contention,
And his mouth calls for blows.

7 [a]A fool's mouth *is* his destruction,
And his lips *are* the snare of his
[b]soul.

8 [a]The words of a [1]talebearer *are* like
[2]tasty trifles,
And they go down into the [3]inmost
body.

9 He who is slothful in his work
Is a brother to him who is a great
destroyer.

10 The name of the LORD *is* a strong
[a]tower;
The righteous run to it and are
[1]safe.

11 The rich man's wealth *is* his
strong city,
And like a high wall in his own
esteem.

12 [a]Before destruction the heart of a
man is haughty,
And before honor *is* humility.

13 He who answers a matter before
he hears *it*,
It *is* folly and shame to him.

14 The spirit of a man will sustain
him in sickness,
But who can bear a broken spirit?

15 The heart of the prudent acquires
knowledge,
And the ear of the wise seeks
knowledge.

16 [a]A man's gift makes room for
him,
And brings him before great
men.

17 The first *one* to plead his cause
seems right,
Until his neighbor comes and
examines him.

18 Casting [a]lots causes contentions
to cease,
And keeps the mighty apart.

19 A brother offended *is harder to
win* than a strong city,
And contentions *are* like the bars of
a castle.

20 [a]A man's stomach shall be satisfied
from the fruit of his mouth;
From the produce of his lips he
shall be filled.

21 [a]Death and life *are* in the power
of the tongue,
And those who love it will eat its
fruit.

22 [a]*He who* finds a wife finds a good
thing,
And obtains favor from the LORD.

23 The poor *man* uses entreaties,
But the rich answers [a]roughly.

24 A man *who has* friends [1]must
himself be friendly,
[a]But there is a friend *who* sticks
closer than a brother.

19 Better [a]*is* the poor who walks in
his integrity
Than *one who is* perverse in his
lips, and is a fool.

2 Also it is not good *for* a soul *to be*
without knowledge,
And he sins who hastens with *his*
feet.

3 The foolishness of a man twists his
way,
And his heart frets against the
LORD.

4 [a]Wealth makes many friends,
But the poor is separated from his
friend.

5 A [a]false witness will not go
unpunished,
And *he who* speaks lies will not
escape.

6 Many entreat the favor of the
nobility,
And every man *is* a friend to one
who gives gifts.

7 [a]All the brothers of the poor hate
him;
How much more do his friends go
[b]far from him!

---

4 a Prov. 10:11 b [James 3:17]
5 a Prov. 17:15
7 a Prov. 10:14 b Eccl. 10:12
8 a Prov. 12:18 *1 gossip* or *slanderer* *2* A Jewish tradition *wounds* *3* Lit. *rooms of the belly*
10 a 2 Sam. 22:2, 3, 33 *1 secure,* lit. *set on high*
12 a Prov. 15:33; 16:18
16 a Gen. 32:20, 21
18 a [Prov. 16:33]
20 a Prov. 12:14; 14:14
21 a Matt. 12:37
22 a [Prov. 12:4; 19:14]
23 a James 2:3, 6
24 a Prov. 17:17 *1* So with Gr. mss., Syr., Tg., Vg.; MT *may come to ruin*

CHAPTER 19
1 a Prov. 28:6
4 a Prov. 14:20
5 a Ex. 23:1
7 a Prov. 14:20 b Ps. 38:11

Proverbs 18:21

Dear Woman of Destiny,

Did you know that "death and life are in the power of the tongue"? You will reap the rewards or suffer the consequences of words spoken yesterday. Careless, idle words can be reversed by speaking words of life—words of victory.

My life is a portrait of the power of the tongue. Even today, I can hear his deep bass voice reverberate in my head: "You can do anything you make up your mind to do." As a young girl, I answered silently, "Yeah, sure. That may be true for others, but not for me." To cover up my insecurities I made cute, disparaging remarks about myself. I was positive that others knew what I had always known—that I should never have been born.

At the age of 17, I made a vow to serve God, a vow easily forgotten over the next few years. I was married, and taking care of a home and four children consumed my life. A few months after the birth of our last baby on a gray winter's day, I prayed a desperate prayer; and God drew me out of depression into the light of His glorious love. Sorrow turned to joy, and night turned to day. I began reading the Bible—God's love letter to me—and my thought patterns were turned upside down. As I searched the Scriptures, my belief system was transformed; and everyday melancholy, pessimistic conversations changed to hope for the future.

If you are saying, "I can't," practice saying, "I can do all things through Christ who strengthens me" (Phil. 4:13). If you feel that your life has no purpose, remind yourself, "God chose me before the foundation of the world" (see Eph. 1:4). If you have a fear of rejection, replace it with, "I am accepted in the Beloved" (see Eph. 1:6). You may be suffering emotional pain; accept the anointing that is upon Jesus to heal you. You were born for such a time as this. The Holy Spirit is your Helper, and He will teach you to speak blessings over yourself and your family.

The tongue is a small member in the body, but it has great significance. Just as a rudder steers a ship or a bridle directs a horse, the tongue controls your life. Your choice of life or death is determined by your words. The words you speak can tear down, or accomplish great things. Words wound; words heal. Words ensnare; words liberate you. Words destroy relationships, and words restore relationships. Confession is made to salvation. Words shape our destiny.

Words may be the most powerful force on earth. God has set before us life and death. Words activate the law of the Spirit of life in Christ Jesus or the law of sin and death. As you speak words of life, God's destiny for you will take shape. God is faithful, and He continues to enrich my speech. The words that I speak about others and myself are God's Word, and my destiny of blessings and blessing others continues to unfold.

Germaine Copeland

He may pursue *them with* words,
yet they [1]abandon *him*.

8 He who gets [1]wisdom loves his own soul;
He who keeps understanding [a]will find good.

9 A false witness will not go unpunished,
And *he who* speaks lies shall perish.

10 Luxury is not fitting for a fool,
Much less [a]for a servant to rule over princes.

11 [a]The discretion of a man makes him slow to anger,
[b]And his glory *is* to overlook a transgression.

12 [a]The king's wrath *is* like the roaring of a lion,
But his favor *is* [b]like dew on the grass.

13 [a]A foolish son *is* the ruin of his father,
[b]And the contentions of a wife *are* a continual [1]dripping.

14 [a]Houses and riches *are* an inheritance from fathers,
But [b]a prudent wife *is* from the LORD.

15 [a]Laziness casts *one* into a deep sleep,
And an idle person will [b]suffer hunger.

16 [a]He who keeps the commandment keeps his soul,
But he who [1]is careless of his ways will die.

17 [a]He who has pity on the poor lends to the LORD,
And He will pay back what he has given.

18 [a]Chasten your son while there is hope,
And do not set your heart [1]on his destruction.

19 *A man of* great wrath will suffer punishment;
For if you rescue *him,* you will have to do it again.

20 Listen to counsel and receive instruction,
That you may be wise [a]in your latter days.

21 There are many plans in a man's heart,
[a]Nevertheless the LORD's counsel—that will stand.

22 What is desired in a man is [1]kindness,
And a poor man is better than a liar.

23 [a]The fear of the LORD *leads* to life,
And *he who has it* will abide in satisfaction;
He will not be visited with evil.

24 [a]A lazy *man* buries his hand in the [1]bowl,
And will not so much as bring it to his mouth again.

25 Strike a scoffer, and the simple [a]will become wary;
[b]Rebuke one who has understanding, *and* he will discern knowledge.

26 He who mistreats *his* father *and* chases away *his* mother
Is [a]a son who causes shame and brings reproach.

27 Cease listening to instruction, my son,
And you will stray from the words of knowledge.

Lord, may ____ have pity on the poor, for they that have pity on the poor lend to You, and You will pay back what ____ has given.
FROM PROVERBS 19:17

28 A [1]disreputable witness scorns justice,
And [a]the mouth of the wicked devours iniquity.

29 Judgments are prepared for scoffers,
[a]And beatings for the backs of fools.

20

Wine [a]*is* a mocker,
Strong drink *is* a brawler,
And whoever is led astray by it is not wise.

---

7 [1]Lit. *are not*
8 [a]Prov. 16:20 [1]Lit. *heart*
10 [a]Prov. 30:21, 22
11 [a]James 1:19 [b]Eph. 4:32
12 [a]Prov. 16:14 [b]Hos. 14:5
13 [a]Prov. 10:1 [b]Prov. 21:9, 19 [1]Irritation
14 [a]2 Cor. 12:14 [b]Prov. 18:22
15 [a]Prov. 6:9 [b]Prov. 10:4
16 [a]Luke 10:28; 11:28 [1]Is reckless, lit. *despises*
17 [a][2 Cor. 9:6–8]
18 [a]Prov. 13:24 [1]Lit. *to put him to death;* a Jewish tradition *on his crying*
20 [a]Ps. 37:37
21 [a]Heb. 6:17
22 [1]Lit. *loving-kindness*
23 [a][1 Tim. 4:8]
24 [a]Prov. 15:19 [1]LXX, Syr. *bosom;* Tg., Vg. *armpit*
25 [a]Deut. 13:11 [b]Prov. 9:8
26 [a]Prov. 17:2
28 [a]Job 15:16 [1]Lit. *witness of Belial, worthless witness*
29 [a]Prov. 26:3
CHAPTER 20
1 [a]Gen. 9:21

2 The [1]wrath of a king *is* like the roaring of a lion;
Whoever provokes him to anger sins *against* his own life.

3 [a]*It is* honorable for a man to stop striving,
Since any fool can start a quarrel.

4 [a]The lazy *man* will not plow because of winter;
[b]He will beg during harvest and *have* nothing.

5 Counsel in the heart of man *is like* deep water,
But a man of understanding will draw it out.

6 Most men will proclaim each his own [1]goodness,
But who can find a faithful man?

7 [a]The righteous *man* walks in his integrity;
[b]His children *are* blessed after him.

8 A king who sits on the throne of judgment
Scatters all evil with his eyes.

9 [a]Who can say, "I have made my heart clean,
I am pure from my sin"?

10 [a]Diverse weights *and* diverse measures,
They *are* both alike, an abomination to the LORD.

11 Even a child is [a]known by his deeds,
Whether what he does *is* pure and right.

12 [a]The hearing ear and the seeing eye,
The LORD has made them both.

13 [a]Do not love sleep, lest you come to poverty;
Open your eyes, *and* you will be satisfied with bread.

14 "*It is* [1]good for nothing," cries the buyer;
But when he has gone his way, then he boasts.

15 There is gold and a multitude of rubies,
But [a]the lips of knowledge *are* a precious jewel.

16 [a]Take the garment of one who is surety *for* a stranger,
And hold it as a pledge *when it* is for a seductress.

17 [a]Bread gained by deceit *is* sweet to a man,
But afterward his mouth will be filled with gravel.

18 [a]Plans are established by counsel;
[b]By wise counsel wage war.

19 [a]He who goes about *as* a talebearer reveals secrets;
Therefore do not associate with one [b]who flatters with his lips.

20 [a]Whoever curses his father or his mother,
[b]His lamp will be put out in deep darkness.

21 [a]An inheritance gained hastily at the beginning
[b]Will not be blessed at the end.

22 [a]Do not say, "I will [1]recompense evil";
[b]Wait for the LORD, and He will save you.

23 Diverse weights *are* an abomination to the LORD,
And dishonest scales *are* not good.

24 A man's steps *are* of the LORD;
How then can a man understand his own way?

25 *It is* a snare for a man to devote rashly *something as* holy,
And afterward to reconsider *his* vows.

26 [a]A wise king sifts out the wicked,
And brings the threshing wheel over them.

27 [a]The spirit of a man *is* the lamp of the LORD,
Searching all the [1]inner depths of his heart.

28 [a]Mercy and truth preserve the king,
And by [1]lovingkindness he upholds his throne.

29 The glory of young men *is* their strength,
And [a]the splendor of old men *is* their gray head.

---

2 [1] Lit. *fear* or *terror,* produced by the king's wrath
3 a Prov. 17:14
4 a Prov. 10:4 b Prov. 19:15
6 [1] Lit. *mercy*
7 a 2 Cor. 1:12 b Ps. 37:26
9 a [1 Kin. 8:46]
10 a Deut. 25:13
11 a Matt. 7:16
12 a Ex. 4:11
13 a Rom. 12:11
14 [1] Lit. *evil, evil*
15 a [Prov. 3:13–15]
16 a Prov. 22:26
17 a Prov. 9:17
18 a Prov. 24:6 b Luke 14:31
19 a Prov. 11:13 b Rom. 16:18
20 a Matt. 15:4 b Job 18:5, 6
21 a Prov. 28:20 b Hab. 2:6
22 a [Rom. 12:17–19] b 2 Sam. 16:12 [1] *repay*
26 a Ps. 101:8
27 a 1 Cor. 2:11 [1] Lit. *rooms of the belly*
28 a Prov. 21:21 [1] *mercy*
29 a Prov. 16:31

30 Blows that hurt cleanse away evil,
As *do* stripes the [1]inner depths of the heart.

CHAPTER 21

21 The king's heart *is* in the hand of the LORD,
Like the [1]rivers of water; He turns it wherever He wishes.

2 [a]Every way of a man *is* right in his own eyes,
[b]But the LORD weighs the hearts.

3 [a]To do righteousness and justice
Is more acceptable to the LORD than sacrifice.

4 [a]A haughty look, a proud heart,
And the [1]plowing of the wicked *are* sin.

5 [a]The plans of the diligent *lead* surely to plenty,
But *those of* everyone *who is* hasty, surely to poverty.

6 [a]Getting treasures by a lying tongue
[1]*Is* the fleeting fantasy of those who seek death.

7 The violence of the wicked will [1]destroy them,
Because they refuse to do justice.

8 The way of [1]a guilty man *is* perverse;
But *as for* the pure, his work *is* right.

9 Better to dwell in a corner of a housetop,
Than in a house shared with [a]a contentious woman.

10 [a]The soul of the wicked desires evil;
His neighbor finds no favor in his eyes.

11 When the scoffer is punished, the simple is made wise;
But when the [a]wise is instructed, he receives knowledge.

12 The righteous *God* wisely considers the house of the wicked,
Overthrowing the wicked for *their* wickedness.

13 [a]Whoever shuts his ears to the cry of the poor
Will also cry himself and not be heard.

14 A gift in secret pacifies anger,
And a bribe [1]behind the back, strong wrath.

15 *It is* a joy for the just to do justice,
But destruction *will come* to the workers of iniquity.

16 A man who wanders from the way of understanding
Will rest in the assembly of the [a]dead.

17 He who loves pleasure *will be* a poor man;
He who loves wine and oil will not be rich.

18 The wicked *shall be* a ransom for the righteous,
And the unfaithful for the upright.

19 Better to dwell [1]in the wilderness,
Than with a contentious and angry woman.

20 [a]*There is* desirable treasure,
And oil in the dwelling of the wise,
But a foolish man squanders it.

21 [a]He who follows righteousness and mercy
Finds life, righteousness and honor.

22 A [a]wise *man* [1]scales the city of the mighty,
And brings down the trusted stronghold.

23 [a]Whoever guards his mouth and tongue
Keeps his soul from troubles.

24 A proud *and* haughty *man*—
"Scoffer" *is* his name;
He acts with arrogant pride.

25 The [a]desire of the lazy *man* kills him,
For his hands refuse to labor.

26 He covets greedily all day long,
But the righteous [a]gives and does not spare.

27 [a]The sacrifice of the wicked *is* an abomination;
How much more *when* he brings it with wicked intent!

28 A false witness shall perish,
But the man who hears *him* will speak endlessly.

---

30 [1] Lit. *rooms of the belly*

CHAPTER 21

1 [1] *channels*

2 [a] Prov. 16:2 [b] Prov. 24:12

3 [a] 1 Sam. 15:22

4 [a] Prov. 6:17 [1] Or *lamp*

5 [a] Prov. 10:4

6 [a] 2 Pet. 2:3 [1] LXX *Pursue vanity on the snares of death;* Vg. *Is vain and foolish, and shall stumble on the snares of death;* Tg. *They shall be destroyed, and they shall fall who seek death*

7 [1] Lit. *drag them away*

8 [1] Or *The way of a man is perverse and strange;*

9 [a] Prov. 19:13

10 [a] James 4:5

11 [a] Prov. 19:25

13 [a] [Matt. 7:2; 18:30–34]

14 [1] Under cover, lit. *in the bosom*

16 [a] Ps. 49:14

19 [1] Lit. *in the land of the desert*

20 [a] Ps. 112:3

21 [a] Matt. 5:6

22 [a] Prov. 24:5 [1] Climbs over the walls of

23 [a] [James 3:2]

25 [a] Prov. 13:4

26 [a] [Prov. 22:9]

27 [a] Jer. 6:20

PROVERBS 21:1, 2

Dear Woman of Destiny,

After the experience of surviving a heart attack, I gained a personal understanding of the meaning of pain and appreciated the sound of a heartbeat, which I had so often taken for granted. I believe that anyone who has lived through a heart attack or has felt severe chest pain has had to reflect on God, even if only for a few seconds. The pain feels like an elephant has sat on your chest and has started moving around. All you can hear is your heartbeat. You quickly know who is in control.

Twenty years ago I felt completely out of control. As a victim of satanic ritual abuse, I was trapped and controlled by fear. The painful memories of mistakes that opened the door to years of depression and guilt tore at my heart. Yet even then, my heart was in the hand of the Lord. After completely surrendering to Jesus, He lifted me from the ashes of sexual abuse, took a heart scarred by the occult, and gave me a new servant's heart.

Proverbs 21:2 tells us that "the LORD weighs the hearts." We may try to cover personal flaws exposed by our actions and displayed in our thoughts, but God takes notice of the motives of our heart. He is our heart specialist, and He is the only One who can do spiritual heart surgery. When you feel your heart has hardened or been abused, the Lord says, "I will give you a new heart and put a new spirit within you; I will take the heart of stone out of your flesh and give you a heart of flesh" (Ezek. 36:26).

Just as a physical heart attack occurs when there is a stoppage or clot in the flow of blood, a spiritual heart attack can occur when there is a lack of the Holy Spirit flowing in our lives. Sometimes a spiritual heart attack can shatter the heart into a thousand pieces, and the hurt is so deep that it surpasses any degree of physical pain. A divorce, a broken dream, an abortion, a bankruptcy, or the death of a loved one can be an experience that makes us question whether God is listening or if He really cares. Just as a medical doctor might recommend a heart surgery or transplant in cases of extreme heart damage, so God is eager to heal and restore your heart, or to even give you a new one. When you suffer a spiritual heart attack, only God Almighty can bring healing.

When we understand that the Lord weighs our hearts and we begin to trust Him, then it becomes easy to yield to the Holy Spirit. He can easily separate our thoughts and our emotions, which can change like the wind, from the true posture of the heart. As Proverbs 21:2 tells us, we often make choices that are right in our own eyes. But only the Lord knows the motives of our heart, and He alone can transform our hearts to beat in accordance with His.

A. G. Rodriguez

29 A wicked man hardens his face,
But *as for* the upright, he
[1]establishes his way.

30 [a]*There is* no wisdom or
understanding
Or counsel against the LORD.

31 The horse *is* prepared for the day
of battle,
But [a]deliverance *is* of the LORD.

22 A [a]*good* name is to be chosen
rather than great riches,
Loving favor rather than silver and
gold.

2 The [a]rich and the poor have this in
common,
The [b]LORD *is* the maker of them all.

3 A prudent *man* foresees evil and
hides himself,
But the simple pass on and are
[a]punished.

4 By humility *and* the fear of the
LORD
Are riches and honor and life.

5 Thorns *and* snares *are* in the way
of the perverse;
He who guards his soul will be far
from them.

I pray, heavenly Father, that ____ will train up their children in the way they should go, so that even when their children are old, they will not depart from it.
FROM PROVERBS 22:6

6 [a]Train up a child in the way he
should go,
[1]And when he is old he will not
depart from it.

7 The [a]rich rules over the poor,
And the borrower *is* servant to the
lender.

8 He who sows iniquity will reap
[a]sorrow,[1]
And the rod of his anger will fail.

29 *1* Or., LXX *understands*
30 a [Jer. 9:23, 24]
31 a Ps. 3:8
CHAPTER 22
1 a Eccl. 7:1
2 a Prov. 29:13
b Job 31:15
3 a Prov. 27:12
6 a Eph. 6:4
1 Even
7 a James 2:6
8 a Job 4:8
1 trouble
9 a 2 Cor. 9:6
b [Prov. 19:17]
1 Lit. *good*
10 a Ps. 101:5
11 a Ps. 101:6
13 a Prov. 26:13
14 a Prov. 2:16; 5:3; 7:5
b Eccl. 7:26
15 a Prov. 13:24; 23:13, 14
21 a Luke 1:3, 4
b 1 Pet. 3:15
1 Or *send you*
22 a Ex. 23:6

9 [a]He who has a [1]generous eye will
be [b]blessed,
For he gives of his bread to the
poor.

10 [a]Cast out the scoffer, and
contention will leave;
Yes, strife and reproach will cease.

11 [a]He who loves purity of heart
And has grace on his lips,
The king *will be* his friend.

12 The eyes of the LORD preserve
knowledge,
But He overthrows the words of the
faithless.

13 [a]The lazy *man* says, "*There is* a
lion outside!
I shall be slain in the streets!"

14 [a]The mouth of an immoral woman
is a deep pit;
[b]He who is abhorred by the LORD
will fall there.

15 Foolishness *is* bound up in the
heart of a child;
[a]The rod of correction will drive it
far from him.

16 He who oppresses the poor to
increase his *riches,*
And he who gives to the rich, *will*
surely *come* to poverty.

Sayings of the Wise

17 Incline your ear and hear the
words of the wise,
And apply your heart to my
knowledge;
18 For *it is* a pleasant thing if you
keep them within you;
Let them all be fixed upon your
lips,
19 So that your trust may be in the
LORD;
I have instructed you today, even
you.
20 Have I not written to you
excellent things
Of counsels and knowledge,
21 [a]That I may make you know the
certainty of the words of truth,
[b]That you may answer words of
truth
To those who [1]send to you?

22 Do not rob the [a]poor because he
is poor,

Proverbs 22:6

Dear Woman of Destiny,

Are you a mother? Now more than ever, mothers need to understand their high position in God's kingdom. Training, nurturing, and teaching children God's Word and His ways are perhaps the most important jobs on the face of the earth. The children are our future leaders, the next generation that will take the baton of the gospel to all nations.

Throughout the Bible, when God wanted to do something great in the world, He usually chose a youth. In Joseph, Moses, David, and Gideon, God saw destiny. When David wanted to fight Goliath, Saul said, "He is only a child," but God saw that child and put courage in him to do what the whole Israelite army could not do—fight and defeat a Philistine giant.

We may see our child or teenager who doesn't clean his room; God sees a giant slayer in His kingdom. We see the seed; God sees the mighty tree that comes from that one tiny seed. God always sees the potential within the child. He sees the dreams that He imparted within them.

But a child needs direction and guidance. Contrary to our society's belief that young children should make their own decisions, the Bible clearly says that a child left to himself disgraces his mother (see Prov. 29:15). Children are not born with self-control and wisdom; they must be trained.

And whose responsibility is it to train these little giant slayers? An expert in child-rearing? Someone with experience? Not usually! Not even God Himself takes responsibility for child training. He puts it in the hands of the parents. You are the ones! He has chosen you for this incredible task.

Training means to instruct and to inspect what you have instructed. It means to build and mold a child's heart and conscience. You make him do what he doesn't want to do and teach him the moral reason why. You are shaping his moral character. It demands time, work, sacrifice, and consistency. It is a process that doesn't happen overnight. Do you see your child as an interruption in your time schedule or an investment in your life?

Beloved mother, you may be exhausted from feeding a crying baby in the middle of the night or bored by the mundane aspects of your diaper-filled days. You may be shocked and overwhelmed by your child's constantly challenging your authority. But remember, God sees your sacrifices, and He will reward you. God chose you and not another to train your little one. Pray and believe scriptures over him. Don't be discouraged by what you see on the outside. See your child through the eyes of faith. Ask for God's vision for your child, that you may see his destiny—what he was born to do. Enjoy every stage of motherhood, from rocking a soft, sweet-scented newborn to making a heart connection with a precious teenager. Use your courage, energy, time, and education to pour into your greatest asset—not your possessions, not your career, but the gift and reward God has given you—your child. In the end the fruits of your labor will rise and give you praise.

Katie Luce

Nor oppress the afflicted at the
gate;
23 [a]For the LORD will plead their
cause,
And plunder the soul of those who
plunder them.

24 Make no friendship with an angry
man,
And with a [a]furious man do not go,
25 Lest you learn his ways
And set a snare for your soul.

26 [a]Do not be one of those who
[1]shakes hands in a pledge,
One of those who is [2]surety for
debts;
27 If you have nothing *with which* to
pay,
Why should he take away your bed
from under you?

28 [a]Do not remove the ancient
[1]landmark
Which your fathers have set.
29 Do you see a man *who* [1]excels in
his work?
He will stand before kings;
He will not stand before [2]unknown
men.

23 When you sit down to eat with a
ruler,
Consider carefully what *is* before
you;
2 And put a knife to your throat
If you *are* a man given to appetite.
3 Do not desire his delicacies,
For they *are* deceptive food.

4 [a]Do not overwork to be rich;
[b]Because of your own understanding,
cease!
5 [1]Will you set your eyes on that
which is not?
For *riches* certainly make
themselves wings;
They fly away like an eagle *toward*
heaven.

6 Do not eat the bread of [a]a[1] miser,
Nor desire his delicacies;
7 For as he thinks in his heart, so *is*
he.
"Eat and drink!" [a]he says to you,
But his heart is not with you.
8 The morsel you have eaten, you
will vomit up,
And waste your pleasant words.

23 a 1 Sam. 24:12
24 a Prov. 29:22
26 a Prov. 11:15 *1* Lit. *strikes* *2* *guaranty*
28 a Deut. 19:14; 27:17 *1* *boundary*
29 *1* *is prompt in his business* *2* *obscure*

CHAPTER 23
4 a [1 Tim. 6:9, 10] b Rom. 12:16
5 *1* Lit. *Will you cause your eyes to fly upon it and it is not?*
6 a Deut. 15:9 *1* Lit. *one who has an evil eye*
7 a Prov. 12:2
9 a Matt. 7:6
10 *1* *boundary*
11 a Prov. 22:23
13 a Prov. 13:24
14 *1* Or *Sheol*
16 *1* Lit. *kidneys*
17 a Ps. 37:1 b Prov. 28:14
18 a [Ps. 37:37] *1* Future, lit. *latter end*
20 a Is. 5:22
22 a Prov. 1:8

9 [a]Do not speak in the hearing of a
fool,
For he will despise the wisdom of
your words.

10 Do not remove the ancient
[1]landmark,
Nor enter the fields of the
fatherless;
11 [a]For their Redeemer *is* mighty;
He will plead their cause against
you.

12 Apply your heart to instruction,
And your ears to words of
knowledge.

13 [a]Do not withhold correction from a
child,
For *if* you beat him with a rod, he
will not die.
14 You shall beat him with a rod,
And deliver his soul from [1]hell.

15 My son, if your heart is wise,
My heart will rejoice—indeed, I
myself;
16 Yes, my [1]inmost being will rejoice
When your lips speak right things.

17 [a]Do not let your heart envy
sinners,
But [b]*be zealous* for the fear of the
LORD all the day;
18 [a]For surely there is a [1]hereafter,
And your hope will not be cut off.

The ultimate purpose for each of us who knows God is to love Him and enjoy His presence.

MADAME JEANNE GUYON

19 Hear, my son, and be wise;
And guide your heart in the way.
20 [a]Do not mix with winebibbers,
Or with gluttonous eaters of meat;
21 For the drunkard and the glutton
will come to poverty,
And drowsiness will clothe *a man*
with rags.

22 [a]Listen to your father who begot
you,

And do not despise your mother
when she is old.

23 [a]Buy the truth, and do not sell *it,*
Also wisdom and instruction and
understanding.

24 [a]The father of the righteous will
greatly rejoice,
And he who begets a wise *child* will
delight in him.

25 Let your father and your mother
be glad,
And let her who bore you rejoice.

26 My son, give me your heart,
And let your eyes observe my ways.

27 [a]For a harlot *is* a deep pit,
And a seductress *is* a narrow well.

28 [a]She also lies in wait as *for* a
victim,
And increases the unfaithful among
men.

29 [a]Who has woe?
Who has sorrow?
Who has contentions?
Who has complaints?
Who has wounds without cause?
Who [b]has redness of eyes?

30 [a]Those who linger long at the
wine,
Those who go in search of [b]mixed
wine.

31 Do not look on the wine when it
is red,
When it sparkles in the cup,
When it [1]swirls around smoothly;

32 At the last it bites like a serpent,
And stings like a viper.

33 Your eyes will see strange things,
And your heart will utter perverse
things.

34 Yes, you will be like one who lies
down in the [1]midst of the sea,
Or like one who lies at the top of
the mast, *saying:*

35 "They[a] have struck me, *but* I was
not hurt;
They have beaten me, but I did not
feel *it.*
When shall [b]I awake, that I may
seek another *drink?*"

24

Do not be [a]envious of evil men,
Nor desire to be with them;

2 For their heart devises violence,
And their lips talk of
troublemaking.

3 Through wisdom a house is built,
And by understanding it is
established;

4 By knowledge the rooms are filled
With all precious and pleasant
riches.

Lord, through wisdom may ____ build their house, and by understanding may it be established. By knowledge may the rooms be filled with all precious and pleasant riches.

FROM PROVERBS 24:3, 4

5 [a]A wise man *is* strong,
Yes, a man of knowledge increases
strength;

6 [a]For by wise counsel you will wage
your own war,
And in a multitude of counselors
there is safety.

7 [a]Wisdom *is* too lofty for a fool;
He does not open his mouth in the
gate.

8 He who [a]plots to do evil
Will be called a [1]schemer.

9 The devising of foolishness *is* sin,
And the scoffer *is* an abomination
to men.

10 *If* you [a]faint in the day of
adversity,
Your strength *is* small.

11 [a]Deliver *those who* are drawn
toward death,
And hold back *those* stumbling to
the slaughter.

12 If you say, "Surely we did not
know this,"
Does not [a]He who weighs the
hearts consider *it?*
He who keeps your soul, does He
not know *it?*
And will He *not* render to *each*
man [b]according to his deeds?

13 My son, [a]eat honey because *it is*
good,

23 a [Matt. 13:44]
24 a Prov. 10:1
27 a Prov. 22:14
28 a Prov. 7:12
29 a Is. 5:11, 22 b Gen. 49:12
30 a [Eph. 5:18] b Ps. 75:8
31 *1 goes around*
34 *1* Lit. *heart*
35 a Jer. 5:3 b Eph. 4:19
CHAPTER 24
1 a Ps. 1:1; 37:1
5 a Prov. 21:22
6 a Luke 14:31
7 a Ps. 10:5
8 a Rom. 1:30 *1* Lit. *master of evil plots*
10 a Heb. 12:3
11 a Ps. 82:4
12 a Prov. 21:2 b Ps. 62:12
13 a Song 5:1

And the honeycomb *which is* sweet
to your taste;
14 [a]So *shall* the knowledge of wisdom
be to your soul;
If you have found *it,* there is a
[1]prospect,
And your hope will not be cut off.

15 Do not lie in wait, O wicked *man,*
against the dwelling of the
righteous;
Do not plunder his resting place;
16 [a]For a righteous *man* may fall
seven times
And rise again,
[b]But the wicked shall fall by
calamity.

17 [a]Do not rejoice when your enemy
falls,
And do not let your heart be glad
when he stumbles;
18 Lest the LORD see *it,* and [1]it
displease Him,
And He turn away His wrath from
him.

19 [a]Do not fret because of evildoers,
Nor be envious of the wicked;
20 For there will be no prospect for
the evil *man;*
The lamp of the wicked will be put
out.

21 My son, [a]fear the LORD and the
king;
Do not associate with those given
to change;
22 For their calamity will rise
suddenly,
And who knows the ruin those two
can bring?

Further Sayings of the Wise

23 These *things* also *belong* to the wise:
[a]*It is* not good to [1]show partiality in
judgment.
24 [a]He who says to the wicked, "You
are righteous,"
Him the people will curse;
Nations will abhor him.
25 But those who rebuke *the wicked*
will have [a]delight,
And a good blessing will come upon
them.

26 He who gives a right answer
kisses the lips.

27 [a]Prepare your outside work,
Make it fit for yourself in the field;

14 a Ps. 19:10; 58:11
1 Lit. *latter end*
16 a [Mic. 7:8]
b Esth. 7:10
17 a Obad. 12
18 1 Lit. *it be evil in His eyes*
19 a Ps. 37:1
21 a [1 Pet. 2:17]
23 a Lev. 19:15
1 Lit. *recognize faces*
24 a Is. 5:23
25 a Prov. 28:23
27 a Prov. 27:23–27
28 a Eph. 4:25
1 LXX, Vg. *Do not deceive*
29 a [Prov. 20:22]
31 a Gen. 3:18
33 a Prov. 6:9, 10
34 a Prov. 6:9–11
1 Lit. *one who walks about*
2 Lit. *a man with a shield*

CHAPTER 25
1 a 1 Kin. 4:32
2 a Deut. 29:29
4 a 2 Tim. 2:21
5 a Prov. 16:12; 20:8
7 a Luke 14:7–11

And afterward build your house.

28 [a]Do not be a witness against your
neighbor without cause,
[1]For would you deceive with your
lips?
29 [a]Do not say, "I will do to him just
as he has done to me;
I will render to the man according
to his work."

30 I went by the field of the lazy
man,
And by the vineyard of the man
devoid of understanding;
31 And there it was, [a]all overgrown
with thorns;
Its surface was covered with nettles;
Its stone wall was broken down.
32 When I saw *it,* I considered *it*
well;
I looked on *it and* received
instruction:
33 [a]A little sleep, a little slumber,
A little folding of the hands to rest;
34 [a]So shall your poverty come *like* [1]a
prowler,
And your need like [2]an armed man.

Further Wise Sayings of Solomon

25 These[a] also *are* proverbs of Solomon which the men of Hezekiah
king of Judah copied:

2 [a]*It is* the glory of God to conceal a
matter,
But the glory of kings *is* to search
out a matter.
3 *As* the heavens for height and the
earth for depth,
So the heart of kings *is*
unsearchable.

4 [a]Take away the dross from silver,
And it will go to the silversmith *for*
jewelry.
5 Take away the wicked from before
the king,
And his throne will be established
in [a]righteousness.

6 Do not exalt yourself in the
presence of the king,
And do not stand in the place of
the great;
7 [a]For *it is* better that he say to you,
"Come up here,"
Than that you should be put lower
in the presence of the prince,

Whom your eyes have seen.

8 [a]Do not go hastily to [1]court;
For what will you do in the end,
When your neighbor has put you to
shame?

9 [a]Debate your case with your
neighbor,
And do not disclose the secret to
another;

10 Lest he who hears *it* expose your
shame,
And [1]your reputation be ruined.

11 A word fitly [a]spoken *is like* apples
of gold
In settings of silver.

12 *Like* an earring of gold and an
ornament of fine gold
Is a wise rebuker to an obedient
ear.

13 [a]Like the cold of snow in time of
harvest
Is a faithful messenger to those
who send him,
For he refreshes the soul of his
masters.

14 [a]Whoever falsely boasts of giving
Is like [b]clouds and wind without
rain.

15 [a]By long forbearance a ruler is
persuaded,
And a gentle tongue breaks a bone.

16 Have you found honey?
Eat only as much as you need,
Lest you be filled with it and vomit.

17 Seldom set foot in your neighbor's
house,
Lest he become weary of you and
hate you.

18 [a]A man who bears false witness
against his neighbor
Is like a club, a sword, and a sharp
arrow.

19 Confidence in an unfaithful *man*
in time of trouble
Is like a bad tooth and a foot out of
joint.

20 *Like* one who takes away a
garment in cold weather,
And like vinegar on soda,
Is one who [a]sings songs to a heavy
heart.

21 [a]If your enemy is hungry, give him
bread to eat;
And if he is thirsty, give him water
to drink;

22 For *so* you will heap coals of fire
on his head,
[a]And the LORD will reward you.

23 The north wind brings forth rain,
And [a]a backbiting tongue an angry
countenance.

24 [a]*It is* better to dwell in a corner of
a housetop,
Than in a house shared with a
contentious woman.

25 *As* cold water to a weary soul,
So *is* [a]good news from a far
country.

26 A righteous *man* who falters
before the wicked
Is like a murky spring and a
[1]polluted well.

27 *It is* not good to eat much honey;
So [a]to seek one's own glory *is not*
glory.

28 [a]Whoever *has* no rule over his own
spirit
Is like a city broken down, without
walls.

26

As snow in summer [a]and rain in
harvest,
So honor is not fitting for a fool.

2 Like a flitting sparrow, like a flying
swallow,
So [a]a curse without cause shall not
alight.

3 [a]A whip for the horse,
A bridle for the donkey,
And a rod for the fool's back.

4 Do not answer a fool according to
his folly,
Lest you also be like him.

5 [a]Answer a fool according to his
folly,
Lest he be wise in his own eyes.

6 He who sends a message by the
hand of a fool
Cuts off *his own* feet *and* drinks
violence.

7 *Like* the legs of the lame that hang
limp
Is a proverb in the mouth of fools.

8 Like one who binds a stone in a
sling
Is he who gives honor to a fool.

9 *Like* a thorn *that* goes into the
hand of a drunkard

---

8 a Matt. 5:25 *1* Lit. *contend* or *bring a lawsuit*
9 a [Matt. 18:15]
10 *1 the evil report concerning you not pass away*
11 a Prov. 15:23
13 a Prov. 13:17
14 a Prov. 20:6 b Jude 12
15 a Prov. 15:1
18 a Ps. 57:4
20 a Dan. 6:18
21 a Rom. 12:20
22 a 2 Sam. 16:12
23 a Ps. 101:5
24 a Prov. 19:13
25 a Prov. 15:30
26 *1 ruined*
27 a Prov. 27:2
28 a Prov. 16:32

CHAPTER 26
1 a 1 Sam. 12:17
2 a Deut. 23:5
3 a Ps. 32:9
5 a Matt. 16:1–4

Is a proverb in the mouth of fools.
10 [1]The great *God* who formed everything
Gives the fool *his* hire and the transgressor *his* wages.
11 [a]As a dog returns to his own vomit,
[b]*So* a fool repeats his folly.
12 [a]Do you see a man wise in his own eyes?
There is more hope for a fool than for him.
13 The lazy *man* says, "*There is* a lion in the road!
A fierce lion *is* in the [1]streets!"
14 *As* a door turns on its hinges,
So *does* the lazy *man* on his bed.
15 The [a]lazy *man* buries his hand in the [1]bowl;
It wearies him to bring it back to his mouth.
16 The lazy *man is* wiser in his own eyes
Than seven men who can answer sensibly.
17 He who passes by *and* meddles in a quarrel not his own
Is like one who takes a dog by the ears.
18 Like a madman who throws firebrands, arrows, and death,
19 *Is* the man *who* deceives his neighbor,
And says, [a]"I was only joking!"
20 Where *there is* no wood, the fire goes out;
And where *there is* no [1]talebearer, strife ceases.
21 [a]*As* charcoal *is* to burning coals, and wood to fire,
So *is* a contentious man to kindle strife.
22 The words of a [1]talebearer *are* like [2]tasty trifles,
And they go down into the [3]inmost body.
23 Fervent lips with a wicked heart
Are like earthenware covered with silver dross.
24 He who hates, disguises *it* with his lips,
And lays up deceit within himself;
25 [a]When [1]he speaks kindly, do not believe him,

10 [1]Heb. difficult in v. 10; ancient and modern translators differ greatly
11 [a]2 Pet. 2:22 [b]Ex. 8:15
12 [a][Rev. 3:17]
13 [1]Or *plazas, squares*
15 [a]Prov. 19:24 [1]LXX, Syr. *bosom;* Tg., Vg. *armpit*
19 [a]Eph. 5:4
20 [1]*gossip* or *slanderer,* lit. *whisperer*
21 [a]Prov. 15:18
22 [1]*gossip* or *slanderer* [2]A Jewish tradition *wounds* [3]Lit. *rooms of the belly*
25 [a]Ps. 28:3 [1]Lit. *his voice is gracious*
27 [a]Ps. 7:15
28 [a]Prov. 29:5
CHAPTER 27
1 [a]James 4:13–16
2 [a]Prov. 25:27
4 [a]1 John 3:12
5 [a][Prov. 28:23]
6 [a]Matt. 26:49
7 [1]*tramples on*
9 [1]Lit. *counsel of the soul*
10 [a]Prov. 17:17; 18:24
11 [a]Prov. 10:1; 23:15–26

For *there are* seven abominations in his heart;
26 *Though his* hatred is covered by deceit,
His wickedness will be revealed before the assembly.
27 [a]Whoever digs a pit will fall into it,
And he who rolls a stone will have it roll back on him.
28 A lying tongue hates *those who are* crushed by it,
And a flattering mouth works [a]ruin.

27 Do[a] not boast about tomorrow,
For you do not know what a day may bring forth.
2 [a]Let another man praise you, and not your own mouth;
A stranger, and not your own lips.
3 A stone *is* heavy and sand *is* weighty,
But a fool's wrath *is* heavier than both of them.
4 Wrath *is* cruel and anger a torrent,
But [a]who *is* able to stand before jealousy?
5 [a]Open rebuke *is* better
Than love carefully concealed.
6 Faithful *are* the wounds of a friend,
But the kisses of an enemy *are* [a]deceitful.
7 A satisfied soul [1]loathes the honeycomb,
But to a hungry soul every bitter thing *is* sweet.
8 Like a bird that wanders from its nest
Is a man who wanders from his place.
9 Ointment and perfume delight the heart,
And the sweetness of a man's friend *gives delight* by [1]hearty counsel.
10 Do not forsake your own friend or your father's friend,
Nor go to your brother's house in the day of your calamity;
[a]Better *is* a neighbor nearby than a brother far away.
11 My son, be wise, and make my heart glad,
[a]That I may answer him who reproaches me.

12 A prudent *man* foresees evil *and* hides himself;
The simple pass on *and* are [a]punished.

13 Take the garment of him who is surety for a stranger,
And hold it in pledge *when* he is surety for a seductress.

14 He who blesses his friend with a loud voice, rising early in the morning,
It will be counted a curse to him.

When God opens our eyes that we may know the intent of our heart and the deepest thought within us in the measure that He Himself knows us—this is revelation. As we are naked and laid bare before Him, so are we before ourselves as we receive revelation. This is revelation: for us to be allowed to see what our Lord sees.

WATCHMAN NEE

15 A [a]continual dripping on a very rainy day
And a contentious woman are alike;
16 Whoever [1]restrains her restrains the wind,
And grasps oil with his right hand.

17 *As* iron sharpens iron,
So a man sharpens the countenance of his friend.

18 [a]Whoever [1]keeps the fig tree will eat its fruit;
So he who waits on his master will be honored.

19 As in water face *reflects* face,
So a man's heart *reveals* the man.

20 [a]Hell[1] and [2]Destruction are never full;
So [b]the eyes of man are never satisfied.

21 [a]The refining pot *is* for silver and the furnace for gold,
And a man *is valued* by what others say of him.

22 [a]Though you grind a fool in a mortar with a pestle along with crushed grain,
Yet his foolishness will not depart from him.

23 Be diligent to know the state of your [a]flocks,
And attend to your herds;
24 For riches *are* not forever,
Nor does a crown *endure* to all generations.
25 [a]*When* the hay is removed, and the tender grass shows itself,
And the herbs of the mountains are gathered in,
26 The lambs *will provide* your clothing,
And the goats the price of a field;
27 *You shall have* enough goats' milk for your food,
For the food of your household,
And the nourishment of your maidservants.

28

The [a]wicked flee when no one pursues,
But the righteous are bold as a lion.

2 Because of the transgression of a land, many *are* its princes;
But by a man of understanding *and* knowledge
Right will be prolonged.

3 [a]A poor man who oppresses the poor
Is like a driving rain [1]which leaves no food.

4 [a]Those who forsake the law praise the wicked,
[b]But such as keep the law contend with them.

5 [a]Evil men do not understand justice,
But [b]those who seek the LORD understand all.

6 Better *is* the poor who walks in his integrity

---

12 a Prov. 22:3
15 a Prov. 19:13
16 *1* Lit. *hides*
18 a [1 Cor. 3:8; 9:7–13] *1 protects* or *tends*
20 a Hab. 2:5 b Eccl. 1:8; 4:8 *1* Or *Sheol* *2* Heb. *Abaddon*
21 a Prov. 17:3
22 a Jer. 5:3
23 a Prov. 24:27
25 a Ps. 104:14

CHAPTER 28
1 a Ps. 53:5
3 a Matt. 18:28 *1* Lit. *and there is no bread*
4 a Ps. 49:18 b 1 Kin. 18:18
5 a Ps. 92:6 b John 17:17

Than one perverse *in his* ways,
though he *be* rich.

7 Whoever keeps the law *is* a
discerning son,
But a companion of gluttons
shames his father.

8 One who increases his possessions
by usury and extortion
Gathers it for him who will pity the
poor.

9 One who turns away his ear from
hearing the law,
[a]Even his prayer *is* an abomination.

10 [a]Whoever causes the upright to go
astray in an evil way,
He himself will fall into his own
pit;
[b]But the blameless will inherit good.

11 The rich man *is* wise in his own
eyes,
But the poor who has
understanding searches him out.

12 When the righteous rejoice, *there
is* great [a]glory;
But when the wicked arise, men
[1]hide themselves.

13 [a]He who covers his sins will not
prosper,
But whoever confesses and forsakes
them will have mercy.

14 Happy *is* the man who is always
reverent,
But he who hardens his heart will
fall into calamity.

15 [a]*Like* a roaring lion and a charging
bear
[b]*Is* a wicked ruler over poor people.

16 A ruler who lacks understanding *is*
a great [a]oppressor,
But he who hates covetousness will
prolong *his* days.

17 [a]A man burdened with bloodshed
will flee into a pit;
Let no one help him.

18 Whoever walks blamelessly will be
[1]saved,
But *he who is* perverse *in his* ways
will suddenly fall.

19 [a]He who tills his land will have
plenty of bread,
But he who follows frivolity will
have poverty enough!

20 A faithful man will abound with
blessings,
[a]But he who hastens to be rich will
not go unpunished.

21 [a]To [1]show partiality *is* not good,
[b]Because for a piece of bread a man
will transgress.

22 A man with an evil eye hastens
after riches,
And does not consider that [a]poverty
will come upon him.

The main secret of success in the development of the blessing is the exercise of a humble dependence on the Lord.

ANDREW MURRAY

23 [a]He who rebukes a man will find
more favor afterward
Than he who flatters with the
tongue.

24 Whoever robs his father or his
mother,
And says, "*It is* no transgression,"
The same [a]*is* companion to a
destroyer.

25 [a]He who is of a proud heart stirs
up strife,
[b]But he who trusts in the LORD will
be prospered.

26 He who [a]trusts in his own heart is
a fool,
But whoever walks wisely will be
delivered.

27 [a]He who gives to the poor will not
lack,
But he who hides his eyes will have
many curses.

28 When the wicked arise, [a]men hide
themselves;
But when they perish, the righteous
increase.

29 He[a] who is often rebuked, *and*
hardens *his* neck,
Will suddenly be destroyed, and
that without remedy.

---

9 a Prov. 15:8
10 a Prov. 26:27 b [Matt. 6:33]
12 a Prov. 11:10; 29:2 1 Lit. *will be searched for*
13 a Ps. 32:3–5
15 a 1 Pet. 5:8 b Matt. 2:16
16 a Eccl. 10:16
17 a Gen. 9:6
18 1 *delivered*
19 a Prov. 12:11; 20:13
20 a 1 Tim. 6:9
21 a Prov. 18:5 b Ezek. 13:19 1 Lit. *recognize faces*
22 a Prov. 21:5
23 a Prov. 27:5, 6
24 a Prov. 18:9
25 a Prov. 13:10 b 1 Tim. 6:6
26 a Prov. 3:5
27 a Deut. 15:7
28 a Job 24:4
CHAPTER 29
1 a 2 Chr. 36:16

2 When the righteous [1]are in
authority, the [a]people rejoice;
But when a wicked *man* rules, [b]the
people groan.

3 Whoever loves wisdom makes his
father rejoice,
But a companion of harlots wastes
his wealth.

4 The king establishes the land by
justice,
But he who receives bribes
overthrows it.

5 A man who [a]flatters his neighbor
Spreads a net for his feet.

6 By transgression an evil man is
snared,
But the righteous sings and
rejoices.

7 The righteous [a]considers the cause
of the poor,
But the wicked does not understand
such knowledge.

8 Scoffers [a]set a city aflame,
But wise *men* turn away wrath.

9 *If* a wise man contends with a
foolish man,
[a]Whether *the fool* rages or laughs,
there is no peace.

10 [a]The bloodthirsty hate the
blameless,
But the upright seek his
[1]well-being.

11 A fool vents all his [a]feelings,[1]
But a wise *man* holds them back.

12 If a ruler pays attention to lies,
All his servants *become* wicked.

13 The poor *man* and the oppressor
have this in common:
[a]The LORD gives light to the eyes of
both.

14 The king who judges the [a]poor
with truth,
His throne will be established
forever.

15 The rod and rebuke give [a]wisdom,
But a child left *to himself* brings
shame to his mother.

16 When the wicked are multiplied,
transgression increases;
But the righteous will see their
[a]fall.

2 [a] Prov. 28:12 [b] Esth. 4:3 [1] *become great*
5 [a] Prov. 26:28
7 [a] Job 29:16
8 [a] Prov. 11:11
9 [a] Matt. 11:17
10 [a] 1 John 3:12 [1] Lit. *soul* or *life*
11 [a] Prov. 14:33 [1] Lit. *spirit*
13 [a] [Matt. 5:45]
14 [a] Is. 11:4
15 [a] Prov. 22:15
16 [a] Ps. 37:34
18 [a] 1 Sam. 3:1 [b] John 13:17 [1] *prophetic vision*
20 [a] Prov. 26:12
22 [a] Prov. 26:21
23 [a] Is. 66:2
24 [a] Lev. 5:1 [1] Lit. *hears the adjuration* or *oath*
25 [a] Gen. 12:12; 20:2 [1] *secure*, lit. *set on high*
26 [a] Ps. 20:9 [1] Lit. *face*
CHAPTER 30
2 [a] Ps. 73:22
3 [a] [Prov. 9:10]

17 Correct your son, and he will give
you rest;
Yes, he will give delight to your
soul.

18 [a]Where *there is* no [1]revelation, the
people cast off restraint;
But [b]happy *is* he who keeps the
law.

19 A servant will not be corrected by
mere words;
For though he understands, he will
not respond.

20 Do you see a man hasty in his
words?
[a]*There is* more hope for a fool than
for him.

21 He who pampers his servant from
childhood
Will have him as a son in the end.

22 [a]An angry man stirs up strife,
And a furious man abounds in
transgression.

23 [a]A man's pride will bring him low,
But the humble in spirit will retain
honor.

24 Whoever is a partner with a thief
hates his own life;
[a]He [1]swears to tell the truth, but
reveals nothing.

25 [a]The fear of man brings a snare,
But whoever trusts in the LORD
shall be [1]safe.

26 [a]Many seek the ruler's [1]favor,
But justice for man *comes* from the
LORD.

27 An unjust man *is* an abomination
to the righteous,
And *he who is* upright in the way *is*
an abomination to the wicked.

The Wisdom of Agur

30 The words of Agur the son of Jakeh, *his* utterance. This man declared to Ithiel—to Ithiel and Ucal:

2 [a]Surely I *am* more stupid than *any*
man,
And do not have the understanding
of a man.

3 I neither learned wisdom
Nor have [a]knowledge of the Holy
One.

4 [a]Who has ascended into heaven, or
descended?
[b]Who has gathered the wind in His
fists?
Who has bound the waters in a
garment?
Who has established all the ends of
the earth?
What *is* His name, and what *is* His
Son's name,
If you know?

5 [a]Every word of God *is* [1]pure;
[b]He *is* a shield to those who put
their trust in Him.
6 [a]Do not add to His words,
Lest He rebuke you, and you be
found a liar.

7 Two *things* I request of You
(Deprive me not before I die):
8 Remove falsehood and lies far from
me;
Give me neither poverty nor
riches—
[a]Feed me with the food allotted to
me;
9 [a]Lest I be full and deny *You,*
And say, "Who *is* the LORD?"
Or lest I be poor and steal,
And profane the name of my God.

10 Do not malign a servant to his
master,
Lest he curse you, and you be
found guilty.

11 *There is* a generation *that* curses
its [a]father,
And does not bless its mother.
12 *There is* a generation [a]*that is* pure
in its own eyes,
Yet is not washed from its
filthiness.
13 *There is* a generation—oh, how
[a]lofty are their eyes!
And their eyelids are [1]lifted up.
14 [a]*There is* a generation whose teeth
are like swords,
And whose fangs *are like* knives,
[b]To devour the poor from off the
earth,
And the needy from *among* men.

15 The leech has two daughters—
Give *and* Give!

There are three *things that* are
never satisfied,
Four never say, "Enough!":
16 [a]The[1] grave,
The barren womb,
The earth *that* is not satisfied with
water—
And the fire never says, "Enough!"

17 [a]The eye *that* mocks *his* father,
And scorns obedience to *his*
mother,
The ravens of the valley will pick it
out,
And the young eagles will eat it.

18 There are three *things which* are
too wonderful for me,
Yes, four *which* I do not
understand:
19 The way of an eagle in the air,
The way of a serpent on a rock,
The way of a ship in the [1]midst of
the sea,
And the way of a man with a virgin.

20 This *is* the way of an adulterous
woman:
She eats and wipes her mouth,
And says, "I have done no
wickedness."

21 For three *things* the earth is
perturbed,
Yes, for four it cannot bear up:
22 [a]For a servant when he reigns,
A fool when he is filled with food,
23 A [1]hateful *woman* when she is
married,
And a maidservant who succeeds
her mistress.

24 There are four *things which* are
little on the earth,
But they *are* exceedingly wise:
25 [a]The ants *are* a people not strong,
Yet they prepare their food in the
summer;
26 [a]The [1]rock badgers are a feeble
folk,
Yet they make their homes in the
crags;
27 The locusts have no king,
Yet they all advance in ranks;
28 The [1]spider skillfully grasps with
its hands,
And it is in kings' palaces.

29 There are three *things which* are
majestic in pace,
Yes, four *which* are stately in walk:
30 A lion, *which is* mighty among
beasts
And does not turn away from any;
31 A [1]greyhound,

---

4 a [John 3:13] b Job 38:4
5 a Ps. 12:6; 19:8; 119:140 b Ps. 18:30; 84:11; 115:9–11 *1 tested, refined, found pure*
6 a Deut. 4:2; 12:32
8 a Matt. 6:11
9 a Deut. 8:12–14
11 a Ex. 21:17
12 a Luke 18:11
13 a Prov. 6:17 *1* In arrogance
14 a Job 29:17 b Amos 8:4
16 a Prov. 27:20 *1* Or *Sheol*
17 a Gen. 9:22
19 *1* Lit. *heart*
22 a Prov. 19:10
23 *1* Or *hated*
25 a Prov. 6:6
26 a Ps. 104:18 *1 rock hyraxes*
28 *1* Or *lizard*
31 *1* Or perhaps *strutting rooster,* lit. *girded of waist*

PROVERBS 31:10–31

Dear Woman of Destiny,

Let God expand your vision of the Proverbs 31 woman. Meditate upon the powerful spiritual significance of these verses.

Note the meaning of the word *virtuous, chayil* in Hebrew. It means "force, whether of men, means, or other resources," and "strength, able, might, power" (Strong's #2428). Men of war in the Bible were called *chayil* men, valiant men, men of great strength (see 1 Chr. 5:18). This word shares the same consonantal root as the word that means "to twist or whirl, writhe in pain as in childbirth, bear or bring forth."

Put all these words together and we have a powerful description of a godly woman. She is a "warrior woman"! She is an intercessor, a woman of might and power uniquely designed by God to birth His will and purposes on the earth, particularly concerning, but not limited to, her family. The virtuous woman is busy with her hands, two kinds of which are mentioned in these verses. Both can have intercessory implications. *Kaph* hands can indicate beseeching God for favor toward those for whom one prays (see Ex. 9:29). *Yad* hands can refer to warring hands (see Ps. 144:1). Foundational to all of her activity is her intimate knowledge of and identification with God's heart, gained through personal prayer and study of His Word.

The worth of the virtuous woman to her husband, family, and beyond is so high it is said to be "far above rubies" (Prov. 31:10). Incredibly, this is the same inestimable value placed on godly wisdom in Proverbs 3:15 and 8:11.

"The heart of her husband safely trusts her; so he will have no lack of gain" (Prov. 31:11). Scripture frequently speaks of putting our trust solely in God (see Ps. 62:8), but here we are told that a man who has found a godly wife can also trust his heart to her. *Safely trust* means "to run to for refuge, to be confident and sure or secure, a place of safety" (Strong's #982; [1]TWOT #233). A godly woman will help provide a trusting framework in which her husband will be able to share his innermost person with her so that together they will mature and reach their full potential. God declares that the husband who has such a wife will "have no lack of gain" as he grows with her in this safe environment.

The virtuous woman is confident in the things that matter most in life. "She is not afraid of snow for her household, for all her household is clothed with scarlet" (Prov. 31:21). "She shall rejoice [laugh] in time to come" (v. 25). These verses refer to the coming judgment of God that every person will ultimately face. Being "clothed with scarlet" is symbolic of being covered in Christ's blood, the only acceptable provision for our sin. Because of the virtuous woman's intercession, she has confidence that God has heard her prayers, and she knows He is moving in the hearts of her loved ones.

These verses boldly assert that if the virtuous woman will give herself to her God-called work, she will be successful in her efforts. There is no equivocating on God's part here. Ultimately He will "give her of the fruit of her hands, and let her own works praise her in the gates" (Prov. 31:31).

Jane Hansen

[1]TWOT: *Theological Wordbook of the Old Testament*

A male goat also,
And [2]a king *whose* troops *are* with
him.

32 If you have been foolish in
exalting yourself,
Or if you have devised evil, [a]*put
your* hand on *your* mouth.

33 For *as* the churning of milk
produces butter,
And wringing the nose produces
blood,
So the forcing of wrath produces
strife.

The Words of King Lemuel's Mother

31 The words of King Lemuel, the utterance which his mother taught him:

2 What, my son?
And what, son of my womb?
And what, [a]son of my vows?

3 [a]Do not give your strength to
women,
Nor your ways [b]to that which
destroys kings.

4 [a]*It is* not for kings, O Lemuel,
It is not for kings to drink wine,
Nor for princes intoxicating drink;

5 [a]Lest they drink and forget the law,
And pervert the justice of all [1]the
afflicted.

6 [a]Give strong drink to him who is
perishing,
And wine to those who are bitter of
heart.

7 Let him drink and forget his
poverty,
And remember his misery no more.

8 [a]Open your mouth for the
speechless,
In the cause of all *who are*
[1]appointed to die.

9 Open your mouth, [a]judge
righteously,
And [b]plead the cause of the poor
and needy.

The Virtuous Wife

10 [a]Who[1] can find a [2]virtuous wife?
For her worth *is* far above rubies.

11 The heart of her husband safely
trusts her;
So he will have no lack of gain.

12 She does him good and not evil
All the days of her life.

13 She seeks wool and flax,
And willingly works with her hands.

14 She is like the merchant ships,
She brings her food from afar.

15 [a]She also rises while it is yet night,
And [b]provides food for her
household,
And a portion for her maidservants.

16 She considers a field and buys it;
From [1]her profits she plants a
vineyard.

17 She girds herself with strength,
And strengthens her arms.

18 She perceives that her
merchandise *is* good,
And her lamp does not go out by
night.

19 She stretches out her hands to the
distaff,
And her hand holds the spindle.

*I pray, O Lord, for _____.
May strength and honor be
her clothing, and may she
rejoice in the time to come.
May she open her mouth
with wisdom, and may
the law of kindness be
on her tongue.*

FROM PROVERBS 31:25, 26

20 [a]She extends her hand to the poor,
Yes, she reaches out her hands to
the needy.

21 She is not afraid of snow for her
household,
For all her household *is* clothed
with scarlet.

22 She makes tapestry for herself;
Her clothing *is* fine linen and
purple.

23 [a]Her husband is known in the
gates,
When he sits among the elders of
the land.

24 She makes linen garments and
sells *them*,

---

31 [2]A Jewish tradition *a king against whom there is no uprising*
32 [a]Mic. 7:16

CHAPTER 31
2 [a]Is. 49:15
3 [a]Prov. 5:9 [b]Deut. 17:17
4 [a]Eccl. 10:17
5 [a]Hos. 4:11 [1]Lit. *sons of affliction*
6 [a]Ps. 104:15
8 [a]Job 29:15, 16 [1]Lit. *sons of passing away*
9 [a]Lev. 19:15 [b]Jer. 22:16
10 [a]Prov. 12:4; 19:14 [1]Vv. 10–31 are an alphabetic acrostic in Hebrew; cf. Ps. 119 [2]Lit. *a wife of valor,* in the sense of all forms of excellence
15 [a]Rom. 12:11 [b]Luke 12:42
16 [1]Lit. *the fruit of her hands*
20 [a]Eph. 4:28
23 [a]Prov. 12:4

And supplies sashes for the
merchants.
25 Strength and honor *are* her
clothing;
She shall rejoice in time to come.
26 She opens her mouth with
wisdom,
And on her tongue *is* the law of
kindness.
27 She watches over the ways of her
household,
And does not eat the bread of
idleness.

28 Her children rise up and call her
blessed;
Her husband *also,* and he praises
her:
29 "Many daughters have done well,
But you excel them all."
30 Charm *is* deceitful and beauty *is*
passing,
But a woman *who* fears the LORD,
she shall be praised.
31 Give her of the fruit of her hands,
And let her own works praise her in
the gates.

AUTHOR:	*Traditionally Solomon, but May Be the Work of a Teacher Who Calls Himself Qoheleth; Otherwise Unknown to Us*
DATE:	*Traditionally, Near Solomon's Death (Approximately 930 B.C.), Though Many Consider It Much Later*
THEME:	*A Quest for Something of True Value in This Life*
KEY WORDS:	*Profit, Vanity, Under the Sun, Grasping After Wind*

ECCLESIASTES

Dear Woman of Destiny,

In Ecclesiastes, we see the futility of the world's ways. Solomon had prospered greatly through God's wisdom, but he was in despair without Him. To be truly successful women, we need to realize that all good things come from the Father. Let the Holy Spirit minister to you the very truths that brought Solomon back to God—and you will be greatly enriched.

His love and mine,

Marilyn Hickey

The Vanity of Life

The words of the Preacher, the son of David, [a]king in Jerusalem.

2 "Vanity[a][1] of vanities," says the
Preacher;
"Vanity of vanities, [b]all *is* vanity."

3 [a]What profit has a man from all his
labor
In which he [1]toils under the sun?
4 *One* generation passes away, and
another generation comes;
[a]But the earth abides forever.
5 [a]The sun also rises, and the sun
goes down,
And [1]hastens to the place where it
arose.
6 [a]The wind goes toward the south,
And turns around to the north;
The wind whirls about continually,
And comes again on its circuit.
7 [a]All the rivers run into the sea,
Yet the sea *is* not full;
To the place from which the rivers
come,
There they return again.
8 All things *are* [1]full of labor;
Man cannot express *it.*
[a]The eye is not satisfied with seeing,
Nor the ear filled with hearing.

Live in such a way as to pass something tangible to a new generation.

LILLIAN TRASHER

9 [a]That which has been *is* what will
be,
That which *is* done is what will be
done,
And *there is* nothing new under the
sun.
10 Is there anything of which it may
be said,
"See, this *is* new"?
It has already been in ancient times
before us.
11 *There is* [a]no remembrance of
former *things,*
Nor will there be any remembrance
of *things* that are to come
By *those* who will come after.

The Grief of Wisdom

12 I, the Preacher, was king over Israel
in Jerusalem. 13 And I set my heart to seek
and [a]search out by wisdom concerning all
that is done under heaven; [b]this burdensome task God has given to the sons of
man, by which they may be [1]exercised. 14 I
have seen all the works that are done under the sun; and indeed, all *is* vanity and
grasping for the wind.

15 [a]*What is* crooked cannot be made
straight,
And what is lacking cannot be
numbered.

16 I communed with my heart, saying,
"Look, I have attained greatness, and have
gained [a]more wisdom than all who were
before me in Jerusalem. My heart has
[1]understood great wisdom and knowledge." 17 [a]And I set my heart to know wisdom and to know madness and folly. I
perceived that this also is grasping for the
wind.

18 For [a]in much wisdom *is* much
grief,
And he who increases knowledge
increases sorrow.

The Vanity of Pleasure

2 I said [a]in my heart, "Come now, I will
test you with [b]mirth;[1] therefore enjoy
pleasure"; but surely, [c]this also *was* vanity. 2 I said of laughter—"Madness!"; and
of mirth, "What does it accomplish?" 3 [a]I
searched in my heart *how* [1]to gratify my
flesh with wine, while guiding my heart
with wisdom, and how to lay hold on folly,
till I might see what *was* [b]good for the
sons of men to do under heaven all the
days of their lives.

4 I made my works great, I built myself
[a]houses, and planted myself vineyards. 5 I
made myself gardens and orchards, and I
planted all *kinds* of fruit trees in them. 6 I
made myself water pools from which to
[1]water the growing trees of the grove. 7 I
acquired male and female servants, and
had [1]servants born in my house. Yes, I
had greater possessions of herds and
flocks than all who were in Jerusalem before me. 8 [a]I also gathered for myself silver
and gold and the special treasures of kings

CHAPTER 1
1 [a] Prov. 1:1
2 [a] Ps. 39:5, 6; 62:9; 144:4 [b] [Rom. 8:20, 21] [1] Or *Absurdity, Frustration, Futility, Nonsense;* and so throughout the book
3 [a] Eccl. 2:22; 3:9 [1] *labors*
4 [a] Ps. 104:5; 119:90
5 [a] Ps. 19:4–6 [1] Is eager for, lit. *panting*
6 [a] John 3:8
7 [a] [Jer. 5:22]
8 [a] Prov. 27:20 [1] *wearisome*
9 [a] Eccl. 3:15
11 [a] Eccl. 2:16
13 [a] [Eccl. 7:25; 8:16, 17] [b] Eccl. 3:10 [1] Or *afflicted*
15 [a] Eccl. 7:13
16 [a] 1 Kin. 3:12, 13 [1] Lit. *seen*
17 [a] Eccl. 2:3, 12; 7:23, 25
18 [a] Eccl. 12:12

CHAPTER 2
1 [a] Luke 12:19 [b] [Eccl. 7:4; 8:15] [c] Eccl. 1:2 [1] *gladness*
3 [a] Eccl. 1:17 [b] [Eccl. 3:12, 13; 5:18; 6:12] [1] Lit. *to draw my flesh*
4 [a] 1 Kin. 7:1–12
6 [1] *irrigate*
7 [1] Lit. *sons of my house*
8 [a] 1 Kin. 9:28; 10:10, 14, 21

and of the provinces. I acquired male and
female singers, the delights of the sons
of men, *and* [1]musical instruments of all
kinds.

9 [a]So I became great and [1]excelled
[b]more than all who were before me in
Jerusalem. Also my wisdom remained
with me.

10 Whatever my eyes desired I did
not keep from them.
I did not withhold my heart from
any pleasure,
For my heart rejoiced in all my
labor;
And [a]this was my [1]reward from all
my labor.
11 Then I looked on all the works
that my hands had done
And on the labor in which I had
toiled;
And indeed all *was* [a]vanity and
grasping for the wind.
There was no profit under the sun.

The End of the Wise and the Fool

12 Then I turned myself to consider
wisdom [a]and madness and folly;
For what *can* the man *do* who
succeeds the king?—
Only what he has already [b]done.
13 Then I saw that wisdom [a]excels
folly
As light excels darkness.
14 [a]The wise man's eyes *are* in his
head,
But the fool walks in darkness.
Yet I myself perceived
That [b]the same event happens to
them all.

15 So I said in my heart,
"As it happens to the fool,
It also happens to me,
And why was I then more wise?"
Then I said in my heart,
"This also *is* vanity."
16 For *there is* [a]no more
remembrance of the wise than of
the fool forever,
Since all that now *is* will be
forgotten in the days to come.
And how does a wise *man* die?
As the fool!

17 Therefore I hated life because the work
that was done under the sun *was* distressing to me, for all *is* vanity and grasping for
the wind.

18 Then I hated all my labor in which I
had toiled under the sun, because [a]I must
leave it to the man who will come after
me. 19 And who knows whether he will be
wise or a fool? Yet he will rule over all my
labor in which I toiled and in which I have
shown myself wise under the sun. This
also *is* vanity. 20 Therefore I turned my
heart and despaired of all the labor in
which I had toiled under the sun. 21 For
there is a man whose labor *is* with wisdom, knowledge, and skill; yet he must
leave his [1]heritage to a man who has not
labored for it. This also *is* vanity and a
great evil. 22 [a]For what has man for all his
labor, and for the striving of his heart
with which he has toiled under the sun?
23 For all his days *are* [a]sorrowful, and his
work burdensome; even in the night his
heart takes no rest. This also is vanity.

24 [a]Nothing *is* better for a man *than* that
he should eat and drink, and *that* his soul
should enjoy good in his labor. This also,
I saw, was from the hand of God. 25 For
who can eat, or who can have enjoyment,
[1]more than I? 26 For *God* gives [a]wisdom
and knowledge and joy to a man who *is*
good in His sight; but to the sinner He
gives the work of gathering and collecting, that [b]he may give to *him who is* good
before God. This also *is* vanity and grasping for the wind.

Lord, _____ is in the depths of despair, hating life and feeling as though all of their work has been in vain. I pray that You would meet them, Lord, comfort and restore them.

FROM ECCLESIASTES 2:17

Everything Has Its Time

3 To everything *there is* a season,
A [a]time for every purpose under
heaven:

2 A time [1]to be born,
And [a]a time to die;
A time to plant,

8 [1]Exact meaning unknown
9 [a]Eccl. 1:16 [b]2 Chr. 9:22 [1]Lit. *increased*
10 [a]Eccl. 3:22; 5:18; 9:9 [1]Lit. *portion*
11 [a]Eccl. 1:3, 14
12 [a]Eccl. 1:17; 7:25 [b]Eccl. 1:9
13 [a]Eccl. 7:11, 14, 19; 9:18; 10:10
14 [a]Prov. 17:24 [b]Ps. 49:10
16 [a]Eccl. 1:11; 4:16
18 [a]Ps. 49:10
21 [1]Lit. *portion*
22 [a]Eccl. 1:3; 3:9
23 [a]Job 5:7; 14:1
24 [a]Eccl. 3:12, 13, 22
25 [1]So with MT, Tg., Vg.; some Heb. mss., LXX, Syr. *without Him*
26 [a]Prov. 2:6 [b]Prov. 28:8
CHAPTER 3
1 [a]Eccl. 3:17; 8:6
2 [a]Heb. 9:27 [1]Lit. *to bear*

ECCLESIASTES 3:1–8

Dear Woman of Destiny,

Have you been holding on to a promise from God? Do you know that everything in our lives must be in sequence with God's predetermined time so we can be effective and fruitful? Do you know that promises come with pain? God talked to Eve about pain. "In pain you shall bring forth children" (Gen. 3:16). He said He would bless her, but it was going to hurt. We want to embrace God's promises, but we don't want to pay the price for them.

To realize God's promises in our lives we must set ourselves to God's beat. His beat is His rhythm, sequence, order, structure, and timing for our lives. If we miss His timing by moving too fast or too slow we'll fall out of step, and that will affect everything else.

We are not flowing in His rhythm when we figure we can help God birth His promises with our own reasoning; when we get out of step because we are not listening to His voice; when we move to someone else's beat or constantly seek others' advice. Listening to others can result in being manipulated by another person's sequence.

For years I watched women of God around me flowing mightily in harmony with God's music for them. I was tempted to dance to their music when it was not for me. My prayer became "Lord, teach me the timing and sequence You have set for my life so I may dance to Your beat for me."

For every problem and situation you and I are praying about, there is a set time for its answer. We may have to step back and watch others flow with their music, rejoicing with them as we support them with our giftings, knowing that our own appointed time is yet to come. Know that the same God who has called their season today will call you tomorrow. Refuse to get ahead of God's timing.

You may have to wait for God, because what He is going to do in your life is all a matter of timing—His timing. You may be asking God for an answer right now, and He is thinking beyond your anxious heart about your request. Or, His purpose may be to fine-tune you through adversity. Out of your brokenness is coming something invaluable—the creation of a woman of excellence with an excellent spirit, reproducing other women who will rise up into a whole new level of excellence. These women in turn will dance to the music of their Beloved. When He moves, they move—in the same direction at the same time.

If we want to walk in the Spirit, we need to hear His rhythm, accept it, and walk in obedience to it. The key is obedient listening, for the Lord wants to speak a life-changing word into your spirit; and, as you dance to the dance of your Beloved, everything God has promised you is going to come to pass. It's simply a matter of time.

Ginger Lindsay

And a time to pluck *what is*
planted;
3 A time to kill,
And a time to heal;
A time to break down,
And a time to build up;
4 A time to [a]weep,
And a time to laugh;
A time to mourn,
And a time to dance;
5 A time to cast away stones,
And a time to gather stones;
[a]A time to embrace,
And a time to refrain from
embracing;
6 A time to gain,
And a time to lose;
A time to keep,
And a time to throw away;
7 A time to tear,
And a time to sew;
[a]A time to keep silence,
And a time to [b]speak;
8 A time to love,
And a time to [a]hate;
A time of war,
And a time of peace.

The God-Given Task

9 [a]What profit has the worker from that
in which he labors? 10 [a]I have seen the
God-given task with which the sons of
men are to be occupied. 11 He has made
everything beautiful in its time. Also He
has put eternity in their hearts, except
that [a]no one can find out the work that
God does from beginning to end.
12 I know that nothing *is* [a]better for
them than to rejoice, and to do good in
their lives, 13 and also that [a]every man
should eat and drink and enjoy the good
of all his labor—it *is* the gift of God.

14 I know that whatever God does,
It shall be forever.
[a]Nothing can be added to it,
And nothing taken from it.
God does *it,* that men should fear
before Him.
15 [a]That which is has already been,
And what is to be has already been;
And God [1]requires an account of
[2]what is past.

Injustice Seems to Prevail

16 Moreover [a]I saw under the sun:

In the place of [1]judgment,
Wickedness *was* there;
And *in* the place of righteousness,
[2]Iniquity *was* there.

17 I said in my heart,
[a]"God shall judge the righteous and
the wicked,
For *there is* a time there for every
[1]purpose and for every work."

18 I said in my heart, "Concerning the condition of the sons of men, God tests them,
that they may see that they themselves are
like animals." 19 [a]For what happens to the
sons of men also happens to animals; one
thing befalls them: as one dies, so dies the
other. Surely, they all have one breath;
man has no advantage over animals, for
all *is* vanity. 20 All go to one place: [a]all are
from the dust, and all return to dust.
21 [a]Who[1] knows the spirit of the sons of
men, which goes upward, and the spirit of
the animal, which goes down to the earth?
22 [a]So I perceived that nothing *is* better
than that a man should rejoice in his own
works, for [b]that *is* his [1]heritage. [c]For who
can bring him to see what will happen
after him?

4 Then I returned and considered all
the [a]oppression that is done under
the sun:

And look! The tears of the
oppressed,
But they have no comforter—
[1]On the side of their oppressors
there is power,
But they have no comforter.
2 [a]Therefore I praised the dead who
were already dead,
More than the living who are still
alive.
3 [a]Yet, better than both *is he* who has
never existed,
Who has not seen the evil work
that is done under the sun.

The Vanity of Selfish Toil

4 Again, I saw that for all toil and every
skillful work a man is envied by his neighbor. This also *is* vanity and grasping for
the wind.

5 [a]The fool folds his hands
And consumes his own flesh.
6 [a]Better a handful *with* quietness
Than both hands full, *together with*
toil and grasping for the wind.

7 Then I returned, and I saw vanity under the sun:

---

4 [a]Rom. 12:15
5 [a]Joel 2:16
7 [a]Amos 5:13 [b]Prov. 25:11
8 [a]Luke 14:26
9 [a]Eccl. 1:3
10 [a]Eccl. 1:13
11 [a]Rom. 11:33
12 [a]Eccl. 2:3, 24
13 [a]Eccl. 2:24
14 [a]James 1:17
15 [a]Eccl. 1:9 [1]Lit. *seeks* [2]*what is pursued*
16 [a]Eccl. 5:8 [1]*justice* [2]*Wickedness*
17 [a][Rom. 2:6–10] [1]*desire*
19 [a][Eccl. 2:16]
20 [a]Gen. 3:19
21 [a]Eccl. 12:7 [1]LXX, Syr., Tg., Vg. *Who knows whether the spirit . . . goes upward, and whether . . . goes downward to the earth?*
22 [a]Eccl. 2:24; 5:18 [b]Eccl. 2:10 [c]Eccl. 6:12; 8:7 [1]*portion* or *lot*

CHAPTER 4
1 [a]Eccl. 3:16; 5:8 [1]Lit. *At the hand*
2 [a]Job 3:17, 18
3 [a]Job 3:11–22
5 [a]Prov. 6:10; 24:33
6 [a]Prov. 15:16, 17; 16:8

8 There is one alone, without
[1]companion:
He has neither son nor brother.
Yet *there is* no end to all his labors,
Nor is his [a]eye satisfied with riches.
But [b]*he never asks,*
"For whom do I toil and deprive
myself of [c]good?"
This also *is* vanity and a [2]grave
misfortune.

The Value of a Friend

9 Two *are* better than one,
Because they have a good reward
for their labor.
10 For if they fall, one will lift up his
companion.
But woe to him *who is* alone when
he falls,
For *he has* no one to help him up.
11 Again, if two lie down together,
they will keep warm;
But how can one be warm *alone?*
12 Though one may be overpowered
by another, two can withstand
him.
And a threefold cord is not quickly
broken.

Popularity Passes Away

13 Better a poor and wise youth
Than an old and foolish king who
will be admonished no more.
14 For he comes out of prison to be
king,
Although [1]he was born poor in his
kingdom.
15 I saw all the living who walk
under the sun;
They were with the second youth
who stands in his place.
16 *There was* no end of all the people
[1]over whom he was made king;
Yet those who come afterward will
not rejoice in him.
Surely this also *is* vanity and
grasping for the wind.

Fear God, Keep Your Vows

5 Walk [a]prudently when you go to the
house of God; and draw near to hear
rather [b]than to give the sacrifice of fools,
for they do not know that they do evil.

2 Do not be [a]rash with your mouth,
And let not your heart utter
anything hastily before God.
For God *is* in heaven, and you on
earth;
Therefore let your words [b]be few.
3 For a dream comes through much
activity,
And [a]a fool's voice *is known* by *his*
many words.

4 [a]When you make a vow to God, do
not delay to [b]pay it;
For *He has* no pleasure in fools.
Pay what you have vowed—
5 [a]Better not to vow than to vow and
not pay.

The nearer your spirit draws to God, the further you become separated from soulish demands.

MADAME JEANNE GUYON

6 Do not let your [a]mouth cause your flesh
to sin, [b]nor say before the messenger *of*
God that it *was* an error. Why should God
be angry at your [1]excuse and destroy the
work of your hands? 7 For in the multitude
of dreams and many words *there is* also
vanity. But [a]fear God.

The Vanity of Gain and Honor

8 If you [a]see the oppression of the poor,
and the violent [1]perversion of justice and
righteousness in a province, do not marvel at the matter; for [b]high official watches over high official, and higher officials
are over them.
9 Moreover the profit of the land is for
all; *even* the king is served from the field.

10 He who loves silver will not be
satisfied with silver;
Nor he who loves abundance, with
increase.
This also *is* vanity.

11 When goods increase,
They increase who eat them;
So what profit have the owners
Except to see *them* with their eyes?

12 The sleep of a laboring man *is*
sweet,

---

8 a [1 John 2:16] b Ps. 39:6 c Eccl. 2:18–21 1 Lit. *a second* 2 Lit. *evil task*
14 1 The youth
16 1 Lit. *to all before whom he was to be*
CHAPTER 5
1 a Ex. 3:5 b [1 Sam. 15:22]
2 a Prov. 20:25 b Matt. 6:7
3 a Prov. 10:19
4 a Num. 30:2 b Ps. 66:13, 14
5 a Acts 5:4
6 a Prov. 6:2 b 1 Cor. 11:10 1 Lit. *voice*
7 a [Eccl. 12:13]
8 a Eccl. 3:16 b [Ps. 12:5; 58:11; 82:1] 1 *wresting*

Whether he eats little or much;
But the abundance of the rich will
not permit him to sleep.

13 [a]There is a severe evil *which* I have
seen under the sun:
Riches kept for their owner to his
hurt.
14 But those riches perish through
[1]misfortune;
When he begets a son, *there is*
nothing in his hand.
15 [a]As he came from his mother's
womb, naked shall he return,
To go as he came;
And he shall take nothing from his
labor
Which he may carry away in his
hand.
16 And this also *is* a severe evil—
Just exactly as he came, so shall he
go.
And [a]what profit has he [b]who has
labored for the wind?
17 All his days [a]he also eats in
darkness,
And *he has* much sorrow and
sickness and anger.

18Here is what I have seen: [a]*It is* good
and fitting *for one* to eat and drink, and to
enjoy the good of all his labor in which he
toils under the sun all the days of his life
which God gives him; [b]for it *is* his [1]heri-
tage. 19As for [a]every man to whom God
has given riches and wealth, and given
him power to eat of it, to receive his [1]heri-
tage and rejoice in his labor—this *is* the
[b]gift of God. 20For he will not dwell undu-
ly on the days of his life, because God
keeps *him* busy with the joy of his heart.

6 There[a] is an evil which I have seen
under the sun, and it *is* common
among men: 2A man to whom God has
given riches and wealth and honor, [a]so
that he lacks nothing for himself of all he
desires; [b]yet God does not give him power
to eat of it, but a foreigner consumes it.
This *is* vanity, and it *is* an evil [1]affliction.
3If a man begets a hundred *children*
and lives many years, so that the days of
his years are many, but his soul is not
satisfied with goodness, or [a]indeed he has
no burial, I say *that* [b]a [1]stillborn child *is*
better than he— 4for it comes in vanity
and departs in darkness, and its name is
covered with darkness. 5Though it has not
seen the sun or known *anything,* this has
more rest than that man, 6even if he lives
a thousand years twice—but has not seen
goodness. Do not all go to one [a]place?

7 [a]All the labor of man *is* for his
mouth,
And yet the soul is not satisfied.
8 For what more has the wise *man*
than the fool?
What does the poor man have,
Who knows *how* to walk before the
living?
9 Better *is* [1]the [a]sight of the eyes
than the wandering of [2]desire.
This also *is* vanity and grasping for
the wind.

10 Whatever one is, he has been
named [a]already,
For it is known that he *is* man;
[b]And he cannot contend with Him
who is mightier than he.
11 Since there are many things that
increase vanity,
How *is* man the better?

12For who knows what *is* good for man
in life, [1]all the days of his [2]vain life which
he passes like [a]a shadow? [b]Who can tell a
man what will happen after him under the
sun?

The Value of Practical Wisdom

7 A [a]good name *is* better than precious
ointment,
And the day of death than the day
of one's [b]birth;
2 Better to go to the house of
mourning
Than to go to the house of feasting,
For that *is* the end of all men;
And the living will take *it* to [a]heart.
3 [1]Sorrow *is* better than laughter,
[a]For by a sad countenance the heart
is made [2]better.
4 The heart of the wise *is* in the
house of mourning,
But the heart of fools *is* in the
house of mirth.
5 [a]*It is* better to [1]hear the rebuke of
the wise
Than for a man to hear the song of
fools.
6 [a]For like the [1]crackling of thorns
under a pot,
So *is* the laughter of the fool.
This also is vanity.

13 [a]Eccl. 6:1, 2
14 [1]Lit. *bad business*
15 [a]1 Tim. 6:7
16 [a]Eccl. 1:3 [b]Prov. 11:29
17 [a]Ps. 127:2
18 [a][1 Tim. 6:17] [b]Eccl. 2:10; 3:22 [1]Lit. *portion*
19 [a][Eccl. 6:2] [b]Eccl. 2:24; 3:13 [1]Lit. *portion*

CHAPTER 6
1 [a]Eccl. 5:13
2 [a]Job 21:10 [b]Luke 12:20 [1]*disease*
3 [a]Is. 14:19, 20 [b]Job 3:16 [1]Or *miscarriage*
6 [a]Eccl. 2:14, 15
7 [a]Prov. 16:26
9 [a]Eccl. 11:9 [1]What the eyes see [2]Lit. *soul*
10 [a]Eccl. 1:9; 3:15 [b]Job 9:32
12 [a]James 4:14 [b]Eccl. 3:22 [1]Lit. *the number of the days* [2]*futile*

CHAPTER 7
1 [a]Prov. 22:1 [b]Eccl. 4:2
2 [a][Ps. 90:12]
3 [a][2 Cor. 7:10] [1]*Vexation* or *Grief* [2]*well* or *pleasing*
5 [a]Ps. 141:5 [1]*listen to*
6 [a]Eccl. 2:2 [1]Lit. *sound*

7 Surely oppression destroys a wise *man's* reason,
[a]And a bribe [1]debases the heart.
8 The end of a thing *is* better than its beginning;
[a]The patient in spirit *is* better than the proud in spirit.
9 [a]Do not hasten in your spirit to be angry,
For anger rests in the bosom of fools.
10 Do not say,
"Why were the former days better than these?"
For you do not inquire wisely concerning this.

11 Wisdom *is* good with an inheritance,
And profitable [a]to those who see the sun.
12 For wisdom *is* [1]a [a]defense *as* money *is* a defense,
But the [2]excellence of knowledge *is that* wisdom gives [b]life to those who have it.

13 Consider the work of God;
For [a]who can make straight what He has made crooked?
14 [a]In the day of prosperity be joyful,
But in the day of adversity consider:
Surely God has appointed the one [1]as well as the other,
So that man can find out nothing *that will come* after him.

15 I have seen everything in my days of
vanity:

[a]There is a just *man* who perishes in his righteousness,
And there is a wicked *man* who prolongs *life* in his wickedness.
16 [a]Do not be overly righteous,
[b]Nor be overly wise:
Why should you destroy yourself?
17 Do not be overly wicked,
Nor be foolish:
[a]Why should you die before your time?
18 *It is* good that you grasp this,
And also not remove your hand from the other;
For he who [a]fears God will [1]escape them all.

19 [a]Wisdom strengthens the wise
More than ten rulers of the city.
20 [a]For *there is* not a just man on earth who does good
And does not sin.

Lord, I pray that You would give _____ Your wisdom; for wisdom strengthens the wise more than ten rulers of the city.

FROM ECCLESIASTES 7:19

21 Also do not take to heart everything people say,
Lest you hear your servant cursing you.
22 For many times, also, your own heart has known
That even you have cursed others.

We know most when we know least, when all that we would like to be is swallowed up in God.

SMITH WIGGLESWORTH

23 All this I have [1]proved by wisdom.
[a]I said, "I will be wise";
But it *was* far from me.
24 [a]As for that which is far off and [b]exceedingly deep,
Who can find it out?
25 [a]I applied my heart to know,
To search and seek out wisdom and the reason *of things,*
To know the wickedness of folly,
Even of foolishness *and* madness.
26 [a]And I find more bitter than death
The woman whose heart *is* snares and nets,
Whose hands *are* fetters.
[1]He who pleases God shall escape from her,
But the sinner shall be trapped by her.

7 [a]Ex. 23:8 [1]*destroys*
8 [a]Prov. 14:29
9 [a]James 1:19
11 [a]Eccl. 11:7
12 [a]Eccl. 9:18 [b]Prov. 3:18 [1]A protective shade, lit. *shadow* [2]*advantage* or *profit*
13 [a]Job 12:14
14 [a]Deut. 28:47 [1]*alongside*
15 [a]Eccl. 8:12–14
16 [a]Prov. 25:16 [b]Rom. 12:3
17 [a]Job 15:32
18 [a]Eccl. 3:14; 5:7; 8:12, 13 [1]Lit. *come forth from all of them*
19 [a]Prov. 21:22
20 [a]1 John 1:8
23 [a]Rom. 1:22 [1]*tested*
24 [a]1 Tim. 6:16 [b]Rom. 11:33
25 [a]Eccl. 1:17
26 [a]Prov. 5:3, 4 [1]Lit. *He who is good before God*

27 "Here is what I have found," says
[a]the Preacher,
"*Adding* one thing to the other to
find out the reason,
28 Which my soul still seeks but I
cannot find:
[a]One man among a thousand I have
found,
But a woman among all these I
have not found.
29 Truly, this only I have found:
[a]That God made man upright,
But [b]they have sought out many
schemes."

8 Who *is* like a wise *man?*
And who knows the interpretation
of a thing?
[a]A man's wisdom makes his face
shine,
And [b]the [1]sternness of his face is
changed.

Obey Authorities for God's Sake

[2]I *say,* "Keep the king's commandment
[a]for the sake of your oath to God. [3][a]Do
not be hasty to go from his presence. Do
not take your stand for an evil thing, for
he does whatever pleases him."

4 Where the word of a king *is, there*
is power;
And [a]who may say to him, "What
are you doing?"
5 He who keeps his command will
experience nothing harmful;
And a wise man's heart [1]discerns
both time and judgment,
6 Because [a]for every matter there is
a time and judgment,
Though the misery of man
[1]increases greatly.
7 [a]For he does not know what will
happen;
So who can tell him when it will
occur?
8 [a]No one has power over the spirit to
retain the spirit,
And no one has power in the day of
death.
There is [b]no release from that war,
And wickedness will not deliver
those who are given to it.

[9]All this I have seen, and applied my
heart to every work that is done under the
sun: *There is* a time in which one man
rules over another to his own hurt.

Death Comes to All

[10]Then I saw the wicked buried, who
had come and gone from the place of holiness, and they were [a]forgotten[1] in the city
where they had so done. This also *is* vanity. [11][a]Because the sentence against an evil
work is not executed speedily, therefore
the heart of the sons of men is fully set in
them to do evil. [12][a]Though a sinner does
evil a hundred *times,* and his *days* are
prolonged, yet I surely know that [b]it will
be well with those who fear God, who fear
before Him. [13]But it will not be well with
the wicked; nor will he prolong *his* days,
which are as a shadow, because he does
not fear before God.

[14]There is a vanity which occurs on
earth, that there are just *men* to whom it
[a]happens according to the work of the
wicked; again, there are wicked *men* to
whom it happens according to the work
of the [b]righteous. I said that this also *is*
vanity.

[15][a]So I commended enjoyment, because a man has nothing better under the
sun than to eat, drink, and be merry; for
this will remain with him in his labor *all*
the days of his life which God gives him
under the sun.

[16]When I applied my heart to know wisdom and to see the business that is done
on earth, even though one sees no sleep
day or night, [17]then I saw all the work
of God, that [a]a man cannot find out the
work that is done under the sun. For
though a man labors to discover *it,* yet he
will not find *it;* moreover, though a wise
man attempts to know *it,* he will not be
able to find *it.*

9 For I [1]considered all this in my heart,
so that I could declare it all: [a]that the
righteous and the wise and their works
are in the hand of God. People know neither love nor hatred *by* anything *they see*
before them. [2][a]All things *come* alike to
all:

One event *happens* to the righteous
and the wicked;
To the [1]good, the clean, and the
unclean;
To him who sacrifices and him who
does not sacrifice.
As is the good, so *is* the sinner;
He who takes an oath as *he* who
fears an oath.

[3]This *is* an evil in all that is done under
the sun: that one thing *happens* to all.

27 [a] Eccl. 1:1, 2
28 [a] Job 33:23
29 [a] Gen. 1:27 [b] Gen. 3:6, 7

CHAPTER 8
1 [a] Acts 6:15 [b] Deut. 28:50 [1] Lit. *strength*
2 [a] 1 Chr. 29:24
3 [a] Eccl. 10:4
4 [a] Job 34:18
5 [1] Lit. *knows*
6 [a] Eccl. 3:1, 17 [1] *is great upon him*
7 [a] Eccl. 6:12
8 [a] Ps. 49:6, 7 [b] Deut. 20:5–8
10 [a] Eccl. 2:16; 9:5 [1] Some Heb. mss., LXX, Vg. *praised*
11 [a] Is. 26:10
12 [a] Is. 65:20 [b] [Is. 3:10]
14 [a] Ps. 73:14 [b] Eccl. 2:14; 7:15; 9:1–3
15 [a] Eccl. 2:24
17 [a] Rom. 11:33

CHAPTER 9
1 [a] Eccl. 8:14 [1] Lit. *put*
2 [a] Mal. 3:15 [1] LXX, Syr., Vg. *good and bad,*

Truly the hearts of the sons of men are
full of evil; madness *is* in their hearts
while they live, and after that *they go* to
the dead. 4But for him who is joined to all
the living there is hope, for a living dog is
better than a dead lion.

5 For the living know that they will
die;
But [a]the dead know nothing,
And they have no more reward,
For [b]the memory of them is
forgotten.
6 Also their love, their hatred, and
their envy have now perished;
Nevermore will they have a share
In anything done under the sun.

7 Go, [a]eat your bread with joy,
And drink your wine with a merry
heart;
For God has already accepted your
works.
8 Let your garments always be white,
And let your head lack no oil.

9[1]Live joyfully with the wife whom you
love all the days of your vain life which He
has given you under the sun, all your days
of vanity; [a]for that *is* your portion in life,
and in the labor which you perform under
the sun.
10[a]Whatever your hand finds to do, do
it with your [b]might; for *there is* no work
or device or knowledge or wisdom in the
grave where you are going.
11I returned [a]and saw under the sun
that—

The race *is* not to the swift,
Nor the battle to the strong,
Nor bread to the wise,
Nor riches to men of
understanding,
Nor favor to men of skill;
But time and [b]chance happen to
them all.
12 For [a]man also does not know his
time:
Like fish taken in a cruel net,
Like birds caught in a snare,
So the sons of men *are* [b]snared in
an evil time,
When it falls suddenly upon them.

Wisdom Superior to Folly

13This wisdom I have also seen under
the sun, and it *seemed* great to me:
14[a]*There was* a little city with few men in
it; and a great king came against it, besieged it, and built great [1]snares around
it. 15Now there was found in it a poor wise
man, and he by his wisdom delivered the
city. Yet no one remembered that same
poor man.
16Then I said:

"Wisdom *is* better than [a]strength.
Nevertheless [b]the poor man's
wisdom *is* despised,
And his words are not heard.
17 Words of the wise, *spoken* quietly,
should be heard
Rather than the shout of a ruler of
fools.
18 Wisdom *is* better than weapons of
war;
But [a]one sinner destroys much
good."

10

Dead[1] flies [2]putrefy the
perfumer's ointment,
And cause it to give off a foul odor;
So does a little folly to one
respected for wisdom *and* honor.
2 A wise man's heart *is* at his right
hand,
But a fool's heart at his left.
3 Even when a fool walks along the
way,
He lacks wisdom,
[a]And he shows everyone *that* he *is* a
fool.
4 If the spirit of the ruler rises
against you,
[a]Do not leave your post;
For [b]conciliation[1] pacifies great
offenses.
5 There is an evil I have seen under
the sun,
As an error proceeding from the
ruler:
6 [a]Folly is set in [1]great dignity,
While the rich sit in a lowly place.
7 I have seen servants [a]on horses,
While princes walk on the ground
like servants.

8 [a]He who digs a pit will fall into it,
And whoever breaks through a wall
will be bitten by a serpent.
9 He who quarries stones may be
hurt by them,
And he who splits wood may be
endangered by it.
10 If the ax is dull,
And one does not sharpen the edge,
Then he must use more strength;
But wisdom [1]brings success.

---

5 a Is. 63:16 b Is. 26:14
7 a Eccl. 8:15
9 a Eccl. 2:10 1 Lit. *See life*
10 a [Col. 3:17] b Rom. 12:11
11 a Amos 2:14, 15 b 1 Sam. 6:9
12 a Eccl. 8:7 b Prov. 29:6
14 a 2 Sam. 20:16–22 1 LXX, Syr., Vg. *bulwarks*
16 a Eccl. 7:12, 19 b Mark 6:2, 3
18 a Josh. 7:1–26

CHAPTER 10
1 1 Lit. *Flies of death* 2 Tg., Vg. omit *putrefy*
3 a Prov. 13:16; 18:2
4 a Eccl. 8:3 b 1 Sam. 25:24–33 1 Lit. *healing, health*
6 a Esth. 3:1 1 *exalted positions*
7 a Prov. 19:10; 30:22
8 a Prov. 26:27
10 1 Lit. *is a successful advantage*

11 A serpent may bite [a]when *it is* not
charmed;
The [1]babbler is no different.
12 [a]The words of a wise man's mouth
are gracious,
But [b]the lips of a fool shall swallow
him up;
13 The words of his mouth begin
with foolishness,
And the end of his talk *is* raving
madness.
14 [a]A fool also multiplies words.
No man knows what is to be;
Who can tell him [b]what will be
after him?
15 The labor of fools wearies them,
For they do not even know how to
go to the city!

16 [a]Woe to you, O land, when your
king *is* a child,
And your princes feast in the
morning!
17 Blessed *are* you, O land, when
your king *is* the son of nobles,
And your [a]princes feast at the
proper time—
For strength and not for
drunkenness!
18 Because of laziness the [1]building
decays,
And [a]through idleness of hands the
house leaks.
19 A feast is made for laughter,
And [a]wine makes merry;
But money answers everything.

20 [a]Do not curse the king, even in
your thought;
Do not curse the rich, even in your
bedroom;
For a bird of the air may carry your
voice,
And a bird in flight may tell the
matter.

The Value of Diligence

11 Cast your bread [a]upon the
waters,
[b]For you will find it after many days.
2 [a]Give a serving [b]to seven, and also
to eight,
[c]For you do not know what evil will
be on the earth.

3 If the clouds are full of rain,
They empty *themselves* upon the
earth;
And if a tree falls to the south or
the north,
In the place where the tree falls,
there it shall lie.
4 He who observes the wind will not
sow,
And he who regards the clouds will
not reap.

5 As [a]you do not know what *is* the
way of the [1]wind,
[b]*Or* how the bones *grow* in the
womb of her who is with child,
So you do not know the works of
God who makes everything.
6 In the morning sow your seed,
And in the evening do not withhold
your hand;
For you do not know which will
prosper,
Either this or that,
Or whether both alike *will be* good.

7 Truly the light is sweet,
And *it is* pleasant for the eyes [a]to
behold the sun;
8 But if a man lives many years
And [a]rejoices in them all,
Yet let him [b]remember the days of
darkness,
For they will be many.
All that is coming *is* vanity.

Seek God in Early Life

9 Rejoice, O young man, in your
youth,
And let your heart cheer you in the
days of your youth;
[a]Walk in the [1]ways of your heart,
And [2]in the sight of your eyes;
But know that for all these
[b]God will bring you into judgment.
10 Therefore remove [1]sorrow from
your heart,
And [a]put away evil from your flesh,
[b]For childhood and [2]youth *are*
vanity.

12 Remember[a] now your Creator in
the days of your youth,
Before the [1]difficult days come,
And the years draw near [b]when you
say,
"I have no pleasure in them":
2 While the sun and the light,
The moon and the stars,
Are not darkened,
And the clouds do not return after
the rain;

---

11 a Jer. 8:17 *1* Lit. *master of the tongue*
12 a Prov. 10:32 b Prov. 10:14
14 a [Prov. 15:2] b Eccl. 3:22; 8:7
16 a Is. 3:4, 5; 5:11
17 a Prov. 31:4
18 a Prov. 24:30–34 *1* Lit. *rafters sink*
19 a Ps. 104:15
20 a Acts 23:5

CHAPTER 11
1 a Is. 32:20 b [Deut. 15:10]
2 a [1 Tim. 6:18, 19] b Mic. 5:5 c Eph. 5:16
5 a John 3:8 b Ps. 139:14 *1* Or *spirit*
7 a Eccl. 7:11
8 a Eccl. 9:7 b Eccl. 12:1
9 a Num. 15:39 b Eccl. 3:17; 12:14 *1* Impulses *2* As you see to be best
10 a 2 Cor. 7:1 b Ps. 39:5 *1* *vexation* *2* Prime of life

CHAPTER 12
1 a Lam. 3:27 b 2 Sam. 19:35 *1* Lit. *evil*

3 In the day when the keepers of the
house tremble,
And the strong men bow down;
When the grinders cease because
they are few,
And those that look through the
windows grow dim;
4 When the doors are shut in the
streets,
And the sound of grinding is low;
When one rises up at the sound of
a bird,
And all [a]the daughters of music are
brought low.
5 Also they are afraid of height,
And of terrors in the way;
When the almond tree blossoms,
The grasshopper is a burden,
And desire fails.
For man goes to [a]his eternal home,
And [b]the mourners go about the
streets.

6 *Remember your Creator* before the
silver cord is [1]loosed,
Or the golden bowl is broken,
Or the pitcher shattered at the
fountain,
Or the wheel broken at the well.
7 [a]Then the dust will return to the
earth as it was,
[b]And the spirit will return to God
[c]who gave it.

8 "Vanity[a] of vanities," says the
Preacher,
"All *is* vanity."

The Whole Duty of Man

9And moreover, because the Preacher
was wise, he still taught the people knowledge; yes, he pondered and sought out
and [a]set[1] in order many proverbs. 10The
Preacher sought to find [1]acceptable
words; and *what was* written *was* upright—words of truth. 11The words of the
wise are like goads, and the words of
[1]scholars are like well-driven nails, given
by one Shepherd. 12And further, my son,
be admonished by these. Of making many
books *there is* no end, and [a]much study *is*
wearisome to the flesh.

O God, may I fear You and keep Your commandments, for this is the whole duty of man. For You, O Lord, will bring every work into judgment, including every secret thing, whether it is good or whether it is evil.

FROM ECCLESIASTES 12:13, 14

13Let us hear the conclusion of the
whole matter:

[a]Fear God and keep His
commandments,
For this is man's all.
14 For [a]God will bring every work
into judgment,
Including every secret thing,
Whether good or evil.

4 a 2 Sam. 19:35
5 a Job 17:13 b Jer. 9:17
6 1 So with Qr., Tg.; Kt. *removed;* LXX, Vg. *broken*
7 a Gen. 3:19 b Eccl. 3:21 c Job 34:14
8 a Ps. 62:9
9 a 1 Kin. 4:32 1 *arranged*
10 1 Lit. *delightful*
11 1 Lit. *masters of assemblies*
12 a Eccl. 1:18
13 a [Deut. 6:2; 10:12]
14 a Matt. 12:36

AUTHOR: *Attributed to Solomon*
DATE: *Solomon Reigned 970–930 B.C.*
THEME: *The Quest for Authentic Love*
KEY WORDS: *Love, Garden, Mother's House*

SONG OF SOLOMON

Dear Woman of Destiny,

How we women enjoy hearing tales of true love! In the Song of Solomon, we revel in the moving story of the Shulamite woman and the shepherd. Their love endured through temptation and opposition, a beautiful analogy of the love between Jesus and the bride of Christ. Curl up with the *good book* and soak up the sweet words of the great lover of your soul, Jesus.

His love and mine,

Marilyn Hickey

The [a]song of songs, which *is* Solomon's.

The Banquet

THE [1]SHULAMITE

2 Let him kiss me with the kisses of his mouth—
[a]For [2]your love *is* better than wine.
3 Because of the fragrance of your good ointments,
Your name *is* ointment poured forth;
Therefore the virgins love you.
4 [a]Draw me away!

THE DAUGHTERS OF JERUSALEM

[b]We will run after [1]you.

THE SHULAMITE

The king [c]has brought me into his chambers.

THE DAUGHTERS OF JERUSALEM

We will be glad and rejoice in [2]you.

We will remember your love more than wine.

THE SHULAMITE

Rightly do they love you.

5 I *am* dark, but lovely,
O daughters of Jerusalem,
Like the tents of Kedar,
Like the curtains of Solomon.
6 Do not look upon me, because I *am* dark,
Because the sun has [1]tanned me.
My mother's sons were angry with me;
They made me the keeper of the vineyards,
But my own [a]vineyard I have not kept.

(TO HER BELOVED)

7 Tell me, O you whom I love,
Where you feed *your flock,*
Where you make *it* rest at noon.
For why should I be as one who [1]veils herself
By the flocks of your companions?

THE BELOVED

8 If you do not know, [a]O fairest among women,
[1]Follow in the footsteps of the flock,
And feed your little goats
Beside the shepherds' tents.
9 I have compared you, [a]my love,
[b]To my filly among Pharaoh's chariots.
10 [a]Your cheeks are lovely with ornaments,
Your neck with chains *of gold.*

THE DAUGHTERS OF JERUSALEM

11 We will make [1]you ornaments of gold
With studs of silver.

THE SHULAMITE

12 While the king *is* at his table,
My [1]spikenard sends forth its fragrance.
13 A bundle of myrrh *is* my beloved to me,
That lies all night between my breasts.
14 My beloved *is* to me a cluster of henna *blooms*
In the vineyards of En Gedi.

THE BELOVED

15 [a]Behold, you *are* fair, [1]my love!
Behold, you *are* fair!
You *have* dove's eyes.

THE SHULAMITE

16 Behold, you *are* [a]handsome, my beloved!
Yes, pleasant!
Also our [1]bed *is* green.
17 The beams of our houses *are* cedar,
And our rafters of fir.

2 I *am* the rose of Sharon,
And the lily of the valleys.

THE BELOVED

2 Like a lily among thorns,
So is my love among the daughters.

THE SHULAMITE

3 Like an apple tree among the trees of the woods,
So *is* my beloved among the sons.
I sat down in his shade with great delight,
And [a]his fruit *was* sweet to my taste.

CHAPTER 1
1 a 1 Kin. 4:32
2 a Song 4:10 1 A Palestinian young woman, Song 6:13. The speaker and audience are identified according to the number, gender, and person of the Hebrew words. Occasionally the identity is not certain. 2 Masc. sing.: the Beloved
4 a Hos. 11:4 b Phil. 3:12–14 c Ps. 45:14, 15 1 Masc. sing.: the Beloved 2 Fem. sing.: the Shulamite
6 a Song 8:11, 12 1 Lit. *looked upon me*
7 1 LXX, Syr., Vg. *wanders*
8 a Song 5:9 1 Lit. *Go out*
9 a Song 2:2, 10, 13; 4:1, 7 b 2 Chr. 1:16
10 a Ezek. 16:11
11 1 Fem. sing.: the Shulamite
12 1 *perfume*
15 a Song 4:1; 5:12 1 *my companion, friend*
16 a Song 5:10–16 1 *couch*
CHAPTER 2
3 a Rev. 22:1, 2

Song of Solomon 1:3, 4

Dear Woman of Destiny,

As worshipers we need to get to know that great worship book, the Song of Solomon. Get to know it until it becomes part of you. After a while it will almost feel as if you wrote it. You'll begin to think Solomon just got a little ahead of you and put down your feelings on paper. At first, you may wish you had the ability to write such words. Later, as you enter more and more into worship, you will know you could have written it because you will have those same experiences—where God causes the "lips of sleepers" to speak (see Song 7:9). God will open your heart and touch the depth of your being in exactly that way.

Fall in love with Jesus so much that you will be careful when you speak His name. Always say it with love and fullness of expression. Sometimes the greatest worship is just whispering, "Jesus," saying His name and letting the fragrance of His name fill your soul. In certain environments, God's fragrance has been known to suddenly fill an auditorium. He has walked among His people as they spoke His name. When the fragrance of Christ fills a room, there is a profound and beautiful sense of the glory of God.

When we worship God, we are pouring out the fragrance of the Lord. Let's not be skimpy, just giving Him a dab or two. Let's be lavish. Let's be generous. Let's let love flow out of the depths of our being. Let's worship Him with words and songs of love.

God will teach us how to worship. He will anoint us to worship. He will create worship within us. He will touch the deepest part of us and allow us to be those who truly worship Him in spirit and in truth.

Worship is an attitude of the heart in which the heart bows down before God. No one else is present. There are no thoughts in your mind other than God. You haven't come with a petition. You haven't come with a request. You haven't come because you need healing. You haven't come because of some other need. You have come because you love Him so much and are compelled to express that love. Worship is a time of love. He pours out His love on us, and we pour out our love to Him.

The Lord wants you to know Him so intimately that you can present Him to others and describe Him from personal experience—from having seen Him, from having heard His voice, from having felt His touch. He wants you to look upon His face. He wants you to gaze into His eyes. He wants you to see the tears of love on His cheeks. He wants you to know Him in ways you have not known Him until now.

God wants to awaken your heart to love. He wants to awaken your heart to adoration. He wants to awaken in you the ability to truly worship Him.

Ruth Ward Heflin

THE SHULAMITE TO THE DAUGHTERS OF JERUSALEM

4 He brought me to the [1]banqueting house,
And his banner over me *was* love.
5 Sustain me with cakes of raisins,
Refresh me with apples,
For I *am* lovesick.

6 [a]His left hand *is* under my head,
And his right hand embraces me.
7 [a]I [1]charge you, O daughters of Jerusalem,
By the gazelles or by the does of the field,
Do not stir up nor awaken love
Until it pleases.

The Beloved's Request

THE SHULAMITE

8 The voice of my beloved!
Behold, he comes
Leaping upon the mountains,
Skipping upon the hills.
9 [a]My beloved is like a gazelle or a young stag.
Behold, he stands behind our wall;
He is looking through the windows,
Gazing through the lattice.

10 My beloved spoke, and said to me:
"Rise up, my love, my fair one,
And come away.
11 For lo, the winter is past,
The rain is over *and* gone.
12 The flowers appear on the earth;
The time of singing has come,
And the voice of the turtledove
Is heard in our land.
13 The fig tree puts forth her green figs,
And the vines *with* the tender grapes
Give a good smell.
Rise up, my love, my fair one,
And come away!

14 "O my [a]dove, in the clefts of the rock,
In the secret *places* of the cliff,
Let me see your [1]face,
[b]Let me hear your voice;
For your voice *is* sweet,
And your face *is* lovely."

HER BROTHERS

15 Catch us [a]the foxes,
The little foxes that spoil the vines,
For our vines *have* tender grapes.

THE SHULAMITE

16 [a]My beloved *is* mine, and I *am* his.
He feeds *his flock* among the lilies.

(TO HER BELOVED)

17 [a]Until the day breaks
And the shadows flee away,
Turn, my beloved,
And be [b]like a gazelle
Or a young stag
Upon the mountains of [1]Bether.

What a privilege to have intimate fellowship with the Father. To hear the whispers of God's love, our ears must be clean and ready to listen to His voice.

CHARLES H. SPURGEON

A Troubled Night

THE SHULAMITE

3 By [a]night on my bed I sought the one I love;
I sought him, but I did not find him.
2 "I will rise now," *I said,*
"And go about the city;
In the streets and in the squares
I will seek the one I love."
I sought him, but I did not find him.
3 [a]The watchmen who go about the city found me;
I said,
"Have you seen the one I love?"

4 Scarcely had I passed by them,
When I found the one I love.
I held him and would not let him go,
Until I had brought him to the [a]house of my mother,
And into the [1]chamber of her who conceived me.

4 [1] Lit. *house of wine*
6 [a] Song 8:3
7 [a] Song 3:5; 8:4 [1] *adjure*
9 [a] Song 2:17
14 [a] Song 5:2 [b] Song 8:13 [1] Lit. *appearance*
15 [a] Ezek. 13:4
16 [a] Song 6:3
17 [a] Song 4:6 [b] Song 8:14 [1] Lit. *Separation*

CHAPTER 3
1 [a] Is. 26:9
3 [a] Song 5:7
4 [a] Song 8:2 [1] *room*

Song of Solomon 2:15

Dear Woman of Destiny,

God created us to be relational—first with Him and then with one another. As long as the relationship takes top priority, we seem to do well. But eventually, our personal desires and frustrations begin to speak to us more convincingly than the voice of wisdom. Look around you—you'll see it everywhere. Families breaking up because of alcohol, unfaithfulness, pornography. Children who've gone into the "far country" of drugs, sex, abortion. I'm talking about Christians—people who love God! How can it be?

I know what I've seen in my own life. I'm going to be as candid as possible with you, because I want you to know that the things I am sharing I struggle with myself. When I really look at these situations, the problem is not so much circumstances or other people as it is my own heart attitude. Most sin doesn't come at us with a big red ID tag on it. It sneaks up on us a little at a time, usually when we're offended, wounded, lonely, or afraid. Song of Solomon 2:15 says that the "little foxes" are the ones who spoil the vines. When we give a foothold to "little foxes," they begin to grow and soon crowd out and consume all the good fruit.

In marriage, it is so important to communicate openly and honestly with each other. It's not always easy to do. When I am hurt, frustrated, or irritated, I tend to pull away and get very distant. It is a real challenge for me to lay aside my rights for the sake of the relationship. Yet the Book of Romans clearly says that to follow Jesus I must die to myself (see Rom. 6:1–13) When I cling to my own rights, I become self-seeking and judgmental. Choosing to let go of my irritation and frustration is a real challenge, and it is not without cost.

I worry that we have been selling a cheap gospel lately; not clearly defining the cost of being committed to Christ. Galatians 2:20 says, "I have been crucified with Christ; it is no longer I who live, but Christ lives in me; and the life which I now live in the flesh I live by faith in the Son of God, who loved me and gave Himself for me." In other words, my agenda and my rights were nailed to the cross with Christ when I committed my life to Him. Dying to self is a daily choice that is never more challenged than in my relationships with others.

When the enemy can't find a way to attack me personally, you can bet the next place he'll try is my relationships with others. By staying in God's Word, praying, and routing out those "little foxes" whenever they appear, we build a wall of protection around our hearts and our loved ones. It's not something we do once and are done with. It requires attention. Stay vigilant!

Terry Meeuwsen

5 [a]I [1]charge you, O daughters of Jerusalem,
By the gazelles or by the does of the field,
Do not stir up nor awaken love
Until it pleases.

The Coming of Solomon

THE SHULAMITE

6 [a]Who *is* this coming out of the wilderness
Like pillars of smoke,
Perfumed with myrrh and frankincense,
With all the merchant's fragrant powders?
7 Behold, it *is* Solomon's couch,
With sixty valiant men around it,
Of the valiant of Israel.
8 They all hold swords,
Being expert in war.
Every man *has* his sword on his thigh
Because of fear in the night.

9 Of the wood of Lebanon
Solomon the King
Made himself a [1]palanquin:
10 He made its pillars *of* silver,
Its support *of* gold,
Its seat *of* purple,
Its interior paved *with* love
By the daughters of Jerusalem.
11 Go forth, O daughters of Zion,
And see King Solomon with the crown
With which his mother crowned him
On the day of his wedding,
The day of the gladness of his heart.

The Bridegroom Praises the Bride

THE BELOVED

4 Behold, [a]you *are* fair, my love!
Behold, you *are* fair!
You *have* dove's eyes behind your veil.
Your hair *is* like a [b]flock of goats,
Going down from Mount Gilead.
2 [a]Your teeth *are* like a flock of shorn *sheep*
Which have come up from the washing,
Every one of which bears twins,
And none *is* [1]barren among them.

5 [a] Song 2:7; 8:4
[1] adjure

6 [a] Song 8:5

9 [1] A portable enclosed chair

CHAPTER 4
1 [a] Song 1:15; 5:12
[b] Song 6:5

2 [a] Song 6:6
[1] bereaved

3 [a] Song 6:7

4 [a] Song 7:4
[b] Neh. 3:19
[1] Small shields

5 [a] Song 7:3

6 [a] Song 2:17

7 [a] Eph. 5:27

8 [a] Deut. 3:9

10 [a] Song 1:2, 4
[1] fragrance

3 Your lips *are* like a strand of scarlet,
And your mouth is lovely.
[a]Your temples behind your veil
Are like a piece of pomegranate.
4 [a]Your neck *is* like the tower of David,
Built [b]for an armory,
On which hang a thousand [1]bucklers,
All shields of mighty men.
5 [a]Your two breasts *are* like two fawns,
Twins of a gazelle,
Which feed among the lilies.

6 [a]Until the day breaks
And the shadows flee away,
I will go my way to the mountain of myrrh
And to the hill of frankincense.
7 [a]You *are* all fair, my love,
And *there is* no spot in you.
8 Come with me from Lebanon, *my* spouse,
With me from Lebanon.
Look from the top of Amana,
From the top of Senir [a]and Hermon,
From the lions' dens,
From the mountains of the leopards.

I have long since chosen Him for my only good, my all; my pleasure, my happiness in this world as in the world to come.

SUSANNA WESLEY

9 You have ravished my heart,
My sister, *my* spouse;
You have ravished my heart
With one *look* of your eyes,
With one link of your necklace.
10 How fair is your love,
My sister, *my* spouse!
[a]How much better than wine is your love,
And the [1]scent of your perfumes
Than all spices!
11 Your lips, O *my* spouse,
Drip as the honeycomb;

[a]Honey and milk *are* under your
tongue;
And the fragrance of your garments
Is [b]like the fragrance of Lebanon.

12 A garden [1]enclosed
Is my sister, *my* spouse,
A spring shut up,
A fountain sealed.
13 Your plants *are* an orchard of
pomegranates
With pleasant fruits,
Fragrant henna with spikenard,
14 Spikenard and saffron,
Calamus and cinnamon,
With all trees of frankincense,
Myrrh and aloes,
With all the chief spices—
15 A fountain of gardens,
A well of [a]living waters,
And streams from Lebanon.

THE SHULAMITE

16 Awake, O north *wind,*
And come, O south!
Blow upon my garden,
That its spices may flow out.
[a]Let my beloved come to his garden
And eat its pleasant [b]fruits.

THE BELOVED

5 I [a]have come to my garden, my [b]sister, *my* spouse;
I have gathered my myrrh with my
spice;
[c]I have eaten my honeycomb with
my honey;
I have drunk my wine with my
milk.

(TO HIS FRIENDS)

Eat, O [d]friends!
Drink, yes, drink deeply,
O beloved ones!

The Shulamite's Troubled Evening

THE SHULAMITE

2 I sleep, but my heart is awake;
It is the voice of my beloved!
[a]He knocks, *saying,*
"Open for me, my sister, [1]my love,
My dove, my perfect one;
For my head is covered with dew,
My [2]locks with the drops of the
night."

3 I have taken off my robe;
How can I put it on *again?*
I have washed my feet;
How can I [1]defile them?
4 My beloved put his hand
By the [1]latch *of the door,*
And my heart yearned for him.
5 I arose to open for my beloved,
And my hands dripped *with* myrrh,
My fingers with liquid myrrh,
On the handles of the lock.

O dear heart, if you have hunger, cherish and encourage that hunger as you would your life. It is put there by the Holy Spirit to lead you closer to God.

AIMEE SEMPLE MCPHERSON

6 I opened for my beloved,
But my beloved had turned away
and was gone.
My [1]heart leaped up when he
spoke.
[a]I sought him, but I could not find
him;
I called him, but he gave me no
answer.
7 [a]The watchmen who went about the
city found me.
They struck me, they wounded me;
The keepers of the walls
Took my veil away from me.
8 I charge you, O daughters of
Jerusalem,
If you find my beloved,
That you tell him I *am* lovesick!

THE DAUGHTERS OF JERUSALEM

9 What *is* your beloved
More than *another* beloved,
[a]O fairest among women?
What *is* your beloved
More than *another* beloved,
That you so [1]charge us?

THE SHULAMITE

10 My beloved *is* white and ruddy,
[1]Chief among ten thousand.
11 His head *is like* the finest gold;

---

11 a Prov. 24:13, 14 b Hos. 14:6, 7
12 *1 locked* or *barred*
15 a Zech. 14:8
16 a Song 5:1 b Song 7:13

CHAPTER 5
1 a Song 4:16 b Song 4:9 c Song 4:11 d Luke 15:7, 10
2 a Rev. 3:20 *1 my companion, friend* *2 curls* or *hair*
3 *1 dirty*
4 *1 opening*
6 a Song 3:1 *1* Lit. *soul*
7 a Song 3:3
9 a Song 1:8; 6:1 *1 adjure*
10 *1 Distinguished*

His locks *are* wavy,
And black as a raven.
12 [a]His eyes *are* like doves
By the rivers of waters,
Washed with milk,
And [1]fitly set.
13 His cheeks *are* like a bed of spices,
Banks of scented herbs.
His lips *are* lilies,
Dripping liquid myrrh.

14 His hands *are* rods of gold
Set with beryl.
His body *is* carved ivory
Inlaid *with* sapphires.
15 His legs *are* pillars of marble
Set on bases of fine gold.
His countenance *is* like Lebanon,
Excellent as the cedars.
16 His mouth *is* most sweet,
Yes, he *is* altogether lovely.
This *is* my beloved,
And this *is* my friend,
O daughters of Jerusalem!

THE DAUGHTERS OF JERUSALEM

6 Where has your beloved gone,
[a]O fairest among women?
Where has your beloved turned aside,
That we may seek him with you?

THE SHULAMITE

2 My beloved has gone to his [a]garden,
To the beds of spices,
To feed *his flock* in the gardens,
And to gather lilies.
3 [a]I *am* my beloved's,
And my beloved *is* mine.
He feeds *his flock* among the lilies.

Praise of the Shulamite's Beauty

THE BELOVED

4 O my love, you *are as* beautiful as Tirzah,
Lovely as Jerusalem,
Awesome as *an army* with banners!
5 Turn your eyes away from me,
For they have [1]overcome me.
Your hair *is* [a]like a flock of goats
Going down from Gilead.
6 [a]Your teeth *are* like a flock of sheep
Which have come up from the washing;
Every one bears twins,
And none *is* [1]barren among them.
7 [a]Like a piece of pomegranate
Are your temples behind your veil.

8 There are sixty queens
And eighty concubines,
And [a]virgins without number.
9 My dove, my [a]perfect one,
Is the only one,
The only one of her mother,
The favorite of the one who bore her.
The daughters saw her
And called her blessed,
The queens and the concubines,
And they praised her.

10 Who is she who looks forth as the morning,
Fair as the moon,
Clear as the sun,
[a]Awesome as *an army* with banners?

THE SHULAMITE

11 I went down to the garden of nuts
To see the verdure of the valley,
[a]To see whether the vine had budded
And the pomegranates had bloomed.
12 Before I was even aware,
My soul had made me
As the chariots of [1]my noble people.

THE BELOVED AND HIS FRIENDS

13 Return, return, O Shulamite;
Return, return, that we may look upon you!

THE SHULAMITE

What would you see in the Shulamite—
As it were, the dance of [1]the two camps?

Expressions of Praise

THE BELOVED

7 How beautiful are your feet in sandals,
[a]O prince's daughter!
The curves of your thighs *are* like jewels,
The work of the hands of a skillful workman.
2 Your navel *is* a rounded goblet;
It lacks no [1]blended beverage.
Your waist *is* a heap of wheat

12 [a]Song 1:15; 4:1 [1]*sitting in a setting*

CHAPTER 6
1 [a]Song 1:8; 5:9
2 [a]Song 4:16; 5:1
3 [a]Song 2:16; 7:10
5 [a]Song 4:1 [1]*overwhelmed*
6 [a]Song 4:2 [1]*bereaved*
7 [a]Song 4:3
8 [a]Song 1:3
9 [a]Song 2:14; 5:2
10 [a]Song 6:4
11 [a]Song 7:12
12 [1]Heb. *Ammi Nadib*
13 [1]Heb. *Mahanaim*

CHAPTER 7
1 [a]Ps. 45:13
2 [1]Lit. *mixed* or *spiced drink*

Song of Solomon 7:10

Dear Woman of Destiny,

Our precious Savior and Lord Jesus Christ is our Beloved Bridegroom and we, the Church, are represented as the Shulamite bride in the Song of Solomon. Our Beloved has a fiery, passionate love for you—so intense that He gave up everything and left His heavenly home to walk and live among sinful humankind. He willingly experienced unfathomable suffering and poured out His blood for you on the cross two thousand years ago. If you were the only one on earth for whom Jesus had to die, He would do it all over again.

Christ's experience on the cross was the ultimate example of selflessness and the epitome of passion. The word *passion* means "to endure and to suffer." It connotes an overwhelming intensity of feeling, emotion, and affection. I believe that Jesus' passion was motivated by His deep devotion and obedience to the Father. He and the Father are one. The desires of the Father's heart are His. His love for the Father was expressed in His complete trust in and commitment to Him.

Now He desires an intimate relationship with His children. In order to become intimate, you must trust. But you say, "I can't trust. I have been betrayed and violated!" So was Jesus—on the cross, for your sake and mine! Ask Him for the grace to help you trust Him. He will neither leave you nor forsake you as others have and will. Open up your heart, and let Him in on your most secret thoughts and failures. You are accepted in the Beloved no matter what you have been through. He has plans to do you good and not harm, and to prosper you in all your ways for all of your days (see Jer. 29:11).

Jesus never had a thought, word, or deed that was contrary or out of alignment with the Father's will; and this is His desire for you. He made the choice to do whatever was necessary to win you and have you as His own. The word for *desire* in Strong's (#8669) carries the sense of stretching out after, longing for, running after, overflowing—like water. Our Beloved is stretching out after you, calling you to come spend time with Him and get to know Him better. Are you close enough that you sense the throbbing of His heartbeat for the lost? Are you still enough in His presence to hear the sound of His voice of wisdom, counsel, and correction in a whisper?

You can enjoy sweet fellowship with Him and, in time, become more like Him. If you wait for Him and persevere in His presence, you will find that He will flow over you with His Holy Spirit like a refreshing, cleansing stream.

The Beloved takes great delight in you, Woman of Destiny. Every time He glances into your eyes, you make His heart beat faster!

Pat Chen

Set about with lilies.
3 [a]Your two breasts *are* like two fawns,
Twins of a gazelle.
4 [a]Your neck *is* like an ivory tower,
Your eyes *like* the pools in Heshbon
By the gate of Bath Rabbim.
Your nose *is* like the tower of Lebanon
Which looks toward Damascus.
5 Your head *crowns* you like *Mount* Carmel,
And the hair of your head *is* like purple;
A king *is* held captive by *your* tresses.
6 How fair and how pleasant you are,
O love, with your delights!
7 This stature of yours is like a palm tree,
And your breasts *like* its clusters.
8 I said, "I will go up to the palm tree,
I will take hold of its branches."
Let now your breasts be like clusters of the vine,
The fragrance of your [1]breath like apples,
9 And the roof of your mouth like the best wine.

THE SHULAMITE

The wine goes *down* smoothly for my beloved,
[1]Moving gently the [2]lips of sleepers.
10 [a]I *am* my beloved's,
And [b]his desire *is* toward me.

Christ is seeking the affection of mankind, the union of their spirit with His.

JOHN G. LAKE

11 Come, my beloved,
Let us go forth to the field;
Let us lodge in the villages.
12 Let us get up early to the vineyards;
Let us [a]see if the vine has budded,
Whether the grape blossoms are open,
And the pomegranates are in bloom.
There I will give you my love.
13 The [a]mandrakes give off a fragrance,
And at our gates [b]*are* pleasant *fruits,*
All manner, new and old,
Which I have laid up for you, my beloved.

8 Oh, that you were like my brother,
Who nursed at my mother's breasts!
If I should find you outside,
I would kiss you;
I would not be despised.
2 I would lead you *and* bring you
Into the [a]house of my mother,
She *who* used to instruct me.
I would cause you to drink of [b]spiced wine,
Of the juice of my pomegranate.

(TO THE DAUGHTERS OF JERUSALEM)

3 [a]His left hand *is* under my head,
And his right hand embraces me.
4 [a]I charge you, O daughters of Jerusalem,
Do not stir up nor awaken love
Until it pleases.

Love Renewed in Lebanon

A RELATIVE

5 [a]Who *is* this coming up from the wilderness,
Leaning upon her beloved?
I awakened you under the apple tree.
There your mother brought you forth;
There she *who* bore you brought *you* forth.

THE SHULAMITE TO HER BELOVED

6 [a]Set me as a seal upon your heart,
As a seal upon your arm;
For love *is as* strong as death,
[b]Jealousy *as* [1]cruel as [2]the grave;
Its flames *are* flames of fire,
[3]A most vehement flame.
7 Many waters cannot quench love,
Nor can the floods drown it.
[a]If a man would give for love
All the wealth of his house,
It would be utterly despised.

3 [a]Song 4:5
4 [a]Song 4:4
8 [1]Lit. *nose*
9 [1]*Gliding over* [2]LXX, Syr., Vg. *lips and teeth.*
10 [a]Song 2:16; 6:3 [b]Ps. 45:11
12 [a]Song 6:11
13 [a]Gen. 30:14 [b]Matt. 13:52
CHAPTER 8
2 [a]Song 3:4 [b]Prov. 9:2
3 [a]Song 2:6
4 [a]Song 2:7; 3:5
5 [a]Song 3:6
6 [a]Jer. 22:24 [b]Prov. 6:34, 35 [1]*severe,* lit. *hard* [2]Or *Sheol* [3]Lit. *A flame of YAH,* poetic form of *YHWH, the LORD*
7 [a]Prov. 6:35

Song of Solomon 8:4

Dear Woman of Destiny,

I realize this article may be probing into a very personal part of your life, but this is one area where we should all do some deep thinking. After all, the whole human race began with a relationship; and for the time being, it looks like it is going to continue that way!

If you are unmarried and have been facing the possibility of choosing a lifelong mate, let me caution you: Walk with your feet on the ground and your eyes on the Lord. Next to making a commitment to follow Jesus, the marriage commitment is, without a doubt, the most important decision you will ever make!

Love is a commitment, and no one can make a faithful and unwavering commitment to someone they don't know. Many attractions are completely foolish. Often people find themselves daydreaming about someone they've seen once or twice at school or work. The daydreamer begins carrying on an imaginary relationship in her head with this person. The entire basis of her affections is founded on what she *imagines* that person to be like, instead of what they really are.

But other times attractions can be more serious. Occasionally these desires toward the opposite sex can seem overpowering, but the only way to control these feelings is by making the right choices and drawing closer to God. Though it is not a sin to be attracted to someone, what you decide to do with that attraction can be. Since our romantic desires are often stronger than we are, the first thing you should do if you like someone is talk to your Father about it. No, I didn't say, "Talk to your best friend about it . . . "; I said talk to your Father in heaven about it. Ask His permission. Oftentimes we run to our friends because we want their approval; we long to hear them say, "Oh, the two of you would go so well together!" But what we should really be seeking is God's opinion—His counsel. All too often we are afraid He'll just say, "Wait," or worse, "This person is not the right one for you." Yet, if we are not interested in obeying God, all the counsel in heaven will do us no good!

If you really want to do what's right, then don't feed your desire; yield it to God. I recently heard somebody say, "The quickest way to let something die is to quit feeding it." You should also go and get counsel from a pastor, or an older brother or sister in the Lord, for "by pride comes nothing but strife, but with the well-advised is wisdom" (Prov. 13:10).

God has made available to us a love that "never fails," but many of us have mixed it with our foolish romantic notions and desires. If while reading this article you have found yourself guilty of any of the mistakes mentioned, then ask God to forgive you, and change your ways—and for God's sake, become part of the solution! By becoming "imitators of God as dear children . . . walk in love, as Christ also has loved us and given Himself for us, an offering and a sacrifice to God for a sweet-smelling aroma" (Eph. 5:1, 2).

Kathleen Dillard

THE SHULAMITE'S BROTHERS

8 [a]We have a little sister,
And she has no breasts.
What shall we do for our sister
In the day when she is spoken for?

Lord, thank You that many waters cannot quench love, nor can the floods drown it. I pray that You would strengthen the love between _____ and their spouse. Lord, bless their marriage!

FROM SONG OF SOLOMON 8:7

9 If she *is* a wall,
We will build upon her
A battlement of silver;
And if she *is* a door,
We will enclose her
With boards of cedar.

THE SHULAMITE

10 I *am* a wall,
And my breasts like towers;
Then I became in his eyes
As one who found peace.
11 Solomon had a vineyard at Baal
Hamon;
[a]He leased the vineyard to keepers;
Everyone was to bring for its fruit
A thousand silver coins.

(TO SOLOMON)

12 My own vineyard *is* before me.
You, O Solomon, *may have* a
thousand,
And those who tend its fruit two
hundred.

THE BELOVED

13 You who dwell in the gardens,
The companions listen for your
voice—
[a]Let me hear it!

THE SHULAMITE

14 [a]Make[1] haste, my beloved,
And [b]be like a gazelle
Or a young stag
On the mountains of spices.

Many waters cannot quench this little spark which the Lord hath kindled, neither shall the floods of persecution drown it.

CHARLES WESLEY

8 a Ezek. 23:33
11 a Matt. 21:33
13 a Song 2:14
14 a Rev. 22:17, 20 b Song 2:7, 9, 17
1 *Hurry*, lit. *Flee*

AUTHOR: *Isaiah*
DATE: *Approximately 700–690 B.C.*
THEME: *Salvation*
KEY IDEAS: *Judgment of Sin, Messianic Promise*
KEY WORDS: *Salvation, Redeemer, Righteousness, Peace, Comfort*

ISAIAH

Dear Woman of Destiny,

In the Book of Isaiah we find a "miniature Bible": The first division has thirty-nine chapters—the number of Old Testament books—and emphasizes judgment; the second division has twenty-seven chapters—the number of New Testament books—and stresses grace. Let Isaiah's prophetic presentation of the Messiah and His mercy touch the deep places in your heart as you read and meditate.

His love and mine,

Marilyn Hickey

The [a]vision of Isaiah the son of Amoz, which he saw concerning Judah and Jerusalem in the [b]days of Uzziah, Jotham, Ahaz, *and* Hezekiah, kings of Judah.

The Wickedness of Judah

2 [a]Hear, O heavens, and give ear,
O earth!
For the LORD has spoken:
"I have nourished and brought up
children,
And they have rebelled against Me;
3 [a]The ox knows its owner
And the donkey its master's [1]crib;
But Israel [b]does not know,
My people do not [2]consider."

4 Alas, sinful nation,
A people [1]laden with iniquity,
[a]A [2]brood of evildoers,
Children who are corrupters!
They have forsaken the LORD,
They have provoked to anger
The Holy One of Israel,
They have turned away backward.

5 [a]Why should you be stricken again?
You will revolt more and more.
The whole head is sick,
And the whole heart faints.
6 From the sole of the foot even to
the head,
There is no soundness in it,
But wounds and bruises and
putrefying sores;
They have not been closed or bound
up,
Or soothed with ointment.

7 [a]Your country *is* desolate,
Your cities *are* burned with fire;
Strangers devour your land in your
presence;
And *it is* desolate, as overthrown by
strangers.
8 So the daughter of Zion is left [a]as
a [1]booth in a vineyard,
As a hut in a garden of cucumbers,
[b]As a besieged city.
9 [a]Unless the LORD of hosts
Had left to us a very small
remnant,
We would have become like
[b]Sodom,
We would have been made like
Gomorrah.

10 Hear the word of the LORD,
You rulers [a]of Sodom;
Give ear to the law of our God,
You people of Gomorrah:
11 "To what purpose *is* the multitude
of your [a]sacrifices to Me?"
Says the LORD.
"I have had enough of burnt
offerings of rams
And the fat of fed cattle.
I do not delight in the blood of
bulls,
Or of lambs or goats.

12 "When you come [a]to appear before
Me,
Who has required this from your
hand,
To trample My courts?
13 Bring no more [a]futile[1] sacrifices;
Incense is an abomination to Me.
The New Moons, the Sabbaths, and
[b]the calling of assemblies—
I cannot endure iniquity and the
sacred meeting.
14 Your [a]New Moons and your
[b]appointed feasts
My soul hates;
They are a trouble to Me,
I am weary of bearing *them.*
15 [a]When you [1]spread out your hands,
I will hide My eyes from you;
[b]Even though you make many
prayers,
I will not hear.
Your hands are full of [2]blood.

16 "Wash[a] yourselves, make yourselves
clean;
Put away the evil of your doings
from before My eyes.
[b]Cease to do evil,
17 Learn to do good;
Seek justice,
Rebuke [1]the oppressor;
[2]Defend the fatherless,
Plead for the widow.

18 "Come now, and let us [a]reason
together,"
Says the LORD,
"Though your sins are like scarlet,
[b]They shall be as white as snow;
Though they are red like crimson,
They shall be as wool.
19 If you are willing and obedient,
You shall eat the good of the land;
20 But if you refuse and rebel,
You shall be devoured by the
sword";
[a]For the mouth of the LORD has
spoken.

CHAPTER 1
1 a Num. 12:6 b 2 Chr. 26—32
2 a Jer. 2:12
3 a Jer. 8:7 b Jer. 9:3, 6 *1 manger* or *feed trough* *2 understand*
4 a Matt. 3:7 *1* Lit. *heavy, weighed down* *2 offspring, seed*
5 a Jer. 5:3
7 a Deut. 28:51, 52
8 a Job 27:18 b Jer. 4:17 *1 shelter*
9 a Lam. 3:22 b Gen. 19:24
10 a Deut. 32:32
11 a [1 Sam. 15:22]
12 a Ex. 23:17
13 a Matt. 15:9 b Joel 1:14 *1 worthless*
14 a Num. 28:11 b Lam. 2:6
15 a Prov. 1:28 b Mic. 3:4 *1* Pray *2 bloodshed*
16 a Jer. 4:14 b Rom. 12:9
17 *1* Some ancient vss. *the oppressed* *2 Vindicate*
18 a Is. 43:26 b Ps. 51:7
20 a [Titus 1:2]

Isaiah 1:18

Dear Woman of Destiny,

Have you ever tried to compare yourself with women of the Bible? I have, but I never measure up to such "greats" as Ruth, Esther, Sarah or Mary, the mother of Jesus. I identify more with the woman Jesus met at the well, the other Mary, Mary Magdalene, or the woman caught in the act of adultery—yes, all the "scarlet women."

Thank God for Isaiah 1:18! This scripture is an Old Testament forecast of what happens when Jesus' blood is applied to our sins. The "scarlet" and "crimson" in this verse refer to the double-dye process used to permanently color fabric in Bible days—to make white wool such a deep red, the color would not fade, no matter how many times it was washed.

This is how I felt. No matter how many showers I took, I could not clean myself up. My sin had become permanent, destroying my life. At the age of 14 I fell into a life of sex, drugs, and rock 'n' roll. Longing for love and acceptance I married at 17; but instead of cherishing and nurturing me, my husband physically and emotionally abused me. The woman at the well had five husbands; by the time I was 22, I had had five abortions. My life was more like that of the woman, caught in the "very act" of adultery, whom the scribes and the Pharisees brought to Jesus, than like that of a woman of God. I did not feel worthy to come to Jesus. In no way did I feel like a "woman of destiny."

On Easter Sunday, 1989, I wandered into a wonderful church and heard the pastor tell me that I could be forgiven and saved by grace; I didn't have to do it myself. That day my sins, which were permanently double-dyed like scarlet, became white as snow. And for the next ten years, I went through God's training program, conducted by the people of the church. Little did I know that God was preparing me to speak to millions of women and that I would be an instrument to help heal their scars from abortion, drugs, and sinful living. Nor did I know that He was also preparing me to be the wife of Jim Bakker. But I'm beginning to learn that broken and wounded people make the best healers.

Woman of Destiny, Jesus can do the same for you. One of the most awesome Scriptures, and one of my favorites is: "And you, who once were alienated and enemies in your mind by wicked works, yet now He has reconciled in the body of His flesh through [Christ's death on the cross], to present you holy, and blameless, and above reproach in His sight" (Col. 1:21, 22). Yes, Jesus will heal your sin and make you holy, blameless, and above reproach through His blood, not your works. No matter what you have done, when you seek and accept the Lord's forgiveness, you are clean. You are made whiter than snow! Jesus makes life new. Believe it and receive it!

Lori Graham Bakker

The Degenerate City

21 [a]How the faithful city has become
a [1]harlot!
It was full of justice;
Righteousness lodged in it,
But now [b]murderers.
22 [a]Your silver has become dross,
Your wine mixed with water.
23 [a]Your princes *are* rebellious,
And [b]companions of thieves;
[c]Everyone loves bribes,
And follows after rewards.
They [d]do not defend the fatherless,
Nor does the cause of the widow
come before them.

24 Therefore the Lord says,
The LORD of hosts, the Mighty One
of Israel,
"Ah, [a]I will [1]rid Myself of My
adversaries,
And [2]take vengeance on My
enemies.
25 I will turn My hand against you,
And [a]thoroughly[1] purge away your
dross,
And take away all your alloy.
26 I will restore your judges [a]as at
the first,
And your counselors as at the
beginning.
Afterward [b]you shall be called the
city of righteousness, the faithful
city."

27 Zion shall be redeemed with
justice,
And her [1]penitents with
righteousness.
28 The [a]destruction of transgressors
and of sinners *shall be* together,
And those who forsake the LORD
shall be consumed.
29 For [1]they shall be ashamed of the
[2]terebinth trees
Which you have desired;
And you shall be embarrassed
because of the gardens
Which you have chosen.
30 For you shall be as a terebinth
whose leaf fades,
And as a garden that has no water.
31 [a]The strong shall be as tinder,
And the work of it as a spark;
Both will burn together,
And no one shall [b]quench *them.*

21 [a]Jer. 2:20 [b]Mic. 3:1–3 [1]Unfaithful
22 [a]Jer. 6:28
23 [a]Hos. 9:15 [b]Prov. 29:24 [c]Jer. 22:17 [d]Jer. 5:28
24 [a]Deut. 28:63 [1]*be relieved of* [2]*avenge Myself*
25 [a]Mal. 3:3 [1]*refine with lye*
26 [a]Jer. 33:7–11 [b]Zech. 8:3
27 [1]Lit. *returners*
28 [a][2 Thess. 1:8, 9]
29 [1]So with MT, LXX, Vg.; some Heb. mss., Tg. *you* [2]Sites of pagan worship
31 [a]Ezek. 32:21 [b]Mark 9:43

CHAPTER 2
2 [a]Mic. 4:1 [b]Gen. 49:1 [c]Ps. 68:15
3 [a]Jer. 50:5 [b]Luke 24:47
4 [1]*knives*
5 [a]Eph. 5:8
6 [a]Num. 23:7 [b]Deut. 18:14 [c]Ps. 106:35 [1]Or *clap, shake hands to make bargains with the children*
7 [a]Deut. 17:16
8 [a]Jer. 2:28

The Future House of God

2 The word that Isaiah the son of Amoz
saw concerning Judah and Jerusalem.

2 Now [a]it shall come to pass [b]in the
latter days
[c]*That* the mountain of the LORD's
house
Shall be established on the top of
the mountains,
And shall be exalted above the hills;
And all nations shall flow to it.
3 Many people shall come and say,
[a]"Come, and let us go up to the
mountain of the LORD,
To the house of the God of Jacob;
He will teach us His ways,
And we shall walk in His paths."
[b]For out of Zion shall go forth the
law,
And the word of the LORD from
Jerusalem.
4 He shall judge between the
nations,
And rebuke many people;
They shall beat their swords into
plowshares,
And their spears into pruning
[1]hooks;
Nation shall not lift up sword
against nation,
Neither shall they learn war
anymore.

The Day of the Lord

5 O house of Jacob, come and let us
[a]walk
In the light of the LORD.
6 For You have forsaken Your people,
the house of Jacob,
Because they are filled [a]with
eastern ways;
They *are* [b]soothsayers like the
Philistines,
[c]And they [1]are pleased with the
children of foreigners.
7 [a]Their land is also full of silver and
gold,
And there is no end to their
treasures;
Their land is also full of horses,
And there is no end to their
chariots.
8 [a]Their land is also full of idols;
They worship the work of their own
hands,
That which their own fingers have
made.

9 People bow down,
And each man humbles himself;
Therefore do not forgive them.

10 [a]Enter into the rock, and hide in the dust,
From the terror of the LORD
And the glory of His majesty.
11 The [1]lofty looks of man shall be [a]humbled,
The haughtiness of men shall be bowed down,
And the LORD alone shall be exalted [b]in that day.

12 For the day of the LORD of hosts
Shall come upon everything proud and lofty,
Upon everything lifted up—
And it shall be brought low—
13 Upon all [a]the cedars of Lebanon *that are* high and lifted up,
And upon all the oaks of Bashan;
14 [a]Upon all the high mountains,
And upon all the hills *that are* lifted up;
15 Upon every high tower,
And upon every fortified wall;
16 [a]Upon all the ships of Tarshish,
And upon all the beautiful sloops.
17 The [1]loftiness of man shall be bowed down,
And the haughtiness of men shall be brought low;
The LORD alone will be exalted in that day,
18 But the idols [1]He shall utterly abolish.
19 They shall go into the [a]holes of the rocks,
And into the caves of the [1]earth,
[b]From the terror of the LORD
And the glory of His majesty,
When He arises [c]to shake the earth mightily.
20 In that day a man will cast away his idols of silver
And his idols of gold,
Which they made, *each* for himself to worship,
To the moles and bats,
21 To go into the clefts of the rocks,
And into the crags of the rugged rocks,
From the terror of the LORD
And the glory of His majesty,
When He arises to shake the earth mightily.

10 a Rev. 6:15, 16
11 a Prov. 16:5 b Hos. 2:16 1 *proud*
13 a Zech. 11:1, 2
14 a Is. 30:25
16 a 1 Kin. 10:22
17 1 *pride*
18 1 Or *shall utterly vanish*
19 a Hos. 10:8 b [2 Thess. 1:9] c Hag. 2:6, 7 1 Lit. *dust*
22 a Jer. 17:5 b Job 27:3 1 Lit. *Cease yourselves from the man* 2 Lit. *in what is he to be esteemed*

CHAPTER 3
1 a Jer. 37:21 b Lev. 26:26 1 Every support
2 a 2 Kin. 24:14
3 1 Eminent looking men
4 a Eccl. 10:16 1 *boys* 2 Or *capricious ones*
5 1 *aged* 2 *despised, lightly esteemed*
6 1 Lit. *hand*
8 a Mic. 3:12
9 a Gen. 13:13

22 [a]Sever[1] yourselves from such a man,
Whose [b]breath *is* in his nostrils;
For [2]of what account is he?

Judgment on Judah and Jerusalem

3 For behold, the Lord, the LORD of hosts,
[a]Takes away from Jerusalem and from Judah
[b]The[1] stock and the store,
The whole supply of bread and the whole supply of water;
2 [a]The mighty man and the man of war,
The judge and the prophet,
And the diviner and the elder;
3 The captain of fifty and the [1]honorable man,
The counselor and the skillful artisan,
And the expert enchanter.

4 "I will give [a]children[1] *to be* their princes,
And [2]babes shall rule over them.
5 The people will be oppressed,
Every one by another and every one by his neighbor;
The child will be insolent toward the [1]elder,
And the [2]base toward the honorable."

6 When a man takes hold of his brother
In the house of his father, *saying*,
"You have clothing;
You be our ruler,
And *let* these ruins *be* under your [1]power,"
7 In that day he will protest, saying,
"I cannot cure *your* ills,
For in my house *is* neither food nor clothing;
Do not make me a ruler of the people."

8 For [a]Jerusalem stumbled,
And Judah is fallen,
Because their tongue and their doings
Are against the LORD,
To provoke the eyes of His glory.
9 The look on their countenance witnesses against them,
And they declare their sin as [a]Sodom;

They do not hide *it*.
Woe to their soul!
For they have brought evil upon
themselves.

10 "Say to the righteous [a]that *it shall be* well *with them,*
[b]For they shall eat the fruit of their doings.
11 Woe to the wicked! [a]*It shall be* ill *with him,*
For the reward of his hands shall be [1]given him.
12 *As for* My people, children *are* their oppressors,
And women rule over them.
O My people! [a]Those who lead you [1]cause *you* to err,
And destroy the way of your paths."

Oppression and Luxury Condemned

13 The LORD stands up [a]to [1]plead,
And stands to judge the people.
14 The LORD will enter into judgment
With the elders of His people
And His princes:
"For you have [1]eaten up [a]the vineyard;
The plunder of the poor *is* in your houses.
15 What do you mean by [a]crushing My people
And grinding the faces of the poor?"
Says the Lord GOD of hosts.

16 Moreover the LORD says:

"Because the daughters of Zion are haughty,
And walk with [1]outstretched necks
And [2]wanton eyes,
Walking and [3]mincing *as* they go,
Making a jingling with their feet,
17 Therefore the Lord will strike with [a]a scab
The crown of the head of the daughters of Zion,
And the LORD will [b]uncover their secret parts."

18 In that day the Lord will take away the finery:
The jingling anklets, the [1]scarves, and the [a]crescents;
19 The pendants, the bracelets, and the veils;
20 The headdresses, the leg ornaments, and the headbands;
The perfume boxes, the charms,
21 and the rings;
The nose jewels,
22 the festal apparel, and the mantles;
The outer garments, the purses,
23 and the mirrors;
The fine linen, the turbans, and the robes.

24 And so it shall be:

Instead of a sweet smell there will be a stench;
Instead of a sash, a rope;
Instead of well-set hair, [a]baldness;
Instead of a rich robe, a girding of sackcloth;
And [1]branding instead of beauty.
25 Your men shall fall by the sword,
And your [1]mighty in the war.
26 [a]Her gates shall lament and mourn,
And she *being* desolate [b]shall sit on the ground.

4 And [a]in that day seven women shall
take hold of one man, saying,

"We will [b]eat our own food and wear our own apparel;
Only let us be called by your name,
To take away [c]our reproach."

The Renewal of Zion

2 In that day [a]the Branch of the LORD shall be beautiful and glorious;
And the fruit of the earth *shall be* excellent and appealing
For those of Israel who have escaped.

3 And it shall come to pass that *he who*
is left in Zion and remains in Jerusalem
[a]will be called holy—everyone who is [b]re-
corded among the living in Jerusalem.
4 When [a]the Lord has washed away the
filth of the daughters of Zion, and purged
the [1]blood of Jerusalem from her midst,
by the spirit of judgment and by the spirit
of burning, 5 then the LORD will create
above every dwelling place of Mount Zion,
and above her assemblies, [a]a cloud and
smoke by day and [b]the shining of a flaming fire by night. For over all the glory
there *will be* a [1]covering. 6 And there will
be a tabernacle for shade in the daytime
from the heat, [a]for a place of refuge, and
for a shelter from storm and rain.

---

10 a [Eccl. 8:12] b Ps. 128:2
11 a [Ps. 11:6] *1 done to him*
12 a Is. 9:16 *1 lead you astray*
13 a Mic. 6:2 *1 contend, plead His case*
14 a Matt. 21:33 *1 burned*
15 a Mic. 3:2, 3
16 *1* Head held high *2 seductive, ogling* *3 tripping* or *skipping*
17 a Deut. 28:27 b Jer. 13:22
18 a Judg. 8:21, 26 *1 headbands*
24 a Is. 22:12 *1 burning scar*
25 *1* Lit. *strength*
26 a Jer. 14:2 b Lam. 2:10

CHAPTER 4
1 a Is. 2:11, 17 b 2 Thess. 3:12 c Luke 1:25
2 a [Jer. 23:5]
3 a Is. 60:21 b Phil. 4:3
4 a Mal. 3:2, 3 *1 bloodshed*
5 a Ex. 13:21, 22 b Zech. 2:5 *1 canopy*
6 a Is. 25:4

God's Disappointing Vineyard

5 Now let me sing to my Well-beloved
A song of my Beloved [a]regarding
His vineyard:

My Well-beloved has a vineyard
[1]On a very fruitful hill.
2 He dug it up and cleared out its
stones,
And planted it with the choicest
vine.
He built a tower in its midst,
And also [1]made a winepress in it;
[a]So He expected *it* to bring forth
good grapes,
But it brought forth wild grapes.

3 "And now, O inhabitants of
Jerusalem and men of Judah,
[a]Judge, please, between Me and My
vineyard.
4 What more could have been done
to My vineyard
That I have not done in [a]it?
Why then, when I expected *it* to
bring forth *good* grapes,
Did it bring forth wild grapes?
5 And now, please let Me tell you
what I will do to My vineyard:
[a]I will take away its hedge, and it
shall be burned;
And break down its wall, and it
shall be trampled down.
6 I will lay it [a]waste;
It shall not be pruned or [1]dug,
But there shall come up briers and
[b]thorns.
I will also command the clouds
That they rain no rain on it."

7 For the vineyard of the LORD of
hosts *is* the house of Israel,
And the men of Judah are His
pleasant plant.
He looked for justice, but behold,
oppression;
For righteousness, but behold, [1]a
cry *for help*.

Impending Judgment on Excesses

8 Woe to those who [1]join [a]house to
house;
They add field to field,
Till *there is* no place
Where they may dwell alone in the
midst of the land!
9 [a]In my hearing the LORD of hosts
said,
"Truly, many houses shall be
desolate,
Great and beautiful ones, without
inhabitant.
10 For ten acres of vineyard shall
yield one [a]bath,[1]
And a homer of seed shall yield one
[2]ephah."

11 [a]Woe to those who rise early in the
morning,
That they may [1]follow intoxicating
drink;
Who continue until night, *till* wine
inflames them!
12 [a]The harp and the strings,
The tambourine and flute,
And wine are in their feasts;
But [b]they do not regard the work
of the LORD,
Nor consider the operation of His
hands.

13 [a]Therefore my people have gone
into captivity,
Because *they have* no [b]knowledge;
Their honorable men *are* famished,
And their multitude dried up with
thirst.
14 Therefore Sheol has enlarged itself
And opened its mouth beyond
measure;
Their glory and their multitude and
their pomp,
And he who is jubilant, shall
descend into it.
15 People shall be brought down,
[a]Each man shall be humbled,
And the eyes of the lofty shall be
humbled.
16 But the LORD of hosts shall be
[a]exalted in judgment,
And God who is holy shall be
hallowed in righteousness.
17 Then the lambs shall feed in their
pasture,
And in the waste places of [a]the [1]fat
ones strangers shall eat.

18 Woe to those who [1]draw iniquity
with cords of [2]vanity,
And sin as if with a cart rope;
19 [a]That say, "Let Him make speed
and hasten His work,
That we may see *it;*
And let the counsel of the Holy One
of Israel draw near and come,
That we may know *it*."

CHAPTER 5
1 [a]Matt. 21:33 [1]Lit. *In a horn, the son of fatness*
2 [a]Deut. 32:6 [1]Lit. *hewed out*
3 [a][Rom. 3:4]
4 [a]2 Chr. 36:15, 16
5 [a]Ps. 80:12; 89:40, 41
6 [a]2 Chr. 36:19–21 [b]Is. 7:19–25 [1]*hoed*
7 [1]*wailing*
8 [a]Mic. 2:2 [1]Accumulate houses
9 [a]Is. 22:14
10 [a]Ezek. 45:11 [1]1 bath = 1/10 homer [2]1 ephah = 1/10 homer
11 [a]Prov. 23:29, 30 [1]*pursue*
12 [a]Amos 6:5 [b]Job 34:27
13 [a]2 Kin. 24:14–16 [b]Hos. 4:6
15 [a]Is. 2:9, 11
16 [a]Is. 2:11
17 [a]Is. 10:16 [1]Lit. *fatlings*, rich ones
18 [1]*drag* [2]*emptiness* or *falsehood*
19 [a]Jer. 17:15

20 Woe to those who call evil good,
and good evil;
Who put darkness for light, and
light for darkness;
Who put bitter for sweet, and sweet
for bitter!

21 Woe to *those who are* [a]wise in
their own eyes,
And prudent in their own sight!

22 Woe to men mighty at drinking
wine,
Woe to men valiant for mixing
intoxicating drink,

23 Who [a]justify the wicked for a
bribe,
And take away justice from the
righteous man!

24 Therefore, [a]as the [1]fire devours
the stubble,
And the flame consumes the chaff,
So [b]their root will be as rottenness,
And their blossom will ascend like
dust;
Because they have rejected the law
of the LORD of hosts,
And despised the word of the Holy
One of Israel.

25 [a]Therefore the anger of the LORD is
aroused against His people;
He has stretched out His hand
against them
And stricken them,
And [b]the hills trembled.
Their carcasses *were* as refuse in
the midst of the streets.

[c]For all this His anger is not turned
away,
But His hand *is* stretched out still.

26 [a]He will lift up a banner to the
nations from afar,
And will [b]whistle to them from [c]the
end of the earth;
Surely [d]they shall come with speed,
swiftly.

27 No one will be weary or stumble
among them,
No one will slumber or sleep;
Nor [a]will the belt on their loins be
loosed,
Nor the strap of their sandals be
broken;

28 [a]Whose arrows *are* sharp,
And all their bows bent;
Their horses' hooves will [1]seem like
flint,
And their wheels like a whirlwind.

21 [a]Rom. 1:22; 12:16
23 [a]Prov. 17:15
24 [a]Ex. 15:7 [b]Job 18:16 [1]Lit. *tongue of fire*
25 [a]2 Kin. 22:13, 17 [b]Jer. 4:24 [c]Is. 9:12, 17
26 [a]Is. 11:10, 12 [b]Is. 7:18 [c]Mal. 1:11 [d]Joel 2:7
27 [a]Dan. 5:6
28 [a]Jer. 5:16 [1]Lit. *be regarded as*
30 [a]Is. 8:22 [1]*distress*

CHAPTER 6
1 [a]2 Kin. 15:7 [b]John 12:41
2 [a]Ezek. 1:11
3 [a]Rev. 4:8 [b]Num. 14:21
5 [a]Ex. 6:12, 30 [1]*destroyed, cut off*
6 [a]Rev. 8:3
7 [a]Jer. 1:9 [1]*atoned for*
8 [a]Gen. 1:26
9 [a]Matt. 13:14

29 Their roaring *will be* like a lion,
They will roar like young lions;
Yes, they will roar
And lay hold of the prey;
They will carry *it* away safely,
And no one will deliver.

30 In that day they will roar against
them
Like the roaring of the sea.
And if *one* [a]looks to the land,
Behold, darkness *and* [1]sorrow;
And the light is darkened by the
clouds.

Isaiah Called to Be a Prophet

6 In the year that [a]King Uzziah died,
I [b]saw the Lord sitting on a throne,
high and lifted up, and the train of His
robe filled the temple. 2 Above it stood seraphim; each one had six wings: with two
he covered his face, [a]with two he covered
his feet, and with two he flew. 3 And one
cried to another and said:

[a]"Holy, holy, holy *is* the LORD of
hosts;
[b]The whole earth *is* full of His
glory!"

4 And the posts of the door were shaken by
the voice of him who cried out, and the
house was filled with smoke.
5 So I said:

"Woe *is* me, for I am [1]undone!
Because I *am* a man of [a]unclean
lips,
And I dwell in the midst of a people
of unclean lips;
For my eyes have seen the King,
The LORD of hosts."

6 Then one of the seraphim flew to me,
having in his hand a live coal *which* he
had taken with the tongs from [a]the altar.
7 And he [a]touched my mouth *with it,* and
said:

"Behold, this has touched your lips;
Your iniquity is taken away,
And your sin [1]purged."

8 Also I heard the voice of the Lord,
saying:

"Whom shall I send,
And who will go for [a]Us?"

Then I said, "Here *am* I! Send me."
9 And He said, "Go, and [a]tell this people:

Isaiah 6:8

Dear Woman of Destiny,

At some time in your walk with Jesus, you will hear God's call to follow Him in a given area—minister, missionary, helpmate to a godly husband and full-time mother, teacher, writer, musician, artist, businesswoman. To answer the call may not always come easy.

Such a call came to young Isaiah who lived around 700 B.C. When Isaiah began to make excuses, it took a sovereign act of God to change his mind and his direction (see Is. 6:6–8). Isaiah served under four kings and became the greatest Old Testament prophet and the most quoted in the New Testament. He wrote the most awesome single Old Testament chapter (53), prophesying the Messiah's atoning work. His book is full of hope, promised restoration, and redemption, the coming of the Messiah, the salvation of all nations, including the Gentiles, and the triumph of our Lord in the end. Had Isaiah not answered God's call, just think how much millions living after him would have missed!

I remember when my late husband and I were pastoring in Ashland, Oregon, a beautiful mountain town. Our church was located on Main Street about two blocks from downtown. It was free of debt and had grown steadily since our coming. Our monthly salary was larger than the district superintendent's, who was over 153 churches. Our attendance was as large as any in the state. At the last scheduled meeting, the board voted we were to be their pastors as long as we chose, without any additional board confirmations. They had purchased a large, roomy, beautiful parsonage nearby for us and had renovated it.

I had just come home from the hospital that night, after giving birth to my third child, Dennis. Grateful, as I lay in bed, I thanked God for His goodness, and told Him, "This is exactly what I've always wanted. My three children, when they grow up, can go to the college one mile from here. This is where You'll find me when the rapture takes place."

To my great surprise, less than two years later, our family of five was all packed up in a sixteen-foot mobile home, to answer God's call to help evangelize the nations for Jesus! Was it easy? No, a thousand times, no! Tears flowed as we hugged our wonderful church members. But we knew we were obeying God.

What has happened since? We founded Christ For the Nations that helped build over ten thousand churches overseas; Gordon wrote two hundred fifty books, now translated in seventy-eight languages—millions have been sent free worldwide; we built our Bible school in Dallas, Texas, that has trained twenty-seven thousand students from over a hundred nations; and helped found forty other Bible schools in twenty-nine countries. Since Gordon's sudden homegoing twenty-six years ago, this work has more than quadrupled. All three of my children are college graduates, in full-time ministry. And my eight grandchildren are all serving God. We give Jesus all the glory!

It pays to answer: "Here am I. Send me."

Freda Lindsay

'Keep on hearing, but do not
understand;
Keep on seeing, but do not
perceive.'

10 "Make [a]the heart of this people
dull,
And their ears heavy,
And shut their eyes;
[b]Lest they see with their eyes,
And hear with their ears,
And understand with their heart,
And return and be healed."

Lord, may _____ hear Your voice saying, "Whom shall I send, and who will go for Us?" Then let them answer You, like Isaiah, saying, "Here am I! Send me.

FROM ISAIAH 6:8

11 Then I said, "Lord, how long?"
And He answered:

[a]"Until the cities are laid waste and
without inhabitant,
The houses are without a man,
The land is utterly desolate,
12 [a]The LORD has removed men far
away,
And the forsaken places *are* many
in the midst of the land.
13 But yet a tenth *will be* in it,
And will return and be for
consuming,
As a terebinth tree or as an oak,
Whose stump *remains* when it is
cut down.
So [a]the holy seed *shall be* its
stump."

Isaiah Sent to King Ahaz

7 Now it came to pass in the days of
[a]Ahaz the son of Jotham, the son of
Uzziah, king of Judah, *that* Rezin king of
Syria and Pekah the son of Remaliah, king
of Israel, went up to Jerusalem to *make*
war against [b]it, but could not [1]prevail
against it. 2 And it was told to the house
of David, saying, "Syria's forces are [1]de-
ployed in Ephraim." So his heart and the
heart of his people were moved as the

10 a Ps. 119:70 b Jer. 5:21
11 a Mic. 3:12
12 a 2 Kin. 25:21
13 a Ezra 9:2
CHAPTER 7
1 a 2 Chr. 28 b 2 Kin. 16:5, 9 *1 conquer it*
2 1 Lit. *settled upon*
3 1 Lit. *A Remnant Shall Return*
4 a Is. 30:15 *1 Be careful* *2 be calm*
6 *1 cause a sickening dread*
7 a Is. 8:10
8 a 2 Sam. 8:6 1 Lit. *shattered*
9 a 2 Chr. 20:20
11 a Matt. 12:38 1 Lit. *make the request deep or make it high above*
14 a Matt. 1:23 b [Is. 9:6] c Is. 8:8, 10 1 Lit. *God-With-Us*
16 a Is. 8:4 b 2 Kin. 15:30
17 a 2 Chr. 28:19, 20 b 1 Kin. 12:16

trees of the woods are moved with the
wind.
3 Then the LORD said to Isaiah, "Go out
now to meet Ahaz, you and [1]Shear-
Jashub your son, at the end of the aqueduct from the upper pool, on the highway
to the Fuller's Field, 4 and say to him:
[1]'Take heed, and [2]be [a]quiet; do not fear
or be fainthearted for these two stubs of
smoking firebrands, for the fierce anger of
Rezin and Syria, and the son of Remaliah.
5 Because Syria, Ephraim, and the son of
Remaliah have plotted evil against you,
saying, 6 "Let us go up against Judah and
[1]trouble it, and let us make a gap in its
wall for ourselves, and set a king over
them, the son of Tabel"— 7 thus says the
Lord GOD:

[a]"It shall not stand,
Nor shall it come to pass.
8 [a]For the head of Syria *is* Damascus,
And the head of Damascus *is* Rezin.
Within sixty-five years Ephraim will
be [1]broken,
So that it will not *be* a people.
9 The head of Ephraim *is* Samaria,
And the head of Samaria *is*
Remaliah's son.
[a]If you will not believe,
Surely you shall not be
established."'"

The Immanuel Prophecy

10 Moreover the LORD spoke again to
Ahaz, saying, 11 [a]"Ask a sign for yourself
from the LORD your God; [1]ask it either in
the depth or in the height above."
12 But Ahaz said, "I will not ask, nor will
I test the LORD!"
13 Then he said, "Hear now, O house of
David! *Is it* a small thing for you to weary
men, but will you weary my God also?
14 Therefore the Lord Himself will give you
a sign: [a]Behold, the virgin shall conceive
and bear [b]a Son, and shall call His name
[c]Immanuel.[1] 15 Curds and honey He shall
eat, that He may know to refuse the evil
and choose the good. 16 [a]For before the
Child shall know to refuse the evil and
choose the good, the land that you dread
will be forsaken by [b]both her kings.
17 [a]The LORD will bring the king of Assyria
upon you and your people and your father's house—days that have not come
since the day that [b]Ephraim departed
from Judah."

18 And it shall come to pass in that day
That the LORD [a]will whistle for the fly
That *is* in the farthest part of the rivers of Egypt,
And for the bee that *is* in the land of Assyria.
19 They will come, and all of them will rest
In the desolate valleys and in [a]the clefts of the rocks,
And on all thorns and in all pastures.

20 In the same day the Lord will shave with a [a]hired [b]razor,
With those from beyond [1]the River, with the king of Assyria,
The head and the hair of the legs,
And will also remove the beard.

21 It shall be in that day
That a man will keep alive a young cow and two sheep;
22 So it shall be, from the abundance of milk they give,
That he will eat curds;
For curds and honey everyone will eat who is left in the land.

23 It shall happen in that day,
That wherever there could be a thousand vines
Worth a thousand *shekels* of silver,
[a]It will be for briers and thorns.
24 With arrows and bows men will come there,
Because all the land will become briers and thorns.

25 And to any hill which could be dug with the hoe,
You will not go there for fear of briers and thorns;
But it will become a range for oxen
And a place for sheep to roam.

Assyria Will Invade the Land

8 Moreover the LORD said to me, "Take
a large scroll, and [a]write on it with
a man's pen concerning [1]Maher-Shalal-
Hash-Baz. 2 And I will take for Myself
faithful witnesses to record, [a]Uriah the
priest and Zechariah the son of Jebere-
chiah."
3 Then I went to the prophetess, and she
conceived and bore a son. Then the LORD
said to me, "Call his name Maher-Shalal-
Hash-Baz; 4 [a]for before the child [1]shall
have knowledge to cry 'My father' and 'My
mother,' [b]the riches of Damascus and the
[2]spoil of Samaria will be taken away before the king of Assyria."
5 The LORD also spoke to me again,
saying:

6 "Inasmuch as these people refused
The waters of [a]Shiloah that flow softly,
And rejoice [b]in Rezin and in Remaliah's son;
7 Now therefore, behold, the Lord brings up over them
The waters of [1]the River, strong and mighty—
The king of Assyria and all his glory;
He will [2]go up over all his channels
And go over all his banks.
8 He will pass through Judah,
He will overflow and pass over,
[a]He will reach up to the neck;
And the stretching out of his wings
Will [1]fill the breadth of Your land,
O [b]Immanuel.[2]

9 "Be[a] shattered, O you peoples, and be broken in pieces!
Give ear, all you from far countries.
Gird yourselves, but be broken in pieces;
Gird yourselves, but be broken in pieces.
10 [a]Take counsel together, but it will come to nothing;
Speak the word, [b]but it will not stand,
[c]For [1]God *is* with us."

Fear God, Heed His Word

11 For the LORD spoke thus to me with
[1]a strong hand, and instructed me that I
should not walk in the way of this people,
saying:

12 "Do not say, 'A conspiracy,'
Concerning all that this people call a conspiracy,
Nor be afraid of their [1]threats, nor be [2]troubled.
13 The LORD of hosts, Him you shall hallow;
Let Him *be* your fear,
And *let* Him *be* your dread.
14 [a]He will be as a [1]sanctuary,
But [b]a stone of stumbling and a rock of [2]offense
To both the houses of Israel,

18 a Is. 5:26
19 a Jer. 16:16
20 a Is. 10:5, 15 b 2 Kin. 16:7 *1* The Euphrates
23 a Is. 5:6

CHAPTER 8
1 a Hab. 2:2 *1* Lit. *Speed the Spoil, Hasten the Booty*
2 a 2 Kin. 16:10
4 a 2 Kin. 17:6; Is. 7:16 b 2 Kin. 15:29 *1 knows how* *2 plunder*
6 a John 9:7 b Is. 7:1, 2
7 *1* The Euphrates *2* Overflow
8 a Is. 30:28 b Is. 7:14 *1* Lit. *be the fullness of* *2* Lit. *God-With-Us*
9 a Joel 3:9
10 a Is. 7:7 b Is. 7:14 c Rom. 8:31 *1* Heb. *Immanuel*
11 *1* Mighty power
12 *1* Lit. *fear or terror* *2* Lit. *in dread*
14 a Ezek. 11:16 b Luke 2:34; 20:17 *1 holy abode* *2 stumbling over*

As a trap and a snare to the
inhabitants of Jerusalem.
15 And many among them shall
[a]stumble;
They shall fall and be broken,
Be snared and [1]taken."

16 Bind up the testimony,
Seal the law among my disciples.
17 And I will wait on the LORD,
Who [a]hides His face from the house
of Jacob;
And I [b]will hope in Him.
18 [a]Here am I and the children whom
the LORD has given me!
We [b]*are* for signs and wonders in
Israel
From the LORD of hosts,
Who dwells in Mount Zion.

19And when they say to you, [a]"Seek
those who are mediums and wizards,
[b]who whisper and mutter," should not a
people seek their God? *Should they* [c]*seek*
the dead on behalf of the living? 20[a]To the
law and to the testimony! If they do not
speak according to this word, *it is* because
[b]*there*[1] *is* no light in them.
21They will pass through it hard-
pressed and hungry; and it shall happen,
when they are hungry, that they will be
enraged and [a]curse [1]their king and their
God, and look upward. 22Then they will
look to the earth, and see trouble and
darkness, gloom of anguish; and *they will
be* driven into darkness.

The Government of the Promised Son

9 Nevertheless [a]the gloom *will* not *be*
upon her who *is* distressed,
As when at [b]first He lightly
esteemed
The land of Zebulun and the land
of Naphtali,
And [c]afterward more heavily
oppressed *her,*
By the way of the sea, beyond the
Jordan,
In Galilee of the Gentiles.
2 [a]The people who walked in darkness
Have seen a great light;
Those who dwelt in the land of the
shadow of death,
Upon them a light has shined.

3 You have multiplied the nation
And [1]increased its joy;
They rejoice before You
According to the joy of harvest,
As *men* rejoice [a]when they divide
the spoil.
4 For You have broken the yoke of
his burden
And the staff of his shoulder,
The rod of his oppressor,
As in the day of [a]Midian.
5 For every warrior's [1]sandal from
the noisy battle,
And garments rolled in blood,
[a]Will be used for burning *and* fuel
[2]of fire.

6 [a]For unto us a Child is born,
Unto us a [b]Son is given;
And [c]the government will be upon
His shoulder.
And His name will be called
[d]Wonderful, Counselor, [e]Mighty God,
Everlasting Father, [f]Prince of
Peace.
7 Of the increase of *His* government
and peace
[a]*There will be* no end,
Upon the throne of David and over
His kingdom,
To order it and establish it with
judgment and justice
From that time forward, even
forever.
The [b]zeal of the Lord of hosts will
perform this.

The Punishment of Samaria

8 The LORD sent a word against
[a]Jacob,
And it has fallen on Israel.
9 All the people will know—
Ephraim and the inhabitant of
Samaria—
Who say in pride and arrogance of
heart:
10 "The bricks have fallen down,
But we will rebuild with hewn
stones;
The sycamores are cut down,
But we will replace *them* with
cedars."
11 Therefore the LORD shall set up
The adversaries of Rezin against
him,
And spur his enemies on,
12 The Syrians before and the
Philistines behind;
And they shall devour Israel with an
open mouth.

15 a Matt. 21:44
1 captured
17 a Is. 54:8
b Hab. 2:3
18 a Heb. 2:13
b Ps. 71:7
19 a 1 Sam. 28:8
b Is. 29:4
c Ps. 106:28
20 a Luke 16:29
b Mic. 3:6
1 Or they have no dawn
21 a Rev. 16:11
1 Or by their king and by their God

CHAPTER 9
1 a Is. 8:22
b 2 Kin. 15:29
c Matt. 4:13–16
2 a Matt. 4:16
3 a Judg. 5:30
1 So with Qr., Tg.; Kt., Vg. not increased joy; LXX Most of the people You brought down in Your joy
4 a Judg. 7:22
5 a Is. 66:15
1 boot
2 for the fire
6 a [Luke 2:11]
b [John 3:16]
c [Matt. 28:18]
d Judg. 13:18
e Titus 2:13
f Eph. 2:14
7 a Dan. 2:44
b Is. 37:32
8 a Gen. 32:28

For all this His anger is not turned
away,
But His hand *is* [1]stretched out still.

13 For the people do not turn to Him
who strikes them,
Nor do they seek the LORD of hosts.
14 Therefore the LORD will cut off
head and tail from Israel,
Palm branch and bulrush [a]in one
day.
15 The elder and honorable, he *is* the
head;
The prophet who teaches lies, he *is*
the tail.
16 For [a]the leaders of this people
cause *them* to err,
And *those who are* led by them are
destroyed.
17 Therefore the Lord [a]will have no
joy in their young men,
Nor have mercy on their fatherless
and widows;
For everyone *is* a hypocrite and an
evildoer,
And every mouth speaks [1]folly.
[b]For all this His anger is not turned
away,
But His hand *is* stretched out still.

18 For wickedness [a]burns as the fire;
It shall devour the briers and
thorns,
And kindle in the thickets of the
forest;
They shall mount up *like* rising
smoke.
19 Through the wrath of the LORD of
hosts
[a]The land is burned up,
And the people shall be as fuel for
the fire;
[b]No man shall spare his brother.
20 And he shall [1]snatch on the right
hand
And be hungry;
He shall devour on the left hand
[a]And not be satisfied;
[b]Every man shall eat the flesh of his
own arm.
21 Manasseh *shall devour* Ephraim,
and Ephraim Manasseh;
Together they *shall be* [a]against
Judah.

[b]For all this His anger is not turned
away,
But His hand *is* stretched out still.

12 [1] In judgment
14 [a] Rev. 18:8
16 [a] Is. 3:12
17 [a] Ps. 147:10 [b] Is. 5:25 [1] *foolishness*
18 [a] Mal. 4:1
19 [a] Is. 8:22 [b] Mic. 7:2, 6
20 [a] Lev. 26:26 [b] Jer. 19:9 [1] *slice off* or *tear*
21 [a] 2 Chr. 28:6, 8 [b] Is. 9:12, 17

CHAPTER 10
1 [a] Ps. 58:2
3 [a] Job 31:14 [b] Hos. 9:7 [c] Is. 5:26
4 [a] Is. 24:22 [b] Is. 5:25 [1] Lit. *under*
5 [a] Jer. 51:20
6 [a] Is. 9:17 [b] Jer. 34:22
7 [a] Gen. 50:20
8 [a] 2 Kin. 19:10
9 [a] Amos 6:2 [b] 2 Chr. 35:20 [c] 2 Kin. 16:9

10 "Woe to those who [a]decree
unrighteous decrees,
Who write misfortune,
Which they have prescribed
2 To rob the needy of justice,
And to take what is right from the
poor of My people,
That widows may be their prey,
And *that* they may rob the
fatherless.
3 [a]What will you do in [b]the day of
punishment,
And in the desolation *which* will
come from [c]afar?
To whom will you flee for help?
And where will you leave your
glory?
4 Without Me they shall bow down
among the [a]prisoners,
And they shall fall [1]among the
slain."

[b]For all this His anger is not turned
away,
But His hand *is* stretched out still.

Arrogant Assyria Also Judged

5 "Woe to Assyria, [a]the rod of My
anger
And the staff in whose hand is My
indignation.
6 I will send him against [a]an
ungodly nation,
And against the people of My wrath
I will [b]give him charge,
To seize the spoil, to take the prey,
And to tread them down like the
mire of the streets.
7 [a]Yet he does not mean so,
Nor does his heart think so;
But *it is* in his heart to destroy,
And cut off not a few nations.
8 [a]For he says,
'*Are* not my princes altogether
kings?
9 *Is* not [a]Calno [b]like Carchemish?
Is not Hamath like Arpad?
Is not Samaria [c]like Damascus?
10 As my hand has found the
kingdoms of the idols,
Whose carved images excelled those
of Jerusalem and Samaria,
11 As I have done to Samaria and her
idols,
Shall I not do also to Jerusalem
and her idols?' "

[12]Therefore it shall come to pass, when the Lord has [1]performed all His work [a]on Mount Zion and on Jerusalem, *that He will say,* [b]"I will punish the fruit of the arrogant heart of the king of Assyria, and the glory of his haughty looks."
[13][a]For he says:

"By the strength of my hand I have
done *it,*
And by my wisdom, for I am
prudent;
Also I have removed the boundaries
of the people,
And have robbed their treasuries;
So I have put down the inhabitants
like a [1]valiant *man.*
14 [a]My hand has found like a nest the
riches of the people,
And as one gathers eggs *that are*
left,
I have gathered all the earth;
And there was no one who moved
his wing,
Nor opened *his* mouth with even a
peep."

15 Shall [a]the ax boast itself against
him who chops with it?
Or shall the saw exalt itself against
him who saws with it?
As if a rod could wield *itself* against
those who lift it up,
Or as if a staff could lift up, *as if it*
were not wood!
16 Therefore the Lord, the [1]Lord of
hosts,
Will send leanness among his fat
ones;
And under his glory
He will kindle a burning
Like the burning of a fire.
17 So the Light of Israel will be for a
fire,
And his Holy One for a flame;
[a]It will burn and devour
His thorns and his briers in one
day.
18 And it will consume the glory of
his forest and of [a]his fruitful
field,
Both soul and body;
And they will be as when a sick
man wastes away.
19 Then the rest of the trees of his
forest
Will be so few in number
That a child may write them.

12 a 2 Kin. 19:31 b Jer. 50:18 1 *completed*
13 a Is. 37:24–27 1 *mighty*
14 a Job 31:25
15 a Jer. 51:20
16 1 So with Bg.; MT, DSS *YHWH (the* LORD*)*
17 a Is. 9:18
18 a 2 Kin. 19:23
20 a 2 Kin. 16:7 1 Lit. *struck*
21 a [Is. 9:6]
22 a Rom. 9:27, 28 b Is. 6:13
23 a Dan. 9:27
24 a Is. 7:4; 12:2 b Ex. 14
25 a Dan. 11:36
26 a 2 Kin. 19:35 b Is. 9:4 c Ex. 14:26, 27 1 *arouse*
27 a Ps. 105:15
29 a 1 Sam. 13:23 b 1 Sam. 11:4 1 Or *over the pass*
30 a 1 Sam. 25:44 b Judg. 18:7 1 Or *Cry shrilly* 2 So with MT, Tg., Vg.; LXX, Syr. *Listen to her, O Anathoth*
31 a Josh. 15:31

The Returning Remnant of Israel

20 And it shall come to pass in that
day
That the remnant of Israel,
And such as have escaped of the
house of Jacob,
[a]Will never again depend on him
who [1]defeated them,
But will depend on the LORD, the
Holy One of Israel, in truth.
21 The remnant will return, the
remnant of Jacob,
To the [a]Mighty God.
22 [a]For though your people, O Israel,
be as the sand of the sea,
[b]A remnant of them will return;
The destruction decreed shall
overflow with righteousness.
23 [a]For the Lord GOD of hosts
Will make a determined end
In the midst of all the land.

[24]Therefore thus says the Lord GOD of
hosts: "O My people, who dwell in Zion,
[a]do not be afraid of the Assyrian. He shall
strike you with a rod and lift up his staff
against you, in the manner of [b]Egypt.
[25]For yet a very little while [a]and the indignation will cease, as will My anger in their
destruction." [26]And the LORD of hosts will
[1]stir up [a]a scourge for him like the
slaughter of [b]Midian at the rock of Oreb;
[c]*as* His rod was on the sea, so will He lift
it up in the manner of Egypt.

27 It shall come to pass in that day
That his burden will be taken away
from your shoulder,
And his yoke from your neck,
And the yoke will be destroyed
because of [a]the anointing oil.

28 He has come to Aiath,
He has passed Migron;
At Michmash he has attended to his
equipment.
29 They have gone [1]along [a]the ridge,
They have taken up lodging at
Geba.
Ramah is afraid,
[b]Gibeah of Saul has fled.
30 [1]Lift up your voice,
O daughter [a]of Gallim!
Cause it to be heard as far as
[b]Laish—
[2]O poor Anathoth!
31 [a]Madmenah has fled,

Isaiah 10:27

Dear Woman of Destiny,

Having been brought up in a preacher's home and having a father who is a student of Bible prophecy, I was taught that Isaiah 10:22–27 is believed by many Bible scholars to be a direct reference to the Battle of Armageddon—when Christ (the Anointed One) will come to destroy the Antichrist, remove the burden, and destroy the yoke the Antichrist has placed on the nation of Israel during the days of the Tribulation.

However, I was also taught and believe that Isaiah 10:27 has a spiritual principle for every Christian who believes in the power of the Holy Spirit.

The anointing will remove any burden and every yoke of bondage that the enemy may have placed or is trying to place upon your life. This is what Jesus came to do.

In Luke 4:18, 19, Christ, the Anointed One, says, "The Spirit of the LORD is upon Me, because He has anointed Me to preach the gospel to the poor; He has sent Me to heal the brokenhearted, to proclaim liberty to the captives and recovery of sight to the blind, to set at liberty those who are oppressed; to proclaim the acceptable year of the LORD."

In the summer of 1954, my parents were pastoring their first church located in Jacksonville, Florida. It was a small but godly congregation—the type of people who, when challenged by my parents to fast for a week, did so. If the congregation was called to a week of prayer meetings at the church, they were there.

My mom visited a doctor because she had been hemorrhaging for six weeks. She was diagnosed as having a tubal pregnancy, ordered to bed, and scheduled for surgery. She did, however, attend the church services in which my dad requested prayer for her without divulging the problem. (Forty-five years ago people were rather private about their medical problems.) "Sister Mac," a middle-aged woman married to a chronic alcoholic and having little of this world's goods, was a godly, praying woman. She stood during "testimony time" the following Wednesday. "Sister, sister," she said to my mother (in those days people did not have first names), "your husband requested prayer for you last Sunday. Honey, you're healed! I don't know what your problem was, but honey, you're healed! Oh, glory! Oh, hallelujah! I'm a-telling you, you're healed. As I was a-praying for you, the glory of God came down all over me. I'm a-telling you . . . I'm a-telling you, you're healed!"

My mom went to the doctor supposedly to be admitted to the hospital for surgery. When the doctor examined her, he found there was nothing wrong with her, and the surgery was cancelled. The anointing had broken the yoke.

Regardless of what circumstances you are facing—whether it be a spiritual, physical, emotional, or financial need—know that when you allow Christ, the Anointed One, to live within you, and as you learn to dwell in His presence, the anointing will break those yokes of bondage and make you whole in every area of your life.

May the Lord's presence be continually upon you.

Suzanne Hinn

The inhabitants of Gebim seek
refuge.
32 As yet he will remain [a]at Nob that
day;
He will [b]shake his fist at the mount
of [c]the daughter of Zion,
The hill of Jerusalem.

33 Behold, the Lord,
The LORD of hosts,
Will lop off the bough with terror;
[a]Those of high stature *will be* hewn
down,
And the haughty will be humbled.
34 He will cut down the thickets of
the forest with iron,
And Lebanon will fall by the Mighty
One.

The Reign of Jesse's Offspring

11 There [a]shall come forth a [1]Rod
from the [2]stem of [b]Jesse,
And [c]a Branch shall [3]grow out of
his roots.
2 [a]The Spirit of the LORD shall rest
upon Him,
The Spirit of wisdom and
understanding,
The Spirit of counsel and might,
The Spirit of knowledge and of the
fear of the LORD.

3 His delight *is* in the fear of the
LORD,
And He shall not judge by the sight
of His eyes,
Nor decide by the hearing of His
ears;
4 But [a]with righteousness He shall
judge the poor,
And decide with equity for the
meek of the earth;
He shall [b]strike the earth with the
rod of His mouth,
And with the breath of His lips He
shall slay the wicked.
5 Righteousness shall be the belt of
His loins,
And faithfulness the belt of His
waist.

6 "The[a] wolf also shall dwell with the
lamb,
The leopard shall lie down with the
young goat,
The calf and the young lion and the
fatling together;
And a little child shall lead them.
7 The cow and the bear shall graze;

32 a 1 Sam. 21:1
b Is. 13:2
c Is. 37:22

33 a Amos 2:9

CHAPTER 11
1 a [Zech. 6:12]
b [Acts 13:23]
c Is. 4:2
1 Shoot
2 stock or *trunk*
3 be fruitful

2 a [John 1:32]

4 a Rev. 19:11
b Job 4:9

6 a Hos. 2:18

9 a Job 5:23
b Hab. 2:14

10 a Is. 2:11
b Rom. 15:12
c Is. 27:12, 13
d Rom. 15:10

11 a Zech. 10:10
1 Or *coastlands*

12 a John 7:35
1 gather
2 Lit. *wings*

13 a Jer. 3:18

14 a Dan. 11:41
1 Lit. *sons*

15 a Zech. 10:10, 11
1 So with MT, Vg.; LXX, Syr., Tg. *dry up*

Their young ones shall lie down
together;
And the lion shall eat straw like the
ox.
8 The nursing child shall play by the
cobra's hole,
And the weaned child shall put his
hand in the viper's den.
9 [a]They shall not hurt nor destroy in
all My holy mountain,
For [b]the earth shall be full of the
knowledge of the LORD
As the waters cover the sea.

10 "And[a] in that day [b]there shall be a
Root of Jesse,
Who shall stand as a [c]banner to the
people;
For the [d]Gentiles shall seek Him,
And His resting place shall be
glorious."

11 It shall come to pass in that day
That the Lord shall set His hand
again the second time
To recover the remnant of His
people who are left,
[a]From Assyria and Egypt,
From Pathros and Cush,
From Elam and Shinar,
From Hamath and the [1]islands of
the sea.

12 He will set up a banner for the
nations,
And will [1]assemble the outcasts of
Israel,
And gather together [a]the dispersed
of Judah
From the four [2]corners of the
earth.
13 Also [a]the envy of Ephraim shall
depart,
And the adversaries of Judah shall
be cut off;
Ephraim shall not envy Judah,
And Judah shall not harass
Ephraim.
14 But they shall fly down upon the
shoulder of the Philistines
toward the west;
Together they shall plunder the
[1]people of the East;
[a]They shall lay their hand on Edom
and Moab;
And the people of Ammon shall
obey them.
15 The LORD [a]will utterly [1]destroy
the tongue of the Sea of Egypt;

With His mighty wind He will
shake His fist over [2]the River,
And strike it in the seven streams,
And make *men* cross over [3]dryshod.
16 [a]There will be a highway for the
remnant of His people
Who will be left from Assyria,
[b]As it was for Israel
In the day that he came up from
the land of Egypt.

O Lord, I pray that ____ would understand that You are their salvation; may they trust in You and not be afraid. Be their strength and song; O God, become their salvation.

FROM ISAIAH 12:2

A Hymn of Praise

12 And [a]in that day you will say:
"O LORD, I will praise You;
Though You were angry with me,
Your anger is turned away, and You
comfort me.
2 Behold, God *is* my salvation,
I will trust and not be afraid;
[a]'For [b]YAH, the LORD, *is* my strength
and song;
He also has become my salvation.' "

Trust God. Everything will be all right. Face life with a heart of trust.

LILLIAN HUNT

3 Therefore with joy you will draw
[a]water
From the wells of salvation.

15 [2]The Euphrates [3]Lit. *in sandals*
16 [a]Is. 19:23 [b]Ex. 14:29
CHAPTER 12
1 [a]Is. 2:11
2 [a]Ps. 83:18 [b]Ex. 15:2
3 [a][John 4:10, 14; 7:37, 38]
4 [a]1 Chr. 16:8 [b]Ps. 145:4–6 [c]Ps. 34:3
5 [a]Ex. 15:1
6 [a]Zeph. 3:14, 15 [b]Ps. 89:18
CHAPTER 13
1 [a]Jer. 50; 51 [1]*oracle, prophecy*
2 [a]Is. 18:3 [b]Jer. 51:25 [c]Is. 10:32
3 [a]Joel 3:11 [b]Ps. 149:2 [1]*consecrated* or *set apart*
4 [a]Is. 17:12
5 [a]Is. 42:13 [b]Is. 24:1; 34:2 [1]Or *instruments*
6 [a]Zeph. 1:7 [b]Joel 1:15
8 [a]Ps. 48:6 [1]*Sharp pains*

4 And in that day you will say:
[a]"Praise the LORD, call upon His
name;
[b]Declare His deeds among the
peoples,
Make mention that His [c]name is
exalted.
5 [a]Sing to the LORD,
For He has done excellent things;
This *is* known in all the earth.
6 [a]Cry out and shout, O inhabitant of
Zion,
For great *is* [b]the Holy One of Israel
in your midst!"

Proclamation Against Babylon

13 The [a]burden[1] against Babylon
which Isaiah the son of Amoz saw.

2 "Lift[a] up a banner [b]on the high
mountain,
Raise your voice to them;
[c]Wave your hand, that they may
enter the gates of the nobles.
3 I have commanded My [1]sanctified
ones;
I have also called [a]My mighty ones
for My anger—
Those who [b]rejoice in My
exaltation."
4 The [a]noise of a multitude in the
mountains,
Like that of many people!
A tumultuous noise of the
kingdoms of nations gathered
together!
The LORD of hosts musters
The army for battle.
5 They come from a far country,
From the end of heaven—
The [a]LORD and His [1]weapons of
indignation,
To destroy the whole [b]land.
6 Wail, [a]for the day of the LORD *is* at
hand!
[b]It will come as destruction from the
Almighty.
7 Therefore all hands will be limp,
Every man's heart will melt,
8 And they will be afraid.
[a]Pangs[1] and sorrows will take hold
of *them;*
They will be in pain as a woman in
childbirth;
They will be amazed at one
another;

Their faces *will be like* flames.

9 Behold, [a]the day of the LORD comes,
Cruel, with both wrath and fierce anger,
To lay the land desolate;
And He will destroy [b]its sinners from it.
10 For the stars of heaven and their constellations
Will not give their light;
The sun will be [a]darkened in its going forth,
And the moon will not cause its light to shine.

This is a wicked and sinful world, and our children are not safe outside of Jesus Christ.

MAE ELEANOR FREY

11 "I will [a]punish the world for *its* evil,
And the wicked for their iniquity;
[b]I will halt the arrogance of the proud,
And will lay low the haughtiness of the [1]terrible.
12 I will make a mortal more rare than fine gold,
A man more than the golden wedge of Ophir.
13 [a]Therefore I will shake the heavens,
And the earth will move out of her place,
In the wrath of the LORD of hosts
And in [b]the day of His fierce anger.
14 It shall be as the hunted gazelle,
And as a sheep that no man [1]takes up;
[a]Every man will turn to his own people,
And everyone will flee to his own land.
15 Everyone who is found will be thrust through,
And everyone who is captured will fall by the sword.
16 Their children also will be [a]dashed to pieces before their eyes;
Their houses will be plundered
And their wives [b]ravished.
17 "Behold,[a] I will stir up the Medes against them,
Who will not [1]regard silver;
And *as for* gold, they will not delight in it.
18 Also *their* bows will dash the young men to pieces,
And they will have no pity on the fruit of the womb;
Their eye will not spare children.
19 [a]And Babylon, the glory of kingdoms,
The beauty of the Chaldeans' pride,
Will be as when God overthrew
[b]Sodom and Gomorrah.
20 [a]It will never be inhabited,
Nor will it be settled from generation to generation;
Nor will the Arabian pitch tents there,
Nor will the shepherds make their sheepfolds there.
21 [a]But wild beasts of the desert will lie there,
And their houses will be full of [1]owls;
Ostriches will dwell there,
And wild goats will caper there.
22 The hyenas will howl in their citadels,
And jackals in their pleasant palaces.
[a]Her time *is* near to come,
And her days will not be prolonged."

Mercy on Jacob

14 For the LORD [a]will have mercy on
Jacob, and [b]will still choose Israel,
and settle them in their own land. [c]The
strangers will be joined with them, and
they will cling to the house of Jacob.
2 Then people will take them [a]and bring
them to their place, and the house of Israel will possess them for servants and
maids in the land of the LORD; they will
take them captive whose captives they
were, [b]and rule over their oppressors.

Fall of the King of Babylon

3 It shall come to pass in the day the
LORD gives you rest from your sorrow, and
from your fear and the hard bondage in
which you were made to serve, 4 that you

---

9 a Mal. 4:1 b Prov. 2:22
10 a Joel 2:31
11 a Is. 26:21 b [Is. 2:17] *1* Or *tyrants*
13 a Hag. 2:6 b Lam. 1:12
14 a Jer. 50:16; 51:9 *1 gathers*
16 a Nah. 3:10 b Zech. 14:2
17 a Dan. 5:28, 31 *1 esteem*
19 a Is. 14:4 b Gen. 19:24
20 a Jer. 50:3
21 a Is. 34:11–15 *1* Or *howling creatures*
22 a Jer. 51:33

CHAPTER 14
1 a Ps. 102:13 b Zech. 1:17; 2:12 c Is. 60:4, 5, 10
2 a Is. 49:22; 60:9; 66:20 b Is. 60:14

[a]will take up this proverb against the king of Babylon, and say:

"How the oppressor has ceased,
The [b]golden[1] city ceased!
5 The LORD has broken [a]the staff of the wicked,
The scepter of the rulers;
6 He who struck the people in wrath with a continual stroke,
He who ruled the nations in anger,
Is persecuted *and* no one hinders.
7 The whole earth is at rest *and* quiet;
They break forth into singing.
8 [a]Indeed the cypress trees rejoice over you,
And the cedars of Lebanon,
Saying, 'Since you [1]were cut down,
No woodsman has come up against us.'

9 "Hell[a1] from beneath is excited about you,
To meet *you* at your coming;
It stirs up the dead for you,
All the chief ones of the earth;
It has raised up from their thrones
All the kings of the nations.
10 They all shall [a]speak and say to you:
'Have you also become as weak as we?
Have you become like us?
11 Your pomp is brought down to Sheol,
And the sound of your stringed instruments;
The maggot is spread under you,
And worms cover you.'

The Fall of Lucifer

12 "How[a] you are fallen from heaven,
O [1]Lucifer, son of the morning!
How you are cut down to the ground,
You who weakened the nations!
13 For you have said in your heart:
[a]'I will ascend into heaven,
[b]I will exalt my throne above the stars of God;
I will also sit on the [c]mount of the congregation
[d]On the farthest sides of the north;
14 I will ascend above the heights of the clouds,
[a]I will be like the Most High.'
15 Yet you [a]shall be brought down to Sheol,
To the [1]lowest depths of the Pit.

16 "Those who see you will gaze at you,
And consider you, *saying:*
'*Is* this the man who made the earth tremble,
Who shook kingdoms,
17 Who made the world as a wilderness
And destroyed its cities,
Who [1]did not open the house of his prisoners?'

18 "All the kings of the nations,
All of them, sleep in glory,
Everyone in his own house;
19 But you are cast out of your grave
Like an [1]abominable branch,
Like the garment of those who are slain,
[2]Thrust through with a sword,
Who go down to the stones of the pit,
Like a corpse trodden underfoot.
20 You will not be joined with them in burial,
Because you have destroyed your land
And slain your people.
[a]The brood of evildoers shall never be named.
21 Prepare slaughter for his children
[a]Because of the iniquity of their fathers,
Lest they rise up and possess the land,
And fill the face of the world with cities."

Babylon Destroyed

22 "For I will rise up against them,"
says the LORD of hosts,
"And cut off from Babylon [a]the name and [b]remnant,
[c]And offspring and posterity," says the LORD.
23 "I will also make it a possession for the [a]porcupine,
And marshes of muddy water;
I will sweep it with the broom of destruction," says the LORD of hosts.

Assyria Destroyed

24 The LORD of hosts has sworn, saying,

---

4 [a]Hab. 2:6 [b]Rev. 18:16 [1]Or *insolent*
5 [a]Ps. 125:3
8 [a]Ezek. 31:16 [1]*have lain down*
9 [a]Ezek. 32:21 [1]Or *Sheol*
10 [a]Ezek. 32:21
12 [a]Is. 34:4 [1]Lit. *Day Star*
13 [a]Ezek. 28:2 [b]Dan. 8:10 [c]Ezek. 28:14 [d]Ps. 48:2
14 [a]2 Thess. 2:4
15 [a]Matt. 11:23 [1]Lit. *recesses*
17 [1]Would not release
19 [1]*despised* [2]*Pierced*
20 [a]Ps. 21:10; 109:13
21 [a]Ex. 20:5
22 [a]Prov. 10:7 [b]1 Kin. 14:10 [c]Job 18:19
23 [a]Zeph. 2:14

"Surely, as I have thought, so it
shall come to pass,
And as I have purposed, *so* it shall
[a]stand:
25 That I will break the [a]Assyrian in
My land,
And on My mountains tread him
underfoot.
Then [b]his yoke shall be removed
from them,
And his burden removed from their
shoulders.
26 This *is* the [a]purpose that is
purposed against the whole
earth,
And this *is* the hand that is
stretched out over all the
nations.
27 For the LORD of hosts has
[a]purposed,
And who will annul *it?*
His hand *is* stretched out,
And who will turn it back?"

Philistia Destroyed

28 This is the [1]burden which came in the
year that [a]King Ahaz died.

29 "Do not rejoice, all you of Philistia,
[a]Because the rod that struck you is
broken;
For out of the serpent's roots will
come forth a viper,
[b]And its offspring *will be* a fiery
flying serpent.
30 The firstborn of the poor will feed,
And the needy will lie down in
safety;
I will kill your roots with famine,
And it will slay your remnant.
31 Wail, O gate! Cry, O city!
All you of Philistia *are* dissolved;
For smoke will come from the
north,
And no one *will be* alone in his
[1]appointed times."
32 What will they answer the
messengers of the nation?
That [a]the LORD has founded Zion,
And [b]the poor of His people shall
take refuge in it.

Proclamation Against Moab

15 The [a]burden[1] against Moab.

Because in the night [b]Ar of [c]Moab
is laid waste
And destroyed,
Because in the night Kir of Moab is
laid waste
And destroyed,
2 He has gone up to the [1]temple and
Dibon,
To the high places to weep.
Moab will wail over Nebo and over
Medeba;
[a]On all their heads *will be* baldness,
And every beard cut off.
3 In their streets they will clothe
themselves with sackcloth;
On the tops of their houses
And in their streets
Everyone will wail, [a]weeping
bitterly.
4 Heshbon and Elealeh will cry out,
Their voice shall be heard as far as
[a]Jahaz;
Therefore the [1]armed soldiers of
Moab will cry out;
His life will be burdensome to him.

5 "My[a] heart will cry out for Moab;
His fugitives *shall flee* to Zoar,
Like [1]a three-year-old heifer.
For [b]by the Ascent of Luhith
They will go up with weeping;
For in the way of Horonaim
They will raise up a cry of
destruction,
6 For the waters [a]of Nimrim will be
desolate,
For the green grass has withered
away;
The grass fails, there is nothing
green.
7 Therefore the abundance they have
gained,
And what they have laid up,
They will carry away to the Brook
of the Willows.
8 For the cry has gone all around
the borders of Moab,
Its wailing to Eglaim
And its wailing to Beer Elim.
9 For the waters of [1]Dimon will be
full of blood;
Because I will bring more upon
[1]Dimon,
[a]Lions upon him who escapes from
Moab,
And on the remnant of the land."

Moab Destroyed

16 Send [a]the lamb to the ruler of
the land,
[b]From [1]Sela to the wilderness,

14:24 a Is. 43:13
25 a Mic. 5:5, 6 b Is. 10:27
26 a Is. 23:9
27 a Dan. 4:31, 35
28 a 2 Kin. 16:20 1 *oracle, prophecy*
29 a 2 Chr. 26:6 b 2 Kin. 18:8
31 1 Or *ranks*
32 a Ps. 87:1, 5 b Zech. 11:11

CHAPTER 15
1 a 2 Kin. 3:4 b Deut. 2:9 c Amos 2:1–3 1 *oracle, prophecy*
2 a Lev. 21:5 1 Heb. *bayith,* lit. *house*
3 a Jer. 48:38
4 a Jer. 48:34 1 So with MT, Tg., Vg.; LXX, Syr. *loins*
5 a Jer. 48:31 b Jer. 48:5 1 Or *The Third Eglath,* an unknown city, Jer. 48:34
6 a Num. 32:36
9 a 2 Kin. 17:25 1 So with MT, Tg.; DSS, Vg. *Dibon;* LXX *Rimon*

CHAPTER 16
1 a 2 Kin. 3:4 b 2 Kin. 14:7 1 Lit. *Rock*

To the mount of the daughter of
 Zion.
2 For it shall be as a [a]wandering bird
 thrown out of the nest;
So shall be the daughters of Moab
 at the fords of the [b]Arnon.

3 "Take counsel, execute judgment;
Make your shadow like the night in
 the middle of the day;
Hide the outcasts,
Do not betray him who escapes.
4 Let My outcasts dwell with you,
 O Moab;
Be a shelter to them from the face
 of the [1]spoiler.
For the extortioner is at an end,
Devastation ceases,
The oppressors are consumed out of
 the land.
5 In mercy [a]the throne will be
 established;
And One will sit on it in truth, in
 the tabernacle of David,
[b]Judging and seeking justice and
 hastening [c]righteousness."

6 We have heard of the [a]pride of
 Moab—
He is very proud—
Of his haughtiness and his pride
 and his wrath;
[b]*But* his [1]lies *shall* not *be* so.
7 Therefore Moab shall [a]wail for
 Moab;
Everyone shall wail.
For the foundations [b]of Kir
 Hareseth you shall mourn;
Surely *they are* stricken.

8 For [a]the fields of Heshbon
 languish,
And [b]the vine of Sibmah;
The lords of the nations have
 broken down its choice plants,
Which have reached to Jazer
And wandered through the
 wilderness.
Her branches are stretched out,
They are gone over the [c]sea.
9 Therefore I will bewail the vine of
 Sibmah,
With the weeping of Jazer;
I will drench you with my tears,
[a]O Heshbon and Elealeh;
For [1]battle cries have fallen
Over your summer fruits and your
 harvest.

10 [a]Gladness is taken away,
And joy from the plentiful field;
In the vineyards there will be no
 singing,
Nor will there be shouting;
No treaders will tread out wine in
 the presses;
I have made their shouting cease.
11 Therefore [a]my [1]heart shall
 resound like a harp for Moab,
And my inner being for [2]Kir Heres.

12 And it shall come to pass,
When it is seen that Moab is weary
 on [a]the high place,
That he will come to his sanctuary
 to pray;
But he will not prevail.

13 This *is* the word which the LORD has
spoken concerning Moab since that time.
14 But now the LORD has spoken, saying,
"Within three years, [a]as the years of a
hired man, the glory of Moab will be despised with all that great multitude, and
the remnant *will be* very small *and*
feeble."

Proclamation Against Syria and Israel

17 The [a]burden[1] against Damascus.

"Behold, Damascus will cease from
 being a city,
And it will be a ruinous heap.
2 [1]The cities of [a]Aroer *are* forsaken;
They will be for flocks
Which lie down, and [b]no one will
 make *them* afraid.
3 [a]The fortress also will cease from
 Ephraim,
The kingdom from Damascus,
And the remnant of Syria;
They will be as the glory of the
 children of Israel,"
Says the LORD of hosts.

4 "In that day it shall come to pass
That the glory of Jacob will [1]wane,
And [a]the fatness of his flesh grow
 lean.
5 [a]It shall be as when the harvester
 gathers the grain,
And reaps the heads with his arm;
It shall be as he who gathers heads
 of grain
In the Valley of Rephaim.
6 [a]Yet gleaning grapes will be left in
 it,

---

2 a Prov. 27:8 b Num. 21:13
4 *1 devastator*
5 a [Dan. 7:14] b Ps. 72:2 c Is. 9:7
6 a Jer. 48:29 b Is. 28:15 *1* Lit. *vain talk*
7 a Jer. 48:20 b 2 Kin. 3:25
8 a Is. 24:7 b Is. 16:9 c Jer. 48:32
9 a Is. 15:4 *1* Or *shouting has*
10 a Is. 24:8
11 a Jer. 48:36 *1* Lit. *belly* *2 Kir Hareseth,* v. 7
12 a Is. 15:2
14 a Is. 21:16

CHAPTER 17
1 a Zech. 9:1 *1 oracle, prophecy*
2 a Num. 32:34 b Jer. 7:33 *1* So with MT, Vg.; LXX *It shall be forsaken forever;* Tg. *Its cities shall be forsaken and desolate*
3 a Is. 7:16; 8:4
4 a Is. 10:16 *1 fade*
5 a Jer. 51:33
6 a Is. 24:13

Like the shaking of an olive tree,
Two *or* three olives at the top of the uppermost bough,
Four *or* five in its most fruitful branches,"
Says the LORD God of Israel.

7 In that day a man will [a]look to his Maker,
And his eyes will have respect for the Holy One of Israel.
8 He will not look to the altars,
The work of his hands;
He will not respect what his [a]fingers have made,
Nor the [1]wooden images nor the incense altars.

9 In that day his strong cities will be as a forsaken [1]bough
And [2]an uppermost branch,
Which they left because of the children of Israel;
And there will be desolation.

10 Because you have forgotten [a]the God of your salvation,
And have not been mindful of the Rock of your [1]stronghold,
Therefore you will plant pleasant plants
And set out foreign seedlings;
11 In the day you will make your plant to grow,
And in the morning you will make your seed to flourish;
But the harvest *will be* a heap of ruins
In the day of grief and desperate sorrow.

12 Woe to the multitude of many people
Who make a noise [a]like the roar of the seas,
And to the rushing of nations
That make a rushing like the rushing of mighty waters!
13 The nations will rush like the rushing of many waters;
But *God* will [a]rebuke them and they will flee far away,
And [b]be chased like the chaff of the mountains before the wind,
Like a rolling thing before the whirlwind.
14 Then behold, at eventide, trouble!
And before the morning, he *is* no more.

7 a Mic. 7:7

8 a Is. 2:8; 31:7
1 Heb. *Asherim,* Canaanite deities

9 1 LXX *Hivites;* Tg. *laid waste;* Vg. *as the plows*
2 LXX *Amorites;* Tg. *in ruins;* Vg. *corn*

10 a Ps. 68:19
1 *refuge*

12 a Jer. 6:23

13 a Ps. 9:5
b Hos. 13:3

CHAPTER 18
1 a Zeph. 2:12; 3:10
1 Heb. *Cush*

3 a Is. 5:26

4 1 *watch*

7 a Zeph. 3:10
1 So with DSS, LXX, Vg.; MT omits *From;* Tg. *To*

This *is* the portion of those who plunder us,
And the lot of those who rob us.

Proclamation Against Ethiopia

18 Woe [a]to the land shadowed with buzzing wings,
Which *is* beyond the rivers of [1]Ethiopia,
2 Which sends ambassadors by sea,
Even in vessels of reed on the waters, *saying,*
"Go, swift messengers, to a nation tall and smooth *of skin,*
To a people terrible from their beginning onward,
A nation powerful and treading down,
Whose land the rivers divide."

3 All inhabitants of the world and dwellers on the earth:
[a]When he lifts up a banner on the mountains, you see *it;*
And when he blows a trumpet, you hear *it.*
4 For so the LORD said to me,
"I will take My rest,
And I will [1]look from My dwelling place
Like clear heat in sunshine,
Like a cloud of dew in the heat of harvest."
5 For before the harvest, when the bud is perfect
And the sour grape is ripening in the flower,
He will both cut off the sprigs with pruning hooks
And take away *and* cut down the branches.
6 They will be left together for the mountain birds of prey
And for the beasts of the earth;
The birds of prey will summer on them,
And all the beasts of the earth will winter on them.

7 In that time [a]a present will be brought to the LORD of hosts
[1]From a people tall and smooth *of skin,*
And from a people terrible from their beginning onward,
A nation powerful and treading down,
Whose land the rivers divide—

To the place of the name of the LORD of hosts,
To Mount Zion.

Proclamation Against Egypt

19 The [a]burden[1] against Egypt.

Behold, the LORD [b]rides on a swift cloud,
And will come into Egypt;
[c]The idols of Egypt will [2]totter at His presence,
And the heart of Egypt will melt in its midst.

2 "I will [a]set Egyptians against Egyptians;
Everyone will fight against his brother,
And everyone against his neighbor,
City against city, kingdom against kingdom.
3 The spirit of Egypt will fail in its midst;
I will destroy their counsel,
And they will [a]consult the idols and the charmers,
The mediums and the sorcerers.
4 And the Egyptians I will give
[a]Into the hand of a cruel master,
And a fierce king will rule over them,"
Says the Lord, the LORD of hosts.

5 [a]The waters will fail from the sea,
And the river will be wasted and dried up.
6 The rivers will turn foul;
The brooks [a]of defense will be emptied and dried up;
The reeds and rushes will wither.
7 The papyrus reeds by [1]the River, by the mouth of the River,
And everything sown by the River,
Will wither, be driven away, and be no more.
8 The fishermen also will mourn;
All those will lament who cast hooks into the River,
And they will languish who spread nets on the waters.
9 Moreover those who work in [a]fine flax
And those who weave fine fabric will be ashamed;
10 And its foundations will be broken.
All who make wages *will be* troubled of soul.

11 Surely the princes of [a]Zoan *are* fools;
Pharaoh's wise counselors give foolish counsel.
[b]How do you say to Pharaoh, "I *am* the son of the wise,
The son of ancient kings?"
12 [a]Where *are* they?
Where are your wise men?
Let them tell you now,
And let them know what the LORD of hosts has [b]purposed against Egypt.
13 The princes of Zoan have become fools;
[a]The princes of [1]Noph are deceived;
They have also [2]deluded Egypt,
Those who are the [3]mainstay of its tribes.
14 The LORD has mingled [a]a perverse spirit in her midst;
And they have caused Egypt to err in all her work,
As a drunken man staggers in his vomit.
15 Neither will there be *any* work for Egypt,
Which [a]the head or tail,
Palm branch or bulrush, may do.

16 In that day Egypt will [a]be like women,
and will be afraid and fear because of the
waving of the hand of the LORD of hosts,
[b]which He waves over it. 17 And the land of
Judah will be a terror to Egypt; everyone
who makes mention of it will be afraid in
himself, because of the counsel of the
LORD of hosts which He has [a]determined
against it.

Egypt, Assyria, and Israel Blessed

18 In that day five cities in the land of
Egypt will [a]speak the language of Canaan
and [b]swear by the LORD of hosts; one will
be called the City of [1]Destruction.
19 In that day [a]there will be an altar to
the LORD in the midst of the land of Egypt,
and a pillar to the [b]LORD at its border.
20 And [a]it will be for a sign and for a witness to the LORD of hosts in the land of
Egypt; for they will cry to the LORD because of the oppressors, and He will send
them a [b]Savior and a Mighty One, and He
will deliver them. 21 Then the LORD will be
known to Egypt, and the Egyptians will
[a]know the LORD in that day, and [b]will
make sacrifice and offering; yes, they will

CHAPTER 19
1 a Joel 3:19 b Ps. 18:10; 104:3 c Jer. 43:12 *1 oracle, prophecy* 2 Lit. *shake*
2 a Judg. 7:22
3 a Is. 8:19; 47:12
4 a Ezek. 29:19
5 a Jer. 51:36
6 a 2 Kin. 19:24
7 *1* The Nile
9 a Prov. 7:16
11 a Num. 13:22 b 1 Kin. 4:29, 30
12 a 1 Cor. 1:20 b Ps. 33:11
13 a Jer. 2:16 *1* Ancient Memphis *2* Lit. *caused to stagger* *3 cornerstone*
14 a Is. 29:10
15 a Is. 9:14–16
16 a Nah. 3:13 b Is. 11:15
17 a Dan. 4:35
18 a Zeph. 3:9 b Is. 45:23 *1* Some Heb. mss., Arab., DSS, Tg., Vg. *Sun;* LXX *Asedek,* lit. *Righteousness*
19 a Ex. 24:4 b Ps. 68:31
20 a Josh. 4:20; 22:27 b Is. 43:11
21 a [Is. 2:3, 4; 11:9] b Mal. 1:11

make a vow to the LORD and perform *it.*
22 And the LORD will strike Egypt, He will
strike and [a]heal *it;* they will return to the
LORD, and He will be entreated by them
and heal them.

23 In that day [a]there will be a highway
from Egypt to Assyria, and the Assyrian
will come into Egypt and the Egyptian
into Assyria, and the Egyptians will [b]serve
with the Assyrians.

24 In that day Israel will be one of three
with Egypt and Assyria—a blessing in the
midst of the land, 25 whom the LORD of
hosts shall bless, saying, "Blessed *is* Egypt
My people, and Assyria [a]the work of My
hands, and Israel My inheritance."

The Sign Against Egypt and Ethiopia

20 In the year that [a]Tartan[1] came to
Ashdod, when Sargon the king of
Assyria sent him, and he fought against
Ashdod and took it, 2 at the same time the
LORD spoke by Isaiah the son of Amoz,
saying, "Go, and remove [a]the sackcloth
from your [1]body, and take your sandals off
your feet." And he did so, [b]walking naked
and barefoot.

3 Then the LORD said, "Just as My servant Isaiah has walked naked and barefoot
three years [a]*for* a sign and a wonder
against Egypt and Ethiopia, 4 so shall the
[a]king of Assyria lead away the Egyptians
as prisoners and the Ethiopians as captives, young and old, naked and barefoot,
[b]with their buttocks uncovered, to the
shame of Egypt. 5 [a]Then they shall be
afraid and ashamed of Ethiopia their expectation and Egypt their glory. 6 And the
inhabitant of this territory will say in that
day, 'Surely such *is* our expectation,
wherever we flee for [a]help to be delivered
from the king of Assyria; and how shall we
escape?' "

The Fall of Babylon Proclaimed

21 The [1]burden against the Wilderness of the Sea.

As [a]whirlwinds in the South pass
through,
So it comes from the desert, from a
terrible land.
2 A distressing vision is declared to
me;
[a]The treacherous dealer deals
treacherously,
And the plunderer plunders.
[b]Go up, O Elam!
Besiege, O Media!
All its sighing I have made to cease.

3 Therefore [a]my loins are filled with
pain;
[b]Pangs have taken hold of me, like
the pangs of a woman in labor.
I was [1]distressed when *I* heard *it;*
I was dismayed when *I* saw *it.*
4 My heart wavered, fearfulness
frightened me;
[a]The night for which I longed He
turned into fear for me.
5 [a]Prepare the table,
Set a watchman in the tower,
Eat and drink.
Arise, you princes,
Anoint the shield!

6 For thus has the Lord said to me:
"Go, set a watchman,
Let him declare what he sees."
7 And he saw a chariot *with* a pair of
horsemen,
A chariot of donkeys, *and* a chariot
of camels,
And he listened earnestly with great
care.
8 [1]Then he cried, "A lion, my Lord!
I stand continually on the
[a]watchtower in the daytime;
I have sat at my post every night.
9 And look, here comes a chariot of
men *with* a pair of horsemen!"
Then he answered and said,
[a]"Babylon is fallen, is fallen!
And [b]all the carved images of her
gods
He has broken to the ground."
10 [a]Oh, my threshing and the grain of
my floor!
That which I have heard from the
LORD of hosts,
The God of Israel,
I have declared to you.

Proclamation Against Edom

11 [a]The [1]burden against Dumah.

He calls to me out of [b]Seir,
"Watchman, what of the night?
Watchman, what of the night?"
12 The watchman said,
"The morning comes, and also the
night.

---

22 a Deut. 32:39
23 a Is. 11:16; 35:8; 49:11; 62:10 b Is. 27:13
25 a Is. 29:23

CHAPTER 20
1 a 2 Kin. 18:17 *1* Or *the Commander in Chief*
2 a Zech. 13:4 b 1 Sam. 19:24 *1* Lit. *loins*
3 a Is. 8:18
4 a Is. 19:4 b Jer. 13:22
5 a 2 Kin. 18:21
6 a Is. 30:5, 7

CHAPTER 21
1 a Zech. 9:14 *1 oracle, prophecy*
2 a Is. 33:1 b Jer. 49:34
3 a Is. 15:5; 16:11 b Is. 13:8 *1* Lit. *bowed*
4 a Deut. 28:67
5 a Dan. 5:5
8 a Hab. 2:1 *1* DSS *Then the observer cried, "My Lord!*
9 a Jer. 51:8 b Is. 46:1
10 a Jer. 51:33
11 a Gen. 25:14 b Gen. 32:3 *1 oracle, prophecy*

If you will inquire, inquire;
Return! Come back!"

Proclamation Against Arabia

13 [a]The [1]burden against Arabia.

In the forest in Arabia you will
lodge,
O you traveling companies [b]of
Dedanites.
14 O inhabitants of the land of Tema,
Bring water to him who is thirsty;
With their bread they met him who
fled.
15 For they fled from the swords,
from the drawn sword,
From the bent bow, and from the
distress of war.

16 For thus the LORD has said to me:
"Within a year, [a]according to the year of
a hired man, all the glory of [b]Kedar will
fail; 17 and the remainder of the number of
archers, the mighty men of the people of
Kedar, will be diminished; for the LORD
God of Israel has spoken *it*."

Proclamation Against Jerusalem

22 The [1]burden against the Valley of
Vision.

What ails you now, that you have
all gone up to the housetops,
2 You who are full of noise,
A [1]tumultuous city, [a]a joyous city?
Your slain *men are* not slain with
the sword,
Nor dead in battle.
3 All your rulers have fled together;
They are captured by the archers.
All who are found in you are bound
together;
They have fled from afar.
4 Therefore I said, "Look away from
me,
[a]I will weep bitterly;
Do not labor to comfort me
Because of the plundering of the
daughter of my people."

5 [a]For *it is* a day of trouble and
treading down and perplexity
[b]By the Lord GOD of hosts
In the Valley of Vision—
Breaking down the walls
And of crying to the mountain.
6 [a]Elam bore the quiver

13 [a] Jer. 25:24; 49:28 [b] 1 Chr. 1:9, 32 [1] *oracle, prophecy*
16 [a] Is. 16:14 [b] Ps. 120:5
CHAPTER 22
1 [1] *oracle, prophecy*
2 [a] Is. 32:13 [1] *boisterous*
4 [a] Jer. 4:19
5 [a] Is. 37:3 [b] Lam. 1:5; 2:2
6 [a] Jer. 49:35 [b] Is. 15:1
8 [a] 2 Kin. 18:15, 16 [b] 1 Kin. 7:2; 10:17 [1] Lit. *covering*
9 [a] 2 Kin. 20:20 [1] Lit. *breaches* in the city walls
11 [a] Neh. 3:16 [b] 2 Chr. 32:3, 4
12 [a] Joel 1:13; 2:17 [b] Mic. 1:16
13 [a] Luke 17:26–29 [b] 1 Cor. 15:32
14 [a] Is. 5:9 [b] Ezek. 24:13
15 [a] Is. 36:3

With chariots of men *and*
horsemen,
And [b]Kir uncovered the shield.
7 It shall come to pass *that* your
choicest valleys
Shall be full of chariots,
And the horsemen shall set
themselves in array at the gate.

8 [a]He removed the [1]protection of
Judah.
You looked in that day to the
armor [b]of the House of the
Forest;
9 [a]You also saw the [1]damage to the
city of David,
That it was great;
And you gathered together the
waters of the lower pool.
10 You numbered the houses of
Jerusalem,
And the houses you broke down
To fortify the wall.
11 [a]You also made a reservoir between
the two walls
For the water of the old [b]pool.
But you did not look to its Maker,
Nor did you have respect for Him
who fashioned it long ago.

12 And in that day the Lord GOD of
hosts
[a]Called for weeping and for
mourning,
[b]For baldness and for girding with
sackcloth.
13 But instead, joy and gladness,
Slaying oxen and killing sheep,
Eating meat and [a]drinking wine:
[b]"Let us eat and drink, for tomorrow
we die!"

14 [a]Then it was revealed in my
hearing by the LORD of hosts,
"Surely for this iniquity there [b]will
be no atonement for you,
Even to your death," says the Lord
GOD of hosts.

The Judgment on Shebna

15 Thus says the Lord GOD of hosts:

"Go, proceed to this steward,
To [a]Shebna, who *is* over the house,
and say:
16 'What have you here, and whom
have you here,
That you have hewn a sepulcher
here,

As he [a]who hews himself a
sepulcher on high,
Who carves a tomb for himself in a
rock?
17 Indeed, the LORD will throw you
away violently,
O mighty man,
[a]And will surely seize you.
18 He will surely turn violently and
toss you like a ball
Into a large country;
There you shall die, and there
[a]your glorious chariots
Shall be the shame of your master's
house.
19 So I will drive you out of your
office,
And from your position [1]he will
pull you down.

20 'Then it shall be in that day,
That I will call My servant [a]Eliakim
the son of Hilkiah;
21 I will clothe him with your robe
And strengthen him with your belt;
I will commit your responsibility
into his hand.
He shall be a father to the
inhabitants of Jerusalem
And to the house of Judah.
22 The key of the house of David
I will lay on his [a]shoulder;
So he shall [b]open, and no one shall
shut;
And he shall shut, and no one shall
open.
23 I will fasten him *as* [a]a peg in a
secure place,
And he will become a glorious
throne to his father's house.

24 'They will hang on him all the glory of
his father's house, the offspring and the
posterity, all vessels of small quantity,
from the cups to all the pitchers. 25 In that
day,' says the LORD of hosts, 'the peg that
is fastened in the secure place will be removed and be cut down and fall, and the
burden that *was* on it will be cut off; for
the LORD has spoken.' "

Proclamation Against Tyre

23 The [a]burden[1] against Tyre.

Wail, you ships of Tarshish!
For it is laid waste,
So that there is no house, no
harbor;
From the land of [2]Cyprus it is
revealed to them.

2 Be still, you inhabitants of the
coastland,
You merchants of Sidon,
[1]Whom those who cross the sea have
filled.
3 And on great waters the grain of
Shihor,
The harvest of [1]the River, *is* her
revenue;
And [a]she is a marketplace for the
nations.

4 Be ashamed, O Sidon;
For the sea has spoken,
The strength of the sea, saying,
"I do not labor, nor bring forth
children;
Neither do I rear young men,
Nor bring up virgins."
5 [a]When the report *reaches* Egypt,
They also will be in agony at the
report of Tyre.

6 Cross over to Tarshish;
Wail, you inhabitants of the
coastland!
7 *Is* this your [a]joyous *city,*
Whose antiquity *is* from ancient
days,
Whose feet carried her far off to
dwell?
8 Who has taken this counsel against
Tyre, [a]the crowning *city,*
Whose merchants *are* princes,
Whose traders *are* the honorable of
the earth?
9 The LORD of hosts has [a]purposed
it,
To [1]bring to dishonor the [b]pride of
all glory,
To bring into contempt all the
honorable of the earth.

10 Overflow through your land like
[1]the River,
O daughter of Tarshish;
There is no more [2]strength.
11 He stretched out His hand over
the sea,
He shook the kingdoms;
The LORD has given a
commandment [a]against Canaan
To destroy its strongholds.
12 And He said, "You will rejoice no
more,
O you oppressed virgin daughter of
Sidon.

16 a Matt. 27:60
17 a Esth. 7:8
18 a Is. 2:7
19 1 LXX omits *he will pull you down;* Syr., Tg., Vg. *I will pull you down*
20 a 2 Kin. 18:18
22 a Is. 9:6 b Job 12:14; Rev. 3:7
23 a Ezra 9:8

CHAPTER 23
1 a Zech. 9:2, 4 *1 oracle, prophecy* 2 Heb. *Kittim,* western lands, especially Cyprus
2 1 So with MT, Vg.; LXX, Tg. *Passing over the water;* DSS *Your messengers passing over the sea*
3 a Ezek. 27:3–23 1 The Nile
5 a Is. 19:16
7 a Is. 22:2; 32:13
8 a Ezek. 28:2, 12
9 a Is. 14:26 b Dan. 4:37 *1 pollute*
10 1 The Nile *2 restraint,* lit. *belt*
11 a Zech. 9:2–4

Arise, [a]cross over to Cyprus;
There also you will have no rest."

13 Behold, the land of the
[a]Chaldeans,
This people *which* was not;
Assyria founded it for [b]wild beasts
of the desert.
They set up its towers,
They raised up its palaces,
And brought it to ruin.

14 [a]Wail, you ships of Tarshish!
For your strength is laid waste.

15 Now it shall come to pass in that day
that Tyre will be forgotten seventy years,
according to the days of one king. At the
end of seventy years it will happen to Tyre
as *in* the song of the harlot:

16 "Take a harp, go about the city,
You forgotten harlot;
Make sweet melody, sing many
songs,
That you may be remembered."

17 And it shall be, at the end of seventy
years, that the LORD will deal with Tyre.
She will return to her hire, and [a]commit
fornication with all the kingdoms of the
world on the face of the earth. 18 Her gain
and her pay [a]will be set apart for the LORD;
it will not be treasured nor laid up, for her
gain will be for those who dwell before the
LORD, to eat sufficiently, and for [1]fine
clothing.

Impending Judgment on the Earth

24 Behold, the LORD makes the
earth empty and makes it
waste,
Distorts its surface
And scatters abroad its inhabitants.
2 And it shall be:
As with the people, so with the
[a]priest;
As with the servant, so with his
master;
As with the maid, so with her
mistress;
[b]As with the buyer, so with the
seller;
As with the lender, so with the
borrower;
As with the creditor, so with the
debtor.

3 The land shall be entirely emptied
and utterly plundered,
For the LORD has spoken this word.
4 The earth mourns *and* fades away,
The world languishes *and* fades
away;
The [a]haughty[1] people of the earth
languish.
5 [a]The earth is also defiled under its
inhabitants,
Because they have [b]transgressed the
laws,
Changed the ordinance,
Broken the [c]everlasting covenant.
6 Therefore [a]the curse has devoured
the earth,
And those who dwell in it are
[1]desolate.
Therefore the inhabitants of the
earth are [b]burned,
And few men *are* left.

7 [a]The new wine fails, the vine
languishes,
All the merry-hearted sigh.
8 The mirth [a]of the tambourine
ceases,
The noise of the jubilant ends,
The joy of the harp ceases.
9 They shall not drink wine with a
song;
Strong drink is bitter to those who
drink it.
10 The city of confusion is broken
down;
Every house is shut up, so that
none may go in.
11 *There is* a cry for wine in the
streets,
All joy is darkened,
The mirth of the land is gone.
12 In the city desolation is left,
And the gate is stricken with
destruction.
13 When it shall be thus in the midst
of the land among the people,
[a]*It shall be* like the shaking of an
olive tree,
Like the gleaning of grapes when
the vintage is done.
14 They shall lift up their voice, they
shall sing;
For the majesty of the LORD
They shall cry aloud from the sea.
15 Therefore [a]glorify the LORD in the
dawning light,
[b]The name of the LORD God of Israel
in the coastlands of the sea.

---

12 a Rev. 18:22
13 a Is. 47:1 b Ps. 72:9
14 a Ezek. 27:25–30
17 a Rev. 17:2
18 a Zech. 14:20, 21 *1 choice*

CHAPTER 24
2 a Hos. 4:9 b Ezek. 7:12, 13
4 a Is. 25:11 *1 proud*
5 a Num. 35:33 b Is. 59:12 c 1 Chr. 16:14–19
6 a Mal. 4:6 b Is. 9:19 *1 Or held guilty*
7 a Joel 1:10, 12
8 a Ezek. 26:13
13 a [Is. 17:5, 6; 27:12]
15 a Is. 25:3 b Mal. 1:11

16 From the ends of the earth we have heard songs:
"Glory to the righteous!"
But I said, [1]"I am ruined, ruined!
Woe to me!
[a]The treacherous dealers have dealt treacherously,
Indeed, the treacherous dealers have dealt very treacherously."

17 [a]Fear and the pit and the snare
Are upon you, O inhabitant of the earth.
18 And it shall be
That he who flees from the noise of the fear
Shall fall into the pit,
And he who comes up from the midst of the pit
Shall be [1]caught in the snare;
For [a]the windows from on high are open,
And [b]the foundations of the earth are shaken.

19 [a]The earth is violently broken,
The earth is split open,
The earth is shaken exceedingly.
20 The earth shall [a]reel[1] to and fro like a drunkard,
And shall totter like a hut;
Its transgression shall be heavy upon it,
And it will fall, and not rise again.

21 It shall come to pass in that day
That the LORD will punish on high the host of exalted ones,
And on the earth [a]the kings of the earth.
22 They will be gathered together,
As prisoners are gathered in the [1]pit,
And will be shut up in the prison;
After many days they will be punished.
23 Then the [a]moon will be disgraced
And the sun ashamed;
For the LORD of hosts will [b]reign
On [c]Mount Zion and in Jerusalem
And before His elders, gloriously.

Praise to God

25 O LORD, You *are* my God.
[a]I will exalt You,
I will praise Your name,
[b]For You have done wonderful *things;*
[c]*Your* counsels of old *are* faithfulness *and* truth.
2 For You have made [a]a city a ruin,
A fortified city a ruin,
A palace of foreigners to be a city no more;
It will never be rebuilt.
3 Therefore the strong people will [a]glorify You;
The city of the [1]terrible nations will fear You.
4 For You have been a strength to the poor,
A strength to the needy in his distress,
[a]A refuge from the storm,
A shade from the heat;
For the blast of the terrible ones *is* as a storm *against* the wall.
5 You will reduce the noise of aliens,
As heat in a dry place;
As heat in the shadow of a cloud,
The song of the terrible ones will be [1]diminished.

Father, ___ has waited for You, and You will save them. Let them be glad and rejoice in Your salvation.
FROM ISAIAH 25:9

6 And in [a]this mountain
[b]The LORD of hosts will make for [c]all people
A feast of [1]choice pieces,
A feast of [2]wines on the lees,
Of fat things full of marrow,
Of well-refined wines on the lees.
7 And He will destroy on this mountain
The surface of the covering cast over all people,
And [a]the veil that is spread over all nations.
8 He will [a]swallow up death forever,
And the Lord GOD will [b]wipe away tears from all faces;
The rebuke of His people
He will take away from all the earth;
For the LORD has spoken.

---

16 a Jer. 3:20; 5:11 1 Lit. *Leanness to me, leanness to me*
17 a Jer. 48:43
18 a Gen. 7:11 b Ps. 18:7; 46:2 1 Lit. *taken*
19 a Jer. 4:23
20 a Is. 19:14; 24:1; 28:7 1 *stagger*
21 a Ps. 76:12
22 1 *dungeon*
23 a Is. 13:10; 60:19 b Rev. 19:4, 6 c [Heb. 12:22]

CHAPTER 25
1 a Ex. 15:2 b Ps. 98:1 c Num. 23:19
2 a Jer. 51:37
3 a Is. 24:15 1 *terrifying*
4 a Is. 4:6
5 1 *humbled*
6 a [Is. 2:2–4; 56:7] b Prov. 9:2 c [Dan. 7:14] 1 Lit. *fat things* 2 *wines matured on the sediment*
7 a [Eph. 4:18]
8 a [Hos. 13:14] b Rev. 7:17; 21:4

9 And it will be said in that day:
"Behold, this *is* our God;
[a]We have waited for Him, and He will save us.
This *is* the LORD;
We have waited for Him;
[b]We will be glad and rejoice in His salvation."

10 For on this mountain the hand of the LORD will rest,
And [a]Moab shall be trampled down under Him,
As straw is trampled down for the refuse heap.
11 And He will spread out His hands in their midst
As a swimmer reaches out to swim,
And He will bring down their [a]pride
Together with the trickery of their hands.
12 The [a]fortress of the high fort of your walls
He will bring down, lay low,
And bring to the ground, down to the dust.

A Song of Salvation

26 In [a]that day this song will be sung in the land of Judah:

"We have a strong city;
[b]*God* will appoint salvation *for* walls and bulwarks.
2 [a]Open the gates,
That the righteous nation which [1]keeps the truth may enter in.
3 You will keep *him* in perfect [a]peace,
Whose mind *is* stayed *on You,*
Because he trusts in You.

4 Trust in the LORD forever,
[a]For in YAH, the LORD, *is* [1]everlasting strength.
5 For He brings [1]down those who dwell on high,
[a]The lofty city;
He lays it low,
He lays it low to the ground,
He brings it down to the dust.
6 The foot shall [1]tread it down—
The feet of the poor
And the steps of the needy."

Lord, keep ____ in perfect peace, whose mind is stayed on You, because they trust You.

FROM ISAIAH 26:3

Perfect peace is God's gift, but our minds stayed on Him is our responsibility. Always have within you the knowledge that you are acting on the Word of God. You cannot depend on feelings, or on what you see, or on anything else. Have no confidence in anything which is on a natural plane.

SMITH WIGGLESWORTH

7 The way of the just *is* uprightness;
[a]O Most Upright,
You [1]weigh the path of the just.
8 Yes, [a]in the way of Your judgments,
O LORD, we have [b]waited for You;
The desire of *our* soul *is* for Your name
And for the remembrance of You.
9 [a]With my soul I have desired You in the night,
Yes, by my spirit within me I will seek You early;
For when Your judgments *are* in the earth,
The inhabitants of the world will learn righteousness.

10 [a]Let grace be shown to the wicked,
Yet he will not learn righteousness;
In [b]the land of uprightness he will deal unjustly,
And will not behold the majesty of the LORD.

9 a Gen. 49:18 b Ps. 20:5
10 a Amos 2:1–3
11 a Is. 24:4; 26:5
12 a Is. 26:5
CHAPTER 26
1 a Is. 2:11; 12:1 b Is. 60:18
2 a Ps. 118:19, 20 *1* Or *remains faithful*
3 a Is. 57:19
4 a Is. 12:2; 45:17 *1* Or *Rock of Ages*
5 a Is. 25:11, 12 *1 low*
6 *1 trample*
7 a Ps. 37:23 *1* Or *make level*
8 a Is. 64:5 b Is. 25:9; 33:2
9 a Ps. 63:6
10 a [Rom. 2:4] b Ps. 143:10

ISAIAH 26:3

Dear Woman of Destiny,

While on a ministry trip to Great Britain, a phone call brought the devastating news that a fire had destroyed my home. The Lord immediately reminded me "that all things work together for good to those who love God" (Rom. 8:28) and that the thief has to repay sevenfold. Turmoil flooded my mind when I thought of my great loss. Yet when I was able to tame my thought and "stay" (fix) my mind on the Lord and His promises, I had total peace. Many items were recovered. Eventually God abundantly restored and fulfilled all He had promised. During that time, however, I had walked in both panic and peace. Peace was so much better.

In another traumatic situation, the Lord spoke peace once again. This was impossible in the natural. I amplified my problems as I informed Him about my terrible situation, expecting sympathy and comfort. Instead, He said, "You can *choose* peace." As I made that choice, a mantle of incredible serenity seemed to surround me. The situation didn't change for several months, but my peace was not dependent on circumstances. Serenity was much more pleasant than stress. How amazing to realize that the peace that surpasses all human reasoning was actually guarding my heart and mind! (see Phil. 4:7).

Yahweh Shalom has made a covenant of peace with us that can never be broken. Perfect peace is promised, but not perfect circumstances. This promise often seems so difficult to attain, yet the Bible exhorts us to pursue peace. And God wouldn't have made a promise He didn't intend to keep. Why do we struggle so much instead of just receiving the abundant life He offers? Why do we choose to dwell on our difficulties instead of accepting and appropriating this precious gift?

Peace seems so hard to maintain when the storms of life are swirling around us. But remember, we serve the Waymaker who makes a way where there seems to be no way. A jet pilot doesn't purposely remain in turbulent weather. He flies far above the storm. There is a place of peace in the midst of the storm just as there is an eye of calm in the center of a hurricane. We can choose to dwell on our difficulties or look up to the One who spoke peace to the storm. We can dwell in perfect peace in God's presence *if* we keep our mind on Him.

The Prince of Peace desires to lead you beside still, quiet waters today. Cares, anxieties, and fears will try to block your way as you seek Him. But you can choose to cast all your cares on the One who cares for you (see 1 Pet. 5:7). Didn't He command you to be anxious for nothing? (see Phil. 4:6, 7). If you keep your mind on Jesus, remaining stayed (firmly fixed, steadfast, rooted, immovable), you will have perfect peace. He said so.

Sally Horton

11 LORD, *when* Your hand is lifted
up, [a]they will not see.
But they will see and be ashamed
For [1]*their* envy of people;
Yes, the fire of Your enemies shall
devour them.

12 LORD, You will establish peace for
us,
For You have also done all our
works [1]in us.
13 O LORD our God, [a]masters besides
You
Have had dominion over us;
But by You only we make mention
of Your name.
14 *They are* dead, they will not live;
They are deceased, they will not
rise.
Therefore You have punished and
destroyed them,
And made all their memory to
[a]perish.
15 You have increased the nation,
O LORD,
You have [a]increased the nation;
You are glorified;
You have expanded all the [1]borders
of the land.

16 LORD, [a]in trouble they have visited
You,
They poured out a prayer *when*
Your chastening *was* upon them.
17 As [a]a woman with child
Is in pain and cries out in her
[1]pangs,
When she draws near the time of
her delivery,
So have we been in Your sight,
O LORD.
18 We have been with child, we have
been in pain;
We have, as it were, [1]brought forth
wind;
We have not accomplished any
deliverance in the earth,
Nor have [a]the inhabitants of the
world fallen.

19 [a]Your dead shall live;
Together with [1]my dead body they
shall arise.
[b]Awake and sing, you who dwell in
dust;
For your dew *is like* the dew of
herbs,
And the earth shall cast out the
dead.

11 a Is. 5:12 1 Or *Your zeal for the people*
12 1 Or *for us*
13 a 2 Chr. 12:8
14 a Eccl. 9:5
15 a Is. 9:3 1 Or *ends*
16 a Hos. 5:15
17 a [John 16:21] 1 *sharp pains*
18 a Ps. 17:14 1 *given birth to*
19 a [Ezek. 37:1–14] b [Dan. 12:2] 1 So with MT, Vg.; Syr., Tg. *their dead bodies;* LXX *those in the tombs*
20 a Ex. 12:22, 23 b [Ps. 30:5]
21 a Mic. 1:3 1 Or *bloodshed*

CHAPTER 27
1 a Ps. 74:13, 14 b Is. 51:9
2 a Is. 5:1 b Is. 5:7 1 So with MT (Kittel's *Biblia Hebraica*), Bg., Vg.; MT (*Biblia Hebraica Stuttgartensia*), some Heb. mss., LXX *delight;* Tg. *choice vineyard*
3 a Is. 31:5
4 a 2 Sam. 23:6
5 a Is. 25:4 b Job 22:21
6 a Is. 37:31
7 a Is. 10:12, 17; 30:30–33 1 Lit. *him*
8 a Job 23:6 b [Ps. 78:38]

Take Refuge from the Coming Judgment

20 Come, my people, [a]enter your
chambers,
And shut your doors behind you;
Hide yourself, as it were, [b]for a
little moment,
Until the indignation is past.
21 For behold, the LORD [a]comes out
of His place
To punish the inhabitants of the
earth for their iniquity;
The earth will also disclose her
[1]blood,
And will no more cover her slain.

27 In that day the LORD with His
severe sword, great and strong,
Will punish Leviathan the fleeing
serpent,
[a]Leviathan that twisted serpent;
And He will slay [b]the reptile that *is*
in the sea.

The Restoration of Israel

2 In that day [a]sing to her,
[b]"A vineyard of [1]red wine!
3 [a]I, the LORD, keep it,
I water it every moment;
Lest any hurt it,
I keep it night and day.
4 Fury *is* not in Me.
Who would set [a]briers *and* thorns
Against Me in battle?
I would go through them,
I would burn them together.
5 Or let him take hold [a]of My
strength,
That he may [b]make peace with Me;
And he shall make peace with Me."

6 Those who come He shall cause
[a]to take root in Jacob;
Israel shall blossom and bud,
And fill the face of the world with
fruit.

7 [a]Has He struck [1]Israel as He struck
those who struck him?
Or has He been slain according to
the slaughter of those who were
slain by Him?
8 [a]In measure, by sending it away,
You contended with it.
[b]He removes *it* by His rough wind
In the day of the east wind.
9 Therefore by this the iniquity of
Jacob will be covered;

And this *is* all the fruit of taking
away his sin:
When he makes all the stones of
the altar
Like chalkstones that are beaten to
dust,
[1]Wooden images and incense altars
shall not stand.

10 Yet the fortified city *will be*
[a]desolate,
The habitation forsaken and left like
a wilderness;
There the calf will feed, and there it
will lie down
And consume its branches.
11 When its boughs are withered,
they will be broken off;
The women come *and* set them on
fire.
For [a]it *is* a people of no
understanding;
Therefore He who made them will
[b]not have mercy on them,
And [c]He who formed them will
show them no favor.

12 And it shall come to pass in that
day
That the LORD will thresh,
From the channel of [1]the River to
the Brook of Egypt;
And you will be [a]gathered one by
one,
O you children of Israel.

13 [a]So it shall be in that day:
[b]The great trumpet will be blown;
They will come, who are about to
perish in the land of Assyria,
And they who are outcasts in the
land of [c]Egypt,
And shall [d]worship the LORD in the
holy mount at Jerusalem.

Woe to Ephraim and Jerusalem

28 Woe to the crown of pride, to the
drunkards of Ephraim,
Whose glorious beauty *is* a fading
flower
Which *is* at the head of the
[1]verdant valleys,
To those who are overcome with
wine!
2 Behold, the Lord has a mighty and
strong one,
[a]Like a tempest of hail and a
destroying storm,

9 [1] Heb. *Asherim,* Canaanite deities
10 [a] Is. 5:6, 17; 32:14
11 [a] Deut. 32:28 [b] Is. 9:17 [c] Deut. 32:18
12 [a] [Is. 11:11; 56:8] [1] The Euphrates
13 [a] Is. 2:11 [b] Rev. 11:15 [c] Is. 19:21, 22 [d] Zech. 14:16

CHAPTER 28
1 [1] Lit. *valleys of fatness*
2 [a] Ezek. 13:11
4 [1] Lit. *valley of fatness*
7 [a] Hos. 4:11 [b] Is. 56:10, 12
9 [a] Jer. 6:10
10 [a] [2 Chr. 36:15]
11 [a] 1 Cor. 14:21
12 [a] Is. 30:15

Like a flood of mighty waters
overflowing,
Who will bring *them* down to the
earth with *His* hand.
3 The crown of pride, the drunkards
of Ephraim,
Will be trampled underfoot;
4 And the glorious beauty is a fading
flower
Which *is* at the head of the
[1]verdant valley,
Like the first fruit before the
summer,
Which an observer sees;
He eats it up while it is still in his
hand.

5 In that day the LORD of hosts will
be
For a crown of glory and a diadem
of beauty
To the remnant of His people,
6 For a spirit of justice to him who
sits in judgment,
And for strength to those who turn
back the battle at the gate.

7 But they also [a]have erred through
wine,
And through intoxicating drink are
out of the way;
[b]The priest and the prophet have
erred through intoxicating drink,
They are swallowed up by wine,
They are out of the way through
intoxicating drink;
They err in vision, they stumble *in*
judgment.
8 For all tables are full of vomit *and*
filth;
No place *is clean.*

9 "Whom[a] will he teach knowledge?
And whom will he make to
understand the message?
Those *just* weaned from milk?
Those *just* drawn from the breasts?
10 [a]For precept *must be* upon precept,
precept upon precept,
Line upon line, line upon line,
Here a little, there a little."

11 For with [a]stammering lips and
another tongue
He will speak to this people,
12 To whom He said, "This *is* the
[a]rest *with which*
You may cause the weary to rest,"
And, "This *is* the refreshing";
Yet they would not hear.

13 But the word of the LORD was to
them,
"Precept upon precept, precept upon
precept,
Line upon line, line upon line,
Here a little, there a little,"
That they might go and fall
backward, and be broken
And snared and caught.

14 Therefore hear the word of the
LORD, you scornful men,
Who rule this people who *are* in
Jerusalem,
15 Because you have said, "We have
made a covenant with death,
And with Sheol we are in
agreement.
When the overflowing scourge
passes through,
It will not come to us,
[a]For we have made lies our refuge,
And under falsehood we have
hidden ourselves."

A Cornerstone in Zion

16 Therefore thus says the Lord GOD:

"Behold, I lay in Zion [a]a stone for a
foundation,
A tried stone, a precious
cornerstone, a sure foundation;
Whoever believes will not act
hastily.
17 Also I will make justice the
measuring line,
And righteousness the plummet;
The hail will sweep away the refuge
of lies,
And the waters will overflow the
hiding place.
18 Your covenant with death will be
annulled,
And your agreement with Sheol will
not stand;
When the overflowing scourge
passes through,
Then you will be trampled down by
it.
19 As often as it goes out it will take
you;
For morning by morning it will
pass over,
And by day and by night;
It will be a terror just to
understand the report."

20 For the bed is too short to stretch
out *on*,
And the covering so narrow that
one cannot wrap himself *in it*.
21 For the LORD will rise up as *at*
Mount [a]Perazim,
He will be angry as in the Valley of
[b]Gibeon—
That He may do His work, [c]His
awesome work,
And bring to pass His act, His
[1]unusual act.
22 Now therefore, do not be mockers,
Lest your bonds be made strong;
For I have heard from the Lord
GOD of hosts,
[a]A [1]destruction determined even
upon the whole earth.

Listen to the Teaching of God

23 Give ear and hear my voice,
Listen and hear my speech.
24 Does the plowman keep plowing
all day to sow?
Does he keep turning his soil and
breaking the clods?
25 When he has leveled its surface,
Does he not sow the black cummin
And scatter the cummin,
Plant the wheat in rows,
The barley in the appointed place,
And the [1]spelt in its place?
26 For He instructs him in right
judgment,
His God teaches him.

27 For the black cummin is not
threshed with a threshing sledge,
Nor is a cartwheel rolled over the
cummin;
But the black cummin is beaten out
with a stick,
And the cummin with a rod.
28 Bread *flour* must be ground;
Therefore he does not thresh it
forever,
Break *it with* his cartwheel,
Or crush it *with* his horsemen.
29 This also comes from the LORD of
hosts,
[a]*Who* is wonderful in counsel *and*
excellent in [1]guidance.

Woe to Jerusalem

29 "Woe [a]to [1]Ariel, to Ariel, the city
[b]*where* David dwelt!
Add year to year;
Let feasts come around.
2 Yet I will distress Ariel;

15 [a]Is. 9:15
16 [a]Matt. 21:42
21 [a]2 Sam. 5:20 [b]Josh. 10:10, 12 [c][Lam. 3:33] [1]Lit. *foreign*
22 [a]Is. 10:22 [1]Lit. *complete end*
25 [1]*rye*
29 [a]Ps. 92:5 [1]*sound wisdom*

CHAPTER 29
1 [a]Ezek. 24:6, 9 [b]2 Sam. 5:9 [1]Jerusalem, lit. *Lion of God*

There shall be heaviness and
sorrow,
And it shall be to Me as Ariel.
3 I will encamp against you all
around,
I will lay siege against you with a
mound,
And I will raise siegeworks against
you.
4 You shall be brought down,
You shall speak out of the ground;
Your speech shall be low, out of the
dust;
Your voice shall be like a medium's,
[a]out of the ground;
And your speech shall whisper out
of the dust.

5 "Moreover the multitude of your
[a]foes
Shall be like fine dust,
And the multitude of the terrible
ones
Like [b]chaff that passes away;
Yes, it shall be [c]in an instant,
suddenly.
6 [a]You will be punished by the LORD
of hosts
With thunder and [b]earthquake and
great noise,
With storm and tempest
And the flame of devouring fire.
7 [a]The multitude of all the nations
who fight against [1]Ariel,
Even all who fight against her and
her fortress,
And distress her,
Shall be [b]as a dream of a night
vision.
8 [a]It shall even be as when a hungry
man dreams,
And look—he eats;
But he awakes, and his soul is still
empty;
Or as when a thirsty man dreams,
And look—he drinks;
But he awakes, and indeed *he is*
faint,
And his soul still craves:
So the multitude of all the nations
shall be,
Who fight against Mount Zion."

The Blindness of Disobedience

9 Pause and wonder!
Blind yourselves and be blind!
[a]They are drunk, [b]but not with wine;
They stagger, but not with
intoxicating drink.
10 For [a]the LORD has poured out on
you
The spirit of deep sleep,
And has [b]closed your eyes, namely,
the prophets;
And He has covered your heads,
namely, [c]the seers.

[11]The whole vision has become to you
like the words of a [1]book [a]that is sealed,
which *men* deliver to one who is literate,
saying, "Read this, please."
[b]And he says, "I cannot, for it *is* sealed."
[12]Then the book is delivered to one who
[1]is illiterate, saying, "Read this, please."
And he says, "I am not literate."
[13]Therefore the Lord said:

[a]"Inasmuch as these people draw near
with their mouths
And honor Me [b]with their lips,
But have removed their hearts far
from Me,
And their fear toward Me is taught
by the commandment of men,
14 [a]Therefore, behold, I will again do
a marvelous work
Among this people,
A marvelous work and a wonder;
[b]For the wisdom of their wise *men*
shall perish,
And the understanding of their
prudent *men* shall be hidden."

15 [a]Woe to those who seek deep to
hide their counsel far from the
LORD,
And their works are in the dark;
[b]They say, "Who sees us?" and, "Who
knows us?"
16 Surely you have things turned
around!
Shall the potter be esteemed as the
clay;
For shall the [a]thing made say of
him who made it,
"He did not make me"?
Or shall the thing formed say of
him who formed it,
"He has no understanding"?

Future Recovery of Wisdom

17 *Is* it not yet a very little while
Till [a]Lebanon shall be turned into a
fruitful field,
And the fruitful field be esteemed as
a forest?

4 a Is. 8:19
5 a Is. 25:5 b Job 21:18 c Is. 30:13; 47:11
6 a Is. 28:2; 30:30 b Rev. 16:18, 19
7 a Mic. 4:11, 12 b Job 20:8 *1* Jerusalem
8 a Ps. 73:20
9 a Is. 28:7, 8 b Is. 51:21
10 a Rom. 11:8 b Ps. 69:23 c Is. 44:18
11 a Is. 8:16 b Dan. 12:4, 9 *1 scroll*
12 *1* Lit. *does not know books*
13 a Ezek. 33:31 b Col. 2:22
14 a Hab. 1:5 b Jer. 49:7
15 a Is. 30:1 b Ps. 10:11; 94:7
16 a Is. 45:9
17 a Is. 32:15

18 [a]In that day the deaf shall hear the
words of the book,
And the eyes of the blind shall see
out of obscurity and out of
darkness.
19 [a]The humble also shall increase
their joy in the LORD,
And [b]the poor among men shall
rejoice
In the Holy One of Israel.
20 For the [1]terrible one is brought to
nothing,
[a]The scornful one is consumed,
And all who [b]watch for iniquity are
cut off—
21 Who make a man an offender by a
word,
And [a]lay a snare for him who
reproves in the gate,
And turn aside the just [b]by empty
words.

22Therefore thus says the LORD, [a]who
redeemed Abraham, concerning the
house of Jacob:

"Jacob shall not now be [b]ashamed,
Nor shall his face now grow pale;
23 But when he sees his children,
[a]The work of My hands, in his
midst,
They will hallow My name,
And hallow the Holy One of Jacob,
And fear the God of Israel.
24 These also [a]who erred in spirit
will come to understanding,
And those who complained will
learn doctrine."

Futile Confidence in Egypt

30 "Woe to the rebellious children,"
says the LORD,
[a]"Who take counsel, but not of Me,
And who [1]devise plans, but not of
My Spirit,
[b]That they may add sin to sin;
2 [a]Who walk to go down to Egypt,
And [b]have not asked My advice,
To strengthen themselves in the
strength of Pharaoh,
And to trust in the shadow of
Egypt!
3 [a]Therefore the strength of Pharaoh
Shall be your shame,
And trust in the shadow of Egypt
Shall be *your* humiliation.
4 For his princes were at [a]Zoan,
And his ambassadors came to
Hanes.

18 a Is. 35:5
19 a [Is. 11:4; 61:1] b [James 2:5]
20 a Is. 28:14 b Mic. 2:1 *1 terrifying*
21 a Amos 5:10, 12 b Prov. 28:21
22 a Josh. 24:3 b Is. 45:17
23 a [Is. 45:11; 49:20–26]
24 a Is. 28:7
CHAPTER 30
1 a Is. 29:15 b Deut. 29:19 *1* Lit. *weave a web*
2 a Is. 31:1 b Josh. 9:14
3 a Is. 20:5
4 a Is. 19:11
5 a Jer. 2:36
6 a Is. 57:9 b Deut. 8:15 *1 oracle, prophecy*
7 a Jer. 37:7 *1* Lit. *Rahab Sits Idle*
8 a Hab. 2:2
9 a Is. 1:2, 4; 65:2
10 a Jer. 11:21 b 1 Kin. 22:8, 13
12 a Is. 5:24
13 a Ps. 62:3, 4 b Is. 29:5
14 a Jer. 19:11

5 [a]They were all ashamed of a people
who could not benefit them,
Or be help or benefit,
But a shame and also a reproach."

6[a]The [1]burden against the beasts of the
South.

Through a land of trouble and
anguish,
From which *came* the lioness and
lion,
[b]The viper and fiery flying serpent,
They will carry their riches on the
backs of young donkeys,
And their treasures on the humps
of camels,
To a people *who* shall not profit;
7 [a]For the Egyptians shall help in
vain and to no purpose.
Therefore I have called her
[1]Rahab-Hem-Shebeth.

A Rebellious People

8 Now go, [a]write it before them on a
tablet,
And note it on a scroll,
That it may be for time to come,
Forever and ever:
9 That [a]this *is* a rebellious people,
Lying children,
Children *who* will not hear the law
of the LORD;
10 [a]Who say to the seers, "Do not
see,"
And to the prophets, "Do not
prophesy to us right things;
[b]Speak to us smooth things,
prophesy deceits.
11 Get out of the way,
Turn aside from the path,
Cause the Holy One of Israel
To cease from before us."

12Therefore thus says the Holy One of
Israel:

"Because you [a]despise this word,
And trust in oppression and
perversity,
And rely on them,
13 Therefore this iniquity shall be to
you
[a]Like a breach ready to fall,
A bulge in a high wall,
Whose breaking [b]comes suddenly,
in an instant.
14 And [a]He shall break it like the
breaking of the potter's vessel,
Which is broken in pieces;

He shall not spare.
So there shall not be found among its fragments
[1]A shard to take fire from the hearth,
Or to take water from the cistern."

15 For thus says the Lord GOD, the Holy One of Israel:

[a]"In returning and rest you shall be saved;
In quietness and confidence shall be your strength."
[b]But you would not,
16 And you said, "No, for we will flee on horses"—
Therefore you shall flee!
And, "We will ride on swift *horses*"—
Therefore those who pursue you shall be swift!

17 [a]One thousand *shall flee* at the threat of one,
At the threat of five you shall flee,
Till you are left as a [1]pole on top of a mountain
And as a banner on a hill.

God Will Be Gracious

18 Therefore the LORD will wait, that He may be [a]gracious to you;
And therefore He will be exalted, that He may have mercy on you.
For the LORD *is* a God of justice;
[b]Blessed *are* all those who [c]wait for Him.

19 For the people [a]shall dwell in Zion at Jerusalem;
You shall [b]weep no more.
He will be very gracious to you at the sound of your cry;
When He hears it, He will [c]answer you.
20 And *though* the Lord gives you
[a]The bread of adversity and the water of [1]affliction,
Yet [b]your teachers will not be moved into a corner anymore,
But your eyes shall see your teachers.
21 Your ears shall hear a word behind you, saying,
"This *is* the way, walk in it,"
Whenever you [a]turn to the right hand
Or whenever you turn to the left.

14 [1]A piece of broken pottery
15 [a]Is. 7:4; 28:12 [b]Matt. 23:37
17 [a]Josh. 23:10 [1]A tree stripped of branches
18 [a]Is. 33:2 [b]Jer. 17:7 [c]Is. 26:8
19 [a]Is. 65:9 [b]Is. 25:8 [c]Is. 65:24
20 [a]1 Kin. 22:27 [b]Amos 8:11 [1]*oppression*
21 [a]Josh. 1:7
22 [a]Is. 2:20; 31:7 [b]Hos. 14:8
23 [a][Matt. 6:33] [1]*rich*
25 [a]Is. 2:14, 15 [b]Is. 2:10–21; 34:2
26 [a][Is. 60:19, 20]
28 [a]Is. 11:4 [b]Is. 8:8 [c]Is. 37:29

22 [a]You will also defile the covering of your images of silver,
And the ornament of your molded images of gold.
You will throw them away as an unclean thing;
[b]You will say to them, "Get away!"

23 [a]Then He will give the rain for your seed
With which you sow the ground,
And bread of the increase of the earth;
It will be [1]fat and plentiful.
In that day your cattle will feed
In large pastures.
24 Likewise the oxen and the young donkeys that work the ground
Will eat cured fodder,
Which has been winnowed with the shovel and fan.
25 There will be [a]on every high mountain
And on every high hill
Rivers *and* streams of waters,
In the day of the [b]great slaughter,
When the towers fall.
26 Moreover [a]the light of the moon will be as the light of the sun,
And the light of the sun will be sevenfold,
As the light of seven days,
In the day that the LORD binds up the bruise of His people
And heals the stroke of their wound.

Judgment on Assyria

27 Behold, the name of the LORD comes from afar,
Burning *with* His anger,
And *His* burden *is* heavy;
His lips are full of indignation,
And His tongue like a devouring fire.
28 [a]His breath is like an overflowing stream,
[b]Which reaches up to the neck,
To sift the nations with the sieve of futility;
And *there shall be* [c]a bridle in the jaws of the people,
Causing *them* to err.
29 You shall have a song
As in the night *when* a holy festival is kept,
And gladness of heart as when one goes with a flute,

To come into [a]the mountain of the
LORD,
To [1]the Mighty One of Israel.
30 [a]The LORD will cause His glorious
voice to be heard,
And show the descent of His arm,
With the indignation of *His* anger
And the flame of a devouring fire,
With scattering, tempest, [b]and
hailstones.
31 For [a]through the voice of the
LORD
Assyria will be [1]beaten down,
As He strikes with the [b]rod.
32 And *in* every place where the staff
of punishment passes,
Which the LORD lays on him,
It will be with tambourines and
harps;
And in battles of [a]brandishing He
will fight with it.
33 [a]For Tophet *was* established of old,
Yes, for the king it is prepared.
He has made *it* deep and large;
Its pyre *is* fire with much wood;
The breath of the LORD, like a
stream of brimstone,
Kindles it.

The Folly of Not Trusting God

31 Woe to those [a]who go down to
Egypt for help,
And [b]rely on horses,
Who trust in chariots because *they*
are many,
And in horsemen because they are
very strong,
But who do not look to the Holy
One of Israel,
[c]Nor seek the LORD!
2 Yet He also *is* wise and will bring
disaster,
And [a]will not [1]call back His words,
But will arise against the house of
evildoers,
And against the help of those who
work iniquity.
3 Now the Egyptians *are* men, and
not God;
And their horses are flesh, and not
spirit.
When the LORD stretches out His
hand,
Both he who helps will fall,
And he who is helped will fall
down;
They all will perish [a]together.

God Will Deliver Jerusalem

4 For thus the LORD has spoken to me:
[a]"As a lion roars,
And a young lion over his prey
(When a multitude of shepherds is
summoned against him,
He will not be afraid of their voice
Nor be disturbed by their noise),
So the LORD of hosts will come
down
To fight for Mount Zion and for its
hill.
5 [a]Like birds flying about,
So will the LORD of hosts defend
Jerusalem.
Defending, He will also deliver *it;*
Passing over, He will preserve *it.*"

6 Return *to Him* against whom the children of Israel have [a]deeply revolted. 7 For
in that day every man shall [a]throw away
his idols of silver and his idols of gold—
[b]sin, which your own hands have made
for yourselves.

8 "Then Assyria shall [a]fall by a sword
not of man,
And a sword not of mankind shall
[b]devour him.
But he shall flee from the sword,
And his young men shall become
forced labor.
9 [a]He shall cross over to his
stronghold for fear,
And his princes shall be afraid of
the banner,"
Says the LORD,
Whose fire *is* in Zion
And whose furnace *is* in Jerusalem.

A Reign of Righteousness

32 Behold, [a]a king will reign in
righteousness,
And princes will rule with justice.
2 A man will be as a hiding place
from the wind,
And [a]a [1]cover from the tempest,
As rivers of water in a dry place,
As the shadow of a great rock in a
weary land.
3 [a]The eyes of those who see will not
be dim,
And the ears of those who hear will
listen.
4 Also the heart of the [1]rash will
[a]understand knowledge,
And the tongue of the stammerers
will be ready to speak plainly.

---

29 [a][Is. 2:3] [1]Lit. *the Rock*
30 [a]Is. 29:6 [b]Is. 28:2
31 [a]Is. 14:25; 37:36 [b]Is. 10:5, 24 [1]Lit. *shattered*
32 [a]Is. 11:15
33 [a]Jer. 7:31

CHAPTER 31
1 [a]Is. 30:1, 2 [b]Ps. 20:7 [c]Dan. 9:13
2 [a]Num. 23:19 [1]*retract*
3 [a]Is. 20:6
4 [a]Hos. 11:10
5 [a]Deut. 32:11
6 [a]Hos. 9:9
7 [a]Is. 2:20; 30:22 [b]1 Kin. 12:30
8 [a]2 Kin. 19:35, 36 [b]Is. 37:36
9 [a]Is. 37:37

CHAPTER 32
1 [a]Ps. 45:1
2 [a]Is. 4:6 [1]*shelter*
3 [a]Is. 29:18; 35:5
4 [a]Is. 29:24 [1]*hasty*

5 The foolish person will no longer
be called [1]generous,
Nor the miser said *to be* bountiful;
6 For the foolish person will speak
foolishness,
And his heart will work [a]iniquity:
To practice ungodliness,
To utter error against the LORD,
To keep the hungry unsatisfied,
And he will cause the drink of the
thirsty to fail.
7 Also the schemes of the schemer
are evil;
He devises wicked plans
To destroy the poor with [a]lying
words,
Even when the needy speaks
justice.
8 But a [1]generous man devises
generous things,
And by generosity he shall stand.

Consequences of Complacency

9 Rise up, you women [a]who are at
ease,
Hear my voice;
You complacent daughters,
Give ear to my speech.
10 In a year and *some* days
You will be troubled, you
complacent women;
For the vintage will fail,
The gathering will not come.
11 Tremble, you *women* who are at
ease;
Be troubled, you complacent ones;
Strip yourselves, make yourselves
bare,
And gird *sackcloth* on *your* waists.
12 People shall mourn upon their
breasts
For the pleasant fields, for the
fruitful vine.
13 [a]On the land of my people will
come up thorns *and* briers,
Yes, on all the happy homes *in* [b]the
joyous city;
14 [a]Because the palaces will be
forsaken,
The bustling city will be deserted.
The forts and towers will become
lairs forever,
A joy of wild donkeys, a pasture of
flocks—
15 Until [a]the Spirit is poured upon
us from on high,
And [b]the wilderness becomes a
fruitful field,
And the fruitful field is counted as
a forest.

The Peace of God's Reign

16 Then justice will dwell in the
wilderness,
And righteousness remain in the
fruitful field.
17 [a]The work of righteousness will be
peace,
And the effect of righteousness,
quietness and assurance forever.
18 My people will dwell in a peaceful
habitation,
In secure dwellings, and in quiet
[a]resting places,
19 [a]Though hail comes down [b]on the
forest,
And the city is brought low in
humiliation.
20 Blessed *are* you who sow beside
all waters,
Who send out freely the feet of [a]the
ox and the donkey.

A Prayer in Deep Distress

33 Woe to you [a]who plunder,
though you *have* not *been*
plundered;
And you who deal treacherously,
though they have not dealt
treacherously with you!
[b]When you cease plundering,
You will be [c]plundered;
When you make an end of dealing
treacherously,
They will deal treacherously with
you.
2 O LORD, be gracious to us;
[a]We have waited for You.
Be [1]their arm every morning,
Our salvation also in the time of
trouble.
3 At the noise of the tumult the
people [a]shall flee;
When You lift Yourself up, the
nations shall be scattered;
4 And Your plunder shall be gathered
Like the gathering of the
caterpillar;
As the running to and fro of
locusts,
He shall run upon them.

---

5 [1] noble
6 [a] Prov. 24:7–9
7 [a] Jer. 5:26–28
8 [1] noble
9 [a] Amos 6:1
13 [a] Hos. 9:6 [b] Is. 22:2
14 [a] Is. 27:10
15 [a] [Joel 2:28] [b] Is. 29:17
17 [a] James 3:18
18 [a] [Zech. 2:5; 3:10]
19 [a] Is. 30:30 [b] Zech. 11:2
20 [a] Is. 30:23, 24

CHAPTER 33
1 [a] Hab. 2:8 [b] Rev. 13:10 [c] Is. 10:12; 14:25; 31:8
2 [a] Is. 25:9; 26:8 [1] LXX omits *their;* Syr., Tg., Vg. *our*
3 [a] Is. 17:13

5 [a]The LORD is exalted, for He dwells on high;
He has filled Zion with justice and righteousness.
6 Wisdom and knowledge will be the stability of your times,
And the strength of salvation;
The fear of the LORD *is* His treasure.

7 Surely their valiant ones shall cry outside,
[a]The ambassadors of peace shall weep bitterly.
8 [a]The highways lie waste,
The traveling man ceases.
[b]He has broken the covenant,
[1]He has despised the [2]cities,
He regards no man.
9 [a]The earth mourns *and* languishes,
Lebanon is shamed *and* shriveled;
Sharon is like a wilderness,
And Bashan and Carmel shake off *their fruits.*

Impending Judgment on Zion

10 "Now[a] I will rise," says the LORD;
"Now I will be exalted,
Now I will lift Myself up.
11 [a]You shall conceive chaff,
You shall bring forth stubble;
Your breath, *as* fire, shall devour you.
12 And the people shall be *like* the burnings of lime;
[a]*Like* thorns cut up they shall be burned in the fire.
13 Hear, [a]you *who are* afar off, what I have done;
And you *who are* near, acknowledge My might."

14 The sinners in Zion are afraid;
Fearfulness has seized the hypocrites:
"Who among us shall dwell with the devouring [a]fire?
Who among us shall dwell with everlasting burnings?"
15 He who [a]walks righteously and speaks uprightly,
He who despises the gain of oppressions,
Who gestures with his hands, refusing bribes,
Who stops his ears from hearing of bloodshed,
And [b]shuts his eyes from seeing evil:

16 He will dwell on [1]high;
His place of defense *will be* the fortress of rocks;
Bread will be given him,
His water *will be* sure.

The Land of the Majestic King

17 Your eyes will see the King in His [a]beauty;
They will see the land that is very far off.
18 Your heart will meditate on terror:
[a]"Where *is* the scribe?
Where *is* he who weighs?
Where *is* he who counts the towers?"
19 [a]You will not see a fierce people,
[b]A people of obscure speech, beyond perception,
Of a [1]stammering tongue *that you* cannot understand.

20 [a]Look upon Zion, the city of our appointed feasts;
Your eyes will see [b]Jerusalem, a quiet home,
A tabernacle *that* will not be taken down;
[c]Not one of [d]its stakes will ever be removed,
Nor will any of its cords be broken.
21 But there the majestic LORD *will be* for us
A place of broad rivers *and* streams,
In which no [1]galley with oars will sail,
Nor majestic ships pass by
22 (For the LORD *is* our [a]Judge,
The LORD *is* our [b]Lawgiver,
[c]The LORD *is* our King;
He will save us);
23 Your tackle is loosed,
They could not strengthen their mast,
They could not spread the sail.

Then the prey of great plunder is divided;
The lame take the prey.
24 And the inhabitant will not say, "I am sick";
[a]The people who dwell in it *will be* forgiven *their* iniquity.

Judgment on the Nations

34 Come [a]near, you nations, to hear;

5 [a]Ps. 97:9
7 [a]2 Kin. 18:18, 37
8 [a]Judg. 5:6 [b]2 Kin. 18:13–17 [1]Tg. *They have been removed from their cities* [2]So with MT, Vg.; DSS *witnesses;* LXX omits *cities*
9 [a]Is. 24:4
10 [a]Ps. 12:5
11 [a][Ps. 7:14]
12 [a]Is. 9:18
13 [a]Is. 49:1
14 [a]Heb. 12:29
15 [a]Ps. 15:2; 24:3, 4 [b]Ps. 119:37
16 [1]Lit. *heights*
17 [a]Ps. 27:4
18 [a]1 Cor. 1:20
19 [a]2 Kin. 19:32 [b]Jer. 5:15 [1]Unintelligible speech
20 [a]Ps. 48:12 [b]Ps. 46:5; 125:1 [c]Is. 37:33 [d]Is. 54:2
21 [1]*ship*
22 [a][Acts 10:42] [b]James 4:12 [c]Ps. 89:18
24 [a]Is. 40:2
CHAPTER 34
1 [a]Ps. 49:1

And heed, you people!
[b]Let the earth hear, and all that is in it,
The world and all things that come forth from it.
2 For the indignation of the LORD *is* against all nations,
And *His* fury against all their armies;
He has utterly destroyed them,
He has given them over to the [a]slaughter.
3 Also their slain shall be thrown out;
[a]Their stench shall rise from their corpses,
And the mountains shall be melted with their blood.
4 [a]All the host of heaven shall be dissolved,
And the heavens shall be rolled up like a scroll;
[b]All their host shall fall down
As the leaf falls from the vine,
And as [c]*fruit* falling from a fig tree.

5 "For [a]My sword shall be bathed in heaven;
Indeed it [b]shall come down on Edom,
And on the people of My curse, for judgment.
6 The [a]sword of the LORD is filled with blood,
It is made [1]overflowing with fatness,
With the blood of lambs and goats,
With the fat of the kidneys of rams.
For [b]the LORD has a sacrifice in Bozrah,
And a great slaughter in the land of Edom.
7 The wild oxen shall come down with them,
And the young bulls with the mighty bulls;
Their land shall be soaked with blood,
And their dust [1]saturated with fatness."

8 For *it is* the day of the LORD's [a]vengeance,
The year of recompense for the cause of Zion.

1 b Deut. 32:1
2 a Is. 13:5
3 a Joel 2:20
4 a Is. 13:13 b Is. 14:12 c Rev. 6:12–14
5 a Jer. 46:10 b Mal. 1:4
6 a Is. 66:16 b Zeph. 1:7 1 Lit. *fat*
7 1 Lit. *made fat*
8 a Is. 63:4
9 a Deut. 29:23
10 a Rev. 14:11; 18:18; 19:3 b Mal. 1:3, 4
11 a Zeph. 2:14 b Lam. 2:8 1 Or *owl* 2 Or *hedgehog*
13 a Is. 32:13 b Is. 13:21
14 1 Lit. *howling creatures* 2 Heb. *lilith*
16 a [Mal. 3:16]

9 [a]Its streams shall be turned into pitch,
And its dust into brimstone;
Its land shall become burning pitch.
10 It shall not be quenched night or day;
[a]Its smoke shall ascend forever.
[b]From generation to generation it shall lie waste;
No one shall pass through it forever and ever.
11 [a]But the [1]pelican and the [2]porcupine shall possess it,
Also the owl and the raven shall dwell in it.
And [b]He shall stretch out over it
The line of confusion and the stones of emptiness.
12 They shall call its nobles to the kingdom,
But none *shall be* there, and all its princes shall be nothing.

13 And [a]thorns shall come up in its palaces,
Nettles and brambles in its fortresses;
[b]It shall be a habitation of jackals,
A courtyard for ostriches.
14 The wild beasts of the desert shall also meet with the [1]jackals,
And the wild goat shall bleat to its companion;
Also [2]the night creature shall rest there,
And find for herself a place of rest.
15 There the arrow snake shall make her nest and lay *eggs*
And hatch, and gather *them* under her shadow;
There also shall the hawks be gathered,
Every one with her mate.

16 "Search from [a]the book of the LORD, and read:
Not one of these shall fail;
Not one shall lack her mate.
For My mouth has commanded it, and His Spirit has gathered them.
17 He has cast the lot for them,
And His hand has divided it among them with a measuring line.
They shall possess it forever;
From generation to generation they shall dwell in it."

The Future Glory of Zion

35 The [a]wilderness and the [1]wasteland shall be glad for them,
And the [b]desert[2] shall rejoice and blossom as the rose;
2 [a]It shall blossom abundantly and rejoice,
Even with joy and singing.
The glory of Lebanon shall be given to it,
The excellence of Carmel and Sharon.
They shall see the [b]glory of the LORD,
The excellency of our God.

Father, strengthen the weak hands of ____ and make firm her feeble knees. Though she is fearful, enable her to be strong and not fear! For You, Lord, will come and save her.

FROM ISAIAH 35:3, 4

3 [a]Strengthen the [1]weak hands,
And make firm the [2]feeble knees.
4 Say to those *who are* fearful-hearted,
"Be strong, do not fear!
Behold, your God will come *with* [a]vengeance,
With the recompense of God;
He will come and [b]save you."
5 Then the [a]eyes of the blind shall be opened,
And [b]the ears of the deaf shall be unstopped.
6 Then the [a]lame shall leap like a deer,
And the [b]tongue of the dumb sing.
For [c]waters shall burst forth in the wilderness,
And streams in the desert.
7 The parched ground shall become a pool,
And the thirsty land springs of water;
In [a]the habitation of jackals, where each lay,
There shall be grass with reeds and rushes.
8 A [a]highway shall be there, and a road,
And it shall be called the Highway of Holiness.
[b]The unclean shall not pass over it,
But it *shall be* for others.
Whoever walks the road, although a fool,
Shall not go astray.
9 [a]No lion shall be there,
Nor shall *any* ravenous beast go up on it;
It shall not be found there.
But the redeemed shall walk *there,*
10 And the [a]ransomed of the LORD shall return,
And come to Zion with singing,
With everlasting joy on their heads.
They shall obtain joy and gladness,
And [b]sorrow and sighing shall flee away.

Though you may be untrue, Christ is your truth; though you may be unclean, Christ is your chastity; though you may be dishonest, Christ is your honesty; though you may be insincere, Christ is your sincerity.

CATHERINE BOOTH

Sennacherib Boasts Against the Lord

36 Now [a]it came to pass in the fourteenth year of King Hezekiah *that* Sennacherib king of Assyria came up against all the fortified cities of Judah and took them. 2Then the king of Assyria sent *the* [1]Rabshakeh with a great army from Lachish to King Hezekiah at Jerusalem. And he stood by the aqueduct from the upper pool, on the highway to the Fuller's

CHAPTER 35
1 a Is. 32:15; 55:12 b Is. 41:19; 51:3 *1 desert* *2* Heb. *arabah*
2 a Is. 32:15 b Is. 40:5
3 a Heb. 12:12 *1* Lit. *sinking* *2 tottering* or *stumbling*
4 a Is. 34:8 b Is. 33:22
5 a Is. 29:18 b [Matt. 11:5]
6 a Acts 8:7 b Is. 32:4 c [John 7:38]
7 a Is. 34:13
8 a Is. 19:23 b Joel 3:17
9 a Lev. 26:6
10 a Is. 51:11 b [Rev. 7:17; 21:4]

CHAPTER 36
1 a 2 Chr. 32:1
2 *1* A title, probably *Chief of Staff* or *Governor*

Field. 3 And [a]Eliakim the son of Hilkiah, who was over the household, [b]Shebna the scribe, and Joah the son of Asaph, the recorder, came out to him.

4 [a]Then *the* Rabshakeh said to them, "Say now to Hezekiah, 'Thus says the great king, the king of Assyria: "What confidence is this in which you trust? 5 I say you speak of having plans and power for war; but *they are* [1]mere words. Now in whom do you trust, that you rebel against me? 6 Look! You are trusting in the [a]staff of this broken reed, Egypt, on which if a man leans, it will go into his hand and pierce it. So *is* Pharaoh king of Egypt to all who [b]trust in him.

7 "But if you say to me, 'We trust in the LORD our God,' *is it* not He whose high places and whose altars Hezekiah has taken away, and said to Judah and Jerusalem, 'You shall worship before this altar'?" ' 8 Now therefore, I urge you, give a pledge to my master the king of Assyria, and I will give you two thousand horses—if you are able on your part to put riders on them! 9 How then will you repel one captain of the least of my master's servants, and put your trust in Egypt for chariots and horsemen? 10 Have I now come up without the LORD against this land to destroy it? The LORD said to me, 'Go up against this land, and destroy it.' "

11 Then Eliakim, Shebna, and Joah said to *the* Rabshakeh, "Please speak to your servants in Aramaic, for we understand *it;* and do not speak to us in [1]Hebrew in the hearing of the people who *are* on the wall."

12 But *the* Rabshakeh said, "Has my master sent me to your master and to you to speak these words, and not to the men who sit on the wall, who will eat and drink their own waste with you?"

13 Then *the* Rabshakeh stood and called out with a loud voice in Hebrew, and said, "Hear the words of the great king, the king of Assyria! 14 Thus says the king: 'Do not let Hezekiah deceive you, for he will not be able to deliver you; 15 nor let Hezekiah make you trust in the LORD, saying, "The LORD will surely deliver us; this city will not be given into the hand of the king of Assyria." ' 16 Do not listen to Hezekiah; for thus says the king of Assyria: 'Make *peace* with me *by a* present and come out to me; [a]and every one of you eat from his own vine and every one from his own fig tree, and every one of you drink the waters of his own cistern; 17 until I come and take you away to a land like your own land, a land of grain and new wine, a land of bread and vineyards. 18 *Beware* lest Hezekiah persuade you, saying, "The LORD will deliver us." Has any one of the [a]gods of the nations delivered its land from the hand of the king of Assyria? 19 Where *are* the gods of Hamath and Arpad? Where *are* the gods of Sepharvaim? Indeed, have they delivered [a]Samaria from my hand? 20 Who among all the gods of these lands have delivered their countries from my hand, that the LORD should deliver Jerusalem from my hand?' "

21 But they [1]held their peace and answered him not a word; for the king's commandment was, "Do not answer him." 22 Then Eliakim the son of Hilkiah, who *was* over the household, Shebna the scribe, and Joah the son of Asaph, the recorder, came to Hezekiah with *their* clothes torn, and told him the words of *the* Rabshakeh.

Isaiah Assures Deliverance

37 And [a]so it was, when King Hezekiah heard *it,* that he tore his clothes, covered himself with sackcloth, and went into the house of the LORD. 2 Then he sent Eliakim, who *was* over the household, Shebna the scribe, and the elders of the priests, covered with sackcloth, to Isaiah the prophet, the son of Amoz. 3 And they said to him, "Thus says Hezekiah: 'This day *is* a day of [a]trouble and rebuke and [1]blasphemy; for the children have come to birth, but *there is* no strength to bring them forth. 4 It may be that the LORD your God will hear the words of *the* Rabshakeh, whom his master the king of Assyria has sent to [a]reproach the living God, and will rebuke the words which the LORD your God has heard. Therefore lift up *your* prayer for the remnant that is left.' "

5 So the servants of King Hezekiah came to Isaiah. 6 And Isaiah said to them, "Thus you shall say to your master, 'Thus says the LORD: "Do not be afraid of the words which you have heard, with which the servants of the king of Assyria have blasphemed Me. 7 Surely I will send a spirit upon him, and he shall hear a rumor and return to his own land; and I will cause him to fall by the sword in his own land." ' "

---

3 a Is. 22:20 b Is. 22:15
4 a 2 Kin. 18:19
5 1 Lit. *a word of the lips*
6 a Ezek. 29:6 b Ps. 146:3
11 1 Lit. *Judean*
16 a Zech. 3:10
18 a Is. 37:12
19 a 2 Kin. 17:6
21 1 *were silent*

CHAPTER 37
1 a 2 Kin. 19:1–37
3 a Is. 22:5; 26:16; 33:2 1 *contempt*
4 a Is. 36:15, 18, 20

Sennacherib's Threat and Hezekiah's Prayer

8 Then *the* Rabshakeh returned, and
found the king of Assyria warring against
Libnah, for he heard that he had departed
from Lachish. 9 And the king heard concerning Tirhakah king of Ethiopia, "He
has come out to make war with you." So
when he heard *it,* he sent messengers to
Hezekiah, saying, 10 "Thus you shall speak
to Hezekiah king of Judah, saying: 'Do not
let your God in whom you trust deceive
you, saying, "Jerusalem shall not be given
into the hand of the king of Assyria."
11 Look! You have heard what the kings of
Assyria have done to all lands by utterly
destroying them; and shall you be delivered? 12 Have the [a]gods of the nations delivered those whom my fathers have
destroyed, Gozan and Haran and Rezeph,
and the people of Eden who *were* in Telassar? 13 Where *is* the king of [a]Hamath, the
king of Arpad, and the king of the city of
Sepharvaim, Hena, and Ivah?' "
14 And Hezekiah received the letter from
the hand of the messengers, and read it;
and Hezekiah went up to the house of the
LORD, and spread it before the LORD.
15 Then Hezekiah prayed to the LORD, saying: 16 "O LORD of hosts, God of Israel, *the*
One who dwells *between* the cherubim,
You *are* God, You [a]alone, of all the kingdoms of the earth. You have made heaven
and earth. 17 [a]Incline Your ear, O LORD,
and hear; open Your eyes, O LORD, and
see; and [b]hear all the words of Sennacherib, which he has sent to reproach the living God. 18 Truly, LORD, the kings of
Assyria have laid waste all the nations and
their [a]lands, 19 and have cast their gods
into the fire; for they *were* [a]not gods, but
the work of men's hands—wood and
stone. Therefore they destroyed them.
20 Now therefore, O LORD our God, [a]save
us from his hand, that all the kingdoms of
the earth may [b]know that You *are* the
LORD, You alone."

The Word of the Lord Concerning Sennacherib

21 Then Isaiah the son of Amoz sent to
Hezekiah, saying, "Thus says the LORD
God of Israel, 'Because you have prayed to
Me against Sennacherib king of Assyria,
22 this *is* the word which the LORD has spo-
ken concerning him:

"The virgin, the daughter of Zion,
Has despised you, laughed you to scorn;
The daughter of Jerusalem
Has shaken *her* head behind your back!

23 "Whom have you reproached and blasphemed?
Against whom have you raised *your* voice,
And lifted up your eyes on high?
Against the Holy One of Israel.
24 By your servants you have reproached the Lord,
And said, 'By the multitude of my chariots
I have come up to the height of the mountains,
To the limits of Lebanon;
I will cut down its tall cedars
And its choice cypress trees;
I will enter its farthest height,
To its fruitful forest.
25 I have dug and drunk water,
And with the soles of my feet I have dried up
All the brooks of [1]defense.'

26 "Did you not hear [a]long ago
How I made it,
From ancient times that I formed it?
Now I have brought it to pass,
That you should be
For crushing fortified cities *into* heaps of ruins.
27 Therefore their inhabitants *had* little power;
They were dismayed and confounded;
They were *as* the grass of the field
And the green herb,
As the grass on the housetops
And grain blighted before it is grown.

28 "But I know your dwelling place,
Your going out and your coming in,
And your rage against Me.
29 Because your rage against Me and your tumult
Have come up to My ears,
Therefore [a]I will put My hook in your nose
And My bridle in your lips,
And I will [b]turn you back
By the way which you came." '

---

12 a Is. 36:18, 19
13 a Is. 49:23
16 a Is. 43:10, 11
17 a Dan. 9:18 b Ps. 74:22
18 a 2 Kin. 15:29; 16:9; 17:6, 24
19 a Is. 40:19, 20
20 a Is. 33:22 b Ps. 83:18
25 *1* Or perhaps *Egypt*
26 a Is. 25:1; 40:21; 45:21
29 a Is. 30:28 b Ezek. 38:4; 39:2

30"This *shall be* a sign to you:

You shall eat this year such as
grows of itself,
And the second year what springs
from the same;
Also in the third year sow and reap,
Plant vineyards and eat the fruit of
them.
31 And the remnant who have
escaped of the house of Judah
Shall again take root downward,
And bear fruit upward.
32 For out of Jerusalem shall go a
remnant,
And those who escape from Mount
Zion.
The [a]zeal of the LORD of hosts will
do this.

33"Therefore thus says the LORD concerning the king of Assyria:

'He shall not come into this city,
Nor shoot an arrow there,
Nor come before it with shield,
Nor build a siege mound against it.
34 By the way that he came,
By the same shall he return;
And he shall not come into this
city,'
Says the LORD.
35 'For I will [a]defend this city, to save
it
For My own sake and for My
servant [b]David's sake.' "

Sennacherib's Defeat and Death

36Then the [a]angel[1] of the LORD went
out, and [2]killed in the camp of the Assyrians one hundred and eighty-five thousand; and when *people* arose early in the
morning, there were the corpses—all
dead. 37So Sennacherib king of Assyria departed and went away, returned *home,*
and remained at Nineveh. 38Now it came
to pass, as he was worshiping in the house
of Nisroch his god, that his sons Adrammelech and Sharezer struck him down
with the sword; and they escaped into the
land of Ararat. Then [a]Esarhaddon his son
reigned in his place.

Hezekiah's Life Extended

38 In [a]those days Hezekiah was sick
and near death. And Isaiah the
prophet, the son of Amoz, went to him
and said to him, "Thus says the LORD:
[b]'Set your house in order, for you shall die
and not live.' "

2Then Hezekiah turned his face toward
the wall, and prayed to the LORD, 3and
said, [a]"Remember now, O LORD, I pray,
how I have walked before You in truth and
with a [1]loyal heart, and have done *what is*
good in Your [b]sight." And Hezekiah wept
bitterly.

4And the word of the LORD came to Isaiah, saying, 5"Go and tell Hezekiah, 'Thus
says the LORD, the God of David your father: "I have heard your prayer, I have
seen your tears; surely I will add to your
days fifteen years. 6I will deliver you and
this city from the hand of the king of Assyria, and [a]I will defend this city." ' 7And
this *is* [a]the sign to you from the LORD,
that the LORD will do this thing which He
has spoken: 8Behold, I will bring the shadow on the sundial, which has gone down
with the sun on the sundial of Ahaz, ten
degrees backward." So the sun returned
ten degrees on the dial by which it had
gone down.

9This is the writing of Hezekiah king of
Judah, when he had been sick and had
recovered from his sickness:

10 I said,
"In the prime of my life
I shall go to the gates of Sheol;
I am deprived of the remainder of
my years."
11 I said,
"I shall not see [1]YAH,
The LORD [a]in the land of the living;
I shall observe man no more
[2]among the inhabitants of [3]the
world.
12 [a]My life span is gone,
Taken from me like a shepherd's
tent;
I have cut off my life like a weaver.
He cuts me off from the loom;
From day until night You make an
end of me.
13 I have considered until morning—
Like a lion,
So He breaks all my bones;
From day until night You make an
end of me.
14 Like a crane *or* a swallow, so I
chattered;
[a]I mourned like a dove;
My eyes fail *from looking* upward.
O [1]LORD, I am oppressed;
[2]Undertake for me!

32 [a]2 Kin. 19:31
35 [a]Is. 31:5; 38:6 [b]1 Kin. 11:13
36 [a]2 Kin. 19:35 [1]Or *Angel* [2]Lit. *struck*
38 [a]Ezra 4:2

CHAPTER 38
1 [a]2 Chr. 32:24 [b]2 Sam. 17:23
3 [a]Neh. 13:14 [b]2 Kin. 18:5, 6 [1]*whole* or *peaceful*
6 [a]Is. 31:5; 37:35
7 [a]Is. 7:11
11 [a]Ps. 27:13; 116:9 [1]Heb. YAH, YAH [2]LXX omits *among the inhabitants of the world* [3]So with some Heb. mss.; MT, Vg. *rest;* Tg. *land*
12 [a]Job 7:6
14 [a]Is. 59:11 [1]So with Bg.; MT, DSS *Lord* [2]*Be my surety*

15 "What shall I say?
[1]He has both spoken to me,
And He Himself has done *it*.
I shall walk carefully all my years
[a]In the bitterness of my soul.
16 O Lord, by these *things men* live;
And in all these *things is* the life of
my spirit;
So You will restore me and make
me live.
17 Indeed *it was* for *my own* peace
That I had great bitterness;
But You have lovingly *delivered* my
soul from the pit of corruption,
For You have cast all my sins
behind Your back.
18 For [a]Sheol cannot thank You,
Death cannot praise You;
Those who go down to the pit
cannot hope for Your truth.
19 The living, the living man, he
shall praise You,
As I *do* this day;
[a]The father shall make known Your
truth to the children.

Lord, like Hezekiah, You have lovingly delivered _____ from the pit of corruption, for You have cast all their sins behind Your back.

FROM ISAIAH 38:17

20 "The LORD *was ready* to save me;
Therefore we will sing my songs
with stringed instruments
All the days of our life, in the
house of the LORD."

21 Now [a]Isaiah had said, "Let them take
a lump of figs, and apply *it* as a poultice on
the boil, and he shall recover."
22 And [a]Hezekiah had said, "What *is* the
sign that I shall go up to the house of the
LORD?"

The Babylonian Envoys

39 At [a]that time [1]Merodach-Baladan
the son of Baladan, king of Babylon, sent letters and a present to Hezekiah, for he heard that he had been sick
and had recovered. 2 [a]And Hezekiah was
pleased with them, and showed them the
house of his treasures—the silver and
gold, the spices and precious ointment,
and all his armory—all that was found
among his treasures. There was nothing
in his house or in all his dominion that
Hezekiah did not show them.
3 Then Isaiah the prophet went to King
Hezekiah, and said to him, "What did
these men say, and from where did they
come to you?"
So Hezekiah said, "They came to me
from a [a]far country, from Babylon."
4 And he said, "What have they seen in
your house?"
So Hezekiah answered, "They have seen
all that *is* in my house; there is nothing
among my treasures that I have not
shown them."
5 Then Isaiah said to Hezekiah, "Hear
the word of the LORD of hosts: 6 'Behold,
the days are coming [a]when all that *is* in
your house, and what your fathers have
accumulated until this day, shall be carried to Babylon; nothing shall be left,' says
the LORD. 7 'And they shall take away *some*
of your [a]sons who will descend from you,
whom you will beget; and they shall be
eunuchs in the palace of the king of Babylon.' "
8 So Hezekiah said to Isaiah, [a]"The word
of the LORD which you have spoken *is*
good!" For he said, "At least there will be
peace and truth in my days."

God's People Are Comforted

40 "Comfort, yes, comfort My
people!"
Says your God.
2 "Speak [1]comfort to Jerusalem, and
cry out to her,
That her warfare is ended,
That her iniquity is pardoned;
[a]For she has received from the
LORD's hand
Double for all her sins."
3 [a]The voice of one crying in the
wilderness:
[b]"Prepare the way of the LORD;
[c]Make straight [1]in the desert
A highway for our God.
4 Every valley shall be exalted
And every mountain and hill
brought low;
[a]The crooked places shall be made
[1]straight
And the rough places smooth;

15 a Job 7:11; 10:1 *1* So with MT, Vg.; DSS, Tg. *And shall I say to Him;* LXX omits first half of this verse
18 a Ps. 6:5; 30:9; 88:11; 115:17
19 a Deut. 4:9; 6:7
21 a 2 Kin. 20:7
22 a 2 Kin. 20:8

CHAPTER 39
1 a 2 Kin. 20:12–19 *1 Berodach-Baladan,* 2 Kin. 20:12
2 a 2 Chr. 32:25, 31
3 a Deut. 28:49
6 a Jer. 20:5
7 a Dan. 1:1–7
8 a 1 Sam. 3:18

CHAPTER 40
2 a Is. 61:7 *1* Lit. *to the heart of*
3 a Matt. 3:3 b [Mal. 3:1; 4:5, 6] c Ps. 68:4 *1* So with MT, Tg., Vg.; LXX omits *in the desert*
4 a Is. 45:2 *1* Or *a plain*

5 The [a]glory of the LORD shall be revealed,
And all flesh shall see *it* together;
For the mouth of the LORD has spoken."

6 The voice said, "Cry out!"
And [1]he said, "What shall I cry?"

[a]"All flesh *is* grass,
And all its loveliness *is* like the flower of the field.
7 The grass withers, the flower fades,
Because the breath of the LORD blows upon it;
Surely the people *are* grass.
8 The grass withers, the flower fades,
But [a]the word of our God stands forever."

O Lord, my God, though the grass withers and the flower fades, may _____ know that Your word stands forever.

FROM ISAIAH 40:8

9 O Zion,
You who bring good tidings,
Get up into the high mountain;
O Jerusalem,
You who bring good tidings,
Lift up your voice with strength,
Lift *it* up, be not afraid;
Say to the cities of Judah, "Behold your God!"
10 Behold, the Lord GOD shall come [1]with a strong *hand,*
And [a]His arm shall rule for Him;
Behold, [b]His reward *is* with Him,
And His [2]work before Him.
11 He will [a]feed His flock like a shepherd;
He will gather the lambs with His arm,
And carry *them* in His bosom,
And gently lead those who are with young.

12 [a]Who has measured the [1]waters in the hollow of His hand,
Measured heaven with a [2]span
And calculated the dust of the earth in a measure?
Weighed the mountains in scales
And the hills in a balance?
13 [a]Who has directed the Spirit of the LORD,
Or *as* His counselor has taught Him?
14 With whom did He take counsel, and *who* instructed Him,
And [a]taught Him in the path of justice?
Who taught Him knowledge,
And showed Him the way of understanding?

15 Behold, the nations *are* as a drop in a bucket,
And are counted as the small dust on the scales;
Look, He lifts up the isles as a very little thing.
16 And Lebanon *is* not sufficient to burn,
Nor its beasts sufficient for a burnt offering.
17 All nations before Him *are* as [a]nothing,
And [b]they are counted by Him less than nothing and worthless.

18 To whom then will you [a]liken God?
Or what likeness will you compare to Him?
19 [a]The workman molds an image,
The goldsmith overspreads it with gold,
And the silversmith casts silver chains.
20 Whoever *is* too impoverished for *such* [1]a contribution
Chooses a tree *that* will not rot;
He seeks for himself a skillful workman
[a]To prepare a carved image *that* will not totter.

21 [a]Have you not known?
Have you not heard?
Has it not been told you from the beginning?
Have you not understood from the foundations of the earth?
22 *It is* He who sits above the circle of the earth,
And its inhabitants *are* like grasshoppers,
Who [a]stretches out the heavens like a curtain,

---

5 a Is. 35:2
6 a Job 14:2 *1* So with MT, Tg.; DSS, LXX, Vg. *I*
8 a [John 12:34]
10 a Is. 59:16, 18 b Is. 62:11 *1 in strength* *2 recompense*
11 a [John 10:11, 14–16]
12 a Prov. 30:4 *1* So with MT, LXX, Vg.; DSS adds *of the sea;* Tg. adds *of the world* *2* A span = 1/2 cubit, 9 inches; or the width of His hand
13 a [1 Cor. 2:16]
14 a Job 36:22, 23
17 a Dan. 4:35 b Ps. 62:9
18 a Is. 46:5
19 a Is. 41:7; 44:10
20 a Is. 41:7; 46:7 *1 an offering*
21 a Rom. 1:19
22 a Jer. 10:12

And spreads them out like a [b]tent
to dwell in.
23 He [1]brings the [a]princes to
nothing;
He makes the judges of the earth
useless.

24 Scarcely shall they be planted,
Scarcely shall they be sown,
Scarcely shall their stock take root
in the earth,
When He will also blow on them,
And they will wither,
And the whirlwind will take them
away like stubble.

25 "To[a] whom then will you liken Me,
Or *to whom* shall I be equal?" says
the Holy One.
26 Lift up your eyes on high,
And see who has created these
things,
Who brings out their host by
number;
[a]He calls them all by name,
By the greatness of His might
And the strength of *His* power;
Not one is missing.

27 [a]Why do you say, O Jacob,
And speak, O Israel:
"My way is hidden from the LORD,
And my just claim is passed over by
my God"?
28 Have you not known?
Have you not heard?
The everlasting God, the LORD,
The Creator of the ends of the
earth,
Neither faints nor is weary.
[a]His understanding is unsearchable.
29 He gives power to the weak,
And to *those who have* no might
He increases strength.
30 Even the youths shall faint and be
weary,
And the young men shall utterly
fall,
31 But those who [a]wait on the LORD
[b]Shall renew *their* strength;
They shall mount up with wings
like eagles,
They shall run and not be weary,
They shall walk and not faint.

Israel Assured of God's Help

41 "Keep [a]silence before Me,
O coastlands,

22 [b]Ps. 19:4
23 [a]Ps. 107:40
[1]reduces
25 [a]Is. 40:18
26 [a]Ps. 147:4
27 [a]Is. 54:7, 8
28 [a]Rom. 11:33
31 [a]Is. 30:15; 49:23
[b]Ps. 103:5

CHAPTER 41
1 [a]Zech. 2:13
[b]Is. 1:18
2 [a]Is. 46:11
[b]Is. 45:1, 13
3 [1]Lit. *in peace*
4 [a]Is. 41:26
[b]Rev. 1:8, 17; 22:13
[c]Is. 43:10; 44:6
6 [a]Is. 40:19
[1]Lit. *Be strong*
7 [a]Is. 44:13
[b]Is. 40:19
[1]refiner

A vision puts enthusiasm in you, a thrilling understanding of God's Word, and you soar above in tremendous ecstasy; then you come down and run without being weary, then you come to the grandest days and walk without fainting.

OSWALD CHAMBERS

And let the people renew *their*
strength!
Let them come near, then let them
speak;
Let us [b]come near together for
judgment.

2 "Who raised up one [a]from the east?
Who in righteousness called him to
His feet?
Who [b]gave the nations before him,
And made *him* rule over kings?
Who gave *them* as the dust *to* his
sword,
As driven stubble to his bow?
3 Who pursued them, *and* passed
[1]safely
By the way *that* he had not gone
with his feet?
4 [a]Who has performed and done *it,*
Calling the generations from the
beginning?
'I, the LORD, am [b]the first;
And with the last I *am* [c]He.' "
5 The coastlands saw *it* and feared,
The ends of the earth were afraid;
They drew near and came.
6 [a]Everyone helped his neighbor,
And said to his brother,
[1]"Be of good courage!"
7 [a]So the craftsman encouraged the
[b]goldsmith;[1]
He who smooths *with* the hammer
inspired him who strikes the
anvil,

Saying, [2]"It *is* ready for the
soldering";
Then he fastened it with pegs,
[c]*That* it might not totter.

8 "But you, Israel, *are* My servant,
Jacob whom I have [a]chosen,
The descendants of Abraham My
[b]friend.
9 *You* whom I have taken from the
ends of the earth,
And called from its farthest regions,
And said to you,
'You *are* My servant,
I have chosen you and have not
cast you away:
10 [a]Fear not, [b]for I *am* with you;
Be not dismayed, for I *am* your
God.
I will strengthen you,
Yes, I will help you,
I will uphold you with My righteous
right hand.'

Father, may ____ fear not, for You are with them. May they not be dismayed, for You are their God. Strengthen them, help them, and uphold them with Your righteous right hand.

FROM ISAIAH 41:10

11 "Behold, all those who were
incensed against you
Shall be [a]ashamed and disgraced;
They shall be as nothing,
And those who strive with you shall
perish.
12 You shall seek them and not find
them—
[1]Those who contended with you.
Those who war against you
Shall be as nothing,
As a nonexistent thing.
13 For I, the LORD your God, will
hold your right hand,
Saying to you, 'Fear not, I will help
you.'

14 "Fear not, you [a]worm Jacob,
You men of Israel!
I will help you," says the LORD
And your Redeemer, the Holy One
of Israel.
15 "Behold, [a]I will make you into a
new threshing sledge with sharp
teeth;
You shall thresh the mountains and
beat *them* small,
And make the hills like chaff.
16 You shall [a]winnow them, the wind
shall carry them away,
And the whirlwind shall scatter
them;
You shall rejoice in the LORD,
And [b]glory in the Holy One of
Israel.

17 "The poor and needy seek water,
but *there is* none,
Their tongues fail for thirst.
I, the LORD, will hear them;
I, the God of Israel, will not
[a]forsake them.
18 I will open [a]rivers in desolate
heights,
And fountains in the midst of the
valleys;
I will make the [b]wilderness a pool
of water,
And the dry land springs of water.
19 I will plant in the wilderness the
cedar and the acacia tree,
The myrtle and the oil tree;
I will set in the [a]desert the cypress
tree *and* the pine
And the box tree together,
20 [a]That they may see and know,
And consider and understand
together,
That the hand of the LORD has done
this,
And the Holy One of Israel has
created it.

The Futility of Idols

21 "Present your case," says the LORD.
"Bring forth your strong *reasons,*"
says the [a]King of Jacob.
22 "Let[a] them bring forth and show
us what will happen;
Let them show the [b]former things,
what they *were,*
That we may [1]consider them,
And know the latter end of them;
Or declare to us things to come.
23 [a]Show the things that are to come
hereafter,
That we may know that you *are*
gods;

7 c Is. 40:20 2 Or *The soldering is good*
8 a Deut. 7:6; 10:15 b James 2:23
10 a Is. 41:13, 14; 43:5 b [Deut. 31:6]
11 a Zech. 12:3
12 1 Lit. *Men of your strife*
14 a Job 25:6
15 a Mic. 4:13
16 a Jer. 51:2 b Is. 45:25
17 a Rom. 11:2
18 a Is. 35:6, 7; 43:19; 44:3 b Ps. 107:35
19 a Is. 35:1
20 a Job 12:9
21 a Is. 43:15
22 a Is. 45:21 b Is. 43:9 1 Lit. *set our heart on them*
23 a [John 13:19]

Yes, [b]do good or do evil,
That we may be dismayed and see *it* together.
24 Indeed [a]you *are* nothing,
And your work *is* nothing;
He who chooses you *is* an abomination.

25 "I have raised up one from the north,
And he shall come;
From the [1]rising of the sun [a]he shall call on My name;
[b]And he shall come against princes as *though* mortar,
As the potter treads clay.
26 [a]Who has declared from the beginning, that we may know?
And former times, that we may say,
'*He is* righteous'?
Surely *there is* no one who shows,
Surely *there is* no one who declares,
Surely *there is* no one who hears your words.
27 [a]The first time [b]*I said* to Zion,
'Look, there they are!'
And I will give to Jerusalem one who brings good tidings.
28 [a]For I looked, and *there was* no man;
I looked among them, but *there was* no counselor,
Who, when I asked of them, could answer a word.
29 [a]Indeed they *are* all [1]worthless;
Their works *are* nothing;
Their molded images *are* wind and confusion.

The Servant of the Lord

42 "Behold! [a]My Servant whom I uphold,
My [1]Elect One *in whom* My soul [b]delights!
[c]I have put My Spirit upon Him;
He will bring forth justice to the Gentiles.
2 He will not cry out, nor raise *His voice,*
Nor cause His voice to be heard in the street.
3 A bruised reed He will not break,
And [1]smoking flax He will not [2]quench;
He will bring forth justice for truth.
4 He will not fail nor be discouraged,
Till He has established justice in the earth;
[a]And the coastlands shall wait for His law."

5 Thus says God the LORD,
[a]Who created the heavens and stretched them out,
Who spread forth the earth and that which comes from it,
[b]Who gives breath to the people on it,
And spirit to those who walk on it:
6 "I,[a] the LORD, have called You in righteousness,
And will hold Your hand;
I will keep You [b]and give You as a covenant to the people,
As [c]a light to the Gentiles,
7 [a]To open blind eyes,
To [b]bring out prisoners from the prison,
Those who sit in [c]darkness from the prison house.
8 I *am* the LORD, that *is* My name;
And My [a]glory I will not give to another,
Nor My praise to carved images.
9 Behold, the former things have come to pass,
And new things I declare;
Before they spring forth I tell you of them."

Praise to the Lord

10 [a]Sing to the LORD a new song,
And His praise from the ends of the earth,
[b]You who go down to the sea, and [1]all that is in it,
You coastlands and you inhabitants of them!
11 Let the wilderness and its cities lift up *their voice,*
The villages *that* Kedar inhabits.
Let the inhabitants of Sela sing,
Let them shout from the top of the mountains.
12 Let them give glory to the LORD,
And declare His praise in the coastlands.
13 The LORD shall go forth like a mighty man;
He shall stir up *His* zeal like a man of war.
He shall cry out, [a]yes, shout aloud;
He shall prevail against His enemies.

---

23 b Jer. 10:5
24 a [1 Cor. 8:4]
25 a Ezra 1:2 b Is. 41:2 1 East
26 a Is. 43:9
27 a Is. 41:4 b Is. 40:9
28 a Is. 63:5
29 a Is. 41:24 1 So with MT, Vg.; DSS, Syr., Tg. *nothing;* LXX omits first line

CHAPTER 42
1 a [Phil. 2:7] b Matt. 3:17; 17:5 c [Is. 11:2] 1 *Chosen*
3 1 *dimly burning* 2 *extinguish*
4 a [Gen. 49:10]
5 a Zech. 12:1 b Acts 17:25
6 a Is. 43:1 b Is. 49:8 c Luke 2:32
7 a Is. 35:5 b Luke 4:18 c Is. 9:2
8 a Is. 48:11
10 a Ps. 33:3; 40:3; 98:1 b Ps. 107:23 1 Lit. *its fullness*
13 a Is. 31:4

Isaiah 42:9

Dear Woman of Destiny,

Have you ever wished you could start all over? Do you ever look back longingly and say, "If only . . . "? The expression "Hindsight has 20/20 vision" is certainly true. Regret and shame have a powerful way of pulling us into the past. They are enemies to our future, and they show no mercy.

Isaiah has some good news for us: "Behold the former things have come to pass." In other words, the past is over. Jesus said, "It is finished!" (John 19:30). Not only was the suffering of the crucifixion over, but your past sins and mine were completely obliterated. Jesus finished our past for us on Calvary! Paul reminds us to forget what lies behind (see Phil. 3:13). We can't take hold of our future—the new thing or season—until we let go of our past. If you close yesterday's door, you will receive a double portion of the presence of God in exchange for your regrets and humiliation (see Is. 61:7).

Consider this: The ladies who left Egypt and followed Moses into the wilderness offered up their mirrors to build the laver in the tabernacle (see Ex. 38:8). As an act of worship, these women gave up the right to look upon themselves for the greater purpose of looking upon God and serving Him. That which once reflected the image of a woman now reflected the fire of the sacrifice upon the altar. Many times our own image of ourselves keeps us from our destiny of serving God and reflecting Him. If we will stop gazing upon ourselves and our past, and begin to behold Him, we will be changed. The glory of the Lord will change us into His image as we look into the mirror of His Word (see 2 Cor. 3:18).

God has a message for you today. He is declaring new things for your life. One definition of the word *new* is "not existing before." The creative power of the Lord is about to do some things in your life that have never been done before! By the way, when we turn to Jesus and give Him our lives, "all things have become new"! (2 Cor. 5:17).

Would you be willing to give Jesus your mirror—your image—your past? If you will look upon His finished work of the cross, your life will reflect the fiery passion of His sacrifice. The past, with all of its pain, will lose its power; and you will be free to be all that He has destined you to be.

LaNora Van Arsdall

Promise of the Lord's Help

14 "I have held My peace a long time,
I have been still and restrained Myself.
Now I will cry like a woman in [1]labor,
I will pant and gasp at once.
15 I will lay waste the mountains and hills,
And dry up all their vegetation;
I will make the rivers coastlands,
And I will dry up the pools.
16 I will bring the blind by a way they did not know;
I will lead them in paths they have not known.
I will make darkness light before them,
And crooked places straight.
These things I will do for them,
And not forsake them.
17 They shall be [a]turned back,
They shall be greatly ashamed,
Who trust in carved images,
Who say to the molded images,
'You *are* our gods.'

18 "Hear, you deaf;
And look, you blind, that you may see.
19 [a]Who *is* blind but My servant,
Or deaf as My messenger *whom* I send?
Who *is* blind as *he who is* perfect,
And blind as the LORD's servant?
20 Seeing many things, [a]but you do not observe;
Opening the ears, but he does not hear."

Israel's Obstinate Disobedience

21 The LORD is well pleased for His righteousness' sake;
He will exalt the law and make *it* honorable.
22 But this *is* a people robbed and plundered;
All of them are [1]snared in holes,
And they are hidden in prison houses;
They are for prey, and no one delivers;
For plunder, and no one says, "Restore!"

23 Who among you will give ear to this?
Who will listen and hear for the time to come?
24 Who gave Jacob for plunder, and Israel to the robbers?
Was it not the LORD,
He against whom we have sinned?
[a]For they would not walk in His ways,
Nor were they obedient to His law.
25 Therefore He has poured on him the fury of His anger
And the strength of battle;
[a]It has set him on fire all around,
[b]Yet he did not know;
And it burned him,
Yet he did not take *it* to [c]heart.

The Redeemer of Israel

43 But now, thus says the LORD, who created you, O Jacob,
And He who formed you, O Israel:
"Fear not, [a]for I have redeemed you;
[b]I have called *you* by your name;
You *are* Mine.
2 [a]When you pass through the waters, [b]I *will be* with you;
And through the rivers, they shall not overflow you.
When you [c]walk through the fire, you shall not be burned,
Nor shall the flame scorch you.
3 For I *am* the LORD your God,
The Holy One of Israel, your Savior;
[a]I gave Egypt for your ransom,
Ethiopia and Seba in your place.
4 Since you were precious in My sight,
You have been honored,
And I have [a]loved you;
Therefore I will give men for you,
And people for your life.
5 [a]Fear not, for I *am* with you;
I will bring your descendants from the east,
And [b]gather you from the west;
6 I will say to the [a]north, 'Give them up!'
And to the south, 'Do not keep them back!'
Bring My sons from afar,
And My daughters from the ends of the earth—
7 Everyone who is [a]called by My name,
Whom [b]I have created for My glory;
I have formed him, yes, I have made him."

---

14 [1] childbirth
17 [a] Ps. 97:7
19 [a] [John 9:39, 41]
20 [a] Rom. 2:21
22 [1] Or *trapped in caves*
24 [a] Is. 65:2
25 [a] 2 Kin. 25:9 [b] Hos. 7:9 [c] Is. 29:13

CHAPTER 43
1 [a] Is. 43:5; 44:6 [b] Is. 42:6; 45:4
2 [a] [Ps. 66:12; 91:3] [b] [Deut. 31:6] [c] Dan. 3:25
3 [a] [Prov. 11:8; 21:18]
4 [a] Is. 63:9
5 [a] Is. 41:10; 44:2 [b] Is. 54:7
6 [a] Is. 49:12
7 [a] James 2:7 [b] [2 Cor. 5:17]

8 [a]Bring out the blind people who
have eyes,
And the [b]deaf who have ears.
9 Let all the nations be gathered
together,
And let the people be assembled.
[a]Who among them can declare this,
And show us former things?
Let them bring out their witnesses,
that they may be justified;
Or let them hear and say, "*It is*
truth."
10 "You[a] *are* My witnesses," says the
LORD,
[b]"And My servant whom I have
chosen,
That you may know and [c]believe
Me,
And understand that I *am* He.
Before Me there was no God
formed,
Nor shall there be after Me.
11 I, *even* I, [a]*am* the LORD,
And besides Me *there is* no savior.
12 I have declared and saved,
I have proclaimed,
And *there was* no [a]foreign *god*
among you;
[b]Therefore you *are* My witnesses,"
Says the LORD, "that I *am* God.
13 [a]Indeed before the day *was,* I *am*
He;
And *there is* no one who can
deliver out of My hand;
I work, and who will [b]reverse it?"
14 Thus says the LORD, your
Redeemer,
The Holy One of Israel:
"For your sake I will send to
Babylon,
And bring them all down as
fugitives—
The Chaldeans, who rejoice in their
ships.
15 I *am* the LORD, your Holy One,
The Creator of Israel, your [a]King."
16 Thus says the LORD, who [a]makes a
way in the sea
And a [b]path through the mighty
waters,
17 Who [a]brings forth the chariot and
horse,
The army and the power
(They shall lie down together, they
shall not rise;
They are extinguished, they are
quenched like a wick):
18 "Do[a] not remember the former
things,
Nor consider the things of old.
19 Behold, I will do a [a]new thing,
Now it shall spring forth;
Shall you not know it?
[b]I will even make a road in the
wilderness
And rivers in the desert.
20 The beast of the field will honor
Me,
The jackals and the ostriches,
Because [a]I give waters in the
wilderness
And rivers in the desert,
To give drink to My people, My
chosen.
21 [a]This people I have formed for
Myself;
They shall declare My [b]praise.

Pleading with Unfaithful Israel

22 "But you have not called upon Me,
O Jacob;
And you [a]have been weary of Me,
O Israel.
23 [a]You have not brought Me the
sheep for your burnt offerings,
Nor have you honored Me with
your sacrifices.
I have not caused you to serve with
grain offerings,
Nor wearied you with incense.
24 You have bought Me no sweet
cane with money,
Nor have you satisfied Me with the
fat of your sacrifices;
But you have burdened Me with
your sins,
You have [a]wearied Me with your
iniquities.
25 "I, *even* I, *am* He who [a]blots out
your transgressions [b]for My own
sake;
[c]And I will not remember your sins.
26 Put Me in remembrance;
Let us contend together;
State your *case,* that you may be
[1]acquitted.
27 Your first father sinned,
And your [1]mediators have
transgressed against Me.
28 Therefore I will profane the
princes of the sanctuary;
[a]I will give Jacob to the curse,
And Israel to reproaches.

8 a Ezek. 12:2 b Is. 29:18
9 a Is. 41:21, 22, 26
10 a Is. 44:8 b Is. 55:4 c Is. 41:4; 44:6
11 a Hos. 13:4
12 a Deut. 32:16 b Is. 44:8
13 a Ps. 90:2 b Job 9:12
15 a Is. 41:20, 21
16 a Ex. 14:16, 21, 22 b Josh. 3:13
17 a Ex. 14:4–9, 25
18 a Jer. 16:14
19 a [2 Cor. 5:17] b Ex. 17:6
20 a Is. 48:21
21 a Ps. 102:18 b Jer. 13:11
22 a Mal. 1:13; 3:14
23 a Amos 5:25
24 a Is. 1:14; 7:13
25 a Jer. 50:20 b Ezek. 36:22 c Is. 1:18
26 *1 justified*
27 *1 interpreters*
28 a Dan. 9:11

God's Blessing on Israel

44 "Yet hear me now, O Jacob My servant,
And Israel whom I have chosen.
2 Thus says the LORD who made you
And formed you from the womb, *who* will help you:
'Fear not, O Jacob My servant;
And you, Jeshurun, whom I have chosen.
3 For I will pour water on him who is thirsty,
And floods on the dry ground;
I will pour My Spirit on your descendants,
And My blessing on your offspring;
4 They will spring up among the grass
Like willows by the watercourses.'
5 One will say, 'I *am* the LORD's';
Another will call *himself* by the name of Jacob;
Another will write *with* his hand, 'The LORD's,'
And name *himself* by the name of Israel.

There Is No Other God

6 "Thus says the LORD, the King of Israel,
And his Redeemer, the LORD of hosts:
[a]'I *am* the First and I *am* the Last;
Besides Me *there is* no God.
7 And [a]who can proclaim as I do?
Then let him declare it and set it in order for Me,
Since I appointed the ancient people.
And the things that are coming and shall come,
Let them show these to them.
8 Do not fear, nor be afraid;
[a]Have I not told you from that time, and declared *it?*
[b]You *are* My witnesses.
Is there a God besides Me?
Indeed [c]*there is* no other Rock;
I know not *one.*' "

Idolatry Is Foolishness

9 [a]Those who make an image, all of them *are* useless,
And their precious things shall not profit;
They *are* their own witnesses;
[b]They neither see nor know, that they may be ashamed.
10 Who would form a god or mold an image
[a]*That* profits him nothing?
11 Surely all his companions would be [a]ashamed;
And the workmen, they *are* mere men.
Let them all be gathered together,
Let them stand up;
Yet they shall fear,
They shall be ashamed together.

12 [a]The blacksmith with the tongs works one in the coals,
Fashions it with hammers,
And works it with the strength of his arms.
Even so, he is hungry, and his strength fails;
He drinks no water and is faint.

13 The craftsman stretches out *his* rule,
He marks one out with chalk;
He fashions it with a plane,
He marks it out with the compass,
And makes it like the figure of a man,
According to the beauty of a man, that it may remain in the house.
14 He cuts down cedars for himself,
And takes the cypress and the oak;
He [1]secures *it* for himself among the trees of the forest.
He plants a pine, and the rain nourishes *it.*
15 Then it shall be for a man to burn,
For he will take some of it and warm himself;
Yes, he kindles *it* and bakes bread;
Indeed he makes a god and worships *it;*
He makes it a carved image, and falls down to it.
16 He burns half of it in the fire;
With this half he eats meat;
He roasts a roast, and is satisfied.
He even warms *himself* and says,
"Ah! I am warm,
I have seen the fire."
17 And the rest of it he makes into a god,
His carved image.

CHAPTER 44
6 [a]Is. 41:4
7 [a]Is. 41:4, 22, 26
8 [a]Is. 41:22 [b]Is. 43:10, 12 [c]1 Sam. 2:2
9 [a]Is. 41:24 [b]Ps. 115:4
10 [a]Hab. 2:18
11 [a]Ps. 97:7
12 [a]Jer. 10:3–5
14 [1]Lit. *appropriates*

He falls down before it and
worships *it,*
Prays to it and says,
"Deliver me, for you *are* my god!"

18 [a]They do not know nor understand;
For [b]He has [1]shut their eyes, so
that they cannot see,
And their hearts, so that they
cannot [c]understand.
19 And no one [a]considers in his
heart,
Nor *is there* knowledge nor
understanding to say,
"I have burned half of it in the fire,
Yes, I have also baked bread on its
coals;
I have roasted meat and eaten *it;*
And shall I make the rest of it an
abomination?
Shall I fall down before a block of
wood?"
20 He feeds on ashes;
[a]A deceived heart has turned him
aside;
And he cannot deliver his soul,
Nor say, "*Is there* not a [b]lie in my
right hand?"

Israel Is Not Forgotten

21 "Remember these, O Jacob,
And Israel, for you *are* My servant;
I have formed you, you *are* My
servant;
O Israel, you will not be [a]forgotten
by Me!
22 [a]I have blotted out, like a thick
cloud, your transgressions,
And like a cloud, your sins.
Return to Me, for [b]I have redeemed
you."

23 [a]Sing, O heavens, for the LORD has
done *it!*
Shout, you lower parts of the earth;
Break forth into singing, you
mountains,
O forest, and every tree in it!
For the LORD has redeemed Jacob,
And [b]glorified Himself in Israel.

Judah Will Be Restored

24 Thus says the LORD, [a]your
Redeemer,
And [b]He who formed you from the
womb:
"I *am* the LORD, who makes all
things,

[c]Who stretches out the heavens [1]all
alone,
Who spreads abroad the earth by
Myself;
25 Who [a]frustrates the signs [b]of the
babblers,
And drives diviners mad;
Who turns wise men backward,
[c]And makes their knowledge
foolishness;
26 [a]Who confirms the word of His
servant,
And performs the counsel of His
messengers;
Who says to Jerusalem, 'You shall
be inhabited,'
To the cities of Judah, 'You shall be
built,'
And I will raise up her waste places;
27 [a]Who says to the deep, 'Be dry!
And I will dry up your rivers';
28 Who says of [a]Cyrus, '*He is* My
shepherd,
And he shall perform all My
pleasure,
Saying to Jerusalem, [b]"You shall be
built,"
And to the temple, "Your
foundation shall be laid." '

Cyrus, God's Instrument

45 "Thus says the LORD to His
anointed,
To [a]Cyrus, whose [b]right hand I
have [1]held—
[c]To subdue nations before him
And [d]loose the armor of kings,
To open before him the double
doors,
So that the gates will not be shut:
2 'I will go before you
[a]And[1] make the [2]crooked places
straight;
[b]I will break in pieces the gates of
bronze
And cut the bars of iron.
3 I will give you the treasures of
darkness
And hidden riches of secret places,
[a]That you may know that I, the
LORD,
Who [b]call *you* by your name,
Am the God of Israel.
4 For [a]Jacob My servant's sake,
And Israel My elect,
I have even called you by your
name;

18 [a]Is. 45:20 [b]Is. 6:9, 10; 29:10 [c]Jer. 10:14 [1]Lit. *smeared over*

19 [a]Is. 46:8

20 [a]2 Thess. 2:11 [b]Rom. 1:25

21 [a]Is. 49:15

22 [a]Is. 43:25 [b]1 Cor. 6:20

23 [a]Ps. 69:34 [b]Is. 49:3; 60:21

24 [a]Is. 43:14 [b]Is. 43:1 [c]Job 9:8 [1]By Himself

25 [a]Is. 47:13 [b]Jer. 50:36 [c]1 Cor. 1:20, 27

26 [a]Zech. 1:6

27 [a]Jer. 50:38; 51:36

28 [a]Ezra 1:1 [b]Ezra 6:7

CHAPTER 45
1 [a]Is. 44:28 [b]Is. 41:13 [c]Dan. 5:30 [d]Job 12:21 [1]*strengthened* or *sustained*

2 [a]Is. 40:4 [b]Ps. 107:16 [1]Tg. *I will trample down the walls;* Vg. *I will humble the great ones of the earth* [2]DSS, LXX *mountains*

3 [a]Is. 41:23 [b]Ex. 33:12

4 [a]Is. 44:1

I have named you, though you have
not known Me.
5 I [a]*am* the LORD, and [b]*there is* no
other;
There is no God besides Me.
[c]I will gird you, though you have
not known Me,
6 [a]That they may [b]know from the
rising of the sun to its setting
That *there is* none besides Me.
I *am* the LORD, and *there is* no
other;
7 I form the light and create
darkness,
I make peace and [a]create calamity;
I, the LORD, do all these *things*.'

8 "Rain[a] down, you heavens, from
above,
And let the skies pour down
righteousness;
Let the earth open, let them bring
forth salvation,
And let righteousness spring up
together.
I, the LORD, have created it.

9 "Woe to him who strives with [a]his
Maker!
Let the potsherd *strive* with the
potsherds of the earth!
[b]Shall the clay say to him who
forms it, 'What are you making?'
Or shall your handiwork *say*, 'He
has no hands'?
10 Woe to him who says to *his*
father, 'What are you begetting?'
Or to the woman, 'What have you
brought forth?' "

11 Thus says the LORD,
The Holy One of Israel, and his
Maker:
[a]"Ask Me of things to come
concerning [b]My sons;
And concerning [c]the work of My
hands, you command Me.
12 [a]I have made the earth,
And [b]created man on it.
I—My hands—stretched out the
heavens,
And [c]all their host I have
commanded.
13 [a]I have raised him up in
righteousness,
And I will [1]direct all his ways;
He shall [b]build My city
And let My exiles go free,
[c]Not for price nor reward,"
Says the LORD of hosts.

The Lord, the Only Savior

14 Thus says the LORD:

[a]"The labor of Egypt and merchandise
of Cush
And of the Sabeans, men of stature,
Shall come over to you, and they
shall be yours;
They shall walk behind you,
They shall come over [b]in chains;
And they shall bow down to you.
They will make supplication to you,
saying, [c]'Surely God *is* in you,
And *there is* no other;
[d]*There is* no other God.' "

15 Truly You *are* God, [a]who hide
Yourself,
O God of Israel, the Savior!
16 They shall be [a]ashamed
And also disgraced, all of them;
They shall go in confusion together,
Who are makers of idols.
17 [a]*But* Israel shall be saved by the
LORD
With an [b]everlasting salvation;
You shall not be ashamed or
[c]disgraced
Forever and ever.

18 For thus says the LORD,
[a]Who created the heavens,
Who is God,
Who formed the earth and made it,
Who has established it,
Who did not create it [1]in vain,
Who formed it to be [b]inhabited:
[c]"I *am* the LORD, and *there is* no
other.
19 I have not spoken in [a]secret,
In a dark place of the earth;
I did not say to the seed of Jacob,
'Seek Me [1]in vain';
[b]I, the LORD, speak righteousness,
I declare things that are right.

20 "Assemble yourselves and come;
Draw near together,
You *who have* escaped from the
nations.
[a]They have no knowledge,
Who carry the wood of their carved
image,
And pray to a god *that* cannot save.
21 Tell and bring forth *your case;*
Yes, let them take counsel together.
[a]Who has declared this from ancient
time?
Who has told it from that time?
Have not I, the LORD?

5 [a]Deut. 4:35; 32:39 [b]Is. 45:14, 18 [c]Ps. 18:32
6 [a]Mal. 1:11 [b][Is. 11:9; 52:10]
7 [a]Amos 3:6
8 [a]Ps. 85:11
9 [a]Is. 64:8 [b]Jer. 18:6
11 [a]Is. 8:19 [b]Jer. 31:9 [c]Is. 29:23; 60:21; 64:8
12 [a]Is. 42:5 [b]Gen. 1:26 [c]Gen. 2:1
13 [a]Is. 41:2 [b]2 Chr. 36:22 [c][Rom. 3:24] [1]Or *make all his ways straight*
14 [a]Zech. 8:22, 23 [b]Ps. 149:8 [c]1 Cor. 14:25 [d]Is. 45:5
15 [a]Ps. 44:24
16 [a]Is. 44:11
17 [a]Is. 26:4 [b]Is. 51:6 [c]Is. 29:22
18 [a]Is. 42:5 [b]Ps. 115:16 [c]Is. 45:5 [1]Or *empty, a waste*
19 [a]Deut. 30:11 [b]Ps. 19:8 [1]Or *in a waste place*
20 [a]Is. 44:9; 46:7
21 [a]Is. 41:22; 43:9

[b]And *there is* no other God besides
Me,
A just God and a Savior;
There is none besides Me.

Heavenly Father, may _____ look to You and be saved; for You are God, and there is no other!

FROM ISAIAH 45:22

22 "Look to Me, and be saved,
[a]All you ends of the earth!
For I *am* God, and *there is* no
other.
23 [a]I have sworn by Myself;
The word has gone out of My
mouth *in* righteousness,
And shall not return,
That to Me every [b]knee shall bow,
[c]Every tongue shall take an oath.
24 He shall say,
[1]'Surely in the LORD I have
[a]righteousness and strength.
To Him *men* shall come,
And [b]all shall be ashamed
Who are incensed against Him.
25 [a]In the LORD all the descendants of
Israel
Shall be justified, and [b]shall
glory.' "

Dead Idols and the Living God

46 Bel [a]bows down, Nebo stoops;
Their idols were on the beasts
and on the cattle.
Your carriages *were* heavily loaded,
[b]A burden to the weary *beast.*
2 They stoop, they bow down
together;
They could not deliver the burden,
[a]But have themselves gone into
captivity.

3 "Listen to Me, O house of Jacob,
And all the remnant of the house of
Israel,
[a]Who have been upheld *by Me* from
[1]birth,
Who have been carried from the
womb:

21 **b** Is. 44:8
22 **a** Ps. 22:27; 65:5
23 **a** [Heb. 6:13] **b** Rom. 14:11 **c** Deut. 6:13
24 **a** [1 Cor. 1:30] **b** Is. 41:11 *1 Or Only in the LORD are all righteousness and strength*
25 **a** Is. 45:17 **b** 1 Cor. 1:31
CHAPTER 46
1 **a** Jer. 50:2 **b** Jer. 10:5
2 **a** Jer. 48:7
3 **a** Ps. 71:6 *1* Lit. *the belly*
4 **a** Mal. 3:6 **b** Ps. 48:14
5 **a** Is. 40:18, 25
6 **a** Is. 40:19; 41:6 **b** Is. 44:12
7 **a** Jer. 10:5 **b** Is. 45:20
8 **a** Is. 44:19 *1 be men,* take courage
9 **a** Deut. 32:7 **b** Is. 45:5, 21
10 **a** Is. 45:21; 48:3 **b** Ps. 33:11
11 **a** Is. 41:2, 25 **b** Is. 44:28 **c** Num. 23:19
12 **a** Ps. 76:5 **b** [Rom. 10:3]
13 **a** [Rom. 1:17] **b** Hab. 2:3 **c** Is. 62:11 *1 delay*

4 Even to *your* old age, [a]I *am* He,
And *even* to gray hairs [b]I will carry
you!
I have made, and I will bear;
Even I will carry, and will deliver
you.

5 "To[a] whom will you liken Me, and
make *Me* equal
And compare Me, that we should be
alike?
6 [a]They lavish gold out of the bag,
And weigh silver on the scales;
They hire a [b]goldsmith, and he
makes it a god;
They prostrate themselves, yes, they
worship.
7 [a]They bear it on the shoulder, they
carry it
And set it in its place, and it stands;
From its place it shall not move.
Though [b]*one* cries out to it, yet it
cannot answer
Nor save him out of his trouble.

8 "Remember this, and [1]show
yourselves men;
[a]Recall to mind, O you
transgressors.
9 [a]Remember the former things of
old,
For I *am* God, and [b]*there is* no
other;
I am God, and *there is* none like
Me,
10 [a]Declaring the end from the
beginning,
And from ancient times *things* that
are not *yet* done,
Saying, [b]'My counsel shall stand,
And I will do all My pleasure,'
11 Calling a bird of prey [a]from the
east,
The man [b]who executes My
counsel, from a far country.
Indeed [c]I have spoken *it;*
I will also bring it to pass.
I have purposed *it;*
I will also do it.

12 "Listen to Me, you [a]stubborn-
hearted,
[b]Who *are* far from righteousness:
13 [a]I bring My righteousness near, it
shall not be far off;
My salvation [b]shall not [1]linger.
And I will place [c]salvation in Zion,
For Israel My glory.

ISAIAH 46:8–10

Dear Woman of Destiny,

As I ponder your future and consider your purpose in this life, I recall the words of the prophet Isaiah, "Remember the former things of old, for I am God, and there is no other; I am God, and there is none like Me, declaring the end from the beginning, and from ancient times things that are not yet done, saying, 'My counsel shall stand, and I will do all My pleasure,' calling a bird of prey from the east, the man who executes My counsel, from a far country. Indeed I have spoken it; I will also bring it to pass. I have purposed it; I will also do it" (Is. 46:9–11).

Our mighty God determined your end before you began. Psalm 139:15, 16 tell us that: "My frame was not hidden from You, when I was made in secret . . . Your eyes saw my substance, being yet unformed. And in Your book they were all written, the days fashioned for me, when as yet there were none of them." In Ephesians 1:4, you can read that God chose you "in Him before the foundation of the world." Then He planted a holy seed of destiny in your very makeup long before you were born. It is interwoven in the very substance of your bones. As this seed is watered with faith and the word of the Lord, you'll find it blossoming with the full evidence of your purpose in this life. Our Father has written in His own handwriting "the days fashioned for [you], when as yet there were none of them" (Ps. 139:16).

As an acorn has a full-grown oak tree designed into its being, so you have a full-blown destiny within you. The acorn does not struggle to become a tree; neither do you need to struggle to become a woman of God. Allow the Lord to develop and change you.

As you follow God's will for your life, He may lead you through seasons or situations that don't seem to make sense. When you encounter such times, remember that they are necessary steps on your way to His plan for you and that they are *part* of that plan. At a later date, you are likely to look back on these times with gratitude for the lessons you learned, for the obstacles you overcame, for the display of God's faithfulness to you during that season, or for the joy of coming to understand yet more about His character. You may later discover that those times were crucial moments in fulfilling His destiny for your life.

As you daily yield to the word of the Lord, the unfolding purpose of God is taking place deep within you. As you worship Him and seek His face, the light of His favor shines upon you and draws you forth. Slowly but surely you are becoming a woman of destiny. Slowly but steadily you are becoming established. The Lord is breathing upon you His kind breath of love until all the fear of failure and loss falls away. Trust Him. He will never fail you. He will never leave you. Let His word be implanted in the deepest part of you heart.

I think you'll be delighted with what develops. I know He already is.

Mary Glazier

The Humiliation of Babylon

47 "Come [a]down and [b]sit in the
dust,
O virgin daughter of [c]Babylon;
Sit on the ground without a throne,
O daughter of the Chaldeans!
For you shall no more be called
Tender and [1]delicate.
2 [a]Take the millstones and grind
meal.
Remove your veil,
Take off the skirt,
Uncover the thigh,
Pass through the rivers.
3 [a]Your nakedness shall be uncovered,
Yes, your shame will be seen;
[b]I will take vengeance,
And I will not arbitrate with a
man."
4 *As for* [a]our Redeemer, the LORD of
hosts *is* His name,
The Holy One of Israel.
5 "Sit in [a]silence, and go into
darkness,
O daughter of the Chaldeans;
[b]For you shall no longer be called
The Lady of Kingdoms.
6 [a]I was angry with My people;
[b]I have profaned My inheritance,
And given them into your hand.
You showed them no mercy;
[c]On the elderly you laid your yoke
very heavily.
7 And you said, 'I shall be [a]a lady
forever,'
So that you did not [b]take these
things to heart,
[c]Nor remember the latter end of
them.
8 "Therefore hear this now, *you who
are* given to pleasures,
Who dwell securely,
Who say in your heart, 'I *am,* and
there is no one else besides me;
I shall not sit *as* a widow,
Nor shall I know the loss of
children';
9 But these two *things* shall come to
you
[a]In a moment, in one day:
The loss of children, and
widowhood.
They shall come upon you in their
fullness
Because of the multitude of your
sorceries,
For the great abundance of your
enchantments.
10 "For you have trusted in your
wickedness;
You have said, 'No one [a]sees me';
Your wisdom and your knowledge
have [1]warped you;
And you have said in your heart,
'I *am,* and *there is* no one else
besides me.'
11 Therefore evil shall come upon
you;
You shall not know from where it
arises.
And trouble shall fall upon you;
You will not be able [1]to put it off.
And [a]desolation shall come upon
you [b]suddenly,
Which you shall not know.
12 "Stand now with your
enchantments
And the multitude of your
sorceries,
In which you have labored from
your youth—
Perhaps you will be able to profit,
Perhaps you will prevail.
13 [a]You are wearied in the multitude
of your counsels;
Let now [b]the[1] astrologers, the
stargazers,
And [2]the monthly prognosticators
Stand up and save you
From what shall come upon you.
14 Behold, they shall be [a]as stubble,
The fire shall [b]burn them;
They shall not deliver themselves
From the power of the flame;
It shall not *be* a coal to be warmed
by,
Nor a fire to sit before!
15 Thus shall they be to you
With whom you have labored,
[a]Your merchants from your youth;
They shall wander each one to his
[1]quarter.
No one shall save you.

Israel Refined for God's Glory

48 "Hear this, O house of Jacob,
Who are called by the name of
Israel,
And have come forth from the
wellsprings of Judah;
Who swear by the name of the
LORD,

CHAPTER 47
1 [a]Jer. 48:18 [b]Is. 3:26 [c]Jer. 25:12; 50:1—51:64 [1]*dainty*
2 [a]Ex. 11:5
3 [a]Is. 3:17; 20:4 [b][Rom. 12:19]
4 [a]Jer. 50:34
5 [a]1 Sam. 2:9 [b][Dan. 2:37]
6 [a]2 Sam. 24:14 [b]Is. 43:28 [c]Deut. 28:49, 50
7 [a]Rev. 18:7 [b]Is. 42:25; 46:8 [c]Deut. 32:29
9 [a]1 Thess. 5:3
10 [a]Is. 29:15 [1]*led you astray*
11 [a]1 Thess. 5:3 [b]Is. 29:5 [1]Lit. *to cover it or atone for it*
13 [a]Is. 57:10 [b]Dan. 2:2, 10 [1]Lit. *viewers of the heavens* [2]Lit. *those giving knowledge for new moons*
14 [a]Nah. 1:10 [b]Jer. 51:58
15 [a]Rev. 18:11 [1]*own side* or *way*

And make mention of the God of Israel,
But [a]not in truth or in righteousness;
2 For they call themselves [a]after the holy city,
And [b]lean on the God of Israel;
The LORD of hosts *is* His name:
3 "I have [a]declared the former things from the beginning;
They went forth from My mouth, and I caused them to hear it.
Suddenly I did *them,* [b]and they came to pass.
4 Because I knew that you *were* [1]obstinate,
And [a]your neck *was* an iron sinew,
And your brow bronze,
5 Even from the beginning I have declared *it* to you;
Before it came to pass I proclaimed *it* to you,
Lest you should say, 'My idol has done them,
And my carved image and my molded image
Have commanded them.'
6 "You have heard;
See all this.
And will you not declare *it?*
I have made you hear new things from this time,
Even hidden things, and you did not know them.
7 They are created now and not from the beginning;
And before this day you have not heard them,
Lest you should say, 'Of course I knew them.'
8 Surely you did not hear,
Surely you did not know;
Surely from long ago your ear was not opened.
For I knew that you would deal very treacherously,
And were called [a]a transgressor from the womb.
9 "For[a] My name's sake [b]I will [1]defer My anger,
And *for* My praise I will restrain it from you,
So that I do not cut you off.
10 Behold, [a]I have refined you, but not as silver;
I have tested you in the [b]furnace of affliction.

CHAPTER 48
1 [a]Jer. 4:2; 5:2
2 [a]Is. 52:1; 64:10 [b]Mic. 3:11
3 [a]Is. 44:7, 8; 46:10 [b]Josh. 21:45
4 [a]Deut. 31:27 [1]Heb. *hard*
8 [a]Ps. 58:3
9 [a]Ezek. 20:9, 14, 22, 44 [b]Ps. 78:38 [1]*delay*
10 [a]Ps. 66:10 [b]Deut. 4:20
11 [a]Ezek. 20:9 [b]Is. 42:8
12 [a]Deut. 32:39 [b][Rev. 22:13]
13 [a]Ps. 102:25 [b]Is. 40:26
14 [a]Is. 45:1 [b]Is. 44:28; 47:1–15
15 [a]Is. 45:1, 2
16 [a]Is. 45:19 [b]Zech. 2:8, 9, 11 [1]Heb. verb is sing.; or *Has sent Me and His Spirit*
17 [a]Is. 43:14 [b]Ps. 32:8
18 [a]Ps. 81:13 [b]Ps. 119:165
19 [a]Gen. 22:17

11 For My own sake, for My own sake, I will do *it;*
For [a]how should *My name* be profaned?
And [b]I will not give My glory to another.

God's Ancient Plan to Redeem Israel

12 "Listen to Me, O Jacob,
And Israel, My called:
I *am* He, [a]I *am* the [b]First,
I *am* also the Last.
13 Indeed [a]My hand has laid the foundation of the earth,
And My right hand has stretched out the heavens;
When [b]I call to them,
They stand up together.
14 "All of you, assemble yourselves, and hear!
Who among them has declared these *things?*
[a]The LORD loves him;
[b]He shall do His pleasure on Babylon,
And His arm *shall be against* the Chaldeans.
15 I, *even* I, have spoken;
Yes, [a]I have called him,
I have brought him, and his way will prosper.
16 "Come near to Me, hear this:
[a]I have not spoken in secret from the beginning;
From the time that it was, I *was* there.
And now [b]the Lord GOD and His Spirit
[1]Have sent Me."
17 Thus says [a]the LORD, your Redeemer,
The Holy One of Israel:
"I *am* the LORD your God,
Who teaches you to profit,
[b]Who leads you by the way you should go.
18 [a]Oh, that you had heeded My commandments!
[b]Then your peace would have been like a river,
And your righteousness like the waves of the sea.
19 [a]Your descendants also would have been like the sand,

And the offspring of your body like
the grains of sand;
His name would not have been cut
off
Nor destroyed from before Me."

20 [a]Go forth from Babylon!
Flee from the Chaldeans!
With a voice of singing,
Declare, proclaim this,
Utter it to the end of the earth;
Say, "The LORD has [b]redeemed
His servant Jacob!"
21 And they [a]did not thirst
When He led them through the
deserts;
He [b]caused the waters to flow from
the rock for them;
He also split the rock, and the
waters gushed out.

22 "There[a] *is* no peace," says the
LORD, "for the wicked."

The Servant, the Light to the Gentiles

49 "Listen, [a]O coastlands, to Me,
And take heed, you peoples from
afar!
[b]The LORD has called Me from the
womb;
From the [1]matrix of My mother He
has made mention of My name.
2 And He has made [a]My mouth like
a sharp sword;
[b]In the shadow of His hand He has
hidden Me,
And made Me [c]a polished shaft;
In His quiver He has hidden Me."

What is the greatest secret of life? Is it not that the Creator has a plan for every person born into the world?

GORDON LINDSAY

3 "And He said to me,
[a]'You *are* My servant, O Israel,
[b]In whom I will be glorified.'
4 [a]Then I said, 'I have labored in vain,
I have spent my strength for
nothing and in vain;
Yet surely my [1]just reward *is* with
the LORD,
And my [2]work with my God.'"

5 "And now the LORD says,
Who formed Me from the womb *to
be* His Servant,
To bring Jacob back to Him,
So that Israel [a]is [1]gathered to Him
(For I shall be glorious in the eyes
of the LORD,
And My God shall be My strength),
6 Indeed He says,
'It is too small a thing that You
should be My Servant
To raise up the tribes of Jacob,
And to restore the preserved ones of
Israel;
I will also give You as a [a]light to
the Gentiles,
That You should be My salvation to
the ends of the earth.'"

7 Thus says the LORD,
The Redeemer of Israel, [1]their Holy
One,
[a]To Him [2]whom man despises,
To Him whom the nation abhors,
To the Servant of rulers:
[b]"Kings shall see and arise,
Princes also shall worship,
Because of the LORD who is faithful,
The Holy One of Israel;
And He has chosen You."

8 Thus says the LORD:
"In an [a]acceptable[1] time I have
heard You,
And in the day of salvation I have
helped You;
I will [2]preserve You [b]and give You
As a covenant to the people,
To restore the earth,
To cause them to inherit the
desolate [3]heritages;
9 That You may say [a]to the
prisoners, 'Go forth,'
To those who *are* in darkness,
'Show yourselves.'

"They shall feed along the roads,
And their pastures *shall be* on all
desolate heights.
10 They shall neither [a]hunger nor
thirst,
[b]Neither heat nor sun shall strike
them;
For He who has mercy on them
[c]will lead them,

---

20 a Zech. 2:6, 7 b [Ex. 19:4–6]
21 a [Is. 41:17, 18] b Ex. 17:6
22 a [Is. 57:21]

CHAPTER 49
1 a Is. 41:1 b Jer. 1:5 *1 Lit. inward parts*
2 a Rev. 1:16; 2:12 b Is. 51:16 c Ps. 45:5
3 a [Zech. 3:8] b Is. 44:23
4 a [Ezek. 3:19] *1 justice* *2 recompense*
5 a Matt. 23:37 *1* Qr., DSS, LXX *gathered to Him;* Kt. *not gathered*
6 a [Luke 2:32]
7 a [Is. 53:3] b [Is. 52:15] *1* Lit. *his* or *its* *2* Lit. *who is despised of soul*
8 a 2 Cor. 6:2 b Is. 42:6 *1 favorable* *2 keep* *3 inheritances*
9 a Is. 61:1
10 a Rev. 7:16, 17 b Ps. 121:6 c Ps. 23:2

Even by the springs of water He
will guide them.
11 [a]I will make each of My mountains
a road,
And My highways shall be elevated.
12 Surely [a]these shall come from
afar;
Look! Those from the north and
the west,
And these from the land of Sinim."

13 [a]Sing, O heavens!
Be joyful, O earth!
And break out in singing,
O mountains!
For the LORD has comforted His
people,
And will have mercy on His
afflicted.

God Will Remember Zion

14 [a]But Zion said, "The LORD has
forsaken me,
And my Lord has forgotten me."

15 "Can[a] a woman forget her nursing
child,
[1]And not have compassion on the
son of her womb?
Surely they may forget,
[b]Yet I will not forget you.
16 See, [a]I have inscribed you on the
palms *of My hands;*
Your walls *are* continually before
Me.
17 Your [1]sons shall make haste;
Your destroyers and those who laid
you waste
Shall go away from you.
18 [a]Lift up your eyes, look around and
see;
All these gather together *and* come
to you.
As I live," says the LORD,
"You shall surely clothe yourselves
with them all [b]as an ornament,
And bind them *on you* as a bride
does.

19 "For your waste and desolate
places,
And the land of your destruction,
[a]Will even now be too small for the
inhabitants;
And those who swallowed you up
will be far away.
20 [a]The children you will have,
[b]After you have lost the others,
Will say again in your ears,
'The place *is* too small for me;
Give me a place where I may dwell.'
21 Then you will say in your heart,
'Who has begotten these for me,
Since I have lost my children and
am desolate,
A captive, and wandering to and
fro?
And who has brought these up?
There I was, left alone;
But these, where *were* they?' "

22 [a]Thus says the Lord GOD:

"Behold, I will lift My hand in an
oath to the nations,
And set up My [1]standard for the
peoples;
They shall bring your sons in *their*
[2]arms,
And your daughters shall be carried
on *their* shoulders;
23 [a]Kings shall be your foster fathers,
And their queens your nursing
mothers;
They shall bow down to you with
their faces to the earth,
And [b]lick up the dust of your feet.
Then you will know that I *am* the
LORD,
[c]For they shall not be ashamed who
wait for Me."

24 [a]Shall the prey be taken from the
mighty,
Or the captives [1]of the righteous be
delivered?

25 But thus says the LORD:

"Even the captives of the mighty
shall be taken away,
And the prey of the terrible be
delivered;
For I will contend with him who
contends with you,
And I will save your children.
26 I will [a]feed those who oppress you
with their own flesh,
And they shall be drunk with their
own [b]blood as with sweet wine.
All flesh [c]shall know
That I, the LORD, *am* your Savior,
And your Redeemer, the Mighty
One of Jacob."

---

11 a Is. 40:4
12 a Is. 43:5, 6
13 a Is. 44:23
14 a Is. 40:27
15 a Ps. 103:13 b Rom. 11:29 *1* Lit. *From having compassion*
16 a Song 8:6
17 *1* DSS, LXX, Tg., Vg. *builders*
18 a Is. 60:4 b Prov. 17:6
19 a Zech. 10:10
20 a Is. 60:4 b [Rom. 11:11]
22 a Is. 60:4 *1 banner* *2* Lit. *bosom*
23 a Is. 52:15 b Ps. 72:9 c [Rom. 5:5]
24 a Luke 11:21, 22 *1* So with MT, Tg.; DSS, Syr., Vg. *of the mighty;* LXX *unjustly*
26 a Is. 9:20 b Rev. 14:20 c Ps. 9:16

The Servant, Israel's Hope

50 Thus says the LORD:

"Where *is* [a]the certificate of your
mother's divorce,
Whom I have put away?
Or which of My [b]creditors *is it* to
whom I have sold you?
For your iniquities [c]you have sold
yourselves,
And for your transgressions your
mother has been put away.
2 Why, when I came, *was there* no
man?
Why, when I called, *was there* none
to answer?
Is My hand shortened at all that it
cannot redeem?
Or have I no power to deliver?
Indeed with My [a]rebuke I dry up
the sea,
I make the rivers a wilderness;
Their fish stink because *there is* no
water,
And die of thirst.
3 [a]I clothe the heavens with
blackness,
[b]And I make sackcloth their
covering."

4 "The[a] Lord GOD has given Me
The tongue of the learned,
That I should know how to speak
A word in season to *him who is*
[b]weary.
He awakens Me morning by
morning,
He awakens My ear
To hear as the learned.
5 The Lord GOD [a]has opened My ear;
And I was not [b]rebellious,
Nor did I turn away.
6 [a]I gave My back to those who struck
Me,
And [b]My cheeks to those who
plucked out the beard;
I did not hide My face from shame
and [c]spitting.

7 "For the Lord GOD will help Me;
Therefore I will not be disgraced;
Therefore [a]I have set My face like a
flint,
And I know that I will not be
ashamed.
8 [a]*He is* near who justifies Me;
Who will contend with Me?
Let us stand together.
Who *is* [1]My adversary?
Let him come near Me.
9 Surely the Lord GOD will help Me;
Who *is* he *who* will condemn Me?
[a]Indeed they will all grow old like a
garment;
[b]The moth will eat them up.

10 "Who among you fears the LORD?
Who obeys the voice of His
Servant?
Who [a]walks in darkness
And has no light?
[b]Let him trust in the name of the
LORD
And rely upon his God.
11 Look, all you who kindle a fire,
Who encircle *yourselves* with
sparks:
Walk in the light of your fire and in
the sparks you have kindled—
[a]This you shall have from My hand:
You shall lie down [b]in torment.

The Lord Comforts Zion

51 "Listen to Me, [a]you who [1]follow
after righteousness,
You who seek the LORD:
Look to the rock *from which* you
were hewn,
And to the hole of the pit *from
which* you were dug.
2 [a]Look to Abraham your father,
And to Sarah *who* bore you;
[b]For I called him alone,
And [c]blessed him and increased
him."
3 For the LORD will [a]comfort Zion,
He will comfort all her waste
places;
He will make her wilderness like
Eden,
And her desert [b]like the garden of
the LORD;
Joy and gladness will be found in it,
Thanksgiving and the voice of
melody.

4 "Listen to Me, My people;
And give ear to Me, O My nation:
[a]For law will proceed from Me,
And I will make My justice rest
[b]As a light of the peoples.
5 [a]My righteousness *is* near,
My salvation has gone forth,
[b]And My arms will judge the
peoples;
[c]The coastlands will wait upon Me,
And [d]on My arm they will trust.

CHAPTER 50
1 a Deut. 24:1 b Deut. 32:30; 2 Kin. 4:1 c Is. 52:3
2 a Nah. 1:4
3 a Ex. 10:21 b Rev. 6:12
4 a Ex. 4:11 b Matt. 11:28
5 a Ps. 40:6 b Matt. 26:39
6 a Matt. 27:26 b Matt. 26:67; 27:30 c Lam. 3:30
7 a Ezek. 3:8, 9
8 a [Rom. 8:32–34] *1* Lit. *master of My judgment*
9 a Job 13:28 b Is. 51:6, 8
10 a Ps. 23:4 b 2 Chr. 20:20
11 a [John 9:39] b Ps. 16:4

CHAPTER 51
1 a [Rom. 9:30–32] *1 pursue*
2 a Heb. 11:11 b Gen. 12:1 c Gen. 24:35
3 a Is. 40:1; 52:9 b Gen. 13:10
4 a Is. 2:3 b Is. 42:6
5 a Is. 46:13 b Ps. 67:4 c Is. 60:9 d [Rom. 1:16]

6 [a]Lift up your eyes to the heavens,
And look on the earth beneath.
For [b]the heavens will vanish away
like smoke,
[c]The earth will grow old like a
garment,
And those who dwell in it will die
in like manner;
But My salvation will be [d]forever,
And My righteousness will not be
[1]abolished.

7 "Listen to Me, you who know
righteousness,
You people [a]in whose heart *is* My
law:
[b]Do not fear the reproach of men,
Nor be afraid of their insults.
8 For [a]the moth will eat them up
like a garment,
And the worm will eat them like
wool;
But My righteousness will be
forever,
And My salvation from generation
to generation."

9 [a]Awake, awake, [b]put on strength,
O arm of the LORD!
Awake [c]as in the ancient days,
In the generations of old.
[d]*Are* You not *the arm* that cut
[e]Rahab apart,
And wounded the [f]serpent?
10 *Are* You not *the One* who [a]dried
up the sea,
The waters of the great deep;
That made the depths of the sea a
road
For the redeemed to cross over?
11 So [a]the ransomed of the LORD
shall return,
And come to Zion with singing,
With everlasting joy on their heads.
They shall obtain joy and gladness;
Sorrow and sighing shall flee away.

12 "I, *even* I, *am* He [a]who comforts
you.
Who *are* you that you should be
afraid
[b]Of a man *who* will die,
And of the son of a man *who* will
be made [c]like grass?
13 And [a]you forget the LORD your
Maker,
[b]Who stretched out the heavens
And laid the foundations of the
earth;

6 [a]Is. 40:26 [b]Matt. 24:35 [c]Is. 24:19, 20; 50:9 [d]Is. 45:17 *[1]broken*
7 [a]Ps. 37:31 [b][Matt. 5:11, 12; 10:28]
8 [a]Is. 50:9
9 [a]Ps. 44:23 [b]Ps. 93:1 [c]Ps. 44:1 [d]Job 26:12 [e]Ps. 87:4 [f]Ps. 74:13
10 [a]Ex. 14:21
11 [a]Is. 35:10
12 [a]2 Cor. 1:3 [b]Ps. 118:6 [c]Is. 40:6, 7
13 [a]Is. 17:10 [b]Ps. 104:2 [c]Job 20:7
14 [a]Zech. 9:11
15 [a]Job 26:12
16 [a]Deut. 18:18 [b]Is. 49:2 [c]Is. 65:17 *[1]establish*
17 [a]Is. 52:1 [b]Job 21:20
19 [a]Is. 47:9 [b]Amos 7:2
20 [a]Lam. 2:11
21 [a]Lam. 3:15

You have feared continually every
day
Because of the fury of the
oppressor,
When *he has* prepared to destroy.
[c]And where *is* the fury of the
oppressor?
14 The captive exile hastens, that he
may be loosed,
[a]That he should not die in the pit,
And that his bread should not fail.
15 But I *am* the LORD your God,
Who [a]divided the sea whose waves
roared—
The LORD of hosts *is* His name.
16 And [a]I have put My words in your
mouth;
[b]I have covered you with the shadow
of My hand,
[c]That I may [1]plant the heavens,
Lay the foundations of the earth,
And say to Zion, 'You *are* My
people.'"

God's Fury Removed

17 [a]Awake, awake!
Stand up, O Jerusalem,
You who [b]have drunk at the hand
of the LORD
The cup of His fury;
You have drunk the dregs of the
cup of trembling,
And drained *it* out.
18 *There is* no one to guide her
Among all the sons she has brought
forth;
Nor *is there any* who takes her by
the hand
Among all the sons she has brought
up.
19 [a]These two *things* have come to
you;
Who will be sorry for you?—
Desolation and destruction, famine
and sword—
[b]By whom will I comfort you?
20 [a]Your sons have fainted,
They lie at the head of all the
streets,
Like an antelope in a net;
They are full of the fury of the
LORD,
The rebuke of your God.

21 Therefore please hear this, you
afflicted,
And drunk [a]but not with wine.
22 Thus says your Lord,

The LORD and your God,
Who [a]pleads the cause of His people:
"See, I have taken out of your hand
The cup of trembling,
The dregs of the cup of My fury;
You shall no longer drink it.
23 [a]But I will put it into the hand of those who afflict you,
Who have said to [1]you,
'Lie down, that we may walk over you.'
And you have laid your body like the ground,
And as the street, for those who walk over."

How beautiful upon the mountains are the feet of those who bring good news! Lord, may _____ be one who proclaims peace, who brings glad tidings of good things, who proclaims salvation, for You reign, O God!

FROM ISAIAH 52:7

God Redeems Jerusalem

52 Awake, awake!
Put on your strength, O Zion;
Put on your beautiful garments,
O Jerusalem, the holy city!
For the uncircumcised [a]and the unclean
Shall no longer come to you.
2 [a]Shake yourself from the dust, arise;
Sit down, O Jerusalem!
[b]Loose yourself from the bonds of your neck,
O captive daughter of Zion!

3 For thus says the LORD:

[a]"You have sold yourselves for nothing,
And you shall be redeemed
[b]without money."

4 For thus says the Lord GOD:

"My people went down at first
Into [a]Egypt to [1]dwell there;
Then the Assyrian oppressed them without cause.
5 Now therefore, what have I here,"
says the LORD,
"That My people are taken away for nothing?
Those who rule over them
[1]Make them wail," says the LORD,
"And My name *is* [a]blasphemed continually every day.
6 Therefore My people shall know My name;
Therefore *they shall know* in that day
That I *am* He who speaks:
'Behold, *it is* I.' "

7 [a]How beautiful upon the mountains
Are the feet of him who brings good news,
Who proclaims peace,
Who brings glad tidings of good *things,*
Who proclaims salvation,
Who says to Zion,
[b]"Your God reigns!"
8 Your watchmen shall lift up *their* voices,
With their voices they shall sing together;
For they shall see eye to eye
When the LORD brings back Zion.
9 Break forth into joy, sing together,
You waste places of Jerusalem!
For the LORD has comforted His people,
He has redeemed Jerusalem.
10 [a]The LORD has [1]made bare His holy arm
In the eyes of [b]all the nations;
And all the ends of the earth shall see
The salvation of our God.

11 [a]Depart! Depart! Go out from there,
Touch no unclean *thing;*
Go out from the midst of her,
[b]Be clean,
You who bear the vessels of the LORD.
12 For [a]you shall not go out with haste,
Nor go by flight;
[b]For the LORD will go before you,
[c]And the God of Israel *will be* your rear guard.

---

22 a Jer. 50:34
23 a Zech. 12:2 *1* Lit. *your soul*
CHAPTER 52
1 a [Rev. 21:2–27]
2 a Is. 3:26 b Zech. 2:7
3 a Ps. 44:12 b Is. 45:13
4 a Gen. 46:6 *1* As resident aliens
5 a Ezek. 36:20, 23 *1* DSS *Mock;* LXX *Marvel and wail;* Tg. *Boast themselves;* Vg. *Treat them unjustly*
7 a Rom. 10:15 b Ps. 93:1
10 a Ps. 98:1–3 b Luke 3:6 *1* Revealed His power
11 a Is. 48:20 b Lev. 22:2
12 a Ex. 12:11, 33 b Mic. 2:13 c Ex. 14:19, 20

The Sin-Bearing Servant

13 Behold, [a]My Servant shall [1]deal
prudently;
[b]He shall be exalted and [2]extolled
and be very high.
14 Just as many were astonished at
you,
So His [a]visage[1] was marred more
than any man,
And His form more than the sons
of men;
15 [a]So shall He [1]sprinkle many
nations.
Kings shall shut their mouths at
Him;
For [b]what had not been told them
they shall see,
And what they had not heard they
shall consider.

53 Who [a]has believed our report?
And to whom has the arm of the
LORD been revealed?
2 For He shall grow up before Him
as a tender plant,
And as a root out of dry ground.
He has no [1]form or [2]comeliness;
And when we see Him,
There is no [3]beauty that we should
desire Him.
3 [a]He is despised and [1]rejected by
men,
A Man of [2]sorrows and [b]acquainted
with [3]grief.
And we hid, as it were, *our* faces
from Him;
He was despised, and [c]we did not
esteem Him.

4 Surely [a]He has borne our [1]griefs
And carried our [2]sorrows;
Yet we [3]esteemed Him stricken,
[4]Smitten by God, and afflicted.
5 But He *was* [a]wounded[1] for our
transgressions,
He was [2]bruised for our iniquities;
The chastisement for our peace *was*
upon Him,
And by His [b]stripes[3] we are healed.
6 All we like sheep have gone astray;
We have turned, every one, to his
own way;
And the LORD [1]has laid on Him the
iniquity of us all.

7 He was oppressed and He was
afflicted,
Yet [a]He opened not His mouth;
[b]He was led as a lamb to the
slaughter,
And as a sheep before its shearers is
silent,
So He opened not His mouth.
8 He was [a]taken from [1]prison and
from judgment,
And who will declare His
generation?
For [b]He was cut off from the land
of the living;
For the transgressions of My people
He was stricken.
9 [a]And [1]they made His grave with the
wicked—
But with the rich at His death,
Because He had done no violence,
Nor *was any* [b]deceit in His mouth.

10 Yet it pleased the LORD to [1]bruise
Him;
He has put *Him* to grief.
When You make His soul [a]an
offering for sin,
He shall see *His* seed, He shall
prolong *His* days,
And the pleasure of the LORD shall
prosper in His hand.
11 [1]He shall see the labor of His soul,
and be satisfied.
By His knowledge [a]My righteous
[b]Servant shall [c]justify many,
For He shall bear their iniquities.
12 [a]Therefore I will divide Him a
portion with the great,
[b]And He shall divide the [1]spoil with
the strong,

---

13 a Is. 42:1 b Phil. 2:9 *1 prosper* 2 Lit. *be lifted up*
14 a Ps. 22:6, 7 *1 appearance*
15 a Ezek. 36:25 b Rom. 15:21 1 Or *startle*

CHAPTER 53
1 a John 12:38
2 1 Stately form *2 splendor* 3 Lit. *appearance*
3 a Ps. 22:6 b [Heb. 4:15] c [John 1:10, 11] 1 Or *forsaken* 2 Lit. *pains* 3 Lit. *sickness*
4 a [Matt. 8:17] 1 Lit. *sicknesses* 2 Lit. *pains* *3 reckoned* *4 Struck down*
5 a [Rom. 4:25] b [1 Pet. 2:24, 25] 1 Or *pierced through* *2 crushed* 3 Blows that cut in
6 1 Lit. *has caused to land on Him*
7 a Matt. 26:63; 27:12–14 b Acts 8:32, 33
8 a Luke 23:1–25 b [Dan. 9:26] *1 confinement*
9 a Matt. 27:57–60 b 1 Pet. 2:22 1 Lit. *he* or *He*
10 a [2 Cor. 5:21] *1 crush*
11 a [1 John 2:1] b Is. 42:1 c [Rom. 5:15–19] 1 So with MT, Tg., Vg.; DSS, LXX *From the labor of His soul He shall see light*
12 a Ps. 2:8 b Col. 2:15 *1 plunder*

Oh, for more men who will be simple enough to get in touch with God, and give them the mastery of their whole lives, and learn His will, and then give themselves, as Jesus gave Himself, to the sacred service of intercession.

S. D. GORDON

Because He [c]poured out His soul
unto death,
And He was [d]numbered with the
transgressors,
And He bore the sin of many,
And [e]made intercession for the
transgressors.

A Perpetual Covenant of Peace

54 "Sing, O [a]barren,
You *who* have not borne!
Break forth into singing, and cry
aloud,
You *who* have not labored with
child!
For more *are* the children of the
desolate
Than the children of the married
woman," says the LORD.

2 "Enlarge[a] the place of your tent,
And let them stretch out the
curtains of your dwellings;
Do not spare;
Lengthen your cords,
And strengthen your stakes.

3 For you shall expand to the right
and to the left,
And your descendants will [a]inherit
the nations,
And make the desolate cities
inhabited.

4 "Do[a] not fear, for you will not be
ashamed;
Neither be disgraced, for you will
not be put to shame;
For you will forget the shame of
your youth,
And will not remember the
reproach of your widowhood
anymore.

5 [a]For your Maker *is* your husband,
The LORD of hosts *is* His name;
And your Redeemer *is* the Holy One
of Israel;
He is called [b]the God of the whole
earth.

6 For the LORD [a]has called you
Like a woman forsaken and grieved
in spirit,
Like a youthful wife when you were
refused,"
Says your God.

7 "For[a] a mere moment I have
forsaken you,
But with great mercies [b]I will
gather you.

8 With a little wrath I hid My face
from you for a moment;
[a]But with everlasting kindness I will
have mercy on you,"
Says the LORD, your Redeemer.

9 "For this *is* like the waters of [a]Noah
to Me;
For as I have sworn
That the waters of Noah would no
longer cover the earth,
So have I sworn
That I would not be angry with
[b]you, nor rebuke you.

10 For [a]the mountains shall depart
And the hills be removed,
[b]But My kindness shall not depart
from you,
Nor shall My covenant of peace be
removed,"
Says the LORD, who has mercy on
you.

11 "O you afflicted one,
Tossed with tempest, *and* not
comforted,
Behold, I will lay your stones with
[a]colorful gems,
And lay your foundations with
sapphires.

12 I will make your pinnacles of
rubies,
Your gates of crystal,
And all your walls of precious
stones.

13 All your children *shall be*
[a]taught by the LORD,
And [b]great *shall be* the peace of
your children.

14 In righteousness you shall be
established;
You shall be far from oppression,
for you shall not fear;
And from terror, for it shall not
come near you.

15 Indeed they shall surely assemble,
but not because of Me.
Whoever assembles against you
shall [a]fall for your sake.

16 "Behold, I have created the
blacksmith
Who blows the coals in the fire,
Who brings forth an [1]instrument
for his work;
And I have created the [2]spoiler to
destroy.

17 No weapon formed against you
shall [a]prosper,

12 [c]Is. 50:6 [d]Matt. 27:38 [e]Luke 23:34
CHAPTER 54
1 [a]Gal. 4:27
2 [a]Is. 49:19, 20
3 [a]Is. 14:2; 49:22, 23; 60:9
4 [a]Is. 41:10
5 [a]Jer. 3:14 [b]Zech. 14:9
6 [a]Is. 62:4
7 [a]Is. 26:20; 60:10 [b][Is. 43:5; 56:8]
8 [a]Jer. 31:3
9 [a]Gen. 8:21; 9:11 [b]Ezek. 39:29
10 [a]Is. 51:6 [b]Ps. 89:33, 34
11 [a]Rev. 21:18, 19
13 [a][John 6:45] [b]Ps. 119:165
15 [a]Is. 41:11–16
16 [1]Or *weapon* [2]*destroyer*
17 [a]Is. 17:12–14; 29:8

Isaiah 54:13

Dear Woman of Destiny,

Isaiah 54:13—one of my favorite verses—reminds us as mothers that God really is our children's ultimate teacher. Many times I've prayed this scripture for my children, and have encouraged others to do the same. One day in my prayer time I paraphrased the verse something like this: "My son shall be taught of the Lord, and great shall be his peace."

Suddenly I was aware of God's still, small voice speaking to my heart: "If you want Me to be his teacher, then you must get out of the way."

I responded by explaining to God that this headstrong 17-year-old was on a collision course with a brick wall. Because of a bad report from his teacher, I had set an appointment for my son to meet with a tutor who would coach him for his final algebra exam. Claiming the problems were his teacher's fault, he had declared angrily that he wouldn't go to a tutor.

"Maybe hitting a brick wall is the only way he will learn," the Holy Spirit whispered. "After all, how did you learn your lessons?"

It's true for most of us—we learn best by hard experience. I agonized over the consequences my son would face later if he failed algebra, but I obeyed the Lord and cancelled the appointment. I discovered how painful it is to truly commit your child into God's hands.

Sure enough, my son failed his final exam in algebra. He barely passed the course with the lowest grade he had ever made in any class. Almost a year went by before the consequences became apparent.

He had applied to a top university for admission and a scholarship. He passed several levels of the acceptance process, and was in the pool of candidates for the few slots open in the school of architecture. But in the final cut he didn't make it. I was sure it was because of his low grade in eleventh-grade algebra.

The day he came home and found his rejection letter, he stormed upstairs in a fit of anger and disappointment. "Oh Lord," I prayed, "I know he had to learn this lesson, but it's so painful to see him devastated like this."

The Lord spoke to me very gently in the midst of my tears. "Don't worry, I won't hurt him any more than I have to; he was Mine before he was yours, and I love him more than you do."

God was gracious to open another opportunity for my son to study architecture and has faithfully continued to be his teacher. But for me, that experience was the beginning of a "letting go" process that has continued through the years. Yes, Woman of Destiny, as you commit your children to Him, you *can* trust God to be their teacher.

Ruthanne Garlock

And every tongue *which* rises
against you in judgment
You shall condemn.
This *is* the heritage of the servants
of the LORD,
[b]And their righteousness *is* from
Me,"
Says the LORD.

Holy Father, I thank You that no weapon formed against _____ shall prosper, and every tongue which rises against them in judgment You shall condemn. For this is the heritage of the servants of the Lord, and their righteousness is from You.

FROM ISAIAH 54:17

An Invitation to Abundant Life

55 "Ho! [a]Everyone who thirsts,
Come to the waters;
And you who have no money,
[b]Come, buy and eat.
Yes, come, buy wine and milk
Without money and without price.
2 Why do you [1]spend money for
what is not bread,
And your wages for *what* does not
satisfy?
Listen carefully to Me, and eat *what
is* good,
And let your soul delight itself in
abundance.
3 Incline your ear, and [a]come to Me.
Hear, and your soul shall live;
[b]And I will make an everlasting
covenant with you—
The [c]sure mercies of David.
4 Indeed I have given him *as* [a]a
witness to the people,
[b]A leader and commander for the
people.
5 [a]Surely you shall call a nation you
do not know,
[b]And nations *who* do not know you
shall run to you,
Because of the LORD your God,
And the Holy One of Israel;
[c]For He has glorified you."

6 [a]Seek the LORD while He may be
[b]found,
Call upon Him while He is near.
7 [a]Let the [1]wicked forsake his way,
And the unrighteous man [b]his
thoughts;
Let him return to the LORD,
[c]And He will have mercy on him;
And to our God,
For He will abundantly pardon.

8 "For[a] My thoughts *are* not your
thoughts,
Nor *are* your ways My ways," says
the LORD.
9 "For[a] *as* the heavens are higher
than the earth,
So are My ways higher than your
ways,
And My thoughts than your
thoughts.

10 "For [a]as the rain comes down, and
the snow from heaven,
And do not return there,
But water the earth,
And make it bring forth and bud,
That it may give seed to the sower
And bread to the eater,
11 [a]So shall My word be that goes
forth from My mouth;
It shall not return to Me [1]void,
But it shall accomplish what I
please,
And it shall [b]prosper *in the thing*
for which I sent it.

Never compromise with those who water down the Word of God to human experience.

OSWALD CHAMBERS

12 "For[a] you shall go out with joy,
And be led out with peace;
The mountains and the hills
Shall [b]break forth into singing
before you,
And [c]all the trees of the field shall
clap *their* hands.

54:17 b Is. 45:24, 25; 54:14

CHAPTER 55

1 a [John 4:14; 7:37] b [Rev. 3:18]

2 1 Lit. *weigh out silver*

3 a Matt. 11:28 b Jer. 32:40 c 2 Sam. 7:8

4 a [Rev. 1:5] b [Dan. 9:25]

5 a Eph. 2:11, 12 b Is. 60:5 c Is. 60:9

6 a [Heb. 3:13] b Ps. 32:6

7 a Is. 1:16 b Zech. 8:17 c Jer. 3:12 1 Lit. *man of iniquity*

8 a 2 Sam. 7:19

9 a Ps. 103:11

10 a Deut. 32:2

11 a Is. 45:23 b Is. 46:9–11 1 *empty,* without fruit

12 a Is. 35:10 b Ps. 98:8 c 1 Chr. 16:33

13 [a]Instead of [b]the thorn shall come
up the cypress tree,
And instead of the brier shall come
up the myrtle tree;
And it shall be to the LORD [c]for a
name,
For an everlasting sign *that* shall
not be cut off."

Salvation for the Gentiles

56 Thus says the LORD:

"Keep justice, and do righteousness,
[a]For My salvation *is* about to come,
And My righteousness to be
revealed.
2 Blessed *is* the man *who* does this,
And the son of man *who* lays hold
on it;
[a]Who keeps from defiling the
Sabbath,
And keeps his hand from doing any
evil."

3 Do not let [a]the son of the
foreigner
Who has joined himself to the LORD
Speak, saying,
"The LORD has utterly separated me
from His people";
Nor let the [b]eunuch say,
"Here I am, a dry tree."
4 For thus says the LORD:
"To the eunuchs who keep My
Sabbaths,
And choose what pleases Me,
And hold fast My covenant,
5 Even to them I will give in [a]My
house
And within My walls a place [b]and a
name
Better than that of sons and
daughters;
I will give [1]them an everlasting
name
That shall not be cut off.

6 "Also the sons of the foreigner
Who join themselves to the LORD,
to serve Him,
And to love the name of the LORD,
to be His servants—
Everyone who keeps from defiling
the Sabbath,
And holds fast My covenant—
7 Even them I will [a]bring to My holy
mountain,
And make them joyful in My [b]house
of prayer.
[c]Their burnt offerings and their
sacrifices
Will be [d]accepted on My altar;
For [e]My house shall be called a
house of prayer [f]for all nations."
8 The Lord GOD, [a]who gathers the
outcasts of Israel, says,
[b]"Yet I will gather to him
Others besides those who are
gathered to him."

Israel's Irresponsible Leaders

9 [a]All you beasts of the field, come to
devour,
All you beasts in the forest.
10 His watchmen *are* [a]blind,
They are all ignorant;
[b]They *are* all dumb dogs,
They cannot bark;
[1]Sleeping, lying down, loving to
slumber.
11 Yes, *they are* [a]greedy[1] dogs
Which [b]never[2] have enough.
And they *are* shepherds
Who cannot understand;
They all look to their own way,
Every one for his own gain,
From his *own* territory.
12 "Come," *one says,* "I will bring
wine,
And we will fill ourselves with
intoxicating [a]drink;
[b]Tomorrow will be [c]as today,
And much more abundant."

Israel's Futile Idolatry

57 The righteous perishes,
And no man takes *it* to heart;
[a]Merciful men *are* taken away,
[b]While no one considers
That the righteous is taken away
from [1]evil.
2 He shall enter into peace;
They shall rest in [a]their beds,
Each one walking *in* his
uprightness.

3 "But come here,
[a]You sons of the sorceress,
You offspring of the adulterer and
the harlot!
4 Whom do you ridicule?
Against whom do you make a wide
mouth
And stick out the tongue?
Are you not children of
transgression,
Offspring of falsehood,

13 [a]Is. 41:19 [b]Mic. 7:4 [c]Jer. 13:11

CHAPTER 56
1 [a]Matt. 3:2; 4:17
2 [a]Is. 58:13
3 [a][Eph. 2:12–19] [b]Acts 8:27
5 [a]1 Tim. 3:15 [b][1 John 3:1, 2] [1]Lit. *him*
7 [a][Is. 2:2, 3; 60:11] [b]Mark 11:17 [c][Rom. 12:1] [d]Is. 60:7 [e]Matt. 21:13 [f][Mal. 1:11]
8 [a]Is. 11:12; 27:12; 54:7 [b][John 10:16]
9 [a]Jer. 12:9
10 [a]Matt. 15:14 [b]Phil. 3:2 [1]Or *Dreaming*
11 [a][Mic. 3:5, 11] [b]Ezek. 34:2–10 [1]Lit. *strong of soul* [2]Lit. *do not know satisfaction*
12 [a]Is. 28:7 [b]Luke 12:19 [c]2 Pet. 3:4

CHAPTER 57
1 [a]Ps. 12:1 [b]1 Kin. 14:13 [1]Lit. *the face of evil*
2 [a]2 Chr. 16:14
3 [a]Matt. 16:4

5 Inflaming yourselves with gods
[a]under every green tree,
[b]Slaying the children in the valleys,
Under the clefts of the rocks?
6 Among the smooth [a]*stones* of the
stream
Is your portion;
They, they, *are* your lot!
Even to them you have poured a
drink offering,
You have offered a grain offering.
Should I receive comfort in [b]these?

7 "On[a] a lofty and high mountain
You have set [b]your bed;
Even there you went up
To offer sacrifice.
8 Also behind the doors and their
posts
You have set up your remembrance;
For you have uncovered yourself *to*
those other than Me,
And have gone up to them;
You have enlarged your bed
And [1]made *a covenant* with them;
[a]You have loved their bed,
Where you saw *their* [2]nudity.
9 [a]You went to the king with
ointment,
And increased your perfumes;
You sent your [b]messengers far off,
And *even* descended to Sheol.
10 You are wearied in the length of
your way;
[a]*Yet* you did not say, 'There is no
hope.'
You have found the life of your
hand;
Therefore you were not grieved.

11 "And [a]of whom have you been
afraid, or feared,
That you have lied
And not remembered Me,
Nor taken *it* to your heart?
Is it not because [b]I have [1]held My
peace from of old
That you do not fear Me?
12 I will declare your righteousness
And your works,
For they will not profit you.
13 When you cry out,
Let your collection *of idols* deliver
you.
But the wind will carry them all
away,
A breath will take *them*.
But he who puts his trust in Me
shall possess the land,
And shall inherit My holy
mountain."

Healing for the Backslider

14 And one shall say,
[a]"Heap it up! Heap it up!
Prepare the way,
Take the stumbling block out of the
way of My people."

> *Between the humble and contrite heart and the majesty of heaven there are no barriers; the only password is prayer.*
>
> HOSEA BALLOU

15 For thus says the High and Lofty
One
Who inhabits eternity, [a]whose name
is Holy:
[b]"I dwell in the high and holy *place*,
[c]With him *who* has a contrite and
humble spirit,
[d]To revive the spirit of the humble,
And to revive the heart of the
contrite ones.
16 [a]For I will not contend forever,
Nor will I always be angry;
For the spirit would fail before Me,
And the souls [b]*which* I have made.
17 For the iniquity of [a]his
covetousness
I was angry and struck him;
[b]I hid and was angry,
[c]And he went on [1]backsliding in the
way of his heart.
18 I have seen his ways, and [a]will
heal him;
I will also lead him,
And restore comforts to him
And to [b]his mourners.

19 "I create [a]the fruit of the lips:
Peace, peace [b]to *him who is* far off
and to *him who is* near,"
Says the LORD,
"And I will heal him."
20 [a]But the wicked *are* like the
troubled sea,
When it cannot rest,
Whose waters cast up mire and dirt.

5 [a] 2 Kin. 16:4 [b] Jer. 7:31
6 [a] Jer. 3:9 [b] Jer. 5:9, 29; 9:9
7 [a] Ezek. 16:16 [b] Ezek. 23:41
8 [a] Ezek. 16:26 *1* Lit. *cut* *2* Lit. *hand,* a euphemism
9 [a] Hos. 7:11 [b] Ezek. 23:16, 40
10 [a] Jer. 2:25; 18:12
11 [a] Is. 51:12, 13 [b] Ps. 50:21 *1 remained silent*
14 [a] Is. 40:3; 62:10
15 [a] Job 6:10 [b] Zech. 2:13 [c] Ps. 34:18; 51:17 [d] Is. 61:1–3
16 [a] [Mic. 7:18] [b] Num. 16:22
17 [a] Jer. 6:13 [b] Is. 8:17; 45:15; 59:2 [c] Is. 9:13 *1* Or *turning back*
18 [a] Jer. 3:22 [b] Is. 61:2
19 [a] Heb. 13:15 [b] Eph. 2:17
20 [a] Job 15:20

21 "There[a] *is* no peace,"
Says my God, "for the wicked."

Fasting that Pleases God

58 "Cry aloud, [1]spare not;
Lift up your voice like a trumpet;
[a]Tell My people their transgression,
And the house of Jacob their sins.
2 Yet they seek Me daily,
And delight to know My ways,
As a nation that did righteousness,
And did not forsake the ordinance
of their God.
They ask of Me the ordinances of
justice;
They take delight in approaching
God.
3 'Why[a] have we fasted,' *they say,*
'and You have not seen?
Why have we [b]afflicted our souls,
and You take no notice?'

"In fact, in the day of your fast you
find pleasure,
And [1]exploit all your laborers.
4 [a]Indeed you fast for strife and
debate,
And to strike with the fist of
wickedness.
You will not fast as *you do* this day,
To make your voice heard on high.
5 Is [a]it a fast that I have chosen,
[b]A day for a man to afflict his soul?
Is it to bow down his head like a
bulrush,
And [c]to spread out sackcloth and
ashes?
Would you call this a fast,
And an acceptable day to the LORD?

6 "*Is* this not the fast that I have
chosen:
To [a]loose the bonds of wickedness,
[b]To undo the [1]heavy burdens,
[c]To let the oppressed go free,
And that you break every yoke?
7 *Is it* not [a]to share your bread with
the hungry,
And that you bring to your house
the poor who are [1]cast out;
[b]When you see the naked, that you
cover him,
And not hide yourself from [c]your
own flesh?
8 [a]Then your light shall break forth
like the morning,
Your healing shall spring forth
speedily,
And your righteousness shall go
before you;
[b]The glory of the LORD shall be your
rear guard.
9 Then you shall call, and the LORD
will answer;
You shall cry, and He will say,
'Here I *am.*'

"If you take away the yoke from
your midst,
The [1]pointing of the finger, and
[a]speaking wickedness,
10 *If* you extend your soul to the
hungry
And satisfy the afflicted soul,
Then your light shall dawn in the
darkness,
And your [1]darkness shall *be* as the
noonday.
11 The LORD will guide you
continually,
And satisfy your soul in drought,
And strengthen your bones;
You shall be like a watered garden,
And like a spring of water, whose
waters do not fail.
12 Those from among you
[a]Shall build the old waste places;
You shall raise up the foundations
of many generations;
And you shall be called the Repairer
of the Breach,
The Restorer of [1]Streets to Dwell
In.

13 "If [a]you turn away your foot from
the Sabbath,
From doing your pleasure on My
holy day,
And call the Sabbath a delight,
The holy *day* of the LORD
honorable,
And shall honor Him, not doing
your own ways,
Nor finding your own pleasure,
Nor speaking *your own* words,
14 [a]Then you shall delight yourself in
the LORD;
And I will cause you to [b]ride on the
high hills of the earth,
And feed you with the heritage of
Jacob your father.
[c]The mouth of the LORD has
spoken."

Separated from God

59 Behold, the LORD's hand is not
[a]shortened,

21 [a]Is. 48:22

CHAPTER 58
1 [a]Mic. 3:8 [1]*do not hold back*
3 [a]Mal. 3:13–18 [b]Lev. 16:29; 23:27 [1]Lit. *drive hard*
4 [a]1 Kin. 21:9
5 [a]Zech. 7:5 [b]Lev. 16:29 [c]Esth. 4:3
6 [a]Luke 4:18, 19 [b]Neh. 5:10–12 [c]Jer. 34:9 [1]Lit. *bonds of the yoke*
7 [a]Ezek. 18:7 [b]Job 31:19–22 [c]Neh. 5:5 [1]*wandering*
8 [a]Job 11:17 [b]Ex. 14:19
9 [a]Ps. 12:2 [1]Lit. *sending out of*
10 [1]Or *gloom*
12 [a]Is. 61:4 [1]Lit. *Paths*
13 [a]Is. 56:2, 4, 6
14 [a]Job 22:26 [b]Deut. 32:13; 33:29 [c]Is. 1:20; 40:5

CHAPTER 59
1 [a]Num. 11:23

Isaiah 58:10–14

Dear Woman of Destiny,

I can feel the heart of the Father today, and He wants us to know His great love. He wants to change us into His likeness. He created us in His likeness and in His image, but somehow the image was marred and the likeness lost its resemblance. So He sent Jesus into the world to bring us back to His likeness, to bring us back filled with His love. More than just wanting to have us be born again, He wants to repair us until there's not a mar in us, until we resemble His love and His glory.

We need to realize that we do not have to be hindered by circumstances. Those same circumstances can transform our lives through Jesus Christ, who has called us from glory to glory and who changes our countenance (see 2 Cor. 3:18). When we have heavy hearts, we show it. But when we have the joy of the Lord—when He changes our hearts—we show it. We need to be a people not hindered by the circumstances, but recognizing the reason God placed a difficult circumstance in front of us is so we can overcome it. We are not to be overcome by it, but are to overcome it through Christ.

Today He is saying to you, "Don't just open your heart, but open your life and let Me fill you with My love." He isn't going to put it in there with darkness. He's not going to put it in there with you running your life. He will only put His love there when He's in charge. When we permit Him to have charge of our lives, we can trust Him. We have a very mighty promise: "Then you shall delight yourself in the LORD; and I will cause you to ride on the high hills of the earth, and feed you with the heritage of Jacob your father" (Is. 58:14).

The Lord says, "Trust Me. I'll give you *My* love. *My* love never fails. I'll give you *My* hope, and *My* hope never fails. I'll give you the Truth, and the Truth never fails." Can you trust Him? He wants to fill you with His love. You can hinder Him, or you can open up and say, "Lord, I trust You."

The love I'm talking about takes the willingness to lay all of your life in His hands. That kind of love goes beyond your flesh and reaches out to the spirits of the unknown people who pass you every day. Our own love will not do it. Only God's love will reach the world. He still loves this world that He created. He loves the billions out there who don't know Him yet. And I believe He's going now to meet the needs of those people with His love and His glory, for "the mouth of the LORD has spoken" (Is. 58:14).

Agnes Numer

That it cannot save;
Nor His ear heavy,
That it cannot hear.
2 But your iniquities have separated
you from your God;
And your sins have hidden *His* face
from you,
So that He will [a]not hear.
3 For [a]your hands are defiled with
[1]blood,
And your fingers with iniquity;
Your lips have spoken lies,
Your tongue has muttered
perversity.
4 No one calls for justice,
Nor does *any* plead for truth.
They trust in [a]empty words and
speak lies;
[b]They conceive [1]evil and bring forth
iniquity.
5 They hatch vipers' eggs and weave
the spider's web;
He who eats of their eggs dies,
And *from* that which is crushed a
viper breaks out.
6 [a]Their webs will not become
garments,
Nor will they cover themselves with
their works;
Their works *are* works of iniquity,
And the act of violence *is* in their
hands.
7 [a]Their feet run to evil,
And they make haste to shed
[b]innocent blood;
[c]Their thoughts *are* thoughts of
iniquity;
Wasting and [d]destruction *are* in
their paths.
8 The way of [a]peace they have not
known,
And *there is* no justice in their
ways;
[b]They have made themselves crooked
paths;
Whoever takes that way shall not
know peace.

Sin Confessed

9 Therefore justice is far from us,
Nor does righteousness overtake us;
[a]We look for light, but there is
darkness!
For brightness, *but* we walk in
blackness!
10 [a]We grope for the wall like the
blind,
And we grope as if *we had* no eyes;
We stumble at noonday as at
twilight;
We are as dead *men* in desolate
places.
11 We all growl like bears,
And [a]moan sadly like doves;
We look for justice, but *there is*
none;
For salvation, *but* it is far from us.
12 For our [a]transgressions are
multiplied before You,
And our sins testify against us;
For our transgressions *are* with us,
And *as for* our iniquities, we know
them:
13 In transgressing and lying against
the LORD,
And departing from our God,
Speaking oppression and revolt,
Conceiving and uttering [a]from the
heart words of falsehood.
14 Justice is turned back,
And righteousness stands afar off;
For truth is fallen in the street,
And equity cannot enter.
15 So truth fails,
And he *who* departs from evil
makes himself a [a]prey.

The Redeemer of Zion

Then the LORD saw *it,* and [1]it
displeased Him
That *there was* no justice.
16 [a]He saw that *there was* no man,
And [b]wondered that *there was* no
intercessor;
[c]Therefore His own arm brought
salvation for Him;
And His own righteousness, it
sustained Him.
17 [a]For He put on righteousness as a
breastplate,
And a helmet of salvation on His
head;
He put on the garments of
vengeance for clothing,
And was clad with zeal as a cloak.
18 [a]According to *their* deeds,
accordingly He will repay,
Fury to His adversaries,
Recompense to His enemies;
The coastlands He will fully repay.
19 [a]So shall they fear
The name of the LORD from the
west,
And His glory from the rising of
the sun;

2 [a]Is. 1:15
3 [a]Ezek. 7:23 [1]*bloodshed*
4 [a]Jer. 7:4 [b]Job 15:35 [1]*trouble*
6 [a]Job 8:14
7 [a]Rom. 3:15 [b]Prov. 6:17 [c]Is. 55:7 [d]Rom. 3:16, 17
8 [a]Is. 57:20, 21 [b]Prov. 2:15
9 [a]Jer. 8:15
10 [a]Job 5:14
11 [a]Ezek. 7:16
12 [a]Is. 24:5; 58:1
13 [a]Matt. 12:34
15 [a]Is. 5:23; 10:2; 29:21; 32:7 [1]Lit. *it was evil in His eyes*
16 [a]Ezek. 22:30 [b]Mark 6:6 [c]Ps. 98:1
17 [a]Eph. 6:14, 17
18 [a]Is. 63:6
19 [a]Mal. 1:11

When the enemy comes in [b]like a flood,
The Spirit of the LORD will lift up a standard against him.

20 "The[a] Redeemer will come to Zion,
And to those who turn from transgression in Jacob,"
Says the LORD.

21"As[a] for Me," says the LORD, "this *is*
My covenant with them: My Spirit who *is*
upon you, and My words which I have put
in your mouth, shall not depart from your
mouth, nor from the mouth of your descendants, nor from the mouth of your
descendants' descendants," says the LORD,
"from this time and forevermore."

The Gentiles Bless Zion

60 Arise, [a]shine;
For your light has come!
And [b]the glory of the LORD is risen upon you.
2 For behold, the darkness shall cover the earth,
And deep darkness the people;
But the LORD will arise over you,
And His glory will be seen upon you.
3 The [a]Gentiles shall come to your light,
And kings to the brightness of your rising.

4 "Lift[a] up your eyes all around, and see:
They all gather together, [b]they come to you;
Your sons shall come from afar,
And your daughters shall be nursed at *your* side.
5 Then you shall see and become radiant,
And your heart shall swell with joy;
Because [a]the abundance of the sea shall be turned to you,
The wealth of the Gentiles shall come to you.
6 The multitude of camels shall cover your *land,*
The dromedaries of Midian and [a]Ephah;
All those from [b]Sheba shall come;
They shall bring [c]gold and incense,
And they shall proclaim the praises of the LORD.
7 All the flocks of [a]Kedar shall be gathered together to you,
The rams of Nebaioth shall minister to you;
They shall ascend with [b]acceptance on My altar,
And [c]I will glorify the house of My glory.

8 "Who *are* these *who* fly like a cloud,
And like doves to their roosts?
9 [a]Surely the coastlands shall wait for Me;
And the ships of Tarshish *will come* first,
[b]To bring your sons from afar,
[c]Their silver and their gold with them,
To the name of the LORD your God,
And to the Holy One of Israel,
[d]Because He has glorified you.

10 "The[a] sons of foreigners shall build up your walls,
[b]And their kings shall minister to you;
For [c]in My wrath I struck you,
[d]But in My favor I have had mercy on you.
11 Therefore your gates [a]shall be open continually;
They shall not be shut day or night,
That *men* may bring to you the wealth of the Gentiles,
And their kings in procession.
12 [a]For the nation and kingdom which will not serve you shall perish,
And *those* nations shall be utterly ruined.

13 "The[a] glory of Lebanon shall come to you,
The cypress, the pine, and the box tree together,
To beautify the place of My sanctuary;
And I will make [b]the place of My feet glorious.
14 Also the sons of those who afflicted you
Shall come [a]bowing to you,
And all those who despised you shall [b]fall prostrate at the soles of your feet;
And they shall call you The City of the LORD,
[c]Zion of the Holy One of Israel.

15 "Whereas you have been forsaken and hated,
So that no one went through *you,*

19 [b]Rev. 12:15
20 [a]Rom. 11:26
21 [a][Heb. 8:10; 10:16]

CHAPTER 60
1 [a]Eph. 5:14 [b]Mal. 4:2
3 [a]Is. 49:6, 23
4 [a]Is. 49:18 [b]Is. 49:20–22
5 [a][Rom. 11:25–27]
6 [a]Gen. 25:4 [b]Ps. 72:10 [c]Matt. 2:11
7 [a]Gen. 25:13 [b]Is. 56:7 [c]Hag. 2:7, 9
9 [a]Ps. 72:10 [b][Gal. 4:26] [c]Jer. 3:17 [d]Is. 55:5
10 [a]Zech. 6:15 [b]Rev. 21:24 [c]Is. 57:17 [d]Is. 54:7, 8
11 [a]Rev. 21:25, 26
12 [a]Zech. 14:17
13 [a]Is. 35:2 [b]1 Chr. 28:2
14 [a]Is. 45:14 [b]Rev. 3:9 [c][Heb. 12:22]

I will make you an eternal
excellence,
A joy of many generations.
16 You shall drink the milk of the
Gentiles,
[a]And milk the breast of kings;
You shall know that [b]I, the LORD,
am your Savior
And your Redeemer, the Mighty
One of Jacob.

17 "Instead of bronze I will bring gold,
Instead of iron I will bring silver,
Instead of wood, bronze,
And instead of stones, iron.
I will also make your officers peace,
And your magistrates righteousness.
18 Violence shall no longer be heard
in your land,
Neither [1]wasting nor destruction
within your borders;
But you shall call [a]your walls
Salvation,
And your gates Praise.

God the Glory of His People

19 "The [a]sun shall no longer be your
light by day,
Nor for brightness shall the moon
give light to you;
But the LORD will be to you an
everlasting light,
And [b]your God your glory.
20 [a]Your sun shall no longer go down,
Nor shall your moon withdraw
itself;
For the LORD will be your
everlasting light,
And the days of your mourning
shall be ended.
21 [a]Also your people *shall* all *be*
righteous;
[b]They shall inherit the land forever,
[c]The branch of My planting,
[d]The work of My hands,
That I may be glorified.
22 [a]A little one shall become a
thousand,
And a small one a strong nation.
I, the LORD, will hasten it in its
time."

The Good News of Salvation

61 "The [a]Spirit of the Lord GOD
is upon Me,
Because the LORD [b]has anointed Me
To preach good tidings to the poor;

16 [a]Is. 49:23 [b]Is. 43:3
18 [a]Is. 26:1 [1] *devastation*
19 [a]Rev. 21:23; 22:5 [b]Zech. 2:5
20 [a]Amos 8:9
21 [a]Rev. 21:27 [b]Ps. 37:11 [c]Is. 61:3 [d][Eph. 2:10]
22 [a]Matt. 13:31, 32
CHAPTER 61
1 [a]Luke 4:18, 19 [b]Luke 7:22 [c]Ps. 147:3 [d]Is. 42:7 [1] Lit. *bind up*
2 [a]Lev. 25:9 [b]Is. 34:8 [c]Matt. 5:4
3 [a]Ps. 30:11 [b]Is. 60:21 [c][John 15:8] [1] Lit. *appoint*
4 [a]Ezek. 36:33
5 [a][Eph. 2:12]
6 [a]Ex. 19:6 [b]Is. 60:5, 11

He has sent Me [c]to [1]heal the
brokenhearted,
To proclaim [d]liberty to the captives,
And the opening of the prison to
those who are bound;
2 [a]To proclaim the acceptable year of
the LORD,
And [b]the day of vengeance of our
God;
[c]To comfort all who mourn,
3 To [1]console those who mourn in
Zion,
[a]To give them beauty for ashes,
The oil of joy for mourning,
The garment of praise for the spirit
of heaviness;
That they may be called trees of
righteousness,
[b]The planting of the LORD, [c]that He
may be glorified."

Lord, as You did for Israel, so do for ____. Console them as they mourn, give them beauty for ashes, the oil of joy for mourning, and the garment of praise for the spirit of heaviness. May they be called trees of righteousness that You may be glorified.

FROM ISAIAH 61:3

4 And they shall [a]rebuild the old
ruins,
They shall raise up the former
desolations,
And they shall repair the ruined
cities,
The desolations of many
generations.
5 [a]Strangers shall stand and feed your
flocks,
And the sons of the foreigner
Shall be your plowmen and your
vinedressers.
6 [a]But you shall be named the priests
of the LORD,
They shall call you the servants of
our God.
[b]You shall eat the riches of the
Gentiles,

Isaiah 61:1–3

Dear Woman of Destiny,

This prophecy reaches beyond Isaiah's anointing to proclaim liberty to the Jews in Babylon, and points to the coming ministry of the Messiah. Jesus quoted it in Luke 4 and declared, "Today this Scripture is fulfilled in your hearing" (v. 21).

That God anointed Jesus was obvious throughout His entire ministry. He didn't have to repeatedly refer to the moment of the dove resting on Him at baptism or remind others of the voice that declared Him to be pleasing to the Father. He walked in the anointing. The Spirit was always present in Christ, and therefore He was able to bring victory to every situation.

It is important for us to understand that our calling is not because of anything we are or have done, but is simply that the Spirit of the Lord God is upon us, because the Lord has anointed us (see Is. 61:1).

Too many of us feel the need to explain God's use of us. Whether in an attempt at humility and declaration of our unworthiness or in a braggadocio recounting of a glorious spiritual experience, we are wrong to see our position as anything but His anointing by His choice.

To truly know this is to be free of worry about inadequacy for the tasks and teaches us to be totally dependent on the Spirit of God.

We are taught to study the Word that we might rightly declare it, to apply our faith that we may receive all God has for us. We are to pray, praise, and worship at all times and to share our hope with all who will hear. None of these qualify us to preach, heal the sick, set the captive free, bring comfort to the hurting, or promise beauty for ashes. This is the work of the Spirit.

If we are to be used by God for His continuing work on earth we must be qualified the same as Jesus was and be able to say as He said, "The Spirit of the Lord GOD is upon Me, because the LORD has anointed Me."

Sometimes we do it other times. It also prevents us from believing that we somehow have attained it by something we have or have not done.

It's not about us; it's all about Him. I can see the need for ministry and the places of need and can use natural resources and talents to attempt to meet those needs and still fall short of God's goal for me and for others. I can declare peace to the troubled; but unless the God of peace is present, there is no peace. I can long for miracles to be demonstrated; but until the God of miracles is present, the desire is unfulfilled.

Our involvement is simple. We speak what He says, do what He instructs, and add nothing to it.

The ultimate goal is that both we and they to whom we minister may be called "trees of righteousness, the planting of the LORD, that He may be glorified" (v. 3).

Iverna Tompkins

And in their glory you shall boast.
7 [a]Instead of your shame *you shall have* double *honor,*
And *instead of* confusion they shall rejoice in their portion.
Therefore in their land they shall possess double;
Everlasting joy shall be theirs.

8 "For [a]I, the LORD, love justice;
[b]I hate robbery [1]for burnt offering;
I will direct their work in truth,
[c]And will make with them an everlasting covenant.
9 Their descendants shall be known among the Gentiles,
And their offspring among the people.
All who see them shall acknowledge them,
[a]That they *are* the posterity *whom* the LORD has blessed."

10 [a]I will greatly rejoice in the LORD,
My soul shall be joyful in my God;
For [b]He has clothed me with the garments of salvation,
He has covered me with the robe of righteousness,
[c]As a bridegroom decks *himself* with ornaments,
And as a bride adorns *herself* with her jewels.
11 For as the earth brings forth its bud,
As the garden causes the things that are sown in it to spring forth,
So the Lord GOD will cause [a]righteousness and [b]praise to spring forth before all the nations.

Assurance of Zion's Salvation

62 For Zion's sake I will not [1]hold My peace,
And for Jerusalem's sake I will not rest,
Until her righteousness goes forth as brightness,
And her salvation as a lamp *that* burns.
2 [a]The Gentiles shall see your righteousness,
And all [b]kings your glory.
[c]You shall be called by a new name,
Which the mouth of the LORD will name.
3 You shall also be [a]a crown of glory
In the hand of the LORD,
And a royal diadem
In the hand of your God.
4 [a]You shall no longer be termed [b]Forsaken,[1]
Nor shall your land any more be termed [c]Desolate;[2]
But you shall be called [3]Hephzibah, and your land [4]Beulah;
For the LORD delights in you,
And your land shall be married.
5 For *as* a young man marries a virgin,
So shall your sons marry you;
And *as* the bridegroom rejoices over the bride,
[a]*So* shall your God rejoice over you.

6 [a]I have set watchmen on your walls, O Jerusalem;
They shall [1]never hold their peace day or night.
You who [2]make mention of the LORD, do not keep silent,
7 And give Him no rest till He establishes
And till He makes Jerusalem [a]a praise in the earth.

8 The LORD has sworn by His right hand
And by the arm of His strength:
"Surely I will no longer [a]give your grain
As food for your enemies;
And the sons of the foreigner shall not drink your new wine,
For which you have labored.
9 But those who have gathered it shall eat it,
And praise the LORD;
Those who have brought it together shall drink it [a]in My holy courts."

10 Go through,
Go through the gates!
[a]Prepare the way for the people;
Build up,
Build up the highway!
Take out the stones,
[b]Lift up a banner for the peoples!
11 Indeed the LORD has proclaimed
To the end of the world:
[a]"Say to the daughter of Zion,
'Surely your salvation is coming;
Behold, His [b]reward *is* with Him,
And His [1]work before Him.' "

---

7 a Zech. 9:12
8 a Ps. 11:7 b Is. 1:11, 13 c Is. 55:3 *1* Or *in*
9 a Is. 65:23
10 a Hab. 3:18 b Ps. 132:9, 16 c Is. 49:18
11 a Ps. 72:3; 85:11 b Is. 60:18; 62:7

CHAPTER 62
1 *1 keep silent*
2 a Is. 60:3 b Ps. 102:15, 16; 138:4, 5; 148:11, 13 c Is. 62:4, 12; 65:15
3 a Zech. 9:16
4 a Hos. 1:10 b Is. 49:14; 54:6, 7 c Is. 54:1 *1* Heb. *Azubah* *2* Heb. *Shemamah* *3* Lit. *My Delight Is in Her* *4* Lit. *Married*
5 a Is. 65:19
6 a Ezek. 3:17; 33:7 *1 not be silent* *2 remember*
7 a Zeph. 3:19, 20
8 a Deut. 28:31, 33
9 a Deut. 12:12; 14:23, 26
10 a Is. 40:3; 57:14 b Is. 11:12
11 a Zech. 9:9 b [Rev. 22:12] *1 recompense*

12 And they shall call them The Holy People,
The Redeemed of the LORD;
And you shall be called Sought Out,
A City Not Forsaken.

The Lord in Judgment and Salvation

63 Who *is* this who comes from Edom,
With dyed garments from Bozrah,
This *One who is* [1]glorious in His apparel,
Traveling in the greatness of His strength?—

"I who speak in righteousness, mighty to save."

2 Why [a]*is* Your apparel red,
And Your garments like one who treads in the winepress?

3 "I have [a]trodden the winepress alone,
And from the peoples no one *was* with Me.
For I have trodden them in My anger,
And trampled them in My fury;
Their blood is sprinkled upon My garments,
And I have stained all My robes.
4 For the [a]day of vengeance *is* in My heart,
And the year of My redeemed has come.
5 [a]I looked, but [b]*there was* no one to help,
And I wondered
That *there was* no one to uphold;
Therefore My own [c]arm brought salvation for Me;
And My own fury, it sustained Me.
6 I have trodden down the peoples in My anger,
Made them drunk in My fury,
And brought down their strength to the earth."

God's Mercy Remembered

7 I will mention the lovingkindnesses of the LORD
And the praises of the LORD,
According to all that the LORD has bestowed on us,
And the great goodness toward the house of Israel,
Which He has bestowed on them according to His mercies,
According to the multitude of His lovingkindnesses.
8 For He said, "Surely they *are* My people,
Children *who* will not lie."
So He became their Savior.
9 [a]In all their affliction He was [1]afflicted,
[b]And the Angel of His Presence saved them;
[c]In His love and in His pity He redeemed them;
And [d]He bore them and carried them
All the days of old.
10 But they [a]rebelled and [b]grieved His Holy Spirit;
[c]So He turned Himself against them as an enemy,
And He fought against them.
11 Then he [a]remembered the days of old,
Moses *and* his people, *saying:*
"Where *is* He who [b]brought them up out of the sea
With the [1]shepherd of His flock?
[c]Where *is* He who put His Holy Spirit within them,
12 Who led *them* by the right hand of Moses,
[a]With His glorious arm,
[b]Dividing the water before them
To make for Himself an everlasting name,
13 [a]Who led them through the deep,
As a horse in the wilderness,
That they might not stumble?"

14 As a beast goes down into the valley,
And the Spirit of the LORD causes him to rest,
So You lead Your people,
[a]To make Yourself a glorious name.

A Prayer of Penitence

15 [a]Look down from heaven,
And see [b]from Your habitation, holy and glorious.
Where *are* Your zeal and Your strength,
The yearning [c]of Your heart and Your mercies toward me?
Are they restrained?
16 ❦ [a]Doubtless You *are* our Father,

CHAPTER 63
1 *1 Or adorned*
2 a [Rev. 19:13, 15]
3 a Rev. 14:19, 20; 19:15
4 a Is. 34:8; 35:4; 61:2
5 a Is. 41:28; 59:16 b [John 16:32] c Ps. 98:1
9 a Judg. 10:16 b Ex. 14:19 c Deut. 7:7 d Ex. 19:4 *1 Kt., LXX, Syr. not afflicted*
10 a Ex. 15:24 b Ps. 78:40 c Ex. 23:21
11 a Ps. 106:44, 45 b Ex. 14:30 c Num. 11:17, 25, 29 *1 MT, Vg. shepherds*
12 a Ex. 15:6 b Ex. 14:21, 22
13 a Ps. 106:9
14 a 2 Sam. 7:23
15 a Deut. 26:15 b Ps. 33:14 c Jer. 31:20
16 a Deut. 32:6

Isaiah 63:16

Dear Woman of Destiny,

From the beginning, family has been the centerpiece of God's creation. God is first of all a Father. All of His characteristics—His love, His gentleness, His mercy, His grace—are attributes of a Father for His children, attributes that He intended to reproduce in them. He wanted all of creation, especially "the principalities and powers in the heavenly places" (Eph. 3:10) to be able to look at His family and recognize that He is indeed their Father.

God not only wanted to reproduce Himself and fill the earth with His likeness, He also longed for a family. He wanted children with whom He could share His life. He wanted a people who would love and respond to Him, a people who would have the capacity to know Him and have intimate fellowship with Him. So God gifted humanity—male and female together—with the privilege of expanding His family.

Family is God's design for men and women. Family is a place where they can belong, know love, be affirmed, and experience intimacy. It is a place where their children can receive a name and an identity, all as an expression of God's heart.

The church is the fulfillment of God's plan to have a family for Himself. Here, no one is left out. The broken, the hurting, the single person, the widow, and the orphaned all have a place. But the greatest revelation of the heart of God regarding family came in the Person of His Son, Jesus—the One who came to earth to reveal the Father to us. Jesus was the embodiment of the way, the truth, and the life. Yet He was born into a humble family, where He lived for thirty years before He ever taught or performed a miracle. By placing His own Son within its protective, nurturing walls, God gave the family His highest endorsement.

"The strength of a nation is the strength of its families," states Pastor Mike McIntosh, of Federal Way, Washington. "It is not a strong nation that makes families safe. It is the strong families that make a nation prosperous. The family is both a refuge and a launching point for change in society."

The health of society, therefore, depends upon the health of families. God's own family has suffered alienation, divorce, and family breakdown. His Word tells us that the place where He will begin to set things in right order will be His house (see 1 Pet. 4:17).

God is moving by His Holy Spirit in a strategic way. The reconciliation movement that has begun between races and denominations is a foretaste of even greater things to come. God is wanting to heal the rupture between male and female, the first relationship—not only in individual couples, but in the corporate church, the family of God. Here we will begin to see His glorious purposes unfold as we move toward the end of time.

Jane Hansen

Though Abraham [b]was ignorant of us,
And Israel does not acknowledge us.
You, O LORD, *are* our Father;
Our Redeemer from Everlasting *is* Your name.
17 O LORD, why have You [a]made us stray from Your ways,
And hardened our heart from Your fear?
Return for Your servants' sake,
The tribes of Your inheritance.
18 [a]Your holy people have possessed *it* but a little while;
[b]Our adversaries have trodden down Your sanctuary.
19 We have become *like* those of old, over whom You never ruled,
Those who were never called by Your name.

64 Oh, that You would [1]rend the heavens!
That You would come down!
That the mountains might shake at Your [a]presence—
2 As fire burns brushwood,
As fire causes water to boil—
To make Your name known to Your adversaries,
That the nations may tremble at Your presence!
3 When [a]You did awesome things *for which* we did not look,
You came down,
The mountains shook at Your presence.
4 For since the beginning of the world
[a]*Men* have not heard nor perceived by the ear,
Nor has the eye seen any God besides You,
Who acts for the one who waits for Him.
5 You meet him who rejoices and does righteousness,
Who remembers You in Your ways.
You are indeed angry, for we have sinned—
[a]In these ways we continue;
And we need to be saved.

6 But we are all like an unclean *thing,*
And all [a]our righteousnesses *are* like [1]filthy rags;
We all [b]fade as a leaf,
And our iniquities, like the wind,
Have taken us away.
7 And *there is* no one who calls on Your name,
Who stirs himself up to take hold of You;
For You have hidden Your face from us,
And have [1]consumed us because of our iniquities.

8 But now, O LORD,
You *are* our Father;
We *are* the clay, and You our [a]potter;
And all we *are* the work of Your hand.
9 Do not be furious, O LORD,
Nor remember iniquity forever;
Indeed, please look—we all *are* Your people!
10 Your holy cities are a wilderness,
Zion is a wilderness,
Jerusalem a desolation.
11 Our holy and beautiful [1]temple,
Where our fathers praised You,
Is burned up with fire;
And all [a]our pleasant things [2]are laid waste.
12 [a]Will You restrain Yourself because of these *things,* O LORD?
[b]Will You [1]hold Your peace, and afflict us very severely?

The Righteousness of God's Judgment

65 "I was [a]sought by *those who* did not ask *for Me;*
I was found by *those who* did not seek Me.
I said, 'Here I am, here I am,'
To a nation *that* [b]was not called by My name.
2 [a]I have stretched out My hands all day long to a [b]rebellious people,
Who [c]walk in a way *that is* not good,
According to their own thoughts;
3 A people [a]who provoke Me to anger continually to My face;
[b]Who sacrifice in gardens,
And burn incense on altars of brick;
4 [a]Who sit among the graves,
And spend the night in the tombs;
[b]Who eat swine's flesh,
And the broth of [1]abominable things is *in* their vessels;
5 [a]Who say, 'Keep to yourself,
Do not come near me,

---

16 b Job 14:21
17 a John 12:40
18 a Deut. 7:6 b Ps. 74:3–7

CHAPTER 64
1 a Mic. 1:3, 4 *1 tear open*
3 a Ex. 34:10
4 a Ps. 31:19
5 a Mal. 3:6
6 a [Phil. 3:9] b Ps. 90:5, 6 *1* Lit. *a filthy garment*
7 *1* Lit. *caused us to melt*
8 a Is. 29:16; 45:9
11 a Ezek. 24:21 *1* Lit. *house* *2 have become a ruin*
12 a Is. 42:14 b Ps. 83:1 *1 keep silent*

CHAPTER 65
1 a Rom. 9:24; 10:20 b Is. 63:19
2 a Rom. 10:21 b Is. 1:2, 23 c Is. 42:24
3 a Deut. 32:21 b Is. 1:29
4 a Deut. 18:11 b Is. 66:17 *1* Unclean meats, Lev. 7:18; 19:7
5 a Matt. 9:11

For I am holier than you!'
These [1]*are* smoke in My nostrils,
A fire that burns all the day.

6 "Behold, [a]*it is* written before Me:
[b]I will not keep silence, [c]but will
repay—
Even repay into their bosom—
7 Your iniquities and [a]the iniquities
of your fathers together,"
Says the LORD,
[b]"Who have burned incense on the
mountains
[c]And blasphemed Me on the hills;
Therefore I will measure their
former work into their bosom."

8 Thus says the LORD:

"As the new wine is found in the
cluster,
And *one* says, 'Do not destroy it,
For [a]a blessing *is* in it,'
So will I do for My servants' sake,
That I may not destroy them [b]all.
9 I will bring forth descendants from
Jacob,
And from Judah an heir of My
mountains;
My [a]elect shall inherit it,
And My servants shall dwell there.
10 [a]Sharon shall be a fold of flocks,
And [b]the Valley of Achor a place for
herds to lie down,
For My people who have [c]sought
Me.

11 "But you *are* those who forsake the
LORD,
Who forget [a]My holy mountain,
Who prepare [b]a table for [1]Gad,
And who furnish a drink offering
for [2]Meni.
12 Therefore I will number you for
the sword,
And you shall all bow down to the
slaughter;
[a]Because, when I called, you did not
answer;
When I spoke, you did not hear,
But did evil before My eyes,
And chose *that* in which I do not
delight."

13 Therefore thus says the Lord GOD:

"Behold, My servants shall eat,
But you shall be hungry;
Behold, My servants shall drink,
But you shall be thirsty;
Behold, My servants shall rejoice,
But you shall be ashamed;
14 Behold, My servants shall sing for
joy of heart,
But you shall cry for sorrow of
heart,
And [a]wail for [1]grief of spirit.
15 You shall leave your name [a]as a
curse to [b]My chosen;
For the Lord GOD will slay you,
And [c]call His servants by another
name;
16 [a]So that he who blesses himself in
the earth
Shall bless himself in the God of
truth;
And [b]he who swears in the earth
Shall swear by the God of truth;
Because the former troubles are
forgotten,
And because they are hidden from
My eyes.

The Glorious New Creation

17 "For behold, I create [a]new heavens
and a new earth;
And the former shall not be
remembered or [1]come to mind.
18 But be glad and rejoice forever in
what I create;
For behold, I create Jerusalem *as* a
rejoicing,
And her people a joy.
19 [a]I will rejoice in Jerusalem,
And joy in My people;
The [b]voice of weeping shall no
longer be heard in her,
Nor the voice of crying.

20 "No more shall an infant from
there *live but a few* days,
Nor an old man who has not
fulfilled his days;
For the child shall die one hundred
years old,
[a]But the sinner *being* one hundred
years old shall be accursed.
21 [a]They shall build houses and
inhabit *them;*
They shall plant vineyards and eat
their fruit.
22 They shall not build and another
inhabit;
They shall not plant and [a]another
eat;
For [b]as the days of a tree, *so shall
be* the days of My people,
And [c]My elect shall long enjoy the
work of their hands.

5 [1] Cause My wrath to smoke
6 [a] Deut. 32:34 [b] Ps. 50:3 [c] Ps. 79:12
7 [a] Ex. 20:5 [b] Ezek. 18:6 [c] Ezek. 20:27, 28
8 [a] Joel 2:14 [b] Is. 1:9
9 [a] Matt. 24:22
10 [a] Is. 33:9 [b] Josh. 7:24 [c] Is. 55:6
11 [a] Is. 56:7 [b] Ezek. 23:41 [1] Lit. *Troop* or *Fortune;* a pagan deity [2] Lit. *Number* or *Destiny;* a pagan deity
12 [a] Prov. 1:24
14 [a] Matt. 8:12 [1] Or *a broken spirit*
15 [a] Jer. 29:22 [b] Is. 65:9, 22 [c] [Acts 11:26]
16 [a] Jer. 4:2 [b] Zeph. 1:5
17 [a] Rev. 21:1 [1] Lit. *come upon the heart*
19 [a] Is. 62:4, 5 [b] Rev. 7:17; 21:4
20 [a] Eccl. 8:12, 13
21 [a] Amos 9:14
22 [a] Is. 62:8, 9 [b] Ps. 92:12 [c] Is. 65:9, 15

Isaiah 65:8

Dear Woman of Destiny,

I'd like to help you understand something I believe the Holy Spirit is doing in the earth today. It's called "the cluster anointing," which you might also call a corporate anointing. I want to sow it deeply into your spirits because the body of Christ is in transition right now, and this cluster anointing is crucial to understand. God wants to give us a cluster thinking. He wants us to learn to move in Him *together* and not independently of our brothers and sisters in Christ.

Isaiah 65:8 prophetically represents the cluster anointing—a mingling of anointings that produces a greater anointing than any one person could have alone.

It's fascinating; if you study this passage, you see that new wine exists not only in the cluster, but also somehow in the individual grape. The individual grape retains its identity, its shape, its taste, its texture—everything about itself. But it contains new wine, and the new wine represents the powerful corporate anointing that transcends an individual. In the natural, one grape does not contain enough wine to have much effect on anybody. But when many grapes contribute to the wine, then there is enough to make a big impact. We are being crushed together in the winepress. And the Holy Spirit Himself is treading out the wine. He is treading out the grapes in our hearts.

When the cluster comes together and each grape retains its individual distinctions, the anointing is found. This happens while the cluster is still on the branch, abiding in the vine. Spiritually, when a cluster anointing exists, it causes you to dream bigger dreams than you can dream by yourself. It enables you to be a part of accomplishing something for God that is larger than anything you could do alone. It transforms your thinking.

I tell you, dream big dreams. Be willing to have your anointing mingled with someone else's or with the anointing of many people. Satan's strategy would cause us to want to be isolated, to operate by ourselves. But God blesses unity. He gives an unusual measure of glory to those who come together. Jesus Himself prayed for His people in John 17:21, "that they all may be one, as You, Father, are in Me, and I in You; that they also may be one in Us." You will always have the God-given qualities that make you who you are. The mingling of the anointings will not strip your individuality. You may even be able to do great things for God all by yourself. But if you will function as part of a cluster, you will see amazing spiritual breakthrough as the big dreams get bigger and the great things greater.

Cindy Jacobs

23 They shall not labor in vain,
[a]Nor bring forth children for trouble;
For [b]they *shall be* the descendants of the blessed of the LORD,
And their offspring with them.

24 "It shall come to pass
That [a]before they call, I will answer;
And while they are still speaking, I will [b]hear.
25 The [a]wolf and the lamb shall feed together,
The lion shall eat straw like the ox,
[b]And dust *shall be* the serpent's food.
They shall not hurt nor destroy in all My holy mountain,"
Says the LORD.

True Worship and False

66 Thus says the LORD:

[a]"Heaven *is* My throne,
And earth *is* My footstool.
Where *is* the house that you will build Me?
And where *is* the place of My rest?
2 For all those *things* My hand has made,
And all those *things* exist,"
Says the LORD.
[a]"But on this *one* will I look:
[b]On *him who is* poor and of a contrite spirit,
And who trembles at My word.

3 "He[a] who kills a bull *is as if* he slays a man;
He who sacrifices a lamb, *as if* he [b]breaks a dog's neck;
He who offers a grain offering, *as if he offers* swine's blood;
He who burns incense, *as if* he blesses an idol.
Just as they have chosen their own ways,
And their soul delights in their abominations,
4 So will I choose their delusions,
And bring their fears on them;
[a]Because, when I called, no one answered,
When I spoke they did not hear;
But they did evil before My eyes,
And chose *that* in which I do not delight."

23 a Hos. 9:12
b Is. 61:9
24 a Is. 58:9
b Dan. 9:20–23
25 a Is. 11:6–9
b Gen. 3:14
CHAPTER 66
1 a 1 Kin. 8:27
2 a [Is. 57:15; 61:1]
b Ps. 34:18; 51:17
3 a [Is. 1:10–17; 58:1–7]
b Deut. 23:18
4 a Is. 65:12
5 a Is. 60:15
b Is. 5:19
c [Titus 2:13]
12 a Is. 48:18; 60:5
b Is. 60:16
c Is. 49:22; 60:4
13 a Is. 51:3

The Lord Vindicates Zion

5 Hear the word of the LORD,
You who tremble at His word:
"Your brethren who [a]hated you,
Who cast you out for My name's sake, said,
[b]'Let the LORD be glorified,
That [c]we may see your joy.'
But they shall be ashamed."

6 The sound of noise from the city!
A voice from the temple!
The voice of the LORD,
Who fully repays His enemies!

7 "Before she was in labor, she gave birth;
Before her pain came,
She delivered a male child.
8 Who has heard such a thing?
Who has seen such things?
Shall the earth be made to give birth in one day?
Or shall a nation be born at once?
For as soon as Zion was in labor,
She gave birth to her children.
9 Shall I bring to the time of birth, and not cause delivery?" says the LORD.
"Shall I who cause delivery shut up *the womb?*" says your God.
10 "Rejoice with Jerusalem,
And be glad with her, all you who love her;
Rejoice for joy with her, all you who mourn for her;
11 That you may feed and be satisfied
With the consolation of her bosom,
That you may drink deeply and be delighted
With the abundance of her glory."

12 For thus says the LORD:

"Behold, [a]I will extend peace to her like a river,
And the glory of the Gentiles like a flowing stream.
Then you shall [b]feed;
On *her* sides shall you be [c]carried,
And be dandled on *her* knees.
13 As one whom his mother comforts,
So I will [a]comfort you;
And you shall be comforted in Jerusalem."

The Reign and Indignation of God

14 When you see *this,* your heart
shall rejoice,
And [a]your bones shall flourish like
grass;
The hand of the LORD shall be
known to His servants,
And *His* indignation to His
enemies.
15 [a]For behold, the LORD will come
with fire
And with His chariots, like a
whirlwind,
To render His anger with fury,
And His rebuke with flames of fire.
16 For by fire and by [a]His sword
The LORD will judge all flesh;
And the slain of the LORD shall be
[b]many.
17 "Those[a] who sanctify themselves
and purify themselves,
To go to the gardens
[1]After an *idol* in the midst,
Eating swine's flesh and the
abomination and the mouse,
Shall [2]be consumed together," says
the LORD.

18"For I *know* their works and their
[a]thoughts. It shall be that I will [b]gather
all nations and tongues; and they shall
come and see My glory. 19[a]I will set a sign
among them; and those among them who
escape I will send to the nations: *to* Tarshish and [1]Pul and Lud, who draw the
bow, and Tubal and Javan, *to* the coastlands afar off who have not heard My fame
nor seen My glory. [b]And they shall declare
My glory among the Gentiles. 20Then they
shall [a]bring all your brethren [b]for an offering to the LORD out of all nations, on
horses and in chariots and in litters, on
mules and on camels, to My holy mountain Jerusalem," says the LORD, "as the
children of Israel bring an offering in a
clean vessel into the house of the LORD.
21And I will also take some of them for
[a]priests *and* Levites," says the LORD.

22 "For as [a]the new heavens and the
new earth
Which I will make shall remain
before Me," says the LORD,
"So shall your descendants and your
name remain.
23 And [a]it shall come to pass
That from one New Moon to
another,
And from one Sabbath to another,
[b]All flesh shall come to worship
before Me," says the LORD.

24 "And they shall go forth and look
Upon the corpses of the men
Who have transgressed against Me.
For their [a]worm does not die,
And their fire is not quenched.
They shall be an abhorrence to all
flesh."

14 [a]Ezek. 37:1
15 [a]Is. 9:5
16 [a]Is. 27:1 [b]Is. 34:6
17 [a]Is. 65:3–8 [1]Lit. *After one* [2]*come to an end*
18 [a]Is. 59:7 [b]Jer. 3:17
19 [a]Luke 2:34 [b]Mal. 1:11 [1]So with MT, Tg.; LXX *Put* (cf. Jer. 46:9)
20 [a]Is. 49:22 [b][Rom. 15:16]
21 [a]Ex. 19:6
22 [a]Rev. 21:1
23 [a]Zech. 14:16 [b]Zech. 14:17–21
24 [a]Mark 9:44, 46, 48

AUTHOR: *Jeremiah*
DATE: *626–586 B.C.*
THEME: *Failure to Repent Will Lead to Destruction*
KEY WORDS: *Repentance, Restoration*

JEREMIAH

Dear Woman of Destiny,

Have you ever been overwhelmed by compassion for loved ones who are lost or backslidden? Most women have, at one time or another, wept over God's people as Jeremiah did. Our compassion is evidence of the heart of Jesus and holds the promise of God's desire and ability to restore the lives of those we love. As you read and pray, know that your tears are not in vain.

His love and mine,

Marilyn Hickey

The words of Jeremiah the son of
Hilkiah, of the priests who *were* [a]in
Anathoth in the land of Benjamin,
2 to whom the word of the LORD came in
the days of [a]Josiah the son of Amon, king
of Judah, [b]in the thirteenth year of his
reign. 3 It came also in the days of [a]Jehoia-
kim the son of Josiah, king of Judah,
[b]until the end of the eleventh year of
Zedekiah the son of Josiah, king of Judah,
[c]until the carrying away of Jerusalem captive [d]in the fifth month.

The Prophet Is Called

4 Then the word of the LORD came to
me, saying:

5 "Before I [a]formed you in the womb
[b]I knew you;
Before you were born I [c]sanctified[1] you;
I [2]ordained you a prophet to the nations."

6 Then said I:

[a]"Ah, Lord GOD!
Behold, I cannot speak, for I *am* a youth."

Lord, as You called Jeremiah, You have called ____ in their youth. Lord, may they not hold back from going to all the places to which You will send them and saying all that You command.

FROM JEREMIAH 1:7

7 But the LORD said to me:

"Do not say, 'I *am* a youth,'
For you shall go to all to whom I send you,
And [a]whatever I command you, you shall speak.
8 [a]Do not be afraid of their faces,
For [b]I *am* with you to deliver you,"
says the LORD.

9 Then the LORD put forth His hand and
[a]touched my mouth, and the LORD said
to me:

"Behold, I have [b]put My words in your mouth.
10 [a]See, I have this day set you over
the nations and over the kingdoms,
To [b]root out and to pull down,
To destroy and to throw down,
To build and to plant."

11 Moreover the word of the LORD came
to me, saying, "Jeremiah, what do you
see?"
And I said, "I see a [1]branch of an almond tree."
12 Then the LORD said to me, "You have
seen well, for I am [1]ready to perform My
word."
13 And the word of the LORD came to me
the second time, saying, "What do you
see?"
And I said, "I see [a]a boiling pot, and it
is facing away from the north."
14 Then the LORD said to me:

"Out of the [a]north calamity shall break forth
On all the inhabitants of the land.
15 For behold, I am [a]calling
All the families of the kingdoms of the north," says the LORD;
"They shall come and [b]each one set his throne
At the entrance of the gates of Jerusalem,
Against all its walls all around,
And against all the cities of Judah.
16 I will utter My judgments
Against them concerning all their wickedness,
Because [a]they have forsaken Me,
Burned [b]incense to other gods,
And worshiped the works of their own [c]hands.

17 "Therefore [a]prepare yourself and arise,
And speak to them all that I command you.
[b]Do not be dismayed before their faces,
Lest I dismay you before them.
18 For behold, I have made you this day
[a]A fortified city and an iron pillar,
And bronze walls against the whole land—
Against the kings of Judah,
Against its princes,
Against its priests,
And against the people of the land.

CHAPTER 1
1 [a]Josh. 21:18
2 [a]2 Kin. 21:24 [b]Jer. 25:3
3 [a]2 Kin. 23:34 [b]Jer. 39:2 [c]Jer. 52:12 [d]2 Kin. 25:8
5 [a]Is. 49:1, 5 [b]Ex. 33:12 [c][Luke 1:15] [1] *set you apart* [2] *appointed*
6 [a]Ex. 4:10; 6:12, 30
7 [a]Num. 22:20, 38
8 [a]Ezek. 2:6; 3:9 [b]Ex. 3:12
9 [a]Is. 6:7 [b]Is. 51:16
10 [a]1 Kin. 19:17 [b][2 Cor. 10:4, 5]
11 [1] Lit. *rod*
12 [1] Lit. *watching*
13 [a]Ezek. 11:3; 24:3
14 [a]Jer. 6:1
15 [a]Jer. 6:22; 25:9 [b]Jer. 39:3
16 [a]Deut. 28:20 [b]Jer. 7:9 [c]Is. 37:19
17 [a]Job 38:3 [b]Ezek. 2:6
18 [a]Is. 50:7

19 They will fight against you,
But they shall not prevail against you.
For I *am* with you," says the LORD,
"to deliver you."

God's Case Against Israel

2 Moreover the word of the LORD came
to me, saying, 2"Go and cry in the
hearing of Jerusalem, saying, 'Thus says
the LORD:

"I remember you,
The kindness of your [a]youth,
The love of your betrothal,
[b]When you [1]went after Me in the wilderness,
In a land not sown.
3 [a]Israel *was* holiness to the LORD,
[b]The firstfruits of His increase.
[c]All that devour him will offend;
Disaster will [d]come upon them,"
says the LORD.' "

Holiness is the symmetry of the soul.
PHILIP HENRY

4Hear the word of the LORD, O house of
Jacob and all the families of the house of
Israel. 5Thus says the LORD:

[a]"What injustice have your fathers found in Me,
That they have gone far from Me,
[b]Have followed [1]idols,
And have become idolaters?
6 Neither did they say, 'Where *is* the LORD,
Who [a]brought us up out of the land of Egypt,
Who led us through [b]the wilderness,
Through a land of deserts and pits,
Through a land of drought and the shadow of death,
Through a land that no one crossed
And where no one dwelt?'
7 I brought you into [a]a bountiful country,
To eat its fruit and its goodness.
But when you entered, you [b]defiled My land
And made My heritage an abomination.
8 The priests did not say, 'Where *is* the LORD?'
And those who handle the [a]law did not know Me;
The rulers also transgressed against Me;
[b]The prophets prophesied by Baal,
And walked after *things that* do not profit.

9 "Therefore [a]I will yet [1]bring charges against you," says the LORD,
"And against your children's children I will bring charges.
10 For pass beyond the coasts of [1]Cyprus and see,
Send to [2]Kedar and consider diligently,
And see if there has been such *a* [a]*thing.*
11 [a]Has a nation changed *its* gods,
Which *are* [b]not gods?
[c]But My people have changed their Glory
For *what* does not profit.
12 Be astonished, O heavens, at this,
And be horribly afraid;
Be very desolate," says the LORD.
13 "For My people have committed two evils:
They have forsaken Me, the [a]fountain of living waters,
And hewn themselves cisterns—broken cisterns that can hold no water.

14 "*Is* Israel [a]a servant?
Is he a homeborn *slave?*
Why is he plundered?
15 [a]The young lions roared at him, *and* growled;
They made his land waste;
His cities are burned, without inhabitant.
16 Also the people of [1]Noph and [a]Tahpanhes
Have [2]broken the crown of your head.
17 [a]Have you not brought this on yourself,
In that you have forsaken the LORD your God
When [b]He led you in the way?

CHAPTER 2
2 [a]Ezek. 16:8 [b]Deut. 2:7 [1] *followed*
3 [a][Ex. 19:5, 6] [b]Rev. 14:4 [c]Jer. 12:14 [d]Is. 41:11
5 [a]Is. 5:4 [b]2 Kin. 17:15 [1] *vanities* or *futilities*
6 [a]Is. 63:11 [b]Deut. 8:15; 32:10
7 [a]Num. 13:27 [b]Num. 35:33
8 [a]Rom. 2:20 [b]Jer. 23:13
9 [a]Mic. 6:2 [1] *contend with*
10 [a]Jer. 18:13 [1] Heb. *Kittim,* representative of western cultures [2] In northern Arabian desert, representative of eastern cultures
11 [a]Mic. 4:5 [b]Is. 37:19 [c]Rom. 1:23
13 [a]Ps. 36:9
14 [a][Ex. 4:22]
15 [a]Is. 1:7
16 [a]Jer. 43:7–9 [1] Memphis in ancient Egypt [2] Or *grazed*
17 [a]Jer. 4:18 [b]Deut. 32:10

18 And now why take [a]the road to
Egypt,
To drink the waters of [b]Sihor?
Or why take the road to [c]Assyria,
To drink the waters of [1]the River?
19 Your own wickedness will [a]correct
you,
And your backslidings will rebuke
you.
Know therefore and see that *it is* an
evil and bitter *thing*
That you have forsaken the LORD
your God,
And the [1]fear of Me *is* not in you,"
Says the Lord GOD of hosts.
20 "For of old I have [a]broken your
yoke *and* burst your bonds;
And [b]you said, 'I will not
[1]transgress,'
When [c]on every high hill and under
every green tree
You lay down, [d]playing the harlot.
21 Yet I had [a]planted you a noble
vine, a seed of highest quality.
How then have you turned before
Me
Into [b]the degenerate plant of an
alien vine?
22 For though you wash yourself
with lye, and use much soap,
Yet your iniquity is [a]marked[1]
before Me," says the Lord GOD.
23 "How[a] can you say, 'I am not
[1]polluted,
I have not gone after the Baals'?
See your way in the valley;
Know what you have done:
You are a swift dromedary breaking
loose in her ways,
24 A wild donkey used to the
wilderness,
That sniffs at the wind in her
desire;
In her time of mating, who can
turn her away?
All those who seek her will not
weary themselves;
In her month they will find her.
25 Withhold your foot from being
unshod, and your throat from
thirst.
But you said, [a]'There is no hope.
No! For I have loved [b]aliens, and
after them I will go.'
26 "As the thief is ashamed when he is
found out,
So is the house of Israel ashamed;
They and their kings and their
princes, and their priests and
their [a]prophets,
27 Saying to a tree, 'You *are* my
father,'
And to a [a]stone, 'You gave birth to
me.'
For they have turned *their* back to
Me, and not *their* face.
But in the time of their [b]trouble
They will say, 'Arise and save us.'
28 But [a]where *are* your gods that
you have made for yourselves?
Let them arise,
If they [b]can save you in the time of
your [1]trouble;
For [c]*according to* the number of
your cities
Are your gods, O Judah.
29 "Why will you plead with Me?
You all have transgressed against
Me," says the LORD.
30 "In vain I have [a]chastened your
children;
They [b]received no correction.
Your sword has [c]devoured your
prophets
Like a destroying lion.
31 "O generation, see the word of the
LORD!
Have I been a wilderness to Israel,
Or a land of darkness?
Why do My people say, 'We [1]are
lords;
[a]We will come no more to You'?
32 Can a virgin forget her ornaments,
Or a bride her attire?
Yet My people [a]have forgotten Me
days without number.
33 "Why do you beautify your way to
seek love?
Therefore you have also taught
The wicked women your ways.
34 Also on your skirts is found
[a]The blood of the lives of the poor
innocents.
I have not found it by [1]secret
search,
But plainly on all these things.
35 [a]Yet you say, 'Because I am
innocent,
Surely His anger shall turn from
me.'
Behold, [b]I will plead My case
against you,
[c]Because you say, 'I have not
sinned.'

18 [a]Is. 30:1–3 [b]Josh. 13:3 [c]Hos. 5:13 [1]The Euphrates
19 [a]Jer. 4:18 [1]*dread*
20 [a]Lev. 26:13 [b]Judg. 10:16 [c]Deut. 12:2 [d]Ex. 34:15 [1]Kt. *serve*
21 [a]Ex. 15:17 [b]Is. 5:4
22 [a]Job 14:16, 17 [1]*stained*
23 [a]Prov. 30:12 [1]*defiled*
25 [a]Jer. 18:12 [b]Jer. 3:13
26 [a]Is. 28:7
27 [a]Jer. 3:9 [b]Is. 26:16
28 [a]Judg. 10:14 [b]Is. 45:20 [c]Jer. 11:13 [1]Or *evil*
30 [a]Is. 9:13 [b]Jer. 5:3; 7:28 [c]Neh. 9:26
31 [a]Deut. 32:15 [1]*have dominion*
32 [a]Ps. 106:21
34 [a]Ps. 106:38 [1]*digging*
35 [a]Jer. 2:23, 29 [b]Jer. 2:9 [c][Prov. 28:13]

36 [a]Why do you gad about so much to
change your way?
Also [b]you shall be ashamed of
Egypt [c]as you were ashamed of
Assyria.
37 Indeed you will go forth from him
With your hands on [a]your head;
For the LORD has rejected your
trusted allies,
And you will [b]not prosper by them.

Israel Is Shameless

3 "They say, 'If a man divorces his wife,
And she goes from him
And becomes another man's,
[a]May he return to her again?'
Would not that [b]land be greatly
polluted?
But you have [c]played the harlot
with many lovers;
[d]Yet return to Me," says the LORD.
2 "Lift up your eyes to [a]the desolate
heights and see:
Where have you not [1]lain *with
men?*
[b]By the road you have sat for them
Like an Arabian in the wilderness;
[c]And you have polluted the land
With your harlotries and your
wickedness.
3 Therefore the [a]showers have been
withheld,
And there has been no latter rain.
You have had a [b]harlot's forehead;
You refuse to be ashamed.
4 Will you not from this time cry to
Me,
'My Father, You *are* [a]the guide of
[b]my youth?
5 [a]Will He remain angry forever?
Will He keep it to the end?'
Behold, you have spoken and done
evil things,
As you were able."

A Call to Repentance

6The LORD said also to me in the days
of Josiah the king: "Have you seen what
[a]backsliding Israel has done? She has
[b]gone up on every high mountain and under every green tree, and there played the
harlot. 7[a]And I said, after she had done all
these *things,* 'Return to Me.' But she did
not return. And her treacherous [b]sister
Judah saw it. 8Then I saw that [a]for all the
causes for which backsliding Israel had
committed adultery, I had [b]put her away
and given her a certificate of divorce; [c]yet
her treacherous sister Judah did not fear,
but went and played the harlot also. 9So it
came to pass, through her casual harlotry,
that she [a]defiled the land and committed
adultery with [b]stones and trees. 10And yet
for all this her treacherous sister Judah
has not turned to Me [a]with her whole
heart, but in pretense," says the LORD.
11Then the LORD said to me, [a]"Backsliding Israel has shown herself more
righteous than treacherous Judah. 12Go
and proclaim these words toward [a]the
north, and say:

'Return, backsliding Israel,' says the
LORD;
'I will not cause My anger to fall on
you.
For I *am* [b]merciful,' says the LORD;
'I will not remain angry forever.
13 [a]Only acknowledge your iniquity,
That you have transgressed against
the LORD your God,
And have [b]scattered your [1]charms
To [c]alien deities [d]under every green
tree,
And you have not obeyed My voice,'
says the LORD.

14"Return, O backsliding children,"
says the LORD; [a]"for I am married to you.
I will take you, [b]one from a city and two
from a family, and I will bring you to
[c]Zion. 15And I will give you [a]shepherds
according to My heart, who will [b]feed you
with knowledge and understanding.
16"Then it shall come to pass, when you
are multiplied and [a]increased in the land
in those days," says the LORD, "that they
will say no more, 'The ark of the covenant
of the LORD.' [b]It shall not come to mind,
nor shall they remember it, nor shall they
visit *it,* nor shall it be made anymore.
17"At that time Jerusalem shall be
called The Throne of the LORD, and all the
nations shall be gathered to it, [a]to the
name of the LORD, to Jerusalem. No more
shall they [b]follow[1] the dictates of their
evil hearts.
18"In those days [a]the house of Judah
shall walk with the house of Israel, and
they shall come together out of the land
of [b]the north to [c]the land that I have giv-
en as an inheritance to your fathers.
19"But I said:

'How can I put you among the
children
And give you [a]a pleasant land,

---

36 a Hos. 5:13; 12:1 b Is. 30:3 c 2 Chr. 28:16
37 a 2 Sam. 13:19 b Jer. 37:7–10
CHAPTER 3
1 a Deut. 24:1–4 b Jer. 2:7 c Ezek. 16:26 d [Zech. 1:3]
2 a Deut. 12:2 b Prov. 23:28 c Jer. 2:7 *1* Kt. *been violated*
3 a Lev. 26:19 b Zeph. 3:5
4 a Prov. 2:17 b Jer. 2:2
5 a [Is. 57:16]
6 a Jer. 7:24 b Jer. 2:20
7 a 2 Kin. 17:13 b Ezek. 16:47, 48
8 a Ezek. 23:9 b 2 Kin. 17:6 c Ezek. 23:11
9 a Jer. 2:7 b Jer. 2:27
10 a Jer. 12:2
11 a Ezek. 16:51, 52
12 a 2 Kin. 17:6 b Ps. 86:15
13 a Deut. 30:1, 2 b Ezek. 16:15 c Jer. 2:25 d Deut. 12:2 *1* Lit. *ways*
14 a Hos. 2:19, 20 b Jer. 31:6 c [Rom. 11:5]
15 a Eph. 4:11 b Acts 20:28
16 a Is. 49:19 b Is. 65:17
17 a Is. 60:9 b Deut. 29:19; Jer. 7:24 *1 walk after the stubbornness* or *imagination*
18 a Is. 11:13 b Jer. 31:8 c Amos 9:15
19 a Ps. 106:24

A beautiful heritage of the hosts of
nations?'

"And I said:
'You shall call Me, [b]"My Father,"
And not turn away from Me.'
20 Surely, *as* a wife treacherously
departs from her [1]husband,
So [a]have you dealt treacherously
with Me,
O house of Israel," says the LORD.

21 A voice was heard on [a]the desolate
heights,
Weeping *and* supplications of the
children of Israel.
For they have perverted their way;
They have forgotten the LORD their
God.

22 "Return, you backsliding children,
And I will [a]heal your backslidings."

"Indeed we do come to You,
For You are the LORD our God.
23 [a]Truly, in vain *is salvation hoped
for* from the hills,
And from the multitude of
mountains;
[b]Truly, in the LORD our God
Is the salvation of Israel.
24 [a]For shame has devoured
The labor of our fathers from our
youth—
Their flocks and their herds,
Their sons and their daughters.
25 We lie down in our shame,
And our [1]reproach covers us.
[a]For we have sinned against the
LORD our God,
We and our fathers,
From our youth even to this day,
And [b]have not obeyed the voice of
the LORD our God."

4 "If you will return, O Israel," says the
LORD,
[a]"Return to Me;
And if you will put away your
abominations out of My sight,
Then you shall not be moved.
2 [a]And you shall swear, 'The LORD
lives,'
[b]In truth, in [1]judgment, and in
righteousness;
[c]The nations shall bless themselves
in Him,
And in Him they shall [d]glory."

3For thus says the LORD to the men of
Judah and Jerusalem:

[a]"Break up your [1]fallow ground,
And [b]do not sow among thorns.
4 [a]Circumcise yourselves to the LORD,
And take away the foreskins of your
hearts,
You men of Judah and inhabitants
of Jerusalem,
Lest My fury come forth like fire,
And burn so that no one can
quench *it*,
Because of the evil of your doings."

An Imminent Invasion

5Declare in Judah and proclaim in Jerusalem, and say:

[a]"Blow the trumpet in the land;
Cry, 'Gather together,'
And say, [b]'Assemble yourselves,
And let us go into the fortified
cities.'
6 Set up the [1]standard toward Zion.
Take refuge! Do not delay!
For I will bring disaster from the
[a]north,
And great destruction."

7 [a]The lion has come up from his
thicket,
And [b]the destroyer of nations is on
his way.
He has gone forth from his place
[c]To make your land desolate.
Your cities will be laid waste,
Without inhabitant.
8 For this, [a]clothe yourself with
sackcloth,
Lament and wail.
For the fierce anger of the LORD
Has not turned back from us.

9 "And it shall come to pass in that
day," says the LORD,
"*That* the heart of the king shall
perish,
And the heart of the princes;
The priests shall be astonished,
And the prophets shall wonder."

10 Then I said, "Ah, Lord GOD!
[a]Surely You have greatly deceived
this people and Jerusalem,
[b]Saying, 'You shall have peace,'
Whereas the sword reaches to the
[1]heart."
11 At that time it will be said
To this people and to Jerusalem,
[a]"A dry wind of the desolate heights
blows in the wilderness

---

19 b Is. 63:16
20 a Is. 48:8 *1 Lit. companion*
21 a Is. 15:2
22 a Hos. 6:1; 14:4
23 a Ps. 121:1, 2 b Ps. 3:8
24 a Hos. 9:10
25 a Ezra 9:6, 7 b Jer. 22:21 *1 disgrace*

CHAPTER 4
1 a Joel 2:12
2 a Deut. 10:20 b Zech. 8:8 c [Gen. 22:18] d 1 Cor. 1:31 *1 justice*
3 a Hos. 10:12 b Matt. 13:7 *1 untilled*
4 a Deut. 10:16; 30:6
5 a Hos. 8:1 b Jer. 8:14
6 a Jer. 1:13–15; 6:1, 22; 50:17 *1 banner*
7 a Dan. 7:4 b Jer. 25:9 c Is. 1:7; 6:11
8 a Is. 22:12
10 a Ezek. 14:9 b Jer. 5:12; 14:13 *1 Lit. soul*
11 a Hos. 13:15

Toward the daughter of My people—
Not to fan or to cleanse—
12 A wind too strong for these will come for Me;
Now [a]I will also speak judgment against them."

13 "Behold, he shall come up like clouds,
And [a]his chariots like a whirlwind.
[b]His horses are swifter than eagles.
Woe to us, for we are plundered!"

14 O Jerusalem, [a]wash your heart from wickedness,
That you may be saved.
How long shall your evil thoughts lodge within you?
15 For a voice declares [a]from Dan
And proclaims [1]affliction from Mount Ephraim:
16 "Make mention to the nations,
Yes, proclaim against Jerusalem,
That watchers come from a [a]far country
And raise their voice against the cities of Judah.
17 [a]Like keepers of a field they are against her all around,
Because she has been rebellious against Me," says the LORD.
18 "Your[a] ways and your doings
Have procured these *things* for you.
This *is* your wickedness,
Because it is bitter,
Because it reaches to your heart."

Sorrow for the Doomed Nation

19 O my [a]soul, my soul!
I am pained in my very heart!
My heart makes a noise in me;
I cannot hold my peace,
Because you have heard, O my soul,
The sound of the trumpet,
The alarm of war.
20 [a]Destruction upon destruction is cried,
For the whole land is plundered.
Suddenly [b]my tents are plundered,
And my curtains in a moment.
21 How long will I see the [1]standard,
And hear the sound of the trumpet?

22 "For My people *are* foolish,
They have not known Me.
They *are* [1]silly children,
And they have no understanding.
[a]They *are* wise to do evil,
But to do good they have no knowledge."

23 [a]I beheld the earth, and indeed *it was* [b]without form, and void;
And the heavens, they *had* no light.
24 [a]I beheld the mountains, and indeed they trembled,
And all the hills moved back and forth.
25 I beheld, and indeed *there was* no man,
And [a]all the birds of the heavens had fled.
26 I beheld, and indeed the fruitful land *was* a [a]wilderness,
And all its cities were broken down
At the presence of the LORD,
By His fierce anger.

27 For thus says the LORD:

"The whole land shall be desolate;
[a]Yet I will not make a full end.
28 For this [a]shall the earth mourn,
And [b]the heavens above be black,
Because I have spoken.
I have [c]purposed and [d]will not relent,
Nor will I turn back from it.
29 The whole city shall flee from the noise of the horsemen and bowmen.
They shall go into thickets and climb up on the rocks.
Every city *shall be* forsaken,
And not a man shall dwell in it.

30 "And *when* you *are* plundered,
What will you do?
Though you clothe yourself with crimson,
Though you adorn *yourself* with ornaments of gold,
[a]Though you enlarge your eyes with paint,
In vain you will make yourself fair;
[b]*Your* lovers will despise you;
They will seek your life.

31 "For I have heard a voice as of a woman in [1]labor,
The anguish as of her who brings forth her first child,
The voice of the daughter of Zion bewailing herself;
She [a]spreads her hands, *saying,*
'Woe *is* me now, for my soul is [2]weary
Because of murderers!'

---

12 a Jer. 1:16
13 a Is. 5:28 b Deut. 28:49
14 a James 4:8
15 a Jer. 8:16; 50:17 1 Or *wickedness*
16 a Is. 39:3
17 a 2 Kin. 25:1, 4
18 a Is. 50:1
19 a Is. 15:5; 16:11; 21:3; 22:4
20 a Ezek. 7:26 b Jer. 10:20
21 1 *banner*
22 a Rom. 16:19 1 *foolish*
23 a Is. 24:19 b Gen. 1:2
24 a Ezek. 38:20
25 a Zeph. 1:3
26 a Jer. 9:10
27 a Jer. 5:10, 18; 30:11; 46:28
28 a Hos. 4:3 b Is. 5:30; 50:3 c [Dan. 4:35] d [Num. 23:19]
30 a 2 Kin. 9:30 b Jer. 22:20, 22
31 a Lam. 1:17 1 *childbirth* 2 *faint*

The Justice of God's Judgment

5 "Run to and fro through the streets
of Jerusalem;
See now and know;
And seek in her open places
[a]If you can find a man,
[b]If there is *anyone* who executes
[1]judgment,
Who seeks the truth,
[c]And I will pardon her.
2 [a]Though they say, '*As* [b]the LORD
lives,'
Surely they [c]swear falsely."

3 O LORD, *are* not [a]Your eyes on the
truth?
You have [b]stricken them,
But they have not grieved;
You have consumed them,
But [c]they have refused to receive
correction.
They have made their faces harder
than rock;
They have refused to return.
4 Therefore I said, "Surely these *are*
poor.
They are foolish;
For [a]they do not know the way of
the LORD,
The judgment of their God.
5 I will go to the great men and
speak to them,
For [a]they have known the way of
the LORD,
The judgment of their God."

But these have altogether [b]broken
the yoke
And burst the bonds.
6 Therefore [a]a lion from the forest
shall slay them,
[b]A wolf of the deserts shall destroy
them;
[c]A leopard will watch over their
cities.
Everyone who goes out from there
shall be torn in pieces,
Because their transgressions are
many;
Their backslidings have increased.

7 "How shall I pardon you for this?
Your children have forsaken Me
And [a]sworn by *those* [b]*that are* not
gods.
[c]When I had fed them to the full,
Then they committed adultery
And assembled themselves by troops
in the harlots' houses.

CHAPTER 5
1 a Ezek. 22:30 b Gen. 18:23–32 c Gen. 18:26 1 *justice*
2 a Titus 1:16 b Jer. 4:2 c Jer. 7:9
3 a [2 Chr. 16:9] b Is. 1:5; 9:13 c Zeph. 3:2
4 a Jer. 8:7
5 a Mic. 3:1 b Ps. 2:3
6 a Jer. 4:7 b Zeph. 3:3 c Hos. 13:7
7 a Zeph. 1:5 b Deut. 32:21 c Deut. 32:15
8 a Ezek. 22:11
9 a Jer. 9:9
10 a Jer. 4:27 1 *completely destroy*
11 a Jer. 3:6, 7, 20
12 a 2 Chr. 36:16 b Jer. 23:17 c Jer. 14:13 1 *disaster*
14 a Jer. 1:9; 23:29
15 a Deut. 28:49 b Jer. 4:16
17 a Lev. 26:16
18 a Jer. 30:11 1 *completely destroy*
19 a Deut. 29:24–29

8 [a]They were *like* well-fed lusty
stallions;
Every one neighed after his
neighbor's wife.
9 Shall I not punish *them* for these
things?" says the LORD.
"And shall I not [a]avenge Myself on
such a nation as this?

10 "Go up on her walls and destroy,
But do not [1]make a [a]complete end.
Take away her branches,
For they *are* not the LORD's.
11 For [a]the house of Israel and the
house of Judah
Have dealt very treacherously with
Me," says the LORD.
12 [a]They have lied about the LORD,
And said, [b]"*It is* not He.
[c]Neither will [1]evil come upon us,
Nor shall we see sword or famine.
13 And the prophets become wind,
For the word *is* not in them.
Thus shall it be done to them."

14 Therefore thus says the LORD God of
hosts:

"Because you speak this word,
[a]Behold, I will make My words in
your mouth fire,
And this people wood,
And it shall devour them.
15 Behold, I will bring a [a]nation
against you [b]from afar,
O house of Israel," says the LORD.
"It *is* a mighty nation,
It *is* an ancient nation,
A nation whose language you do
not know,
Nor can you understand what they
say.
16 Their quiver *is* like an open tomb;
They *are* all mighty men.
17 And they shall eat up your
[a]harvest and your bread,
Which your sons and daughters
should eat.
They shall eat up your flocks and
your herds;
They shall eat up your vines and
your fig trees;
They shall destroy your fortified
cities,
In which you trust, with the sword.

18 "Nevertheless in those days," says the
LORD, "I [a]will not [1]make a complete end
of you. 19 And it will be when you say,
[a]'Why does the LORD our God do all these

things to us?' then you shall answer them,
'Just as you have [b]forsaken Me and served
foreign gods in your land, so [c]you shall
serve aliens in a land *that is* not yours.'

20 "Declare this in the house of Jacob
And proclaim it in Judah, saying,
21 'Hear this now, O [a]foolish people,
Without [1]understanding,
Who have eyes and see not,
And who have ears and hear not:
22 [a]Do you not fear Me?' says the LORD.
'Will you not tremble at My presence,
Who have placed the sand as the [b]bound of the sea,
By a perpetual decree, that it cannot pass beyond it?
And though its waves toss to and fro,
Yet they cannot prevail;
Though they roar, yet they cannot pass over it.
23 But this people has a defiant and rebellious heart;
They have revolted and departed.
24 They do not say in their heart,
"Let us now fear the LORD our God,
[a]Who gives rain, both the [b]former and the latter, in its season.
[c]He reserves for us the appointed weeks of the harvest."
25 [a]Your iniquities have turned these *things* away,
And your sins have withheld good from you.
26 'For among My people are found wicked *men;*
They [a]lie in wait as one who sets snares;
They set a trap;
They catch men.
27 As a cage is full of birds,
So their houses *are* full of deceit.
Therefore they have become great and grown rich.
28 They have grown [a]fat, they are sleek;
Yes, they [1]surpass the deeds of the wicked;
They do not plead [b]the cause,
The cause of the fatherless;
[c]Yet they prosper,
And the right of the needy they do not defend.
29 [a]Shall I not punish *them* for these *things?*' says the LORD.
'Shall I not avenge Myself on such a nation as this?'

30 "An astonishing and [a]horrible thing
Has been committed in the land:
31 The prophets prophesy [a]falsely,
And the priests rule by their *own* power;
And My people [b]love *to have it* so.
But what will you do in the end?

Impending Destruction from the North

6 "O you children of Benjamin,
Gather yourselves to flee from the midst of Jerusalem!
Blow the trumpet in Tekoa,
And set up a signal-fire in [a]Beth Haccerem;
[b]For disaster appears out of the north,
And great destruction.
2 I have likened the daughter of Zion
To a lovely and delicate woman.
3 The [a]shepherds with their flocks shall come to her.
They shall pitch *their* tents against her all around.
Each one shall pasture in his own place."

4 "Prepare[a] war against her;
Arise, and let us go up [b]at noon.
Woe to us, for the day goes away,
For the shadows of the evening are lengthening.
5 Arise, and let us go by night,
And let us destroy her palaces."

6 For thus has the LORD of hosts said:

"Cut down trees,
And build a mound against Jerusalem.
This *is* the city to be punished.
She *is* full of oppression in her midst.
7 [a]As a fountain [1]wells up with water,
So she wells up with her wickedness.
[b]Violence and plundering are heard in her.
Before Me continually *are* [2]grief and wounds.
8 Be instructed, O Jerusalem,
Lest [a]My soul depart from you;
Lest I make you desolate,
A land not inhabited."

19 [b]Jer. 1:16; 2:13 [c]Deut. 28:48
21 [a]Matt. 13:14 [1]Lit. *heart*
22 [a][Rev. 15:4] [b]Job 26:10
24 [a]Acts 14:17 [b]Joel 2:23 [c][Gen. 8:22]
25 [a]Jer. 3:3
26 [a]Hab. 1:15
28 [a]Deut. 32:15 [b]Zech. 7:10 [c]Job 12:6 [1]Or *pass over* or *overlook*
29 [a]Mal. 3:5
30 [a]Hos. 6:10
31 [a]Ezek. 13:6 [b]Mic. 2:11
CHAPTER 6
1 [a]Neh. 3:14 [b]Jer. 4:6
3 [a]2 Kin. 25:1–4
4 [a]Joel 3:9 [b]Jer. 15:8
7 [a]Is. 57:20 [b]Ps. 55:9 [1]*gushes* [2]*sickness*
8 [a]Hos. 9:12

9Thus says the LORD of hosts:

"They shall thoroughly glean as a
vine the remnant of Israel;
As a grape-gatherer, put your hand
back into the branches."
10 To whom shall I speak and give
warning,
That they may hear?
Indeed their [a]ear *is* uncircumcised,
And they cannot give heed.
Behold, [b]the word of the LORD is a
reproach to them;
They have no delight in it.
11 Therefore I am full of the fury of
the LORD.
[a]I am weary of holding *it* in.
"I will pour it out [b]on the children
outside,
And on the assembly of young men
together;
For even the husband shall be
taken with the wife,
The aged with *him who is* full of
days.
12 And [a]their houses shall be turned
over to others,
Fields and wives together;
For I will stretch out My hand
Against the inhabitants of the land,"
says the LORD.
13 "Because from the least of them
even to the greatest of them,
Everyone *is* given to [a]covetousness;
And from the prophet even to the
[b]priest,
Everyone deals falsely.
14 They have also [a]healed the [1]hurt
of My people [2]slightly,
[b]Saying, 'Peace, peace!'
When *there is* no peace.
15 Were they [a]ashamed when they
had committed abomination?
No! They were not at all ashamed;
Nor did they know how to blush.
Therefore they shall fall among
those who fall;
At the time I punish them,
They shall be cast down," says the
LORD.

16Thus says the LORD:

"Stand in the ways and see,
And ask for the [a]old paths, where
the good way *is*,
And walk in it;
Then you will find [b]rest for your
souls.
But they said, 'We will not walk *in*
it.'
17 Also, I set [a]watchmen over you,
saying,
[b]'Listen to the sound of the trumpet!'
But they said, 'We will not listen.'
18 Therefore hear, you nations,
And know, O congregation, what *is*
among them.
19 [a]Hear, O earth!
Behold, I will certainly bring
[b]calamity on this people—
[c]The fruit of their thoughts,
Because they have not heeded My
words
Nor My law, but rejected it.
20 [a]For what purpose to Me
Comes frankincense [b]from Sheba,
And [c]sweet cane from a far
country?
[d]Your burnt offerings *are* not
acceptable,
Nor your sacrifices sweet to Me."

21Therefore thus says the LORD:

"Behold, I will lay stumbling blocks
before this people,
And the fathers and the sons
together shall fall on them.
The neighbor and his friend shall
perish."

22Thus says the LORD:

"Behold, a people comes from the
[a]north country,
And a great nation will be raised
from the farthest parts of the
earth.
23 They will lay hold on bow and
spear;
They *are* cruel and have no mercy;
Their voice [a]roars like the sea;
And they ride on horses,
As men of war set in array against
you, O daughter of Zion."
24 We have heard the report of it;
Our hands grow feeble.
[a]Anguish has taken hold of us,
Pain as of a woman in [1]labor.
25 Do not go out into the field,
Nor walk by the way.
Because of the sword of the enemy,
Fear *is* on every side.
26 O daughter of my people,
[a]Dress in sackcloth
[b]And roll about in ashes!
[c]Make mourning *as for* an only son,
most bitter lamentation;

10 a [Acts 7:51] b Jer. 8:9; 20:8
11 a Jer. 20:9 b Jer. 9:21
12 a Deut. 28:30
13 a Is. 56:11; Jer. 8:10; 22:17 b Jer. 5:31; 23:11
14 a Jer. 8:11–15 b Jer. 4:10; 23:17 *1* Lit. *crushing* *2* Superficially
15 a Jer. 3:3; 8:12
16 a Jer. 18:15 b Matt. 11:29
17 a Hab. 2:1 b Deut. 4:1
19 a Is. 1:2 b Jer. 19:3, 15 c Prov. 1:31
20 a Mic. 6:6, 7 b Is. 60:6 c Is. 43:24 d Jer. 7:21–23
22 a Jer. 1:15; 10:22; 50:41–43
23 a Is. 5:30
24 a Jer. 4:31; 13:21; 49:24 *1* childbirth
26 a Jer. 4:8 b Mic. 1:10 c [Zech. 12:10]

For the plunderer will suddenly
come upon us.

27 "I have set you *as* an assayer *and*
[a]a fortress among My people,
That you may know and test their
way.
28 [a]They *are* all stubborn rebels,
[b]walking as slanderers.
They are [c]bronze and iron,
They *are* all corrupters;
29 The bellows blow fiercely,
The lead is consumed by the fire;
The smelter refines in vain,
For the wicked are not drawn off.
30 *People* will call them [a]rejected
silver,
Because the LORD has rejected
them."

Trusting in Lying Words

7 The word that came to Jeremiah from the LORD, saying, 2[a]"Stand in the gate of the LORD's house, and proclaim there this word, and say, 'Hear the word of the LORD, all *you of* Judah who enter in at these gates to worship the LORD!' " 3Thus says the LORD of hosts, the God of Israel: [a]"Amend your ways and your doings, and I will cause you to dwell in this place. 4[a]Do not trust in these lying words, saying, 'The temple of the LORD, the temple of the LORD, the temple of the LORD *are* these.'

5"For if you thoroughly amend your ways and your doings, if you thoroughly [a]execute [1]judgment between a man and his neighbor, 6*if* you do not oppress the stranger, the fatherless, and the widow, and do not shed innocent blood in this place, [a]or walk after other gods to your hurt, 7[a]then I will cause you to dwell in this place, in [b]the land that I gave to your fathers forever and ever.

8"Behold, you trust in [a]lying words that cannot profit. 9[a]Will you steal, murder, commit adultery, swear falsely, burn incense to Baal, and [b]walk after other gods whom you do not know, 10[a]and *then* come and stand before Me in this house [b]which is called by My name, and say, 'We are delivered to do all these abominations'? 11Has [a]this house, which is called by My name, become a [b]den of thieves in your eyes? Behold, I, even I, have seen *it*," says the LORD.

12"But go now to [a]My place which *was* in Shiloh, [b]where I set My name at the first, and see [c]what I did to it because of the wickedness of My people Israel. 13And now, because you have done all these works," says the LORD, "and I spoke to you, [a]rising up early and speaking, but you did not hear, and I [b]called you, but you did not answer, 14therefore I will do to the house which is called by My name, in which you trust, and to this place which I gave to you and your fathers, as I have done to [a]Shiloh. 15And I will cast you out of My sight, [a]as I have cast out all your brethren—[b]the whole posterity of Ephraim.

16"Therefore [a]do not pray for this people, nor lift up a cry or prayer for them, nor make intercession to Me; [b]for I will not hear you. 17Do you not see what they do in the cities of Judah and in the streets of Jerusalem? 18[a]The children gather wood, the fathers kindle the fire, and the women knead dough, to make cakes for the queen of heaven; and *they* [b]pour out drink offerings to other gods, that they may provoke Me to anger. 19[a]Do they provoke Me to anger?" says the LORD. "*Do they* not *provoke* themselves, to the shame of their own faces?"

20Therefore thus says the Lord GOD: "Behold, My anger and My fury will be poured out on this place—on man and on beast, on the trees of the field and on the fruit of the ground. And it will burn and not be quenched."

21Thus says the LORD of hosts, the God of Israel: [a]"Add your burnt offerings to your sacrifices and eat meat. 22[a]For I did not speak to your fathers, or command them in the day that I brought them out of the land of Egypt, concerning burnt offerings or sacrifices. 23But this is what I commanded them, saying, [a]'Obey My voice, and [b]I will be your God, and you shall be My people. And walk in all the ways that I have commanded you, that it may be well with you.' 24[a]Yet they did not obey or incline their ear, but [b]followed[1] the counsels *and* the [2]dictates of their evil hearts, and [c]went[3] backward and not forward. 25Since the day that your fathers came out of the land of Egypt until this day, I have even [a]sent to you all My servants the prophets, daily rising up early and sending *them*. 26[a]Yet they did not obey Me or incline their ear, but [b]stiffened their neck. [c]They did worse than their fathers.

27 a Jer. 1:18
28 a Jer. 5:23 b Jer. 9:4 c Ezek. 22:18
30 a Is. 1:22

CHAPTER 7
2 a Jer. 17:19; 26:2
3 a Jer. 4:1; 18:11; 26:13
4 a Mic. 3:11
5 a Jer. 21:12; 22:3 *1 justice*
6 a Deut. 6:14, 15
7 a Deut. 4:40 b Jer. 3:18
8 a Jer. 5:31; 14:13, 14
9 a 1 Kin. 18:21 b Ex. 20:3
10 a Ezek. 23:39 b Jer. 7:11, 14; 32:34; 34:15
11 a Is. 56:7 b Matt. 21:13
12 a Josh. 18:1 b Deut. 12:11 c 1 Sam. 4:10
13 a 2 Chr. 36:15 b Prov. 1:24
14 a 1 Sam. 4:10, 11
15 a 2 Kin. 17:23 b Ps. 78:67
16 a Ex. 32:10; Jer. 11:14 b Jer. 15:1
18 a Jer. 44:17 b Jer. 19:13
19 a Deut. 32:16, 21
21 a Jer. 6:20
22 a [Hos. 6:6]
23 a Deut. 6:3 b [Ex. 19:5, 6]
24 a Ps. 81:11 b Deut. 29:19 c Jer. 32:33 *1 walked in* *2 stubbornness* or *imagination* *3* Lit. *they were*
25 a 2 Chr. 36:15
26 a Jer. 11:8 b Neh. 9:17 c Jer. 16:12

27“Therefore [a]you shall speak all these words to them, but they will not obey you. You shall also call to them, but they will not answer you.

Judgment on Obscene Religion

28“So you shall say to them, ‘This *is* a nation that does not obey the voice of the LORD their God [a]nor receive correction. [b]Truth has perished and has been cut off from their mouth. 29[a]Cut off your hair and cast *it* away, and take up a lamentation on the desolate heights; for the LORD has rejected and forsaken the generation of His wrath.’ 30For the children of Judah have done evil in My sight,” says the LORD. [a]“They have set their abominations in the house which is called by My name, to [1]pollute it. 31And they have built the [a]high places of Tophet, which *is* in the Valley of the Son of Hinnom, to [b]burn their sons and their daughters in the fire, [c]which I did not command, nor did it come into My heart.

32“Therefore behold, [a]the days are coming,” says the LORD, “when it will no more be called Tophet, or the Valley of the Son of Hinnom, but the Valley of Slaughter; [b]for they will bury in Tophet until there is no room. 33The [a]corpses of this people will be food for the birds of the heaven and for the beasts of the earth. And no one will frighten *them away.* 34Then I will cause to [a]cease from the cities of Judah and from the streets of Jerusalem the voice of mirth and the voice of gladness, the voice of the bridegroom and the voice of the bride. For [b]the land shall be desolate.

8 “At that time,” says the LORD, “they shall bring out the bones of the kings of Judah, and the bones of its princes, and the bones of the priests, and the bones of the prophets, and the bones of the inhabitants of Jerusalem, out of their graves. 2They shall spread them before the sun and the moon and all the host of heaven, which they have loved and which they have served and after which they have walked, which they have sought and [a]which they have worshiped. They shall not be gathered [b]nor buried; they shall be like refuse on the face of the earth. 3Then [a]death shall be chosen rather than life by all the [1]residue of those who remain of this evil family, who remain in all the places where I have driven them,” says the LORD of hosts.

The Peril of False Teaching

4“Moreover you shall say to them, ‘Thus says the LORD:

“Will they fall and not rise?
Will one turn away and not return?
5 Why has this people [a]slidden back,
Jerusalem, in a perpetual
backsliding?
[b]They hold fast to deceit,
[c]They refuse to return.
6 [a]I listened and heard,
But they do not speak aright.
[b]No man repented of his wickedness,
Saying, ‘What have I done?’
Everyone turned to his own course,
As the horse rushes into the battle.

7 “Even [a]the stork in the heavens
Knows her appointed times;
And the turtledove, the swift, and
the swallow
Observe the time of their coming.
But [b]My people do not know the
judgment of the LORD.

8 “How can you say, ‘We *are* wise,
[a]And the law of the LORD *is* with
us’?
Look, the false pen of the scribe
certainly works falsehood.
9 [a]The wise men are ashamed,
They are dismayed and taken.
Behold, they have rejected the word
of the LORD;
So [b]what wisdom do they have?
10 Therefore [a]I will give their wives
to others,
And their fields to those who will
inherit *them;*
Because from the least even to the
greatest
Everyone is given to [b]covetousness;
From the prophet even to the priest
Everyone deals falsely.
11 For they have [a]healed the hurt of
the daughter of My people
[1]slightly,
Saying, [b]‘Peace, peace!’
When *there is* no peace.
12 Were they [a]ashamed when they
had committed abomination?
No! They were not at all ashamed,
Nor did they know how to blush.
Therefore they shall fall among
those who fall;
In the time of their punishment
They shall be cast down,” says the
LORD.

---

27 a Ezek. 2:7
28 a Jer. 5:3 b Jer. 9:3
29 a Mic. 1:16
30 a Dan. 9:27; 11:31 *1 defile*
31 a 2 Kin. 23:10 b Ps. 106:38 c Deut. 17:3
32 a Jer. 19:6 b 2 Kin. 23:10
33 a Jer. 9:22; 19:11
34 a Is. 24:7, 8 b Lev. 26:33

CHAPTER 8
2 a 2 Kin. 23:5 b Jer. 22:19
3 a Rev. 9:6 *1 remnant*
5 a Jer. 7:24 b Jer. 9:6 c Jer. 5:3
6 a Ps. 14:2 b Mic. 7:2
7 a Song 2:12 b Jer. 5:4; 9:3
8 a Rom. 2:17
9 a Jer. 6:15 b Jer. 4:22
10 a Deut. 28:30 b Is. 56:11; 57:17
11 a Jer. 6:14 b Ezek. 13:10 *1 Superficially*
12 a Jer. 3:3; 6:15

13 "I will surely [1]consume them," says
the LORD.
"No grapes *shall be* [a]on the vine,
Nor figs on the [b]fig tree,
And the leaf shall fade;
And *the things* I have given them
shall [c]pass away from them." ' "

14 "Why do we sit still?
[a]Assemble yourselves,
And let us enter the fortified cities,
And let us be silent there.
For the LORD our God has put us to
silence
And given us [b]water[1] of gall to
drink,
Because we have sinned against the
LORD.

15 "*We* [a]looked for peace, but no good
came;
And for a time of health, and there
was trouble!
16 The snorting of His horses was
heard from [a]Dan.
The whole land trembled at the
sound of the neighing of His
[b]strong ones;
For they have come and devoured
the land and all that is in it,
The city and those who dwell in it."

17 "For behold, I will send serpents
among you,
Vipers which cannot be [a]charmed,
And they shall bite you," says the
LORD.

The Prophet Mourns for the People

18 I would comfort myself in sorrow;
My heart *is* faint in me.
19 Listen! The voice,
The cry of the daughter of my
people
From [a]a far country:
"*Is* not the LORD in Zion?
Is not her King in her?"

"Why have they provoked Me to
anger
With their carved images—
With foreign idols?"

20 "The harvest is past,
The summer is ended,
And we are not saved!"

21 [a]For the hurt of the daughter of
my people I am hurt.
I am [b]mourning;
Astonishment has taken hold of me.
22 *Is there* no [a]balm in Gilead,
Is there no physician there?
Why then is there no recovery
For the health of the daughter of
my people?

9 Oh, [a]that my head were waters,
And my eyes a fountain of tears,
That I might weep day and night
For the slain of the daughter of my
people!
2 Oh, that I had in the wilderness
A lodging place for travelers;
That I might leave my people,
And go from them!
For [a]they *are* all adulterers,
An assembly of treacherous men.

3 "And *like* their bow [a]they have bent
their tongues *for* lies.
They are not valiant for the truth
on the earth.
For they proceed from [b]evil to evil,
And they [c]do not know Me," says
the LORD.
4 "Everyone[a] take heed to his
[1]neighbor,
And do not trust any brother;
For every brother will utterly
supplant,
And every neighbor will [b]walk with
slanderers.
5 Everyone will [a]deceive his
neighbor,
And will not speak the truth;
They have taught their tongue to
speak lies;
They weary themselves to commit
iniquity.
6 Your dwelling place *is* in the midst
of deceit;
Through deceit they refuse to know
Me," says the LORD.

7 Therefore thus says the LORD of hosts:

"Behold, [a]I will refine them and [1]try
them;
[b]For how shall I deal with the
daughter of My people?
8 Their tongue *is* an arrow shot out;
It speaks [a]deceit;
One speaks [b]peaceably to his
neighbor with his mouth,
But [1]in his heart he [2]lies in wait.
9 [a]Shall I not punish them for these
things?" says the LORD.
"Shall I not avenge Myself on such a
nation as this?"

---

13 a Joel 1:17 b Matt. 21:19 c Deut. 28:39, 40 *1 Or take them away*
14 a Jer. 4:5 b Jer. 9:15 *1 Bitter or poisonous water*
15 a Jer. 14:19
16 a Jer. 4:15 b Jer. 47:3
17 a Ps. 58:4, 5
19 a Is. 39:3
21 a Jer. 9:1 b Joel 2:6
22 a Jer. 46:11

CHAPTER 9
1 a Is. 22:4
2 a Jer. 5:7, 8; 23:10
3 a Ps. 64:3 b Jer. 4:22; 13:23 c 1 Sam. 2:12
4 a Mic. 7:5, 6 b Jer. 6:28 *1 friend*
5 a Is. 59:4
7 a Is. 1:25 b Hos. 11:8 *1 test*
8 a Ps. 12:2 b Ps. 55:21 *1 Inwardly he 2 sets his ambush*
9 a Jer. 5:9, 29

10 I will take up a weeping and
wailing for the mountains,
And [a]for the [1]dwelling places of the
wilderness a lamentation,
Because they are burned up,
So that no one can pass through;
Nor can *men* hear the voice of the
cattle.
[b]Both the birds of the heavens and
the beasts have fled;
They are gone.

11 "I will make Jerusalem [a]a heap of
ruins, [b]a den of jackals.
I will make the cities of Judah
desolate, without an inhabitant."

12 [a]Who *is* the wise man who may understand this? And *who is he* to whom the
mouth of the LORD has spoken, that he
may declare it? Why does the land perish
and burn up like a wilderness, so that no
one can pass through?
13 And the LORD said, "Because they
have forsaken My law which I set before
them, and have [a]not obeyed My voice, nor
walked according to it, 14 but they have
[a]walked according to the [1]dictates of their
own hearts and after the Baals, [b]which
their fathers taught them," 15 therefore
thus says the LORD of hosts, the God of
Israel: "Behold, I will [a]feed them, this
people, [b]with wormwood, and give them
[1]water of gall to drink. 16 I will [a]scatter
them also among the Gentiles, whom neither they nor their fathers have known.
[b]And I will send a sword after them until
I have consumed them."

The People Mourn in Judgment

17 Thus says the LORD of hosts:

"Consider and call for [a]the
mourning women,
That they may come;
And send for skillful wailing
women,
That they may come.
18 Let them make haste
And take up a wailing for us,
That [a]our eyes may run with tears,
And our eyelids gush with water.
19 For a voice of wailing is heard
from Zion:
'How we are plundered!
We are greatly ashamed,
Because we have forsaken the land,

10 [a]Hos. 4:3 [b]Jer. 4:25 [1]Or *pastures*
11 [a]Is. 25:2 [b]Is. 13:22; 34:13
12 [a]Hos. 14:9
13 [a]Jer. 3:25; 7:24
14 [a]Jer. 7:24; 11:8 [b]Gal. 1:14 [1]*stubbornness* or *imagination*
15 [a]Ps. 80:5 [b]Lam. 3:15 [1]Bitter or poisonous water
16 [a]Lev. 26:33 [b]Ezek. 5:2
17 [a]2 Chr. 35:25
18 [a]Jer. 9:1; 14:17
19 [a]Lev. 18:28
21 [a]Jer. 6:11; 18:21 [1]Lit. *from outside* [2]Lit. *from the square*
22 [a]Jer. 8:1, 2
23 [a][Eccl. 9:11] [b]Ps. 33:16–18
24 [a]1 Cor. 1:31 [b]Mic. 7:18 [1]*justice*

Because we have been cast out of
[a]our dwellings.' "
20 Yet hear the word of the LORD,
O women,
And let your ear receive the word of
His mouth;
Teach your daughters wailing,
And everyone her neighbor a
lamentation.
21 For death has come through our
windows,
Has entered our palaces,
To kill off [a]the children—[1]*no
longer to be* outside!
And the young men—[2]*no longer*
on the streets!

22 Speak, "Thus says the LORD:
'Even the carcasses of men shall fall
[a]as refuse on the open field,
Like cuttings after the harvester,
And no one shall gather *them*.' "

23 Thus says the LORD:

[a]"Let not the wise *man* glory in his
wisdom,
Let not the mighty *man* glory in
his [b]might,
Nor let the rich *man* glory in his
riches;
24 But [a]let him who glories glory in
this,
That he understands and knows Me,
That I *am* the LORD, exercising
lovingkindness, [1]judgment, and
righteousness in the earth.
[b]For in these I delight," says the
LORD.

May ____ be wise and not glory in their wisdom, might, or riches, but let them glory in understanding and knowing You, O God, that You are the Lord, exercising lovingkindness, judgment, and righteousness in the earth, for in these You delight.

FROM JEREMIAH 9:23, 24

JEREMIAH 9:17

Dear Woman of Destiny,

In reflecting upon Jeremiah 9:17, I am reminded of a wonderful "divine appointment." Through a unique set of circumstances, I found myself, along with two other pastors' wives from America, preparing for a trip to Kishinev, Moldova. We were to be part of an intercessory prayer support team with an international messianic outreach ministry.

Moldova is a small country in the former USSR. In the short time I had before leaving, I endeavored to learn as much as I could about the intended ministry and specifically about the nation of Moldova. Except for the geographical location I had found on a world map and a sketchy description of our duties, I did not know what to expect. However I became greatly stirred upon hearing from the intercession coordinator. She had discovered that she would be traveling without her usual American intercessors, but the Lord gave her Jeremiah 9:17, "Call for the mourning women."

In obedience to the Word, she began to pray for these women to join the team. Without any previous knowledge of one another, the Lord graciously answered; and we quickly bonded and set out on our God-ordained adventure.

Jeremiah 9:17's request seems to be a curious one; but upon examining the entire context, I became quite excited when I learned the history of the city the crusade would be held in. The Jewish citizens of Kishinev had experienced terrible persecution during the Holocaust, and all but a few of the Jewish people had been executed. The once thriving Jewish community of 250,000 had been reduced to approximately five hundred who had managed to escape. These same people then had had to endure decades of hardship under the communist regime. Now, after many years, some of these same people were hearing of Yeshua their Messiah for the first time.

One evening of the crusade would be dedicated to honoring the families and survivors of the Holocaust atrocities. The meetings were being held in a large outdoor arena, and the staff had cordoned off a section for these special guests. After the messianic ministry performed traditional dances and Jewish songs, affirming that to embrace Yeshua would not compromise their Jewish culture, the simple gospel was presented. Approximately 75 to 85 percent received salvation; and while we prayed for the people who came forward, many tears were shed.

I know we were not the first "mourning women" that God has called to intercede on behalf of this nation. No doubt there have been many closeted mourners, weeping and wailing through the decades for God to intervene. We serve a God who not only hears but answers prayer in His perfect timing. The psalmist wrote wonderful words of encouragement for us in Psalm 126:6, "He who continually goes forth weeping, bearing seed for sowing, shall doubtless come again with rejoicing, bringing his sheaves with him."

Lila Terhune

[25]"Behold, the days are coming," says
the LORD, "that [a]I will punish all *who are*
circumcised with the uncircumcised—
[26]Egypt, Judah, Edom, the people of
Ammon, Moab, and all *who are* in the
[a]farthest corners, who dwell in the
wilderness. For all *these* nations *are* uncircumcised, and all the house of Israel
are [b]uncircumcised in the heart."

Idols and the True God

10 Hear the word which the LORD speaks to you, O house of Israel.

[2]Thus says the LORD:

[a]"Do not learn the way of the
Gentiles;
Do not be dismayed at the signs of
heaven,
For the Gentiles are dismayed at
them.
3 For the customs of the peoples *are*
[1]futile;
For [a]*one* cuts a tree from the
forest,
The work of the hands of the
workman, with the ax.
4 They decorate it with silver and
gold;
They [a]fasten it with nails and
hammers
So that it will not topple.
5 They *are* upright, like a palm tree,
And [a]they cannot speak;
They must be [b]carried,
Because they cannot go *by*
themselves.
Do not be afraid of them,
For [c]they cannot do evil,
Nor can they do any good."

6 Inasmuch as *there is* none [a]like
You, O LORD
(You *are* great, and Your name *is*
great in might),
7 [a]Who would not fear You, O King of
the nations?
For this is Your rightful due.
For [b]among all the wise *men* of the
nations,
And in all their kingdoms,
There is none like You.
8 But they are altogether
[a]dull-hearted and foolish;
A wooden idol *is* a [1]worthless
doctrine.
9 Silver is beaten into plates;
It is brought from Tarshish,
And [a]gold from Uphaz,
The work of the craftsman
And of the hands of the metalsmith;
Blue and purple *are* their clothing;
They *are* all [b]the work of skillful
men.
10 But the LORD *is* the true God;
He *is* [a]the living God and the
[b]everlasting King.
At His wrath the earth will tremble,
And the nations will not be able to
endure His indignation.

[11]Thus you shall say to them: [a]"The
gods that have not made the heavens and
the earth [b]shall perish from the earth and
from under these heavens."

12 He [a]has made the earth by His
power,
He has [b]established the world by
His wisdom,
And [c]has stretched out the heavens
at His discretion.
13 [a]When He utters His voice,
There is a [1]multitude of waters in
the heavens:
[b]"And He causes the vapors to ascend
from the ends of the earth.
He makes lightning for the rain,
He brings the wind out of His
treasuries."
14 [a]Everyone is [b]dull-hearted, without
knowledge;
[c]Every metalsmith is put to shame
by an image;
[d]For his molded image *is* falsehood,
And *there is* no breath in them.
15 They *are* futile, a work of errors;
In the time of their punishment
they shall perish.
16 [a]The Portion of Jacob *is* not like
them,
For He *is* the Maker of all *things,*
And [b]Israel *is* the tribe of His
inheritance;
[c]The LORD of hosts *is* His name.

The Coming Captivity of Judah

17 [a]Gather up your wares from the
land,
O [1]inhabitant of the fortress!

[18]For thus says the LORD:

"Behold, I will [a]throw out at this
time
The inhabitants of the land,

25 a [Rom. 2:28, 29]
26 a Jer. 25:23 b [Rom. 2:28]
CHAPTER 10
2 a [Lev. 18:3; 20:23]
3 a Is. 40:19; 45:20 *1* Lit. *vanity*
4 a Is. 41:7
5 a Ps. 115:5 b Ps. 115:7 c Is. 41:23, 24
6 a Ex. 15:11
7 a Rev. 15:4 b Ps. 89:6
8 a Hab. 2:18 *1 vain teaching*
9 a Dan. 10:5 b Ps. 115:4
10 a 1 Tim. 6:17 b Ps. 10:16
11 a Ps. 96:5 b Zeph. 2:11
12 a Jer. 51:15 b Ps. 93:1 c Job 9:8
13 a Job 38:34 b Ps. 135:7 *1* Or *noise*
14 a Jer. 51:17 b Prov. 30:2 c Is. 42:17; 44:11 d Hab. 2:18
16 a Lam. 3:24 b Deut. 32:9 c Is. 47:4
17 a Jer. 6:1 *1* Or *you who dwell under siege*
18 a 1 Sam. 25:29

And will distress them,
[b]That they may find *it so.*"

19 [a]Woe is me for my hurt!
My wound is severe.
But I say, [b]"Truly this *is* an infirmity,
And [c]I must bear it."
20 [a]My tent is plundered,
And all my cords are broken;
My children have gone from me,
And they *are* [b]no more.
There is no one to pitch my tent anymore,
Or set up my curtains.

21 For the shepherds have become dull-hearted,
And have not sought the LORD;
Therefore they shall not prosper,
And all their flocks shall be [a]scattered.
22 Behold, the noise of the report has come,
And a great commotion out of the [a]north country,
To make the cities of Judah desolate, a [b]den of jackals.

23 O LORD, I know the [a]way of man *is* not in himself;
It is not in man who walks to direct his own steps.
24 O LORD, [a]correct me, but with justice;
Not in Your anger, lest You bring me to nothing.
25 [a]Pour out Your fury on the Gentiles, [b]who do not know You,
And on the families who do not call on Your name;
For they have eaten up Jacob,
[c]Devoured him and consumed him,
And made his dwelling place desolate.

The Broken Covenant

11 The word that came to Jeremiah
from the LORD, saying, [2]"Hear the
words of this covenant, and speak to the
men of Judah and to the inhabitants of
Jerusalem; [3]and say to them, 'Thus says
the LORD God of Israel: [a]"Cursed *is* the
man who does not obey the words of this
covenant [4]which I commanded your fathers in the day I brought them out of the
land of Egypt, [a]from the iron furnace, saying, [b]'Obey My voice, and do according to
all that I command you; so shall you be
My people, and I will be your God,' [5]that
I may establish the [a]oath which I have
sworn to your fathers, to give them [b]'a
land flowing with milk and honey,' as *it is*
this day." ' "
And I answered and said, [1]"So be it,
LORD."
[6]Then the LORD said to me, "Proclaim
all these words in the cities of Judah and
in the streets of Jerusalem, saying: 'Hear
the words of this covenant [a]and do them.
[7]For I earnestly exhorted your fathers in
the day I brought them up out of the land
of Egypt, until this day, [a]rising early and
exhorting, saying, "Obey My voice." [8][a]Yet
they did not obey or incline their ear, but
[b]everyone [1]followed the dictates of his
evil heart; therefore I will bring upon
them all the words of this covenant,
which I commanded *them* to do, but
which they have not done.' "
[9]And the LORD said to me, [a]"A conspiracy has been found among the men of Judah and among the inhabitants of
Jerusalem. [10]They have turned back to
[a]the iniquities of their forefathers who refused to hear My words, and they have
gone after other gods to serve them; the
house of Israel and the house of Judah
have broken My covenant which I made
with their fathers."
[11]Therefore thus says the LORD: "Behold, I will surely bring calamity on them
which they will not be able to [1]escape; and
[a]though they cry out to Me, I will not listen to them. [12]Then the cities of Judah
and the inhabitants of Jerusalem will go
and [a]cry out to the gods to whom they
offer incense, but they will not save them
at all in the time of their trouble. [13]For
according to the number of your [a]cities
were your gods, O Judah; and *according
to* the number of the streets of Jerusalem
you have set up altars to *that* shameful
thing, altars to burn incense to Baal.
[14]"So [a]do not pray for this people, or lift
up a cry or prayer for them; for I will not
hear *them* in the time that they cry out to
Me because of their trouble.

15 "What[a] has My beloved to do in My house,
Having [b]done lewd deeds with many?
And [c]the holy flesh has passed from you.
When you do evil, then you [d]rejoice.
16 The LORD called your name,

18 [b]Ezek. 6:10
19 [a]Jer. 8:21 [b]Ps. 77:10 [c]Mic. 7:9
20 [a]Jer. 4:20 [b]Jer. 31:15
21 [a]Jer. 23:2
22 [a]Jer. 5:15 [b]Jer. 9:11
23 [a]Prov. 16:1; 20:24
24 [a]Jer. 30:11
25 [a]Ps. 79:6, 7 [b]Job 18:21 [c]Jer. 8:16

CHAPTER 11
3 [a]Deut. 27:26
4 [a]Deut. 4:20 [b]Lev. 26:3
5 [a]Ps. 105:9 [b]Ex. 3:8 [1]Heb. *Amen*
6 [a][Rom. 2:13]
7 [a]Jer. 35:15
8 [a]Jer. 7:26 [b]Jer. 13:10 [1]*walked in the stubbornness* or *imagination*
9 [a]Ezek. 22:25
10 [a]Ezek. 20:18
11 [a]Prov. 1:28 [1]Lit. *go out*
12 [a]Deut. 32:37
13 [a]Jer. 2:28
14 [a]Ex. 32:10
15 [a]Ps. 50:16 [b]Ezek. 16:25 [c][Titus 1:15] [d]Prov. 2:14

[a]Green Olive Tree, Lovely *and* of
Good Fruit.
With the noise of a great tumult
He has kindled fire on it,
And its branches are broken.

17"For the LORD of hosts, [a]who planted
you, has pronounced doom against you
for the evil of the house of Israel and of
the house of Judah, which they have done
against themselves to provoke Me to anger in offering incense to Baal."

Jeremiah's Life Threatened

18Now the LORD gave me knowledge *of*
it, and I know *it;* for You showed me their
doings. 19But I *was* like a docile lamb
brought to the slaughter; and I did not
know that they had devised schemes
against me, *saying,* "Let us destroy the
tree with its fruit, [a]and let us cut him off
from [b]the land of the living, that his name
may be remembered no more."

20 But, O LORD of hosts,
You who judge righteously,
[a]Testing the [1]mind and the heart,
Let me see Your [b]vengeance on
them,
For to You I have revealed my
cause.

21"Therefore thus says the LORD concerning the men of [a]Anathoth who seek
your life, saying, [b]'Do not prophesy in the
name of the LORD, lest you die by our
hand'— 22therefore thus says the LORD of
hosts: 'Behold, I will punish them. The
young men shall die by the sword, their
sons and their daughters shall [a]die by
famine; 23and there shall be no remnant
of them, for I will bring catastrophe on
the men of Anathoth, *even* [a]the year of
their punishment.' "

Jeremiah's Question

12 Righteous [a]*are* You, O LORD,
when I plead with You;
Yet let me talk with You about
Your judgments.
[b]Why does the way of the wicked
prosper?
Why are those happy who deal so
treacherously?
2 You have planted them, yes, they
have taken root;
They grow, yes, they bear fruit.
[a]You *are* near in their mouth
But far from their [1]mind.

16 a Ps. 52:8
17 a Is. 5:2
19 a Ps. 83:4 b Ps. 27:13
20 a Ps. 7:9 b Jer. 15:15 *1* Most secret parts, lit. *kidneys*
21 a Jer. 1:1; 12:5, 6 b Mic. 2:6
22 a Jer. 9:21
23 a Jer. 23:12

CHAPTER 12
1 a Ps. 51:4 b Mal. 3:15
2 a Matt. 15:8 *1* Most secret parts, lit. *kidneys*
3 a Ps. 17:3 b Jer. 11:20 c James 5:5
4 a Hos. 4:3 b Jer. 9:10 c Ps. 107:34
5 a Josh. 3:15 *1* Or *thicket*
6 a Jer. 9:4, 5 b Prov. 26:25 *1* Or *abundantly* *2* Lit. *good*
8 a Hos. 9:15
9 a Lev. 26:22 *1 inheritance*
10 a Jer. 6:3; 23:1 b Is. 5:1–7 c Is. 63:18 *1* Lit. *shepherds* or *pastors* *2 desired portion* of land

3 But You, O LORD, [a]know me;
You have seen me,
And You have [b]tested my heart
toward You.
Pull them out like sheep for the
slaughter,
And prepare them for [c]the day of
slaughter.
4 How long will [a]the land mourn,
And the herbs of every field wither?
[b]The beasts and birds are consumed,
[c]For the wickedness of those who
dwell there,
Because they said, "He will not see
our final end."

The LORD Answers Jeremiah

5 "If you have run with the footmen,
and they have wearied you,
Then how can you contend with
horses?
And *if* in the land of peace,
In which you trusted, *they wearied*
you,
Then how will you do in [a]the
[1]floodplain of the Jordan?
6 For even [a]your brothers, the house
of your father,
Even they have dealt treacherously
with you;
Yes, they have called [1]a multitude
after you.
[b]Do not believe them,
Even though they speak [2]smooth
words to you.

7 "I have forsaken My house, I have
left My heritage;
I have given the dearly beloved of
My soul into the hand of her
enemies.
8 My heritage is to Me like a lion in
the forest;
It cries out against Me;
Therefore I have [a]hated it.
9 My [1]heritage *is* to Me *like* a
speckled vulture;
The vultures all around *are* against
her.
Come, assemble all the beasts of
the field,
[a]Bring them to devour!
10 "Many [a]rulers[1] have destroyed [b]My
vineyard,
They have [c]trodden My portion
underfoot;
They have made My [2]pleasant
portion a desolate wilderness.

11 They have made it [a]desolate;
Desolate, it mourns to Me;
The whole land is made desolate,
Because [b]no one takes *it* to heart.
12 The plunderers have come
On all the desolate heights in the wilderness,
For the sword of the LORD shall devour
From *one* end of the land to the *other* end of the land;
No flesh shall have peace.
13 [a]They have sown wheat but reaped thorns;
They have [1]put themselves to pain *but* do not profit.
But be ashamed of your harvest
Because of the fierce anger of the LORD."

14Thus says the LORD: "Against all My evil neighbors who [a]touch the inheritance which I have caused My people Israel to inherit—behold, I will [b]pluck them out of their land and pluck out the house of Judah from among them. 15[a]Then it shall be, after I have plucked them out, that I will return and have compassion on them [b]and bring them back, everyone to his heritage and everyone to his land. 16And it shall be, if they will learn carefully the ways of My people, [a]to swear by My name, 'As the LORD lives,' as they taught My people to swear by Baal, then they shall be [b]established in the midst of My people. 17But if they do not [a]obey, I will utterly pluck up and destroy that nation," says the LORD.

Symbol of the Linen Sash

13 Thus the LORD said to me: "Go and get yourself a linen sash, and put it [1]around your waist, but do not put it in water." 2So I got a [1]sash according to the word of the LORD, and put *it* around my waist.

3And the word of the LORD came to me the second time, saying, 4"Take the [1]sash that you acquired, which *is* [2]around your waist, and arise, go to the [3]Euphrates, and hide it there in a hole in the rock." 5So I went and hid it by the Euphrates, as the LORD commanded me.

6Now it came to pass after many days that the LORD said to me, "Arise, go to the Euphrates, and take from there the sash which I commanded you to hide there." 7Then I went to the Euphrates and dug, and I took the [1]sash from the place where I had hidden it; and there was the sash, ruined. It was profitable for nothing.

8Then the word of the LORD came to me, saying, 9"Thus says the LORD: 'In this manner [a]I will ruin the pride of Judah and the great [b]pride of Jerusalem. 10This evil people, who [a]refuse to hear My words, who [b]follow[1] the dictates of their hearts, and walk after other gods to serve them and worship them, shall be just like this sash which is profitable for nothing. 11For as the sash clings to the waist of a man, so I have caused the whole house of Israel and the whole house of Judah to cling to Me,' says the LORD, 'that [a]they may become My people, [b]for renown, for praise, and for [c]glory; but they would [d]not hear.'

Symbol of the Wine Bottles

12"Therefore you shall speak to them this word: 'Thus says the LORD God of Israel: "Every bottle shall be filled with wine." '

"And they will say to you, 'Do we not certainly know that every bottle will be filled with wine?'

13"Then you shall say to them, 'Thus says the LORD: "Behold, I will fill all the inhabitants of this land—even the kings who sit on David's throne, the priests, the prophets, and all the inhabitants of Jerusalem—[a]with drunkenness! 14And [a]I will dash them [1]one against another, even the fathers and the sons together," says the LORD. "I will not pity nor spare nor have mercy, but will destroy them." ' "

Pride Precedes Captivity

15 Hear and give ear:
Do not be proud,
For the LORD has spoken.
16 [a]Give glory to the LORD your God
Before He causes [b]darkness,
And before your feet stumble
On the dark mountains,
And while you are [c]looking for light,
He turns it into [d]the shadow of death
And makes *it* dense darkness.
17 But if you will not hear it,
My soul will [a]weep in secret for *your* pride;
My eyes will weep bitterly
And run down with tears,
Because the LORD's flock has been taken captive.

---

11 a Jer. 10:22; 22:6 b Is. 42:25
13 a Hag. 1:6 1 Or *strained*
14 a Zech. 2:8 b Deut. 30:3
15 a Ezek. 28:25 b Amos 9:14
16 a [Jer. 4:2] b [1 Pet. 2:5]
17 a Is. 60:12

CHAPTER 13
1 1 Lit. *upon your loins*
2 1 *waistband*
4 1 *waistband* 2 Lit. *upon your loins* 3 Heb. *Perath*
7 1 *waistband*
9 a Lev. 26:19 b Zeph. 3:11
10 a Jer. 16:12 b Jer. 7:24; 16:12 1 *walk in the stubbornness or imagination*
11 a [Ex. 19:5, 6] b Jer. 33:9 c Is. 43:21 d Jer. 7:13, 24, 26
13 a Is. 51:17; 63:6
14 a Jer. 19:9–11 1 Lit. *a man against his brother*
16 a Josh. 7:19 b Amos 8:9 c Is. 59:9 d Ps. 44:19
17 a Jer. 9:1; 14:17

18 Say to [a]the king and to the queen
mother,
"Humble yourselves;
Sit down,
For your rule shall collapse, the
crown of your glory."
19 The cities of the South shall be
shut up,
And no one shall open *them;*
Judah shall be carried away captive,
all of it;
It shall be wholly carried away
captive.

20 Lift up your eyes and see
Those who come from the [a]north.
Where *is* the flock *that* was given
to you,
Your beautiful sheep?
21 What will you say when He
punishes you?
For you have taught them
To be chieftains, to be head over
you.
Will not [a]pangs seize you,
Like a woman in [1]labor?
22 And if you say in your heart,
[a]"Why have these things come upon
me?"
For the greatness of your iniquity
[b]Your skirts have been uncovered,
Your heels [1]made bare.
23 Can the Ethiopian change his skin
or the leopard its spots?
Then may you also do good who
are accustomed to do evil.

24 "Therefore I will [a]scatter them
[b]like stubble
That passes away by the wind of the
wilderness.
25 [a]This is your lot,
The portion of your measures from
Me," says the LORD,
"Because you have forgotten Me
And trusted in [b]falsehood.
26 Therefore [a]I will uncover your
skirts over your face,
That your shame may appear.
27 I have seen your adulteries
And your *lustful* [a]neighings,
The lewdness of your harlotry,
Your abominations [b]on the hills in
the fields.
Woe to you, O Jerusalem!
Will you still not be made clean?"

18 a Jer. 22:26
20 a Jer. 10:22; 46:20
21 a Jer. 6:24 *1 childbirth*
22 a Jer. 16:10 b Is. 47:2 *1* Lit. *suffer violence*
24 a Jer. 9:16 b Hos. 13:3
25 a Job 20:29 b Jer. 10:14
26 a Lam. 1:8
27 a Jer. 5:7, 8 b Is. 65:7; Ezek. 6:13
CHAPTER 14
2 a Is. 3:26 b Jer. 8:21 c 1 Sam. 5:12
3 a Ps. 40:14 b 2 Sam. 15:30
4 a Jer. 3:3
5 *1 abandoned* her young
6 a Jer. 2:24
7 a Ps. 25:11
8 a Jer. 17:13
9 a Is. 59:1 b Ex. 29:45
10 a Jer. 2:23–25

Sword, Famine, and Pestilence

14 The word of the LORD that came
to Jeremiah concerning the
droughts.

2 "Judah mourns,
And [a]her gates languish;
They [b]mourn for the land,
And [c]the cry of Jerusalem has gone
up.
3 Their nobles have sent their lads
for water;
They went to the cisterns *and*
found no water.
They returned with their vessels
empty;
They were [a]ashamed and
confounded
[b]And covered their heads.
4 Because the ground is parched,
For there was [a]no rain in the land,
The plowmen were ashamed;
They covered their heads.
5 Yes, the deer also gave birth in the
field,
But [1]left because there was no
grass.
6 And [a]the wild donkeys stood in the
desolate heights;
They sniffed at the wind like
jackals;
Their eyes failed because *there was*
no grass."

7 O LORD, though our iniquities
testify against us,
Do it [a]for Your name's sake;
For our backslidings are many,
We have sinned against You.
8 [a]O the Hope of Israel, his Savior in
time of trouble,
Why should You be like a stranger
in the land,
And like a traveler *who* turns aside
to tarry for a night?
9 Why should You be like a man
astonished,
Like a mighty one [a]*who* cannot
save?
Yet You, O LORD, [b]*are* in our midst,
And we are called by Your name;
Do not leave us!

10 Thus says the LORD to this people:
[a]"Thus they have loved to wander;
They have not restrained their feet.

Therefore the LORD does not accept
them;
[b]He will remember their iniquity
now,
And punish their sins."

11 Then the LORD said to me, [a]"Do not
pray for this people, for *their* good.
12 [a]When they fast, I will not hear their
cry; and [b]when they offer burnt offering
and grain offering, I will not accept them.
But [c]I will consume them by the sword,
by the famine, and by the pestilence."
13 [a]Then I said, "Ah, Lord GOD! Behold,
the prophets say to them, 'You shall not
see the sword, nor shall you have famine,
but I will give you [1]assured [b]peace in this
place.' "
14 And the LORD said to me, [a]"The
prophets prophesy lies in My name. [b]I
have not sent them, commanded them,
nor spoken to them; they prophesy to you
a false vision, [1]divination, a worthless
thing, and the [c]deceit of their heart.
15 Therefore thus says the LORD concerning the prophets who prophesy in My
name, whom I did not send, [a]and who say,
'Sword and famine shall not be in this
land'—'By sword and famine those
prophets shall be consumed! 16 And the
people to whom they prophesy shall be
cast out in the streets of Jerusalem because of the famine and the sword; [a]they
will have no one to bury them—them nor
their wives, their sons nor their daughters—for I will pour their wickedness on
them.'
17 "Therefore you shall say this word to
them:

[a]'Let my eyes flow with tears night
and day,
And let them not cease;
[b]For the virgin daughter of my
people
Has been broken with a mighty
stroke, with a very severe blow.
18 If I go out to [a]the field,
Then behold, those slain with the
sword!
And if I enter the city,
Then behold, those sick from
famine!
Yes, both prophet and [b]priest go
about in a land they do not
know.' "

10 [b]Hos. 8:13
11 [a]Ex. 32:10
12 [a]Ezek. 8:18 [b]Jer. 6:20 [c]Jer. 9:16
13 [a]Jer. 4:10 [b]Jer. 8:11; 23:17 [1]*true*
14 [a]Jer. 27:10 [b]Jer. 29:8, 9 [c]Jer. 23:16 [1]Telling the future by signs and omens
15 [a]Ezek. 14:10
16 [a]Ps. 79:2, 3
17 [a]Jer. 9:1; 13:17 [b]Jer. 8:21
18 [a]Ezek. 7:15 [b]Jer. 23:11
19 [a]Lam. 5:22 [b]Jer. 15:18 [c]Jer. 8:15
20 [a]Jer. 3:25 [b]Dan. 9:8
21 [a]Ps. 106:45
22 [a]Zech. 10:1 [b]Deut. 32:21 [c]Jer. 5:24 [d]Ps. 135:7

CHAPTER 15
1 [a]Ezek. 14:14 [b]Ex. 32:11–14 [c]1 Sam. 7:9 [1]Lit. *soul was not toward*
2 [a]Zech. 11:9 [b]Jer. 9:16; 16:13
3 [a]Ezek. 14:21 [b]Jer. 7:33
4 [a]Deut. 28:25 [b]2 Kin. 24:3, 4

The People Plead for Mercy

19 [a]Have You utterly rejected Judah?
Has Your soul loathed Zion?
Why have You stricken us so that
[b]*there is* no healing for us?
[c]We looked for peace, but *there was*
no good;
And for the time of healing, and
there was trouble.
20 We acknowledge, O LORD, our
wickedness
And the iniquity of our [a]fathers,
For [b]we have sinned against You.
21 Do not abhor *us,* for Your name's
sake;
Do not disgrace the throne of Your
glory.
[a]Remember, do not break Your
covenant with us.
22 [a]Are there any among [b]the idols of
the nations that can cause [c]rain?
Or can the heavens give showers?
[d]*Are* You not He, O LORD our God?
Therefore we will wait for You,
Since You have made all these.

The Lord Will Not Relent

15 Then the LORD said to me, [a]"*Even*
if [b]Moses and [c]Samuel stood before Me, My [1]mind *would* not *be* favorable
toward this people. Cast *them* out of My
sight, and let them go forth. 2 And it shall
be, if they say to you, 'Where should we
go?' then you shall tell them, 'Thus says
the LORD:

[a]"Such as *are* for death, to death;
And such as *are* for the sword, to
the sword;
And such as *are* for the famine, to
the famine;
And such as *are* for the [b]captivity,
to the captivity." '

3 "And I will [a]appoint over them four
forms *of destruction,*" says the LORD: "the
sword to slay, the dogs to drag, [b]the birds
of the heavens and the beasts of the earth
to devour and destroy. 4 I will hand them
over to [a]trouble, to all kingdoms of the
earth, because of [b]Manasseh the son of
Hezekiah, king of Judah, for what he did
in Jerusalem.

5 "For who will have pity on you,
O Jerusalem?
Or who will bemoan you?
Or who will turn aside to ask how
you are doing?

6 [a]You have forsaken Me," says the
LORD,
"You have [b]gone backward.
Therefore I will stretch out My
hand against you and destroy
you;
[c]I am [1]weary of relenting!
7 And I will winnow them with a
winnowing fan in the gates of
the land;
I will [a]bereave *them* of children;
I will destroy My people,
Since they [b]do not return from
their ways.
8 Their widows will be increased to
Me more than the sand of the
seas;
I will bring against them,
Against the mother of the young
men,
A plunderer at noonday;
I will cause anguish and terror to
fall on them [a]suddenly.

9 "She[a] languishes who has borne
seven;
She has breathed her last;
[b]Her sun has gone down
While *it was* yet day;
She has been ashamed and
confounded.
And the remnant of them I will
deliver to the sword
Before their enemies," says the
LORD.

Jeremiah's Dejection

10 [a]Woe is me, my mother,
That you have borne me,
A man of strife and a man of
contention to the whole [1]earth!
I have neither lent for interest,
Nor have men lent to me for
interest.
Every one of them curses me.

11 The LORD said:

"Surely it will be well with your
remnant;
Surely I will cause [a]the enemy to
intercede with you
In the time of adversity and in the
time of affliction.
12 Can anyone break iron,
The northern iron and the bronze?
13 Your wealth and your treasures
I will give as [a]plunder without
price,
Because of all your sins,
Throughout your territories.
14 And I will [1]make *you* cross over
with your enemies
[a]Into a land *which* you do not know;
For a [b]fire is kindled in My anger,
Which shall burn upon you."

15 O LORD, [a]You know;
Remember me and [1]visit me,
And [b]take vengeance for me on my
persecutors.
In Your enduring patience, do not
take me away.
Know that [c]for Your sake I have
suffered rebuke.
16 Your words were found, and I [a]ate
them,
And [b]Your word was to me the joy
and rejoicing of my heart;
For I am called by Your name,
O LORD God of hosts.
17 [a]I did not sit in the assembly of the
mockers,
Nor did I rejoice;
I sat alone because of Your hand,
For You have filled me with
indignation.
18 Why is my [a]pain perpetual
And my wound incurable,
Which refuses to be healed?
Will You surely be to me [b]like an
unreliable stream,
As waters *that* [1]fail?

The LORD Reassures Jeremiah

19 Therefore thus says the LORD:

[a]"If you return,
Then I will bring you back;
You shall [b]stand before Me;
If you [c]take out the precious from
the vile,
You shall be as My mouth.
Let them return to you,
But you must not return to them.
20 And I will make you to this people
a fortified bronze [a]wall;
And they will fight against you,
But [b]they shall not prevail against
you;
For I *am* with you to save you
And deliver you," says the LORD.
21 "I will deliver you from the hand of
the wicked,
And I will redeem you from the
grip of the terrible."

6 [a]Jer. 2:13 [b]Jer. 7:24 [c]Jer. 20:16 [1]*tired*
7 [a]Jer. 18:21 [b]Is. 9:13
8 [a]Is. 29:5
9 [a]1 Sam. 2:5 [b]Amos 8:9
10 [a]Job 3:1 [1]Or *land*
11 [a]Jer. 40:4, 5
13 [a]Ps. 44:12
14 [a]Jer. 16:13 [b]Deut. 32:22 [1]So with MT, Vg.; LXX, Syr., Tg. *cause you to serve* (cf. 17:4)
15 [a]Jer. 12:3 [b]Jer. 20:12 [c]Ps. 69:7–9 [1]*attend to*
16 [a]Ezek. 3:1, 3 [b][Job 23:12]
17 [a]Ps. 26:4, 5
18 [a]Jer. 10:19; 30:15 [b]Job 6:15 [1]Or *cannot be trusted*
19 [a]Zech. 3:7 [b]Jer. 15:1 [c]Ezek. 22:26; 44:23
20 [a]Ezek. 3:9 [b]Jer. 1:8, 19; 20:11; 37:21; 38:13; 39:11, 12

Jeremiah's Life-Style and Message

16 The word of the LORD also came to
me, saying, 2"You shall not take a
wife, nor shall you have sons or daughters
in this place." 3For thus says the LORD
concerning the sons and daughters who
are born in this place, and concerning
their mothers who bore them and their
fathers who begot them in this land:
4"They shall die [a]gruesome deaths; they
shall not be [b]lamented nor shall they be
[c]buried, *but* they shall be [d]like refuse on
the face of the earth. They shall be consumed by the sword and by famine, and
their [e]corpses shall be meat for the birds
of heaven and for the beasts of the earth."
5For thus says the LORD: [a]"Do not enter
the house of mourning, nor go to lament
or bemoan them; for I have taken away My
peace from this people," says the LORD,
"lovingkindness and mercies. 6Both the
great and the small shall die in this land.
They shall not be buried; [a]neither shall
men lament for them, [b]cut themselves,
nor [c]make themselves bald for them. 7Nor
shall *men* break *bread* in mourning for
them, to comfort them for the dead; nor
shall *men* give them the cup of consolation to [a]drink for their father or their
mother. 8Also you shall not go into the
house of feasting to sit with them, to eat
and drink."
9For thus says the LORD of hosts, the
God of Israel: "Behold, [a]I will cause to
cease from this place, before your eyes
and in your days, the voice of [1]mirth and
the voice of gladness, the voice of the
bridegroom and the voice of the bride.
10"And it shall be, when you show this
people all these words, and they say to
you, [a]'Why has the LORD pronounced all
this great disaster against us? Or what *is*
our iniquity? Or what *is* our sin that we
have committed against the LORD our
God?' 11then you shall say to them, [a]'Because your fathers have forsaken Me,' says
the LORD; 'they have walked after other
gods and have served them and worshiped
them, and have forsaken Me and not kept
My law. 12And you have done [a]worse than
your fathers, for behold, [b]each one [1]fol-
lows the dictates of his own evil heart, so
that no one listens to Me. 13[a]Therefore I
will cast you out of this land [b]into a land
that you do not know, neither you nor
your fathers; and there you shall serve
other gods day and night, where I will not
show you favor.'

God Will Restore Israel

14"Therefore behold, the [a]days are coming," says the LORD, "that it shall no more
be said, 'The LORD lives who brought up
the children of Israel from the land of
Egypt,' 15but, 'The LORD lives who
brought up the children of Israel from the
land of the [a]north and from all the lands
where He had driven them.' For [b]I will
bring them back into their land which I
gave to their fathers.
16"Behold, I will send for many [a]fisher-
men," says the LORD, "and they shall fish
them; and afterward I will send for many
hunters, and they shall hunt them from
every mountain and every hill, and out of
the holes of the rocks. 17For My [a]eyes *are*
on all their ways; they are not hidden
from My face, nor is their iniquity hidden
from My eyes. 18And first I will repay
[a]double for their iniquity and their sin,
because [b]they have defiled My land; they
have filled My inheritance with the carcasses of their detestable and abominable
idols."

19 O LORD, [a]my strength and my
fortress,
[b]My refuge in the day of affliction,
The Gentiles shall come to You
From the ends of the earth and say,
"Surely our fathers have inherited
lies,
Worthlessness and [c]unprofitable
things."
20 Will a man make gods for himself,
[a]Which *are* not gods?

21 "Therefore behold, I will this once
cause them to know,
I will cause them to know
My hand and My might;
And they shall know that [a]My name
is the LORD.

Judah's Sin and Punishment

17 "The sin of Judah *is* [a]written
with a [b]pen of iron;
With the point of a diamond *it is*
[c]engraved
On the tablet of their heart,
And on the horns of your altars,
2 While their children remember
Their altars and their [a]wooden
images[1]

CHAPTER 16
4 a Jer. 15:2 b Jer. 22:18; 25:33 c Jer. 14:16; 19:11 d Ps. 83:10 e Ps. 79:2
5 a Ezek. 24:17, 22, 23
6 a Jer. 22:18 b Deut. 14:1 c Is. 22:12
7 a Prov. 31:6
9 a Rev. 18:23 *1 rejoicing*
10 a Deut. 29:24
11 a Jer. 22:9
12 a Jer. 7:26 b Jer. 3:17; 18:12 *1 walks after the stubbornness* or *imagination*
13 a Deut. 4:26; 28:36, 63 b Jer. 15:14
14 a Jer. 23:7, 8
15 a Jer. 3:18 b Jer. 24:6; 30:3; 32:37
16 a Amos 4:2
17 a Heb. 4:13
18 a Jer. 17:18 b [Ezek. 43:7]
19 a Ps. 18:1, 2 b Jer. 17:17 c Is. 44:10
20 a Gal. 4:8
21 a Amos 5:8

CHAPTER 17
1 a Jer. 2:22 b Job 19:24 c 2 Cor. 3:3
2 a Judg. 3:7 *1 Heb. Asherim,* Canaanite deities

By the green trees on the high
hills.
3 O My mountain in the field,
I will give as plunder your wealth,
all your treasures,
And your high places of sin within
all your borders.
4 And you, even yourself,
Shall let go of your heritage which
I gave you;
And I will cause you to serve your
enemies
In [a]the land which you do not
know;
For [b]you have kindled a fire in My
anger *which* shall burn forever."

5 Thus says the LORD:
[a]"Cursed *is* the man who trusts in
man
And makes [b]flesh his [1]strength,
Whose heart departs from the LORD.
6 For he shall be [a]like a shrub in the
desert,
And [b]shall not see when good
comes,
But shall inhabit the parched places
in the wilderness,
[c]*In* a salt land *which is* not
inhabited.

7 "Blessed[a] *is* the man who trusts in
the LORD,
And whose hope is the LORD.
8 For he shall be [a]like a tree planted
by the waters,
Which spreads out its roots by the
river,
And will not [1]fear when heat
comes;
But its leaf will be green,
And will not be anxious in the year
of drought,
Nor will cease from yielding fruit.

9 "The [a]heart *is* deceitful above all
things,
And [1]desperately wicked;
Who can know it?
10 I, the LORD, [a]search the heart,
I test the [1]mind,
[b]Even to give every man according
to his ways,
According to the fruit of his doings.

11 "*As* a partridge that [1]broods but
does not hatch,
So is he who gets riches, but not
by right;

4 a Jer. 16:13 b Jer. 15:14
5 a Is. 30:1, 2; 31:1 b Is. 31:3 *1 Lit. arm*
6 a Jer. 48:6 b Job 20:17 c Deut. 29:23
7 a [Is. 30:18]
8 a [Ps. 1:3] *1 Qr., Tg. see*
9 a [Eccl. 9:3] *1 Or incurably sick*
10 a Rev. 2:23 b Rom. 2:6 *1 Most secret parts, lit. kidneys*
11 a Ps. 55:23 b Luke 12:20 *1 Sits on eggs*
13 a Jer. 14:8 b [Is. 1:28] c Luke 10:20 d Jer. 2:13
14 a Deut. 10:21
15 a Is. 5:19
16 a Jer. 1:4–12
17 a Jer. 16:19
18 a Ps. 35:4; 70:2 b Ps. 25:2 c Jer. 11:20 *1 Lit. crush*

It [a]will leave him in the midst of
his days,
And at his end he will be [b]a fool."

12 A glorious high throne from the
beginning
Is the place of our sanctuary.
13 O LORD, [a]the hope of Israel,
[b]All who forsake You shall be
ashamed.

"Those who depart from Me
Shall be [c]written in the earth,
Because they have forsaken the
LORD,
The [d]fountain of living waters."

Heal O God, and they shall be healed; save them and they shall be saved, for You are their praise.

FROM JEREMIAH 17:14

Jeremiah Prays for Deliverance

14 Heal me, O LORD, and I shall be
healed;
Save me, and I shall be saved,
For [a]You *are* my praise.
15 Indeed they say to me,
[a]"Where *is* the word of the LORD?
Let it come now!"
16 As for me, [a]I have not hurried
away from *being* a shepherd *who*
follows You,
Nor have I desired the woeful day;
You know what came out of my
lips;
It was right there before You.
17 Do not be a terror to me;
[a]You *are* my hope in the day of
doom.
18 [a]Let them be ashamed who
persecute me,
But [b]do not let me be put to
shame;
Let them be dismayed,
But do not let me be dismayed.
Bring on them the day of doom,
And [c]destroy[1] them with double
destruction!

Hallow the Sabbath Day

[19]Thus the LORD said to me: "Go and stand in the gate of the children of the people, by which the kings of Judah come in and by which they go out, and in all the gates of Jerusalem; [20]and say to them, [a]'Hear the word of the LORD, you kings of Judah, and all Judah, and all the inhabitants of Jerusalem, who enter by these gates. [21]Thus says the LORD: [a]"Take heed to yourselves, and bear no burden on the Sabbath day, nor bring *it* in by the gates of Jerusalem; [22]nor carry a burden out of your houses on the Sabbath day, nor do any work, but hallow the Sabbath day, as I [a]commanded your fathers. [23][a]But they did not obey nor incline their ear, but [1]made their neck stiff, that they might not hear nor receive instruction.

[24]"And it shall be, [a]if you heed Me carefully," says the LORD, "to bring no burden through the gates of this city on the [b]Sabbath day, but hallow the Sabbath day, to do no work in it, [25][a]then shall enter the gates of this city kings and princes sitting on the throne of David, riding in chariots and on horses, they and their princes, accompanied by the men of Judah and the inhabitants of Jerusalem; and this city shall remain forever. [26]And they shall come from the cities of Judah and from [a]the places around Jerusalem, from the land of Benjamin and from [b]the [1]lowland, from the mountains and from [c]the [2]South, bringing burnt offerings and sacrifices, grain offerings and incense, bringing [d]sacrifices of praise to the house of the LORD.

[27]"But if you will not heed Me to hallow the Sabbath day, such as not carrying a burden when entering the gates of Jerusalem on the Sabbath day, then [a]I will kindle a fire in its gates, [b]and it shall devour the palaces of Jerusalem, and it shall not be [c]quenched." ' "

The Potter and the Clay

18 The word which came to Jeremiah from the LORD, saying: [2]"Arise and go down to the potter's house, and there I will cause you to hear My words." [3]Then I went down to the potter's house, and there he was, making something at the [1]wheel. [4]And the vessel that he [1]made of clay was [2]marred in the hand of the potter; so he made it again into another vessel, as it seemed good to the potter to make.

[5]Then the word of the LORD came to me, saying: [6]"O house of Israel, [a]can I not do with you as this potter?" says the LORD. "Look, [b]as the clay *is* in the potter's hand, so *are* you in My hand, O house of Israel! [7]The instant I speak concerning a nation and concerning a kingdom, to [a]pluck up, to pull down, and to destroy *it,* [8][a]if that nation against whom I have spoken turns from its evil, [b]I will relent of the disaster that I thought to bring upon it. [9]And the instant I speak concerning a nation and concerning a kingdom, to build and to plant *it,* [10]if it does evil in My sight so that it does not obey My voice, then I will relent concerning the good with which I said I would benefit it.

Accept me, Lord, as I am and make me such as Thou wouldst have me to be.

MARY LIVINGSTONE

[11]"Now therefore, speak to the men of Judah and to the inhabitants of Jerusalem, saying, 'Thus says the LORD: "Behold, I am fashioning a disaster and devising a plan against you. [a]Return now every one from his evil way, and make your ways and your doings [b]good." ' "

God's Warning Rejected

[12]And they said, [a]"That is hopeless! So we will walk according to our own plans, and we will every one [1]obey the [b]dictates[2] of his evil heart."

[13]Therefore thus says the LORD:

[a]"Ask now among the Gentiles,
Who has heard such things?
The virgin of Israel has done [b]a
very horrible thing.
14 Will *a man* [1]leave the snow water
of Lebanon,
Which comes from the rock of the
field?
Will the cold flowing waters be
forsaken for strange waters?
15 "Because My people have forgotten
[a]Me,

---

20 a Jer. 19:3, 4
21 a Neh. 13:19
22 a Ex. 20:8; 31:13
23 a Jer. 7:24, 26 *1 Were stubborn*
24 a Jer. 11:4; 26:3 b Ex. 16:23–30; 20:8–10
25 a Jer. 22:4
26 a Jer. 33:13 b Zech. 7:7 c Judg. 1:9 d Ps. 107:22; 116:17 *1* Heb. *shephelah* *2* Heb. *Negev*
27 a Lam. 4:11 b 2 Kin. 25:9 c Jer. 7:20

CHAPTER 18
3 *1* Potter's wheel
4 *1 was making* *2 ruined*
6 a Rom. 9:20, 21 b Is. 64:8
7 a Jer. 1:10
8 a [Ezek. 18:21; 33:11] b Jer. 26:3
11 a 2 Kin. 17:13 b Jer. 7:3–7
12 a Jer. 2:25 b Jer. 3:17; 23:17 *1* Lit. *do* *2 stubbornness* or *imagination*
13 a Jer. 2:10, 11 b Jer. 5:30
14 *1 forsake*
15 a Jer. 2:13, 32

They have burned incense to
worthless idols.
And they have caused themselves to
stumble in their ways,
From the [b]ancient paths,
To walk in pathways and not on a
highway,
16 To make their land [a]desolate *and*
a perpetual [b]hissing;
Everyone who passes by it will be
astonished
And shake his head.
17 [a]I will scatter them [b]as with an
east wind before the enemy;
[c]I will [1]show them the back and not
the face
In the day of their calamity."

Jeremiah Persecuted

18 Then they said, [a]"Come and let us devise plans against Jeremiah; [b]for the law
shall not perish from the priest, nor counsel from the wise, nor the word from the
prophet. Come and let us attack him with
the tongue, and let us not give heed to any
of his words."

19 Give heed to me, O LORD,
And listen to the voice of those who
contend with me!
20 [a]Shall evil be repaid for good?
For they have [b]dug a pit for my
life.
Remember that I [c]stood before You
To speak good [1]for them,
To turn away Your wrath from
them.
21 Therefore [a]deliver up their
children to the famine,
And pour out their *blood*
By the force of the sword;
Let their wives *become* widows
And [b]bereaved of their children.
Let their men be put to death,
Their young men *be* slain
By the sword in battle.
22 Let a cry be heard from their
houses,
When You bring a troop suddenly
upon them;
For they have dug a pit to take me,
And hidden snares for my feet.
23 Yet, LORD, You know all their
counsel
Which is against me, to slay *me*.
[a]Provide no atonement for their
iniquity,
Nor blot out their sin from Your
sight;
But let them be overthrown before
You.
Deal *thus* with them
In the time of Your [b]anger.

The Sign of the Broken Flask

19 Thus says the LORD: "Go and get
a potter's earthen flask, and *take*
some of the elders of the people and some
of the elders of the priests. 2 And go out to
[a]the Valley of the Son of Hinnom, which
is by the entry of the Potsherd Gate; and
proclaim there the words that I will tell
you, 3 [a]and say, 'Hear the word of the
LORD, O kings of Judah and inhabitants
of Jerusalem. Thus says the LORD of
hosts, the God of Israel: "Behold, I will
bring such a catastrophe on this place,
that whoever hears of it, his ears will
[b]tingle.
4 "Because they [a]have forsaken Me and
made this an alien place, because they
have burned incense in it to other gods
whom neither they, their fathers, nor the
kings of Judah have known, and have
filled this place with [b]the blood of the innocents 5 [a](they have also built the high
places of Baal, to burn their sons with fire
for burnt offerings to Baal, [b]which I did
not command or speak, nor did it come
into My mind), 6 therefore behold, the
days are coming," says the LORD, "that
this place shall no more be called Tophet
or [a]the Valley of the Son of Hinnom, but
the Valley of Slaughter. 7 And I will make
void the counsel of Judah and Jerusalem
in this place, [a]and I will cause them to fall
by the sword before their enemies and by
the hands of those who seek their lives;
their [b]corpses I will give as meat for the
birds of the heaven and for the beasts of
the earth. 8 I will make this city [a]desolate
and a hissing; everyone who passes by it
will be astonished and hiss because of all
its plagues. 9 And I will cause them to eat
the [a]flesh of their sons and the flesh of
their daughters, and everyone shall eat
the flesh of his friend in the siege and in
the desperation with which their enemies
and those who seek their lives shall drive
them to despair." '
10 [a]"Then you shall break the flask in
the sight of the men who go with you,

15 [b]Jer. 6:16
16 [a]Jer. 19:8 [b]1 Kin. 9:8
17 [a]Jer. 13:24 [b]Ps. 48:7 [c]Jer. 2:27 [1]So with LXX, Syr., Tg., Vg.; MT *look them in*
18 [a]Jer. 11:19 [b]Lev. 10:11
20 [a]Ps. 109:4 [b]Jer. 5:26 [c]Jer. 14:7—15:1 [1]*concerning*
21 [a]Ps. 109:9–20 [b]Jer. 15:7, 8
23 [a]Ps. 35:14; 109:14 [b]Jer. 7:20

CHAPTER 19
2 [a]Josh. 15:8
3 [a]Jer. 17:20 [b]1 Sam. 3:11
4 [a]Is. 65:11 [b]2 Kin. 21:12
5 [a]Jer. 7:31; 32:35 [b]Lev. 18:21
6 [a]Josh. 15:8
7 [a]Lev. 26:17 [b]Ps. 79:2
8 [a]Jer. 18:16; 49:13; 50:13
9 [a]Lev. 26:29
10 [a]Jer. 51:63, 64

11 and say to them, 'Thus says the LORD of
hosts: [a]"Even so I will break this people
and this city, as *one* breaks a potter's vessel, which cannot be [1]made whole again;
and they shall [b]bury *them* in Tophet till
there is no place to bury. 12 Thus I will do
to this place," says the LORD, "and to its
inhabitants, and make this city like Tophet. 13 And the houses of Jerusalem and
the houses of the kings of Judah shall be
defiled [a]like the place of Tophet, because
of all the houses on whose [b]roofs they
have burned incense to all the host of
heaven, and [c]poured out drink offerings
to other gods." ' "
14 Then Jeremiah came from Tophet,
where the LORD had sent him to prophesy;
and he stood in [a]the court of the Lord's
house and said to all the people, 15 "Thus
says the LORD of hosts, the God of Israel:
'Behold, I will bring on this city and on all
her towns all the doom that I have pronounced against it, because [a]they have
stiffened their necks that they might not
hear My words.' "

The Word of God to Pashhur

20 Now [a]Pashhur the son of [b]Immer,
the priest who *was* also chief governor in the house of the LORD, heard that
Jeremiah prophesied these things. 2 Then
Pashhur struck Jeremiah the prophet,
and put him in the stocks that *were* in the
high [a]gate of Benjamin, which *was* by the
house of the LORD.
3 And it happened on the next day that
Pashhur brought Jeremiah out of the
stocks. Then Jeremiah said to him, "The
LORD has not called your name Pashhur,
but [1]Magor-Missabib. 4 For thus says the
LORD: 'Behold, I will make you a terror to
yourself and to all your friends; and they
shall fall by the sword of their enemies,
and your eyes shall see *it*. I will [a]give all
Judah into the hand of the king of Babylon, and he shall carry them captive to
Babylon and slay them with the sword.
5 Moreover I [a]will deliver all the wealth of
this city, all its produce, and all its precious things; all the treasures of the kings
of Judah I will give into the hand of their
enemies, who will plunder them, seize
them, and [b]carry them to Babylon. 6 And
you, Pashhur, and all who dwell in your
house, shall go into captivity. You shall go
to Babylon, and there you shall die, and be
buried there, you and all your friends, to
whom you have [a]prophesied lies.' "

Jeremiah's Unpopular Ministry

7 O LORD, You [1]induced me, and I
was persuaded;
[a]You are stronger than I, and have
prevailed.
[b]I am [2]in derision daily;
Everyone mocks me.
8 For when I spoke, I cried out;
[a]I shouted, "Violence and plunder!"
Because the word of the LORD was
made to me
A reproach and a derision daily.
9 Then I said, "I will not make
mention of Him,
Nor speak anymore in His name."
But *His word* was in my heart like
a [a]burning fire
Shut up in my bones;
I was weary of holding *it* back,
And [b]I could not.
10 [a]For I heard many [1]mocking:
"Fear on every side!"
"Report," *they say,* "and we will
report it!"
[b]All my acquaintances watched for
my stumbling, *saying,*
"Perhaps he can be induced;
Then we will prevail against him,
And we will take our revenge on
him."
11 But the LORD *is* [a]with me as a
mighty, awesome One.
Therefore my persecutors will
stumble, and will not [b]prevail.
They will be greatly ashamed, for
they will not prosper.
Their [c]everlasting confusion will
never be forgotten.
12 But, O LORD of hosts,
You who [a]test the righteous,
And see the [1]mind and heart,
[b]Let me see Your vengeance on
them;
For I have pleaded my cause before
You.
13 Sing to the LORD! Praise the LORD!
For [a]He has delivered the life of the
poor
From the hand of evildoers.
14 [a]Cursed *be* the day in which I was
born!
Let the day not be blessed in which
my mother bore me!
15 Let the man *be* cursed

---

11 [a]Is. 30:14 [b]Jer. 7:32 [1]*restored*
13 [a]2 Kin. 23:10 [b]Zeph. 1:5 [c]Jer. 7:18
14 [a]2 Chr. 20:5
15 [a]Neh. 9:17, 29

CHAPTER 20
1 [a]Ezra 2:37, 38 [b]1 Chr. 24:14
2 [a]Jer. 37:13
3 [1]Lit. *Fear on Every Side*
4 [a]Jer. 21:4–10
5 [a]2 Kin. 20:17 [b]Is. 39:6
6 [a]Jer. 14:13–15
7 [a]Jer. 1:6, 7 [b]Lam. 3:14 [1]*enticed* or *persuaded* [2]Lit. *a laughingstock all the day*
8 [a]Jer. 6:7
9 [a]Ps. 39:3 [b]Job 32:18
10 [a]Ps. 31:13 [b]Ps. 41:9; 55:13, 14 [1]*slandering*
11 [a]Jer. 1:18, 19 [b]Jer. 15:20; 17:18 [c]Jer. 23:40
12 [a][Jer. 11:20; 17:10] [b]Ps. 54:7; 59:10 [1]Most secret parts, lit. *kidneys*
13 [a]Ps. 35:9, 10; 109:30, 31
14 [a]Job 3:3

Who brought news to my father,
saying,
"A male child has been born to you!"
Making him very glad.
16 And let that man be like the cities
Which the LORD [a]overthrew, and
did not relent;
Let him [b]hear the cry in the
morning
And the shouting at noon,
17 [a]Because he did not kill me from
the womb,
That my mother might have been
my grave,
And her womb always enlarged *with*
me.
18 [a]Why did I come forth from the
womb to [b]see [1]labor and sorrow,
That my days should be consumed
with shame?

Jerusalem's Doom Is Sealed

21 The word which came to Jeremiah
from the LORD when [a]King Zedekiah sent to him [b]Pashhur the son of Mel-
chiah, and [c]Zephaniah the son of
Maaseiah, the priest, saying, 2[a]"Please inquire of the LORD for us, for [1]Nebuchad-
nezzar king of Babylon makes war against
us. Perhaps the LORD will deal with us according to all His wonderful works, that
the king may go away from us."
3Then Jeremiah said to them, "Thus
you shall say to Zedekiah, 4'Thus says the
LORD God of Israel: "Behold, I will turn
back the weapons of war that *are* in your
hands, with which you fight against the
king of Babylon and the [1]Chaldeans who
besiege you outside the walls; and [a]I will
assemble them in the midst of this city. 5I
[a]Myself will fight against you with an
[b]outstretched hand and with a strong
arm, even in anger and fury and great
wrath. 6I will strike the inhabitants of this
city, both man and beast; they shall die of
a great pestilence. 7And afterward," says
the LORD, [a]"I will deliver Zedekiah king of
Judah, his servants and the people, and
such as are left in this city from the pestilence and the sword and the famine, into
the hand of Nebuchadnezzar king of Babylon, into the hand of their enemies, and
into the hand of those who seek their life;
and he shall strike them with the edge of
the sword. [b]He shall not spare them, or
have pity or mercy." '
8"Now you shall say to this people,
'Thus says the LORD: "Behold, [a]I set before
you the way of life and the way of death.
9He who [a]remains in this city shall die by
the sword, by famine, and by pestilence;
but he who goes out and [1]defects to the
Chaldeans who besiege you, he shall [b]live,
and his life shall be as a prize to him.
10For I have [a]set My face against this city
for adversity and not for good," says the
LORD. [b]"It shall be given into the hand of
the king of Babylon, and he shall [c]burn it
with fire." '

Message to the House of David

11"And concerning the house of the
king of Judah, *say,* 'Hear the word of the
LORD, 12O house of David! Thus says the
LORD:

[a]"Execute[1] judgment [b]in the
morning;
And deliver *him who is* plundered
Out of the hand of the oppressor,
Lest My fury go forth like fire
And burn so that no one can
quench *it,*
Because of the evil of your doings.

13 "Behold, [a]I *am* against you,
O [1]inhabitant of the valley,
And rock of the plain," says the
LORD,
"Who say, [b]'Who shall come down
against us?
Or who shall enter our dwellings?'
14 But I will punish you according to
the [a]fruit of your [1]doings," says
the LORD;
"I will kindle a fire in its forest,
And [b]it shall devour all things
around it." ' "

22 Thus says the LORD: "Go down to
the house of the king of Judah, and
there speak this word, 2and say, [a]'Hear
the word of the LORD, O king of Judah,
you who sit on the throne of David, you
and your servants and your people who
enter these gates! 3Thus says the LORD:
[a]"Execute[1] judgment and righteousness,
and deliver the plundered out of the hand
of the oppressor. Do no wrong and do no
violence to the stranger, the [b]fatherless,
or the widow, nor shed innocent blood
in this place. 4For if you indeed do this
thing, [a]then shall enter the gates of this
house, riding on horses and in chariots,
accompanied by servants and people,
kings who sit on the throne of David. 5But

---

16 a Gen. 19:25 b Jer. 18:22
17 a Job 3:10, 11
18 a Job 3:20 b Lam. 3:1 1 *toil*

CHAPTER 21
1 a 2 Kin. 24:17, 18 b Jer. 38:1 c 2 Kin. 25:18
2 a Jer. 37:3, 7 1 Heb. *Nebuchadrezzar,* and so elsewhere in the book
4 a Is. 13:4 1 Or *Babylonians,* and so elsewhere in the book
5 a Is. 63:10 b Ex. 6:6
7 a Jer. 37:17; 39:5; 52:9 b 2 Chr. 36:17
8 a Deut. 30:15, 19
9 a Jer. 38:2 b Jer. 39:18 1 Lit. *falls away to*
10 a Amos 9:4 b Jer. 38:3 c Jer. 34:2, 22; 37:10
12 a Zech. 7:9 b Ps. 101:8 1 *Dispense justice*
13 a [Ezek. 13:8] b Jer. 49:4 1 *dweller*
14 a Is. 3:10, 11 b 2 Chr. 36:19 1 *deeds*

CHAPTER 22
2 a Jer. 17:20
3 a Jer. 21:12 b Jer. 7:6 1 *Dispense justice*
4 a Jer. 17:25

if you will not [1]hear these words, [a]I swear
by Myself," says the LORD, "that this house
shall become a desolation." ' "
[6]For thus says the LORD to the house of
the king of Judah:

"You *are* [a]Gilead to Me,
The head of Lebanon;
Yet I surely will make you a
wilderness,
Cities *which* are not inhabited.
7 I will prepare destroyers against
you,
Everyone with his weapons;
They shall cut down [a]your choice
cedars
[b]And cast *them* into the fire.

[8]And many nations will pass by this city;
and everyone will say to his neighbor,
[a]'Why has the LORD done so to this great
city?' [9]Then they will answer, [a]'Because
they have forsaken the covenant of the
LORD their God, and worshiped other gods
and served them.' "

10 Weep not for [a]the dead, nor
bemoan him;
Weep bitterly for him [b]who goes
away,
For he shall return no more,
Nor see his native country.

Message to the Sons of Josiah

[11]For thus says the LORD concerning
[a]Shallum[1] the son of Josiah, king of Judah, who reigned instead of Josiah his father, [b]who went from this place: "He shall
not return here anymore, [12]but he shall
die in the place where they have led him
captive, and shall see this land no more.

13 "Woe[a] to him who builds his house
by unrighteousness
And his [1]chambers by injustice,
[b]*Who* uses his neighbor's service
without wages
And gives him nothing for his
work,
14 Who says, 'I will build myself a
wide house with spacious
[1]chambers,
And cut out windows for it,
Paneling *it* with cedar
And painting *it* with vermilion.'
15 "Shall you reign because you
enclose *yourself* in cedar?
Did not your father eat and drink,
And do justice and righteousness?
Then [a]*it was* well with him.
16 He [1]judged the cause of the poor
and needy;
Then *it was* well.
Was not this knowing Me?" says the
LORD.
17 "Yet[a] your eyes and your heart *are*
for nothing but your
covetousness,
For shedding innocent blood,
And practicing oppression and
violence."

[18]Therefore thus says the LORD concerning Jehoiakim the son of Josiah, king
of Judah:

[a]"They shall not lament for him,
Saying, [b]'Alas, my brother!' or
'Alas, my sister!'
They shall not lament for him,
Saying, 'Alas, master!' or 'Alas, his
glory!'
19 [a]He shall be buried with the burial
of a donkey,
Dragged and cast out beyond the
gates of Jerusalem.

20 "Go up to Lebanon, and cry out,
And lift up your voice in Bashan;
Cry from Abarim,
For all your lovers are destroyed.
21 I spoke to you in your prosperity,
But you said, 'I will not hear.'
[a]This *has been* your manner from
your youth,
That you did not obey My voice.
22 The wind shall eat up all [a]your
[1]rulers,
And your lovers shall go into
captivity;
Surely then you will be ashamed
and humiliated
For all your wickedness.
23 O inhabitant of Lebanon,
Making your nest in the cedars,
How gracious will you be when
pangs come upon you,
Like [a]the pain of a woman in
[1]labor?

Message to Coniah

[24]"*As* I live," says the LORD, [a]"though
[1]Coniah the son of Jehoiakim, king of Judah, [b]were the [2]signet on My right hand,
yet I would pluck you off; [25a]and I will give
you into the hand of those who seek your
life, and into the hand *of those* whose face
you fear—the hand of Nebuchadnezzar

5 a Heb. 6:13, 17 1 Obey
6 a Song 4:1
7 a Is. 37:24 b Jer. 21:14
8 a Deut. 29:24–26
9 a 2 Chr. 34:25
10 a 2 Kin. 22:20 b Jer. 14:17; 22:11
11 a 1 Chr. 3:15 b 2 Kin. 23:34 1 Or *Jehoahaz*
13 a 2 Kin. 23:35 b James 5:4 1 Lit. *roof chambers, upper chambers*
14 1 Lit. *roof chambers, upper chambers*
15 a Ps. 128:2
16 1 Defended
17 a Ezek. 19:6
18 a Jer. 16:4, 6 b 1 Kin. 13:30
19 a Jer. 36:30
21 a Jer. 3:24, 25; 32:30
22 a Jer. 23:1 1 Lit. *shepherds*
23 a Jer. 6:24 1 *childbirth*
24 a 2 Kin. 24:6, 8 b Hag. 2:23 1 Or *Jeconiah* or *Jehoiachin* 2 *signet ring*
25 a Jer. 34:20

king of Babylon and the hand of the
[1]Chaldeans. 26 [a]So I will cast you out, and
your mother who bore you, into another
country where you were not born; and
there you shall die. 27 But to the land to
which they desire to return, there they
shall not return.

28 "Is this man [1]Coniah a despised,
broken idol—
[a]A vessel in which *is* no pleasure?
Why are they cast out, he and his
descendants,
And cast into a land which they do
not know?
29 [a]O earth, earth, earth,
Hear the word of the LORD!
30 Thus says the LORD:
'Write this man down as [a]childless,
A man *who* shall not prosper in his
days;
For [b]none of his descendants shall
prosper,
Sitting on the throne of David,
And ruling anymore in Judah.' "

The Branch of Righteousness

23 "Woe [a]to the shepherds who destroy and scatter the sheep of My
pasture!" says the LORD. 2 Therefore
thus says the LORD God of Israel against
the shepherds who feed My people: "You
have scattered My flock, driven them
away, and not attended to them. [a]Behold,
I will attend to you for the evil of your
doings," says the LORD. 3 "But [a]I will gather the remnant of My flock out of all countries where I have driven them, and bring
them back to their folds; and they shall be
fruitful and increase. 4 I will set up [a]shep-
herds over them who will feed them; and
they shall fear no more, nor be dismayed,
nor shall they be lacking," says the LORD.

5 "Behold, [a]*the* days are coming," says
the LORD,
"That I will raise to David a Branch
of righteousness;
A King shall reign and [1]prosper,
[b]And execute [2]judgment and
righteousness in the [3]earth.
6 [a]In His days Judah will be saved,
And Israel [b]will dwell safely;
Now [c]this *is* His name by which He
will be called:

[1]THE LORD OUR RIGHTEOUSNESS.

7 "Therefore, behold, [a]*the* days are coming," says the LORD, "that they shall no
longer say, 'As the LORD lives who brought
up the children of Israel from the land
of Egypt,' 8 but, 'As the LORD lives who
brought up and led the descendants of the
house of Israel from the north country
[a]and from all the countries where I had
driven them.' And they shall dwell in their
own [b]land."

False Prophets and Empty Oracles

9 My heart within me is broken
Because of the prophets;
[a]All my bones shake.
I am like a drunken man,
And like a man whom wine has
overcome,
Because of the LORD,
And because of His holy words.
10 For [a]the land is full of adulterers;
For [b]because of a curse the land
mourns.
[c]The pleasant places of the
wilderness are dried up.
Their course of life is evil,
And their might *is* not right.

11 "For [a]both prophet and priest are
profane;
Yes, [b]in My house I have found
their wickedness," says the LORD.
12 "Therefore[a] their way shall be to
them
Like slippery *ways;*
In the darkness they shall be driven
on
And fall in them;
For I [b]will bring disaster on them,
The year of their punishment," says
the LORD.
13 "And I have seen [1]folly in the
prophets of Samaria:
[a]They prophesied by Baal
And [b]caused My people Israel to
err.
14 Also I have seen a horrible thing
in the prophets of Jerusalem:
[a]They commit adultery and walk in
lies;
They also [b]strengthen the hands of
evildoers,
So that no one turns back from his
wickedness.
All of them are like [c]Sodom to Me,
And her inhabitants like Gomorrah.

15 "Therefore thus says the LORD of
hosts concerning the prophets:

---

25 [1]Or *Babylonians*
26 [a]2 Kin. 24:15
28 [a]Hos. 8:8 [1]See note at v. 24
29 [a]Deut. 32:1
30 [a]Matt. 1:12 [b]Jer. 36:30

CHAPTER 23
1 [a]Jer. 10:21
2 [a]Ex. 32:34
3 [a]Jer. 32:37
4 [a]Jer. 3:15
5 [a]Jer. 33:14 [b]Ps. 72:2 [1]*act wisely* [2]*justice* [3]*land*
6 [a]Zech. 14:11 [b]Jer. 32:37 [c][1 Cor. 1:30] [1]Heb. *YHWH Tsidkenu*
7 [a]Jer. 16:14
8 [a]Is. 43:5, 6 [b]Gen. 12:7
9 [a]Hab. 3:16
10 [a]Jer. 9:2 [b]Hos. 4:2 [c]Jer. 9:10
11 [a]Zeph. 3:4 [b]Jer. 7:30; 32:34
12 [a][Prov. 4:19] [b]Jer. 11:23
13 [a]Jer. 2:8 [b]Is. 9:16 [1]Lit. *distastefulness*
14 [a]Jer. 29:23 [b]Ezek. 13:22, 23 [c]Is. 1:9, 10

Jeremiah 23:1

Dear Woman of Destiny,

Spiritual adultery is when two people, either of whom are married to another person, form a bond in which they think more about another person than their own spouse. Years ago I related on a regular basis to a male leader from another ministry. After a few months, I found myself looking forward to his calls. Each conversation was spiritually and intellectually interesting. In the meantime, my husband Mike was busy working at a job that took him away from home from 7:00 A.M. until around 8:00 or 9:00 P.M.

Please understand, I never held this man's hand, kissed him, or even considered it. However, the pull was strong. I slipped into a mode in my thought life where he filled a space in my emotions that only my husband was supposed to fill.

Mike and I have always had the kind of relationship in which we can be open about anything with one another. One day Mike said, "Honey, this guy calls and asks about you when you're on the road. He wants to know if you have arrived safely and how the ministry is going. I think he cares for you a little too much."

At that moment I had a huge reality check. I shared with Mike that I felt I was somewhat wrapped up with this other man in my emotions and was shocked to come to that realization. We prayed together, and I asked God to forgive me. Mike and I then discussed how we could improve our communication.

What I hadn't understood was that intimate conversation breeds intimacy. Be careful about intimate sharing. Intimate conversations can lead to emotional entanglement. When having conversations with those of the opposite sex, it's very important to maintain a brother-to-sister relationship. This is especially important with prayer partners. A good safeguard is to ask yourself this question: "Why am I calling this person? Is this something God wants me to do or am I drawn on a personal level?"

Afterward, I thought it would be quite easy to break the tie I had formed with the other guy. Wrong! Although I stopped talking to this man on the phone, the pull I felt toward him was tremendous. Finally, one day I cried out to the Lord for help. The Lord gently spoke to me in my spirit that a major reason I was so emotionally entangled with the other guy was that I had lost my first love for Him. The Lord could have kept me emotionally pure and unentangled if I had spent more intimate time in worship and prayer. Wow, was that a revelation!

I closed my eyes and imagined myself in the throne room of heaven, gave God all my needs and empty places, and asked Him to fill them up with His presence and love. Immediately, I sensed a sweet presence of the Lord, and His answering touch permeated my soul. What happened next took me by surprise. Suddenly, I had a vision of Mike and me dancing together, and a song that was special to me when we first fell in love poured from my memory. At that moment, all the first-love emotions I had for Mike poured through my heart. I fell in love with my husband all over again.

Cindy Jacobs

'Behold, I will feed them with
[a]wormwood,
And make them drink the water of
gall;
For from the prophets of Jerusalem
[1]Profaneness has gone out into all
the land.' "

16Thus says the LORD of hosts:

"Do not listen to the words of the
prophets who prophesy to you.
They make you worthless;
[a]They speak a vision of their own
heart,
Not from the mouth of the LORD.
17 They continually say to those who
despise Me,
'The LORD has said, [a]"You shall have
peace" ';
And to everyone who [b]walks
according to the [1]dictates of his
own heart, they say,
[c]'No evil shall come upon you.' "
18 For [a]who has stood in the counsel
of the LORD,
And has perceived and heard His
word?
Who has marked His word and
heard *it?*
19 Behold, a [a]whirlwind of the LORD
has gone forth in fury—
A violent whirlwind!
It will fall violently on the head of
the wicked.
20 The [a]anger of the LORD will not
turn back
Until He has executed and
performed the thoughts of His
heart.
[b]In the latter days you will
understand it perfectly.
21 "I[a] have not sent these prophets,
yet they ran.
I have not spoken to them, yet they
prophesied.
22 But if they had stood in My
counsel,
And had caused My people to hear
My words,
Then they would have [a]turned
them from their evil way
And from the evil of their doings.
23 "*Am* I a God near at hand," says
the LORD,
"And not a God afar off?
24 Can anyone [a]hide himself in
secret places,
So I shall not see him?" says the
LORD;
[b]"Do I not fill heaven and earth?"
says the LORD.

25"I have heard what the prophets have
said who prophesy lies in My name, saying, 'I have dreamed, I have dreamed!'
26How long will *this* be in the heart of the
prophets who prophesy lies? Indeed *they*
are prophets of the deceit of their own
heart, 27who try to make My people forget
My name by their dreams which everyone
tells his neighbor, [a]as their fathers forgot
My name for Baal.

Let ____ who has Your word speak Your word faithfully.

FROM JEREMIAH 23:28

28 "The prophet who has a dream, let
him tell a dream;
And he who has My word, let him
speak My word faithfully.
What *is* the chaff to the wheat?"
says the LORD.
29 "*Is* not My word like a [a]fire?" says
the LORD,
"And like a hammer *that* breaks the
rock in pieces?

30"Therefore behold, [a]I *am* against the
prophets," says the LORD, "who steal My
words every one from his neighbor. 31Be-
hold, I *am* [a]against the prophets," says the
LORD, "who use their tongues and say, 'He
says.' 32Behold, I *am* against those who
prophesy false dreams," says the LORD,
"and tell them, and cause My people to err
by their [a]lies and by [b]their recklessness.
Yet I did not send them or command
them; therefore they shall not [c]profit this
people at all," says the LORD.
33"So when these people or the prophet
or the priest ask you, saying, 'What is [a]the
[1]oracle of the LORD?' you shall then say to
them, [2]'What oracle?' I will even forsake
you," says the LORD. 34"And *as for* the
prophet and the priest and the people who
say, 'The [1]oracle of the LORD!' I will even
punish that man and his house. 35Thus
every one of you shall say to his neighbor,
and every one to his brother, 'What has

15 a Jer. 9:15
1 Or *Pollution*
16 a Jer. 14:14
17 a Ezek. 13:10
b Deut. 29:19; Jer. 3:17
c Mic. 3:11
1 *stubbornness* or *imagination*
18 a [1 Cor. 2:16]
19 a Amos 1:14
20 a Jer. 30:24
b Gen. 49:1
21 a Jer. 14:14; 23:32; 27:15
22 a Jer. 25:5
24 a [Ps. 139:7]
b [1 Kin. 8:27]
27 a Judg. 3:7
29 a Jer. 5:14
30 a Deut. 18:20
31 a Ezek. 13:9
32 a Lam. 2:14; 3:37
b Zeph. 3:4
c Jer. 7:8
33 a Mal. 1:1
1 *burden, prophecy*
2 LXX, Tg., Vg. *'You are the burden.'*
34 1 *burden, prophecy*

the LORD answered?' and, 'What has the
LORD spoken?' 36And the [1]oracle of the
LORD you shall mention no more. For every man's word will be his oracle, for you
have [a]perverted the words of the living
God, the LORD of hosts, our God. 37Thus
you shall say to the prophet, 'What has the
LORD answered you?' and, 'What has the
LORD spoken?' 38But since you say, 'The
[1]oracle of the LORD!' therefore thus says
the LORD: 'Because you say this word,
"The oracle of the LORD!" and I have sent
to you, saying, "Do not say, 'The oracle of
the LORD!' " 39therefore behold, I, even I,
[a]will utterly forget you and forsake you,
and the city that I gave you and your fathers, and *will cast you* out of My presence. 40And I will bring [a]an everlasting
reproach upon you, and a perpetual
[b]shame, which shall not be forgotten.' "

The Sign of Two Baskets of Figs

24 The [a]LORD showed me, and there
were two baskets of figs set before
the temple of the LORD, after Nebuchadnezzar [b]king of Babylon had carried away
captive [c]Jeconiah the son of Jehoiakim,
king of Judah, and the princes of Judah
with the craftsmen and smiths, from Jerusalem, and had brought them to Babylon.
2One basket *had* very good figs, like the
figs *that are* first ripe; and the other basket *had* very bad figs which could not be
eaten, they were so [a]bad. 3Then the LORD
said to me, "What do you see, Jeremiah?"
And I said, "Figs, the good figs, very
good; and the bad, very bad, which cannot
be eaten, they are so bad."
4Again the word of the LORD came to
me, saying, 5"Thus says the LORD, the God
of Israel: 'Like these good figs, so will I
[1]acknowledge those who are carried away
captive from Judah, whom I have sent out
of this place for *their own* good, into the
land of the Chaldeans. 6For I will set My
eyes on them for good, and [a]I will bring
them back to this land; [b]I will build them
and not pull *them* down, and I will plant
them and not pluck *them* up. 7Then I will
give them [a]a heart to know Me, that I *am*
the LORD; and they shall be [b]My people,
and I will be their God, for they shall return to Me [c]with their whole heart.
8'And as the bad [a]figs which cannot be
eaten, they are so bad'—surely thus says
the LORD—'so will I give up Zedekiah the
king of Judah, his princes, the [b]residue of
Jerusalem who remain in this land, and
[c]those who dwell in the land of Egypt. 9I
will deliver them to [a]trouble into all the
kingdoms of the earth, for *their* harm, [b]*to
be* a reproach and a byword, a taunt and
a curse, in all places where I shall drive
them. 10And I will send the sword, the
famine, and the pestilence among them,
till they are [1]consumed from the land that
I gave to them and their fathers.' "

Seventy Years of Desolation

25 The word that came to Jeremiah
concerning all the people of Judah,
[a]in the fourth year of [b]Jehoiakim the son
of Josiah, king of Judah (which *was* the
first year of Nebuchadnezzar king of Babylon), 2which Jeremiah the prophet spoke
to all the people of Judah and to all the
inhabitants of Jerusalem, saying: 3[a]"From
the thirteenth year of Josiah the son of
Amon, king of Judah, even to this day, this
is the twenty-third year in which the
word of the LORD has come to me; and
I have spoken to you, rising early and
speaking, [b]but you have not listened.
4And the LORD has sent to you all His servants the prophets, [a]rising early and sending *them,* but you have not listened nor
inclined your ear to hear. 5They said,
[a]'Repent now everyone of his evil way and
his evil doings, and dwell in the land that
the LORD has given to you and your fathers forever and ever. 6Do not go after
other gods to serve them and worship
them, and do not provoke Me to anger
with the works of your hands; and I will
not harm you.' 7Yet you have not listened
to Me," says the LORD, "that you might
[a]provoke Me to anger with the works of
your hands to your own hurt.
8"Therefore thus says the LORD of hosts:
'Because you have not heard My words,
9behold, I will send and take [a]all the families of the north,' says the LORD, 'and Nebuchadnezzar the king of Babylon, [b]My
servant, and will bring them against this
land, against its inhabitants, and against
these nations all around, and will utterly
destroy them, and [c]make them an astonishment, a hissing, and perpetual desolations. 10Moreover I will [1]take from them
the [a]voice of mirth and the voice of gladness, the voice of the bridegroom and the
voice of the bride, [b]the sound of the millstones and the light of the lamp. 11And
this whole land shall be a desolation *and*
an astonishment, and these nations shall

36 a Deut. 4:2 *1 burden, prophecy*
38 *1 burden, prophecy*
39 a Hos. 4:6
40 a Jer. 20:11 b Mic. 3:5–7

CHAPTER 24
1 a Amos 7:1, 4; 8:1 b 2 Kin. 24:12–16 c Jer. 22:24–28; 29:2
2 a Jer. 29:17
5 *1 regard*
6 a Jer. 12:15; 29:10 b Jer. 32:41; 33:7; 42:10
7 a [Deut. 30:6] b Jer. 30:22; 31:33; 32:38 c Jer. 29:13
8 a Jer. 29:17 b Jer. 39:9 c Jer. 44:1, 26–30
9 a Deut. 28:25, 37 b Ps. 44:13, 14
10 *1 destroyed*

CHAPTER 25
1 a Jer. 36:1 b 2 Kin. 24:1, 2
3 a Jer. 1:2 b Jer. 7:13; 11:7, 8, 10
4 a Jer. 7:13, 25
5 a Jer. 18:11
7 a Deut. 32:21
9 a Jer. 1:15 b Is. 45:1 c Jer. 18:16
10 a Rev. 18:23 b Eccl. 12:4 *1 Lit. cause to perish from them*

serve the king of Babylon seventy [a]years.
12'Then it will come to pass, [a]when
[1]seventy years are completed, *that* I will
punish the king of Babylon and that nation, the land of the Chaldeans, for their
iniquity,' says the LORD; [b]'and I will make
it a perpetual desolation. 13So I will bring
on that land all My words which I have
pronounced against it, all that is written
in this book, which Jeremiah has prophesied concerning all the nations. 14[a](For
many nations [b]and great kings shall [c]be
served by them also; [d]and I will repay
them according to their deeds and according to the works of their own hands.)' "

Judgment on the Nations

15For thus says the LORD God of Israel
to me: "Take this [a]wine cup of [1]fury from
My hand, and cause all the nations, to
whom I send you, to drink it. 16And [a]they
will drink and stagger and go mad because
of the sword that I will send among
them."
17Then I took the cup from the LORD's
hand, and made all the nations drink, to
whom the LORD had sent me: 18Jerusalem
and the cities of Judah, its kings and its
princes, to make them [a]a desolation, an
astonishment, a hissing, and [b]a curse, as
it is this day; 19Pharaoh king of Egypt, his
servants, his princes, and all his people;
20all the mixed multitude, all the kings of
[a]the land of Uz, all the kings of the land
of the [b]Philistines (namely, Ashkelon,
Gaza, Ekron, and [c]the remnant of Ashdod); 21[a]Edom, Moab, and the people of
Ammon; 22all the kings of [a]Tyre, all the
kings of Sidon, and the kings of the coastlands which *are* across the [b]sea; 23[a]Dedan,
Tema, Buz, and all *who are* in the farthest
corners; 24all the kings of Arabia and all
the kings of the [a]mixed multitude who
dwell in the desert; 25all the kings of Zimri, all the kings of [a]Elam, and all the kings
of the [b]Medes; 26[a]all the kings of the
north, far and near, one with another; and
all the kingdoms of the world which *are*
on the face of the earth. Also the king of
[1]Sheshach shall drink after them.
27"Therefore you shall say to them,
'Thus says the LORD of hosts, the God of
Israel: [a]"Drink, [b]be drunk, and vomit! Fall
and rise no more, because of the sword
which I will send among you." ' 28And it
shall be, if they refuse to take the cup
from your hand to drink, then you shall
say to them, 'Thus says the LORD of hosts:
"You shall certainly drink! 29For behold,
[a]I begin to bring calamity on the city
[b]which is called by My name, and should
you be utterly unpunished? You shall not
be unpunished, for [c]I will call for a sword
on all the inhabitants of the earth," says
the LORD of hosts.'
30"Therefore prophesy against them all
these words, and say to them:

'The LORD will [a]roar from on high,
And utter His voice from [b]His holy
habitation;
He will roar mightily against [c]His
fold.
He will give [d]a shout, as those who
tread *the grapes,*
Against all the inhabitants of the
earth.
31 A noise will come to the ends of
the earth—
For the LORD has [a]a controversy
with the nations;
[b]He will plead His case with all
flesh.
He will give those *who are* wicked
to the sword,' says the LORD."

32Thus says the LORD of hosts:

"Behold, disaster shall go forth
From nation to nation,
And [a]a great whirlwind shall be
raised up
From the farthest parts of the
earth.

33[a]"And at that day the slain of the LORD
shall be from *one* end of the earth even to
the *other* end of the earth. They shall not
be [b]lamented, [c]or gathered, or buried;
they shall become refuse on the ground.

34 "Wail,[a] shepherds, and cry!
Roll about *in the ashes,*
You leaders of the flock!
For the days of your slaughter and
your dispersions are fulfilled;
You shall fall like a precious vessel.
35 And the shepherds will have no
[1]way to flee,
Nor the leaders of the flock to
escape.
36 A voice of the cry of the
shepherds,
And a wailing of the leaders to the
flock *will be heard.*
For the LORD has plundered their
pasture,
37 And the peaceful dwellings are cut
down

11 [a]Jer. 29:10
12 [a]Ezra 1:1 [b]Is. 13:20 [1]Beginning circa 605 B.C. (2 Kin. 24:1) and ending circa 536 B.C. (Ezra 1:1)
14 [a]Jer. 50:9; 51:27, 28 [b]Jer. 51:27 [c]Jer. 27:7 [d]Jer. 50:29; 51:6, 24
15 [a]Rev. 14:10 [1]*wrath*
16 [a]Nah. 3:11
18 [a]Jer. 25:9, 11 [b]Jer. 24:9
20 [a]Job 1:1 [b]Jer. 47:1–7 [c]Is. 20:1
21 [a]Jer. 49:7
22 [a]Jer. 47:4 [b]Jer. 49:23
23 [a]Jer. 49:7, 8
24 [a]Ezek. 30:5
25 [a]Jer. 49:34 [b]Jer. 51:11, 28
26 [a]Jer. 50:9 [1]A code word for Babylon, Jer. 51:41
27 [a]Hab. 2:16 [b]Is. 63:6
29 [a]Ezek. 9:6 [b]Dan. 9:18 [c]Ezek. 38:21
30 [a]Amos 1:2 [b]Ps. 11:4 [c]1 Kin. 9:3 [d]Is. 16:9
31 [a]Mic. 6:2 [b]Is. 66:16
32 [a]Jer. 23:19; 30:23
33 [a]Is. 34:2, 3; 66:16 [b]Jer. 16:4, 6 [c]Ps. 79:3
34 [a]Jer. 4:8; 6:26
35 [1]Or *refuge*

Because of the fierce anger of the
LORD.
38 He has left His lair like the lion;
For their land is desolate
Because of the fierceness of the
Oppressor,
And because of His fierce anger."

Jeremiah Saved from Death

26 In the beginning of the reign of Jehoiakim the son of Josiah, king of
Judah, this word came from the LORD,
saying, 2"Thus says the LORD: 'Stand in
[a]the court of the LORD's house, and speak
to all the cities of Judah, which come to
worship *in* the LORD's house, [b]all the
words that I command you to speak to
them. [c]Do not diminish a word. 3[a]Per-
haps everyone will listen and turn from
his evil way, that I may [b]relent concerning the calamity which I purpose to bring
on them because of the evil of their doings.' 4And you shall say to them, 'Thus
says the LORD: [a]"If you will not listen to
Me, to walk in My law which I have set
before you, 5to heed the words of My servants the prophets [a]whom I sent to you,
both rising up early and sending *them*
(but you have not heeded), 6then I will
make this house like [a]Shiloh, and will
make this city [b]a curse to all the nations
of the earth." ' "
7So the priests and the prophets and all
the people heard Jeremiah speaking these
words in the house of the LORD. 8Now it
happened, when Jeremiah had made an
end of speaking all that the LORD had
commanded *him* to speak to all the people, that the priests and the prophets and
all the people seized him, saying, "You
will surely die! 9Why have you prophesied
in the name of the LORD, saying, 'This
house shall be like Shiloh, and this city
shall be [a]desolate, without an inhabitant'?" And all the people were gathered
against Jeremiah in the house of the
LORD.
10When the princes of Judah heard
these things, they came up from the
king's house to the house of the LORD and
sat down in the entry of the New Gate of
the LORD's *house.* 11And the priests and
the prophets spoke to the princes and all
the people, saying, [1]"This man deserves to
[a]die! For he has prophesied against this
city, as you have heard with your ears."
12Then Jeremiah spoke to all the princes and all the people, saying: "The LORD
sent me to prophesy against this house
and against this city with all the words
that you have heard. 13Now therefore,
[a]amend your ways and your doings, and
obey the voice of the LORD your God; then
the LORD will relent concerning the doom
that He has pronounced against you. 14As
for me, here [a]I am, in your hand; do with
me as seems good and [1]proper to you.
15But know for certain that if you put me
to death, you will surely bring innocent
blood on yourselves, on this city, and on
its inhabitants; for truly the LORD has sent
me to you to speak all these words in your
hearing."
16So the princes and all the people said
to the priests and the prophets, "This man
does not deserve to die. For he has spoken
to us in the name of the LORD our God."
17[a]Then certain of the elders of the land
rose up and spoke to all the assembly of
the people, saying: 18[a]"Micah of Moresheth prophesied in the days of Hezekiah
king of Judah, and spoke to all the people
of Judah, saying, 'Thus says the LORD of
hosts:

[b]"Zion shall be plowed *like* a field,
Jerusalem shall become [c]heaps of
ruins,
And the mountain of the [1]temple
Like the [2]bare hills of the forest." '

19Did Hezekiah king of Judah and all Judah ever put him to death? [a]Did he not
fear the LORD and [b]seek the LORD's favor?
And the LORD [c]relented concerning the
doom which He had pronounced against
them. [d]But we are doing great evil against
ourselves."
20Now there was also a man who prophesied in the name of the LORD, Urijah the
son of Shemaiah of Kirjath Jearim, who
prophesied against this city and against
this land according to all the words of Jeremiah. 21And when Jehoiakim the king,
with all his mighty men and all the princes, heard his words, the king sought to
put him to death; but when Urijah heard
it, he was afraid and fled, and went to
Egypt. 22Then Jehoiakim the king sent
men to Egypt: Elnathan the son of Achbor, and *other* men *who went* with him to
Egypt. 23And they brought Urijah from
Egypt and brought him to Jehoiakim the
king, who killed him with the sword and
cast his dead body into the graves of the
[1]common people.

CHAPTER 26
2 [a]Jer. 19:14 [b]Matt. 28:20 [c]Acts 20:27
3 [a]Jer. 36:3–7 [b]Jer. 18:8
4 [a]Lev. 26:14, 15
5 [a]Jer. 25:4; 29:19
6 [a]1 Sam. 4:10, 11 [b]Is. 65:15
9 [a]Jer. 9:11
11 [a]Jer. 38:4 [1]Lit. *A judgment of death to this man*
13 [a]Jer. 7:3
14 [a]Jer. 38:5 [1]*right*
17 [a]Acts 5:34
18 [a]Mic. 1:1 [b]Mic. 3:12 [c]Jer. 9:11 [1]Lit. *house* [2]Lit. *high places*
19 [a]2 Chr. 32:26 [b]2 Kin. 20:1–19 [c]Ex. 32:14 [d][Acts 5:39]
23 [1]Lit. *sons of the people*

24 Nevertheless [a]the hand of Ahikam the son of Shaphan was with Jeremiah, so that they should not give him into the hand of the people to put him to death.

Symbol of the Bonds and Yokes

27 In[1] the beginning of the reign of [2]Jehoiakim the son of Josiah, [a]king of Judah, this word came to Jeremiah from the LORD, saying, 2 "Thus says the LORD to me: 'Make for yourselves bonds and yokes, [a]and put them on your neck, 3 and send them to the king of Edom, the king of Moab, the king of the Ammonites, the king of Tyre, and the king of Sidon, by the hand of the messengers who come to Jerusalem to Zedekiah king of Judah. 4 And command them to say to their masters, "Thus says the LORD of hosts, the God of Israel—thus you shall say to your masters: 5 [a]'I have made the earth, the man and the beast that *are* on the ground, by My great power and by My outstretched arm, and [b]have given it to whom it seemed proper to Me. 6 [a]And now I have given all these lands into the hand of Nebuchadnezzar the king of Babylon, [b]My servant; and [c]the beasts of the field I have also given him to serve him. 7 [a]So all nations shall serve him and his son and his son's son, [b]until the time of his land comes; [c]and then many nations and great kings shall make him serve them. 8 And it shall be, *that* the nation and kingdom which will not serve Nebuchadnezzar the king of Babylon, and which will not put its neck under the yoke of the king of Babylon, that nation I will punish,' says the LORD, 'with the sword, the famine, and the pestilence, until I have consumed them by his hand. 9 Therefore do not listen to your prophets, your diviners, your [1]dreamers, your soothsayers, or your sorcerers, who speak to you, saying, "You shall not serve the king of Babylon." 10 For they prophesy a [a]lie to you, to remove you far from your land; and I will drive you out, and you will perish. 11 But the nations that bring their necks under the yoke of the king of Babylon and serve him, I will let them remain in their own land,' says the LORD, 'and they shall till it and dwell in it.' " ' "

12 I also spoke to [a]Zedekiah king of Judah according to all these words, saying, "Bring your necks under the yoke of the king of Babylon, and serve him and his people, and live! 13 [a]Why will you die, you and your people, by the sword, by the famine, and by the pestilence, as the LORD has spoken against the nation that will not serve the king of Babylon? 14 Therefore [a]do not listen to the words of the prophets who speak to you, saying, 'You shall not serve the king of Babylon,' for they prophesy [b]a lie to you; 15 for I have [a]not sent them," says the LORD, "yet they prophesy a lie in My name, that I may drive you out, and that you may perish, you and the prophets who prophesy to you."

16 Also I spoke to the priests and to all this people, saying, "Thus says the LORD: 'Do not listen to the words of your prophets who prophesy to you, saying, "Behold, [a]the vessels of the LORD's house will now shortly be brought back from Babylon"; for they prophesy a lie to you. 17 Do not listen to them; serve the king of Babylon, and live! Why should this city be laid waste? 18 But if they *are* prophets, and if the word of the LORD is with them, let them now make intercession to the LORD of hosts, that the vessels which are left in the house of the LORD, *in* the house of the king of Judah, and at Jerusalem, do not go to Babylon.'

19 "For thus says the LORD of hosts [a]concerning the pillars, concerning the Sea, concerning the carts, and concerning the remainder of the vessels that remain in this city, 20 which Nebuchadnezzar king of Babylon did not take, when he carried away [a]captive Jeconiah the son of Jehoiakim, king of Judah, from Jerusalem to Babylon, and all the nobles of Judah and Jerusalem— 21 yes, thus says the LORD of hosts, the God of Israel, concerning the [a]vessels that remain in the house of the LORD, and in the house of the king of Judah and of Jerusalem: 22 'They shall be [a]carried to Babylon, and there they shall be until the day that I [b]visit them,' says the LORD. 'Then [c]I will bring them up and restore them to this place.' "

Hananiah's Falsehood and Doom

28 And [a]it happened in the same year, at the beginning of the reign of Zedekiah king of Judah, in the [b]fourth year *and* in the fifth month, *that* Hananiah the son of [c]Azur the prophet, who *was* from Gibeon, spoke to me in the house of the LORD in the presence of the priests and of all the people, saying, 2 "Thus speaks the LORD of hosts, the God of Isra-

---

24 a 2 Kin. 22:12–14

CHAPTER 27
1 a Jer. 27:3, 12, 20; 28:1
1 LXX omits v. 1.
2 So with MT, Tg., Vg.; some Heb. mss., Arab., Syr. *Zedekiah* (cf. 27:3, 12; 28:1)
2 a Jer. 28:10, 12
5 a Is. 45:12 b Dan. 4:17, 25, 32
6 a Jer. 28:14 b Jer. 25:9; 43:10 c Dan. 2:38
7 a 2 Chr. 36:20 b [Dan. 5:26] c Jer. 25:14
9 *1* Lit. *dreams*
10 a Jer. 23:16, 32; 28:15
12 a Jer. 28:1; 38:17
13 a [Ezek. 18:31]
14 a Jer. 23:16 b Jer. 14:14; 23:21; 29:8, 9
15 a Jer. 23:21; 29:9
16 a Dan. 1:2
19 a 2 Kin. 25:13–17
20 a Jer. 24:1
21 a Jer. 20:5
22 a 2 Kin. 25:13 b 2 Chr. 36:21; Jer. 29:10; 32:5 c Ezra 1:7; 7:19

CHAPTER 28
1 a Jer. 27:1 b Jer. 51:59 c Ezek. 11:1

el, saying: 'I have broken [a]the yoke of the
king of Babylon. 3[a]Within two full years I
will bring back to this place all the vessels
of the LORD's house, that Nebuchadnezzar
king of Babylon [b]took away from this
place and carried to Babylon. 4And I will
bring back to this place [1]Jeconiah the son
of Jehoiakim, king of Judah, with all the
captives of Judah who went to Babylon,'
says the LORD, 'for I will break the yoke of
the king of Babylon.' "
5Then the prophet Jeremiah spoke to
the prophet Hananiah in the presence of
the priests and in the presence of all the
people who stood in the house of the
LORD, 6and the prophet Jeremiah said,
[a]"Amen! The LORD do so; the LORD perform your words which you have prophesied, to bring back the vessels of the
LORD's house and all who were carried
away captive, from Babylon to this place.
7Nevertheless hear now this word that I
speak in your hearing and in the hearing
of all the people: 8The prophets who have
been before me and before you of old
prophesied against many countries and
great kingdoms—of war and disaster and
pestilence. 9As for [a]the prophet who
prophesies of [b]peace, when the word of
the prophet comes to pass, the prophet
will be known *as* one whom the LORD has
truly sent."
10Then Hananiah the prophet took the
[a]yoke off the prophet Jeremiah's neck and
broke it. 11And Hananiah spoke in the
presence of all the people, saying, "Thus
says the LORD: 'Even so I will break the
yoke of Nebuchadnezzar king of Babylon
[a]from the neck of all nations within the
space of two full years.' " And the prophet
Jeremiah went his way.
12Now the word of the LORD came to
Jeremiah, after Hananiah the prophet had
broken the yoke from the neck of the
prophet Jeremiah, saying, 13"Go and tell
Hananiah, saying, 'Thus says the LORD:
"You have broken the yokes of wood, but
you have made in their place yokes of
iron." 14For thus says the LORD of hosts,
the God of Israel: [a]"I have put a yoke of
iron on the neck of all these nations, that
they may serve Nebuchadnezzar king of
Babylon; and they shall serve him. [b]I have
given him the beasts of the field also." ' "
15Then the prophet Jeremiah said to
Hananiah the prophet, "Hear now, Hananiah, the LORD has not sent you, but [a]you
make this people trust in a [b]lie. 16There-
fore thus says the LORD: 'Behold, I will
cast you from the face of the earth. This
year you shall [a]die, because you have
taught [b]rebellion against the LORD.' "
17So Hananiah the prophet died the
same year in the seventh month.

Jeremiah's Letter to the Captives

29 Now these *are* the words of the letter that Jeremiah the prophet sent
from Jerusalem to the remainder of the
elders who were [a]carried away captive—
to the priests, the prophets, and all the
people whom Nebuchadnezzar had carried away captive from Jerusalem to Babylon. 2(This happened after [a]Jeconiah[1]
the king, the [b]queen mother, the [2]eu-
nuchs, the princes of Judah and Jerusalem, the craftsmen, and the smiths had
departed from Jerusalem.) 3*The letter was
sent* by the hand of Elasah the son of
[a]Shaphan, and Gemariah the son of Hilkiah, whom Zedekiah king of Judah sent to
Babylon, to Nebuchadnezzar king of Babylon, saying,

4 Thus says the LORD of hosts, the
God of Israel, to all who were carried away captive, whom I have
caused to be carried away from Jerusalem to Babylon:

5 Build houses and dwell *in them;*
plant gardens and eat their fruit.
6Take wives and beget sons and
daughters; and take wives for your
sons and give your daughters to
husbands, so that they may bear
sons and daughters—that you may
be increased there, and not diminished. 7And seek the peace of the
city where I have caused you to be
carried away captive, [a]and pray to
the LORD for it; for in its peace you
will have peace. 8For thus says the
LORD of hosts, the God of Israel: Do
not let your prophets and your diviners who are in your midst [a]de-
ceive you, nor listen to your dreams
which you cause to be dreamed.
9For they prophesy [a]falsely to you
in My name; I have not sent them,
says the LORD.

10 For thus says the LORD: After
[a]seventy years are completed at
Babylon, I will visit you and perform My good word toward you,

2 [a]Jer. 27:12
3 [a]Jer. 27:16 [b]Dan. 1:2
4 [1] *Jehoiachin,* 2 Kin. 24:12
6 [a]1 Kin. 1:36
9 [a]Deut. 18:22 [b]Jer. 23:17
10 [a]Jer. 27:2
11 [a]Jer. 27:7
14 [a]Deut. 28:48 [b]Jer. 27:6
15 [a]Ezek. 13:22 [b]Jer. 27:10; 29:9
16 [a]Jer. 20:6 [b]Deut. 13:5

CHAPTER 29
1 [a]Jer. 27:20
2 [a]2 Kin. 24:12–16 [b]Jer. 13:18 [1] *Jehoiachin,* 2 Kin. 24:12; 2 Chr. 36:10 [2] Or *officers*
3 [a]2 Chr. 34:8
7 [a]1 Tim. 2:2
8 [a]Eph. 5:6
9 [a]Jer. 28:15; 37:19
10 [a]Dan. 9:2

and cause you to [b]return to this
place. 11 For I know the thoughts
that I think toward you, says the
LORD, thoughts of peace and not of
evil, to give you a future and a
hope. 12 Then you will [a]call upon
Me and go and pray to Me, and I
will [b]listen to you. 13 And [a]you will
seek Me and find *Me,* when you
search for Me [b]with all your heart.
14 [a]I will be found by you, says the
LORD, and I will bring you back
from your captivity; [b]I will gather
you from all the nations and from
all the places where I have driven
you, says the LORD, and I will bring
you to the place from which I cause
you to be carried away captive.

Father, the thoughts that
You think toward ____ are
thoughts of peace and not
of evil, to give her a future
and a hope.

FROM JEREMIAH 29:11

15 Because you have said, "The LORD
has raised up prophets for us in
Babylon"— 16 [a]therefore thus says
the LORD concerning the king who
sits on the throne of David, concerning all the people who dwell in
this city, and concerning your
brethren who have not gone out
with you into captivity— 17 thus
says the LORD of hosts: Behold, I
will send on them the sword, the
famine, and the pestilence, and will
make them like [a]rotten figs that
cannot be eaten, they are so bad.
18 And I will pursue them with the
sword, with famine, and with pestilence; and I [a]will deliver them to
trouble among all the kingdoms of
the earth—to be [b]a curse, an astonishment, a hissing, and a reproach among all the nations where
I have driven them, 19 because they
have not heeded My words, says the
LORD, which [a]I sent to them by My
servants the prophets, rising up
early and sending *them;* neither

10 [b] [Jer. 24:6, 7]
12 [a] Ps. 50:15 [b] Ps. 145:19
13 [a] Deut. 30:1–3 [b] Jer. 24:7
14 [a] [Is. 55:6, 7] [b] Jer. 23:8; 32:37
16 [a] Jer. 38:2, 3, 17–23
17 [a] Jer. 24:3, 8–10
18 [a] Deut. 28:25 [b] Jer. 26:6; 42:18
19 [a] Jer. 25:4; 26:5; 35:15
21 [a] Lam. 2:14
22 [a] Is. 65:15 [b] Dan. 3:6, 21
23 [a] Jer. 23:14 [b] [Prov. 5:21]
25 [a] Jer. 21:1
26 [a] Jer. 20:1 [b] John 10:20 [c] Jer. 20:1, 2
31 [a] Jer. 28:15

would you heed, says the LORD.
20 Therefore hear the word of the
LORD, all you of the captivity,
whom I have sent from Jerusalem
to Babylon.

21 Thus says the LORD of hosts, the
God of Israel, concerning Ahab the
son of Kolaiah, and Zedekiah the
son of Maaseiah, who prophesy a
[a]lie to you in My name: Behold, I
will deliver them into the hand of
Nebuchadnezzar king of Babylon,
and he shall slay them before your
eyes. 22 [a]And because of them a
curse shall be taken up by all the
captivity of Judah who *are* in Babylon, saying, "The LORD make you
like Zedekiah and Ahab, [b]whom the
king of Babylon roasted in the fire";
23 because [a]they have done disgraceful things in Israel, have committed
adultery with their neighbors'
wives, and have spoken lying words
in My name, which I have not commanded them. Indeed I [b]know, and
am a witness, says the LORD.

24 You shall also speak to Shemaiah
the Nehelamite, saying, 25 Thus
speaks the LORD of hosts, the God
of Israel, saying: You have sent letters in your name to all the people
who *are* at Jerusalem, [a]to Zephaniah the son of Maaseiah the priest,
and to all the priests, saying, 26 "The
LORD has made you priest instead
of Jehoiada the priest, so that there
should be [a]officers *in* the house of
the LORD over every man *who* is
[b]demented and considers himself a
prophet, that you should [c]put him
in prison and in the stocks. 27 Now
therefore, why have you not rebuked Jeremiah of Anathoth who
makes himself a prophet to you?
28 For he has sent to us *in* Babylon,
saying, 'This *captivity is* long; build
houses and dwell *in them,* and
plant gardens and eat their fruit.' "

29 Now Zephaniah the priest read
this letter in the hearing of Jeremiah the prophet. 30 Then the word of
the LORD came to Jeremiah, saying:
31 Send to all those in captivity, saying, Thus says the LORD concerning
Shemaiah the Nehelamite: Because
Shemaiah has prophesied to you,
[a]and I have not sent him, and he

Jeremiah 29:11

Dear Woman of Destiny,

I had a dream years ago in which thousands gathered in a large coliseum to observe a king's court proceedings. Every woman was given a number; mine was 29. A woman was there who was consumed with doing the most demeaning things to revile me, but I ran from her evil intentions. No one had known it, but that day the king's son was going to choose his bride. He had been watching the previous encounter between this woman and myself, and had seen me run from evil. When he was asked who his choice was, he answered, "Number 29!" Everyone was startled and began asking where I was. I suddenly reentered the court dressed in regal clothes and with an expression of confidence on my face. I walked down the steps to the king's son, and he leaned over and kissed me. He handed me a scepter, and we both turned and sat in the two throne chairs. That's where the dream ended.

For years afterward I kept asking the Lord, "What does the number 29 mean?" One night He clearly said, "It's Jeremiah 29." I knew then that the dream was not about me, but about the bride of Christ. It was a picture of how the world hates the bride, how a war is raging between the kingdoms of this world and the kingdom of our Christ. Jesus, our Groom, is watching and waiting for our wedding day when He gets to embrace us as His own.

Verse 11 of Jeremiah 29 contains the heart of what God was trying to tell me, because it speaks of purpose and destiny. The plans of the devil are to make us feel discouraged and hopeless so that we will miss the truth of God's all-consuming love for each of us. The devil wants us to feel forgotten and abandoned. We must walk through the difficulties and challenges of life, keeping our eyes fixed on Him and His promise that He knows the thoughts and plans He has for us.

In my searching, I discovered the number 29 to mean "being chosen by God"; and soon afterward, the Lord began unearthing other "29" scriptures such as Esther 2:9, Psalm 29, 1 Peter 2:9, and Acts "29," which is the church of today continuing on in the faith from Acts 28.

The bottom line is this: God wants us to know beyond a shadow of a doubt that He chose us, He loves us, and we must fight the fight of faith that believes His Word at all costs, at all times, regardless what situation we may find ourselves in. He knows all about our destinies and our callings, and He has not forgotten. He will be faithful to each one of us, to give us hope in our final outcome. Oh how great is His love!

Michal Ann Goll

has caused you to trust in a [b]lie—
[32]therefore thus says the LORD: Behold, I will punish Shemaiah the
Nehelamite and his [1]family: he
shall not have anyone to dwell
among this people, nor shall he see
the good that I will do for My people, says the LORD, [a]because he has
taught rebellion against the LORD.

Restoration of Israel and Judah

30 The word that came to Jeremiah
from the LORD, saying, [2]"Thus
speaks the LORD God of Israel, saying:
'Write in a book for yourself all the words
that I have spoken to you. [3]For behold,
the days are coming,' says the LORD, 'that
[a]I will bring back from captivity My people Israel and Judah,' says the LORD. [b]'And
I will cause them to return to the land
that I gave to their fathers, and they shall
possess it.' "
[4]Now these *are* the words that the LORD
spoke concerning Israel and Judah.
[5]"For thus says the LORD:

'We have heard a voice of trembling,
Of [1]fear, and not of peace.
6 Ask now, and see,
Whether a [1]man is ever in [2]labor
with child?
So why do I see every man *with* his
hands on his loins
[a]Like a woman in labor,
And all faces turned pale?
7 [a]Alas! For that day *is* great,
[b]So that none *is* like it;
And it *is* the time of Jacob's
trouble,
But he shall be saved out of it.

8 'For it shall come to pass in that
day,'
Says the LORD of hosts,
'*That* I will break his yoke from
your neck,
And will burst your bonds;
Foreigners shall no more enslave
them.
9 But they shall serve the LORD their
God,
And [a]David their king,
Whom I will [b]raise up for them.

10 'Therefore [a]do not fear, O My
servant Jacob,' says the LORD,
'Nor be dismayed, O Israel;

31 [b] Ezek. 13:8–16, 22, 23
32 [a] Jer. 28:16 [1] *descendants,* lit. *seed*
CHAPTER 30
3 [a] Ezek. 39:25 [b] Jer. 16:15
5 [1] *dread*
6 [a] Jer. 4:31; 6:24 [1] Lit. *male can give birth* [2] *childbirth*
7 [a] Amos 5:18 [b] Dan. 9:12; 12:1
9 [a] Hos. 3:5 [b] [Luke 1:69]
10 [a] Is. 41:13; 43:5; 44:2 [b] Jer. 3:18
11 [a] [Is. 43:2–5] [b] Amos 9:8 [c] Jer. 4:27; 46:27, 28 [d] Ps. 6:1
12 [a] Jer. 15:18
13 [a] Jer. 8:22
14 [a] Lam. 1:2 [b] Job 13:24; 16:9; 19:11 [c] Job 30:21 [d] Jer. 5:6
15 [a] Jer. 15:18
16 [a] Jer. 10:25 [b] Is. 14:2 [c] Ezek. 39:10 [d] Jer. 2:3
17 [a] Jer. 33:6

For behold, I will save you from
afar,
And your seed [b]from the land of
their captivity.
Jacob shall return, have rest and be
quiet,
And no one shall make *him* afraid.
11 For I *am* with [a]you,' says the
LORD, 'to save you;
[b]Though I make a full end of all
nations where I have scattered
you,
[c]Yet I will not make a complete end
of you.
But I will correct you [d]in justice,
And will not let you go altogether
unpunished.'

[12]"For thus says the LORD:

[a]'Your affliction *is* incurable,
Your wound *is* severe.
13 *There is* no one to plead your
cause,
That you may be bound up;
[a]You have no healing medicines.
14 [a]All your lovers have forgotten you;
They do not seek you;
For I have wounded you with the
wound [b]of an enemy,
With the chastisement [c]of a cruel
one,
For the multitude of your
iniquities,
[d]*Because* your sins have increased.
15 Why [a]do you cry about your
affliction?
Your sorrow *is* incurable.
Because of the multitude of your
iniquities,
Because your sins have increased,
I have done these things to you.

16 'Therefore all those who devour
you [a]shall be devoured;
And all your adversaries, every one
of them, shall go into [b]captivity;
Those who plunder you shall
become [c]plunder,
And all who prey upon you I will
make a [d]prey.
17 [a]For I will restore health to you
And heal you of your wounds,' says
the LORD,
'Because they called you an outcast
saying:
"This *is* Zion;
No one seeks her." '

[18]"Thus says the LORD:

'Behold, I will bring back the captivity of Jacob's tents,
And [a]have mercy on his dwelling places;
The city shall be built upon its own [1]mound,
And the palace shall remain according to its own plan.
19 Then [a]out of them shall proceed thanksgiving
And the voice of those who make merry;
[b]I will multiply them, and they shall not diminish;
I will also glorify them, and they shall not be small.
20 Their children also shall be [a]as before,
And their congregation shall be established before Me;
And I will punish all who oppress them.
21 Their nobles shall be from among them,
[a]And their governor shall come from their midst;
Then I will [b]cause him to draw near,
And he shall approach Me;
For who *is* this who pledged his heart to approach Me?' says the LORD.
22 'You shall be [a]My people,
And I will be your God.' "

Clothe yourself with the silk of piety, with the satin of sanctity, with the purple of modesty, so God Himself shall be your suitor.

TERTULLIAN

23 Behold, the [a]whirlwind of the LORD
Goes forth with fury,
A [1]continuing whirlwind;
It will fall violently on the head of the wicked.
24 The fierce anger of the LORD will not return until He has done it,
And until He has performed the intents of His heart.
[a]In the latter days you will consider it.

The Remnant of Israel Saved

31 "At [a]the same time," says the LORD,
[b]"I will be the God of all the families of Israel, and they shall be My people."
2 Thus says the LORD:

"The people who survived the sword
Found grace in the wilderness—
Israel, when [a]I went to give him rest."
3 The LORD has appeared [1]of old to me, *saying:*
"Yes, [a]I have loved you with [b]an everlasting love;
Therefore with lovingkindness I have [c]drawn you.
4 Again [a]I will build you, and you shall be rebuilt,
O virgin of Israel!
You shall again be adorned with your [b]tambourines,
And shall go forth in the dances of those who rejoice.
5 [a]You shall yet plant vines on the mountains of Samaria;
The planters shall plant and [1]eat *them* as ordinary food.
6 For there shall be a day
When the watchmen will cry on Mount Ephraim,
[a]'Arise, and let us go up *to* Zion,
To the LORD our God.' "
7 For thus says the LORD:

[a]"Sing with gladness for Jacob,
And shout among the chief of the nations;
Proclaim, give praise, and say,
'O LORD, save Your people,
The remnant of Israel!'
8 Behold, I will bring them [a]from the north country,
And [b]gather them from the ends of the earth,
Among them the blind and the lame,
The woman with child
And the one who labors with child, together;
A great throng shall return there.
9 [a]They shall come with weeping,
And with supplications I will lead them.
I will cause them to walk [b]by the rivers of waters,

18 a Ps. 102:13 1 *ruins*
19 a Is. 51:11 b Zech. 10:8
20 a Is. 1:26
21 a Gen. 49:10 b Num. 16:5
22 a Ezek. 36:28
23 a Jer. 23:19, 20; 25:32 1 Or *sweeping*
24 a Gen. 49:1

CHAPTER 31
1 a Jer. 30:24 b Jer. 30:22
2 a Num. 10:33
3 a Mal. 1:2 b Rom. 11:28 c Hos. 11:4 1 Lit. *from afar*
4 a Jer. 33:7 b Judg. 11:34
5 a Amos 9:14 1 Lit. *treat them as common*
6 a [Mic. 4:2]
7 a Is. 12:5, 6
8 a Jer. 3:12, 18; 23:8 b Ezek. 20:34, 41; 34:13
9 a [Jer. 50:4] b Is. 35:8; 43:19; 49:10, 11

In a straight way in which they
shall not stumble;
For I am a Father to Israel,
And Ephraim *is* My [c]firstborn.

10 "Hear the word of the LORD,
O nations,
And declare *it* in the [1]isles afar off,
and say,
'He who scattered Israel [a]will gather
him,
And keep him as a shepherd *does*
his flock.'
11 For [a]the LORD has redeemed
Jacob,
And ransomed him [b]from the hand
of one stronger than he.
12 Therefore they shall come and
sing in [a]the height of Zion,
Streaming to [b]the goodness of the
LORD—
For wheat and new wine and oil,
For the young of the flock and the
herd;
Their souls shall be like a
[c]well-watered garden,
[d]And they shall sorrow no more at
all.

13 "Then shall the virgin rejoice in
the dance,
And the young men and the old,
together;
For I will turn their mourning to
joy,
Will comfort them,
And make them rejoice rather than
sorrow.
14 I will [1]satiate the soul of the
priests with abundance,
And My people shall be satisfied
with My goodness, says the
LORD."

Mercy on Ephraim

15 Thus says the LORD:
[a]"A voice was heard in [b]Ramah,
Lamentation *and* bitter [c]weeping,
Rachel weeping for her children,
Refusing to be comforted for her
children,
Because [d]they *are* no more."

16 Thus says the LORD:
"Refrain your voice from [a]weeping,
And your eyes from tears;
For your work shall be rewarded,
says the LORD,
And they shall come back from the
land of the enemy.
17 There is [a]hope in your future, says
the LORD,
That *your* children shall come back
to their own border.

18 "I have surely heard Ephraim
bemoaning himself:
'You have [a]chastised me, and I was
chastised,
Like an untrained bull;
[b]Restore me, and I will return,
For You *are* the LORD my God.
19 Surely, [a]after my turning, I
repented;
And after I was instructed, I struck
myself on the thigh;
I was [b]ashamed, yes, even
humiliated,
Because I bore the reproach of my
youth.'
20 *Is* Ephraim My dear son?
Is he a pleasant child?
For though I spoke against him,
I earnestly remember him still;
[a]Therefore My [1]heart yearns for him;
[b]I will surely have mercy on him,
says the LORD.

21 "Set up signposts,
Make landmarks;
[a]Set your heart toward the highway,
The way in *which* you went.
[1]Turn back, O virgin of Israel,
Turn back to these your cities.
22 How long will you [a]gad about,
O you [b]backsliding daughter?
For the LORD has created a new
thing in the earth—
A woman shall encompass a man."

Future Prosperity of Judah

23 Thus says the LORD of hosts, the God
of Israel: "They shall again use this speech
in the land of Judah and in its cities, when
I bring back their captivity: [a]'The LORD
bless you, O home of justice, *and* [b]moun-
tain of holiness!' 24 And there shall dwell
in Judah itself, and [a]in all its cities together, farmers and those going out with
flocks. 25 For I have [1]satiated the weary
soul, and I have replenished every sorrowful soul."
26 After this I awoke and looked around,
and my sleep was [a]sweet to me.
27 "Behold, the days are coming, says
the LORD, that [a]I will sow the house of
Israel and the house of Judah with the

9 c Ex. 4:22
10 a Is. 40:11 1 Or *coastlands*
11 a Is. 44:23; 48:20 b Is. 49:24
12 a Ezek. 17:23 b Hos. 3:5 c Is. 58:11 d Is. 35:10; 65:19
14 1 Fill to the full
15 a Matt. 2:17, 18 b Josh. 18:25 c Gen. 37:35 d Jer. 10:20
16 a [Is. 25:8; 30:19]
17 a Jer. 29:11
18 a Ps. 94:12 b Lam. 5:21
19 a Deut. 30:2 b Ezek. 36:31
20 a Is. 63:15 b [Hos. 14:4] 1 Lit. *inward parts*
21 a Jer. 50:5 1 Or *Return*
22 a Jer. 2:18, 23, 36 b Jer. 3:6, 8, 11, 12, 14, 22
23 a Is. 1:26 b [Zech. 8:3]
24 a Jer. 33:12
25 1 *fully satisfied*
26 a Prov. 3:24
27 a Ezek. 36:9–11

seed of man and the seed of beast. 28And
it shall come to pass, *that* as I have
[a]watched over them [b]to pluck up, to
break down, to throw down, to destroy,
and to afflict, so I will watch over them [c]to
build and to plant, says the LORD. 29[a]In
those days they shall say no more:

'The fathers have eaten sour grapes,
And the children's teeth are set on
edge.'

30[a]But every one shall die for his own
iniquity; every man who eats the sour
grapes, his teeth shall be set on edge.

A New Covenant

31"Behold, the [a]days are coming, says
the LORD, when I will make a new covenant with the house of Israel and with
the house of Judah— 32not according to
the covenant that I made with their fathers in the day *that* [a]I took them by the
hand to lead them out of the land of
Egypt, My covenant which they broke,
[1]though I was a husband to them, says the
LORD. 33[a]But this *is* the covenant that I
will make with the house of Israel after
those days, says the LORD: [b]I will put My
law in their minds, and write it on their
[1]hearts; [c]and I will be their God, and they
shall be My people. 34No more shall every
man teach his neighbor, and every man
his brother, saying, 'Know the LORD,' for
[a]they all shall know Me, from the least of
them to the greatest of them, says the
LORD. For [b]I will forgive their iniquity,
and their sin I will remember no more."

35 Thus says the LORD,
[a]Who gives the sun for a light by
day,
The ordinances of the moon and
the stars for a light by night,
Who disturbs [b]the sea,
And its waves roar
[c](The LORD of hosts *is* His name):

36 "If [a]those ordinances depart
From before Me, says the LORD,
Then the seed of Israel shall also
cease
From being a nation before Me
forever."

37Thus says the LORD:

[a]"If heaven above can be measured,
And the foundations of the earth
searched out beneath,
I will also [b]cast off all the seed of
Israel
For all that they have done, says
the LORD.

38"Behold, the days are coming, says
the LORD, that the city shall be built for
the LORD [a]from the Tower of Hananel to
the Corner Gate. 39[a]The surveyor's line
shall again extend straight forward over
the hill Gareb; then it shall turn toward
Goath. 40And the whole valley of the dead
bodies and of the ashes, and all the fields
as far as the Brook Kidron, [a]to the corner
of the Horse Gate toward the east, [b]*shall
be* holy to the LORD. It shall not be
plucked up or thrown down anymore forever."

Jeremiah Buys a Field

32 The word that came to Jeremiah
from the LORD [a]in the tenth year of
Zedekiah king of Judah, which was the
eighteenth year of Nebuchadnezzar. 2For
then the king of Babylon's army besieged
Jerusalem, and Jeremiah the prophet was
shut up [a]in the court of the prison, which
was in the king of Judah's house. 3For
Zedekiah king of Judah had shut him up,
saying, "Why do you [a]prophesy and say,
'Thus says the LORD: [b]"Behold, I will give
this city into the hand of the king of Babylon, and he shall take it; 4and Zedekiah
king of Judah [a]shall not escape from the
hand of the Chaldeans, but shall surely be
delivered into the hand of the king of Babylon, and shall speak with him [1]face to
face, and see him [b]eye to eye; 5then he
shall [a]lead Zedekiah to Babylon, and there
he shall be [b]until I visit him," says the
LORD; [c]"though you fight with the Chaldeans, you shall not succeed" '?"

6And Jeremiah said, "The word of the
LORD came to me, saying, 7'Behold, Hanamel the son of Shallum your uncle will
come to you, saying, "Buy my field which
is in Anathoth, for the [a]right of redemption *is* yours to buy *it*." ' 8Then Hanamel
my uncle's son came to me in the court of
the prison according to the word of the
LORD, and said to me, 'Please buy my field
that *is* in Anathoth, which *is* in the country of Benjamin; for the right of inheritance *is* yours, and the redemption yours;
buy *it* for yourself.' Then I knew that this
was the word of the LORD. 9So I bought
the field from Hanamel, the son of my

28 a Jer. 44:27 b Jer. 1:10; 18:7 c Jer. 24:6
29 a Ezek. 18:2, 3
30 a [Gal. 6:5, 7]
31 a Heb. 8:8–12; 10:16, 17
32 a Deut. 1:31 *1* So with MT, Tg., Vg.; LXX, Syr. *and I turned away from them*
33 a Jer. 32:40 b Ps. 40:8 c Jer. 24:7; 30:22; 32:38 *1* Lit. *inward parts*
34 a [John 6:45] b [Rom. 11:27]
35 a Gen. 1:14–18 b Is. 51:15 c Jer. 10:16
36 a Ps. 148:6
37 a Jer. 33:22 b [Rom. 11:2–5, 26, 27]
38 a Zech. 14:10
39 a Zech. 2:1, 2
40 a Neh. 3:28 b [Joel 3:17]

CHAPTER 32
1 a Jer. 39:1, 2
2 a Jer. 33:1; 37:21; 39:14
3 a Jer. 26:8, 9 b Jer. 21:3–7; 34:2
4 a Jer. 34:3; 38:18, 23; 39:5; 52:9 b Jer. 39:5 *1* Lit. *mouth to mouth*
5 a Ezek. 12:12, 13 b Jer. 27:22 c Jer. 21:4; 33:5
7 a Ruth 4:4

uncle who *was* in Anathoth, and [a]weighed
out to him the money—seventeen shekels of silver. 10And I signed the [1]deed and
sealed *it,* took witnesses, and weighed the
money on the scales. 11So I took the purchase deed, *both* that which was sealed
according to the law and custom, and that
which was open; 12and I gave the purchase
deed to [a]Baruch the son of Neriah, son of
Mahseiah, in the presence of Hanamel my
uncle's *son,* and in the presence of the
[b]witnesses who signed the purchase deed,
before all the Jews who sat in the court of
the prison.
13"Then I charged [a]Baruch before
them, saying, 14'Thus says the LORD of
hosts, the God of Israel: "Take these
deeds, both this purchase deed which is
sealed and this deed which is open, and
put them in an earthen vessel, that they
may last many days." 15For thus says the
LORD of hosts, the God of Israel: "Houses

9 [a]Zech. 11:12
10 [1]Lit. *book*
12 [a]Jer. 36:4 [b]Is. 8:2
13 [a]Jer. 36:4

Anne Hutchinson

More than any other woman during America's colonial period, Anne Hutchinson (1591–1643) paved the way for religious freedom in the young nation now called the United States. Anne's mother was of Puritan descent, while her father, Rev. Francis Marbury, was a minister in the Church of England, though not always agreeable to church practices. The Cambridge-educated Marbury recognized Anne's quick mind and intellectual promise. He invested large amounts of time and energy teaching Anne and made his library available to her at all times, constantly encouraging her to read everything she could and to devote herself to the Scriptures.

In 1612, Anne married textile merchant William Hutchinson. They traveled frequently to the village of Boston, England, in order to listen to the young, energetic minister John Cotton. Cotton was as controversial as he was popular and preached the Puritan message with boldness, to the dismay of officials in the Church of England. Anne Hutchinson believed, like Cotton, in a "Covenant of Grace" as opposed to a "Covenant of Works." She believed that people were saved by God's grace and not by their own good works. She also believed that people should judge themselves with God's love as their standard instead of being judged by the church with its legalistic rules as their standard. Furthermore, she believed that people could pray and hear from God for themselves instead of looking to church authorities to interpret the will and ways of God.

As religious persecution increased against the Puritans, Anne and her family decided to leave England and follow John Cotton to America in search of religious freedom. But Anne's hopes were short-lived. She soon found as much narrow-mindedness among some of the Puritans in America as she had endured from Church of England people before moving to America. In fact, she encountered so much opposition to her beliefs that she was eventually arrested and put on trial for heresy. The courts found her guilty and banished her from her home in the Massachusetts Bay Colony. She lived the rest of her life in Rhode Island, having lost her court battle, but having won a great personal victory by remaining true to her convictions.

Jeremiah 33:3–9

Dear Woman of Destiny,

In my opinion, the theme of Jeremiah 33:3–9 is found in the word "restoration." I believe there is a powerful truth waiting to manifest in our lives through our understanding of what it means to be restored. When I studied this word in the Scriptures, I found a pattern that unleashed something very strong in my spirit.

Psalm 107:20 says, "He sent His word and healed them, and delivered them from their destructions." Destruction is a pretty miserable word. The people of Israel were definitely at a point of destruction when the prophet Jeremiah spoke these words in chapter 33. Destruction means to bow down to superiority or to wallow in that superiority or the superiority of someone else. There are only two other times in the Old Testament that the root for this word *destruction* is translated this way. Aside from Psalm 107:20, Lamentations 4:20 also mentions destruction. The word used there is *pits*. Israel was definitely in the pits.

The absolute opposite of destruction is restoration. We all know that whatever God intended and created, Satan has a counterfeit. But whatever Satan has, God has a fix for it. Whatever the devil does to you, God has an answer. In Jeremiah 30:17, God says to His people, "I will restore health to you and heal you of your wounds." Out of the pit of destruction, God has promised to restore you.

Satan comes to destroy you, to make you bow down to sin, sickness, poverty, and disease to the point of destruction in your life. Hosea 4:6 says, "My people are destroyed for lack of knowledge." Another way of translating that is to say, "My people are being pulverized beyond recognition." Much of Christianity has been pulverized beyond recognition. Many Christians have been so pulverized by Satan's schemes of attack that it's hard to even recognize the Christianity left in them.

But God's opposite word is available to you. The word *restore* means "to ascend, to rise up." That is the exact opposite of bowing down. When Satan wants us to bow down to the effects of sickness or to the effects of sin, remember God wants to see us restored. *Restore* also means "to continually convert, deliver, fetch back home again, recompense, recover, relieve, return, rescue, retrieve, or reward." God says He will restore. He wants us to recover. He wants to bring it all back. He wants to exalt us, to elevate us, not for the sake of our being exalted, but to further our destiny in Him. When He restores us, we can go on ministering or preaching or doing whatever it is we're called to do.

How are we restored? The answer is stated simply in Jeremiah 33:3: "Call to Me, and I will answer you." We have to reach out and call upon God. Not only do I believe God can restore us, I believe He watches over His Word to perform it. Nothing else can restore us. And "this is the confidence that we have in Him, that if we ask anything according to His will, He hears us. And if we know that He hears us, whatever we ask, we know that we have the petitions that we have asked of Him" (1 John 5:14, 15).

Even when Satan has sent destruction your way, God has restoration. He is our God of restoration.

Lindsay Roberts

also be broken with David My servant, so
that he shall not have a son to reign on his
throne, and with the Levites, the priests,
My ministers. 22 As [a]the host of heaven
cannot be numbered, nor the sand of the
sea measured, so will I [b]multiply the descendants of David My servant and the
[c]Levites who minister to Me.' "
23 Moreover the word of the LORD came
to Jeremiah, saying, 24 "Have you not considered what these people have spoken,
saying, 'The two families which the LORD
has chosen, He has also cast them off'?
Thus they have [a]despised My people, as if
they should no more be a nation before
them.
25 "Thus says the LORD: 'If [a]My covenant
is not with day and night, *and if* I have not
[b]appointed the ordinances of heaven and
earth, 26 [a]then I will [b]cast away the descendants of Jacob and David My servant,
so that I will not take *any* of his descendants *to be* rulers over the descendants
of Abraham, Isaac, and Jacob. For I will
cause their captives to return, and will
have mercy on them.' "

Zedekiah Warned by God

34 The word which came to Jeremiah
from the LORD, [a]when Nebuchadnezzar king of Babylon and all his army,
[b]all the kingdoms of the earth under his
dominion, and all the people, fought
against Jerusalem and all its cities, saying,
2 "Thus says the LORD, the God of Israel:
'Go and [a]speak to Zedekiah king of Judah
and tell him, "Thus says the LORD: 'Behold, [b]I will give this city into the hand of
the king of Babylon, and he shall burn it
with fire. 3 And [a]you shall not escape from
his hand, but shall surely be taken and
delivered into his hand; your eyes shall
see the eyes of the king of Babylon, he
shall speak with you [b]face[1] to face, and
you shall go to Babylon.' " ' 4 Yet hear the
word of the LORD, O Zedekiah king of Judah! Thus says the LORD concerning you:
'You shall not die by the sword. 5 You shall
die in peace; as in [a]the ceremonies of your
fathers, the former kings who were before
you, [b]so they shall burn incense for you
and [c]lament for you, *saying,* "Alas, lord!"
For I have pronounced the word, says the
LORD.' "
6 Then Jeremiah the prophet spoke all
these words to Zedekiah king of Judah in
Jerusalem, 7 when the king of Babylon's
army fought against Jerusalem and all the

22 [a]Gen. 15:5; 22:17 [b]Jer. 30:19 [c]Is. 66:21
24 [a]Esth. 3:6–8
25 [a]Gen. 8:22 [b]Ps. 74:16; 104:19
26 [a]Jer. 31:37 [b]Rom. 11:1, 2

CHAPTER 34
1 [a]2 Kin. 25:1 [b]Jer. 1:15; 25:9
2 [a]2 Chr. 36:11, 12 [b]Jer. 21:10; 32:3, 28
3 [a]2 Kin. 25:4, 5 [b]Jer. 32:4; 39:5, 6 [1]Lit. *mouth to mouth*
5 [a]2 Chr. 16:14; 21:19 [b]Dan. 2:46 [c]Jer. 22:18
7 [a]2 Kin. 18:13; 19:8
8 [a]Ex. 21:2
9 [a]Neh. 5:11 [b]Lev. 25:39–46
13 [a]Ex. 24:3, 7, 8
14 [a]Deut. 15:12 [1]Or *sold himself*
15 [a]Neh. 10:29 [b]Jer. 7:10 [1]Lit. *today*
16 [a]Ex. 20:7
17 [a][Matt. 7:2] [b]Jer. 32:24, 36 [c]Deut. 28:25, 64

cities of Judah that were left, against Lachish and Azekah; for *only* [a]these fortified
cities remained of the cities of Judah.

Treacherous Treatment of Slaves

8 *This is* the word that came to Jeremiah
from the LORD, after King Zedekiah had
made a covenant with all the people who
were at Jerusalem to proclaim [a]liberty to
them: 9 [a]that every man should set free his
male and female slave—a Hebrew man or
woman—[b]that no one should keep a Jewish brother in bondage. 10 Now when all
the princes and all the people, who had
entered into the covenant, heard that everyone should set free his male and female
slaves, that no one should keep them in
bondage anymore, they obeyed and let
them go. 11 But afterward they changed
their minds and made the male and female slaves return, whom they had set
free, and brought them into subjection as
male and female slaves.
12 Therefore the word of the LORD came
to Jeremiah from the LORD, saying,
13 "Thus says the LORD, the God of Israel:
'I made a [a]covenant with your fathers in
the day that I brought them out of the
land of Egypt, out of the house of bondage, saying, 14 "At the end of [a]seven years
let every man set free his Hebrew brother,
who [1]has been sold to him; and when he
has served you six years, you shall let him
go free from you." But your fathers did
not obey Me nor incline their ear. 15 Then
you [1]recently turned and did what was
right in My sight—every man proclaiming liberty to his neighbor; and you [a]made
a covenant before Me [b]in the house which
is called by My name. 16 Then you turned
around and [a]profaned My name, and every
one of you brought back his male and female slaves, whom you had set at liberty,
at their pleasure, and brought them back
into subjection, to be your male and female slaves.'
17 "Therefore thus says the LORD: 'You
have not obeyed Me in proclaiming liberty, every one to his brother and every one
to his neighbor. [a]Behold, I proclaim liberty to you,' says the LORD—[b]'to the sword,
to pestilence, and to famine! And I will
deliver you to [c]trouble among all the
kingdoms of the earth. 18 And I will give
the men who have transgressed My covenant, who have not performed the words
of the covenant which they made before

Me, when [a]they cut the calf in two and
passed between the parts of it— [19]the
princes of Judah, the princes of Jerusalem, the [1]eunuchs, the priests, and all the
people of the land who passed between the
parts of the calf— [20]I will [a]give them into
the hand of their enemies and into the
hand of those who seek their life. Their
[b]dead bodies shall be for meat for the
birds of the heaven and the beasts of the
earth. [21]And I will give Zedekiah king of
Judah and his princes into the hand of
their enemies, into the hand of those who
seek their life, and into the hand of the
king of Babylon's army [a]which has gone
back from you. [22][a]Behold, I will command,' says the LORD, 'and cause them to
return to this city. They will fight against
it [b]and take it and burn it with fire; and [c]I
will make the cities of Judah a desolation
without inhabitant.' "

The Obedient Rechabites

35 The word which came to Jeremiah
from the LORD in the days of Jehoiakim the son of Josiah, king of Judah, saying, [2]"Go to the house of the [a]Rechabites,
speak to them, and bring them into the
house of the LORD, into one of [b]the chambers, and give them wine to drink."

[3]Then I took Jaazaniah the son of Jeremiah, the son of Habazziniah, his
brothers and all his sons, and the whole
house of the Rechabites, [4]and I brought
them into the house of the LORD, into the
chamber of the sons of Hanan the son of
Igdaliah, a man of God, which *was* by the
chamber of the princes, above the chamber of Maaseiah the son of Shallum, [a]the
keeper of the [1]door. [5]Then I set before the
sons of the house of the Rechabites bowls
full of wine, and cups; and I said to them,
"Drink wine."

[6]But they said, "We will drink no wine,
for [a]Jonadab the son of Rechab, our father, commanded us, saying, 'You shall
drink [b]no wine, you nor your sons, forever. [7]You shall not build a house, sow seed,
plant a vineyard, nor have *any of these;*
but all your days you shall dwell in tents,
[a]that you may live many days in the land
where you are sojourners.' [8]Thus we have
[a]obeyed the voice of Jonadab the son of
Rechab, our father, in all that he charged
us, to drink no wine all our days, we, our
wives, our sons, or our daughters, [9]nor to
build ourselves houses to dwell in; nor do
we have vineyard, field, or seed. [10]But we
have dwelt in tents, and have obeyed and
done according to all that Jonadab our
father commanded us. [11]But it came to
pass, when Nebuchadnezzar king of Babylon came up into the land, that we said,
'Come, let us [a]go to Jerusalem for fear of
the army of the Chaldeans and for fear of
the army of the Syrians.' So we dwell at
Jerusalem."

[12]Then came the word of the LORD to
Jeremiah, saying, [13]"Thus says the LORD
of hosts, the God of Israel: 'Go and tell the
men of Judah and the inhabitants of Jerusalem, "Will you not [a]receive instruction
to [1]obey My words?" says the LORD. [14]"The
words of Jonadab the son of Rechab,
which he commanded his sons, not to
drink wine, are performed; for to this day
they drink none, and obey their father's
commandment. [a]But although I have
spoken to you, [b]rising early and speaking,
you did not [1]obey Me. [15]I have also sent to
you all My [a]servants the prophets, rising
up early and sending *them,* saying, [b]'Turn
now everyone from his evil way, amend
your doings, and do not go after other
gods to serve them; then you will [c]dwell
in the land which I have given you and
your fathers.' But you have not inclined
your ear, nor obeyed Me. [16]Surely the
sons of Jonadab the son of Rechab have
performed the commandment of their
[a]father, which he commanded them, but
this people has not obeyed Me." '

[17]"Therefore thus says the LORD God of
hosts, the God of Israel: 'Behold, I will
bring on Judah and on all the inhabitants
of Jerusalem all the doom that I have pronounced against them; [a]because I have
spoken to them but they have not heard,
and I have called to them but they have
not answered.' "

[18]And Jeremiah said to the house of the
Rechabites, "Thus says the LORD of hosts,
the God of Israel: 'Because you have
obeyed the commandment of Jonadab
your father, and kept all his precepts and
done according to all that he commanded
you, [19]therefore thus says the LORD of
hosts, the God of Israel: "Jonadab the son
of Rechab shall not lack a man to [a]stand
before Me forever." ' "

The Scroll Read in the Temple

36 Now it came to pass in the [a]fourth
year of Jehoiakim the son of Josiah, king of Judah, *that* this word came to

---

18 [a]Gen. 15:10, 17
19 [1]Or *officers*
20 [a]Jer. 22:25 [b]Jer. 7:33; 16:4; 19:7
21 [a]Jer.37:5–11; 39:4–7
22 [a]Jer. 37:8, 10 [b]Jer. 38:3; 39:1, 2, 8; 52:7, 13 [c]Jer. 9:11; 44:2, 6

CHAPTER 35
2 [a]1 Chr. 2:55 [b]1 Kin. 6:5, 8
4 [a]1 Chr. 9:18, 19 [1]Lit. *threshold*
6 [a]2 Kin. 10:15, 23 [b]Luke 1:15
7 [a]Ex. 20:12
8 [a][Col. 3:20]
11 [a]Jer. 4:5–7; 8:14
13 [a]Jer. 6:10; 17:23; 32:33 [1]*listen to*
14 [a]2 Chr. 36:15 [b]Jer. 7:13; 25:3 [1]*listen to*
15 [a]Jer. 26:4, 5; 29:19 [b]Jer. 18:11; 25:5, 6 [c]Jer. 7:7; 25:5, 6
16 [a][Heb. 12:9]
17 [a]Prov. 1:24
19 [a]Jer. 15:19

CHAPTER 36
1 [a]Jer. 25:1, 3; 45:1

Jeremiah from the LORD, saying: 2"Take a
[a]scroll of a book and [b]write on it all the
words that I have spoken to you against
Israel, against Judah, and against [c]all the
nations, from the day I spoke to you, from
the days of [d]Josiah even to this day. 3It
[a]may be that the house of Judah will hear
all the adversities which I purpose to
bring upon them, that everyone may
[b]turn from his evil way, that I may forgive
their iniquity and their sin."
4Then Jeremiah [a]called Baruch the son
of Neriah; and [b]Baruch wrote on a scroll
of a book, [1]at the instruction of Jeremiah,
all the words of the LORD which He had
spoken to him. 5And Jeremiah commanded Baruch, saying, "I *am* confined, I cannot go into the house of the LORD. 6You
go, therefore, and read from the scroll
which you have written [1]at my instruction, the words of the LORD, in the hearing
of the people in the LORD's house on [a]the
day of fasting. And you shall also read
them in the hearing of all Judah who
come from their cities. 7It may be that
they will present their supplication before
the LORD, and everyone will turn from his
evil way. For great *is* the anger and the
fury that the LORD has pronounced
against this people." 8And Baruch the son
of Neriah did according to all that Jeremiah the prophet commanded him, reading
from the book the words of the LORD in
the LORD's house.
9Now it came to pass in the fifth year of
Jehoiakim the son of Josiah, king of Judah, in the ninth month, *that* they proclaimed a fast before the LORD to all the
people in Jerusalem, and to all the people
who came from the cities of Judah to Jerusalem. 10Then Baruch read from the
book the words of Jeremiah in the house
of the LORD, in the chamber of Gemariah
the son of Shaphan the scribe, in the upper court at the [a]entry of the New Gate of
the LORD's house, in the [1]hearing of all
the people.

The Scroll Read in the Palace

11When Michaiah the son of Gemariah,
the son of Shaphan, heard all the words of
the LORD from the book, 12he then went
down to the king's house, into the scribe's
chamber; and there all the princes were
sitting—[a]Elishama the scribe, Delaiah
the son of Shemaiah, [b]Elnathan the son of
Achbor, Gemariah the son of Shaphan,
Zedekiah the son of Hananiah, and all the
princes. 13Then Michaiah declared to
them all the words that he had heard
when Baruch read the book in the hearing
of the people. 14Therefore all the princes
sent Jehudi the son of Nethaniah, the son
of Shelemiah, the son of Cushi, to Baruch,
saying, "Take in your hand the scroll from
which you have read in the hearing of the
people, and come." So Baruch the son of
Neriah took the scroll in his hand and
came to them. 15And they said to him, "Sit
down now, and read it in our hearing." So
Baruch read *it* in their hearing.
16Now it happened, when they had
heard all the words, that they looked in
fear from one to another, and said to Baruch, "We will surely tell the king of all
these words." 17And they asked Baruch,
saying, "Tell us now, how did you write all
these words—[1]at his instruction?"
18So Baruch answered them, "He proclaimed with his mouth all these words to
me, and I wrote *them* with ink in the
book."
19Then the princes said to Baruch, "Go
and hide, you and Jeremiah; and let no
one know where you are."

The King Destroys Jeremiah's Scroll

20And they went to the king, into the
court; but they stored the scroll in the
chamber of Elishama the scribe, and told
all the words in the hearing of the king.
21So the king sent Jehudi to bring the
scroll, and he took it from Elishama the
scribe's chamber. And Jehudi read it in
the hearing of the king and in the hearing
of all the princes who stood beside the
king. 22Now the king was sitting in [a]the
winter house in the ninth month, with *a
fire* burning on the hearth before him.
23And it happened, when Jehudi had read
three or four columns, *that the king* cut
it with the scribe's knife and cast *it* into
the fire that *was* on the hearth, until all
the scroll was consumed in the fire that
was on the hearth. 24Yet they were [a]not
afraid, nor did they [b]tear their garments,
the king nor any of his servants who heard
all these words. 25Nevertheless Elnathan,
Delaiah, and Gemariah implored the king
not to burn the scroll; but he would not
listen to them. 26And the king commanded Jerahmeel [1]the king's son, Seraiah the
son of Azriel, and Shelemiah the son of
Abdeel, to seize Baruch the scribe and

2 a Zech. 5:1 b Jer. 30:2 c Jer. 25:15 d Jer. 25:3
3 a Jer. 26:3 b Jon. 3:8
4 a Jer. 32:12 b Jer. 45:1 1 Lit. *from Jeremiah's mouth*
6 a Acts 27:9 1 Lit. *from my mouth*
10 a Jer. 26:10 1 Lit. *ears*
12 a Jer. 41:1 b Jer. 26:22
17 1 Lit. *with his mouth*
22 a Amos 3:15
24 a [Ps. 36:1] b Is. 36:22; 37:1
26 1 Or *son of Hammelech*

Jeremiah the prophet, but the LORD hid them.

Jeremiah Rewrites the Scroll

[27]Now after the king had burned the scroll with the words which Baruch had written [1]at the instruction of Jeremiah, the word of the LORD came to Jeremiah, saying: [28]"Take yet another scroll, and write on it all the former words that were in the first scroll which Jehoiakim the king of Judah has burned. [29]And you shall say to Jehoiakim king of Judah, 'Thus says the LORD: "You have burned this scroll, saying, [a]'Why have you written in it that the king of Babylon will certainly come and destroy this land, and cause man and beast to [b]cease from here?' " [30]Therefore thus says the LORD concerning Jehoiakim king of Judah: [a]"He shall have no one to sit on the throne of David, and his dead body shall be [b]cast out to the heat of the day and the frost of the night. [31]I will punish him, his [1]family, and his servants for their iniquity; and I will bring on them, on the inhabitants of Jerusalem, and on the men of Judah all the doom that I have pronounced against them; but they did not heed." ' "

[32]Then Jeremiah took another scroll and gave it to Baruch the scribe, the son of Neriah, who wrote on it [1]at the instruction of Jeremiah all the words of the book which Jehoiakim king of Judah had burned in the fire. And besides, there were added to them many similar words.

Zedekiah's Vain Hope

37 Now King [a]Zedekiah the son of Josiah reigned instead of Coniah the son of Jehoiakim, whom Nebuchadnezzar king of Babylon made king in the land of Judah. [2][a]But neither he nor his servants nor the people of the land gave heed to the words of the LORD which He spoke by the prophet Jeremiah.

[3]And Zedekiah the king sent Jehucal the son of Shelemiah, and [a]Zephaniah the son of Maaseiah, the priest, to the prophet Jeremiah, saying, [b]"Pray now to the LORD our God for us." [4]Now Jeremiah was coming and going among the people, for they had not *yet* put him in prison. [5]Then [a]Pharaoh's army came up from Egypt; and when the Chaldeans who were besieging Jerusalem heard news of them, they departed from Jerusalem.

[6]Then the word of the LORD came to the prophet Jeremiah, saying, [7]"Thus says the LORD, the God of Israel, 'Thus you shall say to the king of Judah, [a]who sent you to Me to inquire of Me: "Behold, Pharaoh's army which has come up to help you will return to Egypt, to their own land. [8][a]And the Chaldeans shall come back and fight against this city, and take it and burn it with fire." ' [9]Thus says the LORD: 'Do not deceive yourselves, saying, "The Chaldeans will surely depart from us," for they will not depart. [10][a]For though you had defeated the whole army of the Chaldeans who fight against you, and there remained *only* wounded men among them, they would rise up, every man in his tent, and burn the city with fire.' "

Jeremiah Imprisoned

[11]And it happened, when the army of the Chaldeans left *the siege* of Jerusalem for fear of Pharaoh's army, [12]that Jeremiah went out of Jerusalem to go into the land of Benjamin to claim his property there among the people. [13]And when he was in the Gate of Benjamin, a captain of the guard *was* there whose name *was* Irijah the son of Shelemiah, the son of Hananiah; and he seized Jeremiah the prophet, saying, "You are defecting to the Chaldeans!"

[14]Then Jeremiah said, [1]"False! I am not defecting to the Chaldeans." But he did not listen to him.

So Irijah seized Jeremiah and brought him to the princes. [15]Therefore the princes were angry with Jeremiah, and they struck him [a]and put him in prison in the [b]house of Jonathan the scribe. For they had made that the prison.

[16]When Jeremiah entered [a]the dungeon and the cells, and Jeremiah had remained there many days, [17]then Zedekiah the king sent and took him *out*. The king asked him secretly in his house, and said, "Is there *any* word from the LORD?"

And Jeremiah said, "There is." Then he said, "You shall be [a]delivered into the hand of the king of Babylon!"

[18]Moreover Jeremiah said to King Zedekiah, "What offense have I committed against you, against your servants, or against this people, that you have put me in prison? [19]Where now *are* your prophets who prophesied to you, saying, 'The king of Babylon will not come against you or against this land'? [20]Therefore please hear

27 [1] Lit. *from Jeremiah's mouth*
29 [a] Jer. 32:3 [b] Jer. 25:9–11; 26:9
30 [a] Jer. 22:30 [b] Jer. 22:19
31 [1] Lit. *seed*
32 [1] Lit. *from Jeremiah's mouth*

CHAPTER 37
1 [a] 2 Kin. 24:17
2 [a] 2 Chr. 36:12–16
3 [a] Jer. 21:1, 2; 29:25; 52:24 [b] Jer. 42:2
5 [a] Ezek. 17:15
7 [a] Jer. 21:2
8 [a] Jer. 34:22
10 [a] Jer. 21:4, 5
14 [1] *a lie*
15 [a] Jer. 20:2 [b] Jer. 38:26
16 [a] Jer. 38:6
17 [a] Jer. 21:7

now, O my lord the king. Please, let my petition be accepted before you, and do not make me return to the house of Jonathan the scribe, lest I die there."

21 Then Zedekiah the king commanded that they should commit Jeremiah [a]to the court of the prison, and that they should give him daily a piece of bread from the bakers' street, [b]until all the bread in the city was gone. Thus Jeremiah remained in the court of the prison.

Jeremiah in the Dungeon

38 Now Shephatiah the son of Mattan, Gedaliah the son of Pashhur, [a]Jucal[1] the son of Shelemiah, and [b]Pashhur the son of Malchiah [c]heard the words that Jeremiah had spoken to all the people, saying, 2 "Thus says the LORD: [a]'He who remains in this city shall die by the sword, by famine, and by pestilence; but he who goes over to the Chaldeans shall live; his life shall be as a prize to him, and he shall live.' 3 Thus says the LORD: [a]'This city shall surely be [b]given into the hand of the king of Babylon's army, which shall take it.' "

4 Therefore the princes said to the king, "Please, [a]let this man be put to death, for thus he [1]weakens the hands of the men of war who remain in this city, and the hands of all the people, by speaking such words to them. For this man does not seek the [2]welfare of this people, but their harm."

5 Then Zedekiah the king said, "Look, he *is* in your hand. For the king can *do* nothing against you." 6 [a]So they took Jeremiah and cast him into the dungeon of Malchiah [1]the king's son, which *was* in the court of the prison, and they let Jeremiah down with ropes. And in the dungeon *there was* no water, but mire. So Jeremiah sank in the mire.

7 [a]Now Ebed-Melech the Ethiopian, one of the [1]eunuchs, who was in the king's house, heard that they had put Jeremiah in the dungeon. When the king was sitting at the Gate of Benjamin, 8 Ebed-Melech went out of the king's house and spoke to the king, saying: 9 "My lord the king, these men have done evil in all that they have done to Jeremiah the prophet, whom they have cast into the dungeon, and he is likely to die from hunger in the place where he is. For *there is* [a]no more bread in the city." 10 Then the king commanded Ebed-Melech the Ethiopian, saying, "Take from here thirty men with you, and lift Jeremiah the prophet out of the dungeon before he dies." 11 So Ebed-Melech took the men with him and went into the house of the king under the treasury, and took from there old clothes and old rags, and let them down by ropes into the dungeon to Jeremiah. 12 Then Ebed-Melech the Ethiopian said to Jeremiah, "Please put these old clothes and rags under your armpits, under the ropes." And Jeremiah did so. 13 So they pulled Jeremiah up with ropes and lifted him out of the dungeon. And Jeremiah remained [a]in the court of the prison.

Zedekiah's Fears and Jeremiah's Advice

14 Then Zedekiah the king sent and had Jeremiah the prophet brought to him at the third entrance of the house of the LORD. And the king said to Jeremiah, "I will [a]ask you something. Hide nothing from me."

15 Jeremiah said to Zedekiah, "If I declare *it* to you, will you not surely put me to death? And if I give you advice, you will not listen to me."

16 So Zedekiah the king swore secretly to Jeremiah, saying, "*As* the LORD lives, [a]who made our very souls, I will not put you to death, nor will I give you into the hand of these men who seek your life."

17 Then Jeremiah said to Zedekiah, "Thus says the LORD, the God of hosts, the God of Israel: 'If you surely [a]surrender[1] [b]to the king of Babylon's princes, then your soul shall live; this city shall not be burned with fire, and you and your house shall live. 18 But if you do not [1]surrender to the king of Babylon's princes, then this city shall be given into the hand of the Chaldeans; they shall burn it with fire, and [a]you shall not escape from their hand.' "

19 And Zedekiah the king said to Jeremiah, "I am afraid of the Jews who have [a]defected to the Chaldeans, lest they deliver me into their hand, and they [b]abuse me."

20 But Jeremiah said, "They shall not deliver *you*. Please, obey the voice of the LORD which I speak to you. So it shall be [a]well with you, and your soul shall live. 21 But if you refuse to [1]surrender, this *is* the word that the LORD has shown me: 22 'Now behold, all the [a]women who are left in the king of Judah's house *shall be*

21 [a] Jer. 32:2; 38:13, 28 [b] Jer. 38:9; 52:6

CHAPTER 38
1 [a] Jer. 37:3 [b] Jer. 21:1 [c] Jer. 21:8 [1] *Jehucal,* Jer. 37:3
2 [a] Jer. 21:9
3 [a] Jer. 21:10; 32:3 [b] Jer. 34:2
4 [a] Jer. 26:11 [1] Is discouraging [2] Well-being; lit. *peace*
6 [a] Jer. 37:21 [1] Or *son of Hammelech*
7 [a] Jer. 39:16 [1] Or *officers*
9 [a] Jer. 37:21
13 [a] Jer. 37:21
14 [a] Jer. 21:1, 2; 37:17
16 [a] Is. 57:16
17 [a] 2 Kin. 24:12 [b] Jer. 39:3 [1] Lit. *go out*
18 [a] Jer. 32:4; 34:3 [1] Lit. *go out*
19 [a] Jer. 39:9 [b] 1 Sam. 31:4
20 [a] Jer. 40:9
21 [1] Lit. *go out*
22 [a] Jer. 8:10

surrendered to the king of Babylon's
princes, and those *women* shall say:

"Your close friends have [1]set upon
 you
And prevailed against you;
Your feet have sunk in the mire,
And they have [2]turned away again."

[23]'So they shall surrender all your wives
and [a]children to the Chaldeans. [b]You
shall not escape from their hand, but shall
be taken by the hand of the king of Babylon. And you shall cause this city to be
burned with fire.' "
[24]Then Zedekiah said to Jeremiah, "Let
no one know of these words, and you shall
not die. [25]But if the princes hear that I
have talked with you, and they come to
you and say to you, 'Declare to us now
what you have said to the king, and also
what the king said to you; do not hide *it*
from us, and we will not put you to death,'
[26]then you shall say to them, [a]'I presented
my request before the king, that he would
not make me return [b]to Jonathan's house
to die there.' "
[27]Then all the princes came to Jeremiah and asked him. And he told them according to all these words that the king
had commanded. So they stopped speaking with him, for the conversation had
not been heard. [28]Now [a]Jeremiah remained in the court of the prison until the
day that Jerusalem was taken. And he was
there when Jerusalem was taken.

The Fall of Jerusalem

39 In the [a]ninth year of Zedekiah king
of Judah, in the tenth month, Nebuchadnezzar king of Babylon and all his
army came against Jerusalem, and besieged it. [2]In the [a]eleventh year of Zedekiah, in the fourth month, on the ninth *day*
of the month, the [1]city was penetrated.
[3][a]Then all the princes of the king of
Babylon came in and sat in the Middle
Gate: Nergal-Sharezer, Samgar-Nebo,
Sarsechim, [1]Rabsaris, Nergal-Sarezer,
[2]Rabmag, with the rest of the princes of
the king of Babylon.
[4][a]So it was, when Zedekiah the king of
Judah and all the men of war saw them,
that they fled and went out of the city by
night, by way of the king's garden, by the
gate between the two walls. And he went
out by way of the [1]plain. [5]But the Chaldean army pursued them and [a]overtook
Zedekiah in the plains of Jericho. And
when they had captured him, they
brought him up to Nebuchadnezzar king
of Babylon, to [b]Riblah in the land of Hamath, where he pronounced judgment on
him. [6]Then the king of Babylon killed the
sons of Zedekiah before his [a]eyes in Riblah; the king of Babylon also killed all the
[b]nobles of Judah. [7]Moreover [a]he put out
Zedekiah's eyes, and bound him with
bronze [1]fetters to carry him off to Babylon. [8][a]And the Chaldeans burned the
king's house and the houses of the people
with [b]fire, and broke down the [c]walls of
Jerusalem. [9][a]Then Nebuzaradan the captain of the guard carried away captive to
Babylon the remnant of the people who
remained in the city and those who [b]de-
fected to him, with the rest of the people
who remained. [10]But Nebuzaradan the
captain of the guard left in the land of
Judah the [a]poor people, who had nothing,
and gave them vineyards and fields [1]at the
same time.

Jeremiah Goes Free

[11]Now Nebuchadnezzar king of Babylon gave charge concerning Jeremiah to
Nebuzaradan the captain of the guard,
saying, [12]"Take him and look after him,
and do him no [a]harm; but do to him just
as he says to you." [13]So Nebuzaradan the
captain of the guard sent Nebushasban,
Rabsaris, Nergal-Sharezer, Rabmag, and
all the king of Babylon's chief officers;
[14]then they sent *someone* [a]to take Jeremiah from the court of the prison, and committed him [b]to Gedaliah the son of
[c]Ahikam, the son of Shaphan, that he
should take him home. So he dwelt
among the people.
[15]Meanwhile the word of the LORD had
come to Jeremiah while he was shut up in
the court of the prison, saying, [16]"Go and
speak to [a]Ebed-Melech the Ethiopian,
saying, 'Thus says the LORD of hosts, the
God of Israel: "Behold, [b]I will bring My
words upon this city for adversity and not
for good, and they shall be *performed* in
that day before you. [17]But I will deliver
you in that day," says the LORD, "and you
shall not be given into the hand of the
men of whom you *are* afraid. [18]For I will
surely deliver you, and you shall not fall
by the sword; but [a]your life shall be as a
prize to you, [b]because you have put your
trust in Me," says the LORD.' "

22 [1] Or *misled* [2] Deserted you
23 a Jer. 39:6; 41:10 b Jer. 39:5
26 a Jer. 37:20 b Jer. 37:15
28 a Jer. 37:21; 39:14

CHAPTER 39
1 a 2 Kin. 25:1–12
2 a Jer. 1:3 [1] *city wall was breached*
3 a Jer. 1:15; 38:17 [1] A title, probably *Chief Officer;* also v. 13 [2] A title, probably *Troop Commander;* also v. 13
4 a Jer. 52:7 [1] Or *Arabah;* the Jordan Valley
5 a Jer. 21:7; 32:4; 38:18, 23 b 2 Kin. 23:33
6 a Deut. 28:34 b Jer. 34:19–21
7 a Ezek. 12:13 [1] *chains*
8 a 2 Kin. 25:9 b Jer. 21:10 c Neh. 1:3
9 a 2 Kin. 25:8, 11, 12, 20 b Jer. 38:19
10 a Jer. 40:7 [1] Lit. *on that day*
12 a Jer. 1:18, 19; 15:20, 21
14 a Jer. 38:28 b Jer. 40:5 c Jer. 26:24
16 a Jer. 38:7, 12 b [Dan. 9:12]
18 a Jer. 21:9; 45:5 b Ps. 37:40

Jeremiah with Gedaliah the Governor

40 The word that came to Jeremiah from the LORD [a]after Nebuzaradan the captain of the guard had let him go from Ramah, when he had taken him bound in chains among all who were carried away captive from Jerusalem and Judah, who were carried away captive to Babylon.

[2]And the captain of the guard took Jeremiah and [a]said to him: "The LORD your God has pronounced this doom on this place. [3]Now the LORD has brought *it,* and has done just as He said. [a]Because you *people* have sinned against the LORD, and not obeyed His voice, therefore this thing has come upon you. [4]And now look, I free you this day from the chains that [1]*were* on your hand. [a]If it seems good to you to come with me to Babylon, come, and I will look after you. But if it seems wrong for you to come with me to Babylon, remain here. See, [b]all the land *is* before you; wherever it seems good and convenient for you to go, go there."

[5]Now while Jeremiah had not yet gone back, *Nebuzaradan said,* "Go back to [a]Gedaliah the son of Ahikam, the son of Shaphan, [b]whom the king of Babylon has made governor over the cities of Judah, and dwell with him among the people. Or go wherever it seems convenient for you to go." So the captain of the guard gave him rations and a gift and let him go. [6a]Then Jeremiah went to Gedaliah the son of Ahikam, to [b]Mizpah, and dwelt with him among the people who were left in the land.

[7a]And when all the captains of the armies who *were* in the fields, they and their men, heard that the king of Babylon had made Gedaliah the son of Ahikam governor in the land, and had committed to him men, women, children, and [b]the poorest of the land who had not been carried away captive to Babylon, [8]then they came to Gedaliah at Mizpah—[a]Ishmael the son of Nethaniah, [b]Johanan and Jonathan the sons of Kareah, Seraiah the son of Tanhumeth, the sons of Ephai the Netophathite, and [c]Jezaniah[1] the son of a [d]Maachathite, they and their men. [9]And Gedaliah the son of Ahikam, the son of Shaphan, took an oath before them and their men, saying, "Do not be afraid to serve the Chaldeans. Dwell in the land and serve the king of Babylon, and it shall be [a]well with you. [10]As for me, I will indeed dwell at Mizpah and serve the Chaldeans who come to us. But you, gather wine and summer fruit and oil, put *them* in your vessels, and dwell in your cities that you have taken." [11]Likewise, when all the Jews who *were* in Moab, among the Ammonites, in Edom, and who *were* in all the countries, heard that the king of Babylon had left a remnant of Judah, and that he had set over them Gedaliah the son of Ahikam, the son of Shaphan, [12]then all the Jews [a]returned out of all places where they had been driven, and came to the land of Judah, to Gedaliah at Mizpah, and gathered wine and summer fruit in abundance.

[13]Moreover Johanan the son of Kareah and all the captains of the forces that *were* in the fields came to Gedaliah at Mizpah, [14]and said to him, [1]"Do you certainly know that [a]Baalis the king of the Ammonites has sent Ishmael the son of Nethaniah to murder you?" But Gedaliah the son of Ahikam did not believe them.

[15]Then Johanan the son of Kareah spoke secretly to Gedaliah in Mizpah, saying, "Let me go, please, and I will kill Ishmael the son of Nethaniah, and no one will know *it.* Why should he murder you, so that all the Jews who are gathered to you would be scattered, and the [a]remnant in Judah perish?"

[16]But Gedaliah the son of Ahikam said to Johanan the son of Kareah, "You shall not do this thing, for you speak falsely concerning Ishmael."

Insurrection Against Gedaliah

41 Now it came to pass in the seventh month [a]*that* Ishmael the son of Nethaniah, the son of Elishama, of the royal [1]family and of the officers of the king, came with ten men to Gedaliah the son of Ahikam, at [b]Mizpah. And there they ate bread together in Mizpah. [2]Then Ishmael the son of Nethaniah, and the ten men who were with him, arose and [a]struck Gedaliah the son of [b]Ahikam, the son of Shaphan, with the sword, and killed him whom the king of Babylon had made [c]governor over the land. [3]Ishmael also struck down all the Jews who were with him, *that is,* with Gedaliah at Mizpah, and the Chaldeans who were found there, the men of war.

CHAPTER 40
1 a Jer. 39:9, 11
2 a Jer. 50:7
3 a Dan. 9:11
4 a Jer. 39:12 b Gen. 20:15 *1 Or are*
5 a Jer. 39:14 b Jer. 41:10
6 a Jer. 39:14 b Judg. 20:1
7 a 2 Kin. 25:23, 24 b Jer. 39:10
8 a Jer. 41:1–10 b Jer. 41:11; 43:2 c Jer. 42:1 d Deut. 3:14 *1 Jaazaniah,* 2 Kin. 25:23
9 a Jer. 27:11; 38:17–20
12 a Jer. 43:5
14 a Jer. 41:10 *1 Or Certainly you know that*
15 a Jer. 42:2

CHAPTER 41
1 a 2 Kin. 25:25 b Jer. 40:6, 10 *1 Lit. seed*
2 a 2 Kin. 25:25 b Jer. 26:24 c Jer. 40:5

4And it happened, on the second day
after he had killed Gedaliah, when as yet
no one knew *it,* 5that certain men came
from Shechem, from Shiloh, and from Samaria, eighty men [a]with their beards
shaved and their clothes torn, having cut
themselves, with offerings and incense in
their hand, to bring *them* to [b]the house of
the LORD. 6Now Ishmael the son of Nethaniah went out from Mizpah to meet them,
weeping as he went along; and it happened as he met them that he said to
them, "Come to Gedaliah the son of Ahikam!" 7So it was, when they came into the
midst of the city, that Ishmael the son of
Nethaniah [a]killed them *and cast them*
into the midst of a [1]pit, he and the men
who were with him. 8But ten men were
found among them who said to Ishmael,
"Do not kill us, for we have treasures of
wheat, barley, oil, and honey in the field."
So he desisted and did not kill them
among their brethren. 9Now the [1]pit into
which Ishmael had cast all the dead bodies
of the men whom he had slain, because of
Gedaliah, *was* [a]the same one Asa the king
had made for fear of Baasha king of Israel.
Ishmael the son of Nethaniah filled it with
the slain. 10Then Ishmael carried away
captive all the [a]rest of the people who
were in Mizpah, [b]the king's daughters and
all the people who remained in Mizpah,
[c]whom Nebuzaradan the captain of the
guard had committed to Gedaliah the son
of Ahikam. And Ishmael the son of Nethaniah carried them away captive and departed to go over to [d]the Ammonites.

11But when [a]Johanan the son of Kareah
and all the captains of the forces that *were*
with him heard of all the evil that Ishmael
the son of Nethaniah had done, 12they
took all the men and went to fight with
Ishmael the son of Nethaniah; and they
found him by [a]the great pool that *is* in
Gibeon. 13So it was, when all the people
who *were* with Ishmael saw Johanan the
son of Kareah, and all the captains of the
forces who *were* with him, that they were
glad. 14Then all the people whom Ishmael
had carried away captive from Mizpah
turned around and came back, and went
to Johanan the son of Kareah. 15But Ishmael the son of Nethaniah escaped from
Johanan with eight men and went to the
Ammonites.

16Then Johanan the son of Kareah, and
all the captains of the forces that were
with him, took from Mizpah all the [a]rest
of the people whom he had recovered
from Ishmael the son of Nethaniah after
he had murdered Gedaliah the son of Ahikam—the mighty men of war and the
women and the children and the eunuchs,
whom he had brought back from Gibeon.
17And they departed and dwelt in the habitation of [a]Chimham, which is near Bethlehem, as they went on their way to
[b]Egypt, 18because of the Chaldeans; for
they were afraid of them, because Ishmael
the son of Nethaniah had murdered Gedaliah the son of Ahikam, [a]whom the king
of Babylon had made governor in the
land.

> *If our petitions are in accordance with His will, and if we seek His glory in the asking, the answers will come in ways that will astonish us and fill our hearts with songs of thanksgiving.*
>
> J. KENNEDY MACLEAN

The Flight to Egypt Forbidden

42 Now all the captains of the forces,
[a]Johanan the son of Kareah, Jezaniah the son of Hoshaiah, and all the people, from the least to the greatest, came
near 2and said to Jeremiah the prophet,
[a]"Please, let our petition be acceptable to
you, and [b]pray for us to the LORD your
God, for all this remnant (since we are left
but [c]a few of many, as you can see), 3that
the LORD your God may show us [a]the way
in which we should walk and the thing we
should do."

4Then Jeremiah the prophet said to
them, "I have heard. Indeed, I will pray
to the LORD your God according to your
words, and it shall be, *that* [a]whatever the
LORD answers you, I will declare *it* to you.
I will [b]keep nothing back from you."

5So they said to Jeremiah, [a]"Let the
LORD be a true and faithful witness between us, if we do not do according to
everything which the LORD your God
sends us by you. 6Whether *it is* [1]pleasing

5 [a]Deut. 14:1 [b]1 Sam. 1:7
7 [a]Ps. 55:23 [1]Or *cistern*
9 [a]1 Kin. 15:22 [1]Or *cistern*
10 [a]Jer. 40:11, 12 [b]Jer. 43:6 [c]Jer. 40:7 [d]Jer. 40:14
11 [a]Jer. 40:7, 8, 13–16
12 [a]2 Sam. 2:13
16 [a]Jer. 40:11, 12; 43:4–7
17 [a]2 Sam. 19:37, 38 [b]Jer. 43:7
18 [a]Jer. 40:5
CHAPTER 42
1 [a]Jer. 40:8, 13; 41:11
2 [a]Jer. 15:11 [b]Is. 37:4 [c]Lev. 26:22
3 [a]Ezra 8:21
4 [a]1 Kin. 22:14 [b]1 Sam. 3:17, 18
5 [a]Gen. 31:50
6 [1]Lit. *good*

or [2]displeasing, we will [a]obey the voice of
the LORD our God to whom we send you,
[b]that it may be well with us when we obey
the voice of the LORD our God."
7And it happened after ten days that
the word of the LORD came to Jeremiah.
8Then he called Johanan the son of Kareah, all the captains of the forces which
were with him, and all the people from
the least even to the greatest, 9and said to
them, "Thus says the LORD, the God of
Israel, to whom you sent me to present
your petition before Him: 10'If you will
still remain in this land, then [a]I will build
you and not pull *you* down, and I will
plant you and not pluck *you* up. For I [b]re-
lent concerning the disaster that I have
brought upon you. 11Do not be afraid of
the king of Babylon, of whom you are
afraid; do not be afraid of him,' says the
LORD, [a]'for I *am* with you, to save you and
deliver you from his hand. 12And [a]I will
show you mercy, that he may have mercy
on you and cause you to return to your
own land.'
13"But if [a]you say, 'We will not dwell
in this land,' disobeying the voice of the
LORD your God, 14saying, 'No, but we will
go to the land of [a]Egypt where we shall
see no war, nor hear the sound of the
trumpet, nor be hungry for bread, and
there we will dwell'— 15Then hear now
the word of the LORD, O remnant of Judah! Thus says the LORD of hosts, the God
of Israel: 'If you [a]wholly[1] set [b]your faces
to enter Egypt, and go to dwell there,
16then it shall be *that* the [a]sword which
you feared shall overtake you there in the
land of Egypt; the famine of which you
were afraid shall follow close after you
there *in* Egypt; and there you shall die.
17So shall it be with all the men who set
their faces to go to Egypt to dwell there.
They shall die by the sword, by famine,
and by pestilence. And [a]none of them
shall remain or escape from the disaster
that I will bring upon them.'
18"For thus says the LORD of hosts, the
God of Israel: 'As My anger and My fury
have been [a]poured out on the inhabitants
of Jerusalem, so will My fury be poured
out on you when you enter Egypt. And
[b]you shall be an oath, an astonishment, a
curse, and a reproach; and you shall see
this place no more.'
19"The LORD has said concerning you,
O remnant of Judah, [a]'Do not go to
Egypt!' Know certainly that I have [1]ad-
monished you this day. 20For you [1]were
hypocrites in your hearts when you sent
me to the LORD your God, saying, 'Pray for
us to the LORD our God, and according to
all that the LORD your God says, so declare
to us and we will do *it*.' 21And I have this
day declared *it* to you, but you have [a]not
obeyed the voice of the LORD your God, or
anything which He has sent you by me.
22Now therefore, know certainly that you
[a]shall die by the sword, by famine, and by
pestilence in the place where you desire to
go to dwell."

Jeremiah Taken to Egypt

43 Now it happened, when Jeremiah
had stopped speaking to all the
people all the [a]words of the LORD their
God, for which the LORD their God had
sent him to them, all these words, 2[a]that
Azariah the son of Hoshaiah, Johanan the
son of Kareah, and all the proud men
spoke, saying to Jeremiah, "You speak
falsely! The LORD our God has not sent
you to say, 'Do not go to Egypt to dwell
there.' 3But [a]Baruch the son of Neriah has
[1]set you against us, to deliver us into the
hand of the Chaldeans, that they may put
us to death or carry us away captive to
Babylon." 4So Johanan the son of Kareah,
all the captains of the forces, and all the
people would [a]not obey the voice of the
LORD, to remain in the land of Judah. 5But
Johanan the son of Kareah and all the captains of the forces took [a]all the remnant
of Judah who had returned to dwell in the
land of Judah, from all nations where they
had been driven— 6men, women, children, [a]the king's daughters, [b]and every
person whom Nebuzaradan the captain of
the guard had left with Gedaliah the son
of Ahikam, the son of Shaphan, and Jeremiah the prophet and Baruch the son of
Neriah. 7[a]So they went to the land of
Egypt, for they did not obey the voice of
the LORD. And they went as far as [b]Tah-
panhes.
8Then the [a]word of the LORD came to
Jeremiah in Tahpanhes, saying, 9"Take
large stones in your hand, and hide them
in the sight of the men of Judah, in the
[1]clay in the brick courtyard which *is* at
the entrance to Pharaoh's house in Tahpanhes; 10and say to them, 'Thus says the
LORD of hosts, the God of Israel: "Behold,
I will send and bring Nebuchadnezzar the
king of Babylon, [a]My servant, and will set
his throne above these stones that I have

6 [a]Ex. 24:7 [b]Jer. 7:23 [2]Lit. *evil*
10 [a]Jer. 24:6; 31:28; 33:7 [b][Jer. 18:8]
11 [a]Rom. 8:31
12 [a]Ps. 106:46
13 [a]Jer. 44:16
14 [a]Jer. 41:17; 43:7
15 [a]Deut. 17:16 [b]Luke 9:51 [1]Or *surely*
16 [a]Ezek. 11:8
17 [a]Jer. 44:14, 28
18 [a]Jer. 7:20 [b]Is. 65:15
19 [a]Deut. 17:16 [1]*warned*
20 [1]Lit. *used deceit against your souls*
21 [a]Is. 30:1–7
22 [a]Ezek. 6:11

CHAPTER 43
1 [a]Jer. 42:9–18
2 [a]Jer. 42:1
3 [a]Jer. 36:4; 45:1 [1]Or *incited*
4 [a]2 Kin. 25:26
5 [a]Jer. 40:11, 12
6 [a]Jer. 41:10 [b]Jer. 39:10; 40:7
7 [a]Jer. 42:19 [b]Jer. 2:16; 44:1
8 [a]Jer. 44:1–30
9 [1]Or *mortar*
10 [a]Jer. 25:9; 27:6

hidden. And he will spread his royal pavilion over them. 11 [a]When he comes, he
shall strike the land of Egypt *and deliver*
to death [b]*those appointed* for death, and
to captivity *those appointed* for captivity,
and to the sword *those appointed* for the
sword. 12 [1]I will kindle a fire in the houses
of [a]the gods of Egypt, and he shall burn
them and carry them away captive. And he
shall array himself with the land of Egypt,
as a shepherd puts on his garment, and he
shall go out from there in peace. 13 He
shall also break the *sacred* pillars of [1]Beth
Shemesh that *are* in the land of Egypt;
and the houses of the gods of the Egyptians he shall burn with fire." ' "

Israelites Will Be Punished in Egypt

44 The word that came to Jeremiah
concerning all the Jews who dwell
in the land of Egypt, who dwell at [a]Mig-
dol, at [b]Tahpanhes, at [c]Noph,[1] and in the
country of [d]Pathros, saying, 2 "Thus says
the LORD of hosts, the God of Israel: 'You
have seen all the calamity that I have
brought on Jerusalem and on all the cities
of Judah; and behold, this day they *are* [a]a
desolation, and no one dwells in them,
3 because of their wickedness which they
have committed to provoke Me to anger,
in that they went [a]to burn incense *and*
to [b]serve other gods whom they did not
know, they nor you nor your fathers.
4 However [a]I have sent to you all My servants the prophets, rising early and sending *them,* saying, "Oh, do not do this
abominable thing that I hate!" 5 But they
did not listen or incline their ear to turn
from their wickedness, to burn no incense
to other gods. 6 So My fury and My anger
were poured out and kindled in the cities
of Judah and in the streets of Jerusalem;
and they [1]are wasted *and* desolate, as it is
this day.'

7 "Now therefore, thus says the LORD,
the God of hosts, the God of Israel: 'Why
do you commit *this* great evil [a]against
yourselves, to cut off from you man and
woman, child and infant, out of Judah,
leaving none to remain, 8 in that you [a]pro-
voke Me to wrath with the works of your
hands, burning incense to other gods in
the land of Egypt where you have gone to
dwell, that you may cut yourselves off and
be [b]a curse and a reproach among all the
nations of the earth? 9 Have you forgotten
the wickedness of your fathers, the wickedness of the kings of Judah, the wickedness of their wives, your own wickedness,
and the wickedness of your wives, which
they committed in the land of Judah and
in the streets of Jerusalem? 10 They have
not been [a]humbled,[1] to this day, nor have
they [b]feared; they have not walked in My
law or in My statutes that I set before you
and your fathers.'

11 "Therefore thus says the LORD of
hosts, the God of Israel: 'Behold, [a]I will
set My face against you for catastrophe
and for [1]cutting off all Judah. 12 And I will
take the remnant of Judah who have set
their faces to go into the land of Egypt to
dwell there, and [a]they shall all be consumed *and* fall in the land of Egypt. They
shall be consumed by the sword *and* by
famine. They shall die, from the least to
the greatest, by the sword and by famine;
and [b]they shall be an oath, an astonishment, a curse and a reproach! 13 [a]For I will
punish those who dwell in the land of
Egypt, as I have punished Jerusalem, by
the sword, by famine, and by pestilence,
14 so that none of the remnant of Judah
who have gone into the land of Egypt to
dwell there shall escape or survive, lest
they return to the land of Judah, to which
they [a]desire[1] to return and dwell. For
[b]none shall return except those who escape.' "

15 Then all the men who knew that their
wives had burned incense to other gods,
with all the women who stood by, a great
multitude, and all the people who dwelt in
the land of Egypt, in Pathros, answered
Jeremiah, saying: 16 "*As for* the word that
you have spoken to us in the name of the
LORD, [a]we will not listen to you! 17 But we
will certainly do [a]whatever has gone out
of our own mouth, to burn incense to the
[b]queen of heaven and pour out drink offerings to her, as we have done, we and
our fathers, our kings and our princes, in
the cities of Judah and in the streets of
Jerusalem. For *then* we had plenty of
[1]food, were well-off, and saw no trouble.
18 But since we stopped burning incense
to the queen of heaven and pouring out
drink offerings to her, we have lacked everything and have been consumed by the
sword and by famine."

19 *The women also said,* [a]"And when we
burned incense to the queen of heaven
and poured out drink offerings to her, did
we make cakes for her, to worship her,

11 [a]Jer. 25:15–19; 44:13; 46:1, 2, 13–26 [b]Jer. 15:2
12 [a]Jer. 46:25 [1]So with MT, Tg.; LXX, Syr., Vg. *He*
13 [1]Lit. *House of the Sun,* ancient On, later called Heliopolis

CHAPTER 44
1 [a]Jer. 46:14 [b]Jer. 43:7 [c]Is. 19:13 [d]Ezek. 29:14; 30:14 [1]Ancient Memphis
2 [a]Jer. 4:7; 9:11; 34:22
3 [a]Jer. 19:4 [b]Deut. 13:6; 32:17
4 [a]Jer. 7:25; 25:4; 26:5; 29:19
6 [1]Or *became a ruin*
7 [a]Num. 16:38
8 [a]Jer. 25:6, 7; 44:3 [b]Jer. 42:18
10 [a]Jer. 6:15; 8:12 [b][Prov. 28:14] [1]Lit. *crushed*
11 [a]Amos 9:4 [1]*destroying*
12 [a]Jer. 42:15–17, 22 [b]Is. 65:15
13 [a]Jer. 43:11
14 [a]Jer. 22:26, 27 [b]Jer. 44:28 [1]Lit. *lift up their soul*
16 [a]Jer. 6:16
17 [a]Num. 30:12 [b]Jer. 7:18 [1]Lit. *bread*
19 [a]Jer. 7:18

and pour out drink offerings to her without our husbands' *permission*?"
20Then Jeremiah spoke to all the people—the men, the women, and all the
people who had given him *that* answer—
saying: 21"The incense that you burned in
the cities of Judah and in the streets of
Jerusalem, you and your fathers, your
kings and your princes, and the people
of the land, did not the LORD remember
them, and did it *not* come into His mind?
22So the LORD could no longer bear *it*, because of the evil of your doings *and* because of the abominations which you
committed. Therefore your land is a desolation, an astonishment, a curse, and
without an inhabitant, [a]as *it is* this day.
23Because you have burned incense and
because you have sinned against the
LORD, and have not obeyed the voice of
the LORD or walked in His law, in His statutes or in His testimonies, [a]therefore this
calamity has happened to you, as *at* this
day."
24Moreover Jeremiah said to all the
people and to all the women, "Hear the
word of the LORD, all Judah who *are* in the
land of Egypt! 25Thus says the LORD of
hosts, the God of Israel, saying: 'You and
your wives have spoken with your mouths
and fulfilled with your hands, saying, "We
will surely keep our vows that we have
made, to burn incense to the queen of
heaven and pour out drink offerings to
her." You will surely keep your vows and
perform your vows!' 26Therefore hear the
word of the LORD, all Judah who dwell in
the land of Egypt: 'Behold, [a]I have sworn
by My [b]great name,' says the LORD, 'that
[c]My name shall no more be named in the
mouth of any man of Judah in all the land
of Egypt, saying, "The Lord GOD lives."
27Behold, I will watch over them for adversity and not for good. And all the men
of Judah who *are* in the land of Egypt
[a]shall be consumed by the sword and by
famine, until there is an end to them.
28Yet [a]a small number who escape the
sword shall return from the land of Egypt
to the land of Judah; and all the remnant
of Judah, who have gone to the land of
Egypt to dwell there, shall know whose
words will stand, Mine or theirs. 29And
this *shall be* a sign to you,' says the LORD,
'that I will punish you in this place, that
you may know that My words will surely
[a]stand against you for adversity.'
30"Thus says the LORD: 'Behold, [a]I will
give Pharaoh Hophra king of Egypt into
the hand of his enemies and into the hand
of those who seek his life, as I gave [b]Zede-
kiah king of Judah into the hand of Nebuchadnezzar king of Babylon, his enemy
who sought his life.' "

Assurance to Baruch

45 The [a]word that Jeremiah the
prophet spoke to [b]Baruch the son
of Neriah, when he had written these
words in a book [1]at the instruction of Jeremiah, in the [c]fourth year of Jehoiakim
the son of Josiah, king of Judah, saying,
2"Thus says the LORD, the God of Israel, to
you, O Baruch: 3'You said, "Woe is me
now! For the LORD has added grief to my
sorrow. I [a]fainted in my sighing, and I
find no rest." '
4"Thus you shall say to him, 'Thus says
the LORD: "Behold, [a]what I have built I
will break down, and what I have planted
I will pluck up, that is, this whole land.
5And do you seek great things for yourself? Do not seek *them*; for behold, [a]I will
bring adversity on all flesh," says the
LORD. "But I will give your [b]life to you as
a prize in all places, wherever you go." ' "

Judgment on Egypt

46 The word of the LORD which came
to Jeremiah the prophet against
[a]the nations. 2Against [a]Egypt.
[b]Concerning the army of Pharaoh Necho, king of Egypt, which was by the River
Euphrates in Carchemish, and which
Nebuchadnezzar king of Babylon [c]defeat-
ed in the [d]fourth year of Jehoiakim the
son of Josiah, king of Judah:

3 "Order[1] the [2]buckler and shield,
And draw near to battle!
4 Harness the horses,
And mount up, you horsemen!
Stand forth with *your* helmets,
Polish the spears,
[a]Put on the armor!
5 Why have I seen them dismayed
and turned back?
Their mighty ones are beaten down;
They have speedily fled,
And did not look back,
For [a]fear *was* all around," says the
LORD.
6 "Do not let the swift flee away,
Nor the mighty man escape;
They will [a]stumble and fall

22 a Jer. 25:11, 18, 38
23 a Dan. 9:11, 12
26 a Heb. 6:13 b Jer. 10:6 c Ezek. 20:39
27 a Ezek. 7:6
28 a Is. 10:19; 27:12, 13
29 a [Ps. 33:11]
30 a Ezek. 29:3; 30:21 b Jer. 39:5

CHAPTER 45
1 a Jer. 36:1, 4, 32 b Jer. 32:12, 16; 43:3 c Jer. 25:1; 36:1; 46:2 *1 Lit. from Jeremiah's mouth*
3 a Ps. 6:6; 69:3
4 a Is. 5:5
5 a Jer. 25:17–26 b Jer. 21:9; 38:2; 39:18

CHAPTER 46
1 a Jer. 25:15
2 a Jer. 25:17–19 b 2 Kin. 23:33–35 c 2 Chr. 35:20 d Jer. 45:1
3 *1 Set in order 2 A small shield*
4 a Jer. 51:11, 12
5 a Jer. 49:29
6 a Dan. 11:19

Toward the north, by the River
Euphrates.

7 "Who *is* this coming up [a]like a
flood,
Whose waters move like the rivers?
8 Egypt rises up like a flood,
And *its* waters move like the rivers;
And he says, 'I will go up *and* cover
the earth,
I will destroy the city and its
inhabitants.'
9 Come up, O horses, and rage,
O chariots!
And let the mighty men come
forth:
[1]The Ethiopians and [2]the Libyans
who handle the shield,
And the Lydians [a]who handle *and*
bend the bow.
10 For this *is* [a]the day of the Lord
GOD of hosts,
A day of vengeance,
That He may avenge Himself on His
adversaries.
[b]The sword shall devour;
It shall be [1]satiated and made
drunk with their blood;
For the Lord GOD of hosts [c]has a
sacrifice
In the north country by the River
Euphrates.

11 "Go[a] up to Gilead and take balm,
[b]O virgin, the daughter of Egypt;
In vain you will use many
medicines;
[c]You shall not be cured.
12 The nations have heard of your
[a]shame,
And your cry has filled the land;
For the mighty man has stumbled
against the mighty;
They both have fallen together."

Babylonia Will Strike Egypt

13The word that the LORD spoke to Jeremiah the prophet, how Nebuchadnezzar
king of Babylon would come *and* [a]strike
the land of Egypt.

14 "Declare in Egypt, and proclaim in
[a]Migdol;
Proclaim in [1]Noph and in
[b]Tahpanhes;
Say, 'Stand fast and prepare
yourselves,
For the sword devours all around
you.'

7 a Jer. 47:2
9 a Is. 66:19 *1* Heb. *Cush* *2* Heb. *Put*
10 a Joel 1:15 b Deut. 32:42 c Is. 34:6 *1* Filled to the full
11 a Jer. 8:22 b Is. 47:1 c Ezek. 30:21
12 a Jer. 2:36
13 a Is. 19:1
14 a Jer. 44:1 b Ezek. 30:18 *1* Ancient Memphis
16 a Lev. 26:36, 37 b Jer. 51:9
18 a Jer. 48:15
19 a Jer. 48:18 b Is. 20:4 *1* Ancient Memphis
20 a Hos. 10:11 b Jer. 1:14
21 a [Ps. 37:13] *1* Lit. *calves of the stall*
22 a [Is. 29:4]
23 a Is. 10:34 b Judg. 6:5; 7:12
24 a Jer. 1:15
25 a Ezek. 30:14–16 b Jer. 43:12, 13 *1* A sun god *2* Ancient Thebes

15 Why are your valiant *men* swept
away?
They did not stand
Because the LORD drove them away.
16 He made many fall;
Yes, [a]one fell upon another.
And they said, 'Arise!
[b]Let us go back to our own people
And to the land of our nativity
From the oppressing sword.'
17 They cried there,
'Pharaoh, king of Egypt, *is but* a
noise.
He has passed by the appointed
time!'
18 "*As* I live," says the King,
[a]Whose name *is* the LORD of hosts,
"Surely as Tabor *is* among the
mountains
And as Carmel by the sea, *so* he
shall come.
19 O [a]you daughter dwelling in
Egypt,
Prepare yourself [b]to go into
captivity!
For [1]Noph shall be waste and
desolate, without inhabitant.

20 "Egypt *is* a very pretty [a]heifer,
But destruction comes, it comes
[b]from the north.
21 Also her mercenaries are in her
midst like [1]fat bulls,
For they also are turned back,
They have fled away together.
They did not stand,
For [a]the day of their calamity had
come upon them,
The time of their punishment.
22 [a]Her noise shall go like a serpent,
For they shall march with an army
And come against her with axes,
Like those who chop wood.

23 "They shall [a]cut down her forest,"
says the LORD,
"Though it cannot be searched,
Because they *are* innumerable,
And more numerous than
[b]grasshoppers.
24 The daughter of Egypt shall be
ashamed;
She shall be delivered into the hand
Of [a]the people of the north."

25The LORD of hosts, the God of Israel,
says: "Behold, I will bring punishment on
[1]Amon of [a]No,[2] and Pharaoh and Egypt,
[b]with their gods and their kings—

Pharaoh and those who [c]trust in him.
26[a]And I will deliver them into the hand of those who seek their lives, into the hand of Nebuchadnezzar king of Babylon and the hand of his servants. [b]Afterward it shall be inhabited as in the days of old," says the LORD.

God Will Preserve Israel

27 "But[a] do not fear, O My servant Jacob,
And do not be dismayed, O Israel!
For behold, I will [b]save you from afar,
And your offspring from the land of their captivity;
Jacob shall return, have rest and be at ease;
No one shall make *him* afraid.
28 Do not fear, O Jacob My servant," says the LORD,
"For I *am* with you;
For I will make a complete end of all the nations
To which I have driven you,
But I will not make [a]a complete end of you.
I will rightly [b]correct you,
For I will not leave you wholly unpunished."

Judgment on Philistia

47 The word of the LORD that came to Jeremiah the prophet [a]against the Philistines, [b]before Pharaoh attacked Gaza.
2Thus says the LORD:

"Behold, [a]waters rise [b]out of the north,
And shall be an overflowing flood;
They shall overflow the land and all that is in it,
The city and those who dwell within;
Then the men shall cry,
And all the inhabitants of the land shall wail.
3 At the [a]noise of the stamping hooves of his strong horses,
At the rushing of his chariots,
At the rumbling of his wheels,
The fathers will not look back for *their* children,
[1]Lacking courage,
4 Because of the day that comes to plunder all the [a]Philistines,
To cut off from [b]Tyre and Sidon every helper who remains;
For the LORD shall plunder the Philistines,
[c]The remnant of the country of [d]Caphtor.[1]
5 [a]Baldness has come upon Gaza,
[b]Ashkelon is cut off
With the remnant of their valley.
How long will you cut yourself?

6 "O you [a]sword of the LORD,
How long until you are quiet?
Put yourself up into your scabbard,
Rest and be still!
7 How can [1]it be quiet,
Seeing the LORD has [a]given it a charge
Against Ashkelon and against the seashore?
There He has [b]appointed it."

Judgment on Moab

48 Against [a]Moab.
Thus says the LORD of hosts, the God of Israel:

"Woe to [b]Nebo!
For it is plundered,
[c]Kirjathaim is shamed *and* taken;
[1]The high stronghold is shamed and dismayed—
2 [a]No more praise of Moab.
In [b]Heshbon they have devised evil against her:
'Come, and let us cut her off as a nation.'
You also shall be cut down, O [c]Madmen![1]
The sword shall pursue you;
3 A voice of crying *shall be* from [a]Horonaim:
'Plundering and great destruction!'

4 "Moab is destroyed;
[1]Her little ones have caused a cry to be heard;
5 [a]For in the Ascent of Luhith they ascend with continual weeping;
For in the descent of Horonaim the enemies have heard a cry of destruction.

6 "Flee, save your lives!
And be like [1]the [a]juniper in the wilderness.
7 For because you have trusted in your works and your [a]treasures,
You also shall be taken.

---

25 c Is. 30:1–5; 31:1–3
26 a Ezek. 32:11 b Ezek. 29:8–14
27 a Is. 41:13, 14; 43:5; 44:2 b Is. 11:11
28 a Amos 9:8, 9 b Jer. 30:11

CHAPTER 47
1 a Zeph. 2:4, 5 b Amos 1:6
2 a Is. 8:7, 8 b Jer. 1:14
3 a Jer. 8:16 1 Lit. *From sinking hands*
4 a Is. 14:29–31 b Jer. 25:22 c Ezek. 25:16 d Gen. 10:14 1 Cappadocia in Asia Minor
5 a Mic. 1:16 b Jer. 25:20
6 a Ezek. 21:3–5
7 a Ezek. 14:17 b Mic. 6:9 1 Lit. *you*

CHAPTER 48
1 a Is. 15:1—16:14; 25:10 b Is. 15:2 c Num. 32:37 1 Heb. *Misgab*
2 a Is. 16:14 b Jer. 49:3 c Is. 10:31 1 A city of Moab
3 a Is. 15:5
4 1 So with MT, Tg., Vg.; LXX *Proclaim it in Zoar*
5 a Is. 15:5
6 a Jer. 17:6 1 Or *Aroer,* a city of Moab
7 a Jer. 9:23

And [b]Chemosh shall go forth into
captivity,
His [c]priests and his princes
together.
8 And [a]the plunderer shall come
against every city;
No one shall escape.
The valley also shall perish,
And the plain shall be destroyed,
As the LORD has spoken.

9 "Give[a] wings to Moab,
That she may flee and get away;
For her cities shall be desolate,
Without any to dwell in them.
10 [a]Cursed *is* he who does the work of
the LORD deceitfully,
And cursed *is* he who keeps back
his sword from blood.

11 "Moab has been at ease from [1]his
youth;
He [a]has settled on his dregs,
And has not been emptied from
vessel to vessel,
Nor has he gone into captivity.
Therefore his taste remained in
him,
And his scent has not changed.
12 "Therefore behold, the days are
coming," says the LORD,
"That I shall send him
[1]wine-workers
Who will tip him over
And empty his vessels
And break the bottles.
13 Moab shall be ashamed of
[a]Chemosh,
As the house of Israel [b]was
ashamed of [c]Bethel, their
confidence.

14 "How can you say, [a]'We *are* mighty
And strong men for the war'?
15 Moab is plundered and gone up
from her cities;
Her chosen young men have [a]gone
down to the slaughter," says [b]the
King,
Whose name *is* the LORD of hosts.

16 "The calamity of Moab *is* near at
hand,
And his affliction comes quickly.
17 Bemoan him, all you who are
around him;
And all you who know his name,
Say, [a]'How the strong staff is
broken,
The beautiful rod!'

7 b Jer. 48:13 c Jer. 49:3
8 a Jer. 6:26
9 a Ps. 55:6
10 a 1 Sam. 15:3, 9
11 a Zeph. 1:12 1 Heb. uses masc. and fem. pronouns interchangeably in this chapter.
12 1 Lit. *tippers* of wine bottles
13 a 1 Kin. 11:7 b Hos. 10:6 c 1 Kin. 12:29; 13:32–34
14 a Is. 16:6
15 a Jer. 50:27 b Jer. 46:18; 51:57
17 a Is. 9:4; 14:4, 5
18 a Is. 47:1 b Is. 15:2
19 a Deut. 2:36 b 1 Sam. 4:13, 14, 16
20 a Is. 16:7 b Num. 21:13
24 a Amos 2:2
25 a Ps. 75:10 b Ezek. 30:21 1 Strength
26 a Jer. 25:15
27 a Zeph. 2:8 b Jer. 2:26 c Lam. 2:15
28 a Ps. 55:6, 7 b Song 2:14
29 a Is. 16:6 b Jer. 49:16
30 a Jer. 50:36 1 *idle talk*

18 "O [a]daughter inhabiting [b]Dibon,
Come down from *your* glory,
And sit in thirst;
For the plunderer of Moab has
come against you,
He has destroyed your strongholds.
19 O inhabitant of [a]Aroer,
[b]Stand by the way and watch;
Ask him who flees
And her who escapes;
Say, 'What has happened?'
20 Moab is shamed, for he is broken
down.
[a]Wail and cry!
Tell it in [b]Arnon, that Moab is
plundered.

21 "And judgment has come on the
plain country:
On Holon and Jahzah and
Mephaath,
22 On Dibon and Nebo and Beth
Diblathaim,
23 On Kirjathaim and Beth Gamul
and Beth Meon,
24 On [a]Kerioth and Bozrah,
On all the cities of the land of
Moab,
Far or near.
25 [a]The [1]horn of Moab is cut off,
And his [b]arm is broken," says the
LORD.

26 "Make[a] him drunk,
Because he exalted *himself* against
the LORD.
Moab shall wallow in his vomit,
And he shall also be in derision.
27 For [a]was not Israel a derision to
you?
[b]Was he found among thieves?
For whenever you speak of him,
You shake *your head in* [c]*scorn*.
28 You who dwell in Moab,
Leave the cities and [a]dwell in the
rock,
And be like [b]the dove *which* makes
her nest
In the sides of the cave's mouth.

29 "We have heard the [a]pride of Moab
(He *is* exceedingly proud),
Of his loftiness and arrogance and
[b]pride,
And of the haughtiness of his
heart."

30 "I know his wrath," says the LORD,
"But it *is* not right;
[a]His [1]lies have made nothing right.

31 Therefore [a]I will wail for Moab,
And I will cry out for all Moab;
[1]I will mourn for the men of Kir Heres.
32 [a]O vine of Sibmah! I will weep for you with the weeping of [b]Jazer.
Your plants have gone over the sea,
They reach to the sea of Jazer.
The plunderer has fallen on your summer fruit and your vintage.
33 [a]Joy and gladness are taken
From the plentiful field
And from the land of Moab;
I have caused wine to [1]fail from the winepresses;
No one will tread with joyous shouting—
Not joyous shouting!

34 "From[a] the cry of Heshbon to [b]Elealeh and to Jahaz
They have uttered their voice,
[c]From Zoar to Horonaim,
Like [1]a three-year-old heifer;
For the waters of Nimrim also shall be desolate.

35 "Moreover," says the LORD,
"I will cause to cease in Moab
[a]The one who offers *sacrifices* in the [1]high places
And burns incense to his gods.
36 Therefore [a]My heart shall wail like flutes for Moab,
And like flutes My heart shall wail
For the men of Kir Heres.
Therefore [b]the riches they have acquired have perished.

37 "For [a]every head *shall be* bald, and every beard clipped;
On all the hands *shall be* cuts, and [b]on the loins sackcloth—
38 A general lamentation
On all the [a]housetops of Moab,
And in its streets;
For I have [b]broken Moab like a vessel in which *is* no pleasure,"
says the LORD.
39 "They shall wail:
'How she is broken down!
How Moab has turned her back with shame!'
So Moab shall be a derision
And a dismay to all those about her."

40 For thus says the LORD:

"Behold, [a]one shall fly like an eagle,
And [b]spread his wings over Moab.

31 [a]Is. 15:5; 16:7, 11 [1]So with DSS, LXX, Vg.; MT *He*

32 [a]Is. 16:8, 9 [b]Num. 21:32

33 [a]Joel 1:12 [1]*cease*

34 [a]Is. 15:4–6 [b]Num. 32:3, 37 [c]Is. 15:5, 6 [1]Or *The Third Eglath,* an unknown city, Is. 15:5

35 [a]Is. 15:2; 16:12 [1]Places for pagan worship

36 [a]Is. 15:5; 16:11 [b]Is. 15:7

37 [a]Is. 15:2, 3 [b]Gen. 37:34

38 [a]Is. 15:3 [b]Jer. 22:28

40 [a]Deut. 28:49 [b]Is. 8:8

41 [a]Is. 13:8; 21:3

42 [a]Ps. 83:4

43 [a]Is. 24:17, 18

44 [a]Is. 24:18 [b]Jer. 11:23

45 [a]Num. 21:28, 29 [b]Ps. 135:11 [c]Num. 24:17

46 [a]Num. 21:29

47 [a]Jer. 49:6, 39

CHAPTER 49

1 [a]Ezek. 21:28–32; 25:1–7 [b]Amos 1:13–15 [1]Heb. *Malcam,* lit. *their king;* an Ammonite god, 1 Kin. 11:5; *Molech,* Lev. 18:21

2 [a]Amos 1:13–15 [b]Ezek. 25:5

41 Kerioth is taken,
And the strongholds are surprised;
[a]The mighty men's hearts in Moab on that day shall be
Like the heart of a woman in birth pangs.
42 And Moab shall be destroyed [a]as a people,
Because he exalted *himself* against the LORD.
43 [a]Fear and the pit and the snare *shall be* upon you,
O inhabitant of Moab," says the LORD.
44 "He who flees from the fear shall fall into the pit,
And he who gets out of the pit shall be caught in the [a]snare.
For upon Moab, upon it [b]I will bring
The year of their punishment," says the LORD.

45 "Those who fled stood under the shadow of Heshbon
Because of exhaustion.
But [a]a fire shall come out of Heshbon,
A flame from the midst of [b]Sihon,
And [c]shall devour the brow of Moab,
The crown of the head of the sons of tumult.
46 [a]Woe to you, O Moab!
The people of Chemosh perish;
For your sons have been taken captive,
And your daughters captive.

47 "Yet I will bring back the captives of Moab
[a]In the latter days," says the LORD.
Thus far *is* the judgment of Moab.

Judgment on Ammon

49 Against the [a]Ammonites.
Thus says the LORD:

"Has Israel no sons?
Has he no heir?
Why *then* does [1]Milcom inherit [b]Gad,
And his people dwell in its cities?
2 [a]Therefore behold, the days are coming," says the LORD,
"That I will cause to be heard an alarm of war
In [b]Rabbah of the Ammonites;
It shall be a desolate mound,

And her [1]villages shall be burned
with fire.
Then Israel shall take possession of
his inheritance," says the LORD.

3 "Wail, O [a]Heshbon, for Ai is
plundered!
Cry, you daughters of Rabbah,
[b]Gird yourselves with sackcloth!
Lament and run to and fro by the
walls;
For [1]Milcom shall go into captivity
With his [c]priests and his princes
together.
4 Why [a]do you boast in the valleys,
[1]Your flowing valley, O [b]backsliding
daughter?
Who trusted in her [c]treasures,
[d]*saying,*
'Who will come against me?'
5 Behold, I will bring fear upon you,"
Says the Lord GOD of hosts,
"From all those who are around you;
You shall be driven out, everyone
headlong,
And no one will gather those who
wander off.
6 But [a]afterward I will bring back
The captives of the people of
Ammon," says the LORD.

Judgment on Edom

7 [a]Against Edom.
Thus says the LORD of hosts:
[b]"*Is* wisdom no more in Teman?
[c]Has counsel perished from the
prudent?
Has their wisdom [d]vanished?
8 Flee, turn back, dwell in the
depths, O inhabitants of [a]Dedan!
For I will bring the calamity of
Esau upon him,
The time *that* I will punish him.
9 [a]If grape-gatherers came to you,
Would they not leave *some* gleaning
grapes?
If thieves by night,
Would they not destroy until they
have enough?
10 [a]But I have made Esau bare;
I have uncovered his secret places,
And he shall not be able to hide
himself.
His descendants are plundered,
His brethren and his neighbors,
And [b]he *is* no more.
11 Leave your fatherless children,
I will preserve *them* alive;
And let your widows trust in Me."

12 For thus says the LORD: "Behold,
[a]those whose judgment *was* not to drink
of the cup have assuredly drunk. And *are*
you the one who will altogether go unpunished? You shall not go unpunished,
but you shall surely drink *of it*. 13 For [a]I
have sworn by Myself," says the LORD,
"that [b]Bozrah shall become a desolation,
a reproach, a [1]waste, and a curse. And all
its cities shall be perpetual [2]wastes."

14 [a]I have heard a message from the
LORD,
And an ambassador has been sent
to the nations:
"Gather together, come against her,
And rise up to battle!

15 "For indeed, I will make you small
among nations,
Despised among men.
16 Your fierceness has deceived you,
The [a]pride of your heart,
O you who dwell in the clefts of the
rock,
Who hold the height of the hill!
[b]Though you make your [c]nest as
high as the eagle,
[d]I will bring you down from there,"
says the LORD.

17 "Edom also shall be an
astonishment;
[a]Everyone who goes by it will be
astonished
And will hiss at all its plagues.
18 [a]As in the overthrow of Sodom and
Gomorrah
And their neighbors," says the
LORD,
"No one shall remain there,
Nor shall a son of man dwell in it.

19 "Behold,[a] he shall come up like a
lion from [b]the [1]floodplain of the
Jordan
Against the dwelling place of the
strong;
But I will suddenly make him run
away from her.
And who *is* a chosen *man that* I
may appoint over her?
For [c]who *is* like Me?
Who will arraign Me?
And [d]who *is* that shepherd
Who will withstand Me?"

2 [1] Lit. *daughters*
3 [a] Jer. 48:2 [b] Is. 32:11 [c] Jer. 48:7 [1] See v. 1
4 [a] Jer. 9:23 [b] Jer. 3:14 [c] Jer. 48:7 [d] Jer. 21:13 [1] Lit. *Your valley is flowing*
6 [a] Jer. 48:47
7 [a] Ezek. 25:12–14; 35:1–15 [b] Gen. 36:11 [c] Is. 19:11 [d] Jer. 8:9
8 [a] Jer. 25:23
9 [a] Obad. 5, 6
10 [a] Mal. 1:3 [b] Is. 17:14
12 [a] Jer. 25:29
13 [a] Amos 6:8 [b] Is. 34:6; 63:1 [1] *ruin* [2] *ruins*
14 [a] Obad. 1–4
16 [a] Jer. 48:29 [b] Obad. 3, 4 [c] Job 39:27 [d] Amos 9:2
17 [a] Jer. 18:16; 49:13; 50:13
18 [a] Deut. 29:23
19 [a] Jer. 50:44 [b] Jer. 12:5 [c] Ex. 15:11 [d] Job 41:10 [1] Or *thicket*

20 [a]Therefore hear the counsel of the LORD that He has taken against Edom,
And His purposes that He has proposed against the inhabitants of Teman:
Surely the least of the flock shall [1]draw them out;
Surely He shall make their dwelling places desolate with them.
21 [a]The earth shakes at the noise of their fall;
At the cry its noise is heard at the Red Sea.
22 Behold, [a]He shall come up and fly like the eagle,
And spread His wings over Bozrah;
The heart of the mighty men of Edom in that day shall be
Like the heart of a woman in birth pangs.

Judgment on Damascus

23[a]Against Damascus.

[b]"Hamath and Arpad are shamed,
For they have heard bad news.
They are fainthearted;
[c]*There is* [1]trouble on the sea;
It cannot be quiet.
24 Damascus has grown feeble;
She turns to flee,
And fear has seized *her.*
[a]Anguish and sorrows have taken her like a woman in [1]labor.
25 Why is [a]the city of praise not deserted, the city of My joy?
26 [a]Therefore her young men shall fall in her streets,
And all the men of war shall be cut off in that day," says the LORD of hosts.
27 "I[a] will kindle a fire in the wall of Damascus,
And it shall consume the palaces of Ben-Hadad."

Judgment on Kedar and Hazor

28[a]Against Kedar and against the kingdoms of Hazor, which Nebuchadnezzar
king of Babylon shall strike.
Thus says the LORD:

"Arise, go up to Kedar,
And devastate [b]the men of the East!
29 Their [a]tents and their flocks they shall take away.
They shall take for themselves their curtains,
All their vessels and their camels;
And they shall cry out to them,
[b]'Fear *is* on every side!'
30 "Flee, get far away! Dwell in the depths,
O inhabitants of Hazor!" says the LORD.
"For Nebuchadnezzar king of Babylon has taken counsel against you,
And has conceived a plan against you.
31 "Arise, go up to [a]the wealthy nation that dwells securely," says the LORD,
"Which has neither gates nor bars,
[b]Dwelling alone.
32 Their camels shall be for booty,
And the multitude of their cattle for plunder.
I will [a]scatter to all winds those [1]in the farthest corners,
And I will bring their calamity from all its sides," says the LORD.
33 "Hazor [a]shall be a dwelling for jackals, a desolation forever;
No one shall reside there,
Nor son of man dwell in it."

Judgment on Elam

34The word of the LORD that came to
Jeremiah the prophet against [a]Elam, in
the [b]beginning of the reign of Zedekiah
king of Judah, saying, 35"Thus says the
LORD of hosts:

'Behold, I will break [a]the [1]bow of Elam,
The foremost of their might.
36 Against Elam I will bring the four winds
From the four quarters of heaven,
And scatter them toward all those winds;
There shall be no nations where the outcasts of Elam will not go.
37 For I will cause Elam to be dismayed before their enemies
And before those who seek their life.
[a]I will bring disaster upon them,
My fierce anger,' says the LORD;
'And I will send the sword after them
Until I have consumed them.

20 [a]Jer. 50:45 [1]Or *drag them away*
21 [a]Jer. 50:46
22 [a]Jer. 48:40, 41
23 [a]Amos 1:3, 5 [b]Jer. 39:5 [c][Is. 57:20] [1]*anxiety*
24 [a]Is. 13:8 [1]*childbirth*
25 [a]Jer. 33:9
26 [a]Jer. 50:30
27 [a]Amos 1:4
28 [a]Ezek. 27:21 [b]Judg. 6:3
29 [a]Ps. 120:5 [b]Jer. 46:5
31 [a]Ezek. 38:11 [b]Num. 23:9
32 [a]Ezek. 5:10 [1]Lit. *cut off at the corner,* Jer. 9:26; 25:23
33 [a]Mal. 1:3
34 [a]Jer. 25:25 [b]2 Kin. 24:17, 18
35 [a]Is. 22:6 [1]Power
37 [a]Jer. 9:16

38 I will [a]set My throne in Elam,
And will destroy from there the king and the princes,' says the LORD.

39 'But it shall come to pass [a]in the latter days:
I will bring back the captives of Elam,' says the LORD."

Judgment on Babylon and Babylonia

50 The word that the LORD spoke [a]against Babylon *and* against the land of the Chaldeans by Jeremiah the prophet.

2 "Declare among the nations,
Proclaim, and [1]set up a standard;
Proclaim—do not conceal *it*—
Say, 'Babylon is [a]taken, [b]Bel is shamed.
[2]Merodach is broken in pieces;
[c]Her idols are humiliated,
Her images are broken in pieces.'
3 [a]For out of the north [b]a nation comes up against her,
Which shall make her land desolate,
And no one shall dwell therein.
They shall [1]move, they shall depart,
Both man and beast.

4 "In those days and in that time," says the LORD,
"The children of Israel shall come,
[a]They and the children of Judah together;
[b]With continual weeping they shall come,
[c]And seek the LORD their God.
5 They shall ask the way to Zion,
With their faces toward it, *saying,*
'Come and let us join ourselves to the LORD
In [a]a perpetual covenant
That will not be forgotten.'

6 "My people have been [a]lost sheep.
Their shepherds have led them [b]astray;
They have turned them away *on* [c]the mountains.
They have gone from mountain to hill;
They have forgotten their resting place.
7 All who found them have [a]devoured them;
And [b]their adversaries said, [c]'We have not offended,
Because they have sinned against the LORD, [d]the habitation of justice,
The LORD, [e]the hope of their fathers.'

8 "Move[a] from the midst of Babylon,
Go out of the land of the Chaldeans;
And be like the [1]rams before the flocks.
9 [a]For behold, I will raise and cause to come up against Babylon
An assembly of great nations from the north country,
And they shall array themselves against her;
From there she shall be captured.
Their arrows *shall be* like *those* of [1]an expert warrior;
[b]None shall return in vain.
10 And Chaldea shall become plunder;
[a]All who plunder her shall be satisfied," says the LORD.

11 "Because[a] you were glad, because you rejoiced,
You destroyers of My heritage,
Because you have grown fat [b]like a heifer threshing grain,
And you [1]bellow like bulls,
12 Your mother shall be deeply ashamed;
She who bore you shall be ashamed.
Behold, the least of the nations *shall be* a [a]wilderness,
A dry land and a desert.
13 Because of the wrath of the LORD
She shall not be inhabited,
[a]But she shall be wholly desolate.
[b]Everyone who goes by Babylon shall be horrified
And hiss at all her plagues.

14 "Put[a] yourselves in array against Babylon all around,
All you who bend the bow;
Shoot at her, spare no arrows,
For she has sinned against the LORD.
15 Shout against her all around;
She has [a]given her hand,
Her foundations have fallen,
[b]Her walls are thrown down;
For [c]it *is* the vengeance of the LORD.
Take vengeance on her.
As she has done, so do to her.

38 a Jer. 43:10
39 a Jer. 48:47
CHAPTER 50
1 a Is. 13:1; 47:1
2 a Is. 21:9 b Is. 46:1 c Jer. 43:12, 13 *1 lift* *2* Or *Marduk;* a Babylonian god
3 a Jer. 51:48 b Is. 13:17, 18, 20 *1* Or *wander*
4 a Hos. 1:11 b Ezra 3:12, 13 c Hos. 3:5
5 a Jer. 31:31
6 a Is. 53:6 b Jer. 23:1 c [Jer. 2:20; 3:6, 23]
7 a Ps. 79:7 b Zech. 11:5 c Jer. 2:3 d [Ps. 90:1; 91:1] e Ps. 22:4
8 a Is. 48:20 *1 male goats*
9 a Jer. 15:14; 51:27 b 2 Sam. 1:22 *1* So with some Heb. mss., LXX, Syr.; MT, Tg., Vg. *a warrior who makes childless*
10 a [Rev. 17:16]
11 a Is. 47:6 b Hos. 10:11 *1* Or *neigh like steeds*
12 a Jer. 51:43
13 a Jer. 25:12 b Jer. 49:17
14 a Jer. 51:2
15 a Lam. 5:6 b Jer. 51:58 c Jer. 51:6, 11

16 Cut off the sower from Babylon,
And him who handles the sickle at harvest time.
For fear of the oppressing sword
[a]Everyone shall turn to his own people,
And everyone shall flee to his own land.

17 "Israel *is* like [a]scattered sheep;
[b]The lions have driven *him* away.
First [c]the king of Assyria devoured him;
Now at last this [d]Nebuchadnezzar king of Babylon has broken his bones."

18 Therefore thus says the LORD of hosts, the God of Israel:

"Behold, I will punish the king of Babylon and his land,
As I have punished the king of [a]Assyria.
19 [a]But I will bring back Israel to his home,
And he shall feed on Carmel and Bashan;
His soul shall be satisfied on Mount Ephraim and Gilead.
20 In those days and in that time,"
says the LORD,
[a]"The iniquity of Israel shall be sought, but *there shall be* none;
And the sins of Judah, but they shall not be found;
For I will pardon those [b]whom I preserve.

21 "Go up against the land of Merathaim, against it,
And against the inhabitants of [a]Pekod.
[1]Waste and utterly destroy them,"
says the LORD,
"And do [b]according to all that I have commanded you.
22 [a]A sound of battle *is* in the land,
And of great destruction.
23 How [a]the hammer of the whole earth has been cut apart and broken!
How Babylon has become a desolation among the nations!
I have laid a snare for you;
24 You have indeed been [a]trapped, O Babylon,
And you were not aware;
You have been found and also caught,
Because you have [b]contended against the LORD.
25 The LORD has opened His armory,
And has brought out [a]the weapons of His indignation;
For this *is* the work of the Lord GOD of hosts
In the land of the Chaldeans.
26 Come against her from the farthest border;
Open her storehouses;
Cast her up as heaps of ruins,
And destroy her utterly;
Let nothing of her be left.
27 Slay all her [a]bulls,
Let them go down to the slaughter.
Woe to them!
For their day has come, the time of [b]their punishment.
28 The voice of those who flee and escape from the land of Babylon
[a]Declares in Zion the vengeance of the LORD our God,
The vengeance of His temple.

29 "Call together the archers against Babylon.
All you who bend the bow, encamp against it all around;
Let none of them [1]escape.
[a]Repay her according to her work;
According to all she has done, do to her;
[b]For she has been proud against the LORD,
Against the Holy One of Israel.
30 [a]Therefore her young men shall fall in the streets,
And all her men of war shall be cut off in that day," says the LORD.

31 "Behold, I *am* against you,
O most haughty one!" says the Lord GOD of hosts;
"For your day has come,
[1]The time *that* I will punish you.
32 The most [a]proud shall stumble and fall,
And no one will raise him up;
[b]I will kindle a fire in his cities,
And it will devour all around him."

33 Thus says the LORD of hosts:
"The children of Israel *were* oppressed,
Along with the children of Judah;
All who took them captive have held them fast;
They have refused to let them go.
34 [a]Their Redeemer *is* strong;

---

16 [a] Is. 13:14
17 [a] 2 Kin. 24:10, 14 [b] Jer. 2:15 [c] 2 Kin. 15:29; 17:6; 18:9–13 [d] 2 Kin. 24:10–14; 25:1–7
18 [a] Ezek. 31:3, 11, 12
19 [a] Is. 65:10
20 [a] [Jer. 31:34] [b] Is. 1:9
21 [a] Ezek. 23:23 [b] 2 Sam. 16:11 [1] Or *Attack with the sword*
22 [a] Jer. 51:54
23 [a] Jer. 51:20–24
24 [a] Dan. 5:30 [b] [Is. 45:9]
25 [a] Is. 13:5
27 [a] Is. 34:7 [b] Jer. 48:44
28 [a] Jer. 51:10
29 [a] Jer. 51:56 [b] [Is. 47:10] [1] Qr., some Heb. mss., LXX, Tg. add *to her*
30 [a] Jer. 49:26; 51:4
31 [1] So with MT, Tg.; LXX, Vg. *The time of your punishment*
32 [a] Mal. 4:1 [b] Jer. 21:14
34 [a] Rev. 18:8

[b]The LORD of hosts *is* His name.
He will thoroughly plead their
[c]case,
That He may give rest to the land,
And disquiet the inhabitants of
Babylon.

35 "A sword *is* against the Chaldeans,"
says the LORD,
"Against the inhabitants of Babylon,
And [a]against her princes and [b]her
wise men.
36 A sword *is* [a]against the
soothsayers, and they will be
fools.
A sword *is* against her mighty men,
and they will be dismayed.
37 A sword *is* against their horses,
Against their chariots,
And against all [a]the mixed peoples
who *are* in her midst;
And [b]they will become like women.
A sword *is* against her treasures,
and they will be robbed.
38 [a]A [1]drought *is* against her waters,
and they will be dried up.
For it *is* the land of carved images,
And they are insane with *their*
idols.

39 "Therefore[a] the wild desert beasts
shall dwell *there* with the jackals,
And the ostriches shall dwell in it.
[b]It shall be inhabited no more
forever,
Nor shall it be dwelt in from
generation to generation.
40 [a]As God overthrew Sodom and
Gomorrah
And their neighbors," says the
LORD,
"*So* no one shall reside there,
Nor son of man [b]dwell in it.

41 "Behold,[a] a people shall come from
the north,
And a great nation and many kings
Shall be raised up from the ends of
the earth.
42 [a]They shall hold the bow and the
lance;
[b]They *are* cruel and shall not show
mercy.
[c]Their voice shall roar like the sea;
They shall ride on horses,
Set in array, like a man for the
battle,
Against you, O daughter of Babylon.

34 [b]Is. 47:4 [c]Jer. 51:36; Mic. 7:9
35 [a]Dan. 5:30 [b]Is. 47:13
36 [a]Is. 44:25
37 [a]Jer. 25:20 [b]Jer. 51:30
38 [a]Rev. 16:12 [1]So with MT, Tg., Vg.; Syr. *sword;* LXX omits *A drought is*
39 [a]Rev. 18:2 [b]Is. 13:20
40 [a]Is. 13:19 [b]Is. 13:20
41 [a]Jer. 6:22; 25:14; 51:27
42 [a]Jer. 6:23 [b]Is. 13:18 [c]Is. 5:30
43 [a]Jer. 51:31 [b]Jer. 6:24
44 [a]Jer. 49:19–21 [b]Job 41:10 [1]Or *thicket*
45 [a]Jer. 51:10, 11 [b]Jer. 51:29 [c]Jer. 49:19, 20
46 [a]Rev. 18:9

CHAPTER 51
1 [a]Is. 47:1 [b]Jer. 4:11 [1]Lit. *The Midst of Those Who Rise Up Against Me;* a code word for Chaldea, Babylonia
2 [a]Jer. 15:7 [b]Jer. 50:14
3 [a]Jer. 50:14, 29 [b]Jer. 50:21

43 "The king of Babylon has [a]heard
the report about them,
And his hands grow feeble;
Anguish has taken hold of him,
Pangs as of a woman in [b]childbirth.

44 "Behold,[a] he shall come up like a
lion from the [1]floodplain of the
Jordan
Against the dwelling place of the
strong;
But I will make them suddenly run
away from her.
And who *is* a chosen *man that* I
may appoint over her?
For who *is* like Me?
Who will arraign Me?
And [b]who *is* that shepherd
Who will withstand Me?"

45 Therefore hear [a]the counsel of the
LORD that He has taken against
Babylon,
And His [b]purposes that He has
proposed against the land of the
Chaldeans:
[c]Surely the least of the flock shall
draw them out;
Surely He will make their dwelling
place desolate with them.
46 [a]At the noise of the taking of
Babylon
The earth trembles,
And the cry is heard among the
nations.

The Utter Destruction of Babylon

51 Thus says the LORD:

"Behold, I will raise up against
[a]Babylon,
Against those who dwell in [1]Leb
Kamai,
[b]A destroying wind.
2 And I will send [a]winnowers to
Babylon,
Who shall winnow her and empty
her land.
[b]For in the day of doom
They shall be against her all
around.
3 Against *her* [a]let the archer bend
his bow,
And lift himself up against *her* in
his armor.
Do not spare her young men;
[b]Utterly destroy all her army.

4 Thus the slain shall fall in the land
of the Chaldeans,
[a]And *those* thrust through in her
streets.
5 For Israel is [a]not forsaken, nor
Judah,
By his God, the LORD of hosts,
Though their land was filled with
sin against the Holy One of
Israel."

6 [a]Flee from the midst of Babylon,
And every one save his life!
Do not be cut off in her iniquity,
For [b]this *is* the time of the LORD's
vengeance;
[c]He shall recompense her.
7 [a]Babylon *was* a golden cup in the
LORD's hand,
That made all the earth drunk.
[b]The nations drank her wine;
Therefore the nations [c]are
deranged.
8 Babylon has suddenly [a]fallen and
been destroyed.
[b]Wail for her!
[c]Take balm for her pain;
Perhaps she may be healed.
9 We would have healed Babylon,
But she is not healed.
Forsake her, and [a]let us go
everyone to his own country;
[b]For her judgment reaches to
heaven and is lifted up to the
skies.
10 The LORD has [a]revealed our
righteousness.
Come and let us [b]declare in Zion
the work of the LORD our God.

11 [a]Make[1] the arrows bright!
Gather the shields!
[b]The LORD has raised up the spirit of
the kings of the Medes.
[c]For His plan *is* against Babylon to
destroy it,
Because it *is* [d]the vengeance of the
LORD,
The vengeance for His temple.
12 [a]Set up the standard on the walls
of Babylon;
Make the guard strong,
Set up the watchmen,
Prepare the ambushes.
For the LORD has both devised and
done
What He spoke against the
inhabitants of Babylon.
13 [a]O you who dwell by many waters,
Abundant in treasures,
Your end has come,
The measure of your covetousness.
14 [a]The LORD of hosts has sworn by
Himself:
"Surely I will fill you with men, [b]as
with locusts,
And they shall lift [c]up a shout
against you."

15 [a]He has made the earth by His
power;
He has established the world by His
wisdom,
And [b]stretched out the heaven by
His understanding.
16 When He utters *His* voice—
There is a multitude of waters in
the heavens:
[a]"He causes the vapors to ascend
from the ends of the earth;
He makes lightnings for the rain;
He brings the wind out of His
treasuries."

17 [a]Everyone is dull-hearted, without
knowledge;
Every metalsmith is put to shame
by the carved image;
[b]For his molded image *is* falsehood,
And *there is* no breath in them.
18 They *are* futile, a work of errors;
In the time of their punishment
they shall perish.
19 The Portion of Jacob *is* not like
them,
For He *is* the Maker of all things;
And *Israel is* the tribe of His
inheritance.
The LORD of hosts *is* His name.

20 "You[a] *are* My battle-ax *and*
weapons of war:
For with you I will break the nation
in pieces;
With you I will destroy kingdoms;
21 With you I will break in pieces the
horse and its rider;
With you I will break in pieces the
chariot and its rider;
22 With you also I will break in
pieces man and woman;
With you I will break in pieces [a]old
and young;
With you I will break in pieces the
young man and the maiden;
23 With you also I will break in
pieces the shepherd and his
flock;

4 a Jer. 49:26; 50:30, 37
5 a [Jer. 33:24–26; 46:28]
6 a Rev. 18:4 b Jer. 50:15 c Jer. 25:14
7 a Rev. 17:4 b Rev. 14:8 c Jer. 25:16
8 a Is. 21:9 b Rev. 18:9, 11, 19 c Jer. 46:11
9 a Is. 13:14 b Rev. 18:5
10 a Ps. 37:6 b Jer. 50:28
11 a Jer. 46:4, 9 b Is. 13:17 c Jer. 50:45 d Jer. 50:28 *1 Polish the arrows!*
12 a Nah. 2:1; 3:14
13 a Rev. 17:1, 15
14 a Jer. 49:13 b Nah. 3:15 c Jer. 50:15
15 a Gen. 1:1, 6 b Job 9:8
16 a Ps. 135:7
17 a Jer. 10:14 b Jer. 50:2
20 a Is. 10:5, 15
22 a 2 Chr. 36:17

With you I will break in pieces the
farmer and his yoke of oxen;
And with you I will break in pieces
governors and rulers.

24 "And[a] I will repay Babylon
And all the inhabitants of Chaldea
For all the evil they have done
In Zion in your sight," says the
LORD.

25 "Behold, I *am* against you,
[a]O destroying mountain,
Who destroys all the earth," says
the LORD.
"And I will stretch out My hand
against you,
Roll you down from the rocks,
[b]And make you a burnt mountain.
26 They shall not take from you a
stone for a corner
Nor a stone for a foundation,
[a]But you shall be desolate forever,"
says the LORD.

27 [a]Set up a banner in the land,
Blow the trumpet among the
nations!
[b]Prepare the nations against her,
Call [c]the kingdoms together against
her:
Ararat, Minni, and Ashkenaz.
Appoint a general against her;
Cause the horses to come up like
the bristling locusts.
28 Prepare against her the nations,
With the kings of the Medes,
Its governors and all its rulers,
All the land of his dominion.
29 And the land will tremble and
sorrow;
For every [a]purpose of the LORD
shall be performed against
Babylon,
[b]To make the land of Babylon a
desolation without inhabitant.
30 The mighty men of Babylon have
ceased fighting,
They have remained in their
strongholds;
Their might has failed,
[a]They became *like* women;
They have burned her dwelling
places,
[b]The bars of her *gate* are broken.
31 [a]One runner will run to meet
another,
And one messenger to meet
another,

To show the king of Babylon that
his city is taken on *all* sides;
32 [a]The passages are blocked,
The reeds they have burned with
fire,
And the men of war are terrified.

33 For thus says the LORD of hosts, the
God of Israel:

"The daughter of Babylon *is* [a]like a
threshing floor
When [b]*it is* time to thresh her;
Yet a little while
[c]And the time of her harvest will
come."

34 "Nebuchadnezzar the king of
Babylon
Has [a]devoured me, he has crushed
me;
He has made me an [b]empty vessel,
He has swallowed me up like a
monster;
He has filled his stomach with my
delicacies,
He has spit me out.
35 Let the violence *done* to me and
my flesh *be* upon Babylon,"
The inhabitant of Zion will say;
"And my blood be upon the
inhabitants of Chaldea!"
Jerusalem will say.

36 Therefore thus says the LORD:

"Behold, [a]I will plead your case and
take vengeance for you.
[b]I will dry up her sea and make her
springs dry.
37 [a]Babylon shall become a heap,
A dwelling place for jackals,
[b]An astonishment and a hissing,
Without an inhabitant.
38 They shall roar together like lions,
They shall growl like lions' whelps.
39 In their excitement I will prepare
their feasts;
[a]I will make them drunk,
That they may rejoice,
And sleep a perpetual sleep
And not awake," says the LORD.
40 "I will bring them down
Like lambs to the slaughter,
Like rams with male goats.

41 "Oh, how [a]Sheshach[1] is taken!
Oh, how [b]the praise of the whole
earth is seized!
How Babylon has become desolate
among the nations!

24 a Jer. 50:15, 29
25 a Zech. 4:7 b Rev. 8:8
26 a Jer. 50:26, 40
27 a Is. 13:2 b Jer. 25:14 c Jer. 50:41, 42
29 a Jer. 50:45 b Jer. 50:13; 51:26, 43
30 a Is. 19:16 b Lam. 2:9
31 a Jer. 50:24
32 a Jer. 50:38
33 a Is. 21:10 b Hab. 3:12 c Rev. 14:15
34 a Jer. 50:17 b Is. 24:1–3
36 a Jer. 50:34 b Jer. 50:38
37 a Is. 13:22 b Jer. 25:9, 11
39 a Jer. 51:57
41 a Jer. 25:26 b Is. 13:19 *1* A code word for Babylon, Jer. 25:26

42 [a]The sea has come up over
Babylon;
She is covered with the multitude
of its waves.
43 [a]Her cities are a desolation,
A dry land and a wilderness,
A land where [b]no one dwells,
Through which no son of man
passes.
44 I will punish [a]Bel[1] in Babylon,
And I will bring out of his mouth
what he has swallowed;
And the nations shall not stream to
him anymore.
Yes, [b]the wall of Babylon shall fall.

45 "My[a] people, go out of the midst of
her!
And let everyone deliver [1]himself
from the fierce anger of the
LORD.
46 And lest your heart faint,
And you fear [a]for the rumor that
will be heard in the land
(A rumor will come *one* year,
And after that, in *another* year
A rumor *will come,*
And violence in the land,
Ruler against ruler),
47 Therefore behold, the days are
coming
That I will bring judgment on the
carved images of Babylon;
Her whole land shall be ashamed,
And all her slain shall fall in her
midst.
48 Then [a]the heavens and the earth
and all that *is* in them
Shall sing joyously over Babylon;
[b]For the plunderers shall come to
her from the north," says the
LORD.

49 As Babylon *has caused* the slain of
Israel to fall,
So at Babylon the slain of all the
earth shall fall.
50 [a]You who have escaped the sword,
Get away! Do not stand still!
[b]Remember the LORD afar off,
And let Jerusalem come to your
mind.

51 [a]We are ashamed because we have
heard reproach.
Shame has covered our faces,
For strangers [b]have come into the
[1]sanctuaries of the LORD's house.

42 [a]Is. 8:7, 8
43 [a]Jer. 50:39, 40 [b]Is. 13:20
44 [a]Jer. 50:2 [b]Jer. 50:15 [1]A Babylonian god
45 [a][Rev. 18:4] [1]Lit. *his soul*
46 [a]2 Kin. 19:7
48 [a]Is. 44:23; 48:20; 49:13 [b]Jer. 50:3, 41
50 [a]Jer. 44:28 [b][Deut. 4:29–31]
51 [a]Ps. 44:15; 79:4 [b]Lam. 1:10 [1]*holy places*
53 [a]Amos 9:2 [1]*ascend*
54 [a]Jer. 50:22
56 [a]Jer. 50:29
57 [a]Jer. 50:35 [b]Jer. 46:18; 48:15
58 [a]Jer. 50:15 [b]Hab. 2:13 [1]Lit. *laid utterly bare*
59 [a]Jer. 32:12
60 [a]Jer. 36:2

52 "Therefore behold, the days are
coming," says the LORD,
"That I will bring judgment on her
carved images,
And throughout all her land the
wounded shall groan.
53 [a]Though Babylon were to [1]mount
up to heaven,
And though she were to fortify the
height of her strength,
Yet from Me plunderers would
come to her," says the LORD.

54 [a]The sound of a cry *comes* from
Babylon,
And great destruction from the land
of the Chaldeans,
55 Because the LORD is plundering
Babylon
And silencing her loud voice,
Though her waves roar like great
waters,
And the noise of their voice is
uttered,
56 Because the plunderer comes
against her, against Babylon,
And her mighty men are taken.
Every one of their bows is broken;
[a]For the LORD *is* the God of
recompense,
He will surely repay.

57 "And I will make drunk
Her princes and [a]wise men,
Her governors, her deputies, and
her mighty men.
And they shall sleep a perpetual
sleep
And not awake," says [b]the King,
Whose name *is* the LORD of hosts.

58 Thus says the LORD of hosts:

"The broad walls of Babylon shall be
utterly [a]broken,[1]
And her high gates shall be burned
with fire;
[b]The people will labor in vain,
And the nations, because of the fire;
And they shall be weary."

Jeremiah's Command to Seraiah

59 The word which Jeremiah the prophet commanded Seraiah the son of [a]Neri-
ah, the son of Mahseiah, when he went
with Zedekiah the king of Judah to Babylon in the fourth year of his reign. And
Seraiah *was* the quartermaster. 60 So Jeremiah [a]wrote in a book all the evil that

would come upon Babylon, all these words that are written against Babylon. [61]And Jeremiah said to Seraiah, "When you arrive in Babylon and see it, and read all these words, [62]then you shall say, 'O LORD, You have spoken against this place to cut it off, so that [a]none shall remain in it, neither man nor beast, but it shall be desolate forever.' [63]Now it shall be, when you have finished reading this book, [a]*that* you shall tie a stone to it and throw it out into the Euphrates. [64]Then you shall say, 'Thus Babylon shall sink and not rise from the catastrophe that I will bring upon her. And they shall be weary.' "

Thus far *are* the words of Jeremiah.

The Fall of Jerusalem Reviewed

52 Zedekiah *was* [a]twenty-one years old when he became king, and he reigned eleven years in Jerusalem. His mother's name *was* Hamutal the daughter of Jeremiah of [b]Libnah. [2]He also did evil in the sight of the LORD, according to all that Jehoiakim had done. [3]For because of the anger of the LORD *this* happened in Jerusalem and Judah, till He finally cast them out from His presence. Then Zedekiah [a]rebelled against the king of Babylon.

[4]Now it came to pass in the [a]ninth year of his reign, in the tenth month, on the tenth *day* of the month, *that* Nebuchadnezzar king of Babylon and all his army came against Jerusalem and encamped against it; and *they* built a siege wall against it all around. [5]So the city was besieged until the eleventh year of King Zedekiah. [6]By the fourth month, on the ninth day of the month, the famine had become so severe in the city that there was no food for the people of the land. [7]Then the city wall was broken through, and all the men of war fled and went out of the city at night by way of the gate between the two walls, which *was* by the king's garden, even though the Chaldeans *were* near the city all around. And they went by way of the [1]plain.

[8]But the army of the Chaldeans pursued the king, and they overtook Zedekiah in the plains of Jericho. All his army was scattered from him. [9][a]So they took the king and brought him up to the king of Babylon at Riblah in the land of Hamath, and he pronounced judgment on him. [10][a]Then the king of Babylon killed the sons of Zedekiah before his eyes. And he killed all the princes of Judah in Riblah. [11]He also [a]put out the eyes of Zedekiah; and the king of Babylon bound him in [1]bronze fetters, took him to Babylon, and put him in prison till the day of his death.

The Temple and City Plundered and Burned

[12][a]Now in the fifth month, on the tenth *day* of the month ([b]which *was* the nineteenth year of King Nebuchadnezzar king of Babylon), [c]Nebuzaradan, the captain of the guard, *who* served the king of Babylon, came to Jerusalem. [13]He burned the house of the LORD and the king's house; all the houses of Jerusalem, that is, all the houses of the great, he burned with fire. [14]And all the army of the Chaldeans who *were* with the captain of the guard broke down all the walls of Jerusalem all around. [15][a]Then Nebuzaradan the captain of the guard carried away captive *some* of the poor people, the rest of the people who remained in the city, the defectors who had deserted to the king of Babylon, and the rest of the craftsmen. [16]But Nebuzaradan the captain of the guard left *some* of the poor of the land as vinedressers and farmers.

[17][a]The [b]bronze pillars that *were* in the house of the LORD, and the carts and the bronze Sea that *were* in the house of the LORD, the Chaldeans broke in pieces, and carried all their bronze to Babylon. [18]They also took away [a]the pots, the shovels, the trimmers, the [1]bowls, the spoons, and all the bronze utensils with which the priests ministered. [19]The basins, the firepans, the bowls, the pots, the lampstands, the spoons, and the cups, whatever *was* solid gold and whatever *was* solid silver, the captain of the guard took away. [20]The two pillars, one Sea, the twelve bronze bulls which *were* under *it, and* the carts, which King Solomon had made for the house of the LORD—[a]the bronze of all these articles was beyond measure. [21]Now *concerning* the [a]pillars: the height of one pillar *was* eighteen [1]cubits, a measuring line of twelve cubits could measure its circumference, and its thickness *was* [2]four fingers; *it was* hollow. [22]A capital of bronze *was* on it; and the height of one capital *was* five cubits, with a network and pomegranates all around the capital, all of bronze. The second pillar, with pome-

62 a Jer. 50:3, 39
63 a Rev. 18:21

CHAPTER 52
1 a 2 Kin. 24:18 b Josh. 10:29
3 a 2 Chr. 36:13
4 a Jer. 39:1
7 *1* Or *Arabah;* the Jordan Valley
9 a Jer. 32:4; 39:5
10 a Ezek. 12:13
11 a Ezek. 12:13 *1 shackles*
12 a 2 Kin. 25:8–21 b Jer. 52:29 c Jer. 39:9
15 a Jer. 39:9
17 a Jer. 27:19 b 1 Kin. 7:15, 23, 27, 50
18 a Ex. 27:3 *1 basins*
20 a 1 Kin. 7:47
21 a 2 Kin. 25:17 *1* 18 inches each *2* 3 inches

granates was the same. 23There were
ninety-six pomegranates on the sides; [a]all
the pomegranates, all around on the network, *were* one hundred.

The People Taken Captive to Babylonia

24[a]The captain of the guard took Seraiah the chief priest, [b]Zephaniah the second priest, and the three doorkeepers.
25He also took out of the city an [1]officer
who had charge of the men of war, seven
men of the king's close associates who
were found in the city, the principal scribe
of the army who mustered the people of
the land, and sixty men of the people of
the land who were found in the midst of
the city. 26And Nebuzaradan the captain
of the guard took these and brought them
to the king of Babylon at Riblah. 27Then
the king of Babylon struck them and put
them to death at Riblah in the land of Hamath. Thus Judah was carried away captive from its own land.

28[a]These *are* the people whom Nebuchadnezzar carried away captive: [b]in the
seventh year, [c]three thousand and
twenty-three Jews; 29[a]in the eighteenth
year of Nebuchadnezzar he carried away
captive from Jerusalem eight hundred
and thirty-two persons; 30in the twenty-
third year of Nebuchadnezzar, Nebuzaradan the captain of the guard carried away
captive of the Jews seven hundred and
forty-five persons. All the persons *were*
four thousand six hundred.

Jehoiachin Released from Prison

31[a]Now it came to pass in the thirty-
seventh year of the captivity of Jehoiachin
king of Judah, in the twelfth month, on
the twenty-fifth *day* of the month, *that*
[1]Evil-Merodach king of Babylon, in the
first *year* of his reign, [b]lifted[2] up the head
of Jehoiachin king of Judah and brought
him out of prison. 32And he spoke kindly
to him and gave him a more prominent
seat than those of the kings who *were*
with him in Babylon. 33So [1]Jehoiachin
changed from his prison garments, [a]and
he ate bread regularly before the king all
the days of his life. 34And as for his provisions, there was a regular ration given
him by the king of Babylon, a portion for
each day until the day of his death, all the
days of his life.

23 [a] 1 Kin. 7:20
24 [a] 2 Kin. 25:18 [b] Jer. 21:1; 29:25
25 [1] Lit. *eunuch*
28 [a] 2 Kin. 24:2 [b] 2 Kin. 24:12 [c] 2 Kin. 24:14
29 [a] Jer. 39:9
31 [a] 2 Kin. 25:27–30 [b] Gen. 40:13, 20 [1] Or *Awil-Marduk;* lit. *The Man of Marduk* [2] Showed favor to
33 [a] 2 Sam. 9:7, 13 [1] Lit. *he*

AUTHOR: *Probably Jeremiah*
DATE: *587 B.C.*
THEME: *Suffering as Punishment for Sin*
KEY WORDS: *Hardship, Sorrow, Sin, Prayer*

LAMENTATIONS

Dear Woman of Destiny,

The grief of Jeremiah over the destruction of the beloved city of Jerusalem called God's people to repentance after years of disobedience. Despite sin's devastation, we see God's wonderful compassion and mercy in sparing His people, whom He loved above all. We partake of this mercy today. No matter how devastating the sin, He invites us to repent and be healed by His forgiveness.

His love and mine,

Marilyn Hickey

Jerusalem in Affliction

How lonely sits the city
That was full of people!
[a]*How* like a widow is she,
Who *was* great among the nations!
The [b]princess among the provinces
Has become a [1]slave!

2 She [a]weeps bitterly in the [b]night,
Her tears *are* on her cheeks;
Among all her lovers
She has none to comfort *her.*
All her friends have dealt
treacherously with her;
They have become her enemies.

3 [a]Judah has gone into captivity,
Under affliction and hard servitude;
[b]She dwells among the [1]nations,
She finds no [c]rest;
All her persecutors overtake her in
dire straits.

4 The roads to Zion mourn
Because no one comes to the [1]set
feasts.
All her gates are [a]desolate;
Her priests sigh,
Her virgins are afflicted,
And she *is* in bitterness.

5 Her adversaries [a]have become [1]the
master,
Her enemies prosper;
For the LORD has afflicted her
[b]Because of the multitude of her
transgressions.
Her [c]children have gone into
captivity before the enemy.

6 And from the daughter of Zion
All her splendor has departed.
Her princes have become like deer
That find no pasture,
That [1]flee without strength
Before the pursuer.

7 In the days of her affliction and
roaming,
Jerusalem [a]remembers all her
pleasant things
That she had in the days of old.
When her people fell into the hand
of the enemy,
With no one to help her,
The adversaries saw her
And mocked at her [1]downfall.

8 [a]Jerusalem has sinned gravely,
Therefore she has become [1]vile.
All who honored her despise her
Because [b]they have seen her
nakedness;
Yes, she sighs and turns away.

9 Her uncleanness *is* in her skirts;
She [a]did not consider her destiny;
Therefore her collapse was
awesome;
She had no comforter.
"O LORD, behold my affliction,
For *the* enemy is exalted!"

10 The adversary has spread his hand
Over all her [1]pleasant things;
For she has seen [a]the nations enter
her [2]sanctuary,
Those whom You commanded
[b]Not to enter Your assembly.

11 All her people sigh,
[a]They [1]seek bread;
They have given their [2]valuables for
food to restore life.
"See, O LORD, and consider,
For I am scorned."

12 "*Is it* nothing to you, all you who
[1]pass by?
Behold and see
[a]If there is any sorrow like my
sorrow,
Which has been brought on me,
Which the LORD has inflicted
In the day of His fierce anger.

13 "From above He has sent fire into
my bones,
And it overpowered them;
He has [a]spread a net for my feet
And turned me back;
He has made me desolate
And faint all the day.

14 "The[a] yoke of my transgressions
was [1]bound;
They were woven together by His
hands,
And thrust upon my neck.
He made my strength fail;
The Lord delivered me into the
hands of *those whom* I am not
able to withstand.

15 "The Lord has trampled underfoot
all my mighty *men* in my midst;
He has called an assembly against
me
To crush my young men;
[a]The Lord trampled *as* in a
winepress
The virgin daughter of Judah.

CHAPTER 1
1 [a]Is. 47:7–9 [b]Ezra 4:20 [1]Lit. *forced laborer*
2 [a]Jer. 13:17 [b]Job 7:3
3 [a]Jer. 52:27 [b]Lam. 2:9 [c]Deut. 28:65 [1]*Gentiles*
4 [a]Is. 27:10 [1]*appointed*
5 [a]Deut. 28:43 [b]Dan. 9:7, 16 [c]Jer. 52:28 [1]Lit. *her head*
6 [1]Lit. *are gone*
7 [a]Ps. 137:1 [1]Vg. *Sabbaths*
8 [a][1 Kin. 8:46] [b]Ezek. 16:37 [1]LXX, Vg. *moved* or *removed*
9 [a]Is. 47:7
10 [a]Jer. 51:51 [b]Deut. 23:3 [1]*desirable* [2]*holy place,* the temple
11 [a]Jer. 38:9; 52:6 [1]*hunt food* [2]*desirable things*
12 [a]Dan. 9:12 [1]Lit. *pass by this way*
13 [a]Ezek. 12:13; 17:20
14 [a]Deut. 28:48 [1]So with MT, Tg.; LXX, Syr., Vg. *watched over*
15 [a][Rev. 14:19]

16 "For these *things* I weep;
My eye, [a]my eye overflows with water;
Because the comforter, who should restore my life,
Is far from me.
My children are desolate
Because the enemy prevailed."

17 [a]Zion [1]spreads out her hands,
But no one comforts her;
The LORD has commanded concerning Jacob
That those [b]around him *become* his adversaries;
Jerusalem has become an unclean thing among them.

18 "The LORD is [a]righteous,
For I [b]rebelled against His [1]commandment.
Hear now, all peoples,
And behold my sorrow;
My virgins and my young men
Have gone into captivity.

19 "I called for my lovers,
But they deceived me;
My priests and my elders
Breathed their last in the city,
While they sought food
To restore their life.

20 "See, O LORD, that I *am* in distress;
My [a]soul[1] is troubled;
My heart is overturned within me,
For I have been very rebellious.
[b]Outside the sword bereaves,
At home *it is* like death.

21 "They have heard that I sigh,
But no one comforts me.
All my enemies have heard of my trouble;
They are [a]glad that You have done *it.*
Bring on [b]the day You have [1]announced,
That they may become like me.

22 "Let[a] all their wickedness come before You,
And do to them as You have done to me
For all my transgressions;
For my sighs *are* many,
And my heart *is* faint."

God's Anger with Jerusalem

2 How the Lord has covered the daughter of Zion
With a [a]cloud in His anger!
[b]He cast down from heaven to the earth
[c]The beauty of Israel,
And did not remember [d]His footstool
In the day of His anger.

2 The Lord has swallowed up and has [a]not pitied
All the dwelling places of Jacob.
He has thrown down in His wrath
The strongholds of the daughter of Judah;
He has brought *them* down to the ground;
[b]He has profaned the kingdom and its princes.

3 He has cut off in fierce anger
Every [1]horn of Israel;
[a]He has drawn back His right hand
From before the enemy.
[b]He has blazed against Jacob like a flaming fire
Devouring all around.

4 [a]Standing like an enemy, He has bent His bow;
With His right hand, like an adversary,
He has slain [b]all *who were* pleasing to His eye;
On the tent of the daughter of Zion,
He has poured out His fury like fire.

5 [a]The Lord was like an enemy.
He has swallowed up Israel,
He has swallowed up all her palaces;
[b]He has destroyed her strongholds,
And has increased mourning and lamentation
In the daughter of Judah.

6 He has done violence [a]to His [1]tabernacle,
[b]*As if it were* a garden;
He has destroyed His place of assembly;
The LORD has caused
The appointed feasts and Sabbaths to be forgotten in Zion.
In His burning indignation He has [c]spurned the king and the priest.

7 The Lord has spurned His altar,
He has [a]abandoned His sanctuary;

16 [a]Eccl. 4:1
17 [a]Jer. 4:31 [b]2 Kin. 24:2–4 [1]Prays
18 [a]Dan. 9:7, 14 [b]1 Sam. 12:14, 15 [1]Lit. *mouth*
20 [a]Is. 16:11 [b]Ezek. 7:15 [1]Lit. *inward parts*
21 [a]Ps. 35:15 [b][Jer. 46] [1]*proclaimed*
22 [a]Ps. 109:15; 137:7, 8

CHAPTER 2
1 [a][Lam. 3:44] [b]Matt. 11:23 [c]2 Sam. 1:19 [d]Ps. 99:5
2 [a]Lam. 3:43 [b]Ps. 89:39, 40
3 [a]Ps. 74:11 [b]Ps. 89:46 [1]Strength
4 [a]Is. 63:10 [b]Ezek. 24:25
5 [a]Jer. 30:14 [b]Jer. 52:13
6 [a]Ps. 80:12; 89:40 [b]Is. 1:8 [c]Is. 43:28 [1]Lit. *booth*
7 [a]Ezek. 24:21

He has [1]given up the walls of her
palaces
Into the hand of the enemy.
[b]They have made a noise in the
house of the LORD
As on the day of a set feast.

8 The LORD has [1]purposed to destroy
The [a]wall of the daughter of Zion.
[b]He has stretched out a line;
He has not withdrawn His hand
from destroying;
Therefore He has caused the
rampart and wall to lament;
They languished together.

9 Her gates have sunk into the
ground;
He has destroyed and [a]broken her
bars.
[b]Her king and her princes *are*
among the [1]nations;
[c]The Law *is* no *more,*
And her [d]prophets find no [2]vision
from the LORD.

10 The elders of the daughter of Zion
[a]Sit on the ground *and* keep silence;
[1]They [b]throw dust on their heads
And [c]gird themselves with
sackcloth.
The virgins of Jerusalem
Bow their heads to the ground.

11 [a]My eyes fail with tears,
My [1]heart is troubled;
[b]My [2]bile is poured on the ground
Because of the destruction of the
daughter of my people,
Because [c]the children and the
infants
Faint in the streets of the city.

12 They say to their mothers,
"Where *is* grain and wine?"
As they swoon like the wounded
In the streets of the city,
As their life is poured out
In their mothers' bosom.

13 How shall I [a]console[1] you?
To what shall I liken you,
O daughter of Jerusalem?
What shall I compare with you, that
I may comfort you,
O virgin daughter of Zion?
For your ruin *is* spread wide as the
sea;
Who can heal you?

14 Your [a]prophets have seen for you
False and deceptive visions;
They have not [b]uncovered your
iniquity,
To bring back your captives,
But have envisioned for you false
[c]prophecies and delusions.

15 All who [1]pass by [a]clap *their* hands
at you;
They hiss [b]and shake their heads
At the daughter of Jerusalem:
"*Is* this the city that is called
[c]'The perfection of beauty,
The joy of the whole earth'?"

16 [a]All your enemies have opened
their mouth against you;
They hiss and gnash *their* teeth.
They say, [b]"We have swallowed *her*
up!
Surely this *is* the [c]day we have
waited for;
We have found *it,* [d]we have seen
it!"

17 The LORD has done what He
[a]purposed;
He has fulfilled His word
Which He commanded in days of
old.
He has thrown down and has not
pitied,
And He has caused an enemy to
[b]rejoice over you;
He has exalted the [1]horn of your
adversaries.

18 Their heart cried out to the Lord,
"O wall of the daughter of Zion,
[a]Let tears run down like a river day
and night;
Give yourself no relief;
Give [1]your eyes no rest.

19 "Arise, [a]cry out in the night,
At the beginning of the watches;
[b]Pour out your heart like water
before the face of the Lord.
Lift your hands toward Him
For the life of your young children,
Who faint from hunger [c]at the head
of every street."

20 "See, O LORD, and consider!
To whom have You done this?
[a]Should the women eat their
offspring,
The children [1]they have cuddled?
Should the priest and prophet be
slain
In the sanctuary of the Lord?

7 b Ps. 74:3–8 1 *delivered*
8 a Jer. 52:14 b [Is. 34:11] 1 *determined*
9 a Jer. 51:30 b Deut. 28:36 c 2 Chr. 15:3 d Ps. 74:9 1 *Gentiles* 2 Prophetic revelation
10 a Is. 3:26 b Job 2:12 c Is. 15:3 1 A sign of mourning
11 a Lam. 3:48 b Job 16:13 c Lam. 4:4 1 Lit. *inward parts* 2 Lit. *liver*
13 a Lam. 1:12 1 Or *bear witness to*
14 a Jer. 2:8; 23:25–29; 29:8, 9; 37:19 b Is. 58:1 c Jer. 23:33–36
15 a Ezek. 25:6 b Ps. 44:14 c [Ps. 48:2; 50:2] 1 Lit. *pass by this way*
16 a Job 16:9, 10 b Ps. 56:2; 124:3 c Lam. 1:21 d Ps. 35:21
17 a Lev. 26:16 b Ps. 38:16 1 Strength
18 a Jer. 14:17 1 Lit. *the daughter of your eye*
19 a Ps. 119:147 b Ps. 42:4; 62:8 c Is. 51:20
20 a Lev. 26:29 1 Vg. *a span long*

21 "Young[a] and old lie
On the ground in the streets;
My virgins and my young men
Have fallen by the [b]sword;
You have slain *them* in the day of Your anger,
You have slaughtered *and* not pitied.

22 "You have invited as to a feast day
[a]The terrors that surround me.
In the day of the LORD's anger
There was no refugee or survivor.
[b]Those whom I have borne and brought up
My enemies have [c]destroyed."

The Prophet's Anguish and Hope

3 I *am* the man *who* has seen affliction by the rod of His wrath.
2 He has led me and made *me* walk
In darkness and not *in* light.
3 Surely He has turned His hand against me
Time and time again throughout the day.

4 He has aged [a]my flesh and my skin,
And [b]broken my bones.
5 He has besieged me
And surrounded *me* with bitterness and [1]woe.
6 [a]He has set me in dark places
Like the dead of long ago.

7 [a]He has hedged me in so that I cannot get out;
He has made my chain heavy.
8 Even [a]when I cry and shout,
He shuts out my prayer.
9 He has blocked my ways with hewn stone;
He has made my paths crooked.

10 [a]He *has been* to me a bear lying in wait,
Like a lion in [1]ambush.
11 He has turned aside my ways and [a]torn me in pieces;
He has made me desolate.
12 He has bent His bow
And [a]set me up as a target for the arrow.

13 He has caused [a]the [1]arrows of His quiver
To pierce my [2]loins.

21 a 2 Chr. 36:17 b Jer. 18:21
22 a Ps. 31:13 b Hos. 9:12 c Jer. 16:2–4; 44:7
CHAPTER 3
4 a Job 16:8 b Ps. 51:8
5 *1 hardship* or *weariness*
6 a [Ps. 88:5, 6; 143:3]
7 a Hos. 2:6
8 a Job 30:20
10 a Is. 38:13 *1* Lit. *secret places*
11 a Hos. 6:1
12 a Job 7:20; 16:12
13 a Job 6:4 *1* Lit. *sons of* *2* Lit. *kidneys*
14 a Jer. 20:7 b Job 30:9
15 a Jer. 9:15
16 a [Prov. 20:17] *1* Lit. *bent me down in*
17 *1* Lit. *good*
18 a Ps. 31:22
19 a Jer. 9:15 *1 bitterness*
20 *1* Lit. *bowed down*
21 a Ps. 130:7
22 a [Mal. 3:6] b Ps. 78:38
23 a Is. 33:2
24 a Ps. 16:5; 73:26; 119:57 b Mic. 7:7
25 a Is. 30:18
26 a [Rom. 4:16–18] b Ps. 37:7
27 a Ps. 94:12
28 a Jer. 15:17
29 a Job 42:6

14 I have become the [a]ridicule of all my people—
[b]Their taunting song all the day.
15 [a]He has filled me with bitterness,
He has made me drink wormwood.

16 He has also broken my teeth [a]with gravel,
And [1]covered me with ashes.
17 You have moved my soul far from peace;
I have forgotten [1]prosperity.
18 [a]And I said, "My strength and my hope
Have perished from the LORD."

Through Your mercies, Lord, ____ is not consumed, because Your compassions fail not. They are new every morning; great is Your faithfulness.

FROM LAMENTATIONS 3:22, 23

19 Remember my affliction and roaming,
[a]The wormwood and the [1]gall.
20 My soul still remembers
And [1]sinks within me.
21 This I recall to my mind,
Therefore I have [a]hope.

22 [a]*Through* the LORD's mercies we are not consumed,
Because His compassions [b]fail not.
23 *They are* new [a]every morning;
Great *is* Your faithfulness.
24 "The LORD *is* my [a]portion," says my soul,
"Therefore I [b]hope in Him!"

25 The LORD *is* good to those who [a]wait for Him,
To the soul *who* seeks Him.
26 *It is* good that *one* should [a]hope [b]and wait quietly
For the salvation of the LORD.
27 [a]*It is* good for a man to bear
The yoke in his youth.

28 [a]Let him sit alone and keep silent,
Because *God* has laid *it* on him;
29 [a]Let him put his mouth in the dust—

Lamentations 3:21–25

Dear Woman of Destiny,

Have you ever felt the fog of a broken heart? God, by His Holy Spirit, reaches out to you in Lamentations 3:21–25 with medicine for your soul. He tells you that when you turn to Him you will find help. God will empower you so that you can endure the pain day by day.

God is a gentle shepherd and will never turn away one of His children. Jesus told us when we are burdened we need to come to Him to find rest for our souls (see Matt. 11:28–30). Have you put your burden into the nail-pierced hands of your Savior, Jesus Christ? He knows all about your burden and lovingly waits for you to bring it to Him. Whatever your pain is today, the loving Shepherd waits for you to bring it to Him. Not only does He want to carry your burden, He also wants to carry you through your fog of a broken heart.

What are the types of fog that slyly imprison a Christian's soul? At times it seems there is no way to escape this pain. It is a dark cloud that often comes unexpectedly like a silent mist. Every Christian has experienced his own personal fog; it is how we respond that makes all of the difference in the world. The fog may take the form of depression, discouragement, doubt, or disappointment. Such a fog disorients our lives and makes it hard for us to see the road ahead.

Have you ever been betrayed by a child, spouse, parent, neighbor, friend, or employer? Do you feel like earnest words of help are just vacant phrases from a friend or loved one who doesn't understand? If you feel like you stand alone in this fog, Christian, know that you are never alone. The Holy Spirit is with you in your painful fog. He is your Comforter. God has sent Him to abide with you forever! We don't know how to pray or what to pray. Yet the beloved third Person of the Trinity helps you in your weakness and makes intercession for you (see Rom. 8:26, 27). You are a beloved child of God through your faith in Jesus Christ. He will supply all of your needs and direct your paths.

I believe we see God best in the fog of our pain. I've had serious cancer surgery twice, and just knowing that God was in those traumas with me was a comfort. I have found He can give me peace in my pain and sorrow. In my suffering I have seen God more clearly than when all is going well in my life.

God also has given this precious gift of the presence of the Holy Spirit to encourage every Christian. Thus you are enabled to minister to others who are suffering, for you have been there. You can tell anyone that your Savior carried you through many trials, and He wants to do this for them as well. He is waiting to hear praise from our lips! "His compassions fail not. They are new every morning; great is Your faithfulness" (Lam. 3:22, 23).

Doris Greig

There may yet be hope.
30 [a]Let him give *his* cheek to the one
who strikes him,
And be full of reproach.
31 [a]For the Lord will not cast off
forever.
32 Though He causes grief,
Yet He will show compassion
According to the multitude of His
mercies.
33 For [a]He does not afflict [1]willingly,
Nor grieve the children of men.

34 To crush under one's feet
All the prisoners of the earth,
35 To turn aside the justice *due* a
man
Before the face of the Most High,
36 Or subvert a man in his cause—
[a]The Lord does not approve.

37 Who *is* he [a]*who* speaks and it
comes to pass,
When the Lord has not commanded
it?
38 *Is it* not from the mouth of the
Most High
That [a]woe and well-being proceed?
39 [a]Why should a living man
[1]complain,
[b]A man for the punishment of his
sins?

40 Let us search out and examine
our ways,
And turn back to the LORD;
41 [a]Let us lift our hearts and hands
To God in heaven.
42 [a]We have transgressed and rebelled;
You have not pardoned.

43 You have covered *Yourself* with
anger
And pursued us;
You have slain *and* not pitied.
44 You have covered Yourself with a
cloud,
That prayer should not pass
through.
45 You have made us an [a]offscouring
and refuse
In the midst of the peoples.

46 [a]All our enemies
Have opened their mouths against
us.
47 [a]Fear and a snare have come upon
us,
[b]Desolation and destruction.

30 a Is. 50:6
31 a Ps. 77:7; 94:14
33 a [Ezek. 33:11] *1* Lit. *from His heart*
36 a [Hab. 1:13]
37 a [Ps. 33:9–11]
38 a Job 2:10
39 a Prov. 19:3 b Mic. 7:9 *1* Or *murmur*
41 a Ps. 86:4
42 a Dan. 9:5
45 a 1 Cor. 4:13
46 a Lam. 2:16
47 a Is. 24:17, 18 b Is. 51:19
48 a Jer. 4:19; 14:17
49 a Jer. 14:17
50 a Is. 63:15
52 a Ps. 35:7, 19
53 a Jer. 37:16 b Dan. 6:17 *1* LXX *put to death* *2* Lit. *a stone on*
54 a Ps. 69:2 b Is. 38:10
55 a Ps. 130:1 b Jer. 38:6–13
56 a Ps. 3:4
57 a James 4:8 b Is. 41:10, 14
58 a Jer. 51:36 b Ps. 71:23
59 a Ps. 9:4 *1* Lit. *my wrong*
60 a Jer. 11:19

48 [a]My eyes overflow with rivers of
water
For the destruction of the daughter
of my people.

49 [a]My eyes flow and do not cease,
Without interruption,
50 Till the LORD from heaven
[a]Looks down and sees.
51 My eyes bring suffering to my soul
Because of all the daughters of my
city.

52 My enemies [a]without cause
Hunted me down like a bird.
53 They [1]silenced my life [a]in the pit
And [b]threw [2]stones at me.
54 [a]The waters flowed over my head;
[b]I said, "I am cut off!"

O Lord, may ____ call on Your name from the lowest pit. For You will hear their voice and not hide Your ear from their sighing, from their cry for help. Draw near on the day they call on You and say, "Do not fear!"

FROM LAMENTATIONS 3:55–57

55 [a]I called on Your name, O LORD,
From the lowest [b]pit.
56 [a]You have heard my voice:
"Do not hide Your ear
From my sighing, from my cry for
help."
57 You [a]drew near on the day I
called on You,
And said, [b]"Do not fear!"

58 O Lord, You have [a]pleaded the
case for my soul;
[b]You have redeemed my life.
59 O LORD, You have seen [1]*how* I am
wronged;
[a]Judge my case.
60 You have seen all their vengeance,
All their [a]schemes against me.

61 You have heard their reproach,
O LORD,
All their schemes against me,
62 The lips of my enemies

And their whispering against me all
the day.
63 Look at their [a]sitting down and
their rising up;
I *am* their taunting song.

64 [a]Repay them, O LORD,
According to the work of their
hands.
65 Give them [1]a veiled heart;
Your curse *be* upon them!
66 In Your anger,
Pursue and destroy them
[a]From under the heavens of the
[b]LORD.

The Degradation of Zion

4 How the gold has become dim!
How changed the fine gold!
The stones of the sanctuary are
[1]scattered
At the head of every street.

2 The precious sons of Zion,
[1]Valuable as fine gold,
How they are [2]regarded [a]as clay
pots,
The work of the hands of the
potter!

3 Even the jackals present their
breasts
To nurse their young;
But the daughter of my people *is*
cruel,
[a]Like ostriches in the wilderness.

4 The tongue of the infant clings
To the roof of its mouth for thirst;
[a]The young children ask for bread,
But no one breaks *it* for them.

5 Those who ate delicacies
Are desolate in the streets;
Those who were brought up in
scarlet
[a]Embrace ash heaps.

6 The punishment of the iniquity of
the daughter of my people
Is greater than the punishment of
the [a]sin of Sodom,
Which was [b]overthrown in a
moment,
With no hand to help her!

7 Her [1]Nazirites were [2]brighter than
snow
And whiter than milk;
They were more ruddy in body than
rubies,
Like sapphire in their [3]appearance.

8 *Now* their appearance is blacker
than soot;
They go unrecognized in the
streets;
[a]Their skin clings to their bones,
It has become as dry as wood.

9 *Those* slain by the sword are better
off
Than *those* who die of hunger;
For these [a]pine away,
Stricken *for lack* of the fruits of the
[b]field.

10 The hands of the [a]compassionate
women
Have [1]cooked their [b]own children;
They became [c]food for them
In the destruction of the daughter
of my people.

11 The LORD has fulfilled His fury,
[a]He has poured out His fierce anger.
[b]He kindled a fire in Zion,
And it has devoured its foundations.

12 The kings of the earth,
And all inhabitants of the world,
Would not have believed
That the adversary and the enemy
Could [a]enter the gates of
Jerusalem—

13 [a]Because of the sins of her
prophets
And the iniquities of her priests,
[b]Who shed in her midst
The blood of the just.

14 They wandered blind in the
streets;
[a]They have defiled themselves with
blood,
[b]So that no one would touch their
garments.

15 They cried out to them,
"Go away, [a]unclean!
Go away, go away,
Do not touch us!"
When they fled and wandered,
Those among the nations said,
"They shall no longer dwell *here.*"

16 The [1]face of the LORD scattered
them;
He no longer regards them.

---

63 a Ps. 139:2
64 a Ps. 28:4
65 *1* A Jewish tradition *sorrow of*
66 a Deut. 25:19 b Ps. 8:3

CHAPTER 4
1 *1* Lit. *poured out*
2 a Is. 30:14 *1* Lit. *Weighed against* *2 reckoned*
3 a Job 39:14–17
4 a Ps. 22:15
5 a Job 24:8
6 a Ezek. 16:48 b Gen. 19:25
7 *1* Or *nobles* *2* Or *purer* *3* Lit. *polishing*
8 a Ps. 102:5
9 a Lev. 26:39 b Jer. 16:4
10 a Lam. 2:20 b Is. 49:15 c Deut. 28:57 *1 boiled*
11 a Jer. 7:20 b Deut. 32:22
12 a Jer. 21:13
13 a Jer. 5:31 b Matt. 23:31
14 a Jer. 2:34 b Num. 19:16
15 a Lev. 13:45, 46
16 *1* Tg. *anger*

[a]*The people* do not respect the priests
Nor show favor to the elders.

17 Still [a]our eyes failed us,
Watching vainly for our help;
In our watching we watched
For a nation *that* could not save *us*.

18 [a]They [1]tracked our steps
So that we could not walk in our streets.
[b]Our end was near;
Our days were over,
For our end had come.

19 Our pursuers were [a]swifter
Than the eagles of the heavens.
They pursued us on the mountains
And lay in wait for us in the wilderness.

20 The [a]breath of our nostrils, the anointed of the LORD,
[b]Was caught in their pits,
Of whom we said, "Under his shadow
We shall live among the nations."

21 Rejoice and be glad, O daughter of [a]Edom,
You who dwell in the land of Uz!
[b]The cup shall also pass over to you
And you shall become drunk and make yourself naked.

22 [a]*The punishment of* your iniquity [1]is accomplished,
O daughter of Zion;
He will no longer send you into captivity.
[b]He will punish your iniquity,
O daughter of Edom;
He will uncover your sins!

A Prayer for Restoration

5 Remember, [a]O LORD, what has come upon us;
Look, and behold [b]our reproach!
2 [a]Our inheritance has been turned over to aliens,
And our houses to foreigners.
3 We have become orphans and waifs,
Our mothers *are* like [a]widows.

4 We pay for the water we drink,
And our wood comes at a price.
5 [a]*They* pursue at our [1]heels;
We labor *and* have no rest.
6 [a]We have given our hand [b]*to* the Egyptians
And the [c]Assyrians, to be satisfied with bread.
7 [a]Our fathers sinned *and are* no more,
But we bear their iniquities.
8 Servants rule over us;
There is none to deliver *us* from their hand.
9 We get our bread *at the risk* of our lives,
Because of the sword in the wilderness.

10 Our skin is hot as an oven,
Because of the fever of famine.
11 They [a]ravished the women in Zion,
The maidens in the cities of Judah.
12 Princes were hung up by their hands,
And elders were not respected.
13 Young men [a]ground at the millstones;
Boys staggered under *loads of* wood.
14 The elders have ceased *gathering at* the gate,
And the young men from their [a]music.

15 The joy of our heart has ceased;
Our dance has turned into [a]mourning.
16 [a]The crown has fallen *from* our head.
Woe to us, for we have sinned!
17 Because of this our heart is faint;
[a]Because of these *things* our eyes grow dim;
18 Because of Mount Zion which is [a]desolate,
With foxes walking about on it.

There is a point beyond wavering, and it is that moment when you know that God cannot be unfaithful.

PHOEBE PALMER

16 [a]Lam. 5:12
17 [a]2 Kin. 24:7
18 [a]2 Kin. 25:4 [b]Ezek. 7:2, 3, 6 [1]Lit. *hunted*
19 [a]Deut. 28:49
20 [a]Gen. 2:7 [b]Jer. 52:9
21 [a]Ps. 83:3–6 [b]Jer. 25:15
22 [a][Is. 40:2] [b]Ps. 137:7 [1]*has been completed*

CHAPTER 5
1 [a]Ps. 89:50 [b]Lam. 2:15
2 [a]Ps. 79:1
3 [a]Jer. 15:8; 18:21
5 [a]Jer. 28:14 [1]Lit. *necks*
6 [a]Gen. 24:2 [b]Hos. 9:3; 12:1 [c]Hos. 5:13
7 [a]Jer. 31:29
11 [a]Zech. 14:2
13 [a]Judg. 16:21
14 [a]Jer. 7:34
15 [a]Amos 8:10
16 [a]Ps. 89:39
17 [a]Ps. 6:7
18 [a]Is. 27:10

19 You, O LORD, [a]remain forever;
[b]Your throne from generation to generation.
20 [a]Why do You forget us forever,
And forsake us for so long a time?

21 [a]Turn us back to You, O LORD, and we will be [1]restored;
Renew our days as of old,
22 Unless You have utterly rejected us,
And are very angry with us!

19 [a] Ps. 9:7 [b] Ps. 45:6
20 [a] Ps. 13:1; 44:24
21 [a] Jer. 31:18 *1 returned*

AUTHOR: *Ezekiel*
DATE: *593–573 B.C.*
THEME: *Destruction of Jerusalem and Its Restoration*
KEY WORDS: *Judgment, Blessing, Individual Moral Responsibility*

EZEKIEL

Dear Woman of Destiny,

As women who depend on God's presence to sustain us, we can relate to Ezekiel. His visions stretched from horror to hope, and he was the first to receive the revelation of Yahweh Shammah, "The LORD Is There"—the presence who is always with us. Through all of Israel's ritual, ceremony and rebellion, God was there, revealing the day when hearts would be filled with Jesus Christ. As you read, rejoice that the prophecy is fulfilled in your life!

His love and mine,

Marilyn Hickey

Ezekiel's Vision of God

Now it came to pass in the thirtieth
year, in the fourth *month,* on the
fifth *day* of the month, as I *was*
among the captives by [a]the River Chebar,
that [b]the heavens were opened and I saw
[c]visions[1] of God. 2 On the fifth *day* of the
month, which *was* in the fifth year of King
Jehoiachin's captivity, 3 the word of the
LORD came expressly to Ezekiel the priest,
the son of Buzi, in the land of the [1]Chal-
deans by the River Chebar; and [a]the hand
of the LORD was upon him there.

4 Then I looked, and behold, [a]a whirlwind was coming [b]out of the north, a
great cloud with raging fire engulfing itself; and brightness *was* all around it and
radiating out of its midst like the color of
amber, out of the midst of the fire. 5 [a]Also
from within it *came* the likeness of four
living creatures. And [b]this *was* their appearance: they had [c]the likeness of a
man. 6 Each one had four faces, and each
one had four wings. 7 Their [1]legs *were*
straight, and the soles of their feet *were*
like the soles of calves' feet. They sparkled
[a]like the color of burnished bronze. 8 [a]The
hands of a man *were* under their wings on
their four sides; and each of the four had
faces and wings. 9 Their wings touched
one another. *The creatures* did not turn
when they went, but each one went
straight [a]forward.

10 As for [a]the likeness of their faces,
each [b]had the face of a man; each of the
four had [c]the face of a lion on the right
side, [d]each of the four had the face of an
ox on the left side, [e]and each of the four
had the face of an eagle. 11 Thus *were* their
faces. Their wings stretched upward; two
wings of each one touched one another,
and [a]two covered their bodies. 12 And
[a]each one went straight forward; they
went wherever the spirit wanted to go,
and they did not turn when they went.

13 As for the likeness of the living creatures, their appearance *was* like burning
coals of fire, [a]like the appearance of torches going back and forth among the living
creatures. The fire was bright, and out of
the fire went lightning. 14 And the living
creatures ran back and forth, [a]in appearance like a flash of lightning.

15 Now as I looked at the living creatures, behold, [a]a wheel *was* on the earth
beside each living creature with its four
faces. 16 [a]The appearance of the wheels
and their workings *was* [b]like the color of
beryl, and all four had the same likeness.
The appearance of their workings *was,* as
it were, a wheel in the middle of a wheel.
17 When they moved, they went toward
any one of four directions; they did not
turn aside when they went. 18 As for their
rims, they were so high they were awesome; and their rims *were* [a]full of eyes, all
around the four of them. 19 [a]When the living creatures went, the wheels went beside them; and when the living creatures
were lifted up from the earth, the wheels
were lifted up. 20 Wherever the spirit wanted to go, they went, *because* there the
spirit went; and the wheels were lifted together with them, [a]for the spirit of the
[1]living creatures *was* in the wheels.
21 When those went, *these* went; when
those stood, *these* stood; and when those
were lifted up from the earth, the wheels
were lifted up together with them, for the
spirit of the [1]living creatures *was* in the
wheels.

22 [a]The likeness of the [1]firmament
above the heads of the [2]living creatures
was like the color of an awesome [b]crystal,
stretched out [a]over their heads. 23 And under the firmament their wings *spread out*
straight, one toward another. Each one
had two which covered one side, and each
one had two which covered the other side
of the body. 24 [a]When they went, I heard
the noise of their wings, [b]like the noise of
many waters, like [c]the voice of the Almighty, a tumult like the noise of an
army; and when they stood still, they let
down their wings. 25 A voice came from
above the firmament that *was* over their
heads; whenever they stood, they let down
their wings.

26 [a]And above the firmament over their
heads *was* the likeness of a throne, [b]in
appearance like a sapphire stone; on the
likeness of the throne *was* a likeness with
the appearance of a man high above [c]it.
27 Also from the appearance of His waist
and upward [a]I saw, as it were, the color
of amber with the appearance of fire all
around within it; and from the appearance
of His waist and downward I saw, as it
were, the appearance of fire with brightness all around. 28 [a]Like the appearance of
a rainbow in a cloud on a rainy day, so
was the appearance of the brightness all
around it. [b]This *was* the appearance of the
likeness of the glory of the LORD.

CHAPTER 1
1 [a] Ezek. 3:15, 23; 10:15 [b] Rev. 4:1; 19:11 [c] Ezek. 8:3 [1] So with MT, LXX, Vg.; Syr., Tg. *a vision*
3 [a] Ezek. 3:14, 22 [1] Or *Babylonians,* and so elsewhere in the book
4 [a] Jer. 23:19; 25:32 [b] Jer. 1:14
5 [a] Rev. 4:6–8 [b] Ezek. 10:8 [c] Ezek. 10:14
7 [a] Dan. 10:6 [1] Lit. *feet*
8 [a] Ezek. 10:8, 21
9 [a] Ezek. 1:12; 10:20–22
10 [a] Rev. 4:7 [b] Num. 2:10 [c] Num. 2:3 [d] Num. 2:18 [e] Num. 2:25
11 [a] Is. 6:2
12 [a] Ezek. 10:11, 22
13 [a] Rev. 4:5
14 [a] [Matt. 24:27]
15 [a] Ezek. 10:9
16 [a] Ezek. 10:9, 10 [b] Dan. 10:6
18 [a] Ezek. 10:12
19 [a] Ezek. 10:16, 17
20 [a] Ezek. 10:17 [1] Lit. *living creature;* LXX, Vg. *spirit of life;* Tg. *creatures*
21 [1] See note at v. 20
22 [a] Ezek. 10:1 [b] Rev. 4:6 [1] Or *expanse* [2] So with LXX, Tg., Vg.; MT *living creature*
24 [a] Ezek. 3:13; 10:5 [b] Rev. 1:15 [c] Job 37:4, 5
26 [a] Ezek. 10:1 [b] Ex. 24:10, 16 [c] Ezek. 8:2
27 [a] Ezek. 8:2
28 [a] Rev. 4:3; 10:1 [b] Ezek. 3:23; 8:4

Ezekiel Sent to Rebellious Israel

So when I saw *it,* [c]I fell on my face, and
I heard a voice of One speaking.

2 And He said to me, "Son of man,
[a]stand on your feet, and I will speak to
you." 2Then [a]the Spirit entered me when
He spoke to me, and set me on my feet;
and I heard Him who spoke to me. 3And
He said to me: "Son of man, I am sending
you to the children of Israel, to a rebellious nation that has [a]rebelled against Me;
[b]they and their fathers have transgressed
against Me to this very day. 4[a]For *they are*
[1]impudent and stubborn children. I am
sending you to them, and you shall say
to them, 'Thus says the Lord GOD.' 5[a]As
for them, whether they hear or whether
they refuse—for they *are* a [b]rebellious
house—yet they [c]will know that a prophet has been among them.
6"And you, son of man, [a]do not be
afraid of them nor be afraid of their words,
though [b]briers and thorns *are* with you
and you dwell among scorpions; [c]do not
be afraid of their words or dismayed by
their looks, [d]though they *are* a rebellious
house. 7[a]You shall speak My words to
them, whether they hear or whether they
refuse, for they *are* rebellious. 8But you,
son of man, hear what I say to you. Do not
be rebellious like that rebellious house;
open your mouth and [a]eat what I give
you."
9Now when I looked, there was [a]a hand
stretched out to me; and behold, [b]a scroll
of a book *was* in it. 10Then He spread it
before me; and *there was* writing on the
inside and on the outside, and written on
it *were* lamentations and mourning and
woe.

3 Moreover He said to me, "Son of man,
eat what you find; [a]eat this scroll, and
go, speak to the house of Israel." 2So I
opened my mouth, and He caused me to
eat that scroll.
3And He said to me, "Son of man, feed
your belly, and fill your stomach with this
scroll that I give you." So I [a]ate, and it was
in my mouth [b]like honey in sweetness.
4Then He said to me: "Son of man, go
to the house of Israel and speak with My
words to them. 5For you *are* not sent to a
people of unfamiliar speech and of hard
language, *but* to the house of Israel, 6not
to many people of unfamiliar speech and
of hard language, whose words you cannot understand. Surely, [a]had I sent you to
them, they would have listened to you.
7But the house of Israel will not listen to
you, [a]because they will not listen to Me;
[b]for all the house of Israel *are* [1]impudent
and hard-hearted. 8Behold, I have made
your face strong against their faces, and
your forehead strong against their foreheads. 9[a]Like adamant stone, harder than
flint, I have made your forehead; [b]do
not be afraid of them, nor be dismayed at
their looks, though they *are* a rebellious
house."

Father, may ____ receive into their heart all the words that You speak.

FROM EZEKIEL 3:10

10Moreover He said to me: "Son of man,
receive into your heart all My words that
I speak to you, and hear with your ears.
11And go, get to the captives, to the children of your people, and speak to them
and tell them, [a]'Thus says the Lord GOD,'
whether they hear, or whether they refuse."

There is great value in searching the Scriptures. There may be a promise in the Word that exactly fits your situation, but if you are unaware of it, you will be like a prisoner in a dungeon.

CHARLES H. SPURGEON

12Then [a]the Spirit lifted me up, and I
heard behind me a great thunderous
voice: "Blessed *is* the [b]glory of the LORD
from His place!" 13*I* also *heard* the [a]noise
of the wings of the living creatures that
touched one another, and the noise of the
wheels beside them, and a great thunderous noise. 14So the Spirit lifted me up and

28 [c]Dan. 8:17

CHAPTER 2
1 [a]Dan. 10:11
2 [a]Ezek. 3:24
3 [a]Ezek. 5:6; 20:8, 13, 18 [b]Jer. 3:25
4 [a]Ezek. 3:7 [1]Lit. *stiff-faced and hard-hearted sons*
5 [a]Ezek. 3:11, 26, 27 [b]Ezek. 3:26 [c]Ezek. 33:33
6 [a]Jer. 1:8, 17 [b]Mic. 7:4 [c][1 Pet. 3:14] [d]Ezek. 3:9, 26, 27
7 [a]Jer. 1:7, 17
8 [a]Rev. 10:9
9 [a][Ezek. 8:3] [b]Ezek. 3:1

CHAPTER 3
1 [a]Ezek. 2:8, 9
3 [a]Rev. 10:9 [b]Ps. 19:10; 119:103
6 [a]Matt. 11:21
7 [a]John 15:20, 21 [b]Ezek. 2:4 [1]Lit. *strong of forehead*
9 [a]Mic. 3:8 [b]Jer. 1:8, 17
11 [a]Ezek. 2:5, 7
12 [a]Acts 8:39 [b]Ezek. 1:28; 8:4
13 [a]Ezek. 1:24; 10:5

took me away, and I went in bitterness, in
the [1]heat of my spirit; but [a]the hand of
the LORD was strong upon me. 15Then I
came to the captives at Tel Abib, who
dwelt by the River Chebar; and [a]I sat
where they sat, and remained there astonished among them seven days.

Ezekiel Is a Watchman

16Now it [a]came to pass at the end of
seven days that the word of the LORD came
to me, saying, 17 [a]"Son of man, I have
made you [b]a watchman for the house of
Israel; therefore hear a word from My
mouth, and give them [c]warning from
Me: 18When I say to the wicked, 'You
shall surely die,' and you give him no
warning, nor speak to warn the wicked
from his wicked way, to save his life, that
same wicked *man* [a]shall die in his iniquity; but his blood I will require at your
hand. 19Yet, if you warn the wicked, and
he does not turn from his wickedness, nor
from his wicked way, he shall die in his
iniquity; [a]but you have delivered your
soul.
20"Again, when a [a]righteous *man* turns
from his righteousness and commits iniquity, and I lay a stumbling block before
him, he shall die; because you did not give
him warning, he shall die in his sin, and
his righteousness which he has done shall
not be remembered; but his blood I will
require at your hand. 21Nevertheless if
you warn the righteous *man* that the
righteous should not sin, and he does not
sin, he shall surely live because he took
warning; also you will have delivered your
soul."
22[a]Then the hand of the LORD was upon
me there, and He said to me, "Arise, go
out [b]into the plain, and there I shall talk
with you."
23So I arose and went out into the plain,
and behold, [a]the glory of the LORD stood
there, like the glory which I [b]saw by the
River Chebar; [c]and I fell on my face.
24Then [a]the Spirit entered me and set me
on my feet, and spoke with me and said to
me: "Go, shut yourself inside your house.
25And you, O son of man, surely [a]they will
put ropes on you and bind you with them,
so that you cannot go out among them.
26[a]I will make your tongue cling to the
roof of your mouth, so that you shall be
mute and [b]not be [1]one to rebuke them,
[c]for they *are* a rebellious house. 27[a]But
when I speak with you, I will open your
mouth, and you shall say to them, [b]'Thus
says the Lord GOD.' He who hears, let him
hear; and he who refuses, let him refuse;
for they *are* a rebellious house.

The Siege of Jerusalem Portrayed

4 "You also, son of man, take a clay
tablet and lay it before you, and portray on it a city, Jerusalem. 2[a]Lay siege
against it, build a [b]siege wall against it,
and heap up a mound against it; set camps
against it also, and place battering rams
against it all around. 3Moreover take
for yourself an iron plate, and set it *as* an
iron wall between you and the city. Set
your face against it, and it shall be [a]be-
sieged, and you shall lay siege against it.
[b]This *will be* a sign to the house of Israel.
4"Lie also on your left side, and lay the
iniquity of the house of Israel upon it. *According* to the number of the days that
you lie on it, you shall bear their iniquity.
5For I have laid on you the years of their
iniquity, according to the number of the
days, three hundred and ninety days; [a]so
you shall bear the iniquity of the house of
Israel. 6And when you have completed
them, lie again on your right side; then
you shall bear the iniquity of the house of
Judah forty days. I have laid on you a day
for each year.
7"Therefore you shall set your face toward the siege of Jerusalem; your arm
shall be uncovered, and you shall prophesy against it. 8[a]And surely I will [1]restrain
you so that you cannot turn from one side
to another till you have ended the days of
your siege.
9"Also take for yourself wheat, barley,
beans, lentils, millet, and spelt; put them
into one vessel, and make bread of them
for yourself. *During* the number of days
that you lie on your side, three hundred
and ninety days, you shall eat it. 10And
your food which you eat *shall be* by
weight, twenty shekels a day; from time
to time you shall eat it. 11You shall also
drink water by measure, one-sixth of a
hin; from time to time you shall drink.
12And you shall eat it *as* barley cakes; and
bake it using fuel of human waste in their
sight."
13Then the LORD said, "So [a]shall the
children of Israel eat their defiled bread
among the Gentiles, where I will drive
them."

14 [a]2 Kin. 3:15 [1]Or *anger*
15 [a]Job 2:13
16 [a]Jer. 42:7
17 [a]Ezek. 33:7–9 [b]Jer. 6:17 [c][Lev. 19:17]
18 [a][John 8:21, 24]
19 [a]Acts 18:6; 20:26
20 [a]Ezek. 18:24; 33:18
22 [a]Ezek. 1:3 [b]Ezek. 8:4
23 [a]Ezek. 1:28 [b]Ezek. 1:1 [c]Ezek. 1:28
24 [a]Ezek. 2:2
25 [a]Ezek. 4:8
26 [a]Luke 1:20, 22 [b]Hos. 4:17 [c]Ezek. 2:5–7 [1]Lit. *one who rebukes*
27 [a]Ezek. 24:27; 33:22 [b]Ezek. 3:11

CHAPTER 4
2 [a]Jer. 6:6 [b]2 Kin. 25:1
3 [a]Jer. 39:1, 2 [b]Ezek. 12:6, 11; 24:24, 27
5 [a]Num. 14:34
8 [a]Ezek. 3:25 [1]Lit. *put ropes on*
13 [a]Hos. 9:3

Ezekiel 3:17

Dear Woman of Destiny,

Let me encourage you today as to why you can rejoice that you have been created a woman and destined to live in this generation. When God made Eve, she was called the mother of all the living. Woman's physiology reflects her spiritual destiny to bring forth and to defend life. Woman is designed by God to nurture, surround, protect, counsel, companion, and empower. From the beginning woman was named "helper." Her mettle is strength and insight. Her destiny is to be blessed or "straight," as an arrow, according to the praise for virtuous women in Proverbs 31. These qualities are the unique characteristics of the supreme Helper, the Holy Spirit. He dwells in you to fully manifest this great design!

To "help" in the most effective and classical definition is to stand in the gap. To help is to be strength for the weak or defenseless point of a life, a family, a ministry, a city, or a nation. To help is to be what the Bible calls a "watchman." More than ever before, our God and our world cry out today for one who will stand in the gap. Like Jesus, who lives forever daily interceding before the throne of God on our behalf, every woman on earth is called to take her place on the wall and in the gap to defend against the armies of satanic darkness, which strive earnestly to overwhelm our next generation. The prophet Jeremiah spoke of our day and said, "For the LORD has created a new thing in the earth—a woman shall encompass a man" (Jer. 31:22).

The effectiveness of the watchman is the knitting of her soul to the saving of her people. As Christ came in the flesh and gave Himself so as to identify with mortal man and save him, so the watchman takes her place to become a wall of strength around those for whom she has been called to give of herself. There God causes her to hear the word from His mouth and opens her mouth to give His word to her people (see Ezek. 3:17).

You are equipped for strength against the enemy of our souls. The fact that this letter has made its way into your hands today indicates that like Esther, you have been created, called, anointed, and, yes, destined, for spiritual greatness in such a time as this. No less than Miriam, Deborah, Mary the mother of Jesus, Joan of Arc, or Mother Teresa, you are born to godly significance. No less than Rahab, your intervention and intercession can save your whole house and bring forth an entire generation! Let me exhort you to respond. Esther presented herself in her hour of destiny's call, saying, "If I perish, I perish, but I have not shirked from God's appointment for me" (see Esth. 4:16).

As God said to His watchman Ezekiel, "Son of man, stand on your feet, and I will speak to you" (Ezek. 2:1), so He speaks to you. Forget yesterday, take today as seated with Christ in the heavens through the victory we have in His blood, and cast your vision upon the horizon of your future and glorious call and reward in God. Arise, woman! Awake, watchman; and lift up your voice in strength!

Bonnie Chavda

Ezekiel 4:1, 2

Dear Woman of Destiny,

The Lord's words to Ezekiel in 4:1, 2 are a very clear directive for using prayer tools, such as maps of a city, country, or general region of the world. The Lord says to Ezekiel, "Take a clay tablet (the equivalent of a piece of paper today) . . . and draw a map of Jerusalem on it . . . then lay siege to it." God was suggesting to Ezekiel that before He would work His will *in* the city, the prophet had to declare it *over* the city, using the map.

Thus, Ezekiel was to draw a map of the city and pray over it in very specific ways, as implied by the use of the word *siege*. Find a map of your city to pray over as a starting point in praying over your area.

Siege, from the Hebrew word *matsowr*, means "the surrounding and blockading of a town or fortress by an army bent on capturing it." This suggests that we need a *strategy* when praying for our communities. Find out different facts about your city—its spiritual climate, strongholds in certain parts of town, political structures that need prayer. Then build a strategy for praying for your city, watching for changes as your prayers are answered. There are programs in place in some cities to adopt a policeman, fireman, or political leader for prayer. If not, lead the way in establishing such programs. This helps focus specific prayer for a particular person in your city as representative of your city's needs. Sometimes it's easier and more effective to pray for one person in particular than for the whole city at large.

Siege also means "a prolonged period." This suggests *duration*. We are not to give up after a short period of time, becoming discouraged when answers don't come immediately. The old-fashioned word *tarry* has disappeared from our vocabulary. We are an instant generation, wanting everything "right now" or not at all. But God's timing is certainly not ours. We need to persevere in our pursuit of God's will for our city.

An ancient definition for *siege* is "a seat of rule" or throne. This implies *authority*. We have the authority, as God's children, to pray with boldness over our city. This gives us faith to believe that our prayers make a difference. It also makes us realize that one person can make a difference. Just as one person on a throne is the authority figure for a nation, so one person coming to the throne of God with petitions for a community is an authority figure for that area.

All of this can be applied to the concerns we as women have in every part of our lives. We can pray over ("lay siege to") pictures of our children as they are growing up. For those with problem children, the idea of duration—a prolonged season of time—can help us not to give up in prayer for them. In the stresses of juggling the duties of spouse, Mom, woman in the workplace, spiritual mentor to others, and all that impacts our lives, having a God-given "siege" strategy in place to handle all of this can bring healing to our harried lives.

Dee Eastman

14So I said, [a]"Ah, Lord GOD! Indeed I have never defiled myself from my youth till now; I have never eaten [b]what died of itself or was torn by beasts, nor has [c]abominable[1] flesh ever come into my mouth."

15Then He said to me, "See, I am giving you cow dung instead of human waste, and you shall prepare your bread over it."

16Moreover He said to me, "Son of man, surely I will cut off the [a]supply of bread in Jerusalem; they shall [b]eat bread by weight and with anxiety, and shall [c]drink water by measure and with dread, 17that they may lack bread and water, and be dismayed with one another, and [a]waste away because of their iniquity.

A Sword Against Jerusalem

5 "And you, son of man, take a sharp sword, take it as a barber's razor, [a]and pass *it* over your head and your beard; then take scales to weigh and divide the hair. 2[a]You shall burn with fire one-third in the midst of [b]the city, when [c]the days of the siege are finished; then you shall take one-third and strike around *it* with the sword, and one-third you shall scatter in the wind: I will draw out a sword after [d]them. 3[a]You shall also take a small number of them and bind them in the edge of your *garment.* 4Then take some of them again and [a]throw them into the midst of the fire, and burn them in the fire. From there a fire will go out into all the house of Israel.

5"Thus says the Lord GOD: 'This *is* Jerusalem; I have set her in the midst of the nations and the countries all around her. 6She has rebelled against My judgments by doing wickedness more than the nations, and against My statutes more than the countries that *are* all around her; for they have refused My judgments, and they have not walked in My statutes.' 7Therefore thus says the Lord GOD: 'Because you have [1]multiplied *disobedience* more than the nations that *are* all around you, have not walked in My statutes [a]nor kept My judgments, [2]nor even done according to the judgments of the nations that *are* all around you'— 8therefore thus says the Lord GOD: 'Indeed I, even I, *am* against you and will execute judgments in your midst in the sight of the nations. 9[a]And I will do among you what I have never done, and the like of which I will never do again, because of all your abominations. 10Therefore fathers [a]shall eat *their* sons in your midst, and sons shall eat their fathers; and I will execute judgments among you, and all of you who remain I will [b]scatter to all the winds.

11'Therefore, *as* I live,' says the Lord GOD, 'surely, because you have [a]defiled My sanctuary with all your [b]detestable things and with all your abominations, therefore I will also diminish *you;* [c]My eye will not spare, nor will I have any pity. 12[a]One-third of you shall die of the pestilence, and be consumed with famine in your midst; and one-third shall fall by the sword all around you; and [b]I will scatter another third to all the winds, and I will draw out a sword after [c]them.

13'Thus shall My anger [a]be spent, and I will [b]cause My fury to rest upon them, [c]and I will be avenged; [d]and they shall know that I, the LORD, have spoken *it* in My zeal, when I have spent My fury upon them. 14Moreover [a]I will make you a waste and a reproach among the nations that *are* all around you, in the sight of all who pass by.

15'So [1]it shall be a [a]reproach, a taunt, a [b]lesson, and an astonishment to the nations that *are* all around you, when I execute judgments among you in anger and in fury and in [c]furious rebukes. I, the LORD, have spoken. 16When I [a]send against them the terrible arrows of famine which shall be for destruction, which I will send to destroy you, I will increase the famine upon you and cut off your [b]supply of bread. 17So I will send against you famine and [a]wild beasts, and they will bereave you. [b]Pestilence and blood shall pass through you, and I will bring the sword against you. I, the LORD, have spoken.' "

Judgment on Idolatrous Israel

6 Now the word of the LORD came to me, saying: 2"Son of man, [a]set your face toward the [b]mountains of Israel, and prophesy against them, 3and say, 'O mountains of Israel, hear the word of the Lord GOD! Thus says the Lord GOD to the mountains, to the hills, to the ravines, and to the valleys: "Indeed I, *even* I, will bring a sword against you, and [a]I will destroy your [1]high places. 4Then your altars shall be desolate, your incense altars shall be broken, and [a]I will cast down your slain *men* before your idols. 5And I will lay the corpses of the children of Israel before

---

14 a Acts 10:14 b Lev. 17:15; 22:8 c Deut. 14:3 *1* Ritually unclean flesh, Lev. 7:18
16 a Is. 3:1 b Ezek. 4:10, 11; 12:19 c Ezek. 4:11
17 a Lev. 26:39

CHAPTER 5
1 a Is. 7:20
2 a Ezek. 5:12 b Ezek. 4:1 c Ezek. 4:8, 9 d Lev. 26:25
3 a Jer. 40:6; 52:16
4 a Jer. 41:1, 2; 44:14
7 a Jer. 2:10, 11 *1* Or *raged* *2* So with MT, LXX, Tg., Vg.; many Heb. mss., Syr. *but have done* (cf. 11:12)
9 a [Amos 3:2]
10 a Jer. 19:9 b Zech. 2:6; 7:14
11 a [Jer. 7:9–11] b Ezek. 11:21 c Ezek. 7:4, 9; 8:18; 9:10
12 a Ezek. 6:12 b Jer. 9:16 c Jer. 43:10, 11; 44:27
13 a Lam. 4:11 b Ezek. 21:17 c Is. 1:24 d Ezek. 36:6; 38:19
14 a Lev. 26:31
15 a Jer. 24:9 b [Is. 26:9] c Ezek. 5:8; 25:17 *1* LXX, Syr., Tg., Vg. *you*
16 a Deut. 32:23 b Lev. 26:26
17 a Lev. 26:22 b Ezek. 38:22

CHAPTER 6
2 a Ezek. 20:46; 21:2; 25:2 b Ezek. 36:1
3 a Lev. 26:30 *1* Places for pagan worship
4 a Lev. 26:30

their idols, and I will scatter your bones
all around your altars. 6 In all your dwelling places the cities shall be laid waste,
and the [1]high places shall be desolate, so
that your altars may be laid waste and
made desolate, your idols may be broken
and made to cease, your incense altars
may be cut down, and your works may be
abolished. 7 The slain shall fall in your
midst, and [a]you shall know that I *am* the
LORD.

8 [a]"Yet I will leave a remnant, so that
you may have *some* who escape the sword
among the nations, when you are [b]scat-
tered through the countries. 9 Then those
of you who escape will [a]remember Me
among the nations where they are carried
captive, because [b]I was crushed by their
adulterous heart which has departed from
Me, and [c]by their eyes which play the
harlot after their idols; [d]they will loathe
themselves for the evils which they committed in all their abominations. 10 And
they shall know that I *am* the LORD; I have
not said in vain that I would bring this
calamity upon them."

11 "Thus says the Lord GOD: [a]"Pound[1]
your fists and stamp your feet, and say,
'Alas, for all the evil abominations of the
house of Israel! [b]For they shall fall by the
sword, by famine, and by pestilence. 12 He
who is far off shall die by the pestilence,
he who is near shall fall by the sword, and
he who remains and is besieged shall die
by the famine. [a]Thus will I spend My fury
upon them. 13 Then you shall know that I
am the LORD, when their slain are among
their idols all around their altars, [a]on every high hill, [b]on all the mountaintops,
[c]under every green tree, and under every
thick oak, wherever they offered sweet incense to all their idols. 14 So I will [a]stretch
out My hand against them and make the
land desolate, yes, more desolate than the
wilderness toward [b]Diblah, in all their
dwelling places. Then they shall know
that I *am* the LORD.' " ' "

Judgment on Israel Is Near

7 Moreover the word of the LORD came
to me, saying, 2 "And you, son of man,
thus says the Lord GOD to the land of Israel:

[a]'An end! The end has come upon
the four corners of the land.
3 Now the end *has come* upon you,
And I will send My anger against
you;
I will judge you [a]according to your
ways,
And I will repay you for all your
abominations.
4 [a]My eye will not spare you,
Nor will I have pity;
But I will repay your ways,
And your abominations will be in
your midst;
[b]Then you shall know that I *am* the
LORD!'

5 "Thus says the Lord GOD:

'A disaster, a singular [a]disaster;
Behold, it has come!
6 An end has come,
The end has come;
It has dawned for you;
Behold, it has come!
7 [a]Doom has come to you, you who
dwell in the land;
[b]The time has come,
A day of trouble *is* near,
And not of rejoicing in the
mountains.
8 Now upon you I will soon [a]pour
out My fury,
And spend My anger upon you;
I will judge you according to your
ways,
And I will repay you for all your
abominations.
9 'My eye will not spare,
Nor will I have pity;
I will [1]repay you according to your
ways,
And your abominations will be in
your midst.
Then you shall know that I *am* the
LORD who strikes.

10 'Behold, the day!
Behold, it has come!
[a]Doom has gone out;
The rod has blossomed,
Pride has budded.
11 [a]Violence has risen up into a rod of
wickedness;
None of them *shall remain,*
None of their multitude,
None of [1]them;
[b]Nor *shall there be* wailing for them.
12 The time has come,
The day draws near.
'Let not the buyer [a]rejoice,
Nor the seller [b]mourn,

6 [1] Places for pagan worship
7 [a] Ezek. 7:4, 9
8 [a] Jer. 44:28 [b] Ezek. 5:12
9 [a] [Deut. 4:29] [b] Ps. 78:40 [c] Ezek. 20:7, 24 [d] Ezek. 20:43; 36:31
11 [a] Ezek. 21:14 [b] Ezek. 5:12 [1] Lit. *Strike your hands*
12 [a] Ezek. 5:13
13 [a] Jer. 2:20; 3:6 [b] Hos. 4:13 [c] Is. 57:5
14 [a] Is. 5:25 [b] Num. 33:46

CHAPTER 7
2 [a] Amos 8:2, 10
3 [a] [Rom. 2:6]
4 [a] Ezek. 5:11 [b] Ezek. 12:20
5 [a] 2 Kin. 21:12, 13
7 [a] Ezek. 7:10 [b] Zeph. 1:14, 15
8 [a] Ezek. 20:8, 21
9 [1] Lit. *give*
10 [a] Ezek. 7:7
11 [a] Jer. 6:7 [b] Jer. 16:5, 6 [1] Or *their wealth*
12 [a] Prov. 20:14 [b] Is. 24:2

For wrath *is* on their whole
multitude.
13 For the seller shall not return to
what has been sold,
Though he may still be alive;
For the vision concerns the whole
multitude,
And it shall not turn back;
No one will strengthen himself
Who lives in iniquity.

14 'They have blown the trumpet and
made everyone ready,
But no one goes to battle;
For My wrath *is* on all their
multitude.
15 [a]The sword *is* outside,
And the pestilence and famine
within.
Whoever *is* in the field
Will die by the sword;
And whoever *is* in the city,
Famine and pestilence will devour
him.
16 'Those who [a]survive will escape
and be on the mountains
Like doves of the valleys,
All of them mourning,
Each for his iniquity.
17 Every [a]hand will be feeble,
And every knee will be *as* weak *as*
water.
18 They will also [a]be girded with
sackcloth;
Horror will cover them;
Shame *will be* on every face,
Baldness on all their heads.

19 'They will throw their silver into
the streets,
And their gold will be like refuse;
Their [a]silver and their gold will not
be able to deliver them
In the day of the wrath of the
LORD;
They will not satisfy their souls,
Nor fill their stomachs,
Because it became their stumbling
block of iniquity.
20 'As for the beauty of his
ornaments,
He set it in majesty;
[a]But they made from it
The images of their abominations—
Their detestable things;
Therefore I have made it
Like refuse to them.
21 I will give it as [a]plunder

15 a Jer. 14:18
16 a Ezek. 6:8; 14:22
17 a Is. 13:7
18 a Amos 8:10
19 a Zeph. 1:18
20 a Jer. 7:30
21 a 2 Kin. 24:13
23 a 2 Kin. 21:16
24 a Ezek. 21:31; 28:7 b Ezek. 24:21
25 *1* Lit. *Shuddering*
26 a Jer. 4:20 b Ps. 74:9
CHAPTER 8
1 a Ezek. 14:1; 20:1; 33:31 b Ezek. 1:3; 3:22
2 a Ezek. 1:26, 27 b Ezek. 1:4, 27
3 a Dan. 5:5 b Ezek. 3:14 c Ezek. 11:1, 24; 40:2

Into the hands of strangers,
And to the wicked of the earth as
spoil;
And they shall defile it.
22 I will turn My face from them,
And they will defile My secret place;
For robbers shall enter it and defile
it.

23 'Make a chain,
For [a]the land is filled with crimes
of blood,
And the city is full of violence.
24 Therefore I will bring the [a]worst
of the Gentiles,
And they will possess their houses;
I will cause the pomp of the strong
to cease,
And their holy places shall be
[b]defiled.
25 [1]Destruction comes;
They will seek peace, but *there
shall be* none.
26 [a]Disaster will come upon disaster,
And rumor will be upon rumor.
[b]Then they will seek a vision from a
prophet;
But the law will perish from the
priest,
And counsel from the elders.
27 'The king will mourn,
The prince will be clothed with
desolation,
And the hands of the common
people will tremble.
I will do to them according to their
way,
And according to what they deserve
I will judge them;
Then they shall know that I *am* the
LORD!' "

Abominations in the Temple

8 And it came to pass in the sixth year,
in the sixth *month,* on the fifth *day* of
the month, as I sat in my house with [a]the
elders of Judah sitting before me, that
[b]the hand of the Lord GOD fell upon me
there. 2 [a]Then I looked, and there was a
likeness, like the appearance of fire—
from the appearance of His waist and
downward, fire; and from His waist and
upward, like the appearance of brightness,
[b]like the color of amber. 3 He [a]stretched
out the form of a hand, and took me
by a lock of my hair; and [b]the Spirit lifted me up between earth and heaven,
and [c]brought me in visions of God to

Jerusalem, to the door of the north gate
of the inner *court,* [d]where the seat of the
image of jealousy *was,* which [e]provokes[1]
to jealousy. 4And behold, the [a]glory of the
God of Israel *was* there, like the vision
that I [b]saw in the plain.
5Then He said to me, "Son of man, lift
your eyes now toward the north." So I lifted my eyes toward the north, and there,
north of the altar gate, was this image of
jealousy in the entrance.
6Furthermore He said to me, "Son of
man, do you see what they are doing, the
great [a]abominations that the house of Israel commits here, to make Me go far
away from My sanctuary? Now turn again,
you will see greater abominations." 7So
He brought me to the door of the court;
and when I looked, there was a hole in the
wall. 8Then He said to me, "Son of man,
dig into the wall"; and when I dug into the
wall, there was a door.
9And He said to me, "Go in, and see the
wicked abominations which they are doing there." 10So I went in and saw, and
there—every [a]sort of [b]creeping thing,
abominable beasts, and all the idols of the
house of Israel, [1]portrayed all around on
the walls. 11And there stood before them
[a]seventy men of the elders of the house of
Israel, and in their midst stood Jaazaniah
the son of Shaphan. Each man had a censer in his hand, and a thick cloud of incense went up. 12Then He said to me,
"Son of man, have you seen what the elders of the house of Israel do in the dark,
every man in the room of his idols? For
they say, [a]'The LORD does not see us, the
LORD has forsaken the land.' "
13And He said to me, "Turn again, *and*
you will see greater abominations that
they are doing." 14So He brought me to
the door of the north gate of the LORD's
house; and to my dismay, women were
sitting there weeping for [1]Tammuz.
15Then He said to me, "Have you seen
this, O son of man? Turn again, you will
see greater abominations than these."
16So He brought me into the inner court
of the LORD's house; and there, at the door
of the temple of the LORD, [a]between the
porch and the altar, [b]*were* about twenty-
five men [c]with their backs toward the
temple of the LORD and their faces toward
the east, and they were worshiping [d]the
sun toward the east.
17And He said to me, "Have you seen
this, O son of man? Is it a trivial thing to
the house of Judah to commit the abominations which they commit here? For
they have [a]filled the land with violence;
then they have returned to provoke Me to
anger. Indeed they put the branch to their
nose. 18[a]Therefore I also will act in fury.
My [b]eye will not spare nor will I have pity;
and though they [c]cry in My ears with a
loud voice, I will not hear them."

The Wicked Are Slain

9 Then He called out in my hearing
with a loud voice, saying, "Let those
who have charge over the city draw near,
each *with* a [1]deadly weapon in his hand."
2And suddenly six men came from the
direction of the upper gate, which faces
north, each with his [1]battle-ax in his
hand. [a]One man among them *was* clothed
with linen and had a writer's inkhorn [2]at
his side. They went in and stood beside
the bronze altar.
3Now [a]the glory of the God of Israel had
gone up from the cherub, where it had
been, to the threshold of the [1]temple. And
He called to the man clothed with linen,
who *had* the writer's inkhorn at his side;
4and the LORD said to him, "Go through
the midst of the city, through the midst of
Jerusalem, and put [a]a mark on the foreheads of the men [b]who sigh and cry over
all the abominations that are done within it."
5To the others He said in my [1]hearing,
"Go after him through the city and [a]kill;[2]
[b]do not let your eye spare, nor have any
pity. 6[a]Utterly[1] slay old *and* young men,
maidens and little children and women;
but [b]do not come near anyone on whom
is the mark; and [c]begin at My sanctuary."
[d]So they began with the elders who *were*
before the [2]temple. 7Then He said to
them, "Defile the [1]temple, and fill the
courts with the slain. Go out!" And they
went out and killed in the city.
8So it was, that while they were killing
them, I was left *alone;* and I [a]fell on my
face and cried out, and said, [b]"Ah, Lord
GOD! Will You destroy all the remnant of
Israel in pouring out Your fury on Jerusalem?"
9Then He said to me, "The iniquity of
the house of Israel and Judah *is* exceedingly great, and [a]the land is full of bloodshed, and the city full of perversity; for
they say, [b]'The LORD has forsaken the
land, and [c]the LORD does not see!' 10And
as for Me also, My [a]eye will neither spare,

3 d Ezek. 5:11 e Deut. 32:16, 21 *1* Arouses the LORD's jealousy
4 a Ezek. 3:12; 9:3 b Ezek. 1:28; 3:22, 23
6 a 2 Kin. 23:4, 5
10 a Ex. 20:4 b Rom. 1:23 *1* Or *carved*
11 a Num. 11:16, 25
12 a Ezek. 9:9
14 *1* A Sumerian fertility god similar to the Gr. god Adonis
16 a Joel 2:17 b Ezek. 11:1 c Jer. 2:27; 32:33 d Deut. 4:19
17 a Ezek. 9:9
18 a Ezek. 5:13; 16:42; 24:13 b Ezek. 5:11; 7:4, 9; 9:5, 10 c Mic. 3:4

CHAPTER 9
1 *1* Or *destroying*
2 a Lev. 16:4 *1* Lit. *shattering weapon* *2* Lit. *upon his loins*
3 a Ezek. 3:23; 8:4; 10:4, 18; 11:22, 23 *1* Lit. *house*
4 a Rev. 7:2, 3; 9:4; 14:1 b Jer. 13:17
5 a Ezek. 7:9 b Ezek. 5:11 *1* Lit. *ears* *2* Lit. *strike*
6 a 2 Chr. 36:17 b Rev. 9:4 c Jer. 25:29 d Ezek. 8:11, 12, 16 *1* Lit. *Slay to destruction* *2* Lit. *house*
7 *1* Lit. *house*
8 a Josh. 7:6 b Ezek. 11:13
9 a 2 Kin. 21:16 b Ezek. 8:12 c Is. 29:15
10 a Ezek. 5:11; 7:4; 8:18

nor will I have pity, *but* [b]I will recompense their deeds on their own head."
11 Just then, the man clothed with lin-
en, who *had* the inkhorn at his side, reported back and said, "I have done as You
commanded me."

The Glory Departs from the Temple

10 And I looked, and there in the [a]fir-
mament[1] that was above the head
of the cherubim, there appeared something like a sapphire stone, having the
appearance of the likeness of a throne.
2 [a]Then He spoke to the man clothed with
linen, and said, "Go in among the wheels,
under the cherub, fill your hands with
[b]coals of fire from among the cherubim,
and [c]scatter *them* over the city." And he
went in as I watched.
3 Now the cherubim were standing on
the [1]south side of the [2]temple when the
man went in, and the [a]cloud filled the inner court. 4 [a]Then the glory of the LORD
went up from the cherub, *and paused*
over the threshold of the [1]temple; and
[b]the house was filled with the cloud, and
the court was full of the brightness of the
LORD's [c]glory. 5 And the [a]sound of the
wings of the cherubim was heard *even*
in the outer court, like [b]the voice of Almighty God when He speaks.
6 Then it happened, when He commanded the man clothed in linen, saying,
"Take fire from among the wheels, from
among the cherubim," that he went in
and stood beside the wheels. 7 And the
cherub stretched out his hand from
among the cherubim to the fire that *was*
among the cherubim, and took *some of it*
and put *it* into the hands of the *man*
clothed with linen, who took *it* and went
out. 8 [a]The cherubim appeared to have the
form of a man's hand under their wings.
9 [a]And when I looked, there were four
wheels by the cherubim, one wheel by one
cherub and another wheel by each other
cherub; the wheels appeared *to have* the
color of a [b]beryl stone. 10 *As for* their appearance, all four looked alike—as it
were, a wheel in the middle of a wheel.
11 [a]When they went, they went toward *any*
of their four directions; they did not turn
aside when they went, but followed in the
direction the head was facing. They did
not turn aside when they went. 12 And
their whole body, with their back, their
hands, their wings, and the wheels that
the four had, *were* [a]full of eyes all around.
13 As for the wheels, they were called in my
[1]hearing, "Wheel."
14 [a]Each one had four faces: the first
face *was* the face of a cherub, the second
face the face of a man, the third the face
of a lion, and the fourth the face of an
eagle. 15 And the cherubim were lifted up.
This *was* [a]the living creature I saw by the
River Chebar. 16 [a]When the cherubim
went, the wheels went beside them; and
when the cherubim lifted their wings to
mount up from the earth, the same
wheels also did not turn from beside
them. 17 [a]When [1]*the cherubim* stood still,
the wheels stood still, and when [2]*one* was
lifted up, [3]*the other* lifted itself up, for the
spirit of the living creature *was* in them.
18 Then [a]the glory of the LORD [b]depart-
ed from the threshold of the [1]temple and
stood over the cherubim. 19 And [a]the cherubim lifted their wings and mounted up
from the earth in my sight. When they
went out, the wheels *were* beside them;
and they stood at the door of the [b]east
gate of the LORD's house, and the glory of
the God of Israel *was* above them.
20 [a]This *is* the living creature I saw under the God of Israel [b]by the River Chebar,
and I knew they *were* cherubim. 21 [a]Each
one had four faces and each one four
wings, and the likeness of the hands of a
man *was* under their wings. 22 And [a]the
likeness of their faces *was* the same *as* the
faces which I had seen by the River Chebar, their appearance and their persons.
[b]They each went straight forward.

Judgment on Wicked Counselors

11 Then [a]the Spirit lifted me up and
brought me to [b]the East Gate of
the LORD's house, which faces eastward;
and there [c]at the door of the gate were
twenty-five men, among whom I saw Jaazaniah the son of Azzur, and Pelatiah the
son of Benaiah, princes of the people.
2 And He said to me: "Son of man, these
are the men who devise iniquity and give
wicked [1]counsel in this city, 3 who say,
'*The time is* not [a]near to build houses;
[b]this *city is* the [1]caldron, and we *are* the
meat.' 4 Therefore prophesy against them,
prophesy, O son of man!"
5 Then [a]the Spirit of the LORD fell upon
me, and said to me, "Speak! 'Thus says the
LORD: "Thus you have said, O house of Israel; for [b]I know the things that come into

---

10 [b]Ezek. 11:21

CHAPTER 10
1 [a]Ezek. 1:22, 26 [1]*expanse*
2 [a]Dan. 10:5 [b]Ezek. 1:13 [c]Rev. 8:5
3 [a]1 Kin. 8:10, 11 [1]Lit. *right* [2]Lit. *house*
4 [a]Ezek. 1:28 [b]Ezek. 43:5 [c]Ezek. 11:22, 23 [1]Lit. *house*
5 [a]Ezek. 1:24 [b][Ps. 29:3]
8 [a]Ezek. 1:8; 10:21
9 [a]Ezek. 1:15 [b]Ezek. 1:16
11 [a]Ezek. 1:17
12 [a]Rev. 4:6, 8
13 [1]Lit. *ears*
14 [a]Ezek. 1:6, 10, 11
15 [a]Ezek. 1:3, 5
16 [a]Ezek. 1:19
17 [a]Ezek. 1:12, 20, 21 [1]Lit. *they* [2]Lit. *they were* [3]Lit. *they lifted them*
18 [a]Ezek. 10:4 [b]Hos. 9:12 [1]Lit. *house*
19 [a]Ezek. 11:22 [b]Ezek. 11:1
20 [a]Ezek. 1:22 [b]Ezek. 1:1
21 [a]Ezek. 1:6, 8; 10:14; 41:18, 19
22 [a]Ezek. 1:10 [b]Ezek. 1:9, 12

CHAPTER 11
1 [a]Ezek. 3:12, 14 [b]Ezek. 10:19 [c]Ezek. 8:16
2 [1]Advice
3 [a]2 Pet. 3:4 [b]Jer. 1:13 [1]Pot
5 [a]Ezek. 2:2; 3:24 [b][Jer. 16:17; 17:10]

your mind. 6[a]You have multiplied your
slain in this city, and you have filled its
streets with the slain." 7Therefore thus
says the Lord GOD: [a]"Your slain whom
you have laid in its midst, they *are* the
meat, and this *city is* the caldron; [b]but I
shall bring you out of the midst of it. 8You
have [a]feared the sword; and I will bring
a sword upon you," says the Lord GOD.
9"And I will bring you out of its midst, and
deliver you into the hands of strangers,
and [a]execute judgments on you. 10[a]You
shall fall by the sword. I will judge you
at [b]the border of Israel. [c]Then you shall
know that I *am* the LORD. 11[a]This *city*
shall not be your [1]caldron, nor shall you
be the meat in its midst. I will judge you
at the border of Israel. 12And you shall
know that I *am* the LORD; for you have not
walked in My statutes nor executed My
judgments, but [a]have done according to
the customs of the Gentiles which *are* all
around you." ' "
13Now it happened, while I was prophesying, that [a]Pelatiah the son of Benaiah
died. Then [b]I fell on my face and cried
with a loud voice, and said, "Ah, Lord
GOD! Will You make a complete end of the
remnant of Israel?"

God Will Restore Israel

14Again the word of the LORD came to
me, saying, 15"Son of man, your brethren,
your relatives, your countrymen, and all
the house of Israel in its entirety, *are*
those about whom the inhabitants of Jerusalem have said, 'Get far away from the
LORD; this land has been given to us as a
possession.' 16Therefore say, 'Thus says
the Lord GOD: "Although I have cast them
far off among the Gentiles, and although
I have scattered them among the countries, [a]yet I shall be a little [1]sanctuary for
them in the countries where they have
gone." ' 17Therefore say, 'Thus says the
Lord GOD: [a]"I will gather you from the
peoples, assemble you from the countries
where you have been scattered, and I will
give you the land of Israel." ' 18And they
will go there, and they will take away all
its [a]detestable things and all its abominations from there. 19 Then [a]I will give
them one heart, and I will put [b]a new spirit within [1]them, and take [c]the stony heart
out of their flesh, and give them a heart of
flesh, 20[a]that they may walk in My statutes
and keep My judgments and do them;
[b]and they shall be My people, and I will be
their God. 21But *as for those* whose
hearts follow the desire for their detestable things and their abominations, [a]I will
recompense their deeds on their own
heads," says the Lord GOD.
22So the cherubim [a]lifted up their
wings, with the wheels beside them, and
the glory of the God of Israel *was* high
above them. 23And [a]the glory of the LORD
went up from the midst of the city and
stood [b]on the mountain, [c]which *is* on the
east side of the city.
24Then [a]the Spirit took me up and
brought me in a vision by the Spirit of
God into [1]Chaldea, to those in captivity.
And the vision that I had seen went up
from me. 25So I spoke to those in captivity
of all the things the LORD had shown me.

Judah's Captivity Portrayed

12 Now the word of the LORD came
to me, saying: 2"Son of man, you
dwell in the midst of [a]a rebellious house,
which [b]has eyes to see but does not see,
and ears to hear but does not hear; [c]for
they *are* a rebellious house.
3"Therefore, son of man, prepare your
belongings for captivity, and go into captivity by day in their sight. You shall go
from your place into captivity to another
place in their sight. It may be that they
will consider, though they *are* a rebellious
house. 4By day you shall bring out your
belongings in their sight, as though going
into captivity; and at evening you shall go
in their sight, like those who go into captivity. 5Dig through the wall in their
sight, and carry your belongings out
through it. 6In their sight you shall bear
them on *your* shoulders *and* carry *them*
out at twilight; you shall cover your face,
so that you cannot see the ground, [a]for I
have made you a sign to the house of Israel."
7So I did as I was commanded. I
brought out my belongings by day, as
though going into captivity, and at evening I dug through the wall with my
hand. I brought *them* out at twilight, *and*
I bore *them* on *my* shoulder in their sight.
8And in the morning the word of the
LORD came to me, saying, 9"Son of man,
has not the house of Israel, [a]the rebellious
house, said to you, [b]'What are you doing?'
10Say to them, 'Thus says the Lord GOD:
"This [a]burden[1] *concerns* the prince in Jerusalem and all the house of Israel who
are among them." ' 11Say, [a]'I *am* a sign to

6 [a]Ezek. 7:23; 22:2–6, 9, 12, 27
7 [a]Mic. 3:2, 3 [b]Ezek. 11:9
8 [a]Jer. 42:16
9 [a]Ezek. 5:8
10 [a]Jer. 39:6; 52:10 [b]2 Kin. 14:25 [c]Ps. 9:16
11 [a]Ezek. 11:3, 7 [1]Pot
12 [a]Deut. 12:30, 31
13 [a]Acts 5:5 [b]Ezek. 9:8
16 [a]Is. 8:14 [1]*holy place*
17 [a]Jer. 3:12, 18; 24:5
18 [a]Ezek. 37:23
19 [a]Jer. 32:39 [b]Ezek. 18:31 [c]Zech. 7:12 [1]Lit. *you* (pl.)
20 [a]Ps. 105:45 [b]Jer. 24:7
21 [a]Ezek. 9:10
22 [a]Ezek. 1:19
23 [a]Ezek. 8:4; 9:3 [b]Zech. 14:4 [c]Ezek. 43:2
24 [a]Ezek. 8:3 [1]Or *Babylon,* and so elsewhere in the book

CHAPTER 12
2 [a]Ezek. 2:3, 6–8 [b]Jer. 5:21 [c]Ezek. 2:5
6 [a]Ezek. 4:3; 24:24
9 [a]Ezek. 2:5 [b]Ezek. 17:12; 24:19
10 [a]Mal. 1:1 [1]*oracle, prophecy*
11 [a]Ezek. 12:6

Ezekiel 11:19, 20

Dear Woman of Destiny,

As a heavenly Father who desperately loves us and wants to share His heart with us, God is looking for women with pure hearts who are able to receive all that He has planned for us.

In the Beatitudes, Jesus says that God blesses those with pure hearts, for they will see God (see Matt. 5:8). One day as I was spending time with the Lord, I realized He wouldn't have said this if it weren't actually possible. God sent Jesus into this world to cleanse us from *all* sin and put His Holy Spirit within us—a gift not by works but by grace. We receive a clean heart because His blood cleanses us from all sin.

As we grow in our intimacy with God and ask Him to show us areas in our hearts that are impure, divided, and idolatrous, purity becomes a process, which results in our becoming more tender toward Him. In His presence we can be free to expose ourselves and deal with issues of the heart such as pride, jealousy, covetousness, and idol worship (that is, materialism, the worship of our own bodies, intellectualism, money, lust).

When we ask the Father to reveal these areas—not that we might be self-righteous or spiritual, but that we would receive and walk in greater intimacy—He lovingly brings circumstances into our lives to expose the hardened places of our hearts. The more we allow Him into our hearts, sharing our most secret thoughts in the true essence of intimacy, the more we "see" God. He is the One we go to. He shares our joys and sorrows, and we can confess our sins to Him, receiving forgiveness and healing without condemnation.

This has given me new understanding as to what Jesus meant in the parable of the sower and the seed in Mark 4. He said that when we hear His word and it is crowded out by the cares of this life, the lure of wealth, and the desire for nice things, then nothing is produced. Besides this, there also comes a breach in our relationship. He is the One who makes us pure as gold. The softest, most pliable, translucent, and brightly shining gold is that which has had all of the impurities removed.

Woman of Destiny, I dare you to take the risk and expose your heart to the Father. Unless we see sin as God sees it and realize that it is a roadblock in our relationship with Him, we end up as hearers of the Word, but not doers. God has secrets and special things in His heart to share with each of us; but if we are to receive them, we must draw nearer to Him. The intimacy and love you receive will enable you to have a tender heart. He will then also trust His secrets to you, revealing His heart. Intimacy results in true worship and praise, bringing glory to Him.

Betty Thiessen

you. As I have done, so shall it be done to
them; [b]they shall be carried away into
captivity.' 12 And [a]the prince who *is*
among them shall bear *his belongings* on
his shoulder at twilight and go out. They
shall dig through the wall to carry *them*
out through it. He shall cover his face, so
that he cannot see the ground with *his*
eyes. 13 I will also spread My [a]net over him,
and he shall be caught in My snare. [b]I will
bring him to Babylon, *to* the land of the
Chaldeans; yet he shall not see it, though
he shall die there. 14 [a]I will scatter to every
wind all who *are* around him to help him,
and all his troops; and [b]I will draw out the
sword after them.
15 [a]"Then they shall know that I *am* the
LORD, when I scatter them among the nations and disperse them throughout the
countries. 16 [a]But I will spare a few of their
men from the sword, from famine, and
from pestilence, that they may declare all
their abominations among the Gentiles
wherever they go. Then they shall know
that I *am* the LORD."

Judgment Not Postponed

17 Moreover the word of the LORD came
to me, saying, 18 "Son of man, [a]eat your
bread with [1]quaking, and drink your water with trembling and anxiety. 19 And say
to the people of the land, 'Thus says the
Lord GOD to the inhabitants of Jerusalem
and to the land of Israel: "They shall eat
their bread with anxiety, and drink their
water with dread, so that her land may [a]be
emptied of all who are in it, [b]because of
the violence of all those who dwell in it.
20 Then the cities that are inhabited shall
be laid waste, and the land shall become
desolate; and you shall know that I *am* the
LORD." ' "
21 And the word of the LORD came to me,
saying, 22 "Son of man, what *is* this proverb *that* you *people* have about the land of
Israel, which says, [a]'The days are prolonged, and every vision fails'? 23 Tell them
therefore, 'Thus says the Lord GOD: "I will
lay this proverb to rest, and they shall no
more use it as a proverb in Israel." But say
to them, [a]"The days are at hand, and the
[1]fulfillment of every vision. 24 For [a]no
more shall there be any [b]false[1] vision or
flattering divination within the house of
Israel. 25 For I *am* the LORD. I speak, and
[a]the word which I speak will come to pass;
it will no more be postponed; for in your
days, O rebellious house, I will say the
word and [b]perform it," says the Lord
GOD.' "
26 Again the word of the LORD came to
me, saying, 27 [a]"Son of man, look, the
house of Israel is saying, 'The vision that
he sees *is* [b]for many days *from now,* and
he prophesies of times far off.' 28 [a]There-
fore say to them, 'Thus says the Lord GOD:
"None of My words will be postponed any
more, but the word which I speak [b]will be
done," says the Lord GOD.' "

Woe to Foolish Prophets

13 And the word of the LORD came to
me, saying, 2 "Son of man, prophesy [a]against the prophets of Israel who
prophesy, and say to [b]those who prophesy
out of their own [c]heart,[1] 'Hear the word
of the LORD!' "
3 Thus says the Lord GOD: "Woe to the
foolish prophets, who follow their own
spirit and have seen [1]nothing! 4 O Israel,
your prophets are [a]like foxes in the deserts. 5 You [a]have not gone up into the
[1]gaps to build a wall for the house of Israel to stand in battle on the day of the
LORD. 6 [a]They have envisioned futility and
false divination, saying, 'Thus says the
LORD!' But the LORD has [b]not sent them;
yet they hope that the word may [1]be confirmed. 7 Have you not seen a futile vision,
and have you not spoken false divination?
You say, 'The LORD says,' but I have not
spoken."
8 Therefore thus says the Lord GOD:
"Because you have spoken nonsense and
envisioned lies, therefore I *am* indeed
against you," says the Lord GOD. 9 "My
hand will be [a]against the prophets who
envision futility and who [b]divine lies; they
shall not be in the assembly of My people,
[c]nor be written in the record of the house
of Israel, [b]nor shall they enter into the
land of Israel. [d]Then you shall know that
I *am* the Lord GOD.
10 "Because, indeed, because they have
seduced My people, saying, [a]'Peace!' when
there is no peace—and one builds a wall,
and they [b]plaster[1] it with untempered
mortar— 11 say to those who plaster *it*
with untempered *mortar,* that it will fall.
[a]There will be flooding rain, and you,
O great hailstones, shall fall; and a stormy
wind shall tear *it* down. 12 Surely, when

11 [b] 2 Kin. 25:4, 5, 7
12 [a] Jer. 39:4; 52:7
13 [a] Jer. 52:9 [b] Jer. 52:11
14 [a] Ezek. 5:10 [b] Ezek. 5:2, 12
15 [a] Ezek. 6:7, 14; 12:16, 20
16 [a] Ezek. 6:8–10
18 [a] Ezek. 4:16 [1] *shaking*
19 [a] Zech. 7:14 [b] Ps. 107:34
22 [a] Ezek. 11:3; 12:27
23 [a] Zeph. 1:14 [1] Lit. *word*
24 [a] Ezek. 13:6 [b] Lam. 2:14 [1] Lit. *vain*
25 [a] [Luke 21:33] [b] [Is. 14:24]
27 [a] Ezek. 12:22 [b] Dan. 10:14
28 [a] Ezek. 12:23, 25 [b] Jer. 4:7

CHAPTER 13
2 [a] Ezek. 22:25–28 [b] Ezek. 13:17 [c] Jer. 14:14; 23:16, 26 [1] Inspiration
3 [1] No vision
4 [a] Song 2:15
5 [a] Ps. 106:23 [1] *breaches*
6 [a] Ezek. 22:28 [b] Jer. 27:8–15 [1] Come true
9 [a] Jer. 23:30 [b] Jer. 20:3–6 [c] Ezra 2:59, 62 [d] Ezek. 11:10, 12
10 [a] Jer. 6:14; 8:11 [b] Ezek. 22:28 [1] Or *whitewash*
11 [a] Ezek. 38:22

the wall has fallen, will it not be said to
you, 'Where *is* the mortar with which you
plastered *it?*' "
13Therefore thus says the Lord GOD: "I
will cause a stormy wind to break forth in
My fury; and there shall be a flooding rain
in My anger, and great hailstones in fury
to consume *it.* 14So I will break down the
wall you have plastered with untempered
mortar, and bring it down to the ground,
so that its foundation will be uncovered; it
will fall, and you shall be consumed in the
midst of it. [a]Then you shall know that I
am the LORD.
15"Thus will I accomplish My wrath on
the wall and on those who have plastered
it with untempered *mortar;* and I will say
to you, 'The wall *is* no *more,* nor those
who plastered it, 16*that is,* the prophets of
Israel who prophesy concerning Jerusalem, and who [a]see visions of peace for her
when *there is* no peace,' " says the Lord
GOD.
17"Likewise, son of man, [a]set your face
against the daughters of your people,
[b]who prophesy out of their own [1]heart;
prophesy against them, 18 and say,
'Thus says the Lord GOD: "Woe to the
women who sew *magic* charms [1]on their
sleeves and make veils for the heads of
people of every height to hunt souls! Will
you [a]hunt the souls of My people, and
keep yourselves alive? 19And will you
profane Me among My people [a]for handfuls of barley and for pieces of bread, killing people who should not die, and
keeping people alive who should not live,
by your lying to My people who listen to
lies?"
20'Therefore thus says the Lord GOD:
"Behold, I *am* against your *magic* charms
by which you hunt souls there like [1]birds.
I will tear them from your arms, and let
the souls go, the souls you hunt like birds.
21I will also tear off your veils and deliver
My people out of your hand, and they shall
no longer be as prey in your hand. [a]Then
you shall know that I *am* the LORD.
22"Because with [a]lies you have made
the heart of the righteous sad, whom I
have not made sad; and you have
[b]strengthened the hands of the wicked, so
that he does not turn from his wicked way
to save his life. 23Therefore [a]you shall no
longer envision futility nor practice divination; for I will deliver My people out of
your hand, and you shall know that I *am*
the LORD." ' "

Idolatry Will Be Punished

14 Now [a]some of the elders of Israel
came to me and sat before me.
2And the word of the LORD came to me,
saying, 3"Son of man, these men have set
up their idols in their hearts, and put before them [a]that which causes them to
stumble into iniquity. [b]Should I let Myself
be inquired of at all by them?
4"Therefore speak to them, and say to
them, 'Thus says the Lord GOD: "Everyone
of the house of Israel who sets up his idols
in his heart, and puts before him what
causes him to stumble into iniquity, and
then comes to the prophet, I the LORD will
answer him who comes, according to the
multitude of his idols, 5that I may seize
the house of Israel by their heart, because
they are all estranged from Me by their
idols." '

In the children of God, repentance and faith exactly answer each other. By repentance we feel the sin remaining in our hearts, and cleaving to our words and actions; by faith, we receive the power of God in Christ, purifying our hearts, and cleansing our hands.

JOHN WESLEY

6"Therefore say to the house of Israel,
'Thus says the Lord GOD: "Repent, turn
away from your idols, and [a]turn your faces away from all your abominations. 7For
anyone of the house of Israel, or of the
strangers who dwell in Israel, who separates himself from Me and sets up his
idols in his heart and puts before him
what causes him to stumble into iniquity,
then comes to a prophet to inquire of him
concerning Me, I the LORD will answer
him by Myself. 8[a]I will set My face against
that man and make him a [b]sign and a
proverb, and I will cut him off from the

14 [a]Ezek. 13:9, 21, 23; 14:8
16 [a]Jer. 6:14; 8:11; 28:9
17 [a]Ezek. 20:46; 21:2 [b]Ezek. 13:2 [1]Inspiration
18 [a][2 Pet. 2:14] [1]Lit. *over all the joints of My hands;* Vg. *under every elbow;* LXX, Tg. *on all elbows of the hands*
19 [a]Mic. 3:5
20 [1]Lit. *flying ones*
21 [a]Ezek. 13:9
22 [a]Jer. 28:15 [b]Jer. 23:14
23 [a]Mic. 3:5, 6

CHAPTER 14
1 [a]Ezek. 8:1; 20:1; 33:31
3 [a]Ezek. 7:19 [b]Ezek. 20:3, 31
6 [a]Is. 2:20; 30:22; 55:6, 7
8 [a]Jer. 44:11 [b]Num. 26:10

Ezekiel 13:18

Dear Woman of Destiny,

We are living in an age of great uncertainties concerning the future. People are looking for instant answers. Sadly, most people no longer take time to seek the Lord or to meditate upon His Word. They have lost the art of godly meditation and instead are looking to the occult for answers.

In our instant society where television, media, and computers dictate so much of our lifestyle, the occult is running rampant. Psychics, fortune-tellers, and Eastern cults and religions have come to the forefront of society as never before in history. They prey on those who are seeking truth but don't know where to find it, and on those who know the truth but do not fear the living God.

Leaders in the occult profess to have immediate answers for everything from sex to religion. They are truly false prophets in every sense of the word. The sad thing is that so many people get involved through a lack of knowledge of God's Word. They don't realize that He considers this practice an abomination.

Ezekiel 13:18 refers to an occult act in which false prophetesses made cushions to sit or lean on and draped their arms over them to lure the people. Superstitious belief was that those who received their advice would enter into a place of perfect tranquility. This produced a false sense of peace, security, and comfort.

The veils were considered magical and put over the heads of those being consulted. The word *veil* figuratively means a net used in hunting to trap a victim. These veils were worn by women of stature. However, when they were placed on other women, they stirred pride in their hearts and prepared them to be taken into a trance.

Veils were also worn by false prophetesses and were believed to render them more mysterious and enticing. This was done in order to successfully hunt or lure souls into idolatry.

False prophetesses kept people in awe and terrified them with their predictions. They beguiled people, pretending to save their souls and promising eternal life to the unrepentant.

Times have changed and customs are different, but Satan still has traps today in which he entices people into his net. He appeals to their pride and lures them through sex, false prophecy, and the occult.

In our instant society, be instant in prayer and quick to mediate upon God's Word. When you feel uncertain and you are looking for answers, look to the Lord, search the Scriptures, and trust the Holy Spirit to lead you into all truth. True peace, security, and comfort come from the Lord. Jesus is the only answer for the world today.

Beth Alves

midst of My people. [c]Then you shall know that I *am* the LORD.

9"And if the prophet is induced to speak anything, I the LORD [a]have induced that prophet, and I will stretch out My hand against him and destroy him from among My people Israel. 10And they shall bear their iniquity; the punishment of the prophet shall be the same as the punishment of the one who inquired, 11that the house of Israel may [a]no longer stray from Me, nor be profaned anymore with all their transgressions, [b]but that they may be My people and I may be their God," says the Lord GOD.' "

Judgment on Persistent Unfaithfulness

12The word of the LORD came again to me, saying: 13"Son of man, when a land sins against Me by persistent unfaithfulness, I will stretch out My hand against it; I will cut off its [a]supply of bread, send famine on it, and cut off man and beast from it. 14[a]Even *if* these three men, Noah, Daniel, and Job, were in it, they would deliver *only* themselves [b]by their righteousness," says the Lord GOD.

15"If I cause [a]wild beasts to pass through the land, and they [1]empty it, and make it so desolate that no man may pass through because of the beasts, 16*even* [a]*though* these three men *were* [1]in it, *as* I live," says the Lord GOD, "they would deliver neither sons nor daughters; only they would be delivered, and the land would be [b]desolate.

17"Or *if* [a]I bring a sword on that land, and say, 'Sword, go through the land,' and I [b]cut off man and beast from it, 18even [a]*though* these three men *were* in it, *as* I live," says the Lord GOD, "they would deliver neither sons nor daughters, but only they themselves would be delivered.

19"Or *if* I send [a]a pestilence into that land and [b]pour out My fury on it in blood, and cut off from it man and beast, 20even [a]*though* Noah, Daniel, and Job *were* in it, *as* I live," says the Lord GOD, "they would deliver neither son nor daughter; they would deliver *only* themselves by their righteousness."

21For thus says the Lord GOD: "How much more it shall be when [a]I send My four [1]severe judgments on Jerusalem—the sword and famine and wild beasts and pestilence—to cut off man and beast from it? 22[a]Yet behold, there shall be left in it a remnant who will be [b]brought out, *both* sons and daughters; surely they will come out to you, and [c]you will see their ways and their doings. Then you will be comforted concerning the disaster that I have brought upon Jerusalem, all that I have brought upon it. 23And they will comfort you, when you see their ways and their doings; and you shall know that I have done nothing [a]without cause that I have done in it," says the Lord GOD.

The Outcast Vine

15 Then the word of the LORD came to me, saying: 2"Son of man, how is the wood of the vine *better* than any other wood, the vine branch which is among the trees of the forest? 3Is wood taken from it to make any object? Or can *men* make a peg from it to hang any vessel on? 4Instead, [a]it is thrown into the fire for fuel; the fire devours both ends of it, and its middle is burned. Is it useful for *any* work? 5Indeed, when it was whole, no object could be made from it. How much less will it be useful for *any* work when the fire has devoured it, and it is burned?

6"Therefore thus says the Lord GOD: 'Like the wood of the vine among the trees of the forest, which I have given to the fire for fuel, so I will give up the inhabitants of Jerusalem; 7and [a]I will set My face against them. [b]They will go out from *one* fire, but *another* fire shall devour them. [c]Then you shall know that I *am* the LORD, when I set My face against them. 8Thus I will make the land desolate, because they have persisted in unfaithfulness,' says the Lord GOD."

God's Love for Jerusalem

16 Again the word of the LORD came to me, saying, 2"Son of man, [a]cause Jerusalem to know her abominations, 3and say, 'Thus says the Lord GOD to Jerusalem: "Your [1]birth [a]and your nativity *are* from the land of Canaan; [b]your father *was* an Amorite and your mother a Hittite. 4*As for* your nativity, [a]on the day you were born your navel cord was not cut, nor were you washed in water to cleanse *you;* you were not rubbed with salt nor wrapped in swaddling cloths. 5No eye pitied you, to do any of these things for you, to have compassion on you; but

8 [c]Ezek. 6:7; 13:14
9 [a]2 Thess. 2:11
11 [a]2 Pet. 2:15 [b]Ezek. 11:20; 37:27
13 [a]Is. 3:1
14 [a]Jer. 15:1 [b][Prov. 11:4]
15 [a]Lev. 26:22 [1]Lit. *bereave it* of children
16 [a]Ezek. 14:14, 18, 20 [b]Ezek. 15:8; 33:28, 29 [1]Lit. *in the midst of it*
17 [a]Lev. 26:25 [b]Zeph. 1:3
18 [a]Ezek. 14:14
19 [a]2 Sam. 24:15 [b]Ezek. 7:8
20 [a]Ezek. 14:14
21 [a]Ezek. 5:17; 33:27 [1]Lit. *evil*
22 [a]Ezek. 12:16; 36:20 [b]Ezek. 6:8 [c]Ezek. 20:43
23 [a]Jer. 22:8, 9

CHAPTER 15
4 [a][John 15:6]
7 [a]Ezek. 14:8 [b]Is. 24:18 [c]Ezek. 7:4

CHAPTER 16
2 [a]Ezek. 20:4; 22:2
3 [a]Ezek. 21:30 [b]Ezek. 16:45 [1]*origin and your birth*
4 [a]Hos. 2:3

you were thrown out into the open field,
when you yourself were [1]loathed on the
day you were born.
6"And when I passed by you and saw
you struggling in your own blood, I said
to you in your blood, 'Live!' Yes, I said to
you in your blood, 'Live!' 7[a]I made you
[1]thrive like a plant in the field; and you
grew, matured, and became very beautiful. *Your* breasts were formed, your hair
grew, but you *were* naked and bare.
8"When I passed by you again and
looked upon you, indeed your time *was*
the time of love; [a]so I spread [1]My wing
over you and covered your nakedness.
Yes, I [b]swore an oath to you and entered
into a [c]covenant with you, and [d]you became Mine," says the Lord GOD.
9"Then I washed you in water; yes, I
thoroughly washed off your blood, and I
anointed you with oil. 10I clothed you in
embroidered cloth and gave you sandals
of [1]badger skin; I clothed you with fine
linen and covered you with silk. 11I
adorned you with ornaments, [a]put bracelets on your wrists, [b]and a chain on your
neck. 12And I put a [1]jewel in your nose,
earrings in your ears, and a beautiful
crown on your head. 13Thus you were
adorned with gold and silver, and your
clothing *was of* fine linen, silk, and embroidered cloth. [a]You ate *pastry of* fine
flour, honey, and oil. You were exceedingly [b]beautiful, and succeeded to royalty.
14[a]Your fame went out among the nations
because of your beauty, for it *was* perfect
through My splendor which I had bestowed on you," says the Lord GOD.

Jerusalem's Harlotry

15[a]"But you trusted in your own beauty,
[b]played the harlot because of your fame,
and poured out your harlotry on everyone
passing by who *would have* it. 16[a]You took
some of your garments and adorned multicolored [1]high places for yourself, and
played the harlot on them. *Such* things
should not happen, nor be. 17You have
also taken your beautiful jewelry from My
gold and My silver, which I had given you,
and made for yourself male images and
played the harlot with them. 18You took
your embroidered garments and covered
them, and you set My oil and My incense
before them. 19Also [a]My food which I gave
you—the pastry of fine flour, oil, and
honey *which* I fed you—you set it before
them as [1]sweet incense; and *so* it was,"
says the Lord GOD.
20[a]"Moreover you took your sons and
your daughters, whom you bore to Me,
and these you sacrificed to them to be devoured. *Were* your *acts* of harlotry a small
matter, 21that you have slain My children
and offered them up to them by causing
them to pass through *the* [a]*fire?* 22And in
all your abominations and acts of harlotry
you did not remember the days of your
[a]youth, [b]when you were naked and bare,
struggling in your blood.
23"Then it was so, after all your wickedness—'Woe, woe to you!' says the Lord
GOD— 24*that* [a]you also built for yourself
a shrine, and [b]made a [1]high place for
yourself in every street. 25You built your
high places [a]at the head of every road, and
made your beauty to be abhorred. You offered yourself to everyone who passed by,
and multiplied your acts of harlotry.
26You also committed harlotry with [a]the
Egyptians, your very fleshly neighbors,
and increased your acts of harlotry to
[b]provoke Me to anger.
27"Behold, therefore, I stretched out My
hand against you, diminished your [1]allot-
ment, and gave you up to the will of those
who hate you, [a]the daughters of the Philistines, who were ashamed of your lewd
behavior. 28You also played the harlot
with the [a]Assyrians, because you were in-
satiable; indeed you played the harlot with
them and still were not satisfied. 29More-
over you multiplied your acts of harlotry
as far as the land of the trader, [a]Chaldea;
and even then you were not satisfied.
30"How degenerate is your heart!" says
the Lord GOD, "seeing you do all these
things, the deeds of a brazen harlot.

Jerusalem's Adultery

31[a]"You erected your shrine at the head
of every road, and built your [1]high place
in every street. Yet you were not like a
harlot, because you scorned [b]payment.
32*You are* an adulterous wife, *who* takes
strangers instead of her husband. 33Men
make payment to all harlots, but [a]you
made your payments to all your lovers,
and [1]hired them to come to you from all
around for your harlotry. 34You are the
opposite of *other* women in your harlotry,
because no one solicited you to be a harlot. In that you gave payment but no payment was given you, therefore you are the
opposite."

5 [1] *abhorred*
7 [a] Ex. 1:7 [1] Lit. *a myriad*
8 [a] Ruth 3:9 [b] Gen. 22:16–18 [c] Ex. 24:6–8 [d] [Ex. 19:5] [1] Or *the corner of My garment*
10 [1] Or *dolphin* or *dugong*
11 [a] Gen. 24:22, 47 [b] Prov. 1:9
12 [1] Lit. *ring*
13 [a] Deut. 32:13, 14 [b] Ps. 48:2
14 [a] Lam. 2:15
15 [a] Mic. 3:11 [b] Is. 1:21; 57:8
16 [a] Ezek. 7:20 [1] Places for pagan worship
19 [a] Hos. 2:8 [1] Or *a sweet aroma*
20 [a] Jer. 7:31
21 [a] Jer. 19:5
22 [a] Jer. 2:2 [b] Ezek. 16:4–6
24 [a] Jer. 11:13 [b] Jer. 2:20; 3:2 [1] Place for pagan worship
25 [a] Prov. 9:14
26 [a] Ezek. 16:26; 20:7, 8 [b] Deut. 31:20
27 [a] Ezek. 16:57 [1] Allowance of food
28 [a] Jer. 2:18, 36
29 [a] Ezek. 23:14–17
31 [a] Ezek. 16:24, 39 [b] Is. 52:3 [1] Place for pagan worship
33 [a] Hos. 8:9, 10 [1] Or *bribed*

Jerusalem's Lovers Will Abuse Her

35'Now then, O harlot, hear the word of
the LORD! 36Thus says the Lord GOD: "Because your filthiness was poured out and
your nakedness uncovered in your harlotry with your lovers, and with all your
abominable idols, and because of [a]the
blood of your children which you gave to
them, 37surely, therefore, [a]I will gather all
your lovers with whom you took pleasure,
all those you loved, *and* all those you hated; I will gather them from all around
against you and will uncover your nakedness to them, that they may see all your
nakedness. 38And I will judge you as
[a]women who break wedlock or [b]shed
blood are judged; I will bring blood upon
you in fury and jealousy. 39I will also give
you into their hand, and they shall throw
down your shrines and break down [a]your

36 a Jer. 2:34
37 a Lam. 1:8
38 a Lev. 20:10 b Gen. 9:6
39 a Ezek. 16:24, 31

AMY CARMICHAEL

God's destiny for Amy Carmichael's life (1867–1951) can be summed up in two words: "Go ye." One of the best-known missionaries in Christian history, Amy was born into a devout Irish Christian family. From childhood, she demonstrated the spunk, courage, and dedication to Jesus that would later enable her to do great exploits in His name.

Amy possessed enormous compassion—always comparing her struggles to the greater sufferings of Jesus Christ. In comparison to His sacrifice, she reasoned, no sacrifice of hers could cost too much. So sacrifice she did.

While still of prime marriageable age, Amy made the difficult and deliberate choice to be fully consecrated to God and His purposes, vowing to remain single for the rest of her life. Letting go of her dreams was agonizing; but in the end, she enjoyed a deeply intimate walk with God and became a spiritual mother to hundreds of children.

Amy gained strength to follow through with difficult decisions by reminding herself that "He goeth before." These words encouraged her to go first to Japan, then briefly to China, to Ceylon (modern-day Sri Lanka), and finally to India. In each place, she met unique struggles. She suffered from illnesses and physical challenges all of her adult life, with problems so severe in Japan that she was forced to leave—but not without making an impact by confronting the sin of idolatry and encouraging new Christians to burn their idols. In Ceylon, she continued that campaign by risking her life to visit Buddhist priests.

She moved from Ceylon to India and became a champion of children—rescuing them from the prostitution and ritual sacrifice practiced by the Hindus. This work incurred their wrath and brought Amy more than her share of lawsuits, threats, and unfriendly visits from Hindus demanding that the children be returned to their heinous duties in the temple. But Amy stood firm and became a refuge for countless children, snatching them from the kingdom of darkness and leading them into the kingdom of light.

Against seemingly unbeatable odds, Amy Carmichael gave her life to prayer, to winning souls for her beloved Jesus, and to one courageous act of mercy after another.

[1]high places. [b]They shall also strip you of
your clothes, take your beautiful jewelry,
and leave you naked and bare.
40[a]"They shall also bring up an assembly against you, [b]and they shall stone you
with stones and thrust you through with
their swords. 41They shall [a]burn your
houses with fire, and [b]execute judgments
on you in the sight of many women; and
I will make you [c]cease playing the harlot,
and you shall no longer hire lovers. 42So
[a]I will lay to rest My fury toward you, and
My jealousy shall depart from you. I will
be quiet, and be angry no more. 43Because
[a]you did not remember the days of your
youth, but [1]agitated Me with all these
things, surely [b]I will also recompense
your [2]deeds on *your own* head," says the
Lord GOD. "And you shall not commit
lewdness in addition to all your abominations.

More Wicked than Samaria and Sodom

44"Indeed everyone who quotes proverbs will use *this* proverb against you:
'Like mother, like daughter!' 45You *are*
your mother's daughter, [1]loathing husband and children; and you *are* the [a]sister
of your sisters, who loathed their husbands and children; [b]your mother *was* a
Hittite and your father an Amorite.
46"Your elder sister *is* Samaria, who
dwells with her daughters to the north of
you; and [a]your younger sister, who dwells
to the south of you, *is* Sodom and her
daughters. 47You did not walk in their
ways nor act according to their abominations; but, as *if that were* too little, [a]you
became more corrupt than they in all
your ways.
48"*As* I live," says the Lord GOD, "neither [a]your sister Sodom nor her daughters have done as you and your daughters
have done. 49Look, this was the iniquity of
your sister Sodom: She and her daughter
had pride, [a]fullness of food, and abundance of idleness; neither did she
strengthen the hand of the poor and
needy. 50And they were haughty and
[a]committed abomination before Me;
therefore [b]I took them away as [1]I saw *fit.*
51"Samaria did not commit [a]half of
your sins; but you have multiplied your
abominations more than they, and [b]have
justified your sisters by all the abominations which you have done. 52You who
judged your sisters, bear your own shame
also, because the sins which you committed were more abominable than theirs;
they are more righteous than you. Yes, be
disgraced also, and bear your own shame,
because you justified your sisters.
53[a]"When I bring back their captives,
the captives of Sodom and her daughters,
and the captives of Samaria and her
daughters, then *I will also bring back* [b]the
captives of your captivity among them,
54that you may bear your own shame and
be disgraced by all that you did when [a]you
comforted them. 55When your sisters,
Sodom and her daughters, return to their
former state, and Samaria and her daughters return to their former state, then you
and your daughters will return to your
former state. 56For your sister Sodom was
not a byword in your mouth in the days of
your pride, 57before your wickedness was
uncovered. It was like the time of the [a]re-
proach of the daughters of [1]Syria and all
those around her, and of [b]the daughters
of the Philistines, who despise you everywhere. 58[a]You have paid for your lewdness
and your abominations," says the LORD.
59For thus says the Lord GOD: "I will deal
with you as you have done, who [a]despised
[b]the oath by breaking the covenant.

An Everlasting Covenant

60"Nevertheless I will [a]remember My
covenant with you in the days of your
youth, and I will establish [b]an everlasting
covenant with you. 61Then [a]you will remember your ways and be ashamed, when
you receive your older and your younger
sisters; for I will give them to you for
[b]daughters, [c]but not because of My covenant with you. 62[a]And I will establish My
covenant with you. Then you shall know
that I *am* the LORD, 63that you may [a]re-
member and be ashamed, [b]and never
open your mouth anymore because of
your shame, when I provide you an atonement for all you have done," says the Lord
GOD.' "

The Eagles and the Vine

17 And the word of the LORD came to
me, saying, 2"Son of man, pose a
riddle, and speak a [a]parable to the house
of Israel, 3and say, 'Thus says the Lord
GOD:

[a]"A great eagle with large wings and
long pinions,

39 b Hos. 2:3 *1* Places for pagan worship
40 a Ezek. 23:45–47 b John 8:5, 7
41 a Deut. 13:16 b Ezek. 5:8; 23:10, 48 c Ezek. 23:27
42 a Ezek. 5:13; 21:17
43 a Ps. 78:42 b Ezek. 9:10; 11:21; 22:31 *1* So with LXX, Syr., Tg., Vg.; MT *were agitated with Me* *2* Lit. *way*
45 a Ezek. 23:2–4 b Ezek. 16:3 *1* Or *despising*
46 a Is. 1:10
47 a Ezek. 5:6, 7
48 a Matt. 10:15; 11:24
49 a Gen. 13:10
50 a Gen. 13:13; 18:20; 19:5 b Gen. 19:24 *1* Vg. *you saw;* LXX *he saw;* Tg. *as was revealed to Me*
51 a Ezek. 23:11 b Jer. 3:8–11
53 a Is. 1:9 b Jer. 20:16
54 a Ezek. 14:22
57 a 2 Kin. 16:5 b Ezek. 16:27 *1* Heb. *Aram;* so with MT, LXX, Tg., Vg.; many Heb. mss., Syr. *Edom*
58 a Ezek. 23:49
59 a Ezek. 17:13 b Deut. 29:12
60 a Ps. 106:45 b Is. 55:3
61 a Ezek. 20:43; 36:31 b [Gal. 4:26] c Jer. 31:31
62 a Hos. 2:19, 20
63 a Ezek. 36:31, 32 b [Rom. 3:19]

CHAPTER 17
2 a Ezek. 20:49; 24:3 **3** a Ezek. 17:12

Full of feathers of various colors,
Came to Lebanon
And [b]took from the cedar the
highest branch.
4 He cropped off its topmost young
twig
And carried it to a land of trade;
He set it in a city of merchants.
5 Then he took some of the seed of
the land
And planted it in [a]a fertile field;
He placed *it* by abundant waters
And set it [b]like a willow tree.
6 And it grew and became a
spreading vine [a]of low stature;
Its branches turned toward him,
But its roots were under it.
So it became a vine,
Brought forth branches,
And put forth shoots.

7 "But there was [1]another great eagle
with large wings and many
feathers;
And behold, [a]this vine bent its
roots toward him,
And stretched its branches toward
him,
From the garden terrace where it
had been planted,
That he might water it.
8 It was planted in [1]good soil by
many waters,
To bring forth branches, bear fruit,
And become a majestic vine." '

9"Say, 'Thus says the Lord GOD:

"Will it thrive?
[a]Will he not pull up its roots,
Cut off its fruit,
And leave it to wither?
All of its spring leaves will wither,
And no great power or many people
Will be needed to pluck it up by its
roots.
10 Behold, *it is* planted,
Will it thrive?
[a]Will it not utterly wither when the
east wind touches it?
It will wither in the garden terrace
where it grew." ' "

11Moreover the word of the LORD came
to me, saying, 12"Say now to [a]the rebellious house: 'Do you not know what these
things mean?' Tell *them,* 'Indeed [b]the
king of Babylon went to Jerusalem and
took its king and princes, and led them
with him to Babylon. 13[a]And he took the
king's offspring, made a covenant with
him, [b]and put him under oath. He also
took away the mighty of the land, 14that
the kingdom might be [a]brought low and
not lift itself up, *but* that by keeping his
covenant it might stand. 15But [a]he rebelled against him by sending his ambassadors to Egypt, [b]that they might give
him horses and many people. [c]Will he
prosper? Will he who does such *things* escape? Can he break a covenant and still be
delivered?

16'*As* I live,' says the Lord GOD, 'surely
[a]in the place *where* the king *dwells* who
made him king, whose oath he despised
and whose covenant he broke—with him
in the midst of Babylon he shall die.
17[a]Nor will Pharaoh with *his* mighty army
and great company do anything in the
war, [b]when they heap up a siege mound
and build a [1]wall to cut off many persons.
18Since he despised the oath by breaking
the covenant, and in fact [a]gave[1] his hand
and still did all these *things,* he shall not
escape.' "

19Therefore thus says the Lord GOD: "*As*
I live, surely My oath which he despised,
and My covenant which he broke, I will
recompense on his own head. 20I will
[a]spread My net over him, and he shall be
taken in My snare. I will bring him to Babylon and [b]try him there for the [1]treason
which he committed against Me. 21[a]All
his [1]fugitives with all his troops shall fall
by the sword, and those who remain shall
be [b]scattered to every wind; and you shall
know that I, the LORD, have spoken."

Israel Exalted at Last

22Thus says the Lord GOD: "I will take
also *one* of the highest [a]branches of the
high cedar and set *it* out. I will crop off
from the topmost of its young twigs [b]a
tender one, and will [c]plant *it* on a high
and prominent mountain. 23[a]On the
mountain height of Israel I will plant it;
and it will bring forth boughs, and bear
fruit, and be a majestic cedar. [b]Under it
will dwell birds of every sort; in the shadow of its branches they will dwell. 24And
all the trees of the field shall know that I,
the LORD, [a]have brought down the high
tree and exalted the low tree, dried up the
green tree and made the dry tree flourish;
[b]I, the LORD, have spoken and have
done *it.*"

3 b 2 Kin. 24:12
5 a Deut. 8:7–9 b Is. 44:4
6 a Ezek. 17:14
7 a Ezek. 17:15 1 So with LXX, Syr., Vg.; MT, Tg. *one*
8 1 Lit. *a good field*
9 a 2 Kin. 25:7
10 a Hos. 13:15
12 a Ezek. 2:3–5; 12:9 b 2 Kin. 24:11–16
13 a 2 Kin. 24:17 b 2 Chr. 36:13
14 a Ezek. 29:14
15 a 2 Kin. 24:20 b Deut. 17:16 c Ezek. 17:9
16 a Ezek. 12:13
17 a Jer. 37:7 b Jer. 52:4 1 Or *siege wall*
18 a 1 Chr. 29:24 1 Took an oath
20 a Ezek. 12:13 b Ezek. 20:36 1 Lit. *unfaithful act*
21 a Ezek. 12:14 b Ezek. 12:15; 22:15 1 So with MT, Vg.; many Heb. mss., Syr. *choice men;* Tg. *mighty men;* LXX omits *All his fugitives*
22 a [Zech. 3:8] b Is. 53:2 c [Ps. 2:6]
23 a [Is. 2:2, 3] b Dan. 4:12
24 a Amos 9:11 b Ezek. 22:14

A False Proverb Refuted

18 The word of the LORD came to me
again, saying, 2"What do you mean
when you use this proverb concerning the
land of Israel, saying:

'The [a]fathers have eaten sour
grapes,
And the children's teeth are set on
edge'?

3"*As* I live," says the Lord GOD, "you
shall no longer use this proverb in Israel.

4 "Behold, all souls are [a]Mine;
The soul of the father
As well as the soul of the son is
Mine;
[b]The soul who sins shall die.
5 But if a man is just
And does what is lawful and right;
6 [a]If he has not eaten [1]on the
mountains,
Nor lifted up his eyes to the idols of
the house of Israel,
Nor [b]defiled his neighbor's wife,
Nor approached [c]a woman during
her impurity;
7 If he has not [a]oppressed anyone,
But has restored to the debtor his
[b]pledge;
Has robbed no one by violence,
But has [c]given his bread to the
hungry
And covered the naked with
[d]clothing;
8 If he has not [1]exacted [a]usury
Nor taken any increase,
But has withdrawn his hand from
iniquity
And [b]executed true [2]judgment
between man and man;
9 *If* he has walked in My statutes
And kept My judgments faithfully—
He *is* just;
He shall surely [a]live!"
Says the Lord GOD.

10 "If he begets a son *who is* a robber
Or [a]a shedder of blood,
Who does any of these *things*
11 And does none of those *duties,*
But has eaten [1]on the mountains
Or defiled his neighbor's wife;
12 If he has oppressed the poor and
needy,
Robbed by violence,
Not restored the pledge,
Lifted his eyes to the idols,
Or [a]committed abomination;

CHAPTER 18
2 a Lam. 5:7
4 a Num. 16:22; 27:16
b [Rom. 6:23]
6 a Ezek. 22:9
b Lev. 18:20; 20:10
c Lev. 18:19; 20:18
1 At the mountain shrines
7 a Ex. 22:21
b Deut. 24:12
c Deut. 15:7, 11
d Is. 58:7
8 a Ex. 22:25
b Zech. 8:16
1 Lent money at interest
2 *justice*
9 a Amos 5:4
10 a Num. 35:31
11 1 At the mountain shrines
12 a Ezek. 8:6, 17
13 a Lev. 20:9, 11–13, 16, 27
15 a Ezek. 18:6
1 At the mountain shrines
17 1 So with MT, Tg., Vg.; LXX *iniquity* (cf. v. 8)
18 a Ezek. 3:18
19 a Ex. 20:5

13 If he has exacted usury
Or taken increase—
Shall he then live?
He shall not live!
If he has done any of these
abominations,
He shall surely die;
[a]His blood shall be upon him.

14 "*If,* however, he begets a son
Who sees all the sins which his
father has done,
And considers but does not do
likewise;
15 [a]*Who* has not eaten [1]on the
mountains,
Nor lifted his eyes to the idols of
the house of Israel,
Nor defiled his neighbor's wife;
16 Has not oppressed anyone,
Nor withheld a pledge,
Nor robbed by violence,
But has given his bread to the
hungry
And covered the naked with
clothing;
17 *Who* has withdrawn his hand from
[1]the poor
And not received usury or increase,
But has executed My judgments
And walked in My statutes—
He shall not die for the iniquity of
his father;
He shall surely live!

18 "*As for* his father,
Because he cruelly oppressed,
Robbed his brother by violence,
And did what *is* not good among
his people,
Behold, [a]he shall die for his
iniquity.

But if our Leader
we pursue
We every evil shun.

CHARLES WESLEY

Turn and Live

19"Yet you say, 'Why [a]should the son
not bear the guilt of the father?' Because

the son has done what is lawful and right,
and has kept all My statutes and observed
them, he shall surely live. [20][a]The soul
who sins shall die. [b]The son shall not bear
the guilt of the father, nor the father bear
the guilt of the son. [c]The righteousness
of the righteous shall be upon himself,
[d]and the wickedness of the wicked shall
be upon himself.

I pray that ____ will repent, and turn from all their transgressions, so that iniquity will not be their ruin. May they cast away all the transgressions they have committed, and get a new heart and a new spirit.

FROM EZEKIEL 18:30, 31

[21]"But [a]if a wicked man turns from all
his sins which he has committed, keeps
all My statutes, and does what is lawful
and right, he shall surely live; he shall not
die. [22][a]None of the transgressions which
he has committed shall be remembered
against him; because of the righteousness
which he has done, he shall [b]live. [23][a]Do I
have any pleasure at all that the wicked
should die?" says the Lord GOD, *"and* not
that he should turn from his ways and
live?

[24]"But [a]when a righteous man turns
away from his righteousness and commits
iniquity, and does according to all the
abominations that the wicked *man* does,
shall he live? [b]All the righteousness which
he has done shall not be remembered; because of the unfaithfulness of which he is
guilty and the sin which he has committed, because of them he shall die.

[25]"Yet you say, [a]'The way of the Lord is
not fair.' Hear now, O house of Israel, is it
not My way which is fair, and your ways
which are not fair? [26][a]When a righteous
man turns away from his righteousness,
commits iniquity, and dies in it, it is because of the iniquity which he has done
that he dies. [27]Again, [a]when a wicked *man*
turns away from the wickedness which he
committed, and does what is lawful and
right, he preserves himself alive. [28]Be-
cause he [a]considers and turns away from
all the transgressions which he committed, he shall surely live; he shall not die.
[29][a]Yet the house of Israel says, 'The way of
the Lord is not fair.' O house of Israel, is
it not My ways which are fair, and your
ways which are not fair?

[30][a]"Therefore I will judge you, O house
of Israel, every one according to his ways,"
says the Lord GOD. [b]"Repent, and turn
from all your transgressions, so that iniquity will not be your ruin. [31][a]Cast away
from you all the transgressions which you
have committed, and get yourselves a
[b]new heart and a new spirit. For why
should you die, O house of Israel? [32]For [a]I
have no pleasure in the death of one who
dies," says the Lord GOD. "Therefore turn
and [b]live!"

Israel Degraded

19 "Moreover [a]take up a lamentation
for the princes of Israel, [2]and say:

'What *is* your mother? A lioness:
She lay down among the lions;
Among the young lions she
nourished her cubs.
3 She brought up one of her cubs,
And [a]he became a young lion;
He learned to catch prey,
And he devoured men.
4 The nations also heard of him;
He was trapped in their pit,
And they brought him with chains
to the land of [a]Egypt.
5 'When she saw that she waited, *that*
her hope was lost,
She took [a]another of her cubs *and*
made him a young lion.
6 [a]He roved among the lions,
And [b]became a young lion;
He learned to catch prey;
He devoured men.
7 [1]He knew their desolate places,
And laid waste their cities;
The land with its fullness was
desolated
By the noise of his roaring.
8 [a]Then the nations set against him
from the provinces on every side,
And spread their net over him;
[b]He was trapped in their pit.
9 [a]They put him in a cage with
[1]chains,
And brought him to the king of
Babylon;

---

20 a Ezek. 18:4 b Deut. 24:16 c Is. 3:10, 11 d Rom. 2:6–9
21 a Ezek. 18:27; 33:12, 19
22 a Ezek. 18:24; 33:16 b [Ps. 18:20–24]
23 a [Ezek. 18:32; 33:11]
24 a Ezek. 3:20; 18:26; 33:18 b [2 Pet. 2:20]
25 a Ezek. 18:29; 33:17, 20
26 a Ezek. 18:24
27 a Ezek. 18:21
28 a Ezek. 18:14
29 a Ezek. 18:25
30 a Ezek. 7:3; 33:20 b Matt. 3:2
31 a Eph. 4:22, 23 b Jer. 32:39
32 a Lam. 3:33 b [Prov. 4:2, 5, 6]

CHAPTER 19
1 a Ezek. 26:17; 27:2
3 a 2 Kin. 23:31, 32
4 a 2 Kin. 23:33, 34
5 a 2 Kin. 23:34
6 a 2 Kin. 24:8, 9 b Ezek. 19:3
7 1 LXX *He stood in insolence;* Tg. *He destroyed its palaces;* Vg. *He learned to make widows*
8 a 2 Kin. 24:2, 11 b Ezek. 19:4
9 a 2 Chr. 36:6 1 Or *hooks*

They brought him in nets,
That his voice should no longer be
heard on [b]the mountains of
Israel.

10 'Your mother *was* [a]like a vine in
your [1]bloodline,
Planted by the waters,
[b]Fruitful and full of branches
Because of many waters.
11 She had strong branches for
scepters of rulers.
[a]She towered in stature above the
thick branches,
And was seen in her height amid
the [1]dense foliage.
12 But she was [a]plucked up in fury,
She was cast down to the ground,
And the [b]east wind dried her fruit.
Her strong branches were broken
and withered;
The fire consumed them.
13 And now she *is* planted in the
wilderness,
In a dry and thirsty land.
14 [a]Fire has come out from a rod of
her branches
And devoured her fruit,
So that she has no strong branch—
a scepter for ruling.' "

[b]This *is* a lamentation, and has become
a lamentation.

The Rebellions of Israel

20 It came to pass in the seventh year,
in the fifth *month,* on the tenth
day of the month, *that* [a]certain of the elders of Israel came to inquire of the LORD,
and sat before me. 2Then the word of the
LORD came to me, saying, 3"Son of man,
speak to the elders of Israel, and say to
them, 'Thus says the Lord GOD: "Have you
come to inquire of Me? *As* I live," says the
Lord GOD, [a]"I will not be inquired of by
you." ' 4Will you judge them, son of man,
will you judge *them?* Then [a]make known
to them the abominations of their fathers.
5"Say to them, 'Thus says the Lord GOD:
"On the day when [a]I chose Israel and
raised My hand in an oath to the descendants of the house of Jacob, and made Myself [b]known to them in the land of Egypt,
I raised My hand in an oath to them, saying, [c]'I *am* the LORD your God.' 6On that
day I raised My hand in an oath to them,
[a]to bring them out of the land of Egypt
into a land that I had searched out for
them, [b]'flowing with milk and honey,'
[c]the glory of all lands. 7Then I said to
them, 'Each of you, [a]throw away [b]the
abominations which are before his eyes,
and do not defile yourselves with [c]the
idols of Egypt. I *am* the LORD your God.'
8But they rebelled against Me and would
not [1]obey Me. They did not all cast away
the abominations which were before their
eyes, nor did they forsake the idols of
Egypt. Then I said, 'I will [a]pour out My
fury on them and fulfill My anger against
them in the midst of the land of Egypt.'
9[a]But I acted for My name's sake, that it
should not be profaned before the Gentiles among whom they *were,* in whose
sight I had made Myself [b]known to them,
to bring them out of the land of Egypt.
10"Therefore I [a]made them go out of
the land of Egypt and brought them into
the wilderness. 11[a]And I gave them My
statutes and [1]showed them My judgments, [b]'which, *if* a man does, he shall
live by them.' 12Moreover I also gave them
My [a]Sabbaths, to be a sign between them
and Me, that they might know that I *am*
the LORD who sanctifies them. 13Yet the
house of Israel [a]rebelled against Me in
the wilderness; they did not walk in My
statutes; they [b]despised My judgments,
[c]'which, *if* a man does, he shall live by
them'; and they greatly [d]defiled My Sabbaths. Then I said I would pour out My
fury on them in the [e]wilderness, to consume them. 14[a]But I acted for My name's
sake, that it should not be profaned before
the Gentiles, in whose sight I had brought
them out. 15So [a]I also raised My hand in
an oath to them in the wilderness, that I
would not bring them into the land which
I had given *them,* [b]'flowing with milk and
honey,' [c]the glory of all lands, 16[a]because
they despised My judgments and did not
walk in My statutes, but profaned My Sabbaths; for [b]their heart went after their
idols. 17[a]Nevertheless My eye spared them
from destruction. I did not make an end
of them in the wilderness.
18"But I said to their children in the
wilderness, 'Do not walk in the statutes
of your fathers, nor observe their judgments, nor defile yourselves with their
idols. 19I *am* the LORD your God: [a]Walk in
My statutes, keep My judgments, and do
them; 20[a]hallow My Sabbaths, and they
will be a sign between Me and you, that
you may know that I *am* the LORD your
God.'

9 [b]Ezek. 6:2
10 [a]Ezek. 17:6 [b]Deut. 8:7–9 [1]Lit. *blood,* so with MT, Syr., Vg.; LXX *like a flower on a pomegranate tree;* Tg. *in your likeness*
11 [a]Dan. 4:11 [1]Or *many branches*
12 [a]Jer. 31:27, 28 [b]Hos. 13:5
14 [a]Judg. 9:15 [b]Lam. 2:5

CHAPTER 20
1 [a]Ezek. 8:1, 11, 12; 14:1
3 [a]Ezek. 7:26; 14:3
4 [a]Ezek. 16:2; 22:2
5 [a]Ex. 6:6–8 [b]Deut. 4:34 [c]Ex. 20:2
6 [a]Jer. 32:22 [b]Ex. 3:8 [c]Jer. 11:5; 32:22
7 [a]Ezek. 18:31 [b]2 Chr. 15:8 [c]Lev. 18:3
8 [a]Ezek. 7:8 [1]Lit. *listen to*
9 [a]Num. 14:13 [b]Josh. 2:10; 9:9, 10
10 [a]Ex. 13:18
11 [a]Neh. 9:13 [b]Lev. 18:5 [1]Lit. *made known to*
12 [a]Deut. 5:12
13 [a]Num. 14:22 [b]Prov. 1:25 [c]Lev. 18:5 [d]Ex. 16:27 [e]Num. 14:29
14 [a]Ezek. 20:9, 20
15 [a]Num. 14:28 [b]Ex. 3:8 [c]Ezek. 20:6
16 [a]Ezek. 20:13, 24 [b]Amos 5:25
17 [a][Ps. 78:38]
19 [a]Deut. 5:32
20 [a]Jer. 17:22

21"Notwithstanding, [a]the children rebelled against Me; they did not walk in My statutes, and were not careful to observe My judgments, [b]'which, *if* a man does, he shall live by them'; but they profaned My Sabbaths. Then I said I would pour out My fury on them and fulfill My anger against them in the wilderness. 22Nevertheless I [1]withdrew My hand and acted for My name's sake, that it should not be profaned in the sight of the Gentiles, in whose sight I had brought them out. 23Also I raised My hand in an oath to those in the wilderness, that [a]I would scatter them among the Gentiles and disperse them throughout the countries, 24[a]because they had not executed My judgments, but had despised My statutes, profaned My Sabbaths, and [b]their eyes were fixed on their fathers' idols.

25"Therefore [a]I also gave them up to statutes *that were* not good, and judgments by which they could not live; 26and I pronounced them unclean because of their ritual gifts, in that they caused all [1]their firstborn to pass [a]through *the fire,* that I might make them desolate and that they [b]might know that I am the LORD." '

> *Be much in secret fellowship with God. . . . Let prayer be the key of the morning and the bolt at night.*
>
> PHILIP HENRY

27"Therefore, son of man, speak to the house of Israel, and say to them, 'Thus says the Lord GOD: "In this too your fathers have [a]blasphemed Me, by being unfaithful to Me. 28When I brought them into the land *concerning* which I had raised My hand in an oath to give them, and [a]they saw all the high hills and all the thick trees, there they offered their sacrifices and provoked Me with their offerings. There they also sent up their [b]sweet aroma and poured out their drink offerings. 29Then I said to them, 'What *is* this [1]high place to which you go?' So its name is called [2]Bamah to this day." ' 30Therefore say to the house of Israel, 'Thus says the Lord GOD: "Are you defiling yourselves in the manner of your [a]fathers, and committing harlotry according to their [b]abominations? 31For when you offer [a]your gifts and make your sons pass through the fire, you defile yourselves with all your idols, even to this day. So shall I be inquired of by you, O house of Israel? *As* I live," says the Lord GOD, "I will [b]not be inquired of by you. 32[a]What you have in your mind shall never be, when you say, 'We will be like the Gentiles, like the families in other countries, serving wood and stone.'

God Will Restore Israel

33"*As* I live," says the Lord GOD, "surely with a mighty hand, [a]with an outstretched arm, and with fury poured out, I will rule over you. 34I will bring you out from the peoples and gather you out of the countries where you are scattered, with a mighty hand, with an outstretched arm, and with fury poured out. 35And I will bring you into the wilderness of the peoples, and there [a]I will plead My case with you face to face. 36[a]Just as I pleaded My case with your fathers in the wilderness of the land of Egypt, so I will plead My case with you," says the Lord GOD.

37"I will make you [a]pass under the rod, and I will bring you into the bond of the [b]covenant; 38[a]I will purge the rebels from among you, and those who transgress against Me; I will bring them out of the country where they dwell, but [b]they shall not enter the land of Israel. Then you will know that I *am* the LORD.

39"As for you, O house of Israel," thus says the Lord GOD: [a]"Go, serve every one of you his idols—and hereafter—if you will not obey Me; [b]but profane My holy name no more with your gifts and your idols. 40For [a]on My holy mountain, on the mountain height of Israel," says the Lord GOD, "there [b]all the house of Israel, all of them in the land, shall serve Me; there [c]I will accept them, and there I will require your offerings and the firstfruits of your [1]sacrifices, together with all your holy things. 41I will accept you as a [a]sweet aroma when I bring you out from the peoples and gather you out of the countries where you have been scattered; and I will be hallowed in you before the Gentiles. 42[a]Then you shall know that I *am* the LORD, [b]when I bring you into the land of Israel, into the country *for* which I raised My hand in an oath to give to your fathers. 43And [a]there

21 a Num. 25:1 b Lev. 18:5
22 *1* Refrained from judgment
23 a Lev. 26:33
24 a Ezek. 20:13, 16 b Ezek. 6:9
25 a Rom. 1:24
26 a Jer. 32:35 b Ezek. 6:7; 20:12, 20 *1* Lit. *that open the womb*
27 a Rom. 2:24
28 a Ezek. 6:13 b Ezek. 16:19
29 *1* Place for pagan worship *2* Lit. *High Place*
30 a Judg. 2:19 b Jer. 7:26; 16:12
31 a Ezek. 16:20; 20:26 b Ezek. 20:3
32 a Ezek. 11:5
33 a Jer. 21:5
35 a Jer. 2:9, 35; Ezek. 17:20
36 a Num. 14:21–23, 28
37 a Lev. 27:32 b Ps. 89:30–34
38 a Ezek. 34:17 b Jer. 44:14
39 a Amos 4:4 b Is. 1:13–15
40 a Is. 2:2, 3 b Ezek. 37:22 c Zech. 8:20–22 *1 offerings*
41 a Phil. 4:18
42 a Ezek. 36:23; 38:23 b Ezek. 11:17; 34:13; 36:24
43 a Ezek. 16:61

you shall remember your ways and all
your doings with which you were defiled;
and [b]you shall [1]loathe yourselves in your
own sight because of all the evils that you
have committed. 44[a]Then you shall know
that I *am* the LORD, when I have dealt with
you [b]for My name's sake, not according to
your wicked ways nor according to your
corrupt doings, O house of Israel," says
the Lord GOD.' "

Fire in the Forest

45Furthermore the word of the LORD
came to me, saying, 46[a]"Son of man, set
your face toward the south; [1]preach
against the south and prophesy against
the forest land, the [2]South, 47and say to
the forest of the South, 'Hear the word of
the LORD! Thus says the Lord GOD: "Behold, [a]I will kindle a fire in you, and it
shall devour [b]every green tree and every
dry tree in you; the blazing flame shall not
be quenched, and all faces [c]from the
south to the north shall be scorched by it.
48All flesh shall see that I, the LORD, have
kindled it; it shall not be quenched." ' "
49Then I said, "Ah, Lord GOD! They say
of me, 'Does he not speak [a]parables?' "

Babylon, the Sword of God

21 And the word of the LORD came
to me, saying, 2[a]"Son of man, set
your face toward Jerusalem, [b]preach[1]
against the holy places, and prophesy
against the land of Israel; 3and say to the
land of Israel, 'Thus says the LORD: "Behold, I *am* [a]against you, and I will draw
My sword out of its sheath and cut off
both [b]righteous and wicked from you.
4Because I will cut off both righteous and
wicked from you, therefore My sword
shall go out of its sheath against all flesh
[a]from south *to* north, 5that all flesh may
know that I, the LORD, have drawn My
sword out of its sheath; it [a]shall not return anymore." ' 6[a]Sigh therefore, son of
man, with [1]a breaking heart, and sigh
with bitterness before their eyes. 7And it
shall be when they say to you, 'Why are
you sighing?' that you shall answer, 'Because of the news; when it comes, every
heart will melt, [a]all hands will be feeble,
every spirit will faint, and all knees will be
weak *as* water. Behold, it is coming and
shall be brought to pass,' says the Lord
GOD."

8Again the word of the LORD came to
me, saying, 9"Son of man, prophesy and
say, 'Thus says the LORD!' Say:

[a]'A sword, a sword is sharpened
And also polished!
10 Sharpened to make a dreadful
slaughter,
Polished to flash like lightning!
Should we then make mirth?
It despises the scepter of My son,
As it does all wood.
11 And He has given it to be
polished,
That it may be handled;
This sword is sharpened, and it is
polished
To be given into the hand of [a]the
slayer.'

12 "Cry and wail, son of man;
For it will be against My people,
Against all the princes of Israel.
Terrors including the sword will be
against My people;
Therefore [a]strike *your* thigh.
13 "Because *it is* [a]a testing,
And what if *the sword* despises even
the scepter?
[b]*The scepter* shall be no *more*,"

says the Lord GOD.

14 "You therefore, son of man,
prophesy,
And [a]strike *your* hands together.
The third time let the sword do
double *damage*.
It *is* the sword *that* slays,
The sword that slays the great *men*,
That enters their [b]private chambers.
15 I have set the point of the sword
against all their gates,
That the heart may melt and many
may stumble.
Ah! [a]*It is* made bright;
It is grasped for slaughter:
16 "Swords[a][1] at the ready!
Thrust right!
Set your blade!
Thrust left—
Wherever your [2]edge is ordered!
17 "I also will [a]beat My fists together,
And [b]I will cause My fury to rest;
I, the LORD, have spoken."

18The word of the LORD came to me
again, saying: 19"And son of man, appoint
for yourself two ways for the sword of the

---

43 b Lev. 26:39 · *1* Or *despise*
44 a Ezek. 24:24 · b Ezek. 36:22
46 a Ezek. 21:2 · *1* *proclaim*, lit. *drop* · *2* Heb. *Negev*
47 a Jer. 21:14 · b Luke 23:31 · c Ezek. 21:4
49 a Ezek. 12:9; 17:2

CHAPTER 21
2 a Ezek. 20:46 · b Amos 7:16 · *1* *proclaim*, lit. *drop*
3 a Ezek. 5:8 · b Job 9:22
4 a Ezek. 20:47
5 a [Is. 45:23; 55:11]
6 a Is. 22:4 · *1* Emotional distress, lit. *the breaking of your loins*
7 a Ezek. 7:17
9 a Deut. 32:41
11 a Ezek. 21:19
12 a Jer. 31:19
13 a Job 9:23 · b Ezek. 21:27
14 a Num. 24:10 · b 1 Kin. 20:30
15 a Ezek. 21:10, 28
16 a Ezek. 14:17 · *1* Lit. *Sharpen yourself!* or *Unite yourself!* · *2* Lit. *face*
17 a Ezek. 22:13 · b Ezek. 5:13; 16:42; 24:13

king of Babylon to go; both of them shall
go from the same land. Make a sign; put
it at the head of the road to the city. 20Ap-
point a road for the sword to go to [a]Rab-
bah of the Ammonites, and to Judah, into
fortified Jerusalem. 21For the king of Babylon stands at the parting of the road, at
the fork of the two roads, to use divination: he shakes the arrows, he consults
the [1]images, he looks at the liver. 22In his
right hand is the divination for Jerusalem:
to set up battering rams, to call for a
slaughter, to [a]lift the voice with shouting,
[b]to set battering rams against the gates,
to heap up a *siege* mound, and to build a
wall. 23And it will be to them like a false
divination in the eyes of those who [a]have
sworn oaths with them; but he will bring
their iniquity to remembrance, that they
may be taken.
24"Therefore thus says the Lord GOD:
'Because you have made your iniquity to
be remembered, in that your transgressions are uncovered, so that in all your
doings your sins appear—because you
have come to remembrance, you shall be
taken in hand.
25'Now to you, O [a]profane, wicked
prince of Israel, [b]whose day has come,
whose iniquity *shall* end, 26thus says the
Lord GOD:

"Remove the turban, and take off the
crown;
Nothing *shall remain* the same.
[a]Exalt the humble, and humble the
exalted.
27 [1]Overthrown, overthrown,
I will make it overthrown!
[a]It shall be no *longer,*
Until He comes whose right it is,
And I will give it *to* [b]*Him.*" '

A Sword Against the Ammonites

28"And you, son of man, prophesy and
say, 'Thus says the Lord GOD [a]concerning
the Ammonites and concerning their reproach,' and say:

'A sword, a sword *is* drawn,
Polished for slaughter,
For consuming, for flashing—
29 While they [a]see false visions for
you,
While they divine a lie to you,
To bring you on the necks of the
wicked, the slain
[b]Whose day has come,
Whose iniquity *shall* end.
30 'Return[a] *it* to its sheath.
[b]I will judge you
In the place where you were
created,
[c]In the land of your [1]nativity.
31 I will [a]pour out My indignation on
you;
I will [b]blow against you with the
fire of My wrath,
And deliver you into the hands of
brutal men *who are* skillful to
[c]destroy.
32 You shall be fuel for the fire;
Your blood shall be in the midst of
the land.
[a]You shall not be remembered,
For I the LORD have spoken.' "

Sins of Jerusalem

22 Moreover the word of the LORD
came to me, saying, 2"Now, son of
man, [a]will you judge, will you judge [b]the
bloody city? Yes, show her all her abominations! 3Then say, 'Thus says the Lord
GOD: "The city sheds [a]blood in her own
midst, that her time may come; and she
makes idols within herself to defile herself. 4You have become guilty by the blood
which you have [a]shed, and have defiled
yourself with the idols which you have
made. You have caused your days to draw
near, and have come to *the end of* your
years; [b]therefore I have made you a reproach to the nations, and a mockery to
all countries. 5*Those* near and *those* far
from you will mock you as [1]infamous *and*
full of tumult.
6"Look, [a]the princes of Israel: each one
has used his [1]power to shed blood in you.
7In you they have [a]made light of father
and mother; in your midst they have [b]op-
pressed the stranger; in you they have
mistreated the [1]fatherless and the widow.
8You have despised My holy things and
[a]profaned My Sabbaths. 9In you are [a]men
who slander to cause bloodshed; [b]in you
are those who eat on the mountains; in
your midst they commit lewdness. 10In
you men [a]uncover their fathers' nakedness; in you they violate women who are
[b]set apart during their impurity. 11One
commits abomination [a]with his neighbor's wife; [b]another lewdly defiles his
daughter-in-law; and another in you vio-
lates his sister, his father's [c]daughter. 12In
you [a]they take bribes to shed blood; [b]you

20 [a]Jer. 49:2
21 [1]Heb. *teraphim*
22 [a]Jer. 51:14 [b]Ezek. 4:2
23 [a]Ezek. 17:16, 18
25 [a]Jer. 52:2 [b]Ezek. 21:29
26 [a]Luke 1:52
27 [a][Luke 1:32, 33] [b][Jer. 23:5, 6] [1]Or *Distortion, Ruin*
28 [a]Ezek. 25:1–7
29 [a]Ezek. 12:24; 13:6–9; 22:28 [b]Job 18:20
30 [a]Jer. 47:6, 7 [b]Gen. 15:14 [c]Ezek. 16:3 [1]Or *origin*
31 [a]Ezek. 7:8 [b]Ezek. 22:20, 21 [c]Hab. 1:6–10
32 [a]Ezek. 25:10

CHAPTER 22
2 [a]Ezek. 20:4 [b]Nah. 3:1
3 [a]Ezek. 24:6, 7
4 [a]2 Kin. 21:16 [b]Deut. 28:37
5 [1]Lit. *defiled of name*
6 [a]Is. 1:23 [1]Lit. *arm*
7 [a]Lev. 20:9 [b]Ex. 22:22 [1]Lit. *orphan*
8 [a]Lev. 19:30
9 [a]Lev. 19:16 [b]Ezek. 18:6, 11
10 [a]Lev. 18:7, 8 [b]Lev. 18:19; 20:18
11 [a]Ezek. 18:11 [b]Lev. 18:15 [c]Lev. 18:9
12 [a]Ex. 23:8 [b]Ex. 22:25

take usury and increase; you have made profit from your neighbors by extortion, and [c]have forgotten Me," says the Lord GOD.

13"Behold, therefore, I [a]beat My fists at the dishonest profit which you have made, and at the bloodshed which has been in your midst. 14[a]Can your heart endure, or can your hands remain strong, in the days when I shall deal with you? [b]I, the LORD, have spoken, and will do *it.* 15[a]I will scatter you among the nations, disperse you throughout the countries, and [b]remove your filthiness completely from you. 16You shall defile yourself in the sight of the nations; then [a]you shall know that I *am* the LORD." ' "

Israel in the Furnace

17The word of the LORD came to me, saying, 18"Son of man, [a]the house of Israel has become dross to Me; they *are* all bronze, tin, iron, and lead, in the midst of a [b]furnace; they have become dross from silver. 19Therefore thus says the Lord GOD: 'Because you have all become dross, therefore behold, I will gather you into the midst of Jerusalem. 20*As men* gather silver, bronze, iron, lead, and tin into the midst of a furnace, to blow fire on it, to [a]melt *it;* so I will gather *you* in My anger and in My fury, and I will leave *you there* and melt you. 21Yes, I will gather you and blow on you with the fire of My wrath, and you shall be melted in its midst. 22As silver is melted in the midst of a furnace, so shall you be melted in its midst; then you shall know that I, the LORD, have [a]poured out My fury on you.' "

Israel's Wicked Leaders

23And the word of the LORD came to me, saying, 24"Son of man, say to her: 'You *are* a land that is [a]not [1]cleansed or rained on in the day of indignation.' 25[a]The conspiracy of her [1]prophets in her midst is like a roaring lion tearing the prey; they [b]have devoured [2]people; [c]they have taken treasure and precious things; they have made many widows in her midst. 26[a]Her priests have [1]violated My law and [b]profaned My holy things; they have not [c]distinguished between the holy and unholy, nor have they made known *the difference* between the unclean and the clean; and they have hidden their eyes from My Sabbaths, so that I am profaned among them. 27Her [a]princes in her midst *are* like wolves tearing the prey, to shed blood, to destroy [1]people, and to get dishonest gain. 28[a]Her prophets plastered them with untempered *mortar,* [b]seeing false visions, and divining [c]lies for them, saying, 'Thus says the Lord GOD,' when the LORD had not spoken. 29The people of the land have used oppressions, committed robbery, and mistreated the poor and needy; and they wrongfully [a]oppress the stranger. 30[a]So I sought for a man among them who would [b]make a wall, and [c]stand in the gap before Me on behalf of the land, that I should not destroy it; but I found no one. 31Therefore I have [a]poured out My indignation on them; I have consumed them with the fire of My wrath; and I have recompensed [b]their deeds on their own heads," says the Lord GOD.

Two Harlot Sisters

23 The word of the LORD came again to me, saying:

2 "Son of man, there were [a]two
women,
The daughters of one mother.
3 [a]They committed harlotry in Egypt,
They committed harlotry in [b]their
youth;
Their breasts were there embraced,
Their virgin bosom was there
pressed.
4 Their names: [1]Oholah the elder
and [2]Oholibah [a]her sister;
[b]They were Mine,
And they bore sons and daughters.
As for their names,
Samaria *is* Oholah, and Jerusalem
is Oholibah.

The Older Sister, Samaria

5 "Oholah played the harlot even
though she was Mine;
And she lusted for her lovers, the
neighboring [a]Assyrians,
6 *Who were* clothed in purple,
Captains and rulers,
All of them desirable young men,
Horsemen riding on horses.
7 Thus she committed her harlotry
with them,
All of them choice men of Assyria;
And with all for whom she lusted,
With all their idols, she defiled
herself.
8 She has never given up her
harlotry *brought* [a]from Egypt,

12 [c]Ezek. 23:35
13 [a]Ezek. 21:17
14 [a]Ezek. 21:7 [b]Ezek. 17:24
15 [a]Deut. 4:27 [b]Ezek. 23:27, 48
16 [a]Ps. 9:16
18 [a]Is. 1:22 [b]Prov. 17:3
20 [a]Is. 1:25
22 [a]Ezek. 20:8, 33
24 [a]Ezek. 24:13 [1]So with MT, Syr., Vg.; LXX *showered upon*
25 [a]Hos. 6:9 [b]Matt. 23:14 [c]Mic. 3:11 [1]So with MT, Vg.; LXX *princes;* Tg. *scribes* [2]Lit. *souls*
26 [a]Mal. 2:8 [b]1 Sam. 2:29 [c]Lev. 10:10 [1]Lit. *done violence to*
27 [a]Is. 1:23 [1]Lit. *souls*
28 [a]Ezek. 13:10 [b]Ezek. 13:6, 7 [c]Jer. 23:25–32
29 [a]Ex. 23:9
30 [a]Jer. 5:1 [b]Ezek. 13:5 [c]Ps. 106:23
31 [a]Ezek. 22:22 [b]Ezek. 9:10

CHAPTER 23
2 [a]Ezek. 16:44–46
3 [a]Lev. 17:7 [b]Ezek. 16:22
4 [a]Jer. 3:6, 7 [b]Ezek. 16:8, 20 [1]Lit. *Her Own Tabernacle* [2]Lit. *My Tabernacle Is in Her*
5 [a]Hos. 5:13; 8:9, 10
8 [a]Ezek. 23:3, 19

Ezekiel 22:30

Dear Woman of Destiny,

This familiar passage presents us with undeniable proof that the great works of God—and even His judgments—are influenced by the prayers of His people. It is also a vivid reminder that unless His people press in to know His thoughts, they risk praying amiss. These two principles, fully embraced, will revolutionize any prayer life.

Why have we been given such authority to influence the destiny of peoples and lands? When God first created Adam and Eve, He charged them with the responsibility of governing the earth. Even when they sinned and opened the door to demonic activity and authority (creating a gap between man and his maker), God remained faithful to His original plan. Today an omnipotent God waits for us to call down His power and mercy upon the earth. Could it be that He places limitations upon Himself that we might yet be trained to rule and reign in the spiritual realm?

Grave and sorrowful consequences result from our failure to grasp God's need of us at crucial moments in history. In this situation God's justice called for the destruction of a people given over to injustice, oppression, corruption, and idolatry. Still, God desired to show mercy. He searched for a solitary intercessor willing to seek out the deep longings of His heart. And He searches still—not for eloquent intercessors, but for attentive ones. God gives the answer to prayer, but He also gives the prayer itself.

Our natural eyes see lands and people deserving of judgment. But this human response to a world often lacks divine perspective. Our limited perspective yields presumptuous prayers. We pray that which is obvious to us, missing the nuances of the situation or the deep feelings of God. Though we may secretly congratulate ourselves for devoting large quantities of time to these prayers, they bear little fruit.

Thankfully, God promises to reveal that which is beyond human reasoning—His very heart. It is this revelation that lifts our intercession above the vain, repetitious praying that characterizes so many of the world's religions. The good news is that we serve a God who longs to be known and heard.

As we sharpen our listening skills, we must not neglect obedience. To know His heart and not be moved to action belies indifference. We must hear, but we must also hearken. It is a matter of harnessing our God-given authority to His supercharged passion for people (see Jer. 1:9, 10). These are the prayers that change the world.

According to Andrew Murray in *With Christ in the School of Prayer,* the Father's heart is revealed "to the man who withdraws himself from all that is of the world and waits for God alone." We live fast-paced lives overflowing with daily demands. Too often prayer becomes a task we must tend to—yet another job to do. Today as you pray, settle yourself and look heavenward to a God who searches the earth for those courageous and sensitive enough to stand in the gap.

Lisa Otis

For in her youth they had lain with her,
Pressed her virgin bosom,
And poured out their immorality upon her.

9 "Therefore I have delivered her
Into the hand of her lovers,
Into the hand of the [a]Assyrians,
For whom she lusted.
10 They uncovered her nakedness,
Took away her sons and daughters,
And slew her with the sword;
She became a byword among women,
For they had executed judgment on her.

The Younger Sister, Jerusalem

11"Now [a]although her sister Oholibah
saw *this,* [b]she became more corrupt in
her lust than she, and in her harlotry
more corrupt than her sister's harlotry.

12 "She lusted for the neighboring [a]Assyrians,
[b]Captains and rulers,
Clothed most gorgeously,
Horsemen riding on horses,
All of them desirable young men.
13 Then I saw that she was defiled;
Both *took* the same way.
14 But she increased her harlotry;
She looked at men portrayed on the wall,
Images of [a]Chaldeans portrayed in vermilion,
15 Girded with belts around their waists,
Flowing turbans on their heads,
All of them looking like captains,
In the manner of the Babylonians of Chaldea,
The land of their nativity.
16 [a]As soon as her eyes saw them,
She lusted for them
And sent [b]messengers to them in Chaldea.

17 "Then the [1]Babylonians came to her, into the bed of love,
And they defiled her with their immorality;
So she was defiled by them, [a]and alienated herself from them.
18 She revealed her harlotry and uncovered her nakedness.
Then [a]I [b]alienated Myself from her,
As I had alienated Myself from her sister.

19 "Yet she multiplied her harlotry
In calling to remembrance the days of her youth,
[a]When she had played the harlot in the land of Egypt.
20 For she lusted for her [1]paramours,
Whose flesh *is like* the flesh of donkeys,
And whose issue *is like* the issue of horses.
21 Thus you called to remembrance the lewdness of your youth,
When the [a]Egyptians pressed your bosom
Because of your youthful breasts.

Judgment on Jerusalem

22"Therefore, Oholibah, thus says the
Lord GOD:

[a]'Behold, I will stir up your lovers against you,
From whom you have alienated yourself,
And I will bring them against you from every side:
23 The Babylonians,
All the Chaldeans,
[a]Pekod, Shoa, Koa,
[b]All the Assyrians with them,
All of them desirable young men,
Governors and rulers,
Captains and men of renown,
All of them riding on horses.
24 And they shall come against you
With chariots, wagons, and war-horses,
With a horde of people.
They shall array against you
Buckler, shield, and helmet all around.

'I will delegate judgment to them,
And they shall judge you according to their judgments.
25 I will set My [a]jealousy against you,
And they shall deal furiously with you;
They shall remove your nose and your ears,
And your remnant shall fall by the sword;
They shall take your sons and your daughters,
And your remnant shall be devoured by fire.

9 [a] 2 Kin. 17:3
11 [a] Jer. 3:8 [b] Jer. 3:8–11
12 [a] 2 Kin. 16:7, 8 [b] Ezek. 23:6, 23
14 [a] Ezek. 8:10; 16:29
16 [a] 2 Kin. 24:1 [b] Is. 57:9
17 [a] Ezek. 23:22, 28 [1] Lit. *sons of Babel*
18 [a] Jer. 6:8 [b] Jer. 12:8
19 [a] Ezek. 23:2
20 [1] Illicit lovers
21 [a] Ezek. 16:26
22 [a] Ezek. 16:37–41; 23:28
23 [a] Jer. 50:21 [b] Ezek. 23:12
25 [a] Ex. 34:14

26 [a]They shall also strip you of your
clothes
And take away your beautiful
jewelry.
27 ‘Thus [a]I will make you cease your
lewdness and your [b]harlotry
Brought from the land of Egypt,
So that you will not lift your eyes
to them,
Nor remember Egypt anymore.’

28“For thus says the Lord GOD: ‘Surely
I will deliver you into the hand of [a]those
you hate, into the hand *of those* [b]from
whom you alienated yourself. 29[a]They will
deal hatefully with you, take away all you
have worked for, and [b]leave you naked
and bare. The nakedness of your harlotry
shall be uncovered, both your lewdness
and your harlotry. 30I will do these *things*
to you because you have [a]gone as a harlot
after the Gentiles, because you have become defiled by their idols. 31You have
walked in the way of your sister; therefore
I will put her [a]cup in your hand.’
32“Thus says the Lord GOD:

‘You shall drink of your sister’s cup,
The deep and wide one;
[a]You shall be laughed to scorn
And held in derision;
It contains much.
33 You will be filled with
drunkenness and sorrow,
The cup of horror and desolation,
The cup of your sister Samaria.
34 You shall [a]drink and drain it,
You shall break its [1]shards,
And tear at your own breasts;
For I have spoken,’
Says the Lord GOD.

35“Therefore thus says the Lord GOD:

‘Because you [a]have forgotten Me
and [b]cast Me behind your back,
Therefore you shall bear the
penalty
Of your lewdness and your
harlotry.’ ”

Both Sisters Judged

36The LORD also said to me: “Son of
man, will you [a]judge Oholah and Oholibah? Then [b]declare to them their abominations. 37For they have committed
adultery, and [a]blood *is* on their hands.
They have committed adultery with their
idols, and even sacrificed their sons
[b]whom they bore to Me, passing them
through *the fire,* to devour *them.* 38More-
over they have done this to Me: They have
[a]defiled My sanctuary on the same day
and [b]profaned My Sabbaths. 39For after
they had slain their children for their
idols, on the same day they came into My
sanctuary to profane it; and indeed [a]thus
they have done in the midst of My house.
40“Furthermore you sent for men to
come from afar, [a]to whom a messenger
was sent; and there they came. And you
[b]washed yourself for them, [c]painted your
eyes, and adorned yourself with ornaments. 41You sat on a stately [a]couch, with
a table prepared before it, [b]on which you
had set My incense and My oil. 42The
sound of a carefree multitude *was* with
her, and [1]Sabeans *were* brought from the
wilderness with men of the common sort,
who put bracelets on their [2]wrists and
beautiful crowns on their heads. 43Then I
said concerning *her who had grown* old
in adulteries, ‘Will they commit harlotry
with her now, and she *with them?*’ 44Yet
they went in to her, as men go in to a
woman who plays the harlot; thus they
went in to Oholah and Oholibah, the lewd
women. 45But righteous men will [a]judge
them after the manner of adulteresses,
and after the manner of women who shed
blood, because they *are* adulteresses, and
[b]blood *is* on their hands.
46“For thus says the Lord GOD: [a]‘Bring
up an assembly against them, give them
up to trouble and plunder. 47[a]The assembly shall stone them with stones and [1]exe-
cute them with their swords; [b]they shall
slay their sons and their daughters, and
burn their houses with fire. 48Thus [a]I will
cause lewdness to cease from the land,
[b]that all women may be taught not to
practice your lewdness. 49They shall repay
you for your lewdness, and you shall [a]pay
for your idolatrous sins. [b]Then you shall
know that I *am* the Lord GOD.’ ”

Symbol of the Cooking Pot

24 Again, in the ninth year, in the
tenth month, on the tenth *day* of
the month, the word of the LORD came to
me, saying, 2“Son of man, write down the
name of the day, this very day—the king
of Babylon started his siege against Jerusalem [a]this very day. 3[a]And utter a parable

26 a Is. 3:18–23
27 a Ezek. 16:41; 22:15 b Ezek. 23:3, 19
28 a Ezek. 16:37–41 b Ezek. 23:17
29 a Deut. 28:48 b Ezek. 16:39
30 a Ezek. 6:9
31 a Jer. 7:14, 15; 25:15
32 a Ezek. 22:4, 5
34 a Is. 51:17 *1* Earthenware fragments
35 a Jer. 3:21 b 1 Kin. 14:9
36 a Ezek. 20:4; 22:2 b Is. 58:1
37 a Ezek. 16:38 b Ezek. 16:20, 21, 36, 45; 20:26, 31
38 a 2 Kin. 21:4, 7 b Ezek. 22:8
39 a 2 Kin. 21:2–8
40 a Is. 57:9 b Ruth 3:3 c Jer. 4:30
41 a Is. 57:7 b Prov. 7:17
42 *1* Or *drunkards* *2* Lit. *hands*
45 a Ezek. 16:38 b Ezek. 23:37
46 a Ezek. 16:40
47 a Ezek. 16:40 b Ezek. 24:21 *1* Lit. *cut down*
48 a Ezek. 22:15 b Deut. 13:11
49 a Ezek. 23:35 b Ezek. 20:38, 42, 44; 25:5

CHAPTER 24
2 a 2 Kin. 25:1
3 a Ezek. 17:12

to the rebellious house, and say to them,
'Thus says the Lord GOD:

[b]"Put on a pot, set *it* on,
And also pour water into it.
4 Gather pieces *of meat* in it,
Every good piece,
The thigh and the shoulder.
Fill *it* with choice [1]cuts;
5 Take the choice of the flock.
Also pile *fuel* bones under it,
Make it boil well,
And let the cuts simmer in it."

6 'Therefore thus says the Lord GOD:

"Woe to [a]the bloody city,
To the pot whose scum *is* in it,
And whose scum is not gone from
it!
Bring it out piece by piece,
On which no [b]lot has fallen.
7 For her blood is in her midst;
She set it on top of a rock;
[a]She did not pour it on the ground,
To cover it with dust.
8 That it may raise up fury and take
vengeance,
[a]I have set her blood on top of a
rock,
That it may not be covered."

9 'Therefore thus says the Lord GOD:

[a]"Woe to the bloody city!
I too will make the pyre great.
10 Heap on the wood,
Kindle the fire;
Cook the meat well,
Mix in the spices,
And let the [1]cuts be burned up.
11 "Then set the pot empty on the
coals,
That it may become hot and its
bronze may burn,
That [a]its filthiness may be melted
in it,
That its scum may be consumed.
12 She has [1]grown weary with [2]lies,
And her great scum has not gone
from her.
Let her scum *be* in the fire!
13 In your [a]filthiness *is* lewdness.
Because I have cleansed you, and
you were not cleansed,
You will [b]not be cleansed of your
filthiness anymore,
[c]Till I have caused My fury to rest
upon you.
14 [a]I, the LORD, have spoken *it;*
[b]It shall come to pass, and I will do
it;
I will not hold back,
[c]Nor will I spare,
Nor will I relent;
According to your ways
And according to your deeds
[1]They will judge you,"
Says the Lord GOD.'"

The Prophet's Wife Dies

15 Also the word of the LORD came to
me, saying, 16 "Son of man, behold, I take
away from you the desire of your eyes with
one stroke; yet you shall [a]neither mourn
nor weep, nor shall your tears run down.
17 Sigh in silence, [a]make no mourning for
the dead; [b]bind your turban on your head,
and [c]put your sandals on your feet; [d]do
not cover *your* [1]lips, and do not eat man's
bread *of sorrow.*"
18 So I spoke to the people in the morning, and at evening my wife died; and the
next morning I did as I was commanded.
19 And the people said to me, [a]"Will you
not tell us what these *things signify* to us,
that you behave so?"
20 Then I answered them, "The word of
the LORD came to me, saying, 21 'Speak to
the house of Israel, "Thus says the Lord
GOD: 'Behold, [a]I will profane My sanctuary, [1]your arrogant boast, the desire of
your eyes, the [2]delight of your soul; [b]and
your sons and daughters whom you left
behind shall fall by the sword. 22 And you
shall do as I have done; [a]you shall not
cover *your* [1]lips nor eat man's bread *of
sorrow.* 23 Your turbans shall be on your
heads and your sandals on your feet; [a]you
shall neither mourn nor weep, but [b]you
shall pine away in your iniquities and
mourn with one another. 24 Thus [a]Ezekiel
is a sign to you; according to all that he
has done you shall do; [b]and when this
comes, [c]you shall know that I *am* the
Lord GOD.'"
25 'And you, son of man—*will it* not *be*
in the day when I take from them [a]their
stronghold, their joy and their glory, the
desire of their eyes, and [1]that on which
they set their minds, their sons and their
daughters: 26 *that* on that day [a]one who
escapes will come to you to let *you* hear *it*
with *your* ears? 27 [a]On that day your mouth
will be opened to him who has escaped; you
shall speak and no longer be mute. Thus
you will be a sign to them, and they shall
know that I *am* the LORD.'"

3 [b]Jer. 1:13
4 [1]Lit. *bones*
6 [a]Ezek. 22:2, 3, 27 [b]Nah. 3:10
7 [a]Lev. 17:13
8 [a][Matt. 7:2]
9 [a]Hab. 2:12
10 [1]Lit. *bones*
11 [a]Ezek. 22:15
12 [1]Or *wearied Me* [2]Or *toil*
13 [a]Ezek. 23:36–48 [b]Jer. 6:28–30 [c]Ezek. 5:13; 8:18; 16:42
14 [a][1 Sam. 15:29] [b]Is. 55:11 [c]Ezek. 5:11 [1]LXX, Syr., Tg., Vg. *I*
16 [a]Jer. 16:5
17 [a]Jer. 16:5 [b]Lev. 10:6; 21:10 [c]2 Sam. 15:30 [d]Mic. 3:7 [1]Lit. *moustache*
19 [a]Ezek. 12:9; 37:18
21 [a]Jer. 7:14 [b]Ezek. 23:25, 47 [1]Lit. *the pride of your strength* [2]Lit. *compassion*
22 [a]Jer. 16:6, 7 [1]Lit. *moustache*
23 [a]Job 27:15 [b]Lev. 26:39
24 [a]Is. 20:3 [b]Jer. 17:15 [c]Ezek. 6:7; 25:5
25 [a]Ezek. 24:21 [1]Lit. *the lifting up of their soul*
26 [a]Ezek. 33:21
27 [a]Ezek. 3:26; 33:22

Proclamation Against Ammon

25 The word of the LORD came to me,
saying, 2"Son of man, [a]set your
face [b]against the Ammonites, and prophesy against them. 3Say to the Ammonites,
'Hear the word of the Lord GOD! Thus says
the Lord GOD: [a]"Because you said, 'Aha!'
against My sanctuary when it was profaned, and against the land of Israel when
it was desolate, and against the house of
Judah when they went into captivity, 4in-
deed, therefore, I will deliver you as a possession to the [1]men of the East, and they
shall set their encampments among you
and make their dwellings among you;
they shall eat your fruit, and they shall
drink your milk. 5And I will make [a]Rab-
bah [b]a stable for camels and Ammon a
resting place for flocks. [c]Then you shall
know that I *am* the LORD."

6'For thus says the Lord GOD: "Because
you [a]clapped *your* hands, stamped your
feet, and [b]rejoiced in heart with all your
disdain for the land of Israel, 7indeed,
therefore, I will [a]stretch out My hand
against you, and give you as plunder to
the nations; I will cut you off from the
peoples, and I will cause you to perish
from the countries; I will destroy you, and
you shall know that I *am* the LORD."

Proclamation Against Moab

8'Thus says the Lord GOD: "Because
[a]Moab and [b]Seir say, 'Look! The house of
Judah *is* like all the nations,' 9therefore,
behold, I will clear the territory of Moab
of cities, of the cities on its frontier, the
glory of the country, Beth Jeshimoth,
Baal Meon, and [a]Kirjathaim. 10[a]To the
men of the East I will give it as a possession, together with the Ammonites, that
the Ammonites [b]may not be remembered
among the nations. 11And I will execute
judgments upon Moab, and they shall
know that I *am* the LORD."

Proclamation Against Edom

12'Thus says the Lord GOD: [a]"Because of
what Edom did against the house of Judah
by taking vengeance, and has greatly offended by avenging itself on them,"
13therefore thus says the Lord GOD: "I will
also stretch out My hand against Edom,
cut off man and beast from it, and make
it desolate from Teman; [1]Dedan shall fall
by the sword. 14[a]I will lay My vengeance
on Edom by the hand of My people Israel,
that they may do in Edom according to
My anger and according to My fury; and
they shall know My vengeance," says the
Lord GOD.

Proclamation Against Philistia

15'Thus says the Lord GOD: [a]"Because
[b]the Philistines dealt vengefully and took
vengeance with [1]a spiteful heart, to destroy because of the [2]old hatred," 16there-
fore thus says the Lord GOD: [a]"I will
stretch out My hand against the Philistines, and I will cut off the [b]Cherethites
[c]and destroy the remnant of the seacoast.
17I will [a]execute great vengeance on them
with furious rebukes; [b]and they shall
know that I *am* the LORD, when I lay My
vengeance upon them." ' "

Proclamation Against Tyre

26 And it came to pass in the eleventh
year, on the first *day* of the month,
that the word of the LORD came to me,
saying, 2"Son of man, [a]because Tyre has
said against Jerusalem, [b]'Aha! She is broken who *was* the gateway of the peoples;
now she is turned over to me; I shall be
filled; she is laid waste.'

3"Therefore thus says the Lord GOD:
'Behold, I *am* against you, O Tyre, and
will cause many nations to come up
against you, as the sea causes its waves to
come up. 4And they shall destroy the walls
of Tyre and break down her towers; I will
also scrape her dust from her, and [a]make
her like the top of a rock. 5It shall be *a*
place for spreading nets [a]in the midst of
the sea, for I have spoken,' says the Lord
GOD; 'it shall become plunder for the nations. 6Also her daughter *villages* which
are in the fields shall be slain by the
sword. [a]Then they shall know that I am
the LORD.'

7"For thus says the Lord GOD: 'Behold,
I will bring against Tyre from the north
[a]Nebuchadnezzar[1] king of Babylon, [b]king
of kings, with horses, with chariots, and
with horsemen, and an army with many
people. 8He will slay with the sword your
daughter *villages* in the fields; he will
[a]heap up a siege mound against you, build
a wall against you, and raise a [1]defense
against you. 9He will direct his battering
rams against your walls, and with his axes
he will break down your towers. 10Be-
cause of the abundance of his horses,

CHAPTER 25
2 [a]Ezek. 35:2 [b]Jer. 49:1
3 [a]Ezek. 26:2
4 [1]Lit. *sons*
5 [a]Ezek. 21:20 [b]Is. 17:2 [c]Ezek. 24:24
6 [a]Job 27:23 [b]Ezek. 36:5
7 [a]Ezek. 35:3
8 [a]Amos 2:1, 2 [b]Ezek. 35:2, 5
9 [a]Jer. 48:23
10 [a]Ezek. 25:4 [b]Ezek. 21:32
12 [a]Obad. 10–14
13 [1]Or *even to Dedan they shall fall*
14 [a]Is. 11:14
15 [a]Jer. 25:20 [b]2 Chr. 28:18 [1]Lit. *spite in soul* [2]Or *perpetual*
16 [a]Zeph. 2:4 [b]1 Sam. 30:14 [c]Jer. 47:4
17 [a]Ezek. 5:15 [b]Ps. 9:16

CHAPTER 26
2 [a]Jer. 25:22 [b]Ezek. 25:3
4 [a]Ezek. 26:14
5 [a]Ezek. 27:32
6 [a]Ezek. 25:5
7 [a]Jer. 27:3–6 [b]Dan. 2:37, 47 [1]Heb. *Nebuchadrezzar,* and so elsewhere in the book
8 [a]Ezek. 21:22 [1]Lit. *a large shield*

their dust will cover you; your walls will
shake at the noise of the horsemen, the
wagons, and the chariots, when he enters
your gates, as men enter a city that has
been breached. 11 With the hooves of his
[a]horses he will trample all your streets; he
will slay your people by the sword, and
your strong pillars will fall to the ground.
12 They will plunder your riches and pillage your merchandise; they will break
down your walls and destroy your pleasant houses; they will lay your stones, your
timber, and your soil in the [a]midst of the
water. 13 [a]I will put an end to the sound of
[b]your songs, and the sound of your harps
shall be heard no more. 14 [a]I will make you
like the top of a rock; you shall be *a place
for* spreading nets, and you shall never be
rebuilt, for I the LORD have spoken,' says
the Lord GOD.

15 "Thus says the Lord GOD to Tyre: 'Will
the coastlands not [a]shake at the sound of
your fall, when the wounded cry, when
slaughter is made in the midst of you?
16 Then all the [a]princes of the sea will
[b]come down from their thrones, lay aside
their robes, and take off their embroidered garments; they will clothe themselves with trembling; [c]they will sit on the
ground, [d]tremble *every* moment, and [e]be
astonished at you. 17 And they will take up
a [a]lamentation for you, and say to you:

"How you have perished,
O one inhabited by seafaring men,
O renowned city,
Who was [b]strong at sea,
She and her inhabitants,
Who caused their terror *to be* on
all her inhabitants!
18 Now [a]the coastlands tremble on
the day of your fall;
Yes, the coastlands by the sea are
troubled at your departure." '

19 "For thus says the Lord GOD: 'When I
make you a desolate city, like cities that
are not inhabited, when I bring the deep
upon you, and great waters cover you,
20 then I will bring you down [a]with those
who descend into the Pit, to the people of
old, and I will make you dwell in the lowest part of the earth, in places desolate
from antiquity, with those who go down
to the Pit, so that you may never be inhabited; and I shall establish glory [b]in the
land of the living. 21 [a]I will make you a
terror, and you *shall be* no *more;* [b]though
you are sought for, you will never be
found again,' says the Lord GOD."

Lamentation for Tyre

27 The word of the LORD came again
to me, saying, 2 "Now, son of man,
[a]take up a lamentation for Tyre, 3 and say
to Tyre, [a]'You who [1]are situated at the
entrance of the sea, [b]merchant of the peoples on many coastlands, thus says the
Lord GOD:

"O Tyre, you have said,
[c]'I *am* perfect in beauty.'
4 Your borders *are* in the midst of
the seas.
Your builders have perfected your
beauty.
5 They [1]made all *your* planks of fir
trees from [a]Senir;
They took a cedar from Lebanon to
make you a mast.
6 *Of* [a]oaks from Bashan they made
your oars;
The company of Ashurites have
inlaid your planks
With ivory from [b]the coasts of
[1]Cyprus.
7 Fine embroidered linen from Egypt
was what you spread for your
sail;
Blue and purple from the coasts of
Elishah was what covered you.

8 "Inhabitants of Sidon and Arvad
were your oarsmen;
Your wise men, O Tyre, were in
you;
They became your pilots.
9 Elders of [a]Gebal and its wise men
Were in you to caulk your seams;
All the ships of the sea
And their oarsmen were in you
To market your merchandise.

10 "Those from Persia, [1]Lydia, and
[2]Libya
Were in your army as men of war;
They hung shield and helmet in
you;
They gave splendor to you.
11 Men of Arvad with your army *were*
on your walls *all* around,
And the men of Gammad were in
your towers;
They hung their shields on your
walls *all* around;
They made [a]your beauty perfect.

11 a Hab. 1:8
12 a Ezek. 27:27, 32
13 a Is. 14:11; 24:8 b Rev. 18:22
14 a Ezek. 26:4, 5
15 a Jer. 49:21
16 a Is. 23:8 b Jon. 3:6 c Job 2:13 d Ezek. 32:10 e Ezek. 27:35
17 a Ezek. 27:2–36 b Is. 23:4
18 a Ezek. 26:15
20 a Ezek. 32:18 b Ezek. 32:23
21 a Ezek. 27:36; 28:19 b Ps. 37:10, 36
CHAPTER 27
2 a Ezek. 26:17
3 a Ezek. 26:17; 28:2 b Is. 23:3 c Ezek. 28:12 *1* Lit. *sit* or *dwell*
5 a Deut. 3:9 *1 built*
6 a Is. 2:12, 13 b Jer. 2:10 *1* Heb. *Kittim,* western lands, especially Cyprus
9 a 1 Kin. 5:18
10 *1* Heb. *Lud* *2* Heb. *Put*
11 a Ezek. 27:3

12[a]“Tarshish *was* your merchant because of your many luxury goods. They
gave you silver, iron, tin, and lead for your
goods. 13[a]Javan, Tubal, and Meshech *were*
your traders. They bartered [b]human lives
and vessels of bronze for your merchandise. 14Those from the house of [a]Togar-
mah traded for your wares with horses,
steeds, and mules. 15The men of [a]Dedan
were your traders; many isles *were* the
market of your hand. They brought you
ivory tusks and ebony as payment. 16Syria
was your merchant because of the abundance of goods you made. They gave you
for your wares emeralds, purple, embroidery, fine linen, corals, and rubies. 17Ju-
dah and the land of Israel *were* your
traders. They traded for your merchandise
wheat of [a]Minnith, millet, honey, oil, and
[b]balm. 18Damascus *was* your merchant
because of the abundance of goods you
made, because of your many luxury items,
with the wine of Helbon and with white
wool. 19Dan and Javan paid for your
wares, [1]traversing back and forth.
Wrought iron, cassia, and cane were
among your merchandise. 20[a]Dedan *was*
your merchant in saddlecloths for riding.
21Arabia and all the princes of [a]Kedar
were your regular merchants. They traded
with you in lambs, rams, and goats. 22The
merchants of [a]Sheba and Raamah *were*
your merchants. They traded for your
wares the choicest spices, all kinds of precious stones, and gold. 23[a]Haran, Canneh,
Eden, the merchants of [b]Sheba, Assyria,
and Chilmad *were* your merchants.
24These *were* your merchants in choice
items—in purple clothes, in embroidered
garments, in chests of multicolored apparel, in sturdy woven cords, which were
in your marketplace.

25 “The [a]ships of Tarshish were
carriers of your merchandise.
You were filled and very glorious
[b]in the midst of the seas.
26 Your oarsmen brought you into
many waters,
But [a]the east wind broke you in the
midst of the seas.

27 “Your [a]riches, wares, and
merchandise,
Your mariners and pilots,
Your caulkers and merchandisers,
All your men of war who *are* in
you,
And the entire company which *is* in
your midst,
Will fall into the midst of the seas
on the day of your ruin.
28 The [a]common-land[1] will shake at
the sound of the cry of your
pilots.

29 “All [a]who handle the oar,
The mariners,
All the pilots of the sea
Will come down from their ships
and stand on the [1]shore.
30 They will make their voice heard
because of you;
They will cry bitterly and [a]cast dust
on their heads;
They [b]will roll about in ashes;
31 They will [a]shave themselves
completely bald because of you,
Gird themselves with sackcloth,
And weep for you
With bitterness of heart *and* bitter
wailing.
32 In their wailing for you
They will [a]take up a lamentation,
And lament for you:
[b]‘What *city is* like Tyre,
Destroyed in the midst of the sea?

33 ‘When[a] your wares went out by
sea,
You satisfied many people;
You enriched the kings of the earth
With your many luxury goods and
your merchandise.
34 But [a]you are broken by the seas
in the depths of the waters;
[b]Your merchandise and the entire
company will fall in your midst.
35 [a]All the inhabitants of the isles will
be astonished at you;
Their kings will be greatly afraid,
And *their* countenance will be
troubled.
36 The merchants among the peoples
[a]will hiss at you;
[b]You will become a horror, and *be*
no [c]more forever.’ ” ’ ”

Proclamation Against the King of Tyre

28 The word of the LORD came to me
again, saying, 2“Son of man, say to
the prince of Tyre, ‘Thus says the Lord
GOD:

“Because your heart *is* [a]lifted[1] up,
And [b]you say, ‘I *am* a god,

12 a Gen. 10:4
13 a Gen. 10:2 b Rev. 18:13
14 a Gen. 10:3
15 a Gen. 10:7
17 a Judg. 11:33 b Jer. 8:22
19 1 LXX, Syr. *from Uzal*
20 a Gen. 25:3
21 a Is. 60:7
22 a Gen. 10:7
23 a 2 Kin. 19:12 b Gen. 25:3
25 a Is. 2:16 b Ezek. 27:4
26 a Ps. 48:7
27 a [Prov. 11:4]
28 a Ezek. 26:15 1 *open lands* or *pasture-lands*
29 a Rev. 18:17 1 Lit. *land*
30 a Rev. 18:19 b Jer. 6:26
31 a Ezek. 29:18
32 a Ezek. 26:17 b Rev. 18:18
33 a Rev. 18:19
34 a Ezek. 26:19 b Ezek. 27:27
35 a Ezek. 26:15, 16
36 a Jer. 18:16 b Ezek. 26:2 c Ps. 37:10, 36

CHAPTER 28
2 a Jer. 49:16 b Ezek. 28:9 1 Proud

I sit *in* the seat of gods,
[c]In the midst of the seas,'
[d]Yet you *are* a man, and not a god,
Though you set your heart as the
heart of a god
3 (Behold, [a]you *are* wiser than
Daniel!
There is no secret that can be
hidden from you!
4 With your wisdom and your
understanding
You have gained [a]riches for
yourself,
And gathered gold and silver into
your treasuries;
5 [a]By your great wisdom in trade you
have increased your riches,
And your heart is lifted up because
of your riches),"

6 'Therefore thus says the Lord GOD:

"Because you have set your heart as
the heart of a god,
7 Behold, therefore, I will bring
[a]strangers against you,
[b]The most terrible of the nations;
And they shall draw their swords
against the beauty of your
wisdom,
And defile your splendor.
8 They shall throw you down into
the [a]Pit,
And you shall die the death of the
slain
In the midst of the seas.
9 "Will you still [a]say before him who
slays you,
'I *am* a god'?
But you *shall be* a man, and not a
god,
In the hand of him who slays you.
10 You shall die the death of [a]the
uncircumcised
By the hand of aliens;
For I have spoken," says the Lord
GOD.' "

Lamentation for the King of Tyre

11 Moreover the word of the LORD came
to me, saying, 12 "Son of man, [a]take up a
lamentation for the king of Tyre, and say
to him, 'Thus says the Lord GOD:

[b]"You *were* the seal of perfection,
Full of wisdom and perfect in
beauty.
13 You were in [a]Eden, the garden of
God;
Every precious stone *was* your
covering:
The sardius, topaz, and diamond,
Beryl, onyx, and jasper,
Sapphire, turquoise, and emerald
with gold.
The workmanship of [b]your timbrels
and pipes
Was prepared for you on the day
you were created.
14 "You *were* the anointed [a]cherub
who covers;
I established you;
You were on [b]the holy mountain of
God;
You walked back and forth in the
midst of fiery stones.
15 You *were* perfect in your ways
from the day you were created,
Till [a]iniquity was found in you.
16 "By the abundance of your trading
You became filled with violence
within,
And you sinned;
Therefore I cast you as a profane
thing
Out of the mountain of God;
And I destroyed you, [a]O covering
cherub,
From the midst of the fiery stones.
17 "Your [a]heart was [1]lifted up because
of your beauty;
You corrupted your wisdom for the
sake of your splendor;
I cast you to the ground,
I laid you before kings,
That they might gaze at you.
18 "You defiled your sanctuaries
By the multitude of your iniquities,
By the iniquity of your trading;
Therefore I brought fire from your
midst;
It devoured you,
And I turned you to ashes upon the
earth
In the sight of all who saw you.
19 All who knew you among the
peoples are astonished at you;
[a]You have become a horror,
And *shall be* no [b]more forever." ' "

Proclamation Against Sidon

20 Then the word of the LORD came to
me, saying, 21 "Son of man, [a]set your face

2 [c]Ezek. 27:3, 4 [d]Is. 31:3
3 [a]Dan. 1:20; 2:20–23, 28; 5:11, 12
4 [a]Zech. 9:1–3
5 [a]Ps. 62:10
7 [a]Ezek. 26:7 [b]Ezek. 7:24; 21:31; 30:11
8 [a]Is. 14:15
9 [a]Ezek. 28:2
10 [a]Ezek. 31:18; 32:19, 21, 25, 27
12 [a]Ezek. 27:2 [b]Ezek. 27:3; 28:3
13 [a]Ezek. 31:8, 9; 36:35 [b]Ezek. 26:13
14 [a]Ex. 25:20 [b]Ezek. 20:40
15 [a][Is. 14:12]
16 [a]Ezek. 28:14
17 [a]Ezek. 28:2, 5 [1]Proud
19 [a]Ezek. 26:21 [b]Ezek. 27:36
21 [a]Ezek. 6:2; 25:2; 29:2

Ezekiel 28:15–17

Dear Woman of Destiny,

In Ezekiel 28:15–17 the prophet Ezekiel gives us one of the most vivid portraits of the archenemy of God. Satan once had great power before the throne of God. He was a beautiful creature, according to the prophet, perfect in all his ways until iniquity was found in him. His heart was filled with pride because of his beauty. He was called profane and cast out of the holy mountain. His beauty was defiled when he betrayed God with his desire to be exalted above Him. Satan challenged the holy nature of God. Such insurrection and rebellion was intolerable in the presence of God. Do you know who Satan really is?—an unemployed cherub.

Originally, God created this beautiful archangel to gather up praise and worship before the throne of God. Music was formed in and through him. Now, as God's enemy, Satan's ultimate desire is to divert worship from God and receive worship for himself.

He tried to entice Jesus to worship him, declaring, "All these things I will give you if You will fall down and worship me" (Matt. 4:9). When he was in the Garden of Eden, this fallen cherub tempted Adam and Eve (see Ezek. 28:13). His desire was for them to defy the command of God so that they could become gods (see Gen. 3:5). He had failed in his own attempt to ascend and dethrone God, but he had not given up his iniquitous thought and way.

How is it possible that one as beautiful, intelligent, and privileged as Lucifer could turn so viciously against the One who created him? Ministering in worship around the throne of God stirred a jealousy, an ambition in Lucifer's heart to be like the Most High (see Ezek. 28:15–17).

Giftings, beauty, privilege, opportunity—none of these make us immune to an iniquitous heart that craves self-exaltation. It is important to know that our exalted position of authority in serving God does not prevent us from selfish ambition. In fact, because of the Adamic nature we were all born with, we are predisposed to the desire to be "like gods."

Satan is called the prince of this world. For that reason he was able to offer the kingdoms of this world to Jesus during His wilderness temptation. But as the church takes a stand in Jesus' name confronting the enemy, the ground Satan has taken in the world will be returned. It is the responsibility of the church to unmask Satan, identify him, and reclaim the souls of men for the kingdom of God through the authority Jesus has given us.

The end of Satan is a cause of great rejoicing for all Christians. Scripture reveals that after Jesus returns for His bride, He will set up His reign on this earth for a thousand years. During that time Satan will be bound (see Rev. 20:1, 2). After that millennium, though Satan will be loosed for a short while to continue his deceiving work (see Rev. 20:7, 8), the appointed time for his end will finally come, and he will be judged and put away forever (see Rev. 20:10). It is hard to imagine what joy and rejoicing we will know in the day we are freed forever from this tireless enemy.

Sue Curran

[b]toward Sidon, and prophesy against her, 22and say, 'Thus says the Lord GOD:

[a]"Behold, I *am* against you, O Sidon;
I will be glorified in your midst;
And [b]they shall know that I *am* the
LORD,
When I execute judgments in her
and am [c]hallowed in her.
23 [a]For I will send pestilence upon
her,
And blood in her streets;
The wounded shall be judged in her
midst
By the sword against her on every
side;
Then they shall know that I *am* the
LORD.

24"And there shall no longer be a pricking brier or [a]a painful thorn for the house of Israel from among all *who are* around them, who [b]despise them. Then they shall know that I *am* the Lord GOD."

Israel's Future Blessing

25'Thus says the Lord GOD: "When I have [a]gathered the house of Israel from the peoples among whom they are scattered, and am [b]hallowed in them in the sight of the Gentiles, then they will dwell in their own land which I gave to My servant Jacob. 26And they will [a]dwell [1]safely there, [b]build houses, and [c]plant vineyards; yes, they will dwell securely, when I execute judgments on all those around them who despise them. Then they shall know that I *am* the LORD their God." ' "

Proclamation Against Egypt

29 In the tenth year, in the tenth *month,* on the twelfth *day* of the month, the word of the LORD came to me, saying, 2"Son of man, [a]set your face against Pharaoh king of Egypt, and prophesy against him, and [b]against all Egypt. 3Speak, and say, 'Thus says the Lord GOD:

[a]"Behold, I *am* against you,
O Pharaoh king of Egypt,
O great [b]monster who lies in the
midst of his rivers,
[c]Who has said, 'My [1]River *is* my
own;
I have made *it* for myself.'
4 But [a]I will put hooks in your jaws,
And cause the fish of your rivers to
stick to your scales;
I will bring you up out of the midst
of your rivers,
And all the fish in your rivers will
stick to your scales.
5 I will leave you in the wilderness,
You and all the fish of your rivers;
You shall fall on the [1]open [a]field;
[b]You shall not be picked up or
[2]gathered.
[c]I have given you as food
To the beasts of the field
And to the birds of the heavens.

6 "Then all the inhabitants of Egypt
Shall know that I *am* the LORD,
Because they have been a [a]staff of
reed to the house of Israel.
7 [a]When they took hold of you with
the hand,
You broke and tore all their
[1]shoulders;
When they leaned on you,
You broke and made all their backs
quiver."

8'Therefore thus says the Lord GOD: "Surely I will bring [a]a sword upon you and cut off from you man and beast. 9And the land of Egypt shall become [a]desolate and waste; then they will know that I *am* the LORD, because he said, 'The River *is* mine, and I have made *it*.' 10Indeed, therefore, I *am* against you and against your rivers, [a]and I will make the land of Egypt utterly waste and desolate, [b]from [1]Migdol *to* Syene, as far as the border of Ethiopia. 11[a]Neither foot of man shall pass through it nor foot of beast pass through it, and it shall be uninhabited forty years. 12[a]I will make the land of Egypt desolate in the midst of the countries *that are* desolate; and among the cities *that are* laid waste, her cities shall be desolate forty years; and I will [b]scatter the Egyptians among the nations and disperse them throughout the countries."

13'Yet, thus says the Lord GOD: "At the [a]end of forty years I will gather the Egyptians from the peoples among whom they were scattered. 14I will bring back the captives of Egypt and cause them to return to the land of Pathros, to the land of their origin, and there they shall be a [a]lowly kingdom. 15It shall be the lowliest of kingdoms; it shall never again exalt itself above the nations, for I will diminish them so that they will not rule over the nations anymore. 16No longer shall it be [a]the confidence of the house of Israel, but

21 [b]Is. 23:2, 4, 12
22 [a]Ex. 14:4, 17 [b]Ps. 9:16 [c]Ezek. 28:25
23 [a]Ezek. 38:22
24 [a]Josh. 23:13 [b]Ezek. 16:57; 25:6, 7
25 [a]Is. 11:12, 13 [b]Ezek. 28:22
26 [a]Jer. 23:6 [b]Amos 9:13, 14 [c]Jer. 31:5 [1]*securely*

CHAPTER 29
2 [a]Ezek. 28:21 [b]Is. 19:1
3 [a]Jer. 44:30 [b]Ps. 74:13, 14 [c]Ezek. 28:2 [1]The Nile
4 [a]Ezek. 38:4
5 [a]Ezek. 32:4–6 [b]Jer. 8:2; 16:4; 25:33 [c]Jer. 7:33; 34:20 [1]Lit. *face of the field* [2]So with MT, LXX, Vg.; some Heb. mss., Tg. *buried*
6 [a]Is. 36:6
7 [a]Ezek. 17:17 [1]So with MT, Vg.; LXX, Syr. *hand*
8 [a]Ezek. 14:17; 32:11–13
9 [a]Ezek. 30:7, 8
10 [a]Ezek. 30:12 [b]Ezek. 30:6 [1]Or *the tower*
11 [a]Ezek. 32:13
12 [a]Ezek. 30:7, 26 [b]Ezek. 30:23, 26
13 [a]Jer. 46:26
14 [a]Ezek. 17:6, 14
16 [a]Is. 30:2, 3; 36:4, 6

will remind them of *their* iniquity when they turned to follow them. Then they shall know that I *am* the Lord GOD." ' "

Babylonia Will Plunder Egypt

17And it came to pass in the twenty-seventh year, in the first *month,* on the first *day* of the month, *that* the word of the LORD came to me, saying, 18"Son of man, [a]Nebuchadnezzar king of Babylon caused his army to labor strenuously against Tyre; every head *was* made [b]bald, and every shoulder rubbed raw; yet neither he nor his army received wages from Tyre, for the labor which they expended on it. 19Therefore thus says the Lord GOD: 'Surely I will give the land of Egypt to [a]Nebuchadnezzar king of Babylon; he shall take away her wealth, carry off her spoil, and remove her pillage; and that will be the wages for his army. 20I have given him the land of Egypt *for* his labor, because they [a]worked for Me,' says the Lord GOD.

21'In that day [a]I will cause the [1]horn of the house of Israel to spring forth, and I will [b]open your mouth to speak in their midst. Then they shall know that I *am* the LORD.' "

Egypt and Her Allies Will Fall

30 The word of the LORD came to me again, saying, 2"Son of man, prophesy and say, 'Thus says the Lord GOD:

[a]"Wail, 'Woe to the day!'
3 For [a]the day *is* near,
Even the day of the LORD *is* near;
It will be a day of clouds, the time
of the Gentiles.
4 The sword shall come upon Egypt,
And great anguish shall be in
[1]Ethiopia,
When the slain fall in Egypt,
And they [a]take away her wealth,
And [b]her foundations are broken
down.

5"Ethiopia, [1]Libya, [2]Lydia, [a]all the mingled people, Chub, and the men of the lands who are allied, shall fall with them by the sword."

6'Thus says the LORD:

"Those who uphold Egypt shall fall,
And the pride of her power shall
come down.
[a]From [1]Migdol *to* Syene
Those within her shall fall by the
sword,"
Says the Lord GOD.

7 "They[a] shall be desolate in the
midst of the desolate countries,
And her cities shall be in the midst
of the cities *that are* laid waste.
8 Then they will know that I *am* the
LORD,
When I have set a fire in Egypt
And all her helpers are destroyed.
9 On that day [a]messengers shall go
forth from Me in ships
To make the [1]careless Ethiopians
afraid,
And great anguish shall come upon
them,
As on the day of Egypt;
For indeed it is coming!"

10'Thus says the Lord GOD:

[a]"I will also make a multitude of
Egypt to cease
By the hand of Nebuchadnezzar
king of Babylon.
11 He and his people with him, [a]the
most terrible of the nations,
Shall be brought to destroy the
land;
They shall draw their swords
against Egypt,
And fill the land with the slain.
12 [a]I will make the rivers dry,
And [b]sell the land into the hand of
the wicked;
I will make the land waste, and all
that is in it,
By the hand of aliens.
I, the LORD, have spoken."

13'Thus says the Lord GOD:

"I will also [a]destroy the idols,
And cause the images to cease from
[1]Noph;
[b]There shall no longer be princes
from the land of Egypt;
[c]I will put fear in the land of Egypt.
14 I will make [a]Pathros desolate,
Set fire to [b]Zoan,
[c]And execute judgments in [1]No.
15 I will pour My fury on [1]Sin, the
strength of Egypt;

18 a Jer. 25:9; 27:6 b Ezek. 27:31
19 a Jer. 43:10–13
20 a Jer. 25:9
21 a Ps. 92:10; 132:17 b Ezek. 24:27 *1* Strength
CHAPTER 30
2 a Is. 13:6; 15:2
3 a Joel 2:1
4 a Ezek. 29:19 b Jer. 50:15 *1* Heb. *Cush*
5 a Jer. 25:20, 24 *1* Heb. *Put* *2* Heb. *Lud*
6 a Ezek. 29:10 *1* Or *the tower*
7 a Ezek. 29:12
9 a Is. 18:1, 2 *1* Or *secure*
10 a Ezek. 29:19
11 a Ezek. 28:7; 31:12
12 a Is. 19:5, 6 b Is. 19:4
13 a Is. 19:1 b Zech. 10:11 c Is. 19:16 *1* Ancient Memphis
14 a Ezek. 29:14 b Ps. 78:12, 43 c Nah. 3:8–10 *1* Ancient Thebes
15 *1* Ancient Pelusium

[a]I will cut off the multitude of [2]No,
16 And [a]set a fire in Egypt;
Sin shall have great pain,
No shall be split open,
And Noph *shall be in* distress daily.
17 The young men of [1]Aven and Pi Beseth shall fall by the sword,
And these *cities* shall go into captivity.
18 [a]At [1]Tehaphnehes the day shall also be [2]darkened,
When I break the yokes of Egypt there.
And her arrogant strength shall cease in her;
As for her, a cloud shall cover her,
And her daughters shall go into captivity.
19 Thus I will [a]execute judgments on Egypt,
Then they shall know that I *am* the LORD." ' "

Proclamation Against Pharaoh

20And it came to pass in the eleventh
year, in the first *month,* on the seventh
day of the month, *that* the word of the
LORD came to me, saying, 21"Son of man,
I have [a]broken the arm of Pharaoh king of
Egypt; and see, [b]it has not been bandaged
for healing, nor a [1]splint put on to bind it,
to make it strong enough to hold a sword.
22Therefore thus says the Lord GOD:
'Surely I *am* [a]against Pharaoh king of
Egypt, and will [b]break his arms, both
the strong one and the one that was broken; and I will make the sword fall out
of his hand. 23[a]I will scatter the Egyptians among the nations, and disperse
them throughout the countries. 24I will
strengthen the arms of the king of Babylon and put My sword in his hand; but I
will break Pharaoh's arms, and he will
groan before him with the groanings of
a mortally wounded *man.* 25Thus I will
strengthen the arms of the king of Babylon, but the arms of Pharaoh shall fall
down; [a]they shall know that I *am* the
LORD, when I put My sword into the hand
of the king of Babylon and he stretches it
out against the land of Egypt. 26[a]I will
scatter the Egyptians among the nations
and disperse them throughout the countries. Then they shall know that I *am* the
LORD.' "

15 [a]Jer. 46:25 [2]Ancient Thebes
16 [a]Ezek. 30:8
17 [1]Ancient On, Heliopolis
18 [a]Jer. 2:16 [1]*Tahpanhes,* Jer. 43:7 [2]So with many Heb. mss., Bg., LXX, Syr., Tg., Vg.; MT *refrained*
19 [a][Ps. 9:16]
21 [a]Jer. 48:25 [b]Jer. 46:11 [1]Lit. *bandage*
22 [a]Jer. 46:25 [b]Ps. 37:17
23 [a]Ezek. 29:12; 30:17, 18, 26
25 [a]Ps. 9:16
26 [a]Ezek. 29:12
CHAPTER 31
1 [a]Ezek. 30:20; 32:1
2 [a]Ezek. 31:18
3 [a]Dan. 4:10, 20–23
4 [a]Jer. 51:36 [1]Or *channels*
5 [a]Dan. 4:11
6 [a]Dan. 4:12, 21 [1]Lit. *dwelled*
8 [a]Gen. 2:8, 9; 13:10 [1]Or *plane,* Heb. *armon*

Egypt Cut Down Like a Great Tree

31 Now it came to pass in the [a]elev-
enth year, in the third *month,* on
the first *day* of the month, *that* the word
of the LORD came to me, saying, 2"Son of
man, say to Pharaoh king of Egypt and to
his multitude:

[a]'Whom are you like in your greatness?
3 [a]Indeed Assyria *was* a cedar in Lebanon,
With fine branches that shaded the forest,
And of high stature;
And its top was among the thick boughs.
4 [a]The waters made it grow;
Underground waters gave it height,
With their rivers running around the place where it was planted,
And sent out [1]rivulets to all the trees of the field.
5 'Therefore [a]its height was exalted above all the trees of the field;
Its boughs were multiplied,
And its branches became long because of the abundance of water,
As it sent them out.
6 All the [a]birds of the heavens made their nests in its boughs;
Under its branches all the beasts of the field brought forth their young;
And in its shadow all great nations [1]made their home.
7 'Thus it was beautiful in greatness and in the length of its branches,
Because its roots reached to abundant waters.
8 The cedars in the [a]garden of God could not hide it;
The fir trees were not like its boughs,
And the [1]chestnut trees were not like its branches;
No tree in the garden of God was like it in beauty.
9 I made it beautiful with a multitude of branches,
So that all the trees of Eden envied it,
That *were* in the garden of God.'

10"Therefore thus says the Lord GOD:
'Because you have increased in height,
and it set its top among the thick boughs,
and [a]its heart was [1]lifted up in its height,
11therefore I will deliver it into the hand
of the [a]mighty one of the nations, and he
shall surely deal with it; I have driven it
out for its wickedness. 12And aliens, [a]the
most terrible of the nations, have cut it
down and left it; its branches have fallen
[b]on the mountains and in all the valleys;
its boughs lie [c]broken by all the rivers of
the land; and all the peoples of the earth
have gone from under its shadow and
left it.

13 'On [a]its ruin will remain all the
birds of the heavens,
And all the beasts of the field will
come to its branches—

14'So that no trees by the waters may ever
again exalt themselves for their height,
nor set their tops among the thick
boughs, that no tree which drinks water
may ever be high enough to reach up to
them.

'For [a]they have all been delivered to
death,
[b]To the depths of the earth,
Among the children of men who go
down to the Pit.'

15"Thus says the Lord GOD: 'In the day
when it [a]went down to [1]hell, I caused
mourning. I covered the deep because of
it. I restrained its rivers, and the great waters were held back. I caused Lebanon to
[2]mourn for it, and all the trees of the field
wilted because of it. 16I made the nations
[a]shake at the sound of its fall, when I [b]cast
it down to [1]hell together with those who
descend into the Pit; and [c]all the trees of
Eden, the choice and best of Lebanon, all
that drink water, [d]were comforted in the
depths of the earth. 17They also went
down to hell with it, with those *slain* by
the sword; and *those who were* its *strong*
arm [a]dwelt in its shadows among the nations.

18[a]'To which of the trees in Eden will
you then be likened in glory and greatness? Yet you shall be brought down with
the trees of Eden to the depths of the
earth; [b]you shall lie in the midst of the
uncircumcised, with *those* slain by the
sword. This *is* Pharaoh and all his multitude,' says the Lord GOD."

Lamentation for Pharaoh and Egypt

32 And it came to pass in the twelfth
year, in the [a]twelfth *month,* on the
first *day* of the month, *that* the word of
the LORD came to me, saying, 2"Son of
man, [a]take up a lamentation for Pharaoh
king of Egypt, and say to him:

[b]'You are like a young lion among
the nations,
And [c]you *are* like a monster in the
seas,
[d]Bursting forth in your rivers,
Troubling the waters with your feet,
And [e]fouling their rivers.'

3"Thus says the Lord GOD:

'I will therefore [a]spread My net over
you with a company of many
people,
And they will draw you up in My
net.
4 Then [a]I will leave you on the land;
I will cast you out on the open
fields,
[b]And cause to [1]settle on you all the
birds of the heavens.
And with you I will fill the beasts of
the whole earth.
5 I will lay your flesh [a]on the
mountains,
And fill the valleys with your
carcass.
6 'I will also water the land with the
flow of your blood,
Even to the mountains;
And the riverbeds will be full of
you.
7 When *I* put out your light,
[a]I will cover the heavens, and make
its stars dark;
I will cover the sun with a cloud,
And the moon shall not give her
light.
8 All the [1]bright lights of the
heavens I will make dark over
you,
And bring darkness upon your
land,'
Says the Lord GOD.

9'I will also trouble the hearts of many
peoples, when I bring your destruction
among the nations, into the countries
which you have not known. 10Yes, I will
make many peoples astonished at you,
and their kings shall be horribly afraid

10 [a]Dan. 5:20 [1]Proud
11 [a]Ezek. 30:10
12 [a]Ezek. 28:7; 30:11; 32:12 [b]Ezek. 32:5; 35:8 [c]Ezek. 30:24, 25
13 [a]Is. 18:6
14 [a]Ps. 82:7 [b]Ezek. 32:18
15 [a]Ezek. 32:22, 23 [1]Or *Sheol* [2]Lit. *be darkened*
16 [a]Ezek. 26:15 [b]Is. 14:15 [c]Is. 14:8 [d]Ezek. 32:31 [1]Or *Sheol*
17 [a]Lam. 4:20
18 [a]Ezek. 32:19 [b]Ezek. 28:10; 32:19, 21

CHAPTER 32
1 [a]Ezek. 31:1; 33:21
2 [a]Ezek. 27:2 [b]Ezek. 19:2–6 [c]Ezek. 29:3 [d]Jer. 46:7, 8 [e]Ezek. 34:18
3 [a]Ezek. 12:13; 17:20
4 [a]Ezek. 29:5 [b]Is. 18:6; Ezek. 31:13 [1]Lit. *sit* or *dwell*
5 [a]Ezek. 31:12
7 [a]Rev. 6:12, 13; 8:12
8 [1]Or *shining*

of you when I brandish My sword before
them; and [a]they shall tremble *every* moment,
every man for his own life, in the
day of your fall.'

11 [a]"For thus says the Lord GOD: 'The
sword of the king of Babylon shall come
upon you. 12 By the swords of the mighty
warriors, all of them [a]the most terrible of
the nations, I will cause your multitude to
fall.

[b]'They shall plunder the pomp of
Egypt,
And all its multitude shall be
destroyed.
13 Also I will destroy all its animals
From beside its great waters;
[a]The foot of man shall muddy them
no more,
Nor shall the hooves of animals
muddy them.
14 Then I will make their waters
[1]clear,
And make their rivers run like oil,'
Says the Lord GOD.
15 'When I make the land of Egypt
desolate,
And the country is destitute of all
that once filled it,
When I strike all who dwell in it,
[a]Then they shall know that I *am* the
LORD.
16 'This *is* the [a]lamentation
With which they shall lament her;
The daughters of the nations shall
lament her;
They shall lament for her, for
Egypt,
And for all her multitude,'
Says the Lord GOD."

Egypt and Others Consigned to the Pit

17 It came to pass also in the twelfth
year, on the fifteenth *day* of the month,
[a]*that* the word of the LORD came to me,
saying:

18 "Son of man, wail over the
multitude of Egypt,
And [a]cast them down to the depths
of the earth,
Her and the daughters of the
famous nations,
With those who go down to the Pit:
19 'Whom [a]do you surpass in beauty?
[b]Go down, be placed with the
uncircumcised.'
20 "They shall fall in the midst of
those slain by the sword;
She is delivered to the sword,
[a]Drawing her and all her multitudes.
21 [a]The strong among the mighty
Shall speak to him out of the midst
of hell
With those who help him:
'They have [b]gone down,
They lie with the uncircumcised,
slain by the sword.'
22 "Assyria[a] *is* there, and all her
company,
With their graves all around her,
All of them slain, fallen by the
sword.
23 [a]Her graves are set in the recesses
of the Pit,
And her company is all around her
grave,
All of them slain, fallen by the
sword,
Who [b]caused terror in the land of
the living.
24 "There *is* [a]Elam and all her
multitude,
All around her grave,
All of them slain, fallen by the
sword,
Who have [b]gone down
uncircumcised to the lower parts
of the earth,
[c]Who caused their terror in the land
of the living;
Now they bear their shame with
those who go down to the Pit.
25 They have set her [a]bed in the
midst of the slain,
With all her multitude,
With her graves all around it,
All of them uncircumcised, slain by
the sword;
Though their terror was caused
In the land of the living,
Yet they bear their shame
With those who go down to the Pit;
It was put in the midst of the slain.
26 "There *are* [a]Meshech and Tubal
and all their multitudes,
With all their graves around it,
All of them [b]uncircumcised, slain
by the sword,
Though they caused their terror in
the land of the living.
27 [a]They do not lie with the mighty
Who are fallen of the
uncircumcised,

10 a Ezek. 26:16
11 a Jer. 46:26
12 a Ezek. 28:7; 30:11; 31:12 b Ezek. 29:19
13 a Ezek. 29:11
14 1 Lit. *sink; settle, grow clear*
15 a Ps. 9:16
16 a Ezek. 26:17
17 a Ezek. 32:1; 33:21
18 a Ezek. 26:20; 31:14
19 a Ezek. 31:2, 18 b Ezek. 28:10
20 a Ps. 28:3
21 a Is. 1:31; 14:9, 10 b Ezek. 32:19, 25
22 a Ezek. 31:3, 16
23 a Is. 14:15 b Ezek. 32:24–27, 32
24 a Jer. 25:25; 49:34–39 b Ezek. 32:21 c Ezek. 32:23
25 a Ps. 139:8
26 a Gen. 10:2 b Ezek. 32:19
27 a Is. 14:18, 19

Who have gone down to hell with
their weapons of war;
They have laid their swords under
their heads,
But their iniquities will be on their
bones,
Because of the terror of the mighty
in the land of the living.

28 Yes, you shall be broken in the
midst of the uncircumcised,
And lie with *those* slain by the
sword.

29 “There *is* [a]Edom,
Her kings and all her princes,
Who despite their might
Are laid beside *those* slain by the
sword;
They shall lie with the uncircumcised,
And with those who go down to the
Pit.

30 [a]There *are* the princes of the
north,
All of them, and all the [b]Sidonians,
Who have gone down with the slain
In shame at the terror which they
caused by their might;
They lie uncircumcised with *those*
slain by the sword,
And bear their shame with those
who go down to the Pit.

31 “Pharaoh will see them
And be [a]comforted over all his
multitude,
Pharaoh and all his army,
Slain by the sword,”
Says the Lord GOD.

32 “For I have caused My terror in the
land of the living;
And he shall be placed in the midst
of the uncircumcised
With *those* slain by the sword,
Pharaoh and all his multitude,”
Says the Lord GOD.

The Watchman and His Message

33 Again the word of the LORD came
to me, saying, 2“Son of man, speak
to [a]the children of your people, and say to
them: [b]‘When I bring the sword upon a
land, and the people of the land take a
man from their territory and make him
their [c]watchman, 3when he sees the
sword coming upon the land, if he blows
the trumpet and warns the people, 4then
whoever hears the sound of the trumpet
and does [a]not take warning, if the sword
comes and takes him away, [b]his blood
shall be on his *own* head. 5He heard the
sound of the trumpet, but did not take
warning; his blood shall be upon himself.
But he who takes warning will [1]save his
life. 6But if the watchman sees the sword
coming and does not blow the trumpet,
and the people are not warned, and the
sword comes and takes *any* person from
among them, [a]he is taken away in his iniquity; but his blood I will require at the
watchman’s hand.’

Lord, as you called Ezekiel,
You have called ____ to be a
watchman for Your people.
May she hear a word from
Your mouth and faithfully
warn them for You.
FROM EZEKIEL 33:7

7[a]“So you, son of man: I have made you
a watchman for the house of Israel; therefore you shall hear a word from My mouth
and warn them for Me. 8When I say to the
wicked, ‘O wicked *man,* you shall surely
die!’ and you do not speak to warn the
wicked from his way, that wicked *man*
shall die in his iniquity; but his blood I
will require at your hand. 9Nevertheless if
you warn the wicked to turn from his way,
and he does not turn from his way, he
shall die in his iniquity; but you have [1]de-
livered your soul.
10“Therefore you, O son of man, say to
the house of Israel: ‘Thus you say, “If our
transgressions and our sins *lie* upon us,
and we [a]pine[1] away in them, [b]how can we
then live?” ’ 11Say to them: ‘*As* I live,’ says
the Lord GOD, [a]‘I have no pleasure in the
death of the wicked, but that the wicked
[b]turn from his way and live. Turn, turn
from your evil ways! For [c]why should you
die, O house of Israel?’

The Fairness of God’s Judgment

12“Therefore you, O son of man, say to
the children of your people: ‘The [a]righ-
teousness of the righteous man shall not

---

29 a Ezek. 25:12–14
30 a Jer. 1:15; 25:26 b Ezek. 28:21–23
31 a Ezek. 14:22; 31:16
CHAPTER 33
2 a Ezek. 3:11 b Ezek. 14:17 c 2 Sam. 18:24, 25
4 a Zech. 1:4 b [Acts 18:6]
5 *1* Or *deliver his soul*
6 a Ezek. 33:8
7 a Is. 62:6
9 *1* Or *saved your life*
10 a Ezek. 24:23 b Is. 49:14 *1* Or *waste away*
11 a [2 Sam. 14:14] b [Acts 3:19] c Ezek. 18:30, 31
12 a Ezek. 3:20; 18:24, 26

deliver him in the day of his transgression; as for the wickedness of the wicked,
[b]he shall not fall because of it in the day
that he turns from his wickedness; nor
shall the righteous be able to live because
of *his righteousness* in the day that he
sins.' [13]When I say to the righteous *that*
he shall surely live, [a]but he trusts in his
own righteousness and commits iniquity,
none of his righteous works shall be remembered; but because of the iniquity
that he has committed, he shall die.
[14]Again, [a]when I say to the wicked, 'You
shall surely die,' if he turns from his sin
and does [1]what is lawful and [2]right, [15]*if*
the wicked [a]restores the pledge, [b]gives
back what he has stolen, and walks in [c]the
statutes of life without committing iniquity, he shall surely live; he shall not die.
[16][a]None of his sins which he has committed shall be remembered against him; he
has done what is lawful and right; he shall
surely live.

[17][a]"Yet the children of your people say,
'The way of the LORD is not [1]fair.' But it
is their way which is not fair! [18][a]When the
righteous turns from his righteousness
and commits iniquity, he shall die because of it. [19]But when the wicked turns
from his wickedness and does what is lawful and right, he shall live because of it.
[20]Yet you say, [a]'The way of the LORD is not
[1]fair.' O house of Israel, I will judge every
one of you according to his own ways."

The Fall of Jerusalem

[21]And it came to pass in the twelfth year
[a]of our captivity, in the tenth *month,* on
the fifth *day* of the month, [b]*that* one who
had escaped from Jerusalem came to me
and said, [c]"The city has been [1]captured!"
[22]Now [a]the hand of the LORD had been
upon me the evening before the man
came who had escaped. And He had
[b]opened my mouth; so when he came to
me in the morning, my mouth was
opened, and I was no longer mute.

The Cause of Judah's Ruin

[23]Then the word of the LORD came to
me, saying: [24]"Son of man, [a]they who inhabit those [b]ruins in the land of Israel are
saying, [c]'Abraham was only one, and he
inherited the land. [d]But we *are* many; the
land has been given to us as a [e]posses-
sion.'

[25]"Therefore say to them, 'Thus says the
Lord GOD: [a]"You eat *meat* with blood, you
[b]lift up your eyes toward your idols, and
[c]shed blood. Should you then possess the
[d]land? [26]You rely on your sword, you
commit abominations, and you [a]defile
one another's wives. Should you then possess the land?" '

[27]"Say thus to them, 'Thus says the
Lord GOD: "*As* I live, surely [a]those who *are*
in the ruins shall fall by the sword, and
the one who *is* in the open field [b]I will give
to the beasts to be devoured, and those
who *are* in the strongholds and [c]caves
shall die of the pestilence. [28][a]For I will
make the land most desolate, [1]her [b]arro-
gant strength shall cease, and [c]the mountains of Israel shall be so desolate that no
one will pass through. [29]Then they shall
know that I *am* the LORD, when I have
made the land most desolate because of all
their abominations which they have committed." '

Hearing and Not Doing

[30]"As for you, son of man, the children
of your people are talking about you beside the walls and in the doors of the
houses; and they [a]speak to one another,
everyone saying to his brother, 'Please
come and hear what the word is that
comes from the LORD.' [31]So [a]they come to
you as people do, they [b]sit before you *as*
My people, and they [c]hear your words, but
they do not do them; [d]for with their
mouth they show much love, *but* [e]their
hearts pursue their *own* gain. [32]Indeed
you *are* to them as a very lovely song of
one who has a pleasant voice and can play
well on an instrument; for they hear your
words, but they do [a]not do them. [33][a]And
when this comes to pass—surely it will
come—then [b]they will know that a
prophet has been among them."

Irresponsible Shepherds

34 And the word of the LORD came
to me, saying, [2]"Son of man,
prophesy against the shepherds of Israel,
prophesy and say to them, 'Thus says the
Lord GOD to the shepherds: [a]"Woe to the
shepherds of Israel who feed themselves!
Should not the shepherds feed the
flocks? [3][a]You eat the fat and clothe
yourselves with the wool; you [b]slaughter
the fatlings, *but* you do not feed the flock.

12 b [2 Chr. 7:14]
13 a Ezek. 3:20; 18:24
14 a Ezek. 3:18, 19; 18:27 *1 justice* *2 righteousness*
15 a Ezek. 18:7 b Lev. 6:2, 4, 5 c Ezek. 20:11, 13, 21
16 a [Is. 1:18; 43:25]
17 a Ezek. 18:25, 29 *1* Or *equitable*
18 a Ezek. 18:26
20 a Ezek. 18:25, 29 *1* Or *equitable*
21 a Ezek. 1:2 b Ezek. 24:26 c 2 Kin. 25:4 *1* Lit. *struck down*
22 a Ezek. 1:3; 8:1; 37:1 b Ezek. 24:27
24 a Ezek. 34:2 b Ezek. 36:4 c Is. 51:2 d [Matt. 3:9] e Ezek. 11:15
25 a Lev. 3:17; 7:26; 17:10–14; 19:26 b Ezek. 18:6 c Ezek. 22:6, 9 d Deut. 29:28
26 a Ezek. 18:6; 22:11
27 a Ezek. 33:24 b Ezek. 39:4 c 1 Sam. 13:6
28 a Jer. 44:2, 6, 22 b Ezek. 7:24; 24:21 c Ezek. 6:2, 3, 6 *1* Lit. *pride of her strength*
30 a Is. 29:13
31 a Ezek. 14:1 b Ezek. 8:1 c Is. 58:2 d Ps. 78:36, 37 e [Matt. 13:22]
32 a [Matt. 7:21–28]
33 a 1 Sam. 3:20 b Ezek. 2:5

CHAPTER 34
2 a Zech. 11:17
3 a Zech. 11:16 b Ezek. 33:25, 26

EZEKIEL 34:2–10

Dear Woman of Destiny,

I'd like to share some things with you about what I believe is one of the most important areas of the Christian life—your relationship with a local church. When you join a church, you make a covenant not only with the local body of Christ, but also with God to obey the leadership of that church. Conversely, the leadership has a responsibility before God to keep watch over your soul. Any pastor who truly understands his role in the church will take his oversight of the sheep very seriously. Many members do not realize how heavily this responsibility can weigh on their pastor. It is painful for leaders of a church when church people reject the counsel and wisdom they could receive through local church leadership.

One little-understood concept in the church today is that of honoring those in authority over us. Of course, we are not to venerate or worship the leaders over us, but we do need to understand how to esteem and respect them. We honor them not just as people, but we also honor the positions in which the Lord has put them. At times, you may find yourself in a difference of opinion with a person in leadership, but you still need to submit to that person's position of authority unless it is unbiblical.

Unfortunately, there are situations when abuse does occur in a church setting. Abuse is not healthy, nor is it God's will, so what do you do if you are in a truly abusive spiritual situation? First of all, seek the Lord regarding whether you are to go or to stay. If you believe you are to leave that church or ministry, do it correctly. In other words, do everything you can to receive a blessing when you leave. Don't just run off without saying good-bye.

The balance between not submitting to abuse and keeping our attitude right can be delicate. When we have an adverse reaction to something a leader tells us, it is time to search our own hearts. We need to ask: Am I reacting out of past hurts and wounds, or is this really abuse? The truth may not be evident at first, but may require a prayerful time of seeking the Lord.

First Chronicles 16:22 has been a great blessing to persecuted leaders, but has also been taken out of context and used to "beat the sheep": It says, "Do not touch My anointed ones, and do My prophets no harm." This has wrongly been taken to mean that people in the congregation cannot think for themselves or question anything a leader says. This is not what the verse means, and is, in fact, dysfunctional. It *does* mean that even in the midst of our questionings, we need to keep our hearts right and not attack. If we come against a leader unjustly, God will protect and take care of the leader and we will answer to the Lord for what we've done.

The body of Christ is a beautiful place. I pray that God would heal you of any wounds that have been inflicted by or in the church, and that He would allow you to enjoy the fellowship He desires among His people.

Cindy Jacobs

4 [a]The weak you have not strengthened,
nor have you healed those who were sick,
nor bound up the broken, nor brought
back what was driven away, nor [b]sought
what was lost; but with [c]force and [1]cruel-
ty you have ruled them. 5 [a]So they were
[b]scattered because *there was* no shepherd; [c]and they became food for all the
beasts of the field when they were scattered. 6 My sheep [a]wandered through all
the mountains, and on every high hill;
yes, My flock was scattered over the whole
face of the earth, and no one was seeking
or searching *for them.*"
7 'Therefore, you shepherds, hear the
word of the LORD: 8 "*As* I live," says the
Lord GOD, "surely because My flock became a prey, and My flock [a]became food
for every beast of the field, because *there
was* no shepherd, nor did My shepherds
search for My flock, [b]but the shepherds
fed themselves and did not feed My
flock"— 9 therefore, O shepherds, hear
the word of the LORD! 10 Thus says the
Lord GOD: "Behold, I *am* [a]against the
shepherds, and [b]I will require My flock at
their hand; I will cause them to cease
feeding the sheep, and the shepherds shall
[c]feed themselves no more; for I will [d]de-
liver My flock from their mouths, that
they may no longer be food for them."

God, the True Shepherd

11 'For thus says the Lord GOD: "Indeed
I Myself will search for My sheep and seek
them out. 12 As a [a]shepherd seeks out his
flock on the day he is among his scattered
sheep, so will I seek out My sheep and
deliver them from all the places where
they were scattered on [b]a cloudy and dark
day. 13 And [a]I will bring them out from the
peoples and gather them from the countries, and will bring them to their own
land; I will feed them on the mountains of
Israel, [1]in the valleys and in all the inhabited places of the country. 14 [a]I will feed
them in good pasture, and their fold shall
be on the high mountains of Israel.
[b]There they shall lie down in a good fold
and feed in rich pasture on the mountains
of Israel. 15 I will feed My flock, and I will
make them lie down," says the Lord GOD.
16 [a]"I will seek what was lost and bring
back what was driven away, bind up the
broken and strengthen what was sick; but
I will destroy [b]the fat and the strong, and
feed them [c]in judgment."

17 'And *as for* you, O My flock, thus says
the Lord GOD: [a]"Behold, I shall judge between sheep and sheep, between rams and
goats. 18 *Is it* too little for you to have eat-
en up the good pasture, that you must
tread down with your feet the [1]residue of
your pasture—and to have drunk of the
clear waters, that you must foul the residue with your feet? 19 And *as for* My flock,
they eat what you have trampled with
your feet, and they drink what you have
fouled with your feet."
20 'Therefore thus says the Lord GOD to
them: [a]"Behold, I Myself will judge between the fat and the lean sheep. 21 Because you have pushed with side and
shoulder, butted all the weak ones with
your horns, and scattered them abroad,
22 therefore I will save My flock, and they
shall no longer be a prey; and I will judge
between sheep and sheep. 23 I will establish one [a]shepherd over them, and he
shall feed them—[b]My servant David. He
shall feed them and be their shepherd.
24 And [a]I, the LORD, will be their God, and
My servant David [b]a prince among them;
I, the LORD, have spoken.
25 [a]"I will make a covenant of peace with
them, and [b]cause wild beasts to cease
from the land; and they [c]will dwell safely
in the wilderness and sleep in the woods.
26 I will make them and the places all
around [a]My hill [b]a blessing; and I will
[c]cause showers to come down in their
season; there shall be [d]showers of blessing. 27 Then [a]the trees of the field shall
yield their fruit, and the earth shall yield
her increase. They shall be safe in their
land; and they shall know that I *am* the
LORD, when I have [b]broken the bands
of their yoke and delivered them from
the hand of those who [c]enslaved them.
28 And they shall no longer be a prey for
the nations, nor shall beasts of the land
devour them; but [a]they shall dwell safely,
and no one shall make *them* afraid. 29 I
will raise up for them a [a]garden[1] of renown, and they shall [b]no longer be consumed with hunger in the land, [c]nor
bear the shame of the Gentiles anymore.
30 Thus they shall know that [a]I, the LORD
their God, *am* with them, and they, the
house of Israel, *are* [b]My people," says the
Lord GOD.' "
31 "You are My [a]flock, the flock of My
pasture; you *are* men, *and* I *am* your
God," says the Lord GOD.

---

4 a Zech. 11:16 b Luke 15:4 c [1 Pet. 5:3] *1 harshness* or *rigor*
5 a Ezek. 33:21 b Matt. 9:36 c Is. 56:9
6 a 1 Pet. 2:25
8 a Ezek. 34:5, 6 b Ezek. 34:2, 10
10 a Jer. 21:13; 52:24–27 b Heb. 13:17 c Ezek. 34:2, 8 d Ezek. 13:23
12 a Jer. 31:10 b Ezek. 30:3
13 a Jer. 23:3 *1* Or *by the streams*
14 a [John 10:9] b Jer. 33:12
16 a Mic. 4:6 b Is. 10:16 c Jer. 10:24
17 a [Matt. 25:32]
18 *1 remainder*
20 a Ezek. 34:17
23 a [Is. 40:11] b Jer. 30:9
24 a Ex. 29:45 b Ezek. 37:24, 25
25 a Ezek. 37:26 b Is. 11:6–9 c Jer. 23:6
26 a Is. 56:7 b Zech. 8:13 c Lev. 26:4 d Ps. 68:9
27 a Is. 4:2 b Jer. 2:20 c Jer. 25:14
28 a Jer. 30:10
29 a [Is. 11:1] b Ezek. 36:29 c Ezek. 36:3, 6, 15 *1* Lit. *planting place*
30 a Ezek. 34:24 b Ezek. 14:11; 36:28
31 a Ps. 100:3

Judgment on Mount Seir

35 Moreover the word of the LORD came to me, saying, 2“Son of man, set your face against [a]Mount Seir and [b]prophesy against it, 3and say to it, ‘Thus says the Lord GOD:

“Behold, O Mount Seir, I *am* against
you;
[a]I will stretch out My hand against
you,
And make you [1]most desolate;
4 I shall lay your cities waste,
And you shall be desolate.
Then you shall know that I *am* the
LORD.

5[a]“Because you have had an [1]ancient hatred, and have shed *the blood of* the children of Israel by the power of the sword at the time of their calamity, [b]*when* their iniquity *came to an* end, 6therefore, *as* I live,” says the Lord GOD, “I will prepare you for [a]blood, and blood shall pursue you; [b]since you have not hated [1]blood, therefore blood shall pursue you. 7Thus I will make Mount Seir [1]most desolate, and cut off from it the [a]one who leaves and the one who returns. 8And I will fill its mountains with the slain; on your hills and in your valleys and in all your ravines those who are slain by the sword shall fall. 9[a]I will make you [1]perpetually desolate, and your cities shall be uninhabited; [b]then you shall know that I *am* the LORD.

10“Because you have said, ‘These two nations and these two countries shall be mine, and we will [a]possess them,’ although [b]the LORD was there, 11therefore, *as* I live,” says the Lord GOD, “I will do [a]according to your anger and according to the envy which you showed in your hatred against them; and I will make Myself known among them when I judge you. 12[a]Then you shall know that I *am* the LORD. I have [b]heard all your [c]blasphemies which you have spoken against the mountains of Israel, saying, ‘They are desolate; they are given to us to consume.’ 13Thus [a]with your mouth you have [1]boasted against Me and multiplied your [b]words against Me; I have heard *them.*”

14‘Thus says the Lord GOD: [a]“The whole earth will rejoice when I make you desolate. 15[a]As you rejoiced because the inheritance of the house of Israel was desolate, [b]so I will do to you; you shall be desolate, O Mount Seir, as well as all of Edom—all of it! Then they shall know that I *am* the LORD.” ’

CHAPTER 35
2 a Ezek. 25:12–14 b Amos 1:11
3 a Ezek. 6:14 *1* Lit. *a desolation and a waste*
5 a Ezek. 25:12 b Ps. 137:7 *1* Or *everlasting*
6 a Is. 63:1–6 b Ps. 109:17 *1* Or *bloodshed*
7 a Judg. 5:6 *1* Lit. *a waste and a desolation*
9 a Jer. 49:13 b Ezek. 36:11 *1* Lit. *desolated forever*
10 a Ps. 83:4–12 b [Ps. 48:1–3; 132:13, 14]
11 a [James 2:13]
12 a Ps. 9:16 b Zeph. 2:8 c Is. 52:5
13 a [1 Sam. 2:3] b Ezek. 36:3 *1* Lit. *made yourself great*
14 a Is. 65:13, 14
15 a Obad. 12, 15 b Lam. 4:21

CHAPTER 36
1 a Ezek. 6:2, 3
2 a Ezek. 25:3; 26:2 b Deut. 32:13 c Ezek. 35:10 *1* Or *everlasting*
3 a Deut. 28:37 b Ezek. 35:13
4 a Ezek. 34:8, 28 b Ps. 79:4 *1* Or *ravines*
5 a Deut. 4:24 b Ezek. 35:10, 12 *1* Lit. *scorning souls*
6 a Ps. 74:10; 123:3, 4
7 a Ezek. 20:5 b Jer. 25:9, 15, 29
10 a Amos 9:14
11 a Jer. 31:27; 33:12 b Is. 51:3 c Ezek. 35:9; 37:6, 13

Blessing on Israel

36 “And you, son of man, prophesy to the [a]mountains of Israel, and say, ‘O mountains of Israel, hear the word of the LORD! 2Thus says the Lord GOD: “Because [a]the enemy has said of you, ‘Aha! [b]The [1]ancient heights [c]have become our possession,’ ” ’ 3therefore prophesy, and say, ‘Thus says the Lord GOD: “Because they made *you* desolate and swallowed you up on every side, so that you became the possession of the rest of the nations, [a]and you are taken up by the lips of [b]talkers and slandered by the people”— 4therefore, O mountains of Israel, hear the word of the Lord GOD! Thus says the Lord GOD to the mountains, the hills, the [1]rivers, the valleys, the desolate wastes, and the cities that have been forsaken, which [a]became plunder and [b]mockery to the rest of the nations all around— 5therefore thus says the Lord GOD: [a]“Surely I have spoken in My burning jealousy against the rest of the nations and against all Edom, [b]who gave My land to themselves as a possession, with wholehearted joy *and* [1]spiteful minds, in order to plunder its open country.” ’

6“Therefore prophesy concerning the land of Israel, and say to the mountains, the hills, the rivers, and the valleys, ‘Thus says the Lord GOD: “Behold, I have spoken in My jealousy and My fury, because you have [a]borne the shame of the nations.” 7Therefore thus says the Lord GOD: “I have [a]raised My hand in an oath that surely the nations that *are* around you shall [b]bear their own shame. 8But you, O mountains of Israel, you shall shoot forth your branches and yield your fruit to My people Israel, for they are about to come. 9For indeed I *am* for you, and I will turn to you, and you shall be tilled and sown. 10I will multiply men upon you, all the house of Israel, all of it; and the cities shall be inhabited and [a]the ruins rebuilt. 11[a]I will multiply upon you man and beast; and they shall increase and [1]bear young; I will make you inhabited as in former times, and do [b]better *for you* than at your beginnings. [c]Then you shall know

1 Lit. *be fruitful*

that I *am* the LORD. 12Yes, I will cause men to walk on you, My people Israel; [a]they shall take possession of you, and you shall be their inheritance; no more shall you [b]bereave them *of children.*"

13"Thus says the Lord GOD: "Because they say to you, [a]'You devour men and bereave your nation *of children,*' 14therefore you shall devour men no more, nor bereave your nation anymore," says the Lord GOD. 15[a]Nor will I let you hear the taunts of the nations anymore, nor bear the reproach of the peoples anymore, nor shall you cause your nation to stumble anymore," says the Lord GOD.' "

O Lord, cleanse ___ from their filthiness and their idols. Give them a new heart and put a new spirit within them; take their heart of stone and give them a heart of flesh.

FROM EZEKIEL 36:25, 26

The Renewal of Israel

16Moreover the word of the LORD came to me, saying: 17"Son of man, when the house of Israel dwelt in their own land, [a]they defiled it by their own ways and deeds; to Me their way was like [b]the uncleanness of a woman in her customary impurity. 18Therefore I poured out My fury on them [a]for the blood they had shed on the land, and for their idols *with which* they had defiled it. 19So I [a]scattered them among the nations, and they were dispersed throughout the countries; I judged them [b]according to their ways and their deeds. 20When they came to the nations, wherever they went, they [a]profaned My holy name—when they said of them, 'These *are* the people of the LORD, *and* yet they have gone out of His land.' 21But I had concern [a]for My holy name, which the house of Israel had profaned among the nations wherever they went.

22"Therefore say to the house of Israel, 'Thus says the Lord GOD: "I do not do *this* for your sake, O house of Israel, [a]but for My holy name's sake, which you have profaned among the nations wherever you went. 23And I will sanctify My great name, which has been profaned among the nations, which you have profaned in their midst; and the nations shall know that I *am* the LORD," says the Lord GOD, "when I am [a]hallowed in you before their eyes. 24For [a]I will take you from among the nations, gather you out of all countries, and bring you into your own land. 25[a]Then I will sprinkle clean water on you, and you shall be clean; I will cleanse you [b]from all your filthiness and from all your idols. 26I will give you a [a]new heart and put a new spirit within you; I will take the heart of stone out of your flesh and give you a heart of flesh. 27I will put My [a]Spirit within you and cause you to walk in My statutes, and you will keep My judgments and do *them.* 28[a]Then you shall dwell in the land that I gave to your fathers; [b]you shall be My people, and I will be your God. 29I will [a]deliver you from all your uncleannesses. [b]I will call for the grain and multiply it, and [c]bring no famine upon you. 30[a]And I will multiply the fruit of your trees and the increase of your fields, so that you need never again bear the reproach of famine among the nations. 31Then [a]you will remember your evil ways and your deeds that *were* not good; and you [b]will [1]loathe yourselves in your own sight, for your iniquities and your abominations. 32[a]Not for your sake do I do *this,*" says the Lord GOD, "let it be known to you. Be ashamed and confounded for your own ways, O house of Israel!"

33"Thus says the Lord GOD: "On the day that I cleanse you from all your iniquities, I will also enable *you* to dwell in the cities, [a]and the ruins shall be rebuilt. 34The desolate land shall be tilled instead of lying desolate in the sight of all who pass by. 35So they will say, 'This land that was desolate has become like the garden of [a]Eden; and the wasted, desolate, and ruined cities *are now* fortified *and* inhabited.' 36Then the nations which are left all around you shall know that I, the LORD, have rebuilt the ruined places *and* planted what was desolate. [a]I, the LORD, have spoken *it,* and I will do *it.*"

37"Thus says the Lord GOD: [a]"I will also let the house of Israel inquire of Me to do this for them: I will [b]increase their men like a flock. 38Like a [1]flock *offered as* holy *sacrifices,* like the flock at Jerusalem on its [2]feast days, so shall the ruined cities be

12 a Obad. 17 b Jer. 15:7
13 a Num. 13:32
15 a Ezek. 34:29
17 a Jer. 2:7 b Lev. 15:19
18 a Ezek. 16:36, 38; 23:37
19 a Deut. 28:64 b [Rom. 2:6]
20 a Rom. 2:24
21 a Ezek. 20:9, 14
22 a Ps. 106:8
23 a Ezek. 20:41; 28:22
24 a Ezek. 34:13; 37:21
25 a Heb. 9:13, 19; 10:22 b Jer. 33:8
26 a Ezek. 11:19
27 a Ezek. 11:19; 37:14
28 a Ezek. 28:25; 37:25 b Jer. 30:22
29 a [Rom. 11:26] b Ps. 105:16 c Ezek. 34:27, 29
30 a Ezek. 34:27
31 a Ezek. 16:61, 63 b Ezek. 6:9; 20:43 *1 despise*
32 a Deut. 9:5
33 a Ezek. 36:10
35 a Joel 2:3
36 a Ezek. 17:24; 22:14; 37:14
37 a Ezek. 14:3; 20:3, 31 b Ezek. 36:10
38 *1* Lit. *holy flock* *2 appointed feasts*

filled with flocks of men. Then they shall
know that I *am* the LORD." ' "

The Dry Bones Live

37 The [a]hand of the LORD came
upon me and brought me out [b]in
the Spirit of the LORD, and set me down
in the midst of the valley; and it *was* full
of bones. 2Then He caused me to pass by
them all around, and behold, *there were*
very many in the open valley; and indeed
they were very dry. 3And He said to me,
"Son of man, can these bones live?"
So I answered, "O Lord GOD, [a]You
know."
4Again He said to me, "Prophesy to
these bones, and say to them, 'O dry
bones, hear the word of the LORD!
5Thus says the Lord GOD to these bones:
"Surely I will [a]cause breath to enter into
you, and you shall live. 6I will put sinews
on you and bring flesh upon you, cover
you with skin and put breath in you; and
you shall live. [a]Then you shall know that
I *am* the LORD." ' "
7So I prophesied as I was commanded;
and as I prophesied, there was a noise, and
suddenly a rattling; and the bones came
together, bone to bone. 8Indeed, as I
looked, the sinews and the flesh came
upon them, and the skin covered them
over; but *there was* no breath in them.
9Also He said to me, "Prophesy to the
breath, prophesy, son of man, and say to
the [1]breath, 'Thus says the Lord GOD:
[a]"Come from the four winds, O breath,
and breathe on these slain, that they may
live." ' " 10So I prophesied as He commanded me, [a]and [1]breath came into
them, and they lived, and stood upon their
feet, an exceedingly great army.
11Then He said to me, "Son of man,
these bones are the [a]whole house of Israel. They indeed say, [b]'Our bones are dry,
our hope is lost, and we ourselves are
cut off!' 12Therefore prophesy and say to
them, 'Thus says the Lord GOD: "Behold,
[a]O My people, I will open your graves and
cause you to come up from your graves,
and [b]bring you into the land of Israel.
13Then you shall know that I *am* the
LORD, when I have opened your graves,
O My people, and brought you up from
your graves. 14I [a]will put My Spirit in you,
and you shall live, and I will place you in
your own land. Then you shall know that
I, the LORD, have spoken *it* and performed
it," says the LORD.' "

CHAPTER 37
1 a Ezek. 1:3 b Ezek. 3:14; 8:3; 11:24
3 a [1 Sam. 2:6]
5 a Ps. 104:29, 30
6 a Joel 2:27; 3:17
9 a [Ps. 104:30] *1* Breath of life
10 a Rev. 11:11 *1* Breath of life
11 a Ezek. 36:10 b Ps. 141:7
12 a Is. 26:19; 66:14 b Ezek. 36:24
14 a Ezek. 36:27
16 a Num. 17:2, 3 b 2 Chr. 11:12, 13, 16; 15:9; 30:11, 18
17 a Hos. 1:11
18 a Ezek. 12:9; 24:19
19 a Zech. 10:6 b Ezek. 37:16, 17
20 a Ezek. 12:3
21 a Ezek. 36:24
22 a Jer. 3:18 b Ezek. 34:23
23 a Ezek. 36:25 b Ezek. 36:28, 29
24 a Is. 40:11 b [John 10:16] c Ezek. 36:27
25 a Ezek. 36:28 b Is. 60:21 c John 12:34
26 a Is. 55:3 b Ezek. 36:10 c [2 Cor. 6:16] *1* Lit. *cut*
27 a [John 1:14] b Ezek. 11:20

One Kingdom, One King

15Again the word of the LORD came to
me, saying, 16"As for you, son of man,
[a]take a stick for yourself and write on it:
'For Judah and for [b]the children of Israel,
his companions.' Then take another stick
and write on it, 'For Joseph, the stick of
Ephraim, and *for* all the house of Israel,
his companions.' 17Then [a]join them one
to another for yourself into one stick, and
they will become one in your hand.
18"And when the children of your people speak to you, saying, [a]'Will you not
show us what you *mean* by these?'—
19[a]say to them, 'Thus says the Lord GOD:
"Surely I will take [b]the stick of Joseph,
which *is* in the hand of Ephraim, and the
tribes of Israel, his companions; and I will
join them with it, with the stick of Judah,
and make them one stick, and they will be
one in My hand." ' 20And the sticks on
which you write will be in your hand [a]be-
fore their eyes.
21"Then say to them, 'Thus says the
Lord GOD: "Surely [a]I will take the children of Israel from among the nations,
wherever they have gone, and will gather
them from every side and bring them into
their own land; 22and [a]I will make them
one nation in the land, on the mountains
of Israel; and [b]one king shall be king over
them all; they shall no longer be two nations, nor shall they ever be divided into
two kingdoms again. 23[a]They shall not defile themselves anymore with their idols,
nor with their detestable things, nor with
any of their transgressions; but [b]I will deliver them from all their dwelling places
in which they have sinned, and will
cleanse them. Then they shall be My people, and I will be their God.
24"[a]David My servant *shall be* king over
them, and [b]they shall all have one shepherd; [c]they shall also walk in My judgments and observe My statutes, and do
them. 25[a]Then they shall dwell in the land
that I have given to Jacob My servant,
where your fathers dwelt; and they shall
dwell there, they, their children, and their
children's children, [b]forever; and [c]My servant David *shall be* their prince forever.
26Moreover I will [1]make [a]a covenant of
peace with them, and it shall be an everlasting covenant with them; I will establish them and [b]multiply them, and I will
set My [c]sanctuary in their midst forevermore. 27[a]My tabernacle also shall be with
them; indeed I will be [b]their God, and

Ezekiel 37:1–4

Dear Woman of Destiny,

Every successful woman of God goes through times of dryness. When that happens, we're usually bewildered by God's silence. Where is God in the midst of all this? Will I ever feel His presence again? Is He angry with me? I feel like a failure. Why can't I hear His voice? Day after day the questions go unanswered. One yearns to leave the desert and experience the refreshing river of God.

I remember times of dryness in my own life. Although those seasons seemed so long at the moment, I now realize how short they really were. The Lord knows what He is doing. He also knows how long it takes to do the work in me that must be done.

During dry seasons, the Lord will set you on a path toward restoration. He wants to free you from the pain and disappointment of the past as much as you want Him to! God will do His part, but you must do yours. One of the important things to do during seasons of dryness is to prophesy. Prophecy will revive the dry, dead places in your life.

The Hebrew word for prophesy is *naba'*. It means "to bubble or flow forth; to gush; to flow; to boil up or over." *Naba'* is the word used in Ezekiel when he was commanded by the Lord to speak to the dry bones: "Prophesy to these bones, and say to them, 'O dry bones, hear the word of the LORD!'" (v. 4).

God promised that the dry bones would be raised from their graves, brought back to life, and restored to their inheritance. You have the same promise from the Lord. You have a divine inheritance. Ask Him to show you the heritage He has for you. Then speak to the dry places that are holding back your restoration. Don't wait for the next prophet to come to town and do what you are able to do. Prophecy is simply "speaking forth the mind of God." Once the Lord reveals His will for the restoration He has for you, speak forth His mind.

As the prophetic word is released from your mouth, rivers will break out in your desert. "Behold, I will do a new thing, now it shall spring forth; . . . I will even make a road in the wilderness and rivers in the desert" (Is. 43:19).

Woman of Destiny, there is a river inside you, waiting to be released. Prophesy, and the Lord will begin to reveal to you how great your restoration will be.

Barbara Wentroble

they shall be My people. 28[a]The nations also will know that I, the LORD, [b]sanctify Israel, when My sanctuary is in their midst forevermore." ' "

Gog and Allies Attack Israel

38 Now the word of the LORD came to me, saying, 2[a]"Son of man, [b]set your face against [c]Gog, of the land of [d]Magog, [1]the prince of Rosh, [e]Meshech, and Tubal, and prophesy against him, 3and say, 'Thus says the Lord GOD: "Behold, I *am* against you, O Gog, the prince of Rosh, Meshech, and Tubal. 4[a]I will turn you around, put hooks into your jaws, and [b]lead you out, with all your army, horses, and horsemen, [c]all splendidly clothed, a great company *with* bucklers and shields, all of them handling swords. 5Persia, [1]Ethiopia, and [2]Libya are with them, all of them *with* shield and helmet; 6[a]Gomer and all its troops; the house of [b]Togarmah *from* the far north and all its troops—many people *are* with you.

7[a]"Prepare yourself and be ready, you and all your companies that are gathered about you; and be a guard for them. 8[a]After many days [b]you will be visited. In the latter years you will come into the land of those brought back from the sword [c]*and* gathered from many people on [d]the mountains of Israel, which had long been desolate; they were brought out of the nations, and now all of them [e]dwell safely. 9You will ascend, coming [a]like a storm, covering the [b]land like a cloud, you and all your troops and many peoples with you."

10"Thus says the Lord GOD: "On that day it shall come to pass *that* thoughts will arise in your mind, and you will make an evil plan: 11You will say, 'I will go up against a land of [a]unwalled villages; I will [b]go to a peaceful people, [c]who dwell [1]safely, all of them dwelling without walls, and having neither bars nor gates'— 12to take plunder and to take booty, to stretch out your hand against the waste places *that are again* inhabited, [a]and against a people gathered from the nations, who have acquired livestock and goods, who dwell in the midst of the land. 13[a]Sheba, [b]Dedan, the merchants [c]of Tarshish, and all [d]their young lions will say to you, 'Have you come to take plunder? Have you gathered your army to take booty, to carry away silver and gold, to take away livestock and goods, to take great plunder?' " '

14"Therefore, son of man, prophesy and say to Gog, 'Thus says the Lord GOD: [a]"On that day when My people Israel [b]dwell safely, will you not know *it?* 15[a]Then you will come from your place out of the far north, you and many peoples with you, all of them riding on horses, a great company and a mighty army. 16You will come up against My people Israel like a cloud, to cover the land. It will be in the latter days that I will bring you against My land, so that the nations may [a]know Me, when I am [b]hallowed in you, O Gog, before their eyes." 17Thus says the Lord GOD: "Are *you* he of whom I have spoken in former days by My servants the prophets of Israel, who prophesied for years in those days that I would bring you against them?

Judgment on Gog

18"And it will come to pass at the same time, when Gog comes against the land of Israel," says the Lord GOD, "*that* My fury will show in My face. 19For [a]in My jealousy [b]*and* in the fire of My wrath I have spoken: [c]'Surely in that day there shall be a great [1]earthquake in the land of Israel, 20so that [a]the fish of the sea, the birds of the heavens, the beasts of the field, all creeping things that creep on the earth, and all men who *are* on the face of the earth shall shake at My presence. [b]The mountains shall be thrown down, the steep places shall fall, and every wall shall fall to the ground.' 21I will [a]call for [b]a sword against Gog throughout all My mountains," says the Lord GOD. [c]"Every man's sword will be against his brother. 22And I will [a]bring him to judgment with [b]pestilence and bloodshed; [c]I will rain down on him, on his troops, and on the many peoples who *are* with him, flooding rain, [d]great hailstones, fire, and brimstone. 23Thus I will magnify Myself and [a]sanctify Myself, [b]and I will be known in the eyes of many nations. Then they shall know that I *am* the LORD." '

Gog's Armies Destroyed

39 "And [a]you, son of man, prophesy against Gog, and say, 'Thus says the Lord GOD: "Behold, I *am* against you, O Gog, [1]the prince of Rosh, Meshech, and Tubal; 2and I will [a]turn you around and lead you on, [b]bringing you up from the far

28 a Ezek. 36:23 b Ezek. 20:12

CHAPTER 38
2 a Ezek. 39:1 b Ezek. 35:2, 3 c Rev. 20:8 d Gen. 10:2 e Ezek. 32:26 *1* Tg., Vg., Aquila *the chief prince of Meshech,* also v. 3
4 a 2 Kin. 19:28 b Is. 43:17 c Ezek. 23:12
5 *1* Heb. *Cush* *2* Heb. *Put*
6 a Gen. 10:2 b Ezek. 27:14
7 a Is. 8:9, 10
8 a Is. 24:22 b Is. 29:6 c Ezek. 34:13 d Ezek. 36:1, 4 e Ezek. 34:25; 39:26
9 a Is. 28:2 b Jer. 4:13
11 a Zech. 2:4 b Jer. 49:31 c Ezek. 38:8 *1 securely*
12 a Ezek. 38:8
13 a Ezek. 27:22 b Ezek. 27:15, 20 c Ezek. 27:12 d Ezek. 19:3, 5
14 a Is. 4:1 b Ezek. 38:8, 11
15 a Ezek. 39:2
16 a Ezek. 35:11 b Ezek. 28:22
19 a Ezek. 36:5, 6 b Ps. 89:46 c Rev. 16:18 *1* Lit. *shaking*
20 a Hos. 4:3 b Jer. 4:24
21 a Ps. 105:16 b Ezek. 14:17 c 1 Sam. 14:20
22 a Is. 66:16 b Ezek. 5:17 c Ps. 11:6 d Rev. 16:21
23 a Ezek. 36:23 b Ezek. 37:28; 38:16

CHAPTER 39
1 a Ezek. 38:2, 3 *1* Tg., Vg., Aquila *the chief prince of Meshech*

2 a Ezek. 38:8 b Ezek. 38:15

north, and bring you against the mountains of Israel. [3]Then I will knock the bow
out of your left hand, and cause the arrows to fall out of your right hand. [4][a]You
shall [1]fall upon the mountains of Israel,
you and all your troops and the peoples
who *are* with you; [b]I will give you to birds
of prey of every sort and *to* the beasts of
the field to be devoured. [5]You shall [1]fall
on [2]the open field; for I have spoken," says
the Lord GOD. [6][a]"And I will send fire on
Magog and on those who live [1]in security
in [b]the coastlands. Then they shall know
that I *am* the LORD. [7][a]So I will make My
holy name known in the midst of My people Israel, and I will not *let them* [b]profane
My holy name anymore. [c]Then the nations shall know that *I am* the LORD, the
Holy One in Israel. [8][a]Surely it is coming,
and it shall be done," says the Lord GOD.
"This *is* the day [b]of which I have spoken.
[9]"Then those who dwell in the cities of
Israel will go out and set on fire and burn
the weapons, both the shields and bucklers, the bows and arrows, the [1]javelins
and spears; and they will make fires with
them for seven years. [10]They will not take
wood from the field nor cut down *any*
from the forests, because they will make
fires with the weapons; [a]and they will
plunder those who plundered them, and
pillage those who pillaged them," says the
Lord GOD.

The Burial of Gog

[11]"It will come to pass in that day *that*
I will give Gog a burial place there in Israel, the valley of those who pass by east of
the sea; and it will obstruct travelers,
because there they will bury Gog and all
his multitude. Therefore they will call *it*
the Valley of [1]Hamon Gog. [12]For seven
months the house of Israel will be burying
them, [a]in order to cleanse the land. [13]In-
deed all the people of the land will be
burying, and they will gain [a]renown for it
on the day that [b]I am glorified," says the
Lord GOD. [14]"They will set apart men regularly employed, with the help of [1]a
search party, to pass through the land
and bury those bodies remaining on the
ground, in order [a]to cleanse it. At the end
of seven months they will make a search.
[15]The search party will pass through the
land; and *when anyone* sees a man's bone,
he shall [1]set up a marker by it, till the
buriers have buried it in the Valley of Hamon Gog. [16]*The* name of *the* city *will* also
be [1]Hamonah. Thus they shall [a]cleanse
the land." '

A Triumphant Festival

[17]"And as for you, son of man, thus says
the Lord GOD, [a]'Speak to every sort of bird
and to every beast of the field:

[b]"Assemble yourselves and come;
Gather together from all sides to
My [c]sacrificial meal
Which I am sacrificing for you,
A great sacrificial meal [d]on the
mountains of Israel,
That you may eat flesh and drink
blood.
18 [a]You shall eat the flesh of the mighty,
Drink the blood of the princes of
the earth,
Of rams and lambs,
Of goats and bulls,
All of them [b]fatlings of Bashan.
19 You shall eat fat till you are full,
And drink blood till you are drunk,
At My sacrificial meal
Which I am sacrificing for you.
20 [a]You shall be filled at My table
With horses and riders,
[b]With mighty men
And with all the men of war," says
the Lord GOD.

Israel Restored to the Land

[21][a]"I will set My glory among the nations; all the nations shall see My judgment which I have executed, and [b]My
hand which I have laid on them. [22][a]So the
house of Israel shall know that I *am* the
LORD their God from that day forward.
[23][a]The Gentiles shall know that the house
of Israel went into captivity for their iniquity; because they were unfaithful to Me,
therefore [b]I hid My face from them. I
[c]gave them into the hand of their enemies, and they all fell by the sword. [24][a]Ac-
cording to their uncleanness and
according to their transgressions I have
dealt with them, and hidden My face from
them." '
[25]"Therefore thus says the Lord GOD:
[a]'Now I will bring back the captives of Jacob, and have mercy on the [b]whole house
of Israel; and I will be jealous for My holy
name— [26][a]after they have borne their
shame, and all their unfaithfulness in
which they were unfaithful to Me, when
they [b]dwelt safely in their *own* land and

4 a Ezek. 38:4, 21 b Ezek. 33:27 *1* Be slain
5 *1* Be slain *2* Lit. *the face of the field*
6 a Amos 1:4, 7, 10 b Ps. 72:10 *1 securely* or *confidently*
7 a Ezek. 39:25 b Lev. 18:21 c Ezek. 38:16
8 a Rev. 16:17; 21:6 b Ezek. 38:17
9 *1* Lit. *hand staffs*
10 a Is. 14:2; 33:1
11 *1* Lit. *The Multitude of Gog*
12 a Deut. 21:23
13 a Zeph. 3:19, 20 b Ezek. 28:22
14 a Ezek. 39:12 *1* Lit. *those who pass through*
15 *1 build*
16 a Ezek. 39:12 *1* Lit. *Multitude*
17 a Rev. 19:17, 18 b Is. 18:6 c Zeph. 1:7 d Ezek. 39:4
18 a Rev. 19:18 b Deut. 32:14
20 a Ps. 76:5, 6 b Rev. 19:18
21 a Ezek. 36:23; 38:23 b Ex. 7:4
22 a Ex. 39:7, 28
23 a Ezek. 36:18–20, 23 b Is. 1:15; 59:2 c Lev. 26:25
24 a Ezek. 36:19
25 a Ezek. 34:13; 36:24 b Hos. 1:11
26 a Dan. 9:16 b Lev. 26:5, 6

no one made *them* afraid. 27 [a]When I have
brought them back from the peoples and
gathered them out of their enemies'
lands, and I [b]am hallowed in them in the
sight of many nations, 28 [a]then they shall
know that I *am* the LORD their God, who
sent them into captivity among the nations, but also brought them back to their
land, and left none of them [1]captive any
longer. 29 [a]And I will not hide My face
from them anymore; for I shall have
[b]poured out My Spirit on the house of Israel,' says the Lord GOD."

A New City, a New Temple

40 In the twenty-fifth year of our captivity, at the beginning of the year,
on the tenth *day* of the month, in the
fourteenth year after [a]the city was [1]cap-
tured, on the very same day [b]the hand of
the LORD was upon me; and He took me
there. 2 [a]In the visions of God He took me
into the land of Israel and [b]set me on a
very high mountain; on it toward the
south *was* something like the structure of
a city. 3 He took me there, and behold,
there was a man whose appearance *was*
[a]like the appearance of bronze. [b]He had a
line of flax [c]and a measuring rod in his
hand, and he stood in the gateway.

4 And the man said to me, [a]"Son of man,
look with your eyes and hear with your
ears, and [1]fix your mind on everything I
show you; for you *were* brought here so
that I might show *them* to you. [b]Declare
to the house of Israel everything you see."
5 Now there was [a]a wall all around the outside of the [1]temple. In the man's hand was
a measuring rod six [2]cubits *long, each being a* cubit and a handbreadth; and he
measured the width of the wall structure,
one rod; and the height, one rod.

The Eastern Gateway of the Temple

6 Then he went to the gateway which
faced [a]east; and he went up its stairs and
measured the threshold of the gateway,
which was one rod wide, and the other
threshold *was* one rod wide. 7 Each gate
chamber *was* one rod long and one rod
wide; between the gate chambers *was a
space of* five cubits; and the threshold of
the gateway by the vestibule of the inside
gate *was* one rod. 8 He also measured the
vestibule of the inside gate, one rod.
9 Then he measured the vestibule of the
gateway, eight cubits; and the gateposts,
two cubits. The vestibule of the gate *was*
on the inside. 10 In the eastern gateway
were three gate chambers on one side and
three on the other; the three *were* all the
same size; also the gateposts were of the
same size on this side and that side.

11 He measured the width of the entrance to the gateway, ten cubits; *and*
the length of the gate, thirteen cubits.
12 *There was* a [1]space in front of the gate
chambers, one cubit *on this side* and one
cubit on that side; the gate chambers *were*
six cubits on this side and six cubits on
that side. 13 Then he measured the gateway from the roof of *one* gate chamber
to the roof of the other; the width *was*
twenty-five cubits, as door faces door.
14 He measured the gateposts, sixty cubits
high, and the court all around the gateway *extended* to the gatepost. 15 *From* the
front of the entrance gate to the front of
the vestibule of the inner gate *was* fifty
cubits. 16 *There were* [a]beveled window
frames in the gate chambers and in their
intervening archways on the inside of the
gateway all around, and likewise in the
vestibules. *There were* windows all
around on the inside. And on each gatepost *were* [b]palm trees.

The Outer Court

17 Then he brought me into [a]the outer
court; and *there were* [b]chambers and a
pavement made all around the court;
[c]thirty chambers faced the pavement.
18 The pavement was by the side of the
gateways, corresponding to the length of
the gateways; *this was* the lower pavement. 19 Then he measured the width
from the front of the lower gateway to the
front of the inner court exterior, one hundred cubits toward the east and the north.

The Northern Gateway

20 On the outer court was also a gateway
facing north, and he measured its length
and its width. 21 Its gate chambers, three
on this side and three on that side, its
gateposts and its archways, had the same
measurements as the first gate; its length
was fifty cubits and its width twenty-five
cubits. 22 Its windows and those of its
archways, and also its palm trees, *had* the
same measurements as the gateway facing
east; it was ascended by seven steps, and
its archway *was* in front of it. 23 A gate of
the inner court was opposite the northern

27 [a]Ezek. 28:25, 26 [b]Ezek. 36:23, 24; 38:16
28 [a]Ezek. 34:30 [1]Lit. *there*
29 [a]Is. 54:8, 9 [b][Joel 2:28]
CHAPTER 40
1 [a]Ezek. 33:21 [b]Ezek. 1:3; 3:14, 22; 37:1 [1]Lit. *struck*
2 [a]Ezek. 1:1; 3:14; 8:3; 37:1 [b]Rev. 21:10
3 [a]Dan. 10:6 [b]Ezek. 47:3 [c]Rev. 11:1; 21:15
4 [a]Ezek. 44:5 [b]Ezek. 43:10 [1]Lit. *set your heart*
5 [a]Ezek. 42:20 [1]Lit. *house* [2]A royal cubit of about 21 inches
6 [a]Ezek. 43:1
12 [1]Lit. *border*
16 [a]1 Kin. 6:4 [b]1 Kin. 6:29, 32, 35
17 [a]Rev. 11:2 [b]1 Kin. 6:5 [c]Ezek. 45:5

gateway, just as the eastern *gateway;* and he measured from gateway to gateway, one hundred cubits.

The Southern Gateway

24After that he brought me toward the south, and there a gateway was facing south; and he measured its gateposts and archways according to these same measurements. 25*There were* windows in it and in its archways all around like those windows; its length *was* fifty cubits and its width twenty-five cubits. 26Seven steps led up to it, and its archway *was* in front of them; and it had palm trees on its gateposts, one on this side and one on that side. 27*There was* also a gateway on the inner court, facing south; and he measured from gateway to gateway toward the south, one hundred cubits.

Gateways of the Inner Court

28Then he brought me to the inner court through the southern gateway; he measured the southern gateway according to these same measurements. 29Also its gate chambers, its gateposts, and its archways *were* according to these same measurements; *there were* windows in it and in its archways all around; *it was* fifty cubits long and twenty-five cubits wide. 30*There were* archways all around, [a]twenty-five cubits long and five cubits wide. 31Its archways faced the outer court, palm trees *were* on its gateposts, and going up to it *were* eight steps.

32And he brought me into the inner court facing east; he measured the gateway according to these same measurements. 33Also its gate chambers, its gateposts, and its archways *were* according to these same measurements; and *there were* windows in it and in its archways all around; *it was* fifty cubits long and twenty-five cubits wide. 34Its archways faced the outer court, and palm trees *were* on its gateposts on this side and on that side; and going up to it *were* eight steps.

35Then he brought me to the north gateway and measured *it* according to these same measurements— 36also its gate chambers, its gateposts, and its archways. It had windows all around; its length *was* fifty cubits and its width twenty-five cubits. 37Its gateposts faced the outer court, palm trees *were* on its gateposts on this side and on that side, and going up to it *were* eight steps.

Where Sacrifices Were Prepared

38*There was* a chamber and its entrance by the gateposts of the gateway, where they [a]washed the burnt offering. 39In the vestibule of the gateway *were* two tables on this side and two tables on that side, on which to slay the burnt offering, [a]the sin offering, and [b]the trespass offering. 40At the outer side of the vestibule, as one goes up to the entrance of the northern gateway, *were* two tables; and on the other side of the vestibule of the gateway *were* two tables. 41Four tables *were* on this side and four tables on that side, by the side of the gateway, eight tables on which they slaughtered *the sacrifices.* 42*There were* also four tables of hewn stone for the burnt offering, one cubit and a half long, one cubit and a half wide, and one cubit high; on these they laid the instruments with which they slaughtered the burnt offering and the sacrifice. 43Inside *were* hooks, a handbreadth wide, fastened all around; and the flesh of the sacrifices *was* on the tables.

Chambers for Singers and Priests

44Outside the inner gate *were* the chambers for [a]the singers in the inner court, one facing south at the side of the northern gateway, and the other facing north at the side of the southern gateway. 45Then he said to me, "This chamber which faces south *is* for [a]the priests who have charge of the temple. 46The chamber which faces north *is* for the priests [a]who have charge of the altar; these *are* the sons of [b]Zadok, from the sons of Levi, who come near the LORD to minister to Him."

Dimensions of the Inner Court and Vestibule

47And he measured the court, one hundred cubits long and one hundred cubits wide, foursquare. The altar *was* in front of the temple. 48Then he brought me to the [a]vestibule of the temple and measured the doorposts of the vestibule, five cubits on this side and five cubits on that side; and the width of the gateway was three cubits on this side and three cubits on that side.

30 [a] Ezek. 40:21, 25, 33, 36
38 [a] 2 Chr. 4:6
39 [a] Lev. 4:2, 3 [b] Lev. 5:6; 6:6; 7:1
44 [a] 1 Chr. 6:31, 32; 16:41–43; 25:1–7
45 [a] Lev. 8:35
46 [a] Num. 18:5 [b] 1 Kin. 2:35
48 [a] 1 Kin. 6:3

[49][a]The length of the vestibule *was* twenty cubits, and the width eleven cubits; and by the steps which led up to it *there were* [b]pillars by the doorposts, one on this side and another on that side.

Dimensions of the Sanctuary

41 Then he [a]brought me into the [1]sanctuary and measured the doorposts, six cubits wide on one side and six cubits wide on the other side—the width of the tabernacle. [2]The width of the entryway *was* ten cubits, and the side walls of the entrance *were* five cubits on this side and five cubits on the other side; and he measured its length, forty cubits, and its width, twenty cubits.

[3]Also he went inside and measured the doorposts, two cubits; and the entrance, six cubits *high;* and the width of the entrance, seven cubits. [4][a]He measured the length, twenty cubits; and the width, twenty cubits, beyond the sanctuary; and he said to me, "This *is* the Most Holy *Place.*"

The Side Chambers on the Wall

[5]Next, he measured the wall of the [1]temple, six cubits. The width of each side chamber all around the temple *was* four cubits on every side. [6][a]The side chambers *were* in three stories, one above the other, thirty chambers in each story; they rested on [1]ledges which *were* for the side chambers all around, that they might be supported, but [b]not fastened to the wall of the temple. [7]As one went up from story to story, the side chambers [a]became wider all around, because their supporting ledges in the wall of the temple ascended like steps; therefore the width of the structure increased as one went up *from* the lowest *story* to the highest by way of the middle one. [8]I also saw an elevation all around the temple; it was the foundation of the side chambers, [a]a full rod, *that is,* six cubits *high.* [9]The thickness of the outer wall of the side chambers *was* five cubits, and so also the remaining terrace by the place of the side chambers of the [1]temple. [10]And between *it and* the *wall* chambers was a width of twenty cubits all around the temple on every side. [11]The doors of the side chambers opened on the terrace, one door toward the north and another toward the south; and the width of the terrace *was* five cubits all around.

The Building at the Western End

[12]The building that faced the separating courtyard at its western end *was* seventy cubits wide; the wall of the building *was* five cubits thick all around, and its length ninety cubits.

Dimensions and Design of the Temple Area

[13]So he measured the temple, one [a]hundred cubits long; and the separating courtyard with the building and its walls *was* one hundred cubits long; [14]also the width of the eastern face of the temple, including the separating courtyard, *was* one hundred cubits. [15]He measured the length of the building behind it, facing the separating courtyard, with its [a]galleries on the one side and on the other side, one hundred cubits, as well as the inner [1]temple and the porches of the court, [16]their doorposts and [a]the beveled window frames. And the galleries all around their three stories opposite the threshold were paneled with [b]wood from the ground to the windows—the windows were covered— [17]from the space above the door, even to the inner [1]room, as well as outside, and on every wall all around, inside and outside, by measure.

[18]And *it was* made [a]with cherubim and [b]palm trees, a palm tree between cherub and cherub. *Each* cherub had two faces, [19][a]so that the face of a man *was* toward a palm tree on one side, and the face of a young lion toward a palm tree on the other side; thus *it was* made throughout the temple all around. [20]From the floor to the space above the door, and on the wall of the sanctuary, cherubim and palm trees *were* carved.

[21]The [a]doorposts of the temple *were* square, *as was* the front of the sanctuary; their appearance was similar. [22][a]The altar *was* of wood, three cubits high, and its length two cubits. Its corners, its length, and its sides *were* of wood; and he said to me, "This *is* [b]the table that *is* [c]before the LORD."

[23][a]The temple and the sanctuary had two doors. [24]The doors had two [a]panels

---

49 a 1 Kin. 6:3 b 1 Kin. 7:15–22

CHAPTER 41
1 a Ezek. 40:2, 3, 17
1 Heb. *heykal;* the main room in the temple, the holy place, Ex. 26:33
4 a 1 Kin. 6:20
5 *1* Lit. *house*
6 a 1 Kin. 6:5–10 b 1 Kin. 6:6, 10 *1* Lit. *the wall*
7 a 1 Kin. 6:8
8 a Ezek. 40:5
9 *1* Lit. *house*
13 a Ezek. 40:47
15 a Ezek. 42:3, 5 *1* Or *sanctuary*
16 a Ezek. 40:16, 25 b 1 Kin. 6:15
17 *1* Lit. *house;* the Most Holy Place
18 a 1 Kin. 6:29 b Ezek. 40:16
19 a Ezek. 1:10; 10:14
21 a 1 Kin. 6:33
22 a Ex. 30:1–3 b Ex. 25:23, 30 c Ex. 30:8
23 a 1 Kin. 6:31–35
24 a 1 Kin. 6:34

apiece, two folding panels: two *panels* for
one door and two panels for the other
door. 25Cherubim and palm trees *were*
carved on the doors of the temple just as
they *were* carved on the walls. A wooden
canopy *was* on the front of the vestibule
outside. 26*There were* [a]beveled window
frames and palm trees on one side and on
the other, on the sides of the vestibule—
also on the side chambers of the temple
and on the canopies.

The Chambers for the Priests

42 Then he [a]brought me out into the
outer court, by the way toward the
[b]north; and he brought me into [c]the
chamber which *was* opposite the separating courtyard, and which *was* opposite the
building toward the north. 2Facing the
length, *which was* one hundred cubits
(the width was fifty cubits), was the north
door. 3Opposite the inner court of twenty
cubits, and opposite the [a]pavement of the
outer court, *was* [b]gallery against gallery
in three *stories.* 4In front of the chambers,
toward the inside, *was* a walk ten cubits
wide, at a distance of one cubit; and their
doors faced north. 5Now the upper chambers *were* shorter, because the galleries
took away *space* from them more than
from the lower and middle stories of the
building. 6For they *were* in three *stories*
and did not have pillars like the pillars of
the courts; therefore *the upper level* was
[1]shortened more than the lower and middle levels from the ground up. 7And a wall
which *was* outside ran parallel to the
chambers, at the front of the chambers,
toward the outer court; its length *was* fifty
cubits. 8The length of the chambers toward the outer court *was* fifty cubits,
whereas that facing the temple *was* one
[a]hundred cubits. 9At the lower chambers
was the entrance on the east side, as one
goes into them from the outer court.

10Also *there were* chambers in the
thickness of the wall of the court toward
the east, opposite the separating courtyard and opposite the building. 11[a]*There
was* a walk in front of them also, and their
appearance *was* like the chambers which
were toward the north; they *were* as long
and as wide as the others, and all their
exits and entrances *were* according to
plan. 12And corresponding to the doors of
the chambers that *were* facing south, as
one enters them, *there was* a door in front
of the walk, the way directly in front of the
wall toward the east.

13Then he said to me, "The north chambers *and* the south chambers, which *are*
opposite the separating courtyard, *are* the
holy chambers where the priests who approach the LORD [a]shall eat the most holy
offerings. There they shall lay the most
holy offerings—[b]the grain offering, the
sin offering, and the trespass offering—
for the place *is* holy. 14[a]When the priests
enter them, they shall not go out of the
holy *chamber* into the outer court; but
there they shall leave their garments in
which they minister, for they *are* holy.
They shall put on other garments; then
they may approach *that* which *is* for the
people."

Outer Dimensions of the Temple

15Now when he had finished measuring
the inner [1]temple, he brought me out
through the gateway that faces toward the
[a]east, and measured it all around. 16He
measured the east side with the [1]measur-
ing rod, five hundred rods by the measuring rod all around. 17He measured the
north side, five hundred rods by the measuring rod all around. 18He measured the
south side, five hundred rods by the measuring rod. 19He came around to the west
side *and* measured five hundred rods by
the measuring rod. 20He measured it on
the four sides; [a]it had a wall all around,
[b]five hundred *cubits* long and five hundred wide, to separate the holy areas from
the [1]common.

The Temple, the Lord's Dwelling Place

43 Afterward he brought me to the
gate, the gate [a]that faces toward
the east. 2[a]And behold, the glory of the
God of Israel came from the way of the
east. [b]His voice *was* like the sound of
many waters; [c]and the earth shone with
His glory. 3*It was* [a]like the appearance of
the vision which I saw—like the vision
which I saw when [1]I came [b]to destroy the
city. The visions *were* like the vision
which I saw [c]by the River Chebar; and I
fell on my face. 4[a]And the glory of the
LORD came into the [1]temple by way of the

---

26 a Ezek. 40:16

CHAPTER 42
1 a Ezek. 41:1 b Ezek. 40:20 c Ezek. 41:12, 15
3 a Ezek. 40:17 b Ezek. 41:15, 16; 42:5
6 1 Or *narrowed*
8 a Ezek. 41:13, 14
11 a Ezek. 42:4
13 a Lev. 6:16, 26; 24:9 b Lev. 2:3, 10; 6:14, 17, 25
14 a Ezek. 44:19
15 a Ezek. 40:6; 43:1 1 Lit. *house*
16 1 About 10.5 feet, Ezek. 40:5
20 a Ezek. 40:5 b Ezek. 45:2 1 Or *profane*

CHAPTER 43
1 a Ezek. 10:19; 46:1
2 a Ezek. 11:23 b Rev. 1:15; 14:2 c Rev. 18:1
3 a Ezek. 1:4–28 b Jer. 1:10 c Ezek. 1:28; 3:23 1 Some Heb. mss., Vg. *He*
4 a Ezek. 10:19; 11:23 1 Lit. *house*

gate which faces toward the east. 5 [a]The
Spirit lifted me up and brought me into
the inner court; and behold, [b]the glory of
the LORD filled the [1]temple.
6 Then I heard *Him* speaking to me from
the temple, while [a]a man stood beside me.
7 And He said to me, "Son of man, *this is*
[a]the place of My throne and [b]the place of
the soles of My feet, [c]where I will dwell in
the midst of the children of Israel forever.
[d]No more shall the house of Israel defile
My holy name, they nor their kings, by
their [1]harlotry or with [e]the carcasses of
their kings on their high places. 8 [a]When
they set their threshold by My threshold,
and their doorpost by My doorpost, with a
wall between them and Me, they defiled
My holy name by the abominations which
they committed; therefore I have consumed them in My anger. 9 Now let them
put their harlotry and the carcasses of
their kings far away from Me, and I will
dwell in their midst forever.
10 "Son of man, [a]describe the [1]temple
to the house of Israel, that they may be
ashamed of their iniquities; and let them
measure the pattern. 11 And if they are
ashamed of all that they have done, make
known to them the design of the [1]temple
and its arrangement, its exits and its entrances, its entire design and all its [a]ordi-
nances, all its forms and all its laws. Write
it down in their sight, so that they may
keep its whole design and all its ordinances, and [b]perform them. 12 This *is* the law of
the [1]temple: The whole area surrounding
[a]the mountaintop *is* most holy. Behold,
this *is* the law of the temple.

Dimensions of the Altar

13 "These are the measurements of the
[a]altar in cubits [b](the [1]*cubit is* one cubit
and a handbreadth): the base one cubit
high and one cubit wide, with a rim all
around its edge of one span. This *is* the
height of the altar: 14 from the base on the
ground to the lower ledge, two cubits; the
width of the ledge, one cubit; from
the smaller ledge to the larger ledge, four
cubits; and the width of the ledge, *one*
cubit. 15 The altar hearth *is* four cubits
high, with four [a]horns extending upward
from the [1]hearth. 16 The altar hearth *is*
twelve cubits long, twelve wide, [a]square at
its four corners; 17 the ledge, fourteen *cubits* long and fourteen wide on its four
sides, with a rim of half a cubit around it;
its base, one cubit all around; and [a]its
steps face toward the east."

Consecrating the Altar

18 And He said to me, "Son of man, thus
says the Lord GOD: 'These *are* the ordinances for the altar on the day when it is
made, for sacrificing [a]burnt offerings on
it, and for [b]sprinkling blood on it. 19 You
shall give [a]a young bull for a sin offering
to [b]the priests, the Levites, who are of the
seed of [c]Zadok, who approach Me to minister to Me,' says the Lord GOD. 20 You
shall take some of its blood and put *it* on
the four horns of the altar, on the four
corners of the ledge, and on the rim
around it; thus you shall cleanse it and
make atonement for it. 21 Then you shall
also take the bull of the sin offering, and
[a]burn it in the appointed place of the
[1]temple, [b]outside the sanctuary. 22 On the
second day you shall offer a kid of the
goats without blemish for a sin offering;
and they shall cleanse the altar, as they
cleansed *it* with the bull. 23 When you have
finished cleansing *it*, you shall offer a
young bull without blemish, and a ram
from the flock without blemish. 24 When
you offer them before the LORD, [a]the
priests shall throw salt on them, and they
will offer them up *as* a burnt offering to
the LORD. 25 Every day for [a]seven days you
shall prepare a goat *for* a sin offering; they
shall also prepare a young bull and a ram
from the flock, both without blemish.
26 Seven days they shall make atonement
for the altar and purify it, and so [1]conse-
crate [2]*it*. 27 [a]When these days are over it
shall be, on the eighth day and thereafter,
that the priests shall offer your burnt offerings and your peace offerings on the
altar; and I will [b]accept you,' says the Lord
GOD."

The East Gate and the Prince

44 Then He brought me back to the
outer gate of the sanctuary [a]which
faces toward the east, but it *was* shut.
2 And the LORD said to me, "This gate shall
be shut; it shall not be opened, and no
man shall enter by it, [a]because the LORD
God of Israel has entered by it; therefore
it shall be shut. 3 *As for* the [a]prince, *because* he *is* the prince, he may sit in it to
[b]eat bread before the LORD; he shall enter
by way of the vestibule of the gateway, and
go out the same way."

---

5 [a]Ezek. 3:12, 14; 8:3 [b]1 Kin. 8:10, 11 [1]Lit. *house*
6 [a]Ezek. 1:26; 40:3
7 [a]Ps. 99:1 [b]1 Chr. 28:2 [c]Joel 3:17 [d]Ezek. 39:7 [e]Lev. 26:30 [1]*Unfaithful idolatry*
8 [a]Ezek. 8:3; 23:39; 44:7
10 [a]Ezek. 40:4 [1]Lit. *house*
11 [a]Ezek. 44:5 [b]Ezek. 11:20 [1]Lit. *house*
12 [a]Ezek. 40:2 [1]Lit. *house*
13 [a]Ex. 27:1–8 [b]Ezek. 41:8 [1]A royal cubit of about 21 inches
15 [a]Ex. 27:2 [1]Heb. *ariel*
16 [a]Ex. 27:1
17 [a]Ex. 20:26
18 [a]Ex. 40:29 [b]Lev. 1:5, 11
19 [a]Lev. 8:14 [b]Ezek. 44:15, 16 [c]Ezek. 40:46
21 [a]Ex. 29:14 [b]Heb. 13:11 [1]Lit. *house*
24 [a]Lev. 2:13
25 [a]Ex. 29:35
26 [1]Lit. *fill its hands* [2]LXX, Syr. *themselves*
27 [a]Lev. 9:1–4 [b]Ezek. 20:40, 41

CHAPTER 44
1 [a]Ezek. 43:1
2 [a]Ezek. 43:2–4
3 [a]Gen. 31:54 [b]Ezek. 46:2, 8

Those Admitted to the Temple

4 Also He brought me by way of the north gate to the front of the [1]temple; so I looked, and [a]behold, the glory of the LORD filled the house of the LORD; [b]and I fell on my face. 5 And the LORD said to me, [a]"Son of man, [1]mark well, see with your eyes and hear with your ears, all that I say to you concerning all the [b]ordinances of the house of the LORD and all its laws. Mark well who may enter the house and all who go out from the sanctuary.

6 "Now say to the [a]rebellious, to the house of Israel, 'Thus says the Lord GOD: "O house of Israel, [b]let Us have no more of all your abominations. 7 [a]When you brought in [b]foreigners, [c]uncircumcised in heart and uncircumcised in flesh, to be in My sanctuary to defile it—My house—and when you offered [d]My food, [e]the fat and the blood, then they broke My covenant because of all your abominations. 8 And you have not [a]kept charge of My holy things, but you have set *others* to keep charge of My sanctuary for you." 9 Thus says the Lord GOD: [a]"No foreigner, uncircumcised in heart or uncircumcised in flesh, shall enter My sanctuary, including any foreigner who *is* among the children of Israel.

Laws Governing Priests

10 [a]"And the Levites who went far from Me, when Israel went astray, who strayed away from Me after their idols, they shall bear their iniquity. 11 Yet they shall be ministers in My sanctuary, [a]*as* gatekeepers of the house and ministers of the house; [b]they shall slay the burnt offering and the sacrifice for the people, and [c]they shall stand before them to minister to them. 12 Because they ministered to them before their idols and [a]caused[1] the house of Israel to fall into iniquity, therefore I have [b]raised My hand in an oath against them," says the Lord GOD, "that they shall bear their iniquity. 13 [a]And they shall not come near Me to minister to Me as priest, nor come near any of My holy things, nor into the Most Holy *Place;* but they shall [b]bear their shame and their abominations which they have committed. 14 Nevertheless I will make them [a]keep charge of the temple, for all its work, and for all that has to be done in it.

15 [a]"But the priests, the Levites, [b]the sons of Zadok, who kept charge of My sanctuary [c]when the children of Israel went astray from Me, they shall come near Me to minister to Me; and they [d]shall stand before Me to offer to Me the [e]fat and the blood," says the Lord GOD. 16 "They shall [a]enter My sanctuary, and they shall come near [b]My table to minister to Me, and they shall keep My charge. 17 And it shall be, whenever they enter the gates of the inner court, that [a]they shall put on linen garments; no wool shall come upon them while they minister within the gates of the inner court or within the house. 18 [a]They shall have linen turbans on their heads and linen trousers on their bodies; they shall not clothe themselves with *anything that causes* sweat. 19 When they go out to the outer court, to the *outer* court to the people, [a]they shall take off their garments in which they have ministered, leave them in the holy chambers, and put on other garments; and in their holy garments they shall [b]not sanctify the people.

20 [a]"They shall neither shave their heads, nor let their hair grow [b]long, but they shall keep their hair well trimmed. 21 [a]No priest shall drink wine when he enters the inner court. 22 They shall not take as wife a [a]widow or a divorced woman, but take virgins of the descendants of the house of Israel, or widows of priests.

23 "And [a]they shall teach My people *the difference* between the holy and the unholy, and cause them to [b]discern between the unclean and the clean. 24 [a]In controversy they shall stand as judges, *and* judge it according to My judgments. They shall keep My laws and My statutes in all My appointed meetings, [b]and they shall hallow My Sabbaths.

25 "They shall not defile *themselves* by coming near a dead person. Only for father or mother, for son or daughter, for brother or unmarried sister may they defile themselves. 26 [a]After he is cleansed, they shall count seven days for him. 27 And on the day that he goes to the sanctuary to minister in the sanctuary, [a]he must offer his sin offering [b]in the inner court," says the Lord GOD.

28 "It shall be, in regard to their inheritance, *that* I [a]*am* their inheritance. You shall give them no [b]possession in Israel, for I *am* their possession. 29 [a]They shall eat the grain offering, the sin offering, and the trespass offering; [b]every dedicated thing in Israel shall be theirs. 30 The [a]best[1]

---

4 a Ezek. 3:23; 43:5 b Ezek. 1:28; 43:3 *1* Lit. *house*
5 a Ezek. 40:4 b Ezek. 43:10, 11 *1* Lit. *set your heart*
6 a Ezek. 2:5 b 1 Pet. 4:3
7 a Acts 21:28 b Lev. 22:25 c Lev. 26:41 d Lev. 21:17 e Lev. 3:16
8 a Lev. 22:2
9 a Ezek. 44:7
10 a 2 Kin. 23:8
11 a 1 Chr. 26:1–19 b 2 Chr. 29:34; 30:17 c Num. 16:9
12 a Is. 9:16 b Ps. 106:26 *1* Lit. *became a stumbling block of iniquity to the house of Israel*
13 a 2 Kin. 23:9 b Ezek. 32:30
14 a Num. 18:4
15 a Ezek. 40:46 b [1 Sam. 2:35] c Ezek. 44:10 d Deut. 10:8 e Ezek. 44:7
16 a Num. 18:5, 7, 8 b Ezek. 41:22
17 a Ex. 28:39–43; 39:27–29
18 a Ex. 28:40; 39:28
19 a Ezek. 42:14 b Lev. 6:27
20 a Lev. 21:5 b Num. 6:5
21 a Lev. 10:9
22 a Lev. 21:7, 13, 14
23 a Mal. 2:6–8 b Lev. 20:25
24 a Deut. 17:8, 9 b Ezek. 22:26
26 a Num. 6:10; 19:11, 13–19
27 a Lev. 5:3, 6 b Ezek. 44:17
28 a Num. 18:20 b Ezek. 45:4
29 a Lev. 7:6 b Lev. 27:21, 28
30 a Num. 3:13; 18:12 *1* Lit. *first*

of all firstfruits of any kind, and every sacrifice of any kind from all your sacrifices,
shall be the priest's; also you [b]shall give to
the priest the first of your ground meal,
[c]to cause a blessing to rest on your house.
31The priests shall not eat anything, bird
or beast, that [a]died naturally or was torn
by wild beasts.

The Holy District

45 "Moreover, when you [a]divide the
land by lot into inheritance, you
shall [b]set apart a district for the LORD, a
holy section of the land; its length *shall be*
twenty-five thousand *cubits,* and the
width ten thousand. It *shall be* holy
throughout its territory all around. 2Of
this there shall be a square plot for the
sanctuary, [a]five hundred by five hundred
rods, with fifty cubits around it for an
open space. 3So this is the district you
shall measure: twenty-five thousand *cubits* long and ten thousand wide; [a]in it
shall be the sanctuary, the Most Holy
Place. 4It shall be [a]a holy *section* of the
land, belonging to the priests, the ministers of the sanctuary, who come near to
minister to the LORD; it shall be a place for
their houses and a holy place for the sanctuary. 5[a]*An area* twenty-five thousand *cubits* long and ten thousand wide shall
belong to the Levites, the ministers of the
[1]temple; they shall have [b]twenty[2] chambers as a possession.

Properties of the City and the Prince

6[a]"You shall appoint as the property of
the city *an area* five thousand *cubits* wide
and twenty-five thousand long, adjacent
to the district of the holy *section;* it shall
belong to the whole house of Israel.
7[a]"The prince shall have *a section* on
one side and the other of the holy district
and the city's property; and bordering on
the holy district and the city's property,
extending westward on the west side and
eastward on the east side, the length *shall
be* side by side with one of the *tribal* portions, from the west border to the east
border. 8The land shall be his possession
in Israel; and [a]My princes shall no more
oppress My people, but they shall give *the
rest of* the land to the house of Israel, according to their tribes."

Laws Governing the Prince

9'Thus says the Lord GOD: [a]"Enough,
O princes of Israel! [b]Remove violence and
plundering, execute justice and righteousness, and stop dispossessing My people," says the Lord GOD. 10"You shall have
[a]honest scales, an honest ephah, and an
honest bath. 11The ephah and the bath
shall be of the same measure, so that the
bath contains one-tenth of a homer, and
the ephah one-tenth of a homer; their
measure shall be according to the homer.
12The [a]shekel *shall be* twenty gerahs;
twenty shekels, twenty-five shekels, *and*
fifteen shekels shall be your mina.
13"This *is* the offering which you shall
offer: you shall give one-sixth of an ephah
from a homer of wheat, and one-sixth of
an ephah from a homer of barley. 14The
ordinance concerning oil, the bath of oil,
is one-tenth of a bath from a kor. A kor *is*
a homer or ten baths, for ten baths *are*
a homer. 15And one lamb shall be given
from a flock of two hundred, from the rich
pastures of Israel. These shall be for grain
offerings, burnt offerings, and peace offerings, [a]to make atonement for them," says
the Lord GOD. 16"All the people of the land
shall give this offering for the prince in
Israel. 17Then it shall be the [a]prince's part
to give burnt offerings, grain offerings,
and drink offerings, at the feasts, the New
Moons, the Sabbaths, and at all the appointed seasons of the house of Israel. He
shall prepare the sin offering, the grain
offering, the burnt offering, and the peace
offerings to make atonement for the
house of Israel."

Keeping the Feasts

18"Thus says the Lord GOD: "In the first
month, on the first *day* of the month, you
shall take a young bull without blemish
and [a]cleanse the sanctuary. 19[a]The priest
shall take some of the blood of the sin
offering and put *it* on the doorposts of the
[1]temple, on the four corners of the ledge
of the altar, and on the gateposts of the
gate of the inner court. 20And so you shall
do on the seventh *day* of the month [a]for
everyone who has sinned unintentionally
or in ignorance. Thus you shall make
atonement for the temple.
21[a]"In the first *month,* on the fourteenth day of the month, you shall observe the Passover, a feast of seven days;
unleavened bread shall be eaten. 22And
on that day the prince shall prepare for

---

30 b Neh. 10:37 c [Mal. 3:10]
31 a Lev. 22:8

CHAPTER 45
1 a Ezek. 47:22 b Ezek. 48:8, 9
2 a Ezek. 42:20
3 a Ezek. 48:10
4 a Ezek. 48:10, 11
5 a Ezek. 48:13 b Ezek. 40:17 *1* Lit. *house* *2* So with MT, Tg., Vg.; LXX *a possession, cities of dwelling*
6 a Ezek. 48:15
7 a Ezek. 48:21
8 a Ezek. 22:27
9 a Ezek. 44:6 b Jer. 22:3
10 a Lev. 19:36
12 a Ex. 30:13
15 a Lev. 1:4; 6:30
17 a Ezek. 46:4–12
18 a Lev. 16:16, 33
19 a Ezek. 43:20 *1* Lit. *house*
20 a Lev. 4:27
21 a Ex. 12:18

himself and for all the people of the land [a]a bull *for* a sin offering. 23On the [a]seven days of the feast he shall prepare a burnt offering to the LORD, seven bulls and seven rams without blemish, daily for seven days, [b]and a kid of the goats daily *for* a sin offering. 24[a]And he shall prepare a grain offering of one ephah for each bull and one ephah for each ram, together with a hin of oil for each ephah.

25"In the seventh *month,* on the fifteenth day of the month, at the [a]feast, he shall do likewise for seven days, according to the sin offering, the burnt offering, the grain offering, and the oil."

The Manner of Worship

46 "Thus says the Lord GOD: "The gateway of the inner court that faces toward the east shall be shut the six [a]working days; but on the Sabbath it shall be opened, and on the day of the New Moon it shall be opened. 2[a]The prince shall enter by way of the vestibule of the gateway from the outside, and stand by the gatepost. The priests shall prepare his burnt offering and his peace offerings. He shall worship at the threshold of the gate. Then he shall go out, but the gate shall not be shut until evening. 3Likewise the people of the land shall worship at the entrance to this gateway before the LORD on the Sabbaths and the New Moons. 4The burnt offering that [a]the prince offers to the LORD on the [b]Sabbath day *shall be* six lambs without blemish, and a ram without blemish; 5[a]and the grain offering *shall be one* ephah for a ram, and the grain offering for the lambs, [1]as much as he wants to give, as well as a hin of oil with every ephah. 6On the day of the New Moon *it shall be* a young bull without blemish, six lambs, and a ram; they shall be without blemish. 7He shall prepare a grain offering of an ephah for a bull, an ephah for a ram, [1]as much as he wants to give for the lambs, and a hin of oil with every ephah. 8[a]When the prince enters, he shall go in by way of the vestibule of the gateway, and go out the same way.

9"But when the people of the land [a]come before the LORD on the appointed feast days, whoever enters by way of the north [b]gate to worship shall go out by way of the south gate; and whoever enters by way of the south gate shall go out by way of the north gate. He shall not return by way of the gate through which he came, but shall go out through the opposite gate. 10The prince shall then be in their midst. When they go in, he shall go in; and when they go out, he shall go out. 11At the festivals and the appointed feast days [a]the grain offering shall be an ephah for a bull, an ephah for a ram, as much as he wants to give for the lambs, and a hin of oil with every ephah.

12"Now when the prince makes a voluntary burnt offering or voluntary peace offering to the LORD, the gate that faces toward the east [a]shall then be opened for him; and he shall prepare his burnt offering and his peace offerings as he did on the Sabbath day. Then he shall go out, and after he goes out the gate shall be shut.

13[a]"You shall daily make a burnt offering to the LORD *of* a lamb of the first year without blemish; you shall prepare it [1]every morning. 14And you shall prepare a grain offering with it every morning, a sixth of an ephah, and a third of a hin of oil to moisten the fine flour. This grain offering is a perpetual ordinance, to be made regularly to the LORD. 15Thus they shall prepare the lamb, the grain offering, and the oil, *as* a [a]regular burnt offering every morning."

The Prince and Inheritance Laws

16"Thus says the Lord GOD: "If the prince gives a gift *of some* of his inheritance to any of his sons, it shall belong to his sons; it is their possession by inheritance. 17But if he gives a gift of some of his inheritance to one of his servants, it shall be his until [a]the year of liberty, after which it shall return to the prince. But his inheritance shall belong to his sons; it shall become theirs. 18Moreover [a]the prince shall not take any of the people's inheritance by evicting them from their property; he shall provide an inheritance for his sons from his own property, so that none of My people may be scattered from his property." ' "

How the Offerings Were Prepared

19Now he brought me through the entrance, which *was* at the side of the gate, into the holy [a]chambers of the priests which face toward the north; and there a place *was* situated at their extreme western end. 20And he said to me, "This *is* the

---

22 [a]Lev. 4:14
23 [a]Lev. 23:8 [b]Num. 28:15, 22, 30; 29:5, 11, 16, 19
24 [a]Ezek. 46:5, 7
25 [a]Num. 29:12

CHAPTER 46
1 [a]Ex. 20:9
2 [a]Ezek. 44:3
4 [a]Ezek. 45:17 [b]Num. 28:9, 10
5 [a]Ezek. 45:24; 46:7, 11 [1]Lit. *the gift of his hand*
7 [1]Lit. *as much as his hand can reach*
8 [a]Ezek. 44:3; 46:2
9 [a]Ex. 23:14–17; 34:23 [b]Ezek. 48:31, 33
11 [a]Ezek. 46:5, 7
12 [a]Ezek. 44:3;46:1, 2, 8
13 [a]Num. 28:3–5 [1]Lit. *morning by morning*
15 [a]Ex. 29:42
17 [a]Lev. 25:10
18 [a]Ezek. 45:8
19 [a]Ezek. 42:13

place where the priests shall [a]boil the
trespass offering and the sin offering, *and*
where they shall [b]bake the grain offering,
so that they do not bring *them* out into
the outer court [c]to sanctify the people."
21 Then he brought me out into the outer court and caused me to pass by the four
corners of the court; and in fact, in every
corner of the court *there was another*
court. 22 In the four corners of the court
were enclosed courts, forty *cubits* long
and thirty wide; all four corners *were* the
same size. 23 *There was* a row *of building*
stones all around in them, all around the
four of them; and [1]cooking hearths were
made under the rows of stones all around.
24 And he said to me, "These *are* the
[1]kitchens where the ministers of the
[2]temple shall [a]boil the sacrifices of the
people."

The Healing Waters and Trees

47 Then he brought me back to the
door of the [1]temple; and there was
[a]water, flowing from under the threshold
of the temple toward the east, for the
front of the temple faced east; the water
was flowing from under the right side of
the temple, south of the altar. 2 He
brought me out by way of the north gate,
and led me around on the outside to the
outer gateway that faces [a]east; and there
was water, running out on the right side.
3 And when [a]the man went out to the
east with the line in his hand, he measured one thousand cubits, and he
brought me through the waters; the water
came up to my ankles. 4 Again he measured one thousand and brought me
through the waters; the water *came up to*
my knees. Again he measured one thousand and brought me through; the water
came up to my waist. 5 Again he measured
one thousand, *and it was* a river that I
could not cross; for the water was too
deep, water in which one must swim, a
river that could not be crossed. 6 He said
to me, "Son of man, have you seen *this?*"
Then he brought me and returned me to
the bank of the river.
7 When I returned, there, along the
bank of the river, *were* very many [a]trees
on one side and the other. 8 Then he said
to me: "This water flows toward the eastern region, goes down into the [1]valley,
and enters the sea. *When it* reaches the
sea, *its* waters are healed. 9 And it shall be
that every living thing that moves, wherever [1]the rivers go, will live. There will be
a very great multitude of fish, because
these waters go there; for they will be
healed, and everything will live wherever
the river goes. 10 It shall be *that* fishermen
will stand by it from En Gedi to En Eglaim; they will be *places* for spreading their
nets. Their fish will be of the same kinds
as the fish [a]of the Great Sea, exceedingly
many. 11 But its swamps and marshes will
not be healed; they will be given over to
salt. 12 [a]Along the bank of the river, on this
side and that, will grow all *kinds of* trees
used for food; [b]their leaves will not wither, and their fruit will not fail. They will
bear fruit every month, because their water flows from the sanctuary. Their fruit
will be for food, and their leaves for [c]med-
icine."[1]

Borders of the Land

13 Thus says the Lord GOD: "These *are*
the [a]borders by which you shall divide the
land as an inheritance among the twelve
tribes of Israel. [b]Joseph *shall have two*
portions. 14 You shall inherit it equally
with one another; for I [a]raised My hand in
an oath to give it to your fathers, and this
land shall [b]fall to you as your inheritance.
15 "This *shall be* the border of the land
on the north: from the Great Sea, *by* [a]the
road to Hethlon, as one goes to [b]Zedad,
16 [a]Hamath, [b]Berothah, Sibraim (which *is*
between the border of Damascus and the
border of Hamath), to Hazar Hatticon
(which *is* on the border of Hauran).
17 Thus the boundary shall be from the Sea
to [a]Hazar Enan, the border of Damascus;
and as for the north, northward, it is the
border of Hamath. *This is* the north side.
18 "On the east side you shall mark out
the border from between Hauran and Damascus, and between Gilead and the land
of Israel, along the Jordan, and along the
eastern side of the sea. *This is* the east
side.
19 "The south side, toward the [1]South,
shall be from Tamar to [a]the waters of
[2]Meribah by Kadesh, along the brook to
the Great Sea. *This is* the south side, toward the South.
20 "The west side *shall be* the Great Sea,
from the *southern* boundary until one
comes to a point opposite Hamath. This *is*
the west side.
21 "Thus you shall [a]divide this land
among yourselves according to the tribes

20 a 2 Chr. 35:13 b Lev. 2:4, 5, 7 c Ezek. 44:19
23 1 Lit. *boiling places*
24 a Ezek. 46:20 1 Lit. *house of those who boil* 2 Lit. *house*
CHAPTER 47
1 a Joel 3:18 1 Lit. *house*
2 a Ezek. 44:1, 2
3 a Ezek. 40:3
7 a [Rev. 22:2]
8 1 Or *Arabah*, the Jordan Valley
9 1 Lit. *two rivers*
10 a Num. 34:3
12 a Ezek. 47:7 b [Jer. 17:8] c [Rev. 22:2] 1 Or *healing*
13 a Num. 34:1–29 b Gen. 48:5
14 a Ezek. 20:5, 6, 28, 42 b Ezek. 48:29
15 a Ezek. 48:1 b Num. 34:7, 8
16 a Num. 34:8 b 2 Sam. 8:8
17 a Num. 34:9
19 a Ps. 81:7 1 Heb. *Negev* 2 Lit. *Strife*
21 a Ezek. 45:1

of Israel. 22 It shall be that you will divide it by [a]lot as an inheritance for yourselves, [b]and for the strangers who dwell among you and who bear children among you. [c]They shall be to you as native-born among the children of Israel; they shall have an inheritance with you among the tribes of Israel. 23 And it shall be *that* in whatever tribe the stranger dwells, there you shall give *him* his inheritance," says the Lord GOD.

Division of the Land

48 "Now these *are* the names of the tribes: [a]From the northern border along the road to Hethlon at the entrance of Hamath, to Hazar Enan, the border of Damascus northward, in the direction of Hamath, *there shall be* one *section for* [b]Dan from its east to its west side; 2 by the border of Dan, from the east side to the west, one *section for* [a]Asher; 3 by the border of Asher, from the east side to the west, one *section for* [a]Naphtali; 4 by the border of Naphtali, from the east side to the west, one *section for* [a]Manasseh; 5 by the border of Manasseh, from the east side to the west, one *section for* [a]Ephraim; 6 by the border of Ephraim, from the east side to the west, one *section for* [a]Reuben; 7 by the border of Reuben, from the east side to the west, one *section for* [a]Judah; 8 by the border of Judah, from the east side to the west, shall be [a]the district which you shall set apart, twenty-five thousand *cubits* in width, and *in* length the same as one of the *other* portions, from the east side to the west, with the [b]sanctuary in the center.

9 "The district that you shall set apart for the LORD *shall be* twenty-five thousand *cubits* in length and ten thousand in width. 10 To these—to the priests—the holy district shall belong: on the north twenty-five thousand *cubits in length,* on the west ten thousand in width, on the east ten thousand in width, and on the south twenty-five thousand in length. The sanctuary of the LORD shall be in the center. 11 [a]*It shall be* for the priests of the sons of Zadok, who are sanctified, who have kept My charge, who did not go astray when the children of Israel went astray, [b]as the Levites went astray. 12 And *this* district of land that is set apart shall be to them a thing most [a]holy by the border of the Levites.

13 "Opposite the border of the priests, the [a]Levites *shall have an area* twenty-five thousand *cubits* in length and ten thousand in width; its entire length *shall be* twenty-five thousand and its width ten thousand. 14 [a]And they shall not sell or exchange any of it; they may not alienate this best *part* of the land, for *it is* holy to the LORD.

15 [a]"The five thousand *cubits* in width that remain, along the edge of the twenty-five thousand, shall be [b]for general use by the city, for dwellings and common-land; and the city shall be in the center. 16 These *shall be* its measurements: the north side four thousand five hundred *cubits,* the south side four thousand five hundred, the east side four thousand five hundred, and the west side four thousand five hundred. 17 The common-land of the city shall be: to the north two hundred and fifty *cubits,* to the south two hundred and fifty, to the east two hundred and fifty, and to the west two hundred and fifty. 18 The rest of the length, alongside the district of the holy *section, shall be* ten thousand *cubits* to the east and ten thousand to the west. It shall be adjacent to the district of the holy *section,* and its produce shall be food for the workers of the city. 19 [a]The workers of the city, from all the tribes of Israel, shall cultivate it. 20 The entire district *shall be* twenty-five thousand *cubits* by twenty-five thousand *cubits,* foursquare. You shall set apart the holy district with the property of the city.

21 [a]"The rest *shall belong* to the prince, on one side and on the other of the holy district and of the city's property, next to the twenty-five thousand *cubits* of the *holy* district as far as the eastern border, and westward next to the twenty-five thousand as far as the western border, adjacent to the *tribal* portions; *it shall belong* to the prince. It shall be the holy district, [b]and the sanctuary of the [1]temple *shall be* in the center. 22 Moreover, apart from the possession of the Levites and the possession of the city *which are* in the midst of what *belongs* to the prince, *the area* between the border of Judah and the border of [a]Benjamin shall belong to the prince.

23 "As for the rest of the tribes, from the east side to the west, Benjamin *shall have* one *section;* 24 by the border of Benjamin, from the east side to the west, [a]Simeon *shall have* one *section;* 25 by the border of

---

22 [a]Num. 26:55, 56 [b][Eph. 3:6] [c][Col. 3:11]

CHAPTER 48

1 [a]Ezek. 47:15 [b]Josh. 19:40–48

2 [a]Josh. 19:24–31

3 [a]Josh. 19:32–39

4 [a]Josh. 13:29–31; 17:1–11, 17, 18

5 [a]Josh. 16:5–10; 17:8–10, 14–18

6 [a]Josh. 13:15–23

7 [a]Josh. 15:1–63; 19:9

8 [a]Ezek. 45:1–6 [b][Is. 12:6; 33:20–22]

11 [a]Ezek. 40:46; 44:15 [b]Ezek. 44:10, 12

12 [a]Ezek. 45:4

13 [a]Ezek. 45:5

14 [a]Lev. 27:10, 28, 33

15 [a]Ezek. 45:6 [b]Ezek. 42:20

19 [a]Ezek. 45:6

21 [a]Ezek. 34:24; 45:7; 48:22 [b]Ezek. 48:8, 10 [1]Lit. *house*

22 [a]Josh. 18:21–28

24 [a]Josh. 19:1–9

Simeon, from the east side to the west,
[a]Issachar *shall have* one *section;* 26by the
border of Issachar, from the east side to
the west, [a]Zebulun *shall have* one *sec-*
tion; 27by the border of Zebulun, from the
east side to the west, [a]Gad *shall have* one
section; 28by the border of Gad, on the
south side, toward the [1]South, the border
shall be from Tamar *to* [a]the waters of
[2]Meribah *by* Kadesh, along the brook to
the [b]Great Sea. 29[a]This *is* the land which
you shall divide by lot as an inheritance
among the tribes of Israel, and these *are*
their portions," says the Lord GOD.

The Gates of the City and Its Name

30"These *are* the exits of the city. On the
north side, measuring four thousand five
hundred *cubits* 31[a](the gates of the city
shall be named after the tribes of Israel),
the three gates northward: one gate for
Reuben, one gate for Judah, and one gate
for Levi; 32on the east side, four thousand
five hundred *cubits,* three gates: one gate
for Joseph, one gate for Benjamin, and
one gate for Dan; 33on the south side,
measuring four thousand five hundred
cubits, three gates: one gate for Simeon,
one gate for Issachar, and one gate for
Zebulun; 34on the west side, four thousand five hundred *cubits* with their three
gates: one gate for Gad, one gate for
Asher, and one gate for Naphtali. 35All
the way around *shall be* eighteen thousand *cubits;* [a]and the name of the city
from *that* day *shall be:* [b]THE[1] LORD *IS*
THERE."

25 a Josh. 19:17–23
26 a Josh. 19:10–16
27 a Josh. 13:24–28
28 a Ezek. 47:19 b Ezek. 47:10, 15, 19, 20 1 Heb. *Negev* 2 Lit. *Strife*
29 a Ezek. 47:14, 21, 22
31 a [Rev. 21:10–14]
35 a Jer. 23:6; 33:16 b Joel 3:21 1 Heb. *YHWH Shammah*

AUTHOR: *Daniel*
DATE: *Late Sixth Century B.C.*
THEME: *God Controls the Destiny of All Nations*
KEY WORDS: *Kings, Kingdoms, Visions, Dreams*

DANIEL

Dear Woman of Destiny,

Because of the destiny placed in our hearts, we desire a life characterized by purpose, prayer, perception, and power. Daniel lived such a life. In the first chapter, we read that *"Daniel purposed in his heart."* In time, four nations would be changed. As we purpose in our own hearts and proceed in prayer, we, too, will continue in wise perception and power, as Daniel did. Let this book lead you to a deeper revelation of your own inspired destiny.

His love and mine,

Marilyn Hickey

Daniel and His Friends Obey God

In the third year of the reign of [a]Jehoiakim king of Judah, Nebuchadnezzar king of Babylon came to Jerusalem and besieged it. 2And the Lord gave Jehoiakim king of Judah into his hand, with [a]some of the articles of [1]the house of God, which he carried [b]into the land of Shinar to the house of his god; [c]and he brought the articles into the treasure house of his god.

3Then the king instructed Ashpenaz, the master of his eunuchs, to bring [a]some of the children of Israel and some of the king's descendants and some of the nobles, 4young men [a]in whom *there was* no blemish, but good-looking, gifted in all wisdom, possessing knowledge and quick to understand, who *had* ability to serve in the king's palace, and [b]whom they might teach the language and [1]literature of the Chaldeans. 5And the king appointed for them a daily provision of the king's delicacies and of the wine which he drank, and three years of training for them, so that at the end of *that time* they might [a]serve before the king. 6Now from among those of the sons of Judah were Daniel, Hananiah, Mishael, and Azariah. 7 [a]To them the chief of the eunuchs gave names: [b]he gave Daniel *the name* Belteshazzar; to Hananiah, Shadrach; to Mishael, Meshach; and to Azariah, Abed-Nego.

8But Daniel purposed in his heart that he would not defile himself [a]with the portion of the king's delicacies, nor with the wine which he drank; therefore he requested of the chief of the eunuchs that he might not defile himself. 9Now [a]God had brought Daniel into the favor and [1]goodwill of the chief of the eunuchs. 10And the chief of the eunuchs said to Daniel, "I fear my lord the king, who has appointed your food and drink. For why should he see your faces looking worse than the young men who *are* your age? Then you would endanger my head before the king."

11So Daniel said to [1]the steward whom the chief of the eunuchs had set over Daniel, Hananiah, Mishael, and Azariah, 12"Please test your servants for ten days, and let them give us vegetables to eat and water to drink. 13Then let our appearance be examined before you, and the appearance of the young men who eat the portion of the king's delicacies; and as you see fit, *so* deal with your servants." 14So he consented with them in this matter, and tested them ten days.

15And at the end of ten days their features appeared better and fatter in flesh than all the young men who ate the portion of the king's delicacies. 16Thus [1]the steward took away their portion of delicacies and the wine that they were to drink, and gave them vegetables.

17As for these four young men, [a]God gave them [b]knowledge and skill in all literature and wisdom; and Daniel had [c]understanding in all visions and dreams.

> *God has called us to shine, just as much as Daniel was sent into Babylon to shine. Let no one say that he cannot shine because he has not so much influence as some others may have. What God wants you to do is to use the influence you have. Daniel probably did not have much influence down in Babylon at first, but God soon gave him more because he was faithful and used what he had.*
>
> DWIGHT L. MOODY

18Now at the end of the days, when the king had said that they should be brought in, the chief of the eunuchs brought them in before Nebuchadnezzar. 19Then the king [1]interviewed them, and among them all none was found like Daniel, Hananiah, Mishael, and Azariah; therefore [a]they served before the king. 20[a]And in all matters of wisdom *and* understanding about which the king examined them, he found them ten times better than all the

CHAPTER 1
1 a 2 Kin. 24:1, 2
2 a Jer. 27:19, 20 b Zech. 5:11 c 2 Chr. 36:7 1 The temple
3 a Is. 39:7
4 a Lev. 24:19, 20 b Acts 7:22 1 Lit. *writing* or *book*
5 a Dan. 1:19
7 a 2 Kin. 24:17 b Dan. 2:26; 4:8; 5:12
8 a Hos. 9:3
9 a Gen. 39:21 1 *kindness*
11 1 Or *Melzar*
16 1 Or *Melzar*
17 a [James 1:5–7] b Acts 7:22 c 2 Chr. 26:5
19 a Gen. 41:46 1 Lit. *talked with them*
20 a 1 Kin. 10:1

Daniel 1:7

Dear Woman of Destiny,

I believe that you are a woman of destiny and that God has a special plan and unique purpose for your life. He has something very specific for you and is calling you forward to fulfill this destiny!

All over the earth there is a deep cry in the hearts of people to know the purpose they are to fulfill. Have you sensed a stirring in your own heart to understand the plan for your life? That stirring is the Holy Spirit drawing you and calling you closer so that your desires, motives, attitudes, and actions agree with God's specific plan for your life. In Jeremiah 29:11, the Lord says that He has thoughts of peace toward you and plans to give you a future and a hope. Since the beginning of time God has had a specific and special plan for you to fulfill.

One of the enemy's tactics to distract us from the Lord's plans is tempting us to compare our lives and circumstances with those around us. It is important to understand what God has and has not gifted, equipped, and called us to do. I can't look at how anointed my friend is at leading worship and decide that is what I want to do. God did not give me the talents or voice to lead others into His presence through music. I am one who makes a joyful noise to the Lord! To grow in our understanding of the destiny God has for us, we need to seek Him through prayer, His Word, and wise counsel.

We are in a time when God is moving His people into their appointed positions. We must seek the Lord to know where He is asking us to go. Now is a time to stay flexible and willing to adjust to any changes that God is bringing into our lives.

Daniel 1:7 reveals that when Daniel was taken captive, his captors changed his name to one that reflected their pagan beliefs, but Daniel purposed in his heart not to let his new name or difficult circumstances define his future (see Dan. 1:8). He knew his circumstances would not hinder the plan of God for his life. Daniel didn't let the pressures of captivity deflate his hopes and dreams for God's plans for him to be fulfilled. I believe that living with the stresses and temptations of this age, we need the tenacious attitude that is so evident in Daniel. He refused to fall into the snare of doubt and think that God's plan for his life wouldn't come to pass just because times got a little tough.

You might find yourself in very difficult situations and in your own personal "captivity." The enemy wants to hinder your journey of fulfilling your destiny by distracting you with doubt, fear, and unbelief. *God has not forgotten you*. Let me assure you that the plans to see you through this time of captivity are in motion. The Lord wants you to resist thoughts of fear and doubt and tenaciously believe that you are going to fulfill His plan for you as a woman of destiny!

Mary Forsythe

magicians *and* astrologers who *were* in all
his realm. [21][a]Thus Daniel continued until
the first year of King Cyrus.

Lord God, I pray that you would give great wisdom and understanding to _____ even as you did to Daniel.

FROM DANIEL 1:20

Nebuchadnezzar's Dream

2 Now in the second year of Nebuchadnezzar's reign, Nebuchadnezzar had
dreams; [a]and his spirit was *so* troubled
that [b]his sleep left him. [2][a]Then the king
gave the command to call the magicians,
the astrologers, the sorcerers, and the
Chaldeans to tell the king his dreams. So
they came and stood before the king. [3]And
the king said to them, "I have had a
dream, and my spirit is anxious to [1]know
the dream."

[4]Then the Chaldeans spoke to the king
in Aramaic, [a]"O[1] king, live forever! Tell
your servants the dream, and we will give
the interpretation."

[5]The king answered and said to the
Chaldeans, "My [1]decision is firm: if you do
not make known the dream to me, and its
interpretation, you shall be [a]cut in pieces,
and your houses shall be made an ash
heap. [6][a]However, if you tell the dream and
its interpretation, you shall receive from
me gifts, rewards, and great honor. Therefore tell me the dream and its interpretation."

[7]They answered again and said, "Let the
king tell his servants the dream, and we
will give its interpretation."

[8]The king answered and said, "I know
for certain that you would gain time, because you see that my decision is firm: [9]if
you do not make known the dream to me,
there is only one decree for you! For you
have agreed to speak lying and corrupt
words before me till the [1]time has
changed. Therefore tell me the dream,
and I shall know that you can [2]give me its
interpretation."

[10]The Chaldeans answered the king,
and said, "There is not a man on earth
who can tell the king's matter; therefore
no king, lord, or ruler has *ever* asked such
things of any magician, astrologer, or
Chaldean. [11]*It is* a [1]difficult thing that the
king requests, and there is no other who
can tell it to the king [a]except the gods,
whose dwelling is not with flesh."

[12]For this reason the king was angry
and very furious, and gave the command
to destroy all the wise *men* of Babylon.
[13]So the decree went out, and they began
killing the wise *men;* and they sought
[a]Daniel and his companions, to kill *them.*

God Reveals Nebuchadnezzar's Dream

[14]Then with counsel and wisdom Daniel answered Arioch, the captain of the
king's guard, who had gone out to kill the
wise *men* of Babylon; [15]he answered and
said to Arioch the king's captain, "Why is
the decree from the king so [1]urgent?"
Then Arioch made the decision known to
Daniel.

[16]So Daniel went in and asked the king
to give him time, that he might tell the
king the interpretation. [17]Then Daniel
went to his house, and made the decision
known to Hananiah, Mishael, and Azariah, his companions, [18][a]that they might
seek mercies from the God of heaven concerning this secret, so that Daniel and his
companions might not perish with the
rest of the wise *men* of Babylon. [19]Then
the secret was revealed to Daniel [a]in a
night vision. So Daniel blessed the God of
heaven.

[20]Daniel answered and said:

[a]"Blessed be the name of God forever
and ever,
[b]For wisdom and might are His.
21 And He changes [a]the times and
the seasons;
[b]He removes kings and raises up
kings;
[c]He gives wisdom to the wise
And knowledge to those who have
understanding.
22 [a]He reveals deep and secret things;
[b]He knows what *is* in the darkness,
And [c]light dwells with Him.
23 "I thank You and praise You,
O God of my fathers;
You have given me wisdom and
might,
And have now made known to me
what we [a]asked of You,

---

21 a Dan. 6:28; 10:1
CHAPTER 2
1 a Gen. 40:5–8; 41:1, 8 b Esth. 6:1
2 a Ex. 7:11
3 *1* Or *understand*
4 a Dan. 3:9; 5:10; 6:6, 21 *1* The original language of Daniel 2:4b through 7:28 is Aramaic.
5 a Ezra 6:11 *1* The command
6 a Dan. 5:16
9 *1* Situation *2* Or *declare to me*
11 a Dan. 5:11 *1* Or *rare*
13 a Dan. 1:19, 20
15 *1* Or *harsh*
18 a [Matt. 18:19]
19 a Job 33:15
20 a Ps. 113:2 b [Jer. 32:19]
21 a Esth. 1:13 b [Ps. 75:6, 7] c [James 1:5]
22 a Ps. 25:14 b [Heb. 4:13] c Dan. 5:11, 14
23 a Dan. 2:18, 29, 30

For You have made known to us
the king's [1]demand."

Daniel Explains the Dream

24 Therefore Daniel went to Arioch,
whom the king had appointed to destroy
the wise *men* of Babylon. He went and
said thus to him: "Do not destroy the wise
men of Babylon; take me before the king,
and I will tell the king the interpretation."
25 Then Arioch quickly brought Daniel
before the king, and said thus to him, "I
have found a man of the [1]captives of Judah, who will make known to the king the
interpretation."

> *Appropriating faith cannot go beyond our knowledge of the revealed will of God.*
>
> F. F. BOSWORTH

26 The king answered and said to Daniel,
whose name *was* Belteshazzar, "Are you
able to make known to me the dream
which I have seen, and its interpretation?"
27 Daniel answered in the presence of
the king, and said, "The secret which the
king has demanded, the wise *men,* the astrologers, the magicians, and the soothsayers cannot declare to the king. 28 [a]But
there is a God in heaven who reveals secrets, and He has made known to King
Nebuchadnezzar [b]what will be in the latter days. Your dream, and the visions of
your head upon your bed, were these: 29 As
for you, O king, thoughts came *to* your
mind while on your bed, *about* what
would come to pass after this; [a]and He
who reveals secrets has made known to
you what will be. 30 [a]But as for me, this
secret has not been revealed to me because I have more wisdom than anyone
living, but for *our* sakes who make known
the interpretation to the king, [b]and that
you may [1]know the thoughts of your
heart.
31 "You, O king, were watching; and behold, a great image! This great image,
whose splendor *was* excellent, stood before you; and its form *was* awesome.
32 [a]This image's head *was* of fine gold, its
chest and arms of silver, its belly and
[1]thighs of bronze, 33 its legs of iron, its feet
partly of iron and partly of [1]clay. 34 You
watched while a stone was cut out [a]with-
out hands, which struck the image on its
feet of iron and clay, and broke them in
pieces. 35 [a]Then the iron, the clay, the
bronze, the silver, and the gold were
crushed together, and became [b]like chaff
from the summer threshing floors; the
wind carried them away so that [c]no trace
of them was found. And the stone that
struck the image [d]became a great mountain [e]and filled the whole earth.
36 "This *is* the dream. Now we will tell
the interpretation of it before the king.
37 [a]You, O king, *are* a king of kings. [b]For
the God of heaven has given you a kingdom, power, strength, and glory; 38 [a]and
wherever the children of men dwell, or
the beasts of the field and the birds of the
heaven, He has given *them* into your
hand, and has made you ruler over them
all—[b]you *are* this head of gold. 39 But after you shall arise [a]another kingdom [b]in-
ferior to yours; then another, a third
kingdom of bronze, which shall rule over
all the earth. 40 And [a]the fourth kingdom
shall be as strong as iron, inasmuch as
iron breaks in pieces and shatters everything; and like iron that crushes, *that*
kingdom will break in pieces and crush all
the others. 41 Whereas you saw the feet
and toes, partly of potter's clay and partly
of iron, the kingdom shall be divided; yet
the strength of the iron shall be in it, just
as you saw the iron mixed with ceramic
clay. 42 And *as* the toes of the feet *were*
partly of iron and partly of clay, [a]*so* the
kingdom shall be partly strong and partly
[1]fragile. 43 As you saw iron mixed with ceramic clay, they will mingle with the seed
of men; but they will not adhere to one
another, just as iron does not mix with
clay. 44 And in the days of these kings [a]the
God of heaven will set up a kingdom
[b]which shall never be destroyed; and the
kingdom shall not be left to other people;
[c]it shall [1]break in pieces and [2]consume all
these kingdoms, and it shall stand forever.
45 [a]Inasmuch as you saw that the stone
was cut out of the mountain without
hands, and that it broke in pieces the iron,
the bronze, the clay, the silver, and the
gold—the great God has made known to
the king what will come to pass after this.

---

23 [1] Lit. *word*

25 [1] Lit. *sons of the captivity*

28 [a] Gen. 40:8 [b] Gen. 49:1

29 [a] [Dan. 2:22, 28]

30 [a] Acts 3:12 [b] Dan. 2:47 [1] Understand

32 [a] Dan. 2:38, 45 [1] Or *sides*

33 [1] Or *baked clay,* also vv. 34, 35, 42

34 [a] [Zech. 4:6]

35 [a] [Rev. 16:14] [b] Hos. 13:3 [c] Ps. 37:10, 36 [d] [Is. 2:2, 3] [e] Ps. 80:9

37 [a] Jer. 27:6, 7 [b] Ezra 1:2

38 [a] Dan. 4:21, 22 [b] Dan. 2:32

39 [a] Dan. 5:28, 31 [b] Dan. 2:32

40 [a] Dan. 7:7, 23

42 [a] Dan. 7:24 [1] Or *brittle*

44 [a] Dan. 2:28, 37 [b] [Luke 1:32, 33] [c] Is. 60:12 [1] Or *crush* [2] Lit. *put an end to*

45 [a] Dan. 2:35

The dream is certain, and its interpretation is sure."

Daniel and His Friends Promoted

46 [a]Then King Nebuchadnezzar fell on
his face, prostrate before Daniel, and commanded that they should present an offering [b]and incense to him. 47 The king
answered Daniel, and said, "Truly [a]your
God *is* the God of [b]gods, the Lord of kings,
and a revealer of secrets, since you could
reveal this secret." 48 [a]Then the king promoted Daniel [b]and gave him many great
gifts; and he made him ruler over the
whole province of Babylon, and [c]chief ad-
ministrator over all the wise *men* of Babylon. 49 Also Daniel petitioned the king,
[a]and he set Shadrach, Meshach, and
Abed-Nego over the affairs of the province
of Babylon; but Daniel [b]*sat* in [1]the gate of
the king.

The Image of Gold

3 Nebuchadnezzar the king made an
image of gold, whose height *was* [1]six-
ty cubits *and* its width six cubits. He set
it up in the plain of Dura, in the province
of Babylon. 2 And King Nebuchadnezzar
sent *word* to gather together the satraps,
the administrators, the governors, the
counselors, the treasurers, the judges, the
magistrates, and all the officials of the
provinces, to come to the dedication of
the image which King Nebuchadnezzar
had set up. 3 So the satraps, the administrators, the governors, the counselors, the
treasurers, the judges, the magistrates,
and all the officials of the provinces gathered together for the dedication of the image that King Nebuchadnezzar had set up;
and they stood before the image that Nebuchadnezzar had set up. 4 Then a herald
cried [1]aloud: "To you it is commanded,
[a]O peoples, nations, and languages, 5 *that*
at the time you hear the sound of the
horn, flute, harp, lyre, *and* psaltery, in
symphony with all kinds of music, you
shall fall down and worship the gold image that King Nebuchadnezzar has set up;
6 and whoever does not fall down and worship shall [a]be cast immediately into the
midst of a burning fiery furnace."

7 So at that time, when all the people
heard the sound of the horn, flute, harp,
and lyre, in symphony with all kinds of
music, all the people, nations, and languages fell down *and* worshiped the gold
image which King Nebuchadnezzar had
set up.

Daniel's Friends Disobey the King

8 Therefore at that time certain Chaldeans [a]came forward and accused the Jews.
9 They spoke and said to King Nebuchadnezzar, [a]"O king, live forever! 10 You,
O king, have made a decree that everyone
who hears the sound of the horn, flute,
harp, lyre, *and* psaltery, in symphony with
all kinds of music, shall fall down and
worship the gold image; 11 and whoever
does not fall down and worship shall be
cast into the midst of a burning fiery furnace. 12 [a]There are certain Jews whom you
have set over the affairs of the province of
Babylon: Shadrach, Meshach, and Abed-
Nego; these men, O king, have [b]not paid
due regard to you. They do not serve your
gods or worship the gold image which you
have set up."

Let your mind soak in the deliverance of God.

OSWALD CHAMBERS

13 Then Nebuchadnezzar, in [a]rage and
fury, gave the command to bring Shadrach, Meshach, and Abed-Nego. So they
brought these men before the king.
14 Nebuchadnezzar spoke, saying to them,
"*Is it* true, Shadrach, Meshach, and Abed-
Nego, *that* you do not serve my gods or
worship the gold image which I have set
up? 15 Now if you are ready at the time you
hear the sound of the horn, flute, harp,
lyre, *and* psaltery, in symphony with all
kinds of music, and you fall down and
worship the image which I have made,
[a]*good!* But if you do not worship, you
shall be cast immediately into the midst of
a burning fiery furnace. [b]And who *is* the
god who will deliver you from my hands?"

16 Shadrach, Meshach, and Abed-Nego
answered and said to the king,
"O Nebuchadnezzar, [a]we have no need to

---

46 a Acts 10:25; 14:13 b Ezra 6:10
47 a Dan. 3:28, 29; 4:34–37 b [Deut. 10:17]
48 a [Prov. 14:35; 21:1] b Dan. 2:6 c Dan. 4:9; 5:11
49 a Dan. 1:7; 3:12 b Esth. 2:19, 21; 3:2 *1* The king's court
CHAPTER 3
1 *1* About 90 feet
4 a Dan. 4:1; 6:25 *1* Lit. *with strength*
6 a Jer. 29:22
8 a Dan. 6:12, 13
9 a Dan. 2:4; 5:10; 6:6, 21
12 a Dan. 2:49 b Dan. 1:8; 6:12, 13
13 a Dan. 2:12; 3:19
15 a Luke 13:9 b Ex. 5:2
16 a [Matt. 10:19]

answer you in this matter. 17 If that *is the*
case, our [a]God whom we serve is able to
[b]deliver us from the burning fiery furnace, and He will deliver *us* from your
hand, O king. 18 But if not, let it be known
to you, O king, that we do not serve your
gods, nor will we [a]worship the gold image
which you have set up."

O God, as Your servant ____ faces persecution, I ask that You would enable them to stand and put their trust in You, for You are able to deliver. May those around them know that they will not serve other gods nor will they worship idols.

FROM DANIEL 3:17, 18

Saved in Fiery Trial

19 Then Nebuchadnezzar was full of
fury, and the expression on his face
changed toward Shadrach, Meshach, and
Abed-Nego. He spoke and commanded
that they heat the furnace seven times
more than it was usually heated. 20 And he
commanded certain mighty men of valor
who *were* in his army to bind Shadrach,
Meshach, and Abed-Nego, *and* cast *them*
into the burning fiery furnace. 21 Then
these men were bound in their coats,
their trousers, their turbans, and their
other garments, and were cast into the
midst of the burning fiery furnace.
22 Therefore, because the king's command
was [1]urgent, and the furnace exceedingly
hot, the flame of the fire killed those men
who took up Shadrach, Meshach, and
Abed-Nego. 23 And these three men, Shadrach, Meshach, and Abed-Nego, fell
down bound into the midst of the burning
fiery furnace.
24 Then King Nebuchadnezzar was astonished; and he rose in haste *and* spoke,
saying to his [1]counselors, "Did we not
cast three men bound into the midst of
the fire?"
They answered and said to the king,
"True, O king."
25 "Look!" he answered, "I see four men
loose, [a]walking in the midst of the fire;
and they are not hurt, and the form of the
fourth is like [b]the[1] Son of God."

Nebuchadnezzar Praises God

26 Then Nebuchadnezzar went near the
[1]mouth of the burning fiery furnace *and*
spoke, saying, "Shadrach, Meshach, and
Abed-Nego, servants of the [a]Most High
God, come out, and come *here.*" Then
Shadrach, Meshach, and Abed-Nego came
from the midst of the fire. 27 And the satraps, administrators, governors, and the
king's counselors gathered together, and
they saw these men [a]on whose bodies the
fire had no power; the hair of their head
was not singed nor were their garments
affected, and the smell of fire was not on
them.
28 Nebuchadnezzar spoke, saying,
"Blessed be the God of Shadrach, Meshach, and Abed-Nego, who sent His [a]An-
gel[1] and delivered His servants who
trusted in Him, and they have frustrated
the king's word, and yielded their bodies,
that they should not serve nor worship
any god except their own God! 29 [a]There-
fore I make a decree that any people, nation, or language which speaks anything
amiss against the [b]God of Shadrach, Meshach, and Abed-Nego shall be [c]cut in
pieces, and their houses shall be made an
ash heap; [d]because there is no other God
who can deliver like this."
30 Then the king [1]promoted Shadrach,
Meshach, and Abed-Nego in the province
of Babylon.

Nebuchadnezzar's Second Dream

4 Nebuchadnezzar the king,

[a]To all peoples, nations, and languages that dwell in all the earth:

Peace be multiplied to you.

2 I thought it good to declare the
signs and wonders [a]that the Most
High God has worked for me.

3 [a]How great *are* His signs,
And how mighty His wonders!
His kingdom *is* [b]an everlasting
kingdom,
And His dominion *is* from
generation to generation.

17 a[Is. 26:3, 4] b1 Sam. 17:37
18 aJob 13:15
22 *1* Or *harsh*
24 *1* High officials
25 aIs. 43:2 b[Ps. 34:7] *1* Or *a son of the gods*
26 a[Dan. 4:2, 3, 17, 34, 35] *1* Lit. *door*
27 aHeb. 11:34
28 a[Ps. 34:7, 8] *1* Or *angel*
29 aDan. 6:26 bDan. 2:46, 47; 4:34–37 cDan. 2:5 dDan. 6:27
30 *1* Lit. *caused to prosper*
CHAPTER 4
1 aDan. 3:4; 6:25
2 aDan. 3:26
3 a2 Sam. 7:16 b[Dan. 2:44; 4:34; 6:26]

4 I, Nebuchadnezzar, was at rest in
my house, and flourishing in my
palace. 5 I saw a dream which made
me afraid, [a]and the thoughts on my
bed and the visions of my head
[b]troubled me. 6 Therefore I issued a
decree to bring in all the wise *men*
of Babylon before me, that they
might make known to me the interpretation of the dream. 7 [a]Then the
magicians, the astrologers, the
Chaldeans, and the soothsayers
came in, and I told them the
dream; but they did not make
known to me its interpretation.
8 But at last Daniel came before me
[a](his name *is* Belteshazzar, according to the name of my god; [b]in him
is the Spirit of the Holy God), and I
told the dream before him, *saying:*
9 "Belteshazzar, [a]chief of the magicians, because I know that the Spirit of the Holy God *is* in you, and no
secret troubles you, explain to me
the visions of my dream that I have
seen, and its interpretation.

10 "These *were* the visions of my
head *while* on my bed:

I was looking, and behold,
[a]A tree in the midst of the earth,
And its height was great.
11 The tree grew and became strong;
Its height reached to the heavens,
And it could be seen to the ends of
all the earth.
12 Its leaves *were* lovely,
Its fruit abundant,
And in it *was* food for all.
[a]The beasts of the field found shade
under it,
The birds of the heavens dwelt in
its branches,
And all flesh was fed from it.

13 "I saw in the visions of my head
while on my bed, and there was [a]a
watcher, [b]a holy one, coming down
from heaven. 14 He cried [1]aloud and
said thus:

[a]'Chop down the tree and cut off its
branches,
Strip off its leaves and scatter its
fruit.
[b]Let the beasts get out from under
it,
And the birds from its branches.
15 Nevertheless leave the stump and
roots in the earth,
Bound with a band of iron and
bronze,
In the tender grass of the field.
Let it be wet with the dew of
heaven,
And *let* him graze with the beasts
On the grass of the earth.
16 Let his heart be changed from
that of a man,
Let him be given the heart of a
beast,
And let seven [a]times[1] pass over
him.

17 'This decision *is* by the decree of
the watchers,
And the sentence by the word of
the holy ones,
In order [a]that the living may know
[b]That the Most High rules in the
kingdom of men,
[c]Gives it to whomever He will,
And sets over it the [d]lowest of
men.'

18 "This dream I, King Nebuchadnezzar, have seen. Now you, Belteshazzar, declare its interpretation,
[a]since all the wise *men* of my kingdom are not able to make known to
me the interpretation; but you *are*
able, [b]for the Spirit of the Holy God
is in you."

Daniel Explains the Second Dream

19 Then Daniel, [a]whose name was
Belteshazzar, was astonished for a
time, and his thoughts [b]troubled
him. *So* the king spoke, and said,
"Belteshazzar, do not let the dream
or its interpretation trouble you."
Belteshazzar answered and said,
"My lord, *may* [c]the dream [1]concern
those who hate you, and its interpretation [2]concern your enemies!

20 [a]"The tree that you saw, which
grew and became strong, whose
height reached to the heavens and
which *could be seen* by all the
earth, 21 whose leaves *were* lovely
and its fruit abundant, in which
was food for all, under which the
beasts of the field dwelt, and in
whose branches the birds of the
heaven had their home— 22 [a]it *is*

---

5 a Dan. 2:28, 29 b Dan. 2:1
7 a Dan. 2:2
8 a Dan. 1:7 b Dan. 2:11; 4:18; 5:11, 14
9 a Dan. 2:48; 5:11
10 a Ezek. 31:3
12 a Lam. 4:20
13 a [Dan. 4:17, 23] b Deut. 33:2
14 a Ezek. 31:10–14 b Ezek. 31:12, 13 1 Lit. *with strength*
16 a Dan. 11:13; 12:7 1 Possibly *years*
17 a Ps. 9:16; 83:18 b Dan. 2:21; 4:25, 32; 5:21 c Jer. 27:5–7 d 1 Sam. 2:8
18 a Gen. 41:8, 15 b Dan. 4:8, 9; 5:11, 14
19 a Dan. 4:8 b Dan. 7:15, 28; 8:27 c 2 Sam. 18:32 1 *be for* 2 *for*
20 a Dan. 4:10–12
22 a Dan. 2:37, 38

you, O king, who have grown and
become strong; for your greatness
has grown and reaches to the heavens, [b]and your dominion to the end
of the earth.

23 [a]"And inasmuch as the king saw a
watcher, a holy one, coming down
from heaven and saying, 'Chop
down the tree and destroy it, but
leave its stump and roots in the
earth, *bound* with a band of iron
and bronze in the tender grass of
the field; let it be wet with the dew
of heaven, [b]and let him graze with
the beasts of the field, till seven
[1]times pass over him'; [24]this is the
interpretation, O king, and this is
the decree of the Most High, which
has come upon my lord the king:
[25]They shall [a]drive you from men,
your dwelling shall be with the
beasts of the field, and they shall
make you [b]eat grass like oxen. They
shall wet you with the dew of heav-
en, and seven [1]times shall pass over
you, [c]till you know that the Most
High rules in the kingdom of men,
and [d]gives it to whomever He
chooses.

26 "And inasmuch as they gave the
command to leave the stump *and*
roots of the tree, your kingdom
shall be assured to you, after you
come to know that [a]Heaven[1] rules.
[27]Therefore, O king, let my advice
be acceptable to you; [a]break off
your sins by *being* righteous, and
your iniquities by showing mercy to
the poor. [b]Perhaps there may be [c]a
[1]lengthening of your prosperity."

Nebuchadnezzar's Humiliation

28 All *this* came upon King Nebuchadnezzar. [29]At the end of the
twelve months he was walking
[1]about the royal palace of Babylon.
[30]The king [a]spoke, saying, "Is not
this great Babylon, that I have built
for a royal dwelling by my mighty
power and for the honor of my
majesty?"

31 [a]While the word *was still* in the
king's mouth, [b]a voice fell from
heaven: "King Nebuchadnezzar, to
you it is spoken: the kingdom has
departed from you! [32]And [a]they
shall drive you from men, and your
dwelling *shall be* with the beasts of
the field. They shall make you eat
grass like oxen; and seven [1]times
shall pass over you, until you know
that the Most High rules in the
kingdom of men, and gives it to
whomever He chooses."

33 That very hour the word was fulfilled concerning Nebuchadnezzar;
he was driven from men and ate
grass like oxen; his body was wet
with the dew of heaven till his hair
had grown like eagles' *feathers* and
his nails like birds' *claws.*

Nebuchadnezzar Praises God

34 And [a]at the end of the [1]time I,
Nebuchadnezzar, lifted my eyes to
heaven, and my understanding re-
turned to me; and I blessed the
Most High and praised and honored
Him [b]who lives forever:

For His dominion *is* [c]an everlasting
dominion,
And His kingdom *is* from
generation to generation.

35 [a]All the inhabitants of the earth
are reputed as nothing;
[b]He does according to His will in
the army of heaven
And *among* the inhabitants of the
earth.
[c]No one can restrain His hand
Or say to Him, [d]"What have You
done?"

36 At the same time my reason returned to me, [a]and for the glory of
my kingdom, my honor and splendor returned to me. My counselors
and nobles resorted to me, I was
[b]restored to my kingdom, and excellent majesty was [c]added to me.
[37]Now I, Nebuchadnezzar, [a]praise
and extol and honor the King of
heaven, [b]all of whose works *are*
truth, and His ways justice. [c]And
those who walk in pride He is able
to put down.

Belshazzar's Feast

5 Belshazzar the king [a]made a great
feast for a thousand of his lords, and
drank wine in the presence of the thou-

22 [b]Jer. 27:6–8
23 [a]Dan. 4:13–15 [b]Dan. 5:21 *[1] Possibly years*
25 [a]Dan. 4:32; 5:21 [b]Ps. 106:20 [c]Dan. 4:2, 17, 32 [d]Jer. 27:5 *[1] Possibly years*
26 [a]Matt. 21:25 [1]God
27 [a][1 Pet. 4:8] [b][Ps. 41:1–3] [c]1 Kin. 21:29 *[1] prolonging*
29 [1] Or *upon*
30 [a]Prov. 16:18
31 [a]Luke 12:20 [b]Dan. 4:24
32 [a][Dan. 4:25] *[1] Possibly years*
34 [a]Dan. 4:26 [b][Rev. 4:10] [c][Luke 1:33] [1] Lit. *days*
35 [a]Is. 40:15, 17 [b]Ps. 115:3; 135:6 [c]Job 34:29 [d]Rom. 9:20
36 [a]Dan. 4:26 [b]2 Chr. 20:20 [c][Prov. 22:4]
37 [a]Dan. 2:46, 47; 3:28, 29 [b][Ps. 33:4] [c]Ex. 18:11

CHAPTER 5
1 [a]Esth. 1:3

sand. 2While he tasted the wine, Belshazzar gave the command to bring the gold and silver vessels [a]which his [1]father Nebuchadnezzar had taken from the temple which *had been* in Jerusalem, that the king and his lords, his wives, and his concubines might drink from them. 3Then they brought the gold [a]vessels that had been taken from the temple of the house of God which *had been* in Jerusalem; and the king and his lords, his wives, and his concubines drank from them. 4They drank wine, [a]and praised the gods of gold and silver, bronze and iron, wood and stone.

5[a]In the same hour the fingers of a man's hand appeared and wrote opposite the lampstand on the plaster of the wall of the king's palace; and the king saw the part of the hand that wrote. 6Then the king's countenance changed, and his thoughts troubled him, so that the joints of his hips were loosened and his [a]knees knocked against each other. 7[a]The king cried [1]aloud to bring in [b]the astrologers, the Chaldeans, and the soothsayers. The king spoke, saying to the wise *men* of Babylon, "Whoever reads this writing, and tells me its interpretation, shall be clothed with purple and *have* a chain of gold around his neck; [c]and he shall be the third ruler in the kingdom." 8Now all the king's wise *men* came, [a]but they could not read the writing, or make known to the king its interpretation. 9Then King Belshazzar was greatly [a]troubled, his countenance was changed, and his lords were [1]astonished.

10The queen, because of the words of the king and his lords, came to the banquet hall. The queen spoke, saying, "O king, live forever! Do not let your thoughts trouble you, nor let your countenance change. 11[a]There is a man in your kingdom in whom *is* the Spirit of the Holy God. And in the days of your [1]father, light and understanding and wisdom, like the wisdom of the gods, were found in him; and King Nebuchadnezzar your father—your father the king—made him chief of the magicians, astrologers, Chaldeans, *and* soothsayers. 12Inasmuch as an excellent spirit, knowledge, understanding, interpreting dreams, solving riddles, and [1]explaining enigmas were found in this Daniel, [a]whom the king named Belteshazzar, now let Daniel be called, and he will give the interpretation."

The Writing on the Wall Explained

13Then Daniel was brought in before the king. The king spoke, and said to Daniel, "*Are* you that Daniel [1]who is one of the captives from Judah, whom my [2]father the king brought from Judah? 14I have heard of you, that [a]the [1]Spirit of God *is* in you, and *that* light and understanding and excellent wisdom are found in you. 15Now [a]the wise *men,* the astrologers, have been brought in before me, that they should read this writing and make known to me its interpretation, but they could not give the interpretation of the thing. 16And I have heard of you, that you can give interpretations and [1]explain enigmas. [a]Now if you can read the writing and make known to me its interpretation, you shall be clothed with purple and *have* a chain of gold around your neck, and shall be the third ruler in the kingdom."

17Then Daniel answered, and said before the king, "Let your gifts be for yourself, and give your rewards to another; yet I will read the writing to the king, and make known to him the interpretation. 18O king, [a]the Most High God gave Nebuchadnezzar your [1]father a kingdom and majesty, glory and honor. 19And because of the majesty that He gave him, [a]all peoples, nations, and languages trembled and feared before him. Whomever he wished, he [b]executed; whomever he wished, he kept alive; whomever he wished, he set up; and whomever he wished, he put down. 20[a]But when his heart was lifted up, and his spirit was hardened in pride, he was deposed from his kingly throne, and they took his glory from him. 21Then he was [a]driven from the sons of men, his heart was made like the beasts, and his dwelling *was* with the wild donkeys. They fed him with grass like oxen, and his body was wet with the dew of heaven, [b]till he [1]knew that the Most High God rules in the kingdom of men, and appoints over it whomever He chooses.

22"But you his son, Belshazzar, [a]have not humbled your heart, although you knew all this. 23[a]And you have [1]lifted yourself up against the Lord of heaven. They have brought the [b]vessels of [2]His house before you, and you and your lords, your wives and your concubines, have drunk wine from them. And you have praised the gods of silver and gold, bronze

---

2 a Dan. 1:2 *1* Or *ancestor*
3 a 2 Chr. 36:10
4 a Rev. 9:20
5 a Dan. 4:31
6 a Ezek. 7:17; 21:7
7 a Dan. 4:6,7; 5:11, 15 b Is. 47:13 c Dan. 6:2, 3 *1* Lit. *with strength*
8 a Dan. 2:27; 4:7; 5:15
9 a Dan. 2:1; 5:6 *1 perplexed*
11 a Dan. 2:48; 4:8, 9, 18 *1* Or *ancestor*
12 a Dan. 1:7; 4:8 *1* Lit. *untying knots*
13 *1* Lit. *who is of the sons of the captivity* *2* Or *ancestor*
14 a Dan. 4:8, 9, 18; 5:11, 12 *1* Or *spirit of the gods*
15 a Dan. 5:7, 8
16 a Dan. 5:7, 29 *1* Lit. *untie knots*
18 a Dan. 2:37, 38; 4:17, 22, 25 *1* Or *ancestor*
19 a Jer. 27:7 b Dan. 2:12, 13; 3:6
20 a Dan. 4:30, 37
21 a Dan. 4:32, 33 b Ezek. 17:24 *1* Recognized
22 a 2 Chr. 33:23; 36:12
23 a Dan. 5:3, 4 b Ex. 40:9 *1* Exalted *2* The temple

and iron, wood and stone, [c]which do not
see or hear or know; and the God who
holds your breath in His hand [d]and owns
all your ways, you have not glorified.
24Then the [1]fingers of the hand were sent
from Him, and this writing was written.
25"And this is the inscription that was
written:

[1]MENE, MENE, [2]TEKEL, [3]UPHARSIN.

26This *is* the interpretation of *each* word.
MENE: God has numbered your kingdom,
and finished it; 27TEKEL: [a]You have been
weighed in the balances, and found wanting; 28PERES: Your kingdom has been divided, and given to the [a]Medes and
[b]Persians."[1] 29Then Belshazzar gave the
command, and they clothed Daniel with
purple and *put* a chain of gold around his
neck, and made a proclamation concerning him [a]that he should be the third ruler
in the kingdom.

Belshazzar's Fall

30[a]That very night Belshazzar, king of
the Chaldeans, was slain. 31[a]And Darius
the Mede received the kingdom, *being*
about sixty-two years old.

The Plot Against Daniel

6 It pleased Darius to set over the kingdom one hundred and twenty satraps,
to be over the whole kingdom; 2and over
these, three governors, of whom Daniel
was one, that the satraps might give account to them, so that the king would
suffer no loss. 3Then this Daniel
distinguished himself above the governors and satraps, [a]because an excellent
spirit *was* in him; and the king gave
thought to setting him over the whole
realm. 4[a]So the governors and satraps
sought to find *some* charge against Daniel
concerning the kingdom; but they could
find no charge or fault, because he *was*
faithful; nor was there any error or fault
found in him. 5Then these men said, "We
shall not find any charge against this Daniel unless we find *it* against him concerning the law of his God."
6So these governors and satraps
thronged before the king, and said thus to
him: [a]"King Darius, live forever! 7All the
governors of the kingdom, the administrators and satraps, the counselors and
advisors, have [a]consulted together to establish a royal statute and to make a firm
decree, that whoever petitions any god or
man for thirty days, except you, O king,
shall be cast into the den of lions. 8Now,
O king, establish the decree and sign the
writing, so that it cannot be changed, according to the [a]law of the Medes and Persians, which [1]does not alter." 9Therefore
King Darius signed the written decree.

Daniel in the Lions' Den

10Now when Daniel knew that the writing was signed, he went home. And in his
upper room, with his windows open [a]to-
ward Jerusalem, he knelt down on his
knees [b]three times that day, and prayed
and gave thanks before his God, as was his
custom since early days.
11Then these men assembled and found
Daniel praying and making supplication
before his God. 12[a]And they went before
the king, and spoke concerning the king's
decree: "Have you not signed a decree that
every man who petitions any god or man
within thirty days, except you, O king,
shall be cast into the den of lions?"
The king answered and said, "The thing
is true, [b]according to the law of the Medes
and Persians, which [1]does not alter."
13So they answered and said before the
king, "That Daniel, [a]who is [1]one of the
captives from Judah, [b]does not show due
regard for you, O king, or for the decree
that you have signed, but makes his petition three times a day."
14And the king, when he heard *these*
words, [a]was greatly displeased with himself, and set *his* heart on Daniel to deliver
him; and he [1]labored till the going down
of the sun to deliver him. 15Then these
men [1]approached the king, and said to the
king, "Know, O king, that *it is* [a]the law of
the Medes and Persians that no decree or
statute which the king establishes may be
changed."

The den of lions is as safe a place as any.
CHARLES WESLEY

---

23 c Ps. 115:5, 6 d [Jer. 10:23]
24 1 Lit. *palm*
25 1 Lit. *a mina* (50 shekels) from the verb "to number" 2 Lit. *a shekel* from the verb "to weigh" 3 Lit. *and half-shekels* from the verb "to divide"; pl. of *Peres,* v. 28
27 a Ps. 62:9
28 a Dan. 5:31; 9:1 b Dan. 6:28 1 Aram. *Paras,* consonant with *Peres*
29 a Dan. 5:7, 16
30 a Jer. 51:31, 39, 57
31 a Dan. 2:39; 9:1

CHAPTER 6
3 a Dan. 5:12
4 a Eccl. 4:4
6 a Neh. 2:3
7 a Ps. 59:3; 62:4; 64:2–6
8 a Esth. 1:19; 8:8 1 Lit. *does not pass away*
10 a Jon. 2:4 b Ps. 55:17
12 a Dan. 3:8–12 b Dan. 6:8, 15 1 Lit. *does not pass away*
13 a Dan. 1:6; 5:13 b Dan. 3:12 1 Lit. *of the sons of the captivity*
14 a Mark 6:26 1 *strove*
15 a Dan. 6:8, 12 1 Lit. *thronged before*

Daniel 6:15–23

Dear Woman of Destiny,

God's Word tells us to flee temptations and face troubles, but we often see women doing the opposite. Troubles are common and are used by God to develop our character as we press in to find His purpose for us—our destiny. Destiny sometimes comes dressed in troubles. God wants to turn your troubles around and make them part of His purpose for you.

Temptations, on the other hand, are used by Satan to defeat us and block us from achieving our life's purpose. Daniel fled from temptations, not even allowing the king's food to be brought to him. He steadfastly prayed many times each day to keep himself pure from the wicked culture of the country where he'd been taken in his youth as a slave.

Earlier in history, Joseph had set the example by fleeing the house of Potiphar when Potiphar's wife tried to seduce him (see Gen. 39). Paul later commanded his young protégé Timothy, "Flee also youthful lusts" (2 Tim. 2:22). We are not to face alluring temptations, but to turn away from them completely.

My husband, Edwin, and I have watched many young Christians become discouraged and even fall away when they tried to face temptations and instead gave in to them. Sin is contagious, but righteousness is not. And "evil company corrupts good habits" (1 Cor. 15:33).

While we should escape *temptations*, women who try to escape from *troubles* generally compound them. How many women do you know who tried to flee a troubled relationship and ended up in another one? Or who tried to flee their troubled pasts by running into drugs or a bad marriage?

Crisis is normal in our lives and can be important as we find our way to destiny. Your destiny will only be reached by way of crisis. By facing crisis and overcoming it, you qualify yourself to achieve your destiny, which is right on the other side of the crisis.

Edwin and I first started pastoring in the small mountain community of Sonora, California. After agreeing in the summer to receive a percentage of the church income, we moved, settled in, and financed a car. That winter we discovered that most of our church members were in the lumber industry and didn't work during the winter! As a result, our finances were depleted to the point that we were forced to sell the car. I'll never forget the old clunker we traded our beautiful car for.

Crises like that molded and shaped our characters, cemented our marriage bond, and propelled us toward the destiny in ministry that God had for us. Our destiny was clothed with difficulties, but none could deter us.

What is there to fear in any difficulty when we center our lives on Christ, the Risen Savior? As Daniel was lowered into the den of lions, he may not have known whether God would actually close the mouths of the lions. But he did know that in every crisis of his life, God revealed more of his personal destiny. Armed with that knowledge, Daniel didn't fear what the lions could do.

God's Word tells us not to fear what man can do, but to fear God only, because He has the power over eternal life or death (see Matt. 10:28). Fear God enough to flee temptations (see Prov. 16:6). Fear God by trusting Him more than you trust the troubles you see. Crisis is just the garment worn by destiny.

Nancy Corbett Cole

16 So the king gave the command, and they brought Daniel and cast *him* into the den of lions. *But* the king spoke, saying to Daniel, "Your God, whom you serve continually, He will deliver you." 17 [a]Then a stone was brought and laid on the mouth of the den, [b]and the king sealed it with his own signet ring and with the signets of his lords, that the purpose concerning Daniel might not be changed.

Daniel Saved from the Lions

18 Now the king went to his palace and spent the night fasting; and no [1]musicians were brought before him. [a]Also his sleep [2]went from him. 19 Then the [a]king arose very early in the morning and went in haste to the den of lions. 20 And when he came to the den, he cried out with a [1]lamenting voice to Daniel. The king spoke, saying to Daniel, "Daniel, servant of the living God, [a]has your God, whom you serve continually, been able to deliver you from the lions?"

21 Then Daniel said to the king, [a]"O king, live forever! 22 [a]My God sent His angel and [b]shut the lions' mouths, so that they have not hurt me, because I was found innocent before Him; and also, O king, I have done no wrong before you."

23 Now the king was exceedingly glad for him, and commanded that they should take Daniel up out of the den. So Daniel was taken up out of the den, and no injury whatever was found on him, [a]because he believed in his God.

Darius Honors God

24 And the king gave the command, [a]and they brought those men who had accused Daniel, and they cast *them* into the den of lions—them, [b]their children, and their wives; and the lions overpowered them, and broke all their bones in pieces before they ever came to the bottom of the den.

25 [a]Then King Darius wrote:

To all peoples, nations, and languages that dwell in all the earth:

Peace be multiplied to you.

26 [a]I make a decree that in every dominion of my kingdom *men must*
[b]tremble and fear before the God of Daniel.

[c]For He *is* the living God,
And steadfast forever;
His kingdom *is the one* which shall not be [d]destroyed,
And His dominion *shall endure* to the end.

27 He delivers and rescues,
[a]And He works signs and wonders
In heaven and on earth,
Who has delivered Daniel from the [1]power of the lions.

28 So this Daniel prospered in the reign of Darius [a]and in the reign of [b]Cyrus the Persian.

Living God, You deliver and rescue; You work signs and wonders in heaven and on earth. Deliver ____, even as You delivered Daniel from the power of the lions.

FROM DANIEL 6:27

Vision of the Four Beasts

7 In the first year of Belshazzar king of Babylon, [a]Daniel [1]had a dream and [b]visions of his head *while* on his bed. Then he wrote down the dream, telling [2]the main facts.

2 Daniel spoke, saying, "I saw in my vision by night, and behold, the four winds of heaven were stirring up the Great Sea. 3 And four great beasts [a]came up from the sea, each different from the other. 4 The first *was* [a]like a lion, and had eagle's wings. I watched till its wings were plucked off; and it was lifted up from the earth and made to stand on two feet like a man, and a [b]man's heart was given to it.

5 [a]"And suddenly another beast, a second, like a bear. It was raised up on one side, and *had* three ribs in its mouth between its teeth. And they said thus to it: 'Arise, devour much flesh!'

6 "After this I looked, and there was another, like a leopard, which had on its back four wings of a bird. The beast also had [a]four heads, and dominion was given to it.

7 "After this I saw in the night visions, and behold, [a]a fourth beast, dreadful and terrible, exceedingly strong. It had huge iron teeth; it was devouring, breaking in

17 a Lam. 3:53 b Matt. 27:66
18 a Dan. 2:1 *1* Exact meaning unknown *2* Or *fled*
19 a Dan. 3:24
20 a Dan. 3:17 *1* Or *grieved*
21 a Dan. 2:4; 6:6
22 a Dan. 3:28 b Heb. 11:33
23 a Heb. 11:33
24 a Deut. 19:18, 19 b Deut. 24:16
25 a Dan. 4:1
26 a Dan. 3:29 b Ps. 99:1 c Dan. 4:34; 6:20 d Dan. 2:44; 4:3; 7:14, 27
27 a Dan. 4:2, 3 *1* Lit. *hand*
28 a Dan. 1:21 b Ezra 1:1, 2
CHAPTER 7
1 a [Amos 3:7] b [Dan. 2:28] *1* Lit. *saw* *2* Lit. *the head* or *chief of the words*
3 a Rev. 13:1; 17:8
4 a Deut. 28:49 b Dan. 4:16, 34
5 a Dan. 2:39
6 a Dan. 8:8, 22
7 a Dan. 2:40

pieces, and trampling the residue with its
feet. It *was* different from all the beasts
that *were* before it, [b]and it had ten horns.
[8]I was considering the horns, and [a]there
was another horn, a little one, coming up
among them, before whom three of the
first horns were plucked out by the roots.
And there, in this horn, *were* eyes like the
eyes [b]of a man, [c]and a mouth speaking
[1]pompous words.

Vision of the Ancient of Days

9 "I[a] watched till thrones were [1]put
in place,
And [b]the Ancient of Days was
seated;
[c]His garment *was* white as snow,
And the hair of His head *was* like
pure wool.
His throne *was* a fiery flame,
[d]Its wheels a burning fire;
10 [a]A fiery stream issued
And came forth from before Him.
[b]A thousand thousands ministered to
Him;
Ten thousand times ten thousand
stood before Him.
[c]The [1]court was seated,
And the books were opened.

7 [b]Rev. 12:3; 13:1
8 [a]Dan. 8:9 [b]Rev. 9:7 [c]Rev. 13:5, 6 [1]Lit. *great things*
9 [a][Rev. 20:4] [b]Ps. 90:2 [c]Rev. 1:14 [d]Ezek. 1:15 [1]Or *set up*
10 [a]Is. 30:33; 66:15 [b]Rev. 5:11 [c][Rev. 20:11–15] [1]Or *judgment*

MARIA WOODWORTH-ETTER

It didn't make sense when God called Maria Woodworth-Etter (1844–1924) to evangelize the lost at the young age of 13. First, she was a woman, living in an era when women weren't allowed to vote, much less preach. The thought of a single woman serving in the ministry was unheard of. In addition, Maria had no formal Christian schooling. She often prayed, "Lord, I can't preach, I don't know what to say, and I don't have any education."

Even with all these strikes against her, Maria expected a life of "normal" Christian service when she married P.H. Woodworth. Tragedy struck the family, but Maria did not become bitter; and she continued to feel God's call on her life. In a vision, she saw fields of grain swaying in the wind. She began to preach, and she watched as the grain fell like sheaves. She believed Jesus told her that just as the sheaves fell, people would fall as the words of the Spirit left her mouth.

In obedience, Maria gathered a small crowd of relatives; and as she opened her mouth, they began to weep and fall on the floor. Word quickly spread that the hand of God was on her; and in a short time, she had held nine revivals, preached two hundred sermons and started two churches.

At 40, Maria was at the forefront of the Pentecostal Movement. But with her prominence came a bombardment of criticism and attack. Doctors attended her meetings, intent on proving her healings fake. Hired thugs came to disrupt the services. Mentally disturbed individuals were planted to suggest that Maria drove people to insanity. Even fellow ministers publicly rebuked her. Through all of these setbacks, Maria rarely defended herself, but continued to trust God.

In a time when the mainstream church sat rigid in its pews, Maria brought signs, wonders, healings, and an exuberant life. Thousands were saved. She broke through the religious walls that prevented women from fulfilling their destiny in God and, as a result, impacted an entire nation.

[11]"I watched then because of the sound of the [1]pompous words which the horn was speaking; [a]I watched till the beast was slain, and its body destroyed and given to the burning flame. [12]As for the rest of the beasts, they had their dominion taken away, yet their lives were prolonged for a season and a time.

13 "I was watching in the night
visions,
And behold, [a]*One* like the Son of
Man,
Coming with the clouds of heaven!
He came to the Ancient of Days,
And they brought Him near before
Him.
14 [a]Then to Him was given dominion
and glory and a kingdom,
That all [b]peoples, nations, and
languages should serve Him.
His dominion *is* [c]an everlasting
dominion,
Which shall not pass away,
And His kingdom *the one*
Which shall not be destroyed.

Daniel's Visions Interpreted

[15]"I, Daniel, was grieved in my spirit [1]within *my* body, and the visions of my head troubled me. [16]I came near to one of those who stood by, and asked him the truth of all this. So he told me and made known to me the interpretation of these things: [17]'Those great beasts, which are four, *are* four [1]kings *which* arise out of the earth. [18]But [a]the saints of the Most High shall receive the kingdom, and possess the kingdom forever, even forever and ever.'

[19]"Then I wished to know the truth about the fourth beast, which was different from all the others, exceedingly dreadful, *with* its teeth of iron and its nails of bronze, *which* devoured, broke in pieces, and trampled the residue with its feet; [20]and the ten horns that *were* on its head, and the other *horn* which came up, before which three fell, namely, that horn which had eyes and a mouth which spoke [1]pompous words, whose appearance *was* greater than his fellows.

[21]"I was watching; [a]and the same horn was making war against the saints, and prevailing against them, [22]until the Ancient of Days came, [a]and a judgment was made *in favor* of the saints of the Most High, and the time came for the saints to possess the kingdom.

[23]"Thus he said:

'The fourth beast shall be
[a]A fourth kingdom on earth,
Which shall be different from all
other kingdoms,
And shall devour the whole earth,
Trample it and break it in pieces.
24 [a]The ten horns *are* ten kings
Who shall arise from this kingdom.
And another shall rise after them;
He shall be different from the first
ones,
And shall subdue three kings.
25 [a]He shall speak *pompous* words
against the Most High,
Shall [b]persecute[1] the saints of the
Most High,
And shall [c]intend to change times
and law.
Then [d]*the saints* shall be given into
his hand
[e]For a time and times and half a
time.

26 'But[a] the court shall be seated,
And they shall [b]take away his
dominion,
To consume and destroy *it* forever.
27 Then the [a]kingdom and dominion,
And the greatness of the kingdoms
under the whole heaven,
Shall be given to the people, the
saints of the Most High.
[b]His kingdom *is* an everlasting
kingdom,
[c]And all dominions shall serve and
obey Him.'

[28]"This *is* the end of the [1]account. As for me, Daniel, [a]my thoughts greatly troubled me, and my countenance changed; but I [b]kept the matter in my heart."

Vision of a Ram and a Goat

8 In[1] the third year of the reign of King Belshazzar a vision appeared *to* me—to me, Daniel—after the one that appeared to me [a]the first time. [2]I saw in the vision, and it so happened while I was looking, that I *was* in [a]Shushan,[1] the [2]citadel, which *is* in the province of Elam; and I saw in the vision that I was by the River Ulai. [3]Then I lifted my eyes and saw, and there, standing beside the river, was a ram which had two horns, and the two horns

11 [a][Rev. 19:20; 20:10] [1]Lit. *great*
13 [a][Matt. 24:30; 26:64]
14 [a][John 3:35, 36] [b]Dan. 3:4 [c]Mic. 4:7
15 [1]Lit. *in the midst of its sheath*
17 [1]Representing their kingdoms, v. 23
18 [a]Is. 60:12–14
20 [1]Lit. *great things*
21 [a]Rev. 11:7; 13:7; 17:14
22 [a][Rev. 1:6]
23 [a]Dan. 2:40
24 [a]Rev. 13:1; 17:12
25 [a]Rev. 13:1–6 [b]Rev. 17:6 [c]Dan. 2:21 [d]Rev. 13:7; 18:24 [e]Rev. 12:14 [1]Lit. *wear out*
26 [a][Dan. 2:35; 7:10, 22] [b]Rev. 19:20
27 [a]Dan. 7:14, 18, 22 [b][Luke 1:33, 34] [c]Is. 60:12
28 [a]Dan. 8:27 [b]Luke 2:19, 51 [1]Lit. *word*

CHAPTER 8
1 [a]Dan. 7:1 [1]The Hebrew language resumes in Dan. 8:1.
2 [a]Esth. 1:2; 2:8 [1]Or *Susa* [2]Or *fortified palace*

were high; but one *was* [a]higher than the
other, and the higher *one* came up last. 4I
saw the ram pushing westward, northward, and southward, so that no animal
could [1]withstand him; nor *was there any*
that could deliver from his hand, [a]but
he did according to his will and became
great.
5And as I was considering, suddenly a
male goat came from the west, across the
surface of the whole earth, without touching the ground; and the goat *had* a notable [a]horn between his eyes. 6Then he
came to the ram that had two horns,
which I had seen standing beside the river, and ran at him with furious power.
7And I saw him confronting the ram; he
was moved with rage against him, [1]at-
tacked the ram, and broke his two horns.
There was no power in the ram to withstand him, but he cast him down to the
ground and trampled him; and there was
no one that could deliver the ram from his
hand.
8Therefore the male goat grew very
great; but when he became strong, the
large horn was broken, and in place of it
[a]four notable ones came up toward the
four winds of heaven. 9[a]And out of one of
them came a little horn which grew exceedingly great toward the south, [b]toward
the east, and toward the [c]Glorious *Land.*
10[a]And it grew up to [b]the host of heaven;
and [c]it cast down *some* of the host and
some of the stars to the ground, and trampled them. 11[a]He even exalted *himself* as
high as [b]the Prince of the host; [c]and by
him [d]the daily *sacrifices* were taken away,
and the place of [1]His sanctuary was cast
down. 12Because of transgression, [a]an
army was given over *to the horn* to oppose
the daily *sacrifices;* and he cast [b]truth
down to the ground. He [c]did *all this* and
prospered.
13Then I heard [a]a holy one speaking;
and *another* holy one said to that certain
one who was speaking, "How long *will* the
vision *be, concerning* the daily *sacrifices*
and the transgression [1]of desolation, the
giving of both the sanctuary and the host
to be trampled underfoot?"
14And he said to me, "For two thousand
three hundred [1]days; then the sanctuary
shall be cleansed."

Gabriel Interprets the Vision

15Then it happened, when I, Daniel, had
seen the vision and [a]was seeking the
meaning, that suddenly there stood before me [b]one having the appearance of a
man. 16And I heard a man's voice [a]be-
tween *the banks of* the Ulai, who called,
and said, [b]"Gabriel, make this *man* understand the vision." 17So he came near
where I stood, and when he came I was
afraid and [a]fell on my face; but he said to
me, "Understand, son of man, that the vision *refers* to the time of the end."
18[a]Now, as he was speaking with me, I
was in a deep sleep with my face to the
ground; [b]but he touched me, and stood
me upright. 19And he said, "Look, I am
making known to you what shall happen
in the latter time of the indignation; [a]for
at the appointed time the end *shall be.*
20The ram which you saw, having the two
horns—*they are* the kings of Media and
Persia. 21And the [1]male goat *is* the [2]king-
dom of Greece. The large horn that *is* between its eyes [a]*is* the first king. 22[a]As for
the broken *horn* and the four that stood
up in its place, four kingdoms shall arise
out of that nation, but not with its power.

23 "And in the latter time of their
kingdom,
When the transgressors have
reached their fullness,
A king shall arise,
[a]Having fierce [1]features,
Who understands sinister schemes.
24 His power shall be mighty, [a]but
not by his own power;
He shall destroy [1]fearfully,
[b]And shall prosper and thrive;
[c]He shall destroy the mighty, and
also the holy people.

25 "Through[a] his cunning
He shall cause deceit to prosper
under his [1]rule;
[b]And he shall exalt *himself* in his
heart.
He shall destroy many in *their*
prosperity.
[c]He shall even rise against the
Prince of princes;
But he shall be [d]broken without
human means.

26 "And the vision of the evenings and
mornings
Which was told is true;
[a]Therefore seal up the vision,
For *it refers* to many days *in the
future.*"

3 [a]Dan. 7:5
4 [a]Dan. 5:19 [1]Lit. *stand before him*
5 [a]Dan. 8:8, 21; 11:3
7 [1]Lit. *struck*
8 [a]Dan. 7:6; 8:22; 11:4
9 [a]Dan. 11:21 [b]Dan. 11:25 [c]Ps. 48:2
10 [a]Dan. 11:28 [b]Is. 14:13 [c]Rev. 12:4
11 [a]Dan. 8:25; 11:36, 37 [b]Josh. 5:14 [c]Dan. 11:31; 12:11 [d]Ex. 29:38 [1]The temple
12 [a]Dan. 11:31 [b]Is. 59:14 [c]Dan. 8:4; 11:36
13 [a]Dan. 4:13, 23 [1]Or *making desolate*
14 [1]Lit. *evening-mornings*
15 [a]1 Pet. 1:10 [b]Ezek. 1:26
16 [a]Dan. 12:6, 7 [b]Luke 1:19, 26
17 [a]Rev. 1:17
18 [a]Luke 9:32 [b]Ezek. 2:2
19 [a]Hab. 2:3
21 [a]Dan. 11:3 [1]*shaggy male* [2]Lit. *king,* representing his kingdom, Dan. 7:17, 23
22 [a]Dan. 11:4
23 [a]Deut. 28:50 [1]Lit. *countenance*
24 [a]Rev. 17:13 [b]Dan. 11:36 [c]Dan. 7:25 [1]Or *extraordinarily*
25 [a]Dan. 11:21 [b]Dan. 8:11–13; 11:36; 12:7 [c]Rev. 19:19, 20 [d]Job 34:20 [1]Lit. *hand*
26 [a]Ezek. 12:27

27[a]And I, Daniel, fainted and was sick
for days; afterward I arose and went about
the king's business. I was [1]astonished by
the vision, but no one understood it.

Daniel's Prayer for the People

9 In the first year [a]of Darius the son
of Ahasuerus, of the lineage of the
Medes, who was made king over the realm
of the Chaldeans— 2in the first year of his
reign I, Daniel, understood by the books
the number of the years *specified* by the
word of the LORD through [a]Jeremiah the
prophet, that He would accomplish seventy years in the desolations of Jerusalem.

Lord, may ____ take their place as an intercessor for Your people, as Daniel did, with prayer, supplications, and fasting, praying that Your word and purposes would be accomplished.

FROM DANIEL 9:2, 3

3[a]Then I set my face toward the Lord
God to make request by prayer and supplications, with fasting, sackcloth, and ashes. 4And I prayed to the LORD my God, and
made confession, and said, "O [a]Lord,
great and awesome God, who keeps His
covenant and mercy with those who love
Him, and with those who keep His commandments, 5[a]we have sinned and committed iniquity, we have done wickedly
and rebelled, even by departing from Your
precepts and Your judgments. 6[a]Neither
have we heeded Your servants the prophets, who spoke in Your name to our kings
and our princes, to our fathers and all the
people of the land. 7O Lord, [a]righteous-
ness *belongs* to You, but to us shame of
face, as *it is* this day—to the men of Judah, to the inhabitants of Jerusalem and
all Israel, those near and those far off in
all the countries to which You have driv-
en them, because of the unfaithfulness which they have committed against
You.
8"O Lord, to us *belongs* shame of face,
to our kings, our princes, and our fathers,
because we have sinned against You. 9[a]To
the Lord our God *belong* mercy and forgiveness, though we have rebelled against
Him. 10We have not obeyed the voice of
the LORD our God, to walk in His laws,
which He set before us by His servants the
prophets. 11Yes, [a]all Israel has transgressed Your law, and has departed so as
not to obey Your voice; therefore the
curse and the oath written in the [b]Law
of Moses the servant of God have been
poured out on us, because we have sinned
against Him. 12And He has [a]confirmed
His words, which He spoke against us and
against our judges who judged us, by
bringing upon us a great disaster; [b]for under the whole heaven such has never been
done as what has been done to Jerusalem.

O, dear, disappointed one, have you given up expecting things from God and settled down into the ordinary Christian life? Let us stir ourselves to prayer, as Daniel, and God will surely hear.

MARGARET GORDON

13[a]"As *it is* written in the Law of Moses,
all this disaster has come upon us; [b]yet we
have not made our prayer before the LORD
our God, that we might turn from our
iniquities and understand Your truth.
14Therefore the LORD has [a]kept the disaster in mind, and brought it upon us; for
[b]the LORD our God *is* righteous in all the
works which He does, though we have not
obeyed His voice. 15And now, O Lord our
God, [a]who brought Your people out of the
land of Egypt with a mighty hand, and
made Yourself [b]a name, as *it is* this day—
we have sinned, we have done wickedly!
16"O Lord, [a]according to all Your righteousness, I pray, let Your anger and Your
fury be turned away from Your city Jerusalem, [b]Your holy mountain; because for
our sins, [c]and for the iniquities of our fathers, [d]Jerusalem and Your people [e]*are* a

27 a Dan. 7:28; 8:17
1 *amazed*

CHAPTER 9
1 a Dan. 1:21
2 a 2 Chr. 36:21
3 a Neh. 1:4
4 a Ex. 20:6
5 a 1 Kin. 8:47, 48
6 a 2 Chr. 36:15
7 a Neh. 9:33
9 a [Ps. 130:4, 7]
11 a Is. 1:3–6 b Lev. 26:14
12 a Zech. 1:6 b Lam. 1:12; 2:13
13 a Deut. 28:15–68 b Is. 9:13
14 a Jer. 31:28; 44:27 b Neh. 9:33
15 a Neh. 1:10 b Neh. 9:10
16 a 1 Sam. 12:7 b Zech. 8:3 c Ex. 20:5 d Lam. 2:16 e Ps. 79:4

reproach to all *those* around us. 17Now
therefore, our God, hear the prayer of
Your servant, and his supplications, [a]and
[b]for the Lord's sake [1]cause Your face to
shine on [2]Your sanctuary, [c]which is desolate. 18[a]O my God, incline Your ear and
hear; open Your eyes [b]and see our desolations, and the city [c]which is called by
Your name; for we do not present our supplications before You because of our righteous deeds, but because of Your great
mercies. 19O Lord, hear! O Lord, forgive!
O Lord, listen and act! Do not delay for
Your own sake, my God, for Your city and
Your people are called by Your name."

The Seventy-Weeks Prophecy

20Now while I *was* speaking, praying,
and confessing my sin and the sin of my
people Israel, and presenting my supplication before the LORD my God for the holy
mountain of my God, 21yes, while I *was*
speaking in prayer, the man [a]Gabriel,
whom I had seen in the vision at the beginning, [1]being caused to fly swiftly,
reached me about the time of the evening
offering. 22And he informed *me,* and
talked with me, and said, "O Daniel, I
have now come forth to give you skill to
understand. 23At the beginning of your
supplications the [1]command went out,
and I have come to tell *you,* for you *are*
greatly [a]beloved; therefore [b]consider the
matter, and understand the vision:

24 "Seventy [1]weeks are determined
For your people and for your holy
city,
To finish the transgression,
[2]To make an end of sins,
[a]To make reconciliation for iniquity,
[b]To bring in everlasting
righteousness,
To seal up vision and prophecy,
[c]And to anoint [3]the Most Holy.

25 "Know therefore and understand,
That from the going forth of the
command
To restore and build Jerusalem
Until [a]Messiah [b]the Prince,
There shall be seven weeks and
sixty-two weeks;
The [1]street shall be built again, and
the [2]wall,
Even in troublesome times.

26 "And after the sixty-two weeks
[a]Messiah shall [1]be cut off, [b]but not
for Himself;
And [c]the people of the prince who
is to come
[d]Shall destroy the city and the
sanctuary.
The end of it *shall be* with a flood,
And till the end of the war
desolations are determined.

27 Then he shall confirm [a]a
[1]covenant with [b]many for one
week;
But in the middle of the week
He shall bring an end to sacrifice
and offering.
And on the wing of abominations
shall be one who makes desolate,
[c]Even until the consummation,
which is determined,
Is poured out on the [2]desolate."

Vision of the Glorious Man

10 In the third year of Cyrus king of
Persia a message was revealed to
Daniel, whose [a]name was called Belteshazzar. The message *was* true, [1]but the
appointed time *was* long; and he understood the message, and had understanding of the vision. 2In those days I, Daniel,
was mourning three full weeks. 3I ate no
[1]pleasant food, no meat or wine came into
my mouth, nor did I anoint myself at all,
till three whole weeks were fulfilled.
4Now on the twenty-fourth day of the
first month, as I was by the side of the
great river, that *is,* the [1]Tigris, 5I lifted my
eyes and looked, and behold, a certain
man clothed in [a]linen, whose waist *was*
[b]girded with gold of Uphaz! 6His body *was*
like beryl, his face like the appearance of
lightning, his eyes like torches of fire, his
arms and feet like burnished bronze in
color, [a]and the sound of his words like the
voice of a multitude.
7And I, Daniel, alone saw the vision, for
the men who were with me did not see the
vision; but a great terror fell upon them,
so that they fled to hide themselves.
8Therefore I was left alone when I saw this
great vision, and no strength remained in
me; for my [1]vigor was turned to [2]frailty in
me, and I retained no strength. 9Yet I
heard the sound of his words; and while I
heard the sound of his words I was in a
deep sleep on my face, with my face to the
ground.

17 [a]Num. 6:24–26 [b]Lam. 5:18 [c][John 16:24] [1]Be gracious [2]The temple

18 [a]Is. 37:17 [b]Ex. 3:7 [c]Jer. 25:29

21 [a]Dan. 8:16 [1]Or *being weary with weariness*

23 [a]Dan. 10:11, 19 [b]Matt. 24:15 [1]Lit. *word*

24 [a][Is. 53:10] [b]Rev. 14:6 [c]Ps. 45:7 [1]Lit. *sevens,* and so throughout the chapter [2]So with Qr., LXX, Syr., Vg.; Kt., Theodotion *To seal up* [3]The Most Holy Place

25 [a]John 1:41; 4:25 [b]Is. 55:4 [1]Or *open square* [2]Or *moat*

26 [a][Is. 53:8] [b][1 Pet. 2:21] [c]Matt. 22:7 [d]Luke 19:43, 44 [1]Suffer the death penalty

27 [a]Is. 42:6 [b][Matt. 26:28] [c]Dan. 11:36 [1]Or *treaty* [2]Or *desolator*

CHAPTER 10

1 [a]Dan. 1:7 [1]Or *and of great conflict;*

3 [1]*desirable*

4 [1]Heb. *Hiddekel*

5 [a]Ezek. 9:2; 10:2 [b]Rev. 1:13; 15:6

6 [a][Rev. 1:15]

8 [1]Lit. *splendor* [2]Lit. *ruin*

Prophecies Concerning Persia and Greece

10[a]Suddenly, a hand touched me, which
made me tremble on my knees and *on* the
palms of my hands. 11And he said to
me, "O Daniel, [a]man greatly beloved, understand the words that I speak to you,
and stand upright, for I have now been
sent to you." While he was speaking this
word to me, I stood trembling.
12Then he said to me, [a]"Do not fear,
Daniel, for from the first day that you set
your heart to understand, and to humble
yourself before your God, [b]your words
were heard; and I have come because of
your words. 13[a]But the prince of the
kingdom of Persia withstood me twenty-
one days; and behold, [b]Michael, one of the
chief princes, came to help me, for I had
been left alone there with the kings of
Persia. 14Now I have come to make you
understand what will happen to your people [a]in the latter days, [b]for the vision *refers* to *many* days yet *to come.*"
15When he had spoken such words to
me, [a]I [1]turned my face toward the ground
and became speechless. 16And suddenly,
[a]*one* having the likeness of the [1]sons of
men [b]touched my lips; then I opened my
mouth and spoke, saying to him who
stood before me, "My lord, because of the
vision [c]my sorrows have [2]overwhelmed
me, and I have retained no strength. 17For
how can this servant of my lord talk with
you, my lord? As for me, no strength remains in me now, nor is any breath left
in me."
18Then again, *the one* having the likeness of a man touched me and strengthened me. 19[a]And he said, "O man greatly
beloved, [b]fear not! Peace *be* to you; be
strong, yes, be strong!"
So when he spoke to me I was strengthened, and said, "Let my lord speak, for you
have strengthened me."
20Then he said, "Do you know why I
have come to you? And now I must return
to fight [a]with the prince of Persia; and
when I have gone forth, indeed the prince
of Greece will come. 21But I will tell you
what is noted in the Scripture of Truth.
(No one upholds me against these, [a]ex-
cept Michael your prince.

11 "Also [a]in the first year of [b]Darius
the Mede, I, *even* I, stood up to
confirm and strengthen him.) 2And now I
will tell you the truth: Behold, three more
kings will arise in Persia, and the fourth
shall be far richer than *them* all; by his
strength, through his riches, he shall stir
up all against the realm of Greece. 3Then
[a]a mighty king shall arise, who shall rule
with great dominion, and [b]do according
to his will. 4And when he has arisen, [a]his
kingdom shall be broken up and divided
toward the four winds of heaven, but not
among his posterity [b]nor according to his
dominion with which he ruled; for his
kingdom shall be uprooted, even for others besides these.

Warring Kings of North and South

5"Also the king of the South shall become strong, as well as *one* of his princes;
and he shall gain power over him and
have dominion. His dominion *shall be* a
great dominion. 6And at the end of *some*
years they shall join forces, for the daughter of the king of the South shall go to the
king of the North to make an agreement;
but she shall not retain the power of her
[1]authority, and neither he nor his authority shall stand; but she shall be given up,
with those who brought her, and with
him who begot her, and with him who
strengthened her in *those* times. 7But
from a branch of her roots *one* shall arise
in his place, who shall come with an army,
enter the fortress of the king of the North,
and deal with them and prevail. 8And he
shall also carry their gods captive to
Egypt, with their [1]princes *and* their precious articles of silver and gold; and he
shall continue *more* years than the king
of the North.
9"Also *the king of the North* shall come
to the kingdom of the king of the South,
but shall return to his own land. 10Howev-
er his sons shall stir up strife, and assemble a multitude of great forces; and *one*
shall certainly come [a]and overwhelm and
pass through; then he shall return [b]to his
fortress and stir up strife.
11"And the king of the South shall be
[a]moved with rage, and go out and fight
with him, with the king of the North, who
shall muster a great multitude; but the
[b]multitude shall be given into the hand of
his *enemy.* 12When he has taken away the
multitude, his heart will be [1]lifted up; and
he will cast down tens of thousands, but
he will not prevail. 13For the king of
the North will return and muster a multitude greater than the former, and shall

---

10 a Dan. 9:21
11 a Dan. 9:23
12 a Rev. 1:17 b Acts 10:4
13 a Dan. 10:20 b Dan. 10:21; 12:1
14 a Dan. 2:28 b Dan. 8:26; 10:1
15 a Dan. 8:18; 10:9 *1* Lit. *set*
16 a Dan. 8:15 b Jer. 1:9 c Dan. 10:8, 9 *1* Theodotion, Vg. *the son;* LXX *a hand* *2* Or *turned upon*
19 a Dan. 10:11 b Judg. 6:23
20 a Dan. 10:13
21 a [Rev. 12:7]

CHAPTER 11
1 a Dan. 9:1 b Dan. 5:31
3 a Dan. 7:6; 8:5 b Dan. 8:4; 11:16, 36
4 a Zech. 2:6 b Dan. 8:22
6 *1* Lit. *arm*
8 *1* Or *molded images*
10 a Is. 8:8 b Dan. 11:7
11 a Prov. 16:14 b [Ps. 33:10, 16]
12 *1* Proud

DANIEL 10:11,12

Dear Woman of Destiny,

Recently, in a time of intensely seeking the Lord's face, I began to search for answers for a breakthrough we needed in the ministry. One day as I was reading in the Book of Daniel, the words "from the first day . . . your words were heard" (10:12) leapt out at me. God is not deaf; He hears and sends the answer from the first day. But this passage reminded me that interference often comes from powers of darkness in heavenly places to hinder the arrival of the answer. Satan tries in many ways to stop us from hearing God's voice when we need direction.

While many pray and others even use the weapons of binding and loosing, there is one secret piece of spiritual armament we often overlook—the weapon of strategic fasting. I am convinced that there are many mountains in our lives that would be removed if we would fast on a regular basis.

Isn't it interesting that sin entered the world over food? Adam and Eve lost their innocence over a piece of fruit, and Esau lost his birthright over a pot of stew. It may be that we cannot control our flesh because we have not learned the lesson of self-denial. Yet Jesus instructed His disciples, saying, "*When* you fast," not *if* you fast (Matt. 6:16). Perhaps this is one reason the body of Christ is so weak.

If you have never fasted before, you have missed out on a great adventure with God. Perhaps you ought to begin by asking His forgiveness for not loving Him more than your necessary food (see Job 23:12). Fasting is actually a form of worship unto God.

First, decide what kind of fast God is leading you to do. A total fast consists of water or other liquids, but no solid food. A Daniel fast is fruit and vegetables. A partial fast may involve eating only once a day, while a denial fast may mean that you will abstain from eating certain specific foods such as sweets, breads, potatoes, or something you normally enjoy. You might also be led to deny yourself television, videos, or reading material other than the Bible.

After you have determined how long the fast should be, plan to spend as much time as possible in the Word. You will be amazed at the revelation that comes when your mind is not distracted with food or food preparation.

Make a list of specific prayer requests or needs. Isaiah 58:6–8 encourages us that the right kind of fasting will change us and the lives of those around us. It will:

Loose bonds of wickedness
Lift heavy burdens
Free the oppressed
Break yokes
Bring healing

You will find that the blessings of truly spiritual fasting will linger long after the fast ends. The answers you have sought will break through the spiritual darkness, and the glory of the Lord will be revealed to you.

Cindy Jacobs

certainly come at the end of some years with a great army and much equipment.

14“Now in those times many shall rise up against the king of the South. Also, [1]violent men of your people shall exalt themselves [2]in fulfillment of the vision, but they shall [a]fall. 15So the king of the North shall come and [a]build a siege mound, and take a fortified city; and the [1]forces of the South shall not withstand *him.* Even his choice troops *shall have* no strength to resist. 16But he who comes against him [a]shall do according to his own will, and [b]no one shall stand against him. He shall stand in the Glorious Land with destruction in his [1]power.

17“He shall also [a]set his face to enter with the strength of his whole kingdom, and [1]upright ones with him; thus shall he do. And he shall give him the daughter of women to destroy it; but she shall not stand *with him,* [b]or be for him. 18After this he shall turn his face to the coastlands, and shall take many. But a ruler shall bring the reproach against them to an end; and with the reproach removed, he shall turn back on him. 19Then he shall turn his face toward the fortress of his own land; but he shall [a]stumble and fall, [b]and not be found.

20“There shall arise in his place one who imposes taxes *on* the glorious kingdom; but within a few days he shall be destroyed, but not in anger or in battle. 21And in his place [a]shall arise a vile person, to whom they will not give the honor of royalty; but he shall come in peaceably, and seize the kingdom by intrigue. 22With the [1]force of a [a]flood they shall be swept away from before him and be broken, [b]and also the prince of the covenant. 23And after the league *is made* with him [a]he shall act deceitfully, for he shall come up and become strong with a small *number of* people. 24He shall enter peaceably, even into the richest places of the province; and he shall do *what* his fathers have not done, nor his forefathers: he shall disperse among them the plunder, [1]spoil, and riches; and he shall devise his plans against the strongholds, but *only* for a time.

25“He shall stir up his power and his courage against the king of the South with a great army. And the king of the South shall be stirred up to battle with a very great and mighty army; but he shall not stand, for they shall devise plans against him. 26Yes, those who eat of the portion of his delicacies shall destroy him; his army shall [1]be swept away, and many shall fall down slain. 27Both these kings' hearts *shall be* bent on evil, and they shall speak lies at the same table; but it shall not prosper, for the end *will* still *be* at the [a]appointed time. 28While returning to his land with great riches, his heart shall be *moved* against the holy covenant; so he shall do *damage* and return to his own land.

The Northern King's Blasphemies

29“At the appointed time he shall return and go toward the south; but it shall not be like the former or the latter. 30[a]For ships from [1]Cyprus shall come against him; therefore he shall be grieved, and return in rage against the holy covenant, and do *damage.*

“So he shall return and show regard for those who forsake the holy covenant. 31And [1]forces shall be mustered by him, [a]and they shall defile the sanctuary fortress; then they shall take away the daily *sacrifices,* and place *there* the abomination of desolation. 32Those who do wickedly against the covenant he shall [1]corrupt with flattery; but the people who know their God shall be strong, and carry out *great exploits.* 33And those of the people who understand shall instruct many; yet *for many* days they shall fall by sword and flame, by captivity and plundering. 34Now when they fall, they shall be aided with a little help; but many shall join with them by [1]intrigue. 35And *some* of those of understanding shall fall, [a]to refine them, purify *them,* and make *them* white, *until* the time of the end; because *it is* still for the appointed time.

Expect great things from God; attempt great things for God.

WILLIAM CAREY

14 a Job 9:13 *1* Or *robbers,* lit. *sons of breakage* *2* Lit. *to establish*
15 a Ezek. 4:2; 17:17 *1* Lit. *arms*
16 a Dan. 8:4, 7 b Josh. 1:5 *1* Lit. *hand*
17 a 2 Chr. 20:3 b Dan. 9:26 *1* Or *bring equitable terms*
19 a Jer. 46:6 b Ps. 37:36
21 a Dan. 7:8
22 a Dan. 9:26 b Dan. 8:10, 11 *1* Lit. *arms*
23 a Dan. 8:25
24 *1 booty*
26 *1* Or *overflow*
27 a Hab. 2:3
30 a Jer. 2:10 *1* Heb. *Kittim,* western lands, especially Cyprus
31 a Dan. 8:11–13; 12:11 *1* Lit. *arms*
32 *1 pollute*
34 *1* Or *slipperiness, flattery*
35 a Dan. 12:10

36"Then the king shall do according to his own will: he shall [a]exalt and magnify himself above every god, shall speak blasphemies against the God of gods, and shall prosper till the wrath has been accomplished; for what has been determined shall be done. 37He shall regard neither the [1]God of his fathers nor the desire of women, [a]nor regard any god; for he shall exalt himself above *them* all. 38But in their place he shall honor a god of fortresses; and a god which his fathers did not know he shall honor with gold and silver, with precious stones and pleasant things. 39Thus he shall act against the strongest fortresses with a foreign god, which he shall acknowledge, *and* advance *its* glory; and he shall cause them to rule over many, and divide the land for [1]gain.

The Northern King's Conquests

40"At the [a]time of the end the king of the South shall attack him; and the king of the North shall come against him [b]like a whirlwind, with chariots, [c]horsemen, and with many ships; and he shall enter the countries, overwhelm *them,* and pass through. 41He shall also enter the Glorious Land, and many *countries* shall be overthrown; but these shall escape from his hand: [a]Edom, Moab, and the [1]prominent people of Ammon. 42He shall stretch out his hand against the countries, and the land of [a]Egypt shall not escape. 43He shall have power over the treasures of gold and silver, and over all the precious things of Egypt; also the Libyans and Ethiopians *shall follow* [a]at his heels. 44But news from the east and the north shall trouble him; therefore he shall go out with great fury to destroy and annihilate many. 45And he shall plant the tents of his palace between the seas and [a]the glorious holy mountain; [b]yet he shall come to his end, and no one will help him.

Prophecy of the End Time

12 "At that time Michael shall stand
up,
The great prince who stands *watch*
over the sons of your people;
[a]And there shall be a time of
trouble,
Such as never was since there was
a nation,
Even to that time.
And at that time your people [b]shall
be delivered,
Every one who is found [c]written in
the book.
2 And many of those who sleep in
the dust of the earth shall awake,
[a]Some to everlasting life,
Some to shame [b]*and* everlasting
[1]contempt.
3 Those who are wise shall [a]shine
Like the brightness of the
firmament,
[b]And those who turn many to
righteousness
[c]Like the stars forever and ever.

4"But you, Daniel, [a]shut up the words, and seal the book until the time of the end; many shall [b]run to and fro, and knowledge shall increase."

5Then I, Daniel, looked; and there stood two others, one on this riverbank and the other on that [a]riverbank. 6And *one* said to the man clothed in [a]linen, who *was* above the waters of the river, [b]"How long shall the fulfillment of these wonders *be?*"

History is fulfilling prophecy all the time.
OSWALD CHAMBERS

7Then I heard the man clothed in linen, who *was* above the waters of the river, when he [a]held up his right hand and his left hand to heaven, and swore by Him [b]who lives forever, [c]that *it shall be* for a time, times, and half *a time;* [d]and when the power of [e]the holy people has been completely shattered, all these *things* shall be finished.

8Although I heard, I did not understand. Then I said, "My lord, what *shall be* the end of these *things?*"

9And he said, "Go *your way,* Daniel, for the words *are* closed up and sealed till the time of the end. 10[a]Many shall be purified, made white, and refined, [b]but the wicked shall do wickedly; and none of the wicked shall understand, but [c]the wise shall understand.

---

36 a Dan. 7:8, 25
37 a Is. 14:13 *1* Or *gods*
39 *1 profit*
40 a Dan. 11:27, 35; 12:4, 9 b Is. 21:1 c Rev. 9:16
41 a Is. 11:14 *1* Lit. *chief of the sons of Ammon*
42 a Joel 3:19
43 a Ex. 11:8
45 a Ps. 48:2 b Rev. 19:20
CHAPTER 12
1 a Jer. 30:7 b Rom. 11:26 c Ex. 32:32
2 a [John 5:28, 29] b [Is. 66:24] *1* Lit. *abhorrence*
3 a Matt. 13:43 b [James 5:19, 20] c 1 Cor. 15:41
4 a Rev. 22:10 b Amos 8:12
5 a Dan. 10:4
6 a Ezek. 9:2 b Dan. 8:13; 12:8
7 a Deut. 32:40 b Dan. 4:34 c Dan. 7:25 d Luke 21:24 e Dan. 8:24
10 a Zech. 13:9 b Is. 32:6, 7 c John 7:17; 8:47

[11]"And from the time *that* the daily *sacrifice* is taken away, and the abomination of desolation is set up, *there shall be* one thousand two hundred and ninety days.
[12]Blessed *is* he who waits, and comes to the one thousand three hundred and thirty-five days.
[13]"But you, go *your way* till the end; [a]for you shall rest, [b]and will arise to your inheritance at the end of the days."

13 [a]Rev. 14:13 [b]Ps. 1:5

AUTHOR: *Hosea*
DATE: *Approximately 750 B.C.*
THEME: *Return to God*
KEY WORDS: *Sin, Judgment, Love*

HOSEA

Dear Woman of Destiny,

Hosea is one of the most beautiful books in the Bible—a word picture of God's unconditional love and mercy toward ancient Israel and His people throughout the ages. See the redemptive work of Jesus through Hosea's unswerving dedication to his wayward wife, and bask in the knowledge of the depth of God's love for *you*.

His love and mine,

Marilyn Hickey

The word of the LORD that came to Hosea the son of Beeri, in the days of [a]Uzziah, [b]Jotham, [c]Ahaz, *and* [d]Hezekiah, kings of Judah, and in the days of [e]Jeroboam the son of Joash, king of Israel.

The Family of Hosea

2 When the LORD began to speak by Hosea, the LORD said to Hosea:

[a]"Go, take yourself a wife of harlotry
And children of harlotry,
For [b]the land has committed great
[1]harlotry
By departing from the LORD."

3 So he went and took Gomer the daughter
of Diblaim, and she conceived and bore
him a son. 4 Then the LORD said to him:

"Call his name Jezreel,
For in a little *while*
[a]I will avenge the bloodshed of
Jezreel on the house of Jehu,
[b]And bring an end to the kingdom
of the house of Israel.
5 [a]It shall come to pass in that day
That I will break the bow of Israel
in the Valley of Jezreel."

6 And she conceived again and bore a
daughter. Then *God* said to him:

"Call her name [1]Lo-Ruhamah,
[a]For I will no longer have mercy on
the house of Israel,
[2]But I will utterly take them away.
7 [a]Yet I will have mercy on the house
of Judah,
Will save them by the LORD their
God,
And [b]will not save them by bow,
Nor by sword or battle,
By horses or horsemen."

8 Now when she had weaned Lo-
Ruhamah, she conceived and bore a son.
9 Then *God* said:

"Call his name [1]Lo-Ammi,
For you *are* not My people,
And I will not be your *God.*

The Restoration of Israel

10 "Yet [a]the number of the children
of Israel
Shall be as the sand of the sea,
Which cannot be measured or
numbered.
[b]And it shall come to pass
In the place where it was said to
them,
'You *are* [1]not My [c]people,'
There it shall be said to them,
'*You are* [d]sons of the living God.'
11 [a]Then the children of Judah and
the children of Israel
Shall be gathered together,
And appoint for themselves one
head;
And they shall come up out of the
land,
For great *will be* the day of Jezreel!

2 Say to your brethren, [1]'My people,'
And to your sisters, [2]'Mercy *is*
shown.'

God's Unfaithful People

2 "Bring[1] charges against your
mother, [2]bring charges;
For [a]she *is* not My wife, nor *am* I
her Husband!
Let her put away her [b]harlotries
from her sight,
And her adulteries from between
her breasts;
3 Lest [a]I strip her naked
And expose her, as in the day she
was [b]born,
And make her like a wilderness,
And set her like a dry land,
And slay her with [c]thirst.
4 "I will not have mercy on her
children,
For they *are* the [a]children of
harlotry.
5 For their mother has played the
harlot;
She who conceived them has
behaved shamefully.
For she said, 'I will go after my
lovers,
[a]Who give *me* my bread and my
water,
My wool and my linen,
My oil and my drink.'

6 "Therefore, behold,
[a]I will hedge up your way with
thorns,
And [1]wall her in,
So that she cannot find her paths.
7 She will [1]chase her lovers,
But not overtake them;
Yes, she will seek them, but not
find *them.*
Then she will say,

CHAPTER 1
1 [a]Amos 1:1 [b]2 Chr. 27 [c]2 Chr. 28 [d]2 Chr. 29:1—32:33 [e]2 Kin. 13:13;14:23–29
2 [a]Hos. 3:1 [b]Jer. 2:13 [1]Spiritual adultery
4 [a]2 Kin. 10:11 [b]2 Kin.15:8–10; 17:6, 23; 18:11
5 [a]2 Kin. 15:29
6 [a]2 Kin. 17:6 [1]Lit. *No-Mercy* [2]Or *That I may forgive them at all*
7 [a]2 Kin. 19:29–35 [b][Zech. 4:6]
9 [1]Lit. *Not-My-People*
10 [a]Gen. 22:17; 32:12 [b]1 Pet. 2:10 [c]Rom. 9:26 [d][John 1:12] [1]Heb. *lo-ammi,* v. 9
11 [a]Is. 11:11–13

CHAPTER 2
1 [1]Heb. *Ammi,* Hos. 1:9, 10 [2]Heb. *Ruhamah,* Hos. 1:6
2 [a]Is. 50:1 [b]Ezek. 16:25 [1]Or *Contend with* [2]Or *contend*
3 [a]Jer. 13:22, 26 [b]Ezek. 16:4–7, 22 [c]Amos 8:11–13
4 [a]John 8:41
5 [a]Hos. 2:8, 12
6 [a]Lam. 3:7, 9 [1]Lit. *wall up her wall*
7 [1]Or *pursue*

[a]'I will go and return to my [b]first
husband,
For then *it was* better for me than
now.'
8 For she did not [a]know
That I gave her grain, new wine,
and oil,
And multiplied her silver and
gold—
Which they prepared for Baal.

9 "Therefore I will return and take
away
My grain in its time
And My new wine in its season,
And will take back My wool and My
linen,
Given to cover her nakedness.
10 Now [a]I will uncover her lewdness
in the sight of her lovers,
And no one shall deliver her from
My hand.
11 [a]I will also cause all her mirth to
cease,
Her feast days,
Her New Moons,
Her Sabbaths—
All her appointed feasts.

12 "And I will destroy her vines and
her fig trees,
Of which she has said,
'These *are* my wages that my lovers
have given me.'
So I will make them a forest,
And the beasts of the field shall eat
them.
13 I will punish her
For the days of the Baals to which
she burned incense.
She decked herself with her
earrings and jewelry,
And went after her lovers;
But Me she forgot," says the LORD.

God's Mercy on His People

14 "Therefore, behold, I will allure
her,
Will bring her into the wilderness,
And speak [1]comfort to her.
15 I will give her her vineyards
from there,
And [a]the Valley of Achor as a door
of hope;
She shall sing there,
As in [b]the days of her youth,
[c]As in the day when she came up
from the land of Egypt.

7 [a]Luke 15:17, 18 [b]Ezek. 16:8; 23:4
8 [a]Is. 1:3
10 [a]Ezek. 16:37
11 [a]Amos 5:21; 8:10
14 [1]Lit. *to her heart*
15 [a]Josh. 7:26 [b]Ezek. 16:8–14 [c]Ex. 15:1
16 [1]Heb. *Ishi* [2]Heb. *Baali*
17 [a]Ex. 23:13
18 [a]Job 5:23 [b]Is. 2:4 [c]Lev. 26:5
20 [a][Jer. 31:33, 34]
21 [a]Zech. 8:12
22 [1]Lit. *God Will Sow*
23 [a]Jer. 31:27 [b]Hos. 1:6 [c]Hos. 1:10 [1]Heb. *lo-ruhamah* [2]Heb. *lo-ammi* [3]Heb. *ammi*

16 "And it shall be, in that day,"
Says the LORD,
"*That* you will call Me [1]'My
Husband,'
And no longer call Me [2]'My Master,'
17 For [a]I will take from her mouth
the names of the Baals,
And they shall be remembered by
their name no more.
18 In that day I will make a
[a]covenant for them
With the beasts of the field,
With the birds of the air,
And *with* the creeping things of the
ground.
Bow and sword of battle [b]I will
shatter from the earth,
To make them [c]lie down safely.

Betroth ____ to Yourself forever, O Lord; betroth them in righteousness and justice, in lovingkindness and mercy; betroth them to You in faithfulness, and they shall know You.

FROM HOSEA 2:19, 20

19 "I will betroth you to Me forever;
Yes, I will betroth you to Me
In righteousness and justice,
In lovingkindness and mercy;
20 I will betroth you to Me in
faithfulness,
And [a]you shall know the LORD.

21 "It shall come to pass in that day
That [a]I will answer," says the LORD;
"I will answer the heavens,
And they shall answer the earth.
22 The earth shall answer
With grain,
With new wine,
And with oil;
They shall answer [1]Jezreel.
23 Then [a]I will sow her for Myself in
the earth,
[b]And I will have mercy on *her who
had* [1]not obtained mercy;
Then [c]I will say to *those who were*
[2]not My people,
'You *are* [3]My people!'

Hosea 2:15

Dear Woman of Destiny,

Are you struggling right now with some heavy burden—a troubled marriage, a financial setback, a prolonged illness—where everything seems impossible? God promises to exchange trouble for a door of hope. He did it for Hosea.

At God's request, Hosea married into a seemingly hopeless situation. His marriage was in shambles. His wife was a former prostitute, and she worshiped foreign gods. Yet, in the midst of this, the Lord promised that He would make a way where there seemed to be no way: "I will give her . . . the Valley of Achor as a door of hope" (Hos. 2:15).

You might not understand the richness of this promise if you do not know what the Valley of Achor, or "Troubling," meant to Hosea. This valley was the scene of a national disaster in the history of Israel. The tremendous victory over Jericho was nullified by the sin of one man, Achan, who was responsible for causing God to remove His blessing over the nation. The place where this man was stoned for the remission of his sin was named the Valley of Achor ("Troubling").

Essentially, the Lord was saying to Hosea, "Son, I'm going to turn the curse into a blessing. This woman who seems like such trouble to you, which is a prophetic picture of the whole nation, will become a blessing. There is hope for you and your land."

Did this promise automatically turn the circumstance around? Not at all. The crisis required action. What God was saying was, "I will, if you will." Hosea still had to forgive his wife and take her back.

You, too, may have to close the door to the trouble, hurt, and pain of yesterday. The Lord wants to open a door of opportunity to you; but unresolved issues, unforgiveness, and the woundedness from relational problems may be hindering His blessing.

How do you close the door to the past? First, seek the Lord's face regarding your life. Spend time with Him in reviewing past years. Is there anyone you need to forgive? Have you allowed time for old wounds to heal? Second, release the circumstances, disappointments, and unmet expectations to your heavenly Father. Then, ask Him for a new strategy.

Our nation, too, is suffering from corporate sin. Pray for our leaders. Pray that the Lord will speak to our leaders about gathering together for a solemn assembly, where they would ask Him to forgive us and heal our land.

Satan is at work to steal, kill, and destroy. He is busy trying to destroy families, marriages, relationships, finances, and governments. But with God, no situation is hopeless. He wants to open a door of hope before you. When God opens a door, no man will be able to shut it; and you will experience the restoration of those things that seemed lost and beyond repair both for you and for the nation.

Cindy Jacobs

And they shall say, *'You are* my
God!' "

Israel Will Return to God

3 Then the LORD said to me, "Go again,
love a woman *who is* loved by a [a]lov-
er[1] and is committing adultery, just like
the love of the LORD for the children of
Israel, who look to other gods and love *the*
raisin cakes *of the pagans.*"

There is a Power that man can wield when mortal aid is vain. There is a Love that never fails when human strength gives way. That Power is prayer through Jesus Christ the Lord, and that Love is God Himself, the Hand that moves the world to help a soul.

KATHRYN KUHLMAN

2 So I bought her for myself for fifteen
shekels of silver, and one and one-half ho-
mers of barley. 3 And I said to her, "You
shall [a]stay with me many days; you shall
not play the harlot, nor shall you have a
man—so, too, *will* I *be* toward you."
4 For the children of Israel shall abide
many days [a]without king or prince, without sacrifice or *sacred* pillar, without
[b]ephod or [c]teraphim. 5 Afterward the children of Israel shall return and [a]seek the
LORD their God and [b]David their king.
They shall fear the LORD and His goodness
in the [c]latter days.

God's Charge Against Israel

4 Hear the word of the LORD,
You children of Israel,
For the LORD *brings* a [a]charge[1]
against the inhabitants of the
land:
"There is no truth or mercy
Or [b]knowledge of God in the land.
2 *By* swearing and lying,
Killing and stealing and committing
adultery,
They break all restraint,
With bloodshed [1]upon bloodshed.
3 Therefore [a]the land will mourn;
And [b]everyone who dwells there
will waste away
With the beasts of the field
And the birds of the air;
Even the fish of the sea will be
taken away.

4 "Now let no man contend, or
rebuke another;
For your people *are* like those [a]who
contend with the priest.
5 Therefore you shall stumble [a]in the
day;
The prophet also shall stumble with
you in the night;
And I will destroy your mother.
6 [a]My people are destroyed for lack of
knowledge.
Because you have rejected
knowledge,
I also will reject you from being
priest for Me;
[b]Because you have forgotten the law
of your God,
I also will forget your children.

7 "The more they increased,
The more they sinned against Me;
[a]I[1] will change [2]their glory into
shame.
8 They eat up the sin of My people;
They set their [1]heart on their
iniquity.
9 And it shall be: [a]like people, like
priest.
So I will punish them for their
ways,
And [1]reward them for their deeds.
10 For [a]they shall eat, but not have
enough;
They shall commit harlotry, but not
increase;
Because they have ceased obeying
the LORD.

The Idolatry of Israel

11 "Harlotry, wine, and new wine
[a]enslave the heart.
12 My people ask counsel from their
[a]wooden *idols,*
And their [1]staff informs them.
For [b]the spirit of harlotry has
caused *them* to stray,

CHAPTER 3
1 [a]Jer. 3:20 [1]Lit. *friend* or *husband*
3 [a]Deut. 21:13
4 [a]Hos. 10:3 [b]Ex. 28:4–12 [c]Judg. 17:5; 18:14, 17
5 [a]Jer. 50:4 [b]Jer. 30:9 [c][Is. 2:2, 3]

CHAPTER 4
1 [a]Is. 1:18 [b]Jer. 4:22 [1]A legal complaint
2 [1]Lit. *touching*
3 [a]Amos 5:16; 8:8 [b]Zeph. 1:3
4 [a]Deut. 17:12
5 [a]Jer. 15:8
6 [a]Is. 5:13 [b]Ezek. 22:26
7 [a]1 Sam. 2:30 [1]So with MT, LXX, Vg.; scribal tradition, Syr., Tg. *They will change* [2]So with MT, LXX, Syr., Tg., Vg.; scribal tradition *My glory*
8 [1]Desires
9 [a]Is. 24:2 [1]*repay*
10 [a]Lev. 26:26
11 [a]Is. 5:12; 28:7
12 [a]Jer. 2:27 [b]Is. 44:19, 20 [1]Diviner's rod

And they have played the harlot
against their God.

13 [a]They offer sacrifices on the
mountaintops,
And burn incense on the hills,
Under oaks, poplars, and terebinths,
Because their shade *is* good.
[b]Therefore your daughters commit
harlotry,
And your brides commit adultery.

14 "I will not punish your daughters
when they commit harlotry,
Nor your brides when they commit
adultery;
For *the men* themselves go apart
with harlots,
And offer sacrifices with a [a]ritual
harlot.
Therefore people *who* do not
understand will be trampled.

15 "Though you, Israel, play the
harlot,
Let not Judah offend.
[a]Do not come up to Gilgal,
Nor go up to [b]Beth[1] Aven,
[c]Nor swear an oath, *saying,* 'As the
LORD lives'—

16 "For Israel [a]is stubborn
Like a stubborn calf;
Now the LORD will let them forage
Like a lamb in [1]open country.

17 "Ephraim *is* joined to idols,
[a]Let him alone.
18 Their drink [1]is rebellion,
They commit harlotry continually.
[a]Her [2]rulers [3]dearly love dishonor.
19 [a]The wind has wrapped her up in
its wings,
And [b]they shall be ashamed because
of their sacrifices.

Impending Judgment on Israel and Judah

5 "Hear this, O priests!
Take heed, O house of Israel!
Give ear, O house of the king!
For [1]yours *is* the judgment,
Because [a]you have been a snare to
Mizpah
And a net spread on Tabor.
2 The revolters are [a]deeply involved
in slaughter,
Though I rebuke them all.
3 [a]I know Ephraim,
And Israel is not hidden from Me;
For now, O Ephraim, [b]you commit
harlotry;
Israel is defiled.

4 "They[1] do not direct their deeds
Toward turning to their God,
For [a]the spirit of harlotry is in
their midst,
And they do not know the LORD.
5 The [a]pride of Israel testifies to his
face;
Therefore Israel and Ephraim
stumble in their iniquity;
Judah also stumbles with them.

6 "With their flocks and herds
[a]They shall go to seek the LORD,
But they will not find *Him;*
He has withdrawn Himself from
them.
7 They have [a]dealt treacherously
with the LORD,
For they have begotten [1]pagan
children.
Now a New Moon shall devour
them and their heritage.

8 "Blow[a] the ram's horn in Gibeah,
The trumpet in Ramah!
[b]Cry aloud *at* [c]Beth Aven,
'*Look* behind you, O Benjamin!'
9 Ephraim shall be desolate in the
day of rebuke;
Among the tribes of Israel I make
known what is sure.

10 "The princes of Judah are like
those who [a]remove a landmark;
I will pour out My wrath on them
like water.
11 Ephraim is [a]oppressed *and* broken
in judgment,
Because he willingly walked by
[b]*human* precept.
12 Therefore I *will be* to Ephraim
like a moth,
And to the house of Judah [a]like
rottenness.
13 "When Ephraim saw his sickness,
And Judah *saw* his [a]wound,
Then Ephraim went [b]to Assyria
And sent to King Jareb;
Yet he cannot cure you,
Nor heal you of your wound.
14 For [a]I *will be* like a lion to
Ephraim,
And like a young lion to the house
of Judah.
[b]I, *even* I, will tear *them* and go
away;

13 [a] Is. 1:29; 57:5, 7 [b] Amos 7:17
14 [a] Deut. 23:18
15 [a] Hos. 9:15; 12:11 [b] 1 Kin. 12:29 [c] Amos 8:14 [1] Lit. *House of Idolatry* or *Wickedness*
16 [a] Jer. 3:6; 7:24; 8:5 [1] Lit. *a large place*
17 [a] Matt. 15:14
18 [a] Mic. 3:11 [1] Or *has turned aside* [2] Lit. *shields* [3] Heb. difficult; a Jewish tradition *shamefully love, 'Give!'*
19 [a] Jer. 51:1 [b] Is. 1:29

CHAPTER 5
1 [a] Hos. 6:9 [1] Or *to you*
2 [a] Is. 29:15
3 [a] Amos 3:2; 5:12 [b] Hos. 4:17
4 [a] Hos. 4:12 [1] Or *Their deeds will not allow them to turn*
5 [a] Hos. 7:10
6 [a] Prov. 1:28
7 [a] Jer. 3:20 [1] Lit. *strange*
8 [a] Joel 2:1 [b] Is. 10:30 [c] Josh. 7:2
10 [a] Deut. 19:14; 27:17
11 [a] Deut. 28:33 [b] Mic. 6:16
12 [a] Prov. 12:4
13 [a] Jer. 30:12–15 [b] 2 Kin. 15:19
14 [a] Lam. 3:10 [b] Ps. 50:22

I will take *them* away, and no one
shall rescue.
15 I will return again to My place
Till they [1]acknowledge their
offense.
Then they will seek My face;
In their affliction they will earnestly
seek Me."

A Call to Repentance

6 [a]Come, and let us return to the
LORD;
For [b]He has torn, but [c]He will heal
us;
He has stricken, but He will [1]bind
us up.
2 [a]After two days He will revive us;
On the third day He will raise us
up,
That we may live in His sight.
3 [a]Let us know,
Let us pursue the knowledge of the
LORD.
His going forth is established [b]as
the morning;
[c]He will come to us [d]like the rain,
Like the latter *and* former rain to
the earth.

Impenitence of Israel and Judah

4 "O Ephraim, what shall I do to you?
O Judah, what shall I do to you?
For your faithfulness is like a
morning cloud,
And like the early dew it goes away.
5 Therefore I have hewn *them* by the
prophets,
I have slain them by [a]the words of
My mouth;
And [1]your judgments *are like* light
that goes forth.
6 For I desire [a]mercy[1] and [b]not
sacrifice,
And the [c]knowledge of God more
than burnt offerings.

7 "But like [1]men they transgressed
the covenant;
There they dealt treacherously with
Me.
8 [a]Gilead *is* a city of evildoers
And [1]defiled with blood.
9 As bands of robbers lie in wait for
a man,
So the company of [a]priests [b]murder
on the way to Shechem;
Surely they commit [c]lewdness.

15 [1] Lit. *become guilty* or *bear punishment*

CHAPTER 6
1 [a] Is. 1:18 [b] Deut. 32:39 [c] Jer. 30:17 [1] Bandage
2 [a] [1 Cor. 15:4]
3 [a] Is. 54:13 [b] 2 Sam. 23:4 [c] Ps. 72:6 [d] Job 29:23
5 [a] [Jer. 23:29] [1] Or *the judgments on you*
6 [a] Matt. 9:13; 12:7 [b] [Mic. 6:6–8] [c] [John 17:3] [1] Or *faithfulness* or *loyalty*
7 [1] Or *Adam*
8 [a] Hos. 12:11 [1] Lit. *foot-tracked*
9 [a] Hos. 5:1 [b] Jer. 7:9, 10 [c] Ezek. 22:9; 23:27
10 [1] Spiritual adultery

CHAPTER 7
1 [a] Hos. 5:1 [1] *plunders*
2 [a] Jer. 14:10; 17:1 [1] Lit. *do not say to*
3 [a] Hos. 1:1 [b] [Rom. 1:32]
4 [a] Jer. 9:2; 23:10
5 [a] Is. 28:1, 7 [1] Lit. *with the heat of*
6 [1] So with MT, Vg.; Syr., Tg. *Their anger;* LXX *Ephraim*
7 [a] Is. 64:7
8 [a] Ps. 106:35
9 [a] Hos. 8:7
10 [a] Hos. 5:5

10 I have seen a horrible thing in the
house of Israel:
There *is* the [1]harlotry of Ephraim;
Israel is defiled.
11 Also, O Judah, a harvest is
appointed for you,
When I return the captives of My
people.

7 "When I would have healed Israel,
Then the iniquity of Ephraim was
uncovered,
And the wickedness of Samaria.
For [a]they have committed fraud;
A thief comes in;
A band of robbers [1]takes spoil
outside.
2 They [1]do not consider in their
hearts
That [a]I remember all their
wickedness;
Now their own deeds have
surrounded them;
They are before My face.
3 They make a [a]king glad with their
wickedness,
And princes [b]with their lies.

4 "They[a] *are* all adulterers.
Like an oven heated by a baker—
He ceases stirring *the fire* after
kneading the dough,
Until it is leavened.
5 In the day of our king
Princes have made *him* sick,
[1]inflamed with [a]wine;
He stretched out his hand with
scoffers.
6 They prepare their heart like an
oven,
While they lie in wait;
[1]Their baker sleeps all night;
In the morning it burns like a
flaming fire.
7 They are all hot, like an oven,
And have devoured their judges;
All their kings have fallen.
[a]None among them calls upon Me.

8 "Ephraim [a]has mixed himself
among the peoples;
Ephraim is a cake unturned.
9 [a]Aliens have devoured his strength,
But he does not know *it;*
Yes, gray hairs are here and there
on him,
Yet he does not know *it*.
10 And the [a]pride of Israel testifies to
his face,

Hosea 6:1

Dear Woman of Destiny,

The first time I read the sixth chapter of Hosea, I was a young Christian with very little understanding of the nature of God. The words, "Come, and let us return to the LORD; for He has torn, but He will heal us; He has stricken, but He will bind us up" (v. 1) baffled me. Surely this couldn't be true! Why would God strike me just to bind me up afterward? It just didn't make sense to me.

Then I heard the story of David's dilemma in 2 Samuel 24. When David sinned against God, the Lord sent the prophet Gad to confront him with a choice of consequences. In verse 13, Gad lists David's options: "Shall seven years of famine come to you in your land? Or shall you flee three months before your enemies, while they pursue you? Or shall there be three days' plague in your land? Now consider and see what answer I should take back to Him who sent me."

David didn't even hesitate before replying, "I am in great distress. Please let us fall into the hand of the LORD, for His mercies are great; but do not let me fall into the hand of man" (v. 14). David knew he could submit to God and receive mercy even though he deserved justice. He understood that if he received discipline from God, he would also receive healing from Him.

Like David, we are often led by our unbelief into places God never planned for us to go. When I was in my twenties, I received a devastating lie from the enemy that led me into an eighteen-month prison of unbelief. The deeper I fell into that prison, the more hopeless my life seemed to be. I felt so separated from God that I even began to contemplate suicide.

I am happy to say that my Father had other plans. In Hosea 6:2, we see that it is God's desire to revive us and raise us up so "that we may live in His sight." Once the sovereign hand of God secured my deliverance from darkness, He then began the painstaking process of restoring me into fellowship with Him. I had to learn all over again how to "pursue the knowledge of the LORD" (v. 3) and replace eighteen months of lies with Truth.

We can know, just as Hosea says, that "He will come to us like the rain, like the latter and former rain to the earth" (v. 3). He will nourish and hydrate us by His Spirit until the barren places are saturated and bursting again with life.

Pam Pierce

But [b]they do not return to the
LORD their God,
Nor seek Him for all this.

Futile Reliance on the Nations

11 "Ephraim[a] also is like a silly dove,
without [1]sense—
[b]They call to Egypt,
They go to [c]Assyria.
12 Wherever they go, I will [a]spread
My net on them;
I will bring them down like birds of
the air;
I will chastise them
[b]According to what their
congregation has heard.

13 "Woe to them, for they have fled
from Me!
Destruction to them,
Because they have transgressed
against Me!
Though [a]I redeemed them,
Yet they have spoken lies against
Me.
14 [a]They did not cry out to Me with
their heart
When they wailed upon their beds.

"They [1]assemble together for grain
and new [b]wine,
[2]They rebel against Me;
15 Though I disciplined *and*
strengthened their arms,
Yet they devise evil against Me;
16 They return, *but* not [1]to the Most
High;
[a]They are like a treacherous bow.
Their princes shall fall by the sword
For the [b]cursings of their tongue.
This *shall be* their derision [c]in the
land of Egypt.

The Apostasy of Israel

8 "*Set* the [1]trumpet to your mouth!
He shall come [a]like an eagle
against the house of the LORD,
Because they have transgressed My
covenant
And rebelled against My law.
2 [a]Israel will cry to Me,
'My God, [b]we know You!'
3 Israel has rejected the good;
The enemy will pursue him.

4 "They[a] set up kings, but not by Me;
They made princes, but I did not
acknowledge *them*.
From their silver and gold
They made idols for themselves—
That they might be cut off.
5 Your [1]calf [2]is rejected, O Samaria!
My anger is aroused against
them—
[a]How long until they attain to
innocence?
6 For from Israel *is* even this:
A [a]workman made it, and it *is* not
God;
But the calf of Samaria shall be
broken to pieces.

7 "They[a] sow the wind,
And reap the whirlwind.
The stalk has no bud;
It shall never produce meal.
If it should produce,
[b]Aliens would swallow it up.
8 [a]Israel is swallowed up;
Now they are among the Gentiles
[b]Like a vessel in which *is* no
pleasure.
9 For they have gone up to Assyria,
Like [a]a wild donkey alone by itself;
Ephraim [b]has hired lovers.
10 Yes, though they have hired
among the nations,
Now [a]I will gather them;
And they shall [1]sorrow a little,
Because of the [2]burden of [b]the king
of princes.

11 "Because Ephraim has made many
altars for sin,
They have become for him altars
for sinning.
12 I have written for him [a]the great
things of My law,
But they were considered a strange
thing.
13 *For* the sacrifices of My offerings
[a]they sacrifice flesh and eat *it*,
[b]*But* the LORD does not accept them.
[c]Now He will remember their
iniquity and punish their sins.
They shall return to Egypt.

14 "For[a] Israel has forgotten [b]his
Maker,
And has built [1]temples;
Judah also has multiplied [c]fortified
cities;
But [d]I will send fire upon his cities,
And it shall devour his [2]palaces."

10 [b]Is. 9:13
11 [a]Hos. 11:11 [b]Is. 30:3 [c]Hos. 5:13; 8:9 [1]Lit. *heart*
12 [a]Ezek. 12:13 [b]Lev. 26:14
13 [a]Mic. 6:4
14 [a]Job 35:9, 10 [b]Amos 2:8 [1]So with MT, Tg.; Vg. *thought upon;* LXX *slashed themselves for* (cf. 1 Kin. 18:28) [2]So with MT, Syr., Tg.; LXX omits *They rebel against Me;* Vg. *They departed from Me*
16 [a]Ps. 78:57 [b]Ps. 73:9 [c]Hos. 8:13; 9:3 [1]Or *upward*

CHAPTER 8
1 [a]Deut. 28:49 [1]*ram's horn,* Heb. *shophar*
2 [a]Ps. 78:34 [b]Titus 1:16
4 [a]2 Kin. 15:23, 25
5 [a]Jer. 13:27 [1]Golden calf image [2]Or *has rejected you*
6 [a]Is. 40:19
7 [a]Prov. 22:8 [b]Hos. 7:9
8 [a]2 Kin. 17:6 [b]Jer. 22:28; 25:34
9 [a]Jer. 2:24 [b]Ezek. 16:33, 34
10 [a]Ezek. 16:37; 22:20 [b]Is. 10:8 [1]Or *begin to diminish* [2]Or *oracle* or *proclamation*
12 [a][Deut. 4:6–8]
13 [a]Zech. 7:6 [b]Jer. 14:10 [c]Amos 8:7
14 [a]Deut. 32:18 [b]Is. 29:23 [c]Num. 32:17 [d]Jer. 17:27 [1]Or *palaces* [2]Or *citadels*

Judgment of Israel's Sin

9 Do[a] not rejoice, O Israel, with joy
like *other* peoples,
For you have played the harlot
against your God.
You have made love *for* [b]hire on
every threshing floor.
2 The threshing floor and the
winepress
Shall not feed them,
And the new wine shall fail in her.

3 They shall not dwell in [a]the LORD's
land,
[b]But Ephraim shall return to Egypt,
And [c]shall eat unclean *things* in
Assyria.
4 They shall not offer wine *offerings*
to the LORD,
Nor [a]shall their [b]sacrifices be
pleasing to Him.
It shall be like bread of mourners
to them;
All who eat it shall be defiled.
For their bread *shall be* for their
own life;
It shall not come into the house of
the LORD.

5 What will you do in the appointed
day,
And in the day of the feast of the
LORD?
6 For indeed they are gone because
of destruction.
Egypt shall gather them up;
Memphis shall bury them.
[a]Nettles shall possess their valuables
of silver;
Thorns *shall be* in their tents.

7 The [a]days of punishment have
come;
The days of recompense have come.
Israel knows!
The prophet *is* a [b]fool,
[c]The spiritual man *is* insane,
Because of the greatness of your
iniquity and great enmity.
8 The [a]watchman of Ephraim *is* with
my God;
But the prophet *is* a [1]fowler's snare
in all his ways—
Enmity in the house of his God.
9 [a]They are deeply corrupted,
As in the days of [b]Gibeah.
He will remember their iniquity;
He will punish their sins.

10 "I found Israel
Like grapes in the [a]wilderness;
I saw your fathers
As the [b]firstfruits on the fig tree in
its first season.
But they went to [c]Baal Peor,
And [1]separated themselves *to that*
shame;
[d]They became an abomination like
the thing they loved.
11 *As for* Ephraim, their glory shall
fly away like a bird—
No birth, no pregnancy, and no
conception!
12 Though they bring up their
children,
Yet I will bereave them to the last
man.
Yes, [a]woe to them when I depart
from them!
13 Just [a]as I saw Ephraim like Tyre,
planted in a pleasant place,
So Ephraim will bring out his
children to the murderer."

14 Give them, O LORD—
What will You give?
Give them [a]a miscarrying womb
And dry breasts!

15 "All their wickedness *is* in [a]Gilgal,
For there I hated them.
Because of the evil of their deeds
I will drive them from My house;
I will love them no more.
[b]All their princes *are* rebellious.
16 Ephraim is [a]stricken,
Their root is dried up;
They shall bear no fruit.
Yes, were they to bear children,
I would kill the darlings of their
womb."

17 My God will [a]cast them away,
Because they did not obey Him;
And they shall be [b]wanderers
among the nations.

Israel's Sin and Captivity

10 Israel [a]empties *his* vine;
He brings forth fruit for himself.
According to the multitude of his
fruit
[b]He has increased the altars;
According to the bounty of his land
They have embellished *his sacred*
pillars.
2 Their heart is [a]divided;[1]
Now they are held guilty.

CHAPTER 9
1 [a] Is. 22:12, 13 [b] Jer. 44:17
3 [a] [Lev. 25:23] [b] Hos. 7:16; 8:13 [c] Ezek. 4:13
4 [a] Jer. 6:20 [b] Hos. 8:13
6 [a] Is. 5:6; 7:23
7 [a] Is. 10:3 [b] Lam. 2:14 [c] Mic. 2:11
8 [a] Ezek. 3:17; 33:7 [1] One who catches birds in a trap or snare
9 [a] Hos. 10:9 [b] Judg. 19:22
10 [a] Jer. 2:2 [b] Is. 28:4 [c] Num. 25:3 [d] Ps. 81:12 [1] Or *dedicated*
12 [a] Deut. 31:17
13 [a] Ezek. 26—28
14 [a] Luke 23:29
15 [a] Hos. 4:15; 12:11 [b] Is. 1:23
16 [a] Hos. 5:11
17 [a] [Zech. 10:6] [b] Lev. 26:33

CHAPTER 10
1 [a] Nah. 2:2 [b] Jer. 2:28
2 [a] 1 Kin. 18:21 [1] Divided in loyalty

He will break down their altars;
He will ruin their *sacred* pillars.
3 For now they say,
"We have no king,
Because we did not fear the LORD.
And as for a king, what would he do for us?"
4 They have spoken words,
Swearing falsely in making a covenant.
Thus judgment springs up [a]like hemlock in the furrows of the field.
5 The inhabitants of Samaria fear
Because of the [a]calf[1] of Beth Aven.
For its people mourn for it,
And [2]its priests shriek for it—
Because its [b]glory has departed from it.
6 *The idol* also shall be carried to Assyria
As a present for King [a]Jareb.
Ephraim shall receive shame,
And Israel shall be ashamed of his own counsel.

7 *As for* Samaria, her king is cut off
Like a twig on the water.
8 Also the [a]high places of [1]Aven,
[b]the sin of Israel,
Shall be destroyed.
The thorn and thistle shall grow on their altars;
[c]They shall say to the mountains, "Cover us!"
And to the hills, "Fall on us!"

9 "O Israel, you have sinned from the days of [a]Gibeah;
There they stood.
The [b]battle in Gibeah against the children of [1]iniquity
Did not [2]overtake them.
10 When *it is* My desire, I will chasten them.
[a]Peoples shall be gathered against them
When I bind them [1]for their two transgressions.
11 Ephraim *is* [a]a trained heifer
That loves to thresh *grain;*
But I harnessed her fair neck,
I will make Ephraim [1]pull *a plow.*
Judah shall plow;
Jacob shall break his clods."

12 Sow for yourselves righteousness;
Reap in mercy;
[a]Break up your fallow ground,
For *it is* time to seek the LORD,
Till He [b]comes and rains righteousness on you.

13 [a]You have plowed wickedness;
You have reaped iniquity.
You have eaten the fruit of lies,
Because you trusted in your own way,
In the multitude of your mighty men.
14 Therefore tumult shall arise among your people,
And all your fortresses shall be plundered
As Shalman plundered Beth Arbel in the day of battle—
A mother dashed in pieces upon *her* children.
15 Thus it shall be done to you,
O Bethel,
Because of your great wickedness.
At dawn the king of Israel
Shall be cut off utterly.

I pray that ____ would sow righteousness and reap mercy; may they break up the fallow ground of their heart, for it is time to seek You.

FROM HOSEA 10:12

God's Continuing Love for Israel

11 "When Israel *was* a [1]child, I loved him,
And out of Egypt [a]I called My [b]son.
2 [1]*As* they called them,
So they [a]went [2]from them;
They sacrificed to the Baals,
And burned incense to carved images.

3 "I[a] taught Ephraim to walk,
Taking them by [1]their arms;
But they did not know that [b]I healed them.
4 I drew them with [1]gentle cords,
With bands of love,

4 a Amos 5:7
5 a Hos. 8:5, 6; 13:2 b Hos. 9:11 1 Lit. *calves, images* 2 *idolatrous priests*
6 a Hos. 5:13
8 a Hos. 4:15 b 1 Kin. 13:34 c Luke 23:30 1 Lit. *Idolatry* or *Wickedness*
9 a Hos. 9:9 b Judg. 20 1 So with many Heb. mss., LXX, Vg.; MT *unruliness* 2 Or *overcome*
10 a Jer. 16:16 1 Or *in their two habitations*
11 a [Mic. 4:13] 1 Lit. *to ride*
12 a Jer. 4:3 b Hos. 6:3
13 a [Prov. 22:8]
CHAPTER 11
1 a Matt. 2:15 b Ex. 4:22, 23 1 Or *youth*
2 a 2 Kin. 17:13–15 1 So with MT, Vg.; LXX *Just as I called them;* Tg. interprets as *I sent prophets to a thousand of them.* 2 So with MT, Tg., Vg.; LXX *from My face*
3 a Deut. 1:31; 32:10, 11 b Ex. 15:26 1 Some Heb. mss., LXX, Syr., Vg. *My arms*
4 1 Lit. *cords of a man*

And [a]I was to them as those who
take the yoke from their [2]neck.
[b]I stooped *and* fed them.

5 "He shall not return to the land of
Egypt;
But the Assyrian shall be his king,
Because they refused to repent.
6 And the sword shall slash in his
cities,
Devour his districts,
And consume *them,*
Because of their own counsels.
7 My people are bent on [a]backsliding
from Me.
Though [1]they call [2]to the Most
High,
None at all exalt *Him.*

8 "How[a] can I give you up, Ephraim?
How can I hand you over, Israel?
How can I make you like [b]Admah?
How can I set you like Zeboiim?
My heart [1]churns within Me;
My sympathy is stirred.
9 I will not execute the fierceness of
My anger;
I will not again destroy Ephraim.
[a]For I *am* God, and not man,
The Holy One in your midst;
And I will not [1]come with terror.

10 "They shall walk after the LORD.
[a]He will roar like a lion.
When He roars,
Then *His* sons shall come trembling
from the west;
11 They shall come trembling like a
bird from Egypt,
[a]Like a dove from the land of
Assyria.
[b]And I will let them dwell in their
houses,"
Says the LORD.

God's Charge Against Ephraim

12 "Ephraim has encircled Me with
lies,
And the house of Israel with deceit;
But Judah still walks with God,
Even with the [1]Holy One *who is*
faithful.

12 "Ephraim [a]feeds on the wind,
And pursues the east wind;
He daily increases lies and
[1]desolation.
[b]Also they make a [2]covenant with
the Assyrians,
And [c]oil is carried to Egypt.

2 "The[a] LORD also *brings* a [1]charge
against Judah,
And will punish Jacob according to
his ways;
According to his deeds He will
recompense him.
3 He took his brother [a]by the heel in
the womb,
And in his strength he [b]struggled
with God.
4 Yes, he struggled with the Angel
and prevailed;
He wept, and sought favor from
Him.
He found Him *in* [a]Bethel,
And there He spoke to us—
5 That is, the LORD God of hosts.
The LORD *is* His [a]memorable name.
6 [a]So you, by *the help of* your God,
return;
Observe mercy and justice,
And wait on your God
continually.

Mercy imitates God and disappoints Satan.

ST. JOHN CHRYSOSTOM

7 "A cunning [1]Canaanite!
[a]Deceitful scales *are* in his hand;
He loves to oppress.
8 And Ephraim said,
[a]'Surely I have become rich,
I have found wealth for myself;
In all my labors
They shall find in me no iniquity
that *is* sin.'

9 "But I *am* the LORD your God,
Ever since the land of Egypt;
[a]I will again make you dwell in
tents,
As in the days of the appointed
feast.
10 [a]I have also spoken by the
prophets,
And have multiplied visions;
I have given [1]symbols [2]through the
witness of the prophets."

4 a Lev. 26:13 b Ps. 78:25 *2* Lit. *jaws*

7 a Jer. 3:6, 7; 8:5 *1* The prophets *2* Or *upward*

8 a Jer. 9:7 b Gen. 14:8; 19:24, 25 *1* Lit. *turns over*

9 a Num. 23:19 *1* Or *enter a city*

10 a [Joel 3:16]

11 a Is. 11:11; 60:8 b Ezek. 28:25, 26; 34:27, 28

12 *1* Or *holy ones*

CHAPTER 12

1 a Job 15:2, 3 b 2 Kin. 17:4 c Is. 30:6 *1 ruin* *2* Or *treaty*

2 a Mic. 6:2 *1* A legal complaint

3 a Gen. 25:26 b Gen. 32:24–28

4 a [Gen. 28:12–19; 35:9–15]

5 a Ex. 3:15

6 a Mic. 6:8

7 a Amos 8:5 *1* Or *merchant*

8 a Rev. 3:17

9 a Lev. 23:42

10 a 2 Kin. 17:13 *1* Or *parables* *2* Lit. *by the hand*

Hosea 12:6

Dear Woman of Destiny,

Too often we feel stagnant and ineffective while waiting for the fulfillment of the promises of God. We need not get discouraged or yield to passivity. There are many appropriate ways to wait on the Lord.

- We should wait *prayerfully* on Him (see Ps. 25:1–3).
- In our prayerful attitude, we must wait *expectantly*, knowing that He hears our cries of intercession and in due time He will answer (see Ps. 31:24).
- And most of all, we should *patiently* wait for the Lord's answer (see Ps. 37:7–9).

But why does the Father make us wait sometimes for long periods of time for the answer? There are two reasons I believe He allows this to happen.

First, the Lord asks us to wait in order for Him to develop our character. Like Abraham, we receive rich promises from the Lord, but the promise generally precedes the supply. So we must wait. Remember, however, that periods of darkness often follow God's promises. God develops our character in direct proportion to our willingness to wait for His timing. We should never try to help God fulfill His Word.

When the Lord gives us a promise, He knows that our disposition must match His revelation. To accomplish this, He resorts to silence to remove our self-sufficiency. God's "silent treatment" is an act of His discipline, not His displeasure. The higher the calling of service, the greater the level of integrity that is required. So the Lord uses testing to form the character of Christ in our lives.

Second, we must learn to wait for the Holy Spirit to empower us. As the 120 disciples waited in the Upper Room following Christ's resurrection, we, too, must learn to wait for the Spirit's empowerment. As He used them powerfully in the days that followed, He will use us in the days to come.

Empowering comes as we meditate on God's Word (see Ps. 77:11–13; 119:12–14). To meditate is to contemplate, to ponder, or to become absorbed in thought. The famous revivalist and preacher C.H. Spurgeon reportedly said that meditation for a believer is like a cow chewing her cud. Meditation draws the sweetness and spiritual nutrition of every morsel of God's Word into our hearts and lives. By it, we digest the Scripture so spiritual growth can occur.

Waiting on God cultivates intimacy (see Ps. 42:1, 2, 7, 8). An elderly lady told Duncan Campbell, the famous traveling evangelist from the nineteenth century, what to do one day. He sarcastically answered back to her, "If God wants me to do that, why didn't He tell me?" She said, "Because you don't live close enough to Him to hear Him." We would do well to patiently wait so we can learn to hear Him better. Woman of Destiny, if we do not grow weary in doing well, we will receive the promises!

Alice Smith

11 Though [a]Gilead *has* idols—
Surely they are [1]vanity—
Though they sacrifice bulls in
[b]Gilgal,
Indeed their altars *shall be* heaps in
the furrows of the field.

12 Jacob [a]fled to the country of
Syria;
[b]Israel served for a spouse,
And for a wife he tended *sheep.*
13 [a]By a prophet the LORD brought
Israel out of Egypt,
And by a prophet he was preserved.
14 Ephraim [a]provoked *Him* to anger
most bitterly;
Therefore his Lord will leave the
guilt of his bloodshed upon him,
[b]And return his reproach upon him.

Relentless Judgment on Israel

13 When Ephraim spoke, trembling,
He exalted *himself* in Israel;
But when he offended through Baal
worship, he died.
2 Now they sin more and more,
And have made for themselves
molded images,
Idols of their silver, according to
their skill;
All of it *is* the work of craftsmen.
They say of them,
"Let [1]the men who sacrifice [2]kiss
the calves!"
3 Therefore they shall be like the
morning cloud
And like the early dew that passes
away,
[a]Like chaff blown off from a
threshing floor
And like smoke from a chimney.

4 "Yet [a]I *am* the LORD your God
Ever since the land of Egypt,
And you shall know no God but Me;
For [b]*there is* no savior besides Me.
5 [a]I [1]knew you in the wilderness,
[b]In the land of [2]great drought.
6 [a]When they had pasture, they were
filled;
They were filled and their heart was
exalted;
Therefore they forgot Me.

7 "So [a]I will be to them like a lion;
Like [b]a leopard by the road I will
lurk;
8 I will meet them [a]like a bear
deprived *of her cubs;*

11 [a]Hos. 6:8 [b]Hos. 9:15 [1]*worthless*
12 [a]Gen. 28:5 [b]Gen. 29:20, 28
13 [a]Ex. 12:50, 51; 13:3
14 [a]Ezek. 18:10–13 [b]Dan. 11:18

CHAPTER 13
2 [1]Or *those who offer human sacrifice* [2]Worship with kisses
3 [a]Dan. 2:35
4 [a]Is. 43:11 [b]Is. 43:11; 45:21, 22
5 [a]Deut. 2:7; 32:10 [b]Deut. 8:15 [1]Cared for you [2]Lit. *droughts*
6 [a]Deut. 8:12, 14; 32:13–15
7 [a]Lam. 3:10 [b]Jer. 5:6
8 [a]2 Sam. 17:8 [1]Lit. *beast of the field*
9 [1]Lit. *it* or *he destroyed you* [2]Lit. *in your help*
10 [a]Deut. 32:38 [b]1 Sam. 8:5, 6 [1]LXX, Syr., Tg., Vg. *Where is your king?*
11 [a]1 Sam. 8:7; 10:17–24
12 [a]Deut. 32:34, 35
13 [a]Is. 13:8
14 [a][1 Cor. 15:54, 55] [b]Jer. 15:6 [1]Lit. *hand* [2]Or *Sheol* [3]LXX *where is your punishment?* [4]Or *Sheol* [5]LXX *where is your sting?*
15 [a]Jer. 4:11, 12
16 [a]2 Kin. 18:12 [1]LXX *shall be disfigured*

I will tear open their rib cage,
And there I will devour them like a
lion.
The [1]wild beast shall tear them.

9 "O Israel, [1]you are destroyed,
But [2]your help *is* from Me.
10 [1]I will be your King;
[a]Where *is any other,*
That he may save you in all your
cities?
And your judges to whom [b]you
said,
'Give me a king and princes'?
11 [a]I gave you a king in My anger,
And took *him* away in My wrath.

12 "The[a] iniquity of Ephraim *is* bound
up;
His sin *is* stored up.
13 [a]The sorrows of a woman in
childbirth shall come upon him.
He *is* an unwise son,
For he should not stay long where
children are born.

Father, ransom —— from the power of the grave; redeem them from death.

FROM HOSEA 13:14

14 "I will ransom them from the
[1]power of [2]the grave;
I will redeem them from death.
[a]O Death, [3]I will be your plagues!
O [4]Grave, [5]I will be your
destruction!
[b]Pity is hidden from My eyes."

15 Though he is fruitful among *his*
brethren,
[a]An east wind shall come;
The wind of the LORD shall come
up from the wilderness.
Then his spring shall become dry,
And his fountain shall be dried up.
He shall plunder the treasury of
every desirable prize.
16 Samaria [1]is held guilty,
For she has [a]rebelled against her
God.
They shall fall by the sword,
Their infants shall be dashed in
pieces,

And their women with child [b]ripped open.

Israel Restored at Last

14 O Israel, [a]return to the LORD your God,
For you have stumbled because of your iniquity;
2 Take words with you,
And return to the LORD.
Say to Him,
"Take away all iniquity;
Receive *us* graciously,
For we will offer the [a]sacrifices[1] of our lips.
3 Assyria shall [a]not save us,
[b]We will not ride on horses,
Nor will we say anymore to the work of our hands, '*You are* our gods.'
[c]For in You the fatherless finds mercy."

4 "I will heal their [a]backsliding,
I will [b]love them freely,
For My anger has turned away from him.
5 I will be like the [a]dew to Israel;
He shall [1]grow like the lily,
And [2]lengthen his roots like Lebanon.
6 His branches shall [1]spread;
[a]His beauty shall be like an olive tree,
And [b]his fragrance like Lebanon.
7 [a]Those who dwell under his shadow shall return;
They shall be revived *like* grain,
And [1]grow like a vine.
Their [2]scent *shall be* like the wine of Lebanon.

Lord, I pray that ____ will return to You, for they have stumbled because of their iniquity.

FROM HOSEA 14:1

8 "Ephraim *shall say,* 'What have I to do anymore with idols?'
I have heard and observed him.
I *am* like a green cypress tree;
[a]Your fruit is found in Me."

9 Who *is* wise?
Let him understand these things.
Who is prudent?
Let him know them.
For [a]the ways of the LORD *are* right;
The righteous walk in them,
But transgressors stumble in them.

16 [b]2 Kin. 15:16

CHAPTER 14
1 [a][Joel 2:13]
2 [a][Heb. 13:15] [1]Lit. *bull calves;* LXX *fruit*
3 [a]Hos. 7:11; 10:13; 12:1 [b][Ps. 33:17] [c]Ps. 10:14; 68:5
4 [a]Jer. 14:7 [b][Eph. 1:6]
5 [a]Prov. 19:12 [1]Lit. *bud* or *sprout* [2]Lit. *strike*
6 [a]Ps. 52:8; 128:3 [b]Gen. 27:27 [1]Lit. *go*
7 [a]Dan. 4:12 [1]Lit. *bud* or *sprout* [2]Lit. *remembrance*
8 [a][John 15:4]
9 [a][Prov. 10:29]

AUTHOR: *Joel*
DATE: *Probably 835–805 B.C.*
THEME: *The Judgment and Grace of God*
KEY WORDS: *Great and Awesome Day of the Lord*

JOEL

Dear Woman of Destiny,

The Book of Joel calls Israel to repentance and provides an overview from Joel's time through the establishment of the Millennium. Joel presents Jesus Christ as El Shaddai (God Almighty) and prophesies the outpouring of the Holy Spirit on all flesh. Allow the Spirit of God to minister the fullness of your *personal* destiny as you read His faithful words.

His love and mine,

Marilyn Hickey

The word of the LORD that came to [a]Joel the son of Pethuel.

The Land Laid Waste

2 Hear this, you elders,
And give ear, all you inhabitants of the land!
[a]Has *anything like* this happened in your days,
Or even in the days of your fathers?
3 [a]Tell your children about it,
Let your children *tell* their children,
And their children another generation.

4 [a]What the chewing [1]locust left, the [b]swarming locust has eaten;
What the swarming locust left, the crawling locust has eaten;
And what the crawling locust left, the consuming locust has eaten.

5 Awake, you [a]drunkards, and weep;
And wail, all you drinkers of wine,
Because of the new wine,
[b]For it has been cut off from your mouth.
6 For [a]a nation has come up against My land,
Strong, and without number;
[b]His teeth *are* the teeth of a lion,
And he has the fangs of a [1]fierce lion.
7 He has [a]laid waste My vine,
And [1]ruined My fig tree;
He has stripped it bare and thrown *it* away;
Its branches are made white.

8 [a]Lament like a virgin girded with sackcloth
For [b]the husband of her youth.
9 [a]The grain offering and the drink offering
Have been cut off from the house of the LORD;
The priests [b]mourn, who minister to the LORD.
10 The field is wasted,
[a]The land mourns;
For the grain is ruined,
[b]The new wine is dried up,
The oil fails.

11 [a]Be ashamed, you farmers,
Wail, you vinedressers,
For the wheat and the barley;
Because the harvest of the field has perished.
12 [a]The vine has dried up,
And the fig tree has withered;
The pomegranate tree,
The palm tree also,
And the apple tree—
All the trees of the field are withered;
Surely [b]joy has withered away from the sons of men.

Self-effacement and repentance, acceptance of extended mercies, and unwavering dependence on God's promises is the only highway to genuine spiritual exultation.

CHARLES F. PARHAM

Mourning for the Land

13 [a]Gird yourselves and lament, you priests;
Wail, you who minister before the altar;
Come, lie all night in sackcloth,
You who minister to my God;
For the grain offering and the drink offering
Are withheld from the house of your God.
14 [a]Consecrate a fast,
Call [b]a sacred assembly;
Gather the elders
And [c]all the inhabitants of the land
Into the house of the LORD your God,
And cry out to the LORD.

15 [a]Alas for the day!
For [b]the day of the LORD *is* at hand;
It shall come as destruction from the Almighty.
16 Is not the food [a]cut off before our eyes,
[b]Joy and gladness from the house of our God?
17 The seed shrivels under the clods,
Storehouses are in shambles;
Barns are broken down,

CHAPTER 1
1 a Acts 2:16
2 a Joel 2:2
3 a Ps. 78:4
4 a Deut. 28:38 b Is. 33:4 *1* Exact identity of these locusts unknown
5 a Is. 5:11; 28:1 b Is. 32:10
6 a Joel 2:2, 11, 25 b Rev. 9:8 *1* Or *lioness*
7 a Is. 5:6 *1* Or *splintered*
8 a Is. 22:12 b Jer. 3:4
9 a Joel 1:13; 2:14 b Joel 2:17
10 a Jer. 12:11 b Is. 24:7
11 a Jer. 14:3, 4
12 a Joel 1:10 b Jer. 48:33
13 a Jer. 4:8
14 a Joel 2:15, 16 b Lev. 23:36 c 2 Chr. 20:13
15 a [Jer. 30:7] b Is. 13:6
16 a Is. 3:1 b Deut. 12:7

Joel 1:13, 14

Dear Woman of Destiny,

"A funny story is told of a woman who had received a remarkable healing in her body. She wrote the pastor to tell him of this wonderful experience. As she concluded her letter she wrote, 'Do you think God would do anything about my overweight?' He wrote back, 'This kind goeth out only by fasting'" (Milburn H. Miller's *Notes and Quotes*). Don't we all wish we could get rid of a few extra pounds by a quick healing from the Lord?

On a serious note, what is fasting? Fasting is abstinence from food in order to accomplish a spiritual goal. Fasting is to the soul what food is to the body. When we deny ourselves food, coupled with time in prayer, the benefits can be endless.

The prophet Joel announced the eminent destruction of Judah by Babylon's army if the people of Judah did not repent. The urgency of Joel's message made it clear that Israel's suffering was due to her backsliding.

In their day of desperation, Joel directed Judah to take drastic measures:

- Consecrate a fast, and
- Proclaim a solemn assembly.

The Hebrew word for *proclaim* is *qara'*, meaning to force a response by crying out the message. A solemn assembly was a day of repentance and restraint. The people were to fast and repent. The priests were to cry out for mercy.

Doesn't Joel's admonition apply to us today? We are living in desperate times. Immorality abounds. Immorality and apathy have left the church impotent. The destiny of any immoral nation is clear: destruction! We are women of destiny, meaning that our destiny and the destiny of our children are in our hands. We must purify ourselves and move from apathy and passivity to action. Prayer and fasting must become part of the fabric of our very lives!

You say, "But who am I that God could use me?" May I remind you that:

- Moses was busy with the sheep at Horeb when God called him (see Ex. 3:1).
- Deborah was holding court as a judge in Israel when God called her to fight the Canaanites (see Judg. 4:4, 5).
- Gideon was threshing wheat by the winepress when God called him to fight against the Midianites (see Judg. 6:11).
- David was in the hills shepherding his father's flock when Samuel sent for him. Then Samuel anointed him king of Israel (see 1 Sam. 16:11–13).
- Peter, Andrew, James, and John were fishing when Jesus said, "Follow Me" (see Matt. 4:18–22).

What are you doing right now? Can you hear His call? Are you willing to be a woman of destiny?

Alice Smith

For the grain has withered.
18 How [a]the animals groan!
The herds of cattle are restless,
Because they have no pasture;
Even the flocks of sheep [1]suffer punishment.

19 O LORD, [a]to You I cry out;
For [b]fire has devoured the [1]open pastures,
And a flame has burned all the trees of the field.
20 The beasts of the field also [a]cry out to You,
For [b]the water brooks are dried up,
And fire has devoured the [1]open pastures.

The Day of the Lord

2 Blow [a]the [1]trumpet in Zion,
And [b]sound an alarm in My holy mountain!
Let all the inhabitants of the land tremble;
For [c]the day of the LORD is coming,
For it is at hand:
2 [a]A day of darkness and gloominess,
A day of clouds and thick darkness,
Like the morning *clouds* spread over the mountains.
[b]A people *come,* great and strong,
[c]The like of whom has never been;
Nor will there ever be any *such* after them,
Even for many successive generations.

3 A fire devours before them,
And behind them a flame burns;
The land *is* like [a]the Garden of Eden before them,
[b]And behind them a desolate wilderness;
Surely nothing shall escape them.
4 [a]Their appearance is like the appearance of horses;
And like [1]swift steeds, so they run.
5 [a]With a noise like chariots
Over mountaintops they leap,
Like the noise of a flaming fire that devours the stubble,
Like a strong people set in battle array.

6 Before them the people writhe in pain;
[a]All faces [1]are drained of color.
7 They run like mighty men,
They climb the wall like men of war;
Every one marches in formation,
And they do not break [a]ranks.
8 They do not push one another;
Every one marches in his own [1]column.
Though they lunge between the weapons,
They are not [2]cut down.
9 They run to and fro in the city,
They run on the wall;
They climb into the houses,
They [a]enter at the windows [b]like a thief.

10 [a]The earth quakes before them,
The heavens tremble;
[b]The sun and moon grow dark,
And the stars diminish their brightness.
11 [a]The LORD gives voice before His army,
For His camp is very great;
[b]For strong *is the One* who executes His word.
For the [c]day of the LORD *is* great and very terrible;
[d]Who can endure it?

O Lord, may ____ turn to You with all their heart, with fasting, with weeping, and with mourning. For You, O Lord, are gracious and merciful, slow to anger, and of great kindness.

FROM JOEL 2:12, 13

A Call to Repentance

12 "Now, therefore," says the LORD,
[a]"Turn to Me with all your heart,
With fasting, with weeping, and with mourning."
13 So [a]rend your heart, and not [b]your garments;
Return to the LORD your God,
For He *is* [c]gracious and merciful,
Slow to anger, and of great kindness;
And He relents from doing harm.

---

18 a Hos. 4:3 *1* LXX, Vg. *are made desolate*
19 a [Ps. 50:15] b Jer. 9:10 *1* Lit. *pastures of the wilderness*
20 a Ps. 104:21; 147:9 b 1 Kin. 17:7; 18:5 *1* Lit. *pastures of the wilderness*

CHAPTER 2
1 a Jer. 4:5 b Num. 10:5 c [Obad. 15] *1 ram's horn*
2 a Amos 5:18 b Joel 1:6; 2:11, 25 c Dan. 9:12; 12:1
3 a Is. 51:3 b Zech. 7:14
4 a Rev. 9:7 *1* Or *horsemen*
5 a Rev. 9:9
6 a Nah. 2:10 *1* LXX, Tg., Vg. *gather blackness*
7 a Prov. 30:27
8 *1* Lit. *highway* *2* Halted by losses
9 a Jer. 9:21 b John 10:1
10 a Ps. 18:7 b Is. 13:10; 34:4
11 a Jer. 25:30 b Rev. 18:8 c Amos 5:18 d [Mal. 3:2]
12 a Jer. 4:1
13 a [Ps. 34:18; 51:17] b Gen. 37:34 c [Ex. 34:6]

14 [a]Who knows *if* He will turn and relent,
And leave [b]a blessing behind Him—
[c]A grain offering and a drink offering
For the LORD your God?

15 [a]Blow the [1]trumpet in Zion,
[b]Consecrate a fast,
Call a sacred assembly;
16 Gather the people,
[a]Sanctify the congregation,
Assemble the elders,
Gather the children and nursing babes;
[b]Let the bridegroom go out from his chamber,
And the bride from her dressing room.
17 Let the priests, who minister to the LORD,
Weep [a]between the porch and the altar;
Let them say, [b]"Spare Your people, O LORD,
And do not give Your heritage to reproach,
That the nations should [1]rule over them.
[c]Why should they say among the peoples,
'Where *is* their God?' "

The Land Refreshed

18 Then the LORD will [a]be zealous for His land,
And pity His people.
19 The LORD will answer and say to His people,
"Behold, I will send you [a]grain and new wine and oil,
And you will be satisfied by them;
I will no longer make you a reproach among the nations.

20 "But [a]I will remove far from you [b]the northern *army,*
And will drive him away into a barren and desolate land,
With his face toward the eastern sea
And his back [c]toward the western sea;
His stench will come up,
And his foul odor will rise,
Because he has done [1]monstrous things."

14 [a]Jer. 26:3 [b]Hag. 2:19 [c]Joel 1:9, 13
15 [a]Num. 10:3 [b]Joel 1:14 [1]*ram's horn*
16 [a]Ex. 19:10 [b]Ps. 19:5
17 [a]Matt. 23:35 [b]Ex. 32:11, 12 [c]Ps. 42:10 [1]Or *speak a proverb against them*
18 [a][Is. 60:10; 63:9, 15]
19 [a][Mal. 3:10]
20 [a]Ex. 10:19 [b]Jer. 1:14, 15 [c]Deut. 11:24 [1]Lit. *great*
21 [1]Lit. *great*
22 [a]Joel 1:19
23 [a]Is. 41:16 [b]Lev. 26:4 [1]Or *teacher of righteousness*
25 [a]Joel 1:4–7; 2:2–11 [1]Exact identity of these locusts unknown
26 [a]Lev. 26:5 [b]Is. 45:17
27 [a]Lev. 26:11, 12 [b][Is. 45:5, 6]

21 Fear not, O land;
Be glad and rejoice,
For the LORD has done [1]marvelous things!
22 Do not be afraid, you beasts of the field;
For [a]the open pastures are springing up,
And the tree bears its fruit;
The fig tree and the vine yield their strength.
23 Be glad then, you children of Zion,
And [a]rejoice in the LORD your God;
For He has given you the [1]former rain faithfully,
And He [b]will cause the rain to come down for you—
The former rain,
And the latter rain in the first *month.*
24 The threshing floors shall be full of wheat,
And the vats shall overflow with new wine and oil.

The miracle of the grace of God is that He can make the past as though it had never been.

OSWALD CHAMBERS

25 "So I will restore to you the years [a]that the swarming [1]locust has eaten,
The crawling locust,
The consuming locust,
And the chewing locust,
My great army which I sent among you.
26 You shall [a]eat in plenty and be satisfied,
And praise the name of the LORD your God,
Who has dealt wondrously with you;
And My people shall never be put to [b]shame.
27 Then you shall know that I *am* [a]in the midst of Israel:
[b]I *am* the LORD your God
And there is no other.

Joel 2:25

Dear Woman of Destiny,

When I was a freshman in high school, my family moved from New England to a small town in South Carolina. Although my dad was stationed at an Air Force base in a neighboring city, he chose this town for our family because of a treasure he'd discovered there: an old house in need of restoration.

You see, an apparent "lost cause" was something my dad could not resist. Where someone else saw a run-down house with an overgrown yard, he saw a masterpiece of Southern architecture. Over the next three years, my dad transformed that drafty old house into a work of art. He ripped out the acoustical tiles to reveal high ceilings, so essential in the South Carolina heat. He replaced plumbing and wiring, painted and papered the walls, and repaired French doors and windows. The trees and shrubs that had overgrown the front porch columns were pruned or removed, and the rest of the property was reclaimed from the kudzu vines.

Almost thirty years later, when I see the word *restoration*, I see that house and realize that I was once a "lost cause" as well. Our aunt and uncle had adopted my sister and me when I was twelve. After an erratic childhood, we suddenly found ourselves in a Christian home with, of all things, an Air Force sergeant for a father. My undisciplined existence came to a screeching halt, but not without some resistance on my part. Fortunately, my dad decided that I needed to learn the value of hard work and responsibility. That proved to be a turning point in my life. For the first time in my twelve years, I discovered that I was a person of value who could actually make a contribution to my small corner of the world.

My heavenly Father has been even more determined to restore to me "the years that the . . . locust has eaten." I used to resent the missed years of childhood and felt robbed by circumstances beyond my control. Now, through the miracle of restoration, God has given me childlike faith, a loving husband, and a house full of children. It is as though the love of the Father has worked backwards through time, returning to me what I never had, simply because it is His good pleasure to do so.

Restoration begins with vision. My dad's vision for that old house only went as far as restoring the structure to its former beauty. The Father's vision for His children goes beyond restoring to us what we lost through earthly circumstances. His desire is to restore us to the original blueprint: communion with our Designer. Prophetic revelation directs us as we cooperate with the Master Architect. He is constantly giving us instructions as He performs His perfect work in us. Every time we obey, we see His transforming hand working in our lives. Release to Him your past and rejoice in His plan of restoration for you, His beautiful daughter!

Pam Pierce

My people shall never be put to
shame.

God's Spirit Poured Out

28 "And[a] it shall come to pass
afterward
That [b]I will pour out My Spirit on
all flesh;
[c]Your sons and your [d]daughters
shall prophesy,
Your old men shall dream dreams,
Your young men shall see
visions.
29 And also on *My* [a]menservants and
on *My* maidservants
I will pour out My Spirit in those
days.

*Mighty God, I pray that
You would pour out Your
Spirit on _____.*

FROM JOEL 2:28

30 "And [a]I will show wonders in the
heavens and in the earth:
Blood and fire and pillars of smoke.
31 [a]The sun shall be turned into
darkness,
And the moon into blood,
[b]Before the coming of the great and
awesome day of the LORD.
32 And it shall come to pass
That [a]whoever calls on the name of
the LORD
Shall be [1]saved.
For [b]in Mount Zion and in
Jerusalem there shall be
[2]deliverance,
As the LORD has said,
Among [c]the remnant whom the
LORD calls.

God Judges the Nations

3 "For behold, [a]in those days and at
that time,
When I bring back the captives of
Judah and Jerusalem,
2 [a]I will also gather all nations,
And bring them down to the Valley
of Jehoshaphat;
And I [b]will enter into judgment
with them there

28 [a]Ezek. 39:29 [b]Zech. 12:10 [c]Is. 54:13 [d]Acts 21:9
29 [a][Gal. 3:28]
30 [a]Matt. 24:29
31 [a]Is. 13:9, 10; 34:4 [b][Mal. 4:1, 5, 6]
32 [a]Rom. 10:13 [b]Is. 46:13 [c][Mic. 4:7] [1]*Or delivered* [2]Or *salvation*

CHAPTER 3
1 [a]Jer. 30:3
2 [a]Zech. 14:2 [b]Is. 66:16
3 [a]Nah. 3:10
4 [a]Amos 1:6–8 [1]Or *render Me repayment* [2]Or *repay Me* [3]Or *repayment*
5 [1]Lit. *precious good things*
7 [a]Jer. 23:8 [1]Or *repayment*
8 [a]Ezek. 23:42 [b]Jer. 6:20 [1]Lit. *Shebaites,* Is. 60:6; Ezek. 27:22
9 [a]Ezek. 38:7
10 [a][Is. 2:4] [b]Zech. 12:8 [1]*pruning knives*
11 [a]Is. 13:3

On account of My people, My
heritage Israel,
Whom they have scattered among
the nations;
They have also divided up My land.
3 They have [a]cast lots for My people,
Have given a boy *as payment* for a
harlot,
And sold a girl for wine, that they
may drink.

4 "Indeed, what have you to do with
Me,
[a]O Tyre and Sidon, and all the
coasts of Philistia?
Will you [1]retaliate against Me?
But if you [2]retaliate against Me,
Swiftly and speedily I will return
your [3]retaliation upon your own
head;
5 Because you have taken My silver
and My gold,
And have carried into your temples
My [1]prized possessions.
6 Also the people of Judah and the
people of Jerusalem
You have sold to the Greeks,
That you may remove them far
from their borders.

7 "Behold, [a]I will raise them
Out of the place to which you have
sold them,
And will return your [1]retaliation
upon your own head.
8 I will sell your sons and your
daughters
Into the hand of the people of
Judah,
And they will sell them to the
[a]Sabeans,[1]
To a people [b]far off;
For the LORD has spoken."

9 [a]Proclaim this among the nations:
"Prepare for war!
Wake up the mighty men,
Let all the men of war draw near,
Let them come up.
10 [a]Beat your plowshares into swords
And your [1]pruning hooks into
spears;
[b]Let the weak say, 'I *am* strong.' "
11 Assemble and come, all you
nations,
And gather together all around.
Cause [a]Your mighty ones to go
down there, O LORD.

Joel 2:28

Dear Woman of Destiny,

We are living in the days of Joel 2:28. The Father is calling both His sons and His daughters to prophesy. Some prophesy publicly, while others may prophesy in hidden ways, such as intercession. Regardless of the way God desires to use you, He will always deal with the issue of integrity. Those who prophesy must be pure-hearted and trustworthy to the core. If the Lord is going to trust *His* words to specific people to speak, then those people must first be faithful in giving *their* word.

Following are five specific areas in which God commonly works to establish the integrity of those who prophesy. This is not an exhaustive list, so as you grow in the prophetic, seek the Lord for other aspects of your life to which He may want to bring integrity.

Not exaggerating. The prophet must learn to speak only what God tells him or her and no more. One temptation is to make the prophetic word more exciting, more fruitful, or more dramatic than it actually was. Be assured, God knows exactly what to say to the person and how to communicate it. He knows that different personalities perceive things in different ways, so trust Him to speak in the way that is exactly right for the person and situation as He ministers through you.

Understanding timing and being on time for commitments. Timing is important in both the spiritual and the natural realm. The old saying is true. "God is never late." His timing may be confusing or even frustrating; but He is the One who knows the beginning from the end, and He does all things according to His perfect plan. Do not move ahead of God or lag behind Him as you speak His word. Instead, learn to hear to the heartbeat of the Lord and walk to its rhythm.

Keeping your word. If you can't be trusted to keep a promise, then how can you be trusted to receive a prophecy from God? At night, before you go to bed, ask the Lord to remind you of any forgotten commitments or broken promises, and make a note to yourself so you won't forget again!

Proper handling of money. Prophetic leaders should pay their bills promptly, control their use of credit, and not live beyond their means. More importantly, they must never solicit funds as a prerequisite for giving a prophetic word from God. The gift of prophecy cannot be bought or sold, and those who engage in such activity fall into divination as did Balaam the seer (see Num. 22—24: compare Acts18—23).

Speaking the pure Word from God. Receiving a pure prophetic word of God can be a powerful experience. It is beautiful to see a person's life changed by a word that comes straight from the heart of God. But it is possible for the prophetic word to be "tainted." In other words, only part of what the prophet is saying may actually come from God, while the rest may be distorted by sin, inconsistency, or other issues in the person's life. Be aware of your personal weaknesses, prejudices, and temptations. Pursue purity and holiness in every area of your life, and continue to walk tenderly in the fear of the Lord.

Cindy Jacobs

12 "Let the nations be wakened, and
come up to the Valley of
Jehoshaphat;
For there I will sit to [a]judge all the
surrounding nations.
13 [a]Put in the sickle, for [b]the harvest
is ripe.
Come, go down;
For the [c]winepress is full,
The vats overflow—
For their wickedness *is* great."

14 Multitudes, multitudes in the
valley of decision!
For [a]the day of the LORD *is* near in
the valley of decision.
15 The sun and moon will grow dark,
And the stars will diminish their
brightness.
16 The LORD also will roar from Zion,
And utter His voice from Jerusalem;
The heavens and earth will shake;
[a]But the LORD will be a shelter for
His people,
And the strength of the children of
Israel.

17 "So you shall know that I *am* the
LORD your God,
Dwelling in Zion My [a]holy
mountain.

12 [a]Is. 2:4
13 [a]Rev. 14:15 [b]Jer. 51:33 [c][Is. 63:3]
14 [a]Joel 2:1
16 [a][Is. 51:5, 6]
17 [a]Zech. 8:3
18 [a]Ezek. 47:1 [1]Heb. *Shittim*
21 [a]Is. 4:4

Then Jerusalem shall be holy,
And no aliens shall ever pass
through her again."

God Blesses His People

18 And it will come to pass in that
day
That the mountains shall drip with
new wine,
The hills shall flow with milk,
And all the brooks of Judah shall be
flooded with water;
A [a]fountain shall flow from the
house of the LORD
And water the Valley of [1]Acacias.

19 "Egypt shall be a desolation,
And Edom a desolate wilderness,
Because of violence *against* the
people of Judah,
For they have shed innocent blood
in their land.
20 But Judah shall abide forever,
And Jerusalem from generation to
generation.
21 For I will [a]acquit them of the
guilt of bloodshed, whom I had
not acquitted;
For the LORD dwells in Zion."

AUTHOR: *Amos*
DATE: *760–750 B.C.*
THEME: *The Judgment of God Is About to Fall on Israel*
KEY WORDS: *Judgment, Righteousness, Justice*

AMOS

Dear Woman of Destiny,

In Amos we see the prophecy of judgment on Israel for worldliness and idolatry, yet we are reminded that God preserves the humble and promises enduring hope for the remnant. We women of destiny are part of that remnant—a generation chosen to receive from God the restoration and supernatural abundance Amos saw as he looked ahead to Christ.

His love and mine,

Marilyn Hickey

The words of Amos, who was among the [a]sheepbreeders of [b]Tekoa, which he saw concerning Israel in the days of [c]Uzziah king of Judah, and in the days of [d]Jeroboam the son of Joash, king of Israel, two years before the [e]earthquake.

2 And he said:

"The LORD [a]roars from Zion,
And utters His voice from
Jerusalem;
The pastures of the shepherds
mourn,
And the top of [b]Carmel withers."

Judgment on the Nations

3 Thus says the LORD:

"For three transgressions of
[a]Damascus, and for four,
I will not turn away its
punishment,
Because they have [b]threshed Gilead
with implements of iron.
4 [a]But I will send a fire into the
house of Hazael,
Which shall devour the palaces of
[b]Ben-Hadad.
5 I will also break the *gate* [a]bar of
Damascus,
And cut off the inhabitant from the
Valley of Aven,
And the one who [1]holds the scepter
from [2]Beth Eden.
The people of Syria shall go captive
to Kir,"
Says the LORD.

6 Thus says the LORD:

"For three transgressions of [a]Gaza,
and for four,
I will not turn away its
punishment,
Because they took captive the whole
captivity
To deliver *them* up to Edom.
7 [a]But I will send a fire upon the wall
of Gaza,
Which shall devour its palaces.
8 I will cut off the inhabitant [a]from
Ashdod,
And the one who holds the scepter
from Ashkelon;
I will [b]turn My hand against Ekron,
And [c]the remnant of the Philistines
shall perish,"
Says the Lord GOD.

9 Thus says the LORD:

"For three transgressions of [a]Tyre,
and for four,
I will not turn away its
punishment,
Because they delivered up the
whole captivity to Edom,
And did not remember the covenant
of brotherhood.
10 But I will send a fire upon the
wall of Tyre,
Which shall devour its palaces."

11 Thus says the LORD:

"For three transgressions of [a]Edom,
and for four,
I will not turn away its
punishment,
Because he pursued his [b]brother
with the sword,
And cast off all pity;
His anger tore perpetually,
And he kept his wrath forever.
12 But [a]I will send a fire upon
Teman,
Which shall devour the palaces of
Bozrah."

13 Thus says the LORD:

"For three transgressions of [a]the
people of Ammon, and for four,
I will not turn away its
punishment,
Because they ripped open the
women with child in Gilead,
That they might enlarge their
territory.
14 But I will kindle a fire in the wall
of [a]Rabbah,
And it shall devour its palaces,
[b]Amid shouting in the day of battle,
And a tempest in the day of the
whirlwind.
15 [a]Their king shall go into captivity,
He and his princes together,"
Says the LORD.

2 Thus says the LORD:

[a]"For three transgressions of Moab,
and for four,
I will not turn away its
punishment,
Because he [b]burned the bones of
the king of Edom to lime.
2 But I will send a fire upon Moab,
And it shall devour the palaces of
[a]Kerioth;

CHAPTER 1
1 [a]2 Kin. 3:4; Amos 7:14 [b]2 Sam. 14:2 [c]2 Chr. 26:1–23 [d]Amos 7:10 [e]Zech. 14:5
2 [a]Joel 3:16 [b]1 Sam. 25:2
3 [a]Is. 8:4; 17:1–3 [b]2 Kin. 10:32, 33
4 [a]Jer. 49:27; 51:30 [b]2 Kin. 6:24
5 [a]Jer. 51:30 [1]Rules [2]Lit. *House of Eden*
6 [a]Jer. 47:1, 5
7 [a]Jer. 47:1
8 [a]Zeph. 2:4 [b]Ps. 81:14 [c]Ezek. 25:16
9 [a]Is. 23:1–18
11 [a]Is. 21:11 [b]Obad. 10–12
12 [a]Obad. 9, 10
13 [a]Ezek. 25:2
14 [a]Deut. 3:11 [b]Amos 2:2
15 [a]Jer. 49:3
CHAPTER 2
1 [a]Zeph. 2:8–11 [b]2 Kin. 3:26, 27
2 [a]Jer. 48:24, 41

Moab shall die with tumult,
With shouting *and* trumpet sound.
3 And I will cut off [a]the judge from its midst,
And slay all its princes with him,"
Says the LORD.

Judgment on Judah

[4]Thus says the LORD:

"For three transgressions of [a]Judah, and for four,
I will not turn away its *punishment,*
[b]Because they have despised the law of the LORD,
And have not kept His commandments.
[c]Their lies lead them astray,
Lies [d]which their fathers followed.
5 [a]But I will send a fire upon Judah,
And it shall devour the palaces of Jerusalem."

Judgment on Israel

[6]Thus says the LORD:

"For three transgressions of [a]Israel, and for four,
I will not turn away its *punishment,*
Because [b]they sell the righteous for silver,
And the [c]poor for a pair of sandals.
7 They [1]pant after the dust of the earth *which is* on the head of the poor,
And [a]pervert the way of the humble.
[b]A man and his father go in to the *same* girl,
[c]To defile My holy name.
8 They lie down [a]by every altar on clothes [b]taken in pledge,
And drink the wine of [1]the condemned *in* the house of their god.
9 "Yet *it was* I *who* destroyed the [a]Amorite before them,
Whose height *was* like the [b]height of the cedars,
And he *was as* strong as the oaks;
Yet I [c]destroyed his fruit above
And his roots beneath.
10 Also *it was* [a]I *who* brought you up from the land of Egypt,
And [b]led you forty years through the wilderness,

3 [a]Num. 24:17
4 [a]Hos. 12:2 [b]Lev. 26:14 [c]Jer. 16:19 [d]Ezek. 20:13, 16, 18
5 [a]Hos. 8:14
6 [a]2 Kin. 17:7–18; 18:12 [b]Is. 29:21 [c]Amos 4:1; 5:11; 8:6
7 [a]Amos 5:12 [b]Ezek. 22:11 [c]Lev. 20:3 [1]*Or trample on*
8 [a]1 Cor. 8:10 [b]Ex. 22:26 [1]*Or those punished by fines*
9 [a]Num. 21:25 [b]Ezek. 31:3 [c][Mal. 4:1]
10 [a]Ex. 12:51 [b]Deut. 2:7
11 [a]Num. 12:6 [b]Num. 6:2, 3
12 [a]Is. 30:10
13 [a]Is. 1:14 [1]Or *tottering under* [2]Or *totters*
14 [a]Jer. 46:6 [b]Ps. 33:16 [1]Or *the place of refuge* [2]Lit. *save his soul* or *life*
15 [1]Or *save*
16 [1]Lit. *strong of his heart among the mighty*
CHAPTER 3
2 [a][Deut. 7:6] [b][Rom. 2:9]
4 [1]Lit. *give his voice*
5 [1]Or *bait* or *lure*

To possess the land of the Amorite.
11 I raised up some of your sons as [a]prophets,
And some of your young men as [b]Nazirites.
Is it not so, O you children of Israel?"
Says the LORD.
12 "But you gave the Nazirites wine to drink,
And commanded the prophets [a]saying,
'Do not prophesy!'
13 "Behold,[a] I am [1]weighed down by you,
As a cart full of sheaves [2]is weighed down.
14 [a]Therefore [1]flight shall perish from the swift,
The strong shall not strengthen his power,
[b]Nor shall the mighty [2]deliver himself;
15 He shall not stand who handles the bow,
The swift of foot shall not [1]escape,
Nor shall he who rides a horse deliver himself.
16 The most [1]courageous men of might
Shall flee naked in that day,"
Says the LORD.

Authority of the Prophet's Message

3 Hear this word that the LORD has spoken against you, O children of Israel, against the whole family which I brought up from the land of Egypt, saying:

2 "You[a] only have I known of all the families of the earth;
[b]Therefore I will punish you for all your iniquities."

3 Can two walk together, unless they are agreed?
4 Will a lion roar in the forest, when he has no prey?
Will a young lion [1]cry out of his den, if he has caught nothing?
5 Will a bird fall into a snare on the earth, where there is no [1]trap for it?
Will a snare spring up from the earth, if it has caught nothing at all?

6 If a [1]trumpet is blown in a city,
will not the people be afraid?
[a]If there is calamity in a city, will
not the LORD have done *it?*

7 Surely the Lord GOD does nothing,
Unless [a]He reveals His secret to His
servants the prophets.
8 A lion has roared!
Who will not fear?
The Lord GOD has spoken!
[a]Who can but prophesy?

Punishment of Israel's Sins

9 "Proclaim in the palaces at [1]Ashdod,
And in the palaces in the land of
Egypt, and say:
'Assemble on the mountains of
Samaria;
See great tumults in her midst,
And the [2]oppressed within her.
10 For they [a]do not know to do
right,'
Says the LORD,
'Who store up violence and [1]robbery
in their palaces.' "

11 Therefore thus says the Lord GOD:

"An adversary *shall be* all around the
land;
He shall sap your strength from
you,
And your palaces shall be
plundered."

12 Thus says the LORD:

"As a shepherd [1]takes from the
mouth of a lion
Two legs or a piece of an ear,
So shall the children of Israel be
taken out
Who dwell in Samaria—
In the corner of a bed and [2]on the
edge of a couch!
13 Hear and testify against the house
of Jacob,"
Says the Lord GOD, the God of
hosts,
14 "That in the day I punish Israel for
their transgressions,
I will also visit *destruction* on the
altars of [a]Bethel;
And the horns of the altar shall be
cut off
And fall to the ground.
15 I will [1]destroy [a]the winter house
along with [b]the summer house;
The [c]houses of ivory shall perish,
And the great houses shall have an
end,"
Says the LORD.

4 Hear this word, you [a]cows of
Bashan, who *are* on the
mountain of Samaria,
Who oppress the [b]poor,
Who crush the needy,
Who say to [1]your husbands, "Bring
wine, let us [c]drink!"
2 [a]The Lord GOD has sworn by His
holiness:
"Behold, the days shall come upon
you
When He will take you away [b]with
fishhooks,
And your posterity with fishhooks.
3 [a]You will go out *through* broken
walls,
Each one straight ahead of her,
And you will [1]be cast into
Harmon,"
Says the LORD.

4 "Come[a] to Bethel and transgress,
At [b]Gilgal multiply transgression;
[c]Bring your sacrifices every
morning,
[d]Your tithes every three [1]days.
5 [a]Offer a sacrifice of thanksgiving
with leaven,
Proclaim *and* announce [b]the
freewill offerings;
For this you love,
You children of Israel!"
Says the Lord GOD.

Israel Did Not Accept Correction

6 "Also I gave you [1]cleanness of teeth
in all your cities.
And lack of bread in all your places;
[a]Yet you have not returned to Me,"
Says the LORD.

7 "I also withheld rain from you,
When *there were* still three months
to the harvest.
I made it rain on one city,
I withheld rain from another city.
One part was rained upon,
And where it did not rain the part
withered.
8 So two *or* three cities wandered to
another city to drink water,
But they were not satisfied;
Yet you have not returned to Me,"
Says the LORD.

6 [a]Is. 45:7 [1]*ram's horn*
7 [a][John 15:15]
8 [a]Acts 4:20
9 [1]So with MT; LXX *Assyria* [2]Or *oppression*
10 [a]Jer. 4:22 [1]Or *devastation*
12 [1]Or *snatches* [2]Heb. uncertain, possibly *on the cover*
14 [a]Amos 4:4
15 [a]Jer. 36:22 [b]Judg. 3:20 [c]1 Kin. 22:39 [1]Lit. *strike*

CHAPTER 4
1 [a]Ps. 22:12 [b]Amos 2:6 [c]Prov. 23:20 [1]Lit. *their masters* or *lords*
2 [a]Ps. 89:35 [b]Jer. 16:16
3 [a]Ezek. 12:5 [1]Or *cast them*
4 [a]Ezek. 20:39 [b]Hos. 4:15 [c]Num. 28:3 [d]Deut. 14:28 [1]Or *years,* Deut. 14:28
5 [a]Lev. 7:13 [b]Lev. 22:18
6 [a]Jer. 5:3 [1]Hunger

9 "I[a] blasted you with blight and
mildew.
When your gardens increased,
Your vineyards,
Your fig trees,
And your olive trees,
[b]The locust devoured *them;*
Yet you have not returned to Me,"
Says the LORD.

10 "I sent among you a plague [a]after
the manner of Egypt;
Your young men I killed with a
sword,
Along with your captive horses;
I made the stench of your camps
come up into your nostrils;
Yet you have not returned to Me,"
Says the LORD.

11 "I overthrew *some* of you,
As God overthrew [a]Sodom and
Gomorrah,
And you were like a firebrand
plucked from the burning;
Yet you have not returned to Me,"
Says the LORD.

12 "Therefore thus will I do to you,
O Israel;
Because I will do this to you,
[a]Prepare to meet your God,
O Israel!"

13 For behold,
He who forms mountains,
And creates the [1]wind,
[a]Who declares to man what [2]his
thought *is,*
And makes the morning darkness,
[b]Who treads the high places of the
earth—
[c]The LORD God of hosts *is* His name.

A Lament for Israel

5 Hear this word which I [a]take up
against you, a lamentation, O house
of Israel:

2 The virgin of Israel has fallen;
She will rise no more.
She lies forsaken on her land;
There is no one to raise her up.

3 For thus says the Lord GOD:

"The city that goes out by a
thousand
Shall have a hundred left,
And that which goes out by a
hundred
Shall have ten left to the house of
Israel."

A Call to Repentance

4 For thus says the LORD to the house of
Israel:

[a]"Seek Me [b]and live;
5 But do not seek [a]Bethel,
Nor enter Gilgal,
Nor pass over to [b]Beersheba;
For Gilgal shall surely go into
captivity,
And [c]Bethel shall come to nothing.
6 [a]Seek the LORD and live,
Lest He break out like fire *in* the
house of Joseph,
And devour *it,*
With no one to quench *it* in
Bethel—
7 You who [a]turn justice to
wormwood,
And lay righteousness to rest in the
earth!"

They never sought in vain that sought the Lord aright.

ROBERT BURNS

8 He made the [a]Pleiades and Orion;
He turns the shadow of death into
morning
[b]And makes the day dark as night;
He [c]calls for the waters of the sea
And pours them out on the face of
the earth;
[d]The LORD *is* His name.
9 He [1]rains ruin upon the strong,
So that fury comes upon the
fortress.

10 [a]They hate the one who rebukes in
the gate,
And they [b]abhor the one who
speaks uprightly.
11 [a]Therefore, because you [1]tread
down the poor
And take grain [2]taxes from him,
Though [b]you have built houses of
hewn stone,

---

9 a Hag. 2:17 b Joel 1:4, 7
10 a Ps. 78:50
11 a Is. 13:19
12 a Jer. 5:22
13 a Ps. 139:2 b Mic. 1:3 c Is. 47:4 *1 Or spirit* *2 Or His*

CHAPTER 5
1 a Jer. 7:29; 9:10, 17
4 a [Jer. 29:13] b [Is. 55:3]
5 a Amos 4:4 b Amos 8:14 c Hos. 4:15
6 a [Is. 55:3, 6, 7]
7 a Amos 6:12
8 a Job 9:9; 38:31 b Ps. 104:20 c Job 38:34 d [Amos 4:13]
9 *1 Or flashes forth destruction*
10 a Is. 29:21; 66:5 b 1 Kin. 22:8
11 a Amos 2:6 b Mic. 6:15 *1 trample* *2 Or tribute*

Yet you shall not dwell in them;
You have planted [3]pleasant vineyards,
But you shall not drink wine from them.
12 For I [a]know your manifold transgressions
And your mighty sins:
[b]Afflicting the just *and* taking bribes;
[c]Diverting the poor *from justice* at the gate.
13 Therefore [a]the prudent keep silent at that time,
For it *is* an evil time.

I pray that ____ will seek good and not evil, that they may live; so You, the Lord God of hosts, will be with them.

FROM AMOS 5:14

14 Seek good and not evil,
That you may live;
So the LORD God of hosts will be with you,
[a]As you have spoken.
15 [a]Hate evil, love good;
Establish justice in the gate.
[b]It may be that the LORD God of hosts
Will be gracious to the remnant of Joseph.

God acts so excellently in us and for us. To hate sin is to hate it as God does.

MADAME JEANNE GUYON

The Day of the Lord

16Therefore the LORD God of hosts, the Lord, says this:

"*There shall be* wailing in all streets,
And they shall say in all the highways,
'Alas! Alas!'
They shall call the farmer to mourning,
[a]And skillful lamenters to wailing.
17 In all vineyards *there shall be* wailing,
For [a]I will pass through you,"
Says the LORD.
18 [a]Woe to you who desire the day of the LORD!
For what good *is* [b]the day of the LORD to you?
It *will be* darkness, and not light.
19 It *will be* [a]as though a man fled from a lion,
And a bear met him!
Or *as though* he went into the house,
Leaned his hand on the wall,
And a serpent bit him!
20 *Is* not the day of the LORD darkness, and not light?
Is it not very dark, with no brightness in it?
21 "I[a] hate, I despise your feast days,
And [b]I do not savor your sacred assemblies.
22 [a]Though you offer Me burnt offerings and your grain offerings,
I will not accept *them,*
Nor will I regard your fattened peace offerings.
23 Take away from Me the noise of your songs,
For I will not hear the melody of your stringed instruments.
24 [a]But let justice run down like water,
And righteousness like a mighty stream.
25 "Did[a] you offer Me sacrifices and offerings
In the wilderness forty years,
O house of Israel?
26 You also carried [1]Sikkuth[2] [a]your king
And Chiun, your idols,
The star of your gods,
Which you made for yourselves.
27 Therefore I will send you into captivity [a]beyond Damascus,"
Says the LORD, [b]whose name *is* the God of hosts.

11 [3] *desirable*
12 [a] Hos. 5:3 [b] Amos 2:6 [c] Is. 29:21
13 [a] Amos 6:10
14 [a] Mic. 3:11
15 [a] Rom. 12:9 [b] Joel 2:14
16 [a] Jer. 9:17
17 [a] Ex. 12:12
18 [a] Is. 5:19 [b] Joel 2:2
19 [a] Jer. 48:44
21 [a] Is. 1:11–16 [b] Lev. 26:31
22 [a] Mic. 6:6, 7
24 [a] Mic. 6:8
25 [a] Deut. 32:17
26 [a] 1 Kin. 11:33 [1] LXX, Vg. *tabernacle of Moloch* [2] A pagan deity
27 [a] 2 Kin. 17:6 [b] Amos 4:13

Amos 5:14, 15, 24

Dear Woman of Destiny,

We'd just turned on to the most gorgeous road in the world—17 Mile Drive in Carmel, California. Opening the windows, we were immediately assaulted by a foul, putrid odor. *These poor people,* I thought. *How can they live with this nauseating smell?* We drove on holding our breath. Suddenly, my husband said, "Honey, that stink may be us." *Impossible,* I thought. *How could it* possibly *be us?*

My husband (who knows all things mechanical) was clueless. After asphyxiating the tourist population of Carmel, we found a station and fearfully opened the hood. It *was* us. The battery was spewing out sulfuric acid fumes. It was ready to blow up any second and could blind anyone standing near.

We desperately needed a good diagnostician, someone who wouldn't mince words. "This is what's wrong, and this is how you fix it. Hurry, there isn't much time!"

In Amos 5, God is the diagnostician, scrubbed and ready for emergency operations. His diagnosis: "You are seeped in idolatry, you disregard the poor, you afflict the just and take bribes." The cure is quick and to the point, "Seek Me and live" (v. 4).

We might dismiss the warning. We think, "Hey, I go to church, I tithe, I pray, I am even on the worship team. This couldn't possibly apply to me!" But when we come to severe passages like this, our hearts must stand at attention and salute. We must listen.

We do have idols. Dostoevsky said, "Man cannot live without worshiping something." We worship at the altar of our own inadequacies. We collapse into the laps of smooth gods of comfort and ease. We loan our eyes happily to the god of entertainment. The muscular god of sport claims our passion and drains our vision. Our gods exhaust us.

We dishonor the poor, and we shy away from urban ghettos. Yet God measures our love for Him by the way we treat them. They are the divine litmus test. Do the poor make a regular appearance in your prayer life? Do you ask God for ways to touch fatherless children in your city? Do you know who they are?

We are apathetic to the appalling injustice of racism. I believe God weeps that Sunday morning is the most segregated hour of the American week. We would do well to weep with Him. We are reeking with sin, and God loves us too much to let us go on smelling.

God comes to cure, with the antidote always being Himself. "Seek Me and live." The phrase thunders repeatedly through Amos 5. It's the four-word cure for everything wrong, everywhere. "Look to Me, and be saved, all you ends of the earth!" Isaiah shouts (Is. 45:22).

How do we seek Him? By esteeming His words (even the difficult ones) more than our necessary food (see Job 23:12); by allowing His Words spacious room in our thought life; by obeying Him. We seek Him like a paleontologist, willing to dig in the hot sun, joyfully looking for the slightest clue about His character and personality. We seek Him, dear one, with confidence, because He said, "And you will seek Me and find Me, when you search for Me with all your heart" (Jer. 29:13).

May you, beloved, be a woman who wholeheartedly seeks God. Life will follow you. That's His promise.

Fawn Parish

Warnings to Zion and Samaria

6 Woe [a]to you *who are* at [b]ease in
Zion,
And [c]trust in Mount Samaria,
Notable persons in the [d]chief
nation,
To whom the house of Israel
comes!
2 [a]Go over to [b]Calneh and see;
And from there go to [c]Hamath the
great;
Then go down to Gath of the
Philistines.
[d]*Are you* better than these
kingdoms?
Or is their territory greater than
your territory?
3 *Woe to* you who [a]put far off the
day of [b]doom,
[c]Who cause [d]the seat of violence to
come near;
4 Who lie on beds of ivory,
Stretch out on your couches,
Eat lambs from the flock
And calves from the midst of the
stall;
5 [a]Who sing idly to the sound of
stringed instruments,
And invent for yourselves [b]musical
instruments [c]like David;
6 Who [a]drink wine from bowls,
And anoint yourselves with the best
ointments,
[b]But are not grieved for the
affliction of Joseph.
7 Therefore they shall now go
[a]captive as the first of the
captives,
And those who recline at banquets
shall be removed.

8 [a]The Lord GOD has sworn by
Himself,
The LORD God of hosts says:
"I abhor [b]the pride of Jacob,
And hate his palaces;
Therefore I will deliver up *the* city
And all that is in it."

9Then it shall come to pass, that if ten
men remain in one house, they shall die.
10And when [1]a relative *of the dead,* with
one who will burn *the bodies,* picks up the
[2]bodies to take them out of the house, he
will say to one inside the house, "*Are
there* any more with you?"
Then someone will say, "None."
And he will say, [a]"Hold your tongue!
[b]For we dare not mention the name of the
LORD."

11 For behold, [a]the LORD gives a
command:
[b]He will break the great house into
bits,
And the little house into pieces.

12 Do horses run on rocks?
Does *one* plow *there* with oxen?
Yet [a]you have turned justice into
gall,
And the fruit of righteousness into
wormwood,
13 You who rejoice over [1]Lo Debar,
Who say, "Have we not taken
[2]Karnaim for ourselves
By our own strength?"

14 "But, behold, [a]I will raise up a
nation against you,
O house of Israel,"
Says the LORD God of hosts;
"And they will afflict you from the
[b]entrance of Hamath
To the Valley of the Arabah."

Vision of the Locusts

7 Thus the Lord GOD showed me: Behold, He formed locust swarms at the
[1]beginning of the late crop; indeed *it was*
the late crop after the king's mowings.
2And so it was, when they had finished
eating the grass of the land, that I said:

"O Lord GOD, forgive, I pray!
[a]Oh,[1] that Jacob may stand,
For he *is* small!"
3 *So* [a]the LORD relented concerning
this.
"It shall not be," said the LORD.

Vision of the Fire

4Thus the Lord GOD showed me: Behold, the Lord GOD called [1]for conflict by
fire, and it consumed the great deep and
devoured the [2]territory. 5Then I said:

"O Lord GOD, cease, I pray!
[a]Oh, that Jacob may stand,
For he *is* small!"
6 *So* the LORD relented concerning
this.
"This also shall not be," said the
Lord GOD.

CHAPTER 6
1 a Luke 6:24 b Zeph. 1:12 c Is. 31:1 d Ex. 19:5
2 a Jer. 2:10 b Is. 10:9 c 2 Kin. 18:34 d Nah. 3:8
3 a Is. 56:12 b Amos 5:18 c Amos 5:12 d Ps. 94:20
5 a Is. 5:12; Amos 5:23 b 1 Chr. 15:16; 16:42 c 1 Chr. 23:5
6 a Amos 2:8; 4:1 b Gen. 37:25
7 a Amos 5:27
8 a Jer. 51:14 b Amos 8:7
10 a Amos 5:13 b Amos 8:3 1 Lit. *his loved one* or *uncle* 2 Lit. *bones*
11 a Is. 55:11 b Amos 3:15
12 a Hos. 10:4
13 1 Lit. *Nothing* 2 Lit. *Horns,* a symbol of strength
14 a Jer. 5:15 b 1 Kin. 8:65

CHAPTER 7
1 1 Lit. *beginning of the sprouting of*
2 a Is. 51:19 1 Or *How shall Jacob stand*
3 a Jon. 3:10
4 1 *to contend* 2 Lit. *portion*
5 a Amos 7:2, 3

Vision of the Plumb Line

7 Thus He showed me: Behold, the Lord
stood on a wall *made* with a plumb line,
with a plumb line in His hand. 8 And the
LORD said to me, "Amos, what do you
see?"

And I said, "A plumb line."
Then the Lord said:

"Behold, [a]I am setting a plumb line
In the midst of My people Israel;
[b]I will not pass by them anymore.
9 [a]The [1]high places of Isaac shall be
desolate,
And the [2]sanctuaries of Israel shall
be laid waste.
[b]I will rise with the sword against
the house of Jeroboam."

Amaziah's Complaint

10 Then Amaziah the [a]priest of [b]Bethel
sent to [c]Jeroboam king of Israel, saying,
"Amos has conspired against you in the
midst of the house of Israel. The land is
not able to [1]bear all his words. 11 For thus
Amos has said:

'Jeroboam shall die by the sword,
And Israel shall surely be led away
[a]captive
From their own land.' "

12 Then Amaziah said to Amos:

"Go, you seer!
Flee to the land of Judah.
There eat bread,
And there prophesy.
13 But [a]never again prophesy at
Bethel,
[b]For it *is* the king's [1]sanctuary,
And it *is* the royal [2]residence."

14 Then Amos answered, and said to Amaziah:

"I *was* no prophet,
Nor *was* I [a]a son of a prophet,
But I *was* a [b]sheepbreeder
And a tender of sycamore fruit.
15 Then the LORD took me [1]as I
followed the flock,
And the LORD said to me,
'Go, [a]prophesy to My people Israel.'
16 Now therefore, hear the word of
the LORD:
You say, 'Do not prophesy against
Israel,
And [a]do not [1]spout against the
house of Isaac.'

8 [a] 2 Kin. 21:13 [b] Mic. 7:18
9 [a] Gen. 46:1 [b] 2 Kin.15:8–10 *1* Places of pagan worship *2* Or *holy places*
10 [a] 1 Kin. 12:31, 32; 13:33 [b] Amos 4:4 [c] 2 Kin. 14:23 *1* Or *endure*
11 [a] Amos 5:27; 6:7
13 [a] Amos 2:12 [b] 1 Kin. 12:29, 32 *1* Or *holy place* *2* Lit. *house*
14 [a] 1 Kin. 20:35 [b] Zech. 13:5
15 [a] Amos 3:8 *1* Lit. *from behind*
16 [a] Ezek. 21:2 *1* Lit. *drip*
17 [a] Jer. 28:12; 29:21, 32 [b] Zech. 14:2 [c] Hos. 9:3

CHAPTER 8
2 [a] Ezek. 7:2 [b] Amos 7:8
3 [a] Amos 5:23 [b] Amos 6:9, 10
4 *1* Or *trample on,* Amos 2:7
5 [a] Neh. 13:15 [b] Mic. 6:10, 11 [c] Lev. 19:35, 36 *1* Lit. *open*
6 [a] Amos 2:6
7 [a] Amos 6:8 [b] Hos. 7:2; 8:13
8 [a] Hos. 4:3 [b] Amos 9:5 *1* The Nile; some Heb. mss., LXX, Tg., Syr., Vg. *River* (cf. 9:5); MT *the light*

17 "Therefore[a] thus says the LORD:

[b]'Your wife shall be a harlot in the
city;
Your sons and daughters shall fall
by the sword;
Your land shall be divided by *survey*
line;
You shall die in a [c]defiled land;
And Israel shall surely be led away
captive
From his own land.' "

Vision of the Summer Fruit

8 Thus the Lord GOD showed me: Be-
hold, a basket of summer fruit. 2 And
He said, "Amos, what do you see?"
So I said, "A basket of summer fruit."
Then the LORD said to me:

[a]"The end has come upon My people
Israel;
[b]I will not pass by them anymore.
3 And [a]the songs of the temple
Shall be wailing in that day,"
Says the Lord GOD—
"Many dead bodies everywhere,
[b]They shall be thrown out in
silence."

4 Hear this, you who [1]swallow up
the needy,
And make the poor of the land fail,

5 Saying:

"When will the New Moon be past,
That we may sell grain?
And [a]the Sabbath,
That we may [1]trade wheat?
[b]Making the ephah small and the
shekel large,
Falsifying the scales by [c]deceit,
6 That we may buy the poor for
[a]silver,
And the needy for a pair of
sandals—
Even sell the bad wheat?"

7 The LORD has sworn by [a]the pride
of Jacob:
"Surely [b]I will never forget any of
their works.
8 [a]Shall the land not tremble for this,
And everyone mourn who dwells in
it?
All of it shall swell like [1]the River,
Heave and subside
[b]Like the River of Egypt.

9 "And it shall come to pass in that
day," says the Lord GOD,
[a]"That I will make the sun go down
at noon,
And I will darken the earth in
[1]broad daylight;
10 I will turn your feasts into
[a]mourning,
[b]And all your songs into
lamentation;
[c]I will bring sackcloth on every
waist,
And baldness on every head;
I will make it like mourning for an
only *son,*
And its end like a bitter day.

11 "Behold, the days are coming," says
the Lord GOD,
"That I will send a famine on the
land,
Not a famine of bread,
Nor a thirst for water,
But [a]of hearing the words of the
LORD.
12 They shall wander from sea to sea,
And from north to east;
They shall run to and fro, seeking
the word of the LORD,
But shall [a]not find *it.*

13 "In that day the fair virgins
And strong young men
Shall faint from thirst.
14 Those who [a]swear by [b]the [1]sin of
Samaria,
Who say,
'As your god lives, O Dan!'
And, 'As the way of [c]Beersheba
lives!'
They shall fall and never rise
again."

The Destruction of Israel

9 I saw the Lord standing by the altar,
and He said:

"Strike the [1]doorposts, that the
thresholds may shake,
And [a]break them on the heads of
them all.
I will slay the last of them with the
sword.
[b]He who flees from them shall not
get away,
And he who escapes from them
shall not be delivered.

2 "Though[a] they dig into [1]hell,
From there My hand shall take
them;
[b]Though they climb up to heaven,
From there I will bring them down;
3 And though they [a]hide themselves
on top of Carmel,
From there I will search and take
them;
Though they hide from My sight at
the bottom of the sea,
From there I will command the
serpent, and it shall bite them;
4 Though they go into captivity
before their enemies,
From there [a]I will command the
sword,
And it shall slay them.
[b]I will set My eyes on them for harm
and not for good."

The more my Lord prolongs His stay
The more my duty is to pray
And watch and labor on.

CHARLES WESLEY

5 The Lord GOD of hosts,
He who touches the earth and it
[a]melts,
[b]And all who dwell there mourn;
All of it shall swell like [1]the River,
And subside like the River of Egypt.
6 He who builds His [a]layers[1] in the
sky,
And has founded His strata in the
earth;
Who [b]calls for the waters of the
sea,
And pours them out on the face of
the earth—
[c]The LORD *is* His name.

7 "*Are* you not like the [1]people of
Ethiopia to Me,
O children of Israel?" says the
LORD.
"Did I not bring up Israel from the
land of Egypt,
The [a]Philistines from [b]Caphtor,[2]
And the Syrians from [c]Kir?

8:9 a Job 5:14 *1* Lit. *a day of light*
10 a Ezek. 7:18 b Ezek. 27:31 c [Zech. 12:10]
11 a Ezek. 7:26
12 a Hos. 5:6
14 a Hos. 4:15 b Deut. 9:21 c Amos 5:5 *1* Or *Ashima,* a Syrian goddess

CHAPTER 9
1 a Hab. 3:13 b Amos 2:14 *1* Capitals of the pillars
2 a Ps. 139:8 b Jer. 51:53 *1* Or *Sheol*
3 a Jer. 23:24
4 a Lev. 26:33 b Jer. 21:10; 39:16; 44:11
5 a Mic. 1:4 b Amos 8:8 *1* The Nile
6 a Ps. 104:3, 13 b Amos 5:8 c Amos 4:13; 5:27 *1* Or *stairs*
7 a Jer. 47:4 b Deut. 2:23 c Amos 1:5 *1* Lit. *sons of the Ethiopians* *2* Crete

8 "Behold, [a]the eyes of the Lord GOD
are on the sinful kingdom,
And I [b]will destroy it from the face
of the earth;
Yet I will not utterly destroy the
house of Jacob,"
Says the LORD.

9 "For surely I will command,
And will [1]sift the house of Israel
among all nations,
As *grain* is sifted in a sieve;
[a]Yet not the smallest [2]grain shall fall
to the ground.
10 All the sinners of My people shall
die by the sword,
[a]Who say, 'The calamity shall not
overtake nor confront us.'

Israel Will Be Restored

11 "On[a] that day I will raise up
The [1]tabernacle of David, which has
fallen down,
And [2]repair its damages;
I will raise up its ruins,
And rebuild it as in the days of old;
12 [a]That they may possess the
remnant of [b]Edom,[1]
And all the Gentiles who are called
by My name,"
Says the LORD who does this thing.

13 "Behold, [a]the days are coming,"
says the LORD,
"When the plowman shall overtake
the reaper,
And the treader of grapes him who
sows seed;
[b]The mountains shall drip with
sweet wine,
And all the hills shall flow *with it.*
14 [a]I will bring back the captives of
My people Israel;
[b]They shall build the waste cities
and inhabit *them;*
They shall plant vineyards and
drink wine from them;
They shall also make gardens and
eat fruit from them.
15 I will plant them in their land,
[a]And no longer shall they be pulled
up
From the land I have given them,"
Says the LORD your God.

8 [a] Amos 9:4 [b] Jer. 5:10; 30:11
9 [a] [Is. 65:8–16] [1] *shake* [2] Lit. *pebble*
10 [a] Amos 6:3
11 [a] Acts 15:16–18 [1] Lit. *booth;* a figure of a deposed dynasty [2] Lit. *wall up its breaches*
12 [a] Obad. 19 [b] Num. 24:18 [1] LXX *mankind*
13 [a] Lev. 26:5 [b] Joel 3:18
14 [a] Jer. 30:3, 18 [b] Is. 61:4
15 [a] Ezek. 34:28; 37:25

AUTHOR: *Obadiah*
DATE: *Shortly After 586 B.C.*
THEME: *God's Judgment on Edom*
KEY WORDS: *Day, Day of the Lord*

OBADIAH

Dear Woman of Destiny,

It's so good to know Yahweh is for us! In Obadiah, God deals with the pride and cruelty of Israel's enemies and rises in defense of His people. When the enemy rises against you, take heart. The God of all creation will be your protection and will preserve your destiny. As you read and pray, meditate on His outstanding faithfulness.

His love and mine,

Marilyn Hickey

The Coming Judgment on Edom

1 The vision of Obadiah.

Thus says the Lord GOD
[a]concerning Edom
[b](We have heard a report from the LORD,
And a messenger has been sent among the nations, *saying,*
"Arise, and let us rise up against her for battle"):

2 "Behold, I will make you small among the nations;
You shall be greatly despised.
3 The [a]pride of your heart has deceived you,
You who dwell in the clefts of the rock,
Whose habitation is high;
[b]*You* who say in your heart, 'Who will bring me down to the ground?'
4 [a]Though you ascend *as* high as the eagle,
And though you [b]set your nest among the stars,
From there I will bring you down,"
says the LORD.

Father, keep pride far from the heart of ___ that they would not be deceived.

FROM OBADIAH 3

5 "If [a]thieves had come to you,
If robbers by night—
Oh, how you will be cut off!—
Would they not have stolen till they had enough?
If grape-gatherers had come to you,
[b]Would they not have left *some* gleanings?

6 "Oh, how Esau shall be searched out!
How his hidden treasures shall be sought after!
7 All the men in your confederacy
Shall force you to the border;
[a]The men at peace with you
Shall deceive you *and* prevail against you.
Those who eat your bread shall lay a [1]trap for you.
[b]No[2] one is aware of it.
8 "Will[a] I not in that day," says the LORD,
"Even destroy the wise *men* from Edom,
And understanding from the mountains of Esau?
9 Then your [a]mighty men,
O [b]Teman, shall be dismayed,
To the end that everyone from the mountains of Esau
May be cut off by slaughter.

Stop beholding your business . . . pleasure . . . neighbors . . . earthly cares and duties. Whatever thing may be absorbing your attention, stop beholding that thing, and instead, behold, the Man!

AIMEE SEMPLE MCPHERSON

Edom Mistreated His Brother

10 "For [a]violence against your brother Jacob,
Shame shall cover you,
And [b]you shall be cut off forever.
11 In the day that you [a]stood on the other side—
In the day that strangers carried captive his forces,
When foreigners entered his gates
And [b]cast lots for Jerusalem—
Even you *were* as one of them.

12 "But you should not have [a]gazed[1] on the day of your brother
[2]In the day of his captivity;
Nor should you have [b]rejoiced over the children of Judah
In the day of their destruction;
Nor should you have spoken proudly
In the day of distress.

1 a Is. 21:11 b Jer. 49:14–16
3 a Jer. 49:16 b Rev. 18:7
4 a Job 20:6 b Hab. 2:9
5 a Jer. 49:9 b Deut. 24:21
7 a Jer. 38:22 b Is. 19:11 *1* Or *wound* or *plot* *2* Or *There is no understanding in him*
8 a [Job 5:12–14]
9 a Ps. 76:5 b Jer. 49:7
10 a Gen. 27:41 b Ezek. 35:9
11 a Ps. 83:5–8 b Nah. 3:10
12 a Mic. 4:11; 7:10 b [Prov. 17:5] *1* Gloated over *2* Lit. *On the day he became a foreigner*

Obadiah 3, 4

Dear Woman of Destiny,

Several years ago a tragedy happened. A talented pastor with a church of more than four thousand people swapped his moral authority for an adulterous relationship. Those who loved him were speechless as they tried to hold together the fragile, shattered pieces of his success.

The pastors in that city prayed and wondered how God would have them respond. They wrote a letter to the congregation. They said, "We love you; we're praying for you. We don't want to profit from your calamity. We don't want to increase our congregations at your expense. Please stay together and believe God will bring good out of this." A similar letter was sent to the editor of the city newspaper.

The pastors could have said, "That church sprung up overnight. We lost a lot of our congregation when they came to town. God was simply judging their pride." The pastors could have salivated over the spoils other churches would inherit—talented people, sound-systems, chairs, church facility items that would be on the cheap—if the church folded.

Instead of gloating, the pastors adopted the heart of God. They spent themselves in prayer for the congregation, they felt the grief of God, and covenanted together to see God restore the church under new leadership.

In Obadiah, God is judging the Edomites for their pride in adopting a spectator status while their brothers were being destroyed in front of them. Instead of rushing to help, the Edomites greedily eyed the spoil. They "made big their mouth" (literal translation of v. 12). They even handed over some of the Judeans who were trying to flee to the Babylonians.

Obadiah teaches us an important lesson in the fascinating character and personality of God. Even when God declares judgment on His people by captivity, He judges the oppressor's attitudes, as well as those of the people who stand and watch. We are not to be people of retribution, but people who reconcile and restore. We are not allowed to wrap our righteous robes about ourselves, to stand aloof, and to gloat about pigpen histories like the prodigal son's older brother.

I once walked into the house of a man watching a special on AIDS. He was well respected in the Christian community. He prided himself on the famous leaders he knew and hung their pictures conspicuously in his den. He said to me with great excitement, "Just think, Fawn, this virus seems to attack mainly homosexuals. Isn't that great?" I was aghast. He was clueless as to how his speech betrayed him.

A pastor was discussing with his elder board someone who had fallen into sin. The pastor canvassed each of the members: "Are you capable of ever committing a sin like this?" One after another they vehemently denied they could do something so disgraceful. Then the last elder spoke. "You know, if I were tired enough, and if the temptation came in just the right package, yes, I think I am definitely capable of doing that sin." The pastor said solemnly, "Then you are the one who can restore him." That elder understood that each of us is capable of the most heinous of sins.

May you, loved one, be known as a restorer and reconciler who rushes to aid those under judgment. And may your tribe increase.

Fawn Parish

13 You should not have entered the
gate of My people
In the day of their calamity.
Indeed, you should not have [1]gazed
on their affliction
In the day of their calamity,
Nor laid *hands* on their substance
In the day of their calamity.
14 You should not have stood at the
crossroads
To cut off those among them who
escaped;
Nor should you have [1]delivered up
those among them who remained
In the day of distress.

15 "For[a] the day of the LORD upon all
the nations *is* near;
[b]As you have done, it shall be done
to you;
Your [1]reprisal shall return upon
your own head.
16 [a]For as you drank on My holy
mountain,
So shall all the nations drink
continually;
Yes, they shall drink, and swallow,
And they shall be as though they
had never been.

Israel's Final Triumph

17 "But on Mount Zion there [a]shall be
[1]deliverance,
And there shall be holiness;
The house of Jacob shall possess
their possessions.
18 The house of Jacob shall be a fire,
And the house of Joseph [a]a flame;
But the house of Esau *shall be*
stubble;
They shall kindle them and devour
them,
And no survivor shall *remain* of the
house of Esau,"
For the LORD has spoken.

19 The [1]South [a]shall possess the
mountains of Esau,
[b]And the Lowland shall possess
Philistia.
They shall possess the fields of
Ephraim
And the fields of Samaria.
Benjamin *shall possess* Gilead.
20 And the captives of this host of
the children of Israel
Shall possess the land of the
Canaanites
As [a]far as Zarephath.
The captives of Jerusalem who are
in Sepharad
[b]Shall possess the cities of the
[1]South.
21 Then [a]saviors[1] shall come to
Mount Zion
To judge the mountains of Esau,
And the [b]kingdom shall be the
LORD's.

13 [1] Gloated over
14 [1] Handed over to the enemy
15 [a] Ezek. 30:3 [b] Hab. 2:8 [1] Or *reward*
16 [a] Joel 3:17
17 [a] Amos 9:8 [1] Or *salvation*
18 [a] Zech. 12:6
19 [a] Is. 11:14 [b] Zeph. 2:7 [1] Heb. *Negev*
20 [a] 1 Kin. 17:9 [b] Jer. 32:44 [1] Heb. *Negev*
21 [a] [James 5:20] [b] [Rev. 11:15] [1] *deliverers*

AUTHOR: *Jonah or Narrator*
DATE: *Approximately 760 B.C. or After 612 B.C.*
THEME: *God's Compassion for Everyone*
KEY WORDS: *Arise, Prepared, Relent*

JONAH

Dear Woman of Destiny,

At the heart of the Book of Jonah lies the revelation of the rich, enduring mercy of God. Jonah was the prophet called to speak against Nineveh, but he ran from God and ultimately despised God's mercy for the Ninevites. Then, as today, God required not only obedience, but compassion for others. Read on with joy as this book illustrates the power of resurrection and brings our focus to the great commission "to preach the gospel to every creature."

His love and mine,

Marilyn Hickey

Jonah's Disobedience

Now the word of the LORD came to
[a]Jonah the son of Amittai, saying,
2"Arise, go to [a]Nineveh, that
[b]great city, and cry out against it; for
[c]their wickedness has come up before
Me." 3But Jonah arose to flee to Tarshish
from the presence of the LORD. He went
down to [a]Joppa, and found a ship going to
Tarshish; so he paid the fare, and went
down into it, to go with them to [b]Tarshish
[c]from the presence of the LORD.

The Storm at Sea

4But [a]the LORD [1]sent out a great wind
on the sea, and there was a mighty tempest on the sea, so that the ship was about
to be broken up.
5Then the mariners were afraid; and every man cried out to his god, and threw

CHAPTER 1
1 a 2 Kin. 14:25
2 a Is. 37:37
b Gen. 10:11, 12
c Gen. 18:20
3 a Josh. 19:46
b Is. 23:1
c Gen. 4:16
4 a Ps. 107:25
1 Lit. *hurled*

AIMEE SEMPLE MCPHERSON

With Maria Woodworth-Etter before her and Kathryn Kuhlman behind her, it seems that Aimee Semple McPherson (1890–1944) received the mantle of a powerful miracle ministry from Maria and passed it on to Kathryn. Aimee became a Christian at age 17 while attending services of evangelist Robert Semple. She and Robert married a year later and immediately started traveling and preaching. In 1910, they sailed to Hong Kong to minister among the Chinese people. Two months later, Robert died of malaria, leaving Aimee a widow in a foreign land.

After she later married Harold McPherson, Aimee began to sense God speaking to her, "Preach the Word! Will you go?" The call burned in her heart, but seemed impossible to answer because women were not allowed to preach at that time. The longer she waited, the more she felt like Jonah—running from God.

She finally began preaching in 1915 and became a national phenomenon. Her ministry was characterized by passionate evangelism and was known for miraculous healings. Her radical commitment to seeing sinners saved took her to witness in nightclubs and dance halls and led her to befriend prostitutes, alcoholics, and outcasts for the purpose of sharing Jesus.

Aimee attained Hollywood-like star status and, with it, a Hollywood-like life. She endured several unpleasant incidents: two divorces, betrayal by friends and by her own mother, and her mysterious apparent kidnapping in 1926. Despite the turmoil, Aimee continued to break new ground for the cause of Jesus Christ. She built Angeles Temple and, in 1923, founded the International Church of the Foursquare Gospel. She also started the world's first Christian radio station. Often accused of being too flamboyant and dramatic in her church services, Aimee refused to stop short of using every possible means to bring people to salvation.

May God raise up in our generation a company of women like Maria Woodworth-Etter, Aimee Semple McPherson, and Kathryn Kuhlman. May we, too, be known for our passion to see salvations increase and miracles abound. And may we walk in the powerful anointing of the sisters who have gone before us.

the cargo that *was* in the ship into the sea,
to lighten [1]the load. But Jonah had gone
down [a]into the lowest parts of the ship,
had lain down, and was fast asleep.
6So the captain came to him, and said
to him, "What do you mean, sleeper?
Arise, [a]call on your God; [b]perhaps your
God will consider us, so that we may not
perish."
7And they said to one another, "Come,
let us [a]cast lots, that we may know for
whose cause this trouble *has come* upon
us." So they cast lots, and the lot fell on
Jonah. 8Then they said to him, [a]"Please
tell us! For whose cause *is* this trouble
upon us? What is your occupation? And
where do you come from? What is your
country? And of what people are you?"
9So he said to them, "I *am* a Hebrew;
and I fear [1]the LORD, the God of heaven,
[a]who made the sea and the dry *land*."

Jonah Thrown into the Sea

10Then the men were exceedingly
afraid, and said to him, "Why have you
done this?" For the men knew that he fled
from the presence of the LORD, because he
had told them. 11Then they said to him,
"What shall we do to you that the sea may
be calm for us?"—for the sea was growing
more tempestuous.
12And he said to them, [a]"Pick me up
and [1]throw me into the sea; then the sea
will become calm for you. For I know that
this great tempest *is* because of me."
13Nevertheless the men rowed hard to
return to land, [a]but they could not, for
the sea continued to grow more tempestuous against them. 14Therefore they
cried out to the LORD and said, "We pray,
O LORD, please do not let us perish for
this man's life, and [a]do not charge us with
innocent blood; for You, O LORD, [b]have
done as it pleased You." 15So they picked
up Jonah and threw him into the sea,
[a]and the sea ceased from its raging.
16Then the men [a]feared the LORD exceedingly, and offered a sacrifice to the LORD
and took vows.

Jonah's Prayer and Deliverance

17Now the LORD had prepared a great
fish to swallow Jonah. And [a]Jonah was in
the belly of the fish three days and three
nights.

2 Then Jonah prayed to the LORD his
God from the fish's belly. 2And he
said:

"I [a]cried out to the LORD because of
my affliction,
[b]And He answered me.

"Out of the belly of Sheol I cried,
And You heard my voice.
3 [a]For You cast me into the deep,
Into the heart of the seas,
And the floods surrounded me;
[b]All Your billows and Your waves
passed over me.
4 [a]Then I said, 'I have been cast out
of Your sight;
Yet I will look again [b]toward Your
holy temple.'
5 The [a]waters surrounded me, *even*
to my soul;
The deep closed around me;
Weeds were wrapped around my
head.
6 I went down to the [1]moorings of
the mountains;
The earth with its bars *closed*
behind me forever;
Yet You have brought up my [a]life
from the pit,
O LORD, my God.

As soon as you know your sins are forgiven, be sure that you make your "back-tracks" as clean and straight as possible . . . get the love of God into your heart.

AIMEE SEMPLE MCPHERSON

7 "When my soul fainted within me,
I remembered the LORD;
[a]And my prayer went *up* to You,
Into Your holy temple.
8 "Those who regard [a]worthless idols
Forsake their own [1]Mercy.
9 But I will [a]sacrifice to You
With the voice of thanksgiving;

5 [a]1 Sam. 24:3 [1]Lit. *from upon them*
6 [a]Ps. 107:28 [b]Joel 2:14
7 [a]Josh. 7:14
8 [a]Josh. 7:19
9 [a][Neh. 9:6] [1]Heb. *YHWH*
12 [a]John 11:50 [1]Lit. *hurl*
13 [a][Prov. 21:30]
14 [a]Deut. 21:8 [b]Ps. 115:3
15 [a][Ps. 89:9; 107:29]
16 [a]Acts 5:11
17 [a][Matt. 12:40]

CHAPTER 2
2 [a]Ps. 120:1 [b]Ps. 65:2
3 [a]Ps. 88:6 [b]Ps. 42:7
4 [a]Ps. 31:22 [b]1 Kin. 8:38
5 [a]Lam. 3:54
6 [a][Ps. 16:10] [1]*foundations* or *bases*
7 [a]Ps. 18:6
8 [a]Jer. 10:8 [1]Or *Lovingkindness*
9 [a]Hos. 14:2

Jonah 3:10

Dear Woman of Destiny,

As we visit the childhood Bible story of Jonah and the great fish, let's view the prophet Jonah from an alternate adult perspective. Jonah was a Jew and a loyal lover of Israel; a patriot who was also a prophet—the only prophet sent to preach to the Gentiles. The Ninevites were Assyrians (Gentiles) and noted enemies of Israel. How could it be that the God of Israel would ask him, a Jew, to deliver a message with a conditional promise of mercy to a Gentile city immersed in sin? The manifold grace of God is uniquely revealed in the Book of Jonah.

"Now the word of the LORD came to Jonah the son of Amittai, saying, 'Arise, go to Nineveh, that great city, and cry out against it; for their wickedness has come up before Me'" (Jon. 1:1, 2). Jonah was clearly chosen for a specific task—one he could not agree with, because his mind-set was that forgiveness for the Ninevites meant for them to attack his beloved Israel. He simply could not trust God with the outcome, so he fled. Can you relate to this? I can. There have been times in my life when I have been tempted to reject a godly directive because I feared what I perceived the result would look like. God, with His infinite love and wisdom, provided a way of escape in spite of Jonah's willful disobedience.

Now the Lord had prepared a great fish to swallow Jonah. Those three days and nights in the fish's belly captured Jonah's full attention. He began to cry out prayers of repentance, thanksgiving, and rededication. So the Lord, the One in control of Jonah's circumstances, delivered him from himself once again.

When the word of the Lord came to Jonah the second time to arise and go to Nineveh, he went. Godly discipline from a loving father yields good fruit. The anointing was strong on this vessel who was reluctant to be obedient, but God used Jonah in spite of himself. Sound familiar? Praise God that the Word tells us the gifts and callings are irrevocable! The Holy Spirit did not cease His work. He continued to intervene in Jonah's life until God's will was fulfilled. God is the same today as yesterday. He wants to do this for us!

Jonah delivered the prophetic mandate, and the anointing broke the yoke of sin over Nineveh. Within a matter of days, the entire city responded to God's charge of repentance from the greatest to the least of them. Overcoming victory for an entire city came through the anointing that was released when one prophet surrendered his opinion and obeyed.

Nineveh is a divine paradox. The prophet of God with his belief system and strong will was unwilling to obey God, whereas the ungodly Assyrians were quick to repent and turn from their wicked ways. Jonah 3:10 says, "Then God saw . . . God relented . . . and He did not do it." The Lord's mercy triumphed over judgment; and where sin had abounded in Jonah and in Nineveh, grace abounded more!

Jill Griffith

I will pay what I have [b]vowed.
[c]Salvation *is* of the [d]LORD."

10 So the LORD spoke to the fish, and it
vomited Jonah onto dry *land*.

When the soul of ____
faints within her, may she
remember You, O Lord; may
she lift her prayer to You.

FROM JONAH 2:7

Jonah Preaches at Nineveh

3 Now the word of the LORD came to
Jonah the second time, saying,
2 "Arise, go to Nineveh, that great city, and
preach to it the message that I tell you."
3 So Jonah arose and went to Nineveh, according to the word of the LORD. Now
Nineveh was an exceedingly great city, [1]a
three-day journey *in extent*. 4 And Jonah
began to enter the city on the first day's
walk. Then [a]he cried out and said, "Yet
forty days, and Nineveh shall be overthrown!"

The People of Nineveh Believe

5 So the [a]people of Nineveh believed
God, proclaimed a fast, and put on sackcloth, from the greatest to the least of
them. 6 Then word came to the king of
Nineveh; and he arose from his throne
and laid aside his robe, covered *himself*
with sackcloth [a]and sat in ashes. 7 [a]And he
caused *it* to be proclaimed and published
throughout Nineveh by the decree of the
king and his [1]nobles, saying,

> Let neither man nor beast, herd
> nor flock, taste anything; do not let
> them eat, or drink water. 8 But let
> man and beast be covered with
> sackcloth, and cry mightily to God;
> yes, [a]let every one turn from his
> evil way and from [b]the violence
> that is in his hands. 9 [a]Who can tell
> *if* God will turn and relent, and
> turn away from His fierce anger, so
> that we may not perish?

10 [a]Then God saw their works, that
they turned from their evil way; and God
relented from the disaster that He had
said He would bring upon them, and He
did not do it.

Jonah's Anger and God's Kindness

4 But it displeased Jonah exceedingly,
and he became angry. 2 So he prayed
to the LORD, and said, "Ah, LORD, was not
this what I said when I was still in my
country? Therefore I [a]fled previously to
Tarshish; for I know that You *are* a [b]gra-
cious and merciful God, slow to anger and
abundant in lovingkindness, One who relents from doing harm. 3 [a]Therefore now,
O LORD, please take my life from me, for
[b]*it is* better for me to die than to live!"
4 Then the LORD said, "*Is it* right for you
to be angry?"
5 So Jonah went out of the city and sat
on the east side of the city. There he made
himself a shelter and sat under it in the
shade, till he might see what would become of the city. 6 And the LORD God prepared a [1]plant and made it come up over
Jonah, that it might be shade for his head
to deliver him from his misery. So Jonah
[2]was very grateful for the plant. 7 But as
morning dawned the next day God prepared a worm, and it *so* damaged the plant
that it withered. 8 And it happened, when
the sun arose, that God prepared a vehement east wind; and the sun beat on Jonah's head, so that he grew faint. Then he
wished death for himself, and said, [a]"*It is*
better for me to die than to live."
9 Then God said to Jonah, "*Is it* right for
you to be angry about the plant?"
And he said, "*It is* right for me to be
angry, even to death!"
10 But the LORD said, "You have had pity
on the plant for which you have not labored, nor made it grow, which [1]came up
in a night and perished in a night. 11 And
should I not pity Nineveh, [a]that great city,
in which are more than one hundred and
twenty thousand persons [b]who cannot
discern between their right hand and
their left—and much livestock?"

---

9 b [Eccl. 5:4, 5] c Ps. 3:8 d [Jer. 3:23]

CHAPTER 3

3 *1* Exact meaning unknown
4 a [Deut. 18:22]
5 a [Matt. 12:41]
6 a Job 2:8
7 a 2 Chr. 20:3 *1* Lit. *great ones*
8 a Is. 58:6 b Is. 59:6
9 a Joel 2:14
10 a Jer. 18:8

CHAPTER 4

2 a Jon. 1:3 b Joel 2:13
3 a 1 Kin. 19:4 b Jon. 4:8
6 *1* Heb. *kikayon,* exact identity unknown *2* Lit. *rejoiced with great joy*
8 a Jon. 4:3
10 *1* Lit. *was a son of a night*
11 a Jon. 1:2; 3:2, 3 b Deut. 1:39

AUTHOR: *Micah*
DATE: *704–696 B.C.*
THEME: *Incomparability of the Compassionate Lord*
KEY WORDS: *Sin, Daughter of Zion, Remnant, Compassion*

MICAH

Dear Woman of Destiny,

This book is a compilation of Micah's sermons and deals with the moral, civil, and economic situations of his time. Micah warned of God's judgment against sin and offered the hope of the coming Deliverer who would restore not only Israel, but all mankind. It is good to know that in every situation, God has a plan to bring restoration to your present situation and hope to your future. Woman of Destiny, press in to the rich goodness of God day by day.

His love and mine,

Marilyn Hickey

The word of the LORD that came to [a]Micah of Moresheth in the days of [b]Jotham, Ahaz, *and* Hezekiah, kings of Judah, which he saw concerning Samaria and Jerusalem.

The Coming Judgment on Israel

2 Hear, all you peoples!
Listen, O earth, and all that is in it!
Let the Lord GOD be a witness
against you,
The Lord from [a]His holy temple.

3 For behold, the LORD is coming
out of His place;
He will come down
And tread on the high places of the
earth.
4 [a]The mountains will melt under
Him,
And the valleys will split
Like wax before the fire,
Like waters poured down a steep
place.
5 All this is for the transgression of
Jacob
And for the sins of the house of
Israel.
What *is* the transgression of Jacob?
Is it not Samaria?
And what *are* the [a]high places of
Judah?
Are they not Jerusalem?

6 "Therefore I will make Samaria [a]a
heap of ruins in the field,
Places for planting a vineyard;
I will pour down her stones into
the valley,
And I will [b]uncover her
foundations.
7 All her carved images shall be
beaten to pieces,
And all her [a]pay as a harlot shall be
burned with the fire;
All her idols I will lay desolate,
For she gathered *it* from the pay of
a harlot,
And they shall return to the [b]pay of
a harlot."

Mourning for Israel and Judah

8 Therefore I will wail and howl,
I will go stripped and naked;
[a]I will make a wailing like the
jackals
And a mourning like the ostriches,
9 For her wounds *are* incurable.
For [a]it has come to Judah;
It has come to the gate of My
people—
To Jerusalem.

10 [a]Tell *it* not in Gath,
Weep not at all;
In [1]Beth Aphrah
Roll yourself in the dust.
11 Pass by in naked shame, you
inhabitant of [1]Shaphir;
The inhabitant of [2]Zaanan does not
go out.
Beth Ezel mourns;
Its place to stand is taken away
from you.

12 For the inhabitant of [1]Maroth
[2]pined for good,
But [a]disaster came down from the
LORD
To the gate of Jerusalem.
13 O inhabitant of [a]Lachish,
Harness the chariot to the swift
steeds
(She *was* the beginning of sin to
the daughter of Zion),
For the transgressions of Israel
were [b]found in you.

14 Therefore you shall [a]give presents
to [1]Moresheth Gath;
The houses of [b]Achzib[2] *shall be* a
lie to the kings of Israel.
15 I will yet bring an heir to you,
O inhabitant of [a]Mareshah;[1]
The glory of Israel shall come to
[b]Adullam.[2]
16 Make yourself [a]bald and cut off
your hair,
Because of your [b]precious children;
Enlarge your baldness like an eagle,
For they shall go from you into
[c]captivity.

Woe to Evildoers

2 Woe to those who devise iniquity,
And [1]work out evil on their beds!
At [a]morning light they practice it,
Because it is in the power of their
hand.
2 They [a]covet fields and take *them*
by violence,
Also houses, and seize *them*.
So they oppress a man and his
house,
A man and his inheritance.

CHAPTER 1
1 [a]Jer. 26:18 [b]Is. 1:1
2 [a][Ps. 11:4]
4 [a]Amos 9:5
5 [a]Deut. 32:13; 33:29
6 [a]2 Kin. 19:25 [b]Ezek. 13:14
7 [a]Hos. 2:5 [b]Deut. 23:18
8 [a]Ps. 102:6
9 [a]2 Kin. 18:13
10 [a]2 Sam. 1:20 [1]Lit. *House of Dust*
11 [1]Lit. *Beautiful* [2]Lit. *Going Out*
12 [a]Is. 59:9–11 [1]Lit. *Bitterness* [2]Lit. *was sick*
13 [a]Is. 36:2 [b]Ezek. 23:11
14 [a]2 Sam. 8:2 [b]Josh. 15:44 [1]Lit. *Possession of Gath* [2]Lit. *Lie*
15 [a]Josh. 15:44 [b]2 Chr. 11:7 [1]Lit. *Inheritance* [2]Lit. *Refuge*
16 [a]Job 1:20 [b]Lam. 4:5 [c]Amos 7:11, 17

CHAPTER 2
1 [a]Hos. 7:6, 7 [1]Plan
2 [a]Is. 5:8

3 Therefore thus says the LORD:

"Behold, against this [a]family I am
devising [b]disaster,
From which you cannot remove
your necks;
Nor shall you walk haughtily,
For this *is* an evil time.
4 In that day *one* shall take up a
proverb against you,
And [a]lament with a bitter
lamentation, saying:
'We are utterly destroyed!
He has changed the [1]heritage of my
people;
How He has removed *it* from me!
To [2]a turncoat He has divided our
fields.' "

5 Therefore you will have no [1]one to
determine boundaries by lot
In the assembly of the LORD.

Lying Prophets

6 "Do not prattle," *you say to those*
who [1]prophesy.
So they shall not prophesy [2]to you;
[3]They shall not return insult for
insult.
7 *You who are* named the house of
Jacob:
"Is the Spirit of the LORD restricted?
Are these His doings?
Do not My words do good
To him who walks uprightly?

8 "Lately My people have risen up as
an enemy—
You pull off the robe with the
garment
From those who trust *you,* as they
pass by,
Like men returned from war.
9 The women of My people you cast
out
From their pleasant houses;
From their children
You have taken away My glory
forever.

10 "Arise and depart,
For this *is* not *your* [a]rest;
Because it is [b]defiled, it shall
destroy,
Yes, with utter destruction.
11 If a man should walk in a false
spirit
And speak a lie, *saying,*
'I will [1]prophesy to you [2]of wine
and drink,'

3 a Jer. 8:3
b Amos 5:13

4 a 2 Sam. 1:17
1 Lit. *portion*
2 Lit. *one turning back,* an apostate

5 1 Lit. *one casting a surveyor's line*

6 1 Or *preach,* lit. *drip* words
2 Lit. *to these*
3 Vg. *He shall not take shame*

10 a Deut. 12:9
b Lev. 18:25

11 a Is. 30:10
1 Or *preach,* lit. *drip*
2 *concerning*

12 a [Mic. 4:6, 7]
b Jer. 31:10
c Ezek. 33:22; 36:37
1 Heb. *Bozrah*

13 a [Hos. 3:5]
b Is. 52:12

CHAPTER 3
1 a Ezek. 22:27
b Jer. 5:4, 5

2 1 Lit. *them*

3 a Ps. 14:4; 27:2
b Ezek. 11:3, 6, 7

4 a Jer. 11:11

Without Jesus Christ man must be in vice and misery; with Jesus Christ man is free from vice and misery; in Him is all our virtue and all our happiness.

BLAISE PASCAL

Even he would be the [a]prattler of
this people.

Israel Restored

12 "I[a] will surely assemble all of you,
O Jacob,
I will surely gather the remnant of
Israel;
I will put them together [b]like sheep
of [1]the fold,
Like a flock in the midst of their
pasture;
[c]They shall make a loud noise
because of *so many* people.
13 The one who breaks open will
come up before them;
They will break out,
Pass through the gate,
And go out by it;
[a]Their king will pass before them,
[b]With the LORD at their head."

Wicked Rulers and Prophets

3 And I said:

"Hear now, O heads of Jacob,
And you [a]rulers of the house of
Israel:
[b]*Is it* not for you to know justice?
2 You who hate good and love evil;
Who strip the skin from [1]My
people,
And the flesh from their bones;
3 Who also [a]eat the flesh of My
people,
Flay their skin from them,
Break their bones,
And chop *them* in pieces
Like *meat* for the pot,
[b]Like flesh in the caldron."

4 Then [a]they will cry to the LORD,
But He will not hear them;

He will even hide His face from
them at that time,
Because they have been evil in their
deeds.

5 Thus says the LORD [a]concerning
the prophets
Who make my people stray;
Who chant [1]"Peace"
[2]While they [b]chew with their teeth,
But who prepare war against him
[c]Who puts nothing into their
mouths:
6 "Therefore[a] you shall have night
without [1]vision,
And you shall have darkness
without divination;
The sun shall go down on the
prophets,
And the day shall be dark for
[b]them.
7 So the seers shall be ashamed,
And the diviners abashed;
Indeed they shall all cover their
lips;
[a]For *there is* no answer from God."

Lord, may _____ be full of power by the Spirit of the Lord, and full of justice and might to declare truth.

FROM MICAH 3:8

8 But truly I am full of power by the
Spirit of the LORD,
And of justice and might,
[a]To declare to Jacob his
transgression
And to Israel his sin.
9 Now hear this,
You heads of the house of Jacob
And rulers of the house of Israel,
Who abhor justice
And [1]pervert all equity,
10 [a]Who build up Zion with
[b]bloodshed
And Jerusalem with iniquity:
11 [a]Her heads judge for a bribe,
[b]Her priests teach for pay,
And her prophets divine for
[1]money.
[c]Yet they lean on the LORD, and say,
"Is not the LORD among us?
No harm can come upon us."
12 Therefore because of you
Zion shall be [a]plowed *like* a field,
[b]Jerusalem shall become heaps of
ruins,
And [c]the mountain of the [1]temple
Like the bare hills of the forest.

I want to move you to a greater hunger for holiness and purity. The moment you look up when you are in the place of affection with the Lord Jesus, the heavens are opened.

SMITH WIGGLESWORTH

The Lord's Reign in Zion

4 Now [a]it shall come to pass in the
latter days
That the mountain of the LORD's
house
Shall be established on the top of
the mountains,
And shall be exalted above the hills;
And peoples shall flow to it.
2 Many nations shall come and say,
"Come, and let us go up to the
mountain of the LORD,
To the house of the God of Jacob;
He will teach us His ways,
And we shall walk in His paths."
For out of Zion the law shall go
forth,
And the word of the LORD from
Jerusalem.
3 He shall judge between many
peoples,
And rebuke strong nations afar off;
They shall beat their swords into
[a]plowshares,
And their spears into [1]pruning
hooks;
Nation shall not lift up sword
against nation,
[b]Neither shall they learn war
anymore.
4 [a]But everyone shall sit under his
vine and under his fig tree,

5 [a]Ezek. 13:10, 19 [b]Matt. 7:15 [c]Ezek. 13:18 [1]All is well [2]For those who feed them
6 [a]Is. 8:20–22; 29:10–12 [b]Is. 29:10 [1]Prophetic revelation
7 [a]Amos 8:11
8 [a]Is. 58:1
9 [1]Lit. *twist*
10 [a]Jer. 22:13, 17 [b]Hab. 2:12
11 [a]Is. 1:23 [b]Jer. 6:13 [c]Is. 48:2 [1]Lit. *silver*
12 [a]Jer. 26:18 [b]Ps. 79:1 [c]Mic. 4:1, 2 [1]Lit. *house*
CHAPTER 4
1 [a]Is. 2:2–4
3 [a]Is. 2:4 [b]Ps. 72:7 [1]*pruning knives*
4 [a]Zech. 3:10

And no one shall make *them* afraid;
For the mouth of the LORD of hosts
has spoken.
5 For all people walk each in the
name of his god,
But [a]we will walk in the name of
the LORD our God
Forever and ever.

Zion's Future Triumph

6 "In that day," says the LORD,
[a]"I will assemble the lame,
[b]I will gather the outcast
And those whom I have afflicted;
7 I will make the lame [a]a remnant,
And the outcast a strong nation;
So the LORD [b]will reign over them
in Mount Zion
From now on, even forever.
8 And you, O tower of the flock,
The stronghold of the daughter of
Zion,
To you shall it come,
Even the former dominion shall
come,
The kingdom of the daughter of
Jerusalem."

9 Now why do you cry aloud?
[a]*Is there* no king in your midst?
Has your counselor perished?
For [b]pangs have seized you like a
woman in [1]labor.
10 Be in pain, and labor to bring
forth,
O daughter of Zion,
Like a woman in birth pangs.
For now you shall go forth from
the city,
You shall dwell in the field,
And to [a]Babylon you shall go.
There you shall be delivered;
There the [b]LORD will [c]redeem you
From the hand of your enemies.

11 [a]Now also many nations have
gathered against you,
Who say, "Let her be defiled,
And let our eye [b]look upon Zion."
12 But they do not know [a]the
thoughts of the LORD,
Nor do they understand His
counsel;
For He will gather them [b]like
sheaves to the threshing floor.

13 "Arise[a] and [b]thresh, O daughter of
Zion;
For I will make your horn iron,
And I will make your hooves
bronze;
You shall [c]beat in pieces many
peoples;
[d]I will consecrate their gain to the
LORD,
And their substance to [e]the Lord of
the whole earth."

5 Now gather yourself in troops,
O daughter of troops;
He has laid siege against us;
They will [a]strike the judge of Israel
with a rod on the cheek.

The Coming Messiah

2 "But you, [a]Bethlehem [b]Ephrathah,
Though you are little [c]among the
[d]thousands of Judah,
Yet out of you shall come forth to
Me
The One to be [e]Ruler in Israel,
[f]Whose goings forth *are* from of old,
From [1]everlasting."

No, there is none but Christ, none but Christ. . . . Oh let us love Him much for we have much forgiven.

SUSANNA WESLEY

3 Therefore He shall give them up,
Until the time *that* [a]she who is in
labor has given birth;
Then [b]the remnant of His brethren
Shall return to the children of
Israel.
4 And He shall stand and [a]feed[1] *His
flock*
In the strength of the LORD,
In the majesty of the name of the
LORD His God;
And they shall abide,
For now He [b]shall be great
To the ends of the earth;
5 And this *One* [a]shall be peace.

Judgment on Israel's Enemies

When the Assyrian comes into our
land,
And when he treads in our palaces,
Then we will raise against him

5 [a] Zech. 10:12
6 [a] Ezek. 34:16 [b] Ps. 147:2
7 [a] Mic. 2:12 [b] [Is. 9:6; 24:23]
9 [a] Jer. 8:19 [b] Is. 13:8 [1] *childbirth*
10 [a] Amos 5:27 [b] [Is. 45:13] [c] Ps. 18:17
11 [a] Lam. 2:16 [b] Obad. 12
12 [a] [Is. 55:8, 9] [b] Is. 21:10
13 [a] Jer. 51:33 [b] Is. 41:15 [c] Dan. 2:44 [d] Is. 18:7 [e] Zech. 4:14
CHAPTER 5
1 [a] Lam. 3:30
2 [a] John 7:42 [b] Gen. 35:19; 48:7; [c] 1 Sam. 23:23 [d] Ex. 18:25 [e] [Is. 9:6] [f] Ps. 90:2 [1] Lit. *the days of eternity*
3 [a] Mic. 4:10 [b] Mic. 4:7; 7:18
4 [a] [Is. 40:11; 49:9] [b] Ps. 72:8 [1] *shepherd*
5 [a] [Is. 9:6]

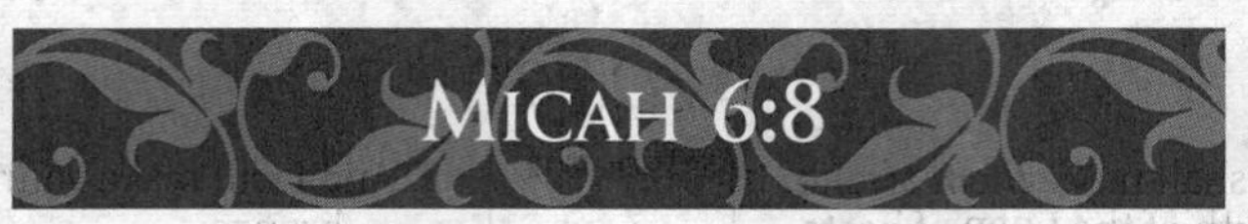

MICAH 6:8

Dear Woman of Destiny,

You and I are living in a day when many are asking, "What is Good?" Unregenerate men and women will answer: "There are no absolutes. Everything is relative. Each person must decide what is right. If it feels good, do it!"

This is a dangerous course, more so for women than for men, for it is often still true that she who rocks the cradle rules the world. Never has there been such a time of opportunity for women in every walk of life.

Unfortunately, this is not true for all women. A tenth of the world's population are Muslim women—most of whom are living in bondage and servitude today. Their restrictions are beyond comprehension for Western women. Most are not allowed to drive a car or eat with men. Some are killed for uncovering even a part of their face. Girls who are raped are summarily disowned and killed by their families. This I learned when visiting shelters in Bangladesh. Only when they were given an opportunity to hear the gospel and accept Jesus as Lord and Savior did their faces light up.

American women may not suffer such injustice, but unless we live by Micah's standard of excellence—"to do justly, to love mercy, and to walk humbly with [our] God"—and teach our children to follow our example, this generation will be forever lost. What about the 1.3 million women who abort their babies in the U.S. each year? What about the 56 percent of girls under age 18 who engage in sexual intercourse? Are we making certain our children and grandchildren, or those of their friends, are not exposed to pornography in our homes or wherever they meet? Are we making sure they aren't allowed to be close companions with drug-using, drinking, smoking, homosexual, lawless, evil companions?

What is the answer? Open your home to your children's friends. Pray daily with them, and teach them to lead in prayer. Pray over your meals. Join the PUSH group—Pray Until Something Happens. Read the Bible to them daily, and encourage them to do the same. (I began reading my Bible through each year when I was in Bible school. This year I'm reading it through the sixty-fourth time. Three chapters a day and five on Sundays will do it!) Have a family altar in your home. Practice worship and praise daily. Attend and be sure the children in your lives are regular attendees of a good, Spirit-led church. Spend quality time with each of your family members—husband and children. Pray with your family—sure—but play with them, too. Always keep them looking forward to something special—a trip, camping, tennis, an evening of clean fun. Develop a grateful spirit.

So what is Good? It's living God's way. It will provide peace and joy in this life and the promise of a glorious eternity with Jesus!

Freda Lindsay

Seven shepherds and eight princely
men.
6 They shall [1]waste with the sword
the land of Assyria,
And the land of [a]Nimrod at its
entrances;
Thus He shall [b]deliver *us* from the
Assyrian,
When he comes into our land
And when he treads within our
borders.

7 Then [a]the remnant of Jacob
Shall be in the midst of many
peoples,
[b]Like dew from the LORD,
Like showers on the grass,
That [1]tarry for no man
Nor [2]wait for the sons of men.
8 And the remnant of Jacob
Shall be among the Gentiles,
In the midst of many peoples,
Like a [a]lion among the beasts of
the forest,
Like a young lion among flocks of
sheep,
Who, if he passes through,
Both treads down and tears in
pieces,
And none can deliver.
9 Your hand shall be lifted against
your adversaries,
And all your enemies shall be [1]cut
off.

10 "And it shall be in that day," says
the LORD,
"That I will [a]cut[1] off your [b]horses
from your midst
And destroy your [c]chariots.
11 I will cut off the cities of your
land
And throw down all your
strongholds.
12 I will cut off sorceries from your
hand,
And you shall have no [a]soothsayers.
13 [a]Your carved images I will also cut
off,
And your sacred pillars from your
midst;
You shall [b]no more worship the
work of your hands;
14 I will pluck your [1]wooden images
from your midst;
Thus I will destroy your cities.
15 And I will [a]execute vengeance in
anger and fury

6 a Gen. 10:8–11 b Is. 14:25 1 *devastate*
7 a Mic. 5:3 b Deut. 32:2 1 *wait* 2 *delay*
8 a Num. 24:9
9 1 *destroyed*
10 a Zech. 9:10 b Deut. 17:16 c Is. 2:7; 22:18 1 *destroy*
12 a Is. 2:6
13 a Zech. 13:2 b Is. 2:8
14 1 Heb. *Asherim,* Canaanite deities
15 a [2 Thess. 1:8] 1 *obeyed*

CHAPTER 6
2 a Ps. 50:1, 4 b Hos. 12:2 c [Is. 1:18] 1 *bring charges against*
3 a Jer. 2:5, 31 b Is. 43:22, 23
4 a [Deut. 4:20]
5 a Num. 22:5, 6 b Judg. 5:11 1 Heb. *Shittim,* Num. 25:1; Josh. 2:1; 3:1
7 a Is. 1:11 b Job 29:6 c 2 Kin. 16:3 1 My own child
8 a [Deut. 10:12] b Gen. 18:19 1 Or *lovingkindness*

On the nations that have not
[1]heard."

God Pleads with Israel

6 Hear now what the LORD says:

"Arise, plead your case before the
mountains,
And let the hills hear your voice.
2 [a]Hear, O you mountains, [b]the
LORD's complaint,
And you strong foundations of the
earth;
For [c]the LORD has a complaint
against His people,
And He will [1]contend with Israel.

3 "O My people, what [a]have I done to
you?
And how have I [b]wearied you?
Testify against Me.
4 [a]For I brought you up from the
land of Egypt,
I redeemed you from the house of
bondage;
And I sent before you Moses, Aaron,
and Miriam.
5 O My people, remember now
What [a]Balak king of Moab
counseled,
And what Balaam the son of Beor
answered him,
From [1]Acacia Grove to Gilgal,
That you may know [b]the
righteousness of the LORD."

6 With what shall I come before the
LORD,
And bow myself before the High
God?
Shall I come before Him with burnt
offerings,
With calves a year old?
7 [a]Will the LORD be pleased with
thousands of rams,
Ten thousand [b]rivers of oil?
[c]Shall I give my firstborn *for* my
transgression,
[1]The fruit of my body *for* the sin of
my soul?
8 He has [a]shown you, O man,
what *is* good;
And what does the LORD require of
you
But [b]to do justly,
To love [1]mercy,
And to walk humbly with your
God?

Father, I ask that You would show ______ what is good and what You require of them: to do justly, to love mercy, and to walk humbly with their God.

FROM MICAH 6:8

Punishment of Israel's Injustice

9 The LORD's voice cries to the
city—
Wisdom shall see Your name:

"Hear the rod!
Who has appointed it?
10 Are there yet the treasures of
wickedness
In the house of the wicked,
And the short measure *that is* an
abomination?
11 Shall I count pure *those* with [a]the
wicked scales,
And with the bag of deceitful
weights?
12 For her rich men are full of
[a]violence,
Her inhabitants have spoken lies,
And [b]their tongue is deceitful in
their mouth.
13 "Therefore I will also [a]make *you*
sick by striking you,
By making *you* desolate because of
your sins.
14 [a]You shall eat, but not be satisfied;
[1]Hunger *shall be* in your midst.
[2]You may carry *some* away, but shall
not save *them;*
And what you do rescue I will give
over to the sword.
15 "You shall [a]sow, but not reap;
You shall tread the olives, but not
anoint yourselves with oil;
And *make* sweet wine, but not
drink wine.
16 For the statutes of [a]Omri are [b]kept;
All the works of Ahab's house *are*
done;
And you walk in their counsels,
That I may make you a [1]desolation,
And your inhabitants a hissing.
Therefore you shall bear the
[c]reproach of [2]My people."

Sorrow for Israel's Sins

7 Woe is me!
For I am like those who gather
summer fruits,
Like those who [a]glean vintage
grapes;
There is no cluster to eat
Of the first-ripe fruit *which* [b]my
soul desires.
2 The [a]faithful[1] *man* has perished
from the earth,
And *there is* no one upright among
men.
They all lie in wait for blood;
[b]Every man hunts his brother with a
net.
3 That they may successfully do evil
with both hands—
The prince asks *for gifts,*
The judge *seeks* a [a]bribe,
And the great *man* utters his evil
desire;
So they scheme together.
4 The best of them *is* [a]like a brier;
The most upright *is sharper* than a
thorn hedge;
The day of your watchman and your
punishment comes;
Now shall be their perplexity.

5 [a]Do not trust in a friend;
Do not put your confidence in a
companion;
Guard the doors of your mouth
From her who lies in your [b]bosom.
6 For [a]son dishonors father,
Daughter rises against her mother,
Daughter-in-law against her
mother-in-law;
A man's enemies *are* the men of his
own household.
7 Therefore I will look to the LORD;
I will [a]wait for the God of my
salvation;
My God will hear me.

Israel's Confession and Comfort

8 [a]Do not rejoice over me, my
enemy;
[b]When I fall, I will arise;
When I sit in darkness,
The LORD *will be* a light to me.

11 [a]Hos. 12:7
12 [a]Mic. 2:1, 2 [b]Jer. 9:2–6, 8
13 [a]Lev. 26:16
14 [a]Lev. 26:26 *1* Or *Emptiness* or *Humiliation* *2* Tg., Vg. *You shall take hold*
15 [a]Amos 5:11
16 [a]1 Kin. 16:25, 26 [b]Hos. 5:11 [c]Is. 25:8 *1* Or *object of horror* *2* So with MT, Tg., Vg.; LXX *nations*

CHAPTER 7
1 [a]Is. 17:6 [b]Is. 28:4
2 [a]Is. 57:1 [b]Hab. 1:15 *1* Or *loyal*
3 [a]Mic. 3:11
4 [a]Ezek. 2:6
5 [a]Jer. 9:4 [b]Deut. 28:56
6 [a]Matt. 10:36
7 [a]Is. 25:9
8 [a]Prov. 24:17 [b][Prov. 24:16]

MICAH 7:8

Dear Woman of Destiny,

When I was two months old, my parents proudly took me to our family church to be dedicated to God. Before the pastor prayed over me, he uttered words my parents felt were prophetic: "This little girl has been born to be a bulwark against sin and the devil."

Fourteen years later, my life was anything but a bulwark or defense against evil. By 22, I was a hopeless drug addict. The little girl who carried a baby doll with her at all times by then had experienced five abortions and a complete hysterectomy.

I was angry with God, though I knew it was my own rebellion that took my dreams away. To fill the hurt and void I went deeper into alcohol and drugs, and at 27 ended an abusive marriage through divorce. I felt so sinful and hopeless that God would not hear my prayers.

Do you feel like your prayers hit the ceiling? The enemy of your soul reminds you of your sins and says you are not good enough for God to hear your prayers. Can you identify with David when he cried, "How long, O LORD? Will You forget me forever? How long will You hide Your face from me?" (Ps. 13:1).

God is not playing some high-stakes hiding game with us. In fact, He says in Hebrews 13:5, "I will never leave you nor forsake you." My husband showed me the meaning of *never* in Greek as used in this verse. He suggested the verse should read like this: "I will never, not at all, by no means, in no case, not ever, not at all in any wise leave you, and I will never, not at all, by no means, in no case, not ever, not at all in any wise forsake you." It is settled in heaven and in the mind of God. He will never leave you!

At 31, my night turned into day when God's light of salvation came into my life. Perhaps you feel in the dark, in a situation so awful you can't solve it and God doesn't see you. I have good news: Jesus has come right now and He's caused you to read my letter. "The LORD upholds all who fall, and raises up all who are bowed down" (Ps. 145:14). When you are down, when heaven feels like brass, and the enemy is whispering in your ear, proclaim Micah 7:8.

What you are going through now may mean God is teaching you, getting you ready for a special work. Hebrews 12:6–8 proclaims: "'For whom the LORD loves He chastens, and scourges every son whom He receives.' If you endure chastening, God deals with you as with sons; for what son is there whom a father does not chasten? But if you are without chastening . . . then you are illegitimate and not sons." All God's children must go through times of training. The Word declares that even the trial of our faith is more precious than gold (see 1 Pet. 1:7).

I have been put back together, forgiven of all my sins, delivered from drugs and alcohol, given a wonderful home, husband, and a ministry beyond my wildest dream.

Woman of Destiny, your time has come—you will arise!

Lori Graham Bakker

9 [a]I will bear the indignation of the
LORD,
Because I have sinned against Him,
Until He pleads my [b]case
And executes justice for me.
He will bring me forth to the light;
I will see His righteousness.
10 Then *she who is* my enemy will
see,
And [a]shame will cover her who said
to me,
[b]"Where is the LORD your God?"
My eyes will see her;
Now she will be trampled down
Like mud in the streets.

11 *In* the day when your [a]walls are to
be built,
In that day [1]the decree shall go far
and wide.
12 *In* that day [a]they[1] shall come to
you
From Assyria and the [2]fortified
cities,
From the [3]fortress to [4]the River,
From sea to sea,
And mountain *to* mountain.
13 Yet the land shall be desolate
Because of those who dwell in it,
And [a]for the fruit of their deeds.

God Will Forgive Israel

14 Shepherd Your people with Your
staff,
The flock of Your heritage,
Who dwell [1]solitarily *in* a
[a]woodland,
In the midst of Carmel;
Let them feed *in* Bashan and
Gilead,
As in days of old.

15 "As[a] in the days when you came
out of the land of Egypt,

9 a Lam. 3:39, 40 b Jer. 50:34
10 a Ps. 35:26 b Ps. 42:3
11 a [Amos 9:11] 1 Or *the boundary shall be extended*
12 a [Is. 11:16; 19:23–25] 1 Lit. *he,* collective of the captives 2 Heb. *arey mazor,* possibly *cities of Egypt* 3 Heb. *mazor,* possibly *Egypt* 4 The Euphrates
13 a Jer. 21:14
14 a Is. 37:24 1 Alone
15 a Ps. 68:22; 78:12 b Ex. 34:10 1 Lit. *him,* collective for the captives
16 a Is. 26:11 b Job 21:5
17 a [Is. 49:23] b Ps. 18:45 c Jer. 33:9 1 Lit. *crawlers*
18 a Ex. 15:11 b Ex. 34:6, 7, 9 c Mic. 4:7 d Ps. 103:8, 9, 13 e [Ezek. 33:11] 1 Or *loving-kindness*
19 1 Lit. *their*
20 a Luke 1:72, 73 b Ps. 105:9 1 Or *loving-kindness*

I will show [1]them [b]wonders."
16 The nations [a]shall see and be
ashamed of all their might;
[b]They shall put *their* hand over *their*
mouth;
Their ears shall be deaf.
17 They shall lick the [a]dust like a
serpent;
[b]They shall crawl from their holes
like [1]snakes of the earth.
[c]They shall be afraid of the LORD our
God,
And shall fear because of You.
18 [a]Who *is* a God like You,
[b]Pardoning iniquity
And passing over the transgression
of [c]the remnant of His heritage?
[d]He does not retain His anger
forever,
Because He delights *in* [e]mercy.[1]
19 He will again have compassion on
us,
And will subdue our iniquities.

Who is a God like You, pardoning iniquity? Lord, have compassion on ____ and subdue their iniquities.

FROM MICAH 7:18, 19

You will cast all [1]our sins
Into the depths of the sea.
20 [a]You will give truth to Jacob
And [1]mercy to Abraham,
[b]Which You have sworn to our
fathers
From days of old.

AUTHOR: *Nahum*
DATE: *Shortly Before 612 B.C.*
THEME: *God's Judgment on the City of Nineveh*
KEY WORDS: *Evil, Cut Off, "I Am Against You"*

NAHUM

Dear Woman of Destiny,

Nahum teaches us that although God is merciful, He will judge sin. In Jonah's time, Nineveh had repented; but a century later, their return to sin and rebellion brought God's wrath. Those who trust God know His justice is unerring. Take courage today; and remember that, in every situation, God is truly in control.

His love and mine,

Marilyn Hickey

The [1]burden [a]against Nineveh. The book of the vision of Nahum the Elkoshite.

God's Wrath on His Enemies

2 God *is* [a]jealous, and the LORD avenges;
The LORD avenges and *is* furious.
The LORD will take vengeance on His adversaries,
And He reserves *wrath* for His enemies;
3 The LORD *is* [a]slow to anger and [b]great in power,
And will not at all acquit *the wicked.*

[c]The LORD has His way
In the whirlwind and in the storm,
And the clouds *are* the dust of His feet.
4 [a]He rebukes the sea and makes it dry,
And dries up all the rivers.
[b]Bashan and Carmel wither,
And the flower of Lebanon wilts.
5 The mountains quake before Him,
The hills melt,
And the earth [1]heaves at His presence,
Yes, the world and all who dwell in it.

6 Who can stand before His indignation?
And [a]who can endure the fierceness of His anger?
His fury is poured out like fire,
And the rocks are thrown down by Him.

You are good, O Lord, a stronghold in the day of trouble. You know _____, for they trust in You.

FROM NAHUM 1:7

7 [a]The LORD *is* good,
A stronghold in the day of trouble;
And [b]He knows those who trust in Him.
8 But with an overflowing flood
He will make an utter end of its place,
And darkness will pursue His enemies.

9 [a]What do you [1]conspire against the LORD?
[b]He will make an utter end *of it.*
Affliction will not rise up a second time.
10 For while tangled [a]*like* thorns,
[b]And while drunken *like* drunkards,
[c]They shall be devoured like stubble fully dried.
11 From you comes forth *one*
Who plots evil against the LORD,
A [1]wicked counselor.

12 Thus says the LORD:

"Though *they are* [1]safe, and likewise many,
Yet in this manner they will be [a]cut down
When he passes through.
Though I have afflicted you,
I will afflict you no more;
13 For now I will break off his yoke from you,
And burst your bonds apart."

14 The LORD has given a command concerning you:
[1]"Your name shall be perpetuated no longer.
Out of the house of your gods
I will cut off the carved image and the molded image.
I will dig your [a]grave,
For you are [b]vile."[2]

15 Behold, on the mountains
The [a]feet of him who brings good tidings,
Who proclaims peace!
O Judah, keep your appointed feasts,
Perform your vows.
For the [1]wicked one shall no more pass through you;
He is [b]utterly cut off.

The Destruction of Nineveh

2 He[1] who scatters has come up before your face.
Man the fort!
Watch the road!
Strengthen *your* flanks!
Fortify *your* power mightily.

2 For the LORD will restore the excellence of Jacob

CHAPTER 1
1 **a** Zeph. 2:13 *1 oracle, prophecy*
2 **a** Ex. 20:5
3 **a** Ex. 34:6, 7 **b** [Job 9:4] **c** Ps. 18:17
4 **a** Matt. 8:26 **b** Is. 33:9
5 *1* Tg. *burns*
6 **a** [Mal. 3:2]
7 **a** [Jer. 33:11] **b** 2 Tim. 2:19
9 **a** Ps. 2:1 **b** 1 Sam. 3:12 *1* Or *devise*
10 **a** 2 Sam. 23:6 **b** Nah. 3:11 **c** Mal. 4:1
11 *1* Lit. *counselor of Belial*
12 **a** [Is. 10:16–19, 33, 34] *1* Or *at peace* or *complete*
14 **a** Ezek. 32:22, 23 **b** Nah. 3:6 *1* Lit. *No more of your name shall be fruitful* *2* Or *contemptible*
15 **a** Rom. 10:15 **b** Is. 29:7, 8 *1* Lit. *one of Belial*

CHAPTER 2
1 *1* Vg. *He who destroys*

NAHUM 1:7

Dear Woman of Destiny,

We all face trouble in our lives. Even little children find trouble in their lives. Their first encounter with trouble comes on the day they are born. Leaving their mother's protective womb is not an easy task; a baby is completely comfortable there. But one day the unusual trauma begins. All that takes care of him starts telling him that is the time to go. The baby feels uneasy; he sees trouble up front. New experiences are sensed as trouble—as disturbances to "the way it has always been." They are a cause of worry, uneasiness, and inconvenience.

Have you ever been in a place or time where you felt as if nobody was there for you? Have you felt as if you had to care for yourself in every way? As I meditated in this passage and reflected on the times men and women in the Bible have felt this way, I was impressed by the amazing love of the Father for His creation, us.

Look at Esther. The times were hard; she had all the pressure of the world on her, as she was the only one who could save her people from destruction. In those days of trouble, Esther probably felt she was totally alone in this endeavor. She could only ask for prayer to find favor before the king (see Esth. 4:14). But "the LORD is good, a stronghold in the day of trouble" (Nah. 1:7). This is a truth we need to have embedded in our lives.

The Lord is good. We have a good God. His mercy is upon us, and His love for His creation is so great we cannot even imagine it. First Chronicles 16:34 says to "give thanks to the LORD, for He is good! For His mercy endures forever." David admonished us to "taste and see that the LORD is good; blessed is the man who trusts in Him!" (Ps. 34:8). And again in Psalm 100:5, we read, "For the LORD is good; His mercy is everlasting, and His truth endures to all generations."

Our Lord is also a stronghold in the day of trouble. Remember David when he was hiding from Saul? David hid in strongholds while Saul sought for him every day, but God covered him, and he was not found (see 1 Sam. 23:14). He wrote about this in Psalm 27:5, saying, "For in the time of trouble He shall hide me in His pavilion; in the secret place of His tabernacle He shall hide me; He shall set me high upon a rock."

Oh, the mercy of the LORD! Oh, His love toward us! Oh, His care that makes me want to get closer to Him that I may know Him more deeply—always remembering that He is with me and that He is my stronghold.

The next time you are in trouble and feel all alone, remember that God has a pavilion for you—the secret place of His tabernacle where you can hide and feel His protection. That is where you can hide and hear from Him, being sure that He will set you upon the Rock, Jesus Christ.

I pray that the Lord will keep you from harm and that, in the day of trouble when you feel in despair, He becomes real to you and that He becomes your stronghold.

Cecilia Caballeros

Like the excellence of Israel,
For the emptiers have emptied
them out
And ruined their vine branches.

Professing Christian, is sin subdued in you? If your life is unholy, your heart unchanged, you are not saved. Grace that does not make you holy is a worthless counterfeit.

CHARLES H. SPURGEON

3 The shields of his mighty men *are*
made red,
The valiant men *are* in scarlet.
The chariots *come* with flaming
torches
In the day of his preparation,
And [1]the spears are brandished.
4 The chariots rage in the streets,
They jostle one another in the
broad roads;
They seem like torches,
They run like lightning.

5 He remembers his nobles;
They stumble in their walk;
They make haste to her walls,
And the defense is prepared.
6 The gates of the rivers are opened,
And the palace is dissolved.
7 [1]It is decreed:
She shall be led away captive,
She shall be brought up;
And her maidservants shall lead *her*
as with the voice of doves,
Beating their breasts.

8 Though Nineveh of old *was* like a
pool of water,
Now they flee away.
[1]"Halt! Halt!" *they cry;*
But no one turns back.
9 [1]Take spoil of silver!
Take spoil of [a]gold!
There is no end of treasure,
Or wealth of every desirable prize.
10 She is empty, desolate, and waste!
The heart melts, and the knees
shake;
Much pain *is* in every side,
And all their faces [1]are drained of
color.

11 Where *is* the dwelling of the
[a]lions,
And the feeding place of the young
lions,
Where the lion walked, the lioness
and lion's cub,
And no one made *them* afraid?
12 The lion tore in pieces enough for
his cubs,
[1]Killed for his lionesses,
[a]Filled his caves with prey,
And his dens with [2]flesh.

13 "Behold, [a]I *am* against you," says the
LORD of hosts, "I will burn [1]your chariots
in smoke, and the sword shall devour your
young lions; I will cut off your prey from
the earth, and the voice of your [b]messen-
gers shall be heard no more."

The Woe of Nineveh

3 Woe to the [a]bloody city!
It *is* all full of lies *and* robbery.
Its [1]victim never departs.
2 The noise of a whip
And the noise of rattling wheels,
Of galloping horses,
Of [1]clattering chariots!
3 Horsemen charge with bright
sword and glittering spear.
There is a multitude of slain,
A great number of bodies,
Countless corpses—
They stumble over the corpses—
4 Because of the multitude of
[1]harlotries of the [2]seductive
harlot,
[a]The mistress of sorceries,
Who sells nations through her
harlotries,
And families through her sorceries.

5 "Behold, I *am* [a]against you," says
the LORD of hosts;
[b]"I will lift your skirts over your face,
I will show the nations your
nakedness,
And the kingdoms your shame.
6 I will cast abominable filth upon
you,
Make you [a]vile,[1]
And make you [b]a spectacle.
7 It shall come to pass *that* all who
look upon you
[a]Will flee from you, and say,
[b]'Nineveh is laid waste!

---

3 [1] Lit. *the cypresses are shaken;* LXX, Syr. *the horses rush about;* Vg. *the drivers are stupefied*
7 [1] Heb. *Huzzab*
8 [1] Lit. *Stand*
9 [a] Zeph. 1:18 [1] *Plunder*
10 [1] LXX, Tg., Vg. *gather blackness;* Joel 2:6
11 [a] Job 4:10, 11
12 [a] Jer. 51:34 [1] Lit. *Strangled* [2] Torn flesh
13 [a] Nah. 3:5 [b] 2 Kin. 18:17–25; 19:9–13, 23 [1] Lit. *her*

CHAPTER 3
1 [a] Hab. 2:12 [1] Lit. *prey*
2 [1] *bounding* or *jolting*
4 [a] Is. 47:9–12 [1] Spiritual unfaithfulness [2] Lit. *goodly charm,* in a bad sense
5 [a] Nah. 2:13 [b] Is. 47:2, 3
6 [a] Nah. 1:14 [b] Heb. 10:33 [1] *despicable*
7 [a] Rev. 18:10 [b] Jon. 3:3; 4:11

[c]Who will bemoan her?'
Where shall I seek comforters for
you?"

8 [a]Are you better than [b]No[1] Amon
That was situated by the [2]River,
That had the waters around her,
Whose rampart *was* the sea,
Whose wall *was* the sea?
9 Ethiopia and Egypt *were* her
strength,
And *it was* boundless;
[a]Put and Lubim were [1]your helpers.
10 Yet she *was* carried away,
She went into captivity;
[a]Her young children also were
dashed to pieces
[b]At the head of every street;
They [c]cast lots for her honorable
men,
And all her great men were bound
in chains.
11 You also will be [a]drunk;
You will be hidden;
You also will seek refuge from the
enemy.

12 All your strongholds *are* [a]fig trees
with ripened figs:
If they are shaken,
They fall into the mouth of the
eater.
13 Surely, [a]your people in your midst
are women!
The gates of your land are wide
open for your enemies;
Fire shall devour the [b]bars of your
gates.

14 Draw your water for the siege!
[a]Fortify your strongholds!
Go into the clay and tread the
mortar!
Make strong the brick kiln!
15 There the fire will devour you,
The sword will cut you off;
It will eat you up like a [a]locust.

Make yourself many—like the
locust!
Make yourself many—like the
swarming locusts!
16 You have multiplied your
[a]merchants more than the stars
of heaven.
The locust plunders and flies away.
17 [a]Your commanders *are* like
swarming locusts,
And your generals like great
grasshoppers,
Which camp in the hedges on a
cold day;
When the sun rises they flee away,
And the place where they *are* is not
known.

18 [a]Your shepherds slumber, O [b]king
of Assyria;
Your nobles rest *in the dust.*
Your people are [c]scattered on the
mountains,
And no one gathers them.
19 Your injury *has* no healing,
[a]Your wound is severe.
[b]All who hear news of you
Will clap *their* hands over you,
For upon whom has not your
wickedness passed continually?

---

7 [c]Jer. 15:5
8 [a]Amos 6:2 [b]Jer. 46:25 [1]Ancient Thebes; Tg., Vg. *populous Alexandria* [2]Lit. *rivers,* the Nile and the surrounding canals
9 [a]Ezek. 27:10 [1]LXX *her*
10 [a]Hos. 13:16 [b]Lam. 2:19 [c]Joel 3:3
11 [a]Nah. 1:10
12 [a]Rev. 6:12, 13
13 [a]Is. 19:16 [b]Jer. 51:30
14 [a]Nah. 2:1
15 [a]Joel 1:4
16 [a]Rev. 18:3, 11–19
17 [a]Rev. 9:7
18 [a]Ps. 76:5, 6 [b]Jer. 50:18 [c]1 Kin. 22:17
19 [a]Mic. 1:9 [b]Lam. 2:15

AUTHOR: *Habakkuk*
DATE: *Approximately 600 B.C.*
THEME: *The Just Shall Live by Faith*
KEY WORDS: *Faith, Why?, Woe*

HABAKKUK

Dear Woman of Destiny,

Habakkuk contains a truth central to the salvation message: *"The just shall live by his faith"* (Hab. 2:4). When Habakkuk struggled in his faith, God made it clear that His children must look beyond the natural realm and seek Him for the truth in every situation. Let your faith increase and your heart be quickened as you read on.

His love and mine,

Marilyn Hickey

The [1]burden which the prophet Habakkuk saw.

The Prophet's Question

2 O LORD, how long shall I cry,
[a]And You will not hear?
Even cry out to You, [b]"Violence!"
And You will [c]not save.
3 Why do You show me iniquity,
And cause *me* to see [1]trouble?
For plundering and violence *are* before me;
There is strife, and contention arises.
4 Therefore the law is powerless,
And justice never goes forth.
For the [a]wicked surround the righteous;
Therefore perverse judgment proceeds.

The Lord's Reply

5 "Look[a] among the nations and watch—
Be utterly astounded!
For *I will* work a work in your days
Which you would not believe, though it were told *you*.
6 For indeed I am [a]raising up the Chaldeans,
A bitter and hasty [b]nation
Which marches through the breadth of the earth,
To possess dwelling places *that are* not theirs.
7 They are terrible and dreadful;
Their judgment and their dignity proceed from themselves.
8 Their horses also are [a]swifter than leopards,
And more fierce than evening wolves.
Their [1]chargers [2]charge ahead;
Their cavalry comes from afar;
They fly as the [b]eagle *that* hastens to eat.

9 "They all come for violence;
Their faces are set *like* the east wind.
They gather captives like sand.
10 They scoff at kings,
And princes are scorned by them.
They deride every stronghold,
For they heap up earthen *mounds* and seize it.
11 Then *his* [1]mind changes, and he transgresses;
He commits offense,
[a]*Ascribing* this power to his god."

The Prophet's Second Question

12 Are You not [a]from everlasting,
O LORD my God, my Holy One?
We shall not die.
O LORD, [b]You have appointed them for judgment;
O Rock, You have marked them for [c]correction.
13 *You are* of purer eyes than to behold evil,
And cannot look on wickedness.
Why do You look on those who deal treacherously,
And hold Your tongue when the wicked devours
A *person* more righteous than he?
14 *Why* do You make men like fish of the sea,
Like creeping things *that have* no ruler over them?
15 They take up all of them with a hook,
They catch them in their net,
And gather them in their dragnet.
Therefore they rejoice and are glad.
16 Therefore [a]they sacrifice to their net,
And burn incense to their dragnet;
Because by them their share *is* [1]sumptuous
And their food plentiful.
17 Shall they therefore empty their net,
And continue to slay nations without pity?

2 I will [a]stand my watch
And set myself on the rampart,
And watch to see what He will say to me,
And what I will answer when I am corrected.

The Just Live by Faith

2 Then the LORD answered me and said:

[a]"Write the vision
And make *it* plain on tablets,
That he may run who reads it.
3 For [a]the vision *is* yet for an appointed time;

CHAPTER 1
1 [1] *oracle, prophecy*
2 [a] Lam. 3:8 [b] Mic. 2:1, 2; 3:1–3 [c] [Job 21:5–16]
3 [1] Or *toil*
4 [a] Jer. 12:1
5 [a] Is. 29:14
6 [a] 2 Kin. 24:2 [b] Ezek. 7:24; 21:31
8 [a] Jer. 4:13 [b] Hos. 8:1 [1] Lit. *horsemen* [2] Lit. *spring about*
11 [a] Dan. 5:4 [1] Lit. *spirit* or *wind*
12 [a] Ps. 90:2; 93:2 [b] Is. 10:5–7 [c] Jer. 25:9
16 [a] Deut. 8:17 [1] Lit. *fat*

CHAPTER 2
1 [a] Is. 21:8, 11
2 [a] Is. 8:1
3 [a] Dan. 8:17, 19; 10:14

Habakkuk 2:2, 3

Dear Woman of Destiny,

God has a vision for your life; and until you discover it, the world will go on without the gift you can impart. However, your destiny will only be experienced and fulfilled outside of your comfort zone, which stretches your faith. Step out. Rely on faith; it is a friend of the spirit. Rely on God to meet you as you walk out His plan for you. One of the keys to walking victoriously in God's plan will be choosing to walk in love and forgiveness and discovering the power in that choice. Beware of what stops you. Don't let fear become your friend, for fear will only sabotage your future.

I challenge you to love the way you want to be loved. Stop waiting to be rescued and begin to reach out. It's impossible to harvest something you don't plant. Sow it to reap it. In spite of rejection, Jesus forgave, and because of that, was free to love. I testify that forgiveness will free you to discover new dimensions of your destiny. Begin to make choices that contribute to a future worth having. Begin to serve others unselfishly. Give and expect nothing in return except from the Lord Himself.

Like Eve, you are a woman of great significance. God's vision and destiny for your life is very special. Eve did not have "plain vision" (see Hab. 2:2), and she compromised her inheritance by letting the enemy question her validity. Our world is full of right answers to wrong questions, and that is where most of us are deceived and misguided.

Do you know who God created you to be? What vision has His Spirit birthed in your heart? Habakkuk encourages us to "write the vision and make it plain" (v. 2). We must begin to see our lives and our purpose as God does. Go ahead and keep a spiritual journal. Go ahead and write your vision. If you misunderstand or miscommunicate His vision for you, He will straighten you out!

Women still face the great problem of entertaining illegitimate questions, suspicious speculations, and all sorts of accusations from the enemy. Because of our ability to incubate, we must be cautious of entertaining and nurturing those conversations. If you will "write the vision," you can refer to it, and it will enable you to stand against the taunts of the enemy.

Life can be like a sport if you choose to view it as such, but it is a serious sport with a series of games to play and win. Being a spectator will always leave you out, feeling unimportant and insignificant. Looking at life through the lenses of timidity and cowardice incapacitates you, paralyzes you, and renders you ineffective. Participate, enroll, and register your active presence. Stop apologizing for your uniqueness. Stop selling out and compromising the destiny of God in you. Embrace His vision for your life and make your contribution. Begin to give yourself in a new way!

His grace is sufficient for you to maximize every opportunity to extend yourself. Run the race. Go the distance, and begin to live beyond the familiar. Be risky! Take the leap of faith! Step out and step into the abundance of His grace. Fulfill your destiny!

Gina Pearson

But at the end it will speak, and it
will [b]not lie.
Though it tarries, [c]wait for it;
Because it will [d]surely come,
It will not tarry.

Be very patient and very confident in Him.

OSWALD CHAMBERS

4 "Behold the proud,
His soul is not upright in him;
But the [a]just shall live by his
faith.

I pray that ____ will be among the just who live by faith, O Lord.

FROM HABAKKUK 2:4

Woe to the Wicked

5 "Indeed, because he transgresses by
wine,
He is a proud man,
And he does not stay at home.
Because he [a]enlarges his desire as
[1]hell,
And he *is* like death, and cannot be
satisfied,
He gathers to himself all nations
And heaps up for himself all
peoples.

6 "Will not all these [a]take up a
proverb against him,
And a taunting riddle against him,
and say,
'Woe to him who increases
What is not his—how long?
And to him who loads himself with
[1]many pledges'?
7 Will not [1]your creditors rise up
suddenly?
Will they not awaken who oppress
you?
And you will become their booty.
8 [a]Because you have plundered many
nations,
All the remnant of the people shall
plunder you,
Because of men's [1]blood
And the violence of the land *and*
the city,
And of all who dwell in it.

9 "Woe to him who covets evil gain
for his house,
That he may [a]set his nest on high,
That he may be delivered from the
[1]power of disaster!
10 You give shameful counsel to your
house,
Cutting off many peoples,
And sin *against* your soul.
11 For the stone will cry out from
the wall,
And the beam from the timbers will
answer it.

12 "Woe to him who builds a town
with bloodshed,
Who establishes a city by iniquity!
13 Behold, *is it* not of the LORD of
hosts
That the peoples labor [1]to feed the
fire,
And nations weary themselves in
vain?
14 For the earth will be filled
With the knowledge of the glory of
the LORD,
As the waters cover the sea.

15 "Woe to him who gives drink to his
neighbor,
[1]Pressing *him to* your [a]bottle,
Even to make *him* drunk,
That you may look on [2]his
nakedness!
16 You are filled with shame instead
of glory.
You also—drink!
And [1]be exposed as uncircumcised!
The cup of the LORD's right hand
will be turned against you,
And utter shame will be on your
glory.
17 For the violence *done to* Lebanon
will cover you,
And the plunder of beasts *which*
made them afraid,
Because of men's blood
And the violence of the land *and*
the city,
And of all who dwell in it.

3 [b] Ezek. 12:24, 25 [c] [Heb. 10:37, 38] [d] [2 Pet. 3:9]
4 [a] [John 3:36]; Rom. 1:17
5 [a] Is. 5:11–15 [1] Or *Sheol*
6 [a] Mic. 2:4 [1] Syr., Vg. *thick clay*
7 [1] Lit. *those who bite you*
8 [a] Is. 33:1 [1] Or *bloodshed*
9 [a] Obad. 4 [1] Lit. *hand of evil*
13 [1] Lit. *for what satisfies fire,* for what is of no lasting value
15 [a] Hos. 7:5 [1] Lit. *Attaching* or *Joining* [2] Lit. *their*
16 [1] DSS, LXX *reel!*; Syr., Vg. *fall fast asleep!*

Habakkuk 2:4

Dear Woman of Destiny,

God is a good God, who always provides for us, even when we can't see it with our natural eyes. How I've learned the walk of faith over the years!

When my husband Edwin and I launched into ministry over forty years ago, I was pregnant with my second child, Lois, and we were completely without income. One day I went for my regular checkup, and my doctor asked me for payment of his bill. It was $150.00, which represented a fortune to us!

Edwin was taking speaking engagements whenever and wherever he could. That weekend, as Edwin went off to minister, I stayed home and prayed for three days, desperately asking God for the payment for the doctor. I fully believed that Edwin would come home with a check from the congregation where he ministered that would miraculously be the exact amount we needed.

Instead, Edwin came home with only $7.00 and a fruitcake in a tin that smelled so bad we couldn't even eat it. Seven dollars and a fruitcake! Where was the money for the doctor's bill? Where was the food? Where was the provision God promised?

Today I don't even remember how we paid that doctor's bill. (It hardly matters since Lois is over forty and she's none the worse!) All I remember is the disappointment I experienced. The principle is, disappointments are not based on what we find, but on what we expect to find.

When I prayed "by faith," I had it all figured out how God would answer me. Instead, He surprised me, and He is still full of surprises!

Another time, Edwin and I could only afford to go to the regional camp meeting if he worked while we were there. The job they gave him was cleaning the latrines. He was embarrassed when some young ministers who had much larger churches made a comment to him as he cleaned the bathrooms.

"God, let my latter years of ministry be greater than this humble start," he cried out to the Lord.

When we returned home, we had no money to feed our family. But as we pushed open the front door, we saw an envelope on the floor. Inside was $25.00 cash and a note from a friend who said he dropped by to see us; and when we weren't there, he wanted to bless us with a gift. What a miracle!

God is faithful. Not only does He provide for us, He hears and answers *every* prayer! Today, forty years after Edwin's frustrated prayer in that dirty latrine, we're in a vibrant international ministry that far exceeds anything we thought or imagined (see Eph. 3:20). The proud, the arrogant, the greedy—none of these have a promise from God, but the righteous can assuredly live by faith!

Nancy Corbett Cole

18 "What profit is the image, that its
maker should carve it,
The molded image, a teacher of lies,
That the maker of its mold should
trust in it,
To make mute idols?
19 Woe to him who says to wood,
'Awake!'
To silent stone, 'Arise! It shall
teach!'
Behold, it is overlaid with gold and
silver,
Yet in it there is no breath at all.
20 "But[a] the LORD is in His holy
temple.
Let all the earth keep silence before
Him."

The Prophet's Prayer

3 A prayer of Habakkuk the prophet, on
[1]Shigionoth.

2 O LORD, I have heard Your speech
and was afraid;
O LORD, revive Your work in the
midst of the years!
In the midst of the years make *it*
known;
In wrath remember mercy.

3 God came from Teman,
The Holy One from Mount Paran.
Selah
His glory covered the heavens,
And the earth was full of His praise.
4 *His* brightness was like the light;
He had rays *flashing* from His
hand,
And there His power *was* hidden.
5 Before Him went pestilence,
And fever followed at His feet.
6 He stood and measured the earth;
He looked and startled the nations.
[a]And the everlasting mountains were
scattered,
The perpetual hills bowed.
His ways *are* everlasting.
7 I saw the tents of Cushan in
affliction;
The curtains of the land of Midian
trembled.

8 O LORD, were *You* displeased with
the rivers,
Was Your anger against the rivers,
Was Your wrath against the sea,
That You rode on Your horses,
Your chariots of salvation?
9 Your bow was made quite ready;
Oaths were sworn over *Your*
[1]arrows. Selah
You divided the earth with rivers.
10 The mountains saw You *and*
trembled;
The overflowing of the water passed
by.
The deep uttered its voice,
And [a]lifted its hands on high.
11 The [a]sun and moon stood still in
their habitation;
At the light of Your arrows they
went,
At the shining of Your glittering
spear.

We are conscious of the need of constant prayer for more and yet more of the Holy Spirit's presence and power. But as we give ourselves yet more and more to prayer, we shall see greater and more glorious revivals.

STANLEY FRODSHAM

12 You marched through the land in
indignation;
You [1]trampled the nations in anger.
13 You went forth for the salvation of
Your people,
For salvation with Your Anointed.
You struck the head from the house
of the wicked,
By laying bare from foundation to
neck. Selah
14 You thrust through with his own
arrows
The head of his villages.
They came out like a whirlwind to
scatter me;
Their rejoicing was like feasting on
the poor in secret.
15 [a]You walked through the sea with
Your horses,
Through the heap of great waters.

20 [a]Zeph. 1:7

CHAPTER 3
1 [1]Exact meaning unknown

6 [a]Nah. 1:5

9 [1]Lit. *tribes* or *rods*, cf. v. 14

10 [a]Ex. 14:22

11 [a]Josh. 10:12–14

12 [1]Or *threshed*

15 [a]Ps. 77:19

Habakkuk 3:17–19

Dear Woman of Destiny,

Have you ever been in terrible circumstances and thought there was no way things could get any worse? I certainly have. While serving a five-year prison sentence, I was transferred to a holding facility to await a court appearance. I was overwhelmed by the humiliation and emotional pressure of being shackled, chained, strip-searched, and given the standard orange jumpsuit to wear. The atmosphere of that place was demonic, and the treatment was inhumane. I felt like an animal.

On the day I had to appear in court (yes, in the orange jumpsuit), I had to wait in an isolated holding cell. I had never experienced such hopelessness and extreme despair. I was almost lifeless sitting in that cell, knowing I was about to face the same judge who had sentenced me.

But I began to hear the faint whisper of the Holy Spirit. In my heart, I heard Him say, "Walk around this cell with hands raised, giving praise to Me." I thought, *No way. Not here. Not now*. I was physically and emotionally crushed, barely able to walk, and certainly in no condition to raise my hands. But the prompting would not stop. God would not allow me to focus on my weaknesses. Then I remembered other times in prison when I had been devastated—when my fiancé left me, when I found out that the presidential pardon promising my release had fallen through, when a guard put me into a drainage pit. In each situation, the Holy Spirit had led me to "praise my way through it." These circumstances were much worse, but the Lord was asking for the same response. Could rejoicing in Him make any difference?

I began to hum and walk slowly around that prison cell. I turned my thoughts toward the Lord's faithfulness to me. I gradually took my focus off the orange jumpsuit and my weakened physical condition, and I looked to the Lord. My circumstances did not change, but something inside of me did. A strength, a source of life, began to touch me that hadn't been there before. Instead of humming, I allowed a song to come out of my mouth as I raised my hands and thanked God for His protection and love. I was so amazed as hope began to return and the heavy oppression began to lift. When the guards came to escort me into the courtroom where I would face the Judge and prosecutors who had sentenced me, I had the strength of His presence and the reassurance of His love.

You might not be in a desolate physical prison cell, but your circumstances could seem just as hopeless and lifeless. Habakkuk 3:17–19 tells us that, in desperate and barren circumstances, the response that will enable us to go on with strength is to rejoice in the Lord. Even in the midst of tremendous pressures and difficulties, we can rise above them if we choose to focus on the unchanging faithfulness and endless love of God with praise and worship. Disappointments and unfilled expectations may be your closest friends—and I understand what that feels like—but there is great strength and comfort in turning to Jesus. I encourage you to respond to your difficult circumstances with rejoicing and praise. His strength and peace await you.

Mary Forsythe

16 When I heard, [a]my body trembled;
My lips quivered at *the* voice;
Rottenness entered my bones;
And I trembled in myself,
That I might rest in the day of trouble.
When he comes up to the people,
He will invade them with his troops.

16 a Ps. 119:120

A Hymn of Faith

17 Though the fig tree may not blossom,
Nor fruit be on the vines;
Though the labor of the olive may fail,
And the fields yield no food;
Though the flock may be cut off from the fold,
And there be no herd in the stalls—
18 Yet I will [a]rejoice in the LORD,
I will joy in the God of my salvation.

18 a Is. 41:16; 61:10

Lord God, though ____ may be surrounded by fruitlessness and destruction, yet may they rejoice in You, the God of their salvation. Be their strength; and make their feet like deer's feet to walk on high hills.

FROM HABAKKUK 3:17–19

19 [1]The LORD God is my strength;
He will make my feet like [a]deer's *feet,*
And He will make me [b]walk on my high hills.

To the Chief Musician. With my stringed instruments.

19 a 2 Sam. 22:34 b Deut. 32:13; 33:29 1 Heb. *YHWH Adonai*

AUTHOR: *Zephaniah*
DATE: *Approximately 630 B.C.*
THEME: *The Wrath of a Loving God*
KEY WORDS: *The Day of the Lord, The Lord Is in Your Midst*

ZEPHANIAH

Dear Woman of Destiny,

The God of mercy is a holy God. In Zephaniah, He presents a choice—be holy or be judged. By His mercy, a righteous remnant would survive, and all who called upon Him, whether Jew or Gentile, would be blessed. The book ends with the promise of the Christ to come—the same great hope that transforms the lives of men and women of destiny today.

His love and mine,

Marilyn Hickey

The word of the LORD which came to Zephaniah the son of Cushi, the son of Gedaliah, the son of Amariah, the son of Hezekiah, in the days of [a]Josiah the son of Amon, king of Judah.

The Great Day of the Lord

2 "I will [1]utterly consume everything
From the face of the land,"
Says the LORD;
3 "I[a] will consume man and beast;
I will consume the birds of the heavens,
The fish of the sea,
And the [1]stumbling blocks along with the wicked.
I will cut off man from the face of the [2]land,"
Says the LORD.

4 "I will stretch out My hand against Judah,
And against all the inhabitants of Jerusalem.
[1]I will cut off every trace of Baal from this place,
The names of the [a]idolatrous[2] priests with the *pagan* priests—
5 Those [a]who worship the host of heaven on the housetops;
Those who worship and swear *oaths* by the LORD,
But who *also* swear [b]by [1]Milcom;
6 [a]Those who have turned back from *following* the LORD,
And [b]have not sought the LORD, nor inquired of Him."

7 [a]Be silent in the presence of the Lord GOD;
[b]For the day of the LORD *is* at hand,
For [c]the LORD has prepared a sacrifice;
He has [1]invited His guests.

8 "And it shall be,
In the day of the LORD's sacrifice,
That I will punish [a]the princes and the king's children,
And all such as are clothed with foreign apparel.
9 In the same day I will punish
All those who [a]leap over the threshold,
Who fill their masters' houses with violence and deceit.

10 "And there shall be on that day," says the LORD,
"The sound of a mournful cry from [a]the Fish Gate,
A wailing from the Second Quarter,
And a loud crashing from the hills.
11 [a]Wail, you inhabitants of [1]Maktesh!
For all the merchant people are cut down;
All those who handle money are cut off.

Holding a feast with Him in our hearts, worshiping Him, loving Him, adoring Him, conscious of His presence continually—here is the instrument perfectly adjusted to the Master's touch.

ZELMA ARGUE

12 "And it shall come to pass at that time
That I will search Jerusalem with lamps,
And punish the men
Who are [a]settled[1] in complacency,
[b]Who say in their heart,
'The LORD will not do good,
Nor will He do evil.'
13 Therefore their goods shall become booty,
And their houses a desolation;
They shall build houses, but not inhabit *them;*
They shall plant vineyards, but [a]not drink their wine."

14 [a]The great day of the LORD *is* near;
It is near and hastens quickly.
The noise of the day of the LORD is bitter;
There the mighty men shall cry out.
15 [a]That day *is* a day of wrath,
A day of trouble and distress,
A day of devastation and desolation,
A day of darkness and gloominess,
A day of clouds and thick darkness,
16 A day of [a]trumpet and alarm
Against the fortified cities
And against the high towers.

CHAPTER 1
1 a 2 Kin. 22:1, 2
2 1 Lit. *make a complete end of,* Jer. 8:13
3 a Hos. 4:3 1 Idols 2 *ground*
4 a Hos. 10:5 1 Fulfilled in 2 Kin. 23:4, 5 2 Heb. *chemarim*
5 a 2 Kin. 23:12 b Josh. 23:7 1 Or *Malcam,* an Ammonite god, 1 Kin. 11:5; Jer. 49:1; *Molech,* Lev. 18:21
6 a Is. 1:4 b Hos. 7:7
7 a Zech. 2:13 b Is. 13:6 c Jer. 46:10 1 Lit. *set apart, consecrated*
8 a Jer. 39:6
9 a 1 Sam. 5:5
10 a 2 Chr. 33:14
11 a James 5:1 1 A market district of Jerusalem, lit. *Mortar*
12 a Jer. 48:11 b Ps. 94:7 1 Lit. *on their lees;* like the dregs of wine
13 a Deut. 28:39
14 a Joel 2:1, 11
15 a Is. 22:5
16 a Jer. 4:19

17 "I will bring distress upon men,
And they shall [a]walk like blind
men,
Because they have sinned against
the LORD;
Their blood shall be poured out like
dust,
And their flesh like refuse."

18 [a]Neither their silver nor their gold
Shall be able to deliver them
In the day of the LORD's wrath;
But the whole land shall be
devoured
By the fire of His jealousy,
For He will make speedy riddance
Of all those who dwell in the land.

A Call to Repentance

2 Gather[a] yourselves together, yes,
gather together,
O [1]undesirable nation,
2 Before the decree is issued,
Or the day passes like chaff,
Before the LORD's fierce anger
comes upon you,
Before the day of the LORD's anger
comes upon you!
3 [a]Seek the LORD, [b]all you meek of
the earth,
Who have upheld His justice.
Seek righteousness, seek humility.
[c]It may be that you will be hidden
In the day of the LORD's anger.

Judgment on Nations

4 For [a]Gaza shall be forsaken,
And Ashkelon desolate;
They shall drive out Ashdod [b]at
noonday,
And Ekron shall be uprooted.
5 Woe to the inhabitants of [a]the
seacoast,
The nation of the Cherethites!
The word of the LORD *is* against
you,
O [b]Canaan, land of the Philistines:
"I will destroy you;
So there shall be no inhabitant."

6 The seacoast shall be pastures,
With [1]shelters for shepherds [a]and
folds for flocks.
7 The coast shall be for [a]the
remnant of the house of Judah;
They shall feed *their* flocks there;
In the houses of Ashkelon they
shall lie down at evening.
For the LORD their God will
[b]intervene[1] for them,
And [c]return their captives.
8 "I[a] have heard the reproach of
Moab,
And [b]the insults of the people of
Ammon,
With which they have reproached
My people,
And [c]made arrogant threats against
their borders.
9 Therefore, as I live,"
Says the LORD of hosts, the God of
Israel,
"Surely [a]Moab shall be like Sodom,
And [b]the people of Ammon like
Gomorrah—
[c]Overrun[1] with weeds and saltpits,
And a [2]perpetual desolation.
The residue of My people shall
plunder them,
And the remnant of My people shall
possess them."

10 This they shall have [a]for their
pride,
Because they have reproached and
made arrogant threats
Against the people of the LORD of
hosts.
11 The LORD *will be* awesome to
them,
For He will reduce to nothing all
the gods of the earth;
[a]*People* shall worship Him,
Each one from his place,
Indeed all [b]the shores of the
nations.

12 "You[a] Ethiopians also,
You shall be slain by [b]My sword."

13 And He will stretch out His hand
against the north,
[a]Destroy Assyria,
And make Nineveh a desolation,
As dry as the wilderness.
14 The herds shall lie down in her
midst,
[a]Every beast of the nation.
Both the [b]pelican and the bittern
Shall lodge on the capitals *of* her
pillars;
Their voice shall sing in the
windows;
Desolation *shall be* at the
threshold;
For He will lay bare the [c]cedar
work.

17 a Deut. 28:29
18 a Ezek. 7:19
CHAPTER 2
1 a Joel 1:14; 2:16 *1* Or *shameless*
3 a Amos 5:6 b Ps. 76:9 c Amos 5:14, 15
4 a Zech. 9:5 b Jer. 6:4
5 a Ezek. 25:15–17 b Josh. 13:3
6 a Is. 17:2 *1* Underground huts or cisterns, lit. *excavations*
7 a [Mic. 5:7, 8] b Luke 1:68 c Jer. 29:14 *1* Lit. *visit them*
8 a Jer. 48:27 b Ezek. 25:3 c Jer. 49:1
9 a Is. 15:1–9 b Amos 1:13 c Deut. 29:23 *1* Lit. *Possessed by nettles* *2* Or *permanent ruin*
10 a Is. 16:6
11 a Mal. 1:11 b Gen. 10:5
12 a Is. 18:1–7 b Ps. 17:13
13 a Is.10:5–27; 14:24–27
14 a Is. 13:21 b Is. 14:23; 34:11 c Jer. 22:14

Zephaniah 3:5

Dear Woman of Destiny,

God's love story stays faithfully with us, even in the midst of evil, in the midst of rebellion, in the midst of the most unpromising circumstances. When we believe His love is diminished, it's a sign there's something happening with us, not with Him.

As I passed through midlife, with all its emotional and physical upheavals, I prayed as always, yet felt like I was getting nowhere with God. It was as if His face were veiled from me.

My husband, Edwin, was deeply concerned for me, so he took me with him to a campground where he was scheduled to minister. We were assigned to a rustic cabin in the woods beneath towering trees that produced a delightful, woodsy scent. After a morning session, I slipped down the path to the cabin, while Edwin stayed behind to pray with people at the altars. As I knelt down and once again bared my heart to God in prayer, I sensed Him smiling at me and saying, "I'm not hiding behind a newspaper." It took me aback until I caught the revelation.

You see, when I was growing up, my mother was essentially the leader of our household, leaving my father without a lot to say about the children. Every evening Daddy would come home, bury his head in the newspaper, and peer over it blankly when addressed. He wasn't a bad father, just somewhat absent.

When Edwin joined me after his teaching session, I shared it with him, and we prayed and cried together beneath those glorious trees on that marvelous bare plank floor! What I'd never known before was that I had always seen God in the same way as my earthly father, as one who peered at me blankly if I called to Him, but who wasn't truly interested in the details of my life. Nothing could be further from the truth!

God loved us as sinners. How much more does He care for us now! God perfects the things that concern us. He is deeply interested in every detail of our lives. God lavishes us with His love, never being absent, always giving to us without making us beg for His attention. The love of God Himself fills our heart (see Rom. 5:5).

As I told Edwin that day, God was not hiding Himself from me, but my perception of Him hindered me from seeing Him when He showed Himself to me.

How do you see God? Do you realize that the Creator of the universe wants to have a close relationship with you? He is with you right now, ready to right the most extreme wrong, ready to rescue the most wickedly rebellious, ready to love the most despicably hateful.

An old hymn about God's love has verses like this:

"The love of God is greater far than tongue or pen can ever tell . . . Were every stalk on earth a quill, and every man a scribe by trade; to write the love of God above would drain the ocean dry; nor could the scroll contain the whole, though stretched from sky to sky."

How great is God's love! How great is His faithfulness to you!

Nancy Corbett Cole

15 This is the rejoicing city
[a]That dwelt securely,
[b]That said in her heart,
"I *am it,* and *there is* none besides
me."
How has she become a desolation,
A place for beasts to lie down!
Everyone who passes by her
[c]Shall hiss and [d]shake his fist.

The Wickedness of Jerusalem

3 Woe to her who is rebellious and
polluted,
To the oppressing city!
2 She has not obeyed *His* voice,
She has not received correction;
She has not trusted in the LORD,
She has not drawn near to her God.

3 [a]Her princes in her midst *are*
roaring lions;
Her judges *are* [b]evening wolves
That leave not a bone till morning.
4 Her [a]prophets are insolent,
treacherous people;
Her priests have [1]polluted the
sanctuary,
They have done [b]violence to the
law.
5 The LORD *is* righteous in her
midst,
He will do no unrighteousness.
[1]Every morning He brings His
justice to light;
He never fails,
But [a]the unjust knows no shame.

6 "I have cut off nations,
Their fortresses are devastated;
I have made their streets desolate,
With none passing by.
Their cities are destroyed;
There is no one, no inhabitant.
7 [a]I said, 'Surely you will fear Me,
You will receive instruction'—
So that her dwelling would not be
cut off,
Despite everything for which I
punished her.
But [1]they rose early and [b]corrupted
all their deeds.

A Faithful Remnant

8 "Therefore [a]wait for Me," says the
LORD,
"Until the day I rise up [1]for plunder;
My determination *is* to [b]gather the
nations
To My assembly of kingdoms,
To pour on them My indignation,
All My fierce anger;
All the earth [c]shall be devoured
With the fire of My jealousy.

God wants us of one accord; hearts running together like drops of water. A little company like that could shake a city in a day.

MARIA WOODWORTH-ETTER

9 "For then I will restore to the
peoples [a]a pure [1]language,
That they all may call on the name
of the LORD,
To serve Him with one accord.
10 [a]From beyond the rivers of
Ethiopia
My worshipers,
The daughter of My dispersed ones,
Shall bring My offering.
11 In that day you shall not be
shamed for any of your deeds
In which you transgress against Me;
For then I will take away from your
midst
Those who [a]rejoice in your pride,
And you shall no longer be haughty
In My holy mountain.
12 I will leave in your midst
[a]A meek and humble people,
And they shall trust in the name of
the LORD.
13 [a]The remnant of Israel [b]shall do no
unrighteousness
[c]And speak no lies,
Nor shall a deceitful tongue be
found in their mouth;
For [d]they shall feed *their* flocks and
lie down,
And no one shall make *them*
afraid."

Joy in God's Faithfulness

14 [a]Sing, O daughter of Zion!
Shout, O Israel!
Be glad and rejoice with all *your*
heart,
O daughter of Jerusalem!
15 The LORD has taken away your
judgments,

---

15 [a]Is. 47:8 [b]Rev. 18:7 [c]Lam. 2:15 [d]Nah. 3:19

CHAPTER 3
3 [a]Ezek. 22:27 [b]Hab. 1:8
4 [a]Hos. 9:7 [b]Ezek. 22:26 [1]*Or profaned*
5 [a]Jer. 3:3 [1]Lit. *Morning by morning*
7 [a]Jer. 8:6 [b]Gen. 6:12 [1]They were eager
8 [a]Hab. 2:3 [b]Joel 3:2 [c]Zeph. 1:18 [1]LXX, Syr. *for witness;* Tg. *for the day of My revelation for judgment;* Vg. *for the day of My resurrection that is to come*
9 [a]Is. 19:18; 57:19 [1]Lit. *lip*
10 [a]Ps. 68:31
11 [a]Is. 2:12; 5:15
12 [a]Is. 14:32
13 [a][Mic. 4:7] [b]Is. 60:21 [c]Rev. 14:5 [d]Ezek. 34:13–15, 28
14 [a]Is. 12:6

ZEPHANIAH 3:17

Dear Woman of Destiny,

In *The Hippopotamus Postman*, Joseph Ozawa tells an unforgettable story. Joe dreams of appearing before God. He assumes the most appropriate thing would be to start apologizing, so he says, "God, forgive me for not praying enough." God replies, "Praying is important, but it's not the most important thing." Joseph thinks for a moment and says, "Well, I apologize for being selfish." God says, "Being selfless is good, but it is not the most important thing." Joseph mournfully mounts apology after apology. He apologizes for not giving more to the poor, for not having enough faith. God keeps saying the same thing: "That's important, but it's not the most important thing." It was getting pretty annoying.

Finally Joseph thinks of the ultimate apology. "I am sorry, God; I wasn't very nice to my wife." God, of course, likes men to be nice to their wives. But again He says, "That's important, but it's not the most important thing."

God was frustrating Joe. He finally whines like a little spoiled child, "What do you want from me anyway?"

God replies, "When you appear before Me the final time, I will only have one question to ask of you: Did you learn to receive My love?"

That is the question for you, beloved. This passage in Zephaniah 3:17 is staggering in describing God's love for Israel. It's instructive to us as well. By observing how God loves Israel, we learn how He loves us, because He's grafted us in with them.

God is absolutely, irrepressibly, in love with His chosen people. Israel *is* God's love letter to the world. By observing God's continual commitment to Israel, through centuries of joy and heartbreak, we can be confident that God will never forsake *us* no matter where we're from or what we've done.

In watching Israel, we see that no matter how outlandish God's promises are, He always fulfills them. God's love means He is faithful to do *all* He's promised. God chose Israel to be the chief story, the premiere illustration of how He loves. Because He's kept His promise to Israel, you can be sure He'll keep His promise to you.

God loves us so much He wants to be near—right in the *middle* of us. This is a staggering thought. Jesus chose the Twelve to be *with* Him. For the children of Israel in the wilderness, God's actual presence was *with* them in the fire and the cloud. Jesus came and dwelt *among* us, and we beheld His glory.

The one true, pure, and holy God spends His affections, desires, and attention on *us*. We are not merely some philanthropic project to Him. We are the consuming focus of His energy and passion.

God's love is not only near; it is potent. He is no local deity only powerful in certain jurisdictions. The fact that He brings all Israel back from being scattered all over the world shows that He is the God above all gods. Nothing is too difficult for Him.

God's love for Israel and for you is joyful, expressive, emotive. He sings, He dances, He is completely involved in loving you. This is no detached God.

Which brings us back to our original question: Have you learned to receive His love? Your answer determines your joy.

Fawn Parish

He has cast out your enemy.
[a]The King of Israel, the LORD, [b]*is* in your midst;
You shall [1]see disaster no more.

16 In that day [a]it shall be said to Jerusalem:
"Do not fear;
Zion, [b]let not your hands be weak.
17 The LORD your God [a]in your midst,
The Mighty One, will save;
[b]He will rejoice over you with gladness,
He will quiet *you* with His love,
He will rejoice over you with singing."

18 "I will gather those who [a]sorrow over the appointed assembly,
Who are among you,
To whom its reproach *is* a burden.
19 Behold, at that time
I will deal with all who afflict you;
I will save the [a]lame,
And gather those who were driven out;
I will appoint them for praise and fame
In every land where they were put to shame.
20 At that time [a]I will bring you back,
Even at the time I gather you;
For I will give you [1]fame and praise
Among all the peoples of the earth,
When I return your captives before your eyes,"
Says the LORD.

15 a[John 1:49]
b Ezek. 48:35
1 So with Heb. mss., LXX, Bg.; MT, Vg. *fear*
16 a Is. 35:3, 4
b Heb. 12:12
17 a Zeph. 3:5, 15
b Is. 62:5; 65:19
18 a Lam. 2:6
19 a [Mic. 4:6, 7]
20 a Is. 11:12
1 Lit. *a name*

O Lord God, You are in our midst. Mighty One, I pray that You will save _____. Rejoice over her with gladness; quiet her with Your love. Rejoice over her with singing.

FROM ZEPHANIAH 3:17

AUTHOR: *Haggai*
DATE: *520 B.C.*
THEME: *Rebuilding the Temple*
KEY WORDS: *The Lord's House, Consider, Glory*

HAGGAI

Dear Woman of Destiny,

Thank God for His Word that strengthens us in the face of opposition. Haggai preached to the Jews, whose personal issues hindered the rebuilding of the temple. As Haggai stirred their hearts to return to their purpose, he stirs us to greater focus and commitment. No matter what the conflict, or how intense the distraction, as we seek God first, we *will* complete our divine assignments.

His love and mine,

Marilyn Hickey

The Command to Build God's House

In [a]the second year of King Darius, in
the sixth month, on the first day of
the month, the word of the LORD
came by [b]Haggai the prophet to [c]Ze-
rubbabel the son of Shealtiel, governor
of Judah, and to [d]Joshua the son of
[e]Jehozadak, the high priest, saying,
2“Thus speaks the LORD of hosts, saying:
‘This people says, “The time has not come,
the time that the LORD's house should be
built.” ’ ”
3Then the word of the LORD [a]came by
Haggai the prophet, saying, 4“*Is it* [a]time
for you yourselves to dwell in your paneled houses, and this [1]temple *to lie* in ruins?” 5Now therefore, thus says the LORD
of hosts: [a]“Consider your ways!

6 “You have [a]sown much, and bring
in little;
You eat, but do not have enough;
You drink, but you are not filled
with drink;
You clothe yourselves, but no one
is warm;
And [b]he who earns wages,
Earns wages *to put* into a bag with
holes.”

You have to bring your mind to the Word of God and not try to bring the Word of God to your mind.

SMITH WIGGLESWORTH

7Thus says the LORD of hosts: “Consider
your ways! 8Go up to the [a]mountains and
bring wood and build the [1]temple, that I
may take pleasure in it and be glorified,”
says the LORD. 9[a]“*You* looked for much,
but indeed *it came to* little; and when you
brought it home, [b]I blew it away. Why?”
says the LORD of hosts. “Because of My
house that *is in* ruins, while every one of
you runs to his own house. 10Therefore
[a]the heavens above you withhold the dew,
and the earth withholds its fruit. 11For I
[a]called for a drought on the land and the
mountains, on the grain and the new wine
and the oil, on whatever the ground
brings forth, on men and livestock, and
on [b]all the labor of *your* hands.”

The People's Obedience

12[a]Then Zerubbabel the son of Shealtiel, and Joshua the son of Jehozadak, the
high priest, with all the remnant of the
people, obeyed the voice of the LORD their
God, and the words of Haggai the prophet,
as the LORD their God had sent him; and
the people feared the presence of the
LORD. 13Then Haggai, the LORD's messenger, spoke the LORD's message to the people, saying, [a]“I *am* with you, says the
LORD.” 14So [a]the LORD stirred up the spirit
of Zerubbabel the son of Shealtiel, [b]gover-
nor of Judah, and the spirit of Joshua the
son of Jehozadak, the high priest, and the
spirit of all the remnant of the people;
[c]and they came and worked on the house
of the LORD of hosts, their God, 15on the
twenty-fourth day of the sixth month, in
the second year of King Darius.

The Coming Glory of God's House

2 In the seventh *month,* on the twenty-
first of the month, the word of the
LORD came [1]by Haggai the prophet, saying: 2“Speak now to Zerubbabel the son of
Shealtiel, governor of Judah, and to Joshua the son of Jehozadak, the high priest,
and to the remnant of the people, saying:
3[a]‘Who is left among you who saw this
[1]temple in its former glory? And how do
you see it now? In comparison with it, [b]*is
this* not in your eyes as nothing? 4Yet now
[a]be strong, Zerubbabel,’ says the LORD;
‘and be strong, Joshua, son of Jehozadak,
the high priest; and be strong, all you people of the land,’ says the LORD, ‘and work;
for I *am* with you,’ says the LORD of hosts.
5[a]‘*According to* the word that I covenanted with you when you came out of
Egypt, so [b]My Spirit remains among you;
do not fear!’
6 “For thus says the LORD of hosts:
[a]‘Once more (it *is* a little while) [b]I will
shake heaven and earth, the sea and dry
land; 7and I will shake all nations, and
they shall come to [a]the [1]Desire of All Nations, and I will fill this [2]temple with [b]glo-
ry,’ says the LORD of hosts. 8‘The silver *is*
Mine, and the gold *is* Mine,’ says the LORD
of hosts. 9[a]‘The glory of this latter [1]tem-
ple shall be greater than the former,’ says

CHAPTER 1
1 [a]Ezra 4:24 [b]Ezra 5:1; 6:14 [c]Ezra 2:2 [d]Ezra 5:2, 3 [e]1 Chr. 6:15
3 [a]Ezra 5:1
4 [a]2 Sam. 7:2 [1]Lit. *house*
5 [a]Lam. 3:40
6 [a]Deut. 28:38–40 [b]Zech. 8:10
8 [a]Ezra 3:7 [1]Lit. *house*
9 [a]Hag. 2:16 [b]Hag. 2:17
10 [a]Deut. 28:23
11 [a]1 Kin. 17:1 [b]Hag. 2:17
12 [a]Ezra 5:2
13 [a][Matt. 28:20]
14 [a]Ezra 1:1 [b]Hag. 2:21 [c]Ezra 5:2, 8

CHAPTER 2
1 [1]Lit. *by the hand of*
3 [a]Ezra 3:12, 13 [b]Zech. 4:10 [1]Lit. *house*
4 [a]Zech. 8:9
5 [a]Ex. 29:45, 46 [b][Neh. 9:20]
6 [a]Heb. 12:26 [b][Joel 3:16]
7 [a]Gen. 49:10 [b]Is. 60:7 [1]Or *desire of all nations* [2]Lit. *house*
9 [a][John 1:14] [1]Lit. *house*

Haggai 2:6–9

Dear Woman of Destiny,

Are you experiencing a "whole lotta shaking going on" in your Christian life? If so, hang on! You are normal, because the Christian life can be compared to living on God's fault line. However, the shaking that God does is constructive, not destructive.

Haggai told his audience in 520 B.C. that God would "once more . . . shake heaven and earth, the sea and dry land" (Hag. 2:6). He said that He would "shake all nations" (Hag. 2:7). God had shaken the earth in the past at Sinai, but the Book of Hebrews says that this second "once more" shaking happened when the New Covenant was established through Christ (see Heb. 12:18–29, especially verses 27–29). It is going on now and will reach its climax at the Second Coming. This shaking occurs so that all that is made or created is removed and only the unshakeable remains. The "unshakeable" that is left is the kingdom of God.

God is committed to establishing His kingdom in our lives. This is our destiny! To achieve this He will shake us so that everything that is not of His kingdom is removed, like dead autumn leaves stripped off trees by the wind. In Exodus 19 and 20, God visited His chosen people, the nation of Israel. What took place were earthshaking events in Israel's history. The comparison is that the same type of earthshaking events are taking place in our daily lives as we are being conformed to the image of Christ.

The Jews who originally heard Haggai prophesy had just undergone a shaking. God had confronted them about their complacency and disobedience to His specific command to rebuild the temple in Jerusalem. Haggai records that they got back on track and began rebuilding so that they could once again have a place of worship, a temple (see Hag. 1:14). It seems, however, that God wanted these rebuilders to understand that their building project was not His ultimate goal. He had a future building in mind that would not be made of stones and mortar. Now we know that this future temple is glorious, more glorious than Solomon's temple. And it involves the nations. It is where God's glory will dwell, and it will be a place of peace (see Hag. 2:9). Ultimately, that temple is God's people. His glory dwells in you (see 1 Cor. 3:16, 17; 6:19; 2 Cor. 6:16; Eph. 2:19–22; 1 Tim. 3:15; 1 Pet. 2:4).

So the kingdom of God is not about buildings, but people—people of all nations. Buildings are not the dwelling place that God desires. How impersonal. No, He wants to get much closer than that. God's people are the treasures of His spiritual temple.

As a woman of destiny, you are involved in the Lord's ongoing building project. You are called to build into your life and into the lives of others the unshakeable kingdom of God.

Judy Smith

Lord, draw the nations to Yourself. May _____ and her people be counted among those who come. Desire of All Nations, as You promised to fill the temple, Lord, fill Your church.

FROM HAGGAI 2:7

the LORD of hosts. 'And in this place I will
give [b]peace,' says the LORD of hosts."

The People Are Defiled

10On the twenty-fourth *day* of the
ninth *month,* in the second year of Darius, the word of the LORD came by Haggai
the prophet, saying, 11"Thus says the
LORD of hosts: 'Now, [a]ask the priests *concerning the* law, saying, 12"If one carries
holy meat in the fold of his garment, and
with the edge he touches bread or stew,
wine or oil, or any food, will it become
holy?" ' "
Then the priests answered and
said, "No."
13And Haggai said, "If *one who is* [a]un-
clean *because* of a dead body touches any
of these, will it be unclean?"
So the priests answered and said, "It
shall be unclean."
14Then Haggai answered and said,
[a]" 'So is this people, and so is this nation
before Me,' says the LORD, 'and so is every
work of their hands; and what they offer
there is unclean.

Promised Blessing

15'And now, carefully [a]consider from
this day forward: from before stone was
laid upon stone in the temple of the
LORD— 16since those *days,* [a]when *one*
came to a heap of twenty ephahs, there
were *but* ten; when *one* came to the wine
vat to draw out fifty baths from the press,
there were *but* twenty. 17[a]I struck you
with blight and mildew and hail [b]in all the
labors of your hands; [c]yet you did not
turn to Me,' says the LORD. 18'Consider
now from this day forward, from the
twenty-fourth day of the ninth month,
from [a]the day that the foundation of the
LORD's temple was laid—consider it: 19[a]Is
the seed still in the barn? As yet the vine,
the fig tree, the pomegranate, and the olive tree have not yielded *fruit. But* from
this day I will [b]bless *you.*' "

Zerubbabel Chosen as a Signet

20And again the word of the LORD came
to Haggai on the twenty-fourth day of the
month, saying, 21"Speak to Zerubbabel,
[a]governor of Judah, saying:

[b]'I will shake heaven and earth.
22 [a]I will overthrow the throne of
kingdoms;
I will destroy the strength of the
Gentile kingdoms.
[b]I will overthrow the chariots
And those who ride in them;
The horses and their riders shall
come down,
Every one by the sword of his
brother.

23'In that day,' says the LORD of hosts, 'I
will take you, Zerubbabel My servant, the
son of Shealtiel,' says the LORD, [a]'and will
make you like a signet *ring;* for [b]I have
chosen you,' says the LORD of hosts."

9 b Ps. 85:8, 9
11 a Mal. 2:7
13 a Num. 19:11, 22
14 a [Titus 1:15]
15 a Hag. 1:5, 7; 2:18
16 a Zech. 8:10
17 a Deut. 28:22 b Hag. 1:11 c Amos 4:6–11
18 a Zech. 8:9
19 a Zech. 8:12 b [Mal. 3:10]
21 a Zech. 4:6–10 b Hag. 2:6, 7
22 a [Dan. 2:44] b Mic. 5:10
23 a Song 8:6 b Is. 42:1; 43:10

AUTHOR: *Zechariah*
DATE: *520–475 B.C.*
THEME: *The Lord Remembers Zion*
KEY WORDS: *Jerusalem, The Day of the Lord, That Day*

ZECHARIAH

Dear Woman of Destiny,

Like Haggai, Zechariah delivered a message of encouragement. Prompted by his faith, the Israelites completed the temple, preparing hearts for the fullness of God's glory—the coming Messiah. Zechariah foreshadows a clear and powerful picture of Jesus—the One who would dwell, not in temples made with hands, but within the hearts of men. Rejoice as your heart is filled with the good news today!

His love and mine,

Marilyn Hickey

A Call to Repentance

In the eighth month [a]of the second
year of Darius, the word of the LORD
came [b]to Zechariah the son of Berechiah, the son of [c]Iddo the prophet, saying, 2"The LORD has been very angry with
your fathers. 3Therefore say to them,
'Thus says the LORD of hosts: "Return [a]to
Me," says the LORD of hosts, "and I will
return to you," says the LORD of hosts.
4"Do not be like your fathers, [a]to whom
the former prophets preached, saying,
'Thus says the LORD of hosts: [b]"Turn now
from your evil ways and your evil deeds." '
But they did not hear nor heed Me," says
the LORD.

When coming back to God for pardon, come with all you have. Lay it at His feet. Come with your body to offer as a living sacrifice upon His altar. Come with your soul and all its powers, and yield them in willing consecration to your God and Savior. Come with your spirit and yield it to His spirit.

MRS. F. F. BOSWORTH

5 "Your fathers, where *are* they?
And the prophets, do they live
forever?
6 Yet surely [a]My words and My
statutes,
Which I commanded My servants
the prophets,
Did they not overtake your fathers?

"So they returned and said:

[b]'Just as the LORD of hosts
determined to do to us,
According to our ways and
according to our deeds,
So He has dealt with us.' " ' "

Vision of the Horses

7On the twenty-fourth day of the eleventh month, which is the month Shebat,
in the second year of Darius, the word of
the LORD came to Zechariah the son of
Berechiah, the son of Iddo the prophet: 8I
saw by night, and behold, [a]a man riding
on a red horse, and it stood among the
myrtle trees in the hollow; and behind
him *were* [b]horses: red, sorrel, and white.
9Then I said, [a]"My lord, what *are* these?"
So the angel who talked with me said to
me, "I will show you what they *are*."
10And the man who stood among the
myrtle trees answered and said, [a]"These
are the ones whom the LORD has sent to
walk to and fro throughout the earth."
11[a]So they answered the Angel of the
LORD, who stood among the myrtle trees,
and said, "We have walked to and fro
throughout the earth, and behold, all the
earth is [1]resting quietly."

The Lord Will Comfort Zion

12Then the Angel of the LORD answered
and said, "O LORD of hosts, [a]how long will
You not have mercy on Jerusalem and on
the cities of Judah, against which You
were angry [b]these seventy years?"
13And the LORD answered the angel who
talked to me, *with* [a]good *and* comforting
words. 14So the angel who spoke with me
said to me, [1]"Proclaim, saying, 'Thus says
the LORD of hosts:

"I am [a]zealous[2] for Jerusalem
And for Zion with great [3]zeal.
15 I am exceedingly angry with the
nations at ease;
For [a]I was a little angry,
And they helped—*but* with evil
intent."

16'Therefore thus says the LORD:

[a]"I am returning to Jerusalem with
mercy;
My [b]house [c]shall be built in it,"
says the LORD of hosts,
"And [d]a *surveyor's* line shall be
stretched out over Jerusalem." '

17"Again proclaim, saying, 'Thus says
the LORD of hosts:

"My cities shall again [1]spread out
through prosperity;
[a]The LORD will again comfort Zion,
And [b]will again choose
Jerusalem." ' "

CHAPTER 1
1 a Zech. 7:1 b Matt. 23:35 c Neh. 12:4, 16
3 a [Mal. 3:7–10]
4 a 2 Chr. 36:15, 16 b Is. 31:6
6 a [Is. 55:11] b Lam. 1:18; 2:17
8 a [Rev. 6:4] b [Zech. 6:2–7]
9 a Zech. 4:4, 5, 13; 6:4
10 a [Heb. 1:14]
11 a [Ps. 103:20, 21] *1* Lit. *sitting and quiet*
12 a Ps. 74:10 b Jer. 25:11, 12; 29:10
13 a Jer. 29:10
14 a Zech. 8:2 *1* Lit. *Cry out* *2* Or *jealous* *3* Or *jealousy*
15 a Is. 47:6
16 a [Zech. 2:10; 8:3] b Ezra 6:14, 15 c Is. 44:28 d Zech. 2:1–3
17 a [Is. 40:1, 2; 51:3] b Zech. 2:12 *1* Or *overflow with good*

Vision of the Horns

18Then I raised my eyes and looked, and
there *were* four [a]horns. 19And I said to the
angel who talked with me, "What *are*
these?"

So he answered me, [a]"These *are* the
[1]horns that have scattered Judah, Israel,
and Jerusalem."

20Then the LORD showed me four
craftsmen. 21And I said, "What are these
coming to do?"

So he said, "These *are* the [a]horns that
scattered Judah, so that no one could lift
up his head; but [1]the craftsmen are coming to terrify them, to cast out the horns
of the nations that [b]lifted up *their* horn
against the land of Judah to scatter it."

Vision of the Measuring Line

2 Then I raised my eyes and looked, and
behold, [a]a man with a measuring line
in his hand. 2So I said, "Where are you
going?"

And he said to me, [a]"To measure Jerusalem, to see what *is* its width and what *is*
its length."

3And there *was* the angel who talked
with me, going out; and another angel
was coming out to meet him, 4who said to
him, "Run, speak to this young man, saying: [a]'Jerusalem shall be inhabited *as*
towns without walls, because of the multitude of men and livestock in it. 5For I,'
says the LORD, 'will be [a]a wall of fire all
around her, [b]and I will be the glory in her
midst.' "

Future Joy of Zion and Many Nations

6"Up, up! Flee [a]from the land of the
north," says the LORD; "for I have [b]spread
you abroad like the four winds of heaven,"
says the LORD. 7"Up, Zion! [a]Escape, you
who dwell with the daughter of Babylon."

8For thus says the LORD of hosts: "He
sent Me after glory, to the nations which
plunder you; for he who [a]touches you
touches the [1]apple of His eye. 9For surely
I will [a]shake My hand against them, and
they shall become [1]spoil for their servants. Then [b]you will know that the LORD
of hosts has sent Me.

10[a]"Sing and rejoice, O daughter of
Zion! For behold, I am coming and I [b]will
dwell in your midst," says the LORD.
11[a]"Many nations shall be joined to the
LORD [b]in that day, and they shall become
[c]My people. And I will dwell in your midst.
Then [d]you will know that the LORD of
hosts has sent Me to you. 12And the LORD
will [a]take possession of Judah as His inheritance in the Holy Land, and will again
choose Jerusalem. 13[a]Be silent, all flesh,
before the LORD, for He is aroused [b]from
His holy habitation!"

> *Peace like a river—undisturbed by anything—this is your inheritance. If you had 10 million pounds at your disposal, you could not buy it. It comes to the broken and contrite heart—the heart that says an inward "amen" to God and will not withdraw that "amen" for anything.*
>
> SMITH WIGGLESWORTH

Vision of the High Priest

3 Then he showed me [a]Joshua the high
priest standing before the Angel of the
LORD, and [b]Satan[1] standing at his right
hand to oppose him. 2And the LORD said
to Satan, [a]"The LORD rebuke you, Satan!
The LORD who [b]has chosen Jerusalem rebuke you! [c]*Is* this not a brand plucked
from the fire?"

3Now Joshua was clothed with [a]filthy
garments, and was standing before the
Angel.

4Then He answered and spoke to those
who stood before Him, saying, "Take away
the filthy garments from him." And to
him He said, "See, I have removed your
iniquity from you, [a]and I will clothe you
with rich robes."

5And I said, "Let them put a clean [a]tur-
ban on his head."

So they put a clean turban on his head,
and they put the clothes on him. And the
Angel of the LORD stood by.

---

18 a [Lam. 2:17]
19 a Ezra 4:1, 4, 7 *1* Kingdoms or powers
21 a [Ps. 75:10] b Ps. 75:4, 5 *1* Lit. *these*

CHAPTER 2
1 a Jer. 31:39
2 a Rev. 11:1
4 a Jer. 31:27
5 a [Is. 26:1] b [Is. 60:19]
6 a Is. 48:20 b Deut. 28:64
7 a Is. 48:20
8 a Deut. 32:10 *1* Lit. *pupil*
9 a Is. 19:16 b Zech. 4:9 *1 booty* or *plunder*
10 a Is. 12:6 b [Lev. 26:12]
11 a [Is. 2:2, 3] b Zech. 3:10 c Ex. 12:49 d Ezek. 33:33
12 a [Deut. 32:9]
13 a Hab. 2:20 b Ps. 68:5

CHAPTER 3
1 a Hag. 1:1 b Ps. 109:6 *1* Lit. *the Adversary*
2 a [Jude 9] b [Rom. 8:33] c Amos 4:11
3 a Is. 64:6
4 a Is. 61:10
5 a Ex. 29:6

The Coming Branch

6Then the Angel of the LORD admonished Joshua, saying, 7"Thus says the
LORD of hosts:

'If you will walk in My ways,
And if you will [a]keep My command,
Then you shall also [b]judge My
house,
And likewise have charge of My
courts;
I will give you places to walk
Among these who [c]stand here.

8 'Hear, O Joshua, the high priest,
You and your companions who sit
before you,
For they are [a]a[1] wondrous sign;
For behold, I am bringing forth
[b]My Servant the [c]BRANCH.
9 For behold, the stone
That I have laid before Joshua:
[a]Upon the stone *are* [b]seven eyes.
Behold, I will engrave its
inscription,'
Says the LORD of hosts,
'And [c]I will remove the iniquity of
that land in one day.
10 [a]In that day,' says the LORD of
hosts,
'Everyone will invite his neighbor
[b]Under his vine and under his fig
tree.' "

Vision of the Lampstand and Olive Trees

4 Now [a]the angel who talked with me
came back and wakened me, [b]as a
man who is wakened out of his sleep. 2And
he said to me, "What do you see?"
So I said, "I am looking, and there *is* [a]a
lampstand of solid gold with a bowl on top
of it, [b]and on the *stand* seven lamps with
seven pipes to the seven lamps. 3[a]Two olive trees *are* by it, one at the right of the
bowl and the other at its left." 4So I answered and spoke to the angel who talked
with me, saying, "What *are* these, my
lord?"
5Then the angel who talked with me
answered and said to me, "Do you not
know what these are?"
And I said, "No, my lord."
6So he answered and said to me:

"This *is* the word of the LORD to
[a]Zerubbabel:
[b]'Not by might nor by power, but by
My Spirit,'
Says the LORD of hosts.
7 'Who *are* you, [a]O great mountain?
Before Zerubbabel *you shall
become* a plain!
And he shall bring forth [b]the
capstone
[c]With shouts of "Grace, grace to
it!" ' "

May ____ be reminded that it is not by might nor by power, but by Your Spirit, O Lord.

FROM ZECHARIAH 4:6

8Moreover the word of the LORD came
to me, saying:

9 "The hands of Zerubbabel
[a]Have laid the foundation of this
[1]temple;
His hands [b]shall also finish *it*.
Then [c]you will know
That the [d]LORD of hosts has sent
Me to you.
10 For who has despised the day of
[a]small things?
For these seven rejoice to see
The [1]plumb line in the hand of
Zerubbabel.
[b]They are the eyes of the LORD,
Which scan to and fro throughout
the whole earth."

11Then I answered and said to him,
"What *are* these [a]two olive trees—at the
right of the lampstand and at its left?"
12And I further answered and said to him,
"What *are these* two olive branches that
drip [1]into the receptacles of the two gold
pipes from which the golden *oil* drains?"
13Then he answered me and said, "Do
you not know what these *are?*"
And I said, "No, my lord."
14So he said, [a]"These *are* the two
[1]anointed ones, [b]who stand beside the
Lord of the whole earth."

Vision of the Flying Scroll

5 Then I turned and raised my eyes, and
saw there a flying [a]scroll.
2And he said to me, "What do you see?"

7 [a]Lev. 8:35 [b]Deut. 17:9, 12 [c]Zech. 3:4

8 [a]Ps. 71:7 [b]Is. 42:1 [c]Is. 11:1; 53:2 [1]Lit. *men of a sign* or *wonder*

9 [a][Zech. 4:10] [b]Ps. 118:22 [c]Jer. 31:34; 50:20

10 [a]Zech. 2:11 [b]Is. 36:16

CHAPTER 4

1 [a]Zech. 1:9; 2:3 [b]Dan. 8:18

2 [a]Rev. 1:12 [b][Rev. 4:5]

3 [a]Rev. 11:3, 4

6 [a]Hag. 1:1 [b]Hos. 1:7

7 [a]Jer. 51:25 [b]Ps. 118:22 [c]Ezra 3:10, 11, 13

9 [a]Ezra 3:8–10; 5:16 [b]Ezra 6:14, 15 [c]Zech. 2:9, 11; 6:15 [d][Is. 43:16] [1]Lit. *house*

10 [a]Hag. 2:3 [b]2 Chr. 16:9 [1]Lit. *plummet stone*

11 [a]Zech. 4:3

12 [1]Lit. *into the hands of*

14 [a]Rev. 11:4 [b]Zech. 3:1–7 [1]Lit. *sons of fresh oil*

CHAPTER 5

1 [a]Ezek. 2:9

Zechariah 4:10

Dear Woman of Destiny,

When Jack and I began in ministry, we had no idea what God was going to do with us. We were just willing to do whatever He asked and go wherever He led.

As we look back on it now, we wonder why anyone would have listened to two youngsters. We were inexperienced both as ministers and in life itself. We had been married only a couple of years, had just graduated from Bible college, and still had no children. But, in our youthful zeal and enthusiasm, we were ready to "save the world." I have often thought that if young people who enter the ministry did not have that "all-conquering" feeling, they couldn't stand when the hard times come.

Our first pastorate was in Fort Wayne, Indiana. Supposedly, there were thirty to thirty-five people in town who wanted a Foursquare Church, but that is not what we found when we arrived. There were only five or six very elderly people who attended a small service in the YMCA every Sunday afternoon. Now, I love the elderly and prize their wisdom and experience, but these were folk who came to the service only because a free dinner was served at the Y that day. Not an ideal group to launch a church.

Shortly after our arrival in Fort Wayne, we found a little building to house our flock. It was up to Jack and me to do everything! We cleaned the church, taught Sunday school, led the music, played the piano, preached, and did all the yard work. One time Jack even painted the outside of the church, and another dear lady and I made all the curtains for the sanctuary.

We have often said that we would be happy to do it all over again if the Lord led. We also know that He did not put us in Fort Wayne for what we could do for Him, but rather for what He could teach us during our time there. We are so thankful for the experience of those first four years in ministry because that is when we were really educated.

We learned to study, to counsel, to love people even at their most unlovable. We learned to trust the Lord for everything—food, housing, bill-paying, and taking care of our little ones as they came along (two of our four children were born there). We learned to stand against the devil when attacks of loneliness came or when we were faced with doubt and questioning. We learned to stay in the place God had sent us when everything in us wanted to jump and run.

Dear Woman of Destiny, don't despise your day of "small things." It's the hard times that make us strong. And it's the "small things" that will prepare you for the bigger things God has in store for you.

Anna Hayford

So I answered, "I see a flying scroll. Its length *is* twenty cubits and its width ten cubits."

3Then he said to me, "This *is* the [a]curse that goes out over the face of the whole earth: 'Every thief shall be expelled,' according *to* this side of *the scroll;* and, 'Every perjurer shall be expelled,' according *to* that side of it."

4 "I will send out *the curse,*" says the
LORD of hosts;
"It shall enter the house of the
[a]thief
And the house of [b]the one who
swears falsely by My name.
It shall remain in the midst of his
house
And consume [c]it, with its timber
and stones."

Vision of the Woman in a Basket

5Then the angel who talked with me came out and said to me, "Lift your eyes now, and see what this *is* that goes forth."

6So I asked, "What *is* it?" And he said, "It *is* a [1]basket that is going forth."

He also said, "This *is* their resemblance throughout the earth: 7Here *is* a lead disc lifted up, and this *is* a woman sitting inside the basket"; 8then he said, "This *is* Wickedness!" And he thrust her down into the basket, and threw the lead [1]cover over its mouth. 9Then I raised my eyes and looked, and there *were* two women, coming with the wind in their wings; for they had wings like the wings of a [a]stork, and they lifted up the basket between earth and heaven.

10So I said to the [a]angel who talked with me, "Where are they carrying the basket?"

11And he said to me, "To [a]build a house for it in [b]the land of [1]Shinar; when it is ready, *the basket* will be set there on its base."

Vision of the Four Chariots

6 Then I turned and raised my eyes and looked, and behold, four chariots *were* coming from between two mountains, and the mountains *were* mountains of bronze. 2With the first chariot *were* [a]red horses, with the second chariot [b]black horses, 3with the third chariot white horses, and with the fourth chariot dappled horses—strong *steeds.* 4Then I answered [a]and said to the angel who talked with me, "What *are* these, my lord?"

5And the angel answered and said to me, [a]"These *are* four spirits of heaven, who go out from *their* [b]station before the Lord of all the earth. 6[1]The one with the black horses is going to [a]the north country, the white are going after them, and the dappled are going toward the south country." 7Then the strong *steeds* went out, eager to go, that they might [a]walk to and fro throughout the earth. And He said, "Go, walk to and fro throughout the earth." So they walked to and fro throughout the earth. 8And He called to me, and spoke to me, saying, "See, those who go toward the north country have given rest to My [a]Spirit in the north country."

The Command to Crown Joshua

9Then the word of the LORD came to me, saying: 10"Receive *the gift* from the captives—from Heldai, Tobijah, and Jedaiah, who have come from Babylon—and go the same day and enter the house of Josiah the son of Zephaniah. 11Take the silver and gold, make [a]an[1] elaborate crown, and set *it* on the head of [b]Joshua the son of Jehozadak, the high priest. 12Then speak to him, saying, 'Thus says the LORD of hosts, saying:

"Behold, [a]the Man whose name *is*
the [b]BRANCH!
From His place He shall [1]branch
out,
[c]And He shall build the temple of
the LORD;
13 Yes, He shall build the temple of
the LORD.
He [a]shall bear the glory,
And shall sit and rule on His
throne;
So [b]He shall be a priest on His
throne,
And the counsel of peace shall be
between [1]them both." '

14"Now the [1]elaborate crown shall be [a]for a memorial in the temple of the LORD [2]for Helem, Tobijah, Jedaiah, and Hen the son of Zephaniah. 15Even [a]those from afar shall come and build the temple of the LORD. Then you shall know that the LORD of hosts has sent Me to you. And *this* shall come to pass if you diligently obey the voice of the LORD your God."

---

3 a Mal. 4:6
4 a Ex. 20:15 b Lev. 19:12 c Lev. 14:34, 35
6 *1* Heb. *ephah,* a measuring container, and so elsewhere
8 *1* Lit. *stone*
9 a Lev. 11:13, 19
10 a Zech. 5:5
11 a Jer. 29:5, 28 b Gen. 10:10 *1* Babylon

CHAPTER 6
2 a Zech. 1:8 b Rev. 6:5
4 a Zech. 5:10
5 a [Heb. 1:7, 14] b Dan. 7:10
6 a Jer. 1:14 *1* The chariot
7 a Zech. 1:10
8 a Eccl. 10:4
11 a Ex. 29:6 b Hag. 1:1 *1* Lit. *crowns*
12 a John 1:45 b Zech. 3:8 c [Eph. 2:20] *1* Lit. *sprout up*
13 a Is. 22:24 b Ps. 110:4 *1* Both offices
14 a Ex. 12:14 *1* Lit. *crowns* *2* So with MT, Tg., Vg.; Syr. *for Heldai* (cf. v. 10); LXX *for the patient ones*
15 a Is. 57:19

Obedience Better than Fasting

7 Now in the fourth year of King Darius it came to pass *that* the word of the LORD came to Zechariah, on the fourth day of the ninth month, Chislev, 2when [1]*the people* sent [2]Sherezer, with Regem-Melech and his men, *to* [3]the house of God, [4]to pray before the LORD, 3*and* to [a]ask the priests who *were* in the house of the LORD of hosts, and the prophets, saying, "Should I weep in [b]the fifth month and [1]fast as I have done for so many years?"

4Then the word of the LORD of hosts came to me, saying, 5"Say to all the people of the land, and to the priests: 'When you [a]fasted and mourned in the fifth [b]and seventh *months* [c]during those seventy years, did you really fast [d]for Me—for Me? 6[a]When you eat and when you drink, do you not eat and drink *for yourselves?* 7*Should you* not *have obeyed* the words which the LORD proclaimed through the [a]former prophets when Jerusalem and the cities around it were inhabited and prosperous, and [b]the [1]South and the Lowland were inhabited?' "

Father, may ____ execute true justice and show mercy and compassion. May they not oppress the widow or the fatherless, the alien or the poor. May they not plan evil in their hearts against another.

FROM ZECHARIAH 7:9, 10

Disobedience Resulted in Captivity

8Then the word of the LORD came to Zechariah, saying, 9"Thus says the LORD of hosts:

[a]'Execute true justice,
Show [1]mercy and compassion
Everyone to his brother.
10 [a]Do not oppress the widow or the fatherless,
The alien or the poor.
[b]Let none of you plan evil in his heart
Against his brother.'

11But they refused to heed, [a]shrugged[1] their shoulders, and [b]stopped[2] their ears so that they could not hear. 12Yes, they made their [a]hearts like flint, [b]refusing to hear the law and the words which the LORD of hosts had sent by His Spirit through the former prophets. [c]Thus great wrath came from the LORD of hosts. 13Therefore it happened, *that* just as He proclaimed and they would not hear, so [a]they called out and I would not listen," says the LORD of hosts. 14"But [a]I scattered them with a whirlwind among all the nations which they had not known. Thus the land became desolate after them, so that no one passed through or returned; for they made the pleasant land desolate."

Jerusalem, Holy City of the Future

8 Again the word of the LORD of hosts came, saying, 2"Thus says the LORD of hosts:

[a]'I am [1]zealous for Zion with great [2]zeal;
With great [3]fervor I am zealous for her.'

3"Thus says the LORD:

[a]'I will return to Zion,
And [b]dwell in the midst of Jerusalem.
Jerusalem [c]shall be called the City of Truth,
[d]The Mountain of the LORD of hosts,
[e]The Holy Mountain.'

4"Thus says the LORD of hosts:

[a]'Old men and old women shall again sit
In the streets of Jerusalem,
Each one with his staff in his hand
Because of [1]great age.
5 The streets of the city
Shall be [a]full of boys and girls
Playing in its streets.'

6"Thus says the LORD of hosts:

'If it is [1]marvelous in the eyes of the remnant of this people in these days,
[a]Will it also be marvelous in My eyes?'
Says the LORD of hosts.

CHAPTER 7
2 *1* Lit. *they,* cf. v. 5 *2* Or *Sar-Ezer* *3* Heb. *Bethel* *4* Or *to entreat the favor of*
3 a Mal. 2:7 b Zech. 8:19 *1* Lit. *consecrate myself*
5 a [Is. 58:1–9] b Jer. 41:1 c Zech. 1:12 d [Rom. 14:6]
6 a 1 Chr. 29:22
7 a Zech. 1:4 b Jer. 17:26 *1* Heb. *Negev*
9 a Jer. 7:28 *1* Or *loving-kindness*
10 a Ex. 22:22 b Mic. 2:1
11 a Neh. 9:29 b Jer. 17:23 *1* Lit. *gave a stubborn* or *rebellious shoulder* *2* Lit. *made their ears heavy*
12 a Ezek. 11:19 b Neh. 9:29, 30 c Dan. 9:11, 12
13 a Prov. 1:24–28
14 a Deut. 4:27; 28:64

CHAPTER 8
2 a Zech. 1:14 *1* Or *jealous* *2* Or *jealousy* *3* Lit. *heat* or *rage*
3 a Zech. 1:16 b Zech. 2:10, 11 c Is. 1:21 d [Is. 2:2, 3] e Jer. 31:23
4 a Is. 65:20 *1* Lit. *many days*
5 a Jer. 30:19, 20
6 a [Luke 1:37] *1* Or *wonderful*

7“Thus says the LORD of hosts:

‘Behold, [a]I will save My people from
the land of the [1]east
And from the land of the [2]west;
8 I will [a]bring them *back*,
And they shall dwell in the midst of
Jerusalem.
[b]They shall be My people
And I will be their God,
[c]In truth and righteousness.’

9“Thus says the LORD of hosts:

[a]‘Let your hands be strong,
You who have been hearing in
these days
These words by the mouth of [b]the
prophets,
Who *spoke* in [c]the day the
foundation was laid
For the house of the LORD of hosts,
That the temple might be built.
10 For before these days
There were no [a]wages for man nor
any hire for beast;
There was no peace from the
enemy for whoever went out or
came in;
For I set all men, everyone, against
his neighbor.

11[a]But now I *will* not *treat* the remnant of
this people as in the former days,’ says the
LORD of hosts.

12 ‘For[a] the [1]seed *shall be*
prosperous,
The vine shall give its fruit,
[b]The ground shall give her increase,
And [c]the heavens shall give their
dew—
I will cause the remnant of this
people
To possess all these.
13 And it shall come to pass
That just as you were [a]a curse
among the nations,
O house of Judah and house of
Israel,
So I will save you, and [b]you shall
be a blessing.
Do not fear,
Let your hands be strong.’

14“For thus says the LORD of hosts:

[a]‘Just as I determined to [1]punish you
When your fathers provoked Me to
wrath,’
Says the LORD of hosts,
[b]‘And I would not relent,
15 So again in these days
I am determined to do good
To Jerusalem and to the house of
Judah.
Do not fear.
16 These *are* the things you shall
[a]do:
[b]Speak each man the truth to his
neighbor;
Give judgment in your gates for
truth, justice, and peace;
17 [a]Let none of you think evil in
[1]your heart against your
neighbor;
And do not love a false oath.
For all these *are things* that I hate,’
Says the LORD.”

18Then the word of the LORD of hosts
came to me, saying, 19“Thus says the LORD
of hosts:

[a]‘The fast of the fourth *month*,
[b]The fast of the fifth,
[c]The fast of the seventh,
[d]And the fast of the tenth,
Shall be [e]joy and gladness and
cheerful feasts
For the house of Judah.
[f]Therefore love truth and peace.’

20“Thus says the LORD of hosts:

‘Peoples shall yet come,
Inhabitants of many cities;
21 The inhabitants of one *city* shall
go to another, saying,
[a]“Let us continue to go and pray
before the LORD,
And seek the LORD of hosts.
I myself will go also.”
22 Yes, [a]many peoples and strong
nations
Shall come to seek the LORD of
hosts in Jerusalem,
And to pray before the LORD.’

23“Thus says the LORD of hosts: ‘In
those days ten men [a]from every language
of the nations shall [b]grasp the [1]sleeve of
a Jewish man, saying, “Let us go with you,
for we have heard [c]*that* God *is* with
you.” ’ ”

Israel Defended Against Enemies

9 The [1]burden of the word of the
LORD
Against the land of Hadrach,
And [a]Damascus its resting place

7 [a]Is. 11:11 [1]Lit. *rising sun* [2]Lit. *setting sun*
8 [a]Zeph. 3:20 [b][Jer. 30:22; 31:1, 33] [c]Jer. 4:2
9 [a]Hag. 2:4 [b]Ezra 5:1, 2; 6:14 [c]Hag. 2:18
10 [a]Hag. 1:6, 9
11 [a]Hag. 2:15–19
12 [a]Joel 2:22 [b]Ps. 67:6 [c]Hag. 1:10 [1]Lit. *seed of peace*
13 [a]Jer. 42:18 [b]Gen. 12:2
14 [a]Jer. 31:28 [b][2 Chr. 36:16] [1]Lit. *bring calamity to you*
16 [a]Zech. 7:9, 10 [b][Eph. 4:25]
17 [a]Prov. 3:29 [1]Lit. *his*
19 [a]Jer. 52:6 [b]Jer. 52:12 [c]2 Kin. 25:25 [d]Jer. 52:4 [e]Esth. 8:17 [f]Zech. 8:16
21 [a][Is. 2:2, 3]
22 [a]Is. 60:3; 66:23
23 [a]Is. 3:6 [b][Is. 45:14] [c]1 Cor. 14:25 [1]Lit. *wing, corner of a garment*

CHAPTER 9
1 [a]Is. 17:1 [1]*oracle, prophecy*

Zechariah 8:20, 21

Dear Woman of Destiny,

When we think of city-reaching, sometimes we think of huge meetings and extensive programs. We can easily lose sight of individuals in our rush to convert the masses. This, in turn, can create an impersonal approach to reaching the lost in our communities and neighborhoods.

Yet the very foundations of reaching cities for Christ depend upon relationship—connecting with the hearts of people. Prayer evangelism, which is really just talking to God about your neighbor before talking to your neighbor about God, is built upon four principles, found in Luke 10:5–9.

1) Bless them (v. 5): Do you speak curses against your friends or neighbors without realizing it? When you complain or say something like, "That man is an alcoholic, and he's on his way to getting cirrhosis of the liver," you are speaking curses. Come against that spirit by speaking peace and blessing instead.
2) Fellowship with them (v. 7): When Jesus broke bread with sinners and tax collectors, He was saying to them, "I accept you the way you are, and I want to be your friend." Do you send signals to others that say, "I care about you," or are you looking for conversions for your evangelical scorecard? People know the difference. Take time to get to know them.
3) Pray for their felt needs (v. 9): Do you remember the first time God answered a prayer for you? It may have been a small request or a mighty miracle, but the point is, you knew God cared. Pray for what is important to them, whether it be the need of a job, a lost pet, or a shaky marriage. Choose to be the one to open the door of God's mercy and love to those who are ill or hurting.
4) Preach the gospel (v. 9): Once you have laid the foundations of relationship in the lives of those in your circle of influence, then (and only then!) are you really able to share the gospel with effectiveness. Because their needs have been met in a way that is meaningful to them, it is only natural to reveal the source of their provision and introduce them to Christ.

Did you know the first city-reacher mentioned in the New Testament was a woman? That's right; the woman Jesus met at the well was responsible for bringing the men of her city to Christ. No big programs or events. Just a woman who had been given a drink of living water wanting to share her newfound treasure with her entire city.

No matter who you are, God can use you to light the fuse of revival for your city if you are willing to be an instrument of His love and mercy to the lost.

Friend, city-reaching is nothing more than people-touching. Begin to bless those around you, seeing neighbors, coworkers, and strangers with eyes that look past their daily nods and greetings to their heart needs. Ask God to provide opportunities to build relationship based on the four-step model above, and then watch what God will do!

Ruth Silvoso

(For [b]the eyes of men
And all the tribes of Israel
Are on the LORD);
2 Also *against* [a]Hamath, *which*
borders on it,
And *against* [b]Tyre and [c]Sidon,
though they are very [d]wise.
3 For Tyre built herself a tower,
Heaped up silver like the dust,
And gold like the mire of the
streets.
4 Behold, [a]the LORD will cast her
out;
He will destroy [b]her power in the
sea,
And she will be devoured by fire.
5 Ashkelon shall see *it* and fear;
Gaza also shall be very sorrowful;
And [a]Ekron, for He dried up her
expectation.
The king shall perish from Gaza,
And Ashkelon shall not be
inhabited.
6 "A[1] mixed race shall settle [a]in
Ashdod,
And I will cut off the pride of the
[b]Philistines.
7 I will take away the blood from his
mouth,
And the abominations from between
his teeth.
But he who remains, even he *shall*
be for our God,
And shall be like a leader in Judah,
And Ekron like a Jebusite.
8 [a]I will camp around My house
Because of the army,
Because of him who passes by and
him who returns.
No more shall an oppressor pass
through them,
For now I have seen with My eyes.

The Coming King

9 "Rejoice [a]greatly, O daughter of
Zion!
Shout, O daughter of Jerusalem!
Behold, [b]your King is coming to
you;
He *is* just and having salvation,
Lowly and riding on a donkey,
A colt, the foal of a donkey.
10 I [a]will cut off the chariot from
Ephraim
And the horse from Jerusalem;
The [b]battle bow shall be cut off.
He shall speak peace to the nations;
His dominion *shall be* [c]'from sea to
sea,
And from the River to the ends of
the earth.'

God Will Save His People

11 "As for you also,
Because of the blood of your
covenant,
I will set your [a]prisoners free from
the waterless pit.
12 Return to the stronghold,
[a]You prisoners of hope.
Even today I declare
That I will restore [b]double to you.
13 For I have bent Judah, My *bow,*
Fitted the bow with Ephraim,
And raised up your sons, O Zion,
Against your sons, O Greece,
And made you like the sword of a
mighty man."
14 Then the LORD will be seen over
them,
And [a]His arrow will go forth like
lightning.
The Lord GOD will blow the
trumpet,
And go [b]with whirlwinds from the
south.
15 The LORD of hosts will [a]defend
them;
They shall devour and subdue with
slingstones.
They shall drink *and* roar as if with
wine;
They shall be filled *with blood* like
[1]basins,
Like the corners of the altar.
16 The LORD their God will [a]save
them in that day,
As the flock of His people.
For [b]they *shall be like* the [1]jewels
of a crown,
[c]Lifted like a banner over His land—
17 For [a]how great is [1]its goodness
And how great [1]its [b]beauty!
[c]Grain shall make the young men
thrive,
And new wine the young women.

Restoration of Judah and Israel

10 Ask [a]the LORD for [b]rain
In [c]the time of the [1]latter rain.
The LORD will make [2]flashing
clouds;

1 [b]Amos 1:3–5
2 [a]Jer. 49:23 [b]Is. 23 [c]1 Kin. 17:9 [d]Ezek. 28:3
4 [a]Is. 23:1 [b]Ezek. 26:17
5 [a]Zeph. 2:4, 5
6 [a]Amos 1:8 [b]Ezek. 25:15–17 [1]Lit. *An illegitimate one*
8 [a][Ps. 34:7]
9 [a]Zech. 2:10 [b][Jer. 23:5, 6]
10 [a]Hos. 1:7 [b]Hos. 2:18 [c]Ps. 72:8
11 [a]Is. 42:7
12 [a]Is. 49:9 [b]Is. 61:7
14 [a]Ps. 18:14 [b]Is. 21:1
15 [a]Zech. 12:8 [1]Sacrificial basins
16 [a]Jer. 31:10, 11 [b]Is. 62:3 [c]Is. 11:12 [1]Lit. *stones*
17 [a][Ps. 31:19] [b][Ps. 45:1–16] [c]Joel 3:18 [1]Lit. *His*

CHAPTER 10
1 [a][Jer. 14:22] [b][Deut. 11:13, 14] [c][Joel 2:23] [1]Spring rain [2]Or *lightning flashes*

He will give them showers of rain,
Grass in the field for everyone.

2 For the [a]idols[1] speak delusion;
The diviners envision [b]lies,
And tell false dreams;
They [c]comfort in vain.
Therefore *the people* wend their
way like [d]sheep;
They are [2]in trouble [e]because *there*
is no shepherd.

3 "My anger is kindled against the
[a]shepherds,
[b]And I will punish the [1]goatherds.
For the LORD of hosts [c]will visit His
flock,
The house of Judah,
And [d]will make them as His royal
horse in the battle.
4 From him comes [a]the cornerstone,
From him [b]the tent peg,
From him the battle bow,
From him every [1]ruler together.
5 They shall be like mighty men,
Who [a]tread down *their enemies*
In the mire of the streets in the
battle.
They shall fight because the LORD is
with them,
And the riders on horses shall be
put to shame.

6 "I will strengthen the house of
Judah,
And I will save the house of Joseph.
[a]I will bring them back,
Because I [b]have mercy on them.
They shall be as though I had not
cast them aside;
For I *am* the LORD their God,
And I [c]will hear them.
7 *Those of* Ephraim shall be like a
mighty man,
And their [a]heart shall rejoice as if
with wine.
Yes, their children shall see *it* and
be glad;
Their heart shall rejoice in the
LORD.
8 I will [a]whistle for them and gather
them,
For I will redeem them;
[b]And they shall increase as they once
increased.

9 "I[a] will [1]sow them among the
peoples,
And they shall [b]remember Me in far
countries;
They shall live, together with their
children,
And they shall return.
10 [a]I will also bring them back from
the land of Egypt,
And gather them from Assyria.
I will bring them into the land of
Gilead and Lebanon,
[b]Until no *more room* is found for
them.
11 [a]He shall pass through the sea with
affliction,
And strike the waves of the sea:
All the depths of [1]the River shall
dry up.
Then [b]the pride of Assyria shall be
brought down,
And [c]the scepter of Egypt shall
depart.
12 "So I will strengthen them in the
LORD,
And [a]they shall walk up and down
in His name,"
Says the LORD.

Desolation of Israel

11 Open [a]your doors, O Lebanon,
That fire may devour your
cedars.
2 Wail, O cypress, for the [a]cedar has
fallen,
Because the mighty *trees* are
ruined.
Wail, O oaks of Bashan,
[b]For the thick forest has come
down.
3 *There is* the sound of wailing
[a]shepherds!
For their glory is in ruins.
There is the sound of roaring lions!
For the [1]pride of the Jordan is in
ruins.

Prophecy of the Shepherds

4Thus says the LORD my God, "Feed
the flock for slaughter, 5whose owners
slaughter them and [a]feel no guilt; those
who sell them [b]say, 'Blessed be the LORD,
for I am rich'; and their shepherds do [c]not
pity them. 6For I will no longer pity the
inhabitants of the land," says the LORD.
"But indeed I will give everyone into his
neighbor's hand and into the hand of his
king. They shall [1]attack the land, and I
will not deliver *them* from their hand."
7So I fed the flock for slaughter, [1]in
particular [a]the poor of the flock. I took for

2 a Jer. 10:8 b Jer. 27:9 c Job 13:4 d Jer. 50:6, 17 e Ezek. 34:5–8 *1* Heb. *teraphim* *2 afflicted*
3 a Jer. 25:34–36 b Ezek. 34:17 c Luke 1:68 d Song 1:9 *1* Leaders
4 a Is. 28:16 b Is. 22:23 *1* Or *despot*
5 a Ps. 18:42
6 a Jer. 3:18 b Hos. 1:7 c Zech. 13:9
7 a Ps. 104:15
8 a Is. 5:26 b Ezek. 36:37
9 a Hos. 2:23 b Deut. 30:1 *1* Or *scatter*
10 a Is. 11:11 b Is. 49:19, 20
11 a Is. 11:15 b Zeph. 2:13 c Ezek. 30:13 *1* The Nile
12 a Mic. 4:5
CHAPTER 11
1 a Zech. 10:10
2 a Ezek. 31:3 b Is. 32:19
3 a Jer. 25:34–36 *1* Or *floodplain, thicket*
5 a [Jer. 2:3]; 50:7 b Hos. 12:8 c Ezek. 34:2, 3
6 *1* Lit. *strike*
7 a Zeph. 3:12 *1* So with MT, Tg., Vg.; LXX *for the Canaanites*

myself two staffs: the one I called [2]Beauty,
and the other I called [3]Bonds; and I fed
the flock. 8I [1]dismissed the three shepherds [a]in one month. My soul loathed
them, and their soul also abhorred me.
9Then I said, "I will not feed you. [a]Let
what is dying die, and what is perishing
perish. Let those that are left eat each other's flesh." 10And I took my staff, [1]Beauty,
and cut it in two, that I might break the
covenant which I had made with all the
peoples. 11So it was broken on that day.
Thus [a]the[1] poor of the flock, who were
watching me, knew that it *was* the word
of the LORD. 12Then I said to them, "If it
is [1]agreeable to you, give *me* my wages;
and if not, refrain." So they [a]weighed out
for my wages thirty *pieces* of silver.

13And the LORD said to me, "Throw it to
the [a]potter"—that princely price they set
on me. So I took the thirty *pieces* of silver
and threw them into the house of the
LORD for the potter. 14Then I cut in two
my other staff, [1]Bonds, that I might break
the brotherhood between Judah and Israel.

15And the LORD said to me, [a]"Next, take
for yourself the implements of a foolish
shepherd. 16For indeed I will raise up a
shepherd in the land *who* will not care for
those who are cut off, nor seek the young,
nor heal those that are broken, nor feed
those that still stand. But he will eat the
flesh of the fat and tear their hooves in
[a]pieces.

17 "Woe[a] to the worthless shepherd,
Who leaves the flock!
A sword *shall be* against his arm
And against his right eye;
His arm shall completely wither,
And his right eye shall be totally
blinded."

The Coming Deliverance of Judah

12 The [1]burden of the word of the
LORD against Israel. Thus says the
LORD, [a]who stretches out the heavens,
lays the foundation of the earth, and
[b]forms the spirit of man within him: 2"Behold, I will make Jerusalem [a]a cup of
[1]drunkenness to all the surrounding peoples, when they lay siege against Judah
and Jerusalem. 3[a]And it shall happen in
that day that I will make Jerusalem [b]a
very heavy stone for all peoples; all who
would heave it away will surely be cut in
pieces, though all nations of the earth are
gathered against it. 4In that day," says the
LORD, [a]"I will strike every horse with confusion, and its rider with madness; I will
open My eyes on the house of Judah, and
will strike every horse of the peoples with
blindness. 5And the governors of Judah
shall say in their heart, 'The inhabitants of
Jerusalem *are* my strength in the LORD of
hosts, their God.' 6In that day I will make
the governors of Judah [a]like a firepan in
the woodpile, and like a fiery torch in the
sheaves; they shall devour all the surrounding peoples on the right hand and
on the left, but Jerusalem shall be inhabited again in her own place—Jerusalem.

7"The LORD will save the tents of Judah
first, so that the glory of the house of David and the glory of the inhabitants of Jerusalem shall not become greater than
that of Judah. 8In that day the LORD will
defend the inhabitants of Jerusalem; the
one who is feeble among them in that day
shall be like David, and the house of David
shall be like God, like the Angel of the
LORD before them. 9It shall be in that day
that I will seek to [a]destroy all the nations
that come against Jerusalem.

Mourning for the Pierced One

10 [a]"And I will pour on the house of
David and on the inhabitants of Jerusalem
the Spirit of grace and supplication; then
they will [b]look on Me whom they pierced.
Yes, they will mourn for Him [c]as one
mourns for *his* only *son,* and grieve for
Him as one grieves for a firstborn. 11In
that day there shall be a great [a]mourning
in Jerusalem, [b]like the mourning at Hadad Rimmon in the plain of [1]Megiddo.
12[a]And the land shall mourn, every family
by itself: the family of the house of David
by itself, and their wives by themselves;
the family of the house of [b]Nathan by itself, and their wives by themselves; 13the
family of the house of Levi by itself, and
their wives by themselves; the family of
Shimei by itself, and their wives by themselves; 14all the families that remain, every family by itself, and their wives by
themselves.

Idolatry Cut Off

13 "In that [a]day [b]a fountain shall be
opened for the house of David and
for the inhabitants of Jerusalem, for sin
and for [c]uncleanness.

7 [2]Or *Grace* [3]Or *Unity*
8 [a]Hos. 5:7 [1]Or *destroyed,* lit. *cut off*
9 [a]Jer. 15:2
10 [1]Or *Grace*
11 [a]Zeph. 3:12 [1]So with MT, Tg., Vg.; LXX *the Canaanites*
12 [a]Ex. 21:32 [1]*good in your sight*
13 [a]Matt. 27:3–10
14 [1]Or *Unity*
15 [a]Is. 56:11
16 [a]Ezek. 34:1–10
17 [a]Jer. 23:1

CHAPTER 12
1 [a]Is. 42:5; 44:24 [b][Is. 57:16] [1]*oracle, prophecy*
2 [a]Is. 51:17 [1]Lit. *reeling*
3 [a]Zech. 12:4, 6, 8; 13:1 [b]Matt. 21:44
4 [a]Ezek. 38:4
6 [a]Obad. 18
9 [a]Hag. 2:22
10 [a][Joel 2:28, 29] [b]John 19:34, 37; 20:27 [c]Jer. 6:26
11 [a][Rev. 1:7] [b]2 Kin. 23:29 [1]Heb. *Megiddon*
12 [a][Matt. 24:30] [b]Luke 3:31

CHAPTER 13
1 [a][Rev. 21:6, 7] [b][Heb. 9:14] [c]Ezek. 36:25

ZECHARIAH 12:10

Dear Woman of Destiny,

No one understands the pain of grief like a mother who has lost a child. Yet it is in this place of deep mourning that the wonderful grace of God abounds. . . .

The casket is so small, I thought to myself as the pastor spoke his words of comfort. The tiny box that had captured my attention held my firstborn child—a stillborn daughter. Without any warning or explanation, she had died within my womb. It all seemed so unreal. I felt a wave of overwhelming grief engulf my body—the kind of grief the prophet describes in this passage. But this passage also links mourning with God's wonderful Spirit of grace.

My husband, Jack, and I felt that grace when our daughter was born. As we stared at what appeared to be a perfect little face, we could see peace in her sweet expression. Our child was with the Lord. We felt the Lord speak to us that her name was to be Anna Jean. We later discovered that *Anna* means "Grace," and that *Jean* means "God's Gracious Gift." Through Anna's death, God had somehow given us the gift of grace.

In the months that followed, my pain came in waves. But so did the grace of God. In the heaviness of mourning, His presence never subsided. Jack was often God's most tender instrument of grace as he pushed his own grief aside and ministered to me for hours at a time, often late into the night.

As the weeks passed, my emotions turned to anger. Anger at God. But even in that I learned a great lesson about our Creator. He could take it. He did not remove His hand from me, nor punish me for it. Instead, He loved me through it. I also learned that when I was angry enough to stop praying, grief would overtake me. But when I expressed my anger to Him, the comfort He extended eventually soothed my raw emotion. I could once again feel His grace. I knew that God had heard my prayers and that He somehow mourned with me. My pain and anger did not offend Him; it touched Him. Not one tear had gone unnoticed.

Why did Anna die? I don't know. But I do see the fruit of Anna's short life. My husband and I are much closer. People's lives, some non-Christians, have been touched through Anna's story. I have a greater understanding of eternity. Jack and I rejoice in knowing that Anna is already experiencing the joy of resurrection life. I have a deep joy in watching my son, Nicholas, born one year after Anna, grow and flourish. I now know a dimension of the grace of God that I might never have known.

In the story of my life, 1997 will be marked by a tragic loss. Even so, I am deeply thankful for a simple yet profound attribute of God called grace. My heart echoes the words of the familiar hymn "Amazing Grace": "Through many dangers, toils and snares, I have already come. 'Tis grace hath brought me safe thus far, and grace will lead me home."

Rebecca Wagner Sytsema

2"It shall be in that day," says the LORD
of hosts, "*that* I will [a]cut off the names of
the idols from the land, and they shall no
longer be remembered. I will also cause
[b]the prophets and the unclean spirit to
depart from the land. 3It shall come to
pass *that* if anyone still prophesies, then
his father and mother who begot him will
say to him, 'You shall [a]not live, because
you have spoken lies in the name of the
LORD.' And his father and mother who begot him [b]shall thrust him through when
he prophesies.
4"And it shall be in that day *that* [a]every
prophet will be ashamed of his vision
when he prophesies; they will not wear [b]a
robe of coarse hair to deceive. 5[a]But he
will say, 'I *am* no prophet, I *am* a farmer;
for a man taught me to keep cattle from
my youth.' 6And *one* will say to him,
'What are these wounds between your
[1]arms?' Then he will answer, '*Those* with
which I was wounded in the house of my
friends.'

Lord, like the remnant, when ____ is refined as silver and tested as gold, may they call on Your name. You will answer them, saying, "They are My people"; and they will say, "The Lord is my God.

FROM ZECHARIAH 13:9

The Shepherd Savior

7 "Awake, O sword, against [a]My
Shepherd,
Against the Man [b]who is My
Companion,"
Says the LORD of hosts.
[c]"Strike the Shepherd,
And the sheep will be scattered;
Then I will turn My hand against
[d]the little ones.
8 And it shall come to pass in all the
land,"
Says the LORD,
"*That* [a]two-thirds in it shall be cut
off *and* die,
[b]But *one*-third shall be left in it:
9 I will bring the *one*-third [a]through
the fire,
Will [b]refine them as silver is
refined,
And test them as gold is tested.
[c]They will call on My name,
And I will answer them.
[d]I will say, 'This *is* My people';
And each one will say, 'The LORD *is*
my God.'"

The Day of the Lord

14 Behold, [a]the day of the LORD is
coming,
And your [1]spoil will be divided in
your midst.
2 For [a]I will gather all the nations to
battle against Jerusalem;
The city shall be taken,
The houses [1]rifled,
And the women ravished.
Half of the city shall go into
captivity,
But the remnant of the people shall
not be cut off from the city.

3 Then the LORD will go forth
And fight against those nations,
As He fights in the day of battle.
4 And in that day His feet will stand
[a]on the Mount of Olives,
Which faces Jerusalem on the east.
And the Mount of Olives shall be
split in two,
From east to west,
[b]*Making* a very large valley;
Half of the mountain shall move
toward the north
And half of it toward the south.
5 Then you shall flee *through* My
mountain valley,
For the mountain valley shall reach
to Azal.
Yes, you shall flee
As you fled from the [a]earthquake
In the days of Uzziah king of Judah.

[b]Thus the LORD my God will come,
And [c]call the saints with [1]You.
6 It shall come to pass in that day
That there will be no light;
The [1]lights will diminish.
7 It shall be one day
[a]Which is known to the LORD—
Neither day nor night.
But at [b]evening time it shall
happen
That it will be light.

2 [a] Ex. 23:13 [b] Jer. 23:14, 15
3 [a] Deut. 18:20 [b] Deut. 13:6–11
4 [a] [Mic. 3:6, 7] [b] 2 Kin. 1:8
5 [a] Amos 7:14
6 [1] Or *hands*
7 [a] Is. 40:11 [b] [John 10:30] [c] Matt. 26:31, 56, 67 [d] Luke 12:32
8 [a] Ezek. 5:2, 4, 12 [b] [Rom. 11:5]
9 [a] Is. 48:10 [b] 1 Pet. 1:6, 7 [c] Ps. 50:15 [d] Hos. 2:23
CHAPTER 14
1 [a] [Is. 13:6, 9] [1] *plunder* or *booty*
2 [a] Zech. 12:2, 3 [1] Or *plundered*
4 [a] Ezek. 11:23 [b] Joel 3:12
5 [a] Amos 1:1 [b] Matt. 24:30, 31; 25:31 [c] Joel 3:11 [1] Or *you;* LXX, Tg., Vg. *Him*
6 [1] Lit. *glorious ones*
7 [a] Matt. 24:36 [b] Is. 30:26

8 And in that day it shall be
That living [a]waters shall flow from
Jerusalem,
Half of them toward [1]the eastern
sea
And half of them toward [2]the
western sea;
In both summer and winter it shall
occur.
9 And the LORD shall be [a]King over
all the earth.
In that day it shall be—
[b]"The LORD *is* one,"
And His name one.

10All the land shall be turned into a
plain from Geba to Rimmon south of Jerusalem. [1]*Jerusalem* shall be raised up
and [a]inhabited in her place from Benjamin's Gate to the place of the First Gate
and the Corner Gate, [b]and *from* the Tower
of Hananel to the king's winepresses.

11 *The people* shall dwell in it;
And [a]no longer shall there be utter
destruction,
[b]But Jerusalem shall be safely
inhabited.

12And this shall be the plague with
which the LORD will strike all the people
who fought against Jerusalem:

Their flesh shall [1]dissolve while
they stand on their feet,
Their eyes shall dissolve in their
sockets,
And their tongues shall dissolve in
their mouths.

13 It shall come to pass in that day
That [a]a great panic from the LORD
will be among them.
Everyone will seize the hand of his
neighbor,
And raise [b]his hand against his
neighbor's hand;

8 **a** Ezek. 47:1–12 *1* The Dead Sea *2* The Mediterranean Sea
9 **a** [Rev. 11:15] **b** Deut. 6:4
10 **a** Zech. 12:6 **b** Jer. 31:38 *1* Lit. *She*
11 **a** Jer. 31:40 **b** Jer. 23:6
12 *1* Lit. *decay*
13 **a** 1 Sam. 14:15, 20 **b** Judg. 7:22
14 **a** Ezek. 39:10, 17
15 **a** Zech. 14:12
16 **a** [Is. 2:2, 3; 60:6–9; 66:18–21] **b** Is. 27:13 **c** Lev. 23:34–44
17 **a** Is. 60:12
18 **a** Is. 19:21 **b** Deut. 11:10
19 *1* Lit. *sin*
20 **a** Is. 23:18 **b** Ezek. 46:20
21 **a** Is. 35:8 **b** [Eph. 2:19–22] *1* Or *on every pot . . . shall be engraved "HOLINESS TO THE LORD OF HOSTS"*

14 Judah also will fight at Jerusalem.
[a]And the wealth of all the
surrounding nations
Shall be gathered together:
Gold, silver, and apparel in great
abundance.

15 [a]Such also shall be the plague
On the horse *and* the mule,
On the camel and the donkey,
And on all the cattle that will be in
those camps.
So *shall* this plague *be*.

The Nations Worship the King

16And it shall come to pass *that* everyone who is left of all the nations which
came against Jerusalem shall [a]go up from
year to year to [b]worship the King, the
LORD of hosts, and to keep [c]the Feast of
Tabernacles. 17[a]And it shall be *that*
whichever of the families of the earth do
not come up to Jerusalem to worship the
King, the LORD of hosts, on them there
will be no rain. 18If the family of [a]Egypt
will not come up and enter in, [b]they *shall*
have no *rain;* they shall receive the plague
with which the LORD strikes the nations
who do not come up to keep the Feast of
Tabernacles. 19This shall be the [1]punish-
ment of Egypt and the punishment of all
the nations that do not come up to keep
the Feast of Tabernacles.
20In that day [a]"HOLINESS TO THE
LORD" shall be *engraved* on the bells of
the horses. The [b]pots in the LORD's house
shall be like the bowls before the altar.
21Yes, [1]every pot in Jerusalem and Judah
shall be holiness to the LORD of hosts. Everyone who sacrifices shall come and take
them and cook in them. In that day there
shall no longer be a [a]Canaanite [b]in the
house of the LORD of hosts.

AUTHOR: *Malachi*
DATE: *Approximately 450 B.C.*
THEME: *Reassurance of God's Love and Justice*
KEY WORDS: *Messenger, Priests, Sun of Righteousness, Day of Judgment*

MALACHI

Dear Woman of Destiny,

Women all over the world are standing in the gap for their nations, praying for hearts to turn to Jesus Christ. Malachi's message was clear to Israel in its time, and it is just as potent today: Whether a nation prospers or falls depends upon obedience to God's laws. Woman of Destiny, you are the salt of the earth, preserving those around you through fervent prayer and the touch of God's awesome love as you reach out with the hands of Jesus Christ today.

His love and mine,

Marilyn Hickey

The [1]burden of the word of the LORD to Israel [2]by Malachi.

Israel Beloved of God

2 "I[a] have loved you," says the LORD.
"Yet you say, 'In what way have You loved us?'
Was not Esau Jacob's brother?"
Says the LORD.
"Yet [b]Jacob I have loved;
3 But Esau I have hated,
And [a]laid waste his mountains and his heritage
For the jackals of the wilderness."
4 Even though Edom has said,
"We have been impoverished,
But we will return and build the desolate places,"

Thus says the LORD of hosts:

"They may build, but I will [a]throw down;
They shall be called the Territory of Wickedness,
And the people against whom the LORD will have indignation forever.
5 Your eyes shall see,
And you shall say,
[a]'The LORD is magnified beyond the border of Israel.'

Polluted Offerings

6 "A son [a]honors *his* father,
And a servant *his* master.
[b]If then I am the Father,
Where *is* My honor?
And if I *am* a Master,
Where *is* My reverence?
Says the LORD of hosts
To you priests who despise My name.
[c]Yet you say, 'In what way have we despised Your name?'
7 "You offer [a]defiled food on My altar,
But say,
'In what way have we defiled You?'
By saying,
[b]'The table of the LORD is [1]contemptible.'
8 And [a]when you offer the blind as a sacrifice,
Is it not evil?
And when you offer the lame and sick,
Is it not evil?
Offer it then to your governor!
Would he be pleased with you?
Would he [b]accept[1] you favorably?"
Says the LORD of hosts.
9 "But now entreat God's favor,
That He may be gracious to us.
[a]*While* this is being *done* by your hands,
Will He accept you favorably?"
Says the LORD of hosts.
10 "Who *is there* even among you who would shut the doors,
[a]So that you would not kindle fire *on* My altar in vain?
I have no pleasure in you,"
Says the LORD of hosts,
[b]"Nor will I accept an offering from your hands.
11 For [a]from the rising of the sun, even to its going down,
My name *shall be* great [b]among the Gentiles;
[c]In every place [d]incense *shall be* offered to My name,
And a pure offering;
[e]For My name shall be great among the nations,"
Says the LORD of hosts.
12 "But you profane it,
In that you say,
[a]'The table of the [1]LORD is defiled;
And its fruit, its food, *is* contemptible.'
13 You also say,
'Oh, what a [a]weariness!'
And you sneer at it,"
Says the LORD of hosts.
"And you bring the stolen, the lame, and the sick;
Thus you bring an offering!
[b]Should I accept this from your hand?"
Says the LORD.
14 "But cursed *be* [a]the deceiver
Who has in his flock a male,
And takes a vow,
But sacrifices to the Lord [b]what is blemished—
For [c]I *am* a great King,"
Says the LORD of hosts,
"And My name *is to be* feared among the nations.

Corrupt Priests

2 "And now, O [a]priests, this commandment is for you.
2 [a]If you will not hear,

CHAPTER 1
1 [1] *oracle, prophecy* [2] Lit. *by the hand of*
2 a Deut. 4:37; 7:8; 23:5 b Rom. 9:13
3 a Jer. 49:18
4 a Jer. 49:16–18
5 a Ps. 35:27
6 a [Ex. 20:12] b Luke 6:46 c Mal. 2:14
7 a Deut. 15:21 b Ezek. 41:22 [1] Or *to be despised*
8 a Lev. 22:22 b [Job 42:8] [1] Lit. *lift up your face*
9 a Hos. 13:9
10 a 1 Cor. 9:13 b Is. 1:11
11 a Is. 59:19 b Is. 60:3, 5 c 1 Tim. 2:8 d Rev. 8:3 e Is. 66:18, 19
12 a Mal. 1:7 [1] So with Bg.; MT *Lord*
13 a Is. 43:22 b Lev. 22:20
14 a Mal. 1:8 b Lev. 22:18–20 c Ps. 47:2
CHAPTER 2
1 a Mal. 1:6
2 a [Deut. 28:15]

And if you will not take *it* to heart,
To give glory to My name,"
Says the LORD of hosts,
"I will send a curse upon you,
And I will curse your blessings.
Yes, I have cursed them [b]already,
Because you do not take *it* to heart.

3 "Behold, I will rebuke your descendants
And spread [a]refuse on your faces,
The refuse of your solemn feasts;
And *one* will [b]take you away [1]with it.
4 Then you shall know that I have sent this commandment to you,
That My covenant with Levi may continue,"
Says the LORD of hosts.
5 "My[a] covenant was with him, *one* of life and peace,
And I gave them to him [b]*that he might* fear *Me;*
So he feared Me
And was reverent before My name.
6 [a]The[1] law of truth was in his mouth,
And [2]injustice was not found on his lips.
He walked with Me in peace and equity,
And [b]turned many away from iniquity.

7 "For[a] the lips of a priest should keep knowledge,
And *people* should seek the law from his mouth;
[b]For he is the messenger of the LORD of hosts.
8 But you have departed from the way;
You [a]have caused many to stumble at the law.
[b]You have corrupted the covenant of Levi,"
Says the LORD of hosts.
9 "Therefore [a]I also have made you contemptible and base
Before all the people,
Because you have not kept My ways
But have shown [b]partiality in the law."

Treachery of Infidelity

10 [a]Have we not all one Father?
[b]Has not one God created us?
Why do we deal treacherously with one another
By profaning the covenant of the fathers?
11 Judah has dealt treacherously,
And an abomination has been committed in Israel and in Jerusalem,
For Judah has [a]profaned
The LORD's holy *institution* which He loves:
He has married the daughter of a foreign god.
12 May the LORD cut off from the tents of Jacob
The man who does this, being [1]awake and aware,
Yet [a]who brings an offering to the LORD of hosts!

13 And this is the second thing you do:
You cover the altar of the LORD with tears,
With weeping and crying;
So He does not regard the offering anymore,
Nor receive *it* with goodwill from your hands.
14 Yet you say, "For what reason?"
Because the LORD has been witness
Between you and [a]the wife of your youth,
With whom you have dealt treacherously;
[b]Yet she is your companion
And your wife by covenant.
15 But [a]did He not make *them* one,
Having a remnant of the Spirit?
And why one?
He seeks [b]godly offspring.
Therefore take heed to your spirit,
And let none deal treacherously with the wife of his youth.

16 "For [a]the LORD God of Israel says
That He hates divorce,
For it covers one's garment with violence,"
Says the LORD of hosts.
"Therefore take heed to your spirit,
That you do not deal treacherously."

17 [a]You have wearied the LORD with your words;
Yet you say,
"In what way have we wearied *Him?*"
In that you say,
[b]"Everyone who does evil
Is good in the sight of the LORD,

---

2 [b]Mal. 3:9
3 [a]Ex. 29:14 [b]1 Kin. 14:10 [1]Lit. *to it*
5 [a]Num. 25:12 [b]Deut. 33:9
6 [a]Deut. 33:10 [b]Jer. 23:22 [1]Or *True instruction* [2]Or *unrighteousness*
7 [a]Deut. 17:8–11 [b][Gal. 4:14]
8 [a]Jer. 18:15 [b]Neh. 13:29
9 [a]1 Sam. 2:30 [b]Deut. 1:17
10 [a]1 Cor. 8:6 [b]Job 31:15
11 [a]Ezra 9:1, 2
12 [a]Neh. 13:29 [1]Talmud, Vg. *teacher and student*
14 [a]Mal. 3:5 [b]Prov. 2:17
15 [a]Matt. 19:4, 5 [b][1 Cor. 7:14]
16 [a][Matt. 5:31; 19:6–8]
17 [a]Is. 43:22, 24 [b]Is. 5:20

MALACHI 3:2, 3

Dear Woman of Destiny,

I am probably the least qualified to write to you about holiness, except that my husband and I have been touched by the Refiner's fire. In May 1997, the Lord captured my husband's attention for six days and spoke to him about the condition of His church. The Lord told him, "Ninety-eight percent holiness is not enough. My church has allowed poison in their minds—sin in their life." Pure is not pure unless it is 100 percent.

You can imagine the burden of sharing that message with others. You begin to ask yourself, "Lord, but how can I be 100 percent holy, especially since I am telling others of their need to be so." Just this year, the Lord in His mercy, called me into an extended fast. It was my experience that the farther I got away from food and my fleshly desires, the closer I got to Him.

I gained a new perspective during that fast. I realized in a very personal way there was nothing in my flesh I could do to make myself more acceptable to Him. There was no list of "Do's and Don'ts" that could make me more like Him. I was reminded again that holiness is not a list, but a Person, Jesus Christ. It is only when His fire purifies us and His sanctification is imparted to us that we can even be near Him.

But the Refiner's fire and His sanctification are things reserved for those who fear Him. His eyes are always looking for the humble. I like to think about God writing a book of remembrance for those who fear Him, and imagine Him writing my name there! (see Mal. 3:16).

The apostle Paul was able to say, "My conscience does not condemn me" (see 2 Tim. 1:3), and he called others to follow him as he followed Christ. It is only with humility that we could think of asking others to imitate us. We must learn to teach and preach holiness with tears in our eyes.

We need to stay humble and pliable in His presence. When we fail, we repent and allow Him to purify us and remove our sin. I am not talking about living any sort of sinful life and then relying on His grace to fix things up. Grac does not cover sin we refuse to confess and renounce.

Women of God, I desire for each of you this blessing spoken in 1 Thessalonians 5:23, 24: "Now may the God of peace Himself sanctify you completely; and may your whole spirit, soul, and body be preserved blamele at the coming of our Lord Jesus Christ. He who calls you is faithful, who als will do it."

Kathleen Scataglini

And He delights in them,"
Or, "Where *is* the God of justice?"

The Coming Messenger

3 "Behold, [a]I send My messenger,
And he will [b]prepare the way before
Me.
And the Lord, whom you seek,
Will suddenly come to His temple,
[c]Even the Messenger of the
covenant,
In whom you delight.
Behold, [d]He is coming,"
Says the LORD of hosts.

2 "But who can endure [a]the day of
His coming?
And [b]who can stand when He
appears?
For [c]He *is* like a refiner's fire
And like launderers' soap.
3 [a]He will sit as a refiner and a
purifier of silver;
He will purify the sons of Levi,
nd [1]purge them as gold and silver,
t they may [b]offer to the LORD
ffering in righteousness.

farther we get in
hotter the fire
use the infini-
requires a
t it out of

AM

nd

CHAPTER 3
1 [a]Matt. 11:10
[b][Is. 40:3]
[c]Is. 63:9
[d]Hab. 2:7
2 [a][Mal. 4:1]
[b]Rev. 6:17
[c][Matt. 3:10–12]
3 [a]Is. 1:25
[b][1 Pet. 2:5]
[1] Or *refine*
4 [a]Mal. 1:11
[1] *pleasing*
5 [a]Zech. 5:4
[b]James 5:4
[c]Ex. 22:22
6 [a][Rom. 11:29]
[b][Lam. 3:22]
7 [a]Acts 7:51
[b]Zech. 1:3
[c]Mal. 1:6
8 [a]Neh. 13:10–12
Prov. 3:9,
26:20
11
10
11 [a]Amos 4:9

Says the LORD of hosts.

6 "For I *am* the LORD, [a]I do not
change;
[b]Therefore you are not consumed,
O sons of Jacob.
7 Yet from the days of [a]your fathers
You have gone away from My
ordinances
And have not kept *them.*
[b]Return to Me, and I will return to
you,"
Says the LORD of hosts.
[c]"But you said,
'In what way shall we return?'

Do Not Rob God

8 "Will a man rob God?
Yet you have robbed Me!
But you say,
'In what way have we robbed You?'
[a]In tithes and offerings.
9 You are cursed with a curse,
For you have robbed Me,
Even this whole nation.
10 [a]Bring all the tithes into the
[b]storehouse,
That there may be food in My
house,
And try Me now in this,"
Says the LORD of hosts,
"If I will not open for you the
[c]windows of heaven
And [d]pour out for you *such*
blessing
That *there will* not *be room* enough
to receive it.

Father, I pray that ____ will bring all their tithes into the storehouse, for You will open for them the windows of heaven and pour out for them such a blessing that there will not be room enough to receive it.

FROM MALACHI 3:10

11 "And I will rebuke [a]the devourer
for your sakes,
So that he will not destroy the fruit
of your ground,

Malachi 3:6–11

Dear Woman of Destiny,

This passage has much to tell us about God's abundant blessings and the extravagant promises He has for those who tithe. This is one area in which God does not hold back.

In Malachi 3, God is telling His people that they are under a curse because they have neglected their responsibility to give tithes and offerings. God even refers to this error as stealing from Him! Giving is an area of the Christian life that God takes very seriously and, consequently, He rewards our obedience lavishly.

In marriage, giving is often left to the husband. However, God has joined the husband and the wife together as one. Because of this, it is important for wives to become involved in tithing and offering with their husbands. Giving expresses a joint statement about you as a couple. Seeking God together regarding your tithes and offerings magnifies a godly marriage. If your husband will not allow you to give financially, consider other ways you might give of yourself to the kingdom of God.

If we are listening to God and giving our tithes, the promises of Malachi 3:10 are ours. In fact, giving is such an important part of the Christian life that God tells us we can actually test Him on His reciprocal promises. In this verse, we read, "'And try Me now in this,' says the LORD of hosts, 'if I will not open for you the windows of heaven and pour out for you such blessing that there will not be room enough to receive it.'"

Our gracious and generous God gives more promises for our tithe. Malachi 3:11 reads, "And I will rebuke the devourer for your sakes, so that he will not destroy the fruit of your ground; nor shall the vine fail to bear fruit for you in the field." This promise covers a multitude of areas in our lives. God says He will protect us from the devourer, Satan. He will protect us from the pestilence of this world and provide a covering of protection over us and our families.

God's promises are based on a spiritual principle found in 2 Corinthians 9:6: "He who sows sparingly will also reap sparingly, and he who sows bountifully will also reap bountifully." This verse tells us we are rewarded according to what we have given. If we give generously, we will be generously rewarded. You cannot give to God without receiving back from Him. Jesus tells us in Luke 6:38, "Give, and it will be given to you."

We have a God who exercises extravagant giving. Take, for example, the gift of His only Son, Jesus, who selflessly gave His life in obedience so we might live. Giving is imbedded deep in the character of God. He is our great example of what we are to model and reflect on earth. God not only wants us to give, but to give liberally. Giving shows the love of God in our actions as it displays the gospel to the world. We serve a mighty God who is waiting in heaven to bestow upon us the blessings He has stored up for us!

Megan Doyle

Malachi 4:2

Dear Woman of Destiny,

How many years of my life were spent trying to overcome the stronghold of fear! Fear hounded me when I was awake, and I had terrifying nightmares when I was asleep. It seemed there was no escape.

I remember attending camp as a child and attempting to climb the steps of a forest tower. After only about three steps, I carefully backed down, gripped with fear.

More than the fear of heights was my fear of people. It was impossible for me to speak in front of a group. Even as an adult, my voice would close off if I tried to address a group of more than three people. Somehow, I had convinced myself that some people were just born this way. Some people were extroverted; others were shy and timid. I considered myself one of the latter. After all, I had been that way all my life.

Years later, I attended a conference where my whole life was changed. In speaking of the fear of the Lord, a woman made a statement that pierced my heart: "You will never walk in the fear of the Lord until you lose the fear of man." That statement grabbed me! I truly wanted the fear of the Lord in my life. It never occurred to me that my timidity and shyness, really the fear of man, could separate me from the fear of the Lord.

Pondering the message of the speaker, I realized why it had been difficult for me to witness to people. My life had many boundaries established by fear.

After repenting to the Lord for yielding to fear, I asked Him to put the fear of the Lord in me. My concern would then be what the Lord thought about me rather than what man thought. Pleasing the Lord became the most important goal in my life.

Reaching that goal was not easy. Each time I was asked to speak to a group, I would sense a tightening in my throat. On the inside, I would hear the Lord's gentle questioning, "Barbara, is this the fear of the Lord or the fear of man?" I then had to make a choice. Which fear would I submit to?

It took several years of continuously yielding to the fear of the Lord and resisting the fear of man before I was free. Today, I can speak and witness without my throat tightening up. What a joy to walk in freedom!

So can you, Woman of Destiny. Each time fear attempts to hinder your obedience to the Lord, use your authority in Jesus and bind the fear of man, yielding to the fear of God. "But to you who fear My name the Sun of Righteousness shall arise with healing in His wings" (Mal. 4:2).

Barbara Wentroble

Nor shall the vine fail to bear fruit
for you in the field,"
Says the LORD of hosts;
12 And all nations will call you
blessed,
For you will be [a]a delightful land,"
Says the LORD of hosts.

The People Complain Harshly

13 "Your[a] words have been [1]harsh
against Me,"
Says the LORD,
"Yet you say,
'What have we spoken against You?'
14 [a]You have said,
'It is useless to serve God;
What profit *is it* that we have kept
His ordinance,
And that we have walked as
mourners
Before the LORD of hosts?
15 So now [a]we call the proud
blessed,
For those who do wickedness are
[1]raised up;
They even [b]tempt God and go
free.' "

A Book of Remembrance

16 Then those [a]who feared the LORD
[b]spoke to one another,
And the LORD listened and heard
them;
So [c]a book of remembrance was
written before Him
For those who fear the LORD
And who [1]meditate on His name.

17 "They[a] shall be Mine," says the
LORD of hosts,
"On the day that I make them My
[b]jewels.[1]
And [c]I will spare them
As a man spares his own son who
serves him."
18 [a]Then you shall again discern
Between the righteous and the
wicked,
Between one who serves God
And one who does not serve Him.

12 [a]Dan. 8:9
13 [a]Mal. 2:17 *[1]* Lit. *strong*
14 [a]Job 21:14
15 [a]Ps. 73:12 [b]Ps. 95:9 *[1]* Lit. *built*
16 [a]Ps. 66:16 [b]Heb. 3:13 [c]Ps. 56:8 *[1]* Or *esteem*
17 [a]Ex. 19:5 [b]Is. 62:3 [c]Ps. 103:13 *[1]* Lit. *special treasure*
18 [a][Ps. 58:11]
CHAPTER 4
1 [a][2 Pet. 3:7] [b]Mal. 3:18 [c]Obad. 18 [d]Amos 2:9
2 [a]Mal. 3:16 [b]Luke 1:78
3 [a]Mic. 7:10
4 [a]Ex. 20:3 [b]Deut. 4:10
5 [a][Matt. 11:14;17:10–13] [b]Joel 2:31
6 [a]Zech. 14:12 [b]Zech. 5:3

The Great Day of God

4 "For behold, [a]the day is coming,
Burning like an oven,
And all [b]the proud, yes, all who do
wickedly will be [c]stubble.
And the day which is coming shall
burn them up,"
Says the LORD of hosts,
"That will [d]leave them neither root
nor branch.
2 But to you who [a]fear My name
The [b]Sun of Righteousness shall
arise
With healing in His wings;
And you shall go out
And grow fat like stall-fed calves.
3 [a]You shall trample the wicked,
For they shall be ashes under the
soles of your feet
On the day that I do *this,*"
Says the LORD of hosts.

Lord, to ____ who fears Your name, may You, the Sun of Righteousness, arise with healing in Your wings.

FROM MALACHI 4:2

4 "Remember the [a]Law of Moses, My
servant,
Which I commanded him in Hor
for all Israel,
With [b]*the* statutes and judgme
5 Behold, I will send you [a]Elijah
prophet
[b]Before the coming of the gre
dreadful day of the LORD.
6 And he will turn
The hearts of the fathers t
children,
And the hearts of the chil
their fathers,
Lest I come and [a]strike
with [b]a curse."

eb

nts.
the

at and

the

dren to

the earth

The New Testament

AUTHOR: *Anonymous, But Early Tradition Unanimously Ascribes It to Matthew*

DATE: *A.D. 50–75*

THEME: *Jesus Is the Fulfillment of Old Testament Prophecies Concerning the Messiah; His Disciples Are Called to a New Covenant, to Live at a Higher Dimension Than the Old Ever Realized*

KEY WORDS: *Fulfill, Kingdom of Heaven, Son of Man, Son of God*

MATTHEW

Dear Woman of Destiny,

From the wonderful account of the Messiah's birth to the torn temple veil, the Book of Matthew shows Jesus Christ as the fulfillment of many Old Testament prophecies. Just look at the unique and powerful way women were treated in the text. God sent an angel to visit Joseph so Mary would not be stoned. Jesus took time to heal Peter's mother-in-law; and He even touched her, something unheard of for any rabbi. The woman with the issue of blood was singled out from the crowd and healed. Even a little girl was important enough for Jesus to take time to raise her from the dead. Jesus loves you as much today as He loved these women.

With His love,

Cindy Jacobs

The Genealogy of Jesus Christ

1 The book of the [a]genealogy[1] of Jesus Christ, [b]the Son of David, [c]the Son of Abraham:

2 [a]Abraham begot Isaac, [b]Isaac begot Jacob, and Jacob begot [c]Judah and his brothers. 3 [a]Judah begot Perez and Zerah by Tamar, [b]Perez begot Hezron, and Hezron begot Ram. 4 Ram begot Amminadab, Amminadab begot Nahshon, and Nahshon begot Salmon. 5 Salmon begot [a]Boaz by Rahab, Boaz begot Obed by Ruth, Obed begot Jesse, 6 and [a]Jesse begot David the king.

[b]David the king begot Solomon by her [1]*who had been the wife* of Uriah. 7 [a]Solomon begot Rehoboam, Rehoboam begot [b]Abijah, and Abijah begot [1]Asa. 8 Asa begot [a]Jehoshaphat, Jehoshaphat begot Joram, and Joram begot [b]Uzziah. 9 Uzziah begot Jotham, Jotham begot [a]Ahaz, and Ahaz begot Hezekiah. 10 [a]Hezekiah begot Manasseh, Manasseh begot [1]Amon, and Amon begot [b]Josiah. 11 [a]Josiah begot [1]Jeconiah and his brothers about the time they were [b]carried away to Babylon.

12 And after they were brought to Babylon, [a]Jeconiah begot Shealtiel, and Shealtiel begot [b]Zerubbabel. 13 Zerubbabel begot Abiud, Abiud begot Eliakim, and Eliakim begot Azor. 14 Azor begot Zadok, Zadok begot Achim, and Achim begot Eliud. 15 Eliud begot Eleazar, Eleazar begot Matthan, and Matthan begot Jacob. 16 And Jacob begot Joseph the husband of [a]Mary, of whom was born Jesus who is called Christ.

17 So all the generations from Abraham to David *are* fourteen generations, from David until the captivity in Babylon *are* fourteen generations, and from the captivity in Babylon until the Christ *are* fourteen generations.

Christ Born of Mary

18 Now the [a]birth of Jesus Christ was as follows: After His mother Mary was betrothed to Joseph, before they came together, she was found with child [b]of the Holy Spirit. 19 Then Joseph her husband, being [1]a just *man,* and not wanting [a]to make her a public example, was minded to put her away secretly. 20 But while he thought about these things, behold, an angel of the Lord appeared to him in a dream, saying, "Joseph, son of David, do not be afraid to take to you Mary your wife, [a]for that which is [1]conceived in her is of the Holy Spirit. 21 [a]And she will bring forth a Son, and you shall call His name [1]JESUS, [b]for He will save His people from their sins."

22 So all this was done that it might be fulfilled which was spoken by the Lord through the prophet, saying: 23 [a]*"Behold,*[1] *the virgin shall be with child, and bear a Son, and they shall call His name Immanuel,"* which is translated, "God with us."

24 Then Joseph, being aroused from sleep, did as the angel of the Lord commanded him and took to him his wife, 25 and [1]did not know her till she had brought forth [a]her[2] firstborn Son. And he called His name JESUS.

Wise Men from the East

2 Now after [a]Jesus was born in Bethlehem of Judea in the days of Herod the king, behold, [1]wise men [b]from the East came to Jerusalem, 2 saying, [a]"Where is He who has been born King of the Jews? For we have seen [b]His star in the East and have come to worship Him."

3 When Herod the king heard *this,* he was troubled, and all Jerusalem with him. 4 And when he had gathered all [a]the chief priests and [b]scribes of the people together, [c]he inquired of them where the Christ was to be born.

5 So they said to him, "In Bethlehem of Judea, for thus it is written by the prophet:

6 *'But[a] you, Bethlehem, in the land*
of Judah,
Are not the least among the rulers
of Judah;
For out of you shall come a Ruler
[b]*Who will shepherd My people*
Israel.' "

7 Then Herod, when he had secretly called the [1]wise men, determined from them what time the [a]star appeared. 8 And he sent them to Bethlehem and said, "Go and search carefully for the young Child, and when you have found *Him,* bring back word to me, that I may come and worship Him also."

9 When they heard the king, they departed; and behold, the star which they had seen in the East went before them, till it came and stood over where the young Child was. 10 When they saw the star, they

CHAPTER 1
1 [a] Luke 3:23 [b] John 7:42 [c] Gen. 12:3; 22:18 [1] Lit. *generation*
2 [a] Gen. 21:2, 12 [b] Gen. 25:26; 28:14 [c] Gen. 29:35
3 [a] Gen. 38:27; 49:10 [b] Ruth 4:18–22
5 [a] Ruth 2:1; 4:1–13
6 [a] 1 Sam. 16:1 [b] 2 Sam. 7:12; 12:24 [1] Words in italic type have been added for clarity. They are not found in the original Greek.
7 [a] 1 Chr. 3:10 [b] 2 Chr. 11:20 [1] NU *Asaph*
8 [a] 1 Chr. 3:10 [b] 2 Kin. 15:13
9 [a] 2 Kin. 15:38
10 [a] 2 Kin. 20:21 [b] 1 Kin. 13:2 [1] NU *Amos*
11 [a] 1 Chr. 3:15, 16 [b] 2 Kin. 24:14–16 [1] Or *Coniah* or *Jehoiachin*
12 [a] 1 Chr. 3:17 [b] Ezra 3:2
16 [a] Matt. 13:55
18 [a] Luke 1:27 [b] Luke 1:35
19 [a] Deut. 24:1 [1] *an upright*
20 [a] Luke 1:35 [1] Lit. *begotten*
21 [a] Luke 1:31; 2:21 [b] John 1:29 [1] Lit. *Savior*
23 [a] Is. 7:14 [1] Words in oblique type in the New Testament are quoted from the Old Testament.
25 [a] Luke 2:7, 21 [1] Kept her a virgin [2] NU *a Son*

CHAPTER 2
1 [a] Luke 2:4–7 [b] Gen. 25:6 [1] Gr. *magoi*
2 [a] Luke 2:11 [b] [Num. 24:17]
4 [a] 2 Chr. 36:14 [b] 2 Chr. 34:13 [c] Mal. 2:7
6 [a] Mic. 5:2 [b] [Rev. 2:27]
7 [a] Num. 24:17 [1] Gr. *magoi*

rejoiced with exceedingly great joy. 11 And
when they had come into the house, they
saw the young Child with Mary His
mother, and fell down and worshiped
Him. And when they had opened their
treasures, [a]they presented gifts to Him:
gold, frankincense, and myrrh.
12 Then, being divinely warned [a]in a
dream that they should not return to Herod, they departed for their own country
another way.

The Flight into Egypt

13 Now when they had departed, behold,
an angel of the Lord appeared to Joseph in
a dream, saying, "Arise, take the young
Child and His mother, flee to Egypt, and
stay there until I bring you word; for Herod will seek the young Child to destroy
Him."
14 When he arose, he took the young
Child and His mother by night and departed for Egypt, 15 and was there until the
death of Herod, that it might be fulfilled
which was spoken by the Lord through
the prophet, saying, [a]*"Out of Egypt I
called My Son."*

Massacre of the Innocents

16 Then Herod, when he saw that he was
deceived by the wise men, was exceedingly
angry; and he sent forth and put to death
all the male children who were in Bethlehem and in all its districts, from two years
old and under, according to the time
which he had determined from the wise
men. 17 Then was fulfilled what was spoken by Jeremiah the prophet, saying:

18 *"A[a] voice was heard in Ramah,*
Lamentation, weeping, and great
mourning,
Rachel weeping for her children,
Refusing to be comforted,
Because they are no more."

The Home in Nazareth

19 Now when Herod was dead, behold,
an angel of the Lord appeared in a dream
to Joseph in Egypt, 20 [a]saying, "Arise, take
the young Child and His mother, and go
to the land of Israel, for those who
[b]sought the young Child's life are dead."
21 Then he arose, took the young Child and
His mother, and came into the land of
Israel.
22 But when he heard that Archelaus
was reigning over Judea instead of his fa-

11 a Is. 60:6
12 a Matt. 1:20
15 a Hos. 11:1
18 a Jer. 31:15
20 a Luke 2:39 b Matt. 2:16
22 a Matt. 2:12, 13, 19 b Luke 2:39
23 a John 1:45, 46 b Judg. 13:5

CHAPTER 3
1 a Mark 1:3–8 b Josh. 14:10
2 a Dan. 2:44
3 a Is. 40:3 b Luke 1:76
4 a Mark 1:6 b Lev. 11:22 c 1 Sam. 14:25, 26
5 a Mark 1:5
6 a Acts 19:4, 18
7 a Matt. 12:34 b [1 Thess. 1:10]
9 a John 8:33
10 a Matt. 7:19
11 a Luke 3:16 b [Acts 2:3, 4] *1* M omits *and fire*
12 a Mal. 3:3 b Matt. 13:30
13 a Mark 1:9–11 b Matt. 2:22

ther Herod, he was afraid to go there. And
being warned by God in a [a]dream, he
turned aside [b]into the region of Galilee.
23 And he came and dwelt in a city called
[a]Nazareth, that it might be fulfilled
[b]which was spoken by the prophets, "He
shall be called a Nazarene."

John the Baptist Prepares the Way

3 In those days [a]John the Baptist came
preaching [b]in the wilderness of Judea,
2 and saying, "Repent, for [a]the kingdom of
heaven is at hand!" 3 For this is he who
was spoken of by the prophet Isaiah,
saying:

[a]*"The voice of one crying in the*
wilderness:
[b]*'Prepare the way of the LORD;*
Make His paths straight.'"

4 Now [a]John himself was clothed in
camel's hair, with a leather belt around
his waist; and his food was [b]locusts and
[c]wild honey. 5 [a]Then Jerusalem, all Judea,
and all the region around the Jordan went
out to him 6 [a]and were baptized by him in
the Jordan, confessing their sins.
7 But when he saw many of the Pharisees and Sadducees coming to his baptism, he said to them, [a]"Brood of vipers!
Who warned you to flee from [b]the wrath
to come? 8 Therefore bear fruits worthy of
repentance, 9 and do not think to say to
yourselves, [a]'We have Abraham as *our* father.' For I say to you that God is able to
raise up children to Abraham from these
stones. 10 And even now the ax is laid to
the root of the trees. [a]Therefore every tree
which does not bear good fruit is cut
down and thrown into the fire. 11 [a]I indeed
baptize you with water unto repentance,
but He who is coming after me is mightier
than I, whose sandals I am not worthy to
carry. [b]He will baptize you with the Holy
Spirit [1]and fire. 12 [a]His winnowing fan *is*
in His hand, and He will thoroughly clean
out His threshing floor, and gather His
wheat into the barn; but He will [b]burn up
the chaff with unquenchable fire."

John Baptizes Jesus

13 [a]Then Jesus came [b]from Galilee to
John at the Jordan to be baptized by him.
14 And John *tried to* prevent Him, saying,
"I need to be baptized by You, and are You
coming to me?"

15 But Jesus answered and said to him,
"Permit *it to be so* now, for thus it is fit-
ting for us to fulfill all righteousness."
Then he allowed Him.

Let no one pray for a
mighty baptism of power
who is not prepared for
deep heart searchings and
confession of sin.

EVAN ROBERTS

16 [a]When He had been baptized, Jesus
came up immediately from the water; and
behold, the heavens were opened to Him,
and [1]He saw [b]the Spirit of God descending like a dove and alighting upon Him.
17 [a]And suddenly a voice *came* from heav-
en, saying, [b]"This is My beloved Son, in
whom I am well pleased."

Satan Tempts Jesus

4 Then [a]Jesus was led up by [b]the Spirit
into the wilderness to be tempted by
the devil. 2 And when He had fasted forty
days and forty nights, afterward He was
hungry. 3 Now when the tempter came to
Him, he said, "If You are the Son of God,
command that these stones become
bread."
4 But He answered and said, "It is written, [a]*'Man shall not live by bread alone,
but by every word that proceeds from the
mouth of God.'* "
5 Then the devil took Him up [a]into the
holy city, set Him on the pinnacle of the
temple, 6 and said to Him, "If You are the
Son of God, throw Yourself down. For it is
written:

[a]*'He shall give His angels charge*
over you,'

and,

[b]*'In their hands they shall bear you*
up,
Lest you dash your foot against a
stone.' "

7 Jesus said to him, "It is written again,
[a]*'You shall not [1]tempt the* LORD *your
God.'* "

8 Again, the devil took Him up on an
exceedingly high mountain, and [a]showed
Him all the kingdoms of the world and
their glory. 9 And he said to Him, "All
these things I will give You if You will fall
down and worship me."
10 Then Jesus said to him, [1]"Away with
you, Satan! For it is written, [a]*'You shall
worship the* LORD *your God, and Him only
you shall serve.'* "
11 Then the devil [a]left Him, and behold,
[b]angels came and ministered to Him.

Dare to look up to God
and say, "Make use
of me for the future
as Thou wilt."

EPICTETUS

Jesus Begins His Galilean Ministry

12 [a]Now when Jesus heard that John had
been put in prison, He departed to Galilee.
13 And leaving Nazareth, He came and
dwelt in Capernaum, which is by the sea,
in the regions of Zebulun and Naphtali,
14 that it might be fulfilled which was spoken by Isaiah the prophet, saying:

15 *"The[a] land of Zebulun and the*
land of Naphtali,
By the way of the sea, beyond the
Jordan,
Galilee of the Gentiles:
16 [a]*The people who sat in darkness*
have seen a great light,
And upon those who sat in the
region and shadow of death
Light has dawned."

17 [a]From that time Jesus began to
preach and to say, [b]"Repent, for the kingdom of heaven [1]is at hand."

Four Fishermen Called as Disciples

18 [a]And Jesus, walking by the Sea of Galilee, saw two brothers, Simon [b]called Peter, and Andrew his brother, casting a net
into the sea; for they were fishermen.
19 Then He said to them, "Follow Me, and

16 a Mark 1:10 b John 1:32 1 Or *he*
17 a John 12:28 b Ps. 2:7

CHAPTER 4
1 a Mark 1:12 b Ezek. 3:14
4 a Deut. 8:3
5 a Neh. 11:1, 18
6 a Ps. 91:11 b Ps. 91:12
7 a Deut. 6:16 1 *test*
8 a [1 John 2:15–17]
10 a Deut. 6:13; 10:20 1 M *Get behind Me*
11 a [James 4:7] b [Heb. 1:14]
12 a John 4:43
15 a Is. 9:1, 2
16 a Luke 2:32
17 a Mark 1:14, 15 b Matt. 3:2; 10:7 1 *has drawn near*
18 a Mark 1:16–20 b John 1:40–42

[a]I will make you fishers of men." 20 [a]They
immediately left *their* nets and followed
Him.
21 [a]Going on from there, He saw two
other brothers, James *the son* of Zebedee,
and John his brother, in the boat with
Zebedee their father, mending their nets.
He called them, 22 and immediately they
left the boat and their father, and followed
Him.

Jesus Heals a Great Multitude

23 And Jesus went about all Galilee,
[a]teaching in their synagogues, preaching
[b]the gospel of the kingdom, [c]and healing
all kinds of sickness and all kinds of disease among the people. 24 Then [1]His fame
went throughout all Syria; and they
[a]brought to Him all sick people who were
afflicted with various diseases and torments, and those who were demon-
possessed, epileptics, and paralytics; and
He healed them. 25 [a]Great multitudes followed Him—from Galilee, and *from* [1]De-
capolis, Jerusalem, Judea, and beyond the
Jordan.

The Beatitudes

5 And seeing the multitudes, [a]He went
up on a mountain, and when He was
seated His disciples came to Him. 2 Then
He opened His mouth and [a]taught them,
saying:

Lord, bless ____ who is poor in spirit, for You have promised that theirs is the kingdom of heaven.

FROM MATTHEW 5:3

3 "Blessed[a] *are* the poor in spirit,
For theirs is the kingdom of heaven.
4 [a]Blessed *are* those who mourn,
For they shall be comforted.
5 [a]Blessed *are* the meek,
For [b]they shall inherit the [1]earth.
6 Blessed *are* those who [a]hunger and thirst for righteousness,
[b]For they shall be filled.
7 Blessed *are* the merciful,
[a]For they shall obtain mercy.
8 [a]Blessed *are* the pure in heart,
For [b]they shall see God.
9 Blessed *are* the peacemakers,
For they shall be called sons of God.
10 [a]Blessed *are* those who are persecuted for righteousness' sake,
For theirs is the kingdom of heaven.

To hunger and thirst after righteousness is when nothing in the world can fascinate us so much as being near to God.

SMITH WIGGLESWORTH

11 [a]"Blessed are you when they revile and
persecute you, and say all kinds of [b]evil
against you falsely for My sake. 12 [a]Rejoice
and be exceedingly glad, for great *is* your
reward in heaven, for [b]so they persecuted
the prophets who were before you.

Believers Are Salt and Light

13 "You are the salt of the earth; [a]but
if the salt loses its flavor, how shall it be
seasoned? It is then good for nothing but
to be thrown out and trampled underfoot
by men.
14 [a]"You are the light of the world. A city
that is set on a hill cannot be hidden.
15 Nor do they [a]light a lamp and put it
under a basket, but on a lampstand, and it
gives light to all *who are* in the house.

Faith, like light, should always be simple and unbending; while love, like warmth, should beam forth on every side, and bend to every necessity of our brethren.

MARTIN LUTHER

19 a Luke 5:10
20 a Mark 10:28
21 a Mark 1:19
23 a Matt. 9:35 b [Matt. 24:14] c Mark 1:34
24 a Luke 4:40 1 Lit. *the report of Him*
25 a Mark 3:7, 8 1 Lit. *Ten Cities*

CHAPTER 5
1 a Mark 3:13
2 a [Matt. 7:29]
3 a Luke 6:20–23
4 a Rev. 21:4
5 a Ps. 37:11 b [Rom. 4:13] 1 Or *land*
6 a Luke 1:53 b [Is. 55:1; 65:13]
7 a Ps. 41:1
8 a Ps. 15:2; 24:4 b 1 Cor. 13:12
10 a 1 Pet. 3:14
11 a Luke 6:22 b 1 Pet. 4:14
12 a 1 Pet. 4:13, 14 b Acts 7:52
13 a Luke 14:34
14 a [John 8:12]
15 a Luke 8:16

Matthew 5:13–15

Dear Woman of Destiny,

Jesus calls His people to be the salt of the earth. Salt (a Christian) is a preservative that retards decay. When the sprinkling of this "salt" begins, Christ's followers are observed seeking ways to preserve others! In times of chaos, it is so fulfilling to be a preserver, allowing God to sprinkle us into the situation as His Spirit's "sodium chloride," bringing healing and preservation.

Salt is a clear, brittle mineral used to flavor, preserve, and deice. Obtained by mining and evaporation, it must be crushed and ground before it can be very useful. Like salt, Christians must often be crushed before we can be of much use in God's kingdom and be a preserving force on the earth. Interestingly, the Hebrew word for salt, *melach*, actually means "easily pulverized and dissolved." The Greek word for salt in Matthew 5:13 is from *halas*, which figuratively means "prudence." Could it be that calamitous experiences pulverize our own foundations, fracturing our idols of self-trust, wealth, intelligence, and talents? The persecuted churches of China, Pakistan, North Africa, and others graphically demonstrate the intangible value of pulverization. In being crushed, these courageous Christians have become salty savor indeed!

If we answer this call and let our values and priorities dissolve like salt into our Father's heart, then His agenda, His nature will emerge and He can sprinkle us into the wounds of people's crises. And, since salt deices, our effective presence in the midst of an emergency can melt hearts that have been cold to the gospel!

The Scriptures reveal that Father God has pain in His heart today. Centuries ago, He said to Jeremiah, "Say this word to them: 'Let my eyes flow with tears night and day, and let them not cease; for the virgin daughter of my people has been broken with a mighty stroke, with a very severe blow'" (Jer. 14:17). Jeremiah's crying is God's crying.

How can we get God's cry into our hearts? To even hear His cry, we must allow God to circumcise our hearts, cutting away the concerns of this world, the deceitfulness of riches, the desires for more and more *things*—even the preoccupation with our personal well-being. Being consumed by such pursuits, we are forced to ignore the needs of millions who suffer without knowing how God's heart-cry moved Him to send Jesus to relieve their suffering! When we do not reach out, rescue, and serve those around us, we fail to be salt and fall short of our destiny. Perhaps now is a good time to think about what we can give up to intensify our saltiness.

Can we Christians feel the anguish in the heart of God? Can we as women hear His cry? If we would only allow God Almighty to put His passion inside of us, His nature would so fill us that we would have to explode in service to others, or rupture ourselves. And then, we would be salt.

How awesome to partner with God to bless others! We can make deliberate choices to do so. We can be ready with natural and spiritual skills. We can preserve physical and spiritual life! We can be salt and light!

Betsy Neuenschwander

16 Let your light so shine before men,
[a]that they may see your good works and
[b]glorify your Father in heaven.

Christ Fulfills the Law

17 [a]"Do not think that I came to destroy
the Law or the Prophets. I did not come
to destroy but to fulfill. 18 For assuredly, I
say to you, [a]till heaven and earth pass
away, one [1]jot or one [2]tittle will by no
means pass from the law till all is fulfilled.
19 [a]Whoever therefore breaks one of the
least of these commandments, and teaches men so, shall be called least in the kingdom of heaven; but whoever does and
teaches *them,* he shall be called great in
the kingdom of heaven. 20 For I say to you,
that unless your righteousness exceeds
[a]*the righteousness* of the scribes and
Pharisees, you will by no means enter the
kingdom of heaven.

Murder Begins in the Heart

21 "You have heard that it was said to
those [1]of old, [a]*'You shall not murder,* and
whoever murders will be in danger of the
judgment.' 22 But I say to you that [a]who-
ever is angry with his brother [1]without a
cause shall be in danger of the judgment.
And whoever says to his brother, [b]'Raca!'[2]
shall be in danger of the council. But
whoever says, [3]'You fool!' shall be in danger of [4]hell fire. 23 Therefore [a]if you bring
your gift to the altar, and there remember
that your brother has something against
you, 24 [a]leave your gift there before the altar, and go your way. First be reconciled
to your brother, and then come and offer
your gift. 25 [a]Agree with your adversary
quickly, [b]while you are on the way with
him, lest your adversary deliver you to the
judge, the judge hand you over to the officer, and you be thrown into prison. 26 Assuredly, I say to you, you will by no means
get out of there till you have paid the last
penny.

Adultery in the Heart

27 "You have heard that it was said [1]to
those of old, [a]*'You shall not commit adultery.'* 28 But I say to you that whoever
[a]looks at a woman to lust for her has already committed adultery with her in his
heart. 29 [a]If your right eye causes you to
[1]sin, [b]pluck it out and cast *it* from you; for
it is more profitable for you that one of
your members perish, than for your whole
body to be cast into hell. 30 And if your
right hand causes you to [1]sin, cut it off
and cast *it* from you; for it is more profitable for you that one of your members
perish, than for your whole body to be
cast into hell.

Remember that your thoughts are heard aloud in heaven. Cultivate the habit of governing the thoughts and imaginations. Do not suffer them to wander.

RAYMOND T. RICHEY

Marriage Is Sacred and Binding

31 "Furthermore it has been said,
[a]'Whoever divorces his wife, let him give
her a certificate of divorce.' 32 But I say to
you that [a]whoever divorces his wife for
any reason except [1]sexual immorality
causes her to commit adultery; and whoever marries a woman who is divorced
commits adultery.

Jesus Forbids Oaths

33 "Again you have heard that [a]it was
said to those of [1]old, [b]'You shall not swear
falsely, but [c]shall perform your oaths to
the Lord.' 34 But I say to you, [a]do not
swear at all: neither by heaven, for it is
[b]God's throne; 35 nor by the earth, for it is
His footstool; nor by Jerusalem, for it is
the city of [a]the great King. 36 Nor shall you
swear by your head, because you cannot
make one hair white or black. 37 [a]But let
[1]your 'Yes' be 'Yes,' and your 'No,' 'No.'
For whatever is more than these is from
the evil one.

Go the Second Mile

38 "You have heard that it was said, [a]*'An
eye for an eye and a tooth for a tooth.'*
39 [a]But I tell you not to resist an evil person. [b]But whoever slaps you on your right
cheek, turn the other to him also. 40 If anyone wants to sue you and take away your
tunic, let him have *your* cloak also. 41 And

16 a 1 Pet. 2:12 b [John 15:8]
17 a Rom. 10:4
18 a Luke 16:17 *1* Gr. *iota,* Heb. *yod,* the smallest letter *2* The smallest stroke in a Heb. letter
19 a [James 2:10]
20 a [Rom. 10:3]
21 a Ex. 20:13; Deut. 5:17 *1 in ancient times*
22 a [1 John 3:15] b [James 2:20; 3:6] *1* NU omits *without a cause* *2* Lit., in Aram., *Empty head* *3* Gr. *More* *4* Gr. *Gehenna*
23 a Matt. 8:4
24 a [Job 42:8]
25 a Luke 12:58, 59 b [Is. 55:6]
27 a Ex. 20:14; Deut. 5:18 *1* NU, M omit *to those of old*
28 a Prov. 6:25
29 a Mark 9:43 b [Col. 3:5] *1* Lit. *stumble* or *offend*
30 *1* Lit. *stumble* or *offend*
31 a Deut. 24:1
32 a [Luke 16:18] *1* Or *fornication*
33 a Matt. 23:16 b Lev. 19:12 c Deut. 23:23 *1 ancient times*
34 a James 5:12 b Is. 66:1
35 a Ps. 48:2
37 a [Col. 4:6] *1* Lit. *your word be yes yes*
38 a Ex. 21:24; Lev. 24:20; Deut. 19:21
39 a Luke 6:29 b Is. 50:6

whoever [a]compels you to go one mile, go
with him two. 42Give to him who asks you,
and [a]from him who wants to borrow from
you do not turn away.

Love Your Enemies

43"You have heard that it was said,
[a]'*You shall love your neighbor* [b]and hate
your enemy.' 44[1]But I say to you, [a]love
your enemies, bless those who curse you,
[b]do good to those who hate you, and pray
[c]for those who spitefully use you and persecute you, 45that you may be sons of your
Father in heaven; for [a]He makes His sun
rise on the evil and on the good, and sends
rain on the just and on the unjust. 46[a]For
if you love those who love you, what reward have you? Do not even the tax collectors do the same? 47And if you greet your
[1]brethren only, what do you do more *than
others?* Do not even the [2]tax collectors do
so? 48[a]Therefore you shall be perfect, just
[b]as your Father in heaven is perfect.

Do Good to Please God

6 "Take heed that you do not do your
charitable deeds before men, to be
seen by them. Otherwise you have no reward from your Father in heaven. 2There-
fore, [a]when you do a charitable deed, do
not sound a trumpet before you as the
hypocrites do in the synagogues and in

Our Father in heaven,
hallowed be Your name.
Your kingdom come. Your
will be done on earth as it is
in heaven. Give _____ this
day their daily bread. And
forgive them their debts, as
they forgive their debtors.
And do not lead _____ into
temptation, but deliver them
from the evil one. For Yours
is the kingdom and the
power and the glory forever.
Amen.

FROM MATTHEW 6:9–13

the streets, that they may have glory from
men. Assuredly, I say to you, they have
their reward. 3But when you do a charitable deed, do not let your left hand know
what your right hand is doing, 4that your
charitable deed may be in secret; and your
Father who sees in secret [a]will Himself
reward you [1]openly.

The Model Prayer

5"And when you pray, you shall not be
like the [1]hypocrites. For they love to pray
standing in the synagogues and on the
corners of the streets, that they may be
seen by men. Assuredly, I say to you, they
have their reward. 6But you, when you
pray, [a]go into your room, and when you
have shut your door, pray to your Father
who *is* in the secret *place;* and your Father who sees in secret will reward you
[1]openly. 7And when you pray, [a]do not use
vain repetitions as the heathen *do.* [b]For
they think that they will be heard for their
many words.

Reading God's Word
regularly and praying
habitually in the secret
place of the Most High
puts one where he is
absolutely safe from the
attacks of the Enemy
of souls.

E. M. BOUNDS

8"Therefore do not be like them. For
your Father [a]knows the things you have
need of before you ask Him. 9In this
[a]manner, therefore, pray:

[b]Our Father in heaven,
Hallowed be Your [c]name.
10 Your kingdom come.
[a]Your will be done
On earth [b]as *it is* in heaven.
11 Give us this day our [a]daily bread.
12 And [a]forgive us our debts,
As we forgive our debtors.
13 [a]And do not lead us into
temptation,
But [b]deliver us from the evil one.

41 a Matt. 27:32
42 a Luke 6:30–34
43 a Lev. 19:18 b Deut. 23:3–6
44 a Luke 6:27 b [Rom. 12:20] c Acts 7:60 *1* NU *But I say to you, love your enemies and pray for those who persecute you*
45 a Job 25:3
46 a Luke 6:32
47 *1* M *friends* *2* NU *Gentiles*
48 a [Col. 1:28; 4:12] b Eph. 5:1

CHAPTER 6
2 a Rom. 12:8
4 a Luke 14:12–14 *1* NU omits *openly*
5 *1 pretenders*
6 a 2 Kin. 4:33 *1* NU omits *openly*
7 a Eccl. 5:2 b 1 Kin. 18:26
8 a [Rom. 8:26, 27]
9 a Luke 11:2–4 b [Matt. 5:9, 16] c Mal. 1:11
10 a Matt. 26:42 b Ps. 103:20
11 a Prov. 30:8
12 a [Matt. 18:21, 22]
13 a [2 Pet. 2:9] b John 17:15

MATTHEW 6:12

Dear Woman of Destiny,

One of Satan's most destructive lies is that forgiveness is optional. It is not. While it is true that we have to make the choice to forgive or not to forgive, it is not true that the choice we make will have no effect on our lives and the lives of those around us. The fact is, whether or not we forgive determines our forgiveness from the Father (see v. 14). That is why Jesus taught us to pray, "Forgive us our debts, as we forgive our debtors" (v. 12).

Forgiveness is the very essence of the gospel. Jesus prayed while He hung on the cross, "Father, forgive them, for they do not know what they do" (Luke 23:34). If Jesus had not forgiven us, there would be no gospel—no good news.

Why is it that forgiveness is so difficult at times? It even seems that perhaps God was not aware of the atrocities man would commit when He required us to forgive. How could He ask us to forgive such cruelties? Yet forgiveness is the most Godlike thing that man can do on earth because it involves the ultimate giving of oneself. It is like the fragrance of the violet on the sole of the shoe that crushed it.

In Matthew 18, Jesus deals with the issue of forgiveness. He discusses offense, which is the seed of unforgiveness. He tells us that when we are offended, we should go to the person who offended us and talk with him or her about it. If the person is not receptive, we should return, taking someone with us to mediate the reconciliation. Then if the person still refuses to hear, we should tell it to the church.

The end of the matter is that as Christians, we must be reconciled to one another (see vv. 19, 20). Otherwise, we have the awesome power to bring bondage into the spiritual atmosphere of the church.

I have had the privilege of witnessing several revivals during my years in the ministry. The simple action of one person going to another and acknowledging their wrong and then being forgiven by the other person would often be the catalyst that released the Spirit of God to move in revival among us. I have seen one act of forgiveness release persons who have been held captive to bitterness for years, thus opening the way for their deliverance and healing.

And I have often said that if I had not learned about the power of forgiveness to heal emotional wounds, I would not be in the ministry today. We must never suppose that Jesus does not know the pain we are going through. It is *because* people are cruel and life's situations are painful that we have been given the remedy of forgiveness.

Forgiveness really has nothing to do with an emotional feeling or with another person asking us to forgive. We need not worry that we don't "feel" like forgiving. Forgiveness is not a feeling; it is a decision—our decision. That is why Jesus can command it of those who follow Him.

Woman of Destiny, if you are holding a grudge against anyone who has wronged you, let it go today. Release the spirit of reconciliation that will bring your healing.

Sue Curran

[1]For Yours is the kingdom and the
power and the glory forever.
Amen.

14[a]"For if you forgive men their trespasses, your heavenly Father will also forgive you. 15But [a]if you do not forgive men
their trespasses, neither will your Father
forgive your trespasses.

If Thy will is done in me, I shall be whole.

CHARLES PARHAM

Fasting to Be Seen Only by God

16"Moreover, [a]when you fast, do not be
like the [1]hypocrites, with a sad countenance. For they disfigure their faces that
they may appear to men to be fasting. Assuredly, I say to you, they have their reward. 17But you, when you fast, [a]anoint
your head and wash your face, 18so that
you do not appear to men to be fasting,
but to your Father who *is* in the secret
place; and your Father who sees in secret
will reward you [1]openly.

Lay Up Treasures in Heaven

19[a]"Do not lay up for yourselves treasures on earth, where moth and rust destroy and where thieves break in and steal;
20[a]but lay up for yourselves treasures in
heaven, where neither moth nor rust destroys and where thieves do not break in
and steal. 21For where your treasure is,
there your heart will be also.

The Lamp of the Body

22[a]"The lamp of the body is the eye. If
therefore your eye is [1]good, your whole
body will be full of light. 23But if your eye
is [1]bad, your whole body will be full of
darkness. If therefore the light that is in
you is darkness, how great *is* that darkness!

You Cannot Serve God and Riches

24[a]"No one can serve two masters; for
either he will hate the one and love the
other, or else he will be loyal to the one
and despise the other. [b]You cannot serve
God and [1]mammon.

Do Not Worry

25"Therefore I say to you, [a]do not worry
about your life, what you will eat or what
you will drink; nor about your body, what
you will put on. Is not life more than food
and the body more than clothing? 26[a]Look
at the birds of the air, for they neither sow
nor reap nor gather into barns; yet your
heavenly Father feeds them. Are you not
of more value than they? 27Which of you
by worrying can add one [1]cubit to his
[2]stature?

28"So why do you worry about clothing?
Consider the lilies of the field, how they
grow: they neither toil nor spin; 29and yet
I say to you that even Solomon in all his
glory was not [1]arrayed like one of these.
30Now if God so clothes the grass of the
field, which today is, and tomorrow is
thrown into the oven, *will He* not much
more *clothe* you, O you of little faith?

Enough for today is all we can enjoy. We cannot eat or drink or wear more than today's supply of food and clothing. When our Father does not give you more, be content with your daily allowance.

CHARLES H. SPURGEON

31"Therefore do not worry, saying,
'What shall we eat?' or 'What shall we
drink?' or 'What shall we wear?' 32For after all these things the Gentiles seek. For
your heavenly Father knows that you
need all these things. 33 But [a]seek first
the kingdom of God and His righteousness, and all these things shall be added to
you. 34Therefore do not worry about tomorrow, for tomorrow will worry about

13 [1] NU omits the rest of v. 13.
14 [a] Mark 11:25
15 [a] Matt. 18:35
16 [a] Is. 58:3–7 [1] *pretenders*
17 [a] Ruth 3:3
18 [1] NU, M omit *openly*
19 [a] Prov. 23:4
20 [a] Matt. 19:21
22 [a] Luke 11:34, 35 [1] Clear, or healthy
23 [1] Evil, or unhealthy
24 [a] Luke 16:9, 11, 13 [b] [Gal. 1:10] [1] Lit., in Aram., *riches*
25 [a] Luke 12:22
26 [a] Luke 12:24
27 [1] About 18 inches [2] *height*
29 [1] *dressed*
33 [a] [1 Tim. 4:8]

MATTHEW 6:33

Dear Woman of Destiny,

In considering seeking the kingdom of God, the main thing we need to understand is that the kingdom of God is not heaven. It's not way out there in the blue somewhere. The kingdom of God is immediately accessible to its residents, which is who we are if we have accepted the Lord into our hearts. Matthew 12:28 says the "kingdom of God has come upon you." And in Luke 17:21, we read that the "kingdom of God is within you." Those Scriptures say to me that the kingdom is immediately available—you can touch it and feel it. You are living in it now.

As women, it is not always easy for us to seek God's kingdom first. Everything in our lives seems to rear its head when it's time for us to seek the Lord. The children need us, our husbands need us, the doorbell or the phone rings.

When my children were small and there was no time to close my eyes to "seek" without a catastrophe taking place, I learned to not whistle while I worked, but to pray while I worked—or at least keep my eyes on the little ones while I prayed.

It's surprising how little brainpower it took to vacuum or iron. Those two chores especially were conducive to spending time with the Lord. He and I talked a lot during those times. I could sing, praise, and worship, and at the same time be an influence on the children as they listened.

The Lord always seems to meet us where we are, and so graciously encourages us with "pats on the back" just when we need them most.

"And His righteousness" simply means to do things right. It is not impossible to do things right when we seek the Lord and His kingdom. One habit I had when I was a teenager was to drop to my knees as soon as I got out of bed and ask the Lord to cover my day. It's an important few seconds to start your day right.

When we seek His kingdom, He adds all "these things" to us. What are "these things"? They are whatever you have need of. He promised to supply all our needs (see Phil. 4:19).

When I was a small girl, visiting my aunt, I was surprised to find she did not have the ingredients to make gravy to go with the potatoes she was preparing for our dinner. This was following the Great Depression, so there were many people in similar situations. We had never been without gravy in spite of our own financial difficulties. When I mentioned this to my mother on my return home, she said, "Honey, remember it's God who gives the gravy." I understood in that moment that He was the provider not only of our absolute "needs," but also of the things that make life more enjoyable and tasty.

All we have to do is seek His kingdom, and He will add and add and add!

Anna Hayford

its own things. Sufficient for the day *is* its
own trouble.

Do Not Judge

7 "Judge[1] [a]not, that you be not judged.
2For with what [1]judgment you judge,
you will be judged; [a]and with the measure
you use, it will be measured back to you.
3[a]And why do you look at the speck in
your brother's eye, but do not consider
the plank in your own eye? 4Or how can
you say to your brother, 'Let me remove
the speck from your eye'; and look, a
plank *is* in your own eye? 5Hypocrite!
First remove the plank from your own
eye, and then you will see clearly to remove the speck from your brother's eye.
6[a]"Do not give what is holy to the dogs;
nor cast your pearls before swine, lest
they trample them under their feet, and
turn and tear you in pieces.

Keep Asking, Seeking, Knocking

7[a]"Ask, and it will be given to you; seek,
and you will find; knock, and it will be
opened to you. 8For [a]everyone who asks
receives, and he who seeks finds, and to
him who knocks it will be opened. 9[a]Or
what man is there among you who, if his
son asks for bread, will give him a stone?
10Or if he asks for a fish, will he give him
a serpent? 11If you then, [a]being evil, know
how to give good gifts to your children,
how much more will your Father who is
in heaven give good things to those who
ask Him! 12Therefore, [a]whatever you want
men to do to you, do also to them, for
[b]this is the Law and the Prophets.

The Narrow Way

13[a]"Enter by the narrow gate; for wide
is the gate and broad *is* the way that leads
to destruction, and there are many who
go in by it. 14[1]Because narrow *is* the gate
and [2]difficult *is* the way which leads to
life, and there are few who find it.

You Will Know Them by Their Fruits

15[a]"Beware of false prophets, [b]who
come to you in sheep's clothing, but inwardly they are ravenous wolves. 16[a]You
will know them by their fruits. [b]Do men
gather grapes from thornbushes or figs
from thistles? 17Even so, [a]every good tree
bears good fruit, but a bad tree bears bad
fruit. 18A good tree cannot bear bad fruit,
nor *can* a bad tree bear good fruit. 19[a]Ev-
ery tree that does not bear good fruit is
cut down and thrown into the fire.
20Therefore by their fruits you will know
them.

I Never Knew You

21"Not everyone who says to Me, [a]'Lord,
Lord,' shall enter the kingdom of heaven,
but he who [b]does the will of My Father in
heaven. 22Many will say to Me in that day,
'Lord, Lord, have we [a]not prophesied in
Your name, cast out demons in Your
name, and done many wonders in Your
name?' 23And [a]then I will declare to them,
'I never knew you; [b]depart from Me, you
who practice lawlessness!'

Lord, may ______ hear Your word and do it that they may be like the wise person who built their house upon the rock. Though the floods come and the winds blow, their house will stand.

FROM MATTHEW 7:24, 25

Build on the Rock

24"Therefore [a]whoever hears these sayings of Mine, and does them, I will liken
him to a wise man who built his house on
the rock: 25and the rain descended, the
floods came, and the winds blew and beat
on that house; and it did not fall, for it was
founded on the rock.
26"But everyone who hears these sayings of Mine, and does not do them, will
be like a foolish man who built his house
on the sand: 27and the rain descended, the
floods came, and the winds blew and beat
on that house; and it fell. And great was its
fall."
28And so it was, when Jesus had ended
these sayings, that [a]the people were astonished at His teaching, 29[a]for He taught
them as one having authority, and not as
the scribes.

CHAPTER 7
1 a Rom. 14:3
1 Condemn
2 a Luke 6:38
1 Condemnation
3 a Luke 6:41
6 a Prov. 9:7, 8
7 a [Mark 11:24]
8 a Prov. 8:17
9 a Luke 11:11
11 a Gen. 6:5; 8:21
12 a Luke 6:31
b Gal. 5:14
13 a Luke 13:24
14 1 NU, M *How narrow. . . !*
2 *confined*
15 a Jer. 23:16
b Mic. 3:5
16 a Matt. 7:20; 12:33
b Luke 6:43
17 a Matt. 12:33
19 a [John 15:2, 6]
21 a Luke 6:46
b Rom. 2:13
22 a Num. 24:4
23 a [2 Tim. 2:19]
b Ps. 5:5; 6:8
24 a Luke 6:47–49
28 a Matt. 13:54
29 a [John 7:46]

Jesus Cleanses a Leper

8 When He had come down from the mountain, great multitudes followed Him. 2[a]And behold, a leper came and [b]worshiped Him, saying, "Lord, if You are willing, You can make me clean."

3Then Jesus put out *His* hand and touched him, saying, "I am willing; be cleansed." Immediately his leprosy [a]was cleansed.

4And Jesus said to him, [a]"See that you tell no one; but go your way, show yourself to the priest, and offer the gift that [b]Moses [c]commanded, as a testimony to them."

Jesus Heals a Centurion's Servant

5[a]Now when Jesus had entered Capernaum, a [b]centurion came to Him, pleading with Him, 6saying, "Lord, my servant is lying at home paralyzed, dreadfully tormented."

7And Jesus said to him, "I will come and heal him."

8The centurion answered and said, "Lord, [a]I am not worthy that You should come under my roof. But only [b]speak a word, and my servant will be healed. 9For I also am a man under authority, having soldiers under me. And I say to this *one,* 'Go,' and he goes; and to another, 'Come,' and he comes; and to my servant, 'Do this,' and he does *it.*"

10When Jesus heard *it,* He marveled, and said to those who followed, "Assuredly, I say to you, I have not found such great faith, not even in Israel! 11And I say to you that [a]many will come from east and west, and sit down with Abraham, Isaac, and Jacob in the kingdom of heaven. 12But [a]the sons of the kingdom [b]will be cast out into outer darkness. There will be weeping and gnashing of teeth." 13Then Jesus said to the centurion, "Go your way; and as you have believed, *so* let it be done for you." And his servant was healed that same hour.

Peter's Mother-in-Law Healed

14[a]Now when Jesus had come into Peter's house, He saw [b]his wife's mother lying sick with a fever. 15So He touched her hand, and the fever left her. And she arose and served [1]them.

Many Healed After Sabbath Sunset

16[a]When evening had come, they brought to Him many who were demon-possessed. And He cast out the spirits with a word, and healed all who were sick, 17that it might be fulfilled which was spoken by Isaiah the prophet, saying:

[a]*"He Himself took our infirmities*
And bore our sicknesses."

After being sufficiently enlightened, our attitude toward sickness should be the same as our attitude toward sin.

F. F. Bosworth

The Cost of Discipleship

18And when Jesus saw great multitudes about Him, He gave a command to depart to the other side. 19[a]Then a certain scribe came and said to Him, "Teacher, I will follow You wherever You go."

20And Jesus said to him, "Foxes have holes and birds of the air *have* nests, but the Son of Man has nowhere to lay *His* head."

21[a]Then another of His disciples said to Him, "Lord, [b]let me first go and bury my father."

22But Jesus said to him, "Follow Me, and let the dead bury their own dead."

Wind and Wave Obey Jesus

23Now when He got into a boat, His disciples followed Him. 24[a]And suddenly a great tempest arose on the sea, so that the boat was covered with the waves. But He was asleep. 25Then His disciples came to *Him* and awoke Him, saying, "Lord, save us! We are perishing!"

26But He said to them, "Why are you fearful, O you of little faith?" Then [a]He arose and rebuked the winds and the sea, and there was a great calm. 27So the men marveled, saying, [1]"Who can this be, that even the winds and the sea obey Him?"

CHAPTER 8
2 a Mark 1:40–45 b John 9:38
3 a Luke 4:27
4 a Mark 5:43 b Luke 5:14 c Deut. 24:8
5 a Luke 7:1–3 b Matt. 27:54
8 a Luke 15:19, 21 b Ps. 107:20
11 a Mal. 1:11
12 a [Matt. 21:43] b Luke 13:28
14 a Mark 1:29–31 b 1 Cor. 9:5
15 1 NU, M *Him*
16 a Luke 4:40, 41
17 a Is. 53:4
19 a Luke 9:57, 58
21 a Luke 9:59, 60 b 1 Kin. 19:20
24 a Mark 4:37
26 a Ps. 65:7; 89:9; 107:29
27 1 Lit. *What sort of man is this*

MATTHEW 8:18–27

Dear Woman of Destiny,

Have you ever wondered why Jesus would have to *command* His disciples, several of whom were fishermen, to cross the Sea of Galilee? Being sons of fishermen, they would have grown up on those waters. Crossing it would have been second nature to them. Later in the story, we find that as they were crossing the sea, a violent storm arose. I believe that Jesus *commanded* them to cross because they could all see that a storm was developing. Being fishermen, they would have known how extremely dangerous it would be to follow Jesus across that darkening sea. They would have known it could cost them their very lives. But the story does not stop there—Jesus drives the issue of radical discipleship still deeper.

A scribe approaches Jesus and asks if he can follow Him. Jesus' answer implies that to follow Him, he must be willing to become like Him. Jesus had given up the comfort, security, and status that accompany the place where we "lay our head." To follow Jesus, the scribe would have to do likewise. Another disciple wanted to bury his father before following Jesus. In that day, to do so would have been culturally and religiously expected of him. Jesus' answer clearly placed following Him above cultural, traditional, and even religious norms. Following Jesus requires nothing less than radical discipleship!

Jesus' call to those disciples is the same call to you and to me today. The Lord may call you to follow Him across the street to your neighbor or to the coworker at the office. The Lord may be calling you to follow Him, as He did me, to some remote region of the earth. The issue, however, is not so much a geographical one as it is an issue of the heart. Radical discipleship is really radical obedience. When He asks us to follow Him in the face of potential danger, will we go? Will we follow and obey when it means giving up the comfort and status of our belongings? Will we follow Him when it cuts across our cultural, traditional, or even religious preconceptions? Will we follow if it means we might be misunderstood? Self-preservation, comfort, houses, culture, and religious traditions are not wrong in themselves. The heart of the matter lies in whether or not these things are keeping us from following Jesus.

Take a moment and invite the Lord to search your heart. Allow Him to show you if there is anything in your life that would keep you from following Him and obeying Him fully. Ask for His forgiveness, entrust those things to Him, and ask Him to be Lord over those areas of your life. There is nothing more exciting, challenging, and fulfilling than following Jesus with your whole heart. Radical discipleship means radical obedience to the One whose lovingkindness and faithfulness will never fail you.

Leslyn Musch

Two Demon-Possessed Men Healed

28[a]When He had come to the other side, to the country of the [1]Gergesenes, there met Him two demon-possessed *men,* coming out of the tombs, exceedingly fierce, so that no one could pass that way. 29And suddenly they cried out, saying, "What have we to do with You, Jesus, You Son of God? Have You come here to torment us before the time?"

30Now a good way off from them there was a herd of many swine feeding. 31So the demons begged Him, saying, "If You cast us out, [1]permit us to go away into the herd of swine."

32And He said to them, "Go." So when they had come out, they went into the herd of swine. And suddenly the whole herd of swine ran violently down the steep place into the sea, and perished in the water.

33Then those who kept *them* fled; and they went away into the city and told everything, including what *had happened* to the demon-possessed *men.* 34And behold, the whole city came out to meet Jesus. And when they saw Him, [a]they begged *Him* to depart from their region.

Thank You, Lord, that You desire mercy and not sacrifice. Lord, ____ is walking in sin. In Your mercy, call them to repentance.

FROM MATTHEW 9:13

Jesus Forgives and Heals a Paralytic

9 So He got into a boat, crossed over, [a]and came to His own city. 2[a]Then behold, they brought to Him a paralytic lying on a bed. [b]When Jesus saw their faith, He said to the paralytic, "Son, be of good cheer; your sins are forgiven you."

3And at once some of the scribes said within themselves, "This Man blasphemes!"

4But Jesus, [a]knowing their thoughts, said, "Why do you think evil in your hearts? 5For which is easier, to say, '*Your* sins are forgiven you,' or to say, 'Arise and walk'? 6But that you may know that the Son of Man has power on earth to forgive sins"—then He said to the paralytic, "Arise, take up your bed, and go to your house." 7And he arose and departed to his house.

8Now when the multitudes saw *it,* they [a]marveled[1] and glorified God, who had given such power to men.

Matthew the Tax Collector

9[a]As Jesus passed on from there, He saw a man named Matthew sitting at the tax office. And He said to him, "Follow Me." So he arose and followed Him.

10[a]Now it happened, as Jesus sat at the table in the house, *that* behold, many tax collectors and sinners came and sat down with Him and His disciples. 11And when the Pharisees saw *it,* they said to His disciples, "Why does your Teacher eat with [a]tax collectors and [b]sinners?"

12When Jesus heard *that,* He said to them, "Those who are well have no need of a physician, but those who are sick. 13But go and learn what *this* means: [a]'*I desire mercy and not sacrifice.*' For I did not come to call the righteous, [b]but sinners, [1]to repentance."

Jesus Is Questioned About Fasting

14Then the disciples of John came to Him, saying, [a]"Why do we and the Pharisees fast [1]often, but Your disciples do not fast?"

15And Jesus said to them, "Can [a]the [1]friends of the bridegroom mourn as long as the bridegroom is with them? But the days will come when the bridegroom will be taken away from them, and [b]then they will fast. 16No one puts a piece of unshrunk cloth on an old garment; for [1]the patch pulls away from the garment, and the tear is made worse. 17Nor do they put new wine into old wineskins, or else the wineskins [1]break, the wine is spilled, and the wineskins are ruined. But they put new wine into new wineskins, and both are preserved."

A Girl Restored to Life and a Woman Healed

18[a]While He spoke these things to them, behold, a ruler came and worshiped Him, saying, "My daughter has just died,

---

28 a Mark 5:1–4 *1* NU *Gadarenes*
31 *1* NU *send us into*
34 a Luke 5:8; Acts 16:39

CHAPTER 9
1 a Matt. 4:13; 11:23
2 a Luke 5:18–26 b Matt. 8:10
4 a Matt. 12:25
8 a John 7:15 *1* NU *were afraid*
9 a Luke 5:27
10 a Mark 2:15
11 a Matt. 11:19 b [Gal. 2:15]
13 a Hos. 6:6 b 1 Tim. 1:15 *1* NU omits *to repentance*
14 a Luke 5:33–35; 18:12 *1* NU brackets *often* as disputed.
15 a John 3:29 b Acts 13:2, 3; 14:23 *1* Lit. *sons of the bridechamber*
16 *1* Lit. *that which is put on*
17 *1 burst*
18 a Luke 8:41–56

but come and lay Your hand on her and
she will live." 19So Jesus arose and followed him, and so *did* His [a]disciples.
20[a]And suddenly, a woman who had a
flow of blood for twelve years came from
behind and [b]touched the hem of His garment. 21For she said to herself, "If only I
may touch His garment, I shall be made
well." 22But Jesus turned around, and
when He saw her He said, "Be of good
cheer, daughter; [a]your faith has made you
well." And the woman was made well from
that hour.
23[a]When Jesus came into the ruler's
house, and saw [b]the flute players and the
noisy crowd wailing, 24He said to them,
[a]"Make room, for the girl is not dead, but
sleeping." And they ridiculed Him. 25But
when the crowd was put outside, He went
in and [a]took her by the hand, and the girl
arose. 26And the [a]report of this went out
into all that land.

Two Blind Men Healed

27When Jesus departed from there,
[a]two blind men followed Him, crying out
and saying, [b]"Son of David, have mercy
on us!"
28And when He had come into the
house, the blind men came to Him. And
Jesus said to them, "Do you believe that I
am able to do this?"
They said to Him, "Yes, Lord."
29Then He touched their eyes, saying,
"According to your faith let it be to you."
30And their eyes were opened. And Jesus
sternly warned them, saying, [a]"See *that*
no one knows *it.*" 31[a]But when they had
departed, they [1]spread the news about
Him in all that [2]country.

A Mute Man Speaks

32[a]As they went out, behold, they
brought to Him a man, mute and demon-
possessed. 33And when the demon was
cast out, the mute spoke. And the multitudes marveled, saying, "It was never seen
like this in Israel!"
34But the Pharisees said, [a]"He casts out
demons by the ruler of the demons."

The Compassion of Jesus

35Then Jesus went about all the cities
and villages, [a]teaching in their synagogues, preaching the gospel of the kingdom, and healing every sickness and every
disease [1]among the people. 36[a]But when
He saw the multitudes, He was moved
with compassion for them, because they
were [1]weary and scattered, [b]like sheep
having no shepherd. 37Then He said to His
disciples, [a]"The harvest truly *is* plentiful,
but the laborers *are* few. 38[a]Therefore
pray the Lord of the harvest to send out
laborers into His harvest."

I can get more out of God by believing Him for one minute than by shouting at Him all night.

SMITH WIGGLESWORTH

The Twelve Apostles

10 And [a]when He had called His
twelve disciples to *Him,* He gave
them power *over* unclean spirits, to cast
them out, and to heal all kinds of sickness
and all kinds of disease. 2Now the names
of the twelve apostles are these: first, Simon, [a]who is called Peter, and Andrew his
brother; James the *son* of Zebedee, and
John his brother; 3Philip and Bartholomew; Thomas and Matthew the tax collector; James the *son* of Alphaeus, and
[1]Lebbaeus, whose surname was Thaddaeus; 4[a]Simon the [1]Cananite, and Judas [b]Is-
cariot, who also betrayed Him.

Sending Out the Twelve

5These twelve Jesus sent out and commanded them, saying: [a]"Do not go into
the way of the Gentiles, and do not enter
a city of [b]the Samaritans. 6[a]But go rather
to the [b]lost sheep of the house of Israel.
7[a]And as you go, preach, saying, [b]'The
kingdom of heaven [1]is at hand.' 8Heal the
sick, [1]cleanse the lepers, [2]raise the dead,
cast out demons. [a]Freely you have received, freely give. 9[a]Provide neither gold
nor silver nor [b]copper in your money
belts, 10nor bag for *your* journey, nor two
tunics, nor sandals, nor staffs; [a]for a
worker is worthy of his food.
11[a]"Now whatever city or town you enter, inquire who in it is worthy, and stay
there till you go out. 12And when you go

19 a Matt. 10:2–4
20 a Luke 8:43 b Matt. 14:36; 23:5
22 a Luke 7:50; 8:48; 17:19; 18:42
23 a Mark 5:38 b 2 Chr. 35:25
24 a Acts 20:10
25 a Mark 1:31
26 a Matt. 4:24
27 a Matt. 20:29–34 b Luke 18:38, 39
30 a Matt. 8:4
31 a Mark 7:36 *1* Lit. *made Him known* *2* Lit. *land*
32 a Matt. 12:22, 24
34 a Luke 11:15
35 a Matt. 4:23 *1* NU omits *among the people*
36 a Mark 6:34 b Num. 27:17 *1* NU, M *harassed*
37 a Luke 10:2
38 a 2 Thess. 3:1

CHAPTER 10
1 a Luke 6:13
2 a John 1:42
3 *1* NU omits *Lebbaeus, whose surname was*
4 a Acts 1:13 b John 13:2, 26 *1* NU *Cananaean*
5 a Matt. 4:15 b John 4:9
6 a Matt. 15:24 b Jer. 50:6
7 a Luke 9:2 b Matt. 3:2 *1* has drawn near
8 a [Acts 8:18] *1* NU *raise the dead, cleanse the lepers* *2* M omits *raise the dead*
9 a 1 Sam. 9:7 b Mark 6:8
10 a 1 Tim. 5:18
11 a Luke 10:8

into a household, greet it. [13][a]If the household is worthy, let your peace come upon
it. [b]But if it is not worthy, let your peace
return to you. [14][a]And whoever will not
receive you nor hear your words, when
you depart from that house or city, [b]shake
off the dust from your feet. [15]Assuredly, I
say to you, [a]it will be more tolerable for
the land of Sodom and Gomorrah in the
day of judgment than for that city!

Persecutions Are Coming

[16][a]"Behold, I send you out as sheep in
the midst of wolves. [b]Therefore be wise as
serpents and [c]harmless[1] as doves. [17]But
beware of men, for [a]they will deliver you
up to councils and [b]scourge you in their
synagogues. [18][a]You will be brought before
governors and kings for My sake, as a testimony to them and to the Gentiles.
[19][a]But when they deliver you up, do not
worry about how or what you should
speak. For [b]it will be given to you in that
hour what you should speak; [20][a]for it is
not you who speak, but the Spirit of your
Father who speaks in you.

[21][a]"Now brother will deliver up brother
to death, and a father *his* child; and children will rise up against parents and
cause them to be put to death. [22]And [a]you
will be hated by all for My name's sake.
[b]But he who endures to the end will be
saved. [23][a]When they persecute you in this
city, flee to another. For assuredly, I say to
you, you will not have [b]gone through the
cities of Israel [c]before the Son of Man
comes.

[24][a]"A disciple is not above *his* teacher,
nor a servant above his master. [25]It is
enough for a disciple that he be like his
teacher, and a servant like his master. If
[a]they have called the master of the house
[1]Beelzebub, how much more *will they
call* those of his household! [26]Therefore
do not fear them. [a]For there is nothing
covered that will not be revealed, and hidden that will not be known.

Jesus Teaches the Fear of God

[27]"Whatever I tell you in the dark,
[a]speak in the light; and what you hear in
the ear, preach on the housetops. [28][a]And
do not fear those who kill the body but
cannot kill the soul. But rather [b]fear Him
who is able to destroy both soul and body
in [1]hell. [29]Are not two [a]sparrows sold for
a [1]copper coin? And not one of them falls
to the ground apart from your Father's
will. [30][a]But the very hairs of your head are
all numbered. [31]Do not fear therefore; you
are of more value than many sparrows.

Confess Christ Before Men

[32][a]"Therefore whoever confesses Me
before men, [b]him I will also confess before My Father who is in heaven. [33][a]But
whoever denies Me before men, him I
will also deny before My Father who is in
heaven.

Christ Brings Division

[34][a]"Do not think that I came to bring
peace on earth. I did not come to bring
peace but a sword. [35]For I have come to
[a]'*set*[1] *a man against his father, a daughter
against her mother, and a daughter-in-
law against her mother-in-law*'; [36]and [a]'*a
man's enemies will be those of his own
household*.' [37][a]He who loves father or
mother more than Me is not worthy of
Me. And he who loves son or daughter
more than Me is not worthy of Me. [38][a]And
he who does not take his cross and follow
after Me is not worthy of Me. [39][a]He who
finds his life will lose it, and he who loses
his life for My sake will find it.

> *Christ is not valued at all unless He be valued above all.*
>
> St. Augustine

A Cup of Cold Water

[40][a]"He who receives you receives Me,
and he who receives Me receives Him who
sent Me. [41][a]He who receives a prophet
in the name of a prophet shall receive a
prophet's reward. And he who receives a
righteous man in the name of a righteous
man shall receive a righteous man's reward. [42][a]And whoever gives one of these
little ones only a cup of cold *water* in the
name of a disciple, assuredly, I say to you,
he shall by no means lose his reward."

---

13 a Luke 10:5 b Ps. 35:13
14 a Mark 6:11 b Acts 13:51
15 a Matt. 11:22, 24
16 a Luke 10:3 b Eph. 5:15 c [Phil. 2:14–16] *1 innocent*
17 a Mark 13:9 b Acts 5:40; 22:19; 26:11
18 a 2 Tim. 4:16
19 a Luke 12:11, 12; 21:14, 15 b Ex. 4:12
20 a 2 Sam. 23:2
21 a Mic. 7:6
22 a Luke 21:17 b Mark 13:13
23 a Acts 8:1 b [Mark 13:10] c Matt. 16:28
24 a John 15:20
25 a John 8:48, 52 *1* NU, M *Beelzebul;* a Philistine deity, 2 Kin. 1:2, 3
26 a Mark 4:22
27 a Acts 5:20
28 a Luke 12:4 b Luke 12:5 *1* Gr. *Gehenna*
29 a Luke 12:6, 7 *1* Gr. *assarion,* a coin worth about 1/16 of a denarius
30 a Luke 21:18
32 a Luke 12:8 b [Rev. 3:5]
33 a 2 Tim. 2:12
34 a [Luke 12:49]
35 a Mic. 7:6 *1 alienate a man from*
36 a John 13:18
37 a Luke 14:26
38 a [Mark 8:34]
39 a John 12:25
40 a Luke 9:48
41 a 1 Kin. 17:10
42 a Mark 9:41

John the Baptist Sends Messengers to Jesus

11 Now it came to pass, when Jesus finished commanding His twelve disciples, that He departed from there to [a]teach and to preach in their cities.

2 [a]And when John had heard [b]in prison about the works of Christ, he [1]sent two of his disciples 3 and said to Him, "Are You [a]the Coming One, or do we look for another?"

4 Jesus answered and said to them, "Go and tell John the things which you hear and see: 5 [a]*The* blind see and *the* lame walk; *the* lepers are cleansed and *the* deaf hear; *the* dead are raised up and [b]*the* poor have the gospel preached to them. 6 And blessed is he who is not [a]offended because of Me."

7 [a]As they departed, Jesus began to say to the multitudes concerning John: "What did you go out into the wilderness to see? [b]A reed shaken by the wind? 8 But what did you go out to see? A man clothed in soft garments? Indeed, those who wear soft *clothing* are in kings' houses. 9 But what did you go out to see? A prophet? Yes, I say to you, [a]and more than a prophet. 10 For this is *he* of whom it is written:

[a]'Behold, I send My messenger
before Your face,
Who will prepare Your way before
You.'

11 "Assuredly, I say to you, among those born of women there has not risen one greater than John the Baptist; but he who is least in the kingdom of heaven is greater than he. 12 [a]And from the days of John the Baptist until now the kingdom of heaven suffers violence, and the violent take it by force. 13 [a]For all the prophets and the law prophesied until John. 14 And if you are willing to receive *it,* he is [a]Elijah who is to come. 15 [a]He who has ears to hear, let him hear!

16 [a]"But to what shall I liken this generation? It is like children sitting in the marketplaces and calling to their companions, 17 and saying:

'We played the flute for you,
And you did not dance;
We mourned to you,
And you did not [1]lament.'

18 For John came neither eating nor drinking, and they say, 'He has a demon.' 19 The Son of Man came eating and drinking, and they say, 'Look, a glutton and a [1]winebibber, [a]a friend of tax collectors and sinners!' [b]But wisdom is justified by her [2]children."

Woe to the Impenitent Cities

20 [a]Then He began to rebuke the cities in which most of His mighty works had been done, because they did not repent: 21 "Woe to you, Chorazin! Woe to you, Bethsaida! For if the mighty works which were done in you had been done in Tyre and Sidon, they would have repented long ago [a]in sackcloth and ashes. 22 But I say to you, [a]it will be more tolerable for Tyre and Sidon in the day of judgment than for you. 23 And you, Capernaum, [a]who[1] are exalted to heaven, will be brought down to Hades; for if the mighty works which were done in you had been done in Sodom, it would have remained until this day. 24 But I say to you [a]that it shall be more tolerable for the land of Sodom in the day of judgment than for you."

Jesus Gives True Rest

25 [a]At that time Jesus answered and said, "I thank You, Father, Lord of heaven and earth, that [b]You have hidden these things from *the* wise and prudent [c]and have revealed them to babes. 26 Even so, Father, for so it seemed good in Your sight. 27 [a]All things have been delivered to Me by My Father, and no one knows the Son except the Father. [b]Nor does anyone know the Father except the Son, and *the one* to whom the Son wills to reveal *Him.* 28 Come to [a]Me, all *you* who labor and are heavy laden, and I will give you rest. 29 Take My yoke upon you [a]and learn from Me, for I am [1]gentle and [b]lowly in heart, [c]and you will find rest for your souls. 30 [a]For My yoke *is* easy and My burden is light."

Jesus Is Lord of the Sabbath

12 At that time [a]Jesus went through the grainfields on the Sabbath. And His disciples were hungry, and began to [b]pluck heads of grain and to eat. 2 And when the Pharisees saw *it,* they said to Him, "Look, Your disciples are doing what is not lawful to do on the Sabbath!"

3 But He said to them, "Have you not read [a]what David did when he was hungry, he and those who were with him: 4 how he entered the house of God and ate

CHAPTER 11
1 a Luke 23:5
2 a Luke 7:18–35 b Matt. 4:12; 14:3 *1 NU sent by his*
3 a John 6:14
5 a Is. 29:18; 35:4–6 b Is. 61:1
6 a [Rom. 9:32]
7 a Luke 7:24 b [Eph. 4:14]
9 a Luke 1:76; 20:6
10 a Mal. 3:1
12 a Luke 16:16
13 a Mal. 4:4–6
14 a Luke 1:17
15 a Luke 8:8
16 a Luke 7:31
17 *1 Lit. beat your breast*
19 a Matt. 9:10 b Luke 7:35 *1 wine drinker* *2 NU works*
20 a Luke 10:13–15, 18
21 a Jon. 3:6–8
22 a Matt. 10:15; 11:24
23 a Is. 14:13 *1 NU will you be exalted to heaven? No, you will be*
24 a Matt. 10:15
25 a Luke 10:21, 22 b Ps. 8:2 c Matt. 16:17
27 a Matt. 28:18 b John 1:18; 6:46; 10:15
28 a [John 6:35–37]
29 a [Phil. 2:5] b Zech. 9:9 c Jer. 6:16 *1 meek*
30 a [1 John 5:3]

CHAPTER 12
1 a Luke 6:1–5 b Deut. 23:25
3 a 1 Sam. 21:6

MATTHEW 11:28–30

Dear Woman of Destiny,

Your pace of living is probably like mine—hectic and stressful at times. You have to get children ready for school. Don't forget their homework and nutritious lunches. (Right? Or did that New Year's resolution go out the door with the new exercise program?) You're rushing to work so you won't be late another morning. Then you've got to squeeze in some errands on your lunch break. Race to piano lessons and baseball practice. Rush home; cook one of those ten-minute ready-for-the-table meals; help with homework; throw laundry into the washer; and then sit down to have a few minutes with Jesus when you suddenly find yourself already in "la-la land."

We live in an age with more technology, more appliances, and more conveniences, but yet our lives are more stressful than probably any other time in history. But Jesus' words in Matthew 11:28–30, "Come to Me, all you who labor and are heavy laden, and I will give you rest," are as appropriate for this time as any other century. Our busyness and hectic schedules actually can become the enemy of our souls. Then you add any extra problems such as teenage rebellion, marriage conflicts, financial pressures, or serious diseases, and you have one depleted life. You start to wonder where is that "abundant life" Jesus promised to us.

First, we must come to Him. Then, as verse 29 tells us, we must take His yoke upon us. Upon first reading this, you might think, *Yoke—yuck!* A yoke is a piece of wood that harnesses together a pair of oxen for the purpose of labor. Because of Jesus' death on the cross we now can be harnessed with Him to help in our labors and with the stresses we face each day. In our busy lives we must remember to continually cast all our cares upon Him so that He carries the brunt of the heavy load.

Jesus' yoke is not a legalistic religious system, but it is a bonded relationship with Him that helps keep our daily priorities in right perspective and our lives directed with eternal purpose. And the fruit of that harnessing together is rest for our souls. The word in Greek for "rest" is *anapauo*. *Ana* means "up" and *pauo* means "to make to cease." Rest is not just getting enough sleep, but we need "rest" in our souls from the emotional turmoil and mental aggravations of life. When we reach our arms up to our loving Savior and feel His embrace, we can expect a cessation from our stress and tension.

I recently heard an angry remark come out of my mouth—and it shocked me! I had been carrying a particular burden for a long time without seeing a change in the situation. I discovered I was carrying the yoke in my own strength and wisdom. I was weighed down with the burden and had allowed frustration to develop into anger. I was reminded again how much I need Jesus to be my Burden-Carrier. He has much bigger shoulders than we do to carry our everyday "crosses."

Judy Radachy

[a]the showbread which was not lawful for him to eat, nor for those who were with him, [b]but only for the priests? 5 Or have you not read in the [a]law that on the Sabbath the priests in the temple [1]profane the Sabbath, and are blameless? 6 Yet I say to you that in this place there is [a]*One* greater than the temple. 7 But if you had known what *this* means, [a]'*I desire mercy and not sacrifice,*' you would not have condemned the guiltless. 8 For the Son of Man is Lord [1]even of the Sabbath."

Healing on the Sabbath

9 [a]Now when He had departed from there, He went into their synagogue. 10 And behold, there was a man who had a withered hand. And they asked Him, saying, [a]"Is it lawful to heal on the Sabbath?"—that they might accuse Him.

11 Then He said to them, "What man is there among you who has one sheep, and if it falls into a pit on the Sabbath, will not lay hold of it and lift *it* out? 12 Of how much more value then is a man than a sheep? Therefore it is lawful to do good on the Sabbath." 13 Then He said to the man, "Stretch out your hand." And he stretched *it* out, and it was restored as whole as the other. 14 Then [a]the Pharisees went out and plotted against Him, how they might destroy Him.

Behold, My Servant

15 But when Jesus knew *it,* [a]He withdrew from there. [b]And great [1]multitudes followed Him, and He healed them all. 16 Yet He [a]warned them not to make Him known, 17 that it might be fulfilled which was spoken by Isaiah the prophet, saying:

18 *"Behold![a] My Servant whom I*
have chosen,
My Beloved [b]in whom My soul is
well pleased!
I will put My Spirit upon Him,
And He will declare justice to the
Gentiles.
19 *He will not quarrel nor cry out,*
Nor will anyone hear His voice in
the streets.
20 *A bruised reed He will not break,*
And smoking flax He will not
quench,
Till He sends forth justice to
victory;
21 *And in His name Gentiles will*
trust."

A House Divided Cannot Stand

22 [a]Then one was brought to Him who was demon-possessed, blind and mute; and He healed him, so that the [1]blind and mute man both spoke and saw. 23 And all the multitudes were amazed and said, "Could this be the [a]Son of David?"

24 [a]Now when the Pharisees heard *it* they said, "This *fellow* does not cast out demons except by [1]Beelzebub, the ruler of the demons."

25 But Jesus [a]knew their thoughts, and said to them: "Every kingdom divided against itself is brought to desolation, and every city or house divided against itself will not stand. 26 If Satan casts out Satan, he is divided against himself. How then will his kingdom stand? 27 And if I cast out demons by Beelzebub, by whom do your sons cast *them* out? Therefore they shall be your judges. 28 But if I cast out demons by the Spirit of God, [a]surely the kingdom of God has come upon you. 29 [a]Or how can one enter a strong man's house and plunder his goods, unless he first binds the strong man? And then he will plunder his house. 30 He who is not with Me is against Me, and he who does not gather with Me scatters abroad.

The Unpardonable Sin

31 "Therefore I say to you, [a]every sin and blasphemy will be forgiven men, [b]but the blasphemy *against* the Spirit will not be forgiven men. 32 Anyone who [a]speaks a word against the Son of Man, [b]it will be forgiven him; but whoever speaks against the Holy Spirit, it will not be forgiven him, either in this age or in the *age* to come.

A Tree Known by Its Fruit

33 "Either make the tree good and [a]its fruit good, or else make the tree bad and its fruit bad; for a tree is known by *its* fruit. 34 [a]Brood[1] of vipers! How can you, being evil, speak good things? [b]For out of the abundance of the heart the mouth speaks. 35 A good man out of the good treasure [1]of his heart brings forth good things, and an evil man out of the evil treasure brings forth evil things. 36 But I say to you that for every idle word men may speak, they will give account of it in the day of judgment. 37 For by your words

4 a Lev. 24:5 b Ex. 29:32
5 a Num. 28:9 *1 desecrate*
6 a [Is. 66:1, 2]
7 a [Hos. 6:6]
8 *1* NU, M omit *even*
9 a Mark 3:1–6
10 a John 9:16
14 a Mark 3:6
15 a Mark 3:7 b Matt. 19:2 *1* NU brackets *multitudes* as disputed.
16 a Matt. 8:4; 9:30; 17:9
18 a Is. 42:1–4; 49:3 b Matt. 3:17; 17:5
22 a Luke 11:14, 15 *1* NU omits *blind and*
23 a Matt. 9:27; 21:9
24 a Matt. 9:34 *1* NU, M *Beelzebul,* a Philistine deity
25 a Matt. 9:4
28 a [Dan. 2:44; 7:14]
29 a Is. 49:24
31 a Mark 3:28–30 b Acts 7:51
32 a John 7:12, 52 b 1 Tim. 1:13
33 a Matt. 7:16–18
34 a Matt. 3:7; 23:33 b Luke 6:45 *1 Offspring*
35 *1* NU, M omit *of his heart*

you will be justified, and by your words
you will be condemned."

The Scribes and Pharisees Ask for a Sign

38 [a]Then some of the scribes and Pharisees answered, saying, "Teacher, we want
to see a sign from You."
39 But He answered and said to them,
"An evil and [a]adulterous generation seeks
after a sign, and no sign will be given to
it except the sign of the prophet Jonah.
40 [a]For as Jonah was three days and three
nights in the belly of the great fish, so will
the Son of Man be three days and three
nights in the heart of the earth. 41 [a]The
men of Nineveh will rise up in the judgment with this generation and [b]condemn
it, [c]because they repented at the preaching of Jonah; and indeed a greater than
Jonah *is* here. 42 [a]The queen of the South
will rise up in the judgment with this generation and condemn it, for she came
from the ends of the earth to hear the
wisdom of Solomon; and indeed a greater
than Solomon *is* here.

An Unclean Spirit Returns

43 [a]"When an unclean spirit goes out of
a man, [b]he goes through dry places, seeking rest, and finds none. 44 Then he says,
'I will return to my house from which I
came.' And when he comes, he finds *it*
empty, swept, and put in order. 45 Then he
goes and takes with him seven other spirits more wicked than himself, and they
enter and dwell there; [a]and the last *state*
of that man is worse than the first. So
shall it also be with this wicked generation."

Jesus' Mother and Brothers Send for Him

46 While He was still talking to the multitudes, [a]behold, His mother and
[b]brothers stood outside, seeking to speak
with Him. 47 Then one said to Him, "Look,
[a]Your mother and Your brothers are
standing outside, seeking to speak with
You."
48 But He answered and said to the one
who told Him, "Who is My mother and
who are My brothers?" 49 And He stretched
out His hand toward His disciples and
said, "Here are My mother and My
[a]brothers! 50 For [a]whoever does the will of
My Father in heaven is My brother and
sister and mother."

The Parable of the Sower

13 On the same day Jesus went out
of the house [a]and sat by the sea.
2 [a]And great multitudes were gathered together to Him, so that [b]He got into a boat
and sat; and the whole multitude stood on
the shore.
3 Then He spoke many things to them in
parables, saying: [a]"Behold, a sower went
out to sow. 4 And as he sowed, some *seed*
fell by the wayside; and the birds came
and devoured them. 5 Some fell on stony
places, where they did not have much
earth; and they immediately sprang up because they had no depth of earth. 6 But
when the sun was up they were scorched,
and because they had no root they withered away. 7 And some fell among thorns,
and the thorns sprang up and choked
them. 8 But others fell on good ground
and yielded a crop: some [a]a hundredfold,
some sixty, some thirty. 9 [a]He who has
ears to hear, let him hear!"

Never dig up in unbelief what you have sown in faith.

GORDON LINDSAY

The Purpose of Parables

10 And the disciples came and said to
Him, "Why do You speak to them in parables?"
11 He answered and said to them, "Because [a]it has been given to you to know
the [1]mysteries of the kingdom of heaven,
but to them it has not been given. 12 [a]For
whoever has, to him more will be given,
and he will have abundance; but whoever
does not have, even what he has will be
taken away from him. 13 Therefore I speak
to them in parables, because seeing they
do not see, and hearing they do not hear,
nor do they understand. 14 And in them
the prophecy of Isaiah is fulfilled, which
says:

38 a Mark 8:11
39 a Matt. 16:4
40 a Jon. 1:17
41 a Luke 11:32 b Jer. 3:11 c Jon. 3:5
42 a 1 Kin. 10:1–13
43 a Luke 11:24–26 b [1 Pet. 5:8]
45 a [2 Pet. 2:20–22]
46 a Luke 8:19–21 b John 2:12; 7:3, 5
47 a Matt. 13:55, 56
49 a John 20:17
50 a John 15:14
CHAPTER 13
1 a Mark 4:1–12
2 a Luke 8:4 b Luke 5:3
3 a Luke 8:5
8 a Gen. 26:12
9 a Matt. 11:15
11 a Mark 4:10, 11 *1 secret* or *hidden truths*
12 a Matt. 25:29

[a]*'Hearing you will hear and shall not*
understand,
And seeing you will see and not
[b]*perceive;*
15 *For the hearts of this people have*
grown dull.
Their ears [a]*are hard of hearing,*
And their eyes they have [b]*closed,*
Lest they should see with their eyes
and hear with their ears,
Lest they should understand with
their hearts and turn,
So that I [1]*should* [c]*heal them.'*

16 But [a]blessed *are* your eyes for they see,
and your ears for they hear; 17 for assuredly, I say to you [a]that many prophets and
righteous *men* desired to see what you
see, and did not see *it,* and to hear what
you hear, and did not hear *it.*

The Parable of the Sower Explained

18 [a]"Therefore hear the parable of the
sower: 19 When anyone hears the word [a]of
the kingdom, and does not understand *it,*
then the wicked *one* comes and snatches
away what was sown in his heart. This
is he who received seed by the wayside.
20 But he who received the seed on stony
places, this is he who hears the word and
immediately [a]receives it with joy; 21 yet he
has no root in himself, but endures only
for a while. For when [a]tribulation or persecution arises because of the word, immediately [b]he stumbles. 22 Now [a]he who
received seed [b]among the thorns is he
who hears the word, and the cares of this
world and the deceitfulness of riches
choke the word, and he becomes unfruitful. 23 But he who received seed on the
good ground is he who hears the word and
understands *it,* who indeed bears [a]fruit
and produces: some a hundredfold, some
sixty, some thirty."

The Parable of the Wheat and the Tares

24 Another parable He put forth to them,
saying: "The kingdom of heaven is like a
man who sowed good seed in his field;
25 but while men slept, his enemy came
and sowed tares among the wheat and
went his way. 26 But when the grain had
sprouted and produced a crop, then the
tares also appeared. 27 So the servants of
the owner came and said to him, 'Sir, did
you not sow good seed in your field? How
then does it have tares?' 28 He said to
them, 'An enemy has done this.' The servants said to him, 'Do you want us then to
go and gather them up?' 29 But he said,
'No, lest while you gather up the tares you
also uproot the wheat with them. 30 Let
both grow together until the harvest, and
at the time of harvest I will say to the
reapers, "First gather together the tares
and bind them in bundles to burn them,
but [a]gather the wheat into my barn." ' "

The Parable of the Mustard Seed

31 Another parable He put forth to them,
saying: [a]"The kingdom of heaven is like
a mustard seed, which a man took and
sowed in his field, 32 which indeed is the
least of all the seeds; but when it is grown
it is greater than the herbs and becomes
a [a]tree, so that the birds of the air come
and nest in its branches."

The Parable of the Leaven

33 [a]Another parable He spoke to them:
"The kingdom of heaven is like leaven,
which a woman took and hid in three
[1]measures of meal till [b]it was all leavened."

Prophecy and the Parables

34 [a]All these things Jesus spoke to the
multitude in parables; and without a parable He did not speak to them, 35 that it
might be fulfilled which was spoken by
the prophet, saying:

[a]*"I will open My mouth in parables;*
[b]*I will utter things kept secret from*
the foundation of the world."

The Parable of the Tares Explained

36 Then Jesus sent the multitude away
and went into the house. And His disciples
came to Him, saying, "Explain to us the
parable of the tares of the field."
37 He answered and said to them: "He
who sows the good seed is the Son of Man.
38 [a]The field is the world, the good seeds
are the sons of the kingdom, but the tares
are [b]the sons of the wicked *one.* 39 The enemy who sowed them is the devil, [a]the
harvest is the end of the age, and the reapers are the angels. 40 Therefore as the tares
are gathered and burned in the fire, so it

---

14 a Is. 6:9, 10 b [John 3:36]
15 a Heb. 5:11 b Luke 19:42 c Acts 28:26, 27 *1* NU, M *would*
16 a Luke 10:23, 24
17 a Heb. 11:13
18 a Mark 4:13–20
19 a Matt. 4:23
20 a Is. 58:2
21 a [Acts 14:22] b Matt. 11:6
22 a 1 Tim. 6:9 b Jer. 4:3
23 a Col. 1:6
30 a Matt. 3:12
31 a Luke 13:18, 19
32 a Ezek. 17:22–24; 31:3–9
33 a Luke 13:20, 21 b [1 Cor. 5:6] *1* Gr. *sata,* same as a Heb. *seah;* approximately 2 pecks in all
34 a Mark 4:33, 34
35 a Ps. 78:2 b Eph. 3:9
38 a Rom. 10:18 b John 8:44
39 a Rev. 14:15

will be at the end of this age. 41The Son of
Man will send out His angels, [a]and they
will gather out of His kingdom all things
that offend, and those who practice lawlessness, 42[a]and will cast them into the
furnace of fire. [b]There will be wailing and
gnashing of teeth. 43[a]Then the righteous
will shine forth as the sun in the kingdom
of their Father. [b]He who has ears to hear,
let him hear!

The Parable of the Hidden Treasure

44"Again, the kingdom of heaven is like
treasure hidden in a field, which a man
found and hid; and for joy over it he goes
and [a]sells all that he has and [b]buys that
field.

The Parable of the Pearl of Great Price

45"Again, the kingdom of heaven is like
a merchant seeking beautiful pearls,
46who, when he had found [a]one pearl of
great price, went and sold all that he had
and bought it.

The Parable of the Dragnet

47"Again, the kingdom of heaven is like
a dragnet that was cast into the sea and
[a]gathered some of every kind, 48which,
when it was full, they drew to shore; and
they sat down and gathered the good into
vessels, but threw the bad away. 49So it
will be at the end of the age. The angels
will come forth, [a]separate the wicked
from among the just, 50and cast them into
the furnace of fire. There will be wailing
and gnashing of teeth."

51[1]Jesus said to them, "Have you understood all these things?"

They said to Him, "Yes, [2]Lord."

52Then He said to them, "Therefore every [1]scribe instructed [2]concerning the
kingdom of heaven is like a householder
who brings out of his treasure [a]*things*
new and old."

Jesus Rejected at Nazareth

53Now it came to pass, when Jesus had
finished these parables, that He departed
from there. 54[a]When He had come to His
own country, He taught them in their
synagogue, so that they were astonished
and said, "Where did this *Man* get this
wisdom and *these* mighty works? 55[a]Is
this not the carpenter's son? Is not His
mother called Mary? And [b]His brothers
[c]James, [1]Joses, Simon, and Judas? 56And
His sisters, are they not all with us?
Where then did this *Man* get all these
things?" 57So they [a]were offended at Him.

But Jesus said to them, [b]"A prophet
is not without honor except in his own
country and in his own house." 58Now
[a]He did not do many mighty works there
because of their unbelief.

John the Baptist Beheaded

14 At that time [a]Herod the tetrarch
heard the report about Jesus 2and
said to his servants, "This is John the Baptist; he is risen from the dead, and therefore these powers are at work in him."
3[a]For Herod had laid hold of John and
bound him, and put *him* in prison for the
sake of Herodias, his brother Philip's wife.
4Because John had said to him, [a]"It is not
lawful for you to have her." 5And although
he wanted to put him to death, he feared
the multitude, [a]because they counted
him as a prophet.

6But when Herod's birthday was celebrated, the daughter of Herodias danced
before them and pleased Herod. 7There-
fore he promised with an oath to give her
whatever she might ask.

8So she, having been prompted by her
mother, said, "Give me John the Baptist's
head here on a platter."

9And the king was sorry; nevertheless,
because of the oaths and because of those
who sat with him, he commanded *it* to be
given to *her*. 10So he sent and had John
beheaded in prison. 11And his head was
brought on a platter and given to the girl,
and she brought *it* to her mother. 12Then
his disciples came and took away the body
and buried it, and went and told Jesus.

Feeding the Five Thousand

13[a]When Jesus heard *it*, He departed
from there by boat to a deserted place by
Himself. But when the multitudes heard
it, they followed Him on foot from the
cities. 14And when Jesus went out He saw
a great multitude; and He [a]was moved
with compassion for them, and healed
their sick. 15[a]When it was evening, His
disciples came to Him, saying, "This is a
deserted place, and the hour is already
late. Send the multitudes away, that they
may go into the villages and buy themselves food."

41 [a] Matt. 18:7
42 [a] Rev. 19:20; 20:10 [b] Matt. 8:12; 13:50
43 [a] [Dan. 12:3] [b] Matt. 13:9
44 [a] Phil. 3:7, 8 [b] [Is. 55:1]
46 [a] Prov. 2:4; 3:14, 15; 8:10, 19
47 [a] Matt. 22:9, 10
49 [a] Matt. 25:32
51 [1] NU omits *Jesus said to them* [2] NU omits *Lord*
52 [a] Song 7:13 [1] A scholar of the Old Testament [2] Or *for*
54 [a] Luke 4:16
55 [a] John 6:42 [b] Matt. 12:46 [c] Mark 15:40 [1] NU *Joseph*
57 [a] Matt. 11:6 [b] Luke 4:24
58 [a] Mark 6:5, 6

CHAPTER 14
1 [a] Mark 6:14–29
3 [a] Luke 3:19, 20
4 [a] Lev. 18:16; 20:21
5 [a] Luke 20:6
13 [a] John 6:1, 2
14 [a] Mark 6:34
15 [a] Luke 9:12

16But Jesus said to them, "They do not need to go away. You give them something to eat."

17And they said to Him, "We have here only five loaves and two fish."

18He said, "Bring them here to Me." 19Then He commanded the multitudes to sit down on the grass. And He took the five loaves and the two fish, and looking up to heaven, [a]He blessed and broke and gave the loaves to the disciples; and the disciples gave to the multitudes. 20So they all ate and were filled, and they took up twelve baskets full of the fragments that remained. 21Now those who had eaten were about five thousand men, besides women and children.

Jesus Walks on the Sea

22Immediately Jesus [1]made His disciples get into the boat and go before Him to the other side, while He sent the multitudes away. 23[a]And when He had sent the multitudes away, He went up on the mountain by Himself to pray. [b]Now when evening came, He was alone there. 24But the boat was now [1]in the middle of the sea, tossed by the waves, for the wind was contrary.

> *If He prayed who was without sin, how much more it becometh a sinner to pray.*
>
> St. Cyprian

25Now in the fourth watch of the night Jesus went to them, walking on the sea. 26And when the disciples saw Him [a]walking on the sea, they were troubled, saying, "It is a ghost!" And they cried out for fear.

27But immediately Jesus spoke to them, saying, [1]"Be of good [a]cheer! [2]It is I; do not be afraid."

28And Peter answered Him and said, "Lord, if it is You, command me to come to You on the water."

29So He said, "Come." And when Peter had come down out of the boat, he walked on the water to go to Jesus. 30But when he saw [1]that the wind *was* boisterous, he was afraid; and beginning to sink he cried out, saying, "Lord, save me!"

31And immediately Jesus stretched out *His* hand and caught him, and said to him, "O you of [a]little faith, why did you doubt?" 32And when they got into the boat, the wind ceased.

33Then those who were in the boat [1]came and worshiped Him, saying, "Truly [a]You are the Son of God."

> *As we unflinchingly take our stand on the naked promise, there springs up within us the "faith of God" which makes walking on the water a delight.*
>
> Dr. Lilian B. Yeomans

Many Touch Him and Are Made Well

34[a]When they had crossed over, they came [1]to the land of Gennesaret. 35And when the men of that place recognized Him, they sent out into all that surrounding region, brought to Him all who were sick, 36and begged Him that they might only [a]touch the hem of His garment. And [b]as many as touched *it* were made perfectly well.

Defilement Comes from Within

15 Then [a]the scribes and Pharisees who were from Jerusalem came to Jesus, saying, 2[a]"Why do Your disciples transgress the tradition of the elders? For they do not wash their hands when they eat bread."

3He answered and said to them, "Why do you also transgress the commandment of God because of your tradition? 4For God commanded, saying, [a]*'Honor your father and your mother'*; and, [b]*'He who curses father or mother, let him be put to death.'* 5But you say, 'Whoever says to his father or mother, [a]"Whatever profit you might have received from me *is* a gift *to God*"— 6then he need not honor his father [1]or mother.' Thus you have made the [2]commandment of God of no effect by

19 a Matt. 15:36; 26:26
22 1 *invited, strongly urged*
23 a Mark 6:46 b John 6:16
24 1 NU *many furlongs away from the land*
26 a Job 9:8
27 a Acts 23:11; 27:22, 25, 36 1 *Take courage* 2 Lit. *I am*
30 1 NU brackets *that* and *boisterous* as disputed.
31 a Matt. 6:30; 8:26
33 a Ps. 2:7 1 NU omits *came and*
34 a Mark 6:53 1 NU *to land at*
36 a [Mark 5:24–34] b [Luke 6:19]

CHAPTER 15
1 a Mark 7:1
2 a Mark 7:5
4 a [Deut. 5:16] b Ex. 21:17
5 a Mark 7:11, 12
6 1 NU omits *or mother* 2 NU *word*

your tradition. [7][a]Hypocrites! Well did Isaiah prophesy about you, saying:

8 *'These[a] people [1]draw near to Me*
with their mouth,
And honor Me with their lips,
But their heart is far from Me.
9 *And in vain they worship Me,*
[a]Teaching as doctrines the
commandments of men.' "

[10][a]When He had called the multitude to *Himself,* He said to them, "Hear and understand: [11][a]Not what goes into the mouth defiles a man; but what comes out of the mouth, this defiles a man."

[12]Then His disciples came and said to Him, "Do You know that the Pharisees were offended when they heard this saying?"

[13]But He answered and said, [a]"Every plant which My heavenly Father has not planted will be uprooted. [14]Let them alone. [a]They are blind leaders of the blind. And if the blind leads the blind, both will fall into a ditch."

[15][a]Then Peter answered and said to Him, "Explain this parable to us."

[16]So Jesus said, [a]"Are you also still without understanding? [17]Do you not yet understand that [a]whatever enters the mouth goes into the stomach and is eliminated? [18]But [a]those things which proceed out of the mouth come from the heart, and they defile a man. [19][a]For out of the heart proceed evil thoughts, murders, adulteries, fornications, thefts, false witness, blasphemies. [20]These are *the things* which defile a man, but to eat with unwashed hands does not defile a man."

A Gentile Shows Her Faith

[21][a]Then Jesus went out from there and departed to the region of Tyre and Sidon. [22]And behold, a woman of Canaan came from that region and cried out to Him, saying, "Have mercy on me, O Lord, [a]Son of David! My daughter is severely demon-possessed."

[23]But He answered her not a word.

And His disciples came and urged Him, saying, "Send her away, for she cries out after us."

[24]But He answered and said, [a]"I was not sent except to the lost sheep of the house of Israel."

[25]Then she came and worshiped Him, saying, "Lord, help me!"

[26]But He answered and said, "It is not good to take the children's bread and throw *it* to the little [a]dogs."

[27]And she said, "Yes, Lord, yet even the little dogs eat the crumbs which fall from their masters' table."

[28]Then Jesus answered and said to her, "O woman, [a]great *is* your faith! Let it be to you as you desire." And her daughter was healed from that very hour.

The life of faith does not earn eternal life: it is eternal life. And Christ is its vehicle.

WILLIAM TEMPLE

Jesus Heals Great Multitudes

[29][a]Jesus departed from there, [b]skirted the Sea of Galilee, and went up on the mountain and sat down there. [30][a]Then great multitudes came to Him, having with them *the* lame, blind, mute, [1]maimed, and many others; and they laid them down at Jesus' [b]feet, and He healed them. [31]So the multitude marveled when they saw *the* mute speaking, *the* [1]maimed made whole, *the* lame walking, and *the* blind seeing; and they [a]glorified the God of Israel.

Feeding the Four Thousand

[32][a]Now Jesus called His disciples to *Himself* and said, "I have compassion on the multitude, because they have now continued with Me three days and have nothing to eat. And I do not want to send them away hungry, lest they faint on the way."

[33][a]Then His disciples said to Him, "Where could we get enough bread in the wilderness to fill such a great multitude?"

[34]Jesus said to them, "How many loaves do you have?"

And they said, "Seven, and a few little fish."

[35]So He commanded the multitude to sit down on the ground. [36]And [a]He took the seven loaves and the fish and [b]gave

---

7 a Mark 7:6
8 a Is. 29:13 *1* NU omits *draw near to Me with their mouth, And*
9 a [Col. 2:18–22]
10 a Mark 7:14
11 a [Acts 10:15]
13 a [John 15:2]
14 a Luke 6:39
15 a Mark 7:17
16 a Matt. 16:9
17 a [1 Cor. 6:13]
18 a [James 3:6]
19 a Prov. 6:14
21 a Mark 7:24–30
22 a Matt. 1:1; 22:41, 42
24 a Matt. 10:5, 6
26 a Matt. 7:6
28 a Luke 7:9
29 a Mark 7:31–37 b Matt. 4:18
30 a Is. 35:5, 6 b Luke 7:38; 8:41; 10:39 *1 crippled*
31 a Luke 5:25, 26; 19:37, 38 *1 crippled*
32 a Mark 8:1–10
33 a 2 Kin. 4:43
36 a Matt. 14:19; 26:27 b Luke 22:19

thanks, broke *them* and gave *them* to His
disciples; and the disciples *gave* to the
multitude. 37So they all ate and were
filled, and they took up seven large baskets full of the fragments that were left.
38Now those who ate were four thousand
men, besides women and children. 39[a]And
He sent away the multitude, got into the
boat, and came to the region of [1]Magdala.

The Pharisees and Sadducees Seek a Sign

16 Then the [a]Pharisees and Sadducees came, and testing Him asked
that He would show them a sign from
heaven. 2He answered and said to them,
"When it is evening you say, *'It will be* fair
weather, for the sky is red'; 3and in the
morning, *'It will be* foul weather today,
for the sky is red and threatening.' [1]Hypo-
crites! You know how to discern the face
of the sky, but you cannot *discern* the
signs of the times. 4[a]A wicked and adulterous generation seeks after a sign, and
no sign shall be given to it except the sign
of [1]the prophet Jonah." And He left them
and departed.

Heavenly Father, I pray that You would reveal to ______, as You did to Peter, that Jesus is the Christ, the Son of the living God.

FROM MATTHEW 16:16

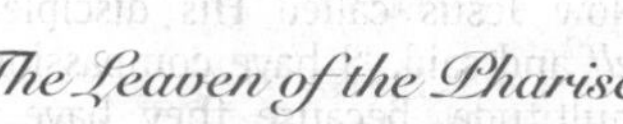

The Leaven of the Pharisees and Sadducees

5Now [a]when His disciples had come to
the other side, they had forgotten to take
bread. 6Then Jesus said to them, [a]"Take
heed and beware of the [1]leaven of the
Pharisees and the Sadducees."

7And they reasoned among themselves,
saying, *"It is* because we have taken no
bread."

8But Jesus, being aware of *it,* said to
them, "O you of little faith, why do you
reason among yourselves because you
[1]have brought no bread? 9[a]Do you not yet
understand, or remember the five loaves
of the five thousand and how many baskets you took up? 10[a]Nor the seven loaves
of the four thousand and how many large
baskets you took up? 11How is it you do
not understand that I did not speak to you
concerning bread?—*but* to beware of the
[1]leaven of the Pharisees and Sadducees."
12Then they understood that He did not
tell *them* to beware of the leaven of bread,
but of the [1]doctrine of the Pharisees and
Sadducees.

Peter Confesses Jesus as the Christ

13When Jesus came into the region of
Caesarea Philippi, He asked His disciples,
saying, [a]"Who do men say that I, the Son
of Man, am?"

14So they said, [a]"Some *say* John the
Baptist, some Elijah, and others Jeremiah
or [b]one of the prophets."

15He said to them, "But who do [a]you
say that I am?"

16Simon Peter answered and said,
[a]"You are the Christ, the Son of the living
God."

17Jesus answered and said to him,
"Blessed are you, Simon Bar-Jonah, [a]for
flesh and blood has not revealed *this* to
you, but [b]My Father who is in heaven.
18And I also say to you that [a]you are Peter,
and [b]on this rock I will build My church,
and [c]the gates of Hades shall not [1]prevail
against it. 19[a]And I will give you the keys
of the kingdom of heaven, and whatever
you bind on earth [1]will be bound in heav-
en, and whatever you loose on earth will
be loosed in heaven."

20[a]Then He commanded His disciples
that they should tell no one that He was
Jesus the Christ.

Jesus Predicts His Death and Resurrection

21From that time Jesus began [a]to show
to His disciples that He must go to Jerusalem, and suffer many things from the elders and chief priests and scribes, and be
killed, and be raised the third day.

22Then Peter took Him aside and began
to rebuke Him, saying, [1]"Far be it from
You, Lord; this shall not happen to You!"

23But He turned and said to Peter, "Get
behind Me, [a]Satan! [b]You are [1]an offense
to Me, for you are not mindful of the
things of God, but the things of men."

---

39 [a] Mark 8:10 [1] NU *Magadan*

CHAPTER 16

1 [a] Mark 8:11

3 [1] NU omits *Hypocrites*

4 [a] Matt. 12:39 [1] NU omits *the prophet*

5 [a] Mark 8:14

6 [a] Luke 12:1 [1] *yeast*

8 [1] NU *have no bread*

9 [a] Matt. 14:15–21

10 [a] Matt. 15:32–38

11 [1] *yeast*

12 [1] *teaching*

13 [a] Luke 9:18

14 [a] Matt. 14:2 [b] Matt. 21:11

15 [a] John 6:67

16 [a] Acts 8:37; 9:20

17 [a] [Eph. 2:8] [b] Gal. 1:16

18 [a] John 1:42 [b] [Eph. 2:20] [c] Is. 38:10 [1] *be victorious*

19 [a] Matt. 18:18 [1] *Or will have been bound . . . will have been loosed*

20 [a] Luke 9:21

21 [a] Luke 9:22; 18:31; 24:46

22 [1] Lit. *Merciful to You,* (May God be merciful)

23 [a] Matt. 4:10 [b] [Rom. 8:7] [1] *a stumbling block*

Take Up the Cross and Follow Him

24[a]Then Jesus said to His disciples, "If
anyone desires to come after Me, let him
deny himself, and take up his cross, and
[b]follow Me. 25For [a]whoever desires to save
his life will lose it, but whoever loses his
life for My sake will find it. 26For what
[a]profit is it to a man if he gains the whole
world, and loses his own soul? Or [b]what
will a man give in exchange for his soul?
27For [a]the Son of Man will come in the
glory of His Father [b]with His angels, [c]and
then He will reward each according to his
works.

Jesus Transfigured on the Mount

28Assuredly, I say to you, [a]there are some
standing here who shall not taste death
till they see the Son of Man coming in His
kingdom."

17 Now [a]after six days Jesus took Peter, James, and John his brother,
led them up on a high mountain by themselves; 2and He was transfigured before
them. His face shone like the sun, and His
clothes became as white as the light. 3And
behold, Moses and Elijah appeared to
them, talking with Him. 4Then Peter answered and said to Jesus, "Lord, it is good
for us to be here; if You wish, [1]let us make
here three tabernacles: one for You, one
for Moses, and one for Elijah."

5[a]While he was still speaking, behold,
a bright cloud overshadowed them; and
suddenly a voice came out of the cloud,
saying, [b]"This is My beloved Son, [c]in
whom I am well pleased. [d]Hear Him!"
6[a]And when the disciples heard *it,* they
fell on their faces and were greatly afraid.
7But Jesus came and [a]touched them and
said, "Arise, and do not be afraid." 8When
they had lifted up their eyes, they saw no
one but Jesus only.

9Now as they came down from the
mountain, Jesus commanded them, saying, "Tell the vision to no one until the
Son of Man is risen from the dead."

10And His disciples asked Him, saying,
[a]"Why then do the scribes say that Elijah
must come first?"

11Jesus answered and said to them, "Indeed, Elijah is coming [1]first and will [a]re-
store all things. 12[a]But I say to you that
Elijah has come already, and they [b]did not
know him but did to him whatever they
wished. Likewise [c]the Son of Man is also
about to suffer at their hands." 13[a]Then
the disciples understood that He spoke to
them of John the Baptist.

A Boy Is Healed

14[a]And when they had come to the multitude, a man came to Him, kneeling
down to Him and saying, 15"Lord, have
mercy on my son, for he is [1]an epileptic
and suffers severely; for he often falls into
the fire and often into the water. 16So I
brought him to Your disciples, but they
could not cure him."

17Then Jesus answered and said,
"O [1]faithless and [a]perverse generation,
how long shall I be with you? How long
shall I bear with you? Bring him here to
Me." 18And Jesus [a]rebuked the demon,
and it came out of him; and the child was
cured from that very hour.

19Then the disciples came to Jesus privately and said, "Why could we not cast it
out?"

20So Jesus said to them, "Because of
your [1]unbelief; for assuredly, I say to you,
[a]if you have faith as a mustard seed, you
will say to this mountain, 'Move from here
to there,' and it will move; and nothing
will be impossible for you. 21[1]However,
this kind does not go out except by prayer
and fasting."

It is great to be faced with the impossible, for nothing is impossible if one is meant to do it. Wisdom will be given, and strength. When the Lord leads, He always strengthens.

AMY CARMICHAEL

Jesus Again Predicts His Death and Resurrection

22[a]Now while they were [1]staying in Galilee, Jesus said to them, "The Son of Man
is about to be betrayed into the hands of
men, 23and they will kill Him, and the

24 a [2 Tim. 3:12] b [1 Pet. 2:21]
25 a John 12:25
26 a Luke 12:20, 21 b Ps. 49:7, 8
27 a Mark 8:38 b [Dan. 7:10] c Rom. 2:6
28 a Luke 9:27

CHAPTER 17
1 a Mark 9:2–8
4 1 NU *I will make*
5 a 2 Pet. 1:17 b Mark 1:11 c Matt. 3:17; 12:18 d [Deut. 18:15, 19]
6 a 2 Pet. 1:18
7 a Dan. 8:18
10 a Mal. 4:5
11 a [Mal. 4:6] 1 NU omits *first*
12 a Mark 9:12, 13 b Matt. 14:3, 10 c Matt. 16:21
13 a Matt. 11:14
14 a Mark 9:14–28
15 1 Lit. *moonstruck*
17 a Phil. 2:15 1 *unbelieving*
18 a Luke 4:41
20 a Luke 17:6 1 NU *little faith*
21 1 NU omits v. 21.
22 a Mark 8:31 1 NU *gathering together*

third day He will be raised up." And they
were exceedingly [a]sorrowful.

Peter and His Master Pay Their Taxes

24 [a]When they had come to [1]Caperna-
um, those who received the [2]*temple* tax
came to Peter and said, "Does your Teacher not pay the *temple* tax?"
25 He said, "Yes."
And when he had come into the house,
Jesus anticipated him, saying, "What do
you think, Simon? From whom do the
kings of the earth take customs or taxes,
from their sons or from [a]strangers?"
26 Peter said to Him, "From strangers."
Jesus said to him, "Then the sons are
free. 27 Nevertheless, lest we offend them,
go to the sea, cast in a hook, and take the
fish that comes up first. And when you
have opened its mouth, you will find a
[1]piece of money; take that and give it to
them for Me and you."

O Lord, I cry out for ______
that they will be converted
and become as a little child,
for You have said that unless
they do, they will by no
means enter the kingdom
of heaven.

FROM MATTHEW 18:3, 4

Who Is the Greatest?

18 At [a]that time the disciples came
to Jesus, saying, "Who then is
greatest in the kingdom of heaven?"
2 Then Jesus called a little [a]child to
Him, set him in the midst of them, 3 and
said, "Assuredly, I say to you, [a]unless you
are converted and become as little children, you will by no means enter the kingdom of heaven. 4 [a]Therefore whoever
humbles himself as this little child is the
greatest in the kingdom of heaven.
5 [a]Whoever receives one little child like
this in My name receives Me.

Jesus Warns of Offenses

6 [a]"Whoever causes one of these little
ones who believe in Me to sin, it would be
better for him if a millstone were hung
around his neck, and he were drowned in
the depth of the sea. 7 Woe to the world
because of [1]offenses! For [a]offenses must
come, but [b]woe to that man by whom the
offense comes!
8 [a]"If your hand or foot causes you to
sin, cut it off and cast *it* from you. It is
better for you to enter into life lame or
maimed, rather than having two hands or
two feet, to be cast into the everlasting
fire. 9 And if your eye causes you to sin,
pluck it out and cast *it* from you. It is
better for you to enter into life with one
eye, rather than having two eyes, to be
cast into [1]hell fire.

The Parable of the Lost Sheep

10 "Take heed that you do not despise
one of these little ones, for I say to you
that in heaven [a]their angels always [b]see
the face of My Father who is in heaven.
11 [a]For[1] the Son of Man has come to save
that which was lost.
12 [a]"What do you think? If a man has
a hundred sheep, and one of them goes
astray, does he not leave the ninety-nine
and go to the mountains to seek the one
that is straying? 13 And if he should find it,
assuredly, I say to you, he rejoices more
over that *sheep* than over the ninety-nine
that did not go astray. 14 Even so it is not
the [a]will of your Father who is in heaven
that one of these little ones should perish.

Dealing with a Sinning Brother

15 "Moreover [a]if your brother sins
against you, go and tell him his fault between you and him alone. If he hears you,
[b]you have gained your brother. 16 But if he
will not hear, take with you one or two
more, that [a]'*by the mouth of two or three*
witnesses every word may be established.'
17 And if he refuses to hear them, tell *it* to
the church. But if he refuses even to hear
the church, let him be to you like a [a]hea-
then and a tax collector.
18 "Assuredly, I say to you, [a]whatever
you bind on earth will be bound in heav-
en, and whatever you loose on earth will
be loosed in heaven.
19 [a]"Again[1] I say to you that if two of you
agree on earth concerning anything that

23 a John 16:6; 19:30
24 a Mark 9:33 *1* NU *Capharnaum,* here and elsewhere *2* Lit. *double drachma*
25 a [Is. 60:10–17]
27 *1* Gr. *stater,* the exact temple tax for two

CHAPTER 18
1 a Luke 9:46–48; 22:24–27
2 a Matt. 19:14
3 a Luke 18:16
4 a [Matt. 20:27; 23:11]
5 a [Matt. 10:42]
6 a Mark 9:42
7 a [1 Cor. 11:19] b Matt. 26:24; 27:4, 5 *1 enticements to sin*
8 a Matt. 5:29, 30
9 *1* Gr. *Gehenna*
10 a [Heb. 1:14] b Luke 1:19
11 a Luke 9:56 *1* NU omits v. 11.
12 a Luke 15:4–7
14 a [1 Tim. 2:4]
15 a Lev. 19:17 b [James 5:20]
16 a Deut. 17:6; 19:15
17 a [2 Thess. 3:6, 14]
18 a [John 20:22, 23]
19 a [1 Cor. 1:10] *1* NU, M *Again, assuredly, I say*

MATTHEW 18:1–5

Dear Woman of Destiny,

Don't you love how eloquently Jesus illustrates His point in Matthew 18:1–5, using a *child* in response to the disciples' question? It must have stunned them. Let's look at it phrase by phrase and determine how it relates to *you*, to *children*, and then to *children and you*.

Jesus begins, "I say to you, unless you are converted." The first thing I think of from this phrase is change. To be converted is to change your ways, to walk away from the old and start anew. Change—where better things begin.

"And become as little children": If you will make the changes necessary to become childlike in your faith, I believe you'll hear Him say, "Welcome to the kingdom, Woman of Destiny." Jesus equates childlikeness with humility. How would the disciples score on it? How would you? Change, childlikeness, humility—do these words encourage you to do some soul searching? Then follow through because your appointed destiny is worth it.

"Is the greatest in the kingdom of heaven": Humility and greatness? Just think. Wouldn't it be "great" to have less pride, fewer doubts, and more dependence on God and to forgive more easily? My conclusion: Humility *is* greatness.

Jesus' use of a child to exemplify a right spirit isn't surprising. Was he a "good boy"? Is that why Jesus called him? No. Jesus simply underscores the guilelessness of all children, which meets His standard for kingdom greatness. He continues, "Whoever receives one little child like this in My name receives Me." Beyond the child's physical frame and intellect into his inner self, Jesus recognizes the child's spiritual greatness and points out the necessity for childlike dependence on the Father.

Here's where you and children meet. Woman's nurturing nature is inherent. Children thrive on it. It's a perfect and natural combination. In nurturing their whole personhood, you receive them wholly, and you receive Jesus.

However, whether God's destiny for you includes physical motherhood or not, nurturing children physically and mentally, though honorable, is temporal. What about the eternal? So often, we adults discover pieces of eternity in children. Their insights are simply profound. They love to pray . . . and pray! They're spiritually attuned, full of faith, amazingly prophetic, concerned about the world, and ceaselessly eager to lay their sovereignly anointed hands on everyone. Eternal things, indeed.

Back to the beginning of the story. "Then Jesus called a little child to Him, set him in the midst of them": Imagine how that child must have felt! Jesus still "calls" children today. Children among us. I call it "Intergenerational Ministry." I've lived in this part of the passage for years, working with children from around the world. I say to them, "Welcome! I respect you. You are very important. God's Spirit in you is mighty and awesome. I want to be just like you so I can 'enter the kingdom.'" It utterly delights them. It's inviting. It releases them to be "spiritual." And it's revolutionary.

A child was near Jesus. That's a lesson in itself! How did he get there? Let's assume his mother had brought him. Woman and child, close to Jesus, in the right place at the right time, together; called, humble, chosen for eternally meaningful moment. Talk about destiny!

Esther Ilnisky

Matthew 18:23–27

Dear Woman of Destiny,

Jesus tells the story of an ungrateful servant who owed a huge debt, worth a great many millions of dollars. When he asked for mercy, it was given, and the debt was erased. That same servant, however, refused to forgive a smaller debt, a few months' wages, when he was asked for an extension on the loan. In fact, he grabbed the debtor by the throat and threw him into prison.

That servant represents you and me; we are the debtors with the huge debt of sin we cannot pay. And Jesus has forgiven us. Though we deserve to perish in hell, our sins have all been washed away by the precious blood of Jesus. How, then, do we dare not forgive the lesser debts owed to us?

When Jesus came, He instituted a whole new order of relationships among God's people. Forgiveness is the manner of the kingdom. The "eye for an eye" of the Old Testament law became the "love your enemies" of the Sermon on the Mount. In that teaching in Matthew 5, Jesus was not expounding an ivory tower idea; He was describing the way of life in His kingdom!

If forgiveness is the kingdom lifestyle, what sort of picture does our unforgiveness paint? Do we sometimes find ourselves displaying the attitude of the unmerciful servant, taking our debtors by the throat? Unforgiveness chokes the body of Christ. Let us pray that our fingerprints cannot be found on the throats of our brothers and sisters.

Furthermore, Jesus likens our unforgiving attitudes to casting our victims into prison. The irony is that it is impossible for a person to repay a debt while he is in prison. In harboring unforgiveness, we put people into impossible situations in which they are helpless to resolve the problems they may have caused.

Jesus described the servant who cast his debtor into prison as a "wicked servant" (v. 32). *Wicked* means "perverse" or "twisted." If we refuse to forgive after we have been forgiven so much by God, we are twisted—wicked. Unforgiveness perverts the true gospel.

But it doesn't end there. The end of the story reveals the complex effect of unforgiveness. The wicked servant was turned over to the tormentors until he could pay off the original debt he had been forgiven. Likewise, if we refuse to forgive, the Father will turn us over to the tormentors of guilt, oppression, fear, hatred, bitterness, and even physical torment that results from emotional turmoil. When there is unforgiveness, no one goes free.

God calls us to unconditional forgiveness—the very means by which we will be released from torment. We can't afford the cost of harboring unforgiveness. If Christians keep one another in the cruel prison of unforgiveness and suffer torment themselves, then who will reap the harvest of souls waiting for salvation? Who will preach the gospel, bind up the brokenhearted, and set the captives free?

Why don't we just let everyone out of prison? Jesus is saying, "Remember? I cancelled all that debt of yours . . . 'Should you not also have had compassion on your fellow servant, just as I had pity on you?'" (v. 33).

Sue Curran

they ask, [b]it will be done for them by My
Father in heaven. 20 For where two or
three are gathered [a]together in My name,
I am there in the midst of them."

The Parable of the Unforgiving Servant

21 Then Peter came to Him and said,
"Lord, how often shall my brother sin
against me, and I forgive him? [a]Up to sev-
en times?"

He who cannot forgive breaks the bridge over which he himself must pass.

THOMAS FULLER

22 Jesus said to him, "I do not say to you,
[a]up to seven times, but up to seventy
times seven. 23 Therefore the kingdom
of heaven is like a certain king who wanted to settle accounts with his servants.
24 And when he had begun to settle accounts, one was brought to him who owed
him ten thousand talents. 25 But as he was
not able to pay, his master commanded
[a]that he be sold, with his wife and children and all that he had, and that payment be made. 26 The servant therefore
fell down before him, saying, 'Master,
have patience with me, and I will pay you
all.' 27 Then the master of that servant was
moved with compassion, released him,
and forgave him the debt.

28 "But that servant went out and found
one of his fellow servants who owed him
a hundred denarii; and he laid hands on
him and took *him* by the throat, saying,
'Pay me what you owe!' 29 So his fellow
servant fell down [1]at his feet and begged
him, saying, 'Have patience with me, and
I will pay you [2]all.' 30 And he would not,
but went and threw him into prison till he
should pay the debt. 31 So when his fellow
servants saw what had been done, they
were very grieved, and came and told their
master all that had been done. 32 Then his
master, after he had called him, said to
him, 'You wicked servant! I forgave you
[a]all that debt because you begged me.
33 Should you not also have had compassion on your fellow servant, just as I had
pity on you?' 34 And his master was angry,
and delivered him to the torturers until
he should pay all that was due to him.

35 [a]"So My heavenly Father also will do
to you if each of you, from his heart, does
not forgive his brother [1]his trespasses."

We owe to everyone the debt of love, and as we yield to the Holy Ghost, who sheds abroad in our hearts the love of Christ, He will enable us to pay it.

CARRIE JUDD MONTGOMERY

Marriage and Divorce

19 Now it came to pass, [a]when Jesus
had finished these sayings, *that* He
departed from Galilee and came to the region of Judea beyond the Jordan. 2 [a]And
great multitudes followed Him, and He
healed them there.

3 The Pharisees also came to Him, testing Him, and saying to Him, "Is it lawful
for a man to divorce his wife for *just* any
reason?"

4 And He answered and said to them,
"Have you not read that He who [1]made
them at the beginning [a]*'made them male
and female,'* 5 and said, [a]*'For this reason
a man shall leave his father and mother
and be joined to his wife, and* [b]*the two
shall become one flesh'*? 6 So then, they
are no longer two but one flesh. Therefore
what God has joined together, let not man
separate."

7 They said to Him, [a]"Why then did Moses command to give a certificate of divorce, and to put her away?"

8 He said to them, "Moses, because of
the [a]hardness of your hearts, permitted
you to divorce your [b]wives, but from the
beginning it was not so. 9 [a]And I say to
you, whoever divorces his wife, except for
[1]sexual immorality, and marries another,
commits adultery; and whoever marries
her who is divorced commits adultery."

19 b [1 John 3:22; 5:14]
20 a Acts 20:7
21 a Luke 17:4
22 a Col. 3:13
25 a 2 Kin. 4:1
29 *1* NU omits *at his feet* *2* NU, M omit *all*
32 a Luke 7:41–43
35 a James 2:13 *1* NU omits *his trespasses*

CHAPTER 19
1 a Mark 10:1–12
2 a Matt. 12:15
4 a Gen. 1:27; 5:2 *1* NU *created*
5 a Gen. 2:24 b [1 Cor. 6:16; 7:2]
7 a Deut. 24:1–4
8 a Heb. 3:15 b Mal. 2:16
9 a [Matt. 5:32] *1* Or *fornication*

Matthew 19:5

Dear Woman of Destiny,

We are told in Genesis 2 that the woman was taken from the side of man. She was his own body, an extension of himself. She was, in fact, his other self. Something of Adam's own self was removed from him and returned to him in a very different package.

When God created Adam, he was created fully in the image of God. When the woman was taken out of him, the image of God was not added to or subtracted from. It was divided. Now the image of God was male and female. Yet they were one.

Because sin had not yet made its entrance, there was no fear or hesitation within them. Neither of them felt threatened. There were no "control" issues, no calculating, no "game playing." They were open, naked, and transparent in each other's presence. There was an awareness that God had made them for each other, that He had specifically fashioned this union to be interdependent.

The union between the man and woman was to be inseparable. They were to know intimacy in the fullest sense of the word, far beyond the "one flesh" relationship. Sexual intimacy was given to be the seal, the celebration, of a much greater intimacy, which was intended to follow—that of heart, soul, and spirit. This kind of relationship would reflect not only union with one another, but also with God. It is a mystery, yet God's design is that something of Christ's love—His commitment and faithfulness to us, His bride, and our union with Him—would be displayed in the marriage union. It would showcase to the world His care and provision for His own and the high place of honor He has prepared for us.

The woman is to become the priority relationship in her husband's life because of the significance of this union. He is to cleave to his wife, not only for her sake, to nourish and cherish her, but for his own sake as well, acknowledging that, in marriage, what was taken out of him long ago in Adam is being returned to him again—to help him.

Some have assumed that the woman was merely brought forth to enable procreation, thereby resolving Adam's solitary condition. Nothing, however, in the Hebrew definition of the word for *help* remotely refers to the act of reproduction. The word *help* in the Hebrew means "to surround, to protect, to aid, to succor." It is an extremely strong word, used twenty-one times in Scripture. Eve was both human help and divine help because she came from the hand of God.

She was created for Adam, not to be a mother over him to babysit, nor to be as a child under him, dominated by him. She would be a wife—someone who would be like him, yet different. Someone on an equal par—his other self, taken from his side—who would stand "boldly out opposite" him and call him forth in a way no one else could.

She was designed to talk to him, to comfort, encourage, confront, and challenge him in love, using life-giving words. God intended her to surround and protect something of His creation that was very precious to Him—the heart of man.

Jane Hansen

10His disciples said to Him, [a]"If such is
the case of the man with *his* wife, it is
better not to marry."

Jesus Teaches on Celibacy

11But He said to them, [a]"All cannot accept this saying, but only *those* to whom
it has been given: 12For there are [1]eu-
nuchs who were born thus from *their*
mother's womb, and [a]there are eunuchs
who were made eunuchs by men, and
there are eunuchs who have made themselves eunuchs for the kingdom of heav-
en's sake. He who is able to accept *it,* let
him accept *it.*"

Jesus Blesses Little Children

13[a]Then little children were brought
to Him that He might put *His* hands on
them and pray, but the disciples rebuked
them. 14But Jesus said, "Let the little children come to Me, and do not forbid them;
for [a]of such is the kingdom of heaven."
15And He laid *His* hands on them and departed from there.

Jesus Counsels the Rich Young Ruler

16[a]Now behold, one came and said to
Him, [b]"Good[1] Teacher, what good thing
shall I do that I may have eternal life?"
17So He said to him, [1]"Why do you call
Me good? [2]No one *is* [a]good but One, *that
is,* God. But if you want to enter into life,
[b]keep the commandments."
18He said to Him, "Which ones?"
Jesus said, [a]"*'You shall not murder,'
'You shall not commit adultery,' 'You
shall not steal,' 'You shall not bear false
witness,'* 19[a]*'Honor your father and your
mother,'* and, [b]*'You shall love your neighbor as yourself.'* "
20The young man said to Him, "All
these things I have [a]kept [1]from my youth.
What do I still lack?"
21Jesus said to him, "If you want to be
perfect, [a]go, sell what you have and give
to the poor, and you will have treasure in
heaven; and come, follow Me."
22But when the young man heard that
saying, he went away sorrowful, for he
had great possessions.

With God All Things Are Possible

23Then Jesus said to His disciples, "Assuredly, I say to you that [a]it is hard for a
rich man to enter the kingdom of heaven.
24And again I say to you, it is easier for a
camel to go through the eye of a needle
than for a rich man to enter the kingdom
of God."
25When His disciples heard *it,* they were
greatly astonished, saying, "Who then can
be saved?"
26But Jesus looked at *them* and said
to them, "With men this is impossible,
but [a]with God all things are possible."
27Then Peter answered and said to Him,
"See, [a]we have left all and followed You.
Therefore what shall we have?"
28So Jesus said to them, "Assuredly I
say to you, that in the regeneration, when
the Son of Man sits on the throne of His
glory, [a]you who have followed Me will also
sit on twelve thrones, judging the twelve
tribes of Israel. 29[a]And everyone who has
left houses or brothers or sisters or father
or mother [1]or wife or children or [2]lands,
for My name's sake, shall receive a
hundredfold, and inherit eternal life.
30[a]But many *who are* first will be last, and
the last first.

The Parable of the Workers in the Vineyard

20 "For the kingdom of heaven is like
a landowner who went out early in
the morning to hire laborers for his vineyard. 2Now when he had agreed with the
laborers for a denarius a day, he sent them
into his vineyard. 3And he went out about
the third hour and saw others standing
idle in the marketplace, 4and said to
them, 'You also go into the vineyard, and
whatever is right I will give you.' So they
went. 5Again he went out about the sixth
and the ninth hour, and did likewise. 6And
about the eleventh hour he went out and
found others standing [1]idle, and said to
them, 'Why have you been standing here
idle all day?' 7They said to him, 'Because
no one hired us.' He said to them, 'You
also go into the vineyard, [1]and whatever is
right you will receive.'
8"So when evening had come, the owner of the vineyard said to his steward, 'Call
the laborers and give them *their* wages,
beginning with the last to the first.' 9And
when those came who *were hired* about
the eleventh hour, they each received a
denarius. 10But when the first came, they
supposed that they would receive more;
and they likewise received each a denarius. 11And when they had received *it,* they

10 a [Prov. 21:19]
11 a [1 Cor. 7:2, 7, 9, 17]
12 a [1 Cor. 7:32] *1* Emasculated men
13 a Luke 18:15
14 a Matt. 18:3, 4
16 a Mark 10:17–30 b Luke 10:25 *1* NU omits *Good*
17 a Nah. 1:7 b Lev. 18:5 *1* NU *Why do you ask Me about what is good?* *2* NU *There is One who is good. But*
18 a Ex. 20:13–16
19 a Ex. 20:12–16; Deut. 5:16–20 b Lev. 19:18
20 a [Phil. 3:6, 7] *1* NU omits *from my youth*
21 a Acts 2:45; 4:34, 35
23 a [1 Tim. 6:9]
26 a Jer. 32:17
27 a Deut. 33:9
28 a Luke 22:28–30
29 a Mark 10:29, 30 *1* NU omits *or wife* *2* Lit. *fields*
30 a Luke 13:30

CHAPTER 20
6 *1* NU omits *idle*
7 *1* NU omits the rest of v. 7.

Matthew 19:26

Dear Woman of Destiny,

When anyone tells you they heard God speak, it becomes highly subjective—you know, raised eyebrows and visions of the Hale-Bopp comet. But one day, His voice was so clear—not audible, but loud and plain—and this is what I heard: "Cathy, you are living in the *possible.*" I fell to my knees and began crying out to God, "Thank You, Lord. Thank You for Your love and affirmation."

But He was giving me a rebuke, not a compliment.

I began to understand that living in the possible is where most of God's people live. We can stay there if we want to. But if we desire those things that we have seen by His Spirit, and if we desire to be a part of His great end-time move, then we must leave the possible and live where He is. As long as we stay in the possible, *we* are lord. But if we are willing to step out, He is Lord of the impossible.

One morning, I sensed I would be getting a call from the adoption agency. I heard the Lord speak to my heart, "They have a mixed-race infant girl for you. My hand is on her, and I have a great destiny for this child. I desire for you and Randi to adopt her and raise her for My kingdom. Call her name *Lydia.*"

That very morning the phone rang. A biracial baby girl had been born over the weekend and needed a home. Would we be interested in adopting her? I was stunned. I remember thinking, *We have no room, no time, no money, no strength, or energy. Yup, sounds just like God.* When it is most inconvenient and when you are just starting to find your comfort zone, God says, "It's time to stretch again."

Just days later, I boarded an airplane, headed to a three-day conference with Lydia in my arms. I had a message to call my husband when we checked into the hotel. He told me that our attorney needed five thousand dollars immediately in order to cover the expenses of Lydia's birth.

My first inclination was to cry out, "Oh God, why did You leave me? I trusted You and said yes." I almost returned to the possible because of my problem. We had four hours to get five thousand dollars. It did not seem possible.

During that conference, I never mentioned my "problem" to anyone. At the last Sunday morning service, the pastor asked me to bring Lydia to the platform to be prayed for. He handed me an envelope—a gift for the baby. I was thinking, *A twenty-dollar gift certificate to Sears,* which would have been most welcome.

Later, the pastor told me the Holy Spirit had been prompting him throughout the previous night to bless Lydia and asked me to open the envelope. Inside was a check for five thousand dollars. I fell to the floor weeping—not only because God had met our need, but in shame for my lack of trust in the Lord of the impossible.

Not everyone is called to adopt little children. However, *everyone* is called to walk in the impossible. We can remain distant, safely ensconced in our little world of the possible. Or we can step over into the impossible realm, where it's really scary.

Cathy Lechner

[1]complained against the landowner, 12 saying, 'These last *men* have worked *only* one hour, and you made them equal to us who have borne the burden and the heat of the day.' 13 But he answered one of them and said, 'Friend, I am doing you no wrong. Did you not agree with me for a denarius? 14 Take *what is* yours and go your way. I wish to give to this last man *the same* as to you. 15 [a]Is it not lawful for me to do what I wish with my own things? Or [b]is your eye evil because I am good?' 16 [a]So the last will be first, and the first last. [b]For[1] many are called, but few chosen."

Jesus a Third Time Predicts His Death and Resurrection

17 [a]Now Jesus, going up to Jerusalem, took the twelve disciples aside on the road and said to them, 18 [a]"Behold, we are going up to Jerusalem, and the Son of Man will be betrayed to the chief priests and to the scribes; and they will condemn Him to death, 19 [a]and deliver Him to the Gentiles to [b]mock and to [c]scourge and to [d]crucify. And the third day He will [e]rise again."

Greatness Is Serving

20 [a]Then the mother of [b]Zebedee's sons came to Him with her sons, kneeling down and asking something from Him.

21 And He said to her, "What do you wish?"

She said to Him, "Grant that these two sons of mine [a]may sit, one on Your right hand and the other on the left, in Your kingdom."

22 But Jesus answered and said, "You do not know what you ask. Are you able to drink [a]the cup that I am about to drink, [1]and be baptized with [b]the baptism that I am baptized with?"

They said to Him, "We are able."

23 So He said to them, [a]"You will indeed drink My cup, [1]and be baptized with the baptism that I am baptized with; but to sit on My right hand and on My left is not Mine to give, but *it is for those* for whom it is prepared by My Father."

24 [a]And when the ten heard *it,* they were greatly displeased with the two brothers. 25 But Jesus called them to *Himself* and said, "You know that the rulers of the Gentiles lord it over them, and those who are great exercise authority over them. 26 Yet [a]it shall not be so among you; but [b]whoever desires to become great among you, let him be your servant. 27 [a]And whoever desires to be first among you, let him be your slave— 28 [a]just as the [b]Son of Man did not come to be served, [c]but to serve, and [d]to give His life a ransom [e]for many."

Lord God, may ____ learn that to become great in Your kingdom they must be a servant.

FROM MATTHEW 20:26

Two Blind Men Receive Their Sight

29 [a]Now as they went out of Jericho, a great multitude followed Him. 30 And behold, [a]two blind men sitting by the road, when they heard that Jesus was passing by, cried out, saying, "Have mercy on us, O Lord, [b]Son of David!"

31 Then the multitude [a]warned them that they should be quiet; but they cried out all the more, saying, "Have mercy on us, O Lord, Son of David!"

32 So Jesus stood still and called them, and said, "What do you want Me to do for you?"

33 They said to Him, "Lord, that our eyes may be opened." 34 So Jesus had [a]compassion and touched their eyes. And immediately their eyes received sight, and they followed Him.

The Triumphal Entry

21 Now [a]when they drew near Jerusalem, and came to [1]Bethphage, at [b]the Mount of Olives, then Jesus sent two disciples, 2 saying to them, "Go into the village opposite you, and immediately you will find a donkey tied, and a colt with her. Loose *them* and bring *them* to Me. 3 And if anyone says anything to you, you shall say, 'The Lord has need of them,' and immediately he will send them."

4 [1]All this was done that it might be fulfilled which was spoken by the prophet, saying:

5 *"Tell[a] the daughter of Zion,*
'Behold, your King is coming to
you,

---

11 [1] *grumbled*
15 [a] [Rom. 9:20, 21] [b] Deut. 15:9
16 [a] Matt. 19:30 [b] Matt. 22:14 [1] NU omits the rest of v. 16.
17 [a] Mark 10:32–34
18 [a] Matt. 16:21; 26:47–57
19 [a] Matt. 27:2 [b] Matt. 26:67, 68; 27:29, 41 [c] Matt. 27:26 [d] Acts 3:13–15 [e] Matt. 28:5, 6
20 [a] Mark 10:35–45 [b] Matt. 4:21; 10:2
21 [a] [Matt. 19:28]
22 [a] Luke 22:42 [b] Luke 12:50 [1] NU omits *and be baptized with the baptism that I am baptized with*
23 [a] [Acts 12:2] [1] NU omits *and be baptized with the baptism that I am baptized with*
24 [a] Mark 10:41
26 [a] [1 Pet. 5:3] [b] Matt. 23:11
27 [a] [Matt. 18:4]
28 [a] John 13:4 [b] [Phil. 2:6, 7] [c] Luke 22:27 [d] [Is. 53:10–12] [e] [Rom. 5:15, 19]
29 [a] Mark 10:46–52
30 [a] Matt. 9:27 [b] [Ezek. 37:21–25]
31 [a] Matt. 19:13
34 [a] Matt. 9:36; 14:14; 15:32; 18:27

CHAPTER 21
1 [a] Luke 19:29–38 [b] [Zech. 14:4] [1] M *Bethsphage*
4 [1] NU omits *All*
5 [a] Zech. 9:9

Lowly, and sitting on a donkey,
A colt, the foal of a donkey.' "

6[a]So the disciples went and did as Jesus
commanded them. 7They brought the
donkey and the colt, [a]laid their clothes on
them, [1]and set *Him* on them. 8And a very
great multitude spread their clothes on
the road; [a]others cut down branches from
the trees and spread *them* on the road.
9Then the multitudes who went before
and those who followed cried out, saying:

"Hosanna to the Son of David!
[a]*'Blessed is He who comes in the*
name of the LORD!'
Hosanna in the highest!"

10[a]And when He had come into Jerusalem, all the city was moved, saying, "Who
is this?"

11So the multitudes said, "This is Jesus,
[a]the prophet from Nazareth of Galilee."

Jesus Cleanses the Temple

12[a]Then Jesus went into the temple [1]of
God and drove out all those who bought
and sold in the temple, and overturned
the tables of the [b]money changers and the
seats of those who sold doves. 13And He
said to them, "It is written, [a]*'My house*
shall be called a house of prayer,' but you
have made it a [b]*'den of thieves.'* "

14Then *the* blind and *the* lame came to
Him in the temple, and He healed them.
15But when the chief priests and scribes
saw the wonderful things that He did, and
the children crying out in the temple and
saying, "Hosanna to the [a]Son of David!"
they were [1]indignant 16and said to Him,
"Do You hear what these are saying?"

And Jesus said to them, "Yes. Have you
never read,

[a]*'Out of the mouth of babes and*
nursing infants
You have perfected praise'?"

17Then He left them and [a]went out of
the city to Bethany, and He lodged there.

The Fig Tree Withered

18[a]Now in the morning, as He returned
to the city, He was hungry. 19[a]And seeing
a fig tree by the road, He came to it and
found nothing on it but leaves, and said to
it, "Let no fruit grow on you ever again."
Immediately the fig tree withered away.

The Lesson of the Withered Fig Tree

20[a]And when the disciples saw *it,* they
marveled, saying, "How did the fig tree
wither away so soon?"

21So Jesus answered and said to them,
"Assuredly, I say to you, [a]if you have faith
and [b]do not doubt, you will not only do
what was done to the fig tree, [c]but also if
you say to this mountain, 'Be removed
and be cast into the sea,' it will be done.
22And [a]whatever things you ask in prayer,
believing, you will receive."

When the church of God is aroused to its obligation and duties and right faith to claim what Christ has promised—"all things whatsoever" (Matt. 21:22)—a revolution will take place.

JOHN FOSTER

Jesus' Authority Questioned

23[a]Now when He came into the temple,
the chief priests and the elders of the people confronted Him as He was teaching,
and [b]said, "By what authority are You doing these things? And who gave You this
authority?"

24But Jesus answered and said to them,
"I also will ask you one thing, which if you
tell Me, I likewise will tell you by what
authority I do these things: 25The [a]bap-
tism of [b]John—where was it from? From
heaven or from men?"

And they reasoned among themselves,
saying, "If we say, 'From heaven,' He will
say to us, 'Why then did you not believe
him?' 26But if we say, 'From men,' we
[a]fear the multitude, [b]for all count John as
a prophet." 27So they answered Jesus and
said, "We do not know."

And He said to them, "Neither will I tell
you by what authority I do these things.

The Parable of the Two Sons

28"But what do you think? A man had
two sons, and he came to the first and

6 a Mark 11:4
7 a 2 Kin. 9:13 1 NU *and He sat*
8 a Lev. 23:40
9 a Ps. 118:26; Matt. 23:39
10 a John 2:13, 15
11 a John 6:14; 7:40; 9:17
12 a Mark 11:15–18 b Deut. 14:25 1 NU omits *of God*
13 a Is. 56:7 b Jer. 7:11
15 a John 7:42 1 *angry*
16 a Ps. 8:2
17 a John 11:1, 18; 12:1
18 a Mark 11:12–14, 20–24
19 a Mark 11:13
20 a Mark 11:20
21 a Matt. 17:20 b James 1:6 c 1 Cor. 13:2
22 a Matt. 7:7–11
23 a Luke 20:1–8 b Ex. 2:14
25 a [John 1:29–34] b John 1:15–28
26 a Matt. 14:5; 21:46 b Mark 6:20

said, 'Son, go, work today in my [a]vine-
yard.' 29He answered and said, 'I will not,'
but afterward he regretted it and went.
30Then he came to the second and said
likewise. And he answered and said, 'I *go,*
sir,' but he did not go. 31Which of the two
did the will of *his* father?"
They said to Him, "The first."
Jesus said to them, [a]"Assuredly, I say to
you that tax collectors and harlots enter
the kingdom of God before you. 32For
[a]John came to you in the way of righteousness, and you did not believe him;
[b]but tax collectors and harlots believed
him; and when you saw *it,* you did not
afterward [1]relent and believe him.

The Parable of the Wicked Vinedressers

33"Hear another parable: There was a
certain landowner [a]who planted a vineyard and set a hedge around it, dug a
winepress in it and built a tower. And he
leased it to vinedressers and [b]went into
a far country. 34Now when vintage-time
drew near, he sent his servants to the
vinedressers, that they might receive its
fruit. 35[a]And the vinedressers took his servants, beat one, killed one, and stoned
another. 36Again he sent other servants,
more than the first, and they did likewise
to them. 37Then last of all he sent his [a]son
to them, saying, 'They will respect my
son.' 38But when the vinedressers saw the
son, they said among themselves, [a]'This is
the heir. [b]Come, let us kill him and seize
his inheritance.' 39[a]So they took him and
cast *him* out of the vineyard and killed
him.
40"Therefore, when the owner of the
vineyard comes, what will he do to those
vinedressers?"
41[a]They said to Him, [b]"He will destroy
those wicked men miserably, [c]and lease
his vineyard to other vinedressers who
will [1]render to him the fruits in their seasons."
42Jesus said to them, "Have you never
read in the Scriptures:

[a]*'The stone which the builders*
rejected
Has become the chief cornerstone.
This was the LORD*'s doing,*
And it is marvelous in our eyes'?

43"Therefore I say to you, [a]the kingdom
of God will be taken from you and given
to a nation bearing the fruits of it. 44And
[a]whoever falls on this stone will be broken; but on whomever it falls, [b]it will
grind him to powder."
45Now when the chief priests and Pharisees heard His parables, they [1]perceived
that He was speaking of them. 46But when
they sought to lay hands on Him, they
[a]feared the multitudes, because [b]they
took Him for a prophet.

The Parable of the Wedding Feast

22 And Jesus answered [a]and spoke to
them again by parables and said:
2"The kingdom of heaven is like a certain
king who arranged a marriage for his son,
3and sent out his servants to call those
who were invited to the wedding; and they
were not willing to come. 4Again, he sent
out other servants, saying, 'Tell those who
are invited, "See, I have prepared my dinner; [a]my oxen and fatted cattle *are* killed,
and all things *are* ready. Come to the wedding." ' 5But they made light of it and
went their ways, one to his own farm, another to his business. 6And the rest seized
his servants, treated *them* [1]spitefully, and
killed *them.* 7But when the king heard
about it, he was furious. And he sent out
[a]his armies, destroyed those murderers,
and burned up their city. 8Then he said to
his servants, 'The wedding is ready, but
those who were invited were not [a]worthy.
9Therefore go into the highways, and as
many as you find, invite to the wedding.'
10So those servants went out into the
highways and [a]gathered together all
whom they found, both bad and good. And
the wedding *hall* was filled with guests.
11"But when the king came in to see the
guests, he saw a man there [a]who did not
have on a wedding garment. 12So he said
to him, 'Friend, how did you come in here
without a wedding garment?' And he was
[a]speechless. 13Then the king said to the
servants, 'Bind him hand and foot, [1]take
him away, and cast *him* [a]into outer darkness; there will be weeping and gnashing
of teeth.'
14[a]"For many are called, but few *are*
chosen."

The Pharisees: Is It Lawful to Pay Taxes to Caesar?

15[a]Then the Pharisees went and plotted
how they might entangle Him in *His* talk.
16And they sent to Him their disciples

28 a Matt. 20:1; 21:33
31 a Luke 7:29, 37–50
32 a Luke 3:1–12; 7:29 b Luke 3:12, 13 *1 regret it*
33 a Luke 20:9–19 b Matt. 25:14
35 a [1 Thess. 2:15]
37 a [John 3:16]
38 a [Heb. 1:2] b John 11:53
39 a [Acts 2:23]
41 a Luke 20:16 b [Luke 21:24] c [Acts 13:46] *1 give*
42 a Ps. 118:22, 23
43 a [Matt. 8:12]
44 a Is. 8:14, 15 b [Dan. 2:44]
45 *1 knew*
46 a Matt. 21:26 b Matt. 21:11
CHAPTER 22
1 a [Rev. 19:7–9]
4 a Prov. 9:2
6 *1 insolently*
7 a [Dan. 9:26]
8 a Matt. 10:11
10 a Matt. 13:38, 47, 48
11 a [Col. 3:10, 12]
12 a [Rom. 3:19]
13 a Matt. 8:12; 25:30 *1* NU omits *take him away, and*
14 a Matt. 20:16
15 a Mark 12:13–17

with the [a]Herodians, saying, "Teacher, we
know that You are true, and teach the way
of God in truth; nor do You care about
anyone, for You do not [1]regard the person
of men. 17 Tell us, therefore, what do You
think? Is it lawful to pay taxes to Caesar,
or not?"
18 But Jesus [1]perceived their wickedness, and said, "Why do you test Me, *you*
hypocrites? 19 Show Me the tax money."
So they brought Him a denarius.
20 And He said to them, "Whose image
and inscription *is* this?"
21 They said to Him, "Caesar's."
And He said to them, [a]"Render[1] therefore to Caesar the things that are [b]Cae-
sar's, and to God the things that are
[c]God's." 22 When they had heard *these
words,* they marveled, and left Him and
went their way.

The Sadducees: What About the Resurrection?

23 [a]The same day the Sadducees, [b]who
say there is no resurrection, came to Him
and asked Him, 24 saying: "Teacher, [a]Mo-
ses said that if a man dies, having no children, his brother shall marry his wife and
raise up offspring for his brother. 25 Now
there were with us seven brothers. The
first died after he had married, and having
no offspring, left his wife to his brother.
26 Likewise the second also, and the third,
even to the seventh. 27 Last of all the woman died also. 28 Therefore, in the resurrection, whose wife of the seven will she be?
For they all had her."
29 Jesus answered and said to them,
"You are [1]mistaken, [a]not knowing the
Scriptures nor the power of God. 30 For in
the resurrection they neither marry nor
are given in marriage, but [a]are like angels
[1]of God in heaven. 31 But concerning the
resurrection of the dead, have you not
read what was spoken to you by God, saying, 32 [a]*'I am the God of Abraham, the God
of Isaac, and the God of Jacob'*? God is not
the God of the dead, but of the living."
33 And when the multitudes heard *this,*
[a]they were astonished at His teaching.

The Scribes: Which Is the First Commandment of All?

34 [a]But when the Pharisees heard that
He had silenced the Sadducees, they gathered together. 35 Then one of them, [a]a law-

16 a Mark 3:6; 8:15; 12:13 1 Lit. *look at the face of*
18 1 *knew*
21 a Matt. 17:25 b [Rom. 13:1–7] c [1 Cor. 3:23; 6:19, 20; 12:27] 1 *Pay*
23 a Luke 20:27–40 b Acts 23:8
24 a Deut. 25:5
29 a John 20:9 1 *deceived*
30 a [1 John 3:2] 1 NU omits *of God*
32 a Ex. 3:6, 15
33 a Matt. 7:28
34 a Mark 12:28–31
35 a Luke 7:30; 10:25; 11:45, 46, 52; 14:3
37 a Deut. 6:5; 10:12; 30:6
39 a Lev. 19:18
40 a [Matt. 7:12]
41 a Luke 20:41–44
42 a Matt. 1:1; 21:9
44 a Ps. 110:1
46 a Luke 14:6 b Mark 12:34
CHAPTER 23
2 a Neh. 8:4, 8
3 a [Rom. 2:19] 1 NU omits *to observe*
4 a Luke 11:46

yer, asked *Him a question,* testing Him,
and saying, 36 "Teacher, which *is* the great
commandment in the law?"

> *It is a grace that loves God for Himself and our neighbors for God.*
>
> JEREMY TAYLOR

37 Jesus said to him, [a]"*'You shall love
the* LORD *your God with all your heart,
with all your soul, and with all your
mind.'* 38 This is *the* first and great commandment. 39 And *the* second *is* like it:
[a]*'You shall love your neighbor as yourself.'* 40 [a]On these two commandments
hang all the Law and the Prophets."

Jesus: How Can David Call His Descendant Lord?

41 [a]While the Pharisees were gathered
together, Jesus asked them, 42 saying,
"What do you think about the Christ?
Whose Son is He?"
They said to Him, *"The* [a]*Son* of David."
43 He said to them, "How then does David in the Spirit call Him *'Lord,'* saying:
44 *'The*[a] LORD *said to my Lord,*
"Sit at My right hand,
Till I make Your enemies Your
footstool"'?
45 If David then calls Him *'Lord,'* how is He
his Son?" 46 [a]And no one was able to answer Him a word, [b]nor from that day on
did anyone dare question Him anymore.

Woe to the Scribes and Pharisees

23 Then Jesus spoke to the multitudes
and to His disciples, 2 saying: [a]"The
scribes and the Pharisees sit in Moses'
seat. 3 Therefore whatever they tell you [1]to
observe, *that* observe and do, but do not
do according to their works; for [a]they say,
and do not do. 4 [a]For they bind heavy burdens, hard to bear, and lay *them* on men's
shoulders; but they *themselves* will not
move them with one of their fingers. 5 But

all their works they do to [a]be seen by men. They make their phylacteries broad and enlarge the borders of their garments. 6[a]They love the [1]best places at feasts, the best seats in the synagogues, 7greetings in the marketplaces, and to be called by men, 'Rabbi, Rabbi.' 8[a]But you, do not be called 'Rabbi'; for One is your [1]Teacher, [2]the Christ, and you are all brethren. 9Do not call anyone on earth your father; [a]for One is your Father, He who is in heaven. 10And do not be called teachers; for One is your Teacher, the Christ. 11But [a]he who is greatest among you shall be your servant. 12[a]And whoever exalts himself will be [1]humbled, and he who humbles himself will be [2]exalted.

13"But [a]woe to you, scribes and Pharisees, hypocrites! For you shut up the kingdom of heaven against men; for you neither go in *yourselves,* nor do you allow those who are entering to go in. 14[1]Woe to you, scribes and Pharisees, hypocrites! [a]For you devour widows' houses, and for a pretense make long prayers. Therefore you will receive greater condemnation.

15"Woe to you, scribes and Pharisees, hypocrites! For you travel land and sea to win one proselyte, and when he is won, you make him twice as much a son of [1]hell as yourselves.

16"Woe to you, [a]blind guides, who say, [b]'Whoever swears by the temple, it is nothing; but whoever swears by the gold of the temple, he is obliged *to perform it.*' 17Fools and blind! For which is greater, the gold [a]or the temple that [1]sanctifies the gold? 18And, 'Whoever swears by the altar, it is nothing; but whoever swears by the gift that is on it, he is obliged *to perform it.*' 19Fools and blind! For which is greater, the gift [a]or the altar that sanctifies the gift? 20Therefore he who [1]swears by the altar, swears by it and by all things on it. 21He who swears by the temple, swears by it and by [a]Him who [1]dwells in it. 22And he who swears by heaven, swears by [a]the throne of God and by Him who sits on it.

23"Woe to you, scribes and Pharisees, hypocrites! [a]For you pay tithe of mint and anise and cummin, and [b]have neglected the weightier *matters* of the law: justice and mercy and faith. These you ought to have done, without leaving the others undone. 24Blind guides, who strain out a gnat and swallow a camel!

25"Woe to you, scribes and Pharisees, hypocrites! [a]For you cleanse the outside of the cup and dish, but inside they are full of extortion and [1]self-indulgence. 26Blind Pharisee, first cleanse the inside of the cup and dish, that the outside of them may be clean also.

27"Woe to you, scribes and Pharisees, hypocrites! [a]For you are like whitewashed tombs which indeed appear beautiful outwardly, but inside are full of dead *men's* bones and all uncleanness. 28Even so you also outwardly appear righteous to men, but inside you are full of hypocrisy and lawlessness.

We must always be on our guard lest, under the pretext of keeping one commandment, we be found breaking another.

St. Basil the Great

29[a]"Woe to you, scribes and Pharisees, hypocrites! Because you build the tombs of the prophets and [1]adorn the monuments of the righteous, 30and say, 'If we had lived in the days of our fathers, we would not have been partakers with them in the blood of the prophets.'

31"Therefore you are witnesses against yourselves that [a]you are sons of those who murdered the prophets. 32[a]Fill up, then, the measure of your fathers' *guilt.* 33Serpents, [a]brood[1] of vipers! How can you escape the condemnation of hell? 34[a]Therefore, indeed, I send you prophets, wise men, and scribes: [b]*some* of them you will kill and crucify, and [c]*some* of them you will scourge in your synagogues and persecute from city to city, 35[a]that on you may come all the righteous blood shed on the earth, [b]from the blood of righteous Abel to [c]the blood of Zechariah, son of Berechiah, whom you murdered between the temple and the altar. 36Assuredly, I say to you, all these things will come upon this generation.

Jesus Laments over Jerusalem

37[a]"O Jerusalem, Jerusalem, the one who kills the prophets [b]and stones those

5 a [Matt. 6:1–6, 16–18]
6 a Luke 11:43; 20:46 1 Or *place of honor*
8 a [James 3:1] 1 *Leader* 2 NU omits *the Christ*
9 a [Mal. 1:6]
11 a Matt. 20:26, 27
12 a Luke 14:11; 18:14 1 *put down* 2 *lifted up*
13 a Luke 11:52
14 a Mark 12:40 1 NU omits v. 14.
15 1 Gr. *Gehenna*
16 a Matt. 15:14; 23:24 b [Matt. 5:33, 34]
17 a Ex. 30:29 1 NU *sanctified*
19 a Ex. 29:37
20 1 Swears an oath
21 a 1 Kin. 8:13 1 M *dwelt*
22 a Matt. 5:34
23 a Luke 11:42; 18:12 b [Hos. 6:6]
25 a Luke 11:39 1 M *unrighteousness*
27 a Acts 23:3
29 a Luke 11:47, 48 1 *decorate*
31 a [Acts 7:51, 52]
32 a [1 Thess. 2:16]
33 a Matt. 3:7; 12:34 1 *offspring*
34 a Luke 11:49 b Acts 7:54–60; 22:19 c 2 Cor. 11:24, 25
35 a Rev. 18:24 b Gen. 4:8 c 2 Chr. 24:20, 21
37 a Luke 13:34, 35 b 2 Chr. 24:20, 21; 36:15, 16

who are sent to her! How often [c]I wanted
to gather your children together, as a hen
gathers her chicks [d]under *her* wings, but
you were not willing! 38See! Your house is
left to you desolate; 39for I say to you,
you shall see Me no more till you say,
[a]*'Blessed is He who comes in the name of*
the LORD*!'* "

Jesus Predicts the Destruction of the Temple

24 Then [a]Jesus went out and departed
from the temple, and His disciples
came up to show Him the buildings of the
temple. 2And Jesus said to them, "Do you
not see all these things? Assuredly, I say to
you, [a]not *one* stone shall be left here upon
another, that shall not be thrown down."

The Signs of the Times and the End of the Age

3Now as He sat on the Mount of Olives,
[a]the disciples came to Him privately, saying, [b]"Tell us, when will these things be?
And what *will be* the sign of Your coming,
and of the end of the age?"

Heavenly Father, may
____ take heed that no one
deceives them. For Jesus said
that many will come in His
name, saying, "I am the
Christ," and will deceive
many.

FROM MATTHEW 24:4, 5

4And Jesus answered and said to them:
[a]"Take heed that no one deceives you.
5For [a]many will come in My name, saying, 'I am the Christ,' [b]and will deceive
many. 6And you will hear of [a]wars and
rumors of wars. See that you are not troubled; for [1]all *these things* must come to
pass, but the end is not yet. 7For [a]nation
will rise against nation, and kingdom
against kingdom. And there will be [b]fam-
ines, [1]pestilences, and earthquakes in various places. 8All these *are* the beginning
of sorrows.

9[a]"Then they will deliver you up to tribulation and kill you, and you will be hated
by all nations for My name's sake. 10And
then many will be offended, will betray
one another, and will hate one another.
11Then [a]many false prophets will rise up
and [b]deceive many. 12And because lawlessness will abound, the love of many will
grow [a]cold. 13[a]But he who endures to the
end shall be saved. 14And this [a]gospel of
the kingdom [b]will be preached in all the
world as a witness to all the nations, and
then the end will come.

The Great Tribulation

15[a]"Therefore when you see the
[b]*'abomination of desolation,'* spoken of by
Daniel the prophet, standing in the holy
place" [c](whoever reads, let him understand), 16"then let those who are in Judea
flee to the mountains. 17Let him who is on
the housetop not go down to take anything out of his house. 18And let him who
is in the field not go back to get his
clothes. 19But [a]woe to those who are pregnant and to those who are nursing babies
in those days! 20And pray that your flight
may not be in winter or on the Sabbath.
21For [a]then there will be great tribulation, such as has not been since the beginning of the world until this time, no, nor
ever shall be. 22And unless those days
were shortened, no flesh would be saved;
[a]but for the [1]elect's sake those days will
be shortened.

23[a]"Then if anyone says to you, 'Look,
here *is* the Christ!' or 'There!' do not believe *it.* 24For [a]false christs and false
prophets will rise and show great signs
and wonders to deceive, [b]if possible, even
the elect. 25See, I have told you beforehand.

26"Therefore if they say to you, 'Look,
He is in the desert!' do not go out; *or*
'Look, *He is* in the inner rooms!' do not
believe *it.* 27[a]For as the lightning comes
from the east and flashes to the west, so
also will the coming of the Son of Man be.
28[a]For wherever the carcass is, there the
eagles will be gathered together.

The Coming of the Son of Man

29[a]"Immediately after the tribulation of
those days [b]the sun will be darkened, and
the moon will not give its light; the stars
will fall from heaven, and the powers of

37 c Deut. 32:11, 12 d Ps. 17:8; 91:4
39 a Ps. 118:26
CHAPTER 24
1 a Mark 13:1
2 a Luke 19:44
3 a Mark 13:3 b [1 Thess. 5:1–3]
4 a [Col. 2:8, 18]
5 a John 5:43 b Matt. 24:11
6 a [Rev. 6:2–4] *1* NU omits *all*
7 a Hag. 2:22 b Rev. 6:5, 6 *1* NU omits *pestilences*
9 a Matt. 10:17
11 a 2 Pet. 2:1 b [1 Tim. 4:1]
12 a [2 Thess. 2:3]
13 a Matt. 10:22
14 a Matt. 4:23 b Rom. 10:18
15 a Mark 13:14 b Dan. 9:27; 11:31; 12:11 c Dan. 9:23
19 a Luke 23:29
21 a Dan. 9:26
22 a Is. 65:8, 9 *1 chosen ones'*
23 a Luke 17:23
24 a [2 Thess. 2:9] b [2 Tim. 2:19]
27 a Luke 17:24
28 a Luke 17:37
29 a [Dan. 7:11] b Ezek. 32:7

the heavens will be shaken. 30[a]Then the
sign of the Son of Man will appear in heav-
en, [b]and then all the tribes of the earth
will mourn, and they will see the Son of
Man coming on the clouds of heaven with
power and great glory. 31[a]And He will
send His angels with a great sound of a
trumpet, and they will gather together
His [1]elect from the four winds, from one
end of heaven to the other.

The Parable of the Fig Tree

32"Now learn [a]this parable from the fig
tree: When its branch has already become
tender and puts forth leaves, you know
that summer *is* near. 33So you also, when
you see all these things, know [a]that [1]it is
near—at the doors! 34Assuredly, I say to
you, [a]this generation will by no means
pass away till all these things take place.
35[a]Heaven and earth will pass away, but
My words will by no means pass away.

No One Knows the Day or Hour

36[a]"But of that day and hour no one
knows, not even the angels of [1]heaven,
[b]but My Father only. 37But as the days of
Noah *were,* so also will the coming of the
Son of Man be. 38[a]For as in the days before
the flood, they were eating and drinking,
marrying and giving in marriage, until
the day that Noah entered the ark, 39and
did not know until the flood came and
took them all away, so also will the coming of the Son of Man be. 40[a]Then two
men will be in the field: one will be taken
and the other left. 41Two *women will be*
grinding at the mill: one will be taken and
the other left. 42[a]Watch therefore, for you
do not know what [1]hour your Lord is
coming. 43[a]But know this, that if the master of the house had known what [1]hour
the thief would come, he would have
watched and not allowed his house to be
broken into. 44[a]Therefore you also be
ready, for the Son of Man is coming at an
hour you do not expect.

The Faithful Servant and the Evil Servant

45[a]"Who then is a faithful and wise servant, whom his master made ruler over
his household, to give them food [1]in due
season? 46[a]Blessed *is* that servant whom
his master, when he comes, will find so
doing. 47Assuredly, I say to you that [a]he
will make him ruler over all his goods.
48But if that evil servant says in his heart,
'My master [a]is delaying [1]his coming,'
49and begins to beat *his* fellow servants,
and to eat and drink with the drunkards,
50the master of that servant will come on
a day when he is not looking for *him* and
at an hour that he is [a]not aware of, 51and
will cut him in two and appoint *him* his
portion with the hypocrites. [a]There shall
be weeping and gnashing of teeth.

The Parable of the Wise and Foolish Virgins

25 "Then the kingdom of heaven shall
be likened to ten virgins who took
their lamps and went out to meet [a]the
bridegroom. 2[a]Now five of them were
wise, and five *were* foolish. 3Those who
were foolish took their lamps and took no
oil with them, 4but the wise took oil in
their vessels with their lamps. 5But while
the bridegroom was delayed, [a]they all
slumbered and slept.

6"And at midnight [a]a cry was *heard:*
'Behold, the bridegroom [1]is coming; go
out to meet him!' 7Then all those virgins
arose and [a]trimmed their lamps. 8And the
foolish said to the wise, 'Give us *some* of
your oil, for our lamps are going out.'
9But the wise answered, saying, '*No,* lest
there should not be enough for us and
you; but go rather to those who sell, and
buy for yourselves.' 10And while they went
to buy, the bridegroom came, and those
who were ready went in with him to the
wedding; and [a]the door was shut.

11"Afterward the other virgins came
also, saying, [a]'Lord, Lord, open to us!'
12But he answered and said, 'Assuredly, I
say to you, [a]I do not know you.'

13[a]"Watch therefore, for you [b]know
neither the day nor the hour [1]in which
the Son of Man is coming.

The Parable of the Talents

14[a]"For *the kingdom of heaven is* [b]like
a man traveling to a far country, *who*
called his own servants and delivered his
goods to them. 15And to one he gave five
talents, to another two, and to another
one, [a]to each according to his own ability;

30 a [Dan. 7:13, 14] b Zech. 12:12
31 a [1 Cor. 15:52] *1 chosen ones*
32 a Luke 21:29
33 a [James 5:9] *1* Or *He*
34 a [Matt. 10:23; 16:28; 23:36]
35 a Luke 21:33
36 a Acts 1:7 b Zech. 14:7 *1* NU adds *nor the Son*
38 a [Gen. 6:3–5]
40 a Luke 17:34
42 a Matt. 25:13 *1* NU *day*
43 a Luke 12:39 *1* Lit. *watch of the night*
44 a [1 Thess. 5:6]
45 a Luke 12:42–46 *1 at the right time*
46 a Rev. 16:15
47 a Matt. 25:21, 23
48 a [2 Pet. 3:4–9] *1* NU omits *his coming*
50 a Mark 13:32
51 a Matt. 8:12; 25:30

CHAPTER 25
1 a [Eph. 5:29, 30]
2 a Matt. 13:47; 22:10
5 a 1 Thess. 5:6
6 a [1 Thess. 4:16] *1* NU omits *is coming*
7 a Luke 12:35
10 a Luke 13:25
11 a [Matt. 7:21–23]
12 a [Hab. 1:13]
13 a Mark 13:35 b Matt. 24:36, 42 *1* NU omits the rest of v. 13.
14 a Luke 19:12–27 b Matt. 21:33
15 a [Rom. 12:6]

and immediately he went on a journey.
16Then he who had received the five talents went and traded with them, and
made another five talents. 17And likewise
he who *had received* two gained two more
also. 18But he who had received one went
and dug in the ground, and hid his lord's
money. 19After a long time the lord of
those servants came and settled accounts
with them.
20"So he who had received five talents
came and brought five other talents, saying, 'Lord, you delivered to me five talents; look, I have gained five more talents
besides them.' 21His lord said to him,
'Well *done,* good and faithful servant; you
were [a]faithful over a few things, [b]I will
make you ruler over many things. Enter
into [c]the joy of your lord.' 22He also who
had received two talents came and said,
'Lord, you delivered to me two talents;
look, I have gained two more talents besides them.' 23His lord said to him, [a]'Well
done, good and faithful servant; you have
been faithful over a few things, I will make
you ruler over many things. Enter into
[b]the joy of your lord.'
24"Then he who had received the one
talent came and said, 'Lord, I knew you to
be a hard man, reaping where you have
not sown, and gathering where you have
not scattered seed. 25And I was afraid, and
went and hid your talent in the ground.
Look, *there* you have *what is* yours.'
26"But his lord answered and said to
him, 'You [a]wicked and lazy servant, you
knew that I reap where I have not sown,
and gather where I have not scattered
seed. 27So you ought to have deposited my
money with the bankers, and at my coming I would have received back my own
with interest. 28So take the talent from
him, and give *it* to him who has ten talents.
29[a]'For to everyone who has, more will
be given, and he will have abundance; but
from him who does not have, even what
he has will be taken away. 30And cast the
unprofitable servant [a]into the outer darkness. [b]There will be weeping and [c]gnash-
ing of teeth.'

The Son of Man Will Judge the Nations

31[a]"When the Son of Man comes in His
glory, and all the [1]holy angels with Him,
then He will sit on the throne of His glory.
32[a]All the nations will be gathered before
Him, and [b]He will separate them one
from another, as a shepherd divides *his*
sheep from the goats. 33And He will set
the [a]sheep on His right hand, but the
goats on the left. 34Then the King will say
to those on His right hand, 'Come, you
blessed of My Father, [a]inherit the kingdom [b]prepared for you from the foundation of the world: 35[a]for I was hungry and
you gave Me food; I was thirsty and you
gave Me drink; [b]I was a stranger and you
took Me in; 36I *was* [a]naked and you
clothed Me; I was sick and you visited Me;
[b]I was in prison and you came to Me.'
37"Then the righteous will answer Him,
saying, 'Lord, when did we see You hungry and feed *You,* or thirsty and give *You*
drink? 38When did we see You a stranger
and take *You* in, or naked and clothe *You?*
39Or when did we see You sick, or in prison, and come to You?' 40And the King will
answer and say to them, 'Assuredly, I say
to you, [a]inasmuch as you did *it* to one of
the least of these My brethren, you did *it*
to Me.'

> *May my Lord never let me grow cold in my longing to be a cup in His hand for the quenching of His own royal thirst.*
>
> OSWALD CHAMBERS

41"Then He will also say to those on the
left hand, [a]'Depart from Me, you cursed,
[b]into the everlasting fire prepared for [c]the
devil and his angels: 42for I was hungry
and you gave Me no food; I was thirsty and
you gave Me no drink; 43I was a stranger
and you did not take Me in, naked and you
did not clothe Me, sick and in prison and
you did not visit Me.'
44"Then they also will answer [1]Him,
saying, 'Lord, when did we see You hungry or thirsty or a stranger or naked or
sick or in prison, and did not minister to
You?' 45Then He will answer them, saying,
'Assuredly, I say to you, [a]inasmuch as you
did not do *it* to one of the least of these,
you did not do *it* to Me.' 46And [a]these will
go away into everlasting punishment, but
the righteous into eternal life."

21 [a] [1 Cor. 4:2] [b] [Luke 12:44; 22:29, 30] [c] [Heb. 12:2]
23 [a] Matt. 24:45, 47; 25:21 [b] [Ps. 16:11]
26 [a] Matt. 18:32
29 [a] Matt. 13:12
30 [a] Matt. 8:12; 22:13 [b] Matt. 7:23; 8:12; 24:51 [c] Ps. 112:10
31 [a] [1 Thess. 4:16] [1] NU omits *holy*
32 [a] [2 Cor. 5:10] [b] Ezek. 20:38
33 [a] [John 10:11, 27, 28]
34 [a] [Rom. 8:17] [b] Mark 10:40
35 [a] Is. 58:7 [b] [Heb. 13:2]
36 [a] [James 2:15, 16] [b] 2 Tim. 1:16
40 [a] Mark 9:41
41 [a] Matt. 7:23 [b] Matt. 13:40, 42 [c] [2 Pet. 2:4]
44 [1] NU, M omit *Him*
45 [a] Prov. 14:31
46 [a] [Dan. 12:2]

The Plot to Kill Jesus

26 Now it came to pass, when Jesus
had finished all these sayings, *that*
He said to His disciples, 2[a]"You know that
after two days is the Passover, and the Son
of Man will be delivered up to be crucified."
3[a]Then the chief priests, [1]the scribes,
and the elders of the people assembled at
the palace of the high priest, who was
called Caiaphas, 4and [a]plotted to take Jesus by [1]trickery and kill *Him.* 5But they
said, "Not during the feast, lest there be
an uproar among the [a]people."

The Anointing at Bethany

6And when Jesus was in [a]Bethany at the
house of Simon the leper, 7a woman came
to Him having an alabaster flask of very
costly fragrant oil, and she poured *it* on

CHAPTER 26
2 [a]Luke 22:1, 2
3 [a]John 11:47 [1]NU omits *the scribes*
4 [a]Acts 4:25–28 [1]*deception*
5 [a]Matt. 21:26
6 [a]Mark 14:3–9

Catherine Booth

When Catherine Booth (1829–1890) arrived in a city to preach, advertisements for her meetings read like those for a sideshow: "Come and hear a woman preach!" Such was the stigma of women in Christian ministry during the nineteenth century, but Catherine was instrumental in forwarding the role of women in ministry.

After marrying Salvation Army cofounder William Booth in 1855, the couple lived out of suitcases for their first two years of marriage. They shared a love people envied for thirty-five years. During a time of ill health, William was unable to perform his leadership duties, so Catherine took over his responsibilities, including his preaching obligations. It was immediately obvious that William was not the only Booth who had a mighty call to preach.

By 1864, Catherine was conducting revival meetings of her own; and the following year, she became instrumental in the development of The Christian Mission. The Mission was unlike the stiff churches of the day that often closed their doors to common people. Instead, it targeted the outcasts, holding services in the squalid streets of London amid fistfights and jeering crowds.

In 1878, the Mission changed its name to The Salvation Army and, while expanding at an astounding rate, quickly began an aggressive evangelism effort. In 1880, the Army went international, sending missionaries across the United States, Canada, and Australia and eventually becoming the influential powerhouse of service it is today.

Though Catherine never held an official office in the Army, she was considered the "mother" from its inception and is credited with shaping the organization. Though her willingness to include women among the Army's ministers received great criticism, it also enabled the organization to become a religious phenomenon in the nineteenth century. While others refused to use women ministers and working-class citizens as leaders, the Army succeeded by preaching where churches were afraid to go. Speaking of God's love in theaters and circuses in the common language which secular, working-class people would understand, the Salvation Army, under "Mother" Booth's supervision, changed the spiritual atmosphere of nations and the role of women in ministry into the next century.

His head as He sat *at the table.* 8[a]But
when His disciples saw *it,* they were indignant, saying, "Why this waste? 9For this
fragrant oil might have been sold for
much and given to *the* poor."

10But when Jesus was aware of *it,* He
said to them, "Why do you trouble the
woman? For she has done a good work for
Me. 11[a]For you have the poor with you
always, but [b]Me you do not have always.
12For in pouring this fragrant oil on My
body, she did *it* for My [a]burial. 13Assured-
ly, I say to you, wherever this gospel is
preached in the whole world, what this
woman has done will also be told as a memorial to her."

Judas Agrees to Betray Jesus

14[a]Then one of the twelve, called [b]Judas
Iscariot, went to the chief priests 15and
said, [a]"What are you willing to give me if
I deliver Him to you?" And they counted
out to him thirty pieces of silver. 16So
from that time he sought opportunity to
betray Him.

Jesus Celebrates Passover with His Disciples

17[a]Now on the first *day of the Feast*
of Unleavened Bread the disciples came
to Jesus, saying to Him, "Where do You
want us to prepare for You to eat the Passover?"

18And He said, "Go into the city to a
certain man, and say to him, 'The Teacher
says, [a]"My time is at hand; I will keep the
Passover at your house with My disciples." ' "

8 a John 12:4
11 a [Deut. 15:11] b [John 13:33; 14:19; 16:5, 28; 17:11]
12 a John 19:38–42
14 a Mark 14:10, 11; Luke 22:3–6 b Matt. 10:4
15 a Zech. 11:12
17 a Ex. 12:6, 18–20
18 a Luke 9:51

THE WOMAN AT BETHANY

She had come to anoint His body for burial. Little did she know, it would be a burial that would not last. What did Jesus think about this woman and her desire to anoint Him? He said that, "Wherever this gospel is preached in the whole world, what this woman has done will also be told as a memorial to her" (Matt. 26:13). In other words, His burial might have been just a three-day event, but this nameless woman's actions to prepare Him for it would last a long, long time.

The woman had courage. She was brave enough to enter Simon's house and interrupt what was likely an all-male gathering. She walked straight to Jesus while He was still sitting at the table, broke a flask of very expensive oil, and poured it on His head. The disciples were outraged, but Jesus was pleased.

Jesus understood this woman. He understood that she loved Him without regard for what it cost. He understood the profound gratitude behind her fragrant offering of devotion. He understood the power of sacrifice, the power of loving someone with utter abandon. He understood that she desperately wanted to do something for Him. And He told the critical disciples that it was perfectly acceptable for her to do what she would not have had another opportunity to do instead of selling the oil and giving the money to the poor.

In the case of this woman, and so often in the service of Jesus, the sacrifice outlives the one who sacrifices. Woman of Destiny, Jesus is worth everything. Let us give to Him freely and joyfully, knowing that nothing is too precious for Him. Let us lavish on Him all of our best affections. Let us love Him with as much passion and as much abandon as the woman at Bethany. Let us give to Him the sacrifices that will outlive us.

19 So the disciples did as Jesus had directed them; and they prepared the Passover.

20 [a]When evening had come, He sat down with the twelve. 21 Now as they were eating, He said, "Assuredly, I say to you, one of you will [a]betray Me."

22 And they were exceedingly sorrowful, and each of them began to say to Him, "Lord, is it I?"

23 He answered and said, [a]"He who dipped *his* hand with Me in the dish will betray Me. 24 The Son of Man indeed goes just [a]as it is written of Him, but [b]woe to that man by whom the Son of Man is betrayed! [c]It would have been good for that man if he had not been born."

25 Then Judas, who was betraying Him, answered and said, "Rabbi, is it I?"

He said to him, "You have said it."

Jesus Institutes the Lord's Supper

26 [a]And as they were eating, [b]Jesus took bread, [1]blessed and broke *it,* and gave *it* to the disciples and said, "Take, eat; [c]this is My body."

27 Then He took the cup, and gave thanks, and gave *it* to them, saying, [a]"Drink from it, all of you. 28 For [a]this is My blood [b]of the [1]new covenant, which is shed [c]for many for the [2]remission of sins. 29 But [a]I say to you, I will not drink of this fruit of the vine from now on [b]until that day when I drink it new with you in My Father's kingdom."

30 [a]And when they had sung a hymn, they went out to the Mount of Olives.

Jesus Predicts Peter's Denial

31 Then Jesus said to them, [a]"All of you will [b]be [1]made to stumble because of Me this night, for it is written:

[c]'I will strike the Shepherd,
And the sheep of the flock will be scattered.'

32 But after I have been raised, [a]I will go before you to Galilee."

33 Peter answered and said to Him, "Even if all are [1]made to stumble because of You, I will never be made to stumble."

34 Jesus said to him, [a]"Assuredly, I say to you that this night, before the rooster crows, you will deny Me three times."

35 Peter said to Him, "Even if I have to die with You, I will not deny You!"

And so said all the disciples.

The Prayer in the Garden

36 [a]Then Jesus came with them to a place called Gethsemane, and said to the disciples, "Sit here while I go and pray over there." 37 And He took with Him Peter and [a]the two sons of Zebedee, and He began to be sorrowful and deeply distressed. 38 Then He said to them, [a]"My soul is exceedingly sorrowful, even to death. Stay here and watch with Me."

39 He went a little farther and fell on His face, and [a]prayed, saying, [b]"O My Father, if it is possible, [c]let this cup pass from Me; nevertheless, [d]not as I will, but as You *will.*"

> *True praying is not mere sentiment, poetry, or eloquent speech. Prayer is obedience. Only those who obey have the right to pray.*
>
> E. M. Bounds

40 Then He came to the disciples and found them sleeping, and said to Peter, "What! Could you not watch with Me one hour? 41 [a]Watch and pray, lest you enter into temptation. [b]The spirit indeed *is* willing, but the flesh *is* weak."

42 Again, a second time, He went away and prayed, saying, "O My Father, [1]if this cup cannot pass away from Me unless I drink it, Your will be done." 43 And He came and found them asleep again, for their eyes were heavy.

44 So He left them, went away again, and prayed the third time, saying the same words. 45 Then He came to His disciples and said to them, "Are *you* still sleeping and resting? Behold, the hour [1]is at hand, and the Son of Man is being [a]betrayed into the hands of sinners. 46 Rise, let us be going. See, My betrayer is at hand."

20 a Mark 14:17–21
21 a John 6:70, 71; 13:21
23 a Ps. 41:9
24 a 1 Cor. 15:3 b Luke 17:1 c John 17:12
26 a Mark 14:22–25 b 1 Cor. 11:23–25 c [1 Pet. 2:24] *1 M gave thanks for*
27 a Mark 14:23
28 a [Ex. 24:8] b Jer. 31:31 c Matt. 20:28 *1 NU omits new* *2 forgiveness*
29 a Mark 14:25 b Acts 10:41
30 a Mark 14:26–31
31 a John 16:32 b [Matt. 11:6] c Zech. 13:7 *1 caused to take offense at Me*
32 a Matt. 28:7, 10, 16
33 *1 caused to take offense at You*
34 a John 13:38
36 a Mark 14:32–35
37 a Matt. 4:21; 17:1
38 a John 12:27
39 a [Heb. 5:7–9] b John 12:27 c Matt. 20:22 d John 5:30; 6:38
41 a Luke 22:40, 46 b [Gal. 5:17]
42 *1 NU if this may not pass away unless*
45 a Matt. 17:22, 23; 20:18, 19 *1 has drawn near*

Betrayal and Arrest in Gethsemane

47And [a]while He was still speaking, behold, Judas, one of the twelve, with a great
multitude with swords and clubs, came
from the chief priests and elders of the
people.
48Now His betrayer had given them a
sign, saying, "Whomever I kiss, He is the
One; seize Him." 49Immediately he went
up to Jesus and said, "Greetings, Rabbi!"
[a]and kissed Him.
50But Jesus said to him, [a]"Friend, why
have you come?"
Then they came and laid hands on Jesus
and took Him. 51And suddenly, [a]one of
those *who were* with Jesus stretched out
his hand and drew his sword, struck the
servant of the high priest, and cut off his
ear.
52But Jesus said to him, "Put your
sword in its place, [a]for all who take the
sword will [1]perish by the sword. 53Or do
you think that I cannot now pray to My
Father, and He will provide Me with
[a]more than twelve legions of angels?
54How then could the Scriptures be fulfilled, [a]that it must happen thus?"
55In that hour Jesus said to the multitudes, "Have you come out, as against a
robber, with swords and clubs to take Me?
I sat daily with you, teaching in the temple, and you did not seize Me. 56But all
this was done that the [a]Scriptures of the
prophets might be fulfilled."
Then [b]all the disciples forsook Him and
fled.

Jesus Faces the Sanhedrin

57[a]And those who had laid hold of Jesus
led *Him* away to Caiaphas the high priest,
where the scribes and the elders were assembled. 58But [a]Peter followed Him at a
distance to the high priest's courtyard.
And he went in and sat with the servants
to see the end.
59Now the chief priests, [1]the elders, and
all the council sought [a]false testimony
against Jesus to put Him to death, 60[1]but
found none. Even though [a]many false witnesses came forward, they found none.
But at last [b]two [2]false witnesses came forward 61and said, "This *fellow* said, [a]'I am
able to destroy the temple of God and to
build it in three days.'"
62[a]And the high priest arose and said to
Him, "Do You answer nothing? What *is it*
these men testify against You?" 63But [a]Je-
sus kept silent. And the high priest answered and said to Him, [b]"I put You under
oath by the living God: Tell us if You are
the Christ, the Son of God!"
64Jesus said to him, "*It is as* you said.
Nevertheless, I say to you, [a]hereafter you
will see the Son of Man [b]sitting at the
right hand of the Power, and coming on
the clouds of heaven."
65[a]Then the high priest tore his clothes,
saying, "He has spoken blasphemy! What
further need do we have of witnesses?
Look, now you have heard His [b]blasphe-
my! 66What do you think?"
They answered and said, [a]"He is deserving of death."
67[a]Then they spat in His face and beat
Him; and [b]others struck *Him* with [1]the
palms of their hands, 68saying, [a]"Prophesy
to us, Christ! Who is the one who struck
You?"

Peter Denies Jesus, and Weeps Bitterly

69[a]Now Peter sat outside in the courtyard. And a servant girl came to him, saying, "You also were with Jesus of Galilee."
70But he denied it before *them* all, saying, "I do not know what you are saying."
71And when he had gone out to the
gateway, another *girl* saw him and said to
those *who were* there, "This *fellow* also
was with Jesus of Nazareth."
72But again he denied with an oath, "I
do not know the Man!"
73And a little later those who stood by
came up and said to Peter, "Surely you
also are *one* of them, for your [a]speech betrays you."
74Then [a]he began to [1]curse and [2]swear,
saying, "I do not know the Man!"
Immediately a rooster crowed. 75And
Peter remembered the word of Jesus who
had said to him, [a]"Before the rooster
crows, you will deny Me three times." So
he went out and wept bitterly.

Jesus Handed Over to Pontius Pilate

27 When morning came, [a]all the chief
priests and elders of the people
plotted against Jesus to put Him to death.
2And when they had bound Him, they led
Him away and [a]delivered Him to [1]Pontius
Pilate the governor.

47 a Acts 1:16
49 a 2 Sam. 20:9
50 a Ps. 41:9; 55:13
51 a John 18:10
52 a Rev. 13:10 *1* M *die*
53 a Dan. 7:10
54 a Is. 50:6; 53:2–11
56 a Lam. 4:20 b John 18:15
57 a John 18:12, 19–24
58 a John 18:15, 16
59 a Ps. 35:11 *1* NU omits *the elders*
60 a Mark 14:55 b Deut. 19:15 *1* NU *but found none, even though many false witnesses came forward.* *2* NU omits *false witnesses*
61 a John 2:19
62 a Mark 14:60
63 a Is. 53:7 b Lev. 5:1
64 a Dan. 7:13 b [Acts 7:55]
65 a 2 Kin. 18:37 b John 10:30–36
66 a Lev. 24:16
67 a Is. 50:6; 53:3 b Luke 22:63–65 *1* Or *rods,*
68 a Mark 14:65
69 a John 18:16–18, 25–27
73 a Luke 22:59
74 a Mark 14:71 *1 call down curses* *2* Swear oaths
75 a Matt. 26:34

CHAPTER 27
1 a John 18:28
2 a Acts 3:13 *1* NU omits *Pontius*

Judas Hangs Himself

3[a]Then Judas, His betrayer, seeing that
He had been condemned, was remorseful
and brought back the thirty [b]pieces of silver to the chief priests and elders, 4saying,
"I have sinned by betraying innocent
blood."
And they said, "What *is that* to us? You
see *to it!*"
5Then he threw down the pieces of silver in the temple and [a]departed, and went
and hanged himself.
6But the chief priests took the silver
pieces and said, "It is not lawful to put
them into the treasury, because they are
the price of blood." 7And they consulted
together and bought with them the potter's field, to bury strangers in. 8Therefore
that field has been called [a]the Field of
Blood to this day.
9Then was fulfilled what was spoken by
Jeremiah the prophet, saying, [a]"*And they
took the thirty pieces of silver, the value
of Him who was priced,* whom they of the
children of Israel priced, 10*and* [a]*gave
them for the potter's field, as the* LORD
directed me."

Jesus Faces Pilate

11Now Jesus stood before the governor.
[a]And the governor asked Him, saying,
"Are You the King of the Jews?"
Jesus said to him, [b]"*It is as* you say."
12And while He was being accused by the
chief priests and elders, [a]He answered
nothing.
13Then Pilate said to Him, [a]"Do You not
hear how many things they testify against
You?" 14But He answered him not one
word, so that the governor marveled
greatly.

Taking the Place of Barabbas

15[a]Now at the feast the governor was
accustomed to releasing to the multitude
one prisoner whom they wished. 16And at
that time they had a notorious prisoner
called [1]Barabbas. 17Therefore, when they
had gathered together, Pilate said to
them, "Whom do you want me to release
to you? Barabbas, or Jesus who is called
Christ?" 18For he knew that they had
handed Him over because of [a]envy.
19While he was sitting on the judgment
seat, his wife sent to him, saying, "Have
nothing to do with that just Man, for I
have suffered many things today in a
dream because of Him."
20[a]But the chief priests and elders persuaded the multitudes that they should
ask for Barabbas and destroy Jesus. 21The
governor answered and said to them,
"Which of the two do you want me to release to you?"
They said, [a]"Barabbas!"
22Pilate said to them, "What then shall
I do with Jesus who is called Christ?"
They all said to him, "Let Him be crucified!"
23Then the governor said, [a]"Why, what
evil has He done?"
But they cried out all the more, saying,
"Let Him be crucified!"
24When Pilate saw that he could not
prevail at all, but rather *that* a [1]tumult
was rising, he [a]took water and washed *his*
hands before the multitude, saying, "I am
innocent of the blood of this [2]just Person.
You see *to it.*"
25And all the people answered and said,
[a]"His blood *be* on us and on our children."
26Then he released Barabbas to them;
and when [a]he had [1]scourged Jesus, he delivered *Him* to be crucified.

The Soldiers Mock Jesus

27[a]Then the soldiers of the governor
took Jesus into the [1]Praetorium and gathered the whole [2]garrison around Him.
28And they [a]stripped Him and [b]put a scarlet robe on Him. 29[a]When they had [1]twist-
ed a crown of thorns, they put *it* on His
head, and a reed in His right hand. And
they bowed the knee before Him and
mocked Him, saying, "Hail, King of the
Jews!" 30Then [a]they spat on Him, and
took the reed and struck Him on the head.
31And when they had mocked Him, they
took the robe off Him, put His *own*
clothes on Him, [a]and led Him away to be
crucified.

The King on a Cross

32[a]Now as they came out, [b]they found a
man of Cyrene, Simon by name. Him they
compelled to bear His cross. 33[a]And when
they had come to a place called Golgotha,
that is to say, Place of a Skull, 34[a]they gave
Him [1]sour wine mingled with gall to
drink. But when He had tasted *it,* He
would not drink.
35[a]Then they crucified Him, and divided His garments, casting lots, [1]that it

3 a Matt. 26:14 b Matt. 26:15
5 a Acts 1:18
8 a Acts 1:19
9 a Zech. 11:12
10 a Jer. 32:6–9; Zech. 11:12, 13
11 a Mark 15:2–5 b John 18:37
12 a John 19:9
13 a Matt. 26:62
15 a Luke 23:17–25
16 1 NU *Jesus Barabbas*
18 a Matt. 21:38
20 a Acts 3:14
21 a Acts 3:14
23 a Acts 3:13
24 a Deut. 21:6–8 1 *an uproar* 2 NU omits *just*
25 a Josh. 2:19
26 a [Is. 50:6; 53:5] 1 *flogged* with a Roman scourge
27 a Mark 15:16–20 1 The governor's headquarters 2 *cohort*
28 a John 19:2 b Luke 23:11
29 a Is. 53:3 1 Lit. *woven*
30 a Matt. 26:67
31 a Is. 53:7
32 a Heb. 13:12 b Mark 15:21
33 a John 19:17
34 a Ps. 69:21 1 NU omits *sour*
35 a Luke 23:34 1 NU, M omit the rest of v. 35.

might be fulfilled which was spoken by the prophet:

[b]"They divided My garments among them,
And for My clothing they cast lots."

36[a]Sitting down, they kept watch over Him there. 37And they [a]put up over His head the accusation written against Him:

THIS IS JESUS THE KING OF THE JEWS.

35 [b]Ps. 22:18
36 [a]Matt. 27:54
37 [a]John 19:19
38 [a]Is. 53:9, 12
39 [a]Mark 15:29
40 [a]John 2:19 [b]Matt. 26:63
41 [1]M *scribes, the Pharisees, and the elders*

38[a]Then two robbers were crucified with
Him, one on the right and another on the
left.
39And [a]those who passed by blasphemed Him, wagging their heads 40and
saying, [a]"You who destroy the temple and
build *it* in three days, save Yourself! [b]If
You are the Son of God, come down from
the cross."
41Likewise the chief priests also, mocking with the [1]scribes and elders, said,

Lottie Moon

Lottie Moon was a young and feisty, but attractive, four-foot-three woman who came from a wealthy, aristocratic Virginia family. During her college years, this tiny lady had resisted the gospel of Jesus Christ and said of her salvation experience, " I went to the [church] service to scoff, and returned to my room praying all night." A descendant of the Quaker theologian and preacher Robert Barclay, Lottie was highly educated. In fact, she was one of the first women in the Southern states to earn a master's degree. The great thing about Lottie Moon, though, was that she allowed the Lord to work through her to transform world missions.

For a short season, Lottie was content with tutoring and working to affect social change in the American South. But when her sister left for China in 1872, Lottie's heart turned toward the mission field as well. She devoured her sister's letters and finally received her own call to China in the spring of 1873, after hearing a sermon preached on John 4:35: "Lift up your eyes and look at the fields, for they are already white for harvest!"

In North China, Lottie traveled from village to village in a mule litter and regularly slept in noisy, filthy conditions. Often, the places through which she traveled were so dangerous that her carriers would take the precaution of muffling the mule's bells with straw. She was as fearless and firm as a man, yet altogether feminine.

When revolution broke out in China in 1911, the American Consul and many of Lottie's friends urged her to leave, but she refused. The more her Chinese friends suffered epidemics and poverty during the war, the more of her personal resources Lottie gave to feed the poor. As the famine worsened, Lottie herself stopped eating so that more food would be available for others. When a doctor realized she was starving to death, she was put on a boat to return to the States, but died during the voyage.

May we, as women of destiny, possess the sacrificial love that Lottie Moon demonstrated; and may we willingly give ourselves to the cause of Jesus Christ as selflessly as she did.

42"He [a]saved others; Himself He cannot
save. [1]If He is the King of Israel, let Him
now come down from the cross, and we
will believe [2]Him. 43[a]He trusted in God;
let Him deliver Him now if He will have
Him; for He said, 'I am the Son of God.' "
44[a]Even the robbers who were crucified
with Him reviled Him with the same
thing.

Jesus Dies on the Cross

45[a]Now from the sixth hour until the
ninth hour there was darkness over all the
land. 46And about the ninth hour [a]Jesus
cried out with a loud voice, saying, "Eli,
Eli, lama sabachthani?" that is, [b]*"My God,
My God, why have You forsaken Me?"*
47Some of those who stood there, when
they heard *that,* said, "This Man is calling
for Elijah!" 48Immediately one of them
ran and took a sponge, [a]filled *it* with sour
wine and put *it* on a reed, and offered it to
Him to drink.
49The rest said, "Let Him alone; let us
see if Elijah will come to save Him."
50And Jesus [a]cried out again with a loud
voice, and [b]yielded up His spirit.
51Then, behold, [a]the veil of the temple
was torn in two from top to bottom; and
the earth quaked, and the rocks were split,
52and the graves were opened; and many
bodies of the saints who had fallen asleep
were raised; 53and coming out of the
graves after His resurrection, they went
into the holy city and appeared to many.
54[a]So when the centurion and those
with him, who were guarding Jesus, saw
the earthquake and the things that had
happened, they feared greatly, saying,
[b]"Truly this was the Son of God!"
55And many women [a]who followed
Jesus from Galilee, ministering to
Him, were there looking on from afar,
56[a]among whom were Mary Magdalene,
Mary the mother of James and [1]Joses, and
the mother of Zebedee's sons.

Jesus Buried in Joseph's Tomb

57Now [a]when evening had come, there
came a rich man from Arimathea, named
Joseph, who himself had also become a
disciple of Jesus. 58This man went to Pilate and asked for the body of Jesus. Then
Pilate commanded the body to be given to
him. 59When Joseph had taken the body,
he wrapped it in a clean linen cloth, 60and
[a]laid it in his new tomb which he had
hewn out of the rock; and he rolled a large
stone against the door of the tomb, and
departed. 61And Mary Magdalene was
there, and the other Mary, sitting [1]oppo-
site the tomb.

Pilate Sets a Guard

62On the next day, which followed the
Day of Preparation, the chief priests and
Pharisees gathered together to Pilate,
63saying, "Sir, we remember, while He
was still alive, how that deceiver said, [a]'After three days I will rise.' 64Therefore
command that the tomb be made secure
until the third day, lest His disciples come
[1]by night and steal Him *away,* and say to
the people, 'He has risen from the dead.'
So the last deception will be worse than
the first."
65Pilate said to them, "You have a
guard; go your way, make *it* as secure as
you know how." 66So they went and made
the tomb secure, [a]sealing the stone and
setting the guard.

He Is Risen

28 Now [a]after the Sabbath, as the first
day of the week began to dawn,
Mary Magdalene [b]and the other Mary
came to see the tomb. 2And behold, there
was a great earthquake; for [a]an angel of
the Lord descended from heaven, and
came and rolled back the stone [1]from the
door, and sat on it. 3[a]His countenance
was like lightning, and his clothing as
white as snow. 4And the guards shook for
fear of him, and became like [a]dead *men.*
5But the angel answered and said to the
women, "Do not be afraid, for I know that
you seek Jesus who was crucified. 6He is
not here; for He is risen, [a]as He said.
Come, see the place where the Lord lay.
7And go quickly and tell His disciples that
He is risen from the dead, and indeed [a]He
is going before you into Galilee; there you
will see Him. Behold, I have told you."
8So they went out quickly from the
tomb with fear and great joy, and ran to
bring His disciples word.

The Women Worship the Risen Lord

9And [1]as they went to tell His disciples, behold, [a]Jesus met them, saying,

42 a [John 3:14, 15] *1* NU omits *If* *2* NU, M *in Him*
43 a Ps. 22:8
44 a Luke 23:39–43
45 a Mark 15:33–41
46 a [Heb. 5:7] b Ps. 22:1
48 a Ps. 69:21
50 a Luke 23:46 b [John 10:18]
51 a Ex. 26:31
54 a Mark 15:39 b Matt. 14:33
55 a Luke 8:2, 3
56 a Mark 15:40, 47; 16:9 *1* NU *Joseph*
57 a John 19:38–42
60 a Is. 53:9
61 *1 in front of*
63 a Mark 8:31; 10:34
64 *1* NU omits *by night*
66 a Dan. 6:17
CHAPTER 28
1 a Luke 24:1–10 b Matt. 27:56, 61
2 a Mark 16:5 *1* NU omits *from the door*
3 a Dan. 7:9; 10:6
4 a Rev. 1:17
6 a Matt. 12:40; 16:21; 17:23; 20:19
7 a Mark 16:7
9 a John 20:14 *1* NU omits *as they went to tell His disciples*

Matthew 28:19

Dear Woman of Destiny,

I was eight when my mom started sending me to the store alone. I loved it. Unfortunately, I always returned with the wrong thing. I'd bring home iceberg lettuce (Mom liked romaine). I'd come back with ice cream (Mom had her teeth all set on orange sherbet). You get the picture. I never managed to get the order quite right.

My problem was I *assumed* I knew what she was asking me to do. And I *assumed* that I knew all the possibilities there were to obey successfully. We often make the same mistake in trying to fulfill the Great Commission. We assume we understand the assignment. It seems clear. The temptation is to accept the command and not ask any more questions. I've seen it all over the world—good-hearted lovers of Jesus who seek to fulfill the Great Commission, but without any further discussion with Jesus about how He wants to do it.

I once prayed with a Youth With A Mission team in Micronesia. YWAM people wisely don't assume they know what to pray, so they ask God and wait. Everyone felt God said "India." I rubbed my hands together eager to start. "Oh no," the leader tenderly said. "Now we need to ask God what *exactly* in India He wants us to target." It was one of the most instructive moments of my life.

God has asked us to go into everyman's world and make disciples. But the world is not inhabited by mere statistics; it's inhabited by people God passionately loves and desires, people He understands intimately. And He wants to tell you His heart for them. He wants to give you keys to their hearts. He wants to show you how best to communicate His love.

Joe Aldrich tells of a young Russian woman who led many people to Jesus. When asked her secret, she unfolded this story:

One day she noticed a woman with two children looking longingly through a market window. She followed them home and left some groceries on their step. Then over a period of time, she felt the Lord nudge her to drop off various items. Once, some sweaters for the children . . . another time, some handkerchiefs . . . one day, some shoes, and then, of all things (this is the amazing part of the story), some underwear!

Finally the woman said, "Who is it that tells you my most intimate secrets? Winter was coming, and my boys needed sweaters. I asked my drunken husband if I could buy some. 'Absolutely not!' he thundered. Then you arrived with two sweaters. The boys caught colds, and I wanted to buy them handkerchiefs, but my husband wouldn't allow it. The next day you arrived with handkerchiefs. I was searching for a job when my shoe got caught in the mud as the bus took off. Even though you had no idea what my shoe size was, you brought me a pair of shoes. I landed the job, but was required to have a physical and I needed underwear. Who is it that tells you everything about me?"

People will ask us that question if we are listening to Jesus. There are five important words to remember about the Great Commission. "Do whatever He tells you" (see John 2:5).

You'll never fail if you do.

Fawn Parish

"Rejoice!" So they came and held Him by
the feet and worshiped Him. 10Then Jesus
said to them, "Do not be afraid. Go *and*
tell [a]My brethren to go to Galilee, and
there they will see Me."

The validity of the Christian faith rests on one supreme miracle—the resurrection of Jesus Christ.

KATHRYN KUHLMAN

The Soldiers Are Bribed

11Now while they were going, behold,
some of the guard came into the city
and reported to the chief priests all the
things that had happened. 12When they
had assembled with the elders and consulted together, they gave a large sum
of money to the soldiers, 13saying, "Tell
them, 'His disciples came at night and
stole Him *away* while we slept.' 14And
if this comes to the governor's ears, we
will appease him and make you secure."
15So they took the money and did as they
were instructed; and this saying is commonly reported among the Jews until this
day.

10 [a] John 20:17
16 [a] Matt. 26:32; 28:7, 10
17 [a] John 20:24–29
18 [a] [Dan. 7:13, 14]
19 [a] Mark 16:15 [b] Luke 24:47 [1] M omits *therefore*
20 [a] [Acts 2:42] [b] [Acts 4:31; 18:10; 23:11] [1] NU omits *Amen.*

O Lord, may ____ go and make disciples of all the nations, baptizing them in the name of the Father, the Son, and the Holy Spirit, teaching them to observe all things that You have commanded them. For lo, You will be with them always, even to the end of the age.

FROM MATTHEW 28:19, 20

The Great Commission

16Then the eleven disciples went away
into Galilee, to the mountain [a]which Jesus had appointed for them. 17When they
saw Him, they worshiped Him; but some
[a]doubted.
18And Jesus came and spoke to them,
saying, [a]"All authority has been given to
Me in heaven and on earth. 19 [a]Go
[1]therefore and [b]make disciples of all the
nations, baptizing them in the name of
the Father and of the Son and of the Holy
Spirit, 20[a]teaching them to observe all
things that I have commanded you; and
lo, I am [b]with you always, *even* to the end
of the age." [1]Amen.

AUTHOR: *Mark*
DATE: *A.D. 65–70*
THEME: *The Suffering Son of Man Who Is in Fact the Son of God*
KEY WORDS: *Authority, Son of Man, Son of God, Suffering, Faith, Discipline, Gospel*

MARK

Dear Woman of Destiny,

The Book of Mark is unique in its presentation of Jesus as both the Son of Man and the Son of God. One of its most beautiful lessons comes from the woman who came to Jesus with an alabaster flask of spikenard. Some say this flask would represent a whole year's wages for the woman. This unknown woman gave her *all* for the Lord. The broken flask might represent our lives given in completeness to Him. God wants us to give everything to Him and not hold back a single part of ourselves.

With His love,

Cindy Jacobs

John the Baptist Prepares the Way

The [a]beginning of the gospel of Jesus Christ, [b]the Son of God. 2As it
is written in [1]the Prophets:

[a]*"Behold, I send My messenger*
before Your face,
Who will prepare Your way before
You."

3 *"The[a] voice of one crying in the*
wilderness:
'Prepare the way of the LORD;
Make His paths straight.'"

4[a]John came baptizing in the wilderness and preaching a baptism of repentance [1]for the remission of sins. 5[a]Then
all the land of Judea, and those from Jerusalem, went out to him and were all baptized by him in the Jordan River,
confessing their sins.
6Now John was [a]clothed with camel's
hair and with a leather belt around his
waist, and he ate locusts and wild honey.
7And he preached, saying, [a]"There comes
One after me who is mightier than I,
whose sandal strap I am not worthy to
stoop down and loose. 8[a]I indeed baptized
you with water, but He will baptize you
[b]with the Holy Spirit."

John Baptizes Jesus

9[a]It came to pass in those days *that* Jesus came from Nazareth of Galilee, and
was baptized by John in the Jordan.
10[a]And immediately, coming up [1]from the
water, He saw the heavens [2]parting and
the Spirit [b]descending upon Him like a
dove. 11Then a voice came from heaven,
[a]"You are My beloved Son, in whom I am
well pleased."

Let us take Jesus for our pattern and example and see no man, save Jesus only.

MARIA WOODWORTH-ETTER

Satan Tempts Jesus

12[a]Immediately the Spirit [1]drove Him
into the wilderness. 13And He was there in
the wilderness forty days, tempted by Satan, and was with the wild beasts; [a]and the
angels ministered to Him.

Jesus Begins His Galilean Ministry

14[a]Now after John was put in prison,
Jesus came to Galilee, [b]preaching the gospel [1]of the kingdom of God, 15and saying,
[a]"The time is fulfilled, and [b]the kingdom
of God [1]is at hand. Repent, and believe in
the gospel."

Four Fishermen Called as Disciples

16[a]And as He walked by the Sea of Galilee, He saw Simon and Andrew his
brother casting a net into the sea; for they
were fishermen. 17Then Jesus said to
them, "Follow Me, and I will make you
become [a]fishers of men." 18[a]They immediately left their nets and followed Him.

Lord Jesus, I pray that ______ will follow You as Your disciples did, that they, too, would become fishers of men.

FROM MARK 1:17

19When He had gone a little farther
from there, He saw James the *son* of Zebedee, and John his brother, who also *were*
in the boat mending their nets. 20And immediately He called them, and they left
their father Zebedee in the boat with the
hired servants, and went after Him.

Jesus Casts Out an Unclean Spirit

21[a]Then they went into Capernaum,
and immediately on the Sabbath He entered the [b]synagogue and taught. 22[a]And
they were astonished at His teaching, for
He taught them as one having authority,
and not as the scribes.
23Now there was a man in their synagogue with an [a]unclean spirit. And he

CHAPTER 1
1 a Luke 3:22 b Matt. 14:33
2 a Mal. 3:1 1 NU *Isaiah the prophet*
3 a Is. 40:3
4 a Matt. 3:1 1 *Or because of forgiveness*
5 a Matt. 3:5
6 a Matt. 3:4
7 a John 1:27
8 a Acts 1:5; 11:16 b Is. 44:3
9 a Matt. 3:13–17
10 a Matt. 3:16 b Acts 10:38 1 NU *out of* 2 *torn open*
11 a Matt. 3:17; 12:18
12 a Matt. 4:1–11 1 *sent Him out*
13 a Matt. 4:10, 11
14 a Matt. 4:12 b Matt. 4:23 1 NU omits *of the kingdom*
15 a [Gal. 4:4] b Matt. 3:2; 4:17 1 *has drawn near*
16 a Luke 5:2–11
17 a Matt. 13:47, 48
18 a [Luke 14:26]
21 a Luke 4:31–37 b Matt. 4:23
22 a Matt. 7:28, 29; 13:54
23 a [Matt. 12:43]

cried out, 24 saying, "Let *us* alone! [a]What have we to do with You, Jesus of Nazareth? Did You come to destroy us? I [b]know who You are—the [c]Holy One of God!"

25 But Jesus [a]rebuked him, saying, [1]"Be quiet, and come out of him!" 26 And when the unclean spirit [a]had convulsed him and cried out with a loud voice, he came out of him. 27 Then they were all amazed, so that they questioned among themselves, saying, [1]"What is this? What new [2]doctrine *is* this? For with authority He commands even the unclean spirits, and they obey Him." 28 And immediately His [a]fame spread throughout all the region around Galilee.

Peter's Mother-in-Law Healed

29 [a]Now as soon as they had come out of the synagogue, they entered the house of Simon and Andrew, with James and John. 30 But Simon's wife's mother lay sick with a fever, and they told Him about her at once. 31 So He came and took her by the hand and lifted her up, and immediately the fever left her. And she served them.

Many Healed After Sabbath Sunset

32 [a]At evening, when the sun had set, they brought to Him all who were sick and those who were demon-possessed. 33 And the whole city was gathered together at the door. 34 Then He healed many who were sick with various diseases, and [a]cast out many demons; and He [b]did not allow the demons to speak, because they knew Him.

Preaching in Galilee

35 Now [a]in the morning, having risen a long while before daylight, He went out and departed to a [1]solitary place; and there He [b]prayed. 36 And Simon and those *who were* with Him searched for Him. 37 When they found Him, they said to Him, [a]"Everyone [b]is looking for You."

38 But He said to them, [a]"Let us go into the next towns, that I may preach there also, because [b]for this purpose I have come forth."

39 [a]And He was preaching in their synagogues throughout all Galilee, and [b]casting out demons.

Jesus Cleanses a Leper

40 [a]Now a leper came to Him, imploring Him, kneeling down to Him and saying to Him, "If You are willing, You can make me clean."

41 Then Jesus, moved with [a]compassion, stretched out *His* hand and touched him, and said to him, "I am willing; be cleansed." 42 As soon as He had spoken, [a]immediately the leprosy left him, and he was cleansed. 43 And He strictly warned him and sent him away at once, 44 and said to him, "See that you say nothing to anyone; but go your way, show yourself to the priest, and offer for your cleansing those things [a]which Moses commanded, as a testimony to them."

45 [a]However, he went out and began to proclaim *it* freely, and to spread the matter, so that Jesus could no longer openly enter the city, but was outside in deserted places; [b]and they came to Him from every direction.

Jesus Forgives and Heals a Paralytic

2 And again [a]He entered Capernaum after *some* days, and it was heard that He was in the house. 2 [1]Immediately many gathered together, so that there was no longer room to receive *them*, not even near the door. And He preached the word to them. 3 Then they came to Him, bringing a [a]paralytic who was carried by four *men*. 4 And when they could not come near Him because of the crowd, they uncovered the roof where He was. So when they had broken through, they let down the bed on which the paralytic was lying.

5 When Jesus saw their faith, He said to

24 a Matt. 8:28, 29 b James 2:19 c Ps. 16:10
25 a [Luke 4:39] *1* Lit. *Be muzzled*
26 a Mark 9:20
27 *1* NU *What is this? A new doctrine with authority! He* *2 teaching*
28 a Matt. 4:24; 9:31
29 a Luke 4:38, 39
32 a Matt. 8:16, 17
34 a Luke 13:32 b Acts 16:17, 18
35 a Luke 4:42, 43 b Luke 5:16; 6:12; 9:28, 29 *1 deserted*
37 a John 3:26; 12:19 b [Heb. 11:6]
38 a Luke 4:43 b [Is. 61:1, 2]
39 a Matt. 4:23; 9:35 b Mark 5:8, 13; 7:29, 30
40 a Luke 5:12–14
41 a Luke 7:13
42 a Matt. 15:28
44 a Lev. 14:1–32
45 a Luke 5:15 b Mark 2:2, 13; 3:7

CHAPTER 2
1 a Matt. 9:1
2 *1* NU omits *Immediately*
3 a Matt. 4:24; 8:6

Jesus is the only Physician of souls; His blood the only salve that can heal a wounded conscience.

SUSANNA WESLEY

the paralytic, "Son, your sins are forgiven you."

6And some of the scribes were sitting there and reasoning in their hearts, 7"Why does this *Man* speak blasphemies like this? [a]Who can forgive sins but God alone?"

8But immediately, when Jesus perceived in His spirit that they reasoned thus within themselves, He said to them, "Why do you reason about these things in your hearts? 9[a]Which is easier, to say to the paralytic, '*Your* sins are forgiven you,' or to say, 'Arise, take up your bed and walk'? 10But that you may know that the Son of Man has [1]power on earth to forgive sins"—He said to the paralytic, 11"I say to you, arise, take up your bed, and go to your house." 12Immediately he arose, took up the bed, and went out in the presence of them all, so that all were amazed and [a]glorified God, saying, "We never saw *anything* like this!"

Lord Jesus, may I know that You, the Son of Man, have power to forgive sins.
FROM MARK 2:10

Matthew the Tax Collector

13[a]Then He went out again by the sea; and all the multitude came to Him, and He taught them. 14[a]As He passed by, He saw Levi the *son* of Alphaeus sitting at the tax office. And He said to him, [b]"Follow Me." So he arose and [c]followed Him.

15[a]Now it happened, as He was dining in *Levi's* house, that many tax collectors and sinners also sat together with Jesus and His disciples; for there were many, and they followed Him. 16And when the scribes [1]and Pharisees saw Him eating with the tax collectors and sinners, they said to His disciples, "How *is it* that He eats and drinks with tax collectors and sinners?"

17When Jesus heard *it,* He said to them, [a]"Those who are well have no need of a physician, but those who are sick. I did not come to call *the* righteous, but sinners, [1]to repentance."

Jesus Is Questioned About Fasting

18[a]The disciples of John and of the Pharisees were fasting. Then they came and said to Him, "Why do the disciples of John and of the Pharisees fast, but Your disciples do not fast?"

19And Jesus said to them, "Can the [1]friends of the bridegroom fast while the bridegroom is with them? As long as they have the bridegroom with them they cannot fast. 20But the days will come when the bridegroom will be [a]taken away from them, and then they will fast in those days. 21No one sews a piece of unshrunk cloth on an old garment; or else the new piece pulls away from the old, and the tear is made worse. 22And no one puts new wine into old wineskins; or else the new wine bursts the wineskins, the wine is spilled, and the wineskins are ruined. But new wine must be put into new wineskins."

Jesus Is Lord of the Sabbath

23[a]Now it happened that He went through the grainfields on the Sabbath; and as they went His disciples began [b]to pluck the heads of grain. 24And the Pharisees said to Him, "Look, why do they do what is [a]not lawful on the Sabbath?"

25But He said to them, "Have you never read [a]what David did when he was in need and hungry, he and those with him: 26how he went into the house of God *in the days* of Abiathar the high priest, and ate the showbread, [a]which is not lawful to eat except for the priests, and also gave some to those who were with him?"

27And He said to them, "The Sabbath was made for man, and not man for the [a]Sabbath. 28Therefore [a]the Son of Man is also Lord of the Sabbath."

Healing on the Sabbath

3 And [a]He entered the synagogue again, and a man was there who had a withered hand. 2So they [a]watched Him closely, whether He would [b]heal him on the Sabbath, so that they might [1]accuse Him. 3And He said to the man who had the withered hand, [1]"Step forward." 4Then He said to them, "Is it lawful on the Sabbath to do good or to do evil, to save life or to kill?" But they kept silent. 5And when He had looked around at them with anger, being grieved by the [a]hardness of their

7 a Is. 43:25
9 a Matt. 9:5
10 1 *authority*
12 a [Phil. 2:11]
13 a Matt. 9:9
14 a Luke 5:27–32 b John 1:43; 12:26; 21:22 c Luke 18:28
15 a Matt. 9:10
16 1 NU *of the*
17 a Matt. 9:12, 13; 18:11 1 NU omits *to repentance*
18 a Luke 5:33–38
19 1 Lit. *sons of the bridechamber*
20 a Acts 1:9; 13:2, 3; 14:23
23 a Luke 6:1–5 b Deut. 23:25
24 a Ex. 20:10; 31:15
25 a 1 Sam. 21:1–6
26 a Lev. 24:5–9
27 a Deut. 5:14
28 a Matt. 12:8
CHAPTER 3
1 a Luke 6:6–11
2 a Luke 14:1; 20:20 b Luke 13:14 1 *bring charges against*
3 1 Lit. *Arise into the midst*
5 a Zech. 7:12

hearts, He said to the man, "Stretch out
your hand." And he stretched *it* out, and
his hand was restored [1]as whole as the
other. 6[a]Then the Pharisees went out and
immediately plotted with [b]the Herodians
against Him, how they might destroy
Him.

A Great Multitude Follows Jesus

7But Jesus withdrew with His disciples
to the sea. And a great multitude from
Galilee followed Him, [a]and from Judea
8and Jerusalem and Idumea and beyond
the Jordan; and those from Tyre and Sidon, a great multitude, when they heard
how [a]many things He was doing, came
to Him. 9So He told His disciples that a
small boat should be kept ready for Him
because of the multitude, lest they should
crush Him. 10For He healed [a]many, so
that as many as had afflictions pressed
about Him to [b]touch Him. 11[a]And the unclean spirits, whenever they saw Him, fell
down before Him and cried out, saying,
[b]"You are the Son of God." 12But [a]He
sternly warned them that they should not
make Him known.

The Twelve Apostles

13[a]And He went up on the mountain
and called to *Him* those He Himself wanted. And they came to Him. 14Then He appointed twelve, [1]that they might be with
Him and that He might send them out to
preach, 15and to have [1]power [2]to heal
sicknesses and to cast out demons: 16[1]Si-
mon, [a]to whom He gave the name Peter;
17James the *son* of Zebedee and John the
brother of James, to whom He gave the
name Boanerges, that is, "Sons of Thunder"; 18Andrew, Philip, Bartholomew,
Matthew, Thomas, James the *son* of Alphaeus, Thaddaeus, Simon the Cananite;
19and Judas Iscariot, who also betrayed
Him. And they went into a house.

A House Divided Cannot Stand

20Then the multitude came together
again, [a]so that they could not so much as
eat bread. 21But when His [a]own people
heard *about this,* they went out to lay
hold of Him, [b]for they said, "He is out of
His mind."
22And the scribes who came down from
Jerusalem said, [a]"He has Beelzebub," and,
"By the [b]ruler of the demons He casts out
demons."
23[a]So He called them to *Himself* and
said to them in parables: "How can Satan
cast out Satan? 24If a kingdom is divided
against itself, that kingdom cannot stand.
25And if a house is divided against itself,
that house cannot stand. 26And if Satan
has risen up against himself, and is divided, he cannot stand, but has an end. 27[a]No
one can enter a strong man's house and
plunder his goods, unless he first binds
the strong man. And then he will plunder
his house.

The Unpardonable Sin

28[a]"Assuredly, I say to you, all sins will
be forgiven the sons of men, and whatever
blasphemies they may utter; 29but he who
blasphemes against the Holy Spirit never
has forgiveness, but is subject to eternal
condemnation"— 30because they [a]said,
"He has an unclean spirit."

Jesus' Mother and Brothers Send for Him

31[a]Then His brothers and His mother
came, and standing outside they sent to
Him, calling Him. 32And a multitude was
sitting around Him; and they said to Him,
"Look, Your mother and Your brothers
[1]are outside seeking You."
33But He answered them, saying, "Who
is My mother, or My brothers?" 34And He
looked around in a circle at those who sat
about Him, and said, "Here are My mother
and My brothers! 35For whoever does the
[a]will of God is My brother and My sister
and mother."

The Parable of the Sower

4 And [a]again He began to teach by the
sea. And a great multitude was gathered to Him, so that He got into a boat
and sat *in it* on the sea; and the whole
multitude was on the land facing the sea.
2Then He taught them many things by
parables, [a]and said to them in His
teaching:
3"Listen! Behold, a sower went out to
sow. 4And it happened, as he sowed, *that*
some *seed* fell by the wayside; and the
birds [1]of the air came and devoured it.
5Some fell on stony ground, where it did
not have much earth; and immediately
it sprang up because it had no depth of
earth. 6But when the sun was up it was

---

5 [1]NU omits *as whole as the other*
6 [a]Mark 12:13 [b]Matt. 22:16
7 [a]Luke 6:17
8 [a]Mark 5:19
10 [a]Luke 7:21 [b]Matt. 9:21; 14:36
11 [a]Luke 4:41 [b]Matt. 8:29; 14:33
12 [a]Mark 1:25, 34
13 [a]Luke 9:1
14 [1]NU adds *whom He also named apostles*
15 [1]*authority* [2]NU omits *to heal sicknesses and*
16 [a]John 1:42 [1]NU *and He appointed the twelve: Simon . . .*
20 [a]Mark 6:31
21 [a]Mark 6:3 [b]John 7:5; 10:20
22 [a]Matt. 9:34; 10:25 [b][John 12:31; 14:30; 16:11]
23 [a]Matt. 12:25–29
27 [a][Is. 49:24, 25]
28 [a]Luke 12:10
30 [a]Matt. 9:34
31 [a]Matt. 12:46–50
32 [1]NU, M add *and Your sisters*
35 [a]Eph. 6:6
CHAPTER 4
1 [a]Luke 8:4–10
2 [a]Mark 12:38
4 [1]NU, M omit *of the air*

scorched, and because it had no root it
withered away. 7And some *seed* fell among
thorns; and the thorns grew up and
choked it, and it yielded no [1]crop. 8But
other *seed* fell on good ground and yielded a crop that sprang up, increased and
produced: some thirtyfold, some sixty,
and some a hundred."
9And He said [1]to them, "He who has
ears to hear, let him hear!"

The Purpose of Parables

10[a]But when He was alone, those
around Him with the twelve asked Him
about the parable. 11And He said to them,
"To you it has been given to [a]know the
[1]mystery of the kingdom of God; but to
[b]those who are outside, all things come in
parables, 12so that

[a]'Seeing they may see and not
perceive,
And hearing they may hear and not
understand;
Lest they should turn,
And their sins be forgiven them.' "

> *The devil is busy trying to take from us what we take from God, and so God bids us hold fast.*
>
> MRS. C. NUZUM

The Parable of the Sower Explained

13And He said to them, "Do you not understand this parable? How then will you
understand all the parables? 14[a]The sower
sows the word. 15And these are the ones
by the wayside where the word is sown.
When they hear, Satan comes immediately and takes away the word that was sown
in their hearts. 16These likewise are the
ones sown on stony ground who, when
they hear the word, immediately receive it
with gladness; 17and they have no root in
themselves, and so endure only for a time.
Afterward, when tribulation or persecution arises for the word's sake, immediately they stumble. 18Now these are the ones
sown among thorns; *they are* the ones
who hear the word, 19and the [a]cares of
this world, [b]the deceitfulness of riches,
and the desires for other things entering
in choke the word, and it becomes unfruitful. 20But these are the ones sown on
good ground, those who hear the word,
[1]accept *it,* and bear [a]fruit: some thirtyfold, some sixty, and some a hundred."

Light Under a Basket

21[a]Also He said to them, "Is a lamp
brought to be put under a basket or under
a bed? Is it not to be set on a lampstand?
22[a]For there is nothing hidden which will
not be revealed, nor has anything been
kept secret but that it should come to
light. 23[a]If anyone has ears to hear, let
him hear."
24Then He said to them, "Take heed
what you hear. [a]With the same measure
you use, it will be measured to you; and to
you who hear, more will be given. 25[a]For
whoever has, to him more will be given;
but whoever does not have, even what he
has will be taken away from him."

The Parable of the Growing Seed

26And He said, [a]"The kingdom of God is
as if a man should [1]scatter seed on the
ground, 27and should sleep by night and
rise by day, and the seed should sprout
and [a]grow, he himself does not know how.
28For the earth [a]yields crops by itself: first
the blade, then the head, after that the full
grain in the head. 29But when the grain
ripens, immediately [a]he puts in the sickle,
because the harvest has come."

The Parable of the Mustard Seed

30Then He said, [a]"To what shall we lik-
en the kingdom of God? Or with what
parable shall we picture it? 31*It is* like a
mustard seed which, when it is sown on
the ground, is smaller than all the seeds
on earth; 32but when it is sown, it grows
up and becomes greater than all herbs,
and shoots out large branches, so that the
birds of the air may nest under its shade."

Jesus' Use of Parables

33[a]And with many such parables He
spoke the word to them as they were able
to hear *it.* 34But without a parable He did
not speak to them. And when they were

7 [1] Lit. *fruit*
9 [1] NU, M omit *to them*
10 [a] Luke 8:9
11 [a] [1 Cor. 2:10–16] [b] [Col. 4:5] [1] *secret* or *hidden truths*
12 [a] Is. 6:9, 10; 43:8
14 [a] Matt. 13:18–23
19 [a] Luke 21:34 [b] 1 Tim. 6:9, 10, 17
20 [a] [Rom. 7:4] [1] *receive*
21 [a] Matt. 5:15
22 [a] Matt. 10:26, 27
23 [a] Matt. 11:15; 13:9, 43
24 [a] Matt. 7:2
25 [a] Luke 8:18; 19:26
26 [a] [Matt. 13:24–30, 36–43] [1] *sow*
27 [a] [2 Pet. 3:18]
28 [a] [John 12:24]
29 [a] Rev. 14:15
30 [a] Matt. 13:31, 32
33 [a] Matt. 13:34, 35

alone, [a]He explained all things to His disciples.

Wind and Wave Obey Jesus

35 [a]On the same day, when evening had
come, He said to them, "Let us cross over
to the other side." 36 Now when they had
left the multitude, they took Him along in
the boat as He was. And other little boats
were also with Him. 37 And a great windstorm arose, and the waves beat into the
boat, so that it was already filling. 38 But
He was in the stern, asleep on a pillow.
And they awoke Him and said to Him,
[a]"Teacher, [b]do You not care that we are
perishing?"

The prayer of faith shuts or opens heaven.

LADY MAXWELL OF EDINBURGH

39 Then He arose and [a]rebuked the
wind, and said to the sea, [b]"Peace,[1] be
still!" And the wind ceased and there was
a great calm. 40 But He said to them, "Why
are you so fearful? [a]How[1] *is it* that you
have no faith?" 41 And they feared exceedingly, and said to one another, "Who can
this be, that even the wind and the sea
obey Him!"

A Demon-Possessed Man Healed

5 Then [a]they came to the other side of
the sea, to the country of the [1]Gada-
renes. 2 And when He had come out of the
boat, immediately there met Him out of
the tombs a man with an [a]unclean spirit,
3 who had *his* dwelling among the tombs;
and no one could bind [1]him, not even
with chains, 4 because he had often been
bound with shackles and chains. And the
chains had been pulled apart by him, and
the shackles broken in pieces; neither
could anyone tame him. 5 And always,
night and day, he was in the mountains
and in the tombs, crying out and cutting
himself with stones.

6 When he saw Jesus from afar, he ran
and worshiped Him. 7 And he cried out
with a loud voice and said, "What have I
to do with You, Jesus, Son of the Most
High God? I [a]implore[1] You by God that
You do not torment me."
8 For He said to him, [a]"Come out of the
man, unclean spirit!" 9 Then He asked
him, "What *is* your name?"

And he answered, saying, "My name *is*
Legion; for we are many." 10 Also he
begged Him earnestly that He would not
send them out of the country.
11 Now a large herd of [a]swine was feeding there near the mountains. 12 So all the
demons begged Him, saying, "Send us to
the swine, that we may enter them."
13 And [1]at once Jesus gave them permission. Then the unclean spirits went out
and entered the swine (there were about
two thousand); and the herd ran violently
down the steep place into the sea, and
drowned in the sea.
14 So those who fed the swine fled, and
they told *it* in the city and in the country.
And they went out to see what it was that
had happened. 15 Then they came to Jesus,
and saw the one *who had been* [a]demon-
possessed and had the legion, [b]sitting and
[c]clothed and in his right mind. And they
were afraid. 16 And those who saw it told
them how it happened to him *who had
been* demon-possessed, and about the
swine. 17 Then [a]they began to plead with
Him to depart from their region.
18 And when He got into the boat, [a]he
who had been demon-possessed begged
Him that he might be with Him. 19 However, Jesus did not permit him, but said to
him, "Go home to your friends, and tell
them what great things the Lord has done
for you, and how He has had compassion
on you." 20 And he departed and began to
[a]proclaim in [1]Decapolis all that Jesus had
done for him; and all [b]marveled.

A Girl Restored to Life and a Woman Healed

21 [a]Now when Jesus had crossed over
again by boat to the other side, a great
multitude gathered to Him; and He was
by the sea. 22 [a]And behold, one of the rulers of the synagogue came, Jairus by
name. And when he saw Him, he fell at
His feet 23 and begged Him earnestly, saying, "My little daughter lies at the point of

34 a Luke 24:27, 45
35 a Luke 8:22, 25
38 a [Matt. 23:8–10] b Ps. 44:23
39 a Luke 4:39 b Ps. 65:7; 89:9; 93:4; 104:6, 7 1 Lit. *Be quiet*
40 a Matt. 14:31, 32 1 NU *Have you still no faith?*

CHAPTER 5
1 a Matt. 8:28–34 1 NU *Gerasenes*
2 a Mark 1:23; 7:25
3 1 NU adds *anymore*
7 a Acts 19:13 1 *adjure*
8 a Mark 1:25; 9:25
11 a Deut. 14:8
13 1 NU *He gave*
15 a Matt. 4:24; 8:16 b Luke 10:39 c [Is. 61:10]
17 a Acts 16:39
18 a Luke 8:38, 39
20 a Ps. 66:16 b Matt. 9:8, 33 1 Lit. *Ten Cities*
21 a Luke 8:40
22 a Matt. 9:18–26

death. Come and [a]lay Your hands on her,
that she may be healed, and she will live."
24So *Jesus* went with him, and a great
multitude followed Him and thronged
Him.

25Now a certain woman [a]had a flow of
blood for twelve years, 26and had suffered
many things from many physicians. She
had spent all that she had and was no better, but rather grew worse. 27When she
heard about Jesus, she came behind *Him*
in the crowd and [a]touched His garment.
28For she said, "If only I may touch His
clothes, I shall be made well."

29Immediately the fountain of her
blood was dried up, and she felt in *her*
body that she was healed of the [1]affliction.
30And Jesus, immediately knowing in
Himself that [a]power had gone out of Him,
turned around in the crowd and said,
"Who touched My clothes?"

31But His disciples said to Him, "You
see the multitude thronging You, and You
say, 'Who touched Me?' "

32And He looked around to see her who
had done this thing. 33But the woman,
[a]fearing and trembling, knowing what
had happened to her, came and fell down
before Him and told Him the whole truth.
34And He said to her, "Daughter, [a]your
faith has made you well. [b]Go in peace, and
be healed of your affliction."

35[a]While He was still speaking, *some*
came from the ruler of the synagogue's
house who said, "Your daughter is dead.
Why trouble the Teacher any further?"

36As soon as Jesus heard the word that
was spoken, He said to the ruler of the
synagogue, "Do not be afraid; only [a]be-
lieve." 37And He permitted no one to follow Him except Peter, James, and John
the brother of James. 38Then He came to

23 a Acts 9:17; 28:8
25 a Lev. 15:19, 25
27 a Matt. 14:35, 36
29 1 *suffering*
30 a Luke 6:19; 8:46
33 a [Ps. 89:7]
34 a Matt. 9:22 b Luke 7:50; 8:48
35 a Luke 8:49
36 a [John 11:40]

The Woman with the Flow of Blood

Discouragement can set in when a person has been ill for twelve years. And after twelve years of hemorrhaging, the woman in Mark 5 was probably tired of seeing doctors and not interested in playing games. She needed a miracle, and she did not let her likely discouragement keep her from going after it. Mark 5:27 reports that "when she heard about Jesus" she started toward Him. She didn't question, didn't doubt, but responded immediately and with simple, but profound, faith.

Jesus was in the midst of a multitude of people, and the woman had to make an effort to get to Him. He had not stopped and summoned her, but she had to press through the crowd and make her way to Him. She approached Him from behind—not shouting His name, not demanding His attention, not requiring anything at all of Him—only of herself, to simply touch His clothes.

Jesus knew instantly when healing power had gone out of Him, and He wanted to know who had been healed. The woman was terrified, but overcame her fear, "fell down before Him and told Him the whole truth" (Mark 5:33). He commended her for her faith, declaring that it had been the force that made her well, wished her peace, and sent her on her way—completely healed for the first time in twelve years.

Maybe this woman knew what her destiny was. Maybe she didn't. But she did know that it was not to keep bleeding indefinitely, and she recognized her moment for a miracle and that Jesus could do one for her. May we, too, possess the simple faith for miracles, and may we press through every obstacle to get to Jesus, the Miracle-worker.

the house of the ruler of the synagogue, and saw [1]a tumult and those who [a]wept and wailed loudly. 39When He came in, He said to them, "Why make this commotion and weep? The child is not dead, but [a]sleeping."

Lord, may _____ not be afraid, but only believe.

FROM MARK 5:36

40And they ridiculed Him. [a]But when He had put them all outside, He took the father and the mother of the child, and those *who were* with Him, and entered where the child was lying. 41Then He took the child by the hand, and said to her, "Talitha, cumi," which is translated, "Little girl, I say to you, arise." 42Immediately the girl arose and walked, for she was twelve years *of age.* And they were [a]overcome with great amazement. 43But [a]He commanded them strictly that no one should know it, and said that *something* should be given her to eat.

Jesus Rejected at Nazareth

6 Then [a]He went out from there and came to His own country, and His disciples followed Him. 2And when the Sabbath had come, He began to teach in the synagogue. And many hearing *Him* were [a]astonished, saying, [b]"Where *did* this Man *get* these things? And what wisdom *is* this which is given to Him, that such mighty works are performed by His hands! 3Is this not the carpenter, the Son of Mary, and [a]brother of James, Joses, Judas, and Simon? And are not His sisters here with us?" So they [b]were offended at Him.

4But Jesus said to them, [a]"A prophet is not without honor except in his own country, among his own relatives, and in his own house." 5[a]Now He could do no mighty work there, except that He laid His hands on a few sick people and healed *them.* 6And [a]He marveled because of their unbelief. [b]Then He went about the villages in a circuit, teaching.

Sending Out the Twelve

7[a]And He called the twelve to *Himself,* and began to send them out [b]two *by* two, and gave them power over unclean spirits. 8He commanded them to take nothing for the journey except a staff—no bag, no bread, no copper in *their* money belts—9but [a]to wear sandals, and not to put on two tunics.

10[a]Also He said to them, "In whatever place you enter a house, stay there till you depart from that place. 11[a]And [1]whoever will not receive you nor hear you, when you depart from there, [b]shake off the dust under your feet as a testimony against them. [2]Assuredly, I say to you, it will be more tolerable for Sodom and Gomorrah in the day of judgment than for that city!"

12So they went out and preached that *people* should repent. 13And they cast out many demons, [a]and anointed with oil many who were sick, and healed *them.*

John the Baptist Beheaded

14[a]Now King Herod heard *of Him,* for His name had become well known. And he said, "John the Baptist is risen from the dead, and therefore [b]these powers are at work in him."

15[a]Others said, "It is Elijah."

And others said, "It is [1]the Prophet, [b]or like one of the prophets."

16[a]But when Herod heard, he said, "This is John, whom I beheaded; he has been raised from the dead!" 17For Herod himself had sent and laid hold of John, and bound him in prison for the sake of Herodias, his brother Philip's wife; for he had married her. 18Because John had said to Herod, [a]"It is not lawful for you to have your brother's wife."

19Therefore Herodias [1]held it against him and wanted to kill him, but she could not; 20for Herod [a]feared John, knowing that he *was* a just and holy man, and he protected him. And when he heard him, he [1]did many things, and heard him gladly.

21[a]Then an opportune day came when Herod [b]on his birthday gave a feast for his nobles, the high officers, and the chief *men* of Galilee. 22And when Herodias' daughter herself came in and danced, and pleased Herod and those who sat with him, the king said to the girl, "Ask me whatever you want, and I will give *it* to you." 23He also swore to her, [a]"Whatever you ask me, I will give you, up to half my kingdom."

24So she went out and said to her mother, "What shall I ask?"

38 [a] Acts 9:39 *[1] an uproar*
39 [a] John 11:4, 11
40 [a] Acts 9:40
42 [a] Mark 1:27; 7:37
43 [a] [Matt. 8:4; 12:16–19; 17:9]

CHAPTER 6
1 [a] Matt. 13:54
2 [a] Matt. 7:28 [b] John 6:42
3 [a] Matt. 12:46 [b] [Matt. 11:6]
4 [a] John 4:44
5 [a] Gen. 19:22; 32:25
6 [a] Is. 59:16 [b] Matt. 9:35
7 [a] Mark 3:13, 14 [b] [Eccl. 4:9, 10]
9 [a] [Eph. 6:15]
10 [a] Matt. 10:11
11 [a] Matt. 10:14 [b] Acts 13:51; 18:6 [1] NU *whatever place* [2] NU omits the rest of v. 11.
13 [a] [James 5:14]
14 [a] Luke 9:7–9 [b] Luke 19:37
15 [a] Mark 8:28 [b] Matt. 21:11 [1] NU, M *a prophet, like one*
16 [a] Luke 3:19
18 [a] Lev. 18:16; 20:21
19 *[1] held a grudge*
20 [a] Matt. 14:5; 21:26 [1] NU *was very perplexed, yet*
21 [a] Matt. 14:6 [b] Gen. 40:20
23 [a] Esth. 5:3, 6; 7:2

And she said, "The head of John the
Baptist!"
25 Immediately she came in with haste
to the king and asked, saying, "I want you
to give me at once the head of John the
Baptist on a platter."
26 [a]And the king was exceedingly sorry;
yet, because of the oaths and because of
those who sat with him, he did not want
to refuse her. 27 Immediately the king sent
an executioner and commanded his head
to be brought. And he went and beheaded
him in prison, 28 brought his head on a
platter, and gave it to the girl; and the girl
gave it to her mother. 29 When his disciples heard *of it,* they came and [a]took away
his corpse and laid it in a tomb.

Feeding the Five Thousand

30 [a]Then the apostles gathered to Jesus
and told Him all things, both what they
had done and what they had taught.
31 [a]And He said to them, "Come aside by
yourselves to a deserted place and rest a
while." For [b]there were many coming and
going, and they did not even have time to
eat. 32 [a]So they departed to a deserted
place in the boat by themselves.
33 But [1]the multitudes saw them departing, and many [a]knew Him and ran there
on foot from all the cities. They arrived
before them and came together to Him.
34 [a]And Jesus, when He came out, saw a
great multitude and was moved with compassion for them, because they were like
[b]sheep not having a shepherd. So [c]He began to teach them many things. 35 [a]When
the day was now far spent, His disciples
came to Him and said, "This is a deserted
place, and already the hour *is* late. 36 Send
them away, that they may go into the surrounding country and villages and buy
themselves [1]bread; for they have nothing
to eat."
37 But He answered and said to them,
"You give them something to eat."
And they said to Him, [a]"Shall we go and
buy two hundred denarii worth of bread
and give them *something* to eat?"
38 But He said to them, "How many
loaves do you have? Go and see."
And when they found out they said,
[a]"Five, and two fish."
39 Then He [a]commanded them to make
them all sit down in groups on the green
grass. 40 So they sat down in ranks, in hundreds and in fifties. 41 And when He had
taken the five loaves and the two fish, He
[a]looked up to heaven, [b]blessed and broke
the loaves, and gave *them* to His disciples
to set before them; and the two fish He
divided among *them* all. 42 So they all ate
and were filled. 43 And they took up twelve
baskets full of fragments and of the fish.
44 Now those who had eaten the loaves
were [1]about five thousand men.

Jesus Walks on the Sea

45 [a]Immediately He [1]made His disciples
get into the boat and go before Him to the
other side, to Bethsaida, while He sent the
multitude away. 46 And when He had sent
them away, He [a]departed to the mountain
to pray. 47 Now when evening came, the
boat was in the middle of the sea; and He
was alone on the land. 48 Then He saw
them straining at rowing, for the wind
was against them. Now about the fourth
watch of the night He came to them,
walking on the sea, and [a]would have
passed them by. 49 And when they saw Him
walking on the sea, they supposed it was
a [a]ghost, and cried out; 50 for they all saw
Him and were troubled. But immediately
He talked with them and said to them,
[a]"Be[1] of good cheer! It is I; do not be
[b]afraid." 51 Then He went up into the boat
to them, and the wind [a]ceased. And they
were greatly [b]amazed in themselves beyond measure, and marveled. 52 For [a]they
had not understood about the loaves, because their [b]heart was hardened.

Many Touch Him and Are Made Well

53 [a]When they had crossed over, they
came to the land of Gennesaret and anchored there. 54 And when they came out
of the boat, immediately [1]the people recognized Him, 55 ran through that whole
surrounding region, and began to carry
about on beds those who were sick to
wherever they heard He was. 56 Wherever
He entered, into villages, cities, or the
country, they laid the sick in the marketplaces, and begged Him that [a]they might
just touch the [b]hem of His garment. And
as many as touched Him were made well.

Defilement Comes from Within

7 Then [a]the Pharisees and some of the
scribes came together to Him, having
come from Jerusalem. 2 Now [1]when they
saw some of His disciples eat bread with
defiled, that is, with [a]unwashed hands,

26 a Matt. 14:9
29 a 1 Kin. 13:29, 30
30 a Luke 9:10
31 a Matt. 14:13 b Mark 3:20
32 a Matt. 14:13–21
33 a [Col. 1:6] 1 NU, M *they*
34 a Matt. 9:36; 14:14 b Num. 27:17 c Luke 9:11
35 a Matt. 14:15
36 1 NU *something to eat* and omits the rest of v. 36.
37 a 2 Kin. 4:43
38 a John 6:9
39 a Matt. 15:35
41 a John 11:41, 42 b Matt. 15:36; 26:26
44 1 NU, M omit *about*
45 a John 6:15–21 1 *invited, strongly urged*
46 a Luke 5:16
48 a Luke 24:28
49 a Matt. 14:26
50 a Matt. 9:2 b Is. 41:10 1 *Take courage*
51 a Ps. 107:29 b Mark 1:27; 2:12; 5:42; 7:37
52 a Mark 8:17, 18 b Mark 3:5; 16:14
53 a Matt. 14:34–36
54 1 Lit. *they*
56 a Matt. 9:20 b Num. 15:38, 39

CHAPTER 7
1 a Matt. 15:1–20
2 a Matt. 15:20 1 NU omits *when*

Mark 6:31

Dear Woman of Destiny,

If you're feeling overwhelmed today, you're not alone. There were times when even Jesus had had it. Once He said to His disciples, "Let's get away from the crowds for a while and rest" (Mark 6:31, author's paraphrase).

Jesus had been traveling around the area of His hometown of Nazareth and on to the surrounding villages. After teaching His disciples how to minister, He sent them out on their first ministry tour. At the same time, Jesus received the tragic news that John the Baptist—His cousin, friend, and the man who had really introduced Him to His earthly ministry—was beheaded. But Jesus' personal need for privacy to grieve His cousin's death did not keep the people away. They continued to come from all over with their own unmet needs.

Women often are caught in similar circumstances. We have the responsibility of teaching our children, nurturing our marriage, leading a ladies' Bible study or prayer group, trying to be the Proverbs 31 woman of faith, managing the finances, and being a friendly neighbor. In the midst of all this, aging parents need care and attention, and we become drained emotionally, physically, and spiritually. Your world is crashing in on you, and nobody seems to notice or care.

Then Jesus' loving voice comes to you and gently says, "Let's get away, just you and Me, and get some rest." What a welcome invitation!

"But no," you object, "I would feel too guilty leaving all those who are depending on me to keep the wheels in motion. It couldn't be Jesus saying this; it must be the devil or my flesh! Get thee behind me, Satan!"

But that "still small voice" (1 Kin. 19:12) persists, telling us to take time to sit at Jesus' feet, to be restored. Jesus cares about our bodies. He desires to bring balance to our emotions, to show us His priorities. He wants to restore our souls as the psalmist mentions in Psalm 23:3.

As I meditate on His Word and listen to His voice, I become quiet in my spirit. Then I am able to resume my activities, as Jesus did. After He had rested, He crossed the lake, stepped out of the boat, taught the people, and fed the hungry.

Taking a break is not a waste of time; it is a time for refueling. If you wait too long and get too run down, recovery takes longer. Listen the first time Jesus says to you, "Let's get away together and take a rest." It might be for a few moments, hours, or days; but during that time, the Holy Spirit will impart to you energy, life, and strength.

Look out, devil, here I come in the name of Jesus—anointed, empowered, and ready to do His will!

Betty Thiessen

[2]they found fault. [3]For the Pharisees and
all the Jews do not eat unless they wash
their hands [1]in a special way, holding the
[a]tradition of the elders. [4]*When they come*
from the marketplace, they do not eat unless they wash. And there are many other
things which they have received and hold,
like the washing of cups, pitchers, copper
vessels, and couches.
[5][a]Then the Pharisees and scribes asked
Him, "Why do Your disciples not walk according to the tradition of the elders, but
eat bread with unwashed hands?"
[6]He answered and said to them, "Well
did Isaiah prophesy of you [a]hypocrites, as
it is written:

[b]*'This people honors Me with their*
lips,
But their heart is far from Me.
7 *And in vain they worship Me,*
Teaching as doctrines the
commandments of men.'

[8]For laying aside the commandment of
God, you hold the tradition of men—[1]the
washing of pitchers and cups, and many
other such things you do."
[9]He said to them, "*All too* well [a]you [1]re-
ject the commandment of God, that you
may keep your tradition. [10]For Moses said,
[a]*'Honor your father and your mother'*;
and, [b]*'He who curses father or mother, let*
him be put to death.' [11]But you say, 'If a
man says to his father or mother, [a]"Whatever profit you might have received from
me *is* Corban"—' (that is, a gift *to God*),
[12]then you no longer let him do anything
for his father or his mother, [13]making the
word of God of no effect through your tradition which you have handed down. And
many such things you do."
[14][a]When He had called all the multitude to *Himself,* He said to them, "Hear
Me, everyone, and [b]understand: [15]There is
nothing that enters a man from outside
which can defile him; but the things
which come out of him, those are the
things that [a]defile a man. [16][a]If[1] anyone
has ears to hear, let him hear!"
[17][a]When He had entered a house away
from the crowd, His disciples asked Him
concerning the parable. [18]So He said to
them, [a]"Are you thus without understanding also? Do you not perceive that
whatever enters a man from outside cannot defile him, [19]because it does not enter
his heart but his stomach, and is eliminated, [1]*thus* purifying all foods?" [20]And He
said, [a]"What comes out of a man, that defiles a man. [21][a]For from within, out of the
heart of men, [b]proceed evil thoughts,
[c]adulteries, [d]fornications, murders,
[22]thefts, [a]covetousness, wickedness, [b]de-
ceit, [c]lewdness, an evil eye, [d]blasphemy,
[e]pride, foolishness. [23]All these evil things
come from within and defile a man."

> *O let those who believe in God's precious truths hold fast to the profession of their faith, not doubt His Word, put away all fear, lay aside all preconceived opinions, all traditions that have warped the mind, and believe the whole gospel!*
>
> MRS. EDWARD MIX

A Gentile Shows Her Faith

[24][a]From there He arose and went to the
region of Tyre [1]and Sidon. And He entered a house and wanted no one to know
it, but He could not be [b]hidden. [25]For a
woman whose young daughter had an unclean spirit heard about Him, and she
came and [a]fell at His feet. [26]The woman
was a [1]Greek, a [2]Syro-Phoenician by
birth, and she kept [3]asking Him to cast
the demon out of her daughter. [27]But Jesus said to her, "Let the children be filled
first, for it is not good to take the children's bread and throw *it* to the little
dogs."
[28]And she answered and said to Him,
"Yes, Lord, yet even the little dogs under
the table eat from the children's crumbs."
[29]Then He said to her, "For this saying
go your way; the demon has gone out of
your daughter."
[30]And when she had come to her house,
she found the demon gone out, and her
daughter lying on the bed.

Jesus Heals a Deaf-Mute

[31][a]Again, departing from the region of
Tyre and Sidon, He came through the

---

2 [2] NU omits *they found fault*
3 a Gal. 1:14 · [1] Lit. *with the fist*
5 a Matt. 15:2
6 a Matt. 23:13–29 · b Is. 29:13
8 [1] NU omits the rest of v. 8.
9 a Prov. 1:25 · [1] *set aside*
10 a Ex. 20:12; Deut. 5:16 · b Ex. 21:17
11 a Matt. 15:5; 23:18
14 a Matt. 15:10 · b Matt. 16:9, 11, 12
15 a Is. 59:3
16 a Matt. 11:15 · [1] NU omits v. 16.
17 a Matt. 15:15
18 a [Heb. 5:11–14]
19 [1] NU sets off the final phrase as Mark's comment that Jesus has declared all foods clean.
20 a Ps. 39:1
21 a Gen. 6:5; 8:21 · b [Gal. 5:19–21] · c 2 Pet. 2:14 · d 1 Thess. 4:3
22 a Luke 12:15 · b Rom. 1:28, 29 · c 1 Pet. 4:3 · d Rev. 2:9 · e 1 John 2:16
24 a Matt. 15:21 · b Mark 2:1, 2 · [1] NU omits *and Sidon*
25 a John 11:32
26 [1] *Gentile* · [2] A Syrian of Phoenicia · [3] *begging*
31 a Matt. 15:29

midst of the region of Decapolis to the Sea
of Galilee. 32 Then [a]they brought to Him
one who was deaf and had an impediment
in his speech, and they begged Him to put
His hand on him. 33 And He took him aside
from the multitude, and put His fingers in
his ears, and [a]He spat and touched his
tongue. 34 Then, [a]looking up to heaven,
[b]He sighed, and said to him, "Ephphatha,"
that is, "Be opened."
35 [a]Immediately his ears were opened,
and the [1]impediment of his tongue was
loosed, and he spoke plainly. 36 Then [a]He
commanded them that they should tell no
one; but the more He commanded them,
the more widely they proclaimed *it.* 37 And
they were [a]astonished beyond measure,
saying, "He has done all things well. He
[b]makes both the deaf to hear and the
mute to speak."

Feeding the Four Thousand

8 In those days, [a]the multitude being
very great and having nothing to eat,
Jesus called His disciples *to Him* and said
to them, 2 "I have [a]compassion on the
multitude, because they have now continued with Me three days and have nothing
to eat. 3 And if I send them away hungry to
their own houses, they will faint on the
way; for some of them have come from
afar."
4 Then His disciples answered Him,
"How can one satisfy these people with
bread here in the wilderness?"
5 [a]He asked them, "How many loaves do
you have?"
And they said, "Seven."
6 So He commanded the multitude to
sit down on the ground. And He took the
seven loaves and gave thanks, broke *them*
and gave *them* to His disciples to set before *them;* and they set *them* before the
multitude. 7 They also had a few small fish;
and [a]having blessed them, He said to set
them also before *them.* 8 So they ate and
were filled, and they took up seven large
baskets of leftover fragments. 9 Now those
who had eaten were about four thousand.
And He sent them away, 10 [a]immediately
got into the boat with His disciples, and
came to the region of Dalmanutha.

The Pharisees Seek a Sign

11 [a]Then the Pharisees came out and began to dispute with Him, seeking from
Him a sign from heaven, testing Him.
12 But He [a]sighed deeply in His spirit, and
said, "Why does this generation seek a
sign? Assuredly, I say to you, [b]no sign
shall be given to this generation."

Beware of the Leaven of the Pharisees and Herod

13 And He left them, and getting into the
boat again, departed to the other side.
14 [a]Now [1]the disciples had forgotten to
take bread, and they did not have more
than one loaf with them in the boat.
15 [a]Then He charged them, saying, "Take
heed, beware of the [1]leaven of the Pharisees and the leaven of Herod."
16 And they reasoned among themselves, saying, "*It is* because we have no
bread."
17 But Jesus, being aware of *it,* said to
them, "Why do you reason because you
have no bread? [a]Do you not yet perceive
nor understand? Is your heart [1]still hardened? 18 Having eyes, do you not see? And
having ears, do you not hear? And do you
not remember? 19 [a]When I broke the five
loaves for the five thousand, how many
baskets full of fragments did you take up?"
They said to Him, "Twelve."
20 "Also, [a]when I broke the seven for the
four thousand, how many large baskets
full of fragments did you take up?"
And they said, "Seven."
21 So He said to them, "How *is it* [a]you do
not understand?"

A Blind Man Healed at Bethsaida

22 Then He came to Bethsaida; and they
brought a [a]blind man to Him, and begged
Him to [b]touch him. 23 So He took the
blind man by the hand and led him out of
the town. And when [a]He had spit on his
eyes and put His hands on him, He asked
him if he saw anything.
24 And he looked up and said, "I see men
like trees, walking."
25 Then He put *His* hands on his eyes
again and made him look up. And he was
restored and saw everyone clearly. 26 Then
He sent him away to his house, saying,
[1]"Neither go into the town, [a]nor tell anyone in the town."

Peter Confesses Jesus as the Christ

27 [a]Now Jesus and His disciples went
out to the towns of Caesarea Philippi; and

---

32 a Luke 11:14
33 a Mark 8:23
34 a Mark 6:41 b John 11:33, 38
35 a Is. 35:5, 6 *1 Lit. bond*
36 a Mark 5:43
37 a Mark 6:51; 10:26 b Matt. 12:22

CHAPTER 8
1 a Matt. 15:32–39
2 a Mark 1:41; 6:34
5 a Mark 6:38
7 a Matt. 14:19
10 a Matt. 15:39
11 a Matt. 12:38; 16:1
12 a Mark 7:34 b Matt. 12:39
14 a Matt. 16:5 *1 NU, M they*
15 a Luke 12:1 *1 yeast*
17 a Mark 6:52; 16:14 *1 NU omits still*
19 a Matt. 14:20
20 a Matt. 15:37
21 a [Mark 6:52]
22 a John 9:1 b Luke 18:15
23 a Mark 7:33
26 a Mark 5:43; 7:36 *1 NU "Do not even go into the town."*
27 a Luke 9:18–20

on the road He asked His disciples, saying
to them, "Who do men say that I am?"
28So they answered, [a]"John the Baptist;
but some *say,* [b]Elijah; and others, one of
the prophets."

We know God only by Jesus Christ. All those who have claimed to know God, and to prove Him without Jesus Christ, have only weak proofs.

BLAISE PASCAL

29He said to them, "But who do you say
that I am?"
Peter answered and said to Him, [a]"You
are the Christ."
30[a]Then He strictly warned them that
they should tell no one about Him.

Jesus Predicts His Death and Resurrection

31And [a]He began to teach them that the
Son of Man must suffer many things, and
be [b]rejected by the elders and chief priests
and scribes, and be [c]killed, and after three
days rise again. 32He spoke this word
openly. Then Peter took Him aside and
began to rebuke Him. 33But when He had
turned around and looked at His disciples,
He [a]rebuked Peter, saying, "Get behind
Me, Satan! For you are not [1]mindful of
the things of God, but the things of men."

Take Up the Cross and Follow Him

34When He had called the people to
Himself, with His disciples also, He said to
them, [a]"Whoever desires to come after
Me, let him deny himself, and take up his
cross, and follow Me. 35For [a]whoever desires to save his life will lose it, but whoever loses his life for My sake and the
gospel's will save it. 36For what will it
profit a man if he gains the whole world,
and loses his own soul? 37Or what will a
man give in exchange for his soul? 38[a]For
whoever [b]is ashamed of Me and My words
in this adulterous and sinful generation,
of him the Son of Man also will be
ashamed when He comes in the glory of
His Father with the holy angels."

It is my prayer, Lord, that _____ will deny themselves, take up their cross, and follow You. For whoever desires to save his life will lose it, but whoever loses his life for Your sake and the gospel's will save it.

FROM MARK 8:34, 35

Jesus Transfigured on the Mount

9 And He said to them, [a]"Assuredly, I
say to you that there are some standing here who will not taste death till they
see [b]the kingdom of God [1]present with
power."
2[a]Now after six days Jesus took Peter,
James, and John, and led them up on a
high mountain apart by themselves; and
He was transfigured before them. 3His
clothes became shining, exceedingly
[a]white, like snow, such as no launderer on
earth can whiten them. 4And Elijah appeared to them with Moses, and they were
talking with Jesus. 5Then Peter answered
and said to Jesus, "Rabbi, it is good for us
to be here; and let us make three tabernacles: one for You, one for Moses, and one
for Elijah"— 6because he did not know
what to say, for they were greatly afraid.
7And a [a]cloud came and overshadowed
them; and a voice came out of the cloud,
saying, "This is [b]My beloved Son. [c]Hear
Him!" 8Suddenly, when they had looked
around, they saw no one anymore, but
only Jesus with themselves.
9[a]Now as they came down from the
mountain, He commanded them that
they should tell no one the things they
had seen, till the Son of Man had risen
from the dead. 10So they kept this word to
themselves, questioning [a]what the rising
from the dead meant.

28 a Matt. 14:2 b Luke 9:7, 8
29 a John 1:41; 4:42; 6:69; 11:27
30 a Matt. 8:4; 16:20
31 a Matt. 16:21; 20:19 b Mark 10:33 c Mark 9:31; 10:34
33 a [Rev. 3:19] *1 setting your mind on*
34 a Luke 14:27
35 a John 12:25
38 a Matt. 10:33 b 2 Tim. 1:8, 9; 2:12

CHAPTER 9
1 a Luke 9:27 b [Matt. 24:30] *1 having come*
2 a Matt. 17:1–8
3 a Dan. 7:9
7 a Ex. 40:34 b Mark 1:11 c Acts 3:22
9 a Matt. 17:9–13
10 a John 2:19–22

11And they asked Him, saying, "Why do the scribes say [a]that Elijah must come first?"

12Then He answered and told them, "Indeed, Elijah is coming first and restores all things. And [a]how is it written concerning the Son of Man, that He must suffer many things and [b]be treated with contempt? 13But I say to you that [a]Elijah has also come, and they did to him whatever they wished, as it is written of him."

A Boy Is Healed

14[a]And when He came to the disciples, He saw a great multitude around them, and scribes disputing with them. 15Immediately, when they saw Him, all the people were greatly amazed, and running to *Him,* greeted Him. 16And He asked the scribes, "What are you discussing with them?"

17Then [a]one of the crowd answered and said, "Teacher, I brought You my son, who has a mute spirit. 18And wherever it seizes him, it throws him down; he foams at the mouth, gnashes his teeth, and becomes rigid. So I spoke to Your disciples, that they should cast it out, but they could not."

19He answered him and said, "O [a]faithless[1] generation, how long shall I be with you? How long shall I [2]bear with you? Bring him to Me." 20Then they brought him to Him. And [a]when he saw Him, immediately the spirit convulsed him, and he fell on the ground and wallowed, foaming at the mouth.

21So He asked his father, "How long has this been happening to him?"

And he said, "From childhood. 22And often he has thrown him both into the fire and into the water to destroy him. But if You can do anything, have compassion on us and help us."

23Jesus said to him, [a]"If[1] you can believe, all things *are* possible to him who believes."

24Immediately the father of the child cried out and said with tears, "Lord, I believe; [a]help my unbelief!"

25When Jesus saw that the people came running together, He [a]rebuked the unclean spirit, saying to it, "Deaf and dumb spirit, I command you, come out of him and enter him no more!" 26Then *the spirit* cried out, convulsed him greatly, and came out of him. And he became as one dead, so that many said, "He is dead."

27But Jesus took him by the hand and lifted him up, and he arose.

28[a]And when He had come into the house, His disciples asked Him privately, "Why could we not cast it out?"

29So He said to them, "This kind can come out by nothing but [a]prayer [1]and fasting."

With God all things are possible, and all things are possible to him who believeth, for faith makes room for God to work and thus releases omnipotence.

DR. LILIAN B. YEOMANS

Jesus Again Predicts His Death and Resurrection

30Then they departed from there and passed through Galilee, and He did not want anyone to know *it.* 31[a]For He taught His disciples and said to them, "The Son of Man is being betrayed into the hands of men, and they will [b]kill Him. And after He is killed, He will [c]rise the third day." 32But they [a]did not understand this saying, and were afraid to ask Him.

Who Is the Greatest?

33[a]Then He came to Capernaum. And when He was in the house He asked them, "What was it you [1]disputed among yourselves on the road?" 34But they kept silent, for on the road they had [a]disputed among themselves who *would be the* [b]greatest. 35And He sat down, called the twelve, and said to them, [a]"If anyone desires to be first, he shall be last of all and servant of all." 36Then [a]He took a little child and set him in the midst of them. And when He had taken him in His arms, He said to them, 37"Whoever receives one of these little children in My name receives Me; and [a]whoever receives Me, receives not Me but Him who sent Me."

Jesus Forbids Sectarianism

38[a]Now John answered Him, saying, "Teacher, we saw someone who does not

---

11 a Mal. 4:5
12 a Is. 53:3 b Phil. 2:7
13 a Luke 1:17
14 a Matt. 17:14–19
17 a Luke 9:38
19 a John 4:48 *1 unbelieving* *2 put up with*
20 a Mark 1:26
23 a John 11:40 *1* NU *" 'If You can!' All things*
24 a Luke 17:5
25 a Mark 1:25
28 a Matt. 17:19
29 a [James 5:16] *1* NU omits *and fasting*
31 a Luke 9:44 b Matt. 16:21; 27:50 c 1 Cor. 15:4
32 a Luke 2:50; 18:34
33 a Matt. 18:1–5 *1 discussed*
34 a [Prov. 13:10] b Luke 22:24; 23:46; 24:46
35 a Luke 22:26, 27
36 a Mark 10:13–16
37 a Matt. 10:40
38 a Num. 11:27–29

follow us casting out demons in Your name, and we forbade him because he does not follow us."

39 But Jesus said, "Do not forbid him, [a]for no one who works a miracle in My name can soon afterward speak evil of Me. 40 For [a]he who is not against [1]us is on [2]our side. 41 [a]For whoever gives you a cup of water to drink in My name, because you belong to Christ, assuredly, I say to you, he will by no means lose his reward.

Jesus Warns of Offenses

42 [a]"But whoever causes one of these little ones who believe in Me [1]to stumble, it would be better for him if a millstone were hung around his neck, and he were thrown into the sea. 43 [a]If your hand causes you to sin, cut it off. It is better for you to enter into life [1]maimed, rather than having two hands, to go to [2]hell, into the fire that shall never be quenched— 44 [1]where

> [a]*'Their worm does not die*
> *And the fire is not quenched.'*

45 And if your foot causes you to sin, cut it off. It is better for you to enter life lame, rather than having two feet, to be cast into [1]hell, [2]into the fire that shall never be quenched— 46 where

> [a]*'Their worm does not die*
> *And the fire is not quenched.'*

47 And if your eye causes you to sin, pluck it out. It is better for you to enter the kingdom of God with one eye, rather than having two eyes, to be cast into [1]hell fire— 48 where

> [a]*'Their worm does not die*
> *And the [b]fire is not quenched.'*

Tasteless Salt Is Worthless

49 "For everyone will be [a]seasoned with fire, [b]and[1] every sacrifice will be seasoned with salt. 50 [a]Salt *is* good, but if the salt loses its flavor, how will you season it? [b]Have salt in yourselves, and [c]have peace with one another."

Marriage and Divorce

10 Then [a]He arose from there and came to the region of Judea by the other side of the Jordan. And multitudes gathered to Him again, and as He was accustomed, He taught them again.

2 [a]The Pharisees came and asked Him, "Is it lawful for a man to divorce *his* wife?" testing Him.

3 And He answered and said to them, "What did Moses command you?"

4 They said, [a]"Moses permitted *a man* to write a certificate of divorce, and to dismiss *her.*"

5 And Jesus answered and said to them, "Because of the hardness of your heart he wrote you this [1]precept. 6 But from the beginning of the creation, God [a]*'made them male and female.'* 7 [a]*'For this reason a man shall leave his father and mother and be joined to his wife,* 8 *and the two shall become one flesh'*; so then they are no longer two, but one flesh. 9 Therefore what God has joined together, let not man separate."

10 In the house His disciples also asked Him again about the same *matter.* 11 So He said to them, [a]"Whoever divorces his wife and marries another commits adultery against her. 12 And if a woman divorces her husband and marries another, she commits adultery."

Jesus Blesses Little Children

13 [a]Then they brought little children to Him, that He might touch them; but the disciples rebuked those who brought *them.* 14 But when Jesus saw *it,* He was greatly displeased and said to them, "Let the little children come to Me, and do not forbid them; for [a]of such is the kingdom of God. 15 Assuredly, I say to you, [a]whoever does not receive the kingdom of God as a little child will [b]by no means enter it." 16 And He took them up in His arms, laid *His* hands on them, and blessed them.

Jesus Counsels the Rich Young Ruler

17 [a]Now as He was going out on the road, one came running, knelt before Him, and asked Him, "Good Teacher, what shall I [b]do that I may inherit eternal life?"

18 So Jesus said to him, "Why do you call Me good? No one *is* good but One, *that is,* [a]God. 19 You know the commandments: [a]*'Do not commit adultery,' 'Do not murder,' 'Do not steal,' 'Do not bear false witness,'* 'Do not defraud,' *'Honor your father and your mother.'* "

---

39 [a] 1 Cor. 12:3
40 [a] [Matt. 12:30] [1] M *you* [2] M *your*
41 [a] Matt. 10:42
42 [a] Luke 17:1, 2 [1] To fall into sin
43 [a] Matt. 5:29, 30; 18:8, 9 [1] *crippled* [2] Gr. *Gehenna*
44 [a] Is. 66:24 [1] NU omits v. 44.
45 [1] Gr. *Gehenna* [2] NU omits the rest of v. 45 and all of v. 46.
46 [a] Is. 66:24
47 [1] Gr. *Gehenna*
48 [a] Is. 66:24 [b] Jer. 7:20
49 [a] [Matt. 3:11] [b] Lev. 2:13 [1] NU omits the rest of v. 49.
50 [a] Matt. 5:13 [b] Col. 4:6 [c] Rom. 12:18; 14:19

CHAPTER 10
1 [a] Matt. 19:1–9
2 [a] Matt. 19:3
4 [a] Deut. 24:1–4
5 [1] *command*
6 [a] Gen. 1:27; 5:2
7 [a] Gen. 2:24
11 [a] [Matt. 5:32; 19:9]
13 [a] Luke 18:15–17
14 [a] [1 Pet. 2:2]
15 [a] Matt. 18:3, 4; 19:14 [b] Luke 13:28
17 [a] Matt. 19:16–30 [b] John 6:28
18 [a] 1 Sam. 2:2
19 [a] Ex. 20:12–16; Deut. 5:16–20

Mark 10:13–16

Dear Woman of Destiny,

Do you know that in your hands *right now* is one of God's greatest gifts to change lives? It is the power of *blessing*. We often think of a blessing as a friendly greeting or the words spoken after someone sneezes. But Jesus showed that blessing is the actual *transference of His love* and *transforming power of His life* to those with whom we share it. He gave no greater example of His desire to bless than when He exhorted us to bring the little children to Him.

The blessing of God makes us whole, infusing our spirits with God's favor, joy, and strength. The blessing of God enables us to fully apprehend both the love and presence of the Lord Jesus and His life purpose for us. Blessing is freely given and freely received. Jesus blessed the little children, showing He esteemed as significant that which was rejected and cursed by others.

How easy we forget, as grown-ups, to remain childlike before our heavenly Father. Young children are trusting, completely dependent upon their parents for leadership, provision, and decision making in their lives. No wonder the kingdom of God belongs to such as these.

The wisdom of our Father is to esteem with extravagant worth what the world despises as weak, useless, unimportant. What security for us to become as little children—to fully see and know God, so that we also might value what He values. Like Jesus, what a distinct privilege to honor the youth—receiving them as cherished treasures with unconditional approval, appreciation, and acceptance.

Friend, sister, mother, aunt, grandma, we hold the special power to direct our hearts, our words, our hands—the children. Blessing or cursing. Life or death. Choose. Our words can build up or tear down; our touch can affirm or condemn. Jesus touched each child, communicating with each one as a unique, significant, important gift; and He blessed every one.

Woman of Destiny, may you embrace the mystery and power of blessing to this next generation of history-makers. Pronounce the blessing of God upon their call as they give themselves to the great harvest of souls. Joyfully impart to them the blessing of knowing the Father of love. And remember to continually see yourself as a child in the loving arms of Jesus.

Sue Ahn

20 And he answered and said to Him,
"Teacher, all these things I have [a]kept
from my youth."
21 Then Jesus, looking at him, loved
him, and said to him, "One thing you lack:
Go your way, [a]sell whatever you have and
give to the poor, and you will have [b]trea-
sure in heaven; and come, [c]take up the
cross, and follow Me."
22 But he was sad at this word, and went
away sorrowful, for he had great possessions.

With God All Things Are Possible

23 [a]Then Jesus looked around and said
to His disciples, "How hard it is for those
who have riches to enter the kingdom of
God!" 24 And the disciples were astonished
at His words. But Jesus answered again
and said to them, "Children, how hard it
is [1]for those [a]who trust in riches to enter
the kingdom of God! 25 It is easier for a
camel to go through the eye of a needle
than for a [a]rich man to enter the kingdom
of God."
26 And they were greatly astonished,
saying among themselves, "Who then can
be saved?"
27 But Jesus looked at them and said,
"With men *it is* impossible, but not [a]with
God; for with God all things are possible."
28 [a]Then Peter began to say to Him,
"See, we have left all and followed You."
29 So Jesus answered and said, "Assuredly, I say to you, there is no one who has
left house or brothers or sisters or father
or mother [1]or wife or children or [2]lands,
for My sake and the gospel's, 30 [a]who shall
not receive a hundredfold now in this
time—houses and brothers and sisters
and mothers and children and lands, with
[b]persecutions—and in the age to come,
eternal life. 31 [a]But many *who are* first will
be last, and the last first."

Jesus a Third Time Predicts His Death and Resurrection

32 [a]Now they were on the road, going up
to Jerusalem, and Jesus was going before
them; and they were amazed. And as they
followed they were afraid. [b]Then He took
the twelve aside again and began to tell
them the things that would happen to
Him: 33 "Behold, we are going up to Jerusalem, and the Son of Man will be betrayed to the chief priests and to the
scribes; and they will condemn Him to
death and deliver Him to the Gentiles;
34 and they will mock Him, and [1]scourge
Him, and spit on Him, and kill Him. And
the third day He will rise again."

Greatness Is Serving

35 [a]Then James and John, the sons of
Zebedee, came to Him, saying, "Teacher,
we want You to do for us whatever we
ask."
36 And He said to them, "What do you
want Me to do for you?"
37 They said to Him, "Grant us that we
may sit, one on Your right hand and the
other on Your left, in Your glory."
38 But Jesus said to them, "You do not
know what you ask. Are you able to drink
the [a]cup that I drink, and be baptized with
the [b]baptism that I am baptized with?"
39 They said to Him, "We are able."
So Jesus said to them, [a]"You will indeed drink the cup that I drink, and with
the baptism I am baptized with you will be
baptized; 40 but to sit on My right hand
and on My left is not Mine to give, but *it
is for those* [a]for whom it is prepared."
41 [a]And when the ten heard *it,* they began to be greatly displeased with James
and John. 42 But Jesus called them to *Himself* and said to them, [a]"You know that
those who are considered rulers over the
Gentiles lord it over them, and their great
ones exercise authority over them. 43 [a]Yet
it shall not be so among you; but whoever
desires to become great among you shall
be your servant. 44 And whoever of you desires to be first shall be slave of all. 45 For
even [a]the Son of Man did not come to be
served, but to serve, and [b]to give His life
a ransom for many."

Jesus Heals Blind Bartimaeus

46 [a]Now they came to Jericho. As He
went out of Jericho with His disciples and
a great multitude, blind Bartimaeus, the
son of Timaeus, sat by the road begging.
47 And when he heard that it was Jesus of
Nazareth, he began to cry out and say,
"Jesus, [a]Son of David, [b]have mercy
on me!"
48 Then many warned him to be quiet;
but he cried out all the more, "Son of David, have mercy on me!"
49 So Jesus stood still and commanded
him to be called.

20 a Phil. 3:6
21 a [Luke 12:33; 16:9] b Matt. 6:19, 20; 19:21 c [Mark 8:34]
23 a Matt. 19:23
24 a [1 Tim. 6:17] 1 NU omits *for those who trust in riches*
25 a [Matt. 13:22; 19:24]
27 a Jer. 32:17
28 a Luke 18:28
29 1 NU omits *or wife* 2 Lit. *fields*
30 a Luke 18:29, 30 b [1 Pet. 4:12, 13]
31 a Luke 13:30
32 a Matt. 20:17–19 b Mark 8:31; 9:31
34 1 *flog Him* with a Roman scourge
35 a [James 4:3]
38 a John 18:11 b Luke 12:50
39 a Acts 12:2
40 a [Heb. 11:16]
41 a Matt. 20:24
42 a Luke 22:25
43 a Mark 9:35
45 a [Phil. 2:7, 8] b [Titus 2:14]
46 a Luke 18:35–43
47 a Rev. 22:16 b Matt. 15:22

Then they called the blind man, saying
to him, "Be of good cheer. Rise, He is calling you."
50 And throwing aside his garment, he
rose and came to Jesus.
51 So Jesus answered and said to him,
"What do you want Me to do for you?"
The blind man said to Him, [1]"Rabboni,
that I may receive my sight."
52 Then Jesus said to him, "Go your way;
[a]your faith has [1]made you well." And immediately he received his sight and followed Jesus on the road.

The Triumphal Entry

11 Now [a]when they drew near Jerusalem, to [1]Bethphage and Bethany,
at the Mount of Olives, He sent two of His
disciples; 2 and He said to them, "Go into
the village opposite you; and as soon as
you have entered it you will find a colt
tied, on which no one has sat. Loose it and
bring *it.* 3 And if anyone says to you, 'Why
are you doing this?' say, 'The Lord has
need of it,' and immediately he will send
it here."
4 So they went their way, and found [1]the
colt tied by the door outside on the street,
and they loosed it. 5 But some of those
who stood there said to them, "What are
you doing, loosing the colt?"
6 And they spoke to them just as Jesus
had commanded. So they let them go.
7 Then they brought the colt to Jesus and
threw their clothes on it, and He sat on it.
8 [a]And many spread their clothes on the
road, and others cut down leafy branches
from the trees and spread *them* on the
road. 9 Then those who went before and
those who followed cried out, saying:

"Hosanna!
[a]*'Blessed is He who comes in the*
name of the LORD!'
10 Blessed *is* the kingdom of our
father David
That comes [1]in the name of the
Lord!
[a]Hosanna in the highest!"

11 [a]And Jesus went into Jerusalem and
into the temple. So when He had looked
around at all things, as the hour was already late, He went out to Bethany with
the twelve.

The Fig Tree Withered

12 [a]Now the next day, when they had
come out from Bethany, He was hungry.
13 [a]And seeing from afar a fig tree having
leaves, He went to see if perhaps He would
find something on it. When He came to it,
He found nothing but leaves, for it was
not the season for figs. 14 In response Jesus
said to it, "Let no one eat fruit from you
ever again."
And His disciples heard *it.*

Jesus Cleanses the Temple

15 [a]So they came to Jerusalem. Then Jesus went into the temple and began to
drive out those who bought and sold in
the temple, and overturned the tables of
the money changers and the seats of those
who sold [b]doves. 16 And He would not allow anyone to carry wares through the
temple. 17 Then He taught, saying to
them, "Is it not written, [a]*'My house shall*
be called a house of prayer for all na-
tions'? But you have made it a [b]*'den of*
thieves.' "
18 And [a]the scribes and chief priests
heard it and sought how they might destroy Him; for they feared Him, because
[b]all the people were astonished at His
teaching. 19 When evening had come, He
went out of the city.

The Lesson of the Withered Fig Tree

20 [a]Now in the morning, as they passed
by, they saw the fig tree dried up from the
roots. 21 And Peter, remembering, said to
Him, "Rabbi, look! The fig tree which You
cursed has withered away."
22 So Jesus answered and said to them,
"Have faith in God. 23 For [a]assuredly, I say
to you, whoever says to this mountain, 'Be
removed and be cast into the sea,' and
does not doubt in his heart, but believes
that those things he says will be done, he

It is not what God can do, but what we know He yearns to do, that inspires faith.

F. F. BOSWORTH

---

51 [1]Lit. *My Great One*
52 [a]Matt. 9:22 [1]Lit. *saved you*
CHAPTER 11
1 [a]Matt. 21:1–9 [1]M *Beths-phage*
4 [1]NU, M *a*
8 [a]Matt. 21:8
9 [a]Ps. 118:25, 26
10 [a]Ps. 148:1 [1]NU omits *in the name of the Lord*
11 [a]Matt. 21:12
12 [a]Matt. 21:18–22
13 [a]Matt. 21:19
15 [a]John 2:13–16 [b]Lev. 14:22
17 [a]Is. 56:7 [b]Jer. 7:11
18 [a]Matt. 21:45, 46 [b]Matt. 7:28
20 [a]Matt. 21:19–22
23 [a]Matt. 17:20; 21:21

will have whatever he says. 24 Therefore I say to you, [a]whatever things you ask when you pray, believe that you receive *them,* and you will have *them.*

Forgiveness and Prayer

25 "And whenever you stand praying, [a]if you have anything against anyone, forgive him, that your Father in heaven may also forgive you your trespasses. 26 [1]But [a]if you do not forgive, neither will your Father in heaven forgive your trespasses."

Jesus' Authority Questioned

27 Then they came again to Jerusalem. [a]And as He was walking in the temple, the chief priests, the scribes, and the elders came to Him. 28 And they said to Him, "By what [a]authority are You doing these things? And who gave You this authority to do these things?"

29 But Jesus answered and said to them, "I also will ask you one question; then answer Me, and I will tell you by what authority I do these things: 30 The [a]baptism of John—was it from heaven or from men? Answer Me."

31 And they reasoned among themselves, saying, "If we say, 'From heaven,' He will say, 'Why then did you not believe him?' 32 But if we say, 'From men' "—they feared the people, for [a]all counted John to have been a prophet indeed. 33 So they answered and said to Jesus, "We do not know."

And Jesus answered and said to them, "Neither will I tell you by what authority I do these things."

The Parable of the Wicked Vinedressers

12

Then [a]He began to speak to them in parables: "A man planted a vineyard and set a hedge around *it,* dug *a place for* the wine vat and built a tower. And he leased it to [1]vinedressers and went into a far country. 2 Now at vintage-time he sent a servant to the vinedressers, that he might receive some of the fruit of the vineyard from the vinedressers. 3 And they took *him* and beat him and sent *him* away empty-handed. 4 Again he sent them another servant, [1]and at him they threw stones, wounded *him* in the head, and sent *him* away shamefully treated. 5 And again he sent another, and him they killed; and many others, [a]beating some and killing some. 6 Therefore still having one son, his beloved, he also sent him to them last, saying, 'They will respect my son.' 7 But those [1]vinedressers said among themselves, 'This is the heir. Come, let us kill him, and the inheritance will be ours.' 8 So they took him and [a]killed *him* and cast *him* out of the vineyard.

9 "Therefore what will the owner of the vineyard do? He will come and destroy the vinedressers, and give the vineyard to others. 10 Have you not even read this Scripture:

> [a]*'The stone which the builders rejected*
> *Has become the chief cornerstone.*
> 11 *This was the LORD's doing,*
> *And it is marvelous in our eyes'?"*

12 [a]And they sought to lay hands on Him, but feared the multitude, for they knew He had spoken the parable against them. So they left Him and went away.

The Pharisees: Is It Lawful to Pay Taxes to Caesar?

13 [a]Then they sent to Him some of the Pharisees and the Herodians, to catch Him in *His* words. 14 When they had come, they said to Him, "Teacher, we know that You are true, and [1]care about no one; for You do not [2]regard the person of men, but teach the [a]way of God in truth. Is it lawful to pay taxes to Caesar, or not? 15 Shall we pay, or shall we not pay?"

But He, knowing their [a]hypocrisy, said to them, "Why do you test Me? Bring Me a denarius that I may see *it.*" 16 So they brought *it.*

And He said to them, "Whose image and inscription *is* this?" They said to Him, "Caesar's."

17 And Jesus answered and said to them, [1]"Render to Caesar the things that are Caesar's, and to [a]God the things that are God's."

And they marveled at Him.

The Sadducees: What About the Resurrection?

18 [a]Then *some* Sadducees, [b]who say there is no resurrection, came to Him; and they asked Him, saying: 19 "Teacher, [a]Moses wrote to us that if a man's brother dies, and leaves *his* wife behind, and leaves no children, his brother should take his wife and raise up offspring for his brother.

---

24 a Matt. 7:7
25 a [Col. 3:13]
26 a Matt. 6:15; 18:35 1 NU omits v. 26.
27 a Luke 20:1–8
28 a John 5:27
30 a Luke 7:29, 30
32 a Matt. 3:5; 14:5
CHAPTER 12
1 a Luke 20:9–19 1 *tenant farmers*
4 1 NU omits *and at him they threw stones*
5 a 2 Chr. 36:16
7 1 *tenant farmers*
8 a [Acts 2:23]
10 a Ps. 118:22, 23
12 a John 7:25, 30, 44
13 a Luke 20:20–26
14 a Acts 18:26 1 Court no man's favor 2 Lit. *look at the face of men*
15 a Luke 12:1
17 a [Eccl. 5:4, 5] 1 *Pay*
18 a Luke 20:27–38 b Acts 23:8
19 a Deut. 25:5

20 Now there were seven brothers. The
first took a wife; and dying, he left no offspring. 21 And the second took her, and he
died; nor did he leave any offspring. And
the third likewise. 22 So the seven had her
and left no offspring. Last of all the woman died also. 23 Therefore, in the resurrection, when they rise, whose wife will she
be? For all seven had her as wife."
24 Jesus answered and said to them, "Are
you not therefore [1]mistaken, because you
do not know the Scriptures nor the power
of God? 25 For when they rise from the
dead, they neither marry nor are given in
marriage, but [a]are like angels in heaven.
26 But concerning the dead, that they
[a]rise, have you not read in the book of
Moses, in the *burning* bush *passage,* how
God spoke to him, saying, [b]*'I am the God
of Abraham, the God of Isaac, and the God
of Jacob'* ? 27 He is not the God of the dead,
but the God of the living. You are therefore greatly [1]mistaken."

The Scribes: Which Is the First Commandment of All?

28 [a]Then one of the scribes came, and
having heard them reasoning together,
[1]perceiving that He had answered them
well, asked Him, "Which is the [2]first commandment of all?"

Father, I pray that ____ will love You with all their heart, soul, mind, and strength and love their neighbor as themselves.

FROM MARK 12:30, 31

29 Jesus answered him, "The [1]first of all
the commandments *is:* [a]*'Hear, O Israel,
the LORD our God, the LORD is one.* 30 *And
you shall* [a]*love the LORD your God with all
your heart, with all your soul, with all
your mind, and with all your strength.'*
[1]This *is* the first commandment. 31 And
the second, like *it, is* this: [a]*'You shall love
your neighbor as yourself.'* There is no
other commandment greater than
[b]these."

32 So the scribe said to Him, "Well *said,*
Teacher. You have spoken the truth, for
there is one God, [a]and there is no other
but He. 33 And to love Him with all the
heart, with all the understanding, [1]with
all the soul, and with all the strength, and
to love one's neighbor as oneself, [a]is more
than all the whole burnt offerings and
sacrifices."
34 Now when Jesus saw that he answered wisely, He said to him, "You are
not far from the kingdom of God."
[a]But after that no one dared question
Him.

Jesus: How Can David Call His Descendant Lord?

35 [a]Then Jesus answered and said, while
He taught in the temple, "How *is it* that
the scribes say that the Christ is the Son
of David? 36 For David himself said [a]by the
Holy Spirit:

[b]*'The LORD said to my Lord,*
"Sit at My right hand,
Till I make Your enemies Your
footstool."'

37 Therefore David himself calls Him
'Lord'; how is He *then* his [a]Son?"
And the common people heard Him
gladly.

Beware of the Scribes

38 Then [a]He said to them in His teaching, [b]"Beware of the scribes, who desire to
go around in long robes, [c]*love* greetings
in the marketplaces, 39 the [a]best seats in
the synagogues, and the best places at
feasts, 40 [a]who devour widows' houses, and
[1]for a pretense make long prayers. These
will receive greater condemnation."

The Widow's Two Mites

41 [a]Now Jesus sat opposite the treasury
and saw how the people put money [b]into
the treasury. And many *who were* rich put
in much. 42 Then one poor widow came
and threw in two [1]mites, which make a
[2]quadrans. 43 So He called His disciples to
Himself and said to them, "Assuredly, I
say to you that [a]this poor widow has put
in more than all those who have given to
the treasury; 44 for they all put in out of
their abundance, but she out of her poverty put in all that she had, [a]her whole livelihood."

24 *1 Or deceived*
25 a [1 Cor. 15:42, 49, 52]
26 a [Rev. 20:12, 13] b Ex. 3:6, 15
27 *1 Or deceived*
28 a Matt. 22:34–40 *1 NU seeing* *2 foremost*
29 a Deut. 6:4, 5 *1 foremost*
30 a [Deut. 10:12; 30:6] 1 NU omits the rest of v. 30.
31 a Lev. 19:18 b [Rom. 13:9]
32 a Deut. 4:39
33 a [Hos. 6:6] 1 NU omits *with all the soul*
34 a Matt. 22:46
35 a Luke 20:41–44
36 a 2 Sam. 23:2 b Ps. 110:1
37 a [Acts 2:29–31]
38 a Mark 4:2 b Matt. 23:1–7 c Matt. 23:7
39 a Luke 14:7
40 a Matt. 23:14 *1 for appearance' sake*
41 a Luke 21:1–4 b 2 Kin. 12:9
42 1 Gr. *lepta,* very small copper coins 2 A Roman coin
43 a [2 Cor. 8:12]
44 a Deut. 24:6

I am not a woman with great faith—I am a woman with a little faith in the Great God!

KATHRYN KUHLMAN

Jesus Predicts the Destruction of the Temple

13 Then [a]as He went out of the temple, one of His disciples said to Him, "Teacher, see what manner of stones and what buildings *are here!*"

2 And Jesus answered and said to him, "Do you see these great buildings? [a]Not *one* stone shall be left upon another, that shall not be thrown down."

The Signs of the Times and the End of the Age

3 Now as He sat on the Mount of Olives opposite the temple, [a]Peter, [b]James, [b]John, and [c]Andrew asked Him privately, 4 [a]"Tell us, when will these things be? And what *will be* the sign when all these things will be fulfilled?"

5 And Jesus, answering them, began to say: [a]"Take heed that no one deceives you. 6 For many will come in My name, saying, 'I am *He,*' and will deceive many. 7 But when you hear of wars and rumors of wars, do not be troubled; for *such things* must happen, but the end *is* not yet. 8 For nation will rise against nation, and [a]kingdom against kingdom. And there will be earthquakes in various places, and there will be famines [1]and troubles. [b]These *are* the beginnings of [2]sorrows.

9 "But [a]watch out for yourselves, for they will deliver you up to councils, and you will be beaten in the synagogues. You will [1]be brought before rulers and kings for My sake, for a testimony to them. 10 And [a]the gospel must first be preached to all the nations. 11 [a]But when they arrest *you* and deliver you up, do not worry beforehand, [1]or premeditate what you will speak. But whatever is given you in that hour, speak that; for it is not you who speak, [b]but the Holy Spirit. 12 Now [a]brother will betray brother to death, and a father *his* child; and children will rise up against parents and cause them to be put to death. 13 [a]And you will be hated by all for My name's sake. But [b]he who [1]endures to the end shall be saved.

The Great Tribulation

14 [a]"So when you see the [b]'*abomination of desolation,*' [1]spoken of by Daniel the prophet, standing where it ought not" (let the reader understand), "then [c]let those who are in Judea flee to the mountains. 15 Let him who is on the housetop not go down into the house, nor enter to take anything out of his house. 16 And let him who is in the field not go back to get his clothes. 17 [a]But woe to those who are pregnant and to those who are nursing babies in those days! 18 And pray that your flight may not be in winter. 19 [a]For *in* those days there will be tribulation, such as has not been since the beginning of the creation which God created until this time, nor ever shall be. 20 And unless the Lord had shortened those days, no flesh would be saved; but for the elect's sake, whom He chose, He shortened the days.

21 [a]"Then if anyone says to you, 'Look, here *is* the Christ!' or, 'Look, *He is* there!' do not believe it. 22 For false christs and false prophets will rise and show signs and [a]wonders to deceive, if possible, even the [1]elect. 23 But [a]take heed; see, I have told you all things beforehand.

The Coming of the Son of Man

24 [a]"But in those days, after that tribulation, the sun will be darkened, and the moon will not give its light; 25 the stars of heaven will fall, and the powers in the heavens will be [a]shaken. 26 [a]Then they will see the Son of Man coming in the clouds with great power and glory. 27 And then He will send His angels, and gather together His [1]elect from the four winds, from the farthest part of earth to the farthest part of heaven.

The Parable of the Fig Tree

28 [a]"Now learn this parable from the fig tree: When its branch has already become tender, and puts forth leaves, you know that summer is near. 29 So you also, when you see these things happening, know that [1]it is near—at the doors! 30 Assuredly, I say to you, this generation will by no

CHAPTER 13
1 a Luke 21:5–36
2 a Luke 19:44
3 a Matt. 16:18 b Mark 1:19 c John 1:40
4 a Matt. 24:3
5 a Eph. 5:6
8 a Hag. 2:22 b Matt. 24:8 *1* NU omits *and troubles* *2* Lit. *birth pangs*
9 a Matt. 10:17, 18; 24:9 *1* NU, M *stand*
10 a Matt. 24:14
11 a Luke 12:11; 21:12–17 b Acts 2:4; 4:8, 31 *1* NU omits *or premeditate*
12 a Mic. 7:6
13 a Luke 21:17 b Matt. 10:22; 24:13 *1 bears patiently*
14 a Matt. 24:15 b Dan. 9:27; 11:31; 12:11 c Luke 21:21 *1* NU omits *spoken of by Daniel the prophet*
17 a Luke 21:23
19 a Dan. 9:26; 12:1
21 a Luke 17:23; 21:8
22 a Rev. 13:13, 14 *1 chosen ones*
23 a [2 Pet. 3:17]
24 a Zeph. 1:15
25 a Is. 13:10; 34:4
26 a [Dan. 7:13, 14]
27 *1 chosen ones*
28 a Luke 21:29
29 *1* Or *He*

means pass away till all these things take place. 31Heaven and earth will pass away, but [a]My words will by no means pass away.

No One Knows the Day or Hour

32"But of that day and hour [a]no one knows, not even the angels in heaven, nor the Son, but only the [b]Father. 33[a]Take heed, watch and pray; for you do not know when the time is. 34[a]*It is* like a man going to a far country, who left his house and gave [b]authority to his servants, and to each his work, and commanded the doorkeeper to watch. 35[a]Watch therefore, for you do not know when the master of the house is coming—in the evening, at midnight, at the crowing of the rooster, or in the morning— 36lest, coming suddenly, he find you sleeping. 37And what I say to you, I say to all: Watch!"

The Plot to Kill Jesus

14 After [a]two days it was the Passover and [b]*the Feast* of Unleavened Bread. And the chief priests and the scribes sought how they might take Him by [1]trickery and put *Him* to death. 2But they said, "Not during the feast, lest there be an uproar of the people."

The Anointing at Bethany

3[a]And being in Bethany at the house of Simon the leper, as He sat at the table, a woman came having an alabaster flask of very costly [1]oil of spikenard. Then she broke the flask and poured *it* on His head. 4But there were some who were indignant among themselves, and said, "Why was this fragrant oil wasted? 5For it might have been sold for more than three hundred [a]denarii and given to the poor." And they [b]criticized[1] her sharply.

6But Jesus said, "Let her alone. Why do you trouble her? She has done a good work for Me. 7[a]For you have the poor with you always, and whenever you wish you may do them good; [b]but Me you do not have always. 8She has done what she could. She has come beforehand to anoint My body for burial. 9Assuredly, I say to you, wherever this gospel is [a]preached in the whole world, what this woman has done will also be told as a memorial to her."

Judas Agrees to Betray Jesus

10[a]Then Judas Iscariot, one of the twelve, went to the chief priests to betray Him to them. 11And when they heard *it*, they were glad, and promised to give him money. So he sought how he might conveniently betray Him.

Jesus Celebrates the Passover with His Disciples

12[a]Now on the first day of Unleavened Bread, when they [1]killed the Passover *lamb*, His disciples said to Him, "Where do You want us to go and prepare, that You may eat the Passover?"

13And He sent out two of His disciples and said to them, "Go into the city, and a man will meet you carrying a pitcher of water; follow him. 14Wherever he goes in, say to the master of the house, 'The Teacher says, "Where is the guest room in which I may eat the Passover with My disciples?" ' 15Then he will show you a large upper room, furnished *and* prepared; there make ready for us."

16So His disciples went out, and came into the city, and found it just as He had said to them; and they prepared the Passover.

17[a]In the evening He came with the twelve. 18Now as they sat and ate, Jesus said, "Assuredly, I say to you, [a]one of you who eats with Me will betray Me."

19And they began to be sorrowful, and to say to Him one by one, "*Is* it I?" [1]And another *said*, "*Is* it I?"

20He answered and said to them, "*It is* one of the twelve, who dips with Me in the dish. 21[a]The Son of Man indeed goes just as it is written of Him, but woe to that man by whom the Son of Man is betrayed! It would have been good for that man if he had never been born."

Jesus Institutes the Lord's Supper

22 [a]And as they were eating, Jesus took bread, blessed and broke *it*, and gave *it* to them and said, "Take, [1]eat; this is My [b]body."

23Then He took the cup, and when He had given thanks He gave *it* to them, and they all drank from it. 24And He said to them, "This is My blood of the [1]new covenant, which is shed for many. 25Assuredly, I say to you, I will no longer drink

---

31 a Is. 40:8
32 a Matt. 25:13 b Acts 1:7
33 a 1 Thess. 5:6
34 a Matt. 24:45; 25:14 b [Matt. 16:19]
35 a Matt. 24:42, 44

CHAPTER 14
1 a Luke 22:1, 2 b Ex. 12:1–27 *1 deception*
3 a Luke 7:37 *1* Perfume of pure nard
5 a Matt. 18:28 b John 6:61 *1 scolded*
7 a Deut. 15:11 b [John 7:33; 8:21; 14:2, 12; 16:10, 17, 28]
9 a Luke 24:47
10 a Matt. 10:2–4
12 a Matt. 26:17–19 *1 sacrificed*
17 a Matt. 26:20–24
18 a John 6:70, 71; 13:18
19 *1* NU omits the rest of v. 19.
21 a Luke 22:22
22 a 1 Cor. 11:23–25 b [1 Pet. 2:24] *1* NU omits *eat*
24 *1* NU omits *new*

Mark 14:22–24

Dear Woman of Destiny,

Do you remember your high-school football games? Following the game you probably attended a victory party where each touchdown was smugly replayed. In fact, the greater the victory, the greater the party! Most of the fun was smearing that victory into your defeated rival!

Without sounding irreverent, this is a good picture of family communion. Indeed, two thousand years ago on Calvary's cross a great victory was won on your family's behalf. You not only have a reason to celebrate, but a responsibility to remember. Communion is not just a time to weep over the Cross, but to rejoice over the empty tomb.

I recognize that people in many traditions receive communion only in a church service. However, the first communion was taken in an upper room, likely in a home. When are the appropriate times to receive communion in your home? My husband and I have a conviction that there is great blessing that comes from receiving communion in your home. The whole point of communion is to "remember" Jesus Christ. And what do we remember? That He paid for our healing. Jesus could have suggested, "Serve communion whenever you need to remember Me and the victory that My death at Calvary represents." In times of sickness, "remember Me." During family squabbles, stop fighting and "remember Me." Communion declares that Calvary's victories are greater than any problems your family is experiencing at the moment.

Remembering Him in the Lord's Supper gives us a strength in times of trouble, but should also be encouraged during times of celebration. When your son slam-dunks the winning point, rejoice with the Lord's Supper. This brings focus to God's goodness and reminds your budding athlete that "every good gift and every perfect gift is from above" (James 1:17). When our ministry miraculously secured an additional 530 acres for Texas Bible Institute, we rejoiced with the Lord's Supper.

My husband, Tommy, began a New Year's tradition of family communion when our three children were just toddlers. Abby finger painted with the grape juice, and Peter crumbled crackers on Andrew's head. I would get so angry over their foolishness that Tommy had to serve me communion after our family communion! In spite of it all, communion has now become a bonding family tradition in which we remember all God has done for us and our family. With toddlers or teens, relax, keep it short, and pray with your eyes open!

Some of you may want to invite different family members to take turns serving the Lord's Supper as you open your hearts to each other and remember the Lord's goodness. This idea is especially good for single moms or blended families. The result is often the healing of relationships. "One generation shall praise Your works to another" (Ps. 145:4) becomes a precious reality when Grandma begins to reminisce about her greatest healings. If your daughter is beginning a new junior high school, let her older brother serve the elements and pray for little sis. In their own way and on their own spiritual level, everyone can feel a part of communion. If Dad is able, he should lead the overall communion to reinforce his honored role as head of the home.

Celebrating communion in your home welcomes the victories of Calvary and will bond your family forever. Don't you think God is nudging you to host some remembrance parties of your own? Go for it!

Rachel Burchfield

of the fruit of the vine until that day when I drink it new in the kingdom of God."

26[a]And when they had sung [1]a hymn, they went out to the Mount of Olives.

The blood and the Word are all-powerful, but it takes true faith to set this never-failing power to work.

MRS. C. NUZUM

Jesus Predicts Peter's Denial

27[a]Then Jesus said to them, "All of you will be made to stumble [1]because of Me this night, for it is written:

> [b]'*I will strike the Shepherd,*
> *And the sheep will be scattered.*'

28"But [a]after I have been raised, I will go before you to Galilee."

29[a]Peter said to Him, "Even if all are made to [1]stumble, yet I *will* not *be*."

30Jesus said to him, "Assuredly, I say to you that today, *even* this night, before the rooster crows twice, you will deny Me three times."

31But he spoke more vehemently, "If I have to die with You, I will not deny You!"
And they all said likewise.

The Prayer in the Garden

32[a]Then they came to a place which was named Gethsemane; and He said to His disciples, "Sit here while I pray."
33And He [a]took Peter, James, and John with Him, and He began to be troubled and deeply distressed.
34Then He said to them, [a]"My soul is exceedingly sorrowful, *even* to death. Stay here and watch."

35He went a little farther, and fell on the ground, and prayed that if it were possible, the hour might pass from Him.
36And He said, [a]"Abba, Father, [b]all things *are* possible for You. Take this cup away from Me; [c]nevertheless, not what I will, but what You *will*."

37Then He came and found them sleeping, and said to Peter, "Simon, are you sleeping? Could you not watch one hour?
38[a]Watch and pray, lest you enter into temptation. [b]The spirit indeed *is* willing, but the flesh *is* weak."

39Again He went away and prayed, and spoke the same words.
40And when He returned, He found them asleep again, for their eyes were heavy; and they did not know what to answer Him.

God is better served in resisting a temptation to evil than in many formal prayers.

WILLIAM PENN

41Then He came the third time and said to them, "Are you still sleeping and resting? It is enough! [a]The hour has come; behold, the Son of Man is being betrayed into the hands of sinners.
42[a]Rise, let us be going. See, My betrayer is at hand."

Betrayal and Arrest in Gethsemane

43[a]And immediately, while He was still speaking, Judas, one of the twelve, with a great multitude with swords and clubs, came from the chief priests and the scribes and the elders.
44Now His betrayer had given them a signal, saying, "Whomever I [a]kiss, He is the One; seize Him and lead *Him* away safely."

45As soon as he had come, immediately he went up to Him and said to Him, "Rabbi, Rabbi!" and kissed Him.

46Then they laid their hands on Him and took Him.
47And one of those who stood by drew his sword and struck the servant of the high priest, and cut off his ear.

48[a]Then Jesus answered and said to them, "Have you come out, as against a robber, with swords and clubs to take Me?
49I was daily with you in the temple [a]teaching, and you did not seize Me. But [b]the Scriptures must be fulfilled."

50[a]Then they all forsook Him and fled.

A Young Man Flees Naked

51Now a certain young man followed Him, having a linen cloth thrown around *his* naked *body*. And the young men laid

26 a Matt. 26:30 1 Or *hymns*
27 a Matt. 26:31–35 b Zech. 13:7 1 NU omits *because of Me this night*
28 a Mark 16:7
29 a John 13:37, 38 1 *fall away*
32 a Luke 22:40–46
33 a Mark 5:37; 9:2; 13:3
34 a John 12:27
36 a Gal. 4:6 b [Heb. 5:7] c John 5:30; 6:38
38 a Luke 21:36 b [Rom. 7:18, 21–24]
41 a John 13:1; 17:1
42 a John 13:21; 18:1, 2
43 a Luke 22:47–53
44 a [Prov. 27:6]
48 a Matt. 26:55
49 a Matt. 21:23 b Is. 53:7
50 a Ps. 88:8

hold of him, [52]and he left the linen cloth
and fled from them naked.

Jesus Faces the Sanhedrin

[53a]And they led Jesus away to the high
priest; and with him were [b]assembled all
the [c]chief priests, the elders, and the
scribes. [54]But [a]Peter followed Him at a
distance, right into the courtyard of the
high priest. And he sat with the servants
and warmed himself at the fire.
[55a]Now the chief priests and all the
council sought testimony against Jesus to
put Him to death, but found none. [56]For
many bore [a]false witness against Him, but
their testimonies [1]did not agree.
[57]Then some rose up and bore false witness against Him, saying, [58]"We heard
Him say, [a]'I will destroy this temple made
with hands, and within three days I will
build another made without hands.' "
[59]But not even then did their testimony
agree.
[60a]And the high priest stood up in the
midst and asked Jesus, saying, "Do You
answer nothing? What *is it* these men testify against You?" [61]But [a]He kept silent
and answered nothing.
[b]Again the high priest asked Him, saying to Him, "Are You the Christ, the Son
of the Blessed?"
[62]Jesus said, "I am. [a]And you will see
the Son of Man sitting at the right hand
of the Power, and coming with the clouds
of heaven."
[63]Then the high priest tore his clothes
and said, "What further need do we have
of witnesses? [64]You have heard the [a]blas-
phemy! What do you think?"
And they all condemned Him to be deserving of [b]death.
[65]Then some began to [a]spit on Him,
and to blindfold Him, and to beat Him,
and to say to Him, "Prophesy!" And the
officers [1]struck Him with the palms of
their hands.

Peter Denies Jesus, and Weeps

[66a]Now as Peter was below in the courtyard, one of the servant girls of the high
priest came. [67]And when she saw Peter
warming himself, she looked at him and
said, "You also were with [a]Jesus of Nazareth."
[68]But he denied it, saying, "I neither
know nor understand what you are saying." And he went out on the porch, and
a rooster crowed.
[69a]And the servant girl saw him again,
and began to say to those who stood by,
"This is one of them." [70]But he denied it
again.
[a]And a little later those who stood by
said to Peter again, "Surely you are *one* of
them; [b]for you are a Galilean, [1]and your
[2]speech shows *it*."
[71]Then he began to curse and swear, "I
do not know this Man of whom you
speak!"
[72a]A second time *the* rooster crowed.
Then Peter called to mind the word that
Jesus had said to him, "Before the rooster
crows twice, you will deny Me three
times." And when he thought about it, he
wept.

Jesus Faces Pilate

15 Immediately, [a]in the morning, the
chief priests held a consultation
with the elders and scribes and the whole
council; and they bound Jesus, led *Him*
away, and [b]delivered *Him* to Pilate.
[2a]Then Pilate asked Him, "Are You the
King of the Jews?"
He answered and said to him, *"It is as*
you say."
[3]And the chief priests accused Him of
many things, but He [a]answered nothing.
[4a]Then Pilate asked Him again, saying,
"Do You answer nothing? See how many
things [1]they testify against You!" [5a]But
Jesus still answered nothing, so that Pilate marveled.

Taking the Place of Barabbas

[6]Now [a]at the feast he was accustomed
to releasing one prisoner to them, whomever they requested. [7]And there was one
named Barabbas, *who was* chained with
his fellow rebels; they had committed
murder in the rebellion. [8]Then the multitude, [1]crying aloud, began to ask *him to*
do just as he had always done for them.
[9]But Pilate answered them, saying, "Do
you want me to release to you the King of
the Jews?" [10]For he knew that the chief
priests had handed Him over because of
envy.
[11]But [a]the chief priests stirred up the
crowd, so that he should rather release
Barabbas to them. [12]Pilate answered and
said to them again, "What then do you

53 a Matt. 26:57–68 b Mark 15:1 c John 7:32; 18:3; 19:6
54 a John 18:15
55 a Matt. 26:59
56 a Ex. 20:16 *1 were not consistent*
58 a John 2:19
60 a Matt. 26:62
61 a Is. 53:7 b Luke 22:67–71
62 a Luke 22:69
64 a John 10:33, 36 b John 19:7
65 a Is. 50:6; 52:14 *1* NU *received Him with slaps*
66 a John 18:16–18, 25–27
67 a John 1:45
69 a Matt. 26:71
70 a Luke 22:59 b Acts 2:7 *1* NU omits the rest of v. 70. *2 accent*
72 a Matt. 26:75

CHAPTER 15
1 a Ps. 2:2 b Acts 3:13
2 a Matt. 27:11–14
3 a John 19:9
4 a Matt. 27:13 *1* NU *of which they accuse You*
5 a Is. 53:7
6 a Matt. 27:15–26
8 *1* NU *going up*
11 a Acts 3:14

want me to do *with Him* whom you call the [a]King of the Jews?"

13 So they cried out again, "Crucify Him!"

14 Then Pilate said to them, "Why, [a]what evil has He done?"

But they cried out all the more, "Crucify Him!"

15 [a]So Pilate, wanting to gratify the crowd, released Barabbas to them; and he delivered Jesus, after he had scourged *Him,* to be [b]crucified.

The Soldiers Mock Jesus

16 [a]Then the soldiers led Him away into the hall called [1]Praetorium, and they called together the whole garrison. 17 And they clothed Him with purple; and they twisted a crown of thorns, put it on His *head,* 18 and began to salute Him, "Hail, King of the Jews!" 19 Then they [a]struck Him on the head with a reed and spat on Him; and bowing the knee, they worshiped Him. 20 And when they had [a]mocked Him, they took the purple off Him, put His own clothes on Him, and led Him out to crucify Him.

The King on a Cross

21 [a]Then they compelled a certain man, Simon a Cyrenian, the father of Alexander and Rufus, as he was coming out of the country and passing by, to bear His cross. 22 [a]And they brought Him to the place Golgotha, which is translated, Place of a Skull. 23 [a]Then they gave Him wine mingled with myrrh to drink, but He did not take *it.* 24 And when they crucified Him, [a]they divided His garments, casting lots for them to determine what every man should take.

25 Now [a]it was the third hour, and they crucified Him. 26 And [a]the inscription of His [1]accusation was written above:

THE KING OF THE JEWS.

27 [a]With Him they also crucified two robbers, one on His right and the other on His left. 28 [1]So the Scripture was fulfilled which says, [a]*"And He was numbered with the transgressors."*

29 And [a]those who passed by blasphemed Him, [b]wagging their heads and saying, "Aha! [c]*You* who destroy the temple and build *it* in three days, 30 save Yourself, and come down from the cross!"

31 Likewise the chief priests also, [a]mocking among themselves with the scribes, said, "He saved [b]others; Himself He cannot save. 32 Let the Christ, the King of Israel, descend now from the cross, that we may see and [1]believe."

Even [a]those who were crucified with Him reviled Him.

> *We must ever abide under the shadow of the cross, and the result will be perfect physical, as well as spiritual, victory.*
>
> Dr. Lilian B. Yeomans

Jesus Dies on the Cross

33 Now [a]when the sixth hour had come, there was darkness over the whole land until the ninth hour. 34 And at the ninth hour Jesus cried out with a loud voice, saying, "Eloi, Eloi, lama sabachthani?" which is translated, [a]*"My God, My God, why have You forsaken Me?"*

35 Some of those who stood by, when they heard *that,* said, "Look, He is calling for Elijah!" 36 Then [a]someone ran and filled a sponge full of sour wine, put *it* on a reed, and [b]offered *it* to Him to drink, saying, "Let Him alone; let us see if Elijah will come to take Him down."

37 [a]And Jesus cried out with a loud voice, and breathed His last.

38 Then [a]the veil of the temple was torn in two from top to bottom. 39 So [a]when the centurion, who stood opposite Him, saw that [1]He cried out like this and breathed His last, he said, "Truly this Man was the Son of God!"

40 [a]There were also women looking on [b]from afar, among whom were Mary Magdalene, Mary the mother of James the Less and of Joses, and Salome, 41 who also [a]followed Him and ministered to Him when He was in Galilee, and many other women who came up with Him to Jerusalem.

Jesus Buried in Joseph's Tomb

42 [a]Now when evening had come, because it was the Preparation Day, that is,

12 a Mic. 5:2
14 a 1 Pet. 2:21–23
15 a Matt. 27:26 b [Is. 53:8]
16 a Matt. 27:27–31 *1 The governor's headquarters*
19 a [Is. 50:6; 52:14; 53:5]
20 a Luke 22:63; 23:11
21 a Matt. 27:32
22 a John 19:17–24
23 a Matt. 27:34
24 a Ps. 22:18
25 a John 19:14
26 a Matt. 27:37 *1 crime*
27 a Luke 22:37
28 a Is. 53:12 *1* NU omits v. 28.
29 a Ps. 22:6, 7; 69:7 b Ps. 109:25 c John 2:19–21
31 a Luke 18:32 b John 11:43, 44
32 a Matt. 27:44 *1* M *believe Him*
33 a Luke 23:44–49
34 a Ps. 22:1
36 a John 19:29 b Ps. 69:21
37 a Matt. 27:50
38 a Ex. 26:31–33
39 a Luke 23:47 *1* NU *He thus breathed His last*
40 a Matt. 27:55 b Ps. 38:11
41 a Luke 8:2, 3
42 a John 19:38–42

the day before the Sabbath, 43 Joseph of
Arimathea, a prominent council member,
who [a]was himself waiting for the kingdom of God, coming and taking courage,
went in to Pilate and asked for the body of
Jesus. 44 Pilate marveled that He was already dead; and summoning the centurion, he asked him if He had been dead for
some time. 45 So when he found out from
the centurion, he granted the body to Joseph. 46 [a]Then he bought fine linen, took
Him down, and wrapped Him in the linen.
And he laid Him in a tomb which had
been hewn out of the rock, and rolled a
stone against the door of the tomb. 47 And
Mary Magdalene and Mary *the mother* of
Joses observed where He was laid.

He Is Risen

16 Now [a]when the Sabbath was past,
Mary Magdalene, Mary *the mother*
of James, and Salome [b]bought spices, that
they might come and anoint Him. 2 [a]Very
early in the morning, on the first *day* of
the week, they came to the tomb when the
sun had risen. 3 And they said among
themselves, "Who will roll away the stone
from the door of the tomb for us?" 4 But
when they looked up, they saw that the
stone had been rolled away—for it was

43 [a] Luke 2:25, 38; 23:51
46 [a] Matt. 27:59, 60

CHAPTER 16
1 [a] John 20:1–8 [b] Luke 23:56
2 [a] Luke 24:1

ANNIE ARMSTRONG

In Annie Armstrong's eyes, no one needed more support than missionaries, and her life revolved around spreading the Word of God through missions. Though she spent almost her entire life in Baltimore, her work was felt around the world.

In an era when most children in the United States were raised as Christians, Annie was a late bloomer. Growing up, she enjoyed a good time and feared joining a church would "take the edge off of life." But she noticed the indescribable peace her believing mother exuded even in the midst of trouble. She so wanted the peace and joy her mother had that, at age 20, she accepted Christ. The two attended prayer meetings, where Annie watched her mother kneel and pray with other women. The small group met weekly, praying and sharing the latest reports of a pioneer missionary to China. They eventually became an organization called Woman's Mission to Women and dedicated themselves with the practical needs of missionaries both abroad and within the United States.

Annie's love for missions exploded because of her exposure to these praying women, and she began to use her organizational abilities to garner support for missionaries. Over the next six years, she was elected to prominent leadership positions with both the Woman's Baptist Home Mission Society and the Maryland Mission Rooms.

When the Woman's Missionary Union was formed in 1888, Annie became its secretary and went full steam ahead. Through her selfless efforts of providing everything from prayer to toothbrushes for missionaries, she did more than keep the home fires burning; she spread them across the nations and built an infrastructure of mission support that lasted for more than a century.

In an era when female leadership was especially rare in business affairs, Annie Armstrong emerged as an excellent and efficient manager and fundraiser. As women of destiny today, let us be like Annie Armstrong and use the full range of our gifts and abilities to further the cause of Jesus Christ.

Mark 16:17

Dear Woman of Destiny,

Interestingly enough, there seems to be a distinct difference in the way demons and evil spirits were treated by the believers in the Old Testament and the New Testament. The word *demons* is mentioned only four times in the entire Old Testament, and each time it has to do with sacrifices to idols, stating that those who sacrificed to idols were sacrificing to demons. Apparently idols represent and might even embody demons! The Old Testament also mentions *spirits* in a negative way—lying spirits, familiar spirits, perverse spirits, distressing spirits, unclean spirits, spirits of harlotry, jealousy, heaviness, and pride. It is reasonable to assume that the word *spirit* in these instances could also be used interchangeably with *demon*. But search as we may, we don't seem to find any way that God's children had of dealing with these evil spirits in the Old Testament.

Things radically changed with the coming of Christ, who summoned a clash between the kingdom of darkness and the kingdom of God. Many more are named—spirits of divination, fear, error, infirmity, bondage, stupor, deceiving spirits, unclean spirits, evil spirits, foul spirits and spirits of demons. Also mentioned are spirits of the kingdom of God—gentleness, wisdom, truth, faith, prophecy, ministering spirits, and a gift of the discerning of spirits—in stark contrast to the list of evil spirits.

Jesus commanded His followers to do spiritual warfare, giving them specific instructions in casting them out using two weapons: His authority and His name. After demonstrating how this was to be done, He sent them out. Upon their return, He gave them further instruction. When some unyielding spirits remained entrenched, the disciples were told to use prayer and fasting (see Mark 9:29).

A much wider circle of people is covered in Mark 16:17, 18—"those who believe." One of the clearest examples of casting out a demon is found in the incident with Paul and the girl at Philippi. Paul says to the spirit of divination in her: "'I command you in the name of Jesus Christ to come out of her.' And he came out that very hour" (Acts 16:18). Like Paul, in obedience to Jesus' orders, we, too, should continually be pushing back the kingdom of darkness.

Persons needing deliverance from evil spirits know that they are not in control of some emotion or "besetting sin." They feel totally helpless and say or do things they don't want to do. Past involvement in Satanism, witchcraft, deliberate sins of lust and the like can provide openings for evil spirits to take up residence. Being severely rejected or victimized and hanging on to resulting hatred, anger, bitterness, or unforgiveness also opens the way for demons.

Once forgiveness for past sins has been extended or appropriated, curses and soul ties can be broken through the power given us by Jesus. Then demons usually leave readily when a strong believer addresses the demons causing the problem, one by one, and commands them to come out in the name of Jesus Christ.

Doris Wagner

very large. 5[a]And entering the tomb, they
saw a young man clothed in a long white
robe sitting on the right side; and they
were alarmed.

Lord, I pray that these signs will follow _____ who believe: In Your name they will cast out demons; they will speak with new tongues; they will take up serpents; and if they drink anything deadly, it will by no means hurt them; they will lay hands on the sick, and they will recover.

FROM MARK 16:17, 18

6[a]But he said to them, "Do not be
alarmed. You seek Jesus of Nazareth, who
was crucified. He is risen! He is not here.
See the place where they laid Him. 7But
go, tell His disciples—and Peter—that
He is going [1]before you into Galilee; there
you will see Him, [a]as He said to you."
8So they went out [1]quickly and fled
from the tomb, for they trembled and
were amazed. [a]And they said nothing to
anyone, for they were afraid.

Mary Magdalene Sees the Risen Lord

9[1]Now when *He* rose early on the first
day of the week, He appeared first to Mary
Magdalene, [a]out of whom He had cast sev-
en demons. 10[a]She went and told those
who had been with Him, as they mourned
and wept. 11[a]And when they heard that He
was alive and had been seen by her, they
did not believe.

Jesus Appears to Two Disciples

12After that, He appeared in another
form [a]to two of them as they walked and
went into the country. 13And they went
and told *it* to the rest, *but* they did not
believe them either.

The Great Commission

14[a]Later He appeared to the eleven as
they sat at the table; and He rebuked their
unbelief and hardness of heart, because
they did not believe those who had seen
Him after He had risen. 15[a]And He said to
them, "Go into all the world [b]and preach
the gospel to every creature. 16[a]He who
believes and is baptized will be saved; [b]but
he who does not believe will be condemned. 17 And these [a]signs will follow
those who [1]believe: [b]In My name they will
cast out demons; [c]they will speak with
new tongues; 18[a]they[1] will take up serpents; and if they drink anything deadly,
it will by no means hurt them; [b]they will
lay hands on the sick, and they will recover."

Christ Ascends to God's Right Hand

19So then, [a]after the Lord had spoken
to them, He was [b]received up into heaven,
and [c]sat down at the right hand of God.
20And they went out and preached everywhere, the Lord working with *them* [a]and
confirming the word through the accompanying signs. Amen.

5 a John 20:11, 12
6 a Matt. 28:6
7 a Matt. 26:32; 28:16, 17 1 *ahead of*
8 a Matt. 28:8 1 NU, M omit *quickly*
9 a Luke 8:2 1 Vv. 9–20 are bracketed in NU as not in the original text. They are lacking in Codex Sinaiticus and Codex Vaticanus, although nearly all other mss. of Mark contain them.
10 a Luke 24:10
11 a Luke 24:11, 41
12 a Luke 24:13–35
14 a 1 Cor. 15:5
15 a Matt. 28:19 b [Col. 1:23]
16 a [John 3:18, 36] b [John 12:48]
17 a Acts 5:12 b Luke 10:17 c [Acts 2:4] 1 *have believed*
18 a Acts 28:3–6 b James 5:14 1 NU *and in their hands they will*
19 a Acts 1:2, 3 b Luke 9:51; 24:51 c [Ps. 110:1]
20 a [Heb. 2:4]

AUTHOR: *Luke*
DATE: *A.D. 59–75*
THEME: *Jesus the Savior of the World*
KEY WORDS: *Prayer, Thanksgiving, Joy, Save, Kingdom, Holy Spirit, Repentance*

LUKE

Dear Woman of Destiny,

The Book of Luke is incredibly rich in its stories of women. It begins with an angelic visitation to a barren couple. Elizabeth became pregnant with her son, John, even though she was well advanced in age. Young Mary, most likely around fourteen years of age, received the promise of the Spirit and replied with a statement that should echo from each of our hearts today, "Behold the maidservant of the Lord! Let it be to me according to your word" (Luke 1:38). We also need to believe God's precious Word to us. Remember that you are as special to your Father in heaven as were Elizabeth and young Mary.

With His love,

Cindy Jacobs

Dedication to Theophilus

Inasmuch as many have taken in hand
to set in order a narrative of those
[a]things which [1]have been fulfilled
among us, 2just as those who [a]from the
beginning were [b]eyewitnesses and ministers of the word [c]delivered them to us, 3it
seemed good to me also, having [1]had perfect understanding of all things from the
very first, to write to you an orderly account, [a]most excellent Theophilus, 4[a]that
you may know the certainty of those
things in which you were instructed.

John's Birth Announced to Zacharias

5There was [a]in the days of Herod, the
king of Judea, a certain priest named
Zacharias, [b]of the division of [c]Abijah. His
[d]wife *was* of the daughters of Aaron, and
her name *was* Elizabeth. 6And they were
both righteous before God, walking in all
the commandments and ordinances of the
Lord blameless. 7But they had no child,
because Elizabeth was barren, and they
were both well advanced in years.
8So it was, that while he was serving as
priest before God in the order of his division, 9according to the custom of the
priesthood, [1]his lot fell [a]to burn incense
when he went into the temple of the Lord.
10[a]And the whole multitude of the people
was praying outside at the hour of incense. 11Then an angel of the Lord appeared to him, standing on the right side
of [a]the altar of incense. 12And when Zacharias saw *him,* [a]he was troubled, and fear
fell upon him.
13But the angel said to him, "Do not be
afraid, Zacharias, for your prayer is heard;
and your wife Elizabeth will bear you a
son, and [a]you shall call his name John.
14And you will have joy and gladness, and
[a]many will rejoice at his birth. 15For he
will be [a]great in the sight of the Lord, and
[b]shall drink neither wine nor strong
drink. He will also be filled with the Holy
Spirit, [c]even from his mother's womb.
16And he will turn many of the children of
Israel to the Lord their God. 17[a]He will
also go before Him in the spirit and power
of Elijah, *'to turn the hearts of the fathers
to the children,'* and the disobedient to
the wisdom of the just, to make ready a
people prepared for the Lord."
18And Zacharias said to the angel,
[a]"How shall I know this? For I am an old

CHAPTER 1
1 a John 20:31 *1* Or *are most surely believed*
2 a Acts 1:21, 22 b Acts 1:2 c Heb. 2:3
3 a Acts 1:1 *1* Lit. *accurately followed*
4 a [John 20:31]
5 a Matt. 2:1 b 1 Chr. 24:1, 10 c Neh. 12:4 d Lev. 21:13, 14
9 a Ex. 30:7, 8 *1 he was chosen by lot*
10 a Lev. 16:17
11 a Ex. 30:1
12 a Luke 2:9
13 a Luke 1:57, 60, 63
14 a Luke 1:58
15 a [Luke 7:24–28] b Num. 6:3 c Jer. 1:5
17 a Mal. 4:5, 6; Matt. 3:2; 11:14
18 a Gen. 17:17
19 a Dan. 8:16 b Luke 2:10 *1 this good news*
20 a Ezek. 3:26; 24:27
23 a 2 Kin. 11:5
25 a Gen. 30:23
27 a Matt. 1:18
28 a Dan. 9:23 b Judg. 6:12 *1* NU omits *blessed are you among women*
29 a Luke 1:12 *1* NU omits *when she saw him*
30 a Luke 2:52
31 a Is. 7:14 b Luke 2:21
32 a Mark 5:7 b 2 Sam. 7:12, 13, 16 c 2 Sam. 7:14–17 d Matt. 1:1
33 a [Dan. 2:44]
34 *1* Am a virgin
35 a Matt. 1:20 b [Heb. 1:2, 8]

man, and my wife is well advanced in
years."
19And the angel answered and said to
him, "I am [a]Gabriel, who stands in the
presence of God, and was sent to speak to
you and bring you [1]these glad [b]tidings.
20But behold, [a]you will be mute and not
able to speak until the day these things
take place, because you did not believe my
words which will be fulfilled in their own
time."
21And the people waited for Zacharias,
and marveled that he lingered so long in
the temple. 22But when he came out, he
could not speak to them; and they perceived that he had seen a vision in the
temple, for he beckoned to them and remained speechless.
23So it was, as soon as [a]the days of his
service were completed, that he departed
to his own house. 24Now after those days
his wife Elizabeth conceived; and she hid
herself five months, saying, 25"Thus the
Lord has dealt with me, in the days when
He looked on *me,* to [a]take away my reproach among people."

Christ's Birth Announced to Mary

26Now in the sixth month the angel Gabriel was sent by God to a city of Galilee
named Nazareth, 27to a virgin [a]betrothed
to a man whose name was Joseph, of the
house of David. The virgin's name *was*
Mary. 28And having come in, the angel
said to her, [a]"Rejoice, highly favored *one,*
[b]the Lord *is* with you; [1]blessed *are* you
among women!"
29But [1]when she saw *him,* [a]she was
troubled at his saying, and considered
what manner of greeting this was. 30Then
the angel said to her, "Do not be afraid,
Mary, for you have found [a]favor with God.
31[a]And behold, you will conceive in your
womb and bring forth a Son, and [b]shall
call His name JESUS. 32He will be great,
[a]and will be called the Son of the Highest;
and [b]the Lord God will give Him the
[c]throne of His [d]father David. 33[a]And He
will reign over the house of Jacob forever,
and of His kingdom there will be no end."
34Then Mary said to the angel, "How
can this be, since I [1]do not know a man?"
35And the angel answered and said to
her, [a]"*The* Holy Spirit will come upon
you, and the power of the Highest will
overshadow you; therefore, also, that Holy
One who is to be born will be called [b]the

Son of God. 36Now indeed, Elizabeth your
relative has also conceived a son in her old
age; and this is now the sixth month for
her who was called barren. 37For [a]with
God nothing will be impossible."
38Then Mary said, "Behold the maidservant of the Lord! Let it be to me according to your word." And the angel
departed from her.

Mary Visits Elizabeth

39Now Mary arose in those days and
went into the hill country with haste, [a]to
a city of Judah, 40and entered the house of
Zacharias and greeted Elizabeth. 41And
it happened, when Elizabeth heard the
greeting of Mary, that the babe leaped in
her womb; and Elizabeth was [a]filled with
the Holy Spirit. 42Then she spoke out with
a loud voice and said, [a]"Blessed *are* you
among women, and blessed *is* the fruit of
your womb! 43But why *is* this *granted* to
me, that the mother of my Lord should
come to me? 44For indeed, as soon as the
voice of your greeting sounded in my ears,
the babe leaped in my womb for joy.
45[a]Blessed *is* she who [1]believed, for there

37 [a] Jer. 32:17
39 [a] Josh. 21:9
41 [a] Acts 6:3
42 [a] Judg. 5:24
45 [a] John 20:29 [1] Or *believed that there*

Mary, Mother of Jesus

God had a profound destiny for a young woman named Mary—a destiny unlike any He has ever allowed or will ever allow another woman to fulfill. He handpicked her for the highest honor ever given to a human being. He chose her to be the earthly mother of His only Son.

What was it about her that qualified her to be the mother of Jesus? We know that Mary possessed enormous purity, humility, devotion, and confidence in God. We know that she was "highly favored" of the Lord (Luke 1:28). And we know that when she heard God's holy call, she simply said yes.

Mary could have said no. Her situation must have been unsettling and would certainly make her the talk of the town. When she said to Gabriel, "Let it be to me according to your word" (Luke 1:38), she did not know how her life would change or whether Joseph would be faithful to her; in fact, she had every reason to assume he would break their engagement. Still, Mary chose obedience. Essentially, she told Gabriel, "I belong to the Lord. Whatever He says, I'll do it." She placed her entire life on the altar of God's purpose, and then rejoiced (see Luke 1:46–49), embracing God's destiny for her.

Years later, when Mary and Jesus attended a wedding in Cana, she said to the servants there, "Whatever He says to you, do it" (John 2:5). They began to obey Jesus, and soon His first miracle was performed. Mary knew from experience that it is crucial to do whatever the Lord asks.

Mary, the woman all generations have called "blessed," was the first woman in Scripture to utter the phrase that should stay on the lips of every woman of destiny: "Let it be to me according to your word." She was also the one who gave an indispensable instruction to anyone who wants to fulfill God's destiny for her life: "Whatever He says to you, do it." When God reveals His plans, purposes, and seasons for our lives, may we say to Him with joy, "Lord, let it be to *me* according to Your word!" and may we do, with all of our hearts, whatever He asks.

Father, may ____ magnify You and may her spirit rejoice in God her Savior.

FROM LUKE 1:46

will be a fulfillment of those things which
were told her from the Lord."

The Song of Mary

46 And Mary said:

[a]"My soul [1]magnifies the Lord,
47 And my spirit has [a]rejoiced in
[b]God my Savior.
48 For [a]He has regarded the lowly
state of His maidservant;
For behold, henceforth [b]all
generations will call me blessed.
49 For He who is mighty [a]has done
great things for me,
And [b]holy *is* His name.
50 And [a]His mercy *is* on those who
fear Him
From generation to generation.
51 [a]He has shown strength with His
arm;
[b]He has scattered *the* proud in the
imagination of their hearts.
52 [a]He has put down the mighty from
their thrones,
And exalted *the* lowly.
53 He has [a]filled *the* hungry with
good things,
And *the* rich He has sent away
empty.
54 He has helped His [a]servant Israel,
[b]In remembrance of *His* mercy,
55 [a]As He spoke to our [b]fathers,
To Abraham and to his [c]seed
forever."

56 And Mary remained with her about
three months, and returned to her house.

Birth of John the Baptist

57 Now Elizabeth's full time came for
her to be delivered, and she brought forth
a son. 58 When her neighbors and relatives
heard how the Lord had shown great mercy to her, they [a]rejoiced with her.

46 a 1 Sam. 2:1–10 *1* Declares the greatness of
47 a Hab. 3:18 b 1 Tim. 1:1; 2:3
48 a Ps. 138:6 b Luke 11:27
49 a Ps. 71:19; 126:2, 3 b Ps. 111:9
50 a Ps. 103:17
51 a Ps. 98:1; 118:15 b [1 Pet. 5:5]
52 a 1 Sam. 2:7, 8
53 a [Matt. 5:6]
54 a Is. 41:8 b [Jer. 31:3]
55 a Gen. 17:19 b [Rom. 11:28] c Gen. 17:7
58 a [Rom. 12:15]
59 a Gen. 17:12
60 a Luke 1:13, 63
66 a Luke 2:19 b Acts 11:21
67 a Joel 2:28
68 a 1 Kin. 1:48 b Ex. 3:16
69 a Ps. 132:17
70 a Rom. 1:2 b Acts 3:21
72 a Lev. 26:42
73 a Gen. 12:3; 22:16–18
74 a [Heb. 9:14]
75 a [Eph. 4:24]

Circumcision of John the Baptist

59 So it was, [a]on the eighth day, that
they came to circumcise the child; and
they would have called him by the name
of his father, Zacharias. 60 His mother answered and said, [a]"No; he shall be called
John."

61 But they said to her, "There is no one
among your relatives who is called by this
name." 62 So they made signs to his father—what he would have him called.

63 And he asked for a writing tablet, and
wrote, saying, "His name is John." So they
all marveled. 64 Immediately his mouth
was opened and his tongue *loosed,* and he
spoke, praising God. 65 Then fear came on
all who dwelt around them; and all these
sayings were discussed throughout all the
hill country of Judea. 66 And all those who
heard *them* [a]kept *them* in their hearts,
saying, "What kind of child will this be?"
And [b]the hand of the Lord was with him.

Zacharias' Prophecy

67 Now his father Zacharias [a]was filled
with the Holy Spirit, and prophesied,
saying:

68 "Blessed[a] *is* the Lord God of Israel,
For [b]He has visited and redeemed
His people,
69 [a]And has raised up a horn of
salvation for us
In the house of His servant David,
70 [a]As He spoke by the mouth of His
holy prophets,
Who *have been* [b]since the world
began,
71 That we should be saved from our
enemies
And from the hand of all who hate
us,
72 [a]To perform the mercy *promised* to
our fathers
And to remember His holy
covenant,
73 [a]The oath which He swore to our
father Abraham:
74 To grant us that we,
Being delivered from the hand of
our enemies,
Might [a]serve Him without fear,
75 [a]In holiness and righteousness
before Him all the days of our
life.

76 "And you, child, will be called the
[a]prophet of the Highest;
For [b]you will go before the face of
the Lord to prepare His ways,
77 To give [a]knowledge of salvation to
His people
By the remission of their sins,
78 Through the tender mercy of our
God,
With which the [1]Dayspring from on
high [2]has visited us;
79 [a]To give light to those who sit in
darkness and the shadow of
death,
To [b]guide our feet into the way of
peace."

80 So [a]the child grew and became strong
in spirit, and [b]was in the deserts till the
day of his manifestation to Israel.

Christ Born of Mary

2 And it came to pass in those days *that*
a decree went out from Caesar Augustus that all the world should be registered.
2 [a]This census first took place while Qui-
rinius was governing Syria. 3 So all went
to be registered, everyone to his own city.
4 Joseph also went up from Galilee, out
of the city of Nazareth, into Judea, to [a]the
city of David, which is called Bethlehem,
[b]because he was of the house and lineage
of David, 5 to be registered with Mary, [a]his
betrothed [1]wife, who was with child. 6 So
it was, that while they were there, the days
were completed for her to be delivered.
7 And [a]she brought forth her firstborn
Son, and wrapped Him in swaddling
cloths, and laid Him in a [1]manger, because there was no room for them in the
inn.

Glory in the Highest

8 Now there were in the same country
shepherds living out in the fields, keeping
watch over their flock by night. 9 And [1]be-
hold, an angel of the Lord stood before
them, and the glory of the Lord shone
around them, [a]and they were greatly
afraid. 10 Then the angel said to them,
[a]"Do not be afraid, for behold, I bring you
good tidings of great joy [b]which will be to
all people. 11 [a]For there is born to you this
day in the city of David [b]a Savior, [c]who is
Christ the Lord. 12 And this *will be* the sign
to you: You will find a Babe wrapped in
swaddling cloths, lying in a [1]manger."

13 [a]And suddenly there was with the angel a multitude of the heavenly host praising God and saying:

14 "Glory[a] to God in the highest,
And on earth [b]peace, [c]goodwill[1]
toward men!"

15 So it was, when the angels had gone
away from them into heaven, that the
shepherds said to one another, "Let us
now go to Bethlehem and see this thing
that has come to pass, which the Lord has
made known to us." 16 And they came with
haste and found Mary and Joseph, and the
Babe lying in a manger. 17 Now when they
had seen *Him,* they made [1]widely known
the saying which was told them concerning this Child. 18 And all those who heard
it marveled at those things which were
told them by the shepherds. 19 [a]But Mary
kept all these things and pondered *them*
in her heart. 20 Then the shepherds returned, glorifying and [a]praising God for
all the things that they had heard and
seen, as it was told them.

Circumcision of Jesus

21 [a]And when eight days were completed
[1]for the circumcision of the Child, His
name was called [b]JESUS, the name given
by the angel [c]before He was conceived in
the womb.

Jesus Presented in the Temple

22 Now when [a]the days of her purification according to the law of Moses were
completed, they brought Him to Jerusalem to present *Him* to the Lord 23 [a](as it
is written in the law of the Lord, [b]*"Every
male who opens the womb shall be called
holy to the LORD"*), 24 and to offer a sacrifice according to what is said in the law of
the Lord, [a]*"A pair of turtledoves or two
young pigeons."*

Simeon Sees God's Salvation

25 And behold, there was a man in Jerusalem whose name was Simeon, and this
man was just and devout, [a]waiting for the
Consolation of Israel, and the Holy Spirit
was upon him. 26 And it had been revealed
to him by the Holy Spirit that he would
not [a]see death before he had seen the
Lord's Christ. 27 So he came [a]by the Spirit
into the temple. And when the parents
brought in the Child Jesus, to do for Him
according to the custom of the law, 28 he

76 a Matt. 3:3; 11:9 b Is. 40:3
77 a [Mark 1:4]
78 1 Lit. *Dawn;* the Messiah 2 NU *shall visit*
79 a Is. 9:2 b [John 10:4; 14:27; 16:33]
80 a Luke 2:40 b Matt. 3:1

CHAPTER 2
2 a Acts 5:37
4 a 1 Sam. 16:1 b Matt. 1:16
5 a [Matt. 1:18] 1 NU omits *wife*
7 a Matt. 1:25 1 *feed trough*
9 a Luke 1:12 1 NU omits *behold*
10 a Luke 1:13, 30 b Gen. 12:3
11 a Is. 9:6 b Matt. 1:21 c Acts 2:36
12 1 *feed trough*
13 a Dan. 7:10
14 a Luke 19:38 b Is. 57:19 c [Eph. 2:4, 7] 1 NU *toward men of goodwill*
17 1 NU omits *widely*
19 a Gen. 37:11
20 a Luke 19:37
21 a Lev. 12:3 b [Matt. 1:21] c Luke 1:31 1 NU *for His circumcision*
22 a Lev. 12:2–8
23 a Deut. 18:4 b Ex. 13:2, 12, 15
24 a Lev. 12:2, 8
25 a Mark 15:43
26 a [Heb. 11:5]
27 a Matt. 4:1

took Him up in his arms and blessed God and said:

29 "Lord, [a]now You are letting Your
servant depart in peace,
According to Your word;
30 For my eyes [a]have seen Your
salvation
31 Which You have prepared before
the face of all peoples,
32 [a]A light to *bring* revelation to the
Gentiles,
And the glory of Your people
Israel."

33 [1]And Joseph and His mother marveled at those things which were spoken
of Him. 34 Then Simeon blessed them, and
said to Mary His mother, "Behold, this

29 a Gen. 46:30
30 a [Is. 52:10]
32 a Acts 10:45; 13:47; 28:28
33 1 NU *And His father and mother*
34 a [1 Pet. 2:7, 8] b Acts 4:2; 17:32; 28:22
35 a Ps. 42:10
36 a Josh. 19:24
37 a 1 Tim. 5:5 1 NU *until she was eighty-four*

Child is destined for the [a]fall and rising of
many in Israel, and for [b]a sign which will
be spoken against 35 (yes, [a]a sword will
pierce through your own soul also), that
the thoughts of many hearts may be revealed."

Anna Bears Witness to the Redeemer

36 Now there was one, Anna, a prophetess, the daughter of Phanuel, of the tribe
of [a]Asher. She was of a great age, and had
lived with a husband seven years from her
virginity; 37 and this woman *was* a widow
[1]of about eighty-four years, who did not
depart from the temple, but served *God*
with fastings and prayers [a]night and day.
38 And coming in that instant she gave

ANNA

Anna had been waiting for the Messiah for a long, long time. And all the prayers she had prayed for years were answered with just one look at His tiny, holy face. This prophetess, like the prophets before her, *knew* that Israel's Redeemer would come; and when Mary and Joseph brought Him to the temple, she knew that He *had* come.

Scripture seems to indicate that Anna made her home in the temple, devoting her entire existence to God, serving Him "with fastings and prayers night and day" (Luke 2:37). In her younger days, Anna had been married for about seven years. After her husband died, she spent the rest of her life as a widow. At eighty-four years old, she could be found in the temple demonstrating the great gifts of age—wisdom, faith, perseverance, steadfast devotion—to God's people.

Anna is often mentioned in connection with Simeon, an old Jewish man who, likewise, had been "waiting for [Jesus,] the Consolation of Israel" (2:25). Anna's first look at the infant Messiah happened while Simeon was speaking with Mary and Joseph—praying, prophesying, and blessing them. Instantly, she recognized Him as the One she had anticipated. Immediately, she began praising God and from that moment on, "spoke of Him to all those who looked for redemption in Jerusalem" (2:38).

What joy she must have had in finally being able to see the answer to her prayers—an answer that all of history had waited for. Anna was a true woman of destiny, appointed to fast, pray, and minister in the temple during the most exciting event the world has ever known—the birth of Jesus Christ. She embraced God's purpose for her—never departing from the temple and never remarrying, simply serving faithfully until her eyes had seen what her heart had longed for.

A travailing spirit, the throes of a great burdened desire, belongs to prayer. A fervency strong enough to drive away sleep, which devotes and inflames the spirit, and which retires all earthly ties, all this belongs to wrestling, prevailing prayer. The Spirit, the power, the air and food of prayer is in such a spirit.

ADONIRAM JUDSON

thanks to [1]the Lord, and spoke of Him to all those who [a]looked for redemption in Jerusalem.

The Family Returns to Nazareth

39So when they had performed all things according to the law of the Lord, they returned to Galilee, to their *own* city, Nazareth. 40[a]And the Child grew and became strong [1]in spirit, filled with wisdom; and the grace of God was upon Him.

The Boy Jesus Amazes the Scholars

41His parents went to [a]Jerusalem [b]every year at the Feast of the Passover. 42And when He was twelve years old, they went up to Jerusalem according to the [a]custom of the feast. 43When they had finished the [a]days, as they returned, the Boy Jesus lingered behind in Jerusalem. And [1]Joseph and His mother did not know *it;* 44but supposing Him to have been in the company, they went a day's journey, and sought Him among *their* relatives and acquaintances. 45So when they did not find Him, they returned to Jerusalem, seeking Him. 46Now so it was *that* after three days they found Him in the temple, sitting in the midst of the teachers, both listening to them and asking them questions. 47And [a]all who heard Him were astonished at His understanding and answers. 48So when they saw Him, they were amazed; and His mother said to Him, "Son, why have You done this to us? Look, Your father and I have sought You anxiously."

49And He said to them, "Why did you seek Me? Did you not know that I must be [a]about [b]My Father's business?" 50But [a]they did not understand the statement which He spoke to them.

Jesus Advances in Wisdom and Favor

51Then He went down with them and came to Nazareth, and was [1]subject to them, but His mother [a]kept all these things in her heart. 52And Jesus [a]increased in wisdom and stature, [b]and in favor with God and men.

John the Baptist Prepares the Way

3 Now in the fifteenth year of the reign of Tiberius Caesar, [a]Pontius Pilate being governor of Judea, Herod being tetrarch of Galilee, his brother Philip tetrarch of Iturea and the region of Trachonitis, and Lysanias tetrarch of Abilene, 2[1]while [a]Annas and Caiaphas were high priests, the word of God came to [b]John the son of Zacharias in the wilderness. 3[a]And he went into all the region around the Jordan, preaching a baptism of repentance [b]for the remission of sins, 4as it is written in the book of the words of Isaiah the prophet, saying:

[a]"The voice of one crying in the wilderness:
'Prepare the way of the LORD;
Make His paths straight.
5 *Every valley shall be filled*
And every mountain and hill brought low;
The crooked places shall be made straight
And the rough ways smooth;
6 *And [a]all flesh shall see the salvation of God.' "*

John Preaches to the People

7Then he said to the multitudes that came out to be baptized by him, [a]"Brood[1] of vipers! Who warned you to flee from the wrath to come? 8Therefore bear fruits

38 a Mark 15:43 *1* NU *God*
40 a Luke 1:80; 2:52 *1* NU omits *in spirit*
41 a John 4:20 b Deut. 16:1, 16
42 a Ex. 23:14, 15
43 a Ex. 12:15 *1* NU *His parents*
47 a Matt. 7:28; 13:54; 22:33
49 a John 9:4 b [Luke 4:22, 32]
50 a John 7:15, 46
51 a Dan. 7:28 *1 obedient*
52 a [Col. 2:2, 3] b 1 Sam. 2:26
CHAPTER 3
1 a Matt. 27:2
2 a Acts 4:6 b Luke 1:13 *1* NU, M *in the high priesthood of Annas and Caiaphas*
3 a Mark 1:4 b Luke 1:77
4 a Is. 40:3–5
6 a Is. 52:10
7 a Matt. 3:7; 12:34; 23:33 *1 Offspring*

[a]worthy of repentance, and do not begin
to say to yourselves, 'We have Abraham as
our father.' For I say to you that God is
able to raise up children to Abraham from
these stones. 9And even now the ax is laid
to the root of the trees. Therefore [a]every
tree which does not bear good fruit is cut
down and thrown into the fire."

10So the people asked him, saying,
[a]"What shall we do then?"

11He answered and said to them, [a]"He
who has two tunics, let him give to him
who has none; and he who has food, [b]let
him do likewise."

12Then [a]tax collectors also came to be
baptized, and said to him, "Teacher, what
shall we do?"

13And he said to them, [a]"Collect no
more than what is appointed for you."

14Likewise the soldiers asked him, saying, "And what shall we do?"

So he said to them, "Do not [1]intimidate
anyone [a]or accuse falsely, and be content
with your wages."

15Now as the people were in expectation, and all reasoned in their hearts
about John, whether he was the Christ *or*
not, 16John answered, saying to all, [a]"I
indeed baptize you with water; but One
mightier than I is coming, whose sandal
strap I am not worthy to loose. He will
[b]baptize you with the Holy Spirit and fire.
17His winnowing fan *is* in His hand, and
He will thoroughly clean out His threshing floor, and [a]gather the wheat into His
barn; but the chaff He will burn with unquenchable fire."

18And with many other exhortations he
preached to the people. 19[a]But Herod the
tetrarch, being rebuked by him concerning Herodias, his [1]brother Philip's wife,
and for all the evils which Herod had
done, 20also added this, above all, that he
shut John up in prison.

John Baptizes Jesus

21When all the people were baptized, [a]it
came to pass that Jesus also was baptized;
and while He prayed, the heaven was
opened. 22And the Holy Spirit descended
in bodily form like a dove upon Him, and
a voice came from heaven which said,
"You are My beloved Son; in You I am
[a]well pleased."

The Genealogy of Jesus Christ

23Now Jesus Himself began *His ministry at* [a]about thirty years of age, being (as
was supposed) [b]*the* son of Joseph, *the son*
of Heli, 24*the son* of Matthat, *the son* of
Levi, *the son* of Melchi, *the son* of Janna,
the son of Joseph, 25*the son* of Mattathiah,
the son of Amos, *the son* of Nahum, *the
son* of Esli, *the son* of Naggai, 26*the son* of
Maath, *the son* of Mattathiah, *the son* of
Semei, *the son* of Joseph, *the son* of Judah, 27*the son* of Joannas, *the son* of Rhe-
sa, *the son* of [a]Zerubbabel, *the son* of
Shealtiel, *the son* of Neri, 28*the son* of
Melchi, *the son* of Addi, *the son* of Cosam,
the son of Elmodam, *the son* of Er, 29*the
son* of Jose, *the son* of Eliezer, *the son* of
Jorim, *the son* of Matthat, *the son* of Levi,
30*the son* of Simeon, *the son* of Judah, *the
son* of Joseph, *the son* of Jonan, *the son* of
Eliakim, 31*the son* of Melea, *the son* of
Menan, *the son* of Mattathah, *the son* of
[a]Nathan, [b]*the son* of David, 32[a]*the son*
of Jesse, *the son* of Obed, *the son* of Boaz,
the son of Salmon, *the son* of Nahshon,
33*the son* of Amminadab, *the son* of Ram,
the son of Hezron, *the son* of Perez, *the
son* of Judah, 34*the son* of Jacob, *the son*
of Isaac, *the son* of Abraham, [a]*the son* of
Terah, *the son* of Nahor, 35*the son* of Serug, *the son* of Reu, *the son* of Peleg, *the
son* of Eber, *the son* of Shelah, 36[a]*the son*
of Cainan, *the son* of [b]Arphaxad, [c]*the son*
of Shem, *the son* of Noah, *the son* of
Lamech, 37*the son* of Methuselah, *the
son* of Enoch, *the son* of Jared, *the son* of
Mahalalel, *the son* of Cainan, 38*the son*
of Enosh, *the son* of Seth, *the son* of
Adam, [a]*the son* of God.

Satan Tempts Jesus

4 Then [a]Jesus, being filled with the
Holy Spirit, returned from the Jordan
and [b]was led by the Spirit [1]into the wilderness, 2being [1]tempted for forty days
by the devil. And [a]in those days He ate
nothing, and afterward, when they had
ended, He was hungry.

3And the devil said to Him, "If You are
[a]the Son of God, command this stone to
become bread."

4But Jesus answered him, saying, "It
is written, [a]*'Man shall not live by bread
alone,* [1]*but by every word of God.'* "

5[1]Then the devil, taking Him up on a
high mountain, showed Him all the kingdoms of the world in a moment of time.
6And the devil said to Him, "All this authority I will give You, and their glory; for
[a]*this* has been delivered to me, and I give
it to whomever I wish. 7Therefore, if You

8 a [2 Cor. 7:9–11]
9 a Matt. 7:19
10 a [Acts 2:37, 38; 16:30, 31]
11 a 2 Cor. 8:14 b Is. 58:7
12 a Luke 7:29
13 a Luke 19:8
14 a Ex. 20:16; 23:1 *1* Lit. *shake down* for money
16 a Matt. 3:11, 12 b John 7:39; 20:22
17 a Matt. 13:24–30
19 a Mark 6:17 *1* NU *brother's wife*
21 a Matt. 3:13–17
22 a 2 Pet. 1:17
23 a [Num. 4:3, 35, 39, 43, 47] b John 6:42
27 a Ezra 2:2; 3:8
31 a Zech. 12:12 b 2 Sam. 5:14; 7:12
32 a Ruth 4:18–22
34 a Gen. 11:24, 26–30; 12:3
36 a Gen. 11:12 b Gen. 10:22, 24; 11:10–13 c Gen. 5:6–32; 9:27; 11:10
38 a Gen. 5:1, 2

CHAPTER 4
1 a Matt. 4:1–11 b Luke 2:27 *1* NU *in*
2 a Ex. 34:28 *1 tested*
3 a John 20:31
4 a Deut. 8:3 *1* NU omits *but by every word of God*
5 *1* NU *And taking Him up, he showed Him*
6 a [Rev. 13:2, 7]

Luke 4:2

Dear Woman of Destiny,

As the young woman hangs up the phone she wonders, "How did I let myself get caught up in a gossip session like that? Why, only this morning in my devotional time, I committed my words to the Lord that they would be edifying and pure. Now look what I've done!"

This woman, who genuinely has a heart and passion for Jesus, has just lost a battle with temptation. It didn't seem like a horrible sin at the time, but afterward she feels guilty and defeated. Instead of being an overcomer, she feels overcome. How could she have given in so easily to temptation?

Each day, Christians are faced with the reality of the tension between the kingdom of darkness and the kingdom of light. Just as the Spirit of God draws us to live lives full of righteousness, peace, and joy, so also, the forces of darkness make a bid for our souls. The enemy is subtle, appealing to the intellect, reason, or emotions to establish a stronghold in our lives. We must be able to discern his tactics, choose to deny the comforts of our flesh, and stand firmly upon the truth of God's Word. Temptation is a part of God's growth process in every Christian's life. In Luke 4, Satan subtly came to tempt Jesus by appealing to His flesh at one of His most vulnerable times. Jesus was not subjected to temptation, however, because He had done something wrong. Actually, it was the Spirit of God who led Him into the wilderness for the purpose of facing and overcoming temptation.

This time of temptation was preceded by Jesus' glorious baptism where the Holy Spirit came upon Him as a dove and He heard the Father say, "You are My beloved Son; in You I am well pleased" (Luke 3:22). Jesus was able to face the evil one because He knew who He was to the Father, was full of the Holy Spirit, and was able to trust Him.

Similarly, each one of us must be filled with the power of the Holy Spirit and know that we are "beloved" of the Father. Otherwise the enemy will tempt us to abandon our spiritual inheritance by saying, "What makes you think God loves you or will answer your need?" In realizing our God-ordained identities, we become empowered to trust God and to resist evil.

Jesus did not stand in His own strength, but in the strength of the Word of God. Because of His intimate relationship with the Father, He was able to trust His Word and use it as a weapon of war. Every attempt of Satan to draw Jesus away from God's plan and purpose was thwarted by the Word. He submitted Himself to God through His agreement with the Word; and He resisted the devil, who had to flee! (see James 4:7). This same power is available to each of us. We must simply choose to employ it! As we allow the power of the Holy Spirit, the principles of the Word of God, and a passion for righteousness to reign in our hearts, we will overcome every temptation and manifest the life of Jesus for all to see.

Jane Hamon

will worship before me, all will be Yours."
8 And Jesus answered and said to him,
[1]"Get behind Me, Satan! [2]For it is written,
[a]*'You shall worship the LORD your God,*
and Him only you shall serve.'"
9 [a]Then he brought Him to Jerusalem,
set Him on the pinnacle of the temple,
and said to Him, "If You are the Son of
God, throw Yourself down from here.
10 For it is written:

[a]*'He shall give His angels charge*
over you,
To keep you,'

11 and,

[a]*'In their hands they shall bear you*
up,
Lest you dash your foot against a
stone.'"

12 And Jesus answered and said to him,
"It has been said, [a]*'You shall not [1]tempt*
the LORD your God.'"
13 Now when the devil had ended every
[1]temptation, he departed from Him [a]until
an opportune time.

Jesus Begins His Galilean Ministry

14 [a]Then Jesus returned [b]in the power
of the Spirit to [c]Galilee, and [d]news of Him
went out through all the surrounding region. 15 And He [a]taught in their synagogues, [b]being glorified by all.

Jesus Rejected at Nazareth

16 So He came to [a]Nazareth, where He
had been brought up. And as His custom
was, [b]He went into the synagogue on the
Sabbath day, and stood up to read. 17 And
He was handed the book of the prophet
Isaiah. And when He had opened the
book, He found the place where it was
written:

18 *"The[a] Spirit of the LORD is upon*
Me,
Because He has anointed Me
To preach the gospel to the poor;
He has sent Me [1]to heal the
brokenhearted,
To proclaim liberty to the captives
And recovery of sight to the blind,
To [b]set at liberty those who are
[2]oppressed;
19 *To proclaim the acceptable year of*
the LORD."

8 a Deut. 6:13; 10:20 *1* NU omits *Get behind Me, Satan* *2* NU, M omit *For*
9 a Matt. 4:5–7
10 a Ps. 91:11
11 a Ps. 91:12
12 a Deut. 6:16 *1 test*
13 a [Heb. 4:15] *1 testing*
14 a Matt. 4:12 b John 4:43 c Acts 10:37 d Matt. 4:24
15 a Matt. 4:23 b Is. 52:13
16 a Mark 6:1 b Acts 13:14–16; 17:2
18 a Is. 49:8, 9; 61:1, 2 b [Dan. 9:24] *1* NU omits *to heal the brokenhearted* *2 downtrodden*
21 a Acts 13:29
22 a [Ps. 45:2] b John 6:42
23 a Matt. 4:13; 11:23 b Matt. 13:54 *1* NU *Capharnaum,* here and elsewhere
24 a John 4:44
25 a 1 Kin. 17:9
26 *1* Gr. *Sarepta*
27 a 2 Kin. 5:1–14
28 a Luke 6:11 *1 rage*
29 a John 8:37; 10:31
30 a John 8:59; 10:39
31 a Matt. 4:13
32 a Matt. 7:28, 29 b [John 6:63; 7:46; 8:26, 28, 38, 47; 12:49, 50]
33 a Mark 1:23
34 a Luke 4:41 b Ps. 16:10
35 *1* Lit. *Be muzzled*

20 Then He closed the book, and gave *it*
back to the attendant and sat down. And
the eyes of all who were in the synagogue
were fixed on Him. 21 And He began to say
to them, "Today this Scripture is [a]fulfilled
in your hearing." 22 So all bore witness to
Him, and [a]marveled at the gracious words
which proceeded out of His mouth. And
they said, [b]"Is this not Joseph's son?"
23 He said to them, "You will surely say
this proverb to Me, 'Physician, heal yourself! Whatever we have heard done in
[a]Capernaum,[1] do also here in [b]Your
country.'" 24 Then He said, "Assuredly, I
say to you, no [a]prophet is accepted in his
own country. 25 But I tell you truly, [a]many
widows were in Israel in the days of Elijah,
when the heaven was shut up three years
and six months, and there was a great
famine throughout all the land; 26 but to
none of them was Elijah sent except to
[1]Zarephath, *in the region* of Sidon, to a
woman *who was* a widow. 27 [a]And many
lepers were in Israel in the time of Elisha
the prophet, and none of them was
cleansed except Naaman the Syrian."
28 So all those in the synagogue, when
they heard these things, were [a]filled with
[1]wrath, 29 [a]and rose up and thrust Him
out of the city; and they led Him to the
brow of the hill on which their city was
built, that they might throw Him down
over the cliff. 30 Then [a]passing through
the midst of them, He went His way.

Jesus Casts Out an Unclean Spirit

31 Then [a]He went down to Capernaum,
a city of Galilee, and was teaching them
on the Sabbaths. 32 And they were [a]aston-
ished at His teaching, [b]for His word was
with authority. 33 [a]Now in the synagogue
there was a man who had a spirit of an
unclean demon. And he cried out with a
loud voice, 34 saying, "Let *us* alone! What
have we to do with You, Jesus of Nazareth? Did You come to destroy us? [a]I
know who You are—[b]the Holy One of
God!"
35 But Jesus rebuked him, saying, [1]"Be
quiet, and come out of him!" And when
the demon had thrown him in *their*
midst, it came out of him and did not hurt
him. 36 Then they were all amazed and
spoke among themselves, saying, "What a
word this *is!* For with authority and power
He commands the unclean spirits, and
they come out." 37 And the report about

Him went out into every place in the surrounding region.

Peter's Mother-in-Law Healed

38 [a]Now He arose from the synagogue
and entered Simon's house. But Simon's
wife's mother was [1]sick with a high fever,
and they [b]made request of Him concerning her. 39 So He stood over her and [a]re-
buked the fever, and it left her. And
immediately she arose and served them.

Many Healed After Sabbath Sunset

40 [a]When the sun was setting, all those
who had any that were sick with various
diseases brought them to Him; and He
laid His hands on every one of them and
healed them. 41 [a]And demons also came
out of many, crying out and saying, [b]"You
are [1]the Christ, the Son of God!"
And He, [c]rebuking *them,* did not allow
them to [2]speak, for they knew that He was
the Christ.

Jesus Preaches in Galilee

42 [a]Now when it was day, He departed
and went into a deserted place. And the
crowd sought Him and came to Him, and
tried to keep Him from leaving them;
43 but He said to them, "I must [a]preach
the kingdom of God to the other cities
also, because for this purpose I have been
sent." 44 [a]And He was preaching in the
synagogues of [1]Galilee.

Four Fishermen Called as Disciples

5 So[a] it was, as the multitude pressed
about Him to [b]hear the word of God,
that He stood by the Lake of Gennesaret,
2 and saw two boats standing by the lake;
but the fishermen had gone from them
and were washing *their* nets. 3 Then He
got into one of the boats, which was Simon's, and asked him to put out a little
from the land. And He [a]sat down and
taught the multitudes from the boat.
4 When He had stopped speaking, He
said to Simon, [a]"Launch out into the deep
and let down your nets for a catch."
5 But Simon answered and said to Him,
"Master, we have toiled all night and
caught [a]nothing; nevertheless [b]at Your
word I will let down the net." 6 And when
they had done this, they caught a great
number of fish, and their net was breaking. 7 So they signaled to *their* partners in
the other boat to come and help them.
And they came and filled both the boats,
so that they began to sink. 8 When Simon
Peter saw *it,* he fell down at Jesus' knees,
saying, [a]"Depart from me, for I am a sinful man, O Lord!"
9 For he and all who were with him were
[a]astonished at the catch of fish which they
had taken; 10 and so also *were* James and
John, the sons of Zebedee, who were partners with Simon. And Jesus said to Simon, "Do not be afraid. [a]From now on
you will catch men." 11 So when they had
brought their boats to land, [a]they [1]for-
sook all and followed Him.

Jesus Cleanses a Leper

12 [a]And it happened when He was in a
certain city, that behold, a man who was
full of [b]leprosy saw Jesus; and he fell on
his face and [1]implored Him, saying,
"Lord, if You are willing, You can make
me clean."
13 Then He put out *His* hand and
touched him, saying, "I am willing; be
cleansed." [a]Immediately the leprosy left
him. 14 [a]And He charged him to tell no
one, "But go and show yourself to the
priest, and make an offering for your
cleansing, as a testimony to them, [b]just as
Moses commanded."
15 However, [a]the report went around
concerning Him all the more; and [b]great
multitudes came together to hear, and
to be healed by Him of their infirmities.
16 [a]So He Himself *often* withdrew into the
wilderness and [b]prayed.

Jesus Forgives and Heals a Paralytic

17 Now it happened on a certain day, as
He was teaching, that there were Pharisees and teachers of the law sitting by,
who had come out of every town of Galilee, Judea, and Jerusalem. And the power
of the Lord was *present* [1]to heal them.
18 [a]Then behold, men brought on a bed
a man who was paralyzed, whom they
sought to bring in and lay before Him.
19 And when they could not find how they
might bring him in, because of the crowd,
they went up on the housetop and let him
down with *his* bed through the tiling into
the midst [a]before Jesus.

38 a Mark 1:29–31 b Mark 5:23 *1 afflicted with*
39 a Luke 8:24
40 a Matt. 8:16, 17
41 a Mark 1:34; 3:11 b Mark 8:29 c Mark 1:25, 34; 3:11 *1* NU omits *the Christ* *2* Or *say that they knew*
42 a Mark 1:35–38
43 a [John 9:4]
44 a Matt. 4:23; 9:35 *1* NU *Judea*

CHAPTER 5
1 a Mark 1:16–20 b Acts 13:44
3 a John 8:2
4 a John 21:6
5 a John 21:3 b Ps. 33:9
8 a 1 Kin. 17:18
9 a Mark 5:42; 10:24, 26
10 a Matt. 4:19
11 a Matt. 4:20; 19:27 *1 left behind*
12 a Mark 1:40–44 b Lev. 13:14 *1 begged*
13 a John 5:9
14 a Matt. 8:4 b Lev. 13:1–3; 14:2–32
15 a Mark 1:45 b John 6:2
16 a Luke 9:10 b Matt. 14:23
17 *1* NU *with Him to heal*
18 a Mark 2:3–12
19 a Matt. 15:30

20When He saw their faith, He said to
him, "Man, your sins are forgiven you."
21[a]And the scribes and the Pharisees
began to reason, saying, "Who is this who
speaks blasphemies? [b]Who can forgive
sins but God alone?"
22But when Jesus [a]perceived their
thoughts, He answered and said to them,
"Why are you reasoning in your hearts?
23Which is easier, to say, 'Your sins are
forgiven you,' or to say, 'Rise up and
walk'? 24But that you may know that the
Son of Man has power on earth to forgive
sins"—He said to the man who was paralyzed, [a]"I say to you, arise, take up your
bed, and go to your house."
25Immediately he rose up before them,
took up what he had been lying on, and
departed to his own house, [a]glorifying
God. 26And they were all amazed, and they
[a]glorified God and were filled with fear,
saying, "We have seen strange things
today!"

Matthew the Tax Collector

27[a]After these things He went out and
saw a tax collector named Levi, sitting at
the tax office. And He said to him, [b]"Follow Me." 28So he left all, rose up, and [a]fol-
lowed Him.
29[a]Then Levi gave Him a great feast in
his own house. And [b]there were a great
number of tax collectors and others who
sat down with them. 30[1]And their scribes
and the Pharisees [2]complained against
His disciples, saying, [a]"Why do You eat
and drink with tax collectors and sinners?"
31Jesus answered and said to them,
"Those who are well have no need of a
physician, but those who are sick. 32[a]I
have not come to call *the* righteous, but
sinners, to repentance."

Jesus Is Questioned About Fasting

33Then they said to Him, [a]"Why[1] do the
disciples of John fast often and make
prayers, and likewise those of the Pharisees, but Yours eat and drink?"
34And He said to them, "Can you make
the friends of the bridegroom fast while
the [a]bridegroom is with them? 35But the
days will come when the bridegroom will
be taken away from them; then they will
fast in those days."

21 [a]Mark 2:6, 7 [b]Is. 43:25
22 [a]John 2:25
24 [a]Luke 7:14
25 [a]Acts 3:8
26 [a]Luke 1:65; 7:16
27 [a]Matt. 9:9–17 [b]John 12:26; 21:19, 22
28 [a]Mark 10:28
29 [a]Matt. 9:9, 10 [b]Luke 15:1
30 [a]Luke 15:2 [1]NU *But the Pharisees and their scribes* [2]*grumbled*
32 [a]1 Tim. 1:15
33 [a]Matt. 9:14 [1]NU omits *Why do,* making the verse a statement
34 [a]John 3:29
36 [a]Mark 2:21, 22 [1]NU *tears a piece from a new garment and puts it on an old one*
38 [1]NU omits *and both are preserved*
39 [1]NU omits *immediately* [2]NU *good*
CHAPTER 6
1 [a]Matt. 12:1–8 [1]NU *on a Sabbath that He went*
2 [a]Ex. 20:10
3 [a]1 Sam. 21:6
4 [a]Lev. 24:9
6 [a]Mark 3:1–6
7 [a]Luke 13:14; 14:1–6 [b]Luke 20:20
8 [a]Matt. 9:4
9 [a]John 7:23 [1]M *to kill*
10 [1]NU, M *him* [2]NU omits *as whole as the other*

36[a]Then He spoke a parable to them:
"No one [1]puts a piece from a new garment
on an old one; otherwise the new makes
a tear, and also the piece that was *taken*
out of the new does not match the old.
37And no one puts new wine into old wineskins; or else the new wine will burst the
wineskins and be spilled, and the wineskins will be ruined. 38But new wine must
be put into new wineskins, [1]and both are
preserved. 39And no one, having drunk old
wine, [1]immediately desires new; for he
says, 'The old is [2]better.' "

Jesus Is Lord of the Sabbath

6 Now [a]it happened [1]on the second
Sabbath after the first that He went
through the grainfields. And His disciples
plucked the heads of grain and ate *them,*
rubbing *them* in *their* hands. 2And some
of the Pharisees said to them, "Why are
you doing [a]what is not lawful to do on the
Sabbath?"
3But Jesus answering them said, "Have
you not even read this, [a]what David did
when he was hungry, he and those who
were with him: 4how he went into the
house of God, took and ate the showbread,
and also gave some to those with him,
[a]which is not lawful for any but the
priests to eat?" 5And He said to them,
"The Son of Man is also Lord of the Sabbath."

Healing on the Sabbath

6[a]Now it happened on another Sabbath,
also, that He entered the synagogue and
taught. And a man was there whose right
hand was withered. 7So the scribes and
Pharisees watched Him closely, whether
He would [a]heal on the Sabbath, that they
might find an [b]accusation against Him.
8But He [a]knew their thoughts, and said
to the man who had the withered hand,
"Arise and stand here." And he arose and
stood. 9Then Jesus said to them, "I will
ask you one thing: [a]Is it lawful on the
Sabbath to do good or to do evil, to save
life or [1]to destroy?" 10And when He had
looked around at them all, He said to [1]the
man, "Stretch out your hand." And he did
so, and his hand was restored [2]as whole as
the other. 11But they were filled with rage,
and discussed with one another what they
might do to Jesus.

The Twelve Apostles

12 Now it came to pass in those days that
He went out to the mountain to pray, and
continued all night in [a]prayer to God.
13 And when it was day, He called His disciples to *Himself;* [a]and from them He chose
[b]twelve whom He also named apostles:
14 Simon, [a]whom He also named Peter,
and Andrew his brother; James and John;
Philip and Bartholomew; 15 Matthew and
Thomas; James the *son* of Alphaeus, and
Simon called the Zealot; 16 Judas [a]*the son*
of James, and [b]Judas Iscariot who also became a traitor.

Jesus Heals a Great Multitude

17 And He came down with them and
stood on a level place with a crowd of His
disciples [a]and a great multitude of people
from all Judea and Jerusalem, and from
the seacoast of Tyre and Sidon, who came
to hear Him and be healed of their diseases, 18 as well as those who were tormented
with unclean spirits. And they were
healed. 19 And the whole multitude
[a]sought to [b]touch Him, for [c]power went
out from Him and healed *them* all.

The Beatitudes

20 Then He lifted up His eyes toward His
disciples, and said:

[a]"Blessed *are you* poor,
For yours is the kingdom of God.
21 [a]Blessed *are you* who hunger now,
For you shall be [b]filled.[1]
[c]Blessed *are you* who weep now,
For you shall [d]laugh.
22 [a]Blessed are you when men hate
you,
And when they [b]exclude you,
And revile *you,* and cast out your
name as evil,
For the Son of Man's sake.
23 [a]Rejoice in that day and leap for
joy!
For indeed your reward *is* great
in heaven,
For [b]in like manner their fathers
did to the prophets.

Jesus Pronounces Woes

24 "But[a] woe to you [b]who are rich,
For [c]you have received your
consolation.
25 [a]Woe to you who are full,
For you shall hunger.
[b]Woe to you who laugh now,
For you shall mourn and [c]weep.
26 [a]Woe [1]to you when [2]all men speak
well of you,
For so did their fathers to the
false prophets.

Love Your Enemies

27 [a]"But I say to you who hear: Love
your enemies, do good to those who hate
you, 28 [a]bless those who curse you, and
[b]pray for those who spitefully use you.
29 [a]To him who strikes you on the *one*
cheek, offer the other also. [b]And from him
who takes away your cloak, do not withhold *your* tunic either. 30 [a]Give to everyone who asks of you. And from him who
takes away your goods do not ask *them*
back. 31 [a]And just as you want men to do
to you, you also do to them likewise.
32 [a]"But if you love those who love you,
what credit is that to you? For even sinners love those who love them. 33 And if
you do good to those who do good to you,
what credit is that to you? For even sinners do the same. 34 [a]And if you lend *to
those* from whom you hope to receive
back, what credit is that to you? For even
sinners lend to sinners to receive as much
back. 35 But [a]love your enemies, [b]do good,
and [c]lend, [1]hoping for nothing in return;
and your reward will be great, and [d]you
will be sons of the Most High. For He is
kind to the unthankful and evil. 36 [a]There-
fore be merciful, just as your Father also
is merciful.

Do Not Judge

37 [a]"Judge not, and you shall not be
judged. Condemn not, and you shall not
be condemned. [b]Forgive, and you will be
forgiven. 38 [a]Give, and it will be given to

12 a Mark 1:35
13 a John 6:70 b Matt. 10:1
14 a John 1:42
16 a Jude 1 b Luke 22:3–6
17 a Mark 3:7, 8
19 a Matt. 9:21; 14:36 b Mark 5:27, 28 c Luke 8:46
20 a Matt. 5:3–12; [11:5]
21 a Is. 55:1; 65:13 b [Rev. 7:16] c [Is. 61:3] d Ps. 126:5 *1 satisfied*
22 a 1 Pet. 2:19; 3:14; 4:14 b [John 16:2]
23 a James 1:2 b Acts 7:51
24 a James 5:1–6 b Luke 12:21 c Luke 16:25
25 a [Is. 65:13] b [Prov. 14:13] c James 4:9
26 a [John 15:19] *1* NU, M omit *to you* *2* M omits *all*
27 a Rom. 12:20
28 a Rom. 12:14 b Acts 7:60
29 a Matt. 5:39–42 b [1 Cor. 6:7]
30 a Deut. 15:7, 8
31 a Matt. 7:12
32 a Matt. 5:46
34 a Matt. 5:42
35 a [Rom. 13:10] b Heb. 13:16 c Ps. 37:26 d Matt. 5:46 *1 expecting*
36 a Matt. 5:48
37 a Matt. 7:1–5 b Matt. 18:21–35
38 a [Prov. 19:17; 28:27]

O Lord, I pray that as ____ gives, it will be given to them: good measure, pressed down, shaken together, and running over. For with the same measure they use, it will be measured back to them.

FROM LUKE 6:38

you: good measure, pressed down, shaken
together, and running over will be put
into your [b]bosom. For [c]with the same
measure that you use, it will be measured
back to you."
[39]And He spoke a parable to them:
[a]"Can the blind lead the blind? Will they
not both fall into the ditch? [40][a]A disciple
is not above his teacher, but everyone who
is perfectly trained will be like his teacher.
[41][a]And why do you look at the speck in
your brother's eye, but do not perceive the
plank in your own eye? [42]Or how can you
say to your brother, 'Brother, let me remove the speck that *is* in your eye,' when
you yourself do not see the plank that *is*
in your own eye? Hypocrite! First remove
the plank from your own eye, and then
you will see clearly to remove the speck
that is in your brother's eye.

So long as we are full of self we are shocked at the faults of others. Let us think more often of our own sin, and we shall be lenient to the sins of others.

FENELON

A Tree Is Known by Its Fruit

[43][a]"For a good tree does not bear bad
fruit, nor does a bad tree bear good fruit.
[44]For [a]every tree is known by its own
fruit. For *men* do not gather figs from
thorns, nor do they gather grapes from a
bramble bush. [45][a]A good man out of the
good treasure of his heart brings forth
good; and an evil man out of the evil
[1]treasure of his heart brings forth evil.
For out [b]of the abundance of the heart his
mouth speaks.

Build on the Rock

[46][a]"But why do you call Me 'Lord,
Lord,' and not do the things which I say?
[47][a]Whoever comes to Me, and hears My
sayings and does them, I will show you
whom he is like: [48]He is like a man building a house, who dug deep and laid the
foundation on the rock. And when the
flood arose, the stream beat vehemently
against that house, and could not shake it,
for it was [1]founded on the rock. [49]But he
who heard and did nothing is like a man
who built a house on the earth without a
foundation, against which the stream beat
vehemently; and immediately it [1]fell. And
the ruin of that house was great."

Jesus Heals a Centurion's Servant

7 Now when He concluded all His sayings in the hearing of the people, He
[a]entered Capernaum. [2]And a certain centurion's servant, who was dear to him,
was sick and ready to die. [3]So when he
heard about Jesus, he sent elders of the
Jews to Him, pleading with Him to come
and heal his servant. [4]And when they
came to Jesus, they begged Him earnestly,
saying that the one for whom He should
do this was deserving, [5]"for he loves our
nation, and has built us a synagogue."
[6]Then Jesus went with them. And when
He was already not far from the house, the
centurion sent friends to Him, saying to
Him, "Lord, do not trouble Yourself, for I
am not worthy that You should enter under my roof. [7]Therefore I did not even
think myself worthy to come to You. But
[a]say the word, and my servant will be
healed. [8]For I also am a man placed under
[a]authority, having soldiers under me. And
I say to one, 'Go,' and he goes; and to another, 'Come,' and he comes; and to my
servant, 'Do this,' and he does *it*."
[9]When Jesus heard these things, He
marveled at him, and turned around and
said to the crowd that followed Him, "I say
to you, I have not found such great faith,
not even in Israel!" [10]And those who were
sent, returning to the house, found the
servant well [1]who had been sick.

Jesus Raises the Son of the Widow of Nain

[11]Now it happened, the day after, *that*
He went into a city called Nain; and many
of His disciples went with Him, and a
large crowd. [12]And when He came near
the gate of the city, behold, a dead man
was being carried out, the only son of his
mother; and she was a widow. And a large
crowd from the city was with her. [13]When
the Lord saw her, He had [a]compassion
on her and said to her, [b]"Do not weep."

38 b Ps. 79:12 c James 2:13
39 a Matt. 15:14; 23:16
40 a [John 13:16; 15:20]
41 a Matt. 7:3
43 a Matt. 7:16–18, 20
44 a Matt. 12:33
45 a Matt. 12:35 b Matt. 12:34 *1* NU omits *treasure of his heart*
46 a Mal. 1:6
47 a James 1:22–25
48 *1* NU *well built*
49 *1* NU *collapsed*
CHAPTER 7
1 a Matt. 8:5–13
7 a Ps. 33:9; 107:20
8 a [Mark 13:34]
10 *1* NU omits *who had been sick*
13 a John 11:35 b Luke 8:52

14 Then He came and touched the open
coffin, and those who carried *him* stood
still. And He said, "Young man, I say to
you, [a]arise." 15 So he who was dead [a]sat up
and began to speak. And He [b]presented
him to his mother.
16 [a]Then fear [1]came upon all, and they
[b]glorified God, saying, [c]"A great prophet
has risen up among us"; and, [d]"God has
visited His people." 17 And this report
about Him went throughout all Judea and
all the surrounding region.

John the Baptist Sends Messengers to Jesus

18 [a]Then the disciples of John reported
to him concerning all these things. 19 And
John, calling two of his disciples to *him,*
sent *them* to [1]Jesus, saying, "Are You [a]the
Coming One, or [2]do we look for another?"
20 When the men had come to Him, they
said, "John the Baptist has sent us to You,
saying, 'Are You the Coming One, or do
we look for another?'" 21 And that very
hour He cured many of [1]infirmities, afflictions, and evil spirits; and to many blind
He gave sight.
22 [a]Jesus answered and said to them,
"Go and tell John the things you have
seen and heard: [b]that *the* blind [c]see, *the*
lame [d]walk, *the* lepers are [e]cleansed, *the*
deaf [f]hear, *the* dead are raised, [g]*the* poor
have the gospel preached to them. 23 And
blessed is *he* who is not [1]offended because
of Me."
24 [a]When the messengers of John had
departed, He began to speak to the multitudes concerning John: "What did you go
out into the wilderness to see? A reed
shaken by the wind? 25 But what did you
go out to see? A man clothed in soft garments? Indeed those who are gorgeously
appareled and live in luxury are in kings'
courts. 26 But what did you go out to see?
A prophet? Yes, I say to you, and more
than a prophet. 27 This is *he* of whom it is
written:

[a]*'Behold, I send My messenger*
before Your face,
Who will prepare Your way before
You.'

28 For I say to you, among those born of
women there is [1]not a [a]greater prophet
than John the Baptist; but he who is least
in the kingdom of God is greater than he."
29 And when all the people heard *Him,*
even the tax collectors [1]justified God,
[a]having been baptized with the baptism of
John. 30 But the Pharisees and [1]lawyers rejected [a]the will of God for themselves, not
having been baptized by him.
31 [1]And the Lord said, [a]"To what then
shall I liken the men of this generation,
and what are they like? 32 They are like
children sitting in the marketplace and
calling to one another, saying:

'We played the flute for you,
And you did not dance;
We mourned to you,
And you did not weep.'

33 For [a]John the Baptist came [b]neither
eating bread nor drinking wine, and you
say, 'He has a demon.' 34 The Son of Man
has come [a]eating and drinking, and you
say, 'Look, a glutton and a [1]winebibber,
a friend of tax collectors and sinners!'
35 [a]But wisdom is justified by all her children."

A Sinful Woman Forgiven

36 [a]Then one of the Pharisees asked Him
to eat with him. And He went to the Pharisee's house, and sat down to eat. 37 And
behold, a woman in the city who was a
sinner, when she knew that *Jesus* sat at
the table in the Pharisee's house, brought
an alabaster flask of fragrant oil, 38 and
stood at His feet behind *Him* weeping; and
she began to wash His feet with her tears,
and wiped *them* with the hair of her head;
and she kissed His feet and anointed *them*
with the fragrant oil. 39 Now when the
Pharisee who had invited Him saw *this,* he
spoke to himself, saying, [a]"This Man, if He
were a prophet, would know who and
what manner of woman *this is* who is
touching Him, for she is a sinner."
40 And Jesus answered and said to him,
"Simon, I have something to say to you."
So he said, "Teacher, say it."
41 "There was a certain creditor who had
two debtors. One owed five hundred [a]de-
narii, and the other fifty. 42 And when they
had nothing with which to repay, he freely
forgave them both. Tell Me, therefore,
which of them will love him more?"
43 Simon answered and said, "I suppose
the *one* whom he forgave more."
And He said to him, "You have rightly
judged." 44 Then He turned to the woman
and said to Simon, "Do you see this woman? I entered your house; you gave Me no
[a]water for My feet, but she has washed My
feet with her tears and wiped *them* with

---

14 a Acts 9:40
15 a John 11:44 b 2 Kin. 4:36
16 a Luke 1:65 b Luke 5:26 c Luke 24:19 d Luke 1:68 1 *seized them all*
18 a Matt. 11:2–19
19 a [Zech. 9:9] 1 NU *the Lord* 2 *should we expect*
21 1 *illnesses*
22 a Matt. 11:4 b Is. 35:5 c John 9:7 d Matt. 15:31 e Luke 17:12–14 f Mark 7:37 g [Is. 61:1–3]
23 1 *caused to stumble*
24 a Matt. 11:7
27 a Mal. 3:1
28 a [Luke 1:15] 1 NU *none greater than John;*
29 a Luke 3:12 1 *declared the righteousness of*
30 a Acts 20:27 1 *the experts in the law*
31 a Matt. 11:16 1 NU, M omit *And the Lord said*
33 a Matt. 3:1 b Luke 1:15
34 a Luke 15:2 1 An excessive drinker
35 a Matt. 11:19
36 a John 11:2
39 a Luke 15:2
41 a Matt. 18:28
44 a Gen. 18:4; 19:2; 43:24

the hair of her head. 45You gave Me no [a]kiss, but this woman has not ceased to kiss My feet since the time I came in. 46[a]You did not anoint My head with oil, but this woman has anointed My feet with fragrant oil. 47[a]Therefore I say to you, her sins, *which are* many, are forgiven, for she loved much. But to whom little is forgiven, *the same* loves little."

48Then He said to her, [a]"Your sins are forgiven."

49And those who sat at the table with Him began to say to themselves, [a]"Who is this who even forgives sins?"

50Then He said to the woman, [a]"Your faith has saved you. Go in peace."

Many Women Minister to Jesus

8 Now it came to pass, afterward, that He went through every city and village, preaching and [1]bringing the glad tidings of the kingdom of God. And the twelve *were* with Him, 2and [a]certain women who had been healed of evil spirits and [1]infirmities—Mary called Magdalene, [b]out of whom had come seven demons, 3and Joanna the wife of Chuza, Herod's steward, and Susanna, and many others who provided for [1]Him from their [2]substance.

The Parable of the Sower

4[a]And when a great multitude had gathered, and they had come to Him from every city, He spoke by a parable: 5"A sower went out to sow his seed. And as he sowed, some fell by the wayside; and it was trampled down, and the birds of the air devoured it. 6Some fell on rock; and as soon as it sprang up, it withered away because it lacked moisture. 7And some fell among thorns, and the thorns sprang up with it and choked it. 8But others fell on good ground, sprang up, and yielded [1]a crop a hundredfold." When He had said these things He cried, [a]"He who has ears to hear, let him hear!"

The Purpose of Parables

9[a]Then His disciples asked Him, saying, "What does this parable mean?"

10And He said, "To you it has been given to know the [1]mysteries of the kingdom of God, but to the rest *it is given* in parables, that

[a]*'Seeing they may not see,*
And hearing they may not
understand.'

The Parable of the Sower Explained

11[a]"Now the parable is this: The seed is the [b]word of God. 12Those by the wayside are the ones who hear; then the devil comes and takes away the word out of their hearts, lest they should believe and be saved. 13But the ones on the rock *are those* who, when they hear, receive the word with joy; and these have no root, who believe for a while and in time of [1]temptation fall away. 14Now the ones *that* fell among thorns are those who, when they have heard, go out and are choked with cares, [a]riches, and pleasures of life, and bring no fruit to maturity. 15But the ones *that* fell on the good ground are those who, having heard the word with a noble and good heart, keep *it* and bear fruit with [a]patience.[1]

The Parable of the Revealed Light

16[a]"No one, when he has lit a lamp, covers it with a vessel or puts *it* under a bed, but sets *it* on a lampstand, that those who enter may see the [b]light. 17[a]For nothing is secret that will not be [b]revealed, nor *anything* hidden that will not be known and come to light. 18Therefore take heed how you hear. [a]For whoever has, to him *more* will be given; and whoever does not have, even what he [1]seems to [b]have will be taken from him."

Jesus' Mother and Brothers Come to Him

19[a]Then His mother and brothers came to Him, and could not approach Him because of the crowd. 20And it was told Him *by some,* who said, "Your mother and Your brothers are standing outside, desiring to see You."

21But He answered and said to them, "My mother and My brothers are these who hear the word of God and do it."

Wind and Wave Obey Jesus

22[a]Now it happened, on a certain day, that He got into a boat with His disciples. And He said to them, "Let us cross over to the other side of the lake." And they

45 [a]Rom. 16:16
46 [a]Ps. 23:5
47 [a][1 Tim. 1:14]
48 [a]Matt. 9:2
49 [a]Luke 5:21
50 [a]Matt. 9:22

CHAPTER 8
1 [1]*proclaiming the good news*
2 [a]Matt. 27:55 [b]Mark 16:9 [1]*sicknesses*
3 [1]NU, M *them* [2]*possessions*
4 [a]Mark 4:1–9
8 [a]Luke 14:35 [1]Lit. *fruit*
9 [a]Matt. 13:10–23
10 [a]Is. 6:9 [1]*secret* or *hidden truths*
11 [a][1 Pet. 1:23] [b]Luke 5:1; 11:28
13 [1]*testing*
14 [a]1 Tim. 6:9, 10
15 [a][Heb. 10:36–39] [1]*endurance*
16 [a]Luke 11:33 [b]Matt. 5:14
17 [a]Luke 12:2 [b][2 Cor. 5:10]
18 [a]Matt. 25:29 [b]Matt. 13:12 [1]*thinks that he has*
19 [a]Mark 3:31–35
22 [a]Matt. 8:23–27

launched out. 23But as they sailed He fell
asleep. And a windstorm came down on
the lake, and they were filling *with water,*
and were in [1]jeopardy. 24And they came to
Him and awoke Him, saying, "Master,
Master, we are perishing!"
Then He arose and rebuked the wind
and the raging of the water. And they
ceased, and there was a calm. 25But He
said to them, [a]"Where is your faith?"
And they were afraid, and marveled,
saying to one another, [b]"Who can this be?
For He commands even the winds and water, and they obey Him!"

A Demon-Possessed Man Healed

26[a]Then they sailed to the country of
the [1]Gadarenes, which is opposite Galilee.
27And when He stepped out on the land,
there met Him a certain man from the
city who had demons [1]for a long time.
And he wore no clothes, nor did he live in
a house but in the tombs. 28When he saw
Jesus, he [a]cried out, fell down before Him,
and with a loud voice said, [b]"What have I
to do with [c]You, Jesus, Son of the Most
High God? I beg You, do not torment me!"
29For He had commanded the unclean
spirit to come out of the man. For it had
often seized him, and he was kept under
guard, bound with chains and shackles;
and he broke the bonds and was driven by
the demon into the wilderness.
30Jesus asked him, saying, "What is
your name?"
And he said, "Legion," because many
demons had entered him. 31And they
begged Him that He would not command
them to go out [a]into the abyss.
32Now a herd of many [a]swine was feeding there on the mountain. So they
begged Him that He would permit them
to enter them. And He permitted them.
33Then the demons went out of the man
and entered the swine, and the herd ran
violently down the steep place into the
lake and drowned.
34When those who fed *them* saw what
had happened, they fled and told *it* in the
city and in the country. 35Then they went
out to see what had happened, and came
to Jesus, and found the man from whom
the demons had departed, [a]sitting at the
[b]feet of Jesus, clothed and in his [c]right
mind. And they were afraid. 36They also
who had seen *it* told them by what means
he who had been demon-possessed was
[1]healed. 37[a]Then the whole multitude of
the surrounding region of the [1]Gadarenes
[b]asked Him to [c]depart from them, for
they were seized with great [d]fear. And He
got into the boat and returned.
38Now [a]the man from whom the demons had departed begged Him that he
might be with Him. But Jesus sent him
away, saying, 39"Return to your own
house, and tell what great things God has
done for you." And he went his way and
proclaimed throughout the whole city
what great things Jesus had done for him.

> *I am through forever with everything in life but the proclamation and demonstration of the Gospel of Jesus Christ.*
>
> JOHN G. LAKE

A Girl Restored to Life and a Woman Healed

40So it was, when Jesus returned, that
the multitude welcomed Him, for they
were all waiting for Him. 41[a]And behold,
there came a man named Jairus, and he
was a ruler of the synagogue. And he fell
down at Jesus' feet and begged Him to
come to his house, 42for he had an only
daughter about twelve years of age, and
she [a]was dying.
But as He went, the multitudes
thronged Him. 43[a]Now a woman, having a
[b]flow of blood for twelve years, who had
spent all her livelihood on physicians and
could not be healed by any, 44came from
behind and [a]touched the border of His
garment. And immediately her flow of
blood stopped.
45And Jesus said, "Who touched Me?"
When all denied it, Peter [1]and those
with him said, "Master, the multitudes
throng and press You, [2]and You say, 'Who
touched Me?' "
46But Jesus said, "Somebody touched
Me, for I perceived [a]power going out from
Me." 47Now when the woman saw that she
was not hidden, she came trembling; and
falling down before Him, she declared to
Him in the presence of all the people the

23 [1] *danger*
25 [a] Luke 9:41 [b] Luke 4:36; 5:26
26 [a] Mark 5:1–17 [1] NU *Gerasenes*
27 [1] NU *and for a long time wore no clothes*
28 [a] Mark 1:26; 9:26 [b] Mark 1:23, 24 [c] Luke 4:41
31 [a] [Rev. 20:1, 3]
32 [a] Lev. 11:7
35 [a] [Matt. 11:28] [b] Luke 10:39; 17:16 [c] [2 Tim. 1:7]
36 [1] *delivered*
37 [a] Matt. 8:34 [b] Luke 4:34 [c] Acts 16:39 [d] Luke 5:26 [1] NU *Gerasenes*
38 [a] Mark 5:18–20
41 [a] Mark 5:22–43
42 [a] Luke 7:2
43 [a] Matt. 9:20 [b] Luke 15:19–22
44 [a] Mark 6:56
45 [1] NU omits *and those with him* [2] NU omits the rest of v. 45.
46 [a] Mark 5:30

reason she had touched Him and how she was healed immediately.

48 And He said to her, “Daughter, [1]be of good cheer; [a]your faith has made you well. [b]Go in peace.”

49 [a]While He was still speaking, someone came from the ruler of the synagogue’s *house,* saying to him, “Your daughter is dead. Do not trouble the [1]Teacher.”

50 But when Jesus heard *it,* He answered him, saying, “Do not be afraid; [a]only believe, and she will be made well.” 51 When He came into the house, He permitted no one to go [1]in except [2]Peter, James, and John, and the father and mother of the girl. 52 Now all wept and mourned for her; but He said, [a]“Do not weep; she is not dead, [b]but sleeping.” 53 And they ridiculed Him, knowing that she was dead.

54 But He [1]put them all outside, took her by the hand and called, saying, “Little girl, [a]arise.” 55 Then her spirit returned, and she arose immediately. And He commanded that she be given *something* to eat. 56 And her parents were astonished, but [a]He charged them to tell no one what had happened.

Sending Out the Twelve

9 Then [a]He called His twelve disciples together and [b]gave them power and authority over all demons, and to cure diseases. 2 [a]He sent them to preach the kingdom of God and to heal the sick. 3 [a]And He said to them, “Take nothing for the journey, neither staffs nor bag nor bread nor money; and do not have two tunics apiece.

4 [a]“Whatever house you enter, stay there, and from there depart. 5 [a]And whoever will not receive you, when you go out of that city, [b]shake off the very dust from your feet as a testimony against them.”

6 [a]So they departed and went through the towns, preaching the gospel and healing everywhere.

Herod Seeks to See Jesus

7 [a]Now Herod the tetrarch heard of all that was done by Him; and he was perplexed, because it was said by some that John had risen from the dead, 8 and by some that Elijah had appeared, and by others that one of the old prophets had risen again. 9 Herod said, “John I have beheaded, but who is this of whom I hear such things?” [a]So he sought to see Him.

Feeding the Five Thousand

10 [a]And the apostles, when they had returned, told Him all that they had done. [b]Then He took them and went aside privately into a deserted place belonging to the city called Bethsaida. 11 But when the multitudes knew *it,* they followed Him; and He received them and spoke to them about the kingdom of God, and healed those who had need of healing. 12 [a]When the day began to wear away, the twelve came and said to Him, “Send the multitude away, that they may go into the surrounding towns and country, and lodge and get provisions; for we are in a deserted place here.”

13 [a]But He said to them, “You give them something to eat.”

And they said, “We have no more than five loaves and two fish, unless we go and buy food for all these people.” 14 For there were about five thousand men.

Then He said to His disciples, “Make them sit down in groups of fifty.” 15 And they did so, and made them all sit down.

16 Then He took the five loaves and the two fish, and looking up to heaven, He [a]blessed and broke *them,* and gave *them* to the disciples to set before the multitude. 17 So they all ate and were [1]filled, and twelve baskets of the leftover fragments were taken up by them.

Peter Confesses Jesus as the Christ

18 [a]And it happened, as He was alone praying, *that* His disciples joined Him, and He asked them, saying, “Who do the crowds say that I am?”

19 So they answered and said, [a]“John the Baptist, but some *say* Elijah; and others *say* that one of the old prophets has risen again.”

20 He said to them, “But who do you say that I am?”

[a]Peter answered and said, “The Christ of God.”

Jesus Predicts His Death and Resurrection

21 [a]And He strictly warned and commanded them to tell this to no one, 22 saying, [a]“The Son of Man must suffer many things, and be rejected by the elders and chief priests and scribes, and be killed, and be raised the third day.”

48 a Luke 7:50 b John 8:11 *1 NU omits be of good cheer*
49 a Mark 5:35 *1 NU adds anymore*
50 a [Mark 11:22–24]
51 *1 NU adds with Him 2 NU, M Peter, John, and James*
52 a Luke 7:13 b [John 11:11, 13]
54 a John 11:43 *1 NU omits put them all outside*
56 a Matt. 8:4; 9:30

CHAPTER 9
1 a Matt. 10:1, 2 b [John 14:12]
2 a Matt. 10:7, 8
3 a Luke 10:4–12; 22:35
4 a Mark 6:10
5 a Matt. 10:14 b Acts 13:51
6 a Mark 6:12
7 a Matt. 14:1, 2
9 a Luke 23:8
10 a Mark 6:30 b Matt. 14:13
12 a John 6:1, 5
16 a Luke 22:19; 24:30
17 *1 satisfied*
18 a Matt. 16:13–16
19 a Matt. 14:2
20 a John 6:68, 69
21 a Matt. 8:4; 16:20
22 a Matt. 16:21; 17:22

Luke 9:1, 2

Dear Woman of Destiny,

Jesus had a purpose for everything. First, He performed healing and deliverance; then He sent His followers to do likewise. He was a model of perfect obedience. Whatever He saw the Father do, He did. Whatever He heard the Father say, He said. Jesus longed to see the kingdom established. He knew He would have to duplicate Himself in order to spread the Good News, so He gathered those closest to Him and gave them authority to heal the sick and cast out demons. It is very clear that the message of the kingdom must be more than talk. Until there is a demonstration of God's power, the kingdom message is simply a good theory. It is interesting that the Holy Spirit chose Luke, a physician, to relate this precious truth.

In Luke 8:43–48, the physician relates the story of the woman with the flow of blood. She had spent all her money going to doctors who could not heal her. One touch from Jesus accomplished what no doctor could accomplish. So Jesus sent His disciples out with more than a sermon. He sent them with a message and the power to demonstrate its truth. As disciples in this kingdom, we have a responsibility to give people the whole story.

There are so many voices in the world trying to give people the answers they desperately seek. The kingdom of God is distinguished by the performance of the spoken word. In 1 Corinthians 2:4, 5, Paul told the church that he came to them in the power of the Holy Spirit that their faith should rest in God. He said the gospel was not fully preached until signs and wonders occurred. It is easy to talk about the things of God, but it's time to become a woman of action.

You have been sent to preach the good news of this kingdom. Some of the best sermons are not delivered from a pulpit on Sunday morning. Our lives become the message of God to a lost and suffering world as we reach out our hands to demonstrate His love.

The word *preach* means to proclaim, publish, or publicly declare the Good News. While not all of you will preach from a pulpit, your pulpit may be your neighborhood. The concept of preaching can be intimidating. We seldom see ourselves as messengers of God. The key to the release of God's power through our lives is found in our joyful obedience. The disciples did not go out under their own power; they were sent. You are not limited to what you can produce. You have been sent by God to proclaim His message and perform His word. With God's authority and blessing, we must boldly demonstrate His heart to those who are weak and sick. So let us be bold as a lion as we are sent out to accomplish the purposes of God.

Shirley Arnold

Take Up the Cross and Follow Him

23[a]Then He said to *them* all, "If anyone
desires to come after Me, let him deny
himself, and take up his cross [1]daily, and
follow Me. 24[a]For whoever desires to save
his life will lose it, but whoever loses his
life for My sake will save it. 25[a]For what
profit is it to a man if he gains the whole
world, and is himself destroyed or lost?
26[a]For whoever is ashamed of Me and My
words, of him the Son of Man will be
[b]ashamed when He comes in His *own* glory, and *in His* Father's, and of the holy
angels.

> *We need to be bold for Jesus Christ, never embarrassed to admit that we are His. Jesus will never disgrace us. Let us be careful that we never disgrace Him.*
>
> CHARLES H. SPURGEON

Jesus Transfigured on the Mount

27[a]But I tell you truly, there are some
standing here who shall not taste death
till they see the kingdom of God."
28[a]Now it came to pass, about eight
days after these sayings, that He took Peter, John, and James and went up on the
mountain to pray. 29As He prayed, the appearance of His face was altered, and His
robe *became* white *and* glistening. 30And
behold, two men talked with Him, who
were [a]Moses and [b]Elijah, 31who appeared
in glory and spoke of His [1]decease which
He was about to accomplish at Jerusalem.
32But Peter and those with him [a]were
heavy with sleep; and when they were fully awake, they saw His glory and the two
men who stood with Him. 33Then it happened, as they were parting from Him,
that Peter said to Jesus, "Master, it is good
for us to be here; and let us make three
[1]tabernacles: one for You, one for Moses,
and one for Elijah"—not knowing what
he said.

34While he was saying this, a cloud
came and overshadowed them; and they
were fearful as they entered the [a]cloud.
35And a voice came out of the cloud, saying, [a]"This is [1]My beloved Son. [b]Hear
Him!" 36When the voice had ceased, Jesus
was found alone. [a]But they kept quiet, and
told no one in those days any of the things
they had seen.

A Boy Is Healed

37[a]Now it happened on the next day,
when they had come down from the
mountain, that a great multitude met
Him. 38Suddenly a man from the multitude cried out, saying, "Teacher, I implore
You, look on my son, for he is my only
child. 39And behold, a spirit seizes him,
and he suddenly cries out; it convulses
him so that he foams *at the mouth;* and
it departs from him with great difficulty,
bruising him. 40So I implored Your disciples to cast it out, but they could not."
41Then Jesus answered and said,
"O [1]faithless and perverse generation,
how long shall I be with you and [2]bear
with you? Bring your son here." 42And as
he was still coming, the demon threw him
down and convulsed *him.* Then Jesus rebuked the unclean spirit, healed the child,
and gave him back to his father.

Jesus Again Predicts His Death

43And they were all amazed at the majesty of God.
But while everyone marveled at all the
things which Jesus did, He said to His disciples, 44[a]"Let these words sink down into
your ears, for the Son of Man is about
to be betrayed into the hands of men."
45[a]But they did not understand this saying, and it was hidden from them so that
they did not perceive it; and they were
afraid to ask Him about this saying.

Who Is the Greatest?

46[a]Then a dispute arose among them as
to which of them would be greatest. 47And
Jesus, [a]perceiving the thought of their
heart, took a [b]little child and set him by
Him, 48and said to them, [a]"Whoever receives this little child in My name receives
Me; and [b]whoever receives Me [c]receives
Him who sent Me. [d]For he who is least
among you all will be great."

23 a Matt. 10:38; 16:24 *1* M omits *daily*
24 a [John 12:25]
25 a Mark 8:36
26 a [Rom. 1:16] b Matt. 10:33
27 a Matt. 16:28
28 a Mark 9:2–8
30 a Heb. 11:23–29 b 2 Kin. 2:1–11
31 *1* Death, lit. *departure*
32 a Dan. 8:18; 10:9
33 *1 tents*
34 a Ex. 13:21
35 a [Matt. 3:17; 12:18] b Acts 3:22 *1* NU *My Son, the Chosen One*
36 a Matt. 17:9
37 a Mark 9:14–27
41 *1 unbelieving 2 put up with*
44 a Matt. 17:22
45 a Mark 9:32
46 a Matt. 18:1–5
47 a Matt. 9:4 b Luke 18:17
48 a Matt. 18:5 b John 12:44 c John 13:20 d Eph. 3:8

Jesus Forbids Sectarianism

49[a]Now John answered and said, "Master, we saw someone casting out demons
in Your name, and we forbade him because he does not follow with us."
50But Jesus said to him, "Do not forbid
him, for [a]he who is not against [1]us is on
[2]our side."

A Samaritan Village Rejects the Savior

51Now it came to pass, when the time
had come for [a]Him to be received up, that
He steadfastly set His face to go to Jerusalem, 52and sent messengers before His
face. And as they went, they entered a
village of the Samaritans, to prepare for
Him. 53But [a]they did not receive Him, because His face was *set* for the journey
to Jerusalem. 54And when His disciples
[a]James and John saw *this,* they said,
"Lord, do You want us to command fire to
come down from heaven and consume
them, [1]just as [b]Elijah did?"
55But He turned and rebuked them,
[1]and said, "You do not know what manner
of [a]spirit you are of. 56[1]For [a]the Son of
Man did not come to destroy men's lives
but to save *them.*" And they went to another village.

The Cost of Discipleship

57[a]Now it happened as they journeyed
on the road, *that* someone said to Him,
"Lord, I will follow You wherever You go."

The great word of Jesus to His disciples is Abandon. When God has brought us into the relationship of disciples, we have to venture on His Word; trust entirely to Him and watch that when He brings us to the venture, we take it.

OSWALD CHAMBERS

58And Jesus said to him, "Foxes have
holes and birds of the air *have* nests, but
the Son of Man [a]has nowhere to lay *His*
head."
59[a]Then He said to another, "Follow
Me."
But he said, "Lord, let me first go and
bury my father."
60Jesus said to him, "Let the dead bury
their own dead, but you go and preach the
kingdom of God."
61And another also said, "Lord, [a]I will
follow You, but let me first go *and* bid
them farewell who are at my house."
62But Jesus said to him, "No one, having put his hand to the plow, and looking
back, is [a]fit for the kingdom of God."

The Seventy Sent Out

10 After these things the Lord appointed [1]seventy others also, and
[a]sent them two by two before His face into
every city and place where He Himself was
about to go. 2Then He said to them, [a]"The
harvest truly *is* great, but the laborers *are*
few; therefore [b]pray the Lord of the harvest to send out laborers into His harvest.
3Go your way; [a]behold, I send you out
as lambs among wolves. 4[a]Carry neither
money bag, knapsack, nor sandals; and
[b]greet no one along the road. 5[a]But whatever house you enter, first say, 'Peace to
this house.' 6And if a son of peace is there,
your peace will rest on it; if not, it will
return to you. 7[a]And remain in the same
house, [b]eating and drinking such things
as they give, for [c]the laborer is worthy of
his wages. Do not go from house to house.
8Whatever city you enter, and they receive
you, eat such things as are set before you.
9[a]And heal the sick there, and say to
them, [b]'The kingdom of God has come
near to you.' 10But whatever city you enter, and they do not receive you, go out
into its streets and say, 11[a]'The very dust
of your city which clings to [1]us we wipe
off against you. Nevertheless know this,
that the kingdom of God has come near
you.' 12[1]But I say to you that [a]it will be
more tolerable in that Day for Sodom
than for that city.

Woe to the Impenitent Cities

13[a]"Woe to you, Chorazin! Woe to you,
Bethsaida! [b]For if the mighty works
which were done in you had been done in
Tyre and Sidon, they would have repented
long ago, sitting in sackcloth and ashes.
14But it will be more tolerable for Tyre

---

49 a Mark 9:38–40
50 a Luke 11:23 *1* NU *you* *2* NU *your*
51 a Mark 16:19
53 a John 4:4, 9
54 a Mark 3:17 b 2 Kin. 1:10, 12 *1* NU omits *just as Elijah did*
55 a [2 Tim. 1:7] *1* NU omits the rest of v. 55.
56 a John 3:17; 12:47 *1* NU omits *For the Son of Man did not come to destroy men's lives but to save them.*
57 a Matt. 8:19–22
58 a Luke 2:7; 8:23
59 a Matt. 8:21, 22
61 a 1 Kin. 19:20
62 a 2 Tim. 4:10

CHAPTER 10
1 a Mark 6:7 *1* NU *seventy-two others*
2 a John 4:35 b 2 Thess. 3:1
3 a Matt. 10:16
4 a Luke 9:3–5 b 2 Kin. 4:29
5 a Matt. 10:12
7 a Matt. 10:11 b 1 Cor. 10:27 c 1 Tim. 5:18
9 a Mark 3:15 b Matt. 3:2; 10:7
11 a Acts 13:51 *1* NU *our feet*
12 a Matt. 10:15; 11:24 *1* NU, M omit *But*
13 a Matt. 11:21–23 b Ezek. 3:6

and Sidon at the judgment than for you.
15 [a]And you, Capernaum, [1]who are [b]exalt-
ed to heaven, [c]will be brought down to
Hades. 16 [a]He who hears you hears Me, [b]he
who rejects you rejects Me, and [c]he who
rejects Me rejects Him who sent Me."

The Seventy Return with Joy

17 Then [a]the [1]seventy returned with joy,
saying, "Lord, even the demons are subject to us in Your name."

18 And He said to them, [a]"I saw Satan
fall like lightning from heaven. 19 Behold,
[a]I give you the authority to trample on
serpents and scorpions, and over all the
power of the enemy, and nothing shall by
any means hurt you. 20 Nevertheless do
not rejoice in this, that the spirits are subject to you, but [1]rather rejoice because
[a]your names are written in heaven."

Jesus Rejoices in the Spirit

21 [a]In that hour Jesus rejoiced in the
Spirit and said, "I thank You, Father, Lord
of heaven and earth, that You have hidden
these things from *the* wise and prudent
and revealed them to babes. Even so, Father, for so it seemed good in Your sight.
22 [a]All[1] things have been delivered to Me
by My Father, and [b]no one knows who the
Son is except the Father, and who the Father is except the Son, and *the one* to
whom the Son wills to reveal *Him*."

23 Then He turned to *His* disciples and
said privately, [a]"Blessed *are* the eyes
which see the things you see; 24 for I tell
you [a]that many prophets and kings have
desired to see what you see, and have not
seen *it*, and to hear what you hear, and
have not heard *it*."

The Parable of the Good Samaritan

25 And behold, a certain [1]lawyer stood
up and tested Him, saying, [a]"Teacher,
what shall I do to inherit eternal life?"

26 He said to him, "What is written in
the law? What is your reading *of it?*"

27 So he answered and said, [a]"*'You shall
love the* LORD *your God with all your
heart, with all your soul, with all your
strength, and with all your mind,'* and
[b]*'your neighbor as yourself.'* "

28 And He said to him, "You have answered rightly; do this and [a]you will live."
29 But he, wanting to [a]justify himself,
said to Jesus, "And who is my neighbor?"

30 Then Jesus answered and said: "A certain *man* went down from Jerusalem to
Jericho, and fell among [1]thieves, who
stripped him of his clothing, wounded
him, and departed, leaving *him* half dead.
31 Now by chance a certain priest came
down that road. And when he saw him,
[a]he passed by on the other side. 32 Likewise a Levite, when he arrived at the
place, came and looked, and passed by on
the other side. 33 But a certain [a]Samari-
tan, as he journeyed, came where he was.
And when he saw him, he had [b]compas-
sion. 34 So he went to *him* and bandaged
his wounds, pouring on oil and wine; and
he set him on his own animal, brought
him to an inn, and took care of him. 35 On
the next day, [1]when he departed, he took
out two [a]denarii, gave *them* to the inn-
keeper, and said to him, 'Take care of him;
and whatever more you spend, when I
come again, I will repay you.' 36 So which
of these three do you think was neighbor
to him who fell among the thieves?"

This ability to receive help—allowing another's spirit to touch our spirit—is proof that one is broken.

WATCHMAN NEE

37 And he said, "He who showed mercy
on him."
Then Jesus said to him, [a]"Go and do
likewise."

Mary and Martha Worship and Serve

38 Now it happened as they went that He
entered a certain village; and a certain
woman named [a]Martha welcomed Him
into her house. 39 And she had a sister
called Mary, [a]who also [b]sat at [1]Jesus' feet
and heard His word. 40 But Martha was distracted with much serving, and she approached Him and said, "Lord, do You not
care that my sister has left me to serve
alone? Therefore tell her to help me."

41 And [1]Jesus answered and said to her,
"Martha, Martha, you are worried and
troubled about many things. 42 But [a]one

---

15 a Matt. 11:23 b Is. 14:13–15 c Ezek. 26:20 1 NU *will you be exalted to heaven? You will be thrust down to Hades!*
16 a John 13:20 b 1 Thess. 4:8 c John 5:23
17 a Luke 10:1 1 NU *seventy-two*
18 a John 12:31
19 a Mark 16:18
20 a Is. 4:3 1 NU, M omit *rather*
21 a Matt. 11:25–27
22 a John 3:35; 5:27; 17:2 b [John 1:18; 6:44, 46] 1 M *And turning to the disciples He said, "All*
23 a Matt. 13:16, 17
24 a 1 Pet. 1:10, 11
25 a Matt. 19:16–19; 22:35 1 *expert in the law*
27 a Deut. 6:5 b Lev. 19:18
28 a Ezek. 20:11, 13, 21
29 a Luke 16:15
30 1 *robbers*
31 a Ps. 38:11
33 a John 4:9 b Luke 15:20
35 a Matt. 20:2 1 NU omits *when he departed*
37 a Prov. 14:21
38 a John 11:1; 12:2, 3
39 a [1 Cor. 7:32–40] b Acts 22:3 1 NU *the Lord's*
41 1 NU *the Lord*
42 a [Ps. 27:4]

thing is needed, and Mary has chosen that
good part, which will not be taken away
from her."

God is calling the Marys and the Marthas today all over our land to work in various places of the vineyard of the Lord; God grant that they may respond and say, "Lord, here am I; send me."

MARIA WOODWORTH-ETTER

The Model Prayer

11 Now it came to pass, as He was
praying in a certain place, when He
ceased, *that* one of His disciples said to
Him, "Lord, teach us to pray, as John also
taught his disciples."
2So He said to them, "When you pray,
say:

[a]Our[1] Father [2]in heaven,
Hallowed be Your name.
Your kingdom come.
[3]Your will be done
On earth as *it is* in heaven.
3 Give us day by day our daily bread.
4 And [a]forgive us our sins,
For we also forgive everyone who is indebted to us.
And do not lead us into temptation,
[1]But deliver us from the evil one."

Jesus taught His disciples not how to preach, only how to pray.

ANDREW MURRAY

A Friend Comes at Midnight

5And He said to them, "Which of you
shall have a friend, and go to him at midnight and say to him, 'Friend, lend me
three loaves; 6for a friend of mine has
come to me on his journey, and I have
nothing to set before him'; 7and he will
answer from within and say, 'Do not trouble me; the door is now shut, and my children are with me in bed; I cannot rise and
give to you'? 8I say to you, [a]though he will
not rise and give to him because he is his
friend, yet because of his persistence he
will rise and give him as many as he
needs.

Keep Asking, Seeking, Knocking

9[a]"So I say to you, ask, and it will be
given to you; [b]seek, and you will find;
knock, and it will be opened to you. 10For
everyone who asks receives, and he who
seeks finds, and to him who knocks it will
be opened. 11[a]If a son asks for [1]bread from
any father among you, will he give him a
stone? Or if *he asks* for a fish, will he give
him a serpent instead of a fish? 12Or if he
asks for an egg, will he offer him a scorpion? 13If you then, being evil, know how to
give [a]good gifts to your children, how
much more will *your* heavenly Father
give the Holy Spirit to those who ask
Him!"

A House Divided Cannot Stand

14[a]And He was casting out a demon,
and it was mute. So it was, when the demon had gone out, that the mute spoke;
and the multitudes marveled. 15But some
of them said, [a]"He casts out demons by
[1]Beelzebub, the ruler of the demons."
16Others, testing *Him*, [a]sought from
Him a sign from heaven. 17[a]But [b]He,
knowing their thoughts, said to them:
"Every kingdom divided against itself is
brought to desolation, and a house *divided* against a house falls. 18If Satan also is
divided against himself, how will his kingdom stand? Because you say I cast out demons by Beelzebub. 19And if I cast out
demons by Beelzebub, by whom do your
sons cast *them* out? Therefore they will be
your judges. 20 But if I cast out demons
[a]with the finger of God, surely the kingdom of God has come upon you.
21[a]When a strong man, fully armed,
guards his own palace, his goods are in
peace. 22But [a]when a stronger than he
comes upon him and overcomes him, he

CHAPTER 11
2 [a]Matt. 6:9–13 [1]NU omits *Our* [2]NU omits *in heaven* [3]NU omits the rest of v. 2.
4 [a][Eph. 4:32] [1]NU omits *But deliver us from the evil one*
8 [a][Luke 18:1–5]
9 [a][John 15:7] [b]Is. 55:6
11 [a]Matt. 7:9 [1]NU omits *bread from any father among you, will he give him a stone? Or if he asks for*
13 [a]James 1:17
14 [a]Matt. 9:32–34; 12:22, 24
15 [a]Matt. 9:34; 12:24 [1]NU, M *Beelzebul*
16 [a]Matt. 12:38; 16:1
17 [a]Matt. 12:25–29 [b]John 2:25
20 [a]Ex. 8:19
21 [a]Mark 3:27
22 [a][Is. 53:12]

Luke 11:20

Dear Woman of Destiny,

As I knelt down to pray, the moist, hot air of India hung around me like a blanket. A small boy sat on the ground in the cardboard box that was home to him and his large family. His legs were crippled by disease, and my heart felt as though it would break. Having witnessed God work tremendous miracles of healing and deliverance, I gathered my team around, and we began to pray for this little boy's healing. Filled with faith and compassion, we waited to see what God would do, but nothing happened. That day began a long journey of earnestly seeking the Lord for understanding. I was surprised to find in Luke 11:20 the key that God would use to begin teaching me His ways. Though your circumstances may be different, you, too, may have experienced this dilemma. Why do we see God do miracles sometimes but not at other times?

We know from Scripture that when the kingdom of God comes in its fullness, there will be no more death, sickness, pain, or crying; all of the former things will pass away (see Rev. 21:1–4). We also know that we do not yet live in that future state. Dr. George Ladd, in his work on the kingdom of God, says that we live in an "age of tension." We don't have to look far to see that we are living in an age where sin and evil seem to dominate our present life situation. We live in an age of tension between the victory won through Jesus' death and resurrection and the culmination of that victory when He comes again.

Into this tension, the words of Jesus bring understanding to our dilemma. Jesus is saying that when a deliverance takes place, the future kingdom of God breaks into the present reality of life. When Jesus performed miracles, people experienced the glory of the future kingdom of God firsthand. In Jesus' touch, they were touched by eternity.

Today, by the power of God's Spirit, we continue to see both the reign and the glory of the future kingdom of God breaking into our present life situations; for the kingdom of God is both a present and a future kingdom. We see this when someone is healed, when someone is delivered, and when we see miracles. Why don't we see this happen all the time? Because we still live in this age of tension, affected by evil and sin, experiencing death, pain, and mourning. We have not yet experienced the kingdom in its fullness. God manifests His grace to us when He invades our lives through the miraculous and grants us a taste of eternity. May God place within your heart, as He has in mine, a fresh expectancy and fervency in prayer that His kingdom would come in power and that He would touch His people with eternity.

Leslyn Musch

takes from him all his armor in which he
trusted, and divides his [1]spoils. 23[a]He who
is not with Me is against Me, and he who
does not gather with Me scatters.

An Unclean Spirit Returns

24[a]"When an unclean spirit goes out of
a man, he goes through dry places, seeking rest; and finding none, he says, 'I will
return to my house from which I came.'
25And when he comes, he finds *it* swept
and put in order. 26Then he goes and takes
with *him* seven other spirits more wicked
than himself, and they enter and dwell
there; and [a]the last *state* of that man is
worse than the first."

Keeping the Word

27And it happened, as He spoke these
things, that a certain woman from the
crowd raised her voice and said to Him,
[a]"Blessed *is* the womb that bore You, and
the breasts which nursed You!"
28But He said, [a]"More than that,
blessed *are* those who hear the word of
God and keep it!"

Seeking a Sign

29[a]And while the crowds were thickly
gathered together, He began to say, "This
is an evil generation. It seeks a [b]sign, and
no sign will be given to it except the sign
of Jonah [1]the prophet. 30For as [a]Jonah became a sign to the Ninevites, so also the
Son of Man will be to this generation.
31[a]The queen of the South will rise up in
the judgment with the men of this generation and condemn them, for she came
from the ends of the earth to hear the
wisdom of Solomon; and indeed a [b]great-
er than Solomon *is* here. 32The men of
Nineveh will rise up in the judgment with
this generation and condemn it, for [a]they
repented at the preaching of Jonah; and
indeed a greater than Jonah *is* here.

The Lamp of the Body

33[a]"No one, when he has lit a lamp, puts
it in a secret place or under a [b]basket, but
on a lampstand, that those who come in
may see the light. 34[a]The lamp of the body
is the eye. Therefore, when your eye is
[1]good, your whole body also is full of
light. But when *your eye* is [2]bad, your
body also *is* full of darkness. 35Therefore
take heed that the light which is in you is
not darkness. 36If then your whole body
is full of light, having no part dark, *the*
whole *body* will be full of light, as when
the bright shining of a lamp gives you
light."

Woe to the Pharisees and Lawyers

37And as He spoke, a certain Pharisee
asked Him to dine with him. So He went
in and sat down to eat. 38[a]When the Pharisee saw *it,* he marveled that He had not
first washed before dinner.
39[a]Then the Lord said to him, "Now you
Pharisees make the outside of the cup and
dish clean, but [b]your inward part is full of
[1]greed and wickedness. 40Foolish ones!
Did not [a]He who made the outside make
the inside also? 41[a]But rather give alms of
[1]such things as you have; then indeed all
things are clean to you.
42[a]"But woe to you Pharisees! For you
tithe the mint and rue and all manner of
herbs, and [b]pass by justice and the [c]love
of God. These you ought to have done,
without leaving the others undone.
43[a]Woe to you Pharisees! For you love the
[1]best seats in the synagogues and greetings in the marketplaces. 44[a]Woe to you,
[1]scribes and Pharisees, hypocrites! [b]For
you are like graves which are not seen,
and the men who walk over *them* are not
aware *of them.*"
45Then one of the lawyers answered and
said to Him, "Teacher, by saying these
things You reproach us also."
46And He said, "Woe to you also, lawyers! [a]For you load men with burdens
hard to bear, and you yourselves do not
touch the burdens with one of your fingers. 47[a]Woe to you! For you build the
tombs of the prophets, and your fathers
killed them. 48In fact, you bear witness
that you approve the deeds of your fathers; for they indeed killed them, and you
build their tombs. 49Therefore the wisdom of God also said, [a]'I will send them
prophets and apostles, and *some* of them
they will kill and persecute,' 50that the
blood of all the prophets which was shed
from the foundation of the world may be
required of this generation, 51[a]from the
blood of Abel to [b]the blood of Zechariah
who perished between the altar and the
temple. Yes, I say to you, it shall be required of this generation.
52[a]"Woe to you lawyers! For you have
taken away the key of knowledge. You did

22 [1] *plunder*
23 a Matt. 12:30
24 a Matt. 12:43–45
26 a [2 Pet. 2:20]
27 a Luke 1:28, 48
28 a [Luke 8:21]
29 a Matt. 12:38–42 b 1 Cor. 1:22 [1] NU omits *the prophet*
30 a Jon. 1:17; 2:10; 3:3–10
31 a 1 Kin. 10:1–9 b [Rom. 9:5]
32 a Jon. 3:5
33 a Mark 4:21 b Matt. 5:15
34 a Matt. 6:22, 23 [1] Clear, or healthy [2] Evil, or unhealthy
38 a Mark 7:2, 3
39 a Matt. 23:25 b Titus 1:15 [1] Lit. *eager grasping* or *robbery*
40 a Gen. 1:26, 27
41 a [Luke 12:33; 16:9] [1] Or *what is inside*
42 a Matt. 23:23 b [Mic. 6:7, 8] c John 5:42
43 a Mark 12:38, 39 [1] Or *places of honor*
44 a Matt. 23:27 b Ps. 5:9 [1] NU omits *scribes and Pharisees, hypocrites*
46 a Matt. 23:4
47 a Matt. 23:29
49 a Matt. 23:34
51 a Gen. 4:8 b 2 Chr. 24:20, 21
52 a Matt. 23:13

not enter in yourselves, and those who
were entering in you hindered."
53 [1]And as He said these things to them,
the scribes and the Pharisees began to
assail *Him* vehemently, and to cross-
examine Him about many things, 54 lying
in wait for Him, [1]and [a]seeking to catch
Him in something He might say, [2]that
they might accuse Him.

Beware of Hypocrisy

12 In [a]the meantime, when an innumerable multitude of people had
gathered together, so that they trampled
one another, He began to say to His disciples first *of all,* [b]"Beware of the [1]leaven of
the Pharisees, which is hypocrisy. 2 [a]For
there is nothing covered that will not be
revealed, nor hidden that will not be
known. 3 Therefore whatever you have
spoken in the dark will be heard in the
light, and what you have spoken in the ear
in inner rooms will be proclaimed on the
housetops.

Jesus Teaches the Fear of God

4 [a]"And I say to you, [b]My friends, do not
be afraid of those who kill the body, and
after that have no more that they can do.
5 But I will show you whom you should
fear: Fear Him who, after He has killed,
has power to cast into hell; yes, I say to
you, [a]fear Him!

Loving Lord, You have not forgotten even the sparrows. May _____ know that You have numbered the very hairs on her head. May she not be afraid; for she is of more value than the sparrows.

FROM LUKE 12:6, 7

6 "Are not five sparrows sold for two
[1]copper coins? And [a]not one of them is
forgotten before God. 7 But the very hairs
of your head are all numbered. Do not fear
therefore; you are of more value than
many sparrows.

The Lord has not forgotten you. He who counts the stars will not forget His children. It is as if you were the only creature He ever fashioned, or the only saint He ever loved.

CHARLES H. SPURGEON

Confess Christ Before Men

8 [a]"Also I say to you, whoever confesses
Me [b]before men, him the Son of Man also
will confess before the angels of God. 9 But
he who [a]denies Me before men will be denied before the angels of God.
10 "And [a]anyone who speaks a word
against the Son of Man, it will be forgiven
him; but to him who blasphemes against
the Holy Spirit, it will not be forgiven.
11 [a]"Now when they bring you to the
synagogues and magistrates and authorities, do not worry about how or what you
should answer, or what you should say.
12 For the Holy Spirit will [a]teach you in
that very hour what you ought to say."

The Parable of the Rich Fool

13 Then one from the crowd said to Him,
"Teacher, tell my brother to divide the inheritance with me."
14 But He said to him, [a]"Man, who made
Me a judge or an arbitrator over you?"
15 And He said to them, [a]"Take heed and
beware of [1]covetousness, for one's life
does not consist in the abundance of the
things he possesses."
16 Then He spoke a parable to them, saying: "The ground of a certain rich man
yielded plentifully. 17 And he thought
within himself, saying, 'What shall I do,
since I have no room to store my crops?'
18 So he said, 'I will do this: I will pull
down my barns and build greater, and
there I will store all my crops and my
goods. 19 And I will say to my soul, [a]"Soul,
you have many goods laid up for many
years; take your ease; [b]eat, drink, *and* be

53 [1] NU *And when He left there*
54 [a] Mark 12:13 [1] NU omits *and seeking* [2] NU omits *that they might accuse Him*
CHAPTER 12
1 [a] Mark 8:15 [b] Matt. 16:12 [1] *yeast*
2 [a] Matt. 10:26; [1 Cor. 4:5]
4 [a] Is. 51:7, 8, 12, 13 [b] [John 15:13–15]
5 [a] Ps. 119:120
6 [a] Matt. 6:26 [1] Gr. *assarion,* a coin worth about 1/16 of a denarius
8 [a] Matt. 10:32 [b] Ps. 119:46
9 [a] Matt. 10:33
10 [a] [Matt. 12:31, 32]
11 [a] Mark 13:11
12 [a] [John 14:26]
14 [a] [John 18:36]
15 [a] [1 Tim. 6:6–10] [1] NU *all covetousness*
19 [a] Eccl. 11:9 [b] [Eccl. 2:24; 3:13; 5:18; 8:15]

merry."' 20But God said to him, 'Fool! This night [a]your soul will be required of you; [b]then whose will those things be which you have provided?'

21"So *is* he who lays up treasure for himself, [a]and is not rich toward God."

Do Not Worry

22Then He said to His disciples, "Therefore I say to you, [a]do not worry about your life, what you will eat; nor about the body, what you will put on. 23Life is more than food, and the body *is more* than clothing. 24Consider the ravens, for they neither sow nor reap, which have neither storehouse nor barn; and [a]God feeds them. Of how much more value are you than the birds? 25And which of you by worrying can add one cubit to his stature? 26If you then are not able to do *the* least, why [1]are you anxious for the rest? 27Consider the lilies, how they grow: they neither toil nor spin; and yet I say to you, even [a]Solomon in all his glory was not [1]arrayed like one of these. 28If then God so clothes the grass, which today is in the field and tomorrow is thrown into the oven, how much more *will He clothe* you, O *you* of [a]little faith?

29"And do not seek what you should eat or what you should drink, nor have an anxious mind. 30For all these things the nations of the world seek after, and your Father [a]knows that you need these things. 31[a]But seek [1]the kingdom of God, and all these things shall be added to you.

32"Do not fear, little flock, for [a]it is your Father's good pleasure to give you the kingdom. 33[a]Sell what you have and give [b]alms; [c]provide yourselves money bags which do not grow old, a treasure in the heavens that does not fail, where no thief approaches nor moth destroys. 34For where your treasure is, there your heart will be also.

The Faithful Servant and the Evil Servant

35[a]"Let your waist be girded and [b]*your* lamps burning; 36and you yourselves be like men who wait for their master, when he will return from the wedding, that when he comes and knocks they may open to him immediately. 37[a]Blessed *are* those servants whom the master, when he comes, will find watching. Assuredly, I say to you that he will gird himself and have them sit down *to eat,* and will come and serve them. 38And if he should come in the second watch, or come in the third watch, and find *them* so, blessed are those servants. 39[a]But know this, that if the master of the house had known what hour the thief would come, he would [1]have watched and not allowed his house to be broken into. 40[a]Therefore you also be ready, for the Son of Man is coming at an hour you do not expect."

41Then Peter said to Him, "Lord, do You speak this parable *only* to us, or to all *people?*"

42And the Lord said, [a]"Who then is that faithful and wise steward, whom *his* master will make ruler over his household, to give *them their* portion of food [1]in due season? 43Blessed *is* that servant whom his master will find so doing when he comes. 44[a]Truly, I say to you that he will make him ruler over all that he has. 45[a]But if that servant says in his heart, 'My master is delaying his coming,' and begins to beat the male and female servants, and to eat and drink and be drunk, 46the master of that servant will come on a [a]day when he is not looking for *him,* and at an hour when he is not aware, and will cut him in two and appoint *him* his portion with the unbelievers. 47And [a]that servant who [b]knew his master's will, and did not prepare *himself* or do according to his will, shall be beaten with many *stripes.* 48[a]But he who did not know, yet committed things deserving of stripes, shall be beaten with few. For everyone to whom much is given, from him much will be required; and to whom much has been committed, of him they will ask the more.

Christ Brings Division

49[a]"I came to send fire on the earth, and how I wish it were already kindled! 50But [a]I have a baptism to be baptized with, and how distressed I am till it is [b]accomplished! 51[a]Do *you* suppose that I came to give peace on earth? I tell you, not at all, [b]but rather division. 52[a]For from now on five in one house will be divided: three against two, and two against three. 53[a]Father will be divided against son and son against father, mother against daughter and daughter against mother, mother-in-law against her daughter-in-law and daughter-in-law against her mother-in-law."

---

20 a Ps. 52:7 b Ps. 39:6
21 a [James 2:5; 5:1–5]
22 a Matt. 6:25–33
24 a Job 38:41
26 *1 do you worry*
27 a 1 Kin. 10:4–7 *1 clothed*
28 a Matt. 6:30; 8:26; 14:31; 16:8
30 a Matt. 6:31, 32
31 a Matt. 6:33 *1* NU *His kingdom, and these things*
32 a [Matt. 11:25, 26]
33 a Matt. 19:21 b Luke 11:41 c Matt. 6:20
35 a [1 Pet. 1:13] b [Matt. 25:1–13]
37 a Matt. 24:46
39 a Rev. 3:3; 16:15 *1* NU *not have allowed*
40 a Mark 13:33
42 a Matt. 24:45, 46; 25:21 *1 at the right time*
44 a Matt. 24:47; 25:21
45 a 2 Pet. 3:3, 4
46 a 1 Thess. 5:3
47 a Deut. 25:2 b [James 4:17]
48 a [Lev. 5:17]
49 a Luke 12:51
50 a Mark 10:38 b John 12:27; 19:30
51 a Matt. 10:34–36 b John 7:43; 9:16; 10:19
52 a Mark 13:12
53 a Matt. 10:21, 36

Discern the Time

54 Then He also said to the multitudes,
[a]"Whenever *you see* a cloud rising out of
the west, immediately you say, 'A shower
is coming'; and so it is. 55 And when you
see the [a]south wind blow, you say, 'There
will be hot weather'; and there is. 56 Hypocrites! You can discern the face of the sky
and of the earth, but how *is it* you do not
discern [a]this time?

Make Peace with Your Adversary

57 "Yes, and why, even of yourselves, do
you not judge what is right? 58 [a]When you
go with your adversary to the magistrate,
make every effort [b]along the way to settle
with him, lest he drag you to the judge,
the judge deliver you to the officer, and
the officer throw you into prison. 59 I tell
you, you shall not depart from there till
you have paid the very last mite."

Repent or Perish

13 There were present at that season
some who told Him about the Galileans whose blood Pilate had [1]mingled
with their sacrifices. 2 And Jesus answered
and said to them, "Do you suppose that
these Galileans were worse sinners than
all *other* Galileans, because they suffered
such things? 3 I tell you, no; but unless
you repent you will all likewise perish. 4 Or
those eighteen on whom the tower in Siloam fell and killed them, do you think
that they were worse sinners than all *other* men who dwelt in Jerusalem? 5 I tell
you, no; but unless you repent you will all
likewise perish."

The Parable of the Barren Fig Tree

6 He also spoke this parable: [a]"A certain
man had a fig tree planted in his vineyard,
and he came seeking fruit on it and found
none. 7 Then he said to the keeper of his
vineyard, 'Look, for three years I have
come seeking fruit on this fig tree and
find none. Cut it down; why does it [1]use
up the ground?' 8 But he answered and
said to him, 'Sir, let it alone this year also,
until I dig around it and fertilize *it*. 9 [1]And
if it bears fruit, *well*. But if not, after that
you can [a]cut it down.' "

A Spirit of Infirmity

10 Now He was teaching in one of the
synagogues on the Sabbath. 11 And behold,
there was a woman who had a spirit of
infirmity eighteen years, and was bent
over and could in no way [1]raise *herself* up.
12 But when Jesus saw her, He called *her*
to *Him* and said to her, "Woman, you are
loosed from your [a]infirmity." 13 [a]And He
laid *His* hands on her, and immediately
she was made straight, and glorified God.
14 But the ruler of the synagogue answered with indignation, because Jesus
had [a]healed on the Sabbath; and he said
to the crowd, [b]"There are six days on
which men ought to work; therefore come
and be healed on them, and [c]not on the
Sabbath day."
15 The Lord then answered him and
said, [1]"Hypocrite! [a]Does not each one of
you on the Sabbath loose his ox or donkey
from the stall, and lead *it* away to water
it? 16 So ought not this woman, [a]being a
daughter of Abraham, whom Satan has
bound—think of it—for eighteen years,
be loosed from this bond on the Sabbath?"
17 And when He said these things, all His
adversaries were put to shame; and all the
multitude rejoiced for all the glorious
things that were [a]done by Him.

The Parable of the Mustard Seed

18 [a]Then He said, "What is the kingdom
of God like? And to what shall I compare
it? 19 It is like a mustard seed, which a man
took and put in his garden; and it grew
and became a [1]large tree, and the birds of
the air nested in its branches."

The Parable of the Leaven

20 And again He said, "To what shall I
liken the kingdom of God? 21 It is like
[1]leaven, which a woman took and hid in
three [a]measures[2] of meal till it was all
leavened."

The Narrow Way

22 [a]And He went through the cities and
villages, teaching, and journeying toward
Jerusalem. 23 Then one said to Him, "Lord,
are there [a]few who are saved?"
And He said to them, 24 [a]"Strive to enter
through the narrow gate, for [b]many, I say
to you, will seek to enter and will not
be able. 25 [a]When once the Master of the
house has risen up and [b]shut the door,

---

54 a Matt. 16:2, 3
55 a Job 37:17
56 a Luke 19:41–44
58 a Prov. 25:8 b [Is. 55:6]

CHAPTER 13
1 *1 mixed*
6 a Matt. 21:19
7 *1 waste*
9 a [John 15:2] *1 NU And if it bears fruit after that, well. But if not, you can*
11 *1 straighten up*
12 a Luke 7:21; 8:2
13 a Acts 9:17
14 a [Luke 6:6–11; 14:1–6] b Ex. 20:9; 23:12 c Mark 3:2
15 a Luke 14:5 *1 NU, M Hypocrites*
16 a Luke 19:9
17 a Mark 5:19, 20
18 a Mark 4:30–32
19 *1 NU omits large*
21 a Matt. 13:33 *1 yeast* *2 Gr. sata, same as Heb. seah; approximately 2 pecks in all*
22 a Mark 6:6
23 a [Matt. 7:14; 20:16]
24 a [Matt. 7:13] b [John 7:34; 8:21; 13:33]
25 a Is. 55:6 b Matt. 25:10

and you begin to stand outside and knock
at the door, saying, [c]'Lord, Lord, open for
us,' and He will answer and say to you, [d]'I
do not know you, where you are from,'
26then you will begin to say, 'We ate and
drank in Your presence, and You taught
in our streets.' 27[a]But He will say, 'I tell
you I do not know you, where you are
from. [b]Depart from Me, all you workers of
iniquity.' 28[a]There will be weeping and
gnashing of teeth, [b]when you see Abraham and Isaac and Jacob and all the
prophets in the kingdom of God, and
yourselves thrust out. 29They will come
from the east and the west, from the
north and the south, and sit down in the
kingdom of God. 30[a]And indeed there are
last who will be first, and there are first
who will be last."

31[1]On that very day some Pharisees
came, saying to Him, "Get out and depart
from here, for Herod wants to kill You."

32And He said to them, "Go, tell that
fox, 'Behold, I cast out demons and perform cures today and tomorrow, and the
third *day* [a]I shall be [1]perfected.' 33Never-
theless I must journey today, tomorrow,
and the *day* following; for it cannot be
that a prophet should perish outside of
Jerusalem.

Jesus Laments over Jerusalem

34[a]"O Jerusalem, Jerusalem, the one
who kills the prophets and stones those
who are sent to her! How often I wanted
to gather your children together, as a hen
gathers her brood under *her* wings, but
you were not willing! 35See! [a]Your house
is left to you desolate; and [1]assuredly, I
say to you, you shall not see Me until *the
time* comes when you say, [b]*'Blessed is He
who comes in the name of the LORD!'* "

A Man with Dropsy Healed on the Sabbath

14 Now it happened, as He went into
the house of one of the rulers of
the Pharisees to eat bread on the Sabbath,
that they watched Him closely. 2And behold, there was a certain man before Him
who had dropsy. 3And Jesus, answering,
spoke to the lawyers and Pharisees, saying, [a]"Is it lawful to heal on the [1]Sab-
bath?"

4But they kept silent. And He took *him*
and healed him, and let him go. 5Then He
answered them, saying, [a]"Which of you,
having a [1]donkey or an ox that has fallen
into a pit, will not immediately pull him
out on the Sabbath day?" 6And they could
not answer Him regarding these things.

Take the Lowly Place

7So He told a parable to those who were
invited, when He noted how they chose
the best places, saying to them: 8"When
you are invited by anyone to a wedding
feast, do not sit down in the best place,
lest one more honorable than you be invited by him; 9and he who invited you and
him come and say to you, 'Give place to
this man,' and then you begin with shame
to take the lowest place. 10[a]But when you
are invited, go and sit down in the lowest
place, so that when he who invited you
comes he may say to you, 'Friend, go up
higher.' Then you will have glory in the
presence of those who sit at the table with
you. 11[a]For whoever exalts himself will be
[1]humbled, and he who humbles himself
will be exalted."

12Then He also said to him who invited
Him, "When you give a dinner or a supper, do not ask your friends, your
brothers, your relatives, nor rich neighbors, lest they also invite you back, and
you be repaid. 13But when you give a feast,
invite [a]*the* poor, *the* [1]maimed, *the* lame,
the blind. 14And you will be [a]blessed, because they cannot repay you; for you shall
be repaid at the resurrection of the just."

The Parable of the Great Supper

15Now when one of those who sat at the
table with Him heard these things, he said
to Him, [a]"Blessed *is* he who shall eat
[1]bread in the kingdom of God!"

16[a]Then He said to him, "A certain man
gave a great supper and invited many,
17and [a]sent his servant at supper time to
say to those who were invited, 'Come, for
all things are now ready.' 18But they all
with one *accord* began to make excuses.
The first said to him, 'I have bought a
piece of ground, and I must go and see it.
I ask you to have me excused.' 19And another said, 'I have bought five yoke of
oxen, and I am going to test them. I ask
you to have me excused.' 20Still another
said, 'I have married a wife, and therefore
I cannot come.' 21So that servant came
and reported these things to his master.
Then the master of the house, being an-

25 c Luke 6:46 d Matt. 7:23; 25:12
27 a [Matt. 7:23; 25:41] b Ps. 6:8
28 a Matt. 8:12; 13:42; 24:51 b Matt. 8:11
30 a [Matt. 19:30; 20:16]
31 1 NU *In that very hour*
32 a [Heb. 2:10; 5:9; 7:28] 1 Resurrected
34 a Matt. 23:37–39
35 a Lev. 26:31, 32 b Ps. 118:26; Matt. 21:9 1 NU, M omit *assuredly*

CHAPTER 14
3 a Matt. 12:10 1 NU adds *or not*
5 a [Ex. 23:5] 1 NU, M *son*
10 a Prov. 25:6, 7
11 a Matt. 23:12 1 *put down*
13 a Neh. 8:10, 12 1 *crippled*
14 a [Matt. 25:34–40]
15 a Rev. 19:9 1 M *dinner*
16 a Matt. 22:2–14
17 a Prov. 9:2, 5

gry, said to his servant, 'Go out quickly
into the streets and lanes of the city, and
bring in here *the* poor and *the* [1]maimed
and *the* lame and *the* blind.' 22And the
servant said, 'Master, it is done as you
commanded, and still there is room.'
23Then the master said to the servant, 'Go
out into the highways and hedges, and
compel *them* to come in, that my house
may be filled. 24For I say to you [a]that none
of those men who were invited shall taste
my supper.' "

Leaving All to Follow Christ

25Now great multitudes went with Him.
And He turned and said to them, 26[a]"If
anyone comes to Me [b]and does not hate
his father and mother, wife and children,
brothers and sisters, [c]yes, and his own life
also, he cannot be My disciple. 27And
[a]whoever does not bear his cross and
come after Me cannot be My disciple.
28For [a]which of you, intending to build a
tower, does not sit down first and count
the cost, whether he has *enough* to finish
it— 29lest, after he has laid the foundation, and is not able to finish, all who see
it begin to mock him, 30saying, 'This man
began to build and was not able to finish.'
31Or what king, going to make war against
another king, does not sit down first and
consider whether he is able with ten thousand to meet him who comes against him
with twenty thousand? 32Or else, while
the other is still a great way off, he sends
a delegation and asks conditions of peace.
33So likewise, whoever of you [a]does not
forsake all that he has cannot be My disciple.

Tasteless Salt Is Worthless

34[a]"Salt *is* good; but if the salt has lost
its flavor, how shall it be seasoned? 35It is
neither fit for the land nor for the [1]dung-
hill, *but* men throw it out. He who has
ears to hear, let him hear!"

The Parable of the Lost Sheep

15 Then [a]all the tax collectors and the
sinners drew near to Him to hear
Him. 2And the Pharisees and scribes complained, saying, "This Man [1]receives sinners [a]and eats with them." 3So He spoke
this parable to them, saying:
4[a]"What man of you, having a hundred
sheep, if he loses one of them, does not
leave the ninety-nine in the wilderness,
and go after the one which is lost until he
finds it? 5And when he has found *it,* he
lays *it* on his shoulders, rejoicing. 6And
when he comes home, he calls together
his friends and neighbors, saying to them,
[a]'Rejoice with me, for I have found my
sheep [b]which was lost!' 7I say to you that
likewise there will be more joy in heaven
over one sinner who repents [a]than over
ninety-nine [1]just persons who [b]need no
repentance.

The Parable of the Lost Coin

8"Or what woman, having ten silver
[1]coins, if she loses one coin, does not light
a lamp, sweep the house, and search carefully until she finds *it?* 9And when she has
found *it,* she calls *her* friends and neighbors together, saying, 'Rejoice with me,
for I have found the piece which I lost!'
10Likewise, I say to you, there is joy in the
presence of the angels of God over one
sinner who repents."

The Parable of the Lost Son

11Then He said: "A certain man had
two sons. 12And the younger of them said
to *his* father, 'Father, give me the portion
of goods that falls *to me.*' So he divided
to them [a]*his* livelihood. 13And not many
days after, the younger son gathered all
together, journeyed to a far country, and
there wasted his possessions with [1]prodi-
gal living. 14But when he had spent all,
there arose a severe famine in that land,
and he began to be in want. 15Then he
went and joined himself to a citizen of
that country, and he sent him into his
fields to feed swine. 16And he would gladly
have filled his stomach with the [1]pods
that the swine ate, and no one gave him
anything.
17"But when he came to himself, he
said, 'How many of my father's hired servants have bread enough and to spare, and
I perish with hunger! 18I will arise and go
to my father, and will say to him, "Father,
[a]I have sinned against heaven and before
you, 19and I am no longer worthy to be
called your son. Make me like one of your
hired servants." '
20"And he arose and came to his father.
But [a]when he was still a great way off, his
father saw him and had compassion, and
ran and fell on his neck and kissed him.
21And the son said to him, 'Father, I have
sinned against heaven [a]and in your sight,
and am no longer worthy to be called your
son.'

21 [1] *crippled*
24 [a] [Acts 13:46]
26 [a] Deut. 13:6; 33:9 [b] Rom. 9:13 [c] Rev. 12:11
27 [a] Luke 9:23
28 [a] Prov. 24:27
33 [a] Matt. 19:27
34 [a] [Mark 9:50]
35 [1] *rubbish heap*

CHAPTER 15
1 [a] [Matt. 9:10–13]
2 [a] Gal. 2:12 [1] *welcomes*
4 [a] Matt. 18:12–14
6 [a] [Rom. 12:15] [b] [1 Pet. 2:10, 25]
7 [a] [Luke 5:32] [b] [Mark 2:17] [1] *upright*
8 [1] Gr. *drachma,* a valuable coin often worn in a ten-piece garland by married women
12 [a] Mark 12:44
13 [1] *wasteful*
16 [1] *carob pods*
18 [a] 2 Sam. 12:13; 24:10, 17
20 [a] [Eph. 2:13, 17]
21 [a] Ps. 51:4

Luke 15:11–13

Dear Woman of Destiny,

If you have a prodigal child, take heart. No matter how hopeless your situation seems, God wants to woo your lost, damaged children back to Himself. To do this, He needs us to be faithful in prayer. And we need His wisdom and strength to stand in the gap for our children.

As you read the story of the prodigal son in Luke 15, you can say he was a "give-me son" who demanded his inheritance before it was due him. He took it, went to a distant country, and spent it all on reckless living.

But when he hit rock bottom he *came to his senses* and headed home, willing to be just a servant in his father's household.

When this son was still a long way off, his father saw him coming, was filled with compassion, ran to meet him, threw his arms around him, and kissed him over and over again—before his son had asked him for forgiveness.

The focus of this parable Jesus told is on the compassionate parent. The analogy is clear: If we want to follow our heavenly Father's example, we must forgive and show compassion for our prodigals just as this father did.

Every spiritual battle is different; therefore, we must ask the Holy Spirit to show us how to pray in each situation. While there is no formula for prayer, here are a few helpful ways to pray for prodigals:

- Pray aloud, using applicable Scripture verses, such as 2 Samuel 15:31b, Proverbs 11:21, and Isaiah 54:13;
- Pray in agreement with a prayer partner or support team;
- Pray with faith, not fear and unbelief;
- Pray for your children's friends and others influencing them. I used to pray, "Lord, guard my children from wrong influences, wrong friends, and wrong environments. Bring the right people into their lives at the right time. Keep them from error and from being deceived."

You may want to paraphrase this scripture as a prayer and add the names of your wayward ones.

"[God] grant _____ (name) repentance, so that they may know the truth, and that they may come to their senses and escape the snare of the devil, having been taken captive by him to do his will" (2 Tim. 2:25b, 26). Remember, the prodigal son came to his senses and returned home.

Or use this one:

God, "open their eyes, in order to turn them from darkness to light, and from the power of Satan to God, that they may receive forgiveness of sins and an inheritance among those who are sanctified by faith in [Jesus]" (Acts 26:18).

One mother who went often into her prodigal's empty bedroom spoke aloud to the enemy. "My son is covered by the blood of Jesus, and your plan to keep him in your kingdom of darkness will not succeed. I declare that the blood of Jesus defeats your plan, Satan; and he will repent and come back to God." Three years later, he did and has since led many other youth to Christ.

Just remember, nothing is impossible with God. It is not His will that any perish—and that includes your offspring!

Quin Sherrer

22"But the father said to his servants,
[1]'Bring out the best robe and put *it* on
him, and put a ring on his hand and sandals on *his* feet. 23And bring the fatted calf
here and kill *it,* and let us eat and be merry; 24[a]for this my son was dead and is alive
again; he was lost and is found.' And they
began to be merry.

25"Now his older son was in the field.
And as he came and drew near to the
house, he heard music and dancing. 26So
he called one of the servants and asked
what these things meant. 27And he said to
him, 'Your brother has come, and because
he has received him safe and sound, your
father has killed the fatted calf.'

28"But he was angry and would not go
in. Therefore his father came out and
pleaded with him. 29So he answered and
said to *his* father, 'Lo, these many years
I have been serving you; I never transgressed your commandment at any time;
and yet you never gave me a young goat,
that I might make merry with my friends.
30But as soon as this son of yours came,
who has devoured your livelihood with
harlots, you killed the fatted calf for him.'

31"And he said to him, 'Son, you are
always with me, and all that I have is
yours. 32It was right that we should make
merry and be glad, [a]for your brother was
dead and is alive again, and was lost and
is found.' "

The Parable of the Unjust Steward

16 He also said to His disciples:
"There was a certain rich man who
had a steward, and an accusation was
brought to him that this man was [1]wast-
ing his goods. 2So he called him and said
to him, 'What is this I hear about you?
Give an [a]account of your stewardship, for
you can no longer be steward.'

3"Then the steward said within himself,
'What shall I do? For my master is taking
the stewardship away from me. I cannot
dig; I am ashamed to beg. 4I have resolved
what to do, that when I am put out of the
stewardship, they may receive me into
their houses.'

5"So he called every one of his master's
debtors to *him,* and said to the first, 'How
much do you owe my master?' 6And he
said, 'A hundred [1]measures of oil.' So he
said to him, 'Take your bill, and sit down
quickly and write fifty.' 7Then he said to
another, 'And how much do you owe?' So
he said, 'A hundred [1]measures of wheat.'
And he said to him, 'Take your bill, and
write eighty.' 8So the master commended
the unjust steward because he had dealt
shrewdly. For the sons of this world are
more shrewd in their generation than
[a]the sons of light.

9"And I say to you, [a]make friends for
yourselves by unrighteous [1]mammon,
that when [2]you fail, they may receive you
into an everlasting home. 10[a]He who *is*
faithful in *what is* least is faithful also in
much; and he who is unjust in *what is*
least is unjust also in much. 11Therefore
if you have not been faithful in the unrighteous mammon, who will commit to
your trust the true *riches?* 12And if you
have not been faithful in what is another
man's, who will give you what is your
[a]own?

13[a]"No servant can serve two masters;
for either he will hate the one and love the
other, or else he will be loyal to the one
and despise the other. You cannot serve
God and mammon."

The Law, the Prophets, and the Kingdom

14Now the Pharisees, [a]who were lovers
of money, also heard all these things, and
they [1]derided Him. 15And He said to
them, "You are those who [a]justify yourselves [b]before men, but [c]God knows your
hearts. For [d]what is highly esteemed
among men is an abomination in the
sight of God.

16[a]"The law and the prophets *were* until
John. Since that time the kingdom of God
has been preached, and everyone is pressing into it. 17[a]And it is easier for heaven
and earth to pass away than for one [1]tittle
of the law to fail.

18[a]"Whoever divorces his wife and marries another commits adultery; and whoever marries her who is divorced from *her*
husband commits adultery.

The Rich Man and Lazarus

19"There was a certain rich man who
was clothed in purple and fine linen and
[1]fared sumptuously every day. 20But there
was a certain beggar named Lazarus, full
of sores, who was laid at his gate, 21desir-
ing to be fed with [1]the crumbs which fell
from the rich man's table. Moreover the
dogs came and licked his sores. 22So it was
that the beggar died, and was carried by

22 [1] NU *Quickly bring*

24 [a] Luke 9:60; 15:32

32 [a] Luke 15:24

CHAPTER 16

1 [1] *squandering*

2 [a] [Rom. 14:12]

6 [1] Gr. *batos,* same as Heb. *bath;* 8 or 9 gallons each

7 [1] Gr. *koros,* same as Heb. *kor;* 10 or 12 bushels each

8 [a] [Eph. 5:8]

9 [a] Dan. 4:27 [1] Lit., in Aram., *wealth* [2] NU *it fails*

10 [a] Matt. 25:21

12 [a] [1 Pet. 1:3, 4]

13 [a] Matt. 6:24

14 [a] Matt. 23:14 [1] Lit. *turned up their nose at*

15 [a] Luke 10:29 [b] [Matt. 6:2, 5, 16] [c] Ps. 7:9 [d] 1 Sam. 16:7

16 [a] Matt. 3:1–12; 4:17; 11:12, 13

17 [a] Is. 40:8; 51:6 [1] The smallest stroke in a Heb. letter

18 [a] 1 Cor. 7:10, 11

19 [1] *lived in luxury*

21 [1] NU *what fell*

the angels to [a]Abraham's bosom. The rich man also died and was buried. 23 And being in torments in Hades, he lifted up his eyes and saw Abraham afar off, and Lazarus in his bosom.

24 "Then he cried and said, 'Father Abraham, have mercy on me, and send Lazarus that he may dip the tip of his finger in water and [a]cool my tongue; for I [b]am tormented in this flame.' 25 But Abraham said, 'Son, [a]remember that in your lifetime you received your good things, and likewise Lazarus evil things; but now he is comforted and you are tormented. 26 And besides all this, between us and you there is a great gulf fixed, so that those who want to pass from here to you cannot, nor can those from there pass to us.'

27 "Then he said, 'I beg you therefore, father, that you would send him to my father's house, 28 for I have five brothers, that he may testify to them, lest they also come to this place of torment.' 29 Abraham said to him, [a]'They have Moses and the prophets; let them hear them.' 30 And he said, 'No, father Abraham; but if one goes to them from the dead, they will repent.' 31 But he said to him, [a]'If they do not hear Moses and the prophets, [b]neither will they be persuaded though one rise from the dead.' "

Jesus Warns of Offenses

17 Then He said to the disciples, [a]"It is impossible that no [1]offenses should come, but [b]woe *to him* through whom they do come! 2 It would be better for him if a millstone were hung around his neck, and he were thrown into the sea, than that he should [1]offend one of these little ones. 3 Take heed to yourselves. [a]If your brother sins [1]against you, [b]rebuke him; and if he repents, forgive him. 4 And if he sins against you seven times in a day, and seven times in a day returns [1]to you, saying, 'I repent,' you shall forgive him."

Faith and Duty

5 And the apostles said to the Lord, "Increase our faith."

6 [a]So the Lord said, "If you have faith as a mustard seed, you can say to this mulberry tree, 'Be pulled up by the roots and be planted in the sea,' and it would obey you. 7 And which of you, having a servant plowing or tending sheep, will say to him when he has come in from the field, 'Come at once and sit down to eat'? 8 But will he not rather say to him, 'Prepare something for my supper, and gird yourself [a]and serve me till I have eaten and drunk, and afterward you will eat and drink'? 9 Does he thank that servant because he did the things that were commanded [1]him? I think not. 10 So likewise you, when you have done all those things which you are commanded, say, 'We are [a]unprofitable servants. We have done what was our duty to do.' "

Ten Lepers Cleansed

11 Now it happened [a]as He went to Jerusalem that He passed through the midst of Samaria and Galilee. 12 Then as He entered a certain village, there met Him ten men who were lepers, [a]who stood afar off. 13 And they lifted up *their* voices and said, "Jesus, Master, have mercy on us!"

14 So when He saw *them,* He said to them, [a]"Go, show yourselves to the priests." And so it was that as they went, they were cleansed.

15 And one of them, when he saw that he was healed, returned, and with a loud voice [a]glorified God, 16 and fell down on *his* face at His feet, giving Him thanks. And he was a [a]Samaritan.

17 So Jesus answered and said, "Were there not ten cleansed? But where *are* the nine? 18 Were there not any found who returned to give glory to God except this foreigner?" 19 [a]And He said to him, "Arise, go your way. Your faith has made you well."

The Coming of the Kingdom

20 Now when He was asked by the Pharisees when the kingdom of God would come, He answered them and said, "The kingdom of God does not come with observation; 21 [a]nor will they say, [1]'See here!' or 'See there!' For indeed, [b]the kingdom of God is [2]within you."

22 Then He said to the disciples, [a]"The days will come when you will desire to see one of the days of the Son of Man, and you will not see *it.* 23 [a]And they will say to you, [1]'Look here!' or 'Look there!' Do not go after *them* or follow *them.* 24 [a]For as the lightning that flashes out of one *part* under heaven shines to the other *part* under heaven, so also the Son of Man will be in His day. 25 [a]But first He must suffer many things and be [b]rejected by this generation. 26 [a]And as it [b]was in the [c]days of

22 a Matt. 8:11
24 a Zech. 14:12 b [Mark 9:42–48]
25 a Luke 6:24
29 a Acts 15:21; 17:11
31 a [John 5:46] b John 12:10, 11

CHAPTER 17
1 a [1 Cor. 11:19] b [2 Thess. 1:6] *1 stumbling blocks*
2 *1 cause one of these little ones to stumble*
3 a [Matt. 18:15, 21] b [Prov. 17:10] *1* NU omits *against you*
4 *1* M omits *to you*
6 a [Mark 9:23; 11:23]
8 a [Luke 12:37]
9 *1* NU omits the rest of v. 9; M omits *him*
10 a Rom. 3:12; 11:35
11 a Luke 9:51, 52
12 a Lev. 13:46
14 a Matt. 8:4
15 a Luke 5:25; 18:43
16 a 2 Kin. 17:24
19 a Matt. 9:22
21 a Luke 17:23 b [Rom. 14:17] *1* NU reverses *here* and *there* *2 in your midst*
22 a Matt. 9:15
23 a Matt. 24:23 *1* NU reverses *here* and *there*
24 a Matt. 24:27
25 a Mark 8:31; 9:31; 10:33 b Luke 9:22
26 a Matt. 24:37–39 b [Gen. 6:5–7] c [Gen. 6:8–13]

LUKE 17:11–19

Dear Woman of Destiny,

Giving thanks is an expression of faith. Jesus said in Luke 17:19 to the one thankful leper out of the ten who were cleansed: "Arise, go your way. Your faith has made you well." Faith is being sure of what we hope for and certain of what we do not see, according to Hebrews 11:1. We may not always see the results immediately, as the lepers did, but we believe that the Lord has heard our requests. By giving thanks, we're expressing belief that God has chosen the very best for us, and we receive it gratefully.

The opposite of gratitude is bitterness. Usually we don't even realize we're allowing bitterness to set in. It often begins with comparing ourselves to others; and as we see we do not measure up, we stop giving thanks and begin demanding, and a root of bitterness sets in.

When my husband was serving the Lord as a pastor in Central America, we lived in the parsonage provided by the church. A cheerful little house and very adequate, it was ideally situated three blocks away from the church, and not right next door. We often enjoyed walking there and back. Our four children have wonderful memories of our days there: the two bedrooms they shared and the one bathroom we all shared; sliding around on the wet patio floor in their bathing suits to cool down from the midday heat; the birthday parties out in the backyard; and the parks close by with the different swing sets.

During that time, I joined a Bible study with other missionary wives who were serving in the same capital city. Some of their homes were so beautiful, almost like those in *Better Homes and Gardens*! On returning to our humble abode, I fell into a trap of comparing houses in my mind and felt great unrest in my spirit as a root of bitterness was setting in.

God is faithful. As I confessed to Him my sin and pled forgiveness from Him, He heard me. He answered me by taking me on a tour of our home and reminding me of each item we had gathered along the way and who had given it to us. I began to give thanks to Him for His loving and abundant provision for us. Almost immediately, as I gave Him thanks, the bitterness of my heart left me.

Thankfulness works marvels in many amazing ways. Instead of focusing on what we do not have or do not like, we can turn our circumstances around so that we now see all we have, all we like, and all we can truly thank God for. Believe me, each one of us has so much to thank Him for. As the hymn "Count Your Blessings" tells us, naming our blessings "one by one" helps us to discover the many things our Lord has done for us.

Doris Bush

[d]Noah, so it will be also in the days of the Son of Man: 27They ate, they drank, they married wives, they were given in marriage, until the [a]day that Noah entered the ark, and the flood came and [b]destroyed them all. 28[a]Likewise as it was also in the days of Lot: They ate, they drank, they bought, they sold, they planted, they built; 29but on [a]the day that Lot went out of Sodom it rained fire and brimstone from heaven and destroyed *them* all. 30Even so will it be in the day when the Son of Man [a]is revealed.

If we find the plan of God and work within it, we cannot fail.

E. STANLEY JONES

31"In that day, he [a]who is on the housetop, and his [1]goods *are* in the house, let him not come down to take them away. And likewise the one who is in the field, let him not turn back. 32[a]Remember Lot's wife. 33[a]Whoever seeks to save his life will lose it, and whoever loses his life will preserve it. 34[a]I tell you, in that night there will be two [1]*men* in one bed: the one will be taken and the other will be left. 35[a]Two *women* will be grinding together: the one will be taken and the other left. 36[1]Two *men* will be in the field: the one will be taken and the other left."

37And they answered and said to Him, [a]"Where, Lord?"

So He said to them, "Wherever the body is, there the eagles will be gathered together."

The Parable of the Persistent Widow

18 Then He spoke a parable to them, that men [a]always ought to pray and not lose heart, 2saying: "There was in a certain city a judge who did not fear God nor [1]regard man. 3Now there was a widow in that city; and she came to him, saying, [1]'Get justice for me from my adversary.' 4And he would not for a while; but afterward he said within himself, 'Though I do not fear God nor regard man, 5[a]yet because this widow troubles me I will [1]avenge her, lest by her continual coming she weary me.' "

6Then the Lord said, "Hear what the unjust judge said. 7And [a]shall God not avenge His own elect who cry out day and night to Him, though He bears long with them? 8I tell you [a]that He will avenge them speedily. Nevertheless, when the Son of Man comes, will He really find faith on the earth?"

Father, may ____ always pray and not lose heart.

FROM LUKE 18:1

The Parable of the Pharisee and the Tax Collector

9Also He spoke this parable to some [a]who trusted in themselves that they were righteous, and despised others: 10"Two men went up to the temple to pray, one a Pharisee and the other a tax collector. 11The Pharisee [a]stood and prayed thus with himself, [b]'God, I thank You that I am not like other men—extortioners, unjust, adulterers, or even as this tax collector. 12I fast twice a week; I give tithes of all that I possess.' 13And the tax collector, standing afar off, would not so much as raise *his* eyes to heaven, but beat his breast, saying, 'God, be merciful to me a sinner!' 14I tell you, this man went down to his house justified *rather* than the other; [a]for everyone who exalts himself will be [1]humbled, and he who humbles himself will be exalted."

Merciful Savior, like the tax collector, I pray that ____ would recognize their sin and cry out to You for mercy!

FROM LUKE 18:13

26 [d] 1 Pet. 3:20
27 [a] Gen. 7:1–16 [b] Gen. 7:19–23
28 [a] Gen. 19
29 [a] Gen. 19:16, 24, 29
30 [a] [2 Thess. 1:7]
31 [a] Mark 13:15 [1] *possessions*
32 [a] Gen. 19:26
33 [a] Matt. 10:39; 16:25
34 [a] [1 Thess. 4:17] [1] Or *people*
35 [a] Matt. 24:40, 41
36 [1] NU, M omit v. 36.
37 [a] Matt. 24:28
CHAPTER 18
1 [a] Luke 11:5–10
2 [1] *respect*
3 [1] *Avenge me on*
5 [a] Luke 11:8 [1] *vindicate*
7 [a] Rev. 6:10
8 [a] Heb. 10:37
9 [a] Luke 10:29; 16:15
11 [a] Ps. 135:2 [b] Is. 1:15; 58:2
14 [a] Luke 14:11 [1] *put down*

Luke 18:3–7

Dear Woman of Destiny,

In this parable, the Lord teaches us about a persistent widow who displayed courage, determination, and perseverance. She approached the judge with boldness, and with no fear of man. The judge did not exhibit the fear of the Lord, yet he was used to answer her request and bring blessing to her life.

Years ago, when I first read this parable, I started trusting God to use strangers, even unbelievers, to provide financial and material blessings. Several years ago, hurricane Andrew left my family homeless, with no physical assets. I wanted to go on missionary trips to help those who had lack. We had nothing to sell. All I had to give to the Lord was a heart with a desire to travel and to have a prayer center to help the needy.

Since then, strangers have paid my way on 140 mission trips. That has proven God's provision! The Holy Spirit used people I did not know, and God arranged the divine connections. Sometimes I shared my need, but most of the time I only prayed to God and expected a miracle. One year ago, the Lord blessed us with a 12,000-square-foot prayer center completely furnished and stocked with food, clothes, and household items for distribution to the needy. Every item has been donated, the majority by strangers. This has been a true miracle to prove that God answers prayer and gives us the desires of our hearts. I just followed the example of the determined widow and repeatedly prayed for each blessing until it arrived. Woman of Destiny, do not give up. Keep pressing in; and pray it in!

The Lord is so faithful to answer persistent prayer. He has sent me around the world preaching and teaching, and He has provided the finances that enabled me to go. Several times, I have prayed from an airport or bus station for a return ticket. I then waited on God to speak to strangers who would be His vessels of provision.

Is God stretching your faith today? Renounce your own agenda, and start using the agenda God has prepared for you. Ask Him to send you only to places He wants you to go. We are not all called to be missionaries traveling by faith, but we are all called to share the gospel with others in our own worlds.

When God sends you, He will provide the finances, the agenda, and divine connections with the right people. Everything happens in God's perfect timing. I pray you will see the importance of understanding His timing and the need to seek His face repeatedly until the blessing arrives. The persistent widow continued to seek the judge's face with utter determination until he took the time to grant her request. When you whisper the name of Jesus, He is right there. The Lord has time to listen to you and to grant you your request.

You have received grace from the Lord to prepare you, systematically, to be faithful in prayer. Avoid looking at your circumstances, which might bring discouragement. Only look at Jesus and believe. The widow expected to find favor with the judge, and this teaches us to expect to find favor. When you pray persistently, remember that you are anointed and highly favored of the Lord, and expect His provision.

A. G. Rodriguez

Jesus Blesses Little Children

15[a]Then they also brought infants to
Him that He might touch them; but when
the disciples saw *it,* they rebuked them.
16But Jesus called them to *Him* and said,
"Let the little children come to Me, and do
not forbid them; for [a]of such is the kingdom of God. 17[a]Assuredly, I say to you,
whoever does not receive the kingdom
of God as a little child will by no means
enter it."

Jesus Counsels the Rich Young Ruler

18[a]Now a certain ruler asked Him, saying, "Good Teacher, what shall I do to inherit eternal life?"
19So Jesus said to him, "Why do you call
Me good? No one *is* good but [a]One, *that
is,* God. 20You know the commandments:
[a]*'Do not commit adultery,' 'Do not murder,' 'Do not steal,' 'Do not bear false witness,'* [b]*'Honor your father and your
mother.'* "
21And he said, "All [a]these things I have
kept from my youth."
22So when Jesus heard these things, He
said to him, "You still lack one thing.
[a]Sell all that you have and distribute to
the poor, and you will have treasure in
heaven; and come, follow Me."
23But when he heard this, he became
very sorrowful, for he was very rich.

With God All Things Are Possible

24And when Jesus saw that he became
very sorrowful, He said, [a]"How hard it is
for those who have riches to enter the
kingdom of God! 25For it is easier for a
camel to go through the eye of a needle
than for a rich man to enter the kingdom
of God."
26And those who heard it said, "Who
then can be saved?"
27But He said, [a]"The things which are
impossible with men are possible with
God."
28[a]Then Peter said, "See, we have left
[1]all and followed You."
29So He said to them, "Assuredly, I say
to you, [a]there is no one who has left house
or parents or brothers or wife or children,
for the sake of the kingdom of God,
30[a]who shall not receive many times more
in this present time, and in the age to
come eternal life."

Jesus a Third Time Predicts His Death and Resurrection

31[a]Then He took the twelve aside and
said to them, "Behold, we are going up to
Jerusalem, and all things [b]that are written
by the prophets concerning the Son of
Man will be [1]accomplished. 32For [a]He will
be delivered to the Gentiles and will be
mocked and insulted and spit upon.
33They will scourge *Him* and kill Him.
And the third day He will rise again."
34[a]But they understood none of these
things; this saying was hidden from them,
and they did not know the things which
were spoken.

A Blind Man Receives His Sight

35[a]Then it happened, as He was coming
near Jericho, that a certain blind man sat
by the road begging. 36And hearing a multitude passing by, he asked what it meant.
37So they told him that Jesus of Nazareth
was passing by. 38And he cried out, saying, "Jesus, [a]Son of David, have mercy
on me!"
39Then those who went before warned
him that he should be quiet; but he cried
out all the more, "Son of David, have mercy on me!"
40So Jesus stood still and commanded
him to be brought to Him. And when he
had come near, He asked him, 41saying,
"What do you want Me to do for you?"
He said, "Lord, that I may receive my
sight."
42Then Jesus said to him, "Receive your
sight; [a]your faith has made you well."
43And immediately he received his sight,
and followed Him, [a]glorifying God. And
all the people, when they saw *it,* gave
praise to God.

Jesus Comes to Zacchaeus' House

19 Then *Jesus* entered and passed
through [a]Jericho. 2Now behold,
there was a man named Zacchaeus who
was a chief tax collector, and he was rich.
3And he sought to [a]see who Jesus was, but
could not because of the crowd, for he was
of short stature. 4So he ran ahead and
climbed up into a sycamore tree to see
Him, for He was going to pass that *way.*
5And when Jesus came to the place, He
looked up [1]and saw him, and said to him,

---

15 a Mark 10:13–16
16 a 1 Pet. 2:2
17 a Mark 10:15
18 a Matt. 19:16–29
19 a Ps. 86:5; 119:68
20 a Ex. 20:12–16; Deut. 5:16–20 b Eph. 6:2; Col. 3:20
21 a Phil. 3:6
22 a Matt. 6:19, 20; 19:21
24 a Mark 10:23
27 a Jer. 32:17
28 a Matt. 19:27 *1* NU *our own*
29 a Deut. 33:9
30 a Job 42:10
31 a Matt. 16:21; 17:22; 20:17 b Ps. 22 *1 fulfilled*
32 a Acts 3:13
34 a Luke 2:50; 9:45
35 a Matt. 20:29–34
38 a Matt. 9:27
42 a Luke 17:19
43 a Luke 5:26

CHAPTER 19
1 a Josh. 6:26
3 a John 12:21
5 *1* NU omits *and saw him*

"Zacchaeus, [2]make haste and come down,
for today I must stay at your house." 6So
he [1]made haste and came down, and received Him joyfully. 7But when they saw
it, they all [1]complained, saying, [a]"He has
gone to be a guest with a man who is a
sinner."
8Then Zacchaeus stood and said to the
Lord, "Look, Lord, I give half of my goods
to the [a]poor; and if I have taken anything
from anyone by [b]false accusation, [c]I restore fourfold."
9And Jesus said to him, "Today salvation has come to this house, because [a]he
also is [b]a son of Abraham; 10[a]for the Son
of Man has come to seek and to save that
which was lost."

The Parable of the Minas

11Now as they heard these things, He
spoke another parable, because He was
near Jerusalem and because [a]they
thought the kingdom of God would appear immediately. 12[a]Therefore He said:
"A certain nobleman went into a far country to receive for himself a kingdom and
to return. 13So he called ten of his servants, delivered to them ten [1]minas, and
said to them, 'Do business till I come.'
14[a]But his citizens hated him, and sent a
delegation after him, saying, 'We will not
have this *man* to reign over us.'
15"And so it was that when he returned,
having received the kingdom, he then
commanded these servants, to whom he
had given the money, to be called to him,
that he might know how much every man
had gained by trading. 16Then came the
first, saying, 'Master, your mina has
earned ten minas.' 17And he said to him,
[a]'Well *done,* good servant; because you
were [b]faithful in a very little, have authority over ten cities.' 18And the second
came, saying, 'Master, your mina has
earned five minas.' 19Likewise he said to
him, 'You also be over five cities.'
20"Then another came, saying, 'Master,
here is your mina, which I have kept put
away in a handkerchief. 21[a]For I feared
you, because you are [1]an austere man.
You collect what you did not deposit, and
reap what you did not sow.' 22And he said
to him, [a]'Out of your own mouth I will
judge you, *you* wicked servant. [b]You knew
that I was an austere man, collecting what
I did not deposit and reaping what I did
not sow. 23Why then did you not put my

5 [2] *hurry*
6 [1] *hurried*
7 [a] Luke 5:30; 15:2 [1] *grumbled*
8 [a] [Ps. 41:1] [b] Luke 3:14 [c] Ex. 22:1
9 [a] [Gal. 3:7] [b] [Luke 13:16]
10 [a] Matt. 18:11
11 [a] Acts 1:6
12 [a] Matt. 25:14–30
13 [1] Gr. *mna,* same as Heb. *minah,* each worth about three months' salary
14 [a] [John 1:11]
17 [a] Matt. 25:21, 23 [b] Luke 16:10
21 [a] Matt. 25:24 [1] *a severe*
22 [a] Job 15:6 [b] Matt. 25:26
26 [a] Luke 8:18
28 [a] Mark 10:32
29 [a] Matt. 21:1 [b] John 12:1 [c] Acts 1:12 [1] M *Bethsphage*
32 [a] Luke 22:13
35 [a] 2 Kin. 9:13
37 [a] Luke 13:17; 18:43
38 [a] Ps. 118:26 [b] [Eph. 2:14]
40 [a] Hab. 2:11
41 [a] John 11:35

money in the bank, that at my coming I
might have collected it with interest?'
24"And he said to those who stood by,
'Take the mina from him, and give *it* to
him who has ten minas.' 25(But they said
to him, 'Master, he has ten minas.') 26'For
I say to you, [a]that to everyone who has
will be given; and from him who does not
have, even what he has will be taken away
from him. 27But bring here those enemies
of mine, who did not want me to reign
over them, and slay *them* before me.' "

The Triumphal Entry

28When He had said this, [a]He went on
ahead, going up to Jerusalem. 29[a]And it
came to pass, when He drew near to
[1]Bethphage and [b]Bethany, at the mountain called [c]Olivet, *that* He sent two of His
disciples, 30saying, "Go into the village opposite *you,* where as you enter you will
find a colt tied, on which no one has ever
sat. Loose it and bring *it here.* 31And if
anyone asks you, 'Why are you loosing *it?*'
thus you shall say to him, 'Because the
Lord has need of it.' "
32So those who were sent went their
way and found *it* just [a]as He had said to
them. 33But as they were loosing the colt,
the owners of it said to them, "Why are
you loosing the colt?"
34And they said, "The Lord has need of
him." 35Then they brought him to Jesus.
[a]And they threw their own clothes on the
colt, and they set Jesus on him. 36And as
He went, *many* spread their clothes on
the road.
37Then, as He was now drawing near
the descent of the Mount of Olives, the
whole multitude of the disciples began to
[a]rejoice and praise God with a loud voice
for all the mighty works they had seen,
38saying:

[a]" *'Blessed is the King who comes in*
the name of the LORD!'
[b]Peace in heaven and glory in the
highest!"

39And some of the Pharisees called to
Him from the crowd, "Teacher, rebuke
Your disciples."
40But He answered and said to them, "I
tell you that if these should keep silent,
[a]the stones would immediately cry out."

Jesus Weeps over Jerusalem

41Now as He drew near, He saw the city
and [a]wept over it, 42saying, "If you had

known, even you, especially in this [a]your day, the things *that* [b]*make* for your [c]peace! But now they are hidden from your eyes. 43For days will come upon you when your enemies will [a]build an embankment around you, surround you and close you in on every side, 44[a]and level you, and your children within you, to the ground; and [b]they will not leave in you one stone upon another, [c]because you did not know the time of your visitation."

Jesus Cleanses the Temple

45[a]Then He went into the temple and began to drive out those who [1]bought and sold in it, 46saying to them, "It is written, [a]*'My house [1]is a house of prayer,'* but you have made it a [b]*'den of thieves.'* "

47And He [a]was teaching daily in the temple. But [b]the chief priests, the scribes, and the leaders of the people sought to destroy Him, 48and were unable to do anything; for all the people were very attentive to [a]hear Him.

Jesus' Authority Questioned

20 Now [a]it happened on one of those days, as He taught the people in the temple and preached the gospel, *that* the chief priests and the scribes, together with the elders, confronted *Him* 2and spoke to Him, saying, "Tell us, [a]by what authority are You doing these things? Or who is he who gave You this authority?"

3But He answered and said to them, "I also will ask you one thing, and answer Me: 4The [a]baptism of John—was it from heaven or from men?"

5And they reasoned among themselves, saying, "If we say, 'From heaven,' He will say, 'Why [1]then did you not believe him?' 6But if we say, 'From men,' all the people will stone us, [a]for they are persuaded that John was a prophet." 7So they answered that they did not know where *it was* from.

8And Jesus said to them, "Neither will I tell you by what authority I do these things."

The Parable of the Wicked Vinedressers

9Then He began to tell the people this parable: [a]"A certain man planted a vineyard, leased it to [1]vinedressers, and went into a far country for a long time. 10Now at [1]vintage-time he [a]sent a servant to the vinedressers, that they might give him some of the fruit of the vineyard. But the vinedressers beat him and sent *him* away empty-handed. 11Again he sent another servant; and they beat him also, treated *him* shamefully, and sent *him* away empty-handed. 12And again he sent a third; and they wounded him also and cast *him* out.

13"Then the owner of the vineyard said, 'What shall I do? I will send my beloved son. Probably they will respect *him* when they see him.' 14But when the vinedressers saw him, they reasoned among themselves, saying, 'This is the [a]heir. Come, [b]let us kill him, that the inheritance may be [c]ours.' 15So they cast him out of the vineyard and [a]killed *him*. Therefore what will the owner of the vineyard do to them? 16He will come and destroy those vinedressers and give the vineyard to [a]others."

And when they heard *it* they said, "Certainly not!"

17Then He looked at them and said, "What then is this that is written:

> [a]*'The stone which the builders rejected*
> *Has become the chief cornerstone'*?

18Whoever falls on that stone will be [a]broken; but [b]on whomever it falls, it will grind him to powder."

19And the chief priests and the scribes that very hour sought to lay hands on Him, but they [1]feared the people—for they knew He had spoken this parable against them.

The Pharisees: Is It Lawful to Pay Taxes to Caesar?

20[a]So they watched *Him*, and sent spies who pretended to be righteous, that they might seize on His words, in order to deliver Him to the power and the authority of the governor.

21Then they asked Him, saying, [a]"Teacher, we know that You say and teach rightly, and You do not show personal favoritism, but teach the way of God in truth: 22Is it lawful for us to pay taxes to Caesar or not?"

23But He perceived their craftiness, and said to them, [1]"Why do you test Me? 24Show Me a denarius. Whose image and inscription does it have?"

They answered and said, "Caesar's."

25And He said to them, [a]"Render[1] therefore to Caesar the things that are

42 a Heb. 3:13 b [Acts 10:36] c [Rom. 5:1]
43 a Jer. 6:3, 6
44 a 1 Kin. 9:7, 8 b Matt. 24:2 c [1 Pet. 2:12]
45 a Mark 11:11, 15–17 *1* NU *were selling, saying*
46 a Is. 56:7 b Jer. 7:11 *1* NU *shall be*
47 a Luke 21:37; 22:53 b John 7:19; 8:37
48 a Luke 21:38
CHAPTER 20
1 a Matt. 21:23–27
2 a Acts 4:7; 7:27
4 a John 1:26, 31
5 *1* NU, M omit *then*
6 a Luke 7:24–30
9 a Mark 12:1–12 *1 tenant farmers*
10 a [1 Thess. 2:15] *1* Lit. *the season*
14 a [Heb. 1:1–3] b Matt. 27:21–23 c John 11:47, 48
15 a Luke 23:33
16 a Rom. 11:1, 11
17 a Ps. 118:22
18 a Is. 8:14, 15 b [Dan. 2:34, 35, 44, 45]
19 *1* M *were afraid—for*
20 a Matt. 22:15
21 a Mark 12:14
23 *1* NU omits *Why do you test Me?*
25 a [1 Pet. 2:13–17] *1 Pay*

Caesar's, and to God the things that are
God's."
26But they could not catch Him in His
words in the presence of the people. And
they marveled at His answer and kept silent.

The Sadducees: What About the Resurrection?

27[a]Then some of the Sadducees, [b]who
deny that there is a resurrection, came to
Him and asked Him, 28saying: "Teacher,
Moses wrote to us *that* if a man's brother
dies, having a wife, and he dies without
children, his brother should take his wife
and raise up offspring for his brother.
29Now there were seven brothers. And the
first took a wife, and died without children. 30And the second [1]took her as wife,
and he died childless. 31Then the third
took her, and in like manner the seven
[1]also; and they left no children, and died.
32Last of all the woman died also. 33There-
fore, in the resurrection, whose wife does
she become? For all seven had her as
wife."
34Jesus answered and said to them,
"The sons of this age marry and are given
in marriage. 35But those who are [a]count-
ed worthy to attain that age, and the resurrection from the dead, neither marry
nor are given in marriage; 36nor can they
die anymore, for [a]they are equal to the
angels and are sons of God, [b]being sons
of the resurrection. 37But even Moses
showed in the *burning* bush *passage* that
the dead are raised, when he called the
Lord [a]*'the God of Abraham, the God of
Isaac, and the God of Jacob.'* 38For He is
not the God of the dead but of the living,
for [a]all live to Him."
39Then some of the scribes answered
and said, "Teacher, You have spoken
well." 40But after that they dared not
question Him anymore.

Jesus: How Can David Call His Descendant Lord?

41And He said to them, [a]"How can they
say that the Christ is the Son of David?
42Now David himself said in the Book of
Psalms:

> [a]*'The LORD said to my Lord,*
> *"Sit at My right hand,*
> 43 *Till I make Your enemies Your*
> *footstool."'*

44Therefore David calls Him *'Lord'*; [a]how
is He then his Son?"

Beware of the Scribes

45[a]Then, in the hearing of all the people, He said to His disciples, 46[a]"Beware of
the scribes, who desire to go around in
long robes, [b]love greetings in the marketplaces, the best seats in the synagogues,
and the best places at feasts, 47[a]who devour widows' houses, and for a [b]pretense
make long prayers. These will receive
greater condemnation."

The Widow's Two Mites

21 And He looked up [a]and saw the
rich putting their gifts into the
treasury, 2and He saw also a certain [a]poor
widow putting in two [b]mites.[1] 3So He
said, "Truly I say to you [a]that this poor
widow has put in more than all; 4for all
these out of their abundance have put in
offerings [1]for God, but she out of her poverty put in [a]all the livelihood that she
had."

> *God gives us an opportunity to act our faith. When we give larger as an act of our faith in God's promise, we show confidence that God will not fail us.*
>
> GORDON LINDSAY

Jesus Predicts the Destruction of the Temple

5[a]Then, as some spoke of the temple,
how it was [1]adorned with beautiful stones
and donations, He said, 6"These things
which you see—the days will come in
which [a]not *one* stone shall be left upon
another that shall not be thrown down."

The Signs of the Times and the End of the Age

7So they asked Him, saying, "Teacher,
but when will these things be? And what
sign *will there be* when these things are
about to take place?"

---

27 a Mark 12:18–27 b Acts 23:6, 8
30 *1* NU omits the rest of v. 30.
31 *1* NU, M *also left no children*
35 a Phil. 3:11
36 a [1 John 3:2] b Rom. 8:23
37 a Ex. 3:1–6, 15
38 a [Rom. 6:10, 11; 14:8, 9]
41 a Matt. 22:41–46
42 a Ps. 110:1
44 a Rom. 1:3; 9:4, 5
45 a Matt. 23:1–7
46 a Matt. 23:5 b Luke 11:43; 14:7
47 a Matt. 23:14 b [Matt. 6:5, 6]
CHAPTER 21
1 a Mark 12:41–44
2 a [2 Cor. 6:10] b Mark 12:42 *1* Gr. *lepta,* very small copper coins
3 a [2 Cor. 8:12]
4 a [2 Cor. 8:12] *1* NU omits *for God*
5 a Mark 13:1 *1 decorated*
6 a Luke 19:41–44

Luke 21:1–4

Dear Woman of Destiny,

For many years I pondered the passage in Luke 21:1–4—the account of the widow who gave everything she had to God.

Jesus was watching that day as the people came to drop their money into the temple treasury. Many rich people gave much; but this poor woman put in only two mites, two small coins worth less than a fraction of a penny. Yet Jesus said that she had given more than all the others, for "out of her poverty [she] put in all the livelihood that she had" (Luke 21:4).

How could that be? I wondered. Perhaps it was because her need was greater than the others. Maybe she was really planting a seed of faith, believing God to meet her needs. She was a widow, with no husband to make a living for her. No doubt she had children who required food, clothing, and shelter. Even in the midst of her great need, this woman chose to plant her seed.

When Jesus observed what she did, He was touched by it. He's always touched by our needs. He sees us when we plant a seed of our faith, knowing God will multiply that seed and return it to us in the form that will meet whatever our need is.

God had perhaps the greatest need anyone has ever had. He created human beings who refused to love and worship Him. They would not keep the commandments even though He told them through Moses, His prophet, that He would bless and prosper them if they did (see Deut. 28). Their blood sacrifices were not enough to take away their sins, so He sent His Son to shed His blood to save all who would believe on His name. In return, they would receive eternal life (see John 3:16). God loves us so much that He wants to live with us forever!

The most precious love imaginable is in God's heart for you, Woman of Destiny. When you have a need, show your love for God by giving Him your whole self first. He wants *you—all of you.* Then give of your resources to Him—your time, your talent, your prayers, your money. If all of you belongs to God, then all you possess also belongs to Him. He wants to multiply what you give to meet every need in your life.

Aim your seed toward a *need*. Be specific in telling God just what you need in return for your giving. He is a giving God. He came to give abundant life—not just an existence. He wants you to have good health, a good home, food for your family, spiritual strength, and love for Him as He has for you. I have found in my own experience that you cannot outgive or outlove God. The more you give, the more He will give back!

I bless you today with the love in my heart, and I want to see you prosper in every area of your life.

Evelyn Roberts

8And He said: [a]"Take heed that you not
be deceived. For many will come in My
name, saying, 'I am *He,*' and, 'The time
has drawn near.' [1]Therefore do not [2]go
after them. 9But when you hear of [a]wars
and commotions, do not be terrified; for
these things must come to pass first, but
the end *will not come* immediately."
10[a]Then He said to them, "Nation will
rise against nation, and kingdom against
kingdom. 11And there will be great [a]earth-
quakes in various places, and famines and
pestilences; and there will be fearful
sights and great signs from heaven.
12[a]But before all these things, they will lay
their hands on you and persecute *you,* delivering *you* up to the synagogues and
[b]prisons. [c]You will be brought before
kings and rulers [d]for My name's sake.
13But [a]it will turn out for you as an occasion for testimony. 14[a]Therefore settle *it*
in your hearts not to meditate beforehand
on what you will [1]answer; 15for I will give
you a mouth and wisdom [a]which all your
adversaries will not be able to contradict
or [1]resist. 16[a]You will be betrayed even
by parents and brothers, relatives and
friends; and they will put [b]*some* of you to
death. 17And [a]you will be hated by all for
My name's sake. 18[a]But not a hair of your
head shall be lost. 19By your patience possess your souls.

The Destruction of Jerusalem

20[a]"But when you see Jerusalem surrounded by armies, then know that its
desolation is near. 21Then let those who
are in Judea flee to the mountains, let
those who are in the midst of her depart,
and let not those who are in the country
enter her. 22For these are the days of vengeance, that [a]all things which are written
may be fulfilled. 23[a]But woe to those who
are pregnant and to those who are nursing babies in those days! For there will be
great distress in the land and wrath upon
this people. 24And they will fall by the
edge of the sword, and be led away captive
into all nations. And Jerusalem will be
trampled by Gentiles [a]until the times of
the Gentiles are fulfilled.

The Coming of the Son of Man

25[a]"And there will be signs in the sun,
in the moon, and in the stars; and on the
earth distress of nations, with perplexity,
the sea and the waves roaring; 26men's
hearts failing them from fear and the expectation of those things which are coming on the earth, [a]for the powers of the
heavens will be shaken. 27Then they will
see the Son of Man [a]coming in a cloud
with power and great glory. 28Now when
these things begin to happen, look up and
lift up your heads, because [a]your redemption draws near."

The Parable of the Fig Tree

29[a]Then He spoke to them a parable:
"Look at the fig tree, and all the trees.
30When they are already budding, you see
and know for yourselves that summer is
now near. 31So you also, when you see
these things happening, know that the
kingdom of God is near. 32Assuredly, I say
to you, this generation will by no means
pass away till all things take place.
33[a]Heaven and earth will pass away, but
My [b]words will by no means pass away.

Lord, may ____ take heed to themselves, lest their hearts be weighed down with carousing, drunkenness, and cares of this life.

FROM LUKE 21:34

The Importance of Watching

34"But [a]take heed to yourselves, lest
your hearts be weighed down with [1]ca-
rousing, drunkenness, and [b]cares of this
life, and that Day come on you unexpectedly. 35For [a]it will come as a snare on all
those who dwell on the face of the whole
earth. 36[a]Watch therefore, and [b]pray always that you may [1]be counted [c]worthy to
escape all these things that will come to
pass, and [d]to stand before the Son of
Man."
37[a]And in the daytime He was teaching
in the temple, but [b]at night He went out
and stayed on the mountain called Olivet.
38Then early in the morning all the people
came to Him in the temple to hear Him.

8 a Eph. 5:6 1 NU omits *Therefore* 2 *follow*
9 a Rev. 6:4
10 a Matt. 24:7
11 a Rev. 6:12
12 a [Rev. 2:10] b Acts 4:3; 5:18; 12:4; 16:24 c Acts 25:23 d 1 Pet. 2:13
13 a [Phil. 1:12–14, 28]
14 a Luke 12:11 1 *say in defense*
15 a Acts 6:10 1 *withstand*
16 a Mic. 7:6 b Acts 7:59; 12:2
17 a Matt. 10:22
18 a Matt. 10:30
20 a Mark 13:14
22 a [Dan. 9:24–27]
23 a Matt. 24:19
24 a [Dan. 9:27; 12:7]
25 a [2 Pet. 3:10–12]
26 a Matt. 24:29
27 a Rev. 1:7; 14:14
28 a [Rom. 8:19, 23]
29 a Mark 13:28
33 a Matt. 24:35 b Is. 40:8
34 a 1 Thess. 5:6 b Luke 8:14 1 *dissipation*
35 a Rev. 3:3; 16:15
36 a Matt. 24:42; 25:13 b Luke 18:1 c Luke 20:35 d [Eph. 6:13] 1 NU *have strength to*
37 a John 8:1, 2 b Luke 22:39

The Plot to Kill Jesus

22 Now [a]the Feast of Unleavened
Bread drew near, which is called
Passover. 2And [a]the chief priests and the
scribes sought how they might kill Him,
for they feared the people.
3[a]Then Satan entered Judas, surnamed
Iscariot, who was numbered among the
[b]twelve. 4So he went his way and conferred with the chief priests and captains,
how he might betray Him to them. 5And
they were glad, and [a]agreed to give him
money. 6So he promised and sought opportunity to [a]betray Him to them in the
absence of the multitude.

Jesus and His Disciples Prepare the Passover

7[a]Then came the Day of Unleavened
Bread, when the Passover must be [1]killed.
8And He sent Peter and John, saying, "Go
and prepare the Passover for us, that we
may eat."
9So they said to Him, "Where do You
want us to prepare?"
10And He said to them, "Behold, when
you have entered the city, a man will meet
you carrying a pitcher of water; follow
him into the house which he enters.
11Then you shall say to the master of the
house, 'The Teacher says to you, "Where
is the guest room where I may eat the
Passover with My disciples?"' 12Then he
will show you a large, furnished upper
room; there make ready."
13So they went and [a]found it just as He
had said to them, and they prepared the
Passover.

Jesus Institutes the Lord's Supper

14[a]When the hour had come, He sat
down, and the [1]twelve apostles with Him.
15Then He said to them, "With *fervent* desire I have desired to eat this Passover
with you before I suffer; 16for I say to you,
I will no longer eat of it [a]until it is fulfilled
in the kingdom of God."
17Then He took the cup, and gave
thanks, and said, "Take this and divide *it*
among yourselves; 18for [a]I say to you, [1]I
will not drink of the fruit of the vine until
the kingdom of God comes."
19[a]And He took bread, gave thanks and
broke *it*, and gave *it* to them, saying, "This
is My [b]body which is given for you; [c]do
this in remembrance of Me."
20Likewise He also *took* the cup after
supper, saying, [a]"This cup *is* the new covenant in My blood, which is shed for you.
21[a]But behold, the hand of My betrayer *is*
with Me on the table. 22[a]And truly the Son
of Man goes [b]as it has been determined,
but woe to that man by whom He is betrayed!"
23[a]Then they began to question among
themselves, which of them it was who
would do this thing.

The Disciples Argue About Greatness

24[a]Now there was also a dispute among
them, as to which of them should be considered the greatest. 25[a]And He said to
them, "The kings of the Gentiles exercise
lordship over them, and those who exercise authority over them are called 'benefactors.' 26[a]But not so *among* you; on the
contrary, [b]he who is greatest among you,
let him be as the younger, and he who
governs as he who serves. 27[a]For who *is*
greater, he who sits at the table, or he who
serves? *Is* it not he who sits at the table?
Yet [b]I am among you as the One who
serves.
28"But you are those who have continued with Me in [a]My trials. 29And [a]I bestow
upon you a kingdom, just as My Father
bestowed *one* upon Me, 30that [a]you may
eat and drink at My table in My kingdom,
[b]and sit on thrones judging the twelve
tribes of Israel."

Jesus Predicts Peter's Denial

31[1]And the Lord said, "Simon, Simon!
Indeed, [a]Satan has asked for you, that he
may [b]sift *you* as wheat. 32But [a]I have
prayed for you, that your faith should not
fail; and when you have returned to *Me*,
[b]strengthen your brethren."
33But he said to Him, "Lord, I am ready
to go with You, both to prison and to
death."
34[a]Then He said, "I tell you, Peter, the
rooster shall not crow this day before you
will deny three times that you know Me."

Supplies for the Road

35[a]And He said to them, "When I sent
you without money bag, knapsack, and
sandals, did you lack anything?"
So they said, "Nothing."
36Then He said to them, "But now, he
who has a money bag, let him take *it*, and

CHAPTER 22
1 a Matt. 26:2–5
2 a John 11:47
3 a Mark 14:10, 11 b Matt. 10:2–4
5 a Zech. 11:12
6 a Ps. 41:9
7 a Matt. 26:17–19 1 Sacrificed
13 a Luke 19:32
14 a Mark 14:17 1 NU omits *twelve*
16 a [Rev. 19:9]
18 a Mark 14:25 1 NU adds *from now on*
19 a Matt. 26:26 b [1 Pet. 2:24] c 1 Cor. 11:23–26
20 a 1 Cor. 10:16
21 a John 13:21, 26, 27
22 a Matt. 26:24 b Acts 2:23
23 a John 13:22, 25
24 a Mark 9:34
25 a Mark 10:42–45
26 a [1 Pet. 5:3] b Luke 9:48
27 a [Luke 12:37] b Phil. 2:7
28 a [Heb. 2:18; 4:15]
29 a Matt. 24:47
30 a [Matt. 8:11] b [Rev. 3:21]
31 a 1 Pet. 5:8 b Amos 9:9 1 NU omits *And the Lord said*
32 a [John 17:9, 11, 15] b John 21:15–17
34 a John 13:37, 38
35 a Matt. 10:9

likewise a knapsack; and he who has no
sword, let him sell his garment and buy
one. 37 For I say to you that this which is
written must still be [1]accomplished in
Me: [a]*'And He was numbered with the
transgressors.'* For the things concerning
Me have an end."
38 So they said, "Lord, look, here *are* two
swords."
And He said to them, "It is enough."

The Prayer in the Garden

39 [a]Coming out, [b]He went to the Mount
of Olives, as He was accustomed, and His
disciples also followed Him. 40 [a]When He
came to the place, He said to them, "Pray
that you may not enter into temptation."
41 [a]And He was withdrawn from them
about a stone's throw, and He knelt down
and prayed, 42 saying, "Father, if it is Your
will, take this cup away from Me; nevertheless [a]not My will, but Yours, be done."
43 [1]Then [a]an angel appeared to Him from
heaven, strengthening Him. 44 [a]And being
in agony, He prayed more earnestly. Then
His sweat became like great drops of blood
falling down to the ground.
45 When He rose up from prayer, and
had come to His disciples, He found them
sleeping from sorrow. 46 Then He said to
them, "Why [a]do you sleep? Rise and [b]pray,
lest you enter into temptation."

Betrayal and Arrest in Gethsemane

47 And while He was still speaking, [a]be-
hold, a multitude; and he who was called
[b]Judas, one of the twelve, went before
them and drew near to Jesus to kiss Him.
48 But Jesus said to him, "Judas, are you
betraying the Son of Man with a [a]kiss?"
49 When those around Him saw what
was going to happen, they said to Him,
"Lord, shall we strike with the sword?"
50 And [a]one of them struck the servant of
the high priest and cut off his right ear.
51 But Jesus answered and said, "Permit
even this." And He touched his ear and
healed him.
52 [a]Then Jesus said to the chief priests,
captains of the temple, and the elders who
had come to Him, "Have you come out, as
against a [b]robber, with swords and clubs?
53 When I was with you daily in the [a]tem-
ple, you did not try to seize Me. But this
is your [b]hour, and the power of darkness."

37 [a]Is. 53:12 [1]fulfilled
39 [a]John 18:1 [b]Luke 21:37
40 [a]Mark 14:32–42
41 [a]Matt. 26:39
42 [a]John 4:34; 5:30; 6:38; 8:29
43 [a]Matt. 4:11 [1]NU brackets vv. 43 and 44 as not in the original text.
44 [a][Heb. 5:7]
46 [a]Luke 9:32 [b]Luke 22:40
47 [a]John 18:3–11 [b]Acts 1:16, 17
48 [a][Prov. 27:6]
50 [a]Matt. 26:51
52 [a]Matt. 26:55 [b]Luke 23:32
53 [a]Luke 19:47, 48 [b][John 12:27]
54 [a]Matt. 26:57 [b]John 18:15
55 [a]Mark 14:66–72
57 [1]NU *it*
58 [a]John 18:25
59 [a]Mark 14:70 [b]Acts 1:11; 2:7
60 [1]NU, M *a rooster*
61 [a]Matt. 26:75 [b]John 13:38 [1]NU adds *today*
63 [a]Ps. 69:1, 4, 7–9 [b]Is. 50:6
64 [a]Zech. 13:7 [1]NU *And having blindfolded Him, they asked Him*

> *To pray until hell feels the ponderous stroke, to pray until the iron gates of difficulty are opened, to pray until the mountains of obstacles are removed—this is hard work, but it is God's work and man's best labor.*
>
> E. M. Bounds

Peter Denies Jesus, and Weeps Bitterly

54 [a]Having arrested Him, they led *Him*
and brought Him into the high priest's
house. [b]But Peter followed at a distance.
55 [a]Now when they had kindled a fire in
the midst of the courtyard and sat down
together, Peter sat among them. 56 And a
certain servant girl, seeing him as he sat
by the fire, looked intently at him and
said, "This man was also with Him."
57 But he denied [1]Him, saying, "Woman, I do not know Him."
58 [a]And after a little while another saw
him and said, "You also are of them."
But Peter said, "Man, I am not!"
59 [a]Then after about an hour had passed,
another confidently affirmed, saying,
"Surely this *fellow* also was with Him, for
he is a [b]Galilean."
60 But Peter said, "Man, I do not know
what you are saying!"
Immediately, while he was still speaking, [1]the rooster crowed. 61 And the Lord
turned and looked at Peter. Then [a]Peter
remembered the word of the Lord, how
He had said to him, [b]"Before the rooster
[1]crows, you will deny Me three times."
62 So Peter went out and wept bitterly.

Jesus Mocked and Beaten

63 [a]Now the men who held Jesus
mocked Him and [b]beat Him. 64 [1]And having blindfolded Him, they [a]struck Him on
the face and asked Him, saying, "Prophesy! Who is the one who struck You?"

65 And many other things they blasphe-
mously spoke against Him.

Jesus Faces the Sanhedrin

66 [a]As soon as it was day, [b]the elders of
the people, both chief priests and scribes,
came together and led Him into their
council, saying, 67 [a]"If You are the Christ,
tell us."
But He said to them, "If I tell you, you
will [b]by no means believe. 68 And if I [1]also
ask *you,* you will by no means answer [2]Me
or let *Me* go. 69 [a]Hereafter the Son of Man
will sit on the right hand of the power of
God."
70 Then they all said, "Are You then the
Son of God?"
So He said to them, [a]"You *rightly* say
that I am."
71 [a]And they said, "What further testimony do we need? For we have heard it
ourselves from His own mouth."

Jesus Handed Over to Pontius Pilate

23 Then [a]the whole multitude of
them arose and led Him to [b]Pilate.
2 And they began to [a]accuse Him, saying,
"We found this *fellow* [b]perverting [1]the nation, and [c]forbidding to pay taxes to Caesar, saying [d]that He Himself is Christ, a
King."
3 [a]Then Pilate asked Him, saying, "Are
You the King of the Jews?"
He answered him and said, "*It is as* you
say."
4 So Pilate said to the chief priests and
the crowd, [a]"I find no fault in this Man."
5 But they were the more fierce, saying,
"He stirs up the people, teaching throughout all Judea, beginning from [a]Galilee to
this place."

Jesus Faces Herod

6 When Pilate heard [1]of Galilee, he
asked if the Man were a Galilean. 7 And
as soon as he knew that He belonged to
[a]Herod's jurisdiction, he sent Him to Herod, who was also in Jerusalem at that
time. 8 Now when Herod saw Jesus, [a]he
was exceedingly glad; for he had desired
for a long *time* to see Him, because [b]he
had heard many things about Him, and he
hoped to see some miracle done by Him.
9 Then he questioned Him with many
words, but He answered him [a]nothing.
10 And the chief priests and scribes stood
and vehemently accused Him. 11 [a]Then
Herod, with his [1]men of war, treated Him
with contempt and mocked *Him,* arrayed
Him in a gorgeous robe, and sent Him
back to Pilate. 12 That very day [a]Pilate and
Herod became friends with each other, for
previously they had been at enmity with
each other.

Taking the Place of Barabbas

13 [a]Then Pilate, when he had called together the chief priests, the rulers, and
the people, 14 said to them, [a]"You have
brought this Man to me, as one who mis-
leads the people. And indeed, [b]having examined *Him* in your presence, I have
found no fault in this Man concerning
those things of which you accuse Him;
15 no, neither did Herod, for [1]I sent you
back to him; and indeed nothing deserving of death has been done by Him. 16 [a]I
will therefore chastise Him and release
Him" 17 [a](for[1] it was necessary for him to
release one to them at the feast).
18 And [a]they all cried out at once, saying, "Away with this *Man,* and release to
us Barabbas"— 19 who had been thrown
into prison for a certain rebellion made in
the city, and for murder.
20 Pilate, therefore, wishing to release
Jesus, again called out to them. 21 But they
shouted, saying, "Crucify *Him,* crucify
Him!"
22 Then he said to them the third time,
"Why, what evil has He done? I have found
no reason for death in Him. I will therefore chastise Him and let *Him* go."
23 But they were insistent, demanding
with loud voices that He be crucified. And
the voices of these men [1]and of the chief
priests prevailed. 24 So [a]Pilate gave sentence that it should be as they requested.
25 [a]And he released [1]to them the one they
requested, who for rebellion and murder
had been thrown into prison; but he delivered Jesus to their will.

The King on a Cross

26 [a]Now as they led Him away, they laid
hold of a certain man, Simon a Cyrenian,
who was coming from the country, and on
him they laid the cross that he might bear
it after Jesus.
27 And a great multitude of the people
followed Him, and women who also
mourned and lamented Him. 28 But Jesus,

66 a Matt. 27:1 b Acts 4:26
67 a Matt. 26:63–66 b Luke 20:5–7
68 1 NU omits *also* 2 NU omits the rest of v. 68.
69 a Heb. 1:3; 8:1
70 a Matt. 26:64; 27:11
71 a Mark 14:63

CHAPTER 23
1 a John 18:28 b Luke 3:1; 13:1
2 a Acts 24:2 b Acts 17:7 c Matt. 17:27 d John 19:12 1 NU *our*
3 a 1 Tim. 6:13
4 a [1 Pet. 2:22]
5 a John 7:41
6 1 NU omits *of Galilee*
7 a Luke 3:1; 9:7; 13:31
8 a Luke 9:9 b Matt. 14:1
9 a John 19:9
11 a Is. 53:3 1 *troops*
12 a Acts 4:26, 27
13 a Mark 15:14
14 a Luke 23:1, 2 b Luke 23:4
15 1 NU *he sent Him back to us*
16 a John 19:1
17 a John 18:39 1 NU omits v. 17.
18 a Acts 3:13–15
23 1 NU omits *and of the chief priests*
24 a Mark 15:15
25 a Is. 53:8 1 NU, M omit *to them*
26 a Matt. 27:32

turning to them, said, "Daughters of Jerusalem, do not weep for Me, but weep for
yourselves and for your children. 29 [a]For
indeed the days are coming in which they
will say, 'Blessed *are* the barren, wombs
that never bore, and breasts which never
nursed!' 30 Then they will begin [a]*'to say to
the mountains, "Fall on us!" and to the
hills, "Cover us!"'* 31 [a]For if they do these
things in the green wood, what will be
done in the dry?"

32 [a]There were also two others, criminals, led with Him to be put to death.
33 And [a]when they had come to the place
called Calvary, there they crucified Him,
and the criminals, one on the right hand
and the other on the left. 34 [1]Then Jesus
said, "Father, [a]forgive them, for [b]they do
not know what they do."

And [c]they divided His garments and
cast lots. 35 And [a]the people stood looking
on. But even the [b]rulers with them
sneered, saying, "He saved others; let Him
save Himself if He is the Christ, the chosen of God."

36 The soldiers also mocked Him, coming and offering Him [a]sour wine, 37 and
saying, "If You are the King of the Jews,
save Yourself."

38 [a]And an inscription also was [1]written
over Him in letters of Greek, Latin, and
Hebrew:

THIS IS THE KING OF THE JEWS.

39 [a]Then one of the criminals who were
hanged blasphemed Him, saying, [1]"If You
are the Christ, save Yourself and us."

40 But the other, answering, rebuked
him, saying, "Do you not even fear God,
seeing you are under the same condemnation? 41 And we indeed justly, for we receive the due reward of our deeds; but this
Man has done [a]nothing wrong." 42 Then
he said [1]to Jesus, "Lord, remember me
when You come into Your kingdom."

43 And Jesus said to him, "Assuredly, I
say to you, today you will be with Me in
[a]Paradise."

Jesus Dies on the Cross

44 [a]Now it [1]was about the sixth hour,
and there was darkness over all the earth
until the ninth hour. 45 Then the sun was
[1]darkened, and [a]the veil of the temple was
torn in [2]two. 46 And when Jesus had cried
out with a loud voice, He said, "Father,
[a]*'into Your hands I commit My spirit.'*"
[b]Having said this, He breathed His last.

47 [a]So when the centurion saw what had
happened, he glorified God, saying, "Certainly this was a righteous Man!"

48 And the whole crowd who came together to that sight, seeing what had been
done, beat their breasts and returned.
49 [a]But all His acquaintances, and the
women who followed Him from Galilee,
stood at a distance, watching these things.

Nails were not enough to hold God-and-man nailed and fastened on the Cross, had not love held Him there.

St. Catherine of Siena

Jesus Buried in Joseph's Tomb

50 [a]Now behold, *there was* a man named
Joseph, a council member, a good and just
man. 51 He had not consented to their decision and deed. *He was* from Arimathea,
a city of the Jews, [a]who[1] himself was also
waiting for the kingdom of God. 52 This
man went to Pilate and asked for the body
of Jesus. 53 [a]Then he took it down,
wrapped it in linen, and laid it in a tomb
that was hewn out of the rock, where no
one had ever lain before. 54 That day was
[a]the Preparation, and the Sabbath drew
near.

55 And the women [a]who had come with
Him from Galilee followed after, and
[b]they observed the tomb and how His
body was laid. 56 Then they returned and
[a]prepared spices and fragrant oils. And
they rested on the Sabbath [b]according to
the commandment.

He Is Risen

24 Now [a]on the first *day* of the week,
very early in the morning, they,
[1]and certain *other women* with them,
came to the tomb [b]bringing the spices
which they had prepared. 2 [a]But they
found the stone rolled away from the
tomb. 3 [a]Then they went in and did not
find the body of the Lord Jesus. 4 And it

29 a Matt. 24:19
30 a Hos. 10:8; Rev. 6:16, 17; 9:6
31 a [Jer. 25:29]
32 a Is. 53:9, 12
33 a John 19:17–24
34 a 1 Cor. 4:12 b Acts 3:17 c Matt. 27:35 *1* NU brackets the first sentence as a later addition.
35 a Ps. 22:17 b Matt. 27:39
36 a Ps. 69:21
38 a John 19:19 *1* NU omits *written* and *in letters of Greek, Latin, and Hebrew*
39 a Mark 15:32 *1* NU *Are You not the Christ? Save*
41 a [Heb. 7:26]
42 *1* NU *"Jesus, remember me*
43 a [Rev. 2:7]
44 a Matt. 27:45–56 *1* NU adds *already*
45 a Matt. 27:51 *1* NU *obscured* *2* *the middle*
46 a Ps. 31:5 b John 19:30
47 a Mark 15:39
49 a Ps. 38:11
50 a Matt. 27:57–61
51 a Luke 2:25, 38 *1* NU *who was waiting*
53 a Mark 15:46
54 a Matt. 27:62
55 a Luke 8:2 b Mark 15:47
56 a Mark 16:1 b Ex. 20:10
CHAPTER 24
1 a John 20:1–8 b Luke 23:56

1 NU omits *and certain other women with them*
2 a Mark 16:4 **3** a Mark 16:5

happened, as they were [1]greatly perplexed about this, that [a]behold, two men stood by them in shining garments. 5Then, as they were afraid and bowed *their* faces to the earth, they said to them, "Why do you seek the living among the dead? 6He is not here, but is risen! [a]Remember how He spoke to you when He was still in Galilee, 7saying, 'The Son of Man must be [a]delivered into the hands of sinful men, and be crucified, and the third day rise again.' "

8And [a]they remembered His words. 9[a]Then they returned from the tomb and told all these things to the eleven and to all the rest. 10It was Mary Magdalene, [a]Joanna, Mary *the mother* of James, and the other *women* with them, who told these things to the apostles. 11[a]And their words seemed to them like [1]idle tales, and they did not believe them. 12[a]But Peter arose and ran to the tomb; and stooping down, he saw the linen cloths [1]lying by themselves; and he departed, marveling to himself at what had happened.

The Road to Emmaus

13[a]Now behold, two of them were traveling that same day to a village called Emmaus, which was [1]seven miles from Jerusalem. 14And they talked together of all these things which had happened. 15So it was, while they conversed and reasoned, that [a]Jesus Himself drew near and went with them. 16But [a]their eyes were restrained, so that they did not know Him.

17And He said to them, "What kind of conversation *is* this that you have with one another as you [1]walk and are sad?"

18Then the one [a]whose name was Cleopas answered and said to Him, "Are You the only stranger in Jerusalem, and have You not known the things which happened there in these days?"

19And He said to them, "What things?"

So they said to Him, "The things concerning Jesus of Nazareth, [a]who was a Prophet [b]mighty in deed and word before God and all the people, 20[a]and how the chief priests and our rulers delivered Him to be condemned to death, and crucified Him. 21But we were hoping [a]that it was He who was going to redeem Israel. Indeed, besides all this, today is the third day since these things happened. 22Yes, and [a]certain women of our company, who arrived at the tomb early, astonished us. 23When they did not find His body, they came saying that they had also seen a vision of angels who said He was alive. 24And [a]certain of those *who were* with us went to the tomb and found *it* just as the women had said; but Him they did not see."

25Then He said to them, "O foolish ones, and slow of heart to believe in all that the prophets have spoken! 26[a]Ought not the Christ to have suffered these things and to enter into His [b]glory?" 27And beginning at [a]Moses and [b]all the Prophets, He [1]expounded to them in all the Scriptures the things concerning Himself.

The Disciples' Eyes Opened

28Then they drew near to the village where they were going, and [a]He [1]indicated that He would have gone farther. 29But [a]they constrained Him, saying, [b]"Abide with us, for it is toward evening, and the day is far spent." And He went in to stay with them.

30Now it came to pass, as [a]He sat at the table with them, that He took bread, blessed and broke *it,* and gave it to them. 31Then their eyes were opened and they knew Him; and He vanished from their sight.

32And they said to one another, "Did not our heart burn within us while He talked with us on the road, and while He opened the Scriptures to us?" 33So they rose up that very hour and returned to Jerusalem, and found the eleven and those *who were* with them gathered together, 34saying, "The Lord is risen indeed, and [a]has appeared to Simon!" 35And they told about the things *that had happened* on the road, and how He was [1]known to them in the breaking of bread.

Jesus Appears to His Disciples

36[a]Now as they said these things, Jesus Himself stood in the midst of them, and said to them, "Peace to you." 37But they were terrified and frightened, and supposed they had seen [a]a spirit. 38And He said to them, "Why are you troubled? And why do doubts arise in your hearts? 39Behold My hands and My feet, that it is I Myself. [a]Handle Me and see, for a [b]spirit does not have flesh and bones as you see I have."

4 a John 20:12 *1* NU omits *greatly*
6 a Luke 9:22
7 a Luke 9:44; 11:29, 30; 18:31–33
8 a John 2:19–22
9 a Mark 16:10
10 a Luke 8:3
11 a Luke 24:25 *1 nonsense*
12 a John 20:3–6 *1* NU omits *lying*
13 a Mark 16:12 *1* Lit. *60 stadia*
15 a [Matt. 18:20]
16 a John 20:14; 21:4
17 *1* NU *walk? And they stood still, looking sad.*
18 a John 19:25
19 a Matt. 21:11 b Acts 7:22
20 a Acts 13:27, 28
21 a Luke 1:68; 2:38
22 a Mark 16:10
24 a Luke 24:12
26 a Acts 17:2, 3 b [1 Pet. 1:10–12]
27 a [Deut. 18:15] b [Is. 7:14; 9:6] *1 explained*
28 a Mark 6:48 *1 acted as if*
29 a Gen. 19:2, 3 b [John 14:23]
30 a Matt. 14:19
34 a 1 Cor. 15:5
35 *1 recognized*
36 a Mark 16:14
37 a Mark 6:49
39 a John 20:20, 27 b [1 Cor. 15:50]

40 [1]When He had said this, He showed
them His hands and His feet. 41 But while
they still did not believe [a]for joy, and marveled, He said to them, [b]"Have you any
food here?" 42 So they gave Him a piece
of a broiled fish [1]and some honeycomb.
43 [a]And He took *it* and ate in their presence.

The Scriptures Opened

44 Then He said to them, [a]"These *are*
the words which I spoke to you while I
was still with you, that all things must be
fulfilled which were written in the Law of
Moses and *the* Prophets and *the* Psalms
concerning Me." 45 And [a]He opened their
understanding, that they might comprehend the Scriptures.

46 Then He said to them, [a]"Thus it is
written, [1]and thus it was necessary for the
Christ to suffer and to rise from the dead
the third day, 47 and that repentance and
[a]remission of sins should be preached in
His name [b]to all nations, beginning at
Jerusalem. 48 And [a]you are witnesses of
these things. 49 [a]Behold, I send the Promise of My Father upon you; but tarry in the
city [1]of Jerusalem until you are endued
with power from on high."

The Ascension

50 And He led them out [a]as far as Bethany, and He lifted up His hands and blessed
them. 51 [a]Now it came to pass, while He
blessed them, that He was parted from
them and carried up into heaven. 52 [a]And
they worshiped Him, and returned to Jerusalem with great joy, 53 and were continually [a]in the temple [1]praising and
blessing God. [2]Amen.

40 *1* Some printed New Testaments omit v. 40. It is found in nearly all Gr. mss.

41 a Gen. 45:26 b John 21:5

42 *1* NU omits *and some honeycomb*

43 a Acts 10:39–41

44 a Matt. 16:21; 17:22; 20:18

45 a Acts 16:14

46 a Acts 17:3 *1* NU *that the Christ should suffer and rise*

47 a Acts 5:31; 10:43; 13:38; 26:18 b [Jer. 31:34]

48 a [Acts 1:8]

49 a Joel 2:28 *1* NU omits *of Jerusalem* **50** a Acts 1:12 **51** a Mark 16:19 **52** a Matt. 28:9 **53** a Acts 2:46 *1* NU omits *praising and* *2* NU omits *Amen.*

AUTHOR: *The Apostle John*
DATE: *About A.D. 85*
THEME: *Knowing God by Believing in Jesus Christ*
KEY WORDS: *Believe, Bear Witness, Life*

JOHN

Dear Woman of Destiny,

John's Gospel is full of encouragement for women like us to know God by believing in Jesus Christ as our Savior. Each of us must have a personal relationship with Him. In John 4:1–26, we see the longest theological discussion Jesus had with any person in the Bible, and it was with a Samaritan woman. Not only did the rabbis of the day not discuss theology with women, they considered Samaritan women to be particularly unclean. Maybe you feel like you have done so many bad things in your life that God wouldn't want you for His child. Or perhaps you think yourself too untalented to be used by Him. Nothing could be further from the truth! You are a woman of destiny, especially created by God for this hour.

With His love,

Cindy Jacobs

The Eternal Word

In the beginning [a]was the Word, and the [b]Word was [c]with God, and the Word was [d]God. 2 [a]He was in the beginning with God. 3 [a]All things were made through Him, and without Him nothing was made that was made. 4 [a]In Him was life, and [b]the life was the light of men. 5 And [a]the light shines in the darkness, and the darkness did not [1]comprehend it.

John's Witness: The True Light

6 There was a [a]man sent from God, whose name *was* John. 7 This man came for a [a]witness, to bear witness of the Light, that all through him might [b]believe. 8 He was not that Light, but *was sent* to bear witness of that [a]Light. 9 [a]That [1]was the true Light which gives light to every man coming into the world.

10 He was in the world, and the world was made through Him, and [a]the world did not know Him. 11 [a]He came to His [1]own, and His [2]own did not receive Him. 12 But [a]as many as received Him, to them He gave the [1]right to become children of God, to those who believe in His name: 13 [a]who were born, not of blood, nor of the will of the flesh, nor of the will of man, but of God.

We praise You, Lord Jesus, that to as many as receive You, to them You give the right to become children of God. I pray that ____ would receive You and believe in Your name.

FROM JOHN 1:12

The Word Becomes Flesh

14 [a]And the Word [b]became [c]flesh and dwelt among us, and [d]we beheld His glory, the glory as of the only begotten of the Father, [e]full of grace and truth.

15 [a]John bore witness of Him and cried out, saying, "This was He of whom I said, [b]'He who comes after me [1]is preferred before me, [c]for He was before me.' "

16 [1]And of His [a]fullness we have all received, and grace for grace. 17 For [a]the law was given through Moses, *but* [b]grace and [c]truth came through Jesus Christ. 18 [a]No one has seen God at any time. [b]The only begotten [1]Son, who is in the bosom of the Father, He has declared *Him*.

God's way of saving the soul, of healing the body, and of doing everything else He wants to do, is to send His Word—His promise—and then keep the promise when it produces faith.

F. F. BOSWORTH

A Voice in the Wilderness

19 Now this is [a]the testimony of John, when the Jews sent priests and Levites from Jerusalem to ask him, "Who are you?"

20 [a]He confessed, and did not deny, but confessed, "I am not the Christ."

21 And they asked him, "What then? Are you Elijah?"

He said, "I am not."

"Are you [a]the Prophet?"

And he answered, "No."

22 Then they said to him, "Who are you, that we may give an answer to those who sent us? What do you say about yourself?"

23 He said: [a]"I *am*

[b]*'The voice of one crying in the wilderness:*
"Make straight the way of the LORD," '

as the prophet Isaiah said."

24 Now those who were sent were from the Pharisees. 25 And they asked him, saying, "Why then do you baptize if you are not the Christ, nor Elijah, nor the Prophet?"

26 John answered them, saying, [a]"I baptize with water, [b]but there stands One among you whom you do not know. 27 [a]It is He who, coming after me, [1]is preferred

---

CHAPTER 1
1 a 1 John 1:1 b Rev. 19:13 c [John 17:5] d [1 John 5:20]
2 a Gen. 1:1
3 a [Col. 1:16, 17]
4 a [1 John 5:11] b John 8:12; 9:5; 12:46
5 a [John 3:19] *1 Or overcome*
6 a Matt. 3:1–17
7 a John 3:25–36; 5:33–35 b [John 3:16]
8 a Is. 9:2; 49:6
9 a Is. 49:6 *1 Or That was the true Light which, coming into the world, gives light to every man.*
10 a Heb. 1:2
11 a [Luke 19:14] 1 His own things or domain 2 His own people
12 a Gal. 3:26 *1 authority*
13 a [1 Pet. 1:23]
14 a Rev. 19:13 b Gal. 4:4 c Heb. 2:11 d Is. 40:5 e [John 8:32; 14:6; 18:37]
15 a John 3:32 b [Matt. 3:11] c [Col. 1:17] *1 ranks higher than I*
16 a [Col. 1:19; 2:9] *1 NU For*
17 a [Ex. 20:1] b [Rom. 5:21; 6:14] c [John 8:32; 14:6; 18:37]
18 a Ex. 33:20 b 1 John 4:9 *1 NU God*
19 a John 5:33
20 a Luke 3:15
21 a Deut. 18:15, 18
23 a Matt. 3:3 b Is. 40:3
26 a Matt. 3:11 b Mal. 3:1
27 a Acts 19:4 *1 ranks higher than I*

before me, whose sandal strap I am not
worthy to loose."
28 These things were done [a]in [1]Bethaba-
ra beyond the Jordan, where John was
baptizing.

The Lamb of God

29 The next day John saw Jesus coming
toward him, and said, "Behold! [a]The
Lamb of God [b]who takes away the sin of
the world! 30 This is He of whom I said,
'After me comes a Man who [1]is preferred
before me, for He was before me.' 31 I did
not know Him; but that He should be revealed to Israel, [a]therefore I came baptizing with water."
32 [a]And John bore witness, saying, "I
saw the Spirit descending from heaven
like a dove, and He remained upon Him.
33 I did not know Him, but He who sent
me to baptize with water said to me,
'Upon whom you see the Spirit descending, and remaining on Him, [a]this is He
who baptizes with the Holy Spirit.' 34 And
I have seen and testified that this is the
[a]Son of God."

The First Disciples

35 Again, the next day, John stood with
two of his disciples. 36 And looking at Jesus
as He walked, he said, [a]"Behold the Lamb
of God!"
37 The two disciples heard him speak,
and they [a]followed Jesus. 38 Then Jesus
turned, and seeing them following, said to
them, "What do you seek?"
They said to Him, "Rabbi" (which is to
say, when translated, Teacher), "where
are You staying?"
39 He said to them, "Come and see."
They came and saw where He was staying,
and remained with Him that day (now it
was about the tenth hour).
40 One of the two who heard John *speak,*
and followed Him, was [a]Andrew, Simon
Peter's brother. 41 He first found his own
brother Simon, and said to him, "We have
found the [1]Messiah" (which is translated,
the Christ). 42 And he brought him to
Jesus.
Now when Jesus looked at him, He said,
"You are Simon the son of [1]Jonah. [a]You
shall be called Cephas" (which is translated, [2]A Stone).

Philip and Nathanael

43 The following day Jesus wanted to go
to Galilee, and He found [a]Philip and said
to him, "Follow Me." 44 Now [a]Philip was
from Bethsaida, the city of Andrew and
Peter. 45 Philip found [a]Nathanael and said
to him, "We have found Him of whom
[b]Moses in the law, and also the [c]prophets,
wrote—Jesus [d]of Nazareth, the [e]son of
Joseph."
46 And Nathanael said to him, [a]"Can
anything good come out of Nazareth?"
Philip said to him, "Come and see."
47 Jesus saw Nathanael coming toward
Him, and said of him, "Behold, [a]an Israelite indeed, in whom is no deceit!"
48 Nathanael said to Him, "How do You
know me?"
Jesus answered and said to him, "Before
Philip called you, when you were under
the fig tree, I saw you."
49 Nathanael answered and said to Him,
"Rabbi, [a]You are the Son of God! You are
[b]the King of Israel!"
50 Jesus answered and said to him, "Because I said to you, 'I saw you under the
fig tree,' do you believe? You will see
greater things than these." 51 And He said
to him, "Most assuredly, I say to you,
[a]hereafter[1] you shall see heaven open,
and the angels of God ascending and descending upon the Son of Man."

Water Turned to Wine

2 On the third day there was a [a]wedding
in [b]Cana of Galilee, and the [c]mother
of Jesus was there. 2 Now both Jesus and
His disciples were invited to the wedding.
3 And when they ran out of wine, the
mother of Jesus said to Him, "They have
no wine."
4 Jesus said to her, [a]"Woman, [b]what
does your concern have to do with Me?
[c]My hour has not yet come."
5 His mother said to the servants,
"Whatever He says to you, do *it.*"
6 Now there were set there six waterpots
of stone, [a]according to the manner of purification of the Jews, containing twenty
or thirty gallons apiece. 7 Jesus said to
them, "Fill the waterpots with water." And
they filled them up to the brim. 8 And He
said to them, "Draw *some* out now, and
take *it* to the master of the feast." And
they took *it.* 9 When the master of the feast
had tasted [a]the water that was made wine,
and did not know where it came from (but
the servants who had drawn the water
knew), the master of the feast called the
bridegroom. 10 And he said to him, "Every
man at the beginning sets out the good

28 a Judg. 7:24 *1* NU, M *Bethany*
29 a Rev. 5:6–14 b [1 Pet. 2:24]
30 *1 ranks higher than I*
31 a Matt. 3:6
32 a Mark 1:10
33 a Matt. 3:11
34 a John 11:27
36 a John 1:29
37 a Matt. 4:20, 22
40 a Matt. 4:18
41 *1* Lit. *Anointed One*
42 a Matt. 16:18 *1* NU *John* *2* Gr. *Petros,* usually translated *Peter*
43 a John 6:5; 12:21, 22; 14:8, 9
44 a John 12:21
45 a John 21:2 b Luke 24:27 c [Zech. 6:12] d [Matt. 2:23] e Luke 3:23
46 a John 7:41, 42, 52
47 a Ps. 32:2; 73:1
49 a Matt. 14:33 b Matt. 21:5
51 a Gen. 28:12 *1* NU omits *hereafter*

CHAPTER 2
1 a [Heb. 13:4] b John 4:46 c John 19:25
4 a John 19:26 b 2 Sam. 16:10 c John 7:6, 8, 30; 8:20
6 a [Mark 7:3]
9 a John 4:46

wine, and when the *guests* have well
drunk, then the inferior. You have kept
the good wine until now!"
11 This [a]beginning of signs Jesus did in
Cana of Galilee, [b]and [1]manifested His glory; and His disciples believed in Him.
12 After this He went down to [a]Caperna-
um, He, His mother, [b]His brothers, and
His disciples; and they did not stay there
many days.

Jesus Cleanses the Temple

13 [a]Now the Passover of the Jews was at
hand, and Jesus went up to Jerusalem.
14 [a]And He found in the temple those who
sold oxen and sheep and doves, and the
money changers [1]doing business. 15 When
He had made a whip of cords, He drove
them all out of the temple, with the sheep
and the oxen, and poured out the changers' money and overturned the tables.
16 And He said to those who sold doves,
"Take these things away! Do not make
[a]My Father's house a house of merchandise!" 17 Then His disciples remembered
that it was written, [a]*"Zeal for Your house*
[1]*has eaten Me up."*
18 So the Jews answered and said to
Him, [a]"What sign do You show to us,
since You do these things?"
19 Jesus answered and said to them,
[a]"Destroy this temple, and in three days I
will raise it up."
20 Then the Jews said, "It has taken
forty-six years to build this temple, and
will You raise it up in three days?"
21 But He was speaking [a]of the temple of
His body. 22 Therefore, when He had risen
from the dead, [a]His disciples remembered
that He had said this [1]to them; and they
believed the Scripture and the word
which Jesus had said.

The Discerner of Hearts

23 Now when He was in Jerusalem at the
Passover, during the feast, many believed
in His name when they saw the [a]signs
which He did. 24 But Jesus did not commit
Himself to them, because He [a]knew all
men, 25 and had no need that anyone
should testify of man, for [a]He knew what
was in man.

The New Birth

3 There was a man of the Pharisees
named Nicodemus, a ruler of the
Jews. 2 [a]This man came to Jesus by night
and said to Him, "Rabbi, we know that
You are a teacher come from God; for [b]no
one can do these signs that You do unless
[c]God is with him."
3 Jesus answered and said to him, "Most
assuredly, I say to you, [a]unless one is born
[1]again, he cannot see the kingdom of
God."
4 Nicodemus said to Him, "How can a
man be born when he is old? Can he enter
a second time into his mother's womb
and be born?"
5 Jesus answered, "Most assuredly, I say
to you, [a]unless one is born of water and
the Spirit, he cannot enter the kingdom of
God. 6 That which is born of the flesh is
[a]flesh, and that which is born of the Spirit
is spirit. 7 Do not marvel that I said to you,
'You must be born again.' 8 [a]The wind
blows where it wishes, and you hear the
sound of it, but cannot tell where it comes
from and where it goes. So is everyone
who is born of the Spirit."

> *God does not patch up the old life, or make certain repairs on the old life; He gives a new life, through the new birth.*
>
> KATHRYN KUHLMAN

9 Nicodemus answered and said to Him,
[a]"How can these things be?"
10 Jesus answered and said to him, "Are
you the teacher of Israel, and do not know
these things? 11 [a]Most assuredly, I say to
you, We speak what We know and testify
what We have seen, and [b]you do not receive Our witness. 12 If I have told you
earthly things and you do not believe, how
will you believe if I tell you heavenly
things? 13 [a]No one has ascended to heaven
but He who came down from heaven, *that*
is, the Son of Man [1]who is in heaven.
14 [a]And as Moses lifted up the serpent in
the wilderness, even so [b]must the Son of
Man be lifted up, 15 that whoever [a]believes
in Him should [1]not perish but [b]have eternal life. 16 [a]For God so loved the world
that He gave His only begotten [b]Son, that
whoever believes in Him should not perish but have everlasting life. 17 [a]For God
did not send His Son into the world to

11 a John 4:54 b [John 1:14] *1 revealed*
12 a Matt. 4:13 b Matt. 12:46; 13:55
13 a Deut. 16:1–6
14 a Mark 11:15, 17 *1* Lit. *sitting*
16 a Luke 2:49
17 a Ps. 69:9 *1* NU, M *will eat*
18 a Matt. 12:38
19 a Matt. 26:61; 27:40
21 a [1 Cor. 3:16; 6:19]
22 a Luke 24:8 *1* NU, M omit *to them*
23 a [Acts 2:22]
24 a Rev. 2:23
25 a Matt. 9:4

CHAPTER 3
2 a John 7:50; 19:39 b John 9:16, 33 c [Acts 10:38]
3 a [1 Pet. 1:23] *1 Or from above*
5 a [Acts 2:38]
6 a 1 Cor. 15:50
8 a Eccl. 11:5
9 a John 6:52, 60
11 a [Matt. 11:27] b John 3:32; 8:14
13 a Eph. 4:9 *1* NU omits *who is in heaven*
14 a Num. 21:9 b John 8:28; 12:34; 19:18
15 a John 6:47 b John 3:36 *1* NU omits *not perish but*
16 a Rom. 5:8 b [Is. 9:6]
17 a Luke 9:56

JOHN 3:16

Dear Woman of Destiny,

Did you just pick up this Bible and wonder if it had some answers for you? Or maybe someone gave it to you as a gift. Even the words *Woman of Destiny* may seem to mock you when you look at your life and wonder where is the meaning in all of this. Read on, because there is a destiny and purpose for your life—even an abundant life that God has promised to anyone who will come to Him.

John 3:16 is probably the most quoted verse in the Bible. Jesus spoke these words to a highly respected religious leader, Nicodemus, who was probably affluent and well educated, but did not understand such spiritual concepts as "being born again." Jesus was emphasizing that it was not a religious exercise, but actually a metamorphosis from an earthbound "caterpillarlike" state of being transformed to an eternally freed "butterflylike" new creation.

Many think Jesus is an oppressor of females, but quite the opposite is true. He reached out to the prostitute and restored dignity to her. He lifted up the woman who was downtrodden from her long battle with disease and healed her body. He reached across racial and gender lines to the Samaritan woman to bring forgiveness and new life. To the victimized he gave hope and restoration.

God loves you so much that if you had been the only person on this planet, He still would have sent His only Son, Jesus, to be born of a virgin, live a sacrificial life of reaching out to others, and then make the ultimate sacrifice of hanging on a cross for your sins. Sin, our own selfish choices, separates us from God. It's sin, not God, that causes wars and that causes children to die of starvation. God is a loving Father and desires to have a relationship with us each individually. But He will never force His way into anyone's life. He is a gentleman. He merely stands at the door of our hearts and gently knocks. He never karate-chops the door down, but patiently waits for our response.

God has taken the first two steps toward us: He loved, and He gave His only Son. Now we have to take one step toward Him—to "believe," which is not just a mental assent, but a relying on, trusting in, putting all our confidence in the God of the universe. He promises that, if we allow Him to come into the living room, the basement, the bedroom, all the dirty closets of our lives, He will not only clean the house, but He will redecorate it, too. He will also give us an eternal insurance policy. What a deal!

Do you want that new life while living on this earth—to know you will have eternal life after you die? All you need to do is confess, "Jesus, I have sinned and messed up my life at times. I need Your forgiveness." Then ask Him, "Jesus, will You come into my life and 'clean house'? And will You give me the assurance that I will have eternal life with You in heaven when I die?"

He is waiting. In fact, He's been waiting all your life—all of time—for this moment!

Judy Radachy

*Father, thank You for lov-
ing ____ so much that You
gave Your only begotten Son,
that if ____ would believe in
You they should not perish
but have everlasting life. I
pray that, through Jesus,
____ would be saved.*

FROM JOHN 3:16, 17

condemn the world, but that the world
through Him might be saved.
18[a]"He who believes in Him is not condemned; but he who does not believe is
condemned already, because he has not
believed in the name of the only begotten
Son of God. 19And this is the condemnation, [a]that the light has come into the
world, and men loved darkness rather
than light, because their deeds were evil.
20For [a]everyone practicing evil hates the
light and does not come to the light, lest
his deeds should be exposed. 21But he who
does the truth comes to the light, that his
deeds may be clearly seen, that they have
been [a]done in God."

John the Baptist Exalts Christ

22After these things Jesus and His disciples came into the land of Judea, and
there He remained with them [a]and baptized. 23Now John also was baptizing in
Aenon near [a]Salim, because there was
much water there. [b]And they came and
were baptized. 24For [a]John had not yet
been thrown into prison.
25Then there arose a dispute between
some of John's disciples and the Jews
about purification. 26And they came to
John and said to him, "Rabbi, He who was
with you beyond the Jordan, [a]to whom
you have testified—behold, He is baptizing, and all [b]are coming to Him!"
27John answered and said, [a]"A man can
receive nothing unless it has been given
to him from heaven. 28You yourselves
bear me witness, that I said, [a]'I am not the
Christ,' but, [b]'I have been sent before
Him.' 29[a]He who has the bride is the
bridegroom; but [b]the friend of the bridegroom, who stands and hears him, rejoices greatly because of the bridegroom's
voice. Therefore this joy of mine is fulfilled. 30[a]He must increase, but I *must* decrease. 31[a]He who comes from above [b]is
above all; [c]he who is of the earth is earthly
and speaks of the earth. [d]He who comes
from heaven is above all. 32And [a]what He
has seen and heard, that He testifies; and
no one receives His testimony. 33He who
has received His testimony [a]has certified
that God is true. 34[a]For He whom God has
sent speaks the words of God, for God
does not give the Spirit [b]by measure.
35[a]The Father loves the Son, and has giv-
en all things into His hand. 36[a]He who
believes in the Son has everlasting life;
and he who does not believe the Son shall
not see life, but the [b]wrath of God abides
on him."

A Samaritan Woman Meets Her Messiah

4 Therefore, when the Lord knew that
the Pharisees had heard that Jesus
made and [a]baptized more disciples than
John 2(though Jesus Himself did not baptize, but His disciples), 3He left Judea and
departed again to Galilee. 4But He needed
to go through Samaria.
5So He came to a city of Samaria which
is called Sychar, near the plot of ground
that [a]Jacob [b]gave to his son Joseph. 6Now
Jacob's well was there. Jesus therefore,
being wearied from *His* journey, sat thus
by the well. It was about the sixth hour.
7A woman of Samaria came to draw water. Jesus said to her, "Give Me a drink."
8For His disciples had gone away into the
city to buy food.
9Then the woman of Samaria said to
Him, "How is it that You, being a Jew, ask
a drink from me, a Samaritan woman?"
For [a]Jews have no dealings with [b]Samari-
tans.
10Jesus answered and said to her, "If
you knew the [a]gift of God, and who it is
who says to you, 'Give Me a drink,' you
would have asked Him, and He would
have given you [b]living water."
11The woman said to Him, "Sir, You
have nothing to draw with, and the well is
deep. Where then do You get that living
water? 12Are You greater than our father
Jacob, who gave us the well, and drank
from it himself, as well as his sons and his
livestock?"
13Jesus answered and said to her, "Whoever drinks of this water will thirst again,

18 a John 5:24; 6:40, 47; 20:31
19 a [John 1:4, 9–11]
20 a Eph. 5:11, 13
21 a 1 Cor. 15:10
22 a John 4:1, 2
23 a 1 Sam. 9:4 b Matt. 3:5, 6
24 a Matt. 4:12; 14:3
26 a John 1:7, 15, 27, 34 b Mark 2:2; 3:10; 5:24
27 a 1 Cor. 3:5, 6; 4:7
28 a John 1:19–27 b Mal. 3:1
29 a [2 Cor. 11:2] b Song 5:1
30 a [Is. 9:7]
31 a John 3:13; 8:23 b Matt. 28:18 c 1 Cor. 15:47 d John 6:33
32 a John 3:11; 15:15
33 a 1 John 5:10
34 a John 7:16 b John 1:16
35 a [Heb. 2:8]
36 a John 3:16, 17; 6:47 b Rom. 1:18

CHAPTER 4
1 a John 3:22, 26
5 a Gen. 33:19 b Gen. 48:22
9 a Acts 10:28 b 2 Kin. 17:24
10 a [Rom. 5:15] b Is. 12:3; 44:3

14 but [a]whoever drinks of the water that I
shall give him will never thirst. But the
water that I shall give him [b]will become in
him a fountain of water springing up into
everlasting life."
15 [a]The woman said to Him, "Sir, give
me this water, that I may not thirst, nor
come here to draw."
16 Jesus said to her, "Go, call your husband, and come here."
17 The woman answered and said, "I
have no husband."
Jesus said to her, "You have well said, 'I
have no husband,' 18 for you have had five
husbands, and the one whom you now
have is not your husband; in that you
spoke truly."
19 The woman said to Him, "Sir, [a]I perceive that You are a prophet. 20 Our fathers
worshiped on [a]this mountain, and you
Jews say that in [b]Jerusalem is the place
where one ought to worship."
21 Jesus said to her, "Woman, believe
Me, the hour is coming [a]when you will
neither on this mountain, nor in Jerusalem, worship the Father. 22 You worship
[a]what you do not know; we know what we
worship, for [b]salvation is of the Jews.
23 But the hour is coming, and now is,
when the true worshipers will [a]worship
the Father in [b]spirit [c]and truth; for the
Father is seeking such to worship Him.
24 [a]God *is* Spirit, and those who worship
Him must worship in spirit and truth."
25 The woman said to Him, "I know that
Messiah [a]is coming" (who is called
Christ). "When He comes, [b]He will tell us
all things."
26 Jesus said to her, [a]"I who speak to you
am *He*."

14 a [John 6:35, 58] b John 7:37, 38
15 a John 6:34, 35; 17:2, 3
19 a Luke 7:16, 39; 24:19
20 a Judg. 9:7 b Deut. 12:5, 11
21 a 1 Tim. 2:8
22 a [2 Kin. 17:28–41] b [Rom. 3:1; 9:4, 5]
23 a [Heb. 13:10–14] b Phil. 3:3 c [John 1:17]
24 a 2 Cor. 3:17
25 a Deut. 18:15 b John 4:29, 39
26 a Matt. 26:63, 64

The Samaritan Woman

Jesus took quite a risk when He engaged in conversation with the woman at the well. In New Testament times, Samaritans were especially despised by the Jews; and no respectable rabbi would stoop low enough to speak to a Jewish woman, let alone to a woman from Samaria. Even His disciples "marveled that He talked with a woman" (John 4:27). But Jesus did not always abide by the cultural or religious customs of His day. His single focus was to see people saved, healed, delivered, and made whole. When it came to snatching souls from hell, He had no regard for race, tradition, or gender.

In this, the Bible's supreme example of prophetic evangelism, Jesus captures the woman's attention because He is able to see into her life and tell her "all things that [she] ever did" (4:29). It was this prophetic gift of His that caused her to ask, "Could this be the Christ?" (4:29). The woman knew the Christ was coming, but still, He caught her by surprise when He met her at the well (see 4:25). He spoke to her of His living water and pointed out her sin without being harsh or condescending. He spoke to her of true worship and then identified Himself as the Messiah. She left the well as a changed woman, went into the nearby city, and began spreading the news that the Messiah had finally come.

Jesus is still speaking to women today. He is still revealing Himself to women of every race, tribe, and tongue. No matter what your past has been, take comfort in the fact that He already knows. You have nothing to hide, nothing to be ashamed of in His presence. He knows every sin and secret, and He is eager to be the Living Water you are thirsting for.

JOHN 4:23, 24

Dear Woman of Destiny,

As you go about your daily routine, seeking to be all that God has ordained you to be and to fulfill the call of God on your life, please remember this: He has given you a means by which His presence can be accessed—anytime and anywhere. It's called praise and worship.

In John 4:23, 24, Jesus spoke to the woman at the well about what the Father truly desires from each of us. Worship, which is offered in spirit and truth, is what the Father desires; and praise is the way we get there. How interesting that it was a woman whom Jesus chose to teach this vital lesson. He is looking for true worshipers—those who will worship the Father "in spirit and truth" (v. 24).

Whenever Jesus spoke, it is very evident that He used much wisdom and care in selecting His words, saying only what He heard the Father say. I believe this sovereign way of delivering the Scriptures is seen here in this particular passage. God saw people of many nations, creeds, cultures, traditions, and denominations attempting to worship Him in their own way, making (in their minds) their way of worshiping the "right" and only way to worship, thus alienating from the presence of the Almighty God those who did not worship as they did.

Worship is the destination that God desires us to reach, and praise is merely the vehicle we use to get there. The vehicle (praise) is important, but worship is the ultimate destination. I use the analogy of a vehicle because just as a car is operated by the individual, so praise is operated by the individual. In order to get anywhere in a car, you must first open the door, get in, put the key in the ignition, start the engine, give it some gas, and go. So it is with praise. You must put your key of faith in the ignition, start it up, and then follow the road map given in the Scriptures.

Apparently, from Jesus' words to the woman at the well, not everyone arrives at the destination of worship. Many Christians know how to praise the Lord (they know how to operate the vehicle), but in the midst of praising, they become so preoccupied with the vehicle that they forget they were supposed to be going to a special place, a place of worship. They fall short of ever experiencing what worship is. The very fact that God had to specify that He is looking for them means that true worshipers are few and far between. Anything and anybody can praise the Lord, but it takes someone who has a relationship with Him to truly worship Him.

Woman of Destiny, the Father desires that you come into His presence. He wants to fellowship with you. It's the best experience you will ever have. Psalm 16:11 says that in His presence, there is fullness of joy, and at His right hand there are pleasures forevermore. Enjoy them!

Judith Christie-McAllister

The Whitened Harvest

27 And at this *point* His disciples came,
and they marveled that He talked with a
woman; yet no one said, "What do You
seek?" or, "Why are You talking with her?"
28 The woman then left her waterpot,
went her way into the city, and said to the
men, 29 "Come, see a Man [a]who told me all
things that I ever did. Could this be the
Christ?" 30 Then they went out of the city
and came to Him.
31 In the meantime His disciples urged
Him, saying, "Rabbi, eat."
32 But He said to them, "I have food to
eat of which you do not know."
33 Therefore the disciples said to one another, "Has anyone brought Him *anything* to eat?"
34 Jesus said to them, [a]"My food is to do
the will of Him who sent Me, and to [b]fin-
ish His work. 35 Do you not say, 'There are
still four months and *then* comes [a]the
harvest'? Behold, I say to you, lift up your
eyes and look at the fields, [b]for they are
already white for harvest! 36 [a]And he who
reaps receives wages, and gathers fruit for
eternal life, that [b]both he who sows and
he who reaps may rejoice together. 37 For
in this the saying is true: [a]'One sows and
another reaps.' 38 I sent you to reap that
for which you have not labored; [a]others
have labored, and you have entered into
their labors."

The Savior of the World

39 And many of the Samaritans of that
city believed in Him [a]because of the word
of the woman who testified, "He told me
all that I *ever* did." 40 So when the Samaritans had come to Him, they urged Him to
stay with them; and He stayed there two
days. 41 And many more believed because
of His own [a]word.
42 Then they said to the woman, "Now
we believe, not because of what you said,
for [a]we ourselves have heard *Him* and we
know that this is indeed [1]the Christ, the
Savior of the world."

Welcome at Galilee

43 Now after the two days He departed
from there and went to Galilee. 44 For [a]Je-
sus Himself testified that a prophet has no
honor in his own country. 45 So when He
came to Galilee, the Galileans received
Him, [a]having seen all the things He did in

29 a John 4:25
34 a Ps. 40:7, 8 b [John 6:38; 17:4; 19:30]
35 a Gen. 8:22 b Matt. 9:37
36 a Dan. 12:3 b 1 Thess. 2:19
37 a 1 Cor. 3:5–9
38 a [1 Pet. 1:12]
39 a John 4:29
41 a Luke 4:32
42 a 1 John 4:14 1 NU omits *the Christ*
44 a Matt. 13:57
45 a John 2:13, 23; 3:2 b Deut. 16:16
46 a John 2:1, 11 *1 royal official*
48 a 1 Cor. 1:22
CHAPTER 5
1 a Deut. 16:16 b John 2:13
2 a Neh. 3:1, 32; 12:39 1 NU *Bethzatha*
3 *1 withered* 2 NU omits the rest of v. 3 and all of v. 4.

Jerusalem at the feast; [b]for they also had
gone to the feast.

A Nobleman's Son Healed

46 So Jesus came again to Cana of Galilee [a]where He had made the water wine.
And there was a certain [1]nobleman whose
son was sick at Capernaum. 47 When he
heard that Jesus had come out of Judea
into Galilee, he went to Him and implored
Him to come down and heal his son, for
he was at the point of death. 48 Then Jesus
said to him, [a]"Unless you *people* see signs
and wonders, you will by no means believe."
49 The nobleman said to Him, "Sir,
come down before my child dies!"
50 Jesus said to him, "Go your way; your
son lives." So the man believed the word
that Jesus spoke to him, and he went his
way. 51 And as he was now going down, his
servants met him and told *him,* saying,
"Your son lives!"
52 Then he inquired of them the hour
when he got better. And they said to him,
"Yesterday at the seventh hour the fever
left him." 53 So the father knew that *it was*
at the same hour in which Jesus said to
him, "Your son lives." And he himself believed, and his whole household.
54 This again *is* the second sign Jesus
did when He had come out of Judea into
Galilee.

A Man Healed at the Pool of Bethesda

5 After [a]this there was a feast of the
Jews, and Jesus [b]went up to Jerusalem. 2 Now there is in Jerusalem [a]by the
Sheep *Gate* a pool, which is called in Hebrew, [1]Bethesda, having five porches. 3 In
these lay a great multitude of sick people,
blind, lame, [1]paralyzed, [2]waiting for the
moving of the water. 4 For an angel went
down at a certain time into the pool and
stirred up the water; then whoever
stepped in first, after the stirring of the
water, was made well of whatever disease
he had. 5 Now a certain man was there
who had an infirmity thirty-eight years.
6 When Jesus saw him lying there, and
knew that he already had been *in that
condition* a long time, He said to him, "Do
you want to be made well?"
7 The sick man answered Him, "Sir, I
have no man to put me into the pool when
the water is stirred up; but while I am

JOHN 5:1–9

Dear Woman of Destiny,

You are the answer to somebody's prayer today! Jesus said, "These signs will follow those who believe: . . . they will lay hands on the sick, and they will recover" (Mark 16:17, 18). The man Jesus healed waited for nearly forty years for his miracle. He had been disappointed time after time as he saw the water moving and tried to move his debilitated body to the pool, only to have someone else get in before him! When Jesus came on the scene, there was only one prerequisite for a miracle: "Do you want to be made well?" As you have compassion on the infirm, keep your ministry simple! Don't get caught up in all kinds of special prayers and preparations. Don't put any further yokes on those who need a touch from God. Don't get hung up on your faith or on the sick person's faith. Jesus is the Healer! Our job is to pray for the sick. God's job is to heal them!

If you are waiting for a miracle, today is your day. No matter how long you have waited, what you have already been through, or what you have spent on remedies, "Do you want to be made well?" You need no man to put you "in the water" when Jesus passes by. The man by the pool saw only his infirmity, disappointment, and difficult circumstances until Jesus put the man's attention back on his simple hope in healing. Let Him simply hear, "Lord, I want to be made well." He has compassion for you. He will heal you.

Your miracle may be waiting for you to be the vessel of healing for someone else. I know a dear woman who suffered from debilitating depression that led to many physical infirmities in her body. She spent thousands of dollars on doctors. Years passed. She got sicker. She withdrew from life to the point of barely being able to move from her bed.

One day my friend slowly made her way through the grocery store when she noticed a poorly dressed woman with two small needy children. My friend's heart went out to them. For a moment she forgot about herself. She approached the family and found them desperately in need of food and clothing. My friend decided to buy them some groceries. She drove the woman, her children, and their groceries to their home. Seeing the extent of their want and that they were surrounded by other families in need, my friend stretched out her hands and her faith. She became involved in helping to relieve the suffering of these needy families. After a while she realized her own infirmities, including the dark cloud that previously kept her in her bed for days on end, were leaving her!

Within a few months my friend had organized a ministry outreach for the needy in her community. In the course of a year, she was completely healed and was bringing healing of various kinds to many others. My friend became one of the most joyful, faith-filled Christians one could meet.

Your miracle may be hiding in your act of mercy or kindness for someone else. Whether you are waiting for your miracle or know someone who is, Jesus is passing by today!

Bonnie Chavda

coming, another steps down before me."

[8]Jesus said to him, [a]"Rise, take up your bed and walk." [9]And immediately the man was made well, took up his bed, and walked.

And [a]that day was the Sabbath. [10]The Jews therefore said to him who was cured, "It is the Sabbath; [a]it is not lawful for you to carry your bed."

[11]He answered them, "He who made me well said to me, 'Take up your bed and walk.' "

[12]Then they asked him, "Who is the Man who said to you, 'Take up your bed and walk'?" [13]But the one who was [a]healed did not know who it was, for Jesus had withdrawn, a multitude being in *that* place. [14]Afterward Jesus found him in the temple, and said to him, "See, you have been made well. [a]Sin no more, lest a worse thing come upon you."

[15]The man departed and told the Jews that it was Jesus who had made him well.

Honor the Father and the Son

[16]For this reason the Jews [a]persecuted Jesus, [1]and sought to kill Him, because He had done these things on the Sabbath. [17]But Jesus answered them, [a]"My Father has been working until now, and I have been working."

[18]Therefore the Jews [a]sought all the more to kill Him, because He not only broke the Sabbath, but also said that God was His Father, [b]making Himself equal with God. [19]Then Jesus answered and said to them, "Most assuredly, I say to you, [a]the Son can do nothing of Himself, but what He sees the Father do; for whatever He does, the Son also does in like manner. [20]For [a]the Father loves the Son, and [b]shows Him all things that He Himself does; and He will show Him greater works than these, that you may marvel. [21]For as the Father raises the dead and gives life to *them,* [a]even so the Son gives life to whom He will. [22]For the Father judges no one, but [a]has committed all judgment to the Son, [23]that all should honor the Son just as they honor the Father. [a]He who does not honor the Son does not honor the Father who sent Him.

Life and Judgment Are Through the Son

[24]"Most assuredly, I say to you, [a]he who hears My word and believes in Him who sent Me has everlasting life, and shall not come into judgment, [b]but has passed from death into life. [25]Most assuredly, I say to you, the hour is coming, and now is, when [a]the dead will hear the voice of the Son of God; and those who hear will live. [26]For [a]as the Father has life in Himself, so He has granted the Son to have [b]life in Himself, [27]and [a]has given Him authority to execute judgment also, [b]because He is the Son of Man. [28]Do not marvel at this; for the hour is coming in which all who are in the graves will [a]hear His voice [29][a]and come forth—[b]those who have done good, to the resurrection of life, and those who have done evil, to the resurrection of condemnation. [30][a]I can of Myself do nothing. As I hear, I judge; and My judgment is righteous, because [b]I do not seek My own will but the will of the Father who sent Me.

The Fourfold Witness

[31][a]"If I bear witness of Myself, My witness is not [1]true. [32][a]There is another who bears witness of Me, and I know that the witness which He witnesses of Me is true. [33]You have sent to John, [a]and he has borne witness to the truth. [34]Yet I do not receive testimony from man, but I say these things that you may be saved. [35]He was the burning and [a]shining lamp, and [b]you were willing for a time to rejoice in his light. [36]But [a]I have a greater witness than John's; for [b]the works which the Father has given Me to finish—the very [c]works that I do—bear witness of Me, that the Father has sent Me. [37]And the Father Himself, who sent Me, [a]has testified of Me. You have neither heard His voice at any time, [b]nor seen His form. [38]But you do not have His word abiding in you, because whom He sent, Him you do not believe. [39][a]You search the Scriptures, for in them you think you have eternal life; and [b]these are they which testify of Me. [40][a]But you are not willing to come to Me that you may have life.

[41][a]"I do not receive honor from men. [42]But I know you, that you do not have the love of God in you. [43]I have come in My Father's name, and you do not receive Me; if another comes in his own name, him you will receive. [44][a]How can you believe, who receive honor from one another, and do not seek [b]the honor that *comes*

8 a Luke 5:24
9 a John 9:14
10 a Jer. 17:21, 22
13 a Luke 13:14; 22:51
14 a John 8:11
16 a John 8:37; 10:39 *1* NU omits *and sought to kill Him*
17 a [John 9:4; 17:4]
18 a John 7:1, 19 b John 10:30
19 a John 5:30; 6:38; 8:28; 12:49; 14:10
20 a Matt. 3:17 b [Matt. 11:27]
21 a [John 11:25]
22 a [Acts 17:31]
23 a 1 John 2:23
24 a John 3:16, 18; 6:47 b [1 John 3:14]
25 a [Col. 2:13]
26 a Ps. 36:9 b 1 Cor. 15:45
27 a [Acts 10:42; 17:31] b Dan. 7:13
28 a [1 Thess. 4:15–17]
29 a Is. 26:19 b Dan. 12:2
30 a John 5:19 b Matt. 26:39
31 a John 8:14 *1 valid* as testimony
32 a [Matt. 3:17]
33 a [John 1:15, 19, 27, 32]
35 a 2 Pet. 1:19 b Mark 6:20
36 a 1 John 5:9 b John 3:2; 10:25; 17:4 c John 9:16; 10:38
37 a Matt. 3:17 b 1 John 4:12
39 a Is. 8:20; 34:16 b Luke 24:27
40 a [John 1:11; 3:19]
41 a 1 Thess. 2:6
44 a John 12:43 b [Rom. 2:29]

from the only God? 45 Do not think that I shall accuse you to the Father; [a]there is *one* who accuses you—Moses, in whom you trust. 46 For if you believed Moses, you would believe Me; [a]for he wrote about Me. 47 But if you [a]do not believe his writings, how will you believe My words?"

Feeding the Five Thousand

6 After [a]these things Jesus went over the Sea of Galilee, which is *the Sea* of [b]Tiberias. 2 Then a great multitude followed Him, because they saw His signs which He performed on those who were [a]diseased.[1] 3 And Jesus went up on the mountain, and there He sat with His disciples.

4 [a]Now the Passover, a feast of the Jews, was near. 5 [a]Then Jesus lifted up *His* eyes, and seeing a great multitude coming toward Him, He said to [b]Philip, "Where shall we buy bread, that these may eat?" 6 But this He said to test him, for He Himself knew what He would do.

7 Philip answered Him, [a]"Two hundred denarii worth of bread is not sufficient for them, that every one of them may have a little."

8 One of His disciples, [a]Andrew, Simon Peter's brother, said to Him, 9 "There is a lad here who has five barley loaves and two small fish, [a]but what are they among so many?"

10 Then Jesus said, "Make the people sit down." Now there was much grass in the place. So the men sat down, in number about five thousand. 11 And Jesus took the loaves, and when He had given thanks He distributed *them* [1]to the disciples, and the disciples to those sitting down; and likewise of the fish, as much as they wanted. 12 So when they were filled, He said to His disciples, "Gather up the fragments that remain, so that nothing is lost." 13 Therefore they gathered *them* up, and filled twelve baskets with the fragments of the five barley loaves which were left over by those who had eaten. 14 Then those men, when they had seen the sign that Jesus did, said, "This is truly [a]the Prophet who is to come into the world."

Jesus Walks on the Sea

15 Therefore when Jesus perceived that they were about to come and take Him by force to make Him [a]king, He departed again to the mountain by Himself alone.

16 [a]Now when evening came, His disciples went down to the sea, 17 got into the boat, and went over the sea toward Capernaum. And it was already dark, and Jesus had not come to them. 18 Then the sea arose because a great wind was blowing. 19 So when they had rowed about [1]three or four miles, they saw Jesus walking on the sea and drawing near the boat; and they were [a]afraid. 20 But He said to them, [a]"It is I; do not be afraid." 21 Then they willingly received Him into the boat, and immediately the boat was at the land where they were going.

The Bread from Heaven

22 On the following day, when the people who were standing on the other side of the sea saw that there was no other boat there, except [1]that one [2]which His disciples had entered, and that Jesus had not entered the boat with His disciples, but His disciples had gone away alone— 23 however, other boats came from Tiberias, near the place where they ate bread after the Lord had given thanks— 24 when the people therefore saw that Jesus was not there, nor His disciples, they also got into boats and came to Capernaum, [a]seeking Jesus. 25 And when they found Him on the other side of the sea, they said to Him, "Rabbi, when did You come here?"

26 Jesus answered them and said, "Most assuredly, I say to you, you seek Me, not because you saw the signs, but because you ate of the loaves and were filled. 27 [a]Do not labor for the food which perishes, but [b]for the food which endures to everlasting life, which the Son of Man will give you, [c]because God the Father has set His seal on Him."

28 Then they said to Him, "What shall we do, that we may work the works of God?"

29 Jesus answered and said to them, [a]"This is the work of God, that you believe in Him whom He sent."

30 Therefore they said to Him, [a]"What sign will You perform then, that we may see it and believe You? What work will You do? 31 [a]Our fathers ate the manna in the desert; as it is written, [b]*'He gave them bread from heaven to eat.'* "

32 Then Jesus said to them, "Most assuredly, I say to you, Moses did not give you the bread from heaven, but [a]My Father gives you the true bread from heaven. 33 For the bread of God is He who

45 a Rom. 2:12
46 a Deut. 18:15, 18
47 a Luke 16:29, 31

CHAPTER 6
1 a Mark 6:32 b John 6:23; 21:1
2 a Matt. 4:23; 8:16; 9:35; 14:36; 15:30; 19:2 *1 sick*
4 a Deut. 16:1
5 a Matt. 14:14 b John 1:43
7 a Num. 11:21, 22
8 a John 1:40
9 a 2 Kin. 4:43
11 1 NU omits *to the disciples, and the disciples*
14 a Gen. 49:10
15 a [John 18:36]
16 a Matt. 14:23
19 a Matt. 17:6 1 Lit. *25 or 30 stadia*
20 a Is. 43:1, 2
22 1 NU omits *that* 2 NU omits *which His disciples had entered*
24 a Luke 4:42
27 a Matt. 6:19 b John 4:14 c Acts 2:22
29 a [1 John 3:23]
30 a Matt. 12:38; 16:1
31 a Ex. 16:15 b Ex. 16:4, 15; Neh. 9:15; Ps. 78:24
32 a John 3:13, 16

John 6:15–21

Dear Woman of Destiny,

Part of realizing your destiny is knowing how to continually make progress. Progress requires that we traverse seas of transition as we emerge out of the old and into the new person we are becoming. A transition is the process of moving from one place to another.

John 6:15–21 tells of an incident in which the disciples were crossing the Sea of Galilee on their way to Capernaum. Any crossing from one place to another requires a transition that begins with an ending and ends with a beginning. Leaving the shore represented an ending, catapulting the disciples into a transition—that limbo period between the ending and the new beginning.

Limbo can be likened to being in a boat at sea. The disciples were neither where they started nor where they were going. Their moorings had been cut loose, and they were vulnerable to the elements. A great wind blew up, and the sea became even more unstable, threatening to capsize their boat and abort their arrival at the new place.

In that unstable place, the disciples were confronted with contrary or treacherous winds that threatened to capsize their boat and abort their arriving at the new place. *Contrary* means antagonistic, against, or opposing. The wind was trying to keep the disciples from reaching their destiny. It was a force that opposed them.

In the midst of that threat of aborted destiny, Jesus came to the disciples. At first they did not recognize Him. Often in places of such uncertainty and threat, we cannot recognize Jesus when He comes to us. When they did recognize Him, they let Him into the boat with them—a decision that saved their lives and enabled them to reach their destination, the new place.

When we permit God to "get in our boat," it makes all the difference to the success of our "trip." To acknowledge God in this way is to worship Him—to bow down, to yield, to take our hands off the wheel that is steering our lives. In that act of worship, He overtakes us. Suddenly we see Him for who He is. Doubt and fear are transformed to faith. Revelation is released in that what was unknown to us about God we now see and understand. Revelation releases strategy on how to get to the other side. As Hannah Whitehall Smith wrote many years ago in *The Christian's Secret of Happy Life*, contrary forces are chariots which carry us to God.

From the account in Matthew 14:22–33, we know it was God who sent the disciples across the sea. If He sent them, then He was also committed to their destiny and would release all of the resources necessary for them to get to the other side. When God directs us in a way that leads us into transition, He has already committed Himself to come to us when we reach unstable waters.

Woman of Destiny, don't be afraid. Jesus has promised to rescue you from the stormy seas of your life. Allow Him to get into your boat!

Barbara Yoder

comes down from heaven and gives life to
the world."
34[a]Then they said to Him, "Lord, give
us this bread always."

The things of God are so precious, He will not give them to those who do not greatly desire them. It is those who hunger and thirst who are filled.

MRS. C. NUZUM

35And Jesus said to them, [a]"I am the
bread of life. [b]He who comes to Me shall
never hunger, and he who believes in Me
shall never [c]thirst. 36[a]But I said to you
that you have seen Me and yet [b]do not
believe. 37[a]All that the Father gives Me
will come to Me, and [b]the one who comes
to Me I will [1]by no means cast out. 38For
I have come down from heaven, [a]not to do
My own will, [b]but the will of Him who
sent Me. 39This is the will of the Father
who sent Me, [a]that of all He has given Me
I should lose nothing, but should raise it
up at the last day. 40And this is the will of
Him who sent Me, [a]that everyone who
sees the Son and believes in Him may
have everlasting life; and I will raise him
up at the last day."

Rejected by His Own

41The Jews then [1]complained about
Him, because He said, "I am the bread
which came down from heaven." 42And
they said, [a]"Is not this Jesus, the son of
Joseph, whose father and mother we
know? How is it then that He says, 'I have
come down from heaven'?"
43Jesus therefore answered and said to
them, [1]"Do not murmur among yourselves. 44[a]No one can come to Me unless
the Father who sent Me [b]draws him; and
I will raise him up at the last day. 45It is
written in the prophets, [a]'*And they shall
all be taught by God.*' [b]Therefore everyone
who [1]has heard and learned from the Father comes to Me. 46[a]Not that anyone has
seen the Father, [b]except He who is from
God; He has seen the Father. 47Most assuredly, I say to you, [a]he who believes [1]in
Me has everlasting life. 48[a]I am the bread
of life. 49[a]Your fathers ate the manna in
the wilderness, and are dead. 50[a]This is
the bread which comes down from heav-
en, that one may eat of it and not die. 51I
am the living bread [a]which came down
from heaven. If anyone eats of this bread,
he will live forever; and [b]the bread that I
shall give is My flesh, which I shall give for
the life of the world."
52The Jews therefore [a]quarreled among
themselves, saying, "How can this Man
give us *His* flesh to eat?"
53Then Jesus said to them, "Most assuredly, I say to you, unless [a]you eat the
flesh of the Son of Man and drink His
blood, you have no life in you. 54[a]Whoever
eats My flesh and drinks My blood has
eternal life, and I will raise him up at the
last day. 55For My flesh is [1]food indeed,
and My blood is [2]drink indeed. 56He who
eats My flesh and drinks My blood [a]abides
in Me, and I in him. 57As the living Father
sent Me, and I live because of the Father,
so he who feeds on Me will live because of
Me. 58[a]This is the bread which came down
from heaven—not [b]as your fathers ate
the manna, and are dead. He who eats this
bread will live forever."
59These things He said in the synagogue as He taught in Capernaum.

Many Disciples Turn Away

60[a]Therefore many of His disciples,
when they heard *this,* said, "This is a
[1]hard saying; who can understand it?"
61When Jesus knew in Himself that His
disciples [1]complained about this, He said
to them, "Does this [2]offend you? 62[a]*What*
then if you should see the Son of Man
ascend where He was before? 63[a]It is the
Spirit who gives life; the [b]flesh profits
nothing. The [c]words that I speak to you
are spirit, and *they* are life. 64But [a]there
are some of you who do not believe." For
[b]Jesus knew from the beginning who they
were who did not believe, and who would
betray Him. 65And He said, "Therefore [a]I
have said to you that no one can come to
Me unless it has been granted to him by
My Father."
66[a]From that *time* many of His disciples went [1]back and walked with Him no
more. 67Then Jesus said to the twelve, "Do
you also want to go away?"

34 a John 4:15
35 a John 6:48, 58 b John 4:14; 7:37 c Is. 55:1, 2
36 a John 6:26, 64; 15:24 b John 10:26
37 a John 6:45 b 2 Tim. 2:19 *1 certainly not*
38 a Matt. 26:39 b John 4:34
39 a John 10:28; 17:12; 18:9
40 a John 3:15, 16; 4:14; 6:27, 47, 54
41 *1 grumbled*
42 a Matt. 13:55
43 *1 Stop grumbling*
44 a Song 1:4 b [Phil. 1:29; 2:12, 13]
45 a Is. 54:13 b John 6:37 *1 M hears and has learned*
46 a John 1:18 b Matt. 11:27
47 a [John 3:16, 18] *1 NU omits in Me*
48 a John 6:33, 35
49 a John 6:31, 58
50 a John 6:51, 58
51 a John 3:13 b Heb. 10:5
52 a John 7:43; 9:16; 10:19
53 a Matt. 26:26
54 a John 4:14; 6:27, 40
55 *1 NU true food 2 NU true drink*
56 a [1 John 3:24; 4:15, 16]
58 a John 6:49–51 b Ex. 16:14–35
60 a John 6:66 *1 difficult*
61 *1 grumbled 2 make you stumble*
62 a Acts 1:9; 2:32, 33
63 a 2 Cor. 3:6 b John 3:6 c [John 6:68; 14:24]
64 a John 6:36 b John 2:24, 25; 13:11
65 a John 6:37, 44, 45
66 a Luke 9:62 *1 Or away;* lit. *to the back*

68But Simon Peter answered Him, "Lord, to whom shall we go? You have [a]the words of eternal life. 69[a]Also we have come to believe and know that You are the [1]Christ, the Son of the living God."

70Jesus answered them, [a]"Did I not choose you, the twelve, [b]and one of you is a devil?" 71He spoke of [a]Judas Iscariot, *the son* of Simon, for it was he who would [b]betray Him, being one of the twelve.

Jesus' Brothers Disbelieve

7 After these things Jesus walked in Galilee; for He did not want to walk in Judea, [a]because the [1]Jews sought to kill Him. 2[a]Now the Jews' Feast of Tabernacles was at hand. 3[a]His brothers therefore said to Him, "Depart from here and go into Judea, that Your disciples also may see the works that You are doing. 4For no one does anything in secret while he himself seeks to be known openly. If You do these things, show Yourself to the world." 5For [a]even His [b]brothers did not believe in Him.

6Then Jesus said to them, [a]"My time has not yet come, but your time is always ready. 7[a]The world cannot hate you, but it hates Me [b]because I testify of it that its works are evil. 8You go up to this feast. I am not [1]yet going up to this feast, [a]for My time has not yet fully come." 9When He had said these things to them, He remained in Galilee.

The Heavenly Scholar

10But when His brothers had gone up, then He also went up to the feast, not openly, but as it were in secret. 11Then [a]the Jews sought Him at the feast, and said, "Where is He?" 12And [a]there was much complaining among the people concerning Him. [b]Some said, "He is good"; others said, "No, on the contrary, He deceives the people." 13However, no one spoke openly of Him [a]for fear of the Jews.

14Now about the middle of the feast Jesus went up into the temple and [a]taught. 15[a]And the Jews marveled, saying, "How does this Man know letters, having never studied?"

16[1]Jesus answered them and said, [a]"My doctrine is not Mine, but His who sent Me. 17[a]If anyone wills to do His will, he shall know concerning the doctrine, whether it is from God or *whether* I speak on My own *authority.* 18[a]He who speaks from himself seeks his own glory; but He who [b]seeks the glory of the One who sent Him is true, and [c]no unrighteousness is in Him. 19[a]Did not Moses give you the law, yet none of you keeps the law? [b]Why do you seek to kill Me?"

20The people answered and said, [a]"You have a demon. Who is seeking to kill You?"

21Jesus answered and said to them, "I did one work, and you all marvel. 22[a]Moses therefore gave you circumcision (not that it is from Moses, [b]but from the fathers), and you circumcise a man on the Sabbath. 23If a man receives circumcision on the Sabbath, so that the law of Moses should not be broken, are you angry with Me because [a]I made a man completely well on the Sabbath? 24[a]Do not judge according to appearance, but judge with righteous judgment."

Could This Be the Christ?

25Now some of them from Jerusalem said, "Is this not He whom they seek to [a]kill? 26But look! He speaks boldly, and they say nothing to Him. [a]Do the rulers know indeed that this is [1]truly the Christ? 27[a]However, we know where this Man is from; but when the Christ comes, no one knows where He is from."

28Then Jesus cried out, as He taught in the temple, saying, [a]"You both know Me, and you know where I am from; and [b]I have not come of Myself, but He who sent Me [c]is true, [d]whom you do not know. 29[1]But [a]I know Him, for I am from Him, and He sent Me."

30Therefore [a]they sought to take Him; but [b]no one laid a hand on Him, because His hour had not yet come. 31And [a]many of the people believed in Him, and said, "When the Christ comes, will He do more signs than these which this *Man* has done?"

Jesus and the Religious Leaders

32The Pharisees heard the crowd murmuring these things concerning Him, and the Pharisees and the chief priests sent officers to take Him. 33Then Jesus said [1]to them, [a]"I shall be with you a little while longer, and *then* I [b]go to Him who

68 a Acts 5:20
69 a Luke 9:20 *1* NU *Holy One of God.*
70 a Luke 6:13 b [John 13:27]
71 a John 12:4; 13:2, 26 b Matt. 26:14–16
CHAPTER 7
1 a John 5:18; 7:19, 25; 8:37, 40 *1* The ruling authorities
2 a Lev. 23:34
3 a Matt. 12:46
5 a Ps. 69:8 b Mark 3:21
6 a John 2:4; 8:20
7 a [John 15:19] b John 3:19
8 a John 8:20 *1* NU omits *yet*
11 a John 11:56
12 a John 9:16; 10:19 b Luke 7:16
13 a [John 9:22; 12:42; 19:38]
14 a Mark 6:34
15 a Matt. 13:54
16 a John 3:11 *1* NU, M *So Jesus*
17 a John 3:21; 8:43
18 a John 5:41 b John 8:50 c [2 Cor. 5:21]
19 a Deut. 33:4 b Matt. 12:14
20 a John 8:48, 52
22 a Lev. 12:3 b Gen. 17:9–14
23 a John 5:8, 9, 16
24 a Prov. 24:23
25 a Matt. 21:38; 26:4
26 a John 7:48 *1* NU omits *truly*
27 a Luke 4:22
28 a John 8:14 b John 5:43 c Rom. 3:4 d John 1:18; 8:55
29 a Matt. 11:27 *1* NU, M omit *But* **30** a Mark 11:18 b John 7:32, 44; 8:20; 10:39 **31** a Matt. 12:23 **33** a John 13:33 b [1 Pet. 3:22] *1* NU, M omit *to them*

John 7:8

Dear Woman of Destiny,

Timing is crucial to the plans of God in our lives. Jesus understood times and seasons, and He established a pattern for us to follow. In John 7, Jesus told His brothers that His hour had not yet come. Scripture states that His brothers did not believe in Him, but attempted to force Him prematurely into what was ultimately God's plan for His life. Had Jesus not walked in the will, times, and seasons of the Father for His life, there would have been a "miscarriage" of God's redemptive plan!

We also see this principle in Nehemiah 4:7, 8. The enemies of Israel were fighting and carrying out open opposition to Nehemiah's rebuilding of the walls. The Hebrew word for *hinder* means not only "to delay, retard, and cease"; it also literally means "to cause a miscarriage."

Neither the devil nor the flesh wants to see you give birth to God's will, plan, and purpose for your life. They want you to suffer a "miscarriage." You also must remember that when the "man child" (the will, plan, vision) is birthed, the dragon is waiting to devour it! (see Rev. 12). But thanks be to God, who always causes us to triumph in Christ! (see 2 Cor. 2:14).

Jesus was very conscious of doing things in the timing of Almighty God. He told His brothers they could do whatever they wanted to do anytime (see John 7:6). His life was different. He essentially said, "Because I came to do the will of My Father, My times are in His hands" (see Ps. 31:15).

In Matthew 26:18, Jesus finally said that His hour had come. Just as Jesus' hour came in life, so your hour shall also surely come.

What happened as Jesus saw His hour approaching? The people desired to bring earthly glory to Jesus and themselves by making Him a king. But Jesus knew that only the Father had the right to elevate Him to that position—and it would have to be in God's timing, not man's.

If the people had succeeded in getting Jesus to act outside of God's timing for His life, there would have been no opportunity for salvation! There would have been no cross on Calvary, no precious blood shed, no finished work, and no better covenant.

What do we see Jesus doing when He "knew that His hour had come"? (see John 13:1–17). Is He sitting on a throne being served by humanity, as the people wanted? No! Jesus is a servant. We see Him on His knees, washing His disciples' feet.

What does this scripture tell us? The nearer you approach your hour—and even in the height of your hour—the more you life will consist of servitude. The more you will live to give. The more you will wash feet—even the feet of your betrayers. The peak of your hour is the peak of your servitude.

Relax in God's timing. Your hour will surely come.

Bobbie Jean Merck

sent Me. 34You [a]will seek Me and not find *Me,* and where I am you [b]cannot come."

35Then the Jews said among themselves, "Where does He intend to go that we shall not find Him? Does He intend to go to [a]the Dispersion among the Greeks and teach the Greeks? 36What is this thing that He said, 'You will seek Me and not find Me, and where I am you cannot come'?"

The Promise of the Holy Spirit

37[a]On the last day, that great *day* of the feast, Jesus stood and cried out, saying, [b]"If anyone thirsts, let him come to Me and drink. 38[a]He who believes in Me, as the Scripture has said, [b]out of his heart will flow rivers of living water." 39[a]But this He spoke concerning the Spirit, whom those [1]believing in Him would receive; for the [2]Holy Spirit was not yet *given,* because Jesus was not yet [b]glorified.

Risen Lord, because ____ believes in You, may rivers of living water flow from their heart.

FROM JOHN 7:38

Who Is He?

40Therefore [1]many from the crowd, when they heard this saying, said, "Truly this is [a]the Prophet." 41Others said, "This is [a]the Christ."

But some said, "Will the Christ come out of Galilee? 42[a]Has not the Scripture said that the Christ comes from the seed of David and from the town of Bethlehem, [b]where David was?" 43So [a]there was a division among the people because of Him. 44Now [a]some of them wanted to take Him, but no one laid hands on Him.

Rejected by the Authorities

45Then the officers came to the chief priests and Pharisees, who said to them, "Why have you not brought Him?"

46The officers answered, [a]"No man ever spoke like this Man!"

47Then the Pharisees answered them, "Are you also deceived? 48Have any of the rulers or the Pharisees believed in Him? 49But this crowd that does not know the law is accursed."

50Nicodemus [a](he who came to [1]Jesus [2]by night, being one of them) said to them, 51[a]"Does our law judge a man before it hears him and knows what he is doing?"

52They answered and said to him, "Are you also from Galilee? Search and look, for [a]no prophet [1]has arisen out of Galilee."

An Adulteress Faces the Light of the World

53[1]And everyone went to his *own* house.

8 But Jesus went to the Mount of Olives.

2Now [1]early in the morning He came again into the temple, and all the people came to Him; and He sat down and [a]taught them. 3Then the scribes and Pharisees brought to Him a woman caught in adultery. And when they had set her in the midst, 4they said to Him, "Teacher, [1]this woman was caught in [a]adultery, in the very act. 5[a]Now [1]Moses, in the law, commanded us [2]that such should be stoned. But what do You [3]say?" 6This they said, testing Him, that they [a]might have *something* of which to accuse Him. But Jesus stooped down and wrote on the ground with *His* finger, [1]as though He did not hear.

7So when they continued asking Him, He [1]raised Himself up and said to them, [a]"He who is without sin among you, let him throw a stone at her first." 8And again He stooped down and wrote on the ground. 9Then those who heard *it,* [a]being[1] convicted by *their* conscience, went out one by one, beginning with the oldest *even* to the last. And Jesus was left alone, and the woman standing in the midst. 10When Jesus had raised Himself up [1]and saw no one but the woman, He said to her, "Woman, where are those accusers [2]of yours? Has no one condemned you?"

11She said, "No one, Lord."

And Jesus said to her, [a]"Neither do I condemn you; go [1]and [b]sin no more."

34 a Hos. 5:6 b [Matt. 5:20]
35 a James 1:1
37 a Lev. 23:36 b [Is. 55:1]
38 a Deut. 18:15 b Is. 12:3; 43:20; 44:3; 55:1
39 a Is. 44:3 b John 12:16; 13:31; 17:5 *1* NU *who believed* *2* NU omits *Holy*
40 a Deut. 18:15, 18 *1* NU *some*
41 a John 4:42; 6:69
42 a Mic. 5:2 b 1 Sam. 16:1, 4
43 a John 7:12
44 a John 7:30
46 a Luke 4:22
50 a John 3:1, 2; 19:39 *1* Lit. *Him* *2* NU *before*
51 a Deut. 1:16, 17; 19:15
52 a [Is. 9:1, 2] *1* NU *is to rise*
53 *1* NU brackets 7:53 through 8:11 as not in the original text. They are present in over 900 mss. of John.

CHAPTER 8
2 a John 8:20; 18:20 *1* M *very early*
4 a Ex. 20:14 *1* M *we found this woman*
5 a Lev. 20:10 *1* M *in our law Moses commanded* *2* NU, M *to stone such* *3* M adds *about her*
6 a Matt. 22:15 *1* NU, M omit *as though He did not hear*
7 a Deut. 17:7 *1* M *He looked up*
9 a Rom. 2:22 *1* NU, M omit *being convicted by their conscience*

10 *1* NU omits *and saw no one but the woman;* M *He saw her and said,* *2* NU, M omit *of yours* **11** a [John 3:17] b [John 5:14] *1* NU, M add *from now on*

[12]Then Jesus spoke to them again, saying, [a]"I am the light of the world. He who [b]follows Me shall not walk in darkness, but have the light of life."

Peace is the consequence of forgiveness, God's removal of that which obscures His face and so breaks union with Him.

CHARLES H. BRENT

12 a John 1:4; 9:5; 12:35 b 1 Thess. 5:5

13 a John 5:31 *1 valid* as testimony

14 a John 7:28; 9:29

15 a John 7:24 b [John 3:17; 12:47; 18:36]

16 a John 16:32

17 a Deut. 17:6; 19:15

18 a John 5:37

Jesus Defends His Self-Witness

[13]The Pharisees therefore said to Him,
[a]"You bear witness of Yourself; Your witness is not [1]true."
[14]Jesus answered and said to them,
"Even if I bear witness of Myself, My witness is true, for I know where I came from
and where I am going; but [a]you do not
know where I come from and where I am
going. [15][a]You judge according to the
flesh; [b]I judge no one. [16]And yet if I do
judge, My judgment is true; for [a]I am not
alone, but I *am* with the Father who sent
Me. [17][a]It is also written in your law that
the testimony of two men is true. [18]I am
One who bears witness of Myself, and [a]the
Father who sent Me bears witness of Me."

PANDITA RAMABAI

Pandita Ramabai (1858–1920) was one of the most outstanding Christian educators in history. Called the "mother" of the Pentecostal movement in India, Pandita was born into a high caste family and became a woman of both great intellect and great faith. Although quite controversial, this well-educated woman did impact her society for Jesus Christ.

Pandita was fluent in seven languages and provided the people around her with a translation of the Bible (from the original languages) in their native tongue, Marathi. She also devoted much effort to establishing schools for girls in India. One of her accomplishments included opening a school for child widows, so that they would not fall prey to the Hindu custom of being burned on their husbands' funeral pyres. She was able to open another school in the midst of a severe famine, relying on prayer and God's provision to supply her every need.

But her prayers for God to provide physically for His people were not the only prayers she prayed. She also cried out to God for genuine revival in her nation. She started encouraging people to pray for revival and an outpouring of God's power in January 1905. It happened on June 30 of that same year. Pandita was teaching her girls from John 8 when the Holy Spirit descended and His presence filled the room, almost as dramatically as it did at Pentecost. What followed was a revival characterized by deep repentance and confession of sin, joyous praise and worship, and even supernatural dreams and visions.

Just as Pandita Ramabai courageously plowed new ground for the gospel in India, may we also cry out for a powerful visitation of God's presence and for a revival of His Spirit in the places where we live.

19Then they said to Him, "Where is Your Father?"

Jesus answered, [a]"You know neither Me nor My Father. [b]If you had known Me, you would have known My Father also."

20These words Jesus spoke in [a]the treasury, as He taught in the temple; and [b]no one laid hands on Him, for [c]His hour had not yet come.

Jesus Predicts His Departure

21Then Jesus said to them again, "I am going away, and [a]you will seek Me, and [b]will die in your sin. Where I go you cannot come."

22So the Jews said, "Will He kill Himself, because He says, 'Where I go you cannot come'?"

23And He said to them, [a]"You are from beneath; I am from above. [b]You are of this world; I am not of this world. 24[a]Therefore I said to you that you will die in your sins; [b]for if you do not believe that I am *He,* you will die in your sins."

25Then they said to Him, "Who are You?"

And Jesus said to them, "Just what I [a]have been saying to you from the beginning. 26I have many things to say and to judge concerning you, but [a]He who sent Me is true; and [b]I speak to the world those things which I heard from Him."

27They did not understand that He spoke to them of the Father.

28Then Jesus said to them, "When you [a]lift[1] up the Son of Man, [b]then you will know that I am *He,* and [c]*that* I do nothing of Myself; but [d]as My Father taught Me, I speak these things. 29And [a]He who sent Me is with Me. [b]The Father has not left Me alone, [c]for I always do those things that please Him." 30As He spoke these words, [a]many believed in Him.

The Truth Shall Make You Free

31 Then Jesus said to those Jews who believed Him, "If you [a]abide in My word, you are My disciples indeed. 32And you shall know the [a]truth, and [b]the truth shall make you free."

33They answered Him, [a]"We are Abraham's descendants, and have never been in bondage to anyone. How *can* You say, 'You will be made free'?"

34Jesus answered them, "Most assuredly, I say to you, [a]whoever commits sin is a slave of sin. 35And [a]a slave does not abide in the house forever, *but* a son abides forever. 36[a]Therefore if the Son makes you free, you shall be free indeed.

Lord, I pray that ____ will know the truth and the truth will make them free.

FROM JOHN 8:32

Abraham's Seed and Satan's

37"I know that you are Abraham's descendants, but [a]you seek to kill Me, because My word has no place in you. 38[a]I speak what I have seen with My Father, and you do what you have [1]seen with your father."

39They answered and said to Him, [a]"Abraham is our father."

Jesus said to them, [b]"If you were Abraham's children, you would do the works of Abraham. 40[a]But now you seek to kill Me, a Man who has told you the truth [b]which I heard from God. Abraham did not do this. 41You do the deeds of your father."

Then they said to Him, "We were not born of fornication; [a]we have one Father—God."

42Jesus said to them, [a]"If God were your Father, you would love Me, for [b]I proceeded forth and came from God; [c]nor have I come of Myself, but He sent Me. 43[a]Why do you not understand My speech? Because you are not able to listen to My word. 44[a]You are of *your* father the devil, and the [b]desires of your father you want to [c]do. He was a murderer from the beginning, and [d]does not stand in the truth, because there is no truth in him. When he speaks a lie, he speaks from his own *resources,* for he is a liar and the father of it. 45But because I tell the truth, you do not believe Me. 46Which of you convicts Me of sin? And if I tell the truth, why do you not believe Me? 47[a]He who is of God hears God's words; therefore you do not hear, because you are not of God."

Before Abraham Was, I AM

48Then the Jews answered and said to Him, "Do we not say rightly that You are a Samaritan and [a]have a demon?"

19 a John 16:3 b John 14:7
20 a Mark 12:41, 43 b John 2:4; 7:30 c John 7:8
21 a John 7:34; 13:33 b John 8:24
23 a John 3:31 b 1 John 4:5
24 a John 8:21 b [Mark 16:16]
25 a John 4:26
26 a John 7:28 b John 3:32; 15:15
28 a John 3:14; 12:32; 19:18 b [Rom. 1:4] c John 5:19, 30 d John 3:11 *1* Crucify
29 a John 14:10 b John 8:16; 16:32 c John 4:34; 5:30; 6:38
30 a John 7:31; 10:42; 11:45
31 a [John 14:15, 23]
32 a [John 1:14, 17; 14:6] b [Rom. 6:14, 18, 22]
33 a [Matt. 3:9]
34 a 2 Pet. 2:19
35 a Gal. 4:30
36 a Gal. 5:1
37 a John 7:19
38 a [John 3:32; 5:19, 30; 14:10, 24] *1* NU *heard from*
39 a Matt. 3:9 b [Rom. 2:28]
40 a John 8:37 b John 8:26
41 a Is. 63:16
42 a 1 John 5:1 b John 16:27; 17:8, 25 c Gal. 4:4
43 a [John 7:17]
44 a Matt. 13:38 b 1 John 2:16, 17 c [1 John 3:8–10, 15] d [Jude 6]
47 a 1 John 4:6
48 a John 7:20; 10:20

John 8:31, 32

Dear Woman of Destiny,

Although I was raised a "PK" (pastor's kid) and had a good relationship with my parents, it wasn't until I was sixteen years old that I settled into an absolute surrender of my life to Jesus Christ. At that time, I heard my heart speak so clearly it was as if I heard the audible voice of God. He spoke within my heart and mind, "Read your Bible daily, talk to Me daily," and "I have called you for My purposes." I had thought the Bible was boring before then. But as I read it each day, it became alive and relevant to me.

God's Word is the highest truth (see John 17:17). It is higher than the truth of man's own knowledge or feelings. Jesus said if we would continue in His Word we would come to know the highest truth that would set us free. We don't just receive the truth to set us free when we are saved. We must put His Word of truth in our lives daily. In order to be set free from any sin and change wrong behavior patterns, a person must put God's Word in her or his heart daily. We become free in areas of our lives we never realized we were suffering or bound in because of a lack of knowledge (see Hos. 4:6).

As time progressed, I began to hear men and women of God teach that "faith comes by hearing, and hearing by the word of God" (Rom. 10:17). I also began to realize that some preached words of doubt or uncertainty, and others preached the word of faith and certainty from the Holy Scriptures. We must guard our hearts from listening to nonfaith-building teaching. The reason for this is that our faith in God's Word is our victory to overcome the devil's thoughts and plans against our lives. Faith is also how we receive all of the promises of God.

God's Word shows us a standard of lifestyle different from those of the world around us. Romans 12:1, 2 says that we are to make a decisive dedication of our bodies to God. In order not to remain conformed to the world's ways, we are transformed or changed by renewing our minds to think according to the attitudes and thoughts of God's Word. The psalmist said that the way we keep from sinning is by taking heed to God's Word and hiding it in our hearts (see Ps. 119:9, 11). How do we hide God's Word in our hearts?

1. Reading (see Rev. 1:3)
2. Studying (see 2 Tim. 2:15)
3. Memorizing (see Ps. 119:11)
4. Meditating (see Ps. 1:1–3)
5. Speaking and doing (see Josh. 1:1–8)

When we believe and agree with His Word, God says it "shall not return to Me void, but it shall accomplish what I please, and it shall prosper in the thing for which I sent it" (Is. 55:11).

Sharon Daugherty

49 Jesus answered, "I do not have a demon; but I honor My Father, and [a]you
dishonor Me. 50 And [a]I do not seek My *own*
glory; there is One who seeks and judges.
51 Most assuredly, I say to you, [a]if anyone
keeps My word he shall never see death."
52 Then the Jews said to Him, "Now we
know that You [a]have a demon! [b]Abraham
is dead, and the prophets; and You say, 'If
anyone keeps My word he shall never taste
death.' 53 Are You greater than our father
Abraham, who is dead? And the prophets
are dead. [a]Who do You make Yourself out
to be?"
54 Jesus answered, [a]"If I honor Myself,
My honor is nothing. [b]It is My Father who
honors Me, of whom you say that He is
[1]your God. 55 Yet [a]you have not known
Him, but I know Him. And if I say, 'I do
not know Him,' I shall be a liar like you;
but I do know Him and [b]keep His word.
56 Your father Abraham [a]rejoiced to see
My day, [b]and he saw *it* and was glad."
57 Then the Jews said to Him, "You are
not yet fifty years old, and have You seen
Abraham?"
58 Jesus said to them, "Most assuredly, I
say to you, [a]before Abraham was, [b]I AM."
59 Then [a]they took up stones to throw at
Him; but Jesus hid Himself and went out
of the temple, [b]going[1] through the midst
of them, and so passed by.

A Man Born Blind Receives Sight

9 Now as *Jesus* passed by, He saw a man
who was blind from birth. 2 And His
disciples asked Him, saying, "Rabbi, [a]who
sinned, this man or his parents, that he
was born blind?"
3 Jesus answered, "Neither this man nor
his parents sinned, [a]but that the works of
God should be revealed in him. 4 [a]I[1] must
work the works of Him who sent Me while
it is [b]day; *the* night is coming when no
one can work. 5 As long as I am in the
world, [a]I am the light of the world."
6 When He had said these things, [a]He
spat on the ground and made clay with
the saliva; and He anointed the eyes of the
blind man with the clay. 7 And He said to
him, "Go, wash [a]in the pool of Siloam"
(which is translated, Sent). So [b]he went
and washed, and came back seeing.
8 Therefore the neighbors and those
who previously had seen that he was
[1]blind said, "Is not this he who sat and
begged?"

49 [a]John 5:41
50 [a]John 5:41; 7:18
51 [a]John 5:24; 11:26
52 [a]John 7:20; 10:20 [b]Zech. 1:5
53 [a]John 10:33; 19:7
54 [a]John 5:31, 32 [b]Acts 3:13 [1]NU, M *our*
55 [a]John 7:28, 29 [b][John 15:10]
56 [a]Luke 10:24 [b]Heb. 11:13
58 [a]Mic. 5:2 [b]Rev. 1:8
59 [a]John 10:31; 11:8 [b]Luke 4:30 [1]NU omits the rest of v. 59.

CHAPTER 9
2 [a]John 9:34
3 [a]John 11:4
4 [a][John 4:34; 5:19, 36; 17:4] [b]John 11:9, 10; 12:35 [1]NU *We*
5 [a][John 1:5, 9; 3:19; 8:12; 12:35, 46]
6 [a]Mark 7:33; 8:23
7 [a]Neh. 3:15 [b]2 Kin. 5:14
8 [1]NU *a beggar*
9 [1]NU *"No, but he is like him."*
11 [a]John 9:6, 7 [1]NU omits *the pool of*
16 [a]John 3:2; 9:33 [b]John 7:12, 43; 10:19 [1]*observe*
17 [a][John 4:19; 6:14]

9 Some said, "This is he." Others *said,*
[1]"He is like him."
He said, "I am *he.*"
10 Therefore they said to him, "How
were your eyes opened?"
11 He answered and said, [a]"A Man called
Jesus made clay and anointed my eyes and
said to me, 'Go to [1]the pool of Siloam and
wash.' So I went and washed, and I received sight."
12 Then they said to him, "Where
is He?"
He said, "I do not know."

The Pharisees Excommunicate the Healed Man

13 They brought him who formerly was
blind to the Pharisees. 14 Now it was a Sabbath when Jesus made the clay and
opened his eyes. 15 Then the Pharisees also
asked him again how he had received his
sight. He said to them, "He put clay on my
eyes, and I washed, and I see."
16 Therefore some of the Pharisees said,
"This Man is not from God, because He
does not [1]keep the Sabbath."
Others said, [a]"How can a man who is a
sinner do such signs?" And [b]there was a
division among them.
17 They said to the blind man again,
"What do you say about Him because He
opened your eyes?"
He said, [a]"He is a prophet."

Let us not look at the darkness that is growing continually deeper; but let us look upon the light that is shining brighter and brighter. Let us look on the works of God.

ZELMA ARGUE

18 But the Jews did not believe concerning him, that he had been blind and received his sight, until they called the
parents of him who had received his sight.
19 And they asked them, saying, "Is this
your son, who you say was born blind?
How then does he now see?"
20 His parents answered them and said,
"We know that this is our son, and that he

was born blind; 21but by what means he now sees we do not know, or who opened his eyes we do not know. He is of age; ask him. He will speak for himself." 22His parents said these *things* because [a]they feared the Jews, for the Jews had agreed already that if anyone confessed *that* He *was* Christ, he [b]would be put out of the synagogue. 23Therefore his parents said, "He is of age; ask him."

24So they again called the man who was blind, and said to him, [a]"Give God the glory! [b]We know that this Man is a sinner."

25He answered and said, "Whether He is a sinner *or not* I do not know. One thing I know: that though I was blind, now I see."

26Then they said to him again, "What did He do to you? How did He open your eyes?"

27He answered them, "I told you already, and you did not listen. Why do you want to hear *it* again? Do you also want to become His disciples?"

28Then they reviled him and said, "You are His disciple, but we are Moses' disciples. 29We know that God [a]spoke to [b]Moses; *as for* this *fellow,* [c]we do not know where He is from."

30The man answered and said to them, [a]"Why, this is a marvelous thing, that you do not know where He is from; yet He has opened my eyes! 31Now we know that [a]God does not hear sinners; but if anyone is a worshiper of God and does His will, He hears him. 32Since the world began it has been unheard of that anyone opened the eyes of one who was born blind. 33[a]If this Man were not from God, He could do nothing."

34They answered and said to him, [a]"You were completely born in sins, and are you teaching us?" And they [1]cast him out.

True Vision and True Blindness

35Jesus heard that they had cast him out; and when He had [a]found him, He said to him, "Do you [b]believe in [c]the Son of [1]God?"

36He answered and said, "Who is He, Lord, that I may believe in Him?"

37And Jesus said to him, "You have both seen Him and [a]it is He who is talking with you."

38Then he said, "Lord, I believe!" And he [a]worshiped Him.

39And Jesus said, [a]"For judgment I have come into this world, [b]that those who do not see may see, and that those who see may be made blind."

40Then *some* of the Pharisees who were with Him heard these words, [a]and said to Him, "Are we blind also?"

41Jesus said to them, [a]"If you were blind, you would have no sin; but now you say, 'We see.' Therefore your sin remains.

Jesus the True Shepherd

10 "Most assuredly, I say to you, he who does not enter the sheepfold by the door, but climbs up some other way, the same is a thief and a robber. 2But he who enters by the door is the shepherd of the sheep. 3To him the doorkeeper opens, and the sheep hear his voice; and he calls his own sheep by [a]name and leads them out. 4And when he brings out his own sheep, he goes before them; and the sheep follow him, for they know his voice. 5Yet they will by no means follow a [a]stranger, but will flee from him, for they do not know the voice of strangers." 6Jesus used this illustration, but they did not understand the things which He spoke to them.

Jesus the Good Shepherd

7Then Jesus said to them again, "Most assuredly, I say to you, I am the door of the sheep. 8All who *ever* came [1]before Me are thieves and robbers, but the sheep did not hear them. 9[a]I am the door. If anyone enters by Me, he will be saved, and will go in and out and find pasture. 10The thief does not come except to steal, and to kill, and to destroy. I have come that they may have life, and that they may have *it* more abundantly.

Thank You, Father God,
that Jesus came so that ____
may have life, and that
they may have it more
abundantly.
FROM JOHN 10:10

22 a Acts 5:13 b John 16:2
24 a Josh. 7:19 b John 9:16
29 a Num. 12:6–8 b [John 5:45–47] c John 7:27, 28; 8:14
30 a John 3:10
31 a Zech. 7:13
33 a John 3:2; 9:16
34 a John 9:2 1 Excommunicated him
35 a John 5:14 b John 1:7; 16:31 c Matt. 14:33; 16:16 1 NU *Man*
37 a John 4:26
38 a Matt. 8:2
39 a [John 3:17; 5:22, 27; 12:47] b Matt. 13:13; 15:14
40 a [Rom. 2:19]
41 a John 15:22, 24
CHAPTER 10
3 a John 20:16
5 a [2 Cor. 11:13–15]
8 1 M omits *before Me*
9 a [Eph. 2:18]

11 [a]"I am the good shepherd. The good
shepherd gives His life for the sheep.
12 But a [1]hireling, *he who is* not the shepherd, one who does not own the sheep,
sees the wolf coming and [a]leaves the
sheep and flees; and the wolf catches the
sheep and scatters them. 13 The hireling
flees because he is a hireling and does not
care about the sheep. 14 I am the good
shepherd; and [a]I know My *sheep,* and [b]am
known by My own. 15 [a]As the Father knows
Me, even so I know the Father; [b]and I lay
down My life for the sheep. 16 And [a]other
sheep I have which are not of this fold;
them also I must bring, and they will hear
My voice; [b]and there will be one flock *and*
one shepherd.
17 "Therefore My Father [a]loves Me, [b]be-
cause I lay down My life that I may take it
again. 18 No one takes it from Me, but I lay
it down of Myself. I [a]have power to lay it
down, and I have power to take it again.
[b]This command I have received from My
Father."
19 Therefore [a]there was a division again
among the Jews because of these sayings.
20 And many of them said, [a]"He has a demon and is [1]mad. Why do you listen to
Him?"
21 Others said, "These are not the words
of one who has a demon. [a]Can a demon
[b]open the eyes of the blind?"

The Shepherd Knows His Sheep

22 Now it was the Feast of Dedication in
Jerusalem, and it was winter. 23 And Jesus
walked in the temple, [a]in Solomon's
porch. 24 Then the Jews surrounded Him
and said to Him, "How long do You keep
us in [1]doubt? If You are the Christ, tell us
plainly."
25 Jesus answered them, "I told you, and
you do not believe. [a]The works that I do
in My Father's name, they [b]bear witness
of Me. 26 But [a]you do not believe, because
you are not of My sheep, [1]as I said to you.
27 [a]My sheep hear My voice, and I know
them, and they follow Me. 28 And I give
them eternal life, and they shall never
perish; neither shall anyone snatch them
out of My hand. 29 [a]My Father, [b]who has
given *them* to Me, is greater than all; and
no one is able to snatch *them* out of My
Father's hand. 30 [a]I and *My* Father are
one."

Renewed Efforts to Stone Jesus

31 Then [a]the Jews took up stones again
to stone Him. 32 Jesus answered them,
"Many good works I have shown you from
My Father. For which of those works do
you stone Me?"
33 The Jews answered Him, saying, "For
a good work we do not stone You, but for
[a]blasphemy, and because You, being a
Man, [b]make Yourself God."
34 Jesus answered them, "Is it not written in your law, [a]*'I said, "You are gods"'*?
35 If He called them gods, [a]to whom the
word of God came (and the Scripture
[b]cannot be broken), 36 do you say of Him
[a]whom the Father sanctified and [b]sent
into the world, 'You are blaspheming,'
[c]because I said, 'I am [d]the Son of God'?
37 [a]If I do not do the works of My Father,
do not believe Me; 38 but if I do, though
you do not believe Me, [a]believe the works,
that you may know and [1]believe [b]that the
Father *is* in Me, and I in Him." 39 [a]There-
fore they sought again to seize Him, but
He escaped out of their hand.

The Believers Beyond Jordan

40 And He went away again beyond the
Jordan to the place [a]where John was baptizing at first, and there He stayed. 41 Then
many came to Him and said, "John performed no sign, [a]but all the things that
John spoke about this Man were true."
42 And many believed in Him there.

The Death of Lazarus

11 Now a certain *man* was sick, Lazarus of Bethany, the town of [a]Mary
and her sister Martha. 2 [a]It was *that* Mary
who anointed the Lord with fragrant oil
and wiped His feet with her hair, whose
brother Lazarus was sick. 3 Therefore the
sisters sent to Him, saying, "Lord, behold,
he whom You love is sick."
4 When Jesus heard *that,* He said, "This
sickness is not unto death, but for the glory of God, that the Son of God may be
glorified through it."
5 Now Jesus loved Martha and her sister
and Lazarus. 6 So, when He heard that he
was sick, [a]He stayed two more days in the
place where He was. 7 Then after this He

11 a Is. 40:11
12 a Zech. 11:16, 17 · *1 hired man*
14 a 2 Tim. 2:19 · b 2 Tim. 1:12
15 a Matt. 11:27 · b [John 15:13; 19:30]
16 a Is. 42:6; 56:8 · b Eph. 2:13–18
17 a John 5:20 · b [Heb. 2:9]
18 a [John 2:19; 5:26] · b [John 6:38; 14:31; 17:4; Acts 2:24, 32]
19 a John 7:43; 9:16
20 a John 7:20 · *1 insane*
21 a [Ex. 4:11] · b John 9:6, 7, 32, 33
23 a Acts 3:11; 5:12
24 *1* Suspense
25 a John 5:36; 10:38 · b Matt. 11:4
26 a [John 8:47] · *1* NU omits *as I said to you*
27 a John 10:4, 14
29 a John 14:28 · b [John 17:2, 6, 12, 24]
30 a John 17:11, 21–24
31 a John 8:59
33 a Matt. 9:3 · b John 5:18
34 a Ps. 82:6
35 a Matt. 5:17, 18 · b 1 Pet. 1:25
36 a John 6:27 · b John 3:17 · c John 5:17, 18 · d Luke 1:35
37 a John 10:25; 15:24
38 a John 5:36 · b John 14:10, 11 · *1* NU *understand*
39 a John 7:30, 44
40 a John 1:28
41 a [John 1:29, 36; 3:28–36; 5:33]

CHAPTER 11 **1** a Luke 10:38, 39 · **2** a Matt. 26:7 · **6** a John 10:40

said to *the* disciples, "Let us go to Judea again."

8 *The* disciples said to Him, "Rabbi, lately the Jews sought to [a]stone You, and are You going there again?"

9 Jesus answered, "Are there not twelve hours in the day? [a]If anyone walks in the day, he does not stumble, because he sees the [b]light of this world. 10 But [a]if one walks in the night, he stumbles, because the light is not in him." 11 These things He said, and after that He said to them, "Our friend Lazarus [a]sleeps, but I go that I may wake him up."

12 Then His disciples said, "Lord, if he sleeps he will get well." 13 However, Jesus spoke of his death, but they thought that He was speaking about taking rest in sleep.

14 Then Jesus said to them plainly, "Lazarus is dead. 15 And I am glad for your sakes that I was not there, that you may believe. Nevertheless let us go to him."

16 Then [a]Thomas, who is called the Twin, said to his fellow disciples, "Let us also go, that we may die with Him."

I Am the Resurrection and the Life

17 So when Jesus came, He found that he had already been in the tomb four days. 18 Now Bethany was near Jerusalem, about [1]two miles away. 19 And many of the Jews had joined the women around Martha and Mary, to comfort them concerning their brother.

20 Now Martha, as soon as she heard that Jesus was coming, went and met Him, but Mary was sitting in the house. 21 Now Martha said to Jesus, "Lord, if You had been here, my brother would not have died. 22 But even now I know that [a]whatever You ask of God, God will give You."

23 Jesus said to her, "Your brother will rise again."

24 Martha said to Him, [a]"I know that he will rise again in the resurrection at the last day."

25 Jesus said to her, "I am [a]the resurrection and the life. [b]He who believes in Me, though he may [c]die, he shall live. 26 And whoever lives and believes in Me shall never die. Do you believe this?"

27 She said to Him, "Yes, Lord, [a]I believe that You are the Christ, the Son of God, who is to come into the world."

Jesus and Death, the Last Enemy

28 And when she had said these things, she went her way and secretly called Mary her sister, saying, "The Teacher has come and is calling for you." 29 As soon as she heard *that,* she arose quickly and came to Him. 30 Now Jesus had not yet come into the town, but [1]was in the place where Martha met Him. 31 [a]Then the Jews who were with her in the house, and comforting her, when they saw that Mary rose up quickly and went out, followed her, [1]saying, "She is going to the tomb to weep there."

32 Then, when Mary came where Jesus was, and saw Him, she [a]fell down at His feet, saying to Him, [b]"Lord, if You had been here, my brother would not have died."

33 Therefore, when Jesus saw her weeping, and the Jews who came with her weeping, He groaned in the spirit and was troubled. 34 And He said, "Where have you laid him?"

They said to Him, "Lord, come and see."

35 [a]Jesus wept. 36 Then the Jews said, "See how He loved him!"

37 And some of them said, "Could not this Man, [a]who opened the eyes of the blind, also have kept this man from dying?"

Lazarus Raised from the Dead

38 Then Jesus, again groaning in Himself, came to the tomb. It was a cave, and a [a]stone lay against it. 39 Jesus said, "Take away the stone."

Martha, the sister of him who was dead, said to Him, "Lord, by this time there is a stench, for he has been *dead* four days."

40 Jesus said to her, "Did I not say to you that if you would believe you would [a]see the glory of God?" 41 Then they took away the stone [1]*from the place* where the dead man was lying. And Jesus lifted up *His* eyes and said, "Father, I thank You that You have heard Me. 42 And I know that You always hear Me, but [a]because of the people who are standing by I said *this,* that they may believe that You sent Me." 43 Now when He had said these things, He cried with a loud voice, "Lazarus, come forth!" 44 And he who had died came out bound hand and foot with [a]graveclothes,

8 [a]John 8:59; 10:31
9 [a]John 9:4; 12:35 [b]Is. 9:2
10 [a]John 12:35
11 [a]Matt. 9:24
16 [a]John 14:5; 20:26–28
18 [1]Lit. *15 stadia*
22 [a][John 9:31; 11:41]
24 [a][John 5:29]
25 [a]John 5:21; 6:39, 40, 44 [b]1 John 5:10 [c]1 Cor. 15:22
27 [a]Matt. 16:16
30 [1]NU *was still*
31 [a]John 11:19, 33 [1]NU *supposing that she was going*
32 [a]Rev. 1:17 [b]John 11:21
35 [a]Luke 19:41
37 [a]John 9:6, 7
38 [a]Matt. 27:60, 66
40 [a][John 11:4, 23]
41 [1]NU omits *from the place where the dead man was lying*
42 [a]John 12:30; 17:21
44 [a]John 19:40

John 11:25

Dear Woman of Destiny,

When we think of the resurrection of Jesus Christ, we are reminded of His great sacrifice and love. We are reminded of the words in 1 John 3:8: "For this purpose the Son of God was manifested, that He might destroy the works of the devil."

Friends, think about the full impact of these words coupled with Jesus' actions, of dying but then rising from the dead. That which was dead is now alive—the implications are powerful.

Resurrection is only needed if something is dead. As a woman, many times there is the feeling of being trapped in life. You discover that you are trapped by circumstances, trapped by a lack of finances, or trapped because of a lack of love. Then because of that sense of being trapped, many things seem to "die" inside your heart. Even though you cannot put your finger on the emotions you are going through, still they are felt; and they impact your outlook on life, eating you up on the inside. Ultimately, you cry out, "Oh God, is there any hope?"

Today, the words of Jesus in John 11:25 should cause faith to arise in your spirit. The Holy Spirit is saying to you right now, "Arise, Woman of Destiny, for that which was dead can live again." The resurrection of Jesus is proof that dead things can have life returned to them.

In the Old Testament, we see Ezekiel standing in the valley of dry, dead bones. God asked the ultimate question: "Can these bones live?" (Ezek. 37:3). Ezekiel had the right answer—a nonanswer! "You know," was his only reply to the Omnipotent God. As a test of Ezekiel's faith and a sign of His own power, God instructed the prophet, "Prophesy to these bones" (v. 4). Ezekiel needed to get his eyes off of what seemed to be reality—all those dry, dead bones. For the moment, Ezekiel began to see the situation through God's eyes. He was then freed to act upon the word of the Lord—and things began to change.

This same faith should begin to arise in your spirit right now for your own personal situation. God is speaking a word into your spirit through the resurrection of Jesus. He is saying to you, "All of your dreams that have died, your marriage that seems to have lost its spark and excitement, your hope for joy and fulfillment—they can live again. Where you have lost hope for things passing through the valley of death, allow His resurrection power to begin to flow with revived hope.

Jesus' resurrection tells you even your vision and your ministry that you have buried can be resurrected again. Believe it! All of your days, all of your future will never be the same, because of the fresh awareness of the power of His resurrection.

Today, right now, Jesus is saying to you, "I am the resurrection and the life. That which was dead, shall live again." Therefore, I say to you, in the authority of Jesus' resurrection power, "Be healed, be restored, and reclaim your God-given destiny."

Naomi Dowdy

and [b]his face was wrapped with a cloth.
Jesus said to them, "Loose him, and let
him go."

The Plot to Kill Jesus

45Then many of the Jews who had come
to Mary, [a]and had seen the things Jesus
did, believed in Him. 46But some of them
went away to the Pharisees and [a]told
them the things Jesus did. 47[a]Then the
chief priests and the Pharisees gathered a
council and said, [b]"What shall we do? For
this Man works many signs. 48If we let
Him alone like this, everyone will believe
in Him, and the Romans will come and
take away both our place and nation."
49And one of them, [a]Caiaphas, being
high priest that year, said to them, "You
know nothing at all, 50[a]nor do you consider that it is expedient for [1]us that one man
should die for the people, and not that the
whole nation should perish." 51Now this
he did not say on his own *authority;* but
being high priest that year he prophesied
that Jesus would die for the nation, 52and
[a]not for that nation only, but [b]also that
He would gather together in one the children of God who were scattered abroad.
53Then, from that day on, they plotted
to [a]put Him to death. 54[a]Therefore Jesus
no longer walked openly among the Jews,
but went from there into the country near
the wilderness, to a city called [b]Ephraim,
and there remained with His disciples.
55[a]And the Passover of the Jews was
near, and many went from the country up
to Jerusalem before the Passover, to [b]pu-
rify themselves. 56[a]Then they sought Jesus, and spoke among themselves as they
stood in the temple, "What do you
think—that He will not come to the
feast?" 57Now both the chief priests and
the Pharisees had given a command, that
if anyone knew where He was, he should
report *it,* that they might [a]seize Him.

The Anointing at Bethany

12 Then, six days before the Passover, Jesus came to Bethany,
[a]where Lazarus was [1]who had been dead,
whom He had raised from the dead.
2[a]There they made Him a supper; and
Martha served, but Lazarus was one of
those who sat at the table with Him.
3Then [a]Mary took a pound of very costly
oil of [b]spikenard, anointed the feet of Jesus, and wiped His feet with her hair. And
the house was filled with the fragrance of
the oil.
4But one of His disciples, [a]Judas Iscariot, Simon's *son,* who would betray Him,
said, 5"Why was this fragrant oil not sold
for [1]three hundred denarii and given to
the poor?" 6This he said, not that he cared
for the poor, but because he was a thief,
and [a]had the money box; and he used to
take what was put in it.
7But Jesus said, "Let her alone; [1]she has
kept this for the day of My burial. 8For
[a]the poor you have with you always, but
Me you do not have always."

The Plot to Kill Lazarus

9Now a great many of the Jews knew
that He was there; and they came, not for
Jesus' sake only, but that they might also
see Lazarus, [a]whom He had raised from
the dead. 10[a]But the chief priests plotted
to put Lazarus to death also, 11[a]because
on account of him many of the Jews went
away and believed in Jesus.

The Triumphal Entry

12[a]The next day a great multitude that
had come to the feast, when they heard
that Jesus was coming to Jerusalem,
13took branches of palm trees and went
out to meet Him, and cried out:

"Hosanna!
[a]*'Blessed is He who comes in the*
name of the LORD!'
The King of Israel!"

14[a]Then Jesus, when He had found a
young donkey, sat on it; as it is written:

15 *"Fear[a] not, daughter of Zion;*
Behold, your King is coming,
Sitting on a donkey's colt."

16[a]His disciples did not understand
these things at first; [b]but when Jesus was
glorified, [c]then they remembered that
these things were written about Him and
that they had done these things to Him.
17Therefore the people, who were with
Him when He called Lazarus out of his
tomb and raised him from the dead, bore
witness. 18[a]For this reason the people also
met Him, because they heard that He had
done this sign. 19The Pharisees therefore
said among themselves, [a]"You see that
you are accomplishing nothing. Look, the
world has gone after Him!"

---

44 b John 20:7
45 a John 2:23; 10:42; 12:11, 18
46 a John 5:15
47 a Ps. 2:2 b Acts 4:16
49 a Luke 3:2
50 a John 18:14 1 NU *you*
52 a Is. 49:6 b [Eph. 2:14–17]
53 a Matt. 26:4
54 a John 4:1, 3; 7:1 b 2 Chr. 13:19
55 a John 2:13; 5:1; 6:4 b Num. 9:10, 13; 31:19, 20
56 a John 7:11
57 a Matt. 26:14–16

CHAPTER 12
1 a John 11:1, 43 1 NU omits *who had been dead*
2 a Mark 14:3; Luke 10:38–41
3 a John 11:2 b Song 1:12
4 a John 13:26
5 1 About one year's wages for a worker
6 a John 13:29
7 1 NU *that she may keep*
8 a Mark 14:7
9 a John 11:43, 44
10 a Luke 16:31
11 a John 11:45; 12:18
12 a Matt. 21:4–9
13 a Ps. 118:25, 26
14 a Matt. 21:7
15 a Zech. 9:9
16 a Luke 18:34 b John 7:39; 12:23 c [John 14:26]
18 a John 12:11
19 a John 11:47, 48

JOHN 12:1–7

Dear Woman of Destiny:

There is nothing more intriguing and victorious than a woman who truly knows how to worship. You can almost tell by looking at her that she has been in the presence of the Lord. She is unstoppable, no matter what is thrown her way. She has an uncanny knack for transcending all of the things that attempt to hinder her. In spite of the obstacles, she continues to give God what He is worthy of. She understands that we worship Him because of who He is, not because of who we are.

Let's look for a moment at Mary of Bethany. In John 12:1–7, we see her sacrifice was one of full abandon. It cost her much money; nevertheless, she gave it willingly—denying herself and fully surrendering those things she cherished most to the One she loved the most.

Among the group gathered in the house at Bethany that day was Judas, who missed the point of the lavish worship Mary poured out upon Jesus. Unlike Judas, who later betrayed Jesus, Mary possessed a loyal and devoted love for Him that could not be bought or sold. While it was true the ointment she used could have been sold and the money given to the poor, it served a greater mission—that of showing love and affection to her beloved Jesus and of preparing His body for burial. By this act, she was making a profound statement: Nothing is too good, nothing is too costly for my Savior.

Sometimes it is difficult to really let go and worship the Lord if we are afraid our actions may be criticized or ridiculed by others. The lesson we learn from Mary is that we are not to allow our fear or pride (wanting to be well thought of and respected by others) to stop us from worshiping the Lord the way He deserves. We must not allow anything to become an idol before the Lord.

Hear this, my sister: Whatever stops us from worshiping God, whether we realize it or not, has become an idol because it has become more important to us than He is. Mary's sacrifice should challenge us to give everything that we have in worship to the Lord. I challenge you to begin thinking about what you can sacrifice and to surrender whatever is more dear to you than Jesus. Since the days of burnt offerings, God has smiled on and lovingly received the sacrifices of a heart that loves Him. In spite of what it might cost us, Woman of Destiny, let us all seek to please Him in such a manner.

Judith Christie-McAllister

The Fruitful Grain of Wheat

[20]Now there [a]were certain Greeks among those [b]who came up to worship at the feast. [21]Then they came to Philip, [a]who was from Bethsaida of Galilee, and asked him, saying, "Sir, we wish to see Jesus."

[22]Philip came and told Andrew, and in turn Andrew and Philip told Jesus.

[23]But Jesus answered them, saying, [a]"The hour has come that the Son of Man should be glorified. [24]Most assuredly, I say to you, [a]unless a grain of wheat falls into the ground and dies, it remains alone; but if it dies, it produces much [1]grain. [25][a]He who loves his life will lose it, and he who hates his life in this world will keep it for eternal life. [26]If anyone serves Me, let him [a]follow Me; and [b]where I am, there My servant will be also. If anyone serves Me, him *My* Father will honor.

Jesus Predicts His Death on the Cross

[27][a]"Now My soul is troubled, and what shall I say? 'Father, save Me from this hour'? [b]But for this purpose I came to this hour. [28]Father, glorify Your name."

[a]Then a voice came from heaven, *saying,* "I have both glorified *it* and will glorify *it* again."

[29]Therefore the people who stood by and heard *it* said that it had thundered. Others said, "An angel has spoken to Him."

[30]Jesus answered and said, [a]"This voice did not come because of Me, but for your sake. [31]Now is the judgment of this world; now [a]the ruler of this world will be cast out. [32]And I, [a]if I am [1]lifted up from the earth, will draw [b]all *peoples* to Myself." [33][a]This He said, signifying by what death He would die.

[34]The people answered Him, [a]"We have heard from the law that the Christ remains forever; and how *can* You say, 'The Son of Man must be lifted up'? Who is this Son of Man?"

[35]Then Jesus said to them, "A little while longer [a]the light is with you. [b]Walk while you have the light, lest darkness overtake you; [c]he who walks in darkness does not know where he is going. [36]While you have the light, believe in the light, that you may become [a]sons of light." These things Jesus spoke, and departed, and [b]was hidden from them.

Who Has Believed Our Report?

[37]But although He had done so many [a]signs before them, they did not believe in Him, [38]that the word of Isaiah the prophet might be fulfilled, which he spoke:

> [a]*"Lord, who has believed our report?*
> *And to whom has the arm of the*
> *LORD been revealed?"*

[39]Therefore they could not believe, because Isaiah said again:

> [40] *"He[a] has blinded their eyes and*
> *hardened their hearts,*
> [b]*Lest they should see with their*
> *eyes,*
> *Lest they should understand with*
> *their hearts and turn,*
> *So that I should heal them."*

[41][a]These things Isaiah said [1]when he saw His glory and spoke of Him.

Walk in the Light

[42]Nevertheless even among the rulers many believed in Him, but [a]because of the Pharisees they did not confess *Him,* lest they should be put out of the synagogue; [43][a]for they loved the praise of men more than the praise of God.

[44]Then Jesus cried out and said, [a]"He who believes in Me, [b]believes not in Me [c]but in Him who sent Me. [45]And [a]he who sees Me sees Him who sent Me. [46][a]I have come *as* a light into the world, that whoever believes in Me should not abide in darkness. [47]And if anyone hears My words and does not [1]believe, [a]I do not judge him; for [b]I did not come to judge the world but to save the world. [48][a]He who rejects Me, and does not receive My words, has that which judges him—[b]the word that I have spoken will judge him in the last day. [49]For [a]I have not spoken on My own *authority;* but the Father who sent Me gave Me a command, [b]what I should say and what I should speak. [50]And I know that His command is everlasting life. Therefore, whatever I speak, just as the Father has told Me, so I [a]speak."

---

20 a Acts 17:4 b 1 Kin. 8:41, 42
21 a John 1:43, 44; 14:8–11
23 a John 13:32
24 a 1 Cor. 15:36 *1* Lit. *fruit*
25 a Mark 8:35
26 a [Matt. 16:24] b John 14:3; 17:24
27 a [Matt. 26:38, 39] b Luke 22:53
28 a Matt. 3:17; 17:5
30 a John 11:42
31 a [2 Cor. 4:4]
32 a John 3:14; 8:28 b [Rom. 5:18] *1* Crucified
33 a John 18:32; 21:19
34 a Mic. 4:7
35 a [John 1:9; 7:33; 8:12] b Eph. 5:8 c [1 John 2:9–11]
36 a Luke 16:8 b John 8:59
37 a John 11:47
38 a Is. 53:1
40 a Is. 6:9, 10 b Matt. 13:14
41 a Is. 6:1 *1* NU *because*
42 a John 7:13; 9:22
43 a John 5:41, 44
44 a Mark 9:37 b [John 3:16, 18, 36; 11:25, 26] c [John 5:24]
45 a [John 14:9]
46 a John 1:4, 5; 8:12; 12:35, 36
47 a John 5:45 b John 3:17 *1* NU *keep them*
48 a [Luke 10:16] b Deut. 18:18, 19
49 a John 8:38 b Deut. 18:18
50 a John 5:19; 8:28

Jesus Washes the Disciples' Feet

13 Now [a]before the Feast of the Passover, when Jesus knew that [b]His hour had come that He should depart from this world to the Father, having loved His own who were in the world, He [c]loved them to the end.

2 And [1]supper being ended, [a]the devil having already put it into the heart of Judas Iscariot, Simon's *son,* to betray Him, 3 Jesus, knowing [a]that the Father had given all things into His hands, and that He [b]had come from God and [c]was going to God, 4 [a]rose from supper and laid aside His garments, took a towel and girded Himself. 5 After that, He poured water into a basin and began to wash the disciples' feet, and to wipe *them* with the towel with which He was girded. 6 Then He came to Simon Peter. And *Peter* said to Him, [a]"Lord, are You washing my feet?"

7 Jesus answered and said to him, "What I am doing you [a]do not understand now, [b]but you will know after this."

8 Peter said to Him, "You shall never wash my feet!"

Jesus answered him, [a]"If I do not wash you, you have no part with Me."

9 Simon Peter said to Him, "Lord, not my feet only, but also *my* hands and *my* head!"

10 Jesus said to him, "He who is bathed needs only to wash *his* feet, but is completely clean; and [a]you are clean, but not all of you." 11 For [a]He knew who would betray Him; therefore He said, "You are not all clean."

12 So when He had washed their feet, taken His garments, and sat down again, He said to them, "Do you [1]know what I have done to you? 13 [a]You call Me Teacher and Lord, and you say well, for *so* I am. 14 [a]If I then, *your* Lord and Teacher, have washed your feet, [b]you also ought to wash one another's feet. 15 For [a]I have given you an example, that you should do as I have done to you. 16 [a]Most assuredly, I say to you, a servant is not greater than his master; nor is he who is sent greater than he who sent him. 17 [a]If you know these things, blessed are you if you do them.

Jesus Identifies His Betrayer

18 "I do not speak concerning all of you. I know whom I have chosen; but that the [a]Scripture may be fulfilled, [b]'*He who eats* [1]*bread with Me has lifted up his heel against Me.'* 19 [a]Now I tell you before it comes, that when it does come to pass, you may believe that I am *He.* 20 [a]Most assuredly, I say to you, he who receives whomever I send receives Me; and he who receives Me receives Him who sent Me."

21 [a]When Jesus had said these things, [b]He was troubled in spirit, and testified and said, "Most assuredly, I say to you, [c]one of you will betray Me." 22 Then the disciples looked at one another, perplexed about whom He spoke.

23 Now [a]there was [1]leaning on Jesus' bosom one of His disciples, whom Jesus loved. 24 Simon Peter therefore motioned to him to ask who it was of whom He spoke.

25 Then, leaning [1]back on Jesus' breast, he said to Him, "Lord, who is it?"

26 Jesus answered, "It is he to whom I shall give a piece of bread when I have dipped *it.*" And having dipped the bread, He gave *it* to [a]Judas Iscariot, *the son* of Simon. 27 [a]Now after the piece of bread, Satan entered him. Then Jesus said to him, "What you do, do quickly." 28 But no one at the table knew for what reason He said this to him. 29 For some thought, because [a]Judas had the money box, that Jesus had said to him, "Buy *those things* we need for the feast," or that he should give something to the poor.

30 Having received the piece of bread, he then went out immediately. And it was night.

The New Commandment

31 So, when he had gone out, Jesus said, [a]"Now the Son of Man is glorified, and [b]God is glorified in Him. 32 If God is glorified in Him, God will also glorify Him in Himself, and [a]glorify Him immediately. 33 Little children, I shall be with you a [a]little while longer. You will seek Me; [b]and as I said to the Jews, 'Where I am going, you

Precious Savior, may ___ love others as You have loved them.

FROM JOHN 13:34

CHAPTER 13
1 a Matt. 26:2 b John 12:23; 17:1 c John 15:9
2 a Luke 22:3 *1 NU during supper*
3 a Acts 2:36 b John 8:42; 16:28 c John 17:11; 20:17
4 a [Luke 22:27]
6 a Matt. 3:14
7 a John 12:16; 16:12 b John 13:19
8 a [1 Cor. 6:11]
10 a [John 15:3]
11 a John 6:64; 18:4
12 *1 understand*
13 a Matt. 23:8, 10
14 a Luke 22:27 b [Rom. 12:10]
15 a [1 Pet. 2:21–24]
16 a Matt. 10:24
17 a [James 1:25]
18 a John 15:25; 17:12 b Ps. 41:9 *1 NU My bread has*
19 a John 14:29; 16:4
20 a Matt. 10:40
21 a Luke 22:21 b John 12:27 c 1 John 2:19
23 a John 19:26; 20:2; 21:7, 20 *1 reclining*
25 *1 NU, M add thus*
26 a John 6:70, 71; 12:4
27 a Luke 22:3
29 a John 12:6
31 a John 12:23 b [1 Pet. 4:11]
32 a John 12:23
33 a John 12:35; 14:19; 16:16–19 b [John 7:34; 8:21]

cannot come,' so now I say to you. 34[a]A
new commandment I give to you, that you
love one another; as I have loved you, that
you also love one another. 35[a]By this all
will know that you are My disciples, if you
have love for one another."

Jesus Predicts Peter's Denial

36Simon Peter said to Him, "Lord,
where are You going?"

Jesus answered him, "Where I [a]am going you cannot follow Me now, but [b]you
shall follow Me afterward."

37Peter said to Him, "Lord, why can I
not follow You now? I will [a]lay down my
life for Your sake."

38Jesus answered him, "Will you lay
down your life for My sake? Most assuredly, I say to you, the rooster shall not [a]crow
till you have denied Me three times.

The Way, the Truth, and the Life

14 "Let [a]not your heart be troubled;
you believe in God, believe also in
Me. 2In My Father's house are many
[1]mansions; if *it were* not *so*, [2]I would have
told you. [a]I go to prepare a place for you.
3And if I go and prepare a place for you, [a]I
will come again and receive you to Myself;
that [b]where I am, *there* you may be also.
4And where I go you know, and the way
you know."

5[a]Thomas said to Him, "Lord, we do not
know where You are going, and how can
we know the way?"

6Jesus said to him, "I am [a]the way, [b]the
truth, and [c]the life. [d]No one comes to the
Father [e]except through Me.

Lord Jesus, may ____ know that You are the way, the truth, and the life; for no one comes to the Father except through You.

FROM JOHN 14:6

The Father Revealed

7[a]"If you had known Me, you would
have known My Father also; and from now
on you know Him and have seen Him."

34 a 1 Thess. 4:9
35 a 1 John 2:5
36 a John 13:33; 14:2; 16:5 b 2 Pet. 1:14
37 a Mark 14:29–31
38 a John 18:25–27

CHAPTER 14
1 a [John 14:27; 16:22, 24]
2 a John 13:33, 36 *1* Lit. *dwellings* *2* NU *would I have told you that I go* or *I would have told you; for I go*
3 a [Acts 1:11] b [John 12:26]
5 a Matt. 10:3
6 a [Heb. 9:8; 10:19, 20] b [John 1:14, 17; 8:32; 18:37] c [John 11:25] d 1 Tim. 2:5 e [John 10:7–9]
7 a John 8:19
9 a Col. 1:15
10 a John 10:38; 14:11, 20 b John 5:19; 14:24
11 a John 5:36; 10:38
12 a Luke 10:17
13 a Matt. 7:7 b John 13:31
14 *1* NU *ask Me*
15 a 1 John 5:3 *1* NU *you will keep*
16 a Rom. 8:15 *1 Comforter,* Gr. *Parakletos*
17 a [1 John 4:6; 5:7] b [1 Cor. 2:14]

8Philip said to Him, "Lord, show us the
Father, and it is sufficient for us."

9Jesus said to him, "Have I been with
you so long, and yet you have not known
Me, Philip? [a]He who has seen Me has seen
the Father; so how can you say, 'Show us
the Father'? 10Do you not believe that [a]I
am in the Father, and the Father in Me?
The words that I speak to you [b]I do not
speak on My own *authority;* but the Father who dwells in Me does the works.
11Believe Me that I *am* in the Father and
the Father in Me, [a]or else believe Me for
the sake of the works themselves.

Remain in peace. Move only when Jesus does. In Jesus there is life, and He must give life to every living thing.

MADAME JEANNE GUYON

The Answered Prayer

12[a]"Most assuredly, I say to you, he who
believes in Me, the works that I do he will
do also; and greater *works* than these he
will do, because I go to My Father. 13[a]And
whatever you ask in My name, that I will
do, that the Father may be [b]glorified in
the Son. 14If you [1]ask anything in My
name, I will do *it*.

We can do nothing without the Holy Spirit.

EVAN ROBERTS

Jesus Promises Another Helper

15[a]"If you love Me, [1]keep My commandments. 16 And I will pray the Father, and
[a]He will give you another [1]Helper, that
He may abide with you forever— 17[a]the
Spirit of truth, [b]whom the world cannot

JOHN 14:16

Dear Woman of Destiny,

In over twenty years of full-time ministry (not to mention fifty years of just plain life), I have come to value the gift of true comfort. I have known my share of tragedy and hurt, and with it, deep mourning and despair. I admit to periods of self-pity and complaining. There have been many times when I have cried with the psalmist, "My eyes fail from searching Your word, saying, 'When will You comfort me?'" (Ps. 119:82).

Aloneness does not help in these times. Isolation sharpens the grief and loss. Often, on these occasions, I have thought about the disciples and, with some envy, recalled that they had the comfort of Jesus' physical presence. They walked with Him day by day. They held fast to Him as circumstances grew more frightening. On stormy seas, He calmed the waters. When sickness prevailed, He healed. His words held a power they could not understand. His hands demonstrated that same power. His ways were mysterious, not of their world. They couldn't control Him, direct Him, or predict Him. But with great relief and passion, they came to trust and rely on Him. They eagerly embraced all He stood for, believing in His power, and loving Him and the Father He revealed, even to their very death.

When Jesus began to speak to them about leaving them, they couldn't accept it. They could not imagine life without Him. And Jesus knew their hearts. He knew they could not live without Him. He knew they were still like little children, that when He had ascended to the Father they would need Him and His comfort again, and again, and again. And so He said, "And I will pray the Father, and He will give you another Helper [KJV, "Comforter"], that He may abide with you forever" (John 14:16).

Another Comforter. "Another" means "One like Me." Jesus was about to introduce them to another "like Himself" who had the same ability, compassion, and power to overcome the world. They had to learn to walk all over again, this time with the Holy Spirit.

You and I must learn that same lesson. We cannot see the Holy Spirit with our natural eyes, as the disciples saw Jesus. He cannot physically hold us as Jesus did. His voice doesn't fill the room with comforting resonance when we are so in need. We have to learn to walk with Him in another way. We have to learn to trust and rely on the Holy Spirit and remember that He is another like Jesus, just as Jesus promised.

Just as the disciples learned to trust the quiet wisdom of the stranger from Galilee, we must learn to trust the quiet voice of the Holy Spirit. He will not always tell us what we want to hear. He may move in ways we do not expect. He will not be controlled or manipulated. But He will help, and He will comfort and quiet the raging storms of our lives and guide us into all truth. His comfort is vital to our survival. We always have a choice, each day, between living life and living death. Remember, "It is the Spirit who gives life" (John 6:63a). Choose life!

Lora Allison

receive, because it neither sees Him nor knows Him; but you know Him, for He dwells with you [c]and will be in you. 18[a]I will not leave you orphans; [b]I will come to you.

Lord Jesus, You are the vine and we are the branches. May ____ abide in You and bear much fruit, for without You they can do nothing.

FROM JOHN 15:5

Indwelling of the Father and the Son

19"A little while longer and the world will see Me no more, but [a]you will see Me. [b]Because I live, you will live also. 20At that day you will know that [a]I *am* in My Father, and you in Me, and I in you. 21[a]He who has My commandments and keeps them, it is he who loves Me. And he who loves Me will be loved by My Father, and I will love him and [1]manifest Myself to him."

22[a]Judas (not Iscariot) said to Him, "Lord, how is it that You will manifest Yourself to us, and not to the world?"

23Jesus answered and said to him, "If anyone loves Me, he will keep My word; and My Father will love him, [a]and We will come to him and make Our home with him. 24He who does not love Me does not keep My words; and [a]the word which you hear is not Mine but the Father's who sent Me.

The Gift of His Peace

25"These things I have spoken to you while being present with you. 26But [a]the [1]Helper, the Holy Spirit, whom the Father will [b]send in My name, [c]He will teach you all things, and bring to your [d]remembrance all things that I said to you. 27[a]Peace I leave with you, My peace I give to you; not as the world gives do I give to you. Let not your heart be troubled, neither let it be afraid. 28You have heard Me [a]say to you, 'I am going away and coming *back* to you.' If you loved Me, you would rejoice because [1]I said, [b]'I am going to the Father,' for [c]My Father is greater than I.

29"And [a]now I have told you before it comes, that when it does come to pass, you may believe. 30I will no longer talk much with you, [a]for the ruler of this world is coming, and he has [b]nothing in Me. 31But that the world may know that I love the Father, and [a]as the Father gave Me commandment, so I do. Arise, let us go from here.

The True Vine

15 "I am the true vine, and My Father is the vinedresser. 2[a]Every branch in Me that does not bear fruit He [1]takes away; and every *branch* that bears fruit He prunes, that it may bear [b]more fruit. 3[a]You are already clean because of the word which I have spoken to you. 4[a]Abide in Me, and I in you. As the branch cannot bear fruit of itself, unless it abides in the vine, neither can you, unless you abide in Me.

Our Lord, the beauty of our Lord and His Righteousness—these are our priestly garments. Without that clothing we have no priestly rights, powers or virtues whatsoever. It is just another illustration of "Without Me you can do nothing," be nothing too.

AMY CARMICHAEL

5"I am the vine, you *are* the branches. He who abides in Me, and I in him, bears much [a]fruit; for without Me you can do [b]nothing. 6If anyone does not abide in Me, [a]he is cast out as a branch and is withered; and they gather them and throw *them* into the fire, and they are burned. 7If you abide in Me, and My words [a]abide in you, [b]you[1] will ask what you desire, and it shall be done for you. 8[a]By this My Father is

17 c [1 John 2:27]
18 a [Matt. 28:20] b [John 14:3, 28]
19 a John 16:16, 22 b [1 Cor. 15:20]
20 a John 10:38; 14:11
21 a 1 John 2:5 *1 reveal*
22 a Luke 6:16
23 a Rev. 3:20; 21:3
24 a John 5:19
26 a Luke 24:49 b John 15:26 c 1 Cor. 2:13 d John 2:22; 12:16 *1 Comforter, Gr. Parakletos*
27 a [Phil. 4:7]
28 a John 14:3, 18 b John 16:16 c [Phil. 2:6] *1* NU omits *I said*
29 a John 13:19
30 a [John 12:31] b [Heb. 4:15]
31 a John 10:18
CHAPTER 15
2 a Matt. 15:13 b [Matt. 13:12] *1* Or *lifts up*
3 a [John 13:10; 17:17]
4 a [Col. 1:23]
5 a Hos. 14:8 b 2 Cor. 3:5
6 a Matt. 3:10
7 a 1 John 2:14 b John 14:13; 16:23 *1* NU omits *you will*
8 a [Matt. 5:16]

John 15:4

Dear Woman of Destiny,

Finding our place of rest and abiding in Jesus as we walk in this journey of eternal purpose is a need each of us has. Not a physical place but a place of recognition and surrender to God's will. There we are able to experience a peace and comfort of soul that reflect complete dependence on the Holy Spirit.

In seeking out this needed and desired place, we must go beyond ourselves, our natural capabilities, surrounding circumstances and, especially, the lies and accusations of the enemy. This is a heavenly realm we can share with our Father in heaven. It is in His holy presence, safely tucked under His wings of love, that we receive cleansing, healing, and direction for life's journey. It is there that His will and special secrets are revealed to us.

What a place! Do you want to go there? Today, Jesus is telling you, "Come to Me, all you who labor and are heavy laden, and I will give you rest" (Matt. 11:28). To enter into this rest you must acknowledge Christ's complete work on the Cross. We must cease striving for salvation through our own efforts. We must embrace the truth that Jesus gave His life so that we could be justified through His precious blood. Guilt and shame are removed from you this day so that you may enter with confidence your place of rest in God.

We must learn to retreat to God's presence often, as well as abide in that place of rest. When I was very young, I decided that my life would be used to share the Gospel of Christ. Being a woman of purpose, my nature is goal oriented. I determined to do everything I could to achieve the goals I had set for myself. I accomplished them through prayer and my own efforts. It was not long before I found myself frustrated, mentally exhausted, physically fatigued and wondering if it was all in vain.

If we are to abide in His rest, we must first be totally surrendered and willing to go down the road of brokenness, of dying to ourselves. We must admit to the Lord and to ourselves that we don't know what to do and we do not have the strength to do things in ourselves. Humility is the key that opens this place of rest. When we lose everything for Him, we can find ourselves *in* Him.

The more time I spend in His presence, the more I realize that He is in full control of everything — even when I do not understand what He is doing! It is in that rest that we can hear the call for our specific course of action and receive the strategies He's designed for our involvement in accomplishing His purposes.

The only "striving" or "working" that should be occurring is the daily search for that place of rest. We all have the need to lay down our wishes and desires on God's altar and to rely only on the strength that we receive from Him. This can only happen as we spend time "resting" in Him.

Start today! Make adjustments in your life that will enable you to spend time with the Father—to abide in Him. The more time we spend with Him, the more we will be like Him.

Miriam Witt

glorified, that you bear much fruit; [b]so
you will be My disciples.

Love and Joy Perfected

9"As the Father [a]loved Me, I also have
loved you; abide in My love. 10[a]If you keep
My commandments, you will abide in My
love, just as I have kept My Father's commandments and abide in His love.
11"These things I have spoken to you,
that My joy may remain in you, and [a]*that*
your joy may be full. 12[a]This is My [b]commandment, that you love one another as
I have loved you. 13[a]Greater love has no
one than this, than to lay down one's life
for his friends. 14[a]You are My friends if
you do whatever I command you. 15No
longer do I call you servants, for a servant
does not know what his master is doing;
but I have called you friends, [a]for all
things that I heard from My Father I have
made known to you. 16[a]You did not
choose Me, but I chose you and [b]appointed you that you should go and bear fruit,
and *that* your fruit should remain, that
whatever you ask the Father [c]in My name

8 b John 8:31
9 a John 5:20; 17:26
10 a John 14:15
11 a 1 John 1:4
12 a 1 John 3:11 b Rom. 12:9
13 a 1 John 3:16
14 a [Matt. 12:50; 28:20]
15 a Gen. 18:17
16 a John 6:70; 13:18; 15:19 b [Col. 1:6] c John 14:13; 16:23, 24

Amanda Smith

Among the most noted and courageous African-American women in history was the Methodist revivalist Amanda Smith (1837–1915). Amanda was born a slave in Maryland and worked as a scrubwoman prior to her work in the ministry.

She was a tremendous pioneer who set an example for all the women who would follow her in obeying God's call to their lives. Women in ministry often suffer persecution and even hostility at times, but Amanda encountered particularly fierce opposition.

She defied all the norms of life in post–Civil War America. Not only was she a woman evangelist, she was a black woman evangelist and an ex-slave. She must have been filled with love and grace; because she traveled both north and south, preaching to people of all races and persuasions. She later spent fourteen years evangelizing in England, India, and Africa. To the best of her ability, she fulfilled the Great Commission.

Amanda received opposition from her own African American churches as well as from white people. When her own denomination held their first general conference south of the Mason-Dixon line, Amanda made plans to attend. Her appearance caused quite a stir of gossip, even though she says in her own words: "The thought of ordination had never once entered my mind, for I had received my ordination from Him who said, 'Ye have not chosen me, but I have chosen you, and ordained you, that ye should go and bring forth fruit'" (John 15:16, KJV).

She knew the power and protection of being chosen by God. She traveled the world, preaching with courage and spreading revival. We must know who calls us to ministry. Many women who minister experience some form of rejection, opposition, or misunderstanding. May we, as women of destiny, be strong in the face of opposition and willing to embrace the call of God on our lives, regardless of the cost.

He may give you. [17]These things I command you, that you love one another.

The World's Hatred

[18][a]"If the world hates you, you know that it hated Me before *it hated* you. [19][a]If you were of the world, the world would love its own. Yet [b]because you are not of the world, but I chose you out of the world, therefore the world hates you. [20]Remember the word that I said to you, [a]'A servant is not greater than his master.' If they persecuted Me, they will also persecute you. [b]If they kept My word, they will keep yours also. [21]But [a]all these things they will do to you for My name's sake, because they do not know Him who sent Me. [22][a]If I had not come and spoken to them, they would have no sin, [b]but now they have no excuse for their sin. [23][a]He who hates Me hates My Father also. [24]If I had not done among them [a]the works which no one else did, they would have no sin; but now they have [b]seen and also hated both Me and My Father. [25]But *this happened* that the word might be fulfilled which is written in their law, [a]*'They hated Me without a cause.'*

The Coming Rejection

[26][a]"But when the [1]Helper comes, whom I shall send to you from the Father, the Spirit of truth who proceeds from the Father, [b]He will testify of Me. [27]And [a]you also will bear witness, because [b]you have been with Me from the beginning.

16 "These things I have spoken to you, that you [a]should not be made to stumble. [2][a]They will put you out of the synagogues; yes, the time is coming [b]that whoever kills you will think that he offers God service. [3]And [a]these things they will do [1]to you because they have not known the Father nor Me. [4]But these things I have told you, that when [1]the time comes, you may remember that I told you of them.

"And these things I did not say to you at the beginning, because I was with you.

The Work of the Holy Spirit

[5]"But now I [a]go away to Him who sent Me, and none of you asks Me, 'Where are You going?' [6]But because I have said these things to you, [a]sorrow has filled your heart. [7]Nevertheless I tell you the truth. It is to your advantage that I go away; for if I do not go away, the Helper will not come to you; but [a]if I depart, I will send Him to you. [8]And when He has [a]come, He will convict the world of sin, and of righteousness, and of judgment: [9][a]of sin, because they do not believe in Me; [10][a]of righteousness, [b]because I go to My Father and you see Me no more; [11][a]of judgment, because [b]the ruler of this world is judged.

[12]"I still have many things to say to you, [a]but you cannot bear *them* now. [13]However, when He, [a]the Spirit of truth, has come, [b]He will guide you into all truth; for He will not speak on His own *authority,* but whatever He hears He will speak; and He will tell you things to come. [14][a]He will glorify Me, for He will take of what is Mine and declare *it* to you. [15][a]All things that the Father has are Mine. Therefore I said that He [1]will take of Mine and declare *it* to you.

Sorrow Will Turn to Joy

[16]"A [a]little while, and you will not see Me; and again a little while, and you will see Me, [b]because I go to the Father."

[17]Then *some* of His disciples said among themselves, "What is this that He says to us, 'A little while, and you will not see Me; and again a little while, and you will see Me'; and, 'because I go to the Father'?" [18]They said therefore, "What is this that He says, 'A little while'? We do not [1]know what He is saying."

[19]Now Jesus knew that they desired to ask Him, and He said to them, "Are you inquiring among yourselves about what I said, 'A little while, and you will not see Me; and again a little while, and you will see Me'? [20]Most assuredly, I say to you that you will weep and [a]lament, but the world will rejoice; and you will be sorrowful, but your sorrow will be turned into [b]joy. [21][a]A woman, when she is in labor, has sorrow because her hour has come; but as soon as she has given birth to the child, she no longer remembers the anguish, for joy that a human being has been born into the world. [22]Therefore you now have sorrow; but I will see you again and [a]your heart will rejoice, and your joy no one will take from you.

[23]"And in that day you will ask Me nothing. [a]Most assuredly, I say to you, whatever you ask the Father in My name He will give you. [24]Until now you have asked

18 a 1 John 3:13
19 a 1 John 4:5 b John 17:14
20 a John 13:16 b Ezek. 3:7
21 a Matt. 10:22; 24:9
22 a John 9:41; 15:24 b [James 4:17]
23 a 1 John 2:23
24 a John 3:2 b John 14:9
25 a Ps. 35:19; 69:4; 109:3–5
26 a Luke 24:49 b 1 John 5:6 *1 Comforter,* Gr. *Parakletos*
27 a Luke 24:48 b Luke 1:2

CHAPTER 16
1 a Matt. 11:6
2 a John 9:22 b Acts 8:1
3 a John 8:19; 15:21 *1* NU, M omit *to you*
4 *1* NU *their*
5 a John 7:33; 13:33; 14:28; 17:11
6 a [John 16:20, 22]
7 a Acts 2:33
8 a Acts 1:8; 2:1–4, 37
9 a Acts 2:22
10 a Acts 2:32 b John 5:32
11 a Acts 26:18 b [Luke 10:18]
12 a Mark 4:33
13 a [John 14:17] b John 14:26
14 a John 15:26
15 a Matt. 11:27 *1* NU, M *takes of Mine and will declare*
16 a John 7:33; 12:35; 13:33; 14:19; 19:40–42; 20:19 b John 13:3
18 *1 understand*
20 a Mark 16:10 b Luke 24:32, 41

21 a Is. 13:8; 26:17; 42:14 **22** a 1 Pet. 1:8 **23** a Matt. 7:7

nothing in My name. Ask, and you will
receive, [a]that your joy may be [b]full.

Jesus Christ Has Overcome the World

25“These things I have spoken to you in
figurative language; but the time is coming when I will no longer speak to you in
figurative language, but I will tell you
[a]plainly about the Father. 26In that day
you will ask in My name, and I do not say
to you that I shall pray the Father for you;
27[a]for the Father Himself loves you, because you have loved Me, and [b]have believed that I came forth from God. 28[a]I
came forth from the Father and have
come into the world. Again, I leave the
world and go to the Father.”
29His disciples said to Him, “See, now
You are speaking plainly, and using no
figure of speech! 30Now we are sure that
[a]You know all things, and have no need
that anyone should question You. By this
[b]we believe that You came forth from
God.”
31Jesus answered them, “Do you now
believe? 32[a]Indeed the hour is coming,
yes, has now come, that you will be scattered, [b]each to his [1]own, and will leave Me
alone. And [c]yet I am not alone, because
the Father is with Me. 33These things I
have spoken to you, that [a]in Me you may
have peace. [b]In the world you [1]will have
tribulation; but be of good cheer, [c]I have
overcome the world.”

O Lord, You have spoken these things to _____, that in You they may have peace. In the world they will have tribulation, but help them to be of good cheer, for You have overcome the world.

FROM JOHN 16:33

Jesus Prays for Himself

17 Jesus spoke these words, lifted up
His eyes to heaven, and said: “Father, [a]the hour has come. Glorify Your
Son, that Your Son also may glorify You,
2[a]as You have given Him authority over
all flesh, that He [1]should give eternal life
to as many [b]as You have given Him. 3And
[a]this is eternal life, that they may know
You, [b]the only true God, and Jesus Christ
[c]whom You have sent. 4[a]I have glorified
You on the earth. [b]I have finished the
work [c]which You have given Me to do.
5And now, O Father, glorify Me together
[1]with Yourself, with the glory [a]which I
had with You before the world was.

Jesus Prays for His Disciples

6[a]“I have [1]manifested Your name to the
men [b]whom You have given Me out of the
world. [c]They were Yours, You gave them
to Me, and they have kept Your word.
7Now they have known that all things
which You have given Me are from You.
8For I have given to them the words
[a]which You have given Me; and they have
received *them,* [b]and have known surely
that I came forth from You; and they have
believed that [c]You sent Me.
9“I pray for them. [a]I do not pray for the
world but for those whom You have given
Me, for they are Yours. 10And all Mine are
Yours, and [a]Yours are Mine, and I am glorified in them. 11[a]Now I am no longer in
the world, but these are in the world, and
I come to You. Holy Father, [b]keep[1]
through Your name those whom You
have given Me, that they may be one [c]as
We *are.* 12While I was with them [1]in the
world, [a]I kept them in [2]Your name. Those
whom You gave Me I have kept; and [b]none
of them is [3]lost [c]except the son of [4]perdi-
tion, [d]that the Scripture might be fulfilled. 13But now I come to You, and these
things I speak in the world, that they may
have My joy fulfilled in themselves. 14I
have given them Your word; [a]and the
world has hated them because they are
not of the world, [b]just as I am not of the
world. 15I do not pray that You should
take them out of the world, but [a]that You
should keep them from the evil one.
16They are not of the world, just as I am
not of the world. 17[a]Sanctify[1] them by
Your truth. [b]Your word is truth. 18[a]As
You sent Me into the world, I also have
sent them into the world. 19And [a]for their
sakes I sanctify Myself, that they also may
be sanctified by the truth.

24 [a]John 17:13 [b]John 15:11
25 [a]John 7:13
27 [a][John 14:21, 23] [b]John 3:13
28 [a]John 13:1, 3; 16:5, 10, 17
30 [a]John 21:17 [b]John 17:8
32 [a]Matt. 26:31, 56 [b]John 20:10 [c]John 8:29 [1] *own things* or *place*
33 [a][Eph. 2:14] [b]2 Tim. 3:12 [c]Rom. 8:37 [1] NU, M omit *will*

CHAPTER 17
1 [a]John 12:23
2 [a]John 3:35 [b]John 6:37, 39; 17:6, 9, 24 [1] M *shall*
3 [a]Jer. 9:23, 24 [b]1 Cor. 8:4 [c]John 3:34
4 [a]John 13:31 [b]John 4:34; 19:30 [c]John 14:31
5 [a]Phil. 2:6 [1] Lit. *alongside*
6 [a]Ps. 22:22 [b]John 6:37 [c]Ezek. 18:4 [1] *revealed*
8 [a]John 8:28 [b]John 8:42; 16:27, 30 [c]Deut. 18:15, 18
9 [a][1 John 5:19]
10 [a]John 16:15
11 [a]John 13:1 [b][1 Pet. 1:5] [c]John 10:30 [1] NU, M *keep them through Your name which You have given Me*
12 [a]Heb. 2:13 [b]1 John 2:19 [c]John 6:70 [d]Ps. 41:9; 109:8 [1] NU omits *in the world* [2] NU *Your name which You gave Me. And I guarded them; (*or *it;)* [3] *destroyed* [4] *destruction*
14 [a]John 15:19 [b]John 8:23
15 [a]1 John 5:18
17 [a][Eph. 5:26] [b]Ps. 119:9, 142, 151 [1] *Set them apart*
18 [a]John 4:38; 20:21
19 [a][Heb. 10:10]

Jesus Prays for All Believers

20 "I do not pray for these alone, but also for those who [1]will believe in Me through their word; 21 [a]that they all may be one, as [b]You, Father, *are* in Me, and I in You; that they also may be one in Us, that the world may believe that You sent Me. 22 And the [a]glory which You gave Me I have given them, [b]that they may be one just as We are one: 23 I in them, and You in Me; [a]that they may be made perfect in one, and that the world may know that You have sent Me, and have loved them as You have loved Me.

24 [a]"Father, I desire that they also whom You gave Me may be with Me where I am, that they may behold My glory which You have given Me; [b]for You loved Me before the foundation of the world. 25 O righteous Father! [a]The world has not known You, but [b]I have known You; and [c]these have known that You sent Me. 26 [a]And I have declared to them Your name, and will declare *it,* that the love [b]with which You loved Me may be in them, and I in them."

Betrayal and Arrest in Gethsemane

18 When Jesus had spoken these words, [a]He went out with His disciples over [b]the Brook Kidron, where there was a garden, which He and His disciples entered. 2 And Judas, who betrayed Him, also knew the place; [a]for Jesus often met there with His disciples. 3 [a]Then Judas, having received a detachment *of troops,* and officers from the chief priests and Pharisees, came there with lanterns, torches, and weapons. 4 Jesus therefore, [a]knowing all things that would come upon Him, went forward and said to them, "Whom are you seeking?"

5 They answered Him, [a]"Jesus [1]of Nazareth."

Jesus said to them, "I am *He.*" And Judas, who [b]betrayed Him, also stood with them. 6 Now when He said to them, "I am *He,*" they drew back and fell to the ground.

7 Then He asked them again, "Whom are you seeking?"

And they said, "Jesus of Nazareth."

8 Jesus answered, "I have told you that I am *He.* Therefore, if you seek Me, let these go their way," 9 that the saying might be fulfilled which He spoke, [a]"Of those whom You gave Me I have lost none."

10 [a]Then Simon Peter, having a sword, drew it and struck the high priest's servant, and cut off his right ear. The servant's name was Malchus.

11 So Jesus said to Peter, "Put your sword into the sheath. Shall I not drink [a]the cup which My Father has given Me?"

Before the High Priest

12 Then the detachment *of troops* and the captain and the officers of the Jews arrested Jesus and bound Him. 13 And [a]they led Him away to [b]Annas first, for he was the father-in-law of [c]Caiaphas who was high priest that year. 14 [a]Now it was Caiaphas who advised the Jews that it was [1]expedient that one man should die for the people.

Peter Denies Jesus

15 [a]And Simon Peter followed Jesus, and so *did* [b]another[1] disciple. Now that disciple was known to the high priest, and went with Jesus into the courtyard of the high priest. 16 [a]But Peter stood at the door outside. Then the other disciple, who was known to the high priest, went out and spoke to her who kept the door, and brought Peter in. 17 Then the servant girl who kept the door said to Peter, "You are not also *one* of this Man's disciples, are you?"

He said, "I am [a]not."

18 Now the servants and officers who had made a fire of coals stood there, for it was cold, and they warmed themselves. And Peter stood with them and warmed himself.

Jesus Questioned by the High Priest

19 The high priest then asked Jesus about His disciples and His doctrine.

20 Jesus answered him, [a]"I spoke openly to the world. I always taught [b]in synagogues and [c]in the temple, where [1]the Jews always meet, and in secret I have said nothing. 21 Why do you ask Me? Ask [a]those who have heard Me what I said to them. Indeed they know what I said."

22 And when He had said these things, one of the officers who stood by [a]struck[1] Jesus with the palm of his hand, saying, "Do You answer the high priest like that?"

---

20 *1* NU, M omit *will*
21 a [Gal. 3:28] b John 10:38; 17:11, 23
22 a 1 John 1:3 b [2 Cor. 3:18]
23 a [Col. 3:14]
24 a [1 Thess. 4:17] b John 17:5
25 a John 15:21 b John 7:29; 8:55; 10:15 c John 3:17; 17:3, 8, 18, 21, 23
26 a John 17:6 b John 15:9

CHAPTER 18
1 a Mark 14:26, 32 b 2 Sam. 15:23
2 a Luke 21:37; 22:39
3 a Luke 22:47–53
4 a John 6:64; 13:1, 3; 19:28
5 a Matt. 21:11 b Ps. 41:9 *1* Lit. *the Nazarene*
9 a [John 6:39; 17:12]
10 a Matt. 26:51
11 a Matt. 20:22; 26:39
13 a Matt. 26:57 b Luke 3:2 c Matt. 26:3
14 a John 11:50 *1 advantageous*
15 a Mark 14:54 b John 20:2–5 *1* M *the other*
16 a Matt. 26:69
17 a Matt. 26:34
20 a Luke 4:15 b John 6:59 c Mark 14:49 *1* NU *all the Jews meet*
21 a Mark 12:37
22 a Jer. 20:2 *1* Lit. *gave Jesus a slap,*

23Jesus answered him, "If I have spoken evil, bear witness of the evil; but if well, why do you strike Me?"

24[a]Then Annas sent Him bound to [b]Caiaphas the high priest.

Peter Denies Twice More

25Now Simon Peter stood and warmed himself. [a]Therefore they said to him, "You are not also *one* of His disciples, are you?"

He denied *it* and said, "I am not!"

26One of the servants of the high priest, a relative *of him* whose ear Peter cut off, said, "Did I not see you in the garden with Him?" 27Peter then denied again; and [a]immediately a rooster crowed.

In Pilate's Court

28[a]Then they led Jesus from Caiaphas to the Praetorium, and it was early morning. [b]But they themselves did not go into the [1]Praetorium, lest they should be defiled, but that they might eat the Passover. 29[a]Pilate then went out to them and said, "What accusation do you bring against this Man?"

30They answered and said to him, "If He were not [1]an evildoer, we would not have delivered Him up to you."

31Then Pilate said to them, "You take Him and judge Him according to your law."

Therefore the Jews said to him, "It is not lawful for us to put anyone to death," 32[a]that the saying of Jesus might be fulfilled which He spoke, [b]signifying by what death He would die.

33[a]Then Pilate entered the [1]Praetorium again, called Jesus, and said to Him, "Are You the King of the Jews?"

34Jesus answered him, "Are you speaking for yourself about this, or did others tell you this concerning Me?"

35Pilate answered, "Am I a Jew? Your own nation and the chief priests have delivered You to me. What have You done?"

36[a]Jesus answered, [b]"My kingdom is not of this world. If My kingdom were of this world, My servants would fight, so that I should not be delivered to the Jews; but now My kingdom is not from here."

37Pilate therefore said to Him, "Are You a king then?"

Jesus answered, "You say *rightly* that I am a king. For this cause I was born, and for this cause I have come into the world, [a]that I should bear [b]witness to the truth. Everyone who [c]is of the truth [d]hears My voice."

38Pilate said to Him, "What is truth?" And when he had said this, he went out again to the Jews, and said to them, [a]"I find no fault in Him at all.

Taking the Place of Barabbas

39[a]"But you have a custom that I should release someone to you at the Passover. Do you therefore want me to release to you the King of the Jews?"

40[a]Then they all cried again, saying, "Not this Man, but Barabbas!" [b]Now Barabbas was a robber.

The Soldiers Mock Jesus

19 So then [a]Pilate took Jesus and scourged *Him*. 2And the soldiers twisted a crown of thorns and put *it* on His head, and they put on Him a purple robe. 3[1]Then they said, "Hail, King of the Jews!" And they [a]struck Him with their hands.

4Pilate then went out again, and said to them, "Behold, I am bringing Him out to you, [a]that you may know that I find no fault in Him."

Pilate's Decision

5Then Jesus came out, wearing the crown of thorns and the purple robe. And *Pilate* said to them, "Behold the Man!"

6[a]Therefore, when the chief priests and officers saw Him, they cried out, saying, "Crucify *Him*, crucify *Him!*"

Pilate said to them, "You take Him and crucify *Him*, for I find no fault in Him."

7The Jews answered him, [a]"We have a law, and according to [1]our law He ought to die, because [b]He made Himself the Son of God."

8Therefore, when Pilate heard that saying, he was the more afraid, 9and went again into the Praetorium, and said to Jesus, "Where are You from?" [a]But Jesus gave him no answer.

10Then Pilate said to Him, "Are You not speaking to me? Do You not know that I have [1]power to crucify You, and power to release You?"

11Jesus answered, [a]"You could have no

---

24 [a]Matt. 26:57 [b]John 11:49
25 [a]Luke 22:58–62
27 [a]John 13:38
28 [a]Mark 15:1 [b]Acts 10:28; 11:3 [1]*The governor's headquarters*
29 [a]Matt. 27:11–14
30 [1]*a criminal*
32 [a]Matt. 20:17–19; 26:2 [b]John 3:14; 8:28; 12:32, 33
33 [a]Matt. 27:11 [1]*The governor's headquarters*
36 [a]1 Tim. 6:13 [b][Dan. 2:44; 7:14]
37 [a][Matt. 5:17; 20:28] [b]Is. 55:4 [c][John 14:6] [d]John 8:47; 10:27
38 [a]John 19:4, 6
39 [a]Luke 23:17–25
40 [a]Acts 3:14 [b]Luke 23:19

CHAPTER 19
1 [a]Matt. 20:19; 27:26
3 [a]Is. 50:6 [1]NU *And they came up to Him and said*
4 [a]John 18:33, 38
6 [a]Acts 3:13
7 [a]Lev. 24:16 [b]Matt. 26:63–66 [1]NU *the law*
9 [a]Is. 53:7
10 [1]*authority*
11 [a][Luke 22:53]

power at all against Me unless it had been
given you from above. Therefore [b]the one
who delivered Me to you has the greater
sin."
12From then on Pilate sought to release
Him, but the Jews cried out, saying, "If
you let this Man go, you are not Caesar's
friend. [a]Whoever makes himself a king
speaks against Caesar."
13[a]When Pilate therefore heard that
saying, he brought Jesus out and sat down
in the judgment seat in a place that is
called *The* Pavement, but in Hebrew, Gab-
batha. 14Now [a]it was the Preparation Day
of the Passover, and about the sixth hour.
And he said to the Jews, "Behold your
King!"
15But they cried out, "Away with *Him,*
away with *Him!* Crucify Him!"

Pilate said to them, "Shall I crucify
your King?"

The chief priests answered, [a]"We have
no king but Caesar!"
16[a]Then he delivered Him to them to be
crucified. Then they took Jesus [1]and led
Him away.

The King on a Cross

17[a]And He, bearing His cross, [b]went out
to a place called *the Place* of a Skull,
which is called in Hebrew, Golgotha,
18where they crucified Him, and [a]two others with Him, one on either side, and Jesus in the center. 19[a]Now Pilate wrote a
title and put *it* on the cross. And the writing was:

JESUS OF NAZARETH, THE KING OF
THE JEWS.

20Then many of the Jews read this title,
for the place where Jesus was crucified
was near the city; and it was written in
Hebrew, Greek, *and* Latin.
21Therefore the chief priests of the Jews
said to Pilate, "Do not write, 'The King of
the Jews,' but, 'He said, "I am the King of
the Jews." ' "
22Pilate answered, "What I have written, I have written."
23[a]Then the soldiers, when they had
crucified Jesus, took His garments and
made four parts, to each soldier a part,
and also the tunic. Now the tunic was
without seam, woven from the top in one
piece. 24They said therefore among themselves, "Let us not tear it, but cast lots for
it, whose it shall be," that the Scripture
might be fulfilled which says:

[a]*"They divided My garments among*
them,
And for My clothing they cast lots."

Therefore the soldiers did these things.

Behold Your Mother

25[a]Now there stood by the cross of Jesus
His mother, and His mother's sister, Mary
the *wife* of [b]Clopas, and Mary Magdalene.
26When Jesus therefore saw His mother,
and [a]the disciple whom He loved standing
by, He said to His mother, [b]"Woman, behold your son!" 27Then He said to the disciple, "Behold your mother!" And from
that hour that disciple took her [a]to his
own *home.*

It Is Finished

28After this, Jesus, [1]knowing that all
things were now accomplished, [a]that the
Scripture might be fulfilled, said, "I
thirst!" 29Now a vessel full of sour wine
was sitting there; and [a]they filled a sponge
with sour wine, put *it* on hyssop, and put
it to His mouth. 30So when Jesus had received the sour wine, He said, [a]"It is finished!" And bowing His head, He gave up
His spirit.

Jesus' Side Is Pierced

31[a]Therefore, because it was the Preparation *Day,* [b]that the bodies should not
remain on the cross on the Sabbath (for
that Sabbath was a [c]high day), the Jews
asked Pilate that their legs might be broken, and *that* they might be taken away.
32Then the soldiers came and broke the
legs of the first and of the other who was
crucified with Him. 33But when they
came to Jesus and saw that He was already
dead, they did not break His legs. 34But
one of the soldiers pierced His side with a
spear, and immediately [a]blood and water
came out. 35And he who has seen has testified, and his testimony is [a]true; and he
knows that he is telling the truth, so that
you may [b]believe. 36For these things were
done that the Scripture should be fulfilled, [a]*"Not one of His bones shall be bro-*
ken." 37And again another Scripture says,
[a]*"They shall look on Him whom they*
pierced."

11 b Rom. 13:1
12 a Luke 23:2
13 a 1 Sam. 15:24
14 a Matt. 27:62
15 a [Gen. 49:10]
16 a Luke 23:24 1 NU omits *and led Him away*
17 a Mark 15:21, 22 b Num. 15:36
18 a Is. 53:12
19 a Matt. 27:37
23 a Luke 23:34
24 a Ps. 22:18
25 a Mark 15:40 b Luke 24:18
26 a John 13:23; 20:2; 21:7, 20, 24 b John 2:4
27 a John 1:11; 16:32
28 a Ps. 22:15 1 M *seeing*
29 a Matt. 27:48, 50
30 a John 17:4
31 a Mark 15:42 b Deut. 21:23 c Ex. 12:16
34 a [1 John 5:6, 8]
35 a John 21:24 b [John 20:31]
36 a [Ex. 12:46; Num. 9:12]; Ps. 34:20
37 a Zech. 12:10; 13:6

Jesus Buried in Joseph's Tomb

38[a]After this, Joseph of Arimathea, being a disciple of Jesus, but secretly, [b]for
fear of the Jews, asked Pilate that he
might take away the body of Jesus; and
Pilate gave *him* permission. So he came
and took the body of Jesus. 39And [a]Nico-
demus, who at first came to Jesus by
night, also came, bringing a mixture of
[b]myrrh and aloes, about a hundred
pounds. 40Then they took the body of Jesus, and [a]bound it in strips of linen with
the spices, as the custom of the Jews is to
bury. 41Now in the place where He was
crucified there was a garden, and in the
garden a new tomb in which no one had
yet been laid. 42So [a]there they laid Jesus,
[b]because of the Jews' Preparation *Day,* for
the tomb was nearby.

The Empty Tomb

20 Now the [a]first *day* of the week
Mary Magdalene went to the tomb
early, while it was still dark, and saw *that*
the [b]stone had been taken away from the
tomb. 2Then she ran and came to Simon
Peter, and to the [a]other disciple, [b]whom
Jesus loved, and said to them, "They have
taken away the Lord out of the tomb, and
we do not know where they have laid
Him."

3[a]Peter therefore went out, and the
other disciple, and were going to the
tomb. 4So they both ran together, and the
other disciple outran Peter and came to
the tomb first. 5And he, stooping down
and looking in, saw [a]the linen cloths lying
there; yet he did not go in. 6Then Simon
Peter came, following him, and went into
the tomb; and he saw the linen cloths lying *there,* 7and [a]the [1]handkerchief that
had been around His head, not lying with
the linen cloths, but folded together in a
place by itself. 8Then the [a]other disciple,
who came to the tomb first, went in also;
and he saw and believed. 9For as yet they
did not [1]know the [a]Scripture, that He
must rise again from the dead. 10Then the
disciples went away again to their own
homes.

Mary Magdalene Sees the Risen Lord

11[a]But Mary stood outside by the tomb
weeping, and as she wept she stooped
down *and looked* into the tomb. 12And she
saw two angels in white sitting, one at the
head and the other at the feet, where the
body of Jesus had lain. 13Then they said to
her, "Woman, why are you weeping?"

She said to them, "Because they have
taken away my Lord, and I do not know
where they have laid Him."

14[a]Now when she had said this, she
turned around and saw Jesus standing
there, and [b]did not know that it was Jesus.
15Jesus said to her, "Woman, why are you
weeping? Whom are you seeking?"

She, supposing Him to be the gardener,
said to Him, "Sir, if You have carried Him
away, tell me where You have laid Him,
and I will take Him away."

16Jesus said to her, [a]"Mary!"

She turned and said to [1]Him, "Rabboni!" (which is to say, Teacher).

17Jesus said to her, "Do not cling to Me,
for I have not yet [a]ascended to My Father;
but go to [b]My brethren and say to them,
[c]'I am ascending to My Father and your
Father, and *to* [d]My God and your God.' "

18[a]Mary Magdalene came and told the
[1]disciples that she had seen the Lord, and
that He had spoken these things to her.

The Apostles Commissioned

19[a]Then, the same day at evening, being
the first *day* of the week, when the doors
were shut where the disciples were [1]as-
sembled, for [b]fear of the Jews, Jesus came
and stood in the midst, and said to them,
[c]"Peace *be* with you." 20When He had said
this, He [a]showed them *His* hands and His
side. [b]Then the disciples were glad when
they saw the Lord.

21So Jesus said to them again, "Peace to
you! [a]As the Father has sent Me, I also
send you." 22And when He had said this,
He breathed on *them,* and said to them,
"Receive the Holy Spirit. 23[a]If you forgive
the sins of any, they are forgiven them; if
you retain the *sins* of any, they are retained."

Seeing and Believing

24Now Thomas, [a]called the Twin, one of
the twelve, was not with them when Jesus
came. 25The other disciples therefore said
to him, "We have seen the Lord."

So he said to them, "Unless I see in His
hands the print of the nails, and put my
finger into the print of the nails, and put
my hand into His side, I will not believe."

26And after eight days His disciples
were again inside, and Thomas with them.

38 a Luke 23:50–56 b [John 7:13; 9:22; 12:42]
39 a John 3:1, 2; 7:50 b Matt. 2:11
40 a John 20:5, 7
42 a Is. 53:9 b John 19:14, 31

CHAPTER 20
1 a Matt. 28:1–8 b Matt. 27:60, 66; 28:2
2 a John 21:23, 24 b John 13:23; 19:26; 21:7, 20, 24
3 a Luke 24:12
5 a John 19:40
7 a John 11:44 *1 face cloth*
8 a John 21:23, 24
9 a Ps. 16:10 *1 understand*
11 a Mark 16:5
14 a Matt. 28:9 b John 21:4
16 a John 10:3 *1* NU adds *in Hebrew*
17 a Heb. 4:14 b Heb. 2:11 c John 16:28; 17:11 d Eph. 1:17
18 a Luke 24:10, 23 *1* NU *disciples, "I have seen the Lord,"*
19 a Luke 24:36 b John 9:22; 19:38 c John 14:27; 16:33 *1* NU omits *assembled*
20 a Acts 1:3 b John 16:20, 22
21 a John 17:18, 19
23 a Matt. 16:19; 18:18
24 a John 11:16

Jesus came, the doors being shut, and
stood in the midst, and said, "Peace to
you!" 27Then He said to Thomas, "Reach
your finger here, and look at My hands;
and [a]reach your hand *here,* and put *it* into
My side. Do not be [b]unbelieving, but believing."
28And Thomas answered and said to
Him, "My Lord and my God!"
29Jesus said to him, [1]"Thomas, because
you have seen Me, you have believed.
[a]Blessed *are* those who have not seen and
yet have believed."

27 a 1 John 1:1 b Mark 16:14

29 a 1 Pet. 1:8 1 NU, M omit *Thomas*

Father, Your Word is written that those who read it may believe that Jesus is the Christ, the Son of God. Believing, may ____ have life in His name.

FROM JOHN 20:31

MARY MAGDALENE

Mary Magdalene was a changed woman. This faithful follower of Jesus Christ once had an encounter with Him that changed her life forever. Though Scripture reveals little about her past, we know she had been possessed by seven demons, and therefore, by unimaginable torment. But Jesus delivered her and made possible a life of peace and wholeness. A woman who had once been controlled by evil spirits became a woman consumed by complete devotion and love for Jesus.

Mary Magdalene was one of a small band of women who followed Jesus almost as closely as His twelve disciples. In fact, three of these faithful women made such an impression on Luke that he recorded their names in Scripture: Mary Magdalene, Joanna, and Susanna (see Luke 8:2, 3). According to him, they were among "many others who provided for Him from their substance" (8:3). These women were so dedicated to Jesus and His ministry that they supported Him out of their own personal resources

Throughout the Gospels, Mary Magdalene never seems to be far from Jesus. Whenever a group of women is mentioned, she is in the middle of them (see Matt. 27:55, 56; Mark 15:40; 16:1; Luke 23:55, 56; 24:10). She followed Jesus all the way to Calvary and watched Him breathe His last breath. She followed Him even beyond death, being one of the two women mentioned in the Bible who "observed where He was laid" (Mark 15:47) and bringing spices to anoint His body on resurrection morning (see Mark 16:9).

Mary Magdalene entered the garden probably planning to spend the morning doing one last favor for the One who had given her so much. But instead of being able to honor Jesus by anointing Him, she was honored by being allowed to be the first to witness His resurrection. With the other women, she was among the first to hear the most revolutionary words in history: "He is risen!" In John's account, she was the first to hear the ever-living Lord speak her name; the first to whom He revealed Himself; and the first to hear Him issue the call that still beckons women today: to spread the good news that He is alive!

That You May Believe

30 And [a]truly Jesus did many other signs in the presence of His disciples, which are not written in this book; 31 [a]but these are written that [b]you may believe that Jesus [c]is the Christ, the Son of God, [d]and that believing you may have life in His name.

Breakfast by the Sea

21 After these things Jesus showed Himself again to the disciples at the [a]Sea of Tiberias, and in this way He showed *Himself:* 2 Simon Peter, [a]Thomas called the Twin, [b]Nathanael of [c]Cana in Galilee, [d]the *sons* of Zebedee, and two others of His disciples were together. 3 Simon Peter said to them, "I am going fishing."

They said to him, "We are going with you also." They went out and [1]immediately got into the boat, and that night they caught nothing. 4 But when the morning had now come, Jesus stood on the shore; yet the disciples [a]did not know that it was Jesus. 5 Then [a]Jesus said to them, "Children, have you any food?"

They answered Him, "No."

6 And He said to them, [a]"Cast the net on the right side of the boat, and you will find *some.*" So they cast, and now they were not able to draw it in because of the multitude of fish.

7 Therefore [a]that disciple whom Jesus loved said to Peter, "It is the Lord!" Now when Simon Peter heard that it was the Lord, he put on *his* outer garment (for he had removed it), and plunged into the sea. 8 But the other disciples came in the little boat (for they were not far from land, but about two hundred cubits), dragging the net with fish. 9 Then, as soon as they had come to land, they saw a fire of coals there, and fish laid on it, and bread. 10 Jesus said to them, "Bring some of the fish which you have just caught."

11 Simon Peter went up and dragged the net to land, full of large fish, one hundred and fifty-three; and although there were so many, the net was not broken. 12 Jesus said to them, [a]"Come *and* eat breakfast." Yet none of the disciples dared ask Him, "Who are You?"—knowing that it was the Lord. 13 Jesus then came and took the bread and gave it to them, and likewise the fish.

14 This *is* now [a]the third time Jesus showed Himself to His disciples after He was raised from the dead.

Jesus Restores Peter

15 So when they had eaten breakfast, Jesus said to Simon Peter, "Simon, *son* of [1]Jonah, do you love Me more than these?"

He said to Him, "Yes, Lord; You know that I [2]love You."

He said to him, [a]"Feed My lambs."

16 He said to him again a second time, "Simon, *son* of [1]Jonah, do you love Me?"

He said to Him, "Yes, Lord; You know that I [2]love You."

[a]He said to him, "Tend My [b]sheep."

17 He said to him the third time, "Simon, *son* of [1]Jonah, do you [2]love Me?" Peter was grieved because He said to him the third time, "Do you love Me?"

And he said to Him, "Lord, [a]You know all things; You know that I love You."

Jesus said to him, "Feed My sheep. 18 [a]Most assuredly, I say to you, when you were younger, you girded yourself and walked where you wished; but when you are old, you will stretch out your hands, and another will gird you and carry *you* where you do not wish." 19 This He spoke, signifying [a]by what death he would glorify God. And when He had spoken this, He said to him, [b]"Follow Me."

The Beloved Disciple and His Book

20 Then Peter, turning around, saw the disciple [a]whom Jesus loved following, [b]who also had leaned on His breast at the supper, and said, "Lord, who is the one who betrays You?" 21 Peter, seeing him, said to Jesus, "But Lord, what *about* this man?"

22 Jesus said to him, "If I [1]will that he remain [a]till I come, what *is that* to you? You follow Me."

23 Then this saying went out among the brethren that this disciple would not die. Yet Jesus did not say to him that he would not die, but, "If I will that he remain till I come, what *is that* to you?"

24 This is the disciple who [a]testifies of these things, and wrote these things; and we know that his testimony is true.

25 [a]And there are also many other things that Jesus did, which if they were written one by one, [b]I suppose that even the world itself could not contain the books that would be written. Amen.

---

30 a John 21:25
31 a Luke 1:4 b 1 John 5:13 c Luke 2:11 d John 3:15, 16; 5:24
CHAPTER 21
1 a John 6:1
2 a John 20:24 b John 1:45–51 c John 2:1 d Matt. 4:21
3 *1* NU omits *immediately*
4 a John 20:14
5 a Luke 24:41
6 a Luke 5:4, 6, 7
7 a John 13:23; 20:2
12 a Acts 10:41
14 a John 20:19, 26
15 a Acts 20:28 *1* NU *John* *2 have affection for*
16 a Heb. 13:20 b Ps. 79:13 *1* NU *John* *2 have affection for*
17 a John 2:24, 25; 16:30 *1* NU *John* *2 have affection for*
18 a Acts 12:3, 4
19 a 2 Pet. 1:13, 14 b [Matt. 4:19; 16:24]
20 a John 13:23; 20:2 b John 13:25
22 a [Rev. 2:25; 3:11; 22:7, 20] *1 desire*
24 a John 19:35
25 a John 20:30 b Amos 7:10

AUTHOR: *Historically, Luke*
DATE: *About A.D. 62*
THEME: *The Work of the Holy Spirit in the Early History of Christianity*
KEY WORDS: *Jesus, Spirit, Resurrection, Apostle, Church*

ACTS

Dear Woman of Destiny,

This powerful book contains the fulfillment of the promise given in Joel 2:28 that God would pour out His Spirit upon all flesh—upon boys and girls, as well as upon men and women. None will be left out. All are important to God. The women who were disciples of Christ were present with the men (see Acts 1:14; 2:17, 18). This would most likely have included women, such as Mary of Bethany who sat at Jesus' feet; Mary Magdalene, out of whom Jesus cast seven demons; and even Mary, the mother of Jesus. By including them in the account of the birth of the church, God was making a bold and radical statement in the culture of that day. As He was then, so He is now calling women from all walks of life to follow Christ and make a difference.

With His love,

Cindy Jacobs

Prologue

The former account I made,
O [a]Theophilus, of all that Jesus began both to do and teach, 2 [a]until
the day in which [1]He was taken up, after
He through the Holy Spirit [b]had given
commandments to the apostles whom He
had chosen, 3 [a]to whom He also presented
Himself alive after His suffering by many
[1]infallible proofs, being seen by them during forty days and speaking of the things
pertaining to the kingdom of God.

The Holy Spirit Promised

4 [a]And being assembled together with
them, He commanded them not to depart
from Jerusalem, but to wait for the Promise of the Father, "which," *He said,* "you
have [b]heard from Me; 5 [a]for John truly
baptized with water, [b]but you shall be
baptized with the Holy Spirit not many
days from now." 6 Therefore, when they
had come together, they asked Him, saying, "Lord, will You at this time restore
the kingdom to Israel?" 7 And He said to
them, [a]"It is not for you to [b]know times
or seasons which the Father has put in
His own authority. 8 [a]But you shall receive power [b]when the Holy Spirit has
come upon you; and [c]you shall be [1]wit-
nesses to Me in Jerusalem, and in all Judea and [d]Samaria, and to the [e]end of the
earth."

The Holy Spirit is the Gift of God, which gift is in truth itself equal to the Giver. Therefore, the Holy Spirit also is God, not inferior to the Father and the Son.

St. Augustine

Jesus Ascends to Heaven

9 [a]Now when He had spoken these
things, while they watched, [b]He was taken
up, and a cloud received Him out of their
sight. 10 And while they looked steadfastly
toward heaven as He went up, behold, two
men stood by them [a]in white apparel,
11 who also said, "Men of Galilee, why do
you stand gazing up into heaven? This
same Jesus, who was taken up from you
into heaven, [a]will so come in like manner
as you saw Him go into heaven."

The Upper Room Prayer Meeting

12 [a]Then they returned to Jerusalem
from the mount called Olivet, which is
near Jerusalem, a Sabbath day's journey.
13 And when they had entered, they went
up [a]into the upper room where they were
staying: [b]Peter, James, John, and Andrew;
Philip and Thomas; Bartholomew and
Matthew; James *the son* of Alphaeus and
[c]Simon the Zealot; and [d]Judas *the son* of
James. 14 [a]These all continued with one
[1]accord in prayer [2]and supplication, with
[b]the women and Mary the mother of Jesus, and with [c]His brothers.

Matthias Chosen

15 And in those days Peter stood up in
the midst of the [1]disciples (altogether the
number [a]of names was about a hundred
and twenty), and said, 16 "Men *and* brethren, this Scripture had to be fulfilled,
[a]which the Holy Spirit spoke before by the
mouth of David concerning Judas, [b]who
became a guide to those who arrested Jesus; 17 for [a]he was numbered with us and
obtained a part in [b]this ministry."

18 [a](Now this man purchased a field
with [b]the [1]wages of iniquity; and falling
headlong, he burst open in the middle and
all his [2]entrails gushed out. 19 And it became known to all those dwelling in Jerusalem; so that field is called in their own
language, Akel Dama, that is, Field of
Blood.)

20 "For it is written in the Book of
Psalms:

> [a]*'Let his dwelling place be [1]desolate,*
> *And let no one live in it';*

and,

> [b]*'Let another take his [2]office.'*

21 "Therefore, of these men who have
accompanied us all the time that the Lord
Jesus went in and out among us, 22 beginning from the baptism of John to that day
when [a]He was taken up from us, one of
these must [b]become a witness with us of
His resurrection."

23 And they proposed two: Joseph called
[a]Barsabas, who was surnamed Justus, and

CHAPTER 1
1 a Luke 1:3
2 a Mark 16:19 b Matt. 28:19 *1* He ascended into heaven.
3 a Mark 16:12, 14 *1 unmistakable*
4 a Luke 24:49 b [John 14:16, 17, 26; 15:26]
5 a Matt. 3:11 b [Joel 2:28]
7 a 1 Thess. 5:1 b Matt. 24:36
8 a [Acts 2:1, 4] b Luke 24:49 c Luke 24:48 d Acts 8:1, 5, 14 e Col. 1:23 *1* NU *My witnesses*
9 a Luke 24:50, 51 b Acts 1:2
10 a John 20:12
11 a Dan. 7:13
12 a Luke 24:52
13 a Acts 9:37, 39; 20:8 b Matt. 10:2–4 c Luke 6:15 d Jude 1
14 a Acts 2:1, 46 b Luke 23:49, 55 c Matt. 13:55 *1 purpose* or *mind* *2* NU omits *and supplication*
15 a Rev. 3:4 *1* NU *brethren*
16 a Ps. 41:9 b Luke 22:47
17 a Matt. 10:4 b Acts 1:25
18 a Matt. 27:3–10 b Mark 14:21 *1 reward of unrighteousness* *2 intestines*
20 a Ps. 69:25 b Ps. 109:8 *1 deserted* *2* Gr. *episkopen,* position of overseer
22 a Acts 1:9 b Acts 1:8; 2:32
23 a Acts 15:22

Acts 1:8

Dear Woman of Destiny,

One of the most exciting adventures of my life is my friendship and intimacy with the Holy Spirit! He has revolutionized my whole walk and relationship with the Lord Jesus!

It is so hard to put into words how I feel about Someone I love so deeply. After I was baptized in the Holy Spirit, the Word suddenly became alive and I could feel His tangible presence in my everyday life. The intimacy and love I had for the Lord began to spill out to others around me. My life became Acts 1:8.

The fact that the Holy Spirit is actually a Person with feelings, emotions, and personality was a real revelation to me! I began to interact and communicate with Him as my closest Friend, Counselor, Comforter, Guide, Teacher, and Revealer of the glorious Man Christ Jesus, the Lover of my soul.

Let me ask you some personal questions about your journey in the Lord. Are you personally acquainted with the Holy Spirit? Do you have power in your life to overcome the things that are displeasing to you and to God? Are you in bondage and cannot get free? Can you hear the Lord's voice and prompting in your everyday life, or do you feel isolated and lonely? Do you see significant results from your prayer life? Are you walking with the demonstrations of the power of the Holy Spirit evident in your life? Are you a carrier of God's presence with His glory radiating from you, confronting the darkness all around you?

As you know, accepting Jesus as your Lord and Savior is the most important decision you will ever make. The next crucial decision is to receive the baptism of the Holy Spirit, which is a baptism of divine impartation and revelation. Matthew 3:11 says, "He will baptize you with the Holy Spirit and fire."

When the disciples and all those in the Upper Room met together, "Suddenly there came a sound from heaven, as of a rushing mighty wind, and it filled the whole house where they were sitting" (Acts 2:2). They were baptized in the Holy Spirit, and the church was set ablaze—just like the Lord wants your life to be ignited now!

The baptism of the Holy Spirit is for everyone! All 120 people in the Upper Room received the gift of tongues and the courage to be radical and passionate voluntary lovers of Jesus Christ.

Beloved, I can feel the hunger in your heart to have a vibrant walk with the Lord! If you have not received the baptism of the Holy Spirit and you would like to, then please repeat this prayer out loud: "Come, Holy Spirit, and baptize me. I want Your impartation in every area of my life. Lord, I want to receive everything You have for me. My heart cry is for a radical transformation in my walk with You. Consume me, O God, with Your holy fire!"

As you pray this, continue to worship Him and tell Him how much you love Him. Woman of Destiny, I pray that from this moment on you will experience and enjoy all the fullness of the Holy Spirit in your life.

Jill Austin

Matthias. [24]And they prayed and said,
"You, O Lord, [a]who know the hearts of
all, show which of these two You have
chosen [25][a]to take part in this ministry and
apostleship from which Judas by transgression fell, that he might go to his own
place." [26]And they cast their lots, and the
lot fell on Matthias. And he was numbered
with the eleven apostles.

Coming of the Holy Spirit

2 When [a]the Day of Pentecost had fully
come, [b]they were all [1]with one accord
in one place. [2]And suddenly there came
a sound from heaven, as of a rushing
mighty wind, and [a]it filled the whole
house where they were sitting. [3]Then
there appeared to them [1]divided tongues,
as of fire, and *one* sat upon each of them.
[4]And [a]they were all filled with the Holy
Spirit and began [b]to speak with other
tongues, as the Spirit gave them utterance.

The Crowd's Response

[5]And there were dwelling in Jerusalem
Jews, [a]devout men, from every nation
under heaven. [6]And when this sound

24 a 1 Sam. 16:7
25 a Acts 1:17

CHAPTER 2
1 a Lev. 23:15 b Acts 1:14 1 NU *together*
2 a Acts 4:31
3 1 Or *tongues as of fire, distributed and resting on each*
4 a Acts 1:5 b Mark 16:17
5 a Acts 8:2

Polly Wigglesworth

Few women—few people, for that matter—would have the grit to "out-faith" the legendary Smith Wigglesworth. Yet Mary Jane Featherstone (1860–1913), known to most as Polly, lived such a life of complete reliance on God that it spurred a man renowned for his unshakeable faith to an even stronger trust in God.

Polly committed her life to Christ at age 17 through a Salvation Army evangelist. She quickly put her faith in action as an Army officer and grew in her passion to see the lost saved. At the same time, she was enjoying a blossoming relationship with Wigglesworth. In a few years, they were married in Bradford, England. While he worked incessantly to make money as a plumber and grew colder toward God, Polly gained a reputation as a fiery evangelist. Her heart weighed heavily with compassion for lost souls.

Once, while Polly prayed with a recent convert, the woman's husband barged in and threatened to physically remove Polly if she did not stop praying. Upon her refusal, he picked her up and carried her down five flights of stairs. As they went, she continued praying, "Lord, save this man; save his soul, Lord." At the end of the stairs, the man was kneeling with her, accepting Christ into his life.

Such was the passion Polly had for evangelism. After wooing her husband back into a radical love for God, she continued to spur him to holiness and complete faith in God. Polly was responsible for teaching Wigglesworth to read and write, and even urged him to continue preaching when he repeatedly would become tongue-tied to the point of tears while in front of a congregation. Were it not for Polly's commitment to God and determination to see her husband fulfill God's amazing destiny for his life, we would have no miraculous stories of the signs and wonders that followed the ministry of Smith Wigglesworth. May we, as women of destiny, not only pursue God's call for our own lives, but may we also encourage those around us to embrace God's purpose for their lives.

occurred, the [a]multitude came together,
and were confused, because everyone
heard them speak in his own language.
7 Then they were all amazed and marveled,
saying to one another, "Look, are not all
these who speak [a]Galileans? 8 And how *is*
it that we hear, each in our own [1]lan-
guage in which we were born? 9 Parthians
and Medes and Elamites, those dwelling
in Mesopotamia, Judea and [a]Cappadocia,
Pontus and Asia, 10 Phrygia and Pamphylia, Egypt and the parts of Libya adjoining
Cyrene, visitors from Rome, both Jews
and proselytes, 11 Cretans and [1]Arabs—we
hear them speaking in our own tongues
the wonderful works of God." 12 So they
were all amazed and perplexed, saying to
one another, "Whatever could this
mean?"
13 Others mocking said, "They are full of
new wine."

God expects to be represented by a fiery church or He is not, in any proper sense, represented at all. God Himself is all fire; and His church, if it is to be like Him, must also be like white heat. The only things that His church can afford to be on fire about are the great, eternal interests of heaven-born, God-given faith.

E. M. BOUNDS

Peter's Sermon

14 But Peter, standing up with the elev-
en, raised his voice and said to them,
"Men of Judea and all who dwell in Jerusalem, let this be known to you, and heed
my words. 15 For these are not drunk, as
you suppose, [a]since it is *only* [1]the third
hour of the day. 16 But this is what was
spoken by the prophet Joel:

17 *'And[a] it shall come to pass in the*
last days, says God,
[b]That I will pour out of My Spirit on
all flesh;
Your sons and [c]your daughters
shall prophesy,
Your young men shall see visions,
Your old men shall dream dreams.
18 *And on My menservants and on*
My maidservants
I will pour out My Spirit in those
days;
[a]And they shall prophesy.
19 *[a]I will show wonders in heaven*
above
And signs in the earth beneath:
Blood and fire and vapor of smoke.
20 *[a]The sun shall be turned into*
darkness,
And the moon into blood,
Before the coming of the great and
awesome day of the LORD.
21 *And it shall come to pass*
That [a]whoever calls on the name of
the LORD
Shall be saved.'

22 "Men of Israel, hear these words: Jesus of Nazareth, a Man attested by God
to you [a]by miracles, wonders, and signs
which God did through Him in your
midst, as you yourselves also know—
23 Him, [a]being delivered by the determined purpose and foreknowledge of God,
[b]you [1]have taken by lawless hands, have
crucified, and put to death; 24 [a]whom God
raised up, having [1]loosed the [2]pains of
death, because it was not possible that He
should be held by it. 25 For David says concerning Him:

[a]'I foresaw the LORD *always before*
my face,
For He is at my right hand, that I
may not be shaken.
26 *Therefore my heart rejoiced, and*
my tongue was glad;
Moreover my flesh also will rest in
hope.
27 *For You will not leave my soul in*
Hades,
Nor will You allow Your Holy One
to see [a]corruption.
28 *You have made known to me the*
ways of life;
You will make me full of joy in
Your presence.'

29 "Men *and* brethren, let *me* speak freely to you [a]of the patriarch David, that he

6 a Acts 4:32
7 a Acts 1:11
8 *1 dialect*
9 a 1 Pet. 1:1
11 *1 Arabians*
15 a 1 Thess. 5:7 *1* 9 A.M.
17 a Joel 2:28–32 b Acts 10:45 c Acts 21:9
18 a 1 Cor. 12:10
19 a Joel 2:30
20 a Matt. 24:29
21 a Rom. 10:13
22 a John 3:2; 5:6
23 a Luke 22:22 b Acts 5:30 *1* NU omits *have taken*
24 a [Rom. 8:11] *1 destroyed* or *abolished* *2* Lit. *birth pangs*
25 a Ps. 16:8–11
27 a Acts 13:30–37
29 a Acts 13:36

is both dead and buried, and his tomb is
with us to this day. 30Therefore, being a
prophet, [a]and knowing that God had
sworn with an oath to him that of the fruit
of his body, [1]according to the flesh, He
would raise up the Christ to sit on his
throne, 31he, foreseeing this, spoke concerning the resurrection of the Christ,
[a]that His soul was not left in Hades, nor
did His flesh see corruption. 32[a]This Jesus
God has raised up, [b]of which we are all
witnesses. 33Therefore [a]being exalted [1]to
[b]the right hand of God, and [c]having received from the Father the promise of the
Holy Spirit, He [d]poured out this which
you now see and hear.

34"For David did not ascend into the
heavens, but he says himself:

[a]*'The LORD said to my Lord,*
"Sit at My right hand,
35 *Till I make Your enemies Your*
footstool."'

36"Therefore let all the house of Israel
know assuredly that God has made this
Jesus, whom you crucified, both Lord and
Christ."

37Now when they heard *this,* [a]they were
cut to the heart, and said to Peter and the
rest of the apostles, "Men *and* brethren,
what shall we do?"

Father, may ____ repent and be baptized in the name of Jesus Christ for the remission of sins; and they will receive the gift of the Holy Spirit. For Your promise is to them and to their children, and to all who are afar off, as many as You will call.

FROM ACTS 2:38, 39

38Then Peter said to them, [a]"Repent,
and let every one of you be baptized in the
name of Jesus Christ for the [1]remission of
sins; and you shall receive the gift of the
Holy Spirit. 39For the promise is to you
and [a]to your children, and [b]to all who are
afar off, as many as the Lord our God will
call."

A Vital Church Grows

40And with many other words he testified and exhorted them, saying, "Be saved
from this [1]perverse generation." 41Then
those who [1]gladly received his word were
baptized; and that day about three thousand souls were added *to them.* 42[a]And
they continued steadfastly in the apostles'
[1]doctrine and fellowship, in the breaking
of bread, and in prayers. 43Then fear came
upon every soul, and [a]many wonders and
signs were done through the apostles.
44Now all who believed were together, and
[a]had all things in common, 45and [1]sold
their possessions and goods, and [a]divid-
ed[2] them among all, as anyone had need.
46[a]So continuing daily with one accord
[b]in the temple, and [c]breaking bread from
house to house, they ate their food with
gladness and simplicity of heart, 47prais-
ing God and having favor with all the people. And [a]the Lord added [1]to the church
daily those who were being saved.

A Lame Man Healed

3 Now Peter and John went up together
[a]to the temple at the hour of prayer,
[b]the ninth *hour.* 2And [a]a certain man
lame from his mother's womb was carried, whom they laid daily at the gate of
the temple which is called Beautiful, [b]to
[1]ask alms from those who entered the
temple; 3who, seeing Peter and John
about to go into the temple, asked for
alms. 4And fixing his eyes on him, with
John, Peter said, "Look at us." 5So he gave
them his attention, expecting to receive
something from them. 6Then Peter said,
"Silver and gold I do not have, but what I
do have I give you: [a]In the name of Jesus
Christ of Nazareth, rise up and walk."
7And he took him by the right hand and
lifted *him* up, and immediately his feet
and ankle bones received strength. 8So
he, [a]leaping up, stood and walked and entered the temple with them—walking,
leaping, and praising God. 9[a]And all the
people saw him walking and praising God.
10Then they knew that it was he who [a]sat
begging alms at the Beautiful Gate of the
temple; and they were filled with wonder
and amazement at what had happened to
him.

30 a Ps. 132:11 *1* NU *He would seat one on his throne,*
31 a Ps. 16:10
32 a Acts 2:24 b Acts 1:8; 3:15
33 a [Acts 5:31] b [Heb. 10:12] c [John 14:26] d Acts 2:1–11, 17; 10:45 *1* Possibly *by*
34 a Ps. 68:18; 110:1
37 a Luke 3:10, 12, 14
38 a Luke 24:47 *1 forgiveness*
39 a Joel 2:28, 32 b Eph. 2:13
40 *1 crooked*
41 *1* NU omits *gladly*
42 a Acts 1:14 *1 teaching*
43 a Acts 2:22
44 a Acts 4:32, 34, 37; 5:2
45 a Is. 58:7 *1 would sell 2 distributed*
46 a Acts 1:14 b Luke 24:53 c Acts 2:42; 20:7
47 a Acts 5:14 *1* NU omits *to the church*

CHAPTER 3
1 a Acts 2:46 b Ps. 55:17
2 a Acts 14:8 b John 9:8 *1 Beg*
6 a Acts 4:10
8 a Is. 35:6
9 a Acts 4:16, 21
10 a John 9:8

Preaching in Solomon's Portico

11Now as the lame man who was healed
held on to Peter and John, all the people
ran together to them in the porch [a]which
is called Solomon's, greatly amazed. 12So
when Peter saw *it,* he responded to the
people: "Men of Israel, why do you marvel
at this? Or why look so intently at us, as
though by our own power or godliness we
had made this man walk? 13[a]The God of
Abraham, Isaac, and Jacob, the God of
our fathers, [b]glorified His Servant Jesus,
whom you [c]delivered up and [d]denied in
the presence of Pilate, when he was determined to let *Him* go. 14But you denied
[a]the Holy One [b]and the Just, and [c]asked
for a murderer to be granted to you, 15and
killed the [1]Prince of life, [a]whom God
raised from the dead, [b]of which we are
witnesses. 16[a]And His name, through faith
in His name, has made this man strong,
whom you see and know. Yes, the faith
which *comes* through Him has given him
this perfect soundness in the presence of
you all.

Merciful Father, I pray that ____ will repent and be converted, that their sins may be blotted out, so that times of refreshing may come from Your presence.

FROM ACTS 3:19

17"Yet now, brethren, I know that [a]you
did *it* in ignorance, as *did* also your rulers.
18But [a]those things which God foretold
[b]by the mouth of all His prophets, that
the Christ would suffer, He has thus fulfilled. 19 [a]Repent therefore and be converted, that your sins may be blotted out,
so that times of refreshing may come
from the presence of the Lord, 20and
that He may send [1]Jesus Christ, who was
[2]preached to you before, 21[a]whom heaven
must receive until the times of [b]restora-
tion of all things, [c]which God has spoken
by the mouth of all His holy prophets
since [1]the world began. 22For Moses truly
said to the fathers, [a]*'The* LORD *your God
will raise up for you a Prophet like me
from your brethren. Him you shall hear in
all things, whatever He says to you.* 23*And
it shall be that every soul who will not
hear that Prophet shall be utterly destroyed from among the people.'* 24Yes,
and [a]all the prophets, from Samuel and
those who follow, as many as have spoken,
have also [1]foretold these days. 25[a]You are
sons of the prophets, and of the covenant
which God made with our fathers, saying
to Abraham, [b]*'And in your seed all the
families of the earth shall be blessed.'* 26To
you [a]first, God, having raised up His Servant Jesus, sent Him to bless you, [b]in
turning away every one *of you* from your
iniquities."

Peter and John Arrested

4 Now as they spoke to the people, the
priests, the captain of the temple, and
the [a]Sadducees came upon them, 2being
greatly disturbed that they taught the
people and preached in Jesus the resurrection from the dead. 3And they laid
hands on them, and put *them* in custody
until the next day, for it was already evening. 4However, many of those who heard
the word believed; and the number of the
men came to be about five thousand.

Addressing the Sanhedrin

5And it came to pass, on the next day,
that their rulers, elders, and scribes, 6as
well as [a]Annas the high priest, Caiaphas,
John, and Alexander, and as many as were
of the family of the high priest, were gathered together at Jerusalem. 7And when
they had set them in the midst, they
asked, [a]"By what power or by what name
have you done this?"

8[a]Then Peter, filled with the Holy Spirit, said to them, "Rulers of the people and
elders of Israel: 9If we this day are judged
for a good deed *done* to a helpless man, by
what means he has been made well, 10let
it be known to you all, and to all the people of Israel, [a]that by the name of Jesus
Christ of Nazareth, whom you crucified,
[b]whom God raised from the dead, by Him
this man stands here before you whole.
11This is the [a]*'stone which was rejected by
you builders, which has become the chief
cornerstone.'* 12[a]Nor is there salvation in
any other, for there is no other name under heaven given among men by which we
must be saved."

---

11 a John 10:23
13 a John 5:30 b John 7:39; 12:23; 13:31 c Matt. 27:2 d Matt. 27:20
14 a Mark 1:24 b Acts 7:52 c John 18:40
15 a Acts 2:24 b Acts 2:32 *1* Or *Originator*
16 a Matt. 9:22
17 a Luke 23:34
18 a Acts 26:22 b 1 Pet. 1:10
19 a [Acts 2:38; 26:20]
20 *1* NU, M *Christ Jesus* *2* NU, M *ordained for you before*
21 a Acts 1:11 b Matt. 17:11 c Luke 1:70 *1* Or *time*
22 a Deut. 18:15, 18, 19
24 a Luke 24:25 *1* NU, M *proclaimed*
25 a [Rom. 9:4, 8] b Gen. 12:3; 18:18; 22:18; 26:4; 28:14
26 a [Rom. 1:16; 2:9] b Matt. 1:21

CHAPTER 4
1 a Matt. 22:23
6 a Luke 3:2
7 a Matt. 21:23
8 a Luke 12:11, 12
10 a Acts 2:22; 3:6, 16 b Acts 2:24
11 a Ps. 118:22
12 a [1 Tim. 2:5, 6]

Acts 3:19

Dear Woman of Destiny,

In these days of busy schedules and fast-paced lifestyles, refreshing may be just what you need today. Sometimes you may find it difficult to squeeze in a little time to read your Bible and pray. Have you ever noticed that just about the time you turn your attention to God and to your daily devotions, the phone rings or a child wakes up from a nap?

Whether you work in your home or have an outside career, there are many demands and deadlines. It's hard to fit God in. "Oh well, Lord, You understand . . . I was just too busy today and now I'm so tired. Tomorrow will be better," you say as you drop into bed at night. Sound familiar? Maybe the problem is that you could be trying to fit God into your plans instead of letting yourself fit into God and His plans. After all, Romans 8:28 tells us, "And we know that all things work together for good to those who love God, to those who are the called according to His purpose."

When I think of "times of refreshing," I think of an ice-cold glass of water on a hot summer day or a time of sweet fellowship with a dear friend. I would never think of that glass of water as just one more thing to do. It is necessary for my survival (especially because I live in the desert!). The fellowship with my friend isn't a burden, but a blessing. When I haven't seen my friend for awhile, I thirst for the fellowship. There's always so much to share, and it lifts my spirit. The presence of Jesus is that drink of water to your thirsty soul (see Ps. 42:1, 2). His presence is a fellowship that is so satisfying you will never thirst again (see John 4:14).

Acts 3:19 tells us to repent and return so that we can have "times of refreshing." If you are in a dry time or in a spiritual wilderness, there is a way out. Repentance simply means "turning around and going the other way." John the Baptist brought the message of repentance in the wilderness in order to prepare the way of the Lord (see Luke 3:3, 4). In my experience, I have learned that I must return daily to the Lord. I must live a lifestyle of repentance. This makes a way—a highway in the desert—for the Lord.

Maybe the Lord is talking to you about returning to your "first love" (see Rev. 2:4) and putting Him first. If you "repent . . . and be converted," Jesus will come to you. And that, my friend, is refreshing!

LaNora Van Arsdall

The Name of Jesus Forbidden

13 Now when they saw the boldness of
Peter and John, [a]and perceived that they
were uneducated and untrained men,
they marveled. And they realized that they
had been with Jesus. 14And seeing the
man who had been healed [a]standing with
them, they could say nothing against it.
15But when they had commanded them to
go aside out of the council, they conferred
among themselves, 16saying, [a]"What shall
we do to these men? For, indeed, that a
[1]notable miracle has been done through
them *is* [b]evident[2] to all who dwell in Jerusalem, and we cannot deny *it*. 17But so
that it spreads no further among the people, let us severely threaten them, that
from now on they speak to no man in this
name."

18[a]So they called them and commanded
them not to speak at all nor teach in the
name of Jesus. 19But Peter and John answered and said to them, [a]"Whether it is
right in the sight of God to listen to you
more than to God, you judge. 20[a]For we
cannot but speak the things which [b]we
have seen and heard." 21So when they had
further threatened them, they let them
go, finding no way of punishing them,
[a]because of the people, since they all [b]glo-
rified God for [c]what had been done. 22For
the man was over forty years old on whom
this miracle of healing had been performed.

Prayer for Boldness

23And being let go, [a]they went to their
own *companions* and reported all that the
chief priests and elders had said to them.
24So when they heard that, they raised
their voice to God with one accord and
said: "Lord, [a]You *are* God, who made
heaven and earth and the sea, and all that
is in them, 25who [1]by the mouth of Your
servant David have said:

[a]*'Why did the nations rage,*
And the people plot vain things?
26 *The kings of the earth took their*
stand,
And the rulers were gathered
together
Against the LORD and against His
Christ.'

27"For [a]truly against [b]Your holy Servant Jesus, [c]whom You anointed, both
Herod and Pontius Pilate, with the Gentiles and the people of Israel, were gathered together 28[a]to do whatever Your
hand and Your purpose determined before
to be done. 29Now, Lord, look on their
threats, and grant to Your servants [a]that
with all boldness they may speak Your
word, 30by stretching out Your hand to
heal, [a]and that signs and wonders may be
done [b]through the name of [c]Your holy
Servant Jesus."

Lord God, grant to Your servant _____, that with all boldness they may speak Your word. Lord, stretch out Your hand to heal, and may signs and wonders be done through the name of Your holy Servant Jesus.

FROM ACTS 4:29, 30

31And when they had prayed, [a]the place
where they were assembled together was
shaken; and they were all filled with the
Holy Spirit, [b]and they spoke the word of
God with boldness.

Sharing in All Things

32 Now the multitude of those who
believed [a]were of one heart and one soul;
[b]neither did anyone say that any of the
things he possessed was his own, but they
had all things in common. 33And with
[a]great power the apostles gave [b]witness to
the resurrection of the Lord Jesus. And
[c]great grace was upon them all. 34Nor was
there anyone among them who lacked;
[a]for all who were possessors of lands or
houses sold them, and brought the proceeds of the things that were sold, 35[a]and
laid *them* at the apostles' feet; [b]and they
distributed to each as anyone had need.
36And [1]Joses, who was also named Barnabas by the apostles (which is translated
Son of [2]Encouragement), a Levite of the
country of Cyprus, 37[a]having land, sold *it*,
and brought the money and laid *it* at the
apostles' feet.

---

13 a [1 Cor. 1:27]
14 a Acts 3:11
16 a John 11:47 b Acts 3:7–10 *1 remarkable sign* *2 well known*
18 a Acts 5:28, 40
19 a Acts 5:29
20 a Acts 1:8; 2:32 b [1 John 1:1, 3]
21 a Acts 5:26 b Matt. 15:31 c Acts 3:7, 8
23 a Acts 2:44–46; 12:12
24 a Ex. 20:11
25 a Ps. 2:1, 2 *1* NU *through the Holy Spirit, by the mouth of our father, Your servant David,*
27 a Luke 22:2; 23:1, 8 b [Luke 1:35] c John 10:36
28 a Acts 2:23; 3:18
29 a Acts 4:13, 31; 9:27; 13:46; 14:3; 19:8; 26:26
30 a Acts 2:43; 5:12 b Acts 3:6, 16 c Acts 4:27
31 a Acts 2:2, 4; 16:26 b Acts 4:29
32 a Rom. 15:5, 6 b Acts 2:44
33 a [Acts 1:8] b Acts 1:22 c Rom. 6:15
34 a Acts 2:45
35 a Acts 4:37; 5:2 b Acts 2:45; 6:1
36 *1* NU *Joseph* *2* Or *Consolation*
37 a Acts 4:34, 35; 5:1, 2

Acts 4:13

Dear Woman of Destiny,

Blessings on you and grace for today!

Please allow me to share with you the impact you can have on those around you, just by living in the presence of Jesus. When I was young, I was a rebellious teenager. As you know, teenagers in rebellion do a lot of things their parents don't want them to do. I remember, on one particular occasion, coming home at three o'clock in the morning. My mom was waiting for me. She was sitting on the sofa with her Bible on her knees when I came walking through the door. Do you know what she did? Rather than raise her voice in disgust at my behavior, she softly said, "Good night, honey." And then she went to bed. I remember the presence of Jesus emanating from her life. It was as if she were saying, "Thank You, Jesus, for bringing my daughter home safely. She's home now. You have been with me while I waited. I have been in Your presence. I have been leaning on You." Without even knowing it, my momma had been speaking into my life by radiating her sweet, gentle spirit that came from being with Jesus.

Another example was Helen. She was a little lady who could hardly walk, who worked at the Teen Challenge program where I was a student. Her knees were swollen, her ankles were weak, and she lived with agonizing arthritic pain. I remember her slowly walking down the hall. To me, it was as if she were gliding; the presence of God was all over her. She would come into the classroom, slip her little body into the chair, and begin teaching us the Word of God. The Spirit of God infiltrated our group. Oftentimes, weeping would break out and we would find ourselves on our knees, going after God. I remember thinking, "Someday, I want to be like Sister Helen."

Woman of Destiny, you may ask, "What made the difference in these women's lives?" The answer is clear. My mom spent time with Jesus—alone! And as for Sister Helen, one day I found her on her arthritic knees, in the presence of the Lord, worshiping—all alone. For my mom and Sister Helen, spending time in sweet communion with Jesus was part of their daily routine.

My friend, spend time with Jesus. It will be said of you as it was said of the disciples, "She has been with the Lord."

Keep going after God.

Jeri Hill

Acts 4:32

Dear Woman of Destiny,

Acts 4:32 gives us a beautiful example of the believers who incorporated giving into their lives as a lifestyle. They were of one heart and mind; they did not claim ownership over any of their possessions; and they shared all they had. As a result, there was not anyone in need.

What does it mean for a woman to enter into a lifestyle of giving? First, we must realize that all we have in this world has come from God. All of our material possessions, our occupations, and anything else of value have come from our Father. Psalm 24:1 says, "The earth is the LORD's, and all its fullness, the world and those who dwell therein." God also gives us the power to get wealth, as we see in Deuteronomy 8:18: "And you shall remember the LORD your God, for it is He who gives you power to get wealth, that He may establish His covenant which He swore to your fathers, as it is this day."

The believers in Acts 4:32 fully understood that their possessions were not their own. They were sold out to Jesus. In the persecution of that day, they fully expected to lose everything they had for the cause of Christ. Therefore, it was easier for them to loosely hold onto their belongings. Whether or not we are under persecution for our beliefs, we are to imitate in every way these Christians who have gone before us.

Consider God's call in Romans 12:1: "I beseech you therefore, brethren, by the mercies of God, that you present your bodies a living sacrifice, holy, acceptable to God, which is your reasonable service." We must first submit our bodies and souls for the Lord to use as He determines. Full submission to Christ also implies giving back to God that which He has first given us, which means not only our lives but also all things of value in our lives. This is a voluntary act of worship because we want to glorify the Lord.

Giving is not a single act but a lifestyle of submitting all things to the Lord (recognizing that He gave them to us in the first place) and holding on loosely to our resources. Giving includes every part of our lives: hospitality, automobiles, clothing, finances, as well as our time, talents, and skills. For married women, it is important for us to be in agreement with our spouses in the area of giving, because marriage is a partnership.

As true givers, each year we should try to give more than we gave the year before. The average evangelical Christian gives less than three percent of his or her annual income to the cause of Jesus Christ. As the wealthiest country on earth, Americans are dreadfully undergiving. This is a serious issue for believers, because we miss important blessings by holding back our giving (see Mal. 3)—blessings that we need to fulfill the call of God on our lives.

Have you allowed God to use you through giving in every area of your life? Have you ever asked God if you are giving to your full potential? Giving is an area that needs growth for most Christians. Let us aspire to be mature, productive Christians, with giving as an integral part of our lifestyle.

Megan Doyle

Lying to the Holy Spirit

5 But a certain man named Ananias, with Sapphira his wife, sold a possession. 2And he kept back *part* of the proceeds, his wife also being aware *of it,* and brought a certain part and laid *it* at the apostles' feet. 3[a]But Peter said, "Ananias, why has [b]Satan filled your heart to lie to the Holy Spirit and keep back *part* of the price of the land for yourself? 4While it remained, was it not your own? And after it was sold, was it not in your own control? Why have you conceived this thing in your heart? You have not lied to men but to God."

> *The only way in which we as a church or an individual can successfully put on the wonder-working mantle of the Holy Spirit is to first rend our own garments—our own plans, methods, ideas, desires, schemes . . . in two pieces and strip them away. Then we may put on the mantle of power which our Lord has sent down.*
>
> AIMEE SEMPLE MCPHERSON

5Then Ananias, hearing these words, [a]fell down and breathed his last. So great fear came upon all those who heard these things. 6And the young men arose and [a]wrapped him up, carried *him* out, and buried *him.*

7Now it was about three hours later when his wife came in, not knowing what had happened. 8And Peter answered her, "Tell me whether you sold the land for so much?"

She said, "Yes, for so much."

9Then Peter said to her, "How is it that you have agreed together [a]to test the Spirit of the Lord? Look, the feet of those who have buried your husband *are* at the door, and they will carry you out." 10[a]Then immediately she fell down at his feet and breathed her last. And the young men came in and found her dead, and carrying *her* out, buried *her* by her husband. 11[a]So great fear came upon all the church and upon all who heard these things.

Continuing Power in the Church

12And [a]through the hands of the apostles many signs and wonders were done among the people. [b]And they were all with one accord in Solomon's Porch. 13Yet [a]none of the rest dared join them, [b]but the people esteemed them highly. 14And believers were increasingly added to the Lord, multitudes of both men and women, 15so that they brought the sick out into the streets and laid *them* on beds and couches, [a]that at least the shadow of Peter passing by might fall on some of them. 16Also a multitude gathered from the surrounding cities to Jerusalem, bringing [a]sick people and those who were tormented by unclean spirits, and they were all healed.

Imprisoned Apostles Freed

17[a]Then the high priest rose up, and all those who *were* with him (which is the sect of the Sadducees), and they were filled with [1]indignation, 18[a]and laid their hands on the apostles and put them in the common prison. 19But at night [a]an angel of the Lord opened the prison doors and brought them out, and said, 20"Go, stand in the temple and speak to the people [a]all the words of this life."

21And when they heard *that,* they entered the temple early in the morning and taught. [a]But the high priest and those with him came and called the [1]council together, with all the [2]elders of the children of Israel, and sent to the prison to have them brought.

Apostles on Trial Again

22But when the officers came and did not find them in the prison, they returned and reported, 23saying, "Indeed we found the prison shut securely, and the guards standing [1]outside before the doors; but when we opened them, we found no one inside!" 24Now when [1]the high priest, [a]the

CHAPTER 5
3 [a]Deut. 23:21 [b]Luke 22:3
5 [a]Acts 5:10, 11
6 [a]John 19:40
9 [a]Acts 5:3, 4
10 [a]Acts 5:5
11 [a]Acts 2:43; 5:5; 19:17
12 [a]Acts 2:43; 4:30; 6:8; 14:3; 15:12 [b]Acts 3:11; 4:32
13 [a]John 9:22 [b]Acts 2:47; 4:21
15 [a]Acts 19:12
16 [a]Mark 16:17, 18
17 [a]Acts 4:1, 2, 6 [1]*jealousy*
18 [a]Luke 21:12
19 [a]Acts 12:7; 16:26
20 [a][John 6:63, 68; 17:3]
21 [a]Acts 4:5, 6 [1]Sanhedrin [2]*council of elders* or *senate*
23 [1]NU, M omit *outside*
24 [a]Acts 4:1; 5:26 [1]NU omits *the high priest*

captain of the temple, and the chief
priests heard these things, they wondered
what the outcome would be. 25So one
came and told them, [1]saying, "Look, the
men whom you put in prison are standing
in the temple and teaching the people!"
26Then the captain went with the officers and brought them without violence,
[a]for they feared the people, lest they
should be stoned. 27And when they had
brought them, they set *them* before the
council. And the high priest asked them,
28saying, [a]"Did we not strictly command
you not to teach in this name? And look,
you have filled Jerusalem with your doctrine, [b]and intend to bring this Man's
[c]blood on us!"
29But Peter and the *other* apostles answered and said: [a]"We ought to obey God
rather than men. 30[a]The God of our fathers raised up Jesus whom you murdered
by [b]hanging on a tree. 31[a]Him God has
exalted to His right hand *to be* [b]Prince
and [c]Savior, [d]to give repentance to Israel
and forgiveness of sins. 32And [a]we are His
witnesses to these things, and *so* also *is*
the Holy Spirit [b]whom God has given to
those who obey Him."

Gamaliel's Advice

33When they heard *this,* they were [a]fu-
rious[1] and plotted to kill them. 34Then
one in the council stood up, a Pharisee
named [a]Gamaliel, a teacher of the law
held in respect by all the people, and commanded them to put the apostles outside
for a little while. 35And he said to them:
"Men of Israel, [1]take heed to yourselves
what you intend to do regarding these
men. 36For some time ago Theudas rose
up, claiming to be somebody. A number of
men, about four hundred, [1]joined him.
He was slain, and all who obeyed him
were scattered and came to nothing. 37Af-
ter this man, Judas of Galilee rose up in
the days of the census, and drew away
many people after him. He also perished,
and all who obeyed him were dispersed.
38And now I say to you, keep away from
these men and let them alone; for if this
plan or this work is of men, it will come
to nothing; 39[a]but if it is of God, you cannot overthrow it—lest you even be found
[b]to fight against God."
40And they agreed with him, and when
they had [a]called for the apostles [b]and
beaten *them,* they commanded that they
should not speak in the name of Jesus,
and let them go. 41So they departed from
the presence of the council, [a]rejoicing
that they were counted worthy to suffer
shame for [1]His name. 42And daily [a]in the
temple, and in every house, [b]they did not
cease teaching and preaching Jesus *as* the
Christ.

Seven Chosen to Serve

6 Now in those days, [a]when *the number
of* the disciples was multiplying, there
arose a complaint against the Hebrews by
the [b]Hellenists,[1] because their widows
were neglected [c]in the daily distribution.
2Then the twelve summoned the multitude of the disciples and said, [a]"It is not
desirable that we should leave the word of
God and serve tables. 3Therefore, brethren, [a]seek out from among you seven men
of *good* reputation, full of the Holy Spirit
and wisdom, whom we may appoint over
this [b]business; 4but we [a]will give ourselves continually to prayer and to the
ministry of the word."
5And the saying pleased the whole multitude. And they chose Stephen, [a]a man
full of faith and the Holy Spirit, and [b]Phil-
ip, Prochorus, Nicanor, Timon, Parme-
nas, and [c]Nicolas, a proselyte from
Antioch, 6whom they set before the apostles; and [a]when they had prayed, [b]they
laid hands on them.
7Then [a]the word of God spread, and the
number of the disciples multiplied greatly
in Jerusalem, and a great many [b]of the
priests were obedient to the faith.

Stephen Accused of Blasphemy

8And Stephen, full of [1]faith and power,
did great [a]wonders and signs among the
people. 9Then there arose some from what
is called the Synagogue of the Freedmen
(Cyrenians, Alexandrians, and those from
Cilicia and Asia), disputing with Stephen.
10And [a]they were not able to resist the
wisdom and the Spirit by which he spoke.
11[a]Then they secretly induced men to say,
"We have heard him speak blasphemous
words against Moses and God." 12And they
stirred up the people, the elders, and the
scribes; and they came upon *him,* seized
him, and brought *him* to the council.
13They also set up false witnesses who
said, "This man does not cease to speak
[1]blasphemous words against this holy

25 [1] NU, M omit *saying*
26 a Matt. 21:26
28 a Acts 4:17, 18 b Acts 2:23, 36 c Matt. 23:35
29 a Acts 4:19
30 a Acts 3:13, 15 b [1 Pet. 2:24]
31 a [Acts 2:33, 36] b Acts 3:15 c Matt. 1:21 d Luke 24:47
32 a John 15:26, 27 b Acts 2:4; 10:44
33 a Acts 2:37; 7:54 [1] *cut to the quick*
34 a Acts 22:3
35 [1] *be careful*
36 [1] *followed*
39 a 1 Cor. 1:25 b Acts 7:51; 9:5
40 a Acts 4:18 b Matt. 10:17
41 a [1 Pet. 4:13–16] [1] NU *the name;* M *the name of Jesus*
42 a Acts 2:46 b Acts 4:20, 29

CHAPTER 6
1 a Acts 2:41; 4:4 b Acts 9:29; 11:20 c Acts 4:35; 11:29 [1] *Greek-speaking Jews*
2 a Ex. 18:17
3 a 1 Tim. 3:7 b 1 Tim. 3:8–13
4 a Acts 2:42
5 a Acts 6:3; 11:24 b Acts 8:5, 26; 21:8 c Rev. 2:6, 15
6 a Acts 1:24 b [2 Tim. 1:6]
7 a Acts 12:24 b John 12:42
8 a Acts 2:43; 5:12; 8:15; 14:3 [1] NU *grace*
10 a Luke 21:15
11 a 1 Kin. 21:10, 13
13 [1] NU omits *blasphemous*

place and the law; 14 [a]for we have heard him say that this Jesus of Nazareth will destroy this place and change the customs which Moses delivered to us." 15 And all who sat in the council, looking steadfastly at him, saw his face as the face of an angel.

Stephen's Address: The Call of Abraham

7 Then the high priest said, "Are these things so?"

2 And he said, [a]"Brethren and fathers, listen: The [b]God of glory appeared to our father Abraham when he was in Mesopotamia, before he dwelt in [c]Haran, 3 and said to him, [a]'*Get out of your country and from your relatives, and come to a land that I will show you.*' 4 Then [a]he came out of the land of the Chaldeans and dwelt in Haran. And from there, when his father was [b]dead, He moved him to this land in which you now dwell. 5 And *God* gave him no inheritance in it, not even *enough* to set his foot on. But even when *Abraham* had no child, [a]He promised to give it to him for a possession, and to his descendants after him. 6 But God spoke in this way: [a]that his descendants would dwell in a foreign land, and that they would bring them into [b]bondage and oppress *them* four hundred years. 7 [a]'*And the nation to whom they will be in bondage I will* [b]*judge,*' said God, [c]'*and after that they shall come out and serve Me in this place.*' 8 [a]Then He gave him the covenant of circumcision; [b]and so *Abraham* begot Isaac and circumcised him on the eighth day; [c]and Isaac *begot* Jacob, and [d]Jacob *begot* the twelve patriarchs.

The Patriarchs in Egypt

9 [a]"And the patriarchs, becoming envious, [b]sold Joseph into Egypt. [c]But God was with him 10 and delivered him out of all his troubles, [a]and gave him favor and wisdom in the presence of Pharaoh, king of Egypt; and he made him governor over Egypt and all his house. 11 [a]Now a famine and great [1]trouble came over all the land of Egypt and Canaan, and our fathers found no sustenance. 12 [a]But when Jacob heard that there was grain in Egypt, he sent out our fathers first. 13 And the [a]second *time* Joseph was made known to his brothers, and Joseph's family became known to the Pharaoh. 14 [a]Then Joseph sent and called his father Jacob and [b]all his relatives to *him,* [1]seventy-five people. 15 [a]So Jacob went down to Egypt; [b]and he died, he and our fathers. 16 And [a]they were carried back to Shechem and laid in [b]the tomb that Abraham bought for a sum of money from the sons of Hamor, *the father* of Shechem.

God Delivers Israel by Moses

17 "But when [a]the time of the promise drew near which God had sworn to Abraham, [b]the people grew and multiplied in Egypt 18 till another king [a]arose who did not know Joseph. 19 This man dealt treacherously with our people, and oppressed our forefathers, [a]making them expose their babies, so that they might not live. 20 [a]At this time Moses was born, and [b]was well pleasing to God; and he was brought up in his father's house for three months. 21 But [a]when he was set out, [b]Pharaoh's daughter took him away and brought him up as her own son. 22 And Moses was learned in all the wisdom of the Egyptians, and was [a]mighty in words and deeds.

23 [a]"Now when he was forty years old, it came into his heart to visit his brethren, the children of Israel. 24 And seeing one of *them* suffer wrong, he defended and avenged him who was oppressed, and struck down the Egyptian. 25 For he supposed that his brethren would have understood that God would deliver them by his hand, but they did not understand. 26 And the next day he appeared to two of them as they were fighting, and *tried to* reconcile them, saying, 'Men, you are brethren; why do you wrong one another?' 27 But he who did his neighbor wrong pushed him away, saying, [a]'*Who made you a ruler and a judge over us?* 28 *Do you want to kill me as you did the Egyptian yesterday?*' 29 [a]Then, at this saying, Moses fled and became a dweller in the land of Midian, where he [b]had two sons.

30 [a]"And when forty years had passed, an Angel [1]of the Lord appeared to him in a flame of fire in a bush, in the wilderness of Mount Sinai. 31 When Moses saw *it,* he marveled at the sight; and as he drew near to observe, the voice of the Lord came to him, 32 *saying,* [a]'*I am the God of your fathers—the God of Abraham, the God of*

14 a Acts 10:38; 25:8

CHAPTER 7

2 a Acts 22:1 b Ps. 29:3 c Gen. 11:31, 32
3 a Gen. 12:1
4 a Gen. 11:31; 15:7 b Gen. 11:32
5 a Gen. 12:7; 13:15; 15:3, 18; 17:8; 26:3
6 a Gen. 15:13, 14, 16; 47:11, 12 b Ex. 1:8–14; 12:40, 41
7 a Gen. 15:14 b Ex. 14:13–31 c Ex. 3:12
8 a Gen. 17:9–14 b Gen. 21:1–5 c Gen. 25:21–26 d Gen. 29:31—30:24; 35:18, 22–26
9 a Gen. 37:4, 11, 28 b Gen. 37:28 c Gen. 39:2, 21, 23
10 a Gen. 41:38–44
11 a Gen. 41:54; 42:5 *1 affliction*
12 a Gen. 42:1, 2
13 a Gen. 45:4, 16
14 a Gen. 45:9, 27 b Deut. 10:22 *1* Or *seventy,* Ex. 1:5
15 a Gen. 46:1–7 b Gen. 49:33
16 a Josh. 24:32 b Gen. 23:16
17 a Gen. 15:13 b Ex. 1:7–9
18 a Ex. 1:8
19 a Ex. 1:22
20 a Ex. 2:1, 2 b Heb. 11:23
21 a Ex. 2:3, 4 b Ex. 2:5–10
22 a Luke 24:19
23 a Ex. 2:11, 12
27 a Ex. 2:14
29 a Heb. 11:27 b Ex. 2:15, 21, 22; 4:20; 18:3

30 a Ex. 3:1–10 *1* NU omits *of the Lord* **32** a Ex. 3:6, 15

Isaac, and the God of Jacob.' And Moses trembled and dared not look. 33 [a]*'Then the* LORD *said to him, "Take your sandals off your feet, for the place where you stand is holy ground.* 34 *I have surely* [a]*seen the oppression of My people who are in Egypt; I have heard their groaning and have come down to deliver them. And now come, I will* [b]*send you to Egypt."'*

35 "This Moses whom they rejected, saying, [a]*'Who made you a ruler and a judge?'* is the one God sent *to be* a ruler and a deliverer [b]by the hand of the Angel who appeared to him in the bush. 36 [a]He brought them out, after he had [b]shown wonders and signs in the land of Egypt, [c]and in the Red Sea, [d]and in the wilderness forty years.

Israel Rebels Against God

37 "This is that Moses who said to the children of Israel, [a]*'The* LORD *your God will raise up for you a Prophet like me from your brethren.* [b]*Him*[1] *you shall hear.'*

38 [a]"This is he who was in the [1]congregation in the wilderness with [b]the Angel who spoke to him on Mount Sinai, and *with* our fathers, [c]the one who received the living [d]oracles[2] to give to us, 39 whom our fathers [a]would not obey, but rejected. And in their hearts they turned back to Egypt, 40 [a]saying to Aaron, *'Make us gods to go before us; as for this Moses who brought us out of the land of Egypt, we do not know what has become of him.'* 41 [a]And they made a calf in those days, offered sacrifices to the idol, and [b]rejoiced in the works of their own hands. 42 Then [a]God turned and gave them up to worship [b]the host of heaven, as it is written in the book of the Prophets:

[c]*'Did you offer Me slaughtered*
animals and sacrifices during
forty years in the wilderness,
O house of Israel?
43 *You also took up the tabernacle of*
Moloch,
And the star of your god Remphan,
Images which you made to worship;
And [a]*I will carry you away beyond*
Babylon.'

God's True Tabernacle

44 "Our fathers had the tabernacle of witness in the wilderness, as He appointed, instructing Moses [a]to make it according to the pattern that he had seen, 45 [a]which our fathers, having received it in turn, also brought with Joshua into the land possessed by the Gentiles, [b]whom God drove out before the face of our fathers until the [c]days of David, 46 [a]who found favor before God and [b]asked to find a dwelling for the God of Jacob. 47 [a]But Solomon built Him a house.

48 "However, [a]the Most High does not dwell in temples made with hands, as the prophet says:

49 *'Heaven*[a] *is My throne,*
And earth is My footstool.
What house will you build for Me?
says the LORD,
Or what is the place of My rest?
50 *Has My hand not* [a]*made all these*
things?'

Israel Resists the Holy Spirit

51 "*You* [a]stiff-necked[1] and [b]uncircumcised in heart and ears! You always resist the Holy Spirit; as your fathers *did,* so *do* you. 52 [a]Which of the prophets did your fathers not persecute? And they killed those who foretold the coming of [b]the Just One, of whom you now have become the betrayers and murderers, 53 [a]who have received the law by the direction of angels and have not kept *it.*"

Stephen the Martyr

54 [a]When they heard these things they were [1]cut to the heart, and they gnashed at him with *their* teeth. 55 But he, [a]being full of the Holy Spirit, gazed into heaven and saw the [b]glory of God, and Jesus standing at the right hand of God, 56 and said, "Look! [a]I see the heavens opened and the [b]Son of Man standing at the right hand of God!"

57 Then they cried out with a loud voice, stopped their ears, and ran at him with one accord; 58 and they cast *him* out of the city and stoned *him.* And [a]the witnesses laid down their clothes at the feet of a young man named Saul. 59 And they stoned Stephen as he was calling on *God* and saying, "Lord Jesus, [a]receive my spirit." 60 Then he knelt down and cried out with a loud voice, [a]"Lord, do not charge them with this sin." And when he had said this, he fell asleep.

33 a Ex. 3:5, 7, 8, 10
34 a Ex. 2:24, 25 b Ps. 105:26
35 a Ex. 2:14 b Ex. 14:21
36 a Ex. 12:41; 33:1 b Ps. 105:27 c Ex. 14:21 d Ex. 16:1, 35
37 a Deut. 18:15, 18, 19 b Matt. 17:5 *1* NU, M omit *Him you shall hear*
38 a Ex. 19:3 b Gal. 3:19 c Deut. 5:27 d Heb. 5:12 *1* Gr. *ekklesia, assembly* or *church* *2 sayings*
39 a Ps. 95:8–11
40 a Ex. 32:1, 23
41 a Deut. 9:16 b Ex. 32:6, 18, 19
42 a [2 Thess. 2:11] b 2 Kin. 21:3 c Amos 5:25–27
43 a Jer. 25:9–12
44 a [Heb. 8:5]
45 a Josh. 3:14; 18:1; 23:9 b Ps. 44:2 c 2 Sam. 6:2–15
46 a 2 Sam. 7:1–13 b 1 Chr. 22:7
47 a 1 Kin. 6:1–38; 8:20, 21
48 a 1 Kin. 8:27
49 a Is. 66:1, 2
50 a Ps. 102:25
51 a Ex. 32:9 b Lev. 26:41 *1 stubborn*
52 a 2 Chr. 36:16 b Acts 3:14; 22:14
53 a Ex. 20:1
54 a Acts 5:33 *1 furious*
55 a Acts 6:5 b [Ex. 24:17]
56 a Matt. 3:16 b Dan. 7:13
58 a Acts 22:20
59 a Ps. 31:5
60 a Matt. 5:44

ACTS 7:55

Dear Woman of Destiny,

The New Testament word for glory is *doxa*. It has at least five different meanings. Each aspect of the word expands our understanding of the glory of God as more than a cloud or something so mystical we cannot relate to it. First, *doxa* expresses the majesty and splendor of God. It also means to ascribe to Him the honor and credit for His operation through us.

John declares, "And the Word became flesh and dwelt among us, and we beheld His glory, the glory as of the only begotten of the Father, full of grace and truth" (John 1:14). Jesus was the manifest presence of God on the earth as He walked among us. In His perfect love, He revealed the nature of the Father.

Now follow Christ to the garden of prayer, where He prayed that "the glory which [God the Father] gave Me I have given them [His disciples]" (John 17:22). Later, the apostle Paul declares to us that it is "Christ in you, the hope of glory" (Col. 1:27).

As we yield to the work of the Holy Spirit in our lives, He takes the sword of the Word and divides asunder the veil of flesh that keeps the glory of God from being revealed to the world through us (see Heb. 4:12). As our carnal minds are renewed, our warped emotions restored, and our rebellious wills submit to the law of God, the life of Christ resident within us will be released, and we will reveal the glory of God to the world. Then God will have a glorious church without spot or wrinkle, through which His glory will be manifest. To this end, Paul prayed, "To Him be glory in the church by Christ Jesus to all generations, forever and ever" (Eph. 3:21).

Still another aspect of the word *glory* involves the Spirit of God resting upon us in our trials and testings that are meant to change our character into the character of Christ. The apostle Paul understood this when he wrote, "For I consider that the sufferings of this present time are not worthy to be compared with the glory which shall be revealed in us" (Rom. 8:18). When Peter wrote to Christians concerning "the fiery trial which is to try you" (1 Pet. 4:12), he urged them not to think it strange that they should have to suffer in that way. Instead, he exhorted them to "rejoice to the extent that you partake of Christ's sufferings, that when His glory is revealed, you may also be glad with exceeding joy" (v. 13).

And it is that Spirit of glory that even gives grace for martyrdom. When Stephen was being stoned, he "saw the glory of God, and Jesus standing at the right hand of God."

The Spirit of glory rests on us in our suffering as we yield to Him without rebelling against the trial. The glory of God will be revealed in us as we are victorious in the trials we must endure.

Fuchsia Pickett

Prayer is the lisping of the believing infant, the shout of the fighting believer, the requiem of the dying saint falling asleep in Jesus.

CHARLES H. SPURGEON

Saul Persecutes the Church

8 Now Saul was consenting to his
death.
At that time a great persecution arose
against the church which was at Jerusalem; and [a]they were all scattered throughout the regions of Judea and Samaria,
except the apostles. [2]And devout men carried Stephen *to his burial,* and [a]made
great lamentation over him.
[3]As for Saul, [a]he made havoc of the
church, entering every house, and dragging off men and women, committing
them to prison.

Christ Is Preached in Samaria

[4]Therefore [a]those who were scattered
went everywhere preaching the word.
[5]Then [a]Philip went down to [1]the city of
Samaria and preached Christ to them.
[6]And the multitudes with one accord
heeded the things spoken by Philip, hearing and seeing the miracles which he did.
[7]For [a]unclean spirits, crying with a loud
voice, came out of many who were possessed; and many who were paralyzed and
lame were healed. [8]And there was great
joy in that city.

The Sorcerer's Profession of Faith

[9]But there was a certain man called Simon, who previously [a]practiced [1]sorcery
in the city and [b]astonished the [2]people of
Samaria, claiming that he was someone
great, [10]to whom they all gave heed, from
the least to the greatest, saying, "This
man is the great power of God." [11]And
they heeded him because he had astonished them with his [1]sorceries for a long
time. [12]But when they believed Philip as
he preached the things [a]concerning the
kingdom of God and the name of Jesus
Christ, both men and women were baptized. [13]Then Simon himself also believed;
and when he was baptized he continued
with Philip, and was amazed, seeing the
miracles and signs which were done.

The Sorcerer's Sin

[14]Now when the [a]apostles who were at
Jerusalem heard that Samaria had received the word of God, they sent Peter
and John to them, [15]who, when they had
come down, prayed for them [a]that they
might receive the Holy Spirit. [16]For [a]as
yet He had fallen upon none of them.
[b]They had only been baptized in [c]the
name of the Lord Jesus. [17]Then [a]they laid
hands on them, and they received the
Holy Spirit.
[18]And when Simon saw that through
the laying on of the apostles' hands the
Holy Spirit was given, he offered them
money, [19]saying, "Give me this power
also, that anyone on whom I lay hands
may receive the Holy Spirit."
[20]But Peter said to him, "Your money
perish with you, because [a]you thought
that [b]the gift of God could be purchased
with money! [21]You have neither part nor
portion in this matter, for your [a]heart is
not right in the sight of God. [22]Repent
therefore of this your wickedness, and
pray God [a]if perhaps the thought of your
heart may be forgiven you. [23]For I see that
you are [a]poisoned by bitterness and
bound by iniquity."
[24]Then Simon answered and said,
[a]"Pray to the Lord for me, that none of the
things which you have spoken may come
upon me."
[25]So when they had testified and
preached the word of the Lord, they returned to Jerusalem, preaching the gospel
in many villages of the Samaritans.

Christ Is Preached to an Ethiopian

[26]Now an angel of the Lord spoke to
[a]Philip, saying, "Arise and go toward the
south along the road which goes down
from Jerusalem to Gaza." This is [1]desert.
[27]So he arose and went. And behold, [a]a
man of Ethiopia, a eunuch of great authority under Candace the queen of the
Ethiopians, who had charge of all her
treasury, and [b]had come to Jerusalem to
worship, [28]was returning. And sitting in
his chariot, he was reading Isaiah the

CHAPTER 8
1 a Acts 8:4; 11:19
2 a Gen. 23:2
3 a Phil. 3:6
4 a Matt. 10:23
5 a Acts 6:5; 8:26, 30 *1 Or a*
7 a Mark 16:17
9 a Acts 8:11; 13:6 b Acts 5:36 *1 magic* *2 Or nation*
11 *1 magic arts*
12 a Acts 1:3; 8:4
14 a Acts 5:12, 29, 40
15 a Acts 2:38; 19:2
16 a Acts 19:2 b Matt. 28:19 c Acts 10:48; 19:5
17 a Acts 6:6; 19:6
20 a [Matt. 10:8] b [Acts 2:38; 10:45; 11:17]
21 a Jer. 17:9
22 a 2 Tim. 2:25
23 a Heb. 12:15
24 a James 5:16
26 a Acts 6:5 *1 Or a deserted place*
27 a Ps. 68:31; 87:4 b John 12:20

prophet. 29Then the Spirit said to Philip,
"Go near and overtake this chariot."
30So Philip ran to him, and heard him
reading the prophet Isaiah, and said, "Do
you understand what you are reading?"
31And he said, "How can I, unless someone guides me?" And he asked Philip to
come up and sit with him. 32The place in
the Scripture which he read was this:

> [a]*"He was led as a sheep to the*
> *slaughter;*
> *And as a lamb before its shearer is*
> *silent,*
> [b]*So He opened not His mouth.*
> 33 *In His humiliation His* [a]*justice*
> *was taken away,*
> *And who will declare His*
> *generation?*
> *For His life is* [b]*taken from the*
> *earth."*

34So the eunuch answered Philip and
said, "I ask you, of whom does the prophet
say this, of himself or of some other
man?" 35Then Philip opened his mouth,
[a]and beginning at this Scripture,
preached Jesus to him. 36Now as they
went down the road, they came to some
water. And the eunuch said, "See, *here is*
water. [a]What hinders me from being baptized?"
37[1]Then Philip said, [a]"If you believe
with all your heart, you may."
And he answered and said, [b]"I believe
that Jesus Christ is the Son of God."
38So he commanded the chariot to
stand still. And both Philip and the eunuch went down into the water, and he
baptized him. 39Now when they came up
out of the water, [a]the Spirit of the Lord
caught Philip away, so that the eunuch
saw him no more; and he went on his way
rejoicing. 40But Philip was found at [1]Azo-
tus. And passing through, he preached in
all the cities till he came to [a]Caesarea.

The Damascus Road: Saul Converted

9 Then [a]Saul, still breathing threats
and murder against the disciples of
the Lord, went to the high priest 2and
asked [a]letters from him to the synagogues
of Damascus, so that if he found any who
were of the Way, whether men or women,
he might bring them bound to Jerusalem.
3[a]As he journeyed he came near Damascus, and suddenly a light shone
around him from heaven. 4Then he fell to
the ground, and heard a voice saying to
him, "Saul, Saul, [a]why are you persecuting Me?"
5And he said, "Who are You, Lord?"
Then the Lord said, "I am Jesus, whom
you are persecuting. [1]It *is* hard for you to
kick against the goads."
6So he, trembling and astonished, said,
"Lord, what do You want me to do?"
Then the Lord *said* to him, "Arise and
go into the city, and you will be told what
you must do."
7And [a]the men who journeyed with
him stood speechless, hearing a voice but
seeing no one. 8Then Saul arose from the
ground, and when his eyes were opened
he saw no one. But they led him by the
hand and brought *him* into Damascus.
9And he was three days without sight, and
neither ate nor drank.

Ananias Baptizes Saul

10Now there was a certain disciple at
Damascus [a]named Ananias; and to him
the Lord said in a vision, "Ananias."
And he said, "Here I am, Lord."
11So the Lord *said* to him, "Arise and go
to the street called Straight, and inquire
at the house of Judas for *one* called Saul
[a]of Tarsus, for behold, he is praying.
12And in a vision he has seen a man
named Ananias coming in and putting *his*
hand on him, so that he might receive his
sight."
13Then Ananias answered, "Lord, I have
heard from many about this man, [a]how
much [1]harm he has done to Your saints in
Jerusalem. 14And here he has authority
from the chief priests to bind all [a]who call
on Your name."
15But the Lord said to him, "Go, for [a]he
is a chosen vessel of Mine to bear My
name before [b]Gentiles, [c]kings, and the
[d]children[1] of Israel. 16For [a]I will show
him how many things he must suffer for
My [b]name's sake."
17[a]And Ananias went his way and entered the house; and [b]laying his hands on
him he said, "Brother Saul, the Lord [1]Je-
sus, who appeared to you on the road as
you came, has sent me that you may receive your sight and [c]be filled with the
Holy Spirit." 18Immediately there fell
from his eyes *something* like scales, and
he received his sight at once; and he arose
and was baptized.

---

32 [a]Is. 53:7, 8 [b]John 19:9
33 [a]Luke 23:1–25 [b]Luke 23:33–46
35 [a]Luke 24:27
36 [a]Acts 10:47; 16:33
37 [a][Mark 16:16] [b]Matt. 16:16 [1]NU, M omit v. 37. It is found in Western texts, including the Latin tradition.
39 [a]Ezek. 3:12, 14
40 [a]Acts 21:8 [1]Same as Heb. *Ashdod*

CHAPTER 9
1 [a]Acts 7:57; 8:1, 3; 26:10, 11
2 [a]Acts 22:5
3 [a]1 Cor. 15:8
4 [a][Matt. 25:40]
5 [1]NU, M omit the rest of v. 5 and begin v. 6 with *But arise and go*
7 [a][Acts 22:9; 26:13]
10 [a]Acts 22:12
11 [a]Acts 21:39; 22:3
13 [a]Acts 9:1 [1]*bad things*
14 [a]Acts 7:59; 9:2, 21
15 [a]Eph. 3:7, 8 [b]Rom. 1:5; 11:13 [c]Acts 25:22, 23; 26:1 [d]Rom. 1:16; 9:1–5 [1]Lit. *sons*
16 [a]Acts 20:23 [b]2 Cor. 4:11
17 [a]Acts 22:12, 13 [b]Acts 8:17 [c]Acts 2:4; 4:31; 8:17; 13:52 [1]M omits *Jesus*

19 So when he had received food, he was strengthened. [a]Then Saul spent some days with the disciples at Damascus.

Saul Preaches Christ

20 Immediately he preached [1]the Christ in the synagogues, that He is the Son of God.

21 Then all who heard were amazed, and said, [a]"Is this not he who destroyed those who called on this name in Jerusalem, and has come here for that purpose, so that he might bring them bound to the chief priests?"

22 But Saul increased all the more in strength, [a]and confounded the Jews who dwelt in Damascus, proving that this *Jesus* is the Christ.

Saul Escapes Death

23 Now after many days were past, [a]the Jews plotted to kill him. 24 [a]But their plot became known to Saul. And they watched the gates day and night, to kill him. 25 Then the disciples took him by night and [a]let *him* down through the wall in a large basket.

Saul at Jerusalem

26 And [a]when Saul had come to Jerusalem, he tried to join the disciples; but they were all afraid of him, and did not believe that he was a disciple. 27 [a]But Barnabas took him and brought *him* to the apostles. And he declared to them how he had seen the Lord on the road, and that He had spoken to him, [b]and how he had preached boldly at Damascus in the name of Jesus. 28 So [a]he was with them at Jerusalem, coming in and going out. 29 And he spoke boldly in the name of the Lord Jesus and disputed against the [a]Hellenists,[1] [b]but they attempted to kill him. 30 When the brethren found out, they brought him down to Caesarea and sent him out to Tarsus.

The Church Prospers

31 [a]Then the [1]churches throughout all Judea, Galilee, and Samaria had peace and were [b]edified.[2] And walking in the [c]fear of the Lord and in the [d]comfort of the Holy Spirit, they were [e]multiplied.

Aeneas Healed

32 Now it came to pass, as Peter went [a]through all *parts of the country,* that he also came down to the saints who dwelt in Lydda. 33 There he found a certain man named Aeneas, who had been bedridden eight years and was paralyzed. 34 And Peter said to him, "Aeneas, [a]Jesus the Christ heals you. Arise and make your bed." Then he arose immediately. 35 So all who dwelt at Lydda and [a]Sharon saw him and [b]turned to the Lord.

Dorcas Restored to Life

36 At Joppa there was a certain disciple named [1]Tabitha, which is translated [2]Dorcas. This woman was full [a]of good works and charitable deeds which she did. 37 But it happened in those days that she became sick and died. When they had washed her, they laid *her* in [a]an upper room. 38 And since Lydda was near Joppa, and the disciples had heard that Peter was there, they sent two men to him, imploring *him* not to delay in coming to them. 39 Then Peter arose and went with them. When he had come, they brought *him* to the upper room. And all the widows stood by him weeping, showing the tunics and garments which Dorcas had made while she was with them. 40 But Peter [a]put them all out, and [b]knelt down and prayed. And turning to the body he [c]said, "Tabitha, arise." And she opened her eyes, and when she saw Peter she sat up. 41 Then he gave her *his* hand and lifted her up; and when he had called the saints and widows, he presented her alive. 42 And it became known throughout all Joppa, [a]and many believed on the Lord. 43 So it was that he stayed many days in Joppa with [a]Simon, a tanner.

Cornelius Sends a Delegation

10 There was a certain man in [a]Caesarea called Cornelius, a centurion of what was called the Italian [1]Regiment, 2 [a]a devout *man* and one who [b]feared God with all his household, who gave [1]alms generously to the people, and prayed to God always. 3 About [1]the ninth hour of the day [a]he saw clearly in a vision an angel of God coming in and saying to him, "Cornelius!"

4 And when he observed him, he was afraid, and said, "What is it, lord?"

So he said to him, "Your prayers and your alms have come up for a memorial before God. 5 Now [a]send men to Joppa, and send for Simon whose surname is Peter. 6 He is lodging with [a]Simon, a tanner,

---

19 a Acts 26:20
20 1 NU *Jesus*
21 a Gal. 1:13, 23
22 a Acts 18:28
23 a 2 Cor. 11:26
24 a 2 Cor. 11:32
25 a Josh. 2:15
26 a Acts 22:17–20; 26:20
27 a Acts 4:36; 13:2 b Acts 9:20, 22
28 a Gal. 1:18
29 a Acts 6:1; 11:20 b 2 Cor. 11:26 *1* Greek-speaking Jews
31 a Acts 5:11; 8:1; 16:5 b [Eph. 4:16, 29] c Ps. 34:9 d John 14:16 e Acts 16:5 *1* NU *church . . . was* *2 built up*
32 a Acts 8:14
34 a [Acts 3:6, 16; 4:10]
35 a 1 Chr. 5:16; 27:29 b Acts 11:21; 15:19
36 a 1 Tim. 2:10 *1* Lit., in Aram., *Gazelle* *2* Lit., in Gr., *Gazelle*
37 a Acts 1:13; 9:39
40 a Matt. 9:25 b Acts 7:60 c Mark 5:41, 42
42 a John 11:45
43 a Acts 10:6
CHAPTER 10
1 a Acts 8:40; 23:23 *1 Cohort*
2 a Acts 8:2; 9:22; 22:12 b [Acts 10:22, 35; 13:16, 26] *1 charitable gifts*
3 a Acts 10:30; 11:13 *1* 3 P.M.
5 a Acts 11:13, 14
6 a Acts 9:43

whose house is by the sea. [b]He[1] will tell
you what you must do." 7And when the
angel who spoke to him had departed,
Cornelius called two of his household servants and a devout soldier from among
those who waited on him continually. 8So
when he had explained all *these* things to
them, he sent them to Joppa.

Peter's Vision

9The next day, as they went on their
journey and drew near the city, [a]Peter
went up on the housetop to pray, about
[1]the sixth hour. 10Then he became very
hungry and wanted to eat; but while they
made ready, he fell into a trance 11and
[a]saw heaven opened and an object like a
great sheet bound at the four corners,
descending to him and let down to the
earth. 12In it were all kinds of four-footed
animals of the earth, wild beasts, creeping
things, and birds of the air. 13And a voice
came to him, "Rise, Peter; kill and eat."
14But Peter said, "Not so, Lord! [a]For I
have never eaten anything common or
unclean."
15And a voice *spoke* to him again the
second time, [a]"What God has [1]cleansed
you must not call common." 16This was
done three times. And the object was tak-
en up into heaven again.

Summoned to Caesarea

17Now while Peter [1]wondered within
himself what this vision which he had
seen meant, behold, the men who had
been sent from Cornelius had made inquiry for Simon's house, and stood before

6 [b]Acts 11:14 [1]NU, M omit the rest of v. 6.

9 [a]Acts 10:9–32; 11:5–14 [1]Noon

11 [a]Acts 7:56

14 [a]Deut. 14:3, 7

15 [a][Rom. 14:14] [1]Declared clean

17 [1]*was perplexed*

Dorcas

Some women are born servants, and Dorcas was one of them. The Bible tells us she was "full of good works and charitable deeds" (Acts 9:36); she probably would have been the first to show up with dinner for a bereaved family and the first to knit a blanket for a new baby. When she died, her friends carefully prepared her body for burial, placed her in an upper room, and got busy looking for a miracle.

The situation was urgent, so they sent for Peter, "imploring him not to delay in coming to them" (Acts 9:38). When he arrived at the house where Dorcas's body was, he found a group of women holding things Dorcas had made for them, weeping for this woman who had given so much to so many people. Peter asked the mourners to leave, maybe because he didn't think that mourning was the right atmosphere for a miracle. He then knelt to pray, called Dorcas by her Hebrew name, Tabitha, and spoke one word: "Arise." And she did. She awoke, stood, and was presented to the people alive.

There are dry, dead places inside so many women today—places filled with dreams that have died, hopes that have been destroyed, springs of joy that have dried up. Once-sparkling eyes have grown dull. It is time to speak the word *arise*. Jesus our Lord *is* the resurrection—the One who restores (see John 11:25). And He is longing to revive every lifeless place inside of us. It is time for everything within us to come to life and to be presented to the Lord for His service.

May we as women of destiny begin to speak to the dead places in ourselves and in others. May we speak words of life and hope, words of restoration and encouragement. May we be fully alive, so that we can completely fulfill God's purposes for our lives.

the gate. [18]And they called and asked whether Simon, whose surname was Peter, was lodging there.

[19]While Peter thought about the vision, [a]the Spirit said to him, "Behold, three men are seeking you. [20][a]Arise therefore, go down and go with them, doubting nothing; for I have sent them."

Seeing only what God says will produce and increase faith. Don't doubt your faith, doubt your doubts for they are unreliable.

F. F. BOSWORTH

[21]Then Peter went down to the men [1]who had been sent to him from Cornelius, and said, "Yes, I am he whom you seek. For what reason have you come?"

[22]And they said, "Cornelius *the* centurion, a just man, one who fears God and [a]has a good reputation among all the nation of the Jews, was divinely instructed by a holy angel to summon you to his house, and to hear words from you." [23]Then he invited them in and lodged *them.*

On the next day Peter went away with them, [a]and some brethren from Joppa accompanied him.

Peter Meets Cornelius

[24]And the following day they entered Caesarea. Now Cornelius was waiting for them, and had called together his relatives and close friends. [25]As Peter was coming in, Cornelius met him and fell down at his feet and worshiped *him.* [26]But Peter lifted him up, saying, [a]"Stand up; I myself am also a man." [27]And as he talked with him, he went in and found many who had come together. [28]Then he said to them, "You know how [a]unlawful it is for a Jewish man to keep company with or go to one of another nation. But [b]God has shown me that I should not call any man common or unclean. [29]Therefore I came without objection as soon as I was sent for. I ask, then, for what reason have you sent for me?"

[30]So Cornelius said, [1]"Four days ago I was fasting until this hour; and at the ninth hour I prayed in my house, and behold, [a]a man stood before me [b]in bright clothing, [31]and said, 'Cornelius, [a]your prayer has been heard, and [b]your [1]alms are remembered in the sight of God. [32]Send therefore to Joppa and call Simon here, whose surname is Peter. He is lodging in the house of Simon, a tanner, by the sea. [1]When he comes, he will speak to you.' [33]So I sent to you immediately, and you have done well to come. Now therefore, we are all present before God, to hear all the things commanded you by God."

Preaching to Cornelius' Household

[34]Then Peter opened *his* mouth and said: [a]"In truth I perceive that God shows no partiality. [35]But [a]in every nation whoever fears Him and works righteousness is [b]accepted by Him. [36]The word which *God* sent to the [1]children of Israel, [a]preaching peace through Jesus Christ—[b]He is Lord of all— [37]that word you know, which was proclaimed throughout all Judea, and [a]began from Galilee after the baptism which John preached: [38]how [a]God anointed Jesus of Nazareth with the Holy Spirit and with power, who [b]went about doing good and healing all who were oppressed by the devil, [c]for God was with Him. [39]And we are [a]witnesses of all things which He did both in the land of the Jews and in Jerusalem, whom [1]they [b]killed by hanging on a tree. [40]Him [a]God raised up on the third day, and showed Him openly, [41][a]not to all the people, but to witnesses chosen before by God, *even* to us [b]who ate and drank with Him after He arose from the dead. [42]And [a]He commanded us to preach to the people, and to testify [b]that it is He who was ordained by God *to be* Judge [c]of

In becoming part of the Body of Christ, sickness should have no more mastery over us than it had over the Body of Christ when He was on earth.

GORDON LINDSAY

19 a Acts 11:12
20 a Acts 15:7–9
21 *1* NU, M omit *who had been sent to him from Cornelius*
22 a Acts 22:12
23 a Acts 10:45; 11:12
26 a Acts 14:14, 15
28 a John 4:9; 18:28 b [Acts 10:14, 35; 15:8, 9]
30 a Acts 1:10 b Matt. 28:3 *1* NU *Four days ago to this hour, at the ninth hour*
31 a Dan. 10:12 b Heb. 6:10 *1 charitable gifts*
32 *1* NU omits the rest of v. 32.
34 a Deut. 10:17
35 a [Eph. 2:13] b Ps. 15:1, 2
36 a Is. 57:19 b Rom. 10:12 *1* Lit. *sons*
37 a Luke 4:14
38 a Luke 4:18 b Matt. 4:23 c John 3:2; 8:29
39 a Acts 1:8 b Acts 2:23 *1* NU, M *they also*
40 a Acts 2:24
41 a [John 14:17, 19, 22; 15:27] b Luke 24:30, 41–43
42 a Matt. 28:19 b John 5:22, 27 c 1 Pet. 4:5

the living and the dead. 43[a]To Him all the
prophets witness that, through His name,
[b]whoever believes in Him will receive [c]re-
mission[1] of sins."

Lord, may Your Spirit fall on ____ and on all those who hear Your word.

FROM ACTS 10:44

The Holy Spirit Falls on the Gentiles

44While Peter was still speaking these
words, [a]the Holy Spirit fell upon all those
who heard the word. 45[a]And [1]those of the
circumcision who believed were astonished, as many as came with Peter, [b]be-
cause the gift of the Holy Spirit had been
poured out on the Gentiles also. 46For
they heard them speak with tongues and
magnify God.

Then Peter answered, 47"Can anyone forbid water, that these should not be baptized
who have received the Holy Spirit [a]just as
we *have?*" 48[a]And he commanded them to
be baptized [b]in the name of the Lord. Then
they asked him to stay a few days.

Peter Defends God's Grace

11 Now the apostles and brethren who
were in Judea heard that the Gentiles had also received the word of God.
2And when Peter came up to Jerusalem,
[a]those of the circumcision contended
with him, 3saying, [a]"You went in to uncircumcised men [b]and ate with them!"

4But Peter explained *it* to them [a]in order from the beginning, saying: 5[a]"I was
in the city of Joppa praying; and in a
trance I saw a vision, an object descending
like a great sheet, let down from heaven
by four corners; and it came to me. 6When
I observed it intently and considered, I
saw four-footed animals of the earth, wild
beasts, creeping things, and birds of the
air. 7And I heard a voice saying to me,
'Rise, Peter; kill and eat.' 8But I said, 'Not
so, Lord! For nothing common or unclean
has at any time entered my mouth.' 9But
the voice answered me again from heaven,
'What God has cleansed you must not call
common.' 10Now this was done three
times, and all were drawn up again into
heaven. 11At that very moment, three men
stood before the house where I was, having been sent to me from Caesarea.
12Then [a]the Spirit told me to go with
them, doubting nothing. Moreover [b]these
six brethren accompanied me, and we entered the man's house. 13[a]And he told us
how he had seen an angel standing in his
house, who said to him, 'Send men to Joppa, and call for Simon whose surname is
Peter, 14who will tell you words by which
you and all your household will be saved.'
15And as I began to speak, the Holy Spirit
fell upon them, [a]as upon us at the beginning. 16Then I remembered the word of
the Lord, how He said, [a]'John indeed baptized with water, but [b]you shall be baptized with the Holy Spirit.' 17[a]If therefore
God gave them the same gift as *He gave*
us when we believed on the Lord Jesus
Christ, [b]who was I that I could withstand
God?"

In this age of faith in the natural, and disinclination to the supernatural, we want especially to meet the whole world with this credo: "I believe in the Holy Ghost."

WILLIAM ARTHUR

18When they heard these things they
became silent; and they glorified God, saying, [a]"Then God has also granted to the
Gentiles repentance to life."

Barnabas and Saul at Antioch

19[a]Now those who were scattered after
the persecution that arose over Stephen
traveled as far as Phoenicia, Cyprus, and
Antioch, preaching the word to no one
but the Jews only. 20But some of them
were men from Cyprus and Cyrene, who,
when they had come to Antioch, spoke to
[a]the Hellenists, preaching the Lord Jesus.
21And [a]the hand of the Lord was with
them, and a great number believed and
[b]turned to the Lord.

43 a Zech. 13:1 b Gal. 3:22 c Acts 13:38, 39 *1 forgiveness*
44 a Acts 4:31
45 a Acts 10:23 b Acts 11:18 *1 The Jews*
47 a Acts 2:4; 10:44; 11:17; 15:8
48 a 1 Cor. 1:14–17 b Acts 2:38; 8:16; 19:5

CHAPTER 11
2 a Acts 10:45
3 a Acts 10:28 b Gal. 2:12
4 a Luke 1:3
5 a Acts 10:9
12 a [John 16:13] b Acts 10:23
13 a Acts 10:30
15 a Acts 2:1–4; 15:7–9
16 a John 1:26, 33 b Is. 44:3
17 a [Acts 15:8, 9] b Acts 10:47
18 a Rom. 10:12, 13; 15:9, 16
19 a Acts 8:1, 4
20 a Acts 6:1; 9:29
21 a Luke 1:66 b Acts 9:35; 14:1

[22]Then news of these things came to
the ears of the church in Jerusalem, and
they sent out [a]Barnabas to go as far as
Antioch. [23]When he came and had seen
the grace of God, he was glad, and [a]en-
couraged them all that with purpose of
heart they should continue with the Lord.
[24]For he was a good man, [a]full of the Holy
Spirit and of faith. [b]And a great many people were added to the Lord.
[25]Then Barnabas departed for [a]Tarsus
to seek Saul. [26]And when he had found
him, he brought him to Antioch. So it was
that for a whole year they assembled with
the church and taught a great many people. And the disciples were first called
Christians in Antioch.

Relief to Judea

[27]And in these days [a]prophets came
from Jerusalem to Antioch. [28]Then one
of them, named [a]Agabus, stood up and
showed by the Spirit that there was going
to be a great famine throughout all the
world, which also happened in the days of
[b]Claudius Caesar. [29]Then the disciples,
each according to his ability, determined
to send [a]relief to the brethren dwelling in
Judea. [30][a]This they also did, and sent it to
the elders by the hands of Barnabas and
Saul.

Herod's Violence to the Church

12 Now about that time Herod the
king stretched out *his* hand to harass some from the church. [2]Then he
killed James [a]the brother of John with the
sword. [3]And because he saw that it pleased
the Jews, he proceeded further to seize
Peter also. Now it was *during* [a]the Days of
Unleavened Bread. [4]So [a]when he had arrested him, he put *him* in prison, and delivered *him* to four [1]squads of soldiers to
keep him, intending to bring him before
the people after Passover.

Peter Freed from Prison

[5]Peter was therefore kept in prison, but
[1]constant prayer was offered to God for
him by the church. [6]And when Herod was
about to bring him out, that night Peter
was sleeping, bound with two chains between two soldiers; and the guards before
the door were [1]keeping the prison. [7]Now
behold, [a]an angel of the Lord stood by
him, and a light shone in the prison; and
he struck Peter on the side and raised him
up, saying, "Arise quickly!" And his chains
fell off *his* hands. [8]Then the angel said to
him, "Gird yourself and tie on your sandals"; and so he did. And he said to him,
"Put on your garment and follow me." [9]So
he went out and followed him, and [a]did
not know that what was done by the angel
was real, but thought [b]he was seeing a
vision. [10]When they were past the first and
the second guard posts, they came to the
iron gate that leads to the city, [a]which
opened to them of its own accord; and
they went out and went down one street,
and immediately the angel departed from
him.
[11]And when Peter had come to himself,
he said, "Now I know for certain that [a]the
Lord has sent His angel, and [b]has delivered me from the hand of Herod and *from*
all the expectation of the Jewish people."
[12]So, when he had considered *this,* [a]he
came to the house of Mary, the mother of
[b]John whose surname was Mark, where
many were gathered together [c]praying.
[13]And as Peter knocked at the door of the
gate, a girl named Rhoda came to answer.
[14]When she recognized Peter's voice, because of *her* gladness she did not open the
gate, but ran in and announced that Peter
stood before the gate. [15]But they said to
her, "You are beside yourself!" Yet she
kept insisting that it was so. So they said,
[a]"It is his angel."
[16]Now Peter continued knocking; and
when they opened *the door* and saw him,
they were astonished. [17]But [a]motioning
to them with his hand to keep silent, he
declared to them how the Lord had
brought him out of the prison. And he
said, "Go, tell these things to James and to
the brethren." And he departed and went
to another place.
[18]Then, as soon as it was day, there was
no small [1]stir among the soldiers about
what had become of Peter. [19]But when
Herod had searched for him and not
found him, he examined the guards and
commanded that *they* should be put to
death.
And he went down from Judea to Caesarea, and stayed *there.*

Herod's Violent Death

[20]Now Herod had been very angry with
the people of [a]Tyre and Sidon; but they
came to him with one accord, and having
made Blastus [1]the king's personal aide

22 a Acts 4:36; 9:27
23 a Acts 13:43; 14:22
24 a Acts 6:5 b Acts 5:14; 11:21
25 a Acts 9:11, 30
27 a 1 Cor. 12:28
28 a Acts 21:10 b Acts 18:2
29 a 1 Cor. 16:1
30 a Acts 12:25

CHAPTER 12
2 a Matt. 4:21; 20:23
3 a Ex. 12:15; 23:15
4 a John 21:18 1 Gr. *tetrads,* squads of four
5 1 NU *constantly* or *earnestly*
6 1 *guarding*
7 a Acts 5:19
9 a Ps. 126:1 b Acts 10:3, 17; 11:5
10 a Acts 5:19; 16:26
11 a [Ps. 34:7] b Job 5:19
12 a Acts 4:23 b Acts 13:5, 13; 15:37 c Acts 12:5
15 a [Matt. 18:10]
17 a Acts 13:16; 19:33; 21:40
18 1 *disturbance*
20 a Matt. 11:21 1 *who was in charge of the king's bedchamber*

their friend, they asked for peace, because
[b]their country was [2]supplied with food by
the king's *country.*
21So on a set day Herod, arrayed in royal apparel, sat on his throne and gave an
oration to them. 22And the people kept
shouting, "The voice of a god and not of
a man!" 23Then immediately an angel of
the Lord [a]struck him, because [b]he did not
give glory to God. And he was eaten by
worms and [1]died.
24But [a]the word of God grew and multiplied.

Barnabas and Saul Appointed

25And [a]Barnabas and Saul returned
[1]from Jerusalem when they had [b]fulfilled
their ministry, and they also [c]took with
them [d]John whose surname was Mark.

13 Now [a]in the church that was at Antioch there were certain prophets
and teachers: [b]Barnabas, Simeon who was
called Niger, [c]Lucius of Cyrene, Manaen
who had been brought up with Herod the
tetrarch, and Saul. 2As they ministered to
the Lord and fasted, the Holy Spirit said,
[a]"Now separate to Me Barnabas and Saul
for the work [b]to which I have called
them." 3Then, [a]having fasted and prayed,
and laid hands on them, they sent *them*
away.

Preaching in Cyprus

4So, being sent out by the Holy Spirit,
they went down to Seleucia, and from
there they sailed to [a]Cyprus. 5And when
they arrived in Salamis, [a]they preached
the word of God in the synagogues of the
Jews. They also had [b]John as *their* assistant.
6Now when they had gone through [1]the
island to Paphos, they found [a]a certain
sorcerer, a false prophet, a Jew whose
name *was* Bar-Jesus, 7who was with the
proconsul, Sergius Paulus, an intelligent
man. This man called for Barnabas and
Saul and sought to hear the word of God.
8But [a]Elymas the sorcerer (for so his
name is translated) [1]withstood them,
seeking to turn the proconsul away from
the faith. 9Then Saul, who also *is called*
Paul, [a]filled with the Holy Spirit, looked
intently at him 10and said, "O full of all
deceit and all fraud, [a]*you* son of the devil,
you enemy of all righteousness, will you
not cease perverting the straight ways of
the Lord? 11And now, indeed, [a]the hand of
the Lord *is* upon you, and you shall be
blind, not seeing the sun for a time."
And immediately a dark mist fell on
him, and he went around seeking someone to lead him by the hand. 12Then the
proconsul believed, when he saw what had
been done, being astonished at the teaching of the Lord.

At Antioch in Pisidia

13Now when Paul and his party set sail
from Paphos, they came to Perga in Pamphylia; and [a]John, departing from them,
returned to Jerusalem. 14But when they
departed from Perga, they came to Antioch in Pisidia, and [a]went into the synagogue on the Sabbath day and sat down.
15And [a]after the reading of the Law and
the Prophets, the rulers of the synagogue
sent to them, saying, "Men *and* brethren,
if you have [b]any word of [1]exhortation for
the people, say on."
16Then Paul stood up, and motioning
with *his* hand said, "Men of Israel, and
[a]you who fear God, listen: 17The God of
this people [1]Israel [a]chose our fathers, and
exalted the people [b]when they dwelt as
strangers in the land of Egypt, and with
[2]an uplifted arm He [c]brought them out of
it. 18Now [a]for a time of about forty years
He put up with their ways in the wilderness. 19And when He had destroyed [a]seven
nations in the land of Canaan, [b]He distributed their land to them by allotment.
20"After that [a]He gave *them* judges for
about four hundred and fifty years, [b]until
Samuel the prophet. 21[a]And afterward
they asked for a king; so God gave them
[b]Saul the son of Kish, a man of the tribe
of Benjamin, for forty years. 22And [a]when
He had removed him, [b]He raised up for
them David as king, to whom also He gave
testimony and said, [c]'*I have found David*
the *son* of Jesse, [d]*a man after My own*
heart, who will do all My will.' 23[a]From
this man's seed, according [b]to *the* promise, God raised up for Israel [c]a[1] Savior—
Jesus— 24[a]after John had first preached,
before His coming, the baptism of repentance to all the people of Israel. 25And as
John was finishing his course, he said,
[a]'Who do you think I am? I am not *He.*
But behold, [b]there comes One after me,
the sandals of whose feet I am not worthy
to loose.'

20 [b]Ezek. 27:17 *2* Lit. *nourished*
23 [a]2 Sam. 24:16, 17 [b]Ps. 115:1 *1 breathed his last*
24 [a]Acts 6:7; 19:20
25 [a]Acts 11:30 [b]Acts 11:30 [c]Acts 13:5, 13 [d]Acts 12:12; 15:37 *1* NU, M *to*

CHAPTER 13
1 [a]Acts 14:26 [b]Acts 11:22 [c]Rom. 16:21
2 [a]Gal. 1:15; 2:9 [b]Heb. 5:4
3 [a]Acts 6:6
4 [a]Acts 4:36
5 [a][Acts 13:46] [b]Acts 12:25; 15:37
6 [a]Acts 8:9 *1* NU *the whole island*
8 [a]Ex. 7:11 *1 opposed*
9 [a]Acts 2:4; 4:8
10 [a]Matt. 13:38
11 [a]1 Sam. 5:6
13 [a]Acts 15:38
14 [a]Acts 16:13
15 [a]Luke 4:16 [b]Heb. 13:22 *1 encouragement*
16 [a]Acts 10:35
17 [a]Deut. 7:6–8 [b]Acts 7:17 [c]Ex. 14:8 *1* M omits *Israel* *2* Mighty power
18 [a]Num. 14:34
19 [a]Deut. 7:1 [b]Josh. 14:1, 2; 19:51
20 [a]Judg. 2:16 [b]1 Sam. 3:20
21 [a]1 Sam. 8:5 [b]1 Sam. 10:20–24
22 [a]1 Sam. 15:23, 26, 28 [b]1 Sam. 16:1, 12, 13 [c]Ps. 89:20 [d]1 Sam. 13:14

23 [a]Is. 11:1 [b]Ps. 132:11 [c][Matt. 1:21] *1* M *salvation, after*
24 [a][Luke 3:3] **25** [a]Mark 1:7 [b]John 1:20, 27

26"Men *and* brethren, sons of the [1]fami-
ly of Abraham, and [a]those among you who
fear God, [b]to you the [2]word of this salvation has been sent. 27For those who dwell
in Jerusalem, and their rulers, [a]because
they did not know Him, nor even the voices of the Prophets which are read every
Sabbath, have fulfilled *them* in condemn-
ing *Him.* 28[a]And though they found no
cause for death *in Him,* they asked Pilate
that He should be put to death. 29[a]Now
when they had fulfilled all that was written concerning Him, [b]they took *Him*
down from the tree and laid *Him* in a
tomb. 30[a]But God raised Him from the
dead. 31[a]He was seen for many days by
those who came up with Him from Galilee
to Jerusalem, who are His witnesses to the
people. 32And we declare to you glad tidings—[a]that promise which was made to
the fathers. 33God has fulfilled this for us
their children, in that He has raised up
Jesus. As it is also written in the second
Psalm:

> [a]*'You are My Son,*
> *Today I have begotten You.'*

34And that He raised Him from the dead,
no more to return to [1]corruption, He has
spoken thus:

> [a]*'I will give you the sure [2]mercies of*
> *David.'*

35Therefore He also says in another
Psalm:

> [a]*'You will not allow Your Holy One*
> *to see corruption.'*

36"For David, after he had served [1]his
own generation by the will of God, [a]fell
asleep, was buried with his fathers, and
[2]saw corruption; 37but He whom God
raised up [1]saw no corruption. 38Therefore
let it be known to you, brethren, that
[a]through this Man is preached to you the
forgiveness of sins; 39and [a]by Him everyone who believes is justified from all
things from which you could not be justified by the law of Moses. 40Beware therefore, lest what has been spoken in the
prophets come upon you:

> 41 *'Behold,*[a] *you despisers,*
> *Marvel and perish!*
> *For I work a work in your days,*
> *A work which you will by no means*
> *believe,*
> *Though one were to declare it to*
> *you.'* "

Blessing and Conflict at Antioch

42[1]So when the Jews went out of the
synagogue, the Gentiles begged that these
words might be preached to them the next
Sabbath. 43Now when the congregation
had broken up, many of the Jews and devout proselytes followed Paul and Barnabas, who, speaking to them, [a]persuaded
them to continue in [b]the grace of God.

44On the next Sabbath almost the
whole city came together to hear the word
of God. 45But when the Jews saw the multitudes, they were filled with envy; and
contradicting and blaspheming, they [a]op-
posed the things spoken by Paul. 46Then
Paul and Barnabas grew bold and said,
[a]"It was necessary that the word of God
should be spoken to you first; but [b]since
you reject it, and judge yourselves unworthy of everlasting life, behold, [c]we turn to
the Gentiles. 47For so the Lord has commanded us:

> [a]*'I have set you as a light to the*
> *Gentiles,*
> *That you should be for salvation to*
> *the ends of the earth.'* "

48Now when the Gentiles heard this,
they were glad and glorified the word of
the Lord. [a]And as many as had been appointed to eternal life believed.

49And the word of the Lord was being
spread throughout all the region. 50But
the Jews stirred up the devout and prominent women and the chief men of the city,
[a]raised up persecution against Paul and
Barnabas, and expelled them from their
region. 51[a]But they shook off the dust
from their feet against them, and came to
Iconium. 52And the disciples [a]were filled
with joy and [b]with the Holy Spirit.

Lord, may _____ be filled with joy and with the Holy Spirit regardless of their circumstances.

FROM ACTS 13:52

26 a Ps. 66:16 b Matt. 10:6 *1 stock* *2 message*
27 a Luke 23:34
28 a Matt. 27:22, 23
29 a Luke 18:31 b Matt. 27:57–61
30 a Matt. 12:39, 40; 28:6
31 a Acts 1:3, 11
32 a [Gen. 3:15]
33 a Ps. 2:7
34 a Is. 55:3 *1 the state of decay* *2 blessings*
35 a Ps. 16:10
36 a Acts 2:29 *1 in his* *2 underwent decay*
37 *1 underwent no decay*
38 a Jer. 31:34
39 a [Is. 53:11]
41 a Hab. 1:5
42 *1 Or And when they went out of the synagogue of the Jews; NU And when they went out of the synagogue, they begged*
43 a Acts 11:23 b Titus 2:11
45 a 1 Pet. 4:4
46 a Rom. 1:16 b Ex. 32:10 c Acts 18:6
47 a Is. 42:6; 49:6
48 a [Acts 2:47]
50 a 2 Tim. 3:11
51 a Matt. 10:14
52 a John 16:22 b Acts 2:4; 4:8, 31; 13:9

At Iconium

14 Now it happened in Iconium that
they went together to the synagogue of the Jews, and so spoke that a
great multitude both of the Jews and of
the [a]Greeks believed. 2But the unbelieving Jews stirred up the Gentiles and [1]poi-
soned their [2]minds against the brethren.
3Therefore they stayed there a long time,
speaking boldly in the Lord, [a]who was
bearing witness to the word of His grace,
granting signs and [b]wonders to be done
by their hands.

> *Because Christ lives, our faith is not vain—our preaching is not vain; and wonder of wonders is that this exceeding greatness of power is at our disposal.*
>
> KATHRYN KUHLMAN

4But the multitude of the city was [a]di-
vided: part sided with the Jews, and part
with the [b]apostles. 5And when a violent
attempt was made by both the Gentiles
and Jews, with their rulers, [a]to abuse and
stone them, 6they became aware of it and
[a]fled to Lystra and Derbe, cities of Lycao-
nia, and to the surrounding region. 7And
they were preaching the gospel there.

Idolatry at Lystra

8[a]And in Lystra a certain man without
strength in his feet was sitting, a cripple
from his mother's womb, who had never
walked. 9*This* man heard Paul speaking.
[1]Paul, observing him intently and seeing
that he had faith to be healed, 10said with
a loud voice, [a]"Stand up straight on your
feet!" And he leaped and walked. 11Now
when the people saw what Paul had done,
they raised their voices, saying in the Lyc-
aonian *language,* [a]"The gods have come
down to us in the likeness of men!" 12And
Barnabas they called [1]Zeus, and Paul,
[2]Hermes, because he was the chief speaker. 13Then the priest of Zeus, whose temple was in front of their city, brought oxen
and garlands to the gates, [a]intending to
sacrifice with the multitudes.
14But when the apostles Barnabas and
Paul heard this, [a]they tore their clothes
and ran in among the multitude, crying
out 15and saying, "Men, [a]why are you doing these things? [b]We also are men with
the same nature as you, and preach to you
that you should turn from [c]these useless
things [d]to the living God, [e]who made the
heaven, the earth, the sea, and all things
that are in them, 16[a]who in bygone generations allowed all nations to walk in their
own ways. 17[a]Nevertheless He did not
leave Himself without witness, in that He
did good, [b]gave us rain from heaven and
fruitful seasons, filling our hearts with
[c]food and gladness." 18And with these sayings they could scarcely restrain the multitudes from sacrificing to them.

Stoning, Escape to Derbe

19[a]Then Jews from Antioch and Iconium came there; and having persuaded
the multitudes, [b]they stoned Paul *and*
dragged *him* out of the city, supposing
him to be [c]dead. 20However, when the disciples gathered around him, he rose up
and went into the city. And the next day
he departed with Barnabas to Derbe.

Strengthening the Converts

21And when they had preached the gospel to that city [a]and made many disciples,
they returned to Lystra, Iconium, and Antioch, 22strengthening the souls of the
disciples, [a]exhorting *them* to continue in
the faith, and *saying,* [b]"We must through
many tribulations enter the kingdom of
God." 23So when they had [a]appointed elders in every church, and prayed with
fasting, they commended them to the
Lord in whom they had believed. 24And
after they had passed through Pisidia,
they came to Pamphylia. 25Now when
they had preached the word in Perga, they
went down to Attalia. 26From there they
sailed to Antioch, where they had been
commended to the grace of God for the
work which they had completed.
27Now when they had come and gathered the church together, [a]they reported
all that God had done with them, and that
He had [b]opened the door of faith to the
Gentiles. 28So they stayed there a long
time with the disciples.

CHAPTER 14
1 a Acts 18:4
2 *1 embittered* *2* Lit. *souls*
3 a Heb. 2:4 b Acts 5:12
4 a Luke 12:51 b Acts 13:2, 3
5 a 2 Tim. 3:11
6 a Matt. 10:23
8 a Acts 3:2
9 *1* Lit. *Who*
10 a [Is. 35:6]
11 a Acts 8:10; 28:6
12 *1 Jupiter* *2 Mercury*
13 a Dan. 2:46
14 a Matt. 26:65
15 a Acts 10:26 b James 5:17 c 1 Cor. 8:4 d 1 Thess. 1:9 e Rev. 14:7
16 a Ps. 81:12
17 a Rom. 1:19, 20 b Deut. 11:14 c Ps. 145:16
19 a Acts 13:45, 50; 14:2–5 b 2 Cor. 11:25 c [2 Cor. 12:1–4]
21 a Matt. 28:19
22 a Acts 11:23 b [2 Tim. 2:12; 3:12]
23 a Titus 1:5
27 a Acts 15:4, 12 b 2 Cor. 2:12

Conflict over Circumcision

15 And [a]certain *men* came down from
Judea and taught the brethren,
[b]"Unless you are circumcised according
to the custom of Moses, you cannot be
saved." 2 Therefore, when Paul and Barnabas had no small dissension and dispute
with them, they determined that [a]Paul
and Barnabas and certain others of them
should go up to Jerusalem, to the apostles
and elders, about this question.
3 So, [a]being sent on their way by the
church, they passed through Phoenicia
and Samaria, [b]describing the conversion
of the Gentiles; and they caused great joy
to all the brethren. 4 And when they had
come to Jerusalem, they were received by
the church and the apostles and the elders; and they reported all things that God
had done with them. 5 But some of the
sect of the Pharisees who believed rose up,
saying, "It is necessary to circumcise
them, and to command *them* to keep the
law of Moses."

The Jerusalem Council

6 Now the apostles and elders came together to consider this matter. 7 And when
there had been much dispute, Peter rose
up and said to them: [a]"Men and brethren,
you know that a good while ago God chose
among us, that by my mouth the Gentiles
should hear the word of the gospel and
believe. 8 So God, [a]who knows the heart,
[1]acknowledged them by [b]giving them the
Holy Spirit, just as *He did* to us, 9 [a]and
made no distinction between us and
them, [b]purifying their hearts by faith.
10 Now therefore, why do you test God [a]by
putting a yoke on the neck of the disciples
which neither our fathers nor we were
able to bear? 11 But [a]we believe that
through the grace of the Lord Jesus
[1]Christ we shall be saved in the same
manner as they."
12 Then all the multitude kept silent and
listened to Barnabas and Paul declaring
how many miracles and wonders God had
[a]worked through them among the Gentiles. 13 And after they had [1]become silent,
[a]James answered, saying, "Men *and*
brethren, listen to me: 14 [a]Simon has declared how God at the first visited the
Gentiles to take out of them a people for
His name. 15 And with this the words of
the prophets agree, just as it is written:

16 *'After[a] this I will return*
And will rebuild the tabernacle of
David, which has fallen down;
I will rebuild its ruins,
And I will set it up;
17 *So that the rest of mankind may*
seek the LORD,
Even all the Gentiles who are called
by My name,
Says the [1]LORD who does all these
things.'

18 [1]"Known to God from eternity are all
His works. 19 Therefore [a]I judge that we
should not trouble those from among the
Gentiles who [b]are turning to God, 20 but
that we [a]write to them to abstain [b]from
things polluted by idols, [c]*from* [1]sexual
immorality, [d]*from* things strangled, and
from blood. 21 For Moses has had throughout many generations those who preach
him in every city, [a]being read in the synagogues every Sabbath."

The Jerusalem Decree

22 Then it pleased the apostles and elders, with the whole church, to send chosen men of their own company to Antioch
with Paul and Barnabas, *namely,* Judas
who was also named [a]Barsabas,[1] and Silas, leading men among the brethren.
23 They wrote this *letter* by them:

The apostles, the elders, and the
brethren,

To the brethren who are of the
Gentiles in Antioch, Syria, and Cilicia:

Greetings.

24 Since we have heard that [a]some
who went out from us have troubled you with words, [b]unsettling
your souls, [1]saying, *"You must* be
circumcised and keep the law"—to
whom we gave no *such* commandment— 25 it seemed good to us, being assembled with one [1]accord, to
send chosen men to you with our
beloved Barnabas and Paul, 26 [a]men
who have risked their lives for the
name of our Lord Jesus Christ.
27 We have therefore sent Judas and
Silas, who will also report the same
things by word of mouth. 28 For it
seemed good to the Holy Spirit, and

CHAPTER 15
1 a Gal. 2:12 b Phil. 3:2
2 a Gal. 2:1
3 a Rom. 15:24 b Acts 14:27; 15:4, 12
7 a Acts 10:20
8 a Acts 1:24 b Acts 2:4; 10:44, 47 *1 bore witness to*
9 a Rom. 10:12 b Acts 10:15, 28
10 a Matt. 23:4
11 a Rom. 3:4; 5:15 *1* NU, M omit *Christ*
12 a Acts 14:27; 15:3, 4
13 a Acts 12:17 *1 stopped speaking*
14 a Acts 15:7
16 a Amos 9:11, 12
17 *1* NU *LORD, who makes these things*
18 *1* NU (continuing v. 17) *known from eternity (of old).'*
19 a Acts 15:28; 21:25 b 1 Thess. 1:9
20 a Acts 21:25 b [1 Cor. 8:1; 10:20, 28] c [1 Cor. 6:9] d Lev. 3:17 *1 Or fornication*
21 a Acts 13:15, 27
22 a Acts 1:23 *1* NU, M *Barsabbas*
24 a Titus 1:10, 11 b Gal. 1:7; 5:10 *1* NU omits *saying, "You must be circumcised and keep the law"*
25 *1 purpose or mind*
26 a Acts 13:50; 14:19

to us, to lay upon you no greater
burden than these necessary things:
29[a]that you abstain from things offered to idols, [b]from blood, from
things strangled, and from [c]sexual[1]
immorality. If you keep yourselves
from these, you will do well.

Farewell.

Continuing Ministry in Syria

30So when they were sent off, they came
to Antioch; and when they had gathered
the multitude together, they delivered the
letter. 31When they had read it, they rejoiced over its encouragement. 32Now Judas and Silas, themselves being [a]prophets
also, [b]exhorted and strengthened the
brethren with many words. 33And after
they had stayed *there* for a time, they were
[a]sent back with greetings from the brethren to [1]the apostles.

34[1]However, it seemed good to Silas to
remain there. 35[a]Paul and Barnabas also
remained in Antioch, teaching and
preaching the word of the Lord, with
many others also.

Division over John Mark

36Then after some days Paul said to
Barnabas, "Let us now go back and visit
our brethren in every city where we have
preached the word of the Lord, *and see*
how they are doing." 37Now Barnabas
[1]was determined to take with them [a]John
called Mark. 38But Paul insisted that they
should not take with them [a]the one who
had departed from them in Pamphylia,
and had not gone with them to the work.
39Then the contention became so sharp
that they parted from one another. And so
Barnabas took Mark and sailed to [a]Cy-
prus; 40but Paul chose Silas and departed,
[a]being [1]commended by the brethren to
the grace of God. 41And he went through
Syria and Cilicia, [a]strengthening the
churches.

Timothy Joins Paul and Silas

16 Then he came to [a]Derbe and Lystra. And behold, a certain disciple
was there, [b]named Timothy, [c]*the* son of a
certain Jewish woman who believed, but
his father *was* Greek. 2He was well spoken
of by the brethren who were at Lystra and
Iconium. 3Paul wanted to have him go on
with him. And he [a]took *him* and circumcised him because of the Jews who were in
that region, for they all knew that his
father was Greek. 4And as they went
through the cities, they delivered to them
the [a]decrees to keep, [b]which were determined by the apostles and elders at
Jerusalem. 5[a]So the churches were
strengthened in the faith, and increased
in number daily.

The Macedonian Call

6Now when they had gone through
Phrygia and the region of [a]Galatia, they
were forbidden by the Holy Spirit to
preach the word in [1]Asia. 7After they had
come to Mysia, they tried to go into Bithynia, but the [1]Spirit did not permit
them. 8So passing by Mysia, they [a]came
down to Troas. 9And a vision appeared to
Paul in the night. A [a]man of Macedonia
stood and pleaded with him, saying,
"Come over to Macedonia and help us."
10Now after he had seen the vision, immediately we sought to go [a]to Macedonia,
concluding that the Lord had called us to
preach the gospel to them.

Lydia Baptized at Philippi

11Therefore, sailing from Troas, we ran
a straight course to Samothrace, and the
next *day* came to Neapolis, 12and from
there to [a]Philippi, which is the [1]foremost
city of that part of Macedonia, a colony.
And we were staying in that city for some
days. 13And on the Sabbath day we went
out of the city to the riverside, where
prayer was customarily made; and we sat
down and spoke to the women who met
there. 14Now a certain woman named
Lydia heard *us.* She was a seller of purple
from the city of [a]Thyatira, who worshiped
God. [b]The Lord opened her heart to heed
the things spoken by Paul. 15And when
she and her household were baptized, she
begged *us,* saying, "If you have judged me
to be faithful to the Lord, come to my
house and stay." So [a]she persuaded us.

Paul and Silas Imprisoned

16Now it happened, as we went to
prayer, that a certain slave girl [a]possessed
with a spirit of divination met us, who
brought her masters [b]much profit by
fortune-telling. 17This girl followed Paul
and us, and cried out, saying, "These men
are the servants of the Most High God,
who proclaim to us the way of salvation."
18And this she did for many days.

29 a Acts 15:20; 21:25 b Lev. 17:14 c Col. 3:5 *1* Or *fornication*
32 a Eph. 4:11 b Acts 14:22; 18:23
33 a Heb. 11:31 *1* NU *those who had sent them*
34 *1* NU, M omit v. 34.
35 a Acts 13:1
37 a Acts 12:12, 25 *1 resolved*
38 a Acts 13:13
39 a Acts 4:36; 13:4
40 a Acts 11:23; 14:26 *1 committed*
41 a Acts 16:5

CHAPTER 16
1 a Acts 14:6 b Rom. 16:21 c 2 Tim. 1:5; 3:15
3 a [Gal. 2:3; 5:2]
4 a Acts 15:19–21 b Acts 15:28, 29
5 a Acts 2:47; 15:41
6 a Gal. 1:1, 2 *1* The Roman province of Asia
7 *1* NU adds *of Jesus*
8 a 2 Cor. 2:12
9 a Acts 10:30
10 a 2 Cor. 2:13
12 a Phil. 1:1 *1* Lit. *first*
14 a Rev. 1:11; 2:18, 24 b Luke 24:45
15 a Judg. 19:21
16 a 1 Sam. 28:3, 7 b Acts 19:24

But Paul, [a]greatly [1]annoyed, turned
and said to the spirit, "I command you in
the name of Jesus Christ to come out of
her." [b]And he came out that very hour.
19But [a]when her masters saw that their
hope of profit was gone, they seized Paul
and Silas and [b]dragged *them* into the
marketplace to the authorities.
20And they brought them to the magistrates, and said, "These men, being Jews,
[a]exceedingly trouble our city; 21and they
teach customs which are not lawful for us,
being Romans, to receive or observe."
22Then the multitude rose up together
against them; and the magistrates tore off
their clothes [a]and commanded *them* to be
beaten with rods. 23And when they had
laid many stripes on them, they threw
them into prison, commanding the jailer
to keep them securely. 24Having received
such a charge, he put them into the inner
prison and fastened their feet in the
stocks.

18 [a]Mark 1:25, 34 [b]Mark 16:17 [1] distressed

19 [a]Acts 16:16; 19:25, 26 [b]Matt. 10:18

20 [a]Acts 17:8

22 [a]1 Thess. 2:2

26 [a]Acts 4:31 [b]Acts 5:19; 12:7, 10

The Philippian Jailer Saved

25But at midnight Paul and Silas
were praying and singing hymns to God,
and the prisoners were listening to them.
26[a]Suddenly there was a great earthquake,
so that the foundations of the prison were
shaken; and immediately [b]all the doors
were opened and everyone's chains were
loosed. 27And the keeper of the prison,
awaking from sleep and seeing the prison
doors open, supposing the prisoners had
fled, drew his sword and was about to kill
himself. 28But Paul called with a loud
voice, saying, "Do yourself no harm, for
we are all here."
29Then he called for a light, ran in, and
fell down trembling before Paul and Silas.

Lydia

Lydia is just one reminder that businesswomen have been impacting the kingdom of God since Bible times. Lydia had come from the city of Thyatira in Asia Minor, but met Paul while she was living in the European city of Philippi, and became the first convert in his European ministry. Interestingly enough, Paul and his colleagues had been headed to Asia to spread the gospel when "they were forbidden by the Holy Spirit to preach the word in Asia" (Acts 16:6). They went to Europe instead, and met Lydia there, so he was able to reach an Asian woman with the gospel anyway.

Lydia met Paul in a riverside place where Jewish women regularly gathered to pray. She was a worshiper, but was not baptized until after "the Lord opened her heart to heed the things spoken by Paul" (Acts 16:14). After hearing Paul preach, Lydia and her entire household were saved.

A wealthy woman of significant social status and influence, Lydia made her living selling items that were dyed with a valuable purple dye made from shellfish. She expressed her generosity and hospitality by receiving Paul and Silas as guests in her home (see Acts 16:15). She also started a church in her home for believers nearby, and no doubt continued to use her resources to further the cause of Christ.

Let businesswomen today follow Lydia's example and use every possible means to build the kingdom of God. Whether we can be stewards of wealth, influence, or authority, let us give generously to spread the gospel.

ACTS 16:25, 26

Dear Woman of Destiny,

Praising God is not just for Sunday mornings or moments of spiritual ecstasy. This story of Paul and Silas reveals praise as a wonderful key to releasing the power of God even in times of tremendous adversity. Cruelly beaten and unjustly imprisoned, they sat chained in the stench and darkness of a Roman dungeon. Yet these godly men responded to their dilemma in a way no one could have expected, demonstrating an unlikely but most effective spiritual weapon—praise (see 2 Chr. 20:20–22; Ps. 149:6–9).

The devil had orchestrated this wicked imprisonment to dishearten and silence these men of God. His plot was instantly foiled when Paul and Silas willfully lifted their voices in a true sacrifice of praise and prayer, refusing to give in to discouragement. But that was only the first blow!

As they continued worshiping and praising into the night, Paul and Silas were inviting the kingdom of God to invade their seemingly impossible circumstance. They understood that God is "enthroned in the praises" of His people (Ps. 22:3). When God is invited to enter the scene and given free reign to display His might, everything that can be shaken will be shaken. The very work God had assigned to Paul and Silas—the declaration of the truth of Jesus Christ and the demonstration of His power—was being accomplished in that prison. In fact, they found themselves with a "captive" audience listening to every word as they called out to their mighty deliverer and proclaimed His power and love through their songs. God not only broke the chains that held Paul and Silas, but extended their freedom to those around them. Even one of Satan's pawns, the jailer himself, came to spiritual freedom and salvation, along with his entire family. God has such a marvelous sense of irony!

Thankfully, I have never yet found myself in such dire straits as Paul and Silas did. But I know, as you do, what it is to feel helpless and immobilized in the prison of my own circumstances, facing the darkness of my own midnight hour. My natural reaction at such times may be to complain, doubt, or even give up in despair. Yet Paul and Silas chose to respond by singing out their faith into the face of adversity.

Did Paul and Silas know what God would do? Probably not. But they knew His power and trusted His wisdom and character. Does God always respond to our praise with instant, miraculous intervention? No, sometimes He allows difficult physical circumstances to continue to fulfill His good purposes and, often, to accomplish a greater work in our hearts. But He *always* responds.

As we magnify the Lord, our perspective becomes more accurate. Our circumstances begin to take on their proper proportion to the greatness of God. Our faith is strengthened as we focus on His majesty, might, and mercy. Declare the truth of God's word; it will bring freedom to you and those around you. Lift up the name of Jesus over every difficulty; others will be drawn to Him as they see your deliverance.

Praise God in the dark places as Paul and Silas did. His light will invade, shaking the earth if necessary to break your chains.

Jamie Owens Collins

30 And he brought them out and said,
[a]"Sirs, what must I do to be saved?"
31 So they said, [a]"Believe on the Lord
Jesus Christ, and you will be saved, you
and your household." 32 Then they spoke
the word of the Lord to him and to all who
were in his house. 33 And he took them the
same hour of the night and washed *their*
stripes. And immediately he and all his
family were baptized. 34 Now when he had
brought them into his house, [a]he set food
before them; and he rejoiced, having believed in God with all his household.

Father, may _____ and their household believe on the Lord Jesus Christ and be saved.

FROM ACTS 16:31

Paul Refuses to Depart Secretly

35 And when it was day, the magistrates
sent the [1]officers, saying, "Let those
men go."
36 So the keeper of the prison reported
these words to Paul, saying, "The magistrates have sent to let you go. Now therefore depart, and go in peace."
37 But Paul said to them, "They have
beaten us openly, uncondemned [a]Ro-
mans, *and* have thrown *us* into prison.
And now do they put us out secretly? No
indeed! Let them come themselves and
get us out."
38 And the officers told these words to
the magistrates, and they were afraid
when they heard that they were Romans.
39 Then they came and pleaded with them
and brought *them* out, and [a]asked *them*
to depart from the city. 40 So they went out
of the prison [a]and entered *the house of*
Lydia; and when they had seen the brethren, they encouraged them and departed.

Preaching Christ at Thessalonica

17 Now when they had passed
through Amphipolis and Apollo-
nia, they came to [a]Thessalonica, where
there was a synagogue of the Jews. 2 Then
Paul, as his custom was, [a]went in to them,
and for three Sabbaths [b]reasoned with
them from the Scriptures, 3 explaining
and demonstrating [a]that the Christ had to
suffer and rise again from the dead, and
saying, "This Jesus whom I preach to you
is the Christ." 4 [a]And some of them were
persuaded; and a great multitude of the
devout Greeks, and not a few of the leading women, joined Paul and [b]Silas.

Assault on Jason's House

5 But the Jews [1]who were not persuaded, [2]becoming [a]envious, took some of the
evil men from the marketplace, and gathering a mob, set all the city in an uproar
and attacked the house of [b]Jason, and
sought to bring them out to the people.
6 But when they did not find them, they
dragged Jason and some brethren to the
rulers of the city, crying out, [a]"These who
have turned the world upside down have
come here too. 7 Jason has [1]harbored
them, and these are all acting contrary to
the decrees of Caesar, [a]saying there is another king—Jesus." 8 And they troubled
the crowd and the rulers of the city when
they heard these things. 9 So when they
had taken security from Jason and the
rest, they let them go.

Ministering at Berea

10 Then [a]the brethren immediately sent
Paul and Silas away by night to Berea.
When they arrived, they went into the
synagogue of the Jews. 11 These were more
[1]fair-minded than those in Thessalonica,
in that they received the word with all
readiness, and [a]searched the Scriptures
daily *to find out* whether these things
were so. 12 Therefore many of them believed, and also not a few of the Greeks,
prominent women as well as men. 13 But
when the Jews from Thessalonica learned
that the word of God was preached by Paul
at Berea, they came there also and stirred
up the crowds. 14 [a]Then immediately the
brethren sent Paul away, to go to the sea;
but both Silas and Timothy remained
there. 15 So those who conducted Paul
brought him to Athens; and [a]receiving a
command for Silas and Timothy to come
to him with all speed, they departed.

The Philosophers at Athens

16 Now while Paul waited for them at
Athens, [a]his spirit was provoked within
him when he saw that the city was [1]given

---

30 a Acts 2:37; 9:6; 22:10
31 a [John 3:16, 36; 6:47]
34 a Luke 5:29; 19:6
35 *1 lictors,* lit. *rod bearers*
37 a Acts 22:25–29
39 a Matt. 8:34
40 a Acts 16:14

CHAPTER 17
1 a 1 Thess. 1:1
2 a Luke 4:16 b 1 Thess. 2:1–16
3 a Acts 18:5, 28
4 a Acts 28:24 b Acts 15:22, 27, 32, 40
5 a Acts 13:45 b Rom. 16:21 *1* NU omits *who were not persuaded* *2* M omits *becoming envious*
6 a [Acts 16:20]
7 a 1 Pet. 2:13 *1 welcomed*
10 a Acts 9:25; 17:14
11 a John 5:39 *1* Lit. *noble*
14 a Matt. 10:23
15 a Acts 18:5
16 a 2 Pet. 2:8 *1 full of idols*

over to idols. 17 Therefore he reasoned in
the synagogue with the Jews and with the
Gentile worshipers, and in the marketplace daily with those who happened to be
there. 18 [1]Then certain Epicurean and Stoic philosophers encountered him. And
some said, "What does this [2]babbler want
to say?"

Others said, "He seems to be a proclaimer of foreign gods," because he
preached to them [a]Jesus and the resurrection.

19 And they took him and brought him
to the [1]Areopagus, saying, "May we know
what this new doctrine *is* of which you
speak? 20 For you are bringing some
strange things to our ears. Therefore we
want to know what these things mean."
21 For all the Athenians and the foreigners
who were there spent their time in nothing else but either to tell or to hear some
new thing.

Addressing the Areopagus

22 Then Paul stood in the midst of the
[1]Areopagus and said, "Men of Athens, I
perceive that in all things you are very
religious; 23 for as I was passing through
and considering the objects of your worship, I even found an altar with this inscription:

TO THE UNKNOWN GOD.

Therefore, the One whom you worship
without knowing, Him I proclaim to you:
24 [a]God, who made the world and everything in it, since He is [b]Lord of heaven
and earth, [c]does not dwell in temples
made with hands. 25 Nor is He worshiped
with men's hands, as though He needed
anything, since He [a]gives to all life,
breath, and all things. 26 And He has made
from one [1]blood every nation of men to
dwell on all the face of the earth, and has
determined their preappointed times and
[a]the boundaries of their dwellings, 27 [a]so
that they should seek the Lord, in the
hope that they might grope for Him and
find Him, [b]though He is not far from each
one of us; 28 for [a]in Him we live and move
and have our being, [b]as also some of your
own poets have said, 'For we are also His
offspring.' 29 Therefore, since we are the
offspring of God, [a]we ought not to think
that the Divine Nature is like gold or silver or stone, something shaped by art and
man's devising. 30 Truly, [a]these times of
ignorance God overlooked, but [b]now
commands all men everywhere to repent,
31 because He has appointed a day on
which [a]He will judge the world in righteousness by the Man whom He has ordained. He has given assurance of this to
all by [b]raising Him from the dead."

32 And when they heard of the resurrection of the dead, some mocked, while others said, "We will hear you again on this
matter." 33 So Paul departed from among
them. 34 However, some men joined him
and believed, among them Dionysius the
Areopagite, a woman named Damaris, and
others with them.

Lord, may ____ know that
in You they live and move
and have their being.
FROM ACTS 17:28

Ministering at Corinth

18 After these things Paul departed
from Athens and went to Corinth.
2 And he found a certain Jew named [a]Aqui-
la, born in Pontus, who had recently come
from Italy with his wife Priscilla (because
Claudius had commanded all the Jews to
depart from Rome); and he came to them.
3 So, because he was of the same trade, he
stayed with them [a]and worked; for by occupation they were tentmakers. 4 [a]And he
reasoned in the synagogue every Sabbath,
and persuaded both Jews and Greeks.

5 [a]When Silas and Timothy had come
from Macedonia, Paul was [b]compelled [1]by
the Spirit, and testified to the Jews *that*
Jesus *is* the Christ. 6 But [a]when they opposed him and blasphemed, [b]he shook *his*
garments and said to them, [c]"Your blood
be upon your *own* heads; [d]I *am* clean.
[e]From now on I will go to the Gentiles."
7 And he departed from there and entered
the house of a certain *man* named [1]Jus-
tus, *one* who worshiped God, whose house
was next door to the synagogue. 8 [a]Then
Crispus, the ruler of the synagogue, believed on the Lord with all his household.
And many of the Corinthians, hearing, believed and were baptized.

9 Now [a]the Lord spoke to Paul in the
night by a vision, "Do not be afraid, but
speak, and do not keep silent; 10 [a]for I am

18 a 1 Cor. 15:12 *1* NU, M add *also* *2* Lit. *seed picker,* an idler who makes a living picking up scraps
19 *1* Lit. *Hill of Ares,* or *Mars' Hill*
22 *1* Lit. *Hill of Ares,* or *Mars' Hill*
24 a Acts 14:15 b Matt. 11:25 c Acts 7:48–50
25 a Is. 42:5
26 a Deut. 32:8 *1* NU omits *blood*
27 a [Rom. 1:20] b Jer. 23:23, 24
28 a [Heb. 1:3] b Titus 1:12
29 a Is. 40:18, 19
30 a [Rom. 3:25] b [Titus 2:11, 12]
31 a Acts 10:42 b Acts 2:24

CHAPTER 18
2 a 1 Cor. 16:19
3 a Acts 20:34
4 a Acts 17:2
5 a Acts 17:14, 15 b Acts 18:28 *1* Or *in his spirit* or *in the Spirit*
6 a Acts 13:45 b Neh. 5:13 c 2 Sam. 1:16 d [Ezek. 3:18, 19] e Acts 13:46–48; 28:28
7 *1* NU *Titius Justus*
8 a 1 Cor. 1:14
9 a Acts 23:11
10 a Jer. 1:18, 19

with you, and no one will attack you to
hurt you; for I have many people in this
city." 11And he continued *there* a year and
six months, teaching the word of God
among them.

12When Gallio was proconsul of Achaia,
the Jews with one accord rose up against
Paul and brought him to the [1]judgment
seat, 13saying, "This *fellow* persuades men
to worship God contrary to the law."

14And when Paul was about to open *his*
mouth, Gallio said to the Jews, "If it were
a matter of wrongdoing or wicked crimes,
O Jews, there would be reason why I
should bear with you. 15But if it is a [a]ques-
tion of words and names and your own
law, look *to it* yourselves; for I do not want
to be a judge of such *matters.*" 16And he
drove them from the judgment seat.
17Then [1]all the Greeks took [a]Sosthenes,
the ruler of the synagogue, and beat *him*
before the judgment seat. But Gallio took
no notice of these things.

Paul Returns to Antioch

18So Paul still remained [1]a good while.
Then he took leave of the brethren and
sailed for Syria, and Priscilla and Aquila
were with him. [a]He had *his* hair cut off at
[b]Cenchrea, for he had taken a vow. 19And
he came to Ephesus, and left them there;
but he himself entered the synagogue and
reasoned with the Jews. 20When they
asked *him* to stay a longer time with
them, he did not consent, 21but took leave
of them, saying, [a]"I[1] must by all means
keep this coming feast in Jerusalem; but
I will return again to you, [b]God willing."
And he sailed from Ephesus.

22And when he had landed at [a]Caesarea,
and [1]gone up and greeted the church, he
went down to Antioch. 23After he had
spent some time *there,* he departed and
went over the region of [a]Galatia and
Phrygia [1]in order, [b]strengthening all the
disciples.

Ministry of Apollos

24[a]Now a certain Jew named Apollos,
born at Alexandria, an eloquent man *and*
mighty in the Scriptures, came to Ephesus. 25This man had been instructed in
the way of the Lord; and being [a]fervent in
spirit, he spoke and taught accurately the
things of the Lord, [b]though he knew only
the baptism of John. 26So he began to
speak boldly in the synagogue. When Aquila and Priscilla heard him, they took
him aside and explained to him the way of
God more accurately. 27And when he desired to cross to Achaia, the brethren
wrote, exhorting the disciples to receive
him; and when he arrived, [a]he greatly
helped those who had believed through
grace; 28for he vigorously refuted the Jews
publicly, [a]showing from the Scriptures
that Jesus is the Christ.

Paul at Ephesus

19 And it happened, while [a]Apollos
was at Corinth, that Paul, having
passed through [b]the upper regions, came
to Ephesus. And finding some disciples
2he said to them, "Did you receive the
Holy Spirit when you believed?"

So they said to him, [a]"We have not so
much as heard whether there is a Holy
Spirit."

3And he said to them, "Into what then
were you baptized?"

So they said, [a]"Into John's baptism."

4Then Paul said, [a]"John indeed baptized with a baptism of repentance, saying
to the people that they should believe on
Him who would come after him, that is,
on Christ Jesus."

5When they heard *this,* they were baptized [a]in the name of the Lord Jesus. 6And
when Paul had [a]laid hands on them, the
Holy Spirit came upon them, and [b]they
spoke with tongues and prophesied. 7Now
the men were about twelve in all.

8[a]And he went into the synagogue and
spoke boldly for three months, reasoning
and persuading [b]concerning the things of
the kingdom of God. 9But [a]when some
were hardened and did not believe, but
spoke evil [b]of the Way before the multitude, he departed from them and withdrew the disciples, reasoning daily in the
school of Tyrannus. 10And [a]this continued
for two years, so that all who dwelt in Asia
heard the word of the Lord Jesus, both
Jews and Greeks.

Miracles Glorify Christ

11Now [a]God worked unusual miracles
by the hands of Paul, 12[a]so that even handkerchiefs or aprons were brought from
his body to the sick, and the diseases left
them and the evil spirits went out of them.
13[a]Then some of the itinerant Jewish exor-
cists [b]took it upon themselves to call the
name of the Lord Jesus over those who
had evil spirits, saying, [1]"We [2]exorcise you
by the Jesus whom Paul [c]preaches." 14Also

---

12 [1] Gr. *bema*
15 [a] Acts 23:29; 25:19
17 [a] 1 Cor. 1:1 [1] NU *they all*
18 [a] Acts 21:24 [b] Rom. 16:1 [1] Lit. *many days*
21 [a] Acts 19:21; 20:16 [b] 1 Cor. 4:19 [1] NU omits *I must by all means keep this coming feast in Jerusalem*
22 [a] Acts 8:40 [1] To Jerusalem
23 [a] Gal. 1:2 [b] Acts 14:22; 15:32, 41 [1] *successively*
24 [a] Titus 3:13
25 [a] Rom. 12:11 [b] Acts 19:3
27 [a] 1 Cor. 3:6
28 [a] Acts 9:22; 17:3; 18:5

CHAPTER 19
1 [a] 1 Cor. 1:12; 3:5, 6 [b] Acts 18:23
2 [a] 1 Sam. 3:7
3 [a] Acts 18:25
4 [a] Matt. 3:11
5 [a] Acts 8:12, 16; 10:48
6 [a] Acts 6:6; 8:17 [b] Acts 2:4; 10:46
8 [a] Acts 17:2; 18:4 [b] Acts 1:3; 28:23
9 [a] 2 Tim. 1:15 [b] Acts 9:2; 19:23; 22:4; 24:14
10 [a] Acts 19:8; 20:31
11 [a] Mark 16:20
12 [a] Acts 5:15
13 [a] Matt. 12:27 [b] Mark 9:38 [c] 1 Cor. 1:23; 2:2 [1] NU *I* [2] *adjure,* solemnly command

there were seven sons of Sceva, a Jewish chief priest, who did so.

15 And the evil spirit answered and said, "Jesus I know, and Paul I know; but who are you?"

16 Then the man in whom the evil spirit was leaped on them, [1]overpowered them, and prevailed against [2]them, so that they fled out of that house naked and wounded. 17 This became known both to all Jews and Greeks dwelling in Ephesus; and [a]fear fell on them all, and the name of the Lord Jesus was magnified. 18 And many who had believed came [a]confessing and telling their deeds. 19 Also, many of those who had practiced magic brought their books together and burned *them* in the sight of all. And they counted up the value of them, and *it* totaled fifty thousand *pieces* of silver. 20 [a]So the word of the Lord grew mightily and prevailed.

Lord God, as You did through Your servant Paul, I ask that You would work unusual miracles through ____.

FROM ACTS 19:11

The Riot at Ephesus

21 [a]When these things were accomplished, Paul [b]purposed in the Spirit, when he had passed through [c]Macedonia and Achaia, to go to Jerusalem, saying, "After I have been there, [d]I must also see Rome." 22 So he sent into Macedonia two of those who ministered to him, [a]Timothy and [b]Erastus, but he himself stayed in Asia for a time.

23 And [a]about that time there arose a great commotion about [b]the Way. 24 For a certain man named Demetrius, a silversmith, who made silver shrines of [1]Diana, brought [a]no small profit to the craftsmen. 25 He called them together with the workers of similar occupation, and said: "Men, you know that we have our prosperity by this trade. 26 Moreover you see and hear that not only at Ephesus, but throughout almost all Asia, this Paul has persuaded and turned away many people, saying that [a]they are not gods which are made with hands. 27 So not only is this trade of ours in danger of falling into disrepute, but also the temple of the great goddess Diana may be despised and [1]her magnificence destroyed, whom all Asia and the world worship."

28 Now when they heard *this,* they were full of wrath and cried out, saying, "Great *is* Diana of the Ephesians!" 29 So the whole city was filled with confusion, and rushed into the theater with one accord, having seized [a]Gaius and [b]Aristarchus, Macedonians, Paul's travel companions. 30 And when Paul wanted to go in to the people, the disciples would not allow him. 31 Then some of the [1]officials of Asia, who were his friends, sent to him pleading that he would not venture into the theater. 32 Some therefore cried one thing and some another, for the assembly was confused, and most of them did not know why they had come together. 33 And they drew Alexander out of the multitude, the Jews putting him forward. And [a]Alexander [b]motioned with his hand, and wanted to make his defense to the people. 34 But when they found out that he was a Jew, all with one voice cried out for about two hours, "Great *is* Diana of the Ephesians!"

35 And when the city clerk had quieted the crowd, he said: "Men of Ephesus, what man is there who does not know that the city of the Ephesians is temple guardian of the great goddess [1]Diana, and of the *image* which fell down from [2]Zeus? 36 Therefore, since these things cannot be denied, you ought to be quiet and do nothing rashly. 37 For you have brought these men here who are neither robbers of temples nor blasphemers of [1]your goddess. 38 Therefore, if Demetrius and his fellow craftsmen have a [1]case against anyone, the courts are open and there are proconsuls. Let them bring charges against one another. 39 But if you have any other inquiry to make, it shall be determined in the lawful assembly. 40 For we are in danger of being [1]called in question for today's uproar, there being no reason which we may give to account for this disorderly gathering." 41 And when he had said these things, he dismissed the assembly.

Journeys in Greece

20 After the uproar had ceased, Paul called the disciples to *himself,* embraced *them,* and [a]departed to go to

16 [1] M *and they overpowered them* [2] NU *both of them*
17 a Luke 1:65; 7:16
18 a Matt. 3:6
20 a Acts 6:7; 12:24
21 a Rom. 15:25 b Acts 20:22 c Acts 20:1 d Rom. 1:13; 15:22–29
22 a 1 Tim. 1:2 b Rom. 16:23
23 a 2 Cor. 1:8 b Acts 9:2
24 a Acts 16:16, 19 [1] Gr. *Artemis*
26 a Is. 44:10–20
27 [1] NU *she be deposed from her magnificence*
29 a Rom. 16:23 b Col. 4:10
31 [1] *Asiarchs, rulers of Asia,* the province
33 a 2 Tim. 4:14 b Acts 12:17
35 [1] Gr. *Artemis* [2] *heaven*
37 [1] NU *our*
38 [1] Lit. *matter*
40 [1] Or *charged with rebellion concerning today*

CHAPTER 20
1 a 1 Tim. 1:3

Acts 19:19

Dear Woman of Destiny,

In Acts 19:19, we read that when the people of Ephesus came to Jesus, many brought their magic books to be burned. This demonstrated their renouncing of witchcraft. Why did they burn the books? Aren't books just paper and print?

Magic, or witchcraft, summons demon powers. As flies are attracted to rubbish, so demon spirits flock to devilish acts. Objects, like the magic books, are just material; however, they can possess spiritual powers, based on the authority people give them. There is a parallel in the spiritual realm. As demon spirits are attracted to evil, so the Holy Spirit responds to faith.

In Acts 19:11, 12, Paul, who had the power of the Holy Spirit working within him, gave handkerchiefs and aprons to take to people who were sick or demon-possessed, and they were healed. Here we see objects that carried a transference of the anointing that was upon Paul. His faith was in Jesus' healing power. However, the objects were a focal point. Likewise, in 2 Samuel 6:6, 7, we clearly see the power resident in the ark of the covenant. When Uzzah reached out to steady the ark, he dropped dead. Again, it was not the power of the object, but the power of God flowing through the object.

Objects can receive power by the belief in or the fear of that object. A family in our church once called us to bless their house because they had experienced unusual demonic activity. As my husband prayed, the Holy Spirit quickened him to ask about a bottle of potion brought from another country. The woman was shocked and acknowledged that she had brought home a bottle of potion purchased from a witch doctor in the Philippines. She had hidden it, and no one knew about it except her. They took the bottle, smashed it, and buried it outside. The curse was broken.

There are many objects in our society that have been given over to evil spirits. We must guard ourselves and our children against these things—occult games, programs that emphasize demonic themes, magic (not illusion), pornography, drugs, and movies that contain witchcraft. Actions will also attract these spirits. Lust, perversion, rebellion, and bitterness (just to mention a few) all summon demonic powers that will seek to possess those who partake of and are deceived by them.

"The thief [Satan] does not come except to steal, and to kill, and to destroy" (see John 10:10). What is our defense?

1. Seek the Lord with all your might, ask God to reveal your sin, and repent openly of that sin. Demonic forces attempt to control you through unconfessed sin.
2. Obey the word of the Lord. Remember, "to him who knows to do good and does not do it, to him it is sin" (James 4:17).
3. Fellowship with believers so that you have encouragement and accountability.
4. Each day take time to pray, and give control to Jesus over every area of your life. Let Him cover you with His blood and clothe you in His armor.
5. In prayer, ask God to reveal any articles in your home that have any demonic attachment. Dispose of them in the same way the believers did in Acts 19:19.

Colleen Marocco

Macedonia. 2 Now when he had gone over that region and encouraged them with many words, he came to [a]Greece 3 and stayed three months. And [a]when the Jews plotted against him as he was about to sail to Syria, he decided to return through Macedonia. 4 And Sopater of Berea accompanied him to Asia—also [a]Aristarchus and Secundus of the Thessalonians, and [b]Gaius of Derbe, and [c]Timothy, and [d]Tychicus and [e]Trophimus of Asia. 5 These men, going ahead, waited for us at [a]Troas. 6 But we sailed away from Philippi after [a]the Days of Unleavened Bread, and in five days joined them [b]at Troas, where we stayed seven days.

Ministering at Troas

7 Now on [a]the first *day* of the week, when the disciples came together [b]to break bread, Paul, ready to depart the next day, spoke to them and continued his message until midnight. 8 There were many lamps [a]in the upper room where [1]they were gathered together. 9 And in a window sat a certain young man named Eutychus, who was sinking into a deep sleep. He was overcome by sleep; and as Paul continued speaking, he fell down from the third story and was taken up dead. 10 But Paul went down, [a]fell on him, and embracing *him* said, [b]"Do not trouble yourselves, for his life is in him." 11 Now when he had come up, had broken bread and eaten, and talked a long while, even till daybreak, he departed. 12 And they brought the young man in alive, and they were not a little comforted.

From Troas to Miletus

13 Then we went ahead to the ship and sailed to Assos, there intending to take Paul on board; for so he had [1]given orders, intending himself to go on foot. 14 And when he met us at Assos, we took him on board and came to Mitylene. 15 We sailed from there, and the next *day* came opposite Chios. The following *day* we arrived at Samos and stayed at Trogyllium. The next *day* we came to Miletus. 16 For Paul had decided to sail past Ephesus, so that he would not have to spend time in Asia; for [a]he was hurrying [b]to be at Jerusalem, if possible, on [c]the Day of Pentecost.

2 a Acts 17:15; 18:1
3 a 2 Cor. 11:26
4 a Col. 4:10 b Acts 19:29 c Acts 16:1 d Eph. 6:21 e 2 Tim. 4:20
5 a 2 Tim. 4:13
6 a Ex. 12:14, 15 b 2 Tim. 4:13
7 a 1 Cor. 16:2 b Acts 2:42, 46; 20:11
8 a Acts 1:13 *1* NU, M *we*
10 a 1 Kin. 17:21 b Matt. 9:23, 24
13 *1 arranged it*
16 a Acts 18:21; 19:21; 21:4 b Acts 24:17 c Acts 2:1
18 a Acts 18:19; 19:1, 10; 20:4, 16
19 a Acts 20:3
20 a Acts 20:27
21 a Acts 18:5; 19:10 b Mark 1:15
22 a Acts 19:21
23 a Acts 21:4, 11
24 a Acts 21:13 b 2 Tim. 4:7 c Acts 1:17 d Gal. 1:1 *1* NU *But I do not count my life of any value or dear to myself* *2 course*
26 a Acts 18:6 *1* Lit. *clean*
27 a Luke 7:30 *1 avoided declaring*
28 a 1 Pet. 5:2 b 1 Cor. 12:28 c Eph. 1:7, 14 d Heb. 9:14 *1* M *of the Lord and God*
29 a Matt. 7:15
30 a 1 Tim. 1:20 *1 misleading*
31 a Acts 19:8, 10; 24:17
32 a Heb. 13:9 b Acts 9:31 c [Heb. 9:15]
34 a Acts 18:3 *1* NU, M omit *Yes*
35 a Rom. 15:1

The Ephesian Elders Exhorted

17 From Miletus he sent to Ephesus and called for the elders of the church. 18 And when they had come to him, he said to them: "You know, [a]from the first day that I came to Asia, in what manner I always lived among you, 19 serving the Lord with all humility, with many tears and trials which happened to me [a]by the plotting of the Jews; 20 how [a]I kept back nothing that was helpful, but proclaimed it to you, and taught you publicly and from house to house, 21 [a]testifying to Jews, and also to Greeks, [b]repentance toward God and faith toward our Lord Jesus Christ. 22 And see, now [a]I go bound in the spirit to Jerusalem, not knowing the things that will happen to me there, 23 except that [a]the Holy Spirit testifies in every city, saying that chains and tribulations await me. 24 [1]But [a]none of these things move me; nor do I count my life dear to myself, [b]so that I may finish my [2]race with joy, [c]and the ministry [d]which I received from the Lord Jesus, to testify to the gospel of the grace of God.

25 "And indeed, now I know that you all, among whom I have gone preaching the kingdom of God, will see my face no more. 26 Therefore I testify to you this day that I *am* [a]innocent[1] of the blood of all *men.* 27 For I have not [1]shunned to declare to you [a]the whole counsel of God. 28 [a]Therefore take heed to yourselves and to all the flock, among which the Holy Spirit [b]has made you overseers, to shepherd the church [1]of God [c]which He purchased [d]with His own blood. 29 For I know this, that after my departure [a]savage wolves will come in among you, not sparing the flock. 30 Also [a]from among yourselves men will rise up, speaking [1]perverse things, to draw away the disciples after themselves. 31 Therefore watch, and remember that [a]for three years I did not cease to warn everyone night and day with tears.

32 "So now, brethren, I commend you to God and [a]to the word of His grace, which is able [b]to build you up and give you [c]an inheritance among all those who are sanctified. 33 I have coveted no one's silver or gold or apparel. 34 [1]Yes, you yourselves know [a]that these hands have provided for my necessities, and for those who were with me. 35 I have shown you in every way, [a]by laboring like this, that you must support the weak. And remember the words

ACTS 20:24

Dear Woman of Destiny,

I am constantly challenged by Acts 20:24's words from Paul—a man apprehended by the love of God, a love that transformed his life, changed his course, and thrust him across the known world. His life was poured out as a drink offering so that those "to whom [Jesus] was not announced, they shall see; and those who have not heard shall understand" (Rom. 15:21). Paul was a pioneer, not a settler, and his life was marked by an apostolic passion for God's glory to be spread throughout the earth.

Many times I've thought of these words from Acts that Paul spoke to the elders of the church in Ephesus as he was leaving for the last time. He was on his way to Jerusalem for the Day of Pentecost and then hoped to go to Rome. From there he desired to go to Spain to see God's kingdom established in that yet-unreached area. His passion was to extend God's kingdom. He knew that chains and tribulations were ahead, that suffering awaited him wherever he went; yet he was not moved off the course or distracted from the destiny the Lord had given him. In finishing that race he found great joy. His life was not dear to him; God's purposes mattered—not his own.

I've stood under a blazing hot sun in dust that buried my feet on the outskirts of Laodicea, Turkey; and as I've looked out over the horizon, Paul has come to mind. There was no plane to board, no air-conditioned car awaiting him, just an endless stretch of sometimes-lush, sometimes-barren land separating him from the next city to which the Lord would send him. But he was undeterred, desiring to testify to the gospel of the grace of God.

The Lord is once again calling us as women to a life of apostolic passion, and these words from Paul give us insight into that life. *Webster's Dictionary* defines *passion* as "a suffering or enduring of imposed or inflicted pain." To be passionate is to be willing to suffer bonds and afflictions, even to the point of laying down our lives for a given purpose. To be "apostolic" is to be a pioneer, to be sent, to establish His kingdom where it is not yet, whether that be in the middle of Dallas, Texas, or in Thimphu, Bhutan. We are not all called as apostles as Paul was, but we are all called to be apostolic and as such, to participate in God's global purposes. A life of apostolic passion is one that is abandoned to God's purposes to redeem for Himself a great multitude from every nation, tribe, and tongue, no matter what the cost. This life is not moved off course or deterred by internal or external fires or difficulties. Apostolic passion is born in those arrested by the love of God, and in this life is found great joy.

We live in some of the most exciting days in all of history, a *kairos* season that is divinely ordained by Him. I pray that we might be arrested by God's love in greater measure and recklessly abandon our lives with apostolic passion to see His kingdom extend throughout the nations.

Susan Ryan

> *Lord, I pray that ___ will take heed to themselves and to all the flock, among which the Holy Spirit has made them overseers, to shepherd Your church which You purchased with Your own blood.*
>
> FROM ACTS 20:28

of the Lord Jesus, that He said, 'It is more blessed to give than to receive.' "

36 And when he had said these things, he knelt down and prayed with them all. 37 Then they all [a]wept [1]freely, and [b]fell on Paul's neck and kissed him, 38 sorrowing most of all for the words which he spoke, that they would see his face no more. And they accompanied him to the ship.

Warnings on the Journey to Jerusalem

21 Now it came to pass, that when we had departed from them and set sail, running a straight course we came to Cos, the following *day* to Rhodes, and from there to Patara. 2 And finding a ship sailing over to Phoenicia, we went aboard and set sail. 3 When we had sighted Cyprus, we passed it on the left, sailed to Syria, and landed at Tyre; for there the ship was to unload her cargo. 4 And finding [1]disciples, we stayed there seven days. [a]They told Paul through the Spirit not to go up to Jerusalem. 5 When we had come to the end of those days, we departed and went on our way; and they all accompanied us, with wives and children, till *we were* out of the city. And [a]we knelt down on the shore and prayed. 6 When we had taken our leave of one another, we boarded the ship, and they returned [a]home.

7 And when we had finished *our* voyage from Tyre, we came to Ptolemais, greeted the brethren, and stayed with them one day. 8 On the next *day* we [1]who were Paul's companions departed and came to [a]Caesarea, and entered the house of Philip [b]the evangelist, [c]who was *one* of the seven, and stayed with him. 9 Now this man had four virgin daughters [a]who prophesied. 10 And as we stayed many days, a certain prophet named [a]Agabus came down from Judea. 11 When he had come to us, he took Paul's belt, bound his *own* hands and feet, and said, "Thus says the Holy Spirit, [a]'So shall the Jews at Jerusalem bind the man who owns this belt, and deliver *him* into the hands of the Gentiles.' "

12 Now when we heard these things, both we and those from that place pleaded with him not to go up to Jerusalem. 13 Then Paul answered, [a]"What do you mean by weeping and breaking my heart? For I am ready not only to be bound, but also to die at Jerusalem for the name of the Lord Jesus."

14 So when he would not be persuaded, we ceased, saying, [a]"The will of the Lord be done."

Paul Urged to Make Peace

15 And after those days we [1]packed and went up to Jerusalem. 16 Also some of the disciples from Caesarea went with us and brought with them a certain Mnason of Cyprus, an early disciple, with whom we were to lodge.

17 [a]And when we had come to Jerusalem, the brethren received us gladly. 18 On the following *day* Paul went in with us to [a]James, and all the elders were present. 19 When he had greeted them, [a]he told in detail those things which God had done among the Gentiles [b]through his ministry. 20 And when they heard *it,* they glorified the Lord. And they said to him, "You see, brother, how many myriads of Jews there are who have believed, and they are all [a]zealous for the law; 21 but they have been informed about you that you teach all the Jews who are among the Gentiles to forsake Moses, saying that they ought not to circumcise *their* children nor to walk according to the customs. 22 [1]What then? The assembly must certainly meet, for they will hear that you have come. 23 Therefore do what we tell you: We have four men who have taken a vow. 24 Take them and be purified with them, and pay their expenses so that they may [a]shave *their* heads, and that all may know that those things of which they were informed concerning you are nothing, but *that* you yourself also walk orderly and keep the law. 25 But concerning the Gentiles who believe, [a]we have written *and* decided [1]that they should observe no such thing, except that they should keep themselves

---

37 a Acts 21:13 b Gen. 45:14 *1* Lit. *much*

CHAPTER 21

4 a [Acts 20:23; 21:12] *1* NU *the disciples*

5 a Acts 9:40; 20:36

6 a John 1:11

8 a Acts 8:40; 21:16 b Eph. 4:11 c Acts 6:5 *1* NU omits *who were Paul's companions*

9 a Joel 2:28

10 a Acts 11:28

11 a Acts 20:23; 21:33; 22:25

13 a Acts 20:24, 37

14 a Luke 11:2; 22:42

15 *1 made preparations*

17 a Acts 15:4

18 a Gal. 1:19; 2:9

19 a Rom. 15:18, 19 b Acts 1:17; 20:24

20 a Acts 15:1; 22:3

22 *1* NU *What then is to be done? They will certainly hear*

24 a Acts 18:18

25 a Acts 15:19, 20, 29 *1* NU omits *that they should observe no such thing, except*

from *things* offered to idols, from blood, from things strangled, and from [2]sexual immorality."

Arrested in the Temple

26Then Paul took the men, and the next day, having been purified with them, [a]entered the temple [b]to announce the [1]expiration of the days of purification, at which time an offering should be made for each one of them.

27Now when the seven days were almost ended, [a]the Jews from Asia, seeing him in the temple, stirred up the whole crowd and [b]laid hands on him, 28crying out, "Men of Israel, help! This is the man [a]who teaches all *men* everywhere against the people, the law, and this place; and furthermore he also brought Greeks into the temple and has defiled this holy place." 29(For they had [1]previously seen [a]Trophimus the Ephesian with him in the city, whom they supposed that Paul had brought into the temple.)

30And [a]all the city was disturbed; and the people ran together, seized Paul, and dragged him out of the temple; and immediately the doors were shut. 31Now as they were [a]seeking to kill him, news came to the commander of the [1]garrison that all Jerusalem was in an uproar. 32[a]He immediately took soldiers and centurions, and ran down to them. And when they saw the commander and the soldiers, they stopped beating Paul. 33Then the [a]commander came near and took him, and [b]commanded *him* to be bound with two chains; and he asked who he was and what he had done. 34And some among the multitude cried one thing and some another.

So when he could not ascertain the truth because of the tumult, he commanded him to be taken into the barracks. 35When he reached the stairs, he had to be carried by the soldiers because of the violence of the mob. 36For the multitude of the people followed after, crying out, [a]"Away with him!"

Addressing the Jerusalem Mob

37Then as Paul was about to be led into the barracks, he said to the commander, "May I speak to you?"

He replied, "Can you speak Greek? 38[a]Are you not the Egyptian who some time ago stirred up a rebellion and led the four thousand assassins out into the wilderness?"

39But Paul said, [a]"I am a Jew from Tarsus, in Cilicia, a citizen of no [1]mean city; and I implore you, permit me to speak to the people."

40So when he had given him permission, Paul stood on the stairs and [a]motioned with his hand to the people. And when there was a great silence, he spoke to *them* in the [b]Hebrew language, saying,

22 "Brethren[a] and fathers, hear my defense before you now." 2And when they heard that he spoke to them in the [a]Hebrew language, they kept all the more silent.

Then he said: 3[a]"I am indeed a Jew, born in Tarsus of Cilicia, but brought up in this city [b]at the feet of [c]Gamaliel, taught [d]according to the strictness of our fathers' law, and [e]was zealous toward God [f]as you all are today. 4[a]I persecuted this Way to the death, binding and delivering into prisons both men and women, 5as also the high priest bears me witness, and [a]all the council of the elders, [b]from whom I also received letters to the brethren, and went to Damascus [c]to bring in chains even those who were there to Jerusalem to be punished.

6"Now [a]it happened, as I journeyed and came near Damascus at about noon, suddenly a great light from heaven shone around me. 7And I fell to the ground and heard a voice saying to me, 'Saul, Saul, why are you persecuting Me?' 8So I answered, 'Who are You, Lord?' And He said to me, 'I am Jesus of Nazareth, whom you are persecuting.'

9"And [a]those who were with me indeed saw the light [1]and were afraid, but they did not hear the voice of Him who spoke to me. 10So I said, 'What shall I do, Lord?' And the Lord said to me, 'Arise and go into Damascus, and there you will be told all things which are appointed for you to do.' 11And since I could not see for the glory of that light, being led by the hand of those who were with me, I came into Damascus.

12"Then [a]a certain Ananias, a devout man according to the law, [b]having a good testimony with all the [c]Jews who dwelt *there,* 13came to me; and he stood and said to me, 'Brother Saul, receive your sight.' And at that same hour I looked up at him. 14Then he said, [a]'The God of our fathers [b]has chosen you that you should [c]know

25 [2] *fornication*

26 [a]Acts 21:24; 24:18 [b]Num. 6:13 [1] *completion*

27 [a]Acts 20:19; 24:18 [b]Acts 26:21

28 [a]Acts 6:13; 24:6

29 [a]Acts 20:4 [1] M omits *previously*

30 [a]Acts 16:19; 26:21

31 [a]2 Cor. 11:23 [1] *cohort*

32 [a]Acts 23:27; 24:7

33 [a]Acts 24:7 [b]Acts 20:23; 21:11

36 [a]John 19:15

38 [a]Acts 5:36

39 [a]Acts 9:11; 22:3 [1] *insignificant*

40 [a]Acts 12:17 [b]Acts 22:2

CHAPTER 22

1 [a]Acts 7:2

2 [a]Acts 21:40

3 [a]2 Cor. 11:22 [b]Deut. 33:3 [c]Acts 5:34 [d]Acts 23:6; 26:5 [e]Gal. 1:14 [f][Rom. 10:2]

4 [a]1 Tim. 1:13

5 [a]Acts 23:14; 24:1; 25:15 [b]Luke 22:66 [c]Acts 9:2

6 [a]Acts 9:3; 26:12, 13

9 [a]Acts 9:7 [1] NU omits *and were afraid*

12 [a]Acts 9:17 [b]Acts 10:22 [c]1 Tim. 3:7

14 [a]Acts 3:13; 5:30 [b]Acts 9:15; 26:16 [c]Acts 3:14; 7:52

His will, and [d]see the Just One, [e]and hear
the voice of His mouth. 15[a]For you will be
His witness to all men of [b]what you have
seen and heard. 16And now why are you
waiting? Arise and be baptized, [a]and wash
away your sins, [b]calling on the name of
the Lord.'

Faith begins where the will of God is known.

F. F. BOSWORTH

17"Now [a]it happened, when I returned
to Jerusalem and was praying in the temple, that I was in a trance 18and [a]saw Him
saying to me, [b]'Make haste and get out of
Jerusalem quickly, for they will not receive your testimony concerning Me.'
19So I said, 'Lord, [a]they know that in every
synagogue I imprisoned and [b]beat those
who believe on You. 20[a]And when the
blood of Your martyr Stephen was shed, I
also was standing by [b]consenting [1]to his
death, and guarding the clothes of those
who were killing him.' 21Then He said to
me, 'Depart, [a]for I will send you far from
here to the Gentiles.' "

Paul's Roman Citizenship

22And they listened to him until this
word, and *then* they raised their voices
and said, [a]"Away with such a *fellow* from
the earth, for [b]he is not fit to live!"
23Then, as they cried out and [1]tore off
their clothes and threw dust into the air,
24the commander ordered him to be
brought into the barracks, and said that
he should be examined under scourging,
so that he might know why they shouted
so against him. 25And as they bound him
with thongs, Paul said to the centurion
who stood by, [a]"Is it lawful for you to
scourge a man who is a Roman, and uncondemned?"

26When the centurion heard *that,* he
went and told the commander, saying,
"Take care what you do, for this man is a
Roman."

27Then the commander came and said
to him, "Tell me, are you a Roman?"

He said, "Yes."

28The commander answered, "With a
large sum I obtained this citizenship."

And Paul said, "But I was born *a citizen."*

29Then immediately those who were
about to examine him withdrew from
him; and the commander was also afraid
after he found out that he was a Roman,
and because he had bound him.

The Sanhedrin Divided

30The next day, because he wanted to
know for certain why he was accused by
the Jews, he released him from *his* bonds,
and commanded the chief priests and all
their council to appear, and brought Paul
down and set him before them.

23
Then Paul, looking earnestly at the
council, said, "Men *and* brethren,
[a]I have lived in all good conscience before
God until this day." 2And the high priest
Ananias commanded those who stood by
him [a]to strike him on the mouth. 3Then
Paul said to him, "God will strike you, *you*
whitewashed wall! For you sit to judge me
according to the law, and [a]do you command me to be struck contrary to the
law?"

4And those who stood by said, "Do you
revile God's high priest?"

5Then Paul said, [a]"I did not know,
brethren, that he was the high priest; for
it is written, [b]*'You shall not speak evil of
a ruler of your people.'* "

6But when Paul perceived that one part
were Sadducees and the other Pharisees,
he cried out in the council, "Men *and*
brethren, [a]I am a Pharisee, the son of a
Pharisee; [b]concerning the hope and resurrection of the dead I am being judged!"

7And when he had said this, a dissension arose between the Pharisees and the
Sadducees; and the assembly was divided.
8[a]For Sadducees say that there is no resurrection—and no angel or spirit; but the
Pharisees confess both. 9Then there arose
a loud outcry. And the scribes of the Pharisees' party arose and protested, saying,
[a]"We find no evil in this man; [1]but [b]if a
spirit or an angel has spoken to him, [c]let
us not fight against God."

10Now when there arose a great dissension, the commander, fearing lest Paul
might be pulled to pieces by them, commanded the soldiers to go down and take

14 d 1 Cor. 9:1; 15:8 e Gal. 1:12
15 a Acts 23:11 b Acts 4:20; 26:16
16 a Heb. 10:22 b Rom. 10:13
17 a Acts 9:26; 26:20
18 a Acts 22:14 b Matt. 10:14
19 a Acts 8:3; 22:4 b Matt. 10:17
20 a Acts 7:54—8:1 b Luke 11:48 *1* NU omits *to his death*
21 a Acts 9:15
22 a Acts 21:36 b Acts 25:24
23 *1* Lit. *threw*
25 a Acts 16:37

CHAPTER 23
1 a 2 Tim. 1:3
2 a John 18:22
3 a Deut. 25:1, 2
5 a Lev. 5:17, 18 b Ex. 22:28
6 a Phil. 3:5 b Acts 24:15, 21; 26:6; 28:20
8 a Matt. 22:23
9 a Acts 25:25; 26:31 b Acts 22:6, 7, 17, 18 c Acts 5:39 *1* NU *what if a spirit or an angel has spoken to him?* omitting the last clause

him by force from among them, and bring
him into the barracks.

The Plot Against Paul

11 But [a]the following night the Lord
stood by him and said, [1]"Be of good cheer,
Paul; for as you have testified for Me in
[b]Jerusalem, so you must also bear witness
at [c]Rome."
12 And when it was day, [a]some of the
Jews banded together and bound themselves under an oath, saying that they
would neither eat nor drink till they had
[b]killed Paul. 13 Now there were more than
forty who had formed this conspiracy.
14 They came to the chief priests and [a]elders, and said, "We have bound ourselves
under a great oath that we will eat nothing until we have killed Paul. 15 Now you,
therefore, together with the council, suggest to the commander that he be brought
down to you [1]tomorrow, as though you
were going to make further inquiries concerning him; but we are ready to kill him
before he comes near."
16 So when Paul's sister's son heard of
their ambush, he went and entered the
barracks and told Paul. 17 Then Paul called
one of the centurions to *him* and said,
"Take this young man to the commander,
for he has something to tell him." 18 So he
took him and brought *him* to the commander and said, "Paul the prisoner called
me to *him* and asked *me* to bring this
young man to you. He has something to
say to you."
19 Then the commander took him by the
hand, went aside, and asked privately,
"What is it that you have to tell me?"
20 And he said, [a]"The Jews have agreed
to ask that you bring Paul down to the
council tomorrow, as though they were
going to inquire more fully about him.
21 But do not yield to them, for more than
forty of them lie in wait for him, men who
have bound themselves by an oath that
they will neither eat nor drink till they
have killed him; and now they are ready,
waiting for the promise from you."
22 So the commander let the young man
depart, and commanded *him*, "Tell no one
that you have revealed these things
to me."

Sent to Felix

23 And he called for two centurions,
saying, "Prepare two hundred soldiers,
seventy horsemen, and two hundred
spearmen to go to [a]Caesarea at the third
hour of the night; 24 and provide mounts
to set Paul on, and bring *him* safely to
Felix the governor." 25 He wrote a letter in
the following manner:

26 Claudius Lysias,

To the most excellent governor
Felix:

Greetings.

27 [a]This man was seized by the Jews
and was about to be killed by them.
Coming with the troops I rescued
him, having learned that he was a
Roman. 28 [a]And when I wanted to
know the reason they accused him,
I brought him before their council.
29 I found out that he was accused
[a]concerning questions of their law,
[b]but had nothing charged against
him deserving of death or chains.
30 And [a]when it was told me that
[1]the Jews lay in wait for the man, I
sent him immediately to you, and
[b]also commanded his accusers to
state before you the charges against
him.

Farewell.

31 Then the soldiers, as they were commanded, took Paul and brought *him* by
night to Antipatris. 32 The next day they
left the horsemen to go on with him, and
returned to the barracks. 33 When they
came to [a]Caesarea and had delivered the
[b]letter to the governor, they also presented Paul to him. 34 And when the governor
had read *it*, he asked what province he was
from. And when he understood that *he
was* from [a]Cilicia, 35 he said, [a]"I will hear
you when your accusers also have come."
And he commanded him to be kept in
[b]Herod's [1]Praetorium.

Accused of Sedition

24 Now after [a]five days [b]Ananias the
high priest came down with the elders and a certain orator *named* Tertullus. These gave evidence to the governor
against Paul.
2 And when he was called upon, Tertullus began his accusation, saying: "Seeing
that through you we enjoy great peace,
and [1]prosperity is being brought to this
nation by your foresight, 3 we accept *it* al-

11 a Acts 18:9; 27:23, 24 b Acts 21:18, 19; 22:1–21 c Acts 28:16, 17, 23 *1 Take courage*
12 a Acts 23:21, 30; 25:3 b Acts 9:23, 24; 25:3; 26:21; 27:42
14 a Acts 4:5, 23; 6:12; 22:5; 24:1; 25:15
15 *1* NU omits *tomorrow*
20 a Acts 23:12
23 a Acts 8:40; 23:33
27 a Acts 21:30, 33; 24:7
28 a Acts 22:30
29 a Acts 18:15; 25:19 b Acts 25:25; 26:31
30 a Acts 23:20 b Acts 24:8; 25:6 *1* NU *there would be a plot against the man*
33 a Acts 8:40 b Acts 23:26–30
34 a Acts 6:9; 21:39
35 a Acts 24:1, 10; 25:16 b Matt. 27:27 *1* Headquarters
CHAPTER 24
1 a Acts 21:27 b Acts 23:2, 30, 35; 25:2
2 *1* Or *reforms are*

ways and in all places, most noble Felix,
with all thankfulness. 4Nevertheless, not
to be tedious to you any further, I beg you
to hear, by your [1]courtesy, a few words
from us. 5[a]For we have found this man a
plague, a creator of dissension among all
the Jews throughout the world, and a
ringleader of the sect of the Nazarenes.
6[a]He even tried to profane the temple, and
we seized him, [1]and wanted [b]to judge him
according to our law. 7[a]But the commander Lysias came by and with great
violence took *him* out of our hands,
8[a]commanding his accusers to come to
you. By examining him yourself you may
ascertain all these things of which we accuse him." 9And the Jews also [1]assented,
maintaining that these things were so.

The Defense Before Felix

10Then Paul, after the governor had
nodded to him to speak, answered: "Inasmuch as I know that you have been for
many years a judge of this nation, I do the
more cheerfully answer for myself, 11because you may ascertain that it is no more
than twelve days since I went up to Jerusalem [a]to worship. 12[a]And they neither
found me in the temple disputing with
anyone nor inciting the crowd, either in
the synagogues or in the city. 13Nor can
they prove the things of which they now
accuse me. 14But this I confess to you,
that according to [a]the Way which they
call a sect, so I worship the [b]God of my
fathers, believing all things which are
written in [c]the Law and in the Prophets.
15[a]I have hope in God, which they themselves also accept, [b]that there will be a
resurrection [1]of *the* dead, both of *the* just
and *the* unjust. 16[a]This *being* so, I myself
always strive to have a conscience without
offense toward God and men.

17"Now after many years [a]I came to
bring alms and offerings to my nation,
18[a]in the midst of which some Jews from
Asia found me [b]purified in the temple,
neither with a mob nor with tumult.
19[a]They ought to have been here before
you to object if they had anything against
me. 20Or else let those who are *here* themselves say [1]if they found any wrongdoing
in me while I stood before the council,
21unless *it is* for this one statement which
I cried out, standing among them, [a]'Concerning the resurrection of the dead I am
being judged by you this day.' "

Felix Procrastinates

22But when Felix heard these things,
having more accurate knowledge of *the*
[a]Way, he adjourned the proceedings and
said, "When [b]Lysias the commander
comes down, I will make a decision on
your case." 23So he commanded the centurion to keep Paul and to let *him* have
liberty, and [a]told him not to forbid any of
his friends to provide for or visit him.

24And after some days, when Felix came
with his wife Drusilla, who was Jewish, he
sent for Paul and heard him concerning
the [a]faith in Christ. 25Now as he reasoned
about righteousness, self-control, and the
judgment to come, Felix was afraid and
answered, "Go away for now; when I have
a convenient time I will call for you."
26Meanwhile he also hoped that [a]money
would be given him by Paul, [1]that he
might release him. Therefore he sent for
him more often and conversed with him.

27But after two years Porcius Festus
succeeded Felix; and Felix, [a]wanting to do
the Jews a favor, left Paul bound.

Paul Appeals to Caesar

25 Now when Festus had come to the
province, after three days he went
up from [a]Caesarea to Jerusalem. 2[a]Then
the [1]high priest and the chief men of the
Jews informed him against Paul; and they
petitioned him, 3asking a favor against
him, that he would summon him to Jerusalem—[a]while *they* lay in ambush along
the road to kill him. 4But Festus answered
that Paul should be kept at Caesarea, and
that he himself was going *there* shortly.
5"Therefore," he said, "let those who have
authority among you go down with *me*
and accuse this man, to see [a]if there is any
fault in him."

6And when he had remained among
them more than ten days, he went down
to Caesarea. And the next day, sitting on
the judgment seat, he commanded Paul to
be brought. 7When he had come, the Jews
who had come down from Jerusalem
stood about [a]and laid many serious complaints against Paul, which they could not
prove, 8while he answered for himself,
[a]"Neither against the law of the Jews, nor
against the temple, nor against Caesar
have I offended in anything at all."

4 [1] *graciousness*
5 [a] 1 Pet. 2:12, 15
6 [a] Acts 21:28 [b] John 18:31 [1] NU ends the sentence here and omits the rest of v. 6, all of v. 7, and the first clause of v. 8.
7 [a] Acts 21:33; 23:10
8 [a] Acts 23:30
9 [1] NU, M *joined the attack*
11 [a] Acts 21:15, 18, 26, 27; 24:17
12 [a] Acts 25:8; 28:17
14 [a] Acts 9:2; 24:22 [b] 2 Tim. 1:3 [c] Acts 26:22; 28:23
15 [a] Acts 23:6; 26:6, 7; 28:20 [b] [Dan. 12:2] [1] NU omits *of the dead*
16 [a] Acts 23:1
17 [a] Rom. 15:25–28
18 [a] Acts 21:27; 26:21 [b] Acts 21:26
19 [a] [Acts 23:30; 25:16]
20 [1] NU, M *what wrongdoing they found*
21 [a] [Acts 23:6; 24:15; 28:20]
22 [a] Acts 9:2; 18:26; 19:9, 23; 22:4 [b] Acts 23:26; 24:7
23 [a] Acts 23:16; 27:3; 28:16
24 [a] [Rom. 10:9]
26 [a] Ex. 23:8 [1] NU omits *that he might release him*
27 [a] Acts 12:3; 23:35; 25:9, 14

CHAPTER 25
1 [a] Acts 8:40; 25:4, 6, 13
2 [a] Acts 24:1; 25:15 [1] NU *chief priests*
3 [a] Acts 23:12, 15 **5** [a] Acts 18:14; 25:18 **7** [a] Acts 24:5, 13 **8** [a] Acts 6:13; 24:12; 28:17

9But Festus, [a]wanting to do the Jews a
favor, answered Paul and said, [b]"Are you
willing to go up to Jerusalem and there
be judged before me concerning these
things?"
10So Paul said, "I stand at Caesar's judgment seat, where I ought to be judged. To
the Jews I have done no wrong, as you
very well know. 11[a]For if I am an offender,
or have committed anything deserving of
death, I do not object to dying; but if there
is nothing in these things of which these
men accuse me, no one can deliver me to
them. [b]I appeal to Caesar."
12Then Festus, when he had conferred
with the council, answered, "You have appealed to Caesar? To Caesar you shall go!"

Paul Before Agrippa

13And after some days King Agrippa and
Bernice came to Caesarea to greet Festus.
14When they had been there many days,
Festus laid Paul's case before the king,
saying: [a]"There is a certain man left a
prisoner by Felix, 15[a]about whom the
chief priests and the elders of the Jews
informed *me,* when I was in Jerusalem,
asking for a judgment against him. 16[a]To
them I answered, 'It is not the custom of
the Romans to deliver any man [1]to destruction before the accused meets the accusers face to face, and has opportunity to
answer for himself concerning the charge
against him.' 17Therefore when they had
come together, [a]without any delay, the
next day I sat on the judgment seat and
commanded the man to be brought in.
18When the accusers stood up, they
brought no accusation against him of
such things as I [1]supposed, 19[a]but had
some questions against him about their
own religion and about a certain Jesus,
who had died, whom Paul affirmed to be
alive. 20And because I was uncertain of
such questions, I asked whether he was
willing to go to Jerusalem and there be
judged concerning these matters. 21But
when Paul [a]appealed to be reserved for
the decision of Augustus, I commanded
him to be kept till I could send him to
Caesar."
22Then [a]Agrippa said to Festus, "I also
would like to hear the man myself."
"Tomorrow," he said, "you shall hear
him."
23So the next day, when Agrippa and
Bernice had come with great [1]pomp, and
had entered the auditorium with the commanders and the prominent men of the
city, at Festus' command [a]Paul was
brought in. 24And Festus said: "King
Agrippa and all the men who are here
present with us, you see this man about
whom [a]the whole assembly of the Jews
petitioned me, both at Jerusalem and
here, crying out that he was [b]not fit to live
any longer. 25But when I found that [a]he
had committed nothing deserving of
death, [b]and that he himself had appealed
to Augustus, I decided to send him. 26I
have nothing certain to write to my lord
concerning him. Therefore I have
brought him out before you, and especially before you, King Agrippa, so that after
the examination has taken place I may
have something to write. 27For it seems to
me unreasonable to send a prisoner and
not to specify the charges against him."

Paul's Early Life

26 Then Agrippa said to Paul, "You
are permitted to speak for yourself."
So Paul stretched out his hand and answered for himself: 2"I think myself [a]hap-
py, King Agrippa, because today I shall
answer [b]for myself before you concerning
all the things of which I am [c]accused by
the Jews, 3especially because you are expert in all customs and questions which
have to do with the Jews. Therefore I beg
you to hear me patiently.
4"My manner of life from my youth,
which was spent from the beginning
among my own nation at Jerusalem, all
the Jews know. 5They knew me from the
first, if they were willing to testify, that
according to [a]the strictest sect of our religion I lived a Pharisee. 6[a]And now I stand
and am judged for the hope of [b]the promise made by God to our fathers. 7To this
promise [a]our twelve tribes, earnestly
serving *God* [b]night and day, [c]hope to attain. For this hope's sake, King Agrippa, I
am accused by the Jews. 8Why should it be
thought incredible by you that God raises
the dead?
9[a]"Indeed, I myself thought I must do
many things [1]contrary to the name of [b]Je-
sus of Nazareth. 10[a]This I also did in Jerusalem, and many of the saints I shut up in
prison, having received authority [b]from
the chief priests; and when they were put
to death, I cast my vote against *them.*
11[a]And I punished them often in every
synagogue and compelled *them* to blas-

9 a Acts 12:2; 24:27 b Acts 25:20
11 a Acts 18:14; 23:29; 25:25; 26:31 b Acts 26:32; 28:19
14 a Acts 24:27
15 a Acts 24:1; 25:2, 3
16 a Acts 25:4, 5 *1* NU omits *to destruction,* although it is implied
17 a Acts 25:6, 10
18 *1 suspected*
19 a Acts 18:14, 15; 23:29
21 a Acts 25:11, 12
22 a Acts 9:15
23 a Acts 9:15 *1 pageantry*
24 a Acts 25:2, 3, 7 b Acts 21:36; 22:22
25 a Acts 23:9, 29; 26:31 b Acts 25:11, 12
CHAPTER 26
2 a [1 Pet. 3:14; 4:14] b [1 Pet. 3:15, 16] c Acts 21:28; 24:5, 6
5 a Phil. 3:5
6 a Acts 23:6 b Acts 13:32
7 a James 1:1 b 1 Thess. 3:10 c Phil. 3:11
9 a 1 Tim. 1:12, 13 b Acts 2:22; 10:38 *1 against*
10 a Acts 8:1–3; 9:13 b Acts 9:14
11 a Acts 22:19

pheme; and being exceedingly enraged
against them, I persecuted *them* even to
foreign cities.

Paul Recounts His Conversion

12[a]“While thus occupied, as I journeyed
to Damascus with authority and commission from the chief priests, 13at midday,
O king, along the road I saw a light from
heaven, brighter than the sun, shining
around me and those who journeyed with
me. 14And when we all had fallen to the
ground, I heard a voice speaking to me
and saying in the Hebrew language, ‘Saul,
Saul, why are you persecuting Me? *It is*
hard for you to kick against the goads.’
15So I said, ‘Who are You, Lord?’ And He
said, ‘I am Jesus, whom you are persecuting. 16But rise and stand on your feet; for
I have appeared to you for this purpose,
[a]to make you a minister and a witness
both of the things which you have seen
and of the things which I will yet reveal to
you. 17I will [1]deliver you from the *Jewish*
people, as well as *from* the Gentiles, [a]to
whom I [2]now send you, 18[a]to open their
eyes, *in order* [b]to turn *them* from darkness to light, and *from* the power of Satan
to God, [c]that they may receive forgiveness
of sins and [d]an inheritance among those
who are [e]sanctified[1] by faith in Me.’

Paul’s Post-Conversion Life

19“Therefore, King Agrippa, I was not
disobedient to the heavenly vision, 20but
[a]declared first to those in Damascus and
in Jerusalem, and throughout all the region of Judea, and *then* to the Gentiles,
that they should repent, turn to God, and
do [b]works befitting repentance. 21For
these reasons the Jews seized me in the
temple and tried to kill *me.* 22Therefore,
having obtained help from God, to this
day I stand, witnessing both to small and
great, saying no other things than those
[a]which the prophets and [b]Moses said
would come— 23[a]that the Christ would
suffer, [b]that He would be the first to rise
from the dead, and [c]would proclaim light
to the *Jewish* people and to the Gentiles.”

Agrippa Parries Paul’s Challenge

24Now as he thus made his defense, Festus said with a loud voice, “Paul, [a]you are
beside yourself! Much learning is driving
you mad!”

25But he said, “I am not [1]mad, most
noble Festus, but speak the words of truth
and reason. 26For the king, before whom
I also speak freely, [a]knows these things;
for I am convinced that none of these
things escapes his attention, since this
thing was not done in a corner. 27King
Agrippa, do you believe the prophets? I
know that you do believe.”

28Then Agrippa said to Paul, “You almost persuade me to become a Christian.”

29And Paul said, [a]“I would to God that
not only you, but also all who hear me
today, might become both almost and altogether such as I am, except for these
chains.”

30When he had said these things, the
king stood up, as well as the governor and
Bernice and those who sat with them;
31and when they had gone aside, they
talked among themselves, saying, [a]“This
man is doing nothing deserving of death
or chains.”

32Then Agrippa said to Festus, “This
man might have been set [a]free [b]if he had
not appealed to Caesar.”

The Voyage to Rome Begins

27 And when [a]it was decided that we
should sail to Italy, they delivered
Paul and some other prisoners to *one*
named Julius, a centurion of the Augus-
tan Regiment. 2So, entering a ship of Ad-
ramyttium, we put to sea, meaning to sail
along the coasts of Asia. [a]Aristarchus, a
Macedonian of Thessalonica, was with us.
3And the next *day* we landed at Sidon. And
Julius [a]treated Paul kindly and gave *him*
liberty to go to his friends and receive
care. 4When we had put to sea from there,
we sailed under *the shelter of* Cyprus, because the winds were contrary. 5And when
we had sailed over the sea which is off
Cilicia and Pamphylia, we came to Myra,
a city of Lycia. 6There the centurion
found [a]an Alexandrian ship sailing to Italy, and he put us on board.

7When we had sailed slowly many days,
and arrived with difficulty off Cnidus, the
wind not permitting us to proceed, we
sailed under *the shelter of* [a]Crete off Sal-
mone. 8Passing it with difficulty, we came
to a place called Fair Havens, near the city
of Lasea.

12 a Acts 9:3–8; 22:6–11; 26:12–18
16 a Acts 22:15
17 a Acts 22:21 *1 rescue* 2 NU, M omit *now*
18 a Is. 35:5; 42:7, 16 b 1 Pet. 2:9 c Luke 1:77 d Col. 1:12 e Acts 20:32 *1 set apart*
20 a Acts 9:19, 20, 22; 11:26 b Matt. 3:8
22 a Rom. 3:21 b John 5:46
23 a Luke 24:26 b 1 Cor. 15:20, 23 c Luke 2:32
24 a [1 Cor. 1:23; 2:13, 14; 4:10]
25 *1 out of my mind*
26 a Acts 26:3
29 a 1 Cor. 7:7
31 a Acts 23:9, 29; 25:25
32 a Acts 28:18 b Acts 25:11
CHAPTER 27
1 a Acts 25:12, 25
2 a Acts 19:29
3 a Acts 24:23; 28:16
6 a Acts 28:11
7 a Titus 1:5, 12

Paul's Warning Ignored

9 Now when much time had been spent,
and sailing was now dangerous [a]because
[1]the Fast was already over, Paul advised
them, 10 saying, "Men, I perceive that this
voyage will end with disaster and much
loss, not only of the cargo and ship, but
also our lives." 11 Nevertheless the centurion was more persuaded by the helms-
man and the owner of the ship than by the
things spoken by Paul. 12 And because the
harbor was not suitable to winter in, the
majority advised to set sail from there
also, if by any means they could reach
Phoenix, a harbor of Crete opening toward the southwest and northwest, *and*
winter *there.*

In the Tempest

13 When the south wind blew softly, supposing that they had obtained *their* desire,
putting out to sea, they sailed close by
Crete. 14 But not long after, a tempestuous
head wind arose, called [1]Euroclydon. 15 So
when the ship was caught, and could not
head into the wind, we let *her* [1]drive.
16 And running under *the shelter of* an island called [1]Clauda, we secured the skiff
with difficulty. 17 When they had taken it
on board, they used cables to undergird
the ship; and fearing lest they should run
aground on the [1]Syrtis *Sands,* they struck
sail and so were driven. 18 And because
we were exceedingly tempest-tossed, the
next *day* they lightened the ship. 19 On the
third *day* [a]we threw the ship's tackle overboard with our own hands. 20 Now when
neither sun nor stars appeared for many
days, and no small tempest beat on *us,* all
hope that we would be saved was finally
given up.

21 But after long abstinence from food,
then Paul stood in the midst of them and
said, "Men, you should have listened to
me, and not have sailed from Crete and
incurred this disaster and loss. 22 And now
I urge you to take [1]heart, for there will be
no loss of life among you, but only of the
ship. 23 [a]For there stood by me this night
an angel of the God to whom I belong and
[b]whom I serve, 24 saying, 'Do not be afraid,
Paul; you must be brought before Caesar;
and indeed God has granted you all those
who sail with you.' 25 Therefore take heart,
men, [a]for I believe God that it will be just
as it was told me. 26 However, [a]we must
run aground on a certain island."

27 Now when the fourteenth night had
come, as we were driven up and down in
the Adriatic *Sea,* about midnight the sailors sensed that they were drawing near
some land. 28 And they took soundings and
found *it* to be twenty fathoms; and when
they had gone a little farther, they took
soundings again and found *it* to be fifteen
fathoms. 29 Then, fearing lest we should
run aground on the rocks, they dropped
four anchors from the stern, and [1]prayed
for day to come. 30 And as the sailors were
seeking to escape from the ship, when
they had let down the skiff into the sea,
under pretense of putting out anchors
from the prow, 31 Paul said to the centurion and the soldiers, "Unless these men
stay in the ship, you cannot be saved."
32 Then the soldiers cut away the ropes of
the skiff and let it fall off.

33 And as day was about to dawn, Paul
implored *them* all to take food, saying,
"Today is the fourteenth day you have
waited and continued without food, and
eaten nothing. 34 Therefore I urge you to
take nourishment, for this is for your survival, [a]since not a hair will fall from the
head of any of you." 35 And when he had
said these things, he took bread and [a]gave
thanks to God in the presence of them all;
and when he had broken *it* he began to
eat. 36 Then they were all encouraged, and
also took food themselves. 37 And in all we
were two hundred and seventy-six [a]per-
sons on the ship. 38 So when they had eat-
en enough, they lightened the ship and
threw out the wheat into the sea.

Shipwrecked on Malta

39 When it was day, they did not recognize the land; but they observed a bay
with a beach, onto which they planned to
run the ship if possible. 40 And they [1]let
go the anchors and left *them* in the sea,
meanwhile loosing the rudder ropes; and
they hoisted the mainsail to the wind and
made for shore. 41 But striking [1]a place
where two seas met, [a]they ran the ship
aground; and the prow stuck fast and remained immovable, but the stern was being broken up by the violence of the
waves.

42 And the soldiers' plan was to kill the
prisoners, lest any of them should swim
away and escape. 43 But the centurion,
wanting to save Paul, kept them from
their purpose, and commanded that those
who could swim should jump *overboard*

9 [a]Lev. 16:29–31; 23:27–29 [1]The Day of Atonement, late September or early October

14 [1]A southeast wind that stirs up broad waves; NU *Euraquilon,* a northeaster

15 [1]*be driven*

16 [1]NU *Cauda*

17 [1]M *Syrtes*

19 [a]Jon. 1:5

22 [1]*courage*

23 [a]Acts 18:9; 23:11 [b]Dan. 6:16

25 [a]Rom. 4:20, 21

26 [a]Acts 28:1

29 [1]Or *wished*

34 [a][Matt. 10:30]

35 [a][1 Tim. 4:3, 4]

37 [a]Acts 2:41; 7:14

40 [1]*cast off*

41 [a]2 Cor. 11:25 [1]A reef

first and get to land, [44]and the rest, some on boards and some on *parts* of the ship. And so it was [a]that they all escaped safely to land.

Paul's Ministry on Malta

28 Now when they had escaped, they then found out that [a]the island was called Malta. [2]And the [a]natives[1] showed us unusual kindness; for they kindled a fire and made us all welcome, because of the rain that was falling and because of the cold. [3]But when Paul had gathered a bundle of sticks and laid *them* on the fire, a viper came out because of the heat, and fastened on his hand. [4]So when the natives saw the creature hanging from his hand, they said to one another, "No doubt this man is a murderer, whom, though he has escaped the sea, yet justice does not allow to live." [5]But he shook off the creature into the fire and [a]suffered no harm. [6]However, they were expecting that he would swell up or suddenly fall down dead. But after they had looked for a long time and saw no harm come to him, they changed their minds and [a]said that he was a god.

[7]In that region there was an estate of the [1]leading citizen of the island, whose name was Publius, who received us and entertained us courteously for three days. [8]And it happened that the father of Publius lay sick of a fever and dysentery. Paul went in to him and [a]prayed, and [b]he laid his hands on him and healed him. [9]So when this was done, the rest of those on the island who had diseases also came and were healed. [10]They also honored us in many [a]ways; and when we departed, they provided such things as were [b]necessary.

Arrival at Rome

[11]After three months we sailed in [a]an Alexandrian ship whose figurehead was the [1]Twin Brothers, which had wintered at the island. [12]And landing at Syracuse, we stayed three days. [13]From there we circled round and reached Rhegium. And after one day the south wind blew; and the next day we came to Puteoli, [14]where we found [a]brethren, and were invited to stay with them seven days. And so we went toward Rome. [15]And from there, when the brethren heard about us, they came to meet us as far as Appii Forum and Three Inns. When Paul saw them, he thanked God and took courage.

[16]Now when we came to Rome, the centurion delivered the prisoners to the captain of the guard; but [a]Paul was permitted to dwell by himself with the soldier who guarded him.

Paul's Ministry at Rome

[17]And it came to pass after three days that Paul called the leaders of the Jews together. So when they had come together, he said to them: "Men *and* brethren, [a]though I have done nothing against our people or the customs of our fathers, yet [b]I was delivered as a prisoner from Jerusalem into the hands of the Romans, [18]who, [a]when they had examined me, wanted to let *me* go, because there was no cause for putting me to death. [19]But when the [1]Jews spoke against *it,* [a]I was compelled to appeal to Caesar, not that I had anything of which to accuse my nation. [20]For this reason therefore I have called for you, to see *you* and speak with *you,* because [a]for the hope of Israel I am bound with [b]this chain."

[21]Then they said to him, "We neither received letters from Judea concerning you, nor have any of the brethren who came reported or spoken any evil of you. [22]But we desire to hear from you what you think; for concerning this sect, we know that [a]it is spoken against everywhere."

[23]So when they had appointed him a day, many came to him at *his* lodging, [a]to whom he explained and solemnly testified of the kingdom of God, persuading them concerning Jesus [b]from both the Law of Moses and the Prophets, from morning till evening. [24]And [a]some were persuaded by the things which were spoken, and some disbelieved. [25]So when they did not agree among themselves, they departed after Paul had said one word: "The Holy Spirit spoke rightly through Isaiah the prophet to [1]our fathers, [26]saying,

[a]'Go to this people and say:
"Hearing you will hear, and shall not understand;
And seeing you will see, and not perceive;
27 *For the hearts of this people have grown dull.*
Their ears are hard of hearing,
And their eyes they have closed,
Lest they should see with their eyes and hear with their ears,

44 [a]Acts 27:22, 31
CHAPTER 28
1 [a]Acts 27:26
2 [a]Col. 3:11 [1]Lit. *barbarians*
5 [a]Mark 16:18
6 [a]Acts 12:22; 14:11
7 [1]Magistrate
8 [a][James 5:14, 15] [b]Mark 5:23; 6:5; 7:32; 16:18
10 [a]Matt. 15:6 [b][Phil. 4:19]
11 [a]Acts 27:6 [1]Gr. *Dioskouroi,* Zeus's sons Castor and Pollux
14 [a]Rom. 1:8
16 [a]Acts 23:11; 24:25; 27:3
17 [a]Acts 23:29; 24:12, 13; 26:31 [b]Acts 21:33
18 [a]Acts 22:24; 24:10; 25:8; 26:32
19 [a]Acts 25:11, 21, 25 [1]The ruling authorities
20 [a]Acts 26:6, 7 [b]Eph. 3:1; 4:1; 6:20
22 [a][1 Pet. 2:12; 3:16; 4:14, 16]
23 [a]Luke 24:27 [b]Acts 26:6, 22
24 [a]Acts 14:4; 19:9
25 [1]NU *your*
26 [a]Is. 6:9, 10

Lest they should understand with
their hearts and turn,
So that I should heal them."'

28"Therefore let it be known to you that
the salvation of God has been sent [a]to the
Gentiles, and they will hear it!" 29[1]And
when he had said these words, the Jews
departed and had a great dispute among
themselves.

30Then Paul dwelt two whole years in
his own rented house, and received all
who came to him, 31[a]preaching the kingdom of God and teaching the things
which concern the Lord Jesus Christ with
all confidence, no one forbidding him.

28 a Rom. 11:11
29 *1* NU omits v. 29.
31 a Eph. 6:19

AUTHOR: *Paul*
DATE: *A.D. 56*
THEME: *The Righteousness of God in the Gospel of Christ*
KEY WORDS: *Righteousness, Faith, Justification, Law, Grace*

ROMANS

Dear Woman of Destiny,

The Book of Romans is filled with the glorious truth of our redemption in Christ. Many scholars believe that this book was delivered into the hands of the church at Rome by a woman named Phoebe who was called a servant, or *diakonos* (see Rom. 16:1). This is the same word translated *minister* elsewhere. One of my favorite Scripture passages, Romans 8:28, is found in these pages. It says: "And we know that all things work together for good to those who love God, to those who are the called according to His purpose." We are all born with a purpose and destiny from God. You are not an accident. You were not a mistake or born out of time. You are here on this earth because you have gifts and talents God wanted to be expressed through you to others. Find those gifts and use them as a woman of destiny.

With His love,

Cindy Jacobs

Greeting

Paul, a bondservant of Jesus Christ,
[a]called *to be* an apostle, [b]separated
to the gospel of God 2[a]which He
promised before [b]through His prophets in
the Holy Scriptures, 3concerning His Son
Jesus Christ our Lord, who [1]was [a]born of
the seed of David according to the flesh,
4*and* [a]declared *to be* the Son of God with
power according [b]to the Spirit of holiness,
by the resurrection from the dead.
5Through Him [a]we have received grace
and apostleship for [b]obedience to the faith
among all nations [c]for His name, 6among
whom you also are the called of Jesus
Christ;

7To all who are in Rome, beloved of
God, [a]called *to be* saints:

[b]Grace to you and peace from God our
Father and the Lord Jesus Christ.

Desire to Visit Rome

8First, [a]I thank my God through Jesus
Christ for you all, that [b]your faith is spoken of throughout the whole world. 9For
[a]God is my witness, [b]whom I serve [1]with
my spirit in the gospel of His Son, that
[c]without ceasing I make mention of you
always in my prayers, 10making request if,
by some means, now at last I may find a
way in the will of God to come to you.
11 For I long to see you, that [a]I may impart to you some spiritual gift, so that you
may be established— 12that is, that I
may be encouraged together with you by
[a]the mutual faith both of you and me.

13Now I do not want you to be unaware,
brethren, that I often planned to come to
you (but [a]was hindered until now), that I
might have some [b]fruit among you also,
just as among the other Gentiles. 14I am
a debtor both to Greeks and to barbarians,
both to wise and to unwise. 15So, as much
as is in me, *I am* ready to preach the gospel to you who are in Rome also.

The Just Live by Faith

16 For [a]I am not ashamed of the gospel [1]of Christ, for [b]it is the power of God
to salvation for everyone who believes,
[c]for the Jew first and also for the Greek.
17For [a]in it the righteousness of God is
revealed from faith to faith; as it is written, [b]*"The just shall live by faith."*

God's Wrath on Unrighteousness

18[a]For the wrath of God is revealed
from heaven against all ungodliness and
[b]unrighteousness of men, who [1]suppress
the truth in unrighteousness, 19because
[a]what may be known of God is [1]manifest
[2]in them, for [b]God has shown *it* to them.
20For since the creation of the world [a]His
invisible *attributes* are clearly seen, being
understood by the things that are made,
even His eternal power and [1]Godhead, so
that they are without excuse, 21because,
although they knew God, they did not
glorify *Him* as God, nor were thankful,
but [a]became futile in their thoughts,
and their foolish hearts were darkened.
22[a]Professing to be wise, they became
fools, 23and changed the glory of the [a]in-
corruptible [b]God into an image made like
[1]corruptible man—and birds and four-
footed animals and creeping things.

24[a]Therefore God also gave them up to
uncleanness, in the lusts of their hearts,
[b]to dishonor their bodies [c]among themselves, 25who exchanged [a]the truth of God
[b]for the lie, and worshiped and served the
creature rather than the Creator, who is
blessed forever. Amen.

26For this reason God gave them up to
[a]vile passions. For even their [1]women exchanged the natural use for what is
against nature. 27Likewise also the [1]men,
leaving the natural use of the [2]woman,
burned in their lust for one another, men
with men committing what is shameful,
and receiving in themselves the penalty of
their error which was due.

*May ____ never be
ashamed of the gospel,
O Lord, for it is the power of
God to salvation for everyone
who believes.*

FROM ROMANS 1:16

28And even as they did not like to retain
God in *their* knowledge, God gave them
over to a debased mind, to do those things
[a]which are not fitting; 29being filled with

CHAPTER 1
1 a 1 Tim. 1:11 b Acts 9:15; 13:2
2 a Acts 26:6 b Gal. 3:8
3 a Gal. 4:4 *1 came*
4 a Acts 9:20; 13:33 b [Heb. 9:14]
5 a Eph. 3:8 b Acts 6:7 c Acts 9:15
7 a 1 Cor. 1:2, 24 b 1 Cor. 1:3
8 a 1 Cor. 1:4 b Rom. 16:19
9 a Rom. 9:1 b Acts 27:23 c 1 Thess. 3:10 *1* Or *in*
11 a Rom. 15:29
12 a Titus 1:4
13 a [1 Thess. 2:18] b Phil. 4:17
16 a Ps. 40:9, 10 b 1 Cor. 1:18, 24 c Acts 3:26 *1* NU omits *of Christ*
17 a Rom. 3:21; 9:30 b Hab. 2:4
18 a [Acts 17:30] b 2 Thess. 2:10 *1 hold down*
19 a [Acts 14:17; 17:24] b [John 1:9] *1 evident* *2 among*
20 a Ps. 19:1–6 *1 divine nature, deity*
21 a Jer. 2:5
22 a Jer. 10:14
23 a 1 Tim. 1:17; 6:15, 16 b Deut. 4:16–18 *1 perishable*
24 a Eph. 4:18, 19 b 1 Cor. 6:18 c Lev. 18:22
25 a 1 Thess. 1:9 b Is. 44:20
26 a Lev. 18:22 *1* Lit. *females*
27 *1* Lit. *males* *2* Lit. *female*
28 a Eph. 5:4

ROMANS 1:11

Dear Woman of Destiny,

Have you ever looked at another person and desired to be like her, not out of unhealthy envy, but because you see in her a strength and wisdom and experience with God that you would like in your own life? Perhaps you have breathed a prayer, such as this: "Lord, I wish I could minister the way that lady does." If you have, you are hungry for more of God! One of the ways God brings more of Himself to us is through the lives and giftings of others. This is sometimes called *impartation. To impart* means "to give or share with liberality" (Strong's #3330). Paul not only desired to impart spiritual gifts but his very own life (see 1 Thess. 2:8). Acts 8:18 records that Simon saw that the Spirit was bestowed through the laying on of the apostles' hands and he offered them money for this ability. Probably the most familiar example of impartation is the passing of Elijah's mantle to Elisha (see 2 Kin. 2). Impartation is more than a blessing or the influence of one person on another. Something miraculous happens!

The minister that God used to change my life in this way was Dr. Fuchsia Pickett. She is an accomplished theologian, Bible teacher, and author. She is a beautiful reflection of Jesus and a role model to me. When Dr. Pickett accepted the invitation to come to our church, I felt such a sense of expectancy. I was desperate for a change to come to my life. I loved Jesus and did my best to serve Him, but my message lacked passion and my ministry seemed powerless. I sought the Lord with tears of repentance and prepared my heart. When the anticipated moment came for Dr. Pickett to lay hands on me, I was ready for a breakthrough. Through a humble, yielded servant of God came the most powerful experience I have ever known! The anointing of the Holy Spirit flowed through her like electricity! That moment of impartation changed my life. My heart now beats with a fiery passion for Jesus and God's Word. Sometimes people who know nothing of my experience say that my ministry is similar to hers. When Dr. Pickett laid her hands on me, I not only received a part of her, but more—much more—of Him. Since that day I have found that what I freely received, I can now freely give (see Matt. 10:8).

If I were to define *impartation,* I would say it is the passing of life from one person to another. In this way, the Lord's life is multiplied. Just as Jesus broke the bread from a little boy's lunch and fed the multitudes, He will also take what we offer and bring increase in the lives of others. My prayer for you, Woman of Destiny, is that the life of Jesus will grow in you to such a fullness that you, like me, must pass it on!

LaNora Van Arsdall

Romans 1:16

Dear Woman of Destiny,

There is a high purpose and calling on your life from God. It is activated the instant you place yourself in His hands, accepting His salvation and forgiveness through the sacrifice of Jesus on the cross of Calvary.

You have probably asked yourself many times, "What has God specifically called me to?" You can rejoice! There is good news for you! In the same way that you received His salvation, deliverance, and blessing through grace, God desires for you to accept the calling He has placed on your life, so you can unashamedly share with those around you, being confident in the perfect will of your Father in heaven.

Isaiah 61:1–3 says: "The Spirit of the Lord GOD is upon Me, because the LORD has anointed Me to preach good tidings to the poor; He has sent Me to heal the brokenhearted, to proclaim liberty to the captives, and the opening of the prison to those who are bound; to proclaim the acceptable year of the LORD, and the day of vengeance of our God; to comfort all who mourn, to console those who mourn in Zion, to give them beauty for ashes, the oil of joy for mourning, the garment of praise for the spirit of heaviness; that they may be called trees of righteousness, the planting of the LORD, that He may be glorified."

This same anointing that was upon Christ while He walked the earth can now be upon your life, enabling and preparing you to do the work of God. For this reason, we are not ashamed!

Do not be afraid! It is not by your wisdom, strength, or efforts that God sends you out to speak to the world. It is simply with His anointing that He commissions you under the power of His Holy Spirit, in the same way He commissioned His only Son, Jesus, to bring His word of liberation to His people. God desires to use you, like Jesus, to bring comfort to the afflicted by speaking His word into their lives.

You will be astonished as God confirms His word through signs, wonders, and powerful miracles by His Holy Spirit. All He asks you to do is to believe. He wants to prove to you that the time of miracles has not passed; that in this time of apostasy, unbelief, and worldliness, He has not changed. He continues to manifest His love and power to His creation, not only in the wonderful promise of salvation and eternal life, but also by providing solutions to the daily problems that overwhelm us.

Yet the miracle that continues every day is this: God chooses to love, comfort, heal, set free, and empower those around you *through you!* He has placed a specific calling on your life—to be a bearer of restoration, liberation, and salvation, just as Jesus was and is. You are the hands, the feet, and the heart of Jesus in this hurting world! In the same way that God's heart beats for lost souls, He desires for your tender heart to beat with love and compassion for them, too. Place your head on His breast right now, Woman of Destiny, and align the rhythm of your heart with His as you hear the beat of your life's calling.

Maria Annacondia

all unrighteousness, [1]sexual immorality,
wickedness, [2]covetousness, [3]malicious-
ness; full of envy, murder, strife, deceit,
evil-mindedness; *they are* whisperers,
30 backbiters, haters of God, violent,
proud, boasters, inventors of evil things,
disobedient to parents, 31 [1]undiscerning,
untrustworthy, unloving, [2]unforgiving,
unmerciful; 32 who, [a]knowing the righteous judgment of God, that those who
practice such things [b]are deserving of
death, not only do the same but also [c]ap-
prove of those who practice them.

God's Righteous Judgment

2 Therefore you are [a]inexcusable,
O man, whoever you are who judge,
[b]for in whatever you judge another you
condemn yourself; for you who judge
practice the same things. 2 But we know
that the judgment of God is according to
truth against those who practice such
things. 3 And do you think this, O man,
you who judge those practicing such
things, and doing the same, that you will
escape the judgment of God? 4 Or do you
despise [a]the riches of His goodness, [b]for-
bearance, and [c]longsuffering, [d]not knowing that the goodness of God leads you to
repentance? 5 But in accordance with your
hardness and your [1]impenitent heart
[a]you are [2]treasuring up for yourself wrath
in the day of wrath and revelation of the
righteous judgment of God, 6 who [a]*"will
render to each one according to his
deeds"*: 7 eternal life to those who by patient continuance in doing good seek for
glory, honor, and immortality; 8 but to
those who are self-seeking and [a]do not
obey the truth, but obey unrighteousness—indignation and wrath, 9 tribulation and anguish, on every soul of man
who does evil, of the Jew [a]first and also of
the [1]Greek; 10 [a]but glory, honor, and peace
to everyone who works what is good, to
the Jew first and also to the Greek. 11 For
[a]there is no partiality with God.

12 For as many as have sinned without
law will also perish without law, and as
many as have sinned in the law will be
judged by the law 13 (for [a]not the hearers
of the law *are* just in the sight of God, but
the doers of the law will be justified; 14 for
when Gentiles, who do not have the law,
by nature do the things in the law, these,
although not having the law, are a law to
themselves, 15 who show the [a]work of the
law written in their hearts, their [b]con-
science also bearing witness, and between
themselves *their* thoughts accusing or
else excusing *them*) 16 [a]in the day when
God will judge the secrets of men [b]by Jesus Christ, [c]according to my gospel.

The Jews Guilty as the Gentiles

17 [1]Indeed [a]you are called a Jew, and
[b]rest[2] on the law, [c]and make your boast in
God, 18 and [a]know *His* will, and [b]approve
the things that are excellent, being instructed out of the law, 19 and [a]are confident that you yourself are a guide to the
blind, a light to those who are in darkness,
20 an instructor of the foolish, a teacher of
babes, [a]having the form of knowledge and
truth in the law. 21 [a]You, therefore, who
teach another, do you not teach yourself?
You who preach that a man should not
steal, do you steal? 22 You who say, "Do not
commit adultery," do you commit adultery? You who abhor idols, [a]do you rob
temples? 23 You who [a]make your boast in
the law, do you dishonor God through
breaking the law? 24 For [a]*"the name of
God is* [b]*blasphemed among the Gentiles
because of you,"* as it is written.

Circumcision of No Avail

25 [a]For circumcision is indeed profitable if you keep the law; but if you are a
breaker of the law, your circumcision has
become uncircumcision. 26 Therefore, [a]if
an uncircumcised man keeps the righteous requirements of the law, will not his
uncircumcision be counted as circumcision? 27 And will not the physically uncircumcised, if he fulfills the law, [a]judge
you who, *even* with *your* [1]written *code*
and circumcision, *are* a transgressor of
the law? 28 For [a]he is not a Jew who *is one*
outwardly, nor *is* circumcision that which
is outward in the flesh; 29 but *he is* a Jew
[a]who *is one* inwardly; and [b]circumcision
is that of the heart, [c]in the Spirit, not in
the letter; [d]whose [1]praise *is* not from men
but from God.

God's Judgment Defended

3 What advantage then has the Jew, or
what *is* the profit of circumcision?
2 Much in every way! Chiefly because [a]to
them were committed the [1]oracles of

29 [1] NU omits *sexual immorality* [2] *greed* [3] *malice*
31 [1] *without understanding* [2] NU omits *unforgiving*
32 [a] [Rom. 2:2] [b] [Rom. 6:21] [c] Hos. 7:3

CHAPTER 2
1 [a] [Rom. 1:20] [b] [Matt. 7:1–5]
4 [a] [Eph. 1:7, 18; 2:7] [b] [Rom. 3:25] [c] Ex. 34:6 [d] Is. 30:18
5 [a] [Deut. 32:34] [1] *unrepentant* [2] *storing*
6 [a] Ps. 62:12; Prov. 24:12
8 [a] [2 Thess. 1:8]
9 [a] 1 Pet. 4:17 [1] Gentile
10 [a] [1 Pet. 1:7]
11 [a] Deut. 10:17
13 [a] [James 1:22, 25]
15 [a] 1 Cor. 5:1 [b] Acts 24:25
16 [a] [Matt. 25:31] [b] Acts 10:42; 17:31 [c] 1 Tim. 1:11
17 [a] John 8:33 [b] Mic. 3:11 [c] Is. 48:1, 2 [1] NU *But if* [2] *rely*
18 [a] Deut. 4:8 [b] Phil. 1:10
19 [a] Matt. 15:14
20 [a] [2 Tim. 3:5]
21 [a] Matt. 23:3
22 [a] Mal. 3:8
23 [a] Rom. 2:17; 9:4
24 [a] Ezek. 16:27 [b] Is. 52:5; Ezek. 36:22
25 [a] [Gal. 5:3]
26 [a] [Acts 10:34]
27 [a] Matt. 12:41 [1] Lit. *letter*
28 [a] [Gal. 6:15]
29 [a] [1 Pet. 3:4] [b] Phil. 3:3 [c] Deut. 30:6 [d] [1 Cor. 4:5]
[1] A play on words—*Jew* is literally *praise.*

CHAPTER 3 2 [a] Deut. 4:5–8 [1] *sayings,* Scriptures

God. 3For what if [a]some did not believe?
[b]Will their unbelief make the faithfulness
of God without effect? 4[a]Certainly not! Indeed, let [b]God be [1]true but [c]every man a
liar. As it is written:

[d]*"That You may be justified in Your*
words,
And may overcome when You are
judged."

5But if our unrighteousness demonstrates the righteousness of God, what
shall we say? *Is* God unjust who inflicts
wrath? [a](I speak as a man.) 6Certainly
not! For then [a]how will God judge the
world?

7For if the truth of God has increased
through my lie to His glory, why am I also
still judged as a sinner? 8And *why* not *say,*
[a]"Let us do evil that good may come"?—
as we are slanderously reported and as
some affirm that we say. Their [1]condem-
nation is just.

All Have Sinned

9What then? Are we better *than they?*
Not at all. For we have previously charged
both Jews and Greeks that [a]they are all
under sin.

10As it is written:

[a]*"There is none righteous, no, not*
one;
11 *There is none who understands;*
There is none who seeks after God.
12 *They have all turned aside;*
They have together become
unprofitable;
There is none who does good, no,
not one."
13 *"Their[a] throat is an open [1]tomb;*
With their tongues they have
practiced deceit";
[b]*"The poison of asps is under their*
lips";
14 *"Whose[a] mouth is full of cursing*
and bitterness."
15 *"Their[a] feet are swift to shed*
blood;
16 *Destruction and misery are in*
their ways;
17 *And the way of peace they have*
not known."
18 *"There[a] is no fear of God before*
their eyes."

19Now we know that whatever [a]the law
says, it says to those who are under the
law, that [b]every mouth may be stopped,
and all the world may become [1]guilty
before God. 20Therefore [a]by the deeds of
the law no flesh will be justified in His
sight, for by the law *is* the knowledge of
sin.

God's Righteousness Through Faith

21But now [a]the righteousness of God
apart from the law is revealed, [b]being witnessed by the Law [c]and the Prophets,
22even the righteousness of God, through
faith in Jesus Christ, to all [1]and on all who
believe. For [a]there is no difference; 23for
[a]all have sinned and fall short of the glory
of God, 24being justified [1]freely [a]by His
grace [b]through the redemption that is in
Christ Jesus, 25whom God set forth [a]*as*
a [1]propitiation [b]by His blood, through
faith, to demonstrate His righteousness,
because in His forbearance God had
passed over [c]the sins that were previously
committed, 26to demonstrate at the present time His righteousness, that He
might be just and the justifier of the one
who has faith in Jesus.

The great mystery hid in God in all past ages was that of making Jews and Gentiles one new Body—the Church, which is His Body.

FINIS JENNINGS DAKE

Boasting Excluded

27[a]Where *is* boasting then? It is excluded. By what law? Of works? No, but by the
law of faith. 28Therefore we conclude
[a]that a man is [1]justified by faith apart
from the deeds of the law. 29Or *is He* the
God of the Jews only? *Is He* not also the
God of the Gentiles? Yes, of the Gentiles
also, 30since [a]*there is* one God who will
justify the circumcised by faith and the
uncircumcised through faith. 31Do we
then make void the law through faith?
Certainly not! On the contrary, we establish the law.

3 a Heb. 4:2 b [2 Tim. 2:13]
4 a Job 40:8 b [John 3:33] c Ps. 62:9 d Ps. 51:4 1 Found true
5 a Gal. 3:15
6 a [Gen. 18:25]
8 a Rom. 5:20 1 Lit. *judgment*
9 a Gal. 3:22
10 a Ps. 14:1–3; 53:1–3; Eccl. 7:20
13 a Ps. 5:9 b Ps. 140:3 1 *grave*
14 a Ps. 10:7
15 a Prov. 1:16; Is. 59:7, 8
18 a Ps. 36:1
19 a John 10:34 b Job 5:16 1 *accountable*
20 a [Gal. 2:16]
21 a Acts 15:11 b John 5:46 c 1 Pet. 1:10
22 a [Col. 3:11] 1 NU omits *and on all*
23 a Gal. 3:22
24 a [Eph. 2:8] b [Heb. 9:12, 15] 1 *without any cost*
25 a Lev. 16:15 b Col. 1:20 c Acts 14:16; 17:30 1 *mercy seat*
27 a [1 Cor. 1:29]
28 a Gal. 2:16 1 *declared righteous*
30 a [Gal. 3:8, 20]

Abraham Justified by Faith

4 What then shall we say that [a]Abraham our [b]father[1] has found according to the flesh? [2]For if Abraham was [a]justified by works, he has *something* to boast about, but not before God. [3]For what does the Scripture say? [a]*"Abraham believed God, and it was [1]accounted to him for righteousness."* [4]Now [a]to him who works, the wages are not counted [1]as grace but as debt.

David Celebrates the Same Truth

[5]But to him who [a]does not work but believes on Him who justifies [b]the ungodly, his faith is accounted for righteousness, [6]just as David also [a]describes the blessedness of the man to whom God imputes righteousness apart from works:

7 *"Blessed[a] are those whose lawless*
deeds are forgiven,
And whose sins are covered;
8 *Blessed is the man to whom the*
LORD shall not impute sin."

Abraham Justified Before Circumcision

[9]*Does* this blessedness then *come* upon the circumcised *only,* or upon the uncircumcised also? For we say that faith was accounted to Abraham for righteousness. [10]How then was it accounted? While he was circumcised, or uncircumcised? Not while circumcised, but while uncircumcised. [11]And [a]he received the sign of circumcision, a seal of the righteousness of the faith which *he had while still* uncircumcised, that [b]he might be the father of all those who believe, though they are uncircumcised, that righteousness might be imputed to them also, [12]and the father of circumcision to those who not only *are* of the circumcision, but who also walk in the steps of the faith which our father [a]Abraham *had while still* uncircumcised.

The Promise Granted Through Faith

[13]For the promise that he would be the [a]heir of the world *was* not to Abraham or to his seed through the law, but through the righteousness of faith. [14]For [a]if those who are of the law *are* heirs, faith is made void and the promise made of no effect, [15]because [a]the law brings about wrath; for where there is no law *there is* no transgression.

[16]Therefore *it is* of faith that *it might be* [a]according to grace, [b]so that the promise might be [1]sure to all the seed, not only to those who are of the law, but also to those who are of the faith of Abraham, [c]who is the father of us all [17](as it is written, [a]*"I have made you a father of many nations"*) in the presence of Him whom he believed—God, [b]who gives life to the dead and calls those [c]things which do not exist as though they did; [18]who, contrary to hope, in hope believed, so that he became the father of many nations, according to what was spoken, [a]*"So shall your descendants be."* [19]And not being weak in faith, [a]he did not consider his own body, already dead (since he was about a hundred years old), [b]and the deadness of Sarah's womb. [20]He did not waver at the promise of God through unbelief, but was strengthened in faith, giving glory to God, [21]and being fully convinced that what He had promised [a]He was also able to perform. [22]And therefore [a]*"it was accounted to him for righteousness."*

[23]Now [a]it was not written for his sake alone that it was imputed to him, [24]but also for us. It shall be imputed to us who believe [a]in Him who raised up Jesus our Lord from the dead, [25][a]who was delivered up because of our offenses, and [b]was raised because of our justification.

Faith Triumphs in Trouble

5 Therefore, [a]having been justified by faith, [1]we have [b]peace with God through our Lord Jesus Christ, [2][a]through whom also we have access by faith into this grace [b]in which we stand, and [c]rejoice in hope of the glory of God. [3]And not only *that,* but [a]we also glory in tribulations, [b]knowing that tribulation produces [1]perseverance; [4][a]and perseverance, [1]character; and character, hope. [5][a]Now hope does not disappoint, [b]because the love of God has been poured out in our hearts by the Holy Spirit who was given to us.

Christ in Our Place

[6]For when we were still without strength, [1]in due time [a]Christ died for the ungodly. [7]For scarcely for a righteous

[1] at the right time

CHAPTER 4
1 a Is. 51:2 b James 2:21 1 Or *(fore)father according to the flesh has found?*
2 a Rom. 3:20, 27
3 a Gen. 15:6 1 *imputed, credited, reckoned, counted*
4 a Rom. 11:6 1 *according to*
5 a [Eph. 2:8, 9] b Josh. 24:2
6 a Ps. 32:1, 2
7 a Ps. 32:1, 2
11 a Gen. 17:10 b Luke 19:9
12 a Rom. 4:18–22
13 a Gen. 17:4–6; 22:17
14 a Gal. 3:18
15 a Rom. 3:20
16 a [Rom. 3:24] b [Gal. 3:22] c Is. 51:2 1 *certain*
17 a Gen. 17:5 b [Rom. 8:11] c Rom. 9:26
18 a Gen. 15:5
19 a Gen. 17:17 b Heb. 11:11
21 a [Heb. 11:19]
22 a Gen. 15:6
23 a Rom. 15:4
24 a Acts 2:24
25 a Is. 53:4, 5 b [1 Cor. 15:17]

CHAPTER 5
1 a Is. 32:17 b [Eph. 2:14] 1 Some ancient mss. *let us have*
2 a [Eph. 2:18; 3:12] b 1 Cor. 15:1 c Heb. 3:6
3 a Matt. 5:11, 12 b James 1:3 1 *endurance*
4 a [James 1:12] 1 *approved character*
5 a Phil. 1:20 b 2 Cor. 1:22
6 a [Rom. 4:25; 5:8; 8:32]

man will one die; yet perhaps for a good
man someone would even dare to die.
[8]But [a]God demonstrates His own love toward us, in that while we were still sinners, Christ died for us. [9]Much more then,
having now been justified [a]by His blood,
we shall be saved [b]from wrath through
Him. [10]For [a]if when we were enemies [b]we
were reconciled to God through the death
of His Son, much more, having been reconciled, we shall be saved [c]by His life.
[11]And not only *that,* but we also [a]rejoice
in God through our Lord Jesus Christ,
through whom we have now received the
reconciliation.

When the warmth of God's love melts and dissolves your spirit, it causes your prayer to ascend to God in a sweet aroma.

MADAME JEANNE GUYON

Death in Adam, Life in Christ

[12]Therefore, just as [a]through one man
sin entered the world, and [b]death through
sin, and thus death spread to all men, because all sinned— [13](For until the law sin
was in the world, but [a]sin is not imputed
when there is no law. [14]Nevertheless
death reigned from Adam to Moses, even
over those who had not sinned according
to the likeness of the transgression of
Adam, [a]who is a type of Him who was to
come. [15]But the free gift *is* not like the
[1]offense. For if by the one man's offense
many died, much more the grace of God
and the gift by the grace of the one Man,
Jesus Christ, abounded [a]to many. [16]And
the gift *is* not like *that which came*
through the one who sinned. For the
judgment *which came* from one *offense*
resulted in condemnation, but the free
gift *which came* from many [1]offenses *re-*
sulted in justification. [17]For if by the one
man's [1]offense death reigned through the
one, much more those who receive abundance of grace and of the gift of righteousness will reign in life through the One,
Jesus Christ.)

8 a [John 3:16; 15:13]
9 a Eph. 2:13 b 1 Thess. 1:10
10 a [Rom. 8:32] b 2 Cor. 5:18 c John 14:19
11 a [Gal. 4:9]
12 a [1 Cor. 15:21] b Gen. 2:17
13 a 1 John 3:4
14 a [1 Cor. 15:21, 22]
15 a [Is. 53:11] *1 trespass or false step*
16 *1 trespasses*
17 *1 trespass*
18 a [1 Cor. 15:21, 45] b [John 12:32] *1 Or one trespass* *2 Or one righteous act*
19 a [Phil. 2:8]
20 a John 15:22 b 1 Tim. 1:14
CHAPTER 6
1 a Rom. 3:8; 6:15
2 a [Gal. 2:19]
3 a [Gal. 3:27] b [1 Cor. 15:29]
4 a Col. 2:12 b 1 Cor. 6:14 c John 2:11 d [Gal. 6:15]
5 a Phil. 3:10
6 a Gal. 2:20; 5:24; 6:14 b Col. 2:11 *1 rendered inoperative*
7 a 1 Pet. 4:1 *1 cleared*
8 a 2 Tim. 2:11
9 a Rev. 1:18
10 a Heb. 9:27 b Luke 20:38

[18]Therefore, as through [1]one man's offense *judgment* came to all men, resulting
in condemnation, even so through [a]one[2]
Man's righteous act *the free gift came* [b]to
all men, resulting in justification of life.
[19]For as by one man's disobedience many
were made sinners, so also by [a]one Man's
obedience many will be made righteous.

Thank You, Father, for demonstrating Your own love toward ____, in that while they were still sinners, Christ died for them.

FROM ROMANS 5:8

[20]Moreover [a]the law entered that
the offense might abound. But where
sin abounded, grace [b]abounded much
more, [21]so that as sin reigned in death,
even so grace might reign through righteousness to eternal life through Jesus
Christ our Lord.

Dead to Sin, Alive to God

6 What shall we say then? [a]Shall we
continue in sin that grace may
abound? [2]Certainly not! How shall we
who [a]died to sin live any longer in it? [3]Or
do you not know that [a]as many of us as
were baptized into Christ Jesus [b]were
baptized into His death? [4]Therefore we
were [a]buried with Him through baptism
into death, that [b]just as Christ was raised
from the dead by [c]the glory of the Father,
[d]even so we also should walk in newness
of life.

[5][a]For if we have been united together
in the likeness of His death, certainly we
also shall be *in the likeness* of *His* resurrection, [6]knowing this, that [a]our old man
was crucified with *Him,* that [b]the body of
sin might be [1]done away with, that we
should no longer be slaves of sin. [7]For [a]he
who has died has been [1]freed from sin.
[8]Now [a]if we died with Christ, we believe
that we shall also live with Him, [9]knowing
that [a]Christ, having been raised from the
dead, dies no more. Death no longer has
dominion over Him. [10]For *the death* that
He died, [a]He died to sin once for all; but
the life that He lives, [b]He lives to God.

ROMANS 5:20

Dear Woman of Destiny,

God loved us first. He loved us even when we were unlovable, full of transgressions, sin, and death. This great love of God, combined with His rich mercy, made possible the miracle of salvation for you and me, justified through faith. We have been made new creatures with the total possibility, through the access Jesus Christ gave us by faith, to stand in His grace.

"But God, who is rich in mercy, because of His great love with which He loved us, even when we were dead in trespasses, made us alive together with Christ (by grace you have been saved)" (Eph. 2:4, 5). Paul stated the wonderful truth of our redemption in Romans 5:1, 2: "Therefore, having been justified by faith, we have peace with God through our Lord Jesus Christ, through whom also we have access by faith into this grace in which we stand, and rejoice in hope of the glory of God."

The Lord made it possible for us to stand in grace. To stand is not to be in a lying or sitting down position, but in an upright position—on one's feet. The Lord gave you His grace so you could stand upright and hold a place of dignity, resisting the enemy and fighting strong by knowing who you really are—a new creature in Him.

But what is this grace we now stand in? Grace comes to us with salvation. When we took the step—the best step in our lives—to open our heart to the Lord and renounce the world, making Jesus our Lord and Savior, we started a journey in grace. The Lord, by His mercy, saw us in a new way. We now have a new standing before God as recipients of His favor. All of God's blessings and benefits come through His marvelous grace. We deserve nothing, but He opens His arms to us. He, as a loving daddy, gives us everything. Grace is free, while the eternal and unmerited love and favor of God is poured on us.

The Lord made it possible for us to stand in this grace. But with this comes a responsibility. Second Peter 3:18 tells us to "grow in the grace and knowledge of our Lord and Savior Jesus Christ." We read in John 1:14 that Jesus came from the Father "full of grace." There is a work we have to do in our lives. We have to grow in grace, to walk toward the place of being full of grace just like Jesus. This is achieved by complete dependence upon God by faith. We need to understand that we are nothing without Him. God our Creator is all and the source of all. All the blessings of our life are unmerited favors of God toward us. In the measure that we grow in the understanding of His greatness, we will grow in His grace.

"For the grace of God that brings salvation has appeared to all men, teaching us that, denying ungodliness and worldly lusts, we should live soberly, righteously, and godly in the present age" (Titus 2:11, 12).

Cecilia Caballeros

11 Likewise you also, [1]reckon yourselves to
be [a]dead indeed to sin, but [b]alive to God
in Christ Jesus our Lord.
12 [a]Therefore do not let sin reign in your
mortal body, that you should obey it in its
lusts. 13 And do not present your [a]mem-
bers *as* [1]instruments of unrighteousness
to sin, but [b]present yourselves to God as
being alive from the dead, and your members *as* [1]instruments of righteousness to
God. 14 For [a]sin shall not have dominion
over you, for you are not under law but
under grace.

From Slaves of Sin to Slaves of God

15 What then? Shall we sin [a]because we
are not under law but under grace? Certainly not! 16 Do you not know that [a]to
whom you present yourselves slaves to
obey, you are that one's slaves whom you
obey, whether of sin *leading* to death, or
of obedience *leading* to righteousness?
17 But God be thanked that *though* you
were slaves of sin, yet you obeyed from the
heart [a]that form of doctrine to which you
were [1]delivered. 18 And [a]having been set
free from sin, you became slaves of righteousness. 19 I speak in human *terms* because of the weakness of your flesh. For
just as you presented your members *as*
slaves of uncleanness, and of lawlessness
leading to *more* lawlessness, so now present your members *as* slaves *of* righteousness [1]for holiness.
20 For when you were [a]slaves of sin, you
were free in regard to righteousness.
21 [a]What fruit did you have then in the
things of which you are now ashamed?
For [b]the end of those things *is* death.
22 But now [a]having been set free from sin,
and having become slaves of God, you
have your fruit [1]to holiness, and the end,
everlasting life. 23 For [a]the wages of sin *is*
death, but [b]the [1]gift of God *is* eternal life
in Christ Jesus our Lord.

Freed from the Law

7 Or do you not know, brethren (for I
speak to those who know the law),
that the law [1]has dominion over a man as
long as he lives? 2 For [a]the woman who
has a husband is bound by the law to *her*
husband as long as he lives. But if the
husband dies, she is released from the law
of *her* husband. 3 So then [a]if, while *her*
husband lives, she marries another man,
she will be called an adulteress; but if her
husband dies, she is free from that law, so
that she is no adulteress, though she has
married another man. 4 Therefore, my
brethren, you also have become [a]dead to
the law through the body of Christ, that
you may be married to another—to Him
who was raised from the dead, that we
should [b]bear fruit to God. 5 For when we
were in the flesh, the sinful passions
which were aroused by the law [a]were at
work in our members [b]to bear fruit to
death. 6 But now we have been delivered
from the law, having died to what we were
held by, so that we should serve [a]in the
newness of the Spirit and not *in* the old-
ness of the letter.

> *The plan of God for your life is that you should be held captive by His power, doing that which you in the natural world would never do, but that which you are forced to do by the power of the Holy Ghost moving through you.*
>
> SMITH WIGGLESWORTH

Sin's Advantage in the Law

7 What shall we say then? *Is* the law sin?
Certainly not! On the contrary, [a]I would
not have known sin except through the
law. For I would not have known covetousness unless the law had said, [b]*"You
shall not covet."* 8 But [a]sin, taking opportunity by the commandment, produced in
me all *manner of evil* desire. For [b]apart
from the law sin *was* dead. 9 I was alive
once without the law, but when the commandment came, sin revived and I died.
10 And the commandment, [a]which *was* to
bring life, I found to *bring* death. 11 For
sin, taking occasion by the commandment, deceived me, and by it killed *me.*
12 Therefore [a]the law *is* holy, and the commandment holy and just and good.

11 a [Rom. 6:2; 7:4, 6] b [Gal. 2:19] *1 consider*
12 a Ps. 19:13
13 a Col. 3:5 b 1 Pet. 2:24; 4:2 *1 Or weapons*
14 a [Gal. 5:18]
15 a 1 Cor. 9:21
16 a 2 Pet. 2:19
17 a 2 Tim. 1:13 *1 entrusted*
18 a John 8:32
19 *1 unto sanctification*
20 a John 8:34
21 a Rom. 7:5 b Rom. 1:32
22 a Rom. 6:18; 8:2 *1 unto sanctification*
23 a Gen. 2:17 b 1 Pet. 1:4 *1 free gift*

CHAPTER 7
1 *1 rules*
2 a 1 Cor. 7:39
3 a [Matt. 5:32]
4 a Gal. 2:19; 5:18 b Gal. 5:22
5 a Rom. 6:13 b James 1:15
6 a Rom. 2:29
7 a Rom. 3:20 b Ex. 20:17; Deut. 5:21; Acts 20:33
8 a Rom. 4:15 b 1 Cor. 15:56
10 a Lev. 18:5
12 a Ps. 19:8

Law Cannot Save from Sin

13Has then what is good become death
to me? Certainly not! But sin, that it
might appear sin, was producing death
in me through what is good, so that sin
through the commandment might become exceedingly sinful. 14For we know
that the law is spiritual, but I am carnal,
[a]sold under sin. 15For what I am doing, I
do not understand. [a]For what I will to do,
that I do not practice; but what I hate,
that I do. 16 If, then, I do what I will
not to do, I agree with the law that *it is*
good. 17But now, *it is* no longer I who
do it, but sin that dwells in me. 18For I
know that [a]in me (that is, in my flesh)
nothing good dwells; for to will is present
with me, but *how* to perform what is good
I do not find. 19For the good that I will *to*
do, I do not do; but the evil I will not *to*
do, that I practice. 20Now if I do what I will
not *to do,* it is no longer I who do it, but
sin that dwells in me.

I clearly recognize that all good is in God alone, and that in me, without Divine Grace, there is nothing but deficiency. . . . The one sole thing in myself in which I glory, is that I see in myself nothing in which I can glory.

CATHERINE OF GENOA

21I find then a law, that evil is present
with me, the one who wills to do good.
22For I [a]delight in the law of God according to [b]the inward man. 23But [a]I see another law in [b]my members, warring
against the law of my mind, and bringing
me into captivity to the law of sin which
is in my members. 24O wretched man that
I am! Who will deliver me [a]from this body
of death? 25[a]I thank God—through Jesus
Christ our Lord!

14 a 2 Kin. 17:17
15 a [Gal. 5:17]
18 a [Gen. 6:5; 8:21]
22 a Ps. 1:2 b [2 Cor. 4:16]
23 a [Gal. 5:17] b Rom. 6:13, 19
24 a [1 Cor. 15:51, 52]
25 a 1 Cor. 15:57

CHAPTER 8
1 a Gal. 5:16 *1* NU omits the rest of v. 1.
2 a Rom. 6:18, 22 b [1 Cor. 15:45] c Rom. 7:24, 25
3 a Acts 13:39 b [2 Cor. 5:21]
4 a Gal. 5:16, 25
5 a John 3:6 b [Gal. 5:22–25]
6 a Gal. 6:8 *1 fleshly*
7 a James 4:4 b 1 Cor. 2:14 *1 fleshly*
11 a Acts 2:24 b 1 Cor. 6:14 *1* Or *because of*

So then, with the mind I myself serve
the law of God, but with the flesh the law
of sin.

Free from Indwelling Sin

8 *There* is therefore now no condemnation to those who are in Christ Jesus,
[a]who[1] do not walk according to the flesh,
but according to the Spirit. 2For [a]the law
of [b]the Spirit of life in Christ Jesus has
made me free from [c]the law of sin and
death. 3For [a]what the law could not do in
that it was weak through the flesh, [b]God
did by sending His own Son in the likeness of sinful flesh, on account of sin: He
condemned sin in the flesh, 4that the
righteous requirement of the law might
be fulfilled in us who [a]do not walk according to the flesh but according to the Spirit. 5For [a]those who live according to the
flesh set their minds on the things of the
flesh, but those *who live* according to
the Spirit, [b]the things of the Spirit. 6For
[a]to be [1]carnally minded *is* death, but to be
spiritually minded *is* life and peace. 7Be-
cause [a]the [1]carnal mind *is* enmity against
God; for it is not subject to the law of God,
[b]nor indeed can be. 8So then, those who
are in the flesh cannot please God.

We praise You, Father, that there is therefore now no condemnation for ____ who is in Christ Jesus, for ____ does not walk according to the flesh, but according to the Spirit.

FROM ROMANS 8:1

9But you are not in the flesh but in the
Spirit, if indeed the Spirit of God dwells in
you. Now if anyone does not have the
Spirit of Christ, he is not His. 10And if
Christ *is* in you, the body *is* dead because
of sin, but the Spirit *is* life because of righteousness. 11But if the Spirit of [a]Him who
raised Jesus from the dead dwells in you,
[b]He who raised Christ from the dead will
also give life to your mortal bodies
[1]through His Spirit who dwells in you.

Romans 7:16

Dear Woman of Destiny,

Do you like your body? Are you constantly dieting and wishing you looked like someone else? Do you spend your days thinking about food, weight, and your body? Do you count calories, weigh yourself multiple times a day, and feel "fat" no matter what you weigh? Are you uncomfortable eating a regular meal? Do you make judgments about yourself based on what you eat? Do you think others are judging you by what you eat, and do you feel anxious eating around other people? If you answer "Yes" to these questions, you may be suffering from an eating disorder. More than 11 million women and girls struggle with eating disorders in America today.

Anorexia is a form of self-starvation that can cause severe medical complications including death. This disorder usually begins around puberty and involves extreme weight loss. Young girls become obsessed with food and weight as a cover for other emotional struggles.

Bulimia involves eating large amounts of food and then ridding the body of that food by vomiting, abusing laxatives, exercising excessively, taking diuretics or diet pills, and/or using enemas. This cycle, known as the "binge-purge" cycle is usually done in secret and may cause serious medical complications. Women and girls with bulimia are usually normal weight and ashamed of their behavior.

Compulsive and binge eating occurs when you consume large numbers of calories and feel as if you've lost control over eating. Most women continue to eat even though they are uncomfortably full. The major consequence is weight gain and obesity.

Although food is the substance over which women struggle, food is not the root of the problem. Emotional and spiritual emptiness are the real culprits. There is tremendous pressure from the culture to be thin. Families can be too rigid or too out of control in their structure. The pressure to conform, appear perfect, and not deal with negative emotions plays a role. Developmental issues of facing the physical and emotional changes of adolescence and leaving home also contribute to the development of an eating disorder. Conflict is poorly handled, and food is used to numb negative feelings brought on by interpersonal relationships. Spiritually, deception plays a role leading one to think the perfect body must be attained. Interest in food becomes all-consuming and blocks our relationship with God.

To be free, you must admit to the problem and get help. Confront your hopelessness through the Scriptures. God will help you if you trust Him and ask for His help. The recognition of dependence on Him is a big step toward healing. Next, you must correct your faulty eating habits and develop an appropriate view of food as nourishment. Stop dieting, and learn to eat healthily. Finally, you must work through whatever self, family, and other interpersonal issues exist.

The difficulty overcoming an eating disorder is found in Romans 7:16. Paul says we do what we hate (starving, bingeing, and purging) and don't do what we should (eat healthily). So we must trust God to help us correct our view of self, open our eyes to our true beauty, and develop as mature women of God.

Linda Mintle

Either sin is with you, lying on your shoulders, or it is lying on Christ, the Lamb of God. Now if it is lying on your back, you are lost; but if it is resting on Christ, you are free, and you will be saved. Now choose what you want.

MARTIN LUTHER

Sonship Through the Spirit

12[a]Therefore, brethren, we are debtors—not to the flesh, to live according to
the flesh. 13For [a]if you live according to
the flesh you will die; but if by the Spirit
you [b]put to death the deeds of the body,
you will live. 14For [a]as many as are led by
the Spirit of God, these are sons of God.
15For [a]you did not receive the spirit of
bondage again [b]to fear, but you received
the [c]Spirit of adoption by whom we cry
out, [d]"Abba,[1] Father." 16[a]The Spirit Himself bears witness with our spirit that we
are children of God, 17and if children,
then [a]heirs—heirs of God and joint heirs
with Christ, [b]if indeed we suffer with *Him,*
that we may also be glorified together.

From Suffering to Glory

18For I consider that [a]the sufferings of
this present time are not worthy *to be
compared* with the glory which shall be
revealed in us. 19For [a]the earnest expectation of the creation eagerly waits for the
revealing of the sons of God. 20For [a]the
creation was subjected to futility, not willingly, but because of Him who subjected
it in hope; 21because the creation itself
also will be delivered from the bondage of
[1]corruption into the glorious [a]liberty of
the children of God. 22For we know that
the whole creation [a]groans and labors
with birth pangs together until now.
23Not only *that,* but we also who have [a]the
firstfruits of the Spirit, [b]even we ourselves
groan [c]within ourselves, eagerly waiting
for the adoption, the [d]redemption of our
body. 24For we were saved in this hope,
but [a]hope that is seen is not hope; for why
does one still hope for what he sees? 25But
if we hope for what we do not see, we eagerly wait for *it* with perseverance.

The spirit is a great mystery. It is the part of us that alone can touch the unseen, the unfelt—in short, God and the things of God.

MARY BODDY

26 Likewise the Spirit also helps in
our weaknesses. For [a]we do not know
what we should pray for as we ought, but
[b]the Spirit Himself makes intercession
[1]for us with groanings which cannot be
uttered. 27Now [a]He who searches the
hearts knows what the mind of the Spirit
is, because He makes intercession for the
saints [b]according to *the will of* God.
28 And we know that all things work
together for good to those who love God,
to those [a]who are the called according to
His purpose. 29For whom [a]He foreknew,
[b]He also predestined [c]*to be* conformed to
the image of His Son, [d]that He might be
the firstborn among many brethren.
30Moreover whom He predestined, these
He also [a]called; whom He called, these He
also [b]justified; and whom He justified,
these He also [c]glorified.

God's Everlasting Love

31What then shall we say to these
things? [a]If God *is* for us, who *can be*
against us? 32[a]He who did not spare His
own Son, but [b]delivered Him up for us all,
how shall He not with Him also freely give
us all things? 33Who shall bring a charge
against God's elect? [a]*It is* God who justifies. 34[a]Who *is* he who condemns? *It is*
Christ who died, and furthermore is also
risen, [b]who is even at the right hand of
God, [c]who also makes intercession for us.
35Who shall separate us from the love of
Christ? *Shall* tribulation, or distress, or
persecution, or famine, or nakedness,
or peril, or sword? 36As it is written:

---

12 a [Rom. 6:7, 14]
13 a Gal. 6:8 b Eph. 4:22
14 a [Gal. 5:18]
15 a Heb. 2:15 b 2 Tim. 1:7 c [Is. 56:5] d Mark 14:36 *1 Lit., in Aram., Father*
16 a Eph. 1:13
17 a Acts 26:18 b Phil. 1:29
18 a 2 Cor. 4:17
19 a [2 Pet. 3:13]
20 a Gen. 3:17–19
21 a [2 Cor. 3:17] *1 decay*
22 a Jer. 12:4, 11
23 a 2 Cor. 5:5 b 2 Cor. 5:2, 4 c [Luke 20:36] d Eph. 1:14; 4:30
24 a Heb. 11:1
26 a Matt. 20:22 b Eph. 6:18 *1 NU omits for us*
27 a 1 Chr. 28:9 b 1 John 5:14
28 a 2 Tim. 1:9
29 a 2 Tim. 2:19 b Eph. 1:5, 11 c [2 Cor. 3:18] d Heb. 1:6
30 a [1 Pet. 2:9; 3:9] b [Gal. 2:16] c John 17:22
31 a Num. 14:9
32 a Rom. 5:6, 10 b [Rom. 4:25]
33 a Is. 50:8, 9
34 a John 3:18 b Mark 16:19 c Heb. 7:25; 9:24

Romans 8:26, 27

Dear Woman of Destiny,

I believe one of the most beautifully comforting scriptures in the Bible is Romans 8:26, 27. Hebrews 7:25 tells us, "Therefore He is also able to save to the uttermost those who come to God through Him, since He *always* lives to make intercession for them" (italics mine).

In Hebrews 2:17, 18 we read, "Therefore, in all things He had to be made like His brethren, that He might be a merciful and faithful High Priest in things pertaining to God, to make propitiation for the sins of the people. For in that He Himself has suffered, being tempted, He is able to aid those who are tempted."

We serve a Lord who understands us completely and compassionately and who is able to identify *with* us and intercede *for* us according to the perfect will of God. When our souls melt from heaviness (see Ps. 119:28) and we lose all discernment about what to do or how to pray, the Holy Spirit is there to meet us, to weep and *groan* with us, for us, and at the same time to connect us to the Father by His intercession. "Surely He has borne our griefs and carried our sorrows" (Is. 53:4), and He continues to do so in love.

It was excruciating for our family when my dad developed Alzheimer's disease. We watched helplessly as the lovable and dependable father we had known slowly cracked and crumbled. It seemed like our ardent prayers for his healing weren't being heard as we watched our father become more and more lost from himself and us. We didn't know what more to pray.

One day I talked very straight to God about my feelings, telling Him how hurt and angry I was, declaring how unfair I felt it was that a man who was so good and who had worked so hard was being robbed in his later years of time just to rest and enjoy life. I went on and on about how my parents didn't deserve this, and the Lord was silent. But somehow I felt He was hearing with compassion. I began then to pray simply that God would have mercy on Dad, that either He would heal him completely or take him home. I prayed earnestly that the Lord would release his beautiful spirit from his deteriorating mind and body and set him free to come into his inheritance. I asked the Lord to take him into His loving arms, wipe away his tears, and fill him with the Father's love. I asked Him to let Dad know how much we appreciated the many ways he had laid down his life for us.

The more I prayed, the more I cried, and the better I felt. A peace settled into me. Something inside of me let go. Dad died soon after—not from Alzheimer's but from a series of small strokes. He went home to be with the Father without having to go through all the stages of the disease. He never lost his ability to recognize relatives and close friends. He never completely lost his sense of humor, and he never ceased to be kind. We all wept at his funeral—for ourselves. For him we rejoiced.

Paula Sandford

ROMANS 8:28, 29

Dear Woman of Destiny,

Once I was young; I am now a grandma of nine in my seventies. Looking back I see how God has been with me in all of my joys and sorrows. Nothing is wasted in our lives; He turns it all to His glory. All that comes into our lives has already been filtered through the loving hands of our precious Savior.

God calls us "to be conformed to the image of His Son" (Rom. 8:29). Thus any time of testing, health problems, relational difficulties, death of a loved one, or any other experience cannot separate us from the love of God. Testing and trials only make us more like Jesus Christ.

I know this from personal experience as I look back on the various trials God has permitted to come into my life. Heart trouble kept me flat on my back for a year and on strong heart medication for ten years. A daughter of missionary friends lived with us, and our four children needed me. Two of the girls were in high school, two boys were in junior high school, and our youngest daughter was eight years old. With the help of the Lord and my dear husband, I made it through that difficult year.

A friend visited me. She challenged me with, "You aren't just going to lie there and do nothing! Why don't you write?" In the meantime, another friend who lived thirty-five miles away asked if I would come and teach a new Bible study group when I was able to be up again. For several years prior, I had been a Bible study leader and teacher of four hundred women in my home church. Since I was too weak to write, I dictated the first twenty-eight-lesson course of the *Joy of Living* Bible Study Series.

With no advertising and only personal testimony of how much this method of Bible study had meant in their lives, women began to tell others about the *Joy of Living* courses. Today there are more than eight hundred classes, daytime and evening, for men and women, church school classes, Christian schools, and even in prison ministries. Some courses have been offered by radio with a Bible exposition and call-in interactive format. Courses are now available in Spanish, Russian, and other languages.

God, by the guidance and empowerment of His Holy Spirit, has worked all things together "for good" for me! All of our children are serving the Lord. God is good! Just trust Him in your circumstances. We need to "count it all joy when [we] fall into various trials" (James 1:2). Over the years I have had confirmed in so many ways that joy is **j**ust **o**ur **y**ieldedness, while the loving hand of God works all things together "for good to those who love God, to those who are the called according to His purpose." Look back and see what the Lord had done in your life by the power of His Holy Spirit. You have a mighty God who loves you and cares about you personally in every area and circumstance of your life!

Doris Greig

> [a]*"For Your sake we are killed all day*
> *long;*
> *We are accounted as sheep for the*
> *slaughter."*

Give your all to Him, and He will give His all to you.

AIMEE SEMPLE MCPHERSON

37[a]Yet in all these things we are more than conquerors through Him who loved us. 38For I am persuaded that neither death nor life, nor angels nor [a]principalities nor powers, nor things present nor things to come, 39nor height nor depth, nor any other created thing, shall be able to separate us from the love of God which is in Christ Jesus our Lord.

Israel's Rejection of Christ

9 I [a]tell the truth in Christ, I am not lying, my conscience also bearing me witness in the Holy Spirit, 2[a]that I have great sorrow and continual grief in my heart. 3For [a]I could wish that I myself were accursed from Christ for my brethren, my [1]countrymen according to the flesh, 4who are Israelites, [a]to whom *pertain* the adoption, [b]the glory, [c]the covenants, [d]the giving of the law, [e]the service *of God,* and [f]the promises; 5[a]of whom *are* the fathers and from [b]whom, according to the flesh, Christ *came,* [c]who is over all, *the* eternally blessed God. Amen.

Israel's Rejection and God's Purpose

6[a]But it is not that the word of God has taken no effect. For [b]they *are* not all Israel who *are* of Israel, 7[a]nor *are they* all children because they are the seed of Abraham; but, [b]*"In Isaac your seed shall be called."* 8That is, those who *are* the children of the flesh, these *are* not the children of God; but [a]the children of the promise are counted as the seed. 9For this *is* the word of promise: [a]*"At this time I will come and Sarah shall have a son."*

36 a Ps. 44:22
37 a 1 Cor. 15:57
38 a [Eph. 1:21]

CHAPTER 9
1 a 2 Cor. 1:23
2 a Rom. 10:1
3 a Ex. 32:32 *1 Or relatives*
4 a Ex. 4:22 b 1 Sam. 4:21 c Acts 3:25 d Ps. 147:19 e Heb. 9:1, 6 f [Acts 2:39; 13:32]
5 a Deut. 10:15 b [Luke 1:34, 35; 3:23] c Jer. 23:6
6 a Num. 23:19 b [Gal. 6:16]
7 a [Gal. 4:23] b Gen. 21:12
8 a Gal. 4:28
9 a Gen. 18:10, 14
10 a Gen. 25:21
11 a [Rom. 4:17; 8:28]
12 a Gen. 25:23
13 a Mal. 1:2, 3
14 a Deut. 32:4
15 a Ex. 33:19
17 a Gal. 3:8 b Ex. 9:16
18 a Ex. 4:21
19 a 2 Chr. 20:6
20 a Is. 29:16
21 a Prov. 16:4 b 2 Tim. 2:20
22 a [1 Thess. 5:9] b [1 Pet. 2:8]
23 a [Col. 1:27] b [Rom. 8:28–30]
24 a [Rom. 8:28] b Rom. 3:29
25 a Hos. 2:23
26 a Hos. 1:10

10And not only *this,* but when [a]Rebecca also had conceived by one man, *even* by our father Isaac 11(for *the children* not yet being born, nor having done any good or evil, that the purpose of God according to election might stand, not of works but of [a]Him who calls), 12it was said to her, [a]*"The older shall serve the younger."* 13As it is written, [a]*"Jacob I have loved, but Esau I have hated."*

Israel's Rejection and God's Justice

14What shall we say then? [a]*Is there* unrighteousness with God? Certainly not! 15For He says to Moses, [a]*"I will have mercy on whomever I will have mercy, and I will have compassion on whomever I will have compassion."* 16So then *it is* not of him who wills, nor of him who runs, but of God who shows mercy. 17For [a]the Scripture says to the Pharaoh, [b]*"For this very purpose I have raised you up, that I may show My power in you, and that My name may be declared in all the earth."* 18Therefore He has mercy on whom He wills, and whom He wills He [a]hardens.

19You will say to me then, "Why does He still find fault? For [a]who has resisted His will?" 20But indeed, O man, who are you to reply against God? [a]Will the thing formed say to him who formed *it,* "Why have you made me like this?" 21Does not the [a]potter have power over the clay, from the same lump to make [b]one vessel for honor and another for dishonor?

22*What* if God, wanting to show *His* wrath and to make His power known, endured with much longsuffering [a]the vessels of wrath [b]prepared for destruction, 23and that He might make known [a]the riches of His glory on the vessels of mercy, which He had [b]prepared beforehand for glory, 24*even* us whom He [a]called, [b]not of the Jews only, but also of the Gentiles?

25As He says also in Hosea:

> [a]*"I will call them My people, who*
> *were not My people,*
> *And her beloved, who was not*
> *beloved."*

26 *"And[a] it shall come to pass in the*
> *place where it was said to them,*
> *'You are not My people,'*
> *There they shall be called sons of*
> *the living God."*

27Isaiah also cries out concerning Israel:

[a]"Though the number of the
children of Israel be as the sand
of the sea,
[b]The remnant will be saved.
28 *For [1]He will finish the work and*
cut it short in righteousness,
[a]Because the LORD will make a short
work upon the earth."

29And as Isaiah said before:

[a]"Unless the LORD of [1]Sabaoth had
left us a seed,
[b]We would have become like Sodom,
And we would have been made like
Gomorrah."

Present Condition of Israel

30What shall we say then? [a]That Gentiles, who did not pursue righteousness,
have attained to righteousness, [b]even the
righteousness of faith; 31but Israel, [a]pur-
suing the law of righteousness, [b]has not
attained to the law [1]of righteousness.
32Why? Because *they did* not *seek it* by
faith, but as it were, [1]by the works of the
law. For [a]they stumbled at that stumbling
stone. 33As it is written:

[a]"Behold, I lay in Zion a stumbling
stone and rock of offense,
And [b]whoever believes on Him will
not be put to shame."

Israel Needs the Gospel

10 Brethren, my heart's desire and
prayer to God for [1]Israel is that
they may be saved. 2For I bear them witness [a]that they have a zeal for God, but
not according to knowledge. 3For they being ignorant of [a]God's righteousness, and
seeking to establish their own [b]righteous-
ness, have not submitted to the righteousness of God. 4For [a]Christ *is* the end of the
law for righteousness to everyone who believes.
5For Moses writes about the righteousness which is of the law, [a]*"The man who*
does those things shall live by them." 6But
the righteousness of faith speaks in this
way, [a]*"Do not say in your heart, 'Who will*
ascend into heaven?' " (that is, to bring
Christ down *from above*) 7or, [a]*" 'Who will*
descend into the abyss?' " (that is, to bring
Christ up from the dead). 8But what does
it say? [a]*"The word is near you, in your*
mouth and in your heart" (that is, the
word of faith which we preach): 9that [a]if
you confess with your mouth the Lord Jesus and believe in your heart that God has
raised Him from the dead, you will be
saved. 10For with the heart one believes
unto righteousness, and with the mouth
confession is made unto salvation. 11For
the Scripture says, [a]*"Whoever believes on*
Him will not be put to shame." 12For
[a]there is no distinction between Jew and
Greek, for [b]the same Lord over all [c]is rich
to all who call upon Him. 13For [a]*"whoever*
calls [b]*on the name of the LORD shall be*
saved."

Israel Rejects the Gospel

14How then shall they call on Him in
whom they have not believed? And how
shall they believe in Him of whom they
have not heard? And how shall they hear
[a]without a preacher? 15And how shall they
preach unless they are sent? As it is
written:

[a]"How beautiful are the feet of those
who [1]preach the gospel of peace,
Who bring glad tidings of good
things!"

> *You get faith by studying the Word. Study that Word until something in you "knows that you know" and that you do not just hope that you know.*
>
> CARRIE JUDD MONTGOMERY

16But they have not all obeyed the gospel.
For Isaiah says, [a]*"LORD, who has believed*
our report?" 17So then faith *comes* by
hearing, and hearing by the word of God.
18But I say, have they not heard? Yes
indeed:

[a]"Their sound has gone out to all
the earth,
And their words to the ends of the
world."

19But I say, did Israel not know? First
Moses says:

---

27 a Is. 10:22, 23 b Rom. 11:5
28 a Is. 10:23; 28:22 1 NU *the LORD will finish the work and cut it short upon the earth*
29 a Is. 1:9 b Is. 13:19 1 Lit., in Heb., *Hosts*
30 a Rom. 4:11 b Rom. 1:17; 3:21; 10:6
31 a [Rom. 10:2–4] b [Gal. 5:4] 1 NU omits *of righteousness*
32 a [1 Cor. 1:23] 1 NU *by works,* omitting *of the law*
33 a Is. 8:14; 28:16 b Rom. 5:5; 10:11

CHAPTER 10
1 1 NU *them*
2 a Acts 21:20
3 a [Rom. 1:17] b [Phil. 3:9]
4 a [Gal. 3:24; 4:5]
5 a Lev. 18:5
6 a Deut. 30:12–14
7 a Deut. 30:13
8 a Deut. 30:14
9 a Luke 12:8
11 a Is. 28:16
12 a Rom. 3:22, 29 b Acts 10:36 c Eph. 1:7
13 a Joel 2:32 b Acts 9:14
14 a Titus 1:3
15 a Is. 52:7; Nah. 1:15 1 NU omits *preach the gospel of peace, Who*
16 a Is. 53:1
18 a Ps. 19:4

[a]*"I will provoke you to jealousy by*
those who are not a nation,
I will move you to anger by a
[b]*foolish nation."*

20 But Isaiah is very bold and says:

[a]*"I was found by those who did not*
seek Me;
I was made manifest to those who
did not ask for Me."

21 But to Israel he says:

[a]*"All day long I have stretched out*
My hands
To a disobedient and contrary
people."

Israel's Rejection Not Total

11 I say then, [a]has God cast away His people? [b]Certainly not! For [c]I also am an Israelite, of the seed of Abraham, *of* the tribe of Benjamin. 2 God has not cast away His people whom [a]He foreknew. Or do you not know what the Scripture says of Elijah, how he pleads with God against Israel, saying, 3 [a]*"LORD, they have killed Your prophets and torn down Your altars, and I alone am left, and they seek my life"*? 4 But what does the divine response say to him? [a]*"I have reserved for Myself seven thousand men who have not bowed the knee to Baal."* 5 [a]Even so then, at this present time there is a remnant according to the election of grace. 6 And [a]if by grace, then *it is* no longer of works; otherwise grace is no longer grace. [1]But if *it is* of works, it is no longer grace; otherwise work is no longer work.

7 What then? [a]Israel has not obtained what it seeks; but the elect have obtained it, and the rest were [b]blinded. 8 Just as it is written:

[a]*"God has given them a spirit of*
stupor,
[b]*Eyes that they should not see*
And ears that they should not hear,
To this very day."

9 And David says:

[a]*"Let their table become a snare and*
a trap,
A stumbling block and a
recompense to them.
10 *Let their eyes be darkened, so that*
they do not see,
And bow down their back always."

Israel's Rejection Not Final

11 I say then, have they stumbled that they should fall? Certainly not! But [a]through their [1]fall, to provoke them to [b]jealousy, salvation *has come* to the Gentiles. 12 Now if their [1]fall *is* riches for the world, and their failure riches for the Gentiles, how much more their fullness!

13 For I speak to you Gentiles; inasmuch as [a]I am an apostle to the Gentiles, I magnify my ministry, 14 if by any means I may provoke to jealousy *those who are* my flesh and [a]save some of them. 15 For if their being cast away *is* the reconciling of the world, what *will* their acceptance *be* [a]but life from the dead?

16 For if [a]the firstfruit *is* holy, the lump *is* also *holy;* and if the root *is* holy, so *are* the branches. 17 And if [a]some of the branches were broken off, [b]and you, being a wild olive tree, were grafted in among them, and with them became a partaker of the root and [1]fatness of the olive tree, 18 [a]do not boast against the branches. But if you do boast, *remember that* you do not support the root, but the root supports you.

19 You will say then, "Branches were broken off that I might be grafted in." 20 Well *said.* Because of [a]unbelief they were broken off, and you stand by faith. Do not be haughty, but fear. 21 For if God did not spare the natural branches, He may not spare you either. 22 Therefore consider the goodness and severity of God: on those who fell, severity; but toward you, [1]goodness, [a]if you continue in *His* goodness. Otherwise [b]you also will be cut off. 23 And they also, [a]if they do not continue in unbelief, will be grafted in, for God is able to graft them in again. 24 For if you were cut out of the olive tree which is wild by nature, and were grafted contrary to nature into a cultivated olive tree, how much more will these, who *are* natural *branches,* be grafted into their own olive tree?

25 For I do not desire, brethren, that you should be ignorant of this mystery, lest you should be [a]wise in your own [1]opinion, that [b]blindness in part has happened to Israel [c]until the fullness of the Gentiles has come in. 26 And so all Israel will be [1]saved, as it is written:

[a]*"The Deliverer will come out of*
Zion,

---

19 a Deut. 32:21 b Titus 3:3
20 a Is. 65:1
21 a Is. 65:2

CHAPTER 11
1 a Jer. 46:28 b 1 Sam. 12:22 c 2 Cor. 11:22
2 a [Rom. 8:29]
3 a 1 Kin. 19:10, 14
4 a 1 Kin. 19:18
5 a Rom. 9:27
6 a Rom. 4:4 1 NU omits the rest of v. 6.
7 a Rom. 9:31 b 2 Cor. 3:14
8 a Is. 29:10, 13 b Deut. 29:3, 4
9 a Ps. 69:22, 23
11 a Is. 42:6, 7 b Rom. 10:19 1 *trespass*
12 1 *trespass*
13 a Acts 9:15; 22:21
14 a 1 Cor. 9:22
15 a [Is. 26:16–19]
16 a Lev. 23:10
17 a Jer. 11:16 b [Eph. 2:12] 1 *richness*
18 a [1 Cor. 10:12]
20 a Heb. 3:19
22 a 1 Cor. 15:2 b [John 15:2] 1 NU adds *of God*
23 a [2 Cor. 3:16]
25 a Rom. 12:16 b 2 Cor. 3:14 c Luke 21:24 1 *estimation*
26 a Is. 59:20, 21 1 Or *delivered*

And He will turn away ungodliness
from Jacob;
27 *For* [a]*this is My covenant with*
them,
When I take away their sins."

28 Concerning the gospel *they are* enemies for your sake, but concerning the election *they are* [a]beloved for the sake of the fathers. 29 For the gifts and the calling of God *are* [a]irrevocable. 30 For as you [a]were once disobedient to God, yet have now obtained mercy through their disobedience, 31 even so these also have now been disobedient, that through the mercy shown you they also may obtain mercy. 32 For God has [1]committed them [a]all to disobedience, that He might have mercy on all.

33 Oh, the depth of the riches both of the wisdom and knowledge of God! How unsearchable *are* His judgments and His ways past finding out!

34 *"For who has known the* [a]*mind of*
the LORD?
Or [b]*who has become His*
counselor?"
35 *"Or*[a] *who has first given to Him*
And it shall be repaid to him?"

36 For [a]of Him and through Him and to Him *are* all things, [b]to whom *be* glory forever. Amen.

Conversion is more than letting Jesus come into your heart. It is giving Him not only your heart but also your body, as a living sacrifice.

KATHRYN KUHLMAN

Living Sacrifices to God

12 I [a]beseech[1] you therefore, brethren, by the mercies of God, that you present your bodies [b]a living sacrifice, holy, acceptable to God, *which is* your [2]reasonable service. 2 And [a]do not be conformed to this world, but [b]be transformed by the renewing of your mind, that you may [c]prove what *is* that good and acceptable and perfect will of God.

Serve God with Spiritual Gifts

3 For I say, [a]through the grace given to me, to everyone who is among you, [b]not to think *of himself* more highly than he ought to think, but to think soberly, as God has dealt [c]to each one a measure of faith. 4 For [a]as we have many members in one body, but all the members do not have the same function, 5 so [a]we, *being* many, are one body in Christ, and individually members of one another. 6 Having then gifts differing according to the grace that is [a]given to us, *let us use them:* if prophecy, *let us* [b]*prophesy* in proportion to our faith; 7 or ministry, *let us use it* in *our* ministering; [a]he who teaches, in teaching; 8 [a]he who exhorts, in exhortation; [b]he who gives, with liberality; [c]he who leads, with diligence; he who shows mercy, [d]with cheerfulness.

Father, I pray that ____ will love without hypocrisy. I pray that they will abhor what is evil and cling to what is good.

FROM ROMANS 12:9

Behave Like a Christian

9 [a]*Let* love *be* without hypocrisy. [b]Abhor what is evil. Cling to what is good. 10 [a]*Be* kindly affectionate to one another with brotherly love, [b]in honor giving preference to one another; 11 not lagging in diligence, fervent in spirit, serving the Lord; 12 [a]rejoicing in hope, [b]patient[1] in tribulation, [c]continuing steadfastly in prayer; 13 [a]distributing to the needs of the saints, [b]given[1] to hospitality.

14 [a]Bless those who persecute you; bless and do not curse. 15 [a]Rejoice with those who rejoice, and weep with those who weep. 16 [a]Be of the same mind toward one another. [b]Do not set your mind on high things, but associate with the humble. Do not be wise in your own opinion.

17 [a]Repay no one evil for evil. [b]Have[1] regard for good things in the sight of all men. 18 If it is possible, as much as depends on you, [a]live peaceably with all men. 19 Beloved, [a]do not avenge yourselves,

27 a Is. 27:9
28 a Deut. 7:8; 10:15
29 a Num. 23:19
30 a [Eph. 2:2]
32 a [Gal. 3:22] *1 shut them all up in*
34 a Is. 40:13; Jer. 23:18 b Job 36:22
35 a Job 41:11
36 a Heb. 2:10 b Heb. 13:21

CHAPTER 12
1 a 2 Cor. 10:1–4 b Heb. 10:18, 20 *1 urge* *2 rational*
2 a 1 John 2:15 b Eph. 4:23 c [1 Thess. 4:3]
3 a Gal. 2:9 b Prov. 25:27 c [Eph. 4:7]
4 a 1 Cor. 12:12–14
5 a [1 Cor. 10:17]
6 a [John 3:27] b Acts 11:27
7 a Eph. 4:11
8 a Acts 15:32 b [Matt. 6:1–3] c [Acts 20:28] d 2 Cor. 9:7
9 a 1 Tim. 1:5 b Ps. 34:14
10 a Heb. 13:1 b Phil. 2:3
12 a Luke 10:20 b Luke 21:19 c Luke 18:1 *1 persevering*
13 a 1 Cor. 16:1 b 1 Tim. 3:2 *1 Lit. pursuing*
14 a [Matt. 5:44]
15 a [1 Cor. 12:26]
16 a [Phil. 2:2; 4:2] b Jer. 45:5
17 a [Matt. 5:39] b 2 Cor. 8:21 *1 Or Provide good*
18 a Heb. 12:14
19 a Lev. 19:18

Romans 12:9

Dear Woman of Destiny,

God is a good God, rich in mercy and faithfulness. What infinite patience and love we need every day. And each day we get it—a fresh beginning with God! In turn, we have it to give freely to others.

One of my friends had a demanding daytime job that required every bit of her talent, ability, mental faculties, and patience. To deal with other people in her highly charged work atmosphere, she learned to take each person to the Lord in her private prayer time on a regular basis. When problems arose or tempers flared at work, she was able to see beyond the moment into the life and soul of the person with whom she was working. Because she genuinely cared for them and invested prayer time into them, it was easier to hold her own temper in check, stave off panic, and work through each crisis.

God tells us in Romans 12:6–8 how to exercise our talents, and He encourages us to exercise them. Then He tells us in Romans 12:9–21 how to exercise our love, and encourages us to love. I see the two working hand in hand.

As I meditated on these passages, I could see a woman in my mind's eye who fell short of her goal to live the Christ-life. Finally, she blocked everything from her thoughts in a time of prayer, and set her mind completely on Jesus Christ. In her conscious state, she let all the worries and concerns of this world lift from her. And she was left with just her God and herself. When she finished praying, she was able to move through her day with a heart full of love, serving the Lord enthusiastically in all she did.

If only it were true—what a way to live! Yet can it be true?

I often hear people leave church saying they feel so lighthearted after the worship service. That's because they've left every care with the Lord! Casting their cares on Him, knowing that He cares for them, taking every wayward thought captive to the obedience of Jesus Christ, they can go about the rest of their day with genuine love in their hearts (see 1 Pet. 5:7 and 2 Cor. 10:5).

The problem is, by Monday morning it's worn off! Then what? What woman wants to live her life feeling she must plaster a smile on her face to "look Christian"? No one!

The truth is, we might fall short of the "ideal" woman, but no woman alive has any more of God than you do. No one! If you've received Christ and His Spirit, you've already received God's best. You are now free to live in the fullness of Christ.

Each day you have a fresh start. God's refreshing pool of mercy is new each morning, as if you never used a drop before—fresh, full, ready for you to dive in!

So shake off yesterday. Dive in today! Live with a heart full of love. Commit your talents to Him. Work enthusiastically, as if working directly for Him. And tonight, thank God for all He accomplished through you.

Nancy Corbett Cole

but *rather* give place to wrath; for it is written, [b]*"Vengeance is Mine, I will repay,"* says the Lord. 20 Therefore

[a]*"If your enemy is hungry, feed him;*
If he is thirsty, give him a drink;
For in so doing you will heap coals
of fire on his head."

21 Do not be overcome by evil, but [a]overcome evil with good.

Submit to Government

13 Let every soul be [a]subject to the governing authorities. For there is no authority except from God, and the authorities that exist are appointed by God. 2 Therefore whoever resists [a]the authority resists the ordinance of God, and those who resist will [1]bring judgment on themselves. 3 For rulers are not a terror to good works, but to evil. Do you want to be unafraid of the authority? [a]Do what is good, and you will have praise from the same. 4 For he is God's minister to you for good. But if you do evil, be afraid; for he does not bear the sword in vain; for he is God's minister, an avenger to *execute* wrath on him who practices evil. 5 Therefore [a]*you* must be subject, not only because of wrath [b]but also for conscience' sake. 6 For because of this you also pay taxes, for they are God's ministers attending continually to this very thing. 7 [a]Render therefore to all their due: taxes to whom taxes *are due,* customs to whom customs, fear to whom fear, honor to whom honor.

May _____ owe no one anything except to love one another, Lord, for the one who loves another has fulfilled the law.

FROM ROMANS 13:8

Love Your Neighbor

8 Owe no one anything except to love one another, for [a]he who loves another has fulfilled the law. 9 For the commandments, [a]*"You shall not commit adultery," "You shall not murder," "You shall not steal,"* [1]*"You shall not bear false witness," "You shall not covet,"* and if *there is* any other commandment, are *all* summed up in this saying, namely, [b]*"You shall love your neighbor as yourself."* 10 Love does no harm to a neighbor; therefore [a]love *is* the fulfillment of the law.

Put on Christ

11 And *do* this, knowing the time, that now *it is* high time [a]to awake out of sleep; for now our salvation *is* nearer than when we *first* believed. 12 The night is far spent, the day is at hand. [a]Therefore let us cast off the works of darkness, and [b]let us put on the armor of light. 13 [a]Let us walk [1]properly, as in the day, [b]not in revelry and drunkenness, [c]not in lewdness and lust, [d]not in strife and envy. 14 But [a]put on the Lord Jesus Christ, and [b]make no provision for the flesh, to *fulfill its* lusts.

The more we die to ourselves and yield ourselves to the discipline of the Spirit, the more God's good pleasure and His nearness to the broken in heart will become ours.

ANDREW MURRAY

The Law of Liberty

14 Receive[a] one who is weak in the faith, *but* not to disputes over doubtful things. 2 For one believes he [a]may eat all things, but he who is weak eats *only* vegetables. 3 Let not him who eats despise him who does not eat, and [a]let not him who does not eat judge him who eats; for God has received him. 4 [a]Who are you to judge another's servant? To his own master he stands or falls. Indeed, he will be made to stand, for God is able to make him stand.

5 [a]One person esteems *one* day above another; another esteems every day *alike.* Let each be fully convinced in his own mind. 6 He who [a]observes the day, observes *it* to the Lord; [1]and he who does not observe the day, to the Lord he does not observe *it.* He who eats, eats to the Lord, for [b]he gives God thanks; and he who does not eat, to the Lord he does not eat, and gives God thanks. 7 For [a]none of

---

19 b Deut. 32:35
20 a Prov. 25:21, 22
21 a [Rom. 12:1, 2]

CHAPTER 13
1 a 1 Pet. 2:13
2 a [Titus 3:1] *1* Lit. *receive*
3 a 1 Pet. 2:14
5 a Eccl. 8:2 b [1 Pet. 2:13, 19]
7 a Matt. 22:21
8 a [Gal. 5:13, 14]
9 a Ex. 20:13–17; Deut. 5:17–21 b Lev. 19:18 *1* NU omits *"You shall not bear false witness,"*
10 a [Matt. 7:12; 22:39, 40]
11 a [1 Cor. 15:34]
12 a Eph. 5:11 b [Eph. 6:11, 13]
13 a Phil. 4:8 b Prov. 23:20 c [1 Cor. 6:9] d James 3:14 *1 decently*
14 a Gal. 3:27 b [Gal. 5:16]

CHAPTER 14
1 a [1 Cor. 8:9; 9:22]
2 a [Titus 1:15]
3 a [Col. 2:16]
4 a James 4:11, 12
5 a Gal. 4:10
6 a Gal. 4:10 b [1 Tim. 4:3] *1* NU omits the rest of this sentence.
7 a [Gal. 2:20]

us lives to himself, and no one dies to himself. 8For if we [a]live, we live to the Lord; and if we die, we die to the Lord. Therefore, whether we live or die, we are the Lord's. 9For [a]to this end Christ died [1]and rose and lived again, that He might be [b]Lord of both the dead and the living. 10But why do you judge your brother? Or why do you show contempt for your brother? For [a]we shall all stand before the judgment seat of [1]Christ. 11For it is written:

> [a]*"As I live, says the LORD,*
> *Every knee shall bow to Me,*
> *And every tongue shall confess to*
> *God."*

12So then [a]each of us shall give account of himself to God. 13Therefore let us not judge one another [1]anymore, but rather resolve this, [a]not to put a stumbling block or a cause to fall in *our* brother's way.

The Law of Love

14I know and am convinced by the Lord Jesus [a]that *there is* nothing unclean of itself; but to him who considers anything to be unclean, to him *it is* unclean. 15Yet if your brother is grieved because of *your* food, you are no longer walking in love. [a]Do not destroy with your food the one for whom Christ died. 16[a]Therefore do not let your good be spoken of as evil; 17[a]for the kingdom of God is not eating and drinking, but righteousness and [b]peace and joy in the Holy Spirit. 18For he who serves Christ in [1]these things [a]*is* acceptable to God and approved by men.

Lord, may ____ pursue the things which make for peace and the things by which one may edify another.

FROM ROMANS 14:19

19[a]Therefore let us pursue the things *which make* for peace and the things by which [b]one may [1]edify another. 20[a]Do not destroy the work of God for the sake of food. [b]All things indeed *are* pure, [c]but *it is* evil for the man who eats with [1]offense. 21*It is* good neither to eat [a]meat nor drink wine nor *do anything* by which your brother stumbles [1]or is offended or is made weak. 22[1]Do you have faith? Have *it* to yourself before God. [a]Happy *is* he who does not condemn himself in what he approves. 23But he who doubts is condemned if he eats, because *he does* not *eat* from faith; for [a]whatever *is* not from faith is [1]sin.

Bearing Others' Burdens

15 We [a]then who are strong ought to bear with the [1]scruples of the weak, and not to please ourselves. 2[a]Let each of us please *his* neighbor for *his* good, leading to [1]edification. 3[a]For even Christ did not please Himself; but as it is written, [b]*"The reproaches of those who reproached You fell on Me."* 4For [a]whatever things were written before were written for our learning, that we through the [1]patience and comfort of the Scriptures might have hope. 5[a]Now may the God of patience and comfort grant you to be like-minded toward one another, according to Christ Jesus, 6that you may [a]with one mind *and* one mouth glorify the God and Father of our Lord Jesus Christ.

Glorify God Together

7Therefore [a]receive one another, just [b]as Christ also received [1]us, to the glory of God. 8Now I say that [a]Jesus Christ has become a [1]servant to the circumcision for the truth of God, [b]to confirm the promises *made* to the fathers, 9and [a]that the Gentiles might glorify God for *His* mercy, as it is written:

> [b]*"For this reason I will confess to*
> *You among the Gentiles,*
> *And sing to Your name."*

10And again he says:

> [a]*"Rejoice, O Gentiles, with His*
> *people!"*

11And again:

> [a]*"Praise the LORD, all you Gentiles!*
> *Laud Him, all you peoples!"*

12And again, Isaiah says:

> [a]*"There shall be a root of Jesse;*
> *And He who shall rise to reign over*
> *the Gentiles,*
> *In Him the Gentiles shall hope."*

---

8 [a]2 Cor. 5:14, 15
9 [a]2 Cor. 5:15 [b]Acts 10:36 [1]NU omits *and rose*
10 [a]2 Cor. 5:10 [1]NU *God*
11 [a]Is. 45:23
12 [a]1 Pet. 4:5
13 [a]1 Cor. 8:9 [1]*any longer*
14 [a]1 Cor. 10:25
15 [a]1 Cor. 8:11
16 [a][Rom. 12:17]
17 [a]1 Cor. 8:8 [b][Rom. 8:6]
18 [a]2 Cor. 8:21 [1]NU *this thing*
19 [a]Rom. 12:18 [b]1 Cor. 14:12 [1]*build up*
20 [a]Rom. 14:15 [b]Acts 10:15 [c]1 Cor. 8:9–12 [1]A feeling of giving offense
21 [a]1 Cor. 8:13 [1]NU omits the rest of v. 21.
22 [a][1 John 3:21] [1]NU *The faith which you have—have*
23 [a]Titus 1:15 [1]M puts Rom. 16:25–27 here.

CHAPTER 15
1 [a][Gal. 6:1, 2] [1]*weaknesses*
2 [a]1 Cor. 9:22; 10:24, 33 [1]*building up*
3 [a]Matt. 26:39 [b]Ps. 69:9
4 [a]1 Cor. 10:11 [1]*perseverance*
5 [a]1 Cor. 1:10
6 [a]Acts 4:24
7 [a]Rom. 14:1, 3 [b]Rom. 5:2 [1]NU, M *you*
8 [a]Matt. 15:24 [b]2 Cor. 1:20 [1]*minister*
9 [a]John 10:16 [b]2 Sam. 22:50; Ps. 18:49
10 [a]Deut. 32:43
11 [a]Ps. 117:1
12 [a]Is. 11:1, 10

13 Now may the God of hope fill you with
all [a]joy and peace in believing, that you
may abound in hope by the power of the
Holy Spirit.

May You, the God of
hope, fill _____ with all joy
and peace in believing, that
they may abound in hope by
the power of the Holy Spirit.

FROM ROMANS 15:13

From Jerusalem to Illyricum

14 Now [a]I myself am confident concerning you, my brethren, that you also are
full of goodness, [b]filled with all knowledge, able also to admonish [1]one another.
15 Nevertheless, brethren, I have written
more boldly to you on *some* points, as reminding you, [a]because of the grace given
to me by God, 16 that [a]I might be a minister of Jesus Christ to the Gentiles, ministering the gospel of God, that the
[b]offering [1]of the Gentiles might be acceptable, sanctified by the Holy Spirit.
17 Therefore I have reason to glory in
Christ Jesus [a]in the things *which pertain*
to God. 18 For I will not dare to speak of
any of those things [a]which Christ has not
accomplished through me, in word and
deed, [b]to make the Gentiles obedient—
19 [a]in mighty signs and wonders, by the
power of the Spirit of God, so that from
Jerusalem and round about to Illyricum I
have fully preached the gospel of Christ.
20 And so I have made it my aim to preach
the gospel, not where Christ was named,
[a]lest I should build on another man's
foundation, 21 but as it is written:

> [a]*"To whom He was not announced,*
> *they shall see;*
> *And those who have not heard shall*
> *understand."*

Plan to Visit Rome

22 For this reason [a]I also have been
much hindered from coming to you.
23 But now no longer having a place in
these parts, and [a]having a great desire
these many years to come to you, 24 whenever I journey to Spain, [1]I shall come to
you. For I hope to see you on my journey,
[a]and to be helped on my way there by you,
if first I may [b]enjoy your *company* for a
while. 25 But now [a]I am going to Jerusalem to [1]minister to the saints. 26 For [a]it
pleased those from Macedonia and Achaia
to make a certain contribution for the
poor among the saints who are in Jerusalem. 27 It pleased them indeed, and they
are their debtors. For [a]if the Gentiles have
been partakers of their spiritual things,
[b]their duty is also to minister to them in
material things. 28 Therefore, when I have
performed this and have sealed to them
[a]this fruit, I shall go by way of you to
Spain. 29 [a]But I know that when I come to
you, I shall come in the fullness of the
blessing [1]of the gospel of Christ.

30 Now I beg you, brethren, through the
Lord Jesus Christ, and [a]through the love
of the Spirit, [b]that you strive together
with me in prayers to God for me, 31 [a]that
I may be delivered from those in Judea
who [1]do not believe, and that [b]my service
for Jerusalem may be acceptable to the
saints, 32 [a]that I may come to you with joy
[b]by the will of God, and may [c]be refreshed
together with you. 33 Now [a]the God of
peace *be* with you all. Amen.

And after all, is there
anything in all the world
to be compared with the
joy of doing His will? I
know of no joy like it.

AMY CARMICHAEL

Sister Phoebe Commended

16 I commend to you Phoebe our sister, who is a servant of the church
in [a]Cenchrea, 2 [a]that you may receive her
in the Lord [b]in a manner worthy of the
saints, and assist her in whatever business
she has need of you; for indeed she has
been a helper of many and of myself also.

Greeting Roman Saints

3 Greet [a]Priscilla and Aquila, my fellow
workers in Christ Jesus, 4 who risked their
own necks for my life, to whom not only
I give thanks, but also all the churches of

---

13 a Rom. 12:12; 14:17
14 a 2 Pet. 1:12 b 1 Cor. 1:5; 8:1, 7, 10 *1 M others*
15 a Rom. 1:5; 12:3
16 a Rom. 11:13 b [Is. 66:20] *1* Consisting of
17 a Heb. 2:17; 5:1
18 a Acts 15:12; 21:19 b Rom. 1:5
19 a Acts 19:11
20 a [2 Cor. 10:13, 15, 16]
21 a Is. 52:15
22 a Rom. 1:13
23 a Acts 19:21; 23:11
24 a Acts 15:3 b Rom. 1:12 *1* NU omits *I shall come to you* and joins *Spain* with the next sentence.
25 a Acts 19:21 *1 serve*
26 a 1 Cor. 16:1
27 a Rom. 11:17 b 1 Cor. 9:11
28 a Phil. 4:17
29 a [Rom. 1:11] *1* NU omits *of the gospel*
30 a Phil. 2:1 b 2 Cor. 1:11
31 a 2 Tim. 3:11; 4:17 b 2 Cor. 8:4 *1 are disobedient*
32 a Rom. 1:10 b Acts 18:21 c 1 Cor. 16:18
33 a 1 Cor. 14:33

CHAPTER 16
1 a Acts 18:18
2 a Phil. 2:29 b Phil. 1:27
3 a Acts 18:2, 18, 26

the Gentiles. 5Likewise *greet* [a]the church
that is in their house.
Greet my beloved Epaenetus, who is
[b]the firstfruits of [1]Achaia to Christ. 6Greet
Mary, who labored much for us. 7Greet
Andronicus and Junia, my countrymen
and my fellow prisoners, who are of note
among the [a]apostles, who also [b]were in
Christ before me.
8Greet Amplias, my beloved in the
Lord. 9Greet Urbanus, our fellow worker
in Christ, and Stachys, my beloved.
10Greet Apelles, approved in Christ. Greet
those who are of the *household* of Aristo-
bulus. 11Greet Herodion, my [1]country-
man. Greet those who are of the
household of Narcissus who are in the
Lord.
12Greet Tryphena and Tryphosa, who
have labored in the Lord. Greet the beloved Persis, who labored much in the
Lord. 13Greet Rufus, [a]chosen in the Lord,
and his mother and mine. 14Greet Asyn-
critus, Phlegon, Hermas, Patrobas, Her-
mes, and the brethren who are with them.
15Greet Philologus and Julia, Nereus and
his sister, and Olympas, and all the saints
who are with them.
16[a]Greet one another with a holy kiss.
[1]The churches of Christ greet you.

Avoid Divisive Persons

17Now I urge you, brethren, note those
[a]who cause divisions and offenses, contrary to the doctrine which you learned,
and [b]avoid them. 18For those who are

5 a 1 Cor. 16:19 b 1 Cor. 16:15 *1* NU *Asia*
7 a Acts 1:13, 26 b Gal. 1:22
11 *1* Or *relative*
13 a 2 John 1
16 a 1 Cor. 16:20 *1* NU *All the churches*
17 a [Acts 15:1] b [1 Cor. 5:9]

Phoebe

Many scholars believe that Phoebe was the woman who delivered Paul's letter to the Romans to the church at Rome, spreading the gospel and providing believers there with invaluable spiritual instruction and encouragement. In Romans 16:1, 2, Paul calls her "a servant of the church" in her hometown of Cenchrea and writes that "indeed she has been a helper of many and of myself also."

The same word that describes Phoebe as a "servant" in Romans 16:1 is usually translated "minister" when referring to men, so it is likely that Phoebe was indeed a minister in her church. Whether she served as a minister or a deaconess in her church, she did exhibit a spirit of servanthood and humility as she exercised spiritual leadership.

Phoebe's helpful nature may have also earned her the position of patron in Cenchrea. In such a capacity, she would have been appointed by the leaders of the city to protect the rights of foreign visitors, and to help ensure the welfare during their stay. It seems that Phoebe had a love for people and a desire to serve, which benefited both her community and her church.

May God continue to use women as powerful ministers of the gospel. As women of destiny, may we be like Phoebe—true servants of the church, giving gladly of ourselves to our local congregations and to the body of Christ. May we develop the love out of which true service is born, and may we possess a genuine love for the church—the bride of Jesus Christ, the one for whom He is yearning even this very moment. As we love and care about His church, may we do everything we can to encourage holiness, purity, and unity among the people of God. And may we endeavor to develop and promote passion for Jesus Christ, the head of the church, the glorious Groom who longs to receive His bride.

such do not serve our Lord [1]Jesus Christ,
but [a]their own belly, and [b]by smooth
words and flattering speech deceive the
hearts of the simple. 19 For [a]your obedience has become known to all. Therefore
I am glad on your behalf; but I want you
to be [b]wise in what is good, and [1]simple
concerning evil. 20 And [a]the God of peace
[b]will crush Satan under your feet shortly.
[c]The grace of our Lord Jesus Christ *be*
with you. Amen.

Greetings from Paul's Friends

21 [a]Timothy, my fellow worker, and
[b]Lucius, [c]Jason, and [d]Sosipater, my
countrymen, greet you.
22 I, Tertius, who wrote *this* epistle,
greet you in the Lord.
23 [a]Gaius, my host and *the host* of the
whole church, greets you. [b]Erastus, the
treasurer of the city, greets you, and
Quartus, a brother. 24 [a]The[1] grace of our
Lord Jesus Christ *be* with you all. Amen.

Benediction

25 [1]Now [a]to Him who is able to establish
you [b]according to my gospel and the
preaching of Jesus Christ, [c]according to
the revelation of the mystery [d]kept secret
since the world began 26 but [a]now made
manifest, and by the prophetic Scriptures
made known to all nations, according to
the commandment of the everlasting
God, for [b]obedience to the faith— 27 to
[a]God, alone wise, *be* glory through Jesus
Christ forever. Amen.

18 a Phil. 3:19 b Col. 2:4 1 NU, M omit *Jesus*
19 a Rom. 1:8 b Matt. 10:16 1 *innocent*
20 a Rom. 15:33 b Gen. 3:15 c 1 Cor. 16:23
21 a Acts 16:1 b Acts 13:1 c Acts 17:5 d Acts 20:4
23 a 1 Cor. 1:14 b Acts 19:22
24 a 1 Thess. 5:28 1 NU omits v. 24.
25 a [Eph. 3:20] b Rom. 2:16 c Eph. 1:9 d Col. 1:26; 2:2; 4:3 1 M puts Rom. 16:25–27 after Rom. 14:23. **26** a Eph. 1:9 b Rom. 1:5 **27** a Jude 25

AUTHOR: *Paul*
DATE: *A.D. 56*
THEME: *Resolving Doctrinal and Practical Church Problems and Growth of a Church in Christ*
KEY WORDS: *The Cross, Sexual Sins, Spiritual Gifts, Love, the Resurrection*

1 CORINTHIANS

Dear Woman of Destiny,

The backdrop of this book is the city and culture of Corinth. Corinth was where Aphrodite (Venus), the goddess of licentious love, was worshiped. Her temple was known to have a thousand professional prostitutes attached to it. Even the expression "to Corinthianize" meant to practice prostitution. Many people came to this city seeking immoral love. In the midst of this book, which brings correction to the evil of the day, we find the jewel which speaks of true love, 1 Corinthians 13:8: "Love [God's love] never fails." All of us as women want to love and be loved. Some settle for second best—a worldly kind of love. God wants you to feel His pure and unconditional love and to express it to others, whether in a friendship or with your spouse. Don't settle for less as a woman of destiny.

With His love,

Cindy Jacobs

Greeting

Paul, [a]called *to be* an apostle of Jesus
Christ [b]through the will of God,
and [c]Sosthenes *our* brother,

2To the church of God which is at Corinth, to those who [a]are [1]sanctified in
Christ Jesus, [b]called *to be* saints, with all
who in every place call on the name of
Jesus Christ [c]our Lord, [d]both theirs and
ours:

3[a]Grace to you and peace from God our
Father and the Lord Jesus Christ.

> *I thank You, my God, always concerning ____ for Your grace which was given to them by Christ Jesus.*
>
> FROM 1 CORINTHIANS 1:4

Spiritual Gifts at Corinth

4[a]I thank my God always concerning
you for the grace of God which was given
to you by Christ Jesus, 5that you were enriched in everything by Him [a]in all [1]utter-
ance and all knowledge, 6even as [a]the
testimony of Christ was confirmed [1]in
you, 7so that you come short in no gift,
eagerly [a]waiting for the revelation of our
Lord Jesus Christ, 8[a]who will also confirm
you to the end, [b]*that you may be* blameless in the day of our Lord Jesus Christ.
9[a]God *is* faithful, by whom you were
called into [b]the fellowship of His Son, Jesus Christ our Lord.

> *Let us never rest till we experience all the fullness of Christ Jesus.*
>
> CHARLES WESLEY

Sectarianism Is Sin

10 Now I plead with you, brethren, by
the name of our Lord Jesus Christ, [a]that
you all [1]speak the same thing, and *that*
there be no [2]divisions among you, but
that you be perfectly joined together in
the same mind and in the same judgment. 11For it has been declared to me
concerning you, my brethren, by those of
Chloe's *household,* that there are [1]con-
tentions among you. 12Now I say this, that
[a]each of you says, "I am of Paul," or "I am
of [b]Apollos," or "I am of [c]Cephas," or "I
am of Christ." 13[a]Is Christ divided? Was
Paul crucified for you? Or were you baptized in the name of Paul?

> *In order for a church to prosper, she must obey Jesus' teachings in all things.*
>
> WILLIAM SEYMOUR

14I thank God that I baptized [a]none of
you except [b]Crispus and [c]Gaius, 15lest
anyone should say that I had baptized in
my own name. 16Yes, I also baptized the
household of [a]Stephanas. Besides, I do
not know whether I baptized any other.
17For Christ did not send me to baptize,
but to preach the gospel, [a]not with wisdom of words, lest the cross of Christ
should be made of no effect.

Christ the Power and Wisdom of God

18For the [1]message of the cross is [a]fool-
ishness to [b]those who are perishing, but
to us [c]who are being saved it is the [d]power
of God. 19For it is written:

> [a]*"I will destroy the wisdom of the wise,*
> *And bring to nothing the understanding of the prudent."*

20[a]Where *is* the wise? Where *is* the
scribe? Where *is* the [1]disputer of this age?
[b]Has not God made foolish the wisdom
of this world? 21For since, in the [a]wisdom
of God, the world through wisdom did
not know God, it pleased God through
the foolishness of the message preached
to save those who believe. 22For [a]Jews

CHAPTER 1
1 a Rom. 1:1 b 2 Cor. 1:1 c Acts 18:17
2 a [Acts 15:9] b Rom. 1:7 c [1 Cor. 8:6] d [Rom. 3:22] *1 set apart*
3 a Rom. 1:7
4 a Rom. 1:8
5 a [1 Cor. 12:8] *1 speech*
6 a 2 Tim. 1:8 *1 Or among*
7 a Phil. 3:20
8 a 1 Thess. 3:13; 5:23 b Col. 1:22; 2:7
9 a Is. 49:7 b [John 15:4]
10 a 2 Cor. 13:11 *1* Have a uniform testimony *2 schisms* or *dissensions*
11 *1 quarrels*
12 a 1 Cor. 3:4 b Acts 18:24 c John 1:42
13 a 2 Cor. 11:4
14 a John 4:2 b Acts 18:8 c Rom. 16:23
16 a 1 Cor. 16:15, 17
17 a [1 Cor. 2:1, 4, 13]
18 a 1 Cor. 2:14 b 2 Cor. 2:15 c [1 Cor. 15:2] d Rom. 1:16 *1* Lit. *word*
19 a Is. 29:14
20 a Is. 19:12; 33:18 b Job 12:17 *1 debater*
21 a Dan. 2:20
22 a Matt. 12:38

1 Corinthians 1:10

Dear Woman of Destiny,

Twenty years ago my husband Hal and I cofounded a ministry that today is called BridgeBuilders. We started with only a burning vision from the heart of God—a vision to see pastors cross denominational lines in friendship and love, to see churches come together to work as one body to reach their communities for Christ, and to see the bride of Christ united and experiencing the full power of God.

I believe I now know how Paul felt when he was writing to the Corinthians. The problems that plagued the church of Corinth are the same ones we face today: immaturity, divisions, gossip, jealousy, lawsuits, and marital difficulties.

First Corinthians 1:10 specifically addresses the problem of divisions and sectarianism. A more contemporary word is *cliques.* We find cliques operating among denominations, generations, and races. As women, we know that there are issues regarding gender in the church as well. This disunity in the church is perhaps the greatest stumbling block we present to a lost world. In John 17, Jesus prayed that His disciples would be united that the world might know Him. Is it possible then that the unity of the body of Christ is the missing key to completing the task of fulfilling the Great Commission?

First Corinthians 1:10 speaks of the need for believers to live and work together in agreement (to "speak the same thing"). As in an orchestra, the members may play different instruments and their parts may vary, but everyone is playing the same piece of music. The result is harmony, not cacophony.

Several scriptures in both the Old and New Testaments provide a picture of what happens when the body of Christ operates in unity:

". . . they raised their voice to God with one accord . . . And when they had prayed, the place where they were assembled together was shaken; and they were all filled with the Holy Spirit" (Acts 4:24, 31).

". . . when the trumpeters and singers were as one, to make one sound to be heard in praising and thanking the LORD . . . the house of the LORD was filled with a cloud . . . for the glory of the LORD filled the house of God" (2 Chr. 5:13, 14).

"Five of you shall chase a hundred, and a hundred of you shall put ten thousand to flight" (Lev. 26:8).

When the beloved of Christ is united in heart and purpose, the power and presence of God is released. How then can we choose to remain isolated from other true believers just because they are different from us or because we do not see eye-to-eye on the nonessentials? The Scriptures leave no room for discussion on this issue. Christ is not divided, so how can His people be?

I believe Jesus is asking us to rid our hearts of prejudice, judgmental attitudes, and denominational pride. We must lay down our carnal weapons and pick up the spiritual weapons of forgiveness, reconciliation, and humility. As we take the position of a servant (even to those with whom we do not agree), we will see the presence and power of God released in our homes, churches, and cities. Christ will be glorified, and the gospel will reach to the ends of the earth.

Cheryl Sacks

request a sign, and Greeks seek after wisdom; 23 but we preach Christ crucified, [a]to the Jews a [1]stumbling block and to the [2]Greeks [b]foolishness, 24 but to those who are called, both Jews and Greeks, Christ [a]the power of God and [b]the wisdom of God. 25 Because the foolishness of God is wiser than men, and the weakness of God is stronger than men.

Glory Only in the Lord

26 For [1]you see your calling, brethren, [a]that not many wise according to the flesh, not many mighty, not many [2]noble, *are called.* 27 But [a]God has chosen the foolish things of the world to put to shame the wise, and God has chosen the weak things of the world to put to shame the things which are mighty; 28 and the [1]base things of the world and the things which are despised God has chosen, and the things which are not, to bring to nothing the things that are, 29 that no flesh should glory in His presence. 30 But of Him you are in Christ Jesus, who became for us wisdom from God—and [a]righteousness and sanctification and redemption— 31 that, as it is written, [a]*"He who glories, let him glory in the LORD."*

Christ Crucified

2 And I, brethren, when I came to you, did not come with excellence of speech or of wisdom declaring to you the [1]testimony of God. 2 For I determined not to know anything among you [a]except Jesus Christ and Him crucified. 3 [a]I was with you [b]in weakness, in fear, and in much trembling. 4 And my speech and my preaching [a]*were* not with persuasive words of [1]human wisdom, [b]but in demonstration of the Spirit and of power, 5 that your faith should not be in the wisdom of men but in the [a]power of God.

Spiritual Wisdom

6 However, we speak wisdom among those who are mature, yet not the wisdom of this age, nor of the rulers of this age, who are coming to nothing. 7 But we speak the wisdom of God in a mystery, the hidden *wisdom* which God [1]ordained before the ages for our glory, 8 which none of the rulers of this age knew; for [a]had they known, they would not have [b]crucified the Lord of glory.

9 But as it is written:

[a]*"Eye has not seen, nor ear heard,*
Nor have entered into the heart of man
The things which God has prepared for those who love Him."

10 But [a]God has revealed *them* to us through His Spirit. For the Spirit searches all things, yes, the deep things of God. 11 For what man knows the things of a man except the [a]spirit of the man which is in him? [b]Even so no one knows the things of God except the Spirit of God. 12 Now we have received, not the spirit of the world, but [a]the Spirit who is from God, that we might know the things that have been freely given to us by God.

13 These things we also speak, not in words which man's wisdom teaches but which the [1]Holy Spirit teaches, comparing spiritual things with spiritual. 14 [a]But the natural man does not receive the things of the Spirit of God, for they are foolishness to him; nor can he know *them,* because they are spiritually discerned. 15 But he who is spiritual judges all things, yet he himself is *rightly* judged by no one. 16 For [a]*"who has known the mind of the LORD that he may instruct Him?"* [b]But we have the mind of Christ.

Sectarianism Is Carnal

3 And I, brethren, could not speak to you as to spiritual *people* but as to carnal, as to [a]babes in Christ. 2 I fed you with [a]milk and not with solid food; [b]for until now you were not able *to receive it,* and even now you are still not able; 3 for you are still carnal. For where *there are* envy, strife, and divisions among you, are you not carnal and [1]behaving like *mere* men? 4 For when one says, "I am of Paul," and another, "I *am* of Apollos," are you not carnal?

Watering, Working, Warning

5 Who then is Paul, and who *is* Apollos, but [a]ministers through whom you believed, as the Lord gave to each one? 6 [a]I planted, [b]Apollos watered, [c]but God gave the increase. 7 So then [a]neither he who plants is anything, nor he who waters, but God who gives the increase. 8 Now he who plants and he who waters are one, [a]and each one will receive his own reward according to his own labor.

9 For [a]we are God's fellow workers; you

---

23 [a] Luke 2:34 [b] [1 Cor. 2:14] [1] Gr. *skandalon, offense* [2] NU *Gentiles*
24 [a] [Rom. 1:4] [b] Col. 2:3
26 [a] John 7:48 [1] *consider* [2] *well-born*
27 [a] Matt. 11:25
28 [1] *insignificant* or *lowly*
30 [a] [2 Cor. 5:21]
31 [a] Jer. 9:23, 24

CHAPTER 2
1 [1] NU *mystery*
2 [a] Gal. 6:14
3 [a] Acts 18:1 [b] [2 Cor. 4:7]
4 [a] 2 Pet. 1:16 [b] Rom. 15:19 [1] NU omits *human*
5 [a] 1 Thess. 1:5
7 [1] *predetermined*
8 [a] Luke 23:34 [b] Matt. 27:33–50
9 [a] [Is. 64:4; 65:17]
10 [a] Matt. 11:25; 13:11; 16:17
11 [a] [James 2:26] [b] Rom. 11:33
12 [a] [Rom. 8:15]
13 [1] NU omits *Holy*
14 [a] Matt. 16:23
16 [a] Is. 40:13 [b] [John 15:15]

CHAPTER 3
1 [a] Heb. 5:13
2 [a] 1 Pet. 2:2 [b] John 16:12
3 [1] Lit. *walking according to man*
5 [a] 2 Cor. 3:3, 6; 4:1; 5:18; 6:4
6 [a] Acts 18:4 [b] Acts 18:24–27 [c] [2 Cor. 3:5]
7 [a] [Gal. 6:3]
8 [a] Ps. 62:12
9 [a] 2 Cor. 6:1

are God's field, *you are* [b]God's building.
10 [a]According to the grace of God which
was given to me, as a wise master builder
I have laid [b]the foundation, and another
builds on it. But let each one take heed
how he builds on it. 11 For no other foundation can anyone lay than [a]that which is
laid, [b]which is Jesus Christ. 12 Now if anyone builds on this foundation *with* gold,
silver, precious stones, wood, hay, straw,
13 each one's work will become clear; for
the Day [a]will declare it, because [b]it will be
revealed by fire; and the fire will test each
one's work, of what sort it is. 14 If anyone's
work which he has built on *it* endures, he
will receive a reward. 15 If anyone's work is
burned, he will suffer loss; but he himself
will be saved, yet so as through fire.
16 [a]Do you not know that you are the
temple of God and *that* the Spirit of God
dwells in you? 17 If anyone [1]defiles the
temple of God, God will destroy him. For
the temple of God is holy, which *temple*
you are.

Avoid Worldly Wisdom

18 [a]Let no one deceive himself. If anyone
among you seems to be wise in this age,
let him become a fool that he may become
wise. 19 For the wisdom of this world is
foolishness with God. For it is written,
[a]*"He catches the wise in their own crafti-*
ness"; 20 and again, [a]*"The LORD knows the*
thoughts of the wise, that they are futile."
21 Therefore let no one boast in men. For
[a]all things are yours: 22 whether Paul or
Apollos or Cephas, or the world or life
or death, or things present or things to
come—all are yours. 23 And [a]you *are*
Christ's, and Christ *is* God's.

Stewards of the Mysteries of God

4 Let a man so consider us, as [a]ser-
vants of Christ [b]and stewards of the
mysteries of God. 2 Moreover it is required
in stewards that one be found faithful.
3 But with me it is a very small thing that
I should be judged by you or by a human
[1]court. In fact, I do not even judge myself.
4 For I know of nothing against myself, yet
I am not justified by this; but He who
judges me is the Lord. 5 [a]Therefore judge
nothing before the time, until the Lord
comes, who will both bring to [b]light the
hidden things of darkness and [c]reveal the
[1]counsels of the hearts. [d]Then each one's
praise will come from God.

Fools for Christ's Sake

6 Now these things, brethren, I have figuratively transferred to myself and Apollos for your sakes, that you may learn in
us not to think beyond what is written,
that none of you may be [1]puffed up on
behalf of one against the other. 7 For who
[1]makes you differ *from another?* And
[a]what do you have that you did not receive? Now if you did indeed receive *it,*
why do you boast as if you had not received *it?*
8 You are already full! [a]You are already
rich! You have reigned as kings without
us—and indeed I could wish you did
reign, that we also might reign with you!
9 For I think that God has displayed us,
the apostles, last, as men condemned to
death; for we have been made a [a]specta-
cle[1] to the world, both to angels and to
men. 10 We *are* [a]fools for Christ's sake, but
you *are* wise in Christ! [b]We *are* weak, but
you *are* strong! You *are* distinguished, but
we *are* dishonored! 11 To the present hour
we both hunger and thirst, and we are
poorly clothed, and beaten, and homeless.
12 [a]And we labor, working with our own
hands. [b]Being reviled, we bless; being persecuted, we endure; 13 being defamed, we
[1]entreat. [a]We have been made as the filth
of the world, the offscouring of all things
until now.

Paul's Paternal Care

14 I do not write these things to shame
you, but [a]as my beloved children I warn
you. 15 For though you might have ten
thousand instructors in Christ, yet *you do*
not *have* many fathers; for [a]in Christ Jesus I have begotten you through the gospel. 16 Therefore I urge you, [a]imitate me.
17 For this reason I have sent [a]Timothy to
you, [b]who is my beloved and faithful son
in the Lord, who will [c]remind you of my
ways in Christ, as I [d]teach everywhere [e]in
every church.
18 [a]Now some are [1]puffed up, as though
I were not coming to you. 19 [a]But I will
come to you shortly, [b]if the Lord wills,
and I will know, not the word of those who
are puffed up, but the power. 20 For [a]the
kingdom of God *is* not in word but in
[b]power. 21 What do you want? [a]Shall I
come to you with a rod, or in love and a
spirit of gentleness?

9 b [Eph. 2:20–22]
10 a Rom. 1:5 b 1 Cor. 4:15
11 a Is. 28:16 b Eph. 2:20
13 a 1 Pet. 1:7 b Luke 2:35
16 a 2 Cor. 6:16
17 *1 destroys*
18 a Prov. 3:7
19 a Job 5:13
20 a Ps. 94:11
21 a [2 Cor. 4:5]
23 a 2 Cor. 10:7

CHAPTER 4
1 a Col. 1:25 b Titus 1:7
3 *1 Lit. day*
5 a Matt. 7:1 b Matt. 10:26 c 1 Cor. 3:13 d Rom. 2:29 *1 motives*
6 *1 arrogant*
7 a John 3:27 *1 distinguishes you*
8 a Rev. 3:17
9 a Heb. 10:33 *1 Lit. theater*
10 a Acts 17:18; 26:24 b 2 Cor. 13:9
12 a Acts 18:3; 20:34 b Matt. 5:44
13 a Lam. 3:45 *1 exhort, encourage*
14 a 1 Thess. 2:11
15 a Gal. 4:19
16 a [1 Cor. 11:1]
17 a Acts 19:22 b 1 Tim. 1:2, 18 c 1 Cor. 11:2 d 1 Cor. 7:17 e 1 Cor. 14:33
18 a 1 Cor. 5:2 *1 arrogant*
19 a Acts 19:21; 20:2 b Acts 18:21
20 a 1 Thess. 1:5 b 1 Cor. 2:4
21 a 2 Cor. 10:2

1 Corinthians 4:1, 2

Dear Woman of Destiny,

Several years ago, I learned a valuable lesson from a four-year-old granddaughter. As her mother walked out the door to run some errands, leaving her with me, her words of wisdom, accompanied with a downcast countenance, came slowly and deliberately: "Life just happens, Mimi. You may fall down and skin your knee—'cause life just happens. You may not get what you want—'cause life just happens. Your mother may leave you sometimes—'cause life just happens."

I am sure she gleaned these pearls of wisdom from the little lecture her mother gave her as she protested what her mother thought best for her that day.

Countless times in the years since this happened, I have crowned an event, a disappointment, a hurt, an alarming change, with the wisdom of these words—life just happens. And so it does. Good days, bad days, happy times, sad times, exciting events, and scary situations—they all come in the course of life. But there is one thing you can do—you can stay faithful. Being faithful as a servant of God simply means doing what the Master would expect you to do.

Faithful is a biblical, perhaps even spiritual, word. In the grit, grind, grace, and glory of contemporary life, perhaps commitment is the foundation for biblical faithfulness. Commitment in this sense is the binding allegiance to set a course or purpose in life, regardless of circumstance or consequence!

I have recently learned another valuable lesson. Real commitment is the automatic pilot when the wind has been knocked out of your sails.

A deadening blow hit me on a Saturday afternoon. It was one of my life's greatest disappointments. I wanted life to stop. I wanted to go to sleep and wake up from a terrible dream. I was devastated over a friend's plight. Tears washed away my smile.

But life didn't stop. Life insisted I go on. Monday came, and with it responsibility to a group of faithful people gathered for a retreat who were looking to me for encouragement, renewed purpose, and direction. I didn't know how I could do it. My wind was caught in a web of astounding despair. Alone in my room, I felt paralyzing pain and wondered if I could even meet the people, much less speak. But commitment to the call of responsibility steadied me, strengthened me, and surprised me as the One who called me to be faithful worked through me in a wonderful way. I have no idea how I did it, I just know that I was committed to be faithful in doing as I should.

So what does it mean to be faithful? It is simple, but sure commitment to doing what is right when life just happens.

Faithfulness is the strength of character that compels us to do what is pleasing to our Master regardless of circumstances. Commitment is the determined mind-set that keeps us on course, binding our allegiance to the purpose.

Thetus Tenney

Immorality Defiles the Church

5 It is actually reported *that there is* sexual immorality among you, and such sexual immorality as is not even [1]named among the Gentiles—that a man has his father's [a]wife! 2 [a]And you are [1]puffed up, and have not rather [b]mourned, that he who has done this deed might be taken away from among you. 3 [a]For I indeed, as absent in body but present in spirit, have already judged (as though I were present) him who has so done this deed. 4 In the [a]name of our Lord Jesus Christ, when you are gathered together, along with my spirit, [b]with the power of our Lord Jesus Christ, 5 [a]deliver such a one to [b]Satan for the destruction of the flesh, that his spirit may be saved in the day of the Lord [1]Jesus.

6 [a]Your glorying *is* not good. Do you not know that [b]a little leaven leavens the whole lump? 7 Therefore [1]purge out the old leaven, that you may be a new lump, since you truly are unleavened. For indeed [a]Christ, our [b]Passover, was sacrificed [2]for us. 8 Therefore [a]let us keep the feast, [b]not with old leaven, nor [c]with the leaven of malice and wickedness, but with the unleavened *bread* of sincerity and truth.

Immorality Must Be Judged

9 I wrote to you in my epistle [a]not to [1]keep company with sexually immoral people. 10 Yet *I* certainly *did* not *mean* with the sexually immoral people of this world, or with the covetous, or extortioners, or idolaters, since then you would need to go [a]out of the world. 11 But now I have written to you not to keep company [a]with anyone named a brother, who is sexually immoral, or covetous, or an idolater, or a reviler, or a drunkard, or an extortioner—[b]not even to eat with such a person.

12 For what *have* I *to do* with judging those also who are outside? Do you not judge those who are inside? 13 But those who are outside God judges. Therefore [a]*"put away from yourselves the evil person."*

Do Not Sue the Brethren

6 Dare any of you, having a matter against another, go to law before the unrighteous, and not before the [a]saints? 2 Do you not know that [a]the saints will judge the world? And if the world will be judged by you, are you unworthy to judge the smallest matters? 3 Do you not know that we shall [a]judge angels? How much more, things that pertain to this life? 4 If then you have [1]judgments concerning things pertaining to this life, do you appoint those who are least esteemed by the church to judge? 5 I say this to your shame. Is it so, that there is not a wise man among you, not even one, who will be able to judge between his brethren? 6 But brother goes to law against brother, and that before unbelievers!

7 Now therefore, it is already an utter failure for you that you go to law against one another. [a]Why do you not rather accept wrong? Why do you not rather *let yourselves* be cheated? 8 No, you yourselves do wrong and cheat, and *you do* these things *to your* brethren! 9 Do you not know that the unrighteous will not inherit the kingdom of God? Do not be deceived. [a]Neither fornicators, nor idolaters, nor adulterers, nor [1]homosexuals, nor [2]sodomites, 10 nor thieves, nor covetous, nor drunkards, nor revilers, nor extortioners will inherit the kingdom of God. 11 And such were [a]some of you. [b]But you were washed, but you were [1]sanctified, but you were justified in the name of the Lord Jesus and by the Spirit of our God.

> *Justification is what God does for us, while sanctification is what God does in us.*
>
> P. C. Nelson

Glorify God in Body and Spirit

12 [a]All things are lawful for me, but all things are not [1]helpful. All things are lawful for me, but I will not be brought under the power of [2]any. 13 [a]Foods for the stomach and the stomach for foods, but God will destroy both it and them. Now the body *is* not for [b]sexual immorality but [c]for the Lord, [d]and the Lord for the body.

CHAPTER 5

1 a Lev. 18:6–8 *1* NU omits *named*

2 a 1 Cor. 4:18 b 2 Cor. 7:7–10 *1 arrogant*

3 a Col. 2:5

4 a [Matt. 18:20] b [John 20:23]

5 a 1 Tim. 1:20 b [Acts 26:18] *1* NU omits *Jesus*

6 a 1 Cor. 3:21 b Gal. 5:9

7 a Is. 53:7 b John 19:14 *1 clean out* *2* NU omits *for us*

8 a Ex. 12:15 b Deut. 16:3 c Matt. 16:6

9 a 2 Cor. 6:14 *1 associate*

10 a John 17:15

11 a Matt. 18:17 b Gal. 2:12

13 a Deut. 13:5; 17:7, 12; 19:19; 21:21; 22:21, 24; 24:7

CHAPTER 6

1 a Dan. 7:22

2 a Ps. 49:14

3 a 2 Pet. 2:4

4 *1 courts*

7 a [Prov. 20:22]

9 a Gal. 5:21 *1 catamites,* those submitting to homosexuals *2 male homosexuals*

11 a [1 Cor. 12:2] b Heb. 10:22 *1 set apart*

12 a 1 Cor. 10:23 *1 profitable* *2* Or *anything*

13 a Matt. 15:17 b Gal. 5:19 c 1 Thess. 4:3 d [Eph. 5:23]

14And [a]God both raised up the Lord and
will also raise us up [b]by His power.
15Do you not know that [a]your bodies
are members of Christ? Shall I then take
the members of Christ and make *them*
members of a harlot? Certainly not! 16Or
do you not know that he who is joined to
a harlot is one body *with her?* For [a]*"the*
two," He says, *"shall become one flesh."*
17[a]But he who is joined to the Lord is one
spirit *with Him.*
18[a]Flee sexual immorality. Every sin
that a man does is outside the body, but
he who commits sexual immorality sins
[b]against his own body. 19Or [a]do you not
know that your body is the temple of the
Holy Spirit *who is* in you, whom you have
from God, [b]and you are not your own?
20For [a]you were bought at a price; therefore glorify God in your body [1]and in your
spirit, which are God's.

O Lord, may ______
acknowledge that their body
is the temple of the Holy
Spirit who is in them and
that they are not their own.
FROM 1 CORINTHIANS 6:19

Principles of Marriage

7 Now concerning the things of which
you wrote to me:
[a]*It is* good for a man not to touch a
woman. 2Nevertheless, because of sexual
immorality, let each man have his own
wife, and let each woman have her own
husband. 3[a]Let the husband render to his
wife the affection due her, and likewise
also the wife to her husband. 4The wife
does not have authority over her own
body, but the husband *does.* And likewise
the husband does not have authority over
his own body, but the wife *does.* 5[a]Do not
deprive one another except with consent
for a time, that you may give yourselves to
fasting and prayer; and come together
again so that [b]Satan does not tempt you
because of your lack of self-control. 6But
I say this as a concession, [a]not as a commandment. 7For [a]I wish that all men were
even as I myself. But each one has his own
gift from God, one in this manner and
another in that.
8But I say to the unmarried and to the
widows: [a]It is good for them if they remain even as I am; 9but [a]if they cannot
exercise self-control, let them marry. For
it is better to marry than to burn *with*
passion.

Keep Your Marriage Vows

10Now to the married I command, *yet*
not I but the [a]Lord: [b]A wife is not to depart from *her* husband. 11But even if
she does depart, let her remain unmarried
or be reconciled to *her* husband. And a
husband is not to divorce *his* wife.
12But to the rest I, not the Lord, say: If
any brother has a wife who does not believe, and she is willing to live with him,
let him not divorce her. 13And a woman
who has a husband who does not believe,
if he is willing to live with her, let her not
divorce him. 14For the unbelieving husband is sanctified by the wife, and the
unbelieving wife is sanctified by the
husband; otherwise [a]your children would
be unclean, but now they are holy. 15But
if the unbeliever departs, let him depart;
a brother or a sister is not under bondage
in such *cases.* But God has called us [a]to
peace. 16For how do you know, O wife,
whether you will [a]save *your* husband? Or
how do you know, O husband, whether
you will save *your* wife?

Live as You Are Called

17But as God has distributed to each
one, as the Lord has called each one, so let
him walk. And [a]so I [1]ordain in all the
churches. 18Was anyone called while circumcised? Let him not become uncircumcised. Was anyone called while
uncircumcised? [a]Let him not be circumcised. 19[a]Circumcision is nothing and uncircumcision is nothing, but [b]keeping the
commandments of God *is what matters.*
20Let each one remain in the same calling
in which he was called. 21Were you called
while a slave? Do not be concerned about
it; but if you can be made free, rather use
it. 22For he who is called in the Lord *while*
a slave is [a]the Lord's freedman. Likewise
he who is called *while* free is [b]Christ's
slave. 23[a]You were bought at a price; do
not become slaves of men. 24Brethren, let
each one remain with [a]God in that *state*
in which he was called.

14 a 2 Cor. 4:14 b Eph. 1:19
15 a Rom. 12:5
16 a Gen. 2:24
17 a [John 17:21–23]
18 a Heb. 13:4 b Rom. 1:24
19 a 2 Cor. 6:16 b Rom. 14:7
20 a 2 Pet. 2:1 *1* NU omits the rest of v. 20.

CHAPTER 7
1 a 1 Cor. 7:8, 26
3 a Ex. 21:10
5 a Joel 2:16 b 1 Thess. 3:5
6 a 2 Cor. 8:8
7 a Acts 26:29
8 a 1 Cor. 7:1, 26
9 a 1 Tim. 5:14
10 a Mark 10:6–10 b [Matt. 5:32]
14 a Mal. 2:15
15 a Rom. 12:18
16 a 1 Pet. 3:1
17 a 1 Cor. 4:17 *1 direct*
18 a Acts 15:1
19 a [Gal. 3:28; 5:6; 6:15] b [John 15:14]
22 a [John 8:36] b 1 Pet. 2:16
23 a 1 Pet. 1:18, 19
24 a [Col. 3:22–24]

To the Unmarried and Widows

[25]Now concerning virgins: [a]I have no
commandment from the Lord; yet I give
judgment as one [b]whom the Lord in His
mercy *has made* [c]trustworthy. [26]I suppose therefore that this is good because of
the present distress—[a]that *it is* good for
a man to remain as he is: [27]Are you bound
to a wife? Do not seek to be loosed. Are
you loosed from a wife? Do not seek a wife.
[28]But even if you do marry, you have not
sinned; and if a virgin marries, she has not
sinned. Nevertheless such will have trouble in the flesh, but I would spare you.

[29]But [a]this I say, brethren, the time *is*
short, so that from now on even those
who have wives should be as though they
had none, [30]those who weep as though
they did not weep, those who rejoice as
though they did not rejoice, those who
buy as though they did not possess, [31]and
those who use this world as not [a]misusing
it. For [b]the form of this world is passing
away.

[32]But I want you to be without [1]care.
[a]He who is unmarried [2]cares for the
things of the Lord—how he may please
the Lord. [33]But he who is married cares
about the things of the world—how he
may please *his* wife. [34]There is a difference between a wife and a virgin. The unmarried woman [a]cares about the things of
the Lord, that she may be holy both in
body and in spirit. But she who is married
cares about the things of the world—how
she may please *her* husband. [35]And this I
say for your own profit, not that I may put
a leash on you, but for what is proper, and
that you may serve the Lord without distraction.

[36]But if any man thinks he is behaving
improperly toward his [1]virgin, if she is
past the flower of youth, and thus it must
be, let him do what he wishes. He does not
sin; let them marry. [37]Nevertheless he
who stands steadfast in his heart, having
no necessity, but has power over his own
will, and has so determined in his heart
that he will keep his [1]virgin, does well.
[38][a]So then he who gives [1]*her* in marriage
does well, but he who does not give *her* in
marriage does better.

[39][a]A wife is bound by law as long as her
husband lives; but if her husband dies, she
is at liberty to be married to whom she
wishes, [b]only in the Lord. [40]But she is
happier if she remains as she is, [a]accord-
ing to my judgment—and [b]I think I also
have the Spirit of God.

Be Sensitive to Conscience

8 Now [a]concerning things offered to
idols: We know that we all have
[b]knowledge. [c]Knowledge [1]puffs up, but
love [2]edifies. [2]And [a]if anyone thinks that
he knows anything, he knows nothing yet
as he ought to know. [3]But if anyone loves
God, this one is known by Him.

[4]Therefore concerning the eating of
things offered to idols, we know that [a]an
idol *is* nothing in the world, [b]and that
there is no other God but one. [5]For even
if there are [a]so-called gods, whether in
heaven or on earth (as there are many
gods and many lords), [6]yet [a]for us *there is*
one God, the Father, [b]of whom *are* all
things, and we for Him; and [c]one Lord
Jesus Christ, [d]through whom *are* all
things, and [e]through whom we *live*.

[7]However, *there is* not in everyone that
knowledge; for some, [a]with consciousness
of the idol, until now eat *it* as a thing offered to an idol; and their conscience, being weak, is [b]defiled. [8]But [a]food does not
commend us to God; for neither if we eat
are we the better, nor if we do not eat are
we the worse.

[9]But [a]beware lest somehow this liberty
of yours become [b]a [1]stumbling block to
those who are weak. [10]For if anyone sees
you who have knowledge eating in an
idol's temple, will not [a]the conscience of
him who is weak be emboldened to eat
those things offered to idols? [11]And [a]be-
cause of your knowledge shall the weak
brother perish, for whom Christ died?
[12]But [a]when you thus sin against the
brethren, and wound their weak conscience, you sin against Christ. [13]There-
fore, [a]if food makes my brother stumble,
I will never again eat meat, lest I make my
brother stumble.

A Pattern of Self-Denial

9 Am [a]I not an apostle? Am I not free?
[b]Have I not seen Jesus Christ our
Lord? [c]Are you not my work in the Lord?
[2]If I am not an apostle to others, yet
doubtless I am to you. For you are [a]the
[1]seal of my apostleship in the Lord.

25 a 2 Cor. 8:8 b 1 Tim. 1:13, 16 c 1 Tim. 1:12
26 a 1 Cor. 7:1, 8
29 a 1 Pet. 4:7
31 a 1 Cor. 9:18 b [1 John 2:17]
32 a 1 Tim. 5:5 *1 concern* *2 is concerned about*
34 a Luke 10:40
36 *1 Or virgin daughter*
37 *1 Or virgin daughter*
38 a Heb. 13:4 *1 NU his own virgin*
39 a Rom. 7:2 b 2 Cor. 6:14
40 a 1 Cor. 7:6, 25 b 1 Thess. 4:8

CHAPTER 8
1 a Acts 15:20 b Rom. 14:14 c Rom. 14:3 *1 makes arrogant* *2 builds up*
2 a [1 Cor. 13:8–12]
4 a Is. 41:24 b Deut. 4:35, 39; 6:4
5 a [John 10:34]
6 a Mal. 2:10 b Acts 17:28 c John 13:13 d John 1:3 e Rom. 5:11
7 a [1 Cor. 10:28] b Rom. 14:14, 22
8 a [Rom. 14:17]
9 a Gal. 5:13 b Rom. 14:13, 21 *1 cause of offense*
10 a 1 Cor. 10:28
11 a Rom. 14:15, 20
12 a Matt. 25:40
13 a Rom. 14:21

CHAPTER 9
1 a Acts 9:15 b 1 Cor. 15:8 c 1 Cor. 3:6; 4:15
2 a 2 Cor. 12:12 *1 certification*

1 Corinthians 7:34, 35

Dear Woman of Destiny,

In 1 Corinthians 7:34, 35, Paul speaks about the unique opportunity available to single women, observing that "the unmarried woman cares about the things of the Lord, that she may be holy both in body and spirit." He continues in verse 35 to encourage us to "serve the Lord without distraction." Without distraction and *with* a single focus, a single purpose, a single passion, and a single vision to minister unto Him. These two elements—holiness and serving Him without distraction—combine to compose what I like to call "the consecrated life." And that life is available to anyone—male or female, married or single.

I believe there is a call going out in the Spirit. It is an invitation to consecration. It is the call of the Lord, expressing His desire for holiness among His people. Just as the Old Testament priests were consecrated, or set apart, to minister to the Lord on behalf of the whole nation of Israel, so I believe we as women of destiny are being called into a place of consecration before Him (see Ex. 28, 29; Lev. 8, 9). This consecrated life is a place of absolute abandon, absolute surrender. One of the keys to it is determining not to exercise the option to say no to Him. It is a place where we voluntarily release the things that separate us *from* Him, so that we can embrace the things that separate us *to* Him. It is a process of letting go of everything that is more dear to us than He is. As we do, that which is dear to Him becomes precious to us. When we delight ourselves in Him, He will put His desires in our hearts (see Ps. 37:4).

Among the children of Israel, what was the unique privilege and highest honor of the priests? Being able to enter the most holy place. It only happened once a year, to one sanctified man. Only those "set apart" ones had any hope of ever being in the same room with Him. And that is still the essence and the aim of the consecrated life—being in the presence of the Lord.

Since the death and resurrection of Jesus Christ, and by the ministry of the Holy Spirit, the door to God's presence is flung open. But it is still the consecrated ones who are most intimate with Him, who are near enough to hear His heart beat, who visit Him in His secret place. They are the ones who have set themselves apart for Him, who have paid the price for His presence. And nothing is more beautiful, nothing is more pure; nothing is safer, nothing is sweeter than just being with Him.

So how do we begin the journey toward consecration, this journey that is a series of sprints and stumbles that will continually lead us into deeper experiences in Him and with Him? It starts with a choice. It starts when we simply choose to embrace Him and to say yes to His purpose for our lives. One of the things God asked of the Old Testament priests was that they "distinguish between holy and unholy" (Lev. 10:10). It continues as we make the holy exchanges that He wants us to make—exchanging life for death, faith for fear, wholeness for brokenness, joy over pain, peace over chaos. And it continues further as you surrender, as you draw near to the One who is wooing you, as you daily die to yourself and live to dwell in His presence.

Commit to the consecrated life. God may call you to be single or to be married. Whatever the case, be willing to submit to His plan for you, enjoying every stage of your life in His presence.

Beth Clark

3 My defense to those who examine me is this: 4 [a]Do we have no [1]right to eat and drink? 5 Do we have no right to take along [1]a believing wife, as *do* also the other apostles, [a]the brothers of the Lord, and [b]Cephas? 6 Or *is it* only Barnabas and I [a]*who* have no right to refrain from working? 7 Who ever [a]goes to war at his own expense? Who [b]plants a vineyard and does not eat of its fruit? Or who [c]tends a flock and does not drink of the milk of the flock?

8 Do I say these things as a *mere* man? Or does not the law say the same also? 9 For it is written in the law of Moses, [a]*"You shall not muzzle an ox while it treads out the grain."* Is it oxen God is concerned about? 10 Or does He say *it* altogether for our sakes? For our sakes, no doubt, *this* is written, that [a]he who plows should plow in hope, and he who threshes in hope should be partaker of his hope. 11 [a]If we have sown spiritual things for you, *is it* a great thing if we reap your material things? 12 If others are partakers of *this* right over you, *are* we not even more?

[a]Nevertheless we have not used this right, but endure all things [b]lest we hinder the gospel of Christ. 13 [a]Do you not know that those who minister the holy things eat *of the things* of the [b]temple, and those who serve at the altar partake of *the offerings of* the altar? 14 Even so [a]the Lord has commanded [b]that those who preach the gospel should live from the gospel.

15 But [a]I have used none of these things, nor have I written these things that it should be done so to me; for [b]it *would be* better for me to die than that anyone should make my boasting void. 16 For if I preach the gospel, I have nothing to boast of, for [a]necessity is laid upon me; yes, woe is me if I do not preach the gospel! 17 For if I do this willingly, [a]I have a reward; but if against my will, [b]I have been entrusted with a stewardship. 18 What is my reward then? That [a]when I preach the gospel, I may present the gospel [1]of Christ without charge, that I [b]may not abuse my authority in the gospel.

Serving All Men

19 For though I am [a]free from all *men,* [b]I have made myself a servant to all, [c]that I might win the more; 20 and [a]to the Jews I became as a Jew, that I might win Jews; to those *who are* under the law, as under the [1]law, that I might win those *who are* under the law; 21 [a]to [b]those *who are* without law, as without law [c](not being without [1]law toward God, but under [2]law toward Christ), that I might win those *who are* without law; 22 [a]to the weak I became [1]as weak, that I might win the weak. [b]I have become all things to all *men,* [c]that I might by all means save some. 23 Now this I do for the gospel's sake, that I may be partaker of it with *you.*

Striving for a Crown

24 Do you not know that those who run in a race all run, but one receives the prize? [a]Run in such a way that you may [1]obtain *it.* 25 And everyone who competes *for the prize* [1]is temperate in all things. Now they *do it* to obtain a perishable crown, but we *for* [a]an imperishable *crown.* 26 Therefore I run thus: [a]not with uncertainty. Thus I fight: not as *one who* beats the air. 27 [a]But I discipline my body and [b]bring *it* into subjection, lest, when I have preached to others, I myself should become [c]disqualified.

Old Testament Examples

10 Moreover, brethren, I do not want you to be unaware that all our fathers were under [a]the cloud, all passed through [b]the sea, 2 all were baptized into Moses in the cloud and in the sea, 3 all ate the same [a]spiritual food, 4 and all drank the same [a]spiritual drink. For they drank of that spiritual Rock that followed them, and that Rock was Christ. 5 But with most of them God was not well pleased, for *their bodies* [a]were scattered in the wilderness.

6 Now these things became our examples, to the intent that we should not lust after evil things as [a]they also lusted. 7 [a]And do not become idolaters as *were* some of them. As it is written, [b]*"The people sat down to eat and drink, and rose up to play."* 8 [a]Nor let us commit sexual immorality, as [b]some of them did, and [c]in one day twenty-three thousand fell; 9 nor let us [1]tempt Christ, as [a]some of them also tempted, and [b]were destroyed by serpents; 10 nor complain, as [a]some of them

4 a[1 Thess. 2:6, 9] *1 authority*
5 a Matt. 13:55 b Matt. 8:14 *1 Lit. a sister, a wife*
6 a Acts 4:36
7 a 2 Cor. 10:4 b Deut. 20:6 c John 21:15
9 a Deut. 25:4
10 a 2 Tim. 2:6
11 a Rom. 15:27
12 a[Acts 18:3; 20:33] b 2 Cor. 11:12
13 a Lev. 6:16, 26; 7:6, 31 b Num. 18:8–31
14 a Matt. 10:10 b Rom. 10:15
15 a Acts 18:3; 20:33 b 2 Cor. 11:10
16 a[Rom. 1:14]
17 a 1 Cor. 3:8, 14; 9:18 b Gal. 2:7
18 a 1 Cor. 10:33 b 1 Cor. 7:31; 9:12 *1 NU omits of Christ*
19 a 1 Cor. 9:1 b Gal. 5:13 c Matt. 18:15
20 a Acts 16:3; 21:23–26 *1 NU adds though not being myself under the law*
21 a[Gal. 2:3; 3:2] b[Rom. 2:12, 14] c[1 Cor. 7:22] *1 NU God's law* *2 NU Christ's law*
22 a Rom. 14:1; 15:1 b 1 Cor. 10:33 c Rom. 11:14 *1 NU omits as*
24 a Gal. 2:2 *1 win*
25 a James 1:12 *1 exercises self-control*
26 a 2 Tim. 2:5
27 a[Rom. 8:13] b[Rom. 6:18] c Jer. 6:30

CHAPTER 10 **1** a Ex. 13:21, 22 b Ex. 14:21, 22, 29 **3** a Ex. 16:4, 15, 35 **4** a Ex. 17:5–7 **5** a Num. 14:29, 37; 26:65 **6** a Num. 11:4, 34 **7** a 1 Cor. 5:11; 10:14 b Ex. 32:6 **8** a Rev. 2:14 b Num. 25:1–9 c Ps. 106:29 **9** a Ex. 17:2, 7 b Num. 21:6–9 *1 test* **10** a Ex. 16:2

also complained, and [b]were destroyed by
[c]the destroyer. 11Now [1]all these things
happened to them as examples, and [a]they
were written for our [2]admonition, [b]upon
whom the ends of the ages have come.
12Therefore [a]let him who thinks he
stands take heed lest he fall. 13No temptation has overtaken you except such as is
common to man; but [a]God *is* faithful,
[b]who will not allow you to be tempted
beyond what you are able, but with the
temptation will also make the way of escape, that you may be able to [1]bear *it.*

I thank You, Father, that no temptation has overtaken _____ but such as is common to all people. You are faithful and will not allow _____ to be tempted beyond what they are able. Open their eyes to see the way of escape that You have provided.

FROM 1 CORINTHIANS 10:13

Flee from Idolatry

14Therefore, my beloved, [a]flee from
idolatry. 15I speak as to [a]wise men; judge
for yourselves what I say. 16[a]The cup of
blessing which we bless, is it not the
[1]communion of the blood of Christ? [b]The
bread which we break, is it not the communion of the body of Christ? 17For [a]we,
though many, are one bread *and* one
body; for we all partake of that one bread.
18Observe [a]Israel [b]after the flesh: [c]Are
not those who eat of the sacrifices [1]par-
takers of the altar? 19What am I saying
then? [a]That an idol is anything, or what is
offered to idols is anything? 20Rather, that
the things which the Gentiles [a]sacrifice
[b]they sacrifice to demons and not to God,
and I do not want you to have fellowship
with demons. 21[a]You cannot drink the
cup of the Lord and [b]the cup of demons;
you cannot partake of the [c]Lord's table
and of the table of demons. 22Or do we
[a]provoke the Lord to jealousy? [b]Are we
stronger than He?

Don't say "it doesn't matter" about anything (except your own feelings) for everything matters. Everything is important, even the tiniest thing. If you do everything, whether great or small, for the sake of your Savior and Lord, then you will be ready for whatever work He has chosen for you to do later.

AMY CARMICHAEL

All to the Glory of God

23All things are lawful [1]for me, but not
all things are [a]helpful; all things are lawful for me, but not all things [2]edify. 24Let
no one seek his own, but each one [a]the
other's *well-being.*
25[a]Eat whatever is sold in the meat
market, asking no questions for conscience' sake; 26for [a]*"the earth is the*
LORD's, and all its fullness."
27If any of those who do not believe invites you *to dinner,* and you desire to go,
[a]eat whatever is set before you, asking no
question for conscience' sake. 28But if
anyone says to you, "This was offered to
idols," do not eat it [a]for the sake of the
one who told you, and for conscience'
sake; [1]for [b]*"the earth is the LORD's, and all*
its fullness." 29"Conscience," I say, not
your own, but that of the other. For [a]why
is my liberty judged by another *man's*
conscience? 30But if I partake with
thanks, why am I evil spoken of for *the*
food [a]over which I give thanks?
31[a]Therefore, whether you eat or drink,
or whatever you do, do all to the glory
of God. 32[a]Give no offense, either to the
Jews or to the Greeks or to the church of
God, 33just [a]as I also please all *men* in
all *things,* not seeking my own profit,

10 b Num. 14:37 c Ex. 12:23
11 a Rom. 15:4 b Phil. 4:5 *1* NU omits *all* *2* *instruction*
12 a Rom. 11:20
13 a 1 Cor. 1:9 b Ps. 125:3 *1* *endure*
14 a 2 Cor. 6:17
15 a 1 Cor. 8:1
16 a Matt. 26:26–28 b Acts 2:42 *1* *fellowship* or *sharing*
17 a 1 Cor. 12:12, 27
18 a Rom. 4:12 b Rom. 4:1 c Lev. 3:3; 7:6, 14 *1* *fellowshippers* or *sharers*
19 a 1 Cor. 8:4
20 a Lev. 17:7 b Deut. 32:17
21 a 2 Cor. 6:15, 16 b Deut. 32:38 c [1 Cor. 11:23–29]
22 a Deut. 32:21 b Ezek. 22:14
23 a 1 Cor. 6:12 *1* NU omits *for me* *2* *build up*
24 a Phil. 2:4
25 a [1 Tim. 4:4]
26 a Ps. 24:1
27 a Luke 10:7, 8
28 a [1 Cor. 8:7, 10, 12] b Ps. 24:1 *1* NU omits the rest of v. 28.
29 a Rom. 14:16
30 a Rom. 14:6
31 a Col. 3:17
32 a Rom. 14:13
33 a Rom. 15:2

but the *profit* of many, that they may be saved.

11 Imitate[a] me, just as I also *imitate* Christ.

Head Coverings

[2]Now I praise you, brethren, that you remember me in all things and keep the traditions just as I delivered *them* to you. [3]But I want you to know that [a]the head of every man is Christ, [b]the head of woman *is* man, and [c]the head of Christ *is* God. [4]Every man praying or [a]prophesying, having *his* head covered, dishonors his head. [5]But every woman who prays or prophesies with *her* head uncovered dishonors her head, for that is one and the same as if her head were [a]shaved. [6]For if a woman is not covered, let her also be shorn. But if it is [a]shameful for a woman to be shorn or shaved, let her be covered. [7]For a man indeed ought not to cover *his* head, since [a]he is the image and glory of God; but woman is the glory of man. [8]For man is not from woman, but woman [a]from man. [9]Nor was man created for the woman, but woman [a]for the man. [10]For this reason the woman ought to have *a symbol of* authority on *her* head, because of the angels. [11]Nevertheless, [a]neither *is* man independent of woman, nor woman independent of man, in the Lord. [12]For as woman *came* from man, even so man also *comes* through woman; but all things are from God.

[13]Judge among yourselves. Is it proper for a woman to pray to God with her head uncovered? [14]Does not even nature itself teach you that if a man has long hair, it is a dishonor to him? [15]But if a woman has long hair, it is a glory to her; for *her* hair is given [1]to her for a covering. [16]But [a]if anyone seems to be contentious, we have no such custom, [b]nor *do* the churches of God.

Conduct at the Lord's Supper

[17]Now in giving these instructions I do not praise *you,* since you come together not for the better but for the worse. [18]For first of all, when you come together as a church, [a]I hear that there are divisions among you, and in part I believe it. [19]For [a]there must also be factions among you, [b]that those who are approved may be [1]recognized among you. [20]Therefore when you come together in one place, it is not to eat the Lord's Supper. [21]For in eating, each one takes his own supper ahead of *others;* and one is hungry and [a]another is drunk. [22]What! Do you not have houses to eat and drink in? Or do you despise [a]the church of God and [b]shame [1]those who have nothing? What shall I say to you? Shall I praise you in this? I do not praise *you.*

Institution of the Lord's Supper

[23]For [a]I received from the Lord that which I also delivered to you: [b]that the Lord Jesus on the *same* night in which He was betrayed took bread; [24]and when He had given thanks, He broke *it* and said, [1]"Take, eat; this is My body which is [2]broken for you; do this in remembrance of Me." [25]In the same manner *He* also *took* the cup after supper, saying, "This cup is the new covenant in My blood. This do, as often as you drink *it,* in remembrance of Me."

[26]For as often as you eat this bread and drink this cup, you proclaim the Lord's death [a]till He comes.

Examine Yourself

[27]Therefore whoever eats [a]this bread or drinks *this* cup of the Lord in an unworthy manner will be guilty of the body and [1]blood of the Lord. [28]But [a]let a man examine himself, and so let him eat of the bread and drink of the cup. [29]For he who eats and drinks [1]in an unworthy manner eats and drinks judgment to himself, not discerning the [2]Lord's body. [30]For this reason many *are* weak and sick among you, and many [1]sleep. [31]For [a]if we would judge ourselves, we would not be judged. [32]But when we are judged, [a]we are chastened by the Lord, that we may not be condemned with the world.

[33]Therefore, my brethren, when you [a]come together to eat, wait for one another. [34]But if anyone is hungry, let him eat at home, lest you come together for judgment. And the rest I will set in order when I come.

Spiritual Gifts: Unity in Diversity

12 Now [a]concerning spiritual *gifts,* brethren, I do not want you to be ignorant: [2]You know [a]that[1] you were Gentiles, carried away to these [b]dumb[2] idols, however you were led. [3]Therefore I

CHAPTER 11
1 a Eph. 5:1
3 a Eph. 1:22; 4:15; 5:23 b Gen. 3:16 c John 14:28
4 a 1 Cor. 12:10
5 a Deut. 21:12
6 a Num. 5:18
7 a Gen. 1:26, 27; 5:1; 9:6
8 a Gen. 2:21–23
9 a Gen. 2:18
11 a [Gal. 3:28]
15 *1* M omits *to her*
16 a 1 Tim. 6:4 b 1 Cor. 7:17
18 a 1 Cor. 1:10–12; 3:3
19 a 1 Tim. 4:1 b [Deut. 13:3] *1* Lit. *manifest, evident*
21 a Jude 12
22 a 1 Cor. 10:32 b James 2:6 *1* The poor
23 a 1 Cor. 15:3 b Matt. 26:26–28
24 *1* NU omits *Take, eat* *2* NU omits *broken*
26 a John 14:3
27 a [John 6:51] *1* NU, M *the blood*
28 a 2 Cor. 13:5
29 *1* NU omits *in an unworthy manner* *2* NU omits *Lord's*
30 *1* Are dead
31 a [1 John 1:9]
32 a Ps. 94:12
33 a 1 Cor. 14:26

CHAPTER 12
1 a 1 Cor. 12:4; 14:1, 37
2 a Eph. 2:11 b Ps. 115:5 *1* NU, M *that when* *2 mute, silent*

make known to you that no one speaking
by the Spirit of God calls Jesus [1]accursed,
and [a]no one can say that Jesus is Lord
except by the Holy Spirit.

The Lord Jesus Christ left us a legacy. He has left us gifts of the Holy Ghost, and concerning these spiritual gifts we ought not to be ignorant.

HOWARD CARTER

4[a]There are [1]diversities of gifts, but
[b]the same Spirit. 5[a]There are differences
of ministries, but the same Lord. 6And
there are diversities of activities, but it is
the same God [a]who works [1]all in all. 7But
the manifestation of the Spirit is given to
each one for the profit *of all:* 8for to one
is given [a]the word of wisdom through the
Spirit, to another [b]the word of knowledge
through the same Spirit, 9[a]to another
faith by the same Spirit, to another [b]gifts
of healings by [1]the same Spirit, 10[a]to another the working of miracles, to another
[b]prophecy, to another [c]discerning of spirits, to another [d]*different* kinds of tongues,
to another the interpretation of tongues.
11But one and the same Spirit works all
these things, [a]distributing to each one individually [b]as He wills.

Lord, I ask that ____ would be mindful that the manifestation of the Spirit is given to them for the profit of all.

FROM 1 CORINTHIANS 12:7

Unity and Diversity in One Body

12For [a]as the body is one and has many
members, but all the members of that one
body, being many, are one body, [b]so also
is Christ. 13For [a]by one Spirit we were all
baptized into one body—[b]whether Jews
or Greeks, whether slaves or free—and
[c]have all been made to drink [1]into one
Spirit. 14For in fact the body is not one
member but many.
15If the foot should say, "Because I am
not a hand, I am not of the body," is it
therefore not of the body? 16And if the ear
should say, "Because I am not an eye, I am
not of the body," is it therefore not of the
body? 17If the whole body *were* an eye,
where *would be* the hearing? If the whole
were hearing, where *would be* the smelling? 18But now [a]God has set the members, each one of them, in the body [b]just
as He pleased. 19And if they *were* all one
member, where *would* the body *be?*
20But now indeed *there are* many members, yet one body. 21And the eye cannot
say to the hand, "I have no need of you";
nor again the head to the feet, "I have no
need of you." 22No, much rather, those
members of the body which seem to be
weaker are necessary. 23And those *mem-*
bers of the body which we think to be less
honorable, on these we bestow greater
honor; and our unpresentable *parts* have
greater modesty, 24but our presentable
parts have no need. But God composed
the body, having given greater honor to
that *part* which lacks it, 25that there
should be no [1]schism in the body, but
that the members should have the same
care for one another. 26And if one member
suffers, all the members suffer with *it;* or
if one member is honored, all the members rejoice with *it.*
27Now [a]you are the body of Christ, and
[b]members individually. 28And [a]God has
appointed these in the church: first [b]apos-
tles, second [c]prophets, third teachers, after that [d]miracles, then [e]gifts of healings,
[f]helps, [g]administrations, varieties of
tongues. 29*Are* all apostles? *Are* all prophets? *Are* all teachers? *Are* all workers of
miracles? 30Do all have gifts of healings?
Do all speak with tongues? Do all interpret? 31But [a]earnestly desire the [1]best
gifts. And yet I show you a more excellent
way.

The Greatest Gift

13 Though I speak with the tongues of
men and of angels, but have not
love, I have become sounding brass or a
clanging cymbal. 2And though I have *the*
gift of [a]prophecy, and understand all mysteries and all knowledge, and though I

3 [a]Matt. 16:17 [1]Gr. *anathema*
4 [a]Rom. 12:3–8 [b]Eph. 4:4 [1]*allotments* or *various kinds*
5 [a]Rom. 12:6
6 [a]1 Cor. 15:28 [1]*all things in*
8 [a]1 Cor. 2:6, 7 [b]Rom. 15:14
9 [a]2 Cor. 4:13 [b]Mark 3:15; 16:18 [1]NU *one*
10 [a]Mark 16:17 [b]Rom. 12:6 [c]1 John 4:1 [d]Acts 2:4–11
11 [a]Rom. 12:6 [b][John 3:8]
12 [a]Rom. 12:4, 5 [b][Gal. 3:16]
13 [a][Rom. 6:5] [b]Col. 3:11 [c][John 7:37–39] [1]NU omits *into*
18 [a]1 Cor. 12:28 [b]Rom. 12:3
25 [1]*division*
27 [a]Rom. 12:5 [b]Eph. 5:30
28 [a]Eph. 4:11 [b][Eph. 2:20; 3:5] [c]Acts 13:1 [d]1 Cor. 12:10, 29 [e]1 Cor. 12:9, 30 [f]Num. 11:17 [g]Rom. 12:8
31 [a]1 Cor. 14:1, 39 [1]NU *greater*

CHAPTER 13
2 [a]1 Cor. 12:8–10, 28; 14:1

1 Corinthians 13:13

Dear Woman of Destiny,

At the age of six, I had a powerful example of love shown me. My parents were both born in Russia. When Lenin declared in 1899 that Russia was going to be an atheist nation, my father, who was a firm Lutheran Christian, decided he would not rear his children in a godless nation. So he, his wife, and two little daughters, along with forty-three others, including the pastor, immigrated to Mexico. But unaware they were settling in a malaria-infested area, forty died that first year, among them my dad's first wife, who died while giving birth to a son. Only seven survived—three of whom were my father and his two little girls. They journeyed to Kansas where my dad met and married my mother. Their next stop was in Canada, where I was born. Hard worker that my dad was, he soon prospered on the homestead given him by the Canadian government. After a few years, he sold the farm and, with cash in hand, moved us to Oregon.

There a minister whom he had just met sold my father a farm—an orchard—where apples grew that he could sell "and make a lot of money." My father believed him, because a box of apples we bought at Christmas each year while living in Canada cost a small fortune.

But this was 1919, right after the close of World War I, and it seemed everyone was poor. When my dad took a truckload of apples to Oregon City to sell, they brought only fifty cents a box. Heartbroken, my dad drove back to the farm and fed the apples to the pigs. With our means of livelihood gone, we lost the farm a year later and moved to town. With nine of us children at home and no job, my dad was desperate. We rented a house close to a charismatic church, which we all began to attend. The pastor helped us get credit at a grocery store until my dad found a low-paying job. But God was merciful. Most of my family was filled with the Holy Spirit in that church.

I had a loud voice; and on occasion, the pastor would call me to the platform to sing. This pastor, realizing our desperate financial predicament, came to my parents with this offer: "Allow us to adopt Freda." My little five-foot-two mother replied, "If I have to live on bread and water the rest of my life, not one of our children will leave our home." At age six, I had my first real example of love. My godly mother lived to age 87, and we were very close.

The world's greatest example of love was Jesus. It was He who willingly went to the cross to die for you and me, that we can be saved, bring glory to His name, and spend eternity with Him. No other religion in all the world is built on love. First John 4:8 tells us "God is love." The believer's testimony and message to all humankind is: "Jesus loves you." This is the appropriate, true confession to men, women, boys, and girls.

Develop and practice a life of love, and yours will bear fruit for God and eternity. Start today.

Freda Lindsay

have all faith, [b]so that I could remove mountains, but have not love, I am nothing. 3And [a]though I bestow all my goods to feed *the poor,* and though I give my body [1]to be burned, but have not love, it profits me nothing.

4[a]Love suffers long *and* is [b]kind; love [c]does not envy; love does not parade itself, is not [1]puffed up; 5does not behave rudely, [a]does not seek its own, is not provoked, [1]thinks no evil; 6[a]does not rejoice in iniquity, but [b]rejoices in the truth; 7[a]bears all things, believes all things, hopes all things, endures all things.

Father, may ____ possess love that bears all things, believes all things, hopes all things, endures all things. May ____ have love that never fails.

FROM 1 CORINTHIANS 13:7, 8

8Love never fails. But whether *there are* prophecies, they will fail; whether *there are* tongues, they will cease; whether *there is* knowledge, it will vanish away. 9[a]For we know in part and we prophesy in part. 10But when that which is [1]perfect has come, then that which is in part will be done away.

11When I was a child, I spoke as a child, I understood as a child, I thought as a child; but when I became a man, I put away childish things. 12For [a]now we see in a mirror, dimly, but then [b]face to face. Now I know in part, but then I shall know just as I also am known.

13 And now abide faith, hope, love, these three; but the greatest of these *is* love.

Prophecy and Tongues

14 Pursue love, and [a]desire spiritual *gifts,* [b]but especially that you may prophesy. 2 For he who [a]speaks in a tongue does not speak to men but to God, for no one understands *him;* however, in the spirit he speaks mysteries. 3But he who prophesies speaks [a]edification and [b]exhortation and comfort to men. 4He who speaks in a tongue edifies himself, but he who prophesies edifies the church. 5I wish you all spoke with tongues, but even more that you prophesied; [1]for he who prophesies *is* greater than he who speaks with tongues, unless indeed he interprets, that the church may receive edification.

Tongues Must Be Interpreted

6But now, brethren, if I come to you speaking with tongues, what shall I profit you unless I speak to you either by [a]revelation, by knowledge, by prophesying, or by teaching? 7Even things without life, whether flute or harp, when they make a sound, unless they make a distinction in the sounds, how will it be known what is piped or played? 8For if the trumpet makes an uncertain sound, who will prepare for battle? 9So likewise you, unless you utter by the tongue words easy to understand, how will it be known what is spoken? For you will be speaking into the air. 10There are, it may be, so many kinds of languages in the world, and none of them *is* without [1]significance. 11Therefore, if I do not know the meaning of the language, I shall be a [1]foreigner to him who speaks, and he who speaks *will be* a foreigner to me. 12Even so you, since you are [1]zealous for spiritual *gifts, let it be* for the [2]edification of the church *that* you seek to excel.

Love is the beginning, love is the middle and love is the end. After He comes in, all you see is "Jesus only, Jesus ever."

OSWALD CHAMBERS

13Therefore let him who speaks in a tongue pray that he may [a]interpret. 14For if I pray in a tongue, my spirit prays, but my understanding is unfruitful. 15What is *the conclusion* then? I will pray with the spirit, and I will also pray with the understanding. [a]I will sing with the spirit, and I will also sing [b]with the understanding. 16Otherwise, if you bless with the spirit, how will he who occupies the place of the uninformed say "Amen" [a]at your giving of thanks, since he does not understand

---

2 b Matt. 17:20; 21:21
3 a Matt. 6:1, 2 · *1* NU *so I may boast*
4 a Prov. 10:12; 17:9 · b Eph. 4:32 · c Gal. 5:26 · *1 arrogant*
5 a 1 Cor. 10:24 · *1 keeps no accounts of evil*
6 a Rom. 1:32 · b 2 John 4
7 a Gal. 6:2
9 a 1 Cor. 8:2; 13:12
10 *1 complete*
12 a Phil. 3:12 · b [1 John 3:2]

CHAPTER 14
1 a 1 Cor. 12:31; 14:39 · b Num. 11:25, 29
2 a Acts 2:4; 10:46
3 a Rom. 14:19; 15:2 · b 1 Tim. 4:13
5 *1* NU *and*
6 a 1 Cor. 14:26
10 *1 meaning*
11 *1* Lit. *barbarian*
12 *1 eager* · *2 building up*
13 a 1 Cor. 12:10
15 a Col. 3:16 · b Ps. 47:7
16 a 1 Cor. 11:24

1 Corinthians 14:2

Dear Woman of Destiny,

What are we doing every time we pray in tongues? We're speaking the wisdom of God. We're speaking mysteries. A mystery is just a hidden thing, a secret. God wants to reveal the hidden things, and we should want to see them.

Those words you thought were so insignificant are, in reality, profound mysteries in God. You *can* speak the mysteries of God. Yes, you can. We speak the wisdom of God in a mystery. This has been ordained unto our glory.

When we speak in other tongues, we are speaking mysteries. Many times people have used 1 Corinthians 14:2 as a criticism of speaking in tongues. The apostle Paul is not using this truth negatively; he is saying that this is a plus. He is saying in essence, "Thank God nobody understands. Thank God that you're not just living in the realm of your logic; you're moving over into the spirit man. The spirit is speaking. The spirit is praying. The spirit is understanding."

The eye hasn't seen it. The ear hasn't heard it. The heart of man has not yet perceived what God has planned. But He reveals it by His Spirit.

We are moving, then, into the revelation of God. God reveals it to us by His Spirit. We reach this revelatory realm through prayer in the Spirit. God gives supernatural, revelatory knowledge to those who are seeking Him, praying in the Spirit, letting revelation come. We speak the wisdom of God in a mystery.

God causes us to know by revelation the same mysteries that we were speaking in a language we didn't know. And in the midst of those words was hidden wisdom. Suddenly, we find that we begin to speak forth that wisdom, because the revelation begins to come forth in our lives.

If you want to live in the realm of supernatural revelation, pray in tongues often. Sing in tongues often. You will be filling the well—the depths of your spirit. Jesus said in John 7:38, "He who believes in Me, as the Scripture has said, out of his heart will flow rivers of living water." You will be singing to the well of Living Water that will bring forth that release of information. You will flow in revelation knowledge. It might not happen right at the moment because you don't need it right at the moment. But when you do encounter a situation where you need revelation knowledge, it will be there.

The mysteries of God defy all human understanding, and they are available to those who seek them.

Ruth Ward Heflin

what you say? 17For you indeed give
thanks well, but the other is not edified.
18I thank my God I speak with tongues
more than you all; 19yet in the church I
would rather speak five words with my
understanding, that I may teach others
also, than ten thousand words in a
tongue.

Tongues a Sign to Unbelievers

20Brethren, [a]do not be children in understanding; however, in malice [b]be
babes, but in understanding be mature.
21[a]In the law it is written:

[b]*"With men of other tongues and*
other lips
I will speak to this people;
And yet, for all that, they will not
hear Me,"

says the Lord.
22Therefore tongues are for a [a]sign, not
to those who believe but to unbelievers;
but prophesying is not for unbelievers but
for those who believe. 23Therefore if the
whole church comes together in one
place, and all speak with tongues, and
there come in *those who are* uninformed
or unbelievers, [a]will they not say that you
are [1]out of your mind? 24But if all prophesy, and an unbeliever or an uninformed
person comes in, he is convinced by all, he
is convicted by all. 25[1]And thus the secrets
of his heart are revealed; and so, falling
down on *his* face, he will worship God and
report [a]that God is truly among you.

Order in Church Meetings

26How is it then, brethren? Whenever
you come together, each of you has a
psalm, [a]has a teaching, has a tongue, has
a revelation, has an interpretation. [b]Let
all things be done for [1]edification. 27If
anyone speaks in a tongue, *let there be*
two or at the most three, *each* in turn,
and let one interpret. 28But if there is no
interpreter, let him keep silent in church,
and let him speak to himself and to God.
29Let two or three prophets speak, and
[a]let the others judge. 30But if *anything* is
revealed to another who sits by, [a]let the
first keep silent. 31For you can all prophesy one by one, that all may learn and all
may be encouraged. 32And [a]the spirits of
the prophets are subject to the prophets.
33For God is not *the author* of [1]confu-
sion but of peace, [a]as in all the churches
of the saints.
34 ☙ [a]Let [1]your women keep silent in the
churches, for they are not permitted to
speak; but *they are* to be submissive, as
the [b]law also says. 35And if they want to
learn something, let them ask their own
husbands at home; for it is shameful for
women to speak in church. ❧
36Or did the word of God come *origi-*
nally from you? Or *was it* you only that it
reached? 37[a]If anyone thinks himself to be
a prophet or spiritual, let him acknowledge that the things which I write to you
are the commandments of the Lord. 38But
[1]if anyone is ignorant, let him be ignorant.
39Therefore, brethren, [a]desire earnestly
to prophesy, and do not forbid to speak
with tongues. 40[a]Let all things be done
decently and in order.

The Risen Christ, Faith's Reality

15 Moreover, brethren, I declare to
you the gospel [a]which I preached
to you, which also you received and [b]in
which you stand, 2[a]by which also you are
saved, if you hold fast that word which I
preached to you—unless [b]you believed in
vain.
3For [a]I delivered to you first of all that
[b]which I also received: that Christ died for
our sins [c]according to the Scriptures,
4and that He was buried, and that He rose
again the third day [a]according to the
Scriptures, 5[a]and that He was seen by
[1]Cephas, then [b]by the twelve. 6After that
He was seen by over five hundred brethren at once, of whom the greater part
remain to the present, but some have
[1]fallen asleep. 7After that He was seen by
James, then [a]by all the apostles. 8[a]Then
last of all He was seen by me also, as by
one born out of due time.
9For I am [a]the least of the apostles, who
am not worthy to be called an apostle, because [b]I persecuted the church of God.
10But [a]by the grace of God I am what I am,
and His grace toward me was not in vain;
but I labored more abundantly than they
all, [b]yet not I, but the grace of God *which*
was with me. 11Therefore, whether *it was*
I or they, so we preach and so you believed.

20 [a]Ps. 131:2 [b][1 Pet. 2:2]
21 [a]John 10:34 [b]Is. 28:11, 12
22 [a]Mark 16:17
23 [a]Acts 2:13 [1] *insane*
25 [a]Is. 45:14 [1] NU omits *And thus*
26 [a]1 Cor. 12:8–10; 14:6 [b][2 Cor. 12:19] [1] *building up*
29 [a]1 Cor. 12:10
30 [a][1 Thess. 5:19, 20]
32 [a]1 John 4:1
33 [a]1 Cor. 11:16 [1] *disorder*
34 [a]1 Tim. 2:11 [b]Gen. 3:16 [1] NU omits *your*
37 [a]2 Cor. 10:7
38 [1] NU *if anyone does not recognize this, he is not recognized.*
39 [a]1 Cor. 12:31
40 [a]1 Cor. 14:33

CHAPTER 15
1 [a][Gal. 1:11] [b][Rom. 5:2; 11:20]
2 [a]Rom. 1:16 [b]Gal. 3:4
3 [a]1 Cor. 11:2, 23 [b][Gal. 1:12] [c]Ps. 22:15
4 [a]Ps. 16:9–11; 68:18; 110:1
5 [a]Luke 24:34 [b]Matt. 28:17 [1] Peter
6 [1] Died
7 [a]Acts 1:3, 4
8 [a][Acts 9:3–8; 22:6–11; 26:12–18]
9 [a]Eph. 3:8 [b]Acts 8:3
10 [a]Eph. 3:7, 8 [b]Phil. 2:13

☙ **For explanation of 1 Corinthians 14:34, 35, please see article on page 1595.** ❧

The Risen Christ, Our Hope

12Now if Christ is preached that He has
been raised from the dead, how do some
among you say that there is no resurrection of the dead? 13But if there is no resurrection of the dead, [a]then Christ is not
risen. 14And if Christ is not risen, then our
preaching *is* empty and your faith *is* also
empty. 15Yes, and we are found false witnesses of God, because [a]we have testified
of God that He raised up Christ, whom He
did not raise up—if in fact the dead do not
rise. 16For if *the* dead do not rise, then
Christ is not risen. 17And if Christ is not
risen, your faith *is* futile; [a]you are still in
your sins! 18Then also those who have
[1]fallen [a]asleep in Christ have perished.
19[a]If in this life only we have hope in
Christ, we are of all men the most pitiable.

The Last Enemy Destroyed

20But now [a]Christ is risen from the
dead, *and* has become [b]the firstfruits of
those who have [1]fallen asleep. 21For
[a]since by man *came* death, [b]by Man also
came the resurrection of the dead. 22For
as in Adam all die, even so in Christ all
shall [a]be made alive. 23But [a]each one in
his own order: Christ the firstfruits, afterward those *who are* Christ's at His coming. 24Then *comes* the end, when He
delivers [a]the kingdom to God the Father,
when He puts an end to all rule and all
authority and power. 25For He must reign
[a]till He has put all enemies under His
feet. 26[a]The last enemy *that* will be destroyed *is* death. 27For [a]*"He has put all
things under His feet."* But when He says
"all things are put under *Him,*" *it is* evident that He who put all things under
Him is excepted. 28[a]Now when all things
are made subject to Him, then [b]the Son
Himself will also be subject to Him who
put all things under Him, that God may
be all in all.

Effects of Denying the Resurrection

29Otherwise, what will they do who are
baptized for the dead, if the dead do not
rise at all? Why then are they baptized for
the dead? 30And [a]why do we stand in
[1]jeopardy every hour? 31I affirm, by [a]the
boasting in you which I have in Christ
Jesus our Lord, [b]I die daily. 32If, in the
manner of men, [a]I have fought with
beasts at Ephesus, what advantage *is it* to
me? If *the* dead do not rise, [b]*"Let us eat
and drink, for tomorrow we die!"*
33Do not be deceived: [a]"Evil company
corrupts good habits." 34[a]Awake to righteousness, and do not sin; [b]for some do
not have the knowledge of God. [c]I speak
this to your shame.

A Glorious Body

35But someone will say, [a]"How are the
dead raised up? And with what body do
they come?" 36Foolish one, [a]what you sow
is not made alive unless it dies. 37And
what you sow, you do not sow that body
that shall be, but mere grain—perhaps
wheat or some other *grain.* 38But God
gives it a body as He pleases, and to each
seed its own body.

39All flesh *is* not the same flesh, but
there is one *kind* [1]*of* flesh of men, another
flesh of animals, another of fish, *and* another of birds.
40*There are* also [1]celestial bodies and
[2]terrestrial bodies; but the glory of the celestial *is* one, and the *glory* of the terrestrial *is* another. 41*There is* one glory of the
sun, another glory of the moon, and another glory of the stars; for *one* star differs
from *another* star in glory.

42[a]So also *is* the resurrection of the
dead. *The body* is sown in corruption, it is
raised in incorruption. 43[a]It is sown in
dishonor, it is raised in glory. It is sown
in weakness, it is raised in power. 44It is
sown a natural body, it is raised a spiritual
body. There is a natural body, and there is
a spiritual body. 45And so it is written,
[a]*"The first man Adam became a living
being."* [b]The last Adam *became* [c]a life-
giving spirit.

46However, the spiritual is not first, but
the natural, and afterward the spiritual.
47[a]The first man *was* of the earth, [b]*made*[1]
of dust; the second Man *is* [2]the Lord
[c]from heaven. 48As *was* the [1]*man* of dust,
so also *are* those *who are made* of dust;
[a]and as *is* the heavenly *Man,* so also *are*
those *who are* heavenly. 49And [a]as we
have borne the image of the *man* of dust,
[b]we[1] shall also bear the image of the heavenly *Man.*

Our Final Victory

50Now this I say, brethren, that [a]flesh
and blood cannot inherit the kingdom
of God; nor does corruption inherit in-

---

13 a [1 Thess. 4:14]
15 a Acts 2:24
17 a [Rom. 4:25]
18 a Job 14:12 *1 Died*
19 a 2 Tim. 3:12
20 a 1 Pet. 1:3 b Acts 26:23 *1 Died*
21 a Rom. 5:12; 6:23 b John 11:25
22 a [John 5:28, 29]
23 a [1 Thess. 4:15–17]
24 a [Dan. 2:44; 7:14, 27]
25 a Ps. 110:1
26 a [2 Tim. 1:10]
27 a Ps. 8:6
28 a [Phil. 3:21] b 1 Cor. 3:23; 11:3; 12:6
30 a 2 Cor. 11:26 *1 danger*
31 a 1 Thess. 2:19 b Rom. 8:36
32 a 2 Cor. 1:8 b Is. 22:13; 56:12
33 a [1 Cor. 5:6]
34 a Rom. 13:11 b [1 Thess. 4:5] c 1 Cor. 6:5
35 a Ezek. 37:3
36 a John 12:24
39 *1* NU, M omit *of flesh*
40 *1 heavenly 2 earthly*
42 a [Dan. 12:3]
43 a [Phil. 3:21]
45 a Gen. 2:7 b [Rom. 5:14] c John 5:21; 6:57
47 a John 3:31 b Gen. 2:7; 3:19 c John 3:13 *1 earthy 2* NU omits *the Lord*
48 a Phil. 3:20 *1 earthy*
49 a Gen. 5:3 b Rom. 8:29 *1* M *let us also bear*
50 a [John 3:3, 5]

corruption. 51Behold, I tell you a [1]mystery:
[a]We shall not all sleep, [b]but we shall all be
changed— 52in a moment, in the twinkling of an eye, at the last trumpet. [a]For
the trumpet will sound, and the dead will
be raised incorruptible, and we shall be
changed. 53For this corruptible must put
on incorruption, and [a]this mortal *must*
put on immortality. 54So when this corruptible has put on incorruption, and this
mortal has put on immortality, then shall
be brought to pass the saying that is written: [a]*"Death is swallowed up in victory."*

55 *"O*[a][1] *Death, where is your sting?*
O Hades, where is your victory?"

56The sting of death *is* sin, and [a]the
strength of sin *is* the law. 57[a]But thanks
be to God, who gives us [b]the victory
through our Lord Jesus Christ.
58[a]Therefore, my beloved brethren, be
steadfast, immovable, always abounding
in the work of the Lord, knowing [b]that
your labor is not in vain in the Lord.

51 a [1 Thess. 4:15] b [Phil. 3:21] *1 hidden truth*
52 a Matt. 24:31
53 a 2 Cor. 5:4
54 a Is. 25:8
55 a Hos. 13:14 *1 NU O Death, where is your victory? O Death, where is your sting?*
56 a [Rom. 3:20; 4:15; 7:8] **57** a [Rom. 7:25] b [1 John 5:4]
58 a 2 Pet. 3:14 b [1 Cor. 3:8]

MARY MOFFAT

When Mary Moffat (1795–1870) left England, she was a small, delicate woman, known for her timidity and fragility. But after fifty years in Kuruman, South Africa, as a pioneer missionary with her husband Robert, she had the power and authority of a mother calling her children in with a two-fingered whistle.

Though she was a foreigner among the Bechuana people, Ma-Mary, as she was called, was seen as the mother of the tribe. She defined love in action, taking in people from every tribe and nurturing them. She saved three African children from being buried alive and adopted them, while raising ten children of her own. When an influx of new missionaries to South Africa came, she assumed the role of a mother on whom they could count for help in sickness, for food and supplies, and, most importantly, for counsel, encouragement, and love.

During the Moffats' first twelve years in Kuruman, however, evangelizing the area seemed hopeless. Rather than being greeted with curious questions and open hearts, the missionaries received nothing but ridicule and contempt. They endured the Bechuanas' constant thievery of their crops, sheep, tools, and even the bread from their oven. But when an awakening occurred in 1829, the entire face of the town changed. Aside from taking on the colossal task of translating the Bible into Sechuana, Robert taught the men everything from gardening to carpentry to reading. Mary, meanwhile, showed the women how to treat their children's illnesses, improve their families' diets, make their own clothes, and even how to make candles so they could have light at night.

While Robert Moffat was responsible for Africa's first Bibles, Mary was the strength behind every translated word. "You will never let us lose hope," Robert once said to his wife. "You have saved us from despair again and again by your courage and your unconquerable faith." Out of her frail body, she replied, "Perhaps it is because I am so weak and fearful that I know I have no strength in myself. I have to trust Him or I should die."

Collection for the Saints

16 Now concerning [a]the collection
for the saints, as I have given orders to the churches of Galatia, so you
must do also: 2[a]On the first *day* of the
week let each one of you lay something
aside, storing up as he may prosper, that
there be no collections when I come. 3And
when I come, [a]whomever you approve by
your letters I will send to bear your gift to
Jerusalem. 4[a]But if it is fitting that I go
also, they will go with me.

Personal Plans

5Now I will come to you [a]when I pass
through Macedonia (for I am passing
through Macedonia). 6And it may be that
I will remain, or even spend the winter
with you, that you may [a]send me on my
journey, wherever I go. 7For I do not wish
to see you now on the way; but I hope to
stay a while with you, [a]if the Lord permits.
8But I will tarry in Ephesus until [a]Pen-
tecost. 9For [a]a great and effective door has
opened to me, and [b]*there are* many adversaries.
10And [a]if Timothy comes, see that he
may be with you without fear; for [b]he
does the work of the Lord, as I also *do*.
11[a]Therefore let no one despise him. But
send him on his journey [b]in peace, that he
may come to me; for I am waiting for him
with the brethren.
12Now concerning *our* brother [a]Apol-
los, I strongly urged him to come to you
with the brethren, but he was quite unwilling to come at this time; however, he
will come when he has a convenient time.

1 a Gal. 2:10
2 a Acts 20:7
3 a 2 Cor. 3:1; 8:18
4 a 2 Cor. 8:4, 19
5 a 2 Cor. 1:15, 16
6 a Acts 15:3
7 a James 4:15
8 a Lev. 23:15–22
9 a Acts 14:27 b Acts 19:9
10 a Acts 19:22 b Phil. 2:20
11 a 1 Tim. 4:12 b Acts 15:33
12 a 1 Cor. 1:12; 3:5

PRISCILLA

We rarely think of Priscilla without also thinking of her husband, Aquila. Together they present a powerful picture of team ministry. The couple had lived in Rome, but moved to Corinth in A.D. 49 when the emperor Claudius demanded that all Jews leave the city. The apostle Paul traveled to Corinth in A.D. 50, met them there, and joined them in their tent-making business. From all indications, their lives changed radically after they became acquainted with the apostle. They learned everything they could from Paul; they dedicated themselves wholeheartedly to the gospel; and they got busy spreading the good news together.

As is the case in any marriage, each of them had something to offer the kingdom, and together they likely enjoyed the complementary combination of gifts and strengths that each one brought to their ministry. Together they traveled with Paul to Ephesus; and together they stayed in Ephesus while Paul continued traveling and started a church in their home (see Acts 18:18, 19; 1 Cor. 16:19). Together they became respected teachers in the early church and "explained to [Apollos] the way of God more accurately" (Acts 18:26). And together they "risked their own necks" in order to save Paul's life (see Rom. 16:4).

Team ministry can involve anything from hosting a group of believers in a home to prayer walking a neighborhood to full-time service on the mission field. Whatever the call, may God raise up couples like Aquila and Priscilla among His people today. May He continue to use women of destiny, with their husbands, to build His kingdom together. May those who are called together serve the Lord together!

Final Exhortations

[13][a]Watch, [b]stand fast in the faith, be
brave, [c]be strong. [14][a]Let all *that* you *do* be
done with love.
[15]I urge you, brethren—you know [a]the
household of Stephanas, that it is [b]the
firstfruits of Achaia, and *that* they have
devoted themselves to [c]the ministry of
the saints— [16][a]that you also submit to
such, and to everyone who works and [b]la-
bors with *us*.
[17]I am glad about the coming of Stephanas, Fortunatus, and Achaicus, [a]for what
was lacking on your part they supplied.
[18][a]For they refreshed my spirit and yours.
Therefore [b]acknowledge such men.

Greetings and a Solemn Farewell

[19]The churches of Asia greet you. Aquila and Priscilla greet you heartily in the
Lord, [a]with the church that is in their
house. [20]All the brethren greet you.
[a]Greet one another with a holy kiss.
[21][a]The salutation with my own hand—
Paul's.
[22]If anyone [a]does not love the Lord
Jesus Christ, [b]let him be [1]accursed.
[c]O[2] Lord, come!
[23][a]The grace of our Lord Jesus Christ
be with you. [24]My love *be* with you all in
Christ Jesus. Amen.

Lord, I pray that ____ will watch, stand firm in the faith, be brave, be strong, and that all they do will be done with love.

FROM 1 CORINTHIANS 16:13, 14

13 [a] Matt. 24:42 [b] Phil. 1:27; 4:1 [c] [Eph. 3:16; 6:10]
14 [a] [1 Pet. 4:8]
15 [a] 1 Cor. 1:16 [b] Rom. 16:5 [c] 2 Cor. 8:4
16 [a] Heb. 13:17 [b] [Heb. 6:10]
17 [a] 2 Cor. 11:9
18 [a] Col. 4:8 [b] Phil. 2:29
19 [a] Rom. 16:5
20 [a] Rom. 16:16
21 [a] Col. 4:18
22 [a] Eph. 6:24 [b] Gal. 1:8, 9 [c] Jude 14, 15 [1] Gr. *anathema* [2] Aram. *Marana tha;* possibly *Maran atha, Our Lord has come*
23 [a] Rom. 16:20

AUTHOR: *Paul*
DATE: *A.D. 55–56*
THEME: *Powerful Ministry Through Weak Vessels*
KEY WORDS: *Comfort, Suffering, Ministry, Glory, Power, Weakness*

2 CORINTHIANS

Dear Woman of Destiny,

The Book of 2 Corinthians starts off with a big embrace from God! Right from the start in the greeting of this letter, the Holy Spirit has chosen to address us with the attributes of our heavenly Father as the "God of all comfort" (2 Cor. 1:3). In this letter, Paul confronts the church in Corinth after reestablishing his apostolic authority. In doing so, he recounts how he has suffered for Christ. There are times when all of us, like the apostle Paul, suffer. Paul said that he and his companions were "burdened beyond measure, above strength, so that we despaired even of life" (2 Cor. 1:8). Later he went on to say they were "hard-pressed on every side, yet not crushed; we are perplexed, but not in despair; persecuted, but not forsaken" (2 Cor. 4:8, 9). All of us have hard days where we struggle and feel pressure and stress. Don't lose hope, Woman of Destiny; ask your Father in heaven to be the God of all comfort for you today.

With His love,

Cindy Jacobs

Greeting

Paul, [a]an apostle of Jesus Christ by
the will of God, and [b]Timothy *our*
brother,
To the church of God which is at Corinth, [c]with all the saints who are in all
Achaia:
2[a]Grace to you and peace from God our
Father and the Lord Jesus Christ.

Father of mercies and God of all comfort, please comfort ____ in all their tribulation, that they may be able to comfort those who are in any trouble, with the comfort with which they themselves are comforted by You.

FROM 2 CORINTHIANS 1:3, 4

Comfort in Suffering

3[a]Blessed *be* the God and Father of our
Lord Jesus Christ, the Father of mercies
and God of all comfort, 4who [a]comforts us
in all our tribulation, that we may be able
to comfort those who are in any [1]trouble,
with the comfort with which we ourselves
are comforted by God. 5For as [a]the sufferings of Christ abound in us, so our [1]con-
solation also abounds through Christ.
6Now if we are afflicted, [a]*it is* for your
consolation and salvation, which is effective for enduring the same sufferings
which we also suffer. Or if we are comforted, *it is* for your consolation and salvation. 7And our hope for you *is* steadfast,
because we know that [a]as you are partakers of the sufferings, so also *you will partake* of the consolation.

Delivered from Suffering

8For we do not want you to be ignorant,
brethren, of [a]our [1]trouble which came to
us in Asia: that we were burdened beyond
measure, above strength, so that we despaired even of life. 9Yes, we had the sentence of death in ourselves, that we
should [a]not trust in ourselves but in God
who raises the dead, 10[a]who delivered us
from so great a death, and [1]does deliver
us; in whom we trust that He will still
deliver *us,* 11you also [a]helping together in
prayer for us, that thanks may be given by
many persons on [1]our behalf [b]for the gift
granted to us through many.

Paul's Sincerity

12For our boasting is this: the testimony of our conscience that we conducted
ourselves in the world in [1]simplicity and
[a]godly sincerity, [b]not with fleshly wisdom
but by the grace of God, and more abundantly toward you. 13For we are not writing any other things to you than what you
read or understand. Now I trust you will
understand, even to the end 14(as also you
have understood us in part), [a]that we are
your boast as [b]you also *are* ours, in the
day of the Lord Jesus.

God's promises work their wonders while we see and act on eternal realities and refuse to be affected by temporal things to the contrary.

F. F. BOSWORTH

Sparing the Church

15And in this confidence [a]I intended to
come to you before, that you might have
[b]a second benefit— 16to pass by way of
you to Macedonia, [a]to come again from
Macedonia to you, and be helped by you
on my way to Judea. 17Therefore, when I
was planning this, did I do it lightly? Or
the things I plan, do I plan [a]according to
the flesh, that with me there should be
Yes, Yes, and No, No? 18But *as* God *is*
[a]faithful, our [1]word to you was not Yes
and No. 19For [a]the Son of God, Jesus
Christ, who was preached among you by
us—by me, [b]Silvanus, and [c]Timothy—
was not Yes and No, [d]but in Him was Yes.
20[a]For all the promises of God in Him *are*
Yes, and in Him Amen, to the glory of God
through us. 21Now He who establishes us
with you in Christ and [a]has anointed us *is*
God, 22who [a]also has sealed us and [b]given
us the Spirit in our hearts as a guarantee.

CHAPTER 1
1 a 2 Tim. 1:1 b 1 Cor. 16:10 c Col. 1:2
2 a Rom. 1:7
3 a 1 Pet. 1:3
4 a Is. 51:12; 66:13 *1 tribulation*
5 a 2 Cor. 4:10 *1 comfort*
6 a 2 Cor. 4:15; 12:15
7 a [Rom. 8:17]
8 a Acts 19:23 *1 tribulation*
9 a Jer. 17:5, 7
10 a [2 Pet. 2:9] *1 NU shall*
11 a Rom. 15:30 b 2 Cor. 4:15; 9:11 *1 M your behalf*
12 a 2 Cor. 2:17 b [1 Cor. 2:4] *1 The opposite of duplicity*
14 a 2 Cor. 5:12 b Phil. 2:16
15 a 1 Cor. 4:19 b Rom. 1:11; 15:29
16 a 1 Cor. 16:3–6
17 a 2 Cor. 10:2; 11:18
18 a 1 John 5:20 *1 message*
19 a Mark 1:1 b 1 Pet. 5:12 c 2 Cor. 1:1 d [Heb. 13:8]
20 a [Rom. 15:8, 9]
21 a [1 John 2:20, 27]
22 a [Eph. 4:30] b [Eph. 1:14]

23 Moreover [a]I call God as witness against my soul, [b]that to spare you I came no more to Corinth. 24 Not [a]that we [1]have dominion over your faith, but are fellow workers for your joy; for [b]by faith you stand.

2 But I determined this within myself, [a]that I would not come again to you in sorrow. 2 For if I make you [a]sorrowful, then who is he who makes me glad but the one who is made sorrowful by me?

Forgive the Offender

3 And I wrote this very thing to you, lest, when I came, [a]I should have sorrow over those from whom I ought to have joy, [b]having confidence in you all that my joy is *the joy* of you all. 4 For out of much [1]affliction and anguish of heart I wrote to you, with many tears, [a]not that you should be grieved, but that you might know the love which I have so abundantly for you.

5 But [a]if anyone has caused grief, he has not [b]grieved me, but all of you to some extent—not to be too severe. 6 This punishment which *was inflicted* [a]by the majority *is* sufficient for such a man, 7 [a]so that, on the contrary, you *ought* rather to forgive and comfort *him,* lest perhaps such a one be swallowed up with too much sorrow. 8 Therefore I urge you to reaffirm *your* love to him. 9 For to this end I also wrote, that I might put you to the test, whether you are [a]obedient in all things. 10 Now whom you forgive anything, I also *forgive.* For [1]if indeed I have forgiven anything, I have forgiven that one for your sakes in the presence of Christ, 11 lest Satan should take advantage of us; for we are not ignorant of his devices.

Triumph in Christ

12 Furthermore, [a]when I came to Troas to *preach* Christ's gospel, and [b]a [1]door was opened to me by the Lord, 13 [a]I had no rest in my spirit, because I did not find Titus my brother; but taking my leave of them, I departed for Macedonia.

14 Now thanks *be* to God who always leads us in triumph in Christ, and through us [1]diffuses the fragrance of His knowledge in every place. 15 For we are to God the fragrance of Christ [a]among those who are being saved and [b]among those who are perishing. 16 [a]To the one *we are* the aroma of death *leading* to death, and to the other the aroma of life *leading* to life. And [b]who *is* sufficient for these things? 17 For we are not, as [1]so many, [a]peddling[2] the word of God; but as [b]of sincerity, but as from God, we speak in the sight of God in Christ.

> *The world wants living epistles who will live, weep, act, suffer, and, if need be, die before the people. The testimony of such witnesses will prove a living word indeed, sharper than any two-edged sword.*
>
> CATHERINE BOOTH

Christ's Epistle

3 Do [a]we begin again to commend ourselves? Or do we need, as some *others,* [b]epistles of commendation to you or *letters* of commendation from you? 2 [a]You are our epistle written in our hearts, known and read by all men; 3 clearly *you are* an epistle of Christ, [a]ministered by us, written not with ink but by the Spirit of the living God, not [b]on tablets of stone but [c]on tablets of flesh, *that is,* of the heart.

The Spirit, Not the Letter

4 And we have such trust through Christ toward God. 5 [a]Not that we are sufficient of ourselves to think of anything as *being* from ourselves, but [b]our sufficiency *is* from God, 6 who also made us sufficient as [a]ministers of [b]the new covenant, not [c]of the letter but of the [1]Spirit; for [d]the letter kills, [e]but the Spirit gives life.

Glory of the New Covenant

7 But if [a]the ministry of death, [b]written *and* engraved on stones, was glorious, [c]so that the children of Israel could not look steadily at the face of Moses because of the glory of his countenance, which *glory* was passing away, 8 how will [a]the ministry of the Spirit not be more glorious? 9 For if the ministry of condemnation *had* glory,

---

23 a Gal. 1:20 b 1 Cor. 4:21
24 a [1 Pet. 5:3] b Rom. 11:20 *1 rule*

CHAPTER 2
1 a 2 Cor. 1:23
2 a 2 Cor. 7:8
3 a 2 Cor. 12:21 b Gal. 5:10
4 a [2 Cor. 2:9; 7:8, 12] *1 tribulation*
5 a [1 Cor. 5:1] b Gal. 4:12
6 a 1 Cor. 5:4, 5
7 a Gal. 6:1
9 a 2 Cor. 7:15; 10:6
10 *1* NU *indeed, what I have forgiven, if I have forgiven anything, I did it for your sakes*
12 a Acts 16:8 b 1 Cor. 16:9 *1* Opportunity
13 a 2 Cor. 7:6, 13; 8:6
14 *1 manifests*
15 a [1 Cor. 1:18] b [2 Cor. 4:3]
16 a Luke 2:34 b [1 Cor. 15:10]
17 a 2 Pet. 2:3 b 2 Cor. 1:12 *1* M *the rest* *2 adulterating for gain*

CHAPTER 3
1 a 2 Cor. 5:12; 10:12, 18; 12:11 b Acts 18:27
2 a 1 Cor. 9:2
3 a 1 Cor. 3:5 b Ex. 24:12; 31:18; 32:15 c Ps. 40:8
5 a [John 15:5] b 1 Cor. 15:10
6 a 1 Cor. 3:5 b Jer. 31:31 c Rom. 2:27 d Gal. 3:10 e John 6:63 *1 Or spirit*
7 a Rom. 7:10 b Ex. 34:1 c Ex. 34:29
8 a [Gal. 3:5]

the ministry [a]of righteousness exceeds
much more in glory. 10For even what was
made glorious had no glory in this respect, because of the glory that excels.
11For if what is passing away *was* glorious,
what remains *is* much more glorious.
12Therefore, since we have such hope,
[a]we use great boldness of speech— 13un-
like Moses, [a]*who* put a veil over his face so
that the children of Israel could not look
steadily at [b]the end of what was passing
away. 14But [a]their minds were blinded.
For until this day the same veil remains
unlifted in the reading of the Old Testament, because the *veil* is taken away in
Christ. 15But even to this day, when Moses
is read, a veil lies on their heart. 16Never-
theless [a]when one turns to the Lord, [b]the
veil is taken away. 17Now [a]the Lord is the
Spirit; and where the Spirit of the Lord *is,*
there *is* [b]liberty. 18But we all, with unveiled face, beholding [a]as in a mirror [b]the
glory of the Lord, [c]are being transformed
into the same image from glory to glory,
just as [1]by the Spirit of the Lord.

*Lord, may ____ look to
You with an unveiled face,
beholding as in a mirror the
glory of the Lord. May they
be transformed into the same
image from glory to glory,
just as by the Spirit
of the Lord.*

FROM 2 CORINTHIANS 3:18

The Light of Christ's Gospel

4 Therefore, since we have this ministry, [a]as we have received mercy, we
[b]do not lose heart. 2But we have renounced the hidden things of shame, not
walking in craftiness nor [1]handling the
word of God deceitfully, but by manifestation of the truth [a]commending ourselves
to every man's conscience in the sight of
God. 3But even if our gospel is veiled,
[a]it is veiled to those who are perishing,
4whose minds [a]the god of this age [b]has
blinded, who do not believe, lest [c]the light
of the gospel of the glory of Christ, [d]who
is the image of God, should shine on
them. 5[a]For we do not preach ourselves,
but Christ Jesus the Lord, and [b]ourselves
your bondservants for Jesus' sake. 6For
it is the God [a]who commanded light to
shine out of darkness, who has [b]shone in
our hearts to *give* the light of the knowledge of the glory of God in the face of
Jesus Christ.

Cast Down but Unconquered

7But we have this treasure in earthen
vessels, [a]that the excellence of the power
may be of God and not of us. 8*We are*
[a]hard-pressed on every side, yet not
crushed; *we are* perplexed, but not in despair; 9persecuted, but not [a]forsaken;
[b]struck down, but not destroyed— 10[a]al-
ways carrying about in the body the dying
of the Lord Jesus, [b]that the life of Jesus
also may be manifested in our body. 11For
we who live [a]are always delivered to death
for Jesus' sake, that the life of Jesus also
may be manifested in our mortal flesh.
12So then death is working in us, but life
in you.
13And since we have [a]the same spirit of
faith, according to what is written, [b]*"I believed and therefore I spoke,"* we also believe and therefore speak, 14knowing that
[a]He who raised up the Lord Jesus will also
raise us up with Jesus, and will present *us*
with you. 15For [a]all things *are* for your
sakes, that [b]grace, having spread through
the many, may cause thanksgiving to
abound to the glory of God.

Seeing the Invisible

16Therefore we [a]do not lose heart. Even
though our outward man is perishing, yet
the inward *man* is [b]being renewed day by
day. 17For [a]our light affliction, which is
but for a moment, is working for us a far
more exceeding *and* eternal weight of glory, 18[a]while we do not look at the things
which are seen, but at the things which
are not seen. For the things which are
seen *are* temporary, but the things which
are not seen *are* eternal.

Assurance of the Resurrection

5 For we know that if [a]our earthly
[1]house, *this* tent, is destroyed, we
have a building from God, a house [b]not
made with hands, eternal in the heavens.
2For in this [a]we groan, earnestly desiring
to be clothed with our [1]habitation which
is from heaven, 3if indeed, [a]having been
clothed, we shall not be found naked. 4For

9 a[Rom. 1:17; 3:21]
12 a Eph. 6:19
13 a Ex. 34:33–35 b[Gal. 3:23]
14 a Acts 28:26
16 a Rom. 11:23 b Is. 25:7
17 a[1 Cor. 15:45] b Gal. 5:1, 13
18 a 1 Cor. 13:12 b[2 Cor. 4:4, 6] c[Rom. 8:29, 30] *1 Or from the Lord, the Spirit*

CHAPTER 4
1 a 1 Cor. 7:25 b 2 Cor. 4:16
2 a 2 Cor. 5:11 *1 adulterating the word of God*
3 a[1 Cor. 1:18]
4 a John 12:31 b John 12:40 c[2 Cor. 3:8, 9] d[John 1:18]
5 a 1 Cor. 1:13 b 1 Cor. 9:19
6 a Gen. 1:3 b 2 Pet. 1:19
7 a 1 Cor. 2:5
8 a 2 Cor. 1:8; 7:5
9 a[Heb. 13:5] b Ps. 37:24
10 a Phil. 3:10 b Rom. 8:17
11 a Rom. 8:36
13 a 2 Pet. 1:1 b Ps. 116:10
14 a[Rom. 8:11]
15 a Col. 1:24 b 2 Cor. 1:11
16 a 2 Cor. 4:1 b[Is. 40:29, 31]
17 a Rom. 8:18
18 a[Heb. 11:1, 13]

CHAPTER 5
1 a Job 4:19 b Mark 14:58 *1 Physical body*
2 a Rom. 8:23 *1 dwelling*
3 a Rev. 3:18

2 Corinthians 4:3–6

Dear Woman of Destiny,

Are you "trying" to believe God to save a precious loved one—a relative, even a son or daughter? Many can testify of God's faithfulness to save loved ones, but the pain experienced during the waiting period can be overwhelming at times. However, God can turn your fear into fighting and victory if you can apply some of His principles as you pray and believe for these loved ones.

My husband and I gave our son Jonathan to God before he was ever born, and we raised him in church. However, at the age of 17, through a combination of several well-laid plans of the enemy, he began to wander away from God. It wasn't long before he was living a life of total rebellion, characterized by drugs and all the things that accompany such a lifestyle. At 18, he was diagnosed with diabetes; and at times he would go to the hospital with complications, only to return to hard living.

We were devastated and sometimes frozen with fear; but as we cried out to God, we began to learn more and more. Through intercession with my husband and two friends, God began to give instructions on how to pray, as well as many uplifting promises and words of encouragement. Daily we asked the Holy Spirit to hover around Jonathan's bed as he slept, in his car, wherever he was—and birth life into him. We anointed his room, the doors and windows, his bed, his car, his clothing, and his wallet. Many times I would go into his room and sing in the Spirit for an hour or more. I sang, "The name of Jesus is exalted in this place—over his bed, over these things, these clothes," and "Jonathan has a destiny I know he will fulfill." My friends and I would pray at times for four to six hours.

We prayed over a prayer cloth with our pastor, agreeing that the anointing would break the yoke of drugs, sin, ungodly friends, perversion, and so on. Cutting it into many pieces, we placed them all over his room, in his clothes, in his car . . . . With each one we would declare, "The anointing breaks the yoke." We were releasing the light of the glory of His gospel into every situation.

At times things seemed worse, as it seemed he was on a mission to destroy his life. But we stood fast—loving him, speaking God's plan over his life, anointing and singing over his room and car, interceding daily, and declaring scripture after scripture. The more we did these things, the more our faith grew and fear left.

After more than four years of intercession, we began to see that God was dealing with our son. He wanted his life to be straight; and one night at a prayer meeting in our home, he rededicated his life to Jesus.

God is faithful, and His word is alive and true. If you will believe it and practice prayer, worship, declaring the Word and loving unconditionally, you will see your loved ones come to the God, who gave His life for them and loves them even more than you do.

Polly Simchen

we who are in *this* tent groan, being burdened, not because we want to be unclothed, [a]but further clothed, that
mortality may be swallowed up by life.
5Now He who has prepared us for this very
thing *is* God, who also [a]has given us the
Spirit as [1]a guarantee.
6So *we are* always confident, knowing
that while we are at home in the body we
are absent from the Lord. 7For [a]we walk
by faith, not by sight. 8We are confident,
yes, [a]well pleased rather to be absent from
the body and to be present with the Lord.

The Judgment Seat of Christ

9Therefore we make it our aim, whether present or absent, to be well pleasing to
Him. 10[a]For we must all appear before the
judgment seat of Christ, [b]that each one
may receive the things *done* in the body,
according to what he has done, whether
good or bad. 11Knowing, therefore, [a]the
terror of the Lord, we persuade men; but
we are well known to God, and I also trust
are well known in your consciences.

Be Reconciled to God

12For [a]we do not commend ourselves
again to you, but give you opportunity [b]to
boast on our behalf, that you may have *an
answer* for those who boast in appearance
and not in heart. 13For [a]if we are beside
ourselves, *it is* for God; or if we are of
sound mind, *it is* for you. 14For the love of
Christ compels us, because we judge thus:
that [a]if One died for all, then all died;
15and He died for all, [a]that those who live
should live no longer for themselves, but
for Him who died for them and rose again.
16[a]Therefore, from now on, we regard
no one according to the flesh. Even
though we have known Christ according
to the flesh, [b]yet now we know *Him thus*
no longer. 17Therefore, if anyone [a]*is* in
Christ, *he is* [b]a new creation; [c]old things
have passed away; behold, all things have
become [d]new. 18 Now all things *are* of
God, [a]who has reconciled us to Himself
through Jesus Christ, and has given us
the ministry of reconciliation, 19that is,
that [a]God was in Christ reconciling the
world to Himself, not [1]imputing their
trespasses to them, and has committed to
us the word of reconciliation.
20Now then, we are [a]ambassadors for
Christ, as though God were pleading
through us: we implore *you* on Christ's
behalf, be reconciled to God. 21For [a]He
made Him who knew no sin *to be* sin for
us, that we might become [b]the righteousness of God in Him.

Thank You, Father, that ____ is in Christ and is a new creation; old things have passed away; behold, all things have become new.

FROM 2 CORINTHIANS 5:17

Marks of the Ministry

6 We then, *as* [a]workers together *with
Him* also [b]plead with *you* not to receive the grace of God in vain. 2For He
says:

[a]*"In an acceptable time I have heard
you,
And in the day of salvation I have
helped you."*

Behold, now *is* the accepted time; behold,
now *is* the day of salvation.

The Lord intends to bring us into the place where not only our gospel message and teaching ministry are correct but we as well are right.

WATCHMAN NEE

3[a]We give no offense in anything, that
our ministry may not be blamed. 4But
in all *things* we commend ourselves [a]as
ministers of God: in much [1]patience, in
tribulations, in needs, in distresses, 5[a]in
stripes, in imprisonments, in tumults, in
labors, in sleeplessness, in fastings; 6by
purity, by knowledge, by longsuffering, by
kindness, by the Holy Spirit, by [1]sincere
love, 7[a]by the word of truth, by [b]the power
of God, by [c]the armor of righteousness on
the right hand and on the left, 8by honor
and dishonor, by evil report and good
report; as deceivers, and *yet* true; 9as

4 a 1 Cor. 15:53
5 a Rom. 8:23 *1 down payment, earnest*
7 a Heb. 11:1
8 a Phil. 1:23
10 a Rom. 2:16; 14:10, 12 b Eph. 6:8
11 a [Heb. 10:31; 12:29]
12 a 2 Cor. 3:1 b 2 Cor. 1:14
13 a 2 Cor. 11:1, 16; 12:11
14 a [Rom. 5:15; 6:6]
15 a [Rom. 6:11]
16 a 2 Cor. 10:3 b [Matt. 12:50]
17 a [John 6:63] b [Rom. 8:9] c Is. 43:18; 65:17 d [Rom. 6:3–10]
18 a Rom. 5:10
19 a [Rom. 3:24] *1 reckoning*
20 a Eph. 6:20
21 a Is. 53:6, 9 b [Rom. 1:17; 3:21]

CHAPTER 6
1 a 1 Cor. 3:9 b 2 Cor. 5:20
2 a Is. 49:8
3 a Rom. 14:13
4 a 1 Cor. 4:1 *1 endurance*
5 a 2 Cor. 11:23
6 *1* Lit. *unhypocritical*
7 a 2 Cor. 7:14 b 1 Cor. 2:4 c 2 Cor. 10:4

2 Corinthians 5:18, 19

Dear Woman of Destiny,

It was painful to confess. Prejudice had polluted my heart. As a prayer leader in Southern California, ungodly attitudes curdled my actions. My sin was precisely this: I respected and esteemed pastors of mega-churches, pastors with convening authority, more than pastors of tiny congregations. As I confessed my sin to my friends, we weren't prepared to go where the Holy Spirit seemed bent on taking us.

Fern Noble, a Cree Indian and a reconciliation prayer-leader, grabbed my hands and said, "Don't you get it? You represent the white church, and I represent the Native Americans. You have shut us out because we didn't have convening power, we didn't have letters after our names, we didn't have money, or savvy, or know the protocol. *We couldn't open any doors for you.* You shut us out and wouldn't give us your pulpits. Even when we had the word of the Lord, you wouldn't even open the front door of the church to us because we had no influence. We are nameless and faceless because you refused to ever know or esteem us."

The Holy Spirit was underscoring the grievous sin of exclusion. Fern was right. It *was* the same root sin, and it was odious to God. Whole segments of God's multicolored bride had had no place for expression because we did not respect them; we had not made room for them. We *perceived* they had nothing to give. I said sadly, "Fern, this is not God's way. We have not portrayed Him well to your people. We have sinned in failing to represent God's humility and love."

Later that same day, I thought proudly to myself, *It's true the white church does not tend to seek out and give platform to people of color. But I am glad I'm not like that. I use my influence all the time to promote God's breathtaking multicolored bride.*

I sensed the Holy Spirit quietly interrupting my arrogance. "Yes, and you're proud of it, too." Ouch. It wasn't enough to be a reconciler who opens doors for others. If I was still so awake to our differences, that I had pride about even opening doors, then I obviously knew nothing of the heart of the Reconciling Father.

To move beyond the rhetoric of reconciliation, I had to see my own pride. My posture, my hand movements, my tone of voice, all unconsciously and perpetually declared an air of superiority. The thing that destroyed Satan lurked in me. Pride divides and excludes. Love provides and includes. Reconciliation is that simple.

When God reconciled us to Himself through Christ, He didn't offer graduated levels of acceptance. He made us freely accepted in the Beloved. He didn't just tolerate us. He gave us His name, His inheritance, His future. He fully identified with us without reservation.

Because we have been the recipients of such reconciling generosity, we can become reconcilers who portray God's total and complete acceptance to others, with humility and love.

We can be reconcilers only as we allow Him to be who He is within us—a loving, humble God who reconciles the world to Himself through Christ and through us. May you, loved one, increase His fame by being a reconciler of many to God.

Fawn Parish

unknown, and [a]*yet* well known; [b]as dying,
and behold we live; [c]as chastened, and *yet*
not killed; 10as sorrowful, yet always rejoicing; as poor, yet making many [a]rich;
as having nothing, and *yet* possessing all
things.

Be Holy

11O Corinthians! [1]We have spoken
openly to you, [a]our heart is wide open.
12You are not restricted by us, but [a]you
are restricted by your *own* affections.
13Now in return for the same [a](I speak as
to children), you also be open.

Lord, may ____ not be
unequally yoked together
with unbelievers. For what
fellowship has righteousness
with lawlessness? And what
communion has light
with darkness?
FROM 2 CORINTHIANS 6:14

14[a]Do not be unequally yoked together with unbelievers. For [b]what [1]fellow-
ship has righteousness with lawlessness?
And what [2]communion has light with
darkness? 15And what accord has Christ
with Belial? Or what part has a believer
with an unbeliever? 16And what agreement has the temple of God with idols?
For [a]you[1] are the temple of the living
God. As God has said:

[b]*"I will dwell in them*
And walk among them.
I will be their God,
And they shall be My people."

17Therefore

[a]*"Come out from among them*
And be separate, says the Lord.
Do not touch what is unclean,
And I will receive you."
18 *"I [a]will be a Father to you,*
And you shall be My [b]sons and
daughters,
Says the LORD Almighty."

9 a 2 Cor. 4:2; 5:11 b 1 Cor. 4:9, 11 c Ps. 118:18
10 a [2 Cor. 8:9]
11 a 2 Cor. 7:3 *1 Lit. Our mouth is open*
12 a 2 Cor. 12:15
13 a 1 Cor. 4:14
14 a 1 Cor. 5:9 b Eph. 5:6, 7, 11 *1 in common* *2 fellowship*
16 a [1 Cor. 3:16, 17; 6:19] b Ezek. 37:26, 27 *1* NU *we*
17 a Is. 52:11
18 a 2 Sam. 7:14 b [Rom. 8:14]

CHAPTER 7
1 a [1 John 3:3]
2 a Acts 20:33
3 a 2 Cor. 6:11, 12
4 a 2 Cor. 3:12 b 1 Cor. 1:4 c Phil. 2:17
5 a 2 Cor. 2:13 b 2 Cor. 4:8 c Deut. 32:25
6 a 2 Cor. 1:3, 4 b 2 Cor. 2:13; 7:13
7 *1 comfort*
8 a 2 Cor. 2:2 b 2 Cor. 2:4
10 a Matt. 26:75 b Prov. 17:22

7 Therefore,[a] having these promises,
beloved, let us cleanse ourselves from
all filthiness of the flesh and spirit, perfecting holiness in the fear of God.

The Corinthians' Repentance

2Open *your hearts* to us. We have
wronged no one, we have corrupted no
one, [a]we have cheated no one. 3I do not
say *this* to condemn; for [a]I have said before that you are in our hearts, to die together and to live together. 4[a]Great *is* my
boldness of speech toward you, [b]great *is*
my boasting on your behalf. [c]I am filled
with comfort. I am exceedingly joyful in
all our tribulation.
5For indeed, [a]when we came to Macedonia, our bodies had no rest, but [b]we
were troubled on every side. [c]Outside
were conflicts, inside *were* fears. 6Never-
theless [a]God, who comforts the downcast,
comforted us by [b]the coming of Titus,
7and not only by his coming, but also by
the [1]consolation with which he was comforted in you, when he told us of your
earnest desire, your mourning, your zeal
for me, so that I rejoiced even more.
8For even if I made you [a]sorry with my
letter, I do not regret it; [b]though I did
regret it. For I perceive that the same
epistle made you sorry, though only for a
while. 9Now I rejoice, not that you were
made sorry, but that your sorrow led to
repentance. For you were made sorry in a
godly manner, that you might suffer loss
from us in nothing. 10For [a]godly sorrow
produces repentance *leading* to salvation,
not to be regretted; [b]but the sorrow of the

Repentance is not a
voluntary feeling of any
kind. It is a turning
away from disobedience to
obedience. It is willing
and feeling as God
does concerning sin,
and always implies
forsaking sin.
MRS. F. F. BOSWORTH

2 Corinthians 6:14

Dear Woman of Destiny,

I think it's safe to say most marriages begin with a simple date. But many Christians are deceived about this. They feel all right about dating an unbeliever as long as it doesn't "get too serious." They think, "One or two dates can't hurt. Maybe I can lead him to the Lord. I'm just having fun right now, but I will definitely marry a Christian." The next thing they know they've "fallen in love" and are desperately trying to rationalize their upcoming marriage—to themselves, their friends, and to God.

I'm not exactly sure who came up with the term *missionary dating,* but I love it because it paints such a great picture. Imagine this: A young girl, zealous for God, goes to a remote tribal village to reach the lost. She gets a special burden for the chief's handsome son. He seems interested in Jesus, so she spends a lot of time with him, hoping to win him to the Lord. Soon her friends at the Missionary Society get a postcard saying she's getting married and won't be back. Was he converted? Well, not really—but she is confident he will be shortly. Meanwhile, she's happily getting ready to set up house in his hut full of idols (which, of course, she wouldn't think of worshiping) and dreaming of the wonderful future they'll have together.

What would you say about this girl's chances at real happiness—or her professed love for the Lord?

Marriage is the biggest and most important decision you'll make after your decision to follow Jesus. Spending time with the wrong person opens you up to getting emotionally involved to a point of no return. Once you've given your heart you'll be surprised at how hard it is to take it back—even if you know you should.

Don't wait until it's too late. Any Christian foolish enough to date an unbeliever is foolish enough to marry one! The time to ask Jesus for wisdom is before you start a relationship—not after. Once your own desires demand priority, your zeal to put God first begins to fade. Emotions are a powerful thing, and if you don't control them, they will control you! (see Jer. 17:9).

Women who marry unbelievers will never experience the fullness and richness of marriage as God intended. They won't have someone to love Jesus with and their husbands won't have someone to love the world with. Life will be a continual tug-of-war where no one is free to do what makes him or her happy. Instead of having the blessing of a family united by the common bond of God's love, there will be the "common bondage" of frustration and discontent that may lead to separation or divorce. True intimacy and oneness can only be experienced with someone of "like mind." That is why God commanded us to marry "only in the Lord" (1 Cor. 7:39).

Don't be foolish. Don't settle for anything less than God's very best. If you are called to marriage, God will call a wonderful Christian man to your side. But beware; the enemy is a matchmaker, too.

Melody Green

2 Corinthians 7:1

Dear Woman of Destiny,

In 2 Corinthians 7:2, Paul tells us that through believing and accepting the promises of God's Word daily in our lives, we must choose to "cleanse ourselves from all filthiness of the flesh and spirit, perfecting holiness in the fear of God." *The Living Bible* puts verse 1 this way: "Let us turn away from everything wrong, whether of body or spirit, and purify ourselves, living in the wholesome fear of God, giving ourselves to him alone." First Thessalonians 5:22 says, "Abstain from [or voluntarily do without, hold yourself back, refrain from] every form of evil." If you have any question within your spirit regarding whether something is right or wrong, don't do it.

For example, we've warned friends regarding counseling alone with the opposite sex. We've watched them resist warnings and lose their marriages because of an inappropriate counseling relationship with another person. The act of sin always starts with an attitude of compromise. This attitude says, "I'm okay, I'm handling it well, and others do this and seem to be doing okay." Another example is how others perceive what you do. Romans 14:13 warns us not to put a stumbling block in the way of other Christians or people who might be watching us. For example, some Christians have felt justified in drinking alcohol with their meals. Although they may feel that this is acceptable, the love we have for God and for others supersedes this.

Another area of holiness is evidenced in how we treat others. Hebrews 12:14 tells us that we are to be continually conscious of being peacemakers with all people and are to walk in holiness; otherwise, we will not see the Lord. In verses 12–15, Paul addresses the subject of releasing any hurt or offense that could become bitterness. He says that we are to be healed of any discouragement that may have crippled our strength. Obviously, holiness involves keeping our hearts free from resentments, grudges, bitterness, or strife toward others.

Peter wrote that we are to be holy as Christ is holy (see 1 Pet. 1:15, 16). It is Christ within you who gives you the help and grace to walk out the truths of His Word. He always provides ways of escape from sin if we are open to see them (see 1 Cor. 10:13 and 2 Pet. 1:4). If we do fail or sin, He's provided immediate forgiveness and cleansing if we repent and turn to obey Him. Choose to walk in the mind of Christ.

1. Realize it is because of His grace that you are called to holiness and to His purposes for your life.
2. Believe and receive His holy calling upon your life.
3. Confess these and other scriptures that pertain to who you are in Christ (Rom. 12:21; 1 Cor. 7:30, 31; 2 Cor. 7:1; 2 Tim. 1:9; Heb. 12:14; 2 Pet. 1:3, 4; 1 John 4:4).
4. Read your Bible daily (Ps. 119:9, 11).
5. Have a daily prayer time and determine to listen to and obey His still small voice during your day in the way you respond to others around you.
6. Guard your mind and heart (Prov. 4:23–27). Avoid any situations that would pull you away from Jesus, your first love (1 Thess. 5:22; 2 Tim. 2:22).

Sharon Daugherty

world produces death. 11For observe this
very thing, that you sorrowed in a godly
manner: What diligence it produced in
you, *what* [a]clearing *of yourselves, what*
indignation, *what* fear, *what* vehement
desire, *what* zeal, *what* vindication! In all
things you proved yourselves to be [b]clear
in this matter. 12Therefore, although I
wrote to you, *I did* not *do it* for the sake
of him who had done the wrong, nor for
the sake of him who suffered wrong, [a]but
that our care for you in the sight of God
might appear to you.

The Joy of Titus

13Therefore we have been comforted in
your comfort. And we rejoiced exceedingly more for the joy of Titus, because his
spirit [a]has been refreshed by you all. 14For
if in anything I have boasted to him about
you, I am not ashamed. But as we spoke
all things to you in truth, even so our
boasting to Titus was found true. 15And
his affections are greater for you as he remembers [a]the obedience of you all, how
with fear and trembling you received him.
16Therefore I rejoice that [a]I have confidence in you in everything.

Excel in Giving

8 Moreover, brethren, we make known
to you the grace of God bestowed on
the churches of Macedonia: 2that in a
great trial of affliction the abundance of
their joy and [a]their deep poverty abounded in the riches of their liberality. 3For I
bear witness that according to *their* ability, yes, and beyond *their* ability, *they were*
freely willing, 4imploring us with much
urgency [1]that we would receive the gift
and [a]the fellowship of the ministering to
the saints. 5And not *only* as we had hoped,
but they first [a]gave themselves to the
Lord, and *then* to us by the [b]will of God.
6So [a]we urged Titus, that as he had begun, so he would also complete this grace
in you as well. 7But as [a]you abound in
everything—in faith, in speech, in knowledge, in all diligence, and in your love for
us—*see* [b]that you abound in this grace
also.

Christ Our Pattern

8[a]I speak not by commandment, but I
am testing the sincerity of your love by
the diligence of others. 9For you know the
grace of our Lord Jesus Christ, [a]that
though He was rich, yet for your sakes He
became poor, that you through His poverty might become [b]rich.
10And in this [a]I give advice: [b]It is to
your advantage not only to be doing what
you began and [c]were desiring to do a year
ago; 11but now you also must complete
the doing *of it;* that as *there was* a readiness to desire *it,* so *there* also *may be* a
completion out of what *you* have. 12For [a]if
there is first a willing mind, *it is* accepted
according to what one has, *and* not according to what he does not have.
13For *I do* not *mean* that others should
be eased and you burdened; 14but by an
equality, *that* now at this time your abundance *may supply* their lack, that their
abundance also may supply your lack—
that there may be equality. 15As it is written, [a]*"He who gathered much had*
nothing left over, and he who gathered
little had no lack."

Collection for the Judean Saints

16But thanks *be* to God who [1]puts the
same earnest care for you into the heart of
Titus. 17For he not only accepted the exhortation, but being more diligent, he
went to you of his own accord. 18And we
have sent with him [a]the brother whose
praise *is* in the gospel throughout all the
churches, 19and not only *that,* but who
was also [a]chosen by the churches to travel
with us with this gift, which is administered by us [b]to the glory of the Lord
Himself and *to show* your ready mind,
20avoiding this: that anyone should blame
us in this lavish gift which is administered
by us— 21[a]providing honorable things,
not only in the sight of the Lord, but also
in the sight of men.
22And we have sent with them our
brother whom we have often proved diligent in many things, but now much more
diligent, because of the great confidence
which *we have* in you. 23If *anyone in-*
quires about [a]Titus, *he is* my partner and
fellow worker concerning you. Or if our
brethren *are inquired about, they are*
[b]messengers[1] of the churches, the glory
of Christ. 24Therefore show to them, [1]and
before the churches, the proof of your
love and of our [a]boasting on your behalf.

---

11 a Eph. 5:11 b 2 Cor. 2:5–11
12 a 2 Cor. 2:4
13 a Rom. 15:32
15 a 2 Cor. 2:9
16 a 2 Thess. 3:4

CHAPTER 8
2 a Mark 12:44
4 a Rom. 15:25, 26 1 NU, M omit *that we would receive,* thus changing text to *urgency for the favor and fellowship*
5 a [Rom. 12:1, 2] b [Eph. 6:6]
6 a 2 Cor. 8:17; 12:18
7 a [1 Cor. 1:5; 12:13] b 2 Cor. 9:8
8 a 1 Cor. 7:6
9 a Phil. 2:6, 7 b Rom. 9:23
10 a 1 Cor. 7:25, 40 b [Heb. 13:16] c 2 Cor. 9:2
12 a Mark 12:43, 44
15 a Ex. 16:18
16 1 NU *has put*
18 a 2 Cor. 12:18
19 a 1 Cor. 16:3, 4 b 2 Cor. 4:15
21 a Rom. 12:17
23 a 2 Cor. 7:13, 14 b Phil. 2:25 1 Lit. *apostles,* "sent ones"
24 a 2 Cor. 7:4, 14; 9:2 1 NU, M omit *and*

Administering the Gift

9 Now concerning [a]the ministering to
the saints, it is superfluous for me to
write to you; 2for I know your willingness,
about which I boast of you to the Macedonians, that Achaia was ready a [a]year ago;
and your zeal has stirred up the majority.
3[a]Yet I have sent the brethren, lest our
boasting of you should be in vain in this
respect, that, as I said, you may be ready;
4lest if *some* Macedonians come with me
and find you unprepared, we (not to mention you!) should be ashamed of this [1]con-
fident boasting. 5Therefore I thought it
necessary to [1]exhort the brethren to go to
you ahead of time, and prepare your generous gift beforehand, which *you had* previously promised, that it may be ready
as *a matter of* generosity and not as a
[2]grudging obligation.

O Lord, I pray that ____ will sow bountifully so that they will also reap bountifully. May they give as they purpose in their hearts, not grudgingly or of necessity; for You love a cheerful giver.

FROM 2 CORINTHIANS 9:6, 7

The Cheerful Giver

6[a]But this *I say:* He who sows sparingly
will also reap sparingly, and he who sows
[1]bountifully will also reap bountifully.
7*So let* each one *give* as he purposes in
his heart, [a]not grudgingly or of [1]neces-
sity; for [b]God loves a cheerful giver. 8[a]And
God *is* able to make all grace abound toward you, that you, always having all
sufficiency in all *things,* may have an
abundance for every good work. 9As it is
written:

[a]"*He has dispersed abroad,*
He has given to the poor;
His righteousness endures forever."

10Now [1]may He who [a]supplies seed to
the sower, and bread for food, [2]supply and
multiply the seed you have *sown* and increase the fruits of your [b]righteousness,
11while *you are* enriched in everything for
all liberality, [a]which causes thanksgiving
through us to God. 12For the administration of this service not only [a]supplies the
needs of the saints, but also is abounding
through many thanksgivings to God,
13while, through the proof of this ministry, they [a]glorify God for the obedience of
your confession to the gospel of Christ,
and for *your* liberal [b]sharing with them
and all *men,* 14and by their prayer for you,
who long for you because of the exceeding
[a]grace of God in you. 15Thanks *be* to God
[a]for His indescribable gift!

The Spiritual War

10 Now [a]I, Paul, myself am pleading
with you by the meekness and gentleness of Christ—[b]who in presence *am*
lowly among you, but being absent am
bold toward you. 2But I beg *you* [a]that
when I am present I may not be bold with
that confidence by which I intend to be
bold against some, who think of us as if
we walked according to the flesh. 3For
though we walk in the flesh, we do not
war according to the flesh. 4[a]For the
weapons [b]of our warfare *are* not [1]carnal
but [c]mighty in God [d]for pulling down
strongholds, 5[a]casting down arguments and every high thing that exalts
itself against the knowledge of God,
bringing every thought into captivity to
the obedience of Christ, 6[a]and being ready
to punish all disobedience when [b]your
obedience is fulfilled.

Reality of Paul's Authority

7[a]Do you look at things according to
the outward appearance? [b]If anyone is
convinced in himself that he is Christ's,
let him again consider this in himself,
that just as he *is* Christ's, even [1]so [c]we *are*
Christ's. 8For even if I should boast somewhat more [a]about our authority, which
the Lord gave [1]us for [2]edification and not
for your destruction, [b]I shall not be
ashamed— 9lest I seem to terrify you by
letters. 10"For *his* letters," they say, "*are*
weighty and powerful, but [a]*his* bodily
presence *is* weak, and *his* [b]speech contemptible." 11Let such a person consider
this, that what we are in word by letters
when we are absent, such *we will* also *be*
in deed when we are present.

CHAPTER 9
1 a Gal. 2:10
2 a 2 Cor. 8:10
3 a 2 Cor. 8:6, 17
4 *1* NU *confidence.*
5 *1 encourage* *2* Lit. *covetousness*
6 a Prov. 11:24; 22:9 *1 with blessings*
7 a Deut. 15:7 b Rom. 12:8 *1 compulsion*
8 a [Prov. 11:24]
9 a Ps. 112:9
10 a Is. 55:10 b Hos. 10:12 *1* NU omits *may* *2* NU *will supply*
11 a 2 Cor. 1:11
12 a 2 Cor. 8:14
13 a [Matt. 5:16] b [Heb. 13:16]
14 a 2 Cor. 8:1
15 a [James 1:17]

CHAPTER 10
1 a Rom. 12:1 b 1 Thess. 2:7
2 a 1 Cor. 4:21
4 a Eph. 6:13 b 1 Tim. 1:18 c Acts 7:22 d Jer. 1:10 *1 of the flesh*
5 a 1 Cor. 1:19
6 a 2 Cor. 13:2, 10 b 2 Cor. 7:15
7 a [John 7:24] b 1 Cor. 1:12; 14:37 c 1 Cor. 3:23 *1* NU *as we are.*
8 a 2 Cor. 13:10 b 2 Cor. 7:14 *1* NU omits *us* *2 building up*
10 a Gal. 4:13 b 2 Cor. 11:6

2 Corinthians 10:4

Dear Woman of Destiny,

When was the last time you made a statement like, "My husband will never change," "I'll never lose weight!" or "I can't help my temper—it runs in my family!"

Have you become so resigned to certain "facts" in your life—an addictive behavior, an unhappy marriage, disappointments that have slowly given way to hopelessness and despair—that you are actually building strongholds rather than pulling them down, as the Scriptures instruct us?

What is a stronghold anyway? My husband Ed defines a stronghold as "a mind-set impregnated with hopelessness that causes us to accept as unchangeable situations that we know are contrary to the will of God." I think it's safe to say most of us struggle with hopelessness at one time or another. Perhaps you aren't experiencing intimacy with your husband, and although you've prayed, you have seen little or no change. Or maybe your child has rebelled and turned his back on God.

What is the will of God concerning these situations? That you enjoy intimacy with your husband, and that your rebellious child be reconciled to God and live under His lordship. But have you given up and accepted that there is no hope for change?

Dear friend, please realize that in allowing hopelessness to take hold of your heart, you have become double-minded and have built a stronghold in your mind to help you cope with these apparent contradictions. With every wound, betrayal, and disappointment you encounter along the path of life, these strongholds are only reinforced, giving room for the devil to continue lying to you.

How would you like to be free from the strongholds in your life? Let me suggest the weapon of choice: the Word of God, which is the sword of the Spirit. Remember how Jesus refuted Satan's lies in the wilderness with the words, "It is written . . . "? We can follow His example and shatter the lies of the enemy with the truth of the Word.

When Satan comes at you with the lie that your husband is no good and will never change, stand firm against him and declare, "It is written . . . 'He who finds a wife [or husband] finds a good thing'" (Prov. 18:22). You can do the same thing for any situation you might be facing.

Now the enemy will come back at you to destroy you, but if you will persevere and resist him (see James 4:7), he will flee! Imagine you are having an arm wrestling match. As long as you resist and apply pressure, your opponent cannot defeat you, and will eventually succumb. However, if you become distracted and let up for even a moment, your opponent can take advantage of your momentary instability and overtake you.

Stand firm, my friend; resist the devil so that he will flee, and the strongholds will come tumbling down!

Ruth Silvoso

Limits of Paul's Authority

[12][a]For we dare not class ourselves or
compare ourselves with those who commend themselves. But they, measuring
themselves by themselves, and comparing
themselves among themselves, are not
wise. [13][a]We, however, will not boast beyond measure, but within the limits of
the sphere which God appointed us—a
sphere which especially includes you.
[14]For we are not overextending ourselves
(as though *our authority* did not extend
to you), [a]for it was to you that we came
with the gospel of Christ; [15]not boasting
of things beyond measure, *that is,* [a]in other men's labors, but having hope, *that* as
your faith is increased, we shall be greatly
enlarged by you in our sphere, [16]to preach
the gospel in the *regions* beyond you, *and*
not to boast in another man's sphere of
accomplishment.
[17]But [a]*"he who glories, let him glory in
the LORD."* [18]For [a]not he who commends

12 a 2 Cor. 5:12
13 a 2 Cor. 10:15
14 a 1 Cor. 3:5, 6
15 a Rom. 15:20
17 a Jer. 9:24
18 a Prov. 27:2

HENRIETTA MEARS

Perhaps no one understood the importance of mentoring better than Henrietta Mears (1890–1963). While most have the opportunity to mentor one or two people in a lifetime, Henrietta took the world under her wings, seeing its need for powerful biblical teaching.

Known for her liveliness, wit, and straightforwardness, Henrietta was the ultimate Sunday school teacher. In 1928, she was hired as Director of Christian Education at the First Presbyterian Church in Hollywood, California. She quickly became bothered by the poor, often unscriptural material used to teach children, youth, and families the Word of God, and consequently she and her associates in the Sunday school began to write their own lessons. Within three years, the church's Sunday school attendance skyrocketed from 450 to 4,500, with the new Bible lessons being a primary reason.

For Henrietta, nothing could match the joy of seeing a life lining up in obedience to God's Word. She once remarked, "A bird is free in the air. Place a bird in water, and he has lost his liberty. A fish is free in the water, but leave him on the sand and he perishes. He is out of his realm. So, young people, the Christian is free when he does the will of God and is obedient to God's command. This is as natural a realm for God's child as the water is for the fish, or the air for the bird."

Henrietta's remarkable teaching and communication skills live on through the Sunday school curriculum of Gospel Light Publications, the publishing company she founded. The lessons have also been published in more than twenty languages. Her book, *What the Bible Is All About,* is one of the most popular and best-selling Christian books ever, and has been published in more than twenty-two languages. More importantly, however, Henrietta's passion for the Word lives on through the great men and women of God who have changed the world. Just as Henrietta Mears "multiplied" herself through influencing thousands of fervent Christians, may we as women of destiny start the multiplication process through sharing our gifts and talents with those around us.

himself is approved, but [b]whom the Lord commends.

Concern for Their Faithfulness

11 Oh, that you would bear with me in a little [a]folly—and indeed you do bear with me. 2For I am [a]jealous for you with godly jealousy. For [b]I have betrothed you to one husband, [c]that I may present *you* [d]*as* a chaste virgin to Christ. 3But I fear, lest somehow, as [a]the serpent deceived Eve by his craftiness, so your minds [b]may be corrupted from the [1]simplicity that is in Christ. 4For if he who comes preaches another Jesus whom we have not preached, or *if* you receive a different spirit which you have not received, or a [a]different gospel which you have not accepted—you may well put up with it!

Paul and False Apostles

5For I consider that [a]I am not at all inferior to the most eminent apostles. 6Even though [a]*I am* untrained in speech, yet *I am* not [b]in knowledge. But [c]we have [1]been thoroughly manifested among you in all things.

7Did I commit sin in [1]humbling myself that you might be exalted, because I preached the gospel of God to you [a]free of charge? 8I robbed other churches, taking wages *from them* to minister to you. 9And when I was present with you, and in need, [a]I was a burden to no one, for what I lacked [b]the brethren who came from Macedonia supplied. And in everything I kept myself from being burdensome to you, and so I will keep *myself.* 10[a]As the truth of Christ is in me, [b]no one shall stop me from this boasting in the regions of Achaia. 11Why? [a]Because I do not love you? God knows!

12But what I do, I will also continue to do, [a]that I may cut off the opportunity from those who desire an opportunity to be regarded just as we are in the things of which they boast. 13For such [a]*are* false apostles, [b]deceitful workers, transforming themselves into apostles of Christ. 14And no wonder! For Satan himself transforms himself into [a]an angel of light. 15Therefore *it is* no great thing if his ministers also transform themselves into ministers of righteousness, [a]whose end will be according to their works.

Reluctant Boasting

16I say again, let no one think me a fool. If otherwise, at least receive me as a fool, that I also may boast a little. 17What I speak, [a]I speak not according to the Lord, but as it were, foolishly, in this confidence of boasting. 18Seeing that many boast according to the flesh, I also will boast. 19For you put up with fools gladly, [a]since you *yourselves* are wise! 20For you put up with it [a]if one brings you into bondage, if one devours *you,* if one takes *from you,* if one exalts himself, if one strikes you on the face. 21To *our* shame [a]I say that we were too weak for that! But [b]in whatever anyone is bold—I speak foolishly—I am bold also.

Suffering for Christ

22Are they [a]Hebrews? So *am* I. Are they Israelites? So *am* I. Are they the seed of Abraham? So *am* I. 23Are they ministers of Christ?—I speak as a fool—I *am* more: [a]in labors more abundant, [b]in stripes above measure, in prisons more frequently, [c]in deaths often. 24From the Jews five times I received [a]forty [b]*stripes* minus one. 25Three times I was [a]beaten with rods; [b]once I was stoned; three times I [c]was shipwrecked; a night and a day I have been in the deep; 26*in* journeys often, *in* perils of waters, *in* perils of robbers, [a]*in* perils of *my own* countrymen, [b]*in* perils of the Gentiles, *in* perils in the city, *in* perils in the wilderness, *in* perils in the sea, *in* perils among false brethren; 27in weariness and toil, [a]in sleeplessness often, [b]in hunger and thirst, in [c]fastings often, in cold and nakedness— 28besides the other things, what comes upon me daily: [a]my deep concern for all the churches. 29[a]Who is weak, and I am not weak? Who is made to stumble, and I do not burn *with indignation?*

30If I must boast, [a]I will boast in the things which concern my [1]infirmity. 31[a]The God and Father of our Lord Jesus Christ, [b]who is blessed forever, knows that I am not lying. 32[a]In Damascus the governor, under Aretas the king, was guarding the city of the Damascenes with a garrison, desiring to arrest me; 33but I was let down in a basket through a window in the wall, and escaped from his hands.

18 b Rom. 2:29

CHAPTER 11

1 a 2 Cor. 11:4, 16, 19
2 a Gal. 4:17 b Hos. 2:19 c Col. 1:28 d Lev. 21:13
3 a Gen. 3:4, 13 b Eph. 6:24 *1 NU adds and purity*
4 a Gal. 1:6–8
5 a 2 Cor. 12:11
6 a [1 Cor. 1:17] b [Eph. 3:4] c [2 Cor. 12:12] *1 NU omits been*
7 a 1 Cor. 9:18 *1 putting myself down*
9 a Acts 20:33 b Phil. 4:10
10 a Rom. 1:9; 9:1 b 1 Cor. 9:15
11 a 2 Cor. 6:11; 12:15
12 a 1 Cor. 9:12
13 a Phil. 1:15 b Phil. 3:2
14 a Gal. 1:8
15 a [Phil. 3:19]
17 a 1 Cor. 7:6
19 a 1 Cor. 4:10
20 a [Gal. 2:4; 4:3, 9; 5:1]
21 a 2 Cor. 10:10 b Phil. 3:4
22 a Phil. 3:4–6
23 a 1 Cor. 15:10 b Acts 9:16 c 1 Cor. 15:30
24 a Deut. 25:3 b 2 Cor. 6:5
25 a Acts 16:22, 23; 21:32 b Acts 14:5, 19 c Acts 27:1–44
26 a Acts 9:23, 24; 13:45, 50; 17:5, 13 b Acts 14:5, 19; 19:23; 27:42
27 a Acts 20:31 b 1 Cor. 4:11 c Acts 9:9; 13:2, 3; 14:23
28 a Acts 20:18
29 a [1 Cor. 8:9, 13; 9:22]
30 a [2 Cor. 12:5, 9, 10] *1 weakness*
31 a 1 Thess. 2:5 b Rom. 9:5 32 a Acts 9:19–25

The Vision of Paradise

12 It is [1]doubtless not profitable for
me to boast. I will come to [a]visions
and [b]revelations of the Lord: 2I know a
man [a]in Christ who fourteen years ago—
whether in the body I do not know, or
whether out of the body I do not know,
God knows—such a one [b]was caught up
to the third heaven. 3And I know such a
man—whether in the body or out of the
body I do not know, God knows— 4how
he was caught up into [a]Paradise and
heard inexpressible words, which it is not
lawful for a man to utter. 5Of such a one
I will boast; yet of myself I will not [a]boast,
except in my infirmities. 6For though I
might desire to boast, I will not be a fool;
for I will speak the truth. But I refrain,
lest anyone should think of me above
what he sees me *to be* or hears from me.

The Thorn in the Flesh

7And lest I should be exalted above
measure by the abundance of the revela-
tions, a [a]thorn in the flesh was given to
me, [b]a messenger of Satan to [1]buffet me,
lest I be exalted above measure. 8[a]Con-
cerning this thing I pleaded with the Lord
three times that it might depart from me.
9 And He said to me, "My grace is sufficient for you, for My strength is made perfect in weakness." Therefore most gladly
[a]I will rather boast in my infirmities,
[b]that the power of Christ may rest upon
me. 10Therefore [a]I take pleasure in infirmities, in reproaches, in needs, in persecutions, in distresses, for Christ's sake.
[b]For when I am weak, then I am strong.

Father, Your grace is sufficient for ____, for Your strength is made perfect in weakness. Therefore may they gladly boast in their infirmities, that the power of Christ may rest upon them.

FROM 2 CORINTHIANS 12:9

Signs of an Apostle

11I have become [a]a fool [1]in boasting;
you have compelled me. For I ought to
have been commended by you; for [b]in
nothing was I behind the most eminent
apostles, though [c]I am nothing. 12[a]Truly
the signs of an apostle were accomplished
among you with all perseverance, in signs
and [b]wonders and mighty [c]deeds. 13For
what is it in which you were inferior to
other churches, except that I myself was
not burdensome to you? Forgive me this
wrong!

Love for the Church

14[a]Now *for* the third time I am ready to
come to you. And I will not be burdensome to you; for [b]I do not seek yours, but
you. [c]For the children ought not to lay up
for the parents, but the parents for the
children. 15And I will very gladly spend
and be spent [a]for your souls; though [b]the
more abundantly I love you, the less I am
loved.

16But be that *as it may,* [a]I did not burden you. Nevertheless, being crafty, I
caught you by cunning! 17Did I take advantage of you by any of those whom I
sent to you? 18I urged Titus, and sent our
[a]brother with *him.* Did Titus take advantage of you? Did we not walk in the same
spirit? Did *we* not *walk* in the same steps?

19[a]Again,[1] do you think that we excuse
ourselves to you? [b]We speak before God in
Christ. [c]But *we do* all things, beloved, for
your edification. 20For I fear lest, when I
come, I shall not find you such as I wish,
and *that* [a]I shall be found by you such as
you do not wish; lest *there be* contentions, jealousies, outbursts of wrath, selfish ambitions, backbitings, whisperings,
conceits, tumults; 21lest, when I come
again, my God [a]will humble me among
you, and I shall mourn for many [b]who
have sinned before and have not repented
of the uncleanness, [c]fornication, and
lewdness which they have practiced.

Coming with Authority

13 This *will be* [a]the third *time* I am
coming to you. [b]*"By the mouth of
two or three witnesses every word shall be
established."* 2[a]I have told you before, and
foretell as if I were present the second
time, and now being absent [1]I write to
those [b]who have sinned before, and to all
the rest, that if I come again [c]I will not
spare— 3since you seek a proof of Christ
[a]speaking in me, who is not weak toward

CHAPTER 12
1 a Acts 16:9; 18:9; 22:17, 18; 23:11; 26:13–15; 27:23 b [Gal. 1:12; 2:2] *1* NU *necessary, though not profitable, to boast*
2 a Rom. 16:7 b Acts 22:17
4 a Luke 23:43
5 a 2 Cor. 11:30
7 a Ezek. 28:24 b Job 2:7 *1 beat*
8 a Matt. 26:44
9 a 2 Cor. 11:30 b [1 Pet. 4:14]
10 a [Rom. 5:3; 8:35] b 2 Cor. 13:4
11 a 2 Cor. 5:13; 11:1, 16; 12:6 b 2 Cor. 11:5 c 1 Cor. 3:7; 13:2; 15:9 *1* NU omits *in boasting*
12 a Rom. 15:18 b Acts 15:12 c Acts 14:8–10; 16:16–18; 19:11, 12; 20:6–12; 28:1–10
14 a 2 Cor. 1:15; 13:1, 2 b [1 Cor. 10:24–33] c 1 Cor. 4:14
15 a [2 Tim. 2:10] b 2 Cor. 6:12, 13
16 a 2 Cor. 11:9
18 a 2 Cor. 8:18
19 a 2 Cor. 5:12 b [Rom. 9:1, 2] c 1 Cor. 10:33 *1* NU *You have been thinking for a long time that we*
20 a 1 Cor. 4:21
21 a 2 Cor. 2:1, 4 b 2 Cor. 13:2 c 1 Cor. 5:1

CHAPTER 13
1 a 2 Cor. 12:14 b Deut. 17:6; 19:15
2 a 2 Cor. 10:2 b 2 Cor. 12:21 c 2 Cor. 1:23; 10:11

1 NU omits *I write* **3** a Matt. 10:20

2 Corinthians 12:9, 10

Dear Woman of Destiny,

By the time we reach our teenage years, experts tell us, each of us has formed most of our core beliefs about ourselves. By then, based on our interpretation of the messages around us, we have decided whether we "measure up," and our personal identity is generally firmly in place.

Words spoken by parents, teachers, peers, and even strangers begin to form a picture in our hearts of who we are. Sometimes the messages are derived from the absence of words and warmth. Then there is the message our culture sends, the standards of acceptability communicated loudly and incessantly through the media.

God intended that who we are would be mirrored by others in our lives, affirmed and confirmed by them. He intended that we would communicate to each other His truth about us, "the edifying of itself [each other] in love" (Eph. 4:16).

Unfortunately, the inner picture we have formed of ourselves is flawed, retouched by the "accuser of our brethren," whose job it is to rob, kill, and destroy through deception what God has created. Satan's intent is to cripple us when we are most vulnerable, most insecure, and, thus, most susceptible to his lies.

The snare Satan set for Eve in the garden was to convince her that something was wrong with her, that she was lacking and defective, that this life was about her and what she could accomplish. As a result, she became self-focused, looking to herself to make up the difference. This, in turn, led her away from her true life Source, thus causing her to sin.

Satan uses this same tactic today, and Christians are probably his most specific target. "See," whispers the enemy, "you still don't have it together. Other Christians look better, pray longer, know more scripture, walk in greater victory. The blood of Jesus may get you to heaven, but here on earth . . . you're still not good enough."

So the game becomes: What can I do to keep others from discovering my terrible secret? We do the same thing Adam and Eve did when they believed the lie. We try to make up for the deficit in our own wisdom. We update our wardrobe, upgrade our vehicle, join more committees, earn more degrees, work harder, try to amass more money. Or we drop out altogether: We drink, do drugs, overeat, get depressed or just vegetate in front of the TV.

True freedom comes when we simply admit we really are insufficient and inadequate—that we always have been, are now, and always will be. To admit such deficiency is to die to self. This is precisely what God is after! He wants to bring us to the place of renouncing all our ways of self-relating, self-dependence, and self-sufficiency.

The message that tripped up Eve was not merely that she was insufficient, but also that her condition was flawed and unacceptable. The truth is, weakness and insufficiency are part of our design, primary components of what it means to be human. Insufficient in ourselves, we are perfectly designed to be vessels filled with God, to live and love out of His life, and thereby accomplish His purposes on earth.

Jane Hansen

you, but mighty [b]in you. [4][a]For though He
was crucified in weakness, yet [b]He lives by
the power of God. For [c]we also are weak
in Him, but we shall live with Him by the
power of God toward you.

And Satan trembles when he sees the weakest saint upon his knees.

WILLIAM COWPER

[5]Examine yourselves *as to* whether you
are in the faith. Test yourselves. Do you
not know yourselves, [a]that Jesus Christ is
in you?—unless indeed you [1]are [b]disqual-
ified. [6]But I trust that you will know that
we are not disqualified.

Paul Prefers Gentleness

[7]Now [1]I pray to God that you do no evil,
not that we should appear approved, but
that you should do what is honorable,
though [a]we may seem disqualified. [8]For
we can do nothing against the truth, but
for the truth. [9]For we are glad [a]when we
are weak and you are strong. And this also
we pray, [b]that you may be made complete.
[10][a]Therefore I write these things being
absent, lest being present I should use
sharpness, according to the [b]authority
which the Lord has given me for edification and not for destruction.

Greetings and Benediction

[11]Finally, brethren, farewell. Become
complete. [a]Be of good comfort, be of one
mind, live in peace; and the God of love
[b]and peace will be with you.
[12][a]Greet one another with a holy kiss.
[13]All the saints greet you.
[14][a]The grace of the Lord Jesus Christ,
and the love of God, and [b]the [1]commu-
nion of the Holy Spirit *be* with you all.
Amen.

Be aware of God's presence, without interruption, throughout your entire day. As soon as your eyes close in prayer, you should be blessed by the joy of communion with Him in which external events cannot interrupt.

MADAME JEANNE GUYON

---

3 b[1 Cor. 9:2]
4 a[1 Pet. 3:18] b[Rom. 1:4; 6:4] c[2 Cor. 10:3, 4]
5 a[Gal. 4:19] b1 Cor. 9:27 *1 do not stand the test*
7 a2 Cor. 6:9 *1* NU *we*
9 a1 Cor. 4:10 b[1 Thess. 3:10]
10 a1 Cor. 4:21 b2 Cor. 10:8
11 aRom. 12:16, 18 bRom. 15:33
12 aRom. 16:16
14 aRom. 16:24 bPhil. 2:1 *1 fellowship*

AUTHOR: *Paul*
DATE: *A.D. 55–56*
THEME: *Justification by Faith Alone*
KEY WORDS: *Grace, Gospel, Faith, Justified, Promise, Liberty, Law*

GALATIANS

Dear Woman of Destiny,

Galatians tells us that we are set free from the law in order to pursue our destiny in God. This book was written in the time of Christ when women were not considered to be on a par with men. They were not inheritors in their society. The Holy Spirit makes some radical, revolutionary statements in Galatians, which show that God wanted His daughters to fully partake of His kingdom. In Galatians 3:26, for example, He calls all of us—both men and women—"sons," or inheritors, "through faith in Christ Jesus." Giving us all the status of sonship, His message to us sweeps on through Galatians 3:28, which says, "There is neither Jew nor Greek, there is neither slave nor free, there is neither male nor female; for you are all one in Christ Jesus." Powerful! Amazing! Standing on God's promises, there are no limits to what you can do in His kingdom as a woman of destiny!

With His love,

Cindy Jacobs

Greeting

Paul, an apostle (not from men nor
through man, but [a]through Jesus
Christ and God the Father [b]who
raised Him from the dead), 2and all the
brethren who are with me,

To the churches of Galatia:

3Grace to you and peace from God the
Father and our Lord Jesus Christ, 4[a]who
gave Himself for our sins, that He might
deliver us [b]from this present evil age, according to the will of our God and Father,
5to whom *be* glory forever and ever.
Amen.

Grace to ____ and peace from God the Father and our Lord Jesus Christ, who gave Himself for their sins that He might deliver them from this present evil age, according to the will of our God and Father.

FROM GALATIANS 1:3, 4

Only One Gospel

6I marvel that you are turning away so
soon [a]from Him who called you in the
grace of Christ, to a different gospel,
7[a]which is not another; but there are
some [b]who trouble you and want to [c]per-
vert[1] the gospel of Christ. 8But even if
[a]we, or an angel from heaven, preach any
other gospel to you than what we have
preached to you, let him be [1]accursed.
9As we have said before, so now I say
again, if anyone preaches any other gospel
to you [a]than what you have received, let
him be accursed.

10For [a]do I now [b]persuade men, or
God? Or [c]do I seek to please men? For if
I still pleased men, I would not be a bond-
servant of Christ.

Call to Apostleship

11[a]But I make known to you, brethren,
that the gospel which was preached by me
is not according to man. 12For [a]I neither
received it from man, nor was I taught *it,*
but *it came* [b]through the revelation of Jesus Christ.

13For you have heard of my former conduct in Judaism, how [a]I persecuted the
church of God beyond measure and [b]*tried
to* destroy it. 14And I advanced in Judaism
beyond many of my contemporaries in my
own nation, [a]being more exceedingly
zealous [b]for the traditions of my fathers.

15But when it pleased God, [a]who separated me from my mother's womb and
called *me* through His grace, 16[a]to reveal
His Son in me, that [b]I might preach Him
among the Gentiles, I did not immediately
confer with [c]flesh and blood, 17nor did I
go up to Jerusalem to those *who were*
apostles before me; but I went to Arabia,
and returned again to Damascus.

Contacts at Jerusalem

18Then after three years [a]I went up to
Jerusalem to see [1]Peter, and remained
with him fifteen days. 19But [a]I saw none
of the other apostles except [b]James, the
Lord's brother. 20(Now *concerning* the
things which I write to you, indeed, before
God, I do not lie.)

21[a]Afterward I went into the regions of
Syria and Cilicia. 22And I was unknown by
face to the churches of Judea which [a]*were*
in Christ. 23But they were [a]hearing only,
"He who formerly [b]persecuted us now
preaches the faith which he once *tried to*
destroy." 24And they [a]glorified God in me.

Defending the Gospel

2 Then after fourteen years [a]I went up
again to Jerusalem with Barnabas,
and also took Titus with *me.* 2And I went
up [1]by revelation, and communicated to
them that gospel which I preach among
the Gentiles, but [a]privately to those who
were of reputation, lest by any means [b]I
might run, or had run, in vain. 3Yet not
even Titus who *was* with me, being a
Greek, was compelled to be circumcised.
4And *this occurred* because of [a]false
brethren secretly brought in (who came
in by stealth to spy out our [b]liberty which
we have in Christ Jesus, [c]that they might
bring us into bondage), 5to whom we did
not yield submission even for an hour,
that [a]the truth of the gospel might continue with you.

6But from those [a]who seemed to be
something—whatever they were, it
makes no difference to me; [b]God [1]shows
personal favoritism to no man—for those

CHAPTER 1
1 a Acts 9:6 b Acts 2:24
4 a [Matt. 20:28] b Heb. 2:5
6 a Gal. 1:15; 5:8
7 a 2 Cor. 11:4 b Gal. 5:10, 12 c 2 Cor. 2:17 *1 distort*
8 a 1 Cor. 16:22 *1* Gr. *anathema*
9 a Deut. 4:2
10 a 1 Thess. 2:4 b 1 Sam. 24:7 c 1 Thess. 2:4
11 a 1 Cor. 15:1
12 a 1 Cor. 15:1 b [Eph. 3:3–5]
13 a Acts 9:1 b Acts 8:3; 22:4, 5
14 a Acts 26:9 b Jer. 9:14
15 a Is. 49:1, 5
16 a [2 Cor. 4:5–7] b Acts 9:15 c Matt. 16:17
18 a Acts 9:26 *1* NU *Cephas*
19 a 1 Cor. 9:5 b Matt. 13:55
21 a Acts 9:30
22 a Rom. 16:7
23 a Acts 9:20, 21 b Acts 8:3
24 a Acts 11:18

CHAPTER 2
1 a Acts 15:2
2 a Acts 15:1–4 b Phil. 2:16 *1 because of*
4 a Acts 15:1, 24 b Gal. 3:25; 5:1, 13 c Gal. 4:3, 9
5 a [Gal. 1:6; 2:14; 3:1]
6 a Gal. 2:9; 6:3 b Acts 10:34 *1* Lit. *does not receive the face of a man*

GALATIANS 1:8

Dear Woman of Destiny,

How you align your life with the gospel will greatly impact your destiny. The gospel is not a dogma to be adhered to, but a life-giving force that transforms our lives and brings us into intimate relationship with Almighty God as our loving Father.

The gospel is "the power of God to salvation for everyone who believes" (Rom. 1:16). It is not a message or doctrine delivered by man, but a revelation of Jesus Christ manifested through the Holy Spirit. There is *no other name* and *no other gospel* through which men can be saved, healed, restored, and delivered.

The gospel of Jesus Christ is the strong, immovable foundation upon which your life must be firmly anchored. To fulfill your destiny and experience the fullness of all that God has purposed for your life, the Word must become "flesh" within you. It must be so much a part of your life that there will be a continual transformation taking place within you, whereby you are constantly being changed and conformed into Christ's image.

In Galatians 1, the apostle Paul addresses a serious problem within the churches in Galatia—a problem that we must guard against today. The Christians had turned away from the gospel of Jesus Christ to accept "a different gospel" from teachers who were perverting the true gospel.

There is no other gospel! There is only one. By embracing the false teaching they had heard, these believers were not simply turning away from a doctrine, but from God who had called them to faith in Jesus Christ.

Jesus warned that before His second coming there will be false teachers and prophets within the church who will deceive and seduce Christians away from the truth. Paul warned of "savage wolves" and even men among themselves who would "rise up, speaking perverse things, to draw away the disciples after themselves" (Acts 20:30). He spent three long years agonizing and warning them with tears about this grave danger.

As a woman of destiny, you must establish a standard for your life, whereby you will not accept a "substitute" gospel or any teaching that does not line up with what has been revealed by the Holy Spirit through the Word.

You must refuse to accept a watered down version of the gospel that compromises with the world's standards. When ministering the Word or sharing the gospel, there can be no alternative or substitute for the truth.

The greatest safeguard against deception is to have a passionate love relationship with Christ. When you know Him intimately, He will expose the false and reveal the truth.

To fulfill God's destiny, make the gospel of Jesus Christ the central focus of your life. Submerge yourself in the Word. Align your life, work, and ministry with truth as revealed in His Word. Refuse to compromise.

The gospel is a treasure God has entrusted into your hands to bring salvation, healing, and deliverance to people in your neighborhood, city, and nation. Cherish it, proclaim it, and be willing to die for it.

Connie Broome

who seemed *to be something* [c]added nothing to me. 7But on the contrary, [a]when they saw that the gospel for the uncircumcised [b]had been committed to me, as *the gospel* for the circumcised *was* to Peter 8(for He who worked effectively in Peter for the apostleship to the [a]circumcised [b]also [c]worked effectively in me toward the Gentiles), 9and when James, [1]Cephas, and John, who seemed to be [a]pillars, perceived [b]the grace that had been given to me, they gave me and Barnabas the right hand of fellowship, [c]that we *should go* to the Gentiles and they to the circumcised. 10*They desired* only that we should remember the poor, [a]the very thing which I also was eager to do.

No Return to the Law

11[a]Now when [1]Peter had come to Antioch, I [2]withstood him to his face, because he was to be blamed; 12for before certain men came from James, [a]he would eat with the Gentiles; but when they came, he withdrew and separated himself, fearing [1]those who were of the circumcision. 13And the rest of the Jews also played the hypocrite with him, so that even Barnabas was carried away with their hypocrisy.

14But when I saw that they were not straightforward about [a]the truth of the gospel, I said to Peter [b]before *them* all, [c]"If you, being a Jew, live in the manner of Gentiles and not as the Jews, [1]why do you compel Gentiles to live as [2]Jews? 15[a]We *who are* Jews by nature, and not [b]sinners of the Gentiles, 16[a]knowing that a man is not [1]justified by the works of the law but [b]by faith in Jesus Christ, even we have believed in Christ Jesus, that we might be justified by faith in Christ and not [c]by the works of the law; for by the works of the law no flesh shall be justified.

17"But if, while we seek to be justified by Christ, we ourselves also are found [a]sinners, *is* Christ therefore a minister of sin? Certainly not! 18For if I build again those things which I destroyed, I make myself a transgressor. 19For I [a]through the law [b]died to the law that I might [c]live to God. 20I have been [a]crucified with Christ; it is no longer I who live, but Christ lives in me; and the *life* which I now live in the flesh [b]I live by faith in the Son of God, [c]who loved me and gave Himself for me. 21I do not set aside the grace of God; for [a]if righteousness *comes* through the law, then Christ died [1]in vain."

The secret of Christianity is the secret of Christ possessing the heart of man; man being yielded to Him so that His victory, His consciousness, and His power possess your spirit and mind.

JOHN G. LAKE

Justification by Faith

3 O foolish Galatians! Who has bewitched you [1]that you should not obey the truth, before whose eyes Jesus Christ was clearly portrayed [2]among you as crucified? 2This only I want to learn from you: Did you receive the Spirit by the works of the law, [a]or by the hearing of faith? 3Are you so foolish? [a]Having begun in the Spirit, are you now being made perfect by [b]the flesh? 4[a]Have you suffered so [1]many things in vain—if indeed *it was* in vain?

5Therefore He who supplies the Spirit to you and works miracles among you, *does He do it* by the works of the law, or by the hearing of faith?— 6just as Abraham [a]*"believed God, and it was accounted to him for righteousness."* 7Therefore know that *only* [a]those who are of faith are sons of Abraham. 8And [a]the Scripture, foreseeing that God would justify the Gentiles by faith, preached the gospel to Abraham beforehand, *saying,* [b]*"In you all the nations shall be blessed."* 9So then those who *are* of faith are blessed with believing Abraham.

The Law Brings a Curse

10For as many as are of the works of the law are under the curse; for it is written, [a]*"Cursed is everyone who does not continue in all things which are written in the book of the law, to do them."* 11But

6 c 2 Cor. 11:5; 12:11
7 a Acts 9:15; 13:46; 22:21 b 1 Thess. 2:4
8 a 1 Pet. 1:1 b Acts 9:15 c [Gal. 3:5]
9 a Matt. 16:18 b Rom. 1:5 c Acts 13:3 *1* Peter
10 a Acts 11:30
11 a Acts 15:35 *1* NU *Cephas* *2 opposed*
12 a [Acts 10:28; 11:2, 3] *1* Jewish Christians
14 a Gal. 1:6; 2:5 b 1 Tim. 5:20 c [Acts 10:28] *1* NU *how can you* *2* Some interpreters stop the quotation here.
15 a [Acts 15:10] b Matt. 9:11
16 a Acts 13:38, 39 b Rom. 1:17 c Ps. 143:2 *1 declared righteous*
17 a [1 John 3:8]
19 a Rom. 8:2 b [Rom. 6:2, 14; 7:4] c [Rom. 6:11]
20 a [Rom. 6:6] b 2 Cor. 5:15 c Eph. 5:2
21 a Heb. 7:11 *1 for nothing*

CHAPTER 3
1 *1* NU omits *that you should not obey the truth* *2* NU omits *among you*
2 a Rom. 10:16, 17
3 a [Gal. 4:9] b Heb. 7:16
4 a Heb. 10:35 *1* Or *great*
6 a Gen. 15:6
7 a John 8:39
8 a Rom. 9:17 b Gen. 12:3; 18:18; 22:18; 26:4; 28:14
10 a Deut. 27:26

that no one is [1]justified by the law in the sight of God *is* evident, for [a]*"the just shall live by faith."* 12Yet [a]the law is not of faith, but [b]*"the man who does them shall live by them."*

13[a]Christ has redeemed us from the curse of the law, having become a curse for us (for it is written, [b]*"Cursed is everyone who hangs on a tree"*), 14[a]that the blessing of Abraham might come upon the [b]Gentiles in Christ Jesus, that we might receive [c]the promise of the Spirit through faith.

Father, You have redeemed ____ through Christ from the curse of the law, for He became a curse for them. May the blessing of Abraham come upon them in Christ Jesus, that they might receive the promise of the Spirit through faith.

FROM GALATIANS 3:13, 14

The Changeless Promise

15Brethren, I speak in the manner of men: [a]Though *it is* only a man's covenant, yet *if it is* confirmed, no one annuls or adds to it. 16Now to Abraham and his Seed were the promises made. He does not say, "And to seeds," as of many, but as of [a]one, [b]*"And to your Seed,"* who is [c]Christ. 17And this I say, *that* the law, [a]which was four hundred and thirty years later, cannot annul the covenant that was confirmed before by God [1]in Christ, [b]that it should make the promise of no effect. 18For if [a]the inheritance *is* of the law, [b]*it is* no longer of promise; but God gave *it* to Abraham by promise.

Purpose of the Law

19What purpose then *does* the law *serve?* [a]It was added because of transgressions, till the [b]Seed should come to whom the promise was made; *and it was* [c]appointed through angels by the hand [d]of a mediator. 20Now a mediator does not *mediate* for one *only,* [a]but God is one.

21*Is* the law then against the promises of God? Certainly not! For if there had been a law given which could have given life, truly righteousness would have been by the law. 22But the Scripture has confined [a]all under sin, [b]that the promise by faith in Jesus Christ might be given to those who believe. 23But before faith came, we were kept under guard by the law, [1]kept for the faith which would afterward be revealed. 24Therefore [a]the law was our [1]tutor *to bring us* to Christ, [b]that we might be justified by faith. 25But after faith has come, we are no longer under a tutor.

Sons and Heirs

26For you [a]are all sons of God through faith in Christ Jesus. 27For [a]as many of you as were baptized into Christ [b]have put on Christ. 28[a]There is neither Jew nor Greek, [b]there is neither slave nor free, there is neither male nor female; for you are all [c]one in Christ Jesus. 29And [a]if you *are* Christ's, then you are Abraham's [b]seed, and [c]heirs according to the promise.

4 Now I say *that* the heir, as long as he is a child, does not differ at all from a slave, though he is master of all, 2but is under guardians and stewards until the time appointed by the father. 3Even so we, when we were children, [a]were in bondage under the elements of the world. 4But [a]when the fullness of the time had come, God sent forth His Son, [b]born[1] [c]of a woman, [d]born under the law, 5[a]to redeem those who were under the law, [b]that we might receive the adoption as sons.

6And because you are sons, God has sent forth [a]the Spirit of His Son into your hearts, crying out, [1]"Abba, Father!" 7Therefore you are no longer a slave but a son, [a]and if a son, then an heir [1]of God [2]through Christ.

Fears for the Church

8But then, indeed, [a]when you did not know God, [b]you served those which by nature are not gods. 9But now [a]after you have known God, or rather are known by God, [b]how *is it that* you turn again to [c]the weak and beggarly elements, to which you desire again to be in bondage? 10[a]You observe days and months and seasons and

11 [a] Hab. 2:4 [1] *declared righteous*
12 [a] Rom. 4:4, 5 [b] Lev. 18:5
13 [a] [Rom. 8:3] [b] Deut. 21:23
14 [a] [Rom. 4:1–5, 9, 16] [b] Rom. 3:29, 30 [c] Is. 32:15
15 [a] Heb. 9:17
16 [a] Gen. 22:18 [b] Gen. 12:3, 7; 13:15; 24:7 [c] [1 Cor. 12:12]
17 [a] Ex. 12:40 [b] [Rom. 4:13] [1] NU omits *in Christ*
18 [a] [Rom. 8:17] [b] Rom. 4:14
19 [a] John 15:22 [b] Gal. 4:4 [c] Acts 7:53 [d] Ex. 20:19
20 [a] [Rom. 3:29]
22 [a] Rom. 11:32 [b] Rom. 4:11
23 [1] Lit. *confined*
24 [a] Rom. 10:4 [b] Acts 13:39 [1] In a household, the guardian responsible for the care and discipline of the children
26 [a] John 1:12
27 [a] [Rom. 6:3] [b] Rom. 10:12; 13:14
28 [a] Col. 3:11 [b] [1 Cor. 12:13] [c] [Eph. 2:15, 16]
29 [a] Gen. 21:10 [b] Rom. 4:11 [c] Rom. 8:17

CHAPTER 4
3 [a] Col. 2:8, 20
4 [a] [Gen. 49:10] [b] [John 1:14] [c] Gen. 3:15 [d] Luke 2:21, 27 [1] Or *made*
5 [a] [Matt. 20:28] [b] [John 1:12]
6 [a] [Rom. 5:5; 8:9, 15, 16] [1] Lit., in Aram., *Father*
7 [a] [Rom. 8:16, 17] [1] NU *through God* [2] NU omits *through Christ*
8 [a] Eph. 2:12 [b] Rom. 1:25
9 [a] [1 Cor. 8:3] [b] Col. 2:20 [c] Heb. 7:18
10 [a] Rom. 14:5

GALATIANS 4:4–7

Dear Woman of Destiny,

God is a good God, who sent His Son to be born of a woman, live a sinless life, die for our sins, and rise to live eternally. What a life! And what a picture—for a woman to raise the very Son of God!

The mother and Holy Son together is likely the most painted subject in history. Regardless of how many images we see of movie stars or royalty, the artist's impression of young Mary makes her the most recognizable woman on earth. Why the fame? Because she was a *mother!*

In Galatians 4:4, Paul emphasizes the importance of Jesus having been "born of a woman." From placing the newborn Jesus in a manger to watching each drop of His redeeming blood fall from the cross, Mary understood the God-given intimacy that only a mother can share with her child.

Motherhood provides some of our greatest tests and greatest joys. My initial look at my firstborn, Paul, sent a thrill through me that has never left. Motherhood is a source of pride—a joy! Then I got home from the hospital and there came the tests. First was to give my children a peaceful house. That meant getting along with my husband! Next and most importantly was to ensure they made a choice to follow God wholeheartedly. I wanted my children's choice of a mate, career, and hundreds of life decisions to be based on their first major decision, to follow Christ.

Edwin and I pursued our goals with intense prayer, and now have the joy of seeing our grandchildren also following Christ. But like everyone, we have regrets and realize many mistakes we made. Dozens of mothers have told me they wish they could start over. Hundreds of parents have done "right," yet have seen it blow up and turn out "wrong." If that's you, remember that God never gave up on you. Don't you give up on them!

There is so much to learn, and mothering changes as the child matures. Pointing out our older children's wrongdoing often makes them minimize the negative consequences, which they must acknowledge in order to learn. The worst case is when conflict becomes a test of wills. The mother always loses short-term. The child always loses long-term.

Having the 20–20 vision of retrospect, here are ten things I recommend to mothers overall:

- Keep a godly atmosphere in the home. That comes straight out of your own spirit and devotional time with the Lord.
- Don't miss church. Show by your actions that it is important to you.
- Don't undermine parental authority by disagreeing with your husband in front of your children.
- Refrain from gossip.
- Maintain family devotions.
- Know the young man or woman your child "likes."
- Give children latitude.
- Invite godly people to your home.
- Forgive your children daily.
- Know what your children see on television and the internet.

God honored motherhood by bringing His Son to the earth through an earthly mother. Mary's fame and joy came from her motherhood. You can take joy in your motherhood, too!

Nancy Corbett Cole

years. 11I am afraid for you, [a]lest I have
labored for you in vain.
12Brethren, I urge you to become like
me, for I *became* like you. [a]You have not
injured me at all. 13You know that [a]be-
cause of physical infirmity I preached the
gospel to you at the first. 14And my trial
which was in my flesh you did not despise
or reject, but you received me [a]as an [1]an-
gel of God, [b]*even* as Christ Jesus. 15[1]What
then was the blessing you *enjoyed?* For
I bear you witness that, if possible, you
would have plucked out your own eyes
and given them to me. 16Have I therefore
become your enemy because I tell you the
truth?
17They [a]zealously court you, *but* for no
good; yes, they want to exclude you, that
you may be zealous for them. 18But it is
good to be zealous in a good thing always,
and not only when I am present with you.
19[a]My little children, for whom I labor in
birth again until Christ is formed in you,
20I would like to be present with you now
and to change my tone; for I have doubts
about you.

Two Covenants

21Tell me, you who desire to be under
the law, do you not hear the law? 22For it
is written that Abraham had two sons:
[a]the one by a bondwoman, [b]the other by
a freewoman. 23But he *who was* of the
bondwoman [a]was born according to the
flesh, [b]and he of the freewoman through
promise, 24which things are symbolic. For
these are [1]the two covenants: the one
from Mount [a]Sinai which gives birth to
bondage, which is Hagar— 25for this Hagar is Mount Sinai in Arabia, and corresponds to Jerusalem which now is, and is
in bondage with her children— 26but the
[a]Jerusalem above is free, which is the
mother of us all. 27For it is written:

[a]*"Rejoice, O barren,*
You who do not bear!
Break forth and shout,
You who are not in labor!
For the desolate has many more
children
Than she who has a husband."

28Now [a]we, brethren, as Isaac *was,* are
[b]children of promise. 29But, as [a]he who
was born according to the flesh then persecuted him *who was born* according to
the Spirit, [b]even so *it is* now. 30Neverthe-
less what does [a]the Scripture say? [b]*"Cast*

11 a 1 Thess. 3:5
12 a 2 Cor. 2:5
13 a 1 Cor. 2:3
14 a Mal. 2:7 b [Luke 10:16] *1 Or messenger*
15 *1 NU Where*
17 a Rom. 10:2
19 a 1 Cor. 4:15
22 a Gen. 16:15 b Gen. 21:2
23 a Rom. 9:7, 8 b Heb. 11:11
24 a Deut. 33:2 *1 NU, M omit the*
26 a [Is. 2:2]
27 a Is. 54:1
28 a Gal. 3:29 b Acts 3:25
29 a Gen. 21:9 b Gal. 5:11
30 a [Gal. 3:8, 22] b Gen. 21:10, 12 c [John 8:35]

CHAPTER 5
1 a Phil. 4:1 b Acts 15:10 *1 NU For freedom Christ has made us free; stand fast therefore, and*
2 a Acts 15:1
3 a [Rom. 2:25] *1 obligated*
4 a [Rom. 9:31] b Heb. 12:15
5 a Rom. 8:24
6 a [Gal. 6:15] b 1 Thess. 1:3
7 a 1 Cor. 9:24
9 a 1 Cor. 5:6
11 a 1 Cor. 15:30 b [1 Cor. 1:23]
12 a Josh. 7:25 b Acts 15:1, 2 *1 mutilate themselves*
13 a 1 Cor. 8:9 b 1 Pet. 2:16 c 1 Cor. 9:19
14 a Matt. 7:12; 22:40 b Lev. 19:18

out the bondwoman and her son, for [c]the
son of the bondwoman shall not be heir
with the son of the freewoman." 31So
then, brethren, we are not children of the
bondwoman but of the free.

Christian Liberty

5 Stand[a][1] fast therefore in the liberty
by which Christ has made us free, and
do not be entangled again with a [b]yoke of
bondage. 2Indeed I, Paul, say to you
that [a]if you become circumcised, Christ
will profit you nothing. 3And I testify
again to every man who becomes circumcised [a]that he is [1]a debtor to keep the
whole law. 4[a]You have become estranged
from Christ, you who *attempt to* be justified by law; [b]you have fallen from grace.
5For we through the Spirit eagerly [a]wait
for the hope of righteousness by faith.
6For [a]in Christ Jesus neither circumcision nor uncircumcision avails anything,
but [b]faith working through love.

Love Fulfills the Law

7You [a]ran well. Who hindered you from
obeying the truth? 8This persuasion does
not *come* from Him who calls you. 9[a]A
little leaven leavens the whole lump. 10I
have confidence in you, in the Lord, that
you will have no other mind; but he who
troubles you shall bear his judgment,
whoever he is.
11And I, brethren, if I still preach circumcision, [a]why do I still suffer persecution? Then [b]the offense of the cross has
ceased. 12[a]I could wish that those [b]who
trouble you would even [1]cut themselves
off!

Thank You that _____ has
been called to liberty, Father;
may they not use liberty as
an opportunity for the flesh,
but through love serve others.
FROM GALATIANS 5:13

13For you, brethren, have been called to
liberty; only [a]do not *use* liberty as an [b]op-
portunity for the flesh, but [c]through love
serve one another. 14For [a]all the law is
fulfilled in one word, *even* in this: [b]*"You*

Galatians 5:1

Dear Woman of Destiny,

I love to think about true freedom. I discovered it in the most unlikely place—a federal women's prison. As the Spirit of God began to teach me the real lessons of liberty, I began to see that the spirit of this world is relentlessly bombarding our hearts and minds with images and thoughts of false freedom and liberty. Commercials, movies, and billboards broadcast that "doing your own thing" will give you a life of freedom. Even in the church we hear messages suggesting that freedom is found in what we do and how well we perform.

The gospel declares that freedom is only found in faith in Jesus and the work of the Cross. It is Jesus who has made us free by satisfying the demands of the broken law; and by His authority as King, He has released us from every obligation of the law. Galatians 3:13 says that our freedom from the curse of the law comes only because Jesus took our place and became a curse for us when He hung on a tree. He bore the very curse that we were all destined for. We are not to depend on anything that we do or don't do to acquire our freedom, but are to depend only on our faith in what Jesus has done for us.

Once we depend on Jesus as the sole source of our freedom, our responsibility is to stand fast in that liberty. We must constantly resist any temptation to think that our efforts or accomplishments have contributed to the gift of freedom we can enjoy. Our position in God is not based on how much we pray, fast, tithe, or serve the poor. Our good deeds to others do not qualify as payment for our freedom. The chasm between God and us caused by the fall of man in the Garden cannot be satisfied by anything we do. The only thing that will satisfy the debt that sin has caused is the sinless blood sacrifice of Jesus (see Heb. 9:22).

Jesus is "able to save the uttermost" (Heb. 7:25) but there are multitudes who will profit nothing from His precious sacrifice because they are depending on their own works and performance to "buy" their freedom. The gospel requires that all our hopes be placed in Jesus as the sole source of our freedom and salvation. We must stand fast in our freedom by continually keeping our faith in Jesus and His sacrifice on the cross.

The world and religion encourages you to put on the yoke of performance, but you must stand against this. You might be trapped in the snare of believing that your performance has a part to play in your freedom. The Lord does want us living lives reflecting the fruit of the Spirit, filled with integrity, honesty, and excellence, but we must see that it is only through Jesus that we have true liberty and freedom. Whether you are physically incarcerated or find yourself in an emotional "prison," I pray that the Holy Spirit will stir your faith to fully lean on Jesus, the true source of freedom, and that you will begin to apply God's Word, follow the Holy Spirit, and experience real liberty.

Mary Forsythe

shall love your neighbor as yourself."
15 But if you bite and devour one another,
beware lest you be consumed by one another!

Walking in the Spirit

16 I say then: [a]Walk in the Spirit, and
you shall not fulfill the lust of the flesh.
17 For [a]the flesh lusts against the Spirit,
and the Spirit against the flesh; and these
are contrary to one another, [b]so that you
do not do the things that you wish. 18 But
[a]if you are led by the Spirit, you are not
under the law.
19 Now [a]the works of the flesh are evident, which are: [1]adultery, [2]fornication,
uncleanness, lewdness, 20 idolatry, sorcery, hatred, contentions, jealousies, outbursts of wrath, selfish ambitions,
dissensions, heresies, 21 envy, [1]murders,
drunkenness, revelries, and the like; of
which I tell you beforehand, just as I also
told *you* in time past, that [a]those who
practice such things will not inherit the
kingdom of God.

> *The fruit of the Spirit is the direct result of the life of Christ ministered to the believer by the Spirit.*
>
> DONALD GEE

22 But [a]the fruit of the Spirit is [b]love,
joy, peace, longsuffering, kindness,
[c]goodness, [d]faithfulness, 23 [1]gentleness,
self-control. [a]Against such there is no
law. 24 And those *who are* Christ's [a]have
crucified the flesh with its passions and
desires. 25 [a]If we live in the Spirit, let us
also walk in the Spirit. 26 [a]Let us not become conceited, provoking one another,
envying one another.

Bear and Share the Burdens

6 Brethren, if a man is [1]overtaken in
any trespass, you who *are* spiritual restore such a one in a spirit of [a]gentleness,
considering yourself lest you also be
tempted. 2 [a]Bear one another's burdens,
and so fulfill [b]the law of Christ. 3 For [a]if
anyone thinks himself to be something,
when [b]he is nothing, he deceives himself.
4 But [a]let each one examine his own work,
and then he will have rejoicing in himself
alone, and [b]not in another. 5 For [a]each
one shall bear his own load.

> *Lord, may ____ not grow weary while doing good, for in due season they will reap if they do not lose heart.*
>
> FROM GALATIANS 6:9

Be Generous and Do Good

6 [a]Let him who is taught the word share
in all good things with him who teaches.
7 Do not be deceived, God is not
mocked; for [a]whatever a man sows, that
he will also reap. 8 For he who sows to his
flesh will of the flesh reap corruption, but
he who sows to the Spirit will of the Spirit
reap [a]everlasting life. 9 And [a]let us not
grow weary while doing good, for in due
season we shall reap [b]if we do not lose
heart. 10 [a]Therefore, as we have opportunity, [b]let us do good to all, [c]especially to
those who are of the household of faith.

> *We ought not to be weary of doing little things for the love of God, who regards not the greatness of the work, but the love with which it is performed.*
>
> BROTHER LAWRENCE

Glory Only in the Cross

11 See with what large letters I have
written to you with my own hand! 12 As
many as desire to make a good showing in
the flesh, these *would* compel you to be
circumcised, [a]only that they may not suffer persecution for the cross of Christ.
13 For not even those who are circumcised

---

16 a Rom. 6:12
17 a Rom. 7:18, 22, 23; 8:5 b Rom. 7:15
18 a [Rom. 6:14; 7:4; 8:14]
19 a Eph. 5:3, 11 *1* NU omits *adultery* *2 sexual immorality*
21 a 1 Cor. 6:9, 10 *1* NU omits *murders*
22 a [John 15:2] b [Col. 3:12–15] c Rom. 15:14 d 1 Cor. 13:7
23 a 1 Tim. 1:9 *1 meekness*
24 a Rom. 6:6
25 a [Rom. 8:4, 5]
26 a Phil. 2:3

CHAPTER 6
1 a Eph. 4:2 *1 caught*
2 a Rom. 15:1 b [James 2:8]
3 a Rom. 12:3 b [2 Cor. 3:5]
4 a 1 Cor. 11:28 b Luke 18:11
5 a [Rom. 2:6]
6 a 1 Cor. 9:11, 14
7 a [Rom. 2:6]
8 a [Rom. 6:8]
9 a 1 Cor. 15:58 b [James 5:7, 8]
10 a Prov. 3:27 b Titus 3:8 c Rom. 12:13
12 a Gal. 5:11

Galatians 5:22, 23

Dear Woman of Destiny,

I had always thought God was in control of my life until His plan collided with mine. My plan had seemed great to me: a life of luxury, good wife of a successful businessman, loving mother to model children. I'd planned it that way since childhood and thought my life was shaping up pretty well. Then unexpectedly God called my husband, Terry, and me to start a church; and instead of peace, I felt fear; instead of faith, doubt. Instead of thoughts about God and His kingdom, I was consumed with thoughts of myself and my kingdom. Fear gripped my heart as I focused on my security, my reputation, and everything else I'd grown accustomed to in my comfortable life. God used these circumstances to expose the "fruit" in my life—and it wasn't the fruit of the Spirit.

Desperate and needy, I cried out to God and sought Him through His Word. He met me one day as I was driving in my car. In my heart, I believe I clearly heard His voice say, "I will do it through you." I knew exactly what He meant. I knew He was dealing with my fears and doubts about the task ahead. I burst into tears, and the fear and anxiety were broken. I knew that I could do everything He was calling me to do, because He would do it through me, by the power of the Spirit. Immediately following this intimate and dramatic encounter with Him, the fruit of the Spirit became more evident in my life.

The fruit of the Spirit can begin to blossom and grow when we yield our lives to the Spirit of God. It is called "fruit" because it is the by-product of an intimate relationship with Jesus—our source of life, growth, and fruitfulness.

After many years of pastoring, I am still able to say He is doing it through me. He is faithful. As my relationship with Jesus has grown in intimacy, the fruit of the Spirit in my life has also increased. However, when I begin thinking about myself, focusing on my problems, my weaknesses, what others say or do to me, I find the fruit of the Spirit begins to wither. To stay yielded and focused on Jesus, I spend time in the Bible meditating on His promises, praising and worshiping Him, praying, and blessing others. It is in this place of intimacy that the fruit of the Spirit flourishes. This place is available to you.

Just as the fruit of the Spirit is evident as we spend time in that place of intimacy, the works of the flesh are evident when our thoughts are focused on our circumstances and ourselves.

Jesus is longing to draw you into a place of intimacy where His grace will enable you to yield to the work of His Spirit in your life, whatever challenges you may be facing. He is extending the same promise to you that He did to me: "I will do it through you."

Susan Moore

keep the law, but they desire to have you
circumcised that they may boast in your
flesh. 14But God forbid that I should boast
except in the [a]cross of our Lord Jesus
Christ, by [1]whom the world has been crucified to me, and [b]I to the world. 15For [a]in
Christ Jesus neither circumcision nor uncircumcision avails anything, but a new
creation.

Blessing and a Plea

16And as many as walk according to this
rule, peace and mercy *be* upon them, and
upon the Israel of God.

17From now on let no one trouble me,
for I bear in my body the marks of the
Lord Jesus.

18Brethren, the grace of our Lord Jesus
Christ *be* with your spirit. Amen.

14 a[1 Cor. 1:18] b Col. 2:20 *1* Or *which*, the cross
15 a 1 Cor. 7:19

AUTHOR: *Paul*
DATE: *A.D. 60, 61*
THEME: *The Glorious Church*
KEY WORDS: *Glory, Body, Heavenly Places*

EPHESIANS

Dear Woman of Destiny,

Ephesians has been called the book of the church. It is a wealth of revelation and wisdom which, properly applied, will bring order in every aspect of our lives. The reason order is so important is found at the end of the book, "For we do not wrestle against flesh and blood, but against principalities, against powers, against the rulers of the darkness of this age, against spiritual hosts of wickedness in the heavenly places" (Eph. 6:12). All of us fight daily battles against an unseen enemy. Some days are easy. Other days we may feel like we are battling with Satan himself who wants to hurt our children, our relationships, or us. Make a decision today to recall the spiritual wealth we have in Christ and then to take up your shield of faith and quench the fiery darts of the enemy. Women of destiny are prayer warriors who never give up!

With His love,

Cindy Jacobs

Greeting

Paul, an apostle of Jesus Christ by
the will of God,

To the saints who are in Ephesus, and
faithful in Christ Jesus:

2 Grace to you and peace from God our
Father and the Lord Jesus Christ.

Redemption in Christ

3 [a]Blessed *be* the God and Father of our
Lord Jesus Christ, who has blessed us
with every spiritual blessing in the heavenly *places* in Christ, 4 just as [a]He chose
us in Him [b]before the foundation of the
world, that we should [c]be holy and without blame before Him in love, 5 [a]having
predestined us to [b]adoption as sons by Jesus Christ to Himself, [c]according to the
good pleasure of His will, 6 to the praise
of the glory of His grace, [a]by which He
[1]made us accepted in [b]the Beloved.
7 [a]In Him we have redemption through
His blood, the forgiveness of sins, according to [b]the riches of His grace 8 which He
made to abound toward us in all wisdom
and [1]prudence, 9 [a]having made known to
us the mystery of His will, according to
His good pleasure [b]which He purposed in
Himself, 10 that in the dispensation of [a]the
fullness of the times [b]He might gather together in one [c]all things in Christ, [1]both
which are in heaven and which are on
earth—in Him. 11 [a]In Him also we have
obtained an inheritance, being predestined according to [b]the purpose of Him
who works all things according to the
counsel of His will, 12 [a]that we [b]who first
trusted in Christ should be to the praise of
His glory.
13 In Him you also *trusted,* after you
heard [a]the word of truth, the gospel of
your salvation; in whom also, having believed, [b]you were sealed with the Holy
Spirit of promise, 14 [a]who[1] is the [2]guaran-
tee of our inheritance [b]until the redemption of [c]the purchased possession, [d]to the
praise of His glory.

Prayer for Spiritual Wisdom

15 Therefore I also, [a]after I heard of your
faith in the Lord Jesus and your love for
all the saints, 16 [a]do not cease to give
thanks for you, making mention of you in
my prayers: 17 that [a]the God of our Lord
Jesus Christ, the Father of glory, [b]may
give to you the spirit of wisdom and revelation in the knowledge of Him, 18 [a]the
eyes of your [1]understanding being enlightened; that you may know what is [b]the
hope of His calling, what are the riches of
the glory of His inheritance in the saints,
19 and what *is* the exceeding greatness of
His power toward us who believe, [a]ac-
cording to the working of His mighty
power 20 which He worked in Christ when
[a]He raised Him from the dead and [b]seated
Him at His right hand in the heavenly
places, 21 [a]far above all [b]principality[1] and
[2]power and [3]might and dominion, and every name that is named, not only in this
age but also in that which is to come.

Father of glory, give ____ the spirit of wisdom and revelation in the knowledge of You. May the eyes of their understanding be enlightened; that they may know what is the hope of Your calling, and what are the riches of the glory of Your inheritance in the saints.

FROM EPHESIANS 1:17, 18

22 And [a]He put all *things* under His feet,
and gave Him [b]*to be* head over all *things*
to the church, 23 [a]which is His body, [b]the
fullness of Him [c]who fills all in all.

By Grace Through Faith

2 And [a]you *He made alive,* [b]who were
dead in trespasses and sins, 2 [a]in
which you once walked according to the
[1]course of this world, according to [b]the
prince of the power of the air, the spirit
who now works in [c]the sons of disobedience, 3 [a]among whom also we all once
conducted ourselves in [b]the lusts of our
flesh, fulfilling the desires of the flesh and
of the mind, and [c]were by nature children
of wrath, just as the others.

CHAPTER 1
3 a 2 Cor. 1:3
4 a Rom. 8:28 b 1 Pet. 1:2 c Luke 1:75
5 a [Rom. 8:29] b John 1:12 c [1 Cor. 1:21]
6 a [Rom. 3:24] b Matt. 3:17 *1* Lit. *bestowed grace (favor) upon us*
7 a [Heb. 9:12] b [Rom. 3:24, 25]
8 *1 understanding*
9 a [Rom. 16:25] b [2 Tim. 1:9]
10 a Gal. 4:4 b 1 Cor. 3:22 c [Col. 1:16, 20] *1* NU, M omit *both*
11 a Rom. 8:17 b Is. 46:10
12 a 2 Thess. 2:13 b James 1:18
13 a John 1:17 b [2 Cor. 1:22]
14 a 2 Cor. 5:5 b Rom. 8:23 c [Acts 20:28] d 1 Pet. 2:9 *1* NU *which* *2 down payment, earnest*
15 a Col. 1:4
16 a Rom. 1:9
17 a John 20:17 b Col. 1:9
18 a Acts 26:18 b Eph. 2:12 *1* NU, M *hearts*
19 a Col. 2:12
20 a Acts 2:24 b Ps. 110:1
21 a Phil. 2:9, 10 b [Rom. 8:38, 39] *1 rule* *2 authority* *3 power*
22 a Ps. 8:6; 110:1 b Heb. 2:7
23 a Rom. 12:5 b Col. 2:9 c [1 Cor. 12:6]

CHAPTER 2
1 a Col. 2:13 b Eph. 4:18
2 a Col. 1:21 b Eph. 6:12 c Col. 3:6

1 Gr. *aion,* aeon **3** a 1 Pet. 4:3 b Gal. 5:16 c [Ps. 51:5]

Ephesians 1:4

Dear Woman of Destiny,

Every woman has a divine destiny that a sovereign God determined before the foundation of the world.

God called Sarah to have Isaac, the "Son of Laughter," when her womb was barren to prove once and for all to humanity that "with God nothing will be impossible" (Luke 1:37).

God called Ruth, a Gentile, to leave her country following the death of her husband and to look into the haggard face of her mother-in-law, Naomi, and say, "Entreat me not to leave you, or to turn back from following after you; for wherever you go, I will go; and wherever you lodge, I will lodge; your people shall be my people, and your God, my God" (Ruth 1:16). Ruth's destiny was to demonstrate that God is a God of hope. As a Gentile coming into a Jewish nation, she had no hope. Her destiny was to marry Boaz, a mighty man of wealth, and to have a baby, Obed, an ancestor of Jesus of Nazareth.

God's destiny called Esther to risk her life for those she loved, saying, "If I perish, I perish!" (Esth. 4:16).

God's destiny called Jael to drive a stake through the head of the Syrian general, Sisera, which determined the destiny of Israel (see Judg. 4).

God's destiny called Mary to submit her body, her life, and her reputation to give birth to the Son of God, which determined the destiny of all humankind (see Luke 1).

If you want to reach your divine destiny, remember these requirements: First, you must absolutely obey the voice of God. You know His voice by reading His Word. Second, you must follow faith over feeling—faith in a God who never fails, a God who is too good to be unkind and too wise to make a mistake. Third, you must persist in the way dictated in Ephesians 6—to stand, stand, and stand again. Fourth, you must take bold action. Once you have received God's direction, act on what He has commissioned you to do and watch miracles happen before your eyes.

Finally, know that you are a very important person in the kingdom of God. Even though the plans of women are many, the purposes of God will prevail in your life once you have surrendered yourself to His will (see Prov. 19:21). Your speech will bless your children, your actions will strengthen your marriage, your prayers will move mountains, and your character will influence others for Christ. Identifying these principles as God-given will help you turn the world toward the God of Abraham, Isaac, and Jacob; and beyond a shadow of a doubt, you will know that it does not take a village to raise a child, but a kingdom, the kingdom of God.

Diana Hagee

EPHESIANS 1:17

Dear Woman of Destiny,

We have many needs, but none greater than having a greater revelation of the character of God. That makes the prayer from Ephesians 1:17 of utmost importance.

The main purpose in having a Bible is to get to know the character of the author—God Himself. So every time we read the Word, we need to ask God to reveal to us His character and ways, and we need to believe that He will.

Moses, David, and Paul made the knowledge of God a priority prayer request, and God granted it. More than any other factor, I believe the revelation of who God is enabled them to become mighty instruments in the hand of God to bring blessing to the multitudes.

Never minimize the extent of the powerful influence that can come from your life when you make the pursuit of God Himself a passion. To know God and make Him known becomes your focused goal.

In Jeremiah 9:23, 24, God tells us that we're not to be impressed with those who have acquired a lot of knowledge about earthly things, who are wealthy, and have positions of authority, but that God delights in those who will study His character to know and understand Him.

God's character is multifaceted. Unless we're prepared to study every facet, we'll always have a distorted view of Him. He's something like a gigantic diamond. His true, intrinsic beauty will only be seen by those who take time to have a close-up, concentrated focus on the wonders of His whole Personhood.

I have discovered Him to be the most extraordinary, intriguing, fascinating Being. Intimate friendship with Him totally ruined me for the ordinary. I am captivated by His combination of mystery, majesty, and meekness. The One who has the power to create the universe by spoken words can become the lover of our souls. How indescribably awesome and absolutely exciting! We do ourselves a favor to hotly pursue His friendship.

But have you noticed that it takes time to cultivate a close, in-depth relationship with someone, where you've become secure in the knowledge of his or her character? When we make that effort, we come to understand them—what makes them tick. Only then can we explain to others, who may only know about them.

Want to make God known to others in the power of the Holy Spirit? You're going to have to spend a lot of time with Him. There are no crash courses.

Only an in-depth revelation of the character of God—especially His justice, faithfulness, and love—will cause your faith in Him not to fail when you go through the inevitable fiery trials of life.

The greatest test is the perplexity test. Job had it more than anyone. There may be times when God withholds all understanding of why you're experiencing what you are. That's when you bow to His sovereignty, trust in His flawless character and remember that, at times, "His ways [are] past finding out" (Rom. 11:33).

As with Peter, Jesus is interceding to the Father that your faith in Him will not fail. God answers Jesus' prayers.

Joy Dawson

4But God, [a]who is rich in mercy, because of His [b]great love with which He loved us, 5[a]even when we were dead in trespasses, [b]made us alive together with Christ (by grace you have been saved), 6and raised *us* up together, and made *us* sit together [a]in the heavenly *places* in Christ Jesus, 7that in the ages to come He might show the exceeding riches of His grace in [a]*His* kindness toward us in Christ Jesus. 8[a]For by grace you have been saved [b]through faith, and that not of yourselves; [c]*it is* the gift of God, 9not of [a]works, lest anyone should [b]boast. 10For we are [a]His workmanship, created in Christ Jesus for good works, which God prepared beforehand that we should walk in them.

Brought Near by His Blood

11Therefore remember that you, once Gentiles in the flesh—who are called Uncircumcision by what is called [a]the Circumcision made in the flesh by hands—12that at that time you were without Christ, being aliens from the commonwealth of Israel and strangers from the covenants of promise, having no hope and without God in the world. 13But now in Christ Jesus you who once were far off have been brought near by the blood of Christ.

Christ Our Peace

14For He Himself is our peace, who has made both one, and has broken down the middle wall of separation, 15having abolished in His flesh the enmity, *that is,* the law of commandments *contained* in ordinances, so as to create in Himself one [a]new man *from* the two, *thus* making peace, 16and that He might [a]reconcile them both to God in one body through the cross, thereby [b]putting to death the enmity. 17And He came and preached peace to you who were afar off and to those who were near. 18For [a]through Him we both have access [b]by one Spirit to the Father.

Christ Our Cornerstone

19Now, therefore, you are no longer strangers and foreigners, but fellow citizens with the saints and members of the household of God, 20having been [a]built [b]on the foundation of the [c]apostles and prophets, Jesus Christ Himself being [d]the chief corner*stone,* 21 in whom the whole building, being fitted together, grows into [a]a holy temple in the Lord, 22[a]in whom you also are being built together for a [b]dwelling place of God in the Spirit.

The Mystery Revealed

3 For this reason I, Paul, the prisoner of Christ Jesus for you Gentiles—2if indeed you have heard of the [1]dispensation of the grace of God [a]which was given to me for you, 3[a]how that by revelation [b]He made known to me the mystery (as I have briefly written already, 4by which, when you read, you may understand my knowledge in the mystery of Christ), 5which in other ages was not made known to the sons of men, as it has now been revealed by the Spirit to His holy apostles and prophets: 6that the Gentiles [a]should be fellow heirs, of the same body, and partakers of His promise in Christ through the gospel, 7[a]of which I became a minister [b]according to the gift of the grace of God given to me by [c]the effective working of His power.

Purpose of the Mystery

8To me, [a]who am less than the least of all the saints, this grace was given, that I should preach among the Gentiles [b]the unsearchable riches of Christ, 9and to make all see what *is* the [1]fellowship of the mystery, which from the beginning of the ages has been hidden in God who [a]created all things [2]through Jesus Christ; 10[a]to the intent that now [b]the [1]manifold wisdom of God might be made known by the church [c]to the [2]principalities and powers in the heavenly *places,* 11[a]according to the eternal purpose which He accomplished in Christ Jesus our Lord, 12in whom we have boldness and access [a]with confidence through faith in Him. 13[a]Therefore I ask that you do not lose heart at my tribulations for you, [b]which is your glory.

Appreciation of the Mystery

14For this reason I bow my knees to the [a]Father [1]of our Lord Jesus Christ, 15from whom the whole family in heaven and earth is named, 16that He would grant you, [a]according to the riches of His glory, [b]to be strengthened with might through His Spirit in [c]the inner man, 17[a]that Christ may dwell in your hearts through

---

4 a Rom. 10:12 b John 3:16
5 a Rom. 5:6, 8 b [Rom. 6:4, 5]
6 a Eph. 1:20
7 a Titus 3:4
8 a [2 Tim. 1:9] b Rom. 4:16 c [John 1:12, 13]
9 a Rom. 4:4, 5; 11:6 b Rom. 3:27
10 a Is. 19:25
11 a [Col. 2:11]
15 a Gal. 6:15
16 a [Col. 1:20–22] b [Rom. 6:6]
18 a John 10:9 b 1 Cor. 12:13
20 a 1 Pet. 2:4 b Matt. 16:18 c 1 Cor. 12:28 d Ps. 118:22
21 a 1 Cor. 3:16, 17
22 a 1 Pet. 2:5 b John 17:23

CHAPTER 3
2 a Acts 9:15 *1 stewardship*
3 a Acts 22:17, 21; 26:16 b [Rom. 11:25; 16:25]
6 a Gal. 3:28, 29
7 a Rom. 15:16 b Rom. 1:5 c Rom. 15:18
8 a [1 Cor. 15:9] b [Col. 1:27; 2:2, 3]
9 a Heb. 1:2 *1* NU, M *stewardship* (dispensation) *2* NU omits *through Jesus Christ*
10 a 1 Pet. 1:12 b [1 Tim. 3:16] c Col. 1:16; 2:10, 15 *1 variegated* or *many-sided* *2 rulers*
11 a [Eph. 1:4, 11]
12 a Heb. 4:16; 10:19, 35
13 a Phil. 1:14 b 2 Cor. 1:6
14 a Eph. 1:3 *1* NU omits *of our Lord Jesus Christ*
16 a [Phil. 4:19] b Col. 1:11 c Rom. 7:22
17 a John 14:23

Ephesians 2:21, 22

Dear Woman of Destiny,

God, the Master Builder, covenanted to restore us before He created us. Restoration is not just something on the heart of God; it *is* the heart of God. And it is the reason Jesus came to earth the first time and will come again.

Yet Jesus will not return for a body that is divided, weak, and broken—a body of people who blindly walk in darkness, oblivious to God's plan. He will bring us back to what He purposed for us from before the time of the Fall. His body, His kingdom, will yet be seen as the glorious expression of His life.

God is not reluctant to make His will known to His people. He is always eager to reveal His heart and plan to us so that we might walk with Him in understanding and cooperate with Him. Ephesians 1:11 says, "[He] works all things according to the counsel of His will." *All* things! Not just a few things, not even several things, but all things. *All* means everything, every bit, every part, every one.

One of the "all things" God is working is a global awakening among women. In the Garden, God revealed His plan. Adam initially, then Adam and Eve together, were to represent God on earth and be the expression of His wonderful life to the world around them. They were to be the beginning of a people who would be linked to God in a life-giving, life-sharing union. They were to walk in authority, taking dominion over the earth and over anything that would counter the rule and plan of God. They were to be fruitful and multiply.

The earth had been created for humanity to rule over on God's behalf, but dominion would not come without conflict. God had declared war on His enemy! Satan was to be brought down and trodden underfoot. God would be supremely glorified. In His infinite wisdom, He would use mere humans to subdue the enemy.

But there would be much to learn. God intended that the process of learning to take dominion over the works of His hands would have a twofold purpose for Adam and Eve and their progeny. First, they would grow up into maturity, not only physically and mentally, but also spiritually. Second, they would learn to know their God and become "sons" (and daughters) in the fullest and most intimate sense of the word.

Never in all of history has there been the kind of corporate calling forth or worldwide awakening of women we have seen in the past thirty years. God is up to something. This unprecedented move of God's Spirit is for a purpose. As we listen and learn, He will continue to unfold His plan for restoration between male and female so that, together, we can more effectively represent His complete image and carry out His will in the world. The fracture in the house of the Lord will begin to mend, and the building will rise to new heights.

Jane Hansen

faith; that you, [b]being rooted and grounded in love, 18[a]may be able to comprehend with all the saints [b]what *is* the width and length and depth and height— 19to know the love of Christ which passes knowledge; that you may be filled [a]with all the fullness of God.

I pray, Lord, that _____ may be able to comprehend with all the saints what is the width and length and depth and height—to know the love of Christ which passes knowledge; that they may be filled with all the fullness of God.

FROM EPHESIANS 3:18, 19

20Now [a]to Him who is able to do exceedingly abundantly [b]above all that we ask or think, [c]according to the power that works in us, 21[a]to Him *be* glory in the church by Christ Jesus to all generations, forever and ever. Amen.

Walk in Unity

4 I, therefore, the prisoner [1]of the Lord, [2]beseech you to [a]walk worthy of the calling with which you were called, 2with all lowliness and gentleness, with longsuffering, bearing with one another in love, 3endeavoring to keep the unity of the Spirit [a]in the bond of peace. 4[a]*There is* one body and one Spirit, just as you were called in one hope of your calling; 5[a]one Lord, [b]one faith, [c]one baptism; 6[a]one God and Father of all, who *is* above all, and [b]through all, and in [1]you all.

Spiritual Gifts

7But [a]to each one of us grace was given according to the measure of Christ's gift. 8Therefore He says:

[a]*"When He ascended on high,*
He led captivity captive,
And gave gifts to men."

9[a](Now this, *"He ascended"*—what does it mean but that He also [1]first descended into the lower parts of the earth? 10He who descended is also the One [a]who ascended far above all the heavens, [b]that He might fill all things.)

11And He Himself gave some *to be* apostles, some prophets, some evangelists, and some pastors and teachers, 12for the equipping of the saints for the work of ministry, [a]for the [1]edifying of [b]the body of Christ, 13till we all come to the unity of the faith [a]and of the knowledge of the Son of God, to [b]a perfect man, to the measure of the stature of the fullness of Christ; 14that we should no longer be [a]children, tossed to and fro and carried about with every wind of doctrine, by the trickery of men, in the cunning craftiness of [b]deceitful plotting, 15but, speaking the truth in love, may grow up in all things into Him who is the [a]head—Christ— 16[a]from whom the whole body, joined and knit together by what every joint supplies, according to the effective working by which every part does its share, causes growth of the body for the edifying of itself in love.

The New Man

17This I say, therefore, and testify in the Lord, that you should [a]no longer walk as [1]the rest of the Gentiles walk, in the futility of their mind, 18having their understanding darkened, being alienated from the life of God, because of the ignorance that is in them, because of the [a]blindness of their heart; 19[a]who, being past feeling, [b]have given themselves over to lewdness, to work all uncleanness with greediness. 20But you have not so learned Christ, 21if indeed you have heard Him and have been taught by Him, as the truth is in Jesus: 22that you [a]put off, concerning your former conduct, the old man which grows corrupt according to the deceitful lusts, 23and [a]be renewed in the spirit of your mind, 24and that you [a]put on the new man which was created according to God, in true righteousness and holiness.

Do Not Grieve the Spirit

25Therefore, putting away lying, [a]*"Let each one of you speak truth with his neighbor,"* for [b]we are members of one another. 26 [a]*"Be angry, and do not sin"*: do not let the sun go down on your wrath, 27[a]nor give [1]place to the devil.

17 b Col. 1:23
18 a Eph. 1:18 b Rom. 8:39
19 a Eph. 1:23
20 a Rom. 16:25 b 1 Cor. 2:9 c Col. 1:29
21 a Rom. 11:36

CHAPTER 4
1 a 1 Thess. 2:12 *1 Lit. in* *2 exhort, encourage*
3 a Col. 3:14
4 a Rom. 12:5
5 a 1 Cor. 1:13 b Jude 3 c [Heb. 6:6]
6 a Mal. 2:10 b Rom. 11:36 *1* NU omits *you;* M *us*
7 a [1 Cor. 12:7, 11]
8 a Ps. 68:18
9 a John 3:13; 20:17 *1* NU omits *first*
10 a Acts 1:9 b [Eph. 1:23]
12 a 1 Cor. 14:26 b Col. 1:24 *1 building up*
13 a Col. 2:2 b 1 Cor. 14:20
14 a 1 Cor. 14:20 b Rom. 16:18
15 a Eph. 1:22
16 a Col. 2:19
17 a Eph. 2:2; 4:22 *1* NU omits *the rest of*
18 a Rom. 1:21
19 a 1 Tim. 4:2 b 1 Pet. 4:3
22 a Col. 3:8
23 a [Rom. 12:2]
24 a [Rom. 6:4; 7:6; 12:2]
25 a Zech. 8:16 b Rom. 12:5
26 a Ps. 4:4; 37:8
27 a [Rom. 12:19] *1 an opportunity*

Ephesians 4:26

Dear Woman of Destiny,

For many, anger has become a painful way of life. Our world is immersed in anger, strife, and turmoil. Each day an opportunity to become angry presents itself. What we do with this anger affects those around us, and we cannot escape unscathed either.

I know this because for many years anger was a way of life for me and I felt I had justifications for it. To name a few, I had suffered the loss of an eye to cancer at age five, was raised in a home torn by divorce and alcohol, and had grown up with anger all around me.

We will never change what we excuse in our lives. Excuses just perpetuated the cycle of pain and anger. It wasn't until I had an encounter with truth that I could step into the path of freedom. God showed me that what I justify, I buy. In essence, I was saying I'd earned the right to be this way because of what had been done to me. I also learned that part of taking up my cross and denying myself included denying myself the right to make excuses.

The Bible admonishes us in Ephesians 4:26, 'Be angry, and do not sin': do not let the sun go down on your wrath." Let's treat this verse as two separate yet integrated parts. The first, "Be angry, and do not sin," gives us permission to be angry, but at the same time warns us against being destructive with our anger. Our heavenly Father understands situations will arise where anger is a real and valid response, but we are to handle it responsibly.

James tells us to be "swift to hear, slow to speak, slow to wrath" (James 1:19). I was the very opposite of this. I was slow to listen, quick to speak, and extremely quick to blow up. I attacked people instead of problems. This meant I called names and blamed others. Because I was angry, I wanted them to feel my displeasure or pain. I wanted to punish them. This, of course, is destructive, not constructive anger. It is an example of "be angry, and sin!"

I believe the second part of our verse ("do not let the sun go down on your wrath") is equally as crucial. Too often I found that when I went to sleep angry, I woke up angry. While I slept, the seed of anger had sprouted a root of bitterness. What began as a turned back in the bed had grown into a turned heart in the morning.

God promises His love is steadfast and His mercy new every morning. But, after sleeping with anger I found it hard to sense His mercy, because I was too busy thinking of those who needed to ask for mine.

Reserve your sleep for refreshing and renewal. Settle matters at least in your own heart before you close your eyes so that the Holy Spirit might speak to you in the night watches.

Lisa Bevere

[28]Let him who stole steal no longer, but
rather [a]let him labor, working with *his*
hands what is good, that he may have
something [b]to give him who has need.
[29][a]Let no corrupt word proceed out of
your mouth, but [b]what is good for necessary [1]edification, [c]that it may impart
grace to the hearers. [30]And [a]do not grieve
the Holy Spirit of God, by whom you were
sealed for the day of redemption. [31][a]Let all
bitterness, wrath, anger, [1]clamor, and
[b]evil speaking be put away from you,
[c]with all malice. [32]And [a]be kind to one
another, tenderhearted, [b]forgiving one
another, even as God in Christ forgave
you.

Lord, may _____ put away all bitterness, wrath, anger, clamor, evil speaking, and all malice. May they be kind to others, tenderhearted, forgiving others, just as God in Christ also forgave them.

FROM EPHESIANS 4:31, 32

Walk in Love

5 Therefore[a] be imitators of God as dear
[b]children. [2]And [a]walk in love, [b]as
Christ also has loved us and given Himself
for us, an offering and a sacrifice to God
[c]for a sweet-smelling aroma.
[3]But fornication and all [a]uncleanness
or [b]covetousness, let it not even be named
among you, as is fitting for saints; [4][a]nei-
ther filthiness, nor [b]foolish talking, nor
coarse jesting, [c]which are not fitting, but
rather [d]giving of thanks. [5]For [1]this you
know, that no fornicator, unclean person,
nor covetous man, who is an idolater, has
any [a]inheritance in the kingdom of Christ
and God. [6]Let no one deceive you with
empty words, for because of these things
the wrath of God comes upon the sons of
disobedience. [7]Therefore do not be [a]par-
takers with them.

Walk in Light

[8]For you were once darkness, but now
you are [a]light in the Lord. Walk as children of light [9](for [a]the fruit of the [1]Spirit
is in all goodness, righteousness, and
truth), [10][a]finding out what is acceptable
to the Lord. [11]And have [a]no fellowship
with the unfruitful works of darkness, but
rather [1]expose *them.* [12][a]For it is shameful
even to speak of those things which are
done by them in secret. [13]But [a]all things
that are [1]exposed are made manifest by
the light, for whatever makes manifest is
light. [14]Therefore He says:

[a]"Awake, you who sleep,
Arise from the dead,
And Christ will give you light."

Be loving and tender to all.

JOHN WESLEY

Walk in Wisdom

[15][a]See then that you walk [1]circum-
spectly, not as fools but as wise, [16][a]re-
deeming the time, [b]because the days are
evil.

Lord, I ask that _____ would not be unwise, but understand what Your will is.

FROM EPHESIANS 5:17

[17][a]Therefore do not be unwise, but [b]un-
derstand [c]what the will of the Lord *is.*
[18]And [a]do not be drunk with wine, in
which is dissipation; but be filled with the
Spirit, [19]speaking to one another [a]in
psalms and hymns and spiritual songs,
singing and making [b]melody in your
heart to the Lord, [20][a]giving thanks always

28 a Acts 20:35 b Luke 3:11
29 a Col. 3:8 b 1 Thess. 5:11 c Col. 3:16 *1 building up*
30 a Is. 7:13
31 a Col. 3:8, 19 b James 4:11 c Titus 3:3 *1 loud quarreling*
32 a 2 Cor. 6:10 b [Mark 11:25]

CHAPTER 5
1 a Luke 6:36 b 1 Pet. 1:14–16
2 a 1 Thess. 4:9 b Gal. 1:4 c 2 Cor. 2:14, 15
3 a Col. 3:5–7 b [Luke 12:15]
4 a Matt. 12:34, 35 b Titus 3:9 c Rom. 1:28 d Phil. 4:6
5 a 1 Cor. 6:9, 10 *1 NU know this*
7 a 1 Tim. 5:22
8 a 1 Thess. 5:5
9 a Gal. 5:22 *1 NU light*
10 a [Rom. 12:1, 2]
11 a 2 Cor. 6:14 *1 reprove*
12 a Rom. 1:24
13 a [John 3:20, 21] *1 reproved*
14 a [Is. 26:19; 60:1]
15 a Col. 4:5 *1 carefully*
16 a Col. 4:5 b Eccl. 11:2
17 a Col. 4:5 b [Rom. 12:2] c 1 Thess. 4:3
18 a Prov. 20:1; 23:31
19 a Acts 16:25 b James 5:13
20 a Ps. 34:1

for all things to God the Father [b]in
the name of our Lord Jesus Christ,
21 [a]submitting to one another in the
fear of [1]God.

Marriage—Christ and the Church

22Wives, [a]submit to your own husbands, as to the Lord. 23For [a]the husband
is head of the wife, as also [b]Christ is head
of the church; and He is the Savior of the
body. 24Therefore, just as the church is
subject to Christ, so *let* the wives *be* to
their own husbands [a]in everything.

25[a]Husbands, love your wives, just as
Christ also loved the church and [b]gave
Himself for her, 26that He might [1]sanctify
and cleanse her [a]with the washing of water [b]by the word, 27[a]that He might present her to Himself a glorious church,
[b]not having spot or wrinkle or any such
thing, but that she should be holy and
without blemish. 28So husbands ought to
love their own wives as their own bodies;
he who loves his wife loves himself. 29For
no one ever hated his own flesh, but nourishes and cherishes it, just as the Lord

20 b [1 Pet. 2:5]
21 a [Phil. 2:3] *1* NU *Christ*
22 a Col. 3:18—4:1
23 a [1 Cor. 11:3] b Col. 1:18
24 a Titus 2:4, 5
25 a Col. 3:19 b Acts 20:28
26 a John 3:5 b [John 15:3; 17:17] *1 set it apart*
27 a Col. 1:22 b Song 4:7

Fanny Crosby

A person doesn't need physical sight to behold the glory of God. Such was the case with Fanny Crosby (1820–1915). Blinded as a six-week-old infant, Fanny did not let her inability to see hinder her in any way. She determined at an early age to overcome her limitations and never to succumb to bitterness or resentment. She committed to learn all she could and to develop her mind, continually praying that God would use her in a remarkable way. Fanny had an incredible memory and, reportedly, was able to accurately recite the first four books of both the Old and New Testaments when she was only ten years old.

Fanny entered what was then known as The New York Institution for the Blind in 1835 and excelled as a student and further developed her already blossoming gift for rhyme and poetry. In 1842, she became an instructor at that school and remained a beloved teacher of English, rhetoric, and history until 1858. After she left the school, she devoted her life to writing and to serving the poor.

Fanny Crosby provided the church with some of its best-loved hymns. She wrote more than nine thousand hymns, including "Blessed Assurance," "All the Way My Savior Leads Me," and "To God Be the Glory." Her writing celebrated the faith and trust in God, peace, and joy that characterized her life. She was so in love with Jesus that when asked if she would like to be able to see, she answered that she would not, "because when I get to heaven the first face that shall gladden my sight shall be that of my Savior."

She once wrote: "My ambition was boundless and my desires were intent to live for some great purpose in the world and to make for myself a name that should endure." She did make a name for herself, and her legacy of faith lives on in every glorious word of the hymns she penned. May we, as women of destiny, embrace life as fully as Fanny Crosby did, refusing to let any obstacle stand between us and the fulfillment of God's plan for our lives.

Ephesians 5:21–33

Dear Woman of Destiny,

At one time I felt uncomfortable with the command, "wives, submit to your own husbands" (Eph. 5:22). But now I believe that Paul's instruction to wives and husbands is also a reflection of God's kingdom—of the relationship between God and His people.

Paul begins by addressing the body of Christ: "[Submit] to one another in the fear of God" (v. 21). The key words—*submit* and *Christ*—are woven into the following text, revealing the significance and implications of godly submission as designated to the wife and to the husband.

Paul does instruct the wife to submit to her husband, but he does not leave it there. He compares this submission with submitting "as to the Lord" (v. 22). From the beginning, Paul speaks to women of faith. His instruction of wives submitting to their husbands is based on the premise that they have submitted to the Lord. Just as the wife chooses to follow Christ, so she is to follow her husband, yield to his leadership, and trust his discretion.

What do we do when we, the church, submit to Christ? We choose to be in alignment with His Spirit. We obey His commandments. We have a relationship with Him. We choose to trust Him, serve Him, and honor Him. We are one with Him. So wives are to submit to their husbands as the church submits to Christ.

I find it interesting that following verse 24, Paul says nothing else to the wives about submission. In this fallen world, these words can seem harsh. It is one thing to submit to Jesus Christ, but something else altogether to submit to another human being.

Paul has more to say to the husbands. His first admonition to husbands is to love their wives "just as Christ also loved the church and gave Himself for her" (v. 25). Christ's love is synonymous with servanthood. It is selfless, totally obedient to the will of God, sacrificial, and completely protective for the sake of life—eternal life.

The husband's role is to love his wife as himself. He is to care for her and provide for her as he would for himself (v. 28). This nurturing also parallels Christ and the church, "for we are members of His body" (v. 30). In this is unity. There is a mutual relationship between the husband and wife and Christ and the church. One cannot function effectively without the other. Christ cannot effectively serve us, guide us, and protect us if we are not willing to submit to Him completely. The husband cannot effectively lead if the wife is not willing to trust him. In the same way, the wife is incapable of trusting her husband if he cannot love her.

There is a sense of identity that entails setting aside self-interests for one another. The wife, in her submission to her husband, serves to empower his authority as she blesses him and intercedes for him. For the sake of unity and indentity in marriage, the husband is commanded to leave his father and mother—he is to leave a part of himself, his identity—to "be joined to his wife, and the two shall become one flesh" (v. 31).

I pray that your marriage will be blessed as you enjoy the love, trust, and blessing God intends for you.

Catherine Berg Greig

does the church. 30 For [a]we are members
of His body, [1]of His flesh and of His bones.
31 [a]*"For this reason a man shall leave his
father and mother and be joined to his
wife, and the* [b]*two shall become one
flesh."* 32 This is a great mystery, but I
speak concerning Christ and the church.
33 Nevertheless [a]let each one of you in particular so love his own wife as himself,
and let the wife *see* that she [b]respects *her*
husband.

Children and Parents

6 Children, [a]obey your parents in the
Lord, for this is right. 2 [a]*"Honor your
father and mother,"* which is the first
commandment with promise: 3 *"that it
may be well with you and you may live
long on the earth."*
4 And [a]you, fathers, do not provoke your
children to wrath, but [b]bring them up
in the training and admonition of the
Lord.

Let it be said, that no two things are more essential to a Spirit-filled life than Bible reading and secret prayer.

E. M. BOUNDS

Bondservants and Masters

5 [a]Bondservants, be obedient to those
who are your masters according to the
flesh, [b]with fear and trembling, [c]in sincerity of heart, as to Christ; 6 [a]not with
eyeservice, as men-pleasers, but as bondservants of Christ, doing the will of God
from the heart, 7 with goodwill doing service, as to the Lord, and not to men,
8 [a]knowing that whatever good anyone
does, he will receive the same from the
Lord, whether *he is* a slave or free.
9 And you, masters, do the same things
to them, giving up threatening, knowing
that [1]your own [a]Master also is in heaven,
and [b]there is no partiality with Him.

30 a Gen. 2:23 *1* NU omits the rest of v. 30.
31 a Gen. 2:24 b [1 Cor. 6:16]
33 a Col. 3:19 b 1 Pet. 3:1, 6

CHAPTER 6
1 a Col. 3:20
2 a Deut. 5:16
4 a Col. 3:21 b Gen. 18:19
5 a [1 Tim. 6:1] b 2 Cor. 7:15 c 1 Chr. 29:17
6 a Col. 3:22
8 a Rom. 2:6
9 a Col. 4:1 b Rom. 2:11 *1* NU *He who is both their Master and yours is*
11 a [2 Cor. 6:7] *1 schemings*
12 a Rom. 8:38 b Luke 22:53 *1* NU *this darkness,*
13 a [2 Cor. 10:4] b Eph. 5:16
14 a Is. 11:5 b Is. 59:17
15 a Is. 52:7
16 a 1 John 5:4
17 a 1 Thess. 5:8 b [Heb. 4:12]
18 a Luke 18:1 b [Matt. 26:41] c Phil. 1:4
19 a Col. 4:3
20 a 2 Cor. 5:20
21 a Acts 20:4 b 1 Cor. 4:1, 2

The Whole Armor of God

10 Finally, my brethren, be strong in
the Lord and in the power of His might.
11 [a]Put on the whole armor of God, that
you may be able to stand against the
[1]wiles of the devil. 12 For we do not wrestle
against flesh and blood, but against [a]prin-
cipalities, against powers, against [b]the
rulers of [1]the darkness of this age, against
spiritual *hosts* of wickedness in the heavenly *places.* 13 [a]Therefore take up the
whole armor of God, that you may be able
to withstand [b]in the evil day, and having
done all, to stand.
14 Stand therefore, [a]having girded your
waist with truth, [b]having put on the
breastplate of righteousness, 15 [a]and having shod your feet with the preparation of
the gospel of peace; 16 above all, taking
[a]the shield of faith with which you will be
able to quench all the fiery darts of the
wicked one. 17 And [a]take the helmet of salvation, and [b]the sword of the Spirit, which
is the word of God; 18 [a]praying always with
all prayer and supplication in the Spirit,
[b]being watchful to this end with all perseverance and [c]supplication for all the
saints— 19 and for me, that utterance may
be given to me, [a]that I may open my
mouth boldly to make known the mystery
of the gospel, 20 for which [a]I am an ambassador in chains; that in it I may speak
boldly, as I ought to speak.

Father, may ___ be strong in You and in the power of Your might. May they put on the whole armor of God, that they may be able to stand against the wiles of the devil.

FROM EPHESIANS 6:10, 11

A Gracious Greeting

21 But that you also may know my affairs *and* how I am doing, [a]Tychicus, a
beloved brother and [b]faithful minister in

Ephesians 6:10–13

Dear Woman of Destiny,

When I became a believer, I pictured myself in a long, flowing white dress dancing through a field of flowers on a clear sunny day. I accessorized my carefree wardrobe with a feminine straw hat, sweet little white gloves, a nosegay of spring flowers, and dainty sandals. All the dark clouds of my past left the moment Jesus came into my heart and took over my life. So, when the warfare came, I panicked. I certainly was not dressed for the occasion.

The truth is, we have a real enemy who wants to destroy us. We have a real fight on our hands in the struggle to hold onto our purpose. As citizens of the kingdom of God, we have become a threat. The enemy has been engaged, and the fight is on. My view of lazy days in the sunshine has changed to an attitude of watchful readiness.

And I have traded my flowing dress ensemble for the appropriate uniform of a warrior. I took off the straw hat and covered my head with a helmet called salvation. The strongest battles are fought on the battleground of our minds. The blood of Jesus continually cleanses my mind from thoughts of insecurity, discouragement, fear, and doubt. I am protected by righteousness and truth, because Jesus is my righteousness and He is the truth. We cannot trust in our own good works. The enemy will defeat us if we try to stand on our own righteousness. Our only true freedom comes by hearing and abiding in the truth. That means I am who God says I am. In Him I live and move and have my being!

I have taken off my gloves and laid aside the bouquet of flowers. In one hand, I hold a sword. In the other hand, I hold a shield. We must yield daily to the Holy Spirit who activates the word of God through our faith. Faith is the substance of our hope. When we wield the sword, we do it in faith in God's promise to be faithful to His word. Faith is being persuaded that God is able! God's word will defeat any enemy. I still dance with joy, but I dance with shoes that have been prepared.

In a world of uncertainty and fear, everyone is searching for peace. We have good news to proclaim. God's peace surpasses all understanding. It is not dependent on circumstances or people. We are a part of an unshakable kingdom where peace is a Person named Jesus. The peace of God surrounds me; and everywhere I go, I leave a footprint of peace.

The battle we face daily is not with people or situations. There is an enemy who uses people and circumstances to try to steal our joy and victory. We are already defeated if we try to win this war in our strength with carnal weapons. We must take up the weapons of the Spirit and learn how to stand. We must stand our ground and courageously resist the temptation to surrender.

Dear sister, we are destined for warfare and dressed for battle. Watching in prayer, let us persevere like good soldiers to the victorious end!

Shirley Arnold

the Lord, will make all things known to
you; [22][a]whom I have sent to you for this
very purpose, that you may know our affairs, and *that* he may [b]comfort your
hearts.

[23]Peace to the brethren, and love with
faith, from God the Father and the Lord
Jesus Christ. [24]Grace *be* with all those
who love our Lord Jesus Christ in sincerity. Amen.

22 [a]Col. 4:8
[b]2 Cor. 1:6

AUTHOR: *Paul*
DATE: *A.D. 61*
THEME: *Joy in Christ*
KEY WORDS: *Joy, Rejoice*

PHILIPPIANS

Dear Woman of Destiny,

Philippians is full of the call to persevere! It begins by encouraging us with the promise that we can be confident "that He who has begun a good work in you will complete it until the day of Jesus Christ" (Phil. 1:6). The exhortation to give all for the cause of Christ, holding nothing back, shines through this wonderful book. Why do we do this? So that we may know Him. It is important for us as women to make a conscious decision to give everything we are and everything we have to Him. This includes our possessions, family members, children and/or grandchildren, time, and what we ultimately do with our lives. All of us as women of destiny must be ready to say at anytime, "Here am I! Send me" (Is. 6:8).

With His love,

Cindy Jacobs

Greeting

Paul and Timothy, bondservants of
Jesus Christ,

To all the saints in Christ Jesus who are
in Philippi, with the [1]bishops and [a]dea-
cons:

2 Grace to you and peace from God our
Father and the Lord Jesus Christ.

> *I thank You, God, upon every remembrance of ____, always in every prayer of mine making request for them with joy. For I am confident of this very thing, that You who began a good work in them will complete it until the day of Jesus Christ.*
>
> FROM PHILIPPIANS 1:3, 4, 6

Thankfulness and Prayer

3 [a]I thank my God upon every remembrance of you, 4 always in [a]every prayer of
mine making request for you all with joy,
5 [a]for your fellowship in the gospel from
the first day until now, 6 being confident of this very thing, that He who has
begun [a]a good work in you will complete
it until the day of Jesus Christ; 7 just as
it is right for me to think this of you all,
because I have you in my heart, inasmuch
as both in my chains and in the defense
and confirmation of the gospel, you all are
partakers with me of grace. 8 For God is
my witness, how greatly I long for you all
with the affection of Jesus Christ.

9 And this I pray, that your love may
abound still more and more in knowledge
and all discernment, 10 that you may approve the things that are excellent, that
you may be sincere and without offense
till the day of Christ, 11 being filled with
the fruits of righteousness [a]which *are* by
Jesus Christ, [b]to the glory and praise of
God.

Christ Is Preached

12 But I want you to know, brethren,
that the things *which happened* to me
have actually turned out for the further-
ance of the gospel, 13 so that it has become
evident [a]to the whole [1]palace guard, and
to all the rest, that my chains are in
Christ; 14 and most of the brethren in the
Lord, having become confident by my
chains, are much more bold to speak the
word without fear.

15 Some indeed preach Christ even from
envy and strife, and some also from goodwill: 16 [1]The former preach Christ from
selfish ambition, not sincerely, supposing
to add affliction to my chains; 17 but the
latter out of love, knowing that I am appointed for the defense of the gospel.
18 What then? Only *that* in every way,
whether in pretense or in truth, Christ is
preached; and in this I rejoice, yes, and
will rejoice.

To Live Is Christ

19 For I know that [a]this will turn out for
my deliverance through your prayer and
the supply of the Spirit of Jesus Christ,
20 according to my earnest expectation and
hope that in nothing I shall be ashamed,
but [a]with all boldness, as always, so now
also Christ will be magnified in my body,
whether by life [b]or by death. 21 For to me,
to live *is* Christ, and to die *is* gain. 22 But
if *I* live on in the flesh, this *will mean* fruit
from *my* labor; yet what I shall choose I
[1]cannot tell. 23 [1]For I am hard-pressed between the two, having a [a]desire to depart
and be with Christ, *which is* [b]far better.
24 Nevertheless to remain in the flesh *is*
more needful for you. 25 And being confident of this, I know that I shall remain
and continue with you all for your progress and joy of faith, 26 that [a]your rejoicing
for me may be more abundant in Jesus
Christ by my coming to you again.

Striving and Suffering for Christ

27 Only [a]let your conduct be worthy of
the gospel of Christ, so that whether I
come and see you or am absent, I may
hear of your affairs, that you stand fast in
one spirit, [b]with one mind [c]striving together for the faith of the gospel, 28 and
not in any way terrified by your adversaries, which is to them a proof of perdition,
but [1]to you of salvation, and that from

CHAPTER 1

1 a [1 Tim. 3:8–13] *1* Lit. *overseers*

3 a 1 Cor. 1:4

4 a Eph. 1:16

5 a [Rom. 12:13]

6 a [John 6:29]

11 a Col. 1:6 b John 15:8

13 a Phil. 4:22 *1* Or *Praetorium*

16 *1* NU reverses vv. 16 and 17.

19 a Job 13:16, LXX

20 a Eph. 6:19, 20 b [Rom. 14:8]

22 *1 do not know*

23 a [2 Cor. 5:2, 8] b [Ps. 16:11] *1* NU, M *But*

26 a 2 Cor. 1:14

27 a Eph. 4:1 b Eph. 4:3 c Jude 3

28 *1* NU *of your salvation*

Philippians 1:6

Dear Woman of Destiny,

You are a work in progress. I encourage you to continue pressing forward fervently and with passion, pursuing the depths of who God has created you to be. I further admonish you to take advantage of every opportunity to observe with accuracy who you are now and who you are becoming in Christ. Realize the work God is doing in you is an ongoing, evolving process of growth toward maturity. Release the frustrations you may have about yourself and the fact that you haven't gotten your act together. Let go of the conversation that says, "I should be a lot further along by now." What matters to God is that you transcend the state you are now in and go on to perfection, maturity. Continue to develop, define, and refine your life in the character and virtue of God.

The masterpiece you are being molded into is partly determined by the choices you make in any given moment. Your destiny can only be accomplished moment by moment. How do you respond to someone having a bad day or to others when you're having a bad day? How do you go through life's irritations without becoming irritable or an irritant yourself? Do you react or respond? You'll have repeated opportunities to make choices that count. Consider the choice that will please our Father in heaven and give you peace. I remind you that the *roles you play* as a sister, mother, wife, or aunt *are not who you are*. Monitor your motives, and place your focus on *being* rather than *doing*. God is calling you to a mode of being that represents Himself in you. No matter who you are, I believe He's calling you to a wider and deeper expression of who He is, minus your fears and presupposed judgments.

How are you responding to the will of God? Have you fully yielded in obedience? If your desire is to be used by God as a vehicle through which transformation may occur for others, you then must perpetually yield to the process of personal transformation—going from glory to glory, moment by moment, experience by experience. As you continue to say "yes" to His will and decrease while He increases, He'll have His perfect way in you.

I admonish you to reevaluate what has roadblocked you in the past. Repent, realign your thinking, and receive a fresh endowment of the Father's power. It's yours by choice. Choose life; then live it to its fullest. Have no regrets about how it could have been. The past is under His blood. I call forth from the deepest recesses of your soul the unique contribution you have yet to make to your home, church, and community. The greatest gift you offer to the body of Christ is to discover or recover who you are and to accept and walk in it. Being the best of who you are is your greatest contribution to the kingdom of God.

Come out of your comfort zone. Make a difference by taking a risk to give of yourself without apology. Be bold. Have courage. You're postured and positioned to propel purpose. Create some waves; then ride them. You can do all things through Christ who strengthens (empowers) you. He will complete the good work He began in you!

Gina Pearson

PHILIPPIANS 2:5

Dear Woman of Destiny,

Want to be like Jesus? Sure you do. That's why you're reading this Bible. The more we have of God's mind and heart, the more those desires will be fulfilled. From the context of this scripture, the key is humility.

I believe our spiritual depth is determined by the depth of our genuine humility of heart before God. Jesus said in Matthew 11:29, "Learn from Me, for I am gentle and lowly in heart."

Humility is the least thing sought after with intensity, yet we're exhorted to "seek the LORD, all you meek of the earth, . . . seek humility" (Zeph. 2:3).

The reason for all Jesus' exaltation and honor by the Father is that He became nothing that the Father might become everything.

Until we want to become nothing (living in total dependence upon Him, choosing never to take the glory), He cannot become everything (to us and through us). What a wonderful exchange!

In 1 Corinthians 13:3, God makes it clear that we're totally ineffective if we're not being loving at all times. When we read what love's behavior is like in verses 4–7, it becomes obvious that humility is the basis of it. So humility is one of our greatest needs.

There are no relationship problems that humility cannot solve, provided both parties choose to obey God's Word. Ephesians 4:2 says, "With all lowliness and gentleness, with longsuffering, bearing with one another in love." Colossians 3:13 adds, "As Christ forgave you, so you also must do."

Humility releases God's grace to us in the many difficult situations of life. "God resists the proud, but gives grace to the humble" (James 4:6).

One of the most common forms of pride is the way we make excuses in everyday situations, instead of having the humility of 100 percent honesty. Humility of heart causes us to quickly and easily say, "I'm sorry; I was wrong," or "I failed to do so and so; please forgive me."

Excuses are often a combination of truth and a cover-up. In His special instruction on the fear of the Lord in Psalm 34:11–14, God calls it deceit.

Pride is the most insidious sin—and the ugliest. Humility is the most attractive grace. Pride is the most deeply entrenched sin—the one to which we're the most blind. It's the basis of all deception. "The pride of your heart has deceived you" (Obad. 3a).

If you had an impression you thought was from God when seeking God's guidance, and you later found it wasn't, it is important to humble yourself before God and others to avoid a platform for deception from the enemy.

Pride keeps us from intimate friendship with God. Psalm 138:6 says, "Though the LORD is on high, yet He regards the lowly; but the proud He knows from afar."

I suggest we pray together. "Holy loving God, we welcome every means You use to reveal to us the pride of our hearts, thanking You that, when we repent, You've promised to "revive the spirit of the humble, and to revive the heart of the contrite ones.' We yearn for personal revival. Amen."

Joy Dawson

God. 29 For to you [a]it has been granted on
behalf of Christ, [b]not only to believe in
Him, but also to [c]suffer for His sake,
30 [a]having the same conflict [b]which you
saw in me and now hear *is* in me.

Unity Through Humility

2 Therefore if *there is* any [1]consolation
in Christ, if any comfort of love, if any
fellowship of the Spirit, if any [a]affection
and mercy, 2 [a]fulfill my joy [b]by being like-
minded, having the same love, *being* of
[c]one accord, of one mind. 3 [a]*Let* nothing
be done through selfish ambition or conceit, but [b]in lowliness of mind let each
esteem others better than himself. 4 [a]Let
each of you look out not only for his own
interests, but also for the interests of
[b]others.

O Lord, let ____ do nothing through selfish ambition or conceit, but in lowliness of mind enable ____ to esteem others better than themselves. Let them look out not only for their own interests, but also for the interests of others.

FROM PHILIPPIANS 2:3, 4

The Humbled and Exalted Christ

5 [a]Let this mind be in you which was
also in Christ Jesus, 6 who, [a]being in the
form of God, did not consider it [1]robbery
to be equal with God, 7 [a]but [1]made Himself of no reputation, taking the form [b]of
a bondservant, *and* [c]coming in the likeness of men. 8 And being found in appearance as a man, He humbled Himself and
[a]became [b]obedient to *the point of* death,
even the death of the cross. 9 [a]Therefore
God also [b]has highly exalted Him and
[c]given Him the name which is above every name, 10 [a]that at the name of Jesus
every knee should bow, of those in heav-
en, and of those on earth, and of those
under the earth, 11 and [a]*that* every tongue
should confess that Jesus Christ *is* Lord,
to the glory of God the Father.

29 a [Matt. 5:11, 12] b Eph. 2:8 c [2 Tim. 3:12]
30 a Col. 1:29; 2:1 b Acts 16:19–40

CHAPTER 2
1 a Col. 3:12 *1 Or encouragement*
2 a John 3:29 b Rom. 12:16 c Phil. 4:2
3 a Gal. 5:26 b Rom. 12:10
4 a 1 Cor. 13:5 b Rom. 15:1, 2
5 a [Matt. 11:29]
6 a 2 Cor. 4:4 *1 Or something to be held onto to be equal*
7 a Ps. 22:6 b Is. 42:1 c [John 1:14] *1 emptied Himself* of His privileges
8 a Matt. 26:39 b Heb. 5:8
9 a Heb. 2:9 b Acts 2:33 c Eph. 1:21
10 a Is. 45:23
11 a John 13:13
12 a Phil. 1:5, 6; 4:15 b John 6:27, 29 c Eph. 6:5
13 a Heb. 13:20, 21 b Eph. 1:5
14 a 1 Pet. 4:9 b Rom. 14:1 *1 grumbling* *2 arguing*
15 a Matt. 5:15, 16 *1 innocent*
16 a 2 Cor. 1:14 b Gal. 2:2 c 1 Thess. 3:5
17 a 2 Tim. 4:6 b Rom. 15:16 c 2 Cor. 7:4
19 a Rom. 16:21 *1 condition*
20 a 2 Tim. 3:10
22 a 1 Cor. 4:17
25 a Phil. 4:18 b Philem. 2 c 2 Cor. 8:23 d 2 Cor. 11:9

Light Bearers

12 Therefore, my beloved, [a]as you have
always obeyed, not as in my presence only,
but now much more in my absence,
[b]work out your own salvation with [c]fear
and trembling; 13 for [a]it is God who works
in you both to will and to do [b]for *His* good
pleasure.
14 Do all things [a]without [1]complaining
and [b]disputing,[2] 15 that you may become
blameless and [1]harmless, children of God
without fault in the midst of a crooked
and perverse generation, among whom
you shine as [a]lights in the world, 16 holding fast the word of life, so that [a]I may
rejoice in the day of Christ that [b]I have
not run in vain or labored in [c]vain.
17 Yes, and if [a]I am being poured out *as
a drink offering* on the sacrifice [b]and service of your faith, [c]I am glad and rejoice
with you all. 18 For the same reason you
also be glad and rejoice with me.

Timothy Commended

19 But I trust in the Lord Jesus to send
[a]Timothy to you shortly, that I also may
be encouraged when I know your [1]state.
20 For I have no one [a]like-minded, who
will sincerely care for your state. 21 For all
seek their own, not the things which are
of Christ Jesus. 22 But you know his prov-
en character, [a]that as a son with *his* father
he served with me in the gospel. 23 Therefore I hope to send him at once, as soon
as I see how it goes with me. 24 But I trust
in the Lord that I myself shall also come
shortly.

Epaphroditus Praised

25 Yet I considered it necessary to send
to you [a]Epaphroditus, my brother, fellow
worker, and [b]fellow soldier, [c]but your
messenger and [d]the one who ministered
to my need; 26 [a]since he was longing for
you all, and was distressed because you
had heard that he was sick. 27 For indeed
he was sick almost unto death; but God
had mercy on him, and not only on him
but on me also, lest I should have sorrow
upon sorrow. 28 Therefore I sent him the
more eagerly, that when you see him
again you may rejoice, and I may be less
sorrowful. 29 Receive him therefore in the
Lord with all gladness, and hold such
men in esteem; 30 because for the work
of Christ he came close to death, [1]not

26 a Phil. 1:8 30 *1 risking*

Philippians 3:7–10

Dear Woman of Destiny,

Springtime always brings a special event for high school seniors—graduation. As I recently sat in this noble ceremony with the other dads and moms on a warm June afternoon, my eyes were riveted upon just one: my firstborn and only son. A myriad of emotions filled my heart as I simultaneously observed his every move, awaited the announcement of his name, and flashed back into mental memoirs of his birth and childhood. Quietly, I asked God to keep His hand upon our Gabriel, the son He had so graciously entrusted to us, and that by His grace, our son would walk in a manner worthy of the calling upon his life. I prayed once again, "Lord, I place my son into Your hands. Spend his life for Your utmost glory."

I can identify with the pleasure of our heavenly Father upon His only Son, Jesus. I keep discovering anew the embracing presence of His perfect love in that auditorium seat while rewinding the video of my life, recognizing every time His compassion and commitment have nourished my grave desperation. I am grateful for the life He has blessed me with: parents who modeled God, my loving husband, a healed marriage, the obedient children I enjoy, caring friends, a serving church, health, earthly possessions. Yet I weep over life's single most amazing fact, incomparable to all these: *God's passion for me*. "For God so loved the world that He gave His only begotten Son, that whoever believes in Him should not perish but have everlasting life" (John 3:16).

I've learned that any passion I can offer to my beautiful Lord is solely because of His passion for me. Poverty of the soul causes deep desire to know God and to receive nourishing, eternal life found in His heart. The Father gave us everything in His Son, sent to suffer and die so that He could adopt each of us. This is truly extravagant love. "By this we know love, because He laid down His life for us" (1 John 3:16a). "We love Him because He first loved us" (1 John 4:19).

There is no parent, friend, spouse, no earthly possession that could or should satisfy the deepest longing of the spirit. Any loss of these relationships or lack of intimacy from them is unmatched to the gain of knowing Christ. To know God is to love Him. To love Him is to completely trust Him, this unseen God who knows my every past, present, and future moment; who beckons me into a nearness unlike any other; who covers the nakedness of my shame, fear, and insecurity with the warmth of His kind forgiveness, compassionate grace, and acceptance. By His sacred magnificence He shatters my religiosity, self-performance, earthly mind-sets, and personal agendas. The loss of such false securities brings me to the core of all that really matters: Jesus. He is my all in all. To gain my Lord is my greatest honor. "Yet indeed I also count all things loss for the excellence of the knowledge of Christ Jesus my Lord" (Phil. 3:8a).

As the graduation ceremony is concluding, my son's name is called. He searches the audience for our smile. I'm sure Jesus seated at the right hand of God smiles at His Father, too.

Sue Ahn

regarding his life, [a]to supply what was
lacking in your service toward me.

All for Christ

3 Finally, my brethren, [a]rejoice in the
Lord. For me to write the same things
to you *is* not tedious, but for you *it is* safe.
2 [a]Beware of dogs, beware of [b]evil workers, [c]beware of the mutilation! 3 For we
are [a]the circumcision, [b]who worship
[1]God in the Spirit, rejoice in Christ Jesus,
and have no confidence in the flesh,
4 though [a]I also might have confidence in
the flesh. If anyone else thinks he may
have confidence in the flesh, I [b]more so:
5 circumcised the eighth day, of the stock
of Israel, [a]*of* the tribe of Benjamin, [b]a Hebrew of the Hebrews; concerning the law,
[c]a Pharisee; 6 concerning zeal, [a]persecut-
ing the church; concerning the righteousness which is in the law, blameless.

Nothing can compare with knowing Christ. Lord, teach me to love and I shall understand all Scripture.

FENELON

7 But [a]what things were gain to me,
these I have counted loss for Christ. 8 Yet
indeed I also count all things loss [a]for the
excellence of the knowledge of Christ
Jesus my Lord, for whom I have suffered
the loss of all things, and count them as
rubbish, that I may gain Christ 9 and be
found in Him, not having [a]my own righteousness, which *is* from the law, but
[b]that which *is* through faith in Christ, the
righteousness which is from God by
faith; 10 that I may know Him and the
[a]power of His resurrection, and [b]the fellowship of His sufferings, being conformed
to His death, 11 if, by any means, I
may [a]attain[1] to the resurrection from the
dead.

Pressing Toward the Goal

12 Not that I have already [a]attained,[1] or
am already [b]perfected; but I press on, that
I may lay hold of that for which Christ
Jesus has also laid hold of me. 13 Brethren,
I do not count myself to have [1]apprehend-
ed; but one thing *I do,* [a]forgetting those
things which are behind and [b]reaching
forward to those things which are ahead,
14 [a]I press toward the goal for the prize of
[b]the upward call of God in Christ Jesus.

Father, may ____ forget those things which are behind and reach forward to those things which are ahead. May they press toward the goal for the prize of the upward call of God in Christ Jesus.

FROM PHILIPPIANS 3:13, 14

15 Therefore let us, as many as are [a]ma-
ture, [b]have this mind; and if in anything
you think otherwise, [c]God will reveal even
this to you. 16 Nevertheless, to *the degree*
that we have already [1]attained, [a]let us
walk [b]by the same [2]rule, let us be of the
same mind.

Our Citizenship in Heaven

17 Brethren, [a]join in following my example, and note those who so walk, as
[b]you have us for a pattern. 18 For many
walk, of whom I have told you often, and
now tell you even weeping, *that they are*
[a]the enemies of the cross of Christ:
19 [a]whose end *is* destruction, [b]whose god
is their belly, and [c]*whose* glory *is* in their
shame—[d]who set their mind on earthly
things. 20 For [a]our citizenship is in heav-
en, [b]from which we also [c]eagerly wait for
the Savior, the Lord Jesus Christ, 21 [a]who
will transform our lowly body that it may
be [b]conformed to His glorious body, [c]ac-
cording to the working by which He is
able even to [d]subdue all things to Himself.
4 Therefore, my beloved and [a]longed-
for brethren, [b]my joy and crown, so
[c]stand fast in the Lord, beloved.

30 a 1 Cor. 16:17

CHAPTER 3
1 a 1 Thess. 5:16
2 a Gal. 5:15 b Ps. 119:115 c Rom. 2:28
3 a Deut. 30:6 b Rom. 7:6 *1* NU, M *in the Spirit of God*
4 a 2 Cor. 5:16; 11:18 b 2 Cor. 11:22, 23
5 a Rom. 11:1 b 2 Cor. 11:22 c Acts 23:6
6 a Acts 8:3; 22:4, 5; 26:9–11
7 a Matt. 13:44
8 a Jer. 9:23
9 a Rom. 10:3 b Rom. 1:17
10 a Eph. 1:19, 20 b [Rom. 6:3–5]
11 a Acts 26:6–8 *1* Lit. *arrive at*
12 a [1 Tim. 6:12, 19] b Heb. 12:23 *1 obtained it*
13 a Luke 9:62 b Heb. 6:1 *1 laid hold of it*
14 a 2 Tim. 4:7 b Heb. 3:1
15 a 1 Cor. 2:6 b Gal. 5:10 c Hos. 6:3
16 a Gal. 6:16 b Rom. 12:16; 15:5 *1 arrived* *2* NU omits *rule* and the rest of v. 16.
17 a [1 Cor. 4:16; 11:1] b Titus 2:7, 8
18 a Gal. 1:7
19 a 2 Cor. 11:15 b 1 Tim. 6:5 c Hos. 4:7 d Rom. 8:5
20 a Eph. 2:6, 19 b Acts 1:11 c 1 Cor. 1:7
21 a [1 Cor. 15:43–53] b 1 John 3:2 c Eph. 1:19 d [1 Cor. 15:28]

CHAPTER 4 **1** a Phil. 1:8 b 2 Cor. 1:14 c Phil. 1:27

Philippians 4:6–8

Dear Woman of Destiny,

We all experience anxious moments in our lives. Think about the first time you performed on stage, went out on a date, got married, or gave birth. Anxiety pushed you forward in a healthy and productive way. It came, propelled you to action, and then subsided. But what happens when it doesn't subside? What if the anxious feelings persist and prevent you from doing even the simplest of tasks? What if anxiety pervades your thoughts and you find yourself worrying excessively? When this happens, you may be experiencing an anxiety disorder.

When we have persistent anxiety, our bodies react both physically and emotionally. We can experience a racing heart, shortness of breath, sweating, dry mouth, dizziness, nausea, diarrhea, hot flashes, the "lump in the throat," shaking, restlessness, tiredness, muscle tension, excessive worry, problems concentrating, irritability, and/or difficulty sleeping.

You may wonder why some people experience more anxiety than others. One reason is they may have inherited anxiety responses. Others may have trouble coping with stress and pressure. For some, medical conditions, such as chronic asthma, heart disease, and cancer, can bring on anxiety. Other problems, such as substance abuse, can be factors, too. Many people develop anxiety disorders from an inability to cope with loss and things out of their control.

Over three hundred times in the Bible God tells us not to fear. He knows our human tendency, so He provides help to overcome anxiety. Philippians 4:6–8 gives the formula:

1) *Talk to God* about everything (pray). No matter what the problem, we are told to take it to prayer and to cast all our burdens on the Lord. Unlike people, God does not get overburdened, and He can handle all your cares. He never tires of listening to you.
2) *Make your requests known* (supplication). We have to tell God what it is we need. James 4:2 says we don't have because we don't ask. Matthew 21:22 says, "And whatever things you ask in prayer, believing, you will receive." So be bold and tell Him your specific requests.
3) *Thank Him* for what He's already done. Does this mean we thank God for the horrible situation we may be facing? No. It means we thank Him because He's already done what's necessary to help us. He died on the cross and rose again. He will supply *all* our needs (see Phil 4:19), not just *some*. Give thanks because it's already done!
4) *Believe* God can help you. Notice the scripture says to ask and *believe*. You can't ask and then wonder or doubt. You must trust God to be true to His Word.
5) *Meditate* on the positive and true things of God. Verse 8 tells us what kinds of things to meditate upon. What are the true things? The things God has promised us. When we do this, the promise is we will have the peace of God, and our hearts and minds will be guarded.

God wants to hear our cares and to reassure us that He loves us. No matter what the anxious circumstance, tell God, work the formula, and find His peace.

Linda Mintle

PHILIPPIANS 4:11–13

Dear Woman of Destiny,

You can do it! You have all you need to fulfill your purpose. There is nothing lacking in you. Why? Because God is in you and there is no lack in Him. I know you question your own abilities and giftings. We all face moments when our inadequacy shows, especially when God asks us to do something for Him. I can always think of someone else who could do it better than I. But God doesn't choose His servants based on gifts or talents. He looks for the brave soul who will make herself available to His purpose.

Throughout history, God has delighted in using unlikely people in unlikely ways. Think about Deborah, the judge and prophetess of Israel. She was a mighty woman who led the army with Barak to victory. But there was another woman in that story. Jael, the wife of Heber, struck the final blow for total victory (see Judg. 4:17–22). Even though the armies of Sisera were completely destroyed, Sisera escaped. He came to the tent of Heber and Jael for protection. But Jael knew he was an enemy of God. She dealt a fatal blow to his head while he was sleeping. One woman in the right place at the right time succeeded where all the armies of Israel had failed.

A Samaritan woman was on her way to get water one day. As she approached Jacob's well, she encountered a man named Jesus. She had everything going against her. Jews did not speak to Samaritans. Men had nothing to do with women. And she was a woman of bad reputation. But one conversation with Jesus changed her life. Jesus, a Jew, broke down the barriers of race, gender, and socioeconomic separation. When He saw her desire to be a worshiper, He revealed the greatest revelation concerning worship in the New Testament. It was too much to keep to herself. She laid down her waterpot and ran back to town to tell what had happened to her. A whole city came to know Jesus in one day!

Women like Aimee Semple McPherson, Kathryn Kuhlman, and Catherine Booth did the unthinkable, pioneering ministries in a day when women were not received as ministers. Sister McPherson established a huge church during the Great Depression. Hundreds of thousands of sick people were healed because Kathryn Kuhlman obeyed God. Along with her husband, Catherine Booth raised up a movement called the Salvation Army, establishing places of refuge and assistance.

A woman named Susanna Wesley endured every imaginable hardship. Even though she lost children to death and her home to a fire, she persevered in her purpose of raising her children for Christ. Two of her sons, John and Charles, became great men of God. Both of those young men credited their mother with their spiritual success. As she went about her housework and daily routine, she was planting seeds of destiny.

Precious Woman of Destiny, do not be intimidated. The Greater One lives in you. He chose you for His purpose. Do not lean on your own understanding. Trust the One who made you to enable you. You can do all things through Christ who is your strength. Yes, you can!

Shirley Arnold

Be United, Joyful, and in Prayer

2 I implore Euodia and I implore Syntyche [a]to be of the same mind in the Lord. 3 [1]And I urge you also, true companion, help these women who [a]labored with me in the gospel, with Clement also, and the rest of my fellow workers, whose names *are* in [b]the Book of Life.

4 [a]Rejoice in the Lord always. Again I will say, rejoice!

5 Let your [1]gentleness be known to all men. [a]The Lord *is* at hand.

6 [a]Be anxious for nothing, but in everything by prayer and supplication, with [b]thanksgiving, let your requests be made known to God; 7 and [a]the peace of God, which surpasses all understanding, will guard your hearts and minds through Christ Jesus.

Meditate on These Things

8 Finally, brethren, whatever things are [a]true, whatever things *are* [b]noble, whatever things *are* [c]just, [d]whatever things *are* pure, whatever things *are* [e]lovely, whatever things *are* of good report, if *there is* any virtue and if *there is* anything praiseworthy—meditate on these things. 9 The things which you learned and received and heard and saw in me, these do, and [a]the God of peace will be with you.

Philippian Generosity

10 But I rejoiced in the Lord greatly that now at last [a]your[1] care for me has flourished again; though you surely did care, but you lacked opportunity. 11 Not that I speak in regard to need, for I have learned in whatever state I am, [a]to be content: 12 [a]I know how to [1]be abased, and I know how to [2]abound. Everywhere and in all things I have learned both to be full and to be hungry, both to abound and to suffer need. 13 I can do all things [a]through [1]Christ who strengthens me.

14 Nevertheless you have done well that [a]you shared in my distress. 15 Now you Philippians know also that in the beginning of the gospel, when I departed from Macedonia, [a]no church shared with me concerning giving and receiving but you only. 16 For even in Thessalonica you sent *aid* once and again for my necessities. 17 Not that I seek the gift, but I seek [a]the fruit that abounds to your account. 18 Indeed I [1]have all and abound. I am full, having received from [a]Epaphroditus the things *sent* from you, [b]a sweet-smelling aroma, [c]an acceptable sacrifice, well pleasing to God. 19 And my God [a]shall supply all your need according to His riches in glory by Christ Jesus. 20 [a]Now to our God and Father *be* glory forever and ever. Amen.

O Father, I pray that You will supply all that ______ needs according to Your riches in glory by Christ Jesus.

FROM PHILIPPIANS 4:19

Greeting and Blessing

21 Greet every saint in Christ Jesus. The brethren [a]who are with me greet you. 22 All the saints greet you, but especially those who are of Caesar's household.

23 The grace of our Lord Jesus Christ be with [1]you all. Amen.

---

2 a Phil. 2:2; 3:16
3 a Rom. 16:3 b Luke 10:20 1 NU, M *Yes*
4 a Rom. 12:12
5 a [James 5:7–9] 1 *graciousness or forbearance*
6 a Matt. 6:25 b [1 Thess. 5:17, 18]
7 a [John 14:27]
8 a Eph. 4:25 b 2 Cor. 8:21 c Deut. 16:20 d 1 Thess. 5:22 e 1 Cor. 13:4–7
9 a Rom. 15:33
10 a 2 Cor. 11:9 1 *you have revived your care*
11 a 1 Tim. 6:6, 8
12 a 1 Cor. 4:11 1 *live humbly* 2 *live in prosperity*
13 a John 15:5 1 NU *Him who*
14 a Phil. 1:7
15 a 2 Cor. 11:8, 9
17 a Titus 3:14
18 a Phil. 2:25 b Heb. 13:16 c 2 Cor. 9:12 1 Or *have received all*
19 a Ps. 23:1
20 a Rom. 16:27
21 a Gal. 1:2
23 1 NU *your spirit*

AUTHOR: *Paul*
DATE: *A.D. 61*
THEME: *The Supremacy and Sufficiency of Christ*
KEY WORDS: *Fullness, Wisdom, Knowledge, Mystery*

COLOSSIANS

Dear Woman of Destiny,

The theme of the universal lordship of Christ in Colossians is very important to us in our modern-day cultures. Some of the same false teachings that were beginning to infiltrate the church at Colosse are being encountered by the church today. These come in the form of pluralism, which says that we need to be open to all world religions and that all roads lead to God. This, of course, is heresy. A strong admonition against angel worship is given in 2:18, 19. Today, many non-Christian spiritual practices encourage us to "get in touch with" our angels. Many are being deceived by false doctrines. We, as women of destiny, need to study this book to stay centered in biblical truth.

With His love,

Cindy Jacobs

Greeting

Paul, [a]an apostle of Jesus Christ by
the will of God, and Timothy our
brother,

2To the saints [a]and faithful brethren in
Christ *who are* in Colosse:

[b]Grace to you and peace from God our
Father [1]and the Lord Jesus Christ.

Their Faith in Christ

3[a]We give thanks to the God and Father
of our Lord Jesus Christ, praying always
for you, 4[a]since we heard of your faith in
Christ Jesus and of [b]your love for all the
saints; 5because of the hope [a]which is laid
up for you in heaven, of which you heard
before in the word of the truth of the gospel, 6which has come to you, [a]as *it has*
also in all the world, and [b]is bringing
forth [1]fruit, as *it is* also among you since
the day you heard and knew [c]the grace of
God in truth; 7as you also learned from
[a]Epaphras, our dear fellow servant, who is
[b]a faithful minister of Christ on your behalf, 8who also declared to us your [a]love
in the Spirit.

Preeminence of Christ

9[a]For this reason we also, since the day
we heard it, do not cease to pray for you,
and to ask [b]that you may be filled with
[c]the knowledge of His will [d]in all wisdom
and spiritual understanding; 10[a]that you
may walk worthy of the Lord, [b]fully pleasing *Him,* [c]being fruitful in every good
work and increasing in the [d]knowledge of
God; 11[a]strengthened with all might, according to His glorious power, [b]for all
patience and longsuffering [c]with joy;
12[a]giving thanks to the Father who has
qualified us to be partakers of [b]the inheritance of the saints in the light. 13He has
delivered us from [a]the power of darkness
[b]and [1]conveyed *us* into the kingdom of
the Son of His love, 14[a]in whom we have
redemption [1]through His blood, the forgiveness of sins.

15He is [a]the image of the invisible God,
[b]the firstborn over all creation. 16 For
[a]by Him all things were created that are
in heaven and that are on earth, visible
and invisible, whether thrones or [b]domin-
ions or [1]principalities or [2]powers. All
things were created [c]through Him and for
Him. 17[a]And He is before all things, and
in Him [b]all things consist. 18And [a]He is
the head of the body, the church, who is
the beginning, [b]the firstborn from the
dead, that in all things He may have the
preeminence.

Reconciled in Christ

19For it pleased *the Father that* [a]in Him
all the fullness should dwell, 20and [a]by
Him to reconcile [b]all things to Himself,
by Him, whether things on earth or
things in heaven, [c]having made peace
through the blood of His cross.

21And you, [a]who once were alienated
and enemies in your mind [b]by wicked
works, yet now He has [c]reconciled 22[a]in
the body of His flesh through death, [b]to
present you holy, and blameless, and
above reproach in His sight— 23if indeed
you continue [a]in the faith, grounded and
steadfast, and are [b]not moved away from
the hope of the gospel which you heard,
[c]which was preached to every creature
under heaven, [d]of which I, Paul, became
a minister.

Father, I do not cease to pray for _____. May they be filled with the knowledge of Your will in all wisdom and spiritual understanding; may they have a walk worthy of You, fully pleasing You, being fruitful in every good work and increasing in the knowledge of God.

FROM COLOSSIANS 1:9, 10

Sacrificial Service for Christ

24[a]I now rejoice in my sufferings [b]for
you, and fill up in my flesh [c]what is lacking in the afflictions of Christ, for [d]the
sake of His body, which is the church, 25of
which I became a minister according to
[a]the [1]stewardship from God which was
given to me for you, to fulfill the word of
God, 26[a]the [1]mystery which has been hidden from ages and from generations, [b]but

CHAPTER 1
1 a Eph. 1:1
2 a 1 Cor. 4:17 b Gal. 1:3 *1* NU omits *and the Lord Jesus Christ*
3 a Phil. 1:3
4 a Eph. 1:15 b [Heb. 6:10]
5 a [1 Pet. 1:4]
6 a Matt. 24:14 b John 15:16 c Eph. 3:2 *1* NU, M add *and growing*
7 a Philem. 23 b 2 Cor. 11:23
8 a Rom. 15:30
9 a Eph. 1:15–17 b 1 Cor. 1:5 c [Rom. 12:2] d Eph. 1:8
10 a Eph. 4:1 b 1 Thess. 4:1 c Heb. 13:21 d 2 Pet. 3:18
11 a [Eph. 3:16; 6:10] b Eph. 4:2 c [Acts 5:41]
12 a [Eph. 5:20] b Eph. 1:11
13 a Eph. 6:12 b 2 Pet. 1:11 *1 transferred*
14 a Eph. 1:7 *1* NU, M omit *through His blood*
15 a 2 Cor. 4:4 b Rev. 3:14
16 a Heb. 1:2, 3 b [Eph. 1:20, 21] c Heb. 2:10 *1 rulers* *2 authorities*
17 a [John 17:5] b Heb. 1:3
18 a Eph. 1:22 b Rev. 1:5
19 a John 1:16
20 a Eph. 2:14 b 2 Cor. 5:18 c Eph. 1:10
21 a [Eph. 2:1] b Titus 1:15 c 2 Cor. 5:18, 19
22 a 2 Cor. 5:18 b [Eph. 5:27]
23 a Eph. 3:17 b [John 15:6] c Col. 1:6 d Col. 1:25
24 a 2 Cor. 7:4 b Eph. 3:1, 13 c [2 Cor. 1:5; 12:15] d Eph. 1:23 **25** a Gal. 2:7 *1 dispensation* or *administration* **26** a [1 Cor. 2:7] b [2 Tim. 1:10] *1 secret* or *hidden truth*

COLOSSIANS 1:16

Dear Woman of Destiny,

All creativity comes from God. He is the original creative Genius. Creativity is a part of His divine nature. And since you were created in the image of God, you, too, were born with the ability to create. It is part of your spiritual heritage.

Although you won't find the English word *creativity* in the Scriptures, its principle is often displayed. As with love, joy, and peace, creativity comes from the regenerated spirit of a person. These redemptive qualities do not flow from without, but from within. God at work in you produces these results from the inside. The animal world operates through instinct; the human family was intended to operate by the power of the Holy Spirit working in their own spirits.

Sin, however, severed that life source, disconnecting us from our full capabilities, though many unredeemed people are creative. Men and women living apart from God are still made in His image, with much divine potential that is yet unrealized. We are spirit beings even when we are alienated from God.

If you have been born again, however, you are able to tap back into God's original design for you. His godliness comes back to life in and through you, and you begin the lifelong journey of being conformed to His image, including becoming a joint heir of His creativity.

Creativity is not something given to a few geniuses, a few gifted people, or the highly educated. Compare the dynamic of creativity to other benefits of redeemed living. For example, love is not given to just a few. Love is an expression of God through the One who has come to live in you. So it is with creativity. The same power that enables you to love empowers you with creativity. All creativity flows from His Spirit.

Christ's creative power is limitless. Paul said, "Now to Him who is able to do *exceedingly abundantly above* all that we ask or think, according to the power that works in us" (Eph. 3:20, emphasis added). Whose power? The power of God through His indwelling Spirit.

Learn to develop your fullest potential. A growing child wants to learn and is curious about everything! Godly parents want to pour information into that hungry little mind. We delight in teaching them and watching them apply their new knowledge. God sees His children in the same way. When He looks at you, He says, "Her heart is open. She is studying and learning. She has tasted the joy of knowledge and has discovered how to share it with other people. I will teach her more."

Whatever you need, He has it. Draw from Him, and let His creative wisdom flow through you. Allow His creativity to bloom in your life. It will produce solutions, hope, confidence, and healing. Creativity is energized in you when you come to Christ. When you need an answer, you have it through Him. Tap into it. Exercise and use it. It's yours!

LaDonna Osborn

now has been revealed to His saints. 27[a]To
them God willed to make known what are
[b]the riches of the glory of this mystery
among the Gentiles: [1]which is [c]Christ in
you, [d]the hope of glory. 28Him we preach,
[a]warning every man and teaching every
man in all wisdom, [b]that we may present
every man perfect in Christ Jesus. 29To
this *end* I also labor, striving according
to His working which works in me
[a]mightily.

> *Christ within us can accomplish what we can never hope to do in our own strength; and that continuous walking with Him will change the weakest of us into His image.*
>
> DONALD GEE

Not Philosophy but Christ

2 For I want you to know what a great
[a]conflict[1] I have for you and those in
Laodicea, and *for* as many as have not
seen my face in the flesh, 2that their
hearts may be encouraged, being knit together in love, and *attaining* to all riches
of the full assurance of understanding,
to the knowledge of the mystery of God,
[1]both of the Father and of Christ, 3[a]in
whom are hidden all the treasures of wisdom and knowledge.
4Now this I say [a]lest anyone should deceive you with persuasive words. 5For
[a]though I am absent in the flesh, yet I am
with you in spirit, rejoicing [1]to see [b]your
good order and the [c]steadfastness of your
faith in Christ.
6[a]As you therefore have received Christ
Jesus the Lord, so walk in Him, 7[a]rooted
and built up in Him and established in the
faith, as you have been taught, abounding
[1]in it with thanksgiving.
8Beware lest anyone [1]cheat you
through philosophy and empty deceit, according to [a]the tradition of men, according to the [b]basic principles of the world,
and not according to Christ. 9For [a]in Him
dwells all the fullness of the Godhead
[1]bodily; 10and you are complete in Him,
who is the [a]head of all [1]principality and
power.

Not Legalism but Christ

11In Him you were also [a]circumcised
with the circumcision made without
hands, by [b]putting off the body [1]of the
sins of the flesh, by the circumcision of
Christ, 12[a]buried with Him in baptism,
in which you also were raised with *Him*
through [b]faith in the working of God,
[c]who raised Him from the dead. 13And
you, being dead in your trespasses and the
uncircumcision of your flesh, He has
made alive together with Him, having forgiven you all trespasses, 14[a]having wiped
out the [1]handwriting of requirements
that was against us, which was contrary to
us. And He has taken it out of the way,
having nailed it to the cross. 15[a]Having
disarmed [b]principalities and powers, He
made a public spectacle of them, triumphing over them in it.
16So let no one [a]judge you in food or in
drink, or regarding a [1]festival or a new
moon or sabbaths, 17[a]which are a shadow
of things to come, but the [1]substance is of
Christ. 18Let no one cheat you of your reward, taking delight in *false* humility and
worship of angels, intruding into those
things which he has [1]not seen, vainly
puffed up by his fleshly mind, 19and not
holding fast to [a]the Head, from whom all
the body, nourished and knit together by
joints and ligaments, [b]grows with the increase *that is* from God.

> *Father, as ____ has received Christ Jesus the Lord, so may they walk in Him, rooted and built up in Him and established in the faith, as they have been taught, abounding in it with thanksgiving.*
>
> FROM COLOSSIANS 2:6, 7

20[1]Therefore, if you [a]died with Christ
from the basic principles of the world,
[b]why, as *though* living in the world, do

27 a 2 Cor. 2:14 b Rom. 9:23 c [Rom. 8:10, 11] d 1 Tim. 1:1 *1 M who*
28 a Acts 20:20 b Eph. 5:27
29 a Eph. 3:7

CHAPTER 2
1 a Phil. 1:30 *1 struggle*
2 *1* NU omits *both of the Father and*
3 a 1 Cor. 1:24, 30
4 a Rom. 16:18
5 a 1 Thess. 2:17 b 1 Cor. 14:40 c 1 Pet. 5:9 *1* Lit. *and seeing*
6 a 1 Thess. 4:1
7 a Eph. 2:21 *1* NU omits *in it*
8 a Gal. 1:14 b Gal. 4:3, 9, 10 *1* Lit. *plunder you* or *take you captive*
9 a [John 1:14] *1 in bodily form*
10 a [Eph. 1:20, 21] *1 rule and authority*
11 a Deut. 10:16 b Rom. 6:6; 7:24 *1* NU omits *of the sins*
12 a Rom. 6:4 b Eph. 1:19, 20 c Acts 2:24
14 a [Eph. 2:15, 16] *1 certificate of debt with its*
15 a [Is. 53:12] b Eph. 6:12
16 a Rom. 14:3 *1 feast day*
17 a Heb. 8:5; 10:1 *1* Lit. *body*
18 *1* NU omits *not*
19 a Eph. 4:15 b Eph. 1:23; 4:16
20 a Rom. 6:2–5 b Gal. 4:3, 9 *1* NU, M omit *Therefore*

Colossians 3:8

Dear Woman of Destiny,

Did you know you can influence your own destiny, either for good or for bad? No one else has the power to keep you from fulfilling your destiny. It doesn't matter what others have said about you or what others have done to you. Your gender cannot stop you, your color cannot stop you, and what side of the tracks you were born on cannot stop you from fulfilling your destiny.

However, one tiny thing can stop you right in your tracks. It is called your tongue. The Bible says that your tongue has the power of life and death (see Prov. 18:21). James 3:4 says the tongue is like a rudder on a heavy ship. The rudder steers and sets the course of the ship. So it is with the tongue. What we say about ourselves and our circumstances—what comes out of our mouth—sets the course of our lives.

We can go through hard times and say, "Why me, why, oh why, oh why?" or, "I will never recover from this pit," and we have just set our life's course for destruction. Or we can get into God's Word, the only truth, and find out God's eternal and supernatural perception. Then we can speak life into our pain, and see God change our circumstances. All things work together for good for _____ who loves God (see Rom. 8:28). Plug your name, or the name of one for whom you are praying, right into the scripture, pray out loud in faith, and set your course.

While I was in high school and during part of college, I had an eating disorder called bulimia. It was absolute torture for me. I tried everything under the sun to overcome it; and after five years, I began to lose hope. A friend of mine, Ron Luce (who is now much more than a friend), told me that I needed to say what God was already saying about me. At first, I thought it was hypocritical to say things like, "I am fearfully and wonderfully made," or "I am precious and chosen in God's sight." I felt like an utter failure and very unpleasing to God.

Ron told me that God's Word is more true than what we see in the natural realm of life, and that if He can say something in His Word about us, then we can say it, too. So I began to speak God's Word out of my mouth. I found all kinds of promises, love notes, concerning what God thinks of me. I was astounded at how much He loves even those who have failed Him. I spoke things that were not as though they were, just like Abraham. I began to change.

Eighteen years have passed, and I still walk in complete freedom from overeating. I am confident of who God has made me to be. I continue to pray Scriptures over myself, my husband, our children, our family, and our ministry. I see over and over again God's faithfulness to His word. So get on God's course for your life. Quit complaining, arguing, and speaking negative things, and start speaking His truth; and you will truly become a woman of destiny.

Katie Luce

you subject yourselves to regulations—
21[a]"Do not touch, do not taste, do not
handle," 22which all concern things which
perish with the using—[a]according to the
commandments and doctrines of men?
23[a]These things indeed have an appearance of wisdom in self-imposed religion,
false humility, and [1]neglect of the body,
but are of no value against the indulgence
of the flesh.

Not Carnality but Christ

3 If then you were [a]raised with Christ,
seek those things which are above,
[b]where Christ is, sitting at the right hand
of God. 2Set your mind on things above,
not on things on the [a]earth. 3[a]For you
died, [b]and your life is hidden with Christ
in God. 4[a]When Christ *who is* [b]our life
appears, then you also will appear with
Him in [c]glory.

Be careful not to allow your mind to dwell much on your weaknesses and unworthiness. These excessive feelings spring from a root of pride and a love for our own excellence.

MADAME JEANNE GUYON

5[a]Therefore put to death [b]your members which are on the earth: [c]fornication,
uncleanness, passion, evil desire, and covetousness, [d]which is idolatry. 6[a]Because
of these things the wrath of God is coming
upon [b]the sons of disobedience, 7[a]in
which you yourselves once walked when
you lived in them.
8 [a]But now you yourselves are to put
off all these: anger, wrath, malice, blasphemy, filthy language out of your
mouth. 9Do not lie to one another,
since you have put off the old man with
his deeds, 10and have put on the new *man*
who [a]is renewed in knowledge [b]according
to the image of Him who [c]created him,
11where there is neither [a]Greek nor Jew,
circumcised nor uncircumcised, barbarian, Scythian, slave *nor* free, [b]but Christ *is*
all and in all.

Character of the New Man

12Therefore, [a]as *the* elect of God, holy
and beloved, [b]put on tender mercies,
kindness, humility, meekness, longsuffering; 13[a]bearing with one another, and forgiving one another, if anyone has a
complaint against another; even as Christ
forgave you, so you also *must do.* 14[a]But
above all these things [b]put on love, which
is the [c]bond of perfection. 15And let [a]the
peace of God rule in your hearts, [b]to
which also you were called [c]in one body;
and [d]be thankful. 16Let the word of Christ
dwell in you richly in all wisdom, teaching
and admonishing one another [a]in psalms
and hymns and spiritual songs, singing
with grace in your hearts to the Lord.
17 And [a]*whatever* you do in word or
deed, *do* all in the name of the Lord Jesus,
giving thanks to God the Father through
Him.

I ask that whatever _____ does in word or deed, that it would be done in Your name, Lord Jesus, giving thanks to God the Father.

FROM COLOSSIANS 3:17

The Christian Home

18[a]Wives, submit to your own husbands, [b]as is fitting in the Lord.
19[a]Husbands, love your wives and do
not be [b]bitter toward them.
20[a]Children, obey your parents [b]in all
things, for this is well pleasing to the
Lord.
21[a]Fathers, do not provoke your children, lest they become discouraged.
22[a]Bondservants, obey in all things
your masters according to the flesh, not
with eyeservice, as men-pleasers, but in
sincerity of heart, fearing God. 23[a]And
whatever you do, do it heartily, as to the
Lord and not to men, 24[a]knowing that
from the Lord you will receive the reward
of the inheritance; [b]for[1] you serve the
Lord Christ. 25But he who does wrong will

21 a 1 Tim. 4:3
22 a Titus 1:14
23 a 1 Tim. 4:8 *1 severe treatment, asceticism*

CHAPTER 3
1 a Col. 2:12 b Eph. 1:20
2 a [Matt. 6:19–21]
3 a [Rom. 6:2] b [2 Cor. 5:7]
4 a [1 John 3:2] b John 14:6 c 1 Cor. 15:43
5 a [Rom. 8:13] b [Rom. 6:13] c Eph. 5:3 d Eph. 4:19; 5:3, 5
6 a Rom. 1:18 b [Eph. 2:2]
7 a 1 Cor. 6:11
8 a Eph. 4:22
10 a Rom. 12:2 b [Rom. 8:29] c [Eph. 2:10]
11 a Gal. 3:27, 28 b Eph. 1:23
12 a [1 Pet. 1:2] b 1 John 3:17
13 a [Mark 11:25]
14 a 1 Pet. 4:8 b [1 Cor. 13] c Eph. 4:3
15 a [John 14:27] b 1 Cor. 7:15 c Eph. 4:4 d [1 Thess. 5:18]
16 a Eph. 5:19
17 a 1 Cor. 10:31
18 a 1 Pet. 3:1 b [Eph. 5:22—6:9]
19 a [Eph. 5:25] b Eph. 4:31
20 a Eph. 6:1 b Eph. 5:24
21 a Eph. 6:4
22 a Eph. 6:5
23 a [Eccl. 9:10]
24 a Eph. 6:8 b 1 Cor. 7:22 *1 NU omits for*

Colossians 3:17, 18

Dear Woman of Destiny,

Blessings on you and grace for today!

I believe many of us, as women, miss the true meaning of Colossians 3:17, 18. The phrase "as is fitting in the Lord" can be translated to mean "for that is your duty as Christians," "because this is your service," or "this is what the Lord demands." Over the last twenty years of ministering with my husband, I have learned the true value of my place in the work of God.

Several years ago, I had the opportunity to meet one of the most remarkable women in ministry. Her name is Maria. She is the wife of famed Argentine evangelist Carlos Annacondia. It was 1984; and my husband, Steve, and I were visiting Carlos' crusade in the city of Mar del Plata, Argentina. The crusade was electric with excitement over the thousands of miracles, signs, and wonders that had been occurring. There was a large platform that stood six feet tall, set up at the edge of a huge field in the center of the city. On the platform stood the evangelist, with microphone in hand, preaching the uncompromising word of God. Steve and I drew as close as possible.

When we approached the stage area, I heard a rumbling coming from underneath the platform. About that time, someone came up to me and said, "Do you want to know the secret?" Puzzled and curious, I said, "Sure." It was then that he pulled back a curtain that surrounded the base of the platform. To my amazement, there were about two dozen ladies on their faces moaning, groaning, and weeping for lost souls. The kind gentleman then said, "I want you to meet the leader of these intercessors." He called to Sister Annacondia, who was under the platform.

I was embarrassed to have interrupted her intercession, but she gladly greeted me. She was small in stature, but mighty in God. The mother of nine children, Maria Annacondia has found her place in the ministry. I learned a valuable lesson that day. She wasn't interested in sitting on the platform where she could be seen by man. She was interested in sitting hidden, in obscurity, where she could be seen by God. This was her duty; this was fit in the Lord.

Jeri Hill

be repaid for what he has done, and [a]there
is no partiality.

4 Masters,[a] give your bondservants
what is just and fair, knowing that
you also have a Master in heaven.

Christian Graces

2[a]Continue earnestly in prayer, being
vigilant in it [b]with thanksgiving; 3[a]mean-
while praying also for us, that God would
[b]open to us a door for the word, to speak
[c]the [1]mystery of Christ, [d]for which I am
also in chains, 4that I may make it manifest, as I ought to speak.
5[a]Walk in [b]wisdom toward those *who
are* outside, [c]redeeming the time. 6*Let*
your speech always *be* [a]with grace, [b]sea-
soned with salt, [c]that you may know how
you ought to answer each one.

Heavenly Father, I pray for ____ that their speech would always be with grace, seasoned with salt, that they may know how they ought to answer each one.

FROM COLOSSIANS 4:6

Final Greetings

7[a]Tychicus, a beloved brother, faithful
minister, and fellow servant in the Lord,
will tell you all the news about me. 8[a]I am
sending him to you for this very purpose,
that [1]he may know your circumstances
and comfort your hearts, 9with [a]Onesi-
mus, a faithful and beloved brother, who
is *one* of you. They will make known to
you all things which *are happening* here.
10[a]Aristarchus my fellow prisoner
greets you, with [b]Mark the cousin of Barnabas (about whom you received instructions: if he comes to you, welcome him),
11and Jesus who is called Justus. These
are my only fellow workers for the kingdom of God who are of the circumcision;
they have proved to be a comfort to me.
12[a]Epaphras, who is *one* of you, a bondservant of Christ, greets you, always [b]la-
boring fervently for you in prayers, that
you may stand [c]perfect and [1]complete in
all the will of God. 13For I bear him witness that he has a great [1]zeal for you, and
those who are in Laodicea, and those in
Hierapolis. 14[a]Luke the beloved physician
and [b]Demas greet you. 15Greet the brethren who are in Laodicea, and [1]Nymphas
and [a]the church that *is* in [2]his house.

Closing Exhortations and Blessing

16Now when [a]this epistle is read among
you, see that it is read also in the church
of the Laodiceans, and that you likewise
read the epistle from Laodicea. 17And say
to [a]Archippus, "Take heed to [b]the ministry which you have received in the Lord,
that you may fulfill it."
18[a]This salutation by my own hand—
Paul. [b]Remember my chains. Grace *be*
with you. Amen.

---

25 [a]Rom. 2:11

CHAPTER 4
1 [a]Eph. 6:9
2 [a]Luke 18:1 [b]Col. 2:7
3 [a]Eph. 6:19 [b]1 Cor. 16:9 [c]Eph. 3:3, 4; 6:19 [d]Eph. 6:20 [1]*hidden truth*
5 [a]Eph. 5:15 [b][Matt. 10:16] [c]Eph. 5:16
6 [a]Eccl. 10:12 [b]Mark 9:50 [c]1 Pet. 3:15
7 [a]2 Tim. 4:12
8 [a]Eph. 6:22 [1]NU *you may know our circumstances and he may comfort*
9 [a]Philem. 10
10 [a]Acts 19:29; 20:4; 27:2 [b]2 Tim. 4:11
12 [a]Philem. 23 [b]Rom. 15:30 [c]Matt. 5:48 [1]NU *fully assured*
13 [1]NU *concern*
14 [a]2 Tim. 4:11 [b]2 Tim. 4:10
15 [a]Rom. 16:5 [1]NU *Nympha* [2]NU *her*
16 [a]1 Thess. 5:27
17 [a]Philem. 2 [b]2 Tim. 4:5
18 [a]1 Cor. 16:21 [b]Heb. 13:3

AUTHOR: *Paul*
DATE: *A.D. 50*
THEME: *The Twin Comforts of Past Ministry and the Future Return of the Lord*
KEY WORDS: *Thanks, Coming, Faith/Hope/Love*

1 THESSALONIANS

Dear Woman of Destiny,

The second major church was founded on the European continent in Thessalonica. Among the first converts in this city were leading Greek women (see Acts 17:4). It isn't hard to imagine that these courageous ladies were persecuted for their new beliefs as they cast off idol worship and everything surrounding the pagan worship of the Greek culture. The greeting in the Book of 1 Thessalonians to these new converts, who remained steadfast in the faith, is one with which we should encourage one another today as women of destiny: "We give thanks to God always for you all, making mention of you in our prayers, remembering without ceasing your work of faith, labor of love, and patience of hope in our Lord Jesus Christ in the sight of our God and Father" (1 Thess. 1:2, 3).

With His love,

Cindy Jacobs

Greeting

Paul, [a]Silvanus, and Timothy,

To the church of the [b]Thessalo-
nians in God the Father and the Lord Jesus Christ:

Grace to you and peace [1]from God our
Father and the Lord Jesus Christ.

Father, I give thanks to You always for _____, making mention of them in my prayers, remembering without ceasing their work of faith, labor of love, and patience of hope in our Lord Jesus Christ.

FROM 1 THESSALONIANS 1:2, 3

Their Good Example

2 [a]We give thanks to God always for you
all, making mention of you in our prayers,
3 remembering without ceasing [a]your
work of faith, [b]labor of love, and patience
of hope in our Lord Jesus Christ in the
sight of our God and Father, 4 knowing,
beloved brethren, [a]your election by God.
5 For [a]our gospel did not come to you in
word only, but also in power, [b]and in the
Holy Spirit [c]and in much assurance, as
you know what kind of men we were
among you for your sake.
6 And [a]you became followers of us and
of the Lord, having received the word in
much affliction, [b]with joy of the Holy
Spirit, 7 so that you became examples to
all in Macedonia and Achaia who believe.
8 For from you the word of the Lord [a]has
sounded forth, not only in Macedonia and
Achaia, but also [b]in every place. Your faith
toward God has gone out, so that we do
not need to say anything. 9 For they themselves declare concerning us [a]what manner of entry we had to you, [b]and how you
turned to God from idols to serve the living and true God, 10 and [a]to wait for His
Son from heaven, whom He raised from
the dead, *even* Jesus who delivers us
[b]from the wrath to come.

CHAPTER 1
1 a 1 Pet. 5:12 b Acts 17:1–9 *1* NU omits *from God our Father and the Lord Jesus Christ*
2 a Rom. 1:8
3 a John 6:29 b Rom. 16:6
4 a Col. 3:12
5 a Mark 16:20 b 2 Cor. 6:6 c Heb. 2:3
6 a 1 Cor. 4:16; 11:1 b Acts 5:41; 13:52
8 a Rom. 10:18 b Rom. 1:8; 16:19
9 a 1 Thess. 2:1 b 1 Cor. 12:2
10 a [Rom. 2:7] b Rom. 5:9

CHAPTER 2
2 a Acts 14:5; 16:19–24 b Acts 17:1–9 *1* NU, M omit *even*
3 a 2 Cor. 7:2
4 a 1 Cor. 7:25 b Titus 1:3 c Gal. 1:10 d Prov. 17:3
5 a 2 Cor. 2:17 b Rom. 1:9 *1 pretext for greed*
6 a 1 Tim. 5:17 b 1 Cor. 9:4 c 2 Cor. 11:9 d 1 Cor. 9:1
7 a 1 Cor. 2:3
8 a Rom. 1:11 b 2 Cor. 12:15
9 a Acts 18:3; 20:34, 35 b 2 Cor. 12:13
10 a 1 Thess. 1:5 b 2 Cor. 7:2
11 *1* NU, M *implored*
12 a Eph. 4:1

We must be careful not to think that delays in prayer are denials. Unanswered prayers are not blown away by the wind; they are treasured in the King's archives where every prayer is recorded.

CHARLES H. SPURGEON

Paul's Conduct

2 For you yourselves know, brethren,
that our coming to you was not in
vain. 2 But [1]even after we had suffered before and were spitefully treated at [a]Philip-
pi, as you know, we were [b]bold in our God
to speak to you the gospel of God in much
conflict. 3 [a]For our exhortation *did* not
come from error or uncleanness, nor *was*
it in deceit.
4 But as [a]we have been approved by God
[b]to be entrusted with the gospel, even so
we speak, [c]not as pleasing men, but God
[d]who tests our hearts. 5 For [a]neither at
any time did we use flattering words, as
you know, nor a [1]cloak for covetousness—[b]God *is* witness. 6 [a]Nor did we seek
glory from men, either from you or from
others, when [b]we might have [c]made demands [d]as apostles of Christ. 7 But [a]we
were gentle among you, just as a nursing
mother cherishes her own children. 8 So,
affectionately longing for you, we were
well pleased [a]to impart to you not only
the gospel of God, but also [b]our own lives,
because you had become dear to us. 9 For
you remember, brethren, our [a]labor and
toil; for laboring night and day, [b]that we
might not be a burden to any of you, we
preached to you the gospel of God.
10 [a]You *are* witnesses, and God *also,*
[b]how devoutly and justly and blamelessly
we behaved ourselves among you who believe; 11 as you know how we exhorted, and
comforted, and [1]charged every one of
you, as a father *does* his own children,
12 [a]that you would walk worthy of God

1 Thessalonians 2:12

Dear Woman of Destiny,

The Spirit-led life can only flow from the recreated spirit, your new heart. When God through His Word imparts His nature to you, you become His representative, pulsing with new motivation. Everything is new, flowing from that life source. Enabled by the Spirit from within, you can "walk worthy of God who calls you into His own kingdom and glory."

There is a threefold purpose to the Spirit-led life. You have been called to walk in love, to walk as light, and to walk by faith.

First, we are to walk in love. The word for "imitators" is the Greek word *mimetes*. Its root *mimos* is the word from which the English word *mimic* comes. Young children "mimic" their parents. No mother or father would be critical of such childish efforts. God is not keeping score against you. He watches over you with joy and love.

How can you live this love walk? Begin with a smile. It is hard to think ugly thoughts when you have a smile on your face. Be compassionate. Put yourself in other people's shoes. If they're frowning and full of complaints, maybe it's because they're angry or fearful or ill or broke. So don't judge others. Relax. All that negative stuff will subside and pass away, but love will last. You cannot deny His agape love—His divine love. You cannot can it, bottle it, or fake it if you do not have it. And you cannot hide it if you do. Walk in His love. See things through God's eyes.

Second, we are to walk as light. Light symbolizes understanding, and darkness represents ignorance. To walk as light is to walk in knowledge. It is our responsibility to keep on learning and studying, growing in our insight, becoming receptive to revelation, ever applying truth from God.

Third, we are to walk by faith. All that concerns our redemption, our provision in Christ, can only come to us by faith. Salvation, tranquility, peace, purpose, authority, and dignity—are all received by faith. We do not earn any of it. It is the gift of God.

The Spirit-led life does not mean that you keep your head in the clouds and speak religious-sounding words, or carry an oversized Bible. But you must be ever sensitive to the Spirit of God who rules our lives. He is the source of all new life, energy, and redemption.

To walk where you have never been, you need guidance beyond yourself and your natural abilities. Jesus knew that, so He promised to send the Comforter, the Holy Spirit. The Spirit of Christ is a resident Helper, Advocate, and Comforter who dispenses truth, knowledge, insight, and power. He leads gently and consistently. He will be with you forever. Count on it.

By the power of His indwelling Spirit, He will walk you through everything that God has desired for you to accomplish. You are not alone. Be encouraged and comforted. Jesus has allied Himself with you. He promised!

LaDonna Osborn

[b]who calls you into His own kingdom and
glory.

Their Conversion

[13]For this reason we also thank God
[a]without ceasing, because when you [b]re-
ceived the word of God which you heard
from us, you welcomed *it* [c]not *as* the
word of men, but as it is in truth, the word
of God, which also effectively [d]works in
you who believe. [14]For you, brethren, became imitators [a]of the churches of God
which are in Judea in Christ Jesus. For
[b]you also suffered the same things from
your own countrymen, just as they *did*
from the Judeans, [15][a]who killed both the
Lord Jesus and [b]their own prophets, and
have persecuted us; and they do not please
God [c]and are [1]contrary to all men, [16][a]for-
bidding us to speak to the Gentiles that
they may be saved, so as always [b]to fill up
the measure of their sins; [c]but wrath has
come upon them to the uttermost.

Error of every kind may meet with favor; but the world never did, nor ever will, tolerate real Christianity.

CHARLES WESLEY

Longing to See Them

[17]But we, brethren, having been taken
away from you for a short time [a]in presence, not in heart, endeavored more eagerly to see your face with great desire.
[18]Therefore we wanted to come to you—
even I, Paul, time and again—but [a]Satan
hindered us. [19]For [a]what *is* our hope, or
joy, or [b]crown of rejoicing? *Is it* not even
you in the [c]presence of our Lord Jesus
Christ [d]at His coming? [20]For you are our
glory and joy.

Concern for Their Faith

3 Therefore, when we could no longer
endure it, we thought it good to be
left in Athens alone, [2]and sent [a]Timothy,
our brother and minister of God, and our
fellow laborer in the gospel of Christ, to
establish you and encourage you concerning your faith, [3][a]that no one should be
shaken by these afflictions; for you yourselves know that [b]we are appointed to
this. [4][a]For, in fact, we told you before
when we were with you that we would suffer tribulation, just as it happened, and
you know. [5]For this reason, when I could
no longer endure it, I sent to know your
faith, [a]lest by some means the tempter
had tempted you, and [b]our labor might be
in vain.

Encouraged by Timothy

[6][a]But now that Timothy has come to us
from you, and brought us good news of
your faith and love, and that you always
have good remembrance of us, greatly desiring to see us, [b]as we also *to see* you—
[7]therefore, brethren, in all our affliction
and distress [a]we were comforted concerning you by your faith. [8]For now we live, if
you [a]stand fast in the Lord.
[9]For what thanks can we render to God
for you, for all the joy with which we rejoice for your sake before our God, [10]night
and day praying exceedingly that we may
see your face [a]and perfect what is lacking
in your faith?

Lord Jesus, make ____ increase and abound in love to others. Establish their heart blameless in holiness before our God and Father at Your coming with all Your saints.

FROM 1 THESSALONIANS 3:12, 13

Prayer for the Church

[11]Now may our God and Father Himself, and our Lord Jesus Christ, [a]direct
our way to you. [12]And may the Lord make
you increase and [a]abound in love to one
another and to all, just as we *do* to you,
[13]so that He may establish [a]your hearts
blameless in holiness before our God and
Father at the coming of our Lord Jesus
Christ with all His saints.

---

12 b 1 Cor. 1:9
13 a 1 Thess. 1:2, 3 b Mark 4:20 c [Gal. 4:14] d [1 Pet. 1:23]
14 a Gal. 1:22 b Acts 17:5
15 a Acts 2:23 b Matt. 5:12; 23:34, 35 c Esth. 3:8 *1 hostile*
16 a Luke 11:52 b Gen. 15:16 c Matt. 24:6
17 a 1 Cor. 5:3
18 a Rom. 1:13; 15:22
19 a 2 Cor. 1:14 b Prov. 16:31 c Jude 24 d 1 Cor. 15:23

CHAPTER 3
2 a Rom. 16:21
3 a Eph. 3:13 b Acts 9:16; 14:22
4 a Acts 20:24
5 a 1 Cor. 7:5 b Gal. 2:2
6 a Acts 18:5 b Phil. 1:8
7 a 2 Cor. 1:4
8 a Phil. 4:1
10 a 2 Cor. 13:9
11 a Mark 1:3
12 a Phil. 1:9
13 a 2 Thess. 2:17

1 THESSALONIANS 5:1

Dear Woman of Destiny,

In the New Testament there are two different Greek words for the English word *time*. *Chronos* time is only the succession of minutes and hours, with no inherent challenge or accomplishments at all. The other Greek word for "time" is *kairos*, a season of potential opportunities and achievements.

Kairos time implies that which time gives an opportunity to do. It can be better understood as "opportune time." The necessity of accomplishing the task at hand, whether it is convenient or not, must be seized in order for us to fulfill *kairos* time. *Kairos* time is that wonderful, awesome "God-time," taken out of *chronos* time, that falls into our lives in an unplanned, unexpected way. It is that once-in-a-lifetime opportunity, that second or minute, hour or year, or even longer, when a golden opportunity is sovereignly given to us by the Almighty. What we do with it can change our lives, the lives of others, a nation, and even the world. It might even save a generation of people from destruction, as it did in the story of Queen Esther who had been made queen "for such a time as this" (Esth. 4:14).

Simeon waited all his days for *kairos* time. God had promised him that he would not die until he had seen the Messiah. While routinely walking into the temple one day, he saw the baby Jesus in the arms of His mother Mary and knew his *kairos* time had come. His work was finished. He was ready to go home.

Standing there in the temple, watching all this, was an old woman who had spent most of her life in prayer and fasting on the Holy Mount, waiting for the One who would bring redemption to Israel. When Anna saw what had happened, she gave glory to God and left the prayer room to become a city-wide evangelist, going about the city of Jerusalem, telling everyone who was waiting for the coming of the Messiah that He had arrived. She changed her profession from intercessor to evangelist. She knew she had prayed through. No more time in the prayer room for her! She was going out to visit all her friends and celebrate with them all over Jerusalem. That was the beginning of "women in ministry."

Kairos time is often related to "crisis time." It is important in these last days that we understand God's timetable and be prepared to play our role in God's plan for our destiny. This is *kairos* time for women. Woman of Destiny, this is your golden opportunity to obey that call of God on your life and march with the army of women whom God is calling into the whitened harvest fields and front lines. Come out of your secure hiding place, and walk on the water with Jesus. The thing you fear could turn out to be the greatest experience of your life, your finest hour, your very own God-appointed *kairos* time!

Gwen Shaw

Plea for Purity

4 Finally then, brethren, we urge and
exhort in the Lord Jesus [a]that you
should abound more and more, [b]just as
you received from us how you ought to
walk and to please God; 2for you know
what commandments we gave you
through the Lord Jesus.
3For this is [a]the will of God, [b]your sanctification: [c]that you should abstain from
sexual immorality; 4[a]that each of you
should know how to possess his own vessel in sanctification and honor, 5[a]not in
passion of lust, [b]like the Gentiles [c]who do
not know God; 6that no one should take
advantage of and defraud his brother in
this matter, because the Lord [a]*is* the
avenger of all such, as we also forewarned
you and testified. 7For God did not call us
to uncleanness, [a]but in holiness. 8[a]There-
fore he who rejects *this* does not reject
man, but God, [b]who[1] has also given us
His Holy Spirit.

A Brotherly and Orderly Life

9But concerning brotherly love you
have no need that I should write to you,
for [a]you yourselves are taught by God [b]to
love one another; 10and indeed you do so
toward all the brethren who are in all
Macedonia. But we urge you, brethren,
[a]that you increase more and more; 11that
you also aspire to lead a quiet life, [a]to
mind your own business, and [b]to work
with your own hands, as we commanded
you, 12[a]that you may walk properly toward those who are outside, and *that* you
may lack nothing.

The Comfort of Christ's Coming

13But I do not want you to be ignorant,
brethren, concerning those who have fall-
en [1]asleep, lest you sorrow [a]as others
[b]who have no hope. 14For [a]if we believe
that Jesus died and rose again, even so
God will bring with Him [b]those who
[1]sleep in Jesus.
15For this we say to you [a]by the word of
the Lord, that [b]we who are alive *and* remain until the coming of the Lord will by
no means precede those who are [1]asleep.
16For [a]the Lord Himself will descend from
heaven with a shout, with the voice of an
archangel, and with [b]the trumpet of God.
[c]And the dead in Christ will rise first.
17[a]Then we who are alive *and* remain
shall be caught up together with them [b]in
the clouds to meet the Lord in the air. And
thus [c]we shall always be with the Lord.
18[a]Therefore comfort one another with
these words.

Without persistence, prayers may go unanswered. Importunity is made up of the ability to hold on, to continue, to wait with unrelaxed and unrelaxable grasp, restless desire, and restful patience.

E. M. BOUNDS

The Day of the Lord

5 But concerning [a]the times and the
seasons, brethren, you have no need
that I should write to you. 2For you
yourselves know perfectly that [a]the day of
the Lord so comes as a thief in the night.
3For when they say, "Peace and safety!"
then [a]sudden destruction comes upon
them, [b]as labor pains upon a pregnant
woman. And they shall not escape. 4[a]But
you, brethren, are not in darkness, so that
this Day should overtake you as a thief.
5You are all [a]sons of light and sons of the
day. We are not of the night nor of darkness. 6[a]Therefore let us not sleep, as others *do*, but [b]let us watch and be [1]sober.
7For [a]those who sleep, sleep at night, and
those who get drunk [b]are drunk at night.
8But let us who are of the day be sober,
[a]putting on the breastplate of faith and
love, and *as* a helmet the hope of salvation. 9For [a]God did not appoint us to
wrath, [b]but to obtain salvation through
our Lord Jesus Christ, 10[a]who died for us,
that whether we wake or sleep, we should
live together with Him.
11Therefore [1]comfort each other and
[2]edify one another, just as you also are
doing.

CHAPTER 4
1 a 1 Cor. 15:58 b Phil. 1:27
3 a [Rom. 12:2] b Eph. 5:27 c [1 Cor. 6:15–20]
4 a Rom. 6:19
5 a Col. 3:5 b Eph. 4:17, 18 c 1 Cor. 15:34
6 a 2 Thess. 1:8
7 a Lev. 11:44
8 a Luke 10:16 b 1 Cor. 2:10 *1 NU who also gives*
9 a [Jer. 31:33, 34] b Matt. 22:39
10 a 1 Thess. 3:12
11 a 2 Thess. 3:11 b Acts 20:35
12 a Rom. 13:13
13 a Lev. 19:28 b [Eph. 2:12] *1* Died
14 a 1 Cor. 15:13 b 1 Cor. 15:20, 23 *1* Or *through Jesus sleep*
15 a 1 Kin. 13:17; 20:35 b 1 Cor. 15:51, 52 *1* Dead
16 a [Matt. 24:30, 31] b [1 Cor. 15:52] c [1 Cor. 15:23]
17 a [1 Cor. 15:51–53] b Acts 1:9 c John 14:3; 17:24
18 a 1 Thess. 5:11

CHAPTER 5
1 a Matt. 24:3
2 a [2 Pet. 3:10]
3 a Is. 13:6–9 b Hos. 13:13
4 a 1 John 2:8
5 a Eph. 5:8
6 a Matt. 25:5 b [1 Pet. 5:8] *1 self-controlled*
7 a [Luke 21:34] b Acts 2:15
8 a Eph. 6:14
9 a Rom. 9:22 b [2 Thess. 2:13]
10 a 2 Cor. 5:15
11 *1* Or *encourage* *2 build one another up*

1 Thessalonians 5:24

Dear Woman of Destiny,

The story of my life with my husband, Winkie, is made up of one beautiful account of God's faithfulness after another. Our journey has taken us to many lands and multitudes of people. We have crossed paths with the great and the small of the earth, with the wise and the unwise. In the years of our adventures together with God, time after time we have seen His wonders. We have seen His care and kindness from little unforgettable touches of His provision to momentous events in which a person's entire life hung on His intervention. We have seen Him raise money for a meal, and we have seen Him raise the dead. He is the God who never fails to surprise us with His tenderness and power.

I once stood on the deck of a ship, about to embark on the greatest adventure of my life—leaving my homeland to attend Bible college. Just being on the ship that would carry me to my future ministry was a miracle. I knew my heavenly Father was totally trustworthy and that His kingdom needed to be extended into all the earth. Yet I felt so inadequate. I didn't have the money for the fare. Here I was about to go overseas and not only did I not have enough extra money for the trip, I couldn't even buy the ticket!

I went into the shipping office to tell them I still didn't have the full amount. The man behind the counter said, "You either have the money or you don't! And this is the last day." Here was a great test in my life, of hanging on to the Lord until something happened. And I had done it. I *had* trusted God; I had done what He told me. I *did* believe His promises. And yet here I was, with nothing but an apology to give to the cynical young man at the desk.

I felt devastated. I was so sure the Lord had told me to go and that He would provide. I had to have faith. Despite the embarrassment, I still had full confidence in the Lord's ability to do what I felt He had promised me.

I returned to our car where my mother was waiting and opened the Bible and read again the scriptures God had given me. My mother and I held hands, prayed, and sang a song of victory. Right in the middle of it, there was a knock on our car window. It was a family friend, a man who himself lived by faith. I lowered the window, and he handed me an envelope. He said simply, "God told me to give you this money." It was the *exact amount* I needed to complete my fare.

I returned to the ticket office totally ecstatic. The man behind the counter had no idea my heart was doing somersaults. But the God who could provide so specifically, so directly, so astonishingly, could certainly provide for the rest of my life and ministry.

And He has. He does. For decades now, Winkie and I have traveled that ship of faith. Many ports later, many places and faces across the waters of the world in which God has called us to minister, His faithfulness remains.

Faeona Pratney

Various Exhortations

12 And we urge you, brethren, [a]to recognize those who labor among you, and are
over you in the Lord and [1]admonish you,
13 and to esteem them very highly in love
for their work's sake. [a]Be at peace among
yourselves.

Never stifle the Spirit. Never grieve Him by arguing or disregarding. Quench not the Spirit, vex not the Spirit. All the verbs are gentle. It is as if our God would have us understand that the blessed filling of the Blessed Spirit is a very tender thing, that He is very tender.

AMY CARMICHAEL

14 Now we [1]exhort you, brethren, [a]warn
those who are [2]unruly, [b]comfort the
fainthearted, [c]uphold the weak, [d]be patient with all. 15 [a]See that no one renders
evil for evil to anyone, but always [b]pursue
what is good both for yourselves and for
all.

12 a 1 Cor. 16:18 *1 instruct* or *warn*
13 a Mark 9:50
14 a 2 Thess. 3:6, 7, 11 b Heb. 12:12 c Rom. 14:1; 15:1 d Gal. 5:22 *1 encourage* *2 insubordinate* or *idle*
15 a Lev. 19:18 b Gal. 6:10
16 a [2 Cor. 6:10]
17 a Eph. 6:18
19 a Eph. 4:30
20 a 1 Cor. 14:1, 31
21 a 1 John 4:1 b Phil. 4:8
23 a Phil. 4:9 b 1 Thess. 3:13 c 1 Cor. 1:8, 9 *1 set you apart*
24 a [1 Cor. 10:13] b Phil. 1:6
27 *1 letter* *2* NU omits *holy*

16 [a]Rejoice always, 17 [a]pray without ceasing, 18 in everything give thanks; for this is
the will of God in Christ Jesus for you.
19 [a]Do not quench the Spirit. 20 [a]Do not
despise prophecies. 21 [a]Test all things;
[b]hold fast what is good. 22 Abstain from
every form of evil.

God of peace, I pray that You would sanctify ____ completely; and may their whole spirit, soul, and body be preserved blameless at the coming of our Lord Jesus Christ.

FROM 1 THESSALONIANS 5:23

Blessing and Admonition

23 Now may [a]the God of peace Himself
[b]sanctify[1] you completely; and may your
whole spirit, soul, and body [c]be preserved
blameless at the coming of our Lord Jesus
Christ. 24 He who calls you *is* [a]faithful,
who also will [b]do *it.*
25 Brethren, pray for us.
26 Greet all the brethren with a holy
kiss.
27 I charge you by the Lord that this
[1]epistle be read to all the [2]holy brethren.
28 The grace of our Lord Jesus Christ *be*
with you. Amen.

AUTHOR: *Paul*
DATE: *A.D. 50*
THEME: *The Return of the Lord—Advance Indicators and Lifestyle in the Meanwhile*
KEY WORDS: *Day of the Lord, Man of Sin, Tradition*

2 THESSALONIANS

Dear Woman of Destiny,

Second Thessalonians exhorts us not to let anyone deceive us concerning the end times. It warns us about the coming of the Antichrist and tells us that he will come with lying wonders. Beloved sister, not everything that looks like it comes from God *is* from God. It is wise to make sure that those who come in the name of the Lord are truly sent from Him. Finally, this book is a cry, which still rings from our hearts today, that intercessors will pray for deliverance from unreasonable and wicked people (see 2 Thess. 3:1, 2). All of us women of destiny face times when we need each other's prayers.

With His love,

Cindy Jacobs

Greeting

Paul, Silvanus, and Timothy,
To the church of the Thessaloni-
ans in God our Father and the Lord Jesus
Christ:
2[a]Grace to you and peace from God our
Father and the Lord Jesus Christ.

> *Grace is but glory begun, and glory is but grace perfected.*
>
> JONATHAN EDWARDS

God's Final Judgment and Glory

3We are bound to thank God always for
you, brethren, as it is fitting, because your
faith grows exceedingly, and the love of
every one of you all abounds toward each
other, 4so that [a]we ourselves boast of you
among the churches of God [b]for your patience and faith [c]in all your persecutions
and [1]tribulations that you endure, 5*which*
is [a]manifest[1] evidence of the righteous
judgment of God, that you may be counted worthy of the kingdom of God, [b]for
which you also suffer; 6[a]since *it is* a righteous thing with God to repay with [1]tribu-
lation those who trouble you, 7and to *give*
you who are troubled [a]rest with us when
[b]the Lord Jesus is revealed from heaven
with His mighty angels, 8in flaming fire
taking vengeance on those who do not
know God, and on those who do not obey
the gospel of our Lord Jesus Christ.
9[a]These shall be punished with everlasting destruction from the presence of the
Lord and [b]from the glory of His power,
10when He comes, in that Day, [a]to be
[b]glorified in His saints and to be admired
among all those who [1]believe, because
our testimony among you was believed.
11Therefore we also pray always for you
that our God would [a]count you worthy of
this calling, and fulfill all the good pleasure of *His* goodness and [b]the work of
faith with power, 12[a]that the name of our
Lord Jesus Christ may be glorified in you,
and you in Him, according to the grace of
our God and the Lord Jesus Christ.

The Great Apostasy

2 Now, brethren, [a]concerning the coming of our Lord Jesus Christ [b]and our
gathering together to Him, we ask you,
2[a]not to be soon shaken in mind or troubled, either by spirit or by word or by letter, as if from us, as though the day of
[1]Christ had come. 3Let no one deceive
you by any means; for *that Day will not*
come [a]unless the falling away comes first,
and [b]the man of [1]sin is revealed, [c]the son
of perdition, 4who opposes and [a]exalts
himself [b]above all that is called God or
that is worshiped, so that he sits [1]as God
in the temple of God, showing himself
that he is God.

> *Dearly beloved, once you have given yourself to God, do not take yourself back again. Remember, a gift once presented is no longer at the disposal of the giver.*
>
> MADAME JEANNE GUYON

5Do you not remember that when I was
still with you I told you these things? 6And
now you know what is restraining, that he
may be revealed in his own time. 7For
[a]the [1]mystery of lawlessness is already at
work; only [2]He who now restrains *will do*
so until [2]He is taken out of the way. 8And
then the lawless one will be revealed,
[a]whom the Lord will consume [b]with the
breath of His mouth and destroy [c]with the
brightness of His coming. 9The coming of
the *lawless one* is [a]according to the working of Satan, with all power, [b]signs, and
lying wonders, 10and with all unrighteous
deception among [a]those who perish, because they did not receive [b]the love of the
truth, that they might be saved. 11And
[a]for this reason God will send them
strong delusion, [b]that they should believe
the lie, 12that they all may be condemned

CHAPTER 1
2 a 1 Cor. 1:3
4 a 2 Cor. 7:4 b 1 Thess. 1:3 c 1 Thess. 2:14 *1 afflictions*
5 a Phil. 1:28 b 1 Thess. 2:14 *1 plain*
6 a Rev. 6:10 *1 affliction*
7 a Rev. 14:13 b Jude 14
9 a Phil. 3:19 b Deut. 33:2
10 a Matt. 25:31 b John 17:10 *1* NU, M *have believed*
11 a Col. 1:12 b 1 Thess. 1:3
12 a [Col. 3:17]

CHAPTER 2
1 a [1 Thess. 4:15–17] b Matt. 24:31
2 a Matt. 24:4 *1* NU *the Lord*
3 a 1 Tim. 4:1 b Dan. 7:25; 8:25; 11:36 c John 17:12 *1* NU *lawlessness*
4 a Is. 14:13, 14 b 1 Cor. 8:5 *1* NU omits *as God*
7 a 1 John 2:18 *1 hidden truth* *2 Or he*
8 a Dan. 7:10 b Is. 11:4 c Heb. 10:27
9 a John 8:41 b Deut. 13:1
10 a 2 Cor. 2:15 b 1 Cor. 16:22
11 a Rom. 1:28 b 1 Tim. 4:1

who did not believe the truth but [a]had pleasure in unrighteousness.

Stand Fast

13 But we are [1]bound to give thanks to God always for you, brethren beloved by the Lord, because God [a]from the beginning [b]chose you for salvation [c]through [2]sanctification by the Spirit and belief in the truth, 14 to which He called you by our gospel, for [a]the obtaining of the glory of our Lord Jesus Christ. 15 Therefore, brethren, [a]stand fast and hold [b]the traditions which you were taught, whether by word or our [1]epistle.

16 Now may our Lord Jesus Christ Himself, and our God and Father, [a]who has loved us and given *us* everlasting consolation and [b]good hope by grace, 17 comfort your hearts [a]and [1]establish you in every good word and work.

O God, You have loved ____ and given them everlasting consolation and good hope by grace. Comfort their heart and establish them in every good word and work.

FROM 2 THESSALONIANS 2:16, 17

Pray for Us

3 Finally, brethren, [a]pray for us, that the word of the Lord may run *swiftly* and be glorified, just as *it is* with you, 2 and [a]that we may be delivered from unreasonable and wicked men; [b]for not all have faith.

3 But [a]the Lord is faithful, who will establish you and [b]guard *you* from the evil one. 4 And [a]we have confidence in the Lord concerning you, both that you do and will do the things we command you.

5 Now may [a]the Lord direct your hearts into the love of God and into the patience of Christ.

Warning Against Idleness

6 But we command you, brethren, in the name of our Lord Jesus Christ, [a]that you withdraw [b]from every brother who walks [c]disorderly and not according to the tradition which [1]he received from us. 7 For you yourselves know how you ought to follow us, for we were not disorderly among you; 8 nor did we eat anyone's bread [1]free of charge, but worked with [a]labor and toil night and day, that we might not be a burden to any of you, 9 not because we do not have [a]authority, but to make ourselves an example of how you should follow us.

Father, deliver ____ from unreasonable and wicked people. Establish them and guard them from the evil one. Direct their heart into the love of God and into the patience of Christ.

FROM 2 THESSALONIANS 3:2, 3, 5

10 For even when we were with you, we commanded you this: If anyone will not work, neither shall he eat. 11 For we hear that there are some who walk among you in a disorderly manner, not working at all, but are [a]busybodies. 12 Now those who are such we command and [1]exhort through our Lord Jesus Christ [a]that they work in quietness and eat their own bread.

His peace is a direct gift through the personal presence of the Holy Ghost.

OSWALD CHAMBERS

13 But *as for* you, brethren, [a]do not grow weary *in* doing good. 14 And if anyone does not obey our word in this [1]epistle, note that person and [a]do not keep company with him, that he may be ashamed.

---

12 a Rom. 1:32
13 a Eph. 1:4 b 1 Thess. 1:4 c [1 Pet. 1:2] *1 under obligation* *2 being set apart by*
14 a 1 Pet. 5:10
15 a 1 Cor. 16:13 b 1 Cor. 11:2 *1 letter*
16 a [Rev. 1:5] b 1 Pet. 1:3
17 a 1 Cor. 1:8 *1 strengthen*

CHAPTER 3
1 a Eph. 6:19
2 a Rom. 15:31 b Acts 28:24
3 a 1 Cor. 1:9 b John 17:15
4 a 2 Cor. 7:16
5 a 1 Chr. 29:18
6 a Rom. 16:17 b 1 Cor. 5:1 c 1 Thess. 4:11 *1* NU, M *they*
8 a 1 Thess. 2:9 *1* Lit. *for nothing*
9 a 1 Cor. 9:4, 6–14
11 a 1 Pet. 4:15
12 a Eph. 4:28 *1 encourage*
13 a Gal. 6:9
14 a Matt. 18:17 *1 letter*

[15]a Yet do not count *him* as an enemy, [b]but [1]admonish *him* as a brother.

Benediction

[16]Now may [a]the Lord of peace Himself give you peace always in every way. The Lord *be* with you all.

[17]a The salutation of Paul with my own hand, which is a sign in every [1]epistle; so I write.

[18]a The grace of our Lord Jesus Christ *be* with you all. Amen.

15 a Lev. 19:17 b Titus 3:10 *1 warn*

16 a Rom. 15:33

17 a 1 Cor. 16:21 *1 letter*

18 a Rom. 16:20, 24

AUTHOR: *Paul*
DATE: *About A.D. 64*
THEME: *Removal of False Doctrine, Preservation of Public Worship, and Proper Leadership in the Church*
KEY WORDS: *Carefulness, Watchfulness, Strength, Commitment*

1 TIMOTHY

Dear Woman of Destiny,

The epistle (or letter) of 1 Timothy was written to bring serious correction to the church of Ephesus. Paul, the writer of the letter, obviously trusted young Timothy greatly because he wrote to him as a son (see 1 Tim. 1:2). There is a scene behind this scene we want to look at to understand our role as women in the character development of young leaders. Timothy's grandmother (Lois) and mother (Eunice) raised him in the ways of God. All of us as women of destiny should raise our children, whether they are spiritual or biological children, to follow Christ with all of their hearts and so become men and women God can trust to be leaders.

With His love,

Cindy Jacobs

Greeting

Paul, an apostle of Jesus Christ, by
the commandment of God our Savior and the Lord Jesus Christ, our
hope,

2 To Timothy, a [a]true son in the faith:

[b]Grace, mercy, *and* peace from God our
Father and Jesus Christ our Lord.

No Other Doctrine

3 As I urged you [a]when I went into Macedonia—remain in Ephesus that you may
[1]charge some [b]that they teach no other
doctrine, 4 [a]nor give heed to fables and
endless genealogies, which cause disputes
rather than godly edification which is in
faith. 5 Now [a]the purpose of the commandment is love [b]from a pure heart,
from a good conscience, and *from* [1]sin-
cere faith, 6 from which some, having
strayed, have turned aside to [a]idle talk,
7 desiring to be teachers of the law, understanding neither what they say nor the
things which they affirm.
8 But we know that the law *is* [a]good if
one uses it lawfully, 9 knowing this: that
the law is not made for a righteous person, but for *the* lawless and insubordinate, for *the* ungodly and for sinners, for
the unholy and profane, for murderers of
fathers and murderers of mothers, for
manslayers, 10 for fornicators, for sodomites, for kidnappers, for liars, for perjur-
ers, and if there is any other thing that is
[1]contrary to sound doctrine, 11 according
to the glorious gospel of the [a]blessed God
which was [b]committed to my trust.

Glory to God for His Grace

12 And I thank Christ Jesus our Lord
who has [a]enabled me, [b]because He counted me faithful, [c]putting *me* into the ministry, 13 although [a]I was formerly a
blasphemer, a persecutor, and an [1]inso-
lent man; but I obtained mercy because [b]I
did *it* ignorantly in unbelief. 14 [a]And the
grace of our Lord was exceedingly abundant, [b]with faith and love which are in
Christ Jesus. 15 [a]This *is* a faithful saying
and worthy of all acceptance, that [b]Christ
Jesus came into the world to save sinners,
of whom I am chief. 16 However, for this
reason I obtained mercy, that in me first
Jesus Christ might show all longsuffering,
as a pattern to those who are going to
believe on Him for everlasting life. 17 Now
to [a]the King eternal, [b]immortal, [c]invisi-
ble, to [1]God [d]who alone is wise, [e]*be* honor
and glory forever and ever. Amen.

Fight the Good Fight

18 This [1]charge I commit to you, son
Timothy, according to the prophecies previously made concerning you, that by
them you may wage the good warfare,
19 having faith and a good conscience,
which some having rejected, concerning
the faith have suffered shipwreck, 20 of
whom are [a]Hymenaeus and [b]Alexander,
whom I delivered to Satan that they may
learn not to [c]blaspheme.

It is a great deal better to live a holy life than to talk about it. Lighthouses do not ring bells and fire cannon to call attention to their shining—they just shine.

DWIGHT L. MOODY

Father, teach _____ to pray, intercede, and give thanks for all who are in authority, that they may lead a quiet and peaceable life in all godliness and reverence.

FROM 1 TIMOTHY 2:1, 2

Pray for All Men

2 Therefore I [1]exhort first of all that
supplications, prayers, intercessions,
and giving of thanks be made for all men,
2 [a]for kings and [b]all who are in [1]authority,
that we may lead a quiet and peaceable life
in all godliness and [2]reverence. 3 For this
is [a]good and acceptable in the sight [b]of
God our Savior, 4 [a]who desires all men to
be saved [b]and to come to the knowledge
of the truth. 5 [a]For *there is* one God and
[b]one Mediator between God and men, *the*

CHAPTER 1
2 a Titus 1:4 b Gal. 1:3
3 a Acts 20:1, 3 b Gal. 1:6, 7 1 command
4 a Titus 1:14
5 a Rom. 13:8–10 b Eph. 6:24 1 Lit. *unhypocritical*
6 a 1 Tim. 6:4, 20
8 a Rom. 7:12, 16
10 1 *opposed*
11 a 1 Tim. 6:15 b 1 Cor. 9:17
12 a 1 Cor. 15:10 b 1 Cor. 7:25 c Col. 1:25
13 a Acts 8:3 b John 4:21 1 *violently arrogant*
14 a Rom. 5:20 b 2 Tim. 1:13; 2:22
15 a 2 Tim. 2:11 b Matt. 1:21; 9:13
17 a Ps. 10:16 b Rom. 1:23 c Heb. 11:27 d Rom. 16:27 e 1 Chr. 29:11 1 NU *the only God,*
18 1 *command*
20 a 2 Tim. 2:17, 18 b 2 Tim. 4:14 c Acts 13:45

CHAPTER 2
1 1 *encourage*
2 a Ezra 6:10 b [Rom. 13:1] 1 *a prominent place* 2 *dignity*
3 a Rom. 12:2 b 2 Tim. 1:9
4 a Ezek. 18:23, 32 b [John 17:3]
5 a Gal. 3:20 b [Heb. 9:15]

Man Christ Jesus, 6[a]who gave Himself a
ransom for all, to be testified in due time,
7[a]for which I was appointed a preacher
and an apostle—I am speaking the truth
[1]in Christ *and* not lying—[b]a teacher of
the Gentiles in faith and truth.

Men and Women in the Church

8I desire therefore that the men pray
[a]everywhere, [b]lifting up holy hands, without wrath and doubting; 9in like manner
also, that the [a]women adorn themselves
in modest apparel, with propriety and
[1]moderation, not with braided hair or
gold or pearls or costly clothing, 10[a]but,
which is proper for women professing
godliness, with good works. 11Let a
woman learn in silence with all submission. 12And [a]I do not permit a woman to
teach or to have authority over a man, but
to be in silence. 13For Adam was formed
first, then Eve. 14And Adam was not deceived, but the woman being deceived, fell
into transgression. 15Nevertheless she will
be saved in childbearing if they continue
in faith, love, and holiness, with self-
control.

Qualifications of Overseers

3 This *is* a faithful saying: If a man desires the position of a [1]bishop, he desires a good work. 2A bishop then must be
blameless, the husband of one wife, temperate, sober-minded, of good behavior,
hospitable, able to teach; 3not [1]given to
wine, not violent, [2]not greedy for money,
but gentle, not quarrelsome, not [3]covet-
ous; 4one who rules his own house well,
having *his* children in submission with all
reverence 5(for if a man does not know
how to rule his own house, how will he
take care of the church of God?); 6not a
[1]novice, lest being puffed up with pride he
fall into the *same* condemnation as the
devil. 7Moreover he must have a good testimony among those who are outside, lest
he fall into reproach and the [a]snare of the
devil.

Qualifications of Deacons

8Likewise deacons *must be* reverent,
not double-tongued, [a]not given to much
wine, not greedy for money, 9holding the
[1]mystery of the faith with a pure conscience. 10But let these also first be tested;
then let them serve as deacons, being
found blameless. 11Likewise, *their* wives
must be reverent, not [1]slanderers, temperate, faithful in all things. 12Let deacons
be the husbands of one wife, ruling *their*
children and their own houses well. 13For
those who have served well as deacons
[a]obtain for themselves a good standing
and great boldness in the faith which is in
Christ Jesus.

The Great Mystery

14These things I write to you, though I
hope to come to you shortly; 15but if I am
delayed, *I write* so that you may know how
you ought to conduct yourself in the
house of God, which is the church of the
living God, the pillar and [1]ground of the
truth. 16And without controversy great is
the [1]mystery of godliness:

[a]God[2] was manifested in the flesh,
[b]Justified in the Spirit,
[c]Seen by angels,
[d]Preached among the Gentiles,
[e]Believed on in the world,
[f]Received up in glory.

> *The basic teaching of the Gospels is the presence of God in one Man, while that of the Epistles is God in the church.*
>
> WATCHMAN NEE

The Great Apostasy

4 Now the Spirit [1]expressly says that in
latter times some will depart from the
faith, giving heed [a]to deceiving spirits and
doctrines of demons, 2[a]speaking lies in
hypocrisy, having their own conscience
[b]seared with a hot iron, 3forbidding to
marry, *and commanding* to abstain from
foods which God created to be received
with thanksgiving by those who believe
and know the truth. 4For every creature of
God *is* good, and nothing is to be refused
if it is received with thanksgiving; 5for

---

6 a Mark 10:45
7 a Eph. 3:7, 8 b [Gal. 1:15, 16] *1* NU omits *in Christ*
8 a Luke 23:34 b Ps. 134:2
9 a 1 Pet. 3:3 *1 discretion*
10 a 1 Pet. 3:4
12 a 1 Cor. 14:34

CHAPTER 3
1 *1 Lit. overseer*
3 *1 addicted* *2* NU omits *not greedy for money* *3 loving money*
6 *1 new convert*
7 a 2 Tim. 2:26
8 a Ezek. 44:21
9 *1 hidden truth*
11 *1 malicious gossips*
13 a Matt. 25:21
15 *1 foundation, mainstay*
16 a [John 1:14] b [Matt. 3:16] c Matt. 28:2 d Rom. 10:18 e Col. 1:6, 23 f Luke 24:51 *1 hidden truth* *2* NU *Who*

CHAPTER 4
1 a Rev. 16:14 *1 explicitly*
2 a Matt. 7:15 b Eph. 4:19

For explanation of 1 Timothy 2:11–15, please see article on page 1595.

1 Timothy 4:14

Dear Woman of Destiny,

God has uniquely gifted every person, but few women view themselves as "gifted." Maybe that's not surprising, given the way our society defines "gifted."

Too often "gifted" refers to the brilliant, the elite, the beautiful, the privileged few who appear to have tapped into the primary flow of the gene pool. We have gifted classes for the children in our schools who show academic aptitude—while overlooking the many other areas at which one may excel. We make concessions for those with brilliance, power, or physical beauty—even though they flirt with immorality and exhibit lack of character. We reward people based on performance, daily making determinations on whose life has more value without thought for the talent and creativity inherent in each person.

All of this leaves the "average" woman feeling deficient, inadequate, and overwhelmed. But God has always loved taking the "ordinary" and doing the extraordinary with it (see Mark 1:16–18; Luke 1:26–38; John 2:1–11; 1 Cor. 1:26–31; 2 Cor. 4:7).

The word used here for gift is *charisma*—the same word that is used in 1 Corinthians to describe spiritual gifts. It can be understood as a spiritual endowment, and carries the idea of having been granted as a favor. God fully intends for us to live in thankfulness for His gifts to us . . . and then to use them (see Matt. 25:14–29; Rom. 1:11; 8:6; 1 Cor. 14:1).

The other key word in this scripture is *neglect,* which conveys the idea of being careless with something, or not regarding its proper value. That is a danger for each of us. We look at the number of people we reach and presume it's too small. We develop blurred priorities. We devalue what God is doing in our lives. But the Lord challenges us to not despise the day of small things (see Zech. 4:10).

One woman I knew, who had a unique gift of teaching, is a prime example of using a gift at all points of life. As a young mother, she poured her life and her knowledge of the Word into her own children. As an employee in a home business, she not only trained her workers for the task, but introduced them to Jesus as well. As a church member, she taught small group Bible studies for dozens of years, watching the Lord change women's lives through encounter with Him. Years later, as a widow, she embarked on a national teaching ministry, which she pursued until her death. Throughout the years, her focus of ministry changed and enlarged, but she was always faithful to use "the gift that was in" her.

You, too, have been gifted by God for a purpose (see Rom. 12:6–8; 1 Cor. 12:4; Phil. 3:12). Stir up the gift that He has put in you! (see 2 Tim. 1:6). Use it, nurture it, and thank Him for it! And you *will* see the growth, progress, and consequent ministry that flows in and through your life! (1 Tim. 4:15).

Rebecca Bauer

Father God, I pray that no one will despise _____ for being young. May they be an example to the believers in word, in conduct, in love, in spirit, in faith, and in purity.

FROM 1 TIMOTHY 4:12

it is [1]sanctified by the word of God and
prayer.

A Good Servant of Jesus Christ

6 If you instruct the brethren in these
things, you will be a good minister of Jesus Christ, [a]nourished in the words of
faith and of the good doctrine which you
have carefully followed. 7 But [a]reject profane and old wives' fables, and [b]exercise
yourself toward godliness. 8 For [a]bodily
exercise profits a little, but godliness is
profitable for all things, [b]having promise
of the life that now is and of that which is
to come. 9 This *is* a faithful saying and
worthy of all acceptance. 10 For to this *end*
[1]we both labor and suffer reproach, because we trust in the living God, [a]who is
the Savior of all men, especially of those
who believe. 11 These things command
and teach.

Purity is vital to faith.

SMITH WIGGLESWORTH

Take Heed to Your Ministry

12 Let no one [1]despise your youth, but
be an [a]example to the believers in word,
in conduct, in love, [2]in spirit, in faith, in
purity. 13 Till I come, give attention to
reading, to exhortation, to [1]doctrine.
14 [a]Do not neglect the gift that is in you,
which was given to you by prophecy [b]with
the laying on of the hands of the eldership. 15 Meditate on these things; give
yourself entirely to them, that your progress may be evident to all. 16 Take heed to
yourself and to the doctrine. Continue in
them, for in doing this you will save both
yourself and those who hear you.

God does not give His gifts to be played with, when they are not required. But they are active and ready when the need arises, for those who will put their trust in Him.

GORDON LINDSAY

Treatment of Church Members

5 Do not rebuke an older man, but exhort *him* as a father, younger men
as brothers, 2 older women as mothers,
younger women as sisters, with all purity.

Honor True Widows

3 Honor widows who are really widows.
4 But if any widow has children or grandchildren, let them first learn to show piety
at home and [a]to repay their parents; for
this is [1]good and acceptable before God.
5 Now she who is really a widow, and left
alone, trusts in God and continues in supplications and prayers [a]night and day.
6 But she who lives in [1]pleasure is dead
while she lives. 7 And these things command, that they may be blameless. 8 But if
anyone does not provide for his own, [a]and
especially for those of his household, [b]he
has denied the faith [c]and is worse than an
unbeliever.
9 Do not let a widow under sixty years
old be taken into the number, *and not
unless* she has been the wife of one man,
10 well reported for good works: if she has
brought up children, if she has lodged
strangers, if she has washed the saints'
feet, if she has relieved the afflicted, if she

5 [1] *set apart*
6 [a] 2 Tim. 3:14
7 [a] 2 Tim. 2:16 [b] Heb. 5:14
8 [a] 1 Cor. 8:8 [b] Ps. 37:9
10 [a] Ps. 36:6 [1] NU *we labor and strive,*
12 [a] 1 Pet. 5:3 [1] *look down on your youthfulness* [2] NU omits *in spirit*
13 [1] *teaching*
14 [a] 2 Tim. 1:6 [b] Acts 6:6
CHAPTER 5
4 [a] Gen. 45:10 [1] NU, M omit *good and*
5 [a] Acts 26:7
6 [1] *indulgence*
8 [a] Is. 58:7 [b] 2 Tim. 3:5 [c] Matt. 18:17

has diligently followed every good work.
11But [1]refuse *the* younger widows; for
when they have begun to grow wanton
against Christ, they desire to marry,
12having condemnation because they
have cast off their first [1]faith. 13And besides they learn *to be* idle, wandering
about from house to house, and not only
idle but also gossips and busybodies, saying things which they ought not. 14There-
fore I desire that *the* younger *widows*
marry, bear children, manage the house,
give no opportunity to the adversary to
speak reproachfully. 15For some have already turned aside after Satan. 16If any believing [1]man or woman has widows, let
them [2]relieve them, and do not let the
church be burdened, that it may relieve
those who are really widows.

Honor the Elders

17Let the elders who rule well be counted worthy of double honor, especially
those who labor in the word and doctrine.
18For the Scripture says, [a]*"You shall not*
muzzle an ox while it treads out the
grain," and, [b]"The laborer *is* worthy of his
wages." 19Do not receive an accusation
against an elder except [a]from two or three
witnesses. 20Those who are sinning rebuke in the presence of all, that the rest
also may fear.

> *There is a difference between innocence and purity. Innocence is the characteristic of a child, purity is the characteristic of a man or woman who knows what the tendencies and temptations to go wrong are, and who has overcome them.*
>
> Oswald Chambers

21I charge *you* before God and the Lord
Jesus Christ and the [1]elect angels that you
observe these things without [a]prejudice,
doing nothing with partiality. 22Do not lay
hands on anyone hastily, nor [a]share in
other people's sins; keep yourself pure.
23No longer drink only water, but use a
little wine for your stomach's sake and
your frequent [1]infirmities.
24Some men's sins are [a]clearly evident,
preceding *them* to judgment, but those of
some *men* follow later. 25Likewise, the
good works *of some* are clearly evident,
and those that are otherwise cannot be
hidden.

Honor Masters

6 Let as many [a]bondservants as are under the yoke count their own masters
worthy of all honor, so that the name of
God and *His* doctrine may not be blasphemed. 2And those who have believing
masters, let them not despise *them* because they are brethren, but rather serve
them because those who are benefited are
believers and beloved. Teach and exhort
these things.

Error and Greed

3If anyone teaches otherwise and does
not consent to [a]wholesome words, *even*
the words of our Lord Jesus Christ, [b]and
to the [1]doctrine which accords with godliness, 4he is proud, knowing nothing, but
is obsessed with disputes and arguments
over words, from which come envy, strife,
reviling, evil suspicions, 5[1]useless wranglings of men of corrupt minds and destitute of the truth, who suppose that
godliness is a *means of* gain. [2]From [a]such
withdraw yourself.
6Now godliness with [a]contentment is
great gain. 7For we brought nothing into
this world, [1]*and it is* [a]certain we can carry
nothing out. 8And having food and clothing, with these we shall be [a]content. 9But
those who desire to be rich fall into temptation and a snare, and *into* many foolish
and harmful lusts which drown men in
destruction and perdition. 10For the love
of money is a root of all *kinds of* evil, for
which some have strayed from the faith in
their greediness, and pierced themselves
through with many sorrows.

The Good Confession

11But you, O man of God, flee these
things and pursue righteousness, godliness, faith, love, patience, gentleness.
12Fight the good fight of faith, lay hold on

11 [1] Refuse to enroll
12 [1] Or *solemn promise*
16 [1] NU omits *man or* [2] *give aid to*
18 [a] Deut. 25:4 [b] Luke 10:7
19 [a] Deut. 17:6; 19:15
21 [a] Deut. 1:17 [1] *chosen*
22 [a] Eph. 5:6, 7
23 [1] *illnesses*
24 [a] Gal. 5:19–21
CHAPTER 6
1 [a] Eph. 6:5
3 [a] 2 Tim. 1:13 [b] Titus 1:1 [1] *teaching*
5 [a] 2 Tim. 3:5 [1] NU, M *constant friction* [2] NU omits the rest of v. 5.
6 [a] Heb. 13:5
7 [a] Job 1:21 [1] NU omits *and it is certain*
8 [a] Prov. 30:8, 9

eternal life, to which you were also called
and have confessed the good confession in
the presence of many witnesses. 13I urge
you in the sight of God who gives life to
all things, and *before* Christ Jesus [a]who
witnessed the good confession before
Pontius Pilate, 14that you keep *this* commandment without spot, blameless until our Lord Jesus Christ's appearing,
15which He will manifest in His own time,
He who is the blessed and only [1]Poten-
tate, the King of kings and Lord of lords,
16who alone has immortality, dwelling in
[a]unapproachable light, [b]whom no man
has seen or can see, to whom *be* honor
and everlasting power. Amen.

Instructions to the Rich

17Command those who are rich in this
present age not to be haughty, nor to
trust in uncertain [a]riches but in the living
God, who gives us richly all things [b]to
enjoy. 18*Let them* do good, that they be
rich in good works, ready to give, willing
to share, 19[a]storing up for themselves a
good foundation for the time to come,
that they may lay hold on eternal life.

Guard the Faith

20O Timothy! [a]Guard what was committed to your trust, [b]avoiding the
profane *and* [1]idle babblings and
contradictions of what is falsely called
knowledge— 21by professing it some have
strayed concerning the faith.
Grace *be* with you. Amen.

Lord, I pray that _____ will flee from the love of money and pursue righteousness, godliness, faith, love, patience, and gentleness.

FROM 1 TIMOTHY 6:10, 11

13 a John 18:36, 37

15 1 *Sovereign*

16 a Dan. 2:22 b John 6:46

17 a Jer. 9:23; 48:7 b Eccl. 5:18, 19

19 a [Matt. 6:20, 21; 19:21]

20 a [2 Tim. 1:12, 14] b Titus 1:14 1 *empty chatter*

AUTHOR: *Paul*
DATE: *A.D. 66/67*
THEME: *The Commitment to Ministry*
KEY WORDS: *Fight, Charge, Instruct*

2 TIMOTHY

Dear Woman of Destiny,

The opening chapter of this great book admonishes us not only to safeguard the gospel but also to overcome a stronghold with which we as women often struggle—that of fear. Paul tells Timothy in verse 7 that, "God has not given us a spirit of fear, but of power and of love and of a *sound mind*" (italics mine). This statement was written from the dungeon while Paul was awaiting what would be his sure execution. Sometimes we may feel overwhelmed by life's traumas to the point that we might even think we are about to lose our sanity. Woman of Destiny, we must claim the promises in God's Word to know that He is greater than any situation and will bring peace to the storms that assail us in our minds.

With His love,

Cindy Jacobs

Greeting

Paul, an apostle of [1]Jesus Christ by the will of God, according to the [a]promise of life which is in Christ Jesus,

2 To Timothy, a [a]beloved son:

Grace, mercy, *and* peace from God the Father and Christ Jesus our Lord.

Timothy's Faith and Heritage

3 I thank God, whom I serve with a pure conscience, as *my* [a]forefathers *did,* as without ceasing I remember you in my prayers night and day, 4 greatly desiring to see you, being mindful of your tears, that I may be filled with joy, 5 when I call to remembrance [a]the [1]genuine faith that is in you, which dwelt first in your grandmother Lois and [b]your mother Eunice, and I am persuaded is in you also. 6 Therefore I remind you [a]to stir up the gift of God which is in you through the laying on of my hands. 7 For [a]God has not given us a spirit of fear, [b]but of power and of love and of a sound mind.

You, O Lord, did not give _____ a spirit of fear, but of power and of love and of a sound mind.

FROM 2 TIMOTHY 1:7

Not Ashamed of the Gospel

8 [a]Therefore do not be ashamed of [b]the testimony of our Lord, nor of me [c]His prisoner, but share with me in the sufferings for the gospel according to the power of God, 9 who has saved us and called *us* with a holy calling, [a]not according to our works, but [b]according to His own purpose and grace which was given to us in Christ Jesus [c]before time began, 10 but [a]has now been revealed by the appearing of our Savior Jesus Christ, *who* has abolished death and brought life and immortality to light through the gospel, 11 [a]to which I was appointed a preacher, an apostle, and a teacher [1]of the Gentiles. 12 For this reason I also suffer these things; nevertheless I am not ashamed, [a]for I know whom I have believed and am persuaded that He is able to keep what I have committed to Him until that Day.

Be Loyal to the Faith

13 [a]Hold fast [b]the pattern of [c]sound words which you have heard from me, in faith and love which are in Christ Jesus. 14 That good thing which was committed to you, keep by the Holy Spirit who dwells in us.

15 This you know, that all those in Asia have turned away from me, among whom are Phygellus and Hermogenes. 16 The Lord grant mercy to the [a]household of Onesiphorus, for he often refreshed me, and was not ashamed of my chain; 17 but when he arrived in Rome, he sought me out very zealously and found *me.* 18 The Lord [a]grant to him that he may find mercy from the Lord [b]in that Day—and you know very well how many ways he [c]ministered [1]*to me* at Ephesus.

Be Strong in Grace

2 You therefore, [a]my son, [b]be strong in the grace that is in Christ Jesus. 2 And the things that you have heard from me among many witnesses, commit these to faithful men who will be able to teach others also. 3 You therefore must [a]endure[1] hardship [b]as a good soldier of Jesus Christ. 4 [a]No one engaged in warfare entangles himself with the affairs of *this* life, that he may please him who enlisted him as a soldier. 5 And also [a]if anyone competes in athletics, he is not crowned unless he competes according to the rules. 6 The hardworking farmer must be first to partake of the crops. 7 Consider what I say, and [1]may the Lord [a]give you understanding in all things.

8 Remember that Jesus Christ, [a]of the seed of David, [b]was raised from the dead [c]according to my gospel, 9 [a]for which I suffer trouble as an evildoer, [b]*even* to the point of chains; [c]but the word of God is not chained. 10 Therefore [a]I endure all things for the sake of the [1]elect, [b]that they also may obtain the salvation which is in Christ Jesus with eternal glory.

11 *This is* a faithful saying:

For [a]if we died with *Him,*
We shall also live with *Him.*
12 [a]If we endure,
We shall also reign with *Him.*
[b]If we deny *Him,*

CHAPTER 1
1 a Titus 1:2 1 NU, M *Christ Jesus*
2 a 1 Tim. 1:2
3 a Acts 24:14
5 a 1 Tim. 1:5; 4:6 b Acts 16:1 1 Lit. *unhypocritical*
6 a 1 Tim. 4:14
7 a Rom. 8:15 b [Acts 1:8]
8 a [Rom. 1:16] b 1 Tim. 2:6 c Eph. 3:1
9 a [Rom. 3:20] b Rom. 8:28 c Rom. 16:25
10 a Eph. 1:9
11 a Acts 9:15 1 NU omits *of the Gentiles*
12 a 1 Pet. 4:19
13 a Titus 1:9 b Rom. 2:20; 6:17 c 1 Tim. 6:3
16 a 2 Tim. 4:19
18 a Mark 9:41 b 2 Thess. 1:10 c Heb. 6:10 1 *to me* from Vg., a few Gr. mss.

CHAPTER 2
1 a 1 Tim. 1:2 b Eph. 6:10
3 a 2 Tim. 4:5 b 1 Tim. 1:18 1 NU *You must share*
4 a [2 Pet. 2:20]
5 a [1 Cor. 9:25]
7 a Prov. 2:6 1 NU *the Lord will give you*
8 a Rom. 1:3, 4 b 1 Cor. 15:4 c Rom. 2:16
9 a Acts 9:16 b Eph. 3:1 c Acts 28:31
10 a Eph. 3:13 b 2 Cor. 1:6 1 *chosen ones*
11 a Rom. 6:5, 8
12 a [Rom. 5:17; 8:17] b Matt. 10:33

2 TIMOTHY 1:7

Dear Woman of Destiny,

You probably already have discovered that the area where satanic forces are most likely to attack you is in your mind. Those voices speaking to you, if you heed their message, inevitably will lead you down a road toward doubt, unbelief, and fear.

Many women today seem plagued by fears of all kinds. Fear of failure, financial loss, or the future. Fear of being rejected, disapproved of, left out, unloved, or ignored. Fear of accidents, disease, or death for themselves or their loved ones. Sometimes we fear life itself.

Timothy, a disciple of the apostle Paul, seems to have struggled with this problem of fear and timidity—perhaps because of his youth. You may feel intimidated because you are a woman, or because you feel you lack certain things—a Christian upbringing, a good education, close friends, job skills, attractiveness . . . the list of reasons is endless. But Timothy's mentor wrote to remind him that the remedy for such intimidation was for him to stir up or rekindle the spiritual gift that was in him (see 2 Tim. 1:6). It's good advice for us, too.

The gift God gave this young man is available to every believer. It equips us with power, love, and a sound mind—the direct opposite of fear. But we must embrace the gift, stir it up, and remain focused on what God says instead of listening to the enemy.

I remember once, while praying for a member of my family, all of a sudden I heard a taunting voice in my mind: "What makes you think praying will change anything? He will never change!" Immediately my focus shifted from God's promises to my own shortcomings and my sense of inadequacy as an intercessor. If you're like me, you can be intimidated by a crafty voice like that almost without realizing it.

But then I realized that was not the voice of the Holy Spirit. How dare the enemy interrupt my prayer meeting! I declared aloud, "Satan, the Word says the "fervent prayer of a righteous man avails much' (James 5:16b), and I am righteous because of Jesus. I choose to believe what God says; therefore, my prayer is effective. I refuse to listen to you." Since then I've asked the Lord to help me recognize the enemy's voice, no matter how subtle it is, and never to entertain it.

This verse promises that we need not be timid and fearful of what life brings. Woman of Destiny, I encourage you to keep the fire of the Holy Spirit stirred up within you, and to use the Word of God to resist the enemy's voice (see James 4:7). Then you will function with good judgment and self-control, and make right decisions.

God is for you!

Ruthanne Garlock

2 Timothy 1:9

Dear Woman of Destiny,

For several years after I received Jesus as my Lord and Savior, there were some truths from the Word of God that I did not understand. One of those was the truth of holiness. Some have thought that *holiness* is an out-of-date term, no longer applicable to today's society, or that it is a "religious," "holier-than-thou" way of life. I've come to realize the truth and freedom of understanding holiness. It is not something "spooky" or beyond a Christian's ability to walk in.

Paul wrote that Jesus saved us *and* called us with a *holy calling*. Jesus not only forgave and cleansed you of your sins with His blood, but He also placed a calling upon your life toward Himself. This holy calling is not based upon your own works. Those who've lived a lifestyle of sin would not be able to receive this calling if it was because of their own works. Likewise, those who have been very religious, who have taken pride in themselves because of their good works and have looked down upon others would not be able to qualify for this calling. This holy calling is because of the grace toward our lives. Paul writes that it is according to His own purpose for our lives and His grace. This purpose was given to us in Christ Jesus before the world began. Ephesians 2:8–10 tells us that by grace we are saved through our faith in His gift to us. He goes on to say that "we are His workmanship, created in Christ Jesus for good works, which God prepared beforehand that we should walk in them." Every person born into the world has a purpose in life. Some, however, never discover that purpose in Christ.

Paul encourages Timothy and all of us not to be ashamed of our testimony. It's not because of a person's good works that they're saved and called by God, but it's because of His mercy and grace. Some are so ashamed of their past failures or sin that they believe they can only be saved, but can't see themselves holy or called by God to do great things. God's plans and "purposes for good" are for everyone who can believe. No matter what your past has been, once you accept the saving grace of God, you receive a holy calling to walk in the good things God wants you to do. It's a daily decision to choose to obey His voice instead of the voices of your past or what your flesh is saying to you.

Holiness is an inward consciousness that causes us to walk differently from the world around us. It is having the fear of the Lord (see Prov. 8:13). This is not to be afraid of God, but to have a respect and honor for His presence with you continually. It is taking the time to think about what He would want you to do.

Sharon Daugherty

He also will deny us.
13 If we are faithless,
He remains faithful;
He [a]cannot deny Himself.

Approved and Disapproved Workers

14Remind *them* of these things, [a]charging *them* before the Lord not to [1]strive about words to no profit, to the ruin of the hearers. 15 [a]Be diligent to present yourself approved to God, a worker who does not need to be ashamed, rightly dividing
the word of truth. 16But shun profane *and* [1]idle babblings, for they will [2]increase to more ungodliness. 17And their message will spread like cancer. [a]Hymenaeus and Philetus are of this sort, 18who have strayed concerning the truth, [a]saying that the resurrection is already past; and they overthrow the faith of some. 19Nevertheless [a]the solid foundation of God stands, having this seal: "The Lord [b]knows those who are His," and, "Let everyone who names the name of [1]Christ depart from iniquity."

13 a Num. 23:19
14 a Titus 3:9 *1 battle*
15 a 2 Pet. 1:10
16 *1 empty chatter* *2 lead*
17 a 1 Tim. 1:20
18 a 1 Cor. 15:12
19 a [1 Cor. 3:11] b [Nah. 1:7] *1* NU, M *the Lord*

Lois and Eunice

Mothers and daughters. Grandmothers and granddaughters. Aunts and nieces. There is something strong and unexplainably deep about the generational bonds that exist between women. When the generations come together, there is potential for power. Lois and Eunice were no exception, as together they raised young Timothy to be a faithful disciple and servant of Jesus Christ.

In Paul's second letter to Timothy, he refers to "the genuine faith that is in you, which dwelt first in your grandmother Lois and your mother Eunice" (2 Tim. 1:5). Timothy was heir to a double legacy of genuine faith and godliness from these two women. Among the gifts they gave him was instruction in God's Word that nurtured his faith and gave him a firm foundation on which to build his later ministry.

Generational relationships are possible any time an older person and a younger person are present together and don't necessarily rely on chronological age or blood relationship. They can exist spiritually just as they exist naturally, and many women consider each other spiritual "mothers and daughters." Whatever the case, each generation has treasures to give to the others. Think about the joy that an elderly woman feels as she rocks her great-grandchild to sleep: When she is gone, she can leave that child love to remember and prayers that will continue to be answered in God's timing throughout his life. Older generations connect younger ones to their past; they give them roots and perspective. In turn, the younger generations give the older ones joy, hope for the future, and the confidence that their legacy will outlive them.

May we, as women of destiny today, understand that life is rich and multifaceted, and that each stage of life has something valuable to contribute to the others. May we encourage those who are younger and honor those who are older. May we drink from the wells of wisdom in the older women and feed the spirits of younger women with the Word of God. May we celebrate and embrace the gifts of each generation.

2 Timothy 2:15

Dear Woman of Destiny,

All Bible-believing Christians agree that God has spoken in His Word. Of this we are certain. It follows naturally to ask what He has said. We do not profit when God has spoken if we do not know what He has said. This is the basic task of Bible interpretation, otherwise known as searching the Scriptures.

Bible interpretation should never be considered a purely mechanical or intellectual process; it must involve the Holy Spirit. If we are to know the message of the Bible, to rightly divide it and understand what He is really saying to our spirits, we need the aid of the heavenly Interpreter, the Holy Spirit, who has promised to lead us into all truth. Also keep in mind that the most important tool to be used in the study of the Bible is the Bible itself. Too many people read books about the Bible, but seldom read the Bible itself.

In addition, the following seven characteristics must be present in order to get the most from a study of God's Word: *Receive* the Word with meekness (see James 1:21). Let the Word dwell in you richly (see Col. 3:16). *Keep* the Word tenaciously. *Continue* in the Word untiringly (see John 8:31). *Live* out the Word faithfully. *Hold forth* the Word boldly (see Phil. 2:16). And finally, *meditate* on the Word of God *prayerfully* (see Ps. 1:2).

You will find cleansing, joy, comfort, song, riches, food, light, hope, and peace as you read and understand God's Word. Keep the following guidelines in mind as background for studying a particular passage:

- *The speaker*. Who is speaking—God, an apostle, a prophet, a saint, a sinner, an angel, or Satan? What is the character of the speaker? If he is a man, what is his age, his experience, his background?
- *The addressee*. To whom are the words addressed—God, man, saint, sinner, backslider, individual, or group?
- *The time*. When was it spoken?
- *The place*. Paul wrote to the Ephesians of "spiritual blessing in the heavenly places" (1:3). This becomes particularly meaningful when we realize that Paul was writing from prison.
- *The main theme*. What is the occasion and primary subject of the passage?

The Bible usually means what it says, but Scripture must be compared with Scripture. You will arrive at proper interpretation by studying parallels of passages, of words, and of general teachings. The interpretation of a given verse will depend to a great extent upon *who* said it, *to whom* it was said, and the *occasion* upon which it was said. A concordance and Bible dictionary will help you understand and properly interpret ideas in the Bible expressed by theological words.

The more you read and study the inexhaustible riches of Bible truth, the more you will be convinced that no better investment of time can be made. Read it—slowly, frequently, prayerfully, and reverently. Dig it up, write it down, pray it in, live it out, and pass it on!

Fuchsia Pickett

20But in a great house there are not
only [a]vessels of gold and silver, but also of
wood and clay, some for honor and some
for dishonor. 21Therefore if anyone
cleanses himself from the latter, he will be
a vessel for honor, [1]sanctified and useful
for the Master, [a]prepared for every good
work. 22[a]Flee also youthful lusts; but pursue righteousness, faith, love, peace with
those who call on the Lord out of a pure
heart. 23But avoid foolish and ignorant
disputes, knowing that they generate
strife. 24And [a]a servant of the Lord must
not quarrel but be gentle to all, [b]able to
teach, [c]patient, 25[a]in humility correcting
those who are in opposition, [b]if God perhaps will grant them repentance, [c]so that
they may know the truth, 26and *that* they
may come to their senses *and* [a]*escape* the
snare of the devil, having been taken captive by him to *do* his will.

I pray, Father, that ____ will be diligent to present themselves approved to You, a worker who does not need to be ashamed, rightly dividing the word of truth.

FROM 2 TIMOTHY 2:15

Perilous Times and Perilous Men

3 But know this, that [a]in the last days
[1]perilous times will come: 2For men
will be lovers of themselves, lovers of
money, boasters, proud, blasphemers, disobedient to parents, unthankful, unholy,
3unloving, [1]unforgiving, slanderers, without self-control, brutal, despisers of good,
4[a]traitors, headstrong, haughty, lovers of
pleasure rather than lovers of God, 5[a]hav-
ing a form of godliness but [b]denying its
power. And [c]from such people turn away!
6For [a]of this sort are those who creep into
households and make captives of gullible
women loaded down with sins, led away
by various lusts, 7always learning and never able [a]to come to the knowledge of the
truth. 8[a]Now as Jannes and Jambres resisted Moses, so do these also resist the
truth: [b]men of corrupt minds, [c]disap-
proved concerning the faith; 9but they
will progress no further, for their folly will
be manifest to all, [a]as theirs also was.

The Man of God and the Word of God

10[a]But you have carefully followed my
doctrine, manner of life, purpose, faith,
longsuffering, love, perseverance, 11perse-
cutions, afflictions, which happened to
me [a]at Antioch, [b]at Iconium, [c]at Lystra—
what persecutions I endured. And [d]out of
them all the Lord delivered me. 12Yes, and
[a]all who desire to live godly in Christ Jesus will suffer persecution. 13[a]But evil
men and impostors will grow worse and
worse, deceiving and being deceived.
14But you must [a]continue in the things
which you have learned and been assured
of, knowing from whom you have learned
them, 15and that from childhood you have
known [a]the Holy Scriptures, which are
able to make you wise for salvation
through faith which is in Christ Jesus.
16[a]All Scripture *is* given by inspiration
of God, [b]and *is* profitable for doctrine, for
reproof, for correction, for [1]instruction in
righteousness, 17[a]that the man of God
may be complete, [b]thoroughly equipped
for every good work.

Preach the Word

4 I [a]charge *you* [1]therefore before God
and the Lord Jesus Christ, [b]who will
judge the living and the dead [2]at His appearing and His kingdom: 2 Preach the
word! Be ready in season *and* out of season. [a]Convince, [b]rebuke, [c]exhort, with all
longsuffering and teaching. 3[a]For the

Someone has said that when God calls anyone to do His work, you can hardly get him in the pulpit; but when the devil calls him, you can't keep him out of it.

MARIA WOODWORTH-ETTER

20 a Rom. 9:21
21 a 2 Tim. 3:17 *1 set apart*
22 a 1 Tim. 6:11
24 a Titus 3:2 b Titus 1:9 c 1 Tim. 3:3
25 a Gal. 6:1 b Acts 8:22 c 1 Tim. 2:4
26 a 1 Tim. 3:7

CHAPTER 3
1 a 1 Tim. 4:1 *1 times of stress*
3 *1 irreconcilable*
4 a 2 Pet. 2:10
5 a Titus 1:16 b 1 Tim. 5:8 c 2 Thess. 3:6
6 a Matt. 23:14
7 a 1 Tim. 2:4
8 a Ex. 7:11, 12, 22; 8:7; 9:11 b 1 Tim. 6:5 c Rom. 1:28
9 a Ex. 7:11, 12; 8:18; 9:11
10 a 1 Tim. 4:6
11 a Acts 13:44–52 b Acts 14:1–6, 19 c Acts 14:8–20 d Ps. 34:19
12 a [Ps. 34:19]
13 a 2 Thess. 2:11
14 a 2 Tim. 1:13
15 a John 5:39
16 a [2 Pet. 1:20] b Rom. 4:23; 15:4 *1 training, discipline*
17 a 1 Tim. 6:11 b 2 Tim. 2:21

CHAPTER 4
1 a 1 Tim. 5:21 b Acts 10:42 *1* NU omits *therefore* *2* NU *and by*
2 a Titus 2:15 b 1 Tim. 5:20 c 1 Tim. 4:13
3 a 2 Tim. 3:1

2 Timothy 4:2

Dear Woman of Destiny,

All of us have been influenced by someone in our lives, whether negatively or positively. In a sense, this is what we are talking about when we use the term *mentoring,* or *discipling*. In this context, however, we are referring to intentionally influencing someone toward the goal of becoming more like Jesus. In 2 Timothy 4:2, Paul is instructing Timothy to influence or mentor others. The primary emphasis here is through proclaiming the word. I want to look beyond that, though, to how Timothy is to be a mentor. What is Timothy's approach or attitude to be? The key is found in the word *longsuffering*. Timothy is to instruct and influence others with patience, mercy, and forbearance.

I can think of few other characteristics that are more important in a mentoring relationship than patience, mercy, and longsuffering. I have been mentoring women for the past nineteen years. When I first began, I had a tendency to expect too much too soon; at times, I tried to fill in for the Holy Spirit (a frightening thought!). I lacked the patience and wisdom to seek God for His timing in addressing specific issues in their lives. My attitude was one of, "If I can see it, it should be addressed, and there is no better time than the present!" God, in His grace, still used me, but I have had to go back and ask forgiveness of some of those women. The real change, you see, needed to happen in me. The Lord, in His great mercy, took me on a decade-long journey of learning to be merciful—of instilling within me His compassion and patience.

My approach to mentoring now is one of taking it step by step. When I see areas that need growth in someone's life, my first response is to go to the Lord and pray, to seek His wisdom, His perspective, His timing. Let Him be the One to decide what the next step is to be in the maturing process. I believe that we can often major on the minors, while God's priority is to deal with matters of the heart. Yes, there are times when we need to confront, but it needs to be done in God's timing and with patience and longsuffering, or we may do more damage than good.

You may have been mentored by someone who hurt you and pushed you too hard, too soon. I encourage you to take time to go to the Lord and forgive them; allow the Lord to take any hurt or bitterness from your heart. You may be mentoring someone now and you know that you have not responded to her with patience and mercy. Take time to ask both the Lord and that person for forgiveness. Ask the Lord to work His mercy and compassion into your heart.

May God release you into the fullness of His extraordinary destiny for you!

Leslyn Musch

time will come when they will not endure
[b]sound doctrine, [c]but according to their
own desires, *because* they have itching
ears, they will heap up for themselves
teachers; 4and they will turn *their* ears
away from the truth, and [a]be turned aside
to fables. 5But you be watchful in all
things, [a]endure afflictions, do the work of
[b]an evangelist, fulfill your ministry.

Paul's Valedictory

6For [a]I am already being poured out as
a drink offering, and the time of [b]my departure is at hand. 7[a]I have fought the
good fight, I have finished the race, I have
kept the faith. 8Finally, there is laid up for
me [a]the crown of righteousness, which
the Lord, the righteous [b]Judge, will give
to me [c]on that Day, and not to me only
but also to all who have loved His appearing.

The Abandoned Apostle

9Be diligent to come to me quickly;
10for [a]Demas has forsaken me, [b]having
loved this present world, and has departed
for Thessalonica—Crescens for Galatia,
Titus for Dalmatia. 11Only Luke is with
me. Get [a]Mark and bring him with you,
for he is useful to me for ministry. 12And
[a]Tychicus I have sent to Ephesus. 13Bring
the cloak that I left with Carpus at Troas
when you come—and the books, especially the parchments.
14[a]Alexander the coppersmith did me
much harm. May the Lord repay him according to his works. 15You also must beware of him, for he has greatly resisted
our words.
16At my first defense no one stood with
me, but all forsook me. [a]May it not be
charged against them.

The Lord Is Faithful

17[a]But the Lord stood with me and
strengthened me, [b]so that the message
might be preached fully through me, and
that all the Gentiles might hear. Also I
was delivered [c]out of the mouth of the
lion. 18[a]And the Lord will deliver me from
every evil work and preserve *me* for His
heavenly kingdom. [b]To Him *be* glory forever and ever. Amen!

Come Before Winter

19Greet [a]Prisca and Aquila, and the
household of [b]Onesiphorus. 20[a]Erastus
stayed in Corinth, but [b]Trophimus I have
left in Miletus sick.
21Do your utmost to come before
winter.

O God, I pray that ______ will fight the good fight, finish their race, keep the faith. For You have laid up for them the crown of righteousness, which You, the righteous Judge, will give to them on that Day.

FROM 2 TIMOTHY 4:7, 8

Eubulus greets you, as well as Pudens,
Linus, Claudia, and all the brethren.

Farewell

22The Lord [1]Jesus Christ be with your
spirit. Grace be with you. Amen.

---

3 b 1 Tim. 1:10 c 2 Tim. 3:6
4 a 1 Tim. 1:4
5 a 2 Tim. 1:8 b Acts 21:8
6 a Phil. 2:17 b [Phil. 1:23]
7 a 1 Cor. 9:24–27
8 a James 1:12 b John 5:22 c 2 Tim. 1:12
10 a Col. 4:14 b 1 John 2:15
11 a Acts 12:12, 25; 15:37–39
12 a Acts 20:4
14 a 1 Tim. 1:20
16 a Acts 7:60
17 a Acts 23:11 b Acts 9:15 c 1 Sam. 17:37
18 a Ps. 121:7 b Rom. 11:36
19 a Acts 18:2 b 2 Tim. 1:16
20 a Rom. 16:23 b Acts 20:4; 21:29
22 1 NU omits *Jesus Christ*

AUTHOR: *Paul*
DATE: *Probably A.D. 64*
THEME: *Setting the Church at Crete in Order*
KEY WORDS: *Diligence, Commitment, Responsibility*

TITUS

Dear Woman of Destiny,

The Book of Titus teaches many lessons, such as the need for sound doctrine and holy living. One of the most powerful lessons for us as women focuses on mentoring. Older women must by example teach younger women (see Titus 2:3, 4). Something of a breech has developed between the generations of the older and the younger women in our churches today. Older women need to pray and ask God which of the younger women they can meet with and mentor. Young women should seek out mentors who will befriend them and help guide them with godly wisdom. Women of destiny learn from one another in their respective generations, and the church is strengthened through their relationships.

With His love,

Cindy Jacobs

Greeting

Paul, a bondservant of God and an apostle of Jesus Christ, according to the faith of God's elect and [a]the acknowledgment of the truth [b]which accords with godliness, 2in hope of eternal life which God, who [a]cannot lie, promised before time began, 3but has in due time manifested His word through preaching, which was committed to me according to the commandment of God our Savior;

4To [a]Titus, a true son in *our* common faith:

Grace, mercy, *and* peace from God the Father and [1]the Lord Jesus Christ our Savior.

Qualified Elders

5For this reason I left you in Crete, that you should [a]set in order the things that are lacking, and appoint elders in every city as I commanded you— 6if a man is blameless, the husband of one wife, [a]having faithful children not accused of [1]dissipation or insubordination. 7For a [1]bishop must be blameless, as a steward of God, not self-willed, not quick-tempered, [a]not given to wine, not violent, not greedy for money, 8but hospitable, a lover of what is good, sober-minded, just, holy, self-controlled, 9holding fast the faithful word as he has been taught, that he may be able, by sound doctrine, both to exhort and convict those who contradict.

Father, I pray that ____ will be hospitable, a lover of what is good, sober-minded, just, holy, self-controlled, holding fast the faithful word as they have been taught, that they may be able, by sound doctrine, both to exhort and convict those who contradict.

FROM TITUS 1:8, 9

CHAPTER 1
1 [a]2 Tim. 2:25 [b][1 Tim. 3:16]
2 [a]Num. 23:19
4 [a]2 Cor. 2:13; 8:23 [1]NU *Christ Jesus*
5 [a]1 Cor. 11:34
6 [a]1 Tim. 3:2–4 [1]*debauchery,* lit. *incorrigibility*
7 [a]Lev. 10:9 [1]Lit. *overseer*
10 [a]James 1:26
11 [a]1 Tim. 6:5
12 [a]Acts 17:28
13 [a]2 Cor. 13:10
14 [a]Is. 29:13
15 [a]1 Cor. 6:12
16 [a]Matt. 7:20–23; 25:12 [b][2 Tim. 3:5, 7] [c]Rom. 1:28 [1]*detestable*

CHAPTER 2
5 [a]1 Tim. 5:14 [b]1 Cor. 14:34 [c]Rom. 2:24
7 [a]1 Tim. 4:12 [b]Eph. 6:24 [1]NU omits *incorruptibility*
8 [1]NU, M *us*

The Elders' Task

10For there are many insubordinate, both idle [a]talkers and deceivers, especially those of the circumcision, 11whose mouths must be stopped, who subvert whole households, teaching things which they ought not, [a]for the sake of dishonest gain. 12[a]One of them, a prophet of their own, said, "Cretans *are* always liars, evil beasts, lazy gluttons." 13This testimony is true. [a]Therefore rebuke them sharply, that they may be sound in the faith, 14not giving heed to Jewish fables and [a]commandments of men who turn from the truth. 15[a]To the pure all things are pure, but to those who are defiled and unbelieving nothing is pure; but even their mind and conscience are defiled. 16They profess to [a]know God, but [b]in works they deny Him, being [1]abominable, disobedient, [c]and disqualified for every good work.

The Holy Spirit came to give us power to stand on the infallible Word and overcome false spirits.

WILLIAM SEYMOUR

Qualities of a Sound Church

2 But as for you, speak the things which are proper for sound doctrine: 2that the older men be sober, reverent, temperate, sound in faith, in love, in patience; 3the older women likewise, that they be reverent in behavior, not slanderers, not given to much wine, teachers of good things— 4that they admonish the young women to love their husbands, to love their children, 5to be discreet, chaste, [a]homemakers, good, [b]obedient to their own husbands, [c]that the word of God may not be blasphemed.

6Likewise, exhort the young men to be sober-minded, 7in all things showing yourself *to be* [a]a pattern of good works; in doctrine *showing* integrity, reverence, [b]incorruptibility,[1] 8sound speech that cannot be condemned, that one who is an opponent may be ashamed, having nothing evil to say of [1]you.

Titus 2:3–5

Dear Woman of Destiny,

The Bible is explicit that older women are to train younger women. Today we call this principle *mentoring*.

Mentoring is the passing down of knowledge and training from one who is more experienced to one who is less experienced. A mentor encourages and equips for excellence.

A young, married, working woman once told me what she'd like in a mentor: "Someone who would show me love and acceptance, offer me help, be open to me, have leadership qualities, and be a role model. It would be a win-win situation for both of us, because we would both give to one another."

When I first formed my mentoring group of young single women, I set my own goals as a mentor:

- Help the young women discover their life purposes (see Luke 1:38; Eph. 2:10)
- Encourage and equip them in their own talents and find other women to help me if I was not skilled in what they wanted to learn
- Pray for them individually according to needs and goals
- Encourage discipline in their daily prayer life and Bible reading
- Include homemaking skills, hospitality helps, decorating tips, and cooking shortcuts. By having them in my home every week, I served nourishing meals and showed them various ways to set the table—formal, casual, picnic. Since the Bible says to "practice hospitality," I sometimes let them help me.

In our mobile society with a diversity of cultures, our need for supporting friendships among women—intergenerational bonding—is great. I always hope the young women in whom I invest my time and teaching will outdistance me.

Multitudes of young women are looking for spiritually mature women to speak into their lives. They want someone to help them grow to become all God intends them to be. Maybe you are that mentor who can help one less experienced. If so, ask God to bring the right young woman (or women) into your life. Don't be bashful about asking her to meet you for coffee to discuss the possibility.

Perhaps you are a young woman hungry for the help of a godly woman who will help hold you accountable or even just give you child-care tips. Whatever your need, God has someone who can help meet it. Again, pray for God to show you who that special person is. She may already be in your church or in your neighborhood.

One of my own mentors served breakfast every Tuesday for ten years to a mother of six children who desperately needed the encouragement of an older woman. Today Mary Jo meets once a month with thirty young mothers whom she encourages and prays for; and she lets them ask her questions.

God has given each of us special abilities. We can use them in the body of Christ to help others, bringing them to a higher position of strength and maturity.

Let's be mentors who pass the torch to the next generation—yes, through spiritual insights, but also by sharing practical how-tos for normal nitty-gritty living.

Quin Sherrer

9*Exhort* [a]bondservants to be obedient
to their own masters, to be well pleasing
in all *things,* not answering back, 10not
[1]pilfering, but showing all good [2]fidelity,
that they may adorn the doctrine of God
our Savior in all things.

Trained by Saving Grace

11For [a]the grace of God that brings salvation has appeared to all men, 12teaching
us that, denying ungodliness and worldly
lusts, we should live soberly, righteously,
and godly in the present age, 13[a]looking
for the blessed [b]hope and glorious appearing of our great God and Savior Jesus
Christ, 14[a]who gave Himself for us, that
He might redeem us from every lawless
deed [b]and purify for Himself [c]*His* own
special people, zealous for good works.
15Speak these things, [a]exhort, and rebuke with all authority. Let no one despise you.

> *We are not to be occupied with our feelings or symptoms or our faith, or lack of faith, but only with what God has said.*
>
> GORDON LINDSAY

Graces of the Heirs of Grace

3 Remind them [a]to be subject to rulers
and authorities, to obey, [b]to be ready
for every good work, 2to speak evil of no
one, to be peaceable, gentle, showing all
humility to all men. 3For [a]we ourselves
were also once foolish, disobedient, deceived, serving various lusts and pleasures, living in malice and envy, hateful
and hating one another. 4But when [a]the
kindness and the love of [b]God our Savior
toward man appeared, 5[a]not by works of
righteousness which we have done, but
according to His mercy He saved us,
through [b]the washing of regeneration and
renewing of the Holy Spirit, 6[a]whom He
poured out on us abundantly through Jesus Christ our Savior, 7that having been
justified by His grace [a]we should become
heirs according to the hope of eternal life.
8[a]This is a faithful saying, and these
things I want you to affirm constantly,
that those who have believed in God
should be careful to maintain good works.
These things are good and profitable to
men.

> *The ministry of Christianity is the ministry of the Spirit.*
>
> JOHN G. LAKE

Avoid Dissension

9But [a]avoid foolish disputes, genealogies, contentions, and strivings about the
law; for they are unprofitable and useless.
10[a]Reject a divisive man after the first and
second [1]admonition, 11knowing that such
a person is warped and sinning, being
self-condemned.

> *Lord, in accordance with Your Word, I ask that _____ would avoid foolish disputes, genealogies, contentions, and strivings about the law; for they are unprofitable and useless.*
>
> FROM TITUS 3:9

Final Messages

12When I send Artemas to you, or
[a]Tychicus, be diligent to come to me at
Nicopolis, for I have decided to spend the
winter there. 13Send Zenas the lawyer and
[a]Apollos on their journey with haste, that
they may lack nothing. 14And let our *peo-*
ple also learn to maintain good works, to
meet urgent needs, that they may not be
unfruitful.

Farewell

15All who *are* with me greet you. Greet
those who love us in the faith.
Grace *be* with you all. Amen.

---

9 a 1 Tim. 6:1
10 *1 thieving* *2 honesty*
11 a [Rom. 5:15]
13 a 1 Cor. 1:7 b [Col. 3:4]
14 a Gal. 1:4 b [Heb. 1:3; 9:14] c Ex. 15:16
15 a 2 Tim. 4:2
CHAPTER 3
1 a 1 Pet. 2:13 b Col. 1:10
3 a 1 Cor. 6:11
4 a Titus 2:11 b 1 Tim. 2:3
5 a [Rom. 3:20] b John 3:3
6 a Ezek. 36:26
7 a [Rom. 8:17, 23, 24]
8 a 1 Tim. 1:15
9 a 2 Tim. 2:23
10 a Matt. 18:17 *1 warning*
12 a Acts 20:4
13 a Acts 18:24

AUTHOR: *Paul*
DATE: *A.D. 60–61*
THEME: *Brotherly Love*
KEY WORD: *Brother*

PHILEMON

Dear Woman of Destiny,

Have you ever been in a situation where a relationship was broken and you were the guilty party? Wouldn't it have been wonderful if someone, respected by the person you had wronged, had appealed to them for you? Only this kind of person could go on your behalf to tell them that your heart was truly repentant. That is what Paul did for Onesimus, and we women need to do this for those we love as well. All of us should look for ways to bring restoration and healing to broken relationships between those we love. The good news is that, even if we who don't know a person like Paul who will stand for us, we as women of destiny always have Jesus Christ, our Savior as our mediator and friend.

With His love,

Cindy Jacobs

Greeting

Paul, a [a]prisoner of Christ Jesus, and
Timothy *our* brother,

To Philemon our beloved *friend* and fellow laborer, 2to [1]the beloved Apphia, [a]Ar-
chippus our fellow soldier, and to the
church in your house:

3Grace to you and peace from God our
Father and the Lord Jesus Christ.

For natural ties, apart from religious influences, have their origin and end in the present state; whereas spiritual relationships have their origin in the Eternal God, the Infinite Source of life and happiness, and must, if rightly cherished, endure as long as God Himself endures.

PHOEBE PALMER

Philemon's Love and Faith

4 [a]I thank my God, making mention
of you always in my prayers, 5[a]hearing of
your love and faith which you have toward
the Lord Jesus and toward all the saints,
6that the sharing of your faith may become effective [a]by the acknowledgment of
[b]every good thing which is in [1]you in
Christ Jesus. 7For we [1]have great [2]joy and
[3]consolation in your love, because the
[4]hearts of the saints have been refreshed
by you, brother.

The Plea for Onesimus

8Therefore, though I might be very bold
in Christ to command you what is fitting,
9*yet* for love's sake I rather appeal *to
you*—being such a one as Paul, the aged,
and now also a prisoner of Jesus Christ—
10I appeal to you for my son [a]Onesimus,
whom I have begotten *while* in my chains,
11who once was unprofitable to you, but
now is profitable to you and to me.
12I am sending him [1]back. You therefore receive him, that is, my own [2]heart,
13whom I wished to keep with me, that on
your behalf he might minister to me in
my chains for the gospel. 14But without
your consent I wanted to do nothing,
[a]that your good deed might not be by
compulsion, as it were, but voluntary.

Thank You for ____, Lord, because the hearts of the saints have been refreshed by them as some were by Philemon.

FROM PHILEMON 7

15For perhaps he departed for a while
for this *purpose,* that you might receive
him forever, 16no longer as a slave but
more than a slave—a beloved brother, especially to me but how much more to you,
both in the [a]flesh and in the Lord.

Philemon's Obedience Encouraged

17If then you count me as a partner,
receive him as *you would* me. 18But if he
has wronged you or owes anything, put
that on my account. 19I, Paul, am writing
with my own [a]hand. I will repay—not to
mention to you that you owe me even
your own self besides. 20Yes, brother, let
me have joy from you in the Lord; refresh
my heart in the Lord.

21[a]Having confidence in your obedience, I write to you, knowing that you will
do even more than I say. 22But, meanwhile, also prepare a guest room for me,
for [a]I trust that [b]through your prayers I
shall be granted to you.

Farewell

23[a]Epaphras, my fellow prisoner in
Christ Jesus, greets you, 24*as do* [a]Mark,
[b]Aristarchus, [c]Demas, [d]Luke, my fellow
laborers.

25[a]The grace of our Lord Jesus Christ
be with your spirit. Amen.

1 a Eph. 3:1
2 a Col. 4:17 *1* NU *our sister Apphia*
4 a 2 Thess. 1:3
5 a Col. 1:4
6 a Phil. 1:9 b [1 Thess. 5:18] *1* NU, M *us*
7 *1* NU *had* *2* M *thanksgiving* *3 comfort* *4* Lit. *inward parts,* heart, liver, and lungs
10 a Col. 4:9
12 *1* NU *back to you in person, that is, my own heart,* *2* See v. 7.
14 a 2 Cor. 9:7
16 a Col. 3:22
19 a 1 Cor. 16:21
21 a 2 Cor. 7:16
22 a Phil. 1:25; 2:24 b 2 Cor. 1:11
23 a Col. 1:7; 4:12
24 a Acts 12:12, 25; 15:37–39 b Acts 19:29; 27:2 c Col. 4:14 d 2 Tim. 4:11
25 a 2 Tim. 4:22

Philemon 4–7

Dear Woman of Destiny,

Pray for your nation, and let your prayer and praises be offered not only for yourself, but also for what affects others. This is a very tender thing, so as a woman of destiny, stay tender; and what you desire for yourself, practice and pray on behalf of others.

Offer thanks on behalf of others, and do it with great joy for all the good things you continue to know about them or have heard of them. And let any goodness in them, or done by them or to them, affect your prayers with gratitude. Have a big heart toward others, and pray the "best" things for them, not gold or silver or earthly good, but grace, peace, and favor from God. It's a privilege to bring prayers and praises to God who is the source of all blessings and the author of all good.

Be thankful for others in prayer, especially mentioning brothers and sisters in Christ who labor in the kingdom, faithful to God's work. Pray for those who take pains and endure hardships as they stand at their posts strengthening others' hands and hearts in their holy work and calling. Pray for those who are provided with spiritual weapons and the skill to use them, who watch over others' souls and give an account of them. As they fight the Lord's battles, not entangling themselves in the things of this life, but pleasing God who has chosen them, be thankful for them and pray.

Mention others, not just once or twice, but always. In your private times of thanks and prayers, remember your friends and those you love, who have been in your thoughts. Stay free from repetitive legalistic prayers where you are systematically naming names, but instead pray for others from your love for them. This can be your way of exercising love—through spontaneous prayers that touch God's heart as you obtain good for them.

Woman of Destiny, remember that the deep revelation of Christ is always at work in your life, so readily share your faith. Pray that others' faith will become more productive in loving service and effective witnessing, through the fullness of Christ that promotes deeper insight and fuller understanding of the inheritance we have in Christ. Continue in prayer for the unity of the Spirit working among us all, and understand love through practical grace and mercy. Learn how to yield to all the resources the Holy Spirit wants to bring to you, and practice receiving and applying those benefits. Call forth good things when you pray—for example, restored relationships and all the godly friends you need to fulfill your destiny. Remember, faith and love restore.

Finally, let your prayers compare to Christ's intercession with the Father. In other words, let your intercession be of the same spirit as Christ's is in prayer, that of selfless giving for others, from a full and loving heart. Love through forgiveness in any sensitive situation will win, and the privilege of being cheered up by another Christian's heart will bring refreshing and comfort to you. Great joy comes when you love and pray for others.

Julie Anderson

AUTHOR: *Unknown*
DATE: *Before A.D. 70*
THEME: *The Superiority of Jesus Christ over the Old Covenant*
KEY WORDS: *Better, Let Us*

HEBREWS

Dear Woman of Destiny,

We all have times when our faith is tested. The early Christians were no exception. They were being hotly persecuted and were wavering in their decision for Christ. All of us are assaulted by doubt and unbelief from time to time as to whether or not we will see the promises of God come to pass. Isn't it wonderful that the Holy Spirit included a special section for us as women in the Hebrews 11 "hall of faith"? This book was written about elders in the faith, those to whom we can look as heroines. This chapter inspires us to the faith of Sarah who received strength to conceive when she was past the age of childbearing. Even the harlot Rahab is included in this hall of faith because she received the spies of God. Woman of Destiny, let us live our lives in such a way that we, too, can be in the annals of God's heavenly hall of fame.

With His love,

Cindy Jacobs

God's Supreme Revelation

God, who [1]at various times and [a]in
various ways spoke in time past to
the fathers by the prophets, 2has
in these last days spoken to us by *His* Son,
whom He has appointed heir of all things,
through whom also He made the [1]worlds;
3[a]who being the brightness of *His* glory
and the express [b]image of His person,
and [c]upholding all things by the word of
His power, [d]when He had [1]by Himself
[2]purged [3]our sins, [e]sat down at the right
hand of the Majesty on high, 4having become so much better than the angels, as
[a]He has by inheritance obtained a more
excellent name than they.

The Son Exalted Above Angels

5For to which of the angels did He ever
say:

[a]*"You are My Son,*
Today I have begotten You"?

And again:

[b]*"I will be to Him a Father,*
And He shall be to Me a Son"?

6But when He again brings [a]the firstborn into the world, He says:

[b]*"Let all the angels of God worship*
Him."

7And of the angels He says:

[a]*"Who makes His angels spirits*
And His ministers a flame of fire."

8But to the Son *He says:*

[a]*"Your throne, O God, is forever and*
ever;
A [1]scepter of righteousness is the
scepter of Your kingdom.
9 *You have loved righteousness and*
hated lawlessness;
Therefore God, Your God, [a]has
anointed You
With the oil of gladness more than
Your companions."

10And:

[a]*"You, LORD, in the beginning laid*
the foundation of the earth,
And the heavens are the work of
Your hands.
11 [a]*They will perish, but You remain;*
And [b]they will all grow old like a
garment;
12 *Like a cloak You will fold them*
up,
And they will be changed.
But You are the [a]same,
And Your years will not fail."

13But to which of the angels has He
ever said:

[a]*"Sit at My right hand,*
Till I make Your enemies Your
footstool"?

14[a]Are they not all ministering spirits sent
forth to minister for those who will [b]in-
herit salvation?

Do Not Neglect Salvation

2 Therefore we must give [1]the more
earnest heed to the things we have
heard, lest we drift away. 2For if the word
[a]spoken through angels proved steadfast,
and [b]every transgression and disobedience received a just [1]reward, 3[a]how shall
we escape if we neglect so great a salvation, [b]which at the first began to be spoken by the Lord, and was [c]confirmed to us
by those who heard *Him,* 4[a]God also bearing witness [b]both with signs and wonders,
with various miracles, and [c]gifts[1] of the
Holy Spirit, [d]according to His own will?

Merciful Lord, I cry out
for _____; do not allow
them to neglect so great
a salvation!

FROM HEBREWS 2:3

The Son Made Lower than Angels

5For He has not put [a]the world to
come, of which we speak, in subjection
to angels. 6But one testified in a certain
place, saying:

[a]*"What is man that You are mindful*
of him,
Or the son of man that You take
care of him?
7 *You have made him [1]a little lower*
than the angels;
You have crowned him with glory
and honor,

CHAPTER 1
1 [a]Num. 12:6, 8 [1]Or *in many portions*
2 [1]Or *ages,* Gr. *aiones,* aeons
3 [a]John 1:14 [b]2 Cor. 4:4 [c]Col. 1:17 [d][Heb. 7:27] [e]Ps. 110:1 [1]NU omits *by Himself* [2]*cleansed* [3]NU omits *our*
4 [a][Phil. 2:9, 10]
5 [a]Ps. 2:7 [b]2 Sam. 7:14
6 [a][Rom. 8:29] [b]Deut. 32:43, LXX, DSS; Ps. 97:7
7 [a]Ps. 104:4
8 [a]Ps. 45:6, 7 [1]A ruler's staff
9 [a]Is. 61:1, 3
10 [a]Ps. 102:25–27
11 [a][Is. 34:4] [b]Is. 50:9; 51:6
12 [a]Heb. 13:8
13 [a]Ps. 110:1
14 [a]Ps. 103:20 [b]Rom. 8:17

CHAPTER 2
1 [1]*all the more careful attention*
2 [a]Acts 7:53 [b]Num. 15:30 [1]*retribution* or *penalty*
3 [a]Heb. 10:28 [b]Matt. 4:17 [c]Luke 1:2
4 [a]Mark 16:20 [b]Acts 2:22, 43 [c]1 Cor. 12:4, 7, 11 [d]Eph. 1:5, 9 [1]*distributions*
5 [a][2 Pet. 3:13]
6 [a]Ps. 8:4–6
7 [1]Or *for a little while*

[2]And set him over the works of Your
hands.
8 *[a]You have put all things in*
subjection under his feet."

For in that He put all in subjection under him, He left nothing *that is* not put under him. But now [b]we do not yet see all things put under him. [9]But we see Jesus, [a]who was made [1]a little lower than the angels, for the suffering of death [b]crowned with glory and honor, that He, by the grace of God, might taste death [c]for everyone.

Bringing Many Sons to Glory

[10]For it was fitting for Him, [a]for whom *are* all things and by whom *are* all things, in bringing many sons to glory, to make the captain of their salvation [b]perfect through sufferings. [11]For [a]both He who [1]sanctifies and those who are being sanctified [b]*are* all of one, for which reason [c]He is not ashamed to call them brethren, [12]saying:

[a]"I will declare Your name to My
brethren;
In the midst of the assembly I will
sing praise to You."

[13]And again:

[a]"I will put My trust in Him."

And again:

[b]"Here am I and the children whom
God has given Me."

[14]Inasmuch then as the children have partaken of flesh and blood, He [a]Himself likewise shared in the same, [b]that through death He might destroy him who had the power of [c]death, that is, the devil, [15]and release those who [a]through fear of death were all their lifetime subject to bondage. [16]For indeed He does not [1]give aid to angels, but He does [2]give aid to the seed of Abraham. [17]Therefore, in all things He had [a]to be made like *His* brethren, that He might be [b]a merciful and faithful High Priest in things *pertaining* to God, to make propitiation for the sins of the people. [18][a]For in that He Himself has suffered, being [1]tempted, He is able to aid those who are tempted.

The Son Was Faithful

3 Therefore, holy brethren, partakers of the heavenly calling, consider the Apostle and High Priest of our confession, Christ Jesus, [2]who was faithful to Him who appointed Him, as [a]Moses also *was faithful* in all His house. [3]For this One has been counted worthy of more glory than Moses, inasmuch as [a]He who built the house has more honor than the house. [4]For every house is built by someone, but [a]He who built all things *is* God. [5][a]And Moses indeed *was* faithful in all His house as [b]a servant, [c]for a testimony of those things which would be spoken *afterward,* [6]but Christ as [a]a Son over His own house, [b]whose house we are [c]if we hold fast the confidence and the rejoicing of the hope [1]firm to the end.

Be Faithful

[7]Therefore, as [a]the Holy Spirit says:

[b]"Today, if you will hear His voice,
8 *Do not harden your hearts as in*
the rebellion,
In the day of trial in the wilderness,
9 *Where your fathers tested Me, tried*
Me,
And saw My works forty years.
10 *Therefore I was angry with that*
generation,
And said, 'They always go astray in
their heart,
And they have not known My ways.'
11 *So I swore in My wrath,*
'They shall not enter My rest.' "

[12]Beware, brethren, lest there be in any of you an evil heart of unbelief in departing from the living God; [13]but [1]exhort one another daily, while it is called *"Today,"* lest any of you be hardened through the deceitfulness of sin. [14]For we have become partakers of Christ if we hold the beginning of our confidence steadfast to the end, [15]while it is said:

[a]"Today, if you will hear His voice,
Do not harden your hearts as in the
rebellion."

Failure of the Wilderness Wanderers

[16][a]For who, having heard, rebelled? Indeed, *was it* not all who came out of Egypt, *led* by Moses? [17]Now with whom was He angry forty years? *Was it* not with those who sinned, [a]whose corpses fell in the wilderness? [18]And [a]to whom did He swear that they would not enter His rest, but to those who did not obey? [19]So we see

---

7 [2] NU, M omit the rest of v. 7.
8 [a] Matt. 28:18 [b] 1 Cor. 15:25, 27
9 [a] Phil. 2:7–9 [b] Acts 2:33; 3:13 [c] [John 3:16] [1] Or *for a little while*
10 [a] Col. 1:16 [b] Heb. 5:8, 9; 7:28
11 [a] Heb. 10:10 [b] Acts 17:26 [c] Matt. 28:10 [1] *sets apart*
12 [a] Ps. 22:22
13 [a] 2 Sam. 22:3; Is. 8:17 [b] Is. 8:18
14 [a] John 1:14 [b] Col. 2:15 [c] 2 Tim. 1:10
15 [a] [Luke 1:74]
16 [1] Or *take on* the nature of [2] Or *take on*
17 [a] Phil. 2:7 [b] [Heb. 4:15; 5:1–10]
18 [a] [Heb. 4:15, 16] [1] *tested*

CHAPTER 3
2 [a] Num. 12:7
3 [a] Zech. 6:12, 13
4 [a] [Eph. 2:10]
5 [a] Heb. 3:2 [b] Ex. 14:31 [c] Deut. 18:15, 18, 19
6 [a] Heb. 1:2 [b] [1 Cor. 3:16] [c] [Matt. 10:22] [1] NU omits *firm to the end*
7 [a] Acts 1:16 [b] Ps. 95:7–11
13 [1] *encourage*
15 [a] Ps. 95:7, 8
16 [a] Num. 14:2, 11, 30
17 [a] Num. 14:22, 23
18 [a] Num. 14:30

that they could not enter in because of [a]unbelief.

The Promise of Rest

4 Therefore, since a promise remains of entering His rest, [a]let us fear lest any of you seem to have come short of it. 2For indeed the gospel was preached to us as well as to them; but the word which they heard did not profit them, [1]not being mixed with faith in those who heard *it.* 3For we who have believed do enter that rest, as He has said:

> [a]*"So I swore in My wrath,*
> *'They shall not enter My rest,' "*

although the works were finished from the foundation of the world. 4For He has spoken in a certain place of the seventh *day* in this way: [a]*"And God rested on the seventh day from all His works"*; 5and again in this *place:* [a]*"They shall not enter My rest."*

6Since therefore it remains that some *must* enter it, and those to whom it was first preached did not enter because of disobedience, 7again He designates a certain day, saying in David, *"Today,"* after such a long time, as it has been said:

> [a]*"Today, if you will hear His voice,*
> *Do not harden your hearts."*

8For if [1]Joshua had [a]given them rest, then He would not afterward have spoken of another day. 9There remains therefore a rest for the people of God. 10For he who has entered His rest has himself also ceased from his works as God *did* from His.

The Word Discovers Our Condition

11[a]Let us therefore be diligent to enter that rest, lest anyone fall according to the same example of disobedience. 12For the word of God *is* [a]living and powerful, and [b]sharper than any [c]two-edged sword, piercing even to the division of soul and spirit, and of joints and marrow, and is [d]a discerner of the thoughts and intents of the heart. 13[a]And there is no creature hidden from His sight, but all things *are* [b]naked and open to the eyes of Him to whom we *must give* account.

The Word of God is alive and every part of it is necessary to the perfection of the whole.

HENRIETTA MEARS

Our Compassionate High Priest

14Seeing then that we have a great [a]High Priest who has passed through the heavens, Jesus the Son of God, [b]let us hold fast *our* confession. 15For [a]we do not have a High Priest who cannot sympathize with our weaknesses, but [b]was in all *points* tempted as *we are,* [c]*yet* without sin. 16[a]Let us therefore come boldly to the throne of grace, that we may obtain mercy and find grace to help in time of need.

Father, I come before You in the name of Jesus, our great High Priest who sympathizes with our weaknesses. I come boldly to Your throne of grace to intercede for ____ that they may obtain mercy and find grace to help in time of need.

FROM HEBREWS 4:15, 16

Qualifications for High Priesthood

5 For every high priest taken from among men [a]is appointed for men in things *pertaining* to God, that he may offer both gifts and sacrifices for sins. 2He can [1]have compassion on those who are ignorant and going astray, since he himself is also subject to [a]weakness. 3Because of this he is required as for the people, so also for [a]himself, to offer *sacrifices* for sins. 4And no man takes this honor to himself, but he who is called by God, just as [a]Aaron *was.*

---

19 [a] 1 Cor. 10:11, 12

CHAPTER 4
1 [a] Heb. 12:15
2 [1] NU, M *since they were not united by faith with those who heeded it*
3 [a] Ps. 95:11
4 [a] Gen. 2:2
5 [a] Ps. 95:11
7 [a] Ps. 95:7, 8
8 [a] Josh. 22:4 [1] Gr. *Jesus,* same as Heb. *Joshua*
11 [a] 2 Pet. 1:10
12 [a] Ps. 147:15 [b] Is. 49:2 [c] Eph. 6:17 [d] 1 Cor. 14:24, 25
13 [a] Ps. 33:13–15; 90:8 [b] Job 26:6
14 [a] Heb. 2:17; 7:26 [b] Heb. 10:23
15 [a] Is. 53:3–5 [b] Luke 22:28 [c] 2 Cor. 5:21
16 [a] [Eph. 2:18]

CHAPTER 5
1 [a] Heb. 2:17; 8:3
2 [a] Heb. 7:28 [1] *deal gently with*
3 [a] Lev. 9:7; 16:6
4 [a] Ex. 28:1

Hebrews 4:9–11

Dear Woman of Destiny,

Perhaps you can identify with the young mother of a new baby who, when asked what she wanted for Mother's Day, replied, "A good night's sleep!" Hebrews 4:9–11 sets before us the promise of that elusive treasure so many stressed women, whether mothers or not, only dream about—rest. Because the verb *to rest* means "to cease from labor," we generally associate it with physical rest.

But this passage speaks of rest in a broader sense—based on a root word meaning "to settle into an abode." Previous verses in chapter 4 refer to God's anger against Israel because they refused, through unbelief, to enter in and possess the land He had promised them. Thus God declared they would not enter the rest He had prepared.

Today, because of Christ's provision for us, we have the opportunity to enter into His rest—a place of utter dependence upon God. But we tend to try managing life's responsibilities and pressures on our own, rather than appropriating that place of rest available to us.

Years ago, while I was attending a women's retreat at a guest ranch in the Texas Hill country, our teacher instructed each of us to go outside and find a place of solitude to pray and meditate. At the time, I was struggling with the burden of an assignment I had accepted that seemed overwhelming. Other people's expectations made it even heavier. Though I didn't want to let them down, I was exhausted by the weight of it all.

I climbed a small hill and found a large, flat rock where I sat down to enjoy the expansive view and talk to the Lord. Compared to the majesty of God's creation that surrounded me, somehow my problem didn't seem so enormous after all. As I prayed, the Holy Spirit reminded me of Jesus' words: "Come to Me, all you who labor and are heavy laden, and I will give you rest. . . . For My yoke is easy and My burden is light" (Matt. 11:28, 30).

Realizing the burden I was carrying was of my own making, I repented for my lack of trust in God's promises. I solemnly pledged to the Lord that I would leave my burden on that huge rock I was sitting on and not carry it home with me. I returned from the retreat energized with new faith. Although I still knew I was not equal to the assignment that awaited me, I determined to trust God to equip and enable me to perform it. A great sense of rest and tranquility came to my spirit. And yes, I did complete the job.

Woman of Destiny, I urge you to lay down the weight of tasks you are trying to fulfill in your own strength. Of course, you have responsibilities and duties to perform in many areas of your life. But putting your trust in God and receiving His strength for the doing of those things will give you a great sense of rest. That is His will for you.

Ruthanne Garlock

A Priest Forever

5[a]So also Christ did not glorify Himself
to become High Priest, *but it* was He who
said to Him:

[b]*"You are My Son,*
Today I have begotten You."

6As *He* also *says* in another *place:*

[a]*"You are a priest forever*
According to the order of
Melchizedek";

7who, in the days of His flesh, when He
had [a]offered up prayers and supplications,
[b]with vehement cries and tears to Him
[c]who was able to save Him from death,
and was heard [d]because of His godly fear,
8though He was a Son, *yet* He learned
[a]obedience by the things which He suffered. 9And [a]having been perfected, He
became the author of eternal salvation to
all who obey Him, 10called by God as High
Priest [a]*"according to the order of Mel-*
chizedek," 11of whom [a]we have much to
say, and hard to explain, since you have
become [b]dull of hearing.

Spiritual Immaturity

12For though by this time you ought to
be teachers, you need *someone* to teach
you again the first principles of the [1]ora-
cles of God; and you have come to need
[a]milk and not solid food. 13For everyone
who partakes *only* of milk *is* unskilled in
the word of righteousness, for he is [a]a
babe. 14But solid food belongs to those
who are [1]of full age, *that is,* those who by
reason of [2]use have their senses exercised
[a]to discern both good and evil.

The Peril of Not Progressing

6 Therefore, [a]leaving the discussion of
the elementary *principles* of Christ,
let us go on to [1]perfection, not laying
again the foundation of repentance from
[b]dead works and of faith toward God, 2[a]of
the doctrine of baptisms, [b]of laying on of
hands, [c]of resurrection of the dead, [d]and
of eternal judgment. 3And this [1]we will do
if God permits.

4For *it is* impossible for those who were
once enlightened, and have tasted [a]the
heavenly gift, and [b]have become partakers
of the Holy Spirit, 5and have tasted the
good word of God and the powers of the
age to come, 6[1]if they fall away, to renew
them again to repentance, [a]since they
crucify again for themselves the Son of
God, and put *Him* to an open shame.

7For the earth which drinks in the rain
that often comes upon it, and bears herbs
useful for those by whom it is cultivated,
[a]receives blessing from God; 8[a]but if it
bears thorns and briers, *it is* rejected and
near to being cursed, whose end *is* to be
burned.

Jesus Christ is absolute perfection.

KATHRYN KUHLMAN

A Better Estimate

9But, beloved, we are confident of better things concerning you, yes, things
that accompany salvation, though we
speak in this manner. 10For [a]God *is* not
unjust to forget [b]your work and [1]labor of
love which you have shown toward His
name, *in that* you have [c]ministered to the
saints, and do minister. 11 And we desire
that each one of you show the same diligence [a]to the full assurance of hope until
the end, 12that you do not become [1]slug-
gish, but imitate those who through faith
and patience [a]inherit the promises.

O Lord, You are not unjust to forget the work and labor of love which _____ has shown toward Your name, in that they have ministered and continue to minister to the saints.

FROM HEBREWS 6:10

God's Infallible Purpose in Christ

13For when God made a promise to
Abraham, because He could swear by no

---

5 a John 8:54 b Ps. 2:7
6 a Ps. 110:4
7 a Matt. 26:39, 42, 44 b Ps. 22:1 c Matt. 26:53 d Matt. 26:39
8 a Phil. 2:8
9 a Heb. 2:10
10 a Ps. 110:4
11 a [John 16:12] b [Matt. 13:15]
12 a 1 Cor. 3:1–3 *1 sayings, Scriptures*
13 a Eph. 4:14
14 a Is. 7:15 *1 mature* *2 practice*

CHAPTER 6
1 a Heb. 5:12 b [Heb. 9:14] *1 maturity*
2 a Acts 19:3–5 b [Acts 8:17] c Acts 17:31 d Acts 24:25
3 *1* M *let us do*
4 a [John 4:10] b [Gal. 3:2, 5]
6 a Heb. 10:29 *1* Or *and have fallen away*
7 a Ps. 65:10
8 a Is. 5:6
10 a Rom. 3:4 b 1 Thess. 1:3 c Rom. 15:25 *1* NU omits *labor of*
11 a Col. 2:2
12 a Heb. 10:36 *1 lazy*

Hebrews 6:11, 12

Dear Woman of Destiny,

Perhaps you have heard of a book entitled *The Hiding Place,* which chronicles the life of Corrie ten Boom. Corrie and her family were Dutch believers who hid Jews in their home during the Nazi reign of terror. They were finally arrested and imprisoned for hiding and smuggling Jews to safety. Corrie was her family's only survivor.

When I consider the condition of the world today—the loss of high moral standards, the increasing instances of violence and drug use, and the basic disregard for human life—I am frightened for us as a nation and am deeply concerned for my children. In a world where rules are scorned and personal rights take precedence over all else, how do I teach my children that some things are worth dying for? Stories like Corrie's help me to keep on keeping on in my own faith walk and to encourage my children in theirs.

Years ago, at the age of twenty-two, a friend encouraged me to enter the Miss America Pageant. I wanted to study professionally in New York City, and the pageant scholarship was substantial enough to make that dream a reality.

But there was a process to it. You had to enter a local pageant first. If you won that, you went on to a state competition. If you won that, you competed in Atlantic City, New Jersey, for the Miss America title. Oh, the effort I put into that endeavor! It took hours, days, months of discipline and perseverance. There were mock interviews, rehearsals, and workouts. There were sessions on walking, wardrobe, cosmetics, and speech. And singing, singing, singing.

Ultimately I won, and I was given many opportunities and blessings as a result of being Miss America. But I did all that for a crown that will perish. How much more should I be willing to do for a crown that is imperishable?

The Bible is filled with stories of men and women who, in the face of impossible circumstances, persevered and were mightily used of God. I want to be the kind of woman God can count on. Yet sometimes I look at my own weaknesses or the circumstances around me and am discouraged. I look at my children and the challenges that could face them and am afraid. But then I lift my eyes to my heavenly Father and am reminded that He is strong.

In *The Hiding Place,* Corrie expresses her fear to her father and asks how she can be sure she'll have the courage to walk out her faith if they are caught. Her father replies with a question, "Corrie, when we take a train ride, when do you get the ticket to get on the train?" Corrie answers, "When the train is ready to leave." So it is with our God. We need to keep our heart's attitude right, but the ability and strength to persevere come from Him.

Lord, make me a woman of conviction, willing to pay the price and finish the race. When I am weary, remind me that You are the source of my strength.

Terry Meeuwsen

one greater, [a]He swore by Himself, 14say-
ing, [a]*"Surely blessing I will bless you, and*
multiplying I will multiply you." 15And so,
after he had patiently endured, he obtained the [a]promise. 16For men indeed
swear by the greater, and [a]an oath for
confirmation *is* for them an end of all dispute. 17Thus God, determining to show
more abundantly to [a]the heirs of promise
[b]the [1]immutability of His counsel, [2]con-
firmed *it* by an oath, 18that by two [1]immu-
table things, in which it *is* impossible for
God to [a]lie, we [2]might have strong consolation, who have fled for refuge to lay hold
of the hope [b]set before *us.*

Be patient and so utterly confident in God that you never question His ways or your waiting time.

OSWALD CHAMBERS

19This *hope* we have as an anchor of the
soul, both sure and steadfast, [a]and which
enters the *Presence* behind the veil,
20[a]where the forerunner has entered for
us, *even* Jesus, [b]having become High
Priest forever according to the order of
Melchizedek.

The King of Righteousness

7 For this [a]Melchizedek, king of Salem,
priest of the Most High God, who met
Abraham returning from the slaughter of
the kings and blessed him, 2to whom also
Abraham gave a tenth part of all, first being translated "king of righteousness,"
and then also king of Salem, meaning
"king of peace," 3without father, without
mother, without genealogy, having neither beginning of days nor end of life, but
made like the Son of God, remains a priest
continually.

4Now consider how great this man *was,*
to whom even the patriarch Abraham
gave a tenth of the [1]spoils. 5And indeed
[a]those who are of the sons of Levi, who
receive the priesthood, have a commandment to receive tithes from the people according to the law, that is, from their
brethren, though they have come from
the loins of Abraham; 6but he whose genealogy is not derived from them received
tithes from Abraham [a]and blessed [b]him
who had the promises. 7Now beyond all
contradiction the lesser is blessed by the
better. 8Here mortal men receive tithes,
but there he *receives them,* [a]of whom it is
witnessed that he lives. 9Even Levi, who
receives tithes, paid tithes through Abraham, so to speak, 10for he was still in the
loins of his father when Melchizedek met
him.

Need for a New Priesthood

11[a]Therefore, if perfection were
through the Levitical priesthood (for under it the people received the law), what
further need *was there* that another priest
should rise according to the order of Melchizedek, and not be called according to
the order of Aaron? 12For the priesthood
being changed, of necessity there is also
a change of the law. 13For He of whom
these things are spoken belongs to another tribe, from which no man has [1]officiat-
ed at the altar.

14For *it is* evident that [a]our Lord arose
from [b]Judah, of which tribe Moses spoke
nothing concerning [1]priesthood. 15And it
is yet far more evident if, in the likeness
of Melchizedek, there arises another
priest 16who has come, not according to
the law of a fleshly commandment, but
according to the power of an endless life.
17For [1]He testifies:

[a]*"You are a priest forever*
According to the order of
Melchizedek."

18For on the one hand there is an an-
nulling of the former commandment
because of [a]its weakness and unprofit-
ableness, 19for [a]the law made nothing
[1]perfect; on the other hand, *there is the*
bringing in of [b]a better hope, through
which [c]we draw near to God.

Greatness of the New Priest

20And inasmuch as *He was* not *made*
priest without an oath 21(for they have become priests without an oath, but He with
an oath by Him who said to Him:

[a]*"The LORD has sworn*
And will not relent,
'You are a priest [1]forever
According to the order of
Melchizedek' "),

---

13 a Gen. 22:16, 17
14 a Gen. 22:16, 17
15 a Gen. 12:4; 21:5
16 a Ex. 22:11
17 a Heb. 11:9 b Rom. 11:29 *1 unchangeableness of His purpose* *2 guaranteed*
18 a Num. 23:19 b [Col. 1:5] *1 unchangeable* 2 M omits *might*
19 a Lev. 16:2, 15
20 a [Heb. 4:14] b Heb. 3:1; 5:10, 11

CHAPTER 7
1 a Gen. 14:18–20
4 *1 plunder*
5 a Num. 18:21–26
6 a Gen. 14:19, 20 b [Rom. 4:13]
8 a Heb. 5:6; 6:20
11 a Heb. 7:18; 8:7
13 *1 served*
14 a Is. 1:1 b Matt. 1:2 1 NU *priests*
17 a Ps. 110:4 1 NU *it is testified*
18 a [Rom. 8:3]
19 a [Acts 13:39] b Heb. 6:18, 19 c Rom. 5:2 *1 complete*
21 a Ps. 110:4 1 NU ends the quotation after *forever.*

22 by so much more Jesus has become a [1]surety of a [a]better covenant.

23 Also there were many priests, because they were prevented by death from continuing. 24 But He, because He continues forever, has an unchangeable priesthood. 25 Therefore He is also [a]able to save [1]to the uttermost those who come to God through Him, since He always lives [b]to make intercession for them.

Thank You, Father, that You are able to save _____ to the uttermost if they will come to You through Jesus Christ, since He always lives to make intercession for them.

FROM HEBREWS 7:25

26 For such a High Priest was fitting for us, [a]*who is* holy, [1]harmless, undefiled, separate from sinners, [b]and has become higher than the heavens; 27 who does not need daily, as those high priests, to offer up sacrifices, first for His [a]own sins and then for the people's, for this He did once for all when He offered up Himself. 28 For the law appoints as high priests men who have weakness, but the word of the oath, which came after the law, *appoints* the Son who has been perfected forever.

The New Priestly Service

8 Now *this is* the main point of the things we are saying: We have such a High Priest, [a]who is seated at the right hand of the throne of the Majesty in the heavens, 2 a Minister of [a]the [1]sanctuary and of [b]the true tabernacle which the Lord erected, and not man.

3 For [a]every high priest is appointed to offer both gifts and sacrifices. Therefore [b]*it is* necessary that this One also have something to offer. 4 For if He were on earth, He would not be a priest, since there are priests who offer the gifts according to the law; 5 who serve [a]the copy and [b]shadow of the heavenly things, as Moses was divinely instructed when he was about to make the tabernacle. For He said, [c]*"See that you make all things according to the pattern shown you on the mountain."* 6 But now [a]He has obtained a more excellent ministry, inasmuch as He is also Mediator of a [b]better covenant, which was established on better promises.

A New Covenant

7 For if that [a]first *covenant* had been faultless, then no place would have been sought for a second. 8 Because finding fault with them, He says: [a]*"Behold, the days are coming, says the LORD, when I will make a new covenant with the house of Israel and with the house of Judah— 9 not according to the covenant that I made with their fathers in the day when I took them by the hand to lead them out of the land of Egypt; because they did not continue in My covenant, and I disregarded them, says the LORD. 10 For this is the covenant that I will make with the house of Israel after those days, says the [a]LORD: I will put My laws in their mind and write them on their hearts; and [b]I will be their God, and they shall be My people. 11 [a]None of them shall teach his neighbor, and none his brother, saying, 'Know the [b]LORD,' for all shall know Me, from the least of them to the greatest of them. 12 For I will be merciful to their unrighteousness, [a]and their sins [1]and their lawless deeds I will remember no more."*

13 [a]In that He says, *"A new covenant,"* He has made the first obsolete. Now what is becoming obsolete and growing old is ready to vanish away.

The Earthly Sanctuary

9 Then indeed, even the first *covenant* had ordinances of divine service and [a]the earthly sanctuary. 2 For a tabernacle was prepared: the first *part,* in which *was* the lampstand, the table, and the showbread, which is called the [1]sanctuary; 3 [a]and behind the second veil, the part of the tabernacle which is called the Holiest of All, 4 which had the [a]golden censer and [b]the ark of the covenant overlaid on all sides with gold, in which *were* [c]the golden pot that had the manna, [d]Aaron's rod that budded, and [e]the tablets of the covenant; 5 and [a]above it were the cherubim of glory overshadowing the mercy seat. Of these things we cannot now speak in detail.

---

22 [a]Heb. 8:6 [1]*guarantee*
25 [a]Jude 24 [b]Rom. 8:34 [1]*completely* or *forever*
26 [a]Heb. 4:15 [b]Eph. 1:20 [1]*innocent*
27 [a]Lev. 9:7; 16:6

CHAPTER 8
1 [a]Col. 3:1
2 [a]Heb. 9:8, 12 [b]Heb. 9:11, 24 [1]Lit. *holies*
3 [a]Heb. 5:1; 8:4 [b][Eph. 5:2]
5 [a]Heb. 9:23, 24 [b]Col. 2:17 [c]Ex. 25:40
6 [a][2 Cor. 3:6–8] [b]Heb. 7:22
7 [a]Ex. 3:8; 19:5
8 [a]Jer. 31:31–34
10 [a]Jer. 31:33 [b]Zech. 8:8
11 [a]Is. 54:13 [b]Jer. 31:34
12 [a]Rom. 11:27 [1]NU omits *and their lawless deeds*
13 [a][2 Cor. 5:17]

CHAPTER 9
1 [a]Ex. 25:8
2 [1]*holy place,* lit. *holies*
3 [a]Ex. 26:31–35; 40:3
4 [a]Lev. 16:12 [b]Ex. 25:10 [c]Ex. 16:33 [d]Num. 17:1–10 [e]Ex. 25:16; 34:29
5 [a]Lev. 16:2

HEBREWS 7:25

Dear Woman of Destiny,

Did you know we have an attorney in heaven? That's right. Jesus Christ, the Righteous, sits at the Father's right hand continually interceding on our behalf.

"Why do we need an attorney?" you might ask. We need an attorney for at least two important reasons:

First, because we are sinners. We may be "saved sinners." But we are sinners, nonetheless. And John writes, "My little children, these things I write to you, so that you may not sin. And if anyone sins, we have an Advocate with the Father, Jesus Christ the righteous" (1 John 2:1).

So when we sin (and we will), we need an attorney to represent us in heaven's court. Jesus Christ is that attorney. And what an attorney He is! He has clout. He's the Judge's own Son!

When we are charged with sin, He neither pleads our guilt nor our innocence. He pleads His own blood. In the next verse John writes, "And He Himself [Jesus] is the propitiation for our sins, and not for ours only but also for the whole world" (1 John 2:2). Our attorney, Jesus Christ the Righteous, has never lost a case!

The second reason we need an attorney is that we are continually being brought to trial! And trials abound, don't they? If you are not in a trial, it's probably because you've just concluded one or are about to face one. Life is filled with various kinds of trials. And quite often, *we* are the defendants who are on trial, aren't we? (see 1 Pet. 4:12–16).

When you are facing trial, you need the best attorney money can buy! When we face the trials of life we have the best attorney pleading our case, Jesus Christ the Righteous! Jesus pled Peter's case. "Simon, Simon! Indeed, Satan has asked for you, that he may sift you as wheat. But I have prayed for you, that your faith should not fail" (Luke 22:31, 32a). Jesus pled the case of His disciples. "I pray for them. I do not pray for the world but for those whom You [Father] have given Me, for they are Yours" (John 17:9).

As He represented them in heaven's court, He represents us! Rejoice, Woman of Destiny, because He ever lives to intercede for us!

Alice Smith

HEBREWS 8:6

Dear Woman of Destiny,

Jesus declared, "This cup is the new covenant in My blood, which is shed for you" (Luke 22:20). A covenant was the most solemn, sacred, and binding agreement that could be made as two would give up their own identities to become one in a new relationship. Jesus was saying there would be a *new* way by His blood to enter into a covenant with the Almighty God!

The Old Covenant was established as a blood covenant relationship with humankind when God approached Abram (later called Abraham) in Genesis 15. God instructed Abram to set up a covenant ceremony including split animals. Then God put Abram to sleep. Abram saw someone or something appearing as flame and smoke walking through the ceremony in his place. After all, how could Abram, as a man, enter covenant with God—there was no common ground! Yet, Abram knew the two were being bonded into a mysterious, though very real, oneness. All that each possessed would be part of the other. Eventually, Abraham was given a test of the covenant—would he share in the ultimate sacrifice of God's only Son by his willingness to give up *his* only son, Isaac? We know he passed the test.

God has always been faithful as a covenant partner to His people through the ages, but God's people didn't know how to be faithful. Sin separated humankind from the presence of Holy God. So God gave the Law to show people how to walk as His covenant partners. They would have to transfer their sin to innocent animal sacrifices, spilling blood in those animals' deaths to satisfy judgment against their sin.

How and why is this new covenant better?

- Jesus paid the penalty that transgression of God's law required. When we receive Christ, we are saved from the penalty of our sin, which is eternal death. God sees us as righteous in Christ, as "not with the blood of goats and calves, but with His own blood" Christ paid the penalty for our sin (see Heb. 9:12).
- We are sealed in the New Covenant by the Holy Spirit, sent to dwell in the hearts of believers. Miraculously, the Holy Spirit writes in our inner being how we can live as covenant partners of God Almighty. The Old Covenant was external. In the New Covenant, believers can live by the witness of the Holy Spirit!
- Jesus, as our substitute and representative, becomes our "mediator" with the Father. Could it have been the preincarnate Jesus that Abram saw walking through the covenant ceremony for him? He alone is able to bring us into relationship with God Himself.
- God's faithfulness is everlasting even if we are not faithful. God counts us worthy to be in covenant with Him because we are "in Christ" as believers. Covenant binds us so that we are part of each other, the body of Christ.

As believers, we are in covenant relationship with God through Jesus Christ. This covenant binds you to Him and Him to you for the rest of your earthly life and throughout eternity. You belong to Him forever.

Vicki Bartholomew

Limitations of the Earthly Service

6Now when these things had been thus
prepared, [a]the priests always went into
the first part of the tabernacle, performing *the services.* 7But into the second part
the high priest *went* alone [a]once a year,
not without blood, which he offered for
[b]himself and *for* the people's sins *committed* in ignorance; 8the Holy Spirit indicating this, that [a]the way into the Holiest
of All was not yet made manifest while the
first tabernacle was still standing. 9It *was*
symbolic for the present time in which
both gifts and sacrifices are offered
[a]which cannot make him who performed
the service perfect in regard to the conscience— 10*concerned* only with [a]foods
and drinks, [b]various [1]washings, [c]and
fleshly ordinances imposed until the time
of reformation.

There is a secret place within the holy of holies under the very cover of Christ's wing—a place where we always have access to the mercy seat . . . a place where our spirits are made so spotless by the blood of Jesus that He can always smile upon us.

CARRIE JUDD MONTGOMERY

The Heavenly Sanctuary

11But Christ came *as* High Priest of
[a]the good things [1]to come, with the
greater and more perfect tabernacle not
made with hands, that is, not of this creation. 12Not [a]with the blood of goats and
calves, but [b]with His own blood He entered the Most Holy Place [c]once for all,
[d]having obtained eternal redemption.
13For if [a]the blood of bulls and goats and
[b]the ashes of a heifer, sprinkling the unclean, [1]sanctifies for the [2]purifying of the
flesh, 14how much more shall the blood of
Christ, who through the eternal Spirit offered Himself without [1]spot to God,
[a]cleanse your conscience from [b]dead
works [c]to serve the living God? 15And for
this reason [a]He is the Mediator of the new
covenant, by means of death, for the redemption of the transgressions under the
first covenant, that [b]those who are called
may receive the promise of the eternal inheritance.

The Mediator's Death Necessary

16For where there *is* a testament, there
must also of necessity be the death of the
testator. 17For [a]a testament *is* in force after men are dead, since it has no power at
all while the testator lives. 18[a]Therefore
not even the first *covenant* was dedicated
without blood. 19For when Moses had spoken every [1]precept to all the people according to the law, [a]he took the blood
of calves and goats, [b]with water, scarlet
wool, and hyssop, and sprinkled both the
book itself and all the people, 20saying,
[a]*"This is the* [b]*blood of the covenant which
God has commanded you."* 21Then likewise [a]he sprinkled with blood both the
tabernacle and all the vessels of the ministry. 22 And according to the law almost
all things are [1]purified with blood, and
[a]without shedding of blood there is no
[2]remission.

Lord Jesus, I praise and worship You, for it was not with the blood of goats and calves, but with Your own blood that You entered the Most Holy Place once for all, and obtained eternal redemption for _____.

FROM HEBREWS 9:12

Greatness of Christ's Sacrifice

23Therefore *it was* necessary that [a]the
copies of the things in the heavens should
be [1]purified with these, but the heavenly
things themselves with better sacrifices
than these. 24For [a]Christ has not entered

6 a Num. 18:2–6; 28:3
7 a Ex. 30:10 b Heb. 5:3
8 a [John 14:6]
9 a Heb. 7:19
10 a Col. 2:16 b Num. 19:7 c Eph. 2:15 *1* Lit. *baptisms*
11 a Heb. 10:1 *1* NU *that have come*
12 a Heb. 10:4 b Eph. 1:7 c Zech. 3:9 d [Dan. 9:24]
13 a Lev. 16:14, 15 b Num. 19:2 *1 sets apart 2 cleansing*
14 a 1 John 1:7 b Heb. 6:1 c Luke 1:74 *1 blemish*
15 a Rom. 3:25 b Heb. 3:1
17 a Gal. 3:15
18 a Ex. 24:6
19 a Ex. 24:5, 6 b Lev. 14:4, 7 *1 command*
20 a [Matt. 26:28] b Ex. 24:3–8
21 a Ex. 29:12, 36
22 a Lev. 17:11 *1 cleansed 2 forgiveness*
23 a Heb. 8:5 *1 cleansed*
24 a Heb. 6:20

HEBREWS 9:22

Dear Woman of Destiny,

"It is finished!" Jesus Christ spoke these words to seal for all eternity His accomplishment at the Cross. The power of His blood at Calvary, one drop of His blood, was sufficient to set us free. Heaven was moved, earth was violently shaken, the veil in the temple was torn, and the sins of humanity were nailed to the cross. One can only imagine the pain His mother Mary felt during that moment in time. Her heart shattered when she saw her Son's blood run down His battered body, and heard Jesus' final words spoken, "It is finished!"

Reading Hebrews 9:22, we find that "according to the law almost all things are purified with blood, and without shedding of blood there is no remission." We can understand why His blood was needed to cleanse us. In Old Testament times, animal sacrifice was practiced; and the priest stood in the gap between God and man. The high priest would go into the Most Holy Place, but only once a year on the Day of Atonement. This was strictly observed (see Lev. 23), and no one was permitted to enter the Most Holy Place any other day. The Most Holy Place was the most sacred spot on earth for Jews. In Christ, this system was transformed—Jesus Christ Himself became our High Priest. Now we have the privilege of entering the Most Holy Place on any day of the year and without rituals, because of the shedding of His blood.

After shedding His blood, Christ rose from the grave and proclaimed victory over sin and death. Praise God, we have been redeemed by His blood, which was the only acceptable price allowed in heaven to purchase a sinful and hopeless humanity. The greatest symbol of life is blood, because it keeps us alive. When we comprehend what Jesus accomplished at Calvary, it becomes so easy to praise Him from our innermost being. It was love that kept Him nailed to the cross for you and me.

Ask the Holy Spirit to make Jesus so real to you, that you will feel the Father's love fill every fiber of your heart. I pray that you will understand the depth of the Father's love for you—a love so deep that He gave up His only Son to die for you and me (see John 3:16). Whenever the enemy makes you feel unloved and rejected, remember what Jesus did for you.

There may have been times in life when your heart has been broken and torn in pieces. You may have felt the deep pain of despair, disappointment, and discomfort. You might feel there's no hope, even now as you read these words. But I believe God wants to remind you that Jesus is the source of life, not death. Today you can declare that you are cleansed by His blood and redeemed to be a vessel of honor that God can use. Give glory to God for the victory, for you have been washed by the blood of the Lamb.

A. G. Rodriguez

the holy places made with hands, *which*
are [1]copies of [b]the true, but into heaven
itself, now [c]to appear in the presence of
God for us; 25not that He should offer
Himself often, as [a]the high priest enters
the Most Holy Place every year with blood
of another— 26He then would have had to
suffer often since the foundation of the
world; but now, once at the end of the
ages, He has appeared to put away sin by
the sacrifice of Himself. 27[a]And as it is appointed for men to die once, [b]but after
this the judgment, 28so [a]Christ was [b]of-
fered once to bear the sins [c]of many. To
those who [d]eagerly wait for Him He will
appear a second time, apart from sin, for
salvation.

Animal Sacrifices Insufficient

10 For the law, having a [a]shadow of
the good things to come, *and* not
the very image of the things, [b]can never
with these same sacrifices, which they offer continually year by year, make those
who approach perfect. 2For then would
they not have ceased to be offered? For the
worshipers, once [1]purified, would have
had no more consciousness of sins. 3But
in those *sacrifices there is* a reminder of
sins every year. 4For [a]*it is* not possible
that the blood of bulls and goats could
take away sins.

Christ's Death Fulfills God's Will

5Therefore, when He came into the
world, He said:

[a]*"Sacrifice and offering You did not*
desire,
But a body You have prepared for
Me.
6 *In burnt offerings and sacrifices for*
sin
You had no pleasure.
7 *Then I said, 'Behold, I have*
come—
In the volume of the book it is
written of Me—
To do Your will, O God.' "

8Previously saying, *"Sacrifice and offer-*
ing, burnt offerings, and offerings for sin
You did not desire, nor had pleasure in
them" (which are offered according to the
law), 9then He said, *"Behold, I have come*
to do Your will, [1]O God." He takes away
the first that He may establish the second.
10[a]By that will we have been [1]sanctified
[b]through the offering of the body of Jesus
Christ once *for all.*

Christ's Death Perfects the Sanctified

11And every priest stands [a]ministering
daily and offering repeatedly the same
sacrifices, which can never take away sins.
12[a]But this Man, after He had offered one
sacrifice for sins forever, sat down [b]at the
right hand of God, 13from that time waiting [a]till His enemies are made His footstool. 14For by one offering He has
perfected forever those who are being
[1]sanctified.
15But the Holy Spirit also witnesses to
us; for after He had said before,
16[a]*"This is the covenant that I will*
make with them after those days, says the
LORD: I will put My laws into their hearts,
and in their minds I will write them,"
17*then He adds,* [a]*"Their sins and their*
lawless deeds I will remember no more."
18Now where there is [1]remission of these,
there is no longer an offering for sin.

> *You have just as much right to step into the presence of God Almighty as Jesus has.*
>
> JOHN G. LAKE

Hold Fast Your Confession

19Therefore, brethren, having [a]bold-
ness[1] to enter [b]the Holiest by the blood of
Jesus, 20by a new and [a]living way which
He consecrated for us, through the veil,
that is, His flesh, 21and *having* a High
Priest over the house of God, 22let us
[a]draw near with a true heart [b]in full assurance of faith, having our hearts sprinkled from an evil conscience and our
bodies washed with pure water. 23Let us
hold fast the confession of *our* hope without wavering, for [a]He who promised *is*
faithful. 24And let us consider one another
in order to stir up love and good works,
25[a]not forsaking the assembling of ourselves together, as *is* the manner of some,
but exhorting *one another,* and [b]so

24 b Heb. 8:2 c Rom. 8:34 *1 representations*
25 a Heb. 9:7
27 a Gen. 3:19 b [2 Cor. 5:10]
28 a Rom. 6:10 b 1 Pet. 2:24 c Matt. 26:28 d Titus 2:13

CHAPTER 10
1 a Heb. 8:5 b Heb. 7:19; 9:9
2 *1 cleansed*
4 a Mic. 6:6, 7
5 a Ps. 40:6–8
9 *1* NU, M omit *O God*
10 a John 17:19 b [Heb. 9:12] *1 set apart*
11 a Num. 28:3
12 a Col. 3:1 b Ps. 110:1
13 a Ps. 110:1
14 *1 set apart*
16 a Jer. 31:33, 34
17 a Jer. 31:34
18 *1 forgiveness*
19 a [Eph. 2:18] b Heb. 9:8, 12 *1 confidence*
20 a John 14:6
22 a Heb. 7:19; 10:1 b Eph. 3:12
23 a 1 Cor. 1:9; 10:13
25 a Acts 2:42 b Rom. 13:11

much the more as you see [c]the Day approaching.

The Just Live by Faith

26 For [a]if we sin willfully [b]after we have
received the knowledge of the truth, there
[c]no longer remains a sacrifice for sins,
27 but a certain fearful expectation of judgment, and [a]fiery indignation which will
devour the adversaries. 28 Anyone who has
rejected Moses' law dies without mercy on
the testimony of two or three [a]witnesses.
29 [a]Of how much worse punishment, do
you suppose, will he be thought worthy
who has trampled the Son of God underfoot, [b]counted the blood of the covenant
by which he was sanctified a common
thing, [c]and insulted the Spirit of grace?
30 For we know Him who said, [a]*"Vengeance is Mine, I will repay,"* [1]says the
Lord. And again, [b]*"The LORD will judge
His people."* 31 [a]It is a fearful thing to fall
into the hands of the living God.

O Lord, may ____ hold fast the confession of their hope without wavering, for You who promised are faithful.

FROM HEBREWS 10:23

32 But [a]recall the former days in which,
after you were [1]illuminated, you endured
a great struggle with sufferings: 33 partly
while you were made [a]a spectacle both by
reproaches and tribulations, and partly
while [b]you became companions of those
who were so treated; 34 for you had compassion on [1]me [a]in my chains, and [b]joy-
fully accepted the plundering of your
[2]goods, knowing that [c]you have a better
and an enduring possession for yourselves
[3]in heaven. 35 Therefore do not cast away
your confidence, [a]which has great reward.
36 [a]For you have need of endurance, so
that after you have done the will of God,
[b]you may receive the promise:

37 *"For [a]yet a little while,*
And [b]He[1] who is coming will come
and will not [2]tarry.
38 *Now [a]the[1] just shall live by faith;*
But if anyone draws back,
My soul has no pleasure in him."

39 But we are not of those [a]who draw back
to [1]perdition, but of those who [b]believe to
the saving of the soul.

By Faith We Understand

11 Now faith is the [1]substance of
things hoped for, the [2]evidence [a]of
things not seen. 2 For by it the elders obtained a *good* testimony.
3 By faith we understand that [a]the
[1]worlds were framed by the word of God,
so that the things which are seen were not
made of things which are visible.

There is nothing that so abides with us as what we receive from God; and the reason why the Christians in this day are at such a loss as to some things is that they are contented with what comes from men's mouths, without searching and kneeling before God to know of Him the truth of things.

JOHN BUNYAN

Faith at the Dawn of History

4 By faith [a]Abel offered to God a more
excellent sacrifice than Cain, through
which he obtained witness that he was
righteous, God testifying of his gifts; and
through it he being dead still [b]speaks.
5 By faith Enoch was taken away so that
he did not see death, [a]*"and was not found,
because God had taken him"*; for before he
was taken he had this testimony, that he
pleased God. 6 But without faith *it is* impossible to please *Him,* for he who comes
to God must believe that He is, and *that*
He is a rewarder of those who diligently
seek Him.

---

25 c Phil. 4:5
26 a Num. 15:30 b 2 Pet. 2:20 c Heb. 6:6
27 a Zeph. 1:18
28 a Deut. 17:2–6; 19:15
29 a [Heb. 2:3] b 1 Cor. 11:29 c [Matt. 12:31]
30 a Deut. 32:35 b Deut. 32:36 1 NU omits *says the Lord*
31 a [Luke 12:5]
32 a Gal. 3:4 1 *enlightened*
33 a 1 Cor. 4:9 b Phil. 1:7
34 a 2 Tim. 1:16 b Matt. 5:12 c Matt. 6:20 1 NU *the prisoners* instead of *me in my chains* 2 *possessions* 3 NU omits *in heaven*
35 a Matt. 5:12
36 a Luke 21:19 b [Col. 3:24]
37 a Luke 18:8 b Hab. 2:3, 4 1 Or *that which* 2 *delay*
38 a Rom. 1:17 1 NU *My just one*
39 a 2 Pet. 2:20 b Acts 16:31 1 *destruction*

CHAPTER 11
1 a Rom. 8:24 1 *realization* 2 Or *confidence*
3 a Ps. 33:6 1 Or *ages,* Gr. *aiones,* aeons
4 a Gen. 4:3–5 b Heb. 12:24
5 a Gen. 5:21–24

Hebrews 11:6

Dear Woman of Destiny,

There's nothing in the overall teaching of the Bible to suggest that God is found by, or reveals Himself to, casual inquirers, but only to diligent seekers. When we mean business with God, He'll do business with us. That's a great comfort to me. "When in their trouble they turned to the LORD God of Israel, and sought Him, He was found by them" (2 Chr. 15:4).

It also makes sense. When we stop to think who God is—the Creator and Sustainer of the universe, who has power to snuff out our life's breath at any moment—casualness of approach hardly seems appropriate!

There's nothing casual about God. He's the most intense Being in the universe. In Revelation 3:16, He says He reacts to halfheartedness by throwing up. So let's get serious about seeking Him; as David commanded all the leaders of Israel in 1 Chronicles 22:19, "Now set your heart and your soul to seek the LORD your God."

When you leave the casual inquirers' class and enroll in the diligent seekers' class, you'll want to do what the people of God did under Asa's leadership: "Then they entered into a covenant to seek the LORD God . . . with all their heart and with all their soul" (2 Chr. 15:12). In fact, this group was so radical they agreed with an oath and a lot of noise, that "whoever would not seek the LORD God of Israel was to be put to death, whether small or great, whether man or woman" (v. 13). No wimps among this lot. You can guarantee they got God's attention, approval, and awesome results. Their enemies quit harassing them.

Sometimes God prompts us to fast and pray in order to test our diligence when seeking Him. Moses, Daniel, Nehemiah, Ezra, Hannah, Jehoshaphat, Esther, Mordecai, Paul, Anna, the church leaders at Antioch, and the whole of the city of Nineveh fasted and prayed with mighty results.

Another way God tests our diligence in seeking Him is to temporarily withhold answers from us. In Isaiah 8:17, we read, "I will wait on the LORD, who hides His face from the house of Jacob; and I will hope in Him." Again, in Isaiah 45:15, "Truly You are God, who hide Yourself, O God of Israel, the Savior!"

Don't give up seeking Him. Press in, and hold on. Keep persisting in faith. He's watching. Your reward is coming. "If you will inquire, inquire; return! Come back!" (Is. 21:12). On numerous occasions, my answers from God have come from much persistent inquiry.

Remember the Canaanite woman in Matthew 15:22, who came to Jesus, requesting her daughter's deliverance from an evil spirit? She was tested on her humility, strong persistency, and faith, and came through with flying colors on all counts. She would not be denied, and Jesus gave her His approval, and granted her request. Jacob had to wrestle with God all night before becoming personally and permanently changed. Hannah wept, fasted, withdrew from fellowship with others, poured out her anguished soul before God, despite the taunting by Peninnah and the misunderstandings of her loving husband, Elkanah. As a result, she gave birth to the prophet of God, Samuel, who was used of God to reverse the spiritual climate of the nation of Israel when it was at an all-time low.

God surely rewards diligent seekers of Him.

Joy Dawson

7By faith [a]Noah, being divinely warned
of things not yet seen, moved with godly
fear, [b]prepared an ark for the saving of his
household, by which he condemned the
world and became heir of [c]the righteousness which is according to faith.

Faithful Abraham

8By faith [a]Abraham obeyed when he
was called to go out to the place which he
would receive as an inheritance. And he
went out, not knowing where he was going. 9By faith he dwelt in the land of
promise as *in* a foreign country, [a]dwelling
in tents with Isaac and Jacob, [b]the heirs
with him of the same promise; 10for he
waited for [a]the city which has foundations, [b]whose builder and maker *is* God.
11By faith [a]Sarah herself also received
strength to conceive seed, and [b]she[1] bore
a child when she was past the age, because
she judged Him [c]faithful who had promised. 12Therefore from one man, and him
as good as [a]dead, were born *as many* as
the [b]stars of the sky in multitude—innumerable as the sand which is by the seashore.

The Heavenly Hope

13These all died in faith, [a]not having
received the [b]promises, but [c]having seen
them afar off [1]were assured of them, embraced *them* and [d]confessed that they
were strangers and pilgrims on the earth.
14For those who say such things [a]declare
plainly that they seek a homeland. 15And
truly if they had called to mind [a]that
country from which they had come out,
they would have had opportunity to return. 16But now they desire a better, that
is, a heavenly *country.* Therefore God is
not ashamed [a]to be called their God, for
He has [b]prepared a city for them.

The Faith of the Patriarchs

17By faith Abraham, [a]when he was tested, offered up Isaac, and he who had received the promises offered up his only
begotten *son,* 18[1]of whom it was said, [a]*"In
Isaac your seed shall be called,"* 19con-
cluding that God [a]*was* able to raise *him*
up, even from the dead, from which he
also received him in a figurative sense.
20By faith [a]Isaac blessed Jacob and Esau
concerning things to come.
21By faith Jacob, when he was dying,
[a]blessed each of the sons of Joseph, and
worshiped, *leaning* on the top of his staff.
22By faith [a]Joseph, when he was dying,
made mention of the departure of the
children of Israel, and gave instructions
concerning his bones.

The Faith of Moses

23By faith [a]Moses, when he was born,
was hidden three months by his parents,
because they saw *he was* a beautiful child;
and they were not afraid of the king's
[b]command.
24By faith [a]Moses, when he became of
age, refused to be called the son of Pharaoh's daughter, 25choosing rather to suffer affliction with the people of God than
to enjoy the [1]passing pleasures of sin,
26esteeming [a]the [1]reproach of Christ
greater riches than the treasures [2]in
Egypt; for he looked to the [b]reward.
27By faith [a]he forsook Egypt, not fearing the wrath of the king; for he endured
as seeing Him who is invisible. 28By faith
[a]he kept the Passover and the sprinkling
of blood, lest he who destroyed the firstborn should touch them.
29By faith [a]they passed through the Red
Sea as by dry *land, whereas* the Egyptians,
attempting *to do* so, were drowned.

By Faith They Overcame

30By faith [a]the walls of Jericho fell
down after they were encircled for seven
days. 31By faith [a]the harlot Rahab did not
perish with those who [1]did not believe,
when [b]she had received the spies with
peace.
32And what more shall I say? For the
time would fail me to tell of [a]Gideon and
[b]Barak and [c]Samson and [d]Jephthah, also
of [e]David and [f]Samuel and the prophets:
33who through faith subdued kingdoms,
worked righteousness, obtained promises, [a]stopped the mouths of lions,
34[a]quenched the violence of fire, escaped
the edge of the sword, out of weakness
were made strong, became valiant in battle, turned to flight the armies of the
aliens. 35[a]Women received their dead
raised to life again.
Others were [b]tortured, not accepting
deliverance, that they might obtain a better resurrection. 36Still others had trial of
mockings and scourgings, yes, and [a]of
chains and imprisonment. 37[a]They were

7 a Gen. 6:13–22 b 1 Pet. 3:20 c Rom. 3:22
8 a Gen. 12:1–4
9 a Gen. 12:8; 13:3, 18; 18:1, 9 b Heb. 6:17
10 a [Heb. 12:22; 13:14] b [Rev. 21:10]
11 a Gen. 17:19; 18:11–14; 21:1, 2 b Luke 1:36 c Heb. 10:23 *1* NU omits *she bore a child*
12 a Rom. 4:19 b Gen. 15:5; 22:17; 32:12
13 a Heb. 11:39 b Gen. 12:7 c John 8:56 d Ps. 39:12 *1* NU, M omit *were assured of them*
14 a Heb. 13:14
15 a Gen. 11:31
16 a Ex. 3:6, 15; 4:5 b [Rev. 21:2]
17 a James 2:21
18 a Gen. 21:12 *1 to*
19 a Rom. 4:17
20 a Gen. 27:26–40
21 a Gen. 48:1, 5, 16, 20
22 a Gen. 50:24, 25
23 a Ex. 2:1–3 b Ex. 1:16, 22
24 a Ex. 2:11–15
25 *1 temporary*
26 a Heb. 13:13 b Rom. 8:18 *1 reviling because of* *2* NU, M *of*
27 a Ex. 10:28
28 a Ex. 12:21
29 a Ex. 14:22–29
30 a Josh. 6:20
31 a Josh. 2:9; 6:23 b Josh. 2:1 *1 were disobedient*
32 a Judg. 6:11; 7:1–25 b Judg. 4:6–24 c Judg. 13:24—16:31 d Judg. 11:1–29; 12:1–7 e 1 Sam. 16; 17 f 1 Sam. 7:9–14
33 a Dan. 6:22
34 a Dan. 3:23–28
35 a 1 Kin. 17:22 b Acts 22:25
36 a Gen. 39:20
37 a 1 Kin. 21:13

stoned, they were sawn in two, [1]were
tempted, were slain with the sword. [b]They
wandered about [c]in sheepskins and goat-
skins, being destitute, afflicted, tormented— 38of whom the world was not
worthy. They wandered in deserts and
mountains, [a]*in* dens and caves of the
earth.
39And all these, [a]having obtained a
good testimony through faith, did not receive the promise, 40God having provided
something better for us, that they should
not be [a]made perfect apart from us.

The Race of Faith

12 Therefore we also, since we are
surrounded by so great a cloud of
witnesses, [a]let us lay aside every weight,
and the sin which so easily ensnares *us,*
and [b]let us run [c]with endurance the race
that is set before us, 2looking unto Jesus,
the [1]author and [2]finisher of *our* faith,
[a]who for the joy that was set before Him
[b]endured the cross, despising the shame,
and [c]has sat down at the right hand of the
throne of God.

Father, may _____ lay aside every weight, and the sin which so easily ensnares them, and run with endurance the race that is set before them, looking to Jesus, the author and finisher of their faith.

FROM HEBREWS 12:1, 2

The Discipline of God

3[a]For consider Him who endured such
hostility from sinners against Himself,
[b]lest you become weary and discouraged
in your souls. 4[a]You have not yet resisted
to bloodshed, striving against sin. 5And
you have forgotten the exhortation which
speaks to you as to sons:

[a]*"My son, do not despise the*
[1]chastening of the LORD,
Nor be discouraged when you are
rebuked by Him;

37 b 2 Kin. 1:8 c Zech. 13:4 1 NU omits *were tempted*
38 a 1 Kin. 18:4, 13; 19:9
39 a Heb. 11:2, 13
40 a Heb. 5:9
CHAPTER 12
1 a Col. 3:8 b 1 Cor. 9:24 c Rom. 12:12
2 a Luke 24:26 b Phil. 2:8 c Ps. 110:1 1 *originator* 2 *perfecter*
3 a Matt. 10:24 b Gal. 6:9
4 a [1 Cor. 10:13]
5 a Prov. 3:11, 12 1 *discipline*
6 a Rev. 3:19
7 a Deut. 8:5 b Prov. 13:24; 19:18; 23:13 1 NU, M *It is for discipline that you endure; God*
8 a 1 Pet. 5:9
9 a [Job 12:10]
10 a Lev. 11:44
11 a James 3:17, 18 1 *discipline*
12 a Is. 35:3
14 a Ps. 34:14 b Matt. 5:8
15 a Heb. 4:1 b Deut. 29:18
16 a [1 Cor. 6:13–18] b Gen. 25:33 1 *godless*
17 a Gen. 27:30–40

6 *For [a]whom the LORD loves He*
chastens,
And scourges every son whom He
receives."

7[a]If[1] you endure chastening, God deals
with you as with sons; for what [b]son is
there whom a father does not chasten?
8But if you are without chastening, [a]of
which all have become partakers, then
you are illegitimate and not sons. 9Fur-
thermore, we have had human fathers
who corrected *us,* and we paid *them* respect. Shall we not much more readily be
in subjection to [a]the Father of spirits and
live? 10For they indeed for a few days chastened *us* as seemed *best* to them, but He
for *our* profit, [a]that *we* may be partakers
of His holiness. 11Now no [1]chastening
seems to be joyful for the present, but
painful; nevertheless, afterward it yields
[a]the peaceable fruit of righteousness to
those who have been trained by it.

Whatever fancy name you give it, sin is sin. God looks on the heart and as for holiness, why, without holiness no man shall see the Lord.

AIMEE SEMPLE MCPHERSON

Renew Your Spiritual Vitality

12Therefore [a]strengthen the hands
which hang down, and the feeble knees,
13and make straight paths for your feet, so
that what is lame may not be dislocated,
but rather be healed.
14[a]Pursue peace with all *people,* and
holiness, [b]without which no one will see
the Lord: 15looking carefully lest anyone
[a]fall short of the grace of God; lest any
[b]root of bitterness springing up cause
trouble, and by this many become defiled;
16lest there *be* any [a]fornicator or [1]profane
person like Esau, [b]who for one morsel of
food sold his birthright. 17For you know
that afterward, when he wanted to inherit
the blessing, he was [a]rejected, for he
found no place for repentance, though he
sought it diligently with tears.

Hebrews 12:1, 2

Dear Woman of Destiny,

I hear myself issuing a challenge: run after God, seek His face, pray more, increase your devotions, turn down the radio—enjoy the quiet. But this ultimatum isn't for the ladies in my church or even my Bible study group. It's for me—my life, my walk.

Being a woman, I always have a running list of things to do, goals set, tasks waiting to be accomplished. Just when I have checked off a few, I realize that I've added more to the list—never ending. Thank God that His mercies are never ending as well; grace for the day.

But I still hear this small voice, "Ceci, come away. Come spend some time with Me. Let's enjoy each other's company." Then it's my choice: Come away, or dig deeper into the bottomless list of to-do's.

Thinking about these verses, Hebrews 12:1, 2, I was reminded of something that happened recently. Having moved out of the city and into the country, we felt the need to get a large dog. Sadie, our boxer puppy, is full of energy and bouncing with "let me show you what I can do's."

Behind our home are hiking trails. One day with Sadie up for the challenge to protect us from all would-be predators, I heard the familiar bark. I looked outside only to find Sadie tearing off after a two-legged "predator," a father holding a little girl's hand and carrying another small child on his back. I raced hard down the trail trying to stop my dog, all the time shouting to the man, "She won't hurt you. She's only a puppy!"

Walking back home with the offender in tow, that still small voice was loud and clear: "That's the way I want you to follow Me. Forget all your encumbrances and run from all the things that ensnare you. *Run hard* after Me, and I'll let you catch Me."

Join me. Let's run the race together, laying aside every weight, including the lists of things waiting to be done and the things that keep us from Him. Let's fix our eyes on Jesus, "the author and finisher of our faith, who for the joy that was set before Him endured the cross, despising the shame, and has sat down at the right hand of the throne of God" (Heb. 12:2). Let's *come away* and *run hard* after Him. In doing so we will run straight into Father's loving arms.

Ceci Sheets

The Glorious Company

[18]For you have not come [1]to [a]the
mountain that may be touched and that
burned with fire, and to blackness and
[2]darkness and tempest, [19]and the sound of
a trumpet and the voice of words, so that
those who heard *it* [a]begged that the word
should not be spoken to them anymore.
[20](For they could not endure what was
commanded: [a]*"And if so much as a beast
touches the mountain, it shall be stoned
[1]or shot with an arrow."* [21]And so terrifying was the sight *that* Moses said, [a]*"I am
exceedingly afraid* and trembling.")
[22]But you have come to Mount Zion
and to the city of the living God, the heavenly Jerusalem, to an innumerable company of angels, [23]to the [1]general assembly
and church of [a]the firstborn [b]*who are*
registered in heaven, to God [c]the Judge of
all, to the spirits of just men [d]made perfect, [24]to Jesus [a]the Mediator of the new
covenant, and to [b]the blood of sprinkling
that speaks better things [c]than *that* of
Abel.

Hear the Heavenly Voice

[25]See that you do not refuse Him who
speaks. For [a]if they did not escape who
refused Him who spoke on earth, much
more *shall we not escape* if we turn away
from Him who *speaks* from heaven,
[26]whose voice then shook the earth; but
now He has promised, saying, [a]*"Yet once
more I [1]shake not only the earth, but also
heaven."* [27]Now this, *"Yet once more,"* indicates the [a]removal of those things that
are being shaken, as of things that are
made, that the things which cannot be
shaken may remain.
[28]Therefore, since we are receiving a
kingdom which cannot be shaken, let us
have grace, by which we [1]may [a]serve God
acceptably with reverence and godly fear.
[29]For [a]our God *is* a consuming fire.

Concluding Moral Directions

13 Let [a]brotherly love continue. [2a]Do
not forget to entertain strangers,
for by so *doing* [b]some have unwittingly
entertained angels. [3a]Remember the prisoners as if chained with them—those
who are mistreated—since you yourselves are in the body also.
[4a]Marriage *is* honorable among all, and
the bed undefiled; [b]but fornicators and
adulterers God will judge.
[5]*Let your* conduct *be* without covetousness; *be* content with such things as you
have. For He Himself has said, [a]*"I will
never leave you nor forsake you."* [6]So we
may boldly say:

[a]*"The LORD is my helper;*
I will not fear.
What can man do to me?"

Oh praise the Lord for the wisdom and knowledge, the fellowship and the presence, of the Lord who lives and walks with us continually.

MARIA WOODWORTH-ETTER

Concluding Religious Directions

[7]Remember those who [1]rule over you,
who have spoken the word of God to you,
whose faith follow, considering the outcome of *their* conduct. [8]Jesus Christ *is*
[a]the same yesterday, today, and forever.
[9]Do not be carried [1]about with various
and strange doctrines. For *it is* good that
the heart be established by grace, not with
foods which have not profited those who
have been occupied with them.
[10]We have an altar from which those
who serve the tabernacle have no right to
eat. [11]For the bodies of those animals,
whose blood is brought into the sanctuary
by the high priest for sin, are burned outside the camp. [12]Therefore Jesus also, that
He might [1]sanctify the people with His
own blood, suffered outside the gate.
[13]Therefore let us go forth to Him, outside
the camp, bearing [a]His reproach. [14]For
here we have no continuing city, but we
seek the one to come. [15a]Therefore by
Him let us continually offer [b]the sacrifice
of praise to God, that is, [c]the fruit of *our*
lips, [1]giving thanks to His name. [16a]But
do not forget to do good and to share, for
[b]with such sacrifices God is well pleased.
[17a]Obey those who [1]rule over you, and
be submissive, for [b]they watch out for
your souls, as those who must give account. Let them do so with joy and not

---

18 a Deut. 4:11; 5:22 *1* NU *to that which* *2* NU *gloom*
19 a Ex. 20:18–26
20 a Ex. 19:12, 13 *1* NU, M omit the rest of v. 20.
21 a Deut. 9:19
23 a [James 1:18] b Luke 10:20 c Ps. 50:6; 94:2 d [Phil. 3:12] *1 festal gathering*
24 a Heb. 8:6; 9:15 b Ex. 24:8 c Gen. 4:10
25 a Heb. 2:2, 3
26 a Hag. 2:6 *1* NU *will shake*
27 a [Is. 34:4; 54:10; 65:17]
28 a Heb. 13:15, 21 *1* M omits *may*
29 a Ex. 24:17

CHAPTER 13
1 a Rom. 12:10
2 a Matt. 25:35 b Gen. 18:1–22; 19:1
3 a Matt. 25:36
4 a Prov. 5:18, 19 b 1 Cor. 6:9
5 a Deut. 31:6, 8; Josh. 1:5
6 a Ps. 27:1; 118:6
7 *1 lead*
8 a Heb. 1:12
9 *1* NU, M *away*
12 *1 set apart*
13 a 1 Pet. 4:14
15 a Eph. 5:20 b Lev. 7:12 c Hos. 14:2 *1* Lit. *confessing*
16 a Rom. 12:13 b Phil. 4:18
17 a Phil. 2:29 b Ezek. 3:17 *1 lead*

HEBREWS 12:29

Dear Woman of Destiny,

Our Lord is the same yesterday, today, and forever. Yet, too many of us will quickly disregard the fact that God is still a consuming fire. Erroneous perceptions and interpretations of the Old Testament God continue to die hard—those of a cruel and ruthless God, eternally enraged, standing over His people with a great cosmic club mercilessly waiting to punish. Today these lying perceptions still remain as one of the biggest subterfuges that Satan ever perpetrated on God's people.

Could it be that we have not yet understood one of the greatest and most paradoxical spiritual truths in our lives? We are walking with a God who really is a consuming fire, while simultaneously being consummate love!

That is the ultimate enigma of our God. He is a God who is eternally and unchangingly a consuming fire; at the same time He is perfect and eternal love. These four words—*consuming fire, consummate love*—do more than describe two characteristics and attributes of God. Scripture tells us they are the very essence of who and what God is (see Heb. 12:29; 1 John 4:8).

Does it not then follow that God's consuming fire is also one of consummate love? Does it not follow as well that such a consuming fire will *never* destroy even one of our precious promises for which He died? And does it not also follow that He will consume *everything* that is not of Him that stands in the way of His ultimate best and highest good for us in fulfilling those promises?

Every element of our lives that is *of Him*—every circumstance, event, deed, word, and attitude, given in trust and faith to Him—will never be consumed in any fire. At the same time, all those things that are not wholly of Him will be purged, refined, or consumed.

Today, as never before, the Lord is appearing in the midst of lives as a consuming fire. He is a pillar of fire to all who desire to come closer, hungering after His voice, His ways, and His glory. And just as surely, He is appearing as that same consuming fire to those who do not choose to be involved with a closer walk (see Mal. 3:2, 3).

His holy, consuming fire of glory is burning off all the chaff and removing all the dross in order to shape and manifest His divine character into our transformed lives. As the impurities and contaminants are being purged, purifying our hearts and lives, we realize this has been His divine plan for perfecting His bride from the beginning.

Our explanations for crawling off the altar have been without number. Along the way, there have been fears, hurts, weariness, pride, disappointments, unforgiveness, discouragements, vanity, hopelessness, and lusts, just to name a few. However, God loves us too much to accept even the worst of sins or the best of rationales as justification for lack of fervency, intensity, and total commitment. He is in the process of seeing to it that our flesh *will* die regardless of the reasons. Paradoxically, the *only* safe place for us is on the altar in the midst of His fire.

Margaret Moberly

God of peace, You who brought up our Lord Jesus from the dead, that great Shepherd of the sheep, through the blood of the everlasting covenant, make _____ complete in every good work to do Your will, working in them what is well pleasing in Your sight.

FROM HEBREWS 13:20, 21

with grief, for that would be unprofitable
for you.

Prayer Requested

18[a]Pray for us; for we are confident that
we have [b]a good conscience, in all things
desiring to live honorably. 19But I especially urge *you* to do this, that I may be
restored to you the sooner.

Benediction, Final Exhortation, Farewell

20Now may [a]the God of peace [b]who
brought up our Lord Jesus from the dead,
[c]that great Shepherd of the sheep,
[d]through the blood of the everlasting covenant, 21make you [1]complete in every
good work to do His will, [a]working in
[2]you what is well pleasing in His sight,
through Jesus Christ, to whom *be* glory
forever and ever. Amen.
22And I appeal to you, brethren, bear
with the word of exhortation, for I have
written to you in few words. 23Know that
our brother Timothy has been set free,
with whom I shall see you if he comes
shortly.
24Greet all those who [1]rule over you,
and all the saints. Those from Italy greet
you.
25Grace *be* with you all. Amen.

18 [a] Eph. 6:19 [b] Acts 23:1
20 [a] Rom. 5:1, 2, 10; 15:33 [b] Rom. 4:24 [c] 1 Pet. 2:25; 5:4 [d] Zech. 9:11
21 [a] Phil. 2:13 [1] *perfect* [2] NU, M *us*
24 [1] *lead*

AUTHOR: *James, Brother of Jesus*
DATE: *A.D. 48–62*
THEME: *Faith That Works*
KEY WORD: *Faith, Riches, Tongue, Pride, Prayer*

JAMES

Dear Woman of Destiny,

The Book of James calls all believers to a high standard of ethical living based on the gospel. However, it could have been written for women alone because of its significance to us! It begins with an admonition to "let patience have its perfect work" (James 1:4). Then the next verse flows into the subject of asking God for wisdom. Wisdom. I asked God for that one time with diligence, and after that it seemed like everything in my life began to go wrong. Finally, I grumbled to the Lord (not a good thing to do, by the way), "Lord, ever since I prayed for wisdom, I'm making all kinds of mistakes." He gently spoke to my heart, "Yes, but you will never do those same things again, will you? You will truly become wise." Woman of Destiny, we need to guard what we say with our mouths because the situations we start with them may kindle a forest fire of problems (see James 3:5).

With His love,

Cindy Jacobs

Greeting to the Twelve Tribes

James, [a]a bondservant of God and of
the Lord Jesus Christ,

To the twelve tribes which are scattered
abroad:

Greetings.

Profiting from Trials

[2] My brethren, [a]count it all joy [b]when
you fall into various trials, [3][a]knowing that
the testing of your faith produces [1]pa-
tience. [4]But let patience have *its* perfect
work, that you may be [1]perfect and complete, lacking nothing. [5][a]If any of you
lacks wisdom, [b]let him ask of God, who
gives to all liberally and without reproach,
and [c]it will be given to him. [6][a]But let him
ask in faith, with no doubting, for he who
doubts is like a wave of the sea driven and
tossed by the wind. [7]For let not that man
suppose that he will receive anything
from the Lord; [8]*he is* [a]a double-minded
man, unstable in all his ways.

O Father, enable ____ to count it all joy when they fall into various trials, knowing that the testing of their faith produces patience. May they allow patience to have its perfect work, that they may be perfect and complete, lacking nothing.

FROM JAMES 1:2–4

The Perspective of Rich and Poor

[9]Let the lowly brother glory in his exaltation, [10]but the rich in his humiliation,
because [a]as a flower of the field he will
pass away. [11]For no sooner has the sun
risen with a burning heat than it withers
the grass; its flower falls, and its beautiful
appearance perishes. So the rich man also
will fade away in his pursuits.

Loving God Under Trials

[12][a]Blessed *is* the man who endures
temptation; for when he has been approved, he will receive [b]the crown of life
[c]which the Lord has promised to those
who love Him. [13]Let no one say when he
is tempted, "I am tempted by God"; for
God cannot be tempted by evil, nor does
He Himself tempt anyone. [14]But each one
is tempted when he is drawn away by his
own desires and enticed. [15]Then, [a]when
desire has conceived, it gives birth to sin;
and sin, when it is full-grown, [b]brings
forth death.

The prayer of faith admits no doubt, for where doubt is, there faith is not.

MRS. M. BAXTER

[16]Do not be deceived, my beloved brethren. [17][a]Every good gift and every perfect
gift is from above, and comes down from
the Father of lights, [b]with whom there is
no variation or shadow of turning. [18][a]Of
His own will He brought us forth by the
[b]word of truth, [c]that we might be a kind
of firstfruits of His creatures.

Qualities Needed in Trials

[19][1]So then, my beloved brethren, let every man be swift to hear, [a]slow to speak,
[b]slow to wrath; [20]for the wrath of man
does not produce the righteousness of
God.

Doers—Not Hearers Only

[21]Therefore [a]lay aside all filthiness and
[1]overflow of wickedness, and receive with
meekness the implanted word, [b]which is
able to save your souls.
[22]But [a]be doers of the word, and not
hearers only, deceiving yourselves. [23]For
[a]if anyone is a hearer of the word and
not a doer, he is like a man observing
his natural face in a mirror; [24]for he

CHAPTER 1
1 a Acts 12:17
2 a Acts 5:41 b 1 Pet. 1:6
3 a Rom. 5:3–5 *1 endurance* or *perseverance*
4 *1 mature*
5 a 1 Kin. 3:9 b Matt. 7:7 c Jer. 29:12
6 a [Mark 11:23, 24]
8 a James 4:8
10 a Job 14:2
12 a James 5:11 b [1 Cor. 9:25] c Matt. 10:22
15 a Job 15:35 b [Rom. 5:12; 6:23]
17 a John 3:27 b Num. 23:19
18 a John 1:13 b [1 Pet. 1:3, 23] c [Eph. 1:12, 13]
19 a Prov. 10:19; 17:27 b Prov. 14:17; 16:32 *1* NU *Know this* or *This you know*
21 a Col. 3:8 b Acts 13:26 *1 abundance*
22 a Matt. 7:21–28
23 a Luke 6:47

JAMES 1:2–4

Dear Woman of Destiny,

Trials! Tribulation! Troubles! Joy?

As school students, we all had tests that asked us to look at a series of words and pick the one that did not belong with the others. Remember those? Well, in reading the above scripture, at first glance it appears that James is listing words and concepts that are contradictory. We have to take a closer look to understand the deeper meaning of the verse.

How can we laugh in the face of adversity? How can we rejoice when everything seems to be going against us? Does James really mean "count it all joy"—as in "happy"—and, if so, how is this possible? The two concepts—adversity and joy—seem to be oxymoronic.

In *Strong's Concordance* we find the definition of *joy* to be "calm delight." So that means James is actually telling us that even in times of trial, we can have calm delight. Easier said than done, right? Especially for those of you who have prodigals, or who have had a dream die, suffered the loss of a child or loved one, or faced financial disaster or sickness. You may be asking, "How can I face any of these with calm delight?" And your question is absolutely legitimate!

The calm we have in difficult times comes from knowing that no matter what happens in our lives or on planet earth, God's position never changes. You see, there has never been a survey taken in heaven or earth, no public opinion poll taken, to decide that God is God. He is! That never changes! *He* never changes! He is Lord of heaven and earth. He is our Alpha and Omega, the beginning and the end, which means, my friend, He is the God of the middle, too. He isn't pacing the throne room wondering how it's all going to work out. When an earthly king walks into his throne room and takes his seat, everything in that room comes into order. When God is on the throne of our lives, He brings everything into order. Being in a seated position signifies rest and confidence. When He is seated on the throne, we can be at rest, trusting that God has everything under control. Only when we try to take back the burden does confusion and unbelief enter in. God is ever reminded of the covenant He made with man, and God is not a man that He can lie.

The delight we experience during trials comes from knowing that God designs and allows circumstances in our lives to work a godly maturity in us. How we respond or react to these is our choice. We can learn to embrace trials with delight, because we know whatever comes our way, successes or failures, works a character trait of God in us—endurance, patience, steadfastness. We must have these characteristics and attributes to *finish the race* (see Heb. 12:1).

How can we practically apply this truth to our lives? By striving to embrace each trial as a character-building opportunity.

Nancy Hinkle

observes himself, goes away, and immediately forgets what kind of man he was. 25But [a]he who looks into the perfect law of liberty and continues *in it,* and is not a forgetful hearer but a doer of the work, [b]this one will be blessed in what he does.

26If anyone [1]among you thinks he is religious, and [a]does not bridle his tongue but deceives his own heart, this one's religion *is* useless. 27[a]Pure and undefiled religion before God and the Father is this: [b]to visit orphans and widows in their trouble, [c]*and* to keep oneself unspotted from the world.

Beware of Personal Favoritism

2 My brethren, do not hold the faith of our Lord Jesus Christ, [a]*the Lord* of glory, with [b]partiality. 2For if there should come into your assembly a man with gold rings, in [1]fine apparel, and there should also come in a poor man in [2]filthy clothes, 3and you [1]pay attention to the one wearing the fine clothes and say to him, "You sit here in a good place," and say to the poor man, "You stand there," or, "Sit here at my footstool," 4have you not [1]shown partiality among yourselves, and become judges with evil thoughts?

5Listen, my beloved brethren: [a]Has God not chosen the poor of this world *to be* [b]rich in faith and heirs of the kingdom [c]which He promised to those who love Him? 6But [a]you have dishonored the poor man. Do not the rich oppress you [b]and drag you into the courts? 7Do they not blaspheme that noble name by which you are [a]called?

8If you really fulfill *the* royal law according to the Scripture, [a]*"You shall love your neighbor as yourself,"* you do well; 9but if you [1]show partiality, you commit sin, and are convicted by the law as [a]transgressors. 10For whoever shall keep the whole law, and yet [a]stumble in one *point,* [b]he is guilty of all. 11For He who said, [a]*"Do not commit adultery,"* also said, [b]*"Do not murder."* Now if you do not commit adultery, but you do murder, you have become a transgressor of the law. 12So speak and so do as those who will be judged by [a]the law of liberty. 13For [a]judgment is without mercy to the one who has shown [b]no [c]mercy. [d]Mercy triumphs over judgment.

Faith Without Works Is Dead

14[a]What *does it* profit, my brethren, if someone says he has faith but does not have works? Can faith save him? 15[a]If a brother or sister is naked and destitute of daily food, 16and [a]one of you says to them, "Depart in peace, be warmed and filled," but you do not give them the things which are needed for the body, what *does it* profit? 17Thus also faith by itself, if it does not have works, is dead.

18But someone will say, "You have faith, and I have works." [a]Show me your faith without [1]your works, [b]and I will show you my faith by [2]my works. 19You believe that there is one God. You do well. Even the demons believe—and tremble! 20But do you want to know, O foolish man, that faith without works is [1]dead? 21Was not Abraham our father justified by works [a]when he offered Isaac his son on the altar? 22Do you see [a]that faith was working together with his works, and by [b]works faith was made [1]perfect? 23And the Scripture was fulfilled which says, [a]*"Abraham believed God, and it was [1]accounted to him for righteousness."* And he was called [b]the friend of God. 24You see then that a man is justified by works, and not by faith only.

25Likewise, [a]was not Rahab the harlot also justified by works when she received the messengers and sent *them* out another way?

26For as the body without the spirit is dead, so faith without works is dead also.

The Untamable Tongue

3 My brethren, [a]let not many of you become teachers, [b]knowing that we shall receive a stricter judgment. 2For [a]we all stumble in many things. [b]If anyone does not stumble in word, [c]he *is* a [1]perfect man, able also to bridle the whole body. 3[1]Indeed, [a]we put bits in horses' mouths that they may obey us, and we turn their whole body. 4Look also at ships: although they are so large and are driven by fierce winds, they are turned by a very small rudder wherever the pilot desires. 5Even so [a]the tongue is a little member and [b]boasts great things.

See how great a forest a little fire kindles! 6And [a]the tongue *is* a fire, a world of

25 a James 2:12 b John 13:17
26 a Ps. 34:13 *1* NU omits *among you*
27 a Matt. 25:34–36 b Is. 1:17 c [Rom. 12:2]

CHAPTER 2
1 a 1 Cor. 2:8 b Lev. 19:15
2 *1 bright* *2 vile*
3 *1* Lit. *look upon*
4 *1 differentiated*
5 a 1 Cor. 1:27 b Luke 12:21 c Ex. 20:6
6 a 1 Cor. 11:22 b Acts 13:50
7 a 1 Pet. 4:16
8 a Lev. 19:18
9 a Deut. 1:17 *1* Lit. *receive the face*
10 a Gal. 3:10 b Deut. 27:26
11 a Ex. 20:14; Deut. 5:18 b Ex. 20:13; Deut. 5:17
12 a James 1:25
13 a Job 22:6 b Prov. 21:13 c Mic. 7:18 d Rom. 12:8
14 a Matt. 7:21–23, 26; 21:28–32
15 a Luke 3:11
16 a [1 John 3:17, 18]
18 a Heb. 6:10 b James 3:13 *1* NU omits *your* *2* NU omits *my*
20 *1* NU *useless*
21 a Gen. 22:9, 10, 12, 16–18
22 a Heb. 11:17 b John 8:39 *1 complete*
23 a Gen. 15:6 b 2 Chr. 20:7 *1 credited*
25 a Heb. 11:31

CHAPTER 3
1 a [Matt. 23:8] b Luke 6:37
2 a 1 Kin. 8:46 b Ps. 34:13 c [Matt. 12:34–37] *1 mature*
3 a Ps. 32:9 *1* NU *Now if*
5 a Prov. 12:18; 15:2 b Ps. 12:3; 73:8
6 a Prov. 16:27

[1]iniquity. The tongue is so set among our members that it [b]defiles the whole body, and sets on fire the course of [2]nature; and it is set on fire by [3]hell. 7For every kind of beast and bird, of reptile and creature of the sea, is tamed and has been tamed by mankind. 8But no man can tame the tongue. *It is* an unruly evil, [a]full of deadly poison. 9With it we bless our God and Father, and with it we curse men, who have been made [a]in the [1]similitude of God. 10Out of the same mouth proceed blessing and cursing. My brethren, these things ought not to be so. 11Does a spring send forth fresh *water* and bitter from the same opening? 12Can a [a]fig tree, my brethren, bear olives, or a grapevine bear figs? [1]Thus no spring yields both salt water and fresh.

Heavenly Versus Demonic Wisdom

13[a]Who *is* wise and understanding among you? Let him show by good conduct *that* his works *are done* in the meekness of wisdom. 14But if you have [a]bitter envy and [1]self-seeking in your hearts, [b]do not boast and lie against the truth. 15[a]This wisdom does not descend from above, but *is* earthly, sensual, demonic. 16For [a]where envy and self-seeking *exist,* confusion and every evil thing *are* there. 17But [a]the wisdom that is from above is first pure, then peaceable, gentle, willing to yield, full of mercy and good fruits, [b]without partiality [c]and without hypocrisy. 18[a]Now the fruit of righteousness is sown in peace by those who make peace.

It is no great thing to be humble when you are brought low, but to be humble when you are praised is a great and rare attainment.

BERNARD OF CLAIRVAUX

Pride Promotes Strife

4 Where do [1]wars and fights *come* from among you? Do *they* not *come* from your *desires for* pleasure [a]that war in your members? 2You lust and do not have. You murder and covet and cannot obtain. You fight and [1]war. [2]Yet you do not have because you do not ask. 3[a]You ask and do not receive, [b]because you ask amiss, that you may spend *it* on your pleasures. 4[1]Adulterers and adulteresses! Do you not know that [a]friendship with the world is enmity with God? [b]Whoever therefore wants to be a friend of the world makes himself an enemy of God. 5Or do you think that the Scripture says in vain, [a]"The Spirit who dwells in us yearns jealously"?

6 But He gives more grace. Therefore He says:

[a]*"God resists the proud,*
But gives grace to the humble."

Humility Cures Worldliness

7Therefore submit to God. [a]Resist the devil and he will flee from you. 8[a]Draw near to God and He will draw near to you. [b]Cleanse *your* hands, *you* sinners; and [c]purify *your* hearts, *you* double-minded. 9[a]Lament and mourn and weep! Let your laughter be turned to mourning and *your* joy to gloom. 10[a]Humble yourselves in the sight of the Lord, and He will lift you up.

Lord, I pray that ______ would humble themselves in Your sight, for You will lift them up.

FROM JAMES 4:10

Do Not Judge a Brother

11[a]Do not speak evil of one another, brethren. He who speaks evil of a brother [b]and judges his brother, speaks evil of the law and judges the law. But if you judge the law, you are not a doer of the law but a judge. 12There is one [1]Lawgiver, [a]who is able to save and to destroy. [b]Who[2] are you to judge [3]another?

6 b [Matt. 12:36; 15:11, 18] *1 unrighteousness* *2 existence* *3 Gr. Gehenna*
8 a Ps. 140:3
9 a Gen. 1:26; 5:1; 9:6 *1 likeness*
12 a Matt. 7:16–20 *1 NU Neither can a salty spring produce fresh water.*
13 a Gal. 6:4
14 a Rom. 13:13 b Rom. 2:17 *1 selfish ambition*
15 a Phil. 3:19
16 a 1 Cor. 3:3
17 a 1 Cor. 2:6, 7 b James 2:1 c Rom. 12:9
18 a Prov. 11:18

CHAPTER 4
1 a Rom. 7:23 *1 battles*
2 *1 battle* *2 NU, M omit Yet*
3 a Job 27:8, 9 b [Ps. 66:18]
4 a 1 John 2:15 b Gal. 1:4 *1 NU omits Adulterers and*
5 a Gen. 6:5
6 a Prov. 3:34
7 a [Eph. 4:27; 6:11]
8 a 2 Chr. 15:2 b Is. 1:16 c 1 Pet. 1:22
9 a Matt. 5:4
10 a Job 22:29
11 a 1 Pet. 2:1–3 b [Matt. 7:1–5]
12 a [Matt. 10:28] b Rom. 14:4 *1 NU adds and Judge* *2 NU, M But who* *3 NU a neighbor*

JAMES 4:6–10

Dear Woman of Destiny,

God requires and honors humility! James 4:10 says, "Humble yourselves in the sight of the Lord, and He will lift you up." If you want your life to have significance, then position yourself at the feet of Jesus.

Being a woman in a man's world is a difficult reality for all of us women. Being a woman in ministry is even more of a delicate tightrope to walk! How do we position ourselves in everyday life and in ministry so we can fulfill our destiny in God? As women, we are in spiritual warfare for our destinies!

As I have ministered in conferences throughout the United States and overseas, I've seen many people moving in self-promotion and church politics. I feel that grieves the heart of Jesus. It also challenges our hearts when we are overlooked and others are promoted above us, especially when we see how they do it. The Lord allows these "fires" to work a death in our own hearts, killing our pride and need for position.

There is a price behind the anointing! The years of being overlooked as women are a fiery inferno, but the Lord can use them to work gold in our hearts. The challenge in this lifelong journey is to keep our heart soft, humble, and bowed low before Him. Our gifts will make room for us in due season (see Prov. 18:16). Do we have love and humility, regardless of what has happened to us; or have we become disqualified because of bitterness?

The Holy Spirit is training us in humility to rule and reign with Him as His Bride. She must be equally yoked to the Bridegroom; she must wear the same wedding garments He wears. Jesus was adorned in the beauty of meekness. At the marriage supper of the Lamb, each one of us will have different clothing on, which will be the fruits and rewards of humility and love in our earthly lives.

Another picture of humility is that we are arrayed in many different garments from the wardrobe of the Lord. With His great wisdom, it's as though the outer garment that covered each person was a simple burlap robe, a mantle of humility. We must be clothed in humility! (see 1 Pet. 5:5).

Underneath that robe are the beautiful, colorful royal robes of our giftings and testimony. The Lord displays these at different times, but most of the time they are hidden as a secret testimony between you and the Lord.

Walking in humility is a heart issue, a lifestyle, an attitude that is God-given. An impartation of humility is different from a decision for humility. We must choose humility and bow our hearts before the Lord as the first step, but that alone does not produce a *heart* of humility.

A heart can only be changed by a supernatural impartation of the Lord as He releases His divine touch in response to our yielded hearts. This progressive journey of humility takes years to grow, becoming the very fragrance of Jesus in our hearts.

Beloved, pray for an impartation of humility, that you will be a fragrance to Jesus and to those around you.

Jill Austin

Do Not Boast About Tomorrow

13 Come now, you who say, "Today or
tomorrow [1]we will go to such and such a
city, spend a year there, buy and sell, and
make a profit"; 14 whereas you do not
know what *will happen* tomorrow. For
what *is* your life? [a]It is even a vapor that
appears for a little time and then vanishes
away. 15 Instead you *ought* to say, [a]"If the
Lord wills, we shall live and do this or
that." 16 But now you boast in your arrogance. [a]All such boasting is evil.
17 Therefore, [a]to him who knows to do
good and does not do *it,* to him it is sin.

It is essential to continually submit your will to God's will and renounce every private inclination as soon as it arises—no matter how good it appears. You must want only what God has willed from all eternity.

MADAME JEANNE GUYON

Rich Oppressors Will Be Judged

5 Come now, *you* [a]rich, weep and howl
for your miseries that are coming
upon *you!* 2 Your [a]riches [1]are corrupted,
and [b]your garments are moth-eaten.
3 Your gold and silver are corroded, and
their corrosion will be a witness against
you and will eat your flesh like fire. [a]You
have heaped up treasure in the last days.
4 Indeed [a]the wages of the laborers who
mowed your fields, which you kept back
by fraud, cry out; and [b]the cries of the
reapers have reached the ears of the Lord
of [1]Sabaoth. 5 You have lived on the earth
in pleasure and [1]luxury; you have [2]fat-
tened your hearts [3]as in a day of slaughter. 6 You have condemned, you have
murdered the just; he does not resist you.

Be Patient and Persevering

7 Therefore be patient, brethren, until
the coming of the Lord. See *how* the
farmer waits for the precious fruit of the
earth, waiting patiently for it until it receives the early and latter rain. 8 You also
be patient. Establish your hearts, for the
coming of the Lord [1]is at hand.
9 Do not [1]grumble against one another,
brethren, lest you be [2]condemned. Behold, the Judge is standing at the door!
10 [a]My brethren, take the prophets, who
spoke in the name of the Lord, as an example of suffering and [b]patience. 11 Indeed
[a]we count them blessed who [b]endure.
You have heard of [c]the perseverance of
Job and seen [d]the end *intended by* the
Lord—that [e]the Lord is very compassionate and merciful.
12 But above all, my brethren, [a]do not
swear, either by heaven or by earth or
with any other oath. But let your "Yes" be
"Yes," and *your* "No," "No," lest you fall
into [1]judgment.

Heaven has listening ears only for the wholehearted and the deeply earnest. Energy, courage, and perseverance must back the prayers that heaven respects and that God hears.

E. M. BOUNDS

Meeting Specific Needs

13 Is anyone among you suffering? Let
him [a]pray. Is anyone cheerful? [b]Let him
sing psalms. 14 Is anyone among you sick?
Let him call for the elders of the church,
and let them pray over him, [a]anointing
him with oil in the name of the Lord.
15 And the prayer of faith will save the
sick, and the Lord will raise him up. [a]And
if he has committed sins, he will be forgiven. 16 [1]Confess *your* trespasses to
one another, and pray for one another,
that you may be healed. [a]The effective,

13 [1] M *let us*
14 [a] Job 7:7
15 [a] Acts 18:21
16 [a] 1 Cor. 5:6
17 [a] [Luke 12:47]

CHAPTER 5
1 [a] [Luke 6:24]
2 [a] Matt. 6:19 [b] Job 13:28 [1] *have rotted*
3 [a] Rom. 2:5
4 [a] Lev. 19:13 [b] Deut. 24:15 [1] Lit., in Heb., *Hosts*
5 [1] *indulgence* [2] Lit. *nourished* [3] NU omits *as*
8 [1] *has drawn near*
9 [1] Lit. *groan* [2] NU, M *judged*
10 [a] Matt. 5:12 [b] Heb. 10:36
11 [a] [Ps. 94:12] [b] [James 1:12] [c] Job 1:21, 22; 2:10 [d] Job 42:10 [e] Num. 14:18
12 [a] Matt. 5:34–37 [1] M *hypocrisy*
13 [a] Ps. 50:14, 15 [b] Eph. 5:19
14 [a] Mark 6:13; 16:18
15 [a] Is. 33:24
16 [a] Num. 11:2 [1] NU *Therefore confess your sins* [2] *supplication*

Dear Woman of Destiny,

The circumstances in our home called for a miracle. I asked God to teach me to pray, and He showed me James 5:16. In the beginning, I bypassed the first part of this scripture. I was convinced that if God would change those around me, my life could return to normal. I certainly didn't see that I had done anything wrong.

For a while, I continued going directly to "The effective, fervent prayer of a righteous man avails much." However, when I began praying for those who were unraveling the very seams of my life, it became apparent that I had to be obedient to all of this scripture, which includes: "Confess your trespasses to one another, and pray for one another, that you may be healed."

It is far easier to confess our sins to God. When we acknowledge our sin, calling it by name, "He is faithful and just to forgive us our sins and to cleanse us from all unrighteousness" (1 John 1:9). Isn't it enough that I tell God? No, admitting my sin to another person keeps me free from false pride and positions me for accountability and forgiveness. Receiving forgiveness from others combined with God's forgiveness releases us to forgive those who have wronged us. Then we can pray effectively for others, no longer holding anything against them.

God's intention is for His children to have healthy interdependent relationships, united in love so that the world will know that He sent Jesus. Confessing our faults to each other and praying for one another heals and restores us to a spiritual tone of mind and heart paving the road to unity.

"The effective, fervent prayer of a righteous man avails much." How can you know you are righteous? Christians have been made right with God through Christ. This gives you the right to come into the presence of God just as you are. He is drawing you to Himself with cords of love. The believer seeks first the kingdom of God and His righteousness—His way of doing and being right (see Matt. 6:33).

Praying scriptural prayers releases the will of God in every situation. You determine your destiny as you become more intimately acquainted with the Father through prayer, study, and meditation. The Holy Spirit helps you when you don't know how you should pray. Even though your prayers may be expressed with great emotion, submit to the control of the Holy Spirit, who will help you pray prayers that avail much.

If your prayers are not being answered, reevaluate your life. Have you confessed your sins not only to God, but also to those whom you may have offended? Are you praying for others according to God's will, rather than from your unmet needs and unresolved issues? Are you praying for that one who has confessed his sins to you? God is looking for availability, and if you have accepted Christ and are living according to God's will, you are a channel of prayer. God's timing is not ours. So commit to pray, and don't give up. Your prayers make a difference!

Germaine Copeland

[2]fervent prayer of a righteous man avails
much. 17Elijah was a man [a]with a nature like ours, and [b]he prayed earnestly
that it would not rain; and it did not rain
on the land for three years and six months.
18And he prayed [a]again, and the heav-
en gave rain, and the earth produced its
fruit.

Bring Back the Erring One

19Brethren, if anyone among you wanders from the truth, and someone [a]turns
him back, 20let him know that he who
turns a sinner from the error of his way
[a]will save [1]a soul from death and [b]cover
a multitude of sins.

17 [a]Acts 14:15 [b]1 Kin. 17:1; 18:1
18 [a]1 Kin. 18:1, 42
19 [a]Gal. 6:1
20 [a]Rom. 11:14 [b][1 Pet. 4:8]
[1] NU *his soul*

AUTHOR: *Peter*
DATE: *Early A.D. Sixties*
THEME: *Suffering as a Christian*
KEY WORDS: *Suffer, Suffering*

1 PETER

Dear Woman of Destiny,

What kind of faith do we have? Is it the kind that only works on the days when everything goes right in our lives? First Peter admonishes us to have genuine faith, "being much more precious than gold that perishes, though it is tested by fire" (1 Pet. 1:7). We are not to be like other people who wilt under persecution and act in a prideful manner. This book admonishes us to walk in humility and have a submissive attitude. In today's culture, it seems like submission to authority is not a characteristic to aspire to, but it is one of the highest ones we are to strive for as godly women. Women of destiny are not afraid of suffering and hard times because we know we are refined through trials of persecution to become more Christlike.

With His love,

Cindy Jacobs

Greeting to the Elect Pilgrims

Peter, an apostle of Jesus Christ,

To the [1]pilgrims [a]of the Dispersion in Pontus, Galatia, Cappadocia, Asia, and Bithynia, 2 [a]elect [b]according to the foreknowledge of God the Father, [c]in sanctification of the Spirit, for [d]obedience and [e]sprinkling of the blood of Jesus Christ:

[f]Grace to you and peace be multiplied.

Thank You, Father, that according to Your abundant mercy You have begotten ____ to a living hope through the resurrection of Jesus Christ from the dead, to an inheritance incorruptible and undefiled and that does not fade away, reserved in heaven for them.

FROM 1 PETER 1:3, 4

A Heavenly Inheritance

3 [a]Blessed *be* the God and Father of our Lord Jesus Christ, who [b]according to His abundant mercy [c]has begotten us again to a living hope [d]through the resurrection of Jesus Christ from the dead, 4 to an inheritance [1]incorruptible and undefiled and that does not fade away, [a]reserved in heaven for you, 5 [a]who are kept by the power of God through faith for salvation ready to be revealed in the last time.

6 [a]In this you greatly rejoice, though now [b]for a little while, if need be, [c]you have been [1]grieved by various trials, 7 that [a]the genuineness of your faith, *being* much more precious than gold that perishes, though [b]it is tested by fire, [c]may be found to praise, honor, and glory at the revelation of Jesus Christ, 8 [a]whom having not [1]seen you love. [b]Though now you do not see *Him,* yet believing, you rejoice with joy inexpressible and full of glory, 9 receiving the end of your faith—the salvation of *your* souls.

10 Of this salvation the prophets have inquired and searched carefully, who prophesied of the grace *that would come* to you, 11 searching what, or what manner of time, [a]the Spirit of Christ who was in them was indicating when He testified beforehand the sufferings of Christ and the glories that would follow. 12 To them it was revealed that, not to themselves, but to [1]us they were ministering the things which now have been reported to you through those who have preached the gospel to you by the Holy Spirit sent from heaven—things which [a]angels desire to look into.

Living Before God Our Father

13 Therefore gird up the loins of your mind, be sober, and rest *your* hope fully upon the grace that is to be brought to you at the revelation of Jesus Christ; 14 as obedient children, not [a]conforming yourselves to the former lusts, *as* in your ignorance; 15 [a]but as He who called you *is* holy, you also be holy in all *your* conduct, 16 because it is written, [a]*"Be holy, for I am holy."*

17 And if you call on the Father, who [a]without partiality judges according to each one's work, conduct yourselves throughout the time of your [1]stay *here* in fear; 18 knowing that you were not redeemed with [1]corruptible things, *like* silver or gold, from your aimless conduct *received* by tradition from your fathers, 19 but [a]with the precious blood of Christ, [b]as of a lamb without blemish and without spot. 20 [a]He indeed was foreordained before the foundation of the world, but was [1]manifest [b]in these last times for you 21 who through Him believe in God, [a]who raised Him from the dead and [b]gave Him glory, so that your faith and hope are in God.

The Enduring Word

22 Since you [a]have purified your souls in obeying the truth [1]through the Spirit in [2]sincere [b]love of the brethren, love one another fervently with a pure heart, 23 [a]having been born again, not of [1]corruptible seed but [2]incorruptible, [b]through the word of God which lives and abides [3]forever, 24 because

CHAPTER 1
1 [a] James 1:1 *[1] sojourners,* temporary residents
2 [a] Eph. 1:4 [b] [Rom. 8:29] [c] 2 Thess. 2:13 [d] Rom. 1:5 [e] Heb. 10:22; 12:24 [f] Rom. 1:7
3 [a] Eph. 1:3 [b] Gal. 6:16 [c] [John 3:3, 5] [d] 1 Cor. 15:20
4 [a] Col. 1:5 *[1] imperishable*
5 [a] John 10:28
6 [a] Matt. 5:12 [b] 2 Cor. 4:17 [c] James 1:2 *[1] distressed*
7 [a] James 1:3 [b] Job 23:10 [c] [Rom. 2:7]
8 [a] 1 John 4:20 [b] John 20:29 [1] M *known*
11 [a] 2 Pet. 1:21
12 [a] Eph. 3:10 [1] NU, M *you*
14 [a] [Rom. 12:2]
15 [a] [2 Cor. 7:1]
16 [a] Lev. 11:44, 45; 19:2; 20:7
17 [a] Acts 10:34 *[1] sojourning, dwelling* as resident aliens
18 *[1] perishable*
19 [a] Acts 20:28 [b] Ex. 12:5
20 [a] Rom. 3:25 [b] Gal. 4:4 *[1] revealed*
21 [a] Acts 2:24 [b] Acts 2:33
22 [a] Acts 15:9 [b] Heb. 13:1 [1] NU omits *through the Spirit* [2] Lit. *unhypocritical*
23 [a] John 1:13 [b] James 1:18 *[1] perishable* *[2] imperishable* [3] NU omits *forever*

[a]"*All flesh is as grass,*
And all [1]the glory of man as the
flower of the grass.
The grass withers,
And its flower falls away,
25 [a]*But the [1]word of the* LORD
endures forever."

[b]Now this is the word which by the gospel
was preached to you.

2 Therefore, [a]laying aside all malice, all
deceit, hypocrisy, envy, and all evil
speaking, 2[a]as newborn babes, desire the
pure [b]milk of the word, that you may
grow [1]thereby, 3if indeed you have [a]tasted
that the Lord *is* gracious.

The Chosen Stone and His Chosen People

4Coming to Him *as to* a living stone,
[a]rejected indeed by men, but chosen by
God *and* precious, 5you also, as living
stones, are being built up a spiritual
house, a holy priesthood, to offer up spiritual sacrifices acceptable to God through
Jesus Christ. 6Therefore it is also contained in the Scripture,

[a]"*Behold, I lay in Zion*
A chief cornerstone, elect, precious,
And he who believes on Him will by
no means be put to shame."

7Therefore, to you who believe, *He is*
precious; but to those who [1]are disobedient,

[a]"*The stone which the builders*
rejected
Has become the chief cornerstone,"

8and

[a]"*A stone of stumbling*
And a rock of offense."

[b]They stumble, being disobedient to the
word, [c]to which they also were appointed.
9But you *are* a chosen generation, a
royal priesthood, a holy nation, His own
special people, that you may proclaim
the praises of Him who called you out
of [a]darkness into His marvelous light;
10[a]who once *were* not a people but *are*
now the people of God, who had not obtained mercy but now have obtained
mercy.

Living Before the World

11Beloved, I beg *you* as sojourners and
pilgrims, abstain from fleshly lusts
[a]which war against the soul, 12[a]having
your conduct honorable among the Gentiles, that when they speak against you as
evildoers, [b]they may, by *your* good works
which they observe, glorify God in the day
of visitation.

Submission to Government

13[a]Therefore submit yourselves to every
[1]ordinance of man for the Lord's sake,
whether to the king as supreme, 14or to
governors, as to those who are sent by
him for the punishment of evildoers and
for the praise of those who do good. 15For
this is the will of God, that by doing good
you may put to silence the ignorance of
foolish men— 16[a]as free, yet not [b]using
liberty as a cloak for [1]vice, but as bondservants of God. 17Honor all *people.* Love
the brotherhood. Fear [a]God. Honor the
king.

Submission to Masters

18[a]Servants, *be* submissive to *your*
masters with all fear, not only to the good
and gentle, but also to the harsh. 19For
this *is* [a]commendable, if because of conscience toward God one endures grief,
suffering wrongfully. 20For [a]what credit *is*
it if, when you are beaten for your faults,
you take it patiently? But when you do
good and suffer, if you take it patiently,
this *is* commendable before God. 21For [a]to
this you were called, because Christ also
suffered for [1]us, [b]leaving [2]us an example,
that you should follow His steps:

22 "*Who[a] committed no sin,*
Nor was deceit found in His
mouth";

Praise You, Lord, that ____ is part of a chosen generation, a royal priesthood, a holy nation, Your own special people, that ____ may proclaim Your praises, for You called them out of darkness into Your marvelous light.

FROM 1 PETER 2:9

24 a Is. 40:6–8 1 NU *its glory as*
25 a Is. 40:8 b [John 1:1] 1 *spoken word*

CHAPTER 2
1 a Heb. 12:1
2 a [Matt. 18:3; 19:14] b 1 Cor. 3:2 1 NU adds *up to salvation*
3 a Heb. 6:5
4 a Ps. 118:22
6 a Is. 28:16
7 a Ps. 118:22 1 NU *disbelieve*
8 a Is. 8:14 b 1 Cor. 1:23 c Rom. 9:22
9 a [Acts 26:18]
10 a Hos. 1:9, 10; 2:23
11 a James 4:1
12 a Phil. 2:15 b Matt. 5:16; 9:8
13 a Matt. 22:21 1 *institution*
16 a Rom. 6:14, 20, 22 b Gal. 5:13 1 *wickedness*
17 a Prov. 24:21
18 a Eph. 6:5–8
19 a Matt. 5:10
20 a Luke 6:32–34
21 a Matt. 16:24 b [1 John 2:6] 1 NU *you* 2 NU, M *you*
22 a Is. 53:9

[23a]who, when He was reviled, did not revile in return; when He suffered, He did not threaten, but [b]committed *Himself* to Him who judges righteously; [24a]who Himself bore our sins in His own body on the tree, [b]that we, having died to sins, might live for righteousness—[c]by whose [1]stripes you were healed. [25]For [a]you were like sheep going astray, but have now returned [b]to the Shepherd and [1]Overseer of your souls.

Submission to Husbands

3 Wives, likewise, *be* [a]submissive to your own husbands, that even if some do not obey the word, [b]they, without a word, may [c]be won by the conduct of their wives, [2a]when they observe your chaste conduct *accompanied* by fear. [3][a]Do not let your adornment be *merely* outward—arranging the hair, wearing gold, or putting on *fine* apparel— [4]rather *let it be* [a]the hidden person of the heart, with the [1]incorruptible *beauty* of a gentle and quiet spirit, which is very precious in the sight of God. [5]For in this manner, in former times, the holy women who trusted in God also adorned themselves, being submissive to their own husbands, [6]as Sarah obeyed Abraham, [a]calling him lord, whose daughters you are if you do good and are not afraid with any terror.

A Word to Husbands

[7a]Husbands, likewise, dwell with *them* with understanding, giving honor to the wife, [b]as to the weaker vessel, and as *being* heirs together of the grace of life, [c]that your prayers may not be hindered.

Called to Blessing

[8]Finally, all *of you be* of one mind, having compassion for one another; love as brothers, *be* tenderhearted, *be* [1]courteous; [9a]not returning evil for evil or reviling for reviling, but on the contrary [b]blessing, knowing that you were called to this, [c]that you may inherit a blessing. [10]For

[a]*"He who would love life*
And see good days,
[b]*Let him [1]refrain his tongue from evil,*
And his lips from speaking deceit.
11 *Let him [a]turn away from evil and do good;*
[b]*Let him seek peace and pursue it.*
12 *For the eyes of the LORD are on the righteous,*
[a]*And His ears are open to their prayers;*
But the face of the LORD is against those who do evil."

Suffering for Right and Wrong

[13a]And who *is* he who will harm you if you become followers of what is good? [14a]But even if you should suffer for righteousness' sake, *you are* blessed. [b]*"And do not be afraid of their threats, nor be troubled."* [15]But [1]sanctify [2]the Lord God in your hearts, and always [a]*be* ready to *give* a defense to everyone who asks you a reason for the [b]hope that is in you, with meekness and fear; [16a]having a good conscience, that when they defame you as evildoers, those who revile your good conduct in Christ may be ashamed. [17]For *it is* better, if it is the will of God, to suffer for doing good than for doing evil.

I pray, Father, that ____ would sanctify You in their heart and always be ready to give a defense to everyone who asks them a reason for the hope that is in them, with meekness and fear.

FROM 1 PETER 3:15

Christ's Suffering and Ours

[18]For Christ also suffered once for sins, the just for the unjust, that He might bring [1]us to God, being put to death in the flesh but made alive by the Spirit, [19]by whom also He went and preached to the spirits in prison, [20]who formerly were disobedient, [1]when once the Divine longsuffering waited in the days of Noah, while *the* ark was being prepared, in which a few, that is, eight souls, were saved through water. [21a]There is also an antitype which now saves us—baptism [b](not the removal of the filth of the flesh, [c]but the answer of a good conscience toward God), through the resurrection of Jesus

---

23 a Is. 53:7 b Luke 23:46
24 a [Heb. 9:28] b Rom. 7:6 c Is. 53:5 *1 wounds*
25 a Is. 53:5, 6 b [Ezek. 34:23] *1 Gr. Episkopos*

CHAPTER 3
1 a Eph. 5:22 b 1 Cor. 7:16 c Matt. 18:15
2 a 1 Pet. 2:12; 3:6
3 a 1 Tim. 2:9
4 a Rom. 2:29 *1 imperishable*
6 a Gen. 18:12
7 a [Eph. 5:25] b 1 Cor. 12:23 c Job 42:8
8 *1* NU *humble*
9 a [Prov. 17:13] b Matt. 5:44 c Matt. 25:34
10 a Ps. 34:12–16 b James 1:26 *1 restrain*
11 a Ps. 37:27 b Rom. 12:18
12 a John 9:31
13 a Prov. 16:7
14 a James 1:12 b Is. 8:12
15 a Ps. 119:46 b [Titus 3:7] *1 set apart* *2* NU *Christ as Lord*
16 a Heb. 13:18
18 *1* NU, M *you*
20 *1* NU, M *when the longsuffering of God waited patiently*
21 a Eph. 5:26 b [Titus 3:5] c [Rom. 10:10]

1 Peter 3:1, 3, 4

Dear Woman of Destiny,

Many men, from childhood, have learned strategies to protect themselves from emotions by which they might be labeled as "unmanly." As adults, they have perfected these strategies. Workaholism, alcoholism, preoccupation with sex, money, power, position, recreation, TV, or just plain passivity are ways men have learned to hide from the real issues of life, and thus from the people who are supposed to be closest to them.

For His own purposes, God designed women with an inner need to move past surface relationships. In essence, many women are knocking on the door of their husband's heart, saying, "Will you come out? I need to know you on a deeper level, and I need to know that I am known and cared about on a deeper level, too. I want to know what's in your heart."

God's purpose for the woman in the man's life is to bring him out from that inner place of aloneness where he hides from himself and others, even from God (see Prov. 27:19). In the dynamics of relating to one another—husband to wife, friend to friend—we are continually confronted with what is in our hearts. The heart is the deepest, most inner recess of our being—the place of absolute truth where all masks and pretensions are removed, the place where the real person dwells.

A woman whose center has been turned, who abides in the Holy Spirit, can begin to trust that what is going on inside her is from the Lord—that God is giving her insight and understanding. By exhibiting a "gentle and quiet spirit" (1 Pet. 3:4), she can share these insights with her husband.

If her husband resists her efforts to share, she may become intimidated or seek to retaliate. She may then retreat into self-protective silence or, in self-defense, explode in anger. If so, her divine gifting of words, meant to bring forth life and restoration, can become deadly weapons. She can use them like knives, laying her husband open with ridicule and disrespect, further damaging an already wounded heart.

As a woman whose desire has been turned from man to God, she is to have courage, to use words responsibly, to speak with respect even when disagreeing with her husband. In anger, she is not to sin (see Eph. 4:26). She is to learn to speak "the truth in love" (v. 15), to bind mercy and truth around her neck so that she will "find favor and high esteem in the sight of God and man" (Prov. 3:3, 4).

She is an ambassador of Christ in her marriage. Her submission, like her creation, is initially for the man's sake, to help him. Submission is knowing her purpose from God's viewpoint and then bringing her whole self to the man for his good.

A man who has learned to trust his wife will gain courage to open up about the wounds and failures of the past. As these wounds and failures are brought into the light, real healing can take place. Those years can be left behind forever as he discovers that he is truly loved—not for some image he has felt obligated to project, but for the person he really is. No longer needing to hide, a man is then free to reach beyond himself to others.

Jane Hansen

Christ, 22 who has gone into heaven and [a]is at the right hand of God, [b]angels and authorities and powers having been made subject to Him.

4 Therefore, since Christ suffered [1]for us in the flesh, arm yourselves also with the same mind, for he who has suffered in the flesh has ceased from sin, 2 that he no longer should live the rest of *his* time in the flesh for the lusts of men, [a]but for the will of God. 3 For we *have spent* enough of our past [1]lifetime in doing the will of the Gentiles—when we walked in lewdness, lusts, drunkenness, revelries, drinking parties, and abominable idolatries. 4 In regard to these, they think it strange that you do not run with *them* in the same flood of dissipation, speaking evil of *you*. 5 They will give an account to Him who is ready [a]to judge the living and the dead. 6 For this reason [a]the gospel was preached also to those who are dead, that they might be judged according to men in the flesh, but [b]live according to God in the spirit.

A life of holiness is essential to a life of physical wholeness; and both are ours through faith in the Lamb of God.

DR. LILIAN B. YEOMANS

Serving for God's Glory

7 But [a]the end of all things is at hand; therefore be serious and watchful in your prayers. 8 And above all things have fervent love for one another, for [a]*"love will cover a multitude of sins."* 9 [a]*Be* hospitable to one another [b]without grumbling. 10 [a]As each one has received a gift, minister it to one another, [b]as good stewards of [c]the manifold grace of God. 11 [a]If anyone speaks, *let him speak* as the [1]oracles of God. If anyone ministers, *let him do it* as with the ability which God supplies, that [b]in all things God may be glorified through Jesus Christ, to whom belong the glory and the [2]dominion forever and ever. Amen.

Suffering for God's Glory

12 Beloved, do not think it strange concerning the fiery trial which is to try you, as though some strange thing happened to you; 13 but rejoice [a]to the extent that you partake of Christ's sufferings, that [b]when His glory is revealed, you may also be glad with exceeding joy. 14 If you are [1]reproached for the name of Christ, [a]blessed *are you,* for the Spirit of glory and of God rests upon you. [2]On their part He is blasphemed, [b]but on your part He is glorified. 15 But let none of you suffer as a murderer, a thief, an evildoer, or as a [1]busybody in other people's matters. 16 Yet if *anyone suffers* as a Christian, let him not be ashamed, but let him glorify God in this [1]matter.

A life devoted unto God, looking wholly unto Him in all our actions, and doing all things suitably to His glory, is so far from being dull and uncomfortable, that it creates new comforts in everything that we do.

WILLIAM LAW

17 For the time *has come* [a]for judgment to begin at the house of God; and if *it begins* with us first, [b]what will *be* the end of those who do not obey the gospel of God? 18 Now

> [a]*"If the righteous one is scarcely saved,*
> *Where will the ungodly and the sinner appear?"*

19 Therefore let those who suffer according to the will of God [a]commit their souls *to Him* in doing good, as to a faithful Creator.

Shepherd the Flock

5 The elders who are among you I exhort, I who am a fellow elder and a [a]witness of the sufferings of Christ, and also a partaker of the [b]glory that will be

22 a Ps. 110:1 b Rom. 8:38

CHAPTER 4

1 1 NU omits *for us*

2 a John 1:13

3 1 NU *time*

5 a Acts 10:42

6 a 1 Pet. 1:12; 3:19 b [Rom. 8:9, 13]

7 a Rom. 13:11

8 a [Prov. 10:12]

9 a Heb. 13:2 b 2 Cor. 9:7

10 a Rom. 12:6–8 b 1 Cor. 4:1, 2 c [1 Cor. 12:4]

11 a Eph. 4:29 b [1 Cor. 10:31] 1 *utterances* 2 *sovereignty*

13 a James 1:2 b 2 Tim. 2:12

14 a Matt. 5:11 b Matt. 5:16 1 *insulted* or *reviled* 2 NU omits the rest of v. 14.

15 1 *meddler*

16 1 NU *name*

17 a Is. 10:12 b Luke 10:12

18 a Prov. 11:31

19 a 2 Tim. 1:12

CHAPTER 5

1 a Matt. 26:37 b Rom. 8:17, 18

1 Peter 4:7–11

Dear Woman of Destiny,

First Peter 4:7–11 begins with a definitive call to prayer and concludes with a commissioning prayer filled with rich insight. As women in the army of God, we are called to a disciplined place in our prayer lives. When we stay alert, on guard, and operate from a state of spiritual preparedness, we are taking a strategic offensive position against the powers of darkness. Spiritual victories come in warfare when we can see ahead, like the watchmen of old, and thwart oncoming attacks. Living on the offensive in prayer with God prevents having to be on the defensive in war with the devil.

In the midst of acknowledging the seriousness of our times and the desperate need for prayer, Peter reminds us of the inordinate need for love. The call to love is as paramount as the call to prayer. When love covers, it forgives and disregards the offense of others. We can monitor our spiritual maturity by how readily we take offense. Above *all* things, we are to have fervent love for one another!

First Peter 4:9 says, "Be hospitable to one another without grumbling." As we look at our calls to prayer and to love, we must continually examine our hearts. The Word clearly states that out of the heart, the mouth speaks. James 5:9 gives us the same directive: "Do not grumble against one another." Beloved Woman of God, let us all seek to love our neighbor as ourselves (see Matt. 22:39) and to follow the Golden Rule.

In this passage of Scripture, we have been given a call to prayer, a call to love, and, in verse 10, a call to give. However, here *gift* does not refer to financial giving. This scripture refers to the Greek word for "gift"—*charisma,* which is a gift of grace, a divine gratuity, a spiritual endowment. The Lord desires for us to be good stewards of the spiritual gifts He gives us. Gifts are freely given to be ministered to one another. Lord, give us the freedom to fully release all that we have been entrusted with so we can strengthen and encourage each other. What a joy!

Peter concludes this passage of Scripture with a clear exhortation: "If *anyone* speaks . . . if *anyone* ministers" (italics mine). Woman of God, this is for each one of us, not just for those in fivefold ministry. If we are willing to be the vessels, God eagerly desires to flow through us. He supplies the anointing. We provide the mouth and the hands. The result, amazingly enough, is speaking God's very oracles and ministering with His ability. Isn't it incredible that the God of the universe chooses to release His life and power through us? And that He is glorified when we allow this transference to take place? How humbling. How divine.

As women of destiny, we can rest in the assurance that He has already given us everything we need to fulfill our call to prayer, our call to love, and our call to give. Now, we must go forth and walk in it!

Jill Griffith

1 Peter 4:9

Dear Woman of Destiny,

First Peter 4:9 asks us to be hospitable to one another without grumbling or complaining—a gigantic request for some of us! I believe there is no one more important to whom we should be hospitable than our own families. Making their mealtime as special as if we were cooking and setting the table for guests will pay off in dividends. While they'll look forward to family time around the table, we'll be setting a good role model for their future home-life. God may also want to send others into our lives for us to bless and to bless us.

Hospitality is defined as "behaving in a kind and generous manner toward guests—expressing welcome, generosity." But for the Christian, hospitality is saying, "This home is Yours Lord; use it as You will."

Sometimes when we have unexpected guests for a meal and I'm not sure I have enough to go around, I pray as I prepare the meal, asking God to multiply and bless it. I've seen Him do this time and again.

We don't have to worry about making a good impression on others, whether our home or food is "good enough." No, if Christ is at home in our heart, He'll be at home in our home and ours will be a house that shouts, "Welcome!" People long to be invited to a home where they can experience Christian fellowship. Here are some ideas that might help you:

- Use what you have for serving a meal, without apologies.
- Prepare food ahead of time for expected guests. Don't attempt a menu that is a burden to you—keep it simple.
- Bathe your house in prayer and with Christian music as you prepare your home and heart for guests' arrival.
- If you are hosting overnight guests, sleep in the room yourself first to see if it is comfortable. Does it have a reading light, a mirror, a place for suitcases, closet space for hanging clothes, and towels?
- Show them the way to the bathroom, and tell them with whom they will be sharing it (for example, teens who get up early to go to school).
- Have water and juices available, and a few snacks if they arrive between meals.
- Take time to make guests feel they are not imposing.
- Respect guests' privacy. Do not play your radio or TV so loud that they cannot sleep, pray, or study.

Mary sat at the feet of the Master. Martha served Him. We must do both if we are to be hospitable. And as Jesus cautioned, we can't get distracted with all our preparations.

Francis Shaeffer wrote, "Pray that the Lord will send you the people of His choice. But don't pray that way unless . . . you are willing to take them into your home, have them at your table, introduce them to your family and let them sleep between your sheets."

We can pray, "Lord, help me to be hospitable to those You want to send my way. Give me creative ideas and strength needed to extend my life to others. Help me find a balance in this area. May I be a hostess, Lord, whom my own children will do well to imitate. Amen."

Quin Sherrer

revealed: 2 [a]Shepherd the flock of God
which is among you, serving as overseers,
[b]not by compulsion but [1]willingly, [c]not
for dishonest gain but eagerly; 3 nor as
[a]being [1]lords over [b]those entrusted to
you, but [c]being examples to the flock;
4 and when [a]the Chief Shepherd appears,
you will receive [b]the crown of glory that
does not fade away.

May _____ be sober and vigilant, Father, because their adversary the devil walks about like a roaring lion, seeking whom he may devour. May they resist him, steadfast in the faith, knowing that the same sufferings are experienced by other believers in the world.

FROM 1 PETER 5:8, 9

Submit to God, Resist the Devil

5 Likewise you younger people, submit
yourselves to *your* elders. Yes, [a]all of *you*
be submissive to one another, and be
clothed with humility, for

> [b]*"God resists the proud,*
> *But [c]gives grace to the humble."*

6 Therefore humble yourselves under the
mighty hand of God, that He may exalt
you in due time, 7 casting all your care
upon Him, for He cares for you.
8 Be [1]sober, be [2]vigilant; [3]because
your adversary the devil walks about like
a roaring lion, seeking whom he may devour.
9 Resist him, steadfast in the faith,
knowing that the same sufferings are experienced
by your brotherhood in the
world. 10 But [1]may the God of all grace,
[a]who called [2]us to His eternal glory by
Christ Jesus, after you have suffered a
while, [3]perfect, establish, strengthen, and
settle *you.* 11 [a]To Him *be* the glory and the
dominion forever and ever. Amen.

Farewell and Peace

12 By [a]Silvanus, our faithful brother as I
consider him, I have written to you briefly,
exhorting and testifying [b]that this is
the true grace of God in which you stand.
13 She who is in Babylon, elect together
with *you,* greets you; and *so does* [a]Mark
my son. 14 Greet one another with a kiss of
love.

Peace to you all who are in Christ Jesus.
Amen.

2 a Acts 20:28 b 1 Cor. 9:17 c 1 Tim. 3:3 *1 NU adds according to God*
3 a Ezek. 34:4 b Ps. 33:12 c Phil. 3:17 *1 masters*
4 a Heb. 13:20 b 2 Tim. 4:8
5 a Eph. 5:21 b Prov. 3:34 c Is. 57:15
8 *1 self-controlled 2 watchful* 3 NU, M omit *because*
10 a 1 Cor. 1:9 1 NU *the God of all grace,* 2 NU, M *you* 3 NU *will perfect*
11 a Rev. 1:6
12 a 2 Cor. 1:19 b Acts 20:24
13 a Acts 12:12, 25; 15:37, 39

1 Peter 5:8, 9

Dear Woman of Destiny,

The level of spiritual authority at which you operate is partly determined by the level of integrity and choices you make daily. First Peter 5.8, 9 declares, "Be sober, be vigilant; because your adversary the devil walks about like a roaring lion, seeking whom he may devour. Resist him, steadfast in the faith, knowing that the same sufferings are experienced by your brotherhood in the world."

Understanding godly principles will help you live a victorious lifestyle that will ultimately affect how successful you are at resisting the devil. When you compromise your integrity, you are making a declaration that minimizes your spiritual authority. Satan goes about night and day studying and contriving whom he may ensnare. In this passage, the apostle Peter identifies him as a "roaring lion" to communicate to us that he is strong, cruel, destructive, and a pursuer of souls. We are not to take him lightly and think that we can fool him. We are to be sober and vigilant, meaning we are not to be careless, but rather suspicious of constant danger from the adversary. Sobriety and watchfulness are necessary virtues at all times.

A simple formula that I believe God showed me years ago illustrates how the devil operates and why we end up feeling oppressed. The formula is this: D + C = O. Deception plus Compromise equals Oppression. Usually the first dart that the enemy attacks you with is deception. Then he tries to get you to compromise in some area in your life. The final result of these two (deception plus compromise) will be feeling oppressed. If you continue living in this state of deception, you will end up in bondage and needing deliverance. Every day, you should ask yourself, *In what way is the devil trying to deceive me today?* If you feel you have compromised in a specific area and have a sense of oppression, you need to question where you were first deceived. The enemy is in the business of sending darts that penetrate the mind. We must renew our minds with the cleansing Word of God, in order to discern between truth and deception.

The Scriptures teach us that the devil walks about, seeking whom he may devour. His whole design is to devour and destroy souls. One of his most preferred targets is our faith. If he can weaken and destroy our faith, he knows that we will not be able to please God. For "without faith, it is impossible to please Him" (Heb. 11:6). Every day you choose whether or not to please the Master. Your choices will affect your testimony and let the enemy know where you stand with God. Seek God's face in prayer and declare His promises over your life. God has anointed you with a specific purpose for His kingdom. You are a chosen vessel He wants to use. All you have to do is yield to Him.

A. G. Rodriguez

AUTHOR: *Traditionally Peter*
DATE: *A.D. 65–68*
THEME: *Remaining True to Biblical Faith*
KEY WORDS: *Know, Knowledge, Promise*

2 PETER

Dear Woman of Destiny,

This powerful book reminds us to cultivate Christian maturity, and it reminds us of the sufficiency of God's Word. There are many deceptions that pull against us as women today. Unless we carefully steep ourselves in God's Word, we can be deceived by false doctrine.

As women, we need to faithfully study God's Word every single day. Then, when people who teach false doctrine come our way, we will not be swayed away from the truth. I believe that we are living in the end-times; and so the things 2 Peter warns us about—destructive doctrines, false teachers, and false prophets—have already crept into our society. Christ could return any day now. We must be ready. Remember that God's Word is our daily bread. We cannot live without it.

With His love,

Cindy Jacobs

Greeting the Faithful

Simon Peter, a bondservant and
[a]apostle of Jesus Christ,

To those who have [1]obtained [b]like[2] precious faith with us by the righteousness of
our God and Savior Jesus Christ:

2 [a]Grace and peace be multiplied to you
in the knowledge of God and of Jesus our
Lord, 3 as His [a]divine power has given to
us all things that *pertain* to life and godliness, through the knowledge of Him [b]who
called us by glory and virtue, 4 [a]by which
have been given to us exceedingly great
and precious promises, that through
these you may be [b]partakers of the divine
nature, having escaped the [1]corruption
that is in the world through lust.

Lord, Your divine power has given to ____ all things that pertain to life and godliness, through the knowledge of You who called them by glory and virtue. May ____ receive the exceedingly great and precious promises You have given them.

FROM 2 PETER 1:3, 4

Fruitful Growth in the Faith

5 But also for this very reason, [a]giving
all diligence, add to your faith virtue, to
virtue [b]knowledge, 6 to knowledge self-
control, to self-control [1]perseverance, to
perseverance godliness, 7 to godliness
brotherly kindness, and [a]to brotherly
kindness love. 8 For if these things are
yours and abound, *you will be* neither
[1]barren [a]nor unfruitful in the knowledge
of our Lord Jesus Christ. 9 For he who
lacks these things is [a]shortsighted, even
to blindness, and has forgotten that he
was cleansed from his old sins.
10 Therefore, brethren, be even more
diligent [a]to make your call and election
sure, for if you do these things you will
never stumble; 11 for so an entrance will be
supplied to you abundantly into the everlasting kingdom of our Lord and Savior
Jesus Christ.

Peter's Approaching Death

12 For this reason [a]I will not be negligent to remind you always of these things,
[b]though you know and are established in
the present truth. 13 Yes, I think it is right,
[a]as long as I am in this [1]tent, [b]to stir you
up by reminding *you,* 14 [a]knowing that
shortly I *must* [1]put off my tent, just as
[b]our Lord Jesus Christ showed me.
15 Moreover I will be careful to ensure that
you always have a reminder of these
things after my [1]decease.

The Trustworthy Prophetic Word

16 For we did not follow [a]cunningly devised fables when we made known to you
the [b]power and [c]coming of our Lord Jesus
Christ, but were [d]eyewitnesses of His majesty. 17 For He received from God the Father honor and glory when such a voice
came to Him from the Excellent Glory:
[a]"This is My beloved Son, in whom I am
well pleased." 18 And we heard this voice
which came from heaven when we were
with Him on [a]the holy mountain.
19 [1]And so we have the prophetic word
confirmed, which you do well to heed as
a [a]light that shines in a dark place, [b]until
[c]the day dawns and the morning star rises
in your [d]hearts; 20 knowing this first, that
[a]no prophecy of Scripture is of any private
[1]interpretation, 21 for [a]prophecy never
came by the will of man, [b]but [1]holy men
of God spoke *as they were* moved by the
Holy Spirit.

Remember, the will of man is the biggest hindrance to God.

STANLEY FRODSHAM

Destructive Doctrines

2 But there were also false prophets
among the people, even as there will
be [a]false teachers among you, who will

CHAPTER 1
1 a Gal. 2:8 b Eph. 4:5 *1 received* *2 faith of the same value*
2 a Dan. 4:1
3 a 1 Pet. 1:5 b 1 Thess. 2:12
4 a 2 Cor. 1:20; 7:1 b [2 Cor. 3:18] *1 depravity*
5 a 2 Pet. 3:18 b 2 Pet. 1:2
6 *1 patience*
7 a Gal. 6:10
8 a [John 15:2] *1 useless*
9 a 1 John 2:9–11
10 a 1 John 3:19
12 a Phil. 3:1 b 1 Pet. 5:12
13 a [2 Cor. 5:1, 4] b 2 Pet. 3:1 *1* Body
14 a [2 Tim. 4:6] b John 13:36; 21:18, 19 *1* Die and leave this body
15 *1* Lit. *exodus, departure*
16 a 1 Cor. 1:17 b [Eph. 1:19–22] c [1 Pet. 5:4] d Matt. 17:1–5
17 a Matt. 17:5
18 a Matt. 17:1
19 a [John 1:4, 5, 9] b Prov. 4:18 c Rev. 2:28; 22:16 d [2 Cor. 4:5–7] *1* Or *We also have the more sure prophetic word*
20 a [Rom. 12:6] *1* Or *origin*
21 a [2 Tim. 3:16] b 2 Sam. 23:2 *1* NU *men spoke from God*

CHAPTER 2
1 a 1 Tim. 4:1, 2

2 Peter 2:1

Dear Woman of Destiny,

In 2 Peter 2:1, believers are warned that there may be false prophets and false teachers among them. These individuals teach and prophesy messages that attempt to draw people away from the truth that is found in Jesus Christ (see John 14:6). They are intent upon deceiving others to satisfy their own greed and lust for power. This warning is not given so believers will respond in fear and stop hearing true ministers, but to emphasize the necessity of recognizing the true from the false.

To properly discern truth from error, we must first understand that the devil is an accomplished counterfeiter! Any time God begins to set a plan in motion, Satan, the deceiver, formulates an alternate path, playing on our weaknesses. He is subtle, mixing a formula filled with valid truth, which cleverly disguises the lethal dose of poison made of lies and deceit. (Most carefully concealed deceptions are merely distortions of truth.) The undiscerning person cheerfully ingests the potent combination, believing she is receiving life and freedom. Instead, she has been corrupted by death and destruction.

Satan's most glaring limitation, however, is that he is only a counterfeiter, not a creator! This means he can only mimic something that is real. Criminals who counterfeit money do not make illegitimate three-dollar bills. Why? Because there are no *real* three-dollar bills. Therefore, if there are false teachers and false prophets we should not hear, we must conclude there are also true teachers and true prophets whom we should hear.

In Numbers 22, we find a man named Balaam who gave a true prophecy about the Messiah. Why then does 2 Peter 2:15 refer to him as a false prophet? Balaam followed after greed and led people astray into the ways of unrighteousness. He started out with a true word, but the motive of his heart corrupted his calling as he partnered with darkness rather than light.

When learning to discern, it is important that we recognize God has not left us stumbling about on our own, playing a guessing game where the winners successfully align themselves with righteousness, but the losers fall haphazardly into deception and destruction. No, God has given each believer everything needed to walk in truth, understanding, and wisdom, which yields complete victory in every situation.

God has faithfully given us the road map of His Word to successfully navigate even the most complex circumstances. His Word is truth, and all unrighteousness and falsehood pales in comparison to its light! (see John 17:17). As we read the truth of His Word and allow it to become a part of us, we will immediately be able to identify every counterfeit work.

God has also given us His Holy Spirit, whom John 16:13 refers to as the "Spirit of truth." When we are full of the Holy Spirit, we are guided into truth and are given the ability to discern between what is true and good and what is false and evil. He enables us to hear God's voice and learn His will so that we will never need to grope in the darkness or fear being led astray. As we seek after Him, we shall know the truth and that truth shall make us free! (see John 8:32).

Jane Hamon

secretly bring in destructive heresies, even denying the Lord who bought them, *and* bring on themselves swift destruction. 2And many will follow their destructive ways, because of whom the way of truth will be blasphemed. 3By covetousness they will exploit you with deceptive words; for a long time their judgment has not been idle, and their destruction [1]does not slumber.

Take care the spirit of the world, which is the spirit of slumber and false security, does not seize upon you.

CHARLES WESLEY

Doom of False Teachers

4For if God did not spare the angels who sinned, but cast *them* down to [1]hell and delivered *them* into chains of darkness, to be reserved for judgment; 5and did not spare the ancient world, but saved Noah, *one of* eight *people,* a preacher of righteousness, bringing in the flood on the world of the ungodly; 6and turning the cities of [a]Sodom and Gomorrah into ashes, condemned *them* to destruction, making *them* an example to those who afterward would live ungodly; 7and [a]delivered righteous Lot, *who was* oppressed by the filthy conduct of the wicked 8(for that righteous man, dwelling among them, [a]tormented *his* righteous soul from day to day by seeing and hearing *their* lawless deeds)— 9*then* [a]the Lord knows how to deliver the godly out of temptations and to reserve the unjust under punishment for the day of judgment, 10and especially [a]those who walk according to the flesh in the lust of uncleanness and despise authority. [b]*They are* presumptuous, self-willed. They are not afraid to speak evil of [1]dignitaries, 11whereas [a]angels, who are greater in power and might, do not bring a reviling accusation against them before the Lord.

Depravity of False Teachers

12But these, [a]like natural brute beasts made to be caught and destroyed, speak evil of the things they do not understand, and will utterly perish in their own corruption, 13[a]*and* will receive the wages of unrighteousness, *as* those who count it pleasure [b]to [1]carouse in the daytime. [c]*They are* spots and blemishes, [2]carousing in their own deceptions while [d]they feast with you, 14having eyes full of [1]adultery and that cannot cease from sin, enticing unstable souls. [a]*They have* a heart trained in covetous practices, *and are* accursed children. 15They have forsaken the right way and gone astray, following the way of [a]Balaam the *son* of Beor, who loved the wages of unrighteousness; 16but he was rebuked for his iniquity: a dumb donkey speaking with a man's voice restrained the madness of the prophet.

17[a]These are wells without water, [1]clouds carried by a tempest, for whom is reserved the blackness of darkness [2]forever.

Deceptions of False Teachers

18For when they speak great swelling *words* of emptiness, they allure through the lusts of the flesh, through lewdness, the ones who [1]have actually escaped from those who live in error. 19While they promise them liberty, they themselves are slaves of [1]corruption; [a]for by whom a person is overcome, by him also he is brought into [2]bondage. 20For if, after they [a]have escaped the pollutions of the world through the knowledge of the Lord and Savior Jesus Christ, they are [b]again entangled in them and overcome, the latter end is worse for them than the beginning. 21For [a]it would have been better for them not to have known the way of righteousness, than having known *it,* to turn from the holy commandment delivered to them. 22But it has happened to them according to the true proverb: [a]*"A dog returns to his own vomit,"* and, "a sow, having washed, to her wallowing in the mire."

God's Promise Is Not Slack

3 Beloved, I now write to you this second epistle (in *both of* which [a]I stir up your pure minds by way of reminder), 2that you may be mindful of the words [a]which were spoken before by the holy prophets, [b]and of the commandment of [1]us, the apostles of the Lord and Savior, 3knowing this first: that scoffers will come in the last days, [a]walking according to

---

3 [1] M *will not*
4 [1] Lit. *Tartarus*
6 [a] Gen. 19:1–26
7 [a] Gen. 19:16, 29
8 [a] Ps. 119:139
9 [a] Ps. 34:15–19
10 [a] Jude 4, 7, 8 [b] Jude 8 [1] *glorious ones,* lit. *glories*
11 [a] Jude 9
12 [a] Jude 10
13 [a] Phil. 3:19 [b] Rom. 13:13 [c] Jude 12 [d] 1 Cor. 11:20, 21 [1] *revel* [2] *reveling*
14 [a] Jude 11 [1] Lit. *an adulteress*
15 [a] Num. 22:5, 7
17 [a] Jude 12, 13 [1] NU *and mists* [2] NU omits *forever*
18 [1] NU *are barely escaping*
19 [a] John 8:34 [1] *depravity* [2] *slavery*
20 [a] Matt. 12:45 [b] [Heb. 6:4–6]
21 [a] Luke 12:47
22 [a] Prov. 26:11

CHAPTER 3
1 [a] 2 Pet. 1:13
2 [a] 2 Pet. 1:21 [b] Jude 17 [1] NU, M *the apostles of your Lord and Savior* or *your apostles of the Lord and Savior*
3 [a] 2 Pet. 2:10

2 Peter 3:9

Dear Woman of Destiny,

There were big walls around my broken heart. In search of true love, I had been disappointed. Maybe you can relate. If God wanted, I would gladly stay single my whole life, I told Him. But, in His infinite wisdom, He brought me, at the age of twenty-two, to my husband-to-be. In California, nine time zones away from my native Norway, He found someone with whom He entrusted my heart. Ken has modeled to me how Jesus loves broken lives into wholeness. In spite of our imperfections, we are still a match made in heaven! And to think, I almost missed out for fear of being hurt again!

So many people miss out on knowing Jesus Christ, the one and only true love. The same kind of fear of being hurt keeps them from releasing their hearts to the Lord. The fear of trusting their lives to a God they don't yet know robs so many people of the ultimate fulfillment of a lifelong relationship with Him. God doesn't have love as if it's something He could get and then lose. He *is* love! Everything Jesus did while walking the earth was motivated by love, expressing the very character of God.

I believe it's because of God's love for us that He hasn't yet judged the world, in spite of all the horrendous crimes and evil committed. We all know people who could have died one way or another, but the hand of God reached down and miraculously spared them. In His longsuffering, He extended their life span so they could store up riches in heaven instead of wrath in hell.

How countless and varied are the stories of the road to repentance that could be told by the millions of Christians in heaven and on earth! At this moment, there are multitudes in the valley of decision (see Ezek. 37). Every person alive represents a potential testimony to the saving grace of God: Jesus died on the cross so that none should perish. The rejection of His offer of forgiveness of sins has devastating eternal effects.

While in prayer one day, I believe the Holy Spirit allowed me to feel some of what it would be like to perish. For a span of four or five minutes, my body was in a frozen state. I experienced horrific fear with a sense of being trapped. Panic began to settle in, with grief unbearable, as the message of God's love and grace rolled over and over in my mind. There was a sense that I had rejected the gospel and that it was too late. There was nothing to shelter me from all the surrounding evil. There was no way out! If I had only repented of my sins! If I could just have another chance!

The scene changed. As death lost its grip, an overwhelming feeling of relief and joy overtook me. The Holy Spirit ministered the simple words, "Because of the blood of Jesus, you are able to go into the Holy of Holies." Thank God!

Every day is a gift from God—another chance to know Him and to let Him express His love through us to a dying world. He is not willing for a single soul to perish!

Solveig Henderson

their own lusts, 4and saying, "Where is
the promise of His coming? For since the
fathers fell asleep, all things continue as
they were from the beginning of [a]cre-
ation." 5For this they willfully forget: that
[a]by the word of God the heavens were of
old, and the earth [b]standing out of water
and in the water, 6[a]by which the world
that then existed perished, being flooded
with water. 7But [a]the heavens and the
earth *which* are now preserved by the
same word, are reserved for [b]fire until the
day of judgment and [1]perdition of ungodly men.

Lord, as ___ longs for Your coming, may they remember that with You one day is as a thousand years, and a thousand years as one day. You are not slack concerning Your promise but are longsuffering, not willing that any should perish but that all should come to repentance.

FROM 2 PETER 3:8, 9

8But, beloved, do not forget this one
thing, that with the Lord one day *is* as a
thousand years, and [a]a thousand years as
one day. 9[a]The Lord is not slack concerning *His* promise, as some count slack-
ness, but [b]is longsuffering toward [1]us,
[c]not willing that any should perish but
[d]that all should come to repentance.

The Day of the Lord

10But [a]the day of the Lord will come as
a thief in the night, in which [b]the heavens
will pass away with a great noise, and the
elements will melt with fervent heat; both
the earth and the works that are in it will
be [1]burned up. 11Therefore, since all these
things will be dissolved, what manner *of*
persons ought you to be [a]in holy conduct
and godliness, 12[a]looking for and hastening the coming of the day of God, because
of which the heavens will [b]be dissolved,
being on fire, and the elements will [c]melt
with fervent heat? 13Nevertheless we, according to His promise, look for [a]new
heavens and a [b]new earth in which righteousness dwells.

Endeavor always to remember that you are in the immediate presence of God, and strive to act as you would if you saw the Savior standing by your side.

RAYMOND T. RICHEY

Be Steadfast

14Therefore, beloved, looking forward
to these things, be diligent [a]to be found
by Him in peace, without spot and blameless; 15and consider *that* [a]the longsuffering of our Lord *is* salvation—as also our
beloved brother Paul, according to the
wisdom given to him, has written to you,
16as also in all his [a]epistles, speaking in
them of these things, in which are some
things hard to understand, which un-
taught and unstable *people* twist to their
own destruction, as *they do* also the [b]rest
of the Scriptures.

I must grow in grace; I must love God more; I must feel the power of divine things more.

WILLIAM WILBERFORCE

17You therefore, beloved, [a]since you
know *this* beforehand, [b]beware lest you
also fall from your own steadfastness, being led away with the error of the wicked;
18[a]but grow in the grace and knowledge of
our Lord and Savior Jesus Christ.
[b]To Him *be* the glory both now and forever. Amen.

4 a Gen. 6:1–7
5 a Gen. 1:6, 9 b Ps. 24:2; 136:6
6 a Gen. 7:11, 12, 21–23
7 a 2 Pet. 3:10, 12 b [2 Thess. 1:8] *1 destruction*
8 a Ps. 90:4
9 a Hab. 2:3 b Is. 30:18 c Ezek. 33:11 d [Rom. 2:4] *1* NU *you*
10 a Rev. 3:3; 16:15 b Ps. 102:25, 26 *1* NU *laid bare*, lit. *found*
11 a 1 Pet. 1:15
12 a 1 Cor. 1:7, 8 b Ps. 50:3 c Mic. 1:4
13 a Is. 65:17; 66:22 b Rev. 21:1
14 a 1 Cor. 1:8; 15:58
15 a Rom. 2:4
16 a 1 Cor. 15:24 b 2 Tim. 3:16
17 a Mark 13:23 b Eph. 4:14
18 a Eph. 4:15 b 2 Tim. 4:18

AUTHOR: *The Apostle John*
DATE: *About A.D. 90*
THEME: *Jesus Is the Son of God. Those Who Follow Him Must Live Righteously.*
KEY WORDS: *Love, Know, Life, Light, Fellowship*

1 JOHN

Dear Woman of Destiny,

What rich promises are contained in this book! One of the most powerful is that we can confess our sins and be forgiven. Thank God for the precious blood of the Lamb, which cleanses us from all unrighteousness.

The Holy Spirit warns us in 1 John not to love the world. As women, there seems to be a fine line between appreciating the beautiful things of this earth and loving them to the point of sin.

Other things, such as lust and pride, pull us. It seems that we are assaulted in our lives with the temptation to sin. Don't be deceived by the world and the media who say that sex outside of marriage is permissible if you are in love. The Bible calls such things sin.

I pray that you will learn to live a life of holiness and purity and that you will learn to live in the world in a way that glorifies God.

With His love,

Cindy Jacobs

What Was Heard, Seen, and Touched

That [a]which was from the beginning, which we have heard, which
we have [b]seen with our eyes,
[c]which we have looked upon, and [d]our
hands have handled, concerning the
[e]Word of life— 2 [a]the life [b]was manifested, and we have seen, [c]and bear witness,
and declare to you that eternal life which
was [d]with the Father and was manifested
to us— 3 that which we have seen and
heard we declare to you, that you also may
have fellowship with us; and truly our fellowship *is* [a]with the Father and with His
Son Jesus Christ. 4 And these things we
write to you [a]that [1]your joy may be full.

Fellowship with Him and One Another

5 [a]This is the message which we have
heard from Him and declare to you, that
[b]God is light and in Him is no darkness at
all. 6 [a]If we say that we have fellowship
with Him, and walk in darkness, we lie
and do not practice the truth. 7 But if we
[a]walk in the light as He is in the light, we
have fellowship with one another, and
[b]the blood of Jesus Christ His Son cleanses us from all sin.

I pray that ____ would confess their sins, O Lord, for You are faithful and just to forgive their sins and to cleanse them from all unrighteousness.

FROM 1 JOHN 1:9

8 If we say that we have no sin, we deceive ourselves, and the truth is not in us.
9 If we [a]confess our sins, He is [b]faithful
and just to forgive us *our* sins and to
[c]cleanse us from all unrighteousness.
10 If we say that we have not sinned, we
[a]make Him a liar, and His word is not
in us.

2 My little children, these things I write
to you, so that you may not sin. And
if anyone sins, [a]we have an Advocate with
the Father, Jesus Christ the righteous.
2 And [a]He Himself is the propitiation for
our sins, and not for ours only but [b]also
for the whole world.

God cannot declare one not guilty before he is cleansed from all sin and made holy by the blood of Christ.

FINIS JENNINGS DAKE

The Test of Knowing Him

3 Now by this we know that we know
Him, if we keep His commandments. 4 He
who says, "I know Him," and does not
keep His commandments, is a [a]liar, and
the truth is not in him. 5 But [a]whoever
keeps His word, truly the love of God [1]is
perfected [b]in him. By this we know that
we are in Him. 6 [a]He who says he abides in
Him [b]ought himself also to walk just as
He walked.
7 [1]Brethren, I write no new commandment to you, but an old commandment
which you have had [a]from the beginning.
The old commandment is the word which
you heard [2]from the beginning. 8 Again, [a]a
new commandment I write to you, which
thing is true in Him and in you, [b]because
the darkness is passing away, and [c]the
true light is already shining.
9 [a]He who says he is in the light, and
hates his brother, is in darkness until
now. 10 [a]He who loves his brother abides
in the light, and [b]there is no cause for
stumbling in him. 11 But he who [a]hates
his brother is in darkness and [b]walks in
darkness, and does not know where he is
going, because the darkness has blinded
his eyes.

Their Spiritual State

12 I write to you, little children,
Because [a]your sins are forgiven
you for His name's sake.
13 I write to you, fathers,
Because you have known Him
who is [a]from the beginning.
I write to you, young men,

CHAPTER 1
1 a [John 1:1] b John 1:14 c 2 Pet. 1:16 d Luke 24:39 e [John 1:1, 4, 14]
2 a John 1:4 b Rom. 16:26 c John 21:24 d [John 1:1, 18; 16:28]
3 a 1 Cor. 1:9
4 a John 15:11; 16:24 1 NU, M *our*
5 a 1 John 3:11 b [1 Tim. 6:16]
6 a [1 John 2:9–11]
7 a Is. 2:5 b [1 Cor. 6:11]
9 a Prov. 28:13 b [Rom. 3:24–26] c Ps. 51:2
10 a 1 John 5:10

CHAPTER 2
1 a Heb. 7:25; 9:24
2 a [Rom. 3:25] b John 1:29
4 a Rom. 3:4
5 a John 14:21, 23 b [1 John 4:12] 1 *has been completed*
6 a John 15:4 b 1 Pet. 2:21
7 a 1 John 3:11, 23; 4:21 1 NU *Beloved* 2 NU omits *from the beginning*
8 a John 13:34; 15:12 b Rom. 13:12 c [John 1:9; 8:12; 12:35]
9 a [1 Cor. 13:2]
10 a [1 John 3:14] b 2 Pet. 1:10
11 a [1 John 2:9; 3:15; 4:20] b John 12:35
12 a [1 Cor. 6:11]
13 a John 1:1

1 John 1:9

Dear Woman of Destiny,

One of the most tragic sights in Mexico, the beautiful land where I have labored for more than forty years, is the thousands of devout worshipers, both young and old, who walk for miles, sometimes even crawling on their knees, to a particular shrine or cathedral as an act of penitence. Ingrained into the religious culture is the concept of a God who must be appeased through "sacrifices" and suffering in order to receive forgiveness of sin. However, we don't have to do these things to be forgiven.

The simple message of 1 John 1:9 seems almost too good to be true. Yet it is true. If we confess our sins, He will not only forgive us, but will also cleanse us from all unrighteousness. How simple! How uncomplicated! No human effort or suffering is required to be forgiven. Even a child can understand the meaning.

But what is involved in "confessing our sins"? Surely, it is more than a quick, superficial confession, only to go on living the same lifestyle. Confession must begin with recognizing how sin hurts God. We must hate our sin, have "godly sorrow" (see 2 Cor. 7:9, 10), and then turn away from the sin. Experiencing genuine radical repentance is the only way to live, that our lives might be continually cleansed. Sin breaks our communion with the Father, but confession, which includes repentance, instantly restores this communion.

Once we have come in brokenness and repentance to God, confessing our sin, then we must lift our head, accept His forgiveness, and live guilt-free lives. Psychiatrists and other mental health workers say that unresolved guilt is the root of an assortment of emotional problems. The Word of God has the answer to this situation: Accept the fact that we are guilty; then confess our sin and receive God's pardon.

Like many other women, I have the propensity to feel guilty, usually over self-imposed burdens or religious traditions. But how many times I have come back to the promise of 1 John 1:9 and received the victory.

Several years ago my husband Victor, a well-respected pastor, had a near-burnout experience in which he seriously considered leaving the ministry after years of service. The Lord was gracious and didn't let this happen; instead He took us to some meetings where there was a genuine move of the Holy Spirit. At those meetings, He confronted my husband about his critical spirit toward other servants of the Lord. Upon being confronted through that quiet inner voice, Victor confessed his attitude of sin, truly repented, and immediately received a tremendous outpouring of joy. I can say he has been a new man ever since.

How often the "little foxes" (see Song 2:15), such as unkind attitudes and words, rob our joy and steal our communion with the Lord. We can restore this communion by just confessing our sin and letting Him cleanse us. You don't need to live under a load of guilt any longer. Thank the Lord today for His complete, yet simple, provision for receiving forgiveness.

Gloria Richards

Because you have overcome the
wicked one.
I write to you, little children,
Because you have [b]known the
Father.
14 I have written to you, fathers,
Because you have known Him
who is from the beginning.
I have written to you, young men,
Because [a]you are strong, and the
word of God abides in you,
And you have overcome the
wicked one.

Do Not Love the World

15 [a]Do not love the world or the things
in the world. [b]If anyone loves the world,
the love of the Father is not in him. 16 For
all that *is* in the world—the lust of the
flesh, [a]the lust of the eyes, and the pride
of life—is not of the Father but is of the
world. 17 And [a]the world is passing away,
and the lust of it; but he who does the will
of God abides forever.

O Father, I pray that _____ will not love the world or the things in the world. For all that is in the world—the lust of the flesh, the lust of the eyes, and the pride of life—is not of You but is of the world. May _____ do Your will and abide forever.

FROM 1 JOHN 2:15–17

Deceptions of the Last Hour

18 [a]Little children, [b]it is the last hour;
and as you have heard that [c]the[1] Antichrist is coming, [d]even now many anti-
christs have come, by which we know
[e]that it is the last hour. 19 [a]They went out
from us, but they were not of us; for [b]if
they had been of us, they would have continued with us; but *they went out* [c]that
they might be made manifest, that none
of them were of us.
20 But [a]you have an anointing [b]from the
Holy One, and [c]you[1] know all things. 21 I
have not written to you because you do
not know the truth, but because you know
it, and that no lie is of the truth.
22 [a]Who is a liar but he who denies that
[b]Jesus is the Christ? He is antichrist who
denies the Father and the Son. 23 [a]Whoev-
er denies the Son does not have the [b]Fa-
ther either; [c]he who acknowledges the
Son has the Father also.

The anointing of the Holy Spirit is given to illuminate His Word, to open the Scriptures, and to place the spiritual man in direct communication with the mind of God.

CHARLES F. PARHAM

Let Truth Abide in You

24 Therefore let that abide in you [a]which
you heard from the beginning. If what you
heard from the beginning abides in you,
[b]you also will abide in the Son and in the
Father. 25 [a]And this is the promise that He
has promised us—eternal life.
26 These things I have written to you
concerning those who *try to* [1]deceive you.
27 But the [a]anointing which you have received from Him abides in you, and [b]you
do not need that anyone teach you; but as
the same anointing [c]teaches you concerning all things, and is true, and is not a lie,
and just as it has taught you, you [1]will
abide in Him.

The Children of God

28 And now, little children, abide in
Him, that [1]when He appears, we may have
[a]confidence and not be ashamed before
Him at His coming. 29 [a]If you know that
He is righteous, you know that [b]everyone
who practices righteousness is born of
Him.

3 Behold [a]what manner of love the Father has bestowed on us, that [b]we
should be called children of [1]God! Therefore the world does not know [2]us, [c]be-
cause it did not know Him. 2 Beloved,
[a]now we are children of God; and [b]it has
not yet been revealed what we shall be,
but we know that when He is revealed,
[c]we shall be like Him, for [d]we shall see

13 b [Rom. 8:15–17]
14 a Eph. 6:10
15 a [Rom. 12:2] b James 4:4
16 a [Eccl. 5:10, 11]
17 a 1 Cor. 7:31
18 a John 21:5 b 1 Pet. 4:7 c 2 Thess. 2:3 d 2 John 7 e 1 Tim. 4:1 1 NU omits *the*
19 a Deut. 13:13 b Matt. 24:24 c 1 Cor. 11:19
20 a 2 Cor. 1:21 b Acts 3:14 c [John 16:13] 1 NU *you all know.*
22 a 2 John 7 b 1 John 4:3
23 a John 15:23 b John 5:23 c 1 John 4:15; 5:1
24 a 2 John 5, 6 b John 14:23
25 a John 3:14–16; 6:40; 17:2, 3
26 1 *lead you astray*
27 a [John 14:16; 16:13] b [Jer. 31:33] c [John 14:16] 1 NU omits *will*
28 a 1 John 3:21; 4:17; 5:14 1 NU *if*
29 a Acts 22:14 b 1 John 3:7, 10
CHAPTER 3
1 a [1 John 4:10] b [John 1:12] c John 15:18, 21; 16:3 1 NU adds *And we are.* 2 M *you*
2 a [Rom. 8:15, 16] b [Rom. 8:18, 19, 23] c Rom. 8:29 d [Ps. 16:11]

Him as He is. 3 [a]And everyone who has
this hope in Him purifies himself, just as
He is pure.

Sin and the Child of God

4 Whoever commits sin also commits
lawlessness, and [a]sin is lawlessness. 5 And
you know [a]that He was manifested [b]to
take away our sins, and [c]in Him there is
no sin. 6 Whoever abides in Him does not
sin. Whoever sins has neither seen Him
nor known Him.

7 Little children, let no one deceive you.
He who practices righteousness is righteous, just as He is righteous. 8 [a]He who
sins is of the devil, for the devil has sinned
from the beginning. For this purpose the
Son of God was manifested, [b]that He
might destroy the works of the devil.
9 Whoever has been [a]born of God does not
sin, for [b]His seed remains in him; and he
cannot sin, because he has been born of
God.

The Imperative of Love

10 In this the children of God and the
children of the devil are manifest: Whoever does not practice righteousness is not
of God, nor *is* he who does not love his
brother. 11 For this is the message that
you heard from the beginning, [a]that we
should love one another, 12 not as [a]Cain
who was of the wicked one and murdered
his brother. And why did he murder him?
Because his works were evil and his
brother's righteous.

13 Do not marvel, my brethren, if [a]the
world hates you. 14 We know that we have
passed from death to life, because we love
the brethren. He who does not love [1]*his*
brother abides in death. 15 [a]Whoever hates
his brother is a murderer, and you know
that [b]no murderer has eternal life abiding
in him.

The Outworking of Love

16 [a]By this we know love, [b]because He
laid down His life for us. And we also
ought to lay down *our* lives for the brethren. 17 But [a]whoever has this world's
goods, and sees his brother in need, and
shuts up his heart from him, how does the
love of God abide in him?

18 My little children, [a]let us not love in
word or in tongue, but in deed and in
truth. 19 And by this we [1]know [a]that we
are of the truth, and shall [2]assure our
hearts before Him. 20 [a]For if our heart

3 a 1 John 4:17
4 a Rom. 4:15
5 a 1 John 1:2; 3:8 b John 1:29 c [2 Cor. 5:21]
8 a Matt. 13:38 b Luke 10:18
9 a John 1:3; 3:3 b 1 Pet. 1:23
11 a [John 13:34; 15:12]
12 a Gen. 4:4, 8
13 a [John 15:18; 17:14]
14 1 NU omits *his brother*
15 a Matt. 5:21 b [Gal. 5:20, 21]
16 a [John 3:16] b John 10:11; 15:13
17 a Deut. 15:7
18 a Ezek. 33:31
19 a John 18:37 1 NU *shall know* 2 *persuade, set at rest*
20 a [1 Cor. 4:4, 5]
21 a [1 John 2:28; 5:14]
22 a Ps. 34:15 b John 8:29
23 a Matt. 22:39 1 M omits *us*
24 a John 14:23 b John 14:21; 17:21 c Rom. 8:9, 14, 16

CHAPTER 4
1 a 1 Cor. 14:29 b Matt. 24:5
2 a 1 Cor. 12:3
3 1 NU omits *that* 2 NU omits *Christ has come in the flesh*

condemns us, God is greater than our
heart, and knows all things. 21 Beloved, if
our heart does not condemn us, [a]we have
confidence toward God. 22 And [a]whatever
we ask we receive from Him, because we
keep His commandments [b]and do those
things that are pleasing in His sight.
23 And this is His commandment: that we
should believe on the name of His Son
Jesus Christ [a]and love one another, as He
gave [1]us commandment.

Father, I ask that ____ would keep Your commandment: that they should believe on the name of Your Son Jesus Christ and love one another.

FROM 1 JOHN 3:23

The Spirit of Truth and the Spirit of Error

24 Now [a]he who keeps His commandments [b]abides in Him, and He in him. And
[c]by this we know that He abides in us, by
the Spirit whom He has given us.

If we have the Holy Ghost we can prove the spirits, because everything the Holy Ghost does is confirmed by the Word. . . . everything must be measured by the Word.

MARIA WOODWORTH-ETTER

4 Beloved, do not believe every spirit,
but [a]test the spirits, whether they are
of God; because [b]many false prophets
have gone out into the world. 2 By this you
know the Spirit of God: [a]Every spirit that
confesses that Jesus Christ has come in
the flesh is of God, 3 and every spirit that
does not confess [1]that Jesus [2]Christ has
come in the flesh is not of God. And this

is the *spirit* of the Antichrist, which you
have heard was coming, and is now already in the world.
4You are of God, little children, and
have overcome them, because He who is
in you is greater than [a]he who is in the
world. 5[a]They are of the world. Therefore
they speak *as* of the world, and [b]the world
hears them. 6We are of God. He who
knows God hears us; he who is not of God
does not hear us. [a]By this we know the
spirit of truth and the spirit of error.

Knowing God Through Love

7[a]Beloved, let us love one another, for
love is of God; and everyone who [b]loves is
born of God and knows God. 8He who
does not love does not know God, for God
is love. 9[a]In this the love of God was manifested toward us, that God has sent His
only begotten [b]Son into the world, that
we might live through Him. 10In this is
love, [a]not that we loved God, but that He
loved us and sent His Son [b]*to be* the propitiation for our sins. 11Beloved, [a]if God
so loved us, we also ought to love one another.

O Lord, teach ____ to love others, for love is of You; and everyone who loves is born of You and knows You. He who does not love does not know You, for You are love.

FROM 1 JOHN 4:7, 8

Seeing God Through Love

12[a]No one has seen God at any time. If
we love one another, God abides in us, and
His love has been perfected in us. 13[a]By
this we know that we abide in Him, and
He in us, because He has given us of His
Spirit. 14And [a]we have seen and testify
that [b]the Father has sent the Son *as* Savior of the world. 15[a]Whoever confesses
that Jesus is the Son of God, God abides
in him, and he in God. 16And we have
known and believed the love that God has
for us. God is love, and [a]he who abides in
love abides in God, and God [b]in him.

4 a John 14:30; 16:11
5 a John 3:31 b John 15:19; 17:14
6 a [1 Cor. 2:12–16]
7 a 1 John 3:10, 11, 23 b 1 Thess. 4:9
9 a Rom. 5:8 b John 3:16
10 a Titus 3:5 b 1 John 2:2
11 a Matt. 18:33
12 a John 1:18
13 a John 14:20
14 a John 1:14 b John 3:17; 4:42
15 a [Rom. 10:9]
16 a [1 John 3:24] b [John 14:23]
17 a 1 John 2:28
19 a 1 John 4:10 *1* NU omits *Him*
20 a [1 John 2:4] b 1 John 4:12 *1* NU *he cannot*
21 a [Matt. 5:43, 44; 22:39]
CHAPTER 5
1 a 1 John 2:22; 4:2, 15 b John 1:13

If you want a simple word to characterize the person of God, all you have to do is to take four letters and write them over and over again—the word love—and that's God.

KATHRYN KUHLMAN

The Consummation of Love

17Love has been perfected among us in
this: that [a]we may have boldness in the
day of judgment; because as He is, so are
we in this world. 18 There is no fear
in love; but perfect love casts out fear,
because fear involves torment. But he
who fears has not been made perfect in
love. 19[a]We love [1]Him because He first
loved us.

What makes us love God is that He has first loved us, and loved us with a tender love, like a father pities his children, whose extreme weakness he knows.

FENELON

Obedience by Faith

20[a]If someone says, "I love God," and
hates his brother, he is a liar; for he who
does not love his brother whom he has
seen, [1]how can he love God [b]whom he has
not seen? 21And [a]this commandment we
have from Him: that he who loves God
must love his brother also.

5 Whoever believes that [a]Jesus is the
Christ is [b]born of God, and everyone
who loves Him who begot also loves him
who is begotten of Him. 2By this we know
that we love the children of God, when we

1 John 4:18

Dear Woman of Destiny,

I warn you of an insidious force that stands between you and your destiny in Christ—an adversary so strong it is capable of causing reason and wisdom to flee as it drives us to the brink of unbelief. Our deadly opponent is fear. Fear is not a mental state of mind or a bad attitude. It is a spirit, and it is *not* from God (see 2 Tim. 1:7).

It is sent by the enemy to torment your soul and defile your human spirit. It is after your power, love, and soundness of mind. It is empowered to the degree that you yield to its deception. Imaginary fears can become real if you believe in them. Even the most unfounded ones can alter the course of our lives and, in turn, change our destiny.

But, dear sister, you are not defenseless in this matter. God has provided a strong tower, a shelter of protection and defense from your enemy. There is a haven that fear cannot inhabit. There is no greater protection afforded you than to live in God's love while the love of God resides in you. It is here that you are hidden and inaccessible to the enemy. First John 4:18 tells us, "There is no fear in love; but perfect love casts out fear, because fear involves torment. But he who fears has not been made perfect in love."

The love of God drives or casts out fear. This description confirms that fear is a spiritual force that must be dealt with spiritually. We are to cast out spirits and deny our flesh. Fear is conquered when we resist the base human tendency to preserve ourselves.

The spirit of fear wants to prevent this from happening, so it tries to trick us into believing we must protect our *selves*. But the very nature of love opposes the nature of fear. Love lays down its life while fear tries to preserve it. I have learned that I am incapable of protecting myself. I have tried and failed. But love *never* fails.

Fear and love both operate from belief in the unseen. Love challenges us to doubt what we see and believe what we cannot. Fear urges us to believe what is seen while doubting the unseen. Fear displaces love, and love casts out fear. Fear is the spiritual force that is in direct opposition to God's love and protection in our lives.

Jesus conquered the greatest fear any of us will face—the fear of death. As our High Priest, He was moved with compassion by our weaknesses and understood not only the fear of death, but all our fears. By victoriously facing the greatest fear (death), He conquered all lesser fears and their bondages. This victory over fear, death, and the grave was won when He laid down His life as the supreme example of perfect love.

Woman of Destiny, escape the clutch of fear. Lovingly lay down your life and embrace His.

Lisa Bevere

love God and [a]keep His commandments.
3[a]For this is the love of God, that we keep
His commandments. And [b]His commandments are not burdensome. 4For [a]what-
ever is born of God overcomes the world.
And this is the victory that [b]has overcome
the world—[1]our faith. 5Who is he who
overcomes the world, but [a]he who believes that Jesus is the Son of God?

The Certainty of God's Witness

6This is He who came [a]by water and
blood—Jesus Christ; not only by water,
but by water and blood. [b]And it is the
Spirit who bears witness, because the
Spirit is truth. 7For there are three that
bear witness [1]in heaven: the Father, [a]the
Word, and the Holy Spirit; [b]and these
three are one. 8And there are three that
bear witness on earth: [a]the Spirit, the water, and the blood; and these three agree
as one.
9If we receive [a]the witness of men, the
witness of God is greater; [b]for this is the
witness of [1]God which He has testified of
His Son. 10He who believes in the Son of
God [a]has the witness in himself; he who
does not believe God [b]has made Him a
liar, because he has not believed the testimony that God has given of His Son.
11And this is the testimony: that God has
given us eternal life, and this life is in His
Son. 12[a]He who has the Son has [1]life; he
who does not have the Son of God does
not have life. 13These things I have written to you who believe in the name of the
Son of God, that you may know that you
have eternal life, [1]and that you may *continue to* believe in the name of the Son of
God.

Confidence and Compassion in Prayer

14Now this is the confidence that we
have in Him, that [a]if we ask anything according to His will, He hears us. 15And if
we know that He hears us, whatever we
ask, we know that we have the petitions
that we have asked of Him.
16If anyone sees his brother sinning a
sin *which does* not *lead* to death, he will
ask, and [a]He will give him life for those
who commit sin not *leading* to death.
[b]There is sin *leading* to death. [c]I do not
say that he should pray about that. 17[a]All
unrighteousness is sin, and there is sin
not *leading* to death.

Knowing the True—Rejecting the False

18We know that [a]whoever is born of
God does not sin; but he who has been
born of God [b]keeps[1] [2]himself, and the
wicked one does not touch him.

Thank You, Father, for writing these things to ____ who believes in the name of the Son of God, that they may know that they have eternal life and that they may continue to believe in the name of the Son of God.

FROM 1 JOHN 5:13

19We know that we are of God, and [a]the
whole world lies *under the sway of* the
wicked one.
20And we know that the [a]Son of God
has come and [b]has given us an understanding, [c]that we may know Him who is
true; and we are in Him who is true, in His
Son Jesus Christ. [d]This is the true God
[e]and eternal life.
21Little children, keep yourselves from
idols. Amen.

---

2 [a]John 15:10
3 [a]John 14:15 [b]Matt. 11:30; 23:4
4 [a]John 16:33 [b]1 John 2:13; 4:4 [1]M *your*
5 [a]1 Cor. 15:57
6 [a]John 1:31–34 [b][John 14:17]
7 [a][John 1:1] [b]John 10:30 [1]NU, M omit the words from *in heaven* (v. 7) through *on earth* (v. 8). Only 4 or 5 very late mss. contain these words in Greek.
8 [a]John 15:26
9 [a]John 5:34, 37; 8:17, 18 [b][Matt. 3:16, 17] [1]NU *God, that*
10 [a][Rom. 8:16] [b]John 3:18, 33
12 [a][John 3:15, 36; 6:47; 17:2, 3] [1]Or *the life*
13 [1]NU omits the rest of v. 13.
14 [a][1 John 2:28; 3:21, 22]
16 [a]Job 42:8 [b][Matt. 12:31] [c]Jer. 7:16; 14:11
17 [a]1 John 3:4
18 [a][1 Pet. 1:23] [b]James 1:27 [1]*guards* [2]NU *him*
19 [a]Gal. 1:4
20 [a]1 John 4:2 [b]Luke 24:45 [c]John 17:3 [d]Is. 9:6 [e]1 John 5:11, 12

AUTHOR: *The Apostle John*
DATE: *About A.D. 90*
THEME: *Warning About False Teachers*
KEY WORDS: *Love, Truth*

2 JOHN

Dear Woman of Destiny,

This short but powerful book speaks strongly to women today about the importance of being "gatekeepers" of our homes. The "elect lady" in this letter may have been a group of believers or a particular woman. In either case, she was admonished not to receive anyone into her house who taught deception. Women today need to heed this whether they are single women, wives, or mothers. The influence of television, radio, the Internet, and other media in our homes can create openings in our minds and in the minds of our children to the occult, to violence, and to the view that sexual promiscuity is permissible.

Second John 6 urges us to walk in love. Sometimes the greatest way we can show love is through putting strict standards into place. We need to be constantly alert to the state of our household in the areas of purity and holiness, and we need to guard against the words of the deceiver.

With His love,

Cindy Jacobs

Greeting the Elect Lady

The Elder,

To the [1]elect lady and her children, whom I love in truth, and not only
I, but also all those who have known [a]the
truth, 2because of the truth which abides
in us and will be with us forever:

Be more zealous for holy tempers, for long-suffering, gentleness, meekness, lowliness, and resignation; but be most zealous of all for love, the queen of all graces. . . .

JOHN WESLEY

3[a]Grace, mercy, *and* peace will be with
[1]you from God the Father and from the
Lord Jesus Christ, the Son of the Father,
in truth and love.

Father, help _____ look to themselves, that they do not lose those things they worked for, but that they may receive a full reward.

FROM 2 JOHN 8

Walk in Christ's Commandments

4I [a]rejoiced greatly that I have found
some of your children walking in truth, as
we received commandment from the Father. 5And now I plead with you, lady, not
as though I wrote a new commandment to
you, but that which we have had from the
beginning: [a]that we love one another.
6[a]This is love, that we walk according to
His commandments. This is the commandment, that [b]as you have heard from
the beginning, you should walk in it.

Beware of Antichrist Deceivers

7For [a]many deceivers have gone out
into the world [b]who do not confess Jesus
Christ *as* coming in the flesh. [c]This is a
deceiver and an antichrist. 8[a]Look to
yourselves, [b]that [1]we do not lose those
things we worked for, but *that* we may
receive a full reward.

9[a]Whoever [1]transgresses and does not
abide in the doctrine of Christ does not
have God. He who abides in the doctrine
of Christ has both the Father and the Son.
10If anyone comes to you and [a]does not
bring this doctrine, do not receive him
into your house nor greet him; 11for he
who greets him shares in his evil deeds.

It is the God of love and the Lord of grace who has revealed His Son Jesus Christ in His eternal glory. And I have been such a child of hell that I have dared to sin against this God.

ANDREW MURRAY

John's Farewell Greeting

12[a]Having many things to write to you,
I did not wish *to do so* with paper and ink;
but I hope to come to you and speak face
to face, [b]that our joy may be full.

13[a]The children of your elect sister
greet you. Amen.

1 a Col. 1:5 *1 chosen*
3 a 1 Tim. 1:2 *1* NU, M *us*
4 a 3 John 3, 4
5 a [John 13:34, 35; 15:12, 17]
6 a 1 John 2:5; 5:3 b 1 John 2:24
7 a 1 John 2:19; 4:1 b 1 John 4:2 c 1 John 2:22
8 a Mark 13:9 b Gal. 3:4 *1* NU *you*
9 a John 7:16; 8:31 *1* NU *goes ahead*
10 a Rom. 16:17
12 a 3 John 13, 14 b John 17:13
13 a 1 Pet. 5:13

AUTHOR: *The Apostle John*
DATE: *About A.D. 90*
THEME: *Practicing Hospitality Toward Genuine Christian Teachers*
KEY WORDS: *Love, Truth*

3 JOHN

Dear Woman of Destiny,

This short, but important, book gives us insight into the blessings in which God wants us to walk. These include health, the prosperity of our soul, and emotional stability. In our daily living, many problems come our way that threaten to rob us of these blessings; and no one goes through life without encountering great challenges. It is in these times that we must cling to the promises of God and claim that we are healed, stable and blessed in our finances, and can walk in emotional peace.

Of course, many times it takes a miracle to stand for these things, but then we serve a miracle working God, don't we?

With His love,

Cindy Jacobs

Greeting to Gaius

The Elder,

To the beloved Gaius, [a]whom I
love in truth:

O Lord, I pray that _____
may prosper in all things
and be in health, just as
their soul prospers.
FROM 3 JOHN 2

2 Beloved, I pray that you may prosper in all things and be in health, just as
your soul prospers. 3 For I [a]rejoiced
greatly when brethren came and testified
of the truth *that is* in you, just as you walk
in the truth. 4 I have no greater [a]joy than
to hear that [b]my children walk in [1]truth.

Gaius Commended for Generosity

5 Beloved, you do faithfully whatever
you do for the brethren [1]and for strangers, 6 who have borne witness of your love
before the church. *If* you send them forward on their journey in a manner worthy
of God, you will do well, 7 because they
went forth for His name's sake, [a]taking
nothing from the Gentiles. 8 We therefore
ought to [a]receive[1] such, that we may become fellow workers for the truth.

1 a 2 John 1

3 a 2 John 4

4 a 1 Thess. 2:19, 20 b [1 Cor. 4:15] *1* NU *the truth*

5 *1* NU *and especially for*

7 a 1 Cor. 9:12, 15

8 a Matt. 10:40 *1* NU *support*

10 a Prov. 10:8, 10 *1 talking nonsense*

11 a Ps. 34:14; 37:27 b [1 John 2:29; 3:10] c [1 John 3:10] *1* NU, M omit *but*

12 a 1 Tim. 3:7 b John 19:35; 21:24 *1 testify*

13 a 2 John 12

Diotrephes and Demetrius

9 I wrote to the church, but Diotrephes,
who loves to have the preeminence
among them, does not receive us.
10 Therefore, if I come, I will call to mind
his deeds which he does, [a]prating[1] against
us with malicious words. And not content
with that, he himself does not receive the
brethren, and forbids those who wish to,
putting *them* out of the church.

11 Beloved, [a]do not imitate what is evil,
but what is good. [b]He who does good is of
God, [1]but he who does evil has not seen
[c]God.

12 Demetrius [a]has a *good* testimony
from all, and from the truth itself. And we
also [1]bear witness, [b]and you know that
our testimony is true.

The Holy Scriptures
are our letter from home.
ST. AUGUSTINE

Farewell Greeting

13 [a]I had many things to write, but I do
not wish to write to you with pen and ink;
14 but I hope to see you shortly, and we
shall speak face to face.

Peace to you. Our friends greet you.
Greet the friends by name.

3 John 2

Dear Woman of Destiny,

"I pray that you may you prosper . . . as your soul prospers," John wrote to Gaius. In that statement, there are two inherent implications: first, that Gaius wasn't currently prospering; and second, that Gaius's soul was prospering—to the degree that John prayed the other aspects of his life would do equally well!

All too often, we define prosperity by the things we have or how well our lives are going. But John was writing in a time when the church was facing increasing opposition and persecution. While it is difficult to precisely date the writing of John's epistles, the Roman rulers at the end of the first century seemed to delight in imprisoning, harassing, and killing Christians. This was not what we would typically think of as a "prosperous" environment.

And we all face situations that leave us feeling "less than prosperous."

You may be facing physical or financial challenge. There may have been a recent death in the family, or one of the children may be walking away from the Lord. You may be facing a layoff from your job. You may even be challenged by persecution or false accusation simply because you are a believer. But, like John, in the midst of tough times, we can pray for prosperity.

Interestingly enough, *prosper* literally means "to help on the road" or "to reach successfully." John isn't praying that Gaius will necessarily have riches here on earth, but he is acknowledging that God wants to give us what we need to "help us on the road" so that we can "successfully reach" the destiny He has for us.

God is not intimidated by the things we have, nor does He hold valueless the physical, temporal realm in which we live (see Matt. 6:25–33). But "things" aren't the stuff life is made of. There is a realm He calls us to that is "more real": It is spiritual, it is invisible, and it is eternal (see 2 Cor. 4:18). That is where the real treasure is! (see Matt. 6:19–21).

So what makes us prosper?

First, John says of Gaius that "the truth . . . is in you" and "you walk in the truth" (3 John 3). Gaius didn't just know the Word; he lived it. Second, John writes about Gaius's love for the church (see vv. 5, 6). Third, Paul gives us another hint on how this prosperity of soul can take place. In Philippians 4:12, he says that he has learned "how to be abased, and . . . how to abound." But living in two radically different stages of life is based on *contentment* (see v. 11). Paul isn't looking longingly for "better times ahead," or nostalgically at the "the good ol' days"; he recognizes that wherever he is or whatever is happening, Jesus is at work! (see v. 13).

Don't limit your soul's prosperity by what is happening externally. We all have tough times. But as we allow our souls to prosper—in truth, love, and contentment—we will see prosperity take place in our lives from the inside out!

Rebecca Bauer

AUTHOR: *Jude*
DATE: *A.D. 65–68*
THEME: *Contending for the Faith*
KEY WORDS: *Contend, the Faith, Keep*

JUDE

Dear Woman of Destiny,

Jude admonishes us to contend earnestly for the faith. Evidently there were not only false teachers creeping into the church, but also those who turned from the grace of God to immoral and sensual lifestyles. This happens in the church today. As women of destiny, we must be alert and warn those who are being swayed by humanistic philosophies.

Another important point, especially for those involved in spiritual warfare, is that we are not to arrogantly rebuke Satan. The Bible calls this reviling accusations. While we can take authority over the works of darkness, we must never do so in our own strength or might. This is why it is critical that we learn about brokenness and humility. Pride will get us into trouble. Always remember that we walk in His strength, His name, and His might. Our hope is found in His word, which says that He "is able to keep [us] from stumbling, and to present [us] faultless" before the throne (see v. 24).

With His love,

Cindy Jacobs

Greeting to the Called

Jude, a bondservant of Jesus Christ,
and [a]brother of James,

To those who are [b]called, [1]sanctified by
God the Father, and [c]preserved in Jesus
Christ:

2 Mercy, [a]peace, and love be multiplied
to you.

Contend for the Faith

3 Beloved, while I was very diligent to
write to you [a]concerning our common
salvation, I found it necessary to write to
you exhorting [b]you to contend earnestly
for the faith which was once for all delivered to the saints. 4 For certain men have
crept in unnoticed, who long ago were
marked out for this condemnation, ungodly men, who turn the grace of our God
into lewdness and deny the only Lord
[1]God and our Lord Jesus Christ.

Old and New Apostates

5 But I want to remind you, though you
once knew this, that [a]the Lord, having
saved the people out of the land of Egypt,
afterward destroyed those who did not believe. 6 And the angels who did not keep
their [1]proper domain, but left their own
abode, He has reserved in everlasting
chains under darkness for the judgment
of the great day; 7 as [a]Sodom and Gomorrah, and the cities around them in a
similar manner to these, having given
themselves over to sexual immorality and
gone after strange flesh, are set forth as an
example, suffering the [1]vengeance of eternal fire.
8 [a]Likewise also these dreamers defile
the flesh, reject authority, and [b]speak evil
of [1]dignitaries. 9 Yet Michael the archangel, in [1]contending with the devil,
when he disputed about the body of Moses, dared not bring against him a reviling
accusation, but said, [a]"The Lord rebuke
you!" 10 [a]But these speak evil of whatever they do not know; and whatever they
know naturally, like brute beasts, in these
things they corrupt themselves. 11 Woe to
them! For they have gone in the way [a]of
Cain, [b]have run greedily in the error of
Balaam for profit, and perished [c]in the rebellion of Korah.

Apostates Depraved and Doomed

12 These are [1]spots in your love feasts,
while they feast with you without fear,
serving *only* themselves. *They are* clouds
without water, carried [2]about by the
winds; late autumn trees without fruit,
twice dead, pulled up by the roots; 13 [a]rag-
ing waves of the sea, [b]foaming up their
own shame; wandering stars [c]for whom is
reserved the blackness of darkness forever.

The hardship and suffering involved in real spiritual warfare are too great for any motive but that of love.

CATHERINE BOOTH

14 Now Enoch, the seventh from Adam,
prophesied about these men also, saying,
"Behold, the Lord comes with ten thousands of His saints, 15 to execute judgment
on all, to convict all who are ungodly
among them of all their ungodly deeds
which they have committed in an ungodly
way, and of all the [a]harsh things which
ungodly sinners have spoken against
Him."

Apostates Predicted

16 These are grumblers, complainers,
walking according to their own lusts; and
they [a]mouth great swelling *words*, [b]flat-
tering people to gain advantage. 17 [a]But
you, beloved, remember the words which
were spoken before by the apostles of our
Lord Jesus Christ: 18 how they told you
that [a]there would be mockers in the last
time who would walk according to their
own ungodly lusts. 19 These are [1]sensual
persons, who cause divisions, not having
the Spirit.

Maintain Your Life with God

20 But you, beloved, [a]building yourselves up on your most holy faith, [b]pray-
ing in the Holy Spirit, 21 keep yourselves

1 [a]Acts 1:13 [b]Rom. 1:7 [c]John 17:11, 12 [1]NU *beloved*
2 [a]1 Pet. 1:2
3 [a]Titus 1:4 [b]Phil. 1:27
4 [1]NU omits *God*
5 [a]1 Cor. 10:5–10
6 [1]*own*
7 [a]Gen. 19:24 [1]*punishment*
8 [a]2 Pet. 2:10 [b]Ex. 22:28 [1]*glorious ones*, lit. *glories*
9 [a]Zech. 3:2 [1]*arguing*
10 [a]2 Pet. 2:12
11 [a]Gen. 4:3–8 [b]2 Pet. 2:15 [c]Num. 16:1–3, 31–35
12 [1]*stains*, or *hidden reefs* [2]NU, M *along*
13 [a]Is. 57:20 [b][Phil. 3:19] [c]2 Pet. 2:17
15 [a]1 Sam. 2:3
16 [a]2 Pet. 2:18 [b]Prov. 28:21
17 [a]2 Pet. 3:2
18 [a][1 Tim. 4:1]
19 [1]*soulish* or *worldly*
20 [a]Col. 2:7 [b][Rom. 8:26]

Jude 9

Dear Woman of Destiny,

I can remember misbehaving as a child and hearing my mother telling me to stop. "Why?" I asked. "Because I said so," she replied. "That's why!" Those words sounded so powerful to me. So, when my younger brothers began fighting while I was babysitting them, I tried my mother's technique. "Stop doing that!" I shouted. "Why?" they yelled back. "Because I said so; that's why!" Well, you guessed it, a major war broke out between siblings. My mother's method didn't work for me.

I was trying to overpower my brothers with my own strength, to prove that I was in control, that I was the boss, the one in authority. I was determined to get them to obey me. Crying to my mother, I asked her how to get my brothers to listen to me and obey me while she was gone. She gently whispered in my ear, "Tell them because Mom says so, that's why, and she left me in charge."

As Satan hurls his attacks and threats at you, your family, friends, and others, you must remember a key principle: When Jesus went to heaven, He left us in charge. The Lord has called us to be His representatives and to enforce His kingdom here on earth. Keep this in your heart as you enter into the battle—*Your will, Lord, not mine, be done.*

First, you must come into the presence of the Most High God, seeking His will, purpose and battle plan. Realize you can do nothing without Christ. You walk in danger when you presume to know the will of God without seeking His face. You walk in victory when you draw near to God and humble yourself under His mighty hand. Your motive should be the same as Christ's—to do the will of the Father.

You can enter the battle knowing you have the Victor living in you. Set yourself in agreement with what God says about you. You are His workmanship (see Eph. 2:10). You have the mind of Christ (see 1 Cor. 2:16). You are His hands, feet, and mouth here on earth; and He has given you His authority (see Luke 10:19).

Satan, filled with pride, was cast from heaven. He continues to be motivated by pride and attacks you with this same spirit. You must war in the opposite spirit. Keep in mind, when you fight from a position of humility in Christ, rather than from pride and your own strength, you will see victory. Do not respond with hurt, bitterness, pride, arrogance, or anger—but rather with humility, compassion, love, forgiveness, and confidence in the Lord and His promises.

Your motive for warfare must be to lift Jesus higher. When you walk in humility under the authority of the Lord Jesus, you will walk in true authority. When you speak to the enemy from this position of authority in Christ, he will tremble, flee from you, and be defeated.

Obey the Word, keep yourself pure, walk humbly before God, place yourself under godly leadership, and the Lord will be well pleased to grant you the victory.

Tommi Femrite

To You, Lord, who are able to keep ____ from stumbling and to present them faultless before the presence of Your glory with exceeding joy, to You our Savior, who alone are wise, be glory and majesty, dominion and power, both now and forever. Amen.

FROM JUDE 24, 25

in the love of God, [a]looking for the mercy
of our Lord Jesus Christ unto eternal life.
22 And on some have compassion, [1]mak-
ing a distinction; 23 but [a]others save [1]with
fear, [b]pulling *them* out of the [2]fire, hating
even [c]the garment defiled by the flesh.

Glory to God

24 [a]Now to Him who is able to keep
[1]you from stumbling,
And [b]to present *you* faultless
Before the presence of His glory
with exceeding joy,
25 To [1]God our Savior,
[2]Who alone is wise,
Be glory and majesty,
Dominion and [3]power,
Both now and forever.
Amen.

21 [a] Titus 2:13
22 [1] NU *who are doubting* (or *making distinctions*)
23 [a] Rom. 11:14 [b] Amos 4:11 [c] [Zech. 3:4, 5] [1] NU omits *with fear* [2] NU adds *and on some have mercy with fear*
24 [a] [Eph. 3:20] [b] Col. 1:22 [1] M *them*
25 [1] NU *the only God our* [2] NU *Through Jesus Christ our Lord, Be glory* [3] NU adds *Before all time,*

Author: *The Apostle John*
Date: *A.D. 70–95*
Theme: *The Lord Our God the Almighty Reigns*
Key Words: *Throne, Lamb, Overcomes, Seven, I Saw*

Revelation

Dear Woman of Destiny,

This last and final book of the Bible is an incredibly powerful revelation given to the apostle John during an extremely trying time for the church. It warned of intensified struggle and anti-Christian behavior. Many are suffering from these things today. People are being martyred for Christ today. Some say up to 100,000 or more give their lives for the cause of the gospel each year.

Revelation gives sweeping and powerful promises to those who overcome! In scene after scene, we are caught up and are able to mingle our voices with the throng of heaven, shouting, "Worthy is the Lamb who was slain!" Why don't you take a moment before you study this book to join with the redeemed from many nations and tribes in proclaiming, "Holy are You, Lord God Almighty!"?

Pray with me right now:

Father in heaven, open my eyes to see what You have revealed to us through the Book of Revelation. Give me ears to hear the truths that You whisper in my heart. In Jesus' name, Amen.

With His love,

Cindy Jacobs

Introduction and Benediction

The Revelation of Jesus Christ, [a]which God gave Him to show His servants—things which must [1]shortly take place. And [b]He sent and signified *it* by His angel to His servant John, 2[a]who bore witness to the word of God, and to the testimony of Jesus Christ, to all things [b]that he saw. 3[a]Blessed *is* he who reads and those who hear the words of this prophecy, and keep those things which are written in it; for [b]the time *is* near.

Greeting the Seven Churches

4John, to the seven churches which are in Asia:

Grace to you and peace from Him [a]who is and [b]who was and who is to come, [c]and from the seven Spirits who are before His throne, 5and from Jesus Christ, [a]the faithful [b]witness, the [c]firstborn from the dead, and [d]the ruler over the kings of the earth.

To Him [e]who [1]loved us [f]and washed us from our sins in His own blood, 6and has [a]made us [1]kings and priests to His God and Father, [b]to Him *be* glory and dominion forever and ever. Amen.

7Behold, He is coming with [a]clouds, and every eye will see Him, even [b]they who pierced Him. And all the tribes of the earth will mourn because of Him. Even so, Amen.

8[a]"I am the Alpha and the Omega, [1]*the* Beginning and *the* End," says the [2]Lord, [b]"who is and who was and who is to come, the [c]Almighty."

It is Jesus first, last, and all the time.

MARIA WOODWORTH-ETTER

Vision of the Son of Man

9I, John, [1]both your brother and [a]companion in the tribulation and [b]kingdom and patience of Jesus Christ, was on the island that is called Patmos for the word of God and for the testimony of Jesus Christ. 10[a]I was in the Spirit on [b]the Lord's Day, and I heard behind me [c]a loud voice, as of a trumpet, 11saying, [1]"I am the Alpha and the Omega, the First and the Last," and, "What you see, write in a book and send *it* to the seven churches [2]which are in Asia: to Ephesus, to Smyrna, to Pergamos, to Thyatira, to Sardis, to Philadelphia, and to Laodicea."

12Then I turned to see the voice that spoke with me. And having turned [a]I saw seven golden lampstands, 13[a]and in the midst of the seven lampstands [b]*One* like the Son of Man, [c]clothed with a garment down to the feet and [d]girded about the chest with a golden band. 14His head and [a]hair *were* white like wool, as white as snow, and [b]His eyes like a flame of fire; 15[a]His feet *were* like fine brass, as if refined in a furnace, and [b]His voice as the sound of many waters; 16[a]He had in His right hand seven stars, [b]out of His mouth went a sharp two-edged sword, [c]and His countenance *was* like the sun shining in its strength. 17And [a]when I saw Him, I fell at His feet as dead. But [b]He laid His right hand on me, saying [1]to me, "Do not be afraid; [c]I am the First and the Last. 18[a]I *am* He who lives, and was dead, and behold, [b]I am alive forevermore. Amen. And [c]I have the keys of [1]Hades and of Death. 19[1]Write the things which you have [a]seen, [b]and the things which are, [c]and the things which will take place after this. 20The [1]mystery of the seven stars which you saw in My right hand, and the seven golden lampstands: The seven stars are [a]the [2]angels of the seven churches, and [b]the seven lampstands [3]which you saw are the seven churches.

The Loveless Church

2 "To the [1]angel of the church of Ephesus write,

'These things says [a]He who holds the seven stars in His right hand, [b]who walks in the midst of the seven golden lampstands: 2[a]"I know your works, your labor, your [1]patience, and that you cannot [2]bear those who are evil. And [b]you have tested those [c]who say they are apostles and are not, and have found them liars; 3and you

CHAPTER 1
1 a John 3:32 b Rev. 22:6 *1 quickly* or *swiftly*
2 a 1 Cor. 1:6 b 1 John 1:1
3 a Luke 11:28 b James 5:8
4 a Ex. 3:14 b John 1:1 c [Is. 11:2]
5 a John 8:14 b Is. 55:4 c [Col. 1:18] d Rev. 17:14 e John 13:34 f Heb. 9:14 *1* NU *loves us and freed;* M *loves us and washed*
6 a 1 Pet. 2:5, 9 b 1 Tim. 6:16 *1* NU, M *a kingdom*
7 a Matt. 24:30 b Zech. 12:10–14
8 a Is. 41:4 b Rev. 4:8; 11:17 c Is. 9:6 *1* NU, M omit *the Beginning and the End* *2* NU, M *Lord God*
9 a Phil. 1:7 b [2 Tim. 2:12] *1* NU, M omit *both*
10 a Acts 10:10 b Acts 20:7 c Rev. 4:1
11 *1* NU, M omit *"I am the Alpha and the Omega, the First and the Last," and,* *2* NU, M omit *which are in Asia*
12 a Ex. 25:37
13 a Rev. 2:1 b Ezek. 1:26 c Dan. 10:5 d Rev. 15:6
14 a Dan. 7:9 b Dan. 10:6
15 a Ezek. 1:7 b Ezek. 1:24; 43:2
16 a Rev. 1:20; 2:1; 3:1 b Is. 49:2 c Matt. 17:2
17 a Ezek. 1:28 b Dan. 8:18; 10:10, 12 c Is. 41:4; 44:6; 48:12 *1* NU, M omit *to me*
18 a Rom. 6:9 b Rev. 4:9 c Ps. 68:20 *1* Lit. *Unseen;* the unseen realm
19 a Rev. 1:9–18 b Rev. 2:1 c Rev. 4:1 *1* NU, M *Therefore, write*
20 a Rev. 2:1 b Zech. 4:2 *1 hidden truth* *2* Or *messengers* *3* NU, M omit *which you saw*
CHAPTER 2 **1** a Rev. 1:16 b Rev. 1:13 *1* Or *messenger*
2 a Ps. 1:6 b 1 John 4:1 c 2 Cor. 11:13 *1 perseverance* *2 endure*

have persevered and have patience, and
have labored for My name's sake and have
[a]not become weary. 4 Nevertheless I
have *this* against you, that you have left
your first love. 5Remember therefore
from where you have fallen; repent and do
the first works, [a]or else I will come to you
quickly and remove your lampstand from
its place—unless you repent. 6But this
you have, that you hate the deeds of the
Nicolaitans, which I also hate.
7[a]"He who has an ear, let him hear
what the Spirit says to the churches. To
him who overcomes I will give [b]to eat
from [c]the tree of life, which is in the
midst of the Paradise of God." '

My case is rather like that of the Church of Ephesus; I have not been faithful to the talents committed to my trust, and have lost my first love . . . I do not, I will not, despair; for ever since my sad defection, when I was almost without hope, when I had forgotten God, yet I then found He had not forgotten me.

SUSANNA WESLEY

The Persecuted Church

8"And to the [1]angel of the church in
Smyrna write,
'These things says [a]the First and the
Last, who was dead, and came to life: 9"I
know your works, tribulation, and poverty
(but you are [a]rich); and *I know* the blasphemy of [b]those who say they are Jews
and are not, [c]but *are* a [1]synagogue of Satan. 10[a]Do not fear any of those things
which you are about to suffer. Indeed, the
devil is about to throw *some* of you into
prison, that you may be tested, and you
will have tribulation ten days. [b]Be faithful
until death, and I will give you [c]the crown
of life.
11[a]"He who has an ear, let him hear
what the Spirit says to the churches. He
who overcomes shall not be hurt by [b]the
second death." '

Father, as ___ endures testing through tribulation, may they be faithful until death, for You will give them the crown of life.

FROM REVELATION 2:10

The Compromising Church

12"And to the [1]angel of the church in
Pergamos write,
'These things says [a]He who has the
sharp two-edged sword: 13"I know your
works, and where you dwell, where Satan's throne *is*. And you hold fast to My
name, and did not deny My faith even in
the days in which Antipas *was* My faithful
martyr, who was killed among you, where
Satan dwells. 14But I have a few things
against you, because you have there those
who hold the doctrine of [a]Balaam, who
taught Balak to put a stumbling block before the children of Israel, [b]to eat things
sacrificed to idols, [c]and to commit sexual
immorality. 15Thus you also have those
who hold the doctrine of the Nicolaitans,
[1]which thing I hate. 16Repent, or else I
will come to you quickly and [a]will fight
against them with the sword of My
mouth.
17"He who has an ear, let him hear what
the Spirit says to the churches. To him
who overcomes I will give some of the
hidden [a]manna to eat. And I will give him
a white stone, and on the stone [b]a new
name written which no one knows except
him who receives *it*." '

The Corrupt Church

18"And to the [1]angel of the church in
Thyatira write,
'These things says the Son of God, [a]who
has eyes like a flame of fire, and His feet
like fine brass: 19[a]"I know your works,
love, [1]service, faith, and your [2]patience;
and *as* for your works, the last *are* more

3 a Gal. 6:9
5 a Matt. 21:41
7 a Matt. 11:15 b [Rev. 22:2, 14] c [Gen. 2:9; 3:22]
8 a Rev. 1:8, 17, 18 *1 Or messenger*
9 a Luke 12:21 b Rom. 2:17 c Rev. 3:9 *1 congregation*
10 a Matt. 10:22 b Matt. 24:13 c James 1:12
11 a Rev. 13:9 b [Rev. 20:6, 14; 21:8]
12 a Rev. 1:16; 2:16 *1 Or messenger*
14 a Num. 31:16 b Acts 15:29 c 1 Cor. 6:13
15 *1* NU, M *likewise.*
16 a 2 Thess. 2:8
17 a Ex. 16:33, 34 b Rev. 3:12
18 a Rev. 1:14, 15 *1 Or messenger*
19 a Rev. 2:2 *1* NU, M *faith, service* *2 perseverance*

Revelation 2:4

Dear Woman of Destiny,

At age nine I accepted the Lord into my heart. Subsequent years have continually displayed the wonder of His love. They have also presented a challenge in learning how to respond to this amazing reality.

During the 1960s, my life was filled with the joys and opportunities of being a young wife and mother. As the daughter of a pastor, I knew the importance of seeking God's will for our lives and of being involved in Christian activity. My focus was filled with church, family, and work; but it was in the midst of "the good life" that I lost sight of God's higher vision—the vision of a deep and rich love relationship with Him!

It was not that church activity was the problem, nor other responsibilities. There are many wonderful things that come out of one's consistent commitment to church and family life. The issue was that I had allowed the good to become an enemy to what was best. Even good things can keep us from knowing the Lord as our first love.

When John the apostle wrote Revelation 2:4, it was to address this issue. This passage reveals that the church at Ephesus had become sidetracked in its priorities. The complaint brought by the Lord against the church was not for what they were doing, but for what they were failing to do! They had elevated the activity of kingdom work to a place of honor that belonged only to the King! He was calling them to return to their first love.

Failure to allow Jesus the highest place of honor in our lives will always displease the Father. It will always leave us with a compelling sense of loss, of incompleteness, a void, even an agony of heart that yearns for "something more" while struggling to identify the real issues of inner conflict.

I have discovered we will not reach for more until we are dissatisfied with our current level of relationship. For me, the 1970s challenged the place where I was in spiritual experience. I began to immerse my life in prayer opportunities and the Word. Truth called for repentance. I was filled with a deep hunger and a firm resolve to break free from the grip of mediocrity that always chokes out the best things from God. I prayed earnestly that God would launch me out into the deep with Him—that He would swing me across that huge gulf called the "cares of life," a gulf that so easily separates us from essential steps to furthering our God-ordained destiny. The decade became a season of new beginnings; my heart was being prepared for greater adventures with God.

This is the marvel of it all: Such adventures will always stretch you past yourself, past your fears and inability, past your struggles and bondages, while developing a clearer focus and a stronger faith. You will not only experience more of God's love, but you will be amazed at the exciting ways He arranges for you to share His love and minister in His name. Our vision of life is always limited; His vision is always greater.

Accept the challenge. Be passionate for Jesus. Embrace your first love! Only here will you discover grace perfectly fitted for your future. He is a phenomenal God!

Barbara James

than the first. 20 Nevertheless I have [1]a few things against you, because you allow [2]that woman [a]Jezebel, who calls herself a prophetess, [3]to teach and seduce My servants [b]to commit sexual immorality and eat things sacrificed to idols. 21 And I gave her time [a]to [1]repent of her sexual immorality, and she did not repent. 22 Indeed I will cast her into a sickbed, and those who commit adultery with her into great tribulation, unless they repent of [1]their deeds. 23 I will kill her children with death, and all the churches shall know that I am He who [a]searches[1] the minds and hearts. And I will give to each one of you according to your works.

24 "Now to you I say, [1]and to the rest in Thyatira, as many as do not have this doctrine, who have not known the [a]depths of Satan, as they say, [b]I [2]will put on you no other burden. 25 But hold fast [a]what you have till I come. 26 And he who overcomes, and keeps [a]My works until the end, [b]to him I will give power over the nations—

27 *'He[a] shall rule them with a rod of iron;*
They shall be dashed to pieces like the potter's vessels'—

as I also have received from My Father; 28 and I will give him [a]the morning star.

29 "He who has an ear, let him hear what the Spirit says to the churches." '

The Dead Church

3 "And to the [1]angel of the church in Sardis write,

'These things says He who [a]has the seven Spirits of God and the seven stars: "I know your works, that you have a name that you are alive, but you are dead. 2 Be watchful, and strengthen the things which remain, that are ready to die, for I have not found your works perfect before [1]God. 3 [a]Remember therefore how you have received and heard; hold fast and [b]repent. [c]Therefore if you will not watch, I will come upon you [d]as a thief, and you will not know what hour I will come upon you. 4 [1]You have [a]a few names [2]even in Sardis who have not [b]defiled their garments; and they shall walk with Me [c]in white, for they are worthy. 5 He who overcomes [a]shall be clothed in white garments, and I will not [b]blot out his name from the [c]Book of Life; but [d]I will confess his name before My Father and before His angels.

6 [a]"He who has an ear, let him hear what the Spirit says to the churches." '

The Faithful Church

7 "And to the [1]angel of the church in Philadelphia write,

'These things says [a]He who is holy, [b]He who is true, [c]*"He who has the key of David,* [d]*He who opens and no one shuts, and* [e]*shuts and no one opens"*: 8 [a]"I know your works. See, I have set before you [b]an open door, [1]and no one can shut it; for you have a little strength, have kept My word, and have not denied My name. 9 Indeed I will make [a]*those* of the synagogue of Satan, who say they are Jews and are not, but lie—indeed [b]I will make them come and worship before your feet, and to know that I have loved you. 10 Because you have kept [1]My command to persevere, [a]I also will keep you from the hour of trial which shall come upon [b]the whole world, to test those who dwell [c]on the earth. 11 [1]Behold, [a]I am coming quickly! [b]Hold fast what you have, that no one may take [c]your crown. 12 He who overcomes, I will make him [a]a pillar in the temple of My God, and he shall [b]go out no more. [c]I will write on him the name of My God and the name of the city of My God, the [d]New Jerusalem, which [e]comes down out of heaven from My God. [f]And *I will write on him* My new name.

13 [a]"He who has an ear, let him hear what the Spirit says to the churches." '

The Lukewarm Church

14 "And to the [1]angel of the church [2]of the Laodiceans write,

[a]'These things says the Amen, [b]the Faithful and True Witness, [c]the Beginning of the creation of God: 15 [a]"I know your works, that you are neither cold nor hot. I could wish you were cold or hot. 16 So then, because you are lukewarm, and neither [1]cold nor hot, I will vomit you out of My mouth. 17 Because you say, [a]'I am rich, have become wealthy, and have need of nothing'—and do not know that you are wretched, miserable, poor, blind, and naked— 18 I counsel you [a]to buy from Me

20 a 1 Kin. 16:31; 21:25 b Ex. 34:15 *1* NU, M *against you that you tolerate* *2* M *your wife Jezebel* *3* NU, M *and teaches and seduces*
21 a Rev. 9:20; 16:9, 11 *1* NU, M *repent, and she does not want to repent of her sexual immorality.*
22 *1* NU, M *her*
23 a Jer. 11:20; 17:10 *1 examines*
24 a 2 Tim. 3:1–9 b Acts 15:28 *1* NU, M omit *and* *2* NU, M omit *will*
25 a Rev. 3:11
26 a [John 6:29] b [Matt. 19:28]
27 a Ps. 2:8, 9
28 a 2 Pet. 1:19

CHAPTER 3
1 a Rev. 1:4, 16 *1* Or *messenger*
2 *1* NU, M *My God*
3 a 1 Tim. 6:20 b Rev. 3:19 c Matt. 24:42, 43 d [Rev. 16:15]
4 a Acts 1:15 b [Jude 23] c Rev. 4:4; 6:11 *1* NU, M *Nevertheless you* *2* NU, M omit *even*
5 a [Rev. 19:8] b Ex. 32:32 c Phil. 4:3 d Luke 12:8
6 a Rev. 2:7
7 a Acts 3:14 b 1 John 5:20 c Is. 9:7; 22:22 d [Matt. 16:19] e Job 12:14 *1* Or *messenger*
8 a Rev. 3:1 b 1 Cor. 16:9 *1* NU, M *which no one can shut*
9 a Rev. 2:9 b Is. 45:14; 49:23; 60:14
10 a 2 Pet. 2:9 b Luke 2:1 c Is. 24:17 *1* Lit. *the word of My patience*
11 a Phil. 4:5 b Rev. 2:25 c [Rev. 2:10] *1* NU, M omit *Behold*
12 a 1 Kin. 7:21 b Ps. 23:6 c [Rev. 14:1; 22:4] d [Heb. 12:22] e Rev. 21:2 f [Rev. 2:17; 22:4]
13 a Rev. 2:7
14 a 2 Cor. 1:20 b Rev. 1:5; 3:7; 19:11 c [Col. 1:15] *1* Or *messenger* *2* NU, M *in Laodicea*
15 a Rev. 3:1
16 *1* NU, M *hot nor cold*
17 a Hos. 12:8
18 a Is. 55:1

gold refined in the fire, that you may be
rich; and [b]white garments, that you may
be clothed, *that* the shame of your nakedness may not be revealed; and anoint your
eyes with eye salve, that you may see.
19 [a]As many as I love, I rebuke and [b]chas-
ten.[1] Therefore be [2]zealous and repent.
20 Behold, [a]I stand at the door and knock.
[b]If anyone hears My voice and opens the
door, [c]I will come in to him and dine with
him, and he with Me. 21 To him who overcomes [a]I will grant to sit with Me on My
throne, as I also overcame and sat down
with My Father on His throne.
22 [a]"He who has an ear, let him hear
what the Spirit says to the churches." ' "

Lord, You stand at the door
and knock. May ____ hear
Your voice and open the door,
and You will come in to them
and dine with them, and
they with You.

FROM REVELATION 3:20

The Throne Room of Heaven

4 After these things I looked, and behold, a door *standing* [a]open in heav-
en. And the first voice which I heard *was*
like a [b]trumpet speaking with me, saying,
"Come up here, and I will show you things
which must take place after this."

As you are faithful,
this one thing is certain,
the Lord will show you
great and mighty things
that you know not now.

STANLEY FRODSHAM

2 Immediately [a]I was in the Spirit; and
behold, [b]a throne set in heaven, and *One*
sat on the throne. 3 [1]And He who sat there
was [a]like a jasper and a sardius stone in
appearance; [b]and *there was* a rainbow
around the throne, in appearance like an
emerald. 4 [a]Around the throne *were*
twenty-four thrones, and on the thrones
I saw twenty-four elders sitting, [b]clothed
in white [1]robes; and they had crowns of
gold on their heads. 5 And from the throne
proceeded [a]lightnings, [1]thunderings, and
voices. [b]Seven lamps of fire *were* burning
before the throne, which are [c]the[2] seven
Spirits of God.
6 Before the throne *there* [1]*was* [a]a sea of
glass, like crystal. [b]And in the midst of the
throne, and around the throne, *were* four
living creatures full of eyes in front and in
back. 7 [a]The first living creature *was* like a
lion, the second living creature like a calf,
the third living creature had a face like a
man, and the fourth living creature *was*
like a flying eagle. 8 *The* four living creatures, each having [a]six wings, were full of
eyes around and within. And they do not
rest day or night, saying:

[b]"Holy,[1] holy, holy,
[c]Lord God Almighty,
[d]Who was and is and is to come!"

9 Whenever the living creatures give
glory and honor and thanks to Him who
sits on the throne, [a]who lives forever and
ever, 10 [a]the twenty-four elders fall down
before Him who sits on the throne and
worship Him who lives forever and ever,
and cast their crowns before the throne,
saying:

11 "You[a] are worthy, [1]O Lord,
To receive glory and honor and
power;
[b]For You created all things,
And by [c]Your will they [2]exist and
were created."

The Lamb Takes the Scroll

5 And I saw in the right *hand* of Him
who sat on the throne [a]a scroll written inside and on the back, [b]sealed with
seven seals. 2 Then I saw a strong angel
proclaiming with a loud voice, [a]"Who is
worthy to open the scroll and to loose its
seals?" 3 And no one in heaven or on the
earth or under the earth was able to open
the scroll, or to look at it.
4 So I wept much, because no one was
found worthy to open [1]and read the scroll,
or to look at it. 5 But one of the elders said
to me, "Do not weep. Behold, [a]the Lion of
the tribe of [b]Judah, [c]the Root of David,

18 b 2 Cor. 5:3
19 a Job 5:17 b Heb. 12:6 *1 discipline* *2 eager*
20 a Song 5:2 b Luke 12:36, 37 c [John 14:23]
21 a Matt. 19:28
22 a Rev. 2:7

CHAPTER 4
1 a Ezek. 1:1 b Rev. 1:10
2 a Rev. 1:10 b Is. 6:1
3 a Rev. 21:11 b Ezek. 1:28 1 M omits *And He who sat there was,* making the following a description of the throne.
4 a Rev. 11:16 b Rev. 3:4, 5 1 NU, M *robes, with crowns*
5 a Rev. 8:5; 11:19; 16:18 b Ex. 37:23 c [Rev. 1:4] 1 NU, M *voices, and thunderings.* 2 M omits *the*
6 a Rev. 15:2 b Ezek. 1:5 1 NU, M add *something like*
7 a Ezek. 1:10; 10:14
8 a Is. 6:2 b Is. 6:3 c Rev. 1:8 d Rev. 1:4 1 M has *holy* nine times.
9 a Rev. 1:18
10 a Rev. 5:8, 14; 7:11; 11:16; 19:4
11 a Rev. 1:6; 5:12 b Gen. 1:1 c Col. 1:16 1 NU, M *our Lord and God* 2 NU, M *existed*

CHAPTER 5
1 a Ezek. 2:9, 10 b Is. 29:11
2 a Rev. 4:11; 5:9
4 1 NU, M omit *and read*
5 a Gen. 49:9 b Heb. 7:14 c Is. 11:1, 10

has [d]prevailed to open the scroll [e]and [1]to
loose its seven seals."
6And I looked, [1]and behold, in the
midst of the throne and of the four living
creatures, and in the midst of the elders,
stood [a]a Lamb as though it had been
slain, having seven horns and [b]seven eyes,
which are [c]the seven Spirits of God sent
out into all the earth. 7Then He came and
took the scroll out of the right hand [a]of
Him who sat on the throne.

Worthy Is the Lamb

8Now when He had taken the scroll,
[a]the four living creatures and the twenty-
four elders fell down before the Lamb,
each having a harp, and golden bowls full
of incense, which are the [b]prayers of the
saints. 9And [a]they sang a new song,
saying:

[b]"You are worthy to take the scroll,
And to open its seals;
For You were slain,
And [c]have redeemed us to God [d]by
Your blood
Out of every tribe and tongue and
people and nation,
10 And have made [1]us [a]kings[2] and
[b]priests to our God;
And [3]we shall reign on the earth."

11Then I looked, and I heard the voice
of many angels around the throne, the
living creatures, and the elders; and the
number of them was ten thousand times
ten thousand, and thousands of thousands, 12saying with a loud voice:

"Worthy is the Lamb who was slain
To receive power and riches and
wisdom,
And strength and honor and glory
and blessing!"

13And [a]every creature which is in heav-
en and on the earth and under the earth
and such as are in the sea, and all that are
in them, I heard saying:

[b]"Blessing and honor and glory and
power
Be to Him [c]who sits on the throne,
And to the Lamb, forever and
[1]ever!"

14Then the four living creatures said,
"Amen!" And the [1]twenty-four elders fell
down and worshiped [2]Him who lives forever and ever.

5 [d]Rev. 3:21 [e]Rev. 6:1 [1]NU, M omit *to loose*
6 [a][John 1:29] [b]Zech. 3:9; 4:10 [c]Rev. 1:4; 3:1; 4:5 [1]NU, M *I saw in the midst . . . a Lamb standing*
7 [a]Rev. 4:2
8 [a]Rev. 4:8–10; 19:4 [b]Rev. 8:3
9 [a]Rev. 14:3 [b]Rev. 4:11 [c]John 1:29 [d][Heb. 9:12]
10 [a]Ex. 19:6 [b]Is. 61:6 [1]NU, M *them* [2]NU *a kingdom* [3]NU, M *they*
13 [a]Phil. 2:10 [b]1 Chr. 29:11 [c]Rev. 4:2, 3; 6:16; 20:11 [1]M adds *Amen*
14 [1]NU, M omit *twenty-four* [2]NU, M omit *Him who lives forever and ever*

CHAPTER 6
1 [a][Rev. 5:5–7, 12; 13:8] [b]Rev. 4:7 [1]NU, M *seven seals*
2 [a]Zech. 1:8; 6:3 [b]Ps. 45:4, 5, LXX [c]Zech. 6:11 [d]Matt. 24:5
3 [a]Rev. 4:7 [1]NU, M omit *and see*
4 [a]Zech. 1:8; 6:2 [b]Matt. 24:6, 7
5 [a]Rev. 4:7 [b]Zech. 6:2, 6 [c]Matt. 24:7 [1]*balances*
6 [a]Rev. 7:3; 9:4 [1]Gr. *choinix*, about 1 quart [2]About 1 day's wage for a worker
7 [a]Rev. 4:7
8 [a]Zech. 6:3 [b]Ezek. 5:12, 17; 14:21; 29:5 [c]Lev. 26:22 [1]*authority*

First Seal: The Conqueror

6 Now [a]I saw when the Lamb opened
one of the [1]seals; and I heard [b]one of
the four living creatures saying with a
voice like thunder, "Come and see." 2And
I looked, and behold, [a]a white horse. [b]He
who sat on it had a bow; [c]and a crown was
given to him, and he went out [d]conquer-
ing and to conquer.

Second Seal: Conflict on Earth

3When He opened the second seal, [a]I
heard the second living creature saying,
"Come [1]and see." 4[a]Another horse, fiery
red, went out. And it was granted to the
one who sat on it to [b]take peace from the
earth, and that *people* should kill one another; and there was given to him a great
sword.

Third Seal: Scarcity on Earth

5When He opened the third seal, [a]I
heard the third living creature say, "Come
and see." So I looked, and behold, [b]a black
horse, and he who sat on it had a pair of
[c]scales[1] in his hand. 6And I heard a voice
in the midst of the four living creatures
saying, "A [1]quart of wheat for a [2]denarius,
and three quarts of barley for a denarius;
and [a]do not harm the oil and the wine."

Fourth Seal: Widespread Death on Earth

7When He opened the fourth seal, [a]I
heard the voice of the fourth living creature saying, "Come and see." 8[a]So I
looked, and behold, a pale horse. And the
name of him who sat on it was Death, and
Hades followed with him. And [1]power was
given to them over a fourth of the earth,
[b]to kill with sword, with hunger, with
death, [c]and by the beasts of the earth.

Fifth Seal: The Cry of the Martyrs

9When He opened the fifth seal, I saw
under [a]the altar [b]the souls of those who
had been slain [c]for the word of God and
for [d]the testimony which they held. 10And
they cried with a loud voice, saying,
[a]"How long, O Lord, [b]holy and true, [c]un-
til You judge and avenge our blood on
those who dwell on the earth?" 11Then a

9 [a]Rev. 8:3 [b][Rev. 20:4] [c]Rev. 1:2, 9 [d]2 Tim. 1:8
10 [a]Zech. 1:12 [b]Rev. 3:7 [c]Rev. 11:18

[a]white robe was given to each of them;
and it was said to them [b]that they should
rest a little while longer, until both *the
number of* their fellow servants and their
brethren, who would be killed as they
were, was completed.

Sixth Seal: Cosmic Disturbances

[12]I looked when He opened the sixth
seal, [a]and [1]behold, there was a great
earthquake; and [b]the sun became black as
sackcloth of hair, and the [2]moon became
like blood. [13a]And the stars of heaven fell
to the earth, as a fig tree drops its late figs
when it is shaken by a mighty wind.
[14a]Then the sky [1]receded as a scroll when
it is rolled up, and [b]every mountain and
island was moved out of its place. [15]And
the [a]kings of the earth, the great men,
[1]the rich men, the commanders, the
mighty men, every slave and every free
man, [b]hid themselves in the caves and in
the rocks of the mountains, [16a]and said to
the mountains and rocks, "Fall on us and
hide us from the face of Him who [b]sits on
the throne and from the wrath of the
Lamb! [17]For the great day of His wrath
has come, [a]and who is able to stand?"

The Sealed of Israel

7 After these things I saw four angels
standing at the four corners of the
earth, [a]holding the four winds of the
earth, [b]that the wind should not blow on
the earth, on the sea, or on any tree.
[2]Then I saw another angel ascending from
the east, having the seal of the living God.
And he cried with a loud voice to the four
angels to whom it was granted to harm
the earth and the sea, [3]saying, [a]"Do not
harm the earth, the sea, or the trees till
we have sealed the servants of our God
[b]on their foreheads." [4a]And I heard the
number of those who were sealed. [b]One
hundred *and* forty-four thousand [c]of all
the tribes of the children of Israel *were*
sealed:

5 of the tribe of Judah twelve
thousand *were* sealed;
of the tribe of Reuben twelve
thousand *were* [1]sealed;
of the tribe of Gad twelve thousand
were sealed;
6 of the tribe of Asher twelve
thousand *were* sealed;
of the tribe of Naphtali twelve
thousand *were* sealed;
of the tribe of Manasseh twelve
thousand *were* sealed;
7 of the tribe of Simeon twelve
thousand *were* sealed;
of the tribe of Levi twelve thousand
were sealed;
of the tribe of Issachar twelve
thousand *were* sealed;
8 of the tribe of Zebulun twelve
thousand *were* sealed;
of the tribe of Joseph twelve
thousand *were* sealed;
of the tribe of Benjamin twelve
thousand *were* sealed.

A Multitude from the Great Tribulation

[9]After these things I looked, and behold, [a]a great multitude which no one
could number, [b]of all nations, tribes, peoples, and tongues, standing before the
throne and before the Lamb, [c]clothed
with white robes, with palm branches in
their hands, [10]and crying out with a loud
voice, saying, [a]"Salvation *belongs* to our
God [b]who sits on the throne, and to the
Lamb!" [11a]All the angels stood around the
throne and the elders and the four living
creatures, and fell on their faces before
the throne and [b]worshiped God, [12a]say-
ing:

"Amen! Blessing and glory and
wisdom,
Thanksgiving and honor and power
and might,
Be to our God forever and ever.
Amen."

[13]Then one of the elders answered, saying to me, "Who are these arrayed in
[a]white robes, and where did they come
from?"

[14]And I said to him, [1]"Sir, you know."
So he said to me, [a]"These are the ones
who come out of the great tribulation,
and [b]washed their robes and made them
white in the blood of the Lamb. [15]There-
fore they are before the throne of God,
and serve Him day and night in His temple. And He who sits on the throne will
[a]dwell among them. [16a]They shall neither
hunger anymore nor thirst anymore; [b]the
sun shall not strike them, nor any heat;
[17]for the Lamb who is in the midst of the
throne [a]will shepherd them and lead
them to [1]living fountains of waters. [b]And

11 a Rev. 3:4, 5; 7:9 b Heb. 11:40
12 a Matt. 24:7 b Joel 2:10, 31; 3:15 *1* NU, M omit *behold* *2* NU, M *whole moon*
13 a Rev. 8:10; 9:1
14 a Is. 34:4 b Rev. 16:20 *1* Or *split apart*
15 a Ps. 2:2–4 b Is. 2:10, 19, 21; 24:21 *1* NU, M *the commanders, the rich men,*
16 a Luke 23:29, 30 b Rev. 20:11
17 a Zeph. 1:14

CHAPTER 7
1 a Dan. 7:2 b Rev. 7:3; 8:7; 9:4
3 a Rev. 6:6 b Rev. 22:4
4 a Rev. 9:16 b Rev. 14:1, 3 c Gen. 49:1–27
5 *1* NU, M omit *sealed* in vv. 5b–8b.
9 a Rom. 11:25 b Rev. 5:9 c Rev. 3:5, 18; 4:4; 6:11
10 a Ps. 3:8 b Rev. 5:13
11 a Rev. 4:6 b Rev. 4:11; 5:9, 12, 14; 11:16
12 a Rev. 5:13, 14
13 a Rev. 7:9
14 a Rev. 6:9 b [Heb. 9:14] *1* NU, M *My lord*
15 a Is. 4:5, 6
16 a Is. 49:10 b Ps. 121:6
17 a Ps. 23:1 b Rev. 21:4 *1* NU, M *fountains of the waters of life*

God will wipe away every tear from their eyes."

Seventh Seal: Prelude to the Seven Trumpets

8 When[a] He opened the seventh seal, there was silence in heaven for about half an hour. 2 [a]And I saw the seven angels who stand before God, [b]and to them were given seven trumpets. 3 Then another angel, having a golden censer, came and stood at the altar. He was given much incense, that he should offer *it* with [a]the prayers of all the saints upon [b]the golden altar which was before the throne. 4 And [a]the smoke of the incense, with the prayers of the saints, ascended before God from the angel's hand. 5 Then the angel took the censer, filled it with fire from the altar, and threw *it* to the earth. And [a]there were noises, thunderings, [b]lightnings, [c]and an earthquake.

6 So the seven angels who had the seven trumpets prepared themselves to sound.

First Trumpet: Vegetation Struck

7 The first angel sounded: [a]And hail and fire followed, mingled with blood, and they were thrown [b]to the [1]earth. And a third [c]of the trees were burned up, and all green grass was burned up.

Second Trumpet: The Seas Struck

8 Then the second angel sounded: [a]And *something* like a great mountain burning with fire was thrown into the sea, [b]and a third of the sea [c]became blood. 9 [a]And a third of the living creatures in the sea died, and a third of the ships were destroyed.

Third Trumpet: The Waters Struck

10 Then the third angel sounded: [a]And a great star fell from heaven, burning like a torch, [b]and it fell on a third of the rivers and on the springs of water. 11 [a]The name of the star is Wormwood. [b]A third of the waters became wormwood, and many men died from the water, because it was made bitter.

Fourth Trumpet: The Heavens Struck

12 [a]Then the fourth angel sounded: And a third of the sun was struck, a third of the moon, and a third of the stars, so that a third of them were darkened. A third of the day [1]did not shine, and likewise the night.

13 And I looked, [a]and I heard an [1]angel flying through the midst of heaven, saying with a loud voice, [b]"Woe, woe, woe to the inhabitants of the earth, because of the remaining blasts of the trumpet of the three angels who are about to sound!"

Heap up His praises upon the glowing altar of your soul, and pile His adoration atop of that, crown Him with glory, laud and magnify His name until His burning praises rise as a sweet-smelling savor to be caught in the golden censer of the angel who offers unto the Lord the prayers of all saints upon the golden altar.

AIMEE SEMPLE MCPHERSON

Fifth Trumpet: The Locusts from the Bottomless Pit

9 Then the fifth angel sounded: [a]And I saw a star fallen from heaven to the earth. To him was given the key to [b]the [1]bottomless pit. 2 And he opened the bottomless pit, and smoke arose out of the pit like the smoke of a great furnace. So the [a]sun and the air were darkened because of the smoke of the pit. 3 Then out of the smoke locusts came upon the earth. And to them was given power, [a]as the scorpions of the earth have power. 4 They were commanded [a]not to harm [b]the grass of

CHAPTER 8
1 a Rev. 6:1
2 a [Matt. 18:10] b 2 Chr. 29:25–28
3 a Rev. 5:8 b Ex. 30:1
4 a Ps. 141:2
5 a Rev. 11:19; 16:18 b Rev. 4:5 c 2 Sam. 22:8
7 a Ezek. 38:22 b Rev. 16:2 c Rev. 9:4, 15–18 *1* NU, M add *and a third of the earth was burned up*
8 a Jer. 51:25 b Ex. 7:17 c Ezek. 14:19
9 a Rev. 16:3
10 a Is. 14:12 b Rev. 14:7; 16:4
11 a Ruth 1:20 b Ex. 15:23
12 a Is. 13:10 *1 had no light*
13 a Rev. 14:6; 19:17 b Rev. 9:12; 11:14; 12:12 *1* NU, M *eagle*

CHAPTER 9
1 a Rev. 8:10 b Luke 8:31 *1* Lit. *shaft of the abyss*
2 a Joel 2:2, 10
3 a Judg. 7:12
4 a Rev. 6:6 b Rev. 8:7

the earth, or any green thing, or any tree,
but only those men who do not have [c]the
seal of God on their foreheads. 5And [1]they
were not given *authority* to kill them,
[a]but to torment them *for* five months.
Their torment *was* like the torment of a
scorpion when it strikes a man. 6In those
days [a]men will seek death and will not
find it; they will desire to die, and death
will flee from them.

7[a]The shape of the locusts was like
horses prepared for battle. [b]On their
heads were crowns of something like gold,
[c]and their faces *were* like the faces of
men. 8They had hair like women's hair,
and [a]their teeth were like lions' *teeth.*
9And they had breastplates like breastplates of iron, and the sound of their
wings *was* [a]like the sound of chariots with
many horses running into battle. 10They
had tails like scorpions, and there were
stings in their tails. Their power *was* to
hurt men five months. 11And they had as
king over them [a]the angel of the bottomless pit, whose name in Hebrew *is* [1]Abad-
don, but in Greek he has the name
[2]Apollyon.

12[a]One woe is past. Behold, still two
more woes are coming after these things.

Sixth Trumpet: The Angels from the Euphrates

13Then the sixth angel sounded: And I
heard a voice from the four horns of the
[a]golden altar which is before God, 14say-
ing to the sixth angel who had the trumpet, "Release the four angels who are
bound [a]at the great river Euphrates." 15So
the four angels, who had been prepared
for the hour and day and month and year,
were released to kill a [a]third of mankind.
16Now [a]the number of the army [b]of the
horsemen *was* two hundred million; [c]I
heard the number of them. 17And thus I
saw the horses in the vision: those who sat
on them had breastplates of fiery red, hya-
cinth blue, and sulfur yellow; [a]and the
heads of the horses *were* like the heads of
lions; and out of their mouths came fire,
smoke, and brimstone. 18By these three
plagues a third of mankind was killed—
by the fire and the smoke and the brimstone which came out of their mouths.
19For [1]their power is in their mouth and
in their tails; [a]for their tails *are* like serpents, having heads; and with them they
do harm.

20But the rest of mankind, who were
not killed by these plagues, [a]did not repent of the works of their hands, that they
should not worship [b]demons, [c]and idols
of gold, silver, brass, stone, and wood,
which can neither see nor hear nor walk.
21And they did not repent of their murders [a]or their [1]sorceries or their sexual
immorality or their thefts.

The Mighty Angel with the Little Book

10 I saw still another mighty angel
coming down from heaven,
clothed with a cloud. [a]And a rainbow *was*
on [b]his head, his face *was* like the sun,
and [c]his feet like pillars of fire. 2He had a
little book open in his hand. [a]And he set
his right foot on the sea and *his* left *foot*
on the land, 3and cried with a loud voice,
as *when* a lion roars. When he cried out,
[a]seven thunders uttered their voices.
4Now when the seven thunders [1]uttered
their voices, I was about to write; but I
heard a voice from heaven saying [2]to me,
[a]"Seal up the things which the seven
thunders uttered, and do not write them."

5The angel whom I saw standing on the
sea and on the land [a]raised up his [1]hand
to heaven 6and swore by Him who lives
forever and ever, [a]who created heaven and
the things that are in it, the earth and the
things that are in it, and the sea and the
things that are in it, [b]that there should be
delay no longer, 7but [a]in the days of the
sounding of the seventh angel, when he is
about to sound, the mystery of God would
be finished, as He declared to His servants
the prophets.

John Eats the Little Book

8Then the voice which I heard from
heaven spoke to me again and said, "Go,
take the little book which is open in the
hand of the angel who stands on the sea
and on the earth."

9So I went to the angel and said to him,
"Give me the little book."

And he said to me, [a]"Take and eat it;
and it will make your stomach bitter, but
it will be as sweet as honey in your
mouth."

10Then I took the little book out of the
angel's hand and ate it, [a]and it was as
sweet as honey in my mouth. But when I
had eaten it, [b]my stomach became bitter.
11And [1]he said to me, "You must prophesy

---

4 [c]Rev. 7:2, 3
5 [a][Rev. 9:10; 11:7] [1]The locusts
6 [a]Jer. 8:3
7 [a]Joel 2:4 [b]Nah. 3:17 [c]Dan. 7:8
8 [a]Joel 1:6
9 [a]Joel 2:5–7
11 [a]Eph. 2:2 [1]Lit. *Destruction* [2]Lit. *Destroyer*
12 [a]Rev. 8:13; 11:14
13 [a]Rev. 8:3
14 [a]Rev. 16:12
15 [a]Rev. 8:7–9; 9:18
16 [a]Dan. 7:10 [b]Ezek. 38:4 [c]Rev. 7:4
17 [a]Is. 5:28, 29
19 [a]Is. 9:15 [1]NU, M *the power of the horses*
20 [a]Deut. 31:29 [b]1 Cor. 10:20 [c]Dan. 5:23
21 [a]Rev. 21:8; 22:15 [1]NU, M *drugs*

CHAPTER 10
1 [a]Rev. 4:3 [b]Rev. 1:16 [c]Rev. 1:15
2 [a]Matt. 28:18
3 [a]Ps. 29:3–9
4 [a]Dan. 8:26; 12:4, 9 [1]NU, M *sounded,* [2]NU, M omit *to me*
5 [a]Dan. 12:7 [1]NU, M *right hand*
6 [a]Rev. 4:11 [b]Rev. 16:17
7 [a]Rev. 11:15
9 [a]Jer. 15:16
10 [a]Ezek. 3:3 [b]Ezek. 2:10
11 [1]NU, M *they*

again about many peoples, nations, tongues, and kings."

The Two Witnesses

11 Then I was given [a]a reed like a measuring rod. [1]And the angel stood, saying, [b]"Rise and measure the temple of God, the altar, and those who worship there. 2But leave out [a]the court which is outside the temple, and do not measure it, [b]for it has been given to the Gentiles. And they will [c]tread the holy city underfoot *for* [d]forty-two months. 3And I will give *power* to my two [a]witnesses, [b]and they will prophesy [c]one thousand two hundred and sixty days, clothed in sackcloth."

4These are the [a]two olive trees and the two lampstands standing before the [1]God of the earth. 5And if anyone wants to harm them, [a]fire proceeds from their mouth and devours their enemies. [b]And if anyone wants to harm them, he must be killed in this manner. 6These [a]have power to shut heaven, so that no rain falls in the days of their prophecy; and they have power over waters to turn them to blood, and to strike the earth with all plagues, as often as they desire.

The Witnesses Killed

7When they [a]finish their testimony, [b]the beast that ascends [c]out of the bottomless pit [d]will make war against them, overcome them, and kill them. 8And their dead bodies *will lie* in the street of [a]the great city which spiritually is called Sodom and Egypt, [b]where also [1]our Lord was crucified. 9[a]Then *those* from the peoples, tribes, tongues, and nations [1]will see their dead bodies three-and-a-half days, [b]and not allow their dead bodies to be put into graves. 10[a]And those who dwell on the earth will rejoice over them, make merry, [b]and send gifts to one another, [c]because these two prophets tormented those who dwell on the earth.

The Witnesses Resurrected

11[a]Now after the three-and-a-half days [b]the breath of life from God entered them, and they stood on their feet, and great fear fell on those who saw them. 12And [1]they heard a loud voice from heaven saying to them, "Come up here." [a]And they ascended to heaven [b]in a cloud, [c]and their enemies saw them. 13In the same hour [a]there was a great earthquake, [b]and a tenth of the city fell. In the earthquake seven thousand people were killed, and the rest were afraid [c]and gave glory to the God of heaven.

14[a]The second woe is past. Behold, the third woe is coming quickly.

Seventh Trumpet: The Kingdom Proclaimed

15Then [a]the seventh angel sounded: [b]And there were loud voices in heaven, saying, [c]"The [1]kingdoms of this world have become *the kingdoms* of our Lord and of His Christ, [d]and He shall reign forever and ever!" 16And [a]the twenty-four elders who sat before God on their thrones fell on their faces and [b]worshiped God, 17saying:

"We give You thanks, O Lord God
Almighty,
The One [a]who is and who was [1]and
who is to come,
Because You have taken Your great
power [b]and reigned.
18 The nations were [a]angry, and
Your [1]wrath has come,
And the time of the [b]dead, that
they should be judged,
And that You should reward Your
servants the prophets and the
saints,
And those who fear Your name,
small and great,
And should destroy those who
destroy the earth."

19Then [a]the temple of God was opened in heaven, and the ark of [1]His covenant was seen in His temple. And [b]there were lightnings, noises, thunderings, an earthquake, [c]and great hail.

The Woman, the Child, and the Dragon

12 Now a great sign appeared in heaven: a woman clothed with the sun, with the moon under her feet, and on her head a garland of twelve stars. 2Then being with child, she cried out [a]in labor and in pain to give birth.

3And another sign appeared in heaven: behold, [a]a great, fiery red dragon having seven heads and ten horns, and seven diadems on his heads. 4♀ [a]His tail drew a

CHAPTER 11
1 a Ezek. 40:3—42:20 b Num. 23:18 *1 NU, M omit And the angel stood*
2 a Ezek. 40:17, 20 b Ps. 79:1 c Dan. 8:10 d Rev. 12:6; 13:5
3 a Rev. 20:4 b Rev. 19:10 c Rev. 12:6
4 a Zech. 4:2, 3, 11, 14 *1 NU, M Lord*
5 a 2 Kin. 1:10–12 b Num. 16:29
6 a 1 Kin. 17:1
7 a Luke 13:32 b Rev. 13:1, 11; 17:8 c Rev. 9:1, 2 d Dan. 7:21
8 a Rev. 14:8 b Heb. 13:12 *1 NU, M their*
9 a Rev. 17:15 b Ps. 79:2, 3 *1 NU, M see . . . and will not allow*
10 a Rev. 12:12 b Esth. 9:19, 22 c Rev. 16:10
11 a Rev. 11:9 b Ezek. 37:5, 9, 10
12 a Is. 14:13 b Acts 1:9 c 2 Kin. 2:11, 12 *1 M I*
13 a Rev. 6:12; 8:5; 11:19; 16:18 b Rev. 16:19 c Rev. 14:7; 16:9; 19:7
14 a Rev. 8:13; 9:12
15 a Rev. 8:2; 10:7 b Is. 27:13 c Rev. 12:10 d Ex. 15:18 *1 NU, M kingdom . . . has become the kingdom*
16 a Rev. 4:4 b Rev. 4:11; 5:9, 12, 14; 7:11
17 a Rev. 16:5 b Rev. 19:6 *1 NU, M omit and who is to come*
18 a Ps. 2:1 b Dan. 7:10 *1 anger*
19 a Rev. 4:1; 15:5, 8 b Rev. 8:5 c Rev. 16:21 *1 M the covenant of the Lord*
CHAPTER 12 **2** a Is. 26:17; 66:6–9 **3** a Rev. 13:1; 17:3, 7, 9 **4** a Rev. 9:10, 19

Revelation 12:4

Dear Woman of Destiny,

Satan is the enemy of God, mentioned numerous times in the Bible. He is the enemy who broke God's heart by rebelling in heaven and taking a third of the angels with him when he was cast down to the earth in judgment for his rebellion. Jesus said that Satan came to steal, kill, and destroy (see John 10:10). And his purpose and character are still the same today.

Satan's greatest deception is to get the church to believe he does not exist. If he succeeds in that lie, he convinces the church that we can do nothing about the works of darkness we see all around us. If that deception doesn't work, he tries to convince Christians that his power is much greater than it is; that he is an equal counterpart to the power of God. He is not. He is a created being. Not only is he not omnipotent, he is neither omniscient nor omnipresent. There are many things he does not know and he cannot be in many places at once.

Our walk of faith is more than simply being faithful and obedient to God's Word. The Scriptures speak of the *fight* of faith and teach clearly that we are involved in supernatural warfare. The only way we can expect to be victorious in this battle is first to know who our enemy is.

Our battle is fought in three areas: the world, the flesh, and the devil. While it would be incorrect to blame all our problems on the devil, it is absolutely necessary to understand who he is and how we should deal with his intrusion into our lives.

We can protect ourselves against Satan's attacks if we understand that he works through three basic means: deception, temptation, and accusation. He is called the Tempter, the Father of Lies, an Angel of Light, the Separator, the Murderer, and the Old Serpent—among other titles Scripture attributes to him. Each of these names reveals a facet of his nature and destructive purpose.

As long as we have only a vague picture of who our enemy is, we won't know how to withstand him. Satan is counting on our being indifferent to his existence and his "wiles." We must learn to identify the enemy in order to remain free from his destructive works.

The same enemy who tempted Jesus in the wilderness (see Luke 4:2–13) and used demons to speak through the people Jesus encountered (see Luke 4:33–35) has set himself now to resist the saints. His warfare is with the people of God—those to whom Jesus has committed the work of deliverance from Satan's power (see Dan. 7:25–27).

Jesus defeated Satan on the cross, and the Father gave all authority in heaven and on earth to Him. He transferred that authority to the church: "Behold, I give you the authority to trample on serpents and scorpions, and over all the power of the enemy, and nothing shall by any means hurt you" (Luke 10:19). Jesus gave the church the responsibility of enforcing the victory of Calvary. As we defeat Satan in our own lives, we can then be used to set others free in His name.

Sue Curran

third [b]of the stars of heaven [c]and threw
them to the earth. And the dragon stood
[d]before the woman who was ready to give
birth, [e]to devour her Child as soon as it
was born. 5She bore a male Child [a]who
was to rule all nations with a rod of iron.
And her Child was [b]caught up to God and
His throne. 6Then [a]the woman fled into
the wilderness, where she has a place prepared by God, that they should feed her
there [b]one thousand two hundred and sixty days.

Satan Thrown Out of Heaven

7And war broke out in heaven: [a]Michael
and his angels fought [b]with the dragon;
and the dragon and his angels fought,
8but they [1]did not prevail, nor was a place
found for [2]them in heaven any longer. 9So
[a]the great dragon was cast out, [b]that serpent of old, called the Devil and Satan,
[c]who deceives the whole world; [d]he was
cast to the earth, and his angels were cast
out with him.

Lord, may You give grace and strength to _____ so that they might overcome the accuser of the brethren by the blood of the Lamb and by the word of their testimony, and may they not love their lives even to the death.

FROM REVELATION 12:11

10Then I heard a loud voice saying in
heaven, [a]"Now salvation, and strength,
and the kingdom of our God, and the power of His Christ have come, for the accuser of our brethren, [b]who accused them
before our God day and night, has been
cast down. 11And [a]they overcame him by
the blood of the Lamb and by the word of
their testimony, [b]and they did not love
their lives to the death. 12Therefore [a]re-
joice, O heavens, and you who dwell in
them! [b]Woe to the inhabitants of the
earth and the sea! For the devil has come
down to you, having great wrath, [c]be-
cause he knows that he has a short time."

4 [b]Rev. 8:7, 12 [c]Dan. 8:10 [d]Rev. 12:2 [e]Matt. 2:16
5 [a]Ps. 2:9 [b]Acts 1:9–11
6 [a]Rev. 12:4, 14 [b]Rev. 11:3; 13:5
7 [a]Dan. 10:13, 21; 12:1 [b]Rev. 20:2
8 [1] *were not strong enough* [2] M *him*
9 [a]John 12:31 [b]Gen. 3:1, 4 [c]Rev. 20:3 [d]Rev. 9:1
10 [a]Rev. 11:15 [b]Zech. 3:1
11 [a]Rom. 16:20 [b]Luke 14:26
12 [a]Ps. 96:11 [b]Rev. 8:13 [c]Rev. 10:6
13 [a]Rev. 12:5
14 [a]Ex. 19:4 [b]Rev. 12:6 [c]Rev. 17:3 [d]Dan. 7:25; 12:7
15 [a]Is. 59:19
17 [1] NU, M omit *Christ*

CHAPTER 13
1 [a]Dan. 7:2, 7 [b]Rev. 12:3 [c]Rev. 17:3 [1] NU *he* [2] NU, M *ten horns and seven heads*
2 [a]Rev. 12:3, 9; 13:4, 12
3 [a]Rev. 13:12, 14 [b]Rev. 17:8
4 [a]Rev. 18:18
5 [a]Dan. 7:8, 11, 20, 25; 11:36 [b]Rev. 11:2 [1] M *make war*

The Woman Persecuted

13Now when the dragon saw that he had
been cast to the earth, he persecuted [a]the
woman who gave birth to the male *Child.*
14[a]But the woman was given two wings of
a great eagle, [b]that she might fly [c]into the
wilderness to her place, where she is
nourished [d]for a time and times and half
a time, from the presence of the serpent.
15So the serpent [a]spewed water out of his
mouth like a flood after the woman, that
he might cause her to be carried away
by the flood. 16But the earth helped the
woman, and the earth opened its mouth
and swallowed up the flood which the
dragon had spewed out of his mouth.
17And the dragon was enraged with the
woman, and he went to make war with the
rest of her offspring, who keep the commandments of God and have the testimony of Jesus [1]Christ.

We are familiar with external martyrdom, but inner martyrdom is infinitely more vital.

OSWALD CHAMBERS

The Beast from the Sea

13 Then [1]I stood on the sand of the
sea. And I saw [a]a beast rising up
out of the sea, [b]having [2]seven heads and
ten horns, and on his horns ten crowns,
and on his heads a [c]blasphemous name.
2Now the beast which I saw was like a
leopard, his feet were like *the feet of* a
bear, and his mouth like the mouth of a
lion. The [a]dragon gave him his power, his
throne, and great authority. 3And *I saw*
one of his heads [a]as if it had been mortally
wounded, and his deadly wound was
healed. And [b]all the world marveled and
followed the beast. 4So they worshiped the
dragon who gave authority to the beast;
and they worshiped the beast, saying,
[a]"Who *is* like the beast? Who is able to
make war with him?"
5And he was given [a]a mouth speaking
great things and blasphemies, and he was
given authority to [1]continue for [b]forty-
two months. 6Then he opened his mouth

REVELATION 12:10, 11

Dear Woman of Destiny,

In the summer of 1998, a young woman from Sudan (a country in northeast Africa) was attacked, severely beaten, and raped by Muslims simply because she was wearing a cross. When she tried to escape, her throat was slit and she was stabbed in the back. Her assailants ripped her dress off and proceeded to melt water bottles and pour the hot, liquid plastic onto her skin, leaving it in puddles and scarring her for life. She survived the brutal assault only to become pregnant by the horrible incident and is now raising her child.

Seventy-five percent of the world's Christians live in third-world nations—nations that are predominantly Hindu, Buddhist, and Muslim. Persecution in many nations brings extortion, family division and separation, harassment, and discrimination in employment and education as over 600 millions Christians live as second-class citizens in their societies.

In the Western church today, "intimacy with Jesus" has become a sweet and oft-heard phrase echoing in church halls as believers quote from Philippians 3:10: "That I may know Him and the power of His resurrection . . . ." But they don't finish the verse: " . . . and the fellowship of His sufferings, being conformed to His death."

This is a powerfully ironic revelation—that intimacy comes through suffering! That is why the Holy Spirit chose to use Paul not only to pen these words, but also to demonstrate them though his own life of suffering for the gospel.

The Western church has developed a pacifying theology of telling herself that suffering is not the will of God, but that it is Satan having his way in the life of a believer. Accusations rise up in our hearts against a sovereign God's inability to alleviate pain and suffering in our lives, preventing us from embracing the Cross.

Martyrdom and persecution are on the rise in America and the Western nations. Yet many of us feel still believe that suffering means that we aren't physically comfortable or that persecution means our family thinks we are just too radical when we refuse to watch a certain program on TV!

Yet Jesus paints a different picture in Luke 9:23, 24: "If anyone desires to come after Me, let him deny himself, and take up his cross daily, and follow Me. For whoever desires to save his life will lose it, but whoever loses his life for My sake will save it."

Many will lose their lives and be martyred, but they will overcome their accuser "by the blood of the Lamb and by the word of their testimony," not having loved "their lives to the death" (Rev. 12:11).

I once saw a pastor stand by a large map of the world that was mounted on the wall of his church as the Holy Spirit brooded over the room. In tears, he told the Lord that he would send his sons and daughters from his church to the nations—even if it meant that they would be martyred. Woman of Destiny, release your life to the glorious cause of Christ. Learn to love Him so much that you, too, will join those who have not loved "their lives to the death."

Jill Austin

in blasphemy against God, to blaspheme
His name, [a]His tabernacle, and those who
dwell in heaven. 7It was granted to him
[a]to make war with the saints and to overcome them. And [b]authority was given him
over every [1]tribe, tongue, and nation. 8All
who dwell on the earth will worship him,
[a]whose names have not been written in
the Book of Life of the Lamb slain [b]from
the foundation of the world.
9[a]If anyone has an ear, let him hear.
10[a]He who leads into captivity shall go
into captivity; [b]he who kills with the
sword must be killed with the sword.
[c]Here is the [1]patience and the faith of the
saints.

The Beast from the Earth

11Then I saw another beast [a]coming up
out of the earth, and he had two horns like
a lamb and spoke like a dragon. 12And he
exercises all the authority of the first beast
in his presence, and causes the earth and
those who dwell in it to worship the first
beast, [a]whose deadly wound was healed.
13[a]He performs great signs, [b]so that he
even makes fire come down from heaven
on the earth in the sight of men. 14[a]And
he deceives [1]those who dwell on the earth
[b]by those signs which he was granted to
do in the sight of the beast, telling those
who dwell on the earth to make an image
to the beast who was wounded by the
sword [c]and lived. 15He was granted *power*
to give breath to the image of the beast,
that the image of the beast should both
speak [a]and cause as many as would not
worship the image of the beast to be
killed. 16He causes all, both small and
great, rich and poor, free and slave, [a]to
receive a mark on their right hand or on
their foreheads, 17and that no one may
buy or sell except one who has [1]the mark
or [a]the name of the beast, [b]or the number
of his name.
18[a]Here is wisdom. Let him who has
[b]understanding calculate [c]the number of
the beast, [d]for it is the number of a man:
His number *is* 666.

The Lamb and the 144,000

14 Then I looked, and behold, [1]a
[a]Lamb standing on Mount Zion,
and with Him [b]one hundred *and* forty-
four thousand, [2]having His Father's name
[c]written on their foreheads. 2And I heard
a voice from heaven, [a]like the voice of
many waters, and like the voice of loud
thunder. And I heard the sound of [b]harp-
ists playing their harps. 3They sang as it
were a new song before the throne, before
the four living creatures, and the elders;
and no one could learn that song [a]except
the hundred *and* forty-four thousand who
were redeemed from the earth. 4These
are the ones who were not defiled with
women, [a]for they are virgins. These are
the ones [b]who follow the Lamb wherever
He goes. These [c]were [1]redeemed from
among men, [d]*being* firstfruits to God and
to the Lamb. 5And [a]in their mouth was
found no [1]deceit, for [b]they are without
fault [2]before the throne of God.

The Proclamations of Three Angels

6Then I saw another angel [a]flying in the
midst of heaven, [b]having the everlasting gospel to preach to those who dwell
on the earth—[c]to every nation, tribe,
tongue, and people— 7saying with a loud
voice, [a]"Fear God and give glory to Him,
for the hour of His judgment has come;
[b]and worship Him who made heaven and
earth, the sea and springs of water."
8And another angel followed, saying,
[a]"Babylon[1] is fallen, is fallen, that great
city, because [b]she has made all nations
drink of the wine of the wrath of her fornication."
9Then a third angel followed them, saying with a loud voice, [a]"If anyone worships the beast and his image, and
receives *his* [b]mark on his forehead or on
his hand, 10he himself [a]shall also drink of
the wine of the wrath of God, which is
[b]poured out full strength into [c]the cup of
His indignation. [d]He shall be tormented
with [e]fire and brimstone in the presence
of the holy angels and in the presence of
the Lamb. 11And [a]the smoke of their torment ascends forever and ever; and they
have no rest day or night, who worship
the beast and his image, and whoever receives the mark of his name."
12[a]Here is the [1]patience of the saints;
[b]here[2] *are* those who keep the commandments of God and the faith of Jesus.

6 a [Col. 2:9]
7 a Dan. 7:21 b Rev. 11:18 1 NU, M add *and people*
8 a Ex. 32:32 b Rev. 17:8
9 a Rev. 2:7
10 a Is. 33:1 b Gen. 9:6 c Rev. 14:12 1 *perseverance*
11 a Rev. 11:7
12 a Rev. 13:3, 4
13 a Matt. 24:24 b 1 Kin. 18:38
14 a Rev. 12:9 b 2 Thess. 2:9 c 2 Kin. 20:7 1 M *my own people*
15 a Rev. 16:2
16 a Rev. 7:3; 14:9; 20:4
17 a Rev. 14:9–11 b Rev. 15:2 1 NU, M *the mark, the name*
18 a Rev. 17:9 b [1 Cor. 2:14] c Rev. 15:2 d Rev. 21:17

CHAPTER 14
1 a Rev. 5:6 b Rev. 7:4; 14:3 c Rev. 7:3; 22:4 1 NU, M *the* 2 NU, M add *His name and*
2 a Rev. 1:15; 19:6 b Rev. 5:8
3 a Rev. 5:9
4 a [2 Cor. 11:2] b Rev. 3:4; 7:17 c Rev. 5:9 d James 1:18 1 M adds *by Jesus*
5 a Ps. 32:2 b Eph. 5:27 1 NU, M *falsehood* 2 NU, M omit the rest of v. 5.
6 a Rev. 8:13 b Eph. 3:9 c Rev. 13:7
7 a Rev. 11:18 b Neh. 9:6
8 a Is. 21:9 b Jer. 51:7

1 NU *Babylon the great is fallen, is fallen, which has made;* M *Babylon the great is fallen. She has made* 9 a Rev. 13:14, 15; 14:11 b Rev. 13:16 10 a Ps. 75:8 b Rev. 18:6 c Rev. 16:19 d Rev. 20:10 e 2 Thess. 1:7 11 a Is. 34:8–10 12 a Rev. 13:10 b Rev. 12:17 1 *steadfastness, perseverance* 2 NU, M omit *here are those*

13 Then I heard a voice from heaven saying [1]to me, "Write: [a]'Blessed *are* the dead [b]who die in the Lord from now on.' "

"Yes," says the Spirit, [c]"that they may rest from their labors, and their works follow [d]them."

Reaping the Earth's Harvest

14 Then I looked, and behold, a white cloud, and on the cloud sat *One* like the Son of Man, having on His head a golden crown, and in His hand a sharp sickle. 15 And another angel [a]came out of the temple, crying with a loud voice to Him who sat on the cloud, [b]"Thrust in Your sickle and reap, for the time has come [1]for You to reap, for the harvest [c]of the earth is ripe." 16 So He who sat on the cloud thrust in His sickle on the earth, and the earth was reaped.

Reaping the Grapes of Wrath

17 Then another angel came out of the temple which is in heaven, he also having a sharp sickle.

18 And another angel came out from the altar, [a]who had power over fire, and he cried with a loud cry to him who had the sharp sickle, saying, [b]"Thrust in your sharp sickle and gather the clusters of the vine of the earth, for her grapes are fully ripe." 19 So the angel thrust his sickle into the earth and gathered the vine of the earth, and threw *it* into [a]the great winepress of the wrath of God. 20 And [a]the winepress was trampled [b]outside the city, and blood came out of the winepress, [c]up to the horses' bridles, for one thousand six hundred [1]furlongs.

Prelude to the Bowl Judgments

15 Then [a]I saw another sign in heaven, great and marvelous: [b]seven angels having the seven last plagues, [c]for in them the wrath of God is complete.

2 And I saw *something* like [a]a sea of glass [b]mingled with fire, and those who have the victory over the beast, [c]over his image and [1]over his mark *and* over the [d]number of his name, standing on the sea of glass, [e]having harps of God. 3 They sing [a]the song of Moses, the servant of God, and the song of the [b]Lamb, saying:

[c]"Great and marvelous *are* Your
works,
Lord God Almighty!
[d]Just and true *are* Your ways,
O King of the [1]saints!
4 [a]Who shall not fear You, O Lord,
and glorify Your name?
For *You* alone *are* [b]holy.
For [c]all nations shall come and
worship before You,
For Your judgments have been
manifested."

5 After these things I looked, and [1]behold, [a]the [2]temple of the tabernacle of the testimony in heaven was opened. 6 And out of the [1]temple came the seven angels having the seven plagues, [a]clothed in pure bright linen, and having their chests girded with golden bands. 7 [a]Then one of the four living creatures gave to the seven angels seven golden bowls full of the wrath of God [b]who lives forever and ever. 8 [a]The temple was filled with smoke [b]from the glory of God and from His power, and no one was able to enter the temple till the seven plagues of the seven angels were completed.

16 Then I heard a loud voice from the temple saying [a]to the seven angels, "Go and pour out the [1]bowls [b]of the wrath of God on the earth."

First Bowl: Loathsome Sores

2 So the first went and poured out his bowl [a]upon the earth, and a [1]foul and [b]loathsome sore came upon the men [c]who had the mark of the beast and those [d]who worshiped his image.

Second Bowl: The Sea Turns to Blood

3 Then the second angel poured out his bowl [a]on the sea, and [b]it became blood as of a dead *man;* [c]and every living creature in the sea died.

Third Bowl: The Waters Turn to Blood

4 Then the third angel poured out his bowl [a]on the rivers and springs of water, [b]and they became blood. 5 And I heard the angel of the waters saying:

[a]"You are righteous, [1]O Lord,
The One [b]who is and who [2]was and
who is to be,

13 a Eccl. 4:1, 2 b 1 Cor. 15:18 c Heb. 4:9, 10 d [1 Cor. 3:11–15; 15:58] *1* NU, M omit *to me*
15 a Rev. 16:17 b Joel 3:13 c Jer. 51:33 *1* NU, M omit *for You*
18 a Rev. 16:8 b Joel 3:13
19 a Rev. 19:15
20 a Is. 63:3 b Heb. 13:12 c Is. 34:3 *1* Lit. *stadia,* about 184 miles in all

CHAPTER 15
1 a Rev. 12:1, 3 b Rev. 21:9 c Rev. 14:10
2 a Rev. 4:6 b [Matt. 3:11] c Rev. 13:14, 15 d Rev. 13:17 e Rev. 5:8 *1* NU, M omit *over his mark*
3 a Ex. 15:1–21 b Rev. 15:3 c Deut. 32:3, 4 d Ps. 145:17 *1* NU, M *nations*
4 a Ex. 15:14 b Lev. 11:44 c Is. 66:23
5 a Num. 1:50 *1* NU, M omit *behold* *2 sanctuary,* the inner shrine
6 a Ex. 28:6 *1 sanctuary,* the inner shrine
7 a Rev. 4:6 b 1 Thess. 1:9
8 a Ex. 19:18; 40:34 b 2 Thess. 1:9

CHAPTER 16
1 a Rev. 15:1 b Rev. 14:10 *1* NU, M *seven bowls*
2 a Rev. 8:7 b Ex. 9:9–11 c Rev. 13:15–17; 14:9 d Rev. 13:14 *1 severe and malignant,* lit. *bad and evil*
3 a Rev. 8:8; 11:6 b Ex. 7:17–21
c Rev. 8:9 4 a Rev. 8:10 b Ex. 7:17–20 5 a Rev. 15:3, 4 b Rev. 1:4, 8 *1* NU, M omit *O Lord* *2* NU, M *was, the Holy One*

Because You have judged these
things.
6 For [a]they have shed the blood [b]of
saints and prophets,
[c]And You have given them blood to
drink.
[1]For it is their just due."

7 And I heard [1]another from the altar saying, "Even so, [a]Lord God Almighty, [b]true and righteous *are* Your judgments."

Fourth Bowl: Men Are Scorched

8 Then the fourth angel poured out his bowl [a]on the sun, [b]and power was given to him to scorch men with fire. 9 And men were scorched with great heat, and they [a]blasphemed the name of God who has power over these plagues; [b]and they did not repent [c]and give Him glory.

Fifth Bowl: Darkness and Pain

10 Then the fifth angel poured out his bowl [a]on the throne of the beast, [b]and his kingdom became full of darkness; [c]and they gnawed their tongues because of the pain. 11 They blasphemed the God of heaven because of their pains and their sores, and did not repent of their deeds.

Sixth Bowl: Euphrates Dried Up

12 Then the sixth angel poured out his bowl [a]on the great river Euphrates, [b]and its water was dried up, [c]so that the way of the kings from the east might be prepared. 13 And I saw three unclean [a]spirits like frogs *coming* out of the mouth of [b]the dragon, out of the mouth of the beast, and out of the mouth of [c]the false prophet. 14 For they are spirits of demons, [a]performing signs, *which* go out to the kings [1]of the earth and of [b]the whole world, to gather them to [c]the battle of that great day of God Almighty.

15 [a]"Behold, I am coming as a thief. Blessed *is* he who watches, and keeps his garments, [b]lest he walk naked and they see his shame."

16 [a]And they gathered them together to the place called in Hebrew, [1]Armageddon.

Seventh Bowl: The Earth Utterly Shaken

17 Then the seventh angel poured out his bowl into the air, and a loud voice came out of the temple of heaven, from the throne, saying, [a]"It is done!" 18 And [a]there were noises and thunderings and lightnings; [b]and there was a great earthquake, such a mighty and great earthquake [c]as had not occurred since men were on the earth. 19 Now [a]the great city was divided into three parts, and the cities of the nations fell. And [b]great Babylon [c]was remembered before God, [d]to give her the cup of the wine of the fierceness of His wrath. 20 Then [a]every island fled away, and the mountains were not found. 21 And great hail from heaven fell upon men, *each hailstone* about the weight of a talent. Men blasphemed God because of the plague of the hail, since that plague was exceedingly great.

The Scarlet Woman and the Scarlet Beast

17 Then [a]one of the seven angels who had the seven bowls came and talked with me, saying [1]to me, "Come, [b]I will show you the judgment of [c]the great harlot [d]who sits on many waters, 2 [a]with whom the kings of the earth committed fornication, and [b]the inhabitants of the earth were made drunk with the wine of her fornication."

3 So he carried me away in the Spirit [a]into the wilderness. And I saw a woman sitting [b]on a scarlet beast *which was* full of [c]names of blasphemy, having seven heads and ten horns. 4 The woman [a]was arrayed in purple and scarlet, [b]and adorned with gold and precious stones and pearls, [c]having in her hand a golden cup [d]full of abominations and the filthiness of [1]her fornication. 5 And on her forehead a name *was* written:

[a]MYSTERY, BABYLON THE GREAT,
THE MOTHER OF HARLOTS AND OF
THE ABOMINATIONS OF THE EARTH.

6 I saw [a]the woman, drunk [b]with the blood of the saints and with the blood of [c]the martyrs of Jesus. And when I saw her, I marveled with great amazement.

6 [a]Matt. 23:34 [b]Rev. 11:18 [c]Is. 49:26 [1]NU, M omit *For*
7 [a]Rev. 15:3 [b]Rev. 13:10; 19:2 [1]NU, M omit *another from*
8 [a]Rev. 8:12 [b]Rev. 9:17, 18
9 [a]Rev. 16:11 [b]Dan. 5:22 [c]Rev. 11:13
10 [a]Rev. 13:2 [b]Rev. 8:12; 9:2 [c]Rev. 11:10
12 [a]Rev. 9:14 [b]Jer. 50:38 [c]Is. 41:2, 25; 46:11
13 [a]1 John 4:1 [b]Rev. 12:3, 9 [c]Rev. 13:11, 14; 19:20; 20:10
14 [a]2 Thess. 2:9 [b]Luke 2:1 [c]Rev. 17:14; 19:19; 20:8 [1]NU, M omit *of the earth and*
15 [a]Matt. 24:43 [b]2 Cor. 5:3
16 [a]Rev. 19:19 [1]Lit. *Mount Megiddo;* M *Megiddo*
17 [a]Rev. 10:6; 21:6
18 [a]Rev. 4:5 [b]Rev. 11:13 [c]Dan. 12:1
19 [a]Rev. 14:8 [b]Rev. 17:5, 18 [c]Rev. 14:8; 18:5 [d]Is. 51:17
20 [a]Rev. 6:14; 20:11

CHAPTER 17
1 [a]Rev. 1:1; 21:9 [b]Rev. 16:19 [c]Nah. 3:4 [d]Jer. 51:13 [1]NU, M omit *to me*
2 [a]Rev. 2:22; 18:3, 9 [b]Jer. 51:7
3 [a]Rev. 12:6, 14; 21:10 [b]Rev. 12:3 [c]Rev. 13:1
4 [a]Rev. 18:12, 16 [b]Dan. 11:38 [c]Jer. 51:7 [d]Rev. 14:8

[1]M *the fornication of the earth* 5 [a]2 Thess. 2:7 6 [a]Rev. 18:24 [b]Rev. 13:15 [c]Rev. 6:9, 10

The Meaning of the Woman and the Beast

[7]But the angel said to me, "Why did you
marvel? I will tell you the [1]mystery of the
woman and of the beast that carries her,
which has the seven heads and the ten
horns. [8]The beast that you saw was, and is
not, and [a]will ascend out of the bottomless pit and [b]go to [1]perdition. And those
who [c]dwell on the earth [d]will marvel,
[e]whose names are not written in the Book
of Life from the foundation of the world,
when they see the beast that was, and is
not, and [2]yet is.

[9][a]"Here *is* the mind which has wisdom:
[b]The seven heads are seven mountains on
which the woman sits. [10]There are also
seven kings. Five have fallen, one is, *and*
the other has not yet come. And when he
comes, he must [a]continue a short time.
[11]The [a]beast that was, and is not, is himself also the eighth, and is of the seven,
and is going to [1]perdition.

[12][a]"The ten horns which you saw are
ten kings who have received no kingdom
as yet, but they receive authority for one
hour as kings with the beast. [13]These are
of one mind, and they will give their power and authority to the beast. [14][a]These

7 [1] *hidden truth*
8 [a] Rev. 11:7 [b] Rev. 13:10; 17:11 [c] Rev. 3:10 [d] Rev. 13:3 [e] Rev. 13:8 [1] *destruction* [2] NU, M *shall be present*
9 [a] Rev. 13:18 [b] Rev. 13:1
10 [a] Rev. 13:5
11 [a] Rev. 13:3, 12, 14; 17:8 [1] *destruction*
12 [a] Dan. 7:20
14 [a] Rev. 16:14; 19:19

PERPETUA

One of the earliest female Christian martyrs was Vibia Perpetua (181?–203). A new mother, Perpetua was arrested for her beliefs in Carthage, where Christianity had been preached but prohibited by the emperor. While Perpetua was in prison, God answered her prayer that He would reveal to her the fate of her companions and herself. She knew that they would die.

When the day of the martyrs' honor and glory came, they were led to the arena to be tortured and killed. Ruth A. Tucker and Walter Liefield share the conclusion of Perpetua's story in *Daughters of the Church*. It is worth reading in full: The day of their victory dawned, and with joyful countenances they marched from the prison to the arena as though on their way to heaven. If there was any trembling it was from joy, not fear. Perpetua followed with a quick step as a true spouse of Christ, the darling of God. . .

For the young women the devil had readied a mad cow . . . . Perpetua was tossed first and fell on her back. She sat up, and being more concerned with her sense of modesty than with her pain, covered her thighs with her gown that had been torn down one side. Then finding her hairclip, which had fallen out, she pinned back her loose hair, thinking it not proper for a martyr to suffer with disheveled hair; it might seem that she was mourning in her hour of triumph.

[The women] kissed each other so that their martyrdom would be completely perfected by the rite of the kiss of peace. The others, without making any movement or sounds, were killed by the sword; but Perpetua, in order to feel some of the pain, groaning as she was struck between the ribs, took the gladiator's trembling hand and guided it to her throat. The church father Tertullian added this postscript to Perpetua's life: "O most brave and blessed martyrs, you have gone out of prison rather than into one. Your dungeon is full of darkness, but you yourselves are light. Your dungeon has bonds, but God has made you free."

will make war with the Lamb, and the
Lamb will [b]overcome them, [c]for He is
Lord of lords and King of kings; [d]and
those *who are* with Him *are* called, chosen, and faithful."

Mighty God, You are
Lord of lords and King of
kings; may _____ stand with
You and be called, chosen,
and faithful.

FROM REVELATION 17:14

15Then he said to me, [a]"The waters
which you saw, where the harlot sits, [b]are
peoples, multitudes, nations, and
tongues. 16And the ten horns which you
[1]saw on the beast, [a]these will hate the
harlot, make her [b]desolate [c]and naked,
eat her flesh and [d]burn her with fire.
17[a]For God has put it into their hearts to
fulfill His purpose, to be of one mind, and
to give their kingdom to the beast, [b]until
the words of God are fulfilled. 18And the
woman whom you saw [a]is that great city
[b]which reigns over the kings of the
earth."

The Fall of Babylon the Great

18 After[a] these things I saw another
angel coming down from heaven,
having great authority, [b]and the earth was
illuminated with his glory. 2And he cried
[1]mightily with a loud voice, saying,
[a]"Babylon the great is fallen, is fallen, and
[b]has become a dwelling place of demons,
a prison for every foul spirit, and [c]a cage
for every unclean and hated bird! 3For all
the nations [a]have drunk of the wine of the
wrath of her fornication, the kings of the
earth have committed fornication with
her, [b]and the merchants of the earth have
become rich through the [1]abundance of
her luxury."

4And I heard another voice from heaven
saying, [a]"Come out of her, my people, lest
you share in her sins, and lest you receive
of her plagues. 5[a]For her sins [1]have
reached to heaven, and [b]God has remembered her iniquities. 6[a]Render to her just
as she rendered [1]to you, and repay her
double according to her works; [b]in the
cup which she has mixed, [c]mix double for
her. 7[a]In the measure that she glorified
herself and lived [1]luxuriously, in the same
measure give her torment and sorrow; for
she says in her heart, 'I sit *as* [b]queen, and
am no widow, and will not see sorrow.'
8Therefore her plagues will come [a]in one
day—death and mourning and famine.
And [b]she will be utterly burned with fire,
[c]for strong *is* the Lord God who [1]judges
her.

The World Mourns Babylon's Fall

9[a]"The kings of the earth who committed fornication and lived luxuriously with
her [b]will weep and lament for her, [c]when
they see the smoke of her burning,
10standing at a distance for fear of her torment, saying, [a]'Alas, alas, that great city
Babylon, that mighty city! [b]For in one
hour your judgment has come.'

11"And [a]the merchants of the earth will
weep and mourn over her, for no one buys
their merchandise anymore: 12[a]merchan-
dise of gold and silver, precious stones
and pearls, fine linen and purple, silk and
scarlet, every kind of citron wood, every
kind of object of ivory, every kind of object
of most precious wood, bronze, iron, and
marble; 13and cinnamon and incense, fragrant oil and frankincense, wine and oil,
fine flour and wheat, cattle and sheep,
horses and chariots, and bodies and [a]souls
of men. 14The fruit that your soul longed
for has gone from you, and all the things
which are rich and splendid have [1]gone
from you, and you shall find them no
more at all. 15The merchants of these
things, who became rich by her, will stand
at a distance for fear of her torment,
weeping and wailing, 16and saying, 'Alas,
alas, [a]that great city [b]that was clothed
in fine linen, purple, and scarlet, and
adorned with gold and precious stones
and pearls! 17[a]For in one hour such great
riches [1]came to nothing.' [b]Every ship-
master, all who travel by ship, sailors, and
as many as trade on the sea, stood at a
distance 18[a]and cried out when they saw
the smoke of her burning, saying, [b]'What
is like this great city?'

14 b Rev. 19:20 c 1 Tim. 6:15 d Jer. 50:44
15 a Is. 8:7 b Rev. 13:7
16 a Jer. 50:41 b Rev. 18:17, 19 c Ezek. 16:37, 39 d Rev. 18:8 1 NU, M *saw, and the beast*
17 a 2 Thess. 2:11 b Rev. 10:7
18 a Rev. 11:8; 16:19 b Rev. 12:4

CHAPTER 18
1 a Rev. 17:1, 7 b Ezek. 43:2
2 a Is. 13:19; 21:9 b Is. 13:21; 34:11, 13–15 c Is. 14:23 1 NU, M omit *mightily*
3 a Rev. 14:8 b Is. 47:15 1 Lit. *strengths*
4 a Is. 48:20
5 a Gen. 18:20 b Rev. 16:19 1 NU, M *have been heaped up*
6 a Ps. 137:8 b Rev. 14:10 c Rev. 16:19 1 NU, M omit *to you*
7 a Ezek. 28:2–8 b Is. 47:7, 8 1 *sensually*
8 a Rev. 18:10 b Rev. 17:16 c Jer. 50:34 1 NU, M *has judged*
9 a Ezek. 26:16; 27:35 b Jer. 50:46 c Rev. 19:3
10 a Is. 21:9 b Rev. 18:17, 19
11 a Ezek. 27:27–34
12 a Rev. 17:4
13 a Ezek. 27:13
14 1 NU, M *been lost to you*
16 a Rev. 17:18 b Rev. 17:4
17 a Rev. 18:10 b Is. 23:14 1 *have been laid waste*
18 a Ezek. 27:30 b Rev. 13:4

19[a]“They threw dust on their heads and
cried out, weeping and wailing, and saying, ‘Alas, alas, that great city, in which all
who had ships on the sea became rich by
her wealth! [b]For in one hour she [1]is made
desolate.’
20[a]“Rejoice over her, O heaven, and
you [1]holy apostles and prophets, for [b]God
has avenged you on her!”

Finality of Babylon’s Fall

21Then a mighty angel took up a stone
like a great millstone and threw *it* into the
sea, saying, [a]“Thus with violence the
great city Babylon shall be thrown down,
and [b]shall not be found anymore. 22[a]The
sound of harpists, musicians, flutists, and
trumpeters shall not be heard in you anymore. No craftsman of any craft shall be
found in you anymore, and the sound of
a millstone shall not be heard in you anymore. 23[a]The light of a lamp shall not
shine in you anymore, [b]and the voice of
bridegroom and bride shall not be heard
in you anymore. For [c]your merchants
were the great men of the earth, [d]for by
your sorcery all the nations were deceived. 24And [a]in her was found the blood
of prophets and saints, and of all who
[b]were slain on the earth.”

Heaven Exults over Babylon

19 After these things [a]I [1]heard a loud
voice of a great multitude in heav-
en, saying, “Alleluia! [b]Salvation and glory
and honor and power *belong* to [2]the Lord
our God! 2For [a]true and righteous *are* His
judgments, because He has judged the
great harlot who corrupted the earth with
her fornication; and He [b]has avenged on
her the blood of His servants *shed* by her.”
3Again they said, “Alleluia! [a]Her smoke
rises up forever and ever!” 4And [a]the
twenty-four elders and the four living
creatures fell down and worshiped God
who sat on the throne, saying, [b]“Amen!
Alleluia!” 5Then a voice came from the
throne, saying, [a]“Praise our God, all you
His servants and those who fear Him,
[b]both[1] small and great!”
6[a]And I heard, as it were, the voice of a
great multitude, as the sound of many waters and as the sound of mighty thunderings, saying, “Alleluia! For [b]the[1] Lord God
Omnipotent reigns! 7Let us be glad and
rejoice and give Him glory, for [a]the marriage of the Lamb has come, and His wife
has made herself ready.” 8And [a]to her it
was granted to be arrayed in fine linen,
clean and bright, [b]for the fine linen is the
righteous acts of the saints.

> *He is omnipotent, omnipresent, and omniscient; therefore, He is not limited by time nor is He limited by man’s ideologies, theologies, and preconceived ideas.*
>
> KATHRYN KUHLMAN

9Then he said to me, “Write: [a]‘Blessed
are those who are called to the marriage
supper of the Lamb!’ ” And he said to me,
[b]“These are the true sayings of God.”
10And [a]I fell at his feet to worship him.
But he said to me, [b]“See *that you do* not
do that! I am your [c]fellow servant, and of
your brethren [d]who have the testimony of
Jesus. Worship God! For the [e]testimony
of Jesus is the spirit of prophecy.”

Christ on a White Horse

11[a]Now I saw heaven opened, and behold, [b]a white horse. And He who sat on
him *was* called [c]Faithful and True, and
[d]in righteousness He judges and makes
war. 12[a]His eyes *were* like a flame of fire,
and on His head *were* many crowns. [b]He
[1]had a name written that no one knew
except Himself. 13[a]He *was* clothed with a
robe dipped in blood, and His name is
called [b]The Word of God. 14[a]And the armies in heaven, [b]clothed in [1]fine linen,
white and clean, followed Him on white
horses. 15Now [a]out of His mouth goes a
[1]sharp sword, that with it He should
strike the nations. And [b]He Himself will
rule them with a rod of iron. [c]He Himself
treads the winepress of the fierceness and
wrath of Almighty God. 16And [a]He has on
His robe and on His thigh a name written:

[b]KING OF KINGS AND LORD OF
LORDS.

19 [a]Josh. 7:6 [b]Rev. 18:8 [1]*have been laid waste*
20 [a]Jer. 51:48 [b]Luke 11:49 [1]NU, M *saints and apostles*
21 [a]Jer. 51:63, 64 [b]Rev. 12:8; 16:20
22 [a]Jer. 7:34; 16:9; 25:10
23 [a]Jer. 25:10 [b]Jer. 7:34; 16:9 [c]Is. 23:8 [d]2 Kin. 9:22
24 [a]Rev. 16:6; 17:6 [b]Jer. 51:49

CHAPTER 19
1 [a]Rev. 11:15; 19:6 [b]Rev. 4:11 [1]NU, M add *something like* [2]NU, M omit *the Lord*
2 [a]Rev. 15:3; 16:7 [b]Deut. 32:43
3 [a]Is. 34:10
4 [a]Rev. 4:4, 6, 10 [b]1 Chr. 16:36
5 [a]Ps. 134:1 [b]Rev. 11:18 [1]NU, M omit *both*
6 [a]Ezek. 1:24 [b]Rev. 11:15 [1]NU, M *our*
7 [a][Matt. 22:2; 25:10]
8 [a]Ezek. 16:10 [b]Ps. 132:9
9 [a]Luke 14:15 [b]Rev. 22:6
10 [a]Rev. 22:8 [b]Acts 10:26 [c][Heb. 1:14] [d]1 John 5:10 [e]Luke 24:27
11 [a]Rev. 15:5 [b]Rev. 6:2; 19:19, 21 [c]Rev. 3:7, 14 [d]Is. 11:4
12 [a]Rev. 1:14 [b]Rev. 2:17; 19:16 [1]M adds *names written, and*
13 [a]Is. 63:2, 3 [b][John 1:1, 14]
14 [a]Rev. 14:20 [b]Matt. 28:3 [1]NU, M *pure white linen*

15 [a]Is. 11:4 [b]Ps. 2:8, 9 [c]Is. 63:3–6 [1]M *sharp two-edged*
16 [a]Rev. 2:17; 19:12 [b]Dan. 2:47

The Beast and His Armies Defeated

17 Then I saw an angel standing in the
sun; and he cried with a loud voice, saying
to all the birds that fly in the midst of
heaven, [a]"Come and gather together for
the [1]supper of the great God, 18 [a]that you
may eat the flesh of kings, the flesh of
captains, the flesh of mighty men, the
flesh of horses and of those who sit on
them, and the flesh of all *people,* [1]free and
slave, both small and great."

19 [a]And I saw the beast, the kings of the
earth, and their armies, gathered together
to make war against Him who sat on the
horse and against His army. 20 [a]Then the
beast was captured, and with him the false
prophet who worked signs in his presence, by which he deceived those who received the mark of the beast and [b]those
who worshiped his image. [c]These two
were cast alive into the lake of fire [d]burn-
ing with brimstone. 21 And the rest [a]were
killed with the sword which proceeded
from the mouth of Him who sat on the
horse. [b]And all the birds [c]were filled with
their flesh.

Satan Bound 1000 Years

20 Then I saw an angel coming down
from heaven, [a]having the key to
the bottomless pit and a great chain in his
hand. 2 He laid hold of [a]the dragon, that
serpent of old, who is *the* Devil and Satan,
and bound him for a thousand years; 3 and
he cast him into the bottomless pit, and
shut him up, and [a]set a seal on him, [b]so
that he should deceive the nations no
more till the thousand years were finished. But after these things he must be
released for a little while.

The Saints Reign with Christ 1000 Years

4 And I saw [a]thrones, and they sat on
them, and [b]judgment was committed to
them. Then *I saw* [c]the souls of those who
had been beheaded for their witness to Jesus and for the word of God, [d]who had not
worshiped the beast [e]or his image, and
had not received *his* mark on their foreheads or on their hands. And they [f]lived
and [g]reigned with Christ for [1]a thousand
years. 5 But the rest of the dead did not live
again until the thousand years were finished. This *is* the first resurrection.
6 Blessed and holy *is* he who has part in
the first resurrection. Over such [a]the second death has no power, but they shall be
[b]priests of God and of Christ, [c]and shall
reign with Him a thousand years.

Satanic Rebellion Crushed

7 Now when the thousand years have expired, Satan will be released from his prison 8 and will go out [a]to deceive the nations
which are in the four corners of the earth,
[b]Gog and Magog, [c]to gather them together to battle, whose number *is* as the sand
of the sea. 9 [a]They went up on the breadth
of the earth and surrounded the camp of
the saints and the beloved city. And fire
came down from God out of heaven and
devoured them. 10 The devil, who deceived
them, was cast into the lake of fire and
brimstone [a]where[1] the beast and the false
prophet *are.* And they [b]will be tormented
day and night forever and ever.

The Great White Throne Judgment

11 Then I saw a great white throne and
Him who sat on it, from whose face [a]the
earth and the heaven fled away. [b]And
there was found no place for them. 12 And
I saw the dead, [a]small and great, standing
before [1]God, [b]and books were opened.
And another [c]book was opened, which is
the Book of Life. And the dead were
judged [d]according to their works, by the
things which were written in the books.
13 The sea gave up the dead who were in it,
[a]and Death and Hades delivered up the
dead who were in them. [b]And they were
judged, each one according to his works.
14 Then [a]Death and Hades were cast into
the lake of fire. [b]This is the second [1]death.
15 And anyone not found written in the
Book of Life [a]was cast into the lake of fire.

All Things Made New

21 Now [a]I saw a new heaven and a
new earth, [b]for the first heaven and
the first earth had passed away. Also there
was no more sea. 2 Then I, [1]John, saw [a]the
holy city, New Jerusalem, coming down
out of heaven from God, prepared [b]as a
bride adorned for her husband. 3 And I
heard a loud voice from heaven saying,
"Behold, [a]the tabernacle of God *is* with
men, and He will dwell with them, and
they shall be His people. God Himself will

17 a Ezek. 39:17 *1* NU, M *great supper of God*
18 a Ezek. 39:18–20 *1* NU, M *both free*
19 a Rev. 16:13–16
20 a Rev. 16:13 b Rev. 13:8, 12, 13 c Dan. 7:11 d Rev. 14:10
21 a Rev. 19:15 b Rev. 19:17, 18 c Rev. 17:16

CHAPTER 20
1 a Rev. 1:18; 9:1
2 a 2 Pet. 2:4
3 a Dan. 6:17 b Rev. 12:9; 20:8, 10
4 a Dan. 7:9 b [1 Cor. 6:2, 3] c Rev. 6:9 d Rev. 13:12 e Rev. 13:15 f John 14:19 g Rom. 8:17 *1* M *the*
6 a [Rev. 2:11; 20:14] b Is. 61:6 c Rev. 20:4
8 a Rev. 12:9; 20:3, 10 b Ezek. 38:2; 39:1, 6 c Rev. 16:14
9 a Ezek. 38:9, 16
10 a Rev. 19:20; 20:14, 15 b Rev. 14:10 *1* NU, M *where also*
11 a 2 Pet. 3:7 b Dan. 2:35
12 a Rev. 19:5 b Dan. 7:10 c Ps. 69:28 d Matt. 16:27 *1* NU, M *the throne*
13 a Rev. 1:18; 6:8; 21:4 b Rev. 2:23; 20:12
14 a 1 Cor. 15:26 b Rev. 21:8 *1* NU, M *death, the lake of fire.*
15 a Rev. 19:20

CHAPTER 21
1 a [2 Pet. 3:13] b Rev. 20:11
2 a Is. 52:1 b 2 Cor. 11:2 *1* NU, M omit *John* **3** a Lev. 26:11

be with them *and be* their God. 4[a]And God
will wipe away every tear from their eyes;
[b]there shall be no more death, [c]nor sorrow, nor crying. There shall be no more
pain, for the former things have passed
away."

Lord, I thank You that the day is coming when _____ will dwell with You—when You will wipe every tear from their eyes. There will be no more death, nor sorrow, nor crying; and there will be no more pain, for the former things will have passed away.

FROM REVELATION 21:3, 4

5Then [a]He who sat on the throne said,
[b]"Behold, I make all things new." And He
said [1]to me, "Write, for [c]these words are
true and faithful."
6And He said to me, [a]"It[1] is done! [b]I am
the Alpha and the Omega, the Beginning
and the End. [c]I will give of the fountain of
the water of life freely to him who thirsts.
7He who overcomes [1]shall inherit all
things, and [a]I will be his God and he shall
be My son. 8[a]But the cowardly, [1]unbeliev-
ing, abominable, murderers, sexually immoral, sorcerers, idolaters, and all liars
shall have their part in [b]the lake which
burns with fire and brimstone, which is
the second death."

The New Jerusalem

9Then one of [a]the seven angels who had
the seven bowls filled with the seven last
plagues came [1]to me and talked with me,
saying, "Come, I will show you [b]the
[2]bride, the Lamb's wife." 10And he carried
me away [a]in the Spirit to a great and high
mountain, and showed me [b]the [1]great
city, the [2]holy Jerusalem, descending out
of heaven from God, 11[a]having the glory
of God. Her light *was* like a most precious
stone, like a jasper stone, clear as crystal.
12Also she had a great and high wall with
[a]twelve gates, and twelve angels at the
gates, and names written on them, which
are *the names* of the twelve tribes of the
children of Israel: 13[a]three gates on the
east, three gates on the north, three gates
on the south, and three gates on the
west.
14Now the wall of the city had twelve
foundations, and [a]on them were the
[1]names of the twelve apostles of the
Lamb. 15And he who talked with me [a]had
a gold reed to measure the city, its gates,
and its wall. 16The city is laid out as a
square; its length is as great as its breadth.
And he measured the city with the reed:
twelve thousand [1]furlongs. Its length,
breadth, and height are equal. 17Then he
measured its wall: one hundred *and* forty-
four cubits, *according* to the measure of a
man, that is, of an angel. 18The construction of its wall was *of* jasper; and the city
was pure gold, like clear glass. 19[a]The
foundations of the wall of the city *were*
adorned with all kinds of precious stones:
the first foundation *was* jasper, the second
sapphire, the third chalcedony, the fourth
emerald, 20the fifth sardonyx, the sixth
sardius, the seventh chrysolite, the eighth
beryl, the ninth topaz, the tenth chryso-
prase, the eleventh jacinth, and the
twelfth amethyst. 21The twelve gates *were*
twelve [a]pearls: each individual gate was of
one pearl. [b]And the street of the city *was*
pure gold, like transparent glass.

The Glory of the New Jerusalem

22[a]But I saw no temple in it, for the
Lord God Almighty and the Lamb are its
temple. 23[a]The city had no need of the sun
or of the moon to shine [1]in it, for the
[2]glory of God illuminated it. The Lamb *is*
its light. 24[a]And the nations [1]of those who
are saved shall walk in its light, and the
kings of the earth bring their glory and
honor [2]into it. 25[a]Its gates shall not be
shut at all by day [b](there shall be no night
there). 26[a]And they shall bring the glory
and the honor of the nations into [1]it.
27But [a]there shall by no means enter it
anything [1]that defiles, or causes an abomination or a lie, but only those who are
written in the Lamb's [b]Book of Life.

4 [a]Is. 25:8 [b]1 Cor. 15:26 [c]Is. 35:10; 51:11; 65:19
5 [a]Rev. 4:2, 9; 20:11 [b]Is. 43:19 [c]Rev. 19:9; 22:6 [1]NU, M omit *to me*
6 [a]Rev. 10:6; 16:17 [b]Rev. 1:8; 22:13 [c]John 4:10 [1]M omits *It is done*
7 [a]Zech. 8:8 [1]M *I shall give him these things*
8 [a]1 Cor. 6:9 [b]Rev. 20:14 [1]M adds *and sinners,*
9 [a]Rev. 15:1 [b]Rev. 19:7; 21:2 [1]NU, M omit *to me* [2]M *woman, the Lamb's bride*
10 [a]Rev. 1:10 [b]Ezek. 48 [1]NU, M omit *great* [2]NU, M *holy city, Jerusalem*
11 [a]Rev. 15:8; 21:23; 22:5
12 [a]Ezek. 48:31–34
13 [a]Ezek. 48:31–34
14 [a]Eph. 2:20 [1]NU, M *twelve names*
15 [a]Ezek. 40:3
16 [1]Lit. *stadia,* about 1,380 miles in all
19 [a]Is. 54:11
21 [a]Matt. 13:45, 46 [b]Rev. 22:2
22 [a]John 4:21, 23
23 [a]Is. 24:23; 60:19, 20 [1]NU, M omit *in it* [2]M *very glory*
24 [a]Is. 60:3, 5; 66:12 [1]NU, M omit *of those who are saved* [2]M *of the nations to Him*
25 [a]Is. 60:11 [b]Is. 60:20
26 [a]Rev. 21:24 [1]M adds *that they may enter in.*
27 [a]Joel 3:17 [b]Phil. 4:3 [1]NU, M *profane, nor one who causes*

Revelation 22:1, 2

Dear Woman of Destiny,

As a little girl growing up in church, I really didn't hear much about the healing of nations. It never occurred to me that I could do something that could change my nation. Later, as I was raising my little ones, I started learning to be an intercessor. Phrases like "standing in the gap" began to have great meaning for me.

During this time I started noticing the state of my own nation—the United States. My eyes were opened to the sin and degradation around me. I was appalled at the lack of morality displayed through the media. Many times I would feel frustrated and ask myself the question, "What can I do to stand in the gap for such a huge problem?"

One day in prayer, I said to the Lord, "How has Satan been able to make such huge inroads into the United States?" The answer came back to me as I sensed Him speaking to my heart that Satan had a strategy and the people of God did not. I believed He was leading me to call together His "generals" or prayer leaders to repent for the sins of this nation. I believe He is giving us a strategy to heal this country.

You may think the next thing I asked was a really stupid question, but at that time I didn't understand much about the sins of nations. I queried the Lord with, "What is the sin of my nation?" In my heart, He quietly gave a list of things: slavery, the Trail of Tears, the internment of the Japanese during World War II, and other such atrocities.

From that time, my husband and I began to gather groups of intercessors to do what we do now, called "identificational repentance." We met with leaders of the people groups against whom America had sinned, and we asked their forgiveness. This included the sins of our fathers against different races.

Is this biblical? A resounding yes! Nehemiah said as he prayed for his people, "We have sinned against You. Both my father's house and I have sinned" (Neh. 1:6b). We began crying out to the Lord to heal our land (see 2 Chr. 7:14).

Of course, we also need to repent of other current issues, such as the gross immorality in our land. Have we seen any changes? Yes, we have. Not as many as we would like, but we are believing for God to heal America and other nations as well.

Where is this all headed? We stand in the gap with one major goal in mind—for revival to visit our land. You can help heal your nation through intercession right from your home as you confess the sin of your land. No prayer is too little or too insignificant.

Cindy Jacobs

Revelation 22:20

Dear Woman of Destiny,

This wonderful passage rings out a declaration that should sound from the heart of every woman of God—even so, Lord Jesus, come! So many times we are caught up in the day-to-day cares of the world to such a degree that we do not remember this incredible, exciting truth—Jesus is coming back. He is coming back for us as His glorious bride. Whether or not you have ever been a bride on earth, you will someday be a radiant, glowing bride for the King of Kings and Lord of Lords.

Think of it. Picture yourself preparing as a bride for His coming. One day the trumpet will sound and you will glow with love as you behold Him face-to-face. Your heart will burst with love for your King. The wedding party will be the hosts of heaven. None of us can imagine the wonder of this event. Nothing we will have ever experienced will come near to the union of the heavenly Bridegroom and His bride.

You may have heard the saying, "It is possible to become so heavenly minded that we are of no earthly good." While that may be true, I think that for most of the body of Christ, the opposite is true today—we aren't heavenly minded enough! We need to always keep our earthly lives in perspective with eternity. Everything down here is temporal.

What a great comfort this is to us! There is more beyond this life on earth. We are heaven-bound! This should put the situations that challenge us in life in perspective. This simply isn't the end, but the beginning. Our future with Him is more glorious than we can imagine.

We are in a betrothal time of our lives. We are in a season of courtship between the King, our fiancé, and ourselves. Even though the whole body of Christ is part of the bride, He makes us feel as if we are the only person in relationship with Him. That's how focused and how intense His love is.

Therefore, even as He is preparing for this glorious event, let's prepare ourselves for Him. Our hearts should daily sing with the words, "Come, Lord Jesus." The bride has made herself ready.

Cindy Jacobs

The River of Life

22 And he showed me [a]a [1]pure river of water of life, clear as crystal, proceeding from the throne of God and of the Lamb. 2 [a]In the middle of its street, and on either side of the river, *was* [b]the tree of life, which bore twelve fruits, each *tree* yielding its fruit every month. The leaves of the tree *were* [c]for the healing of the nations. 3 And [a]there shall be no more curse, [b]but the throne of God and of the Lamb shall be in it, and His [c]servants shall serve Him. 4 [a]They shall see His face, and [b]His name *shall be* on their foreheads. 5 [a]There shall be no night there: They need no lamp nor [b]light of the sun, for [c]the Lord God gives them light. [d]And they shall reign forever and ever.

The Time Is Near

6 Then he said to me, [a]"These words *are* faithful and true." And the Lord God of the [1]holy prophets [b]sent His angel to show His servants the things which must [c]shortly take place.

7 [a]"Behold, I am coming quickly! [b]Blessed *is* he who keeps the words of the prophecy of this book."

8 Now I, John, [1]saw and heard these things. And when I heard and saw, [a]I fell down to worship before the feet of the angel who showed me these things.

9 Then he said to me, [a]"See *that you do* not *do that.* [1]For I am your fellow servant, and of your brethren the prophets, and of those who keep the words of this book. Worship God." 10 [a]And he said to me, "Do not seal the words of the prophecy of this book, [b]for the time is at hand. 11 He who is unjust, let him be unjust still; he who is filthy, let him be filthy still; he who is righteous, let him [1]be righteous still; he who is holy, let him be holy still."

Jesus Testifies to the Churches

12 "And behold, I am coming quickly, and [a]My reward *is* with Me, [b]to give to every one according to his work. 13 [a]I am the Alpha and the Omega, *the* [1]Beginning and *the* End, the First and the Last."

14 [a]Blessed *are* those who [1]do His commandments, that they may have the right [b]to the tree of life, [c]and may enter through the gates into the city. 15 [1]But [a]outside *are* [b]dogs and sorcerers and sexually immoral and murderers and idolaters, and whoever loves and practices a lie.

16 [a]"I, Jesus, have sent My angel to testify to you these things in the churches. [b]I am the Root and the Offspring of David, [c]the Bright and Morning Star."

17 And the Spirit and [a]the bride say, "Come!" And let him who hears say, "Come!" [b]And let him who thirsts come. Whoever desires, let him take the water of life freely.

A Warning

18 [1]For I testify to everyone who hears the words of the prophecy of this book: [a]If anyone adds to these things, [2]God will add to him the plagues that are written in this book; 19 and if anyone takes away from the words of the book of this prophecy, [a]God[1] shall take away his part from the [2]Book of Life, from the holy city, and *from* the things which are written in this book.

When our Lord does come, He will come quickly, and we will find that He has been there all the time.

OSWALD CHAMBERS

I Am Coming Quickly

20 He who testifies to these things says, "Surely I am coming quickly."

Amen. Even so, come, Lord Jesus!

21 The grace of our Lord Jesus Christ *be* [1]with you all. Amen.

CHAPTER 22
1 [a]Ezek. 47:1 [1]NU, M omit *pure*
2 [a]Ezek. 47:12 [b]Gen. 2:9 [c]Rev. 21:24
3 [a]Zech. 14:11 [b]Ezek. 48:35 [c]Rev. 7:15
4 [a][Matt. 5:8] [b]Rev. 14:1
5 [a]Rev. 21:23 [b]Rev. 7:15 [c]Ps. 36:9 [d]Dan. 7:18, 27
6 [a]Rev. 19:9 [b]Rev. 1:1 [c]Heb. 10:37 [1]NU, M *spirits of the prophets*
7 [a][Rev. 3:11] [b]Rev. 1:3
8 [a]Rev. 19:10 [1]NU, M *am the one who heard and saw*
9 [a]Rev. 19:10 [1]NU, M omit *For*
10 [a]Dan. 8:26 [b]Rev. 1:3
11 [1]NU, M *do right*
12 [a]Is. 40:10; 62:11 [b]Rev. 20:12
13 [a]Is. 41:4 [1]NU, M *First and the Last, the Beginning and the End.*
14 [a]Dan. 12:12 [b][Prov. 11:30] [c]Rev. 21:27 [1]NU *wash their robes,*
15 [a]1 Cor. 6:9 [b]Phil. 3:2 [1]NU, M omit *But*
16 [a]Rev. 1:1 [b]Rev. 5:5 [c]Num. 24:17
17 [a][Rev. 21:2, 9] [b]Is. 55:1
18 [a]Deut. 4:2; 12:32 [1]NU, M omit *For* [2]M *may God add*
19 [a]Ex. 32:33 [1]M *may God take away* [2]NU, M *tree of life*
21 [1]NU *with all;* M *with all the saints*

APPENDIX

Women in Ministry

CINDY JACOBS

Several years ago my husband Mike was interviewed by a Christian magazine about the Generals of Intercession ministry and me. When asked how he achieved peace concerning God's call upon my life, Mike replied, "Barring all the theological questions, it came down to the basic question of whether Cindy had an anointing from God or not. Once I recognized that she did, I had the responsibility to trust God with it. He's the One who put it there."

I wish such a statement could settle issues of controversy concerning whether a woman can be in spiritual authority or teach men. It seems the major divisive issues, such as tongues, healing, divorce, how to baptize, and other related points of doctrine, no longer stop us from coming together in unity. The main issue of division today is "Can a woman teach?"

The two passages that have brought the greatest confusion and restriction of women's ministry in the church are 1 Corinthians 14:34, 35 and 1 Timothy 2:11–15. While examining the verses in question, allow me to give you four essential principles for interpreting scripture:

1. Determine the author's intent.
2. Determine the context within the chapter, the book, and the rest of the Bible.
3. Determine the historical or cultural setting at the time it was written.
4. Interpret unclear passages in light of passages that are clear.

Using those rules for interpretation, let's begin with 1 Corinthians 14:34, 35. How this passage is interpreted often depends less upon what Paul meant by "keep silent" and "not permitted to speak" than upon the reader's belief system regarding the scope of what a woman can do in the church. This passage has been read by some groups to mean that women should not be allowed to so much as talk out loud in church; other groups have used this passage as a blanket admonition that women should not be allowed to preach. Neither interpretation adequately takes into account Paul's practice of using women in ministry or his intent in this particular context.

The word *silent* has the connotation of "holding one's tongue" (see BAGD Greek-English Lexicon #749d, 1b; see also Strong's concordance # 4601), which fits in with this interpretation. The word *women* (Greek: *gune*) in this passage isn't "women" in general, but "wives" because 1 Corinthians 14:35 specifically mentions husbands. The wives were not conforming to what was right or fitting for the situation.

It is very easy to misread what was happening in the early church through the filter of our own modern-day church buildings and auditoriums. But the early church meetings were mostly in home settings. Even if the homes were large, it would still be quite disruptive for wives to be talking out loud during the meetings. I believe the strongest interpretation is the one concerning disruptions in the Corinthian church caused by women asking questions during the services. I do not believe Paul meant women were not to speak at all because Acts 18:26, 21:9, and 1 Corinthians 11:5 make it clear that they did.

Probably the most controversial and puzzling passage concerning women in the church is 1 Timothy 2:11–15. This time, however, the Greek word used is different from the 1 Corinthians 14:34 word translated "be silent." Although in the Corinthian passage *silent* means "to hold peace," this word *silence* (Greek: *hesuchia*) in 1 Timothy means "stillness" or "quietness" or even "agreement." It expresses the attitude of the learner.

This teachable attitude is the same attitude of humble submission that any male rabbinic scholar was to have in that day. What a beautiful thought! Paul was saying to these women, who were never allowed to be taught in a scholarly way in the Jewish synagogue system, that they could be full-fledged disciples.

So what could 1 Timothy 2:11–15 mean? Rather than completely prohibiting teaching by women, it is possible that Paul was prohibiting their teaching heresy. After all, it was in the very same city of Ephesus that Priscilla, along with her husband Aquila, both well known to Paul (see Rom. 16:3), taught a male Christian leader named Apollos (see Acts 18:24–26). Other admonitions in 1 Timothy suggest that women were going from house to house (or perhaps house church to house church) leading others astray. Paul writes about this in 1 Timothy 5:13 where they are described as "busybodies, saying things which they ought not." In verse 15, Paul warns that "some have already turned aside after Satan" because of the error of their teaching.

One of the most difficult sections of 1 Timothy 2:11–15 is verse 12, because it seems to say that allowing women to teach men would be giving them "authority over a man"—allowing them to take the teaching positions that only men should have. Part of the difficulty arises because the Greek word *authenteō* occurs here and nowhere else in the New Testament. Let's look at this word to try to determine its possible meaning.

There are many interpretations of *authenteō*. One says *authenteō* means "to dominate." Traditionalists use this passage to demonstrate that women should not teach men because they would be "taking authority over men." Other traditionalists say that a woman as a missionary may serve as a leader and teacher, but she may not pastor a church. Some allow a woman to "share" testimonies of great moves of God seen on the mission field as long as the woman doesn't stand in the pulpit. Therefore, the prohibition is not violated because the woman is not "teaching" but "sharing." Other traditionalists say a woman is teaching when she actually opens the Bible to read a scripture along with her speaking time. The line between "teaching" and "sharing" can become very gray indeed. Those who propose this kind of drawing of artificial lines around certain types of teaching and authority are doing "hermeneutical gerrymandering," making distinctions in levels of authority in ministry that are not delineated in the Scriptures.

Furthermore, the traditionalists' viewpoints that limit the setting and to whom a woman can teach do not seem consistent with other Pauline writing, as shown by the example of Priscilla helping to teach Apollos, a Christian leader (see Acts 18:24–26). Another consideration that some may not have considered is the testimony of Mary Magdalene to the Resurrection (see Matt. 28:1–8; Mark 16:9–11; Luke 24:1–10; John 20:11–18). Men everywhere have been taught the glorious fact that He has risen just as He said from the testimony of this woman out of whom Jesus had cast seven demons. Clearly, the Holy Spirit trusted a woman to give this message in a trustworthy fashion, knowing that men everywhere would learn from it. God knew what He was doing and the precedent it would set for the church thereafter!

If Paul did not mean for these texts to universally prohibit women teaching men, then what could he have been saying in these passages? What else could he have been trying to correct in the church? In order to find this out, we need to study the meaning of the word *authenteō* at the time of the first century. Words can take on different meanings even within one generation. Imagine how they can change down through many centuries!

While the word *authenteō* has been translated by the word "authority" in nearly all English versions of the Bible, it is not the same word as *exousia*, the word used for "authority" in many other passages. Studies of the use of *authenteō* in the literature of the day show that the word originally meant "murder." By the second and third century A.D., its connotation had changed to "having authority over." *Authenteō* was also used in connection with sex and murder. Women were known to curse men to death through the use of "curse tablets."

Evidence exists for another possible meaning of *authenteō* from that time period—that of "originator." Gnostic heresy during this time period taught that Eve was the first virgin, the one who had no husband and the originator of all life. She was the "illuminator," full of all wisdom, and Adam was actually given life when she saw her colikeness lying flat upon the earth, whereas she commanded him to live. When he saw her, he said, "You will be called 'the mother of the living' because you are the one who has given me life."

This Gnostic myth is, of course, heresy. The Bible clearly states that Adam was created first and then Eve. The idea that *authenteō* may have the meaning of "originator" instead of "take authority" seems to fit in light of the rest of the passage in 1 Timothy: "For Adam was formed first, then Eve. And Adam was not deceived, but the woman being deceived, fell into transgression" (1 Tim. 2:13, 14).

This passage could very well have been written to attack the Gnostic heresy that Eve was the creator. A further blow is dealt against this error in verse 14, which clearly says that Eve was deceived. The Eve of Gnostic heresy could never have been deceived because she was the illuminator and all-wise. First Timothy 1:17 sets the record straight. Only One is all-wise, and that is God Himself.

As a result of this interpretation, the passage could be translated: "I am not allowing (present tense for that situation) a woman to teach or to proclaim herself the originator of man (*authenteō*). Adam was formed first, then Eve."

In light of the prevailing mother-goddess heresy and emerging Gnosticism in First and Second Timothy and Titus, it seems clear that Paul was bringing correction in 1 Timothy 2:11–15. He was correcting women or possibly "a woman" or even "a wife" who was teaching some kind of heresy. (The word *woman* here can also mean "wife.")

If the admonition for women not to teach was universal, it would have been strengthened with other passages. Instead, we find many passages to show that women did indeed teach men and held significant places as leaders in the church (see Acts 18:26; 21:9; Rom. 16:1, 3, 7). The Old Testament, which was the Bible of the early church, offers clear precedents for women teaching men in a variety of settings in 2 Kings 22:14; Proverbs 1:8; 31:26; and Micah 6:4.

I believe the Lord is clearly speaking to the body of Christ today about the need to reexamine our belief system concerning women teaching. We must open our eyes to the fact that when God anoints women with the gift of teaching, He is releasing great revelation and blessing to the church through them.

I find it interesting that 1 Timothy 2:11–15 and 1 Corinthians 14:34, 35 cause us so many problems when other obscure passages in the Bible don't bother us even though we don't completely understand them. For instance, most Christians don't spend lots of time trying to interpret the verse that deals with baptism for the dead (see 1 Cor. 15:29).

I believe a day is coming when we will look back at the controversy over women teaching in the church and simply shake our heads in wonder that it ever was such a big issue. Years ago when I was lonely and struggling with how to be a woman leader in the midst of rejection and misunderstanding, I made a vow to the Lord that I would do what I could to see that other young women leaders didn't have to suffer as I had. I don't want any young women leaders to have to deal with rejection of their ministries based solely upon their gender.

CONTRIBUTORS

Sue Ahn—Harvest Rock Church; Pasadena, CA

Lora Allison—Celebration International Ministries; La Porte, TX

Beth Alves— Intercessors International; Bulverde, TX

Julie Anderson—Prayer for the Nations; London, England

Maria Annacondia—wife of Carlos Annacondia; Buenos Aires, Argentina

Shirley Arnold—Shirley Arnold Ministries and The Secret Place; Lakeland, FL

Jill Austin—Master Potter Ministries; Kansas City, MO

Lori Graham Bakker—wife of Jim Bakker; Charlotte, NC

Kim Bangs—Gospel Light Publications; Ventura, CA

Vicki Bartholomew—The Master's Plan Bible School; Nashville, TN

Rebecca Hayford Bauer—The Church on the Way; Van Nuys, CA

Naomi Beard—International Church of the Foursquare Gospel; Van Nuys, CA

Lisa Bevere—John Bevere Ministries; Colorado Springs, CO

Connie Broome—Morris Cerullo World Evangelism; San Diego, CA

Rachel Burchfield—Burchfield Ministries, Texas Bible Institute; Columbus, TX

Doris Bush—AD 2000 and Beyond movement; Colorado Springs, CO

Cecilia Caballeros—El Shaddai Church; Guatemala City, Guatemala

Agatha Chan—Revival Fellowship; Hong Kong

Bonnie Chavda—All Nations Church, Watch of the Lord; Charlotte, NC

Pat Chen—First Love Ministries International; San Ramon, CA

Beth Clark—Associate Publisher, Thomas Nelson Bibles; Nashville, TN

Nancy Corbett Cole—Christian Men's Network; Grapevine, TX

Jamie Owens Collins—Singer/Songwriter; Newport Beach, California

Germaine Copeland—Word Ministries; Roswell, GA

Sue Curran— Shekinah Church; Blountville, TN

Sharon Damazio—City Bible Church; Portland, OR

Sharon Daugherty—Victory Christian Center; Tulsa, OK

Joy Dawson—International Bible Teacher, YWAM; Tejunga, CA

Kathleen Dillard—PrayINDIA; Hyderabad, India

Naomi Dowdy—Global Leadership Network; Singapore

Megan Doyle—The Welsh Companies, Nehemiah Partners; Minneapolis, MN

Dee Eastman—Every Home for Christ; Colorado Springs, CO

Tommi Femrite—Intercessors International; Colorado Springs, CO

Mary Forsythe—Sojourn Church; Dallas, TX

Betty Freidzon—King of Kings Church; Buenos Aires, Argentina

Ruthanne Garlock—Garlock Ministries; Bulverde, TX

Mary Glazier—Windwalkers International; Anchorage, AK

Michal Ann Goll—Ministry to the Nations; Nashville, TN

Kathy Gray—Smithton Community Church; Smithton, MO

Melody Green—Writer, Speaker; Aptos, California

Catherine Berg Greig—Writer; Virginia Beach, VA

Doris Greig—Author; Ventura, CA

Jill Griffith—Kingdom Connections International; Houston, TX

Diana Hagee—Cornerstone Church; San Antonio, TX

Jane Hamon—Christian International; Santa Rosa Beach, FL

Jane Hansen—Aglow International; Edmonds, WA

Anna Hayford—The Church on the Way; Van Nuys, CA

Ruth Ward Heflin—Author; Ashland, VA

Solveig Henderson—Singer/Songwriter; Colorado Springs, CO

Marilyn Hickey—Marilyn Hickey Ministries; Englewood, CO

Jeri Hill—Together in the Harvest Ministries; Pensacola, FL

Nancy Hinkle—Scott Hinkle Outreach Ministries; Phoenix, AZ

Suzanne Hinn—Benny Hinn Ministries; Orlando, FL

Sally Horton—Christ for the Nations Institute; Dallas, TX

Esther Ilnisky—The Esther Network International; Palm Beach, FL

Cindy Jacobs—Generals of Intercession; Colorado Springs, CO

Serita Jakes—T. D. Jakes Ministries; Dallas, TX

Barbara James—World Intercession Network (Pentecostal Holiness); Oklahoma City, OK

Brenda Kilpatrick—Brownsville Assembly of God; Pensacola, FL

Cathy Lechner—Covenant Ministries; Jacksonville, FL

Freda Lindsay—Christ for the Nations Institute; Dallas, TX

Ginger Lindsay—Christ for the Nations Institute; Dallas, TX

Katie Luce—Teen Mania; Lindale, TX

Colleen Marocco—Maui First Assembly of God; Maui, HI

Judith Christie-McAllister—Minister of Music, West Angeles Church of God in Christ

Terry Meeuwsen—Cohost, *The 700 Club*; Virginia Beach, VA

Bobbie Jean Merck—A Great Love International; Toccoa, GA

Linda Mintle—Psychologist; Wheaton, IL

Margaret Moberly—Mount Zion Ministries, Word Ministries International, Woman Ministries International; Fort Worth, TX

Susan Moore—Sojourn Church; Dallas, TX

Leslyn Musch—Global Prayer Ministries; Arcadia, CA

Betsy Neuenschwander—Physician; AD 2000 Crisis Relief Task Force; Colorado Springs, CO

Carol Noe—Fuchsia Pickett Ministries; Blountville, TN

Agnes Numer—Somer Haven International Ministries; Palmdale, CA

LaDonna Osborn—Bishop, Int'l Gospel Center Ministries; Tulsa, OK

Lisa Otis—The Sentinel Group; Lynnwood, WA

Carol Owens—Writer/Musician; Colorado Springs, CO

Fawn Parish—International Reconciliation Coalition, Lydia Prayer Fellowship; Camarillo, CA

Gina Pearson—Higher Dimensions Church; Tulsa, OK

Fuchsia Pickett—Fuchsia Pickett Ministries; Blountville, TN

Mary Jean Pidgeon—Christian Men's Network; Grapevine, TX

Pam Pierce—Glory of Zion International Ministries; Colorado Springs, CO

Faeona Pratney—wife of Winkie Pratney; Lindale, TX

Judy Radachy—The Oasis; Hollywood, CA

Gloria Richards—Vino Nuevo; Juarez, Mexico

Evelyn Roberts—Oral Roberts University; Tulsa, OK

Lindsay Roberts—Oral Roberts University; Tulsa, OK

A. G. Rodriguez—It Is Finished Ministries; Nashville, TN

Susan Ryan—World Prayer Center; Colorado Springs, CO

Cheryl Sacks—Bridgebuilders International; Phoenix, AZ

Paula Sandford—Author, Elijah House; Post Falls, ID

Kathleen Scataglini—Puerta de Cielo Church; La Plata, Argentina

Gwen Shaw—End-Time Handmaidens; Jasper, AK

Ceci Sheets—Springs Harvest Fellowship Church; Colorado Springs, CO

Dana Sherrard—The Master's Plan Bible School; Nashville, TN

Quin Sherrer—Author, Speaker; Colorado Springs, CO

Ruth Silvoso—Harvest Evangelism; San Jose, CA

Polly Simchen—Generals of Intercession; Colorado Springs, CO

Alice Smith—Author, US Prayer Track of AD 2000 and Beyond movement; Houston, TX

Judy Smith—International Director; YWAM School of Biblical Studies

Kara Quinn-Smith—Author; Chicago, IL

Rebecca Wagner Sytsema—Global Harvest Ministries; Colorado Springs, CO

Thetus Tenney—United Pentecostal Church; Tioga, LA

Lila Terhune—Brownsville Assembly of God; Pensacola, FL

Betty Thiessen—Host of *It's a New Day* television program; Winnipeg, Canada

Brenda Timberlake—Christian Faith Center; Creedmoor, NC

Iverna Tompkins—Iverna Tompkins Ministries; Phoenix, AZ

LaNora Van Arsdall—Speaker, Sanctuary of the East Valley; Gilbert, AZ

Doris Wagner—Global Harvest Ministries; Colorado Springs, CO

Nola Warren—Centro Cristiano Bethel Norte; Mexico

Joann Cole Webster—Christian Men's Network; Grapevine, TX

Barbara Wentroble—Wentroble Christian Ministries; Duncanville, TX

Miriam Witt—wife of Marcos Witt; Mexico

Barbara Yoder—Author, Senior Pastor, Shekinah Church; Ann Arbor, MI

PERMISSIONS

How to Be Filled with the Holy Spirit
Hickey, Marilyn. *I Can Be Born Again and Spirit Filled* (Denver, CO: Marilyn Hickey Ministries, 1984), pp. 35–44. Reprinted with permission.

The Gifts of the Holy Spirit
Wagner, C. Peter. *Your Spiritual Gifts Can Help Your Church Grow* (Ventura, CA: Regal Books, 1994), pp. 253–258.

God's Plan for Men and Women (Genesis 1:27)
Pickett, Fuchsia. *God's Dream* (Shippensburg, PA: Destiny Image Publishers, 1991), pp. 88–98.

The Desire of the Woman (Genesis 3:16b)
Hansen, Jane with Marie Powers. *Fashioned for Intimacy* (Ventura, CA: Regal Books, 1997), pp. 73–83. Used by permission.

Consecrated to Him (Leviticus 11:44)
Meeuwsen, Terry. *Near to the Heart of God* (Nashville, TN: Thomas Nelson Publishers, 1998), pp. 236–239. Used by permission.

Choosing Life (Deuteronomy 30:19)
Roberts, Lindsay. "What to Do When Satan Comes to Steal." Message preached June 15, 1999, International Charismatic Bible Ministries Conference, Tulsa, OK.

Aiming on Target (Judges 9:50–56)
Sheets, Dutch. *Intercessory Prayer* (Ventura, CA: Regal Publishing, 1996), p. 99.

Giving Your Children to God (1 Samuel 1:25–28)
Sherrer, Quin with Ruthanne Garlock. *How to Pray for Your Children* (Ventura, CA: Regal Books, 1998), pp. 32, 213, 214. Used by permission.

Crying Out to God (1 Samuel 30:6)
Timberlake, Brenda. "Standing in Faith Against Cancer." *SpiritLed Woman,* Dec/Jan 1999, pp. 16–20.

Sharing the Faith (1 Chronicles 16:23, 24)
Meeuwsen, Terry. *Near to the Heart of God* (Nashville, TN: Thomas Nelson Publishers, 1998), pp. 150–152. Used by permission.

The Joy of the Lord (Nehemiah 8:10)
Lechner, Cathy. *I'm Trying to Sit at His Feet, But Who's Going to Cook Dinner?* (Orlando, FL: Creation House, 1995), pp. 11, 12, 51. Used by permission.

Responding to the King (Esther 2:1–18)
Jakes, Serita. *The Princess Within* (Tulsa, OK: Albury Publishing, 1999), pp. 73–97.

Acquainting Yourself with Him (Job 22:21)
Merck, Bobbie Jean. "Acquaint Yourself With Him." *A Great Love Overflow* 21, no. 9 (1998): 1–3. Used by permission.

Overcoming Shame (Psalm 25:2, 3)
Merck, Bobbie Jean. "No Shame." *A Great Love Outpouring* 11, no. 2 (1988): 2, 3. Used by permission.

Waiting on God (Psalm 31:14, 15)
Merck, Bobbie Jean. "God's Timing." *A Great Love Outpouring* 11, no. 4 (1988): 1–7. Used by permission.

The Lord's Protection (Psalm 91)
Houghton, Frank. *Amy Carmichael of Dohnavur* (London: S.P.C.K., 1954) p. 36.

The New Song (Song of Solomon 1:3, 4)
Heflin, Ruth Ward. *Glory* (Hagerstown, MD: McDougal Publishing Company, 1990), pp. 111–126. Used by permission.

Dealing with Little Foxes (Song of Solomon 2:15)
Meeuwsen, Terry. *Near to the Heart of God* (Nashville, TN: Thomas Nelson Publishers, 1998), pp. 138–142. Used by permission.

The Father and His Family (Isaiah 63:16)
Hansen, Jane with Marie Powers. *Fashioned for Intimacy* (Ventura, CA: Regal Books, 1997), pp. 19–27. Used by permission.

Dealing with Spiritual Adultery (Jeremiah 23:1)
Jacobs, Cindy. *Women of Destiny* (Ventura, CA: Regal Books, 1998), pp. 162–164. Used by permission.

An Answer of Restoration (Jeremiah 33:3)
Roberts, Lindsay. "Hour of Healing #394." Aired March 25, 1999.

Standing in the Gap (Ezekiel 22:30)
Murray, Andrew. *With Christ in the School of Prayer* (Springdale, PA: Whitaker House, 1981), p. 25.

Recognizing Spiritual Abuse (Ezekiel 34:2)
Jacobs, Cindy. *The Voice of God* (Ventura, CA: Regal Books, 1995), pp. 146–159. Used by permission.

Breaking Spiritual Strongholds (Daniel 10:11, 12)
Jacobs, Cindy. "Fasting To Break Spiritual Strongholds." *G.I. News* 6, no. 2 (1997): 1, 3. Used by permission.

The Door of Hope (Hosea 2:15)
Jacobs, Cindy. "The Door of Hope." *G.I. News* 5, no. 3 (1996): 1, 3. Used by permission.

Prayer and Fasting (Joel 1:13, 14)
Miller, Milburn H. *Notes and Quotes* (Anderson, IN: The Warner Press, 1960), p. 134.

Prophetic Women (Joel 2:28)
Jacobs, Cindy. *The Voice of God* (Ventura, CA: Regal Books, 1995), pp. 60, 61. Used by permission.

Being Salt and Light (Matthew 5:13–15)
Neuenschwander, Mark and Betsy. *Crisis Evangelism* (Ventura, CA: Regal Books, 1999), pp. 25–32. Used by permission.

Intimacy Beyond Flesh (Matthew 19:5)
Hansen, Jane with Marie Powers. *Fashioned for Intimacy* (Ventura, CA: Regal Books, 1997), pp. 52–60. Used by permission.

All Things Are Possible (Matthew 19:26)
Lechner, Cathy. *I Hope God's Promises Come to Pass Before My Body Parts Go South* (Orlando, FL: Creation House, 1998), pp. 1–10. Used by permission.

Praying for a Prodigal (Luke 15:11–13)
Sherrer, Quin with Ruthanne Garlock. *How to Pray for Your Children* (Ventura, CA: Regal Books, 1998), pp. 93, 94. Used by permission.

Your Appointed Hour (John 7:8)
Merck, Bobbie Jean. "God's Timing." *A Great Love Outpouring* 11, no. 4 (1988): 1–7. Used by permission.

Speaking Mysteries (1 Corinthians 14:2)
Heflin, Ruth Ward. *Glory* (Hagerstown, MD: McDougal Publishing Company, 1990), pp. 172–174. Used by permission.

Picture Perfect (2 Corinthians 12:9, 10)
Hansen, Jane with Marie Powers. *Fashioned for Intimacy* (Ventura, CA: Regal Books, 1997), pp. 100–110. Used by permission.

"Born of a Woman" (Galatians 4:4–7)
Cole, Nancy Corbett. *Tapestry of Life* (Tulsa, OK: Albury Books, 1992), p. 105.

Rebuilding the House (Ephesians 2:21, 22)
Hansen, Jane with Marie Powers. *Fashioned for Intimacy* (Ventura, CA: Regal Books, 1997), pp. 30–36. Used by permission.

Kairos Time (1 Thessalonians 5:1)
Shaw, Gwen. "*Kairos* Time." *End-Time Handmaidens Magazine*, no. 52 (1999):1–20.

Biblical Mentoring (Titus 2:3–5)
From *A Woman's Guide to Spirit-Filled Living*, ©1996 by Quin Sherrer and Ruthanne Garlock. Published by Servant Publications, Box 8617, Ann Arbor, MI 48107. Used with permission.

Persevering for the Prize (Hebrews 6:11, 12)
Meeuwsen, Terry. *Near to the Heart of God* (Nashville, TN: Thomas Nelson Publishers, 1998), pp. 74–76. Used by permission.

The Fire of God (Hebrews 12:29)
Moberly, Margaret Morgan. *FireBride* (Orlando, FL: Creation House, 1999), pp. 11–20. Used by permission.

Revealing the Heart (1 Peter 3:1, 3, 4)
Hansen, Jane with Marie Powers. *Fashioned for Intimacy* (Ventura, CA: Regal Books, 1997), pp. 87–96. Used by permission.

Love Casts Out Fear (1 John 4:18)
Bevere, Lisa. *Out of Control and Loving It!* (Orlando, FL: Creation House, 1996), pp. 105–109. Used by permission.

A diligent effort has been made to secure permission to reprint previously published material. Any oversight should be brought to the attention of the publisher for rectification in a subsequent printing.

CONCORDANCE

A

ABASED
I know how to be *a* .....Phil 4:12

ABBA
And He said, "*A* ......Mark 14:36
whom we cry out, "*A* ...Rom 8:15

ABHOR
Therefore I *a* myself .....Job 42:6

ABHORRED
a His own inheritance ...Ps 106:40

ABIDE
the Most High Shall *a* .....Ps 91:1
Him, "If you *a* ....John 8:31
"If you *a* in Me ....John 15:7
a in My love ....John 15:9

ABIDES
He who *a* in Me ....John 15:5
will of God *a* forever ...1 John 2:17

ABIDING
not have His word *a* ....John 5:38

ABILITY
to his own *a* ....Matt 25:15
a which God supplies ..1 Pet 4:11

ABLE
shall give as he is *a* ....Deut 16:17
whom we serve is *a* ......Dan 3:17
God is *a* to raise up ....Matt 3:9
fear Him who is *a* ....Matt 10:28
you *a* to drink the ......Matt 20:22
that He is *a* ....2 Tim 1:12
learning and never *a* .....2 Tim 3:7
that God was *a* to ....Heb 11:19

ABOLISHED
having *a* in His flesh ......Eph 2:15
Christ, who has *a* ....2 Tim 1:10

ABOMINABLE
deny Him, being *a* ....Titus 1:16
unbelieving, *a* ....Rev 21:8

ABOMINATION
Yes, seven are an *a* .....Prov 6:16
the scoffer is an *a* ....Prov 24:9
prayer is an *a* ....Prov 28:9
and place there the *a* ....Dan 11:31
the *a* of desolation ....Dan 12:11
the *'a of desolation,'* ...Matt 24:15

ABOMINATIONS
delights in their *a* ....Is 66:3
a golden cup full of *a* .....Rev 17:4

ABOUND
the offense might *a* ....Rom 5:20
sin that grace may *a* ....Rom 6:1
to make all grace *a* ....2 Cor 9:8
and I know how to *a* .....Phil 4:12

ABOUNDED
But where sin *a* ....Rom 5:20

ABOUNDING
immovable, always *a* ..1 Cor 15:58

ABOVE
that is in heaven *a* ....Ex 20:4
A it stood seraphim ....Is 6:2
"He who comes from *a* ..John 3:31
I am from *a* ....John 8:23
given you from *a* ....John 19:11
things which are *a* ....Col 3:1
perfect gift is from *a* ...James 1:17

ABSENT
in the body we are *a* .....2 Cor 5:6

ABSTAIN
we write to them to *a* ..Acts 15:20
A from every form ...1 Thess 5:22

ABUNDANCE
put in out of their *a* ...Mark 12:44
not consist in the *a* ....Luke 12:15

ABUNDANT
in labors more *a* ....2 Cor 11:23

ABUNDANTLY
a satisfied with the ....Ps 36:8
may have it more *a* .....John 10:10
to do exceedingly *a* ....Eph 3:20

ACCEPT
offering, I will not *a* .....Jer 14:12
Should I *a* this from ....Mal 1:13

ACCEPTABLE
a time I have heard ....Is 49:8
proclaim the *a* year ....Is 61:2
proclaim the a year ....Luke 4:19
is that good and *a* ....Rom 12:2

ACCEPTABLY
we may serve God *a* ....Heb 12:28

ACCEPTED
Behold, now is the *a* .....2 Cor 6:2
which He made us *a* ....Eph 1:6

ACCESS
whom also we have *a* .....Rom 5:2

ACCOMPLISHED
all things were now *a* ..John 19:28

ACCORD
continued with one *a* .....Acts 1:14

ACCOUNT
they will give *a* ....Matt 12:36
put that on my *a* ....Philem 18

ACCOUNTED
in the LORD, and He *a* ...Gen 15:6
his faith is *a* ....Rom 4:5
God, and it was a ....Gal 3:6
God, and it was a ....James 2:23

ACCURSED
not know the law is *a* ...John 7:49
of God calls Jesus *a* ......1 Cor 12:3
to you, let him be *a* ....Gal 1:8

ACCUSATION
over His head the *a* ....Matt 27:37
they might find an *a* ....Luke 6:7

ACCUSE
they began to *a* Him ......Luke 23:2

ACCUSED
while He was being *a* ..Matt 27:12

ACCUSER
a of our brethren ....Rev 12:10

ACCUSING
their thoughts *a* ....Rom 2:15

ACKNOWLEDGE
a my transgressions ....Ps 51:3
In all your ways *a* ....Prov 3:6

ACKNOWLEDGES
a the Son has the ......1 John 2:23

ACQUAINT
a yourself with Him ....Job 22:21

ACQUAINTED
A Man of sorrows and *a* ...Is 53:3

ACQUIT
at all *a* the wicked ....Nah 1:3

ACT
in the very *a* ....John 8:4

ACTIONS
by Him *a* are weighed ..1 Sam 2:3

ACTS
of Your awesome *a* ....Ps 145:6

ADD
Do not *a* to His words ..Prov 30:6

ADDED
And the Lord *a* to the .....Acts 2:47
It was *a* because of ....Gal 3:19

ADMONISH
a him as a ....2 Thess 3:15

ADMONITION
written for our *a* ....1 Cor 10:11
in the training and *a* ....Eph 6:4

ADOPTION
the Spirit of *a* ....Rom 8:15
waiting for the *a* ....Rom 8:23
to whom pertain the *a* .....Rom 9:4

ADORN
also, that the women *a* ..1 Tim 2:9

ADORNED
God also *a* themselves ....1 Pet 3:5
prepared as a bride *a* .....Rev 21:2

ADRIFT
A among the dead ....Ps 88:5

ADULTERER
The eye of the *a* ....Job 24:15

ADULTERERS
nor idolaters, nor *a* ......1 Cor 6:9
a God will judge ....Heb 13:4

ADULTEROUS
a generation ....Matt 12:39

ADULTERY
You shall not commit *a* . Ex 20:14
already committed *a* ......Matt 5:28

is divorced commits *a* . . Matt 5:32
another commits *a* . . . . Mark 10:11
those who commit *a* . . . . . Rev 2:22

ADVANTAGE

a that I go away . . . . John 16:7
Satan should take *a* . . . 2 Cor 2:11

ADVERSARIES

and there are many *a* . . 1 Cor 16:9
terrified by your *a* . . . . . . Phil 1:28

ADVERSARY

"Agree with your *a* . . . . . Matt 5:25
opportunity to the *a* . . . 1 Tim 5:14
a the devil walks . . . . 1 Pet 5:8

ADVERSITY

I shall never be in *a* . . . . . . Ps 10:6
the day of *a* consider . . . . Eccl 7:14

ADVICE

in this I give my *a* . . . . . 2 Cor 8:10

ADVOCATE

sins, we have an *A* . . . . 1 John 2:1

AFAR

and not a God *a* . . . . Jer 23:23
to you who were *a* . . . . . . Eph 2:17
having seen them *a* . . . . Heb 11:13

AFFAIRS

himself with the *a* . . . . . . 2 Tim 2:4

AFFECTION

to his wife the *a* . . . . 1 Cor 7:3

AFFECTIONATE

Be kindly *a* to one . . . . . Rom 12:10

AFFIRM

you to *a* constantly . . . . . . Titus 3:8

AFFLICT

a Your heritage . . . . Ps 94:5
For He does not *a* . . . . . . Lam 3:33

AFFLICTED

To him who is *a* . . . . Job 6:14
hears the cry of the *a* . . . Job 34:28
days of the *a* are evil . . Prov 15:15
Smitten by God, and *a* . . . . . Is 53:4
"O you *a* one . . . . Is 54:11
being destitute, *a* . . . . . . Heb 11:37

AFFLICTING

A the just and taking . . Amos 5:12

AFFLICTION

is, the bread of *a* . . . . Deut 16:3
a take hold of me . . . . Job 30:16
and it is an evil *a* . . . . Eccl 6:2
For our light *a* . . . . 2 Cor 4:17
supposing to add *a* . . . . . Phil 1:16

AFRAID

garden, and I was *a* . . . . . Gen 3:10
saying, "Do not be *a* . . . . Gen 15:1
none will make you *a* . . . . Lev 26:6
ungodliness made me *a* . . . Ps 18:4
Whenever I am *a* . . . . Ps 56:3
one will make them *a* . . . . . . Is 17:2
do not be *a* . . . . Matt 14:27
if you do evil, be *a* . . . . . Rom 13:4
do good and are not *a* . . . 1 Pet 3:6

AFTERWARD

a receive me to glory . . . . Ps 73:24
you shall follow Me *a* . John 13:36

AGAIN

'You must be born *a* . . . . John 3:7
having been born *a* . . . . 1 Pet 1:23

AGAINST

come to *'set a man a* . . Matt 10:35
or house divided *a* . . . . . Matt 12:25
Me is *a* Me . . . . Matt 12:30
a the Spirit will not . . . . Matt 12:31
lifted up his heel a . . . . John 13:18
LORD and a His Christ . . Acts 4:26
to kick *a* the goads . . . . Acts 9:5
a the promises of God . . . . Gal 3:21
we do not wrestle *a* . . . . . Eph 6:12
I have a few things *a* . . . . Rev 2:20

AGE

the grave at a full *a* . . . . . Job 5:26
and in the *a* to come . . Mark 10:30

AGED

a one as Paul, the *a* . . . . . Philem 9

AGES

ordained before the *a* . . . 1 Cor 2:7

AGONY

And being in *a* . . . . Luke 22:44

AGREE

that if two of you *a* . . . . Matt 18:19

AGREED

unless they are *a* . . . . Amos 3:3

AGREEMENT

what *a* has the temple . 2 Cor 6:16

AIR

the birds of the *a* . . . . Gen 1:26
of the *a* have nests . . . . . Luke 9:58
of the power of the *a* . . . . . Eph 2:2
the Lord in the *a* . . . . 1 Thess 4:17

ALIENATED

darkened, being *a* . . . . Eph 4:18
you, who once were *a* . . . . Col 1:21

ALIENS

A have devoured his . . . . Hos 7:9
Christ, being *a* . . . . Eph 2:12

ALIKE

esteems every day *a* . . . . Rom 14:5

ALIVE

I kill and I make *a* . . . . Deut 32:39
was dead and is *a* . . . . Luke 15:24
presented Himself *a* . . . . . Acts 1:3
indeed to sin, but *a* . . . . . Rom 6:11
all shall be made *a* . . . 1 Cor 15:22
that we who are *a* . . . 1 Thess 4:15
and behold, I am *a* . . . . . . Rev 1:18
These two were cast *a* . . Rev 19:20

ALLELUIA

Again they said, "*A* . . . . . . Rev 19:3

ALLOW

a Your Holy One . . . . Ps 16:10
a My faithfulness . . . . Ps 89:33
a Your Holy One . . . . Acts 2:27

ALLURE

of emptiness, they *a* . . . . 2 Pet 2:18

ALMOND

a tree blossoms . . . . Eccl 12:5

ALMOST

a persuade me to . . . . Acts 26:28

ALOES

of myrrh and *a* . . . . John 19:39

ALPHA

"I am the *A* and the . . . . Rev 1:8
"I am the *A* and the . . . . . Rev 22:13

ALTAR

Then Noah built an *a* . . . Gen 8:20
'An *a* of earth you . . . . Ex 20:24
it to you upon the *a* . . . . Lev 17:11
your gift to the *a* . . . . Matt 5:23
swears by the *a* . . . . Matt 23:18
I even found an *a* . . . . . . Acts 17:23
We have an *a* from . . . . Heb 13:10

ALTARS

Even Your *a*, O LORD . . . . . Ps 84:3
and torn down Your a . . Rom 11:3

ALTERED

of His face was *a* . . . . . . Luke 9:29

ALWAYS

delight, Rejoicing *a* . . . . . Prov 8:30
the poor with you *a* . . . . Matt 26:11
lo, I am with you *a* . . . . Matt 28:20
to them, that men *a* . . . . Luke 18:1
immovable, *a* . . . . 1 Cor 15:58
Rejoice in the Lord *a* . . . . . Phil 4:4
thus we shall *a* . . . . . 1 Thess 4:17
a be ready to give a . . . . . 1 Pet 3:15

AM

to Moses, "I *A* WHO I . . . . Ex 3:14
First and I *a* the Last . . . . . . Is 44:6
in My name, I *a* . . . . Matt 18:20
a the bread of life . . . . John 6:35
a the light of the . . . . John 8:12
I *a* from above . . . . John 8:23
Abraham was, I *A* . . . . . John 8:58
"I *a* the door . . . . John 10:9
a the good shepherd . . . John 10:11
a the resurrection . . . . . John 11:25
to him, "I *a* the way . . . . . John 14:6
of God I *a* what I *a* . . . 1 Cor 15:10

AMBASSADOR

for which I am an *a* . . . . Eph 6:20

AMBASSADORS

we are *a* for Christ . . . . . 2 Cor 5:20

AMBITION

Christ from selfish *a* . . . . . Phil 1:16

AMEN

are Yes, and in Him *A* . 2 Cor 1:20
creatures said, "*A* . . . . Rev 5:14

ANCHOR

hope we have as an *a* . . . Heb 6:19

ANCIENT

Do not remove the *a* . . . Prov 23:10
"until the *A* of Days . . . . Dan 7:22

ANGEL

"Behold, I send an *A* . . . . Ex 23:20
Manoah said to the *A* . Judg 13:17
the *A* of His Presence . . . . . . Is 63:9
things, behold, an *a* . . . . Matt 1:20
for an *a* of the Lord . . . . Matt 28:2
Then an *a* of the Lord . . Luke 1:11
And behold, an *a* . . . . Luke 2:9
a appeared to Him . . . . Luke 22:43
For an *a* went down at . . John 5:4
a has spoken to Him . . John 12:29
But at night an *a* . . . . Acts 5:19
A who appeared to him . Acts 7:35
immediately an *a* . . . . . . Acts 12:23
himself into an *a* . . . . . 2 Cor 11:14
even if we, or an *a* . . . . Gal 1:8
Then I saw a strong *a* . . . . Rev 5:2
Jesus, have sent My *a* . . Rev 22:16

ANGELS

If He charges His *a* . . . . . . Job 4:18
lower than the *a* . . . . Ps 8:5
He shall give His *a* . . . . . . Ps 91:11
He shall give His a . . . . Matt 4:6
not even the *a* . . . . Matt 24:36

and all the holy *a* .... Matt 25:31
twelve legions of *a* .... Matt 26:53
And she saw two *a* .... John 20:12
and worship of *a* .... Col 2:18
much better than the *a* ... Heb 1:4
entertained *a* .... Heb 13:2
things which *a* desire .. 1 Pet 1:12
did not spare the *a* ...... 2 Pet 2:4
a who did not keep .... Jude 6

ANGER
For His *a* is but for a ..... Ps 30:5
gracious, Slow to *a* ...... Ps 103:8
Nor will He keep His *a* .. Ps 103:9
around at them with *a* .. Mark 3:5
bitterness, wrath, *a* ..... Eph 4:31

ANGRY
Cain, "Why are you *a* .... Gen 4:6
"Let not the Lord be *a* . Gen 18:30
the Son, lest He be *a* ...... Ps 2:12
a man stirs up strife ... Prov 29:22
right for you to be *a* ...... Jon 4:4
you that whoever is *a* ... Matt 5:22
"Be a, and do not .... Eph 4:26

ANGUISH
remembers the *a* ...... John 16:21
tribulation and *a* .... Rom 2:9

ANIMAL
of every clean *a* .... Gen 7:2
set him on his own *a* .. Luke 10:34

ANIMALS
of *a* after their kind ..... Gen 6:20
of four-footed *a* .... Acts 10:12

ANNUL
years later, cannot *a* ..... Gal 3:17

ANNULS
is confirmed, no one *a* ... Gal 3:15

ANOINT
a my head with oil .... Ps 23:5
when you fast, *a* .... Matt 6:17
a My body for burial ... Mark 14:8
a your eyes with eye .... Rev 3:18

ANOINTED
"Surely the LORD's *a* .. 1 Sam 16:6
destroy the LORD's *a* .. 2 Sam 1:14
"Do not touch My *a* . 1 Chr 16:22
Because He has a ...... Luke 4:18
but this woman has *a* .. Luke 7:46
a the eyes of the .... John 9:6
that Mary who *a* .... John 11:2
Jesus, whom You *a* ..... Acts 4:27
and has *a* us is God .... 2 Cor 1:21

ANOINTING
But you have an *a* .... 1 John 2:20

ANOTHER
that you love one *a* .... John 13:34

ANSWER
Call, and I will *a* .... Job 13:22
How shall I *a* Him ...... Job 31:14
the day that I call, *a* ..... Ps 102:2
In Your faithfulness *a* ... Ps 143:1
a turns away wrath .... Prov 15:1
a a fool according ...... Prov 26:4
or what you should *a* . Luke 12:11
you may have an *a* .... 2 Cor 5:12

ANT
Go to the *a* .... Prov 6:6

ANTICHRIST
heard that the *A* ...... 1 John 2:18
a who denies the ...... 1 John 2:22
is a deceiver and an *a* ... 2 John 7

ANTITYPE
a which now saves us .. 1 Pet 3:21

ANXIETIES
the multitude of my *a* .... Ps 94:19

ANXIETY
A in the heart of man .. Prov 12:25

ANXIOUS
Be *a* for nothing .... Phil 4:6

APART
justified by faith *a* ...... Rom 3:28

APOSTLE
called to be an *a* .... Rom 1:1
consider the *A* .... Heb 3:1

APOSTLES
of the twelve *a* .... Matt 10:2
He also named *a* .... Luke 6:13
am the least of the *a* ... 1 Cor 15:9
none of the other *a* ...... Gal 1:19
gave some to be *a* ...... Eph 4:11

APOSTLESHIP
in this ministry and *a* ... Acts 1:25
are the seal of my *a* .... 1 Cor 9:2

APPAREL
gold rings, in fine *a* .... James 2:2
or putting on fine *a* ..... 1 Pet 3:3

APPEAL
love's sake I rather *a* .... Philem 9

APPEAR
and let the dry land *a* .... Gen 1:9
also outwardly *a* ...... Matt 23:28
God would *a* .... Luke 19:11
For we must all *a* ...... 2 Cor 5:10

APPEARANCE
Do not look at his *a* ... 1 Sam 16:7
judge according to *a* ... John 7:24
those who boast in *a* ... 2 Cor 5:12
found in *a* as a man ...... Phil 2:8

APPEARED
an angel of the Lord *a* . Luke 1:11
who *a* in glory and ..... Luke 9:31
brings salvation has *a* .. Titus 2:11
of the ages, He has *a* ... Heb 9:26

APPEARING
Lord Jesus Christ's *a* .. 1 Tim 6:14
and the dead at His *a* ... 2 Tim 4:1
who have loved His *a* ... 2 Tim 4:8

APPEARS
can stand when He *a* ..... Mal 3:2
who is our life *a* .... Col 3:4
the Chief Shepherd *a* .... 1 Pet 5:4
that when He *a* .... 1 John 2:28

APPETITE
are a man given to *a* ... Prov 23:2

APPLE
And my law as the *a* .... Prov 7:2

APPLES
fitly spoken is like *a* ... Prov 25:11

APPLIED
a my heart to know ..... Eccl 7:25

APPOINT
For God did not *a* .... 1 Thess 5:9

APPOINTED
And as it is *a* for men ... Heb 9:27

APPROACH
year, make those who *a* . Heb 10:1

APPROACHING
as you see the Day *a* ... Heb 10:25

APPROVE
do the same but also *a* .. Rom 1:32

APPROVED
to God and *a* by men .. Rom 14:18
to present yourself *a* ... 2 Tim 2:15

ARBITRATOR
Me a judge or an *a* .... Luke 12:14

ARCHANGEL
the voice of an *a* .... 1 Thess 4:16

ARGUMENTS
casting down *a* and .... 2 Cor 10:5

ARISE
A, shine .... Is 60:1
But the LORD will *a* .... Is 60:2
you who sleep, *A* .... Eph 5:14

ARK
"Make yourself an *a* .... Gen 6:14
him, she took an *a* .... Ex 2:3
Bezalel made the *a* .... Ex 37:1
in heaven, and the *a* .... Rev 11:19

ARM
with an outstretched *a* ...... Ex 6:6
Have you an *a* like God .. Job 40:9
strength with His *a* .... Luke 1:51
a yourselves also with ... 1 Pet 4:1

ARMED
a strong man, fully *a* .. Luke 11:21

ARMIES
And he sent out his *a* ... Matt 22:7
surrounded by *a* ...... Luke 21:20
And the *a* in heaven .... Rev 19:14
the earth, and their *a* ... Rev 19:19

ARMOR
Put on the whole *a* ...... Eph 6:11

ARMS
are the everlasting *a* .. Deut 33:27
took Him up in his *a* ... Luke 2:28

AROMA
the one we are the *a* ... 2 Cor 2:16
for a sweet-smelling *a* .... Eph 5:2

AROUSED
LORD was greatly *a* .... Num 11:10
Then Joseph, being *a* ... Matt 1:24

ARRAYED
his glory was not *a* ..... Matt 6:29
"Who are these *a* .... Rev 7:13

ARROGANCE
Pride and *a* and the ..... Prov 8:13

ARROW
a that flies by day .... Ps 91:5

ARROWS
a pierce me deeply .... Ps 38:2
Like *a* in the hand of .... Ps 127:4

ASCEND
Who may *a* into the ...... Ps 24:3
If I *a* into heaven .... Ps 139:8
'I will *a* into heaven .... Is 14:13
see the Son of Man *a* ... John 6:62

ASCENDED
You have *a* on high ....Ps 68:18
"No one has *a* ....John 3:13
"When He a on high .....Eph 4:8

ASCENDING
the angels of God *a* ....John 1:51

ASCRIBE
A strength to God ....Ps 68:34

ASHAMED
Let me not be *a* ....Ps 25:2
And Israel shall be *a* ....Hos 10:6
For whoever is *a* ....Mark 8:38
am not *a* of the gospel ...Rom 1:16
Therefore God is not *a* .Heb 11:16

ASHES
become like dust and *a* .Job 30:19
in sackcloth and *a* ....Luke 10:13

ASIDE
lay something *a* ....1 Cor 16:2
lay *a* all filthiness .....James 1:21
Therefore, laying *a* ......1 Pet 2:1

ASK
when your children *a* ....Josh 4:6
"*A* a sign for yourself .....Is 7:11
whatever things you *a* .Matt 21:22
a, and it will be ....Luke 11:9
that whatever You *a* ..John 11:22
a anything in My ......John 14:14
in that day you will *a* ..John 16:23
above all that we *a* ......Eph 3:20
wisdom, let him *a* ....James 1:5
But let him *a* in faith ...James 1:6
because you do not *a* ...James 4:2

ASKS
For everyone who *a* .....Matt 7:8
you who, if his son *a* .....Matt 7:9
Or if he *a* for a fish ....Luke 11:11

ASLEEP
But He was *a* ....Matt 8:24
some have fallen *a* .....1 Cor 15:6
those who are *a* ......1 Thess 4:15

ASSEMBLING
not forsaking the *a* ....Heb 10:25

ASSEMBLY
a I will praise You ....Ps 22:22
fast, Call a sacred *a* .....Joel 1:14
a I will sing praise ......Heb 2:12
to the general *a* ....Heb 12:23

ASSURANCE
riches of the full *a* ....Col 2:2
Spirit and in much *a* ..1 Thess 1:5
to the full *a* of hope ......Heb 6:11

ASSURE
a our hearts before ...1 John 3:19

ASSURED
learned and been *a* ....2 Tim 3:14

ASTONISHED
Just as many were *a* ....Is 52:14
who heard Him were *a* .Luke 2:47

ASTRAY
one of them goes *a* ....Matt 18:12
like sheep going *a* ....1 Pet 2:25

ATONEMENT
the blood that makes *a* .Lev 17:11
for it is the Day of *A* ..Lev 23:28
there will be no *a* ....Is 22:14

ATTAIN
It is high, I cannot *a* .....Ps 139:6
worthy to *a* that age ..Luke 20:35
by any means, I may *a* ..Phil 3:11

ATTENTION
My son, give *a* to my ....Prov 4:20

ATTENTIVE
Let Your ears be *a* ......Ps 130:2

ATTESTED
a Man *a* by God to you .Acts 2:22

AUSTERE
because you are an *a* .Luke 19:21

AUTHOR
For God is not the *a* ..1 Cor 14:33
unto Jesus, the *a* ....Heb 12:2

AUTHORITIES
a that exist are ....Rom 13:1

AUTHORITY
them as one having *a* ...Matt 7:29
"All *a* has been given ..Matt 28:18
a I will give You ....Luke 4:6
and has given Him *a* ...John 5:27
You have given Him *a* ...John 17:2
the flesh, reject *a* ....Jude 8

AUTUMN
a trees without fruit ......Jude 12

AVAILS
of a righteous man *a* ..James 5:16

AVENGE
Beloved, do not *a* .....Rom 12:19
a our blood on those ....Rev 6:10

AVENGER
the Lord is the *a* ......1 Thess 4:6

AWAKE
be satisfied when I *a* ....Ps 17:15
it is high time to *a* ....Rom 13:11
A to righteousness ....1 Cor 15:34

AWAY
the wind drives *a* ....Ps 1:4
Do not cast me *a* ....Ps 51:11
A time to cast *a* ....Eccl 3:5
fair one, And come *a* ....Song 2:10
minded to put her *a* ....Matt 1:19
and earth will pass *a* ..Matt 24:35
"I am going *a* ....John 8:21
they cried out, "*A* .....John 19:15
unless the falling *a* ...2 Thess 2:3
in Asia have turned *a* ..2 Tim 1:15
heard, lest we drift *a* .....Heb 2:1
if they fall *a* ....Heb 6:6
can never take *a* ....Heb 10:11
world is passing *a* .....1 John 2:17
if anyone takes *a* ....Rev 22:19

AWESOME
a is this place ....Gen 28:17
God, the great and *a* ....Deut 7:21
By *a* deeds in ....Ps 65:5
O God, You are more *a* ..Ps 68:35
Your great and *a* name ....Ps 99:3

AWL
his ear with an *a* ....Ex 21:6

AX
If the *a* is dull ....Eccl 10:10
And even now the *a* ....Matt 3:10

B

BABBLER
"What does this *b* .....Acts 17:18

BABBLINGS
the profane and idle *b* .1 Tim 6:20

BABE
the *b* leaped in my .....Luke 1:44
You will find a *B* ....Luke 2:12
for he is a *b* ....Heb 5:13

BABES
Out of the mouth of *b* ......Ps 8:2
revealed them to *b* .....Matt 11:25
of the mouth of b ....Matt 21:16
as to carnal, as to *b* ....1 Cor 3:1
as newborn *b* ....1 Pet 2:2

BACK
for the fool's *b* ....Prov 26:3
I gave My *b* to those ....Is 50:6
plow, and looking *b* .....Luke 9:62
of those who draw *b* ...Heb 10:39
someone turns him *b* ..James 5:19

BACKBITERS
b, haters of God ....Rom 1:30

BACKBITING
b tongue an angry ......Prov 25:23

BACKSLIDER
The *b* in heart will be ..Prov 14:14

BACKSLIDINGS
And I will heal your *b* .....Jer 3:22

BACKWARD
ten degrees *b* ....2 Kin 20:11

BAD
b trees bears *b* fruit ....Matt 7:17

BAG
"nor *b* for your ....Matt 10:10

BAKED
b unleavened cakes .....Ex 12:39

BAKER
the butler and the *b* ....Gen 40:1

BALANCES
Falsifying the *b* ....Amos 8:5

BALD
every head shall be *b* ...Jer 48:37

BALDHEAD
Go up, you *b* ....2 Kin 2:23

BALM
no *b* in Gilead ....Jer 8:22

BANDAGED
and *b* his wounds ......Luke 10:34

BANKERS
my money with the *b* ..Matt 25:27

BANNERS
we will set up our *b* ......Ps 20:5
as an army with *b* ....Song 6:4

BANQUET
b that I have prepared .....Esth 5:4

BANQUETING
He brought me to the *b* ..Song 2:4

BAPTISM
coming to his *b* ....Matt 3:7
b that I am baptized ...Matt 20:22
"But I have a *b* ....Luke 12:50
said, "Into John's *b* ......Acts 19:3
Lord, one faith, one *b* .....Eph 4:5
buried with Him in *b* .....Col 2:12

BAPTISMS
of the doctrine of *b* . . . . Heb 6:2

BAPTIZE
"I indeed *b* you with . . . . Matt 3:11
Himself did not *b* . . . . John 4:2

BAPTIZED
b will be saved . . . . Mark 16:16
every one of you be *b* . . . Acts 2:38
all his family were *b* . . . Acts 16:33
Arise and be *b* . . . . Acts 22:16
were *b* into Christ . . . . Rom 6:3
I thank God that I *b* . . . 1 Cor 1:14
Spirit we were all *b* . . . 1 Cor 12:13

BAPTIZING
b them in the name of . Matt 28:19

BARBARIAN
nor uncircumcised, *b* . . . . Col 3:11

BARLEY
here who has five *b* . . . . . John 6:9

BARN
the wheat into my *b* . . . Matt 13:30

BARNS
reap nor gather into *b* . . Matt 6:26
I will pull down my *b* . Luke 12:18

BARREN
But Sarai was *b* . . . . Gen 11:30
"Sing, O *b* . . . . Is 54:1

BASE
and the *b* things of . . . . 1 Cor 1:28

BASIN
poured water into a *b* . . John 13:5

BASKET
and put it under a *b* . . . . Matt 5:15
I was let down in a *b* . 2 Cor 11:33

BASKETS
they took up twelve *b* . Matt 14:20

BATHED
to him, "He who is *b* . John 13:10

BATS
To the moles and *b* . . . . Is 2:20

BATTLE
b is the LORD's . . . . 1 Sam 17:47
the *b* to the strong . . . . Eccl 9:11
became valiant in *b* . . . . Heb 11:34

BEAR
greater than I can *b* . . . . Gen 4:13
whom Sarah shall *b* . . . . Gen 17:21
not *b* false witness . . . . Ex 20:16
b their iniquities . . . . Is 53:11
child, and b a Son . . . . Matt 1:23
A good tree cannot *b* . . . Matt 7:18
how long shall I *b* . . . . . Matt 17:17
by, to *b* His cross . . . . . . Mark 15:21
whoever does not *b* . . . Luke 14:27
are strong ought to *b* . . . Rom 15:1
B one another's . . . . Gal 6:2
b the sins of many . . . . Heb 9:28

BEARD
the edges of your *b* . . . . Lev 19:27
Running down on the *b* . . Ps 133:2

BEARING
goes forth weeping, *B* . . . Ps 126:6
And He, *b* His cross . . . John 19:17
b His reproach . . . . Heb 13:13

BEARS
Every branch that *b* . . . . John 15:2

BEAST
You preserve man and *b* . . Ps 36:6
And I saw a *b* rising . . . . . Rev 13:1
the mark of the *b* . . . . . . Rev 19:20

BEASTS
like brute *b* . . . . Jude 10

BEAT
b their swords into . . . . Is 2:4
spat in His face and *b* . Matt 26:67

BEATEN
Three times I was *b* . . 2 Cor 11:25

BEAUTIFUL
B in elevation . . . . Ps 48:2
has made everything *b* . . Eccl 3:11
my love, you are as *b* . . . Song 6:4
How *b* upon the . . . . Is 52:7
indeed appear *b* . . . . Matt 23:27

BEAUTIFY
b the place of My . . . . Is 60:13

BEAUTY
"The *b* of Israel is . . . . 2 Sam 1:19
To behold the *b* . . . . Ps 27:4
see the King in His *b* . . . . . Is 33:17
no *b* that we should . . . . Is 53:2

BECAME
b a living being . . . . Gen 2:7
to the Jews I *b* . . . . 1 Cor 9:20

BED
I remember You on my *b* . . Ps 63:6
if I make my *b* in hell . . . . Ps 139:8
"Arise, take up your *b* . . . Matt 9:6
be two men in one *b* . . Luke 17:34
and the *b* undefiled . . . . . . Heb 13:4

BEDS
sing aloud on their *b* . . . . Ps 149:5

BEFOREHAND
up, do not worry *b* . . . . Mark 13:11
told you all things *b* . . Mark 13:23
when He testified *b* . . . . 1 Pet 1:11

BEG
b you as sojourners . . . . 1 Pet 2:11

BEGAN
since the world *b* . . . . . Luke 1:70

BEGGAR
there was a certain *b* . . Luke 16:20

BEGGARLY
weak and *b* elements . . . . Gal 4:9

BEGINNING
b God created the . . . . Gen 1:1
In the *b* was the Word . . . John 1:1
a murderer from the *b* . . John 8:44
True Witness, the *B* . . . . . Rev 3:14
and the Omega, the *B* . . . Rev 21:6

BEGOTTEN
I have *b* You . . . . Ps 2:7
glory as of the only *b* . . . John 1:14
loves him who is *b* . . . . 1 John 5:1

BEGUILING
b unstable souls . . . . 2 Pet 2:14

BEGUN
Having *b* in the Spirit . . . . . Gal 3:3

BEHALF
you on Christ's *b* . . . . . . 2 Cor 5:20

BEHAVE
does not *b* rudely . . . . . 1 Cor 13:5

BEHAVED
blamelessly we *b* . . . . . 1 Thess 2:10

BEHAVIOR
of good *b*, hospitable . . . . 1 Tim 3:2

BEHEADED
and had John *b* . . . . Matt 14:10

BEHOLD
B, the virgin shall . . . . Is 7:14
Judah, "*B* your God . . . . Is 40:9
"*B* the Lamb of God . . . . . . John 1:36
to them, "*B* the Man . . . . John 19:5
B what manner of . . . . . 1 John 3:1

BEHOLDING
with unveiled face, *b* . . 2 Cor 3:18

BEING
move and have our *b* . . Acts 17:28
who, *b* in the form of . . . . . Phil 2:6

BELIEVE
tears, "Lord, I *b* . . . . Mark 9:24
have no root, who *b* . . . . Luke 8:13
slow of heart to *b* . . . . . Luke 24:25
to those who *b* . . . . John 1:12
this, that they may *b* . . John 11:42
that you may *b* . . . . John 20:31
the Lord Jesus and *b* . . . . Rom 10:9
Christ, not only to *b* . . . . . Phil 1:29
comes to God must *b* . . . . Heb 11:6
b that there is one . . . . James 2:19
Even the demons *b* . . . . James 2:19

BELIEVED
And he *b* in the LORD . . . Gen 15:6
Who has *b* our report . . . . . Is 53:1
seen Me, you have *b* . . John 20:29
"Abraham b God . . . . Rom 4:3
whom I have *b* . . . . 2 Tim 1:12

BELIEVERS
example to the *b* . . . . 1 Tim 4:12

BELIEVES
The simple *b* every . . . . Prov 14:15
that whoever *b* in Him . John 3:16
"He who *b* in the Son . . . John 3:36
with the heart one *b* . . . Rom 10:10

BELIEVING
you ask in prayer, *b* . . . Matt 21:22

BELLY
On your *b* you shall go . . . Gen 3:14
and Jonah was in the *b* . . Jon 1:17
whose god is their *b* . . . . . Phil 3:19

BELOVED
so He gives His *b* . . . . Ps 127:2
My *b* is mine . . . . Song 2:16
"This is My *b* . . . . Matt 3:17
us accepted in the *B* . . . . Eph 1:6
Luke the *b* physician . . . . . Col 4:14
"This is My *b* . . . . 2 Pet 1:17

BELT
with a leather *b* . . . . Matt 3:4

BEND
The wicked *b* their bow . . . Ps 11:2

BENEATH
"You are from *b* . . . . John 8:23

BENEFACTORS
them are called '*b* . . . . . Luke 22:25

BENEFIT
have a second *b* . . . . 2 Cor 1:15

BESEECH
b you therefore ....Rom 12:1

BESIDE
He leads me *b* the ....Ps 23:2
"Paul, you are *b* ....Acts 26:24

BEST
desire the *b* ....1 Cor 12:31

BESTOWED
love the Father has *b* ..1 John 3:1

BETRAY
you, one of you will *b* .Matt 26:21

BETRAYED
Man is about to be *b* ..Matt 17:22

BETRAYER
See, My *b* is at ....Matt 26:46

BETRAYING
"Judas, are you *b* .....Luke 22:48

BETRAYS
who is the one who *b* .John 21:20

BETROTH
"I will *b* you to Me ......Hos 2:19

BETROTHED
to a virgin *b* to a man ..Luke 1:27

BETTER
b than sacrifice ....1 Sam 15:22
It is *b* to trust in ....Ps 118:8
For it is *b* to marry .....1 Cor 7:9
Christ, which is far *b* ....Phil 1:23
b than the angels ....Heb 1:4
b things concerning ......Heb 6:9

BEWARE
"*B* of false prophets ....Matt 7:15

BEWITCHED
b you that you should .....Gal 3:1

BEYOND
advanced in Judaism *b* ..Gal 1:14

BILLOWS
b have gone over me .....Ps 42:7

BIND
and whatever you *b* ...Matt 16:19
'*B* him hand and foot ...Matt 22:13

BIRD
soul, "Flee as a *b* ....Ps 11:1

BIRDS
b make their nests ....Ps 104:17
"Look at the *b* ....Matt 6:26
have holes and *b* ....Matt 8:20

BIRTH
the day of one's *b* ....Eccl 7:1
Now the *b* of Jesus .....Matt 1:18
will rejoice at his *b* .....Luke 1:14
conceived, it gives *b* ..James 1:15

BIRTHDAY
was Pharaoh's *b* ....Gen 40:20

BIRTHRIGHT
Esau despised his *b* ....Gen 25:34

BISHOP
the position of a *b* ......1 Tim 3:1
b must be blameless .....Titus 1:7

BIT
and they *b* the people ..Num 21:6

BITE
A serpent may *b* ....Eccl 10:11
But if you *b* and ....Gal 5:15

BITTER
b herbs they ....Ex 12:8
and do not be *b* ....Col 3:19
But if you have *b* .....James 3:14

BITTERLY
And Hezekiah wept *b* ..2 Kin 20:3
went out and wept *b* ...Matt 26:75

BITTERNESS
you are poisoned by *b* ..Acts 8:23
b springing up cause ...Heb 12:15

BLACK
one hair white or *b* ....Matt 5:36
a *b* horse ....Rev 6:5
and the sun became *b* ...Rev 6:12

BLACKNESS
whom is reserved the *b* ...Jude 13

BLACKSMITH
I have created the *b* ......Is 54:16

BLADE
first the *b* ....Mark 4:28

BLAME
be holy and without *b* ....Eph 1:4

BLAMELESS
and that man was *b* ....Job 1:1
body be preserved *b* .1 Thess 5:23

BLAMELESSLY
b we behaved ....1 Thess 2:10

BLASPHEME
b Your name forever ....Ps 74:10
compelled them to *b* ...Acts 26:11
b that noble name .....James 2:7

BLASPHEMED
who passed by *b* Him .Matt 27:39
great heat, and they *b* ...Rev 16:9

BLASPHEMER
I was formerly a *b* ....1 Tim 1:13

BLASPHEMES
b the name of the ......Lev 24:16
"This Man *b* ....Matt 9:3

BLASPHEMIES
is this who speaks *b* ....Luke 5:21

BLASPHEMY
but the *b* against ....Matt 12:31
was full of names of *b* ...Rev 17:3

BLEATING
"What then is this *b* .1 Sam 15:14

BLEMISH
be holy and without *b* ...Eph 5:27
as of a lamb without *b* .1 Pet 1:19

BLEMISHED
to the Lord what is *b* ....Mal 1:14

BLESS
b those who *b* you ......Gen 12:3
You go unless You *b* ...Gen 32:26
"The LORD *b* you and ...Num 6:24
b the LORD at all ....Ps 34:1
b You while I live ....Ps 63:4
b His holy name ....Ps 103:1
b those who curse .....Luke 6:28
B those who ....Rom 12:14
Being reviled, we *b* ....1 Cor 4:12

BLESSED
B is the man who walks ....Ps 1:1
B is the man to whom ....Ps 32:2
B is the nation whose ....Ps 33:12
B is he who comes .....Ps 118:26
rise up and call her *b* ..Prov 31:28
"*B* are the poor in ....Matt 5:3
B are those who mourn ..Matt 5:4
B are the meek ....Matt 5:5
B are those who hunger .Matt 5:6
B are the merciful ....Matt 5:7
B are the pure in ....Matt 5:8
B are the peacemakers ..Matt 5:9
B are those who are ....Matt 5:10
B is He who comes ....Matt 21:9
'It is more *b* to give .....Acts 20:35
B be the God and ....Eph 1:3
"*B* are the dead who ...Rev 14:13

BLESSING
And you shall be a *b* ....Gen 12:2
before you today a *b* ..Deut 11:26
shall be showers of *b* ...Ezek 34:26
and you shall be a *b* ....Zech 8:13
that the *b* of Abraham ...Gal 3:14
with every spiritual *b* ....Eph 1:3

BLIND
To open *b* eyes ....Is 42:7
His watchmen are *b* ....Is 56:10
b leads the *b* ....Matt 15:14
to Him, "Are we *b* .....John 9:40
miserable, poor, *b* ....Rev 3:17

BLINDED
and the rest were *b* .....Rom 11:7

BLINDS
a bribe, for a bribe *b* ..Deut 16:19

BLOOD
of your brother's *b* ......Gen 4:10
b shall be shed ....Gen 9:6
b that makes ....Lev 17:11
hands are full of *b* ....Is 1:15
And the moon into *b* ....Joel 2:31
For this is My *b* ....Matt 26:28
"His *b* be on us and ...Matt 27:25
covenant in My *b* .....Luke 22:20
were born, not of *b* ....John 1:13
b has eternal life ....John 6:54
with His own *b* ....Acts 20:28
propitiation by His *b* ...Rom 3:25
justified by His *b* ....Rom 5:9
through His *b* ....Eph 1:7
brought near by the *b* ...Eph 2:13
against flesh and *b* ....Eph 6:12
peace through the *b* ......Col 1:20
with the precious *b* ....1 Pet 1:19
b of Jesus Christ His ...1 John 1:7
our sins in His own *b* .....Rev 1:5
us to God by Your *b* ......Rev 5:9
them white in the *b* ......Rev 7:14
overcame him by the *b* .Rev 12:11
a robe dipped in *b* .....Rev 19:13

BLOODSHED
me from the guilt of *b* ...Ps 51:14

BLOODTHIRSTY
The LORD abhors the *b* .....Ps 5:6

BLOSSOM
and *b* as the rose ....Is 35:1

BLOT
from my sins, and *b* ......Ps 51:9
and I will not *b* ....Rev 3:5

BLOTTED
your sins may be *b* .....Acts 3:19

BLOW
with a very severe *b* ....Jer 14:17

BLOWS
"The wind *b* where it . . . . John 3:8

BOAST
puts on his armor *b* . . . 1 Kin 20:11
and make your *b* . . . . Rom 2:17
lest anyone should *b* . . . . . Eph 2:9

BOASTERS
God, violent, proud, *b* . . Rom 1:30

BOASTING
Where is *b* then . . . . Rom 3:27

BODIES
b a living sacrifice . . . . . . Rom 12:1
not know that your *b* . . 1 Cor 6:15
wives as their own *b* . . . . Eph 5:28

BODILY
b form like a dove . . . . . Luke 3:22
of the Godhead *b* . . . . Col 2:9

BODY
of the *b* is the eye . . . . . . Matt 6:22
those who kill the *b* . . . Matt 10:28
this is My *b* . . . . Matt 26:26
of the temple of His *b* . . . John 2:21
deliver me from this *b* . . . Rom 7:24
redemption of our *b* . . . . Rom 8:23
members in one *b* . . . . . . Rom 12:4
But I discipline my *b* . . 1 Cor 9:27
b which is broken . . . . 1 Cor 11:24
baptized into one *b* . . . 1 Cor 12:13
are the *b* of Christ . . . . 1 Cor 12:27
though I give my *b* . . . . 1 Cor 13:3
It is sown a natural *b* . 1 Cor 15:44
in the *b* of His flesh . . . . . . Col 1:22
our sins in His own *b* . . . 1 Pet 2:24

BOILS
Job with painful *b* . . . . Job 2:7

BOLDLY
therefore come *b* . . . . Heb 4:16

BOLDNESS
in whom we have *b* . . . . . Eph 3:12
that we may have *b* . . . 1 John 4:17

BOND
love, which is the *b* . . . . . . Col 3:14

BONDAGE
out of the house of *b* . . . . Ex 13:14
again with a yoke of *b* . . . . Gal 5:1

BONDS
"Let us break Their *b* . . . . . . Ps 2:3

BONDSERVANTS
B, be obedient to . . . . Eph 6:5
Masters, give your *b* . . . . . . Col 4:1

BONDWOMAN
the one by a *b* . . . . Gal 4:22

BONE
b clings to my skin . . . . . Job 19:20

BONES
I can count all My *b* . . . . . Ps 22:17
and my *b* waste away . . . Ps 31:10
I kept silent, my *b* . . . . Ps 32:3
the wind, Or how the *b* . Eccl 11:5
say to them, 'O dry *b* . . . Ezek 37:4
of dead men's *b* . . . . Matt 23:27
b shall be broken . . . . . John 19:36

BOOK
are written in the b . . . . . Gal 3:10
in the Lamb's *B* . . . . Rev 21:27
the prophecy of this *b* . . Rev 22:18

BOOKS
b there is no end . . . . . . Eccl 12:12
not contain the *b* . . . . . . John 21:25
and *b* were opened . . . . . Rev 20:12

BOOTH
of Zion is left as a *b* . . . . Is 1:8

BORDERS
and enlarge the *b* . . . . Matt 23:5

BORE
And to Sarah who *b* . . . . Is 51:2
b the sin of many . . . . Is 53:12
b our sicknesses . . . . Matt 8:17
Himself *b* our sins . . . . . . 1 Pet 2:24
b a male Child who was . Rev 12:5

BORN
A time to be *b* . . . . Eccl 3:2
unto us a Child is *b* . . . . Is 9:6
b Jesus who is called . . . Matt 1:16
unless one is *b* again . . . . John 3:3
"That which is *b* . . . . John 3:6
having been *b* again . . . 1 Pet 1:23
who loves is *b* of God . . 1 John 4:7

BORROWER
b is servant to the . . . . . . Prov 22:7

BORROWS
The wicked *b* and does . . Ps 37:21

BOSOM
to Abraham's *b* . . . . Luke 16:22
Son, who is in the *b* . . . . John 1:18

BOTTOMLESS
ascend out of the *b* . . . . . . Rev 17:8
the key to the *b* . . . . Rev 20:1

BOUGHT
b the threshing floor . 2 Sam 24:24
all that he had and *b* . . Matt 13:46
For you were *b* at a . . . . 1 Cor 6:20
denying the Lord who *b* . 2 Pet 2:1

BOUND
on earth will be *b* . . . . . Matt 16:19
And see, now I go *b* . . . Acts 20:22
who has a husband is *b* . . Rom 7:2
Are you *b* to a wife . . . . 1 Cor 7:27
Devil and Satan, and *b* . . Rev 20:2

BOUNTIFULLY
and he who sows *b* . . . . . 2 Cor 9:6

BOW
"You shall not *b* . . . . Ex 23:24
let us worship and *b* . . . . . . Ps 95:6
who sat on it had a *b* . . . . . Rev 6:2

BOWED
stood all around and *b* . . Gen 37:7
And they *b* the knee . . . Matt 27:29

BOWL
and poured out his *b* . . . . Rev 16:2

BOWLS
Go and pour out the *b* . . . Rev 16:1

BOX
had the money *b* . . . . . . John 13:29

BOYS
Shall be full of *b* . . . . Zech 8:5

BRAIDED
not with *b* hair or . . . . . . 1 Tim 2:9

BRANCH
raise to David a *B* . . . . Jer 23:5
forth My Servant the *B* . . Zech 3:8
b that bears fruit He . . . . John 15:2

BRANCHES
vine, you are the *b* . . . . . John 15:5

BRASS
become sounding *b* . . . . 1 Cor 13:1

BRAVE
in the faith, be *b* . . . . . . 1 Cor 16:13

BREAD
brought out *b* . . . . Gen 14:18
shall eat unleavened *b* . . . Ex 23:15
not live by *b* alone . . . . . . Deut 8:3
b eaten in secret is . . . . . Prov 9:17
B gained by deceit is . . Prov 20:17
Cast your *b* upon the . . . . Eccl 11:1
for what is not *b* . . . . Is 55:2
these stones become *b* . . . Matt 4:3
not live by b alone . . . . . . Matt 4:4
this day our daily *b* . . . . . Matt 6:11
eating, Jesus took *b* . . . Matt 26:26
"I am the *b* of life . . . . . . John 6:48
betrayed took *b* . . . . . . 1 Cor 11:23

BREADTH
is as great as its *b* . . . . . . Rev 21:16

BREAK
covenant I will not *b* . . . . Ps 89:34
together to *b* bread . . . . . Acts 20:7

BREAKING
in the *b* of bread . . . . Acts 2:42
b bread from house to . . Acts 2:46

BREAKS
Until the day *b* . . . . Song 2:17

BREAST
back on Jesus' *b* . . . . . . John 13:25

BREASTPLATE
righteousness as a *b* . . . . . Is 59:17
having put on the *b* . . . . . Eph 6:14

BREASTS
Your two *b* are like . . . . . Song 4:5
b which nursed You . . Luke 11:27

BREATH
nostrils the *b* of life . . . . . Gen 2:7
that there was no *b* . . . 1 Kin 17:17
Man is like a *b* . . . . Ps 144:4
everything that has *b* . . . . Ps 150:6
"Surely I will cause *b* . . Ezek 37:5
gives to all life, *b* . . . . . . Acts 17:25
power to give *b* . . . . Rev 13:15

BREATHES
indeed he *b* his last . . . . Job 14:10

BRETHREN
and you are all *b* . . . . Matt 23:8
least of these My *b* . . . . Matt 25:40
among many *b* . . . . Rom 8:29
thus sin against the *b* . . 1 Cor 8:12
over five hundred *b* . . . . 1 Cor 15:6
perils among false *b* . . . 2 Cor 11:26
sincere love of the *b* . . . . 1 Pet 1:22
we love the *b* . . . . 1 John 3:14
our lives for the *b* . . . . 1 John 3:16

BRIBE
you shall take no *b* . . . . Ex 23:8
b blinds the eyes . . . . . . Deut 16:19

BRIBES
hand is full of *b* . . . . Ps 26:10

BRICK
people straw to make *b* . . . . Ex 5:7

BRICKS
"Come, let us make *b* . . . Gen 11:3

BRIDE
I will show you the *b* . . . Rev 21:9
the Spirit and the *b* . . . . Rev 22:17

BRIDEGROOM
And as the *b* rejoices . . . . . . Is 62:5
mourn as long as the *b* . Matt 9:15
went out to meet the *b* . . Matt 25:1
the friend of the *b* . . . . . . John 3:29

BRIDLE
b the whole body . . . . . . James 3:2

BRIER
b shall come up the . . . . . . Is 55:13

BRIERS
there shall come up *b* . . . . . . Is 5:6

BRIGHTER
a light from heaven, *b* . Acts 26:13

BRIGHTNESS
And kings to the *b* . . . . Is 60:3
who being the *b* . . . . Heb 1:3

BRIMSTONE
the lake of fire and *b* . . . Rev 20:10

BRING
b back his soul . . . . Job 33:30
b My righteousness . . . . . . Is 46:13
Who shall *b* a charge . . . . Rom 8:33
b Christ down from . . . . . . Rom 10:6
even so God will *b* . . . 1 Thess 4:14

BROAD
b is the way that . . . . Matt 7:13

BROKE
b them at the foot of . . . . Ex 32:19
He blessed and *b* . . . . . Matt 14:19
b the legs of the . . . . John 19:32

BROKEN
this stone will be *b* . . . . Matt 21:44
Scripture cannot be *b* . John 10:35
body which is *b* . . . . 1 Cor 11:24

BROKENHEARTED
He heals the *b* And . . . . . . Ps 147:3

BRONZE
So Moses made a *b* . . . . . Num 21:9
b walls against the . . . . Jer 1:18
a third kingdom of *b* . . . . . Dan 2:39

BROOD
"*B* of vipers . . . . Matt 12:34
hen gathers her *b* . . . . . Luke 13:34

BROOK
disciples over the *B* . . . . . John 18:1

BROOKS
for the water *b* . . . . Ps 42:1

BROTHER
"Where is Abel your *b* . . . . Gen 4:9
b offended is harder . . Prov 18:19
b will deliver up . . . . Matt 10:21
how often shall my *b* . . Matt 18:21
b will rise again . . . . John 11:23
b goes to law against . . . . 1 Cor 6:6
Whoever hates his *b* . . 1 John 3:15

BROTHERHOOD
Love the *b* . . . . 1 Pet 2:17

BROTHERLY
b love continue . . . . Heb 13:1

BROTHER'S
Am I my *b* keeper . . . . Gen 4:9
at the speck in your *b* . . . . Matt 7:3

BROTHERS
is My mother, or My *b* . Mark 3:33
b are these who hear . . . Luke 8:21

BRUISE
He shall *b* your head . . . . Gen 3:15
the LORD to *b* Him . . . . Is 53:10

BRUISED
He was *b* for our . . . . Is 53:5
b reed He will not . . . . . . Matt 12:20

BUCKLER
be your shield and *b* . . . . . . Ps 91:4

BUFFET
of Satan to *b* me . . . . 2 Cor 12:7

BUILD
b ourselves a city . . . . Gen 11:4
"Would you *b* a house . . 2 Sam 7:5
labor in vain who *b* . . . . . . Ps 127:1
down, And a time to *b* . . . Eccl 3:3
'This man began to *b* . . Luke 14:30
What house will you b . . Acts 7:49
"For if I *b* again . . . . Gal 2:18

BUILDER
foundations, whose *b* . . Heb 11:10

BUILDING
in whom the whole *b* . . . . Eph 2:21

BUILDS
take heed how he *b* . . . . 1 Cor 3:10

BUILT
has *b* her house . . . . Prov 9:1
to a wise man who *b* . . . Matt 7:24
having been *b* on the . . . . Eph 2:20

BULLS
For if the blood of *b* . . . . . Heb 9:13

BULWARKS
Mark well her *b* . . . . Ps 48:13

BUNDLE
man's *b* of money . . . . . . Gen 42:35

BURDEN
Cast your *b* on the . . . . Ps 55:22
easy and My *b* is light . Matt 11:30
we might not be a *b* . . 1 Thess 2:9
on you no other *b* . . . . Rev 2:24

BURDENS
"For they bind heavy *b* . Matt 23:4
Bear one another's *b* . . . . . Gal 6:2

BURDENSOME
I myself was not *b* . . . 2 Cor 12:13
are not *b* . . . . 1 John 5:3

BURIAL
she did it for My *b* . . . . Matt 26:12
for the day of My *b* . . . . John 12:7

BURIED
Therefore we were *b* . . . . Rom 6:4
and that He was *b* . . . . . 1 Cor 15:4
b with Him in baptism . . . Col 2:12

BURN
the bush does not *b* . . . . Ex 3:3
"Did not our heart *b* . . Luke 24:32

BURNED
If anyone's work is *b* . . 1 Cor 3:15
my body to be *b* . . . . 1 Cor 13:3

BURNING
b torch that passed . . . . Gen 15:17
b fire shut up in my . . . . Jer 20:9
plucked from the *b* . . . . Amos 4:11

BURNT
lamb for a *b* offering . . . . Gen 22:7
delight in *b* offering . . . . . Ps 51:16

BURST
the new wine will *b* . . . . Luke 5:37

BURY
and let the dead *b* . . . . . . Matt 8:22

BUSH
from the midst of a *b* . . . . . . Ex 3:2

BUSINESS
about My Father's *b* . . . . Luke 2:49

BUSYBODIES
at all, but are *b* . . . . . . 2 Thess 3:11

BUTLER
b did not remember . . . . . Gen 40:23

BUTTER
were smoother than *b* . . . . Ps 55:21

BUY
Yes, come, *b* wine and . . . . Is 55:1
"I counsel you to *b* . . . . . . Rev 3:18
and that no one may *b* . Rev 13:17

BUYS
has and *b* that field . . . . Matt 13:44

BYWORD
has made me a *b* . . . . Job 17:6

C

CAGE
foul spirit, and a *c* . . . . . . Rev 18:2

CAKE
Ephraim is a *c* . . . . Hos 7:8

CAKES
and love the raisin *c* . . . . . Hos 3:1

CALAMITY
will laugh at your *c* . . . . Prov 1:26

CALCULATED
c the dust of the . . . . Is 40:12

CALDRON
this city is the *c* . . . . Ezek 11:3

CALF
and made a molded *c* . . . . . Ex 32:4
bring the fatted *c* . . . . . Luke 15:23

CALL
C upon Him while He . . . . . Is 55:6
c His name JESUS . . . . Matt 1:21
c the righteous . . . . Matt 9:13
Lord our God will *c* . . . . . Acts 2:39
c them My people . . . . Rom 9:25
c and election sure . . . . . 2 Pet 1:10

CALLED
c the light Day . . . . Gen 1:5
c his wife's name Eve . . . Gen 3:20
I have *c* you by your . . . . . Is 43:1
"*Out of Egypt I c* . . . . Matt 2:15
city *c* Nazareth . . . . Matt 2:23
For many are *c* . . . . Matt 20:16
to those who are the *c* . . Rom 8:28
these He also *c* . . . . Rom 8:30
c children of God . . . . . . 1 John 3:1

CALLING
the gifts and the c .....Rom 11:29
For you see your c ....1 Cor 1:26
remain in the same c ..1 Cor 7:20

CALLS
c them all by name ......Ps 147:4
David himself c ....Mark 12:37
c his own sheep ....John 10:3

CALM
there was a great c .....Matt 8:26

CAMEL
it is easier for a c ....Matt 19:24

CAMP
to Him, outside the c ...Heb 13:13

CAN
I c do all things ....Phil 4:13

CANCER
will spread like c ....2 Tim 2:17

CANOPY
His c around Him was ...Ps 18:11

CAPSTONE
bring forth the c ....Zech 4:7

CAPTAIN
Which, having no c ......Prov 6:7

CAPTIVE
and be led away c ....Luke 21:24
He led captivity c ....Eph 4:8

CAPTIVES
and make c ....2 Tim 3:6

CAPTIVITY
every thought into c ...2 Cor 10:5

CARCASS
"For wherever the c ...Matt 24:28

CARE
"Lord, do You not c ...Luke 10:40
how will he take c ....1 Tim 3:5

CARED
he said, not that he c ...John 12:6

CAREFULLY
I shall walk c all my .....Is 38:15

CARELESS
But he who is c ....Prov 19:16

CARES
No one c for my soul ......Ps 142:4
for He c for you ....1 Pet 5:7

CARNAL
c mind is enmity ....Rom 8:7

CARNALLY
c minded is death ....Rom 8:6

CAROUSE
count it pleasure to c ...2 Pet 2:13

CARPENTER
"Is this not the c ....Mark 6:3

CARRIED
And c our sorrows ....Is 53:4

CARRY
for you to c your bed ...John 5:10
it is certain we can c ....1 Tim 6:7

CARRYING
will meet you c ....Mark 14:13

CASE
Festus laid Paul's c ....Acts 25:14

CASSIA
myrrh and aloes and c ....Ps 45:8

CAST
Why are you c down .....Ps 42:5
whole body to be c .....Matt 5:29
My name they will c ..Mark 16:17
by no means c out ....John 6:37
c their crowns before ....Rev 4:10
the great dragon was c ..Rev 12:9

CASTING
c down arguments .....2 Cor 10:5
c all your care ....1 Pet 5:7

CASTS
perfect love c out .....1 John 4:18

CATCH
c Him in His words ...Mark 12:13
now on you will c ......Luke 5:10

CATCHES
and the wolf c the .....John 10:12
c the wise in their .....1 Cor 3:19

CAUGHT
him was a ram c ....Gen 22:13
her Child was c up ....Rev 12:5

CAUSE
hated Me without a c ..John 15:25
For this c I was born ..John 18:37

CAVES
in dens and c of the ....Heb 11:38

CEASE
and night Shall not c ....Gen 8:22
He makes wars c ....Ps 46:9
tongues, they will c ....1 Cor 13:8

CEASING
pray without c ....1 Thess 5:17

CEDAR
dwell in a house of c ...2 Sam 7:2

CEDARS
the LORD breaks the c .....Ps 29:5

CELESTIAL
but the glory of the c ..1 Cor 15:40

CENSER
Aaron, each took his c ...Lev 10:1

CERTAINTY
you may know the c ....Luke 1:4

CERTIFICATE
a man to write a c ....Mark 10:4

CHAFF
be chased like the c ....Is 17:13
He will burn up the c ....Matt 3:12

CHAIN
pit and a great c ....Rev 20:1

CHAINED
of God is not c ....2 Tim 2:9

CHAINS
And his c fell off ....Acts 12:7
am, except for these c .Acts 26:29

CHAMBERS
brought me into his c ....Song 1:4

CHAMPION
And a c went out .....1 Sam 17:4

CHANGE
now and to c my tone ...Gal 4:20
there is also a c ....Heb 7:12

CHANGED
c the glory of the ....Rom 1:23
but we shall all be c ..1 Cor 15:51

CHANGERS'
and poured out the c ....John 2:15

CHANGES
c the times and the .....Dan 2:21

CHANNELS
c of the sea were seen ...Ps 18:15

CHARIOT
that suddenly a c ....2 Kin 2:11

CHARIOTS
Some trust in c ....Ps 20:7

CHARITABLE
you do not do your c ....Matt 6:1
c deeds which she ....Acts 9:36

CHARM
C is deceitful and .....Prov 31:30

CHARMS
who sew magic c ....Ezek 13:18

CHASE
Five of you shall c ....Lev 26:8

CHASTE
present you as a c ......2 Cor 11:2

CHASTEN
a father does not c ......Heb 12:7
I love, I rebuke and c ....Rev 3:19

CHASTENED
c us as seemed best ....Heb 12:10

CHASTENING
do not despise the c .....Job 5:17
Now no c seems to be ..Heb 12:11

CHASTENS
the LORD loves He c .....Heb 12:6

CHASTISEMENT
The c for our peace ....Is 53:5

CHATTER
c leads only to ....Prov 14:23

CHEAT
Beware lest anyone c .....Col 2:8

CHEATED
let yourselves be c ....1 Cor 6:7

CHEEK
on your right c ....Matt 5:39

CHEEKBONE
my enemies on the c ....Ps 3:7

CHEEKS
His c are like a bed ....Song 5:13

CHEER
"Son, be of good c ......Matt 9:2

CHEERFUL
for God loves a c ....2 Cor 9:7

CHEERFULNESS
shows mercy, with *c* .....Rom 12:8

CHEESE
And curdle me like *c* .....Job 10:10

CHERISHES
but nourishes and *c* .....Eph 5:29

CHERUBIM
above it were the *c* ....Heb 9:5

CHIEF
of whom I am *c* ....1 Tim 1:15
Zion a c cornerstone .....1 Pet 2:6

CHILD
Train up a *c* in the .....Prov 22:6
For unto us a C ....Is 9:6
virgin shall be with c .....Matt 1:23
of God as a little *c* .....Mark 10:15
So the *c* grew and ....Luke 1:80
When I was a *c* ....1 Cor 13:11
She bore a male *C* ....Rev 12:5

CHILDBEARING
she will be saved in *c* . . 1 Tim 2:15

CHILDBIRTH
pain as a woman in *c* ....Is 13:8

CHILDHOOD
c you have known .....2 Tim 3:15

CHILDLESS
give me, seeing I go *c* .....Gen 15:2
this man down as *c* .....Jer 22:30

CHILDREN
c are a heritage ....Ps 127:3
c rise up and call her . . Prov 31:28
and become as little *c* .....Matt 18:3
"Let the little *c* ....Matt 19:14
the right to become *c* .....John 1:12
now we are *c* of God . . 1 John 3:2

CHOOSE
therefore *c* life ....Deut 30:19
"You did not *c* ....John 15:16

CHOSE
just as He *c* us in Him .....Eph 1:4

CHOSEN
servant whom I have *c* .....Is 43:10
whom I have *c* ....John 13:18
c the foolish things .....1 Cor 1:27
Has God not *c* the .....James 2:5

CHRIST
Jesus who is called C . . . Matt 1:16
"You are the C ....Matt 16:16
a Savior, who is C .....Luke 2:11
It is *C* who died ....Rom 8:34
to be justified by *C* ....Gal 2:17
been crucified with *C* .....Gal 2:20
C is head of the ....Eph 5:23
to me, to live is *C* ....Phil 1:21
which is *C* in you ....Col 1:27
C who is our ....Col 3:4
Jesus *C* is the same .....Heb 13:8
C His Son cleanses us . . 1 John 1:7
that Jesus is the *C* .....1 John 5:1

CHRISTIAN
anyone suffers as a *C* . . 1 Pet 4:16

CHRISTIANS
were first called *C* .....Acts 11:26

CHRISTS
"For false *c* and ....Matt 24:24

CHURCH
rock I will build My *c* . Matt 16:18
c daily those who were . Acts 2:47
Himself a glorious *c* ....Eph 5:27
as the Lord does the *c* . . . Eph 5:29
body, which is the *c* .....Col 1:24
assembly and *c* ....Heb 12:23

CHURCHES
these things in the *c* .....Rev 22:16

CIRCLE
who sits above the *c* .....Is 40:22

CIRCUMCISE
is necessary to *c* them . . Acts 15:5

CIRCUMCISED
among you shall be *c* . Gen 17:10
who will justify the *c* . . . Rom 3:30
if you become *c* ....Gal 5:2

CIRCUMCISION
c is that of the heart .....Rom 2:29
C is nothing and .....1 Cor 7:19
Christ Jesus neither *c* .....Gal 5:6

CIRCUMSPECTLY
then that you walk *c* .....Eph 5:15

CISTERN
from your own *c* ....Prov 5:15

CITIES
He overthrew those *c* . . . Gen 19:25
three parts, and the *c* . . . Rev 16:19

CITIZEN
But I was born a *c* .....Acts 22:28

CITIZENS
but fellow *c* with the .....Eph 2:19

CITIZENSHIP
For our *c* is in heaven . . . Phil 3:20

CITY
shall make glad the *c* .....Ps 46:4
c has become a harlot .....Is 1:21
How lonely sits the *c* .....Lam 1:1
c that is set on a ....Matt 5:14
He has prepared a *c* . . . Heb 11:16
have no continuing *c* . . . Heb 13:14
John, saw the holy *c* .....Rev 21:2

CLAP
of the field shall *c* ....Is 55:12

CLAY
pit, out of the miry *c* ....Ps 40:2
We are the *c* ....Is 64:8
blind man with the *c* .....John 9:6
have power over the *c* . . Rom 9:21

CLEAN
He who has *c* hands and . . Ps 24:4
make yourselves *c* ....Is 1:16
c out His threshing .....Matt 3:12
You can make me *c* ....Matt 8:2
"You are not all *c* .....John 13:11
"You are already *c* .....John 15:3

CLEANSE
C me from secret ....Ps 19:12
And *c* me from my sin .....Ps 51:2
How can a young man *c* . Ps 119:9
might sanctify and *c* .....Eph 5:26
us our sins and to *c* . . . 1 John 1:9

CLEANSED
"Were there not ten *c* . Luke 17:17

CLEANSES
Christ His Son *c* ....1 John 1:7

CLEAR
of life, *c* as crystal ....Rev 22:1

CLIFF
secret places of the *c* . . . Song 2:14

CLIMBS
c up some other way . . . John 10:1

CLING
C to what is good ....Rom 12:9

CLINGS
And My tongue *c* ....Ps 22:15

CLOAK
let him have your *c* .....Matt 5:40
using liberty as a *c* .....1 Pet 2:16

CLODS
The *c* of the valley .....Job 21:33

CLOSE
c friends abhor me .....Job 19:19

CLOSED
The deep *c* around me .....Jon 2:5

CLOTH
a piece of unshrunk *c* . . . Matt 9:16

CLOTHE
He not much more *c* .....Matt 6:30

CLOTHED
of skin, and *c* them .....Gen 3:21
A man *c* in soft ....Matt 11:8
naked and you *c* ....Matt 25:36
legion, sitting and *c* .....Mark 5:15
desiring to be *c* ....2 Cor 5:2
that you may be *c* ....Rev 3:18

CLOTHES
c became shining ....Mark 9:3
many spread their *c* . . . Luke 19:36
a poor man in filthy *c* . . James 2:2

CLOTHING
c they cast lots ....Ps 22:18
do you worry about *c* .....Matt 6:28
to you in sheep's *c* .....Matt 7:15
c they cast lots ....John 19:24

CLOTHS
in swaddling *c* ....Luke 2:12

CLOUD
My rainbow in the *c* .....Gen 9:13
day in a pillar of *c* ....Ex 13:21
He led them with the *c* . . . Ps 78:14
behold, a bright *c* ....Matt 17:5
of Man coming in a *c* . Luke 21:27
c received Him out of .....Acts 1:9
by so great a *c* ....Heb 12:1

CLOUDS
Man coming on the *c* . . Matt 24:30
with them in the *c* . . . 1 Thess 4:17
are *c* without water ....Jude 12
He is coming with *c* ....Rev 1:7

CLOUDY
them by day with a *c* .....Neh 9:12

CLOVEN
chew the cud or have *c* . Deut 14:7

CLUSTER
beloved is to me a *c* .....Song 1:14

COAL
in his hand a live *c* ....Is 6:6

COALS
doing you will heap c . . Rom 12:20

COBRA
the lion and the *c* .... Ps 91:13

COBRA'S
shall play by the *c* .... Is 11:8

COFFIN
and he was put in a *c* .. Gen 50:26
touched the open *c* ..... Luke 7:14

COIN
if she loses one *c* ...... Luke 15:8

COLD
and harvest, C and ...... Gen 8:22
of many will grow *c* ... Matt 24:12
that you are neither *c* ... Rev 3:15

COLLECTION
concerning the *c* ...... 1 Cor 16:1

COLT
on a donkey, A *c* .... Zech 9:9
on a donkey, A c .... Matt 21:5

COME
He will *c* and save you .... Is 35:4
who have no money, C ..... Is 55:1
Your kingdom *c* .... Matt 6:10
"C to Me .... Matt 11:28
I have *c* in My .... John 5:43
thirsts, let him *c* .... John 7:37
c as a light into the .... John 12:46
O Lord, *c* .... 1 Cor 16:22
the door, I will *c* .... Rev 3:20

COMELINESS
He has no form or *c* .... Is 53:2

COMES
Lord's death till He *c* . 1 Cor 11:26

COMFORT
and Your staff, they *c* ..... Ps 23:4
yes, *c* My people .... Is 40:1
c each other .... 1 Thess 5:11

COMFORTED
So Isaac was *c* after ... Gen 24:67
Refusing to be *c* .... Jer 31:15

COMFORTER
She had no *c* .... Lam 1:9

COMFORTS
I, even I, am He who *c* ... Is 51:12

COMING
see the Son of Man *c* . Mark 13:26
mightier than I is *c* .... Luke 3:16
are Christ's at His *c* .. 1 Cor 15:23
Behold, I am *c* .... Rev 3:11
"Surely I am *c* .... Rev 22:20

COMMAND
c I have received ...... John 10:18
and I know that His *c* . John 12:50
if you do whatever I *c* . John 15:14

COMMANDED
not endure what was *c* . Heb 12:20

COMMANDMENT
c of the LORD is pure ...... Ps 19:8
which is the great *c* ... Matt 22:36
"A new *c* I give to ...... John 13:34
which is the first *c* .... Eph 6:2
And this is His *c* ..... 1 John 3:23

COMMANDMENTS
covenant, the Ten C ..... Ex 34:28
as doctrines the c ...... Matt 15:9
c hang all the Law ... Matt 22:40
"He who has My *c* .... John 14:21

COMMANDS
with authority He *c* .... Mark 1:27

COMMEND
But food does not *c* ..... 1 Cor 8:8

COMMENDABLE
patiently, this is *c* .... 1 Pet 2:20

COMMENDED
c the unjust steward .... Luke 16:8

COMMENDS
but whom the Lord *c* .. 2 Cor 10:18

COMMIT
"You shall not *c* .... Ex 20:14
into Your hands I c ... Luke 23:46

COMMITS
sin also *c* lawlessness .. 1 John 3:4

COMMITTED
c Himself to Him who ... 1 Pet 2:23

COMMON
c people heard Him .... Mark 12:37
had all things in *c* ...... Acts 2:44
concerning our *c* .... Jude 3

COMMOTION
there arose a great *c* ... Acts 19:23

COMMUNED
I *c* with my heart .... Eccl 1:16

COMMUNION
c of the Holy Spirit ... 2 Cor 13:14

COMPANION
a man my equal, My *c* ... Ps 55:13

COMPANIONS
while you became *c* .... Heb 10:33

COMPANY
Great was the *c* .... Ps 68:11
to an innumerable *c* .... Heb 12:22

COMPARE
c ourselves with ...... 2 Cor 10:12

COMPARED
are not worthy to be *c* .. Rom 8:18

COMPASSION
are a God full of *c* .... Ps 86:15
He was moved with *c* ... Matt 9:36
whomever I will have c . Rom 9:15
He can have *c* on those ..... Heb 5:2

COMPASSIONATE
the Lord is very *c* ..... James 5:11

COMPASSIONS
because His *c* fail not ... Lam 3:22

COMPEL
c them to come in .... Luke 14:23

COMPELS
the love of Christ *c* ... 2 Cor 5:14

COMPLAINED
some of them also *c* .. 1 Cor 10:10

COMPLAINERS
These are grumblers, *c* ... Jude 16

COMPLAINING
all things without *c* ..... Phil 2:14

COMPLAINT
For the LORD has a *c* ..... Mic 6:2

COMPLETE
work in you will *c* .... Phil 1:6
and you are *c* in Him ..... Col 2:10
of God may be *c* ...... 2 Tim 3:17

COMPLETELY
sanctify you *c* .... 1 Thess 5:23

COMPOSED
But God *c* the body ... 1 Cor 12:24

COMPREHEND
which we cannot *c* ...... Job 37:5
the darkness did not *c* ... John 1:5

CONCEAL
of God to *c* a matter .... Prov 25:2

CONCEALED
Than love carefully *c* ... Prov 27:5

CONCEIT
selfish ambition or *c* ..... Phil 2:3

CONCEITED
Let us not become *c* ..... Gal 5:26

CONCEIVE
the virgin shall *c* .... Is 7:14
And behold, you will *c* . Luke 1:31

CONCEIVED
in sin my mother *c* .... Ps 51:5

CONCERN
Neither do I *c* myself .... Ps 131:1

CONCERNED
Is it oxen God is *c* .... 1 Cor 9:9

CONCESSION
But I say this as a *c* ...... 1 Cor 7:6

CONCLUSION
Let us hear the *c* ...... Eccl 12:13

CONDEMN
world to *c* the world .... John 3:17

CONDEMNATION
can you escape the *c* .. Matt 23:33
"And this is the *c* ...... John 3:19
Their *c* is just .... Rom 3:8
therefore now no *c* ...... Rom 8:1

CONDEMNED
does not believe is *c* .... John 3:18
c sin in the flesh .... Rom 8:3

CONDEMNS
Who is he who *c* .... Rom 8:34

CONDUCT
from your aimless *c* ..... 1 Pet 1:8
may be won by the *c* .... 1 Pet 3:1

CONFESS
c my transgressions ...... Ps 32:5
that if you *c* with .... Rom 10:9
every tongue shall c ... Rom 14:11
If we *c* our sins .... 1 John 1:9

CONFESSED
c that He was Christ ... John 9:22

CONFESSES
c that Jesus is the .... 1 John 4:15

CONFESSION
with the mouth *c* ...... Rom 10:10
High Priest of our *c* ...... Heb 3:1
let us hold fast our *c* ..... Heb 4:14

CONFIDENCE
c shall be your ....Is 30:15
Jesus, and have no *c* ......Phil 3:3

CONFINED
the Scripture has *c* ....Gal 3:22

CONFIRM
who will also *c* ....1 Cor 1:8

CONFIRMED
covenant that was *c* ......Gal 3:17
c it by an oath ....Heb 6:17

CONFIRMING
c the word through ... Mark 16:20

CONFLICT
to know what a great *c* ....Col 2:1

CONFLICTS
Outside were *c* ....2 Cor 7:5

CONFORMED
predestined to be *c* .....Rom 8:29
And do not be *c* ....Rom 12:2

CONFUSE
c their language ....Gen 11:7

CONFUSED
the assembly was *c* ....Acts 19:32

CONGREGATION
Nor sinners in the *c* ....Ps 1:5
God stands in the *c* ....Ps 82:1

CONQUER
conquering and to *c* ......Rev 6:2

CONQUERORS
we are more than *c* ....Rom 8:37

CONSCIENCE
convicted by their *c* ......John 8:9
strive to have a *c* ....Acts 24:16

CONSECRATED
c this house which you ..1 Kin 9:3

CONSENT
and does not *c* to ....1 Tim 6:3

CONSENTED
He had not *c* to their ..Luke 23:51

CONSENTING
Now Saul was *c* to his ....Acts 8:1

CONSIDER
When I *c* Your heavens .....Ps 8:3
My people do not *c* ....Is 1:3
C the lilies of the ....Matt 6:28
"*C* the ravens ....Luke 12:24
c Him who endured ....Heb 12:3

CONSIST
in Him all things *c* ....Col 1:17

CONSOLATION
if there is any *c* ....Phil 2:1
us everlasting *c* .....2 Thess 2:16

CONSOLE
c those who mourn ....Is 61:3

CONSTANT
c prayer was ....Acts 12:5

CONSUME
whom the Lord will *c* .2 Thess 2:8

CONSUMED
but the bush was not *c* ....Ex 3:2
mercies we are not *c* ....Lam 3:22
beware lest you be *c* ....Gal 5:15

CONSUMING
our God is a *c* fire .....Heb 12:29

CONTAIN
of heavens cannot *c* ....2 Chr 2:6
c the books that ......John 21:25

CONTEMPT
and be treated with *c* ..Mark 9:12

CONTEMPTIBLE
and his speech *c* ......2 Cor 10:10

CONTEND
c earnestly for the ....Jude 3

CONTENT
state I am, to be *c* ....Phil 4:11
covetousness; be *c* ....Heb 13:5

CONTENTIONS
sorcery, hatred, *c* ....Gal 5:20

CONTENTIOUS
anyone seems to be *c* . 1 Cor 11:16

CONTENTMENT
c is great gain ....1 Tim 6:6

CONTINUAL
a merry heart has a *c* ..Prov 15:15
c coming she weary .....Luke 18:5

CONTINUALLY
heart was only evil *c* ......Gen 6:5
will give ourselves *c* ....Acts 6:4
remains a priest *c* ....Heb 7:3

CONTINUE
Shall we *c* in sin that .....Rom 6:1
C earnestly in prayer ....Col 4:2
Let brotherly love *c* ....Heb 13:1

CONTINUED
c steadfastly in the ......Acts 2:42

CONTRADICTIONS
idle babble and *c* ......1 Tim 6:20

CONTRARY
to worship God *c* ....Acts 18:13

CONTRIBUTION
to make a certain *c* ....Rom 15:26

CONTRITE
A broken and a *c* ....Ps 51:17
poor and of a *c* spirit ....Is 66:2

CONTROVERSY
For the LORD has a *c* .....Jer 25:31

CONVERSION
describing the *c* ....Acts 15:3

CONVERTED
unless you are *c* ....Matt 18:3

CONVICT
He has come, He will *c* . John 16:8

CONVICTS
"Which of you *c* ....John 8:46

CONVINCED
Let each be fully *c* ....Rom 14:5

COOKED
c their own children ....Lam 4:10

COOL
and *c* my tongue ....Luke 16:24

COPIES
necessary that the *c* ......Heb 9:23

COPPER
sold for two *c* coins .....Luke 12:6

COPPERSMITH
c did me much harm ....2 Tim 4:14

COPY
who serve the *c* ....Heb 8:5

CORD
this line of scarlet *c* .....Josh 2:18

CORDS
had made a whip of *c* ..John 2:15

CORNER
was not done in a *c* ....Acts 26:26

CORNERSTONE
become the chief c .....Matt 21:42
in Zion A chief c ....1 Pet 2:6

CORRECT
C your son ....Prov 29:17

CORRECTED
human fathers who *c* .....Heb 12:9

CORRECTION
Do not withhold *c* ......Prov 23:13
for reproof, for *c* ....2 Tim 3:16

CORRECTS
the LORD loves He *c* .... Prov 3:12

CORRODED
and silver are *c* ....James 5:3

CORRUPT
in these things they *c* ......Jude 10

CORRUPTED
for all flesh had *c* ....Gen 6:12
Your riches are *c* ....James 5:2

CORRUPTIBLE
redeemed with *c* ....1 Pet 1:18

CORRUPTION
Your Holy One to see *c* .. Ps 16:10
c inherit incorruption . 1 Cor 15:50
having escaped the *c* .....2 Pet 1:4

COST
and count the *c* ....Luke 14:28

COULD
c remove mountains .....1 Cor 13:2
which no one *c* number ... Rev 7:9

COUNCILS
deliver you up to *c* .....Mark 13:9

COUNSEL
Who walks not in the *c* .....Ps 1:1
We took sweet *c* ....Ps 55:14
guide me with Your *c* .....Ps 73:24
according to the *c* ....Eph 1:11
immutability of His *c* ......Heb 6:17
"I *c* you to buy from ......Rev 3:18

COUNSELOR
be called Wonderful, *C* ......Is 9:6

COUNSELORS
c there is safety ....Prov 11:14

COUNT
c my life dear to ....Acts 20:24
His promise, as some *c* ..2 Pet 3:9

COUNTED
Even a fool is *c* ....Prov 17:28
who rule well be *c* .....1 Tim 5:17

COUNTENANCE
The LORD lift up His *c* ..Num 6:26
with a sad *c* ....Matt 6:16
His *c* was like ....Matt 28:3
of the glory of his *c* .....2 Cor 3:7

COUNTRY
"Get out of your *c* ......Gen 12:1
that is, a heavenly *c* ....Heb 11:16

COUNTRYMEN
for my brethren, my *c* ...Rom 9:3

COURAGE
strong and of good *c* ...Deut 31:6

COURT
They zealously *c* ....Gal 4:17

COURTEOUS
be tenderhearted, be *c* ...1 Pet 3:8

COURTS
and into His *c* ....Ps 100:4

COVENANT
I will establish My *c* ....Gen 6:18
the LORD made a *c* .....Gen 15:18
will show them His *c* ....Ps 25:14
sons will keep My *c* .....Ps 132:12
I will make a new *c* .....Jer 31:31
the Messenger of the *c* ....Mal 3:1
cup is the new *c* ....Luke 22:20
He says, *"A new c* ....Heb 8:13
Mediator of the new *c* ..Heb 12:24
of the everlasting *c* ....Heb 13:20

COVENANTS
the glory, the *c* ....Rom 9:4

COVER
He shall *c* you with ....Ps 91:4
c a multitude of sins ..James 5:20

COVERED
Whose sin is *c* ....Ps 32:1
c all their sin ....Ps 85:2
For there is nothing *c* ..Matt 10:26

COVERING
spread a cloud for a *c* ..Ps 105:39

COVERINGS
and made themselves *c* ...Gen 3:7

COVET
"You shall not *c* ....Ex 20:17

COVETED
c no one's silver ....Acts 20:33

COVETOUS
nor thieves, nor *c* ......1 Cor 6:10

COVETOUSNESS
heed and beware of *c* .Luke 12:15

COWARDLY
the *c*, unbelieving ....Rev 21:8

CRAFTILY
His people, to deal *c* ....Ps 105:25

CRAFTINESS
deceived Eve by his *c* ..2 Cor 11:3
in the cunning *c* ....Eph 4:14

CRAFTSMAN
instructor of every *c* ....Gen 4:22

CRAFTY
the devices of the *c* ......Job 5:12
Nevertheless, being *c* .2 Cor 12:16

CREAM
were bathed with *c* ....Job 29:6

CREATE
peace and *c* calamity ......Is 45:7

CREATED
So God *c* man in His ....Gen 1:27
Has not one God *c* ....Mal 2:10
c in Christ Jesus ....Eph 2:10
new man which was *c* ...Eph 4:24

CREATION
know that the whole *c* ..Rom 8:22
Christ, he is a new *c* ...2 Cor 5:17
anything, but a new *c* ....Gal 6:15

CREATOR
Remember now your *C* .Eccl 12:1
God, the LORD, The *C* .....Is 40:28
rather than the *C* ....Rom 1:25

CREATURE
the gospel to every *c* .Mark 16:15

CREATURES
firstfruits of His *c* .....James 1:18

CREDIT
For what *c* is it if ......1 Pet 2:20

CREDITOR
There was a certain *c* ..Luke 7:41

CREEP
sort are those who *c* ....2 Tim 3:6

CREEPING
c thing and beast of .....Gen 1:24

CREPT
For certain men have *c* ....Jude 4

CRIB
donkey its master's *c* ....Is 1:3

CRIED
the poor who *c* out ....Job 29:12
of the depths I have *c* ....Ps 130:1

CRIES
your brother's blood *c* ..Gen 4:10

CRIMES
land is filled with *c* ....Ezek 7:23

CRIMINALS
also two others, *c* .....Luke 23:32

CROOKED
c places shall be made .....Is 40:4
in the midst of a *c* ....Phil 2:15

CROSS
does not take his *c* .....Matt 10:38
to bear His *c* ....Matt 27:32
down from the *c* ....Matt 27:40
lest the *c* of Christ ....1 Cor 1:17
boast except in the *c* .....Gal 6:14
the enemies of the *c* ......Phil 3:18
Him endured the *c* ......Heb 12:2
shall not follow a *c* ....Ex 23:2

CROWN
c the year with Your .....Ps 65:11
they had twisted a *c* ...Matt 27:29
obtain a perishable *c* ...1 Cor 9:25
laid up for me the *c* .....2 Tim 4:8
on His head a golden *c* .Rev 14:14

CROWNED
angels, And You have *c* ....Ps 8:5
athletics, he is not *c* ....2 Tim 2:5

CROWNS
His head were many *c* ..Rev 19:12

CRUCIFIED
"Let Him be *c* ....Matt 27:22
Calvary, there they *c* ..Luke 23:33
lawless hands, have *c* ...Acts 2:23
that our old man was *c* ...Rom 6:6
Jesus Christ and Him *c* ..1 Cor 2:2
"I have been *c* ....Gal 2:20

CRUCIFY
out again, "*C* Him ....Mark 15:13

CRUEL
hate me with *c* hatred .....Ps 25:19

CRUELTY
the haunts of *c* ....Ps 74:20

CRUSH
of peace will *c* ....Rom 16:20

CRUSHED
every side, yet not *c* ....2 Cor 4:8

CRUST
man is reduced to a *c* ...Prov 6:26

CRY
and their *c* came up to ....Ex 2:23
Does not wisdom *c* ....Prov 8:1
at midnight a *c* ....Matt 25:6
His own elect who *c* ...Luke 18:7

CRYING
nor sorrow, nor *c* ....Rev 21:4

CRYSTAL
a sea of glass, like *c* ......Rev 4:6

CUBIT
can add one *c* ....Matt 6:27

CUNNING
the serpent was more *c* ...Gen 3:1
c craftiness of deceitful ..Eph 4:14

CUP
My *c* runs over ....Ps 23:5
Then He took the *c* ..Matt 26:27
possible, let this *c* ..Matt 26:39
c is the new covenant .Luke 22:20
cannot drink the *c* ....1 Cor 10:21
c is the new ....1 Cor 11:25

CURE
and to *c* diseases ....Luke 9:1

CURES
and perform *c* ....Luke 13:32

CURSE
c the ground for man's ...Gen 8:21
C God and die ....Job 2:9
"I will send a *c* ....Mal 2:2
law are under the *c* ......Gal 3:10

CURSED
c more than all cattle ....Gen 3:14
from Me, you *c* ....Matt 25:41

CURSES
I will curse him who *c* ...Gen 12:3

CURTAIN
the heavens like a *c* ......Ps 104:2

CUSTOM
according to the *c* ....Acts 15:1

CUT
evildoers shall be *c* ....Ps 37:9
the wicked will be *c* ....Prov 2:22

CYMBAL
or a clanging *c* ....1 Cor 13:1

D

DAILY
Give us this day our *d* ..Matt 6:11
take up his cross *d* .....Luke 9:23
the Scriptures *d* ....Acts 17:11

DANCE
mourn, And a time to *d* ..Eccl 3:4
And you did not *d* .....Matt 11:17

DANCED
Then David *d* before ..2 Sam 6:14

DANCING
saw the calf and the *d* ...Ex 32:19
he heard music and *d* .Luke 15:25

DARE
someone would even *d* ...Rom 5:7

DARK
I tell you in the *d* ......Matt 10:27
shines in a *d* place .....2 Pet 1:19

DARKENED
their understanding *d* ...Eph 4:18

DARKNESS
d He called Night ....Gen 1:5
Those who sat in *d* .....Ps 107:10
d Have seen a ....Is 9:2
And deep *d* the people .....Is 60:2
body will be full of *d* ...Matt 6:23
cast out into outer *d* ....Matt 8:12
d rather than light .....John 3:19
For you were once *d* .....Eph 5:8
called you out of *d* ......1 Pet 2:9
d is reserved ....2 Pet 2:17
and in Him is no *d* ....1 John 1:5
d is passing away .....1 John 2:8

DARTS
quench all the fiery *d* ...Eph 6:16

DASH
You shall *d* them to ....Ps 2:9
Lest you d your foot .....Matt 4:6

DASHED
infants shall be *d* ......Hos 13:16

DAUGHTER
"Rejoice greatly, O *d* ....Zech 9:9
"Fear not, d of Zion ...John 12:15
the son of Pharaoh's *d* .Heb 11:24

DAUGHTERS
of God saw the *d* ....Gen 6:2
d shall prophesy ....Acts 2:17

DAY
God called the light *D* ....Gen 1:5
And *d* and night ....Gen 8:22
the Sabbath *d* ....Ex 20:8
For a *d* in Your courts ....Ps 84:10
d the LORD has ....Ps 118:24
not strike you by *d* ......Ps 121:6
For the *d* of the LORD ....Joel 2:11
who can endure the *d* ....Mal 3:2
d our daily bread ....Matt 6:11
sent Me while it is *d* ...John 9:4
person esteems one *d* ...Rom 14:5
D will declare it ....1 Cor 3:13
again the third *d* ....1 Cor 15:4
with the Lord one *d* .....2 Pet 3:8

DAYS
d are swifter than a ....Job 7:6
of woman Is of few *d* ....Job 14:1
The *d* of our lives are ....Ps 90:10
Before the difficult *d* ....Eccl 12:1
shortened those *d* .....Mark 13:20
raise it up in three *d* ....John 2:20

DAYSPRING
With which the *D* ......Luke 1:78

DEACONS
with the bishops and *d* ...Phil 1:1
d must be reverent .....1 Tim 3:8
d be the husbands .....1 Tim 3:12

DEAD
But the *d* know nothing ..Eccl 9:5
d bury their own *d* .....Matt 8:22
not the God of the *d* ...Matt 22:32
this my son was *d* ....Luke 15:24
d will hear the voice ....John 5:25
was raised from the *d* ....Rom 6:4
yourselves to be *d* ....Rom 6:11
be Lord of both the *d* ....Rom 14:9
resurrection of the *d* ..1 Cor 15:12
And the *d* in Christ ..1 Thess 4:16
without works is *d* ....James 2:26
And the *d* were judged .Rev 20:12

DEADLY
drink anything *d* .....Mark 16:18
evil, full of *d* poison ....James 3:8

DEADNESS
the *d* of Sarah's womb ..Rom 4:19

DEAF
d shall be unstopped ......Is 35:5
are cleansed and the *d* ..Matt 11:5

DEAL
My Servant shall *d* ....Is 52:13

DEATH
d parts you and me ....Ruth 1:17
and the shadow of *d* ....Job 10:21
I sleep the sleep of *d* ......Ps 13:3
of the shadow of *d* ....Ps 23:4
house leads down to *d* ..Prov 2:18
who hate me love *d* ....Prov 8:36
swallow up *d* forever ......Is 25:8
no pleasure in the *d* ...Ezek 18:32
who shall not taste *d* ..Matt 16:28
but has passed from *d* ..John 5:24
Nevertheless *d* reigned .Rom 5:14
D no longer has ....Rom 6:9
the wages of sin is *d* ....Rom 6:23
the Lord's *d* ....1 Cor 11:26
since by man came *d* .1 Cor 15:21
D is swallowed up in .1 Cor 15:54
The sting of *d* is sin ..1 Cor 15:56
is sin leading to *d* .....1 John 5:16
Be faithful until *d* ....Rev 2:10
shall be no more *d* ......Rev 21:4
which is the second *d* ...Rev 21:8

DEBTOR
I am a *d* both to ....Rom 1:14
that he is a *d* to keep .....Gal 5:3

DEBTORS
as we forgive our *d* ......Matt 6:12
of his master's *d* ....Luke 16:5
brethren, we are *d* ....Rom 8:12

DECEIT
Nor was any *d* in His ......Is 53:9
philosophy and empty *d* ..Col 2:8
no sin, nor was d ....1 Pet 2:22
mouth was found no *d* ...Rev 14:5

DECEITFUL
deliver me from the *d* .....Ps 43:1
"The heart is *d* ....Jer 17:9
are false apostles, *d* ...2 Cor 11:13

DECEITFULLY
an idol, Nor sworn *d* .....Ps 24:4
the word of God *d* ......2 Cor 4:2

DECEITFULNESS
this world and the *d* ...Matt 13:22

DECEIVE
rise up and *d* many ....Matt 24:11
Let no one *d* you with ....Eph 5:6
we have no sin, we *d* ..1 John 1:8

DECEIVED
"The serpent *d* ....Gen 3:13
the commandment, *d* ...Rom 7:11
deceiving and being *d* .2 Tim 3:13

DECEIVER
how that *d* said ....Matt 27:63
This is a *d* and an ....2 John 7

DECEIVES
heed that no one *d* .....Matt 24:4

DECENTLY
all things be done *d* ...1 Cor 14:40

DECEPTIVE
you with *d* words ....2 Pet 2:3

DECISION
in the valley of *d* ....Joel 3:14

DECLARE
The heavens *d* the ....Ps 19:1
d Your name to My ......Ps 22:22
seen and heard we *d* ...1 John 1:3

DECLARED
and *d* to be the Son of ...Rom 1:4

DECREE
"I will declare the *d* ....Ps 2:7
in those days that a *d* ...Luke 2:1

DEDICATION
it was the Feast of *D* ..John 10:22

DEED
you do in word or *d* .....Col 3:17

DEEDS
because their *d* ....John 3:19
"You do the *d* ....John 8:41
one according to his d ...Rom 2:6
you put to death the *d* ..Rom 8:13

DEEP
LORD God caused a *d* ...Gen 2:21
d uttered its voice ....Hab 3:10
"Launch out into the *d* ..Luke 5:4
I have been in the *d* ..2 Cor 11:25

DEEPER
D than Sheol ....Job 11:8

DEEPLY
But He sighed *d* ....Mark 8:12

DEER
As the *d* pants for the .....Ps 42:1
shall leap like a *d* ....Is 35:6

DEFEATED
and Israel was *d* ......1 Sam 4:10

DEFEND
D the fatherless ....Is 1:17

DEFENSE
For wisdom is a *d* ....Eccl 7:12

am appointed for the *d* . . Phil 1:17
be ready to give a *d* . . . . 1 Pet 3:15

DEFILE

also these dreamers *d* . . . . . Jude 8

DEFILED

lest they should be *d* . . John 18:28
and conscience are *d* . . . Titus 1:15

DEFILES

mouth, this *d* a man . . . Matt 15:11
it anything that *d* . . . . . . Rev 21:27

DEFRAUD

d his brother in this . . . 1 Thess 4:6

DEGREES

go forward ten *d* . . . . . . 2 Kin 20:9

DELICACIES

of the king's *d* . . . . Dan 1:5

DELICATE

a lovely and *d* woman . . . . . Jer 6:2

DELIGHT

But his *d* is in the . . . . Ps 1:2
I *d* to do Your will . . . . Ps 40:8
And I was daily His *d* . . Prov 8:30
And let your soul *d* . . . . Is 55:2
call the Sabbath a *d* . . . . . . Is 58:13
For I *d* in the law of . . . . Rom 7:22

DELIGHTS

For the LORD *d* in you . . . . . Is 62:4

DELIVER

Let Him *d* Him . . . . Ps 22:8
I will *d* him and honor . . . Ps 91:15
into temptation, But *d* . . Matt 6:13
let Him *d* Him now if . . Matt 27:43
And the Lord will *d* . . . 2 Tim 4:18
d the godly out of . . . . 2 Pet 2:9

DELIVERANCE

not accepting *d* . . . . Heb 11:35

DELIVERED

who was *d* up because . . Rom 4:25
was once for all *d* . . . . Jude 3

DELIVERER

D will come out of . . . . Rom 11:26

DELIVERS

even Jesus who *d* . . . . 1 Thess 1:10

DELUSION

send them strong *d* . . 2 Thess 2:11

DEMON

Jesus rebuked the *d* . . . Matt 17:18
and have a *d* . . . . John 8:48

DEMONIC

is earthly, sensual, *d* . . James 3:15

DEMONS

authority over all *d* . . . . . Luke 9:1
the *d* are subject . . . . . . Luke 10:17
Even the *d* believe . . . . James 2:19

DEMONSTRATE

faith, to *d* His . . . . Rom 3:25

DEMONSTRATES

d His own love toward . . . Rom 5:8

DEN

cast him into the *d* . . . . . . Dan 6:16
it a '*d of thieves* . . . . Matt 21:13

DENARIUS

the laborers for a *d* . . . . . Matt 20:2

DENIED

before men will be *d* . . . Luke 12:9
Peter then *d* again . . . . John 18:27
d the Holy One and the . Acts 3:14
things cannot be *d* . . . . Acts 19:36
household, he has *d* . . . . 1 Tim 5:8

DENIES

But whoever *d* . . . . Matt 10:33
d that Jesus is the . . . . 1 John 2:22

DENY

let him *d* himself . . . . . . Matt 16:24
He cannot *d* Himself . . . 2 Tim 2:13

DENYING

but *d* its power . . . . 2 Tim 3:5
d the Lord who bought . . 2 Pet 2:1

DEPART

scepter shall not *d* . . . . . Gen 49:10
on the left hand, '*D* . . . . Matt 25:41
will *d* from the faith . . . . 1 Tim 4:1

DEPARTING

heart of unbelief in *d* . . . Heb 3:12

DEPARTURE

d savage wolves will . . . Acts 20:29
and the time of my *d* . . . 2 Tim 4:6

DEPRESSION

of man causes *d* . . . . Prov 12:25

DEPTH

nor height nor *d* . . . . Rom 8:39
Oh, the *d* of the . . . . Rom 11:33

DEPTHS

our sins Into the *d* . . . . Mic 7:19

DERISION

shall hold them in *d* . . . . Ps 2:4

DESCEND

d now from the cross . Mark 15:32
Lord Himself will *d* . . 1 Thess 4:16

DESCENDANTS

"We are Abraham's *d* . . John 8:33

DESCENDED

He who *d* is also the . . . . Eph 4:10

DESCENDING

God ascending and *d* . . . John 1:51
the holy Jerusalem, *d* . . . Rev 21:10

DESERT

d shall rejoice . . . . Is 35:1
'Look, He is in the *d* . . . Matt 24:26

DESERTED

d place by Himself . . . . Matt 14:13

DESERTS

They wandered in *d* . . . . Heb 11:38

DESIGN

with an artistic *d* . . . . Ex 26:31

DESIRABLE

the eyes, and a tree *d* . . . . Gen 3:6

DESIRE

d shall be for your . . . . . Gen 3:16
Behold, You *d* truth in . . . . Ps 51:6
"Father, I *d* that . . . . John 17:24
all manner of evil *d* . . . . . . Rom 7:8
Brethren, my heart's *d* . . Rom 10:1
d the best gifts . . . . 1 Cor 12:31
the two, having a *d* . . . . . . Phil 1:23

DESIRED

d are they than gold . . . . . Ps 19:10
One thing I have *d* . . . . Ps 27:4

DESIRES

shall give you the *d* . . . . Ps 37:4
the devil, and the *d* . . . . . John 8:44
not come from your *d* . . James 4:1

DESOLATE

any more be termed *D* . . . . Is 62:4
house is left to you *d* . . Matt 23:38

DESOLATION

the '*abomination of* d . Matt 24:15

DESPAIRED

strength, so that we *d* . . . 2 Cor 1:8

DESPISE

one and *d* the other . . . . Matt 6:24
d the riches of His . . . . Rom 2:4

DESPISED

He is *d* and rejected . . . . . . Is 53:3
the things which are *d* . 1 Cor 1:28

DESPISES

d his neighbor sins . . . . Prov 14:21

DESPISING

the cross, *d* the shame . . . Heb 12:2

DESTITUTE

of corrupt minds and *d* . 1 Tim 6:5

DESTROY

Why should you *d* . . . . . . Eccl 7:16
shall not hurt nor *d* . . . . Is 11:9
I did not come to *d* . . . . . . Matt 5:17
Him who is able to *d* . . Matt 10:28
Barabbas and *d* Jesus . Matt 27:20
to save life or to *d* . . . . Luke 6:9
d men's lives but to . . . . Luke 9:56
d the wisdom of the . . . . 1 Cor 1:19
able to save and to *d* . James 4:12

DESTROYED

d all living things . . . . Gen 7:23
house, this tent, is *d* . . . . 2 Cor 5:1

DESTRUCTION

You turn man to *d* . . . . Ps 90:3
d that lays waste . . . . Ps 91:6
your life from *d* . . . . Ps 103:4
Pride goes before *d* . . . . Prov 16:18
whose end is *d* . . . . Phil 3:19
with everlasting *d* . . . . 2 Thess 1:9

DESTRUCTIVE

bring in *d* heresies . . . . . . 2 Pet 2:1

DETERMINED

d their preappointed . . . Acts 17:26
For I *d* not to know . . . . . 1 Cor 2:2

DEVICE

there is no work or *d* . . . Eccl 9:10

DEVICES

not ignorant of his *d* . . . 2 Cor 2:11

DEVIL

to be tempted by the *d* . . . Matt 4:1
prepared for the *d* . . . . . Matt 25:41
of your father the *d* . . . . John 8:44
give place to the *d* . . . . . . Eph 4:27
the snare of the *d* . . . . . . 2 Tim 2:26
the works of the *d* . . . . . 1 John 3:8

DEVIOUS

And who are *d* . . . . Prov 2:15

DEVISES
d wickedness on his . . . . . Ps 36:4
But a generous man *d* . . . . . Is 32:8

DEVOID
who is *d* of wisdom . . . . Prov 11:12

DEVOTED
Your servant, who is *d* . . Ps 119:38

DEVOUR
For you *d* widows' . . . . Matt 23:14
bite and *d* one another . . . Gal 5:15
whom he may *d* . . . . 1 Pet 5:8
d her Child as . . . . Rev 12:4

DEVOURED
wild beast has *d* . . . . Gen 37:20
birds came and *d* them . Matt 13:4
of heaven and *d* them . . . Rev 20:9

DEVOUT
man was just and *d* . . . . Luke 2:25
d soldier from among . . . Acts 10:7

DEW
God give you Of the *d* . . Gen 27:28

DIADEMS
ten horns, and seven *d* . . Rev 12:3

DIAMOND
d it is engraved . . . . Jer 17:1

DICTATES
according to the *d* . . . . . Jer 23:17

DIE
it you shall surely *d* . . . . . Gen 2:17
but a person shall *d* . . . 2 Chr 25:4
I shall not *d* . . . . Ps 118:17
born, And a time to *d* . . . . Eccl 3:2
eat of it and not *d* . . . . . John 6:50
to you that you will *d* . . . John 8:24
though he may *d* . . . . . John 11:25
one man should *d* . . . . . John 11:50
the flesh you will *d* . . . . Rom 8:13
For as in Adam all *d* . . 1 Cor 15:22
and to *d* is gain . . . . Phil 1:21
for men to *d* once . . . . . . Heb 9:27
are the dead who *d* . . . . . Rev 14:13

DIED
And all flesh *d* . . . . Gen 7:21
in due time Christ *d* . . . . . Rom 5:6
Christ *d* for us . . . . Rom 5:8
Now if we *d* with . . . . Rom 6:8
and He *d* for all . . . . . . 2 Cor 5:15
for if we *d* with Him . . . 2 Tim 2:11

DIES
alive unless it *d* . . . . . . 1 Cor 15:36

DIFFERS
for one star *d* from . . . 1 Cor 15:41

DILIGENCE
d it produced in you . . . 2 Cor 7:11

DILIGENT
d makes rich . . . . Prov 10:4

DILIGENTLY
d lest anyone fall . . . . . . Heb 12:15

DIM
His eyes were not *d* . . . . Deut 34:7

DIMLY
we see in a mirror, *d* . 1 Cor 13:12

DINE
come in to him and *d* . . . . Rev 3:20

DINNER
invites you to *d* . . . . 1 Cor 10:27

DIP
d your piece of bread . . . Ruth 2:14

DIPPED
clothed with a robe *d* . . . . Rev 19:13

DIRECT
Now may the Lord *d* . . 2 Thess 3:5

DIRT
cast up mire and *d* . . . . Is 57:20

DISARMED
d principalities . . . . Col 2:15

DISASTER
will end with *d* . . . . Acts 27:10

DISCERN
d the face of the sky . . . . Matt 16:3
senses exercised to *d* . . . . . Heb 5:14

DISCERNED
they are spiritually *d* . . . 1 Cor 2:14

DISCERNER
d of the thoughts . . . . Heb 4:12

DISCERNS
a wise man's heart *d* . . . . . Eccl 8:5

DISCIPLE
he cannot be My *d* . . . . Luke 14:26
d whom Jesus loved . . . . John 21:7

DISCIPLES
word, you are My *d* . . . . John 8:31
but we are Moses' *d* . . . . John 9:28

DISCIPLINES
he who loves him *d* . . . . Prov 13:24

DISCORD
And one who sows *d* . . . Prov 6:19

DISCOURAGED
lest they become *d* . . . . . . Col 3:21
become weary and *d* . . . . . Heb 12:3

DISCRETION
D will preserve you . . . . Prov 2:11

DISFIGURE
d their faces that . . . . Matt 6:16

DISGUISES
And he *d* his face . . . . Job 24:15

DISHONOR
Father, and you *d* Me . . . John 8:49
d their bodies among . . . . Rom 1:24
It is sown in *d* . . . . 1 Cor 15:43

DISHONORED
But you have *d* the . . . . . James 2:6

DISHONORS
For son *d* father . . . . Mic 7:6

DISOBEDIENT
out My hands To a d . . Rom 10:21

DISORDERLY
for this *d* gathering . . . . Acts 19:40

DISPENSATION
d of the fullness of . . . . Eph 1:10

DISPERSION
the pilgrims of the *D* . . . 1 Pet 1:1

DISPLEASE
LORD see it, and it *d* . . . Prov 24:18

DISPLEASED
they were greatly *d* . . . . Matt 20:24
it, He was greatly *d* . . . Mark 10:14

DISPUTE
there was also a *d* . . . . . Luke 22:24

DISPUTER
Where is the *d* of this . . 1 Cor 1:20

DISPUTES
But avoid foolish *d* . . . . . . Titus 3:9

DISQUALIFIED
should become *d* . . . . . . 1 Cor 9:27

DISQUIETED
And why are you *d* . . . . Ps 42:5

DISSENSION
had no small *d* and . . . . . Acts 15:2

DISSIPATION
not accused of *d* . . . . Titus 1:6

DISSOLVED
the heavens will be *d* . . . 2 Pet 3:12

DISTINCTION
compassion, making a *d* . . Jude 22

DISTRESS
d them in His deep . . . . Ps 2:5
tribulation, or *d* . . . . Rom 8:35

DISTRESSED
and deeply *d* . . . . Mark 14:33

DISTRESSES
Bring me out of my *d* . . . Ps 25:17

DISTRIBUTED
and they *d* to each as . . . Acts 4:35

DISTRIBUTING
d to the needs of the . . . Rom 12:13

DITCH
will fall into a *d* . . . . Matt 15:14

DIVERSITIES
There are *d* . . . . 1 Cor 12:4

DIVIDE
d the spoil with the . . . . Prov 16:19
"Take this and *d* . . . . . . Luke 22:17

DIVIDED
and the waters were *d* . . . Ex 14:21
they were not *d* . . . . 2 Sam 1:23
"Every kingdom *d* . . . . . Matt 12:25
Is Christ *d* . . . . 1 Cor 1:13

DIVIDES
at home *d* the spoil . . . . . . Ps 68:12

DIVIDING
rightly *d* the word of . . 2 Tim 2:15

DIVINATION
shall you practice *d* . . . . Lev 19:26
a spirit of *d* met us . . . . Acts 16:16

DIVINE
d service and the . . . . Heb 9:1

DIVISION
So there was a *d* . . . . John 7:43

DIVISIONS
those who cause *d* . . . . . . Rom 16:17
persons, who cause *d* . . . . . Jude 19

DIVISIVE
Reject a *d* man after . . . Titus 3:10

DIVORCE
her a certificate of *d* . . . . Deut 24:1
a certificate of *d* . . . . Mark 10:4

DO
men to *d* to you, *d* . . . . . Matt 7:12
He sees the Father *d* . . . . John 5:19
without Me you can *d* . . John 15:5
"Sirs, what must I *d* . . . Acts 16:30
d evil that good may . . . . . Rom 3:8
or whatever you *d*, *d* . . 1 Cor 10:31

DOCTRINE
What new *d* is this . . . . Mark 1:27
"My *d* is not Mine . . . . . . John 7:16
with every wind of *d* . . . . Eph 4:14
is contrary to sound *d* . 1 Tim 1:10
is profitable for *d* . . . . . 2 Tim 3:16
not endure sound *d* . . . . . 2 Tim 4:3

DOCTRINES
commandments and *d* . . . Col 2:22
various and strange *d* . . . Heb 13:9

DOERS
But be *d* of the word . . James 1:22

DOG
d is better than a . . . . Eccl 9:4
d returns to his own . . . 2 Pet 2:22

DOGS
what is holy to the *d* . . . . . Matt 7:6
d eat the crumbs . . . . . . Matt 15:27
But outside are *d* . . . . Rev 22:15

DOMINION
let them have *d* . . . . Gen 1:26
d is an everlasting . . . . Dan 4:34
sin shall not have *d* . . . . . Rom 6:14
glory and majesty, *D* . . . . . . Jude 25

DONKEY
d its master's crib . . . . Is 1:3
and riding on a *d* . . . . Zech 9:9
colt, the foal of a d . . . . . . Matt 21:5
d speaking with a . . . . 2 Pet 2:16

DOOM
for the day of *d* . . . . Prov 16:4

DOOR
stone against the *d* . . . . Matt 27:60
to you, I am the *d* . . . . John 10:7
before you an open *d* . . . . . Rev 3:8
I stand at the *d* . . . . Rev 3:20

DOORKEEPER
I would rather be a *d* . . . . Ps 84:10

DOORPOSTS
write them on the *d* . . . . . . Deut 6:9

DOORS
up, you everlasting *d* . . . . . Ps 24:7

DOUBLE
from the LORD's hand *D* . . . . Is 40:2
worthy of *d* honor . . . . . 1 Tim 5:17

DOUBLE-MINDED
he is a *d* man . . . . James 1:8

DOUBT
faith, why did you *d* . . . Matt 14:31

DOUBTING
in faith, with no *d* . . . . . James 1:6

DOUBTS
why do *d* arise in . . . . . . Luke 24:38
for I have *d* about you . . . Gal 4:20

DOVE
d found no resting . . . . Gen 8:9
descending like a *d* . . . . . Matt 3:16

DOVES
and harmless as *d* . . . . . Matt 10:16

DOWNCAST
who comforts the *d* . . . . . 2 Cor 7:6

DRAGNET
d that was cast . . . . Matt 13:47

DRAGON
they worshiped the *d* . . . . Rev 13:4
He laid hold of the *d* . . . . Rev 20:2

DRAINED
All faces are *d* . . . . Joel 2:6

DRANK
them, and they all *d* . . Mark 14:23

DRAW
d honey from the . . . . . Deut 32:13
me to *d* near to God . . . . . Ps 73:28
And the years *d* . . . . Eccl 12:1
will *d* all peoples . . . . . . John 12:32
D near to God and He . . James 4:8

DRAWS
your redemption *d* . . . . Luke 21:28

DREAM
Now Joseph had a *d* . . . . Gen 37:5
Your old men shall *d* . . . . . Joel 2:28
to Joseph in a *d* . . . . Matt 2:13
things today in a *d* . . . . Matt 27:19

DREAMERS
d defile the flesh . . . . Jude 8

DREAMS
Nebuchadnezzar had *d* . . . Dan 2:1

DRIED
of her blood was *d* . . . . . Mark 5:29
saw the fig tree *d* . . . . . Mark 11:20

DRIFT
have heard, lest we *d* . . . . Heb 2:1

DRINK
gave me vinegar to *d* . . . . Ps 69:21
Lest they *d* and forget . . Prov 31:5
follow intoxicating *d* . . . . Is 5:11
d the milk of the . . . . Is 60:16
bosom, That you may *d* . . Is 66:11
"Bring wine, let us *d* . . . . Amos 4:1
that day when I *d* . . . . . . Matt 26:29
mingled with gall to *d* . Matt 27:34
with myrrh to *d* . . . . Mark 15:23
to her, "Give Me a *d* . . . . . John 4:7
him come to Me and *d* . John 7:37
do, as often as you *d* . . 1 Cor 11:25
No longer *d* only . . . . 1 Tim 5:23

DRINKS
to her, "Whoever *d* . . . . . John 4:13
d My blood has . . . . John 6:54
he who eats and *d* . . . . . 1 Cor 11:29

DRIPPING
His lips are lilies, *D* . . . . Song 5:13

DROSS
purge away your *d* . . . . Is 1:25

DROUGHT
in the year of *d* . . . . Jer 17:8
"For I called for a *d* . . . . . Hag 1:11

DROVE
So He *d* out the man . . . . Gen 3:24
temple of God and *d* . . . . Matt 21:12

DROWN
Nor can the floods *d* . . . . Song 8:7
harmful lusts which *d* . . . 1 Tim 6:9

DROWSINESS
d will clothe a . . . . Prov 23:21

DRUNK
of the wine and was *d* . . . Gen 9:21
the guests have well *d* . . John 2:10
"For these are not *d* . . . . Acts 2:15
and another is *d* . . . . . . 1 Cor 11:21
I saw the woman, *d* . . . . . . Rev 17:6

DRUNKARD
to and fro like a *d* . . . . Is 24:20
or a reviler, or a *d* . . . . . 1 Cor 5:11

DRUNKEN
I am like a *d* man . . . . Jer 23:9

DRUNKENNESS
will be filled with *d* . . . Ezek 23:33
not in revelry and *d* . . . . Rom 13:13
envy, murders, *d* . . . . Gal 5:21

DRY
place, and let the *d* . . . . Gen 1:9
made the sea into *d* . . . . . Ex 14:21
It was *d* on the fleece . . . Judg 6:40
will be done in the *d* . Luke 23:31

DUE
pay all that was *d* . . . . . Matt 18:34
d time Christ died . . . . Rom 5:6
d season we shall . . . . Gal 6:9
exalt you in *d* time . . . . . . 1 Pet 5:6

DULL
heart of this people *d* . . . . . . Is 6:10
people have grown d . . . Matt 13:15

DUMB
the tongue of the *d* . . . . Is 35:6

DUST
formed man of the *d* . . . . . Gen 2:7
d you shall return . . . . Gen 3:19
And repent in *d* . . . . Job 42:6
that we are *d* . . . . Ps 103:14
counted as the small *d* . . . Is 40:15
city, shake off the *d* . . . Matt 10:14
of the man of *d* . . . . 1 Cor 15:49

DUTY
done what was our *d* . Luke 17:10

DWELL
Who may *d* in Your holy . . Ps 15:1
"I *d* in the high and . . . . . . Is 57:15
"I will d in them . . . . 2 Cor 6:16
that Christ may *d* . . . . Eph 3:17
men, and He will *d* . . . . . Rev 21:3

DWELLING
built together for a *d* . . . . Eph 2:22
a foreign country, *d* . . . . . Heb 11:9

DWELLS
He who *d* in the secret . . . . Ps 91:1
but the Father who *d* . . John 14:10
d all the fullness . . . . Col 2:9
which righteousness *d* . 2 Pet 3:13
you, where Satan *d* . . . . . Rev 2:13

DWELT
became flesh and *d* . . . . John 1:14
By faith he *d* in the . . . . . Heb 11:9

DYING
in the body the *d* . . . . . . 2 Cor 4:10

E

EAGLE
fly away like an *e* . . . . . . Prov 23:5

The way of an *e* .... Prov 30:19
like a flying *e* .... Rev 4:7

EAGLES

up with wings like *e* .... Is 40:31
e will be gathered ...... Matt 24:28

EAGLES'

how I bore you on *e* ...... Ex 19:4

EAR

shall pierce his *e* .... Ex 21:6
And the *e* of the wise .. Prov 18:15
e is uncircumcised .... Jer 6:10
you hear in the *e* ...... Matt 10:27
cut off his right *e* ...... John 18:10
not seen, nor e heard ... 1 Cor 2:9
"He who has an *e* .... Rev 2:7

EARLY

Very *e* in the morning . Mark 16:2
arrived at the tomb *e* .. Luke 24:22

EARNESTLY

He prayed more *e* .... Luke 22:44
e that it would not .... James 5:17
you to contend *e* .... Jude 3

EARS

And hear with their *e* ..... Is 6:10
"He who has *e* .... Matt 11:15
they have itching *e* ..... 2 Tim 4:3

EARTH

to judge the *e* .... 1 Chr 16:33
foundations of the *e* ...... Job 38:4
e is the LORD's .... Ps 24:1
You had formed the *e* ...... Ps 90:2
there was ever an *e* ..... Prov 8:23
e abides forever .... Eccl 1:4
for the meek of the *e* ...... Is 11:4
e is My footstool .... Is 66:1
I will darken the *e* ...... Amos 8:9
shall inherit the *e* .... Matt 5:5
heaven and *e* pass .... Matt 5:18
e as it is in heaven ..... Matt 6:10
treasures on *e* .... Matt 6:19
then shook the *e* .... Heb 12:26
heaven and a new *e* ..... Rev 21:1

EARTHLY

"If I have told you *e* .... John 3:12
that if our *e* house ...... 2 Cor 5:1
their mind on *e* things ... Phil 3:19
from above, but is *e* ... James 3:15

EARTHQUAKE

after the wind an *e* ... 1 Kin 19:11
there was a great *e* ..... Matt 28:2

EARTHQUAKES

And there will be *e* .... Mark 13:8

EASIER

"Which is *e*, to say ..... Mark 2:9
"It is *e* for a camel ..... Mark 10:25

EAST

goes toward the *e* .... Gen 2:14
wise men from the *E* .... Matt 2:1
many will come from *e* . Matt 8:11
will come from the *e* .. Luke 13:29

EAT

you may freely *e* .... Gen 2:16
'You shall not *e* .... Gen 3:17
e this scroll .... Ezek 3:1
life, what you will *e* .... Matt 6:25
give us His flesh to *e* ... John 6:52
one believes he may *e* ... Rom 14:2
e meat nor drink wine . Rom 14:21
I will never again *e* .... 1 Cor 8:13
neither shall he *e* .... 2 Thess 3:10

EATEN

Have you *e* from the .... Gen 3:11
he was *e* by worms .... Acts 12:23

EATS

receives sinners and *e* .. Luke 15:2
"Whoever *e* My flesh ..... John 6:54
e this bread will live .... John 6:58
He who *e*, *e* to the ...... Rom 14:6
unworthy manner *e* ... 1 Cor 11:29

EDIFICATION

has given me for *e* .... 2 Cor 13:10
rather than godly *e* ...... 1 Tim 1:4

EDIFIES

puffs up, but love *e* ..... 1 Cor 8:1

EDIFY

but not all things *e* ... 1 Cor 10:23

EDIFYING

of the body for the *e* .... Eph 4:16

ELDER

against an *e* except .... 1 Tim 5:19

ELDERS

the tradition of the *e* .... Matt 15:2
be rejected by the *e* .... Luke 9:22
they had appointed *e* .. Acts 14:23
e who rule well be ...... 1 Tim 5:17
lacking, and appoint *e* ... Titus 1:5
e obtained a good .... Heb 11:2
e who are among you I .. 1 Pet 5:1
I saw twenty-four *e* .... Rev 4:4

ELDERSHIP

of the hands of the *e* .. 1 Tim 4:14

ELECT

gather together His *e* .. Matt 24:31
e have obtained it ...... Rom 11:7
e according to the .... 1 Pet 1:2
A chief cornerstone, e ... 1 Pet 2:6

ELECTION

call and *e* sure .... 2 Pet 1:10

ELEMENTS

weak and beggarly *e* ..... Gal 4:9
e will melt with .... 2 Pet 3:10

ELEVEN

numbered with the *e* ..... Acts 1:26

ELOQUENT

an *e* man and mighty .. Acts 18:24

EMBALM

to *e* his father .... Gen 50:2

ENCOURAGED

is, that I may be *e* ...... Rom 1:12
and all may be *e* ..... 1 Cor 14:31

END

make me to know my *e* ... Ps 39:4
shall keep it to the *e* ... Ps 119:33
e is the way of death .. Prov 14:12
Declaring the *e* .... Is 46:10
what shall be the *e* .... Dan 12:8
the harvest is the *e* .... Matt 13:39
always, even to the *e* .. Matt 28:20
He loved them to the *e* . John 13:1
For Christ is the *e* .... Rom 10:4
But the *e* of all .... 1 Pet 4:7
the latter *e* is worse .... 2 Pet 2:20
My works until the *e* .... Rev 2:26
Beginning and the *E* ... Rev 22:13

ENDLESS

and *e* genealogies .... 1 Tim 1:4
to the power of an *e* .... Heb 7:16

ENDURANCE

e the race that .... Heb 12:1

ENDURE

as the sun and moon *e* .... Ps 72:5
His name shall *e* .... Ps 72:17
persecuted, we *e* ...... 1 Cor 4:12

ENDURED

he had patiently *e* .... Heb 6:15
e as seeing Him who ... Heb 11:27
consider Him who *e* .... Heb 12:3

ENDURES

And His truth *e* .... Ps 100:5
For His mercy *e* .... Ps 136:1
But he who *e* to the .... Matt 10:22
e only for a while ...... Matt 13:21
for the food which *e* .... John 6:27
he has built on it *e* .... 1 Cor 3:14
hopes all things, *e* ..... 1 Cor 13:7
word of the LORD *e* .... 1 Pet 1:25

ENDURING

the LORD is clean, *e* .... Ps 19:9

ENEMIES

the presence of my *e* ...... Ps 23:5
e will lick the dust .... Ps 72:9
to you, love your *e* ..... Matt 5:44
e will be those .... Matt 10:36
e we were reconciled .... Rom 5:10
till He has put all *e* ... 1 Cor 15:25
were alienated and *e* .... Col 1:21
His *e* are made His .... Heb 10:13

ENEMY

If your *e* is hungry .... Prov 25:21
rejoice over me, my *e* .... Mic 7:8
and hate your *e* .... Matt 5:43
last *e* that will be ..... 1 Cor 15:26
become your *e* because .. Gal 4:16
count him as an *e* ... 2 Thess 3:15
makes himself an *e* .... James 4:4

ENJOY

richly all things to *e* ... 1 Tim 6:17
than to *e* the passing .. Heb 11:25

ENJOYMENT

So I commended *e* ...... Eccl 8:15

ENLIGHTEN

E my eyes .... Ps 13:3

ENLIGHTENED

those who were once *e* ... Heb 6:4

ENMITY

And I will put *e* .... Gen 3:15
the carnal mind is *e* ..... Rom 8:7
in His flesh the *e* .... Eph 2:15

ENRAPTURED

And always be *e* .... Prov 5:19

ENRICHED

while you are *e* .... 2 Cor 9:11

ENSNARED

The wicked is *e* .... Prov 12:13

ENSNARES

sin which so easily *e* .... Heb 12:1

ENTER

E into His gates .... Ps 100:4
you will by no means *e* . Matt 5:20
"*E* by the narrow .... Matt 7:13
e the kingdom of God . Matt 19:24
E into the joy of your .. Matt 25:21
and pray, lest you *e* ... Matt 26:41
"Strive to *e* through ... Luke 13:24
who have believed do *e* .. Heb 4:3
e the temple till the ..... Rev 15:8

ENTERED
Then Satan *e* Judas .... Luke 22:3
through one man sin *e* .. Rom 5:12
ear heard, Nor have e ... 1 Cor 2:9
the forerunner has *e* .... Heb 6:20
e the Most Holy Place .... Heb 9:12

ENTERS
If anyone *e* by Me ...... John 10:9

ENTHRONED
You are holy, *E* in .... Ps 22:3

ENTIRELY
give yourself *e* .... 1 Tim 4:15

ENTREAT
being defamed, we *e* .. 1 Cor 4:13

ENTREATED
e our God for this ...... Ezra 8:23

ENVIOUS
patriarchs, becoming *e* ... Acts 7:9

ENVY
e slays a simple .... Job 5:2
e is rottenness .... Prov 14:30
not let your heart *e* .... Prov 23:17
full of *e* .... Rom 1:29
not in strife and *e* .... Rom 13:13
love does not *e* .... 1 Cor 13:4
e, murders .... Gal 5:21
living in malice and *e* ... Titus 3:3

EPISTLE
You are our *e* written ... 2 Cor 3:2

EPISTLES
as also in all his *e* .... 2 Pet 3:16

ERR
My people Israel to *e* .... Jer 23:13

ERROR
a sinner from the *e* ... James 5:20
led away with the *e* .... 2 Pet 3:17
run greedily in the *e* ..... Jude 11

ERRORS
can understand his *e* .... Ps 19:12

ESCAPE
e all these things ..... Luke 21:36
same, that you will *e* .... Rom 2:3
make the way of *e* .... 1 Cor 10:13
how shall we *e* if we ..... Heb 2:3

ESCAPED
after they have *e* .... 2 Pet 2:20

ESTABLISH
seeking to *e* their own .. Rom 10:3
faithful, who will *e* .... 2 Thess 3:3
E your hearts .... James 5:8
a while, perfect, *e* ...... 1 Pet 5:10

ESTABLISHED
Your throne is *e* .... Ps 93:2
built up in Him and *e* ...... Col 2:7
covenant, which was *e* ... Heb 8:6

ESTEEM
and we did not *e* .... Is 53:3
e others better than ...... Phil 2:3

ESTEEMED
For what is highly *e* ... Luke 16:15

ESTEEMS
One person *e* one day ... Rom 14:5

ETERNAL
e God is your refuge .. Deut 33:27
For man goes to his *e* ... Eccl 12:5
and inherit *e* life ...... Matt 19:29
in the age to come, *e* . Mark 10:30
not perish but have *e* ... John 3:15
you think you have *e* ... John 5:39
I give them *e* life ...... John 10:28
"And this is *e* life ...... John 17:3
the gift of God is *e* ..... Rom 6:23
are not seen are *e* ..... 2 Cor 4:18
lay hold on *e* life ...... 1 Tim 6:12
e life which was .... 1 John 1:2

ETERNITY
Also He has put *e* .... Eccl 3:11
One who inhabits *e* ...... Is 57:15

EUNUCH
of Ethiopia, a *e* .... Acts 8:27

EUNUCHS
made themselves *e* .... Matt 19:12

EVANGELIST
of Philip the *e* .... Acts 21:8
do the work of an *e* .... 2 Tim 4:5

EVANGELISTS
some prophets, some *e* .. Eph 4:11

EVERLASTING
from *E* is Your name ..... Is 63:16
awake, Some to *e* life ... Dan 12:2
not perish but have *e* .. John 3:16
who sent Me has *e* ..... John 5:24
endures to *e* life .... John 6:27
in Him may have *e* ..... John 6:40
believes in Me has *e* .... John 6:47
e destruction from .... 2 Thess 1:9

EVIDENCE
e of things not seen ..... Heb 11:1

EVIDENT
e that our Lord arose .... Heb 7:14

EVIL
of good and *e* .... Gen 2:9
knowing good and *e* ...... Gen 3:5
his heart was only *e* ...... Gen 6:5
I will fear no *e* .... Ps 23:4
e more than good .... Ps 52:3
To do *e* is like sport ..... Prov 10:23
e will bow before the .... Prov 14:19
Keeping watch on the *e* . Prov 15:3
e All the days of her ... Prov 31:12
to those who call *e* .... Is 5:20
of peace and not of *e* .... Jer 29:11
Seek good and not *e* .. Amos 5:14
deliver us from the *e* ..... Matt 6:13
"If you then, being *e* .... Matt 7:11
e treasure brings ...... Matt 12:35
everyone practicing *e* .. John 3:20
done any good or *e* ...... Rom 9:11
Repay no one *e* for ..... Rom 12:17
provoked, thinks no *e* . 1 Cor 13:5

EVILDOER
"If He were not an *e* .. John 18:30
suffer trouble as an *e* ... 2 Tim 2:9

EVILDOERS
e shall be cut off .... Ps 37:9
from me, you *e* .... Ps 119:115
iniquity, A brood of *e* .... Is 1:4
against you as *e* .... 1 Pet 2:12

EXALT
e His name together .... Ps 34:3
E the humble .... Ezek 21:26
And he shall *e* himself .. Dan 8:25

EXALTATION
who rejoice in My *e* .... Is 13:3
brother glory in his *e* ... James 1:9

EXALTED
Let God be *e* .... 2 Sam 22:47
I will be *e* among the .... Ps 46:10
You are *e* far above ...... Ps 97:9
His name alone is *e* .... Ps 148:13
valley shall be *e* .... Is 40:4
"Him God has *e* .... Acts 5:31
And lest I should be *e* . 2 Cor 12:7
also has highly *e* .... Phil 2:9

EXALTS
Righteousness *e* .... Prov 14:34
high thing that *e* .... 2 Cor 10:5
e himself above all .... 2 Thess 2:4

EXAMINE
But let a man *e* .... 1 Cor 11:28
But let each one *e* .... Gal 6:4

EXAMPLE
to make her a public *e* .. Matt 1:19
I have given you an *e* . John 13:15
youth, but be an *e* ..... 1 Tim 4:12
us, leaving us an *e* ..... 1 Pet 2:21
are set forth as an *e* .... Jude 7

EXAMPLES
to them as *e* .... 1 Cor 10:11
to you, but being *e* ...... 1 Pet 5:3

EXCHANGE
give in *e* for his soul ... Matt 16:26

EXCHANGED
Nor can it be *e* .... Job 28:17
e the truth of God for ... Rom 1:25

EXCUSE
now they have no *e* ... John 15:22
they are without *e* .... Rom 1:20

EXCUSES
began to make *e* .... Luke 14:18

EXECUTE
e judgment also .... John 5:27
e wrath on him who .... Rom 13:4

EXECUTES
e justice for me .... Mic 7:9

EXERCISE
e yourself toward .... 1 Tim 4:7

EXHORT
e him as a father .... 1 Tim 5:1
Speak these things, *e* ... Titus 2:15
e one another .... Heb 3:13

EXHORTATION
he who exhorts, in *e* .... Rom 12:8
to reading, to *e* .... 1 Tim 4:13

EXHORTED
know how we *e* ..... 1 Thess 2:11

EXIST
by Your will they *e* ...... Rev 4:11

EXPECT
an hour you do not *e* .. Luke 12:40

EXPECTATION
the people were in *e* ... Luke 3:15
a certain fearful *e* ...... Heb 10:27

EXPLAIN
no one who could *e* .... Gen 41:24
"*E* this parable to us ... Matt 15:15
to say, and hard to *e* ...... Heb 5:11

EXPLAINED
He *e* all things to His .. Mark 4:34

EXPOSED
his deeds should be *e* . . . John 3:20

EXPOUNDED
He *e* to them in all . . . . Luke 24:27

EXPRESS
of His glory and the *e* . . . .Heb 1:3

EXTORTION
they are full of *e* . . . . . .Matt 23:25

EXTORTIONERS
e will inherit . . . . .1 Cor 6:10

EYE
the ear, But now my *e* . . . Job 42:5
guide you with My *e* . . . . . . Ps 32:8
e is not satisfied . . . . .Eccl 1:8
the apple of His *e* . . . . . . .Zech 2:8
if your right *e* . . . . .Matt 5:29
it was said, *'An e* . . . . .Matt 5:38
plank in your own *e* . . . . . .Matt 7:3
e causes you to sin . . . . . .Matt 18:9
Or is your *e* evil . . . . .Matt 20:15
the *e* of a needle . . . . . . .Luke 18:25
the twinkling of an *e* . .1 Cor 15:52
every *e* will see Him . . . . . .Rev 1:7
your eyes with *e* salve . . .Rev 3:18

EYES
e will be opened . . . . .Gen 3:5
And my *e* shall behold . . Job 19:27
e are ever toward the . . . . Ps 25:15
The *e* of the LORD are . . . . Ps 34:15
I will lift up my *e* . . . . .Ps 121:1
but the *e* of a fool . . . . . .Prov 17:24
be wise in his own *e* . . . . .Prov 26:5
You have dove's *e* . . . . . . Song 1:15
e have seen the King . . . . . . .Is 6:5
Who have *e* and see . . . . . . .Jer 5:21
rims were full of *e* . . . . . .Ezek 1:18
You are of purer *e* . . . . .Hab 1:13
blessed are your *e* . . . . . .Matt 13:16
"He put clay on my *e* . . . John 9:15
e they have closed . . . . . . .Acts 28:27
E that they should not . . Rom 11:8
have seen with our *e* . . 1 John 1:1
the lust of the *e* . . . . .1 John 2:16
as snow, and His *e* . . . . . . .Rev 1:14
creatures full of *e* . . . . .Rev 4:6
horns and seven *e* . . . . .Rev 5:6

EYESERVICE
not with *e* . . . . .Eph 6:6

EYEWITNESSES
the beginning were *e* . . . . . Luke 1:2
e of His majesty . . . . .2 Pet 1:16

F

FABLES
nor give heed to *f* . . . . . . .1 Tim 1:4
cunningly devised *f* . . . . .2 Pet 1:16

FACE
"For I have seen God *f* . Gen 32:30
f shone while he . . . . .Ex 34:29
sins have hidden His *f* . . . . . Is 59:2
f shone like the sun . . . . . .Matt 17:2
dimly, but then *f* . . . . . .1 Cor 13:12
with unveiled *f* . . . . .2 Cor 3:18
withstood him to his *f* . . . . Gal 2:11
They shall see His *f* . . . . . Rev 22:4

FADE
We all *f* as a leaf . . . . .Is 64:6
rich man also will *f* . . . . James 1:11
and that does not *f* . . . . 1 Pet 1:4

FADES
withers, the flower *f* . . . . . . .Is 40:7

FAIL
tittle of the law to *f* . . . Luke 16:17
faith should not *f* . . . . . . .Luke 22:32
they will *f* . . . . .1 Cor 13:8
Your years will not f . . . . . Heb 1:12

FAILING
"men's hearts *f* . . . . .Luke 21:26

FAILS
Love never *f* . . . . .1 Cor 13:8

FAINT
shall walk and not *f* . . . . . . .Is 40:31

FAINTS
My soul *f* for Your . . . . . . Ps 119:81
And the whole heart *f* . . . . . .Is 1:5
the earth, Neither *f* . . . . .Is 40:28

FAITH
shall live by his *f* . . . . .Hab 2:4
you, O you of little *f* . . . . .Matt 6:30
not found such great *f* . . . Matt 8:10
that you have no *f* . . . . . . .Mark 4:40
"Increase our *f* . . . . .Luke 17:5
will He really find *f* . . . . . .Luke 18:8
are sanctified by *f* . . . . . .Acts 26:18
God is revealed from *f* . . Rom 1:17
f apart from the deeds . . . Rom 3:28
his *f* is accounted for . . . . . Rom 4:5
those who are of the *f* . . . Rom 4:16
f which we preach . . . . . . .Rom 10:8
f comes by hearing . . . . . . Rom 10:17
and you stand by *f* . . . . . .Rom 11:20
in proportion to our *f* . . . Rom 12:6
Do you have *f* . . . . .Rom 14:22
though I have all *f* . . . . . .1 Cor 13:2
And now abide *f* . . . . .1 Cor 13:13
For we walk by *f* . . . . .2 Cor 5:7
the flesh I live by *f* . . . . . .Gal 2:20
f are sons of Abraham . . . . . Gal 3:7
But after *f* has come . . . . . . Gal 3:25
of the household of *f* . . . . . Gal 6:10
been saved through *f* . . . . . Eph 2:8
one Lord, one *f* . . . . .Eph 4:5
taking the shield of *f* . . . . .Eph 6:16
your work of *f* . . . . .1 Thess 1:3
for not all have *f* . . . . . . .2 Thess 3:2
the mystery of the *f* . . . . . 1 Tim 3:9
I have kept the *f* . . . . .2 Tim 4:7
in our common *f* . . . . Titus 1:4
not being mixed with *f* . . . . Heb 4:2
f is the substance . . . . .Heb 11:1
without *f* it is . . . . .Heb 11:6
says he has *f* . . . . .James 2:14
Show me your *f* . . . . .James 2:18
and not by *f* only . . . . . . .James 2:24
f will save the sick . . . . . .James 5:15
add to your *f* virtue . . . . . . 2 Pet 1:5
the patience and the *f* . . . Rev 13:10

FAITHFUL
God, He is God, the *f* . . Deut 7:9
LORD preserves the *f* . . . . . Ps 31:23
eyes shall be on the *f* . . . . Ps 101:6
But who can find a *f* . . . . Prov 20:6
the Holy One who is *f* . . . Hos 11:12
"Who then is a *f* . . . . .Matt 24:45
good and *f* servant . . . . . .Matt 25:23
"He who is *f* in what . . Luke 16:10
judged me to be *f* . . . . .Acts 16:15
God is *f* . . . . .1 Cor 1:9
is my beloved and *f* . . . . . 1 Cor 4:17
But as God is *f* . . . . 2 Cor 1:18
f brethren in Christ . . . . Col 1:2
who calls you is *f* . . . . . 1 Thess 5:24
This is a *f* saying and . . . 1 Tim 1:15
f High Priest in . . . . Heb 2:17
He who promised is *f* . . Heb 10:23
He is *f* and just to . . . . . . 1 John 1:9
Be *f* until death . . . . Rev 2:10
words are true and *f* . . . . . . Rev 21:5

FAITHFULNESS
I have declared Your *f* . . . Ps 40:10
Your *f* also surrounds . . . . . Ps 89:8
f endures to all . . . . Ps 119:90
Great is Your *f* . . . . Lam 3:23
unbelief make the *f* . . . . . . Rom 3:3

FAITHLESS
"O *f* generation . . . . Mark 9:19
If we are *f* . . . . .2 Tim 2:13

FALL
a deep sleep to *f* . . . . Gen 2:21
Let them *f* by their . . . . Ps 5:10
righteous man may *f* . . Prov 24:16
But the wicked shall *f* . . Prov 24:16
the blind, both will *f* . . . Matt 15:14
the stars will *f* . . . . .Matt 24:29
"I saw Satan *f* . . . . .Luke 10:18
take heed lest he *f* . . . . 1 Cor 10:12
if they *f* away . . . . .Heb 6:6
lest anyone *f* short of . . Heb 12:15
and rocks, "*F* on us . . . . . Rev 6:16

FALLEN
"Babylon is *f* . . . . .Is 21:9
you have *f* from grace . . . . Gal 5:4
"Babylon is *f* . . . . .Rev 14:8

FALLING
great drops of blood *f* . Luke 22:44
f away comes first . . . . .2 Thess 2:3

FALSE
"You shall not bear *f* . . . . Ex 20:16
I hate every *f* way . . . . . Ps 119:104
f witness shall perish . . Prov 21:28
"Beware of *f* prophets . . Matt 7:15
f christs and *f* . . . . .Matt 24:24
and we are found *f* . . . . 1 Cor 15:15
of *f* brethren . . . . Gal 2:4
f prophets have gone . . 1 John 4:1
mouth of the *f* prophet . Rev 16:13

FALSEHOOD
For their deceit is *f* . . . . Ps 119:118
Offspring of *f* . . . . Is 57:4

FALSELY
of evil against you *f* . . . . Matt 5:11
f called knowledge . . . . 1 Tim 6:20

FAMILIES
in you all the *f* . . . . Gen 12:3
the God of all the *f* . . . . . . Jer 31:1
in your seed all the f . . Acts 3:25

FAMILY
shall mourn, every *f* . . . Zech 12:12
f were baptized . . . . .Acts 16:33

FAMINES
And there will be *f* . . . . . Matt 24:7

FAMISH
righteous soul to *f* . . . . . . Prov 10:3

FAMISHED
honorable men are *f* . . . . Is 5:13

FAR
Your judgments are *f* . . . . Ps 10:5
Be not *f* from Me . . . . Ps 22:11
The LORD is *f* from . . . . Prov 15:29
their heart is f from . . . . Matt 15:8
going to a *f* country . . . Mark 13:34
though He is not *f* . . . . . .Acts 17:27
you who once were *f* . . . . Eph 2:13

FARMER
The hard-working *f* . . . . .2 Tim 2:6
See how the *f* waits . . . . James 5:7

FASHIONED
have made me and *f* . . . . . Job 10:8

FASHIONS
He f their hearts .... Ps 33:15

FAST
f as you do this day .... Is 58:4
f that I have chosen .... Is 58:5
"Moreover, when you f . Matt 6:16
disciples do not f .... Matt 9:14
'I f twice a week .... Luke 18:12

FASTED
'When you f and .... Zech 7:5
And when He had f ...... Matt 4:2

FASTING
by prayer and f .... Matt 17:21
give yourselves to f ..... 1 Cor 7:5

FASTINGS
in sleeplessness, in f .... 2 Cor 6:5

FAT
and you will eat the f .. Gen 45:18
f is the LORD's .... Lev 3:16

FATHER
man shall leave his f .... Gen 2:24
and you shall be a f ...... Gen 17:4
I was a f to the poor .... Job 29:16
A f of the fatherless ...... Ps 68:5
f pities his children ..... Ps 103:13
God, Everlasting F .... Is 9:6
You, O LORD, are our F ... Is 63:16
time cry to Me, 'My F ...... Jer 3:4
For I am a F to Israel ..... Jer 31:9
"A son honors his f .... Mal 1:6
Have we not all one F ... Mal 2:10
Our F in heaven .... Matt 6:9
"He who loves f .... Matt 10:37
know the F .... Matt 11:27
'He who curses f .... Matt 15:4
for One is your F .... Matt 23:9
"F will be divided ..... Luke 12:53
F loves the Son .... John 3:35
F raises the dead .... John 5:21
F judges no one .... John 5:22
He has seen the F .... John 6:46
F who sent Me bears .... John 8:18
we have one F .... John 8:41
of your f the devil ...... John 8:44
"I and My F are one .. John 10:30
'I am going to the F .... John 14:28
came forth from the F . John 16:28
that he might be the f ... Rom 4:11
one God and F of all ..... Eph 4:6
"I will be to Him a F ...... Heb 1:5
down from the F ...... James 1:17
if you call on the F ..... 1 Pet 1:17
and testify that the F . 1 John 4:14

FATHERLESS
the helper of the f .... Ps 10:14
He relieves the f .... Ps 146:9
do not defend the f .... Is 1:23
they may rob the f .... Is 10:2
You the f finds mercy ..... Hos 14:3

FATHER'S
you in My F kingdom . Matt 26:29
I must be about My F .. Luke 2:49
F house are many ...... John 14:2
that a man has his f ..... 1 Cor 5:1

FATHERS
the LORD God of our f ... Ezra 7:27
f trusted in You .... Ps 22:4
our ears, O God, our f .... Ps 44:1
f ate the manna .... John 6:31
of whom are the f .... Rom 9:5
unaware that all our f .. 1 Cor 10:1

FATNESS
of the root and f .... Rom 11:17

FAULT
I have found no f ..... Luke 23:14
does He still find f ...... Rom 9:19
of God without f .... Phil 2:15

FAULTLESS
covenant had been f ...... Heb 8:7
to present you f .... Jude 24

FAULTS
"I remember my f .... Gen 41:9
me from secret f .... Ps 19:12

FAVOR
granted me life and f ... Job 10:12
His f is for life .... Ps 30:5
A good man obtains f ... Prov 12:2
and stature, and in f .... Luke 2:52
God and having f .... Acts 2:47

FAVORED
"Rejoice, highly f .... Luke 1:28

FAVORITISM
not show personal f ... Luke 20:21
God shows personal f .... Gal 2:6

FEAR
live, for I f God .... Gen 42:18
to put the dread and f ... Deut 2:25
said, "Does Job f .... Job 1:9
Yes, you cast off f .... Job 15:4
The f of the LORD is .... Ps 19:9
of death, I will f .... Ps 23:4
Whom shall I f .... Ps 27:1
Oh, f the LORD .... Ps 34:9
There is no f of God .... Ps 36:1
The f of the LORD is ...... Ps 111:10
The f of man brings a .. Prov 29:25
F God and keep His .... Eccl 12:13
Let Him be your f .... Is 8:13
"Be strong, do not f .... Is 35:4
who would not f .... Jer 10:7
f Him who is able ...... Matt 10:28
"Do not f .... Luke 12:32
"Do you not even f .. Luke 23:40
And walking in the f .... Acts 9:31
given us a spirit of f ...... 2 Tim 1:7
those who through f ...... Heb 2:15
because of His godly f .... Heb 5:7
F God .... 1 Pet 2:17
love casts out f .... 1 John 4:18

FEARED
He is also to be f ...... 1 Chr 16:25
f God more than .... Neh 7:2
Yourself, are to be f .... Ps 76:7
Then those who f .... Mal 3:16

FEARFUL
It is a f thing to .... Heb 10:31

FEARFULLY
f and wonderfully ...... Ps 139:14

FEARING
sincerity of heart, f ...... Col 3:22
forsook Egypt, not f .... Heb 11:27

FEARS
upright man, one who f ... Job 1:8
me from all my f .... Ps 34:4
nation whoever f .... Acts 10:35
f has not been made .. 1 John 4:18

FEAST
and you shall keep a f . Num 29:12
hate, I despise your f .. Amos 5:21
every year at the F ..... Luke 2:41
when you give a f ..... Luke 14:13
Now the Passover, a f .. John 6:4
great day of the f .... John 7:37

FEASTING
go to the house of f .... Eccl 7:2

FEASTS
the best places at f .... Luke 20:46
spots in your love f .... Jude 12

FED
and f you with manna .... Deut 8:3
f you with milk and ...... 1 Cor 3:2

FEEBLE
strengthened the f .... Job 4:4
And there was none f .... Ps 105:37
And my flesh is f .... Ps 109:24
hang down, and the f .. Heb 12:12

FEED
ravens to f you there ... 1 Kin 17:4
and f your flocks .... Is 61:5
to him, "F My lambs . John 21:15
your enemy hungers, f . Rom 12:20
goods to f the poor ..... 1 Cor 13:3

FEEDS
your heavenly Father f .. Matt 6:26

FEET
all things under his f .... Ps 8:6
He makes my f like the .. Ps 18:33
You have set my f .... Ps 31:8
For their f run to .... Prov 1:16
Her f go down to death .. Prov 5:5
mountains Are the f .... Is 52:7
place of My f glorious ..... Is 60:13
in that day His f .... Zech 14:4
two hands or two f .... Matt 18:8
began to wash His f ..... Luke 7:38
wash the disciples' f .... John 13:5
f are swift to shed .... Rom 3:15
beautiful are the f .... Rom 10:15
things under His f ...... 1 Cor 15:27
and having shod your f .. Eph 6:15
fell at His f as dead ..... Rev 1:17

FELLOW
begins to beat his f .... Matt 24:49
f citizens with the .... Eph 2:19
Gentiles should be f .... Eph 3:6
I am your f servant ..... Rev 19:10

FELLOWSHIP
doctrine and f .... Acts 2:42
were called into the f ... 1 Cor 1:9
f has righteousness ... 2 Cor 6:14
the right hand of f .... Gal 2:9
And have no f with the .. Eph 5:11
of love, if any f .... Phil 2:1
and the f of His .... Phil 3:10
we say that we have f .. 1 John 1:6
the light, we have f .... 1 John 1:7

FERVENT
f prayer of a .... James 5:16
will melt with f .... 2 Pet 3:10

FERVENTLY
love one another f ...... 1 Pet 1:22

FEW
let your words be f .... Eccl 5:2
and there are f .... Matt 7:14
but the laborers are f ... Matt 9:37
called, but f chosen .... Matt 20:16
"Lord, are there f ..... Luke 13:23

FIDELITY
but showing all good f . Titus 2:10

FIELD
Let the f be joyful .... Ps 96:12
"The f is the world ..... Matt 13:38
and buys that f .... Matt 13:44
you are God's f .... 1 Cor 3:9

FIERY
LORD sent *f* serpents . . . . Num 21:6
shall make them as a *f* . . . . Ps 21:9
burning *f* furnace . . . . Dan 3:6
concerning the *f* . . . . 1 Pet 4:12

FIG
f leaves together . . . . Gen 3:7
"Look at the *f* . . . . Luke 21:29
'I saw you under the *f* . . John 1:50

FIGHT
"The LORD will *f* . . . . Ex 14:14
Our God will *f* for us . . . . Neh 4:20
My servants would *f* . . . John 18:36
to him, let us not *f* . . . . . . Acts 23:9
F the good *f* . . . . 1 Tim 6:12
have fought the good *f* . . 2 Tim 4:7

FIGHTS
your God is He who *f* . . Josh 23:10
because my lord *f* . . . . 1 Sam 25:28
f come from among . . . . James 4:1

FIGS
thornbushes or *f* . . . . Matt 7:16
or a grapevine bear *f* . . James 3:12

FILL
f the earth and subdue . . Gen 1:28
"Do I not *f* heaven . . . . . . Jer 23:24
f this temple with . . . . Hag 2:7
"*F* the waterpots . . . . John 2:7
that He might *f* . . . . Eph 4:10

FILLED
the whole earth be *f* . . . . . Ps 72:19
For they shall be *f* . . . . Matt 5:6
"Let the children be *f* . . Mark 7:27
would gladly have *f* . . . Luke 15:16
being *f* with all . . . . Rom 1:29
but be *f* with the . . . . Eph 5:18
be warmed and *f* . . . . . . James 2:16

FILTHY
with *f* garments . . . . Zech 3:3
poor man in *f* clothes . . . James 2:2
oppressed by the *f* . . . . 2 Pet 2:7
let him be *f* . . . . Rev 22:11

FIND
sure your sin will *f* . . . . Num 32:23
waters, For you will *f* . . . Eccl 11:1
seek, and you will *f* . . . . . . Matt 7:7
f a Babe wrapped . . . . . . Luke 2:12
f no fault in this Man . . . Luke 23:4
f grace to help in . . . . Heb 4:16

FINDS
f me *f* life . . . . Prov 8:35
f a wife *f* a good . . . . . . Prov 18:22
and he who seeks *f* . . . . . . Matt 7:8
f his life will lose . . . . . . Matt 10:39
and he who seeks *f* . . . Luke 11:10

FINGER
written with the *f* . . . . Ex 31:18
dip the tip of his *f* . . . . . Luke 16:24
"Reach your *f* . . . . John 20:27

FINISH
he has enough to *f* . . . . Luke 14:28
has given Me to *f* . . . . . . John 5:36

FINISHED
f the work which You . . John 17:4
He said, "It is *f* . . . . John 19:30
I have *f* the race . . . . 2 Tim 4:7

FIRE
rained brimstone and *f* . Gen 19:24
to him in a flame of *f* . . . . . Ex 3:2
who answers by *f* . . . . . 1 Kin 18:24
LORD was not in the *f* . 1 Kin 19:12
We went through *f* . . . . . . Ps 66:12
f goes before Him . . . . Ps 97:3
burns as the *f* . . . . Is 9:18
you walk through the *f* . . . . Is 43:2
f that burns all the . . . . Is 65:5
He break out like *f* . . . . . Amos 5:6
for conflict by *f* . . . . Amos 7:4
like a refiner's *f* . . . . Mal 3:2
the Holy Spirit and *f* . . . . Matt 3:11
f is not quenched . . . . . . Mark 9:44
"I came to send *f* . . . . . Luke 12:49
tongues, as of *f* . . . . Acts 2:3
f taking vengeance . . . . . 2 Thess 1:8
and that burned with *f* . Heb 12:18
And the tongue is a *f* . . . James 3:6
vengeance of eternal *f* . . . . . Jude 7
into the lake of *f* . . . . Rev 20:14

FIRM
of the hope *f* to the . . . . . . Heb 3:6

FIRMAMENT
Thus God made the *f* . . . . Gen 1:7
f shows His handiwork . . . Ps 19:1

FIRST
f father sinned . . . . Is 43:27
desires to be *f* . . . . Matt 20:27
f shall be slave . . . . Mark 10:44
the gospel must *f* . . . . . Mark 13:10
evil, of the Jew *f* . . . . Rom 2:9
f man Adam became . . 1 Cor 15:45
that we who *f* trusted . . . . Eph 1:12
Him because He *f* . . . . . . 1 John 4:19
I am the *F* and the . . . . . . Rev 1:17
you have left your *f* . . . . . . Rev 2:4
is the *f* resurrection . . . . . Rev 20:5

FIRSTBORN
LORD struck all the *f* . . . . . Ex 12:29
brought forth her *f* . . . . . . Matt 1:25
that He might be the *f* . . Rom 8:29
invisible God, the *f* . . . . Col 1:15
the beginning, the *f* . . . . . . Col 1:18
witness, the *f* from . . . . Rev 1:5

FIRSTFRUITS
also who have the *f* . . . . Rom 8:23
and has become the *f* . 1 Cor 15:20
Christ the *f* . . . . 1 Cor 15:23

FISH
had prepared a great *f* . . . Jon 1:17
belly of the great *f* . . . . Matt 12:40
five loaves and two *f* . . Matt 14:17
and likewise the *f* . . . . . . John 21:13

FISHERS
and I will make you *f* . . . Matt 4:19

FIVE
f smooth stones . . . . . . 1 Sam 17:40
about *f* thousand men . Matt 14:21
and *f* were foolish . . . . . . Matt 25:2

FIXED
is a great gulf *f* . . . . Luke 16:26

FLAME
appeared to him in a *f* . . . . . Ex 3:2
tormented in this *f* . . . . Luke 16:24
and His ministers a f . . . . . Heb 1:7
and His eyes like a *f* . . . . . Rev 1:14

FLAMES
the LORD divides the *f* . . . . . Ps 29:7

FLAMING
f sword which turned . . . Gen 3:24
in *f* fire taking . . . . 2 Thess 1:8

FLATTER
They *f* with their . . . . Ps 5:9

FLATTERED
Nevertheless they *f* . . . . . . Ps 78:36

FLATTERING
f speech deceive . . . . Rom 16:18
swelling words, *f* . . . . Jude 16

FLATTERS
f his neighbor Spreads . . Prov 29:5

FLATTERY
shall corrupt with *f* . . . . Dan 11:32

FLAVOR
the salt loses its *f* . . . . Matt 5:13

FLAX
f He will not quench . . . Matt 12:20

FLEE
Or where can I *f* . . . . Ps 139:7
And the shadows *f* . . . . . Song 2:17
who are in Judea *f* . . . . . Matt 24:16
F sexual immorality . . . . 1 Cor 6:18
f these things and . . . . . . 1 Tim 6:11
devil and he will *f* . . . . . . James 4:7

FLESH
bone of my bones And *f* . Gen 2:23
shall become one *f* . . . . . . Gen 2:24
f had corrupted their . . . . Gen 6:12
f I shall see God . . . . Job 19:26
My *f* also will rest in . . . . . . Ps 16:9
is wearisome to the *f* . . . . Eccl 12:12
And all *f* shall see it . . . . Is 40:5
"All *f* is grass . . . . Is 40:6
out My Spirit on all *f* . . . . Joel 2:28
two shall become one f . Matt 19:5
were shortened, no *f* . . . Matt 24:22
shall become one f . . . . . Mark 10:8
the Word became *f* . . . . . . John 1:14
I shall give is My *f* . . . . . John 6:51
f profits nothing . . . . John 6:63
of God, but with the *f* . . . Rom 7:25
on the things of the *f* . . . . Rom 8:5
to the *f* you will die . . . . . Rom 8:13
f should glory in His . . . 1 Cor 1:29
"*shall become one f* . . . . 1 Cor 6:16
For the *f* lusts . . . . Gal 5:17
have crucified the *f* . . . . . . Gal 5:24
may boast in your *f* . . . . . . Gal 6:13
the lust of the *f* . . . . 1 John 2:16
has come in the *f* . . . . 1 John 4:2

FLESHLY
f wisdom but by the . . . 2 Cor 1:12
f lusts which . . . . 1 Pet 2:11

FLIES
Dead *f* putrefy the . . . . . . Eccl 10:1

FLOAT
and he made the iron *f* . . 2 Kin 6:6

FLOCK
lead Joseph like a *f* . . . . . . Ps 80:1
He will feed His *f* . . . . Is 40:11
you do not feed the *f* . . . Ezek 34:3
my God, "Feed the *f* . . . . Zech 11:4
sheep of the f . . . . Matt 26:31
"Do not fear, little *f* . . . Luke 12:32
there will be one *f* . . . . . John 10:16
Shepherd the *f* of God . . . 1 Pet 5:2
examples to the *f* . . . . 1 Pet 5:3

FLOOD
the waters of the *f* . . . . . . Gen 7:10
them away like a *f* . . . . Ps 90:5
the days before the *f* . . . . Matt 24:38
bringing in the *f* . . . . 2 Pet 2:5
of his mouth like a *f* . . . . Rev 12:15

FLOODS
me, And the *f* of . . . . Ps 18:4

f on the dry ground .... Is 44:3
rain descended, the f ... Matt 7:25

FLOURISH

the righteous shall f ...... Ps 72:7

FLOW

of his heart will f .... John 7:38

FLOWER

As a f of the field .... Ps 103:15
beauty is a fading f .... Is 28:4
grass withers, the f .... Is 40:7
of man as the f .... 1 Pet 1:24

FLOWERS

f appear on the earth ... Song 2:12

FLOWING

'a land f with milk .... Deut 6:3
the Gentiles like a f .... Is 66:12

FLUTE

play the harp and f ..... Gen 4:21

FLUTES

instruments and f .... Ps 150:4

FLUTISTS

harpists, musicians, f ... Rev 18:22

FLY

soon cut off, and we f .... Ps 90:10

FOLLOW

f You wherever You go . Matt 8:19
He said to him, "F .... Matt 9:9
up his cross, and f ..... Mark 8:34
will by no means f ...... John 10:5
serves Me, let him f ... John 12:26
that you should f .... 1 Pet 2:21
f the Lamb wherever .... Rev 14:4
and their works f ...... Rev 14:13

FOLLOWED

f the LORD my God ..... Josh 14:8
we have left all and f . Mark 10:28

FOLLOWS

f Me shall not walk .... John 8:12

FOLLY

taken much notice of f .. Job 35:15
not turn back to f .... Ps 85:8
F is joy to him who is . Prov 15:21
F is set in great .... Eccl 10:6

FOOD

you it shall be for f ..... Gen 1:29
that lives shall be f .... Gen 9:3
f which you eat shall ... Ezek 4:10
the fields yield no f ..... Hab 3:17
That there may be f ..... Mal 3:10
to give them f .... Matt 24:45
and you gave Me f ..... Matt 25:35
and he who has f ...... Luke 3:11
have you any f .... John 21:5
they ate their f .... Acts 2:46
our hearts with f ...... Acts 14:17
destroy with your f .... Rom 14:15
f makes my brother .... 1 Cor 8:13
the same spiritual f ..... 1 Cor 10:3
sower, and bread for f . 2 Cor 9:10
And having f and .... 1 Tim 6:8
and not solid f .... Heb 5:12
But solid f belongs to .... Heb 5:14
of f sold his .... Heb 12:16
destitute of daily f .... James 2:15

FOODS

f which God .... 1 Tim 4:3

FOOL

f has said in his .... Ps 14:1
is like sport to a f ..... Prov 10:23
f is right in his own .... Prov 12:15
is too lofty for a f ...... Prov 24:7
whoever says, 'You f .... Matt 5:22
I have become a f .... 2 Cor 12:11

FOOLISH

I was so f and .... Ps 73:22
f pulls it down with .... Prov 14:1
f man squanders it .... Prov 21:20
Has not God made f ... 1 Cor 1:20
O f Galatians .... Gal 3:1
were also once f .... Titus 3:3
But avoid f disputes ...... Titus 3:9

FOOLISHLY

I speak f .... 2 Cor 11:21

FOOLISHNESS

F is bound up in the ... Prov 22:15
devising of f is sin ...... Prov 24:9
of the cross is f .... 1 Cor 1:18
Because the f of God ... 1 Cor 1:25

FOOLS

f despise wisdom .... Prov 1:7
folly of f is deceit .... Prov 14:8
F mock at sin .... Prov 14:9
We are f for Christ's ... 1 Cor 4:10

FOOT

will not allow your f ..... Ps 121:3
f will not stumble ...... Prov 3:23
From the sole of the f ...... Is 1:6
f causes you to sin ...... Matt 18:8
you dash your f .... Luke 4:11
If the f should say .... 1 Cor 12:15

FOOTSTOOL

Your enemies Your f .... Ps 110:1
Your enemies Your f .. Matt 22:44

FORBID

said, "Do not f .... Mark 9:39
"Can anyone f .... Acts 10:47
f that I should boast ..... Gal 6:14

FORBIDDING

f to marry .... 1 Tim 4:3

FOREFATHERS

conscience, as my f ..... 2 Tim 1:3

FOREHEADS

put a mark on the f .... Ezek 9:4
seal of God on their f ...... Rev 9:4
his mark on their f ...... Rev 20:4

FOREIGNER

"I am a f and a .... Gen 23:4
of me, since I am a f .... Ruth 2:10
to God except this f ... Luke 17:18

FOREIGNERS

f who were there ...... Acts 17:21
longer strangers and f ... Eph 2:19

FOREKNEW

For whom He f .... Rom 8:29
His people whom He f .. Rom 11:2

FOREKNOWLEDGE

purpose and f of God ... Acts 2:23

FOREORDAINED

He indeed was f .... 1 Pet 1:20

FORESAW

'I f the LORD .... Acts 2:25

FORESEEING

f that God would .... Gal 3:8

FORESEES

A prudent man f .... Prov 22:3

FORETOLD

have also f these days .... Acts 3:24
killed those who f ...... Acts 7:52

FOREVER

and eat, and live f .... Gen 3:22
to our children f ...... Deut 29:29
LORD sits as King f ...... Ps 29:10
Do not cast us off f ...... Ps 44:23
throne, O God, is f .... Ps 45:6
"You are a priest f ...... Ps 110:4
His mercy endures f .... Ps 136:1
of our God stands f .... Is 40:8
My salvation will be f ..... Is 51:6
will not cast off f .... Lam 3:31
Like the stars f .... Dan 12:3
and the glory f .... Matt 6:13
the Christ remains f ... John 12:34
who is blessed f ..... 2 Cor 11:31
to whom be glory f .... Gal 1:5
generation, f and ever ... Eph 3:21
and Father be glory f .... Phil 4:20
throne, O God, is f .... Heb 1:8
lives and abides f ...... 1 Pet 1:23
of darkness f .... Jude 13
power, Both now and f ... Jude 25
And they shall reign f ... Rev 22:5

FOREVERMORE

Blessed be the LORD f ..... Ps 89:52
this time forth and f ..... Ps 113:2
behold, I am alive f ..... Rev 1:18

FORGAVE

to repay, he freely f .... Luke 7:42
God in Christ f .... Eph 4:32
even as Christ f .... Col 3:13

FORGET

f the LORD who .... Deut 6:12
I will not f Your word .. Ps 119:16
If I f you .... Ps 137:5
My son, do not f .... Prov 3:1
f the LORD your Maker .... Is 51:13
f your work and labor ... Heb 6:10

FORGETFULNESS

in the land of f .... Ps 88:12

FORGETS

and immediately f ..... James 1:24

FORGETTING

f those things which ..... Phil 3:13

FORGIVE

f their sin and heal .... 2 Chr 7:14
good, and ready to f .... Ps 86:5
And f us our debts ...... Matt 6:12
Father will also f .... Matt 6:14
his heart, does not f ... Matt 18:35
Who can f sins but God . Mark 2:7
f the sins of any .... John 20:23
you ought rather to f ..... 2 Cor 2:7
F me this wrong ...... 2 Cor 12:13
f us our sins and to .... 1 John 1:9

FORGIVEN

sins be f them .... Mark 4:12
to whom little is f ...... Luke 7:47
f you all trespasses ...... Col 2:13
your sins are f .... 1 John 2:12

FORGIVENESS

But there is f with .... Ps 130:4
preached to you the f .. Acts 13:38
they may receive f ..... Acts 26:18
His blood, the f .... Eph 1:7

FORGIVES

f all your iniquities ..... Ps 103:3
is this who even f ...... Luke 7:49

FORGIVING
tenderhearted, *f* ... Eph 4:32
and *f* one another ... Col 3:13

FORGOT
Joseph, but *f* ... Gen 40:23
They soon *f* His works .. Ps 106:13

FORGOTTEN
f the God who ... Deut 32:18
not one of them is *f* ... Luke 12:6
f the exhortation ... Heb 12:5
f that he was ... 2 Pet 1:9

FORM
earth was without *f* ... Gen 1:2
Who would *f* a god or ... Is 44:10
f the light and create ... Is 45:7
descended in bodily *f* ... Luke 3:22
time, nor seen His *f* ... John 5:37
For the *f* of this ... 1 Cor 7:31
who, being in the *f* ... Phil 2:6
having a *f* of ... 2 Tim 3:5

FORMED
And the LORD God *f* ... Gen 2:7
f my inward parts ... Ps 139:13
say of him who *f* ... Is 29:16
"Before I *f* you in ... Jer 1:5
Will the thing *f* ... Rom 9:20
until Christ is *f* ... Gal 4:19

FORMER
f days better than ... Eccl 7:10
f rain to the earth ... Hos 6:3
f prophets preached ... Zech 1:4
your *f* conduct ... Eph 4:22
f things have passed ... Rev 21:4

FORMS
clay say to him who *f* ... Is 45:9
f the spirit of man ... Zech 12:1

FORNICATION
"We were not born of *f* . John 8:41
of the wrath of her *f* ... Rev 14:8

FORNICATOR
you know, that no *f* ... Eph 5:5
lest there be any *f* ... Heb 12:16

FORNICATORS
but *f* and adulterers ... Heb 13:4

FORSAKE
But I did not *f* ... Ps 119:87
father, And do not *f* ... Prov 1:8
of you does not *f* ... Luke 14:33
never leave you nor f ... Heb 13:5

FORSAKEN
My God, why have You *f* . Ps 22:1
seen the righteous *f* ... Ps 37:25
a mere moment I have *f* ... Is 54:7
God, why have You f .. Matt 27:46
persecuted, but not *f* ... 2 Cor 4:9
for Demas has *f* ... 2 Tim 4:10

FORSAKING
f the assembling ... Heb 10:25

FORSOOK
f God who made him .. Deut 32:15
all the disciples *f* ... Matt 26:56
with me, but all *f* ... 2 Tim 4:16

FORTRESS
is my rock, my *f* ... 2 Sam 22:2
my rock of refuge, a *f* ... Ps 31:2

FOUND
f a helper comparable ... Gen 2:20
a thousand I have *f* ... Eccl 7:28
LORD while He may be *f* ... Is 55:6
fruit on it and *f* none ... Luke 13:6
he was lost and is *f* ... Luke 15:24
f the Messiah" (which .. John 1:41
and be *f* in Him ... Phil 3:9

FOUNDATION
Of old You laid the *f* ... Ps 102:25
the earth without a *f* ... Luke 6:49
loved Me before the *f* .. John 17:24
I have laid the *f* ... 1 Cor 3:10
f can anyone lay than .. 1 Cor 3:11
us in Him before the *f* ... Eph 1:4
not laying again the *f* ... Heb 6:1
Lamb slain from the *f* .. Rev 13:8

FOUNDATIONS
when I laid the *f* ... Job 38:4
And the *f* of the wall ... Rev 21:19

FOUNTAIN
will become in him a *f* .. John 4:14

FOUNTAINS
on that day all the *f* ... Gen 7:11
lead them to living *f* ... Rev 7:17

FRAGRANCE
was filled with the *f* ... John 12:3
we are to God the *f* ... 2 Cor 2:15

FREE
'You will be made *f* ... John 8:33
And having been set *f* .. Rom 6:18
Jesus has made me *f* ... Rom 8:2
is neither slave nor *f* ... Gal 3:28
Christ has made us *f* ... Gal 5:1
he is a slave or *f* ... Eph 6:8

FREED
has died has been *f* ... Rom 6:7

FREEDMAN
slave is the Lord's *f* ... 1 Cor 7:22

FREELY
the garden you may *f* ... Gen 2:16
F you have received ... Matt 10:8
f give us all ... Rom 8:32
the water of life *f* ... Rev 22:17

FRIEND
of Abraham Your *f* ... 2 Chr 20:7
f who sticks closer ... Prov 18:24
a *f* of tax collectors ... Matt 11:19
of you shall have a *f* ... Luke 11:5
f Lazarus sleeps ... John 11:11
he was called the *f* ... James 2:23
wants to be a *f* ... James 4:4

FRIENDS
My *f* scorn me ... Job 16:20
the rich has many *f* ... Prov 14:20
one's life for his *f* ... John 15:13
I have called you *f* ... John 15:15
to forbid any of his *f* ... Acts 24:23

FROGS
your territory with *f* ... Ex 8:2
f coming out of the ... Rev 16:13

FRUIT
showed them the *f* ... Num 13:26
brings forth its *f* ... Ps 1:3
f is better than gold ... Prov 8:19
with good by the *f* ... Prov 12:14
like the first *f* ... Is 28:4
does not bear good *f* ... Matt 3:10
good tree bears good *f* .. Matt 7:17
not drink of this *f* ... Matt 26:29
and blessed is the *f* ... Luke 1:42
life, and bring no *f* ... Luke 8:14
and he came seeking *f* . Luke 13:6
'And if it bears *f* ... Luke 13:9
branch that bears *f* ... John 15:2
that you bear much *f* ... John 15:8
should go and bear *f* ... John 15:16
God, you have your *f* ... Rom 6:22
that we should bear *f* ... Rom 7:4
But the *f* of the ... Gal 5:22
yields the peaceable *f* . Heb 12:11
Now the *f* of ... James 3:18
autumn trees without *f* ... Jude 12
tree yielding its *f* ... Rev 22:2

FRUITFUL
them, saying, "Be *f* ... Gen 1:22
wife shall be like a *f* ... Ps 128:3
pleasing Him, being *f* ... Col 1:10

FRUITS
Therefore bear *f* ... Matt 3:8
know them by their *f* ... Matt 7:16
of mercy and good *f* .. James 3:17
which bore twelve *f* ... Rev 22:2

FULFILL
for us to *f* all ... Matt 3:15
f the law of Christ ... Gal 6:2
f my joy by being ... Phil 2:2
and *f* all the good ... 2 Thess 1:11
If you really *f* ... James 2:8

FULFILLED
the law till all is *f* ... Matt 5:18
of the Gentiles are *f* ... Luke 21:24
all things must be *f* ... Luke 24:44
of the law might be *f* ... Rom 8:4
loves another has *f* ... Rom 13:8
For all the law is *f* ... Gal 5:14

FULFILLMENT
love is the *f* of the ... Rom 13:10

FULL
and it was *f* of bones .. Ezek 37:1
whole body will be *f* ... Matt 6:22
your joy may be *f* ... John 15:11
You are already *f* ... 1 Cor 4:8
learned both to be *f* ... Phil 4:12

FULLNESS
f we have all received .. John 1:16
But when the *f* of the ... Gal 4:4
filled with all the *f* ... Eph 3:19
Him dwells all the *f* ... Col 2:9

FURNACE
you out of the iron *f* ... Deut 4:20
of a burning fiery *f* ... Dan 3:6
cast them into the *f* ... Matt 13:42
the smoke of a great *f* ... Rev 9:2

FURY
Thus will I spend My *f* . Ezek 6:12
in anger and *f* On the ... Mic 5:15

G

GAIN
and to die is *g* ... Phil 1:21
rubbish, that I may *g* ... Phil 3:8
is a means of *g* ... 1 Tim 6:5
contentment is great *g* .. 1 Tim 6:6
for dishonest *g* ... 1 Pet 5:2

GAINED
g five more talents ... Matt 25:20

GAINS
g the whole world ... Matt 16:26

GALL
They also gave me *g* ... Ps 69:21
wine mingled with *g* ... Matt 27:34

GAP
and stand in the *g* ... Ezek 22:30

GARDEN
LORD God planted a *g* ... Gen 2:8

g enclosed Is my ....Song 4:12
Eden, the g of God ....Ezek 28:13
where there was a g ....John 18:1
g a new tomb in .....John 19:41

GARMENT

the hem of His g ......Matt 9:20
on a wedding g ....Matt 22:11
cloth on an old g ....Mark 2:21
all grow old like a g .....Heb 1:11
hating even the g ....Jude 23

GARMENTS

g did not wear out on ...Deut 8:4
They divide My g ....Ps 22:18
from Edom, With dyed g ..Is 63:1
"Take away the filthy g .Zech 3:4
man clothed in soft g ...Matt 11:8
spread their g on the ...Matt 21:8
and divided His g .....Matt 27:35
by them in shining g ...Luke 24:4
g are moth-eaten ....James 5:2
be clothed in white g .....Rev 3:5

GATE

by the narrow g ....Matt 7:13
by the Sheep G a pool ...John 5:2
laid daily at the g ....Acts 3:2
suffered outside the g ..Heb 13:12

GATES

up your heads, O you g ....Ps 24:7
The LORD loves the g .....Ps 87:2
is known in the g .....Prov 31:23
Go through the g ....Is 62:10
and the g of Hades ....Matt 16:18
wall with twelve g .....Rev 21:12
g were twelve pearls ....Rev 21:21
g shall not be shut .....Rev 21:25

GATHER

And a time to g stones ....Eccl 3:5
g the lambs with His .....Is 40:11
g His wheat into the ....Matt 3:12
sow nor reap nor g .....Matt 6:26
Do men g grapes from ..Matt 7:16
g where I have not .....Matt 25:26
g together His ....Mark 13:27

GATHERED

g some of every kind ..Matt 13:47
the nations will be g ...Matt 25:32

GATHERING

g together of the ....Gen 1:10
g together to Him .....2 Thess 2:1

GATHERS

The Lord GOD, who g .....Is 56:8
together, as a hen g ...Matt 23:37

GAVE

to be with me, she g ....Gen 3:12
g You this authority ....Matt 21:23
that He g His only .....John 3:16
Those whom You g ....John 17:12
but God g the increase ..1 Cor 3:6
g Himself for our sins ....Gal 1:4
g Himself for me ....Gal 2:20
g Himself for it ....Eph 5:25

GENERATION

One g passes away ....Eccl 1:4
who will declare His g .....Is 53:8
and adulterous g ....Matt 12:39
this g will by no ....Matt 24:34
from this perverse g ...Acts 2:40
But you are a chosen g ..1 Pet 2:9

GENERATIONS

be remembered in all g ..Ps 45:17
g will call me blessed ..Luke 1:48

GENEROUS

no longer be called g ....Is 32:5

GENTILES

G were separated ....Gen 10:5
As a light to the G ....Is 42:6
G shall come to your ......Is 60:3
all these things the G ...Matt 6:32
into the way of the G ....Matt 10:5
revelation to the G ....Luke 2:32
G are fulfilled ....Luke 21:24
My name before G ....Acts 9:15
poured out on the G ...Acts 10:45
a light to the G ....Acts 13:47
also the God of the G ....Rom 3:29
mystery among the G ....Col 1:27
a teacher of the G ....1 Tim 2:7

GENTLE

from Me, for I am g ...Matt 11:29
we were g among .....1 Thess 2:7
to be peaceable, g ....Titus 3:2
only to the good and g .1 Pet 2:18
ornament of a g ....1 Pet 3:4

GENTLENESS

love and a spirit of g ....1 Cor 4:21
g, self-control ....Gal 5:23
all lowliness and g ....Eph 4:2
Let your g be known to ...Phil 4:5
love, patience, g ....1 Tim 6:11

GHOST

supposed it was a g ....Mark 6:49

GIFT

it is the g of God ....Eccl 3:13
"If you knew the g ....John 4:10
but the g of God is ....Rom 6:23
each one has his own g ..1 Cor 7:7
though I have the g .....1 Cor 13:2
it is the g of God ....Eph 2:8
Do not neglect the g ....1 Tim 4:14
you to stir up the g ....2 Tim 1:6
tasted the heavenly g ......Heb 6:4
Every good g and ....James 1:17

GIFTS

You have received g ....Ps 68:18
and Seba Will offer g ......Ps 72:10
how to give good g ....Matt 7:11
rich putting their g ....Luke 21:1
g differing ....Rom 12:6
are diversities of g .....1 Cor 12:4
and desire spiritual g ..1 Cor 14:1
captive, And gave g ....Eph 4:8

GIRD

G Your sword upon Your ..Ps 45:3
and another will g .....John 21:18
Therefore g up the ....1 Pet 1:13

GIRDED

a towel and g Himself ..John 13:4

GIVE

g you the desires ....Ps 37:4
Yes, the LORD will g ....Ps 85:12
G me understanding ....Ps 119:34
"G to him who asks .....Matt 5:42
G us this day our ....Matt 6:11
what you have and g ...Matt 19:21
authority I will g ....Luke 4:6
g them eternal life ......John 10:28
commandment I g ....John 13:34
but what I do have I g .....Acts 3:6
g us all things ....Rom 8:32
G no offense ....1 Cor 10:32
g him who has need ....Eph 4:28
g thanks to God ....2 Thess 2:13
g yourself entirely ....1 Tim 4:15

GIVEN

to him more will be g ..Matt 13:12
has, more will be g ......Matt 25:29
to whom much is g ......Luke 12:48

g Me I should lose .....John 6:39
Spirit was not yet g .....John 7:39

GIVES

g life to the world ....John 6:33
"All that the Father g ...John 6:37
The good shepherd g ..John 10:11
not as the world g ....John 14:27
g us richly all things ....1 Tim 6:17
who g to all liberally .....James 1:5
g grace to the humble ..James 4:6

GLAD

streams shall make g ....Ps 46:4
I was g when they said ..Ps 122:1
make merry and be g ..Luke 15:32
he saw it and was g .....John 8:56

GLADNESS

me hear joy and g ....Ps 51:8
Serve the LORD with g ....Ps 100:2

GLORIFIED

and they g the God of ..Matt 15:31
Jesus was not yet g ....John 7:39
when Jesus was g ....John 12:16
this My Father is g ....John 15:8
"I have g You on the .....John 17:4
g His Servant Jesus ....Acts 3:13
these He also g ....Rom 8:30
things God may be g ....1 Pet 4:11

GLORIFY

g your Father in ....Matt 5:16
"Father, g Your name ..John 12:28
"He will g Me ....John 16:14
"And now, O Father, g ..John 17:5
death he would g ....John 21:19
therefore g God in ....1 Cor 6:20
also Christ did not g ....Heb 5:5
ashamed, but let him g ..1 Pet 4:16

GLORIOUS

G things are spoken ....Ps 87:3
g splendor of Your ....Ps 145:5
habitation, holy and g .....Is 63:15
it to Himself a g ....Eph 5:27
be conformed to His g ....Phil 3:21
g appearing of our ....Titus 2:13

GLORY

show me Your g ....Ex 33:18
g has departed from ....1 Sam 4:21
Who is this King of g ....Ps 24:8
Your power and Your g ......Ps 63:2
wise shall inherit g ....Prov 3:35
It is the g of God to .....Prov 25:2
g I will not give ....Is 42:8
that they may have g .....Matt 6:2
the power and the g .....Matt 6:13
g was not arrayed ....Matt 6:29
will come in the g ....Matt 16:27
power and great g ....Matt 24:30
"G to God in the ....Luke 2:14
and we beheld His g .....John 1:14
and manifested His g .....John 2:11
not seek My own g ....John 8:50
"Give God the g ....John 9:24
g which I had with ....John 17:5
g which You gave Me ..John 17:22
he did not give g ....Acts 12:23
doing good seek for g ......Rom 2:7
fall short of the g ....Rom 3:23
in faith, giving g ....Rom 4:20
the adoption, the g ....Rom 9:4
the riches of His g ....Rom 9:23
God, alone wise, be g ..Rom 16:27
who glories, let him g ..1 Cor 1:31
to His riches in g ....Phil 4:19
appear with Him in g ....Col 3:4
For you are our g .....1 Thess 2:20
many sons to g ....Heb 2:10
grass, And all the g ....1 Pet 1:24
to whom belong the g ....1 Pet 4:11
for the Spirit of g ....1 Pet 4:14

the presence of His g ..... Jude 24
O Lord, to receive g ..... Rev 4:11
g of God illuminated ... Rev 21:23

GLORYING
Your g is not good ...... 1 Cor 5:6

GLUTTON
you say, 'Look, a g ..... Luke 7:34

GLUTTONS
g shames his .... Prov 28:7
evil beasts, lazy g ...... Titus 1:12

GNASHING
will be weeping and g .. Matt 8:12

GO
'Let My people g .... Ex 5:1
For wherever you g .... Ruth 1:16
Those who g down to ... Ps 107:23
Where can I g from ..... Ps 139:7
to whom shall we g .... John 6:68
g you cannot come ...... John 8:21
I g to prepare a place ... John 14:2
shall g out no more ...... Rev 3:12

GOADS
to kick against the g ..... Acts 9:5

GOAL
I press toward the g ..... Phil 3:14

GOATS
his sheep from the g ... Matt 25:32
with the blood of g ...... Heb 9:12
g could take away ...... Heb 10:4

GOD
G created the heavens .... Gen 1:1
Abram of G Most .... Gen 14:19
and I will be their G .... Gen 17:8
"I am the LORD your G ... Ex 20:2
G is a consuming fire ... Deut 4:24
If the LORD is G .... 1 Kin 18:21
G is greater than all .... 2 Chr 2:5
You have been My G .... Ps 22:10
G is our refuge .... Ps 46:1
G is in the midst of .... Ps 46:5
me a clean heart, O G ... Ps 51:10
Our G is the G .... Ps 68:20
Who is so great a G ..... Ps 77:13
Restore us, O G .... Ps 80:7
You alone are G .... Ps 86:10
Exalt the LORD our G ...... Ps 99:9
Yes, our G is merciful ... Ps 116:5
For G is in heaven .... Eccl 5:2
Counselor, Mighty G .... Is 9:6
G is my salvation .... Is 12:2
stricken, Smitten by G ...... Is 53:4
"G with us .... Matt 1:23
in G my Savior .... Luke 1:47
the Word was with G .... John 1:1
"For G so loved the .... John 3:16
"G is Spirit .... John 4:24
"My Lord and my G .... John 20:28
Christ is the Son of G ... Acts 8:37
Indeed, let G be true ..... Rom 3:4
If G is for us .... Rom 8:31
G is faithful .... 1 Cor 1:9
G shall supply all .... Phil 4:19
and I will be their G .... Heb 8:10
G is a consuming fire .. Heb 12:29
for G is love .... 1 John 4:8
No one has seen G ... 1 John 4:12
G Himself will be .... Rev 21:3
and I will be his G ...... Rev 21:7

GODDESS
after Ashtoreth the g ... 1 Kin 11:5
of the great g Diana ... Acts 19:35

GODHEAD
eternal power and G .... Rom 1:20
the fullness of the G ...... Col 2:9

GODLINESS
is the mystery of g ..... 1 Tim 3:16
g with contentment ...... 1 Tim 6:6
having a form of g ...... 2 Tim 3:5
to perseverance g .... 2 Pet 1:6

GODLY
who desire to live g ... 2 Tim 3:12
reverence and g fear ... Heb 12:28
to deliver the g .... 2 Pet 2:9

GODS
God is God of g .... Deut 10:17
I said, "You are g .... Ps 82:6
yourselves with g .... Is 57:5
If He called them g .... John 10:35
g have come down to .. Acts 14:11

GOLD
g I do not have .... Acts 3:6
with braided hair or g .. 1 Tim 2:9
a man with g rings ..... James 2:2
Your g and silver are .... James 5:3
more precious than g .... 1 Pet 1:7
like silver or g .... 1 Pet 1:18
of the city was pure g .. Rev 21:21

GONE
like sheep have g .... Is 53:6

GOOD
God saw that it was g ... Gen 1:10
but God meant it for g . Gen 50:20
indeed accept g .... Job 2:10
is none who does g .... Ps 14:1
Truly God is g to .... Ps 73:1
g word makes it glad .. Prov 12:25
on the evil and the g .... Prov 15:3
A merry heart does g .. Prov 17:22
Learn to do g .... Is 1:17
talked to me, with g ..... Zech 1:13
they may see your g .... Matt 5:16
"A g man out of the ... Matt 12:35
No one is g but One ... Matt 19:17
For she has done a g .. Matt 26:10
g works I have shown . John 10:32
went about doing g .... Acts 10:38
g man someone would ... Rom 5:7
in my flesh) nothing g ... Rom 7:18
overcome evil with g .. Rom 12:21
Jesus for g works .... Eph 2:10
fruitful in every g .... Col 1:10
know that the law is g ... 1 Tim 1:8
For this is g and .... 1 Tim 2:3
bishop, he desires a g ... 1 Tim 3:1
for this is g and .... 1 Tim 5:4
prepared for every g ... 2 Tim 2:21
Every g gift and ...... James 1:17

GOODNESS
"I will make all My g .... Ex 33:19
and abounding in g ...... Ex 34:6
"You are my Lord, My g .. Ps 16:2
Surely g and mercy .... Ps 23:6
That I would see the g ... Ps 27:13
the riches of His g .... Rom 2:4
consider the g and ..... Rom 11:22
kindness, g .... Gal 5:22

GOSPEL
The beginning of the g .. Mark 1:1
and believe in the g .... Mark 1:15
g must first be .... Mark 13:10
separated to the g .... Rom 1:1
not ashamed of the g .... Rom 1:16
to a different g .... Gal 1:6
the everlasting g .... Rev 14:6

GOVERNMENT
And the g will be upon ..... Is 9:6

GRACE
But Noah found g .... Gen 6:8
G is poured upon Your .... Ps 45:2
The LORD will give g ..... Ps 84:11
the Spirit of g .... Zech 12:10
and the g of God was .. Luke 2:40
g and truth came .... John 1:17
And great g was upon .. Acts 4:33
receive abundance of g . Rom 5:17
g is no longer g .... Rom 11:6
For you know the g .... 2 Cor 8:9
g is sufficient .... 2 Cor 12:9
The g of the Lord .... 2 Cor 13:14
you have fallen from g ...... Gal 5:4
to the riches of His g ..... Eph 1:7
g you have been .... Eph 2:8
g was given according .... Eph 4:7
G be with all those ...... Eph 6:24
shaken, let us have g ... Heb 12:28
But He gives more g .... James 4:6
but grow in the g .... 2 Pet 3:18

GRACIOUS
he said, "God be g ..... Gen 43:29
I will be g to whom I .... Ex 33:19
at the g words which ... Luke 4:22
that the Lord is g .... 1 Pet 2:3

GRAFTED
in unbelief, will be g ... Rom 11:23

GRAIN
it treads out the g ...... Deut 25:4
be revived like g .... Hos 14:7
to pluck heads of g ..... Matt 12:1
unless a g of wheat .... John 12:24

GRAPES
brought forth wild g .... Is 5:2
have eaten sour g .... Ezek 18:2
Do men gather g .... Matt 7:16
g are fully ripe .... Rev 14:18

GRASS
The g withers .... Is 40:7
so clothes the g .... Matt 6:30
"All flesh is as g .... 1 Pet 1:24

GRAVE
my soul up from the g .... Ps 30:3
And they made His g ...... Is 53:9
the power of the g ...... Hos 13:14

GRAVES
g were opened .... Matt 27:52
g which are not .... Luke 11:44
g will hear His voice ... John 5:28

GRAY
the man of g hairs .... Deut 32:25

GREAT
and make your name g .. Gen 12:2
For the LORD is g ..... 1 Chr 16:25
Who does g things .... Job 5:9
g is the Holy One .... Is 12:6
G is Your faithfulness ... Lam 3:23
he shall be called g .... Matt 5:19
one pearl of g price .... Matt 13:46
desires to become g ... Matt 20:26
g drops of blood ...... Luke 22:44
appearing of our g ..... Titus 2:13
g men, the rich men ..... Rev 6:15
Mystery, Babylon the G . Rev 17:5
the dead, small and g ... Rev 20:12

GREATER
of heaven is g .... Matt 11:11
place there is One g .... Matt 12:6
g than Jonah is here ... Matt 12:41
g than Solomon is ..... Matt 12:42
a servant is not g ..... John 13:16
"G love has no one .... John 15:13
'A servant is not g ..... John 15:20
who prophesies is g ... 1 Cor 14:5
God is g .... 1 John 3:20
witness of God is g ..... 1 John 5:9

GREATEST
little child is the *g* . . . . . . Matt 18:4
but the *g* of these is . . . 1 Cor 13:13

GREATNESS
is the exceeding *g* . . . . Eph 1:19

GREED
part is full of *g* . . . . Luke 11:39

GREEDINESS
all uncleanness with *g* . . . Eph 4:19

GREEDY
of everyone who is *g* . . . Prov 1:19
not violent, not *g* . . . . 1 Tim 3:3

GREEK
written in Hebrew, *G* . . John 19:20
and also for the *G* . . . . . . Rom 1:16
is neither Jew not *G* . . . . Gal 3:28

GREEN
lie down in *g* pastures . . . . Ps 23:2

GRIEF
and acquainted with *g* . . . . . Is 53:3
joy and not with *g* . . . . . Heb 13:17

GRIEVE
g the Holy Spirit . . . . Eph 4:30

GRIEVED
earth, and He was *g* . . . . . . Gen 6:6
g His Holy Spirit . . . . Is 63:10
with anger, being *g* . . . . Mark 3:5

GROAN
even we ourselves *g* . . . . Rom 8:23
who are in this tent *g* . . . 2 Cor 5:4

GROANING
I am weary with my *g* . . . . . Ps 6:6
Then Jesus, again *g* . . . John 11:38

GROANINGS
g which cannot . . . . Rom 8:26

GROUND
"Cursed is the *g* . . . . Gen 3:17
you stand is holy *g* . . . . Ex 3:5
up your fallow *g* . . . . Jer 4:3
others fell on good *g* . . . Matt 13:8
bought a piece of *g* . . . Luke 14:18
God, the pillar and *g* . . 1 Tim 3:15

GROUNDED
being rooted and *g* . . . . Eph 3:17

GROW
truth in love, may *g* . . . . . Eph 4:15
but *g* in the grace and . . 2 Pet 3:18

GRUDGINGLY
in his heart, not *g* . . . . . . 2 Cor 9:7

GUARANTEE
in our hearts as a *g* . . . . 2 Cor 1:22
us the Spirit as a *g* . . . . . 2 Cor 5:5
who is the *g* of our . . . . . . Eph 1:14

GUIDE
He will be our *g* . . . . Ps 48:14
g our feet into the . . . . . . Luke 1:79
has come, He will *g* . . . John 16:13

GUIDES
to you, blind *g* . . . . Matt 23:16

GUILT
of your fathers' *g* . . . . . . Matt 23:32

GUILTLESS
g who takes His name . . . . Ex 20:7
have condemned the *g* . . Matt 12:7

GUILTY
"We are truly *g* . . . . Gen 42:21
world may become *g* . . . Rom 3:19
in one point, he is *g* . . . James 2:10

GULF
you there is a great *g* . Luke 16:26

H

HABITATION
Is God in His holy *h* . . . . . . Ps 68:5
but He blesses the *h* . . . . Prov 3:33
Jerusalem, a quiet *h* . . . . . . Is 33:20
from His holy *h* . . . . Zech 2:13
be clothed with our *h* . . . 2 Cor 5:2

HADES
be brought down to *H* . Matt 11:23
H shall not . . . . Matt 16:18
in torments in *H* . . . . Luke 16:23
not leave my soul in H . . Acts 2:27
I have the keys of *H* . . . . . Rev 1:18
H were cast into the . . . . Rev 20:14

HAIL
of the plague of the *h* . . . Rev 16:21

HAIR
you cannot make one *h* . Matt 5:36
"But not a *h* of your . . . Luke 21:18
not with braided *h* . . . . . . 1 Tim 2:9
h like women's *h* . . . . Rev 9:8

HAIRS
"But the very *h* . . . . Matt 10:30

HALLOWED
the Sabbath day and *h* . . Ex 20:11
who is holy shall be *h* . . . . Is 5:16
heaven, *H* be Your name . Matt 6:9

HAND
the *h* of God was . . . . . 1 Sam 5:11
My times are in Your *h* . . Ps 31:15
"Sit at My right *h* . . . . Ps 110:1
heart is in the *h* . . . . Prov 21:1
Whatever your *h* . . . . Eccl 9:10
is at his right *h* . . . . Eccl 10:2
do not withhold your *h* . . Eccl 11:6
My *h* has laid the . . . . Is 48:13
Behold, the LORD's *h* . . . . Is 59:1
are the work of Your *h* . . . . Is 64:8
"Am I a God near at *h* . . Jer 23:23
of heaven is at *h* . . . . Matt 3:2
if your right *h* . . . . Matt 5:30
do not let your left *h* . . . . . Matt 6:3
h causes you to sin . . . . . Mark 9:43
sitting at the right *h* . . Mark 14:62
at the right *h* of God . . . . Acts 7:55
The Lord is at *h* . . . . Phil 4:5
"Sit at My right h . . . . Heb 1:13
down at the right *h* . . . . Heb 10:12

HANDIWORK
firmament shows His *h* . . . Ps 19:1

HANDLE
H Me and see . . . . Luke 24:39
do not taste, do not *h* . . . . Col 2:21

HANDLED
and our hands have *h* . . 1 John 1:1

HANDS
took his life in his *h* . . . 1 Sam 19:5
but His *h* make whole . . . Job 5:18
They pierced My *h* . . . . Ps 22:16
h formed the dry land . . . . . Ps 95:5
than having two *h* . . . . Matt 18:8
"Behold My *h* and . . . . . Luke 24:39
h the print of the . . . . . . John 20:25

his *h* what is good . . . . . . Eph 4:28
the laying on of the *h* . . 1 Tim 4:14
to fall into the *h* . . . . Heb 10:31

HANDWRITING
having wiped out the *h* . . Col 2:14

HANGED
went and *h* himself . . . . . Matt 27:5

HANGS
h the earth on nothing . . . Job 26:7
is everyone who h . . . . Gal 3:13

HAPPY
H is the man who has . . . Ps 127:5

HARD
I knew you to be a *h* . . Matt 25:24
"This is a *h* saying . . . . . John 6:60
are some things *h* . . . . . . 2 Pet 3:16

HARDEN
But I will *h* his heart . . . . . Ex 4:21
h your hearts as . . . . Heb 3:8

HARDENED
But Pharaoh *h* his . . . . Ex 8:32
their heart was *h* . . . . Mark 6:52
and h their hearts . . . . . . John 12:40
lest any of you be *h* . . . . . Heb 3:13

HARDENS
whom He wills He *h* . . . . Rom 9:18

HARDSHIP
h as a good soldier . . . . . 2 Tim 2:3

HARLOT
of a *h* named Rahab . . . . . Josh 2:1
h is one body with . . . . . 1 Cor 6:16
of the great *h* who . . . . Rev 17:1

HARLOTRIES
Let her put away her *h* . . . Hos 2:2

HARLOTRY
are the children of *h* . . . . Hos 2:4
For the spirit of *h* . . . . Hos 5:4

HARLOTS
h enter the . . . . Matt 21:31
Great, The Mother of *H* . Rev 17:5

HARP
Lamb, each having a *h* . . . Rev 5:8

HARPS
We hung our *h* Upon the . Ps 137:2

HARVEST
Seedtime and *h* . . . . Gen 8:22
"The *h* is past . . . . Jer 8:20
h truly is plentiful . . . . . . Matt 9:37
sickle, because the *h* . . . Mark 4:29
already white for *h* . . . . John 4:35

HASTENS
and he sins who *h* . . . . . . Prov 19:2

HASTILY
utter anything *h* . . . . Eccl 5:2

HASTY
Do you see a man *h* . . . Prov 29:20

HATE
love the LORD, *h* evil . . . . . Ps 97:10
h every false way . . . . . . Ps 119:104
h the double-minded . . . Ps 119:113
I *h* and abhor lying . . . . Ps 119:163
love, And a time to *h* . . . . . Eccl 3:8
You who *h* good and . . . . Mic 3:2
either he will *h* . . . . Matt 6:24

HATED

But Esau I have *h* ... Mal 1:3
"And you will be *h* ... Matt 10:22
have seen and also *h* ... John 15:24
but Esau I have h ... Rom 9:13
For no one ever *h* ... Eph 5:29

HATEFUL

h woman when she is ... Prov 30:23
in malice and envy, *h* ... Titus 3:3

HATERS

backbiters, *h* of God ... Rom 1:30

HATES

six things the LORD *h* ... Prov 6:16
lose it, and he who *h* ... John 12:25
"If the world *h* ... John 15:18
h his brother is ... 1 John 2:11

HAUGHTY

bring down *h* looks ... Ps 18:27
my heart is not *h* ... Ps 131:1
h spirit before a fall ... Prov 16:18

HEAD

He shall bruise your *h* ... Gen 3:15
and gave Him to be *h* ... Eph 1:22
For the husband is *h* ... Eph 5:23

HEAL

O LORD, *h* me ... Ps 6:2
h your backslidings ... Jer 3:22
torn, but He will *h* ... Hos 6:1
"*H* the sick ... Matt 10:8
So that I should h ... Matt 13:15
sent Me to h the ... Luke 4:18
Physician, *h* yourself ... Luke 4:23

HEALED

And return and be *h* ... Is 6:10
His stripes we are *h* ... Is 53:5
"When I would have *h* ... Hos 7:1
and He *h* them ... Matt 4:24
that you may be *h* ... James 5:16
his deadly wound was *h* ... Rev 13:3

HEALING

shall arise With *h* ... Mal 4:2
and *h* all kinds of ... Matt 4:23
tree were for the *h* ... Rev 22:2

HEALINGS

to another gifts of *h* ... 1 Cor 12:9

HEALS

h all your diseases ... Ps 103:3
Jesus the Christ *h* ... Acts 9:34

HEALTH

all things and be in *h* ... 3 John 2

HEAR

"*H*, O Israel ... Deut 6:4
Him you shall *h* ... Deut 18:15
H me when I call ... Ps 4:1
O You who *h* prayer ... Ps 65:2
ear, shall He not *h* ... Ps 94:9
h rather than to give ... Eccl 5:1
'Hearing you will h ... Matt 13:14
heed what you *h* ... Mark 4:24
that God does not *h* ... John 9:31
And how shall they *h* ... Rom 10:14
man be swift to *h* ... James 1:19
h what the Spirit says ... Rev 2:7

HEARD

h their cry because of ... Ex 3:7
that they will be *h* ... Matt 6:7
h the word believed ... Acts 4:4
not seen, nor ear h ... 1 Cor 2:9
things that you have *h* ... 2 Tim 2:2
the word which they *h* ... Heb 4:2
which we have *h* ... 1 John 1:1
Lord's Day, and I *h* ... Rev 1:10

HEARER

if anyone is a *h* ... James 1:23

HEARERS

for not the *h* of the ... Rom 2:13
the word, and not *h* ... James 1:22

HEARING

'Keep on *h* ... Is 6:9
h they do not ... Matt 13:13
h they may hear ... Mark 4:12
or by the *h* of faith ... Gal 3:2

HEARS

out, and the LORD *h* ... Ps 34:17
of God *h* God's words ... John 8:47
"And if anyone *h* ... John 12:47
who is of the truth *h* ... John 18:37
He who knows God *h* ... 1 John 4:6
And let him who *h* ... Rev 22:17

HEART

h was only evil ... Gen 6:5
h rejoices in the LORD ... 1 Sam 2:1
gave him another *h* ... 1 Sam 10:9
LORD looks at the *h* ... 1 Sam 16:7
his wives turned his *h* ... 1 Kin 11:4
He pierces my *h* ... Job 16:13
My *h* also instructs me ... Ps 16:7
h is overflowing ... Ps 45:1
h shall depart from me ... Ps 101:4
look and a proud *h* ... Ps 101:5
with my whole *h* ... Ps 111:1
as he thinks in his *h* ... Prov 23:7
h reveals the man ... Prov 27:19
trusts in his own *h* ... Prov 28:26
The *h* of the wise is ... Eccl 7:4
And a wise man's *h* ... Eccl 8:5
h yearned for him ... Song 5:4
And the whole *h* ... Is 1:5
The yearning of Your *h* ... Is 63:15
h is deceitful above ... Jer 17:9
I will give them a *h* ... Jer 24:7
and take the stony *h* ... Ezek 11:19
yourselves a new *h* ... Ezek 18:31
are the pure in *h* ... Matt 5:8
is, there your *h* ... Matt 6:21
of the *h* proceed evil ... Matt 15:19
h will flow rivers ... John 7:38
"Let not your *h* ... John 14:1
Satan filled your *h* ... Acts 5:3
h that God has raised ... Rom 10:9
refresh my *h* in the ... Philem 20
and shuts up his *h* ... 1 John 3:17

HEARTILY

you do, do it *h* ... Col 3:23

HEARTS

God tests the *h* ... Ps 7:9
And he will turn The *h* ... Mal 4:6
h failing them from ... Luke 21:26
will guard your *h* ... Phil 4:7
of God rule in your *h* ... Col 3:15

HEATHEN

repetitions as the *h* ... Matt 6:7

HEAVEN

called the firmament *H* ... Gen 1:8
LORD looks down from *h* ... Ps 14:2
word is settled in *h* ... Ps 119:89
For God is in *h* ... Eccl 5:2
"*H* is My throne ... Is 66:1
for the kingdom of *h* ... Matt 3:2
your Father in *h* ... Matt 5:16
On earth as it is in *h* ... Matt 6:10
"*H* and earth will ... Matt 24:35
Him a sign from *h* ... Mark 8:11
have sinned against *h* ... Luke 15:18
you shall see *h* ... John 1:51
one has ascended to *h* ... John 3:13
the true bread from *h* ... John 6:32
a voice came from *h* ... John 12:28
sheet, let down from *h* ... Acts 11:5
laid up for you in *h* ... Col 1:5
there was silence in *h* ... Rev 8:1
Now I saw a new *h* ... Rev 21:1

HEAVENLY

your *h* Father will ... Matt 6:14
h host praising God ... Luke 2:13
if I tell you *h* things ... John 3:12
blessing in the *h* ... Eph 1:3
a better, that is, a *h* ... Heb 11:16
the living God, the *h* ... Heb 12:22

HEAVENS

and the highest *h* ... Deut 10:14
h cannot contain ... 1 Kin 8:27
h declare the glory ... Ps 19:1
For as the *h* are high ... Ps 103:11
behold, I create new *h* ... Is 65:17
and behold, the *h* ... Matt 3:16
h will be shaken ... Matt 24:29
h are the work of Your ... Heb 1:10
h will pass away ... 2 Pet 3:10

HEEDS

h counsel is wise ... Prov 12:15

HEEL

you shall bruise His *h* ... Gen 3:15
has lifted up his *h* ... Ps 41:9
Me has lifted up his h ... John 13:18

HEIGHT

nor *h* nor depth ... Rom 8:39
length and depth and *h* ... Eph 3:18

HEIR

He has appointed *h* ... Heb 1:2
world and became *h* ... Heb 11:7

HEIRS

if children, then *h* ... Rom 8:17
should be fellow *h* ... Eph 3:6

HELL

shall be turned into *h* ... Ps 9:17
go down alive into *h* ... Ps 55:15
H and Destruction are ... Prov 27:20
be in danger of *h* fire ... Matt 5:22
to be cast into *h* ... Matt 18:9
condemnation of *h* ... Matt 23:33
power to cast into *h* ... Luke 12:5

HELMET

And take the *h* of ... Eph 6:17
and love, and as a *h* ... 1 Thess 5:8

HELP

May He send you *h* ... Ps 20:2
A very present *h* ... Ps 46:1
He is their *h* and ... Ps 115:9
Our *h* is in the name ... Ps 124:8
h my unbelief ... Mark 9:24
and find grace to *h* ... Heb 4:16

HELPED

fall, but the LORD *h* ... Ps 118:13
of salvation I have *h* ... Is 49:8
h His servant Israel ... Luke 1:54

HELPER

I will make him a *h* ... Gen 2:18
Behold, God is my *h* ... Ps 54:4
give you another *H* ... John 14:16
"But when the *H* ... John 15:26
"The LORD is my h ... Heb 13:6

HELPFUL

all things are not *h* ... 1 Cor 6:12

HELPS

the Spirit also *h* ... Rom 8:26

HEM
and touched the *h* ......Matt 9:20

HERE
Then I said, "*H* am I ....Is 6:8

HERESIES
dissensions, *h* ....Gal 5:20

HERITAGE
for that is his *h* ....Eccl 3:22
This is the *h* of the ....Is 54:17
of My people, My *h* ......Joel 3:2
The flock of Your *h* .....Mic 7:14

HIDDEN
And my sins are not *h* ....Ps 69:5
Your word I have *h* .....Ps 119:11
h that will not ....Matt 10:26
the *h* wisdom which ....1 Cor 2:7
bring to light the *h* .....1 Cor 4:5
have renounced the *h* ...2 Cor 4:2
rather let it be the *h* .....1 Pet 3:4
give some of the *h* ......Rev 2:17

HIDE
H me under the shadow ...Ps 17:8
You shall *h* them in .....Ps 31:20
You *h* Your face ....Ps 104:29
darkness shall not *h* ....Ps 139:12
You are God, who *h* ......Is 45:15
"Fall on us and *h* ....Rev 6:16

HIDES
He *h* His face ....Ps 10:11

HIDING
You are my *h* place ......Ps 32:7

HIGH
priest of God Most *H* ...Gen 14:18
For the LORD Most *H* .....Ps 47:2
"I dwell in the *h* ....Is 57:15
know That the Most *H* ..Dan 4:17
up on a *h* mountain by ..Matt 17:1
your mind on *h* things .Rom 12:16
h thing that exalts .....2 Cor 10:5
and faithful *H* Priest .....Heb 2:17

HIGHER
you, 'Friend, go up *h* ..Luke 14:10

HIGHWAY
in the desert A *h* ....Is 40:3

HIGHWAYS
h shall be elevated ....Is 49:11
go into the *h* ....Matt 22:9

HILL
My King on My holy *h* ....Ps 2:6
h cannot be hidden ......Matt 5:14
and h brought low ....Luke 3:5

HILLS
of the everlasting *h* ....Gen 49:26
of the *h* are His also .....Ps 95:4
up my eyes to the *h* .....Ps 121:1

HINDER
all things lest we *h* .....1 Cor 9:12

HINDERED
Who *h* you from obeying ..Gal 5:7
prayers may not be *h* ....1 Pet 3:7

HOLD
right hand shall *h* ....Ps 139:10
h fast that word ....1 Cor 15:2
h fast and repent ....Rev 3:3

HOLIER
near me, For I am *h* ....Is 65:5

HOLIEST
the way into the *H* ....Heb 9:8

HOLINESS
You, glorious in *h* ....Ex 15:11
I have sworn by My *h* ....Ps 89:35
the Highway of *H* ....Is 35:8
to the Spirit of *h* ....Rom 1:4
spirit, perfecting *h* ......2 Cor 7:1
uncleanness, but in *h* .1 Thess 4:7
be partakers of His *h* ..Heb 12:10

HOLY
where you stand is *h* ......Ex 3:5
day, to keep it *h* ....Ex 20:8
LORD your God am *h* ....Lev 19:2
h seed is mixed ....Ezra 9:2
God sits on His *h* ....Ps 47:8
God, in His *h* mountain ...Ps 48:1
"*H, h, h* ....Is 6:3
child of the *H* Spirit ....Matt 1:18
baptize you with the *H* ..Mark 1:8
who speak, but the *H* . Mark 13:11
H Spirit will come ....Luke 1:35
H Spirit descended ....Luke 3:22
Father give the *H* ....Luke 11:13
H Spirit will teach ....Luke 12:12
H Spirit was not ....John 7:39
H Spirit has come ....Acts 1:8
all filled with the *H* ....Acts 2:4
receive the *H* Spirit .....Acts 19:2
joy in the *H* ....Rom 14:17
H Spirit teaches ....1 Cor 2:13
that we should be *h* .....Eph 1:4
were sealed with the *H* ..Eph 1:13
partakers of the *H* ....Heb 6:4
H Spirit sent from .....1 Pet 1:12
it is written, "*Be h* ....1 Pet 1:16
moved by the *H* Spirit ..2 Pet 1:21
anointing from the *H* . 1 John 2:20
says He who is *h* ....Rev 3:7
For You alone are *h* .....Rev 15:4
is *h*, let him be *h* ....Rev 22:11

HOME
sparrow has found a *h* ....Ps 84:3
to his eternal *h* ....Eccl 12:5
that while we are at *h* ...2 Cor 5:6
to show piety at *h* ....1 Tim 5:4

HOMEMAKERS
be discreet, chaste, *h* .....Titus 2:5

HONEY
and with *h* from the ....Ps 81:16
was locusts and wild *h* ....Matt 3:4

HONEYCOMB
than honey and the *h* ....Ps 19:10
fish and some *h* ....Luke 24:42

HONOR
"*H* your father and your . Ex 20:12
will deliver him and *h* ...Ps 91:15
H and majesty are ....Ps 96:6
H the LORD with your ...Prov 3:9
before *h* is humility ....Prov 15:33
spirit will retain *h* .....Prov 29:23
Father, where is My *h* .....Mal 1:6
is not without *h* ....Matt 13:57
'*H your father and* ....Matt 15:4
h the Son just as they ..John 5:23
"I do not receive *h* ......John 5:41
but I *h* My Father ....John 8:49
"If I *h* Myself ....John 8:54
him My Father will *h* ..John 12:26
to whom fear, *h* ....Rom 13:7
sanctification and *h* ...1 Thess 4:4
alone is wise, be *h* ......1 Tim 1:17
and clay, some for *h* ...2 Tim 2:20
no man takes this *h* ....Heb 5:4
from God the Father *h* .2 Pet 1:17
give glory and *h* ....Rev 4:9

HONORABLE
His work is *h* and ....Ps 111:3
holy day of the LORD *h* ...Is 58:13
providing *h* things ....2 Cor 8:21
Marriage is *h* among .....Heb 13:4
having your conduct *h* .1 Pet 2:12

HONORS
'*This people h Me* ....Mark 7:6
It is My Father who *h* ...John 8:54

HOPE
h He has uprooted ....Job 19:10
also will rest in *h* ....Ps 16:9
My *h* is in You ....Ps 39:7
For You are my *h* ....Ps 71:5
I *h* in Your word ....Ps 119:147
good that one should *h* .Lam 3:26
to *h*, in *h* believed .....Rom 4:18
h does not disappoint .....Rom 5:5
were saved in this *h* .....Rom 8:24
now abide faith, *h* .....1 Cor 13:13
life only we have *h* ....1 Cor 15:19
may know what is the *h* .Eph 1:18
were called in one *h* ....Eph 4:4
Christ in you, the *h* ......Col 1:27
Jesus Christ, our *h* ....1 Tim 1:1
for the blessed *h* ....Titus 2:13
to lay hold of the *h* ....Heb 6:18
in of a better *h* ....Heb 7:19
who has this *h* in Him . 1 John 3:3

HOPED
substance of things *h* ...Heb 11:1

HORSE
and behold, a white *h* ....Rev 6:2
and behold, a white *h* ..Rev 19:11

HOSANNA
H in the highest ....Matt 21:9

HOSPITABLE
Be *h* to one another ....1 Pet 4:9

HOSTS
The LORD of *h* is with .....Ps 46:7
Praise Him, all His *h* ....Ps 148:2
against spiritual *h* ....Eph 6:12

HOUR
is coming at an *h* ......Matt 24:44
"But the *h* is coming .....John 4:23
save Me from this *h* ...John 12:27
keep you from the *h* ......Rev 3:10

HOUSE
as for me and my *h* ....Josh 24:15
Through wisdom a *h* ...Prov 24:3
better to go to the *h* ....Eccl 7:2
h was filled with ....Is 6:4
h divided against ....Matt 12:25
h shall be called a ....Matt 21:13
make My Father's *h* ......John 2:16
h are many mansions ..John 14:2
publicly and from *h* ....Acts 20:20
who rules his own *h* .....1 Tim 3:4
the church in your *h* ....Philem 2
For every *h* is built ....Heb 3:4
His own *h*, whose *h* ......Heb 3:6

HOUSEHOLD
the ways of her *h* ....Prov 31:27
be those of his own h ..Matt 10:36
h were baptized ....Acts 16:15
saved, you and your *h* .Acts 16:31
who are of Caesar's *h* ...Phil 4:22

HOUSEHOLDER
h who brings out of ...Matt 13:52

HOUSES
H and riches are an ....Prov 19:14
who has left *h* or ....Matt 19:29
you devour widows' *h* .Matt 23:14

HOVERING
Spirit of God was *h* . . . . . Gen 1:2

HUMBLE
man Moses was very *h* . Num 12:3
the cry of the *h* . . . . Ps 9:12
h shall hear of it and . . . . . Ps 34:2
contrite and *h* spirit . . . . . . Is 57:15
A meek and *h* people . . . Zeph 3:12
associate with the *h* . . . Rom 12:16
gives grace to the h . . . . James 4:6
H yourselves in the . . . James 4:10
gives grace to the h . . . . . . 1 Pet 5:5
h yourselves under the . . 1 Pet 5:6

HUMBLED
as a man, He *h* Himself . . . Phil 2:8

HUMBLES
h Himself to behold . . . . . Ps 113:6

HUMILITY
the Lord with all *h* . . . . Acts 20:19
delight in false *h* . . . . Col 2:18
mercies, kindness, *h* . . . . . . Col 3:12
h correcting those . . . . . 2 Tim 2:25
gentle, showing all *h* . . . . Titus 3:2
and be clothed with *h* . . . 1 Pet 5:5

HUNGER
They shall neither *h* . . . . . . Is 49:10
are those who *h* . . . . Matt 5:6
for you shall *h* . . . . Luke 6:25
to Me shall never *h* . . . . John 6:35
hour we both *h* . . . . 1 Cor 4:11
"They shall neither *h* . . . . Rev 7:16

HUNGRY
and fills the *h* . . . . Ps 107:9
gives food to the *h* . . . . . . Ps 146:7
'for I was *h* and you . . . Matt 25:35
did we see You *h* . . . . Matt 25:37
to be full and to be *h* . . . . Phil 4:12

HUNTER
Nimrod the mighty *h* . . . . Gen 10:9
Esau was a skillful *h* . . . Gen 25:27

HURT
h a woman with child . . . Ex 21:22
but I was not *h* . . . . Prov 23:35
another to his own *h* . . . . . Eccl 8:9
They shall not *h* . . . . Is 11:9
it will by no means *h* . Mark 16:18
shall not be *h* by the . . . . Rev 2:11

HUSBAND
She also gave to her *h* . . . . Gen 3:6
h safely trusts her . . . . Prov 31:11
your Maker is your *h* . . . . . . Is 54:5
now have is not your *h* . John 4:18
you will save your *h* . . . 1 Cor 7:16
the *h* of one wife . . . . 1 Tim 3:2

HUSBANDS
H, love your wives . . . . . . Eph 5:25
Let deacons be the *h* . . 1 Tim 3:12

HYMN
they had sung a *h* . . . . Matt 26:30

HYMNS
praying and singing *h* . Acts 16:25
in psalms and *h* . . . . Eph 5:19

HYPOCRISY
you are full of *h* . . . . Matt 23:28
Pharisees, which is *h* . . . Luke 12:1
Let love be without *h* . . . Rom 12:9
away with their *h* . . . . Gal 2:13
and without *h* . . . . James 3:17
malice, all deceit, *h* . . . . . 1 Pet 2:1

HYPOCRITE
and the joy of the *h* . . . . . Job 20:5
For everyone is a *h* . . . . Is 9:17
also played the *h* . . . . Gal 2:13

HYPOCRITES
not be like the *h* . . . . Matt 6:5
do you test Me, you *h* . Matt 22:18
and Pharisees, *h* . . . . Matt 23:13

I

IDLE
i person will suffer . . . . Prov 19:15
i word men may . . . . Matt 12:36
saw others standing *i* . . . Matt 20:3
they learn to be *i* . . . . . . 1 Tim 5:13

IDOL
thing offered to an *i* . . . . 1 Cor 8:7
That an *i* is anything . 1 Cor 10:19

IDOLATER
or covetous, or an *i* . . . . 1 Cor 5:11

IDOLATERS
fornicators, nor *i* . . . . . . 1 Cor 6:9
and murderers and *i* . . . Rev 22:15

IDOLATRIES
and abominable *i* . . . . 1 Pet 4:3

IDOLATRY
beloved, flee from *i* . . . 1 Cor 10:14
i, sorcery . . . . Gal 5:20

IDOLS
land is also full of *i* . . . . Is 2:8
in the room of his *i* . . . . Ezek 8:12
who regard worthless *i* . . . . Jon 2:8
You who abhor *i* . . . . Rom 2:22
yourselves from *i* . . . . . 1 John 5:21
worship demons, and *i* . . Rev 9:20

IGNORANCE
that you did it in *i* . . . . . Acts 3:17
i God overlooked . . . . . Acts 17:30
sins committed in *i* . . . . Heb 9:7

IGNORANTLY
because I did it *i* . . . . . . 1 Tim 1:13

ILLUMINATED
after you were *i* . . . . Heb 10:32
and the earth was *i* . . . . . . Rev 18:1
for the glory of God *i* . . . Rev 21:23

IMAGE
Us make man in Our *i* . . . Gen 1:26
since he is the *i* . . . . 1 Cor 11:7
He is the *i* of the . . . . Col 1:15
and not the very *i* . . . . Heb 10:1
the beast and his *i* . . . . Rev 14:9

IMAGINATION
the proud in the *i* . . . . Luke 1:51

IMITATE
as I also *i* Christ . . . . 1 Cor 11:1

IMMANUEL
shall call His name *I* . . . . . . Is 7:14
shall call His name I . . . . Matt 1:23

IMMORAL
murderers, sexually *i* . . . . Rev 21:8

IMMORALITY
except sexual *i* . . . . Matt 5:32
abstain from sexual *i* . 1 Thess 4:3

IMMORTAL
to the King eternal, *i* . . 1 Tim 1:17

IMMORTALITY
mortal must put on *i* . . 1 Cor 15:53
who alone has *i* . . . . 1 Tim 6:16

IMMOVABLE
be steadfast, *i* . . . . 1 Cor 15:58

IMMUTABLE
that by two *i* things . . . . . Heb 6:18

IMPART
that it may *i* grace . . . . . . Eph 4:29

IMPENITENT
i heart you are . . . . Rom 2:5

IMPOSSIBLE
God nothing will be *i* . . . Luke 1:37
without faith it is *i* . . . . . . Heb 11:6

IMPUTE
the LORD does not *i* . . . . Ps 32:2

IMPUTED
might be *i* to them . . . . . . Rom 4:11
but sin is not *i* . . . . Rom 5:13

IMPUTES
i righteousness apart . . . . Rom 4:6

INCORRUPTIBLE
the glory of the *i* . . . . Rom 1:23
dead will be raised *i* . . . 1 Cor 15:52
to an inheritance *i* . . . . . . 1 Pet 1:4

INCORRUPTION
corruption inherit *i* . . . 1 Cor 15:50

INCREASE
Of the *i* of His . . . . Is 9:7
Lord, "*I* our faith . . . . . . Luke 17:5
"He must *i* . . . . John 3:30
but God gave the *i* . . . . . . 1 Cor 3:6

INCREASES
who have no might He *i* . . Is 40:29

INCURABLE
Your sorrow is *i* . . . . Jer 30:15

INDIGNATION
i which will devour . . . Heb 10:27
into the cup of His *i* . . . . Rev 14:10

INEXCUSABLE
Therefore you are *i* . . . . . . Rom 2:1

INEXPRESSIBLE
Paradise and heard *i* . . . 2 Cor 12:4
you rejoice with joy *i* . . . . 1 Pet 1:8

INFALLIBLE
suffering by many *i* . . . . . . Acts 1:3

INFIRMITIES
"He Himself took our i . . Matt 8:17

INHERIT
love me to *i* wealth . . . . . . Prov 8:21
i the kingdom . . . . Matt 25:34
unrighteous will not *i* . . . 1 Cor 6:9
who overcomes shall *i* . . . Rev 21:7

INHERITANCE
"You shall have no *i* . . . Num 18:20
is the place of His *i* . . . . . Deut 32:9
the portion of my *i* . . . . Ps 16:5
i shall be forever . . . . Ps 37:18
He will choose our *i* . . . . Ps 47:4
will arise to your *i* . . . . Dan 12:13
God gave him no *i* . . . . Acts 7:5
and give you an *i* . . . . . . Acts 20:32
For if the *i* is of the . . . . . . Gal 3:18
we have obtained an *i* . . . Eph 1:11

be partakers of the *i* . . . . . Col 1:12
receive as an *i* . . . . Heb 11:8
i incorruptible . . . . 1 Pet 1:4

INIQUITIES

i have overtaken me . . . . . Ps 40:12
forgives all your *i* . . . . Ps 103:3
LORD, should mark *i* . . . . . Ps 130:3
was bruised for our *i* . . . . Is 53:5
He shall bear their *i* . . . . Is 53:11
i have separated you . . . . Is 59:2

INIQUITY

God, visiting the *i* of the . . Ex 20:5
was brought forth in *i* . . . . Ps 51:5
If I regard *i* in my . . . . . . Ps 66:18
i have dominion . . . . Ps 119:133
i will reap sorrow . . . . . . Prov 22:8
A people laden with *i* . . . . Is 1:4
i is taken away . . . . Is 6:7
has laid on Him the *i* . . . . . . Is 53:6
will remember their *i* . . . . . Hos 9:9
to those who devise *i* . . . . . Mic 2:1
like You, Pardoning *i* . . . . Mic 7:18
all you workers of *i* . . . Luke 13:27
a fire, a world of *i* . . . . . . James 3:6

INJUSTICE

i have your fathers . . . . Jer 2:5

INN

room for them in the *i* . . . Luke 2:7
brought him to an *i* . . . Luke 10:34

INNOCENCE

washed my hands in *i* . . . Ps 73:13

INNOCENT

because I was found *i* . . . Dan 6:22
saying, "I am *i* . . . . Matt 27:24
this day that I am *i* . . . . Acts 20:26

INQUIRED

Therefore David *i* . . . . . 1 Sam 23:2
the prophets have *i* . . . . 1 Pet 1:10

INQUIRY

shall make careful *i* . . . Deut 19:18

INSANE

images, And they are *i* . . Jer 50:38

INSPIRATION

is given by *i* of God . . . 2 Tim 3:16

INSTRUCT

I will *i* you and teach . . . . . Ps 32:8
LORD that he may i . . . . 1 Cor 2:16

INSTRUCTED

This man had been *i* . . . Acts 18:25
are excellent, being *i* . . . Rom 2:18
Moses was divinely *i* . . . . . Heb 8:5

INSTRUCTION

seeing you hate *i* . . . . Ps 50:17
Hear *i* and be wise . . . . . Prov 8:33
Give *i* to a wise man . . . . . Prov 9:9
for correction, for *i* . . . . 2 Tim 3:16

INSTRUCTS

My heart also *i* . . . . Ps 16:7

INSTRUMENTS

your members as *i* . . . . Rom 6:13

INSUBORDINATE

for the lawless and *i* . . . . 1 Tim 1:9

INSUBORDINATION

of dissipation or *i* . . . . Titus 1:6

INSULTED

will be mocked and *i* . . Luke 18:32
i the Spirit of grace . . . . Heb 10:29

INSULTS

nor be afraid of their *i* . . . . . Is 51:7

INTEGRITY

In the *i* of my heart . . . . . Gen 20:5
in doctrine showing *i* . . . . Titus 2:7

INTERCEDE

the LORD, who will *i* . . . 1 Sam 2:25

INTERCESSION

of many, And made *i* . . . . . Is 53:12
Spirit Himself makes *i* . . Rom 8:26
always lives to make *i* . . . Heb 7:25

INTERCESSOR

that there was no *i* . . . . Is 59:16

INTEREST

collected it with *i* . . . . Luke 19:23

INTERPRET

Do all *i*? . . . . 1 Cor 12:30
pray that he may *i* . . . . 1 Cor 14:13

INTERPRETATION

to another the *i* . . . . 1 Cor 12:10
of any private *i* . . . . 2 Pet 1:20

INTERPRETATIONS

"Do not *i* belong to . . . . . Gen 40:8

INVISIBLE

of the world His *i* . . . . . . Rom 1:20
is the image of the *i* . . . . . Col 1:15
eternal, immortal, *i* . . . . 1 Tim 1:17
as seeing Him who is *i* . Heb 11:27

INWARD

You have formed my *i* . . Ps 139:13
God according to the *i* . . Rom 7:22
i man is being . . . . 2 Cor 4:16

INWARDLY

i they are . . . . Matt 7:15
is a Jew who is one *i* . . . Rom 2:29

IRON

i sharpens *i* . . . . Prov 27:17
its feet partly of *i* . . . . Dan 2:33

ISRAEL

"Hear, O *I* . . . . Deut 6:4
For they are not all *I* . . . . Rom 9:6
and upon the *I* of God . . . Gal 6:16

ITCHING

they have *i* ears . . . . 2 Tim 4:3

J

JEALOUS

God, am a *j* God . . . . Ex 20:5
a consuming fire, a *j* . . . . Deut 4:24
For I am *j* for you . . . . . 2 Cor 11:2

JEALOUSY

provoked Him to *j* . . . . Deut 32:16
as strong as death, *j* . . . . Song 8:6
for you with godly *j* . . . 2 Cor 11:2

JEOPARDY

stand in *j* every hour . 1 Cor 15:30

JESTING

talking, nor coarse *j* . . . . . . Eph 5:4

JESUS

J Christ was as . . . . Matt 1:18
shall call His name *J* . . . . Matt 1:21
J was led up by the . . . . . . Matt 4:1
and laid hands on *J* . . . . Matt 26:50
and destroy *J* . . . . Matt 27:20
J withdrew with His . . . . . Mark 3:7
J went into . . . . Mark 11:11
they were eating, *J* . . . Mark 14:22
and he delivered *J* . . . . Mark 15:15
truth came through *J* . . . . John 1:17
J lifted up His eyes . . . . . John 6:5
J wept . . . . John 11:35
J was crucified . . . . John 19:20
"This *J* God has raised . . Acts 2:32
of Your holy Servant *J* . . Acts 4:30
believed on the Lord *J* . Acts 11:17
your mouth the Lord *J* . . Rom 10:9
among you except *J* . . . . 1 Cor 2:2
perfect in Christ *J* . . . . Col 1:28
But we see *J* . . . . Heb 2:9
looking unto *J* . . . . Heb 12:2
Revelation of *J* Christ . . . . Rev 1:1
so, come, Lord *J* . . . . Rev 22:20

JOIN

of the rest dared *j* . . . . . . Acts 5:13

JOINED

and mother and be *j* . . . . Gen 2:24
what God has *j* . . . . Matt 19:6
the whole body, *j* . . . . Eph 4:16

JOINT

j as He wrestled . . . . Gen 32:25
My bones are out of *j* . . . . Ps 22:14
j heirs with Christ . . . . . . Rom 8:17

JOINTS

and knit together by *j* . . . . Col 2:19
and spirit, and of *j* . . . . . . Heb 4:12

JOT

one *j* or one tittle . . . . Matt 5:18

JOY

is fullness of *j* . . . . Ps 16:11
j comes in the morning . . . Ps 30:5
j you will draw . . . . Is 12:3
ashes, The oil of *j* . . . . Is 61:3
shall sing for *j* . . . . Is 65:14
receives it with *j* . . . . Matt 13:20
Enter into the *j* . . . . Matt 25:21
in my womb for *j* . . . . Luke 1:44
there will be more *j* . . . . Luke 15:7
did not believe for *j* . . . Luke 24:41
My *j* may remain in . . . . John 15:11
they may have My *j* . . . . John 17:13
the Spirit is love, *j* . . . . Gal 5:22
are our glory and *j* . . 1 Thess 2:20
j that was set before . . . . Heb 12:2
count it all *j* . . . . James 1:2
with exceeding *j* . . . . 1 Pet 4:13

JOYFUL

Make a *j* shout to the . . . . Ps 100:1
And make them *j* . . . . Is 56:7

JUDGE

The LORD *j* between . . . . . Gen 16:5
coming to *j* the earth . 1 Chr 16:33
sword The LORD will *j* . . . . Is 66:16
deliver you to the *j* . . . . . . Matt 5:25
"*J* not . . . . Matt 7:1
who made Me a *j* . . . . . Luke 12:14
j who did not fear God . Luke 18:2
As I hear, I *j* . . . . John 5:30
"Do not *j* according . . . . John 7:24
I *j* no one . . . . John 8:15
j the world but to . . . . . John 12:47
this, O man, you who *j* . . . Rom 2:3
Therefore let us not *j* . . Rom 14:13
Christ, who will *j* . . . . 2 Tim 4:1
But if you *j* the law . . . James 4:11

JUDGES

He makes the *j* of the . . . . Is 40:23
For the Father *j* . . . . John 5:22
he who is spiritual *j* . . . 1 Cor 2:15
j me is the Lord . . . . 1 Cor 4:4
Him who *j* righteously . . 1 Pet 2:23

JUDGMENT

Teach me good *j* . . . . Ps 119:66
from prison and from *j* . . . . Is 53:8
be in danger of the *j* . . . . Matt 5:21
shall not come into *j* . . . . . John 5:24
and My *j* is righteous . . . . John 5:30
if I do judge, My *j* . . . . . . John 8:16
"Now is the *j* . . . . John 12:31
the righteous *j* . . . . Rom 1:32
j which came from one . Rom 5:16
appear before the *j* . . . . 2 Cor 5:10
after this the *j* . . . . Heb 9:27
time has come for *j* . . . . 1 Pet 4:17
a long time their *j* . . . . . . 2 Pet 2:3
darkness for the *j* . . . . Jude 6

JUDGMENTS

The *j* of the LORD are . . . . . Ps 19:9
unsearchable are His *j* . Rom 11:33

JUST

Noah was a *j* man . . . . Gen 6:9
j man who perishes . . . . . Eccl 7:15
j shall live by his . . . . Hab 2:4
her husband, being a *j* . . Matt 1:19
resurrection of the *j* . . . . Luke 14:14
j persons who need no . Luke 15:7
the Holy One and the *J* . Acts 3:14
dead, both of the *j* . . . . . Acts 24:15
j shall live by faith . . . . . . Rom 1:17
that He might be *j* . . . . . . Rom 3:26
j men made perfect . . . . Heb 12:23
have murdered the *j* . . . . James 5:6
He is faithful and *j* . . . . 1 John 1:9

JUSTICE

j as the noonday . . . . Ps 37:6
And Your poor with *j* . . . . . Ps 72:2
j the measuring line . . . . . . Is 28:17
the LORD is a God of *j* . . . . Is 30:18
He will bring forth *j* . . . . . . Is 42:1
J is turned back . . . . Is 59:14
I, the LORD, love *j* . . . . Is 61:8
truth, and His ways *j* . . . . . Dan 4:37
'Execute true *j* . . . . Zech 7:9
"Where is the God of *j* . . . . Mal 2:17
And He will declare j . . Matt 12:18
His humiliation His j . . . . Acts 8:33

JUSTIFICATION

because of our *j* . . . . Rom 4:25
offenses resulted in *j* . . . Rom 5:16

JUSTIFIED

Me that you may be *j* . . . . Job 40:8
words you will be *j* . . . . Matt 12:37
"But wisdom is *j* . . . . Luke 7:35
j rather than the . . . . . . Luke 18:14
who believes is *j* . . . . . . Acts 13:39
"That You may be j . . . . . . Rom 3:4
law no flesh will be *j* . . . . Rom 3:20
j freely by His grace . . . . . Rom 3:24
having been *j* by . . . . Rom 5:1
these He also *j* . . . . Rom 8:30
that we might be *j* . . . . Gal 2:16
no flesh shall be *j* . . . . Gal 2:16
the harlot also *j* . . . . James 2:25

JUSTIFIES

He who *j* the wicked . . . Prov 17:15
It is God who *j* . . . . Rom 8:33

JUSTIFY

wanting to *j* himself . . . Luke 10:29
"You are those who *j* . . Luke 16:15
is one God who will *j* . . . Rom 3:30

K

KEEP

k you wherever you . . . . Gen 28:15
day, to *k* it holy . . . . Ex 20:8
and destroy *k* . . . . Ps 3:6

Let all the earth *k* . . . . . . Hab 2:20
k the commandments . . . Matt 19:17
"If you love Me, *k* . . . . . John 14:15
k through Your name . . John 17:11
orderly and *k* the law . . Acts 21:24
k the unity of the . . . . Eph 4:3
k His commandments . . 1 John 2:3

KEEPER

Am I my brother's *k* . . . . . Gen 4:9
The LORD is your *k* . . . . . Ps 121:5

KEEPS

k truth forever . . . . Ps 146:6
k the commandment . . . Prov 19:16
none of you *k* the law . . . John 7:19
born of God *k* . . . . 1 John 5:18
and *k* his garments . . . . . Rev 16:15

KEPT

For I have *k* the . . . . . . 2 Sam 22:22
these things I have *k* . . . Matt 19:20
love, just as I have *k* . . . John 15:10
k back part of the . . . . Acts 5:2
I have *k* the faith . . . . . . 2 Tim 4:7
who are *k* by the power . 1 Pet 1:5

KEY

taken away the *k* . . . . . Luke 11:52
"He who has the k . . . . Rev 3:7

KEYS

I will give you the *k* . . . Matt 16:19
And I have the *k* . . . . Rev 1:18

KILL

k the Passover . . . . Ex 12:21
I *k* and I make alive . . . Deut 32:39
"Am I God, to *k* . . . . 2 Kin 5:7
A time to *k* . . . . Eccl 3:3
of them they will *k* . . . . Luke 11:49
afraid of those who *k* . . . Luke 12:4
Why do you seek to *k* . . . John 7:19
k and eat . . . . Acts 10:13

KILLED

Abel his brother and *k* . . . Gen 4:8
for Your sake we are *k* . . Ps 44:22
and scribes, and be *k* . . Matt 16:21
Siloam fell and *k* them . Luke 13:4
k the Prince of life . . . . . . Acts 3:15
Your sake we are k . . . . . . Rom 8:36
k both the Lord . . . . . 1 Thess 2:15

KILLS

the one who *k* the . . . . . Matt 23:37
for the letter *k* . . . . 2 Cor 3:6

KIND

animals after their *k* . . . . Gen 6:20
k can come out by . . . . . Mark 9:29
suffers long and is *k* . . . 1 Cor 13:4
And be *k* to one . . . . Eph 4:32

KINDLY

Julius treated Paul *k* . . . Acts 27:3
k affectionate to one . . . Rom 12:10

KINDNESS

For His merciful *k* . . . . Ps 117:2
k shall not depart . . . . Is 54:10
I remember you, The *k* . . . . Jer 2:2
by longsuffering, by *k* . . . 2 Cor 6:6
longsuffering, *k* . . . . Gal 5:22
and to brotherly *k* . . . . . . 2 Pet 1:7

KING

"Yet I have set My *K* . . . . . . Ps 2:6
The LORD is *K* forever . . . Ps 10:16
And the *K* of glory . . . . Ps 24:7
For God is my *K* . . . . Ps 74:12
when your *k* is a child . Eccl 10:16
and the everlasting *K* . . . . Jer 10:10
the LORD shall be *K* . . . . . Zech 14:9
who has been born *K* . . . . Matt 2:2

This Is Jesus The *K* . . . . . Matt 27:37
"Behold your *K* . . . . John 19:14
Now to the *K* eternal . . . . 1 Tim 1:17
only Potentate, the *K* . . . 1 Tim 6:15
this Melchizedek, *k* . . . . . . Heb 7:1
K of Kings and Lord . . . . Rev 19:16

KINGDOM

Yours is the *k* . . . . 1 Chr 29:11
k is the LORD'S . . . . Ps 22:28
the scepter of Your *k* . . . . . Ps 45:6
is an everlasting *k* . . . . . . Ps 145:13
k which shall never be . . . Dan 2:44
High rules in the *k* . . . . . . Dan 4:17
"Repent, for the *k* . . . . Matt 3:2
for Yours is the *k* . . . . Matt 6:13
"But seek first the *k* . . . . Matt 6:33
the mysteries of the *k* . Matt 13:11
are the sons of the *k* . . . Matt 13:38
of such is the *k* . . . . Matt 19:14
back, is fit for the *k* . . . . Luke 9:62
against nation, and *k* . . Luke 21:10
he cannot see the *k* . . . . . John 3:3
he cannot enter the *k* . . . . John 3:5
If My *k* were of this . . . . John 18:36
for the *k* of God is . . . . . . Rom 14:17
will not inherit the *k* . . . . . Gal 5:21
the scepter of Your k . . . . . Heb 1:8
we are receiving a *k* . . . . Heb 12:28

KINGDOMS

the *k* were moved . . . . Ps 46:6
showed Him all the *k* . . . Matt 4:8
have become the *k* . . . . . Rev 11:15

KINGS

The *k* of the earth set . . . . . . Ps 2:2
By me *k* reign . . . . Prov 8:15
governors and *k* . . . . Matt 10:18
k have desired to see . . Luke 10:24
You have reigned as *k* . . . 1 Cor 4:8
and has made us *k* . . . . Rev 1:6
that the way of the *k* . . . . Rev 16:12

KISS

K the Son . . . . Ps 2:12
"You gave Me no *k* . . . . . Luke 7:45
one another with a *k* . . . 1 Pet 5:14

KISSED

they *k* one another . . . . 1 Sam 20:41
and *k* Him . . . . Matt 26:49
and she *k* His feet and . Luke 7:38

KNEE

That to Me every *k* . . . . Is 45:23
have not bowed the k . . . . . Rom 11:4
of Jesus every *k* . . . . Phil 2:10

KNEES

make firm the feeble *k* . . . . . Is 35:3
this reason I bow my *k* . . . Eph 3:14
and the feeble *k* . . . . Heb 12:12

KNEW

in the womb I *k* . . . . Jer 1:5
to them, 'I never *k* . . . . . . Matt 7:23
k what was in man . . . . . . John 2:25
He made Him who *k* . . . . 2 Cor 5:21

KNIT

be encouraged, being *k* . . . . Col 2:2

KNOCK

k, and it will be . . . . Matt 7:7
at the door and *k* . . . . Rev 3:20

KNOW

k good and evil . . . . Gen 3:22
k that I am the LORD . . . . Ex 6:7
k that my Redeemer . . . . Job 19:25
make me to *k* wisdom . . . . . Ps 51:6
Who can *k* it . . . . Jer 17:9
saying, '*K* the LORD . . . . . . Jer 31:34
k what hour your . . . . Matt 24:42

an oath, "I do not *k* . . . Matt 26:72
the world did not *k* . . . . . John 1:10
We speak what We *k* . . . John 3:11
k that You are . . . . John 6:69
My voice, and I *k* . . . . . John 10:27
If you *k* these things . . John 13:17
k whom I have . . . . John 13:18
are sure that You *k* . . . . John 16:30
k that I love You . . . . . . John 21:15
k times or seasons . . . . Acts 1:7
and said, "Jesus I *k* . . . . Acts 19:15
wisdom did not *k* . . . . . . 1 Cor 1:21
nor can he *k* them . . . . . 1 Cor 2:14
For we *k* in part and . . . . 1 Cor 13:9
k the love of Christ . . . . . Eph 3:19
k whom I have . . . . 2 Tim 1:12
we *k* that we *k* Him . . . . 1 John 2:3
and you *k* all things . . 1 John 2:20
By this we *k* love . . . . . 1 John 3:16
k that He abides . . . . . . 1 John 3:24
k that we are of God . . 1 John 5:19
"I *k* your works . . . . Rev 2:2

KNOWLEDGE

and the tree of the *k* . . . . . Gen 2:9
unto night reveals *k* . . . . . . Ps 19:2
k is too wonderful . . . . Ps 139:6
people store up *k* . . . . . . Prov 10:14
k spares his words . . . . . Prov 17:27
and he who increases *k* . Eccl 1:18
k is that wisdom . . . . Eccl 7:12
k shall increase . . . . Dan 12:4
more accurate *k* . . . . Acts 24:22
having the form of *k* . . . . Rom 2:20
law is the *k* of sin . . . . . Rom 3:20
whether there is *k* . . . . . 1 Cor 13:8
Christ which passes *k* . . . Eph 3:19
is falsely called *k* . . . . . 1 Tim 6:20
in the grace and *k* . . . . . 2 Pet 3:18

KNOWN

If you had *k* Me . . . . John 8:19
My sheep, and am *k* . . . John 10:14
The world has not *k* . . . John 17:25
peace they have not k . . Rom 3:17
"For who has k . . . . Rom 11:34
after you have *k* . . . . Gal 4:9
requests be made *k* . . . . Phil 4:6
k the Holy Scriptures . . 2 Tim 3:15

KNOWS

"For God *k* that in . . . . Gen 3:5
k what is in the . . . . Dan 2:22
k the things you have . . . . Matt 6:8
and hour no one *k* . . . . . Matt 24:36
God *k* your hearts . . . . . . Luke 16:15
searches the hearts *k* . . . Rom 8:27
k the things of God . . . . 1 Cor 2:11
k those who are His . . . . 2 Tim 2:19
to him who *k* to do . . . . James 4:17
and *k* all things . . . . . . 1 John 3:20

L

LABOR

Six days you shall *l* . . . . . . Ex 20:9
things are full of *l* . . . . Eccl 1:8
has man for all his *l* . . . . Eccl 2:22
He shall see the *l* . . . . Is 53:11
to Me, all you who *l* . . . Matt 11:28
"Do not *l* for the . . . . John 6:27
knowing that your *l* . . 1 Cor 15:58
but rather let him *l* . . . . . . Eph 4:28
mean fruit from my *l* . . . . . Phil 1:22
your work of faith, *l* . . 1 Thess 1:3
forget your work and *l* . . Heb 6:10
your works, your *l* . . . . Rev 2:2

LABORED

l more abundantly . . . . 1 Cor 15:10
for you, lest I have *l* . . . . . Gal 4:11

LABORERS

but the *l* are few . . . . Matt 9:37

LABORING

l night and day . . . . 1 Thess 2:9

LABORS

entered into their *l* . . . . . . John 4:38
creation groans and *l* . . . Rom 8:22
l more abundant . . . . . . 2 Cor 11:23
may rest from their *l* . . . . Rev 14:13

LACK

What do I still *l* . . . . Matt 19:20
"One thing you *l* . . . . . Mark 10:21

LADDER

and behold, a *l* . . . . Gen 28:12

LAID

the place where they *l* . Mark 16:6
"Where have you *l* . . . . John 11:34

LAKE

cast alive into the *l* . . . . Rev 19:20

LAMB

but where is the *l* . . . . Gen 22:7
He was led as a *l* . . . . Is 53:7
The *L* of God who . . . . John 1:29
the elders, stood a *L* . . . . . . Rev 5:6
"Worthy is the *L* . . . . Rev 5:12
by the blood of the *L* . . . Rev 12:11

LAME

l shall leap like a . . . . Is 35:6
blind see and the *l* . . . . . Matt 11:5
And a certain man *l* . . . . . . Acts 3:2

LAMENTATION

was heard in Ramah, l . . Matt 2:18
and made great *l* . . . . Acts 8:2

LAMP

Your word is a *l* . . . . Ps 119:105
the *l* of the wicked . . . . . . Prov 13:9
his *l* will be put out . . . . Prov 20:20
"Nor do they light a *l* . . . . Matt 5:15
"The *l* of the body . . . . Matt 6:22
when he has lit a *l* . . . . . . Luke 8:16
l gives you light . . . . Luke 11:36
does not light a *l* . . . . Luke 15:8
burning and shining *l* . . John 5:35

LAMPS

he made its seven *l* . . . . . . Ex 37:23
and trimmed their *l* . . . . . Matt 25:7

LAMPSTAND

branches of the *l* . . . . Ex 25:32
a basket, but on a *l* . . . . . Matt 5:15
and remove your *l* . . . . Rev 2:5

LAND

l that I will show you . . . Gen 12:1
l flowing with milk . . . . Ex 3:8
They will see the *l* . . . . Is 33:17
Bethlehem, in the l . . . . Matt 2:6

LANGUAGE

whole earth had one *l* . . . Gen 11:1
speak in his own *l* . . . . Acts 2:6
blasphemy, filthy *l* . . . . Col 3:8

LANGUAGES

according to their *l* . . . . Gen 10:20

LAST

He shall stand at *l* . . . . Job 19:25
First and I am the *L* . . . . Is 44:6
l will be first . . . . Matt 20:16
the First and the *L* . . . . Rev 1:11

LATTER

l times some will . . . . 1 Tim 4:1

LAUGH

"Why did Sarah *l* . . . . . . Gen 18:13
Woe to you who *l* . . . . . . Luke 6:25

LAUGHS

The Lord *l* at him . . . . Ps 37:13

LAUGHTER

your *l* be turned to . . . . . James 4:9

LAW

stones a copy of the *l* . . . Josh 8:32
The *l* of the LORD is . . . . Ps 19:7
I delight in Your *l* . . . . . . Ps 119:70
Oh, how I love Your *l* . . . Ps 119:97
And Your *l* is truth . . . . Ps 119:142
l will proceed from Me . . . . Is 51:4
in whose heart is My *l* . . . . . Is 51:7
The *L* is no more . . . . Lam 2:9
The *l* of truth was in . . . . . Mal 2:6
to destroy the *L* . . . . Matt 5:17
for this is the *L* . . . . Matt 7:12
hang all the *L* and the . . Matt 22:40
"The *l* and the . . . . Luke 16:16
l was given through . . . . John 1:17
"Does our *l* judge a . . . . . John 7:51
l is the knowledge . . . . . . Rom 3:20
because the *l* brings . . . . Rom 4:15
when there is no *l* . . . . . . Rom 5:13
you are not under *l* . . . . . Rom 6:14
For what the *l* could . . . . . Rom 8:3
l that I might live . . . . Gal 2:19
under guard by the *l* . . . . . Gal 3:23
born under the *l* . . . . Gal 4:4
l is fulfilled in one . . . . Gal 5:14
into the perfect *l* . . . . . . James 1:25
fulfill the royal *l* . . . . James 2:8

LAWFUL

Is it *l* to pay taxes . . . . . Matt 22:17
All things are *l* . . . . 1 Cor 6:12

LAWGIVER

There is one *L* . . . . James 4:12

LAWLESS

l one will be revealed . 2 Thess 2:8

LAWLESSNESS

Me, you who practice *l* . Matt 7:23
l is already at work . . . 2 Thess 2:7

LAWYERS

"Woe to you also, *l* . . . Luke 11:46

LAY

nowhere to *l* His head . . Matt 8:20
l hands may receive . . . . . Acts 8:19

LAZINESS

l the building decays . . . Eccl 10:18

LAZY

l man will be put to . . . . Prov 12:24
wicked and *l* servant . . . Matt 25:26
liars, evil beasts, *l* . . . . . . Titus 1:12

LEAD

L me in Your truth and . . . Ps 25:5
And do not *l* us into . . . . . Matt 6:13
"Can the blind *l* . . . . Luke 6:39

LEADS

He *l* me in the paths . . . . Ps 23:3
And if the blind *l* . . . . . . Matt 15:14

LEAF

plucked olive *l* . . . . Gen 8:11

LEAN

all your heart, And *l* . . . . . . Prov 3:5

LEAP

Then the lame shall *l* . . . . . . Is 35:6

LEARN
L to do good . . . . Is 1:17
yoke upon you and *l* . . . Matt 11:29

LEARNED
Me The tongue of the *l* . . . . Is 50:4
have not so *l* Christ . . . . . Eph 4:20
in all things I have *l* . . . . Phil 4:12

LEARNING
l is driving you mad . . . Acts 26:24

LEAST
so, shall be called *l* . . . . . Matt 5:19

LEAVE
a man shall *l* his . . . . Gen 2:24
For You will not *l* . . . . Ps 16:10
"I will never l . . . . Heb 13:5

LEAVEN
of heaven is like *l* . . . . . Matt 13:33
l leavens the whole . . . . . . Gal 5:9

LEAVES
and they sewed fig *l* . . . . . Gen 3:7
The *l* of the tree . . . . Rev 22:2

LED
l them forth by the . . . . . . Ps 107:7
For as many as are *l* . . . . Rom 8:14

LEFT
l hand know what your . . Matt 6:3

LEND
"And if you *l* . . . . Luke 6:34

LENDER
is servant to the *l* . . . . Prov 22:7

LENDS
ever merciful, and *l* . . . . Ps 37:26

LENGTH
is your life and the *l* . . . Deut 30:20

LEOPARD
or the *l* its spots . . . . Jer 13:23

LEPERS
"And many *l* were in . . . Luke 4:27

LET
"*L* there be light . . . . Gen 1:3

LETTER
for the *l* kills . . . . 2 Cor 3:6
or by word or by *l* . . . . 2 Thess 2:2

LETTERS
does this Man know *l* . . John 7:15

LEVIATHAN
"Can you draw out *L* . . . . Job 41:1

LEVITE
"Likewise a *L* . . . . Luke 10:32

LEWDNESS
wickedness, deceit, *l* . . . . Mark 7:22

LIAR
for he is a *l* and the . . . . John 8:44
but every man a *l* . . . . Rom 3:4
we make Him a *l* . . . . . 1 John 1:10
his brother, he is a *l* . . 1 John 4:20

LIARS
"All men are *l* . . . . Ps 116:11
l shall have their . . . . Rev 21:8

LIBERALITY
he who gives, with *l* . . . . Rom 12:8

LIBERALLY
who gives to all *l* . . . . James 1:5

LIBERTY
year, and proclaim *l* . . . . Lev 25:10
'To proclaim l to the . . . . Luke 4:18
into the glorious *l* . . . . . . Rom 8:21
Lord is, there is *l* . . . . . . 2 Cor 3:17
therefore in the *l* . . . . Gal 5:1

LIE
Do not *l* to one . . . . Col 3:9
God, who cannot *l* . . . . Titus 1:2
an abomination or a *l* . . Rev 21:27

LIED
You have not *l* to men . . . Acts 5:4

LIES
sin *l* at the door . . . . Gen 4:7
speaking *l* in . . . . 1 Tim 4:2

LIFE
the breath of *l* . . . . Gen 2:7
'For the *l* of the . . . . Lev 17:11
before you today *l* . . . . Deut 30:15
He will redeem their *l* . . . . Ps 72:14
word has given me *l* . . . . Ps 119:50
She is a tree of *l* . . . . Prov 3:18
finds me finds *l* . . . . Prov 8:35
L is more than . . . . Luke 12:23
l was the light . . . . John 1:4
so the Son gives *l* . . . . John 5:21
spirit, and they are *l* . . . . John 6:63
have the light of *l* . . . . John 8:12
and I lay down My *l* . . . . John 10:15
resurrection and the *l* . . John 11:25
you lay down your *l* . . . John 13:38
l which I now live . . . . Gal 2:20
l is hidden with . . . . Col 3:3
For what is your *l* . . . . . . James 4:14
l was manifested . . . . 1 John 1:2
and the pride of *l* . . . . . 1 John 2:16
has given us eternal *l* . 1 John 5:11
the Lamb's Book of *L* . . . Rev 21:27
right to the tree of *l* . . . Rev 22:14
the water of *l* freely . . . . Rev 22:17
from the Book of *L* . . . . . Rev 22:19

LIFT
I will *l* up my eyes to . . . . Ps 121:1
Lord, and He will *l* . . . . James 4:10

LIFTED
your heart is *l* . . . . Ezek 28:2
in Hades, he *l* up his . . Luke 16:23
the Son of Man be *l* . . . . . John 3:14
"And I, if I am *l* . . . . John 12:32

LIGHT
"Let there be *l* . . . . Gen 1:3
The LORD is my *l* . . . . Ps 27:1
and a *l* to my path . . . . Ps 119:105
The *l* of the righteous . . . Prov 13:9
The LORD gives *l* . . . . Prov 29:13
Truly the *l* is sweet . . . . . . Eccl 11:7
let us walk in the *l* . . . . Is 2:5
l shall break forth . . . . Is 58:8
"You are the *l* . . . . Matt 5:14
"Let your *l* so shine . . . . Matt 5:16
than the sons of *l* . . . . . . Luke 16:8
and the life was the *l* . . . . . John 1:4
darkness rather than *l* . . John 3:19
saying, "I am the *l* . . . . . John 8:12
God who commanded *l* . 2 Cor 4:6
Walk as children of *l* . . . . . Eph 5:8
You are all sons of *l* 1 Thess 5:5
into His marvelous *l* . . . . . 1 Pet 2:9
to you, that God is *l* . . . . 1 John 1:5
l as He is in the . . . . 1 John 1:7
says he is in the *l* . . . . . . 1 John 2:9
The Lamb is its *l* . . . . Rev 21:23

LIGHTNING
"For as the *l* . . . . Matt 24:27
countenance was like *l* . . Matt 28:3

LIGHTNINGS
the throne proceeded *l* . . . Rev 4:5

LIGHTS
"Let there be *l* . . . . Gen 1:14
whom you shine as *l* . . . . Phil 2:15

LIKENESS
according to Our *l* . . . . . . Gen 1:26
carved image—any *l* . . . . . . Ex 20:4
when I awake in Your *l* . . Ps 17:15
and coming in the *l* . . . . . . Phil 2:7

LILY
the *l* of the valleys . . . . . . Song 2:1

LIMIT
to the sea its *l* . . . . Prov 8:29

LINE
upon precept, *L* upon . . . . Is 28:10
I am setting a plumb *l* . . Amos 7:8

LINEN
wrapped Him in the *l* . Mark 15:46

LINGER
salvation shall not *l* . . . . . . Is 46:13

LION
l shall eat straw . . . . Is 11:7

LIONS
the mouths of *l* . . . . Heb 11:33

LIPS
off all flattering *l* . . . . Ps 12:3
The *l* of the righteous . . Prov 10:21
But the *l* of . . . . Prov 20:15
am a man of unclean *l* . . . . . Is 6:5
other l I will speak . . . 1 Cor 14:21
from evil, And his l . . . . 1 Pet 3:10

LISTEN
you are not able to *l* . . . . John 8:43
you who fear God, *l* . . . Acts 13:16

LISTENS
But whoever *l* to me . . . . Prov 1:33

LITTLE
Though you are *l* . . . . Mic 5:2
l ones only a cup . . . . . Matt 10:42
"O you of *l* faith . . . . . . Matt 14:31
to whom *l* is forgiven . . Luke 7:47
faithful in a very *l* . . . . Luke 19:17

LIVE
eat, and *l* forever . . . . Gen 3:22
a man does, he shall *l* . . . Lev 18:5
"Seek Me and *l* . . . . Amos 5:4
But the just shall *l* . . . . Hab 2:4
l by bread alone . . . . Matt 4:4
"for in Him we *l* . . . . Acts 17:28
l peaceably with all . . . . Rom 12:18
the life which I now *l* . . . . Gal 2:20
If we *l* in the Spirit . . . . . . Gal 5:25
to me, to *l* is Christ . . . . . Phil 1:21

LIVED
died and rose and *l* . . . . . Rom 14:9
And they *l* and reigned . . Rev 20:4

LIVES
but man *l* by every . . . . . . Deut 8:3
but Christ *l* in me . . . . Gal 2:20
to lay down our *l* . . . . . 1 John 3:16
"I am He who *l* . . . . Rev 1:18

LIVING
and man became a *l* . . . . . . Gen 2:7
in the light of the *l* . . . . . Ps 56:13

M

MAIDSERVANT
"Behold the *m* . . . . Luke 1:38

MAIDSERVANTS
m I will pour out My . . . . Acts 2:18

MAJESTY
right hand of the *M* . . . . . Heb 1:3
eyewitnesses of His *m* . . 2 Pet 1:16
wise, Be glory and *m* . . . . . Jude 25

MAKE
"Let Us *m* man in Our . . Gen 1:26
m you a great nation . . . . Gen 12:2
"You shall not *m* . . . . Ex 20:4
m Our home with . . . . . John 14:23

MAKER
M is your husband . . . . Is 54:5
has forgotten his *M* . . . . . Hos 8:14
builder and *m* is God . . Heb 11:10

MALICE
in *m* be babes . . . . 1 Cor 14:20
laying aside all *m* . . . . 1 Pet 2:1

MAN
"Let Us make *m* . . . . Gen 1:26
m that You are mindful . . . . . Ps 8:4
of the Son of *M* . . . . Matt 24:27
"Behold the *M* . . . . John 19:5
by *m* came death . . . . . 1 Cor 15:21
our outward *m* . . . . 2 Cor 4:16
the *m* of God may . . . . . 2 Tim 3:17
is the number of a *m* . . . Rev 13:18

MANGER
and laid Him in a *m* . . . . . Luke 2:7

MANIFEST
m Myself to him . . . . . John 14:21

MANIFESTATION
But the *m* of the . . . . 1 Cor 12:7

MANIFESTED
"I have *m* Your name . . John 17:6
God was *m* in the . . . . . 1 Tim 3:16
the life was *m* . . . . 1 John 1:2

MANIFOLD
the *m* wisdom of God . . . . Eph 3:10

MANNA
of Israel ate *m* . . . . Ex 16:35
"Our fathers ate the *m* . John 6:31

MANNER
Is this the *m* of man . . . 2 Sam 7:19
in an unworthy *m* . . . . 1 Cor 11:27
what *m* of love . . . . 1 John 3:1

MANSIONS
house are many *m* . . . . . John 14:2

MANTLE
Then he took the *m* . . . . . 2 Kin 2:14

MARK
And the LORD set a *m* . . . Gen 4:15
receives the *m* . . . . Rev 14:11

MARRED
So His visage was *m* . . . . . Is 52:14

MARRIAGE
M is honorable among . . Heb 13:4

MARRIED
But he who is *m* . . . . 1 Cor 7:33

MARRY
they neither *m* nor . . . . Matt 22:30
forbidding to *m* . . . . 1 Tim 4:3

MARRYING
and drinking, *m* . . . . Matt 24:38

MARTYRS
the blood of the *m* . . . . Rev 17:6

MARVELED
Jesus heard it, He *m* . . . . Matt 8:10
so that Pilate *m* . . . . Mark 15:5

MARVELOUS
It is *m* in our eyes . . . . . . Ps 118:23
of darkness into His *m* . . 1 Pet 2:9

MASTER
a servant like his *m* . . . Matt 10:25
greater than his *m* . . . . John 15:20
and useful for the *M* . . . 2 Tim 2:21

MASTERS
can serve two *m* . . . . . . Luke 16:13
who have believing *m* . . . 1 Tim 6:2

MATTERS
the weightier *m* . . . . Matt 23:23

MATURE
understanding be *m* . . . 1 Cor 14:20
us, as many as are *m* . . . . Phil 3:15

MEANT
but God *m* it for good . . Gen 50:20

MEASURE
a perfect and just *m* . . . Deut 25:15
give the Spirit by *m* . . . . . John 3:34
to each one a *m* . . . . Rom 12:3

MEASURED
m the waters in the . . . . . . Is 40:12
you use, it will be *m* . . . . . Matt 7:2

MEASURES
house differing *m* . . . . . Deut 25:14

MEASURING
behold, a man with a *m* . . Zech 2:1
m themselves by . . . . . 2 Cor 10:12

MEAT
will never again eat *m* . 1 Cor 8:13

MEDIATOR
by the hand of a *m* . . . . . . Gal 3:19
is one God and one *M* . . 1 Tim 2:5
to Jesus the *M* of the . . . Heb 12:24

MEDICINE
does good, like *m* . . . . . Prov 17:22

MEDICINES
you will use many *m* . . . . Jer 46:11

MEDITATE
but you shall *m* . . . . Josh 1:8
M within your heart on . . . . Ps 4:4
I will *m* on Your . . . . Ps 119:15
m beforehand on . . . . . . Luke 21:14
m on these things . . . . Phil 4:8

MEDITATES
in His law he *m* . . . . Ps 1:2

MEDITATION
of my mouth and the *m* . . Ps 19:14
It is my *m* all the day . . . Ps 119:97

MEDIUM
a woman who is a *m* . . . Lev 20:27

MEDIUM'S
shall be like a *m* . . . . Is 29:4

MEDIUMS
"Seek those who are *m* . . . . Is 8:19

MEEK
with equity for the *m* . . . . . . Is 11:4
Blessed are the *m* . . . . Matt 5:5

MEEKNESS
are done in the *m* . . . . . James 3:13

MEET
prepare to *m* your . . . . . Amos 4:12
m the Lord in the . . . . 1 Thess 4:17

MELODY
singing and making *m* . . Eph 5:19

MELT
the elements will *m* . . . . 2 Pet 3:10

MEMBER
body is not one *m* . . . . 1 Cor 12:14

MEMBERS
you that one of your *m* . . Matt 5:29
do not present your *m* . . Rom 6:13
neighbor, for we are *m* . . Eph 4:25

MEMORIAL
and this is My *m* . . . . Ex 3:15
also be told as a *m* . . . . Matt 26:13

MEMORY
The *m* of the righteous . Prov 10:7

MEN
m began to call on the . . Gen 4:26
make you fishers of *m* . . Matt 4:19
goodwill toward *m* . . . . . Luke 2:14
heaven or from *m* . . . . . Luke 20:4
Likewise also the *m* . . . . . Rom 1:27
the Lord, and not to *m* . . . Eph 6:7
between God and *m* . . . . 1 Tim 2:5

MENSERVANTS
And also on My *m* . . . . . . Joel 2:29
And on My m and on . . . Acts 2:18

MERCHANDISE
house a house of *m* . . . . . John 2:16

MERCIES
give you the sure m . . . Acts 13:34

MERCIFUL
LORD, the LORD God, *m* . . . Ex 34:6
He is ever *m* . . . . Ps 37:26
Blessed are the *m* . . . . Matt 5:7
saying, 'God be *m* . . . . Luke 18:13
"For I will be m . . . . Heb 8:12

MERCY
but showing *m* to . . . . Ex 20:6
and abundant in *m* . . . . . Num 14:18
m endures forever . . . . . 1 Chr 16:34
M and truth have met . . . . Ps 85:10
m is everlasting . . . . Ps 100:5
Let not *m* and truth . . . . Prov 3:3
For I desire *m* and not . . . . Hos 6:6
do justly, To love *m* . . . . Mic 6:8
'I desire m and not . . . . . Matt 9:13
And His *m* is on those . . Luke 1:50
"I will have m . . . . Rom 9:15
that He might have *m* . . Rom 11:32
m has made . . . . 1 Cor 7:25
as we have received *m* . . 2 Cor 4:1
God, who is rich in *m* . . . . . Eph 2:4
but I obtained *m* . . . . 1 Tim 1:13
that he may find *m* . . . . . 2 Tim 1:18
to His *m* He saved us . . . . Titus 3:5
that we may obtain *m* . . . . Heb 4:16

MERRY
m heart makes a . . . . Prov 15:13
we should make *m* . . . . Luke 15:32

MESSENGER
"Behold, I send My *m* ....Mal 3:1
'Behold, I send My m ..Matt 11:10

MESSIAH
Until *M* the Prince ......Dan 9:25
"We have found the *M* .John 1:41

MIDST
God is in the *m* ....Ps 46:5
I am there in the *m* ....Matt 18:20

MIGHT
'My power and the *m* ...Deut 8:17
'Not by *m* nor by ....Zech 4:6
in the power of His *m* ...Eph 6:10
honor and power and *m* .Rev 7:12

MIGHTIER
coming after me is *m* ....Matt 3:11

MIGHTY
He was a *m* hunter ......Gen 10:9
m have fallen ....2 Sam 1:19
The LORD *m* in battle ......Ps 24:8
their Redeemer is *m* ...Prov 23:11
m has done great ......Luke 1:49
the flesh, not many *m* .1 Cor 1:26
the working of His *m* ...Eph 1:19

MILK
come, buy wine and *m* .....Is 55:1
shall flow with *m* ....Joel 3:18
have come to need *m*....Heb 5:12
desire the pure *m* ....1 Pet 2:2

MILLSTONE
m were hung around .....Matt 18:6
a stone like a great *m* ..Rev 18:21

MIND
put wisdom in the *m*....Job 38:36
perfect peace, Whose *m* ...Is 26:3
have an anxious *m* .....Luke 12:29
m I myself serve the .....Rom 7:25
who has known the m .Rom 11:34
Be of the same *m* ....Rom 12:16
in his own *m* ....Rom 14:5
has known the m ......1 Cor 2:16
are out of your *m* .....1 Cor 14:23
Let this *m* be in you ....Phil 2:5
love and of a sound *m* ..2 Tim 1:7

MINDFUL
is man that You are *m* ......Ps 8:4
for you are not *m* ....Matt 16:23
is man that You are m.......Heb 2:6

MINDS
put My law in their *m* ...Jer 31:33
I stir up your pure *m* ....2 Pet 3:1

MINISTER
For he is God's *m* ....Rom 13:4
you will be a good *m* ...1 Tim 4:6

MINISTERS
for they are God's *m* .....Rom 13:6
If anyone *m* ....1 Pet 4:11

MINISTRIES
are differences of *m* ...1 Cor 12:5

MINISTRY
But if the *m* of death ....2 Cor 3:7
since we have this *m*....2 Cor 4:1
has given us the *m* ....2 Cor 5:18
for the work of *m* ....Eph 4:12
fulfill your *m* ....2 Tim 4:5
a more excellent *m* ....Heb 8:6

MIRACLE
one who works a *m* ......Mark 9:39

MIRACLES
worked unusual *m* ....Acts 19:11
the working of *m* .....1 Cor 12:10

MISERY
And remember his *m* ...Prov 31:7

MITES
putting in two *m* ....Luke 21:2

MOCK
Fools *m* at sin ....Prov 14:9
to the Gentiles to *m* .....Matt 20:19

MOCKED
noon, that Elijah *m* ...1 Kin 18:27
deceived, God is not *m*.....Gal 6:7

MOCKER
Wine is a *m* ....Prov 20:1

MOCKS
He who *m* the poor .....Prov 17:5

MODERATION
with propriety and *m* ...1 Tim 2:9

MOMENT
In a *m* they die ....Job 34:20
in a *m*, in the ....1 Cor 15:52

MONEY
be redeemed without *m* ....Is 52:3
And you who have no *m* ...Is 55:1
and hid his lord's *m* ....Matt 25:18
to give him *m* ....Mark 14:11
"Carry neither *m* ....Luke 10:4
I sent you without *m* ..Luke 22:35
be purchased with *m*....Acts 8:20
not greedy for *m* ....1 Tim 3:3
m is a root of all ....1 Tim 6:10

MONEYCHANGERS
the tables of the *m* ....Matt 21:12

MOON
until the *m* is no more ....Ps 72:7
m will not give its ....Mark 13:24

MORNING
Evening and *m* and at ...Ps 55:17
Lucifer, son of the *m* ....Is 14:12
very early in the *m* ......Luke 24:1
the Bright and *M* Star ..Rev 22:16

MORTAL
sin reign in your *m* ......Rom 6:12
and this *m* must put ..1 Cor 15:53

MORTALITY
m may be swallowed ....2 Cor 5:4

MOTH
where *m* and rust ....Matt 6:19

MOTHER
because she was the *m* ..Gen 3:20
leave his father and m ..Matt 19:5
"Behold your *m* ....John 19:27
The *M* of Harlots ....Rev 17:5

MOUNT
come up to *M* Sinai .....Ex 19:23
They shall *m* up with ....Is 40:31

MOUNTAIN
to Horeb, the *m* ....Ex 3:1
let us go up to the *m* ....Is 2:3
became a great *m* ....Dan 2:35
are you, O great *m* ....Zech 4:7
you will say to this *m*....Matt 17:20
Him on the holy *m* ....2 Pet 1:18

MOUNTAINS
m were brought forth ....Ps 90:2
m shall depart And the ....Is 54:10
in Judea flee to the *m* .Matt 24:16
that I could remove *m* .1 Cor 13:2

MOURN
A time to *m* ....Eccl 3:4
are those who *m* ....Matt 5:4
of the earth will *m* ....Rev 1:7

MOURNED
and have not rather *m* ..1 Cor 5:2

MOURNING
shall be a great *m* ......Zech 12:11
be turned to *m* and ....James 4:9

MOUTH
"Who has made man's *m* .Ex 4:11
Out of the *m* of babes ......Ps 8:2
knowledge, But the *m* .Prov 10:14
The *m* of an immoral ..Prov 22:14
And a flattering *m* ....Prov 26:28
m speaking pompous ....Dan 7:8
m defiles a man ....Matt 15:11
m I will judge you ....Luke 19:22
I will give you a *m* ....Luke 21:15
m confession is made ..Rom 10:10
m great swelling words ...Jude 16
vomit you out of My *m* ..Rev 3:16

MOVED
she shall not be *m* ....Ps 46:5
spoke as they were *m* ..2 Pet 1:21

MUCH
m study is ....Eccl 12:12
to whom *m* is given ...Luke 12:48

MULTIPLIED
of the disciples *m* ....Acts 6:7
of God grew and *m* ...Acts 12:24

MULTIPLY
"Be fruitful and *m* ......Gen 1:22
m the descendants ....Jer 33:22

MULTITUDE
stars of heaven in *m* ....Deut 1:10
In the *m* of words sin ..Prov 10:19
compassion on the *m* ..Matt 15:32
with the angel a *m* ....Luke 2:13
"love will cover a m ....1 Pet 4:8
and behold, a great *m* .....Rev 7:9

MURDER
"You shall not *m* ....Ex 20:13
'You shall not m ....Matt 5:21
You *m* and covet and ....James 4:2

MURDERED
up Jesus whom you *m* ..Acts 5:30

MURDERER
He was a *m* from the ...John 8:44
his brother is a *m* ....1 John 3:15

MURDERERS
and profane, for *m* .....1 Tim 1:9
abominable, *m* ....Rev 21:8

MURDERS
evil thoughts, *m* ....Matt 15:19

MUSING
while I was *m* ....Ps 39:3

MUTILATION
beware of the *m* ....Phil 3:2

MUZZLE
"You shall not m ....1 Tim 5:18

MYSTERIES
to you to know the *m* ... Matt 13:11
and understand all *m* ... 1 Cor 13:2

MYSTERY
given to know the *m* ... Mark 4:11
wisdom of God in a *m* ... 1 Cor 2:7
I tell you a *m* ... 1 Cor 15:51
made known to us the *m* ... Eph 1:9
the *m* of godliness ... 1 Tim 3:16

N

NAILED
n it to the cross ... Col 2:14

NAKED
And they were both *n* ... Gen 2:25
knew that they were *n* ... Gen 3:7
"*N* I came from my ... Job 1:21
'I was *n* and you ... Matt 25:36
but all things are *n* ... Heb 4:13
brother or sister is *n* ... James 2:15
poor, blind, and *n* ... Rev 3:17

NAKEDNESS
or famine, or *n* ... Rom 8:35
n may not be revealed ... Rev 3:18

NAME
Abram called on the *n* ... Gen 13:4
Israel shall be your *n* ... Gen 35:10
This is My *n* forever ... Ex 3:15
shall not take the *n* ... Ex 20:7
and awesome *n* ... Deut 28:58
excellent is Your *n* ... Ps 8:1
n will put their trust ... Ps 9:10
be His glorious *n* ... Ps 72:19
do not call on Your *n* ... Ps 79:6
to Your *n* give glory ... Ps 115:1
above all Your *n* ... Ps 138:2
A good *n* is to be ... Prov 22:1
what is His Son's *n* ... Prov 30:4
be called by a new *n* ... Is 62:2
Everlasting is Your *n* ... Is 63:16
They will call on My *n* ... Zech 13:9
to you who fear My *n* ... Mal 4:2
Hallowed be Your *n* ... Matt 6:9
prophesied in Your *n* ... Matt 7:22
n Gentiles will trust ... Matt 12:21
together in My *n* ... Matt 18:20
will come in My *n* ... Matt 24:5
who believe in His *n* ... John 1:12
comes in his own *n* ... John 5:43
his own sheep by *n* ... John 10:3
through faith in His *n* ... Acts 3:16
there is no other *n* ... Acts 4:12
which is above every *n* ... Phil 2:9
deed, do all in the *n* ... Col 3:17
a more excellent *n* ... Heb 1:4
you hold fast to My *n* ... Rev 2:13
n that you are alive ... Rev 3:1
having His Father's *n* ... Rev 14:1
and glorify Your *n* ... Rev 15:4
n written that no one ... Rev 19:12

NAMED
I have *n* you ... Is 45:4

NAME'S
saved them for His *n* ... Ps 106:8

NARROW
"Enter by the *n* gate ... Matt 7:13

NATION
make you a great *n* ... Gen 12:2
exalts a *n* ... Prov 14:34
n that was not called ... Is 65:1
make them one *n* ... Ezek 37:22
since there was a *n* ... Dan 12:1
n will rise against ... Matt 24:7
"for he loves our *n* ... Luke 7:5
those who are *not* a *n* ... Rom 10:19
tribe, tongue, and *n* ... Rev 13:7

NATIONS
Why do the *n* rage ... Ps 2:1
I will give You the *n* ... Ps 2:8
n shall serve Him ... Ps 72:11
disciples of all the *n* ... Matt 28:19
who was to rule all *n* ... Rev 12:5
the healing of the *n* ... Rev 22:2

NATURAL
exchanged the *n* ... Rom 1:26
the men, leaving the *n* ... Rom 1:27
did not spare the *n* ... Rom 11:21
n man does not ... 1 Cor 2:14
It is sown a *n* body ... 1 Cor 15:44

NATURE
"We who are Jews by *n* ... Gal 2:15
by *n* children of wrath ... Eph 2:3
of the divine *n* ... 2 Pet 1:4

NEAR
the word is very *n* ... Deut 30:14
upon Him while He is *n* ... Is 55:6
know that it is *n* ... Matt 24:33
kingdom of God is *n* ... Luke 21:31
"The word is n ... Rom 10:8
to those who were *n* ... Eph 2:17
for the time is *n* ... Rev 1:3

NEARER
now our salvation is *n* ... Rom 13:11

NEED
the things you have *n* ... Matt 6:8
supply all your *n* ... Phil 4:19
to help in time of *n* ... Heb 4:16

NEGLECT
if we *n* so great a ... Heb 2:3

NEGLECTED
n the weightier ... Matt 23:23

NEIGHBOR
'you shall love your n ... Lev 19:18
"You shall love your n ... Matt 5:43
"And who is my *n* ... Luke 10:29
"You shall love your n ... Rom 13:9

NEVER
in Me shall *n* thirst ... John 6:35
in Me shall *n* die ... John 11:26
Love *n* fails ... 1 Cor 13:8
n take away sins ... Heb 10:11
"I will n leave you ... Heb 13:5
prophecy *n* came by ... 2 Pet 1:21

NEW
And there is nothing *n* ... Eccl 1:9
"For behold, I create *n* ... Is 65:17
n every morning ... Lam 3:23
wine into *n* wineskins ... Matt 9:17
of the *n* covenant ... Matt 26:28
n commandment I ... John 13:34
he is a *n* creation ... 2 Cor 5:17
when I will make a n ... Heb 8:8
n heavens and a *n* ... 2 Pet 3:13
n name written which ... Rev 2:17
And they sang a *n* ... Rev 5:9
And I saw a *n* heaven ... Rev 21:1
I make all things *n* ... Rev 21:5

NEWNESS
also should walk in *n* ... Rom 6:4

NIGHT
darkness He called *N* ... Gen 1:5
It is a *n* of solemn ... Ex 12:42
pillar of fire by *n* ... Ex 13:22
gives songs in the *n* ... Job 35:10
and continued all *n* ... Luke 6:12
man came to Jesus by *n* ... John 3:2
n is coming when no ... John 9:4
came to Jesus by *n* ... John 19:39
as a thief in the *n* ... 1 Thess 5:2
there shall be no *n* ... Rev 21:25

NINETY-NINE
he not leave the *n* ... Matt 18:12

NOTHING
"I can of Myself do *n* ... John 5:30
Me you can do *n* ... John 15:5
men, it will come to *n* ... Acts 5:38
have not love, I am *n* ... 1 Cor 13:2
Be anxious for *n* ... Phil 4:6
For we brought *n* ... 1 Tim 6:7

NOURISHED
"I have *n* and ... Is 1:2

NOURISHES
n and cherishes it ... Eph 5:29

NUMBER
if a man could *n* ... Gen 13:16
teach us to *n* our days ... Ps 90:12
which no one could *n* ... Rev 7:9
His *n* is 666 ... Rev 13:18

O

OATH
for the sake of your *o* ... Eccl 8:2
he denied with an *o* ... Matt 26:72
o which He swore ... Luke 1:73

OATHS
shall perform your *o* ... Matt 5:33

OBEDIENCE
o many will be made ... Rom 5:19
captivity to the *o* ... 2 Cor 10:5
yet He learned *o* ... Heb 5:8

OBEDIENT
you are willing and *o* ... Is 1:19
of the priests were *o* ... Acts 6:7
make the Gentiles *o* ... Rom 15:18
Himself and became *o* ... Phil 2:8
as *o* children ... 1 Pet 1:14

OBEY
God and *o* His voice ... Deut 4:30
His voice we will *o* ... Josh 24:24
o is better than ... 1 Sam 15:22
o God rather than men ... Acts 5:29
and do not *o* the truth ... Rom 2:8
yourselves slaves to *o* ... Rom 6:16
o your parents in all ... Col 3:20
Bondservants, *o* in all ... Col 3:22
those who do not *o* ... 2 Thess 1:8
O those who rule ... Heb 13:17

OBEYED
of sin, yet you *o* ... Rom 6:17
they have not all *o* ... Rom 10:16
By faith Abraham *o* ... Heb 11:8

OBSERVATION
does not come with *o* ... Luke 17:20

OBSERVE
teaching them to *o* all ... Matt 28:20

OBTAIN
also may *o* mercy ... Rom 11:31
o salvation through ... 1 Thess 5:9

OBTAINED
o a part in this ... Acts 1:17
yet have now *o* mercy ... Rom 11:30
endured, he *o* the ... Heb 6:15

OBTAINS
o favor from the LORD ... Prov 8:35

OFFEND
lest we *o* them ....Matt 17:27
than that he should *o* ..Luke 17:2
them, "Does this *o* .....John 6:61

OFFENDED
they were *o* at Him ....Matt 13:57

OFFENSE
and a rock of *o* ....Is 8:14
You are an *o* to Me ....Matt 16:23
by the one man's *o* ....Rom 5:17
the *o* of the cross ....Gal 5:11
sincere and without *o* ....Phil 1:10
And a rock of o ....1 Pet 2:8

OFFENSES
For *o* must come ....Matt 18:7
impossible that no *o* ....Luke 17:1

OFFER
come and *o* your gift ....Matt 5:24
let us continually *o* ....Heb 13:15

OFFERED
to eat those things *o* ....1 Cor 8:10
so Christ was *o* ....Heb 9:28
o one sacrifice ....Heb 10:12

OFFERING
o You did not require .....Ps 40:6
You make His soul an *o* ..Is 53:10
Himself for us, an *o* ....Eph 5:2
o You did not ....Heb 10:5
o He has perfected .....Heb 10:14

OFFERINGS
and offered burnt *o* .....Gen 8:20
In burnt o ....Heb 10:6

OFFICE
sitting at the tax *o* ....Matt 9:9

OFFSPRING
wife and raise up *o* ....Matt 22:24
we are also His *o* ....Acts 17:28
am the Root and the *O* .Rev 22:16

OFTEN
o I wanted to gather ..Luke 13:34
as *o* as you eat this ...1 Cor 11:26

OIL
a bin, and a little *o* ...1 Kin 17:12
very costly fragrant *o* ...Matt 26:7
anointing him with *o* ..James 5:14
and do not harm the *o* ....Rev 6:6

OLD
young, and now am *o* ....Ps 37:25
was said to those of *o* ...Matt 5:21
but when you are *o* ....John 21:18
Your o men shall dream Acts 2:17
o man was crucified .....Rom 6:6
o things have passed ....2 Cor 5:17
have put off the *o* man ....Col 3:9
that serpent of *o* ....Rev 20:2

OLDER
o shall serve the ....Gen 25:23
not rebuke an *o* man ....1 Tim 5:1

OLDEST
beginning with the *o* ....John 8:9

OLIVE
a freshly plucked *o* ......Gen 8:11
o tree which is wild ....Rom 11:24

OMNIPOTENT
For the Lord God *O* .....Rev 19:6

ONCE
died, He died to sin *o* ....Rom 6:10
for men to die *o* ....Heb 9:27
also suffered *o* ....1 Pet 3:18

ONE
"*O* thing you lack .....Mark 10:21
o thing is needed .....Luke 10:42
I and My Father are *o* .John 10:30
that they may be *o* ....John 17:11
o accord in the temple ..Acts 2:46
for you are all *o* ....Gal 3:28
to create in Himself *o* ....Eph 2:15
o Lord ....Eph 4:5
o faith ....Eph 4:5
o baptism ....Eph 4:5
o God and Father of ....Eph 4:6
For there is *o* God and ...1 Tim 2:5
o Mediator between ....1 Tim 2:5
a thousand years as *o* ....2 Pet 3:8

OPENED
o not His mouth ....Is 53:7
o the Scriptures ....Luke 24:32
o their understanding .Luke 24:45
Now I saw heaven *o* ....Rev 19:11

OPENS
him the doorkeeper *o* ....John 10:3
and shuts and no one o ....Rev 3:7

OPINION
be wise in your own *o* .Rom 11:25

OPINIONS
falter between two *o* ..1 Kin 18:21

OPPORTUNITY
But sin, taking *o* ....Rom 7:8
as we have *o* ....Gal 6:10
but you lacked *o* ....Phil 4:10

OPPRESS
he loves to *o* ....Hos 12:7
o the widow or the .....Zech 7:10
Do not the rich *o* ....James 2:6

OPPRESSED
for all who are *o* ....Ps 103:6
The tears of the *o* ....Eccl 4:1
He was *o* and He was ....Is 53:7
all who were *o* ....Acts 10:38

OPPRESSES
o the poor reproaches .Prov 14:31

OPPRESSION
have surely seen the *o* .....Ex 3:7
their life from *o* ....Ps 72:14
brought low through *o* ..Ps 107:39
me from the *o* ....Ps 119:134
considered all the *o* ......Eccl 4:1
o destroys a wise ....Eccl 7:7
justice, but behold, *o* ....Is 5:7
surely seen the o ....Acts 7:34

ORACLES
received the living *o* ....Acts 7:38
were committed the *o* ...Rom 3:2
principles of the *o* ......Heb 5:12

ORDAINED
o you a prophet ....Jer 1:5
whom He has *o* ....Acts 17:31

ORDER
decently and in *o* .....1 Cor 14:40

ORDERS
o his conduct aright I ....Ps 50:23

ORDINANCE
resists the *o* of God ....Rom 13:2

ORDINANCES
and fleshly *o* imposed ...Heb 9:10

ORPHANS
will not leave you *o* ...John 14:18
to visit *o* and widows .James 1:27

OUGHT
These you *o* to have ...Matt 23:23
pray for as we *o* ....Rom 8:26
persons *o* you to be ....2 Pet 3:11

OUTCAST
they called you an *o* ....Jer 30:17

OUTCASTS
will assemble the *o* ....Is 11:12

OUTRAN
the other disciple *o* .....John 20:4

OUTSIDE
and dish, that the *o* ....Matt 23:26
Pharisees make the *o* .Luke 11:39
toward those who are *o* ...Col 4:5
to Him, *o* the camp ....Heb 13:13
But *o* are dogs and .....Rev 22:15

OUTSTRETCHED
and with an *o* arm ......Deut 26:8

OUTWARD
at the *o* appearance ...1 Sam 16:7
adornment be merely *o* ..1 Pet 3:3

OUTWARDLY
not a Jew who is one *o* .Rom 2:28

OVERCAME
My throne, as I also *o* ...Rev 3:21
"And they *o* him by ....Rev 12:11

OVERCOME
good cheer, I have *o* ...John 16:33
and the Lamb will *o* ....Rev 17:14

OVERCOMES
of God *o* the world ....1 John 5:4
o I will give to eat ....Rev 2:7
o shall not be hurt ....Rev 2:11
o shall inherit all ....Rev 21:7

OVERSEER
to the Shepherd and *O* .1 Pet 2:25

OVERSEERS
you, serving as *o* ....1 Pet 5:2

OVERSHADOW
of the Highest will *o* ....Luke 1:35

OVERTHREW
As God *o* Sodom and ...Jer 50:40

OVERTHROW
o the faith of some .....2 Tim 2:18

OVERTHROWN
and Nineveh shall be *o* ...Jon 3:4

OVERTHROWS
And *o* the mighty ......Job 12:19
o them in the night .....Job 34:25
o the words of the .....Prov 22:12

OVERWHELM
o the fatherless ....Job 6:27

OVERWHELMED
and my spirit was *o* ......Ps 77:3
my spirit is *o* within .....Ps 143:4

OVERWORK
Do not *o* to be rich .....Prov 23:4

OWE
O no one anything ......Rom 13:8

OWED
o him ten thousand . . . . . Matt 18:24

OWN
He came to His *o* . . . . . . John 1:11
having loved His *o* . . . . . John 13:1
would love its *o* . . . . . . John 15:19
you are not your *o* . . . . 1 Cor 6:19
But each one has his *o* . . 1 Cor 7:7
For all seek their *o* . . . . . . Phil 2:21
from our sins in His *o* . . . . Rev 1:5

OX
shall not muzzle an *o* . . . Deut 25:4
o knows its owner . . . . Is 1:3
Sabbath loose his *o* . . . Luke 13:15
shall not muzzle an o . . . 1 Cor 9:9

P

PACIFIES
A gift in secret *p* . . . . Prov 21:14

PAIN
p you shall bring . . . . Gen 3:16
p as a woman in . . . . Is 13:8
Why is my *p* perpetual . . Jer 15:18
shall be no more *p* . . . . . . Rev 21:4

PAINED
My heart is severely *p* . . . . Ps 55:4
I am *p* in my very . . . . Jer 4:19

PAINFUL
for the present, but *p* . . Heb 12:11

PAINS
The *p* of death . . . . Ps 116:3
having loosed the *p* . . . . Acts 2:24

PAINT
your eyes with *p* . . . . Jer 4:30

PALACE
enter the King's *p* . . . . . . Ps 45:15
guards his own *p* . . . . . Luke 11:21
evident to the whole *p* . . . Phil 1:13

PALACES
Out of the ivory *p* . . . . Ps 45:8

PALE
behold, a *p* horse . . . . Rev 6:8

PALM
p branches in their . . . . Rev 7:9

PALMS
struck Him with the *p* . Matt 26:67

PAMPERS
p his servant from . . . . . Prov 29:21

PANGS
The *p* of death . . . . Ps 18:4
labors with birth *p* . . . . . Rom 8:22

PARABLE
do You speak this *p* . . . Luke 12:41

PARABLES
rest it is given in *p* . . . . . Luke 8:10

PARADISE
will be with Me in *P* . . Luke 23:43
in the midst of the *P* . . . . . . Rev 2:7

PARDON
He will abundantly *p* . . . . . . Is 55:7
p all their iniquities . . . . . . Jer 33:8

PARDONING
is a God like You, *p* . . . . . Mic 7:18

PARENTS
will rise up against *p* . . Matt 10:21
has left house or *p* . . . . Luke 18:29
disobedient to *p* . . . . Rom 1:30

PART
chosen that good *p* . . . Luke 10:42
you, you have no *p* . . . . . John 13:8
For we know in *p* . . . . . . 1 Cor 13:9
shall take away his *p* . . . . Rev 22:19

PARTAKE
for we all *p* of that . . . . 1 Cor 10:17

PARTAKER
in hope should be *p* . . . . 1 Cor 9:10
Christ, and also a *p* . . . . . . 1 Pet 5:1

PARTAKERS
Gentiles have been *p* . . . Rom 15:27
know that as you are *p* . 2 Cor 1:7
qualified us to be *p* . . . . Col 1:12

PARTIAL
You shall not be *p* . . . . . Lev 19:15

PARTIALITY
that God shows no *p* . . . Acts 10:34
doing nothing with *p* . . 1 Tim 5:21
good fruits, without *p* . James 3:17

PASS
I will *p* over you . . . . Ex 12:13
When you *p* through the . . . Is 43:2
and earth will *p* . . . . Matt 24:35

PASSED
forbearance God had *p* . Rom 3:25
High Priest who has *p* . . . Heb 4:14
know that we have *p* . 1 John 3:14

PASSES
of Christ which *p* . . . . Eph 3:19

PASSION
uncleanness, *p* . . . . Col 3:5

PASSIONS
gave them up to vile *p* . . Rom 1:26

PASSOVER
It is the LORD's *P* . . . . Ex 12:11
I will keep the *P* . . . . . Matt 26:18
indeed Christ, our *P* . . . . 1 Cor 5:7
By faith he kept the *P* . . Heb 11:28

PASTORS
and some *p* and . . . . Eph 4:11

PASTURE
the sheep of Your *p* . . . . . . Ps 74:1
in and out and find *p* . . . John 10:9

PASTURES
to lie down in green *p* . . . . Ps 23:2

PATH
You will show me the *p* . . Ps 16:11

PATHS
He leads me in the *p* . . . . Ps 23:3
Make His p straight . . . . . Matt 3:3
and make straight *p* . . . Heb 12:13

PATIENCE
'Master, have *p* . . . . Matt 18:26
and bear fruit with *p* . . . Luke 8:15
labor of love, and *p* . . . 1 Thess 1:3
faith, love, *p* . . . . 1 Tim 6:11
your faith produces *p* . . . James 1:3
p have its perfect . . . . . . James 1:4
in the kingdom and *p* . . . . . Rev 1:9

PATIENT
rejoicing in hope, *p* . . . . Rom 12:12
the weak, be *p* . . . . . . 1 Thess 5:14

PATIENTLY
if you take it *p* . . . . 1 Pet 2:20

PATRIARCHS
begot the twelve *p* . . . . Acts 7:8

PATTERN
p which you were . . . . Ex 26:30
as you have us for a *p* . . . Phil 3:17
p shown you on the . . . . . . Heb 8:5

PEACE
you, And give you *p* . . . . Num 6:26
both lie down in *p* . . . . Ps 4:8
p have those who . . . . . Ps 119:165
I am for *p* . . . . Ps 120:7
war, And a time of *p* . . . . . Eccl 3:8
Father, Prince of *P* . . . . Is 9:6
keep him in perfect *p* . . . . . Is 26:3
p they have not . . . . Is 59:8
slightly, Saying, '*P* . . . . Jer 6:14
place I will give *p* . . . . Hag 2:9
is worthy, let your *p* . Matt 10:13
that I came to bring *p* . Matt 10:34
And on earth *p* . . . . Luke 2:14
if a son of *p* is there . . . . Luke 10:6
that make for your *p* . Luke 19:42
leave with you, My *p* . . John 14:27
Me you may have *p* . . . John 16:33
Grace to you and *p* . . . . . . Rom 1:7
by faith, we have *p* . . . . . . Rom 5:1
God has called us to *p* . 1 Cor 7:15
p will be with you . . . . 2 Cor 13:11
Spirit is love, joy, *p* . . . . . . Gal 5:22
He Himself is our *p* . . . . . Eph 2:14
and the *p* of God . . . . Phil 4:7
And let the *p* of God . . . . . Col 3:15
faith, love, *p* . . . . 2 Tim 2:22
meaning "king of *p*," . . . . . . Heb 7:2

PEACEABLE
is first pure, then *p* . . . James 3:17

PEACEABLY
on you, live *p* . . . . Rom 12:18

PEACEFUL
in a *p* habitation . . . . Is 32:18

PEACEMAKERS
Blessed are the *p* . . . . Matt 5:9

PEARL
had found one *p* . . . . . . Matt 13:46

PEARLS
nor cast your *p* . . . . Matt 7:6
gates were twelve *p* . . . . . Rev 21:21

PENTECOST
P had fully come . . . . Acts 2:1

PEOPLE
will take you as My *p* . . . . Ex 6:7
p shall be my *p* . . . . Ruth 1:16
p who know the joyful . . . Ps 89:15
We are His *p* and the . . . . Ps 100:3
"Blessed is Egypt My *p* . . . Is 19:25
to make ready a *p* . . . . . . Luke 1:17
take out of them a *p* . . Acts 15:14
who were not My p . . . . Rom 9:25
they shall be My p . . . . 2 Cor 6:16
LORD will judge His p . . Heb 10:30
but are now the *p* . . . . 1 Pet 2:10
tribe and tongue and *p* . . . . Rev 5:9
they shall be His *p* . . . . . . Rev 21:3

PERCEIVE
seeing, but do not *p* . . . . Is 6:9
may see and not p . . . . . Mark 4:12

PERDITION
except the son of *p* . . . . John 17:12
revealed, the son of *p* . 2 Thess 2:3
who draw back to *p* . . . . Heb 10:39

PERFECT
Noah was a just man, *p* . . Gen 6:9
Father in heaven is *p* . . . Matt 5:48
they may be made *p* . . . John 17:23
and *p* will of God . . . . . Rom 12:2
when that which is *p* . 1 Cor 13:10
present every man *p* . . . . . Col 1:28
good gift and every *p* . James 1:17
in word, he is a *p* . . . . . James 3:2
p love casts out fear . . 1 John 4:18

PERFECTED
third day I shall be *p* . . Luke 13:32
or am already *p* . . . . Phil 3:12
Son who has been *p* . . . . Heb 7:28

PERFECTION
let us go on to *p* . . . . Heb 6:1

PERISH
so that we may not *p* . . . . . Jon 1:6
little ones should *p* . . . . Matt 18:14
in Him should not *p* . . . John 3:16
they shall never *p* . . . . John 10:28
among those who *p* . . 2 Thess 2:10
that any should *p* . . . . 2 Pet 3:9

PERISHABLE
do it to obtain a *p* . . . . 1 Cor 9:25

PERISHED
Truth has *p* and has . . . . . Jer 7:28

PERISHING
We are *p* . . . . Matt 8:25

PERMIT
do not *p* a woman . . . . . 1 Tim 2:12

PERMITS
we will do if God *p* . . . . Heb 6:3

PERMITTED
p no one to do them . . . . Ps 105:14
we are *p* . . . . 2 Cor 4:8

PERSECUTE
when they revile and *p* . Matt 5:11

PERSECUTED
If they *p* Me . . . . John 15:20
p, but not forsaken . . . . . . 2 Cor 4:9

PERSECUTES
wicked in his pride *p* . . . . . Ps 10:2

PERSECUTION
p arises because of . . . . . Matt 13:21
At that time a great *p* . . . . Acts 8:1
do I still suffer *p* . . . . Gal 5:11

PERSECUTOR
a blasphemer, a *p* . . . . . . 1 Tim 1:13

PERSEVERANCE
tribulation produces *p* . . . Rom 5:3

PERSEVERE
kept My command to *p* . . Rev 3:10

PERSISTENCE
p he will rise and . . . . . . Luke 11:8

PERSON
do not regard the *p* . . . . Matt 22:16
express image of His *p* . . . Heb 1:3

PERSUADE
"You almost *p* me . . . . . Acts 26:28

PERSUADED
neither will they be *p* Luke 16:31
p that He is able . . . . 2 Tim 1:12

PERSUASIVE
p words of human . . . . . . 1 Cor 2:4

PERVERSE
your way is *p* . . . . Num 22:32
p man sows strife . . . . . . Prov 16:28
from this *p* generation . . Acts 2:40

PERVERT
"You shall not *p* . . . . . . Deut 16:19
p the gospel of Christ . . . . . Gal 1:7

PERVERTING
will you not cease *p* . . . Acts 13:10

PERVERTS
p his ways will become . Prov 10:9

PESTILENCE
from the perilous *p* . . . . Ps 91:3
Before Him went *p* . . . . Hab 3:5

PESTILENCES
will be famines, *p* . . . . . . Matt 24:7

PETITIONS
p that we have asked . 1 John 5:15

PHARISEE
to pray, one a *P* . . . . . . Luke 18:10

PHILOSOPHERS
p encountered him . . . . Acts 17:18

PHILOSOPHY
cheat you through *p* . . . . . . Col 2:8

PHYSICIAN
have no need of a *p* . . . . Matt 9:12

PHYSICIANS
her livelihood on *p* . . . . . Luke 8:43

PIECES
they took the thirty p . . . Matt 27:9

PIERCE
a sword will *p* . . . . Luke 2:35

PIERCED
p My hands and My feet . Ps 22:16
whom they have *p* . . . . . Zech 12:10
of the soldiers *p* . . . . . . John 19:34
p themselves through . . 1 Tim 6:10
and they also who *p* . . . . . . Rev 1:7

PIERCING
p even to the division . . . Heb 4:12

PILGRIMAGE
heart is set on *p* . . . . Ps 84:5
In the house of my *p* . . . . Ps 119:54

PILGRIMS
we are aliens and *p* . . . 1 Chr 29:15
were strangers and *p* . . . Heb 11:13

PILLAR
and she became a *p* . . . . Gen 19:26
and by night in a *p* . . . . . . Ex 13:21
the living God, the *p* . . . 1 Tim 3:15

PILLARS
break their sacred *p* . . . . . Ex 34:13
Blood and fire and *p* . . . . . . Joel 2:30
and his feet like *p* . . . . Rev 10:1

PIT
who go down to the *p* . . . . . . Ps 28:1
a harlot is a deep *p* . . . . . Prov 23:27
my life in the *p* . . . . Lam 3:53
up my life from the *p* . . . . . . Jon 2:6
into the bottomless *p* . . . . . Rev 20:3

PITIABLE
of all men the most *p* . 1 Cor 15:19

PITS
The proud have dug *p* . . Ps 119:85

PITY
for someone to take *p* . . . Ps 69:20
p He redeemed them . . . . . . Is 63:9
just as I had *p* . . . . Matt 18:33

PLACE
Come, see the *p* . . . . Matt 28:6
My word has no *p* . . . . . John 8:37
I go to prepare a *p* . . . . . John 14:2
might go to his own *p* . . . . Acts 1:25

PLACES
And the rough *p* . . . . Is 40:4
They love the best *p* . . . . Matt 23:6
in the heavenly *p* . . . . Eph 1:3

PLAGUE
bring yet one more *p* . . . . . Ex 11:1

PLAGUES
p that are written . . . . . . Rev 22:18

PLANK
First remove the *p* . . . . Matt 7:5

PLANS
He makes the *p* of the . . . Ps 33:10
that devises wicked *p* . . . Prov 6:18

PLANT
A time to *p* . . . . Eccl 3:2
Him as a tender *p* . . . . Is 53:2
p of an alien vine . . . . Jer 2:21
p which My heavenly . . Matt 15:13

PLANTED
shall be like a tree *p* . . . . Ps 1:3
by the roots and be *p* . . . Luke 17:6
I *p*, Apollos watered . . . . 1 Cor 3:6

PLANTS
neither he who *p* . . . . 1 Cor 3:7

PLATTER
head here on a *p* . . . . Matt 14:8

PLEASANT
food, that it was *p* . . . . Gen 3:6
how good and how *p* . . . . . Ps 133:1

PLEASANTNESS
ways are ways of *p* . . . . . Prov 3:17

PLEASE
in the flesh cannot *p* . . . . . Rom 8:8
p his neighbor for his . . . Rom 15:2
he may *p* the Lord . . . . . 1 Cor 7:32
is impossible to *p* Him . . Heb 11:6

PLEASED
Then You shall be *p* . . . . . Ps 51:19
in whom I am well *p* . . . . Matt 3:17
God was not well *p* . . . . 1 Cor 10:5
testimony, that he *p* . . . . . Heb 11:5

PLEASES
Whatever the LORD *p* . . . . . Ps 135:6

PLEASING
sacrifice, well *p* . . . . Phil 4:18
for this is well *p* . . . . Col 3:20
in you what is well *p* . . . Heb 13:21

PLEASURE
Do good in Your good *p* . Ps 51:18
p will be a poor man . . Prov 21:17

shall perform all My *p* . . . Is 44:28
your Father's good *p* . . Luke 12:32
to the good *p* of His . . . . . . Eph 1:5
for sin You had no p . . . . Heb 10:6
My soul has no p . . . . . . Heb 10:38
p that war in your . . . . . James 4:1

PLEASURES

Your right hand are *p* . . . Ps 16:11
cares, riches, and *p* . . . . Luke 8:14
to enjoy the passing *p* . . Heb 11:25

PLOW

put his hand to the *p* . . . Luke 9:62

PLOWED

You have *p* . . . . Hos 10:13

PLOWMAN

p shall overtake the . . . Amos 9:13

PLUCK

p the heads of grain . . . Mark 2:23

PLUCKED

cheeks to those who *p* . . . . Is 50:6
And His disciples *p* . . . . . Luke 6:1
you would have *p* . . . . Gal 4:15

PLUNDER

p the Egyptians . . . . Ex 3:22
The *p* of the poor is . . . . Is 3:14
house and *p* his goods . Matt 12:29

PLUNDERED

a people robbed and *p* . . . . Is 42:22
"And when you are *p* . . . . Jer 4:30

PLUNDERING

me Because of the *p* . . . . . . Is 22:4
accepted the *p* of your . Heb 10:34

POETS

some of your own *p* . . . Acts 17:28

POISON

"The p of asps is . . . . Rom 3:13

POISONED

p by bitterness . . . . Acts 8:23

POLLUTIONS

have escaped the *p* . . . . . 2 Pet 2:20

POMP

had come with great *p* . Acts 25:23

POMPOUS

and a mouth speaking *p* . . Dan 7:8

PONDER

P the path of your . . . . . . Prov 4:26

PONDERED

p them in her heart . . . . Luke 2:19

PONDERS

p all his paths . . . . Prov 5:21

POOR

p will never cease . . . . . Deut 15:11
So the *p* have hope . . . . . . Job 5:16
I delivered the *p* . . . . Job 29:12
p shall eat and be . . . . Ps 22:26
But I am *p* and needy . . . . Ps 40:17
Let the *p* and needy . . . . . . Ps 74:21
He raises the *p* . . . . Ps 113:7
slack hand becomes *p* . . . Prov 10:4
p man is hated even . . . . Prov 14:20
has mercy on the *p* . . . . . Prov 14:21
who oppresses the *p* . . . . Prov 14:31
p reproaches his . . . . Prov 17:5
Do not rob the *p* . . . . Prov 22:22
that same *p* man . . . . Eccl 9:15
The alien or the *p* . . . . . . Zech 7:10
"Blessed are the *p* . . . . Matt 5:3
p have the gospel . . . . Matt 11:5
"For you have the *p* . . . Matt 26:11
sakes He became *p* . . . . . 2 Cor 8:9
should remember the *p* . . Gal 2:10
God not chosen the *p* . . . . James 2:5
wretched, miserable, *p* . . . Rev 3:17

PORTION

O LORD, You, are the *p* . . . Ps 16:5
heart and my *p* forever . . . Ps 73:26
You are my *p* . . . . Ps 119:57
I will divide Him a *p* . . . . . Is 53:12
rejoice in their *p* . . . . Is 61:7
The *P* of Jacob is not . . . . Jer 10:16
"The LORD is my *p* . . . . . . Lam 3:24
and appoint him his *p* . Matt 24:51
to give them their *p* . . Luke 12:42
give me the *p* . . . . Luke 15:12

POSSESS

descendants shall *p* . . . . Gen 22:17
p the land which . . . . Josh 1:11
"By your patience *p* . . Luke 21:19
p his own vessel . . . . . . 1 Thess 4:4

POSSESSED

"The LORD *p* me at . . . . . . Prov 8:22

POSSESSING

and yet *p* all things . . . 2 Cor 6:10

POSSESSION

as an everlasting *p* . . . . . Gen 17:8
and an enduring *p* . . . . . Heb 10:34

POSSESSIONS

and sold their *p* . . . . Acts 2:45

POSSIBLE

God all things are *p* . . . Matt 19:26
p that the blood . . . . Heb 10:4

POUR

p My Spirit on your . . . . Is 44:3
P out Your fury . . . . Jer 10:25
That I will *p* out My . . . . . Joel 2:28
"And I will *p* . . . . Zech 12:10
angels, "Go and *p* . . . . Rev 16:1

POURED

I am *p* out like water . . . . Ps 22:14
grace is *p* upon Your . . . . . Ps 45:2
strong, Because He *p* . . . . . Is 53:12
and My fury will be *p* . . . . . Jer 7:20
broke the flask and *p* . . . Mark 14:3
I am already being *p* . . . 2 Tim 4:6
whom He *p* out on us . . . . Titus 3:6

POVERTY

leads only to *p* . . . . Prov 14:23
p put in all the . . . . Luke 21:4
and their deep *p* . . . . 2 Cor 8:2
p might become rich . . . . 2 Cor 8:9
tribulation, and *p* . . . . Rev 2:9

POWER

that I may show My *p* . . . Ex 9:16
him who is without *p* . . . . Job 26:2
p who can understand . . . Job 26:14
p belongs to God . . . . Ps 62:11
p Your enemies shall . . . . . . Ps 66:3
gives strength and *p* . . . . . Ps 68:35
a king is, there is *p* . . . . Eccl 8:4
No one has *p* over the . . . . Eccl 8:8
'Not by might nor by *p* . . Zech 4:6
the kingdom and the *p* . . Matt 6:13
the Son of Man has *p* . . . . Matt 9:6
Scriptures nor the *p* . . Matt 22:29
p went out from Him . . . . Luke 6:19
are endued with *p* . . . . . Luke 24:49
I have *p* to lay it . . . . . . John 10:18
"You could have no *p* . John 19:11
you shall receive *p* . . . . . . Acts 1:8
though by our own *p* . . . Acts 3:12
man is the great *p* . . . . . Acts 8:10
"Give me this *p* . . . . Acts 8:19
for it is the *p* . . . . Rom 1:16
saved it is the *p* . . . . 1 Cor 1:18
Greeks, Christ the *p* . . . . 1 Cor 1:24
that the *p* of Christ . . . . 2 Cor 12:9
greatness of His *p* . . . . Eph 1:19
the Lord and in the *p* . . . . Eph 6:10
to His glorious *p* . . . . Col 1:11
the glory of His *p* . . . . . 2 Thess 1:9
of fear, but of *p* . . . . 2 Tim 1:7
by the word of His *p* . . . . . Heb 1:3
p of death, that . . . . Heb 2:14
as His divine *p* . . . . 2 Pet 1:3
Dominion and *p* . . . . Jude 25
to him I will give *p* . . . . . . Rev 2:26
honor and glory and *p* . . Rev 5:13

POWERFUL

of the LORD is *p* . . . . Ps 29:4
of God is living and *p* . . . Heb 4:12

POWERS

principalities and *p* . . . . . . Col 2:15
word of God and the *p* . . . Heb 6:5

PRAISE

p shall be of You in . . . . . . Ps 22:25
the people shall *p* . . . . Ps 45:17
P is awaiting You . . . . Ps 65:1
Let all the peoples *p* . . . . Ps 67:3
p shall be continually . . . . . . Ps 71:6
And the heavens will *p* . . . Ps 89:5
Seven times a day I *p* . . Ps 119:164
that has breath *p* . . . . Ps 150:6
Let another man *p* . . . . . Prov 27:2
let her own works *p* . . . . Prov 31:31
And your gates *P* . . . . Is 60:18
He makes Jerusalem a *p* . . Is 62:7
For You are my *p* . . . . Jer 17:14
Me a name of joy, a *p* . . . . Jer 33:9
give you fame and *p* . . . Zeph 3:20
You have perfected p . . Matt 21:16
men more than the *p* . . John 12:43
p is not from men but . . Rom 2:29
Then each one's *p* . . . . 1 Cor 4:5
should be to the *p* . . . . Eph 1:12
to the glory and *p* . . . . Phil 1:11
I will sing p to You . . . . . Heb 2:12
the sacrifice of *p* . . . . Heb 13:15
and for the *p* of those . . . 1 Pet 2:14
saying, "*P* our God . . . . . . Rev 19:5

PRAISED

daily He shall be *p* . . . . . . Ps 72:15
LORD's name is to be *p* . . Ps 113:3
and greatly to be *p* . . . . . . Ps 145:3
the Most High and *p* . . . . . Dan 4:34

PRAISES

it is good to sing *p* . . . . . . Ps 147:1
and he *p* . . . . Prov 31:28

PRAISEWORTHY

if there is anything *p* . . . . . Phil 4:8

PRAISING

They will still be *p* . . . . Ps 84:4
of the heavenly host *p* . . Luke 2:13
in the temple *p* . . . . Luke 24:53

PRAY

at noon I will *p* . . . . Ps 55:17
who hate you, and *p* . . . . . Matt 5:44
"And when you *p* . . . . Matt 6:5
manner, therefore, *p* . . . . . Matt 6:9
"Watch and *p* . . . . Matt 26:41
"Lord, teach us to *p* . . . . Luke 11:1
"And I will *p* . . . . John 14:16
I do not *p* for the . . . . John 17:9
"I do not *p* for . . . . John 17:20
p without ceasing . . . . . 1 Thess 5:17
Brethren, *p* for us . . . . . 1 Thess 5:25
Let him *p* . . . . James 5:13

to one another, and *p* . James 5:16
say that he should *p* . . 1 John 5:16

PRAYED
p more earnestly . . . . . . Luke 22:44
p earnestly that it . . . . . James 5:17

PRAYER
p made in this place . . . 2 Chr 7:15
And my *p* is pure . . . . . . Job 16:17
A *p* to the God of my . . . . . Ps 42:8
P also will be made . . . . . Ps 72:15
He shall regard the *p* . . . Ps 102:17
to the LORD, But the *p* . . Prov 15:8
go out except by *p* . . . . Matt 17:21
all night in *p* to God . . . . Luke 6:12
continually to *p* . . . . Acts 6:4
where *p* was . . . . Acts 16:13
steadfastly in *p* . . . . Rom 12:12
to fasting and *p* . . . . 1 Cor 7:5
always with all *p* . . . . Eph 6:18
but in everything by *p* . . . . Phil 4:6
the word of God and *p* . . 1 Tim 4:5
And the *p* of faith . . . . James 5:15

PRAYERS
though You make many *p* . Is 1:15
pretense make long *p* . . Matt 23:14
fervently for you in *p* . . . . Col 4:12
p may not be hindered . . . 1 Pet 3:7
which are the *p* . . . . Rev 5:8

PREACH
time Jesus began to *p* . . . Matt 4:17
you hear in the ear, *p* . . Matt 10:27
P the gospel to the . . . . . Luke 4:18
And how shall they *p* . . Rom 10:15
p Christ crucified . . . . . . 1 Cor 1:23
I or they, so we *p* . . . . . 1 Cor 15:11
P the word . . . . 2 Tim 4:2

PREACHED
p that people . . . . Mark 6:12
out and *p* . . . . Mark 16:20
of sins should be *p* . . . . Luke 24:47
p Christ to them . . . . Acts 8:5
lest, when I have *p* . . . . 1 Cor 9:27
than what we have *p* . . . . . Gal 1:8
the gospel was *p* . . . . Heb 4:2
also He went and *p* . . . . 1 Pet 3:19

PREACHER
they hear without a *p* . . Rom 10:14
I was appointed a *p* . . . . 1 Tim 2:7

PREACHES
the Jesus whom Paul *p* Acts 19:13
p another Jesus . . . . 2 Cor 11:4
p any other gospel . . . . Gal 1:9
p the faith which he . . . . . Gal 1:23

PREACHING
p Jesus as the . . . . Acts 5:42
not risen, then our *p* . . 1 Cor 15:14

PRECEPTS
all His *p* are sure . . . . Ps 111:7
how I love Your *p* . . . . . Ps 119:159

PRECIOUS
P in the sight of the . . . . Ps 116:15
She is more *p* than . . . . . Prov 3:15
p things shall not . . . . Is 44:9
if you take out the *p* . . . . Jer 15:19
farmer waits for the *p* . . James 5:7
more *p* than gold . . . . 1 Pet 1:7
who believe, He is *p* . . . . . 1 Pet 2:7
p in the sight of . . . . 1 Pet 3:4

PREDESTINED
foreknew, He also *p* . . . . Rom 8:29
having *p* us to . . . . Eph 1:5
inheritance, being *p* . . . . Eph 1:11

PREEMINENCE
He may have the *p* . . . . . . Col 1:18
loves to have the *p* . . . . . . 3 John 9

PREFERENCE
in honor giving *p* . . . . . . Rom 12:10

PREJUDICE
these things without *p* . 1 Tim 5:21

PREMEDITATE
p what you will . . . . . . Mark 13:11

PREPARATION
Now it was the *P* . . . . . John 19:14
your feet with the *p* . . . . . Eph 6:15

PREPARE
p a table before me in . . . . Ps 23:5
P the way of the LORD . . . Mark 1:3
p a place for you . . . . John 14:2

PREPARED
for whom it is *p* . . . . . . Matt 20:23
Which You have *p* . . . . Luke 2:31
mercy, which He had *p* . Rom 9:23
things which God has p . 1 Cor 2:9
Now He who has *p* . . . . . 2 Cor 5:5
p beforehand that we . . . . Eph 2:10
God, for He has *p* . . . . . . Heb 11:16

PRESENCE
themselves from the *p* . . . . Gen 3:8
went out from the *p* . . . . . Gen 4:16
P will go with you . . . . . . Ex 33:14
afraid in any man's *p* . . Deut 1:17
p is fullness of joy . . . . Ps 16:11
shall dwell in Your *p* . . . Ps 140:13
not tremble at My *p* . . . . . . Jer 5:22
shall shake at My *p* . . . Ezek 38:20
and drank in Your *p* . . . Luke 13:26
full of joy in Your p . . . . Acts 2:28
but his bodily *p* . . . . . . 2 Cor 10:10
obeyed, not as in my *p* . . Phil 2:12

PRESENT
we are all *p* before . . . Acts 10:33
evil is *p* with me . . . . Rom 7:21
p your bodies a living . . Rom 12:1
or death, or things *p* . . . 1 Cor 3:22
absent in body but *p* . . . . 1 Cor 5:3
that He might *p* . . . . Eph 5:27
p you faultless . . . . Jude 24

PRESERVE
He shall *p* your soul . . . . . Ps 121:7
The LORD shall *p* . . . . Ps 121:8
loses his life will *p* . . . Luke 17:33
every evil work and *p* . . 2 Tim 4:18

PRESERVED
soul, and body be *p* . . 1 Thess 5:23

PRESERVES
For the LORD *p* the . . . . . . Ps 31:23
p the souls of His . . . . Ps 97:10
who keeps his way *p* . . . Prov 16:17

PRETENSE
p make long prayers . . Matt 23:14

PRICE
one pearl of great *p* . . . Matt 13:46
were bought at a *p* . . . . 1 Cor 6:20

PRIDE
p serves as . . . . Ps 73:6
By *p* comes nothing . . . . Prov 13:10
P goes before . . . . Prov 16:18
her daughter had *p* . . . . Ezek 16:49
was hardened in *p* . . . . . Dan 5:20
For the *p* of the . . . . Zech 11:3
evil eye, blasphemy, *p* . Mark 7:22
p he fall into the . . . . 1 Tim 3:6
eyes, and the *p* . . . . 1 John 2:16

PRIEST
he was the *p* of God . . . Gen 14:18
p forever According . . . . . Ps 110:4
So He shall be a *p* . . . . . Zech 6:13
and faithful High *P* . . . . . Heb 2:17
we have a great High *P* . Heb 4:14
p forever according . . . . Heb 5:6
Christ came as High *P* . . Heb 9:11

PRIESTHOOD
p being changed . . . . Heb 7:12
has an unchangeable *p* . . Heb 7:24
generation, a royal *p* . . . . 1 Pet 2:9

PRIESTS
to Me a kingdom of *p* . . . . Ex 19:6
Her *p* teach for pay . . . . . Mic 3:11
made us kings and *p* . . . . . Rev 1:6

PRINCE
is the house of the *p* . . . . Job 21:28
Everlasting Father, *P* . . . . Is 9:6
Until Messiah the *P* . . . . . Dan 9:25
days without king or *p* . . . Hos 3:4
p asks for gifts . . . . Mic 7:3
"and killed the *P* . . . . Acts 3:15
His right hand to be *P* . . Acts 5:31
the *p* of the power . . . . Eph 2:2

PRINCES
to put confidence in *p* . . . . Ps 118:9
He brings the *p* . . . . Is 40:23

PRISON
and put him into the *p* . Gen 39:20
Bring my soul out of *p* . . . Ps 142:7
in darkness from the *p* . . . Is 42:7
the opening of the *p* . . . . Is 61:1
John had heard in *p* . . . . Matt 11:2
I was in *p* and you . . . . Matt 25:36

PRIZE
the goal for the *p* . . . . Phil 3:14

PROCEED
of the same mouth *p* . . James 3:10

PROCEEDED
for I *p* forth . . . . John 8:42

PROCEEDS
by every word that *p* . . . . Deut 8:3
by every word that p . . . Matt 4:4
Spirit of truth who *p* . . John 15:26

PROCLAIM
began to *p* it freely . . . . . Mark 1:45
knowing, Him I *p* . . . . . . Acts 17:23
drink this cup, you *p* . 1 Cor 11:26

PROCLAIMED
p the good news . . . . Ps 40:9
he went his way and *p* . Luke 8:39

PROCLAIMER
"He seems to be a *p* . . . . Acts 17:18

PROCLAIMS
good news, Who *p* . . . . Is 52:7

PRODIGAL
with *p* living . . . . Luke 15:13

PROFANE
and priest are *p* . . . . Jer 23:11
tried to *p* the temple . . . . Acts 24:6
But reject *p* and old . . . . . 1 Tim 4:7

PROFANED
and *p* My Sabbaths . . . . . Ezek 22:8

PROFANENESS
of Jerusalem *p* has . . . . . . Jer 23:15

PROFANING
p the covenant of the . . . . . Mal 2:10

PROFESS
They p to know God . . . Titus 1:16

PROFIT
For what p is it to . . . . . Matt 16:26
"For what will it p . . . . . Mark 8:36
"For what p is it to . . . . . Luke 9:25
her masters much p . . . . Acts 16:16
brought no small p . . . . Acts 19:24
what is the p of . . . . Rom 3:1
seeking my own p . . . . 1 Cor 10:33
Christ will p you . . . . Gal 5:2
about words to no p . . . 2 Tim 2:14
them, but He for our p Heb 12:10
What does it p . . . . . . James 2:14
sell, and make a p . . . . James 4:13

PROFITABLE
It is doubtless not p . . . 2 Cor 12:1
of God, and is p . . . . . . 2 Tim 3:16

PROFITS
have not love, it p . . . . . 1 Cor 13:3

PROMISE
"Behold, I send the P . Luke 24:49
but to wait for the P . . . . Acts 1:4
"For the p is to you . . . . . Acts 2:39
for the hope of the p . . . . Acts 26:6
p might be sure . . . . Rom 4:16
Therefore, since a p . . . . . . Heb 4:1
to the heirs of p . . . . Heb 6:17
did not receive the p . . Heb 11:39

PROMISED
faithful who had p . . . . . Heb 11:11

PROMISES
For all the p of God . . . . 2 Cor 1:20
his Seed were the p . . . . . Gal 3:16
having received the p . . Heb 11:13
great and precious p . . . . 2 Pet 1:4

PROPER
you, but for what is p . . 1 Cor 7:35
but, which is p . . . . 1 Tim 2:10

PROPERLY
Let us walk p . . . . Rom 13:13

PROPHECY
to another p . . . . 1 Cor 12:10
for p never came by . . . . 2 Pet 1:21
is the spirit of p . . . . Rev 19:10
of the book of this p . . . . Rev 22:19

PROPHESIED
Lord, have we not p . . . . Matt 7:22
and the law p . . . . Matt 11:13

PROPHESIES
p edifies the church . . . . . 1 Cor 14:4

PROPHESY
prophets, "Do not p . . . . . . Is 30:10
The prophets p falseiy . . . . Jer 5:31
your daughters shall p . . . Joel 2:28
Who can but p . . . . Amos 3:8
saying, "P to us . . . . Matt 26:68
your daughters shall p . . Acts 2:17
in part and we p . . . . 1 Cor 13:9

PROPHET
raise up for you a P . . . Deut 18:15
"I alone am left a p . . . 1 Kin 18:22
I ordained you a p . . . . Jer 1:5
The p is a fool . . . . Hos 9:7
Nor was I a son of a p . Amos 7:14
send you Elijah the p . . . . . . Mal 4:5
p shall receive a . . . . Matt 10:41
p is not without honor . Matt 13:57
by Daniel the p . . . . Mark 13:14
is not a greater p . . . . . . Luke 7:28
it cannot be that a p . . Luke 13:33
who was a P . . . . Luke 24:19
"Are you the P . . . . John 1:21
"This is truly the P . . . . . John 6:14
with him the false p . . . . Rev 19:20

PROPHETIC
p word confirmed . . . . 2 Pet 1:19

PROPHETS
the Law or the P . . . . Matt 5:17
is the Law and the P . . . . Matt 7:12
or one of the p . . . . Matt 16:14
the tombs of the p . . . . . Matt 23:29
indeed, I send you p . . . Matt 23:34
one who kills the p . . . . . Matt 23:37
Then many false p . . . . . . Matt 24:11
Moses and the p . . . . Luke 16:29
are sons of the p . . . . Acts 3:25
p did your fathers not . . . Acts 7:52
"To Him all the p . . . . Acts 10:43
do you believe the p . . . . Acts 26:27
by the Law and the P . . . . Rom 3:21
have killed Your p . . . . . . Rom 11:3
to be apostles, some p . . . . Eph 4:11
this salvation the p . . . . . 1 Pet 1:10
because many false p . . . 1 John 4:1
found the blood of p . . . . Rev 18:24

PROPITIATION
set forth as a p . . . . Rom 3:25
to God, to make p . . . . Heb 2:17
He Himself is the p . . . . . 1 John 2:2
His Son to be the p . . . . 1 John 4:10

PROPRIETY
modest apparel, with p . . . 1 Tim 2:9

PROSPER
they p who love you . . . . . Ps 122:6
of the LORD shall p . . . . . . Is 53:10
against you shall p . . . . Is 54:17
up as he may p . . . . 1 Cor 16:2
I pray that you may p . . . 3 John 2

PROSPERED
since the LORD has p . . . Gen 24:56

PROSPERING
His ways are always p . . . . Ps 10:5

PROSPERITY
p all your days . . . . Deut 23:6
p the destroyer . . . . Job 15:21
Now in my p I said . . . . Ps 30:6
has pleasure in the p . . . . Ps 35:27
When I saw the p . . . . Ps 73:3
I pray, send now p . . . . . . Ps 118:25
that we have our p . . . . . Acts 19:25

PROSPEROUS
will make your way p . . . . . Josh 1:8

PROSPERS
just as your soul p . . . . . . 3 John 2

PROUD
tongue that speaks p . . . . . . Ps 12:3
And fully repays the p . . . Ps 31:23
does not respect the p . . . . Ps 40:4
a haughty look and a p . . Ps 101:5
p He knows from afar . . . Ps 138:6
Everyone p . . . . Prov 16:5
by wine, He is a p . . . . Hab 2:5
He has scattered the p . . Luke 1:51
"God resists the p . . . . . . 1 Pet 5:5

PROVERB
of a drunkard Is a p . . . Prov 26:9
one shall take up a p . . . . . . Mic 2:4
to the true p . . . . 2 Pet 2:22

PROVERBS
three thousand p . . . . . . 1 Kin 4:32
in order many p . . . . Eccl 12:9

PROVIDE
"My son, God will p . . . . Gen 22:8
"P neither gold nor . . . . . Matt 10:9
if anyone does not p . . . . 1 Tim 5:8

PROVIDED
these hands have p . . . . Acts 20:34
p something better . . . . . . Heb 11:40

PROVISION
no p for the flesh . . . . . . Rom 13:14

PROVOKE
"Do they p Me to . . . . Jer 7:19
you, fathers, do not p . . . . Eph 6:4

PROVOKED
p the Most High . . . . Ps 78:56
his spirit was p . . . . Acts 17:16
seek its own, is not p . . . 1 Cor 13:5

PRUDENCE
To give p to the . . . . Prov 1:4
wisdom, dwell with p . . . Prov 8:12
us in all wisdom and p . . . . Eph 1:8

PRUDENT
p man covers shame . . . Prov 12:16
A p man conceals . . . . . Prov 12:23
The wisdom of the p . . . . Prov 14:8
p considers well . . . . Prov 14:15
heart will be called p . . Prov 16:21
p man foresees evil . . . . . Prov 22:3
Therefore the p . . . . Amos 5:13
from the wise and p . . . . Matt 11:25

PRUDENTLY
Servant shall deal p . . . . . . Is 52:13

PRUNES
that bears fruit He p . . . . John 15:2

PSALM
each of you has a p . . . 1 Cor 14:26

PSALMIST
And the sweet p . . . . 2 Sam 23:1

PSALMS
to one another in p . . . . . . Eph 5:19
Let him sing p . . . . James 5:13

PUNISH
p the righteous is . . . . . . Prov 17:26
Shall I not p them for . . . . . Jer 5:9

PUNISHED
p them often in every . . Acts 26:11
These shall be p . . . . 2 Thess 1:9

PUNISHES
will you say when He p . Jer 13:21

PUNISHMENT
p is greater than I . . . . Gen 4:13
you do in the day of p . . . . . Is 10:3
p they shall perish . . . . . . Jer 10:15
not turn away its p . . . . . Amos 1:3
into everlasting p . . . . . . Matt 25:46
p which was inflicted . . . . 2 Cor 2:6
Of how much worse p . . Heb 10:29
sent by him for the p . . . . 1 Pet 2:14
the unjust under p . . . . 2 Pet 2:9

PURE
a mercy seat of p gold . . . Ex 25:17
'My doctrine is p . . . . Job 11:4
that he could be p . . . . Job 15:14
of the LORD are p . . . . Ps 12:6
ways of a man are p . . . Prov 16:2
a generation that is p . . Prov 30:12
things indeed are p . . . . . Rom 14:20
whatever things are p . . . . . Phil 4:8
keep yourself p . . . . 1 Tim 5:22

p all things are p . . . . Titus 1:15
above is first p . . . . James 3:17
babes, desire the p . . . . . . 1 Pet 2:2
just as He is p . . . . 1 John 3:3

PURER
p eyes than to behold . . . Hab 1:13

PURGE
P me with hyssop . . . . Ps 51:7

PURGED
away, And your sin p . . . . . . Is 6:7

PURIFICATION
with the water of p . . . Num 31:23

PURIFIED
all things are p . . . . Heb 9:22
Since you have p . . . . . . 1 Pet 1:22

PURIFIES
hope in Him p himself . 1 John 3:3

PURIFY
and p your hearts . . . . . . James 4:8

PURIFYING
p their hearts by . . . . Acts 15:9
sanctifies for the p . . . . . . Heb 9:13

PURIM
called these days P . . . . . Esth 9:26

PURITY
spirit, in faith, in p . . . . 1 Tim 4:12

PURPOSE
A time for every p . . . . Eccl 3:1
But for this p I came . . John 12:27
by the determined p . . . . Acts 2:23
to fulfill His p . . . . Rev 17:17

PURSUE
p righteousness . . . . Rom 9:30
P love . . . . 1 Cor 14:1

PURSUES
flee when no one p . . . . . Prov 28:1

Q

QUAIL
and it brought q . . . . . . Num 11:31

QUARREL
He will not q nor cry . . . Matt 12:19
the Lord must not q . . . 2 Tim 2:24

QUARRELSOME
but gentle, not q . . . . 1 Tim 3:3

QUEEN
heart, 'I sit as q . . . . Rev 18:7

QUENCH
Many waters cannot q . . . . Song 8:7
flax He will not q . . . . . . Matt 12:20
q all the fiery . . . . Eph 6:16
Do not q the Spirit . . 1 Thess 5:19

QUENCHED
that shall never be q . . . Mark 9:43

QUESTIONS
and asking them q . . . . . . Luke 2:46

QUICKLY
with your adversary q . . Matt 5:25
"Surely I am coming q . . Rev 22:20

QUIET
aspire to lead a q . . . . 1 Thess 4:11
a gentle and q spirit . . . . . 1 Pet 3:4

QUIETNESS
a handful with q . . . . Eccl 4:6
In q and confidence . . . . . . Is 30:15
of righteousness, q . . . . . . Is 32:17
that they work in q . . 2 Thess 3:12

R

RABBI
be called by men, 'R . . . . Matt 23:7

RACA
to his brother, 'R . . . . Matt 5:22

RACE
man to run its r . . . . Ps 19:5
r is not to the swift . . . . . Eccl 9:11
I have finished the r . . . . . 2 Tim 4:7
with endurance the r . . . . Heb 12:1

RAGE
Why do the nations r . . . . . . Ps 2:1
'Why did the nations r . . Acts 4:25

RAIN
had not caused it to r . . . . Gen 2:5
And the r was on the . . . . Gen 7:12
I will r down on him . . Ezek 38:22
given you the former r . . Joel 2:23
the good, and sends r . . . Matt 5:45
"and the r descended . . . Matt 7:25
r that often comes . . . . Heb 6:7
that it would not r . . . . James 5:17

RAINBOW
"I set My r in the . . . . . . Gen 9:13
and there was a r . . . . Rev 4:3

RAINED
r fire and brimstone . . . Luke 17:29

RAINS
r righteousness . . . . Hos 10:12

RAISE
third day He will r . . . . Hos 6:2
in three days I will r . . . John 2:19
and I will r him up at . . . John 6:40
and the Lord will r . . . James 5:15

RAISED
be killed, and be r . . . . . Matt 16:21
just as Christ was r . . . . . . Rom 6:4
Spirit of Him who r . . . . . Rom 8:11
"How are the dead r . . 1 Cor 15:35
the dead will be r . . . . 1 Cor 15:52
and r us up together . . . . . . Eph 2:6

RAISES
"For as the Father r . . . John 5:21
but in God who r . . . . . . 2 Cor 1:9

RAN
You r well . . . . Gal 5:7

RANSOM
to give His life a r . . . . Mark 10:45
who gave Himself a r . . . 1 Tim 2:6

RANSOMED
And the r of the LORD . . . . Is 35:10
redeemed Jacob, And r . . Jer 31:11

RASH
Do not be r with your . . . Eccl 5:2

RASHLY
and do nothing r . . . . . . Acts 19:36

RAVENOUS
inwardly they are r . . . . . Matt 7:15

RAVENS
"Consider the r . . . . Luke 12:24

REACHING
r forward to those . . . . . . Phil 3:13

READ
day, and stood up to r . . Luke 4:16
hearts, known and r . . . . 2 Cor 3:2

READER
the r understand . . . . . Mark 13:14

READINESS
the word with all r . . . . Acts 17:11

READING
r the prophet Isaiah . . . . Acts 8:30

READS
Blessed is he who r . . . . Rev 1:3

READY
and those who were r . Matt 25:10
"Lord, I am r . . . . Luke 22:33
Be r in season and out . . 2 Tim 4:2
and always be r . . . . 1 Pet 3:15

REAP
they neither sow nor r . . Matt 6:26
you knew that I r . . . . . . Matt 25:26

REAPED
You have r iniquity . . . . Hos 10:13

REAPERS
r are the angels . . . . Matt 13:39

REAPING
r what I did not . . . . Luke 19:22

REAPS
sows and another r . . . . . John 4:37

REASON
"Come now, and let us r . . . . Is 1:18
who asks you a r . . . . 1 Pet 3:15

REASONED
for three Sabbaths r . . . . Acts 17:2

REBEL
if you refuse and r . . . . Is 1:20

REBELLING
more against Him By r . . . Ps 78:17

REBELLION
hearts as in the r . . . . Heb 3:8

REBELLIOUS
day long to a r people . . . . . Is 65:2

REBUILD
God, to r its ruins . . . . Ezra 9:9
r it as in the days of . . . . Amos 9:11

REBUKE
Turn at my r . . . . Prov 1:23
R a wise man . . . . Prov 9:8
r is better Than love . . . . Prov 27:5
R the oppressor . . . . Is 1:17
sins against you, r . . . . . . Luke 17:3
Do not r an older man . . . 1 Tim 5:1
who are sinning r . . . . . . 1 Tim 5:20
"The Lord r you . . . . Jude 9
"As many as I love, I r . . Rev 3:19

REBUKED
r the winds and the . . . . . Matt 8:26
r their unbelief . . . . Mark 16:14
but he was r for his . . . . 2 Pet 2:16

REBUKES
ear that hears the r . . . Prov 15:31

RECEIVE
believing, you will r ... Matt 21:22
and His own did not r ... John 1:11
will come again and r ... John 14:3
the world cannot r ... John 14:17
Ask, and you will r ... John 16:24
"R the Holy Spirit ... John 20:22
"Lord Jesus, r ... Acts 7:59
r the Holy Spirit ... Acts 19:2
R one who is weak ... Rom 14:1
r the Spirit by the ... Gal 3:2
suppose that he will r ... James 1:7

RECEIVED
But as many as r ... John 1:12
for God has r him ... Rom 14:3
For I r from the Lord ... 1 Cor 11:23
r Christ ... Col 2:6
R up in glory ... 1 Tim 3:16

RECEIVES
r you r Me ... Matt 10:40
and whoever r Me ... Mark 9:37

RECONCILE
and that He might r ... Eph 2:16

RECONCILED
First be r to your ... Matt 5:24
we were r ... Rom 5:10
Christ's behalf, be r ... 2 Cor 5:20

RECONCILIATION
now received the r ... Rom 5:11
to us the word of r ... 2 Cor 5:19

RECONCILING
cast away is the r ... Rom 11:15
God was in Christ r ... 2 Cor 5:19

REDEEM
But God will r my soul ... Ps 49:15
r their life from ... Ps 72:14
was going to r Israel ... Luke 24:21
r those who were ... Gal 4:5
us, that He might r ... Titus 2:14

REDEEMED
Let the r of the LORD ... Ps 107:2
r shall walk there ... Is 35:9
sea a road For the r ... Is 51:10
And you shall be r ... Is 52:3
and r His people ... Luke 1:68
Christ has r us from ... Gal 3:13
that you were not r ... 1 Pet 1:18
were slain, And have r ... Rev 5:9

REDEEMER
For I know that my R ... Job 19:25
Our R from Everlasting ... Is 63:16

REDEEMING
r the time ... Eph 5:16

REDEMPTION
those who looked for r ... Luke 2:38
your r draws near ... Luke 21:28
grace through the r ... Rom 3:24
the adoption, the r ... Rom 8:23
sanctification and r ... 1 Cor 1:30
In Him we have r ... Eph 1:7
for the day of r ... Eph 4:30
obtained eternal r ... Heb 9:12

REED
r He will not break ... Is 42:3
r shaken by the wind ... Matt 11:7

REFINED
us as silver is r ... Ps 66:10

REFINER
He will sit as a r ... Mal 3:3

REFORMATION
until the time of r ... Heb 9:10

REFRESH
r my heart in the Lord ... Philem 20

REFRESHED
his spirit has been r ... 2 Cor 7:13
for he often r ... 2 Tim 1:16

REFRESHES
r the soul of his ... Prov 25:13

REFRESHING
r may come from the ... Acts 3:19

REFUGE
eternal God is your r ... Deut 33:27
God is our r and ... Ps 46:1
who have fled for r ... Heb 6:18

REGARD
r iniquity in my heart ... Ps 66:18
did not fear God nor r ... Luke 18:2

REGARDED
my hand and no one r ... Prov 1:24
r the lowly state ... Luke 1:48

REGARDS
r a rebuke will be ... Prov 13:18

REGENERATION
to you, that in the r ... Matt 19:28
the washing of r ... Titus 3:5

REGISTERED
So all went to be r ... Luke 2:3

REGRETTED
but afterward he r ... Matt 21:29

REGULATIONS
yourselves to r ... Col 2:20

REIGN
"And He will r ... Luke 1:33
righteousness will r ... Rom 5:17
so grace might r ... Rom 5:21
do not let sin r ... Rom 6:12
For He must r till He ... 1 Cor 15:25
of Christ, and shall r ... Rev 20:6

REIGNED
so that as sin r ... Rom 5:21
You have r as kings ... 1 Cor 4:8
And they lived and r ... Rev 20:4

REIGNS
to Zion, "Your God r ... Is 52:7
Lord God Omnipotent r ... Rev 19:6

REJECT
"All too well you r ... Mark 7:9
R a divisive man ... Titus 3:10

REJECTED
He is despised and r ... Is 53:3
r Has become the ... Matt 21:42
many things and be r ... Luke 17:25
Moses whom they r ... Acts 7:35
to a living stone, r ... 1 Pet 2:4

REJECTION
you shall know My r ... Num 14:34

REJECTS
he who r Me r ... Luke 10:16

REJOICE
R in the LORD ... Ps 33:1
of Your wings I will r ... Ps 63:7
Let them r before God ... Ps 68:3
Let the heavens r ... Ps 96:11
Let the earth r ... Ps 97:1
We will r and be glad ... Ps 118:24
She shall r in time to ... Prov 31:25
R, O young man ... Eccl 11:9
your heart shall r ... Is 66:14
Do not r over me ... Mic 7:8
do not r ... Luke 10:20
you would r ... John 14:28
but the world will r ... John 16:20
and your heart will r ... John 16:22
R with those who ... Rom 12:15
and in this I r ... Phil 1:18
faith, I am glad and r ... Phil 2:17
R in the Lord always ... Phil 4:4
R always ... 1 Thess 5:16
yet believing, you r ... 1 Pet 1:8

REJOICED
And my spirit has r ... Luke 1:47
In that hour Jesus r ... Luke 10:21
Abraham r ... John 8:56

REJOICES
glad, and my glory r ... Ps 16:9
but r in the truth ... 1 Cor 13:6

REJOICING
come again with r ... Ps 126:6
he went on his way r ... Acts 8:39
confidence and the r ... Heb 3:6

RELENT
sworn And will not r ... Ps 110:4
sworn And will not r ... Heb 7:21

RELENTED
and God r from the ... Jon 3:10

RELENTING
I am weary of r ... Jer 15:6

RELIGION
in self-imposed r ... Col 2:23
and undefiled r ... James 1:27

RELIGIOUS
things you are very r ... Acts 17:22

REMAIN
that My joy may r ... John 15:11
your fruit should r ... John 15:16
"If I will that he r ... John 21:22
the greater part r ... 1 Cor 15:6
are alive and r ... 1 Thess 4:15
the things which r ... Rev 3:2

REMAINS
"While the earth r ... Gen 8:22
Therefore your sin r ... John 9:41
There r therefore a ... Heb 4:9

REMEMBER
"R the Sabbath day ... Ex 20:8
But we will r the name ... Ps 20:7
r Your name in the ... Ps 119:55
R now your Creator ... Eccl 12:1
r the former things ... Is 43:18
and their sin I will r ... Jer 31:34
In wrath r mercy ... Hab 3:2
And to r His holy ... Luke 1:72
"R Lot's wife ... Luke 17:32
r the words of the ... Acts 20:35
R that Jesus Christ ... 2 Tim 2:8
R those who rule ... Heb 13:7

REMEMBERED
Then God r Noah ... Gen 8:1
r His covenant with ... Ex 2:24
r His covenant forever ... Ps 105:8
yea, we wept When we r ... Ps 137:1
And Peter r the word ... Matt 26:75
r the word of the Lord ... Acts 11:16

REMEMBRANCE
r my song in the night ... Ps 77:6
Put Me in r ... Is 43:26

REVELATION
Where there is no *r* . . . . Prov 29:18
it came through the *r* . . . . Gal 1:12
spirit of wisdom and *r* . . . Eph 1:17
r He made known to . . . . . Eph 3:3
and glory at the *r* . . . . 1 Pet 1:7

REVERENCE
and *r* My sanctuary . . . . Lev 19:30
God acceptably with *r* . . Heb 12:28

REVERENT
man who is always *r* . . Prov 28:14
their wives must be *r* . . 1 Tim 3:11

REVILE
are you when they *r* . . . . Matt 5:11
r God's high priest . . . . . . Acts 23:4

REVILED
crucified with Him *r* . . Mark 15:32
who, when He was *r* . . . 1 Pet 2:23

REVIVAL
give us a measure of *r* . . . Ezra 9:8

REVIVE
Will You not *r* us . . . . Ps 85:6
two days He will *r* . . . . Hos 6:2

REVIVED
came, sin *r* and I died . . . . Rom 7:9

REWARD
exceedingly great *r* . . . . . . Gen 15:1
look, And see the *r* . . . . Ps 91:8
Behold, His *r* is with . . . . . . Is 40:10
for great is your *r* . . . . . . Matt 5:12
you, they have their *r* . . . . Matt 6:2
no means lose his *r* . . . . Matt 10:42
we receive the due *r* . . . Luke 23:41
will receive his own *r* . . . 1 Cor 3:8
cheat you of your *r* . . . . . . Col 2:18
for he looked to the *r* . . . Heb 11:26
quickly, and My *r* . . . . . . Rev 22:12

REWARDS
Whoever *r* evil for . . . . . . Prov 17:13
And follows after *r* . . . . Is 1:23

RICH
Abram was very *r* . . . . . . Gen 13:2
The *r* and the poor . . . . . . Prov 22:2
r rules over the poor . . . . Prov 22:7
r man is wise in his . . . . Prov 28:11
Do not curse the *r* . . . . . Eccl 10:20
it is hard for a *r* . . . . Matt 19:23
to you who are *r* . . . . Luke 6:24
the *r* man's table . . . . . . Luke 16:21
for he was very *r* . . . . . Luke 18:23
You are already *r* . . . . 1 Cor 4:8
though He was *r* . . . . 2 Cor 8:9
who desire to be *r* . . . . 1 Tim 6:9
of this world to be *r* . . . . James 2:5
you say, 'I am *r* . . . . Rev 3:17

RICHES
R and honor are . . . . Prov 8:18
R do not profit . . . . Prov 11:4
in his *r* will fall . . . . Prov 11:28
of the wise is their *r* . . . Prov 14:24
and *r* are an . . . . Prov 19:14
of the LORD Are *r* . . . . Prov 22:4
r are not forever . . . . Prov 27:24
do you despise the *r* . . . . . Rom 2:4
make known the *r* . . . . Rom 9:23
what are the *r* . . . . Eph 1:18
show the exceeding *r* . . . . . . Eph 2:7
the unsearchable *r* . . . . Eph 3:8
r than the treasures . . . . . . Heb 11:26
To receive power and *r* . . Rev 5:12

RICHLY
Christ dwell in you *r* . . . . . Col 3:16
God, who gives us *r* . . . 1 Tim 6:17

RIGHT
the *r* of the firstborn . . . Deut 21:17
"Is your heart *r* . . . . 2 Kin 10:15
Lord, "Sit at My *r* . . . . Ps 110:1
a way which seems *r* . . . . Prov 14:12
clothed and in his *r* . . . . . Mark 5:15
to them He gave the *r* . . . John 1:12
your heart is not *r* . . . . . . Acts 8:21
seven stars in His *r* . . . . Rev 2:1

RIGHTEOUS
also destroy the *r* . . . . . . Gen 18:23
and they justify the *r* . . . . Deut 25:1
that he could be *r* . . . . Job 15:14
"The *r* see it and . . . . Job 22:19
r shows mercy and . . . . Ps 37:21
I have not seen the *r* . . . . . . Ps 37:25
The LORD loves the *r* . . . Ps 146:8
r is a well of life . . . . Prov 10:11
r will be gladness . . . . . . Prov 10:28
r will be delivered . . . . . . Prov 11:21
r will be recompensed . Prov 11:31
the prayer of the *r* . . . . . . Prov 15:29
r are bold as a lion . . . . . . Prov 28:1
r considers the cause . . . Prov 29:7
Do not be overly *r* . . . . Eccl 7:16
event happens to the *r* . . . . Eccl 9:2
with My *r* right hand . . . . . Is 41:10
By His knowledge My *r* . . . Is 53:11
The *r* perishes . . . . Is 57:1
they sell the *r* . . . . Amos 2:6
not come to call the *r* . . . . Matt 9:13
r men desired to see . . . Matt 13:17
r will shine forth as . . . . Matt 13:43
that they were *r* . . . . Luke 18:9
this was a *r* . . . . Luke 23:47
"There is none r . . . . Rom 3:10
r man will one die . . . . Rom 5:7
Jesus Christ the *r* . . . . . . 1 John 2:1

RIGHTEOUSLY
should live soberly, *r* . . . Titus 2:12
to Him who judges *r* . . . . 1 Pet 2:23

RIGHTEOUSNESS
it to him for *r* . . . . Gen 15:6
I put on *r* . . . . Job 29:14
I call, O God of my *r* . . . . Ps 4:1
from the LORD, And *r* . . . . Ps 24:5
shall speak of Your *r* . . . . . Ps 35:28
the good news of *r* . . . . Ps 40:9
heavens declare His *r* . . . . . . Ps 50:6
R and peace have . . . . Ps 85:10
R will go before Him . . . . . Ps 85:13
r endures forever . . . . Ps 111:3
r delivers from death . . . . Prov 10:2
The *r* of the blameless . . Prov 11:5
the way of *r* is life . . . . . . Prov 12:28
R exalts a nation . . . . Prov 14:34
He who follows *r* . . . . Prov 21:21
R lodged in it . . . . Is 1:21
in the LORD I have *r* . . . . . . Is 45:24
r will be forever . . . . Is 51:8
I will declare your *r* . . . . Is 57:12
r as a breastplate . . . . Is 59:17
r goes forth as . . . . Is 62:1
The Lord Our *R* . . . . Jer 23:6
to David A Branch of *r* . . . Jer 33:15
The *r* of the righteous . Ezek 18:20
who turn many to *r* . . . . Dan 12:3
to fulfill all *r* . . . . Matt 3:15
exceeds the *r* of the . . . . . Matt 5:20
to you in the way of *r* . Matt 21:32
For in it the *r* . . . . Rom 1:17
even the *r* of God . . . . Rom 3:22
accounted to him for r . . . Rom 4:22
r will reign in life . . . . Rom 5:17
might reign through *r* . . . . Rom 5:21
ignorant of God's *r* . . . . Rom 10:3
might become the *r* . . . . . 2 Cor 5:21
the breastplate of *r* . . . . . . Eph 6:14
not having my own *r* . . . . . . Phil 3:9
r which we have . . . . Titus 3:5
not produce the *r* . . . . . . James 1:20
a preacher of *r* . . . . 2 Pet 2:5
a new earth in which *r* . 2 Pet 3:13
who practices *r* . . . . 1 John 2:29
He who practices *r* . . . . 1 John 3:7

RIGHTLY
wise uses knowledge *r* . . . Prov 15:2
r dividing the word . . . . 2 Tim 2:15

RISE
for He makes His sun *r* . Matt 5:45
third day He will *r* . . . . . Matt 20:19
third day He will *r* . . . . . Luke 18:33
be the first to *r* . . . . Acts 26:23
in Christ will *r* . . . . 1 Thess 4:16

RISEN
there has not *r* . . . . Matt 11:11
disciples that He is *r* . . . . . Matt 28:7
"The Lord is *r* . . . . Luke 24:34
then Christ is not *r* . . . 1 Cor 15:13
if Christ is not *r* . . . . . . 1 Cor 15:17
But now Christ is *r* . . . 1 Cor 15:20

RIVER
peace to her like a *r* . . . . . . Is 66:12
he showed me a pure *r* . . Rev 22:1

RIVERS
By the *r* of Babylon . . . . . . Ps 137:1
All the *r* run into the . . . . . Eccl 1:7
his heart will flow *r* . . . . . John 7:38

ROAR
The LORD also will *r* . . . . Joel 3:16

ROARING
and the waves *r* . . . . Luke 21:25
walks about like a *r* . . . . . . 1 Pet 5:8

ROARS
"The LORD *r* from . . . . . . Amos 1:2
as when a lion *r* . . . . Rev 10:3

ROB
"Will a man *r* God . . . . Mal 3:8

ROBBED
r other churches . . . . 2 Cor 11:8

ROBBER
is a thief and a *r* . . . . John 10:1
Barabbas was a *r* . . . . . . John 18:40

ROBBERS
also crucified two *r* . . . Mark 15:27
Me are thieves and *r* . . . John 10:8

ROBBERY
did not consider it *r* . . . . . . Phil 2:6

ROBE
'Bring out the best *r* . . Luke 15:22
on Him a purple *r* . . . . John 19:2
Then a white *r* was . . . . Rev 6:11

ROBES
have stained all My *r* . . . . . . Is 63:3
go around in long *r* . . . . Luke 20:46
clothed with white *r* . . . . Rev 7:9

ROCK
you shall strike the *r* . . . . . Ex 17:6
and struck the *r* . . . . Num 20:11
For their *r* is not . . . . Deut 32:31
"The LORD is my *r* . . . . 2 Sam 22:2
And who is a *r* . . . . 2 Sam 22:32
Blessed be my *R* . . . . . 2 Sam 22:47
For You are my *r* . . . . Ps 31:3
r that is higher than . . . . . . Ps 61:2
been mindful of the *R* . . . . . Is 17:10
shadow of a great *r* . . . . Is 32:2
his house on the *r* . . . . Matt 7:24
r I will build My . . . . Matt 16:18

stumbling stone and r .. Rom 9:33
R that followed them ... 1 Cor 10:4

ROD

Your r and Your staff .... Ps 23:4
shall come forth a R ...... Is 11:1
rule them with a r .... Rev 2:27

ROOM

you a large upper r ... Mark 14:15
no r for them in the ..... Luke 2:7
into the upper r .... Acts 1:13

ROOT

day there shall be a R .... Is 11:10
because they had no r .. Matt 13:6
of money is a r .... 1 Tim 6:10
lest any r of .... Heb 12:15
I am the R and the ..... Rev 22:16

ROOTED

r and built up in Him ..... Col 2:7

ROSE

end Christ died and r ... Rom 14:9
buried, and that He r .. 1 Cor 15:4
Jesus died and r ..... 1 Thess 4:14

RULE

And he shall r .... Gen 3:16
puts an end to all r ... 1 Cor 15:24
let the peace of God r .... Col 3:15
Let the elders who r ... 1 Tim 5:17
Remember those who r .. Heb 13:7

RULER

to Me The One to be r ..... Mic 5:2
by Beelzebub, the r .... Matt 12:24
the r of this world ...... John 12:31
'Who made you a r ..... Acts 7:27

RULERS

And the r take counsel ..... Ps 2:2
"You know that the r ... Matt 20:25
which none of the r .... 1 Cor 2:8
powers, against the r .... Eph 6:12

RULES

That the Most High r .... Dan 4:17
that the Most High r .... Dan 4:32
r his own house well .... 1 Tim 3:4

RULING

r their children .... 1 Tim 3:12

RUMORS

hear of wars and r ...... Matt 24:6

RUN

r and not be weary .... Is 40:31
us, and let us r .... Heb 12:1

S

SABAOTH

S had left us a .... Rom 9:29
ears of the Lord of S ... James 5:4

SABBATH

"Remember the S .... Ex 20:8
S was made for man ... Mark 2:27

SABBATHS

S you shall keep .... Ex 31:13

SACRIFICE

to the LORD than s ...... Prov 21:3
For the LORD has a s ...... Is 34:6
of My offerings they s ... Hos 8:13
LORD has prepared a s ... Zeph 1:7
desire mercy and not s .. Matt 9:13
an offering and a s .... Eph 5:2
put away sin by the s ... Heb 9:26
no longer remains a s .. Heb 10:26
offer the s of praise .... Heb 13:15

SACRIFICED

s their sons And their .... Ps 106:37

SACRIFICES

The s of God are a .... Ps 51:17
multitude of your s .... Is 1:11
priests, to offer up s .... Heb 7:27
s God is well pleased ... Heb 13:16

SAFE

he has received him s . Luke 15:27

SAFELY

make them lie down s ... Hos 2:18

SAFETY

say, "Peace and s ..... 1 Thess 5:3

SAINTS

s who are on the earth .... Ps 16:3
does not forsake His s ... Ps 37:28
Is the death of His s ..... Ps 116:15
war against the s .... Dan 7:21
Jesus, called to be s .... 1 Cor 1:2
the least of all the s .... Eph 3:8
be glorified in His s .. 2 Thess 1:10
all delivered to the s ...... Jude 3
shed the blood of s ...... Rev 16:6

SALT

shall season with s ...... Lev 2:13
"You are the s .... Matt 5:13
s loses its flavor .... Mark 9:50

SALVATION

still, and see the s .... Ex 14:13
S belongs to the LORD .... Ps 3:8
is my light and my s .... Ps 27:1
God is the God of s ...... Ps 68:20
joy in the God of my s .. Hab 3:18
raised up a horn of s ... Luke 1:69
"Nor is there s .... Acts 4:12
the power of God to s .. Rom 1:16
now is the day of s ..... 2 Cor 6:2
work out your own s .... Phil 2:12
chose you for s .... 2 Thess 2:13
neglect so great a s ..... Heb 2:3

SAMARITAN

a drink from me, a S .... John 4:9

SANCTIFICATION

will of God, your s .... 1 Thess 4:3

SANCTIFIED

they also may be s .... John 17:19
but you were s .... 1 Cor 6:11
for it is s by the .... 1 Tim 4:5

SANCTIFIES

For both He who s ...... Heb 2:11

SANCTIFY

s My great name .... Ezek 36:23
"*S them by Your* ...... John 17:17
that He might s .... Eph 5:26

SANCTUARY

let them make Me a s .... Ex 25:8
and the earthly s .... Heb 9:1

SAND

descendants as the s .... Gen 32:12
innumerable as the s ... Heb 11:12

SAT

into heaven, and S .... Mark 16:19
And He who s there was . Rev 4:3

SATAN

before the LORD, and S .... Job 1:6
"Away with you, S .... Matt 4:10
"Get behind Me, S ..... Matt 16:23
"How can S cast out ... Mark 3:23
S has asked for you ... Luke 22:31
to the working of S ... 2 Thess 2:9
known the depths of S .. Rev 2:24
years have expired, S ... Rev 20:7

SATIATED

s the weary soul .... Jer 31:25

SATISFIED

I shall be s when I .... Ps 17:15
that are never s .... Prov 30:15
of His soul, and be s ...... Is 53:11

SATISFIES

s the longing soul .... Ps 107:9

SATISFY

s us early with Your ..... Ps 90:14
long life I will s .... Ps 91:16
for what does not s ...... Is 55:2

SAVE

Oh, s me for Your .... Ps 6:4
s the children of the ...... Ps 72:4
s the souls of the .... Ps 72:13
That it cannot s .... Is 59:1
s you And deliver you ... Jer 15:20
other, That he may s ... Hos 13:10
JESUS, for He will s ...... Matt 1:21
s his life will .... Matt 16:25
s that which was ...... Matt 18:11
let Him s Himself if ... Luke 23:35
but to s the world ...... John 12:47
the world to s sinners . 1 Tim 1:15

SAVED

"He s others .... Matt 27:42
That we should be s .... Luke 1:71
"Your faith has s .... Luke 7:50
might be s .... John 3:17
them, saying, "Be s ..... Acts 2:40
what must I do to be s . Acts 16:30
which also you are s ... 1 Cor 15:2
grace you have been s .... Eph 2:8
to His mercy He s .... Titus 3:5
of those who are s ..... Rev 21:24

SAVES

antitype which now s .. 1 Pet 3:21

SAVIOR

I, the LORD, am your S ..... Is 60:16
rejoiced in God my S ... Luke 1:47
the city of David a S ... Luke 2:11
up for Israel a S .... Acts 13:23
God, who is the S ..... 1 Tim 4:10
and S Jesus Christ ..... Titus 2:13

SAWN

stoned, they were s .... Heb 11:37

SAY

"But I s to you that ..... Matt 5:22
"But who do you s ..... Matt 16:15

SAYING

This is a faithful s ..... 1 Tim 1:15

SAYINGS

whoever hears these s .. Matt 7:24

SCALES

on it had a pair of s ...... Rev 6:5

SCARLET

your sins are like s .... Is 1:18

SCATTER

I will s you among the .. Lev 26:33

SCATTERED

"Israel is like s sheep ... Jer 50:17
the sheep will be s ... Mark 14:27

SCATTERS
not gather with Me *s* . . . Matt 12:30

SCEPTER
s shall not depart . . . . . Gen 49:10

SCHEMER
Will be called a *s* . . . . Prov 24:8

SCHEMES
sought out many *s* . . . . . Eccl 7:29

SCHISM
there should be no *s* . . 1 Cor 12:25

SCHOOL
daily in the *s* of . . . . Acts 19:9

SCOFF
They *s* at kings . . . . Hab 1:10

SCOFFER
"He who corrects a *s* . . . . Prov 9:7
s is an abomination . . . . Prov 24:9

SCOFFERS
s will come in the . . . . 2 Pet 3:3

SCORCHED
And men were *s* with . . . . Rev 16:9

SCORN
My friends *s* me . . . . Job 16:20

SCORNS
He *s* the scornful . . . . Prov 3:34

SCORPIONS
on serpents and *s* . . . . . Luke 10:19
They had tails like *s* . . . . . Rev 9:10

SCOURGE
will mock Him, and *s* . Mark 10:34

SCOURGES
s every son whom . . . . . Heb 12:6

SCRIBES
"Beware of the *s* . . . . . Mark 12:38

SCRIPTURE
S cannot be broken . . . John 10:35
All *S* is given by . . . . . . 2 Tim 3:16

SCRIPTURES
S must be fulfilled . . . . Mark 14:49

SCROLL
eat this *s* . . . . Ezek 3:1
the sky receded as a *s* . . . Rev 6:14

SEA
drowned in the Red *S* . . . . Ex 15:4
who go down to the *s* . . . Ps 107:23
and the *s* obey Him . . . . . Matt 8:27
throne there was a *s* . . . . . . Rev 4:6
there was no more *s* . . . . Rev 21:1

SEAL
stands, having this *s* . . . 2 Tim 2:19

SEALED
by whom you were *s* . . . . Eph 4:30

SEAM
tunic was without *s* . . . John 19:23

SÉANCE
"Please conduct a *s* . . . 1 Sam 28:8

SEARCH
glory of kings is to *s* . . . . Prov 25:2
s the Scriptures . . . . John 5:39

SEARCHED
s the Scriptures . . . . Acts 17:11

SEARCHES
For the Spirit *s* . . . . 1 Cor 2:10

SEASON
Be ready in *s* and out . . . 2 Tim 4:2

SEASONED
how shall it be *s* . . . . Matt 5:13

SEASONS
the times and the *s* . . . 1 Thess 5:1

SEAT
shall make a mercy *s* . . . . Ex 25:17
before the judgment *s* . 2 Cor 5:10

SEATS
at feasts, the best *s* . . . . . Matt 23:6

SECRET
s things belong . . . . Deut 29:29
In the *s* place of His . . . . . . Ps 27:5
Father who is in the *s* . . . . Matt 6:6

SECRETLY
He lies in wait *s* . . . . Ps 10:9

SECRETS
For He knows the *s* . . . . . . Ps 44:21
God will judge the *s* . . . . Rom 2:16

SECT
to the strictest *s* . . . . Acts 26:5

SECURELY
nation that dwells *s* . . . . . Jer 49:31

SEDUCED
flattering lips she *s* . . . . . Prov 7:21

SEE
in my flesh I shall *s* . . . . Job 19:26
For they shall *s* God . . . . . Matt 5:8
seeing they do not *s* . . . Matt 13:13
rejoiced to *s* My day . . . . John 8:56
They shall *s* His face . . . . Rev 22:4

SEED
He shall see His *s* . . . . Is 53:10
S were the promises . . . . . Gal 3:16
you are Abraham's *s* . . . . Gal 3:29

SEEDS
the good *s* are the . . . . . Matt 13:38

SEEK
pray and *s* My face . . . . 2 Chr 7:14
S the LORD while He . . . . . . Is 55:6
s, and you will find . . . . . Matt 7:7
of Man has come to *s* . Luke 19:10
"You will *s* Me and . . . . John 7:34
For all *s* their own . . . . . Phil 2:21
s those things which . . . . . . Col 3:1

SEEKING
like a roaring lion, *s* . . . . . 1 Pet 5:8

SEEKS
There is none who s . . . . Rom 3:11

SEEMS
is a way which *s* . . . . Prov 14:12

SEEN
s God face to face . . . . . Gen 32:30
No one has *s* God at . . . . John 1:18
s Me has *s* the . . . . John 14:9
things which are not *s* . 2 Cor 4:18

SEES
s his brother in need . . 1 John 3:17

SELF-CONFIDENT
a fool rages and is *s* . . . Prov 14:16

SELF-CONTROL
gentleness, *s* . . . . Gal 5:23
to knowledge *s* . . . . 2 Pet 1:6

SELF-CONTROLLED
just, holy, *s* . . . . Titus 1:8

SELF-SEEKING
envy and *s* exist . . . . . . James 3:16

SELL
s whatever you have . . Mark 10:21

SEND
"Behold, I *s* you out . . . Matt 10:16
has sent Me, I also *s* . . . John 20:21

SENSES
of use have their *s* . . . . . . Heb 5:14

SENSIBLY
who can answer *s* . . . . . . Prov 26:16

SENSUAL
but is earthly, *s* . . . . . . James 3:15

SENT
unless they are *s* . . . . . . Rom 10:15

SEPARATED
it pleased God, who *s* . . . . Gal 1:15

SEPARATES
who repeats a matter *s* . Prov 17:9

SEPARATION
the middle wall of *s* . . . . . Eph 2:14

SERAPHIM
Above it stood *s* . . . . Is 6:2

SERIOUS
therefore be *s* and . . . . 1 Pet 4:7

SERPENT
s was more cunning . . . . . . Gen 3:1
"Make a fiery *s* . . . . Num 21:8
Moses lifted up the *s* . . . John 3:14

SERPENTS
be wise as *s* . . . . Matt 10:16

SERVANT
s will rule over a son . . . Prov 17:2
good and faithful *s* . . . . Matt 25:21

SERVANTS
are unprofitable *s* . . . . . Luke 17:10

SERVE
to be served, but to *s* . . Matt 20:28
but through love *s* . . . . Gal 5:13

SERVES
"If anyone *s* Me . . . . John 12:26

SERVICE
is your reasonable *s* . . . . Rom 12:1
with good will doing *s* . . . . Eph 6:7

SERVING
fervent in spirit, *s* . . . . . Rom 12:11

SET
"See, I have *s* . . . . Deut 30:15
s aside the grace . . . . Gal 2:21

SETTLE
"Therefore *s* it in . . . . . . Luke 21:14

SETTLED
O LORD, Your word is *s* . Ps 119:89

SEVEN
s churches which are ..... Rev 1:4

SEVENTY
“S weeks are .... Dan 9:24

SEVERE
not to be too s .... 2 Cor 2:5

SEVERITY
the goodness and s .... Rom 11:22

SHADE
may nest under its s ... Mark 4:32

SHADOW
In the s of His hand .... Is 49:2
the law, having a s ...... Heb 10:1

SHAKE
s the earth .... Is 2:19
I will s all nations .... Hag 2:7

SHAKEN
not to be soon s ...... 2 Thess 2:2

SHAKES
s the Wilderness .... Ps 29:8

SHAME
never be put to s .... Joel 2:26
to put to s the wise .... 1 Cor 1:27
glory is in their s .... Phil 3:19

SHAMEFUL
For it is s even to .... Eph 5:12

SHARE
to do good and to s .... Heb 13:16

SHARING
for your liberal s ...... 2 Cor 9:13

SHARP
S as a two-edged sword .. Prov 5:4

SHARPEN
s their tongue like a ...... Ps 64:3

SHARPENS
My adversary s His ...... Job 16:9

SHARPNESS
I should use s .... 2 Cor 13:10

SHEATH
your sword into the s .. John 18:11

SHEAVES
Bringing his s .... Ps 126:6
gather them like s .... Mic 4:12

SHED
which is s for many ... Matt 26:28

SHEDDING
blood, and without s .... Heb 9:22

SHEEP
s will be scattered ...... Zech 13:7
having a hundred s ...... Luke 15:4
and I know My s ..... John 10:14
“He was led as a s ...... Acts 8:32

SHEEPFOLDS
lie down among the s .... Ps 68:13

SHEET
object like a great s .... Acts 10:11

SHELTER
the LORD will be a s ..... Joel 3:16

SHELTERS
s him all the day long . Deut 33:12

SHEOL
not leave my soul in S ... Ps 16:10
the belly of S I cried ...... Jon 2:2

SHEPHERD
The LORD is my s .... Ps 23:1
His flock like a s .... Is 40:11
'I will strike the S ..... Matt 26:31
“I am the good s ...... John 10:11
the dead, that great S .. Heb 13:20
S the flock of God .... 1 Pet 5:2
when the Chief S .... 1 Pet 5:4

SHEPHERDS
“And I will give you s .... Jer 3:15
s have led them astray ... Jer 50:6

SHIELD
I am your s .... Gen 15:1
truth shall be your s ...... Ps 91:4
all, taking the s .... Eph 6:16

SHINE
LORD make His face s .. Num 6:25
among whom you s .... Phil 2:15

SHINED
them a light has s .... Is 9:2

SHINES
heed as a light that s ... 2 Pet 1:19

SHINING
light is already s ...... 1 John 2:8

SHIPS
down to the sea in s .... Ps 107:23

SHIPWRECK
faith have suffered s ... 1 Tim 1:19

SHOOT
They s out the lip .... Ps 22:7

SHORT
have sinned and fall s .. Rom 3:23

SHORTENED
those days were s ..... Matt 24:22

SHOUT
heaven with a s .... 1 Thess 4:16

SHOW
a land that I will s ...... Gen 12:1
s Him greater works ..... John 5:20

SHOWBREAD
s which was not lawful . Matt 12:4

SHOWERS
make it soft with s ...... Ps 65:10

SHREWDLY
because he had dealt s . Luke 16:8

SHRINES
who made silver s ..... Acts 19:24

SHRIVELED
You have s me up .... Job 16:8

SHUFFLES
with his eyes, He s ..... Prov 6:13

SHUNNED
feared God and s evil ...... Job 1:1

SHUT
For you s up the ...... Matt 23:13

SHUTS
s his eyes from seeing .... Is 33:15
who opens and no one s .. Rev 3:7

SICK
I was s and you .... Matt 25:36
faith will save the s ... James 5:15

SICKLE
“Thrust in Your s ...... Rev 14:15

SICKNESS
will sustain him in s ... Prov 18:14
“This s is not unto ..... John 11:4

SICKNESSES
And bore our s .... Matt 8:17

SIDE
The LORD is on my s ..... Ps 118:6

SIFT
s the nations with the .... Is 30:28

SIGH
our years like a s .... Ps 90:9

SIGHING
For my s comes before ... Job 3:24

SIGHT
and see this great s .... Ex 3:3
by faith, not by s .... 2 Cor 5:7

SIGN
will give you a s .... Is 7:14
seeks after a s .... Matt 12:39
For Jews request a s ... 1 Cor 1:22

SIGNS
and let them be for s .... Gen 1:14
cannot discern the s ...... Matt 16:3
did many other s ...... John 20:30

SILENCE
That You may s .... Ps 8:2
seal, there was s .... Rev 8:1

SILENT
season, and am not s ..... Ps 22:2

SILK
covered you with s ..... Ezek 16:10

SILLY
They are s children .... Jer 4:22

SILVER
may buy the poor for s . Amos 8:6
him thirty pieces of s .. Matt 26:15

SIMILITUDE
been made in the s ..... James 3:9

SIMPLE
making wise the s .... Ps 19:7

SIMPLICITY
corrupted from the s ... 2 Cor 11:3

SIN
and be sure your s ..... Num 32:23
Be angry, and do not s ..... Ps 4:4
s is always before me ..... Ps 51:3
soul an offering for s ...... Is 53:10
And He bore the s .... Is 53:12
who takes away the s .. John 1:29
“He who is without s .... John 8:7
convict the world of s .. John 16:8
s entered the world ..... Rom 5:12
s is not imputed .... Rom 5:13
s shall not have .... Rom 6:14
Shall we s because we .. Rom 6:15
Him who knew no s ... 2 Cor 5:21

man of *s* is revealed ..2 Thess 2:3
we are, yet without *s*.... Heb 4:15
do it, to him it is *s* .... James 4:17
say that we have no *s* .. 1 John 1:8
and he cannot *s* .... 1 John 3:9

SINCERE
and from *s* faith .... 1 Tim 1:5

SINCERITY
simplicity and godly *s* . 2 Cor 1:12

SINFUL
from me, for I am a *s* .... Luke 5:8
become exceedingly *s* .. Rom 7:13

SING
Let him *s* psalms ..... James 5:13

SINGERS
The *s* went before .... Ps 68:25

SINGING
His presence with *s* ...... Ps 100:2
and spiritual songs, *s* .... Eph 5:19

SINISTER
Who understands *s* ..... Dan 8:23

SINK
I *s* in deep mire .... Ps 69:2
to *s* he cried out .... Matt 14:30

SINNED
You only, have I *s* .... Ps 51:4
"Father, I have *s* .... Luke 15:18
for all have *s* and .... Rom 3:23
that we have not *s* .... 1 John 1:10

SINNER
s who repents than ..... Luke 15:7
the ungodly and the s ... 1 Pet 4:18

SINNERS
in the path of *s* .... Ps 1:1
the righteous, but *s* ..... Matt 9:13
while we were still *s* ...... Rom 5:8
many were made *s* ..... Rom 5:19
the world to save *s* .... 1 Tim 1:15
such hostility from *s* .... Heb 12:3

SINS
from presumptuous *s* ..... Ps 19:13
You, Our secret *s* .... Ps 90:8
The soul who *s* shall ... Ezek 18:4
if your brother *s* ...... Matt 18:15
s according to the ..... 1 Cor 15:3
the forgiveness of *s* ...... Eph 1:7
If we confess our *s* .... 1 John 1:9
propitiation for our *s* .. 1 John 2:2

SISTER
is My brother and *s* .... Matt 12:50

SIT
but to *s* on My right ... Matt 20:23
"S at My right hand ..... Heb 1:13
I will grant to *s* .... Rev 3:21

SITS
It is He who *s* above ..... Is 40:22
so that he *s* as God ... 2 Thess 2:4

SITTING
where Christ is, *s* .... Col 3:1

SKILL
hand forget its *s* .... Ps 137:5

SKILLFULNESS
guided them by the *s* .... Ps 78:72

SKIN
God made tunics of *s* .... Gen 3:21

LORD and said, "*S* .... Job 2:4
Ethiopian change his *s* .. Jer 13:23

SKIP
He makes them also *s* ..... Ps 29:6

SKIPPING
upon the mountains, *S* ... Song 2:8

SKULL
to say, Place of a *S* .... Matt 27:33

SKY
s receded as a scroll ..... Rev 6:14

SLACK
The Lord is not *s* .... 2 Pet 3:9

SLAIN
is the Lamb who was *s* .. Rev 5:12

SLANDER
whoever spreads *s* ..... Prov 10:18

SLANDERERS
be reverent, not *s* ..... 1 Tim 3:11

SLANDEROUSLY
as we are *s* reported ...... Rom 3:8

SLAUGHTER
led as a lamb to the *s* ...... Is 53:7
as sheep for the s ...... Rom 8:36

SLAVE
commits sin is a *s* ...... John 8:34

SLAVES
should no longer be *s* .... Rom 6:6

SLAY
s the righteous .... Gen 18:25

SLEEP
God caused a deep *s* .... Gen 2:21
neither slumber nor *s* .... Ps 121:4
He gives His beloved *s* ... Ps 127:2
and many *s* .... 1 Cor 11:30
We shall not all *s* ..... 1 Cor 15:51

SLEEPERS
gently the lips of *s* ...... Song 7:9

SLEEPING
"Are you still *s* .... Matt 26:45

SLEEPLESSNESS
in labors, in *s* .... 2 Cor 6:5

SLEEPS
"Our friend Lazarus *s* . John 11:11

SLEPT
I lay down and *s* .... Ps 3:5

SLIGHTED
is the one who is *s* ..... Prov 12:9

SLING
he had, and his *s* .... 1 Sam 17:40

SLIP
Their foot shall *s* ...... Deut 32:35

SLIPPERY
set them in *s* places ..... Ps 73:18

SLOOPS
all the beautiful *s* .... Is 2:16

SLOW
hear, *s* to speak, *s* ..... James 1:19

SLUGGARD
will you slumber, O *s* .... Prov 6:9

SLUMBERING
upon men, While *s* ..... Job 33:15

SMALL
And I saw the dead, *s* .. Rev 20:12

SMELL
and he smelled the *s* .... Gen 27:27

SMELLS
s the battle from afar ... Job 39:25

SMITTEN
Him stricken, *S* .... Is 53:4

SMOKE
was filled with *s* .... Rev 15:8

SMOOTH
And the rough places *s* .... Is 40:4

SMOOTH-SKINNED
man, and I am a *s* ..... Gen 27:11

SNAIL
s which melts away as .... Ps 58:8

SNARE
is a fowler's *s* .... Hos 9:8
it will come as a *s* .... Luke 21:35
and escape the *s* ...... 2 Tim 2:26

SNARED
All of them are *s* .... Is 42:22

SNARES
who seek my life lay *s* ... Ps 38:12

SNATCH
neither shall anyone *s* . John 10:28

SNATCHES
s away what was ...... Matt 13:19

SNEER
And you *s* at it .... Mal 1:13

SNIFFED
They *s* at the wind .... Jer 14:6

SNORTING
s strikes terror .... Job 39:20

SNOW
shall be whiter than *s* ..... Ps 51:7
shall be as white as *s* ...... Is 1:18

SOAKED
Their land shall be *s* ...... Is 34:7

SOAP
lye, and use much *s* ...... Jer 2:22

SOBER
the older men be *s* ...... Titus 2:2

SOBERLY
think, but to think *s* .... Rom 12:3

SODA
And like vinegar on *s* .. Prov 25:20

SODOMITES
nor homosexuals, nor *s* . 1 Cor 6:9

SOJOURNER
no *s* had to lodge .... Job 31:32

SOJOURNERS
are strangers and *s* ..... Lev 25:23

SOLD
s his birthright .... Gen 25:33

s all that he had . . . . Matt 13:46
but I am carnal, *s* . . . . . . Rom 7:14

SOLDIER
hardship as a good *s* . . . . 2 Tim 2:3

SOLDIERS
s twisted a crown . . . . . . John 19:2

SOLITARILY
heritage, Who dwell *s* . . . Mic 7:14

SOLITARY
God sets the *s* in . . . . Ps 68:6

SOMEBODY
up, claiming to be *s* . . . . Acts 5:36

SOMETHING
thinks himself to be *s* . . . . Gal 6:3

SON
Me, 'You are My *S* . . . . Ps 2:7
is born, Unto us a *S* . . . . Is 9:6
fourth is like the *S* . . . . . . Dan 3:25
will bring forth a *S* . . . . . Matt 1:21
"This is My beloved *S* . . Matt 3:17
Jesus, You *S* of God . . . . . Matt 8:29
are the Christ, the *S* . . . Matt 16:16
Whose *S* is He . . . . Matt 22:42
of the *S* of Man . . . . . . Matt 24:37
'I am the *S* of God . . . . Matt 27:43
of Jesus Christ, the *S* . . . Mark 1:1
out, the only *s* . . . . Luke 7:12
The only begotten *S* . . . . John 1:18
that this is the *S* . . . . John 1:34
of the only begotten *S* . . John 3:18
S can do nothing . . . . John 5:19
s abides forever . . . . John 8:35
you believe in the *S* . . . . John 9:35
I said, 'I am the *S* . . . . . John 10:36
behold your *s* . . . . John 19:26
Jesus Christ is the *S* . . . . Acts 8:37
by sending His own *S* . . . Rom 8:3
not spare His own *S* . . . . Rom 8:32
live by faith in the *S* . . . . Gal 2:20
God sent forth His *S* . . . . . . Gal 4:4
the knowledge of the *S* . . Eph 4:13
"You are My S . . . . Heb 1:5
though He was a *S* . . . . Heb 5:8
but made like the *S* . . . . . . Heb 7:3
"This is My beloved *S* . . 2 Pet 1:17
denies the *S* . . . . 1 John 2:23
One like the *S* of Man . . . . Rev 1:13

SONG
Sing to Him a new *s* . . . . . . Ps 33:3
He has put a new *s* . . . . Ps 40:3
I will sing a new *s* . . . . Ps 144:9
they sang a new *s* . . . . Rev 5:9

SONGS
my Maker, Who gives *s* Job 35:10
and spiritual *s* . . . . Eph 5:19

SONS
s shall come from afar . . . . Is 60:4
He will purify the *s* . . . . . . Mal 3:3
you may become *s* . . . . John 12:36
who are of faith are *s* . . . . . Gal 3:7
the adoption as *s* . . . . Gal 4:5
in bringing many *s* . . . . . . Heb 2:10
speaks to you as to *s* . . . . Heb 12:5

SOON
For it is *s* cut off . . . . Ps 90:10

SOOTHED
or bound up, Or *s* . . . . Is 1:6

SORCERER
But Elymas the *s* . . . . Acts 13:8

SORCERERS
outside are dogs and *s* . . Rev 22:15

SORCERESS
shall not permit a *s* . . . . . Ex 22:18

SORCERY
idolatry, *s* . . . . Gal 5:20

SORES
and putrefying *s* . . . . Is 1:6

SORROW
multiply your *s* . . . . Gen 3:16
s is continually . . . . Ps 38:17
And He adds no *s* . . . . . Prov 10:22
Your *s* is incurable . . . . Jer 30:15
them sleeping from *s* . . Luke 22:45
s will be turned . . . . John 16:20
s produces repentance . . 2 Cor 7:10
s as others who . . . . . 1 Thess 4:13
no more death, nor *s* . . . . Rev 21:4

SORROWFUL
But I am poor and *s* . . . . . . Ps 69:29
he went away *s* . . . . Matt 19:22
soul is exceedingly *s* . . . Matt 26:38
and I may be less *s* . . . . . . Phil 2:28

SORROWS
s shall be multiplied . . . . . . Ps 16:4
by men, A Man of *s* . . . . Is 53:3
are the beginning of *s* . . Matt 24:8

SORRY
s that He had made man . Gen 6:6
For you were made *s* . . . 2 Cor 7:9

SOUGHT
I *s* the LORD . . . . Ps 34:4
s what was lost . . . . Ezek 34:4

SOUL
with all your *s* . . . . Deut 6:5
"My *s* loathes my life . . . . Job 10:1
s draws near the Pit . . . . Job 33:22
will not leave my *s* . . . . . Ps 16:10
converting the *s* . . . . Ps 19:7
He restores my *s* . . . . Ps 23:3
you cast down, O my *s* . . . Ps 42:5
Let my *s* live . . . . Ps 119:175
No one cares for my *s* . . . Ps 142:4
me wrongs his own *s* . . . . Prov 8:36
When You make His *s* . . . . Is 53:10
s delight itself . . . . Is 55:2
The *s* of the father As . . . Ezek 18:4
able to destroy both *s* . Matt 10:28
and loses his own *s* . . . . Matt 16:26
with all your s . . . . Matt 22:37
your whole spirit, *s* . . 1 Thess 5:23
to the saving of the *s* . . . Heb 10:39
his way will save a *s* . . James 5:20
health, just as your *s* . . . . 3 John 2

SOULS
And will save the *s* . . . . . . Ps 72:13
And he who wins *s* . . . . Prov 11:30
unsettling your *s* . . . . Acts 15:24
is able to save your *s* . James 1:21

SOUND
voice was like the *s* . . . . Ezek 43:2
do not *s* a trumpet . . . . . . Matt 6:2
s words which you . . . . 2 Tim 1:13

SOUNDNESS
him this perfect *s* . . . . Acts 3:16

SOUNDS
a distinction in the *s* . . . 1 Cor 14:7

SOW
s trouble reap . . . . Job 4:8
Those who *s* in tears . . . . Ps 126:5
Blessed are you who *s* . . . . Is 32:20
"They *s* the wind . . . . Hos 8:7
s is not made alive . . . . 1 Cor 15:36

SOWER
"Behold, a *s* went . . . . . . Matt 13:3

SOWN
s spiritual things . . . . . . 1 Cor 9:11
of righteousness is *s* . . James 3:18

SOWS
s the good seed is the . . Matt 13:37
'One *s* and another . . . . . John 4:37
for whatever a man *s* . . . . . Gal 6:7

SPARE
He who did not *s* . . . . Rom 8:32
if God did not *s* . . . . 2 Pet 2:4

SPARES
s his rod hates his . . . . . Prov 13:24

SPARK
the work of it as a *s* . . . . Is 1:31

SPARKLES
it is red, When it *s* . . . . Prov 23:31

SPARKS
to trouble, As the *s* . . . . Job 5:7

SPARROW
s has found a home . . . . Ps 84:3

SPARROWS
than many *s* . . . . Matt 10:31

SPAT
Then they *s* on Him . . . Matt 27:30

SPEAK
only the word that I *s* . Num 22:35
oh, that God would *s* . . . Job 11:5
And a time to *s* . . . . Eccl 3:7
s anymore in His name . . Jer 20:9
or what you should *s* . . . Matt 10:19
to you when all men *s* . . Luke 6:26
s what I have seen . . . . . . John 8:38
He hears He will *s* . . . . . John 16:13
Spirit and began to *s* . . . . Acts 2:4

SPEAKING
envy, and all evil *s* . . . . . 1 Pet 2:1

SPEAKS
to face, as a man *s* . . . . . Ex 33:11
God has sent *s* . . . . John 3:34
When he *s* a lie . . . . John 8:44
he being dead still *s* . . . . Heb 11:4
of sprinkling that *s* . . . . . Heb 12:24

SPEAR
His side with a *s* . . . . . . John 19:34

SPEARS
And their *s* into . . . . Is 2:4

SPECK
do you look at the *s* . . . . . Matt 7:3

SPECTACLE
you were made a *s* . . . . . Heb 10:33

SPEECH
one language and one *s* . Gen 11:1
his *s* contemptible . . . . 2 Cor 10:10
s always be with grace . . . . Col 4:6

SPEECHLESS
your mouth for the *s* . . . Prov 31:8

SPEED
they shall come with *s* . . . . Is 5:26

SPEEDILY
I call, answer me *s* . . . . . . Ps 102:2

SPEND
you *s* money for . . . . Is 55:2
amiss, that you may *s* . . James 4:3

SPENT
"But when he had *s* . . . Luke 15:14

SPEW
nor hot, I will *s* . . . . Rev 3:16

SPIDER
s skillfully grasps . . . . . Prov 30:28

SPIES
men who had been *s* . . . . Josh 6:23

SPIN
neither toil nor *s* . . . . Matt 6:28

SPINDLE
her hand holds the *s* . . . Prov 31:19

SPIRIT
And the *S* of God was . . . . Gen 1:2
S shall not strive . . . . Gen 6:3
S that is upon you . . . . Num 11:17
portion of your *s* . . . . 2 Kin 2:9
Then a *s* passed . . . . Job 4:15
hand I commit my *s* . . . . . . Ps 31:5
The *s* of a man is the . . Prov 20:27
s will return to God . . . . . Eccl 12:7
S has gathered them . . . . . Is 34:16
I have put My *S* . . . . Is 42:1
"The *S* of the Lord . . . . Is 61:1
S entered me when He . . Ezek 2:2
and a new *s* . . . . Ezek 18:31
"I will put My *S* . . . . . . Ezek 36:27
walk in a false *s* . . . . Mic 2:11
and He saw the *S* . . . . . . Matt 3:16
I will put My S . . . . Matt 12:18
S descending upon . . . . . . Mark 1:10
s indeed is willing . . . . Mark 14:38
go before Him in the *s* . Luke 1:17
manner of *s* you are of . Luke 9:55
hands I commit My s . . Luke 23:46
they had seen a *s* . . . . . Luke 24:37
"God is *S* . . . . John 4:24
I speak to you are *s* . . . . John 6:63
"the *S* of truth . . . . John 14:17
but if a *s* or an angel . . . . Acts 23:9
the flesh but in the *S* . . . . . Rom 8:9
does not have the *S* . . . . . Rom 8:9
s that we are children . . Rom 8:16
what the mind of the *S* . Rom 8:27
to us through His *S* . . . 1 Cor 2:10
gifts, but the same *S* . . . 1 Cor 12:4
but the *S* gives life . . . . . 2 Cor 3:6
Now the Lord is the *S* . 2 Cor 3:17
Having begun in the *S* . . . . Gal 3:3
has sent forth the *S* . . . . Gal 4:6
with the Holy *S* . . . . Eph 1:13
the unity of the *S* . . . . Eph 4:3
stand fast in one *s* . . . . . . Phil 1:27
S expressly says that . . . 1 Tim 4:1
S who dwells in us . . . . . James 4:5
made alive by the *S* . . . . 1 Pet 3:18
do not believe every *s* . 1 John 4:1
you know the *S* . . . . . . 1 John 4:2
has given us of His *S* . 1 John 4:13
S who bears witness . . . 1 John 5:6
not having the *S* . . . . Jude 19
I was in the *S* on the . . . . . Rev 1:10
him hear what the *S* . . . . . . Rev 2:7
And the *S* and the . . . . . . Rev 22:17

SPIRITS
Who makes His angels *s* . Ps 104:4
heed to deceiving *s* . . . . . 1 Tim 4:1

SPIRITUAL
s judges all things . . . . . 1 Cor 2:15
However, the *s* is not . 1 Cor 15:46
s restore such a one . . . . . . Gal 6:1

SPIRITUALLY
s minded is life . . . . Rom 8:6

SPITEFULLY
for those who *s* . . . . Matt 5:44

SPITTING
face from shame and *s* . . . . Is 50:6

SPLENDOR
on the glorious *s* . . . . Ps 145:5

SPOIL
He shall divide the *s* . . . . . Is 53:12

SPOILER
I have created the *s* . . . . . . Is 54:16

SPOKE
"No man ever *s* . . . . John 7:46
I was a child, I *s* . . . . . . 1 Cor 13:11
in various ways *s* . . . . Heb 1:1
s as they were moved . . 2 Pet 1:21

SPOKEN
I have not *s* in secret . . . . . Is 45:19
why am I evil *s* . . . . 1 Cor 10:30

SPOKESMAN
"So he shall be your *s* . . . . Ex 4:16

SPONGE
them ran and took a *s* . Matt 27:48

SPOT
church, not having *s* . . . . Eph 5:27
Himself without *s* . . . . Heb 9:14

SPOTS
These are *s* in your . . . . . . Jude 12

SPREAD
Then the word of God *s* . . Acts 6:7

SPREADS
s them out like a tent . . . . . Is 40:22

SPRING
Truth shall *s* out of . . . . . Ps 85:11
s send forth fresh . . . . . James 3:11

SPRINGING
a fountain of water *s* . . . John 4:14

SPRINGS
And the thirsty land *s* . . . . . Is 35:7

SPRINKLE
"Then I will *s* . . . . Ezek 36:25

SPRINKLED
having our hearts *s* . . . . Heb 10:22

SPRINKLING
s that speaks . . . . Heb 12:24

SPROUT
and the seed should *s* . . . Mark 4:27

SQUARES
voice in the open *s* . . . . . Prov 1:20

STAFF
this Jordan with my *s* . . Gen 32:10
Your rod and Your *s* . . . . . Ps 23:4
on the top of his *s* . . . . . Heb 11:21

STAGGER
they will drink and *s* . . . . Jer 25:16

STAGGERS
As a drunken man *s* . . . . Is 19:14

STAKES
s will ever be removed . . . Is 33:20

STALLS
be no herd in the *s* . . . . . . Hab 3:17

STAMMERERS
s will be ready . . . . Is 32:4

STAMMERING
s tongue that you . . . . Is 33:19

STAMPING
At the noise of the *s* . . . . . Jer 47:3

STAND
one shall be able to *s* . . . Deut 7:24
lives, And He shall *s* . . . . . Job 19:25
ungodly shall not *s* . . . . Ps 1:5
not lack a man to *s* . . . . . Jer 35:19
And who can *s* when He . . Mal 3:2
that kingdom cannot *s* . Mark 3:24
he will be made to *s* . . . . Rom 14:4
Watch, *s* fast in the . . . 1 Cor 16:13
for by faith you *s* . . . . . . 2 Cor 1:24
having done all, to *s* . . . . Eph 6:13
S therefore . . . . Eph 6:14
of God in which you *s* . . 1 Pet 5:12
"Behold, I *s* at the . . . . Rev 3:20

STANDARD
LORD will lift up a *s* . . . . . Is 59:19

STANDING
they love to pray *s* . . . . . Matt 6:5
and the Son of Man *s* . . . Acts 7:56

STANDS
him who thinks he *s* . . 1 Cor 10:12

STAR
For we have seen His *s* . . Matt 2:2
Bright and Morning *S* . . Rev 22:16

STARS
He made the *s* also . . . . . . Gen 1:16
born as many as the *s* . . Heb 11:12

STATE
learned in whatever *s* . . . Phil 4:11

STATURE
in wisdom and *s* . . . . Luke 2:52

STATUTE
shall be a perpetual *s* . . . . Lev 3:17

STATUTES
the *s* of the LORD are . . . . . Ps 19:8
Teach me Your *s* . . . . Ps 119:12

STAY
S here and watch . . . . . Matt 26:38

STEADFAST
brethren, be *s* . . . . 1 Cor 15:58
soul, both sure and *s* . . . Heb 6:19
Resist him, *s* in the . . . . . . 1 Pet 5:9

STEADFASTLY
s set His face to go . . . . . Luke 9:51
And they continued *s* . . . Acts 2:42

STEADFASTNESS
good order and the *s* . . . . . Col 2:5

STEADILY
could not look *s* . . . . 2 Cor 3:13

STEADY
and his hands were *s* . . . . . Ex 17:12

STEAL
"You shall not *s* . . . . Ex 20:15

thieves break in and *s* . . Matt 6:19
night and *s* Him away . Matt 27:64

STEM

forth a Rod from the *s* . . . . Is 11:1

STENCH

there will be a *s* . . . . Is 3:24
this time there is a *s* . . . John 11:39

STEP

s has turned from the . . . . Job 31:7

STEPS

The *s* of a good man . . . . . Ps 37:23
And established my *s* . . . . . Ps 40:2
the LORD directs his *s* . . . Prov 16:9
should follow His *s* . . . . 1 Pet 2:21

STEWARD

be blameless, as a *s* . . . . . Titus 1:7

STEWARDS

of Christ and *s* . . . . 1 Cor 4:1

STEWARDSHIP

entrusted with a *s* . . . . . 1 Cor 9:17

STICK

'For Joseph, the *s* . . . . . Ezek 37:16

STICKS

a man gathering *s* . . . . . Num 15:32

STIFF

rebellion and your *s* . . . Deut 31:27

STIFF-NECKED

"You *s* and . . . . Acts 7:51

STILL

When I awake, I am *s* . . Ps 139:18
sea, "Peace, be *s* . . . . . . Mark 4:39

STILLBORN

burial, I say that a *s* . . . . . . Eccl 6:3

STINGS

like a serpent, And *s* . . Prov 23:32

STIR

I remind you to *s* . . . . 2 Tim 1:6

STIRRED

So the LORD *s* up the . . . . Hag 1:14

STIRS

It *s* up the dead for . . . . Is 14:9

STOCKS

s that were in the . . . . Jer 20:2

STOIC

and *S* philosophers . . . . Acts 17:18

STOMACH

Foods for the *s* . . . . 1 Cor 6:13

STOMACH'S

little wine for your *s* . . . 1 Tim 5:23

STONE

him, a pillar of *s* . . . . Gen 35:14
s shall be a witness . . . . Josh 24:27
s which the builders . . . . Ps 118:22
I lay in Zion a *s* . . . . Is 28:16
take the heart of *s* . . . . Ezek 36:26
will give him a *s* . . . . Matt 7:9
s will be broken . . . . Matt 21:44
s which the builders . . Luke 20:17
those works do you *s* . . John 10:32
Him as to a living *s* . . . . . 1 Pet 2:4

STONED

s Stephen as he was . . . . Acts 7:59
They were *s* . . . . Heb 11:37

STONES

Abraham from these *s* . . . Matt 3:9
command that these *s* . . . Matt 4:3

STONY

fell on *s* ground . . . . Mark 4:5

STOOPED

And again He *s* down . . . John 8:8

STOPPED

her flow of blood *s* . . . . . Luke 8:44

STORE

exist are kept in *s* . . . . 2 Pet 3:7

STORK

s has her home in the . . . Ps 104:17

STORM

He calms the *s* . . . . Ps 107:29
for a shelter from *s* . . . . Is 4:6

STRAIGHT

Make *s* in the desert A . . . . Is 40:3
and make *s* paths for . . Heb 12:13

STRAIGHTFORWARD

that they were not *s* . . . . . Gal 2:14

STRAIN

"Blind guides, who *s* . . Matt 23:24

STRAITS

and desperate *s* . . . . Deut 28:53

STRANGE

s thing happened . . . . 1 Pet 4:12

STRANGER

and loves the *s* . . . . Deut 10:18
I was a *s* and you . . . . . Matt 25:35

STRANGERS

know the voice of *s* . . . . John 10:5
you are no longer *s* . . . . . Eph 2:19

STRANGLING

that my soul chooses *s* . . . Job 7:15

STRAP

than I, whose sandal *s* . . Mark 1:7

STRAW

stones, wood, hay, *s* . . . 1 Cor 3:12

STRAY

Who make my people *s* . . . Mic 3:5

STRAYED

Yet I have not *s* . . . . . . Ps 119:110
some have *s* . . . . 1 Tim 6:10

STREAM

like a flowing *s* . . . . Is 66:12

STREAMS

He also brought *s* . . . . Ps 78:16

STREET

In the middle of its *s* . . . . Rev 22:2

STREETS

You taught in our *s* . . . Luke 13:26

STRENGTH

s no man shall . . . . 1 Sam 2:9
The LORD is the *s* . . . . Ps 27:1
is our refuge and *s* . . . . Ps 46:1
They go from *s* to . . . . Ps 84:7
S and honor are her . . . Prov 31:25
might He increases *s* . . . . . Is 40:29
O LORD, my *s* and my . . . Jer 16:19

were still without *s* . . . . . Rom 5:6
s is made perfect . . . . . . 2 Cor 12:9

STRENGTHEN

And He shall *s* . . . . Ps 27:14
S the weak hands . . . . Is 35:3
s your brethren . . . . Luke 22:32
s the things . . . . Rev 3:2

STRENGTHENED

unbelief, but was *s* . . . . . Rom 4:20
stood with me and *s* . . . 2 Tim 4:17

STRENGTHENING

s the souls of the . . . . . . Acts 14:22

STRENGTHENS

through Christ who *s* . . . . Phil 4:13

STRETCH

are old, you will *s* . . . . . John 21:18

STRETCHED

I have *s* out my hands . . . . Ps 88:9
"All day long I have s . Rom 10:21

STRETCHES

For he *s* out his hand . . . Job 15:25

STRICKEN

of My people He was *s* . . . . Is 53:8

STRIFE

man stirs up *s* . . . . Prov 15:18
even from envy and *s* . . . Phil 1:15
which come envy, *s* . . . . 1 Tim 6:4

STRIKE

The sun shall not *s* . . . . . . Ps 121:6
"*S* the Shepherd . . . . Zech 13:7
'I will s the Shepherd . . Matt 26:31

STRINGED

of your *s* instruments . . Amos 5:23

STRIP

S yourselves . . . . Is 32:11

STRIPES

s we are healed . . . . Is 53:5
s you were healed . . . . . . 1 Pet 2:24

STRIVE

"My Spirit shall not *s* . . . . Gen 6:3
"*S* to enter through . . . . Luke 13:24
the Lord not to *s* . . . . . . 2 Tim 2:14

STRIVING

for a man to stop *s* . . . . . Prov 20:3

STROKE

with a mighty *s* . . . . Jer 14:17

STRONG

The LORD *s* and mighty . . . Ps 24:8
S is Your hand . . . . Ps 89:13
"When a *s* man . . . . Luke 11:21
We then who are *s* . . . . . . Rom 15:1
weak, then I am *s* . . . . 2 Cor 12:10
my brethren, be *s* . . . . Eph 6:10
were made *s* . . . . Heb 11:34

STRONGHOLD

of my salvation, my *s* . . . . Ps 18:2

STRUCK

s the rock twice . . . . Num 20:11
the hand of God has *s* . . Job 19:21
Behold, He *s* the rock . . . . Ps 78:20
in My wrath I *s* . . . . Is 60:10
s the head from the . . . . . Hab 3:13
took the reed and *s* . . . . Matt 27:30

STUBBLE

do wickedly will be *s* . . . . . Mal 4:1

STUBBORN
"If a man has a *s* . . . . Deut 21:18

STUBBORN-HEARTED
"Listen to Me, you *s* . . . . . . Is 46:12

STUBBORNNESS
do not look on the *s* . . . . Deut 9:27

STUDIED
having never *s* . . . . John 7:15

STUMBLE
have caused many to *s* . . . Mal 2:8
you will be made to *s* . . Matt 26:31
immediately they *s* . . . . Mark 4:17
who believe in Me to *s* . Mark 9:42
For we all *s* in many . . . James 3:2

STUMBLED
s that they should . . . . . Rom 11:11

STUMBLES
immediately he *s* . . . . . Matt 13:21

STUMBLING
the deaf, nor put a *s* . . . . Lev 19:14
But a stone of *s* . . . . Is 8:14
Behold, I will lay *s* . . . . Jer 6:21
I lay in Zion a s . . . . Rom 9:33
this, not to put a *s* . . . . . Rom 14:13
of yours become a *s* . . . . 1 Cor 8:9
and *"A stone of s* . . . . 1 Pet 2:8
to keep you from *s* . . . . Jude 24

STUPID
hates correction is *s* . . . . Prov 12:1

SUBDUE
s all things to . . . . Phil 3:21

SUBJECT
for it is not *s* . . . . Rom 8:7
Let every soul be *s* . . . . Rom 13:1
all their lifetime *s* . . . . Heb 2:15

SUBJECTED
because of Him who *s* . . Rom 8:20

SUBJECTION
put all things in s . . . . Heb 2:8

SUBMISSION
his children in *s* . . . . 1 Tim 3:4

SUBMISSIVE
Yes, all of you be *s* . . . . . . 1 Pet 5:5

SUBMIT
Therefore *s* to God . . . . . James 4:7
s yourselves to every . . . 1 Pet 2:13

SUBSIDED
and the waters *s* . . . . Gen 8:1

SUBSTANCE
Bless his *s* . . . . Deut 33:11

SUCCESS
please give me *s* . . . . . . Gen 24:12
But wisdom brings *s* . . . Eccl 10:10

SUCCESSFUL
Joseph, and he was a *s* . . Gen 39:2

SUDDENLY
s there was with the . . . . Luke 2:13

SUE
s you and take away . . . . Matt 5:40

SUFFER
for the Christ to *s* . . . . . Luke 24:46
Christ, if indeed we *s* . . . Rom 8:17
in Him, but also to *s* . . . . Phil 1:29

SUFFERED
s these things and to . . . Luke 24:26
for whom I have *s* . . . . Phil 3:8
after you have *s* . . . . 1 Pet 5:10

SUFFERING
anyone among you *s* . . James 5:13

SUFFERINGS
I consider that the *s* . . . . Rom 8:18
perfect through *s* . . . . Heb 2:10

SUFFERS
Love *s* long and is . . . . . 1 Cor 13:4

SUFFICIENCY
but our *s* is from God . . . 2 Cor 3:5

SUFFICIENT
S for the day is its . . . . . . Matt 6:34

SUM
How great is the *s* . . . . . . Ps 139:17

SUMMER
and heat, Winter and *s* . . Gen 8:22

SUMPTUOUSLY
fine linen and fared *s* . . Luke 16:19

SUN
So the *s* stood still . . . . . Josh 10:13
s shall not strike you . . . . Ps 121:6
s returned ten degrees . . . . . Is 38:8
The *s* and moon grow . . . . . Joel 2:10
s shall go down on the . . . . Mic 3:6
for He makes His *s* . . . . . Matt 5:45
the *s* was darkened . . . . Luke 23:45
do not let the *s* . . . . Eph 4:26
s became black as . . . . Rev 6:12
had no need of the *s* . . . . . Rev 21:23

SUPPER
to eat the Lord's *S* . . . . 1 Cor 11:20
took the cup after *s* . . . 1 Cor 11:25
together for the *s* . . . . . . Rev 19:17

SUPPLICATION
by prayer and *s* . . . . Phil 4:6

SUPPLIES
by what every joint *s* . . . . Eph 4:16

SUPPLY
And my God shall *s* . . . . . Phil 4:19

SUPPORT
this, that you must *s* . . . Acts 20:35

SUPREME
to the king as *s* . . . . 1 Pet 2:13

SURE
s your sin will find . . . . Num 32:23
call and election *s* . . . . . . 2 Pet 1:10

SURETY
Be *s* for Your servant . . Ps 119:122
Jesus has become a *s* . . . Heb 7:22

SURROUND
LORD, mercy shall *s* . . . . . Ps 32:10

SURROUNDED
also, since we are *s* . . . . . Heb 12:1

SURVIVOR
was no refugee or *s* . . . . Lam 2:22

SUSPICIONS
reviling, evil *s* . . . . 1 Tim 6:4

SUSTAIN
S me with cakes of . . . . . . Song 2:5

SWADDLING
Him in *s* cloths . . . . Luke 2:7

SWALLOW
a gnat and *s* a camel . . Matt 23:24

SWEAR
'You shall not *s* . . . . Matt 5:33
began to curse and *s* . . Matt 26:74

SWEARING
By *s* and lying . . . . Hos 4:2

SWEARS
but whoever *s* by the . . Matt 23:18

SWEAT
His *s* became like . . . . . Luke 22:44

SWEET
s are Your words . . . . . . Ps 119:103
but it will be as *s* . . . . Rev 10:9

SWEETNESS
mouth like honey in *s* . . . Ezek 3:3

SWELLING
they speak great *s* . . . . . 2 Pet 2:18

SWIFT
let every man be *s* . . . . James 1:19

SWIM
night I make my bed *s* . . . . . Ps 6:6

SWOON
As they *s* like the . . . . Lam 2:12

SWORD
s which turned every . . . . Gen 3:24
The *s* of the LORD is . . . . . . Is 34:6
'A *s* is sharpened . . . . Ezek 21:9
Bow and *s* of battle I . . . . . Hos 2:18
to bring peace but a *s* . Matt 10:34
for all who take the *s* . . Matt 26:52
the *s* of the Spirit . . . . Eph 6:17
than any two-edged *s* . . . Heb 4:12
mouth goes a sharp *s* . . Rev 19:15

SWORDS
shall beat their *s* . . . . Is 2:4

SWORE
So I s in My wrath . . . . . . Heb 3:11

SWORN
"By Myself I have *s* . . . . Gen 22:16
"The LORD has s . . . . Heb 7:21

SYMBOLIC
which things are *s* . . . . Gal 4:24

SYMPATHIZE
Priest who cannot *s* . . . . . Heb 4:15

SYMPATHY
My *s* is stirred . . . . Hos 11:8

SYNAGOGUE
but are a *s* of Satan . . . . . . Rev 2:9

T

TABERNACLE
t He shall hide me . . . . Ps 27:5
I will abide in Your *t* . . . . . Ps 61:4
And will rebuild the t . . . Acts 15:16
and more perfect *t* . . . . Heb 9:11

TABERNACLES
Feast of *T* was at hand . . John 7:2

TABLE
prepare a *t* before me . . . . Ps 23:5

dogs under the *t* .... Mark 7:28
of the Lord's *t* .... 1 Cor 10:21

TABLES

and overturned the *t* ... Matt 21:12

TABLET

is engraved On the *t* ..... Jer 17:1

TAIL

t drew a third of the .... Rev 12:4

TAKE

t Your Holy Spirit .... Ps 51:11
"*T* My yoke upon ..... Matt 11:29
and *t* up his cross ..... Mark 8:34
My life that I may *t* ... John 10:17

TAKEN

He was *t* from prison ..... Is 53:8
one will be *t* and the .. Matt 24:40
until He is *t* out of .... 2 Thess 2:7

TALEBEARER

t reveals secrets .... Prov 11:13

TALENT

went and hid your *t* ... Matt 25:25

TALK

shall *t* of them when .... Deut 6:7

TALKED

within us while He *t* .. Luke 24:32

TALKERS

both idle *t* and .... Titus 1:10

TAMBOURINE

The mirth of the *t* .... Is 24:8

TARES

the *t* also appeared .... Matt 13:26

TARGET

You set me as Your *t* .... Job 7:20

TARRY

come and will not t .... Heb 10:37

TASK

this burdensome *t* .... Eccl 1:13

TASTE

Oh, *t* and see that the ..... Ps 34:8
might *t* death for .... Heb 2:9

TASTED

t the heavenly gift .... Heb 6:4

TAUGHT

as His counselor has *t* .... Is 40:13
from man, nor was I *t* ... Gal 1:12

TAUNT

and a byword, a *t* .... Jer 24:9

TAX

t collectors do the ...... Matt 5:46

TAXES

t to whom *t* .... Rom 13:7

TEACH

"Can anyone *t* .... Job 21:22
T me Your paths .... Ps 25:4
t you the fear of the ..... Ps 34:11
t transgressors Your ..... Ps 51:13
So *t* us to number our ... Ps 90:12
t you again the first ..... Heb 5:12

TEACHER

for One is your *T* .... Matt 23:8
know that You are a *t* ... John 3:2
named Gamaliel, a *t* .... Acts 5:34
a *t* of the Gentiles in .... 1 Tim 2:7

TEACHERS

than all my *t* .... Ps 119:99
prophets, third *t* ...... 1 Cor 12:28
and some pastors and *t* . Eph 4:11
desiring to be *t* .... 1 Tim 1:7
there will be false *t* ..... 2 Pet 2:1

TEACHES

the Holy Spirit *t* .... 1 Cor 2:13
the same anointing *t* .. 1 John 2:27

TEACHING

"*t* them to observe all . Matt 28:20
t every man in all .... Col 1:28

TEAR

I, even I, will *t* .... Hos 5:14
will wipe away every *t* .. Rev 21:4

TEARS

my couch with my *t* .... Ps 6:6
mindful of your *t* .... 2 Tim 1:4
it diligently with *t* .... Heb 12:17

TEETH

You have broken the *t* ..... Ps 3:7

TELL

"Who can *t* if God .... Jon 3:9
t him his fault .... Matt 18:15
whatever they *t* .... Matt 23:3
He comes, He will *t* .... John 4:25

TEMPERATE

prize is *t* in all .... 1 Cor 9:25
husband of one wife, *t* .. 1 Tim 3:2

TEMPEST

And suddenly a great *t* . Matt 8:24

TEMPLE

So Solomon built the *t* . 1 Kin 6:14
LORD is in His holy *t* ...... Ps 11:4
One greater than the *t* .. Matt 12:6
"Destroy this *t* .... John 2:19
your body is the *t* ..... 1 Cor 6:19
grows into a holy *t* ..... Eph 2:21
sits as God in the *t* ... 2 Thess 2:4
and the Lamb are its *t* .. Rev 21:22

TEMPLES

t made with hands ..... Acts 7:48

TEMPORARY

which are seen are *t* ... 2 Cor 4:18

TEMPT

t the LORD *your God* .... Matt 4:7
does He Himself *t* .... James 1:13

TEMPTATION

do not lead us into *t* ... Matt 6:13
man who endures *t* ... James 1:12

TEMPTED

forty days, *t* by Satan .. Mark 1:13
lest you also be *t* .... Gal 6:1
in all points *t* .... Heb 4:15

TEMPTER

Now when the *t* came ... Matt 4:3

TENDER

your heart was *t* ..... 2 Kin 22:19

TENDERHEARTED

to one another, *t* .... Eph 4:32

TENDS

t a flock and does not .. 1 Cor 9:7

TENT

earthly house, this *t* .... 2 Cor 5:1

TENTMAKERS

occupation they were *t* .. Acts 18:3

TENTS

Than dwell in the *t* ...... Ps 84:10

TERRESTRIAL

bodies and *t* bodies ... 1 Cor 15:40

TERRIBLE

is great and very *t* ...... Joel 2:11

TERRIFIED

and not in any way *t* .... Phil 1:28

TERRIFY

me with dreams And *t* ... Job 7:14

TERRIFYING

t was the sight .... Heb 12:21

TERROR

are nothing, You see *t* ... Job 6:21
not be afraid of the *t* ..... Ps 91:5

TERRORS

consumed with *t* .... Ps 73:19

TEST

said, "Why do you *t* ... Matt 22:18
T all things .... 1 Thess 5:21
but *t* the spirits .... 1 John 4:1

TESTAMENT

where there is a *t* .... Heb 9:16

TESTED

God *t* Abraham .... Gen 22:1
Where your fathers t ..... Heb 3:9
though it is *t* by fire ..... 1 Pet 1:7

TESTIFIED

who has seen has *t* .... John 19:35
which He has *t* .... 1 John 5:9

TESTIFIES

that the Holy Spirit *t* .. Acts 20:23

TESTIFY

t what We have .... John 3:11
t that the Father ...... 1 John 4:14

TESTIFYING

was righteous, God *t* .... Heb 11:4

TESTIMONIES

those who keep His *t* .... Ps 119:2
t are my meditation .... Ps 119:99

TESTIMONY

two tablets of the *T* ...... Ex 31:18
under your feet as a *t* .. Mark 6:11
no one receives His *t* ... John 3:32
not believed the *t* ...... 1 John 5:10
For the *t* of Jesus is ..... Rev 19:10

TESTING

came to Him, *t* Him ..... Matt 19:3

TESTS

men, but God who *t* .. 1 Thess 2:4

THANK

"I *t* You, Father .... Matt 11:25
t You that I am not ... Luke 18:11

THANKFUL

as God, nor were *t* .... Rom 1:21

THANKFULNESS

Felix, with all *t* .... Acts 24:3

THANKS
the cup, and gave *t* .... Matt 26:27
T be to God for His .... 2 Cor 9:15

THANKSGIVING
His presence with *t* .... Ps 95:2
into His gates with *t* ..... Ps 100:4
supplication, with *t* ...... Phil 4:6

THEATER
and rushed into the *t* .. Acts 19:29

THIEF
do not despise a *t* .... Prov 6:30
because he was a *t* ..... John 12:6
Lord will come as a *t* .. 2 Pet 3:10

THIEVES
And companions of *t* ...... Is 1:23

THINGS
in heaven give good *t* .. Matt 7:11
kept all these *t* .... Luke 2:51
share in all good *t* .... Gal 6:6

THINK
t you have eternal ...... John 5:39
not to *t* of himself ...... Rom 12:3

THINKS
Yet the LORD *t* upon me . Ps 40:17
For as he *t* in his .... Prov 23:7
t he stands take heed . 1 Cor 10:12

THIRST
those who hunger and *t* . Matt 5:6
in Me shall never *t* ...... John 6:35
anymore nor *t* anymore . Rev 7:16

THIRSTS
My soul *t* for God .... Ps 42:2
saying, "If anyone *t* .... John 7:37
freely to him who *t* ..... Rev 21:6

THIRSTY
I was *t* and you gave .. Matt 25:35

THISTLES
or figs from *t* .... Matt 7:16

THORN
a *t* in the flesh was .... 2 Cor 12:7

THORNBUSHES
gather grapes from *t* .... Matt 7:16

THORNS
Both *t* and thistles it .... Gen 3:18
some fell among *t* ...... Matt 13:7
wearing the crown of *t* . John 19:5

THOUGHT
You understand my *t* .... Ps 139:2
I *t* as a child .... 1 Cor 13:11

THOUGHTS
The LORD knows the *t* ... Ps 94:11
unrighteous man his *t* ..... Is 55:7
"For My *t* are not your .... Is 55:8
Jesus, knowing their *t* ... Matt 9:4
heart proceed evil *t* .... Matt 15:19
The LORD knows the t . 1 Cor 3:20

THREAT
shall flee at the *t* .... Is 30:17

THREATEN
suffered, He did not *t* .. 1 Pet 2:23

THREATENING
to them, giving up *t* ...... Eph 6:9

THREATS
still breathing *t* .... Acts 9:1

THREE
hope, love, these *t* .... 1 Cor 13:13

THRESH
it is time to *t* her .... Jer 51:33

THRESHING
t shall last till the .... Lev 26:5

THROAT
t is an open tomb ...... Rom 3:13

THRONE
Your *t*, O God, is .... Ps 45:6
Lord sitting on a *t* .... Is 6:1
"Heaven is My *t* .... Is 66:1
for it is God's *t* .... Matt 5:34
will give Him the *t* ..... Luke 1:32
"Your t, O God, is .... Heb 1:8
come boldly to the *t* .... Heb 4:16
My Father on His *t* ...... Rev 3:21
I saw a great white *t* ... Rev 20:11

THRONES
invisible, whether *t* ...... Col 1:16

THRONG
house of God in the *t* .... Ps 55:14

THROW
t Yourself down .... Matt 4:6

THROWN
neck, and he were *t* .... Mark 9:42

THRUST
and rose up and *t* ...... Luke 4:29

THUNDER
The voice of Your *t* ...... Ps 77:18
the voice of loud *t* ...... Rev 14:2

THUNDERED
"The LORD *t* from .... 2 Sam 22:14

THUNDERINGS
the sound of mighty *t* ... Rev 19:6

THUNDERS
The God of glory *t* .... Ps 29:3

TIDINGS
I bring you good *t* ...... Luke 2:10

TILL
no man to *t* the ground ... Gen 2:5

TILLER
but Cain was a *t* .... Gen 4:2

TILLS
t his land will have .... Prov 28:19

TIME
pray to You In a *t* .... Ps 32:6
for the *t* is near .... Rev 1:3

TIMES
the signs of the *t* ...... Matt 16:3
not for you to know *t* ... Acts 1:7
last days perilous *t* ..... 2 Tim 3:1

TITHE
And he gave him a *t* ... Gen 14:20
For you pay *t* of mint .. Matt 23:23

TITHES
and to bring the *t* ...... Neh 10:37
Bring all the *t* .... Mal 3:10

TITHING
the year of *t* .... Deut 26:12

TITLE
Now Pilate wrote a *t* .. John 19:19

TITTLE
away, one jot or one *t* .. Matt 5:18

TODAY
T I have begotten You ..... Ps 2:7
t you will be with Me . Luke 23:43
"T, if you will hear .... Heb 3:7
the same yesterday, *t* ... Heb 13:8

TOIL
t you shall eat of .... Gen 3:17

TOILED
"Master, we have *t* ...... Luke 5:5

TOLD
Behold, I have *t* .... Matt 28:7
so, I would have *t* ..... John 14:2

TOLERABLE
you, it will be more *t* .. Matt 10:15

TOMB
in the garden a new *t* . John 19:41

TOMBS
like whitewashed *t* .... Matt 23:27

TOMORROW
drink, for *t* we die .... Is 22:13
do not worry about *t* ... Matt 6:34
what will happen *t* .... James 4:14

TONGUE
remember you, Let my *t* . Ps 137:6
forever, But a lying *t* .. Prov 12:19
t breaks a bone .... Prov 25:15
t should confess that .... Phil 2:11
does not bridle his *t* .. James 1:26
no man can tame the *t* . James 3:8
every nation, tribe, *t* .... Rev 14:6

TONGUES
From the strife of *t* ...... Ps 31:20
speak with new *t* ..... Mark 16:17
divided *t*, as of fire ...... Acts 2:3
I speak with the *t* ...... 1 Cor 13:1

TOOTH
eye for an eye and a t .. Matt 5:38

TOPHET
the high places of *T* ...... Jer 7:31

TORCH
and like a fiery *t* .... Zech 12:6

TORCHES
When he had set the *t* . Judg 15:5
come with flaming *t* ...... Nah 2:3

TORMENT
You come here to *t* .... Matt 8:29
t ascends forever ...... Rev 14:11

TORMENTED
And they will be *t* ...... Rev 20:10

TORMENTS
"And being in *t* .... Luke 16:23

TORN
of the temple was *t* .... Matt 27:51

TORTURED
Others were *t* .... Heb 11:35

TOSSED
t to and fro and .... Eph 4:14

TOTTER
drunkard, And shall *t* .... Is 24:20

TOUCH
"If only I may *t* ....Matt 9:21

TOUCHED
t my mouth with it ....Is 6:7

TOUCHES
He *t* the hills ....Ps 104:32

TOWER
t whose top is in the ....Gen 11:4
a watchman in the *t* ....Is 21:5

TRACKED
t our steps So that we ..Lam 4:18

TRADERS
are princes, Whose *t* ....Is 23:8

TRADITION
transgress the *t* ....Matt 15:2
according to the *t* ....Col 2:8

TRAIN
T up a child in the .....Prov 22:6

TRAINED
those who have been *t* .Heb 12:11

TRAINING
bring them up in the *t* ....Eph 6:4

TRAITOR
also became a *t* ....Luke 6:16

TRAITORS
t, headstrong ....2 Tim 3:4

TRAMPLE
serpent you shall *t* ......Ps 91:13
swine, lest they *t* ....Matt 7:6

TRAMPLED
t the Son of God ....Heb 10:29
the winepress was *t* ....Rev 14:20

TRANCE
t I saw a vision ....Acts 11:5

TRANSFIGURED
and was *t* before them ..Matt 17:2

TRANSFORMED
this world, but be *t* .....Rom 12:2

TRANSGRESS
do Your disciples *t* .....Matt 15:2

TRANSGRESSED
"Yes, all Israel has *t* ....Dan 9:11
t your commandment .Luke 15:29

TRANSGRESSES
Whoever *t* and does not .2 John 9

TRANSGRESSION
no law there is no *t* ....Rom 4:15
deceived, fell into *t* ....1 Tim 2:14

TRANSGRESSIONS
mercies, Blot out my *t* ....Ps 51:1
For I acknowledge my *t* ..Ps 51:3
was wounded for our *t* ....Is 53:5
For the *t* of My people ....Is 53:8

TRANSGRESSOR
I make myself a *t* ....Gal 2:18

TRANSGRESSORS
Then I will teach *t* ....Ps 51:13
numbered with the *t* ......Is 53:12

TRAP
of Israel, As a *t* ....Is 8:14

TRAPS
for me, And from the *t* ..Ps 141:9

TRAVEL
you *t* land and sea ....Matt 23:15

TRAVELER
t who turns aside ....Jer 14:8

TRAVELING
lie waste, The *t* ....Is 33:8

TREACHEROUS
are insolent, *t* ....Zeph 3:4

TREACHEROUSLY
"This man dealt *t* ....Acts 7:19

TREAD
You shall *t* upon the ......Ps 91:13

TREADS
an ox while it t ....1 Tim 5:18
t the winepress ....Rev 19:15

TREASURE
and you will have *t* ....Matt 19:21
he who lays up *t* ......Luke 12:21
But we have this *t* ......2 Cor 4:7

TREASURED
t the words of His ......Job 23:12

TREASURER
Erastus, the *t* of the ...Rom 16:23

TREASURES
it more than hidden *t* ....Job 3:21
I will give you the *t* ....Is 45:3
for yourselves *t* ....Matt 6:19
are hidden all the *t* ....Col 2:3
riches than the *t* ....Heb 11:26

TREATY
Now Solomon made a *t* .1 Kin 3:1

TREE
you eaten from the *t* .....Gen 3:11
t Planted by the ....Ps 1:3
like a native green *t* .....Ps 37:35
t bears good fruit ....Matt 7:17
His own body on the *t* .1 Pet 2:24
the river, was the *t* ......Rev 22:2

TREES
late autumn *t* without ....Jude 12
the sea, or the *t* ....Rev 7:3

TREMBLE
That the nations may *t* ....Is 64:2
they shall fear and *t* ....Jer 33:9

TREMBLED
Then everyone who *t* .....Ezra 9:4
the earth shook and *t* .....Ps 18:7
and indeed they *t* ....Jer 4:24

TREMBLING
in fear, and in much *t* ..1 Cor 2:3
t you received ....2 Cor 7:15
flesh, with fear and *t* .....Eph 6:5

TRENCH
and he made a *t* ......1 Kin 18:32

TRESPASSES
forgive men their *t* .....Matt 6:14
not imputing their *t* ...2 Cor 5:19
who were dead in *t* ......Eph 2:1

TRIAL
concerning the fiery *t* ..1 Pet 4:12

TRIBE
the Lion of the *t* ....Rev 5:5
blood Out of every *t* ......Rev 5:9

TRIBES
t which are scattered ...James 1:1

TRIBULATION
there will be great *t* ...Matt 24:21
world you will have *t* ..John 16:33
with her into great *t* ....Rev 2:22
out of the great *t* ....Rev 7:14

TRIBULATIONS
t enter the kingdom ...Acts 14:22
but we also glory in *t* ....Rom 5:3
t that you endure .....2 Thess 1:4

TRIED
A *t* stone, a precious .....Is 28:16

TRIMMED
and *t* their lamps ....Matt 25:7

TRIUMPH
always leads us in *t* ...2 Cor 2:14

TRIUMPHED
the LORD, For He has *t* ...Ex 15:1

TRODDEN
t the winepress alone .....Is 63:3

TROUBLE
few days and full of *t* ....Job 14:1
t He shall hide me ....Ps 27:5
not in *t* as other men ....Ps 73:5
will be with him in *t* ....Ps 91:15
Savior in time of *t* ....Jer 14:8
there are some who *t* .....Gal 1:7

TROUBLED
worried and *t* ....Luke 10:41
shaken in mind or *t* ...2 Thess 2:2

TROUBLES
Out of all their *t* ....Ps 25:22
will be famines and *t* ..Mark 13:8
him out of all his *t* ....Acts 7:10

TROUBLING
wicked cease from *t* .....Job 3:17

TRUE
He who sent Me is *t* ....John 7:28
Indeed, let God be *t* .....Rom 3:4
whatever things are *t* ....Phil 4:8
Him who is *t* ....1 John 5:20
for these words are *t* ....Rev 21:5

TRUMPET
deed, do not sound a *t* ...Matt 6:2
t makes an uncertain ..1 Cor 14:8
For the *t* will sound ..1 Cor 15:52

TRUST
T in the LORD ....Ps 37:3
T in the LORD with all ....Prov 3:5
Do not *t* in a friend ....Mic 7:5
who *t* in riches ....Mark 10:24

TRUSTED
"He *t* in the LORD ....Ps 22:8
"He *t* in God ....Matt 27:43

TRUSTS
But he who *t* in the ......Ps 32:10

TRUTH
led me in the way of *t* ..Gen 24:48
Behold, You desire *t* ......Ps 51:6
t shall be your shield ....Ps 91:4
And Your law is *t* .....Ps 119:142

t is fallen in the .... Is 59:14
called the City of *T* .... Zech 8:3
you shall know the *t* ... John 8:32
"I am the way, the *t* .... John 14:6
He, the Spirit of *t* ..... John 16:13
to Him, "What is *t* ..... John 18:38
who suppress the *t* ..... Rom 1:18
but, speaking the *t* ...... Eph 4:15
your waist with *t* .... Eph 6:14
I am speaking the *t* ..... 1 Tim 2:7
they may know the *t* .. 2 Tim 2:25
the knowledge of the *t* .. 2 Tim 3:7
that we are of the *t* ... 1 John 3:19
the Spirit is *t* .... 1 John 5:6

TRY
which is to *t* you .... 1 Pet 4:12

TUMULT
Your enemies make a *t* ... Ps 83:2

TUNIC
Also he made him a *t* ... Gen 37:3

TUNICS
the LORD God made *t* .... Gen 3:21

TURBAN
"Remove the *t* .... Ezek 21:26

TURN
you shall not *t* .... Deut 17:11
"Repent, *t* away from .. Ezek 14:6
on your right cheek, *t* .. Matt 5:39
t them from darkness .. Acts 26:18

TURNED
The wicked shall be *t* ..... Ps 9:17
of Israel, They have *t* .... Is 1:4
and how you *t* .... 1 Thess 1:9

TURNING
marvel that you are *t* ..... Gal 1:6
or shadow of *t* .... James 1:17

TURNS
A soft answer *t* .... Prov 15:1
that he who *t* .... James 5:20

TURTLEDOVE
t Is heard in our land .. Song 2:12

TUTOR
the law was our *t* .... Gal 3:24

TWIST
unstable people *t* to .... 2 Pet 3:16

TWO
T are better than one ..... Eccl 4:9
t shall become one ..... Matt 19:5
new man from the *t* ..... Eph 2:15

TYPE
of Adam, who is a *t* .... Rom 5:14

U

UNAFRAID
Do you want to be *u* .... Rom 13:3

UNBELIEF
because of their *u* ..... Matt 13:58
help my *u* .... Mark 9:24
did it ignorantly in *u* .. 1 Tim 1:13
enter in because of *u* .... Heb 3:19

UNBELIEVERS
yoked together with *u* . 2 Cor 6:14

UNBELIEVING
Do not be *u* .... John 20:27
u nothing is pure ...... Titus 1:15
"But the cowardly, *u* .... Rev 21:8

UNCIRCUMCISED
not the physically *u* ..... Rom 2:27

UNCLEAN
I am a man of *u* lips .... Is 6:5
man common or *u* ..... Acts 10:28
there is nothing *u* ...... Rom 14:14
that no fornicator, *u* .... Eph 5:5

UNCLEANNESS
men's bones and all *u* . Matt 23:27
flesh in the lust of *u* .... 2 Pet 2:10

UNCLOTHED
we want to be *u* .... 2 Cor 5:4

UNCOVERS
u deep things out of .... Job 12:22

UNDEFILED
incorruptible and *u* ...... 1 Pet 1:4

UNDERMINE
And you *u* your friend ... Job 6:27

UNDERSTAND
if there are any who *u* .. Ps 14:2
hearing, but do not *u* .... Is 6:9
"Why do you not *u* ...... John 8:43
lest they should u ..... Acts 28:27
some things hard to *u* .. 2 Pet 3:16

UNDERSTANDING
His *u* is infinite .... Ps 147:5
lean not on your own *u* .. Prov 3:5
u will find good .... Prov 19:8
His *u* is unsearchable .... Is 40:28
also still without *u* ..... Matt 15:16
also pray with the *u* .. 1 Cor 14:15
the Lord give you *u* ..... 2 Tim 2:7
Who is wise and *u* .... James 3:13

UNDERSTANDS
There is none who u .... Rom 3:11

UNDERSTOOD
Then I *u* their end .... Ps 73:17
clearly seen, being *u* ..... Rom 1:20

UNDESIRABLE
gather together, O *u* ...... Zeph 2:1

UNDIGNIFIED
I will be even more *u* . 2 Sam 6:22

UNDISCERNING
u, untrustworthy .... Rom 1:31

UNDONE
"Woe is me, for I am *u* ...... Is 6:5

UNEDUCATED
that they were *u* .... Acts 4:13

UNFAITHFUL
way of the *u* is hard ... Prov 13:15

UNFAITHFULLY
back and acted *u* .... Ps 78:57

UNFORGIVING
unloving, *u* .... Rom 1:31

UNFORMED
substance, being yet *u* .. Ps 139:16

UNFRUITFUL
and it becomes *u* ...... Mark 4:19

UNGODLINESS
heaven against all *u* .... Rom 1:18

UNGODLY
u shall not stand .... Ps 1:5
Christ died for the *u* ..... Rom 5:6

UNHOLY
the holy and *u* .... Ezek 22:26

UNINFORMED
the place of the *u* ..... 1 Cor 14:16

UNINTENTIONALLY
kills his neighbor *u* ..... Deut 4:42

UNITE
U my heart to fear ...... Ps 86:11

UNITY
to dwell together in *u* .... Ps 133:1
to keep the *u* of the .... Eph 4:3

UNJUST
commended the *u* ...... Luke 16:8
of the just and the *u* ... Acts 24:15
For God is not *u* .... Heb 6:10

UNJUSTLY
long will you judge *u* .... Ps 82:2

UNKNOWN
To The *U* God .... Acts 17:23

UNLEAVENED
the Feast of *U* Bread ...... Ex 12:17

UNLOVING
untrustworthy, *u* .... Rom 1:31

UNMERCIFUL
unforgiving, *u* .... Rom 1:31

UNPREPARED
with me and find you *u* . 2 Cor 9:4

UNPRESENTABLE
u parts have greater .. 1 Cor 12:23

UNPROFITABLE
'We are *u* servants ...... Luke 17:10
for that would be *u* .... Heb 13:17

UNPUNISHED
wicked will not go *u* ... Prov 11:21

UNQUENCHABLE
up the chaff with *u* ..... Matt 3:12

UNRESTRAINED
that the people were *u* ... Ex 32:25

UNRIGHTEOUS
u man his thoughts .... Is 55:7
u will not inherit the .... 1 Cor 6:9

UNRIGHTEOUSNESS
all ungodliness and *u* .... Rom 1:18
cleanse us from all *u* ... 1 John 1:9
All *u* is sin .... 1 John 5:17

UNRULY
those who are *u* ...... 1 Thess 5:14

UNSEARCHABLE
u are His judgments ... Rom 11:33

UNSKILLED
only of milk is *u* .... Heb 5:13

UNSPOTTED
to keep oneself *u* ...... James 1:27

UNSTABLE
U as water .... Gen 49:4

the truth hears My *v* . . John 18:37
If anyone hears My *v* . . . . Rev 3:20

VOICES

And there were loud *v* . . Rev 11:15

VOID

they are a nation *v* . . . . Deut 32:28
heirs, faith is made *v* . . . Rom 4:14

VOLUME

in the v of the book . . . . . Heb 10:7

VOLUNTEERS

Your people shall be *v* . . . Ps 110:3

VOMIT

returns to his own v . . . . 2 Pet 2:22

VOW

for he had taken a *v* . . . Acts 18:18

VOWS

to reconsider his *v* . . . . Prov 20:25

W

WAGE

w the good warfare . . . . 1 Tim 1:18

WAGES

For the *w* of sin is . . . . . . Rom 6:23
Indeed the *w* of the . . . . James 5:4

WAIL

"Son of man, *w* . . . . Ezek 32:18

WAILING

There will be *w* . . . . Matt 13:42

WAIT

w patiently for Him . . . . Ps 37:7
those who *w* on the . . . . . . Is 40:31
To those who eagerly *w* . Heb 9:28

WAITED

w patiently for the . . . . Ps 40:1
Divine longsuffering *w* . 1 Pet 3:20

WAITING

ourselves, eagerly *w* . . . . Rom 8:23
from that time *w* . . . . Heb 10:13

WAITS

the creation eagerly *w* . . Rom 8:19

WAKE

that whether we *w* . . . 1 Thess 5:10

WALK

w before Me and be . . . . Gen 17:1
Yea, though I *w* . . . . Ps 23:4
W prudently when you . . . Eccl 5:1
"This is the way, *w* . . . . . . Is 30:21
be weary, they shall *w* . . . Is 40:31
w humbly with your God . Mic 6:8
W while you have the . John 12:35
so we also should *w* . . . . . Rom 6:4
For we *w* by faith . . . . . . 2 Cor 5:7
W in the Spirit . . . . Gal 5:16
And *w* in love . . . . Eph 5:2
that you may *w* worthy . . Col 1:10
and they shall *w* . . . . Rev 3:4

WALKED

Methuselah, Enoch *w* . . . Gen 5:22
The people who *w* . . . . Is 9:2
in which you once *w* . . . . . Eph 2:2

WALKING

not *w* in craftiness . . . . . . 2 Cor 4:2

WALKS

the LORD your God *w* . . Deut 23:14
is the man Who *w* . . . . Ps 1:1
he who *w* in darkness . John 12:35
adversary the devil *w* . . . 1 Pet 5:8

WALL

then the *w* of the city . . . Josh 6:5
you whitewashed *w* . . . . . Acts 23:3
a window in the *w* . . . . 2 Cor 11:33
Now the *w* of the city . . Rev 21:14

WALLS

By faith the *w* of . . . . Heb 11:30

WANDER

they have loved to *w* . . . . Jer 14:10

WANDERED

They *w* in deserts and . Heb 11:38

WANDERERS

And they shall be *w* . . . . . Hos 9:17

WANDERING

w stars for whom is . . . . . . Jude 13

WANDERS

among you *w* . . . . James 5:19

WANT

I shall not *w* . . . . Ps 23:1

WANTING

balances, and found *w* . . Dan 5:27

WANTON

have begun to grow *w* . 1 Tim 5:11

WAR

"There is a noise of *w* . . . . Ex 32:17
w may rise against . . . . Ps 27:3
shall they learn *w* . . . . Is 2:4
going to make *w* . . . . . . Luke 14:31
You fight and *w* . . . . James 4:2
fleshly lusts which *w* . . . 1 Pet 2:11
judges and makes *w* . . . . Rev 19:11

WARFARE

to her, That her *w* . . . . Is 40:2
w entangles . . . . 2 Tim 2:4

WARMED

in peace, be *w* . . . . James 2:16

WARMING

she saw Peter *w* . . . . . . Mark 14:67

WARMS

w them in the dust . . . . . Job 39:14

WARN

w those who are . . . . . 1 Thess 5:14

WARNED

Then, being divinely *w* . Matt 2:12
Who *w* you to flee . . . . Matt 3:7

WARNING

w every man and . . . . Col 1:28

WARPED

such a person is *w* . . . . . Titus 3:11

WARRING

w against the law of . . . . Rom 7:23

WARRIOR

He runs at me like a *w* . Job 16:14

WARS

you will hear of *w* . . . . . . Matt 24:6
Where do *w* and fights . James 4:1

WASH

w myself with snow . . . . Job 9:30
W me thoroughly . . . . Ps 51:2
w His feet with her . . . . Luke 7:38
said to him, "Go, *w* . . . . . John 9:7
w the disciples' . . . . John 13:5
w away your sins . . . . . . Acts 22:16

WASHED

w his hands before . . . . Matt 27:24
But you were *w* . . . . 1 Cor 6:11
Him who loved us and *w* . Rev 1:5

WASHING

us, through the *w* . . . . Titus 3:5

WASHINGS

and drinks, various *w* . . . Heb 9:10

WASTE

the cities are laid *w* . . . . Is 6:11
"Why this *w* . . . . Matt 26:8

WASTED

this fragrant oil *w* . . . . . Mark 14:4

WASTELAND

w shall be glad . . . . Is 35:1

WASTING

that this man was *w* . . . . Luke 16:1

WATCH

is past, And like a *w* . . . . . Ps 90:4
"*W* therefore . . . . Matt 24:42

WATCHED

he would have *w* . . . . . . Matt 24:43

WATCHES

Blessed is he who *w* . . . . Rev 16:15

WATCHFUL

But you be *w* in all . . . . . 2 Tim 4:5

WATCHING

he comes, will find *w* . Luke 12:37

WATCHMAN

I have made you a *w* . . . . Ezek 3:17

WATCHMEN

I have set *w* on your . . . . . . Is 62:6

WATER

Eden to *w* the garden . . . Gen 2:10
I am poured out like *w* . . . Ps 22:14
For I will pour *w* . . . . Is 44:3
given you living *w* . . . . . John 4:10
rivers of living *w* . . . . John 7:38
can yield both salt *w* . . James 3:12
the Spirit, the *w* . . . . 1 John 5:8
are clouds without *w* . . . . . Jude 12
let him take the *w* . . . . . . Rev 22:17

WATERED

I planted, Apollos *w* . . . . 1 Cor 3:6

WATERS

me beside the still *w* . . . . . . Ps 23:2
Though its *w* roar and . . . . Ps 46:3
your bread upon the *w* . . . Eccl 11:1
thirsts, Come to the *w* . . . . . Is 55:1
fountain of living *w* . . . . . . Jer 2:13
living fountains of *w* . . . . . Rev 7:17

WAVE

Its fruit shall *w* . . . . Ps 72:16

WAVER

He did not *w* at the . . . . . Rom 4:20

WAVERING

of our hope without *w* . Heb 10:23

WAVES
sea, tossed by the *w* . . . Matt 14:24

WAX
My heart is like *w* . . . . Ps 22:14

WAY
As for God, His *w* . . . 2 Sam 22:31
the LORD knows the *w* . . . . Ps 1:6
Teach me Your *w* . . . . Ps 27:11
in the *w* everlasting . . . . Ps 139:24
w that seems right . . . . Prov 14:12
The *w* of the just is . . . . Is 26:7
wicked forsake his *w* . . . . . Is 55:7
And pervert the *w* . . . . . . Amos 2:7
he will prepare the *w* . . . . . Mal 3:1
and broad is the *w* . . . . . . Matt 7:13
will prepare Your w . . . Matt 11:10
to him, "I am the *w* . . . . John 14:6
to him the *w* . . . . Acts 18:26
to have known the *w* . . . 2 Pet 2:21

WAYS
For all His *w* are . . . . Deut 32:4
transgressors Your *w* . . . . . Ps 51:13
w please the LORD . . . . . . Prov 16:7
"Stand in the *w* . . . . Jer 6:16
and owns all your *w* . . . . Dan 5:23
w are everlasting . . . . Hab 3:6
unstable in all his *w* . . . . James 1:8
and true are Your *w* . . . . Rev 15:3

WEAK
gives power to the *w* . . . . . Is 40:29
knee will be as *w* . . . . . . Ezek 7:17
but the flesh is *w* . . . . . . Matt 26:41
Receive one who is *w* . . . . Rom 14:1
God has chosen the *w* . 1 Cor 1:27
We are *w* . . . . 1 Cor 4:10
w I became as *w* . . . . . . 1 Cor 9:22
For when I am *w* . . . . . 2 Cor 12:10

WEAKENED
w my strength in the . . . Ps 102:23

WEAKENS
w the hands of the men . . Jer 38:4

WEAKER
the wife, as to the *w* . . . . . 1 Pet 3:7

WEAKNESS
w were made strong . . . Heb 11:34

WEAKNESSES
also helps in our *w* . . . . . Rom 8:26

WEALTH
W gained by . . . . Prov 13:11

WEALTHY
rich, have become *w* . . . . Rev 3:17

WEANED
w child shall put his . . . . Is 11:8

WEAPON
w formed against you . . . . Is 54:17

WEAPONS
For the *w* of our . . . . 2 Cor 10:4

WEAR
'What shall we *w* . . . . Matt 6:31

WEARIED
You have *w* Me with . . . . . Is 43:24
therefore, being *w* . . . . John 4:6

WEARINESS
say, 'Oh, what a *w* . . . . Mal 1:13

WEARISOME
and much study is *w* . . . Eccl 12:12

WEARY
shall run and not be *w* . . . Is 40:31
And let us not grow *w* . . . . Gal 6:9
do not grow *w* in . . . . 2 Thess 3:13

WEATHER
'It will be fair *w* . . . . Matt 16:2

WEDDING
day there was a *w* . . . . John 2:1

WEEK
the first day of the *w* . . . Matt 28:1

WEEKS
w are determined . . . . . . Dan 9:24

WEEP
A time to *w* . . . . Eccl 3:4
You shall *w* no more . . . . . Is 30:19
are you who *w* . . . . Luke 6:21
do not *w* . . . . Luke 23:28
w with those who *w* . . . Rom 12:15

WEEPING
the noise of the *w* . . . . . . Ezra 3:13
They shall come with *w* . . Jer 31:9
There will be *w* . . . . Matt 8:12
by the tomb *w* . . . . John 20:11

WEIGH
O Most Upright, You *w* . . . Is 26:7

WEIGHED
You have been *w* . . . . Dan 5:27

WEIGHS
eyes, But the LORD *w* . . . Prov 16:2

WEIGHT
us lay aside every *w* . . . . Heb 12:1

WEIGHTIER
have neglected the *w* . . Matt 23:23

WELFARE
does not seek the *w* . . . . . . Jer 38:4

WELL
have done *w* . . . . Prov 31:29
wheel broken at the *w* . . Eccl 12:6
"Those who are *w* . . . . Matt 9:12
said to him, '*W* done . . Matt 25:21

WELLS
These are *w* without . . . 2 Pet 2:17

WENT
They *w* out from us . . . 1 John 2:19

WEPT
out and *w* bitterly . . . . . Matt 26:75
saw the city and *w* . . . . Luke 19:41
Jesus *w* . . . . John 11:35

WET
his body was *w* with . . . . Dan 4:33

WHEAT
w falls into the . . . . John 12:24

WHEEL
in the middle of a *w* . . . . Ezek 1:16

WHEELS
noise of rattling *w* . . . . Nah 3:2

WHERE
not knowing *w* he was . . Heb 11:8

WHIP
A *w* for the horse . . . . . . Prov 26:3

WHIRLWIND
Job out of the *w* . . . . Job 38:1
has His way In the *w* . . . . Nah 1:3

WHISPER
my ear received a *w* . . . . . Job 4:12

WHISPERER
w separates the best . . . Prov 16:28

WHISPERERS
they are *w* . . . . Rom 1:29

WHISPERINGS
backbitings, *w* . . . . 2 Cor 12:20

WHITE
clothed in *w* garments . . . . Rev 3:5
behold, a *w* horse . . . . Rev 6:2
and made them *w* . . . . Rev 7:14

WHOLE
w body were an eye . . 1 Cor 12:17

WHOLESOME
not consent to *w* words . 1 Tim 6:3

WHOLLY
w followed the LORD . . . . Deut 1:36

WICKED
w shall be silent . . . . 1 Sam 2:9
w shall be no more . . . . . . Ps 37:10
if there is any *w* . . . . Ps 139:24
w forsake his way . . . . Is 55:7
And desperately *w* . . . . Jer 17:9
the sway of the *w* . . . . . 1 John 5:19

WICKEDLY
God will never do *w* . . . . Job 34:12

WICKEDNESS
LORD saw that the *w* . . . . Gen 6:5
in the tents of *w* . . . . Ps 84:10
man repented of his *w* . . . . Jer 8:6
is full of greed and *w* . Luke 11:39
sexual immorality, *w* . . . . Rom 1:29
and overflow of *w* . . . . James 1:21

WIDE
open your hand *w* . . . . . . Deut 15:8
w is the gate and . . . . Matt 7:13
to you, our heart is *w* . . 2 Cor 6:11

WIDOW
the fatherless and *w* . . . . . Ps 146:9
How like a *w* is she . . . . . . Lam 1:1
Then one poor *w* . . . . . Mark 12:42
w has children or . . . . 1 Tim 5:4

WIDOW'S
And I caused the *w* . . . . . Job 29:13

WIDOWS
w were neglected . . . . Acts 6:1
visit orphans and *w* . . . James 1:27

WIFE
and be joined to his *w* . . . Gen 2:24
w finds a good thing . . . Prov 18:22
But a prudent *w* . . . . Prov 19:14
"Go, take yourself a *w* . . . Hos 1:2
divorces his *w* . . . . Mark 10:11
'I have married a *w* . . . Luke 14:20
"Remember Lot's *w* . . . Luke 17:32
so love his own *w* . . . . Eph 5:33
the husband of one *w* . . . . Titus 1:6
bride, the Lamb's *w* . . . . . Rev 21:9

WILD
olive tree which is *w* . . . Rom 11:24

WILDERNESS
I will make the *w* . . . . Is 41:18

of one crying in the w ... Matt 3:3
the serpent in the *w* ... John 3:14

WILES

to stand against the *w* ... Eph 6:11

WILL

w be done On earth as .. Matt 6:10
but he who does the *w* .. Matt 7:21
not My *w* .... Luke 22:42
flesh, nor of the *w* ..... John 1:13
not to do My own *w* .... John 6:38
w is present with me .... Rom 7:18
and perfect *w* of God .... Rom 12:2
works in you both to *w* .. Phil 2:13
according to His own *w* .. Heb 2:4
work to do His *w* ...... Heb 13:21

WILLFULLY

For if we sin *w* .... Heb 10:26
For this they *w* .... 2 Pet 3:5

WILLING

If you are *w* and .... Is 1:19
The spirit indeed is *w* . Matt 26:41
w that any should .... 2 Pet 3:9

WILLINGLY

by compulsion but *w* ..... 1 Pet 5:2

WILLOWS

our harps Upon the *w* ... Ps 137:2

WILLS

to whom the Son *w* .... Matt 11:27
it is not of him who *w* .. Rom 9:16
say, "If the Lord *w* .... James 4:15

WIN

to all, that I might *w* .... 1 Cor 9:19

WIND

the chaff which the *w* ...... Ps 1:4
reed shaken by the *w* .... Matt 11:7
"The *w* blows where .... John 3:8
of a rushing mighty *w* ... Acts 2:2

WINDOWS

not open for you the *w* .. Mal 3:10

WINDS

be, that even the *w* ..... Matt 8:27

WINDSTORM

And a great *w* arose ... Mark 4:37

WINE

W is a mocker .... Prov 20:1
love is better than *w* ..... Song 1:2
Yes, come, buy *w* .... Is 55:1
they gave Him sour *w* . Matt 27:34
do not be drunk with *w* .. Eph 5:18
not given to much *w* .... Titus 2:3

WINEBIBBERS

Do not mix with *w* ..... Prov 23:20

WINEPRESS

"I have trodden the *w* ..... Is 63:3
into the great *w* .... Rev 14:19
Himself treads the *w* ... Rev 19:15

WINESKINS

new wine into old *w* .... Matt 9:17

WING

One *w* of the cherub ... 1 Kin 6:24

WINGS

the shadow of Your *w* .... Ps 36:7
With healing in His *w* ...... Mal 4:2

WINNOW

You shall *w* them .... Is 41:16

WINS

w souls is wise .... Prov 11:30

WINTER

For lo, the *w* is past .... Song 2:11
flight may not be in *w* . Matt 24:20

WIPE

w away every tear .... Rev 21:4

WISDOM

for this is your *w* .... Deut 4:6
man who finds *w* .... Prov 3:13
Get *w* .... Prov 4:5
is the beginning of *w* ... Prov 9:10
w is justified by her ... Matt 11:19
Jesus increased in *w* ... Luke 2:52
riches both of the *w* ... Rom 11:33
the gospel, not with *w* . 1 Cor 1:17
w of this world .... 1 Cor 3:19
not with fleshly *w* ...... 2 Cor 1:12
all the treasures of *w* ...... Col 2:3
If any of you lacks *w* .... James 1:5
power and riches and *w* . Rev 5:12

WISE

Do not be *w* in your ...... Prov 3:7
who wins souls is *w* .... Prov 11:30
Therefore be *w* as ...... Matt 10:16
five of them were *w* .... Matt 25:2
to God, alone *w* .... Rom 16:27
Where is the *w* .... 1 Cor 1:20
not as fools but as *w* .... Eph 5:15
able to make you *w* ... 2 Tim 3:15

WISELY

you do not inquire *w* .... Eccl 7:10

WISER

he was *w* than all men . 1 Kin 4:31
of God is *w* than men .. 1 Cor 1:25

WISH

w it were already ..... Luke 12:49

WISHED

Then he *w* death for ...... Jon 4:8

WITCHCRAFT

is as the sin of *w* .... 1 Sam 15:23

WITHDRAW

From such *w* yourself ... 1 Tim 6:5

WITHER

also shall not *w* .... Ps 1:3

WITHERS

The grass *w* .... Is 40:7
The grass w .... 1 Pet 1:24

WITHHELD

And your sins have *w* .... Jer 5:25

WITHHOLD

good thing will He *w* .... Ps 84:11

WITHOUT

pray *w* ceasing ...... 1 Thess 5:17
w works is dead ...... James 2:26

WITHSTAND

you may be able to *w* ... Eph 6:13

WITHSTOOD

I *w* him to his face ...... Gal 2:11

WITNESS

all the world as a *w* ... Matt 24:14
This man came for a *w* .. John 1:7
do not receive Our *w* ... John 3:11
Christ, the faithful *w* ..... Rev 1:5
beheaded for their *w* .... Rev 20:4

WITNESSED

is revealed, being *w* .... Rom 3:21

WITNESSES

"You are My *w* .... Is 43:10
presence of many *w* ... 1 Tim 6:12
so great a cloud of *w* .... Heb 12:1

WIVES

Husbands, love your *w* . Eph 5:25
w must be reverent ..... 1 Tim 3:11

WOLF

The *w* and the lamb .... Is 65:25

WOLVES

out as lambs among *w* . Luke 10:3
savage *w* .... Acts 20:29

WOMAN

She shall be called *W* ... Gen 2:23
whoever looks at a *w* ... Matt 5:28
Then the *w* of Samaria .. John 4:9
"*W*, behold your ..... John 19:26
natural use of the *w* .... Rom 1:27
His Son, born of a *w* .... Gal 4:4
w being deceived ...... 1 Tim 2:14
w clothed with the sun .. Rev 12:1

WOMB

nations are in your *w* . Gen 25:23
in the *w* I knew you .... Jer 1:5
is the fruit of your *w* ... Luke 1:42

WOMEN

O fairest among *w* .... Song 1:8
w will be grinding ..... Matt 24:41
are you among *w* ...... Luke 1:28
admonish the young *w* .. Titus 2:4
times, the holy *w* .... 1 Pet 3:5

WONDER

marvelous work and a *w* . Is 29:14

WONDERFUL

Things too *w* for me ..... Job 42:3
name will be called *W* .... Is 9:6

WONDERFULLY

fearfully and *w* made ... Ps 139:14

WONDERS

"And I will show *w* ...... Joel 2:30
signs, and lying *w* ..... 2 Thess 2:9

WONDROUS

w works declare that ..... Ps 75:1

WONDROUSLY

God, Who has dealt *w* ... Joel 2:26

WOOD

precious stones, *w* ..... 1 Cor 3:12

WOODCUTTERS

but let them be *w* .... Josh 9:21

WOOL

They shall be as *w* .... Is 1:18
hair were white like *w* .. Rev 1:14

WORD

w is very near you .... Deut 30:14
w I have hidden .... Ps 119:11
w is a lamp to my feet . Ps 119:105
Every *w* of God is pure . Prov 30:5
the *w* of our God .... Is 40:8
for every idle *w* .... Matt 12:36
The seed is the *w* ...... Luke 8:11
beginning was the *W* .... John 1:1
W became flesh and ... John 1:14
Your *w* is truth .... John 17:17
Let the *w* of Christ ...... Col 3:16
to you in *w* only .... 1 Thess 1:5

by the *w* of His power . . . . Heb 1:3
For the *w* of God is . . . . . Heb 4:12
does not stumble in *w* . . James 3:2
through the *w* of God . . 1 Pet 1:23
let us not love in *w* . . . 1 John 3:18
name is called The *W* . . Rev 19:13

WORDS

Let the *w* of my mouth . . Ps 19:14
The *w* of the wise are . . Eccl 12:11
pass away, but My *w* . . Matt 24:35
You have the *w* of . . . . . John 6:68
not with wisdom of *w* . . 1 Cor 1:17
those who hear the *w* . . . . Rev 1:3

WORK

day God ended His *w* . . . . Gen 2:2
people had a mind to *w* . . Neh 4:6
the *w* of Your fingers . . . . . . Ps 8:3
Man goes out to his *w* . . Ps 104:23
w is honorable and . . . . . . Ps 111:3
will bring every *w* . . . . . Eccl 12:14
For I will *w* a *w* . . . . Hab 1:5
could do no mighty *w* . . . Mark 6:5
"This is the *w* of God . . . John 6:29
"I must *w* the works . . . . John 9:4
w which You have . . . . . John 17:4
know that all things *w* . . Rom 8:28
w is no longer *w* . . . . Rom 11:6
Do not destroy the *w* . . Rom 14:20
abounding in the *w* . . . 1 Cor 15:58
If anyone will not *w* . 2 Thess 3:10
but a doer of the *w* . . . James 1:25

WORKED

which He *w* in Christ . . . Eph 1:20

WORKER

w is worthy of his . . . . . Matt 10:10
w who does not need . . 2 Tim 2:15

WORKERS

we are God's fellow *w* . . 1 Cor 3:9

WORKING

Father has been *w* . . . . . John 5:17
through faith in the *w* . . . . Col 2:12

WORKMANSHIP

For we are His *w* . . . . Eph 2:10

WORKS

are Your wonderful *w* . . . . Ps 40:5
And let her own *w* . . . . Prov 31:31
"For I know their *w* . . . . . . Is 66:18
show Him greater *w* . . . . John 5:20
w that I do he will do . John 14:12
might stand, not of *w* . . . Rom 9:11
same God who *w* . . . . . . 1 Cor 12:6
not justified by the *w* . . . . Gal 2:16
Now the *w* of the flesh . . . Gal 5:19
not of *w*, lest anyone . . . . Eph 2:9
for it is God who *w* . . . . . Phil 2:13
but does not have *w* . . James 2:14
also justified by *w* . . . . James 2:25
"I know your *w* . . . . Rev 2:2
their *w* follow them . . . . Rev 14:13
according to their *w* . . . . Rev 20:12

WORLD

"The field is the *w* . . . . Matt 13:38
He was in the *w* . . . . John 1:10
God so loved the *w* . . . . John 3:16
His Son into the *w* . . . . John 3:17
w cannot hate you . . . . . John 7:7
You are of this *w* . . . . . . John 8:23
overcome the *w* . . . . John 16:33
w may become guilty . . . Rom 3:19
be conformed to this *w* . Rom 12:2
loved this present *w* . . . 2 Tim 4:10
Do not love the *w* . . . . 1 John 2:15
w is passing away . . . . 1 John 2:17

WORLDS

also He made the *w* . . . . . . Heb 1:2

WORM

But I am a *w* . . . . Ps 22:6
w does not die . . . . Mark 9:44

WORMS

he was eaten by *w* . . . . Acts 12:23

WORMWOOD

of the star is *W* . . . . Rev 8:11

WORRY

to you, do not *w* . . . . Matt 6:25

WORRYING

w can add one . . . . Matt 6:27

WORSE

w than their fathers . . . . . . Jer 7:26

WORSHIP

come to *w* Him . . . . Matt 2:2
w what you do not . . . . . John 4:22
the angels of God w . . . . . . Heb 1:6

WORSHIPED

on their faces and *w* . . . . Rev 11:16

WORSHIPER

if anyone is a *w* . . . . John 9:31

WORTH

make my speech *w* . . . . . Job 24:25

WORTHLESS

Indeed they are all *w* . . . . . Is 41:29

WORTHLESSNESS

long will you love *w* . . . . Ps 4:2

WORTHY

present time are not *w* . . Rom 8:18
to walk *w* . . . . Eph 4:1
the world was not *w* . . . Heb 11:38
"*W* is the Lamb who . . . . Rev 5:12

WOUND

And my *w* incurable . . . . Jer 15:18
and his deadly *w* . . . . Rev 13:3

WOUNDED

But He was *w* for our . . . . . Is 53:5

WOUNDING

killed a man for *w* . . . . . . Gen 4:23

WOUNDS

Faithful are the *w* . . . . . . Prov 27:6

WRANGLINGS

useless *w* of men of . . . . 1 Tim 6:5

WRATH

speak to them in His *w* . . . . Ps 2:5
Surely the *w* of man . . . . . Ps 76:10
So I swore in My *w* . . . . . . Ps 95:11
W is cruel and anger a . Prov 27:4
in My *w* I struck you . . . . . Is 60:10
w remember mercy . . . . . . Hab 3:2
For the *w* of God is . . . . . Rom 1:18
up for yourself *w* . . . . Rom 2:5
nature children of *w* . . . . . Eph 2:3
sun go down on your *w* . Eph 4:26
Let all bitterness, *w* . . . . . Eph 4:31
holy hands, without *w* . . 1 Tim 2:8
So I swore in My w . . . . . Heb 3:11
not fearing the *w* . . . . . . Heb 11:27
for the *w* of man . . . . . . James 1:20
of the wine of the *w* . . . . . Rev 14:8

for in them the *w* . . . . Rev 15:1
fierceness of His *w* . . . . Rev 16:19

WRATHFUL

w man stirs up strife . . Prov 15:18

WRESTLE

For we do not *w* . . . . Eph 6:12

WRETCHED

w man that I am . . . . Rom 7:24
know that you are *w* . . . . Rev 3:17

WRETCHEDNESS

let me see my *w* . . . . . . Num 11:15

WRINGING

w the nose produces . . . Prov 30:33

WRINKLE

not having spot or *w* . . . . Eph 5:27

WRITE

w them on their hearts . . Heb 8:10

WRITING

the *w* was the *w* . . . . Ex 32:16

WRITINGS

do not believe his *w* . . . . John 5:47

WRITTEN

tablets of stone, *w* . . . . Ex 31:18
your names are *w* . . . . Luke 10:20
"What I have *w* . . . . John 19:22

WRONG

done nothing *w* . . . . Luke 23:41
But he who does *w* . . . . . . Col 3:25

WRONGED

We have *w* no one . . . . . . 2 Cor 7:2

WRONGS

me *w* his own soul . . . . . Prov 8:36

WROTE

stooped down and *w* . . . . John 8:6

WROUGHT

And skillfully *w* . . . . Ps 139:15

Y

YEAR

the acceptable *y* . . . . Is 61:2
of sins every *y* . . . . Heb 10:3

YEARS

and for days and *y* . . . . . . Gen 1:14
lives are seventy *y* . . . . Ps 90:10
when He was twelve *y* . Luke 2:42
with Him a thousand *y* . . Rev 20:6

YES

let your '*Y*' be '*Y*,' . . . . . . Matt 5:37

YESTERDAY

For we were born *y* . . . . Job 8:9

YOKE

"Take My *y* upon you . Matt 11:29

YOKED

Do not be unequally *y* . 2 Cor 6:14

YOUNG

I have been *y* . . . . Ps 37:25
she may lay her *y* . . . . Ps 84:3
I write to you, *y* . . . . . . 1 John 2:13

YOUNGER

Likewise you *y* people . . . 1 Pet 5:5

YOURS
the battle is not *y* . . . . 2 Chr 20:15
Y is the kingdom . . . . .Matt 6:13
all Mine are *Y* . . . . John 17:10
for I do not seek *y* . . . . 2 Cor 12:14

YOUTH
the sins of my *y* . . . . Ps 25:7
and *y* are vanity . . . . Eccl 11:10
I have kept from my *y* . Matt 19:20

YOUTHFUL
Flee also *y* lusts . . . . 2 Tim 2:22

YOUTHS
y shall faint and be . . . . Is 40:30

Z

ZEAL
The *z* of the LORD of . . 2 Kin 19:31
"Z for Your house has . John 2:17
that they have a *z* . . . . . . Rom 10:2

ZEALOUS
z for good works . . . . . . Titus 2:14

Hope Chest Journal

The following pages will provide you with an opportunity to journal as you see the plans of God unfold for your life. You might think of this section as your own spiritual "Hope Chest" in which you can store the thoughts, prayers, or other treasures you share with Him.

Here are a few ideas. Perhaps you would like to list scriptures that are especially meaningful to you or to write a prayer, committing yourself to the full purposes of God for your life. Or maybe you just want to pour out your heart to your heavenly Father. Maybe you would like to keep a record of the ways God leads you in His destiny for you, or to write down lessons you have learned from your own mentors. You might also ask one or more of your spiritual mothers to write you a personal letter on these pages.

However you choose to use these pages, may they become a legacy of your deepening relationship with the Lord as you discover and fulfill His special plan for your life.